For Reference

Not to be taken from this room

Places, Towns and Townships
Seventh Edition, 2021

Places, Towns and Townships
Seventh Edition, 2021

Edited by Deirdre A. Gaquin
Mary Meghan Ryan

Lanham, MD

Published by Bernan Press

An imprint of The Rowman & Littlefield Publishing Group, Inc.

4501 Forbes Boulevard, Suite 200, Lanham, Maryland 20706

www.rowman.com

800-462-6420

6 Tinworth Street, London SE11 5AL, United Kingdom

ISBN: 978-1-64143-495-9
E-ISBN: 978-1-64143-496-6

Contents

ABOUT THE EDITORS

Deirdre A. Gaquin has been a data use consultant to private organizations, government agencies, and universities for over 30 years. Prior to that, she was Director of Data Access Services at Data Use & Access Laboratories, a pioneer in private sector distribution of federal statistical data. A former President of the Association of Public Data Users, Ms. Gaquin has served on numerous boards, panels, and task forces concerned with federal statistical data and has worked on five decennial censuses. She holds a Master of Urban Planning (MUP) degree from Hunter College. Ms. Gaquin is also an editor of Bernan Press's *The Who, What, and Where of America: Understanding the American Community Survey; Places, Towns and Townships; The Congressional District Atlas, The Almanac of American Education, Race and Employment in America,* and *the State and Metropolitan Area Data Book.*

Mary Meghan Ryan is the senior research editor for Bernan Press. She is also the editor for the *Handbook of U.S. Labor Statistics, State Profiles,* and the associate editor for *Business Statistics of the United States.*

INTRODUCTION

Places, Towns, and Townships contains statistical information about places in the United States and the people who live in them. Data are presented for all incorporated places, census designated places (CDPs), and consolidated cities—from the largest city to the smallest village. CDPs are unincorporated areas of relatively dense population for which boundaries were established by the Census Bureau in cooperation with state agencies and local census statistical area committees. Data are also provided in this volume for Minor Civil Divisions (MCDs) in the 12 states where MCDs serve as general-purpose local governments. MCDs are primary subdivisions of counties and are often called towns or townships.[1]

This book is divided into three tables. Table A presents data for more than 38,000 places (MCDs, CDPs, and incorporated places) in the United States. Included are the 2019 population estimates; 2010 census population; and age, race, ethnicity, educational attainment and computer availability data from the 2015-2019 5-year American Community Survey.

Table B is limited to places with populations of 10,000 or more and includes data on migration, income, housing value, employment, and household type from the 2015-2019 5-year estimates from the American Community Survey; the most recent available information on crime, residential construction, and local government finances.

Table C, also limited to places with populations of 10,000 or more, contains establishment and employee data from the 2017 Economic Census.

Within each table, data are presented alphabetically by state, with place names listed alphabetically within each state.

What are cities and towns?

About 63 percent of Americans live in incorporated cities, and many others live in unincorporated areas with concentrations of people and businesses. While nearly 60 million people (about 18 percent of the population) lived in the nation's 75 largest cities, 121 million (37 percent) lived in areas that were not incorporated as places in 2019. Incorporation laws and practices vary from state to state, and many of the unincorporated Census Designated Places (CDPs) are large urban centers. Nevada has four unincorporated CDPs with populations over 100,000 in 2010 (there

are no 2019 population estimates for CDPs). About 75 percent of Maryland's residents live outside of incorporated cities, but several of Maryland's CDPs are the principal cities of metropolitan areas. In states where MCDs serve as local governments, many large towns are also incorporated cities, but many towns contain no incorporated cities or several small incorporated villages. On New York's Long Island, four towns have populations over 250,000, ranking them among the 75 most populous cities in the United States, when towns are included in the ranking.

Figure 1 shows the populations of the 10 largest cities—those with one million or more residents. These 10 cities house fully 8 percent of the U.S. population. Thirty-five percent of people live in the 403 cities and towns with more than 100,000 residents.

At the other extreme, a mere 4.4 percent of people live in cities with populations below 2,500, while almost two-thirds of all incorporated places fell into this smallest size category. Eighty-five percent of incorporated places had populations of less than 10,000, but these places include only 8.7 percent of the population. As place size increased, the number of places within the size class dropped markedly. Only 288 incorporated places had populations of 100,000 or more, but nearly 30 percent of Americans live in these 288 cities. Thirty-four cities had populations of 500,000 or more. About 9 percent of people live in the 10 cities with a million or more residents.

The distribution of the population living in incorporated places was quite different from the distribution of the number of places. The largest population grouping consists of persons living in medium-sized places. One out of four persons lived in places of 10,000 to 100,000 in 2019. More than one-third of the population lived outside of incorporated places, ranging from the nearly half a million residents of Hempstead Town NY who lived outside of its 22 incorporated villages, to the 345,000 people in Urban Honolulu CDP, to those who lived outside of any defined urban cluster.

Table 1 provides 2019 population estimates, by state, of the population living in incorporated places of varied sizes and those living outside of places. Table 2 shows the percentage of people in each state by size of place.

Population density varies greatly by state, with the more densely populated states located on the East, West, Gulf, and Great Lakes Coasts. The lower-density Rocky Mountain

---

1 See Appendix A for more complete definitions of CDPs and MCDs and a list of the 12 states for which MCD data are provided.

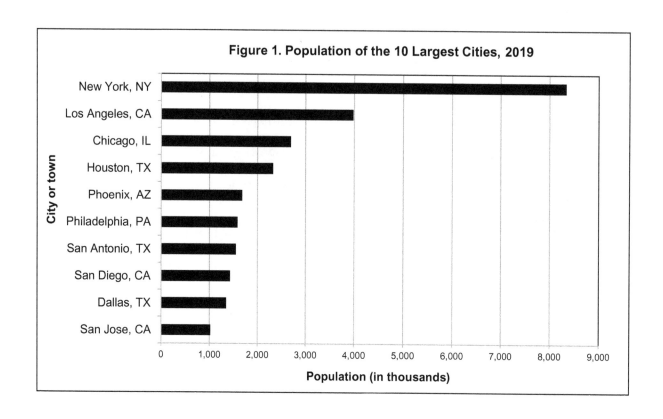

Figure 1. Population of the 10 Largest Cities, 2019

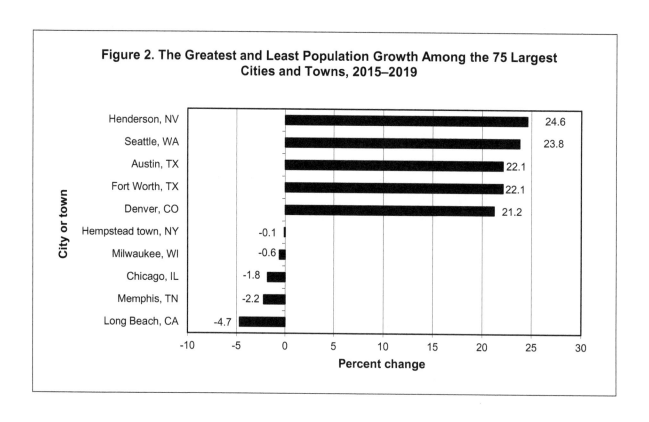

Figure 2. The Greatest and Least Population Growth Among the 75 Largest Cities and Towns, 2015–2019

and Plains states contain many of the places with fewer than 2,500 people. Densely populated states tend to have larger cities. California and Texas each have three cities with more than a million residents, resulting in high densities despite their large land areas.

City size and growth patterns vary from state to state. Most of the older large cities in the East and the Midwest consolidated or annexed territory and grew to their current geographic boundaries more than 100 years ago. In the early years of the 21st century, many of these older cities lost population, while some of their suburban counties experienced high levels of growth. While Chicago's population dropped by almost 7 percent between 2000 and 2010, nearby Kendall county more than doubled its population. At the same time, many large Western cities have continued to annex territory, with development at the edges of these cities helping to accommodate their growing populations. For example, the land area of Phoenix, AZ increased by 8.8 percent between 2000 and 2010 while its population grew by 9.4 percent. Meanwhile, nearby Maricopa city grew by 4,081 percent from 2000 to 2010, reflecting annexations of land that increased its area by 1,070 percent. Some cities have altered their boundaries through consolidation with surrounding areas. In 2003, Louisville, KY, consolidated its governmental functions with the surrounding county, forming the consolidated city Louisville-Jefferson County. Because of this, the Louisville-Jefferson County consolidated city ranked as the 18th most populous city in 2010, jumping from 65th at the time of the 2000 census. The

five boroughs of New York were consolidated into a single incorporated city in 1898, and four of the five, if separate, would be among the top ten cities by 2019 population.

Between 2010 and 2019, Henderson, NV was the fastest growing of the largest cities, increasing by 24.6 percent and moving into the top 75 list to become the 64th largest city. Six other large cities experienced growth rates over 20 percent: Seattle, Austin, Fort Worth, Denver, Charlotte, and Orlando. Eleven of the largest cities lost population. Detroit had the greatest loss at 6.1 percent, followed closely by St. Louis at 5.9 percent. Baltimore and Cleveland suffered losses of 4.4 and 3.9 percent.

New York, Los Angeles, Chicago, Houston, and Phoenix were the five largest cities in 2019, with Phoenix replacing Philadelphia as the fifth largest city. the only change in the top ten. Among the 75 largest cities, 34 experienced growth rates of 10 percent or higher over the 2010-2019 time period.

There were 37 incorporated cities and one town with more than 500,000 people in 2019. These 38 cities and towns represented 24 states, with 6 cities each in Texas and California, 3 in Arizona, 2 each in New York and Tennessee, and 1 each in 18 other states and the District of Columbia. Thirteen percent of the people in the United States lived in these 38 cities and towns. Forty-three percent of New York state's population resided in New York City, and more than a third of Arizona's population lived in either Phoenix, Tucson, or

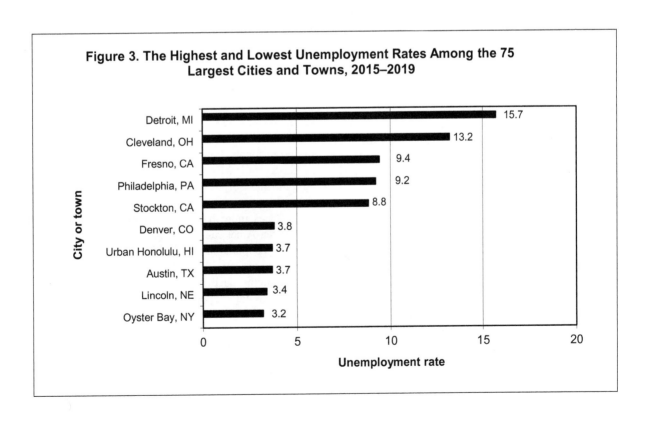

Figure 3. The Highest and Lowest Unemployment Rates Among the 75 Largest Cities and Towns, 2015–2019

Mesa. In California, 21 percent of the population live in its 6 largest cities, and Chicago's population counts for 21 percent of all residents of Illinois.

At the other end of the spectrum are places with very small populations. There were 78 cities, CDPs, or MCDs where no people were counted in the 2010 census. Only four of these were incorporated cities. Some are remote unpopulated MCDs; some are CDPs that had populations in 2000. Three incorporated places had zero population listed in the 2019 estimates: Carbonate, a ghost town in Colorado: Carlton Landing, a newly incorporated town developed in Oklahoma since the 2010 census, and Buffalo Chip, a campground area in South Dakota whose recent incorporation was later declared unlawful by the state Supreme Court. There were 30 incorporated places with 10 or fewer people in 2019. Although these were located in 13 states, there were 7 in South Dakota, 5 in North Dakota, 4 in Oklahoma, 3 in Nebraska, and 2 each in Idaho and Missouri.

Thirty-seven percent of the population of the United States lived outside of incorporated places, but this group included very rural locations as well as major metropolitan areas. In the decennial censuses, census designated places (CDPs) are defined to represent concentrations of population that are identifiable by name but not located in any incorporated place. There are no 2019 population estimates for CDPs but they are included in the American Community Survey (ACS). There has been increasing awareness that some of these CDPs are major residential and commercial centers. In 2000, the Office of Management and Budget issued new guidelines for defining metropolitan areas, and some unincorporated places are now identified as principal cities of metropolitan areas. For example, the CDP Bethesda, MD, together with the incorporated cities of Gaithersburg and Frederick, is now defined as a central city of the Bethesda-Gaithersburg-Frederick, MD Metropolitan Division, in the Washington-Arlington-Alexandria, DC-VA-MD-WV Metropolitan Statistical Area. In the 2010 census, the Bethesda CDP had a population of over 60,000. With a population of over 200,000, Arlington, Virginia—another principal city in this metropolitan area—is also a CDP because it is a county, not an incorporated city.

There are nine CDPs that had more than 100,000 people in 2010. The largest is Urban Honolulu, Hawaii's largest city—Hawaii has no incorporated places. Four of these large CDPs are in Nevada, in the Las Vegas metropolitan area—Enterprise, Paradise, Spring Valley, and Sunrise Manor. Others are large unincorporated places adjacent to large cities—East Los Angeles; Brandon, near St. Petersburg, Florida; Metairie, near New Orleans: and Arlington, Virginia. An additional 56 CDPs had populations of 50,000 or more in the 2010 census. Most of these were suburbs of major metropolitan areas.

Who lives in the cities and towns?

America's cities are home to diverse populations of varied ethnic and racial groups, differing age patterns, and large variations in education, income, and employment.

While 60.7 percent of Americans identified as White alone, not Hispanic or Latino, the 2015-2019 American Community Survey (ACS) estimated over 3,200 places where all of the residents were non-Hispanic White. These were very small towns and villages. Most had fewer than 100 residents and only a few towns had populations of 1,000 or more. More than 10,000 additional places had non-Hispanic white populations of 95 percent or more. Most of these places were very small but there were 9 with populations over 25,000, including The Villages in Florida with nearly 80,000 residents. Among the 75 largest cities, there are four with non-Hispanic White populations of 70 percent or more: Oyster Bay and Brookhaven, two suburban towns near New York City, Lexington-Fayette, Kentucky, and Portland, Oregon. About 10 percent of the residents of Detroit, Michigan and Santa Ana, California are non-Hispanic White.

The predominant ethnic and racial groups estimated by the ACS and included in this book are Hispanic or Latino (18 percent of the United States population); Black alone (12.3 percent); and Asian alone (5.5 percent). Because of small numbers, all other races are combined into a single group in this book: American Indian and Alaska native alone; Native Hawaiian and Other Pacific Islander alone; some other race alone; and two or more races, all not Hispanic or Latino. These combined groups make up 3.5 percent of the U.S. population.

There are 359 places where more than 95 percent of the residents are Latino. Though most are small cities or CDPs, 12 of them have more than 25,000 residents, including Laredo, Texas and Hialeah, Florida, both with more than 200,000 residents. Among the 75 largest cities, El Paso, Texas and Santa Ana, California have the largest concentrations of Latino residents, both close to 80 percent. The proportion is 73 percent in Miami, Florida, and over 60 percent in San Antonio and Corpus Christi, Texas.

In 86 places, more than 95 percent of the residents are Black or African-American. Only one of these—East St. Louis, IL—has a population over 25,000. Among the largest cities, 78 percent of Detroit's residents are Black, while Baltimore and Memphis have African-American populations of 62 and 64 percent, respectively. Black residents number just under 60 percent in New Orleans.

In Hawaii, 37 percent of the people are Asian alone, not of Hispanic or Latino origin. Another 29 percent are in the group that combines native Hawaiians with other racial groups. Twenty-nine places have Non-Hispanic Asian populations of more than 60 percent. While most of these are CDPs with small populations, nine of them are California cities with populations over 25,000. Among the 75 largest cities, Urban Honolulu's population is 52.3 percent Asian, while San Francisco and San Jose are both more than one-third Asian. The Asian population is below two percent in four of the largest cities, only one percent in Miami.

There are 356 cities where 90 percent or more of the residents are in the racial category that combines all other races and two or more races. These small places are mostly located on reservations and only a few have more than 5,000 residents. The largest are Tuba City, Arizona and Shiprock, New Mexico, both in the Navajo Nation, each with about 9,000 residents. Among the 75 largest cities, Urban Honolulu has the largest proportion at 23.1 percent. There, the group consists primarily of Native Hawaiians. Anchorage, Alaska and Tulsa, Oklahoma also have large proportions (18.2 and 11.1 percent respectively) and in those cities the group mainly represents American Indian and Alaskan Native populations.

During the years 2015 through 2019, 13.6 percent of the residents of the United States were born in foreign countries. Some cities have larger immigrant populations than others. In 56 cities—mostly medium-sized cities and CDPs—more than half of the people are foreign-born. About half of these cities are in Florida, and Miami has the highest proportion of the 75 largest cities (58.3 percent). California has 10 cities where more than half of the residents are foreign-born. Among the 75 largest cities, three California cities follow Miami: Santa Ana (43.3 percent), San Jose (39.7 percent), and Los Angeles (36.9 percent). Los Angeles and New York have virtually identical proportions of foreign-born residents—Los Angeles at 36.9 percent and New York at 36.8 percent—but New York has 3.1 million foreign-born residents, more than double the 1.5 million foreign-born residents in Los Angeles.

At the other extreme, there were a few thousand cities where one percent or fewer of the residents were born in foreign countries, including 66 cities with more than 10,000 residents. Among the 75 largest cities, there are five cities where foreign-born residents comprise less than 7 percent of their populations—New Orleans, Cleveland, Cincinnati, Memphis, and Detroit.

The working-age population can be defined to include persons aged 18 to 64, though certainly younger and older persons are often employed. This 18-to-64 age group comprises 61.8 percent of the United States population, while many cities have larger or smaller proportions of working-age adults. While there are about 100 small towns with more than 90 percent of their populations in this age group, the larger of these towns tend to have predominantly student or military populations. At the other extreme are some

small towns with fewer than 25 percent of their residents in the working-age group. Many of these are retirement and age-restricted communities like Sun City, Arizona and The Villages, FL. Among the 75 largest cities, Seattle and Boston both have about 73 percent of their residents in the 18-to-64 age group, and six other cities have levels of 70 percent or more. In Henderson, NV; Mesa, Arizona; and Stockton, California, the proportion is below 60 percent. Henderson and Mesa have high proportions of persons age 65 and older, while Stockton has a high proportion of persons under 18 years old.

Nationally, children under 18 comprise 22.6 percent of the population, but there are communities where more than 70 percent are children, while others have fewer than 10 percent. Most of these are very small cities and towns. Among places with more than 20,000 residents, there are a few where children make up about half of the population: Orthodox Jewish communities in New York and New Jersey, and suburban cities in Utah. Places with low proportions of children tend to have disproportionately large working-age populations or age-restricted retirement communities. Among the largest cities, four California cities have under-18 populations of 28 percent or more. Five have levels of 17 percent or less—generally the same cities with large working-age populations. People age 65 and older make up 15.6 percent of the population, with levels above 70 percent in some places, mainly in Florida and Arizona. Among the 75 largest cities, Urban Honolulu has the highest proportion of retirement-age people at 20 percent. Oyster Bay, NY and Henderson, NV also have high levels, at 19.4 and 18.6 percent.

Education levels vary greatly from city to city. 32.1 percent of persons age 25 and older have earned bachelor's degrees or higher, while 39 percent have never attended college. In 76 cities and towns, more than 90 percent of residents are college graduates, while hundreds of small towns and villages have college-graduate proportions below 5 percent. Of the 75 largest cities, Seattle has the highest proportion of college graduates at 64 percent, with Washington and San Francisco both above 58 percent. Seven more of these largest cities have levels over 50 percent. Stockton, Cleveland, Detroit, and Santa Ana, have college-graduate proportions of 20 percent or below. In Santa Ana, 63.4 percent of residents have no education beyond high school. In Cleveland, Detroit, Stockton, and Miami, more than half of the population have never attended college.

In the five-year period from 2015 through 2019, 63 percent of Americans age 16 and older were in the civilian labor force, and 5.3 percent of the labor force participants were unemployed. The 5.3 percent unemployment rate illustrates one of the issues inherent in using 5-year ACS data. The 2019 national unemployment rate measured by the 1-year ACS data was 4.5 percent, after steadily declining from a

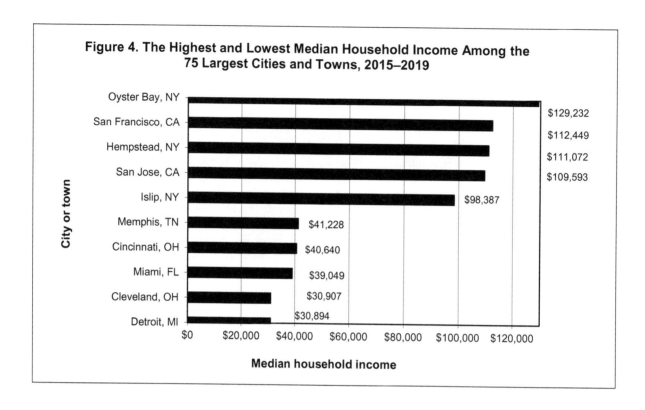

Figure 4. The Highest and Lowest Median Household Income Among the 75 Largest Cities and Towns, 2015–2019

Oyster Bay, NY — $129,232
San Francisco, CA — $112,449
Hempstead, NY — $111,072
San Jose, CA — $109,593
Islip, NY — $98,387
Memphis, TN — $41,228
Cincinnati, OH — $40,640
Miami, FL — $39,049
Cleveland, OH — $30,907
Detroit, MI — $30,894

City or town

Median household income

2015 rate of 6.3 percent. While the 5-year data masks these changes, there is no 1-year data for most of the cities in this book. The official unemployment rate for 2019 was 3.7 percent, as measured by the Current Population Survey.

Labor force participation was over 80 percent in 10 of the cities with populations of 10,000 or more, and 15 of the largest cities had civilian labor force participation of 70 percent or more, led by Minneapolis at 74.4 percent, with Austin and Seattle both over 73 percent. These three cities all had unemployment rates below the national rate of 5.3 percent, with Austin and Seattle well below at 3.7 and 4.1 percent. Three of the largest cities had labor force participation rates below 60 percent: Detroit, Cleveland, and Stockton. Detroit's unemployment rate in the 2015-2019 period was 15.7, the highest among the 75 largest cities, followed by Cleveland at 13.2 percent. Among the 75 largest cities, six had unemployment rates below 4 percent. Oyster Bay Town and Lincoln had the lowest unemployment rates at 3.2 and 3.4 percent.

In the years 2015 through 2019, the median household income in the United States was $62,843. Half of all households had incomes above this level, and half had lower incomes. The median income is calculated from income groupings of $2,500, but the top group is simply "$250,000 or more" so no recorded median is ever over $250,000. This "top code" is necessary to protect the confidentiality of the respondents and to minimize sampling

error because so few households are in this category. There were 47 cities with median incomes of $250,000 or more. Most were very small but five had populations over 10,000: Hillsborough, California; Winnetka, Illinois; Short Hills, New Jersey; Scarsdale, New York; and West University Place, Texas. Among the 75 largest cities, there are four with median incomes over $100,000, topped by Oyster Bay town, New York with a median income of $129,232. The three others are San Francisco and San Jose, California; and Hempstead town, New York. Among cities with populations of 10,000 or more, there are 19 with median incomes below $25,000. Among the 75 largest cities, Detroit and Cleveland had median incomes of just over $30,000.

In 2019, the average poverty threshold for a family of four was $26,172. It can be higher or lower depending on the number of persons in the household. Households with incomes below this level are considered to be in poverty. This poverty-level threshold has no regional variations, though the cost of living can vary dramatically from city to city throughout the nation. Nationally, 12.9 percent of households had incomes below the poverty level. In 7 cities of 10,000 or more population, more than 45 percent of the households had incomes below the poverty level. Some of these are university towns with large student populations. Among the 75 largest cities, Detroit had the highest proportion, at 32.8 percent, followed by Cleveland at 30.9 percent, while Miami, Cincinnati, and New Orleans were only slightly lower. Ten of the largest cities had poverty rates below 10 percent, with Oyster Bay the lowest at 4.6 percent.

Most Americans live in households, and nearly two-thirds of those households are occupied by their owners. The median value of owner-occupied housing units was $2,000,000 or more in 10 cities, all of them in California. The median value was below $50,000 in 12 cities, about half of them in Michigan. Of the 75 largest cities, 13 had median housing values above $500,000 and only Detroit and Cleveland had values below $100,000. San Francisco's median housing value was the highest at $1,097,800.

Access to a computer became more important during the pandemic and about 90 percent of Americans had access to a computer in their households. More than 500 small cities appeared to have 100 percent access, while 20 cities showed computer access for less than a third of their residents. All of the 75 largest cities had computer access levels of 80 percent or higher. More than 95 percent of residents in 6 cities had computers, topped by Plano at 97.7 percent. Memphis had the lowest level among these largest cities, at 80.6 percent.

About two-thirds of all households are family households—people living in the same household who are related by birth, marriage, or adoption. Among cities with populations over 10,000, there are 28 where more than 90 percent of households are family households. These are varied cities, including suburban towns, CDPs with military bases, Orthodox Jewish communities, and cities near the Mexican border. Of the 75 largest cities, Santa Ana, California has the highest proportion of family households at 81.7 percent, and the New York suburbs of Oyster Bay, Hempstead, and Islip all had rates over 75 percent. In a few cities—mostly college towns—family households make up less than 30 percent of all households. Among the largest cities, there are 11 where fewer than half of all households are family households, with Pittsburgh and Atlanta the lowest, both at 42.2 percent.

Persons living alone comprise 27.9 percent of households. Of the cities with 10,000 or more residents, there are 5 where more than half of the households consist of a single person, topped by Laguna Woods and West Hollywood, California, both about 60 percent. One-person households make up more than 40 percent of households in 9 of the 75 largest cities. Atlanta, New Orleans, and St. Louis have the highest levels, all above 45 percent.

What happens in cities and towns?

The FBI's Uniform Crime Reporting (UCR) Program compiles information on crime in the nation. Since the 1930s, they have published data received from over 18,000 city, university/college, county, state, tribal, and federal law enforcement agencies voluntarily participating in the program. Data are not available for many of the cities in this book—they may not have a separate law enforcement agency, they may not participate, or the data may represent only a portion of the entity used here. Nationally in 2018, there were 369 violent crimes and 2200 property crimes per 100,000 persons. In the largest cities—those that were in the database--violent crime ranged from a high of 2008 per 100,000 people in Detroit to a low of 117 per 100,000 in Virginia Beach. Property crime ranged from highs of over 6000 in Memphis and Albuquerque to lows of about 1500 in New York and El Paso.

Data on construction authorized by building permits is compiled by the Census Bureau for about 19,000 permit-issuing places in the United States. Los Angeles and Houston, had the highest construction values at 3.3 and 2.5 billion dollars in 2019, followed by Austin at 2.2 billion and Phoenix at 1.9 billion. Brookhaven had the lowest value of the largest cities, at 1.6 million.

Per capita local taxes are highest in Washington, DC because it has the functions of both a state and a city. Among the largest cities, New York has the highest local taxes, at $6,555, but residents of Nantucket, Massachusetts and three Connecticut cities pay higher per capita local taxes. Among the largest cities, the lowest per capita local taxes are under $400 for residents of Las Vegas and Brookhaven.

As shown in Table 4, the Economic Census provides information about 124,616,999 private nonfarm employees in 18 sectors. Table B includes the number of establishments and employees in each of the cities with 10,000 or more residents. Nationally, Health Care and Social Assistance is the sector with the most employees—16.5 percent of the total—followed by Retail Trade with 12.8 percent. Accommodation and Food Services (11.2 percent), Administrative and Support and Waste Management (9.5 percent) and Manufacturing (9.2 percent) also have large proportions. Each of the other sectors represents less than 8 percent of the national workforce.

Because of its large population, New York City has the most employees in most sectors. For employees in the information sector, San Francisco, Atlanta, Seattle, Boston, and Washington rank considerably higher than their population ranks. The same cities show unusually high proportions of employees in the Professional, Scientific, and Technical sector.

At the state level, Wisconsin and Indiana have nearly double the national proportion of manufacturing employees, both over 18 percent. Wyoming has the highest employment in Mining, Quarrying, and Oil and Gas Extraction, at 9 percent, while this sector represents less than one percent of employment in most states. In Delaware, 11.4 percent of employees work in Finance and Insurance, about double the national level and that of many states. The Accommodation and Food Service sector employs one quarter of Nevada's workforce, compared with 11.2 percent nationally.

SUBJECTS COVERED

A summary of the subjects covered in Tables A and B appears on page xxxv. Page xxxvi show the complete column headings for each table.

RANKINGS

A Rankings section ranks the 75 largest cities by population, land area, population density, population change, race, Hispanic origin, age, education, income, poverty rate, unemployment rate, employee numbers, violent crime rate, and per capita local taxes.

SYMBOLS

D Indicates that the number has been withheld to avoid disclosure of information pertaining to a specific organization or individual, or because the number does not meet statistical standards for publication.

NA Indicates that data are not available.

X Indicates that data are not applicable or are not meaningful for this geographic unit.

In this volume, where a figure is less than half the unit of measure shown, it will appear as zero.

SOURCES

The data in this volume have been obtained from federal government sources. For a complete list of sources, see Appendix B.

Data included in this volume meet the publication standards established by the U.S. Census Bureau and the other federal statistical agencies from which they were obtained. Every effort has been made to select data that are accurate, meaningful, and useful. All data from censuses, surveys, and administrative records are subject to errors arising from factors such as sampling variability, reporting errors, incomplete coverage, nonresponse, imputations, and processing error. Responsibility of the editors and publishers of this volume is limited to reasonable care in the reproduction and presentation of data obtained from sources believed to be reliable.

Table 1. Population by Residence in Incorporated Places and Size of Place, 2019

State	Total Population	500,000 or more	100,000 to 499,999	50,000 to 99,999	10,000 to 49,999	Less than 10,000	Total in incorporated places	Not in incorporated places
United States	328,239,523	44,768,257	50,392,803	32,591,762	50,629,119	28,502,908	206,884,849	121,354,674
Alabama	4,903,185		898,351	327,006	1,017,184	756,446	2,998,987	1,904,198
Alaska	731,545		288,000		73,729	136,105	497,834	233,711
Arizona	7,278,717	2,747,077	1,539,159	645,228	671,626	188,317	5,791,407	1,487,310
Arkansas	3,017,804		197,312	592,119	611,996	599,725	2,001,152	1,016,652
California	39,512,223	8,351,971	11,726,759	7,300,375	5,077,135	509,367	32,965,607	6,546,616
Colorado	5,758,736	727,211	1,999,210	496,726	605,765	450,139	4,279,051	1,479,685
Connecticut	3,565,287		633,960	473,162	249,158	23,163	1,379,443	2,185,844
Delaware	973,764			70,166	118,126	87,824	276,116	697,648
District of Columbia	705,749	705,749					705,749	0
Florida	21,477,737	911,507	3,949,442	2,553,749	2,657,969	700,625	10,773,292	10,704,445
Georgia	10,617,423	506,811	927,645	779,904	1,615,342	855,630	4,685,332	5,932,091
Hawaii	1,415,872		345,064				345,064	1,070,808
Idaho	1,787,065		343,120	379,894	296,003	238,611	1,257,628	529,437
Illinois	12,671,821	2,693,976	974,655	1,375,891	4,185,229	1,810,753	11,040,504	1,631,317
Indiana	6,732,219	876,384	591,475	922,436	1,281,084	834,295	4,505,674	2,226,545
Iowa	3,155,070		449,389	546,669	636,573	891,924	2,524,555	630,515
Kansas	2,913,314		1,004,247	274,229	540,411	599,872	2,418,759	494,555
Kentucky	4,467,673	617,638	323,152	130,674	707,558	694,053	2,473,075	1,994,598
Louisiana	4,648,794		923,677	212,895	538,653	504,037	2,179,262	2,469,532
Maine	1,344,212			66,215	234,453	75,732	376,400	967,812
Maryland	6,045,680	593,490		266,951	364,792	303,627	1,528,860	4,516,820
Massachusetts	6,892,503	692,600	568,958	1,365,104	1,010,096		3,636,758	3,255,745
Michigan	9,986,857	670,031	705,584	1,286,283	1,413,040	976,768	5,051,706	4,935,151
Minnesota	5,639,632		856,637	1,095,212	1,695,379	1,018,260	4,665,488	974,144
Mississippi	2,976,149		160,628	127,485	808,352	409,080	1,505,545	1,470,604
Missouri	6,137,428		1,203,652	549,851	1,252,250	1,061,837	4,067,590	2,069,838
Montana	1,068,778		109,577	133,950	141,727	195,719	580,973	487,805
Nebraska	1,934,408		767,294	104,811	243,898	384,336	1,500,339	434,069
Nevada	3,080,156	651,319	932,770	55,916	77,861	34,339	1,752,205	1,327,951
New Hampshire	1,359,711		112,673	89,355	217,311	8,686	428,025	931,686
New Jersey	8,882,190		818,535	830,988	1,659,452	924,798	4,233,773	4,648,417
New Mexico	2,096,829	560,513	103,432	183,861	369,480	184,963	1,402,249	694,580
New York	19,453,561	8,336,817	803,676	480,607	1,525,640	1,256,608	12,403,348	7,050,213
North Carolina	10,488,084	885,708	1,916,191	773,138	1,409,415	977,749	5,962,201	4,525,883
North Dakota	762,062		124,662	129,368	174,442	164,234	592,706	169,356
Ohio	11,689,100	898,553	1,295,732	557,760	3,485,466	1,366,836	7,604,347	4,084,753
Oklahoma	3,956,971	655,057	636,268	356,840	731,514	664,474	3,044,153	912,818
Oregon	4,217,737	654,741	665,917	415,047	809,821	418,219	2,963,745	1,253,992
Pennsylvania	12,801,989	1,584,064	421,728	395,616	1,116,424	2,068,427	5,586,259	7,215,730
Rhode Island	1,059,361		179,883	234,577	133,271		547,731	511,630
South Carolina	5,148,714		384,622	289,916	763,936	427,088	1,865,562	3,283,152
South Dakota	884,659		183,793	77,503	175,334	189,529	626,159	258,500
Tennessee	6,829,174	1,321,893	675,448	491,500	946,465	661,734	4,097,040	2,732,134
Texas	28,995,881	7,781,315	5,857,065	1,943,536	3,660,128	2,105,726	21,347,770	7,648,111
Utah	3,205,958		568,913	820,049	1,223,915	386,534	2,999,411	206,547
Vermont	623,989				88,254	61,846	150,100	473,889
Virginia	8,535,519		1,641,150	474,560	622,669	353,116	3,091,495	5,444,024
Washington	7,614,893	753,675	1,219,140	1,157,875	1,343,989	495,830	4,970,509	2,644,384
West Virginia	1,792,147			285,375	322,520		607,895	1,184,252
Wisconsin	5,822,434	590,157	364,258	634,599	1,611,364	997,922	4,198,300	1,624,134
Wyoming	578,759			122,166	150,065	125,485	397,716	181,043

Table 2. Percent of Population in Incorporated Places, by Size of Place, 2019

State	Total Population	500,000 or more	100,000 to 499,999	50,000 to 99,999	10,000 to 49,999	Less than 10,000	Total in incorporated places	Not in incorporated places
United States............	100.0	13.6	15.4	9.9	15.4	8.7	63.0	37.0
Alabama	100.0	0.0	18.3	6.7	20.7	15.4	61.2	38.8
Alaska......................	100.0	0.0	39.4	0.0	10.1	18.6	68.1	31.9
Arizona	100.0	37.7	21.1	8.9	9.2	2.6	79.6	20.4
Arkansas...................	100.0	0.0	6.5	19.6	20.3	19.9	66.3	33.7
California	100.0	21.1	29.7	18.5	12.8	1.3	83.4	16.6
Colorado...................	100.0	12.6	34.7	8.6	10.5	7.8	74.3	25.7
Connecticut...............	100.0	0.0	17.8	13.3	7.0	0.6	38.7	61.3
Delaware	100.0	0.0	0.0	7.2	12.1	9.0	28.4	71.6
District of Columbia	100.0	100.0	0.0	0.0	0.0	0.0	100.0	0.0
Florida......................	100.0	4.2	18.4	11.9	12.4	3.3	50.2	49.8
Georgia.....................	100.0	4.8	8.7	7.3	15.2	8.1	44.1	55.9
Hawaii	100.0	0.0	24.4	0.0	0.0	0.0	24.4	75.6
Idaho........................	100.0	0.0	19.2	21.3	16.6	13.4	70.4	29.6
Illinois......................	100.0	21.3	7.7	10.9	33.0	14.3	87.1	12.9
Indiana	100.0	13.0	8.8	13.7	19.0	12.4	66.9	33.1
Iowa.........................	100.0	0.0	14.2	17.3	20.2	28.3	80.0	20.0
Kansas......................	100.0	0.0	34.5	9.4	18.5	20.6	83.0	17.0
Kentucky	100.0	13.8	7.2	2.9	15.8	15.5	55.4	44.6
Louisiana	100.0	0.0	19.9	4.6	11.6	10.8	46.9	53.1
Maine........................	100.0	0.0	0.0	4.9	17.4	5.6	28.0	72.0
Maryland....................	100.0	9.8	0.0	4.4	6.0	5.0	25.3	74.7
Massachusetts............	100.0	10.0	8.3	19.8	14.7	0.0	52.8	47.2
Michigan	100.0	6.7	7.1	12.9	14.1	9.8	50.6	49.4
Minnesota..................	100.0	0.0	15.2	19.4	30.1	18.1	82.7	17.3
Mississippi	100.0	0.0	5.4	4.3	27.2	13.7	50.6	49.4
Missouri	100.0	0.0	19.6	9.0	20.4	17.3	66.3	33.7
Montana....................	100.0	0.0	10.3	12.5	13.3	18.3	54.4	45.6
Nebraska	100.0	0.0	39.7	5.4	12.6	19.9	77.6	22.4
Nevada	100.0	21.1	30.3	1.8	2.5	1.1	56.9	43.1
New Hampshire...........	100.0	0.0	8.3	6.6	16.0	0.6	31.5	68.5
New Jersey.................	100.0	0.0	9.2	9.4	18.7	10.4	47.7	52.3
New Mexico	100.0	26.7	4.9	8.8	17.6	8.8	66.9	33.1
New York....................	100.0	42.9	4.1	2.5	7.8	6.5	63.8	36.2
North Carolina	100.0	8.4	18.3	7.4	13.4	9.3	56.8	43.2
North Dakota	100.0	0.0	16.4	17.0	22.9	21.6	77.8	22.2
Ohio.........................	100.0	7.7	11.1	4.8	29.8	11.7	65.1	34.9
Oklahoma	100.0	16.6	16.1	9.0	18.5	16.8	76.9	23.1
Oregon......................	100.0	15.5	15.8	9.8	19.2	9.9	70.3	29.7
Pennsylvania	100.0	12.4	3.3	3.1	8.7	16.2	43.6	56.4
Rhode Island	100.0	0.0	17.0	22.1	12.6	0.0	51.7	48.3
South Carolina...........	100.0	0.0	7.5	5.6	14.8	8.3	36.2	63.8
South Dakota.............	100.0	0.0	20.8	8.8	19.8	21.4	70.8	29.2
Tennessee	100.0	19.4	9.9	7.2	13.9	9.7	60.0	40.0
Texas	100.0	26.8	20.2	6.7	12.6	7.3	73.6	26.4
Utah.........................	100.0	0.0	17.7	25.6	38.2	12.1	93.6	6.4
Vermont	100.0	0.0	0.0	0.0	14.1	9.9	24.1	75.9
Virginia.....................	100.0	0.0	19.2	5.6	7.3	4.1	36.2	63.8
Washington................	100.0	9.9	16.0	15.2	17.6	6.5	65.3	34.7
West Virginia..............	100.0	0.0	0.0	0.0	15.9	18.0	33.9	66.1
Wisconsin	100.0	10.1	6.3	10.9	27.7	17.1	72.1	27.9
Wyoming....................	100.0	0.0	0.0	21.1	25.9	21.7	68.7	31.3

Table 3. Population Change in the 75 Largest Cities and Towns, 2010–2019

Population rank 2019	City	Population 2019	Population 2010	Population rank 2010	Percent Change 2010–2019
1	New York city, New York	8,336,817	8,175,031	1	2.0
2	Los Angeles city, California	3,979,576	3,793,139	2	4.9
3	Chicago city, Illinois	2,693,976	2,695,652	3	-0.1
4	Houston city, Texas	2,320,268	2,095,517	4	10.7
5	Phoenix city, Arizona	1,680,992	1,446,691	6	16.2
6	Philadelphia city, Pennsylvania	1,584,064	1,526,012	5	3.8
7	San Antonio city, Texas	1,547,253	1,326,161	7	16.7
8	San Diego city, California	1,423,851	1,301,929	8	9.4
9	Dallas city, Texas	1,343,573	1,197,658	9	12.2
10	San Jose city, California	1,021,795	952,528	10	7.3
11	Austin city, Texas	978,908	801,829	14	22.1
12	Jacksonville city, Florida	911,507	821,750	11	10.9
13	Fort Worth city, Texas	909,585	744,824	17	22.1
14	Columbus city, Ohio	898,553	789,018	15	13.9
15	Charlotte city, North Carolina	885,708	735,607	18	20.4
16	San Francisco city, California	881,549	805,184	13	9.5
17	Indianapolis city (balance), Indiana	876,384	820,457	12	6.8
18	Hempstead town, New York	766,980	759,793	16	0.9
19	Seattle city, Washington	753,675	608,661	24	23.8
20	Denver city, Colorado	727,211	599,825	27	21.2
21	Washington city, District of Columbia	705,749	601,767	26	17.3
22	Boston city, Massachusetts	692,600	617,792	23	12.1
23	El Paso city, Texas	681,728	648,245	21	5.2
24	Nashville-Davidson metropolitan government, Tennessee	670,820	603,438	25	11.2
25	Detroit city, Michigan	670,031	713,898	19	-6.1
26	Oklahoma City city, Oklahoma	655,057	580,462	32	12.9
27	Portland city, Oregon	654,741	583,793	31	12.2
28	Las Vegas city, Nevada	651,319	584,489	30	11.4
29	Memphis city, Tennessee	651,073	651,873	20	-0.1
30	Louisville/Jefferson County metro government, Kentucky	617,638	595,710	28	3.7
31	Baltimore city, Maryland	593,490	620,770	22	-4.4
32	Milwaukee city, Wisconsin	590,157	594,498	29	-0.7
33	Albuquerque city, New Mexico	560,513	546,153	33	2.6
34	Tucson city, Arizona	548,073	526,634	34	4.1
35	Fresno city, California	531,576	497,172	35	6.9
36	Mesa city, Arizona	518,012	440,092	41	17.7
37	Sacramento city, California	513,624	466,383	37	10.1
38	Atlanta city, Georgia	506,811	427,059	43	18.7
39	Kansas City city, Missouri	495,327	459,902	39	7.7
40	Brookhaven town, New York	480,763	486,336	36	-1.1
41	Colorado Springs city, Colorado	478,221	417,447	44	14.6
42	Omaha city, Nebraska	478,192	458,989	40	4.2
43	Raleigh city, North Carolina	474,069	404,068	45	17.3
44	Miami city, Florida	467,963	399,481	46	17.1
45	Long Beach city, California	462,628	462,221	38	0.1
46	Virginia Beach city, Virginia	449,974	437,903	42	2.8
47	Oakland city, California	433,031	390,765	49	10.8
48	Minneapolis city, Minnesota	429,606	382,603	50	12.3
49	Tulsa city, Oklahoma	401,190	392,004	48	2.3
50	Tampa city, Florida	399,700	336,150	56	18.9
51	Arlington city, Texas	398,854	365,098	52	9.2
52	New Orleans city, Louisiana	390,144	343,828	54	13.5
53	Wichita city, Kansas	389,938	382,437	51	2.0
54	Bakersfield city, California	384,145	347,817	53	10.4
55	Cleveland city, Ohio	381,009	396,665	47	-3.9
56	Aurora city, Colorado	379,289	324,659	60	16.8
57	Anaheim city, California	350,365	336,109	57	4.2
58	Urban Honolulu CDP, Hawaii	345,064	337,721	55	2.2
59	Santa Ana city, California	332,318	324,774	59	2.3
60	Riverside city, California	331,360	303,933	64	9.0
61	Islip town, New York	329,610	335,298	58	-1.7
62	Corpus Christi city, Texas	326,586	305,226	63	7.0
63	Lexington-Fayette urban county, Kentucky	323,152	295,870	66	9.2
64	Henderson city, Nevada	320,189	257,001	77	24.6
65	Stockton city, California	312,697	292,182	68	7.0
66	St. Paul city, Minnesota	308,096	285,112	71	8.1
67	Cincinnati city, Ohio	303,940	297,025	65	2.3
68	St. Louis city, Missouri	300,576	319,289	61	-5.9
69	Pittsburgh city, Pennsylvania	300,286	305,245	62	-1.6
70	Oyster Bay town, New York	298,391	293,576	67	1.6
71	Greensboro city, North Carolina	296,710	268,936	73	10.3
72	Lincoln city, Nebraska	289,102	258,794	76	11.7
73	Anchorage municipality, Alaska	288,000	291,836	69	-1.3
74	Plano city, Texas	287,677	259,859	75	10.7
75	Orlando city, Florida	287,442	238,836	83	20.4

Table 4. Percent of Private Nonfarm Employment by Industry by State, 2017

State	Private nonfarm employment measured in Economic Census	Percentage of employment by sector							
		Mining, quarrying, and oil and gas extraction	Utilities	Construction	Manufacturing	Wholesale trade	Retail trade	Transportation and ware-housing	Information
United States..................	124,616,999	0.5	0.5	5.3	9.2	5.0	12.8	4.0	2.9
Alabama	1,612,755	0.3	0.8	5.1	15.2	4.7	14.3	3.8	2.1
Alaska*	263,168	4.2	0.8	6.6	4.8	3.3	13.1	7.2	2.5
Arizona*	2,390,553	0.4	0.5	6.3	6.0	4.1	13.6	3.9	2.3
Arkansas.........................	996,438	0.4	0.8	4.6	15.3	5.0	14.3	5.2	2.1
California	14,643,146	0.1	0.4	5.3	7.9	5.9	11.8	3.7	4.6
Colorado	2,302,665	1.1	0.4	7.1	5.3	4.5	12.2	3.1	4.0
Connecticut.....................	1,471,901	0.0	0.6	4.0	10.7	5.2	12.7	3.1	2.9
Delaware*	388,289	0.0	0.7	5.5	7.1	4.5	15.0	2.7	1.8
District of Columbia	488,786	0.0	0.4	2.1	0.2	0.9	4.7	0.8	4.9
Florida.............................	8,105,705	0.0	0.3	5.2	3.7	4.0	13.4	3.3	2.2
Georgia...........................	3,743,509	0.1	0.6	4.8	9.9	5.4	13.0	5.2	3.5
Hawaii*	519,528	0.0	0.7	6.2	2.3	3.7	14.0	6.1	1.6
Idaho...............................	557,497	0.5	0.7	7.3	10.5	5.4	14.8	3.4	2.4
Illinois.............................	5,325,531	0.1	0.6	4.0	9.9	6.3	11.8	4.9	2.5
Indiana............................	2,652,947	0.2	0.6	5.0	18.7	4.6	12.7	4.8	1.8
Iowa	1,295,196	0.2	0.6	5.3	16.3	5.5	14.0	4.4	2.3
Kansas............................	1,155,062	0.6	0.6	5.8	13.5	5.5	13.0	5.0	2.6
Kentucky.........................	1,560,473	0.6	0.6	4.7	15.0	4.6	14.4	6.0	1.9
Louisiana	1,618,613	2.1	0.7	8.6	7.3	4.6	14.4	4.2	1.5
Maine*	489,335	0.0	0.5	5.4	9.9	3.8	16.7	3.5	2.3
Maryland..........................	2,257,496	0.0	0.5	6.9	4.3	4.0	12.9	3.3	2.4
Massachusetts.................	3,147,041	0.0	0.4	4.5	7.4	4.9	11.6	2.9	4.0
Michigan	3,766,830	0.1	0.7	4.0	15.5	4.9	12.5	3.1	1.9
Minnesota	2,603,120	0.2	0.5	4.8	11.9	5.6	11.6	3.4	2.4
Mississippi	890,850	0.4	1.1	4.8	15.5	4.2	15.9	4.5	1.6
Missouri	2,414,947	0.1	0.6	5.4	10.7	5.2	12.9	3.7	2.5
Montana*	368,977	1.5	0.8	7.0	4.9	4.0	16.0	3.2	2.3
Nebraska	801,219	0.1	0.1	5.9	11.7	5.2	13.7	3.7	2.6
Nevada*	1,201,153	1.1	0.4	6.5	3.7	3.2	12.1	4.6	1.5
New Hampshire*..............	573,200	0.1	0.6	4.9	11.4	4.6	16.9	2.4	2.9
New Jersey......................	3,646,674	0.0	0.6	4.5	6.0	7.9	12.9	4.9	2.6
New Mexico*....................	611,162	2.8	0.6	6.6	3.8	3.2	15.1	3.0	2.1
New York.........................	8,029,502	0.0	0.5	4.7	5.1	4.7	11.8	3.2	3.7
North Carolina	3,617,772	0.1	0.6	5.4	11.7	5.4	13.7	3.5	2.6
North Dakota*	339,082	5.3	1.1	7.1	7.1	6.8	14.6	5.1	2.1
Ohio	4,667,086	0.2	0.5	4.2	14.0	5.1	12.6	4.1	2.2
Oklahoma	1,311,609	3.2	0.8	5.6	9.4	4.5	13.8	3.9	2.2
Oregon............................	1,539,242	0.1	0.5	6.2	11.2	5.1	13.7	3.9	2.6
Pennsylvania	5,102,761	0.5	0.6	4.8	10.5	5.1	13.0	4.5	2.2
Rhode Island*	408,347	0.0	0.3	4.6	9.8	5.2	11.9	2.7	1.7
South Carolina................	1,805,382	0.1	0.7	4.8	12.5	4.0	14.0	3.5	2.1
South Dakota..................	348,344	0.3	0.6	5.9	12.3	5.4	15.3	2.9	2.1
Tennessee	2,529,001	0.1	0.1	4.4	12.7	4.7	12.7	5.9	2.0
Texas	10,425,151	2.0	0.6	6.9	7.3	5.1	12.5	4.7	2.4
Utah	1,223,257	0.7	0.3	6.9	9.9	4.5	12.6	5.1	4.3
Vermont*.........................	240,289	0.2	0.5	5.7	11.9	4.6	16.0	2.5	3.4
Virginia............................	3,227,534	0.2	0.5	5.8	7.2	3.3	13.3	3.2	3.3
Washington......................	2,729,865	0.1	0.3	7.1	9.6	5.1	12.7	3.7	5.1
West Virginia...................	532,966	3.6	1.3	4.5	9.1	3.4	15.6	2.8	1.9
Wisconsin	2,486,934	0.2	0.5	4.5	18.3	4.9	12.8	4.2	2.4
Wyoming*	201,948	9.0	1.3	8.9	4.6	3.4	14.7	4.9	2.1

* Includes one or more sectors where the number of employees was withheld to avoid disclosure. For those sectors, a range of employees was used. In this table, the midpoint of the range was used to derive an estimate.

Table 4. Percent of Private Nonfarm Employment by Industry by State, 2017—Continued

State	Percentage of employment by sector									
	Finance and insurance	Real estate and rental and leasing	Professional, scientific, and technical services	Management of companies and enterprises	Administrative and support and waste management and remediation services	Educational services	Health care and social assistance	Arts, entertainment, and recreation	Accommodation and food services	Other services (except public administration)
United States..................	5.2	1.8	7.2	2.9	9.5	0.6	16.5	1.9	11.2	3.0
Alabama	4.5	1.4	6.3	1.4	8.9	0.3	16.0	1.1	11.4	2.4
Alaska*............................	2.8	1.8	6.8	2.8	7.2	0.6	19.8	2.1	11.0	2.8
Arizona*..........................	6.7	2.0	6.1	3.1	11.0	0.6	15.9	2.0	12.5	2.9
Arkansas.........................	3.8	1.3	3.8	4.5	6.5	0.2	18.3	1.0	10.7	2.1
California	4.4	2.1	8.5	2.5	10.7	0.8	14.0	2.4	11.9	3.0
Colorado.........................	4.8	2.1	8.4	2.8	11.3	0.8	13.9	2.5	12.6	3.2
Connecticut.....................	7.9	1.4	7.4	2.4	6.1	0.7	20.0	2.1	10.0	3.2
Delaware*.......................	11.4	1.6	7.7	1.8	7.1	0.5	17.6	2.2	10.3	2.6
District of Columbia	3.9	2.3	22.1	1.7	7.3	1.4	15.2	2.0	14.9	15.1
Florida.............................	4.6	2.2	6.3	1.9	21.3	0.5	13.9	2.6	11.8	2.7
Georgia...........................	5.0	1.7	7.1	3.7	10.3	0.4	13.9	1.4	11.4	2.6
Hawaii*...........................	3.8	2.5	4.4	1.4	10.7	0.6	14.2	2.3	21.7	3.9
Idaho...............................	4.1	1.3	6.0	1.9	7.7	0.4	17.6	1.7	11.7	2.5
Illinois.............................	5.8	1.6	7.6	4.6	9.4	0.6	15.4	1.7	10.1	3.2
Indiana............................	3.9	1.3	4.6	2.2	7.9	0.4	16.5	1.4	10.6	2.8
Iowa	7.5	1.1	4.1	2.1	6.1	0.4	16.8	1.4	9.6	2.4
Kansas............................	5.3	1.3	5.7	2.3	7.3	0.4	17.0	1.5	10.3	2.4
Kentucky.........................	5.0	1.2	4.3	2.4	7.0	0.2	17.2	1.3	11.2	2.4
Louisiana	4.1	1.8	5.9	1.9	6.4	0.4	18.7	1.6	13.3	2.7
Maine*	5.5	1.5	4.8	1.5	5.0	0.5	23.0	1.6	11.4	3.0
Maryland..........................	4.5	2.2	12.6	2.8	9.9	0.7	17.0	1.9	10.5	3.6
Massachusetts.................	6.3	1.7	9.9	3.3	7.0	0.9	20.2	2.1	9.9	3.2
Michigan	4.5	1.5	7.5	3.2	8.9	0.4	16.7	1.3	10.6	2.8
Minnesota	6.4	1.5	7.2	5.1	6.6	0.7	18.2	1.9	9.2	3.0
Mississippi	3.8	1.1	3.4	1.0	5.9	0.2	19.0	0.9	14.6	2.1
Missouri..........................	5.9	1.5	6.7	4.1	7.3	0.4	17.5	1.7	10.9	2.8
Montana*.........................	4.3	1.6	4.8	1.0	7.9	0.5	19.9	2.8	14.2	3.3
Nebraska	8.5	1.4	4.9	2.7	8.1	0.4	16.9	1.9	9.5	2.7
Nevada*..........................	3.2	2.5	5.0	3.1	10.0	0.5	11.0	2.7	26.6	2.4
New Hampshire*..............	5.1	1.4	5.7	1.3	9.8	0.8	16.5	2.2	10.4	3.1
New Jersey......................	5.4	1.7	8.9	3.4	9.6	1.0	16.8	1.8	8.7	3.1
New Mexico*....................	4.1	1.5	9.3	1.1	5.7	0.4	20.9	2.0	15.0	2.9
New York.........................	7.0	2.4	8.3	2.4	8.3	0.8	20.6	2.3	10.3	3.7
North Carolina	5.3	1.6	6.1	2.7	7.8	0.6	16.7	1.9	11.9	2.6
North Dakota*..................	5.3	1.6	4.4	1.3	4.1	0.3	18.4	1.6	10.8	2.9
Ohio.................................	5.6	1.3	5.4	3.4	8.2	0.4	18.4	1.6	10.2	2.7
Oklahoma	4.5	1.7	5.4	3.0	7.8	0.3	17.3	2.0	12.2	2.4
Oregon............................	4.1	1.9	6.0	3.4	7.0	0.6	17.1	1.9	11.9	2.8
Pennsylvania	5.5	1.3	6.7	3.3	6.6	0.5	20.3	2.0	9.4	3.2
Rhode Island*.................	6.6	1.3	5.9	4.3	5.7	0.5	21.4	2.1	12.4	3.4
South Carolina................	4.1	1.5	5.6	1.4	15.3	0.3	13.5	1.6	12.4	2.6
South Dakota...................	7.5	1.2	3.8	2.3	3.4	0.2	20.6	2.0	11.7	2.5
Tennessee.......................	5.1	1.4	4.6	4.0	10.1	0.4	16.4	1.5	11.4	2.4
Texas	5.3	1.9	7.1	3.2	9.7	0.5	15.2	1.5	11.5	2.7
Utah................................	5.5	1.6	7.6	2.2	11.8	0.8	12.0	2.3	9.7	2.4
Vermont*.........................	3.6	1.2	5.2	0.7	3.6	0.8	20.1	3.2	13.7	3.1
Virginia............................	4.8	1.7	14.6	2.4	8.4	0.7	14.1	1.9	11.1	3.7
Washington......................	3.8	2.0	7.9	4.0	6.0	0.7	16.1	2.4	10.6	2.9
West Virginia...................	3.1	1.1	4.3	1.0	6.3	0.2	24.9	1.3	12.8	2.8
Wisconsin	5.9	1.1	4.3	3.1	6.4	0.4	16.8	1.9	9.8	2.5
Wyoming*........................	3.5	2.4	4.7	0.9	3.4	0.6	16.6	2.4	13.5	3.1

* Includes one or more sectors where the number of employees was withheld to avoid disclosure. For those sectors, a range of employees was used. In this table, the midpoint of the range was used to derive an estimate.

75 Largest Cities and Towns by 2019 Population
Selected Rankings

	Population, 2019			Land area, 2010		
Population rank	City	Population [Table A col 2]	Population rank	Land Area rank	City	Land area (square miles) [Table B col 1]
1	New York city, New York	8,336,817	73	1	Anchorage municipality, Alaska	1,706.80
2	Los Angeles city, California	3,979,576	12	2	Jacksonville city, Florida	747.47
3	Chicago city, Illinois	2,693,976	4	3	Houston city, Texas	640.19
4	Houston city, Texas	2,320,268	26	4	Oklahoma City city, Oklahoma	606.45
5	Phoenix city, Arizona	1,680,992	5	5	Phoenix city, Arizona	517.67
6	Philadelphia city, Pennsylvania	1,584,064	7	6	San Antonio city, Texas	485.11
7	San Antonio city, Texas	1,547,253	24	7	Nashville-Davidson metropolitan government	475.54
8	San Diego city, California	1,423,851	2	8	Los Angeles city, California	468.96
9	Dallas city, Texas	1,343,573	17	9	Indianapolis city (balance), Indiana	361.57
10	San Jose city, California	1,021,795	13	10	Fort Worth city, Texas	345.58
11	Austin city, Texas	978,908	9	11	Dallas city, Texas	339.74
12	Jacksonville city, Florida	911,507	8	12	San Diego city, California	325.88
13	Fort Worth city, Texas	909,585	11	13	Austin city, Texas	319.94
14	Columbus city, Ohio	898,553	29	14	Memphis city, Tennessee	317.36
15	Charlotte city, North Carolina	885,708	39	15	Kansas City city, Missouri	314.89
16	San Francisco city, California	881,549	15	16	Charlotte city, North Carolina	307.24
17	Indianapolis city (balance), Indiana	876,384	1	17	New York city, New York	300.38
18	Hempstead town, Nassau County, New York	766,980	63	18	Lexington-Fayette urban county, Kentucky	283.64
19	Seattle city, Washington	753,675	30	19	Louisville/Jefferson County metro government	263.43
20	Denver city, Colorado	727,211	40	20	Brookhaven town, Suffolk County, New York	259.39
21	Washington city, District of Columbia	705,749	23	21	El Paso city, Texas	257.42
22	Boston city, Suffolk County, Massachusetts	692,600	46	22	Virginia Beach city, Virginia	244.72
23	El Paso city, Texas	681,728	34	23	Tucson city, Arizona	238.01
24	Nashville-Davidson metropolitan government (balance)	670,820	3	24	Chicago city, Illinois	227.37
25	Detroit city, Wayne County, Michigan	670,031	14	25	Columbus city, Ohio	219.20
26	Oklahoma City city, Oklahoma	655,057	49	26	Tulsa city, Oklahoma	197.48
27	Portland city, Oregon	654,741	41	27	Colorado Springs city, Colorado	195.00
28	Las Vegas city, Nevada	651,319	33	28	Albuquerque city, New Mexico	187.22
29	Memphis city, Tennessee	651,073	10	29	San Jose city, California	177.81
30	Louisville/Jefferson County metro government (balance)	617,638	52	30	New Orleans city, Louisiana	169.43
31	Baltimore city, Maryland	593,490	53	31	Wichita city, Kansas	161.66
32	Milwaukee city, Milwaukee County, Wisconsin	590,157	62	32	Corpus Christi city, Texas	159.70
33	Albuquerque city, New Mexico	560,513	56	33	Aurora city, Colorado	154.27
34	Tucson city, Arizona	548,073	20	34	Denver city, Colorado	153.29
35	Fresno city, California	531,576	54	35	Bakersfield city, California	149.76
36	Mesa city, Arizona	518,012	43	36	Raleigh city, North Carolina	145.89
37	Sacramento city, California	513,624	28	37	Las Vegas city, Nevada	141.77
38	Atlanta city, Georgia	506,811	42	38	Omaha city, Nebraska	140.98
39	Kansas City city, Missouri	495,327	25	39	Detroit city, Wayne County, Michigan	138.72
40	Brookhaven town, Suffolk County, New York	480,763	36	40	Mesa city, Arizona	138.09
41	Colorado Springs city, Colorado	478,221	38	41	Atlanta city, Georgia	135.74
42	Omaha city, Nebraska	478,192	6	42	Philadelphia city, Pennsylvania	134.28
43	Raleigh city, North Carolina	474,069	27	43	Portland city, Oregon	133.42
44	Miami city, Florida	467,963	71	44	Greensboro city, North Carolina	129.07
45	Long Beach city, California	462,628	18	45	Hempstead town, Nassau County, New York	118.52
46	Virginia Beach city, Virginia	449,974	35	46	Fresno city, California	114.73
47	Oakland city, California	433,031	50	47	Tampa city, Florida	114.02
48	Minneapolis city, Minnesota	429,606	75	48	Orlando city, Florida	110.56
49	Tulsa city, Oklahoma	401,190	64	49	Henderson city, Nevada	106.08
50	Tampa city, Florida	399,700	61	50	Islip town, Suffolk County, New York	103.79
51	Arlington city, Texas	398,854	70	51	Oyster Bay town, Nassau County, New York	103.72
52	New Orleans city, Louisiana	390,144	37	52	Sacramento city, California	97.73
53	Wichita city, Kansas	389,938	72	53	Lincoln city, Nebraska	96.22
54	Bakersfield city, California	384,145	32	54	Milwaukee city, Milwaukee County, Wisconsin	96.18
55	Cleveland city, Ohio	381,009	51	55	Arlington city, Texas	95.78
56	Aurora city, Colorado	379,289	19	56	Seattle city, Washington	83.86
57	Anaheim city, California	350,365	60	57	Riverside city, California	81.26
58	Urban Honolulu CDP, Hawaii	345,064	31	58	Baltimore city, Maryland	80.95
59	Santa Ana city, California	332,318	67	59	Cincinnati city, Ohio	77.84
60	Riverside city, California	331,360	55	60	Cleveland city, Ohio	77.69
61	Islip town, Suffolk County, New York	329,610	74	61	Plano city, Texas	71.68
62	Corpus Christi city, Texas	326,586	65	62	Stockton city, California	62.17
63	Lexington-Fayette urban county, Kentucky	323,152	68	63	St. Louis city, Missouri	61.74
64	Henderson city, Nevada	320,189	21	64	Washington city, District of Columbia	61.14
65	Stockton city, California	312,697	58	65	Urban Honolulu CDP, Hawaii	60.54
66	St. Paul city, Ramsey County, Minnesota	308,096	47	66	Oakland city, California	55.89
67	Cincinnati city, Ohio	303,940	69	67	Pittsburgh city, Allegheny County, Pennsylvania	55.38
68	St. Louis city, Missouri	300,576	48	68	Minneapolis city, Minnesota	54.00
69	Pittsburgh city, Allegheny County, Pennsylvania	300,286	66	69	St. Paul city, Ramsey County, Minnesota	51.98
70	Oyster Bay town, Nassau County, New York	298,391	45	70	Long Beach city, California	50.70
71	Greensboro city, North Carolina	296,710	57	71	Anaheim city, California	50.32
72	Lincoln city, Nebraska	289,102	22	72	Boston city, Suffolk County, Massachusetts	48.34
73	Anchorage municipality, Alaska	288,000	16	73	San Francisco city, California	46.90
74	Plano city, Texas	287,677	44	74	Miami city, Florida	36.00
75	Orlando city, Florida	287,442	59	75	Santa Ana city, California	27.36

75 Largest Cities and Towns by 2019 Population
Selected Rankings

Population density, 2019				Percent population change, 2010–2019			
Population rank	Density rank	City	Density (persons per square mile) [Table B col 5]	Population rank	Percent change rank	City	Percent change [Table A col 3]
1	1	New York city, New York	27754.2	64	1	Henderson city, Nevada	24.6
16	2	San Francisco city, California	18796.4	19	2	Seattle city, Washington	23.8
22	3	Boston city, Suffolk County, Massachusetts	14327.7	11	3	Austin city, Texas	22.1
44	4	Miami city, Florida	12999.0	13	3	Fort Worth city, Texas	22.1
59	5	Santa Ana city, California	12146.1	20	5	Denver city, Colorado	21.2
3	6	Chicago city, Illinois	11848.4	15	6	Charlotte city, North Carolina	20.4
6	7	Philadelphia city, Pennsylvania	11796.7	75	6	Orlando city, Florida	20.4
21	8	Washington city, District of Columbia	11543.2	50	8	Tampa city, Florida	18.9
45	9	Long Beach city, California	9124.8	38	9	Atlanta city, Georgia	18.7
19	10	Seattle city, Washington	8987.3	36	10	Mesa city, Arizona	17.7
2	11	Los Angeles city, California	8486.0	21	11	Washington city, District of Columbia	17.3
48	12	Minneapolis city, Minnesota	7955.7	43	11	Raleigh city, North Carolina	17.3
47	13	Oakland city, California	7747.9	44	13	Miami city, Florida	17.1
31	14	Baltimore city, Maryland	7331.6	56	14	Aurora city, Colorado	16.8
57	15	Anaheim city, California	6962.7	7	15	San Antonio city, Texas	16.7
18	16	Hempstead town, Nassau County, New York	6471.3	5	16	Phoenix city, Arizona	16.2
32	17	Milwaukee city, Milwaukee County, Wisconsin	6136.0	41	17	Colorado Springs city, Colorado	14.6
66	18	St. Paul city, Ramsey County, Minnesota	5927.2	14	18	Columbus city, Ohio	13.9
10	19	San Jose city, California	5746.6	52	19	New Orleans city, Louisiana	13.5
58	20	Urban Honolulu CDP, Hawaii	5699.8	26	20	Oklahoma City city, Oklahoma	12.9
69	21	Pittsburgh city, Allegheny County, Pennsylvania	5422.3	48	21	Minneapolis city, Minnesota	12.3
37	22	Sacramento city, California	5255.5	9	22	Dallas city, Texas	12.2
65	23	Stockton city, California	5029.7	27	22	Portland city, Oregon	12.2
27	24	Portland city, Oregon	4907.4	22	24	Boston city, Suffolk County, Massachusetts	12.1
55	25	Cleveland city, Ohio	4904.2	72	25	Lincoln city, Nebraska	11.7
68	26	St. Louis city, Missouri	4868.4	28	26	Las Vegas city, Nevada	11.4
25	27	Detroit city, Wayne County, Michigan	4830.1	24	27	Nashville-Davidson metropolitan government	11.2
20	28	Denver city, Colorado	4744.0	12	28	Jacksonville city, Florida	10.9
35	29	Fresno city, California	4633.3	47	29	Oakland city, California	10.8
28	30	Las Vegas city, Nevada	4594.2	4	30	Houston city, Texas	10.7
8	31	San Diego city, California	4369.2	74	30	Plano city, Texas	10.7
51	32	Arlington city, Texas	4164.3	54	32	Bakersfield city, California	10.4
14	33	Columbus city, Ohio	4099.2	71	33	Greensboro city, North Carolina	10.3
60	34	Riverside city, California	4077.8	37	34	Sacramento city, California	10.1
74	35	Plano city, Texas	4013.4	16	35	San Francisco city, California	9.5
9	36	Dallas city, Texas	3954.7	8	36	San Diego city, California	9.4
67	37	Cincinnati city, Ohio	3904.7	51	37	Arlington city, Texas	9.2
36	38	Mesa city, Arizona	3751.3	63	37	Lexington-Fayette urban county, Kentucky	9.2
38	39	Atlanta city, Georgia	3733.7	60	39	Riverside city, California	9.0
4	40	Houston city, Texas	3624.3	66	40	St. Paul city, Ramsey County, Minnesota	8.1
50	41	Tampa city, Florida	3505.5	39	41	Kansas City city, Missouri	7.7
42	42	Omaha city, Nebraska	3391.9	10	42	San Jose city, California	7.3
43	43	Raleigh city, North Carolina	3249.5	62	43	Corpus Christi city, Texas	7.0
5	44	Phoenix city, Arizona	3247.2	65	43	Stockton city, California	7.0
7	45	San Antonio city, Texas	3189.5	35	45	Fresno city, California	6.9
61	46	Islip town, Suffolk County, New York	3175.7	17	46	Indianapolis city (balance), Indiana	6.8
11	47	Austin city, Texas	3059.7	23	47	El Paso city, Texas	5.2
64	48	Henderson city, Nevada	3018.4	2	48	Los Angeles city, California	4.9
72	49	Lincoln city, Nebraska	3004.6	42	49	Omaha city, Nebraska	4.2
33	50	Albuquerque city, New Mexico	2993.9	57	49	Anaheim city, California	4.2
15	51	Charlotte city, North Carolina	2882.8	34	51	Tucson city, Arizona	4.1
70	52	Oyster Bay town, Nassau County, New York	2876.9	6	52	Philadelphia city, Pennsylvania	3.8
23	53	El Paso city, Texas	2648.3	30	53	Louisville/Jefferson County metro government	3.7
13	54	Fort Worth city, Texas	2632.1	46	54	Virginia Beach city, Virginia	2.8
75	55	Orlando city, Florida	2599.9	33	55	Albuquerque city, New Mexico	2.6
54	56	Bakersfield city, California	2565.1	49	56	Tulsa city, Oklahoma	2.3
56	57	Aurora city, Colorado	2458.6	59	56	Santa Ana city, California	2.3
41	58	Colorado Springs city, Colorado	2452.4	67	56	Cincinnati city, Ohio	2.3
17	59	Indianapolis city (balance), Indiana	2423.8	58	59	Urban Honolulu CDP, Hawaii	2.2
53	60	Wichita city, Kansas	2412.1	1	60	New York city, New York	2.0
30	61	Louisville/Jefferson County metro government	2344.6	53	60	Wichita city, Kansas	2.0
34	62	Tucson city, Arizona	2302.7	70	62	Oyster Bay town, Nassau County, New York	1.6
52	63	New Orleans city, Louisiana	2302.7	18	63	Hempstead town, Nassau County, New York	0.9
71	64	Greensboro city, North Carolina	2298.8	45	64	Long Beach city, California	0.1
29	65	Memphis city, Tennessee	2051.5	3	65	Chicago city, Illinois	-0.1
62	66	Corpus Christi city, Texas	2045.0	29	65	Memphis city, Tennessee	-0.1
49	67	Tulsa city, Oklahoma	2031.5	32	67	Milwaukee city, Milwaukee County, Wisconsin	-0.7
40	68	Brookhaven town, Suffolk County, New York	1853.4	40	68	Brookhaven town, Suffolk County, New York	-1.1
46	69	Virginia Beach city, Virginia	1838.7	73	69	Anchorage municipality, Alaska	-1.3
39	70	Kansas City city, Missouri	1573.0	69	70	Pittsburgh city, Allegheny County, Pennsylvania	-1.6
24	71	Nashville-Davidson metropolitan government	1410.6	61	71	Islip town, Suffolk County, New York	-1.7
12	72	Jacksonville city, Florida	1219.5	55	72	Cleveland city, Ohio	-3.9
63	73	Lexington-Fayette urban county, Kentucky	1139.3	31	73	Baltimore city, Maryland	-4.4
26	74	Oklahoma City city, Oklahoma	1080.2	68	74	St. Louis city, Missouri	-5.9
73	75	Anchorage municipality, Alaska	168.7	25	75	Detroit city, Wayne County, Michigan	-6.1

75 Largest Cities and Towns by 2019 Population
Selected Rankings

Percent White alone, not Hispanic or Latino 2015-2019				Percent Black alone, not Hispanic or Latino 2015–2019			
Population rank	Non-Hispanic White rank	City	Percent White alone, not Hispanic or Latino [Table A col 5]	Population rank	Non-Hispanic Black rank	City	Percent Black alone, not Hispanic or Latino [Table A col 6]
72	1	Lincoln city, Nebraska	79.6	25	1	Detroit city, Wayne County, Michigan	78.0
70	2	Oyster Bay town, Nassau County, New York	75.5	29	2	Memphis city, Tennessee	63.8
40	3	Brookhaven town, Suffolk County, New York	72.1	31	3	Baltimore city, Maryland	61.8
63	4	Lexington-Fayette urban county, Kentucky	71.0	52	4	New Orleans city, Louisiana	58.9
27	5	Portland city, Oregon	70.6	38	5	Atlanta city, Georgia	50.5
41	6	Colorado Springs city, Colorado	68.6	55	6	Cleveland city, Ohio	48.2
42	7	Omaha city, Nebraska	66.6	68	7	St. Louis city, Missouri	46.2
30	8	Louisville/Jefferson County metro government	65.6	21	8	Washington city, District of Columbia	45.4
69	9	Pittsburgh city, Allegheny County, Pennsylvania	64.7	67	9	Cincinnati city, Ohio	42.0
64	10	Henderson city, Nevada	64.6	71	10	Greensboro city, North Carolina	41.0
19	11	Seattle city, Washington	63.8	6	11	Philadelphia city, Pennsylvania	40.8
53	12	Wichita city, Kansas	62.8	32	12	Milwaukee city, Milwaukee County, Wisconsin	38.3
46	13	Virginia Beach city, Virginia	61.7	15	13	Charlotte city, North Carolina	34.6
36	14	Mesa city, Arizona	61.3	12	14	Jacksonville city, Florida	30.5
48	15	Minneapolis city, Minnesota	60.0	3	15	Chicago city, Illinois	29.2
73	16	Anchorage municipality, Alaska	57.9	14	16	Columbus city, Ohio	28.6
24	17	Nashville-Davidson metropolitan government	55.4	17	17	Indianapolis city (balance), Indiana	28.2
39	18	Kansas City city, Missouri	55.2	43	17	Raleigh city, North Carolina	28.2
14	19	Columbus city, Ohio	55.1	39	19	Kansas City city, Missouri	27.9
17	20	Indianapolis city (balance), Indiana	54.5	24	20	Nashville-Davidson metropolitan government	27.4
61	21	Islip town, Suffolk County, New York	54.3	9	21	Dallas city, Texas	24.0
20	22	Denver city, Colorado	54.2	75	22	Orlando city, Florida	23.5
18	23	Hempstead town, Nassau County, New York	54.0	30	23	Louisville/Jefferson County metro government	23.3
49	23	Tulsa city, Oklahoma	54.0	47	24	Oakland city, California	23.2
26	25	Oklahoma City city, Oklahoma	53.5	69	25	Pittsburgh city, Allegheny County, Pennsylvania	22.8
43	26	Raleigh city, North Carolina	53.1	22	26	Boston city, Suffolk County, Massachusetts	22.7
74	27	Plano city, Texas	52.4	51	27	Arlington city, Texas	22.3
66	28	St. Paul city, Ramsey County, Minnesota	51.4	4	28	Houston city, Texas	22.1
12	29	Jacksonville city, Florida	51.2	50	29	Tampa city, Florida	22.0
11	30	Austin city, Texas	48.3	1	30	New York city, New York	21.8
67	31	Cincinnati city, Ohio	48.2	48	31	Minneapolis city, Minnesota	18.9
50	32	Tampa city, Florida	44.6	13	32	Fort Worth city, Texas	18.5
22	33	Boston city, Suffolk County, Massachusetts	44.5	46	33	Virginia Beach city, Virginia	18.4
56	34	Aurora city, Colorado	44.4	18	34	Hempstead town, Nassau County, New York	16.6
34	35	Tucson city, Arizona	43.9	56	35	Aurora city, Colorado	15.9
68	36	St. Louis city, Missouri	43.6	66	36	St. Paul city, Ramsey County, Minnesota	15.8
28	37	Las Vegas city, Nevada	43.5	49	37	Tulsa city, Oklahoma	15.0
8	38	San Diego city, California	42.8	63	38	Lexington-Fayette urban county, Kentucky	14.5
71	39	Greensboro city, North Carolina	42.6	44	39	Miami city, Florida	14.4
5	40	Phoenix city, Arizona	42.5	26	40	Oklahoma City city, Oklahoma	14.1
15	41	Charlotte city, North Carolina	41.5	37	41	Sacramento city, California	12.7
16	42	San Francisco city, California	40.5	42	42	Omaha city, Nebraska	12.2
13	43	Fort Worth city, Texas	39.2	45	42	Long Beach city, California	12.2
33	44	Albuquerque city, New Mexico	38.9	28	44	Las Vegas city, Nevada	11.6
51	45	Arlington city, Texas	38.6	65	45	Stockton city, California	10.8
38	46	Atlanta city, Georgia	38.3	53	46	Wichita city, Kansas	10.6
21	47	Washington city, District of Columbia	36.6	20	47	Denver city, Colorado	8.9
75	48	Orlando city, Florida	36.5	61	47	Islip town, Suffolk County, New York	8.9
32	49	Milwaukee city, Milwaukee County, Wisconsin	35.1	2	49	Los Angeles city, California	8.6
6	50	Philadelphia city, Pennsylvania	34.5	74	50	Plano city, Texas	8.5
55	51	Cleveland city, Ohio	33.8	11	51	Austin city, Texas	7.4
3	52	Chicago city, Illinois	33.3	19	52	Seattle city, Washington	7.2
54	53	Bakersfield city, California	32.5	54	52	Bakersfield city, California	7.2
37	54	Sacramento city, California	32.4	35	54	Fresno city, California	7.0
1	55	New York city, New York	32.1	5	55	Phoenix city, Arizona	6.7
52	56	New Orleans city, Louisiana	30.7	7	56	San Antonio city, Texas	6.4
60	57	Riverside city, California	29.8	41	57	Colorado Springs city, Colorado	6.1
62	58	Corpus Christi city, Texas	29.5	8	58	San Diego city, California	6.0
9	59	Dallas city, Texas	29.0	60	59	Riverside city, California	5.8
2	60	Los Angeles city, California	28.5	64	60	Henderson city, Nevada	5.7
47	61	Oakland city, California	28.3	27	61	Portland city, Oregon	5.6
45	62	Long Beach city, California	28.2	40	62	Brookhaven town, Suffolk County, New York	5.5
31	63	Baltimore city, Maryland	27.5	73	63	Anchorage municipality, Alaska	5.3
35	64	Fresno city, California	26.9	16	64	San Francisco city, California	5.0
10	65	San Jose city, California	25.7	34	65	Tucson city, Arizona	4.8
29	65	Memphis city, Tennessee	25.7	72	66	Lincoln city, Nebraska	4.2
7	67	San Antonio city, Texas	24.7	36	67	Mesa city, Arizona	4.0
4	68	Houston city, Texas	24.4	62	68	Corpus Christi city, Texas	3.9
57	69	Anaheim city, California	24.2	23	69	El Paso city, Texas	3.2
65	70	Stockton city, California	20.6	10	70	San Jose city, California	2.8
58	71	Urban Honolulu CDP, Hawaii	15.4	33	70	Albuquerque city, New Mexico	2.8
23	72	El Paso city, Texas	12.8	57	72	Anaheim city, California	2.5
44	73	Miami city, Florida	11	70	73	Oyster Bay town, Nassau County, New York	2.2
25	74	Detroit city, Wayne County, Michigan	11	58	74	Urban Honolulu CDP, Hawaii	2.0
59	75	Santa Ana city, California	9	59	75	Santa Ana city, California	1.0

75 Largest Cities and Towns by 2019 Population
Selected Rankings

Population rank	Asian alone not Hispanic or Latino rank	City	Percent Asian alone, not Hispanic or Latino [Table A col 7]	Population rank	All other races or 2 or more races rank	City	Percent All other races or 2 or more races, not Hispanic or Latino [Table A col 8]
58	1	Urban Honolulu CDP, Hawaii	52.3	58	1	Urban Honolulu CDP, Hawaii	23.1
10	2	San Jose city, California	35.7	73	2	Anchorage municipality, Alaska	18.2
16	3	San Francisco city, California	34.1	49	3	Tulsa city, Oklahoma	11.1
74	4	Plano city, Texas	21.1	26	4	Oklahoma City city, Oklahoma	8.2
65	5	Stockton city, California	21.0	37	5	Sacramento city, California	7.4
37	6	Sacramento city, California	18.6	19	6	Seattle city, Washington	7.0
66	6	St. Paul city, Ramsey County, Minnesota	18.6	33	7	Albuquerque city, New Mexico	6.3
57	8	Anaheim city, California	16.6	47	8	Oakland city, California	6.1
8	9	San Diego city, California	16.4	27	9	Portland city, Oregon	6.0
19	10	Seattle city, Washington	15.3	48	10	Minneapolis city, Minnesota	5.6
47	10	Oakland city, California	15.3	16	11	San Francisco city, California	5.2
1	12	New York city, New York	14.0	28	12	Las Vegas city, Nevada	5.1
35	13	Fresno city, California	13.4	46	12	Virginia Beach city, Virginia	5.1
45	14	Long Beach city, California	12.8	65	14	Stockton city, California	5.0
70	15	Oyster Bay town, Nassau County, New York	12.5	36	15	Mesa city, Arizona	4.9
59	16	Santa Ana city, California	11.6	66	15	St. Paul city, Ramsey County, Minnesota	4.9
2	17	Los Angeles city, California	11.5	41	17	Colorado Springs city, Colorado	4.8
22	18	Boston city, Suffolk County, Massachusetts	9.6	64	17	Henderson city, Nevada	4.8
73	19	Anchorage municipality, Alaska	9.4	56	19	Aurora city, Colorado	4.7
27	20	Portland city, Oregon	8.1	34	20	Tucson city, Arizona	4.6
64	20	Henderson city, Nevada	8.1	5	21	Phoenix city, Arizona	4.4
11	22	Austin city, Texas	7.5	8	21	San Diego city, California	4.4
60	23	Riverside city, California	7.4	53	21	Wichita city, Kansas	4.4
54	24	Bakersfield city, California	7.3	14	24	Columbus city, Ohio	4.3
6	25	Philadelphia city, Pennsylvania	7.2	45	25	Long Beach city, California	4.2
4	26	Houston city, Texas	6.7	10	26	San Jose city, California	4.1
28	26	Las Vegas city, Nevada	6.7	72	27	Lincoln city, Nebraska	4.0
46	28	Virginia Beach city, Virginia	6.6	67	28	Cincinnati city, Ohio	3.8
3	29	Chicago city, Illinois	6.5	12	29	Jacksonville city, Florida	3.7
15	29	Charlotte city, North Carolina	6.5	39	30	Kansas City city, Missouri	3.6
51	29	Arlington city, Texas	6.5	55	30	Cleveland city, Ohio	3.6
56	32	Aurora city, Colorado	6.4	63	30	Lexington-Fayette urban county, Kentucky	3.6
18	33	Hempstead town, Nassau County, New York	6.1	69	30	Pittsburgh city, Allegheny County, Pennsylvania	3.6
48	34	Minneapolis city, Minnesota	5.9	71	30	Greensboro city, North Carolina	3.6
14	35	Columbus city, Ohio	5.8	42	35	Omaha city, Nebraska	3.5
69	35	Pittsburgh city, Allegheny County, Pennsylvania	5.8	17	36	Indianapolis city (balance), Indiana	3.4
53	37	Wichita city, Kansas	5.0	20	36	Denver city, Colorado	3.4
71	37	Greensboro city, North Carolina	5.0	22	36	Boston city, Suffolk County, Massachusetts	3.4
12	39	Jacksonville city, Florida	4.7	32	36	Milwaukee city, Milwaukee County, Wisconsin	3.4
43	40	Raleigh city, North Carolina	4.6	60	40	Riverside city, California	3.3
72	40	Lincoln city, Nebraska	4.6	75	40	Orlando city, Florida	3.3
13	42	Fort Worth city, Texas	4.5	15	42	Charlotte city, North Carolina	3.1
26	42	Oklahoma City city, Oklahoma	4.5	21	42	Washington city, District of Columbia	3.1
40	42	Brookhaven town, Suffolk County, New York	4.5	51	42	Arlington city, Texas	3.1
38	45	Atlanta city, Georgia	4.4	74	42	Plano city, Texas	3.1
32	46	Milwaukee city, Milwaukee County, Wisconsin	4.2	1	46	New York city, New York	3.0
50	46	Tampa city, Florida	4.2	2	46	Los Angeles city, California	3.0
75	48	Orlando city, Florida	4.1	24	46	Nashville-Davidson metropolitan government	3.0
21	49	Washington city, District of Columbia	3.9	35	46	Fresno city, California	3.0
42	50	Omaha city, Nebraska	3.8	31	50	Baltimore city, Maryland	2.9
5	51	Phoenix city, Arizona	3.7	43	50	Raleigh city, North Carolina	2.9
63	51	Lexington-Fayette urban county, Kentucky	3.7	6	52	Philadelphia city, Pennsylvania	2.8
20	53	Denver city, Colorado	3.6	11	52	Austin city, Texas	2.8
24	53	Nashville-Davidson metropolitan government	3.6	30	52	Louisville/Jefferson County metro government	2.8
9	55	Dallas city, Texas	3.4	50	52	Tampa city, Florida	2.8
17	55	Indianapolis city (balance), Indiana	3.4	68	52	St. Louis city, Missouri	2.8
49	57	Tulsa city, Oklahoma	3.3	13	57	Fort Worth city, Texas	2.7
68	57	St. Louis city, Missouri	3.3	54	57	Bakersfield city, California	2.7
34	59	Tucson city, Arizona	3.1	38	59	Atlanta city, Georgia	2.5
52	60	New Orleans city, Louisiana	2.9	57	59	Anaheim city, California	2.5
33	61	Albuquerque city, New Mexico	2.8	18	61	Hempstead town, Nassau County, New York	2.4
41	61	Colorado Springs city, Colorado	2.8	3	62	Chicago city, Illinois	2.2
61	61	Islip town, Suffolk County, New York	2.8	25	63	Detroit city, Wayne County, Michigan	2.1
7	64	San Antonio city, Texas	2.7	52	63	New Orleans city, Louisiana	2.1
30	64	Louisville/Jefferson County metro government	2.7	61	65	Islip town, Suffolk County, New York	2.0
39	64	Kansas City city, Missouri	2.7	7	66	San Antonio city, Texas	1.9
31	67	Baltimore city, Maryland	2.6	9	66	Dallas city, Texas	1.9
55	68	Cleveland city, Ohio	2.5	40	66	Brookhaven town, Suffolk County, New York	1.9
62	69	Corpus Christi city, Texas	2.2	4	69	Houston city, Texas	1.8
67	69	Cincinnati city, Ohio	2.2	70	69	Oyster Bay town, Nassau County, New York	1.8
36	71	Mesa city, Arizona	2.1	29	71	Memphis city, Tennessee	1.6
25	72	Detroit city, Wayne County, Michigan	1.7	23	72	El Paso city, Texas	1.4
29	72	Memphis city, Tennessee	1.7	59	73	Santa Ana city, California	1.3
23	74	El Paso city, Texas	1.3	62	74	Corpus Christi city, Texas	1.2
44	75	Miami city, Florida	1.0	44	75	Miami city, Florida	0.7

75 Largest Cities and Towns by 2019 Population
Selected Rankings

Percent Hispanic or Latino,[1] 2015–2019				Percent Foreign-Born, 2015–2019			
Population rank	Hispanic or Latino rank	City	Percent Hispanic or Latino [Table A col 9]	Population rank	Foreign-born rank	City	Percent Foreign-born [Table B col 6]
23	1	El Paso city, Texas	81.4	44	1	Miami city, Florida	58.3
59	2	Santa Ana city, California	76.8	59	2	Santa Ana city, California	43.3
44	3	Miami city, Florida	72.7	10	3	San Jose city, California	39.7
7	4	San Antonio city, Texas	64.2	2	4	Los Angeles city, California	36.9
62	5	Corpus Christi city, Texas	63.2	1	5	New York city, New York	36.8
57	6	Anaheim city, California	54.3	57	6	Anaheim city, California	36.5
60	7	Riverside city, California	53.7	16	7	San Francisco city, California	34.3
54	8	Bakersfield city, California	50.2	4	8	Houston city, Texas	29.3
35	9	Fresno city, California	49.6	22	9	Boston city, Suffolk County, Massachusetts	28.3
33	10	Albuquerque city, New Mexico	49.2	58	10	Urban Honolulu CDP, Hawaii	27.4
2	11	Los Angeles city, California	48.5	74	11	Plano city, Texas	27.0
4	12	Houston city, Texas	45.0	47	12	Oakland city, California	26.8
34	13	Tucson city, Arizona	43.6	8	13	San Diego city, California	26.1
65	14	Stockton city, California	42.7	65	14	Stockton city, California	25.7
5	15	Phoenix city, Arizona	42.6	45	15	Long Beach city, California	25.2
45	15	Long Beach city, California	42.6	9	16	Dallas city, Texas	24.8
9	17	Dallas city, Texas	41.8	23	17	El Paso city, Texas	23.1
13	18	Fort Worth city, Texas	35.1	18	18	Hempstead town, Nassau County, New York	22.7
11	19	Austin city, Texas	33.9	60	19	Riverside city, California	22.6
28	20	Las Vegas city, Nevada	33.1	37	20	Sacramento city, California	22.2
75	21	Orlando city, Florida	32.6	75	21	Orlando city, Florida	22.0
61	22	Islip town, Suffolk County, New York	32.0	61	22	Islip town, Suffolk County, New York	21.1
10	23	San Jose city, California	31.6	28	23	Las Vegas city, Nevada	21.0
8	24	San Diego city, California	30.3	51	24	Arlington city, Texas	20.8
20	25	Denver city, Colorado	29.9	3	25	Chicago city, Illinois	20.6
51	26	Arlington city, Texas	29.6	35	26	Fresno city, California	20.4
1	27	New York city, New York	29.1	56	27	Aurora city, Colorado	20.1
37	28	Sacramento city, California	28.9	66	28	St. Paul city, Ramsey County, Minnesota	20.0
3	29	Chicago city, Illinois	28.8	5	29	Phoenix city, Arizona	19.4
56	30	Aurora city, Colorado	28.6	54	30	Bakersfield city, California	18.9
36	31	Mesa city, Arizona	27.7	11	31	Austin city, Texas	18.8
47	32	Oakland city, California	27.0	19	31	Seattle city, Washington	18.8
50	33	Tampa city, Florida	26.4	50	33	Tampa city, Florida	17.2
18	34	Hempstead town, Nassau County, New York	20.9	13	34	Fort Worth city, Texas	16.8
22	35	Boston city, Suffolk County, Massachusetts	19.8	15	35	Charlotte city, North Carolina	16.7
26	36	Oklahoma City city, Oklahoma	19.7	70	36	Oyster Bay town, Nassau County, New York	16.5
32	37	Milwaukee city, Milwaukee County, Wisconsin	19.0	48	37	Minneapolis city, Minnesota	15.6
41	38	Colorado Springs city, Colorado	17.6	34	38	Tucson city, Arizona	15.3
53	39	Wichita city, Kansas	17.2	20	39	Denver city, Colorado	15.0
64	40	Henderson city, Nevada	16.8	7	40	San Antonio city, Texas	14.3
49	41	Tulsa city, Oklahoma	16.5	6	41	Philadelphia city, Pennsylvania	14.1
40	42	Brookhaven town, Suffolk County, New York	16.0	21	42	Washington city, District of Columbia	13.7
16	43	San Francisco city, California	15.2	27	43	Portland city, Oregon	13.5
74	44	Plano city, Texas	15.0	43	44	Raleigh city, North Carolina	13.4
6	45	Philadelphia city, Pennsylvania	14.7	24	45	Nashville-Davidson metropolitan government	13.3
15	46	Charlotte city, North Carolina	14.3	64	46	Henderson city, Nevada	12.9
42	47	Omaha city, Nebraska	13.9	14	47	Columbus city, Ohio	12.7
55	48	Cleveland city, Ohio	11.9	40	48	Brookhaven town, Suffolk County, New York	12.2
43	49	Raleigh city, North Carolina	11.2	26	49	Oklahoma City city, Oklahoma	11.8
21	50	Washington city, District of Columbia	11.0	36	49	Mesa city, Arizona	11.8
39	51	Kansas City city, Missouri	10.6	12	51	Jacksonville city, Florida	11.3
17	52	Indianapolis city (balance), Indiana	10.5	49	52	Tulsa city, Oklahoma	11.2
24	52	Nashville-Davidson metropolitan government	10.5	71	53	Greensboro city, North Carolina	11.1
12	54	Jacksonville city, Florida	10.0	73	54	Anchorage municipality, Alaska	10.9
27	55	Portland city, Oregon	9.7	42	55	Omaha city, Nebraska	10.7
48	56	Minneapolis city, Minnesota	9.6	53	56	Wichita city, Kansas	10.2
66	57	St. Paul city, Ramsey County, Minnesota	9.2	32	57	Milwaukee city, Milwaukee County, Wisconsin	10.0
73	57	Anchorage municipality, Alaska	9.2	33	58	Albuquerque city, New Mexico	9.9
46	59	Virginia Beach city, Virginia	8.2	17	59	Indianapolis city (balance), Indiana	9.7
70	60	Oyster Bay town, Nassau County, New York	8.1	63	59	Lexington-Fayette urban county, Kentucky	9.7
71	61	Greensboro city, North Carolina	7.9	46	61	Virginia Beach city, Virginia	9.4
25	62	Detroit city, Wayne County, Michigan	7.7	62	62	Corpus Christi city, Texas	9.3
72	63	Lincoln city, Nebraska	7.6	69	63	Pittsburgh city, Allegheny County, Pennsylvania	9.0
58	64	Urban Honolulu CDP, Hawaii	7.3	72	64	Lincoln city, Nebraska	8.5
29	65	Memphis city, Tennessee	7.2	39	65	Kansas City city, Missouri	8.2
63	65	Lexington-Fayette urban county, Kentucky	7.2	31	66	Baltimore city, Maryland	8.1
19	67	Seattle city, Washington	6.7	30	67	Louisville/Jefferson County metro government	7.7
14	68	Columbus city, Ohio	6.2	38	68	Atlanta city, Georgia	7.6
30	69	Louisville/Jefferson County metro government	5.6	41	69	Colorado Springs city, Colorado	7.5
52	70	New Orleans city, Louisiana	5.5	68	70	St. Louis city, Missouri	7.2
31	71	Baltimore city, Maryland	5.3	25	71	Detroit city, Wayne County, Michigan	6.2
38	72	Atlanta city, Georgia	4.3	29	71	Memphis city, Tennessee	6.2
68	73	St. Louis city, Missouri	4.0	67	73	Cincinnati city, Ohio	6.0
67	74	Cincinnati city, Ohio	3.8	55	74	Cleveland city, Ohio	5.9
69	75	Pittsburgh city, Allegheny County, Pennsylvania	3.2	52	75	New Orleans city, Louisiana	5.5

75 Largest Cities and Towns by 2019 Population
Selected Rankings

	Percent under 18 years old, 2015–2019				Percent 65 years old and over, 2015–2019		
Population rank	Under 18 years old rank	City	Percent under 18 years old [Table A col 10]	Population rank	65 years and over rank	City	Percent 65 years old and over [Table A col 11]
54	1	Bakersfield city, California	29.9	58	1	Urban Honolulu CDP, Hawaii	20.0
35	2	Fresno city, California	28.4	64	2	Henderson city, Nevada	19.4
13	3	Fort Worth city, Texas	27.7	70	3	Oyster Bay town, Nassau County, New York	18.6
65	3	Stockton city, California	27.7	44	4	Miami city, Florida	16.9
59	5	Santa Ana city, California	26.9	36	5	Mesa city, Arizona	16.4
23	6	El Paso city, Texas	26.7	18	6	Hempstead town, Nassau County, New York	16.3
5	7	Phoenix city, Arizona	26.1	40	7	Brookhaven town, Suffolk County, New York	15.6
26	8	Oklahoma City city, Oklahoma	25.9	16	8	San Francisco city, California	15.4
32	8	Milwaukee city, Milwaukee County, Wisconsin	25.9	33	9	Albuquerque city, New Mexico	15.1
51	10	Arlington city, Texas	25.6	28	10	Las Vegas city, Nevada	14.9
56	11	Aurora city, Colorado	25.3	30	10	Louisville/Jefferson County metro government	14.9
53	12	Wichita city, Kansas	25.2	69	12	Pittsburgh city, Allegheny County, Pennsylvania	14.7
4	13	Houston city, Texas	25.1	1	13	New York city, New York	14.5
42	13	Omaha city, Nebraska	25.1	34	14	Tucson city, Arizona	14.3
7	15	San Antonio city, Texas	25.0	52	15	New Orleans city, Louisiana	14.1
9	15	Dallas city, Texas	25.0	49	16	Tulsa city, Oklahoma	14.0
25	15	Detroit city, Wayne County, Michigan	25.0	53	16	Wichita city, Kansas	14.0
29	15	Memphis city, Tennessee	25.0	55	16	Cleveland city, Ohio	14.0
66	15	St. Paul city, Ramsey County, Minnesota	25.0	62	19	Corpus Christi city, Texas	13.8
17	20	Indianapolis city (balance), Indiana	24.7	46	20	Virginia Beach city, Virginia	13.7
62	21	Corpus Christi city, Texas	24.6	71	20	Greensboro city, North Carolina	13.7
49	22	Tulsa city, Oklahoma	24.5	25	22	Detroit city, Wayne County, Michigan	13.6
73	22	Anchorage municipality, Alaska	24.5	31	22	Baltimore city, Maryland	13.6
36	24	Mesa city, Arizona	24.3	6	24	Philadelphia city, Pennsylvania	13.4
57	25	Anaheim city, California	24.0	12	24	Jacksonville city, Florida	13.4
28	26	Las Vegas city, Nevada	23.8	41	24	Colorado Springs city, Colorado	13.4
60	26	Riverside city, California	23.8	61	27	Islip town, Suffolk County, New York	13.2
15	28	Charlotte city, North Carolina	23.7	37	28	Sacramento city, California	13.1
41	29	Colorado Springs city, Colorado	23.2	47	28	Oakland city, California	13.1
37	30	Sacramento city, California	23.1	68	28	St. Louis city, Missouri	13.1
39	30	Kansas City city, Missouri	23.1	63	31	Lexington-Fayette urban county, Kentucky	13.0
12	32	Jacksonville city, Florida	22.9	72	31	Lincoln city, Nebraska	13.0
61	32	Islip town, Suffolk County, New York	22.9	39	33	Kansas City city, Missouri	12.9
14	34	Columbus city, Ohio	22.5	27	34	Portland city, Oregon	12.8
30	34	Louisville/Jefferson County metro government	22.5	29	34	Memphis city, Tennessee	12.8
72	34	Lincoln city, Nebraska	22.5	42	34	Omaha city, Nebraska	12.8
74	34	Plano city, Texas	22.5	74	34	Plano city, Texas	12.8
10	38	San Jose city, California	22.4	23	38	El Paso city, Texas	12.7
33	38	Albuquerque city, New Mexico	22.4	8	39	San Diego city, California	12.6
45	38	Long Beach city, California	22.4	10	40	San Jose city, California	12.5
46	41	Virginia Beach city, Virginia	22.3	2	41	Los Angeles city, California	12.4
18	42	Hempstead town, Nassau County, New York	22.1	3	41	Chicago city, Illinois	12.4
55	42	Cleveland city, Ohio	22.1	19	41	Seattle city, Washington	12.4
67	44	Cincinnati city, Ohio	22.0	26	41	Oklahoma City city, Oklahoma	12.4
6	45	Philadelphia city, Pennsylvania	21.9	65	41	Stockton city, California	12.4
71	46	Greensboro city, North Carolina	21.8	50	46	Tampa city, Florida	12.3
50	47	Tampa city, Florida	21.4	17	47	Indianapolis city (balance), Indiana	12.2
64	47	Henderson city, Nevada	21.4	67	47	Cincinnati city, Ohio	12.2
40	49	Brookhaven town, Suffolk County, New York	21.3	21	49	Washington city, District of Columbia	12.1
34	50	Tucson city, Arizona	21.2	7	50	San Antonio city, Texas	12.0
75	51	Orlando city, Florida	21.1	24	51	Nashville-Davidson metropolitan government	11.7
24	52	Nashville-Davidson metropolitan government	21.0	57	52	Anaheim city, California	11.6
3	53	Chicago city, Illinois	20.9	20	53	Denver city, Colorado	11.5
43	53	Raleigh city, North Carolina	20.9	22	53	Boston city, Suffolk County, Massachusetts	11.5
63	53	Lexington-Fayette urban county, Kentucky	20.9	38	53	Atlanta city, Georgia	11.5
1	56	New York city, New York	20.8	45	56	Long Beach city, California	11.4
2	57	Los Angeles city, California	20.7	56	57	Aurora city, Colorado	11.2
31	57	Baltimore city, Maryland	20.7	35	58	Fresno city, California	11.1
70	57	Oyster Bay town, Nassau County, New York	20.7	60	59	Riverside city, California	10.7
11	60	Austin city, Texas	20.4	5	60	Phoenix city, Arizona	10.6
52	61	New Orleans city, Louisiana	20.1	43	60	Raleigh city, North Carolina	10.6
8	62	San Diego city, California	19.9	4	62	Houston city, Texas	10.5
47	62	Oakland city, California	19.9	32	62	Milwaukee city, Milwaukee County, Wisconsin	10.5
20	64	Denver city, Colorado	19.8	66	62	St. Paul city, Ramsey County, Minnesota	10.5
48	64	Minneapolis city, Minnesota	19.8	73	62	Anchorage municipality, Alaska	10.5
68	66	St. Louis city, Missouri	19.4	51	66	Arlington city, Texas	10.4
38	67	Atlanta city, Georgia	18.3	9	67	Dallas city, Texas	10.3
21	68	Washington city, District of Columbia	17.9	14	68	Columbus city, Ohio	10.2
27	69	Portland city, Oregon	17.8	15	68	Charlotte city, North Carolina	10.2
44	70	Miami city, Florida	17.5	75	68	Orlando city, Florida	10.2
58	71	Urban Honolulu CDP, Hawaii	17.1	48	71	Minneapolis city, Minnesota	10.0
22	72	Boston city, Suffolk County, Massachusetts	15.9	54	71	Bakersfield city, California	10.0
69	73	Pittsburgh city, Allegheny County, Pennsylvania	15.1	13	73	Fort Worth city, Texas	9.7
19	74	Seattle city, Washington	15.0	59	74	Santa Ana city, California	9.0
16	75	San Francisco city, California	13.4	11	75	Austin city, Texas	8.9

75 Largest Cities and Towns by 2019 Population
Selected Rankings

Percent age 18 to 64 years old, 2015–2019				Percent of households with a computer, 2015-2019			
Population rank	18 to 64 years old rank	City	Percent 18 to 64 years old [Table A (100- (col 10) - (col 11)]	Population rank	Households with a computer rank	City	Percent of households with a computer [Table A col 16]
19	1	Seattle city, Washington	72.6	74	1	Plano city, Texas	97.7
22	1	Boston city, Suffolk County, Massachusetts	72.6	43	2	Raleigh city, North Carolina	95.9
16	3	San Francisco city, California	71.2	73	2	Anchorage municipality, Alaska	95.9
11	4	Austin city, Texas	70.7	8	4	San Diego city, California	95.3
38	5	Atlanta city, Georgia	70.2	10	5	San Jose city, California	95.2
48	5	Minneapolis city, Minnesota	70.2	19	6	Seattle city, Washington	95.1
69	5	Pittsburgh city, Allegheny County, Pennsylvania	70.2	46	7	Virginia Beach city, Virginia	95.0
21	8	Washington city, District of Columbia	70.0	11	8	Austin city, Texas	94.9
27	9	Portland city, Oregon	69.4	51	9	Arlington city, Texas	94.7
20	10	Denver city, Colorado	68.7	41	10	Colorado Springs city, Colorado	94.5
75	10	Orlando city, Florida	68.7	27	11	Portland city, Oregon	94.3
43	12	Raleigh city, North Carolina	68.5	56	11	Aurora city, Colorado	94.3
8	13	San Diego city, California	67.5	75	13	Orlando city, Florida	94.2
68	13	St. Louis city, Missouri	67.5	15	14	Charlotte city, North Carolina	94.0
14	15	Columbus city, Ohio	67.3	57	15	Anaheim city, California	93.8
24	15	Nashville-Davidson metropolitan government	67.3	60	15	Riverside city, California	93.8
47	17	Oakland city, California	67.0	64	15	Henderson city, Nevada	93.8
2	18	Los Angeles city, California	66.9	70	18	Oyster Bay town, Nassau County, New York	93.7
3	19	Chicago city, Illinois	66.7	63	19	Lexington-Fayette urban county, Kentucky	93.6
50	20	Tampa city, Florida	66.3	37	20	Sacramento city, California	93.5
45	21	Long Beach city, California	66.2	61	20	Islip town, Suffolk County, New York	93.5
15	22	Charlotte city, North Carolina	66.1	72	20	Lincoln city, Nebraska	93.5
63	22	Lexington-Fayette urban county, Kentucky	66.1	18	23	Hempstead town, Nassau County, New York	93.4
52	24	New Orleans city, Louisiana	65.8	20	24	Denver city, Colorado	93.2
67	24	Cincinnati city, Ohio	65.8	16	25	San Francisco city, California	93.1
31	26	Baltimore city, Maryland	65.7	59	26	Santa Ana city, California	93.0
44	27	Miami city, Florida	65.6	13	27	Fort Worth city, Texas	92.8
60	28	Riverside city, California	65.5	40	27	Brookhaven town, Suffolk County, New York	92.8
10	29	San Jose city, California	65.1	45	27	Long Beach city, California	92.8
73	30	Anchorage municipality, Alaska	65.0	48	27	Minneapolis city, Minnesota	92.8
1	31	New York city, New York	64.7	54	27	Bakersfield city, California	92.8
9	31	Dallas city, Texas	64.7	24	32	Nashville-Davidson metropolitan government	92.4
74	31	Plano city, Texas	64.7	36	33	Mesa city, Arizona	92.3
6	31	Philadelphia city, Pennsylvania	64.7	14	34	Columbus city, Ohio	92.2
34	35	Tucson city, Arizona	64.5	50	35	Tampa city, Florida	91.9
66	35	St. Paul city, Ramsey County, Minnesota	64.5	21	36	Washington city, District of Columbia	91.8
71	35	Greensboro city, North Carolina	64.5	28	36	Las Vegas city, Nevada	91.8
72	35	Lincoln city, Nebraska	64.5	2	38	Los Angeles city, California	91.6
4	39	Houston city, Texas	64.4	5	38	Phoenix city, Arizona	91.6
57	39	Anaheim city, California	64.4	66	38	St. Paul city, Ramsey County, Minnesota	91.6
59	41	Santa Ana city, California	64.1	34	41	Tucson city, Arizona	91.3
39	42	Kansas City city, Missouri	64.0	12	42	Jacksonville city, Florida	91.0
46	42	Virginia Beach city, Virginia	64.0	22	42	Boston city, Suffolk County, Massachusetts	91.0
51	42	Arlington city, Texas	64.0	33	44	Albuquerque city, New Mexico	90.7
55	45	Cleveland city, Ohio	63.9	47	44	Oakland city, California	90.7
61	45	Islip town, Suffolk County, New York	63.9	26	46	Oklahoma City city, Oklahoma	90.5
37	47	Sacramento city, California	63.8	38	47	Atlanta city, Georgia	90.1
12	48	Jacksonville city, Florida	63.7	49	48	Tulsa city, Oklahoma	90.0
32	49	Milwaukee city, Milwaukee County, Wisconsin	63.6	7	49	San Antonio city, Texas	89.9
56	50	Aurora city, Colorado	63.5	42	49	Omaha city, Nebraska	89.9
41	51	Colorado Springs city, Colorado	63.4	39	51	Kansas City city, Missouri	89.8
5	52	Phoenix city, Arizona	63.3	35	52	Fresno city, California	89.7
40	53	Brookhaven town, Suffolk County, New York	63.1	58	53	Urban Honolulu CDP, Hawaii	89.4
17	53	Indianapolis city (balance), Indiana	63.1	4	54	Houston city, Texas	89.2
7	55	San Antonio city, Texas	63.0	62	54	Corpus Christi city, Texas	89.2
58	56	Urban Honolulu CDP, Hawaii	62.9	65	54	Stockton city, California	89.2
30	57	Louisville/Jefferson County metro government	62.6	1	57	New York city, New York	89.1
13	57	Fort Worth city, Texas	62.6	30	58	Louisville/Jefferson County metro government	88.8
33	59	Albuquerque city, New Mexico	62.5	53	59	Wichita city, Kansas	88.6
29	60	Memphis city, Tennessee	62.2	69	60	Pittsburgh city, Allegheny County, Pennsylvania	88.3
42	61	Omaha city, Nebraska	62.1	3	61	Chicago city, Illinois	87.9
26	62	Oklahoma City city, Oklahoma	61.7	23	62	El Paso city, Texas	87.3
18	63	Hempstead town, Nassau County, New York	61.6	9	63	Dallas city, Texas	87.2
62	63	Corpus Christi city, Texas	61.6	67	64	Cincinnati city, Ohio	87.1
49	65	Tulsa city, Oklahoma	61.5	71	65	Greensboro city, North Carolina	86.8
25	66	Detroit city, Wayne County, Michigan	61.4	17	66	Indianapolis city (balance), Indiana	86.7
28	67	Las Vegas city, Nevada	61.3	6	67	Philadelphia city, Pennsylvania	86.1
53	68	Wichita city, Kansas	60.8	31	68	Baltimore city, Maryland	85.7
70	69	Oyster Bay town, Nassau County, New York	60.7	32	69	Milwaukee city, Milwaukee County, Wisconsin	85.1
23	70	El Paso city, Texas	60.6	52	69	New Orleans city, Louisiana	85.1
35	71	Fresno city, California	60.5	68	69	St. Louis city, Missouri	85.1
54	72	Bakersfield city, California	60.1	44	72	Miami city, Florida	84.9
65	73	Stockton city, California	59.9	55	73	Cleveland city, Ohio	82.4
36	74	Mesa city, Arizona	59.3	25	74	Detroit city, Wayne County, Michigan	82.2
64	75	Henderson city, Nevada	59.2	29	75	Memphis city, Tennessee	80.6

75 Largest Cities and Towns by 2019 Population
Selected Rankings

Median household income, 2015-2019				Percent of households with income below the poverty level, 2015-2019			
Population rank	Median income rank	City	Median income (dollars) [Table B col 8]	Population rank	Poverty rate rank	City	Poverty rate [Table B col 9]
70	1	Oyster Bay town, Nassau County, New York	129,232	25	1	Detroit city, Wayne County, Michigan	32.8
16	2	San Francisco city, California	112,449	55	2	Cleveland city, Ohio	30.9
18	3	Hempstead town, Nassau County, New York	111,072	44	3	Miami city, Florida	25.3
10	4	San Jose city, California	109,593	67	4	Cincinnati city, Ohio	24.1
61	5	Islip town, Suffolk County, New York	98,387	52	5	New Orleans city, Louisiana	23.8
40	6	Brookhaven town, Suffolk County, New York	96,760	32	6	Milwaukee city, Milwaukee County, Wisconsin	23.2
74	7	Plano city, Texas	95,602	6	7	Philadelphia city, Pennsylvania	22.9
19	8	Seattle city, Washington	92,263	35	8	Fresno city, California	22.5
21	9	Washington city, District of Columbia	86,420	29	9	Memphis city, Tennessee	22.4
73	10	Anchorage municipality, Alaska	84,928	68	10	St. Louis city, Missouri	20.7
8	11	San Diego city, California	79,673	34	11	Tucson city, Arizona	20.6
46	12	Virginia Beach city, Virginia	76,610	31	12	Baltimore city, Maryland	20.0
64	13	Henderson city, Nevada	74,147	69	13	Pittsburgh city, Allegheny County, Pennsylvania	19.7
47	14	Oakland city, California	73,692	23	14	El Paso city, Texas	19.0
57	15	Anaheim city, California	71,763	22	15	Boston city, Suffolk County, Massachusetts	18.7
11	16	Austin city, Texas	71,576	65	16	Stockton city, California	18.1
58	17	Urban Honolulu CDP, Hawaii	71,465	1	17	New York city, New York	17.7
22	18	Boston city, Suffolk County, Massachusetts	71,115	4	17	Houston city, Texas	17.7
27	19	Portland city, Oregon	71,005	49	19	Tulsa city, Oklahoma	17.5
60	20	Riverside city, California	69,045	50	19	Tampa city, Florida	17.5
20	21	Denver city, Colorado	68,592	38	21	Atlanta city, Georgia	17.4
43	22	Raleigh city, North Carolina	67,266	2	22	Los Angeles city, California	17.3
59	23	Santa Ana city, California	66,145	3	22	Chicago city, Illinois	17.3
56	24	Aurora city, Colorado	65,100	7	24	San Antonio city, Texas	16.8
41	25	Colorado Springs city, Colorado	64,712	66	25	St. Paul city, Ramsey County, Minnesota	16.6
1	26	New York city, New York	63,998	17	26	Indianapolis city (balance), Indiana	16.5
54	27	Bakersfield city, California	63,139	48	26	Minneapolis city, Minnesota	16.5
45	28	Long Beach city, California	63,017	71	26	Greensboro city, North Carolina	16.5
15	29	Charlotte city, North Carolina	62,817	9	29	Dallas city, Texas	16.4
48	30	Minneapolis city, Minnesota	62,583	14	30	Columbus city, Ohio	16.3
37	31	Sacramento city, California	62,335	62	30	Corpus Christi city, Texas	16.3
13	32	Fort Worth city, Texas	62,187	75	32	Orlando city, Florida	16.2
2	33	Los Angeles city, California	62,142	33	33	Albuquerque city, New Mexico	16.0
51	34	Arlington city, Texas	60,571	63	34	Lexington-Fayette urban county, Kentucky	15.5
42	35	Omaha city, Nebraska	60,092	5	35	Phoenix city, Arizona	15.4
38	36	Atlanta city, Georgia	59,948	47	35	Oakland city, California	15.4
24	37	Nashville-Davidson metropolitan government	59,828	53	35	Wichita city, Kansas	15.4
3	38	Chicago city, Illinois	58,247	54	38	Bakersfield city, California	15.3
36	39	Mesa city, Arizona	58,181	37	39	Sacramento city, California	15.2
66	40	St. Paul city, Ramsey County, Minnesota	57,876	28	40	Las Vegas city, Nevada	15.0
72	41	Lincoln city, Nebraska	57,746	30	40	Louisville/Jefferson County metro government	15.0
5	42	Phoenix city, Arizona	57,459	26	42	Oklahoma City city, Oklahoma	14.8
63	43	Lexington-Fayette urban county, Kentucky	57,291	39	42	Kansas City city, Missouri	14.8
28	44	Las Vegas city, Nevada	56,354	21	44	Washington city, District of Columbia	14.6
62	45	Corpus Christi city, Texas	56,333	45	44	Long Beach city, California	14.6
26	46	Oklahoma City city, Oklahoma	55,557	59	46	Santa Ana city, California	14.5
12	47	Jacksonville city, Florida	54,701	12	47	Jacksonville city, Florida	13.8
65	48	Stockton city, California	54,614	13	48	Fort Worth city, Texas	13.6
39	49	Kansas City city, Missouri	54,194	27	49	Portland city, Oregon	13.4
50	50	Tampa city, Florida	53,833	57	49	Anaheim city, California	13.4
14	51	Columbus city, Ohio	53,745	60	51	Riverside city, California	13.3
30	52	Louisville/Jefferson County metro government	53,436	24	52	Nashville-Davidson metropolitan government	13.2
33	53	Albuquerque city, New Mexico	52,911	72	53	Lincoln city, Nebraska	13.1
53	54	Wichita city, Kansas	52,620	36	54	Mesa city, Arizona	12.9
9	55	Dallas city, Texas	52,580	42	54	Omaha city, Nebraska	12.9
7	56	San Antonio city, Texas	52,455	51	56	Arlington city, Texas	12.7
4	57	Houston city, Texas	52,338	20	57	Denver city, Colorado	12.1
75	58	Orlando city, Florida	51,757	11	58	Austin city, Texas	11.6
35	59	Fresno city, California	50,432	8	59	San Diego city, California	11.4
31	60	Baltimore city, Maryland	50,379	58	59	Urban Honolulu CDP, Hawaii	11.4
71	61	Greensboro city, North Carolina	48,964	15	61	Charlotte city, North Carolina	11.3
69	62	Pittsburgh city, Allegheny County, Pennsylvania	48,711	41	62	Colorado Springs city, Colorado	11.1
17	63	Indianapolis city (balance), Indiana	47,873	16	63	San Francisco city, California	10.9
49	64	Tulsa city, Oklahoma	47,650	43	64	Raleigh city, North Carolina	10.4
23	65	El Paso city, Texas	47,568	19	65	Seattle city, Washington	10.2
6	66	Philadelphia city, Pennsylvania	45,927	56	66	Aurora city, Colorado	9.7
68	67	St. Louis city, Missouri	43,896	10	67	San Jose city, California	8.6
34	68	Tucson city, Arizona	43,425	64	68	Henderson city, Nevada	8.1
32	69	Milwaukee city, Milwaukee County, Wisconsin	41,838	73	69	Anchorage municipality, Alaska	7.6
52	70	New Orleans city, Louisiana	41,604	61	70	Islip town, Suffolk County, New York	7.3
29	71	Memphis city, Tennessee	41,228	40	71	Brookhaven town, Suffolk County, New York	6.9
67	72	Cincinnati city, Ohio	40,640	74	71	Plano city, Texas	6.9
44	73	Miami city, Florida	39,049	46	73	Virginia Beach city, Virginia	6.8
55	74	Cleveland city, Ohio	30,907	18	74	Hempstead town, Nassau County, New York	6.2
25	75	Detroit city, Wayne County, Michigan	30,894	70	75	Oyster Bay town, Nassau County, New York	4.6

75 Largest Cities and Towns by 2019 Population
Selected Rankings

Percent high school graduates or less, 2015–2019

Population rank	High school graduate or less rank	City	Percent high school graduate or less [Table A col 13]
59	1	Santa Ana city, California	63.4
55	2	Cleveland city, Ohio	51.9
25	3	Detroit city, Wayne County, Michigan	51.6
65	3	Stockton city, California	51.6
44	5	Miami city, Florida	50.5
6	6	Philadelphia city, Pennsylvania	47.9
57	7	Anaheim city, California	46.5
32	8	Milwaukee city, Milwaukee County, Wisconsin	46.2
54	9	Bakersfield city, California	45.8
60	10	Riverside city, California	45.7
62	10	Corpus Christi city, Texas	45.7
35	12	Fresno city, California	45.3
29	13	Memphis city, Tennessee	44.9
9	14	Dallas city, Texas	44.3
4	15	Houston city, Texas	43.9
7	15	San Antonio city, Texas	43.9
31	15	Baltimore city, Maryland	43.9
61	18	Islip town, Suffolk County, New York	43.4
23	19	El Paso city, Texas	42.8
28	19	Las Vegas city, Nevada	42.8
13	21	Fort Worth city, Texas	42.7
17	22	Indianapolis city (balance), Indiana	42.1
1	23	New York city, New York	41.9
2	24	Los Angeles city, California	41.8
5	25	Phoenix city, Arizona	41.7
56	26	Aurora city, Colorado	39.2
26	27	Oklahoma City city, Oklahoma	39.1
30	27	Louisville/Jefferson County metro government	39.1
12	29	Jacksonville city, Florida	39.0
34	30	Tucson city, Arizona	38.6
51	30	Arlington city, Texas	38.6
53	32	Wichita city, Kansas	38.1
40	33	Brookhaven town, Suffolk County, New York	38.0
49	33	Tulsa city, Oklahoma	38.0
45	35	Long Beach city, California	37.9
50	36	Tampa city, Florida	37.7
3	37	Chicago city, Illinois	37.4
52	38	New Orleans city, Louisiana	36.3
67	38	Cincinnati city, Ohio	36.3
68	40	St. Louis city, Missouri	36.2
37	41	Sacramento city, California	36.0
14	42	Columbus city, Ohio	35.7
36	43	Mesa city, Arizona	35.5
39	44	Kansas City city, Missouri	35.3
18	45	Hempstead town, Nassau County, New York	34.5
58	46	Urban Honolulu CDP, Hawaii	34.4
66	47	St. Paul city, Ramsey County, Minnesota	34.0
24	48	Nashville-Davidson metropolitan government	33.5
47	49	Oakland city, California	33.3
33	50	Albuquerque city, New Mexico	32.9
42	51	Omaha city, Nebraska	32.8
75	51	Orlando city, Florida	32.8
22	53	Boston city, Suffolk County, Massachusetts	32.5
69	53	Pittsburgh city, Allegheny County, Pennsylvania	32.5
10	55	San Jose city, California	32.0
64	56	Henderson city, Nevada	31.9
71	57	Greensboro city, North Carolina	31.7
73	58	Anchorage municipality, Alaska	29.5
20	59	Denver city, Colorado	28.8
63	60	Lexington-Fayette urban county, Kentucky	28.4
15	61	Charlotte city, North Carolina	28.0
38	61	Atlanta city, Georgia	28.0
72	61	Lincoln city, Nebraska	28.0
46	64	Virginia Beach city, Virginia	27.4
8	65	San Diego city, California	27.0
70	66	Oyster Bay town, Nassau County, New York	26.6
11	67	Austin city, Texas	26.2
41	68	Colorado Springs city, Colorado	26.0
21	69	Washington city, District of Columbia	25.9
48	70	Minneapolis city, Minnesota	25.2
43	71	Raleigh city, North Carolina	23.8
16	72	San Francisco city, California	23.6
27	73	Portland city, Oregon	22.7
74	74	Plano city, Texas	19.4
19	75	Seattle city, Washington	14.7

Percent college graduates (bachelor's degree or more), 2015–2019

Population rank	College graduate rank	City	Percent college graduates [Table A col 14]
19	1	Seattle city, Washington	64.0
21	2	Washington city, District of Columbia	58.5
16	3	San Francisco city, California	58.1
74	4	Plano city, Texas	57.2
38	5	Atlanta city, Georgia	51.8
11	6	Austin city, Texas	51.7
70	7	Oyster Bay town, Nassau County, New York	51.1
43	8	Raleigh city, North Carolina	50.9
27	9	Portland city, Oregon	50.4
48	9	Minneapolis city, Minnesota	50.4
22	11	Boston city, Suffolk County, Massachusetts	49.7
20	12	Denver city, Colorado	49.4
8	13	San Diego city, California	45.9
69	14	Pittsburgh city, Allegheny County, Pennsylvania	44.6
15	15	Charlotte city, North Carolina	44.3
47	16	Oakland city, California	44.0
10	17	San Jose city, California	43.7
63	18	Lexington-Fayette urban county, Kentucky	43.6
18	19	Hempstead town, Nassau County, New York	41.1
24	19	Nashville-Davidson metropolitan government	41.1
66	21	St. Paul city, Ramsey County, Minnesota	40.8
41	22	Colorado Springs city, Colorado	39.9
72	23	Lincoln city, Nebraska	39.6
3	24	Chicago city, Illinois	39.5
50	25	Tampa city, Florida	38.6
71	26	Greensboro city, North Carolina	38.2
1	27	New York city, New York	38.1
75	27	Orlando city, Florida	38.1
42	29	Omaha city, Nebraska	37.7
52	30	New Orleans city, Louisiana	37.6
58	31	Urban Honolulu CDP, Hawaii	37.2
67	32	Cincinnati city, Ohio	37.1
14	33	Columbus city, Ohio	36.6
68	34	St. Louis city, Missouri	36.3
73	35	Anchorage municipality, Alaska	36.1
46	36	Virginia Beach city, Virginia	36.0
33	37	Albuquerque city, New Mexico	35.2
39	37	Kansas City city, Missouri	35.2
2	39	Los Angeles city, California	34.4
9	40	Dallas city, Texas	33.4
64	40	Henderson city, Nevada	33.4
37	42	Sacramento city, California	33.1
4	43	Houston city, Texas	32.9
40	44	Brookhaven town, Suffolk County, New York	32.6
31	45	Baltimore city, Maryland	31.9
49	46	Tulsa city, Oklahoma	31.5
45	47	Long Beach city, California	31.1
17	48	Indianapolis city (balance), Indiana	30.9
26	49	Oklahoma City city, Oklahoma	30.7
51	50	Arlington city, Texas	30.3
53	51	Wichita city, Kansas	30.1
30	52	Louisville/Jefferson County metro government	29.9
6	53	Philadelphia city, Pennsylvania	29.7
13	53	Fort Worth city, Texas	29.7
56	53	Aurora city, Colorado	29.7
61	53	Islip town, Suffolk County, New York	29.7
44	57	Miami city, Florida	29.6
5	58	Phoenix city, Arizona	28.6
12	58	Jacksonville city, Florida	28.6
34	60	Tucson city, Arizona	27.4
36	60	Mesa city, Arizona	27.4
29	62	Memphis city, Tennessee	26.2
7	63	San Antonio city, Texas	26.0
57	64	Anaheim city, California	25.5
23	65	El Paso city, Texas	25.1
28	66	Las Vegas city, Nevada	24.6
32	66	Milwaukee city, Milwaukee County, Wisconsin	24.6
60	68	Riverside city, California	23.0
62	69	Corpus Christi city, Texas	22.2
35	70	Fresno city, California	21.9
54	70	Bakersfield city, California	21.9
65	72	Stockton city, California	18.3
55	73	Cleveland city, Ohio	17.5
25	74	Detroit city, Wayne County, Michigan	15.3
59	75	Santa Ana city, California	15.0

75 Largest Cities and Towns by 2019 Population
Selected Rankings

Unemployment rate, 2015–2019

Population rank	Unemployment rate rank	City	Unemployment rate [Table B col 13]
25	1	Detroit city, Wayne County, Michigan	15.7
55	2	Cleveland city, Ohio	13.2
35	3	Fresno city, California	9.4
6	4	Philadelphia city, Pennsylvania	9.2
65	5	Stockton city, California	8.8
29	6	Memphis city, Tennessee	8.7
54	7	Bakersfield city, California	8.4
31	8	Baltimore city, Maryland	8.3
3	9	Chicago city, Illinois	8.1
67	10	Cincinnati city, Ohio	8.0
52	11	New Orleans city, Louisiana	7.9
34	12	Tucson city, Arizona	7.8
37	13	Sacramento city, California	7.0
68	13	St. Louis city, Missouri	7.0
21	15	Washington city, District of Columbia	6.9
32	16	Milwaukee city, Milwaukee County, Wisconsin	6.8
28	17	Las Vegas city, Nevada	6.7
22	18	Boston city, Suffolk County, Massachusetts	6.6
60	18	Riverside city, California	6.6
17	20	Indianapolis city (balance), Indiana	6.4
38	20	Atlanta city, Georgia	6.4
1	22	New York city, New York	6.3
2	22	Los Angeles city, California	6.3
49	22	Tulsa city, Oklahoma	6.3
50	22	Tampa city, Florida	6.3
23	26	El Paso city, Texas	6.1
47	26	Oakland city, California	6.1
71	26	Greensboro city, North Carolina	6.1
30	29	Louisville/Jefferson County metro government	6.0
44	29	Miami city, Florida	6.0
45	29	Long Beach city, California	6.0
4	32	Houston city, Texas	5.9
12	32	Jacksonville city, Florida	5.9
8	34	San Diego city, California	5.8
64	34	Henderson city, Nevada	5.8
41	36	Colorado Springs city, Colorado	5.7
73	36	Anchorage municipality, Alaska	5.7
33	38	Albuquerque city, New Mexico	5.6
53	38	Wichita city, Kansas	5.6
69	38	Pittsburgh city, Allegheny County, Pennsylvania	5.6
7	41	San Antonio city, Texas	5.5
14	41	Columbus city, Ohio	5.5
62	41	Corpus Christi city, Texas	5.5
5	44	Phoenix city, Arizona	5.4
13	44	Fort Worth city, Texas	5.4
75	44	Orlando city, Florida	5.4
57	47	Anaheim city, California	5.2
48	48	Minneapolis city, Minnesota	5.1
59	48	Santa Ana city, California	5.1
63	48	Lexington-Fayette urban county, Kentucky	5.1
15	51	Charlotte city, North Carolina	5.0
66	51	St. Paul city, Ramsey County, Minnesota	5.0
36	53	Mesa city, Arizona	4.9
27	54	Portland city, Oregon	4.8
39	54	Kansas City city, Missouri	4.8
9	56	Dallas city, Texas	4.7
10	56	San Jose city, California	4.7
46	58	Virginia Beach city, Virginia	4.6
51	58	Arlington city, Texas	4.6
56	58	Aurora city, Colorado	4.6
40	61	Brookhaven town, Suffolk County, New York	4.4
26	62	Oklahoma City city, Oklahoma	4.3
42	62	Omaha city, Nebraska	4.3
16	64	San Francisco city, California	4.2
18	64	Hempstead town, Nassau County, New York	4.2
19	66	Seattle city, Washington	4.1
24	66	Nashville-Davidson metropolitan government	4.1
43	66	Raleigh city, North Carolina	4.1
61	66	Islip town, Suffolk County, New York	4.1
20	70	Denver city, Colorado	3.8
11	71	Austin city, Texas	3.7
58	71	Urban Honolulu CDP, Hawaii	3.7
74	71	Plano city, Texas	3.7
72	74	Lincoln city, Nebraska	3.4
70	75	Oyster Bay town, Nassau County, New York	3.2

Value of new residential construction authorized by building permits, 2019

Population rank	Value of new residential construction rank	City	Value of new residential construction authorized by building permits [Table B col 19]
2	1	Los Angeles city, California	3,311,094
4	2	Houston city, Texas	2,539,169
11	3	Austin city, Texas	2,157,939
5	4	Phoenix city, Arizona	1,893,626
19	5	Seattle city, Washington	1,693,658
13	6	Fort Worth city, Texas	1,621,821
7	7	San Antonio city, Texas	1,505,994
24	8	Nashville-Davidson metropolitan government	1,430,865
44	9	Miami city, Florida	1,332,215
12	10	Jacksonville city, Florida	1,278,709
20	11	Denver city, Colorado	1,267,641
9	12	Dallas city, Texas	1,068,187
16	13	San Francisco city, California	913,794
3	14	Chicago city, Illinois	913,567
48	15	Minneapolis city, Minnesota	897,180
50	16	Tampa city, Florida	834,087
27	17	Portland city, Oregon	779,225
6	18	Philadelphia city, Pennsylvania	747,902
26	19	Oklahoma City city, Oklahoma	705,270
8	20	San Diego city, California	692,028
51	21	Arlington city, Texas	681,128
21	22	Washington city, District of Columbia	680,539
64	23	Henderson city, Nevada	660,246
37	24	Sacramento city, California	632,277
28	25	Las Vegas city, Nevada	613,199
22	26	Boston city, Suffolk County, Massachusetts	586,333
75	27	Orlando city, Florida	555,715
56	28	Aurora city, Colorado	548,351
36	29	Mesa city, Arizona	513,528
38	30	Atlanta city, Georgia	503,095
23	31	El Paso city, Texas	501,344
14	32	Columbus city, Ohio	468,926
35	33	Fresno city, California	421,046
54	34	Bakersfield city, California	403,835
34	35	Tucson city, Arizona	377,542
47	36	Oakland city, California	360,872
10	37	San Jose city, California	329,550
62	38	Corpus Christi city, Texas	309,595
73	39	Anchorage municipality, Alaska	298,202
72	40	Lincoln city, Nebraska	287,607
49	41	Tulsa city, Oklahoma	246,350
52	42	New Orleans city, Louisiana	244,557
42	43	Omaha city, Nebraska	234,540
45	44	Long Beach city, California	228,993
39	45	Kansas City city, Missouri	225,121
43	46	Raleigh city, North Carolina	222,539
63	47	Lexington-Fayette urban county, Kentucky	217,839
33	48	Albuquerque city, New Mexico	214,597
74	49	Plano city, Texas	178,577
67	50	Cincinnati city, Ohio	170,956
66	51	St. Paul city, Ramsey County, Minnesota	159,855
46	52	Virginia Beach city, Virginia	153,826
71	53	Greensboro city, North Carolina	150,248
53	54	Wichita city, Kansas	143,267
18	55	Hempstead town, Nassau County, New York	127,791
65	56	Stockton city, California	118,076
59	57	Santa Ana city, California	107,820
60	58	Riverside city, California	100,227
70	59	Oyster Bay town, Nassau County, New York	79,878
31	60	Baltimore city, Maryland	77,309
69	61	Pittsburgh city, Allegheny County, Pennsylvania	77,141
25	62	Detroit city, Wayne County, Michigan	54,299
57	63	Anaheim city, California	49,807
68	64	St. Louis city, Missouri	45,033
32	65	Milwaukee city, Milwaukee County, Wisconsin	24,330
61	66	Islip town, Suffolk County, New York	16,944
55	67	Cleveland city, Ohio	12,414
40	68	Brookhaven town, Suffolk County, New York	1,593
1		New York city, New York	NA
15		Charlotte city, North Carolina	NA
17		Indianapolis city (balance), Indiana	NA
29		Memphis city, Tennessee	NA
30		Louisville/Jefferson County metro government	NA
41		Colorado Springs city, Colorado	NA
58		Urban Honolulu CDP, Hawaii	NA

75 Largest Cities and Towns by 2019 Population
Selected Rankings

Per capita local taxes, 2017				Per capita general expenditures, 2017			
Population rank	Per capita local taxes rank	City	Per capita local taxes [Table B col 27]	Population rank	Per capita general expenditures rank	City	Per capita general expenditures [Table B col 27]
21	1	Washington city, District of Columbia	10,729	1	1	New York city, New York	102,551
1	2	New York city, New York	6,555	21	2	Washington city, District of Columbia	13,938
16	3	San Francisco city, California	4,255	16	3	San Francisco city, California	10,297
22	4	Boston city, Suffolk County, Massachusetts	3,439	2	4	Los Angeles city, California	9,618
31	5	Baltimore city, Maryland	2,438	3	5	Chicago city, Illinois	7,769
6	6	Philadelphia city, Pennsylvania	2,346	6	6	Philadelphia city, Pennsylvania	6,861
24	7	Nashville-Davidson metropolitan government	2,329	4	7	Houston city, Texas	4,067
46	8	Virginia Beach city, Virginia	2,107	22	8	Boston city, Suffolk County, Massachusetts	3,729
73	9	Anchorage municipality, Alaska	2,070	31	9	Baltimore city, Maryland	3,479
19	10	Seattle city, Washington	1,966	9	10	Dallas city, Texas	3,236
47	11	Oakland city, California	1,915	20	11	Denver city, Colorado	3,003
20	12	Denver city, Colorado	1,893	24	12	Nashville-Davidson metropolitan government	2,894
68	13	St. Louis city, Missouri	1,875	19	13	Seattle city, Washington	2,586
67	14	Cincinnati city, Ohio	1,810	8	14	San Diego city, California	2,575
39	15	Kansas City city, Missouri	1,513	17	15	Indianapolis city (balance), Indiana	2,462
52	16	New Orleans city, Louisiana	1,416	5	16	Phoenix city, Arizona	2,422
69	17	Pittsburgh city, Allegheny County, Pennsylvania	1,385	7	17	San Antonio city, Texas	2,274
27	18	Portland city, Oregon	1,371	25	18	Detroit city, Wayne County, Michigan	2,109
3	19	Chicago city, Illinois	1,314	11	19	Austin city, Texas	2,010
38	20	Atlanta city, Georgia	1,300	46	20	Virginia Beach city, Virginia	1,859
63	21	Lexington-Fayette urban county, Kentucky	1,277	14	21	Columbus city, Ohio	1,750
55	22	Cleveland city, Ohio	1,225	39	22	Kansas City city, Missouri	1,711
10	23	San Jose city, California	1,200	12	23	Jacksonville city, Florida	1,680
44	24	Miami city, Florida	1,196	45	24	Long Beach city, California	1,648
2	25	Los Angeles city, California	1,184	38	25	Atlanta city, Georgia	1,608
48	26	Minneapolis city, Minnesota	1,120	48	26	Minneapolis city, Minnesota	1,582
12	27	Jacksonville city, Florida	1,114	10	27	San Jose city, California	1,559
25	28	Detroit city, Wayne County, Michigan	1,108	15	28	Charlotte city, North Carolina	1,536
4	29	Houston city, Texas	1,080	27	29	Portland city, Oregon	1,449
14	30	Columbus city, Ohio	1,074	73	30	Anchorage municipality, Alaska	1,395
57	31	Anaheim city, California	1,052	52	31	New Orleans city, Louisiana	1,359
74	32	Plano city, Texas	1,050	47	32	Oakland city, California	1,319
8	33	San Diego city, California	1,001	13	33	Fort Worth city, Texas	1,300
15	34	Charlotte city, North Carolina	999	30	34	Louisville/Jefferson County metro government	1,215
26	34	Oklahoma City city, Oklahoma	999	32	35	Milwaukee city, Milwaukee County, Wisconsin	1,117
9	36	Dallas city, Texas	990	55	36	Cleveland city, Ohio	1,056
49	37	Tulsa city, Oklahoma	967	29	37	Memphis city, Tennessee	1,049
75	38	Orlando city, Florida	954	68	38	St. Louis city, Missouri	1,030
45	39	Long Beach city, California	939	26	39	Oklahoma City city, Oklahoma	1,026
11	40	Austin city, Texas	937	67	40	Cincinnati city, Ohio	929
37	41	Sacramento city, California	913	44	41	Miami city, Florida	894
42	42	Omaha city, Nebraska	898	75	42	Orlando city, Florida	851
70	43	Oyster Bay town, Nassau County, New York	877	33	43	Albuquerque city, New Mexico	814
13	44	Fort Worth city, Texas	875	66	44	St. Paul city, Ramsey County, Minnesota	811
56	45	Aurora city, Colorado	857	28	45	Las Vegas city, Nevada	797
30	46	Louisville/Jefferson County metro government	838	37	46	Sacramento city, California	776
50	47	Tampa city, Florida	791	69	47	Pittsburgh city, Allegheny County, Pennsylvania	757
5	48	Phoenix city, Arizona	767	23	48	El Paso city, Texas	745
43	49	Raleigh city, North Carolina	765	50	49	Tampa city, Florida	733
65	50	Stockton city, California	732	34	50	Tucson city, Arizona	721
62	51	Corpus Christi city, Texas	722	49	51	Tulsa city, Oklahoma	721
51	52	Arlington city, Texas	714	57	52	Anaheim city, California	705
71	53	Greensboro city, North Carolina	709	36	53	Mesa city, Arizona	699
41	54	Colorado Springs city, Colorado	707	18	54	Hempstead town, Nassau County, New York	612
29	55	Memphis city, Tennessee	696	63	55	Lexington-Fayette urban county, Kentucky	590
33	56	Albuquerque city, New Mexico	690	53	56	Wichita city, Kansas	576
60	57	Riverside city, California	686	43	57	Raleigh city, North Carolina	552
23	58	El Paso city, Texas	673	42	58	Omaha city, Nebraska	540
59	59	Santa Ana city, California	634	56	59	Aurora city, Colorado	494
7	60	San Antonio city, Texas	626	41	60	Colorado Springs city, Colorado	481
35	61	Fresno city, California	613	59	61	Santa Ana city, California	471
72	62	Lincoln city, Nebraska	600	54	62	Bakersfield city, California	468
34	63	Tucson city, Arizona	578	51	63	Arlington city, Texas	463
66	64	St. Paul city, Ramsey County, Minnesota	574	35	64	Fresno city, California	441
17	65	Indianapolis city (balance), Indiana	492	62	65	Corpus Christi city, Texas	436
64	65	Henderson city, Nevada	492	71	66	Greensboro city, North Carolina	415
32	67	Milwaukee city, Milwaukee County, Wisconsin	482	60	67	Riverside city, California	404
53	68	Wichita city, Kansas	471	72	68	Lincoln city, Nebraska	374
18	69	Hempstead town, Nassau County, New York	462	74	69	Plano city, Texas	370
54	69	Bakersfield city, California	462	64	70	Henderson city, Nevada	368
36	71	Mesa city, Arizona	439	40	71	Brookhaven town, Suffolk County, New York	338
61	72	Islip town, Suffolk County, New York	407	70	72	Oyster Bay town, Nassau County, New York	334
40	73	Brookhaven town, Suffolk County, New York	396	65	73	Stockton city, California	320
28	74	Las Vegas city, Nevada	354	61	74	Islip town, Suffolk County, New York	202
58	75	Urban Honolulu CDP, Hawaii	NA	58	75	Urban Honolulu CDP, Hawaii	NA

75 Largest Cities and Towns by 2019 Population
Selected Rankings

Number of healthcare and social assistance employees, 2017				Number of professional, scientific, and technical employees, 2017			
Population rank	Healthcare and social assistance employees rank	City	Number of healthcare and social assistance employees [Table C col 20]	Population rank	Professional, scientific, and technical employees rank	City	Number of professional, scientific, and technical employees [Table B col 14]
2	1	Los Angeles city, California	226,723	1	1	New York city, New York	406,156
4	2	Houston city, Texas	220,087	3	2	Chicago city, Illinois	174,661
3	3	Chicago city, Illinois	186,215	2	3	Los Angeles city, California	155,056
6	4	Philadelphia city, Pennsylvania	161,976	4	4	Houston city, Texas	153,689
21	5	Boston city, Massachusetts	133,669	14	5	San Francisco city, California	117,838
9	6	Dallas city, Texas	121,052	8	6	San Diego city, California	115,825
7	7	San Antonio city, Texas	113,466	20	7	Washington city, District of Columbia	108,016
5	8	Phoenix city, Arizona	107,483	21	8	Boston city, Massachusetts	86,292
8	9	San Diego city, California	97,758	11	9	Austin city, Texas	84,531
16	10	Indianapolis city (balance), Indiana	88,524	9	10	Dallas city, Texas	83,897
18	11	Seattle city, Washington	85,733	18	11	Seattle city, Washington	82,213
52	12	Cleveland city, Ohio	79,004	37	12	Atlanta city, Georgia	68,768
30	13	Baltimore city, Maryland	77,508	6	13	Philadelphia city, Pennsylvania	58,180
24	14	Nashville-Davidson metropolitan governme,	75,503	5	14	Phoenix city, Arizona	53,825
20	15	Washington city, District of Columbia	74,134	19	15	Denver city, Colorado	50,003
11	16	Austin city, Texas	71,118	17	16	Charlotte city, North Carolina	47,392
14	17	San Francisco city, California	69,425	74	17	Irvine city, California	47,066
12	18	Jacksonville city, Florida	68,647	7	18	San Antonio city, Texas	46,677
26	19	Portland city, Oregon	67,025	10	19	San Jose city, California	45,002
31	20	Milwaukee city, Wisconsin	61,852	50	20	Tampa city, Florida	41,022
46	21	Minneapolis city, Minnesota	60,986	46	21	Minneapolis city, Minnesota	36,745
17	22	Charlotte city, North Carolina	60,916	12	22	Jacksonville city, Florida	35,882
65	23	Pittsburgh city, Pennsylvania	60,636	26	23	Portland city, Oregon	35,617
15	24	Fort Worth city, Texas	59,067	41	24	Raleigh city, North Carolina	33,853
19	25	Denver city, Colorado	56,165	38	25	Kansas City city, Missouri	32,540
25	26	Memphis city, Tennessee	55,489	69	26	Plano city, Texas	31,565
64	27	Cincinnati city, Ohio	55,181	13	27	Columbus city, Ohio	30,953
27	28	Oklahoma City city, Oklahoma	54,538	65	28	Pittsburgh city, Pennsylvania	30,512
39	29	Omaha city, Nebraska	51,418	24	29	Nashville-Davidson metropolitan governme,	29,524
32	30	Albuquerque city, New Mexico	50,897	43	30	Miami city, Florida	28,985
29	31	Louisville/Jefferson County metro govern,	50,488	30	31	Baltimore city, Maryland	25,853
23	32	Detroit city, Michigan	50,181	27	32	Oklahoma City city, Oklahoma	25,695
35	33	Sacramento city, California	46,565	71	33	Orlando city, Florida	22,012
63	34	St. Paul city, Minnesota	45,769	44	34	Virginia Beach city, Virginia	21,755
47	35	Tulsa city, Oklahoma	45,593	64	35	Cincinnati city, Ohio	20,598
38	36	Kansas City city, Missouri	45,482	42	36	Colorado Springs city, Colorado	20,579
22	37	El Paso city, Texas	45,067	15	37	Fort Worth city, Texas	20,570
33	38	Tucson city, Arizona	44,082	52	38	Cleveland city, Ohio	20,238
37	39	Atlanta city, Georgia	43,378	39	39	Omaha city, Nebraska	19,019
41	40	Raleigh city, North Carolina	43,361	62	40	St. Louis city, Missouri	18,010
43	41	Miami city, Florida	41,128	29	41	Louisville/Jefferson County metro govern,	17,890
62	42	St. Louis city, Missouri	39,629	47	42	Tulsa city, Oklahoma	17,646
28	43	Las Vegas city, Nevada	39,266	31	43	Milwaukee city, Wisconsin	17,420
50	44	Tampa city, Florida	38,844	28	44	Las Vegas city, Nevada	17,301
10	45	San Jose city, California	38,211	35	45	Sacramento city, California	17,260
71	46	Orlando city, Florida	38,074	23	46	Detroit city, Michigan	16,904
34	47	Fresno city, California	35,901	49	47	New Orleans city, Louisiana	15,845
42	48	Colorado Springs city, Colorado	35,415	25	48	Memphis city, Tennessee	14,880
56	49	Urban Honolulu CDP, Hawaii	34,983	45	49	Oakland city, California	14,453
51	50	Wichita city, Kansas	34,913	67	50	Anchorage municipality, Alaska	14,219
60	51	Lexington-Fayette urban county, Kentucky	32,976	56	51	Urban Honolulu CDP, Hawaii	13,894
36	52	Mesa city, Arizona	31,274	33	52	Tucson city, Arizona	12,594
45	53	Oakland city, California	30,875	60	53	Lexington-Fayette urban county, Kentucky	11,126
69	54	Plano city, Texas	29,943	57	54	Santa Ana city, California	10,446
40	55	Long Beach city, California	29,063	51	55	Wichita city, Kansas	10,366
59	56	Corpus Christi city, Texas	27,875	22	56	El Paso city, Texas	9,756
67	57	Anchorage municipality, Alaska	27,333	40	57	Long Beach city, California	8,457
75	58	Durham city, North Carolina	27,001	34	58	Fresno city, California	8,428
54	59	Aurora city, Colorado	26,587	70	59	Lincoln city, Nebraska	8,293
49	60	New Orleans city, Louisiana	26,020	72	60	Newark city, New Jersey	8,271
70	61	Lincoln city, Nebraska	24,568	68	61	Greensboro city, North Carolina	7,972
73	62	Toledo city, Ohio	24,505	54	62	Aurora city, Colorado	7,726
68	63	Greensboro city, North Carolina	24,398	63	63	St. Paul city, Minnesota	7,440
53	64	Bakersfield city, California	23,324	59	64	Corpus Christi city, Texas	7,070
48	65	Arlington city, Texas	22,351	36	65	Mesa city, Arizona	6,599
58	66	Riverside city, California	21,881	48	66	Arlington city, Texas	6,083
44	67	Virginia Beach city, Virginia	21,729	53	67	Bakersfield city, California	5,270
55	68	Anaheim city, California	20,597	58	68	Riverside city, California	5,250
61	69	Stockton city, California	19,134	66	69	Henderson city, Nevada	4,993
72	70	Newark city, New Jersey	18,615	73	70	Toledo city, Ohio	4,285
74	71	Irvine city, California	15,404	61	71	Stockton city, California	2,836
57	72	Santa Ana city, California	14,624	16		Indianapolis city (balance), Indiana	D
66	73	Henderson city, Nevada	12,658	32		Albuquerque city, New Mexico	D
1		New York city, New York	NA	55		Anaheim city, California	D
13		Columbus city, Ohio	NA	75		Durham city, North Carolina	D

75 Largest Cities and Towns by 2019 Population
Selected Rankings

	Number of information employees, 2017				Number of retail trade employees, 2017		
Population rank	Information employees rank	City	Information employees [Table B col 8]	Population rank	Retail trade employees rank	City	Retail trade employees [Table B col 2]
1	1	New York city, New York	208,759	1	1	New York city, New York	353,094
2	2	Los Angeles city, California	88,119	4	2	Houston city, Texas	159,513
14	3	San Francisco city, California	83,500	2	3	Los Angeles city, California	151,931
3	4	Chicago city, Illinois	55,938	3	4	Chicago city, Illinois	97,034
18	5	Seattle city, Washington	34,925	7	5	San Antonio city, Texas	81,646
4	6	Houston city, Texas	34,541	5	6	Phoenix city, Arizona	73,994
11	7	Austin city, Texas	34,334	8	7	San Diego city, California	66,413
37	8	Atlanta city, Georgia	30,644	9	8	Dallas city, Texas	65,708
8	9	San Diego city, California	28,147	11	9	Austin city, Texas	57,095
21	10	Boston city, Massachusetts	26,898	6	10	Philadelphia city, Pennsylvania	53,157
17	11	Charlotte city, North Carolina	24,733	12	11	Jacksonville city, Florida	50,554
20	12	Washington city, District of Columbia	23,787	14	12	San Francisco city, California	49,883
10	13	San Jose city, California	23,324	13	13	Columbus city, Ohio	48,299
9	14	Dallas city, Texas	23,279	17	14	Charlotte city, North Carolina	46,761
19	15	Denver city, Colorado	19,634	16	15	Indianapolis city (balance), Indiana	46,121
6	16	Philadelphia city, Pennsylvania	19,163	10	16	San Jose city, California	43,442
5	17	Phoenix city, Arizona	17,558	15	17	Fort Worth city, Texas	39,925
16	18	Indianapolis city (balance), Indiana	17,408	18	18	Seattle city, Washington	39,883
74	19	Irvine city, California	17,376	26	19	Portland city, Oregon	37,084
7	20	San Antonio city, Texas	16,607	24	20	Nashville-Davidson metropolitan governme,	36,463
12	21	Jacksonville city, Florida	15,113	28	21	Las Vegas city, Nevada	35,708
24	22	Nashville-Davidson metropolitan governme,	14,993	25	22	Memphis city, Tennessee	35,216
46	23	Minneapolis city, Minnesota	12,832	22	23	El Paso city, Texas	34,562
13	24	Columbus city, Ohio	12,717	27	24	Oklahoma City city, Oklahoma	33,933
26	25	Portland city, Oregon	12,270	39	25	Omaha city, Nebraska	33,315
38	26	Kansas City city, Missouri	11,116	43	26	Miami city, Florida	32,942
65	27	Pittsburgh city, Pennsylvania	10,969	19	27	Denver city, Colorado	32,753
50	28	Tampa city, Florida	10,594	32	28	Albuquerque city, New Mexico	32,482
47	29	Tulsa city, Oklahoma	9,497	21	29	Boston city, Massachusetts	32,451
39	30	Omaha city, Nebraska	9,281	29	30	Louisville/Jefferson County metro govern,	32,443
42	31	Colorado Springs city, Colorado	8,939	33	31	Tucson city, Arizona	32,262
71	32	Orlando city, Florida	8,846	71	32	Orlando city, Florida	30,854
41	33	Raleigh city, North Carolina	8,823	41	33	Raleigh city, North Carolina	29,789
69	34	Plano city, Texas	8,403	37	34	Atlanta city, Georgia	28,468
32	35	Albuquerque city, New Mexico	8,164	47	35	Tulsa city, Oklahoma	28,067
64	36	Cincinnati city, Ohio	8,161	56	36	Urban Honolulu CDP, Hawaii	26,810
22	37	El Paso city, Texas	8,145	42	37	Colorado Springs city, Colorado	26,651
27	38	Oklahoma City city, Oklahoma	8,105	51	38	Wichita city, Kansas	26,178
23	39	Detroit city, Michigan	7,045	50	39	Tampa city, Florida	25,775
29	40	Louisville/Jefferson County metro govern,	6,836	38	40	Kansas City city, Missouri	25,405
45	41	Oakland city, California	6,799	34	41	Fresno city, California	25,256
31	42	Milwaukee city, Wisconsin	6,526	44	42	Virginia Beach city, Virginia	24,023
30	43	Baltimore city, Maryland	6,431	69	43	Plano city, Texas	23,966
15	44	Fort Worth city, Texas	6,064	36	44	Mesa city, Arizona	23,696
44	45	Virginia Beach city, Virginia	6,050	20	45	Washington city, District of Columbia	23,133
72	46	Newark city, New Jersey	5,939	60	46	Lexington-Fayette urban county, Kentucky	23,102
62	47	St. Louis city, Missouri	5,891	48	47	Arlington city, Texas	21,315
33	48	Tucson city, Arizona	5,757	30	48	Baltimore city, Maryland	21,064
25	49	Memphis city, Tennessee	5,555	68	49	Greensboro city, North Carolina	20,654
63	50	St. Paul city, Minnesota	5,505	53	50	Bakersfield city, California	20,027
51	51	Wichita city, Kansas	5,491	35	51	Sacramento city, California	19,969
43	52	Miami city, Florida	5,224	70	52	Lincoln city, Nebraska	18,008
28	53	Las Vegas city, Nevada	5,071	59	53	Corpus Christi city, Texas	17,527
68	54	Greensboro city, North Carolina	4,938	54	54	Aurora city, Colorado	17,442
52	55	Cleveland city, Ohio	4,781	65	55	Pittsburgh city, Pennsylvania	17,273
70	56	Lincoln city, Nebraska	4,692	67	56	Anchorage municipality, Alaska	15,445
60	57	Lexington-Fayette urban county, Kentucky	4,558	58	57	Riverside city, California	15,315
56	58	Urban Honolulu CDP, Hawaii	4,498	64	58	Cincinnati city, Ohio	15,048
67	59	Anchorage municipality, Alaska	4,381	49	59	New Orleans city, Louisiana	14,795
35	60	Sacramento city, California	4,151	75	60	Durham city, North Carolina	14,593
34	61	Fresno city, California	3,582	66	61	Henderson city, Nevada	14,462
53	62	Bakersfield city, California	2,638	46	62	Minneapolis city, Minnesota	13,609
48	63	Arlington city, Texas	2,535	40	63	Long Beach city, California	13,603
49	64	New Orleans city, Louisiana	2,412	73	64	Toledo city, Ohio	13,410
40	65	Long Beach city, California	2,365	23	65	Detroit city, Michigan	13,065
55	66	Anaheim city, California	2,034	55	66	Anaheim city, California	12,856
58	67	Riverside city, California	2,011	57	67	Santa Ana city, California	12,828
54	68	Aurora city, Colorado	1,990	61	68	Stockton city, California	11,974
36	69	Mesa city, Arizona	1,967	45	69	Oakland city, California	11,810
57	70	Santa Ana city, California	1,963	74	70	Irvine city, California	11,702
59	71	Corpus Christi city, Texas	1,860	62	71	St. Louis city, Missouri	9,928
73	72	Toledo city, Ohio	1,677	52	72	Cleveland city, Ohio	9,648
61	73	Stockton city, California	1,204	63	73	St. Paul city, Minnesota	9,284
66	74	Henderson city, Nevada	1,100	72	74	Newark city, New Jersey	7,325
75		Durham city, North Carolina	D	31		Milwaukee city, Wisconsin	D

SUBJECTS COVERED, BY PLACE SIZE AND TYPE

	Incorporated places			Minor civil divisions (MCDs)			Census designated places (CDPs)		
	All places	10,000 or more population		All MCDs	10,000 or more population		All CDPs	10,000 or more population	
Subject	Table A	Table B	Table C	Table A	Table B	Table C	Table A	Table B	Table C
Land area		1			1			1	
Population									
Total persons, 2010		2			2			2	
Total persons, 2019	1	3		1	3		1	3	
Percent change, 2010–2019	2	4		2	4		2	4	
Total population estimate, 2015–2019	3			3			3		
Persons per square mile, 2019	4	5		4	5		4	5	
Race and Hispanic origin, 2015–2019	5–9			5–9			5–9		
Age distribution, 2015–2019	10–11			10–11			10–11		
Median age, 2015-2019	12			12			12		
Foreign–born, 2015-2019		6			6			6	
Households									
Total households, 2015–2019	15			15			15		
Family households, 2015–2019		13			13			13	
One–person households, 2015–2019		14			14			14	
Same residence as previous year, 2015–2019		7			7			7	
Value of owner-occupied housing units		10			10			10	
Computer access	16			16			16		
Income									
Median household income, 2015–2019		8			8			8	
Income below poverty level, 2015–2019		9			9			9	
Education									
High school diploma or less, 2015–2019	13			13			13		
Bachelor's degree or more, 2015–2019	14			14			14		
Employment									
Percent in labor force, 2015–2019		11			11			11	
Unemployment rate, 2015–2019		12			12			12	
Crime									
Violent crime number, 2018		15			15			15	
Violent crime rate, 2018		16			16			16	
Property crime number, 2018		17			17			17	
Property crime rate, 2018		18			18			18	
New residential construction									
Value, 2019		19			19			19	
Number of units, 2019		20			20			20	
Percent singe family, 2019		21			21			21	
Local government finance									
General revenue, 2017		22–24			22–24			22–24	
Per capita taxes, 2017		25			25			25	
General expenditure, 2017		26–28			26–28			26–28	
Debt outstanding, 2017		29			29			29	
Retail Trade									
Number of establishments, 2017			1			1			1
Number of employees, 2017			2			2			2
Wholesale Trade									
Number of establishments, 2017			3			3			3
Number of establishments, 2017			4			4			4
Transportation and Warehousing									
Number of establishments, 2017			5			5			5
Number of employees, 2017			6			6			6
Information									
Number of establishments, 2017			7			7			7
Number of employees, 2017			8			8			8
Finance and insurance									
Number of establishments, 2017			9			9			9
Number of employees, 2017			10			10			10
Real Estate and Rental and Leasing									
Number of establishments, 2017			11			11			11
Number of employees, 2017			12			12			12
Professional, scientific, and technical services									
Number of establishments, 2017			13			13			13
Number of employees, 2017			14			14			14
Administration and support and waste management and mediation services									
Number of establishments, 2017			15			15			15
Number of employees, 2017			16			16			16
Educational services									
Number of establishments, 2017			17			17			17
Number of employees, 2017			18			18			18
Health care and social assistance									
Number of establishments, 2017			19			19			19
Number of employees, 2017			20			20			20
Arts, entertainment, and recreation									
Number of establishments, 2017			21			21			21
Number of employees, 2017			22			22			22
Accommodation and food services									
Number of establishments, 2017			23			23			23
Number of employees, 2017			24			24			24
Other services (except public administration)									
Number of establishments, 2017			25			25			25
Number of employees, 2017			26			26			26

COLUMN HEADINGS FOR TABLE A

Table A. All Places — **Population and Housing**

STATE City, town, township, borough, or CDP (county if applicable)	Population				Race and Hispanic or Latino origin (percent)					Age (percent)			Educational attainment of persons age 25 and older		Occupied housing units	
	2010 census total population	2019 estimated population	Percent change 2010–2019	ACS total population estimate 2015–2019	White alone, not Hispanic or Latino	Black alone, not Hispanic or Latino	Asian alone, not Hispanic or Latino	All other races or 2 or more races, not Hispanic or Latino	Hispanic or Latino[1]	Under 18 years old	Age 65 years and older	Median age	Percent High school diploma or less	Percent Bachelor's degree or more	Total	Percent with a computer
	1	2	3	4	5	6	7	8	9	10	11	12	13	14	15	16

COLUMN HEADINGS FOR TABLE B

Table B. Incorporated Places, Census Designated Places (CDPs), and Minor Civil Divisions (MCDs) of 10,000 or More Population — **Land Area, Population, and Households, and Employment**

STATE City, town, township, borough, or CDP (county if applicable)	Land area 2010 (sq mi)	Population				Population characteristics 2015–2019		Income and poverty 2015–2019		Median value of owner-occupied housing units	Employment, 2015–2019		Households, 2015-2019 (percent of households)	
		Total persons 2010	Total persons 2019	Percent change 2010–2019	Persons per square mile, 2019	Percent foreign born	Percent living in the same house as previous year	Median household income	Percent of households with income below poverty level		Percent in civilian labor force	Unemployment rate	Family households	One person households
	1	2	3	4	5	6	7	8	9	10	11	12	13	14

Table B. Incorporated Places, Census Designated Places (CDPs), and Minor Civil Divisions (MCDs) of 10,000 or More Population — **Crime, Residential Construction and Local Government Finance**

STATE City, town, township, borough, or CDP (county if applicable)	Serious crimes known to police, 2018[1]				New residential construction authorized by building permits, 2019			Local government finance, 2017							
	Violent crime		Property crime					General revenue				General expenditure			
									Intergovernmental					Per capita[3]	
	Number	Rate[2]	Number	Rate[2]	Value ($1,000)	Number of housing units	Percent single family	Total (mil dol)	Total (mil dol)	Percent from state gov.	Taxes per capita[3]	Total (mil dol)	Total	Capital outlays	Debt outstanding (mil dol)
	15	16	17	18	19	20	21	22	23	24	25	26	27	28	29

COLUMN HEADINGS FOR TABLE C

Table C. Incorporated Places, Census Designated Places (CDPs), and Minor Civil Divisions (MCDs) of 10,000 or More Population — **Economic Census**

STATE City, town, township, borough, or CDP (county if applicable)	Economic activity by sector, 2017													
	Retail Trade		Wholesale trade[1]		Transportation and warehousing		Information		Finance and insurance		Real estate and rental and leasing		Professional, scientific, and technical services	
	Number of establishments	Number of employees	Number of establishments	Number of employees	Number of establishments	Number of employees	Number of establishments	Number of employees	Number of establishments	Number of employees	Number of establishments	Number of employees	Number of establishments	Number of employees
	1	2	3	4	5	6	7	8	9	10	11	12	13	14

Table C. Incorporated Places, Census Designated Places (CDPs), and Minor Civil Divisions (MCDs) of 10,000 or More Population — **Economic Census**

STATE City, town, township, borough, or CDP (county if applicable)	Economic activity by sector, 2017											
	Administration and support and waste management and mediation services		Educational services		Health care and social assistance		Arts, entertainment, and recreation		Accommodation and food services		Other services (except public administration)	
	Number of establishments	Number of employees	Number of establishments	Number of employees	Number of establishments	Number of employees	Number of establishments	Number of employees	Number of establishments	Number of employees	Number of establishments	Number of employees
	15	16	17	18	19	20	21	22	23	24	25	26

TABLE A.

All Places

(For explanation of symbols see page xvi)

Table A — All Places

Table A. All Places — **Population and Housing**

STATE City, town, township, borough, or CDP (county if applicable)	Population				Race and Hispanic or Latino origin (percent)					Age (percent)			Educational attainment of persons age 25 and older		Occupied housing units	
	2010 census total population	2019 estimated population	Percent change 2010–2019	ACS total population estimate 2015–2019	White alone, not Hispanic or Latino	Black alone, not Hispanic or Latino	Asian alone, not Hispanic or Latino	All other races or 2 or more races, not Hispanic or Latino	Hispanic or Latino[1]	Under 18 years old	Age 65 years and older	Median age	Percent High school diploma or less	Percent Bachelor's degree or more	Total	Percent with a computer
	1	2	3	4	5	6	7	8	9	10	11	12	13	14	15	16
UNITED STATES	305,758,105	328,239,523	7.4	324,697,795	60.7	12.3	5.5	3.5	18.0	22.6	15.6	38.1	39.0	32.1	120,756,048	90.3
ALABAMA	4,780,125	4,903,185	2.6	4,876,250	65.5	26.5	1.3	2.4	4.3	22.5	16.5	39.0	44.6	25.5	1,867,893	85.5
Abanda CDP	192	-	-	176	74.4	25.6	0.0	0.0	0.0	29.5	10.8	32.7	87.3	0.0	53	79.2
Abbeville city	2,705	2,560	-5.4	2,573	51.4	41.5	0.0	1.6	5.5	19.0	26.9	46.9	58.3	11.9	1,029	76.9
Adamsville city	4,506	4,281	-5.0	4,340	47.9	48.2	0.0	3.7	0.2	26.4	18.6	42.3	49.7	15.7	1,471	81.8
Addison town	754	718	-4.8	728	97.4	0.0	0.0	2.6	0.0	19.8	22.0	46.5	63.3	12.4	319	79.0
Akron town	356	328	-7.9	315	25.7	74.3	0.0	0.0	0.0	15.9	12.4	47.3	70.3	4.5	116	62.9
Alabaster city	31,112	33,487	7.6	33,176	70.9	14.5	1.6	3.0	9.9	26.2	12.0	37.5	31.2	35.3	11,568	95.9
Albertville city	21,209	21,711	2.4	21,541	66.0	3.7	0.7	1.4	28.2	30.5	13.2	32.7	54.3	16.0	7,249	87.0
Alexander City city	14,984	14,317	-4.5	14,508	61.3	31.9	0.8	1.3	4.8	24.1	18.4	40.2	48.5	18.2	5,710	87.0
Alexandria CDP	3,917	-	-	4,068	85.4	14.0	0.0	0.6	0.0	21.2	11.2	39.2	37.0	25.3	1,560	95.8
Aliceville city	2,481	2,254	-9.1	2,362	19.6	80.1	0.0	0.3	0.0	20.0	15.5	34.9	66.3	13.9	898	75.5
Allgood town	622	650	4.5	706	39.0	0.0	0.0	2.3	58.8	26.9	12.3	35.7	74.6	3.5	208	65.4
Altoona town	937	913	-2.6	883	95.4	2.3	0.2	1.0	1.1	23.4	16.6	36.2	57.7	7.2	320	81.6
Andalusia city	9,015	8,680	-3.7	8,772	68.4	27.7	0.5	1.3	2.1	21.5	17.8	40.4	48.6	23.4	3,490	83.3
Anderson town	281	267	-5.0	236	94.1	0.0	3.8	0.8	1.3	12.3	26.7	47.5	62.4	11.6	104	65.4
Anniston city	22,987	21,287	-7.4	21,688	41.4	51.4	1.1	3.6	2.5	21.8	20.1	40.8	47.7	20.9	9,277	79.6
Arab city	8,080	8,383	3.8	8,293	93.6	0.8	1.6	2.4	1.7	23.9	20.2	42.3	41.7	23.3	3,177	88.4
Ardmore town	1,194	1,463	22.5	1,350	82.6	11.7	2.5	1.7	1.5	25.2	18.4	38.9	65.0	11.1	520	77.9
Argo town	4,085	4,348	6.4	4,220	89.9	4.8	0.4	0.0	4.9	24.7	10.1	34.3	35.0	16.6	1,348	98.8
Ariton town	762	739	-3.0	837	77.3	12.5	0.0	3.3	6.8	26.0	11.9	35.8	59.3	17.9	272	83.1
Arley town	357	345	-3.4	574	98.4	0.2	0.2	1.2	0.0	23.7	13.4	34.1	59.3	14.6	183	83.6
Ashford town	2,149	2,181	1.5	2,468	70.4	26.4	0.1	0.8	2.3	24.5	17.7	38.8	51.6	13.5	865	73.8
Ashland town	2,039	1,895	-7.1	1,447	67.4	30.7	0.5	0.7	0.8	14.0	27.4	48.4	66.8	9.1	677	77.5
Ashville city	2,231	2,365	6.0	2,380	66.9	29.7	0.0	0.4	2.9	21.7	13.0	41.0	57.0	10.3	778	85.5
Athens city	21,878	27,366	25.1	25,922	71.2	16.7	1.6	3.0	7.5	20.7	18.1	40.6	41.3	30.1	9,397	85.7
Atmore city	10,167	9,107	-10.4	9,495	38.1	58.4	0.1	2.7	0.7	18.2	16.7	38.4	72.5	10.4	2,803	63.5
Attalla city	6,048	5,771	-4.6	5,836	73.8	18.8	0.0	3.3	4.1	26.4	18.9	37.4	54.6	8.9	2,151	89.2
Auburn city	53,439	66,259	24.0	64,054	68.6	18.2	8.6	1.3	3.3	18.3	8.1	24.8	17.2	58.0	23,500	96.4
Autaugaville town	886	871	-1.7	963	26.9	72.7	0.0	0.0	0.4	15.2	22.3	45.6	74.3	8.4	444	74.8
Avon town	496	510	2.8	592	84.3	1.4	0.0	0.0	14.4	22.5	15.2	39.5	60.2	17.0	200	73.5
Axis CDP	757	-	-	1,180	53.3	46.7	0.0	0.0	0.0	36.3	6.9	28.5	45.5	29.9	325	88.9
Babbie town	603	596	-1.2	558	96.2	0.5	0.0	1.3	2.0	22.9	19.4	42.1	52.4	7.8	227	74.9
Baileyton town	606	619	2.1	872	90.3	0.0	0.0	2.2	7.6	20.2	19.3	40.2	59.2	17.2	325	80.0
Bakerhill town	279	252	-9.7	228	62.3	36.4	0.0	0.4	0.9	22.4	20.2	46.5	44.0	20.5	98	90.8
Ballplay CDP	1,580	-	-	1,605	98.1	0.0	0.0	1.9	0.0	22.9	13.5	38.6	46.3	18.6	480	82.5
Banks town	173	164	-5.2	190	78.9	21.1	0.0	0.0	0.0	25.3	11.1	36.4	51.2	27.9	76	81.6
Bay Minette city	8,256	9,354	13.3	9,169	57.2	38.8	0.1	1.7	2.2	23.1	16.8	34.4	54.3	14.6	2,812	89.0
Bayou La Batre city	2,458	2,479	0.9	2,543	63.7	10.1	16.9	3.5	5.8	22.5	15.0	36.3	67.7	8.8	837	86.9
Bear Creek town	1,068	1,068	0.0	1,205	92.0	0.0	0.0	4.1	4.0	25.6	19.0	39.0	65.7	7.1	424	78.3
Beatrice town	302	278	-7.9	221	25.3	74.7	0.0	0.0	0.0	15.8	22.6	43.2	53.5	5.1	97	62.9
Beaverton town	193	187	-3.1	182	92.3	0.0	2.2	3.3	2.2	14.3	28.0	54.4	62.2	16.2	93	72.0
Belgreen CDP	129	-	-	32	100.0	0.0	0.0	0.0	0.0	0.0	15.6	63.2	43.8	12.5	29	51.7
Belk town	215	204	-5.1	238	100.0	0.0	0.0	0.0	0.0	16.4	36.1	49.8	66.1	6.0	94	67.0
Bellamy CDP	543	-	-	466	10.3	89.7	0.0	0.0	0.0	3.9	47.2	61.8	86.4	0.0	208	51.0
Belle Fontaine CDP	608	-	-	564	92.4	0.0	0.0	0.0	7.6	14.7	21.5	44.3	61.6	13.1	213	89.2
Benton town	49	41	-16.3	29	100.0	0.0	0.0	0.0	0.0	20.7	10.3	53.9	26.1	56.5	13	100.0
Berlin town	458	460	0.4	369	98.1	0.0	0.0	0.0	1.9	26.0	13.3	25.6	61.3	0.0	140	90.0
Berry town	1,146	1,095	-4.5	1,345	84.5	4.1	0.1	5.7	5.6	28.1	12.0	35.2	70.2	9.1	489	72.6
Bessemer city	27,667	26,472	-4.3	26,680	20.5	72.4	0.1	2.7	4.3	21.3	18.7	39.5	54.8	14.4	10,492	80.5
Billingsley town	148	142	-4.1	103	57.3	40.8	0.0	1.9	0.0	23.3	30.1	40.5	63.2	4.4	49	75.5
Birmingham city	212,585	209,403	-1.5	212,297	23.8	69.6	1.1	1.7	3.9	20.1	14.9	35.9	41.6	27.4	90,867	83.2
Black town	207	203	-1.9	203	97.5	0.0	0.0	1.5	1.0	20.7	14.8	50.5	63.2	8.4	91	75.8
Blountsville town	1,684	1,670	-0.8	2,262	66.2	1.0	1.1	1.9	29.9	26.4	12.5	30.4	57.9	7.7	702	70.9
Blue Ridge CDP	1,341	-	-	1,490	95.6	1.3	3.1	0.0	0.0	19.7	30.1	53.8	15.8	50.9	589	95.4
Blue Springs town	96	87	-9.4	79	70.9	22.8	6.3	0.0	0.0	10.1	40.5	55.5	62.3	19.7	32	75.0
Boaz city	9,457	9,704	2.6	9,277	86.5	3.1	0.1	1.0	9.3	24.4	18.6	37.7	46.8	19.8	3,494	84.5
Boligee town	328	280	-14.6	441	7.3	92.7	0.0	0.0	0.0	42.4	5.9	28.4	65.4	13.4	177	61.0
Bon Air town	116	110	-5.2	87	57.5	23.0	0.0	8.0	11.5	24.1	17.2	47.8	81.7	6.7	42	76.2
Bon Secour CDP	-	-	-	1,234	75.0	3.1	4.2	6.8	10.9	16.0	18.6	49.1	55.1	24.4	570	85.4
Boykin CDP	275	-	-	269	0.0	100.0	0.0	0.0	0.0	30.9	19.3	47.3	74.0	0.0	120	50.8
Brantley town	807	768	-4.8	1,005	46.2	51.3	0.0	1.5	1.0	31.4	14.7	36.2	59.1	22.8	361	70.6
Brantleyville CDP	884	-	-	860	77.8	2.4	0.0	2.8	17.0	27.2	11.7	34.6	58.6	15.1	333	90.4
Brent city	4,955	4,747	-4.2	4,803	58.2	38.1	0.0	1.0	2.7	17.8	12.6	36.9	74.4	8.2	1,055	86.2
Brewton city	5,406	5,210	-3.6	5,240	54.1	40.4	1.7	1.9	1.8	22.4	18.8	41.6	51.2	22.0	2,050	72.3
Bridgeport city	2,439	2,297	-5.8	2,106	90.4	5.2	0.0	2.6	1.9	19.0	20.7	43.4	64.5	6.9	1,031	75.4
Brighton city	2,945	2,775	-5.8	2,810	5.8	84.9	0.2	1.1	7.9	23.8	19.5	37.6	43.7	13.5	1,180	67.8
Brilliant town	897	873	-2.7	923	97.5	1.8	0.0	0.7	0.0	23.4	18.4	39.6	65.2	1.7	386	80.8
Bristow Cove CDP	683	-	-	668	94.2	0.0	0.0	5.8	0.0	32.9	33.8	35.3	63.6	0.0	221	79.6
Brook Highland CDP	6,746	-	-	7,147	64.1	17.7	6.4	3.1	8.7	16.2	9.6	33.7	14.2	57.0	3,522	97.6
Brookside town	1,364	1,329	-2.6	1,217	74.9	24.3	0.3	0.0	0.4	26.5	16.2	40.1	68.4	6.5	475	85.7
Brookwood town	1,825	1,848	1.3	2,139	86.8	10.3	0.0	0.7	2.2	22.3	9.9	34.9	46.2	18.6	757	92.5
Broomtown CDP	182	-	-	176	76.7	0.0	0.0	0.0	23.3	31.3	12.5	41.6	62.7	9.1	64	100.0
Brundidge city	2,073	1,902	-8.2	2,345	25.7	64.2	0.2	1.8	8.1	19.1	20.1	45.0	65.2	14.4	748	60.6
Bucks CDP	32	-	-	13	0.0	100.0	0.0	0.0	0.0	0.0	100.0	0.0	100.0	0.0	7	0.0
Butler town	1,948	1,721	-11.7	2,419	64.9	32.3	0.2	0.7	1.9	25.8	15.9	38.5	48.1	19.2	928	79.4
Calera city	11,608	14,717	26.8	13,856	62.5	28.3	1.7	2.1	5.4	29.1	10.3	33.1	32.7	30.7	5,100	90.6
Calvert CDP	277	-	-	609	86.4	0.0	0.0	13.6	0.0	52.9	0.0	16.8	89.9	10.1	110	100.0
Camden city	2,041	1,765	-13.5	2,177	39.0	60.3	0.0	0.2	0.4	30.5	17.0	35.6	45.9	24.2	664	76.8
Camp Hill town	1,014	950	-6.3	1,196	6.4	90.5	0.0	0.5	2.6	24.7	12.6	25.5	64.6	9.9	384	72.1
Carbon Hill city	2,025	1,892	-6.6	1,441	88.3	8.0	1.1	2.6	0.0	24.1	16.9	36.7	63.6	9.3	622	78.5
Cardiff town	55	55	0.0	50	100.0	0.0	0.0	0.0	0.0	42.0	12.0	22.7	70.8	16.7	13	84.6
Carlisle-Rockledge CDP	2,137	-	-	2,577	94.6	1.4	0.0	2.0	2.1	27.6	10.6	34.2	58.4	6.8	957	94.5
Carlton CDP	65	-	-	31	0.0	100.0	0.0	0.0	0.0	0.0	80.6	83.7	100.0	0.0	17	0.0
Carolina town	297	295	-0.7	343	94.5	0.0	3.5	2.0	0.0	28.3	13.7	35.6	44.6	12.0	138	73.9
Carrollton town	1,019	943	-7.5	1,055	44.8	40.9	0.0	4.9	9.3	25.4	17.3	31.9	47.2	21.1	353	81.0
Castleberry town	594	540	-9.1	485	73.4	26.0	0.0	0.6	0.0	16.3	27.6	54.1	71.8	8.3	198	51.0
Catherine CDP	22	-	-	-	-	-	-	-	-	-	-	-	-	-	-	-
Cedar Bluff town	1,827	1,823	-0.2	1,999	84.6	14.7	0.0	0.7	0.0	19.8	23.1	50.7	63.4	14.5	876	88.9
Center Point city	16,880	16,110	-4.6	16,353	21.3	72.3	0.1	2.1	4.1	29.0	13.5	34.6	44.5	14.8	6,029	90.1
Centre city	3,496	3,542	1.3	3,525	86.2	10.6	0.0	2.4	0.8	14.2	32.4	53.4	54.8	12.3	1,650	74.1

1 May be of any race.

Table A. All Places — **Population and Housing**

STATE City, town, township, borough, or CDP (county if applicable)	Population: 2010 census total population	Population: 2019 estimated population	Population: Percent change 2010–2019	Population: ACS total population estimate 2015–2019	Race and Hispanic or Latino origin (percent): White alone, not Hispanic or Latino	Black alone, not Hispanic or Latino	Asian alone, not Hispanic or Latino	All other races or 2 or more races, not Hispanic or Latino	Hispanic or Latino[1]	Age (percent): Under 18 years old	Age 65 years and older	Median age	Educational attainment of persons age 25 and older: Percent High school diploma or less	Percent Bachelor's degree or more	Occupied housing units: Total	Percent with a computer
	1	2	3	4	5	6	7	8	9	10	11	12	13	14	15	16
ALABAMA—Con.																
Centreville city	2,788	2,609	-6.4	2,653	78.7	18.4	1.0	0.0	1.9	18.1	23.3	48.1	61.6	16.7	947	69.1
Chatom town	1,284	1,182	-7.9	1,195	57.8	26.8	0.0	7.5	7.9	25.9	13.1	35.7	57.1	13.6	398	67.1
Chelsea city	10,680	14,126	32.3	13,098	88.9	6.1	1.5	2.0	1.4	30.9	12.5	34.9	19.5	44.9	4,508	98.0
Cherokee town	1,048	1,008	-3.8	863	77.9	19.8	0.0	0.0	2.3	20.6	18.9	46.1	53.4	7.9	364	73.4
Chickasaw city	6,101	5,702	-6.5	5,817	47.5	46.0	0.0	4.6	2.0	34.3	12.8	30.2	54.4	12.0	2,134	74.9
Childersburg city	5,161	4,837	-6.3	4,908	54.4	38.0	0.8	2.3	4.4	23.8	16.6	39.2	56.7	12.2	2,175	83.3
Choccolocco CDP	2,804	-	-	3,011	90.9	7.2	1.1	0.8	0.0	20.1	16.0	43.5	27.6	28.2	1,096	91.6
Chunchula CDP	210	-	-	220	0.0	100.0	0.0	0.0	0.0	22.7	18.6	54.3	64.1	14.7	71	100.0
Citronelle city	3,910	3,861	-1.3	3,893	72.5	22.2	0.0	4.9	0.4	31.7	16.2	32.9	59.7	14.9	1,412	90.3
Clanton city	8,640	8,794	1.8	8,700	68.5	21.2	2.2	2.0	6.1	22.9	16.4	39.9	57.5	16.4	3,423	79.8
Clay city	9,966	9,923	-0.4	9,888	59.6	37.5	1.8	0.2	0.9	26.2	18.4	39.9	35.6	27.2	3,555	87.5
Clayhatchee town	596	585	-1.8	644	88.5	3.6	0.3	1.7	5.9	23.9	11.8	42.1	43.8	9.9	261	92.0
Clayton town	3,005	2,847	-5.3	2,884	33.5	63.5	0.0	1.3	1.8	10.9	9.9	38.4	72.9	4.7	569	68.0
Cleveland town	1,306	1,306	0.0	1,334	71.9	0.2	0.4	2.5	24.9	22.3	20.6	42.2	63.9	9.5	522	75.1
Clio city	1,408	1,274	-9.5	1,015	24.5	53.2	0.0	0.0	22.3	28.1	24.5	38.5	66.2	6.6	442	74.4
Coaling town	1,659	1,663	0.2	1,417	82.9	9.1	0.0	1.3	6.7	25.0	9.0	39.3	52.9	18.0	479	92.1
Coats Bend CDP	1,394	-	-	1,358	82.3	6.6	0.0	0.0	11.2	21.2	19.1	45.1	52.9	8.0	570	91.2
Coffee Springs town	223	214	-4.0	177	88.1	11.9	0.0	0.0	0.0	14.7	46.3	60.9	61.4	9.0	77	67.5
Coffeeville town	352	322	-8.5	516	50.8	34.9	0.0	14.3	0.0	28.7	11.8	31.0	50.8	10.9	154	54.5
Coker town	970	964	-0.6	687	94.6	1.3	0.0	1.2	2.9	18.0	16.6	45.1	45.6	21.1	259	93.1
Collinsville town	1,982	2,009	1.4	2,212	42.9	7.7	0.0	4.2	45.3	27.2	16.0	35.1	67.8	9.5	685	73.3
Colony town	270	289	7.0	471	8.7	87.9	0.0	3.4	0.0	19.1	19.5	50.1	59.9	10.5	188	72.9
Columbia town	740	737	-0.4	678	79.5	12.4	0.0	8.1	0.0	13.0	32.4	58.0	51.4	14.7	343	67.9
Columbiana city	4,161	4,550	9.3	4,481	72.1	21.3	0.0	4.9	1.8	17.6	15.3	39.9	58.3	19.0	1,641	75.5
Concord CDP	1,837	-	-	1,616	94.9	0.0	0.4	2.5	2.1	20.4	17.3	43.4	59.7	15.6	631	95.1
Coosada town	1,212	1,298	7.1	1,112	51.1	39.3	0.8	7.2	1.6	23.0	15.8	39.7	41.9	24.2	418	84.2
Cordova city	2,096	1,850	-11.7	2,006	82.5	13.8	0.0	3.7	0.0	20.9	22.4	44.7	60.0	10.5	789	80.0
Cottondale CDP	-	-	-	3,136	58.0	25.7	0.0	3.8	12.5	26.0	11.0	38.4	50.5	9.7	1,050	94.2
Cottonwood town	1,282	1,255	-2.1	1,294	73.9	22.0	0.5	2.6	1.1	24.2	18.6	37.8	59.5	9.5	494	59.7
County Line town	255	265	3.9	256	97.3	0.0	0.8	2.0	0.0	24.6	16.4	43.4	65.1	11.1	97	89.7
Courtland town	617	588	-4.7	760	49.9	48.6	0.0	0.8	0.8	20.3	18.8	42.8	61.9	9.9	321	74.5
Cowarts town	1,905	2,079	9.1	2,142	76.3	13.2	0.3	2.7	7.5	26.9	14.9	36.6	57.2	14.1	734	79.6
Creola city	1,922	2,036	5.9	1,871	79.9	12.6	0.0	7.5	0.0	31.4	12.3	32.5	58.2	15.9	585	88.5
Crossville town	1,864	1,857	-0.4	2,011	85.5	0.7	0.0	7.0	6.8	23.7	20.9	38.1	60.9	14.6	707	76.7
Cuba town	341	290	-15.0	422	87.2	10.7	0.0	2.1	0.0	13.0	29.1	47.7	29.9	45.1	206	90.8
Cullman city	15,158	16,034	5.8	15,729	88.8	1.1	0.6	4.0	5.4	22.2	18.5	38.4	40.6	24.8	6,096	84.8
Cullomburg CDP	171	-	-	229	34.5	65.5	0.0	0.0	0.0	34.1	9.6	41.4	51.7	29.1	87	82.8
Cusseta town	123	124	0.8	90	95.6	3.3	1.1	0.0	0.0	15.6	32.2	52.9	59.4	17.4	41	78.0
Dadeville city	3,232	3,053	-5.5	3,098	48.7	47.8	0.0	0.2	3.3	24.5	15.9	42.4	76.6	5.7	1,044	70.1
Daleville city	5,291	5,102	-3.6	5,123	60.6	21.1	2.6	2.8	12.9	21.5	13.1	35.7	53.3	13.0	1,965	85.4
Daphne city	21,622	26,869	24.3	25,901	74.8	17.6	1.8	3.2	2.7	25.2	16.6	37.9	22.9	41.6	9,457	96.6
Dauphin Island town	1,238	1,335	7.8	1,324	94.6	0.5	0.3	1.9	2.6	8.8	35.6	58.8	26.9	41.2	585	95.2
Daviston town	214	210	-1.9	214	97.7	0.9	0.0	1.4	0.0	26.2	13.6	40.8	35.4	14.6	84	88.1
Dayton town	52	46	-11.5	31	41.9	58.1	0.0	0.0	0.0	35.5	12.9	35.5	29.4	35.3	9	100.0
Deatsville town	1,224	1,237	1.1	1,679	73.3	21.1	0.2	2.4	2.9	32.0	7.5	31.9	31.3	28.5	551	95.1
Decatur city	55,786	54,445	-2.4	54,478	60.8	22.4	0.4	2.9	13.5	23.0	17.6	39.9	44.2	24.7	22,113	84.8
Deer Park CDP	188	-	-	127	65.4	34.6	0.0	0.0	0.0	14.2	14.2	46.6	80.7	0.0	65	32.3
Delta CDP	197	-	-	282	100.0	0.0	0.0	0.0	0.0	10.6	8.9	51.6	94.8	0.0	118	100.0
Demopolis city	7,483	6,612	-11.6	6,807	44.5	52.1	0.0	1.0	2.3	24.0	17.9	38.8	50.3	21.2	2,723	74.3
Detroit town	237	220	-7.2	257	74.7	24.1	0.0	1.2	0.0	11.3	16.7	47.0	67.2	9.1	107	87.9
Dodge City town	603	623	3.3	615	96.1	2.1	0.0	1.8	0.0	22.0	18.0	36.6	57.9	7.0	251	88.8
Dora city	2,043	1,905	-6.8	2,209	71.8	19.6	0.8	7.9	0.0	29.6	19.0	41.9	60.7	14.7	901	84.6
Dothan city	65,922	68,941	4.6	67,894	59.2	33.4	1.2	2.7	3.4	23.0	17.8	39.6	40.8	25.5	26,268	85.9
Double Springs town	1,117	1,062	-4.9	1,610	83.4	1.7	0.0	7.5	7.5	30.9	16.9	36.3	65.7	9.0	564	75.0
Douglas town	744	778	4.6	973	94.2	0.0	0.0	0.0	5.8	31.7	9.5	32.7	56.8	8.6	327	84.1
Dozier town	331	320	-3.3	321	59.5	37.1	0.0	0.0	3.4	27.7	19.9	41.0	61.8	9.8	124	71.8
Dunnavant CDP	981	-	-	957	90.6	1.7	3.3	4.4	0.0	20.8	18.3	44.9	49.6	19.0	365	92.6
Dutton town	327	314	-4.0	382	93.7	0.0	0.0	0.0	6.3	28.3	8.9	30.7	57.2	16.7	133	84.2
East Brewton city	2,479	2,356	-5.0	2,917	66.1	22.9	0.0	0.7	10.3	22.4	12.0	37.5	63.9	6.5	1,052	65.2
East Point CDP	201	-	-	259	100.0	0.0	0.0	0.0	0.0	38.6	12.4	33.6	33.3	0.0	90	87.8
Eclectic town	985	1,013	2.8	1,309	70.2	19.1	0.0	4.4	6.3	33.6	8.9	32.3	44.6	15.9	446	85.4
Edgewater CDP	883	-	-	739	34.5	65.5	0.0	0.0	0.0	33.8	15.4	41.2	46.2	20.1	253	92.9
Edwardsville town	200	196	-2.0	203	100.0	0.0	0.0	0.0	0.0	36.0	11.3	31.8	66.7	4.4	64	79.7
Egypt CDP	932	-	-	1,034	98.3	0.0	0.0	0.0	1.7	27.0	12.0	41.1	67.3	5.2	334	65.9
Elba city	3,937	3,811	-3.2	3,841	57.8	36.6	1.8	3.1	0.7	17.9	18.6	42.2	62.0	10.4	1,427	71.6
Elberta town	1,501	1,746	16.3	1,709	92.5	1.8	0.0	2.2	3.5	15.7	25.9	47.5	52.5	15.5	752	90.2
Eldridge town	130	123	-5.4	153	88.9	7.8	0.0	2.6	0.7	28.8	8.5	28.8	38.8	12.9	50	94.0
Elkmont town	438	510	16.4	540	92.8	2.2	0.0	2.6	2.4	29.6	18.1	32.4	52.1	20.1	158	86.7
Elmore town	1,279	1,348	5.4	1,137	58.6	24.4	0.0	3.3	13.8	20.3	17.5	35.6	66.8	8.3	362	89.8
Emelle town	53	48	-9.4	95	30.5	69.5	0.0	0.0	0.0	9.5	25.3	46.9	26.1	11.6	40	97.5
Emerald Mountain CDP	2,561	-	-	3,472	75.2	17.1	0.3	4.6	2.8	36.8	11.4	33.4	16.5	44.9	1,170	100.0
Enterprise city	26,534	28,376	6.9	27,947	62.0	22.4	1.9	4.6	9.1	26.0	14.6	37.1	31.6	29.8	10,744	92.5
Epes town	373	329	-11.8	614	0.7	99.3	0.0	0.0	0.0	4.9	2.0	41.0	27.5	11.9	227	96.5
Ethelsville town	76	73	-3.9	191	57.6	42.4	0.0	0.0	0.0	36.6	8.9	24.6	81.0	9.5	52	90.4
Eufaula city	13,134	11,709	-10.8	12,065	47.0	45.8	0.9	2.0	4.3	24.6	19.2	38.0	54.1	16.5	4,969	80.9
Eunola CDP	243	-	-	190	100.0	0.0	0.0	0.0	0.0	0.0	51.6	68.1	66.3	0.0	108	100.0
Eutaw town	2,934	2,603	-11.3	2,676	26.7	72.8	0.0	0.0	0.4	22.6	24.2	45.5	51.2	16.2	1,041	67.9
Eva town	508	499	-1.8	545	98.9	0.0	0.6	0.6	0.0	21.3	13.8	43.9	44.2	23.3	195	94.9
Evergreen city	3,952	3,526	-10.8	3,646	35.3	63.9	0.0	0.8	0.0	25.7	20.2	37.7	61.4	12.2	1,441	62.8
Excel town	719	632	-12.1	1,006	87.8	6.5	0.0	5.8	0.0	32.1	10.2	34.0	50.4	16.6	370	65.9
Fairfield city	11,106	10,568	-4.8	10,720	5.9	91.1	0.0	1.8	1.2	19.9	16.2	37.2	46.0	18.5	4,441	79.6
Fairford CDP	186	-	-	110	100.0	0.0	0.0	0.0	0.0	32.7	0.0	41.9	18.9	0.0	42	100.0
Fairhope city	16,265	22,677	39.4	21,083	86.8	4.4	3.0	0.6	5.2	25.9	23.4	43.7	18.5	54.7	7,790	94.0
Fairview town	453	463	2.2	492	80.3	0.0	1.6	6.1	12.0	27.4	18.1	41.4	49.5	16.3	175	86.3
Falkville town	1,279	1,257	-1.7	1,348	92.7	2.9	0.0	3.1	1.3	16.2	28.5	51.1	59.5	13.4	392	84.9
Faunsdale town	102	92	-9.8	23	69.6	30.4	0.0	0.0	0.0	17.4	34.8	47.5	70.6	17.6	16	31.3
Fayette city	4,621	4,275	-7.5	4,364	67.4	25.4	1.3	3.1	2.8	20.1	23.4	43.0	53.5	15.7	1,888	79.4
Fayetteville CDP	1,284	-	-	1,378	94.1	5.9	0.0	0.0	0.0	13.5	39.8	60.1	51.6	9.2	608	80.9
Fitzpatrick CDP	83	-	-	-	-	-	-	-	-	-	-	-	-	-	-	-
Five Points town	141	143	1.4	107	19.6	79.4	0.0	0.9	0.0	2.8	32.7	49.6	73.3	5.9	45	93.3
Flomaton town	1,440	1,393	-3.3	1,652	58.8	33.8	0.0	5.1	2.3	28.6	16.2	38.2	66.8	8.9	608	67.9

1 May be of any race.

Table A. All Places — **Population and Housing**

STATE City, town, township, borough, or CDP (county if applicable)	Population: 2010 census total population	Population: 2019 estimated population	Population: Percent change 2010-2019	Population: ACS total population estimate 2015-2019	Race and Hispanic or Latino origin (percent): White alone, not Hispanic or Latino	Race and Hispanic or Latino origin (percent): Black alone, not Hispanic or Latino	Race and Hispanic or Latino origin (percent): Asian alone, not Hispanic or Latino	Race and Hispanic or Latino origin (percent): All other races or 2 or more races, not Hispanic or Latino	Race and Hispanic or Latino origin (percent): Hispanic or Latino[1]	Age (percent): Under 18 years old	Age (percent): Age 65 years and older	Age (percent): Median age	Educational attainment of persons age 25 and older: Percent High school diploma or less	Educational attainment of persons age 25 and older: Percent Bachelor's degree or more	Occupied housing units: Total	Occupied housing units: Percent with a computer
	1	2	3	4	5	6	7	8	9	10	11	12	13	14	15	16
ALABAMA—Con.																
Florala town	1,981	1,906	-3.8	1,551	81.9	16.3	0.5	1.1	0.3	14.5	32.0	53.9	62.1	7.5	646	63.6
Florence city	39,560	40,797	3.1	40,309	73.4	19.7	0.9	2.0	4.0	18.5	18.5	35.5	41.5	28.1	17,475	85.4
Foley city	15,358	20,391	32.8	18,533	77.6	12.0	1.2	0.8	8.4	16.3	26.1	47.0	41.1	23.5	8,090	87.9
Forestdale CDP	10,162	-	-	8,924	21.8	72.8	0.4	1.6	3.4	19.1	16.9	45.1	35.4	24.6	3,776	86.5
Forkland town	645	588	-8.8	905	19.0	76.5	0.0	4.1	0.4	23.9	22.3	33.8	59.1	6.8	269	61.0
Fort Deposit town	1,347	1,155	-14.3	1,835	15.4	84.6	0.0	0.0	0.0	27.8	6.9	31.9	66.3	14.9	725	75.6
Fort Payne city	14,096	14,074	-0.2	14,115	70.6	3.4	0.1	2.8	23.0	25.7	15.7	38.8	56.8	17.1	5,066	85.7
Fort Rucker CDP	4,636	-	-	5,311	65.7	12.1	2.0	6.1	14.1	32.8	0.0	24.3	17.7	36.3	1,296	99.3
Franklin town	628	512	-18.5	630	10.2	87.8	0.0	1.3	0.8	10.5	26.0	47.7	52.0	30.4	279	83.2
Fredonia CDP	199	-	-	229	76.4	23.6	0.0	0.0	0.0	31.9	29.3	54.0	32.7	14.1	73	74.0
Frisco City town	1,308	1,153	-11.9	1,539	46.7	48.3	1.4	3.6	0.0	25.7	19.9	43.0	58.3	10.3	569	46.7
Fruitdale CDP	185	-	-	104	100.0	0.0	0.0	0.0	0.0	15.4	22.1	27.4	80.0	8.3	54	100.0
Fruithurst town	280	280	0.0	247	97.6	0.0	1.2	0.8	0.4	19.8	12.6	47.1	72.4	7.5	96	87.5
Fulton town	272	246	-9.6	230	46.5	53.5	0.0	0.0	0.0	19.6	21.7	47.4	79.9	0.0	72	65.3
Fultondale city	8,372	9,284	10.9	9,179	64.9	18.0	4.1	2.9	10.2	20.0	14.3	38.3	41.8	23.4	3,879	93.9
Fyffe town	1,018	1,045	2.7	1,203	91.4	0.3	0.0	4.9	3.4	26.1	12.0	36.6	58.0	10.5	422	79.1
Gadsden city	36,964	35,000	-5.3	35,486	54.3	35.5	1.0	2.0	7.1	20.6	18.0	40.2	53.9	15.1	13,766	80.6
Gainesville town	208	183	-12.0	163	12.3	82.2	0.0	5.5	0.0	34.4	4.9	32.5	55.1	17.8	55	87.3
Gallant CDP	855	-	-	833	97.6	0.0	0.0	2.4	0.0	26.4	17.8	43.8	53.1	19.8	265	87.9
Gantt town	219	215	-1.8	158	72.8	27.2	0.0	0.0	0.0	10.8	31.0	50.8	42.3	8.8	61	80.3
Garden City town	494	501	1.4	557	98.9	0.0	0.0	1.1	0.0	24.6	15.6	41.9	59.2	6.8	189	87.8
Gardendale city	13,983	14,177	1.4	14,016	85.3	9.7	1.4	0.8	2.7	24.2	18.7	41.1	33.7	29.4	5,551	91.5
Gaylesville town	144	141	-2.1	171	96.5	0.0	0.0	3.5	0.0	22.8	23.4	45.5	56.3	16.4	65	80.0
Geiger town	170	151	-11.2	239	26.8	51.9	0.0	0.0	21.3	20.9	23.0	34.9	55.3	16.0	88	71.6
Geneva city	4,437	4,289	-3.3	4,340	74.1	18.5	0.0	1.4	6.0	19.0	16.7	47.0	60.5	12.7	1,800	71.3
Georgiana town	1,738	1,608	-7.5	1,806	27.7	68.8	1.1	0.4	1.9	17.4	24.9	50.4	69.4	10.3	524	50.6
Geraldine town	902	898	-0.4	1,116	90.5	0.2	0.0	9.1	0.3	27.1	21.1	37.0	51.2	25.9	445	81.3
Gilbertown town	215	193	-10.2	256	75.0	24.2	0.0	0.8	0.0	23.4	23.8	49.7	50.0	6.6	101	68.3
Glen Allen town	506	480	-5.1	367	82.6	12.5	0.0	4.9	0.0	13.9	25.6	49.1	57.2	16.2	155	78.1
Glencoe city	5,141	5,071	-1.4	5,077	94.9	2.4	0.0	2.1	0.5	21.2	23.8	45.8	39.6	25.2	1,949	86.3
Glenwood town	187	183	-2.1	262	71.8	9.5	11.1	7.6	0.0	24.0	24.4	46.0	32.4	14.3	99	86.9
Goldville town	54	54	0.0	52	96.2	0.0	0.0	0.0	3.8	15.4	30.8	46.5	53.5	18.6	26	65.4
Good Hope city	2,260	2,362	4.5	2,620	76.2	0.0	3.1	0.0	20.8	31.3	13.5	35.9	52.0	7.9	845	86.4
Goodwater town	1,475	1,315	-10.8	1,261	20.7	79.3	0.0	0.0	0.0	25.9	17.9	44.2	67.3	10.2	484	58.9
Gordo town	1,750	1,614	-7.8	1,660	53.5	38.3	0.0	7.3	0.8	20.6	19.8	49.2	55.7	9.2	732	69.8
Gordon town	329	325	-1.2	306	23.5	76.5	0.0	0.0	0.0	8.5	22.9	55.4	78.6	1.6	113	64.6
Gordonville town	325	278	-14.5	182	1.1	90.7	0.0	8.2	0.0	8.2	22.0	46.3	53.5	11.3	81	63.0
Goshen town	266	255	-4.1	224	49.1	46.4	0.0	3.1	1.3	26.3	25.4	53.3	73.4	15.8	79	68.4
Graham CDP	211	-	-	45	100.0	0.0	0.0	0.0	0.0	0.0	35.6	56.4	35.6	46.7	27	66.7
Grand Bay CDP	3,672	-	-	3,897	94.9	2.3	0.0	0.0	2.7	28.6	17.9	39.2	55.4	11.1	1,252	88.4
Grant town	896	916	2.2	1,040	93.6	0.2	1.3	3.3	1.6	24.9	13.3	38.4	48.2	22.0	375	84.5
Grayson Valley CDP	5,736	-	-	6,209	47.3	46.6	1.3	0.9	3.9	23.5	16.5	33.3	33.2	22.9	2,598	93.8
Graysville city	2,183	2,092	-4.2	1,864	65.7	33.6	0.0	0.8	0.0	18.8	24.7	48.3	50.7	15.0	765	84.6
Greensboro city	2,494	2,268	-9.1	3,149	22.5	76.5	0.0	1.0	0.0	25.6	16.9	34.9	66.9	14.6	1,214	62.3
Greenville city	8,132	7,395	-9.1	7,589	40.1	55.9	0.7	2.1	1.3	23.9	18.5	36.8	57.6	21.4	2,356	72.0
Grimes town	558	556	-0.4	717	60.0	26.4	0.0	6.6	7.1	25.7	11.9	37.0	56.4	8.4	290	81.0
Grove Hill town	1,946	1,738	-10.7	1,839	62.6	37.1	0.0	0.3	0.0	22.7	26.4	44.1	50.8	15.9	669	65.6
Guin city	2,379	2,275	-4.4	2,684	77.0	10.5	0.0	4.1	8.3	19.0	20.8	44.3	52.9	10.8	1,038	77.1
Gulfcrest CDP	161	-	-	259	59.1	31.3	0.0	0.0	9.7	31.7	26.6	35.9	80.9	0.0	78	89.7
Gulf Shores city	10,843	12,757	17.7	12,267	95.9	0.3	0.9	0.0	2.9	14.4	23.7	49.6	27.3	35.2	5,810	94.9
Guntersville city	8,247	8,571	3.9	8,468	82.0	12.1	0.9	2.2	2.8	22.9	20.3	42.0	40.9	30.7	3,312	87.6
Gurley town	838	812	-3.1	603	80.9	7.1	0.0	10.1	1.8	25.2	13.9	39.0	55.3	20.4	253	88.9
Gu-Win town	174	174	0.0	123	82.9	2.4	0.0	8.9	5.7	29.3	12.2	28.5	62.7	0.0	52	76.9
Hackleburg town	1,514	1,258	-16.9	1,307	94.6	0.7	0.3	2.3	2.1	21.7	19.5	41.8	54.2	10.3	536	76.1
Hackneyville CDP	347	-	-	416	100.0	0.0	0.0	0.0	0.0	25.2	19.5	41.8	67.5	17.0	158	83.5
Haleburg town	103	100	-2.9	117	100.0	0.0	0.0	0.0	0.0	23.1	23.9	38.8	24.7	23.5	41	95.1
Haleyville city	4,409	4,142	-6.1	4,159	89.9	1.0	0.0	1.0	8.2	27.3	20.9	38.0	59.7	13.0	1,536	80.6
Hamilton city	6,883	6,606	-4.0	6,682	89.2	5.6	0.1	2.8	2.3	19.8	21.0	41.8	59.0	11.1	2,684	83.8
Hammondville town	495	495	0.0	459	95.9	1.3	0.0	2.8	0.0	19.2	24.2	48.4	49.0	11.8	184	75.0
Hanceville city	3,169	3,461	9.2	3,377	87.1	7.1	0.0	0.3	5.5	12.8	24.1	47.7	57.6	10.0	1,263	78.0
Harpersville town	1,659	1,727	4.1	1,483	78.6	20.9	0.0	0.5	0.0	22.2	20.2	46.1	59.7	12.1	562	78.6
Hartford city	2,619	2,578	-1.6	2,586	63.5	30.9	0.0	1.7	3.9	23.7	18.3	41.3	61.5	7.5	934	80.2
Hartselle city	14,281	14,466	1.3	14,428	88.1	5.9	2.5	1.4	2.1	22.4	17.4	41.6	38.8	26.9	5,518	87.4
Harvest CDP	5,281	-	-	5,819	70.3	17.7	3.8	3.7	4.5	26.6	17.6	38.1	28.4	35.1	2,043	96.6
Hatton CDP	261	-	-	70	80.0	0.0	0.0	20.0	0.0	0.0	65.7	66.5	67.1	18.6	34	58.8
Hayden town	1,328	1,343	1.1	1,244	95.6	1.8	0.4	1.4	0.8	22.3	20.4	42.1	52.9	11.8	433	83.1
Hayneville town	933	784	-16.0	872	8.8	91.2	0.0	0.0	0.0	22.2	13.3	39.5	73.9	12.3	358	68.4
Hazel Green CDP	3,630	-	-	3,901	89.7	8.2	1.5	0.0	0.6	22.3	18.0	42.2	54.5	21.2	1,516	86.9
Headland city	4,514	4,712	4.4	4,665	68.4	28.7	0.9	0.2	1.8	25.1	15.7	38.6	48.4	24.2	1,583	92.8
Heath town	256	256	0.0	302	89.4	9.6	0.0	0.0	1.0	33.1	11.9	28.7	42.7	21.9	104	79.8
Heflin city	3,483	3,409	-2.1	3,437	90.5	6.1	0.0	2.6	0.7	24.9	22.9	42.1	50.0	16.1	1,340	80.9
Helena city	16,963	19,925	17.5	18,463	75.0	17.1	1.4	3.8	2.7	25.7	13.1	39.2	21.3	46.8	6,718	96.3
Henagar city	2,347	2,363	0.7	2,184	89.3	0.0	0.0	5.0	5.7	21.9	16.5	41.2	65.0	5.1	833	81.4
Highland Lake town	412	410	-0.5	416	94.5	1.0	0.0	4.6	0.0	16.3	28.4	51.1	41.0	31.8	165	89.1
Highland Lakes CDP	3,926	-	-	5,519	84.4	8.8	3.1	2.8	0.9	24.7	15.5	45.8	9.8	68.5	1,868	99.1
Hillsboro town	553	521	-5.8	593	5.1	93.3	0.0	1.7	0.0	18.2	17.0	47.6	57.6	13.0	226	75.2
Hissop CDP	658	-	-	415	44.3	42.4	0.0	13.3	0.0	13.3	22.7	49.5	75.0	13.9	203	68.5
Hobson CDP	126	-	-	156	100.0	0.0	0.0	0.0	0.0	0.0	35.3	48.7	71.4	28.6	52	34.6
Hobson City town	773	755	-2.3	755	10.3	89.0	0.0	0.7	0.0	15.5	13.6	43.4	46.2	16.0	304	81.9
Hodges town	286	283		270	98.9	0.0	0.7	0.4	0.0	23.0	17.4	43.7	68.5	12.2	108	66.7
Hokes Bluff city	4,281	4,257	-0.6	4,286	98.1	0.0	0.0	0.0	1.9	24.5	19.1	36.9	40.3	18.6	1,610	87.8
Hollins CDP	545	-	-	797	94.4	0.0	1.8	0.0	3.9	22.6	29.1	55.6	71.2	9.3	278	59.0
Hollis Crossroads CDP	608	-	-	679	75.3	0.0	0.0	0.0	24.7	18.0	25.3	43.7	69.6	5.6	240	84.6
Holly Pond town	808	826	2.2	1,064	98.2	0.3	0.0	1.0	0.5	28.4	16.1	35.6	51.3	9.8	368	87.0
Hollywood town	1,003	984	-1.9	1,164	75.5	18.3	0.0	4.8	1.4	20.6	14.0	39.5	64.0	7.0	452	87.4
Holt CDP	3,638	-	-	3,952	28.7	40.4	0.0	0.0	30.9	26.7	10.8	34.3	63.7	4.9	1,210	78.3
Holtville CDP	4,096	-	-	4,449	87.5	11.4	0.0	1.1	0.0	25.3	13.0	38.3	45.1	23.1	1,743	89.5
Homewood city	25,143	25,377	0.9	25,534	74.5	14.1	3.5	2.4	5.5	24.2	10.1	30.8	15.4	64.3	9,566	94.9
Hoover city	80,823	85,768	6.1	85,175	68.0	18.8	5.2	1.9	6.1	26.3	15.5	37.8	16.9	57.6	32,261	96.8
Horn Hill town	228	229	0.4	242	99.2	0.0	0.0	0.0	0.8	21.1	21.1	42.6	54.0	9.2	96	71.9
Hueytown city	16,141	15,322	-5.1	15,540	58.3	40.0	0.1	1.2	0.5	25.0	16.7	36.9	45.7	18.2	5,707	89.2
Huguley CDP	2,540	-	-	2,583	70.3	24.5	3.9	0.6	0.6	16.4	24.9	47.4	54.5	12.3	1,030	85.6

1 May be of any race.

Table A. All Places — **Population and Housing**

STATE City, town, township, borough, or CDP (county if applicable)	Population				Race and Hispanic or Latino origin (percent)					Age (percent)			Educational attainment of persons age 25 and older		Occupied housing units	
	2010 census total population	2019 estimated population	Percent change 2010-2019	ACS total population estimate 2015-2019	White alone, not Hispanic or Latino	Black alone, not Hispanic or Latino	Asian alone, not Hispanic or Latino	All other races or 2 or more races, not Hispanic or Latino	Hispanic or Latino[1]	Under 18 years old	Age 65 years and older	Median age	Percent High school diploma or less	Percent Bachelor's degree or more	Total	Percent with a computer
	1	2	3	4	5	6	7	8	9	10	11	12	13	14	15	16
ALABAMA—Con.																
Huntsville city	180,395	200,574	11.2	196,219	57.7	30.4	2.6	3.1	6.2	20.6	16.1	36.9	27.7	44.1	85,020	91.4
Hurtsboro town	550	589	7.1	535	29.2	69.3	1.5	0.0	0.0	18.7	19.1	44.7	42.1	11.0	221	84.6
Hytop town	431	422	-2.1	424	95.8	0.0	0.0	4.2	0.0	20.0	17.2	38.4	60.3	8.1	173	86.7
Ider town	723	718	-0.7	682	93.5	0.0	0.0	6.5	0.0	16.1	22.6	51.4	59.0	10.5	299	75.9
Indian Springs Village city	2,457	2,559	4.2	2,549	88.0	3.3	5.6	2.3	0.7	22.6	20.6	46.9	13.0	67.0	876	97.6
Irondale city	12,415	12,893	3.9	12,637	48.9	37.3	0.9	4.4	8.5	22.7	14.1	36.6	36.3	35.0	5,161	89.5
Ivalee CDP	879	-	-	887	90.4	1.4	0.0	8.2	0.0	21.9	19.4	37.9	56.2	12.6	341	77.7
Jackson city	5,224	4,642	-11.1	4,781	48.1	51.3	0.5	0.1	0.0	20.3	20.9	43.8	59.3	16.9	1,775	79.5
Jacksons' Gap town	831	827	-0.5	698	90.5	8.9	0.6	0.0	0.0	12.9	19.5	45.8	68.6	5.8	277	77.3
Jacksonville city	13,175	12,544	-4.8	12,651	71.6	23.5	1.2	2.6	1.2	16.3	12.5	28.1	31.2	30.0	4,518	92.0
Jasper city	14,417	13,431	-6.8	13,649	76.7	14.6	1.6	2.4	4.6	24.4	18.4	37.2	45.0	19.0	5,269	85.3
Jemison city	2,615	2,672	2.2	2,630	80.0	16.0	0.0	0.9	3.2	32.4	14.9	34.7	59.7	13.7	946	82.0
Joppa CDP	-	-	-	664	100.0	0.0	0.0	0.0	0.0	2.6	7.1	42.8	61.5	7.1	269	67.3
Kansas town	225	211	-6.2	245	97.6	0.0	0.0	2.4	0.0	34.3	17.1	36.1	51.1	9.5	86	79.1
Kellyton town	217	198	-8.8	172	93.0	7.0	0.0	0.0	0.0	16.9	28.5	51.9	60.6	2.1	68	77.9
Kennedy town	447	421	-5.8	448	69.0	18.5	0.0	0.7	11.8	14.3	27.0	47.6	49.6	21.1	218	75.7
Killen town	993	955	-3.8	1,263	92.8	6.7	0.0	0.0	0.6	23.0	16.2	39.1	43.2	24.3	484	90.7
Kimberly city	3,030	3,593	18.6	3,444	89.3	6.1	0.5	3.9	0.2	29.4	10.2	37.4	41.1	26.5	1,168	95.1
Kinsey town	2,201	2,267	3.0	2,199	42.2	49.9	0.3	3.8	3.9	27.7	13.2	36.8	50.5	10.6	796	86.4
Kinston town	540	547	1.3	741	91.8	0.3	0.0	5.5	2.4	20.6	14.0	37.2	58.3	10.6	276	72.5
Ladonia CDP	3,142	-	-	3,391	73.9	17.4	1.0	5.6	2.1	28.0	17.1	34.0	54.9	16.1	1,364	90.4
La Fayette city	3,003	2,910	-3.1	2,943	34.8	61.0	1.3	0.5	2.4	24.9	12.1	41.8	62.8	10.3	1,017	70.9
Lakeview town	143	139	-2.8	128	100.0	0.0	0.0	0.0	0.0	34.4	21.9	38.5	61.6	8.2	40	80.0
Lake View town	2,008	2,671	33.0	2,452	79.1	14.4	2.9	2.8	0.8	22.3	11.2	34.6	32.7	27.5	777	96.5
Lanett city	6,473	6,151	-5.0	6,271	30.6	59.8	0.0	2.2	7.4	21.1	21.7	44.0	55.8	17.6	2,712	75.4
Langston town	270	262	-3.0	211	89.6	5.2	0.0	1.4	3.8	3.8	43.1	62.1	56.0	19.7	110	79.1
Leeds city	11,772	12,040	2.3	12,600	76.0	18.5	0.1	1.6	3.8	26.3	15.9	36.9	34.5	30.3	4,792	91.0
Leesburg town	1,007	1,013	0.6	946	98.6	0.0	0.0	0.7	0.6	19.5	18.0	40.0	44.9	18.5	381	86.4
Leighton town	773	756	-2.2	971	50.1	48.2	0.0	0.6	1.1	19.1	19.2	40.1	69.8	9.0	368	66.6
Leroy CDP	911	-	-	964	62.0	31.1	0.0	6.2	0.6	19.7	19.1	47.3	38.0	22.4	400	92.0
Lester town	111	131	18.0	157	91.7	1.9	0.6	5.7	0.0	26.1	14.0	39.8	50.9	19.4	45	95.6
Level Plains town	2,068	2,002	-3.2	2,102	57.1	15.2	4.3	10.6	12.7	24.3	11.9	43.4	40.8	18.0	719	91.7
Lexington town	735	709	-3.5	912	95.7	1.3	0.0	1.4	1.5	23.5	18.5	38.4	63.8	9.7	366	80.9
Libertyville town	115	113	-1.7	59	100.0	0.0	0.0	0.0	0.0	13.6	30.5	47.6	44.4	26.7	28	67.9
Lillian CDP	-	-	-	1,728	98.6	0.0	0.0	1.4	0.0	14.8	35.1	53.8	38.8	22.6	662	92.4
Lincoln city	6,244	6,781	8.6	6,681	68.7	27.7	0.5	2.9	0.3	19.0	14.5	42.8	48.6	17.4	2,546	94.5
Linden city	2,123	1,880	-11.4	1,794	62.5	35.1	0.0	0.9	1.6	17.3	27.9	48.7	56.6	12.1	672	73.5
Lineville city	2,423	2,249	-7.2	2,332	52.8	42.5	0.0	1.2	3.5	23.5	20.1	39.7	58.9	12.7	899	85.4
Lipscomb city	2,206	2,139	-3.0	1,873	16.7	59.0	0.0	2.4	21.9	24.1	13.0	36.8	69.8	7.5	737	82.1
Lisman town	548	493	-10.0	580	0.9	96.9	0.0	2.2	0.0	24.8	14.0	41.2	49.3	7.3	192	80.7
Littleville town	1,011	992	-1.9	966	97.3	0.3	0.2	0.8	1.3	24.0	23.4	40.1	65.1	8.3	364	79.7
Livingston city	3,458	3,260	-5.7	3,356	34.1	57.8	8.2	0.0	0.0	21.6	11.4	21.8	35.0	34.5	1,211	78.5
Loachapoka town	180	198	10.0	221	56.1	35.3	4.1	1.4	3.2	19.9	21.3	33.9	36.0	32.3	84	82.1
Lockhart town	516	504	-2.3	290	77.9	16.2	0.0	0.0	5.9	15.9	23.8	48.6	67.1	3.9	129	68.2
Locust Fork town	1,173	1,197	2.0	1,478	99.2	0.0	0.0	0.4	0.4	24.2	21.5	43.6	62.8	9.1	467	82.7
Lookout Mountain CDP	1,621	-	-	1,884	98.4	1.4	0.0	0.0	0.3	25.1	20.0	41.5	57.7	12.8	622	79.7
Louisville town	521	462	-11.3	604	22.5	69.0	0.0	6.8	1.7	24.8	17.1	32.7	71.6	9.0	238	69.3
Lowndesboro town	115	93	-19.1	92	88.0	12.0	0.0	0.0	0.0	2.2	43.5	62.5	17.1	23.2	53	88.7
Loxley town	1,806	3,049	68.8	2,501	85.3	6.9	0.0	4.6	3.2	25.8	9.7	36.2	45.5	29.5	868	87.3
Luverne city	2,817	2,744	-2.6	2,770	55.1	34.2	5.3	5.3	0.1	19.6	23.6	41.8	60.0	19.2	1,005	80.5
Lynn town	658	635	-3.5	635	94.0	0.0	0.0	0.8	5.2	20.3	23.8	47.4	60.6	8.2	274	74.8
McDonald Chapel CDP	717	-	-	573	67.4	30.0	0.0	2.6	0.0	23.4	9.2	40.8	63.5	8.3	224	81.7
Macedonia CDP	292	-	-	200	17.0	81.5	0.0	0.0	1.5	10.0	42.5	55.3	53.9	0.0	146	70.5
McIntosh town	236	215	-8.9	310	27.4	52.9	0.0	19.7	0.0	27.7	19.0	39.4	31.7	32.2	105	93.3
McKenzie town	530	492	-7.2	776	52.1	46.5	0.0	1.4	0.0	40.5	11.1	35.1	50.4	10.3	246	74.4
McMullen town	10	9	-10.0	7	0.0	100.0	0.0	0.0	0.0	0.0	57.1	65.5	57.1	14.3	6	66.7
Madison city	43,192	51,593	19.5	49,327	70.5	14.7	5.8	4.3	4.8	25.2	11.4	39.1	14.8	59.4	18,825	97.6
Madrid town	291	290	-0.3	334	80.8	16.5	0.0	0.0	2.7	28.7	12.0	36.2	53.7	12.7	117	61.5
Magnolia Springs town	723	823	13.8	968	85.3	0.8	0.8	1.7	11.4	8.9	31.1	56.1	29.6	36.8	393	92.9
Malcolm CDP	187	-	-	354	50.8	49.2	0.0	0.0	0.0	62.1	5.6	17.3	60.4	0.0	116	100.0
Malvern town	1,453	1,463	0.7	1,582	89.3	5.1	0.3	0.3	5.2	23.8	16.1	40.1	54.8	13.8	614	78.0
Maplesville town	708	700	-1.1	636	77.2	21.1	0.0	0.9	0.8	30.3	14.3	38.8	71.0	10.0	246	73.2
Marbury CDP	1,418	-	-	1,633	83.0	10.4	1.5	5.1	0.0	21.0	12.2	37.6	59.7	19.0	573	83.9
Margaret town	4,424	5,137	16.1	4,819	59.2	30.0	0.4	0.5	9.9	40.7	6.6	28.5	45.6	17.0	1,256	94.3
Marion city	3,681	3,123	-15.2	3,275	44.2	53.2	0.2	0.1	2.3	19.8	28.1	36.7	55.5	23.8	1,055	56.6
Maytown town	390	371	-4.9	354	89.0	9.6	0.0	0.6	0.8	25.1	16.1	45.8	52.0	9.4	133	85.0
Meadowbrook CDP	8,769	-	-	9,468	91.9	5.5	0.7	0.4	1.6	21.1	14.2	44.3	11.8	59.3	3,360	97.5
Megargel CDP	62	-	-	16	100.0	0.0	0.0	0.0	0.0	0.0	100.0	0.0	100.0	0.0	8	100.0
Memphis town	29	26	-10.3	24	0.0	100.0	0.0	0.0	0.0	0.0	87.5	74.0	87.5	8.3	12	16.7
Mentone town	360	368	2.2	307	97.1	0.0	0.0	2.9	0.0	8.8	41.4	60.8	37.8	32.2	157	86.6
Meridianville CDP	6,021	-	-	7,087	62.9	26.2	5.6	3.0	2.2	23.9	14.8	38.8	27.1	40.2	2,759	92.6
Midfield city	5,339	5,002	-6.3	5,085	12.7	78.7	0.1	1.8	6.8	24.7	12.8	38.2	54.9	17.1	1,855	86.6
Midland City town	2,157	2,358	9.3	1,961	61.5	31.5	0.6	5.5	0.9	34.0	14.1	31.1	52.9	13.9	818	83.7
Midway town	499	466	-6.6	683	3.8	96.2	0.0	0.0	0.0	21.7	11.9	36.2	67.4	7.4	279	61.6
Mignon CDP	1,284	-	-	850	61.8	33.1	0.0	5.2	0.0	21.3	15.4	41.8	42.7	7.8	359	84.7
Millbrook city	14,995	15,896	6.0	15,645	67.5	25.8	0.5	1.4	4.9	24.9	10.5	35.4	35.4	30.1	6,061	90.8
Millerville CDP	278	-	-	186	100.0	0.0	0.0	0.0	0.0	18.3	7.5	53.1	66.7	0.0	90	92.2
Millport town	1,049	980	-6.6	990	67.1	32.9	0.0	0.0	0.0	18.6	22.1	45.8	63.7	15.2	451	56.1
Millry town	546	497	-9.0	697	69.7	26.4	1.0	2.9	0.0	18.5	25.8	51.5	67.6	16.5	241	78.8
Minor CDP	1,094	-	-	843	77.3	17.7	0.0	5.0	0.0	27.8	14.6	33.8	42.1	14.9	315	87.3
Mobile city	194,659	188,720	-3.1	190,432	41.8	51.4	1.9	2.4	2.5	21.2	16.5	37.7	41.3	29.4	78,142	83.8
Monroeville city	6,515	5,718	-12.2	5,898	36.7	61.6	0.5	1.0	0.3	20.1	16.1	43.2	58.6	17.5	2,106	54.1
Montevallo city	6,318	6,738	6.6	6,693	66.9	24.3	1.1	2.6	5.1	12.8	12.4	28.4	40.7	29.9	2,249	89.9
Montgomery city	205,501	198,525	-3.4	199,783	30.7	60.7	2.9	2.0	3.7	23.8	14.3	35.7	38.7	32.8	79,306	87.3
Moody city	11,705	13,065	11.6	12,840	87.5	9.7	1.3	0.9	0.6	24.4	14.7	37.1	40.5	18.8	4,930	89.4
Moores Mill CDP	5,682	-	-	6,882	71.7	19.4	0.2	3.6	5.1	22.3	17.3	43.6	40.8	35.1	2,683	91.8
Mooresville town	53	61	15.1	84	85.7	9.5	2.4	0.0	2.4	19.0	19.0	57.1	17.6	66.2	30	96.7
Morris town	1,921	2,149	11.9	1,841	96.0	2.2	0.3	1.0	0.5	20.7	21.8	46.7	34.9	30.6	751	93.3
Morrison Crossroads CDP	-	-	-	254	90.6	0.0	0.0	0.0	9.4	5.1	49.2	60.9	78.0	4.6	150	51.3
Mosses town	1,030	874	-15.1	846	0.0	99.8	0.0	0.2	0.0	24.5	10.9	37.5	73.8	7.3	367	68.9
Moulton city	3,471	3,241	-6.6	3,285	81.9	13.6	0.2	4.2	0.0	20.1	28.8	49.6	61.5	16.3	1,457	67.9
Moundville town	2,419	2,459	1.7	3,017	53.6	43.4	1.1	1.9	0.0	23.9	12.3	34.9	52.1	16.5	1,072	85.7

1 May be of any race.

Table A. All Places — **Population and Housing**

STATE City, town, township, borough, or CDP (county if applicable)	Population				Race and Hispanic or Latino origin (percent)					Age (percent)			Educational attainment of persons age 25 and older		Occupied housing units	
	2010 census total population	2019 estimated population	Percent change 2010-2019	ACS total population estimate 2015-2019	White alone, not Hispanic or Latino	Black alone, not Hispanic or Latino	Asian alone, not Hispanic or Latino	All other races or 2 or more races, not Hispanic or Latino	Hispanic or Latino[1]	Under 18 years old	Age 65 years and older	Median age	Percent High school diploma or less	Percent Bachelor's degree or more	Total	Percent with a computer
	1	2	3	4	5	6	7	8	9	10	11	12	13	14	15	16
ALABAMA—Con.																
Mountain Brook city	20,467	20,297	-0.8	20,436	96.3	1.1	1.4	0.5	0.7	29.5	18.1	40.4	3.8	85.3	7,284	97.2
Mount Olive CDP	371	-	-	358	57.0	43.0	0.0	0.0	0.0	19.6	22.6	36.6	71.5	13.5	156	80.8
Mount Olive CDP	4,079	-	-	4,387	93.9	5.3	0.0	0.8	0.0	22.6	18.5	42.5	33.9	23.4	1,620	91.2
Mount Vernon town	1,571	1,495	-4.8	1,450	19.9	77.0	0.9	1.8	0.3	18.2	15.4	39.4	70.3	5.8	457	73.3
Movico CDP	305	-	-	86	0.0	100.0	0.0	0.0	0.0	27.9	14.0	29.5	93.5	0.0	46	63.0
Mulga town	835	810	-3.0	856	77.0	16.5	0.0	5.6	0.9	18.9	17.3	43.9	65.6	3.7	359	75.8
Munford town	1,391	1,348	-3.1	1,410	74.3	20.3	0.9	4.1	0.5	23.1	13.2	34.3	50.8	14.8	562	81.5
Muscle Shoals city	13,154	14,575	10.8	14,103	81.6	11.5	1.0	1.7	4.2	24.5	17.5	38.2	42.4	25.6	5,371	87.1
Myrtlewood town	130	116	-10.8	152	88.8	11.2	0.0	0.0	0.0	7.9	15.1	51.0	63.0	5.9	51	84.3
Nanafalia CDP	94	-	-	29	20.7	79.3	0.0	0.0	0.0	0.0	100.0	68.2	79.3	10.3	16	100.0
Nances Creek CDP	407	-	-	476	100.0	0.0	0.0	0.0	0.0	34.5	25.2	42.7	50.3	24.3	178	74.7
Napier Field town	354	344	-2.8	532	61.7	26.3	0.0	3.0	9.0	31.2	5.5	32.3	54.1	7.6	200	86.0
Natural Bridge town	35	35	0.0	4	100.0	0.0	0.0	0.0	0.0	0.0	0.0	0.0	50.0	0.0	2	100.0
Nauvoo town	217	202	-6.9	138	89.1	0.0	0.0	1.4	9.4	16.7	15.9	47.4	69.4	9.2	71	63.4
Nectar town	340	341	0.3	376	99.2	0.0	0.0	0.8	0.0	33.5	16.5	33.4	56.1	10.1	123	87.0
Needham town	94	85	-9.6	73	97.3	0.0	0.0	2.7	0.0	12.3	35.6	58.6	51.6	14.1	39	71.8
Newbern town	186	173	-7.0	228	16.7	83.3	0.0	0.0	0.0	29.4	18.4	36.8	67.9	13.6	77	57.1
New Brockton town	1,142	1,261	10.4	1,146	70.3	18.8	0.4	7.7	2.7	19.6	21.3	44.5	52.1	14.6	508	74.0
New Hope city	2,814	2,916	3.6	2,854	94.7	0.0	0.2	4.4	0.7	24.3	14.8	39.2	52.7	16.9	1,087	89.4
New Market CDP	1,597	-	-	1,122	87.8	0.0	0.0	9.3	2.9	18.5	15.8	45.1	56.5	24.0	475	82.7
New Site town	775	760	-1.9	841	88.5	9.6	0.0	1.1	0.8	24.9	19.3	43.7	53.1	11.9	331	83.7
Newton town	1,511	1,456	-3.6	1,869	82.2	14.8	1.3	1.4	0.3	24.9	16.3	33.9	50.4	12.5	655	90.4
New Union CDP	955	-	-	829	97.1	0.0	0.0	2.9	0.0	8.7	31.1	57.3	59.7	12.8	381	75.3
Newville town	539	512	-5.0	433	62.6	33.7	0.0	2.5	1.2	19.4	20.6	47.1	54.0	15.2	207	79.7
North Courtland town	632	620	-1.9	770	1.7	97.5	0.0	0.0	0.8	20.8	26.0	43.5	77.5	4.0	385	55.3
North Johns town	145	145	0.0	143	61.5	37.1	0.0	1.4	0.0	16.1	18.9	50.6	62.9	4.3	64	81.3
Northport city	23,828	26,115	9.6	25,874	68.6	25.6	0.4	0.7	4.7	26.1	14.3	33.1	32.1	37.3	9,685	90.3
Notasulga town	965	823	-14.7	1,011	41.6	57.4	0.0	0.4	0.6	11.5	13.8	43.4	48.1	12.8	456	86.0
Oak Grove town	533	521	-2.3	562	86.1	11.2	0.0	1.1	1.6	16.4	24.9	51.7	59.7	6.9	238	81.9
Oak Hill town	26	23	-11.5	22	54.5	45.5	0.0	0.0	0.0	0.0	31.8	61.5	27.3	72.7	16	56.3
Oakman town	786	724	-7.9	638	76.0	18.5	0.6	2.5	2.4	26.2	17.9	38.1	58.7	11.1	286	79.0
Odenville town	3,690	3,893	5.5	3,848	94.8	1.3	0.0	1.1	2.8	24.7	11.3	37.1	45.1	20.8	1,381	94.4
Ohatchee town	1,150	1,153	0.3	1,410	95.0	2.1	0.0	2.3	0.6	26.3	20.6	42.6	46.7	17.3	555	94.6
Oneonta city	6,580	6,577	0.0	6,568	80.4	6.9	0.6	4.5	7.7	23.8	24.8	40.6	49.8	18.2	2,565	74.7
Onycha town	184	186	1.1	74	93.2	6.8	0.0	0.0	0.0	24.3	12.2	41.3	68.0	0.0	36	52.8
Opelika city	26,491	30,908	16.7	30,232	49.2	41.9	2.8	2.2	3.9	22.6	14.3	37.7	39.4	29.7	11,866	86.9
Opp city	6,658	6,390	-4.0	6,455	78.2	19.7	0.0	1.1	1.1	23.3	24.8	44.7	55.6	13.5	2,701	74.5
Orange Beach city	5,439	6,235	14.6	6,019	98.0	0.1	0.8	1.0	0.2	12.3	33.5	56.6	26.5	50.8	2,966	97.3
Orrville town	203	168	-17.2	154	46.1	53.9	0.0	0.0	0.0	8.4	43.5	60.7	55.5	13.3	98	34.7
Our Town CDP	641	-	-	688	77.2	11.2	0.0	11.6	0.0	17.4	18.8	47.9	62.9	0.0	251	88.8
Owens Cross Roads town	1,522	2,129	39.9	2,069	85.6	7.2	1.0	4.2	2.0	19.6	15.0	39.6	44.1	23.7	794	95.8
Oxford city	21,533	21,225	-1.4	21,323	71.7	14.6	1.9	1.4	10.4	25.6	14.5	37.6	44.1	22.9	7,871	87.1
Ozark city	14,894	14,284	-4.1	14,413	59.8	30.5	1.5	3.3	4.9	20.8	22.2	44.7	47.2	19.0	5,946	84.3
Paint Rock town	202	197	-2.5	200	94.0	0.0	0.5	5.5	0.0	24.5	18.0	42.5	69.4	6.0	72	90.3
Panola CDP	144	-	-	39	0.0	100.0	0.0	0.0	0.0	0.0	0.0	30.2	20.5	0.0	8	100.0
Parrish town	990	937	-5.4	1,087	70.7	24.5	0.0	2.4	2.4	30.3	11.6	34.3	74.1	2.7	373	78.6
Pelham city	21,466	23,911	11.4	23,428	74.4	11.2	1.3	1.2	12.0	22.8	14.4	40.5	24.4	39.9	9,074	96.4
Pell City city	12,712	14,045	10.5	13,781	85.5	10.7	2.0	0.8	1.0	20.9	19.0	39.8	43.5	18.6	5,801	86.8
Pennington town	225	204	-9.3	321	29.9	69.2	0.0	0.9	0.0	14.3	20.2	48.4	60.3	10.1	119	79.8
Penton CDP	201	-	-	98	81.6	18.4	0.0	0.0	0.0	0.0	80.6	65.9	74.5	12.2	52	25.0
Perdido CDP	-	-	-	795	86.3	7.8	0.0	5.9	0.0	17.4	29.1	49.5	66.4	12.0	272	65.1
Perdido Beach town	562	649	15.5	494	94.9	0.0	0.0	3.8	1.2	7.3	39.7	63.0	40.1	28.0	262	85.9
Peterman CDP	89	-	-	147	100.0	0.0	0.0	0.0	0.0	28.6	51.7	68.6	64.8	16.2	55	43.6
Petrey town	58	56	-3.4	66	90.9	0.0	0.0	9.1	0.0	19.7	30.3	39.5	32.1	34.0	27	88.9
Phenix City city	32,862	36,487	11.0	36,516	44.5	43.7	0.9	4.1	6.9	26.1	12.6	34.2	43.3	22.1	14,716	86.9
Phil Campbell town	1,147	1,071	-6.6	1,009	89.1	1.6	0.0	2.9	6.4	24.5	18.8	40.6	57.2	12.5	385	71.7
Pickensville town	604	578	-4.3	798	37.2	62.5	0.3	0.0	0.0	22.3	20.1	42.2	59.1	8.9	309	68.3
Piedmont city	4,864	4,535	-6.8	4,611	80.5	10.9	0.5	3.0	5.0	22.4	19.3	44.9	54.9	14.3	2,040	81.1
Pike Road town	5,449	10,159	86.4	9,320	59.6	32.3	3.7	2.0	2.3	28.0	10.2	36.8	17.2	55.7	3,328	97.8
Pinckard town	647	630	-2.6	576	79.3	19.8	0.0	0.9	0.0	20.8	24.7	46.0	52.5	13.5	241	75.5
Pine Apple town	153	132	-13.7	129	68.2	29.5	0.0	2.3	0.0	3.9	53.5	65.8	52.6	30.2	67	62.7
Pine Hill town	982	852	-13.2	927	33.1	65.3	0.3	1.3	0.0	28.2	15.5	27.9	61.5	7.1	344	67.2
Pine Level CDP	4,183	-	-	4,484	85.8	6.5	0.6	2.6	4.4	26.0	10.9	33.3	41.8	24.9	1,604	93.8
Pine Ridge town	282	284	0.7	475	59.4	0.0	0.0	0.4	40.2	30.9	7.8	25.9	58.8	10.1	136	91.9
Pinson city	7,148	7,106	-0.6	7,109	69.7	24.5	0.1	1.1	4.7	21.1	13.7	39.2	42.7	21.1	2,711	92.5
Pisgah town	717	692	-3.5	734	94.0	0.0	0.0	4.5	1.5	18.7	21.3	43.6	57.2	14.2	313	80.2
Pleasant Grove city	10,119	9,604	-5.1	9,651	41.7	56.8	0.1	0.8	0.6	19.3	18.6	45.6	37.0	24.3	3,610	93.5
Pleasant Groves town	419	404	-3.6	441	96.4	0.0	0.2	3.4	0.0	22.2	18.4	42.5	71.5	9.4	160	85.6
Point Clear CDP	2,125	-	-	2,652	45.2	50.4	0.0	0.8	3.6	29.6	27.9	42.7	40.5	43.1	793	83.0
Pollard town	137	136	-0.7	126	54.0	14.3	0.0	5.6	26.2	41.3	11.1	31.5	47.3	12.2	38	68.4
Powell town	955	967	1.3	1,261	89.7	3.7	0.2	5.9	0.4	19.6	14.8	41.8	68.2	6.4	359	79.9
Prattville city	34,041	35,957	5.6	35,925	72.9	18.7	1.6	3.0	3.8	24.2	14.9	36.7	40.5	31.6	14,069	91.4
Priceville town	2,683	3,794	41.4	3,475	90.2	6.3	0.7	2.6	0.2	23.1	17.9	42.6	37.1	34.9	1,204	90.0
Prichard city	22,633	21,428	-5.3	21,773	8.9	88.8	0.3	0.9	1.3	27.0	17.4	35.2	60.1	9.2	7,323	69.4
Providence town	220	197	-10.5	158	77.8	20.3	0.0	1.9	0.0	4.4	19.0	48.5	71.0	15.3	75	92.0
Putnam CDP	193	-	-	45	0.0	100.0	0.0	0.0	0.0	24.4	0.0	59.3	100.0	0.0	20	35.0
Ragland town	1,637	1,722	5.2	1,889	83.6	14.0	0.2	1.7	0.5	20.5	15.5	43.4	72.7	6.0	674	79.2
Rainbow City city	9,608	9,611	0.0	9,589	80.5	9.6	2.8	2.0	5.2	23.5	16.7	38.0	37.8	30.0	3,847	90.9
Rainsville city	4,986	5,123	2.7	5,041	78.7	0.9	0.0	4.8	15.6	27.3	14.1	35.8	59.1	8.9	1,894	85.1
Ranburne town	406	398	-2.0	461	92.4	1.7	0.0	4.6	1.3	24.7	23.9	44.1	62.8	9.0	179	73.2
Ray CDP	443	-	-	300	65.3	34.7	0.0	0.0	0.0	17.0	41.7	59.5	39.0	36.5	144	90.3
Red Bay city	3,158	3,085	-2.3	3,114	91.8	0.0	0.1	7.0	1.2	26.5	20.2	36.8	72.5	9.9	1,220	72.5
Redland CDP	3,736	-	-	4,388	87.8	10.8	0.9	0.6	0.0	29.1	12.5	39.0	23.4	50.7	1,485	95.8
Red Level town	487	478	-1.8	385	87.8	12.2	0.0	0.0	0.0	19.5	15.3	39.6	59.1	8.5	159	78.0
Redstone Arsenal CDP	1,946	-	-	1,329	46.3	37.1	2.6	7.6	6.5	23.8	3.5	25.0	18.6	52.0	347	98.8
Reece City town	652	627	-3.8	719	81.8	2.2	3.8	1.8	10.4	21.4	28.7	45.2	59.5	8.4	252	86.9
Reeltown CDP	766	-	-	274	52.9	42.0	5.1	0.0	0.0	39.1	12.8	40.1	71.9	13.2	115	100.0
Reform town	1,697	1,552	-8.5	1,621	39.5	55.3	0.0	3.4	1.7	21.7	19.2	44.9	54.3	11.6	696	83.3
Rehobeth town	1,274	1,657	30.1	2,059	84.8	7.4	0.0	2.2	5.6	34.2	9.3	30.6	42.8	24.0	611	88.1
Repton town	282	258	-8.5	491	52.7	39.7	7.1	0.4	0.0	21.8	7.5	34.6	51.1	31.3	119	66.4
Ridgeville town	114	110	-3.5	86	22.1	77.9	0.0	0.0	0.0	23.3	25.6	33.5	62.5	5.4	32	84.4
River Falls town	526	535	1.7	585	63.2	36.8	0.0	0.0	0.0	21.7	27.5	46.3	66.5	10.8	209	57.9

1 May be of any race.

Table A. All Places — **Population and Housing**

STATE City, town, township, borough, or CDP (county if applicable)	Population				Race and Hispanic or Latino origin (percent)					Age (percent)			Educational attainment of persons age 25 and older		Occupied housing units	
	2010 census total population	2019 estimated population	Percent change 2010-2019	ACS total population estimate 2015-2019	White alone, not Hispanic or Latino	Black alone, not Hispanic or Latino	Asian alone, not Hispanic or Latino	All other races or 2 or more races, not Hispanic or Latino	Hispanic or Latino[1]	Under 18 years old	Age 65 years and older	Median age	Percent High school diploma or less	Percent Bachelor's degree or more	Total	Percent with a computer
	1	2	3	4	5	6	7	8	9	10	11	12	13	14	15	16
ALABAMA—Con.																
Riverside city	2,215	2,377	7.3	3,042	76.7	14.6	4.4	3.0	1.2	26.1	9.7	34.8	47.0	17.6	1,051	93.2
Riverview town	186	181	-2.7	106	87.7	0.0	0.0	1.9	10.4	22.6	33.0	45.4	65.4	3.8	44	63.6
Roanoke city	6,085	5,913	-2.8	5,926	50.3	43.2	0.0	3.0	3.5	18.9	19.6	45.0	53.0	17.4	2,387	89.4
Robertsdale city	5,603	6,815	21.6	6,473	84.5	4.4	0.0	0.6	10.4	30.3	13.2	36.1	51.9	14.1	2,349	88.5
Rock Creek CDP	1,456	-	-	1,508	93.2	1.5	0.0	2.1	3.2	17.2	19.4	50.4	43.2	16.9	645	82.8
Rockford town	477	436	-8.6	838	45.5	51.8	0.0	1.0	1.8	19.7	15.0	43.5	48.2	15.8	261	85.1
Rock Mills CDP	600	-	-	493	100.0	0.0	0.0	0.0	0.0	21.5	28.6	42.2	55.9	16.6	217	93.1
Rockville CDP	43	-	-	12	0.0	100.0	0.0	0.0	0.0	0.0	0.0	0.0	100.0	0.0	6	100.0
Rogersville town	1,258	1,251	-0.6	1,424	81.4	7.2	0.8	2.0	8.6	19.7	19.5	38.6	48.1	18.7	603	75.6
Rosa town	313	319	1.9	431	83.1	1.2	0.0	0.0	15.8	23.7	19.5	38.7	51.2	13.5	134	76.9
Russellville city	9,852	9,737	-1.2	9,781	51.8	9.4	1.1	0.5	37.2	25.5	15.4	32.0	66.2	12.6	3,238	73.7
Rutledge town	470	449	-4.5	357	73.1	20.7	0.0	6.2	0.0	17.4	19.6	47.5	59.8	3.7	141	73.8
St. Florian town	415	670	61.4	470	93.2	5.7	0.2	0.0	0.9	11.7	26.4	58.0	47.3	26.6	225	76.9
St. Stephens CDP	495	-	-	441	69.8	30.2	0.0	0.0	0.0	15.9	25.9	54.6	60.9	5.9	165	94.5
Saks CDP	10,744	-	-	10,645	64.6	25.8	2.2	3.7	3.7	23.8	18.1	41.6	57.1	12.9	4,055	82.3
Samson city	1,943	1,854	-4.6	1,686	74.0	12.1	0.0	8.4	5.5	26.5	20.0	43.1	59.2	10.5	763	75.8
Sand Rock town	580	569	-1.9	458	96.5	0.0	0.0	1.7	1.7	16.2	19.4	49.8	51.6	20.6	190	89.5
Sanford town	256	254	-0.8	249	85.5	4.8	0.0	0.8	8.8	30.1	9.2	38.2	69.8	13.0	89	82.0
Saraland city	13,801	14,649	6.1	14,391	79.5	13.6	1.3	4.5	1.0	25.1	16.0	37.7	49.6	19.4	5,171	86.6
Sardis City town	1,704	1,775	4.2	1,742	97.1	0.0	0.4	1.7	0.7	18.3	23.8	47.0	39.3	20.2	686	90.5
Satsuma city	6,157	6,190	0.5	6,159	89.0	7.7	0.0	2.4	0.9	22.4	19.3	41.0	50.5	21.8	2,205	83.6
Scottsboro city	14,786	14,436	-2.4	14,526	88.4	5.9	1.0	2.2	2.5	20.5	20.2	43.5	48.5	21.6	5,995	85.0
Section town	770	740	-3.9	971	97.2	0.0	0.0	2.8	0.0	26.5	14.7	36.6	52.2	16.3	389	76.3
Selma city	20,756	17,231	-17.0	18,276	15.4	81.8	1.1	0.4	1.2	25.0	16.8	37.7	52.3	17.3	7,612	75.7
Selmont-West Selmont CDP	2,671	-	-	1,812	7.8	91.8	0.0	0.3	0.0	19.9	12.4	40.0	70.5	1.5	769	64.6
Semmes city	4,384	5,594	27.6	5,284	80.1	11.6	0.0	5.2	3.2	17.3	27.1	50.1	61.3	13.9	2,243	78.4
Sheffield city	9,039	8,901	-1.5	8,986	69.7	24.9	0.1	3.1	2.3	20.5	21.4	44.9	52.2	19.8	4,046	75.0
Shelby CDP	1,044	-	-	885	79.1	15.6	1.7	3.6	0.0	17.2	10.7	44.2	42.1	6.2	320	89.7
Shiloh town	276	281	1.8	338	92.6	0.0	0.0	7.4	0.0	20.1	15.1	42.6	49.6	17.1	137	73.7
Shoal Creek CDP	1,400	-	-	1,376	90.3	0.7	0.0	9.0	0.0	22.5	15.4	44.6	10.7	66.5	519	96.7
Shorter town	461	395	-14.3	356	28.1	68.8	2.5	0.6	0.0	17.1	31.2	56.7	60.9	10.6	168	67.9
Silas town	470	430	-8.5	513	65.9	33.7	0.0	0.4	0.0	22.2	26.5	44.8	58.6	12.6	209	78.0
Silverhill town	713	1,170	64.1	645	83.3	0.0	0.0	1.7	15.0	14.9	27.4	52.3	34.9	31.9	303	93.4
Sims Chapel CDP	153	-	-	-	-	-	-	-	-	-	-	-	-	-	-	-
Sipsey town	435	401	-7.8	373	53.4	46.4	0.0	0.3	0.0	28.2	22.5	45.1	54.6	3.4	143	67.1
Skyline town	852	838	-1.6	870	77.6	0.0	0.0	11.4	11.0	24.0	22.2	43.2	68.1	4.0	367	79.3
Slocomb city	1,975	1,898	-3.9	1,852	71.4	22.7	0.0	0.9	4.9	21.7	27.4	45.5	60.6	11.3	844	77.8
Smiths Station city	4,923	5,391	9.5	5,364	80.0	16.3	0.0	2.0	1.7	20.2	20.4	43.2	41.2	21.6	2,151	88.3
Smoke Rise CDP	1,825	-	-	2,101	100.0	0.0	0.0	0.0	0.0	23.4	18.1	39.5	41.6	12.0	662	100.0
Snead town	841	838	-0.4	893	96.3	0.0	1.0	0.4	2.2	11.6	22.7	45.0	50.1	20.0	382	75.4
Somerville town	767	773	0.8	547	88.3	6.8	0.0	2.6	2.4	16.6	18.3	50.7	56.1	14.9	252	84.5
Southside city	8,440	8,905	5.5	8,811	95.3	1.2	0.5	1.4	1.6	20.7	17.9	41.0	29.4	29.3	3,284	95.0
South Vinemont town	723	745	3.0	707	64.6	3.5	2.1	0.6	29.1	23.9	12.9	34.1	57.7	12.6	264	81.8
Spanish Fort city	6,893	9,214	33.7	8,601	86.8	3.7	1.5	1.7	6.3	23.5	15.2	37.9	25.0	44.3	3,278	91.8
Spring Garden CDP	238	-	-	187	100.0	0.0	0.0	0.0	0.0	16.6	0.0	50.0	46.9	14.8	84	100.0
Springville city	4,110	4,304	4.7	4,257	93.4	4.9	0.0	1.6	0.0	28.3	20.2	44.8	36.6	26.1	1,450	96.7
Spruce Pine CDP	222	-	-	178	100.0	0.0	0.0	0.0	0.0	0.0	23.6	53.8	24.2	14.3	96	86.5
Standing Rock CDP	168	-	-	168	100.0	0.0	0.0	0.0	0.0	20.8	12.5	47.8	40.2	9.8	58	100.0
Stapleton CDP	-	-	-	1,421	96.9	0.0	1.5	1.6	0.0	22.4	12.9	46.5	29.4	22.8	559	88.4
Steele town	1,043	1,089	4.4	1,149	84.4	0.0	0.4	0.4	14.7	19.0	17.9	44.7	63.0	9.5	478	82.6
Sterrett CDP	712	-	-	977	89.7	3.5	0.0	6.9	0.0	13.5	21.5	53.0	60.0	18.4	399	79.2
Stevenson city	2,046	1,951	-4.6	1,705	72.5	23.9	0.0	3.6	0.0	26.8	20.8	45.1	67.0	12.3	729	73.0
Stewartville CDP	1,767	-	-	1,634	99.1	0.9	0.0	0.0	0.0	14.2	27.2	51.4	63.3	10.2	605	76.5
Stockton CDP	-	-	-	626	82.9	13.1	0.0	4.0	0.0	30.8	3.5	34.5	36.0	26.1	167	100.0
Sulligent city	1,927	1,834	-4.8	1,917	81.8	15.7	0.0	2.5	0.0	24.3	21.9	44.5	58.2	12.3	884	74.0
Sumiton city	2,515	2,332	-7.3	2,472	87.5	10.5	0.0	1.4	0.7	22.0	21.4	42.2	51.7	8.7	993	83.3
Summerdale town	892	1,681	88.5	1,135	89.1	2.7	0.4	2.6	5.2	25.0	24.1	37.8	49.5	20.3	405	92.1
Susan Moore town	773	776	0.4	849	63.8	0.0	0.0	0.4	35.8	16.0	26.0	41.9	63.0	11.7	317	79.5
Sweet Water town	274	244	-10.9	385	97.4	2.6	0.0	0.0	0.0	41.3	11.7	28.3	26.8	45.9	115	85.2
Sylacauga city	12,803	12,034	-6.0	12,226	62.8	32.8	0.0	2.5	1.9	25.0	16.7	36.9	46.8	17.7	4,943	83.9
Sylvania town	1,861	1,894	1.8	2,546	87.4	0.0	0.0	4.0	8.6	31.8	10.6	34.5	53.4	14.4	829	89.4
Sylvan Springs town	1,542	1,492	-3.2	1,890	87.0	9.3	0.6	3.1	0.0	24.3	18.7	42.4	52.7	16.9	645	91.8
Talladega city	16,054	15,457	-3.7	15,522	44.5	47.7	0.1	1.9	5.7	18.7	16.5	38.3	59.0	14.5	5,553	79.3
Talladega Springs town	166	159	-4.2	161	95.0	3.7	0.0	1.2	0.0	23.0	16.8	40.4	52.3	7.2	61	90.2
Tallassee city	4,682	4,502	-3.8	4,743	68.9	25.4	0.0	0.9	4.8	23.6	18.0	35.4	55.8	13.0	1,905	85.9
Tarrant city	6,382	6,109	-4.3	6,174	33.3	53.1	0.3	2.0	11.4	23.3	14.5	36.8	57.0	10.8	2,206	75.3
Taylor town	2,343	2,428	3.6	2,286	74.7	14.5	0.7	7.1	3.0	30.1	11.5	33.7	56.6	9.3	752	73.8
Theodore CDP	6,130	-	-	6,334	76.8	16.6	3.4	1.4	1.8	30.8	15.6	34.0	57.9	12.9	2,035	86.4
Thomaston town	422	381	-9.7	380	62.1	37.9	0.0	0.0	0.0	13.7	11.1	42.2	54.6	19.7	169	76.9
Thomasville city	4,201	3,836	-8.7	3,928	50.9	47.7	1.1	0.0	0.4	18.5	19.8	42.1	55.7	14.6	1,659	70.8
Thorsby town	2,001	2,057	2.8	1,941	88.6	4.5	0.2	0.6	6.1	24.6	13.9	40.3	55.3	21.4	706	87.0
Tibbie CDP	41	-	-	81	80.2	0.0	0.0	19.8	0.0	56.8	0.0	16.4	0.0	34.3	28	42.9
Tidmore Bend CDP	1,245	-	-	1,221	89.4	7.2	0.0	3.4	0.0	18.9	22.9	44.7	48.4	18.3	475	89.1
Tillmans Corner CDP	17,398	-	-	17,560	63.5	14.6	4.9	4.7	12.3	25.3	15.7	36.6	53.7	15.3	6,400	84.2
Town Creek town	1,100	1,039	-5.5	1,149	57.6	25.9	0.0	12.7	3.7	26.0	18.0	33.8	64.3	13.8	480	80.6
Toxey town	137	124	-9.5	109	77.1	22.9	0.0	0.0	0.0	14.7	33.0	54.4	69.4	7.1	50	58.0
Trafford town	634	617	-2.7	594	84.0	12.6	0.0	3.4	0.0	27.6	22.6	40.9	65.9	11.6	241	66.8
Triana town	512	949	85.4	868	21.4	63.8	1.7	3.8	9.2	18.9	13.4	37.7	38.9	28.9	384	81.0
Trinity town	2,356	2,477	5.1	2,493	76.4	5.9	1.1	4.0	12.6	31.8	11.6	37.3	40.5	19.3	871	89.0
Troy city	18,192	18,957	4.2	19,112	54.5	38.2	3.6	2.2	1.5	17.8	12.0	25.7	41.3	30.2	6,853	77.4
Trussville city	19,874	22,635	13.9	21,876	88.4	5.9	0.8	3.8	1.1	28.1	15.1	39.9	21.2	45.4	7,562	93.5
Tuscaloosa city	90,275	101,129	12.0	99,390	49.1	43.9	2.5	1.2	3.2	18.0	12.2	29.3	38.2	36.9	35,264	86.2
Tuscumbia city	8,576	8,461	-1.3	8,444	62.3	29.5	0.5	3.9	3.9	24.4	16.6	37.0	53.3	16.8	3,304	82.4
Tuskegee city	9,816	8,142	-17.1	8,486	1.6	96.2	0.3	0.4	1.5	16.6	15.3	26.4	41.5	26.5	2,936	76.4
Twin town	398	392	-1.5	387	97.7	0.0	0.3	0.8	1.3	11.1	21.4	50.1	63.0	9.2	170	74.1
Underwood-Petersville CDP	3,247	-	-	3,170	85.3	7.3	3.0	3.8	0.6	21.5	20.4	39.5	61.5	16.4	1,335	88.7
Union town	237	209	-11.8	308	2.6	97.4	0.0	0.0	0.0	8.4	34.1	51.3	57.8	11.1	103	53.4
Union Grove town	77	79	2.6	87	96.6	1.1	0.0	0.0	2.3	11.5	31.0	55.4	36.5	36.5	39	82.1
Union Springs city	3,864	3,410	-11.7	3,514	6.8	92.1	0.3	0.0	0.9	21.6	15.0	31.5	67.9	11.1	1,353	66.7
Uniontown town	2,695	2,227	-17.4	1,880	9.1	90.6	0.0	0.2	0.0	26.0	13.6	34.0	61.2	12.9	704	51.7

1 May be of any race.

Table A. All Places — **Population and Housing**

STATE City, town, township, borough, or CDP (county if applicable)	Population				Race and Hispanic or Latino origin (percent)					Age (percent)			Educational attainment of persons age 25 and older		Occupied housing units	
	2010 census total population	2019 estimated population	Percent change 2010-2019	ACS total population estimate 2015-2019	White alone, not Hispanic or Latino	Black alone, not Hispanic or Latino	Asian alone, not Hispanic or Latino	All other races or 2 or more races, not Hispanic or Latino	Hispanic or Latino[1]	Under 18 years old	Age 65 years and older	Median age	Percent High school diploma or less	Percent Bachelor's degree or more	Total	Percent with a computer
	1	2	3	4	5	6	7	8	9	10	11	12	13	14	15	16
ALABAMA—Con.																
Uriah CDP	294	-	-	318	86.2	5.0	0.0	8.8	0.0	32.4	10.7	39.5	54.0	14.0	86	52.3
Valley city	9,520	9,141	-4.0	9,286	55.9	39.5	1.7	0.6	2.3	23.3	14.3	33.5	50.6	13.6	3,654	85.9
Valley Grande city	4,026	3,570	-11.3	3,708	74.7	24.2	0.0	0.5	0.6	24.4	15.1	41.0	42.9	18.4	1,451	86.6
Valley Head town	556	549	-1.3	699	90.3	0.6	0.0	2.9	6.3	30.6	18.7	39.6	56.0	12.7	252	73.4
Vance town	1,494	1,654	10.7	1,519	86.8	10.9	0.0	1.4	0.9	29.6	10.8	32.4	47.8	20.7	515	89.3
Vandiver CDP	1,135	-	-	949	92.0	3.6	1.5	1.6	1.4	16.6	24.2	50.7	59.8	26.2	438	90.2
Vernon city	2,005	1,850	-7.7	1,961	84.9	13.3	0.0	0.8	1.1	17.7	14.9	44.5	60.4	12.0	923	77.7
Vestavia Hills city	33,766	34,413	1.9	34,307	87.1	5.0	3.5	1.6	2.8	26.1	16.7	39.2	11.5	69.3	13,082	94.1
Vina town	358	356	-0.6	393	98.7	0.0	1.3	0.0	0.0	23.4	20.9	44.8	75.4	7.5	147	59.9
Vincent town	2,087	2,213	6.0	1,918	73.1	23.9	0.0	2.6	0.4	25.7	20.1	39.1	63.5	7.8	722	84.5
Vinegar Bend CDP	192	-	-	383	27.7	72.3	0.0	0.0	0.0	35.8	2.6	29.2	41.4	19.5	126	78.6
Vredenburgh town	312	290	-7.1	241	15.8	84.2	0.0	0.0	0.0	18.7	7.5	40.5	90.2	0.0	54	40.7
Wadley town	751	714	-4.9	829	60.3	32.6	0.0	5.7	1.4	26.1	10.7	20.3	63.0	17.5	229	79.0
Waldo town	277	272	-1.8	235	53.6	44.3	0.0	2.1	0.0	15.3	17.0	46.8	52.8	11.1	110	89.1
Walnut Grove town	696	700	0.6	833	93.2	0.0	0.4	6.5	0.0	25.2	15.0	40.4	58.9	8.3	264	86.0
Warrior city	3,176	3,210	1.1	3,214	84.0	14.6	1.4	0.0	0.0	12.7	29.3	54.8	68.4	6.6	1,647	65.4
Waterloo town	203	197	-3.0	140	96.4	0.0	0.0	1.4	2.1	17.1	32.1	53.0	55.8	15.9	68	75.0
Waverly town	145	144	-0.7	179	99.4	0.0	0.0	0.6	0.0	12.3	22.3	52.6	24.1	51.0	94	95.7
Weaver city	3,057	3,061	0.1	3,077	74.2	12.8	2.9	6.5	3.6	26.6	14.3	36.1	38.8	21.0	1,061	91.0
Webb town	1,421	1,477	3.9	1,427	72.8	18.9	0.1	1.1	7.1	23.4	19.6	38.5	68.1	5.9	481	71.5
Wedowee town	821	794	-3.3	820	57.9	36.2	0.0	2.1	3.8	21.2	28.9	48.8	61.9	16.1	353	64.9
Weogufka CDP	282	-	-	299	76.9	5.0	0.0	0.0	18.1	21.1	3.0	42.1	46.1	0.0	104	90.4
West Blocton town	1,291	1,252	-3.0	1,240	86.1	13.2	0.0	0.6	0.0	19.0	24.4	48.0	71.6	7.4	472	67.8
West End-Cobb Town CDP	3,465	-	-	3,274	74.6	18.5	0.4	1.5	5.0	20.6	18.4	41.5	64.7	5.1	1,258	76.9
West Jefferson town	437	421	-3.7	468	98.7	0.9	0.0	0.4	0.0	26.5	21.6	41.1	56.0	12.3	193	81.3
Westover town	1,280	1,726	34.8	1,660	88.3	1.8	0.2	1.1	8.6	31.3	13.8	34.2	34.7	31.2	573	94.1
West Point town	591	609	3.0	614	94.5	0.0	0.8	0.0	4.7	31.6	12.7	38.7	51.3	14.9	215	70.7
Wetumpka city	6,788	8,371	23.3	8,243	60.7	33.1	0.9	4.2	1.0	19.6	16.4	35.0	49.7	20.7	2,917	79.8
Whatley CDP	150	-	-	280	89.6	10.4	0.0	0.0	0.0	0.0	16.4	54.5	93.1	0.0	139	69.1
White Hall town	870	751	-13.7	711	1.8	95.1	0.0	1.4	1.7	21.4	27.0	49.2	68.0	8.8	351	59.8
White Plains CDP	811	-	-	850	100.0	0.0	0.0	0.0	0.0	20.0	26.1	41.7	45.8	19.0	364	97.0
Whitesboro CDP	2,138	-	-	2,602	90.1	0.0	0.0	9.2	0.7	24.1	17.9	40.8	59.3	11.3	763	89.6
Wilsonville town	1,913	2,056	7.5	2,268	84.2	8.6	0.0	2.2	5.0	21.3	18.1	43.3	47.9	17.1	841	90.1
Wilton town	679	681	0.3	749	71.7	25.0	0.0	0.0	3.3	22.3	15.0	41.7	61.5	14.7	252	85.7
Winfield city	4,714	4,519	-4.1	4,539	92.6	5.1	0.1	0.6	1.5	27.2	21.5	37.7	44.8	19.3	1,627	86.7
Woodland town	184	182	-1.1	240	84.6	15.0	0.0	0.0	0.4	12.5	39.2	54.0	51.8	24.6	98	62.2
Woodstock town	1,425	1,638	14.9	1,972	84.9	2.3	0.0	1.6	11.2	16.0	14.5	41.1	64.4	11.4	565	80.2
Woodville town	751	723	-3.7	794	90.4	0.0	0.3	4.7	4.7	27.2	13.9	37.6	69.5	7.6	275	84.4
Yellow Bluff town	228	202	-11.4	103	1.0	96.1	0.0	2.9	0.0	23.3	25.2	47.5	76.9	1.5	41	41.5
York city	2,538	2,239	-11.8	2,529	12.3	87.4	0.0	0.3	0.0	23.7	14.9	38.7	49.4	14.2	962	75.5
ALASKA	710,249	731,545	3.0	737,068	60.6	3.1	6.1	23.1	7.0	25.0	11.2	34.3	35.2	29.6	253,346	94.1
Adak city	326	326	0.0	226	31.9	4.0	15.5	26.5	22.1	19.9	10.2	33.3	73.9	9.2	58	93.1
Akhiok city	71	68	-4.2	59	3.4	0.0	0.0	88.1	8.5	39.0	0.0	23.6	71.4	0.0	17	88.2
Akiachak CDP	627	-	-	573	1.6	0.2	0.0	97.2	1.0	38.4	6.8	26.3	68.0	3.7	135	78.5
Akiak city	346	394	13.9	381	1.0	0.0	0.0	97.6	1.3	45.1	5.8	23.6	72.0	4.3	78	80.8
Akutan city	1,027	1,041	1.4	731	12.6	11.4	32.3	23.4	20.4	4.0	5.9	42.3	56.7	14.0	65	86.2
Alakanuk city	677	774	14.3	813	0.0	0.0	0.0	100.0	0.0	45.1	6.9	20.5	78.5	3.4	160	80.6
Alatna CDP	37	-	-	13	0.0	0.0	0.0	100.0	0.0	0.0	15.4	38.8	63.6	0.0	6	66.7
Alcan Border CDP	33	-	-	176	22.7	0.0	63.1	13.1	1.1	67.6	0.0	13.9	6.8	43.2	20	100.0
Aleknagik city	220	220	0.0	179	5.0	0.6	0.0	94.4	0.0	30.2	14.0	33.9	55.6	12.1	60	93.3
Aleneva CDP	37	-	-	27	100.0	0.0	0.0	0.0	0.0	0.0	48.1	55.0	100.0	0.0	4	0.0
Allakaket city	171	161	-5.8	213	14.1	0.0	1.9	80.8	3.3	33.3	8.5	27.4	66.4	13.9	63	57.1
Ambler city	258	262	1.6	260	17.3	0.0	0.0	82.7	0.0	30.0	11.2	29.5	59.5	26.4	59	81.4
Anaktuvuk Pass city	324	343	5.9	315	12.4	2.2	0.0	84.1	1.3	43.5	7.9	22.4	58.9	9.2	81	85.2
Anchorage municipality	291,836	288,000	-1.3	293,531	57.9	5.3	9.4	18.2	9.2	24.5	10.5	33.6	29.5	36.1	106,567	95.9
Anchor Point CDP	1,930	-	-	2,129	87.6	0.0	0.0	11.3	1.1	18.6	22.0	48.6	40.9	21.2	800	90.4
Anderson city	246	340	38.2	172	83.1	5.8	0.0	11.0	0.0	16.9	7.0	30.8	35.1	14.4	56	96.4
Angoon city	459	459	0.0	506	17.6	11.3	3.2	55.7	12.3	13.0	15.0	48.6	53.1	5.8	130	81.5
Aniak city	501	549	9.6	526	16.9	1.7	0.0	78.5	2.9	27.8	9.1	36.1	60.8	11.2	149	87.2
Anvik city	85	82	-3.5	105	0.0	0.0	0.0	100.0	0.0	32.4	14.3	31.4	58.9	3.6	38	68.4
Arctic Village CDP	152	-	-	185	4.3	0.0	0.0	95.7	0.0	40.0	4.9	24.8	57.6	6.5	54	74.1
Atka city	61	81	32.8	43	7.0	0.0	0.0	93.0	0.0	34.9	4.7	25.1	68.2	9.1	12	100.0
Atmautluak CDP	277	-	-	189	0.0	0.0	0.0	100.0	0.0	40.7	7.9	25.3	95.8	0.0	43	79.1
Atqasuk city	233	248	6.4	162	1.9	0.0	0.0	98.1	0.0	39.5	8.6	22.8	80.3	2.8	42	88.1
Attu Station CDP	21	-	-	17	47.1	52.9	0.0	0.0	0.0	0.0	0.0	0.0	0.0	100.0	0	0.0
Badger CDP	19,482	-	-	18,911	75.0	3.8	0.9	12.6	7.7	26.0	9.5	31.9	31.0	21.6	6,726	98.2
Bear Creek CDP	1,956	-	-	1,178	80.9	0.0	0.5	15.7	2.9	26.6	15.2	44.8	41.9	20.5	473	96.4
Beaver CDP	84	-	-	70	0.0	0.0	0.0	100.0	0.0	27.1	12.9	34.5	53.2	0.0	29	44.8
Beluga CDP	20	-	-	5	100.0	0.0	0.0	0.0	0.0	0.0	60.0	0.0	100.0	0.0	5	100.0
Bethel city	6,080	6,586	8.3	6,472	20.8	1.8	2.9	68.4	6.0	30.6	7.0	29.2	54.8	20.9	1,934	94.2
Bettles city	13	12	-7.7	84	66.7	0.0	0.0	33.3	0.0	0.0	0.0	37.5	33.3	33.3	0	0.0
Big Delta CDP	591	-	-	556	85.3	0.0	5.8	6.8	2.2	18.7	16.5	39.1	50.6	23.1	236	75.8
Big Lake CDP	3,350	-	-	2,678	78.1	0.0	0.4	15.4	6.0	20.4	18.2	45.7	52.8	13.5	1,060	92.6
Birch Creek CDP	33	-	-	4	0.0	0.0	0.0	100.0	0.0	0.0	0.0	0.0	100.0	0.0	4	50.0
Brevig Mission city	388	401	3.4	384	2.9	0.0	0.0	97.1	0.0	41.1	2.9	24.2	77.1	5.3	96	85.4
Buckland city	416	422	1.4	675	3.7	0.0	0.3	96.0	0.0	42.2	5.0	21.9	78.0	4.3	114	93.0
Buffalo Soapstone CDP	855	-	-	975	86.4	0.0	0.0	10.2	3.5	30.9	11.5	38.7	47.3	24.9	307	91.9
Butte CDP	3,246	-	-	4,015	83.2	0.2	1.7	10.3	4.7	25.3	12.1	36.8	38.9	25.0	1,135	95.6
Cantwell CDP	219	-	-	178	78.1	1.1	0.0	20.8	0.0	13.5	20.8	46.0	49.0	22.8	88	94.3
Central CDP	96	-	-	40	100.0	0.0	0.0	0.0	0.0	0.0	65.0	65.7	61.5	3.9	30	56.7
Chalkyitsik CDP	69	-	-	109	18.3	0.0	0.0	72.5	9.2	18.3	6.4	39.4	45.5	28.6	32	46.9
Chase CDP	34	-	-	-	-	-	-	-	-	-	-	-	-	-	-	-
Chefornak city	418	471	12.7	483	0.0	0.0	0.0	100.0	0.0	38.5	8.1	24.0	72.9	3.5	83	88.0
Chena Ridge CDP	5,791	-	-	6,111	74.6	1.4	1.1	18.3	4.6	23.8	9.2	38.1	15.4	51.6	2,393	98.5
Chenega CDP	76	-	-	68	27.9	0.0	0.0	69.1	2.9	29.4	14.7	31.5	53.5	32.6	13	100.0
Chevak city	933	1,077	15.4	1,037	11.4	0.0	0.0	87.8	0.8	35.9	5.6	28.4	81.4	4.3	181	76.2
Chickaloon CDP	272	-	-	210	87.6	0.0	0.0	11.0	1.4	6.2	33.8	59.0	28.0	16.6	96	91.7
Chicken CDP	7	-	-	12	100.0	0.0	0.0	0.0	0.0	0.0	0.0	0.0	41.7	0.0	7	100.0
Chignik city	92	89	-3.3	57	19.3	0.0	5.3	75.4	0.0	26.3	0.0	30.5	64.7	11.8	18	100.0

1 May be of any race.

Table A. All Places — **Population and Housing**

STATE City, town, township, borough, or CDP (county if applicable)	Population				Race and Hispanic or Latino origin (percent)					Age (percent)			Educational attainment of persons age 25 and older		Occupied housing units	
	2010 census total population	2019 estimated population	Percent change 2010-2019	ACS total population estimate 2015-2019	White alone, not Hispanic or Latino	Black alone, not Hispanic or Latino	Asian alone, not Hispanic or Latino	All other races or 2 or more races, not Hispanic or Latino	Hispanic or Latino[1]	Under 18 years old	Age 65 years and older	Median age	Percent High school diploma or less	Percent Bachelor's degree or more	Total	Percent with a computer
	1	2	3	4	5	6	7	8	9	10	11	12	13	14	15	16
ALASKA—Con.																
Chignik Lagoon CDP	78	-	-	69	20.3	0.0	0.0	79.7	0.0	23.2	5.8	37.5	32.6	6.5	25	100.0
Chignik Lake CDP	73	-	-	49	8.2	0.0	0.0	91.8	0.0	16.3	0.0	50.5	70.6	11.8	23	100.0
Chiniak CDP	47	-	-	-	-	-	-	-	-	-	-	-	-	-	-	-
Chisana CDP	-	-	-	-	-	-	-	-	-	-	-	-	-	-	-	-
Chistochina CDP	93	-	-	80	6.3	0.0	0.0	77.5	16.3	10.0	5.0	48.5	87.1	3.2	14	42.9
Chitina CDP	126	-	-	61	42.6	0.0	0.0	57.4	0.0	16.4	9.8	35.6	79.5	0.0	12	75.0
Chuathbaluk city	116	126	8.6	111	5.4	0.0	0.0	94.6	0.0	28.8	8.1	25.6	69.0	13.8	32	87.5
Circle CDP	104	-	-	64	12.5	0.0	0.0	71.9	15.6	40.6	12.5	26.5	50.0	13.2	21	71.4
Clam Gulch CDP	176	-	-	227	97.4	0.0	0.0	2.6	0.0	14.5	27.3	51.1	36.4	14.2	90	55.6
Clark's Point city	62	62	0.0	44	0.0	0.0	0.0	100.0	0.0	34.1	4.5	27.0	58.3	0.0	17	100.0
Coffman Cove city	178	176	-1.1	152	91.4	0.0	0.0	3.3	5.3	22.4	3.9	40.9	46.9	20.4	71	78.9
Cohoe CDP	1,364	-	-	1,223	80.2	0.0	1.6	15.2	3.0	15.1	21.4	53.2	39.4	23.0	541	89.3
Cold Bay city	108	125	15.7	56	51.8	1.8	12.5	19.6	14.3	5.4	14.3	51.8	20.8	29.2	33	100.0
Coldfoot CDP	10	-	-	156	75.6	0.0	0.6	23.1	0.6	0.0	45.5	56.8	0.8	34.7	0	0.0
College CDP	12,964	-	-	12,791	71.0	2.6	6.2	14.3	5.8	20.9	11.9	31.2	23.0	40.7	4,911	97.0
Cooper Landing CDP	289	-	-	478	92.5	0.0	0.0	7.5	0.0	35.1	17.6	34.7	10.7	58.6	156	88.5
Copper Center CDP	328	-	-	245	26.1	3.3	0.8	62.9	6.9	25.3	7.8	35.0	54.4	8.1	67	94.0
Cordova city	2,239	2,169	-3.1	2,829	62.5	0.5	10.5	21.9	4.5	20.7	12.1	38.2	39.3	29.3	817	99.6
Covenant Life CDP	86	-	-	37	59.5	0.0	0.0	40.5	0.0	0.0	62.2	70.3	37.8	21.6	23	100.0
Craig city	1,201	1,262	5.1	1,189	60.6	0.8	1.7	34.5	2.4	22.6	14.2	38.8	47.0	20.6	476	91.0
Crooked Creek CDP	105	-	-	75	1.3	1.3	0.0	97.3	0.0	24.0	12.0	33.5	63.0	17.4	28	64.3
Crown Point CDP	74	-	-	73	100.0	0.0	0.0	0.0	0.0	24.7	6.8	38.3	49.1	41.8	25	80.0
Deering city	122	123	0.8	143	0.7	0.0	4.2	95.1	0.0	39.9	6.3	26.1	67.6	2.7	34	88.2
Delta Junction city	947	928	-2.0	993	87.1	0.3	0.1	3.6	8.9	28.0	8.5	33.4	34.5	21.5	306	94.8
Deltana CDP	2,251	-	-	2,430	87.4	0.3	0.7	4.7	6.9	33.5	10.7	35.1	44.5	20.1	722	98.5
Denali Park CDP	-	-	-	872	88.6	0.7	2.4	7.5	0.8	2.8	1.4	40.3	20.8	58.4	86	100.0
Diamond Ridge CDP	1,156	-	-	1,245	90.4	0.0	1.9	5.0	2.7	22.2	15.6	46.1	21.2	46.2	481	97.5
Dillingham city	2,327	2,360	1.4	2,215	22.3	1.5	1.9	66.6	7.6	29.5	10.5	31.1	44.0	26.2	742	93.7
Diomede city	115	119	3.5	93	0.0	0.0	0.0	100.0	0.0	40.9	3.2	22.7	80.0	7.5	34	85.3
Dot Lake CDP	13	-	-	-	-	-	-	-	-	-	-	-	-	-	-	-
Dot Lake Village CDP	62	-	-	36	8.3	0.0	0.0	91.7	0.0	11.1	27.8	59.1	65.6	0.0	13	46.2
Dry Creek CDP	94	-	-	119	100.0	0.0	0.0	0.0	0.0	0.0	26.9	52.6	10.4	19.4	48	100.0
Eagle city	84	83	-1.2	86	97.7	0.0	0.0	2.3	0.0	7.0	41.9	63.0	50.0	17.6	38	86.8
Eagle Village CDP	67	-	-	48	45.8	0.0	0.0	54.2	0.0	31.3	8.3	56.7	39.4	6.1	24	62.5
Edna Bay city	42	41	-2.4	35	100.0	0.0	0.0	0.0	0.0	17.1	0.0	37.2	86.2	0.0	7	57.1
Eek city	285	315	10.5	523	0.0	0.0	0.0	95.4	4.6	37.1	8.0	25.2	81.8	0.8	122	82.8
Egegik city	109	106	-2.8	58	55.2	15.5	0.0	29.3	0.0	0.0	8.6	52.3	43.1	17.2	9	55.6
Eielson AFB CDP	2,647	-	-	3,229	77.5	3.0	3.5	4.2	11.8	33.5	0.2	23.7	16.0	35.1	986	98.6
Ekwok city	115	131	13.9	78	1.3	0.0	0.0	98.7	0.0	21.8	14.1	49.5	76.0	0.0	28	75.0
Elfin Cove CDP	20	-	-	4	100.0	0.0	0.0	0.0	0.0	0.0	0.0	0.0	100.0	0.0	4	100.0
Elim city	330	341	3.3	268	1.1	0.0	0.0	98.9	0.0	42.5	3.7	23.2	77.4	0.0	67	89.6
Emmonak city	752	819	8.9	855	0.9	0.4	0.5	98.2	0.0	36.4	8.0	25.6	77.2	4.1	207	77.8
Ester CDP	2,422	-	-	1,622	80.7	1.2	0.1	17.3	0.7	12.9	3.6	38.5	30.8	38.2	518	94.6
Eureka Roadhouse CDP	29	-	-	11	36.4	0.0	0.0	63.6	0.0	0.0	9.1	49.8	27.3	36.4	10	90.0
Evansville CDP	15	-	-	32	37.5	0.0	25.0	37.5	0.0	0.0	0.0	53.0	50.0	12.5	0	0.0
Excursion Inlet CDP	12	-	-													
Fairbanks city	31,556	30,917	-2.0	31,551	60.2	8.2	4.3	17.4	10.0	24.0	8.8	27.6	33.9	27.2	10,866	94.4
False Pass city	35	43	22.9	56	16.1	0.0	3.6	80.4	0.0	23.2	8.9	41.8	73.2	4.9	21	81.0
Farmers Loop CDP	4,853	-	-	5,214	73.7	0.8	1.8	16.9	6.8	27.5	15.4	40.1	21.0	36.1	2,111	89.4
Farm Loop CDP	1,028	-	-	1,170	90.1	0.0	0.2	5.7	4.0	24.5	13.4	39.1	27.8	32.0	350	91.7
Ferry CDP	33	-	-	20	100.0	0.0	0.0	0.0	0.0	0.0	0.0	51.4	46.2	0.0	6	100.0
Fishhook CDP	4,679	-	-	6,788	81.7	2.7	2.2	10.9	2.6	29.1	9.4	35.7	35.0	28.1	1,768	97.9
Flat CDP	-	-	-	-	-	-	-	-	-	-	-	-	-	-	-	-
Fort Greely CDP	539	-	-	144	12.5	0.0	0.0	0.0	87.5	32.6	0.0	23.8	11.8	41.2	34	100.0
Fort Yukon city	583	534	-8.4	561	12.3	0.0	2.1	85.6	0.0	30.8	15.7	36.3	53.7	11.0	219	56.2
Four Mile Road CDP	43	-	-	3	0.0	0.0	0.0	100.0	0.0	0.0	0.0	0.0	100.0	0.0	3	0.0
Fox CDP	417	-	-	448	69.6	0.0	27.7	2.7	0.0	0.0	23.2	59.4	59.6	9.0	228	61.8
Fox River CDP	685	-	-	517	100.0	0.0	0.0	0.0	0.0	46.6	3.9	21.2	71.8	10.5	124	83.9
Fritz Creek CDP	1,932	-	-	2,074	87.7	1.3	2.3	6.6	2.2	19.0	15.5	40.9	30.6	36.8	776	94.6
Funny River CDP	877	-	-	1,331	87.7	6.2	1.1	2.4	2.6	23.5	25.8	46.6	46.7	25.2	488	93.6
Gakona CDP	218	-	-	154	68.2	0.0	0.0	31.8	0.0	20.1	9.1	42.1	52.3	30.8	57	84.2
Galena city	470	450	-4.3	495	32.5	0.0	1.2	64.4	1.8	28.9	11.7	32.1	34.6	30.7	183	84.7
Gambell city	681	700	2.8	591	1.5	0.0	0.0	98.5	0.0	33.3	6.4	25.9	83.2	2.9	152	81.6
Game Creek CDP	18	-	-	-	-	-	-	-	-	-	-	-	-	-	-	-
Gateway CDP	5,552	-	-	7,076	79.7	2.9	0.6	14.1	2.8	29.9	8.0	33.0	29.4	30.4	1,948	98.5
Glacier View CDP	234	-	-	220	89.5	2.7	0.0	4.5	3.2	8.2	31.4	56.1	33.9	39.6	102	98.0
Glennallen CDP	483	-	-	411	64.2	0.0	0.2	35.5	0.0	48.9	1.5	20.5	19.7	58.5	117	100.0
Goldstream CDP	3,557	-	-	3,592	88.3	0.0	1.8	2.9	7.0	14.4	13.2	42.1	16.8	51.3	1,743	100.0
Golovin city	156	161	3.2	142	4.2	0.0	0.0	94.4	1.4	36.6	10.6	25.0	45.1	12.7	47	91.5
Goodnews Bay city	243	277	14.0	182	4.4	0.0	0.0	95.6	0.0	37.9	6.0	26.0	69.9	7.5	44	86.4
Grayling city	194	198	2.1	183	0.5	0.0	0.0	90.7	8.7	37.2	8.7	27.3	89.7	0.0	58	77.6
Gulkana CDP	119	-	-	84	13.1	0.0	0.0	86.9	0.0	21.4	26.2	46.4	80.3	4.5	25	72.0
Gustavus city	442	447	1.1	454	87.0	0.0	0.0	9.7	3.3	11.5	24.2	54.8	21.9	41.0	196	88.8
Haines CDP	1,713	-	-	1,863	75.9	0.0	0.5	19.0	4.6	25.8	21.1	43.4	32.9	34.4	736	95.8
Halibut Cove CDP	76	-	-	91	93.4	0.0	0.0	6.6	0.0	0.0	65.9	68.6	5.5	70.3	52	100.0
Happy Valley CDP	593	-	-	588	84.7	0.0	2.4	8.5	4.4	21.3	27.0	50.9	50.6	12.8	255	86.7
Harding-Birch Lakes CDP	299	-	-	154	91.6	0.0	0.0	4.5	3.9	0.0	48.1	64.0	40.9	55.8	88	87.5
Healy CDP	1,021	-	-	968	81.8	0.8	3.8	13.5	0.0	19.0	12.7	42.2	25.8	33.3	357	95.8
Healy Lake CDP	13	-	-	7	0.0	0.0	0.0	100.0	0.0	57.1	0.0	1.9	66.7	0.0	3	100.0
Hobart Bay CDP	1	-	-	-	-	-	-	-	-	-	-	-	-	-	-	-
Hollis CDP	112	-	-	193	61.1	0.0	2.6	15.5	20.7	31.1	20.7	41.2	27.2	58.4	79	60.8
Holy Cross city	178	164	-7.9	220	4.1	0.0	0.9	90.9	4.1	27.7	9.1	33.0	75.7	4.1	71	78.9
Homer city	5,020	5,922	18.0	5,709	83.9	0.4	1.0	8.5	6.2	19.6	19.5	41.1	26.8	36.0	2,261	93.1
Hoonah city	759	791	4.2	808	21.2	1.0	2.2	67.2	8.4	19.3	18.2	44.0	58.2	14.8	277	86.3
Hooper Bay city	1,093	1,227	12.3	1,141	5.4	0.3	0.0	90.7	3.6	43.8	3.9	23.7	79.2	2.2	204	81.9
Hope CDP	192	-	-	70	75.7	0.0	0.0	24.3	0.0	15.7	0.0	40.3	22.0	37.3	26	100.0
Houston city	1,902	2,412	26.8	1,977	85.6	2.1	0.3	8.6	3.4	24.3	12.4	39.4	50.4	11.7	642	88.9
Hughes city	77	83	7.8	72	0.0	0.0	11.1	88.9	0.0	12.5	16.7	50.3	82.1	0.0	36	36.1
Huslia city	275	258	-6.2	369	4.6	0.0	0.0	88.3	7.0	42.8	11.7	25.7	52.7	7.4	100	70.0
Hydaburg city	375	379	1.1	342	10.2	1.2	0.0	88.6	0.0	28.9	16.1	38.3	53.8	14.2	117	79.5
Hyder CDP	87	-	-	14	100.0	0.0	0.0	0.0	0.0	0.0	100.0	0.0	0.0	100.0	14	100.0
Igiugig CDP	50	-	-	71	9.9	0.0	0.0	90.1	0.0	32.4	15.5	30.9	52.4	16.7	16	81.3

1 May be of any race.

Table A. All Places — **Population and Housing**

STATE City, town, township, borough, or CDP (county if applicable)	Population 2010 census total population	2019 estimated population	Percent change 2010-2019	ACS total population estimate 2015-2019	Race White alone, not Hispanic or Latino	Black alone, not Hispanic or Latino	Asian alone, not Hispanic or Latino	All other races or 2 or more races, not Hispanic or Latino	Hispanic or Latino[1]	Age Under 18 years old	Age 65 years and older	Median age	Educ. Percent High school diploma or less	Percent Bachelor's degree or more	Occupied housing units Total	Percent with a computer
	1	2	3	4	5	6	7	8	9	10	11	12	13	14	15	16
ALASKA—Con.																
Iliamna CDP	109	-	-	55	23.6	0.0	0.0	76.4	0.0	25.5	5.5	34.8	50.0	21.9	18	100.0
Ivanof Bay CDP	7	-	-	-	-	-	-	-	-	-	-	-	-	-	-	-
Juneau city and borough	31,276	31,974	2.2	32,227	64.7	1.0	6.5	21.1	6.8	21.5	12.5	38.1	25.2	38.4	12,676	95.9
Kachemak city	476	490	2.9	474	81.9	0.0	2.5	12.7	3.0	16.5	24.9	48.7	27.9	37.8	200	90.5
Kake city	557	544	-2.3	570	15.4	0.0	0.5	81.9	0.0	23.7	13.2	37.0	56.0	13.2	187	87.2
Kaktovik city	239	254	6.3	178	3.9	1.1	0.0	94.9	0.0	33.7	4.5	26.5	70.7	1.1	56	96.4
Kalifornsky CDP	7,850	-	-	8,581	80.8	0.4	1.3	12.7	4.7	26.4	10.6	34.3	35.5	29.0	3,014	92.7
Kaltag city	190	173	-8.9	180	18.9	0.0	0.0	81.1	0.0	6.7	14.4	45.8	65.7	7.3	56	58.9
Karluk CDP	37	-	-	29	0.0	0.0	0.0	100.0	0.0	24.1	13.8	51.2	25.0	0.0	17	76.5
Kasaan city	49	48	-2.0	72	65.3	0.0	5.6	29.2	0.0	26.4	22.2	35.5	25.5	21.6	33	93.9
Kasigluk CDP	569	-	-	543	0.6	0.0	0.0	99.4	0.0	40.3	5.2	23.6	83.1	0.8	96	93.8
Kasilof CDP	549	-	-	754	100.0	0.0	0.0	0.0	0.0	40.8	17.4	37.7	27.3	35.8	199	100.0
Kenai city	7,114	7,807	9.7	7,742	71.7	0.4	2.7	18.7	6.5	24.6	14.5	37.6	43.8	19.4	3,143	88.2
Kenny Lake CDP	355	-	-	135	100.0	0.0	0.0	0.0	0.0	27.4	17.8	41.5	18.4	81.6	57	89.5
Ketchikan city	8,051	8,284	2.9	8,228	54.9	0.9	12.5	25.5	6.2	21.3	14.7	38.1	40.7	23.0	3,318	91.1
Kiana city	333	338	1.5	285	2.8	0.0	0.7	95.4	1.1	42.1	7.0	23.3	70.1	4.5	69	88.4
King Cove city	938	1,000	6.6	1,147	8.7	1.4	20.7	62.7	6.5	17.9	9.9	41.0	64.9	10.4	311	83.9
King Salmon CDP	374	-	-	361	69.3	1.4	0.6	26.0	2.8	23.3	9.1	38.2	42.9	26.3	130	96.2
Kipnuk CDP	639	-	-	511	0.0	0.4	0.0	99.6	0.0	38.2	6.3	26.5	80.1	0.4	129	83.7
Kivalina city	374	379	1.3	683	6.9	0.0	0.0	93.1	0.0	36.5	10.5	26.4	76.0	13.1	114	80.7
Klawock city	755	787	4.2	831	43.9	0.7	0.7	50.7	4.0	22.5	16.5	44.6	52.0	14.0	288	84.7
Klukwan CDP	95	-	-	72	9.7	0.0	0.0	90.3	0.0	12.5	26.4	49.7	41.9	8.1	32	59.4
Knik-Fairview CDP	14,923	-	-	17,457	79.8	0.7	1.3	13.8	4.3	28.7	9.6	34.4	39.3	20.6	5,090	96.0
Knik River CDP	744	-	-	866	82.1	0.6	0.7	14.7	2.0	31.3	8.9	35.5	43.2	21.3	279	91.0
Kobuk city	151	153	1.3	140	3.6	0.0	0.0	94.3	2.1	52.9	2.1	16.0	85.2	3.7	26	80.8
Kodiak city	6,124	5,813	-5.1	6,022	38.4	0.2	41.2	14.4	5.8	19.5	14.2	38.0	44.7	22.2	1,863	88.5
Kodiak Station CDP	1,301	-	-	1,536	75.7	0.8	1.4	9.9	12.2	40.8	0.0	25.2	24.5	44.6	372	100.0
Kokhanok CDP	170	-	-	180	6.7	0.0	0.0	93.3	0.0	24.4	10.0	35.4	84.6	4.1	51	68.6
Koliganek CDP	209	-	-	202	5.0	0.0	0.0	95.0	0.0	31.7	10.4	25.7	57.1	14.3	58	84.5
Kongiganak CDP	439	-	-	433	0.2	0.0	0.0	97.7	2.1	36.0	5.8	25.3	74.9	2.3	85	85.9
Kotlik city	577	638	10.6	853	0.6	0.0	0.0	99.4	0.0	41.1	5.5	22.4	83.9	1.6	177	87.6
Kotzebue city	3,201	3,246	1.4	3,287	17.5	2.0	2.0	75.8	2.7	29.7	7.8	31.3	51.1	18.4	949	90.8
Koyuk city	332	367	10.5	291	0.7	0.0	0.3	99.0	0.0	37.8	6.9	24.3	38.6	2.1	89	84.3
Koyukuk city	96	92	-4.2	58	0.0	0.0	0.0	100.0	0.0	5.2	19.0	52.5	55.3	8.5	37	45.9
Kupreanof city	26	26	0.0	7	100.0	0.0	0.0	0.0	0.0	0.0	100.0	0.0	0.0	100.0	3	100.0
Kwethluk city	721	762	5.7	613	0.8	0.0	0.2	99.0	0.0	35.2	8.0	25.5	67.6	5.4	141	65.2
Kwigillingok CDP	321	-	-	399	1.3	0.0	0.0	98.7	0.0	42.6	8.8	24.9	66.3	4.0	82	89.0
Lake Louise CDP	46	-	-	-	-	-	-	-	-	-	-	-	-	-	-	-
Lake Minchumina CDP	13	-	-	20	100.0	0.0	0.0	0.0	0.0	0.0	50.0	65.0	30.0	35.0	16	50.0
Lakes CDP	8,364	-	-	10,206	77.0	0.9	1.4	14.3	6.4	27.6	11.8	36.0	34.9	22.9	2,939	96.5
Larsen Bay city	87	83	-4.6	42	26.2	0.0	0.0	64.3	9.5	11.9	19.0	41.5	66.7	9.1	22	90.9
Lazy Mountain CDP	1,479	-	-	1,650	90.8	0.0	1.7	5.6	1.9	21.5	17.8	40.0	28.7	34.5	554	96.0
Levelock CDP	69	-	-	67	1.5	0.0	0.0	97.0	1.5	20.9	17.9	41.5	76.6	2.1	35	71.4
Lime Village CDP	29	-	-	13	0.0	0.0	0.0	100.0	0.0	15.4	15.4	31.8	100.0	0.0	5	60.0
Livengood CDP	13	-	-	11	63.6	0.0	0.0	36.4	0.0	0.0	0.0	60.6	100.0	0.0	8	100.0
Loring CDP	4	-	-	-	-	-	-	-	-	-	-	-	-	-	-	-
Lowell Point CDP	80	-	-	177	92.1	0.0	4.0	4.0	0.0	0.0	0.0	32.9	45.6	27.8	30	100.0
Lower Kalskag city	282	314	11.3	270	2.6	0.0	0.0	97.4	0.0	41.9	4.1	23.0	81.1	2.3	58	82.8
Lutak CDP	49	-	-	158	86.7	0.0	0.0	0.0	13.3	57.6	0.0	15.4	0.0	0.0	31	100.0
McCarthy CDP	28	-	-	-	-	-	-	-	-	-	-	-	-	-	-	-
McGrath city	346	316	-8.7	304	33.6	0.3	0.0	61.5	4.6	32.2	16.4	31.0	53.6	14.8	118	83.1
Manley Hot Springs CDP	89	-	-	44	59.1	0.0	0.0	40.9	0.0	13.6	15.9	54.5	36.8	21.1	24	100.0
Manokotak city	442	440	-0.5	733	17.9	0.0	0.0	82.1	0.0	27.3	6.0	30.6	53.5	28.6	144	81.3
Marshall city	414	461	11.4	261	0.0	0.0	0.0	100.0	0.0	39.1	4.2	23.8	78.4	0.0	61	78.7
Meadow Lakes CDP	7,570	-	-	8,149	82.2	0.3	2.0	10.1	5.4	27.2	12.0	34.1	45.7	16.9	2,537	94.4
Mekoryuk city	191	205	7.3	248	0.4	0.0	0.0	99.6	0.0	27.8	10.9	38.0	66.7	7.9	87	78.2
Mendeltna CDP	39	-	-	24	100.0	0.0	0.0	0.0	0.0	0.0	33.3	0.0	33.3	0.0	24	100.0
Mentasta Lake CDP	112	-	-	266	7.5	0.0	0.0	92.5	0.0	29.7	11.3	31.8	79.8	12.5	73	57.5
Mertarvik CDP	-	-	-	-	-	-	-	-	-	-	-	-	-	-	-	-
Metlakatla CDP	1,405	-	-	1,654	13.0	0.0	2.4	78.7	5.9	28.2	12.9	34.7	47.9	10.4	487	89.9
Minto CDP	210	-	-	177	3.4	0.0	0.0	96.6	0.0	35.0	9.6	28.9	67.3	9.2	63	63.5
Moose Creek CDP	747	-	-	795	74.0	1.6	9.9	11.6	2.9	7.7	5.2	32.7	21.1	21.3	365	100.0
Moose Pass CDP	219	-	-	315	82.5	0.0	0.0	0.0	17.5	15.6	11.1	26.7	48.4	33.2	106	100.0
Mosquito Lake CDP	309	-	-	244	90.6	0.0	0.0	9.4	0.0	19.3	70.5	66.2	53.8	20.8	122	100.0
Mountain Village city	813	877	7.9	784	9.2	0.0	0.0	85.5	5.4	34.1	3.4	28.5	68.1	10.5	168	83.3
Mud Bay CDP	212	-	-	114	86.0	0.0	0.0	14.0	0.0	20.2	32.5	59.3	0.0	100.0	62	100.0
Nabesna CDP	5	-	-	-	-	-	-	-	-	-	-	-	-	-	-	-
Naknek CDP	544	-	-	468	40.6	0.0	0.0	54.7	4.7	20.1	9.8	45.5	42.2	21.1	164	91.5
Nanwalek CDP	254	-	-	212	8.5	0.0	0.5	84.0	7.1	25.9	5.7	41.2	53.7	13.4	56	94.6
Napakiak city	345	370	7.2	386	2.8	0.0	0.0	97.2	0.0	30.6	12.7	27.8	84.5	2.7	117	75.2
Napaskiak city	386	410	6.2	342	0.6	0.0	0.0	99.4	0.0	44.7	5.8	21.3	63.8	4.0	85	69.4
Naukati Bay CDP	113	-	-	126	85.7	0.0	0.0	14.3	0.0	7.1	8.7	58.1	53.0	24.8	74	71.6
Nelchina CDP	59	-	-	116	96.6	0.0	0.0	3.4	0.0	38.8	0.0	36.9	64.8	15.5	28	100.0
Nelson Lagoon CDP	52	-	-	86	27.9	0.0	0.0	72.1	0.0	0.0	24.4	51.3	75.7	2.7	36	91.7
Nenana city	378	357	-5.6	341	53.4	0.0	0.0	46.0	0.6	33.1	21.1	36.9	48.8	16.1	124	79.0
Newhalen city	190	187	-1.6	131	7.6	0.0	0.0	91.6	0.8	28.2	3.8	29.3	63.1	8.3	36	83.3
New Stuyahok city	510	509	-0.2	546	0.4	7.5	0.5	91.6	0.0	36.8	9.2	27.2	60.1	16.6	124	74.2
Newtok CDP	354	-	-	315	0.6	0.0	0.0	99.4	0.0	40.3	10.2	23.1	83.4	3.4	57	89.5
Nightmute city	280	317	13.2	175	0.0	0.0	0.0	100.0	0.0	34.3	10.9	28.3	81.6	1.0	35	82.9
Nikiski CDP	4,493	-	-	4,316	79.3	0.4	0.6	18.0	1.7	22.3	19.8	44.9	44.6	15.5	1,550	83.4
Nikolaevsk CDP	318	-	-	246	89.4	0.0	0.0	4.9	5.7	18.3	8.9	39.7	44.7	15.4	95	82.1
Nikolai city	94	86	-8.5	143	4.2	1.4	0.0	92.3	2.1	16.8	10.5	32.8	77.8	3.0	50	48.0
Nikolski CDP	18	-	-	21	9.5	0.0	0.0	90.5	0.0	23.8	38.1	39.5	87.5	12.5	9	44.4
Ninilchik CDP	883	-	-	836	73.9	0.0	0.7	18.4	6.9	21.4	24.4	52.3	37.2	24.5	344	88.1
Noatak CDP	514	-	-	415	0.7	0.2	0.0	99.0	0.0	34.5	6.7	26.7	85.0	0.0	93	86.0
Nome city	3,595	3,870	7.6	3,850	25.3	1.7	0.7	65.8	6.4	29.0	7.0	31.5	41.4	24.3	1,274	97.1
Nondalton city	136	133	-2.2	110	12.7	0.9	0.0	86.4	0.0	20.0	8.2	37.0	52.1	15.1	44	79.5
Noorvik city	668	675	1.0	623	6.6	0.0	0.0	93.4	0.0	39.5	5.8	25.9	75.2	12.9	116	80.2
North Pole city	2,112	2,094	-0.9	2,740	72.1	8.0	2.4	7.5	10.0	29.4	3.6	26.1	35.4	22.0	977	94.4
Northway CDP	71	-	-	102	3.9	0.0	0.0	96.1	0.0	24.5	5.9	25.0	64.7	7.8	17	58.8
Northway Junction CDP	54	-	-	41	31.7	0.0	0.0	68.3	0.0	26.8	31.7	35.8	63.3	3.3	13	53.8
Northway Village CDP	98	-	-	82	2.4	0.0	0.0	97.6	0.0	36.6	23.2	28.9	95.9	0.0	25	32.0

1 May be of any race.

STATE City, town, township, borough, or CDP (county if applicable)	Population				Race and Hispanic or Latino origin (percent)					Age (percent)			Educational attainment of persons age 25 and older		Occupied housing units	
	2010 census total population	2019 estimated population	Percent change 2010-2019	ACS total population estimate 2015-2019	White alone, not Hispanic or Latino	Black alone, not Hispanic or Latino	Asian alone, not Hispanic or Latino	All other races or 2 or more races, not Hispanic or Latino	Hispanic or Latino[1]	Under 18 years old	Age 65 years and older	Median age	Percent High school diploma or less	Percent Bachelor's degree or more	Total	Percent with a computer
	1	2	3	4	5	6	7	8	9	10	11	12	13	14	15	16
ALASKA—Con.																
Nuiqsut city	402	425	5.7	496	19.2	0.0	0.0	80.8	0.0	35.7	8.1	25.8	60.4	23.8	108	88.9
Nulato city	264	243	-8.0	236	1.7	0.0	0.0	98.3	0.0	21.6	14.0	37.5	53.3	13.3	74	77.0
Nunam Iqua city	187	207	10.7	158	0.0	0.0	3.2	96.8	0.0	42.4	8.9	21.8	68.3	0.0	35	88.6
Nunapitchuk city	496	530	6.9	990	0.0	0.0	0.0	99.4	0.6	40.5	4.3	25.8	75.9	2.0	135	85.2
Old Harbor city	226	215	-4.9	231	21.2	0.0	0.0	77.9	0.9	26.4	8.7	32.3	48.9	17.8	88	61.4
Oscarville CDP	70	-	-	94	10.6	0.0	0.0	89.4	0.0	40.4	6.4	20.0	68.3	17.1	18	61.1
Ouzinkie city	161	153	-5.0	149	2.0	0.0	0.0	96.0	2.0	18.8	12.1	50.3	59.1	1.7	62	88.7
Palmer city	5,928	7,456	25.8	7,131	71.3	3.0	1.2	18.4	6.2	28.1	10.6	30.1	45.9	21.4	2,014	94.0
Paxson CDP	40	-	-	-	-	-	-	-	-	-	-	-	-	-	-	-
Pedro Bay CDP	42	-	-	31	0.0	0.0	0.0	100.0	0.0	6.5	0.0	34.9	55.2	3.4	11	100.0
Pelican city	83	87	4.8	67	65.7	0.0	0.0	34.3	0.0	6.0	13.4	51.1	21.4	44.6	39	100.0
Perryville city	113	-	-	97	1.0	0.0	0.0	99.0	0.0	23.7	7.2	36.3	78.4	2.0	29	75.9
Petersburg CDP	2,948	-	-	3,136	65.0	1.1	4.4	17.5	12.1	20.7	21.5	41.7	43.1	27.5	1,134	93.5
Petersville CDP	4	-	-	-	-	-	-	-	-	-	-	-	-	-	-	-
Pilot Point city	68	65	-4.4	101	29.7	0.0	0.0	70.3	0.0	17.8	9.9	26.9	52.6	32.9	30	73.3
Pilot Station city	568	625	10.0	573	0.3	0.0	0.2	99.5	0.0	42.8	4.5	22.6	80.8	4.2	127	82.7
Pitkas Point CDP	109	-	-	155	0.0	0.0	0.0	100.0	0.0	41.9	5.8	26.1	85.0	1.3	36	75.0
Platinum city	61	67	9.8	13	0.0	0.0	0.0	100.0	0.0	0.0	38.5	52.3	100.0	0.0	5	20.0
Pleasant Valley CDP	725	-	-	614	86.3	0.0	0.0	13.7	0.0	37.3	9.8	30.3	8.8	29.4	201	100.0
Point Baker CDP	15	-	-	-	-	-	-	-	-	-	-	-	-	-	-	-
Point Hope city	674	715	6.1	594	4.2	0.5	0.5	93.1	1.7	42.9	8.8	25.4	67.5	4.0	149	76.5
Point Lay CDP	189	-	-	227	0.4	1.8	0.0	97.8	0.0	47.6	3.5	21.1	69.1	1.1	52	88.5
Point MacKenzie CDP	529	-	-	1,264	60.3	2.8	0.0	35.9	0.9	13.5	2.5	33.6	74.5	5.1	107	94.4
Point Possession CDP	3	-	-	-	-	-	-	-	-	-	-	-	-	-	-	-
Pope-Vannoy Landing CDP	6	-	-	-	-	-	-	-	-	-	-	-	-	-	-	-
Portage Creek CDP	2	-	-	3	0.0	0.0	0.0	100.0	0.0	0.0	0.0	0.0	0.0	0.0	1	100.0
Port Alexander city	52	52	0.0	88	70.5	0.0	0.0	29.5	0.0	29.5	19.3	38.8	36.2	19.0	33	100.0
Port Alsworth CDP	159	-	-	134	73.9	4.5	0.0	21.6	0.0	46.3	8.2	20.5	12.3	63.1	32	100.0
Port Clarence CDP	24	-	-	45	100.0	0.0	0.0	0.0	0.0	0.0	0.0	21.6	0.0	0.0	0	0.0
Port Graham CDP	177	-	-	177	9.0	0.0	0.0	89.3	1.7	23.7	5.6	34.8	74.2	3.9	56	82.1
Port Heiden city	102	109	6.9	88	15.9	0.0	0.0	84.1	0.0	25.0	5.7	28.2	66.7	8.9	29	100.0
Port Lions city	194	184	-5.2	178	23.0	0.0	0.0	74.2	2.8	12.4	14.0	53.1	57.7	12.3	78	92.3
Port Protection CDP	48	-	-	-	-	-	-	-	-	-	-	-	-	-	-	-
Primrose CDP	78	-	-	100	69.0	0.0	0.0	31.0	0.0	0.0	22.0	57.6	47.0	18.0	43	100.0
Prudhoe Bay CDP	2,174	-	-	1,718	79.6	1.6	1.9	13.4	3.5	36.1	4.5	48.4	42.7	21.4	0	0.0
Quinhagak city	669	706	5.5	876	15.8	0.0	0.3	83.9	0.0	36.1	6.3	29.9	57.0	27.9	163	87.1
Rampart CDP	24	-	-	57	0.0	0.0	0.0	75.4	24.6	56.1	14.0	14.3	56.0	0.0	16	75.0
Red Devil CDP	23	-	-	20	20.0	0.0	0.0	80.0	0.0	10.0	35.0	41.5	66.7	0.0	7	28.6
Red Dog Mine CDP	309	-	-	85	60.0	20.0	0.0	0.0	20.0	0.0	18.8	44.4	20.0	38.8	0	0.0
Ridgeway CDP	2,022	-	-	2,702	82.7	0.0	0.0	14.1	3.3	25.6	13.5	41.4	45.3	23.1	862	87.8
Ruby city	166	154	-7.2	185	18.9	0.0	0.0	81.1	0.0	43.2	11.9	23.9	70.0	10.0	59	83.1
Russian Mission city	312	343	9.9	257	0.4	0.0	0.0	99.6	0.0	42.4	5.8	22.4	73.9	1.7	45	93.3
St. George city	102	101	-1.0	76	10.5	0.0	0.0	86.8	2.6	19.7	22.4	39.0	66.7	12.3	26	80.8
St. Mary's city	507	568	12.0	747	2.1	0.0	0.0	97.6	0.3	36.5	5.6	25.1	68.7	4.0	200	82.5
St. Michael city	401	414	3.2	427	0.9	0.0	0.0	99.1	0.0	48.0	3.3	18.9	76.5	1.1	89	93.3
St. Paul city	479	481	0.4	395	10.6	1.8	0.0	85.6	2.0	17.7	12.2	42.8	59.2	12.5	119	84.9
Salamatof CDP	980	-	-	992	65.8	2.3	0.3	27.5	4.0	13.8	13.0	43.4	51.5	8.1	256	85.9
Salcha CDP	1,095	-	-	1,006	91.9	0.0	0.0	6.6	1.5	23.5	8.2	32.6	35.2	36.0	361	98.6
Sand Point city	976	1,064	9.0	1,309	14.7	0.7	14.1	64.9	5.6	17.9	9.7	42.5	52.9	10.9	424	88.9
Savoonga city	671	705	5.1	975	3.0	0.4	0.0	96.6	0.0	41.2	5.9	22.8	84.3	1.6	199	88.9
Saxman city	380	385	1.3	353	18.7	0.0	0.0	78.5	2.8	18.4	15.9	50.2	53.6	9.6	125	88.8
Scammon Bay city	474	534	12.7	594	0.7	0.0	0.0	99.3	0.0	50.2	6.1	17.9	76.7	2.6	121	86.0
Selawik city	829	840	1.3	792	1.6	0.0	0.0	98.4	0.0	46.2	5.4	22.8	85.3	2.9	155	68.4
Seldovia city	255	275	7.8	208	81.3	0.0	0.5	17.3	1.0	19.2	30.3	54.5	33.3	25.9	98	90.8
Seldovia Village CDP	165	-	-	160	55.0	0.0	0.0	43.1	1.9	17.5	22.5	54.6	42.5	16.5	74	85.1
Seward city	2,721	2,796	2.8	2,773	59.2	2.4	7.8	21.5	9.1	21.9	13.1	37.3	50.3	16.9	882	93.4
Shageluk city	83	78	-6.0	61	11.5	0.0	1.6	83.6	3.3	23.0	3.3	29.8	63.2	10.5	24	58.3
Shaktoolik city	251	259	3.2	302	1.3	0.0	0.0	98.7	0.0	39.7	8.3	27.0	79.1	2.5	85	97.6
Shishmaref city	563	613	8.9	498	6.2	0.4	0.0	92.8	0.6	39.6	12.0	27.3	61.7	11.7	136	83.1
Shungnak city	262	264	0.8	292	5.8	0.0	0.0	94.2	0.0	39.4	8.9	27.0	77.7	1.3	58	81.0
Silver Springs CDP	114	-	-	73	100.0	0.0	0.0	0.0	0.0	20.5	4.1	33.6	18.0	58.0	29	89.7
Sitka city and borough	8,881	8,493	-4.4	8,640	61.6	0.7	6.7	24.3	6.8	21.7	15.2	39.5	32.7	33.4	3,547	93.7
Skagway CDP	920	-	-	1,059	82.2	3.5	0.8	7.6	5.9	14.0	11.5	40.3	33.6	29.4	353	95.8
Skwentna CDP	37	-	-	29	100.0	0.0	0.0	0.0	0.0	0.0	51.7	68.1	48.3	0.0	24	83.3
Slana CDP	147	-	-	-	-	-	-	-	-	-	-	-	-	-	-	-
Sleetmute CDP	86	-	-	94	8.5	0.0	0.0	85.1	6.4	31.9	5.3	25.5	77.1	16.7	32	81.3
Soldotna city	4,167	4,719	13.2	4,649	85.3	0.0	0.4	10.2	4.2	19.8	20.0	39.6	36.1	18.7	1,828	93.2
South Naknek CDP	79	-	-	46	10.9	0.0	0.0	89.1	0.0	4.3	17.4	54.5	51.4	10.8	20	75.0
South Van Horn CDP	558	-	-	493	66.9	0.0	0.0	33.1	0.0	30.2	2.8	34.0	38.2	17.5	149	96.0
Stebbins city	556	575	3.4	615	6.5	1.6	0.2	91.7	0.0	41.1	8.8	24.0	66.0	11.8	130	74.6
Steele Creek CDP	6,662	-	-	7,704	72.4	1.6	1.1	14.8	10.2	25.6	11.8	36.8	28.2	31.2	2,834	96.2
Sterling CDP	5,617	-	-	5,169	88.0	0.2	2.2	9.2	0.5	21.9	18.2	45.8	36.7	22.8	2,014	91.6
Stevens Village CDP	78	-	-	15	0.0	0.0	0.0	100.0	0.0	6.7	26.7	52.3	100.0	0.0	8	0.0
Stony River CDP	54	-	-	40	0.0	0.0	0.0	100.0	0.0	50.0	0.0	19.5	100.0	0.0	10	80.0
Sunrise CDP	18	-	-	32	50.0	0.0	0.0	50.0	0.0	0.0	0.0	0.0	0.0	100.0	16	100.0
Susitna CDP	18	-	-	-	-	-	-	-	-	-	-	-	-	-	-	-
Susitna North CDP	1,260	-	-	1,071	77.3	0.0	0.0	16.7	6.0	20.7	21.2	50.1	45.8	16.7	452	92.7
Sutton-Alpine CDP	1,447	-	-	1,458	66.5	0.8	3.3	27.8	1.6	17.7	12.8	40.9	48.8	12.7	366	86.6
Takotna CDP	52	-	-	72	29.2	0.0	0.0	48.6	22.2	58.3	2.8	11.3	70.0	10.0	16	68.8
Talkeetna CDP	876	-	-	1,237	92.7	0.9	0.2	4.8	1.5	31.0	9.8	38.5	24.7	24.2	414	97.8
Tanacross CDP	136	-	-	153	5.2	3.9	0.0	90.8	0.0	19.0	19.0	38.8	72.3	7.9	32	65.6
Tanaina CDP	8,197	-	-	10,464	77.4	0.3	0.7	13.6	8.1	28.3	7.2	30.5	40.5	20.1	2,811	97.6
Tanana city	246	249	1.2	214	10.7	0.5	0.0	87.9	0.9	22.9	20.1	44.2	58.3	11.9	81	63.0
Tatitlek CDP	88	-	-	73	5.5	0.0	0.0	94.5	0.0	9.6	16.4	29.6	79.2	0.0	16	100.0
Tazlina CDP	297	-	-	376	63.0	0.0	0.5	33.2	3.2	34.0	4.0	30.5	53.9	26.0	93	87.1
Teller city	229	237	3.5	193	0.0	1.6	0.0	92.2	6.2	39.4	5.7	27.4	88.5	0.0	60	91.7
Tenakee Springs city	131	135	3.1	137	99.3	0.0	0.0	0.0	0.7	16.8	32.8	55.9	42.1	34.2	67	67.2
Tetlin CDP	127	-	-	223	9.9	0.0	0.0	90.1	0.0	35.4	7.2	28.3	74.3	3.7	44	40.9
Thorne Bay city	471	467	-0.8	533	89.5	0.0	0.0	5.8	4.7	17.6	24.6	54.6	34.4	24.2	260	79.6
Togiak city	817	841	2.9	815	9.9	0.4	2.8	86.9	0.0	33.7	12.5	25.6	54.9	16.5	208	88.5
Tok CDP	1,258	-	-	1,289	74.2	0.0	0.9	24.3	0.6	20.9	18.1	45.1	41.1	21.5	521	95.2

1 May be of any race.

Table A. All Places — **Population and Housing**

STATE City, town, township, borough, or CDP (county if applicable)	Population				Race and Hispanic or Latino origin (percent)					Age (percent)			Educational attainment of persons age 25 and older		Occupied housing units	
	2010 census total population	2019 estimated population	Percent change 2010-2019	ACS total population estimate 2015-2019	White alone, not Hispanic or Latino	Black alone, not Hispanic or Latino	Asian alone, not Hispanic or Latino	All other races or 2 or more races, not Hispanic or Latino	Hispanic or Latino[1]	Under 18 years old	Age 65 years and older	Median age	Percent High school diploma or less	Percent Bachelor's degree or more	Total	Percent with a computer
	1	2	3	4	5	6	7	8	9	10	11	12	13	14	15	16
ALASKA —Con.																
Toksook Bay city	590	673	14.1	546	1.8	0.4	0.0	96.7	1.1	36.4	8.4	27.8	68.7	9.3	121	84.3
Tolsona CDP	30	-	-	-	-	-	-	-	-	-	-	-	-	-	-	-
Tonsina CDP	78	-	-	43	100.0	0.0	0.0	0.0	0.0	0.0	44.2	0.0	0.0	55.8	43	55.8
Trapper Creek CDP	481	-	-	358	79.3	0.0	0.0	19.8	0.8	14.5	21.8	52.8	47.8	16.5	174	91.4
Tuluksak CDP	373	-	-	319	12.5	0.0	0.6	86.8	0.0	36.4	5.0	29.6	71.8	4.0	66	69.7
Tuntutuliak CDP	408	-	-	675	1.0	0.0	0.0	99.0	0.0	44.7	8.1	20.0	75.9	1.7	141	89.4
Tununak CDP	327	-	-	401	1.0	0.0	0.0	99.0	0.0	39.2	7.2	23.6	71.6	4.1	82	96.3
Twin Hills CDP	74	-	-	67	1.5	0.0	0.0	98.5	0.0	34.3	16.4	34.5	78.6	0.0	28	64.3
Two Rivers CDP	719	-	-	663	49.0	0.0	0.0	11.8	39.2	8.4	16.3	49.2	34.8	0.0	248	83.1
Tyonek CDP	171	-	-	399	0.8	0.0	1.3	79.4	18.5	28.6	3.0	36.5	62.9	5.8	105	78.1
Ugashik CDP	12	-	-	9	22.2	0.0	0.0	77.8	0.0	11.1	22.2	55.4	87.5	0.0	3	100.0
Unalakleet city	672	695	3.4	707	16.7	0.0	17.4	65.6	0.3	23.3	11.2	40.5	50.0	29.6	166	77.7
Unalaska city	4,376	4,432	1.3	4,724	23.2	3.2	46.6	11.7	15.4	17.6	5.3	38.1	48.0	17.7	963	94.5
Upper Kalskag city	210	235	11.9	236	8.1	0.4	0.0	90.3	1.3	40.7	3.8	27.2	59.5	4.8	65	80.0
Utqiagvik city	4,212	4,467	6.1	4,416	10.2	2.2	11.0	75.1	1.5	35.8	7.8	28.5	48.4	15.3	1,356	86.7
Valdez city	3,977	3,855	-3.1	3,847	85.8	0.1	0.9	5.4	7.8	21.5	14.4	43.3	24.6	34.1	1,552	94.7
Venetie CDP	166	-	-	125	0.0	0.0	0.0	98.4	1.6	24.0	14.4	42.1	74.1	2.5	48	43.8
Wainwright city	556	587	5.6	494	7.5	0.0	0.0	91.9	0.6	36.8	8.5	30.4	64.9	5.3	135	84.4
Wales city	149	151	1.3	184	0.0	0.0	0.0	100.0	0.0	41.8	3.8	27.0	69.1	0.0	55	78.2
Wasilla city	7,806	10,838	38.8	10,071	76.8	1.2	3.4	12.0	6.6	27.1	15.2	36.7	44.7	16.4	3,192	93.1
Whale Pass city	31	30	-3.2	71	94.4	0.0	0.0	0.0	5.6	16.9	18.3	60.4	69.5	27.1	43	62.8
White Mountain city	190	201	5.8	156	8.3	0.0	0.0	91.7	0.0	26.9	7.1	31.8	47.9	12.5	63	79.4
Whitestone CDP	97	-	-	64	93.8	0.0	0.0	0.0	6.3	34.4	26.6	34.5	30.0	22.5	10	100.0
Whitestone Logging Camp CDP	17	-	-	-	-	-	-	-	-	-	-	-	-	-	-	-
Whittier city	220	205	-6.8	318	48.1	2.5	11.9	33.3	4.1	23.6	10.4	38.1	43.6	17.3	124	91.1
Willow CDP	2,102	-	-	1,987	82.9	0.4	0.5	13.1	3.1	25.4	15.6	40.9	40.5	21.6	724	86.6
Willow Creek CDP	191	-	-	-	-	-	-	-	-	-	-	-	-	-	-	-
Wiseman CDP	14	-	-	10	70.0	0.0	0.0	30.0	0.0	0.0	0.0	0.0	30.0	0.0	3	100.0
Womens Bay CDP	719	-	-	902	77.1	0.0	0.0	22.9	0.0	30.5	12.7	31.4	38.9	23.6	307	100.0
Wrangell city and borough	2,365	2,502	5.8	2,502	61.9	0.0	0.7	32.3	5.0	18.7	22.7	49.4	48.7	19.4	1,027	84.8
Yakutat CDP	662	-	-	649	43.3	0.8	4.9	43.3	7.7	23.1	14.5	36.9	42.3	22.6	219	89.5
ARIZONA	6,392,288	7,278,717	13.9	7,050,299	54.7	4.2	3.2	6.5	31.3	23.2	17.1	37.7	36.7	29.5	2,571,268	91.7
Aguila CDP	798	-	-	888	7.0	0.0	0.0	1.4	91.7	22.5	8.2	30.0	89.2	1.9	170	87.1
Ajo CDP	3,304	-	-	2,841	47.3	0.0	0.3	9.0	43.4	17.9	34.3	50.5	49.3	13.8	1,262	70.9
Ak Chin CDP	30	-	-	-	-	-	-	-	-	-	-	-	-	-	-	-
Ak-Chin Village CDP	862	-	-	1,228	1.0	0.8	0.0	82.6	15.6	31.4	4.1	25.8	74.3	3.5	313	67.7
Alamo Lake CDP	25	-	-	24	100.0	0.0	0.0	0.0	0.0	0.0	54.2	67.5	54.2	0.0	11	100.0
Ali Chuk CDP	161	-	-	178	0.0	0.0	0.0	83.1	16.9	50.0	5.1	16.0	84.3	0.0	37	54.1
Ali Chukson CDP	132	-	-	57	0.0	0.0	0.0	100.0	0.0	54.4	0.0	4.8	73.1	0.0	5	100.0
Ali Molina CDP	71	-	-	61	0.0	0.0	0.0	100.0	0.0	19.7	0.0	20.5	52.4	0.0	21	100.0
Alpine CDP	145	-	-	154	66.9	0.0	0.0	0.0	33.1	14.3	32.5	56.8	17.4	19.7	89	78.7
Amado CDP	295	-	-	33	100.0	0.0	0.0	0.0	0.0	0.0	57.6	0.0	42.4	0.0	19	0.0
Anegam CDP	151	-	-	79	0.0	0.0	0.0	100.0	0.0	8.9	29.1	35.9	65.6	15.6	27	22.2
Antares CDP	126	-	-	166	80.1	0.0	0.0	3.6	16.3	8.4	31.3	62.0	66.4	13.8	75	84.0
Anthem CDP	21,700	-	-	22,468	86.3	1.6	1.2	2.7	8.2	25.8	18.9	43.8	17.5	47.8	8,255	97.9
Apache Junction city	35,709	42,571	19.2	40,592	79.6	1.1	0.9	3.0	15.4	16.4	33.0	52.2	46.0	16.5	17,606	87.0
Arivaca CDP	695	-	-	723	87.4	0.0	0.0	3.6	9.0	2.6	51.3	65.2	49.9	29.2	413	80.6
Arivaca Junction CDP	1,090	-	-	1,248	9.0	0.0	0.8	0.0	90.2	9.9	15.3	47.0	81.0	11.9	360	82.5
Arizona City CDP	10,475	-	-	11,200	50.8	3.3	0.3	5.7	39.9	25.2	23.6	39.2	47.8	13.7	4,548	87.1
Arizona Village CDP	946	-	-	1,117	32.1	0.4	0.0	42.7	24.8	18.8	8.7	42.9	41.6	20.0	400	86.0
Arlington CDP	194	-	-	160	55.0	0.0	0.0	0.0	45.0	6.9	30.0	57.8	37.9	0.0	92	85.9
Ash Fork CDP	396	-	-	698	67.8	0.0	0.0	8.6	23.6	34.4	22.6	40.0	54.1	8.5	247	74.5
Avenue B and C CDP	4,176	-	-	3,797	15.2	0.0	0.6	0.9	83.3	30.4	16.2	31.2	80.3	5.5	1,398	66.6
Avondale city	76,132	87,931	15.5	84,736	31.0	10.2	3.1	3.7	51.9	29.2	8.4	30.8	44.0	18.6	26,067	93.6
Avra Valley CDP	6,050	-	-	6,203	66.2	0.0	1.8	3.2	28.9	24.2	16.2	41.6	54.0	11.0	2,190	93.4
Aztec CDP	47	-	-	-	-	-	-	-	-	-	-	-	-	-	-	-
Bagdad CDP	1,876	-	-	1,774	56.1	0.0	0.0	0.0	43.9	35.7	7.0	24.7	37.5	19.0	633	92.3
Bear Flat CDP	18	-	-	-	-	-	-	-	-	-	-	-	-	-	-	-
Beaver Dam CDP	1,962	-	-	1,349	60.6	0.0	0.0	4.1	35.4	9.4	43.2	61.3	57.4	8.6	835	59.0
Beaver Valley CDP	231	-	-	151	83.4	0.0	0.0	0.0	16.6	6.6	32.5	59.0	33.3	18.4	88	85.2
Benson city	5,103	4,880	-4.4	4,878	65.9	1.5	0.7	3.0	28.9	18.8	34.2	53.4	46.6	19.1	2,312	87.2
Beyerville CDP	177	-	-	33	6.1	0.0	0.0	0.0	93.9	0.0	30.3	58.5	78.8	0.0	22	54.5
Bisbee city	5,578	5,225	-6.3	5,203	64.4	0.7	0.0	3.5	31.4	20.4	31.5	50.8	35.2	28.7	2,455	82.2
Bitter Springs CDP	452	-	-	438	0.0	0.0	0.0	97.7	2.3	32.6	9.6	30.6	78.0	5.4	118	75.4
Black Canyon City CDP	2,837	-	-	2,825	92.9	0.0	0.0	2.3	4.8	11.3	35.3	59.3	37.4	17.4	1,379	82.1
Blackwater CDP	1,062	-	-	1,660	0.6	0.8	0.0	95.9	2.7	28.9	5.4	29.2	76.8	5.2	436	65.8
Bluewater CDP	725	-	-	974	61.4	0.0	0.0	4.9	33.7	18.0	33.2	51.5	50.3	8.7	451	88.2
Bouse CDP	996	-	-	1,108	96.9	0.0	0.8	2.3	0.0	9.6	67.2	72.8	63.9	7.3	557	75.9
Bowie CDP	449	-	-	312	32.7	0.0	0.0	4.2	63.1	17.3	28.8	52.1	78.0	2.8	142	68.3
Brenda CDP	676	-	-	494	100.0	0.0	0.0	0.0	0.0	3.8	90.7	77.4	32.4	18.7	272	91.9
Bryce CDP	175	-	-	103	100.0	0.0	0.0	0.0	0.0	48.5	12.6	25.1	100.0	0.0	32	0.0
Buckeye city	50,851	79,620	56.6	69,744	48.2	7.7	2.2	3.7	38.2	28.0	11.8	34.3	40.2	20.0	18,875	97.3
Buckshot CDP	153	-	-	23	30.4	0.0	0.0	0.0	69.6	0.0	100.0	81.2	100.0	0.0	13	0.0
Bullhead City city	39,541	40,884	3.4	40,252	70.9	1.5	1.3	2.8	23.5	17.5	29.4	51.9	55.3	9.6	17,138	85.3
Burnside CDP	537	-	-	732	2.5	0.0	0.0	96.7	0.8	30.3	6.6	31.1	46.8	16.6	164	61.6
Bylas CDP	1,962	-	-	1,687	0.0	0.0	0.0	93.2	6.8	31.4	10.1	27.3	71.6	3.5	431	62.2
Cactus Flats CDP	1,518	-	-	1,372	70.0	0.0	0.0	0.0	30.0	24.7	17.3	38.7	43.9	10.7	434	98.6
Cactus Forest CDP	594	-	-	876	70.0	3.4	0.0	0.8	25.8	19.5	17.2	43.8	50.3	14.8	367	88.6
Cameron CDP	885	-	-	929	0.6	0.0	0.0	97.5	1.8	26.2	15.3	33.3	70.9	4.2	272	51.1
Campo Bonito CDP	74	-	-	103	100.0	0.0	0.0	0.0	0.0	0.0	61.2	65.2	30.1	0.0	71	100.0
Camp Verde town	10,875	11,187	2.9	11,196	63.0	0.5	0.2	11.5	24.8	24.0	21.2	40.7	44.9	17.2	3,809	89.8
Cane Beds CDP	448	-	-	333	100.0	0.0	0.0	0.0	0.0	46.5	10.8	19.1	60.5	13.2	96	87.5
Canyon Day CDP	1,209	-	-	1,629	0.0	0.0	0.0	97.7	2.3	50.0	7.2	17.9	67.0	6.5	333	62.2
Carefree town	3,368	3,927	16.6	3,811	98.0	0.9	0.0	0.2	0.9	4.1	57.0	67.0	16.9	55.6	1,986	95.2
Carrizo CDP	127	-	-	82	0.0	0.0	0.0	100.0	0.0	34.1	20.7	28.5	41.7	20.8	28	39.3
Casa Blanca CDP	1,388	-	-	1,004	4.1	0.0	0.0	92.2	3.7	22.9	12.0	28.6	76.6	5.4	333	42.0
Casa Grande city	48,564	58,632	20.7	55,653	43.8	2.8	1.6	8.1	43.7	25.6	20.0	37.2	46.8	16.3	18,475	91.2
Casas Adobes CDP	66,795	-	-	70,166	63.6	2.0	3.4	4.3	26.7	18.4	20.7	41.5	27.2	35.0	29,587	94.3
Catalina CDP	7,569	-	-	7,910	77.2	1.1	0.6	2.2	19.0	20.9	25.5	51.3	32.3	26.8	3,164	94.8

1 May be of any race.

STATE City, town, township, borough, or CDP (county if applicable)	2010 census total population	2019 estimated population	Percent change 2010-2019	ACS total population estimate 2015-2019	White alone, not Hispanic or Latino	Black alone, not Hispanic or Latino	Asian alone, not Hispanic or Latino	All other races or 2 or more races, not Hispanic or Latino	Hispanic or Latino[1]	Under 18 years old	Age 65 years and older	Median age	Percent High school diploma or less	Percent Bachelor's degree or more	Occupied housing units Total	Percent with a computer
	1	2	3	4	5	6	7	8	9	10	11	12	13	14	15	16
ARIZONA—Con.																
Catalina Foothills CDP	50,796	-	-	50,454	78.7	1.0	5.2	3.5	11.6	16.7	31.5	53.8	10.9	67.8	23,079	94.9
Cave Creek town	4,807	5,838	21.4	5,670	92.1	0.0	0.0	3.7	4.3	10.2	41.4	61.4	14.8	49.5	2,738	94.8
Cedar Creek CDP	318	-	-	517	0.0	0.0	0.0	100.0	0.0	40.0	4.6	25.8	59.1	0.0	112	73.2
Centennial Park CDP	1,264	-	-	1,366	100.0	0.0	0.0	0.0	0.0	53.7	6.6	16.5	54.8	14.2	197	100.0
Central CDP	645	-	-	323	100.0	0.0	0.0	0.0	0.0	35.3	9.9	40.0	24.4	12.4	118	94.1
Central Heights-Midland City CDP	2,534	-	-	2,774	58.6	0.0	0.0	1.9	39.5	23.2	19.0	43.6	48.6	15.7	1,179	84.0
Chandler city	236,157	261,165	10.6	252,692	58.5	5.4	10.7	4.7	20.8	25.1	11.0	36.3	24.3	44.7	91,216	96.8
Charco CDP	52	-	-	24	0.0	0.0	0.0	100.0	0.0	20.8	0.0	54.0	75.0	0.0	16	25.0
Chiawuli Tak CDP	78	-	-	-	-	-	-	-	-	-	-	-	-	-	-	-
Chilchinbito CDP	506	-	-	926	0.2	0.0	0.0	99.8	0.0	37.1	8.6	25.5	68.1	2.9	258	19.0
Chinle CDP	4,518	-	-	4,879	3.9	0.5	0.0	95.2	0.4	44.5	8.0	22.0	48.6	20.4	1,171	53.5
Chino Valley town	10,817	12,375	14.4	11,670	76.9	0.3	1.9	1.6	19.3	18.1	25.8	51.4	40.8	14.7	4,977	88.2
Chloride CDP	271	-	-	393	90.6	0.0	0.0	1.3	8.1	5.6	49.6	62.9	59.6	11.3	205	76.1
Christopher Creek CDP	156	-	-	123	87.8	0.0	0.0	0.0	12.2	0.0	37.4	64.5	43.1	13.0	66	68.2
Chuichu CDP	269	-	-	338	0.0	0.0	0.0	100.0	0.0	5.3	18.3	46.6	100.0	0.0	78	82.1
Cibecue CDP	1,713	-	-	2,173	0.4	0.0	1.4	97.7	0.5	50.2	4.2	18.0	81.2	2.6	393	59.0
Cibola CDP	250	-	-	355	31.3	0.0	2.8	3.4	62.5	32.7	3.7	34.9	80.3	0.0	124	76.6
Cienega Springs CDP	1,798	-	-	1,830	78.1	1.4	0.0	4.1	16.3	10.2	37.0	59.5	43.6	15.9	916	92.4
Citrus Park CDP	4,028	-	-	5,376	79.7	2.2	2.4	0.2	15.6	23.0	14.5	41.0	26.1	28.0	1,615	99.4
Clacks Canyon CDP	173	-	-	340	97.4	2.6	0.0	0.0	0.0	28.8	14.1	39.7	71.9	20.7	129	100.0
Clarkdale town	4,039	4,391	8.7	4,271	82.7	2.0	1.0	5.4	8.9	17.9	35.8	57.3	42.4	18.7	2,082	88.0
Claypool CDP	1,538	-	-	1,176	36.0	0.0	0.0	4.4	59.6	22.5	28.2	45.4	71.6	4.0	456	61.0
Clay Springs CDP	401	-	-	523	93.7	0.0	0.0	0.0	6.3	27.3	19.7	42.3	48.7	0.0	211	100.0
Clifton town	3,311	3,708	12.0	3,703	36.8	2.7	0.4	4.6	55.5	29.4	8.9	32.1	42.0	15.8	1,148	95.9
Colorado City town	4,820	4,836	0.3	4,836	99.2	0.0	0.0	0.0	0.8	50.0	3.2	18.0	77.3	7.2	556	100.0
Comobabi CDP	8	-	-	-	-	-	-	-	-	-	-	-	-	-	-	-
Concho CDP	38	-	-	-	-	-	-	-	-	-	-	-	-	-	-	-
Congress CDP	1,975	-	-	1,632	96.2	0.0	0.0	3.8	0.0	16.2	49.6	64.7	35.2	16.4	732	85.1
Coolidge city	11,845	13,130	10.8	12,685	38.1	7.7	0.0	9.5	44.6	29.2	11.8	32.0	49.8	14.5	3,371	88.0
Copper Hill CDP	108	-	-	-	-	-	-	-	-	-	-	-	-	-	-	-
Cordes Lakes CDP	2,633	-	-	2,586	68.4	0.6	1.0	5.8	24.2	11.4	33.1	61.1	51.3	9.7	1,266	90.4
Cornfields CDP	255	-	-	260	5.4	1.9	0.0	90.8	1.9	26.5	13.3	33.2	53.5	10.3	49	75.5
Cornville CDP	3,280	-	-	3,351	83.5	0.0	0.0	4.9	11.7	11.3	32.1	54.7	39.6	21.4	1,379	95.9
Corona de Tucson CDP	5,675	-	-	8,470	69.5	3.4	0.8	1.7	24.6	33.5	9.5	35.0	16.0	42.5	2,661	99.5
Cottonwood CDP	226	-	-	207	1.4	0.0	0.0	96.6	1.9	22.2	22.2	33.8	31.0	14.3	74	48.6
Cottonwood city	11,184	12,253	9.6	11,959	77.5	0.7	0.2	3.3	18.2	16.3	27.6	46.0	44.3	17.4	5,478	84.6
Cowlic CDP	135	-	-	106	0.0	0.0	0.0	100.0	0.0	28.3	0.0	22.2	75.0	0.0	29	34.5
Crozier CDP	14	-	-	49	46.9	0.0	0.0	38.8	14.3	10.2	12.2	60.8	39.5	27.9	14	64.3
Crystal Beach CDP	279	-	-	137	83.9	0.0	0.0	0.0	16.1	0.0	48.9	63.9	75.2	0.0	78	85.9
Cutter CDP	74	-	-	45	24.4	0.0	0.0	75.6	0.0	0.0	0.0	61.0	28.9	0.0	12	0.0
Dateland CDP	416	-	-	434	42.2	0.0	0.0	0.0	57.8	26.3	19.8	38.8	47.9	13.6	166	75.3
Deer Creek CDP	216	-	-	182	100.0	0.0	0.0	0.0	0.0	0.0	35.2	57.3	43.4	19.8	110	94.5
Del Muerto CDP	329	-	-	347	0.0	0.0	0.0	100.0	0.0	13.3	24.5	40.9	88.0	0.0	98	31.6
Dennehotso CDP	746	-	-	900	0.0	0.0	0.0	100.0	0.0	23.9	7.7	35.8	82.0	1.9	210	26.7
Desert Hills CDP	2,245	-	-	2,616	79.2	0.2	1.9	0.5	18.1	12.7	38.8	61.0	46.4	14.3	1,224	92.3
Dewey-Humboldt town	3,896	4,137	6.2	4,063	85.4	0.3	0.9	1.8	11.7	15.9	28.2	50.9	30.1	21.0	1,667	90.0
Dilkon CDP	1,184	-	-	1,188	0.0	1.4	2.5	94.5	1.5	41.2	4.5	26.7	60.2	7.9	290	79.0
Dolan Springs CDP	2,033	-	-	2,222	77.2	0.0	0.0	0.0	22.8	16.2	41.0	58.1	47.6	18.6	1,131	84.4
Doney Park CDP	5,395	-	-	5,021	70.8	0.0	0.2	8.6	20.4	21.4	11.5	41.1	27.3	40.8	1,788	95.7
Donovan Estates CDP	1,508	-	-	1,394	6.7	0.0	0.0	0.0	93.3	22.7	18.8	34.6	75.9	0.0	384	87.5
Douglas city	17,509	16,193	-7.5	16,307	14.7	5.1	0.0	3.3	76.9	20.6	10.9	33.2	54.2	10.7	3,993	79.1
Dragoon CDP	209	-	-	14	100.0	0.0	0.0	0.0	0.0	0.0	100.0	-	0.0	100.0	14	100.0
Drexel Heights CDP	27,749	-	-	29,568	17.9	2.1	0.3	3.2	76.5	28.2	13.7	34.5	47.0	13.0	9,436	91.7
Dripping Springs CDP	235	-	-	258	82.9	0.0	0.0	0.0	17.1	21.3	19.8	47.3	50.8	9.0	99	92.9
Drysdale CDP	272	-	-	436	0.0	0.0	0.0	0.0	100.0	28.9	17.9	26.8	69.6	0.0	121	68.6
Dudleyville CDP	959	-	-	1,068	18.0	0.0	0.0	0.0	82.0	38.4	13.9	36.9	64.7	0.0	285	69.5
Duncan town	696	788	13.2	745	76.6	0.0	0.0	1.1	22.3	21.5	21.1	48.9	58.7	10.6	287	81.5
Eagar town	4,891	4,941	1.0	4,890	81.4	0.0	0.0	1.9	16.7	33.0	24.2	37.1	29.4	23.0	1,652	94.1
East Fork CDP	699	-	-	698	0.0	0.0	0.0	100.0	0.0	31.4	12.0	23.9	72.1	6.9	147	41.5
East Globe CDP	226	-	-	171	5.8	0.0	0.0	81.9	12.3	21.1	22.2	36.7	57.0	28.1	64	68.8
East Verde Estates CDP	170	-	-	111	100.0	0.0	0.0	0.0	0.0	0.0	73.9	66.9	29.7	40.5	51	82.4
Ehrenberg CDP	1,470	-	-	1,160	55.2	0.0	0.7	2.6	41.6	15.5	10.8	44.5	62.1	7.4	514	76.5
El Capitan CDP	37	-	-	36	66.7	0.0	0.0	0.0	33.3	0.0	44.4	64.8	69.4	19.4	23	100.0
Elephant Head CDP	612	-	-	844	53.0	0.0	0.0	0.7	46.3	30.2	24.9	39.3	54.7	7.4	297	92.3
Elfrida CDP	459	-	-	403	50.9	0.0	0.0	0.0	49.1	22.1	21.3	42.5	70.5	0.0	162	61.1
Elgin CDP	161	-	-	91	100.0	0.0	0.0	0.0	0.0	0.0	70.3	68.4	22.0	31.9	54	100.0
El Mirage city	31,797	35,753	12.4	35,333	40.3	7.9	1.6	2.9	47.2	30.9	9.1	30.8	51.8	15.3	10,538	92.6
Eloy city	16,665	19,625	17.8	18,666	26.4	7.1	1.9	8.3	56.3	12.5	10.8	35.8	64.4	8.2	3,073	84.5
El Prado Estates CDP	504	-	-	530	5.3	0.0	0.0	0.0	94.7	31.9	12.3	23.8	83.3	0.0	176	100.0
First Mesa CDP	1,555	-	-	1,937	1.2	0.7	3.1	94.2	0.7	30.1	8.6	30.1	60.9	6.9	437	63.2
Flagstaff city	66,006	75,038	13.7	72,402	64.5	1.8	3.0	11.3	19.3	17.9	8.4	25.2	22.4	47.1	23,839	95.5
Florence town	25,452	27,422	7.7	26,420	46.3	6.9	0.5	6.6	39.7	9.0	16.7	39.1	54.7	11.5	4,396	89.7
Flowing Springs CDP	42	-	-	62	50.0	0.0	0.0	0.0	50.0	0.0	69.4	68.5	25.8	61.3	26	100.0
Flowing Wells CDP	16,419	-	-	15,755	44.3	1.3	3.2	2.7	48.6	21.0	17.6	39.6	53.2	11.9	6,177	85.8
Fort Apache CDP	143	-	-	189	6.3	0.0	0.0	90.5	3.2	40.2	8.5	27.4	32.7	9.7	52	76.9
Fort Defiance CDP	3,624	-	-	4,590	2.2	0.0	0.6	96.3	1.0	27.9	13.0	34.4	54.0	13.6	1,139	42.9
Fort Mohave CDP	14,364	-	-	15,593	70.8	1.3	1.7	4.4	21.8	16.9	31.6	51.4	50.5	12.5	6,507	92.7
Fort Thomas CDP	374	-	-	440	97.3	0.0	0.0	0.0	2.7	15.5	21.4	51.7	24.8	15.6	197	100.0
Fortuna Foothills CDP	26,265	-	-	29,955	67.6	1.3	0.9	2.9	27.3	15.6	44.5	60.4	45.8	15.2	13,688	88.7
Fort Valley CDP	779	-	-	1,257	98.6	0.0	0.0	0.0	1.4	23.4	17.1	51.4	12.4	76.6	480	100.0
Fountain Hills town	22,489	25,200	12.1	24,729	91.2	0.4	2.5	1.4	4.6	10.6	38.0	59.4	17.5	48.6	11,918	96.3
Franklin CDP	92	-	-	89	100.0	0.0	0.0	0.0	0.0	10.1	24.7	47.1	63.8	16.3	41	100.0
Fredonia town	1,329	1,281	-3.6	1,040	73.8	0.0	0.0	18.0	8.3	18.1	19.7	45.1	50.8	14.7	430	87.9
Freedom Acres CDP	84	-	-	254	100.0	0.0	0.0	0.0	0.0	16.1	24.8	36.3	40.9	17.5	76	100.0
Gadsden CDP	678	-	-	510	0.0	0.0	0.0	0.0	100.0	26.1	20.6	39.1	73.0	6.5	145	72.4
Ganado CDP	1,210	-	-	980	3.3	0.6	1.0	94.6	0.5	34.4	11.7	30.0	48.3	15.7	292	68.5
Geronimo Estates CDP	60	-	-	-	-	-	-	-	-	-	-	-	-	-	-	-
Gila Bend town	1,921	2,100	9.3	1,853	25.0	3.5	0.0	9.2	62.4	33.7	10.6	32.6	66.5	9.4	625	79.8
Gila Crossing CDP	621	-	-	783	0.0	6.4	5.6	71.4	16.6	30.3	4.0	27.7	47.9	9.5	182	81.3
Gilbert town	208,462	254,114	21.9	243,254	69.4	3.7	5.6	4.2	17.1	29.9	9.4	34.1	20.2	44.4	77,632	98.5
Gisela CDP	570	-	-	458	78.6	0.0	0.0	21.4	0.0	20.3	23.8	47.6	34.9	13.2	166	91.0

1 May be of any race.

Table A. All Places — **Population and Housing**

STATE City, town, township, borough, or CDP (county if applicable)	Population				Race and Hispanic or Latino origin (percent)					Age (percent)			Educational attainment of persons age 25 and older		Occupied housing units	
	2010 census total population	2019 estimated population	Percent change 2010-2019	ACS total population estimate 2015-2019	White alone, not Hispanic or Latino	Black alone, not Hispanic or Latino	Asian alone, not Hispanic or Latino	All other races or 2 or more races, not Hispanic or Latino	Hispanic or Latino[1]	Under 18 years old	Age 65 years and older	Median age	Percent High school diploma or less	Percent Bachelor's degree or more	Total	Percent with a computer
	1	2	3	4	5	6	7	8	9	10	11	12	13	14	15	16
ARIZONA—Con.																
Glendale city	226,172	252,381	11.6	247,813	47.2	6.3	4.2	4.0	38.2	25.5	11.7	34.2	45.1	21.5	82,810	91.3
Globe city	7,515	7,347	-2.2	7,348	50.4	1.6	1.5	6.3	40.1	18.8	21.3	44.0	40.0	20.1	2,962	84.9
Gold Canyon CDP	-	-	-	11,612	88.6	1.5	1.1	1.3	7.5	6.8	50.8	65.2	27.8	38.5	5,570	96.2
Golden Shores CDP	2,047	-	-	945	91.3	0.0	0.0	0.8	7.8	4.3	42.5	64.4	37.4	18.0	633	54.0
Golden Valley CDP	8,370	-	-	9,079	87.1	0.2	0.5	3.6	8.6	11.5	37.6	58.7	57.8	7.4	3,925	78.9
Goodyear city	65,261	86,840	33.1	80,371	55.6	7.5	4.5	4.4	28.0	24.5	15.9	38.7	29.7	31.2	25,524	98.2
Goodyear Village CDP	457	-	-	291	0.0	0.0	0.0	65.3	34.7	17.5	3.4	27.3	83.6	6.6	81	64.2
Grand Canyon Village CDP	2,004	-	-	2,239	47.7	2.5	1.5	38.7	9.7	17.4	5.4	36.6	33.6	19.2	614	78.8
Grand Canyon West CDP	2	-	-	-	-	-	-	-	-	-	-	-	-	-	-	-
Greasewood CDP	547	-	-	454	0.9	0.0	0.0	95.6	3.5	28.9	15.2	37.2	53.4	8.8	113	58.4
Green Valley CDP	21,391	-	-	20,902	93.6	0.2	0.5	0.6	5.0	1.2	79.8	73.1	25.2	42.1	12,722	89.7
Greer CDP	41	-	-	39	100.0	0.0	0.0	0.0	0.0	0.0	100.0	0.0	0.0	53.8	18	100.0
Guadalupe town	5,523	6,631	20.1	6,482	4.6	0.6	0.0	23.3	71.4	28.8	14.3	34.0	71.0	4.3	1,762	73.9
Gu Oidak CDP	188	-	-	139	0.0	0.0	0.0	100.0	0.0	36.7	29.5	40.3	64.8	12.5	31	35.5
Hackberry CDP	68	-	-	136	100.0	0.0	0.0	0.0	0.0	2.9	29.4	63.4	28.8	16.7	81	95.1
Haigler Creek CDP	19	-	-	56	100.0	0.0	0.0	0.0	0.0	0.0	78.6	82.4	41.1	39.3	45	75.6
Haivana Nakya CDP	96	-	-	138	0.0	0.0	0.0	100.0	0.0	26.1	0.0	33.2	83.5	0.0	58	0.0
Hard Rock CDP	94	-	-	53	0.0	0.0	0.0	100.0	0.0	22.6	22.6	38.9	39.4	15.2	19	89.5
Hayden town	662	631	-4.7	525	7.6	0.0	0.8	0.0	91.6	17.7	21.9	47.1	54.7	1.0	190	76.8
Heber-Overgaard CDP	2,822	-	-	2,695	87.5	0.1	0.5	7.5	4.4	16.5	34.2	55.4	44.6	15.4	1,192	84.8
Holbrook city	5,053	5,084	0.6	5,037	40.3	2.6	1.3	28.2	27.6	29.5	10.9	35.3	42.4	15.0	1,539	89.7
Hondah CDP	812	-	-	934	3.0	2.7	0.0	90.0	4.3	23.4	8.8	31.7	50.1	14.6	261	59.0
Hotevilla-Bacavi CDP	957	-	-	1,097	0.8	0.6	0.5	95.0	3.0	30.0	15.3	35.3	60.4	6.9	252	51.6
Houck CDP	1,024	-	-	871	0.5	0.0	0.0	95.9	3.7	22.8	13.1	37.7	57.9	1.7	292	43.8
Huachuca City town	1,853	1,736	-6.3	1,948	55.0	6.1	4.2	9.2	25.5	25.3	15.2	37.6	39.0	12.1	831	85.6
Hunter Creek CDP	48	-	-	16	100.0	0.0	0.0	0.0	0.0	0.0	0.0	0.0	62.5	37.5	6	100.0
Icehouse Canyon CDP	677	-	-	478	90.8	0.0	0.0	2.3	6.9	8.8	49.2	63.7	23.8	20.7	208	91.8
Indian Wells CDP	255	-	-	301	6.0	0.0	1.3	90.4	2.3	26.2	14.6	39.8	68.8	3.5	63	49.2
Jakes Corner CDP	76	-	-	176	100.0	0.0	0.0	0.0	0.0	19.9	43.8	61.3	56.6	0.0	83	65.1
Jeddito CDP	293	-	-	221	0.0	0.0	0.0	86.9	13.1	42.1	9.5	21.3	53.3	4.7	63	57.1
Jerome town	446	455	2.0	474	66.9	0.0	0.0	27.2	5.9	7.6	27.8	53.8	19.4	18.2	232	94.4
Joseph City CDP	1,386	-	-	1,672	65.2	0.0	0.0	22.2	12.6	42.2	7.1	25.7	22.1	17.2	499	91.4
Kachina Village CDP	2,622	-	-	2,932	74.5	0.0	0.0	1.9	23.6	20.8	15.9	38.7	28.1	37.1	1,121	97.1
Kaibab CDP	124	-	-	130	1.5	0.0	3.1	92.3	3.1	22.3	9.2	38.0	58.5	4.9	62	83.9
Kaibito CDP	1,522	-	-	1,657	0.4	0.0	0.0	98.1	1.5	34.8	6.9	26.2	68.1	5.7	374	71.9
Kaka CDP	141	-	-	123	6.5	0.0	4.9	88.6	0.0	22.8	26.0	47.4	78.7	0.0	35	80.0
Katherine CDP	103	-	-	66	100.0	0.0	0.0	0.0	0.0	0.0	90.9	87.3	63.6	0.0	59	23.7
Kayenta CDP	5,189	-	-	5,512	4.4	0.1	0.2	94.4	0.7	34.1	9.0	27.4	56.9	14.5	1,372	27.1
Keams Canyon CDP	304	-	-	305	11.8	0.0	0.0	88.2	0.0	18.4	20.0	53.0	47.5	5.5	76	72.4
Kearny town	1,950	2,168	11.2	2,250	46.5	1.0	2.5	6.7	43.2	26.2	21.5	33.8	51.0	11.3	785	78.6
Kingman city	28,076	31,013	10.5	29,726	76.4	2.0	1.6	5.1	14.9	21.5	23.8	42.4	42.6	18.6	11,843	90.4
Kino Springs CDP	136	-	-	321	48.9	0.0	0.0	6.5	44.5	47.0	5.9	23.6	27.0	30.9	92	100.0
Klagetoh CDP	242	-	-	258	0.0	0.0	0.0	100.0	0.0	36.4	11.2	26.6	61.9	0.0	55	63.6
Kohatk CDP	27	-	-	-	-	-	-	-	-	-	-	-	-	-	-	-
Kohls Ranch CDP	46	-	-	158	63.3	0.0	7.6	0.0	29.1	0.0	40.5	57.4	15.2	36.1	96	100.0
Komatke CDP	821	-	-	915	0.8	0.0	1.5	80.1	17.6	40.1	8.2	24.6	66.0	3.1	226	69.5
Ko Vaya CDP	-	-	-	8	0.0	0.0	0.0	100.0	0.0	0.0	0.0	0.0	50.0	0.0	4	100.0
Kykotsmovi Village CDP	746	-	-	881	0.0	0.0	0.9	98.6	0.5	25.3	16.6	42.4	41.4	12.4	258	82.2
Lake Havasu City city	52,531	55,865	6.3	54,495	79.7	0.3	1.1	2.2	16.7	14.8	33.1	54.2	44.2	15.7	24,448	90.4
Lake Montezuma CDP	4,706	-	-	4,329	76.6	0.0	0.0	9.4	13.9	10.3	26.1	56.3	37.5	18.5	1,997	91.6
Lake of the Woods CDP	4,094	-	-	3,683	74.0	0.0	0.0	3.7	22.3	22.8	25.7	45.9	46.0	16.5	1,495	91.1
La Paz Valley CDP	699	-	-	520	100.0	0.0	0.0	0.0	0.0	0.0	95.8	78.1	33.5	12.2	265	62.3
Lazy Y U CDP	428	-	-	320	94.7	0.0	0.0	0.0	5.3	5.0	14.4	56.7	15.8	48.0	157	100.0
LeChee CDP	1,443	-	-	1,561	0.3	0.4	0.2	95.3	3.8	26.5	7.4	28.5	59.9	6.0	369	77.8
Leupp CDP	951	-	-	1,362	0.4	0.0	1.2	97.9	0.6	30.4	8.8	28.4	51.6	10.7	314	78.0
Linden CDP	2,597	-	-	2,798	89.8	0.0	0.9	3.7	5.6	20.0	22.5	54.3	24.9	22.1	1,072	94.2
Litchfield Park city	4,886	6,436	31.7	6,073	78.4	0.9	3.0	3.9	13.8	20.9	26.0	46.1	15.9	50.1	2,520	93.5
Littlefield CDP	308	-	-	394	0.0	0.0	0.0	0.0	100.0	0.0	0.0	23.8	100.0	0.0	141	100.0
Lower Santan Village CDP	374	-	-	214	0.0	0.0	0.0	100.0	0.0	41.1	4.2	35.5	100.0	0.0	77	58.4
Low Mountain CDP	757	-	-	724	0.0	0.0	0.0	99.7	0.3	27.5	13.0	28.7	62.3	2.6	164	52.4
Lukachukai CDP	1,701	-	-	1,497	0.0	0.0	0.0	100.0	0.0	25.3	12.3	33.3	55.5	7.8	404	49.8
Lupton CDP	25	-	-	19	0.0	0.0	0.0	100.0	0.0	0.0	0.0	24.9	33.3	0.0	6	100.0
McConnico CDP	70	-	-	-	-	-	-	-	-	-	-	-	-	-	-	-
McNary CDP	528	-	-	672	0.7	0.0	0.0	92.9	6.4	42.1	4.6	24.0	56.8	5.8	129	74.4
McNeal CDP	238	-	-	159	97.5	0.0	0.0	0.0	2.5	23.3	33.3	57.8	29.1	26.5	79	77.2
Maish Vaya CDP	158	-	-	137	0.0	0.0	0.0	100.0	0.0	23.4	34.3	56.3	94.0	0.0	45	26.7
Mammoth town	1,494	1,687	12.9	1,653	19.7	0.0	0.0	2.1	78.2	18.9	25.5	45.6	65.2	3.3	539	77.2
Many Farms CDP	1,348	-	-	1,188	5.5	0.2	0.0	91.6	2.8	33.8	9.4	31.8	41.0	23.1	408	51.2
Marana town	34,556	49,030	41.9	45,279	62.5	2.7	4.9	4.3	25.6	24.1	20.3	39.4	21.0	44.9	16,539	96.6
Maricopa city	43,488	52,127	19.9	48,629	49.9	11.6	4.0	5.7	28.7	27.2	13.1	35.7	36.3	24.7	14,987	96.4
Maricopa Colony CDP	709	-	-	607	1.0	0.0	0.0	81.7	17.3	31.1	7.7	27.6	46.9	14.7	157	91.7
Martinez Lake CDP	798	-	-	59	100.0	0.0	0.0	0.0	0.0	0.0	86.4	73.4	61.0	0.0	36	100.0
Mayer CDP	1,497	-	-	1,930	92.0	0.0	0.0	0.0	8.0	19.4	24.3	47.9	52.5	4.6	672	97.3
Mead Ranch CDP	38	-	-	-	-	-	-	-	-	-	-	-	-	-	-	-
Meadview CDP	1,224	-	-	1,211	99.3	0.0	0.0	0.7	0.0	0.7	59.8	68.6	71.1	7.7	676	77.4
Mesa city	440,092	518,012	17.7	499,720	61.3	4.0	2.1	4.9	27.7	24.3	16.4	35.9	35.5	27.4	181,130	92.3
Mesa del Caballo CDP	765	-	-	962	91.6	0.0	1.0	2.1	5.3	33.7	16.0	29.5	51.1	13.1	306	79.4
Mescal CDP	1,812	-	-	1,527	82.6	0.0	1.8	11.2	4.4	19.4	34.4	58.7	31.0	22.9	710	81.0
Mesquite Creek CDP	416	-	-	458	87.3	0.4	1.3	2.0	9.0	5.9	62.4	69.0	53.6	12.3	233	89.3
Miami town	1,838	1,780	-3.2	2,094	34.8	0.4	0.3	3.5	61.0	28.7	14.3	34.8	62.4	12.9	797	75.0
Miracle Valley CDP	644	-	-	764	41.8	2.9	0.0	0.0	55.4	21.3	16.1	43.0	65.8	4.9	276	94.2
Moccasin CDP	89	-	-	101	100.0	0.0	0.0	0.0	0.0	0.0	79.2	76.1	0.0	55.4	39	100.0
Moenkopi CDP	964	-	-	1,252	0.8	0.0	0.0	97.7	1.5	22.6	15.3	33.1	67.8	5.3	317	79.5
Mohave Valley CDP	2,616	-	-	2,675	69.9	0.0	0.0	13.4	16.7	21.3	21.1	42.8	40.4	6.4	1,078	88.6
Mojave Ranch Estates CDP	52	-	-	4	0.0	0.0	0.0	100.0	0.0	0.0	0.0	0.0	0.0	0.0	4	0.0
Morenci CDP	1,489	-	-	1,576	38.8	5.8	1.6	8.8	45.0	31.7	1.6	29.8	41.0	11.4	494	99.4
Morristown CDP	-	-	-	209	84.7	6.2	0.0	0.0	9.1	7.7	14.8	55.3	35.4	16.9	120	96.7
Mountainaire CDP	1,119	-	-	804	80.0	0.0	0.0	2.0	18.0	21.3	9.3	35.4	14.0	44.7	416	100.0
Munds Park CDP	631	-	-	880	89.8	0.0	0.0	5.8	4.4	3.8	37.6	59.9	15.9	65.0	521	89.6
Naco CDP	1,046	-	-	931	11.1	0.0	0.0	0.5	88.4	31.0	20.1	42.2	57.5	11.6	306	85.0

1 May be of any race.

Table A. All Places — Population and Housing

STATE City, town, township, borough, or CDP (county if applicable)	Population 2010 census total population	2019 estimated population	Percent change 2010-2019	ACS total population estimate 2015-2019	Race and Hispanic or Latino origin (percent) White alone, not Hispanic or Latino	Black alone, not Hispanic or Latino	Asian alone, not Hispanic or Latino	All other races or 2 or more races, not Hispanic or Latino	Hispanic or Latino[1]	Age (percent) Under 18 years old	Age 65 years and older	Median age	Educational attainment of persons age 25 and older Percent High school diploma or less	Percent Bachelor's degree or more	Occupied housing units Total	Percent with a computer
	1	2	3	4	5	6	7	8	9	10	11	12	13	14	15	16
ARIZONA—Con.																
Nazlini CDP	489	-	-	522	0.0	0.0	0.0	100.0	0.0	43.9	11.3	20.4	69.5	9.3	111	23.4
Nelson CDP	259	-	-	587	38.0	0.0	0.0	5.8	56.2	51.3	4.1	17.1	46.4	11.9	132	97.0
New Kingman-Butler CDP	12,134	-	-	13,933	87.0	0.8	0.6	3.0	8.6	18.9	23.7	46.1	55.5	7.7	5,602	87.5
New River CDP	14,952	-	-	15,910	89.4	0.2	1.9	1.2	7.3	15.6	21.3	52.4	27.7	32.7	6,192	96.1
Nogales city	20,839	20,103	-3.5	20,201	3.3	0.5	1.5	0.2	94.5	29.1	16.9	35.2	63.8	13.5	6,792	75.4
Nolic CDP	37	-	-	97	9.3	0.0	0.0	90.7	0.0	58.8	9.3	17.3	57.5	0.0	17	47.1
North Fork CDP	1,417	-	-	1,676	2.2	0.0	0.0	97.1	0.7	26.4	10.3	33.0	53.4	9.0	423	59.3
Nutrioso CDP	26	-	-	-	-	-	-	-	-	-	-	-	-	-	-	-
Oak Springs CDP	63	-	-	80	0.0	0.0	0.0	100.0	0.0	22.5	12.5	35.0	51.0	7.8	18	38.9
Oatman CDP	135	-	-	43	41.9	0.0	58.1	0.0	0.0	0.0	41.9	0.0	41.9	58.1	25	100.0
Oljato-Monument Valley CDP	154	-	-	186	0.0	0.0	0.0	100.0	0.0	45.7	4.8	19.4	86.4	0.0	27	18.5
Oracle CDP	3,686	-	-	3,656	58.3	0.0	0.0	7.3	34.4	16.8	38.0	59.4	40.4	18.5	1,480	78.6
Orange Grove Mobile Manor CDP	594	-	-	447	0.0	0.0	0.0	0.0	100.0	31.1	26.2	35.0	84.1	0.0	127	60.6
Oro Valley town	41,045	46,044	12.2	44,630	76.7	1.8	3.1	2.6	15.8	17.4	33.9	54.0	17.7	52.4	19,522	95.5
Oxbow Estates CDP	217	-	-	213	100.0	0.0	0.0	0.0	0.0	17.8	19.2	43.3	55.4	10.3	97	100.0
Padre Ranchitos CDP	171	-	-	49	32.7	0.0	0.0	0.0	67.3	0.0	24.5	59.6	57.1	0.0	18	100.0
Page city	7,268	7,529	3.6	7,531	33.5	0.6	0.0	58.2	7.6	31.3	6.4	28.4	39.4	21.5	2,365	94.8
Palominas CDP	212	-	-	178	100.0	0.0	0.0	0.0	0.0	12.4	27.0	52.6	41.7	13.5	88	100.0
Paradise Valley town	12,755	14,637	14.8	14,362	83.0	0.7	4.7	3.3	8.3	19.7	26.9	53.6	11.0	70.9	5,352	98.4
Parker town	3,083	3,207	4.0	3,132	27.8	5.0	0.1	17.1	49.9	23.6	12.5	31.7	55.2	10.0	960	87.8
Parker Strip CDP	662	-	-	886	82.2	0.0	0.0	5.4	12.4	6.9	55.6	69.9	37.3	18.6	470	90.4
Parks CDP	1,188	-	-	1,496	94.1	0.0	0.9	4.8	0.3	11.0	28.3	57.5	27.2	37.3	716	93.2
Patagonia town	913	874	-4.3	772	51.6	1.3	0.0	14.8	32.4	21.5	28.2	51.0	32.7	39.6	354	83.3
Paulden CDP	5,231	-	-	5,189	74.3	0.0	0.3	2.6	22.7	24.7	20.1	41.3	49.0	10.8	2,058	91.6
Payson town	15,299	15,813	3.4	15,545	85.1	0.7	1.6	5.0	7.5	13.3	37.1	60.0	32.1	25.6	7,002	91.3
Peach Springs CDP	1,090	-	-	1,301	2.1	0.1	0.0	94.0	3.8	35.0	10.5	30.5	61.9	6.8	368	64.4
Peeples Valley CDP	428	-	-	521	95.6	1.5	0.0	0.0	2.9	5.0	60.5	67.0	32.7	25.9	273	76.9
Peoria city	154,048	175,961	14.2	168,196	69.0	2.8	4.1	3.9	20.3	23.7	16.9	39.8	31.1	32.8	59,659	94.8
Peridot CDP	1,350	-	-	1,676	2.6	0.0	0.0	91.7	5.7	36.6	7.7	24.9	71.4	3.5	329	61.1
Phoenix city	1,446,691	1,680,992	16.2	1,633,017	42.5	6.7	3.7	4.4	42.6	26.1	10.6	33.8	41.7	28.6	565,832	91.6
Picacho CDP	471	-	-	430	33.0	0.0	0.0	2.6	64.4	12.8	25.3	50.4	65.9	2.6	128	72.7
Picture Rocks CDP	9,563	-	-	9,653	72.1	0.5	0.0	0.2	27.2	22.9	19.8	44.6	43.6	17.0	3,551	95.3
Pima town	2,375	2,558	7.7	2,513	70.2	0.0	0.1	4.0	25.7	35.3	12.1	30.8	35.9	24.7	758	90.6
Pimaco Two CDP	682	-	-	907	86.4	0.0	0.0	0.0	13.6	29.2	34.2	51.8	48.9	14.8	337	90.5
Pinal CDP	439	-	-	466	64.2	0.0	0.0	0.0	35.8	43.3	26.2	30.6	47.7	14.0	154	66.2
Pine CDP	1,963	-	-	1,817	91.1	0.0	0.0	3.6	5.3	11.2	47.8	62.5	24.6	29.1	934	100.0
Pinedale CDP	487	-	-	246	100.0	0.0	0.0	0.0	0.0	2.4	36.2	60.9	35.7	30.9	156	100.0
Pine Lake CDP	138	-	-	137	100.0	0.0	0.0	0.0	0.0	0.0	48.9	64.9	49.6	0.0	68	100.0
Pinetop Country Club CDP	1,794	-	-	1,437	75.2	0.0	0.0	5.2	19.6	12.5	52.5	66.4	22.6	45.4	686	100.0
Pinetop-Lakeside town	4,282	4,469	4.4	4,370	82.6	0.0	0.6	6.0	10.8	19.0	30.1	53.3	27.5	36.8	1,898	85.9
Pinion Pines CDP	186	-	-	162	100.0	0.0	0.0	0.0	0.0	0.0	48.1	61.9	57.4	8.0	70	71.4
Pinon CDP	904	-	-	889	3.5	0.0	7.3	87.1	2.1	33.2	11.4	32.3	46.1	28.1	252	82.5
Pirtleville CDP	1,744	-	-	1,572	7.6	0.0	0.0	0.0	92.4	26.1	12.2	40.8	66.9	2.2	549	82.7
Pisinemo CDP	321	-	-	301	0.0	0.0	0.0	83.1	16.9	31.2	10.6	23.1	85.0	0.0	72	70.8
Poston CDP	285	-	-	242	6.6	0.0	0.0	31.0	62.4	33.1	4.5	26.0	84.3	0.0	82	86.6
Prescott city	39,770	44,299	11.4	42,785	88.3	0.5	1.3	3.1	6.8	11.9	37.3	58.3	22.4	38.3	19,632	91.7
Prescott Valley town	38,877	46,515	19.6	44,311	74.1	0.7	1.2	3.4	20.6	20.5	25.6	46.1	40.6	21.9	18,327	92.0
Quartzsite town	3,675	3,763	2.4	3,714	86.6	0.0	3.1	0.0	10.3	6.8	58.6	69.2	49.8	16.6	2,120	76.8
Queen Creek town	26,736	50,890	90.3	43,129	75.3	2.5	3.0	3.4	15.8	32.8	9.8	35.1	26.4	38.2	12,849	99.1
Queen Valley CDP	788	-	-	566	100.0	0.0	0.0	0.0	0.0	0.0	61.7	71.0	36.6	19.3	363	84.8
Rainbow City CDP	968	-	-	1,041	0.0	0.0	3.0	90.0	7.0	31.7	6.9	29.7	82.9	1.6	241	68.9
Rancho Mesa Verde CDP	625	-	-	571	0.0	0.0	0.0	0.0	100.0	18.9	4.9	31.1	89.0	0.0	190	86.8
Red Mesa CDP	480	-	-	501	3.8	1.4	0.0	88.8	6.0	23.6	9.6	35.1	37.3	18.2	131	76.3
Red Rock CDP	-	-	-	118	0.0	0.0	0.0	100.0	0.0	16.1	3.4	42.8	55.0	0.0	35	25.7
Red Rock CDP	169	-	-	4,203	69.6	0.2	0.0	7.6	22.6	38.0	7.5	27.4	35.3	23.6	1,199	99.4
Rillito CDP	97	-	-	-	-	-	-	-	-	-	-	-	-	-	-	-
Rincon Valley CDP	5,139	-	-	5,346	80.6	3.3	1.4	2.8	11.9	27.0	19.7	44.7	17.6	53.4	1,879	94.5
Rio Rico CDP	18,962	-	-	19,581	11.4	0.0	0.4	0.3	88.0	28.8	11.3	33.3	49.4	19.7	6,183	90.7
Rio Verde CDP	1,811	-	-	2,180	99.1	0.0	0.0	0.0	0.9	0.0	78.3	71.5	7.4	67.7	1,162	99.0
Rock House CDP	50	-	-	87	82.8	0.0	0.0	0.0	17.2	0.0	39.1	64.4	71.3	9.2	51	86.3
Rock Point CDP	642	-	-	593	0.0	0.0	4.4	95.1	0.5	31.0	11.8	31.2	67.1	15.2	177	38.4
Roosevelt CDP	28	-	-	14	50.0	0.0	0.0	0.0	50.0	0.0	0.0	43.3	50.0	28.6	0	0.0
Rough Rock CDP	414	-	-	428	0.5	0.0	0.0	99.5	0.0	19.9	19.4	44.8	54.5	11.5	168	45.8
Round Rock CDP	789	-	-	654	0.0	0.0	0.0	100.0	0.0	27.2	11.5	32.0	59.7	8.2	153	53.6
Round Valley CDP	487	-	-	754	95.9	0.0	0.0	0.0	4.1	48.8	15.9	22.0	25.6	10.0	220	93.6
Rye CDP	77	-	-	59	98.3	0.0	0.0	1.7	0.0	0.0	39.0	54.4	4.7	41.9	31	25.8
Sacate Village CDP	169	-	-	175	0.0	0.0	0.0	100.0	0.0	37.7	4.0	22.4	100.0	0.0	36	41.7
Sacaton CDP	2,672	-	-	1,824	8.2	0.1	0.5	80.2	11.0	18.8	14.2	34.2	75.8	2.3	650	37.7
Sacaton Flats Village CDP	541	-	-	422	0.0	0.0	0.0	97.2	2.8	19.9	16.6	43.8	88.0	0.0	150	42.0
Saddlebrooke CDP	9,614	-	-	10,945	91.3	0.0	1.6	0.8	6.3	5.2	71.3	70.9	13.2	52.6	5,669	97.2
Safford city	9,564	9,983	4.4	9,749	48.7	3.4	0.0	0.8	47.0	28.4	14.7	32.1	35.2	17.0	3,313	89.4
Sahuarita town	26,000	31,421	20.9	29,905	59.3	2.3	1.6	2.9	34.0	26.6	22.1	38.5	23.8	40.3	10,746	96.2
St. David CDP	1,699	-	-	1,233	85.8	0.0	0.0	0.0	14.2	19.6	20.0	44.5	26.8	29.3	616	86.7
St. Johns city	3,480	3,512	0.9	3,497	47.1	2.9	0.0	6.6	43.4	30.3	11.9	32.2	47.8	4.9	962	81.6
St. Johns CDP	476	-	-	675	0.0	1.2	0.0	83.3	15.6	33.0	7.0	25.1	46.9	17.6	141	90.8
St. Michaels CDP	1,443	-	-	1,125	5.5	0.0	0.2	92.4	2.0	17.6	15.1	46.4	33.1	19.4	342	59.6
Salome CDP	1,530	-	-	1,379	74.4	0.0	0.0	0.0	25.6	12.9	61.3	70.3	66.3	7.7	677	73.4
San Carlos CDP	4,038	-	-	4,451	0.7	0.0	0.6	93.1	5.6	38.0	6.9	25.7	60.5	6.9	1,023	65.4
Sanders CDP	630	-	-	608	10.9	0.0	0.0	82.2	6.9	48.8	12.2	20.3	37.6	9.7	159	71.7
San Jose CDP	506	-	-	718	35.9	0.0	0.0	0.0	64.1	43.7	8.1	29.5	50.8	5.5	194	80.4
San Luis city	27,909	34,778	24.6	32,985	2.3	0.3	0.0	0.4	97.0	29.0	7.6	30.0	68.8	8.4	8,235	81.5
San Manuel CDP	3,551	-	-	3,692	40.0	0.0	0.0	2.8	57.2	20.1	23.2	46.8	49.3	15.2	1,355	79.6
San Miguel CDP	197	-	-	292	0.0	0.0	0.0	100.0	0.0	32.9	3.1	26.3	69.3	0.0	63	69.8
San Simon CDP	165	-	-	183	71.0	0.0	0.0	0.0	29.0	26.2	21.9	40.9	50.9	0.9	83	79.5
Santa Cruz CDP	37	-	-	61	0.0	0.0	0.0	100.0	0.0	0.0	0.0	47.7	100.0	0.0	9	100.0
San Tan Valley CDP	81,321	-	-	96,692	66.0	3.8	2.1	5.2	22.8	31.2	11.4	33.5	37.0	21.3	29,869	96.4
Santa Rosa CDP	628	-	-	536	0.7	0.0	0.0	90.5	8.8	24.4	6.2	38.0	70.9	2.9	183	45.9
Sawmill CDP	748	-	-	775	0.3	0.0	0.0	99.7	0.0	32.4	10.8	25.5	78.9	2.8	156	29.5
Scenic CDP	1,643	-	-	1,701	70.4	0.0	0.0	0.0	29.6	27.3	39.1	56.8	46.8	10.4	577	90.5

1 May be of any race.

STATE City, town, township, borough, or CDP (county if applicable)	2010 census total population	2019 estimated population	Percent change 2010-2019	ACS total population estimate 2015-2019	White alone, not Hispanic or Latino	Black alone, not Hispanic or Latino	Asian alone, not Hispanic or Latino	All other races or 2 or more races, not Hispanic or Latino	Hispanic or Latino[1]	Under 18 years old	Age 65 years and older	Median age	Percent High school diploma or less	Percent Bachelor's degree or more	Total occupied housing units	Percent with a computer
	1	2	3	4	5	6	7	8	9	10	11	12	13	14	15	16
ARIZONA—Con.																
Scottsdale city	217,492	258,069	18.7	250,602	80.4	1.8	4.8	2.8	10.2	15.5	24.3	47.7	15.9	58.4	115,401	96.1
Seba Dalkai CDP	136	-	-	100	2.0	0.0	0.0	98.0	0.0	11.0	17.0	48.0	47.1	10.3	31	67.7
Second Mesa CDP	962	-	-	1,823	0.0	0.0	0.6	99.4	0.0	30.9	10.5	27.2	71.3	1.7	355	49.6
Sedona city	10,034	10,339	3.0	10,322	87.6	0.4	1.4	0.9	9.7	7.5	42.6	61.2	21.8	49.6	5,542	93.8
Sehili CDP	135	-	-	140	0.0	0.0	0.0	100.0	0.0	22.9	15.0	37.8	50.0	0.0	39	12.8
Seligman CDP	445	-	-	776	57.2	0.0	0.0	9.9	32.9	29.5	18.8	36.7	46.5	16.6	287	83.3
Sells CDP	2,495	-	-	2,609	3.1	0.0	0.0	95.6	1.3	35.2	8.5	24.7	70.6	2.7	643	63.9
Seven Mile CDP	707	-	-	950	0.0	0.0	0.0	96.5	3.5	33.1	6.1	26.6	72.0	2.8	189	62.4
Shongopovi CDP	831	-	-	1,017	0.0	0.0	0.0	99.6	0.4	32.4	7.2	26.3	48.1	6.8	219	53.4
Shonto CDP	591	-	-	515	3.5	0.0	0.0	96.5	0.0	30.1	8.0	31.3	56.1	23.4	129	62.8
Show Low city	10,667	11,442	7.3	11,130	75.3	0.4	0.9	3.7	19.7	25.0	23.5	39.7	35.7	22.2	4,377	95.6
Sierra Vista city	45,276	43,045	-4.9	43,398	57.2	6.9	4.5	6.0	25.5	23.0	19.2	36.2	26.5	30.0	17,497	92.9
Sierra Vista Southeast CDP	14,797	-	-	15,841	69.3	1.0	1.5	3.6	24.6	23.8	23.5	46.8	26.9	33.0	6,331	91.0
Six Shooter Canyon CDP	1,019	-	-	1,241	62.9	1.0	0.0	3.2	33.0	28.8	18.6	29.9	53.0	9.6	477	88.1
Snowflake town	5,612	5,995	6.8	5,811	82.7	0.2	0.0	9.2	8.0	39.4	11.4	27.8	27.9	21.0	1,562	88.7
So-Hi CDP	477	-	-	337	100.0	0.0	0.0	0.0	0.0	0.0	40.4	60.4	72.7	0.0	209	65.6
Solomon CDP	426	-	-	522	39.3	0.0	0.0	0.0	60.7	21.6	14.4	36.0	49.7	15.7	143	79.7
Somerton city	14,297	16,554	15.8	16,146	3.1	0.0	0.0	0.8	96.1	33.5	7.4	27.5	63.7	13.0	4,594	79.9
Sonoita CDP	818	-	-	801	91.1	0.9	0.0	0.0	8.0	9.6	46.7	63.3	29.7	32.5	315	94.3
South Komelik CDP	111	-	-	296	0.0	0.0	0.0	80.7	19.3	45.6	3.0	26.3	65.2	13.7	52	78.8
South Tucson city	5,652	5,715	1.1	5,667	10.5	2.7	0.1	16.8	69.9	27.6	11.8	32.6	70.2	5.4	1,840	70.3
Springerville town	1,958	1,978	1.0	2,031	54.5	0.3	0.2	12.9	32.1	31.9	14.6	37.8	40.8	14.0	713	81.2
Spring Valley CDP	1,148	-	-	1,596	94.9	2.4	0.0	0.9	1.8	17.8	33.5	55.0	45.9	11.3	606	85.8
Stanfield CDP	740	-	-	515	0.0	0.0	0.0	29.1	70.9	36.9	4.9	37.9	100.0	0.0	163	67.5
Star Valley town	2,312	2,308	-0.2	1,603	89.6	3.1	0.0	1.1	6.2	10.5	45.0	58.9	26.9	17.4	931	67.0
Steamboat CDP	284	-	-	316	0.0	0.0	0.0	95.9	4.1	25.0	13.3	36.7	60.2	0.0	77	42.9
Stotonic Village CDP	659	-	-	607	0.0	0.0	0.0	89.1	10.9	15.5	10.4	25.5	86.5	0.0	195	41.5
Strawberry CDP	961	-	-	946	98.1	0.0	0.0	0.6	1.3	7.0	53.1	65.6	39.6	25.2	497	98.2
Summerhaven CDP	40	-	-	41	100.0	0.0	0.0	0.0	0.0	0.0	0.0	60.8	58.5	41.5	32	100.0
Summit CDP	5,372	-	-	4,707	15.5	0.5	0.0	0.4	83.6	27.6	11.5	32.8	70.6	3.9	1,400	88.3
Sun City CDP	37,499	-	-	38,877	92.4	1.8	0.9	0.8	4.2	1.0	75.8	73.0	40.6	23.6	23,039	84.7
Sun City West CDP	24,535	-	-	25,544	96.6	0.8	0.6	0.8	1.2	0.1	84.1	75.5	30.0	33.7	15,190	87.3
Sunizona CDP	281	-	-	212	86.3	0.0	0.0	3.3	10.4	10.4	27.4	58.3	48.7	21.9	114	72.8
Sun Lakes CDP	13,975	-	-	14,473	95.2	0.8	0.5	1.1	2.4	0.1	79.6	73.0	26.6	37.1	8,556	92.0
Sun Valley CDP	316	-	-	77	50.6	11.7	0.0	13.0	24.7	0.0	39.0	63.2	88.3	0.0	21	100.0
Sunwest CDP	15	-	-	39	0.0	0.0	0.0	61.5	38.5	0.0	100.0	0.0	0.0	0.0	15	0.0
Supai CDP	208	-	-	-	-	-	-	-	-	-	-	-	-	-	-	-
Superior town	2,878	3,178	10.4	3,071	29.4	0.0	4.5	1.2	64.9	13.5	28.7	54.1	55.8	14.2	1,319	78.6
Surprise city	117,473	141,664	20.6	135,450	68.7	6.1	2.7	2.9	19.6	24.4	22.6	41.4	33.0	28.6	48,618	95.6
Sweet Water Village CDP	83	-	-	8	0.0	0.0	0.0	100.0	0.0	0.0	62.5	0.0	100.0	0.0	8	0.0
Swift Trail Junction CDP	2,935	-	-	2,915	48.0	4.7	1.4	9.5	36.3	16.6	10.8	37.8	44.7	8.9	688	90.0
Tacna CDP	602	-	-	637	35.2	0.0	0.0	0.5	64.4	21.8	10.5	32.8	57.8	11.4	239	77.4
Tanque Verde CDP	16,901	-	-	15,638	85.3	0.5	2.2	2.5	9.4	16.1	31.0	55.6	16.5	55.0	6,315	96.0
Tat Momoli CDP	10	-	-	43	0.0	0.0	0.0	100.0	0.0	0.0	100.0	0.0	100.0	0.0	13	0.0
Taylor town	4,105	4,321	5.3	4,202	78.3	0.0	0.0	9.7	12.0	20.4	18.5	43.0	43.2	11.8	1,515	92.7
Teec Nos Pos CDP	730	-	-	838	0.0	0.0	0.0	100.0	0.0	36.9	11.6	29.0	48.9	9.7	218	45.0
Tees Toh CDP	448	-	-	633	0.8	0.0	0.0	93.2	6.0	25.1	8.7	30.3	54.1	5.6	140	79.3
Tempe city	161,774	195,805	21.0	187,454	56.7	6.5	8.9	5.6	22.2	14.7	10.2	29.5	21.3	46.5	73,032	95.8
Thatcher town	4,826	5,200	7.7	5,047	74.4	1.0	0.7	3.6	20.2	27.5	17.5	33.2	30.5	24.3	1,625	91.8
Theba CDP	90	-	-	90	0.0	0.0	7.8	0.0	92.2	37.8	0.0	27.6	85.4	14.6	24	87.5
Three Points CDP	5,581	-	-	4,801	52.4	1.7	1.4	2.3	42.3	15.0	21.7	48.8	47.7	14.2	1,924	84.4
Tolani Lake CDP	280	-	-	335	0.9	0.6	1.2	94.9	2.4	35.8	9.0	28.2	62.1	1.6	73	83.6
Tolleson city	6,545	7,372	12.6	7,246	3.8	7.4	0.0	2.6	86.3	29.7	10.9	29.0	60.9	7.5	2,046	88.2
Tombstone city	1,387	1,303	-6.1	1,209	76.7	0.0	0.0	0.8	22.5	13.3	42.5	60.0	38.5	13.3	673	81.4
Tonalea CDP	549	-	-	320	0.0	0.0	0.0	100.0	0.0	40.3	15.6	23.2	65.1	6.0	79	75.9
Tonopah CDP	60	-	-	59	100.0	0.0	0.0	0.0	0.0	0.0	16.9	49.2	83.1	16.9	34	100.0
Tonto Basin CDP	1,424	-	-	1,685	98.8	1.2	0.0	0.0	0.0	9.9	48.4	64.6	43.5	11.6	841	77.2
Tonto Village CDP	256	-	-	193	100.0	0.0	0.0	0.0	0.0	20.2	32.6	58.8	11.0	36.4	106	84.0
Topawa CDP	299	-	-	400	0.0	0.0	0.0	97.3	2.8	22.0	19.3	46.2	64.8	11.4	125	57.6
Topock CDP	10	-	-	-	-	-	-	-	-	-	-	-	-	-	-	-
Top-of-the-World CDP	231	-	-	315	72.7	0.0	0.0	11.7	15.6	0.0	33.7	47.9	43.4	29.9	159	100.0
Toyei CDP	13	-	-	-	-	-	-	-	-	-	-	-	-	-	-	-
Truxton CDP	134	-	-	40	32.5	0.0	0.0	67.5	0.0	15.0	22.5	55.8	74.1	0.0	15	93.3
Tsaile CDP	1,205	-	-	1,364	11.3	1.0	1.0	80.4	6.2	24.5	7.3	21.1	45.4	19.9	293	69.3
Tubac CDP	1,191	-	-	1,375	79.1	0.0	0.0	0.0	20.9	5.7	49.9	65.0	18.4	55.3	769	82.7
Tuba City CDP	8,611	-	-	8,609	2.6	0.1	0.4	95.6	1.3	28.8	9.8	31.5	47.3	15.0	2,206	74.5
Tucson city	526,634	548,073	4.1	541,482	43.9	4.8	3.1	4.6	43.6	21.2	14.3	33.7	38.6	27.4	212,491	91.3
Tucson Estates CDP	12,192	-	-	11,960	58.5	2.7	0.7	2.6	35.4	15.8	31.6	53.9	38.7	20.1	5,095	91.9
Tumacacori-Carmen CDP	393	-	-	132	23.5	0.0	0.0	0.0	76.5	0.0	56.8	71.3	64.4	0.0	64	100.0
Turkey Creek CDP	294	-	-	426	0.0	0.0	1.9	98.1	0.0	23.5	4.0	28.5	54.8	6.5	95	69.5
Tusayan town	570	580	1.8	297	49.8	2.4	8.4	16.5	22.9	2.4	10.1	42.3	44.1	24.8	145	93.1
Upper Santan Village CDP	495	-	-	607	0.0	0.0	0.0	95.9	4.1	27.5	4.8	30.6	70.4	7.7	165	43.6
Utting CDP	126	-	-	124	100.0	0.0	0.0	0.0	0.0	0.0	80.6	73.5	47.6	0.0	77	92.2
Vail CDP	10,208	-	-	12,982	74.2	1.6	2.7	3.5	17.9	27.0	14.0	39.3	23.1	36.2	4,409	97.4
Vaiva Vo CDP	128	-	-	-	-	-	-	-	-	-	-	-	-	-	-	-
Valencia West CDP	9,355	-	-	11,796	24.7	1.3	2.5	2.3	69.1	31.9	10.5	32.5	40.8	19.0	3,782	96.2
Valentine CDP	38	-	-	71	50.7	2.8	0.0	46.5	0.0	15.5	50.7	73.3	80.4	8.9	30	93.3
Valle CDP	832	-	-	254	37.8	0.0	0.0	50.0	12.2	0.0	28.3	49.6	44.5	0.0	154	53.2
Valle Vista CDP	1,659	-	-	2,195	83.2	0.0	6.2	5.6	5.0	14.4	41.9	60.5	46.5	18.5	993	86.4
Ventana CDP	49	-	-	107	0.0	0.0	0.0	100.0	0.0	22.4	0.0	32.1	100.0	0.0	15	53.3
Verde Village CDP	11,605	-	-	12,903	72.1	1.6	0.4	2.8	23.2	21.4	22.0	47.5	40.0	19.4	4,912	89.7
Vernon CDP	122	-	-	163	96.9	0.0	0.0	0.0	3.1	41.1	15.3	38.8	44.3	25.0	17	100.0
Vicksburg CDP	597	-	-	647	89.5	0.0	0.0	0.0	10.5	4.0	79.8	73.4	49.8	16.9	379	84.7
Village of Oak Creek (Big Park) CDP	6,147	-	-	6,375	78.2	1.8	1.1	1.6	17.3	8.8	42.2	62.8	20.1	44.1	3,049	92.8
Wagon Wheel CDP	1,652	-	-	1,461	71.6	0.0	0.0	14.4	14.0	21.8	33.5	53.6	37.5	22.3	605	89.4
Wahak Hotrontk CDP	114	-	-	139	0.0	0.0	0.0	100.0	0.0	50.4	4.3	14.0	86.4	0.0	12	58.3
Wall Lane CDP	415	-	-	243	1.6	0.0	0.0	0.0	98.4	7.8	18.9	42.7	86.7	0.0	102	67.6
Walnut Creek CDP	562	-	-	669	71.2	0.0	0.0	23.6	5.2	24.1	26.2	53.3	27.2	6.1	288	93.1
Washington Park CDP	70	-	-	128	100.0	0.0	0.0	0.0	0.0	0.0	43.0	59.6	59.4	11.7	59	100.0
Wellton town	2,882	3,044	5.6	3,007	49.4	0.0	1.4	2.8	46.4	10.4	45.1	62.4	60.2	14.3	1,359	83.9

1 May be of any race.

Table A. All Places — **Population and Housing**

STATE City, town, township, borough, or CDP (county if applicable)	Population				Race and Hispanic or Latino origin (percent)					Age (percent)			Educational attainment of persons age 25 and older		Occupied housing units	
	2010 census total population	2019 estimated population	Percent change 2010-2019	ACS total population estimate 2015-2019	White alone, not Hispanic or Latino	Black alone, not Hispanic or Latino	Asian alone, not Hispanic or Latino	All other races or 2 or more races, not Hispanic or Latino	Hispanic or Latino[1]	Under 18 years old	Age 65 years and older	Median age	Percent High school diploma or less	Percent Bachelor's degree or more	Total	Percent with a computer
	1	2	3	4	5	6	7	8	9	10	11	12	13	14	15	16
ARIZONA—Con.																
Wellton Hills CDP	258	-	-	569	54.3	0.0	0.0	0.0	45.7	27.8	5.4	26.1	48.4	19.7	138	100.0
Wenden CDP	728	-	-	375	34.7	0.0	1.6	10.1	53.6	11.2	36.8	60.5	68.0	16.9	224	60.3
Wet Camp Village CDP	229	-	-	82	0.0	0.0	0.0	59.8	40.2	31.7	20.7	28.5	76.0	0.0	31	38.7
Wheatfields CDP	785	-	-	416	63.5	0.0	0.0	3.4	33.2	0.0	46.4	64.6	61.1	11.8	294	89.5
Whetstone CDP	-	-	-	2,304	83.2	0.6	0.9	10.1	5.2	16.1	26.3	50.0	45.0	10.9	1,032	85.8
Whispering Pines CDP	148	-	-	76	100.0	0.0	0.0	0.0	0.0	0.0	86.8	77.2	11.8	52.6	58	100.0
Whitecone CDP	817	-	-	871	0.0	0.0	0.0	99.2	0.8	31.0	12.6	32.1	62.0	1.8	270	53.0
White Hills CDP	323	-	-	254	79.9	4.7	0.0	0.0	15.4	12.2	27.2	58.9	54.7	34.1	147	87.1
White Mountain Lake CDP	2,205	-	-	2,700	68.6	2.3	0.4	4.3	24.5	16.7	31.3	53.3	51.0	12.9	1,011	86.6
Whiteriver CDP	4,104	-	-	4,296	1.2	0.3	0.0	96.4	2.1	35.7	9.1	28.2	66.2	3.4	972	56.1
Why CDP	-	-	-	148	48.0	0.0	0.0	35.1	16.9	14.9	13.5	38.9	32.5	15.9	39	100.0
Wickenburg town	6,527	8,092	24.0	7,495	87.0	0.0	0.3	6.5	6.2	11.8	40.7	60.6	33.3	30.1	3,634	86.2
Wide Ruins CDP	176	-	-	38	86.8	0.0	0.0	13.2	0.0	0.0	100.0	84.4	10.5	86.8	1	0.0
Wikieup CDP	133	-	-	102	72.5	0.0	0.0	0.0	27.5	20.6	6.9	38.7	61.3	18.7	46	71.7
Wilhoit CDP	868	-	-	1,009	81.3	0.0	0.0	4.0	14.8	11.2	31.4	56.7	54.2	10.4	498	83.9
Willcox city	3,754	3,533	-5.9	3,533	34.4	0.5	0.6	2.7	61.8	31.1	13.7	30.2	63.1	8.9	1,397	84.0
Williams city	3,039	3,248	6.9	3,176	51.3	3.6	0.6	6.9	37.6	26.9	19.6	42.1	39.5	22.7	1,311	89.2
Williamson CDP	5,438	-	-	5,347	91.3	0.0	0.5	1.1	7.1	9.7	46.3	63.5	24.9	37.0	2,508	95.9
Willow Canyon CDP	1	-	-	-	-	-	-	-	-	-	-	-	-	-	-	-
Willow Valley CDP	1,062	-	-	785	85.0	1.0	0.8	3.9	9.3	5.9	47.4	64.3	61.8	4.5	457	75.9
Window Rock CDP	2,712	-	-	2,454	4.1	0.7	0.0	91.2	4.0	25.3	12.8	36.9	41.4	18.5	755	67.8
Winkelman town	356	351	-1.4	293	18.1	0.0	0.0	7.2	74.7	6.5	29.4	52.9	53.4	5.4	127	63.0
Winslow city	9,661	9,338	-3.3	9,476	25.1	3.9	0.1	34.4	36.5	26.4	10.0	33.6	51.3	9.7	2,648	87.1
Winslow West CDP	438	-	-	642	37.5	0.0	0.0	51.1	11.4	28.8	6.5	26.3	48.2	8.4	163	79.8
Wintersburg CDP	136	-	-	25	100.0	0.0	0.0	0.0	0.0	0.0	0.0	48.3	100.0	0.0	8	100.0
Wittmann CDP	763	-	-	693	75.8	0.0	2.3	8.8	13.1	37.7	7.8	24.8	83.4	7.4	180	100.0
Woodruff CDP	191	-	-	111	100.0	0.0	0.0	0.0	0.0	0.0	49.5	65.0	0.0	67.6	56	58.9
Yarnell CDP	649	-	-	739	92.7	0.0	0.0	5.7	1.6	5.5	50.1	65.0	40.7	17.5	403	92.6
York CDP	557	-	-	687	52.8	0.0	0.9	0.7	45.6	30.7	15.1	36.9	46.2	27.2	218	89.4
Young CDP	666	-	-	482	92.1	0.0	0.0	1.7	6.2	13.5	35.7	56.1	30.5	24.8	230	76.5
Youngtown town	6,156	6,859	11.4	6,802	53.2	4.8	1.2	4.9	35.8	25.8	19.0	38.3	52.6	13.6	2,491	87.7
Yucca CDP	126	-	-	65	69.2	0.0	0.0	0.0	30.8	13.8	38.5	64.3	16.1	7.1	42	54.8
Yuma city	90,717	98,285	8.3	96,349	32.6	2.7	2.0	2.8	60.0	26.4	15.2	31.8	45.9	18.5	34,360	88.1
ARKANSAS	2,916,031	3,017,804	3.5	2,999,370	72.4	15.2	1.5	3.4	7.5	23.5	16.6	38.1	47.5	23.0	1,158,071	86.2
Adona city	209	206	-1.4	147	97.3	0.0	0.0	2.7	0.0	25.9	18.4	35.2	58.0	14.0	63	63.5
Alexander city	2,910	3,457	18.8	3,168	43.9	20.3	2.3	5.2	28.4	29.4	8.6	31.4	53.6	19.0	1,034	89.2
Alicia town	139	128	-7.9	140	98.6	0.0	0.0	0.7	0.7	12.1	13.6	41.0	66.1	5.5	56	75.0
Allport town	118	118	0.0	95	8.4	83.2	0.0	5.3	3.2	9.5	14.7	44.9	76.1	7.5	37	48.6
Alma city	5,510	5,864	6.4	5,742	86.9	0.4	0.0	8.5	4.2	27.4	12.9	33.6	52.5	15.6	2,279	90.0
Almyra town	283	262	-7.4	256	100.0	0.0	0.0	0.0	0.0	10.9	18.8	50.2	55.6	13.1	103	83.5
Alpena town	392	397	1.3	309	95.8	0.0	0.3	3.2	0.6	29.1	16.8	38.6	69.3	10.4	116	72.4
Altheimer city	978	811	-17.1	719	7.2	90.7	0.0	0.0	2.1	26.6	15.9	47.9	64.5	8.3	291	58.8
Altus city	754	729	-3.3	825	94.8	0.2	0.0	3.4	1.6	31.0	10.1	31.2	59.8	14.5	329	77.5
Amagon town	98	90	-8.2	85	89.4	0.0	0.0	10.6	0.0	7.1	52.9	65.4	86.8	0.0	46	43.5
Amity city	721	685	-5.0	706	88.4	0.0	0.0	1.7	9.9	27.5	18.7	35.5	55.0	13.4	303	80.5
Anthonyville town	155	147	-5.2	93	2.2	87.1	0.0	10.8	0.0	16.1	25.8	56.3	51.3	11.5	45	57.8
Antoine town	114	108	-5.3	153	81.0	16.3	0.0	2.6	0.0	43.1	13.1	26.5	30.8	0.0	57	70.2
Arkadelphia city	10,704	10,726	0.2	10,670	59.6	32.2	1.4	1.7	5.1	17.4	14.2	23.9	35.5	33.3	3,751	84.3
Arkansas City city	367	315	-14.2	409	41.1	54.8	0.0	4.2	0.0	27.6	16.9	32.6	67.7	13.3	174	82.2
Ashdown city	4,720	4,400	-6.8	4,425	57.2	38.8	0.9	3.0	0.1	26.5	18.3	38.0	52.0	9.9	1,891	88.8
Ash Flat city	1,086	1,098	1.1	1,144	91.6	1.8	0.0	2.4	4.1	14.5	30.9	53.1	55.7	7.5	471	78.6
Atkins city	3,004	3,037	1.1	3,048	97.7	0.0	0.8	1.0	0.5	30.8	16.3	35.9	49.2	20.9	1,164	86.8
Aubrey town	166	138	-16.9	106	84.9	9.4	0.0	0.0	5.7	14.2	24.5	51.0	56.3	13.8	50	82.0
Augusta city	2,247	1,947	-13.4	2,203	53.2	45.7	0.0	1.1	0.0	25.2	20.6	43.2	60.7	13.3	966	57.8
Austin city	2,032	4,079	100.7	3,350	81.9	4.3	0.8	3.5	9.5	33.4	5.1	28.8	35.9	23.7	1,249	95.7
Avilla CDP	896	-	-	1,200	95.8	0.8	0.7	1.4	1.3	28.8	10.2	39.8	33.4	29.5	427	99.1
Avoca town	484	517	6.8	595	72.6	0.0	0.0	0.7	26.7	24.4	16.0	41.2	64.5	9.5	219	87.7
Bald Knob city	2,897	2,868		2,878	84.7	4.1	0.0	7.2	3.9	26.9	17.4	37.0	67.3	8.6	1,123	82.4
Banks town	123	116	-5.7	195	68.2	9.2	0.0	0.0	22.6	24.1	16.9	38.5	46.3	2.2	80	70.0
Barling city	4,696	5,036	7.2	4,910	89.7	1.1	1.5	3.4	4.3	24.7	13.8	33.2	40.9	21.7	1,791	92.9
Bassett town	178	159	-10.7	245	91.4	2.0	0.0	6.1	0.4	29.0	11.0	31.9	73.0	5.1	75	86.7
Batesville city	10,244	10,878	6.2	10,706	77.6	4.2	1.0	2.9	14.3	22.7	16.9	35.1	46.4	25.4	3,985	83.6
Bauxite town	527	548	4.0	713	88.8	7.4	0.0	2.7	1.1	28.1	13.3	34.6	61.9	5.9	214	86.0
Bay city	1,803	1,821	1.0	1,901	90.5	3.2	0.0	3.8	2.5	24.8	16.3	40.2	65.6	9.3	717	88.1
Bearden city	972	858	-11.7	924	64.8	29.3	0.0	0.0	5.8	17.2	13.3	49.1	59.0	10.4	392	77.8
Beaver town	96	95		56	85.7	0.0	0.0	14.3	0.0	3.6	32.1	62.5	30.0	34.0	33	87.9
Beebe city	7,306	8,168	11.8	8,078	92.3	5.3	0.0	0.3	2.0	24.4	17.6	36.4	47.3	29.0	3,198	91.4
Beedeville town	107	97	-9.3	100	93.0	0.0	0.0	7.0	0.0	37.0	11.0	29.0	62.1	0.0	30	53.3
Bella Vista city	26,510	28,872	8.9	28,539	91.3	0.7	1.0	3.4	3.6	17.4	32.5	51.8	30.7	33.3	12,396	95.8
Bellefonte town	440	478	8.6	443	93.9	0.0	0.2	2.5	3.4	22.1	22.8	42.6	53.5	12.5	200	81.5
Belleville city	441	418	-5.2	613	54.2	11.4	12.6	0.0	21.9	30.7	13.5	36.5	62.0	11.7	151	66.9
Ben Lomond town	145	142	-2.1	111	58.6	0.0	0.0	7.2	34.2	34.2	19.8	27.4	62.1	1.7	41	68.3
Benton city	30,766	36,820	19.7	35,679	83.0	8.6	1.8	2.7	3.9	26.1	15.0	36.6	40.9	27.8	13,082	90.0
Bentonville city	35,356	54,909	55.3	49,467	70.2	3.5	12.2	3.9	10.2	28.2	8.2	32.6	26.8	50.2	18,223	94.1
Bergman town	444	510	14.9	774	95.6	0.0	0.3	0.8	3.4	26.6	11.0	28.3	53.9	11.6	251	89.6
Berryville city	5,291	5,550	4.9	5,442	68.2	0.2	3.2	7.9	20.4	24.9	15.7	33.6	60.8	12.3	2,009	78.9
Bethel Heights city	2,320	2,771	19.4	2,638	34.5	5.9	2.3	9.3	47.9	35.3	6.0	28.5	68.3	14.3	771	95.6
Bigelow town	348	345	-0.9	413	93.2	6.8	0.0	0.0	0.0	24.5	9.2	43.1	37.9	24.6	137	83.9
Big Flat town	105	104		23	100.0	0.0	0.0	0.0	0.0	0.0	60.9	70.2	69.6	8.7	12	83.3
Biggers town	347	339	-2.3	335	85.1	12.2	0.0	0.6	2.1	22.7	11.9	35.8	52.1	12.8	152	86.2
Birdsong town	48	42	-12.5	38	0.0	100.0	0.0	0.0	0.0	28.9	28.9	59.5	74.1	7.4	16	68.8
Black Oak town	266	264	-0.8	215	86.0	0.0	0.0	0.0	14.0	26.0	14.4	39.9	55.3	16.7	88	94.3
Black Rock city	661	602	-8.9	827	97.5	0.0	0.0	2.5	0.0	21.4	16.7	35.1	56.4	3.6	313	83.4
Black Springs town	99	92	-7.1	87	92.0	0.0	0.0	5.7	2.3	20.7	17.2	41.3	58.5	13.2	35	65.7
Blevins city	313	301	-3.8	431	49.9	18.1	0.0	0.0	32.0	42.9	15.1	28.2	49.4	13.6	128	86.7
Blue Eye town	35	36	2.9	74	100.0	0.0	0.0	0.0	0.0	51.4	4.1	17.8	100.0	0.0	22	40.9
Blue Mountain town	124	118	-4.8	91	90.1	0.0	0.0	5.5	4.4	15.4	7.7	46.9	67.7	6.2	35	82.9
Bluff City town	127	116	-8.7	116	46.6	53.4	0.0	0.0	0.0	21.6	21.6	52.5	46.1	3.4	50	70.0
Blytheville city	15,614	13,455	-13.8	14,011	28.8	62.4	1.1	4.8	3.0	28.3	14.2	34.2	52.2	18.2	5,674	86.7
Bodcaw town	138	128	-7.2	183	96.7	3.3	0.0	0.0	0.0	39.3	9.8	29.3	42.3	17.5	59	86.4

1 May be of any race.

Table A. All Places — **Population and Housing**

STATE City, town, township, borough, or CDP (county if applicable)	Population: 2010 census total population	Population: 2019 estimated population	Population: Percent change 2010-2019	Population: ACS total population estimate 2015-2019	Race and Hispanic or Latino origin (percent): White alone, not Hispanic or Latino	Race: Black alone, not Hispanic or Latino	Race: Asian alone, not Hispanic or Latino	Race: All other races or 2 or more races, not Hispanic or Latino	Race: Hispanic or Latino[1]	Age (percent): Under 18 years old	Age: Age 65 years and older	Age: Median age	Educational attainment of persons age 25 and older: Percent High school diploma or less	Educational attainment: Percent Bachelor's degree or more	Occupied housing units: Total	Occupied housing units: Percent with a computer
	1	2	3	4	5	6	7	8	9	10	11	12	13	14	15	16
ARKANSAS—Con.																
Bonanza city	567	564	-0.5	491	82.1	0.0	1.0	8.8	8.1	21.6	13.0	40.0	51.6	12.5	196	83.2
Bono city	2,201	2,484	12.9	2,478	89.6	2.3	0.0	3.7	4.4	31.0	11.7	30.9	53.8	11.3	950	90.4
Booneville city	3,979	3,785	-4.9	3,841	88.1	0.2	0.0	5.7	5.9	30.5	14.1	36.3	64.4	10.9	1,439	89.5
Bradford city	749	736	-1.7	744	94.0	0.8	0.0	2.2	3.1	27.0	17.9	35.0	71.0	15.6	283	80.2
Bradley city	623	527	-15.4	471	35.9	59.2	0.0	4.9	0.0	30.8	10.8	34.4	68.5	6.5	206	62.1
Branch city	348	341	-2.0	306	99.0	0.0	0.0	0.7	0.3	11.4	22.2	46.0	66.7	11.4	126	65.1
Briarcliff city	235	240	2.1	288	98.3	0.0	0.3	1.4	0.0	14.6	13.5	50.0	35.1	14.4	115	91.3
Brinkley city	3,193	2,590	-18.9	2,742	36.8	58.6	1.1	2.3	1.2	22.4	21.6	44.6	66.9	9.6	1,179	78.1
Brookland city	1,984	3,674	85.2	3,312	97.7	0.4	0.2	1.0	0.6	28.9	11.2	28.4	40.1	25.6	1,337	94.5
Bryant city	16,666	20,968	25.8	20,231	81.2	12.4	1.4	1.9	3.1	22.4	15.0	38.5	30.7	31.9	8,203	90.4
Buckner city	265	229	-13.6	237	47.3	52.7	0.0	0.0	0.0	19.4	23.6	52.9	54.9	16.8	89	67.4
Bull Shoals city	1,950	1,946	-0.2	2,260	92.0	0.0	0.8	3.5	3.6	16.6	37.9	59.3	46.6	17.7	951	89.1
Burdette town	193	167	-13.5	174	88.5	11.5	0.0	0.0	0.0	21.8	14.4	32.8	51.6	8.9	74	85.1
Cabot city	24,119	26,352	9.3	26,217	86.7	2.4	1.3	3.5	6.2	28.0	10.6	34.5	36.9	26.2	9,780	89.9
Caddo Valley town	691	642	-7.1	688	75.6	19.3	0.0	3.2	1.9	24.3	9.3	34.6	28.7	24.5	275	93.1
Caldwell town	526	456	-13.3	427	60.4	29.3	0.0	0.5	9.8	23.0	30.2	41.4	55.2	13.5	215	89.3
Cale town	76	69	-9.2	86	100.0	0.0	0.0	0.0	0.0	5.8	11.6	53.8	69.9	0.0	43	60.5
Calico Rock city	1,536	1,746	13.7	2,346	85.9	10.1	0.0	1.3	2.7	14.4	15.3	40.8	66.3	9.6	510	92.2
Calion city	498	445	-10.6	510	69.8	30.2	0.0	0.0	0.0	19.2	22.2	49.6	59.1	12.0	229	71.2
Camden city	12,182	10,749	-11.8	10,999	41.4	54.3	0.0	0.8	3.6	27.7	17.3	35.4	54.5	14.1	4,221	75.6
Cammack Village city	778	719	-7.6	757	92.1	1.1	1.7	0.5	4.6	18.1	19.0	35.8	9.3	63.3	362	92.3
Campbell Station city	255	229	-10.2	268	89.6	8.6	0.0	1.9	0.0	11.9	14.2	48.9	56.9	12.3	122	82.8
Caraway city	1,275	1,282	0.5	1,000	87.3	1.4	0.0	2.4	8.9	23.2	18.6	42.6	70.8	12.4	422	81.5
Carlisle city	2,214	2,156	-2.6	2,279	85.5	12.3	0.0	1.0	1.1	24.7	19.0	43.1	60.0	20.1	896	76.7
Carthage city	343	295	-14.0	327	6.1	92.0	1.2	0.0	0.6	18.7	13.5	48.5	75.3	10.9	139	71.2
Casa town	170	167	-1.8	155	83.2	5.8	0.0	11.0	0.0	18.1	21.9	49.8	58.7	7.4	48	87.5
Cash town	344	360	4.7	329	84.8	0.0	0.6	3.6	10.9	35.9	14.9	26.7	69.4	4.7	111	78.4
Caulksville town	217	209	-3.7	234	99.1	0.0	0.0	0.9	0.0	15.8	41.0	57.0	44.6	26.1	100	80.0
Cave City city	1,905	1,927	1.2	2,242	92.0	1.1	0.0	2.4	4.5	27.5	16.9	34.0	60.9	7.7	853	72.3
Cave Springs city	1,939	5,276	172.1	4,359	89.5	0.4	1.8	4.9	3.3	32.9	8.6	32.9	14.1	67.9	1,421	98.9
Cedarville city	1,395	1,410	1.1	1,332	85.1	0.0	0.3	7.7	7.0	23.6	15.9	43.9	54.4	15.5	490	77.3
Center Ridge CDP	388	-	-	365	100.0	0.0	0.0	0.0	0.0	26.3	14.0	41.4	64.3	19.1	125	92.8
Centerton city	9,583	16,244	69.5	14,203	79.0	4.7	3.4	3.9	9.0	31.1	6.4	31.6	29.9	37.3	4,996	94.9
Central City town	502	502	0.0	544	81.3	4.4	0.0	4.4	9.9	21.3	18.8	46.1	41.6	23.7	225	84.9
Charleston city	2,509	2,467	-1.7	2,581	91.7	0.7	0.1	6.1	1.4	23.7	20.2	39.4	47.5	16.4	997	78.7
Cherokee City CDP	72	-	-	49	100.0	0.0	0.0	0.0	0.0	0.0	30.6	50.4	30.6	34.7	32	53.1
Cherokee Village city	4,707	4,661	-	4,973	97.6	0.0	0.0	1.3	1.0	20.0	34.1	54.4	49.8	16.0	2,370	87.2
Cherry Valley city	652	583	-10.6	792	83.6	2.8	0.0	12.8	0.9	34.8	9.1	26.8	59.2	12.0	280	82.5
Chester town	162	157	-3.1	110	95.5	0.0	0.0	0.0	4.5	15.5	38.2	59.5	69.0	6.9	48	77.1
Chidester city	289	260	-10.0	283	27.2	72.1	0.7	0.0	0.0	15.9	20.8	45.8	77.7	4.2	112	70.5
Clarendon city	1,680	1,361	-19.0	1,487	58.0	37.5	0.0	3.6	0.9	18.8	26.0	47.4	60.3	13.0	741	63.7
Clarkedale city	389	360	-7.5	435	68.7	17.7	0.0	8.5	5.1	32.2	11.0	39.4	41.9	22.6	130	93.1
Clarksville city	9,190	9,764	6.2	9,601	62.1	3.9	3.3	4.0	26.6	23.7	15.2	32.8	60.9	16.8	3,456	82.0
Clinton city	2,658	2,520	-5.2	2,547	85.4	0.7	0.3	2.2	11.5	22.8	19.1	37.9	59.8	11.8	942	84.7
Coal Hill city	1,009	1,011	0.2	1,247	96.6	0.0	0.0	2.6	0.8	21.3	19.4	45.9	72.3	10.7	430	73.0
College Station CDP	600	-	-	485	9.5	90.5	0.0	0.0	0.0	29.1	14.4	45.3	56.0	0.0	167	78.4
Colt city	375	329	-12.3	330	69.1	18.2	0.0	3.9	8.8	16.1	20.0	51.6	49.0	12.4	179	87.7
Concord town	244	233	-4.5	174	100.0	0.0	0.0	0.0	0.0	14.4	30.5	49.5	77.2	5.9	83	88.0
Conway city	58,874	67,638	14.9	66,127	72.7	17.2	2.3	3.5	4.3	20.8	10.4	28.9	30.8	39.7	24,320	92.1
Corinth town	70	67	-4.3	43	83.7	0.0	0.0	7.0	9.3	25.6	4.7	29.3	70.0	20.0	17	70.6
Corning city	3,426	3,056	-10.8	3,137	94.8	0.0	0.0	2.1	3.0	23.0	17.9	38.4	56.5	13.0	1,421	82.0
Cotter city	956	950	-0.6	906	94.0	0.0	0.0	1.7	4.3	16.2	31.1	47.2	48.1	21.7	419	91.6
Cotton Plant city	653	574	-12.1	512	27.0	69.5	0.0	3.5	0.0	11.9	23.8	51.5	76.7	2.2	282	44.0
Cove town	390	373	-4.4	255	87.8	0.0	0.0	7.5	4.7	19.2	24.3	49.1	59.6	11.6	121	64.5
Coy town	96	93	-3.1	95	52.6	26.3	0.0	0.0	21.1	13.7	11.6	50.4	67.1	0.0	45	33.3
Crawfordsville town	503	456	-9.3	507	60.4	15.2	0.0	12.8	11.6	21.5	17.9	47.6	50.6	27.1	210	89.5
Crossett city	5,497	4,794	-12.8	4,972	54.8	35.7	0.0	0.5	8.9	25.8	23.0	36.0	57.0	11.7	1,902	71.3
Cushman city	452	459	1.5	438	93.4	0.0	1.4	3.2	2.1	24.0	17.4	38.6	58.1	9.1	161	79.5
Daisy town	115	110	-4.3	71	97.2	0.0	0.0	2.8	0.0	4.2	38.0	55.8	49.2	17.5	36	80.6
Damascus town	389	383	-1.5	431	86.5	0.0	0.0	6.7	6.7	22.7	14.2	31.8	49.8	13.3	158	84.2
Danville city	2,415	2,393	-0.9	2,212	49.0	3.5	2.6	1.6	43.3	32.8	15.3	32.0	60.9	18.0	657	77.9
Dardanelle city	4,745	4,541	-4.3	4,561	58.9	4.3	0.0	0.1	36.7	23.1	15.3	38.4	63.9	11.6	1,609	71.1
Datto town	100	93	-7.0	92	73.9	0.0	0.0	4.3	21.7	25.0	14.1	34.2	89.3	1.8	33	84.8
Decatur city	1,692	1,790	5.8	1,837	57.9	1.4	3.2	11.9	25.7	34.6	6.8	27.9	66.2	17.4	591	83.6
Delaplaine town	112	114	1.8	97	100.0	0.0	0.0	0.0	0.0	11.3	12.4	45.4	46.9	23.4	38	92.1
Delight city	287	271	-5.6	344	89.0	7.0	0.6	1.7	1.7	21.2	25.9	44.5	59.1	10.3	153	83.7
Dell town	222	187	-15.8	218	98.6	0.0	1.4	0.0	0.0	27.5	25.7	40.9	38.2	29.9	88	87.5
Dennard CDP	530	-	-	327	94.8	0.0	0.0	5.2	0.0	15.9	34.9	61.0	80.8	8.8	158	80.4
Denning town	314	248	-21.0	288	88.5	0.0	0.0	11.5	0.0	16.3	10.1	37.3	71.2	3.8	96	68.8
De Queen city	6,578	6,534	-0.7	6,556	30.6	4.9	0.2	2.9	61.4	34.1	10.5	28.8	73.7	12.0	1,865	83.0
Dermott city	2,823	2,483	-12.0	2,810	25.2	72.5	1.1	0.4	0.8	23.5	14.6	34.9	62.9	11.7	810	70.1
Des Arc city	1,716	1,582	-7.8	1,580	85.8	11.4	0.0	1.9	0.9	17.8	24.1	49.4	55.7	12.5	715	77.9
De Valls Bluff city	604	555	-8.1	572	72.6	24.1	0.0	0.0	3.3	28.0	26.6	40.8	74.6	6.8	286	70.6
DeWitt city	3,284	3,005	-8.5	3,091	66.3	24.0	0.0	2.2	7.5	28.1	17.4	34.3	56.6	16.4	1,226	77.7
Diamond City city	782	800	2.3	1,020	96.2	0.0	0.2	1.7	2.0	20.2	33.3	46.0	48.8	11.1	459	87.1
Diaz city	1,323	1,208	-8.7	1,363	57.7	29.4	0.0	4.1	8.7	28.8	12.5	34.2	59.9	12.6	505	80.4
Dierks city	1,127	1,082	-4.0	874	89.7	1.6	0.0	3.5	5.1	16.4	19.7	43.9	65.4	12.4	376	75.5
Donaldson town	300	300	0.0	297	94.3	1.0	0.0	4.7	0.0	26.9	18.5	39.2	55.0	14.3	113	85.8
Dover city	1,381	1,440	4.3	2,045	94.3	0.1	0.0	1.8	3.8	30.8	15.2	34.5	54.0	14.0	718	83.6
Dumas city	4,665	4,046	-13.3	4,173	33.4	56.5	1.2	0.5	8.4	28.7	16.5	35.8	62.0	17.8	1,739	79.2
Dyer city	911	902	-	713	96.5	0.0	0.0	1.7	1.8	25.5	19.1	42.9	52.6	17.9	277	89.5
Dyess town	414	363	-12.3	288	77.4	0.0	0.0	0.0	22.6	25.3	5.2	26.1	78.2	4.1	95	96.8
Earle city	2,399	2,179	-9.2	2,190	17.0	71.6	0.0	10.8	0.6	24.8	14.7	36.0	66.9	9.2	856	79.3
East Camden town	930	818	-12.0	1,022	67.4	24.1	0.6	3.8	4.1	24.9	7.8	28.2	38.4	16.3	444	95.3
East End CDP	6,998	-	-	6,384	93.6	2.8	1.0	1.7	0.8	19.2	19.0	43.8	42.0	21.2	2,401	94.0
Edmondson town	423	391	-7.6	329	14.9	75.1	0.0	9.4	0.6	37.1	15.2	31.6	67.0	16.8	122	51.6
Egypt town	112	109	-2.7	64	100.0	0.0	0.0	0.0	0.0	21.9	20.3	33.5	52.2	23.9	33	90.9
Elaine city	636	499	-21.5	659	38.5	50.4	0.0	3.6	7.4	35.8	8.2	23.7	53.3	9.3	260	75.4
El Dorado city	18,895	17,651	-6.6	17,982	43.5	47.4	1.0	2.3	5.7	26.0	16.2	36.4	50.2	23.5	7,164	71.9
Elkins city	2,683	3,487	30.0	3,139	90.7	0.3	0.4	1.3	7.3	29.8	12.8	32.0	42.1	25.1	1,109	92.9
Elm Springs city	1,876	2,472	31.8	2,399	86.5	1.8	2.3	3.8	5.6	26.2	14.4	43.8	35.1	40.7	819	94.4
Emerson town	369	343	-7.0	218	78.0	16.1	0.5	5.5	0.0	24.8	15.6	39.5	66.1	7.3	89	65.2

1 May be of any race.

Table A. All Places — **Population and Housing**

STATE City, town, township, borough, or CDP (county if applicable)	Population				Race and Hispanic or Latino origin (percent)					Age (percent)			Educational attainment of persons age 25 and older		Occupied housing units	
	2010 census total population	2019 estimated population	Percent change 2010-2019	ACS total population estimate 2015-2019	White alone, not Hispanic or Latino	Black alone, not Hispanic or Latino	Asian alone, not Hispanic or Latino	All other races or 2 or more races, not Hispanic or Latino	Hispanic or Latino[1]	Under 18 years old	Age 65 years and older	Median age	Percent High school diploma or less	Percent Bachelor's degree or more	Total	Percent with a computer
	1	2	3	4	5	6	7	8	9	10	11	12	13	14	15	16
ARKANSAS—Con.																
Emmet city	512	461	-10.0	618	82.4	14.6	0.0	2.8	0.3	22.3	14.4	46.3	61.2	8.4	247	81.8
England city	2,830	2,689	-5.0	2,741	71.2	25.9	0.0	2.7	0.2	27.7	16.4	33.9	53.0	19.8	1,026	79.6
Enola town	339	355	4.7	380	100.0	0.0	0.0	0.0	0.0	26.1	12.1	40.8	49.2	20.5	140	93.6
Etowah town	359	317	-11.7	278	91.4	0.0	0.0	7.9	0.7	15.5	21.6	49.4	67.8	3.3	127	86.6
Eudora city	2,271	1,903	-16.2	2,118	9.0	89.3	0.0	1.7	0.0	26.3	18.2	43.3	57.3	10.6	886	75.1
Eureka Springs city	2,066	2,106	1.9	1,991	83.6	0.6	2.8	6.4	6.6	13.0	25.5	56.4	35.4	36.0	970	90.0
Evening Shade city	440	444	0.9	406	94.6	0.0	0.0	2.5	3.0	15.0	21.9	47.7	59.2	6.7	172	76.2
Everton town	133	135	1.5	64	92.2	0.0	0.0	3.1	4.7	15.6	21.9	52.8	55.8	11.5	28	53.6
Fairfield Bay city	2,336	2,189	-6.3	2,212	95.8	0.3	0.0	0.2	3.8	8.4	53.3	66.0	37.9	26.9	1,186	79.8
Fargo town	93	80	-14.0	75	17.3	82.7	0.0	0.0	0.0	17.3	14.7	47.7	46.3	0.0	36	86.1
Farmington city	5,974	7,400	23.9	6,992	89.2	0.0	0.6	6.0	4.1	29.3	10.4	35.9	39.5	35.5	2,584	94.2
Fayetteville city	73,580	87,590	19.0	85,166	77.4	7.0	3.4	4.7	7.6	17.8	9.0	27.3	23.1	50.2	35,288	95.4
Felsenthal town	150	141	-6.0	42	76.2	21.4	0.0	2.4	0.0	0.0	57.1	68.0	42.5	25.0	28	85.7
Fifty-Six city	177	174	-1.7	118	87.3	0.0	0.0	7.6	5.1	20.3	46.6	61.5	69.6	3.3	54	68.5
Fisher city	223	213	-4.5	226	90.7	2.7	0.0	6.6	0.0	17.3	18.6	46.1	55.4	6.5	98	94.9
Flippin city	1,351	1,322	-2.1	1,471	93.6	0.0	1.6	2.7	2.0	31.8	11.8	31.6	64.2	8.6	594	78.3
Fordyce city	4,309	3,705	-14.0	3,849	36.8	58.8	0.0	2.3	2.1	30.4	17.3	33.5	56.1	8.3	1,398	73.7
Foreman city	1,029	926	-10.0	1,165	49.6	41.7	0.0	4.9	3.8	19.2	21.1	41.7	63.2	15.6	552	70.7
Forrest City city	15,422	13,820	-10.4	14,285	23.8	71.2	0.8	1.5	2.7	23.7	11.9	36.1	54.4	9.4	4,358	79.9
Fort Smith city	86,266	87,891	1.9	87,743	59.4	9.4	6.2	5.5	19.5	24.2	14.7	36.5	48.2	21.8	35,908	86.3
Fouke city	870	878	0.9	808	83.2	3.1	0.0	13.7	0.0	31.1	16.7	32.5	78.6	2.9	281	83.6
Fountain Hill town	171	158	-7.6	161	48.4	46.6	3.7	0.0	1.2	11.2	17.4	54.2	40.4	11.3	86	80.2
Fountain Lake town	549	573	4.4	520	94.8	0.4	0.0	3.3	1.5	24.6	26.5	39.0	63.0	14.8	189	89.4
Fourche town	62	63	1.6	29	100.0	0.0	0.0	0.0	0.0	0.0	34.5	60.6	75.9	13.8	24	50.0
Franklin town	196	191	-2.6	109	85.3	0.0	0.0	11.0	3.7	7.3	23.9	48.8	70.7	4.0	51	78.4
Fredonia (Biscoe) town	372	349	-6.2	300	50.7	48.7	0.0	0.7	0.0	21.0	15.3	47.0	63.3	11.1	138	86.2
Friendship town	188	190	1.1	163	100.0	0.0	0.0	0.0	0.0	28.8	25.2	41.9	63.3	9.2	73	80.8
Fulton town	204	195	-4.4	84	45.2	52.4	0.0	2.4	0.0	15.5	40.5	59.0	65.2	4.3	50	70.0
Garfield town	519	578	11.4	610	97.7	0.2	0.0	1.6	0.5	15.2	27.7	49.3	58.0	15.2	235	89.4
Garland town	240	236	-1.7	351	18.5	80.3	0.0	0.0	1.1	16.8	15.4	32.6	76.4	3.2	133	60.9
Garner town	281	285	1.4	184	90.2	0.0	0.0	0.0	9.8	24.5	15.8	37.8	71.9	4.4	68	88.2
Gassville city	2,076	2,158	3.9	2,557	94.3	1.2	0.5	2.6	1.4	30.8	15.1	34.9	54.3	13.1	942	90.3
Gateway town	430	477	10.9	318	87.7	0.3	0.0	8.2	3.8	15.4	26.1	56.3	66.4	6.3	127	71.7
Gentry city	3,484	4,023	15.5	3,852	78.9	1.6	3.2	3.2	13.0	25.8	15.5	37.2	55.3	16.0	1,449	89.8
Georgetown town	133	132	-0.8	90	96.7	0.0	0.0	3.3	0.0	10.0	41.1	60.0	85.0	2.5	35	45.7
Gibson CDP	3,543	-	-	4,985	64.3	32.8	0.9	0.8	1.2	25.8	11.9	36.2	39.4	22.2	1,617	94.9
Gilbert town	28	26	-7.1	3	100.0	0.0	0.0	0.0	0.0	0.0	66.7	66.5	33.3	33.3	3	100.0
Gillett city	681	680	-0.1	763	76.7	23.3	0.0	0.0	0.0	23.7	20.1	40.7	42.3	16.8	358	71.2
Gillham town	156	157	0.6	293	86.0	0.0	0.0	1.0	13.0	22.2	13.3	38.4	65.2	12.2	96	88.5
Gilmore city	265	246	-7.2	215	34.0	38.1	0.0	25.6	2.3	21.9	11.6	37.8	69.3	10.5	82	62.2
Glenwood city	2,236	2,128	-4.8	1,995	77.3	2.7	0.1	0.3	19.6	22.1	22.9	44.6	51.3	19.8	843	76.5
Goshen town	1,052	1,941	84.5	2,593	90.7	0.3	1.9	2.9	4.2	38.3	7.4	34.3	10.5	68.5	774	99.5
Gosnell city	3,612	3,116	-13.7	3,236	81.6	13.4	0.0	2.9	2.0	24.7	14.3	39.0	59.9	8.6	1,289	92.9
Gould city	839	724	-13.7	663	8.4	89.3	0.0	2.3	0.0	15.4	27.3	52.4	60.3	17.0	408	76.7
Grady city	456	391	-14.3	305	36.1	56.4	0.0	3.9	3.6	20.7	21.3	41.4	56.8	9.7	178	78.1
Grannis city	564	574	1.8	624	73.1	0.0	0.0	7.7	19.2	16.2	20.5	45.9	66.2	8.8	259	83.4
Gravette city	3,155	3,516	11.4	3,381	95.3	0.0	0.3	1.5	2.8	28.3	14.9	33.5	57.1	16.3	1,305	91.0
Greenbrier city	4,715	5,665	20.1	5,478	92.2	1.6	0.0	3.7	2.5	30.6	13.2	30.1	41.3	19.0	2,014	94.3
Green Forest city	2,647	2,749	3.9	2,691	52.0	0.0	0.3	2.3	45.4	29.5	12.4	34.3	74.4	9.3	928	80.1
Greenland city	1,281	1,403	9.5	1,652	93.5	1.3	0.5	4.1	0.6	27.8	12.2	34.1	43.4	24.8	601	95.3
Greenway city	208	189	-9.1	176	97.2	0.0	0.0	1.1	1.7	19.3	15.9	39.1	73.2	6.3	74	89.2
Greenwood city	9,101	9,414	3.4	9,387	93.9	0.2	0.3	2.4	3.2	29.6	13.4	35.2	30.8	26.3	3,492	87.9
Greers Ferry city	886	856	-3.4	940	96.0	0.2	0.0	3.1	0.7	17.2	30.5	52.5	57.3	11.3	451	87.1
Griffithville town	230	225	-2.2	195	100.0	0.0	0.0	0.0	0.0	14.4	9.7	39.3	69.8	7.9	81	86.4
Grubbs city	387	353	-8.8	400	91.3	0.5	0.0	7.5	0.8	20.3	24.5	47.0	73.2	2.7	152	74.3
Guion town	84	83	-1.2	153	81.7	0.0	0.0	18.3	0.0	27.5	13.1	29.3	63.3	15.3	36	100.0
Gum Springs town	120	113	-5.8	134	18.7	48.5	0.0	0.0	32.8	31.3	10.4	36.1	32.9	45.2	53	90.6
Gurdon city	2,237	2,085	-6.8	2,571	47.2	40.1	0.0	2.6	10.2	26.4	9.1	35.1	50.7	13.8	1,016	81.7
Guy city	750	788	5.1	618	94.3	2.3	0.6	1.5	1.3	24.4	16.8	37.6	47.3	23.7	247	82.2
Hackett city	785	844	7.5	894	75.6	0.0	0.8	22.7	0.9	34.1	9.7	25.8	59.5	7.7	350	89.1
Hagarville CDP	129	-	-	41	100.0	0.0	0.0	0.0	0.0	0.0	41.5	64.7	22.0	0.0	29	69.0
Hamburg city	2,884	2,603	-9.7	2,683	49.8	38.4	0.0	0.3	11.5	23.0	17.1	43.4	67.2	14.4	1,104	73.6
Hampton city	1,322	1,258	-4.8	1,490	66.5	29.9	0.0	1.0	2.6	11.5	19.9	45.3	58.0	7.8	619	82.2
Hardy city	767	765	-0.3	597	97.3	0.0	0.0	2.7	0.0	8.7	45.1	60.2	67.0	6.4	352	70.5
Harrell town	256	248	-3.1	393	44.5	52.2	0.0	1.3	2.0	19.8	18.3	47.5	70.9	3.5	131	82.4
Harrisburg city	2,315	2,309	-0.3	2,776	88.4	1.8	0.0	8.0	1.8	26.6	16.2	38.3	65.1	11.8	1,060	83.0
Harrison city	12,949	13,080	1.0	13,063	91.5	0.6	0.4	5.3	2.2	23.3	17.7	36.2	45.9	18.6	5,578	88.3
Hartford city	648	629	-2.9	586	83.6	2.7	0.0	11.4	2.2	27.3	23.4	39.3	56.3	10.7	213	83.6
Hartman city	553	556	0.5	545	87.5	0.0	0.0	4.0	8.4	17.8	22.6	44.5	75.3	4.7	226	80.5
Haskell city	4,011	4,605	14.8	4,543	88.1	4.1	0.2	4.3	3.3	23.9	12.0	33.9	53.5	13.5	1,197	86.7
Hatfield town	410	388	-5.4	494	95.3	0.0	0.0	4.0	0.6	17.2	32.4	46.4	67.5	5.5	210	87.6
Havana city	373	363	-2.7	514	42.4	2.3	0.8	1.0	53.5	50.0	8.9	18.5	77.6	9.0	135	81.5
Haynes town	150	125	-16.7	151	9.3	87.4	0.0	3.3	0.0	15.2	19.9	39.9	59.4	9.9	61	82.0
Hazen city	1,463	1,344	-8.1	1,370	70.2	24.9	0.0	1.0	3.9	20.4	17.7	38.8	52.5	20.3	601	77.9
Heber Springs city	7,242	6,916	-4.5	6,992	91.1	0.8	1.3	1.6	5.3	20.9	22.9	40.2	56.4	16.2	2,868	85.3
Hector town	455	466	2.4	506	89.7	0.0	0.0	4.2	6.1	28.7	15.4	31.9	67.0	14.7	159	79.2
Helena-West Helena city	12,474	10,299	-17.4	10,749	21.5	77.2	0.0	0.4	0.8	28.3	16.4	35.1	53.6	11.3	4,191	74.6
Hensley CDP	139	-	-	56	0.0	100.0	0.0	0.0	0.0	0.0	17.9	52.8	100.0	0.0	44	61.4
Hermitage city	825	771	-6.5	840	26.2	46.8	0.0	0.0	27.0	39.2	3.6	23.8	67.1	4.8	313	79.2
Hickory Ridge city	272	241	-11.4	232	93.1	0.0	0.0	6.9	0.0	17.2	20.3	50.3	60.0	8.8	106	64.2
Higden town	127	122	-3.9	90	100.0	0.0	0.0	0.0	0.0	21.1	28.9	54.3	44.8	16.4	41	90.2
Higginson town	680	731	7.5	686	78.0	7.3	2.9	4.2	7.6	35.3	6.6	30.9	50.3	14.7	211	93.8
Highfill town	579	635	9.7	874	87.1	0.0	7.9	1.0	4.0	22.0	13.6	40.6	40.3	31.3	302	90.7
Highland city	1,051	1,107	5.3	1,092	92.5	1.6	0.0	2.7	3.2	24.5	23.1	45.6	59.7	10.8	454	85.7
Hindsville town	61	65	6.6	34	100.0	0.0	0.0	0.0	0.0	11.8	61.8	70.5	43.3	26.7	16	100.0
Holiday Island CDP	2,373	-	-	2,353	95.8	0.0	0.0	0.0	4.2	10.1	48.8	64.5	25.0	36.2	1,216	95.6
Holland city	533	577	8.3	654	91.3	0.0	0.0	1.2	7.5	17.9	16.7	41.1	52.6	18.9	244	86.1
Holly Grove city	609	528	-13.3	573	3.1	96.2	0.0	0.7	0.0	31.6	18.0	37.0	51.4	11.0	266	65.4
Hope city	10,119	9,599	-5.1	9,768	31.3	44.6	0.1	2.3	21.8	29.9	13.8	36.1	56.9	11.0	3,375	84.5
Horatio city	1,042	1,030	-1.2	989	67.1	0.3	0.0	2.4	30.1	33.0	11.2	31.7	59.4	7.8	375	77.6
Horseshoe Bend city	2,177	2,109	-3.1	2,587	93.2	0.0	0.0	5.4	1.4	19.7	32.0	49.4	48.3	12.6	1,028	86.2
Horseshoe Lake town	296	272	-8.1	432	81.9	3.0	1.9	6.7	6.5	6.9	38.2	60.4	58.7	11.3	220	77.3

1 May be of any race.

Table A. All Places — **Population and Housing**

STATE City, town, township, borough, or CDP (county if applicable)	Population: 2010 census total population	Population: 2019 estimated population	Population: Percent change 2010-2019	Population: ACS total population estimate 2015-2019	Race and Hispanic or Latino origin (percent): White alone, not Hispanic or Latino	Race: Black alone, not Hispanic or Latino	Race: Asian alone, not Hispanic or Latino	Race: All other races or 2 or more races, not Hispanic or Latino	Race: Hispanic or Latino[1]	Age (percent): Under 18 years old	Age: Age 65 years and older	Age: Median age	Educational attainment of persons age 25 and older: Percent High school diploma or less	Educational attainment: Percent Bachelor's degree or more	Occupied housing units: Total	Occupied housing units: Percent with a computer
	1	2	3	4	5	6	7	8	9	10	11	12	13	14	15	16
ARKANSAS—Con.																
Hot Springs city	37,941	38,797	2.3	38,559	67.9	17.1	1.0	4.6	9.3	20.2	21.5	41.9	44.1	19.5	16,163	85.1
Hot Springs Village CDP	12,807	-	-	14,779	95.3	1.0	0.2	0.5	3.0	8.4	59.2	68.0	23.2	41.0	7,279	93.8
Houston town	174	175	0.6	184	100.0	0.0	0.0	0.0	0.0	33.2	15.8	43.3	68.4	4.3	71	66.2
Hoxie city	2,780	2,601	-6.4	2,628	96.7	1.6	0.0	1.3	0.3	23.3	16.9	37.5	60.4	9.2	1,186	76.5
Hughes city	1,447	1,216	-16.0	1,252	26.9	64.1	3.0	0.0	6.0	26.0	15.1	32.5	63.8	4.7	521	65.3
Humnoke city	290	274	-5.5	255	98.4	1.2	0.0	0.4	0.0	19.6	36.5	53.9	76.1	4.1	115	62.6
Humphrey city	550	479	-12.9	464	57.3	41.6	0.0	1.1	0.0	17.5	14.2	46.9	59.2	10.4	213	78.4
Hunter town	105	93	-11.4	151	100.0	0.0	0.0	0.0	0.0	16.6	11.9	40.9	77.1	2.5	72	62.5
Huntington city	633	621	-1.9	499	87.6	1.0	0.8	5.0	5.6	23.2	22.4	40.8	71.4	3.8	203	76.4
Huntsville city	2,435	2,569	5.5	2,513	75.8	0.6	0.0	7.9	15.7	34.6	12.8	29.2	72.9	7.5	866	75.8
Huttig city	595	528	-11.3	721	42.2	57.8	0.0	0.0	0.0	35.2	12.9	35.1	64.8	11.9	225	63.6
Imboden town	678	621	-8.4	712	97.1	0.0	0.0	0.3	2.7	24.3	24.4	44.0	59.1	13.6	294	81.0
Jacksonport town	215	199	-7.4	216	98.1	0.0	0.0	1.9	0.0	38.4	12.5	36.4	66.9	7.6	75	78.7
Jacksonville city	28,354	28,235	-0.4	28,456	49.3	39.2	1.6	3.0	6.9	26.2	13.5	33.5	41.3	18.7	10,333	90.4
Jasper city	525	488	-7.0	742	98.7	0.3	0.0	1.1	0.0	37.2	27.0	37.6	43.6	21.8	240	67.1
Jennette town	124	116	-6.5	69	5.8	94.2	0.0	0.0	0.0	14.5	29.0	58.8	73.2	10.7	42	52.4
Jericho town	113	104	-8.0	40	0.0	90.0	0.0	10.0	0.0	5.0	45.0	62.5	87.5	0.0	21	42.9
Jerome town	36	34	-5.6	43	95.3	0.0	0.0	0.0	4.7	9.3	48.8	61.8	61.5	5.1	21	61.9
Johnson city	3,396	3,742	10.2	3,707	85.6	0.6	2.1	5.7	6.0	27.4	16.0	32.7	18.8	54.2	1,526	93.1
Joiner city	574	500	-12.9	485	37.3	55.5	0.0	7.2	0.0	23.3	16.7	46.4	70.7	8.3	227	68.7
Jonesboro city	67,295	78,394	16.5	76,036	68.5	20.0	1.9	3.4	6.2	25.2	12.5	32.8	41.1	29.5	29,186	91.6
Judsonia city	2,016	1,994	-1.1	2,016	84.8	3.5	0.0	1.2	10.6	25.0	17.7	41.6	70.7	11.7	775	79.0
Junction City city	586	523	-10.8	624	31.3	68.8	0.0	0.0	0.0	28.0	17.3	37.3	46.8	23.9	271	66.8
Keiser city	791	676	-14.5	709	78.6	6.1	0.0	10.4	4.9	33.6	17.5	36.5	70.2	5.5	267	82.8
Kensett city	1,648	1,617	-1.9	1,726	61.9	20.9	0.0	2.8	14.4	22.2	18.4	37.6	73.3	8.8	717	80.9
Keo town	258	251	-2.7	172	72.7	13.4	4.1	0.0	9.9	16.3	27.3	51.0	57.5	23.3	69	62.3
Kibler city	1,020	1,028	0.8	1,137	88.0	0.0	0.2	9.9	1.9	24.9	18.0	38.6	67.4	10.5	429	83.0
Kingsland city	444	400	-9.9	512	65.2	34.2	0.0	0.6	0.0	28.1	15.8	36.0	68.9	5.4	202	83.2
Kirby CDP	786	-	-	878	95.2	0.0	0.0	0.0	4.8	24.4	14.4	37.2	45.1	18.1	313	93.9
Knobel city	283	261	-7.8	184	99.5	0.0	0.0	0.0	0.5	15.8	19.6	42.9	82.6	1.4	87	74.7
Knoxville town	733	756	3.1	833	88.2	0.0	0.6	2.2	9.0	24.5	15.1	41.6	59.7	9.9	315	83.2
Lafe town	452	461	2.0	438	92.5	0.0	0.0	2.1	5.5	21.7	10.5	41.0	65.4	8.1	166	84.9
LaGrange town	85	71	-16.5	37	29.7	70.3	0.0	0.0	0.0	8.1	27.0	31.6	88.2	5.9	19	73.7
Lake City city	2,084	2,650	27.2	2,465	95.9	0.2	0.2	1.7	2.0	21.8	16.1	37.1	62.2	14.9	936	92.4
Lake Hamilton CDP	2,135	-	-	2,240	91.3	0.0	1.1	6.0	1.6	25.1	26.5	57.6	58.0	19.6	962	93.6
Lakeview city	731	719	-1.6	844	94.1	0.0	2.7	2.4	0.8	8.5	49.8	64.9	43.8	10.1	423	87.9
Lake View city	443	358	-19.2	431	1.6	98.1	0.0	0.2	0.0	26.2	17.9	32.6	52.5	9.8	165	59.4
Lake Village city	2,579	2,194	-14.9	2,294	29.9	62.6	1.4	0.7	5.4	20.5	21.2	43.6	54.5	20.3	960	71.1
Lamar city	1,616	1,722	6.6	2,001	87.3	0.5	0.5	5.2	6.5	25.6	18.0	34.4	67.6	16.7	747	75.8
Landmark CDP	3,555	-	-	3,435	64.3	27.5	0.0	2.4	5.9	21.8	20.1	44.0	50.8	17.3	1,324	85.5
Lavaca city	2,297	2,427	5.7	2,545	91.2	0.0	0.0	6.5	2.3	25.8	11.3	33.1	48.0	18.2	951	90.1
Leachville city	2,150	1,864	-13.3	2,952	81.4	0.0	0.0	1.6	17.1	34.1	10.1	29.5	68.4	6.4	971	88.1
Lead Hill town	267	265	-0.7	228	97.8	0.0	0.0	0.0	2.2	22.4	13.2	47.4	75.7	3.3	97	84.5
Leola town	502	500	-0.4	640	50.5	1.1	0.0	3.8	44.7	37.5	4.7	26.7	70.6	4.1	177	90.4
Lepanto city	1,945	1,807	-7.1	1,825	77.3	11.0	0.0	5.6	6.1	25.0	16.6	39.1	58.5	12.2	713	78.8
Leslie city	431	415	-3.7	581	83.8	0.0	2.9	12.7	0.5	15.3	34.3	53.1	63.3	5.9	284	85.6
Letona town	252	244	-3.2	266	94.7	0.0	0.0	5.3	0.0	30.5	9.0	31.0	73.0	2.9	93	87.1
Lewisville city	1,279	1,114	-12.9	924	35.5	50.4	0.0	6.2	7.9	20.6	16.3	42.5	52.1	13.6	360	75.0
Lexa town	293	238	-18.8	188	79.8	10.6	0.0	8.0	1.6	22.9	25.5	39.3	53.8	3.4	78	70.5
Lincoln city	2,285	2,481	8.6	2,444	83.6	1.2	0.0	5.0	10.2	26.1	19.1	38.1	63.0	8.6	937	86.6
Little Flock city	2,524	2,786	10.4	2,766	69.4	1.3	2.7	3.8	22.8	22.2	12.3	30.7	41.1	28.4	1,136	94.6
Little Rock city	193,538	197,312	2.0	197,958	45.1	42.0	3.3	2.2	7.4	23.4	14.1	36.7	31.0	41.8	81,987	89.1
Lockesburg city	731	724		679	89.5	2.2	0.0	2.1	6.2	28.1	13.5	31.4	51.6	10.6	276	85.9
London city	1,040	1,067	2.6	769	94.8	0.9	0.8	2.9	0.7	20.2	17.0	47.2	55.6	19.8	307	90.2
Lonoke city	4,263	4,187	-1.8	4,238	75.4	19.3	0.2	0.4	4.7	23.1	18.1	38.1	53.3	17.2	1,676	88.1
Lonsdale town	94	101	7.4	142	88.0	0.0	0.0	10.6	1.4	33.8	15.5	38.3	57.5	18.4	43	86.0
Lost Bridge Village CDP	434	-	-	292	95.5	0.0	0.0	4.5	0.0	7.9	43.2	60.8	38.8	40.3	141	67.4
Louann town	164	151	-7.9	196	58.2	40.3	1.5	0.0	0.0	30.6	18.9	29.4	67.5	5.8	47	51.1
Lowell city	7,322	9,544	30.3	9,175	67.8	0.5	3.0	3.1	25.6	28.5	7.5	31.6	45.5	30.9	3,277	96.3
Luxora city	1,189	1,027	-13.6	991	39.9	50.5	0.0	3.3	6.4	25.3	10.3	37.9	71.6	4.2	358	65.9
Lynn town	283	264	-6.7	238	97.5	0.0	0.0	2.5	0.0	26.9	22.3	38.8	60.8	20.3	100	65.0
McAlmont CDP	1,873	-	-	1,894	19.2	76.8	0.0	4.0	0.0	32.4	15.2	23.6	66.9	12.7	700	65.4
McCaskill town	96	97	1.0	99	40.4	32.3	0.0	2.0	25.3	18.2	18.2	36.3	87.1	6.5	36	86.1
McCrory city	1,726	1,488	-13.8	1,730	83.7	14.2	0.1	0.3	1.7	22.7	24.8	41.1	65.6	16.0	741	70.0
McDougal town	184	167	-9.2	85	91.8	3.5	0.0	0.0	4.7	5.9	40.0	54.5	81.3	0.0	49	73.5
McGehee city	4,204	3,683	-12.4	3,796	49.9	41.8	0.0	2.5	5.8	27.5	15.3	36.2	55.9	16.6	1,641	84.9
McNab town	68	66	-2.9	47	10.6	89.4	0.0	0.0	0.0	23.4	2.1	56.3	46.4	0.0	23	100.0
McNeil city	513	470	-8.4	507	34.3	64.3	0.0	1.4	0.0	22.3	13.4	39.8	76.5	2.4	220	80.9
McRae city	680	669	-1.6	761	92.0	0.3	0.4	0.4	7.0	24.7	21.9	45.0	64.2	9.3	323	78.6
Madison city	793	686	-13.5	1,043	12.9	54.3	0.0	0.0	32.8	41.8	13.5	36.1	60.7	9.6	399	80.7
Magazine city	870	830	-4.6	792	86.5	2.5	0.0	9.6	1.4	19.8	15.3	39.4	67.5	4.0	309	83.2
Magness town	208	211	1.4	234	99.1	0.0	0.0	0.9	0.0	28.6	6.8	53.3	80.2	4.9	90	75.6
Magnet Cove CDP	5	-	-	544	100.0	0.0	0.0	0.0	0.0	6.4	22.1	50.6	46.9	16.3	185	83.2
Magnolia city	11,559	11,467	-0.8	11,562	49.5	45.1	2.2	0.8	2.4	22.1	17.0	28.4	46.7	20.7	3,935	74.3
Malvern city	10,443	10,931	4.7	10,920	63.1	27.8	0.8	4.0	4.3	15.6	16.6	40.4	55.7	10.5	3,911	77.7
Mammoth Spring city	969	960	-0.9	1,015	96.0	0.0	0.0	4.0	0.0	23.7	23.6	43.6	48.6	11.3	468	80.1
Manila city	3,477	3,357	-3.5	3,371	98.8	0.2	0.0	1.0	0.0	21.7	17.4	43.7	57.7	16.5	1,347	76.3
Mansfield city	1,151	1,096	-4.8	1,398	81.6	0.0	0.4	11.2	6.8	29.1	16.2	32.4	62.1	11.6	473	83.3
Marianna city	4,180	3,402	-18.6	3,575	19.0	79.5	0.0	1.1	0.4	22.0	18.6	42.9	66.9	8.2	1,545	72.9
Marie town	80	71	-11.3	54	98.1	1.9	0.0	0.0	0.0	25.9	7.4	45.3	79.4	0.0	28	64.3
Marion city	12,505	12,310	-1.6	12,404	53.3	34.2	1.1	8.6	2.8	27.8	10.1	34.8	39.1	27.4	4,543	93.2
Marked Tree city	2,563	2,420	-5.6	2,319	69.8	17.1	0.4	9.0	3.7	24.2	17.2	38.8	66.3	10.2	922	79.4
Marmaduke city	1,133	1,251	10.4	1,226	91.7	0.0	0.0	0.7	7.6	23.8	17.4	31.9	62.3	9.6	496	85.9
Marshall city	1,394	1,336	-4.2	1,616	91.8	0.7	0.6	3.0	4.0	18.9	25.7	44.8	57.1	10.5	714	75.5
Marvell city	1,169	916	-21.6	1,244	39.8	54.8	0.0	0.0	5.4	26.2	25.3	42.3	59.7	12.4	488	70.1
Maumelle city	17,170	18,199	6.0	18,142	74.5	14.5	1.8	4.0	5.2	22.4	14.7	39.8	18.8	46.4	7,383	93.0
Mayflower city	2,154	2,391	11.0	2,007	95.2	2.5	0.1	0.9	1.2	18.3	16.3	44.1	56.5	18.7	736	86.0
Maynard town	413	417	1.0	509	97.2	0.0	0.0	0.0	2.8	31.6	16.3	31.1	55.1	6.6	198	76.3
Maysville CDP	130	-	-	467	87.8	0.0	0.0	12.2	0.0	18.6	0.0	27.5	95.0	0.0	159	71.1
Melbourne city	1,942	1,868	-3.8	2,002	98.3	0.6	0.0	1.1	0.0	20.3	25.8	45.6	54.9	20.3	836	82.7
Mena city	5,751	5,490	-4.5	5,558	91.5	0.3	0.9	4.6	2.7	23.3	22.3	40.7	49.5	12.9	2,341	85.8
Menifee town	302	317	5.0	96	9.4	90.6	0.0	0.0	0.0	9.4	13.5	50.7	57.0	22.8	45	75.6

1 May be of any race.

Table A. All Places — **Population and Housing**

STATE City, town, township, borough, or CDP (county if applicable)	Population: 2010 census total population	Population: 2019 estimated population	Population: Percent change 2010-2019	Population: ACS total population estimate 2015-2019	Race and Hispanic or Latino origin (percent): White alone, not Hispanic or Latino	Black alone, not Hispanic or Latino	Asian alone, not Hispanic or Latino	All other races or 2 or more races, not Hispanic or Latino	Hispanic or Latino[1]	Age (percent): Under 18 years old	Age 65 years and older	Median age	Educational attainment of persons age 25 and older: Percent High school diploma or less	Percent Bachelor's degree or more	Occupied housing units: Total	Percent with a computer
	1	2	3	4	5	6	7	8	9	10	11	12	13	14	15	16
ARKANSAS—Con.																
Midland town	334	323	-3.3	273	91.2	0.0	0.0	3.7	5.1	22.3	25.6	45.3	65.1	5.7	118	71.2
Midway CDP	1,084	-	-	1,129	96.6	0.0	1.2	2.2	0.0	22.0	23.5	39.8	47.7	7.4	407	88.0
Midway town	391	391	0.0	536	95.5	0.0	0.0	2.4	2.1	32.1	10.3	30.5	48.4	12.5	173	82.1
Mineral Springs city	1,202	1,148	-4.5	1,135	50.8	41.4	0.0	2.2	5.6	20.4	17.4	38.7	52.5	11.5	470	88.7
Minturn town	113	107	-5.3	68	100.0	0.0	0.0	0.0	0.0	17.6	36.8	52.5	78.2	9.1	33	60.6
Mitchellville city	383	339	-11.5	366	0.0	97.3	0.0	2.7	0.0	37.2	25.7	36.2	75.5	9.5	169	77.5
Monette city	1,535	1,595	3.9	1,678	95.9	0.5	0.0	0.8	2.7	14.3	24.1	49.2	63.9	11.1	730	78.4
Monticello city	9,434	9,372	-0.7	9,508	55.1	39.9	0.1	1.3	3.6	21.1	14.5	29.6	40.5	27.7	3,703	87.3
Montrose city	346	304	-12.1	452	23.2	71.2	0.0	1.3	4.2	32.7	12.4	31.5	64.9	7.1	152	80.3
Moorefield town	135	135	0.0	167	89.2	0.0	0.0	7.8	3.0	28.1	24.0	42.8	44.7	34.2	63	76.2
Moro town	219	178	-18.7	213	96.7	1.4	0.0	0.0	1.9	20.2	29.1	42.4	51.6	14.4	89	74.2
Morrilton city	6,786	6,645	-2.1	6,645	70.1	16.9	0.2	4.0	8.8	25.3	17.8	36.5	58.2	14.3	2,748	81.7
Morrison Bluff town	82	78	-4.9	54	100.0	0.0	0.0	0.0	0.0	11.1	18.5	45.5	52.2	19.6	29	93.1
Mountainburg city	621	613	-1.3	579	79.6	0.0	0.0	20.4	0.0	20.2	18.0	41.0	50.3	12.1	252	80.6
Mountain Home city	12,458	12,569	0.9	12,393	94.3	0.1	0.4	1.3	4.0	18.0	28.8	46.9	44.1	17.7	5,851	87.5
Mountain Pine city	757	783	3.4	776	87.0	7.1	0.0	4.3	1.7	23.7	19.5	44.5	67.6	4.3	284	77.1
Mountain View city	2,755	2,863	3.9	2,848	94.2	0.4	1.4	0.5	3.4	10.1	40.7	56.6	55.9	10.8	1,273	74.9
Mount Ida city	1,069	1,005	-6.0	1,101	95.4	0.9	0.0	2.6	1.1	21.3	28.0	48.5	55.4	19.5	428	81.3
Mount Pleasant town	423	415	-1.9	471	96.6	0.0	0.0	0.0	3.4	20.2	27.2	47.2	59.8	8.3	150	73.3
Mount Vernon town	145	149	2.8	166	97.0	0.0	0.0	0.0	3.0	19.9	16.3	48.7	52.0	12.6	54	81.5
Mulberry city	1,650	1,692	2.5	1,599	95.6	0.6	0.0	2.4	1.4	19.0	24.7	45.7	60.3	7.3	718	75.1
Murfreesboro city	1,681	1,586	-5.7	1,904	76.8	14.4	0.3	2.0	6.5	19.8	23.8	44.9	56.3	10.1	769	68.7
Nashville city	4,622	4,386	-5.1	4,431	41.9	35.1	0.5	3.9	18.6	27.9	15.7	34.9	51.8	13.9	1,733	77.6
Natural Steps CDP	426	-	-	692	84.4	13.3	2.3	0.0	0.0	28.2	14.6	44.6	23.6	44.2	228	100.0
Newark city	1,175	1,199	2.0	1,091	94.1	0.0	0.0	2.1	3.8	22.4	22.4	42.9	62.5	7.4	469	75.9
New Blaine CDP	174	-	-	62	100.0	0.0	0.0	0.0	0.0	0.0	48.4	63.9	33.9	14.5	37	100.0
New Edinburg CDP	127	-	-	198	90.9	9.1	0.0	0.0	0.0	31.8	19.2	33.9	60.7	17.8	74	56.8
Newport city	7,885	7,474	-5.2	7,616	68.2	20.2	0.1	7.6	3.9	14.2	16.9	37.0	61.5	9.8	2,261	78.1
Nimmons town	69	64	-7.2	95	90.5	0.0	0.0	5.3	4.2	11.6	11.6	44.4	77.6	6.6	43	88.4
Norfork city	532	536	0.8	494	94.9	0.0	0.2	4.7	0.2	24.1	18.4	46.5	55.3	14.2	205	85.9
Norman town	387	362	-6.5	423	95.0	0.0	0.0	3.5	1.4	35.2	18.9	39.2	56.5	8.6	152	79.6
Norphlet city	846	782	-7.6	612	93.1	3.1	0.0	2.0	1.8	23.4	14.1	42.5	35.4	20.4	241	79.3
North Crossett CDP	3,119	-	-	2,802	81.4	15.0	0.9	2.7	0.0	18.1	17.6	47.1	68.0	4.2	1,022	80.0
North Little Rock city	62,350	65,903	5.7	66,075	45.8	43.8	0.8	3.3	6.3	25.1	13.8	34.2	42.0	27.6	26,688	86.5
Oak Grove town	390	395	1.3	448	84.2	1.6	1.3	12.3	0.7	33.0	20.8	39.5	68.1	9.2	159	73.6
Oak Grove Heights town	886	1,074	21.2	1,165	95.5	0.0	0.0	2.7	1.7	29.6	7.9	32.0	56.8	12.5	389	95.4
Oakhaven town	63	59	-6.3	111	61.3	0.0	0.0	3.6	35.1	48.6	3.6	22.5	38.2	40.0	27	92.6
Oden town	232	215	-7.3	153	95.4	0.0	0.0	2.0	2.6	23.5	28.8	45.9	35.9	26.2	52	98.1
Ogden city	169	155	-8.3	171	86.5	3.5	0.6	1.2	8.2	29.8	12.3	35.5	65.7	12.0	69	82.6
Oil Trough town	275	274	-0.4	222	93.2	4.5	0.0	2.3	0.0	32.0	17.6	36.6	51.2	10.9	79	92.4
O'Kean town	194	197	1.5	332	100.0	0.0	0.0	0.0	0.0	25.9	27.1	37.5	61.2	6.9	132	83.3
Okolona town	147	137	-6.8	136	61.8	38.2	0.0	0.0	0.0	9.6	16.9	48.0	45.0	9.2	74	78.4
Ola city	1,270	1,209	-4.8	1,193	63.9	0.5	0.0	3.5	32.1	17.5	23.8	43.5	68.5	7.1	481	56.1
Omaha town	173	173	0.0	92	100.0	0.0	0.0	0.0	0.0	37.0	14.1	35.6	62.5	12.5	36	75.0
Oppelo city	779	743	-4.6	669	91.6	0.0	0.0	2.7	5.7	28.3	14.9	35.1	49.7	15.2	239	87.9
Osceola city	7,761	6,638	-14.5	6,908	39.6	51.3	0.6	1.7	6.8	28.0	15.0	36.1	56.6	11.7	2,750	77.4
Oxford city	696	679	-2.4	667	97.8	0.0	0.0	2.2	0.0	20.8	13.8	45.1	49.6	11.1	265	77.4
Ozan town	84	81	-3.6	79	46.8	53.2	0.0	0.0	0.0	13.9	29.1	49.4	66.7	14.3	42	90.5
Ozark city	3,705	3,595	-3.0	3,610	96.8	1.7	0.0	0.7	0.8	23.9	22.4	42.3	61.9	9.0	1,539	78.4
Palestine city	678	576	-15.0	596	88.6	8.4	0.0	0.3	2.7	28.7	21.1	39.0	69.2	4.8	243	72.8
Pangburn city	588	579	-1.5	543	95.0	0.0	0.0	0.4	4.6	24.3	20.4	40.9	69.7	5.3	212	75.9
Paragould city	26,319	28,986	10.1	28,568	91.2	2.9	0.5	2.2	3.2	25.4	14.1	35.5	54.0	18.4	10,755	88.2
Paris city	3,558	3,365	-5.4	3,413	85.7	2.2	5.2	4.6	2.2	21.7	21.9	42.9	57.0	14.4	1,418	83.1
Parkdale city	276	252	-8.7	243	10.7	85.6	0.0	0.0	3.7	15.6	16.0	42.0	73.0	12.9	89	46.1
Parkin city	1,101	990	-10.1	673	24.4	57.1	0.0	17.7	0.9	12.9	25.9	48.3	66.5	3.7	312	59.6
Patmos town	64	60	-6.3	117	81.2	0.0	2.6	13.7	2.6	46.2	14.5	33.8	52.4	17.5	40	75.0
Patterson city	454	391	-13.9	437	71.2	23.1	0.0	5.7	0.0	22.0	20.4	42.6	68.7	7.6	207	60.4
Peach Orchard city	135	125	-7.4	118	95.8	0.0	3.4	0.8	0.0	8.5	33.9	55.0	49.0	16.7	62	83.9
Pea Ridge city	4,741	6,211	31.0	5,717	89.3	0.6	0.0	2.2	7.8	29.7	11.8	33.7	53.4	17.5	2,021	88.8
Perla town	247	247	0.0	265	45.3	49.8	0.0	4.9	0.0	27.2	12.5	36.5	64.3	7.6	98	68.4
Perry town	276	281	1.8	307	88.3	0.3	0.0	1.3	10.1	18.9	16.9	45.8	72.9	3.7	97	66.0
Perrytown town	267	259	-3.0	478	49.0	33.9	1.5	6.5	9.2	34.7	10.9	28.2	51.2	14.2	150	80.7
Perryville city	1,466	1,458	-0.5	1,445	94.0	0.5	0.0	2.3	3.2	24.8	17.4	42.3	59.2	13.5	485	80.6
Piggott city	3,868	3,529	-8.8	3,603	94.6	1.3	0.0	1.6	2.5	22.6	21.2	41.0	54.2	14.1	1,589	76.3
Pindall town	110	105	-4.5	168	74.4	0.0	0.0	25.6	0.0	36.9	8.3	31.8	58.7	8.7	55	65.5
Pine Bluff city	49,066	41,474	-15.5	43,091	20.0	76.5	1.1	0.9	1.5	23.2	14.8	35.5	49.6	19.2	16,966	82.5
Pineville town	228	223	-2.2	175	100.0	0.0	0.0	0.0	0.0	26.3	19.4	44.1	57.8	11.0	63	90.5
Piney CDP	4,699	-	-	4,521	82.7	8.3	0.5	0.8	7.8	24.2	13.4	40.6	45.8	14.7	1,977	93.6
Plainview city	611	579	-5.2	605	99.2	0.0	0.0	0.0	0.8	19.7	13.9	46.9	67.0	7.3	238	68.5
Pleasant Plains town	361	364	0.8	287	93.7	0.0	0.7	0.0	5.6	30.7	12.2	34.8	64.0	13.7	105	79.0
Plumerville city	808	772	-4.5	857	61.5	28.2	0.0	0.0	10.3	15.4	17.2	45.4	66.8	15.0	380	79.2
Pocahontas city	6,637	6,645	0.1	6,528	92.1	1.9	0.3	3.4	2.3	25.2	16.9	35.0	54.3	14.1	2,748	83.2
Pollard city	228	203	-11.0	178	100.0	0.0	0.0	0.0	0.0	19.7	23.0	41.5	73.7	7.5	78	79.5
Portia town	437	405	-7.3	580	98.3	0.3	0.0	1.4	0.0	19.1	21.4	44.5	63.8	7.7	248	64.5
Portland city	432	388	-10.2	355	62.8	34.6	0.0	0.8	1.7	16.9	34.4	57.9	34.8	26.7	178	66.9
Pottsville city	2,798	3,327	18.9	3,183	91.8	0.3	0.2	2.5	5.2	23.8	13.3	34.9	51.6	18.3	1,031	85.5
Powhatan town	68	63	-7.4	69	100.0	0.0	0.0	0.0	0.0	20.3	29.0	39.8	50.0	20.0	32	81.3
Poyen town	287	282	-1.7	308	100.0	0.0	0.0	0.0	0.0	26.0	11.0	34.9	50.0	16.8	103	87.4
Prairie Creek CDP	2,066	-	-	2,421	86.5	0.0	2.1	3.1	8.3	17.7	25.1	47.6	32.1	31.8	1,099	90.7
Prairie Grove city	4,428	6,740	52.2	5,845	90.9	1.3	0.5	3.8	3.6	25.1	15.3	37.7	45.3	18.7	2,175	91.6
Prattsville town	304	306	0.7	331	81.3	11.8	0.0	3.9	3.0	35.0	13.9	34.8	65.1	8.5	101	80.2
Prescott city	3,307	2,989	-9.6	3,035	53.5	44.4	0.0	2.1	0.0	23.7	20.1	36.7	53.4	10.0	1,212	78.5
Pyatt town	231	230	-0.4	277	100.0	0.0	0.0	0.0	0.0	30.0	13.0	38.1	47.0	5.5	101	62.4
Quitman city	762	719	-5.6	733	98.0	0.0	0.0	2.0	0.0	26.6	15.1	35.4	60.1	11.2	311	84.6
Ratcliff city	196	183	-6.6	215	96.3	0.0	0.0	0.0	3.7	16.7	34.4	49.4	69.0	7.5	103	79.6
Ravenden town	476	451	-5.3	469	97.9	0.0	0.9	1.3	0.0	22.0	20.3	46.9	63.6	8.7	202	72.8
Ravenden Springs town	123	121	-1.6	173	100.0	0.0	0.0	0.0	0.0	23.1	11.0	46.6	69.4	3.3	69	65.2
Reader CDP	66	-	-	192	17.7	82.3	0.0	0.0	0.0	0.0	17.7	55.0	56.3	13.3	93	26.9
Rector city	1,965	1,732	-11.9	1,960	97.3	0.0	0.0	2.2	0.5	25.7	22.0	42.0	53.5	10.4	805	75.8
Redfield city	1,292	1,514	17.2	1,614	84.8	8.9	0.6	1.8	3.9	25.3	12.7	38.4	55.4	18.5	640	88.4
Reed town	172	147	-14.5	193	11.4	88.6	0.0	0.0	0.0	13.0	17.6	43.8	77.2	4.8	120	79.2
Reyno city	456	451	-1.1	406	99.3	0.0	0.7	0.0	0.0	19.0	14.0	30.8	51.2	18.6	180	71.7

1 May be of any race.

Table A. All Places — **Population and Housing**

STATE City, town, township, borough, or CDP (county if applicable)	Population				Race and Hispanic or Latino origin (percent)					Age (percent)			Educational attainment of persons age 25 and older		Occupied housing units	
	2010 census total population	2019 estimated population	Percent change 2010-2019	ACS total population estimate 2015-2019	White alone, not Hispanic or Latino	Black alone, not Hispanic or Latino	Asian alone, not Hispanic or Latino	All other races or 2 or more races, not Hispanic or Latino	Hispanic or Latino[1]	Under 18 years old	Age 65 years and older	Median age	Percent High school diploma or less	Percent Bachelor's degree or more	Total	Percent with a computer
	1	2	3	4	5	6	7	8	9	10	11	12	13	14	15	16
ARKANSAS—Con.																
Rison city	1,348	1,212	-10.1	1,317	61.3	37.9	0.0	0.8	0.0	24.3	21.4	36.8	54.7	21.3	498	80.5
Rockport city	700	704	0.6	894	98.3	0.0	0.0	1.7	0.0	23.8	20.2	48.4	56.8	15.0	303	85.1
Rockwell CDP	3,780	-	-	4,744	92.2	5.1	0.0	0.5	2.2	22.1	19.2	42.4	32.1	25.6	1,910	95.4
Roe town	116	96	-17.2	97	96.9	3.1	0.0	0.0	0.0	17.5	30.9	59.4	44.7	26.3	49	69.4
Rogers city	56,109	68,669	22.4	66,344	58.7	1.6	2.3	3.6	33.8	28.0	9.9	33.1	47.0	30.4	24,053	92.4
Roland CDP	746	-	-	590	96.6	2.2	0.0	0.0	1.2	15.8	35.9	51.0	42.6	27.6	266	90.2
Rondo town	201	166	-17.4	156	27.6	69.9	0.0	2.6	0.0	5.1	48.1	64.3	85.3	6.6	83	44.6
Rose Bud town	490	488	-0.4	521	91.6	0.0	0.0	6.5	1.9	22.8	17.7	41.3	59.9	12.7	205	77.6
Rosston town	254	237	-6.7	414	22.7	77.3	0.0	0.0	0.0	41.5	10.1	30.2	52.4	16.6	141	64.5
Rudy town	149	149	0.0	66	95.5	0.0	0.0	0.0	4.5	27.3	16.7	43.5	71.4	0.0	25	100.0
Russell town	220	217	-1.4	260	92.3	0.8	0.0	2.3	4.6	25.0	21.5	43.8	75.5	12.5	125	68.0
Russellville city	28,106	29,175	3.8	29,193	72.4	5.8	1.9	4.1	15.8	21.9	12.0	28.0	44.1	27.6	10,184	92.3
Rye CDP	146	-	-	112	100.0	0.0	0.0	0.0	0.0	42.0	7.1	35.0	29.8	54.4	46	69.6
St. Charles town	229	212	-7.4	337	84.9	0.0	0.0	0.9	14.2	24.9	15.4	38.3	55.9	20.0	118	87.3
St. Francis city	252	228	-9.5	235	98.3	1.3	0.0	0.4	0.0	23.0	23.8	43.8	72.7	6.2	99	78.8
St. Joe town	131	125	-4.6	243	96.7	0.0	0.0	3.3	0.0	30.0	8.6	26.3	38.7	31.5	82	89.0
St. Paul town	99	113	14.1	112	87.5	0.0	0.0	0.0	12.5	20.5	42.9	62.2	43.4	27.7	49	79.6
Salem city	1,643	1,675	1.9	2,033	85.7	0.4	0.0	4.2	9.6	21.9	22.7	43.9	55.6	11.7	818	82.8
Salem CDP	2,607	-	-	1,993	98.5	0.0	1.5	0.0	0.0	17.4	20.6	48.8	39.1	17.0	719	87.1
Salesville city	448	460	2.7	374	87.4	0.0	0.0	1.9	10.7	21.7	23.0	47.8	50.4	12.9	146	83.6
Scott CDP	72	-	-	24	66.7	33.3	0.0	0.0	0.0	0.0	33.3	61.3	33.3	0.0	24	100.0
Scranton city	226	230	1.8	241	95.4	0.0	0.0	4.6	0.0	29.9	10.4	31.2	52.1	14.9	93	76.3
Searcy city	22,849	23,660	3.5	23,767	80.3	9.0	1.3	3.6	5.7	22.4	14.8	28.5	42.5	33.5	8,205	88.9
Sedgwick town	177	167	-5.6	221	85.5	0.0	0.9	8.1	5.4	26.2	17.2	31.7	79.0	5.6	81	82.7
Shannon Hills city	3,122	3,990	27.8	3,837	58.0	35.5	0.0	4.4	2.1	26.7	8.3	32.3	31.4	31.8	1,200	96.8
Sheridan city	4,616	4,929	6.8	4,846	95.2	3.0	0.0	0.0	1.8	25.2	18.2	38.4	45.3	28.5	1,884	90.6
Sherrill town	88	73	-17.0	203	23.2	20.2	0.0	0.0	56.7	53.2	6.9	15.6	80.0	8.4	42	59.5
Sherwood city	29,619	31,436	6.1	31,004	71.1	19.8	1.6	3.4	4.0	22.5	16.6	39.1	33.3	30.8	12,337	89.4
Shirley town	291	275	-5.5	358	95.5	0.0	0.0	0.0	4.5	18.7	22.9	46.2	57.3	16.4	146	80.1
Sidney town	187	189	1.1	179	82.7	0.0	0.0	0.0	17.3	25.1	15.6	42.4	76.8	2.4	77	81.8
Siloam Springs city	15,108	17,101	13.2	16,715	60.1	0.9	1.9	14.7	22.4	28.8	11.2	28.6	49.2	23.1	5,382	91.2
Smackover city	1,863	1,688	-9.4	1,715	66.2	31.4	0.0	1.2	1.2	22.9	14.8	43.6	50.0	16.8	728	73.4
Smithville town	74	69	-6.8	96	100.0	0.0	0.0	0.0	0.0	18.8	9.4	29.9	50.8	23.1	39	76.9
South Lead Hill town	102	98	-3.9	151	94.0	0.0	0.0	6.0	0.0	26.5	6.6	44.1	70.8	2.8	66	83.3
Southside city	3,902	3,989	2.2	3,952	89.7	3.8	0.0	2.5	4.0	23.7	18.4	41.6	54.5	14.8	1,540	90.9
Sparkman city	433	375	-13.4	465	61.3	36.1	0.0	0.4	2.2	19.4	28.0	53.6	72.4	13.7	183	59.0
Springdale city	70,800	81,125	14.6	79,598	47.2	2.6	2.0	10.5	37.6	30.7	9.9	31.7	54.6	20.3	26,547	90.4
Springtown town	87	97	11.5	149	43.0	0.0	0.0	52.3	4.7	12.1	16.1	46.2	87.2	3.7	44	100.0
Stamps city	1,690	1,465	-13.3	1,832	39.1	56.7	0.9	2.2	1.1	20.7	21.2	38.8	66.3	12.5	657	68.6
Star City city	2,275	2,030	-10.8	1,628	85.9	11.1	0.0	0.6	2.3	20.8	30.0	47.5	57.1	12.0	686	69.0
Staves CDP	116	-	-	144	100.0	0.0	0.0	0.0	0.0	11.1	46.5	58.5	70.6	0.0	64	56.3
Stephens city	889	787	-11.5	901	25.6	72.3	0.0	2.1	0.0	19.3	31.7	52.8	66.7	8.5	376	61.2
Strawberry town	296	280	-5.4	264	93.2	0.0	0.0	6.4	0.4	25.4	33.0	40.0	63.7	7.1	125	68.8
Strong city	555	504	-9.2	281	42.7	53.7	0.0	1.1	2.5	9.6	33.1	53.8	82.8	4.5	159	37.7
Stuttgart city	9,328	8,490	-9.0	8,720	60.0	36.3	0.1	1.1	2.5	23.4	18.9	38.7	58.0	14.9	3,607	84.0
Subiaco town	575	558	-3.0	474	86.9	3.0	3.6	2.5	4.0	27.6	19.6	42.7	50.7	22.5	157	94.9
Success town	149	133	-10.7	107	100.0	0.0	0.0	0.0	0.0	14.0	20.6	49.9	72.1	8.1	57	78.9
Sulphur Rock town	455	467	2.6	691	93.1	1.3	0.0	2.6	3.0	29.4	14.2	34.2	55.5	13.2	246	80.1
Sulphur Springs city	519	529	1.9	464	95.7	0.2	0.2	3.9	0.0	16.8	19.8	40.3	72.8	15.7	229	63.8
Sulphur Springs CDP	1,101	-	-	1,189	80.7	13.9	0.0	4.8	0.7	27.0	24.6	46.3	64.1	6.9	467	78.8
Summit city	606	590	-2.6	464	98.3	0.0	0.0	0.0	1.7	28.7	8.0	32.8	64.1	1.7	165	81.2
Sunset town	209	190	-9.1	222	0.9	92.8	0.0	6.3	0.0	7.7	11.3	38.5	65.9	5.3	83	67.5
Sweet Home CDP	849	-	-	1,037	11.8	78.6	0.0	0.0	9.6	28.4	12.2	32.8	48.8	8.7	259	73.7
Swifton city	807	734	-9.0	942	94.2	0.1	0.0	5.7	0.0	31.5	15.7	37.6	58.3	14.3	374	80.2
Taylor city	623	567	-9.0	675	97.8	1.6	0.0	0.4	0.1	36.1	10.1	30.3	61.9	13.5	201	78.1
Texarkana city	29,903	29,657	-0.8	29,901	58.2	33.4	0.2	3.8	4.5	22.9	17.2	39.5	49.4	18.4	11,404	84.0
Thornton city	396	383	-3.3	595	50.6	42.7	0.0	6.7	0.0	37.0	16.3	33.2	57.1	14.9	162	69.8
Tillar city	229	212	-7.4	228	83.8	10.1	0.0	1.8	4.4	22.4	21.5	53.7	65.4	11.7	91	84.6
Tinsman town	45	44	-2.2	83	98.8	0.0	0.0	1.2	0.0	13.3	14.5	50.8	83.1	4.6	31	64.5
Tollette town	257	250	-2.7	244	2.5	95.5	0.0	2.0	0.0	9.0	31.6	53.3	57.6	16.3	108	72.2
Tontitown city	2,428	4,358	79.5	3,677	80.1	0.8	0.1	4.9	14.1	23.3	19.5	41.0	38.6	36.3	1,399	91.3
Traskwood city	518	548	5.8	350	98.6	0.0	0.0	0.0	1.4	14.3	28.3	52.3	65.2	3.7	147	70.7
Trumann city	7,304	6,969	-4.6	7,059	85.4	5.1	0.0	5.6	3.9	28.9	14.6	36.8	61.9	13.1	2,782	83.1
Tuckerman city	1,869	1,682	-10.0	2,035	87.3	1.2	0.0	9.4	2.2	28.4	15.1	36.0	57.0	12.6	857	75.1
Tull town	459	462	0.7	414	94.0	2.9	0.0	1.7	1.4	22.0	18.8	47.5	59.5	11.4	177	71.2
Tumbling Shoals CDP	978	-	-	985	98.3	0.0	0.0	0.0	1.7	17.3	30.3	46.6	57.5	18.3	445	85.8
Tupelo town	186	169	-9.1	74	100.0	0.0	0.0	0.0	0.0	1.4	27.0	54.5	75.0	10.0	41	75.6
Turrell city	610	555	-9.0	564	13.8	69.0	0.0	17.2	0.0	28.2	13.8	38.9	64.2	6.3	243	81.1
Twin Groves town	322	337	4.7	345	38.0	60.9	0.0	0.3	0.9	14.5	24.6	51.3	60.4	5.1	136	70.6
Tyronza city	761	721	-5.3	975	91.4	3.5	0.2	3.8	1.1	29.1	14.1	34.8	62.2	16.1	376	89.6
Ulm town	170	155	-8.8	233	97.4	2.6	0.0	0.0	0.0	17.6	18.5	33.9	44.1	13.6	120	85.0
Valley Springs town	167	169	1.2	231	100.0	0.0	0.0	0.0	0.0	17.3	18.2	41.9	56.4	7.4	81	88.9
Van Buren city	22,811	23,683	3.8	23,413	74.8	2.5	4.2	4.7	13.9	26.8	14.2	33.7	51.6	18.0	8,990	84.5
Vandervoort town	87	86	-1.1	143	90.9	0.0	0.0	0.0	9.1	48.3	0.7	24.1	59.1	21.2	41	90.2
Victoria town	37	32	-13.5	13	76.9	0.0	0.0	0.0	23.1	23.1	38.5	61.5	100.0	0.0	4	25.0
Vilonia city	3,815	4,623	21.2	4,469	98.6	0.9	0.0	0.5	0.0	30.4	10.7	34.2	39.2	21.5	1,432	92.8
Viola town	353	357	1.1	296	99.3	0.0	0.0	0.7	0.0	23.0	23.6	41.3	55.0	5.2	136	82.4
Wabbaseka town	254	218	-14.2	238	18.9	79.0	0.0	0.0	2.1	23.9	16.4	50.6	51.0	16.6	118	60.2
Waldenburg town	61	58	-4.9	48	75.0	0.0	0.0	25.0	0.0	20.8	35.4	56.3	93.5	0.0	21	76.2
Waldo city	1,395	1,265	-9.3	1,208	39.1	59.9	0.0	0.0	1.1	26.1	19.9	38.5	63.1	18.3	558	67.9
Waldron city	3,652	3,374	-7.6	3,405	82.1	0.1	0.9	3.3	13.6	29.0	18.3	35.4	64.2	7.4	1,328	71.8
Walnut Ridge city	5,337	5,062	-5.2	5,098	93.0	2.8	0.1	0.9	3.2	24.1	17.7	34.3	46.2	17.0	1,754	85.7
Ward city	4,076	5,358	31.5	5,060	88.8	1.6	0.9	4.1	4.5	31.3	4.0	28.5	50.9	17.4	1,703	96.3
Warren city	5,993	5,587	-6.8	5,646	34.9	43.5	0.1	0.1	21.3	25.5	17.1	38.4	66.4	11.1	2,153	80.7
Washington city	178	168	-5.6	159	39.6	60.4	0.0	0.0	0.0	13.8	30.8	50.0	53.8	21.5	72	54.2
Watson city	212	180	-15.1	195	74.4	25.6	0.0	0.0	0.0	14.4	41.0	58.7	75.2	11.2	115	76.5
Weiner city	721	674	-6.5	823	92.8	0.4	0.0	3.3	3.5	28.4	16.4	35.0	55.0	18.0	337	87.2
Weldon town	75	68	-9.3	94	90.4	0.0	0.0	9.6	0.0	6.4	27.7	59.5	81.7	6.1	47	70.2
West Crossett CDP	1,256	-	-	1,160	61.2	35.3	0.6	0.3	2.6	25.0	20.4	44.3	66.6	10.1	477	84.1
Western Grove town	385	361	-6.2	587	98.6	0.0	0.0	1.4	0.0	29.8	19.8	34.2	59.9	8.3	186	76.3
West Fork city	2,370	2,655	12.0	2,626	94.8	0.1	1.0	2.6	1.5	27.2	20.0	39.8	41.6	31.4	984	87.6
West Memphis city	26,245	24,402	-7.0	24,823	35.5	57.8	0.5	4.8	1.5	28.0	13.5	33.3	55.4	14.8	9,939	80.4

1 May be of any race.

Table A. All Places — **Population and Housing**

STATE City, town, township, borough, or CDP (county if applicable)	Population: 2010 census total population	Population: 2019 estimated population	Population: Percent change 2010-2019	Population: ACS total population estimate 2015-2019	Race and Hispanic or Latino origin (percent): White alone, not Hispanic or Latino	Black alone, not Hispanic or Latino	Asian alone, not Hispanic or Latino	All other races or 2 or more races, not Hispanic or Latino	Hispanic or Latino[1]	Age (percent): Under 18 years old	Age 65 years and older	Median age	Educational attainment of persons age 25 and older: Percent High school diploma or less	Percent Bachelor's degree or more	Occupied housing units: Total	Percent with a computer
	1	2	3	4	5	6	7	8	9	10	11	12	13	14	15	16
ARKANSAS—Con.																
West Point town	179	178	-0.6	159	84.9	13.2	0.0	1.9	0.0	12.6	18.2	46.6	63.7	4.8	44	86.4
Wheatley city	351	298	-15.1	371	92.7	4.0	0.0	0.0	3.2	24.3	26.7	47.6	64.9	7.1	154	85.7
Whelen Springs town	92	85	-7.6	61	63.9	0.0	0.0	0.0	36.1	45.9	0.0	25.3	61.3	0.0	17	58.8
White Hall city	5,534	4,963	-10.3	5,078	61.9	23.3	2.7	5.1	7.0	29.2	15.8	35.1	42.3	25.6	1,802	94.0
Wickes town	754	747	-0.9	1,033	39.9	0.4	0.0	7.1	52.7	43.1	4.5	26.5	65.9	8.1	302	86.1
Widener town	285	246	-13.7	257	28.4	53.3	5.1	5.1	8.2	21.4	17.9	51.2	65.8	8.0	120	75.8
Wiederkehr Village city	51	46	-9.8	33	100.0	0.0	0.0	0.0	0.0	21.2	0.0	54.1	19.2	53.8	17	100.0
Williford town	82	80	-2.4	57	96.5	0.0	0.0	0.0	3.5	10.5	45.6	61.6	71.4	0.0	35	60.0
Willisville town	152	141	-7.2	270	49.3	50.0	0.0	0.7	0.0	30.7	12.2	52.3	64.1	9.8	130	86.2
Wilmar city	509	485	-4.7	300	11.7	88.3	0.0	0.0	0.0	13.7	18.3	55.3	66.9	8.1	150	61.3
Wilmot city	550	492	-10.5	447	18.6	81.4	0.0	0.0	0.0	29.3	17.7	42.8	75.9	4.7	135	60.0
Wilson city	910	815	-10.4	1,017	70.7	25.0	0.4	3.4	0.5	23.8	16.1	37.5	52.6	23.1	355	86.2
Wilton city	374	347	-7.2	274	52.2	35.8	0.0	1.8	10.2	10.9	28.8	51.1	80.2	0.0	133	71.4
Winchester town	164	159	-3.0	181	9.9	89.0	0.0	1.1	0.0	24.3	20.4	43.3	76.5	11.3	71	57.7
Winslow city	389	424	9.0	398	90.7	1.5	0.3	5.8	1.8	23.6	19.8	42.8	63.1	10.9	157	78.3
Winthrop city	192	180	-6.3	127	92.9	0.0	0.0	1.6	5.5	19.7	26.0	46.1	57.0	4.3	49	95.9
Woodlawn CDP	209	-	-	138	87.0	0.0	0.0	0.0	13.0	18.1	33.3	58.7	70.9	10.7	58	77.6
Woodson CDP	403	-	-	366	18.3	81.7	0.0	0.0	0.0	16.1	10.1	37.6	64.2	7.8	141	84.4
Wooster town	862	1,113	29.1	1,188	89.1	1.3	0.8	6.9	1.9	34.3	10.6	34.5	40.7	26.9	352	94.0
Wrightsville city	2,115	2,131	0.8	1,732	39.0	55.9	0.0	1.2	4.0	5.0	9.5	36.8	74.1	2.2	276	57.2
Wynne city	8,387	7,749	-7.6	7,934	64.4	29.3	0.0	4.3	1.9	24.8	16.9	38.5	51.5	17.3	3,104	83.0
Yarborough Landing CDP	487	-	-	401	94.8	0.0	0.0	5.2	0.0	15.5	53.1	69.5	40.7	33.6	206	94.2
Yellville city	1,198	1,156	-3.5	1,155	85.2	6.1	0.0	3.1	5.6	29.1	19.5	39.2	49.0	6.5	416	78.4
Zinc town	97	101	4.1	81	96.3	0.0	0.0	3.7	0.0	21.0	16.0	40.8	69.5	3.4	32	87.5
CALIFORNIA	37,254,519	39,512,223	6.1	39,283,497	37.2	5.5	14.3	4.0	39.0	23.0	14.0	36.5	37.2	33.9	13,044,266	93.0
Acalanes Ridge CDP	1,137	-	-	1,134	93.3	0.0	3.1	1.7	1.9	31.8	14.0	44.8	0.0	82.7	410	100.0
Acampo CDP	341	-	-	204	90.2	0.0	0.0	0.0	9.8	25.0	53.9	72.1	37.3	28.1	88	100.0
Acton CDP	7,596	-	-	7,232	74.4	0.5	2.4	1.8	20.9	18.9	16.6	49.2	27.4	27.3	2,584	95.2
Adelanto city	31,760	34,049	7.2	33,660	11.8	17.7	1.6	3.0	65.8	34.6	5.6	27.5	61.9	6.0	7,695	92.2
Adin CDP	272	-	-	171	69.6	0.0	0.0	29.2	1.2	5.8	43.3	58.1	48.1	33.3	78	66.7
Agoura Hills city	20,336	20,222	-0.6	20,533	74.3	2.2	8.6	4.3	10.6	21.4	16.0	44.4	15.6	59.5	7,377	96.9
Agua Dulce CDP	3,342	-	-	3,742	71.4	0.0	2.4	3.6	22.6	20.1	17.8	46.1	29.3	27.4	1,118	92.5
Aguanga CDP	1,128	-	-	805	75.3	3.1	0.0	6.0	15.7	27.8	19.0	46.3	39.4	18.8	300	100.0
Ahwahnee CDP	2,246	-	-	2,513	89.8	0.0	0.0	0.9	9.3	12.6	30.8	50.7	31.5	25.5	869	93.9
Airport CDP	1,964	-	-	1,479	15.8	1.2	0.0	0.4	82.6	28.9	2.8	29.8	70.8	4.4	486	81.7
Alameda city	73,812	77,624	5.2	78,522	42.7	7.2	29.9	7.4	12.8	20.3	15.7	40.6	20.7	54.7	30,418	95.6
Alamo CDP	14,570	-	-	14,905	80.2	0.3	8.7	3.9	7.0	22.9	24.0	49.7	6.1	74.2	5,156	96.8
Albany city	18,515	19,696	6.4	19,804	44.1	2.9	29.1	8.9	15.0	26.0	12.0	36.5	12.7	72.9	7,444	96.4
Albion CDP	168	-	-	254	45.3	0.0	17.3	24.4	13.0	0.0	11.8	22.1	41.3	28.8	55	100.0
Alderpoint CDP	186	-	-	156	71.8	0.0	0.0	8.3	19.9	0.0	0.0	53.4	46.2	0.0	59	79.7
Alhambra city	83,119	83,750	0.8	84,647	8.9	2.0	50.9	2.3	35.9	16.9	18.0	40.9	40.7	35.5	29,771	92.3
Alhambra Valley CDP	924	-	-	783	84.4	0.0	0.0	8.8	6.8	25.0	23.0	48.1	17.8	54.0	273	100.0
Aliso Viejo city	47,674	50,887	6.7	50,663	58.8	2.3	15.4	5.3	18.1	24.6	9.0	37.8	14.0	56.2	18,515	98.1
Alleghany CDP	58	-	-	78	100.0	0.0	0.0	0.0	0.0	0.0	39.7	59.6	71.8	0.0	47	53.2
Allendale CDP	1,506	-	-	1,388	78.5	14.0	0.0	0.0	7.4	18.4	21.9	54.4	29.5	29.7	496	96.4
Allensworth CDP	471	-	-	575	0.0	2.6	0.3	0.3	96.7	30.1	8.9	25.5	88.2	1.4	136	66.9
Almanor CDP	-	-	-	-	-	-	-	-	-	-	-	-	-	-	-	-
Alondra Park CDP	8,592	-	-	8,272	19.3	5.9	16.1	3.4	55.3	23.8	14.1	36.5	47.2	26.1	2,692	94.2
Alpaugh CDP	1,026	-	-	1,145	10.0	0.0	0.5	4.0	85.4	40.3	3.2	24.9	83.3	0.0	282	72.7
Alpine CDP	14,236	-	-	14,878	81.5	1.5	1.7	3.4	11.9	23.3	17.5	40.8	23.0	35.6	5,342	97.3
Alpine Village CDP	114	-	-	101	100.0	0.0	0.0	0.0	0.0	16.8	12.9	42.6	26.8	22.5	41	87.8
Alta CDP	610	-	-	566	87.1	0.7	3.9	1.8	6.5	12.7	33.4	56.6	24.9	27.8	233	91.0
Altadena CDP	42,777	-	-	44,850	39.7	21.6	6.3	4.6	27.7	19.6	18.4	44.3	26.4	45.3	15,265	92.7
Alta Sierra CDP	6,911	-	-	7,280	86.6	0.7	0.5	6.1	6.2	20.3	28.1	49.2	22.9	32.1	2,860	94.4
Alto CDP	711	-	-	611	87.4	0.0	2.5	1.3	8.8	19.5	5.6	46.9	5.1	73.6	232	100.0
Alturas city	2,827	2,563	-9.3	2,567	75.2	3.2	0.4	3.4	17.9	21.5	17.5	41.3	45.2	9.2	1,143	77.8
Alum Rock CDP	15,536	-	-	11,551	8.9	1.2	16.0	2.3	71.7	24.6	12.0	32.9	58.6	16.2	2,676	95.7
Amador City city	182	190	4.4	167	66.5	0.0	0.0	12.6	21.0	22.2	13.2	39.1	31.7	26.7	74	87.8
American Canyon city	19,560	20,475	4.7	20,261	21.4	7.6	36.2	6.8	28.0	25.7	12.1	37.9	33.8	29.8	5,296	96.5
Amesti CDP	3,478	-	-	3,163	30.5	0.0	1.5	2.9	65.1	23.0	10.7	30.6	51.6	15.5	822	98.3
Anaheim city	336,109	350,365	4.2	349,964	24.2	2.5	16.6	2.5	54.3	24.0	11.6	34.5	46.5	25.5	101,658	93.8
Anchor Bay CDP	340	-	-	352	90.1	0.0	0.0	0.0	9.9	0.0	73.6	69.2	13.4	32.1	181	100.0
Anderson city	9,968	10,630	6.6	10,407	74.7	1.5	3.4	7.1	13.2	26.0	14.0	34.7	47.2	12.6	4,048	86.1
Angels city	3,812	3,956	3.8	3,875	83.4	0.0	0.4	7.1	9.2	15.1	31.4	54.5	27.8	26.1	1,842	80.9
Angwin CDP	3,051	-	-	3,179	45.7	9.2	15.3	4.4	25.4	10.3	9.5	25.2	25.1	40.9	735	96.5
Antelope CDP	45,770	-	-	48,398	59.1	9.0	11.3	5.9	14.6	29.6	8.5	32.9	37.5	24.7	14,453	97.9
Antioch city	102,745	111,502	8.5	111,200	27.8	21.1	11.4	6.6	33.2	24.8	12.2	36.0	40.2	20.9	34,028	94.0
Anza CDP	3,014	-	-	3,076	75.0	0.0	6.0	5.4	13.6	25.2	15.5	41.5	41.2	18.6	1,015	80.0
Apple Valley town	69,146	73,453	6.2	72,726	47.7	8.4	2.3	3.4	38.1	28.0	16.7	36.7	44.8	17.9	23,842	93.7
Aptos CDP	6,220	-	-	6,387	78.3	0.5	3.7	1.3	16.2	14.6	22.4	51.5	10.4	57.5	2,498	94.9
Aptos Hills-Larkin Valley CDP	2,381	-	-	2,251	68.8	0.0	0.7	5.3	25.2	9.3	30.5	56.5	35.0	41.6	828	100.0
Arbuckle CDP	3,028	-	-	3,809	20.7	0.0	0.0	3.1	76.2	29.9	9.0	30.7	66.0	9.8	1,031	84.9
Arcadia city	56,303	57,939	2.9	58,152	22.1	1.9	61.5	3.4	11.1	22.2	19.1	43.7	22.1	54.8	19,520	95.4
Arcata city	17,410	18,431	5.9	18,178	68.7	2.1	3.9	8.4	16.8	10.0	11.3	26.4	21.6	48.6	7,155	92.7
Arden-Arcade CDP	92,186	-	-	102,864	56.2	9.7	6.2	7.6	20.3	23.3	15.9	36.9	33.4	34.8	42,503	93.9
Armona CDP	4,156	-	-	4,407	15.3	6.9	4.1	3.6	70.2	33.2	10.3	27.5	57.6	9.9	1,197	93.7
Arnold CDP	3,843	-	-	2,291	93.1	0.0	1.4	1.0	4.5	9.6	42.6	61.0	34.7	26.8	1,075	90.2
Aromas CDP	2,650	-	-	2,479	62.4	0.0	1.2	1.3	35.2	18.6	12.8	43.2	26.0	30.4	817	92.7
Arroyo Grande city	17,275	17,976	4.1	18,033	76.5	1.0	4.2	4.1	14.2	19.2	21.8	44.6	30.5	34.2	7,026	92.0
Artesia city	16,522	16,601	0.5	16,758	15.2	5.1	36.0	3.8	39.9	20.2	15.4	38.3	44.7	28.1	4,460	89.9
Artois CDP	295	-	-	311	100.0	0.0	0.0	0.0	0.0	34.7	34.1	40.4	55.5	2.6	108	76.9
Arvin city	19,304	21,851	13.2	21,249	4.3	0.4	0.7	0.2	94.4	36.7	5.2	25.3	83.9	1.9	4,864	81.9
Ashland CDP	21,925	-	-	24,430	11.4	13.9	24.0	5.4	45.4	24.4	8.7	34.2	51.1	20.1	7,695	90.3
Aspen Springs CDP	65	-	-	23	100.0	0.0	0.0	0.0	0.0	0.0	65.2	0.0	0.0	0.0	8	100.0
Atascadero city	28,306	30,075	6.2	30,130	75.5	0.8	1.7	3.6	18.4	21.6	15.6	37.7	28.7	31.8	11,621	94.7
Atherton town	6,919	7,137	3.2	7,168	69.3	0.8	20.7	4.8	4.4	22.3	22.4	47.4	6.1	81.9	2,215	97.6
Atwater city	28,215	29,559	4.8	29,296	32.5	3.8	4.5	2.7	56.5	29.8	11.5	31.6	51.4	14.0	9,161	93.6
Auberry CDP	2,369	-	-	2,009	80.3	0.8	1.2	2.3	15.3	22.4	28.1	50.4	30.2	20.1	837	80.8
Auburn city	13,312	14,195	6.6	14,011	83.4	0.4	1.4	4.5	10.3	17.7	22.8	48.5	22.4	37.6	6,152	92.8

1 May be of any race.

Table A. All Places — **Population and Housing**

STATE City, town, township, borough, or CDP (county if applicable)	Population				Race and Hispanic or Latino origin (percent)					Age (percent)			Educational attainment of persons age 25 and older		Occupied housing units	
	2010 census total population	2019 estimated population	Percent change 2010-2019	ACS total population estimate 2015-2019	White alone, not Hispanic or Latino	Black alone, not Hispanic or Latino	Asian alone, not Hispanic or Latino	All other races or 2 or more races, not Hispanic or Latino	Hispanic or Latino[1]	Under 18 years old	Age 65 years and older	Median age	Percent High school diploma or less	Percent Bachelor's degree or more	Total	Percent with a computer
	1	2	3	4	5	6	7	8	9	10	11	12	13	14	15	16
CALIFORNIA—Con.																
Auburn Lake Trails CDP	3,426	-	-	3,664	94.4	0.0	0.4	2.5	2.6	18.0	22.9	51.6	24.2	32.4	1,454	98.2
August CDP	8,390	-	-	8,405	18.0	5.9	3.4	1.4	71.4	35.7	5.5	26.1	77.5	2.1	2,190	80.5
Avalon city	3,728	3,681	-1.3	3,731	43.3	0.1	0.1	1.3	55.2	26.6	14.7	42.1	38.5	22.7	1,487	95.3
Avenal city	15,504	13,496	-13.0	12,961	9.8	3.2	0.2	1.1	85.7	31.0	5.3	29.1	77.8	3.2	2,489	87.7
Avery CDP	646	-	-	561	94.5	0.0	0.0	0.0	5.5	21.6	34.8	44.2	31.8	25.2	212	85.8
Avila Beach CDP	1,627	-	-	1,311	91.0	0.0	4.6	0.0	4.4	4.4	47.4	63.7	32.1	32.9	731	94.5
Avocado Heights CDP	15,411	-	-	15,426	6.8	0.5	13.5	0.5	78.7	20.0	15.5	38.6	53.4	16.6	3,921	92.7
Azusa city	46,574	49,974	7.3	49,753	19.1	3.2	12.4	2.2	63.1	21.5	9.8	29.8	46.4	24.0	12,811	94.7
Baker CDP	735	-	-	541	18.7	0.0	4.1	0.4	76.9	31.8	3.7	29.2	77.3	1.0	188	86.7
Bakersfield city	347,817	384,145	10.4	377,917	32.5	7.2	7.3	2.7	50.2	29.9	10.0	30.8	45.8	21.9	117,050	92.8
Baldwin Park city	75,397	75,251	-0.2	75,892	3.9	1.3	19.2	1.1	74.5	23.7	12.1	35.0	63.5	13.2	17,988	93.2
Ballard CDP	467	-	-	529	79.2	0.0	0.8	0.0	20.0	13.6	15.7	48.6	26.1	29.5	169	96.4
Ballico CDP	406	-	-	538	46.8	0.0	9.3	2.0	41.8	18.0	4.5	32.7	55.8	8.7	182	97.8
Bangor CDP	646	-	-	429	89.0	0.0	0.0	6.5	4.4	12.4	26.8	58.3	35.4	18.4	162	88.9
Banning city	29,592	31,221	5.5	31,072	36.0	7.8	4.5	4.7	47.0	22.7	27.4	41.5	52.0	15.3	10,991	87.7
Barstow city	22,750	23,915	5.1	23,899	25.3	17.7	2.2	9.0	45.9	31.9	11.6	30.1	52.0	9.2	8,312	86.5
Bass Lake CDP	527	-	-	449	90.0	0.0	0.0	10.0	0.0	6.9	40.8	62.3	24.1	38.1	204	77.9
Bay Point CDP	21,349	-	-	25,808	12.2	9.8	9.4	4.4	64.2	27.5	8.0	32.4	59.7	12.0	6,917	92.3
Bayview CDP	1,754	-	-	1,862	44.7	6.4	17.1	0.0	31.8	18.6	17.6	36.6	43.3	21.2	587	92.7
Bayview CDP	2,510	-	-	2,811	78.3	1.1	1.8	8.9	9.9	24.3	12.5	40.4	41.2	16.2	986	89.4
Beale AFB CDP	1,319	-	-	1,020	65.6	1.8	4.0	6.6	22.1	38.1	0.0	23.6	13.1	34.2	335	100.0
Bear Creek CDP	290	-	-	148	57.4	0.0	0.0	0.0	42.6	10.1	15.5	48.1	56.3	0.0	61	85.2
Bear Valley CDP	121	-	-	59	100.0	0.0	0.0	0.0	0.0	23.7	16.9	44.9	13.3	71.1	26	100.0
Bear Valley CDP	125	-	-	197	55.8	0.0	0.0	3.0	41.1	55.8	9.1	15.5	9.2	16.1	68	60.3
Bear Valley Springs CDP	5,172	-	-	5,292	82.5	1.2	2.4	3.2	10.7	17.7	32.9	56.7	19.7	34.8	2,304	95.7
Beaumont city	36,867	51,063	38.5	47,144	33.6	8.7	8.4	2.8	46.5	29.5	13.5	34.5	39.1	26.1	13,886	95.9
Beckwourth CDP	432	-	-	414	94.0	0.0	0.0	0.0	6.0	19.3	9.2	49.9	11.1	14.7	224	100.0
Belden CDP	22	-	-	-	-	-	-	-	-	-	-	-	-	-	-	-
Bell city	35,469	35,521	0.1	35,682	5.1	1.5	0.5	0.9	91.9	27.5	9.3	30.7	73.4	7.5	8,972	86.2
Bella Vista CDP	2,781	-	-	2,427	86.5	1.1	0.6	4.4	7.4	16.5	28.7	51.7	27.0	19.7	963	90.3
Bell Canyon CDP	2,049	-	-	2,109	63.9	2.8	19.0	4.4	10.0	22.8	15.4	45.8	10.3	68.1	652	100.0
Bellflower city	76,625	76,435	-0.2	77,195	15.9	13.0	12.1	3.2	55.9	25.5	11.1	34.6	48.4	18.5	23,240	90.3
Bell Gardens city	42,053	42,012	-0.1	42,421	2.5	0.8	0.6	0.2	95.8	30.4	8.1	29.5	78.0	5.4	9,823	86.0
Belmont city	25,833	26,941	4.3	27,097	53.9	1.0	27.4	5.6	12.1	23.0	16.7	40.9	13.5	64.7	10,285	95.7
Belvedere city	2,071	2,104	1.6	2,134	92.3	0.0	2.0	0.6	5.1	25.7	29.7	50.7	2.9	85.4	895	93.9
Benbow CDP	321	-	-	118	100.0	0.0	0.0	0.0	0.0	0.0	33.9	50.6	39.3	29.2	56	100.0
Bend CDP	619	-	-	498	82.5	0.0	0.0	0.0	17.5	7.0	55.4	67.5	52.6	19.4	195	82.1
Benicia city	27,035	28,240	4.5	28,192	65.1	3.2	11.2	7.7	12.8	19.8	19.8	46.1	20.5	44.7	11,293	95.3
Ben Lomond CDP	6,234	-	-	6,890	83.8	0.3	1.2	2.5	12.2	18.5	15.3	41.1	19.3	38.9	2,368	96.7
Benton CDP	280	-	-	328	72.6	0.0	0.6	21.6	5.2	2.4	27.1	52.5	21.9	29.4	130	87.7
Berkeley city	112,513	121,363	7.9	121,485	53.3	7.7	20.8	6.8	11.4	12.5	14.3	31.1	9.9	73.8	45,352	96.4
Bermuda Dunes CDP	7,282	-	-	6,704	58.5	1.8	3.5	2.4	33.8	23.1	18.6	38.7	37.5	27.9	2,816	96.3
Berry Creek CDP	1,424	-	-	1,313	86.7	0.0	2.3	4.3	6.6	11.5	27.6	55.5	48.5	8.5	551	83.5
Bertsch-Oceanview CDP	2,436	-	-	1,988	53.0	0.0	6.9	21.9	18.3	21.9	26.5	51.1	55.5	7.5	858	85.2
Bethel Island CDP	2,137	-	-	2,161	66.5	2.3	1.2	1.0	29.0	16.1	22.8	45.5	48.7	11.0	906	77.6
Beverly Hills city	33,921	33,792	-0.4	34,186	77.8	1.9	9.1	5.3	5.9	20.3	21.4	44.8	15.7	63.2	14,769	93.4
Bieber CDP	312	-	-	156	100.0	0.0	0.0	0.0	0.0	12.8	23.1	51.6	34.9	0.0	80	75.0
Big Bear City CDP	12,304	-	-	13,463	68.9	1.2	0.6	2.6	26.8	24.0	19.6	42.2	40.0	17.7	5,375	93.9
Big Bear Lake city	5,037	5,279	4.8	5,241	65.5	0.2	2.6	1.7	30.0	20.1	20.9	43.7	33.1	28.3	2,237	92.3
Big Bend CDP	102	-	-	132	68.9	2.3	0.0	24.2	4.5	22.0	18.9	44.0	42.5	14.9	48	47.9
Big Creek CDP	175	-	-	198	89.9	0.0	2.0	0.0	8.1	42.4	7.6	23.9	28.6	37.8	57	91.2
Biggs city	1,705	1,879	10.2	2,175	38.9	0.0	2.4	6.9	51.8	28.3	14.2	32.1	58.5	6.4	637	95.0
Big Lagoon CDP	93	-	-	100	87.0	0.0	0.0	0.0	13.0	9.0	40.0	62.7	15.4	61.5	46	95.7
Big Pine CDP	1,756	-	-	1,524	54.9	0.9	1.2	28.4	14.5	21.8	23.1	48.6	39.8	19.7	699	90.4
Big River CDP	1,327	-	-	1,149	79.5	0.6	0.4	4.5	14.9	17.8	27.9	56.5	53.1	11.2	526	88.6
Biola CDP	1,623	-	-	1,705	0.9	3.0	11.2	0.0	84.9	33.1	3.5	24.3	68.0	12.3	378	91.0
Bishop city	3,879	3,747	-3.4	3,745	66.4	1.1	5.3	3.5	23.7	18.9	22.1	46.3	35.1	38.5	1,993	92.2
Blackhawk CDP	9,354	-	-	9,604	65.3	1.7	21.4	4.7	6.9	21.0	21.7	50.2	10.1	70.1	3,458	98.4
Blacklake CDP	930	-	-	850	96.0	0.0	0.0	4.0	0.0	5.3	55.1	68.1	9.4	54.7	445	100.0
Black Point-Green Point CDP	1,306	-	-	1,622	80.3	0.0	9.3	3.2	7.2	8.0	29.8	56.1	19.8	56.2	617	98.5
Blairsden CDP	39	-	-	18	100.0	0.0	0.0	0.0	0.0	0.0	50.0	0.0	50.0	0.0	9	100.0
Bloomfield CDP	345	-	-	292	82.5	0.0	0.0	9.6	7.9	0.0	14.4	47.8	8.8	78.4	88	100.0
Bloomington CDP	23,851	-	-	21,847	13.6	1.4	1.0	0.6	83.4	26.6	10.6	32.8	66.7	9.7	5,747	87.5
Blue Lake city	1,253	1,245	-0.6	902	75.2	0.0	1.6	17.6	5.7	11.9	24.1	50.5	25.6	36.6	428	94.6
Bluewater CDP	172	-	-	163	79.1	0.0	0.0	7.4	13.5	16.6	50.3	67.1	51.5	8.8	84	75.0
Blythe city	20,877	19,682	-5.7	19,643	25.9	10.7	2.3	3.9	57.2	20.9	9.8	35.2	56.8	7.8	4,922	81.4
Bodega CDP	220	-	-	892	57.3	2.1	0.0	39.3	1.2	22.4	38.1	45.9	38.5	30.3	241	100.0
Bodega Bay CDP	1,077	-	-	665	92.0	0.0	0.0	0.0	8.0	0.0	58.3	66.8	7.6	68.3	406	92.1
Bodfish CDP	1,956	-	-	2,030	83.3	0.0	0.0	5.1	11.6	23.5	24.0	45.3	56.2	16.1	902	69.0
Bolinas CDP	1,620	-	-	1,074	85.8	0.0	1.2	8.6	4.5	9.8	47.1	62.6	12.7	56.3	528	100.0
Bombay Beach CDP	295	-	-	297	94.6	2.0	3.4	0.0	0.0	0.0	76.1	76.0	32.0	14.8	128	66.4
Bonadelle Ranchos-Madera Ranchos CDP	8,569	-	-	9,551	55.6	1.0	2.9	4.8	35.7	25.1	16.8	41.9	36.4	24.6	3,010	92.6
Bonita CDP	12,538	-	-	12,706	33.0	2.5	14.0	4.6	45.9	18.5	20.4	43.5	27.4	40.4	4,089	98.0
Bonny Doon CDP	2,678	-	-	3,096	82.4	1.1	2.8	5.2	8.6	16.1	22.4	49.8	18.2	50.0	1,108	96.5
Bonsall CDP	3,982	-	-	4,458	63.3	1.2	4.6	3.1	27.8	21.1	20.6	45.0	28.0	36.5	1,604	93.4
Boonville CDP	1,035	-	-	947	36.0	5.9	3.8	1.1	53.2	19.7	19.0	41.3	46.2	20.0	298	98.3
Bootjack CDP	960	-	-	743	76.6	0.0	0.8	13.6	9.0	18.0	31.1	58.0	42.1	25.5	352	83.8
Boron CDP	2,253	-	-	2,221	58.9	3.0	5.4	8.6	24.1	19.4	16.3	37.3	52.9	11.1	943	91.2
Boronda CDP	1,710	-	-	1,763	3.7	0.7	2.0	0.0	93.6	29.7	13.2	37.8	65.9	15.0	410	95.4
Borrego Springs CDP	3,429	-	-	2,145	67.8	5.2	0.0	0.0	27.0	12.0	45.2	62.7	52.7	27.2	1,021	81.8
Bostonia CDP	15,379	-	-	16,603	54.9	6.4	4.9	7.5	26.4	24.0	12.7	33.8	47.8	17.9	5,608	90.2
Boulder Creek CDP	4,923	-	-	5,182	81.9	0.8	0.9	4.7	11.7	17.7	16.1	47.5	15.9	39.0	2,183	95.8
Boulevard CDP	315	-	-	405	95.1	0.0	0.0	4.9	0.0	0.0	66.7	67.1	48.6	15.8	220	72.3
Bowles CDP	166	-	-	272	32.4	0.0	0.0	0.0	67.6	46.0	22.8	31.7	58.9	18.4	50	58.0
Boyes Hot Springs CDP	6,656	-	-	7,728	46.9	1.5	1.5	6.6	43.5	28.8	15.4	36.0	33.8	33.1	2,779	95.7
Bradbury city	1,047	1,070	2.2	833	45.1	1.0	37.5	1.6	14.9	17.4	20.6	46.2	16.9	54.4	270	94.4
Bradley CDP	93	-	-	113	78.8	0.0	0.0	0.0	21.2	13.3	22.1	51.8	88.3	4.3	41	68.3
Brawley city	24,976	26,227	5.0	26,076	12.2	1.2	0.4	2.5	83.7	33.8	12.4	30.6	52.0	11.7	6,887	85.7
Brea city	39,195	43,255	10.4	42,678	41.8	1.7	21.7	3.2	31.7	22.4	14.0	39.5	23.2	45.3	15,246	96.0
Brentwood city	51,627	64,474	24.9	61,961	52.2	7.8	10.5	6.6	22.9	26.5	15.0	40.0	26.6	33.1	19,906	95.8

1 May be of any race.

Table A. All Places — **Population and Housing**

	Population				Race and Hispanic or Latino origin (percent)					Age (percent)			Educational attainment of persons age 25 and older		Occupied housing units	
STATE City, town, township, borough, or CDP (county if applicable)	2010 census total population	2019 estimated population	Percent change 2010-2019	ACS total population estimate 2015-2019	White alone, not Hispanic or Latino	Black alone, not Hispanic or Latino	Asian alone, not Hispanic or Latino	All other races or 2 or more races, not Hispanic or Latino	Hispanic or Latino[1]	Under 18 years old	Age 65 years and older	Median age	Percent High school diploma or less	Percent Bachelor's degree or more	Total	Percent with a computer
	1	2	3	4	5	6	7	8	9	10	11	12	13	14	15	16
CALIFORNIA—Con.																
Bret Harte CDP	5,152	-	-	5,148	10.2	0.0	0.0	0.5	89.3	41.6	4.8	22.1	88.2	1.3	1,259	86.7
Bridgeport CDP	575	-	-	542	91.1	0.7	1.3	4.2	2.6	15.5	33.4	55.2	30.8	31.0	194	99.0
Brisbane city	4,282	4,671	9.1	4,697	43.8	2.8	32.1	4.2	17.2	18.0	17.4	46.6	23.3	54.8	1,892	86.7
Broadmoor CDP	4,176	-	-	5,170	19.6	0.2	47.7	2.5	29.9	16.8	15.9	37.9	31.5	28.7	1,631	91.2
Brookdale CDP	1,991	-	-	1,939	87.6	1.2	0.9	9.2	1.1	13.9	15.8	52.2	32.9	37.9	742	96.8
Brooktrails CDP	3,235	-	-	3,800	78.4	0.0	1.8	5.6	14.2	25.6	18.5	39.0	39.1	24.7	1,531	92.6
Buckhorn CDP	2,429	-	-	2,387	83.7	0.4	4.5	6.0	5.4	13.5	34.6	56.1	35.2	22.2	1,100	85.0
Buck Meadows CDP	31	-	-	10	100.0	0.0	0.0	0.0	0.0	0.0	100.0	0.0	100.0	0.0	10	100.0
Bucks Lake CDP	10	-	-													
Buellton city	4,849	5,102	5.2	5,082	65.8	0.9	1.2	2.8	29.3	26.8	19.4	44.8	29.2	39.9	1,941	95.1
Buena Park city	80,619	81,788	1.5	82,489	23.6	2.9	32.0	3.6	37.9	22.1	13.0	36.8	37.8	30.5	23,680	94.9
Buena Vista CDP	429	-	-	595	76.8	1.7	0.0	7.4	14.1	27.4	18.3	51.9	23.1	14.0	203	92.1
Burbank city	103,357	102,511	-0.8	103,703	56.9	2.7	11.9	5.0	23.5	18.2	15.4	39.8	25.6	42.3	41,797	91.5
Burbank CDP	4,926	-	-	5,022	37.3	0.9	10.4	8.1	43.3	16.8	8.8	39.5	36.4	36.7	1,962	92.9
Burlingame city	28,806	30,889	7.2	30,576	53.3	1.2	27.1	5.7	12.7	23.6	14.4	40.1	13.7	67.8	12,150	96.7
Burney CDP	3,154	-	-	3,965	80.5	1.3	2.1	7.9	8.1	29.0	18.4	35.2	50.9	13.5	1,368	83.7
Burnt Ranch CDP	281	-	-	299	86.6	0.0	0.0	11.7	1.7	0.0	20.4	57.9	49.1	34.8	146	70.5
Butte Creek Canyon CDP.	1,086	-	-	958	79.5	0.0	4.6	11.6	4.3	15.7	48.9	64.3	11.8	59.0	402	99.3
Butte Meadows CDP	40	-	-	41	100.0	0.0	0.0	0.0	0.0	0.0	0.0	0.0	0.0	0.0	41	100.0
Butte Valley CDP	899	-	-	736	76.8	0.0	0.0	21.3	1.9	18.9	26.8	51.1	15.4	35.7	348	79.9
Buttonwillow CDP	1,508	-	-	1,443	15.8	0.5	0.0	4.0	79.8	44.2	5.7	21.2	81.4	3.8	378	65.3
Byron CDP	1,277	-	-	1,304	55.9	3.3	1.6	2.5	36.7	21.8	23.5	40.7	45.9	19.4	439	91.8
Bystrom CDP	4,008	-	-	3,759	11.1	0.1	1.7	2.1	85.0	32.2	8.8	29.3	73.2	7.8	1,085	80.5
Cabazon CDP	2,535	-	-	2,588	36.9	3.0	4.2	11.6	44.4	22.5	10.0	37.2	59.8	11.6	785	80.1
Calabasas city	23,462	23,853	1.7	23,988	75.8	1.6	8.2	5.2	9.1	22.3	18.0	43.6	14.0	61.6	8,764	97.9
Calexico city	38,573	39,825	3.2	39,946	1.0	0.2	0.9	0.1	97.8	29.3	13.9	31.8	54.3	17.8	8,976	85.0
California City city	14,120	14,198	0.6	13,826	36.8	23.9	3.2	5.6	30.6	21.0	11.7	34.9	54.6	11.1	4,222	91.1
California Hot Springs CDP	37	-	-	47	83.0	0.0	17.0	0.0	0.0	8.5	53.2	67.2	41.9	39.5	26	84.6
California Pines CDP	520	-	-	431	56.6	0.0	0.0	16.7	26.7	0.0	46.4	63.7	63.6	9.7	257	66.9
Calimesa city	7,882	9,160	16.2	8,814	63.0	1.2	2.5	2.7	30.5	19.5	27.2	48.0	44.0	18.9	3,235	87.9
Calipatria city	7,694	7,114	-7.5	7,395	5.8	15.0	0.7	2.8	75.7	16.4	5.4	32.5	76.2	1.6	881	81.2
Calistoga city	5,168	5,247	1.5	5,271	61.7	0.0	1.5	0.9	35.9	18.3	22.1	43.4	31.3	32.8	2,124	91.9
Callender CDP	1,262	-	-	1,215	58.2	0.0	2.6	0.0	39.3	17.6	16.9	43.8	16.8	28.6	464	100.0
Calpella CDP	679	-	-	682	49.1	0.0	0.0	0.0	50.9	20.1	40.5	49.8	66.9	11.3	204	95.6
Calpine CDP	205	-	-	182	100.0	0.0	0.0	0.0	0.0	20.9	15.4	50.2	5.7	35.0	85	67.1
Calwa CDP	-	-	-	2,089	4.1	2.8	5.8	0.0	87.3	36.9	4.4	25.7	70.2	0.0	475	81.3
Camanche North Shore CDP	979	-	-	1,139	82.4	0.0	0.0	1.8	15.8	31.5	8.1	32.2	48.6	3.2	367	97.0
Camanche Village CDP	847	-	-	903	89.3	0.0	0.0	3.8	7.0	14.5	18.7	47.0	57.7	22.4	308	81.2
Camarillo city	65,156	69,888	7.3	68,122	57.3	1.6	10.1	3.8	27.2	20.7	20.8	42.3	21.5	41.7	25,033	92.8
Cambria CDP	6,032	-	-	5,647	75.8	0.6	2.9	0.2	20.5	10.1	41.0	60.7	23.5	40.9	2,740	95.1
Cambrian Park CDP	3,282	-	-	3,258	66.2	0.4	8.3	9.3	15.8	23.7	15.6	45.7	23.7	56.3	1,063	99.4
Cameron Park CDP	18,228	-	-	19,171	73.8	0.9	3.4	4.4	17.5	20.2	23.0	45.3	28.2	30.3	7,403	94.2
Camino CDP	1,750	-	-	1,903	84.3	0.0	4.9	5.1	5.7	19.4	22.1	45.6	28.4	29.5	709	89.6
Camino Tassajara CDP	2,197	-	-	4,721	34.4	1.6	48.0	4.9	11.1	36.4	9.0	41.3	18.5	68.1	1,270	98.1
Campbell city	40,580	41,793	3.0	42,221	52.6	2.4	20.7	5.2	19.1	21.5	12.7	38.6	20.3	54.0	16,163	96.0
Camp Nelson CDP	97	-	-													
Campo CDP	2,684	-	-	3,408	47.7	1.3	0.0	2.0	49.0	35.2	9.7	27.1	55.2	19.3	947	96.9
Camp Pendleton North CDP	5,200	-	-	7,367	59.7	3.4	2.6	3.1	31.1	25.4	0.1	21.6	18.9	36.2	1,367	100.0
Camp Pendleton South CDP	10,616	-	-	11,936	61.1	7.9	0.9	5.0	25.2	36.2	0.7	22.6	32.7	27.2	2,944	100.0
Camptonville CDP	158	-	-	339	54.3	0.0	0.0	8.6	37.2	33.3	19.8	40.0	24.4	12.4	117	93.2
Canby CDP	315	-	-	282	53.5	2.1	26.2	0.0	18.1	8.9	79.8	77.2	18.7	56.6	16	100.0
Cantua Creek CDP	466	-	-	379	0.8	0.0	0.0	0.0	99.2	41.2	6.6	34.5	78.1	0.0	96	59.4
Canyondam CDP	31	-	-													
Canyon Lake city	10,553	11,280	6.9	11,170	78.5	0.0	4.3	3.8	13.4	21.1	18.9	45.3	31.7	30.4	4,230	97.9
Capitola city	9,917	10,010	0.9	10,121	64.8	0.6	3.7	6.0	24.9	17.5	23.9	42.2	25.6	34.2	4,461	90.3
Caribou CDP	-	-	-													
Carlsbad city	105,382	115,382	9.5	114,253	73.3	0.8	7.9	4.1	13.9	23.1	17.3	42.9	15.2	59.5	43,531	97.3
Carmel-by-the-Sea city	3,678	3,811	3.6	3,830	84.0	0.1	5.1	2.9	8.0	11.9	43.3	59.6	12.8	66.0	1,927	95.7
Carmel Valley Village CDP	4,407	-	-	4,152	81.8	0.5	1.0	3.0	13.8	19.7	31.3	54.7	16.1	48.9	1,666	94.6
Carmet CDP	47	-	-													
Carmichael CDP	61,762	-	-	64,454	69.6	4.2	4.8	7.2	14.2	20.1	19.4	40.3	28.0	33.5	26,097	94.2
Carnelian Bay CDP	524	-	-	451	82.0	3.5	0.0	5.1	9.3	0.0	36.1	60.4	11.1	54.1	229	94.8
Carpinteria city	13,003	13,385	2.9	13,505	49.4	0.5	2.4	2.1	45.6	19.5	19.2	42.9	34.1	33.6	5,089	94.3
Carrick CDP	131	-	-	92	100.0	0.0	0.0	0.0	0.0	0.0	72.8	80.0	63.0	0.0	74	100.0
Carson city	91,711	91,394	-0.3	92,079	7.0	23.5	26.3	5.9	37.3	20.3	16.7	39.4	40.8	28.3	25,211	92.5
Cartago CDP	92	-	-	5	100.0	0.0	0.0	0.0	0.0	0.0	100.0	0.0	0.0	0.0	5	100.0
Caruthers CDP	2,497	-	-	2,559	22.9	0.0	3.2	2.1	71.8	24.6	15.3	32.8	63.5	13.9	743	84.1
Casa Conejo CDP	3,249	-	-	3,372	67.3	0.0	4.5	6.6	21.6	22.2	13.4	39.6	25.9	32.1	1,078	87.6
Casa de Oro-Mount Helix CDP	18,762	-	-	19,804	62.4	6.2	3.2	4.0	24.2	20.4	20.3	45.2	21.2	44.9	6,918	94.7
Casmalia CDP	138	-	-	144	0.0	6.9	0.0	0.0	93.1	0.0	65.3	68.6	58.8	0.0	69	68.1
Caspar CDP	509	-	-	608	87.7	0.0	7.6	0.0	4.8	26.2	28.8	53.4	29.6	42.4	230	100.0
Cassel CDP	207	-	-	247	100.0	0.0	0.0	0.0	0.0	8.3	42.1	64.7	28.1	22.8	110	76.4
Castaic CDP	19,015	-	-	19,400	53.8	3.8	10.1	4.4	27.9	27.2	9.9	37.4	26.6	36.3	5,877	98.0
Castle Hill CDP	1,299	-	-	1,426	84.6	1.7	4.3	0.0	9.4	35.0	17.5	42.6	1.7	80.1	487	100.0
Castro Valley CDP	61,388	-	-	63,013	43.4	8.0	27.1	6.4	15.0	21.6	16.6	42.1	26.4	44.9	22,357	94.7
Castroville CDP	6,481	-	-	6,521	8.2	0.0	2.6	0.2	89.1	33.4	9.5	27.6	75.6	5.4	1,453	81.5
Cathedral City city	51,230	55,007	7.4	54,357	30.9	2.3	5.8	2.5	58.6	23.2	17.0	39.4	50.1	21.6	18,816	87.3
Catheys Valley CDP	825	-	-	604	94.7	0.0	0.0	0.8	4.5	10.4	25.2	58.4	25.6	22.9	322	78.9
Cayucos CDP	2,592	-	-	2,630	84.9	0.0	1.6	3.2	10.3	11.0	36.2	58.7	21.7	37.4	1,312	92.2
Cazadero CDP	354	-	-	340	89.4	0.0	0.0	0.0	10.6	16.2	24.7	53.0	32.8	22.5	137	89.1
Cedar Ridge CDP	1,132	-	-	1,015	87.6	0.0	0.2	2.7	9.6	14.7	29.2	55.9	33.0	25.8	476	90.8
Cedar Slope CDP	-	-	-													
Cedarville CDP	514	-	-	606	83.0	0.0	0.0	3.5	13.5	34.8	21.5	45.3	41.2	22.0	246	90.2
Centerville CDP	392	-	-	379	53.6	0.0	1.6	1.8	43.0	22.0	20.3	37.5	42.9	4.4	125	84.8
Ceres city	45,843	48,706	6.2	48,214	24.4	3.7	6.7	3.8	61.4	30.9	9.6	30.2	57.9	10.2	12,975	91.3
Cerritos city	49,043	49,859	1.7	50,143	14.0	8.5	58.9	4.9	13.8	18.7	23.2	45.8	20.0	52.9	15,378	94.9
Chalfant CDP	651	-	-	1,005	82.7	0.0	0.0	2.0	15.3	11.3	11.2	46.0	47.5	30.0	255	94.5

1 May be of any race.

Table A. All Places — **Population and Housing**

STATE City, town, township, borough, or CDP (county if applicable)	Population: 2010 census total population	Population: 2019 estimated population	Population: Percent change 2010-2019	Population: ACS total population estimate 2015-2019	Race and Hispanic or Latino origin (percent): White alone, not Hispanic or Latino	Race and Hispanic or Latino origin (percent): Black alone, not Hispanic or Latino	Race and Hispanic or Latino origin (percent): Asian alone, not Hispanic or Latino	Race and Hispanic or Latino origin (percent): All other races or 2 or more races, not Hispanic or Latino	Race and Hispanic or Latino origin (percent): Hispanic or Latino[1]	Age (percent): Under 18 years old	Age (percent): Age 65 years and older	Age (percent): Median age	Educational attainment of persons age 25 and older: Percent High school diploma or less	Educational attainment of persons age 25 and older: Percent Bachelor's degree or more	Occupied housing units: Total	Occupied housing units: Percent with a computer
	1	2	3	4	5	6	7	8	9	10	11	12	13	14	15	16
CALIFORNIA—Con.																
Challenge-Brownsville CDP	1,148	-	-	719	73.6	1.1	0.0	25.3	0.0	20.7	20.0	54.8	22.2	17.3	350	86.3
Channel Islands Beach CDP	3,103	-	-	2,904	78.1	0.4	1.8	4.3	15.4	15.7	16.9	47.5	24.8	43.8	1,194	98.1
Charter Oak CDP	9,310	-	-	10,048	20.6	3.9	13.7	3.7	58.2	24.4	10.5	36.8	37.0	27.0	2,993	94.0
Cherokee CDP	69	-	-	137	100.0	0.0	0.0	0.0	0.0	14.6	21.9	57.5	45.5	6.4	44	100.0
Cherokee Strip CDP	227	-	-	214	18.2	0.0	0.0	0.0	81.8	47.2	8.9	27.5	100.0	0.0	54	13.0
Cherryland CDP	14,728	-	-	16,066	17.6	12.3	10.4	4.2	55.5	24.7	9.8	35.9	55.8	18.4	4,935	93.5
Cherry Valley CDP	6,362	-	-	8,115	64.0	3.7	1.7	5.4	25.2	17.0	27.2	49.8	44.3	18.9	2,903	87.4
Chester CDP	2,144	-	-	2,145	85.5	0.0	0.2	1.2	13.1	12.8	27.9	56.1	37.0	15.9	1,016	90.2
Chico city	86,798	103,301	19.0	94,529	70.6	2.1	4.4	4.5	18.4	19.2	13.0	29.7	24.4	37.4	36,164	94.7
Chilcoot-Vinton CDP	454	-	-	422	42.7	0.0	0.0	57.3	0.0	25.6	26.8	51.1	4.5	39.8	254	66.5
China Lake Acres CDP	1,876	-	-	2,136	41.9	32.6	0.9	4.2	20.4	31.6	18.6	33.6	51.1	22.6	846	70.0
Chinese Camp CDP	126	-	-	174	62.6	0.0	5.2	2.9	29.3	39.1	16.7	21.8	45.8	0.0	60	76.7
Chino city	78,069	94,371	20.9	89,631	24.5	5.3	15.0	4.2	51.0	20.2	11.6	37.6	43.8	23.0	21,918	95.6
Chino Hills city	74,792	83,853	12.1	80,701	29.5	3.5	34.9	3.4	28.8	22.7	11.4	38.0	23.0	46.7	25,289	98.3
Chowchilla city	18,785	18,310	-2.5	18,413	36.5	8.0	3.6	5.0	46.8	19.1	7.4	34.5	52.6	8.5	3,429	86.6
Chualar CDP	1,190	-	-	1,512	0.0	0.0	0.0	0.0	100.0	31.7	5.6	31.1	80.9	4.5	291	78.0
Chula Vista city	243,923	274,492	12.5	268,920	16.8	4.1	15.8	3.6	59.8	25.3	12.1	35.5	37.5	29.4	79,671	92.9
Citrus CDP	10,866	-	-	10,150	13.9	1.0	7.3	1.1	76.6	23.2	10.6	35.8	58.6	12.6	2,461	95.7
Citrus Heights city	83,184	87,796	5.5	87,373	69.2	3.7	3.4	4.5	19.1	20.7	16.2	38.0	34.7	20.4	34,079	93.8
Claremont city	34,878	36,266	4.0	36,090	48.9	5.3	14.1	6.3	25.4	18.4	19.3	40.4	17.9	56.0	11,729	95.5
Clarksburg CDP	418	-	-	456	69.7	0.0	1.5	0.0	28.7	30.3	8.6	37.3	25.5	21.1	176	100.0
Clay CDP	1,195	-	-	1,187	68.8	0.0	2.4	4.0	24.8	20.0	18.3	47.2	26.1	30.4	398	93.7
Clayton city	10,918	12,265	12.3	12,083	74.6	2.3	7.6	5.2	10.3	22.9	17.4	45.9	12.8	57.8	4,232	97.7
Clear Creek CDP	169	-	-	210	77.6	0.0	0.0	8.6	13.8	29.0	13.8	36.2	27.2	24.0	100	88.0
Clearlake city	15,250	15,267	0.1	15,349	58.8	4.1	0.2	8.2	28.8	26.7	17.6	37.5	58.9	7.3	5,805	83.8
Clearlake Oaks CDP	2,359	-	-	2,265	83.6	0.6	1.8	2.5	11.5	10.1	27.3	57.4	46.2	20.0	1,102	84.8
Clearlake Riviera CDP	3,090	-	-	3,930	63.6	8.6	0.0	3.1	24.8	23.2	16.8	38.7	34.3	9.0	1,244	95.1
Cleone CDP	618	-	-	968	60.0	0.0	0.0	0.0	40.0	24.6	24.7	42.5	59.3	14.8	395	70.9
Clio CDP	66	-	-	59	71.2	0.0	0.0	0.0	28.8	10.2	23.7	33.9	0.0	49.1	38	100.0
Clipper Mills CDP	142	-	-	335	75.2	0.0	0.0	11.3	13.4	21.5	59.1	65.5	56.3	21.7	138	100.0
Cloverdale city	8,614	8,656	0.5	8,754	61.8	0.8	4.1	3.3	29.9	24.3	18.9	39.6	35.0	28.1	3,194	95.4
Clovis city	95,980	114,584	19.4	109,160	52.0	2.7	10.6	4.0	30.6	27.7	12.9	34.5	28.6	32.6	37,160	93.3
Clyde CDP	678	-	-	792	75.0	0.0	9.3	10.0	5.7	9.3	11.2	43.4	23.0	20.8	321	92.8
Coachella city	40,708	45,743	12.4	45,181	1.7	0.6	0.2	0.2	97.3	23.9	8.2	34.5	82.4	3.6	15,451	83.8
Coalinga city	18,342	17,179	-6.3	16,906	30.8	2.9	2.3	5.3	58.8	24.4	8.0	32.1	54.2	12.1	4,293	90.8
Coarsegold CDP	1,840	-	-	1,585	72.0	0.0	0.0	4.2	23.8	14.4	40.6	57.7	46.2	17.9	672	83.8
Cobb CDP	1,778	-	-	1,011	95.2	0.0	0.0	0.0	4.8	10.7	25.6	57.1	28.2	21.3	492	100.0
Coffee Creek CDP	217	-	-	197	86.3	0.0	1.5	11.2	1.0	7.6	32.5	56.5	31.5	36.4	105	90.5
Cohasset CDP	847	-	-	631	97.1	0.0	0.0	0.0	2.9	22.3	23.1	46.5	29.0	40.9	251	100.0
Cold Springs CDP	446	-	-	582	91.4	0.0	1.4	0.0	7.2	11.3	26.5	55.0	41.4	27.8	219	83.1
Cold Springs CDP	181	-	-	51	100.0	0.0	0.0	0.0	0.0	0.0	0.0	0.0	0.0	0.0	27	100.0
Coleville CDP	495	-	-	464	72.2	0.0	0.0	3.4	24.4	18.1	0.0	32.4	46.6	22.1	147	100.0
Colfax city	1,950	2,002	2.7	2,057	78.2	3.8	0.0	5.8	12.2	21.9	11.7	35.4	38.2	16.9	873	90.7
College City CDP	290	-	-	170	11.2	0.0	0.0	0.0	88.8	28.2	25.3	30.4	30.9	21.6	58	100.0
Collierville CDP	1,934	-	-	2,698	49.4	0.0	3.3	2.6	44.7	22.7	13.7	31.4	62.2	11.0	769	88.6
Colma town	1,433	1,489	3.9	1,302	25.1	3.1	27.7	4.3	39.8	18.8	17.5	38.8	39.0	26.8	470	93.6
Coloma CDP	529	-	-	427	97.0	0.5	0.0	2.1	0.5	5.2	7.7	56.6	23.2	16.1	205	100.0
Colton city	52,148	54,824	5.1	54,580	17.9	7.1	5.2	1.9	67.9	27.6	10.4	31.4	51.1	17.3	16,689	90.6
Columbia CDP	2,297	-	-	2,226	89.0	0.0	0.4	3.1	7.5	17.8	30.6	45.4	39.6	13.8	1,056	88.4
Colusa city	6,222	6,060	-2.6	6,106	38.4	2.5	0.9	3.6	54.6	25.5	14.5	36.4	44.8	17.2	2,296	88.7
Commerce city	12,840	12,661	-1.4	12,830	1.4	1.5	0.4	1.6	95.0	23.6	13.4	35.5	63.4	11.5	3,537	86.5
Comptche CDP	159	-	-	99	90.9	0.0	0.0	0.0	9.1	18.2	28.3	52.8	19.8	0.0	37	100.0
Compton city	96,404	95,605	-0.8	96,803	1.2	28.4	0.7	1.7	68.0	29.2	9.5	31.2	66.6	8.6	23,742	88.2
Concord city	122,169	129,295	5.8	129,183	48.6	3.2	12.4	5.9	29.9	20.6	15.0	38.9	30.0	36.4	46,455	94.9
Concow CDP	710	-	-	553	62.2	0.0	0.0	20.4	17.4	18.3	16.3	47.8	31.5	24.7	232	78.9
Contra Costa Centre CDP	-	-	-	6,558	54.2	3.5	24.6	6.5	11.2	9.8	8.6	32.8	9.0	75.3	3,611	96.3
Copperopolis CDP	3,671	-	-	4,361	83.0	1.9	1.3	2.0	11.7	18.6	24.7	49.3	40.6	18.9	1,659	93.7
Corcoran city	24,823	21,960	-11.5	22,156	16.3	11.4	0.7	2.2	69.5	18.3	8.2	35.2	71.0	3.6	4,025	80.8
Corning city	7,663	7,710	0.6	7,590	48.7	1.0	0.4	2.1	47.8	27.7	10.9	32.3	57.6	12.0	2,651	82.6
Corona city	152,315	169,868	11.5	166,972	34.7	5.2	11.1	3.3	45.7	25.3	9.9	35.0	38.8	27.0	48,899	94.3
Coronado city	24,701	23,731	-3.9	23,639	74.9	3.1	3.1	3.1	15.9	18.8	20.9	40.6	11.5	64.4	8,435	97.0
Coronita CDP	2,608	-	-	3,383	36.7	0.5	3.1	0.5	59.1	25.6	8.3	30.3	45.5	21.4	743	94.2
Corralitos CDP	2,326	-	-	2,160	82.5	0.0	4.6	4.6	8.2	14.4	20.6	50.3	27.7	46.7	845	97.8
Corte Madera town	9,265	9,751	5.2	9,838	78.5	2.3	6.1	6.0	7.1	25.4	19.3	46.5	10.5	66.7	3,930	95.8
Costa Mesa city	110,078	113,003	2.7	113,159	50.1	1.8	8.4	4.2	35.6	20.3	11.3	35.2	32.1	40.3	40,986	95.2
Cotati city	7,265	7,410	2.0	7,454	74.5	0.6	1.6	4.8	18.4	22.7	13.1	36.0	31.9	31.7	2,758	97.3
Coto de Caza CDP	14,866	-	-	15,056	78.1	1.0	8.1	3.5	9.3	24.5	14.2	46.3	10.2	65.1	4,910	99.5
Cottonwood CDP	3,316	-	-	3,243	87.9	0.0	0.0	4.0	8.0	30.6	7.5	28.8	36.8	11.3	1,307	88.8
Coulterville CDP	201	-	-	60	88.3	0.0	0.0	0.0	11.7	0.0	50.0	64.5	28.3	0.0	43	44.2
Country Club CDP	9,379	-	-	9,977	32.0	7.0	5.7	3.6	51.7	25.0	13.4	34.7	52.6	12.4	3,469	90.9
Courtland CDP	355	-	-	179	66.5	0.0	0.0	5.0	28.5	21.2	15.1	40.2	53.2	34.8	74	100.0
Covelo CDP	1,255	-	-	1,140	38.3	1.5	0.1	26.8	33.3	25.8	22.0	36.1	41.2	20.8	428	85.3
Covina city	47,786	47,450	-0.7	48,095	22.5	3.3	12.7	2.8	58.8	22.6	13.6	37.3	39.4	25.9	15,350	94.1
Cowan CDP	318	-	-	498	30.5	0.0	7.2	4.8	57.4	41.8	15.3	26.7	71.4	0.0	122	76.2
Crescent City city	7,640	6,787	-11.2	6,676	52.9	7.6	3.0	4.1	32.3	13.6	10.3	34.9	66.8	9.1	1,794	82.2
Crescent Mills CDP	196	-	-	93	86.0	0.0	0.0	0.0	14.0	0.0	38.7	62.0	46.2	35.5	62	80.6
Cressey CDP	394	-	-	340	49.1	0.0	0.0	5.3	45.6	31.2	18.8	35.9	40.7	27.0	102	80.4
Crest CDP	2,593	-	-	2,765	73.9	0.7	0.3	2.9	22.1	19.1	17.9	40.6	28.4	25.3	987	97.4
Crestline CDP	10,770	-	-	8,709	77.6	1.9	1.1	2.9	16.5	18.6	16.3	44.0	25.2	26.9	3,524	94.2
Creston CDP	94	-	-	33	0.0	0.0	0.0	33.3	66.7	0.0	42.4	44.8	18.2	24.2	8	100.0
C-Road CDP	150	-	-	140	100.0	0.0	0.0	0.0	0.0	24.3	21.4	29.2	19.8	23.6	51	100.0
Crockett CDP	3,094	-	-	3,265	63.9	7.0	2.7	6.1	20.3	15.9	15.4	46.9	22.8	42.2	1,448	95.0
Cromberg CDP	261	-	-	316	93.4	0.0	0.0	0.0	6.6	17.1	50.3	65.1	26.2	25.4	136	100.0
Crowley Lake CDP	875	-	-	1,077	76.6	0.0	2.9	0.0	20.5	26.2	15.6	42.7	25.3	48.9	348	98.3
Crows Landing CDP	355	-	-	305	14.4	0.0	0.0	0.0	85.6	18.4	19.3	46.1	73.9	0.0	126	58.7
Cudahy city	23,809	23,569		23,890	3.1	0.7	0.5	0.5	95.2	30.7	6.9	29.1	74.8	6.6	5,690	87.5
Culver City city	38,895	39,185	0.7	39,169	45.8	8.7	16.2	5.6	23.7	18.9	16.5	42.3	17.9	58.4	16,796	93.9
Cupertino city	58,559	59,276	1.2	60,257	25.2	0.8	67.4	3.3	3.3	25.7	14.7	41.6	8.3	78.8	20,981	96.4
Cutler CDP	5,000	-	-	5,214	0.9	0.0	0.0	0.0	99.1	35.7	7.7	25.8	84.0	1.3	1,205	81.0
Cutten CDP	3,108	-	-	2,919	90.5	1.0	0.7	2.7	5.1	22.2	20.9	42.1	20.6	54.1	1,136	90.9

1 May be of any race.

Table A. All Places — **Population and Housing**

STATE City, town, township, borough, or CDP (county if applicable)	Population: 2010 census total population	Population: 2019 estimated population	Population: Percent change 2010-2019	Population: ACS total population estimate 2015-2019	Race and Hispanic or Latino origin (percent): White alone, not Hispanic or Latino	Race: Black alone, not Hispanic or Latino	Race: Asian alone, not Hispanic or Latino	Race: All other races or 2 or more races, not Hispanic or Latino	Race: Hispanic or Latino[1]	Age (percent): Under 18 years old	Age: Age 65 years and older	Age: Median age	Educational attainment of persons age 25 and older: Percent High school diploma or less	Educational attainment: Percent Bachelor's degree or more	Occupied housing units: Total	Occupied housing units: Percent with a computer
	1	2	3	4	5	6	7	8	9	10	11	12	13	14	15	16
CALIFORNIA—Con.																
Cuyama CDP	57	-	-	17	17.6	0.0	0.0	0.0	82.4	0.0	100.0	69.6	88.2	0.0	16	12.5
Cypress city	47,865	49,006	2.4	48,893	36.3	3.8	34.9	4.9	20.2	22.9	15.1	41.8	26.0	42.7	15,684	96.4
Daly City city	101,116	106,280	5.1	106,677	12.1	3.2	57.3	4.5	22.9	15.7	17.1	39.9	32.6	37.7	31,796	94.8
Dana Point city	33,290	33,577	0.9	33,769	74.1	1.4	3.6	3.3	17.6	15.5	23.8	50.5	17.6	51.0	14,905	97.3
Danville town	41,865	44,510	6.3	44,605	75.3	1.0	13.2	4.0	6.5	25.1	18.4	45.7	9.5	68.5	16,053	95.0
Daphnedale Park CDP	184	-	-	209	79.4	7.2	0.0	13.4	0.0	35.9	19.1	35.1	76.0	11.6	57	40.4
Darwin CDP	43	-	-	100	67.0	0.0	0.0	33.0	0.0	0.0	46.0	64.8	33.0	22.0	59	100.0
Davenport CDP	408	-	-	368	33.7	0.0	2.2	6.8	57.3	24.5	22.6	47.4	47.0	25.7	132	79.5
Davis city	65,639	69,413	5.7	68,543	55.5	2.1	22.7	6.2	13.6	14.9	11.3	25.5	9.0	73.8	24,630	97.8
Day Valley CDP	3,409	-	-	3,033	87.8	0.3	3.5	1.2	7.2	17.9	27.8	52.0	13.5	58.1	1,108	96.8
Deer Park CDP	1,267	-	-	869	85.8	0.0	7.0	0.9	6.2	12.8	36.9	59.7	14.6	46.2	444	98.6
Del Aire CDP	10,001	-	-	9,990	31.3	8.4	8.0	6.9	45.4	24.2	10.4	35.8	32.0	40.0	3,260	94.8
Delano city	53,044	53,573	1.0	52,886	5.3	3.8	12.1	1.4	77.4	26.4	8.3	30.4	70.5	7.7	11,745	69.5
Delft Colony CDP	454	-	-	715	14.4	0.0	0.0	0.0	85.6	40.6	2.7	19.0	75.2	6.2	149	100.0
Delhi CDP	10,755	-	-	12,301	16.3	0.0	4.1	2.5	77.2	30.9	7.4	30.6	66.2	7.4	2,960	95.0
Delleker CDP	705	-	-	477	88.1	0.0	0.0	0.0	11.9	37.1	18.0	37.1	31.4	18.1	159	76.1
Del Mar city	4,163	4,319	3.7	4,331	82.7	1.2	1.7	3.7	10.7	15.0	27.3	49.4	5.5	75.7	2,008	99.2
Del Monte Forest CDP	4,514	-	-	4,105	72.5	1.4	15.5	2.4	8.2	12.5	40.2	59.6	13.6	63.2	1,752	93.7
Del Rey CDP	1,639	-	-	1,261	1.9	0.0	2.6	0.0	95.5	30.0	10.9	34.5	69.5	12.9	375	83.7
Del Rey Oaks city	1,624	1,654	1.8	1,525	72.1	3.8	6.8	4.9	12.5	17.3	23.2	49.3	19.4	43.7	650	93.5
Del Rio CDP	1,270	-	-	1,592	60.7	0.0	8.5	9.9	20.9	36.3	23.4	35.7	24.1	49.8	490	100.0
Denair CDP	4,404	-	-	5,101	64.9	0.0	3.5	1.0	30.6	26.9	13.7	37.2	53.5	12.4	1,580	97.7
Derby Acres CDP	322	-	-	386	73.3	0.0	0.5	7.5	18.7	26.4	21.5	40.0	58.5	6.2	124	77.4
Descanso CDP	1,423	-	-	1,568	87.8	0.0	0.0	4.7	7.5	22.8	20.2	43.0	25.8	25.3	561	95.7
Desert Center CDP	204	-	-	216	93.1	1.4	0.0	3.2	2.3	2.3	77.8	70.6	16.7	57.1	90	100.0
Desert Edge CDP	3,822	-	-	3,319	68.2	0.0	0.6	0.0	31.2	7.6	56.9	67.2	47.5	16.6	1,791	82.8
Desert Hot Springs city	27,054	28,878	6.7	28,585	30.4	9.2	3.0	2.9	54.5	25.0	13.6	36.8	59.0	12.4	10,476	84.0
Desert Palms CDP	6,957	-	-	6,755	89.9	3.6	0.3	2.2	4.0	0.0	86.2	74.6	21.6	42.2	3,958	96.6
Desert Shores CDP	1,104	-	-	574	2.3	12.4	0.0	0.0	85.4	14.8	17.4	37.6	76.3	17.0	338	77.8
Desert View Highlands CDP	2,360	-	-	2,668	18.6	2.9	5.2	2.9	70.4	20.3	13.8	44.1	58.7	11.6	936	88.8
Diablo CDP	1,158	-	-	448	100.0	0.0	0.0	0.0	0.0	1.6	75.0	70.9	4.8	81.2	228	75.4
Diablo Grande CDP	826	-	-	889	53.1	10.9	4.7	1.7	29.6	19.2	16.6	55.7	34.6	26.5	361	95.3
Diamond Bar city	55,568	55,720	0.3	56,211	17.0	3.5	58.2	2.6	18.6	20.0	16.7	42.6	20.3	54.9	17,904	97.1
Diamond Springs CDP	11,037	-	-	11,731	85.9	0.2	1.7	4.1	8.1	17.1	28.3	52.5	36.3	22.2	4,951	89.8
Dillon Beach CDP	283	-	-	254	82.3	0.0	0.0	0.0	17.7	34.3	14.6	38.9	5.9	56.6	96	100.0
Dinuba city	21,460	24,461	14.0	24,015	10.5	0.3	1.9	1.0	86.2	34.5	8.4	27.7	66.3	8.8	6,174	89.2
Discovery Bay CDP	13,352	-	-	16,159	68.8	4.8	6.1	3.4	16.9	23.1	15.9	41.7	24.6	31.7	5,482	99.3
Dixon city	18,417	20,698	12.4	20,084	45.0	1.9	5.0	5.7	42.4	26.5	13.0	34.0	46.0	19.7	6,062	96.2
Dixon Lane-Meadow Creek CDP	2,645	-	-	2,664	60.7	0.0	1.1	4.1	34.0	20.9	25.5	46.7	45.7	23.4	1,133	95.6
Dobbins CDP	624	-	-	346	84.1	6.1	0.0	0.0	9.8	28.0	8.4	25.6	49.2	7.5	134	74.6
Dogtown CDP	2,506	-	-	2,643	63.0	0.0	5.6	4.1	27.3	19.8	19.4	43.9	51.0	17.7	938	88.8
Dollar Point CDP	1,215	-	-	805	96.5	0.0	0.0	3.5	0.0	3.7	39.3	54.8	27.0	46.7	424	91.5
Dorrington CDP	609	-	-	278	98.2	0.0	1.8	0.0	0.0	6.8	49.6	63.9	28.6	34.7	147	72.1
Dorris city	939	897	-4.5	908	56.3	1.2	0.0	6.4	36.1	27.1	15.1	35.8	68.4	5.5	363	78.5
Dos Palos city	4,950	5,527	11.7	5,351	19.9	1.6	0.6	5.5	72.4	30.2	12.9	30.1	63.4	11.3	1,516	90.6
Dos Palos Y CDP	323	-	-	229	27.1	0.0	0.0	0.0	72.9	18.8	22.7	44.9	77.5	0.0	94	100.0
Douglas City CDP	713	-	-	625	73.6	0.0	11.4	10.6	4.5	17.0	28.0	58.6	45.0	15.5	323	82.0
Downey city	111,775	111,126	-0.6	112,322	14.0	3.3	6.8	1.2	74.8	23.7	12.0	35.6	45.1	23.4	33,045	94.5
Downieville CDP	282	-	-	158	84.2	0.0	0.0	8.2	7.6	20.9	36.1	61.0	28.0	29.6	69	82.6
Doyle CDP	678	-	-	622	97.6	0.0	0.0	0.0	2.4	9.2	17.7	44.5	45.0	5.8	269	84.8
Drytown CDP	167	-	-	21	100.0	0.0	0.0	0.0	0.0	0.0	85.7	72.4	0.0	100.0	20	100.0
Duarte city	21,325	21,271	-0.3	21,559	24.7	5.5	17.1	2.8	49.9	17.6	19.4	42.5	36.2	30.1	7,132	89.1
Dublin city	46,036	64,826	40.8	61,240	32.4	3.5	48.4	5.6	10.1	26.6	9.1	36.7	14.9	66.3	20,235	98.1
Ducor CDP	612	-	-	636	3.6	0.0	0.0	1.4	95.0	32.1	17.1	33.5	74.3	1.6	169	68.6
Dunnigan CDP	1,416	-	-	1,459	44.8	3.7	2.3	0.5	48.6	29.1	17.6	32.4	54.3	19.4	516	89.3
Dunsmuir city	1,640	1,564	-4.6	1,724	77.3	0.0	2.6	5.9	14.2	21.6	23.5	46.1	33.7	22.5	784	90.9
Durham CDP	5,518	-	-	5,987	80.2	1.9	0.7	5.0	12.3	23.5	18.3	42.3	17.5	38.6	2,106	98.7
Dustin Acres CDP	652	-	-	641	88.0	6.2	0.0	0.6	5.1	33.1	9.4	36.5	64.8	2.1	180	97.2
Dutch Flat CDP	160	-	-	178	100.0	0.0	0.0	0.0	0.0	6.2	36.0	60.6	16.9	34.4	105	85.7
Eagleville CDP	59	-	-	52	90.4	0.0	0.0	9.6	0.0	0.0	46.2	63.8	28.8	1.9	23	100.0
Earlimart CDP	8,537	-	-	8,668	0.0	0.0	6.1	0.0	93.9	33.8	7.5	27.3	85.2	2.0	2,084	80.2
East Foothills CDP	8,269	-	-	6,233	44.7	0.9	20.0	2.2	32.2	18.8	18.8	44.8	28.6	42.4	2,018	95.8
East Hemet CDP	17,418	-	-	20,211	40.5	3.8	2.3	4.0	49.4	29.8	11.3	32.9	51.9	11.9	5,556	91.6
East Los Angeles CDP	126,496	-	-	121,187	2.1	0.3	1.1	0.4	96.2	27.4	10.4	32.1	71.3	8.7	31,619	82.1
East Nicolaus CDP	225	-	-	273	96.3	0.0	0.7	0.0	2.9	29.3	20.5	37.3	42.9	15.2	119	93.3
East Oakdale CDP	2,762	-	-	2,839	82.8	0.0	7.9	1.2	8.1	17.4	29.2	55.6	30.1	39.2	1,122	98.8
Easton CDP	2,083	-	-	2,018	27.5	0.4	1.9	1.8	68.4	26.7	12.5	34.3	53.1	18.2	583	82.3
East Orosi CDP	495	-	-	798	0.8	0.0	0.0	0.0	99.2	46.2	5.0	19.1	87.8	0.0	143	76.2
East Palo Alto city	28,155	29,314	4.1	29,593	10.1	10.9	5.1	7.9	66.1	28.3	6.9	30.7	58.7	20.6	7,724	94.4
East Pasadena CDP	6,144	-	-	6,143	24.4	3.2	33.0	2.9	36.5	21.7	17.7	42.1	28.5	44.2	1,936	94.2
East Porterville CDP	6,767	-	-	6,291	19.4	0.0	1.1	0.7	78.8	32.8	10.8	30.1	79.6	3.7	1,621	76.5
East Quincy CDP	2,489	-	-	2,210	82.2	0.0	0.0	6.2	11.6	18.0	18.1	48.1	45.9	9.3	948	80.0
East Rancho Dominguez CDP	15,135	-	-	15,792	1.3	13.6	1.2	1.6	82.3	29.1	8.0	30.3	75.5	4.4	3,407	87.4
East Richmond Heights CDP	3,280	-	-	3,162	53.0	16.0	10.0	5.0	16.0	13.7	24.2	51.4	15.8	56.7	1,360	94.8
East San Gabriel CDP	14,874	-	-	16,256	18.1	1.4	52.3	2.0	26.1	21.8	16.7	40.8	30.8	45.8	5,151	95.2
East Shore CDP	156	-	-	128	100.0	0.0	0.0	0.0	0.0	25.0	41.4	46.3	33.3	31.3	58	100.0
East Sonora CDP	2,266	-	-	2,278	91.2	0.0	0.8	2.9	5.2	7.3	45.8	62.4	41.7	25.5	1,193	93.0
East Tulare Villa CDP	778	-	-	853	21.1	0.0	8.2	2.1	68.6	27.0	15.2	35.1	73.7	4.7	209	89.5
Eastvale city	53,712	64,157	19.4	62,046	21.2	7.9	25.7	5.6	39.5	30.4	7.6	33.1	29.0	37.1	14,749	99.2
East Whittier CDP	-	-	-	10,356	38.2	0.4	5.2	2.0	54.2	20.5	14.9	39.0	37.6	21.7	3,460	92.0
Edgewood CDP	43	-	-	37	78.4	0.0	0.0	0.0	21.6	21.6	21.6	63.5	48.3	31.0	14	100.0
Edmundson Acres CDP	279	-	-	357	17.4	1.4	1.7	6.7	72.8	43.7	8.7	22.6	81.2	9.4	83	79.5
Edna CDP	193	-	-	172	91.9	0.0	8.1	0.0	0.0	12.2	55.2	66.5	31.1	41.1	80	100.0
Edwards AFB CDP	2,063	-	-	2,545	67.7	5.8	4.4	8.1	14.1	43.5	0.0	23.0	9.8	46.6	656	100.0
El Cajon city	99,584	102,708	3.1	103,186	58.5	5.4	3.2	5.1	27.8	25.3	11.7	34.0	43.9	20.9	32,950	93.4
El Centro city	42,588	44,079	3.5	44,003	8.3	1.4	2.2	1.1	87.0	29.4	13.3	32.9	51.9	17.8	11,625	87.3
El Cerrito city	23,585	25,508	8.2	25,398	47.5	4.7	30.3	7.3	10.2	17.7	19.8	42.7	16.2	63.7	10,034	94.6
El Cerrito CDP	5,100	-	-	5,630	35.8	0.5	5.9	3.0	54.9	22.0	13.3	40.3	44.4	25.8	1,517	94.1

1 May be of any race.

Table A. All Places — **Population and Housing**

STATE City, town, township, borough, or CDP (county if applicable)	Population				Race and Hispanic or Latino origin (percent)					Age (percent)			Educational attainment of persons age 25 and older		Occupied housing units	
	2010 census total population	2019 estimated population	Percent change 2010-2019	ACS total population estimate 2015-2019	White alone, not Hispanic or Latino	Black alone, not Hispanic or Latino	Asian alone, not Hispanic or Latino	All other races or 2 or more races, not Hispanic or Latino	Hispanic or Latino[1]	Under 18 years old	Age 65 years and older	Median age	Percent High school diploma or less	Percent Bachelor's degree or more	Total	Percent with a computer
	1	2	3	4	5	6	7	8	9	10	11	12	13	14	15	16
CALIFORNIA—Con.																
El Dorado Hills CDP	42,108	-	-	46,593	74.7	1.3	9.9	5.3	8.8	25.7	16.6	44.6	15.8	55.1	15,777	98.9
Eldridge CDP	1,233	-	-	1,422	72.7	0.0	0.1	14.8	12.4	21.4	19.2	43.3	11.4	47.4	498	100.0
El Granada CDP	5,467	-	-	6,102	78.7	0.6	4.9	2.8	13.0	18.5	15.5	46.8	12.4	61.2	2,202	95.3
Elizabeth Lake CDP	1,756	-	-	1,744	57.4	0.5	3.5	7.6	31.0	19.5	16.5	42.8	46.0	14.3	678	99.7
Elk Creek CDP	163	-	-	183	67.2	0.0	0.0	6.6	26.2	30.6	24.0	32.8	30.9	10.9	70	95.7
Elk Grove city	152,995	174,775	14.2	170,825	34.1	10.9	28.4	8.1	18.5	25.9	12.6	37.5	26.9	36.9	53,182	96.9
Elkhorn CDP	1,565	-	-	1,153	71.9	0.0	2.0	4.9	21.2	11.8	17.3	48.8	36.9	28.5	394	100.0
Elmira CDP	188	-	-	244	46.7	0.0	0.0	0.0	53.3	22.1	7.4	47.1	54.2	9.5	122	71.3
El Monte city	113,531	115,487	1.7	115,517	3.6	0.4	28.7	1.6	65.7	23.0	13.5	35.7	68.2	12.2	29,913	87.5
El Nido CDP	330	-	-	338	17.5	0.0	0.0	0.0	82.5	31.4	5.0	27.3	69.5	2.8	92	87.0
El Paso de Robles (Paso Robles) city	29,747	32,153	8.1	31,822	57.3	1.1	1.8	1.8	38.0	22.5	16.3	38.7	36.1	24.4	12,123	92.9
El Portal CDP	474	-	-	220	100.0	0.0	0.0	0.0	0.0	30.9	9.5	29.5	26.7	33.3	119	73.1
El Rancho CDP	124	-	-	59	0.0	0.0	0.0	0.0	100.0	11.9	23.7	40.8	52.3	0.0	7	100.0
El Rio CDP	7,198	-	-	6,297	16.2	2.8	0.2	1.8	78.9	28.2	12.9	32.7	63.6	9.5	1,559	85.8
El Segundo city	16,656	16,610	-0.3	16,731	62.0	3.7	10.2	7.9	16.2	24.2	10.5	37.3	15.2	58.4	6,417	97.0
El Sobrante CDP	12,669	-	-	13,818	35.4	11.4	17.2	7.3	28.8	18.8	14.1	40.6	30.2	34.8	4,901	95.8
El Sobrante CDP	12,723	-	-	13,881	49.1	8.2	15.9	2.0	24.8	25.3	9.8	38.4	24.1	42.6	4,052	99.1
El Verano CDP	4,123	-	-	3,295	75.7	1.8	0.2	2.1	20.2	15.8	17.3	49.9	31.5	33.6	1,258	98.5
Elverta CDP	5,492	-	-	5,606	70.7	2.4	5.0	5.7	16.2	23.5	16.3	39.9	44.9	16.4	1,736	96.9
Emerald Lake Hills CDP	4,278	-	-	4,721	78.2	0.7	6.2	4.6	10.3	19.3	21.6	49.0	11.2	70.3	1,650	97.5
Emeryville city	10,112	12,086	19.5	11,899	40.3	14.7	28.5	6.9	9.6	8.3	12.8	35.8	12.1	71.5	6,568	94.8
Empire CDP	4,189	-	-	4,051	25.6	1.0	0.0	6.6	66.8	20.8	11.6	37.7	72.1	4.1	1,343	92.4
Encinitas city	59,526	62,709	5.3	62,780	77.9	0.8	4.1	3.4	13.8	20.4	19.4	43.6	13.4	61.9	24,422	95.0
Escalon city	7,123	7,574	6.3	7,538	73.3	0.5	0.9	2.0	23.2	25.7	13.4	36.2	37.5	17.5	2,667	92.5
Escondido city	143,976	151,625	5.3	151,300	35.1	2.0	6.9	4.2	51.7	24.5	12.3	34.4	43.8	23.8	47,101	92.5
Esparto CDP	3,108	-	-	3,272	40.1	0.0	2.2	2.5	55.2	28.2	16.0	33.4	40.9	22.5	1,046	90.4
Etna city	737	718	-2.6	735	84.4	2.4	0.5	7.8	4.9	30.5	26.9	41.2	37.1	13.0	276	90.9
Eucalyptus Hills CDP	5,313	-	-	6,129	72.9	6.2	2.5	4.2	14.2	23.9	14.0	39.8	24.8	34.3	1,833	93.2
Eureka city	27,196	26,710	-1.8	26,966	69.8	2.0	6.6	7.8	13.8	18.9	17.6	38.0	33.4	28.1	11,606	90.8
Exeter city	10,332	10,485	1.5	10,474	47.7	0.8	3.6	2.2	45.7	30.0	13.4	33.3	43.5	15.5	3,427	87.0
Fairbanks Ranch CDP	3,148	-	-	2,085	95.2	0.0	0.0	0.0	4.8	24.1	16.1	45.5	12.3	57.3	641	93.6
Fairfax town	7,444	7,522	1.0	7,578	82.3	0.4	4.3	3.5	9.4	16.7	22.9	47.8	14.8	60.0	3,350	93.6
Fairfield city	105,467	117,133	11.1	115,282	31.5	14.8	16.5	7.9	29.3	25.4	12.2	34.8	34.8	28.3	36,751	94.9
Fairhaven CDP	-	-	-	177	78.5	0.0	1.1	9.0	11.3	10.2	24.3	49.1	52.6	27.7	87	94.3
Fairmead CDP	1,447	-	-	1,105	33.4	0.5	0.6	0.0	65.4	30.1	11.4	36.8	67.1	12.0	313	74.8
Fair Oaks CDP	30,912	-	-	31,032	73.7	2.7	4.9	6.9	11.7	18.8	22.4	46.3	17.3	46.4	12,475	95.3
Fairview CDP	10,003	-	-	10,532	34.6	17.9	17.0	6.9	23.6	16.7	20.8	46.3	24.3	42.1	3,886	96.1
Fallbrook CDP	30,534	-	-	31,701	45.6	2.2	2.4	2.1	47.8	23.8	17.8	36.7	41.2	24.5	10,354	92.9
Fall River Mills CDP	573	-	-	274	73.7	1.1	1.1	11.3	12.8	20.1	42.3	47.5	27.7	20.3	124	87.1
Farmersville city	10,588	10,703	1.1	10,716	9.5	0.6	0.5	0.7	88.6	30.2	8.4	29.5	73.2	3.3	2,912	86.8
Farmington CDP	207	-	-	172	52.3	0.0	32.6	0.0	15.1	19.8	19.8	41.7	52.9	13.0	65	100.0
Fellows CDP	106	-	-	51	100.0	0.0	0.0	0.0	0.0	17.6	15.7	55.2	51.4	2.9	19	52.6
Felton CDP	4,057	-	-	3,633	88.1	0.0	2.1	2.7	7.0	15.7	19.4	46.9	12.2	56.1	1,514	96.2
Ferndale city	1,373	1,352	-1.5	1,377	90.0	0.0	1.1	2.7	6.2	24.6	29.0	40.7	24.3	31.9	566	92.8
Fiddletown CDP	235	-	-	324	98.1	0.0	0.0	0.0	1.9	40.7	0.0	39.1	10.9	0.0	92	100.0
Fieldbrook CDP	859	-	-	880	84.3	0.3	0.7	11.8	2.8	20.6	23.2	48.9	26.3	43.6	337	95.3
Fields Landing CDP	276	-	-	251	100.0	0.0	0.0	0.0	0.0	0.0	22.7	60.4	77.3	22.7	114	100.0
Fillmore city	14,987	15,870	5.9	15,664	21.5	0.3	0.9	2.1	75.2	27.5	12.8	34.6	46.3	15.8	4,431	85.2
Firebaugh city	7,562	8,296	9.7	8,300	8.2	0.0	0.0	0.0	91.8	32.1	7.7	27.8	81.7	5.3	2,100	88.4
Fish Camp CDP	59	-	-	93	100.0	0.0	0.0	0.0	0.0	0.0	86.0	68.8	0.0	86.0	43	100.0
Florence-Graham CDP	63,387	-	-	65,716	0.5	5.9	0.1	0.5	93.0	31.9	6.8	28.8	77.9	5.5	14,630	87.9
Florin CDP	47,513	-	-	47,555	18.5	10.6	32.8	9.1	29.1	25.8	13.8	35.8	52.5	13.4	14,878	91.2
Floriston CDP	73	-	-	-	-	-	-	-	-	-	-	-	-	-	-	-
Flournoy CDP	101	-	-	155	74.8	0.0	0.0	0.0	25.2	25.2	21.9	43.1	59.6	13.5	52	98.1
Folsom city	72,147	81,328	12.7	78,159	61.8	3.3	16.9	5.8	12.2	24.2	12.6	40.7	19.2	51.2	27,836	97.0
Fontana city	196,458	214,547	9.2	210,759	12.9	8.4	6.4	2.7	69.6	28.6	7.8	31.0	52.9	18.1	54,558	95.4
Foothill Farms CDP	33,121	-	-	35,881	51.4	11.7	5.2	7.9	23.9	26.9	9.7	33.0	47.7	15.3	12,097	93.7
Forbestown CDP	320	-	-	413	52.8	0.0	0.0	47.2	0.0	21.3	32.7	49.6	52.9	23.4	210	91.4
Ford City CDP	4,278	-	-	4,753	34.2	0.0	1.9	2.0	61.9	35.6	8.5	25.7	72.1	7.3	1,307	73.4
Foresthill CDP	1,483	-	-	1,856	79.4	0.0	0.0	0.0	20.6	27.2	20.5	47.9	47.0	13.2	773	73.4
Forest Meadows CDP	1,249	-	-	1,327	80.7	0.0	0.9	0.8	17.6	29.3	23.2	33.9	19.5	48.5	484	82.2
Forest Ranch CDP	1,184	-	-	772	78.0	0.0	0.0	6.3	15.7	2.7	31.2	61.6	23.2	32.1	424	100.0
Forestville CDP	3,293	-	-	3,761	79.3	0.2	3.1	6.0	11.3	15.7	22.9	51.4	24.9	39.7	1,671	96.1
Fort Bidwell CDP	173	-	-	192	34.9	0.5	7.3	44.8	12.5	21.4	26.0	34.0	47.4	30.7	76	86.8
Fort Bragg city	7,306	7,291	-0.2	7,302	59.9	1.0	1.0	4.0	34.1	25.4	18.9	39.0	48.8	19.5	2,772	90.2
Fort Dick CDP	-	-	-	1,097	75.1	2.0	0.0	14.9	8.0	13.9	25.3	49.5	39.8	32.6	552	93.7
Fort Irwin CDP	8,845	-	-	9,872	47.9	17.0	7.7	8.9	18.5	36.9	0.9	22.1	25.8	32.0	2,708	99.3
Fort Jones city	710	692	-2.5	689	70.8	0.0	13.8	2.6	12.8	27.0	15.7	39.9	44.8	15.5	274	80.3
Fortuna city	12,039	12,259	1.8	12,210	71.1	0.3	0.6	6.5	21.4	23.5	19.0	40.8	40.1	19.7	4,769	90.3
Fort Washington CDP	233	-	-	540	100.0	0.0	0.0	0.0	0.0	52.6	17.0	10.8	0.0	94.9	147	100.0
Foster City city	30,568	33,901	10.9	33,997	36.9	2.4	47.5	4.7	8.4	21.9	16.8	40.0	10.9	70.3	12,690	98.0
Fountain Valley city	55,360	55,357	0.0	56,026	44.3	0.7	35.5	4.1	15.4	19.7	19.6	44.6	25.9	43.5	18,469	95.6
Fowler city	5,654	6,790	20.1	6,527	18.7	0.3	12.9	4.0	64.2	28.6	14.6	33.6	48.9	20.4	2,075	84.7
Franklin CDP	6,149	-	-	6,929	35.1	0.9	19.0	3.6	41.4	31.8	11.3	32.0	58.5	8.6	1,862	91.5
Franklin CDP	155	-	-	82	100.0	0.0	0.0	0.0	0.0	8.5	23.2	45.9	39.7	8.8	34	100.0
Frazier Park CDP	2,691	-	-	2,587	70.6	0.0	0.5	5.5	23.4	18.2	15.3	47.5	48.7	15.8	1,091	81.5
Freedom CDP	3,070	-	-	3,777	14.3	0.0	3.4	0.6	81.7	26.0	12.6	32.8	58.4	17.4	1,053	76.4
Freeport CDP	38	-	-	70	100.0	0.0	0.0	0.0	0.0	0.0	0.0	55.5	100.0	0.0	48	100.0
Fremont city	214,074	241,110	12.6	235,740	20.2	3.0	59.2	4.8	12.9	22.9	12.7	38.3	23.7	57.0	75,687	96.5
French Camp CDP	3,376	-	-	3,841	21.6	9.4	3.3	3.0	62.7	12.1	8.1	33.4	75.9	6.1	505	82.4
French Gulch CDP	346	-	-	433	86.1	0.0	4.8	3.5	5.5	15.5	22.2	51.8	47.4	15.6	179	83.2
French Valley CDP	23,067	-	-	36,126	43.3	8.8	11.7	8.7	27.5	33.0	8.3	33.0	28.0	30.5	8,943	99.7
Fresno city	497,172	531,576	6.9	525,010	26.9	7.0	13.4	3.0	49.6	28.4	11.1	31.0	45.3	21.9	168,625	89.7
Friant CDP	509	-	-	604	65.1	1.0	0.0	0.0	33.9	22.0	21.4	49.0	28.3	13.7	256	77.3
Fruitdale CDP	935	-	-	961	61.4	1.4	19.5	2.2	15.6	9.9	15.4	46.3	16.6	53.4	414	88.4
Fruitridge Pocket CDP	5,800	-	-	6,116	17.1	19.9	22.8	3.4	36.8	24.7	13.8	35.7	63.5	9.2	1,868	80.1
Fuller Acres CDP	991	-	-	885	9.3	0.0	0.0	0.0	90.7	36.5	8.7	24.4	82.7	2.6	186	68.8
Fullerton city	135,233	138,632	2.5	139,611	32.8	2.3	24.1	3.7	37.1	21.8	13.3	35.4	29.7	42.4	45,814	95.5
Fulton CDP	541	-	-	655	29.5	0.0	0.0	6.1	64.4	31.3	27.0	38.5	59.1	26.3	202	100.0
Furnace Creek CDP	24	-	-	108	57.4	9.3	0.0	23.1	10.2	4.6	4.6	44.3	42.4	27.3	85	77.6
Galt city	23,703	26,536	12.0	25,990	46.5	1.8	4.1	5.1	42.5	26.0	12.8	35.4	46.9	16.5	8,160	93.0

1 May be of any race.

Table A. All Places — **Population and Housing**

STATE City, town, township, borough, or CDP (county if applicable)	Population				Race and Hispanic or Latino origin (percent)					Age (percent)			Educational attainment of persons age 25 and older		Occupied housing units	
	2010 census total population	2019 estimated population	Percent change 2010-2019	ACS total population estimate 2015-2019	White alone, not Hispanic or Latino	Black alone, not Hispanic or Latino	Asian alone, not Hispanic or Latino	All other races or 2 or more races, not Hispanic or Latino	Hispanic or Latino[1]	Under 18 years old	Age 65 years and older	Median age	Percent High school diploma or less	Percent Bachelor's degree or more	Total	Percent with a computer
	1	2	3	4	5	6	7	8	9	10	11	12	13	14	15	16
CALIFORNIA—Con.																
Garberville CDP	913	-	-	913	95.9	0.0	1.1	1.0	2.0	20.7	12.6	31.4	40.4	19.3	481	89.8
Gardena city	58,829	59,329	0.8	59,709	9.4	22.2	24.7	4.4	39.3	19.5	16.8	41.3	42.7	25.4	20,612	89.2
Garden Acres CDP	10,648	-	-	9,972	16.6	1.3	1.2	1.0	79.9	27.8	8.9	33.3	82.8	2.3	2,806	88.2
Garden Farms CDP	386	-	-	403	84.9	0.0	0.0	0.0	15.1	18.6	30.3	52.2	29.1	61.8	178	88.8
Garden Grove city	170,958	171,644	0.4	173,258	19.5	0.9	41.1	2.2	36.4	21.4	14.3	38.5	50.1	22.3	47,761	93.5
Garey CDP	68	-	-	191	19.9	0.0	0.0	0.0	80.1	4.7	6.8	36.2	85.2	5.2	31	100.0
Garnet CDP	7,543	-	-	5,285	22.6	6.2	0.5	2.9	67.8	28.1	12.0	38.5	68.4	10.9	1,660	88.9
Gasquet CDP	661	-	-	685	78.5	0.0	0.0	17.5	3.9	14.5	31.2	53.0	48.4	10.4	252	77.4
Gazelle CDP	70	-	-	56	100.0	0.0	0.0	0.0	0.0	0.0	50.0	65.0	51.9	13.0	36	63.9
Georgetown CDP	2,367	-	-	2,577	85.1	0.3	0.9	1.2	12.5	26.4	13.0	37.4	29.7	16.1	887	91.8
Gerber CDP	1,060	-	-	1,140	21.7	0.0	0.0	20.2	58.2	13.9	19.8	45.7	69.2	10.4	431	74.7
Geyserville CDP	862	-	-	765	46.7	0.0	1.2	3.8	48.4	19.0	11.1	39.5	41.5	22.2	258	95.3
Gilroy city	48,879	59,032	20.8	56,766	28.0	1.1	9.1	2.8	59.1	29.3	10.5	34.4	40.7	27.7	16,126	97.5
Glendale city	191,692	199,303	4.0	200,232	61.7	1.8	16.0	3.1	17.5	17.7	17.6	41.9	33.7	40.5	74,698	87.0
Glendora city	50,267	51,544	2.5	51,801	47.9	1.8	11.3	4.6	34.4	22.8	16.2	41.0	27.6	37.4	16,887	95.4
Glen Ellen CDP	784	-	-	734	87.3	0.0	0.0	8.6	4.1	8.3	27.0	53.6	0.0	61.9	290	100.0
Golden Hills CDP	8,656	-	-	9,351	78.3	0.3	0.7	2.0	18.6	26.8	15.0	35.0	36.0	17.9	3,400	95.0
Gold Mountain CDP	80	-	-	-	-	-	-	-	-	-	-	-	-	-	-	-
Gold River CDP	7,912	-	-	7,538	67.5	2.1	21.1	4.7	4.7	16.5	28.4	52.4	8.3	67.1	3,294	96.0
Goleta city	30,096	30,911	2.7	30,975	51.5	3.1	9.8	3.1	32.5	20.5	16.3	35.8	25.1	47.8	11,019	95.2
Gonzales city	8,149	8,306	1.9	8,375	5.3	0.4	3.2	0.9	90.3	32.2	7.4	30.3	65.5	9.5	2,077	85.5
Good Hope CDP	9,192	-	-	9,195	8.3	1.1	0.0	0.5	90.1	29.3	6.8	29.1	79.9	3.4	2,000	89.4
Goodyears Bar CDP	68	-	-	26	100.0	0.0	0.0	0.0	0.0	0.0	100.0	0.0	46.2	0.0	14	0.0
Goshen CDP	3,006	-	-	3,304	15.4	0.0	5.1	3.5	76.1	30.3	4.3	27.4	71.8	4.2	1,036	92.8
Graeagle CDP	737	-	-	538	92.4	0.0	1.7	0.0	5.9	12.5	44.4	62.6	17.5	43.7	270	96.3
Grand Terrace city	12,040	12,584	4.5	12,510	37.3	4.0	6.6	2.9	49.1	19.6	15.2	37.3	37.2	26.8	4,358	92.5
Grangeville CDP	469	-	-	346	83.2	2.6	2.6	0.0	11.6	32.4	18.8	51.3	15.0	44.4	135	88.1
Granite Bay CDP	20,402	-	-	23,183	73.5	3.5	7.8	5.0	10.2	23.7	18.6	47.1	14.2	55.9	8,231	97.4
Granite Hills CDP	3,035	-	-	3,500	74.6	0.4	1.3	4.1	19.6	14.1	23.3	52.3	31.8	26.9	1,104	98.7
Graniteville CDP	11	-	-	13	38.5	0.0	0.0	0.0	61.5	0.0	0.0	0.0	61.5	38.5	5	100.0
Grass Valley city	12,876	12,817	-0.5	12,891	80.9	0.3	2.2	5.1	11.5	18.7	28.6	46.2	34.2	26.1	6,134	85.6
Graton CDP	1,707	-	-	1,889	77.6	0.0	0.0	9.7	12.7	23.0	16.9	40.1	17.5	47.0	633	90.2
Grayson CDP	952	-	-	1,364	3.2	0.0	0.0	0.0	96.8	34.5	5.6	23.9	83.7	2.1	276	97.1
Greeley Hill CDP	915	-	-	747	87.0	2.1	0.0	10.3	0.5	1.9	46.6	63.5	47.1	20.5	413	81.6
Greenacres CDP	5,566	-	-	5,911	70.5	0.4	0.7	5.9	22.5	25.5	14.9	35.3	44.2	13.9	2,028	89.4
Green Acres CDP	1,805	-	-	2,607	32.8	1.5	1.7	3.0	61.0	29.7	11.9	28.8	66.7	7.6	659	90.7
Greenfield CDP	3,991	-	-	3,899	27.2	1.4	0.0	0.3	71.0	24.6	13.1	40.4	66.3	8.4	1,120	84.6
Greenfield city	16,334	17,516	7.2	17,373	6.1	1.0	0.8	1.0	91.1	35.4	6.4	27.7	78.3	5.2	3,702	78.7
Greenhorn CDP	236	-	-	255	100.0	0.0	0.0	0.0	0.0	8.2	9.4	56.7	34.7	33.3	131	93.9
Green Valley CDP	1,027	-	-	1,124	75.7	0.0	0.8	6.2	17.3	17.8	15.5	45.8	27.9	28.1	463	95.7
Green Valley CDP	1,625	-	-	1,472	83.4	2.2	5.4	3.5	5.5	9.8	30.3	59.4	29.1	43.1	574	94.4
Greenview CDP	201	-	-	229	86.5	0.0	0.0	13.5	0.0	10.0	22.7	59.2	44.8	0.0	95	100.0
Greenville CDP	1,129	-	-	817	75.0	0.0	11.3	12.7	1.0	6.1	33.8	52.5	57.4	10.3	462	75.1
Grenada CDP	367	-	-	398	86.7	0.0	0.0	13.3	0.0	31.2	17.8	46.3	54.3	24.1	134	89.6
Gridley city	6,640	7,246	9.1	6,744	51.7	0.1	2.4	2.7	43.1	30.3	14.5	32.9	46.3	12.9	2,250	92.0
Grimes CDP	391	-	-	305	50.2	0.0	0.0	3.9	45.9	43.9	9.5	27.6	53.2	12.3	106	81.1
Grizzly Flats CDP	1,066	-	-	1,195	73.6	0.0	0.0	10.6	15.7	17.7	35.5	56.0	10.7	25.4	545	89.9
Groveland CDP	601	-	-	247	97.6	0.0	2.4	0.0	0.0	0.0	32.4	54.0	25.5	22.3	158	91.8
Grover Beach city	13,161	13,459	2.3	13,535	60.5	1.6	3.6	2.8	31.5	22.4	16.7	37.2	27.9	31.6	5,307	94.7
Guadalupe city	7,080	7,783	9.9	7,451	5.9	0.4	3.1	0.2	90.4	32.1	10.3	28.5	62.5	9.2	2,030	88.7
Guerneville CDP	4,534	-	-	5,014	82.1	1.1	1.4	3.4	12.0	12.3	25.4	51.3	27.4	34.5	2,457	95.4
Guinda CDP	254	-	-	237	30.4	0.0	0.0	0.0	69.6	26.2	22.4	33.6	41.7	16.6	82	74.4
Gustine city	5,520	5,882	6.6	5,813	44.8	0.0	0.2	0.9	54.1	19.9	14.4	40.4	60.3	12.5	2,054	86.9
Hacienda Heights CDP	54,038	-	-	55,188	11.9	1.0	40.0	1.5	45.5	19.3	18.9	42.9	37.8	34.1	16,320	95.7
Half Moon Bay city	11,324	12,932	14.2	12,834	60.9	0.4	6.2	2.4	30.1	17.7	22.8	46.8	27.8	50.3	4,835	95.6
Hamilton Branch CDP	537	-	-	495	91.7	0.0	0.0	1.6	6.7	13.9	37.2	60.6	33.3	24.4	252	89.3
Hamilton City CDP	1,759	-	-	2,113	14.6	0.0	0.9	0.0	84.6	32.5	8.0	30.4	68.2	10.5	668	77.7
Hanford city	54,436	57,703	6.0	56,475	35.9	4.9	4.5	4.3	50.4	28.2	12.2	33.5	44.0	19.2	18,777	92.1
Happy Camp CDP	1,190	-	-	844	47.9	0.2	1.3	44.0	6.6	18.2	22.6	52.5	54.1	14.5	403	76.9
Harbison Canyon CDP	3,841	-	-	4,155	79.4	0.0	0.4	3.4	16.8	18.5	17.1	44.7	38.0	25.5	1,450	95.0
Hardwick CDP	138	-	-	138	19.6	0.7	0.0	0.0	79.7	21.7	5.8	28.8	79.3	1.1	40	85.0
Hartland CDP	30	-	-	-	-	-	-	-	-	-	-	-	-	-	-	-
Hartley CDP	2,510	-	-	2,960	52.3	7.6	4.1	7.0	29.0	17.6	23.1	46.3	43.0	16.9	988	93.7
Hasley Canyon CDP	1,137	-	-	1,145	73.7	1.8	0.0	2.3	22.2	23.0	11.4	42.6	36.6	28.2	351	97.2
Hat Creek CDP	309	-	-	129	80.6	1.6	3.1	0.0	14.7	0.0	72.9	67.5	19.0	10.3	66	84.8
Hawaiian Gardens city	14,273	14,159	-0.8	14,337	4.3	4.0	9.8	2.0	79.8	27.1	10.4	32.4	67.0	10.4	3,712	88.8
Hawthorne city	84,290	86,068	2.1	87,107	10.3	24.1	7.5	3.2	54.8	25.6	8.9	33.2	46.9	22.3	29,033	92.7
Hayfork CDP	2,368	-	-	2,711	71.6	1.3	3.2	5.3	18.6	18.8	28.8	42.2	52.7	13.4	1,139	78.5
Hayward city	144,427	159,203	10.2	159,293	16.2	9.2	27.0	7.3	40.3	21.4	12.1	35.5	45.2	27.7	47,666	94.7
Healdsburg city	11,255	11,845	5.2	11,845	63.8	0.0	1.7	3.5	31.0	17.7	22.5	47.1	24.2	43.7	4,635	95.2
Heber CDP	4,275	-	-	3,604	0.0	0.0	0.0	0.0	100.0	24.7	18.2	34.6	56.4	9.3	950	93.8
Hemet city	78,630	85,334	8.5	84,542	40.7	7.1	3.0	3.5	45.8	26.2	22.1	38.9	51.9	11.1	28,893	85.2
Herald CDP	1,184	-	-	967	66.0	5.6	2.8	6.8	18.8	14.5	27.2	53.0	33.5	25.1	349	87.1
Hercules city	24,089	26,276	9.1	25,616	19.1	15.0	44.5	5.6	15.8	19.5	15.1	41.2	23.5	43.2	8,402	97.8
Herlong CDP	298	-	-	1,295	31.3	19.8	1.7	9.5	37.8	6.3	1.9	35.9	67.2	3.1	116	92.2
Hermosa Beach city	19,508	19,320	-	19,539	78.0	1.0	5.2	6.5	9.4	17.9	12.4	39.3	8.5	75.7	8,956	97.4
Hesperia city	90,100	95,750	6.3	94,203	33.1	3.9	2.1	2.8	58.1	30.6	10.2	31.2	57.3	11.2	26,738	93.9
Hickman CDP	641	-	-	712	65.2	0.0	2.2	1.1	31.5	26.7	11.8	38.7	59.5	10.2	211	96.2
Hidden Hills city	1,856	1,890	1.8	1,751	85.7	0.0	3.9	0.7	9.7	27.3	17.9	47.3	8.5	70.1	561	98.0
Hidden Meadows CDP	3,485	-	-	3,462	69.5	0.0	12.8	5.8	11.9	16.3	32.5	53.6	18.5	49.7	1,403	98.1
Hidden Valley Lake CDP	5,579	-	-	5,539	83.4	0.0	1.4	3.2	12.0	23.5	18.2	44.5	35.3	18.8	2,068	97.9
Highgrove CDP	3,988	-	-	5,786	23.5	1.3	11.0	1.4	62.8	28.7	9.3	31.2	45.7	20.7	1,560	95.4
Highland city	53,106	55,417	4.4	55,049	25.6	8.1	7.2	4.6	54.5	30.6	9.7	30.9	47.1	21.9	16,138	90.9
Highlands-Baywood Park CDP	4,027	-	-	4,767	54.5	1.5	31.0	6.9	6.0	25.1	18.3	44.9	10.1	65.5	1,570	97.6
Hillsborough town	10,839	11,387	5.1	11,447	56.8	1.1	31.5	6.6	4.1	25.4	21.9	47.9	9.9	78.9	3,633	98.7
Hilmar-Irwin CDP	5,197	-	-	5,755	68.7	0.0	0.0	4.4	27.0	27.3	17.6	37.5	53.2	17.9	1,951	94.6
Hiouchi CDP	301	-	-	244	87.7	0.0	0.0	2.9	9.4	2.0	60.7	67.9	41.0	31.0	133	100.0
Hollister city	34,805	40,740	17.1	38,687	25.4	0.7	2.2	2.4	69.3	28.8	9.5	33.4	49.8	15.0	10,995	95.2
Holtville city	5,947	6,621	11.3	6,527	16.8	0.7	0.0	0.4	82.1	31.9	12.6	32.9	61.4	10.9	1,682	91.2
Home Garden CDP	1,761	-	-	1,521	10.8	5.5	4.2	1.6	78.0	30.0	12.0	28.0	72.7	1.1	393	88.0
Home Gardens CDP	11,570	-	-	12,153	13.2	3.6	4.6	1.9	76.7	26.1	10.3	32.5	62.3	12.5	3,054	91.3

1 May be of any race.

Table A. All Places — **Population and Housing**

STATE City, town, township, borough, or CDP (county if applicable)	Population: 2010 census total population	Population: 2019 estimated population	Population: Percent change 2010-2019	Population: ACS total population estimate 2015-2019	Race and Hispanic or Latino origin (percent): White alone, not Hispanic or Latino	Race and Hispanic or Latino origin (percent): Black alone, not Hispanic or Latino	Race and Hispanic or Latino origin (percent): Asian alone, not Hispanic or Latino	Race and Hispanic or Latino origin (percent): All other races or 2 or more races, not Hispanic or Latino	Race and Hispanic or Latino origin (percent): Hispanic or Latino[1]	Age (percent): Under 18 years old	Age (percent): Age 65 years and older	Age (percent): Median age	Educational attainment of persons age 25 and older: Percent High school diploma or less	Educational attainment of persons age 25 and older: Percent Bachelor's degree or more	Occupied housing units: Total	Occupied housing units: Percent with a computer
	1	2	3	4	5	6	7	8	9	10	11	12	13	14	15	16
CALIFORNIA—Con.																
Homeland CDP	5,969	-	-	7,086	35.4	0.4	0.3	4.4	59.6	28.1	14.9	35.1	64.7	10.2	2,060	89.4
Homestead Valley CDP	3,032	-	-	2,865	73.9	1.0	1.3	5.3	18.5	10.8	26.6	55.5	39.8	16.2	1,391	79.9
Homewood Canyon CDP	44	-	-	69	100.0	0.0	0.0	0.0	0.0	0.0	65.2	68.6	36.2	26.1	46	58.7
Honcut CDP	370	-	-	116	45.7	0.0	0.0	15.5	38.8	12.1	6.0	35.4	76.0	24.0	41	56.1
Hood CDP	271	-	-	313	8.9	0.0	4.2	18.8	68.1	26.2	6.1	38.6	58.9	4.1	103	91.3
Hoopa CDP	-	-	-	3,201	9.5	0.6	0.0	89.6	0.3	30.1	11.7	29.7	44.0	17.5	1,040	72.4
Hopland CDP	756	-	-	920	59.6	0.0	4.5	0.0	36.0	25.3	11.8	31.0	50.0	21.3	283	82.0
Hornbrook CDP	248	-	-	211	89.1	0.0	0.0	4.7	6.2	18.0	42.2	61.4	40.1	9.6	97	84.5
Hornitos CDP	75	-	-	66	59.1	0.0	0.0	0.0	40.9	0.0	15.2	52.1	43.9	0.0	39	100.0
Hughson city	6,649	7,565	13.8	7,460	57.4	0.4	7.8	1.7	32.7	30.5	13.0	32.7	41.4	22.0	2,486	91.5
Humboldt Hill CDP	3,414	-	-	4,315	70.0	0.7	6.1	7.5	15.6	24.1	13.1	37.2	36.9	20.1	1,590	93.0
Huntington Beach city	191,038	199,223	4.3	200,259	61.5	1.3	12.0	5.1	20.2	19.2	17.6	42.4	24.0	42.6	76,911	95.0
Huntington Park city	58,125	57,509	-1.1	58,353	1.5	0.8	0.3	0.3	97.1	28.1	9.2	31.3	76.7	6.4	14,618	86.7
Huron city	6,745	7,281	7.9	7,115	3.8	0.3	0.0	1.8	94.1	36.7	7.0	26.5	84.6	1.1	1,734	71.0
Hyampom CDP	241	-	-	115	100.0	0.0	0.0	0.0	0.0	0.0	23.5	61.2	76.5	23.5	57	100.0
Hydesville CDP	1,237	-	-	1,063	94.4	0.0	0.0	4.5	1.0	16.3	23.9	50.7	31.2	18.4	450	90.2
Idlewild CDP	43	-	-	-	-	-	-	-	-	-	-	-	-	-	-	-
Idyllwild-Pine Cove CDP	3,874	-	-	2,510	77.3	4.2	2.1	0.7	15.7	13.1	26.8	56.0	32.8	38.4	1,196	87.4
Imperial city	14,733	18,120	23.0	17,454	17.1	1.7	2.3	0.9	78.0	36.1	8.6	27.3	38.8	23.1	4,381	95.0
Imperial Beach city	26,329	27,440	4.2	27,315	30.8	4.7	8.4	5.1	51.1	24.0	11.4	32.5	41.1	21.9	9,547	94.1
Independence CDP	669	-	-	603	66.3	0.8	0.5	21.7	10.6	14.3	26.0	44.6	43.1	20.7	286	88.5
Indian Falls CDP	54	-	-	53	52.8	0.0	0.0	47.2	0.0	0.0	0.0	52.1	81.1	0.0	35	100.0
Indianola CDP	823	-	-	739	86.3	0.0	0.8	6.2	6.6	16.6	19.6	47.0	39.6	20.7	362	85.9
Indian Wells city	4,958	5,470	10.3	5,370	88.1	0.9	3.8	1.7	5.4	4.9	58.6	67.9	16.5	55.5	2,778	94.9
Indio city	79,166	91,765	15.9	89,469	29.5	3.1	2.1	1.1	64.2	22.3	19.2	40.0	54.9	17.2	32,470	89.7
Indio Hills CDP	972	-	-	782	19.8	0.0	0.1	0.0	80.1	28.0	7.4	31.5	68.1	4.4	234	79.9
Industry city	217	202	-6.9	373	26.3	0.5	3.2	4.6	65.4	34.9	7.2	26.4	57.0	14.5	85	92.9
Inglewood city	109,649	108,151	-1.4	109,613	4.5	39.6	2.0	3.4	50.6	23.5	12.3	36.1	45.9	21.2	35,997	91.5
Interlaken CDP	7,321	-	-	7,817	20.3	0.8	0.8	3.3	74.8	28.2	7.7	32.2	55.5	16.5	1,951	90.4
Inverness CDP	1,304	-	-	1,097	94.0	0.0	0.0	1.1	4.9	7.5	45.1	62.5	13.1	71.0	632	89.7
Inyokern CDP	1,099	-	-	696	89.2	0.0	0.0	2.0	8.8	26.1	11.2	33.5	30.8	44.5	272	94.9
Ione city	7,913	8,568	8.3	7,753	62.5	9.9	1.0	3.4	23.2	7.7	17.6	46.9	46.3	10.9	1,935	93.6
Iron Horse CDP	297	-	-	191	100.0	0.0	0.0	0.0	0.0	28.8	0.0	37.0	0.0	30.1	95	100.0
Irvine city	212,107	287,401	35.5	273,157	40.3	1.6	42.9	4.9	10.3	22.0	10.2	34.2	11.3	68.9	98,281	97.8
Irwindale city	1,418	1,446	2.0	1,394	8.5	0.0	0.6	0.6	90.3	23.0	15.5	33.9	49.7	15.5	392	88.3
Isla Vista CDP	23,096	-	-	27,707	47.1	3.3	21.2	4.4	24.1	3.1	1.0	20.6	21.1	61.4	5,386	98.6
Isleton city	804	844	5.0	544	49.4	0.0	1.5	6.6	42.5	17.6	17.6	41.3	49.1	5.4	260	92.7
Ivanhoe CDP	4,495	-	-	4,215	13.5	0.0	0.0	0.6	85.8	30.9	12.6	34.2	74.0	5.7	1,188	83.2
Jackson city	4,672	4,840	3.6	4,751	81.2	0.2	3.5	4.4	10.6	17.8	29.4	46.5	41.2	18.0	2,110	94.4
Jacumba CDP	561	-	-	307	37.5	0.0	0.0	11.4	51.1	7.5	52.8	68.1	30.3	5.3	193	82.9
Jamestown CDP	3,433	-	-	3,107	89.3	0.0	0.0	5.3	5.5	18.2	30.6	47.0	29.7	12.4	1,603	90.6
Jamul CDP	6,163	-	-	5,445	74.9	2.1	4.9	3.0	15.1	14.6	24.1	53.8	26.3	43.3	1,916	99.0
Janesville CDP	1,408	-	-	1,409	85.9	0.1	0.9	9.4	3.6	19.1	20.6	38.4	42.1	15.7	588	82.8
Jenner CDP	136	-	-	30	100.0	0.0	0.0	0.0	0.0	0.0	20.0	39.9	23.3	56.7	30	80.0
Johannesburg CDP	172	-	-	119	100.0	0.0	0.0	0.0	0.0	22.7	0.0	31.0	28.3	0.0	58	100.0
Johnstonville CDP	1,024	-	-	1,132	89.7	0.0	0.6	4.5	5.2	27.7	17.7	41.1	26.0	17.3	414	91.5
Johnsville CDP	20	-	-	-	-	-	-	-	-	-	-	-	-	-	-	-
Joshua Tree CDP	7,414	-	-	7,581	72.1	0.9	1.3	4.8	20.8	20.2	18.9	40.1	36.1	19.0	3,089	90.1
Julian CDP	1,502	-	-	1,019	95.4	0.0	0.0	3.8	0.8	10.5	39.3	61.7	25.2	18.9	499	79.0
Junction City CDP	680	-	-	682	77.1	0.0	0.7	9.8	12.3	10.4	33.7	60.2	44.9	24.3	334	82.0
June Lake CDP	629	-	-	390	95.1	0.0	2.1	0.0	2.8	5.6	64.9	66.9	42.1	22.8	187	87.2
Jurupa Valley city	94,986	109,527	15.3	105,653	20.6	3.0	3.5	1.4	71.4	28.0	10.2	32.1	58.7	13.2	24,907	93.4
Keddie CDP	66	-	-	76	100.0	0.0	0.0	0.0	0.0	15.8	50.0	59.5	0.0	90.6	28	100.0
Keeler CDP	66	-	-	10	100.0	0.0	0.0	0.0	0.0	0.0	50.0	0.0	0.0	50.0	10	100.0
Keene CDP	431	-	-	228	82.5	0.0	0.0	0.0	17.5	12.3	28.1	57.5	20.1	59.8	89	100.0
Kelly Ridge CDP	2,544	-	-	2,850	82.6	1.1	0.0	8.9	7.4	19.2	35.1	50.9	43.8	14.3	1,245	89.2
Kelseyville CDP	3,353	-	-	3,560	53.9	1.6	0.0	0.0	44.5	25.8	22.3	37.9	57.8	14.0	1,383	86.3
Kennedy CDP	3,254	-	-	3,356	4.9	4.1	9.0	0.4	81.6	32.2	11.1	30.3	78.4	5.1	859	72.8
Kennedy Meadows CDP	28	-	-	-	-	-	-	-	-	-	-	-	-	-	-	-
Kensington CDP	5,077	-	-	5,329	69.7	2.3	11.7	6.3	10.1	19.9	27.1	50.5	5.1	85.3	2,254	97.3
Kentfield CDP	6,485	-	-	7,020	86.7	0.0	4.0	3.4	5.9	25.5	20.7	45.4	5.4	80.2	2,567	94.9
Kenwood CDP	1,028	-	-	716	80.3	0.0	4.2	13.3	2.2	10.6	37.3	62.9	23.1	68.6	425	78.4
Kerman city	13,567	15,282	12.6	14,816	12.3	0.4	4.2	1.3	81.8	32.6	10.2	27.7	69.8	7.5	3,902	90.2
Kernville CDP	1,395	-	-	663	78.0	0.3	2.9	0.0	18.9	18.1	40.7	61.1	19.9	41.2	386	83.9
Keswick CDP	451	-	-	289	80.3	0.0	11.4	7.3	1.0	19.4	21.5	45.9	52.2	19.4	124	75.0
Kettleman City CDP	1,439	-	-	1,136	1.8	0.0	0.0	0.0	98.2	33.4	6.9	30.3	83.7	0.0	287	65.5
Keyes CDP	5,601	-	-	6,548	22.6	0.4	0.7	2.5	73.8	32.3	8.5	31.0	66.8	6.1	1,704	83.5
King City city	12,874	14,077	9.3	13,921	8.5	1.0	1.7	1.3	87.5	33.6	6.4	28.0	76.9	4.1	3,325	81.4
Kings Beach CDP	3,796	-	-	3,044	64.7	0.0	0.6	2.4	32.3	20.5	12.7	35.3	34.8	27.5	1,305	90.0
Kingsburg city	11,454	12,108	5.7	11,955	47.2	0.3	3.2	4.8	44.5	28.9	13.4	34.8	33.4	30.1	3,996	91.9
Kingvale CDP	143	-	-	71	100.0	0.0	0.0	0.0	0.0	11.3	0.0	35.2	0.0	100.0	32	100.0
Kirkwood CDP	158	-	-	80	55.0	11.3	6.3	0.0	27.5	10.0	6.3	36.0	58.2	34.3	34	100.0
Klamath CDP	779	-	-	632	46.4	0.0	0.0	49.8	3.8	23.1	22.0	47.8	51.4	16.7	250	82.4
Knightsen CDP	1,568	-	-	1,176	72.1	0.0	0.0	1.8	26.1	18.7	21.9	50.2	36.8	18.7	465	98.5
Knights Landing CDP	995	-	-	1,036	7.7	0.0	0.0	0.0	92.3	29.0	18.1	39.4	79.4	12.4	291	73.5
La Cañada Flintridge city	20,256	20,009	-1.2	20,261	54.0	0.8	31.0	4.2	10.0	26.1	18.6	45.1	7.5	75.9	6,423	96.9
La Crescenta-Montrose CDP	19,653	-	-	19,689	50.8	0.3	27.5	5.1	16.3	23.6	16.6	43.0	22.3	51.4	6,917	95.5
Ladera CDP	1,426	-	-	1,607	87.1	0.0	7.5	5.4	0.0	27.8	18.9	43.3	5.4	88.8	508	100.0
Ladera Heights CDP	6,498	-	-	6,620	12.6	70.0	4.9	7.0	5.5	17.6	25.4	49.0	12.9	55.0	2,866	92.8
Ladera Ranch CDP	22,980	-	-	27,277	66.7	0.8	12.4	6.0	14.0	37.0	6.8	34.4	10.4	66.8	8,353	97.6
Lafayette city	23,791	26,638	12.0	26,305	75.2	0.5	11.2	4.5	8.6	25.5	17.9	45.3	7.8	71.6	9,426	97.0
Laguna Beach city	22,733	22,827	0.4	23,036	83.4	0.8	3.7	3.8	8.2	16.6	24.5	51.7	11.1	66.0	10,235	96.2
Laguna Hills city	30,673	31,207	1.7	31,617	57.5	1.5	14.6	4.4	22.0	20.4	17.2	42.8	20.7	50.5	11,037	96.5
Laguna Niguel city	62,989	66,385	5.4	65,808	66.6	1.2	10.2	5.7	16.4	19.6	17.7	45.2	16.9	53.6	25,290	97.3
Laguna Woods city	15,991	15,850	-0.9	16,053	72.0	0.7	19.7	1.8	5.8	0.2	82.8	75.6	21.9	49.3	11,003	87.8
Lagunitas-Forest Knolls CDP	1,819	-	-	1,771	77.0	0.2	0.9	3.2	18.7	22.0	21.7	40.6	19.0	50.7	717	95.3
La Habra city	59,016	60,513	2.5	60,594	25.5	1.3	11.8	1.7	59.7	23.6	12.7	36.0	40.9	28.5	18,416	94.8
La Habra Heights city	6,537	6,492	-0.7	6,574	45.6	0.1	16.9	1.2	36.2	19.1	22.3	46.7	22.4	47.8	2,197	95.8
La Honda CDP	928	-	-	960	92.7	0.1	0.0	6.4	0.8	13.8	15.8	41.7	15.6	65.9	399	100.0

1 May be of any race.

Table A. All Places — **Population and Housing**

STATE City, town, township, borough, or CDP (county if applicable)	Population: 2010 census total population	Population: 2019 estimated population	Population: Percent change 2010-2019	Population: ACS total population estimate 2015-2019	Race and Hispanic or Latino origin (percent): White alone, not Hispanic or Latino	Black alone, not Hispanic or Latino	Asian alone, not Hispanic or Latino	All other races or 2 or more races, not Hispanic or Latino	Hispanic or Latino[1]	Age (percent): Under 18 years old	Age 65 years and older	Median age	Educational attainment of persons age 25 and older: Percent High school diploma or less	Percent Bachelor's degree or more	Occupied housing units: Total	Percent with a computer
	1	2	3	4	5	6	7	8	9	10	11	12	13	14	15	16
CALIFORNIA—Con.																
Lake Almanor Country Club CDP	419	-	-	408	76.5	0.0	0.0	0.0	23.5	11.0	44.6	63.4	13.1	49.3	203	98.0
Lake Almanor Peninsula CDP	356	-	-	366	89.6	0.0	0.0	0.0	10.4	3.8	54.4	65.5	20.4	32.7	184	91.3
Lake Almanor West CDP	270	-	-	224	87.1	0.0	0.0	9.8	3.1	6.7	44.6	57.7	9.6	49.4	108	100.0
Lake Arrowhead CDP	12,424	-	-	8,940	70.9	1.1	1.4	3.9	22.7	19.6	22.7	45.8	31.5	30.6	3,547	95.2
Lake California CDP	3,054	-	-	3,329	78.8	0.6	0.0	2.7	17.8	27.4	20.9	35.2	26.3	21.8	1,207	94.9
Lake City CDP	61	-	-	56	92.9	7.1	0.0	0.0	0.0	0.0	94.6	68.4	28.3	24.5	40	77.5
Lake Davis CDP	45	-	-	52	61.5	0.0	0.0	0.0	38.5	0.0	78.8	77.7	25.0	38.5	34	70.6
Lake Don Pedro CDP	1,077	-	-	901	71.6	0.0	0.0	6.5	21.9	15.2	34.6	55.4	43.9	28.2	430	75.6
Lake Elsinore city	53,313	69,283	30.0	65,817	31.3	6.0	5.9	4.1	52.7	31.9	7.2	30.6	44.8	19.6	17,664	96.0
Lake Forest city	77,445	85,531	10.4	83,974	53.2	1.9	18.5	4.5	21.9	21.8	13.6	39.6	20.5	48.7	29,338	96.1
Lakehead CDP	461	-	-	670	77.8	0.7	8.4	10.3	2.8	18.7	22.2	37.7	42.4	9.9	277	90.6
Lake Hughes CDP	649	-	-	520	81.0	0.0	5.4	0.0	13.7	14.8	15.8	56.9	14.7	39.3	192	94.3
Lake Isabella CDP	3,466	-	-	3,495	81.3	0.0	1.6	3.6	13.4	17.9	22.3	48.6	51.8	9.6	1,542	88.5
Lakeland Village CDP	11,541	-	-	13,002	39.6	2.0	1.9	1.7	54.8	29.1	9.5	33.9	60.0	9.5	3,471	91.9
Lake Los Angeles CDP	12,328	-	-	11,751	32.9	8.8	0.5	1.3	56.5	30.7	11.2	35.1	65.2	7.2	3,355	84.4
Lake Mathews CDP	5,890	-	-	6,792	51.2	4.3	7.2	3.8	33.4	22.8	13.0	40.9	41.8	26.6	1,911	97.7
Lake Nacimiento CDP	2,411	-	-	2,981	76.3	0.0	1.8	9.0	12.9	24.5	15.6	39.9	41.6	17.8	1,194	93.9
Lake of the Pines CDP	3,917	-	-	3,599	81.8	0.0	0.6	4.9	12.7	14.4	27.8	54.2	17.0	45.8	1,541	95.1
Lake of the Woods CDP	917	-	-	931	81.5	0.0	4.3	1.1	13.1	18.9	26.4	55.6	47.9	17.2	386	96.6
Lakeport city	4,754	5,006	5.3	4,910	71.1	0.5	5.7	6.1	16.5	18.8	25.6	51.3	32.2	25.7	2,129	89.3
Lake Riverside CDP	1,173	-	-	1,354	84.9	0.0	0.0	1.6	13.6	28.7	19.2	41.0	35.4	21.6	384	96.4
Lake San Marcos CDP	4,437	-	-	4,713	76.0	2.4	8.4	1.3	11.8	12.6	41.6	61.7	18.4	43.5	2,376	90.2
Lake Sherwood CDP	1,527	-	-	1,677	88.0	0.2	3.0	5.5	3.3	16.8	27.4	51.9	9.5	74.1	624	100.0
Lakeside CDP	20,648	-	-	21,917	74.5	1.7	2.8	4.5	16.6	22.0	15.5	39.3	39.2	17.8	7,403	95.8
Lakeview CDP	2,104	-	-	2,638	18.5	0.0	0.0	0.2	81.3	29.5	9.9	29.0	66.8	9.2	536	91.8
Lake Wildwood CDP	4,991	-	-	5,232	88.5	0.0	0.8	1.5	9.2	13.5	42.7	60.6	21.0	36.2	2,213	96.9
Lakewood city	80,086	79,307	-	80,292	34.3	8.6	18.7	4.6	33.8	21.9	13.4	38.6	30.7	30.8	25,756	94.9
La Mesa city	57,016	59,249	3.9	59,556	55.8	7.7	7.3	5.0	24.2	20.2	14.4	35.7	25.7	37.7	23,288	94.2
La Mirada city	48,527	48,183	-0.7	48,764	31.7	1.8	21.5	3.0	42.0	18.8	17.4	39.6	34.2	32.5	14,217	94.8
Lamont CDP	15,120	-	-	14,799	5.0	0.0	0.5	0.1	94.5	33.8	4.5	26.7	86.1	2.8	3,568	77.4
Lanare CDP	589	-	-	226	4.9	0.0	0.0	0.0	95.1	27.0	3.1	34.5	93.2	0.0	61	100.0
Lancaster city	156,649	157,601	0.6	159,028	30.1	20.5	4.5	3.4	41.5	28.7	9.8	32.6	46.8	17.6	48,083	85.5
La Palma city	15,525	15,428	-0.6	15,604	25.6	4.4	46.4	4.2	19.4	17.9	18.0	43.7	23.7	47.5	4,820	95.5
La Porte CDP	26	-	-	-	-	-	-	-	-	-	-	-	-	-	-	-
La Presa CDP	34,169	-	-	38,227	23.7	11.2	10.5	4.6	50.0	24.4	12.7	34.1	42.5	19.0	10,816	93.4
La Puente city	39,832	39,614	-0.5	40,020	3.7	0.8	11.6	1.0	82.9	24.3	11.2	33.0	66.1	10.9	9,415	91.9
La Quinta city	37,465	41,748	11.4	41,076	57.3	1.7	3.4	2.8	34.7	19.5	26.0	47.9	29.4	36.2	15,948	93.9
La Riviera CDP	10,802	-	-	10,840	48.6	11.7	9.7	6.6	23.4	17.1	15.2	35.0	27.9	32.7	4,384	94.8
Larkfield-Wikiup CDP	8,884	-	-	8,312	65.7	0.0	3.5	5.8	24.9	21.4	19.4	43.5	22.7	32.9	3,340	93.8
Larkspur city	11,908	12,254	2.9	12,319	77.9	0.7	5.4	5.0	11.0	18.0	25.1	49.8	11.1	73.4	5,683	95.7
La Selva Beach CDP	2,843	-	-	2,679	79.2	0.3	0.8	4.3	15.4	16.6	25.4	48.7	14.0	60.3	1,073	96.8
Las Flores CDP	5,971	-	-	5,861	66.3	0.0	15.3	4.4	14.0	30.7	4.7	34.3	11.1	56.2	1,899	100.0
Las Flores CDP	187	-	-	361	53.5	0.0	0.0	0.0	46.5	41.3	6.4	32.7	65.5	0.0	77	100.0
Las Lomas CDP	3,024	-	-	2,924	14.9	0.0	0.1	2.3	82.7	25.5	5.8	30.1	64.6	11.2	650	90.0
Lathrop city	17,589	24,483	39.2	22,341	20.4	6.0	26.3	4.3	43.0	27.7	8.1	32.0	46.7	18.4	5,503	95.8
Laton CDP	1,824	-	-	2,000	19.9	0.0	0.0	0.9	79.2	36.7	7.8	29.4	66.8	1.5	598	73.2
La Verne city	31,096	31,974	2.8	32,211	49.6	3.0	9.2	2.2	36.1	20.4	20.0	45.1	26.0	38.0	11,521	94.7
La Vina CDP	279	-	-	211	0.0	0.0	0.0	0.0	100.0	45.5	16.6	26.1	47.8	27.0	51	100.0
Lawndale city	32,769	32,389	-1.2	32,819	14.6	9.7	10.9	3.3	61.5	23.7	10.3	35.5	51.6	19.9	9,902	94.1
Laytonville CDP	1,227	-	-	1,198	59.0	0.6	0.0	32.1	8.3	20.6	19.7	38.9	45.7	24.5	510	85.1
Lebec CDP	1,468	-	-	1,472	42.5	0.0	11.1	2.3	44.2	14.5	14.1	42.2	61.8	20.5	644	79.3
Lee Vining CDP	222	-	-	98	80.6	5.1	5.1	0.0	9.2	0.0	0.0	59.8	0.0	69.7	62	56.5
Leggett CDP	122	-	-	83	67.5	0.0	0.0	0.0	32.5	22.9	2.4	54.3	34.5	0.0	51	66.7
Le Grand CDP	1,659	-	-	1,739	14.1	0.6	1.2	1.0	83.2	25.2	10.2	35.9	62.6	8.9	529	89.4
Lemon Cove CDP	308	-	-	232	100.0	0.0	0.0	0.0	0.0	19.8	44.4	61.7	32.8	43.7	82	87.8
Lemon Grove city	25,318	26,811	5.9	26,802	28.2	14.4	7.6	5.5	44.3	25.0	13.3	35.6	44.5	18.9	8,494	90.3
Lemon Hill CDP	13,729	-	-	14,733	15.7	11.6	16.1	12.6	43.9	31.4	8.6	30.2	66.6	5.7	4,360	83.9
Lemoore city	24,534	26,725	8.9	26,107	39.7	5.1	7.8	4.5	42.9	27.3	9.4	29.9	38.7	20.1	8,716	92.6
Lemoore Station CDP	7,438	-	-	6,858	50.0	15.9	4.3	6.5	23.3	29.0	0.4	22.5	25.0	24.0	1,603	99.3
Lennox CDP	22,753	-	-	21,818	1.4	3.1	2.8	2.6	90.1	28.8	5.9	29.5	72.4	9.1	5,418	94.2
Lenwood CDP	3,543	-	-	4,122	29.8	5.5	0.6	2.5	61.5	39.8	5.4	24.9	53.0	9.9	1,162	92.3
Leona Valley CDP	1,607	-	-	1,571	83.0	1.0	0.6	3.4	12.0	18.0	26.2	49.6	37.0	15.9	616	92.5
Lewiston CDP	1,193	-	-	1,383	81.6	4.6	0.8	9.8	3.3	12.0	25.3	53.7	45.8	16.3	581	86.1
Lexington Hills CDP	2,421	-	-	2,685	87.4	0.1	4.6	4.4	3.6	24.3	12.0	44.2	19.8	60.3	908	98.7
Likely CDP	63	-	-	-	-	-	-	-	-	-	-	-	-	-	-	-
Lincoln city	42,926	48,275	12.5	47,388	67.8	1.6	6.5	3.0	21.1	22.3	26.9	43.3	27.6	34.2	17,720	95.8
Lincoln Village CDP	4,381	-	-	4,859	46.1	1.9	3.7	5.7	42.6	29.0	17.0	34.5	30.9	33.4	1,675	89.3
Linda CDP	17,773	-	-	20,228	37.6	5.3	13.3	8.0	35.9	31.3	8.8	29.5	46.1	13.4	6,526	91.7
Lindcove CDP	406	-	-	287	36.2	0.0	0.0	1.0	62.7	16.4	15.0	40.4	67.4	9.5	98	77.6
Linden CDP	1,784	-	-	1,547	81.0	0.0	0.5	0.9	17.6	27.0	16.5	40.6	37.3	22.5	541	98.5
Lindsay city	11,756	13,463	14.5	13,310	11.2	0.4	0.9	0.5	87.0	32.8	9.2	29.3	78.6	3.9	3,752	82.3
Linnell Camp CDP	849	-	-	928	0.0	0.0	0.0	0.0	100.0	49.4	1.4	19.2	100.0	0.0	234	94.4
Litchfield CDP	195	-	-	205	90.7	0.0	0.0	0.0	9.3	28.8	22.0	36.3	15.8	29.5	75	100.0
Little Grass Valley CDP	2	-	-	-	-	-	-	-	-	-	-	-	-	-	-	-
Little River CDP	117	-	-	212	95.8	0.0	0.0	0.0	4.2	29.2	33.5	51.5	0.0	19.3	150	100.0
Littlerock CDP	1,377	-	-	786	35.8	0.0	0.0	3.9	60.3	24.3	5.7	32.4	64.9	5.9	227	84.6
Little Valley CDP	-	-	-	26	69.2	0.0	0.0	0.0	30.8	0.0	0.0	57.1	100.0	0.0	13	100.0
Live Oak CDP	17,158	-	-	16,837	59.3	0.6	4.1	3.5	32.7	20.3	16.8	39.8	25.5	38.5	6,226	91.4
Live Oak city	8,465	8,912	5.3	8,679	37.8	2.0	5.8	3.6	50.7	31.0	11.2	32.4	53.7	11.5	2,455	90.4
Livermore city	81,426	90,189	10.8	89,699	61.9	1.8	11.4	5.1	19.8	23.6	13.5	39.8	23.0	44.0	31,747	96.0
Livingston city	13,020	14,896	14.4	14,228	4.4	0.1	21.3	0.7	73.5	30.0	10.7	29.9	60.9	9.7	3,607	90.7
Lockeford CDP	3,233	-	-	3,521	62.7	0.1	0.3	2.6	34.2	30.1	16.0	34.4	43.0	18.8	1,218	85.8
Lockwood CDP	379	-	-	516	85.3	0.0	3.7	0.0	11.0	25.6	11.2	37.5	59.7	10.3	203	97.5
Lodi city	62,121	67,586	8.8	65,846	47.7	1.7	9.6	3.2	37.8	27.8	14.2	35.0	46.5	19.2	23,142	91.0
Lodoga CDP	197	-	-	168	50.0	39.9	0.0	10.1	0.0	10.7	44.0	63.5	70.7	6.4	80	91.3
Loleta CDP	783	-	-	632	78.3	4.1	0.3	5.5	11.7	29.7	10.9	27.9	29.2	33.1	264	85.6
Loma Linda city	23,306	24,482	5.0	24,184	32.3	9.7	24.3	5.4	28.2	18.8	18.8	36.3	28.7	45.2	8,932	89.5
Loma Mar CDP	113	-	-	172	100.0	0.0	0.0	0.0	0.0	0.0	20.3	48.2	62.4	9.7	64	100.0
Loma Rica CDP	2,368	-	-	3,178	71.7	7.5	0.5	6.2	14.1	35.3	8.9	29.8	35.3	20.6	1,073	93.6
Lomita city	20,256	20,320	0.3	20,514	39.5	6.1	15.9	5.2	33.4	21.2	17.3	40.1	36.0	35.3	8,062	93.6

1 May be of any race.

STATE City, town, township, borough, or CDP (county if applicable)	Population				Race and Hispanic or Latino origin (percent)					Age (percent)			Educational attainment of persons age 25 and older		Occupied housing units	
	2010 census total population	2019 estimated population	Percent change 2010-2019	ACS total population estimate 2015-2019	White alone, not Hispanic or Latino	Black alone, not Hispanic or Latino	Asian alone, not Hispanic or Latino	All other races or 2 or more races, not Hispanic or Latino	Hispanic or Latino[1]	Under 18 years old	Age 65 years and older	Median age	Percent High school diploma or less	Percent Bachelor's degree or more	Total	Percent with a computer
	1	2	3	4	5	6	7	8	9	10	11	12	13	14	15	16
CALIFORNIA—Con.																
Lompico CDP	1,137	-	-	1,035	72.9	1.6	6.3	5.4	13.8	14.1	16.5	49.8	23.1	53.6	490	93.5
Lompoc city	42,438	42,853	1.0	43,232	31.7	4.4	3.5	3.8	56.6	27.1	11.2	32.7	50.4	12.6	13,027	89.8
London CDP	1,869	-	-	1,690	7.0	0.7	0.9	0.4	91.1	41.0	6.2	23.6	86.3	2.6	449	72.2
Lone Pine CDP	2,035	-	-	1,807	49.5	0.1	0.7	7.2	42.5	25.2	22.3	43.9	61.5	17.1	758	84.6
Long Barn CDP	155	-	-	102	39.2	0.0	60.8	0.0	0.0	0.0	39.2	60.6	100.0	0.0	71	100.0
Long Beach city	462,221	462,628	0.1	466,776	28.2	12.2	12.8	4.2	42.6	22.4	11.4	34.9	37.9	31.1	166,813	92.8
Lookout CDP	84	-	-	44	100.0	0.0	0.0	0.0	0.0	36.4	0.0	32.5	50.0	0.0	17	100.0
Loomis town	6,417	6,866	7.0	6,790	84.4	0.4	2.0	6.4	6.8	22.8	19.4	46.7	23.5	33.8	2,619	98.7
Los Alamitos city	11,376	11,399	0.2	11,534	47.6	5.8	14.0	5.7	27.0	22.5	16.3	39.7	26.8	45.7	4,092	95.1
Los Alamos CDP	1,890	-	-	1,634	62.7	1.9	4.9	7.6	22.9	25.6	19.7	44.3	59.0	11.6	567	84.8
Los Altos city	29,024	30,089	3.7	30,504	58.1	0.5	31.4	5.5	4.4	25.8	20.0	46.1	4.8	84.2	10,652	97.6
Los Altos Hills town	8,050	8,423	4.6	8,505	59.8	0.6	32.1	3.0	4.5	21.8	27.0	51.1	7.1	85.3	3,016	99.4
Los Angeles city	3,793,139	3,979,576	4.9	3,966,936	28.5	8.6	11.5	3.0	48.5	20.7	12.4	35.6	41.8	34.4	1,383,869	91.6
Los Banos city	35,971	41,036	14.1	38,914	20.2	2.4	2.7	3.0	71.7	34.6	9.5	30.1	60.3	10.5	10,777	92.4
Los Berros CDP	641	-	-	528	53.6	0.4	0.0	0.0	46.0	16.5	19.3	41.4	65.0	15.9	156	82.7
Los Gatos town	29,715	30,222	1.7	30,729	72.3	0.9	14.7	4.2	7.9	22.0	20.8	47.2	11.5	69.8	12,083	95.2
Los Molinos CDP	2,037	-	-	1,746	77.8	0.0	0.9	2.3	19.0	29.3	24.2	38.6	47.8	20.7	724	75.3
Los Olivos CDP	1,132	-	-	791	75.3	0.0	0.0	9.2	15.4	17.2	24.9	50.3	25.5	47.0	367	91.6
Los Osos CDP	14,276	-	-	16,533	75.8	0.2	4.3	3.6	16.1	18.8	25.5	46.9	22.5	42.9	6,392	94.0
Los Ranchos CDP	1,477	-	-	1,639	75.7	0.0	2.9	3.5	18.0	19.2	28.5	54.9	9.0	71.9	631	100.0
Lost Hills CDP	2,412	-	-	1,726	3.4	0.0	0.0	0.0	96.6	35.9	2.2	24.0	85.8	1.3	478	36.2
Lower Lake CDP	1,294	-	-	1,355	64.0	0.0	0.0	1.0	35.1	23.4	27.6	54.1	49.2	5.9	526	84.4
Loyalton city	766	702	-8.4	1,093	81.2	0.1	0.0	0.7	18.0	24.3	26.9	36.4	49.7	4.9	361	88.4
Loyola CDP	3,261	-	-	3,367	59.1	0.1	30.6	6.2	4.0	29.0	20.3	46.8	3.6	89.4	1,115	99.1
Lucas Valley-Marinwood CDP	6,094	-	-	6,686	73.6	0.1	6.0	7.1	13.3	24.2	22.7	47.8	14.1	60.5	2,412	95.6
Lucerne CDP	3,067	-	-	2,896	68.3	3.7	0.0	10.8	17.1	15.5	17.0	37.7	44.6	19.6	1,187	80.3
Lucerne Valley CDP	5,811	-	-	5,956	66.1	2.3	2.2	3.5	25.9	24.3	19.8	40.5	55.6	9.6	2,148	85.2
Lynwood city	69,763	69,887	0.2	70,635	2.4	8.1	0.7	0.8	88.1	28.2	7.5	30.0	72.0	7.7	15,405	91.5
Lytle Creek CDP	701	-	-	673	74.4	0.0	1.3	0.7	23.5	9.5	25.1	54.9	56.8	20.0	361	82.8
Mabie CDP	161	-	-	25	100.0	0.0	0.0	0.0	0.0	0.0	100.0	0.0	44.0	0.0	14	100.0
McArthur CDP	338	-	-	446	50.2	0.0	0.0	2.2	47.5	31.2	16.4	40.5	90.5	0.0	163	76.7
McClellan Park CDP	743	-	-	1,046	40.8	29.2	6.4	7.3	16.3	29.3	14.2	30.9	39.1	19.9	328	100.0
McClenney Tract CDP	10	-	-	47	100.0	0.0	0.0	0.0	0.0	0.0	4.3	25.8	44.1	23.5	26	92.3
McCloud CDP	1,101	-	-	1,020	90.5	0.1	0.0	4.1	5.3	16.7	30.7	52.9	37.5	16.1	494	73.7
Macdoel CDP	133	-	-	54	0.0	0.0	0.0	0.0	100.0	46.3	0.0	49.1	55.2	44.8	16	100.0
McFarland city	12,707	15,506	22.0	14,823	3.4	1.0	0.1	0.7	94.7	34.4	4.4	26.2	79.4	3.4	3,269	69.7
McGee Creek CDP	41	-	-	-	-	-	-	-	-	-	-	-	-	-	-	-
McKinleyville CDP	15,177	-	-	17,208	77.3	0.3	2.7	11.2	8.5	22.8	15.0	35.0	26.5	34.1	6,618	92.1
McKittrick CDP	115	-	-	116	78.4	0.9	0.0	2.6	18.1	16.4	22.4	53.5	46.8	2.1	42	61.9
McSwain CDP	4,171	-	-	4,399	57.0	3.6	11.7	3.4	24.3	23.7	19.2	43.6	33.6	36.2	1,539	96.9
Madera city	61,513	65,860	7.1	64,833	14.6	3.8	1.5	1.7	78.4	34.3	8.7	28.6	63.5	9.5	18,122	86.5
Madera Acres CDP	9,163	-	-	9,857	22.4	2.1	1.0	1.5	73.0	24.9	12.4	36.2	55.3	13.8	2,485	96.2
Madison CDP	503	-	-	581	0.3	0.2	0.2	0.0	99.3	18.6	10.3	35.3	89.6	0.5	193	82.9
Mad River CDP	420	-	-	458	88.6	0.0	0.0	6.6	4.8	26.6	22.9	54.0	45.2	15.2	212	65.1
Magalia CDP	11,310	-	-	11,476	84.5	0.0	0.9	7.0	7.6	15.5	25.1	49.9	36.3	18.7	4,633	94.1
Malaga CDP	947	-	-	1,186	7.3	0.9	0.0	0.0	91.7	29.9	7.8	25.5	72.7	6.3	289	94.5
Malibu city	12,634	11,820	-6.4	12,620	83.3	1.1	2.0	4.6	9.0	15.7	25.5	53.0	10.2	66.0	5,681	97.1
Mammoth Lakes town	8,234	8,235	0.0	8,169	54.9	0.3	3.7	3.7	37.5	22.8	5.1	31.6	33.9	26.6	2,514	92.0
Manchester CDP	195	-	-	218	66.1	0.0	0.0	1.4	32.6	23.4	16.5	43.2	49.7	20.8	86	90.7
Manhattan Beach city	35,131	35,183	0.1	35,500	73.3	0.4	13.4	4.9	8.0	26.7	16.9	44.0	8.1	75.2	13,427	97.8
Manila CDP	784	-	-	793	82.6	1.1	3.0	8.3	4.9	12.9	12.2	42.0	29.8	35.1	346	92.5
Manteca city	67,348	83,028	23.3	79,129	39.9	4.5	9.3	6.5	39.8	26.2	12.9	36.2	47.6	16.7	25,200	92.6
Manton CDP	347	-	-	350	70.3	0.0	0.3	22.0	7.4	32.6	22.9	35.8	35.5	13.3	126	55.6
March ARB CDP	1,159	-	-	989	55.3	5.6	5.3	2.0	31.9	26.8	42.8	46.4	28.0	36.9	476	81.9
Maricopa city	1,154	1,192	3.3	1,229	45.6	0.0	0.7	4.8	48.8	29.8	14.2	33.2	73.9	3.4	403	74.7
Marina city	19,718	22,781	15.5	21,981	35.8	6.4	16.4	10.5	30.9	22.7	14.9	33.9	35.1	28.9	7,771	93.3
Marina del Rey CDP	8,866	-	-	9,852	66.6	7.4	10.5	4.6	10.8	7.3	10.4	38.0	11.0	70.7	5,537	98.8
Marin City CDP	2,666	-	-	3,126	32.9	21.7	6.9	13.8	24.8	27.7	9.8	36.0	31.8	39.3	1,377	89.2
Mariposa CDP	2,173	-	-	1,186	79.8	1.3	0.0	6.6	12.3	11.5	36.2	55.5	27.9	18.6	699	93.7
Markleeville CDP	210	-	-	132	100.0	0.0	0.0	0.0	0.0	0.0	67.4	66.8	12.9	59.8	72	100.0
Martell CDP	282	-	-	400	94.5	0.0	0.0	1.8	3.8	37.5	5.8	29.6	22.6	12.5	99	100.0
Martinez city	36,032	38,297	6.3	38,290	66.3	3.3	8.5	5.2	16.7	19.8	16.2	42.6	22.9	41.6	14,723	95.5
Marysville city	12,072	12,476	3.3	12,327	62.1	2.1	1.5	4.7	29.6	23.6	11.8	31.8	40.6	13.7	4,756	86.3
Matheny CDP	1,212	-	-	1,137	9.9	4.5	0.0	0.8	84.8	37.7	8.3	25.2	68.8	3.8	293	75.4
Mather CDP	4,451	-	-	4,272	54.2	7.8	13.4	10.7	13.8	25.4	10.6	35.0	23.5	38.4	1,388	97.3
Maxwell CDP	1,103	-	-	1,076	40.1	0.0	0.0	4.6	55.3	29.0	10.9	35.4	64.2	8.0	356	80.3
Mayfair CDP	4,589	-	-	4,950	21.1	8.2	4.1	3.8	62.8	30.2	7.1	31.3	47.1	9.4	1,483	92.0
Mayflower Village CDP	5,515	-	-	5,873	25.2	0.5	36.4	4.7	33.2	18.6	18.4	44.3	32.3	37.8	1,836	93.4
Maywood city	27,382	26,973	-1.5	27,332	1.0	0.3	0.2	0.1	98.4	28.2	8.4	30.1	79.9	5.7	6,695	82.6
Meadowbrook CDP	3,185	-	-	3,414	39.8	2.1	2.8	0.2	55.1	22.1	18.2	39.7	60.5	7.3	901	86.6
Meadow Valley CDP	464	-	-	420	96.7	0.0	0.0	0.0	3.3	10.5	33.3	59.9	13.0	28.7	228	89.0
Meadow Vista CDP	3,217	-	-	3,679	87.4	0.0	2.1	3.4	7.1	20.6	20.7	49.3	24.6	35.5	1,389	95.4
Mead Valley CDP	18,510	-	-	20,145	12.3	9.2	2.3	2.0	74.2	29.8	12.0	33.2	71.2	5.2	4,400	91.5
Mecca CDP	8,577	-	-	6,635	0.2	0.0	0.0	0.0	99.8	34.3	6.8	30.2	95.0	0.8	1,860	73.0
Meiners Oaks CDP	3,571	-	-	3,569	63.7	0.5	1.7	5.7	28.4	17.6	15.6	40.0	33.1	36.4	1,190	100.0
Mendocino CDP	894	-	-	855	76.4	0.0	16.8	0.0	6.8	1.6	33.7	55.3	14.0	61.3	451	90.0
Mendota city	11,306	11,511	1.8	11,531	2.9	0.0	0.0	0.2	96.9	36.6	6.4	27.1	87.3	1.5	2,838	77.1
Menifee city	77,382	94,756	22.5	90,349	47.4	5.7	5.3	4.4	37.2	25.1	18.1	37.7	39.9	19.8	29,080	92.6
Menlo Park city	32,019	34,698	8.4	34,138	58.2	4.3	14.8	7.2	15.5	24.9	14.0	37.9	15.3	69.6	11,906	97.8
Mentone CDP	8,720	-	-	9,793	43.3	3.6	7.7	5.6	39.8	23.5	12.2	36.6	37.2	23.1	3,341	92.8
Merced city	78,958	83,676	6.0	82,662	25.8	4.9	11.2	3.0	55.2	29.5	10.1	29.4	50.7	16.5	25,490	90.6
Meridian CDP	358	-	-	371	72.0	3.0	0.8	5.4	18.9	20.8	17.8	49.1	54.7	15.4	153	81.7
Mesa CDP	251	-	-	348	71.8	0.0	0.0	9.8	18.4	17.2	14.9	45.1	31.3	34.4	146	97.3
Mesa Verde CDP	1,023	-	-	913	15.0	0.0	0.0	1.1	83.9	28.4	12.3	36.3	68.5	4.2	228	77.2
Mesa Vista CDP	200	-	-	228	56.1	0.0	0.0	43.9	0.0	9.6	44.7	64.1	51.7	31.0	81	96.3
Mettler CDP	136	-	-	157	6.4	0.0	0.0	0.0	93.6	13.4	14.6	40.0	64.9	3.6	49	79.6
Mexican Colony CDP	281	-	-	423	0.0	0.0	0.0	0.0	100.0	38.1	4.7	27.9	93.9	1.6	115	54.8
Middletown CDP	1,323	-	-	739	53.3	0.0	0.0	1.5	45.2	27.2	16.4	43.5	64.5	2.6	271	100.0
Midpines CDP	1,204	-	-	1,427	80.5	9.3	0.8	5.1	4.2	20.8	14.4	41.9	27.5	34.4	658	87.1
Midway City CDP	8,485	-	-	8,343	12.4	0.3	53.1	2.6	31.6	28.8	13.8	38.8	59.3	18.7	2,432	84.9
Milford CDP	167	-	-	206	100.0	0.0	0.0	0.0	0.0	18.9	31.6	40.0	23.5	21.2	70	100.0

1 May be of any race.

Table A. All Places — **Population and Housing**

STATE City, town, township, borough, or CDP (county if applicable)	Population: 2010 census total population	Population: 2019 estimated population	Population: Percent change 2010-2019	Population: ACS total population estimate 2015-2019	Race and Hispanic or Latino origin (percent): White alone, not Hispanic or Latino	Black alone, not Hispanic or Latino	Asian alone, not Hispanic or Latino	All other races or 2 or more races, not Hispanic or Latino	Hispanic or Latino[1]	Age (percent): Under 18 years old	Age 65 years and older	Median age	Educational attainment of persons age 25 and older: Percent High school diploma or less	Percent Bachelor's degree or more	Occupied housing units: Total	Percent with a computer
	1	2	3	4	5	6	7	8	9	10	11	12	13	14	15	16
CALIFORNIA—Con.																
Millbrae city	21,537	22,394	4.0	22,625	33.9	0.6	48.8	5.4	11.4	19.1	19.1	43.9	23.2	52.3	7,976	95.7
Mill Valley city	13,905	14,259	2.5	14,330	86.2	0.7	5.0	3.8	4.2	22.2	23.7	48.7	6.8	76.5	6,107	95.6
Millville CDP	727	-	-	678	92.3	0.0	0.0	0.6	7.1	24.0	22.0	53.4	20.9	35.3	280	86.4
Milpitas city	66,820	84,196	26.0	79,517	11.1	3.3	66.7	4.7	14.2	21.6	12.2	36.3	27.2	50.7	23,595	97.3
Mineral CDP	123	-	-	359	87.2	0.0	0.0	12.8	0.0	41.5	11.1	40.1	31.4	22.4	137	100.0
Minkler CDP	1,003	-	-	958	96.1	0.0	0.0	1.7	2.2	16.0	21.5	53.2	37.1	25.6	483	87.4
Mira Monte CDP	6,854	-	-	6,633	71.1	0.0	1.4	5.3	22.2	11.4	26.8	51.3	24.0	34.8	2,659	90.4
Miranda CDP	520	-	-	605	64.0	12.7	0.0	0.0	23.3	14.2	15.7	36.2	43.2	11.4	260	76.5
Mission Canyon CDP	2,381	-	-	2,508	86.1	0.4	3.5	3.3	6.7	11.8	28.7	54.1	10.4	68.9	1,027	96.4
Mission Hills CDP	3,576	-	-	3,842	55.8	3.5	4.5	3.3	33.0	21.3	15.8	45.6	32.6	27.7	1,302	96.2
Mission Viejo city	93,103	94,381	1.4	95,516	65.1	1.1	11.7	4.4	17.7	19.4	20.1	45.5	19.3	49.0	33,567	97.0
Mi-Wuk Village CDP	941	-	-	880	96.8	0.0	0.0	0.0	3.2	3.6	28.9	62.0	22.2	0.0	382	94.5
Modesto city	203,114	215,196	5.9	212,616	44.2	4.1	6.9	4.6	40.2	25.5	14.3	35.6	45.9	18.7	72,332	92.8
Mohawk Vista CDP	159	-	-	54	79.6	0.0	0.0	0.0	20.4	0.0	38.9	64.5	57.4	18.5	32	59.4
Mojave CDP	4,238	-	-	3,855	29.8	22.2	0.4	7.3	40.3	22.9	16.1	37.2	59.3	9.3	1,536	76.1
Mokelumne Hill CDP	646	-	-	691	57.7	0.0	0.0	0.0	42.3	23.3	34.3	48.3	20.0	22.5	248	83.5
Monmouth CDP	152	-	-	111	8.1	0.0	5.4	0.0	86.5	29.7	21.6	46.5	73.0	0.0	35	85.7
Mono City CDP	172	-	-	96	78.1	0.0	0.0	0.0	21.9	43.8	0.0	43.2	38.9	61.1	54	100.0
Mono Vista CDP	3,127	-	-	3,446	81.3	0.0	0.4	5.6	12.8	17.1	19.5	43.9	35.8	19.9	1,397	95.8
Monrovia city	36,600	36,331	-0.7	36,816	34.5	5.3	14.7	4.4	41.1	20.5	13.9	40.4	30.4	37.4	12,928	92.8
Monson CDP	188	-	-	283	11.7	7.4	0.0	11.0	70.0	44.5	13.4	26.0	52.1	14.8	47	83.0
Montague city	1,443	1,398	-3.1	1,469	79.8	0.0	0.7	8.4	11.2	19.0	19.1	40.0	37.0	10.2	587	90.3
Montalvin Manor CDP	2,876	-	-	2,852	9.0	10.2	10.2	2.4	68.2	24.3	18.3	36.6	50.8	14.6	816	84.7
Montara CDP	2,909	-	-	2,504	86.1	0.0	1.5	8.3	4.1	8.6	37.1	58.9	24.0	53.4	1,028	85.4
Montclair city	36,645	40,083	9.4	39,155	12.7	3.0	10.4	2.7	71.1	25.8	10.7	32.5	52.6	16.3	10,331	91.5
Montebello city	62,488	61,954	-0.9	62,742	7.0	1.0	13.4	1.2	77.4	22.4	14.8	36.1	53.1	19.8	18,888	85.8
Montecito CDP	8,965	-	-	8,245	84.7	0.7	4.6	1.8	8.2	18.2	32.1	50.8	8.1	72.0	3,102	96.3
Monterey city	27,691	28,178	1.8	28,352	66.7	3.9	7.7	5.5	16.2	15.3	18.2	37.8	18.2	52.8	11,872	92.5
Monterey Park city	60,225	59,669	-0.9	60,439	3.9	0.4	65.3	1.9	28.5	17.3	21.3	44.1	44.3	31.8	19,955	91.3
Monterey Park Tract CDP	133	-	-	272	10.7	0.0	0.0	2.9	86.4	47.1	0.0	19.2	80.4	11.8	59	100.0
Monte Rio CDP	1,152	-	-	977	88.0	0.0	1.8	3.8	6.3	15.9	24.3	51.3	38.2	24.6	489	98.6
Monte Sereno city	3,318	3,427	3.3	3,479	70.6	1.8	18.6	1.8	7.1	26.4	22.1	48.7	3.5	79.1	1,128	96.5
Montgomery Creek CDP	163	-	-	145	89.0	0.0	0.0	2.8	8.3	14.5	45.5	57.5	31.5	26.6	68	89.7
Monument Hills CDP	1,542	-	-	1,466	64.7	0.0	0.0	0.0	35.3	26.1	18.1	38.9	22.1	50.7	486	96.9
Moorpark city	34,523	36,375	5.4	36,372	54.7	1.5	8.5	4.9	30.4	23.6	13.4	39.0	22.4	44.7	11,590	94.4
Morada CDP	3,828	-	-	3,166	84.6	1.0	1.9	4.6	8.0	23.5	21.6	52.1	21.6	46.2	1,100	96.5
Moraga town	16,006	17,783	11.1	17,539	69.9	0.6	15.9	5.9	7.7	21.5	21.3	43.2	7.6	73.6	5,867	96.9
Moreno Valley city	193,305	213,055	10.2	207,289	15.7	17.1	6.0	2.5	58.7	28.1	8.6	30.9	52.5	16.3	50,886	95.2
Morgan Hill city	37,969	45,952	21.0	44,686	49.0	1.7	13.6	4.4	31.3	26.0	14.0	39.3	24.4	43.9	14,854	97.0
Morongo Valley CDP	3,552	-	-	3,090	81.6	0.4	0.6	3.3	14.1	16.9	19.8	50.1	34.7	23.8	1,451	90.8
Morro Bay city	10,235	10,543	3.0	10,578	80.2	1.3	3.4	4.0	11.2	13.6	31.0	50.8	25.7	40.8	4,899	90.5
Moskowite Corner CDP	211	-	-	121	100.0	0.0	0.0	0.0	0.0	23.1	28.9	54.6	52.7	5.4	56	100.0
Moss Beach CDP	3,103	-	-	3,604	61.6	0.5	2.8	9.0	26.1	27.9	15.0	42.9	24.7	54.8	1,244	93.3
Moss Landing CDP	204	-	-	54	68.5	0.0	0.0	0.0	31.5	0.0	27.8	52.7	63.0	11.1	32	100.0
Mountain Center CDP	63	-	-	-	-	-	-	-	-	-	-	-	-	-	-	-
Mountain Gate CDP	943	-	-	952	97.4	0.0	0.7	0.0	1.9	20.2	25.3	47.1	48.5	11.1	400	77.0
Mountain House CDP	9,675	-	-	17,966	25.0	9.6	42.3	8.3	14.8	37.9	5.1	33.1	18.3	47.3	4,732	99.3
Mountain Mesa CDP	777	-	-	1,396	90.1	0.4	0.3	1.9	7.3	30.7	34.4	34.8	41.8	19.4	440	71.6
Mountain Ranch CDP	1,628	-	-	1,141	80.4	0.0	0.0	4.2	15.4	3.6	31.7	60.7	37.5	23.3	557	81.5
Mountain View CDP	2,372	-	-	1,970	59.7	4.8	2.3	4.4	28.7	23.7	4.7	33.0	22.5	25.3	770	97.4
Mountain View city	74,008	82,739	11.8	81,656	43.9	1.4	31.7	4.6	18.3	19.6	11.0	34.8	16.2	69.5	33,756	97.0
Mountain View Acres CDP	3,130	-	-	4,447	23.6	8.0	1.8	1.4	65.1	35.5	12.3	30.6	58.6	12.1	1,124	94.5
Mount Hebron CDP	95	-	-	72	20.8	0.0	0.0	0.0	79.2	18.1	20.8	42.6	67.4	0.0	30	100.0
Mount Hermon CDP	1,037	-	-	1,259	67.5	0.0	0.0	3.7	28.8	31.2	11.1	33.7	19.2	60.0	354	96.6
Mount Laguna CDP	57	-	-	117	100.0	0.0	0.0	0.0	0.0	0.0	20.5	27.7	0.0	100.0	24	100.0
Mount Shasta city	3,392	3,274	-3.5	3,275	86.3	1.5	0.0	1.0	11.2	13.6	28.9	57.5	19.1	33.9	1,823	92.5
Muir Beach CDP	310	-	-	336	88.1	0.0	1.2	3.3	7.4	21.4	22.6	53.3	3.8	72.0	162	100.0
Murphys CDP	2,213	-	-	2,188	90.0	0.0	0.0	5.3	4.7	8.9	45.7	62.1	32.0	24.6	988	85.9
Murrieta city	103,731	116,223	12.0	112,941	48.1	5.5	8.9	6.3	31.3	28.6	12.4	34.2	32.0	30.3	32,175	96.8
Muscoy CDP	10,644	-	-	12,562	6.0	2.5	1.7	0.9	88.9	32.2	7.9	28.8	75.9	6.2	2,711	93.4
Myers Flat CDP	146	-	-	132	100.0	0.0	0.0	0.0	0.0	0.0	35.6	63.5	73.5	0.0	35	100.0
Myrtletown CDP	4,675	-	-	5,222	79.8	0.0	2.2	6.4	11.6	15.7	19.2	44.1	30.4	22.7	2,146	94.5
Napa city	77,088	78,130	1.4	79,074	52.6	0.6	3.1	3.1	40.5	22.7	16.6	38.8	34.1	34.2	28,189	92.8
National City city	58,560	61,394	4.8	61,121	11.6	4.4	18.3	2.3	63.5	20.6	13.4	34.2	53.2	14.2	16,658	86.1
Needles city	4,826	4,976	3.1	4,965	66.6	2.9	0.5	10.9	19.1	26.5	20.8	42.7	56.0	12.5	2,034	82.4
Nevada City city	3,067	3,148	2.6	3,144	83.0	1.5	1.0	8.4	6.1	13.0	25.8	52.8	22.0	35.3	1,462	93.5
Newark city	42,573	49,149	15.4	47,171	23.7	3.9	33.0	4.7	34.8	21.2	12.8	37.1	40.2	33.6	14,047	96.5
Newcastle CDP	1,224	-	-	1,208	84.7	0.3	1.2	8.5	5.3	22.2	31.3	47.7	24.4	31.3	571	92.6
New Cuyama CDP	517	-	-	660	43.8	0.9	0.0	0.8	54.5	35.2	12.4	27.8	49.6	14.0	224	95.5
Newell CDP	449	-	-	566	21.9	0.0	0.0	3.5	74.6	46.6	1.1	19.6	90.9	0.0	132	89.4
Newman city	10,261	11,784	14.8	11,317	26.5	1.9	1.4	0.7	69.5	29.5	11.6	33.6	54.8	11.2	3,299	92.3
New Pine Creek CDP	98	-	-	88	67.0	0.0	0.0	0.0	33.0	33.0	19.3	42.2	88.1	0.0	28	60.7
Newport Beach city	85,211	84,534	-0.8	85,694	79.9	0.8	7.9	2.6	8.8	17.2	23.1	47.2	9.6	67.0	37,605	96.4
Nicasio CDP	96	-	-	71	100.0	0.0	0.0	0.0	0.0	25.4	16.9	49.9	7.5	84.9	25	100.0
Nice CDP	2,731	-	-	2,527	78.0	4.0	0.2	6.9	10.9	20.4	20.5	47.0	40.2	9.9	1,089	83.0
Nicolaus CDP	211	-	-	148	70.3	0.0	0.0	0.0	29.7	11.5	24.3	46.8	37.3	18.6	77	79.2
Niland CDP	1,006	-	-	631	38.0	5.7	0.0	4.8	51.5	52.8	4.8	16.3	79.0	0.0	198	80.8
Nipinnawasee CDP	475	-	-	349	98.6	0.0	0.0	0.0	1.4	20.9	34.1	36.7	70.3	2.3	113	86.7
Nipomo CDP	16,714	-	-	17,601	49.1	1.1	2.8	2.5	44.5	22.0	17.2	39.6	38.5	24.5	5,561	96.0
Norco city	27,212	26,604	-2.2	26,670	55.6	4.5	4.3	2.7	33.0	19.4	13.9	41.2	43.1	20.0	7,119	94.4
Nord CDP	320	-	-	312	82.1	0.0	0.0	4.2	13.8	46.2	8.0	25.5	48.2	2.4	92	96.7
Norris Canyon CDP	957	-	-	897	16.4	0.0	64.7	5.0	13.9	34.3	11.7	44.0	5.1	84.6	285	100.0
North Auburn CDP	13,022	-	-	14,269	75.7	0.5	2.7	4.4	16.7	21.1	24.5	41.8	36.7	24.0	5,426	92.4
North Edwards CDP	1,058	-	-	880	62.4	5.7	4.2	2.7	25.0	14.9	20.8	48.6	50.5	9.4	420	90.2
North El Monte CDP	3,723	-	-	3,933	25.1	1.1	43.6	3.3	26.9	23.8	16.1	40.7	31.3	32.0	1,286	97.9
North Fair Oaks CDP	14,687	-	-	14,372	17.7	1.2	5.7	2.0	73.4	29.2	8.4	33.1	53.9	26.4	4,183	93.6
North Gate CDP	679	-	-	685	62.5	0.0	11.2	3.2	23.1	21.5	18.0	50.3	14.1	74.4	242	100.0
North Highlands CDP	42,694	-	-	47,661	47.9	12.5	6.7	6.7	26.2	27.1	11.5	31.6	50.2	13.6	15,335	92.2
North Lakeport CDP	3,314	-	-	3,351	75.9	0.0	0.7	7.8	15.5	18.8	33.2	51.5	44.1	22.0	1,429	88.0
North Richmond CDP	3,717	-	-	4,085	2.8	21.2	9.0	2.1	64.9	30.4	7.6	33.1	70.8	6.5	1,109	86.9
North San Juan CDP	269	-	-	178	95.5	0.0	0.0	0.0	4.5	0.0	37.6	54.3	55.2	33.1	108	78.7
North Shore CDP	3,477	-	-	2,756	2.4	0.0	0.0	0.6	97.0	19.8	6.0	38.3	94.4	2.2	944	81.5

1 May be of any race.

Table A. All Places — **Population and Housing**

STATE City, town, township, borough, or CDP (county if applicable)	Population: 2010 census total population	Population: 2019 estimated population	Population: Percent change 2010-2019	Population: ACS total population estimate 2015-2019	Race and Hispanic or Latino origin (percent): White alone, not Hispanic or Latino	Black alone, not Hispanic or Latino	Asian alone, not Hispanic or Latino	All other races or 2 or more races, not Hispanic or Latino	Hispanic or Latino[1]	Age (percent): Under 18 years old	Age 65 years and older	Median age	Educational attainment of persons age 25 and older: Percent High school diploma or less	Percent Bachelor's degree or more	Occupied housing units: Total	Percent with a computer
	1	2	3	4	5	6	7	8	9	10	11	12	13	14	15	16
CALIFORNIA—Con.																
North Tustin CDP	24,917	-	-	24,705	68.6	0.5	11.5	3.1	16.4	20.2	22.8	48.3	15.4	58.4	8,435	97.7
Norwalk city	105,549	103,949	-1.5	105,304	10.3	4.5	13.5	2.0	69.7	24.3	11.9	34.9	52.1	18.7	26,964	92.7
Novato city	51,869	55,516	7.0	55,642	63.5	3.4	7.7	6.5	18.9	18.7	20.6	46.9	23.0	46.4	22,325	93.2
Nubieber CDP	50	-	-	35	37.1	0.0	62.9	0.0	0.0	40.0	11.4	40.4	19.0	0.0	16	75.0
Nuevo CDP	6,447	-	-	7,182	36.2	2.5	0.0	1.8	59.5	29.0	12.3	32.5	56.0	15.1	1,878	94.2
Oakdale city	20,744	23,596	13.7	22,936	60.9	0.3	2.2	3.2	33.5	28.7	11.4	35.6	43.5	19.0	7,805	91.0
Oak Glen CDP	638	-	-	430	84.0	2.1	2.3	6.0	5.6	5.3	42.6	60.2	38.3	27.4	162	89.5
Oak Hills CDP	8,879	-	-	10,444	42.9	4.0	5.4	1.6	46.2	19.4	18.1	43.2	47.0	11.3	2,940	88.9
Oakhurst CDP	2,829	-	-	3,446	69.8	0.0	6.4	3.7	20.2	23.3	23.2	39.6	43.4	17.2	1,252	95.0
Oakland city	390,765	433,031	10.8	425,097	28.3	23.2	15.3	6.1	27.0	19.9	13.1	36.5	33.3	44.0	162,419	90.7
Oakley city	35,423	42,543	20.1	41,324	41.2	9.0	6.5	7.5	35.8	29.2	9.3	33.5	39.0	19.9	11,778	96.9
Oak Park CDP	13,811	-	-	13,853	65.2	1.4	18.5	5.4	9.6	25.0	15.3	43.8	9.7	64.6	5,303	97.9
Oak Shores CDP	337	-	-	348	88.8	0.0	0.0	0.0	11.2	16.1	35.9	56.1	27.7	31.2	149	86.6
Oak View CDP	4,066	-	-	4,598	65.2	0.0	0.7	1.2	32.8	22.0	15.6	39.6	39.6	32.3	1,534	97.6
Oakville CDP	71	-	-	91	0.0	0.0	0.0	0.0	100.0	50.5	0.0	13.0	100.0	0.0	21	100.0
Oasis CDP	6,890	-	-	2,857	2.4	0.1	1.9	0.6	95.0	32.2	9.0	31.6	90.0	3.0	992	66.9
Occidental CDP	1,115	-	-	823	83.6	1.5	1.2	6.4	7.3	3.6	49.2	63.9	15.0	49.6	532	92.9
Oceano CDP	7,286	-	-	7,487	45.2	1.0	6.3	2.6	44.9	23.8	18.9	39.0	43.2	18.0	2,634	91.1
Oceanside city	167,547	175,742	4.9	175,622	46.8	4.3	7.2	5.5	36.2	21.5	15.9	37.7	33.7	31.1	61,600	94.7
Ocotillo CDP	266	-	-	89	100.0	0.0	0.0	0.0	0.0	5.6	34.8	59.4	77.4	0.0	55	61.8
Oildale CDP	32,684	-	-	34,763	69.4	1.4	0.9	5.6	22.6	29.0	10.2	31.9	56.5	9.4	12,577	89.0
Ojai city	7,469	7,470	0.0	7,534	80.4	0.2	1.9	2.0	15.4	16.6	27.9	50.4	22.6	47.2	3,086	89.9
Olancha CDP	192	-	-	229	90.8	5.7	0.0	3.5	0.0	3.1	19.2	53.0	59.7	3.8	81	93.8
Old Fig Garden CDP	5,365	-	-	5,850	53.8	1.8	3.8	4.3	36.3	22.5	18.2	39.9	22.8	45.2	2,182	97.7
Old Station CDP	51	-	-	31	100.0	0.0	0.0	0.0	0.0	0.0	54.8	67.1	0.0	29.0	15	100.0
Olivehurst CDP	13,656	-	-	13,464	47.4	1.9	6.5	5.6	38.7	25.9	11.1	33.2	54.9	8.7	4,363	89.6
Ontario city	163,936	185,010	12.9	176,760	15.9	5.1	6.5	2.5	70.0	26.3	9.2	32.4	52.9	17.1	50,621	92.5
Onyx CDP	475	-	-	478	97.9	0.0	0.0	2.1	0.0	4.2	20.7	53.5	52.0	19.7	255	80.4
Orange city	136,776	138,669	1.4	139,887	44.6	1.6	11.8	3.1	38.9	21.3	12.2	35.2	32.3	37.7	43,075	94.9
Orange Cove city	9,735	10,273	5.5	10,274	3.4	1.1	0.0	0.4	95.0	38.9	7.4	25.1	78.1	1.6	2,692	80.3
Orangevale CDP	33,960	-	-	34,824	76.6	1.7	2.9	7.0	11.7	21.1	17.8	41.4	28.7	31.2	13,267	95.0
Orcutt CDP	28,905	-	-	31,118	64.4	1.3	3.2	4.2	26.9	22.3	18.5	39.9	26.7	29.9	10,910	94.0
Orick CDP	357	-	-	389	72.8	0.0	0.0	22.9	4.4	21.1	15.2	39.6	47.8	7.8	149	89.9
Orinda city	17,759	19,926	12.2	19,646	72.0	1.2	16.0	5.5	5.3	23.1	22.6	48.7	4.1	82.6	7,167	97.5
Orland city	7,342	7,827	6.6	7,622	46.1	0.0	1.7	1.2	50.9	31.7	12.6	28.1	58.1	10.0	2,552	89.8
Orosi CDP	8,770	-	-	8,300	3.3	0.0	8.1	4.5	84.1	31.2	10.1	29.4	64.0	7.6	2,150	86.5
Oroville city	18,725	20,737	10.7	19,393	64.2	4.1	8.6	9.4	13.6	24.7	14.9	34.0	44.4	13.2	6,426	88.1
Oroville East CDP	8,280	-	-	7,771	76.8	0.5	6.9	8.1	7.8	17.7	26.4	49.7	39.0	18.3	2,953	94.3
Oxnard city	198,047	208,881	5.5	208,154	14.5	2.4	7.1	2.4	73.6	27.1	9.9	32.3	54.6	18.0	51,424	92.1
Pacheco CDP	3,685	-	-	4,361	47.2	2.7	20.9	6.9	22.3	17.5	15.8	45.8	35.3	29.1	1,692	96.7
Pacifica city	37,338	38,546	3.2	38,984	52.0	2.3	19.8	7.2	18.7	19.2	17.1	42.5	22.0	45.7	13,750	96.5
Pacific Grove city	15,039	15,413	2.5	15,522	79.1	0.9	5.5	4.7	9.8	18.7	27.5	48.9	16.3	54.3	6,839	94.1
Pajaro CDP	3,070	-	-	3,620	2.5	0.6	0.0	4.8	92.1	35.5	2.6	26.4	77.4	4.9	648	86.4
Pajaro Dunes CDP	144	-	-	284	100.0	0.0	0.0	0.0	0.0	0.0	66.9	65.6	39.4	49.3	165	84.2
Pala CDP	-	-	-	1,005	4.0	3.4	6.5	48.9	37.3	34.1	8.5	31.5	60.7	8.3	295	92.2
Palermo CDP	5,382	-	-	5,395	58.4	1.4	4.0	8.3	27.9	27.0	20.9	38.0	55.9	8.5	1,938	85.1
Palmdale city	152,733	155,079	1.5	156,293	20.0	12.7	4.6	2.3	60.4	30.0	9.3	32.0	51.9	15.5	43,404	93.0
Palm Desert city	48,449	53,275	10.0	52,575	66.0	2.8	5.0	2.7	23.5	14.4	36.0	54.5	27.7	36.8	24,396	92.0
Palm Springs city	44,555	48,518	8.9	47,897	61.1	4.3	4.8	3.1	26.8	12.2	31.7	55.4	28.1	39.9	24,136	91.5
Palo Alto city	64,387	65,364	1.5	66,573	54.9	1.8	32.4	5.4	5.6	22.9	19.4	41.8	6.1	82.8	26,161	97.2
Palo Cedro CDP	1,269	-	-	1,143	92.2	1.3	0.5	4.8	1.1	27.8	24.5	47.5	18.6	27.3	385	93.0
Palos Verdes Estates city	13,438	13,273	-1.2	13,434	65.4	0.4	22.9	3.5	7.8	21.4	27.0	52.2	5.6	77.9	4,909	96.5
Palo Verde CDP	171	-	-	65	100.0	0.0	0.0	0.0	0.0	0.0	84.6	69.9	44.6	0.0	55	60.0
Panorama Heights CDP	41	-	-	49	100.0	0.0	0.0	0.0	0.0	0.0	83.7	70.9	38.8	10.2	38	34.2
Paradise town	26,219	4,476	-82.9	22,135	85.2	0.4	1.0	5.5	7.9	18.7	26.1	49.7	33.9	21.3	9,408	91.2
Paradise CDP	153	-	-	172	59.3	0.0	0.0	20.9	19.8	22.7	26.2	48.0	32.4	38.0	64	95.3
Paradise Park CDP	389	-	-	550	86.2	0.0	0.0	11.8	2.0	21.5	29.3	50.1	12.6	53.1	241	95.4
Paramount city	54,098	53,955	-0.3	54,513	5.5	8.8	2.9	1.8	81.0	28.5	8.6	30.9	62.6	11.3	14,207	91.1
Parklawn CDP	1,337	-	-	1,040	5.5	0.0	0.0	0.5	94.0	33.2	11.7	28.0	89.5	4.8	236	81.8
Parksdale CDP	2,621	-	-	2,451	11.1	3.3	0.0	0.4	85.1	26.2	9.9	27.2	70.5	6.0	513	81.1
Parkway CDP	14,670	-	-	15,818	16.5	16.3	16.7	8.8	41.7	30.8	10.3	30.8	56.3	9.8	4,921	91.7
Parkwood CDP	2,268	-	-	2,183	9.3	0.8	0.0	0.0	89.9	39.6	8.8	23.3	60.7	10.1	549	88.9
Parlier city	14,596	15,618	7.0	15,312	0.7	0.0	0.1	0.2	99.0	33.8	8.6	28.9	80.2	4.1	3,901	84.1
Pasadena city	137,114	141,029	2.9	141,258	35.9	8.3	16.9	4.0	34.9	18.2	16.0	38.6	25.8	52.3	55,224	92.3
Pasatiempo CDP	1,041	-	-	1,206	82.2	3.6	3.8	9.5	0.9	16.4	21.8	47.6	9.1	54.1	397	96.2
Paskenta CDP	112	-	-	102	75.5	4.9	0.0	0.0	19.6	20.6	12.7	35.3	57.8	0.0	42	88.1
Patterson city	20,629	22,524	9.2	22,066	20.6	6.1	6.6	3.8	62.9	29.6	9.2	31.1	64.1	10.3	5,958	92.7
Patterson Tract CDP	1,752	-	-	2,085	12.8	0.0	0.0	0.9	86.4	33.2	13.0	29.5	50.4	13.9	631	93.7
Patton Village CDP	702	-	-	630	73.0	12.4	0.0	10.8	3.8	16.7	16.3	35.8	37.6	22.8	275	90.5
Paxton CDP	14	-	-	-	-	-	-	-	-	-	-	-	-	-	-	-
Paynes Creek CDP	57	-	-	78	85.9	0.0	0.0	14.1	0.0	0.0	35.9	58.6	70.5	0.0	50	84.0
Pearsonville CDP	17	-	-	7	100.0	0.0	0.0	0.0	0.0	0.0	0.0	0.0	0.0	0.0	7	100.0
Penngrove CDP	2,522	-	-	2,808	64.8	0.0	4.7	2.8	27.7	22.1	25.7	50.4	25.3	37.2	1,133	96.9
Penn Valley CDP	1,621	-	-	1,341	86.4	0.0	0.7	0.9	12.0	19.7	23.0	44.6	27.4	22.9	563	79.6
Penryn CDP	831	-	-	818	74.3	0.0	0.0	2.4	23.2	15.4	23.3	47.8	37.1	26.5	352	85.2
Perris city	68,564	79,291	15.6	77,290	8.7	9.6	3.4	1.4	76.8	32.2	6.2	28.3	64.6	9.2	17,142	93.9
Pescadero CDP	643	-	-	219	70.3	0.0	0.0	29.7	0.0	31.1	19.6	40.0	34.6	42.1	73	100.0
Petaluma city	57,968	60,520	4.4	60,767	68.1	1.1	4.4	4.6	21.9	21.0	17.6	41.7	26.0	40.4	22,655	94.4
Peters CDP	672	-	-	623	34.0	7.7	3.7	11.4	43.2	16.2	21.2	55.5	45.1	11.5	212	89.2
Phelan CDP	14,304	-	-	15,987	52.8	1.3	2.2	3.3	40.4	28.2	12.0	35.9	49.2	12.2	4,463	92.9
Phillipsville CDP	140	-	-	70	100.0	0.0	0.0	0.0	0.0	0.0	20.0	53.7	57.1	42.9	49	100.0
Philo CDP	349	-	-	175	48.0	0.0	0.0	18.9	33.1	27.4	22.9	54.1	28.7	7.4	79	100.0
Phoenix Lake CDP	4,269	-	-	4,511	89.0	0.9	0.3	4.5	5.4	18.5	29.2	51.6	30.1	22.6	1,867	90.0
Pico Rivera city	62,958	62,027	-1.5	63,001	5.3	0.8	2.6	0.6	90.7	22.7	14.7	37.1	60.6	12.9	16,852	88.6
Piedmont city	10,695	11,135	4.1	11,317	70.9	1.4	17.8	5.7	4.2	24.6	21.5	47.4	5.5	83.4	3,838	97.6
Pierpoint CDP	52	-	-	39	46.2	0.0	0.0	53.8	0.0	0.0	46.2	0.0	0.0	46.2	18	100.0
Pike CDP	134	-	-	159	100.0	0.0	0.0	0.0	0.0	0.0	0.0	41.5	74.8	0.0	63	100.0
Pine Canyon CDP	1,822	-	-	2,369	35.4	0.0	0.4	4.7	59.4	22.9	15.3	40.9	60.2	17.8	722	92.2
Pine Flat CDP	166	-	-	146	87.0	0.0	0.0	13.0	0.0	22.6	33.6	60.3	47.5	31.3	61	78.7
Pine Grove CDP	2,219	-	-	1,762	81.4	0.0	0.0	0.9	17.8	12.2	39.9	62.7	37.9	15.4	733	93.9
Pine Hills CDP	3,131	-	-	3,375	63.6	0.1	6.5	16.6	13.2	22.2	25.3	47.1	34.0	26.5	1,234	92.9
Pine Mountain Club CDP	2,315	-	-	1,751	83.6	0.0	1.9	6.3	8.2	14.6	32.4	58.9	33.1	28.1	886	90.5

1 May be of any race.

Table A. All Places — **Population and Housing**

STATE City, town, township, borough, or CDP (county if applicable)	Population				Race and Hispanic or Latino origin (percent)					Age (percent)			Educational attainment of persons age 25 and older		Occupied housing units	
	2010 census total population	2019 estimated population	Percent change 2010-2019	ACS total population estimate 2015-2019	White alone, not Hispanic or Latino	Black alone, not Hispanic or Latino	Asian alone, not Hispanic or Latino	All other races or 2 or more races, not Hispanic or Latino	Hispanic or Latino[1]	Under 18 years old	Age 65 years and older	Median age	Percent High school diploma or less	Percent Bachelor's degree or more	Total	Percent with a computer
	1	2	3	4	5	6	7	8	9	10	11	12	13	14	15	16
CALIFORNIA—Con.																
Pine Mountain Lake CDP	2,796	-	-	2,772	86.9	0.0	1.4	6.0	5.8	12.3	47.0	63.8	32.2	30.5	1,318	93.8
Pine Valley CDP	1,510	-	-	1,477	77.3	1.2	2.2	2.6	16.8	16.9	17.7	46.7	31.2	31.9	540	91.9
Pinole city	18,330	19,250	5.0	19,279	32.7	11.6	27.1	7.2	21.4	17.2	19.9	43.2	29.3	31.6	6,748	94.4
Pi??on Hills CDP	7,272	-	-	7,661	59.5	0.0	4.5	1.6	34.3	22.7	19.9	43.3	37.0	14.9	2,666	92.5
Pioneer CDP	1,094	-	-	1,386	79.1	0.4	0.0	6.6	13.9	20.3	26.8	44.0	28.4	19.0	569	88.2
Piru CDP	2,063	-	-	1,805	9.3	1.3	0.2	2.8	86.4	31.0	16.2	33.6	59.7	8.2	533	82.0
Pismo Beach city	7,655	8,168	6.7	8,180	80.6	2.8	1.7	2.7	12.2	9.6	33.8	57.5	22.7	46.1	4,213	94.3
Pittsburg city	63,259	72,588	14.7	71,422	19.1	14.9	16.1	6.5	43.4	24.8	11.0	34.7	46.4	21.2	21,357	94.7
Pixley CDP	3,310	-	-	3,347	7.9	3.9	0.0	0.0	88.3	40.6	8.9	26.5	86.2	0.6	894	72.6
Placentia city	50,915	51,233	0.6	51,818	39.2	1.9	16.9	2.8	39.2	23.5	14.4	37.4	29.1	39.3	16,583	96.0
Placerville city	10,488	11,175	6.6	10,970	78.5	0.9	1.6	1.9	17.1	21.1	20.2	42.5	39.5	25.3	4,180	88.4
Plainview CDP	945	-	-	887	8.2	0.0	0.0	0.0	91.8	28.7	12.5	30.6	90.3	1.7	270	71.1
Planada CDP	4,584	-	-	4,418	1.7	0.0	0.0	0.6	97.8	30.3	10.4	30.7	71.9	5.5	1,241	80.5
Pleasant Hill city	33,076	34,839	5.3	34,840	64.4	2.1	12.1	6.8	14.6	19.2	16.1	40.9	14.4	55.0	13,817	96.0
Pleasanton city	70,280	81,777	16.4	81,717	50.1	1.8	34.1	4.5	9.5	24.4	14.7	42.4	13.7	64.9	29,011	97.5
Pleasure Point CDP	-	-	-	6,076	71.4	1.8	2.8	1.2	22.9	16.0	17.4	41.3	28.6	43.5	2,471	84.9
Plumas Eureka CDP	339	-	-	364	94.5	0.0	0.0	0.0	5.5	8.2	50.0	65.0	12.3	50.0	192	100.0
Plumas Lake CDP	5,853	-	-	7,573	57.3	3.9	8.2	9.1	21.4	35.6	6.7	29.7	24.1	25.2	2,212	95.3
Plymouth city	987	1,076	9.0	980	53.6	0.5	0.9	5.3	39.7	26.7	10.7	33.8	51.9	11.5	332	92.5
Point Arena city	449	449	0.0	421	48.9	2.4	2.1	4.3	42.3	26.4	25.2	45.5	54.3	15.2	176	73.9
Point Reyes Station CDP	848	-	-	288	80.9	0.0	0.0	0.0	19.1	0.0	57.6	67.0	26.0	46.2	221	85.5
Pollock Pines CDP	6,871	-	-	7,156	83.5	0.7	1.0	5.9	9.0	23.0	16.5	44.6	35.5	27.1	2,670	92.8
Pomona city	149,061	151,691	1.8	152,209	10.8	5.3	10.1	2.1	71.7	25.0	10.6	32.2	54.3	18.0	39,097	92.7
Ponderosa CDP	16	-	-	18	100.0	0.0	0.0	0.0	0.0	0.0	100.0	0.0	0.0	100.0	18	100.0
Poplar-Cotton Center CDP	2,470	-	-	2,259	10.3	0.0	22.2	4.1	63.4	20.8	10.5	36.4	88.9	0.3	638	83.4
Port Costa CDP	190	-	-	180	100.0	0.0	0.0	0.0	0.0	0.0	0.0	56.8	17.8	35.6	83	100.0
Porterville city	58,104	59,599	2.6	59,697	25.6	0.4	5.0	3.3	65.6	31.2	11.6	30.5	57.1	11.5	17,227	86.3
Port Hueneme city	21,743	21,926	0.8	22,156	27.9	4.9	3.6	2.9	60.7	22.7	12.4	32.7	47.1	20.2	6,627	92.4
Portola city	2,104	1,930	-8.3	1,913	78.9	0.3	2.2	2.4	16.2	22.0	18.7	44.4	32.9	17.0	891	82.3
Portola Valley town	4,353	4,568	4.9	4,592	82.3	0.4	6.5	4.2	6.7	22.9	28.5	52.8	9.2	77.1	1,685	96.9
Posey CDP	10	-	-	-	-	-	-	-	-	-	-	-	-	-	-	-
Poso Park CDP	9	-	-	3	100.0	0.0	0.0	0.0	0.0	0.0	100.0	0.0	0.0	0.0	3	100.0
Potrero CDP	656	-	-	841	22.9	0.0	0.0	0.0	77.1	27.3	8.8	24.8	43.7	35.0	121	100.0
Potter Valley CDP	646	-	-	498	84.5	0.0	0.0	8.0	7.4	20.7	16.9	41.6	28.9	14.7	201	69.7
Poway city	47,805	49,323	3.2	49,701	64.6	1.5	11.6	5.0	17.4	23.7	16.9	40.9	22.6	48.2	15,946	96.8
Prattville CDP	33	-	-	28	100.0	0.0	0.0	0.0	0.0	0.0	78.6	77.8	35.7	14.3	16	100.0
Princeton CDP	303	-	-	382	66.2	0.0	0.0	1.6	32.2	22.5	18.6	47.6	68.0	7.8	150	76.0
Proberta CDP	267	-	-	182	92.9	0.0	0.0	0.0	7.1	27.5	13.2	56.2	70.5	0.0	46	100.0
Prunedale CDP	17,560	-	-	20,327	37.7	1.3	3.6	6.1	51.2	23.4	15.3	40.5	43.7	22.6	5,930	93.8
Quartz Hill CDP	10,912	-	-	10,003	54.2	6.0	3.4	4.6	31.7	25.0	15.1	36.9	36.5	21.8	3,522	91.3
Quincy CDP	1,728	-	-	1,952	79.9	5.6	0.0	6.5	8.0	16.8	17.5	40.6	27.7	30.4	802	89.9
Rackerby CDP	204	-	-	208	73.1	5.8	0.0	5.3	15.9	16.3	26.4	51.6	31.3	13.3	89	95.5
Rail Road Flat CDP	475	-	-	191	86.4	2.6	0.0	11.0	0.0	6.3	42.4	60.2	44.9	11.4	112	100.0
Rainbow CDP	1,832	-	-	2,360	60.5	1.3	2.2	2.9	33.1	17.5	22.6	45.9	41.6	20.3	737	91.7
Raisin City CDP	380	-	-	414	26.8	0.0	1.7	0.7	70.8	27.1	15.9	29.3	77.9	5.2	102	74.5
Ramona CDP	20,292	-	-	21,323	57.9	0.6	1.6	3.9	36.0	21.7	13.9	37.1	43.2	21.9	6,579	96.0
Rancho Calaveras CDP	5,325	-	-	7,026	78.8	1.4	2.9	2.8	14.0	24.2	17.2	44.6	45.8	11.1	2,169	93.7
Rancho Cordova city	64,804	75,087	15.9	73,147	47.9	9.0	13.3	8.4	21.4	24.7	11.7	34.5	36.2	26.9	25,508	94.3
Rancho Cucamonga city	165,380	177,603	7.4	176,379	36.2	9.5	12.6	4.0	37.7	23.7	11.9	35.9	27.6	35.3	56,566	96.5
Rancho Mirage city	17,142	18,528	8.1	18,193	81.2	2.4	4.5	1.9	10.0	7.6	51.7	65.8	21.1	45.1	9,290	93.9
Rancho Murieta CDP	5,488	-	-	5,744	77.0	5.8	2.5	3.2	11.4	18.7	30.1	50.9	11.1	51.3	2,382	99.4
Rancho Palos Verdes city	41,688	41,530	-0.4	42,030	50.3	1.8	31.1	6.4	10.4	21.1	25.5	50.0	11.3	67.6	15,488	96.3
Rancho San Diego CDP	21,208	-	-	21,799	71.6	2.1	3.1	5.0	18.2	19.4	19.4	41.8	21.5	42.9	7,413	95.8
Rancho Santa Fe CDP	3,117	-	-	2,510	82.8	0.0	0.0	0.0	17.2	18.0	29.2	52.0	12.8	65.9	886	100.0
Rancho Santa Margarita city	47,855	47,896	0.1	48,503	60.8	3.1	10.5	4.9	20.6	24.8	9.2	38.5	18.0	51.1	17,192	96.9
Rancho Tehama Reserve CDP	1,485	-	-	1,682	53.5	0.5	0.8	6.1	39.1	16.4	20.0	44.4	74.2	4.0	605	80.2
Randsburg CDP	69	-	-	125	100.0	0.0	0.0	0.0	0.0	0.0	95.2	73.6	76.0	6.4	82	92.7
Red Bluff city	14,071	14,539	3.3	14,264	72.3	1.7	2.5	4.1	19.4	29.1	14.7	32.6	41.6	10.4	5,483	85.6
Red Corral CDP	1,413	-	-	1,787	69.3	0.8	3.1	4.8	22.0	17.9	24.5	48.5	42.0	9.7	627	91.9
Redcrest CDP	89	-	-	24	100.0	0.0	0.0	0.0	0.0	0.0	100.0	68.2	58.3	0.0	14	71.4
Redding city	89,857	92,590	3.0	91,580	77.0	1.5	5.0	5.9	10.7	22.1	18.8	38.1	30.6	25.7	36,836	90.2
Redlands city	68,679	71,513	4.1	71,198	50.6	5.3	8.0	3.5	32.7	22.0	15.8	37.2	29.2	41.8	24,542	90.6
Redondo Beach city	66,931	66,749	-0.3	67,423	60.3	3.1	13.5	7.1	16.0	22.0	13.2	40.7	13.2	60.8	27,663	96.9
Redway CDP	1,225	-	-	1,358	78.8	0.0	0.0	0.0	21.2	17.4	28.6	44.6	31.9	22.5	539	91.7
Redwood City city	76,817	85,925	11.9	85,784	44.1	1.5	14.2	4.8	35.4	21.4	12.7	36.7	28.6	50.2	30,829	95.4
Redwood Valley CDP	1,729	-	-	1,713	82.9	0.0	0.0	0.4	16.7	22.8	10.2	39.7	43.9	25.7	659	94.8
Reedley city	24,306	25,658	5.6	25,591	14.3	1.1	3.5	3.2	77.9	31.4	12.2	31.2	58.7	12.7	7,044	88.6
Reliez Valley CDP	3,101	-	-	3,518	72.9	3.1	13.1	4.1	6.8	18.8	28.2	51.8	12.3	68.0	1,441	93.5
Rialto city	99,103	103,526	4.5	103,045	9.6	12.4	2.4	1.4	74.3	28.1	9.3	30.5	60.8	11.1	26,033	94.6
Richfield CDP	306	-	-	300	60.0	0.0	0.7	0.0	39.3	36.0	17.0	34.3	38.7	26.4	90	96.7
Richgrove CDP	2,882	-	-	2,316	0.0	0.0	0.1	0.0	99.9	26.6	10.4	34.5	88.1	1.5	640	66.3
Richmond city	103,255	110,567	7.1	109,884	17.8	19.5	15.2	5.0	42.5	21.8	13.4	36.0	42.7	28.2	37,088	92.5
Richvale CDP	244	-	-	209	82.3	0.0	0.0	17.7	0.0	0.0	27.3	42.6	22.5	47.5	79	100.0
Ridgecrest city	27,616	28,973	4.9	28,755	64.8	4.1	5.8	3.7	21.6	26.5	13.5	36.0	33.0	28.4	10,974	89.8
Ridgemark CDP	3,016	-	-	2,872	74.6	0.5	1.4	1.4	22.1	17.9	24.8	52.2	22.0	34.8	1,146	96.5
Rio Dell city	3,368	3,349	-0.6	3,373	81.1	0.1	2.4	7.1	9.2	28.8	12.8	34.9	47.0	10.3	1,318	84.8
Rio del Mar CDP	9,216	-	-	9,657	82.5	1.4	3.0	4.5	8.7	17.7	25.5	51.1	11.8	59.9	4,061	95.7
Rio Linda CDP	15,106	-	-	16,359	64.4	2.4	8.4	3.8	21.0	25.4	12.4	37.2	55.1	13.7	4,914	94.7
Rio Oso CDP	356	-	-	350	88.3	0.0	10.3	0.6	0.9	27.7	17.7	37.7	29.7	34.1	110	91.8
Rio Vista city	7,362	9,718	32.0	8,947	74.8	7.6	6.6	3.0	8.1	6.9	48.9	64.4	27.3	33.6	4,792	93.3
Ripley CDP	692	-	-	444	7.2	16.2	0.0	0.0	76.6	40.5	15.1	32.0	89.6	0.0	175	68.6
Ripon city	14,415	16,386	13.7	15,777	64.0	0.4	2.5	3.4	29.7	25.6	15.6	39.2	36.1	23.8	5,350	93.0
Riverbank city	22,675	24,881	9.7	24,482	33.4	1.6	4.9	3.1	56.9	28.6	10.5	32.6	57.3	13.9	7,063	89.9
Riverdale CDP	3,153	-	-	3,433	26.9	0.3	0.0	0.0	72.9	27.4	15.6	31.7	63.4	10.3	980	83.9
Riverdale Park CDP	1,128	-	-	1,033	15.6	0.0	13.5	3.6	67.4	32.9	9.1	30.1	72.5	11.2	260	80.8
River Pines CDP	379	-	-	566	75.1	3.7	0.0	15.2	6.0	3.7	35.0	46.4	51.4	0.0	217	58.5
Riverside city	303,933	331,360	9.0	326,414	29.8	5.8	7.4	3.3	53.7	23.8	10.7	31.6	45.7	23.0	90,722	93.8
Robbins CDP	323	-	-	421	21.6	0.0	0.0	0.0	78.4	23.0	11.2	38.6	65.5	9.0	135	91.9
Robinson Mill CDP	80	-	-	53	100.0	0.0	0.0	0.0	0.0	0.0	62.3	65.4	67.9	0.0	53	69.8
Rocklin city	57,131	68,823	20.5	64,835	70.7	1.8	9.7	5.2	12.6	25.9	12.7	37.5	18.4	46.4	22,360	95.7

1 May be of any race.

Table A. All Places — **Population and Housing**

STATE City, town, township, borough, or CDP (county if applicable)	Population				Race and Hispanic or Latino origin (percent)					Age (percent)			Educational attainment of persons age 25 and older		Occupied housing units	
	2010 census total population	2019 estimated population	Percent change 2010-2019	ACS total population estimate 2015-2019	White alone, not Hispanic or Latino	Black alone, not Hispanic or Latino	Asian alone, not Hispanic or Latino	All other races or 2 or more races, not Hispanic or Latino	Hispanic or Latino[1]	Under 18 years old	Age 65 years and older	Median age	Percent High school diploma or less	Percent Bachelor's degree or more	Total	Percent with a computer
	1	2	3	4	5	6	7	8	9	10	11	12	13	14	15	16
CALIFORNIA—Con.																
Rodeo CDP	8,679	-	-	10,409	22.9	14.4	20.3	10.2	32.2	22.4	13.5	36.8	38.9	23.9	3,384	92.9
Rodriguez Camp CDP	156	-	-	101	0.0	0.0	0.0	0.0	100.0	28.7	0.0	27.2	100.0	0.0	32	53.1
Rohnert Park city	40,818	43,291	6.1	42,902	61.0	2.2	6.6	3.3	26.9	19.7	13.9	35.8	32.2	29.3	16,377	95.7
Rolling Hills city	1,860	1,845	-0.8	1,513	71.3	1.5	15.6	5.8	5.8	18.8	32.9	55.3	11.1	70.4	577	99.5
Rolling Hills CDP	742	-	-	718	69.5	2.8	3.1	4.0	20.6	14.3	32.7	60.1	11.9	40.7	294	100.0
Rolling Hills Estates city	8,060	8,058	0.0	8,169	54.8	1.9	28.8	4.3	10.2	23.3	25.2	50.1	11.6	67.2	2,920	96.7
Rollingwood CDP	2,969	-	-	3,449	8.0	3.5	11.9	3.2	73.3	27.8	7.2	34.2	62.0	9.0	810	99.1
Romoland CDP	1,684	-	-	2,295	14.5	0.0	0.0	1.7	83.8	21.0	12.9	32.5	56.6	8.2	454	89.0
Rosamond CDP	18,150	-	-	20,851	44.3	7.8	1.4	5.5	40.9	30.3	9.0	31.8	49.2	18.3	6,907	91.9
Rosedale CDP	14,058	-	-	16,820	70.3	1.3	1.6	6.1	20.6	24.9	14.0	41.6	33.2	31.3	5,574	97.9
Rose Hills CDP	2,803	-	-	2,771	29.4	0.0	16.9	2.1	51.6	17.4	24.1	46.0	25.0	41.5	1,034	99.1
Rosemead city	53,771	54,058	0.5	54,282	4.1	0.4	61.6	1.3	32.6	19.5	16.9	41.9	60.0	19.8	14,455	91.5
Rosemont CDP	22,681	-	-	23,602	45.9	12.1	11.9	8.1	22.1	22.2	13.2	35.5	31.7	27.4	8,455	93.2
Roseville city	119,277	141,500	18.6	135,637	67.3	2.0	10.7	4.4	15.6	23.6	16.5	39.0	21.7	41.7	49,943	95.4
Ross town	2,421	2,451	1.2	2,290	89.1	3.0	3.8	0.5	3.5	25.9	26.9	48.3	5.3	80.5	812	98.4
Rossmoor CDP	10,244	-	-	11,128	67.7	0.9	12.5	4.7	14.2	24.2	19.6	46.3	16.0	61.0	3,909	96.8
Rough and Ready CDP	963	-	-	499	89.6	0.0	0.0	0.0	10.4	5.0	56.7	67.5	30.8	10.5	318	83.6
Round Mountain CDP	155	-	-	89	53.9	0.0	0.0	34.8	11.2	19.1	14.6	50.7	48.6	4.2	48	77.1
Round Valley CDP	435	-	-	509	52.8	5.1	0.0	10.8	31.2	10.8	8.4	41.6	38.8	25.7	154	98.1
Rouse CDP	2,005	-	-	2,031	6.2	4.9	9.0	3.0	77.1	36.5	6.8	26.5	76.4	4.2	507	81.7
Rowland Heights CDP	48,993	-	-	50,347	8.0	1.4	62.3	2.0	26.4	18.6	18.3	41.4	36.0	39.7	14,724	95.6
Running Springs CDP	4,862	-	-	4,071	74.8	3.3	1.6	7.6	12.7	26.2	20.8	41.8	24.8	27.6	1,598	93.4
Ruth CDP	195	-	-	170	89.4	0.0	0.0	0.0	10.6	4.1	25.9	60.6	44.2	7.1	97	83.5
Rutherford CDP	164	-	-	88	55.7	0.0	0.0	0.0	44.3	8.0	38.6	44.5	38.9	33.3	39	82.1
Sacramento city	466,383	513,624	10.1	500,930	32.4	12.7	18.6	7.4	28.9	23.1	13.1	34.5	36.0	33.1	185,331	93.5
St. Helena city	5,816	6,102	4.9	6,101	65.1	1.6	1.3	1.1	30.9	17.2	26.8	49.9	28.9	50.0	2,702	93.1
Salida CDP	13,722	-	-	14,229	39.0	0.3	4.6	2.0	54.0	27.1	8.2	29.6	53.8	14.7	4,078	92.5
Salinas city	150,607	155,465	3.2	156,143	12.6	1.3	5.1	1.6	79.3	31.0	8.9	30.5	63.2	13.3	40,800	89.0
Salmon Creek CDP	86	-	-	20	100.0	0.0	0.0	0.0	0.0	0.0	100.0	0.0	0.0	100.0	10	100.0
Salton City CDP	3,763	-	-	6,250	26.3	2.5	1.1	1.8	68.3	24.1	16.2	40.5	71.4	9.8	2,133	85.3
Salton Sea Beach CDP	422	-	-	261	82.0	0.0	0.0	0.0	18.0	8.0	14.9	55.2	67.7	0.0	117	77.8
Samoa CDP	258	-	-	212	59.0	0.0	0.0	36.8	4.2	16.0	9.0	34.0	51.1	18.8	71	88.7
San Andreas CDP	2,783	-	-	3,120	76.9	0.3	3.1	8.5	11.2	26.8	16.3	37.1	36.2	10.0	909	98.6
San Anselmo town	12,309	12,476	1.4	12,525	85.9	0.8	3.3	2.9	7.1	22.0	19.0	47.7	8.1	73.3	5,219	98.2
San Antonio Heights CDP	3,371	-	-	3,191	60.3	0.0	9.2	2.7	27.8	15.2	19.6	48.0	25.4	42.2	1,179	97.0
San Ardo CDP	517	-	-	543	14.5	0.0	0.0	0.0	85.5	40.1	6.4	25.3	87.4	8.7	144	62.5
San Bernardino city	210,422	215,784	2.5	216,089	14.4	13.3	3.9	3.3	65.2	29.6	9.0	29.9	59.9	11.9	59,295	90.1
San Bruno city	41,109	42,807	4.1	43,083	32.8	1.0	30.8	8.7	26.8	18.6	14.9	39.3	26.3	43.9	15,063	94.4
San Buenaventura (Ventura) city	107,217	109,106	1.8	109,910	55.7	1.7	3.6	3.0	36.0	21.3	16.7	39.6	28.3	35.7	41,246	92.5
San Carlos city	28,379	30,185	6.4	30,154	67.9	0.7	16.1	6.2	9.1	24.8	15.6	41.8	11.6	68.3	11,223	95.9
San Clemente city	63,500	64,558	1.7	64,878	74.7	0.8	4.2	3.9	16.4	21.4	17.7	44.3	17.3	50.9	24,384	96.8
Sand City city	334	399	19.5	310	58.1	4.8	3.2	3.9	30.0	18.1	10.6	36.4	30.8	39.8	146	95.2
San Diego city	1,301,929	1,423,851	9.4	1,409,573	42.8	6.0	16.4	4.4	30.3	19.9	12.6	34.9	27.0	45.9	507,580	95.3
San Diego Country Estates CDP	10,109	-	-	10,514	82.4	0.6	2.3	2.0	12.8	23.9	14.0	42.4	23.1	34.2	3,454	99.8
San Dimas city	33,375	33,621	0.7	34,048	46.8	1.8	13.8	3.9	33.6	20.9	19.2	41.3	25.8	36.9	11,415	92.1
San Fernando city	23,640	24,322	2.9	24,535	4.1	0.7	1.3	0.7	93.2	24.2	11.0	35.5	65.0	12.9	6,569	86.7
San Francisco city	805,184	881,549	9.5	874,961	40.5	5.0	34.1	5.2	15.2	13.4	15.4	38.2	23.6	58.1	362,354	93.1
San Gabriel city	39,644	39,899	0.6	40,143	10.6	0.6	61.4	1.9	25.5	17.4	16.9	42.4	48.5	32.3	12,401	94.3
Sanger city	24,262	25,339	4.4	25,074	12.4	0.1	2.8	1.9	82.8	30.7	9.8	33.4	58.0	12.2	7,081	85.2
San Geronimo CDP	446	-	-	399	96.0	0.0	0.0	0.0	4.0	28.3	28.6	41.2	26.6	61.9	143	100.0
San Jacinto city	44,213	49,215	11.3	47,989	31.1	6.7	3.3	3.8	55.1	29.3	11.4	31.8	52.3	12.8	12,841	91.3
San Joaquin city	3,994	4,021	0.7	4,020	1.7	1.2	0.0	0.0	97.1	35.6	6.9	27.3	81.9	2.6	987	82.9
San Jose city	952,528	1,021,795	7.3	1,027,690	25.7	2.8	35.7	4.1	31.6	22.4	12.5	36.7	32.0	43.7	325,114	95.2
San Juan Bautista city	1,843	2,104	14.2	2,019	35.2	0.0	4.3	2.4	58.1	26.7	13.6	38.2	38.3	28.7	688	92.2
San Juan Capistrano city	34,426	35,911	4.3	35,922	55.6	0.4	2.4	2.9	38.7	24.3	18.1	41.5	36.1	36.3	12,141	94.3
San Leandro city	84,977	88,815	4.5	90,025	23.2	9.9	34.5	5.3	27.1	19.0	15.1	40.7	40.8	31.7	31,434	92.5
San Lorenzo CDP	23,452	-	-	25,569	25.2	2.6	25.7	5.5	41.1	20.7	14.9	39.7	46.0	25.2	7,574	93.7
San Lucas CDP	269	-	-	543	10.5	0.0	0.0	0.4	89.1	38.5	6.1	25.9	78.3	0.0	110	80.9
San Luis Obispo city	45,121	47,459	5.2	47,302	70.6	1.9	5.3	4.0	18.2	12.9	13.2	26.7	19.1	50.0	18,995	94.7
San Marcos city	83,631	96,664	15.6	95,355	43.6	2.4	9.4	4.7	39.9	26.2	12.9	35.5	33.9	37.0	29,771	95.6
San Marino city	13,101	13,048	-0.4	13,194	28.3	1.9	60.5	3.1	6.3	22.8	20.7	46.9	7.8	78.1	4,487	96.2
San Martin CDP	7,027	-	-	6,803	43.4	1.0	3.3	5.4	46.8	20.6	16.8	43.3	44.8	22.3	1,929	93.7
San Mateo city	97,195	104,430	7.4	104,333	40.9	1.9	23.8	8.4	25.1	20.9	15.4	38.2	23.7	54.2	38,549	95.1
San Miguel CDP	3,392	-	-	3,433	74.0	0.0	12.9	8.3	4.8	24.1	17.0	44.9	10.2	67.6	1,180	98.5
San Miguel CDP	2,336	-	-	2,906	28.0	0.0	2.2	0.9	68.9	28.6	5.8	30.4	60.6	13.5	837	99.2
San Pablo city	29,512	30,990	5.0	30,967	7.7	10.7	17.2	4.3	60.1	24.6	10.1	33.5	60.6	13.1	9,221	92.4
San Pasqual CDP	2,041	-	-	1,970	46.4	4.7	26.4	1.9	20.5	15.9	20.1	46.5	17.7	69.4	919	91.9
San Rafael city	57,698	58,440	1.3	58,775	57.0	1.3	6.7	3.9	31.0	22.0	19.3	41.1	25.6	52.2	23,433	94.2
San Ramon city	71,412	75,995	6.4	75,648	38.6	2.3	46.5	5.6	7.1	28.3	10.5	40.2	11.5	70.6	25,535	98.3
San Simeon CDP	462	-	-	658	21.0	0.0	2.4	0.0	76.6	26.6	14.4	33.5	52.2	12.7	322	82.3
Santa Ana city	324,774	332,318	2.3	332,794	9.4	1.0	11.6	1.3	76.8	26.9	9.0	31.8	63.4	15.0	76,624	93.0
Santa Barbara city	88,380	91,364	3.4	91,376	55.6	1.4	3.8	2.1	37.1	16.9	18.7	39.0	27.0	49.2	37,333	93.1
Santa Clara city	116,453	130,365	11.9	127,721	31.5	2.9	43.1	5.1	17.3	19.8	11.4	33.9	20.1	59.9	44,669	96.3
Santa Clarita city	208,778	212,979	2.0	213,411	47.9	3.7	10.8	4.1	33.5	25.8	11.7	37.0	27.8	36.8	69,046	95.8
Santa Cruz city	59,944	64,608	7.8	64,522	61.6	1.9	10.0	5.5	21.0	12.8	12.3	28.8	18.5	53.8	22,579	96.2
Santa Fe Springs city	16,218	17,630	8.7	17,810	12.9	3.7	6.8	2.2	74.5	22.7	14.1	36.6	49.8	19.1	5,190	94.0
Santa Margarita CDP	1,259	-	-	1,122	94.6	0.0	0.0	0.0	5.4	14.8	1.4	52.7	31.8	33.8	542	75.1
Santa Maria city	99,596	107,263	7.7	106,224	16.4	1.2	5.0	1.4	76.0	31.5	9.8	29.3	60.3	13.8	27,868	89.6
Santa Monica city	89,742	90,401	0.7	91,577	64.6	4.4	9.8	5.8	15.4	15.0	17.8	40.1	13.4	67.9	45,309	94.1
Santa Nella CDP	1,380	-	-	2,135	13.3	0.9	4.3	6.3	75.2	34.4	8.7	30.1	68.2	13.8	558	78.1
Santa Paula city	29,267	29,806	1.8	30,098	15.1	0.2	1.3	1.5	81.9	28.8	11.7	32.1	59.3	14.1	8,615	82.7
Santa Rosa city	175,038	176,753	1.0	179,701	54.6	2.4	5.4	4.8	32.8	21.6	16.7	38.8	33.1	32.6	66,319	94.1
Santa Rosa Valley CDP	3,334	-	-	3,016	81.5	0.7	8.5	6.7	2.7	17.3	29.7	52.7	13.6	52.8	1,084	100.0
Santa Susana CDP	1,037	-	-	935	72.7	0.3	3.0	3.6	20.3	20.9	19.6	50.5	28.4	24.9	376	94.4
Santa Venetia CDP	4,292	-	-	4,474	71.2	3.7	8.8	10.5	5.7	16.0	24.6	49.6	18.3	49.0	1,717	92.3
Santa Ynez CDP	4,418	-	-	4,546	66.0	0.0	3.3	14.1	16.7	23.4	20.2	42.7	25.8	31.5	1,663	98.2
Santee city	53,420	58,081	8.7	57,797	68.8	2.2	5.6	5.5	17.9	22.1	14.0	38.2	32.6	29.5	19,200	94.7
Saranap CDP	5,202	-	-	6,231	77.8	2.2	8.9	2.8	8.3	23.1	18.2	39.7	9.1	69.0	2,418	94.8
Saratoga city	29,995	30,153	0.5	30,697	44.8	0.5	47.7	4.2	2.9	20.6	23.1	50.2	8.6	77.5	11,013	98.0
Saticoy CDP	1,029	-	-	1,242	11.8	0.5	0.0	0.6	87.1	30.0	10.6	32.3	80.1	1.6	268	69.8

1 May be of any race.

STATE City, town, township, borough, or CDP (county if applicable)	Population 2010 census total population	Population 2019 estimated population	Population Percent change 2010-2019	Population ACS total population estimate 2015-2019	Race White alone, not Hispanic or Latino	Race Black alone, not Hispanic or Latino	Race Asian alone, not Hispanic or Latino	Race All other races or 2 or more races, not Hispanic or Latino	Race Hispanic or Latino[1]	Age Under 18 years old	Age 65 years and older	Age Median age	Educ. Percent High school diploma or less	Educ. Percent Bachelor's degree or more	Housing Total	Housing Percent with a computer
	1	2	3	4	5	6	7	8	9	10	11	12	13	14	15	16
CALIFORNIA—Con.																
Sattley CDP	49	-	-	86	72.1	0.0	0.0	27.9	0.0	0.0	46.5	57.9	53.5	0.0	68	58.8
Sausalito city	6,953	7,068	1.7	7,116	86.7	0.9	3.2	1.2	8.1	10.4	30.1	54.9	4.6	68.5	4,030	98.0
Scotia CDP	850	-	-	546	77.7	0.0	0.0	11.9	10.4	25.6	7.7	28.9	40.8	9.2	192	100.0
Scotts Valley city	11,573	11,757	1.6	11,863	78.0	0.6	7.2	3.7	10.6	19.9	17.0	42.9	15.3	54.5	4,420	94.0
Seacliff CDP	3,267	-	-	3,286	76.3	0.7	2.5	3.9	16.7	17.1	18.8	47.1	18.8	41.5	1,543	94.9
Seal Beach city	24,076	23,896	-0.7	24,204	70.6	2.1	11.1	3.8	12.4	12.8	39.9	58.5	17.4	49.0	12,542	88.9
Sea Ranch CDP	1,305	-	-	1,134	82.7	0.0	0.9	0.0	16.4	9.3	53.7	66.1	10.6	67.7	604	97.0
Searles Valley CDP	1,739	-	-	1,689	72.3	6.0	2.0	2.3	17.5	27.3	15.5	40.5	46.7	10.5	745	90.1
Seaside city	33,025	33,748	2.2	33,956	32.1	6.9	9.8	8.2	43.0	24.6	11.0	32.8	44.0	23.3	10,598	90.5
Sebastopol city	7,464	7,674	2.8	7,760	79.1	1.6	2.7	7.2	9.3	16.7	22.3	46.8	17.3	44.9	3,333	96.0
Seeley CDP	1,739	-	-	2,010	5.5	1.3	0.0	4.0	89.2	27.8	10.0	26.8	48.9	9.7	504	83.7
Selma city	23,380	24,825	6.2	24,675	10.9	0.3	3.3	1.5	83.9	30.8	11.0	30.1	59.1	9.5	7,081	84.4
Sequoia Crest CDP	10	-	-	38	100.0	0.0	0.0	0.0	0.0	0.0	100.0	0.0	100.0	0.0	19	100.0
Sereno del Mar CDP	126	-	-	80	100.0	0.0	0.0	0.0	0.0	0.0	46.3	52.7	0.0	68.8	47	100.0
Seville CDP	480	-	-	614	2.4	0.0	0.0	0.2	97.4	49.5	3.3	18.2	86.3	1.6	114	80.7
Shafter city	17,104	20,401	19.3	19,447	12.6	1.9	0.6	0.6	84.2	33.2	7.8	27.2	71.8	9.9	5,081	71.6
Shandon CDP	1,295	-	-	1,085	34.3	1.0	0.0	1.7	63.0	21.5	8.6	42.0	57.9	9.0	425	88.2
Shasta CDP	1,771	-	-	1,573	86.0	1.3	0.0	8.0	4.8	20.4	23.5	47.7	30.3	28.9	601	93.2
Shasta Lake city	10,164	10,413	2.4	10,206	79.5	1.3	0.2	9.0	10.0	24.2	17.0	38.6	39.7	14.9	3,909	91.1
Shaver Lake CDP	634	-	-	473	91.1	0.0	0.6	1.7	6.6	5.7	40.0	62.2	17.6	43.3	248	90.7
Shell Ridge CDP	959	-	-	1,342	55.2	3.8	18.6	8.9	13.5	22.1	15.0	45.2	6.6	80.7	473	100.0
Shelter Cove CDP	693	-	-	580	100.0	0.0	0.0	0.0	0.0	0.0	36.4	56.4	43.4	36.2	377	100.0
Sheridan CDP	1,238	-	-	1,355	87.9	0.0	4.1	4.6	3.4	26.1	18.6	40.5	59.7	23.9	458	84.9
Shingle Springs CDP	4,432	-	-	3,846	87.3	1.0	2.3	1.5	8.0	15.4	12.6	51.6	25.1	27.5	1,453	96.9
Shingletown CDP	2,283	-	-	2,246	92.1	1.0	1.4	3.3	2.2	10.9	39.8	60.8	44.5	16.0	1,008	86.8
Shoshone CDP	31	-	-	17	100.0	0.0	0.0	0.0	0.0	0.0	17.6	39.8	0.0	76.5	13	76.9
Sierra Brooks CDP	478	-	-	292	92.5	0.0	0.0	0.0	7.5	6.8	25.0	59.9	33.8	14.6	125	100.0
Sierra City CDP	221	-	-	126	100.0	0.0	0.0	0.0	0.0	0.0	82.5	69.8	31.7	55.6	60	100.0
Sierra Madre city	10,917	10,793	-1.1	10,932	66.3	0.8	14.6	4.0	14.4	18.2	22.9	49.0	14.4	60.8	4,664	92.3
Sierra Village CDP	456	-	-	169	100.0	0.0	0.0	0.0	0.0	0.0	37.9	60.0	0.0	54.4	113	100.0
Sierraville CDP	200	-	-	85	76.5	1.2	0.0	8.2	14.1	0.0	34.1	62.5	22.9	48.2	50	100.0
Signal Hill city	11,018	11,421	3.7	11,512	29.1	11.0	24.9	3.1	31.9	18.7	12.9	37.9	27.2	46.5	4,719	93.7
Silverado Resort CDP	1,095	-	-	1,018	95.8	1.3	0.0	1.3	1.7	10.6	51.6	65.9	10.0	63.1	507	96.1
Silver City CDP	-	-	-	-	-	-	-	-	-	-	-	-	-	-	-	-
Silver Lakes CDP	5,623	-	-	5,849	64.4	8.2	3.9	4.1	19.4	22.6	24.8	43.5	23.0	27.5	2,353	97.1
Simi Valley city	124,242	125,613	1.1	125,842	59.2	1.3	10.2	3.1	26.2	21.6	14.8	40.6	29.9	33.6	41,986	93.0
Sisquoc CDP	183	-	-	169	57.4	0.0	0.0	3.0	39.6	26.0	14.8	43.2	49.6	11.8	59	96.6
Sky Valley CDP	2,406	-	-	2,227	60.4	0.0	2.0	1.5	36.1	16.3	28.6	51.1	43.0	16.3	963	84.3
Sleepy Hollow CDP	2,384	-	-	2,273	86.2	0.0	2.6	0.9	10.3	21.8	22.5	48.0	11.2	70.3	695	97.1
Smartsville CDP	177	-	-	267	92.5	3.0	0.0	4.5	0.0	33.3	21.0	28.9	63.4	0.7	104	87.5
Smith Corner CDP	524	-	-	486	24.9	0.0	0.0	0.0	75.1	8.6	0.0	26.2	100.0	0.0	100	50.0
Smith River CDP	866	-	-	498	75.3	0.0	0.0	18.5	6.2	15.1	22.7	43.1	37.0	13.6	184	81.0
Snelling CDP	231	-	-	119	62.2	0.0	0.0	7.6	30.3	31.9	18.5	38.5	52.0	12.0	56	89.3
Soda Bay CDP	1,016	-	-	878	80.8	0.0	1.0	0.1	18.1	4.6	31.2	60.5	35.1	28.6	431	100.0
Soda Springs CDP	81	-	-	46	0.0	0.0	100.0	0.0	0.0	0.0	0.0	15.0	100.0	0.0	18	100.0
Solana Beach city	12,867	13,296	3.3	13,356	76.2	0.7	4.9	2.7	15.5	17.9	22.8	45.5	13.5	68.0	5,571	98.2
Soledad city	25,738	25,999	1.0	25,705	13.3	9.4	1.7	3.0	72.5	22.6	6.0	35.8	67.9	6.8	3,674	90.0
Solvang city	5,228	5,838	11.7	5,804	68.1	1.2	2.5	2.2	26.1	19.6	23.2	45.8	22.9	38.2	2,380	95.9
Sonoma city	10,657	11,024	3.4	11,075	73.4	0.1	2.6	3.0	20.8	16.3	30.4	52.3	25.1	42.0	5,125	92.6
Sonora city	4,905	4,864	-0.8	4,844	72.0	1.2	6.9	3.2	16.7	20.3	24.8	42.0	40.5	24.1	2,170	88.0
Soquel CDP	9,644	-	-	10,883	76.2	0.3	2.6	5.0	15.9	20.4	17.1	41.8	20.6	42.0	4,001	95.4
Soulsbyville CDP	2,215	-	-	2,216	77.3	0.0	0.0	6.3	16.4	25.4	14.2	36.2	47.4	15.7	861	90.0
South Dos Palos CDP	1,620	-	-	1,756	5.1	7.3	0.0	0.0	87.6	28.6	4.7	28.4	69.2	9.8	500	90.4
South El Monte city	20,096	20,574	2.4	20,721	2.5	0.3	14.6	0.2	82.3	25.7	11.9	34.4	71.3	10.5	5,072	88.7
South Gate city	94,412	93,444	-1.0	94,642	2.9	0.5	0.5	0.5	95.6	27.0	10.0	31.9	69.1	9.4	24,071	90.1
South Lake Tahoe city	21,397	22,197	3.7	21,939	58.8	1.0	7.1	2.5	30.5	17.0	14.9	37.1	36.7	24.3	8,932	88.7
South Monrovia Island CDP	6,777	-	-	6,572	9.0	9.1	9.9	1.7	70.3	22.1	11.7	34.9	58.9	17.7	1,544	93.1
South Oroville CDP	5,742	-	-	2,906	51.9	0.3	14.5	14.6	18.7	20.0	12.3	35.3	58.8	2.4	924	90.7
South Pasadena city	25,605	25,329	-1.1	25,661	42.7	3.1	30.3	5.4	18.5	24.5	13.9	40.1	11.5	67.4	9,827	95.5
South San Francisco city	63,622	67,789	6.5	67,408	20.1	1.8	40.2	4.7	33.3	18.4	16.2	40.4	35.0	35.6	21,330	92.2
South San Gabriel CDP	8,070	-	-	8,138	6.6	0.2	58.0	0.9	34.3	16.9	19.1	42.0	48.4	26.2	2,140	95.5
South San Jose Hills CDP	20,551	-	-	19,977	2.9	0.7	9.6	0.4	86.4	25.1	12.4	35.3	66.7	10.8	4,133	92.9
South Taft CDP	2,169	-	-	1,768	39.0	0.0	0.0	2.0	59.0	27.7	7.9	32.6	73.8	3.1	609	86.7
South Whittier CDP	57,156	-	-	60,357	13.3	0.7	5.3	2.9	77.7	25.7	11.4	33.4	53.4	15.3	15,471	90.5
Spaulding CDP	178	-	-	108	100.0	0.0	0.0	0.0	0.0	0.0	54.6	66.6	85.2	0.0	76	63.2
Spreckels CDP	673	-	-	414	72.5	0.0	0.0	0.0	27.5	4.1	22.7	47.8	14.5	34.2	148	100.0
Spring Garden CDP	16	-	-	20	100.0	0.0	0.0	0.0	0.0	0.0	100.0	0.0	100.0	0.0	20	100.0
Spring Valley CDP	845	-	-	1,094	65.8	0.0	1.7	1.9	30.5	29.3	16.5	46.2	49.9	9.8	359	92.5
Spring Valley CDP	28,205	-	-	31,650	36.8	13.9	6.3	5.7	37.3	25.4	12.8	35.2	33.1	26.4	9,951	96.3
Spring Valley Lake CDP	8,220	-	-	8,403	67.1	5.3	2.5	2.6	22.5	22.3	18.5	42.4	30.1	29.2	2,817	97.4
Springville CDP	934	-	-	965	89.3	0.0	0.0	0.0	10.7	23.7	26.4	38.4	53.7	14.5	514	65.0
Squaw Valley CDP	3,162	-	-	3,646	71.5	0.8	1.3	1.4	25.0	28.7	17.7	43.2	42.1	23.6	1,198	84.4
Squirrel Mountain Valley CDP	547	-	-	981	94.1	0.0	0.0	5.9	0.0	14.9	36.7	57.2	37.7	19.9	496	87.5
Stallion Springs CDP	2,488	-	-	3,581	73.9	0.0	0.0	6.0	20.1	32.8	16.7	36.8	32.3	13.1	1,231	83.0
Stanford CDP	13,809	-	-	16,326	45.9	3.0	27.8	7.2	16.0	6.1	4.2	22.5	2.7	93.6	3,550	99.9
Stanton city	37,827	38,139	0.8	38,377	18.1	1.1	29.3	3.7	47.8	25.5	12.1	34.9	53.3	19.8	11,282	90.4
Stevenson Ranch CDP	17,557	-	-	19,179	51.2	3.4	24.4	6.4	14.5	26.4	9.5	40.6	16.5	53.7	6,486	97.2
Stevinson CDP	313	-	-	177	55.9	0.0	2.8	15.3	26.0	3.4	19.8	47.8	68.1	9.0	96	75.0
Stinson Beach CDP	632	-	-	600	95.8	0.0	0.0	0.0	4.2	3.2	44.7	59.0	16.0	58.4	336	100.0
Stirling City CDP	295	-	-	374	61.2	0.0	0.0	0.0	38.8	50.0	16.0	25.5	80.7	7.5	97	45.4
Stockton city	292,182	312,697	7.0	309,228	20.6	10.8	21.0	5.0	42.7	27.7	12.4	33.0	51.6	18.3	95,514	89.2
Stonyford CDP	149	-	-	92	95.7	0.0	0.0	0.0	4.3	1.1	40.2	56.5	66.3	18.0	50	54.0
Storrie CDP	4	-	-	-	-	-	-	-	-	-	-	-	-	-	-	-
Stratford CDP	1,277	-	-	901	29.4	0.0	0.0	0.0	70.6	45.4	6.5	21.7	80.0	4.9	196	82.1
Strathmore CDP	2,819	-	-	3,033	15.3	0.0	0.0	0.0	84.7	36.2	9.8	38.3	73.5	6.4	802	79.4
Strawberry CDP	5,393	-	-	5,527	73.3	1.2	12.8	5.1	7.7	20.1	19.3	45.5	8.2	72.7	2,391	97.3
Strawberry CDP	86	-	-	5	60.0	0.0	20.0	0.0	20.0	0.0	100.0	79.5	60.0	0.0	0	0.0
Sugarloaf Mountain Park CDP	-	-	-	-	-	-	-	-	-	-	-	-	-	-	-	-
Sugarloaf Saw Mill CDP	18	-	-	-	-	-	-	-	-	-	-	-	-	-	-	-

1 May be of any race.

Table A. All Places — **Population and Housing**

STATE City, town, township, borough, or CDP (county if applicable)	Population				Race and Hispanic or Latino origin (percent)					Age (percent)			Educational attainment of persons age 25 and older		Occupied housing units	
	2010 census total population	2019 estimated population	Percent change 2010-2019	ACS total population estimate 2015-2019	White alone, not Hispanic or Latino	Black alone, not Hispanic or Latino	Asian alone, not Hispanic or Latino	All other races or 2 or more races, not Hispanic or Latino	Hispanic or Latino[1]	Under 18 years old	Age 65 years and older	Median age	Percent High school diploma or less	Percent Bachelor's degree or more	Total	Percent with a computer
	1	2	3	4	5	6	7	8	9	10	11	12	13	14	15	16
CALIFORNIA—Con.																
Sugarloaf Village CDP	10	-	-	9	100.0	0.0	0.0	0.0	0.0	0.0	88.9	83.5	66.7	22.2	5	100.0
Suisun City city	28,059	29,663	5.7	29,488	26.0	20.9	19.6	6.6	26.8	24.0	11.7	34.4	37.3	21.9	9,310	94.4
Sultana CDP	775	-	-	1,002	8.1	0.0	1.4	1.7	88.8	43.1	5.5	21.8	85.8	2.5	246	85.4
Summerland CDP	1,448	-	-	844	94.2	0.0	0.0	0.0	5.8	1.4	47.4	63.5	13.3	68.9	451	93.1
Sunnyside CDP	4,235	-	-	4,464	42.2	4.2	7.7	3.5	42.4	24.6	16.6	40.3	29.5	38.8	1,569	91.3
Sunnyside-Tahoe City CDP	1,557	-	-	1,164	92.6	0.0	1.3	2.8	3.3	23.3	18.8	41.5	12.0	58.7	503	100.0
Sunny Slopes CDP	182	-	-	67	100.0	0.0	0.0	0.0	0.0	0.0	32.8	63.9	0.0	91.0	52	100.0
Sunnyvale city	140,060	152,703	9.0	152,770	30.7	1.5	46.5	4.8	16.5	21.0	11.8	35.3	17.4	65.1	56,103	96.9
Sunol CDP	913	-	-	850	80.6	0.5	11.4	0.9	6.6	17.5	20.0	50.9	24.6	44.2	316	99.4
Sun Village CDP	11,565	-	-	13,819	23.3	5.4	1.3	3.0	67.1	29.4	12.9	34.2	66.2	5.5	3,471	91.8
Susanville city	17,943	15,010	-16.3	15,064	48.2	14.0	2.1	6.0	29.7	12.3	7.3	31.7	66.5	7.3	3,001	86.4
Sutter CDP	2,904	-	-	3,005	73.7	0.0	3.9	7.5	14.9	25.6	14.8	41.4	46.1	12.5	1,089	92.7
Sutter Creek city	2,523	2,622	3.9	2,573	89.1	0.1	0.3	1.0	9.4	20.7	30.3	50.8	33.2	25.5	1,196	82.9
Swall Meadows CDP	220	-	-	251	98.4	0.0	0.0	0.0	1.6	2.4	67.3	68.6	7.8	61.2	137	88.3
Taft city	9,289	9,272	-0.2	9,372	56.0	1.3	2.8	4.4	35.5	28.1	12.1	34.6	63.4	10.5	3,288	82.6
Taft Heights CDP	1,949	-	-	1,998	70.4	1.2	0.0	1.2	27.3	35.1	8.7	26.8	55.2	5.4	670	93.1
Taft Mosswood CDP	1,530	-	-	1,104	0.8	12.9	9.4	0.7	76.2	19.0	22.0	45.1	73.4	8.1	373	71.3
Tahoe Vista CDP	1,433	-	-	1,158	80.9	0.0	0.0	0.0	19.1	19.9	11.2	34.9	32.4	46.4	491	97.8
Tahoma CDP	1,191	-	-	974	87.6	0.0	3.0	9.4	0.0	24.7	10.2	37.5	26.0	46.8	375	93.3
Talmage CDP	1,130	-	-	1,003	44.0	4.8	26.0	11.5	13.8	16.7	23.0	36.4	37.3	38.3	279	85.3
Tamalpais-Homestead Valley CDP	10,735	-	-	11,689	82.3	1.3	5.8	5.0	5.6	23.7	19.3	47.1	9.1	76.5	4,617	96.5
Tara Hills CDP	5,126	-	-	5,117	21.4	13.7	19.1	5.0	40.8	20.8	12.9	37.8	46.3	15.3	1,678	91.5
Tarpey Village CDP	3,888	-	-	3,609	46.5	1.1	9.0	4.8	38.6	25.7	17.5	36.5	41.2	17.2	1,266	88.9
Taylorsville CDP	140	-	-	198	79.3	0.0	0.0	20.7	0.0	48.5	12.1	38.1	7.8	29.4	53	84.9
Tecopa CDP	150	-	-	168	84.5	0.0	0.0	4.8	10.7	11.3	56.5	67.0	32.7	26.5	102	72.5
Tehachapi city	14,420	13,011	-9.8	12,680	48.6	9.8	2.4	4.2	34.9	18.5	11.9	37.4	50.8	12.8	3,197	82.4
Tehama city	418	373	-10.8	481	74.4	0.0	1.5	7.1	17.0	13.1	24.7	51.0	47.8	11.3	219	83.6
Temecula city	100,013	114,761	14.7	113,381	51.9	4.0	8.8	5.5	29.7	28.9	10.1	34.8	27.0	34.0	33,947	97.8
Temelec CDP	1,441	-	-	1,620	98.7	0.0	0.0	1.3	0.0	0.0	77.8	72.1	12.7	48.9	1,072	86.5
Temescal Valley CDP	-	-	-	27,630	42.3	8.9	10.5	3.7	34.7	27.3	13.6	38.1	29.6	29.0	8,141	97.0
Temple City city	35,554	35,811	0.7	36,042	15.0	0.6	62.4	2.5	19.5	20.4	17.3	43.5	34.8	39.7	11,467	93.1
Templeton CDP	7,674	-	-	7,838	80.3	0.0	1.4	4.9	13.4	25.9	19.2	43.5	24.1	37.7	2,890	94.9
Tennant CDP	41	-	-	26	69.2	0.0	0.0	0.0	30.8	0.0	100.0	73.8	30.8	0.0	17	52.9
Terminous CDP	381	-	-	446	77.8	0.0	3.8	2.2	16.1	7.0	44.8	58.5	50.0	10.3	205	91.2
Terra Bella CDP	3,310	-	-	3,182	6.6	0.0	0.0	0.2	93.3	27.2	10.2	32.9	79.0	1.8	864	83.9
Teviston CDP	1,214	-	-	881	4.7	13.1	3.1	0.0	79.2	29.2	15.6	41.4	79.9	4.5	279	80.6
Thermal CDP	2,865	-	-	1,333	0.6	0.1	0.0	0.0	99.3	29.0	6.8	29.8	86.3	0.0	429	64.3
Thermalito CDP	6,646	-	-	6,894	60.3	1.2	21.1	6.5	10.9	20.1	18.2	39.9	58.4	10.5	2,266	89.3
Thornton CDP	1,131	-	-	1,033	28.2	0.7	3.2	1.7	66.2	36.2	9.8	25.6	79.2	2.3	277	81.6
Thousand Oaks city	126,490	126,813	0.3	127,873	66.8	1.3	9.6	3.0	19.4	21.6	19.0	44.2	19.3	50.8	45,712	95.0
Thousand Palms CDP	7,715	-	-	6,794	46.7	0.4	1.1	0.6	51.3	19.1	27.1	52.0	56.7	12.3	2,607	85.0
Three Rivers CDP	2,182	-	-	2,424	81.9	2.0	5.4	1.4	9.2	15.0	28.5	55.9	18.3	50.8	1,101	91.7
Three Rocks CDP	246	-	-	249	0.0	0.0	0.0	0.0	100.0	0.0	10.4	48.7	100.0	0.0	71	53.5
Tiburon town	8,947	9,084	1.5	9,144	81.6	1.0	2.7	7.1	7.6	21.2	25.7	50.8	6.9	76.2	3,798	98.8
Timber Cove CDP	164	-	-	141	80.1	0.0	2.1	1.4	16.3	5.7	44.0	58.5	15.7	53.5	70	91.4
Tipton CDP	2,543	-	-	3,238	6.8	0.0	0.0	0.2	93.0	39.7	7.6	24.5	82.1	0.2	775	89.9
Tobin CDP	12	-	-	-	-	-	-	-	-	-	-	-	-	-	-	-
Tomales CDP	204	-	-	191	88.5	0.0	11.5	0.0	0.0	0.0	33.0	62.2	11.5	68.6	116	100.0
Tonyville CDP	316	-	-	388	0.0	0.0	0.0	0.0	100.0	34.5	18.3	36.7	82.4	0.0	117	64.1
Tooleville CDP	339	-	-	167	8.4	0.0	0.0	0.0	91.6	21.0	7.2	44.7	88.0	0.0	78	73.1
Topanga CDP	8,289	-	-	7,900	79.6	1.8	6.7	3.0	8.8	17.9	20.5	45.5	8.1	68.6	3,183	98.6
Topaz CDP	50	-	-	126	7.9	0.0	0.0	73.0	19.0	0.0	7.9	46.3	34.3	0.0	70	65.7
Toro Canyon CDP	1,508	-	-	1,728	59.3	0.0	0.5	1.0	39.2	17.4	36.5	56.2	22.7	49.4	658	100.0
Torrance city	145,151	143,592	-1.1	145,492	37.4	2.6	35.6	5.8	18.6	20.6	17.0	41.9	21.7	50.7	54,437	95.2
Tracy city	83,423	94,740	13.6	90,675	33.1	4.4	16.1	6.8	39.6	28.1	8.9	33.9	41.0	22.0	25,854	96.6
Tranquillity CDP	799	-	-	809	7.5	0.0	0.0	0.0	92.5	33.7	15.9	40.6	83.2	0.0	239	74.5
Traver CDP	713	-	-	754	7.8	0.0	0.4	2.9	88.9	31.0	9.4	28.0	84.4	0.5	187	86.1
Tres Pinos CDP	476	-	-	683	61.6	0.0	0.0	2.8	35.6	28.1	17.1	35.8	34.1	24.1	220	95.5
Trinidad city	369	355	-3.8	324	77.2	0.0	2.5	15.1	5.2	12.7	26.9	55.6	5.9	65.5	142	98.6
Trinity Center CDP	267	-	-	154	65.6	0.0	0.0	34.4	0.0	3.9	50.0	64.5	55.0	15.5	81	70.4
Trinity Village CDP	297	-	-	253	94.1	0.0	0.0	5.9	0.0	10.3	49.0	64.6	45.8	13.7	142	58.5
Trona CDP	18	-	-	40	37.5	0.0	0.0	0.0	62.5	35.0	37.5	36.5	100.0	0.0	19	100.0
Trowbridge CDP	226	-	-	254	84.3	2.0	0.0	9.1	4.7	13.0	13.0	42.5	34.3	10.0	93	92.5
Truckee town	16,163	16,735	3.5	16,474	82.0	0.1	0.9	2.1	15.0	24.3	13.2	40.2	15.2	51.9	6,050	97.9
Tulare city	59,293	65,496	10.5	63,547	28.8	3.0	1.4	2.6	64.2	34.1	8.9	28.4	55.7	10.9	18,422	87.9
Tulelake city	1,010	978	-3.2	842	26.0	0.0	0.0	0.0	74.0	32.9	17.6	29.1	70.6	5.7	291	49.5
Tuolumne City CDP	1,779	-	-	1,583	67.7	0.1	2.8	3.1	26.3	25.5	10.2	34.0	50.8	10.3	664	78.5
Tupman CDP	161	-	-	144	81.9	0.0	0.0	7.6	10.4	28.5	4.9	32.3	72.0	18.3	49	83.7
Turlock city	68,712	73,631	7.2	72,904	50.4	2.4	6.0	3.8	37.4	26.6	13.1	34.2	43.0	25.1	25,182	90.2
Tustin city	75,317	79,348	5.4	79,863	31.9	2.4	22.2	3.5	40.0	25.2	10.3	34.4	31.0	43.7	25,697	96.7
Tuttle CDP	103	-	-	94	0.0	0.0	0.0	31.9	68.1	0.0	68.1	75.3	68.1	0.0	48	37.5
Tuttletown CDP	668	-	-	1,003	88.0	0.0	0.0	2.7	9.3	21.8	24.0	39.7	46.0	17.9	385	96.9
Twain CDP	82	-	-	327	43.7	0.0	0.0	56.3	0.0	12.2	12.5	54.7	48.5	10.3	127	65.4
Twain Harte CDP	2,226	-	-	2,311	84.6	0.0	0.6	2.9	11.9	12.0	23.5	56.3	24.9	31.6	1,207	97.3
Twentynine Palms city	25,048	26,073	4.1	26,147	54.7	9.7	3.6	8.5	23.5	27.9	6.0	24.2	33.2	20.5	8,279	92.8
Twin Lakes CDP	4,917	-	-	5,196	67.6	0.7	0.0	4.0	27.6	16.2	18.6	40.2	28.7	41.8	2,332	95.5
Ukiah city	16,083	15,995	-0.5	15,943	51.4	1.1	3.3	5.5	38.7	23.5	14.6	38.1	43.1	21.6	5,992	86.6
Union City city	69,531	74,107	6.6	74,722	15.4	4.9	53.1	6.4	20.2	18.9	16.0	38.4	34.3	40.4	21,852	97.0
University of California-Davis CDP	5,786	-	-	7,311	27.2	1.2	43.7	6.7	21.1	3.1	0.0	19.5	3.4	70.4	964	100.0
University of California-Merced CDP	-	-	-	-	-	-	-	-	-	-	-	-	-	-	-	-
Upland city	73,718	77,140	4.6	76,596	38.6	5.5	9.0	3.8	43.1	21.9	14.8	38.3	30.9	32.4	26,951	92.4
Upper Lake CDP	1,052	-	-	896	76.2	1.7	0.0	1.5	20.6	12.6	11.2	43.8	56.5	8.5	357	82.1
Vacaville city	92,422	100,670	8.9	98,875	50.5	9.5	7.6	7.6	24.8	22.7	14.0	37.5	35.4	23.6	32,698	95.1
Valinda CDP	22,822	-	-	23,705	4.8	1.7	15.1	1.5	77.0	22.4	11.8	36.2	59.2	14.2	5,182	92.6
Vallecito CDP	442	-	-	234	93.2	0.0	0.0	0.0	6.8	2.6	23.1	60.3	20.6	26.3	148	94.6
Vallejo city	115,914	121,692	5.0	121,267	24.1	19.7	23.2	6.7	26.3	20.7	15.8	38.4	37.5	25.8	42,048	93.2
Valle Vista CDP	14,578	-	-	17,663	49.6	4.7	1.7	3.6	40.4	22.8	17.9	40.1	47.5	14.1	5,887	88.7
Valley Acres CDP	527	-	-	656	64.9	0.0	0.0	0.0	35.1	26.2	16.2	43.5	52.1	9.8	239	93.3

1 May be of any race.

Table A. All Places — **Population and Housing**

STATE City, town, township, borough, or CDP (county if applicable)	Population				Race and Hispanic or Latino origin (percent)					Age (percent)			Educational attainment of persons age 25 and older		Occupied housing units	
	2010 census total population	2019 estimated population	Percent change 2010-2019	ACS total population estimate 2015-2019	White alone, not Hispanic or Latino	Black alone, not Hispanic or Latino	Asian alone, not Hispanic or Latino	All other races or 2 or more races, not Hispanic or Latino	Hispanic or Latino[1]	Under 18 years old	Age 65 years and older	Median age	Percent High school diploma or less	Percent Bachelor's degree or more	Total	Percent with a computer
	1	2	3	4	5	6	7	8	9	10	11	12	13	14	15	16
CALIFORNIA—Con.																
Valley Center CDP	9,277	-	-	11,077	60.9	0.8	3.5	7.1	27.6	25.0	15.8	37.8	31.2	35.2	3,169	97.7
Valley Ford CDP	147	-	-	34	100.0	0.0	0.0	0.0	0.0	0.0	0.0	51.4	100.0	0.0	11	100.0
Valley Home CDP	228	-	-	185	88.1	0.0	0.0	2.7	9.2	9.2	28.1	57.5	41.7	12.9	81	100.0
Valley Ranch CDP	109	-	-	-	-	-	-	-	-	-	-	-	-	-	-	-
Valley Springs CDP	3,553	-	-	3,502	79.0	0.0	0.5	3.9	16.6	20.6	24.2	42.9	30.3	13.7	1,336	100.0
Valley Wells CDP	-	-	-	-	-	-	-	-	-	-	-	-	-	-	-	-
Val Verde CDP	2,468	-	-	2,734	26.7	2.4	3.5	1.1	66.3	24.8	10.1	34.2	45.8	13.2	710	97.7
Vandenberg AFB CDP	3,338	-	-	3,387	51.0	10.7	4.7	14.0	19.6	30.6	0.0	23.4	8.5	43.5	1,022	100.0
Vandenberg Village CDP	6,497	-	-	8,114	62.2	4.0	3.2	8.2	22.4	21.2	18.0	41.3	29.9	35.9	2,797	96.7
Verdi CDP	162	-	-	188	100.0	0.0	0.0	0.0	0.0	12.2	40.4	56.3	11.0	16.9	102	100.0
Vernon city	112	110	-1.8	130	6.2	13.8	2.3	0.0	77.7	37.7	3.8	26.5	33.8	13.2	43	95.3
Victor CDP	293	-	-	215	73.5	0.0	0.0	0.0	26.5	28.8	14.9	33.5	49.7	0.0	111	62.2
Victorville city	115,899	122,385	5.6	121,902	22.4	16.0	3.6	3.8	54.3	31.7	9.3	31.0	52.2	12.9	32,699	94.0
View Park-Windsor Hills CDP	11,075	-	-	11,756	6.3	78.0	2.3	5.4	8.0	14.5	22.6	49.8	16.6	52.4	4,834	93.1
Villa Park city	5,822	5,790	-0.5	5,861	67.4	0.5	17.4	2.4	12.3	18.4	27.7	52.2	18.1	54.8	1,988	97.9
Vina CDP	237	-	-	230	73.9	0.0	0.0	0.0	26.1	13.0	24.8	39.0	27.5	54.0	69	69.6
Vincent CDP	-	-	-	16,225	11.4	1.3	9.9	2.7	74.7	24.9	12.6	37.5	55.8	13.8	4,042	94.7
Vine Hill CDP	3,761	-	-	3,886	49.0	0.6	10.0	8.0	32.4	27.9	9.3	34.9	40.1	27.5	1,314	94.9
Vineyard CDP	24,836	-	-	28,386	32.4	8.8	32.2	7.9	18.7	26.5	11.2	35.5	32.5	29.8	8,429	97.7
Visalia city	124,528	134,605	8.1	132,104	38.4	1.8	5.1	2.4	52.2	29.5	11.5	32.0	38.5	23.1	43,250	91.9
Vista city	93,186	101,638	9.1	100,686	39.6	2.9	3.9	2.7	50.9	25.5	10.0	32.9	45.0	23.9	30,168	96.2
Vista Santa Rosa CDP	2,926	-	-	2,739	10.6	0.0	0.0	1.9	87.6	25.5	14.7	37.7	78.5	7.0	805	80.9
Volcano CDP	115	-	-	40	70.0	0.0	30.0	0.0	0.0	0.0	30.0	63.6	0.0	0.0	31	100.0
Volta CDP	246	-	-	128	20.3	10.9	0.0	0.0	68.8	0.0	14.8	40.5	92.9	0.0	69	100.0
Walker CDP	721	-	-	858	73.5	0.0	0.1	18.2	8.2	14.8	39.5	59.7	53.8	12.9	309	96.8
Wallace CDP	403	-	-	944	72.9	0.0	4.7	0.0	22.5	7.3	38.2	55.6	24.6	29.8	299	100.0
Walnut city	29,177	29,685	1.7	29,903	10.4	4.2	62.5	2.6	20.2	18.0	20.4	45.9	22.6	52.7	9,069	97.6
Walnut Creek city	64,157	70,166	9.4	69,567	68.3	1.8	15.2	5.5	9.1	17.0	29.6	47.8	10.8	66.7	31,390	95.4
Walnut Grove CDP	1,542	-	-	1,364	44.1	0.9	3.3	1.6	50.1	20.5	20.0	40.6	50.1	22.7	492	94.9
Walnut Park CDP	15,966	-	-	15,896	1.2	0.0	0.8	0.4	97.5	22.9	11.5	35.7	71.4	8.8	3,775	91.8
Warm Springs CDP	2,676	-	-	1,874	32.4	0.0	0.9	7.3	59.4	24.0	7.8	33.8	75.4	2.4	515	90.3
Warner Valley CDP	2	-	-	-	-	-	-	-	-	-	-	-	-	-	-	-
Wasco city	25,549	28,710	12.4	27,193	9.4	5.9	0.5	1.9	82.2	26.2	6.7	29.7	75.4	3.5	5,960	64.2
Washington CDP	185	-	-	56	100.0	0.0	0.0	0.0	0.0	0.0	87.5	70.5	21.4	28.6	32	34.4
Waterford city	8,461	8,962	5.9	8,877	43.2	0.8	2.1	2.6	51.3	31.7	10.5	33.9	67.3	6.5	2,485	89.3
Waterloo CDP	572	-	-	670	61.8	0.0	1.9	0.0	36.3	17.0	38.2	53.6	45.6	30.9	222	90.5
Watsonville city	51,214	53,856	5.2	53,800	15.2	0.5	2.5	0.6	81.2	30.3	10.2	30.6	64.0	12.3	14,717	81.5
Waukena CDP	108	-	-	149	45.0	0.0	0.0	0.0	55.0	41.6	8.1	27.9	54.9	7.3	49	100.0
Wawona CDP	169	-	-	189	44.4	0.0	0.0	12.7	42.9	25.9	7.4	26.6	0.0	10.7	95	93.7
Weaverville CDP	3,600	-	-	3,158	90.3	0.3	0.0	5.8	3.5	25.0	22.3	45.4	31.5	21.2	1,489	83.1
Weed city	2,967	2,725	-8.2	2,669	59.7	14.3	1.4	5.2	19.3	24.0	19.1	39.8	44.5	11.6	1,129	80.4
Weedpatch CDP	2,658	-	-	2,291	6.3	0.0	0.0	0.0	93.7	37.7	7.8	28.7	91.7	0.5	621	70.2
Weldon CDP	2,642	-	-	2,321	87.9	2.3	0.0	8.4	1.4	13.9	26.7	49.5	54.6	12.4	1,050	74.3
Weott CDP	288	-	-	304	100.0	0.0	0.0	0.0	0.0	21.7	3.9	49.5	46.3	34.1	128	100.0
West Athens CDP	8,729	-	-	9,706	0.5	51.4	0.9	1.2	46.1	23.3	14.3	36.7	49.8	13.8	2,973	88.2
West Bishop CDP	2,607	-	-	2,734	86.9	0.0	0.0	2.0	10.6	23.4	26.3	44.8	25.2	35.5	1,040	96.3
West Carson CDP	21,699	-	-	22,079	16.3	10.1	35.4	4.0	34.3	15.2	23.8	44.9	38.5	35.3	7,483	91.1
West Covina city	106,108	105,101	-0.9	106,589	11.5	4.0	28.6	2.9	53.0	21.0	15.5	38.2	41.2	29.0	30,430	94.5
West Goshen CDP	511	-	-	427	26.7	0.0	0.0	0.0	73.3	33.7	0.0	28.3	67.6	2.9	109	93.6
Westhaven-Moonstone CDP	1,205	-	-	1,110	88.1	0.0	1.0	2.9	8.0	20.5	21.5	43.2	17.1	51.5	458	92.4
West Hollywood city	34,351	36,475	6.2	36,450	75.4	3.6	5.6	5.1	10.3	4.3	14.8	38.7	14.0	62.2	23,369	93.6
Westlake Village city	8,303	8,217	-	8,358	80.1	1.2	7.1	2.3	9.3	19.1	25.9	52.0	13.5	67.3	3,285	97.3
Westley CDP	603	-	-	968	0.0	0.0	0.0	0.0	100.0	35.7	4.9	27.6	76.7	0.0	233	65.2
West Menlo Park CDP	3,659	-	-	4,160	74.4	1.4	15.4	4.6	4.1	31.4	13.8	39.8	5.5	83.2	1,380	97.2
Westminster city	89,619	90,643	1.1	91,137	23.7	1.2	48.1	2.8	24.1	20.1	17.2	41.8	44.0	27.1	27,617	91.9
West Modesto CDP	5,682	-	-	5,762	26.1	1.9	3.4	0.8	67.8	32.9	9.9	31.0	75.9	5.3	1,559	90.9
Westmont CDP	31,853	-	-	35,266	1.2	40.2	0.2	1.2	57.1	30.1	10.8	32.1	61.9	9.2	10,763	86.1
Westmorland city	2,230	2,254	1.1	2,432	10.8	2.5	0.4	3.6	82.6	35.9	12.2	27.0	61.2	6.2	630	83.0
West Park CDP	1,157	-	-	1,071	3.4	1.2	8.6	1.3	85.5	23.9	10.6	30.1	68.4	7.3	258	81.8
West Point CDP	674	-	-	454	85.7	0.0	0.0	10.6	3.7	20.5	31.7	48.6	44.3	8.0	188	64.9
West Puente Valley CDP	22,636	-	-	23,382	3.1	1.4	12.9	0.6	82.0	21.0	14.8	37.3	62.6	13.1	5,057	92.0
West Rancho Dominguez CDP	5,669	-	-	22,901	1.7	42.7	0.9	2.9	51.9	24.1	13.6	36.3	56.5	11.9	6,339	86.4
West Sacramento city	48,744	53,519	9.8	53,151	45.9	4.6	10.5	8.9	30.1	26.1	11.5	34.3	37.9	29.4	18,577	93.7
Westside CDP	-	-	-	80	0.0	0.0	0.0	13.8	86.3	27.5	0.0	27.0	76.5	0.0	27	59.3
West Whittier-Los Nietos CDP	25,540	-	-	26,654	7.9	0.5	1.3	1.0	89.2	22.3	13.4	37.0	56.9	15.7	7,167	94.2
Westwood CDP	1,647	-	-	1,645	86.7	4.0	0.0	3.7	5.6	11.0	26.4	55.6	36.2	18.0	838	73.5
Wheatland city	3,504	3,873	10.5	3,810	73.4	0.2	1.9	8.4	16.2	19.3	13.8	41.6	39.6	18.4	1,407	92.4
Whitehawk CDP	113	-	-	49	100.0	0.0	0.0	0.0	0.0	0.0	83.7	67.4	22.4	38.8	23	100.0
Whitewater CDP	-	-	-	890	42.6	8.9	5.5	2.6	40.4	26.9	10.1	36.1	44.3	24.3	284	82.0
Whitley Gardens CDP	285	-	-	224	93.8	0.0	0.0	6.3	0.0	8.0	0.0	46.2	38.7	16.0	58	100.0
Whittier city	85,313	85,098	-0.3	86,090	24.2	1.0	4.8	2.7	67.3	22.9	14.0	37.0	39.9	26.4	27,419	90.7
Wildomar city	32,210	37,229	15.6	36,445	45.5	3.8	5.5	3.8	41.4	26.9	12.5	34.1	44.1	16.6	10,179	93.7
Wilkerson CDP	563	-	-	519	77.6	0.0	2.5	0.2	19.7	26.0	21.4	49.4	40.1	23.2	180	92.8
Williams city	5,094	5,408	6.2	5,228	15.6	0.2	2.5	0.7	81.0	31.6	10.8	30.3	67.5	10.9	1,491	88.2
Willits city	4,926	4,890	-0.7	4,893	72.3	1.3	0.3	6.8	19.3	24.0	18.0	38.0	37.6	19.5	1,875	86.0
Willowbrook CDP	35,983	-	-	22,811	1.0	16.8	1.2	1.1	79.9	32.7	6.3	27.5	74.7	7.1	5,123	87.3
Willow Creek CDP	1,710	-	-	1,513	82.0	0.0	0.0	9.9	8.1	24.9	18.2	37.3	37.3	23.9	601	91.3
Willows city	6,163	6,072	-1.5	6,013	49.2	1.8	9.9	5.8	33.1	26.5	17.5	38.5	46.9	14.2	2,312	84.2
Wilsonia CDP	5	-	-	-	-	-	-	-	-	-	-	-	-	-	-	-
Wilton CDP	5,363	-	-	5,665	65.1	1.0	8.5	1.3	24.1	22.0	21.7	46.4	30.5	30.2	2,007	97.0
Winchester CDP	2,534	-	-	3,322	40.6	0.3	1.0	2.3	55.8	25.3	18.6	36.5	70.9	4.4	778	91.8
Windsor town	26,791	27,128	1.3	27,447	57.2	0.7	2.6	5.6	33.9	24.5	15.2	40.0	31.9	30.9	9,156	94.2
Winter Gardens CDP	20,631	-	-	23,545	67.7	1.7	2.7	5.7	22.2	21.5	16.1	38.5	45.0	18.1	7,851	95.0
Winterhaven CDP	394	-	-	192	28.1	0.0	0.0	10.9	60.9	0.0	57.3	72.6	100.0	0.0	129	42.6
Winters city	6,624	7,315	10.4	7,197	44.6	0.4	0.0	1.2	53.9	27.3	9.0	36.1	40.4	21.2	2,319	95.6
Winton CDP	10,613	-	-	11,288	18.6	0.5	2.8	2.2	75.9	34.4	10.3	29.8	74.1	5.2	3,196	90.3
Wofford Heights CDP	2,200	-	-	2,336	86.1	0.0	0.0	0.7	13.2	13.5	35.7	56.7	52.9	14.5	1,148	90.7
Woodacre CDP	1,348	-	-	1,171	95.2	0.0	0.0	2.7	2.0	10.9	45.5	64.1	18.6	55.7	615	91.9

1 May be of any race.

Table A. All Places — **Population and Housing**

STATE City, town, township, borough, or CDP (county if applicable)	2010 census total population	2019 estimated population	Percent change 2010-2019	ACS total population estimate 2015-2019	White alone, not Hispanic or Latino	Black alone, not Hispanic or Latino	Asian alone, not Hispanic or Latino	All other races or 2 or more races, not Hispanic or Latino	Hispanic or Latino[1]	Under 18 years old	Age 65 years and older	Median age	Percent High school diploma or less	Percent Bachelor's degree or more	Total	Percent with a computer
	1	2	3	4	5	6	7	8	9	10	11	12	13	14	15	16
CALIFORNIA—Con.																
Woodbridge CDP	3,984	-	-	3,582	66.9	3.8	4.4	5.5	19.5	18.7	25.5	52.1	36.3	32.5	1,424	87.9
Woodcrest CDP	14,347	-	-	17,859	45.0	6.8	3.6	1.7	42.8	23.7	15.0	37.6	34.0	26.5	4,808	96.7
Woodlake city	7,295	7,658	5.0	7,622	5.8	0.0	2.4	1.3	90.4	36.3	9.9	26.6	63.3	10.3	2,120	83.6
Woodland city	55,553	60,548	9.0	59,710	39.3	1.7	7.8	2.9	48.3	24.0	13.9	36.5	42.2	27.3	20,584	90.3
Woodlands CDP	576	-	-	2,028	87.5	0.0	3.3	4.3	4.9	9.4	51.1	65.3	11.9	65.9	935	100.0
Woodside town	5,284	5,458	3.3	5,542	79.0	0.9	7.3	3.7	9.1	24.5	22.3	47.5	7.8	78.7	1,799	99.4
Woodville CDP	1,740	-	-	1,763	6.3	0.0	0.4	0.7	92.6	30.7	7.0	28.9	85.5	3.2	471	75.4
Wrightwood CDP	4,525	-	-	3,984	74.6	0.0	0.5	4.5	20.4	26.7	19.6	38.6	31.3	34.2	1,538	94.0
Yankee Hill CDP	333	-	-	279	73.1	0.0	0.0	1.8	25.1	4.7	29.4	55.4	35.3	32.0	132	84.8
Yettem CDP	211	-	-	516	1.9	0.0	0.0	0.0	98.1	40.1	1.9	21.2	100.0	0.0	109	90.8
Yolo CDP	450	-	-	193	33.7	0.0	0.0	0.0	66.3	7.3	43.5	54.9	67.2	21.2	104	64.4
Yorba Linda city	64,167	67,644	5.4	67,725	58.4	1.3	20.6	3.3	16.5	23.1	18.0	44.2	17.6	54.1	22,649	97.3
Yosemite Lakes CDP	4,952	-	-	5,524	80.5	0.4	1.7	6.5	10.9	24.5	23.1	48.2	28.8	27.5	2,027	98.6
Yosemite Valley CDP	1,035	-	-	1,169	66.2	3.5	4.2	1.9	24.2	1.4	10.9	44.3	37.7	23.4	156	100.0
Yountville city	2,925	2,966	1.4	2,987	73.6	2.5	3.2	3.7	17.0	7.6	48.2	64.4	21.8	41.8	1,372	84.9
Yreka city	7,762	7,518	-3.1	7,562	71.1	1.6	0.3	14.2	12.8	25.1	20.0	36.5	34.3	19.6	3,402	84.9
Yuba City city	65,634	67,010	2.1	66,516	42.5	2.1	19.3	6.3	29.8	25.6	14.6	35.0	45.1	18.9	22,750	88.8
Yucaipa city	51,347	53,921	5.0	53,416	58.9	1.5	3.2	2.3	34.2	24.8	14.5	36.4	39.2	24.4	18,106	92.9
Yucca Valley town	20,652	21,777	5.4	21,622	65.5	6.2	1.4	5.0	21.9	22.6	20.4	42.9	42.6	15.6	8,652	92.1
Zayante CDP	705	-	-	794	88.3	3.0	0.0	5.2	3.5	25.9	24.9	43.7	9.0	27.6	335	96.1
COLORADO	5,029,319	5,758,736	14.5	5,610,349	68.1	3.9	3.1	3.3	21.5	22.5	13.8	36.7	29.6	40.9	2,148,994	93.9
Acres Green CDP	3,007	-	-	3,100	80.5	1.7	5.0	3.1	9.6	20.6	12.6	40.2	21.6	41.9	1,111	98.0
Aetna Estates CDP	834	-	-	1,398	32.0	1.3	0.0	3.3	63.4	45.0	3.4	24.8	70.7	2.8	369	91.6
Aguilar town	537	480	-10.6	477	44.2	0.0	0.0	2.1	53.7	12.6	20.1	47.8	51.0	19.1	257	85.6
Air Force Academy CDP	6,680	-	-	6,512	70.5	8.0	5.3	5.9	10.3	13.2	0.9	21.1	17.2	39.2	629	96.8
Akron town	1,702	1,723	1.2	2,046	78.7	1.1	1.0	1.3	17.9	21.6	18.6	35.6	49.0	12.0	812	89.9
Alamosa city	8,876	9,591	8.1	9,441	39.0	0.6	1.6	4.7	54.2	21.8	10.5	28.4	41.4	24.3	3,828	86.5
Alamosa East CDP	1,458	-	-	1,295	46.9	0.0	0.0	0.0	53.1	26.3	11.1	33.0	37.1	40.8	481	92.5
Allenspark CDP	528	-	-	433	95.4	0.5	0.0	1.6	2.5	16.4	28.6	56.6	21.2	53.3	193	95.9
Alma town	274	313	14.2	377	97.3	2.7	0.0	0.0	0.0	21.2	5.8	38.0	35.3	21.4	147	93.9
Alpine CDP	174	-	-	258	96.5	0.0	0.0	0.0	3.5	22.9	26.0	46.7	21.8	35.6	98	100.0
Altona CDP	501	-	-	513	97.3	0.0	0.0	0.0	2.7	17.3	42.3	61.3	5.9	76.2	244	92.2
Amherst CDP	58	-	-	178	100.0	0.0	0.0	0.0	0.0	23.0	0.0	22.8	48.0	25.3	39	100.0
Antonito town	781	747	-4.4	656	9.6	0.0	0.0	3.7	86.7	19.2	19.2	43.6	48.6	9.8	342	71.9
Applewood CDP	7,160	-	-	8,081	85.2	0.8	1.6	1.4	10.9	21.3	18.6	40.9	18.7	56.0	3,234	91.8
Arboles CDP	280	-	-	326	58.6	0.0	1.5	7.4	32.5	15.6	33.4	53.1	29.4	24.8	169	81.1
Aristocrat Ranchettes CDP	1,344	-	-	1,416	46.0	0.0	0.0	0.4	53.5	26.3	15.5	36.9	65.1	7.7	455	74.5
Arriba town	193	207	7.3	184	89.7	0.0	0.5	6.5	3.3	24.5	16.8	51.5	36.6	21.4	88	75.0
Arvada city	106,760	121,272	13.6	118,746	80.0	1.2	2.0	2.5	14.3	20.9	16.8	40.2	29.0	41.1	47,507	93.7
Aspen city	6,748	7,401	9.7	7,431	86.8	0.5	5.1	1.0	6.6	13.6	19.0	41.8	14.5	66.3	3,356	96.5
Aspen Park CDP	882	-	-	994	88.7	0.0	0.0	4.5	6.7	26.8	3.7	37.3	23.6	45.3	384	100.0
Atwood CDP	133	-	-	193	92.7	0.0	0.0	0.0	7.3	6.7	17.1	41.1	53.7	6.9	92	93.5
Ault town	1,527	1,871	22.5	1,947	63.3	0.3	0.9	1.8	33.7	29.8	13.9	33.8	43.8	19.4	673	87.2
Aurora city	324,659	379,289	16.8	369,111	44.4	15.9	6.4	4.7	28.6	25.3	11.2	34.4	39.2	29.7	130,054	94.3
Avon town	6,396	6,511	1.8	6,539	51.8	3.0	0.9	4.6	39.6	27.3	2.0	32.4	23.7	45.3	2,249	96.8
Avondale CDP	674	-	-	708	32.8	0.0	0.0	0.0	67.2	32.3	3.5	34.3	38.0	5.7	215	84.7
Bark Ranch CDP	213	-	-	75	100.0	0.0	0.0	0.0	0.0	0.0	18.7	63.3	0.0	100.0	44	100.0
Basalt town	3,840	4,157	8.3	3,847	90.1	0.4	0.6	0.6	8.2	17.8	20.5	47.8	16.7	58.8	1,890	98.1
Battlement Mesa CDP	4,471	-	-	5,116	67.2	0.0	0.8	4.6	27.3	28.3	14.5	36.2	49.7	25.5	1,918	94.9
Bayfield town	2,317	2,689	16.1	2,640	75.2	0.0	0.2	6.9	17.8	32.2	9.6	34.4	37.6	29.2	903	94.0
Bennett town	2,300	2,798	21.7	2,358	79.8	0.5	1.7	4.2	13.8	22.6	12.7	37.6	42.1	12.0	834	91.2
Berkley CDP	11,207	-	-	11,879	36.5	2.1	3.4	1.5	56.5	22.0	10.3	33.6	48.3	21.1	3,901	88.6
Berthoud town	5,193	9,094	75.1	7,191	85.4	0.0	0.0	2.1	12.5	23.7	12.7	37.3	30.3	32.8	2,715	98.0
Bethune town	237	235	-0.8	207	70.0	0.0	0.0	2.4	27.5	28.0	18.8	34.6	48.9	11.7	81	80.2
Beulah Valley CDP	556	-	-	780	83.1	0.0	0.0	0.0	16.9	19.1	24.0	50.4	27.3	51.0	267	94.4
Black Forest CDP	13,116	-	-	14,081	85.5	1.0	2.0	3.2	8.3	21.4	17.4	48.3	14.9	58.2	5,104	95.8
Black Hawk city	118	128	8.5	110	57.3	0.0	0.0	0.0	42.7	9.1	15.5	47.5	84.0	8.0	53	88.7
Blanca town	385	406	5.5	498	15.7	0.0	2.2	1.6	80.5	24.5	12.2	38.6	58.1	8.4	173	86.7
Blende CDP	878	-	-	879	51.3	2.2	0.0	0.0	46.5	24.0	20.9	40.3	42.0	13.0	361	78.1
Blue River town	848	921	8.6	652	94.8	0.0	0.0	1.8	3.4	21.9	13.7	42.3	14.3	67.1	247	100.0
Blue Sky CDP	24	-	-	154	25.3	0.0	5.8	0.0	68.8	33.1	23.4	44.1	47.9	31.9	34	52.9
Bonanza town	16	19	18.8	3	100.0	0.0	0.0	0.0	0.0	0.0	0.0	0.0	0.0	0.0	3	100.0
Bonanza Mountain Estates CDP	128	-	-	226	64.6	0.0	0.0	35.4	0.0	8.8	7.1	43.7	0.0	85.9	150	100.0
Boone town	346	367	6.1	233	83.7	1.3	0.0	1.7	13.3	15.0	18.0	43.2	43.1	18.0	97	78.4
Boulder city	97,612	105,673	8.3	106,392	79.6	1.1	5.8	3.8	9.7	12.5	11.2	28.6	9.3	76.0	42,121	97.2
Bow Mar town	844	942	11.6	956	92.2	0.0	1.0	2.8	4.0	32.6	18.7	46.0	8.4	75.5	297	98.0
Brandon CDP	21	-	-	6	100.0	0.0	0.0	0.0	0.0	0.0	100.0	0.0	0.0	50.0	3	100.0
Branson town	74	72	-2.7	72	73.6	0.0	0.0	0.0	26.4	26.4	25.0	46.5	41.5	32.1	38	84.2
Breckenridge town	4,537	4,945	9.0	4,938	93.5	0.3	0.0	2.6	3.6	11.7	6.9	32.2	19.0	50.8	1,695	96.8
Brick Center CDP	107	-	-	138	100.0	0.0	0.0	0.0	0.0	10.1	5.8	49.6	35.0	21.0	49	100.0
Brighton city	33,540	41,554	23.9	39,836	55.6	1.6	3.1	3.2	36.4	27.4	9.9	33.2	46.6	21.0	12,503	91.8
Brookside town	233	262	12.4	216	96.8	0.0	0.0	0.0	3.2	18.5	20.8	51.4	32.9	29.3	88	96.6
Broomfield city	55,861	70,465	26.1	67,886	76.8	1.1	6.5	3.2	12.4	23.2	13.3	37.8	17.5	55.7	27,470	97.5
Brush city	5,473	5,420	-	5,395	72.7	0.0	0.0	2.4	24.9	28.3	17.5	32.2	48.6	21.0	2,188	91.5
Buena Vista town	2,560	2,866	12.0	2,782	97.7	0.0	0.0	0.0	2.3	24.5	19.7	45.4	32.4	34.6	1,143	83.7
Burlington city	4,254	3,140	-26.2	3,457	68.8	5.2	0.1	1.5	24.4	22.2	16.8	38.2	53.3	16.2	1,311	87.0
Byers CDP	1,160	-	-	1,344	72.5	0.0	0.0	4.5	23.0	24.9	18.7	42.1	55.4	15.4	477	99.0
Calhan town	780	834	6.9	704	97.6	0.0	0.0	1.3	1.1	25.9	19.2	42.3	37.6	22.7	298	79.2
Campo town	109	102	-6.4	101	89.1	0.0	0.0	0.0	10.9	20.8	30.7	50.3	38.8	15.0	48	60.4
Cañon City city	16,417	16,725	1.9	16,532	87.2	0.9	0.1	1.6	10.2	22.6	24.6	44.2	39.8	23.6	7,448	89.5
Capulin CDP	200	-	-	202	1.5	0.0	1.0	0.0	97.5	5.9	13.9	47.7	72.7	2.8	53	100.0
Carbondale town	6,447	6,898	7.0	6,785	57.4	1.0	0.2	1.3	40.1	22.3	12.0	36.9	31.1	45.7	2,445	94.7
Carbonate town	-	-	-	-	-	-	-	-	-	-	-	-	-	-	-	-
Cascade-Chipita Park CDP	1,655	-	-	1,233	94.2	0.7	0.0	0.6	4.5	13.5	18.2	53.5	30.3	39.9	595	93.6
Castle Pines city	10,333	10,763	4.2	10,591	86.1	2.5	3.8	1.3	6.4	28.8	12.7	42.2	6.8	71.6	3,437	98.7
Castle Pines Village CDP	-	-	-	4,553	92.6	0.0	3.4	2.6	1.4	25.1	22.1	49.8	3.5	75.8	1,659	99.5
Castle Rock town	48,251	68,484	41.9	62,417	83.8	1.0	1.8	3.0	10.3	28.8	10.0	35.8	16.9	48.2	21,336	96.4

1 May be of any race.

Table A. All Places — **Population and Housing**

STATE City, town, township, borough, or CDP (county if applicable)	Population				Race and Hispanic or Latino origin (percent)					Age (percent)			Educational attainment of persons age 25 and older		Occupied housing units	
	2010 census total population	2019 estimated population	Percent change 2010-2019	ACS total population estimate 2015-2019	White alone, not Hispanic or Latino	Black alone, not Hispanic or Latino	Asian alone, not Hispanic or Latino	All other races or 2 or more races, not Hispanic or Latino	Hispanic or Latino[1]	Under 18 years old	Age 65 years and older	Median age	Percent High school diploma or less	Percent Bachelor's degree or more	Total	Percent with a computer
	1	2	3	4	5	6	7	8	9	10	11	12	13	14	15	16
COLORADO—Con.																
Cathedral CDP	14	-	-	13	69.2	0.0	0.0	30.8	0.0	0.0	84.6	81.8	69.2	15.4	11	63.6
Catherine CDP	228	-	-	320	61.6	0.0	5.6	0.0	32.8	12.5	9.7	38.4	37.3	30.7	134	100.0
Cattle Creek CDP	641	-	-	604	24.2	0.0	0.0	0.0	75.8	30.8	8.4	34.8	47.5	23.1	184	100.0
Cedaredge town	2,251	2,295	2.0	2,412	91.1	0.0	0.4	1.2	7.3	18.2	29.4	48.6	43.1	25.1	1,003	84.7
Centennial city	100,635	110,937	10.2	110,218	79.2	2.9	5.2	3.4	9.3	23.2	15.3	41.3	16.2	57.3	39,851	97.3
Center town	2,241	2,264	1.0	2,207	8.6	1.5	0.0	3.3	86.6	30.2	10.3	32.6	70.9	8.8	828	71.6
Central City city	660	770	16.7	713	90.3	2.2	0.0	2.5	4.9	16.1	19.9	49.6	30.8	29.4	435	94.5
Chacra CDP	329	-	-	372	95.2	0.0	0.0	0.0	4.8	14.0	8.6	44.4	14.1	21.6	171	93.0
Cheraw town	254	249	-2.0	234	68.4	0.0	0.0	0.9	30.8	23.1	16.2	41.3	37.1	25.1	101	86.1
Cherry Creek CDP	11,120	-	-	12,496	77.8	1.4	10.2	2.7	7.9	28.1	11.8	39.5	9.9	70.8	4,500	96.8
Cherry Hills Village city	5,987	6,647	11.0	6,647	94.0	0.3	2.0	1.2	2.6	29.1	18.4	46.4	4.1	84.3	2,243	98.5
Cheyenne Wells town	846	828	-2.1	990	62.8	0.1	4.4	5.4	27.3	26.9	16.5	38.8	48.4	19.2	401	82.8
Cimarron Hills CDP	16,161	-	-	18,727	62.8	4.9	3.5	3.8	25.0	27.7	8.8	32.4	31.9	25.2	6,552	96.3
City of Creede town	290	313	7.9	312	85.9	2.6	0.0	0.0	11.5	11.2	15.1	46.0	34.4	27.7	138	88.4
Clifton CDP	19,889	-	-	20,748	78.0	0.2	0.9	1.7	19.2	26.0	11.4	32.8	49.2	12.4	8,012	95.6
Coal Creek CDP	2,400	-	-	2,313	93.9	0.0	0.4	1.3	4.4	16.0	11.5	45.1	19.2	59.1	1,106	98.4
Coal Creek town	345	350	1.4	355	97.2	0.0	0.0	0.3	2.5	24.5	27.3	41.1	66.1	8.9	137	73.7
Coaldale CDP	255	-	-	350	94.0	0.0	0.0	0.0	6.0	35.1	23.4	36.5	60.9	9.2	134	68.7
Cokedale town	129	120	-7.0	93	65.6	0.0	0.0	17.2	17.2	4.3	24.7	54.4	12.5	17.5	54	88.9
Collbran town	692	698	0.9	605	67.3	8.9	0.0	1.5	22.3	16.9	6.4	21.8	51.4	14.7	136	87.5
Colona CDP	30	-	-	56	100.0	0.0	0.0	0.0	0.0	0.0	28.6	60.4	64.3	0.0	16	100.0
Colorado City CDP	2,193	-	-	2,347	68.6	0.0	1.4	0.7	29.3	29.1	13.8	36.3	40.9	20.3	785	81.9
Colorado Springs city	417,447	478,221	14.6	464,871	68.6	6.1	2.8	4.8	17.6	23.2	13.4	34.7	26.0	39.9	181,478	94.5
Columbine CDP	24,280	-	-	25,332	84.8	0.6	1.9	1.9	10.7	22.1	19.6	43.4	20.0	47.5	9,694	96.5
Columbine Valley town	1,256	1,499	19.3	1,241	96.0	0.5	0.2	1.0	2.3	21.5	27.2	54.4	9.8	73.9	468	97.2
Comanche Creek CDP	369	-	-	182	82.4	0.0	0.0	4.9	12.6	14.3	4.9	48.9	42.5	30.8	62	85.5
Commerce City city	45,864	60,336	31.6	56,448	41.9	4.2	1.8	2.9	49.2	33.0	7.4	31.6	48.0	22.1	16,332	92.7
Conejos CDP	58	-	-	23	60.9	0.0	0.0	0.0	39.1	21.7	39.1	54.7	100.0	0.0	18	0.0
Copper Mountain CDP	385	-	-	571	96.1	0.0	0.0	0.0	3.9	0.0	17.9	48.9	8.8	49.6	344	100.0
Cortez city	8,471	8,736	3.1	8,675	67.2	0.5	1.7	10.8	19.7	24.0	18.5	38.9	37.3	30.4	3,707	85.2
Cotopaxi CDP	47	-	-	9	100.0	0.0	0.0	0.0	0.0	0.0	100.0	0.0	0.0	0.0	9	100.0
Craig city	9,468	9,022	-4.7	8,928	76.3	1.1	0.2	3.9	18.5	24.1	14.0	36.6	51.0	18.5	3,787	88.7
Crawford town	432	433	0.2	279	95.3	0.0	0.0	0.7	3.9	23.3	10.4	43.0	46.2	16.3	126	88.1
Crested Butte town	1,496	1,723	15.2	1,339	95.3	0.0	0.0	1.8	2.9	19.4	10.1	34.4	9.7	63.4	583	97.4
Crestone town	125	140	12.0	86	90.7	0.0	0.0	9.3	0.0	12.8	38.4	53.3	7.1	31.4	59	81.4
Cripple Creek city	1,226	1,258	2.6	1,021	82.5	0.0	0.0	0.4	17.1	8.9	28.3	51.6	58.5	9.6	470	84.7
Crisman CDP	186	-	-	110	100.0	0.0	0.0	0.0	0.0	0.0	59.1	68.2	0.0	75.5	61	70.5
Crook town	110	109	-0.9	190	75.3	0.0	1.1	0.0	23.7	20.0	14.2	30.8	68.7	11.3	54	90.7
Crowley town	176	175	-0.6	246	32.9	0.0	0.0	4.1	63.0	6.9	16.7	29.9	31.7	9.6	62	69.4
Dacono city	4,157	6,034	45.2	5,534	63.8	0.6	2.4	0.6	32.6	28.7	7.8	32.0	47.5	21.0	1,952	94.1
Dakota Ridge CDP	32,005	-	-	34,659	81.4	1.6	1.6	2.8	12.6	21.4	13.2	40.3	22.4	45.1	12,758	98.3
De Beque town	506	518	2.4	518	89.4	0.0	0.0	2.9	7.7	29.3	11.6	37.1	52.9	16.2	191	95.8
Deer Trail town	547	800	46.3	519	97.1	0.0	0.0	1.2	1.7	28.9	12.7	34.9	59.7	8.0	200	94.5
Del Norte town	1,680	1,568	-6.7	1,567	37.7	3.8	0.0	4.8	53.7	17.2	19.5	48.2	55.9	10.9	710	70.4
Delta city	8,884	8,995	1.2	8,829	71.3	0.4	2.1	3.6	22.6	23.5	24.1	43.3	53.4	18.2	3,362	77.4
Denver city	599,825	727,211	21.2	705,576	54.2	8.9	3.6	3.4	29.9	19.8	11.5	34.5	28.8	49.4	301,501	93.2
Derby CDP	7,685	-	-	8,962	24.5	2.9	1.1	0.7	70.7	31.6	7.0	30.2	76.0	5.1	2,339	87.6
Dillon town	903	967	7.1	945	62.9	0.0	1.5	6.3	29.3	16.3	19.9	40.0	15.9	47.3	375	99.7
Dinosaur town	339	332	-2.1	173	89.0	0.0	0.0	0.0	11.0	15.6	16.8	39.9	66.4	10.2	89	64.0
Divide CDP	127	-	-	67	100.0	0.0	0.0	0.0	0.0	26.9	47.8	37.8	0.0	34.7	41	63.4
Dolores town	928	955	2.9	825	74.8	0.0	0.0	0.4	24.8	29.8	12.1	30.9	31.8	38.2	376	89.4
Dotsero CDP	705	-	-	899	23.4	0.0	0.0	0.0	76.6	33.5	0.0	21.8	47.1	16.9	249	100.0
Dove Creek town	724	634	-12.4	648	87.2	0.0	0.0	2.9	9.9	21.3	29.6	52.7	51.8	21.5	272	78.7
Dove Valley CDP	5,243	-	-	5,673	58.5	3.8	9.5	2.5	25.6	28.4	6.2	29.2	18.5	50.5	2,356	99.1
Downieville-Lawson-Dumont CDP	594	-	-	543	65.4	0.0	0.0	0.0	34.6	18.4	16.0	49.1	38.4	44.6	225	83.1
Durango city	16,889	18,973	12.3	18,588	79.7	0.4	0.6	9.8	9.5	15.5	12.2	34.5	15.9	52.7	7,163	92.0
Eads town	609	602	-1.1	795	90.8	0.8	0.0	5.4	3.0	28.7	20.1	37.7	42.7	15.5	310	90.0
Eagle town	6,508	6,986	7.3	6,856	72.2	0.1	0.0	0.0	27.7	32.5	4.1	32.8	23.7	46.9	1,906	95.8
East Pleasant View CDP	356	-	-	226	71.7	1.3	0.0	0.0	27.0	18.6	14.6	50.5	61.7	24.8	100	100.0
Eaton town	4,375	5,738	31.2	5,317	73.1	0.3	0.6	4.1	21.9	25.9	16.6	36.9	32.7	38.1	1,934	93.7
Eckley town	256	258	0.8	333	64.0	0.0	0.0	0.0	36.0	33.3	15.9	28.0	53.3	13.8	117	73.5
Edgewater city	5,172	5,335	3.2	5,328	59.0	2.6	0.0	1.8	36.5	14.8	6.9	33.6	35.1	35.6	2,497	90.3
Edwards CDP	10,266	-	-	9,350	59.9	0.0	1.0	0.0	39.1	21.1	12.3	37.6	34.5	47.9	3,146	96.9
Elbert CDP	230	-	-	202	81.7	0.0	0.0	0.0	18.3	22.8	18.3	39.3	48.0	7.3	70	81.4
Eldora CDP	142	-	-	14	100.0	0.0	0.0	0.0	0.0	0.0	100.0	0.0	0.0	100.0	14	100.0
Eldorado Springs CDP	585	-	-	654	96.3	0.0	0.0	3.7	0.0	13.5	12.5	41.0	12.4	82.2	238	96.2
Elizabeth town	1,361	1,566	15.1	1,125	91.1	0.0	0.4	1.1	7.5	24.2	13.2	40.8	33.4	27.3	439	93.8
El Jebel CDP	3,801	-	-	4,725	58.2	0.0	0.0	0.8	41.0	20.0	10.6	35.9	34.8	42.6	1,224	100.0
Ellicott CDP	1,131	-	-	955	52.5	0.0	0.0	2.4	45.1	40.4	11.6	35.2	46.9	5.3	280	100.0
El Moro CDP	221	-	-	261	66.7	0.0	0.0	0.0	33.3	12.3	19.9	55.9	36.2	25.8	121	85.1
Empire town	282	304	7.8	303	88.4	1.3	1.3	2.3	6.6	15.8	22.1	46.3	26.1	29.0	145	88.3
Englewood city	30,258	34,917	15.4	34,259	75.7	2.5	1.4	3.2	17.3	16.8	13.7	36.4	31.9	40.4	15,529	91.1
Erie town	18,186	27,003	48.5	24,223	82.5	0.2	5.1	2.1	10.2	29.8	9.9	37.1	13.6	62.2	8,256	97.5
Estes Park town	5,938	6,426	8.2	6,377	87.0	0.0	0.0	1.3	11.6	8.2	36.9	61.3	22.6	48.7	3,440	93.7
Evans city	18,505	21,205	14.6	20,533	48.0	1.3	3.4	2.8	44.5	29.1	6.8	29.1	52.7	15.4	6,725	92.9
Evergreen CDP	9,038	-	-	8,885	89.8	0.3	1.3	1.5	7.1	20.6	17.7	46.7	10.0	64.2	3,687	99.5
Fairmount CDP	7,559	-	-	8,606	88.4	0.8	1.2	1.9	7.8	20.0	17.6	43.6	26.0	48.5	3,250	96.6
Fairplay town	696	787	13.1	800	87.6	1.1	0.0	3.8	7.5	29.1	8.1	32.6	41.8	25.8	288	94.1
Federal Heights city	11,461	12,827	11.9	12,745	32.6	1.2	2.4	1.3	62.5	29.5	10.3	30.8	61.8	12.2	4,306	91.3
Firestone town	10,200	16,177	58.6	14,033	75.2	0.1	2.6	4.2	17.9	29.2	9.0	35.3	27.1	33.4	4,479	99.3
Flagler town	561	549	-2.1	464	94.4	0.0	0.0	1.1	4.5	25.2	21.3	48.4	50.6	22.3	228	84.2
Fleming town	405	404	-0.2	602	86.7	0.0	0.0	2.2	11.1	24.8	20.8	39.7	33.5	16.1	222	78.8
Florence city	3,882	3,944	1.6	3,899	89.7	0.3	1.2	1.0	7.8	19.2	22.9	42.3	38.6	21.5	1,751	91.9
Florissant CDP	104	-	-	166	84.9	0.0	0.0	0.0	15.1	5.4	16.3	53.3	24.2	12.1	95	100.0
Floyd Hill CDP	998	-	-	1,102	93.7	0.0	6.3	0.0	0.0	15.7	19.8	46.2	2.1	73.8	502	100.0
Fort Carson CDP	13,813	-	-	14,951	61.0	13.0	1.5	7.0	17.5	28.8	0.0	21.7	26.6	19.5	2,739	98.5
Fort Collins city	144,879	170,243	17.5	165,609	79.9	1.5	3.4	3.6	11.6	18.8	10.6	29.3	18.5	55.5	64,599	96.7
Fort Garland CDP	433	-	-	481	12.9	0.0	0.8	0.0	86.3	31.4	12.7	36.3	56.0	3.9	176	88.6
Fort Lupton city	7,412	8,317	12.2	8,133	41.0	0.8	0.0	1.8	56.4	29.0	12.4	32.6	54.4	13.9	2,574	90.2
Fort Morgan city	11,363	11,463	0.9	11,377	38.3	7.7	0.7	1.5	51.8	27.6	12.5	32.5	58.7	13.4	4,133	85.1
Fountain city	25,905	30,735	18.6	29,784	53.5	8.2	4.6	8.1	25.6	30.3	6.1	29.9	32.5	20.3	9,831	96.1

1 May be of any race.

Table A. All Places — **Population and Housing**

STATE City, town, township, borough, or CDP (county if applicable)	Population: 2010 census total population	Population: 2019 estimated population	Population: Percent change 2010-2019	Population: ACS total population estimate 2015-2019	Race and Hispanic or Latino origin (percent): White alone, not Hispanic or Latino	Black alone, not Hispanic or Latino	Asian alone, not Hispanic or Latino	All other races or 2 or more races, not Hispanic or Latino	Hispanic or Latino[1]	Age (percent): Under 18 years old	Age 65 years and older	Median age	Educational attainment of persons age 25 and older: Percent High school diploma or less	Percent Bachelor's degree or more	Occupied housing units: Total	Percent with a computer
	1	2	3	4	5	6	7	8	9	10	11	12	13	14	15	16
COLORADO—Con.																
Fowler town	1,185	1,141	-3.7	1,229	76.2	0.0	0.0	1.2	22.5	22.9	24.0	42.4	49.7	15.2	519	80.5
Foxfield town	714	782	9.5	610	85.2	4.6	5.4	0.0	4.8	15.1	30.8	55.5	17.9	57.5	236	94.5
Franktown CDP	395	-	-	186	100.0	0.0	0.0	0.0	0.0	32.8	19.9	44.5	25.4	21.2	47	100.0
Fraser town	1,223	1,326	8.4	1,532	71.5	6.2	2.0	1.1	19.3	19.8	5.3	30.9	37.1	35.3	519	93.6
Frederick town	8,665	13,960	61.1	12,767	77.9	0.4	3.2	3.4	15.0	27.5	9.6	35.8	27.9	36.6	4,109	97.4
Frisco town	2,692	3,174	17.9	3,116	90.3	0.0	0.0	5.0	4.7	13.9	10.6	48.0	23.7	55.8	1,237	96.1
Fruita city	12,689	13,478	6.2	13,236	81.5	0.0	0.5	5.0	13.0	26.1	18.2	38.4	35.4	23.6	5,275	92.3
Fruitvale CDP	7,675	-	-	7,874	82.7	0.6	0.6	2.8	13.3	25.4	21.3	40.6	40.4	23.0	3,165	89.5
Fulford CDP	2	-	-	-	-	-	-	-	-	-	-	-	-	-	-	-
Garden City town	250	267	6.8	214	30.4	0.5	0.0	4.2	65.0	10.3	8.9	45.0	67.9	10.3	111	86.5
Garfield CDP	15	-	-	-	-	-	-	-	-	-	-	-	-	-	-	-
Genesee CDP	3,609	-	-	3,910	88.2	0.3	0.2	3.7	7.6	20.4	24.2	53.4	5.2	79.0	1,640	99.5
Genoa town	139	148	6.5	130	95.4	0.0	0.0	3.8	0.8	30.0	21.5	42.0	48.9	11.4	60	81.7
Georgetown town	1,034	1,112	7.5	1,131	84.8	1.1	1.0	5.1	8.0	11.7	20.4	47.1	25.4	35.8	551	92.4
Gerrard CDP	278	-	-	180	93.3	0.0	0.0	0.0	6.7	17.2	42.2	43.7	65.8	8.7	73	100.0
Gilcrest town	1,034	1,106	7.0	938	50.0	0.0	0.0	0.0	50.0	24.3	9.9	32.7	66.1	14.5	295	89.5
Glendale city	4,318	5,141	19.1	5,177	63.9	7.0	4.8	4.9	19.3	5.6	3.8	30.8	23.8	51.5	3,065	94.9
Glendale CDP	69	-	-	120	82.5	0.0	17.5	0.0	0.0	17.5	34.2	42.5	0.0	61.6	80	100.0
Gleneagle CDP	6,611	-	-	6,885	82.6	4.6	2.4	2.1	8.3	23.9	17.9	45.2	14.4	59.0	2,519	98.8
Glenwood Springs city	9,580	9,930	3.7	9,915	67.3	0.9	3.2	1.4	27.2	21.8	13.8	37.1	34.2	40.1	3,957	93.3
Golden city	18,890	20,767	9.9	20,693	85.5	1.8	2.6	2.4	7.7	14.8	11.7	33.5	22.1	56.3	7,618	93.8
Goldfield CDP	49	-	-	36	100.0	0.0	0.0	0.0	0.0	13.9	38.9	42.7	14.8	51.9	22	36.4
Gold Hill CDP	230	-	-	204	100.0	0.0	0.0	0.0	0.0	13.7	35.3	48.1	0.0	94.3	113	100.0
Granada town	517	503	-2.7	589	11.0	0.0	1.7	0.0	87.3	27.0	20.0	41.9	73.7	11.4	229	57.6
Granby town	1,854	2,139	15.4	2,039	91.9	0.7	0.0	0.0	7.4	14.7	20.8	44.7	36.3	34.9	825	90.8
Grand Junction city	59,034	63,597	7.7	62,062	78.3	0.9	1.2	2.6	17.0	20.1	18.2	37.1	34.2	34.7	26,282	90.6
Grand Lake town	469	506	7.9	282	96.1	1.4	0.0	0.0	2.5	6.4	48.9	64.8	1.6	59.3	180	96.1
Grand View Estates CDP	528	-	-	738	69.2	0.0	14.0	7.5	9.3	21.3	14.5	44.6	33.8	45.7	236	97.5
Greeley city	92,950	108,649	16.9	105,888	55.6	2.3	1.3	2.3	38.6	24.8	11.9	31.5	42.7	24.8	36,589	91.3
Green Mountain Falls town	647	722	11.6	563	88.5	0.0	5.3	4.8	1.4	12.4	26.1	55.7	19.9	44.6	298	94.3
Greenwood Village city	13,919	15,735	13.0	15,738	78.8	2.0	11.1	2.6	5.5	23.2	16.6	42.1	7.2	76.3	6,257	98.1
Grover town	139	153	10.1	206	95.1	0.0	0.0	4.9	0.0	22.3	24.3	39.0	55.6	11.8	83	68.7
Guffey CDP	98	-	-	10	100.0	0.0	0.0	0.0	0.0	0.0	0.0	0.0	0.0	0.0	10	100.0
Gunbarrel CDP	9,263	-	-	10,202	89.0	0.3	2.2	1.6	6.9	14.1	15.6	40.2	8.0	71.7	4,506	98.9
Gunnison city	5,842	6,640	13.7	6,403	86.0	0.8	0.0	1.4	11.8	10.4	9.7	25.4	19.8	56.2	2,447	97.0
Gypsum town	6,498	7,375	13.5	7,173	64.1	0.0	0.0	1.1	34.8	25.5	9.7	44.4	43.1	32.2	2,423	96.1
Hartman town	76	75	-1.3	80	72.5	0.0	0.0	7.5	20.0	16.3	8.8	48.8	79.4	3.2	38	94.7
Hasty CDP	144	-	-	129	97.7	0.0	0.0	2.3	0.0	21.7	32.6	44.6	31.7	25.7	68	80.9
Haswell town	68	68	0.0	51	100.0	0.0	0.0	0.0	0.0	17.6	21.6	57.4	50.0	21.4	26	84.6
Haxtun town	946	904	-4.4	854	97.4	0.0	0.0	0.8	1.8	25.4	20.4	45.0	36.4	23.4	380	88.4
Hayden town	1,814	1,979	9.1	2,109	84.4	0.4	0.0	3.3	11.9	22.5	15.1	40.1	41.0	22.4	783	90.5
Heeney CDP	76	-	-	441	92.5	0.0	0.0	0.0	7.5	0.0	6.6	38.1	48.8	25.9	46	100.0
Hidden Lake CDP	31	-	-	-	-	-	-	-	-	-	-	-	-	-	-	-
Highlands Ranch CDP	96,713	-	-	105,631	81.7	1.0	6.1	3.0	8.2	27.1	11.1	39.8	10.8	64.4	37,843	98.4
Hillrose town	256	260	1.6	291	78.0	0.0	0.0	0.0	22.0	15.8	14.4	39.8	53.2	14.4	131	91.6
Hoehne CDP	111	-	-	130	90.8	0.0	0.0	0.0	9.2	19.2	36.9	62.7	41.9	21.0	64	95.3
Holly town	794	774	-2.5	841	41.3	0.0	0.0	0.0	58.7	30.2	20.1	34.3	57.1	13.1	284	79.9
Holly Hills CDP	2,521	-	-	2,835	91.0	1.2	2.2	1.2	4.4	20.4	21.5	45.2	17.4	63.9	1,064	97.7
Holyoke city	2,317	2,208	-4.7	2,484	58.1	0.2	0.9	2.1	38.8	28.7	14.0	32.6	51.0	19.9	943	92.2
Hooper town	103	100	-2.9	81	46.9	0.0	0.0	4.9	48.1	25.9	23.5	57.3	35.6	28.8	40	75.0
Hotchkiss town	922	928	0.7	890	90.6	0.0	0.0	4.5	4.9	33.0	18.5	37.5	41.7	23.0	382	82.5
Hot Sulphur Springs town	679	733	8.0	859	73.1	1.3	14.0	1.6	10.0	25.8	10.8	34.7	43.5	23.9	250	90.8
Howard CDP	723	-	-	906	87.0	0.0	0.0	7.2	5.8	15.8	20.6	41.7	33.4	34.8	391	93.9
Hudson town	2,356	2,767	17.4	2,588	64.6	0.0	0.0	1.0	34.4	27.2	9.3	33.7	50.3	16.3	840	92.1
Hugo town	730	777	6.4	707	83.2	3.0	0.0	5.2	8.6	31.3	24.5	40.8	51.2	16.1	255	88.2
Idaho Springs city	1,722	1,786	3.7	1,858	83.5	3.8	0.0	3.9	8.8	14.3	19.9	43.4	35.5	29.1	908	89.3
Idalia CDP	88	-	-	37	100.0	0.0	0.0	0.0	0.0	51.4	0.0	16.8	21.4	64.3	11	100.0
Idledale CDP	252	-	-	168	94.0	0.0	0.0	6.0	0.0	5.4	0.0	31.5	17.6	69.2	55	100.0
Ignacio town	858	908	5.8	1,259	28.7	0.0	0.4	23.3	47.7	30.6	9.0	34.0	56.6	17.3	429	83.7
Iliff town	266	268	0.8	318	64.5	0.0	0.0	0.3	35.2	21.7	8.8	39.3	36.1	8.7	116	86.2
Indian Hills CDP	1,280	-	-	1,398	87.6	2.9	0.0	5.2	4.3	16.3	21.7	37.3	13.8	49.7	554	100.0
Inverness CDP	1,532	-	-	1,567	71.9	5.8	7.5	6.1	8.7	8.4	7.3	33.8	4.1	71.2	918	100.0
Jackson Lake CDP	154	-	-	174	97.1	0.0	2.9	0.0	0.0	23.0	29.9	39.0	51.9	21.3	77	97.4
Jamestown town	274	249	-9.1	202	92.6	0.0	0.0	2.5	5.0	10.4	18.8	46.5	24.9	55.5	103	86.4
Jansen CDP	112	-	-	285	90.2	0.0	0.0	0.0	9.8	67.7	3.9	12.8	29.3	0.0	64	89.1
Joes CDP	80	-	-	83	100.0	0.0	0.0	0.0	0.0	13.3	37.3	45.8	38.2	4.4	45	91.1
Johnson Village CDP	246	-	-	386	87.0	13.0	0.0	0.0	0.0	15.5	22.8	23.9	63.4	17.2	144	81.9
Johnstown town	9,860	15,198	54.1	14,910	80.2	0.4	3.0	1.2	15.1	26.5	11.8	34.1	30.8	35.0	5,246	96.7
Julesburg town	1,225	1,152	-6.0	1,259	81.8	1.5	0.9	0.0	15.8	25.7	22.8	40.7	41.6	16.2	537	88.6
Keenesburg town	1,124	1,237	10.1	1,312	79.6	0.8	0.0	6.0	13.6	25.3	14.5	37.5	45.8	16.9	441	88.0
Ken Caryl CDP	32,438	-	-	34,040	84.8	0.5	2.5	2.8	9.3	23.0	13.5	41.3	19.7	46.3	13,419	98.1
Kersey town	1,479	1,681	13.7	1,852	61.7	0.3	0.0	4.4	33.6	25.1	6.5	33.5	49.2	15.1	595	91.6
Keystone CDP	1,079	-	-	908	52.1	2.5	1.1	11.1	33.1	2.8	20.9	36.0	12.9	73.5	399	94.0
Kim town	74	70	-5.4	77	77.9	0.0	0.0	0.0	22.1	23.4	27.3	45.8	54.2	16.9	41	87.8
Kiowa town	719	761	5.8	811	81.6	1.1	0.0	2.6	14.7	15.7	13.2	36.9	47.0	20.0	323	92.9
Kirk CDP	59	-	-	80	95.0	0.0	0.0	3.8	1.3	13.8	50.0	64.5	48.5	20.6	44	84.1
Kit Carson town	233	231	-0.9	310	91.6	0.3	0.0	1.6	6.5	42.9	10.3	34.9	38.4	25.0	94	97.9
Kittredge CDP	1,304	-	-	964	95.2	0.0	1.5	0.8	2.5	21.1	3.1	41.0	19.9	57.1	350	96.9
Kremmling town	1,444	1,524	5.5	1,673	76.2	0.0	3.2	0.0	20.6	23.3	11.1	39.2	48.7	20.1	625	84.0
Lafayette city	24,491	30,687	25.3	28,742	74.9	0.6	4.1	4.3	16.1	23.1	13.4	39.3	18.3	57.6	11,856	96.1
Laird CDP	47	-	-	49	30.6	0.0	0.0	69.4	0.0	28.6	0.0	41.7	0.0	0.0	15	100.0
La Jara town	842	817	-3.0	817	35.6	0.0	1.3	0.5	62.5	30.0	15.7	30.8	42.7	23.6	319	76.8
La Junta city	7,073	6,881	-2.7	6,893	50.5	1.1	2.2	4.4	41.8	21.9	19.2	38.9	45.7	20.4	3,185	80.6
La Junta Gardens CDP	153	-	-	119	60.5	0.0	0.0	0.0	39.5	34.5	18.5	37.3	7.7	19.2	41	100.0
Lake City town	410	394	-3.9	436	85.3	0.0	0.9	6.7	7.1	18.3	21.6	51.6	36.9	43.2	188	90.4
Lakeside town	8	8	0.0	7	100.0	0.0	0.0	0.0	0.0	0.0	57.1	70.1	57.1	28.6	7	57.1
Lakewood city	142,600	157,935	10.8	155,146	69.0	1.2	3.6	3.3	23.0	18.4	16.3	38.6	30.6	40.9	66,274	94.0
Lamar city	7,941	7,655	-3.6	7,564	55.4	1.2	0.4	2.5	40.4	26.2	16.5	37.1	45.7	17.9	3,064	84.0
Laporte CDP	2,450	-	-	2,413	81.0	0.0	0.4	3.2	15.3	19.2	20.3	49.3	31.4	35.2	1,066	87.1
Larkspur town	183	212	15.8	278	91.0	0.0	0.0	0.0	9.0	18.0	22.7	47.6	46.4	18.8	127	91.3
La Salle town	1,959	2,342	19.6	2,697	62.8	0.5	0.1	4.1	32.4	33.4	11.2	32.9	52.9	13.0	830	86.7

1 May be of any race.

Table A. All Places — **Population and Housing**

STATE City, town, township, borough, or CDP (county if applicable)	Population: 2010 census total population	Population: 2019 estimated population	Population: Percent change 2010-2019	Population: ACS total population estimate 2015-2019	Race and Hispanic or Latino origin (percent): White alone, not Hispanic or Latino	Black alone, not Hispanic or Latino	Asian alone, not Hispanic or Latino	All other races or 2 or more races, not Hispanic or Latino	Hispanic or Latino[1]	Age (percent): Under 18 years old	Age 65 years and older	Median age	Educational attainment of persons age 25 and older: Percent High school diploma or less	Percent Bachelor's degree or more	Occupied housing units: Total	Percent with a computer
	1	2	3	4	5	6	7	8	9	10	11	12	13	14	15	16
COLORADO—Con.																
Las Animas city	2,410	2,165	-10.2	2,269	55.2	0.0	0.3	1.4	43.1	25.4	22.7	41.1	55.4	12.3	974	79.2
La Veta town	800	811	1.4	873	87.7	0.3	0.0	3.7	8.2	18.8	32.4	50.0	33.0	30.2	413	91.3
Lazy Acres CDP	920	-	-	979	100.0	0.0	0.0	0.0	0.0	15.1	28.7	55.6	7.6	67.5	412	96.8
Leadville city	2,613	2,868	9.8	2,742	66.9	0.3	1.9	4.9	26.0	24.5	11.8	36.0	37.8	35.6	1,143	82.1
Leadville North CDP	1,794	-	-	2,244	79.4	0.0	0.0	2.7	17.9	7.9	10.7	33.5	32.6	38.9	1,037	97.2
Lewis CDP	302	-	-	149	100.0	0.0	0.0	0.0	0.0	14.8	39.6	62.3	59.1	18.1	85	47.1
Leyner CDP	29	-	-	-	-	-	-	-	-	-	-	-	-	-	-	-
Limon town	1,882	1,952	3.7	1,105	85.3	0.0	0.7	1.2	12.8	22.0	28.0	49.7	37.1	14.1	587	88.8
Lincoln Park CDP	3,546	-	-	3,283	93.2	0.1	0.0	0.3	6.4	17.2	25.9	51.1	34.6	22.0	1,603	88.1
Littleton city	41,632	48,065	15.5	47,989	79.5	1.7	2.6	2.4	13.8	19.0	17.2	41.0	22.1	50.2	20,611	95.4
Lochbuie town	4,729	7,304	54.5	6,388	45.4	2.7	0.0	0.0	51.8	32.0	5.9	29.4	54.4	11.8	1,932	91.3
Loghill Village CDP	521	-	-	661	93.2	0.0	0.0	0.0	6.8	7.3	34.8	59.7	5.9	58.9	308	100.0
Log Lane Village town	817	849	3.9	1,217	33.5	0.0	0.0	2.2	64.3	29.0	11.8	33.3	74.6	5.1	416	88.2
Loma CDP	1,293	-	-	941	71.7	0.0	0.0	6.1	22.2	24.0	6.0	42.9	35.0	32.6	383	81.2
Lone Tree city	10,234	13,082	27.8	12,923	75.7	4.0	10.5	3.9	5.9	22.0	13.2	40.0	11.2	70.0	5,310	99.0
Longmont city	86,327	97,261	12.7	94,445	68.1	1.1	3.1	2.5	25.2	23.8	14.5	38.1	28.6	42.9	36,784	93.0
Louisville city	18,408	20,816	13.1	20,860	85.0	0.3	5.1	2.5	7.0	24.0	13.9	41.6	12.0	69.7	8,318	95.9
Louviers CDP	269	-	-	378	58.5	0.0	0.0	11.9	29.6	28.3	11.4	34.6	38.3	18.3	141	94.3
Loveland city	66,992	78,877	17.7	76,972	84.0	0.5	1.0	2.2	12.3	21.1	18.6	39.9	29.0	36.7	31,834	95.5
Lynn CDP	12	-	-	61	13.1	0.0	0.0	0.0	86.9	39.3	26.2	31.1	0.0	29.0	17	47.1
Lyons town	2,119	2,189	3.3	2,228	87.8	1.7	1.0	4.6	4.9	27.5	11.1	41.4	14.7	57.2	809	98.6
McCoy CDP	24	-	-	43	100.0	0.0	0.0	0.0	0.0	0.0	18.6	63.1	37.2	0.0	22	100.0
Manassa town	991	1,001	1.0	996	46.4	1.6	0.0	2.5	49.5	29.9	16.8	36.7	43.2	20.0	377	76.7
Mancos town	1,339	1,430	6.8	1,627	83.1	0.4	0.8	1.7	14.1	25.8	15.4	34.5	31.3	33.6	628	87.4
Manitou Springs city	4,961	5,390	8.6	5,283	91.0	0.9	0.8	3.0	4.3	15.1	21.9	42.7	22.5	48.8	2,483	95.6
Manzanola town	431	417	-3.2	388	38.1	0.0	0.0	0.0	61.9	15.2	29.6	53.5	58.7	14.2	167	83.2
Marble town	119	134	12.6	115	97.4	0.0	0.0	0.0	2.6	7.0	28.7	61.2	37.1	42.9	53	94.3
Maybell CDP	72	-	-	41	36.6	0.0	0.0	12.2	51.2	0.0	82.9	71.3	31.7	0.0	34	23.5
Maysville CDP	135	-	-	122	100.0	0.0	0.0	0.0	0.0	0.0	62.3	67.0	0.0	44.3	69	100.0
Mead town	3,449	4,731	37.2	4,631	78.9	0.0	0.6	1.1	19.5	31.8	12.0	33.8	31.2	34.7	1,451	96.1
Meeker town	2,472	2,252	-8.9	2,415	86.9	0.0	0.0	4.1	9.0	30.1	20.0	38.2	51.9	18.7	945	88.3
Meridian CDP	2,970	-	-	3,640	61.4	6.8	18.8	5.5	7.6	15.3	11.4	32.8	10.3	61.5	1,785	96.6
Merino town	286	281	-1.7	233	61.8	0.0	0.0	13.7	24.5	27.5	10.7	28.5	40.7	11.4	93	93.5
Midland CDP	156	-	-	380	61.1	0.0	0.0	0.0	38.9	36.3	16.8	38.9	5.8	36.0	161	100.0
Milliken town	5,614	8,164	45.4	7,185	71.5	0.2	0.6	2.8	25.0	26.2	11.6	36.3	42.2	20.0	2,489	95.6
Minturn town	1,086	1,145	5.4	1,101	82.6	0.0	0.0	1.4	16.1	5.8	10.8	35.7	17.2	54.2	395	97.2
Moffat town	116	119	2.6	105	97.1	0.0	0.0	2.9	0.0	19.0	13.3	42.1	44.6	15.7	45	95.6
Monte Vista city	4,443	4,138	-6.9	4,157	38.1	0.1	0.0	0.4	61.4	27.8	14.9	38.5	55.2	17.6	1,812	69.4
Montezuma town	69	74	7.2	90	100.0	0.0	0.0	0.0	0.0	18.9	3.3	31.5	37.7	33.3	35	97.1
Montrose city	19,092	19,782	3.6	19,238	75.4	0.1	0.9	2.9	20.7	22.2	24.1	43.6	37.5	27.8	8,110	87.1
Monument town	6,035	8,097	34.2	7,398	79.5	1.4	2.1	5.5	11.6	31.3	7.4	34.8	13.1	61.3	2,431	96.0
Morgan Heights CDP	266	-	-	169	93.5	0.0	2.4	0.0	4.1	2.4	50.3	67.0	20.4	50.0	92	94.6
Morrison town	418	424	1.4	415	92.3	1.0	1.2	0.7	4.8	13.0	48.4	63.5	32.0	34.0	101	89.1
Mountain Meadows CDP	274	-	-	222	100.0	0.0	0.0	0.0	0.0	9.9	33.8	59.1	12.0	88.0	106	100.0
Mountain View town	507	537	5.9	603	70.6	0.0	1.3	2.8	25.2	14.1	9.6	35.2	32.6	44.6	295	93.2
Mountain Village town	1,317	1,426	8.3	1,842	77.4	0.0	3.4	4.4	14.8	15.6	9.1	32.1	17.1	60.0	835	96.4
Mount Crested Butte town	816	876	7.4	989	98.4	0.0	0.0	0.0	1.6	7.7	9.9	39.2	9.7	68.6	424	98.3
Mulford CDP	174	-	-	510	86.5	0.0	1.2	0.0	12.4	27.8	12.4	39.3	9.0	67.7	165	100.0
Naturita town	537	532	-0.9	486	94.0	0.0	0.0	1.9	4.1	11.5	20.0	49.3	62.2	8.8	246	74.4
Nederland town	1,445	1,533	6.1	1,336	92.2	0.0	0.4	1.2	6.2	15.3	9.1	41.6	18.5	52.1	615	89.6
New Castle town	4,518	5,203	15.2	4,875	74.0	0.5	1.3	2.1	22.1	29.6	8.1	32.2	31.4	38.7	1,522	92.7
Niwot CDP	4,006	-	-	3,870	93.4	0.6	0.9	1.3	3.9	21.7	17.1	46.7	10.4	73.9	1,541	100.0
No Name CDP	123	-	-	29	100.0	0.0	0.0	0.0	0.0	0.0	100.0	76.4	31.0	17.2	14	100.0
Norrie CDP	7	-	-	-	-	-	-	-	-	-	-	-	-	-	-	-
Northglenn city	35,758	38,819	8.6	38,973	57.4	2.0	2.5	2.9	35.3	25.6	11.6	32.5	42.6	20.7	13,386	93.7
North La Junta CDP	512	-	-	337	67.7	0.0	0.0	0.0	32.3	23.4	25.5	57.3	40.4	4.4	156	100.0
North Washington CDP	484	-	-	606	43.9	0.0	0.0	0.0	56.1	33.0	14.2	33.4	89.8	2.4	231	100.0
Norwood town	518	579	11.8	581	89.8	0.0	0.0	0.0	10.2	20.8	12.7	44.2	43.3	28.6	222	98.2
Nucla town	712	714	0.3	644	91.0	6.5	0.5	0.0	2.0	26.7	23.3	40.7	54.7	15.8	275	77.8
Nunn town	416	464	11.5	589	82.3	0.5	0.0	3.7	13.4	26.3	12.9	34.7	49.5	9.6	219	91.8
Oak Creek town	899	959	6.7	959	89.6	0.9	0.7	5.4	3.3	20.5	8.8	36.0	40.8	30.8	438	85.4
Olathe town	1,870	1,837	-1.8	1,661	43.3	0.0	0.0	0.4	56.4	22.5	17.7	40.7	70.1	10.6	604	78.1
Olney Springs town	345	340	-1.4	496	72.0	0.0	0.0	2.8	25.2	10.9	13.3	42.1	49.6	14.7	100	65.0
Ophir town	163	184	12.9	193	88.6	0.0	0.0	8.8	2.6	33.2	1.0	45.1	0.8	60.5	72	90.3
Orchard CDP	90	-	-	119	84.9	0.0	0.0	0.0	15.1	10.9	28.6	56.6	53.0	19.0	43	100.0
Orchard City town	3,133	3,212	2.5	3,123	80.5	0.0	1.4	1.8	16.3	17.2	31.0	54.3	43.5	19.9	1,292	86.8
Orchard Mesa CDP	6,836	-	-	6,719	83.3	0.4	0.4	1.7	14.2	23.4	21.9	41.9	34.9	19.5	2,738	94.5
Ordway town	1,080	1,054	-2.4	1,672	68.0	0.6	0.2	2.8	28.4	15.9	17.5	41.6	51.1	14.7	478	77.8
Otis town	473	486	2.7	592	90.0	1.2	0.0	2.7	6.1	33.8	19.4	32.2	37.1	14.0	243	90.5
Ouray city	1,002	1,034	3.2	998	95.7	0.0	3.5	0.6	0.2	11.6	24.8	46.0	19.6	50.4	444	89.6
Ovid town	318	300	-5.7	212	75.9	0.0	0.9	2.4	20.8	14.6	25.0	54.4	59.3	12.4	106	67.9
Padroni CDP	76	-	-	69	94.2	0.0	0.0	0.0	5.8	0.0	40.6	58.4	25.0	14.6	45	62.2
Pagosa Springs town	1,753	2,085	18.9	2,057	52.6	0.0	0.0	5.9	41.5	25.4	15.8	34.3	47.0	23.6	910	85.5
Palisade town	2,663	2,736	2.7	2,696	76.6	0.0	0.6	11.0	11.9	26.7	18.6	38.8	38.5	27.5	1,113	86.3
Palmer Lake town	2,523	2,993	18.6	2,887	78.1	0.6	0.9	2.3	18.1	19.5	12.7	40.1	28.1	34.1	1,176	96.2
Paoli town	34	34	0.0	83	74.7	0.0	0.0	0.0	25.3	14.5	50.6	68.1	61.9	1.6	28	60.7
Paonia town	1,462	1,469	0.5	1,300	89.8	0.0	0.5	1.9	7.8	17.5	33.4	55.9	36.9	34.6	615	89.4
Parachute town	1,077	1,116	3.6	1,312	61.4	2.4	0.2	7.9	28.0	32.2	8.6	32.8	46.9	9.5	498	96.6
Paragon Estates CDP	928	-	-	802	93.5	2.9	2.4	1.2	0.0	14.1	26.8	56.5	10.3	82.3	359	100.0
Parker town	45,357	57,706	27.2	54,352	79.7	1.5	4.8	3.8	10.2	30.2	7.6	34.7	16.3	53.2	18,879	98.9
Parshall CDP	47	-	-	83	100.0	0.0	0.0	0.0	0.0	0.0	100.0	89.4	34.9	0.0	60	51.7
Peetz town	241	235	-2.5	168	91.7	0.0	0.6	2.4	5.4	19.6	13.7	44.7	34.6	11.5	73	90.4
Penrose CDP	3,582	-	-	3,034	89.1	0.6	0.8	0.3	9.3	21.1	22.2	47.5	38.5	24.1	1,316	93.8
Peoria CDP	163	-	-	236	87.7	0.0	2.1	3.8	6.4	19.9	18.6	47.0	22.1	27.3	74	100.0
Perry Park CDP	1,646	-	-	1,972	90.2	0.3	2.4	2.2	4.9	10.9	27.8	58.2	13.5	61.9	880	100.0
Peyton CDP	250	-	-	17	100.0	0.0	0.0	0.0	0.0	0.0	0.0	0.0	0.0	100.0	17	100.0
Phippsburg CDP	-	-	-	227	100.0	0.0	0.0	0.0	0.0	8.8	24.7	37.9	72.0	22.2	123	82.9
Piedra CDP	28	-	-	21	100.0	0.0	0.0	0.0	0.0	0.0	0.0	63.7	0.0	47.6	10	30.0
Pierce town	830	1,133	36.5	1,008	78.1	0.0	0.2	1.0	20.7	22.8	14.1	38.2	63.0	8.4	378	86.8
Pine Brook Hill CDP	983	-	-	925	85.0	1.1	3.6	2.5	7.9	8.8	33.6	54.4	5.0	82.6	435	94.7
Pitkin town	64	69	7.8	91	96.7	0.0	0.0	3.3	0.0	26.4	17.6	30.6	32.3	60.0	30	83.3
Platteville town	2,489	2,760	10.9	2,754	54.2	0.0	0.0	1.1	44.7	25.5	9.6	32.3	52.8	10.1	924	93.4

1 May be of any race.

Table A. All Places — **Population and Housing**

STATE City, town, township, borough, or CDP (county if applicable)	Population				Race and Hispanic or Latino origin (percent)					Age (percent)			Educational attainment of persons age 25 and older		Occupied housing units	
	2010 census total population	2019 estimated population	Percent change 2010-2019	ACS total population estimate 2015-2019	White alone, not Hispanic or Latino	Black alone, not Hispanic or Latino	Asian alone, not Hispanic or Latino	All other races or 2 or more races, not Hispanic or Latino	Hispanic or Latino[1]	Under 18 years old	Age 65 years and older	Median age	Percent High school diploma or less	Percent Bachelor's degree or more	Total	Percent with a computer
	1	2	3	4	5	6	7	8	9	10	11	12	13	14	15	16
COLORADO—Con.																
Poncha Springs town	726	956	31.7	607	83.7	0.0	1.5	0.0	14.8	11.5	30.3	54.0	31.3	33.4	303	88.4
Ponderosa Park CDP	3,232	-	-	3,636	92.8	0.0	0.8	2.0	4.4	19.7	12.5	47.0	30.2	35.5	1,316	99.0
Portland CDP	135	-	-	93	91.4	0.0	0.0	4.3	4.3	7.5	34.4	62.2	12.8	45.3	41	100.0
Pritchett town	140	131	-6.4	114	78.9	0.0	0.0	0.0	21.1	25.4	18.4	37.4	50.0	19.0	53	86.8
Pueblo city	106,542	112,361	5.5	110,841	43.6	1.9	0.6	2.9	51.1	22.4	17.5	37.7	42.6	18.9	44,179	85.2
Pueblo West CDP	29,637	-	-	31,849	68.8	1.3	0.5	3.3	26.2	24.3	17.2	40.4	30.4	28.1	11,443	95.5
Ramah town	123	130	5.7	146	70.5	0.0	0.0	9.6	19.9	19.2	8.2	38.5	47.2	15.1	54	85.2
Rangely town	2,365	2,263	-4.3	2,402	79.9	1.1	0.0	6.8	12.1	21.1	10.3	34.6	31.8	23.9	836	93.1
Raymer (New Raymer) town	98	112	14.3	70	95.7	4.3	0.0	0.0	0.0	15.7	18.6	51.0	29.4	23.5	34	91.2
Red Cliff town	272	282	3.7	345	56.5	0.0	0.0	0.0	43.5	16.2	8.7	40.1	53.1	26.5	101	94.1
Red Feather Lakes CDP	343	-	-	385	84.9	0.0	0.0	2.3	12.7	9.4	63.4	69.6	27.5	31.2	236	77.1
Redlands CDP	8,685	-	-	8,765	93.5	0.0	1.1	1.7	3.8	19.0	27.5	51.5	20.3	45.4	3,544	95.7
Redstone CDP	130	-	-	63	100.0	0.0	0.0	0.0	0.0	0.0	0.0	61.3	0.0	69.8	44	100.0
Redvale CDP	236	-	-	276	94.6	0.0	0.0	5.4	0.0	6.2	26.8	50.7	57.4	20.1	119	68.1
Rico town	265	231	-12.8	195	91.3	0.0	0.0	2.6	6.2	4.1	21.5	46.3	15.5	45.3	105	80.0
Ridgway town	889	1,039	16.9	992	93.4	0.0	0.0	3.0	3.5	14.9	19.6	50.1	14.4	51.0	520	95.2
Rifle city	9,398	9,706	3.3	9,650	65.5	0.1	0.6	3.2	30.7	29.6	10.6	32.4	50.2	16.2	3,411	93.6
Rock Creek Park CDP	58	-	-	128	100.0	0.0	0.0	0.0	0.0	35.2	0.0	32.4	16.9	32.5	41	100.0
Rockvale town	495	519	4.8	499	89.6	0.4	0.0	3.6	6.4	17.2	22.4	52.3	45.9	20.1	228	78.1
Rocky Ford city	3,963	3,815	-3.7	3,824	33.6	0.3	0.0	6.9	59.2	29.3	17.1	34.8	49.8	15.6	1,385	79.6
Rollinsville CDP	181	-	-	271	73.8	0.0	0.0	26.2	0.0	0.0	59.8	65.2	20.7	53.1	141	100.0
Romeo town	404	411	1.7	305	17.7	0.0	0.0	3.3	79.0	22.0	15.4	33.4	68.9	7.7	111	77.5
Roxborough Park CDP	9,099	-	-	9,523	85.6	0.2	1.4	2.9	9.9	24.4	12.0	40.5	16.9	53.9	3,376	99.2
Rye town	156	165	5.8	197	82.7	0.0	0.0	0.0	17.3	23.4	25.4	50.5	34.3	30.1	92	97.8
Saddle Ridge CDP	56	-	-	76	88.2	0.0	0.0	0.0	11.8	19.7	27.6	53.2	18.0	44.3	27	100.0
Saguache town	496	505	1.8	455	63.1	0.0	0.0	2.0	34.9	13.0	18.2	54.3	54.9	15.3	230	78.7
St. Ann Highlands CDP	288	-	-	583	100.0	0.0	0.0	0.0	0.0	13.0	7.7	40.1	15.3	60.1	202	100.0
St. Mary's CDP	283	-	-	620	91.3	0.0	0.0	0.0	8.7	26.6	2.1	37.0	33.4	28.1	252	100.0
Salida city	5,246	6,082	15.9	5,791	74.6	0.1	3.8	4.2	17.3	16.0	24.5	47.2	38.3	33.4	2,507	86.1
Salt Creek CDP	587	-	-	572	5.9	0.0	0.0	7.3	86.7	9.6	20.3	39.9	47.4	6.4	217	65.4
San Acacio CDP	40	-	-	117	76.1	0.0	0.0	17.1	6.8	15.4	36.8	48.8	32.5	9.6	62	100.0
Sanford town	879	887	0.9	1,073	64.4	0.3	0.0	1.6	33.7	34.9	13.4	30.9	39.7	17.9	356	91.6
San Luis town	629	658	4.6	790	6.2	0.0	0.0	1.5	92.3	22.5	32.0	39.8	49.8	10.7	400	64.0
Sawpit town	34	39	14.7	46	100.0	0.0	0.0	0.0	0.0	13.0	23.9	43.0	7.5	67.5	24	100.0
Security-Widefield CDP	32,882	-	-	39,612	62.9	8.8	2.5	6.3	19.5	27.8	11.1	32.9	35.8	22.1	12,725	94.3
Sedalia CDP	206	-	-	133	100.0	0.0	0.0	0.0	0.0	9.8	27.8	51.5	7.2	47.0	64	100.0
Sedgwick town	146	137	-6.2	135	75.6	0.0	4.4	2.2	17.8	17.0	20.0	48.4	49.0	18.4	71	83.1
Segundo CDP	98	-	-	116	85.3	0.0	0.0	0.0	14.7	16.4	31.0	60.9	69.2	7.7	54	88.9
Seibert town	181	213	17.7	142	98.6	0.0	0.0	0.0	1.4	7.7	45.1	55.4	53.7	15.4	95	83.2
Seven Hills CDP	121	-	-	120	100.0	0.0	0.0	0.0	0.0	25.8	42.5	35.5	0.0	100.0	39	100.0
Severance town	3,179	6,494	104.3	4,745	84.4	0.0	0.4	3.0	12.2	31.3	10.4	35.1	22.8	42.6	1,573	97.3
Shaw Heights CDP	5,116	-	-	5,529	54.1	0.4	7.1	1.8	36.6	24.8	13.5	35.7	54.8	19.9	1,694	94.4
Sheridan city	5,623	6,183	10.0	6,089	62.9	3.3	1.2	1.8	30.8	20.7	17.9	36.2	49.4	22.0	2,713	86.7
Sheridan Lake town	83	83	0.0	99	81.8	0.0	0.0	0.0	18.2	49.5	3.0	18.5	21.4	47.6	29	100.0
Sherrelwood CDP	18,287	-	-	19,208	32.5	1.0	1.2	1.3	64.0	24.7	12.2	34.4	53.9	12.8	6,145	93.9
Silt town	2,936	3,190	8.7	3,115	66.0	0.3	0.3	1.0	32.4	32.0	5.5	30.8	42.8	13.7	1,054	94.8
Silver Cliff town	581	667	14.8	565	89.2	0.0	0.0	3.9	6.9	25.0	22.8	47.1	41.2	21.5	278	80.2
Silver Plume town	170	177	4.1	169	98.2	0.0	0.0	0.0	1.8	16.0	28.4	48.1	20.9	51.1	84	95.2
Silverthorne town	3,907	4,898	25.4	4,673	73.1	5.9	0.0	0.0	21.0	20.3	19.7	46.1	36.7	39.5	1,685	94.7
Silverton town	637	663	4.1	534	87.6	0.0	0.0	3.0	9.4	14.2	23.0	49.3	31.6	33.5	253	90.5
Simla town	613	640	4.4	698	85.8	2.7	0.0	3.2	8.3	23.9	16.8	40.4	33.4	29.1	284	78.9
Smeltertown CDP	120	-	-	135	100.0	0.0	0.0	0.0	0.0	25.9	0.0	33.0	17.0	7.0	46	100.0
Snowmass Village town	2,816	2,732	-3.0	2,783	93.2	0.1	0.0	1.7	4.9	10.5	14.9	49.3	24.0	59.5	1,227	100.0
Snyder CDP	132	-	-	145	89.7	0.0	0.0	6.2	4.1	26.2	25.5	42.1	67.3	0.0	46	58.7
Southern Ute CDP	177	-	-	215	42.8	0.0	0.0	39.5	17.7	18.6	25.6	39.0	47.4	5.8	85	72.9
South Fork town	455	425	-6.6	335	87.5	0.0	2.4	3.0	7.2	6.9	47.8	64.2	20.3	36.7	193	93.3
Springfield town	1,451	1,375	-5.2	1,318	85.9	1.9	0.0	2.5	9.7	21.1	23.1	38.8	39.9	22.0	645	85.1
Starkville town	59	54	-8.5	101	16.8	0.0	0.0	5.9	77.2	34.7	19.8	46.1	37.9	10.6	37	59.5
Steamboat Springs city	12,134	13,214	8.9	12,928	86.9	1.5	1.7	0.7	9.2	16.7	12.8	37.0	19.3	56.4	4,912	95.5
Sterling city	14,799	14,495	-2.1	14,478	70.2	1.3	1.1	7.4	20.1	20.4	16.6	34.6	48.0	19.3	5,281	88.4
Stonegate CDP	8,962	-	-	9,847	86.4	0.9	2.4	2.9	7.5	30.7	7.8	35.8	12.0	62.8	3,259	99.4
Stonewall Gap CDP	67	-	-	43	93.0	0.0	0.0	0.0	7.0	0.0	67.4	65.8	20.9	41.9	26	57.7
Strasburg CDP	2,447	-	-	3,013	79.9	0.7	0.0	6.6	12.8	28.5	11.4	39.9	38.8	20.7	1,017	95.4
Stratmoor CDP	6,900	-	-	6,484	53.1	3.5	1.1	11.7	30.7	27.0	12.9	33.2	48.2	19.0	2,206	83.4
Stratton town	661	639	-3.3	676	89.8	1.0	1.5	4.4	3.3	35.4	13.3	31.2	38.2	25.6	249	86.7
Sugar City town	258	253	-1.9	519	65.9	0.0	0.4	2.7	31.0	14.6	10.2	32.6	30.5	26.9	133	94.0
Sugarloaf CDP	261	-	-	353	100.0	0.0	0.0	0.0	0.0	0.0	9.3	40.5	0.0	81.6	158	100.0
Sunshine CDP	230	-	-	168	100.0	0.0	0.0	0.0	0.0	31.5	20.8	41.8	25.2	63.5	57	100.0
Superior town	12,481	13,087	4.9	13,077	71.1	0.4	18.1	3.6	6.8	26.9	7.3	35.9	7.1	76.3	4,596	100.0
Swink town	617	592	-4.1	857	51.7	0.0	0.0	0.0	48.3	37.2	20.1	33.6	40.8	9.5	299	90.0
Tabernash CDP	417	-	-	482	100.0	0.0	0.0	0.0	0.0	16.6	0.0	36.1	21.3	59.4	169	100.0
Tall Timber CDP	208	-	-	156	100.0	0.0	0.0	0.0	0.0	6.4	39.7	62.5	11.0	50.0	81	100.0
Telluride town	2,229	2,479	11.2	1,965	77.5	0.0	3.6	1.1	17.8	19.2	6.4	35.5	10.8	75.0	849	95.8
The Pinery CDP	10,517	-	-	10,806	89.8	0.2	1.1	2.0	6.8	24.8	13.6	47.0	14.0	55.6	3,896	98.1
Thornton city	118,787	141,464	19.1	136,868	56.1	2.0	4.8	3.0	34.2	28.1	9.3	33.8	39.3	29.0	45,676	96.7
Timnath town	643	4,998	677.3	3,476	90.8	0.0	2.4	1.6	5.2	36.9	8.0	35.2	14.6	60.7	1,041	99.3
Todd Creek CDP	3,768	-	-	4,365	80.7	1.1	4.6	2.0	11.6	24.3	11.7	43.4	24.6	37.9	1,312	97.5
Towaoc CDP	1,087	-	-	1,153	2.8	0.0	0.4	94.7	2.1	35.2	4.1	24.9	77.0	4.7	427	78.9
Towner CDP	22	-	-	19	100.0	0.0	0.0	0.0	0.0	10.5	36.8	56.8	17.6	23.5	12	83.3
Trail Side CDP	59	-	-	202	94.1	0.0	0.0	5.9	0.0	27.2	5.9	29.5	29.2	46.7	77	100.0
Trinidad city	9,088	8,200	-9.8	8,080	43.3	0.1	1.6	4.7	50.3	17.8	22.5	41.8	41.5	16.5	3,964	82.3
Twin Lakes CDP	6,101	-	-	8,196	33.0	1.8	1.6	1.8	61.8	20.4	11.9	38.0	57.7	21.2	2,674	86.2
Twin Lakes CDP	171	-	-	196	86.2	0.0	1.5	0.0	12.2	19.4	11.7	46.1	23.7	27.0	105	94.3
Two Buttes town	43	40	-7.0	48	75.0	0.0	0.0	0.0	25.0	0.0	58.3	69.5	56.3	0.0	36	83.3
Upper Bear Creek CDP	1,059	-	-	925	93.9	0.0	0.8	1.3	4.0	16.1	23.8	54.0	23.0	60.9	409	100.0
Vail town	5,307	5,434	2.4	5,479	91.8	0.5	0.9	0.3	6.5	10.5	19.9	43.6	7.3	64.0	2,296	97.9
Valdez CDP	47	-	-	17	0.0	0.0	0.0	0.0	100.0	29.4	0.0	0.0	100.0	0.0	12	0.0
Valmont CDP	59	-	-	96	74.0	0.0	26.0	0.0	0.0	6.3	27.1	28.3	16.4	41.0	48	100.0
Vernon CDP	29	-	-	-	-	-	-	-	-	-	-	-	-	-	-	-
Victor city	413	426	3.1	432	94.4	0.0	0.0	2.5	3.0	8.8	23.1	52.2	38.5	26.5	254	87.0
Vilas town	114	107	-6.1	98	58.2	0.0	0.0	0.0	41.8	49.0	6.1	22.3	50.0	18.2	40	85.0

1 May be of any race.

Table A. All Places — **Population and Housing**

STATE City, town, township, borough, or CDP (county if applicable)	Population 2010 census total population	2019 estimated population	Percent change 2010-2019	ACS total population estimate 2015-2019	Race and Hispanic or Latino origin (percent) White alone, not Hispanic or Latino	Black alone, not Hispanic or Latino	Asian alone, not Hispanic or Latino	All other races or 2 or more races, not Hispanic or Latino	Hispanic or Latino[1]	Age (percent) Under 18 years old	Age 65 years and older	Median age	Educational attainment of persons age 25 and older Percent High school diploma or less	Percent Bachelor's degree or more	Occupied housing units Total	Percent with a computer
	1	2	3	4	5	6	7	8	9	10	11	12	13	14	15	16
COLORADO—Con.																
Vineland CDP	251	-	-	314	79.3	0.0	0.0	8.3	12.4	24.5	22.0	41.9	32.7	31.4	130	81.5
Vona town	106	104	-1.9	110	71.8	0.0	0.0	0.0	28.2	27.3	25.5	39.2	30.6	30.6	43	81.4
Walden town	608	599	-1.5	590	67.3	0.0	0.0	0.0	32.7	12.9	26.8	51.4	49.1	18.6	298	79.9
Walsenburg city	3,063	3,029	-1.1	2,962	45.5	0.0	0.0	3.5	50.9	20.5	27.5	49.8	42.5	19.0	1,463	69.7
Walsh town	546	516	-5.5	524	64.7	0.0	0.0	8.2	27.1	15.3	41.8	57.8	55.1	18.6	273	65.9
Ward town	150	161	7.3	100	92.0	0.0	2.0	0.0	6.0	12.0	26.0	51.0	11.6	36.0	68	76.5
Watkins CDP	-	-	-	670	83.0	0.7	0.0	0.7	15.5	19.1	22.2	52.9	40.9	28.7	265	100.0
Welby CDP	14,846	-	-	16,018	32.7	1.7	2.2	2.8	60.7	24.7	9.3	31.9	57.4	12.2	5,126	92.4
Weldona CDP	139	-	-	182	68.1	2.2	0.0	0.0	29.7	20.3	5.5	42.3	71.2	9.1	77	93.5
Wellington town	6,389	10,437	63.4	9,272	85.2	1.0	0.4	2.8	10.6	29.2	9.4	32.6	24.9	35.3	3,211	96.9
Westcliffe town	571	628	10.0	368	92.9	0.0	0.0	1.4	5.7	14.1	28.5	54.1	27.6	44.1	212	88.7
Westcreek CDP	129	-	-	200	100.0	0.0	0.0	0.0	0.0	30.5	8.0	31.1	47.8	8.1	75	94.7
Westminster city	106,135	113,166	6.6	112,962	67.0	1.7	5.8	3.1	22.3	22.0	13.3	36.6	29.9	38.6	44,092	94.2
Weston CDP	55	-	-	32	28.1	0.0	0.0	0.0	71.9	9.4	50.0	66.0	14.8	18.5	21	61.9
West Pleasant View CDP	3,840	-	-	5,173	80.0	0.3	1.6	0.6	17.5	21.9	6.7	28.3	35.7	38.1	1,750	96.5
Wheat Ridge city	30,176	31,324	3.8	31,331	73.8	1.0	1.1	2.7	21.4	18.5	19.1	41.2	33.8	35.8	14,080	89.6
Wiggins town	886	1,163	31.3	1,201	70.5	0.0	0.0	0.2	29.3	32.6	12.9	34.1	45.9	18.4	390	88.7
Wiley town	405	393	-3.0	344	82.6	0.0	7.6	0.0	9.9	11.3	14.2	46.8	27.5	33.3	167	91.0
Williamsburg town	662	713	7.7	525	91.8	0.0	1.3	1.5	5.3	19.2	29.1	54.6	52.8	15.6	230	87.8
Windsor town	18,649	30,477	63.4	26,806	86.6	0.4	1.9	2.5	8.7	28.4	15.3	38.9	21.9	45.0	9,596	97.0
Winter Park town	1,019	1,090	7.0	659	95.0	2.3	0.0	0.0	2.7	9.0	17.6	39.9	30.3	50.3	341	96.5
Wolcott CDP	15	-	-	-	-	-	-	-	-	-	-	-	-	-	-	-
Woodland Park city	7,138	7,885	10.5	7,555	89.3	0.8	0.8	3.3	5.8	20.9	17.6	46.1	15.7	45.4	3,117	98.4
Woodmoor CDP	8,741	-	-	9,345	84.6	2.2	2.2	4.8	6.3	24.8	15.3	44.0	11.5	63.9	3,110	99.6
Woody Creek CDP	263	-	-	192	100.0	0.0	0.0	0.0	0.0	21.9	41.1	59.7	0.0	87.3	106	100.0
Wray city	2,381	2,349	-1.3	2,536	76.9	0.1	0.0	1.0	22.0	33.0	15.8	36.4	49.5	21.4	1,006	84.4
Yampa town	430	464	7.9	413	87.4	0.0	1.7	2.7	8.2	24.7	18.6	48.9	45.7	27.7	164	89.6
Yuma city	3,518	3,479	-1.1	3,479	58.0	1.3	0.0	1.1	39.6	24.0	19.8	33.2	59.2	20.2	1,375	86.4
CONNECTICUT	3,574,147	3,565,287	-0.2	3,575,074	66.9	9.9	4.5	2.6	16.1	20.8	16.8	41.0	36.2	39.3	1,370,746	90.8
Andover town (Tolland)	3,306	3,236	-2.1	3,203	92.7	3.1	0.0	1.2	3.0	18.5	14.2	45.8	29.2	38.9	1,216	99.3
Ansonia city and town (New Haven)	19,277	18,654	-3.2	18,802	61.3	13.1	1.8	2.5	21.4	20.0	16.2	40.0	48.9	22.7	7,806	86.5
Ashford town (Windham)	4,303	4,255	-1.1	4,236	91.9	0.0	1.2	1.7	5.1	20.8	13.2	43.9	32.4	38.7	1,774	92.1
Avon town (Hartford)	18,091	18,276	1.0	18,312	78.7	0.8	13.1	2.6	4.9	25.0	20.8	45.2	12.7	66.2	6,977	95.6
Baltic CDP	1,250	-	-	1,237	74.1	6.2	2.9	8.6	8.1	23.7	11.9	35.5	55.9	7.2	511	93.3
Bantam borough	759	727	-4.2	660	88.6	0.3	1.7	1.5	7.9	15.9	29.4	46.0	46.4	25.5	337	81.3
Barkhamsted town (Litchfield)	3,796	3,606	-5.0	3,649	94.1	0.1	3.6	1.4	0.9	19.0	19.4	48.4	28.7	41.8	1,336	95.8
Beacon Falls town (New Haven)	6,053	6,222	2.8	6,168	91.6	1.4	0.4	0.7	6.0	20.7	21.1	47.2	36.4	35.5	2,447	96.2
Berlin town (Hartford)	19,874	20,436	2.8	20,484	88.7	1.0	3.4	1.3	5.5	19.9	21.1	47.5	35.3	41.0	8,181	91.2
Bethany town (New Haven)	5,568	5,548	-0.4	5,513	81.4	1.5	7.2	3.2	6.7	20.1	18.9	47.9	28.8	46.7	2,018	94.3
Bethel town (Fairfield)	18,604	19,800	6.4	19,663	80.8	3.9	6.6	1.2	7.6	23.4	15.3	42.9	28.4	45.4	7,164	95.4
Bethel CDP	9,549	-	-	10,012	76.9	5.5	8.0	0.4	9.1	24.0	14.2	42.5	30.1	43.1	4,056	93.9
Bethlehem town (Litchfield)	3,582	3,402	-5.0	3,433	91.2	1.0	2.0	3.4	2.4	23.8	18.0	44.9	30.6	42.5	1,204	92.1
Bethlehem Village CDP	2,021	-	-	1,995	92.2	1.1	0.0	5.2	1.6	21.1	21.9	50.5	34.6	40.8	763	89.4
Bloomfield town (Hartford)	20,480	21,211	3.6	21,022	31.7	55.4	2.1	2.5	8.2	14.5	26.7	51.3	38.0	34.8	8,727	88.4
Blue Hills CDP	2,901	-	-	2,913	5.3	87.4	0.0	5.5	1.8	19.2	23.8	48.1	59.5	13.3	1,053	87.7
Bolton town (Tolland)	4,978	4,884	-1.9	4,911	88.5	1.3	1.5	1.1	7.5	18.8	21.6	46.3	33.2	43.9	1,821	97.6
Bozrah town (New London)	2,627	2,726	3.8	2,589	90.9	2.9	0.6	3.3	2.3	18.9	19.1	45.0	43.6	28.8	986	94.2
Branford town (New Haven)	28,026	27,900	-0.4	28,020	86.4	1.4	4.6	1.5	6.2	16.5	22.8	49.0	32.8	45.0	12,369	91.1
Branford Center CDP	5,819	-	-	6,163	90.0	1.1	6.2	0.3	2.4	14.1	27.4	50.6	33.2	39.5	3,082	90.8
Bridgeport city and town (Fairfield)	144,246	144,399	0.1	145,639	20.1	32.3	3.3	3.6	40.8	23.1	11.3	34.3	56.5	18.8	50,638	86.5
Bridgewater town (Litchfield)	1,733	1,635	-5.7	1,707	89.6	4.5	0.7	2.5	2.8	12.7	31.0	54.9	23.0	56.4	699	94.6
Bristol city and town (Hartford)	60,499	59,947	-0.9	60,218	73.6	4.8	1.5	2.8	17.3	20.3	16.5	40.5	43.5	26.6	24,638	88.9
Broad Brook CDP	4,069	-	-	4,695	72.9	14.0	2.5	2.3	8.4	25.6	11.9	36.3	29.5	38.7	1,628	95.3
Brookfield town (Fairfield)	16,442	16,973	3.2	17,016	86.0	1.3	5.2	1.2	6.3	23.2	19.2	45.5	26.6	50.0	6,200	95.1
Brooklyn CDP	981	-	-	827	65.1	11.9	0.0	3.9	19.2	1.3	26.5	43.4	48.9	14.8	126	90.5
Brooklyn town (Windham)	8,212	8,272	0.7	8,238	89.4	2.0	2.5	1.8	4.3	20.7	18.8	44.3	40.2	22.1	2,915	87.9
Burlington town (Hartford)	9,333	9,704	4.0	9,659	92.8	0.7	2.4	1.8	2.2	23.3	15.7	44.7	23.7	51.1	3,462	94.8
Byram CDP	4,146	-	-	4,560	44.1	4.7	3.4	3.4	44.4	20.0	12.2	41.2	39.4	39.9	1,638	92.2
Canaan CDP	1,212	-	-	1,050	78.0	9.3	0.0	1.5	11.1	16.9	25.6	46.2	55.2	16.6	504	85.3
Canaan town (Litchfield)	1,114	1,053	-5.5	1,143	91.5	4.4	1.2	1.8	1.0	16.6	25.2	53.3	27.1	42.8	507	89.3
Cannondale CDP	141	-	-	8	62.5	12.5	0.0	0.0	25.0	0.0	12.5	48.0	0.0	66.7	0	0.0
Canterbury town (Windham)	5,132	5,079		5,069	96.4	0.7	1.2	0.7	1.1	22.1	17.5	44.7	41.6	22.4	1,916	89.0
Canton town (Hartford)	10,292	10,254	-0.4	10,288	86.1	3.4	4.6	0.9	4.9	21.1	19.6	46.8	17.2	55.4	4,046	94.1
Canton Valley CDP	1,580	-	-	1,651	98.1	0.0	1.3	0.0	0.6	16.1	26.5	52.1	24.5	36.4	791	87.7
Chaplin town (Windham)	2,297	2,239	-2.5	2,489	85.1	0.0	0.4	5.1	9.3	17.2	15.7	46.1	47.7	26.8	988	94.1
Cheshire town (New Haven)	29,279	28,937	-1.2	29,147	82.7	4.3	6.8	2.4	3.7	19.4	18.6	46.2	22.9	55.5	10,169	93.7
Cheshire Village CDP	5,786	-	-	6,082	86.1	0.4	11.0	1.2	1.3	20.6	23.0	47.2	19.9	55.3	2,278	85.9
Chester town (Middlesex)	3,995	4,213	5.5	4,234	96.0	0.5	1.3	0.0	2.2	16.8	25.3	50.0	28.7	37.2	1,772	93.2
Chester Center CDP	1,558	-	-	1,566	94.9	0.7	2.9	0.0	1.5	19.9	22.2	49.4	24.2	43.3	667	98.8
Clinton town (Middlesex)	13,263	12,925	-2.5	12,944	88.4	0.4	0.9	1.7	8.5	18.5	20.9	46.6	32.3	39.1	5,396	93.4
Clinton CDP	3,368	-	-	3,388	90.3	0.1	1.5	0.1	7.9	15.0	20.8	45.8	37.0	34.7	1,548	89.9
Colchester CDP	4,781	-	-	4,788	89.4	3.1	0.2	1.4	6.2	19.6	22.2	44.2	32.4	31.7	2,091	89.0
Colchester town (New London)	16,003	15,809	-1.2	15,860	89.8	1.9	2.3	1.9	4.0	23.5	14.2	42.5	28.7	40.4	5,985	94.5
Colebrook town (Litchfield)	1,480	1,400	-5.4	1,484	97.0	0.5	0.9	0.0	1.5	20.4	14.9	47.5	35.5	31.4	590	90.8
Collinsville CDP	3,746	-	-	3,328	91.0	3.0	2.7	1.5	1.8	22.1	17.4	47.0	12.9	59.2	1,367	95.2
Columbia town (Tolland)	5,482	5,379	-1.9	5,417	91.5	0.3	0.0	0.0	8.3	17.7	21.6	48.6	28.0	46.5	2,156	92.9

1 May be of any race.

Table A. All Places — Population and Housing

STATE City, town, township, borough, or CDP (county if applicable)	Population				Race and Hispanic or Latino origin (percent)					Age (percent)			Educational attainment of persons age 25 and older		Occupied housing units	
	2010 census total population	2019 estimated population	Percent change 2010-2019	ACS total population estimate 2015-2019	White alone, not Hispanic or Latino	Black alone, not Hispanic or Latino	Asian alone, not Hispanic or Latino	All other races or 2 or more races, not Hispanic or Latino	Hispanic or Latino[1]	Under 18 years old	Age 65 years and older	Median age	Percent High school diploma or less	Percent Bachelor's degree or more	Total	Percent with a computer
	1	2	3	4	5	6	7	8	9	10	11	12	13	14	15	16
CONNECTICUT—Con.																
Conning Towers Nautilus Park CDP	8,834	-	-	9,785	68.6	8.4	1.8	4.4	16.8	21.2	5.0	23.6	37.1	18.8	2,532	95.9
Cornwall town (Litchfield) .	1,420	1,362	-4.1	1,291	87.8	0.4	3.6	0.5	7.7	16.4	30.1	57.0	21.3	48.1	598	94.1
Cos Cob CDP	6,770	-	-	6,990	75.4	0.1	10.1	2.6	11.9	27.5	14.3	42.8	16.6	71.2	2,517	96.7
Coventry town (Tolland)....	12,433	12,407	-0.2	12,433	93.7	0.6	1.3	2.0	2.4	21.8	14.9	43.1	29.1	43.0	4,648	95.7
Coventry Lake CDP	2,990	-	-	2,530	88.5	1.6	1.5	1.0	7.4	11.4	17.0	48.2	37.2	34.3	1,089	93.0
Cromwell town (Middlesex)	14,003	13,839	-1.2	13,910	78.3	7.1	4.0	1.7	8.9	20.0	19.4	43.7	27.0	47.2	5,897	90.3
Crystal Lake CDP	1,945	-	-	2,188	92.6	0.9	2.2	2.5	1.8	19.3	16.4	48.5	32.3	44.5	818	97.2
Danbury city and town (Fairfield)	80,893	84,694	4.7	84,619	49.8	9.0	6.3	4.9	30.0	20.1	13.7	38.3	45.0	31.7	30,000	92.2
Danielson borough	4,028	4,012	-0.4	3,993	75.5	1.3	5.5	6.4	11.2	21.0	12.0	39.4	52.1	19.0	1,722	82.9
Darien town (Fairfield)	20,716	21,728	4.9	21,742	87.7	0.8	5.5	2.0	4.1	33.8	11.9	40.1	8.1	82.9	6,895	96.1
Deep River town (Middlesex)	4,628	4,443	-4.0	4,480	90.1	2.9	0.9	1.6	4.4	21.1	18.7	47.1	33.1	41.7	1,883	92.7
Deep River Center CDP ...	2,484	-	-	2,354	90.0	3.9	0.0	0.0	6.1	20.9	17.3	43.6	30.5	42.0	1,101	93.8
Derby city and town (New Haven)	12,876	12,339	-4.2	12,485	63.9	6.7	3.9	3.5	22.0	19.5	17.0	40.0	47.9	20.2	5,146	81.5
Durham CDP	2,933	-	-	2,752	91.8	0.1	4.1	1.6	2.4	19.3	25.8	48.8	34.8	38.9	1,124	91.5
Durham town (Middlesex).	7,387	7,165	-3.0	7,221	96.5	0.2	1.6	0.6	1.1	19.8	20.8	47.1	27.4	49.3	2,768	93.7
East Brooklyn CDP	1,638	-	-	1,521	79.1	4.4	0.0	7.8	8.7	25.6	15.1	38.2	42.0	9.4	652	75.3
Eastford town (Windham) .	1,769	1,790	1.2	1,653	95.0	0.2	0.4	0.4	4.0	14.3	17.9	48.8	34.4	37.1	681	93.5
East Granby town (Hartford)	5,149	5,140	-0.2	5,304	86.7	0.8	2.3	2.0	8.1	23.1	16.6	43.3	23.7	47.0	2,027	93.5
East Haddam town (Middlesex)	9,126	8,997	-1.4	9,007	95.2	0.6	0.1	0.7	3.4	18.3	18.7	48.2	33.3	38.1	3,640	93.6
East Hampton CDP	2,691	-	-	2,969	94.2	1.4	0.3	0.0	4.1	24.4	12.8	38.6	34.0	38.3	1,002	91.6
East Hampton town (Middlesex)	12,960	12,800	-1.2	12,827	90.8	1.1	3.1	2.1	2.8	19.8	17.0	45.2	33.4	37.9	4,831	95.5
East Hartford town (Hartford)	51,254	49,872	-2.7	50,272	33.4	24.4	3.6	2.5	36.1	22.1	14.4	37.8	52.1	19.4	19,046	88.6
East Haven town (New Haven)	29,212	28,569	-2.2	28,742	74.1	3.6	3.6	1.4	17.3	18.4	19.1	43.0	50.5	24.0	11,147	89.6
East Lyme town (New London)	19,164	18,462	-3.7	18,724	82.1	3.5	5.8	2.4	6.2	17.0	23.2	48.2	28.3	46.3	7,345	93.9
Easton town (Fairfield)	7,498	7,521	0.3	7,543	92.4	0.0	1.9	1.9	3.7	21.6	20.4	50.2	17.4	64.3	2,799	96.7
East Windsor town (Hartford)	11,162	11,668	4.5	11,445	77.1	7.3	7.7	2.0	5.9	17.0	17.4	45.3	33.9	37.4	4,855	92.7
Ellington town (Tolland)	15,593	16,467	5.6	16,170	84.1	1.4	6.5	3.4	4.6	21.4	14.2	41.0	30.5	47.0	7,000	92.1
Enfield town (Hartford)	44,653	43,659	-2.2	44,143	76.3	6.7	2.7	3.1	11.2	18.6	16.4	41.0	43.0	27.0	16,744	92.4
Essex town (Middlesex)....	6,679	6,668	-0.2	6,604	86.9	4.0	3.9	2.3	3.0	15.0	31.1	54.6	26.4	52.9	3,074	97.1
Essex Village CDP	2,495	-	-	2,480	79.6	10.6	3.9	5.2	0.7	13.5	36.6	56.9	18.4	58.9	1,181	98.5
Fairfield town (Fairfield)	59,403	62,045	4.4	61,740	84.3	1.9	4.4	2.6	6.9	23.1	16.0	41.4	18.2	66.2	20,641	95.2
Falls Village CDP	538	-	-	451	97.3	0.0	0.0	0.0	2.7	22.2	20.8	52.8	27.0	43.1	182	92.3
Farmington town (Hartford)	25,350	25,497	0.6	25,528	76.3	2.2	12.3	2.7	6.5	20.5	19.8	45.0	19.4	59.7	10,463	92.0
Fenwick borough	43	45	4.7	64	100.0	0.0	0.0	0.0	0.0	0.0	78.1	68.6	19.0	52.4	34	94.1
Franklin town (New London)	1,922	1,920	-0.1	1,778	92.1	0.8	0.3	1.4	5.3	19.7	20.1	48.6	38.9	28.8	717	90.8
Gales Ferry CDP	1,162	-	-	899	89.7	0.0	0.0	2.6	7.8	19.7	27.0	50.9	28.8	36.3	404	100.0
Georgetown CDP	1,805	-	-	1,630	86.7	0.0	11.0	0.0	2.2	24.8	11.8	43.8	16.7	54.6	616	97.1
Glastonbury town (Hartford)	34,427	34,482	0.2	34,564	80.9	2.1	8.7	2.5	5.8	23.2	18.0	45.2	18.1	63.0	13,411	95.3
Glastonbury Center CDP..	7,387	-	-	7,929	79.8	1.2	5.6	4.3	9.2	19.7	20.4	44.7	20.0	56.1	3,392	93.5
Glenville CDP	2,327	-	-	2,538	87.6	3.9	2.5	0.8	5.1	16.8	20.5	47.7	17.3	59.7	1,000	99.2
Goshen town (Litchfield) ..	2,976	2,863	-3.8	2,883	93.0	0.1	0.8	4.1	2.1	18.3	22.9	49.8	19.6	43.9	1,098	95.1
Granby town (Hartford)	11,290	11,507	1.9	11,361	94.9	0.4	1.5	1.2	2.1	22.6	17.9	46.2	21.6	53.4	4,147	94.4
Greenwich town (Fairfield)	61,198	62,840	2.7	62,587	72.9	3.3	7.6	2.5	13.8	25.6	17.5	43.2	18.0	66.6	22,271	96.0
Greenwich CDP	12,942	-	-	13,287	61.7	7.2	7.5	2.8	20.9	23.8	18.1	42.3	22.1	60.3	5,424	93.5
Griswold town (New London)	11,951	11,534	-3.5	11,622	88.1	1.1	2.2	6.1	2.5	21.5	16.3	40.0	45.0	17.8	4,898	88.5
Groton city	9,384	8,911	-5.0	9,030	58.9	8.5	7.4	6.8	18.4	20.8	13.4	35.7	41.1	30.8	4,407	90.5
Groton town (New London)	40,125	38,436	-4.2	38,825	69.3	6.7	5.1	5.2	13.7	19.2	15.3	34.1	35.1	36.1	15,958	90.8
Groton Long Point borough	518	507	-2.1	461	98.3	0.0	0.0	0.0	1.7	10.8	50.3	65.2	6.7	75.2	234	97.4
Guilford town (New Haven)	22,373	22,133	-1.1	22,216	88.3	1.0	4.0	1.9	4.8	21.2	24.0	48.6	20.1	58.4	8,397	94.8
Guilford Center CDP	2,597	-	-	2,689	87.7	0.5	0.5	0.7	10.6	18.8	30.0	52.4	25.0	59.6	1,274	91.5
Haddam town (Middlesex)	8,347	8,193	-1.8	8,227	91.8	1.7	3.2	1.2	2.1	18.2	20.4	48.3	28.9	46.1	3,101	91.5
Hamden town (New Haven)	60,880	60,556	-0.5	60,982	55.6	24.0	5.1	2.8	12.5	17.2	16.1	36.8	31.3	46.1	22,577	91.9
Hampton town (Windham)	1,861	1,842	-	1,830	94.2	0.1	0.5	3.1	2.2	15.0	19.2	51.4	38.6	32.5	785	96.4
Hartford city and town (Hartford)	124,765	122,105	-2.1	123,088	14.8	35.5	2.7	2.7	44.3	23.5	11.3	32.1	58.8	16.9	46,690	83.7
Hartland town (Hartford)...	2,117	2,120	0.1	1,982	90.1	0.3	0.5	9.0	0.1	20.9	19.0	51.0	39.6	29.1	756	94.8
Harwinton town (Litchfield)	5,644	5,420	-4.0	5,456	95.8	1.7	0.5	0.7	1.4	20.7	21.7	47.9	31.4	36.8	1,943	95.0
Hazardville CDP	4,599	-	-	4,615	83.4	2.4	2.2	4.5	7.5	19.6	18.2	42.6	37.9	31.2	1,850	92.6
Hebron town (Tolland)	9,690	9,504	-1.9	9,512	93.9	0.1	1.9	0.9	3.2	22.0	15.6	45.5	23.6	50.8	3,528	93.1
Heritage Village CDP	3,736	-	-	4,156	95.3	3.0	0.2	0.3	1.2	3.0	74.6	73.6	31.6	41.6	2,770	81.0
Higganum CDP	1,698	-	-	1,285	85.4	0.0	10.9	0.9	2.9	16.3	20.5	47.3	24.9	57.5	566	94.9
Jewett City borough	3,487	3,360	-3.6	3,385	80.2	0.0	5.2	10.2	4.3	24.4	11.0	29.8	47.2	6.3	1,509	84.3
Kensington CDP	8,459	-	-	7,971	87.1	0.8	4.7	1.8	5.6	18.4	24.3	46.4	39.2	40.1	3,341	91.3
Kent town (Litchfield)	2,979	2,777	-6.8	2,799	90.5	1.1	3.1	3.1	2.2	14.0	28.2	54.0	30.5	48.4	1,176	91.1
Killingly town (Windham) ..	17,375	17,336	-0.2	17,231	87.7	1.2	2.0	5.0	4.1	20.9	16.1	42.5	47.9	21.7	7,088	88.0
Killingworth town (Middlesex)	6,522	6,364	-2.4	6,392	97.2	0.5	1.3	0.4	0.6	20.5	20.3	48.0	24.2	50.8	2,304	95.4
Lake Pocotopaug CDP	3,436	-	-	3,117	87.5	0.0	6.5	1.4	4.5	13.8	14.1	47.3	36.3	42.1	1,408	95.0
Lakeville CDP	928	-	-	1,040	96.9	0.0	0.0	1.0	2.1	26.1	24.5	45.7	26.2	56.1	460	92.0
Lebanon town (New London)	7,381	7,144	-3.2	7,215	95.1	0.6	1.5	0.8	2.0	20.1	18.5	45.7	34.2	32.5	2,818	93.6

1 May be of any race.

Table A. All Places — **Population and Housing**

STATE City, town, township, borough, or CDP (county if applicable)	2010 census total population	2019 estimated population	Percent change 2010-2019	ACS total population estimate 2015-2019	White alone, not Hispanic or Latino	Black alone, not Hispanic or Latino	Asian alone, not Hispanic or Latino	All other races or 2 or more races, not Hispanic or Latino	Hispanic or Latino[1]	Under 18 years old	Age 65 years and older	Median age	Percent High school diploma or less	Percent Bachelor's degree or more	Total occupied housing units	Percent with a computer
	1	2	3	4	5	6	7	8	9	10	11	12	13	14	15	16
CONNECTICUT—Con.																
Ledyard town (New London)	15,048	14,621	-2.8	14,761	81.2	2.5	4.6	6.4	5.4	22.6	14.6	38.1	24.3	40.9	5,769	95.6
Lisbon town (New London)	4,338	4,220	-2.7	4,247	94.2	0.3	1.7	2.7	1.2	19.2	16.1	44.8	41.0	23.7	1,714	91.0
Litchfield borough	1,258	1,205	-4.2	1,245	93.8	2.4	0.6	0.7	2.4	15.9	39.8	59.5	27.5	39.7	506	86.6
Litchfield town (Litchfield)	8,454	8,094	-4.3	8,147	89.5	1.4	0.9	0.8	7.4	16.7	29.4	53.9	34.0	42.1	3,415	89.3
Long Hill CDP	4,205	-	-	4,369	65.0	5.4	12.0	6.1	11.4	12.3	17.1	33.2	41.9	34.5	2,280	83.9
Lyme town (New London)	2,405	2,316	-3.7	2,499	94.1	2.0	0.5	1.0	2.4	18.7	27.4	51.7	16.8	60.4	1,056	97.2
Madison town (New Haven)	18,258	18,030	-1.2	18,113	91.2	0.4	2.4	3.5	2.5	22.9	23.7	49.3	15.0	64.6	6,912	93.0
Madison Center CDP	2,290	-	-	2,197	94.2	0.3	2.6	0.0	2.9	17.3	36.0	59.3	25.8	55.0	1,167	80.8
Manchester CDP	30,577	-	-	29,972	54.4	18.6	4.9	4.2	17.9	21.5	13.9	35.0	37.6	29.5	12,421	91.1
Manchester town (Hartford)	58,253	57,584	-1.1	57,805	54.7	15.4	11.6	4.9	13.5	21.4	14.6	35.7	32.4	39.9	23,645	93.4
Mansfield town (Tolland)	26,610	25,487	-4.2	25,799	78.3	3.7	10.6	2.0	5.4	8.8	8.5	21.0	21.8	56.0	5,740	94.9
Mansfield Center CDP	947	-	-	939	74.3	0.5	12.8	0.0	12.4	24.1	15.4	35.1	19.9	61.9	342	98.0
Marlborough town (Hartford)	6,390	6,335	-0.9	6,368	91.9	1.3	0.6	0.4	5.7	21.2	17.6	44.6	24.6	50.8	2,331	95.2
Mashantucket CDP	-	-	-	247	11.7	0.8	0.4	85.0	2.0	22.7	15.0	30.9	28.7	25.9	76	97.4
Meriden city and town (New Haven)	60,825	59,395	-2.4	59,676	57.5	9.2	1.7	2.4	29.2	19.4	16.3	40.9	52.0	22.3	25,595	85.0
Middlebury town (New Haven)	7,612	7,798	2.4	7,739	89.6	0.4	3.8	1.7	4.5	19.7	22.0	47.3	24.8	51.2	2,749	89.8
Middlefield town (Middlesex)	4,425	4,374	-1.2	4,381	96.2	0.0	1.9	0.3	1.6	17.4	19.5	48.4	39.3	37.1	1,758	92.4
Middletown city and town (Middlesex)	47,648	46,258	-2.9	46,511	67.0	13.0	5.7	3.1	11.2	17.0	15.3	37.0	35.2	38.0	19,294	87.8
Milford consolidated city and town (New Haven)	52,756	54,747	3.8	54,328	82.7	2.9	6.6	1.9	5.8	17.0	19.4	45.7	30.7	43.0	22,451	91.9
Milford city (balance)	51,261	53,195	3.8	52,732	82.4	3.0	6.8	1.9	5.8	17.0	19.3	45.5	31.1	42.6	21,698	91.9
Monroe town (Fairfield)	19,476	19,434	-0.2	19,546	85.1	1.7	4.4	2.2	6.6	24.8	15.6	43.3	27.1	49.4	6,673	93.8
Montville town (New London)	19,569	18,508	-5.4	18,835	73.1	5.9	4.7	5.3	11.0	16.5	17.1	43.7	48.0	20.1	6,997	92.1
Moodus CDP	1,413	-	-	1,391	88.8	0.0	0.3	0.0	10.9	14.4	17.0	41.8	45.9	23.8	668	94.6
Moosup CDP	3,231	-	-	4,173	84.5	0.0	5.6	0.0	9.9	19.8	14.3	33.7	61.4	10.6	1,400	87.9
Morris town (Litchfield)	2,390	2,254	-5.7	2,205	96.9	0.0	0.0	1.6	1.5	22.0	16.3	46.3	33.6	38.9	854	96.0
Mystic CDP	4,205	-	-	4,249	92.0	1.4	2.4	1.0	3.1	11.5	32.4	54.8	22.9	56.7	2,017	90.1
Naugatuck borough and town (New Haven)	31,872	31,108	-2.4	31,347	72.0	9.1	2.7	3.8	12.5	21.5	14.7	39.9	41.3	27.3	11,589	89.7
New Britain city and town (Hartford)	73,203	72,495	-	72,767	40.0	11.2	2.8	2.7	43.3	23.3	13.1	33.8	55.7	19.9	28,232	83.1
New Canaan town (Fairfield)	19,778	20,233	2.3	20,276	86.3	1.5	5.0	1.8	5.3	29.0	16.3	43.9	8.7	79.5	7,116	96.5
New Fairfield town (Fairfield)	13,890	13,878	-0.1	13,955	87.5	0.6	1.3	1.9	8.7	20.5	17.7	46.4	26.9	49.9	4,971	97.3
New Hartford town (Litchfield)	6,962	6,656	-4.4	6,703	97.2	0.0	0.0	1.2	1.6	23.1	16.8	46.6	24.6	45.1	2,580	93.5
New Hartford Center CDP	1,385	-	-	1,047	91.4	0.0	0.0	4.7	3.9	25.6	11.6	38.5	26.6	34.6	503	88.9
New Haven city and town (New Haven)	129,884	130,250	0.3	130,331	29.5	31.2	4.9	3.1	31.2	22.6	10.3	30.8	46.6	34.9	49,177	87.5
Newington town (Hartford)	30,538	30,014	-1.7	30,234	75.2	4.8	6.8	3.6	9.5	17.7	21.0	45.5	34.0	39.2	12,366	91.3
New London city and town (New London)	27,620	26,858	-2.8	26,966	44.9	12.8	2.3	6.7	33.4	19.2	11.1	31.6	46.4	25.0	10,732	86.5
New Milford CDP	6,523	-	-	6,465	79.2	2.1	4.1	3.9	10.7	18.3	14.6	40.8	42.6	29.3	2,887	91.8
New Milford town (Litchfield)	28,094	26,805	-4.6	27,014	85.5	1.4	3.2	2.6	7.4	19.6	15.1	44.0	31.7	40.3	10,512	95.2
New Preston CDP	1,182	-	-	856	88.1	0.0	2.9	4.7	4.3	16.5	31.0	56.8	28.4	42.4	394	90.9
Newtown borough	1,934	1,960	1.3	1,879	91.7	0.9	4.4	0.4	2.6	25.0	16.8	46.9	17.4	62.4	674	95.3
Newtown town (Fairfield)	27,560	27,891	1.2	27,822	88.5	1.6	2.7	1.9	5.3	23.3	17.1	46.0	23.9	54.4	9,885	93.6
Niantic CDP	3,114	-	-	2,935	92.6	0.1	0.3	3.3	3.6	11.2	30.3	55.3	23.6	47.6	1,457	94.0
Noank CDP	1,796	-	-	1,432	93.9	0.2	0.0	5.0	0.9	11.6	35.0	57.4	14.4	54.4	720	92.1
Norfolk CDP	553	-	-	504	89.9	0.0	0.0	8.5	1.6	16.5	31.7	53.9	36.1	40.0	261	93.1
Norfolk town (Litchfield)	1,709	1,630	-4.6	1,628	92.6	0.4	1.0	3.1	2.9	19.1	28.2	51.9	36.2	42.2	700	93.4
North Branford town (New Haven)	14,424	14,146	-1.9	14,191	91.9	2.2	0.9	1.7	3.4	18.5	21.0	48.1	39.8	34.0	5,339	94.2
North Canaan town (Litchfield)	3,435	3,251	-5.4	3,281	85.2	3.6	0.0	0.8	10.4	15.2	26.1	49.1	51.7	23.5	1,402	87.1
North Granby CDP	1,944	-	-	1,485	98.0	0.2	0.9	0.0	0.9	22.9	19.9	47.4	14.5	67.6	515	97.7
North Grosvenor Dale CDP	1,530	-	-	1,130	88.5	0.0	0.0	3.8	7.7	29.2	9.1	35.4	59.1	12.2	493	89.9
North Haven town (New Haven)	24,088	23,683	-1.7	23,722	83.5	4.3	5.6	1.6	5.1	17.8	22.6	46.8	33.6	43.2	9,064	91.5
North Stonington town (New London)	5,297	5,196	-1.9	5,223	86.0	1.6	2.3	7.0	3.3	24.1	19.6	44.3	39.3	32.2	1,982	94.1
Northwest Harwinton CDP	3,252	-	-	3,011	95.5	2.2	0.8	0.4	1.1	16.5	26.0	51.5	35.4	33.6	1,144	96.9
Norwalk city and town (Fairfield)	85,612	88,816	3.7	88,599	50.8	13.8	5.4	2.3	27.7	20.1	15.4	40.4	34.3	43.4	34,187	93.9
Norwich city and town (New London)	40,493	38,768	-4.3	39,260	61.2	10.0	8.1	6.3	14.4	22.0	16.9	37.9	49.2	20.6	16,121	85.7
Oakville CDP	9,047	-	-	8,799	87.1	2.9	0.2	1.4	8.5	17.6	20.1	47.1	46.9	23.6	3,606	88.3
Old Greenwich CDP	6,611	-	-	6,844	79.0	0.2	4.9	3.8	12.2	32.9	13.7	41.8	8.4	80.2	2,184	97.3
Old Lyme town (New London)	7,608	7,306	-4.0	7,396	91.3	1.5	0.9	1.7	4.6	18.3	26.9	52.7	22.5	54.0	3,197	93.9
Old Mystic CDP	3,554	-	-	3,383	79.9	6.2	4.6	2.7	6.6	19.4	19.8	48.1	28.0	40.5	1,414	92.4
Old Saybrook town (Middlesex)	10,242	10,061	-1.8	10,090	89.5	0.5	2.1	2.1	5.8	16.7	26.8	51.8	26.9	47.8	4,343	94.7
Old Saybrook Center CDP	2,039	-	-	2,296	85.8	0.0	2.7	0.5	11.0	19.0	23.6	48.5	25.7	44.7	1,138	93.1
Orange town (New Haven)	13,955	13,926	-0.2	13,934	85.8	1.9	8.2	2.4	1.6	22.7	22.7	46.2	22.3	59.3	4,974	93.8
Oxford town (New Haven)	12,696	13,255	4.4	13,086	88.7	3.2	0.8	0.8	6.5	21.3	19.6	46.5	31.6	37.3	4,694	94.9
Oxoboxo River CDP	3,165	-	-	2,825	84.6	3.3	0.2	2.0	9.8	15.7	27.3	50.9	48.2	20.8	1,228	91.0
Pawcatuck CDP	5,624	-	-	5,305	86.0	1.6	1.4	4.7	6.3	21.8	18.2	44.1	38.7	34.5	2,478	91.3
Pemberwick CDP	3,680	-	-	4,083	77.2	10.1	7.5	1.5	3.7	20.4	16.5	38.2	30.8	44.5	1,445	98.3

1 May be of any race.

Table A. All Places — **Population and Housing**

STATE City, town, township, borough, or CDP (county if applicable)	2010 census total population	2019 estimated population	Percent change 2010-2019	ACS total population estimate 2015-2019	White alone, not Hispanic or Latino	Black alone, not Hispanic or Latino	Asian alone, not Hispanic or Latino	All other races or 2 or more races, not Hispanic or Latino	Hispanic or Latino[1]	Under 18 years old	Age 65 years and older	Median age	Percent High school diploma or less	Percent Bachelor's degree or more	Total	Percent with a computer
	1	2	3	4	5	6	7	8	9	10	11	12	13	14	15	16
CONNECTICUT—Con.																
Plainfield town (Windham)	15,405	15,125	-1.8	15,105	88.9	1.3	2.1	2.2	5.5	21.1	16.0	40.4	55.8	12.2	5,595	88.6
Plainfield Village CDP	2,557	-	-	1,920	88.8	2.7	0.9	4.1	3.5	11.0	30.6	49.7	65.9	10.1	834	71.8
Plainville town (Hartford)	17,658	17,534	-0.7	17,619	82.0	1.9	3.8	1.0	11.3	18.1	17.6	43.3	43.3	28.4	7,637	90.5
Plantsville CDP	-	-	-	1,692	92.5	2.2	0.0	0.0	5.3	8.0	27.4	56.1	35.9	35.2	935	90.5
Plymouth town (Litchfield)	12,243	11,598	-5.3	11,711	88.1	1.2	0.1	4.4	6.2	16.9	18.1	45.0	44.7	24.2	4,858	91.9
Pomfret town (Windham)	4,247	4,203	-	4,186	93.5	0.7	0.4	2.2	3.2	19.6	18.0	44.6	26.0	47.9	1,647	90.5
Poquonock Bridge CDP	1,727	-	-	2,098	35.4	15.8	13.0	7.7	28.1	33.9	5.8	25.8	57.4	16.1	622	86.7
Portland town (Middlesex)	9,509	9,267	-2.5	9,322	95.8	0.3	0.7	0.5	2.8	21.4	19.1	46.4	35.4	37.3	3,741	91.3
Portland CDP	5,862	-	-	5,552	95.2	0.5	0.2	0.8	3.3	19.1	22.1	45.8	39.9	28.2	2,368	89.1
Preston town (New London)	4,724	4,625	-2.1	4,657	86.2	0.2	4.6	8.0	0.9	20.3	18.6	45.9	38.4	24.5	1,830	91.3
Prospect town (New Haven)	9,424	9,702	2.9	9,705	87.4	6.6	0.5	1.9	3.6	20.8	19.7	45.6	33.0	36.9	3,347	95.8
Putnam CDP	7,214	-	-	6,615	90.2	1.1	0.7	1.8	6.2	18.1	16.0	42.7	44.7	19.9	2,991	86.7
Putnam town (Windham)	9,564	9,389	-1.8	9,361	91.6	0.9	0.7	1.9	4.9	15.6	21.7	48.8	43.3	25.3	4,096	87.4
Quinebaug CDP	1,133	-	-	1,484	99.0	0.0	0.0	1.0	0.0	18.9	20.4	49.5	37.1	24.7	587	84.2
Redding town (Fairfield)	9,143	9,116	-0.3	9,176	92.8	0.3	1.2	1.4	4.4	22.6	20.0	46.6	13.2	67.0	3,452	98.3
Ridgefield CDP	7,645	-	-	8,244	88.1	1.2	3.4	0.9	6.5	26.9	18.4	46.4	11.0	76.0	3,201	95.9
Ridgefield town (Fairfield)	24,645	24,959	1.3	25,042	87.8	1.1	4.0	2.4	4.8	27.7	17.0	45.6	9.9	74.9	9,001	95.7
Riverside CDP	8,416	-	-	8,604	71.7	1.7	12.9	2.2	11.5	31.0	14.1	42.5	11.8	73.3	2,817	96.5
Rockville CDP	7,474	-	-	7,115	66.5	17.6	1.6	1.2	13.0	22.0	12.1	31.4	52.8	16.9	3,198	83.9
Rocky Hill town (Hartford)	19,708	20,115	2.1	20,168	70.0	4.2	18.7	3.2	3.9	17.4	20.5	43.2	27.2	50.5	8,621	91.4
Roxbury town (Litchfield)	2,259	2,152	-4.7	2,105	95.1	0.0	2.5	0.4	1.9	19.1	28.0	53.3	19.6	60.6	892	95.4
Salem town (New London)	4,151	4,083	-1.6	4,112	88.2	2.9	4.6	0.0	4.3	19.9	18.4	45.7	28.6	47.8	1,661	95.7
Salisbury town (Litchfield)	3,746	3,600	-3.9	3,625	95.0	0.6	1.5	0.7	2.3	20.3	37.8	57.1	22.2	60.0	1,700	93.8
Salmon Brook CDP	2,324	-	-	2,294	92.4	0.3	3.7	2.7	1.0	18.2	23.4	50.7	31.7	41.1	1,037	86.7
Saybrook Manor CDP	1,052	-	-	933	89.3	0.0	0.0	0.0	10.7	13.1	23.8	51.2	23.9	48.9	441	92.5
Scotland town (Windham)	1,726	1,672	-3.1	1,569	94.3	0.0	0.1	1.7	3.8	19.6	19.8	46.8	42.7	24.6	614	96.3
Seymour town (New Haven)	16,528	16,437	-0.6	16,508	78.1	2.6	2.6	0.6	16.1	23.1	15.3	41.2	41.1	28.3	6,203	90.4
Sharon CDP	729	-	-	625	79.2	6.6	0.0	14.2	0.0	29.4	18.9	44.8	33.2	52.3	192	91.1
Sharon town (Litchfield)	2,780	2,689	-3.3	2,700	90.3	1.7	1.5	3.3	3.3	14.7	32.9	56.2	35.1	43.8	1,278	93.5
Shelton city and town (Fairfield)	39,558	41,129	4.0	41,141	83.7	1.6	4.3	1.5	8.8	17.4	21.1	47.2	32.0	42.7	16,185	89.5
Sherman town (Fairfield)	3,602	3,630	0.8	3,649	91.8	0.0	2.1	2.7	3.4	19.6	21.3	51.6	25.7	51.2	1,470	98.1
Sherwood Manor CDP	5,410	-	-	5,513	83.6	3.9	5.7	2.0	4.8	18.1	21.9	46.2	40.8	27.2	2,203	93.2
Simsbury town (Hartford)	23,511	25,395	8.0	24,799	87.2	2.1	3.8	2.3	4.7	23.6	18.1	45.4	14.5	65.3	9,583	95.2
Simsbury Center CDP	5,836	-	-	6,154	89.3	1.5	2.6	2.7	3.9	20.5	22.4	49.4	12.0	64.9	2,590	95.4
Somers CDP	1,789	-	-	1,948	92.2	0.5	0.4	0.0	6.8	25.1	21.6	46.2	25.6	49.0	807	88.4
Somers town (Tolland)	11,451	10,784	-5.8	11,005	85.0	5.6	1.6	1.5	6.3	17.5	19.3	47.5	38.1	38.6	3,625	92.1
Southbury town (New Haven)	19,903	19,571	-1.7	19,681	89.8	1.4	2.2	1.3	5.3	20.7	29.8	52.4	27.1	50.2	7,966	90.6
South Coventry CDP	1,483	-	-	1,224	97.9	0.8	0.0	1.3	0.0	12.7	21.9	54.2	28.7	50.0	563	94.5
Southington town (Hartford)	43,103	43,834	1.7	43,781	89.9	1.8	2.5	1.0	4.7	20.6	21.6	45.3	34.8	39.5	17,162	91.6
Southport CDP	1,585	-	-	1,661	86.2	2.2	1.9	0.9	8.8	16.7	29.7	56.3	12.6	74.9	777	98.5
South Windham CDP	1,421	-	-	1,459	74.4	1.6	2.3	1.2	20.5	28.6	14.7	33.0	43.0	21.4	609	86.4
South Windsor town (Hartford)	25,703	26,162	1.8	25,898	75.8	4.1	11.6	2.7	5.8	22.0	17.4	42.3	25.9	49.4	9,783	93.0
Southwood Acres CDP	7,657	-	-	7,473	85.1	2.8	2.3	2.5	7.2	17.8	18.5	43.7	38.7	29.0	3,004	91.2
South Woodstock CDP	1,291	-	-	1,408	100.0	0.0	0.0	0.0	0.0	15.2	19.7	40.9	26.4	41.6	628	95.2
Sprague town (New London)	2,984	2,859	-4.2	2,906	85.6	2.6	1.2	6.6	3.9	22.4	16.4	40.2	47.4	22.3	1,149	91.2
Stafford town (Tolland)	12,080	11,893	-1.5	11,881	92.4	0.6	1.0	2.6	3.5	18.2	17.4	44.3	44.7	21.9	4,707	90.6
Stafford Springs CDP	4,988	-	-	5,023	94.0	0.5	0.2	1.6	3.8	18.6	14.6	40.7	43.7	21.5	2,011	87.5
Stamford city and town (Fairfield)	122,633	129,638	5.7	129,309	49.3	12.8	8.5	2.2	27.2	20.5	14.4	36.9	31.1	50.1	49,141	92.6
Sterling town (Windham)	3,825	3,782	-1.1	3,757	90.0	6.0	0.0	0.5	3.4	24.5	13.6	42.5	42.8	21.6	1,446	93.6
Stonington borough	929	884	-4.8	934	96.4	0.9	2.0	0.7	0.0	9.4	36.3	58.3	15.7	58.6	526	94.7
Stonington town (New London)	18,538	18,559	0.1	18,445	90.1	1.4	2.1	2.3	4.1	17.1	24.8	50.8	28.7	47.1	8,210	93.2
Storrs CDP	15,344	-	-	16,352	76.5	3.8	12.7	1.3	5.6	2.3	4.4	20.4	19.5	61.6	1,956	90.7
Stratford town (Fairfield)	51,380	51,849	0.9	52,120	61.8	15.6	2.3	2.2	18.0	19.0	18.9	42.6	39.6	33.2	19,857	89.9
Suffield town (Hartford)	15,735	15,814	0.5	15,688	79.3	7.2	3.9	1.9	7.8	19.1	15.7	43.5	33.3	43.4	5,158	95.4
Suffield Depot CDP	1,325	-	-	1,227	91.6	4.0	0.0	0.0	4.4	23.7	18.6	46.2	44.5	33.2	486	86.0
Tariffville CDP	1,324	-	-	1,529	77.9	1.4	4.5	4.9	11.2	22.2	8.6	37.6	34.4	34.3	627	97.4
Terramuggus CDP	1,025	-	-	956	100.0	0.0	0.0	0.0	0.0	10.0	15.0	53.9	5.5	68.2	354	100.0
Terryville CDP	5,387	-	-	5,030	88.0	1.3	0.0	4.3	6.3	16.4	16.0	43.6	58.9	19.7	2,324	88.5
Thomaston CDP	1,910	-	-	1,580	95.1	1.5	0.0	0.0	3.5	11.5	29.2	53.4	60.8	21.4	846	86.1
Thomaston town (Litchfield)	7,894	7,535	-4.5	7,599	95.2	0.6	0.8	0.3	3.1	18.8	17.3	45.8	43.4	27.7	3,157	92.8
Thompson town (Windham)	9,491	9,379	-1.2	9,351	94.2	0.1	0.7	1.9	3.1	20.6	15.0	43.5	40.1	28.1	3,569	89.5
Thompsonville CDP	8,577	-	-	8,701	61.3	8.1	3.1	4.2	23.3	22.5	11.9	36.4	52.9	19.9	3,580	91.3
Tolland town (Tolland)	15,056	14,618	-2.9	14,713	91.8	0.7	3.5	2.4	1.6	23.2	15.9	43.4	23.2	49.3	5,252	96.6
Torrington city and town (Litchfield)	36,391	34,044	-6.4	34,489	81.2	2.8	2.9	1.8	11.4	18.6	19.6	44.9	47.8	22.7	14,471	88.8
Trumbull town (Fairfield)	36,005	35,673	-0.9	35,976	79.6	4.5	6.5	2.4	7.0	25.1	18.3	43.0	22.6	55.3	12,190	93.7
Union town (Tolland)	851	839	-1.4	894	95.5	0.0	2.0	2.1	0.3	15.3	29.8	53.3	33.7	38.1	374	91.7
Vernon town (Tolland)	29,183	29,359	0.6	29,232	73.8	7.2	6.5	2.1	10.6	17.7	17.6	37.9	37.6	35.8	13,039	89.9
Voluntown town (New London)	2,603	2,510	-3.6	2,535	93.8	0.0	0.9	2.4	2.9	20.1	14.8	45.7	39.0	23.3	987	88.4
Wallingford town (New Haven)	45,123	44,326	-1.8	44,596	84.3	1.5	4.7	1.0	8.4	18.8	22.1	47.4	39.5	34.7	18,664	88.1
Wallingford Center CDP	18,209	-	-	18,360	77.1	1.9	5.0	1.4	14.6	16.6	19.3	43.4	46.0	28.0	7,886	84.5
Warren town (Litchfield)	1,461	1,395	-4.5	1,457	94.0	1.0	0.8	1.2	3.0	19.3	25.3	51.1	27.5	48.8	593	93.6
Washington town (Litchfield)	3,578	3,428	-4.2	3,450	88.5	1.2	2.0	1.5	6.8	17.4	27.4	53.7	22.8	56.6	1,388	94.8
Waterbury city and town (New Haven)	110,309	107,568	-2.5	108,276	37.8	18.8	2.3	3.6	37.4	24.7	13.3	34.8	57.8	15.7	40,937	82.5
Waterford CDP	2,887	-	-	3,008	80.7	5.3	6.0	1.8	6.2	17.3	25.4	41.6	48.7	23.0	1,335	79.3

1 May be of any race.

Table A. All Places — **Population and Housing**

STATE City, town, township, borough, or CDP (county if applicable)	Population — 2010 census total population	2019 estimated population	Percent change 2010-2019	ACS total population estimate 2015-2019	White alone, not Hispanic or Latino	Black alone, not Hispanic or Latino	Asian alone, not Hispanic or Latino	All other races or 2 or more races, not Hispanic or Latino	Hispanic or Latino[1]	Under 18 years old	Age 65 years and older	Median age	Percent High school diploma or less	Percent Bachelor's degree or more	Occupied housing units — Total	Percent with a computer
	1	2	3	4	5	6	7	8	9	10	11	12	13	14	15	16
Connecticut—Con.																
Waterford town (New London)	19,519	18,746	-4.0	18,935	85.1	2.8	3.3	2.5	6.3	18.4	23.2	48.4	32.8	40.5	7,715	91.4
Watertown CDP	3,574	-	-	3,350	91.3	2.4	1.6	0.0	4.7	14.3	18.1	45.9	23.6	44.4	1,462	88.1
Watertown town (Litchfield)	22,538	21,578	-4.3	21,751	88.3	1.8	2.0	1.2	6.6	17.9	19.1	45.8	38.7	33.8	8,513	89.5
Wauregan CDP	1,205	-	-	1,458	86.5	1.9	0.0	5.8	5.8	35.7	3.6	33.8	52.9	12.7	452	98.2
Weatogue CDP	2,776	-	-	2,738	91.8	0.6	3.2	0.0	4.5	25.4	13.5	41.4	13.0	72.6	973	95.7
Westbrook town (Middlesex)	6,938	6,869		6,903	92.1	1.1	0.9	3.2	2.8	10.4	27.4	54.2	29.7	49.3	3,169	93.4
Westbrook Center CDP	2,413	-	-	2,237	88.2	0.9	0.2	8.1	2.5	8.7	32.1	58.5	33.0	39.9	1,127	94.9
West Hartford town (Hartford)	63,296	62,965	-0.5	63,063	72.9	5.4	7.8	2.7	11.2	22.0	18.4	40.7	18.8	64.7	24,726	92.3
West Haven city and town (New Haven)	55,564	54,620	-1.7	54,763	50.3	18.8	4.1	3.6	23.2	19.7	13.7	36.6	51.4	24.3	19,886	90.9
Weston town (Fairfield)	10,191	10,252	0.6	10,287	83.2	1.7	3.7	5.2	6.3	28.9	14.3	46.8	9.9	78.4	3,447	98.4
Westport town (Fairfield)	26,395	28,491	7.9	28,016	86.0	1.0	6.1	2.4	4.5	27.1	17.1	45.8	10.5	78.0	9,916	97.1
West Simsbury CDP	2,447	-	-	2,764	90.8	0.1	5.0	0.0	4.2	21.2	26.7	50.7	18.2	59.1	900	98.2
Wethersfield town (Hartford)	26,668	26,008	-2.5	26,171	81.8	3.4	4.2	2.6	8.0	19.1	19.3	44.5	32.7	45.3	10,917	89.0
Willimantic CDP	17,737	-	-	17,358	45.0	5.9	2.2	2.6	44.2	17.4	10.3	28.5	57.4	18.2	5,706	85.8
Willington town (Tolland)	6,034	5,864	-2.8	5,893	83.4	1.6	7.5	3.3	4.2	12.6	11.7	33.6	32.0	40.3	2,577	92.3
Wilton town (Fairfield)	18,036	18,343	1.7	18,463	85.2	0.9	8.3	2.0	3.6	28.5	17.0	43.6	10.5	76.3	6,090	97.0
Wilton Center CDP	732	-	-	788	76.3	0.0	13.5	2.2	8.1	17.9	28.4	50.9	11.4	70.5	380	96.1
Winchester town (Litchfield)	11,244	10,604	-5.7	10,730	90.2	0.5	1.2	3.2	4.8	15.9	19.1	47.1	48.7	23.6	4,550	86.1
Windham town (Windham)	25,209	24,561	-2.6	24,655	50.6	4.4	1.7	2.1	41.1	19.8	12.5	30.8	53.5	18.6	8,590	87.9
Windsor town (Hartford)	29,052	28,733	-1.1	28,859	46.8	37.6	4.3	2.4	9.0	18.9	17.7	43.6	30.6	41.0	10,770	93.2
Windsor Locks town (Hartford)	12,498	12,854	2.8	12,671	80.8	5.8	4.6	4.2	4.6	19.6	19.1	43.9	45.7	24.9	5,307	87.8
Winsted CDP	7,712	-	-	7,121	87.9	0.5	0.0	4.9	6.7	18.4	17.5	42.9	54.3	14.9	2,963	81.9
Wolcott town (New Haven)	16,700	16,587	-0.7	16,615	88.1	2.2	1.7	1.4	6.6	21.2	18.9	45.8	39.1	28.9	6,052	91.0
Woodbridge town (New Haven)	8,977	8,750	-2.5	8,827	74.5	3.0	15.7	1.1	5.7	23.2	24.8	49.3	16.4	68.0	2,897	96.5
Woodbury town (Litchfield)	9,978	9,502	-4.8	9,562	91.0	0.5	2.2	1.3	5.0	18.9	23.1	50.3	25.6	47.8	4,129	91.9
Woodbury Center CDP	1,294	-	-	1,194	93.0	0.0	3.4	2.9	0.8	17.1	23.8	49.1	22.8	51.0	616	81.8
Woodmont borough	1,495	1,552	3.8	1,596	90.9	1.3	0.6	2.0	5.3	14.5	21.4	51.0	19.9	55.1	753	91.5
Woodstock town (Windham)	7,964	7,858	-1.3	7,836	98.0	0.0	0.3	1.2	0.5	20.0	17.7	44.5	29.6	41.3	3,249	94.4
DELAWARE	897,937	973,764	8.4	957,248	62.3	21.7	3.8	3.0	9.2	21.3	18.2	40.6	41.3	32.0	363,322	91.6
Arden village	433	440	1.6	380	95.5	2.4	0.8	0.8	0.5	10.8	27.6	55.5	24.7	54.1	181	97.2
Ardencroft village	211	216	2.4	220	90.0	1.4	0.0	2.7	5.9	13.2	24.5	53.9	23.5	47.5	88	95.5
Ardentown village	267	270	1.1	273	93.8	0.7	2.9	1.5	1.1	23.8	28.9	49.6	19.8	51.5	121	86.8
Bear CDP	19,371	-	-	20,850	34.5	37.0	5.1	2.3	21.1	23.3	10.4	36.1	44.4	32.5	7,345	96.1
Bellefonte town	1,193	1,164	-2.4	1,173	89.9	3.2	1.0	4.4	1.5	20.4	11.1	41.9	33.2	41.6	487	93.6
Bethany Beach town	1,055	1,245	18.0	854	96.3	0.0	1.5	0.8	1.4	6.8	61.9	67.6	18.2	58.6	466	89.9
Bethel town	173	201	16.2	268	99.3	0.0	0.0	0.7	0.0	19.0	22.0	48.5	36.0	29.0	100	98.0
Blades town	1,240	1,454	17.3	1,374	38.4	41.0	2.1	4.5	13.9	30.5	15.3	33.6	60.9	8.3	474	81.2
Bowers town	336	374	11.3	319	81.2	4.1	0.3	1.3	13.2	13.5	18.8	43.5	53.0	22.6	145	79.3
Bridgeville town	2,008	2,366	17.8	3,137	50.6	29.6	1.7	3.2	15.0	20.2	35.5	53.8	45.9	29.1	1,292	85.9
Brookside CDP	14,353	-	-	13,396	60.5	16.7	4.1	3.1	15.6	20.8	13.5	35.4	51.5	23.5	4,883	95.7
Camden town	3,440	3,551	3.2	3,484	60.0	22.0	5.5	1.7	10.8	22.9	21.1	41.5	33.0	37.1	1,393	96.4
Cheswold town	1,494	1,695	13.5	1,483	53.3	28.5	2.6	4.2	11.4	26.2	16.6	40.8	56.7	13.6	594	88.7
Claymont CDP	8,253	-	-	9,330	56.8	28.0	5.9	2.5	6.8	21.7	13.0	37.1	44.5	25.2	3,614	90.2
Clayton town	2,935	3,508	19.5	3,282	51.7	36.3	1.3	2.0	8.7	28.5	8.0	34.5	49.7	23.6	1,026	99.1
Dagsboro town	789	927	17.5	986	73.9	8.1	6.0	7.2	4.8	28.5	21.9	38.2	48.2	26.3	352	91.5
Delaware City city	1,776	1,837	3.4	1,771	75.8	14.0	0.0	5.3	5.0	27.6	18.1	39.6	59.8	13.9	647	90.7
Delmar town	1,584	1,822	15.0	1,808	71.5	20.1	2.6	4.8	1.1	25.4	20.1	39.1	58.3	14.4	689	83.7
Dewey Beach town	340	400	17.6	332	97.0	0.0	0.0	1.5	1.5	6.9	41.3	61.3	14.6	62.5	177	92.7
Dover city	35,802	38,166	6.6	37,523	39.3	44.8	2.6	5.6	7.7	21.6	14.4	30.7	41.2	26.3	14,098	88.9
Dover Base Housing CDP	3,450	-	-	3,614	68.8	9.7	0.2	3.0	18.3	33.1	1.0	24.6	18.9	25.8	1,247	100.0
Edgemoor CDP	5,677	-	-	6,934	35.2	49.4	10.6	2.9	1.9	27.2	12.6	37.1	32.6	33.1	2,757	92.6
Ellendale town	370	434	17.3	552	56.2	28.8	0.4	2.0	12.7	28.3	11.8	31.3	62.9	4.0	173	89.6
Elsmere town	6,072	5,872	-3.3	5,943	58.9	12.6	1.0	0.1	27.4	20.6	13.1	34.8	55.3	22.8	2,351	90.7
Farmington town	110	122	10.9	122	95.1	0.0	0.0	0.0	4.9	36.1	9.0	35.4	78.7	2.7	34	94.1
Felton town	1,282	1,414	10.3	1,355	66.2	26.2	0.2	3.7	3.7	21.3	16.3	42.0	36.8	34.0	522	87.0
Fenwick Island town	378	445	17.7	505	96.8	0.0	0.0	3.2	0.0	7.9	53.9	66.8	19.9	54.3	272	95.2
Frankford town	844	987	16.9	867	26.2	36.8	1.5	11.4	24.1	33.6	10.3	30.9	68.3	11.7	266	85.7
Frederica town	760	849	11.7	967	36.9	41.7	2.3	5.3	13.9	29.6	14.0	31.9	63.1	14.9	348	93.4
Georgetown town	6,428	7,563	17.7	7,259	42.2	12.7	4.5	1.7	38.9	28.6	17.7	32.2	59.1	14.8	2,583	78.3
Glasgow CDP	14,303	-	-	14,359	60.9	23.8	6.1	3.1	6.1	22.1	10.5	37.7	29.9	35.4	5,083	97.8
Greenville CDP	2,326	-	-	2,467	78.4	2.6	17.4	0.4	1.2	19.7	24.2	43.4	9.0	76.9	1,120	96.8
Greenwood town	973	1,139	17.1	1,225	54.4	28.7	0.0	1.1	15.8	26.4	11.6	29.9	50.2	9.1	438	91.3
Harrington city	3,561	3,638	2.2	3,652	51.4	38.8	0.1	4.1	5.6	32.0	14.4	28.8	50.3	14.4	1,282	87.6
Hartly town	68	76	11.8	35	100.0	0.0	0.0	0.0	0.0	22.9	5.7	31.9	62.5	8.3	15	66.7
Henlopen Acres town	122	144	18.0	182	100.0	0.0	0.0	0.0	0.0	16.5	42.3	61.9	6.1	73.6	82	98.8
Highland Acres CDP	3,459	-	-	3,446	74.3	14.7	3.1	4.4	3.6	17.6	24.4	51.1	32.8	36.4	1,344	95.8
Hockessin CDP	13,527	-	-	13,157	81.8	4.6	8.6	2.9	2.0	21.2	24.5	48.3	17.1	64.9	4,774	95.6
Houston town	369	405	9.8	452	75.7	12.6	0.0	0.9	10.8	21.5	11.5	39.9	57.9	8.7	163	86.5
Kent Acres CDP	1,890	-	-	2,519	49.8	30.4	1.8	8.6	9.4	29.9	14.3	32.4	46.5	20.9	871	97.7
Kenton town	243	271	11.5	244	79.5	7.4	0.0	4.5	8.6	24.2	7.0	39.7	57.0	10.6	88	85.2
Laurel town	3,718	4,356	17.2	4,179	31.6	51.6	0.0	3.2	13.6	44.0	6.9	22.9	60.4	15.0	1,250	91.2
Leipsic town	186	205	10.2	164	84.1	0.0	0.0	3.0	12.8	22.0	15.2	46.9	59.2	10.4	81	87.7
Lewes city	2,848	3,322	16.6	3,198	89.6	2.5	0.0	5.9	1.9	9.1	53.0	66.0	24.2	48.8	1,565	88.9
Little Creek town	215	235	9.3	239	79.5	0.0	0.0	2.5	18.0	20.1	15.5	37.1	60.6	9.4	92	95.7
Long Neck CDP	1,980	-	-	2,487	91.4	3.3	0.7	1.4	3.2	11.9	38.7	60.4	56.7	16.5	1,146	90.5
Magnolia town	267	289	8.2	337	57.6	40.7	0.0	0.0	1.8	31.2	13.4	30.1	35.0	27.1	98	89.8
Middletown town	18,869	22,900	21.4	21,692	57.3	26.4	4.4	2.3	9.6	27.9	16.3	39.2	30.9	39.9	7,709	96.6
Milford city	9,591	11,732	22.3	11,111	51.9	25.7	1.4	4.9	16.1	26.4	20.6	38.3	40.8	25.1	4,356	87.9
Millsboro town	3,861	4,533	17.4	4,342	67.8	21.9	2.0	0.0	8.3	29.7	22.2	38.9	39.0	32.1	1,594	93.2
Millville town	528	626	18.6	1,755	90.9	0.6	0.5	0.9	7.0	21.1	31.8	54.0	25.5	52.4	746	97.3

1 May be of any race.

Table A. All Places — **Population and Housing**

STATE City, town, township, borough, or CDP (county if applicable)	2010 census total population	2019 estimated population	Percent change 2010-2019	ACS total population estimate 2015-2019	White alone, not Hispanic or Latino	Black alone, not Hispanic or Latino	Asian alone, not Hispanic or Latino	All other races or 2 or more races, not Hispanic or Latino	Hispanic or Latino[1]	Under 18 years old	Age 65 years and older	Median age	Percent High school diploma or less	Percent Bachelor's degree or more	Total	Percent with a computer
	1	2	3	4	5	6	7	8	9	10	11	12	13	14	15	16
DELAWARE—Con.																
Milton town	2,561	3,012	17.6	2,893	80.9	8.1	0.2	3.6	7.3	22.1	35.2	47.4	27.3	39.2	1,372	83.5
Newark city	31,467	33,515	6.5	33,448	72.2	8.6	8.5	3.6	7.1	10.7	13.6	24.8	23.0	53.2	10,737	95.6
New Castle city	5,106	5,392	5.6	5,242	63.6	26.4	1.5	2.2	6.3	10.7	20.8	51.0	45.8	31.1	2,401	90.1
Newport town	1,072	1,039	-3.1	1,182	42.2	23.0	0.3	1.9	32.5	23.5	9.1	32.0	68.3	10.9	480	90.6
North Star CDP	7,980	-	-	7,503	82.2	3.6	9.8	3.7	0.7	19.9	23.5	50.3	17.3	66.0	2,745	98.0
Ocean View town	1,844	2,190	18.8	2,272	91.8	0.0	0.6	3.5	4.1	12.1	37.1	59.4	25.2	43.9	1,060	95.7
Odessa town	362	360	-0.6	511	85.3	12.7	0.0	0.0	2.0	21.1	19.6	47.3	38.8	31.6	199	94.0
Pike Creek CDP	7,898	-	-	7,613	72.9	4.7	18.7	2.1	1.6	21.2	18.2	44.9	16.1	67.8	3,085	99.1
Pike Creek Valley CDP	11,217	-	-	10,989	66.7	15.6	7.7	4.8	5.2	19.6	15.2	39.8	22.4	46.3	4,799	94.6
Rehoboth Beach city	1,319	1,546	17.2	1,400	96.1	0.5	0.6	0.3	2.5	4.6	47.6	64.1	12.5	68.0	763	93.7
Rising Sun-Lebanon CDP	3,391	-	-	4,065	56.0	19.6	1.7	3.1	19.6	29.0	7.5	36.5	37.2	25.3	1,394	98.7
Riverview CDP	2,456	-	-	2,314	71.4	21.7	1.3	5.6	0.0	22.6	15.9	44.4	34.6	37.9	834	96.4
Rodney Village CDP	1,487	-	-	1,304	35.2	57.1	0.8	4.1	2.8	24.8	19.4	41.5	69.5	6.5	504	94.0
St. Georges CDP	-	-	-	767	63.5	22.0	0.0	3.4	11.1	23.1	8.5	44.4	46.7	27.2	299	100.0
Seaford city	6,894	8,013	16.2	7,715	53.4	26.4	2.5	4.3	13.4	22.8	17.3	39.0	55.9	14.8	3,044	79.6
Selbyville town	2,164	2,540	17.4	2,444	75.9	5.5	0.0	0.3	18.3	19.7	18.7	44.6	45.5	23.8	910	86.9
Slaughter Beach town	206	241	17.0	251	90.0	4.4	0.8	2.4	2.4	6.0	39.0	63.3	25.1	48.0	137	88.3
Smyrna town	10,047	11,813	17.6	11,484	61.5	27.9	0.6	4.0	6.0	25.5	12.6	37.6	43.5	25.9	4,327	93.1
South Bethany town	449	530	18.0	426	97.4	0.0	0.7	0.0	1.9	1.2	62.7	69.5	14.7	61.1	249	94.8
Townsend town	2,053	2,659	29.5	2,434	52.3	33.9	1.5	6.3	6.0	32.5	6.1	32.5	34.2	39.5	657	99.7
Viola town	152	165	8.6	147	94.6	0.0	0.0	0.0	5.4	17.0	19.0	59.8	45.2	24.3	55	96.4
Wilmington city	70,875	70,166		70,644	29.2	57.4	1.2	2.0	10.2	22.7	12.9	35.6	51.4	28.0	28,806	84.8
Wilmington Manor CDP	7,889	-	-	7,903	51.9	21.9	1.5	4.1	20.6	24.3	12.8	35.8	58.4	15.3	2,948	93.1
Woodside town	176	193	9.7	149	79.2	8.1	0.0	6.0	6.7	5.4	20.1	55.2	72.5	6.5	71	74.6
Woodside East CDP	2,316	-	-	2,427	50.7	35.4	5.0	8.1	0.8	20.6	12.9	38.7	67.6	13.8	873	84.3
Wyoming town	1,317	1,549	17.6	1,381	63.5	23.6	3.0	5.3	4.6	25.3	10.2	34.6	28.4	30.2	571	91.6
DISTRICT OF COLUMBIA	601,767	705,749	17.3	692,683	36.6	45.4	3.9	3.1	11.0	17.9	12.1	34.0	25.9	58.5	284,386	91.8
Washington city	601,767	705,749	17.3	692,683	36.6	45.4	3.9	3.1	11.0	17.9	12.1	34.0	25.9	58.5	284,386	91.8
FLORIDA	18,804,564	21,477,737	14.2	20,901,636	53.9	15.3	2.7	2.5	25.6	20.0	20.1	42.0	40.4	29.9	7,736,311	91.5
Acacia Villas CDP	427	-	-	381	24.4	0.0	0.0	0.0	75.6	34.1	0.0	20.0	48.0	5.7	115	100.0
Alachua city	9,041	9,899	9.5	9,867	60.6	29.2	1.3	0.8	8.0	27.1	14.3	36.9	32.3	38.3	3,571	93.4
Alafaya CDP	78,113	-	-	91,068	43.3	9.5	7.4	3.7	36.1	22.8	10.2	34.2	25.6	43.2	29,616	96.8
Alford town	482	463	-3.9	630	94.9	0.8	0.0	1.3	3.0	22.5	23.7	47.3	73.5	3.3	250	72.0
Allentown CDP	894	-	-	781	97.8	0.0	0.0	2.2	0.0	16.5	31.8	55.5	40.7	15.6	373	100.0
Altamonte Springs city	41,569	44,143	6.2	43,810	50.0	14.0	3.3	4.4	28.2	18.6	14.4	36.4	25.2	38.5	19,393	95.9
Altha town	512	492	-3.9	514	92.2	0.0	0.0	1.9	5.8	24.7	19.1	40.3	52.9	10.2	190	68.9
Altoona CDP	89	-	-	85	77.6	0.0	0.0	0.0	22.4	27.1	14.1	28.7	23.1	65.4	38	84.2
Alturas CDP	4,185	-	-	3,475	83.4	1.1	0.0	1.5	14.0	19.1	20.1	44.3	63.6	10.8	1,271	97.6
Alva CDP	2,596	-	-	2,952	86.2	2.3	1.1	7.0	3.3	11.7	32.2	55.4	41.9	20.9	1,123	95.0
Andrews CDP	798	-	-	675	78.1	0.0	5.2	15.0	1.8	12.1	27.3	58.4	67.5	0.0	274	94.9
Anna Maria city	1,503	1,762	17.2	719	95.7	0.0	0.1	2.8	1.4	6.1	54.1	67.1	24.9	47.3	384	84.9
Apalachicola city	2,230	2,354	5.6	2,514	65.2	30.4	1.2	0.2	3.1	17.9	22.0	45.2	54.7	22.7	1,088	86.2
Apollo Beach CDP	14,055	-	-	20,947	70.7	7.0	2.1	3.9	16.3	20.8	18.1	45.0	26.2	40.6	8,043	98.2
Apopka city	42,194	53,447	26.7	51,800	43.4	23.1	3.4	2.4	27.8	24.8	12.8	37.3	39.8	27.5	17,184	91.0
Arcadia city	7,627	8,314	9.0	8,072	47.1	24.1	0.1	1.3	27.4	27.5	14.2	32.6	72.5	11.0	2,718	61.6
Archer city	1,111	1,198	7.8	1,262	47.5	36.2	1.5	9.4	5.5	28.5	8.8	32.5	45.8	26.0	470	80.4
Aripeka CDP	308	-	-	109	76.1	0.0	0.0	0.0	23.9	0.0	61.5	71.4	67.9	0.0	63	92.1
Asbury Lake CDP	8,700	-	-	10,160	83.7	6.7	2.5	2.2	5.0	29.0	11.2	38.6	34.2	23.2	3,368	97.0
Astatula town	1,809	2,085	15.3	2,018	72.2	3.9	0.0	1.1	22.9	26.5	14.0	35.1	60.1	11.6	688	85.9
Astor CDP	1,556	-	-	1,595	71.5	0.0	0.0	8.5	20.0	17.2	28.1	55.9	55.3	19.3	683	80.7
Atlantic Beach city	12,671	13,872	9.5	13,575	82.9	7.3	3.1	2.9	3.8	18.1	23.0	47.6	27.3	52.7	6,005	91.7
Atlantis city	1,995	2,129	6.7	1,962	84.9	3.4	3.4	0.3	8.0	11.0	42.0	60.5	17.0	63.3	888	95.2
Auburndale city	13,455	16,650	23.7	15,799	68.9	13.3	0.7	1.2	15.9	25.1	17.0	38.1	49.1	21.4	5,267	84.1
Aucilla CDP	100	-	-	198	68.2	13.1	0.0	0.0	18.7	8.1	3.0	42.0	85.2	3.8	107	100.0
Avalon CDP	679	-	-	556	86.7	0.0	1.4	0.0	11.9	2.3	20.9	29.8	30.9	25.2	265	100.0
Aventura city	35,742	36,987	3.5	37,303	54.9	2.1	1.8	1.2	40.0	14.6	28.8	51.1	17.9	52.7	18,035	91.6
Avon Park city	10,050	10,689	6.4	10,461	37.8	30.9	0.6	2.0	28.8	28.7	20.4	33.6	61.5	10.0	3,421	82.7
Azalea Park CDP	12,556	-	-	14,700	22.3	7.8	3.6	2.0	64.3	22.3	11.5	35.5	56.1	15.6	4,606	95.8
Babson Park CDP	1,356	-	-	1,313	69.1	19.2	1.2	0.0	10.5	19.9	13.7	26.1	56.0	19.6	394	93.4
Bagdad CDP	3,761	-	-	3,728	81.7	4.7	2.6	4.6	6.5	19.2	17.6	38.7	42.7	27.9	1,368	86.9
Baldwin town	1,440	1,489	3.4	1,644	72.9	16.9	0.0	4.4	5.8	25.0	10.3	31.6	64.7	10.3	588	79.6
Bal Harbour village	2,693	2,961	10.0	3,004	57.8	2.2	2.8	1.7	35.5	13.9	36.4	51.6	19.2	61.5	1,424	95.0
Balm CDP	1,457	-	-	4,362	46.6	26.4	2.4	1.7	23.0	25.7	7.4	32.6	38.7	24.6	1,399	97.7
Bardmoor CDP	9,732	-	-	9,373	86.8	2.3	1.8	3.4	5.7	19.6	25.2	46.9	34.1	36.4	3,790	90.5
Bartow city	17,172	20,147	17.3	19,440	54.7	21.5	2.6	2.7	18.4	26.2	16.0	36.6	52.5	19.9	6,633	83.7
Bascom town	120	115	-4.2	56	100.0	0.0	0.0	0.0	0.0	12.5	26.8	58.3	60.0	0.0	34	82.4
Bay Harbor Islands town	5,533	5,793	4.7	5,861	46.9	4.0	1.5	1.6	46.0	27.9	16.0	41.1	13.5	54.2	2,418	97.9
Bay Hill CDP	4,884	-	-	4,909	72.6	0.8	10.8	1.5	14.4	15.6	19.4	51.0	14.3	60.5	1,803	98.1
Bay Lake city	47	53	12.8	61	90.2	0.0	0.0	0.0	9.8	29.5	0.0	33.3	4.7	39.5	24	100.0
Bayonet Point CDP	23,467	-	-	27,418	83.2	2.3	0.8	1.7	12.1	18.5	26.8	48.5	51.7	15.1	11,271	87.9
Bay Pines CDP	2,931	-	-	3,238	82.7	5.1	1.3	6.6	4.3	14.1	26.2	51.6	33.2	28.9	1,482	89.5
Bayport CDP	43	-	-	58	100.0	0.0	0.0	0.0	0.0	34.5	0.0	23.4	0.0	100.0	17	100.0
Bayshore Gardens CDP	16,323	-	-	20,287	62.3	6.9	0.4	2.3	28.0	19.7	24.2	43.5	57.4	16.8	7,810	86.5
Beacon Square CDP	7,224	-	-	6,976	78.8	1.1	0.4	1.3	18.3	19.6	21.5	43.9	53.7	15.5	3,022	83.7
Bear Creek CDP	1,948	-	-	1,709	88.1	1.1	1.6	1.3	7.9	11.9	23.6	55.9	31.8	32.7	769	94.0
Bee Ridge CDP	9,598	-	-	9,958	86.3	0.7	3.0	1.3	8.8	14.4	41.1	59.3	39.0	32.6	4,778	86.3
Bell town	453	498	9.9	582	85.9	0.9	0.0	4.5	8.8	24.7	15.3	30.0	61.5	11.8	193	75.6
Bellair-Meadowbrook Terrace CDP	13,343	-	-	14,800	55.3	18.1	4.5	7.9	14.2	23.4	13.9	33.5	42.4	19.2	5,518	91.6
Belleair town	3,947	4,260	7.9	4,146	91.2	0.2	3.1	1.0	4.5	14.7	35.5	57.7	15.2	55.3	1,701	95.8
Belleair Beach city	1,543	1,603	3.9	1,485	87.1	2.6	1.5	0.0	8.8	11.9	36.5	58.3	19.1	59.3	709	95.3
Belleair Bluffs city	2,119	2,187	3.2	2,329	92.8	1.9	0.3	2.2	2.7	10.7	35.7	60.2	33.0	35.4	1,172	85.4
Belleair Shore town	109	114	4.6	80	96.3	0.0	2.5	0.0	1.3	16.3	30.0	58.5	16.7	57.6	33	87.9
Belle Glade city	18,206	20,134	10.6	19,654	8.3	58.1	0.6	1.3	31.7	26.8	14.2	32.6	70.2	8.1	6,642	54.1
Belle Isle city	5,992	7,240	20.8	7,010	75.3	2.3	4.2	3.4	14.8	14.5	23.2	50.8	26.4	44.7	2,649	95.5
Belleview city	4,540	5,101	12.4	4,927	88.1	1.2	0.7	1.5	8.5	16.4	19.3	44.9	52.3	17.0	2,074	87.6
Bellview CDP	23,355	-	-	21,515	70.5	16.9	3.0	6.9	2.8	18.4	18.5	42.8	36.6	21.6	8,953	93.3
Berrydale CDP	441	-	-	325	77.5	20.0	0.0	2.5	0.0	19.4	15.1	45.6	65.2	14.8	68	88.2

1 May be of any race.

Table A. All Places — **Population and Housing**

STATE City, town, township, borough, or CDP (county if applicable)	Population				Race and Hispanic or Latino origin (percent)					Age (percent)			Educational attainment of persons age 25 and older		Occupied housing units	
	2010 census total population	2019 estimated population	Percent change 2010-2019	ACS total population estimate 2015-2019	White alone, not Hispanic or Latino	Black alone, not Hispanic or Latino	Asian alone, not Hispanic or Latino	All other races or 2 or more races, not Hispanic or Latino	Hispanic or Latino[1]	Under 18 years old	Age 65 years and older	Median age	Percent High school diploma or less	Percent Bachelor's degree or more	Total	Percent with a computer
	1	2	3	4	5	6	7	8	9	10	11	12	13	14	15	16
FLORIDA—Con.																
Beverly Beach town	358	430	20.1	570	95.6	3.2	0.0	0.7	0.5	2.6	45.6	63.9	33.5	29.8	308	92.9
Beverly Hills CDP	8,445	-	-	9,360	85.2	1.7	1.3	2.6	9.2	18.1	27.6	50.1	57.6	7.2	4,185	88.2
Big Coppitt Key CDP	2,458	-	-	2,825	55.1	0.8	0.4	10.5	33.2	22.1	17.3	38.5	35.6	27.0	1,082	98.2
Big Pine Key CDP	4,252	-	-	4,896	80.0	2.0	1.0	0.8	16.1	13.6	24.9	53.6	33.0	30.8	2,065	95.0
Biscayne Park village	3,074	3,065	-0.3	3,124	34.1	25.7	0.5	0.5	39.2	26.2	12.2	39.6	26.2	44.8	1,075	97.0
Bithlo CDP	8,268	-	-	9,627	57.7	8.3	2.9	3.5	27.7	23.4	5.9	33.6	39.2	31.5	2,920	88.5
Black Diamond CDP	1,101	-	-	867	91.1	0.0	8.0	0.0	0.9	5.4	71.6	68.4	17.2	56.1	403	100.0
Black Hammock CDP	1,144	-	-	928	87.9	2.4	4.1	0.0	5.6	20.3	16.3	47.3	37.2	38.0	314	100.0
Bloomingdale CDP	22,711	-	-	24,446	69.2	10.6	1.3	3.1	15.8	23.6	14.9	40.1	26.2	41.5	8,079	98.2
Blountstown city	2,516	2,443	-2.9	2,827	66.3	22.9	0.6	7.9	2.3	23.6	20.8	37.4	60.0	12.9	962	76.6
Boca Raton city	84,409	99,805	18.2	97,468	75.5	4.4	2.9	2.7	14.5	16.8	26.8	48.5	20.7	55.3	41,504	96.1
Bokeelia CDP	1,780	-	-	1,613	90.8	0.0	0.0	1.4	7.9	7.5	50.5	65.2	46.8	24.1	766	94.1
Bonifay city	2,773	2,704	-2.5	2,675	82.5	9.3	0.2	5.0	3.0	23.3	20.3	39.8	58.7	14.4	962	89.4
Bonita Springs city	43,930	59,637	35.8	55,902	72.1	2.7	1.0	0.9	23.3	12.9	41.8	59.0	35.2	37.4	23,450	94.7
Boulevard Gardens CDP	1,274	-	-	1,632	0.0	97.9	0.0	0.0	2.1	23.8	16.4	39.7	69.3	3.5	460	84.8
Bowling Green city	2,937	2,887	-1.7	2,893	22.5	11.4	0.0	4.2	61.9	33.0	11.0	26.3	83.0	8.6	649	60.9
Boynton Beach city	68,293	78,679	15.2	76,832	49.6	29.8	2.4	1.9	16.3	17.3	21.2	42.6	39.2	29.4	29,718	91.8
Bradenton city	49,273	59,439	20.6	56,551	60.7	18.2	1.2	1.7	18.2	20.2	25.4	44.4	45.7	24.0	21,741	89.6
Bradenton Beach city	1,168	1,279	9.5	836	89.6	2.3	0.5	1.3	6.3	8.4	48.9	64.6	33.9	37.3	434	94.9
Bradley Junction CDP	686	-	-	623	24.4	33.9	0.0	4.7	37.1	11.4	32.6	54.8	80.4	0.0	202	73.8
Brandon CDP	103,483	-	-	115,911	47.9	17.5	5.1	3.2	26.3	20.5	12.8	37.1	35.5	31.8	42,821	95.9
Branford town	705	732	3.8	590	80.5	5.9	1.4	3.2	9.0	27.8	19.3	37.8	57.0	13.8	254	79.9
Brent CDP	21,804	-	-	22,337	53.0	31.0	3.5	6.5	5.9	18.8	13.8	29.8	50.7	15.3	7,196	84.2
Briny Breezes town	523	578	10.5	708	98.4	0.0	0.0	0.3	1.3	2.7	70.6	73.4	31.3	40.6	409	87.5
Bristol city	1,015	980	-3.4	1,067	79.3	9.0	1.5	1.1	9.1	23.9	21.4	38.0	60.3	9.2	305	82.3
Broadview Park CDP	7,125	-	-	8,169	18.3	7.2	1.1	0.2	73.1	26.5	12.9	35.8	75.1	9.8	2,418	85.5
Bronson town	1,118	1,147	2.6	1,050	61.6	20.8	1.1	3.4	13.0	30.4	21.0	35.6	60.8	16.7	393	89.6
Brooker town	336	336	0.0	390	94.9	1.5	1.0	0.5	2.1	26.4	18.2	43.8	59.0	8.5	139	89.2
Brookridge CDP	4,420	-	-	4,412	90.5	0.9	0.0	1.6	7.0	8.6	56.0	65.9	53.2	11.5	2,232	89.0
Brooksville city	7,724	8,564	10.9	8,191	74.6	12.3	0.9	4.6	7.6	19.7	29.1	46.6	49.5	21.6	3,872	87.8
Brownsdale CDP	471	-	-	446	100.0	0.0	0.0	0.0	0.0	17.9	13.2	36.4	28.8	24.0	165	100.0
Brownsville CDP	15,313	-	-	17,051	2.9	55.1	0.1	1.5	40.3	29.7	11.6	33.4	67.2	12.7	5,398	76.6
Buckhead Ridge CDP	1,450	-	-	1,634	96.2	0.0	0.0	3.8	0.0	0.0	47.3	63.7	41.2	6.8	763	72.5
Buckingham CDP	4,036	-	-	3,958	95.0	0.9	1.3	0.0	2.8	20.4	16.3	45.3	41.9	27.2	1,353	95.2
Buenaventura Lakes CDP	26,079	-	-	34,784	13.4	9.5	2.0	1.1	74.0	22.1	12.4	36.7	49.0	17.5	9,460	91.4
Bunnell city	2,476	2,943	18.9	2,737	62.6	22.4	2.6	2.5	9.9	23.3	24.6	42.8	53.2	15.1	1,102	70.0
Burnt Store Marina CDP	1,793	-	-	2,057	93.8	1.2	0.4	0.3	4.2	1.1	66.6	70.2	20.9	53.8	1,058	95.2
Bushnell city	3,004	3,183	6.0	3,123	78.4	9.4	0.0	1.2	11.0	19.5	36.3	55.3	57.8	9.3	1,103	88.4
Butler Beach CDP	4,951	-	-	4,716	95.7	0.0	0.8	1.5	2.1	11.5	40.1	60.1	24.5	48.9	2,268	93.0
Cabana Colony CDP	2,391	-	-	2,914	62.3	2.0	7.9	2.7	25.1	21.3	10.4	36.8	37.0	21.7	971	98.0
Callahan town	1,113	1,360	22.2	1,424	82.7	10.8	2.2	1.2	3.1	23.0	15.3	37.4	55.6	12.2	625	86.9
Callaway city	14,318	14,060	-1.8	14,958	60.8	16.9	4.3	9.4	8.6	20.7	15.5	37.8	45.7	11.6	5,397	90.2
Campbell CDP	2,479	-	-	2,323	69.7	5.6	1.1	2.9	20.7	8.6	55.5	69.0	46.8	20.5	1,082	72.6
Campbellton town	230	221	-3.9	251	21.9	76.9	0.0	0.0	1.2	12.7	25.9	43.1	79.0	6.6	97	64.9
Canal Point CDP	367	-	-	563	22.6	14.9	0.0	3.0	59.5	8.5	13.7	46.3	63.4	9.4	165	89.7
Cape Canaveral city	9,987	10,470	4.8	10,377	90.9	1.7	1.4	1.7	4.3	8.8	35.8	57.8	29.8	35.5	5,419	92.1
Cape Coral city	154,309	194,495	26.0	183,942	71.0	4.9	1.8	1.4	20.9	18.2	22.7	46.7	45.6	23.3	65,287	94.7
Captiva CDP	583	-	-	175	49.1	29.1	0.0	0.0	21.7	0.0	32.0	38.9	65.6	16.0	34	88.2
Carrabelle city	2,761	2,820	2.1	2,646	60.8	19.2	0.0	9.2	10.7	16.7	13.9	36.8	64.2	10.1	620	86.0
Carrollwood CDP	33,365	-	-	35,686	51.6	6.8	3.7	3.6	34.4	19.0	19.0	43.5	27.4	42.7	14,403	96.5
Caryville town	412	291	-29.4	179	77.7	21.8	0.0	0.6	0.0	20.7	27.9	45.6	85.8	1.6	84	57.1
Casselberry city	26,032	28,757	10.5	27,950	54.7	10.2	2.7	3.0	29.4	17.3	15.6	37.2	34.2	29.8	11,569	94.8
Cedar Grove CDP	3,397	-	-	3,464	56.6	30.0	1.6	8.3	3.5	20.6	9.5	35.3	62.6	10.0	1,344	94.9
Cedar Key city	731	720	-1.5	773	100.0	0.0	0.0	0.0	0.0	10.0	34.7	53.1	37.6	35.4	312	86.2
Celebration CDP	7,427	-	-	9,923	74.0	1.4	2.3	2.7	19.6	23.6	14.5	40.4	15.3	61.7	3,565	100.0
Center Hill city	996	1,460	46.6	933	54.9	18.5	0.0	0.5	26.0	25.0	16.0	40.7	73.6	7.3	272	76.1
Century town	1,698	1,846	8.7	1,756	38.9	53.4	0.0	5.8	1.9	22.6	24.6	45.8	67.2	6.6	625	77.4
Charleston Park CDP	218	-	-	254	0.0	89.8	0.0	0.0	10.2	0.0	35.8	39.2	61.7	0.0	24	58.3
Charlotte Harbor CDP	3,714	-	-	4,082	86.9	4.5	1.0	3.5	4.2	9.0	54.1	67.8	41.4	25.5	1,910	72.7
Charlotte Park CDP	2,325	-	-	2,401	81.4	0.0	0.3	4.2	14.1	6.2	46.7	62.0	44.2	20.3	1,098	90.1
Chattahoochee city	3,650	3,198	-12.4	3,113	35.7	54.6	0.4	0.4	8.9	15.3	18.1	41.3	65.4	9.3	940	70.9
Cheval CDP	10,702	-	-	10,808	63.0	5.7	5.9	3.3	22.2	24.9	13.5	41.6	21.6	52.3	4,421	96.2
Chiefland city	2,235	2,186	-2.2	2,567	51.3	33.9	1.1	2.7	11.0	27.2	14.3	34.5	59.9	11.0	938	77.2
Chipley city	3,596	3,608	0.3	3,525	55.7	34.6	0.0	0.8	9.0	24.4	10.6	30.9	64.1	14.0	1,226	85.6
Chokoloskee CDP	359	-	-	340	100.0	0.0	0.0	0.0	0.0	13.5	45.9	59.7	49.0	20.1	155	68.4
Christmas CDP	1,146	-	-	1,832	88.6	4.5	0.0	0.0	6.9	10.3	24.6	51.6	47.2	19.3	727	83.9
Chuluota CDP	2,483	-	-	2,629	62.5	0.3	0.5	1.1	35.5	23.9	11.1	33.8	27.0	29.3	864	100.0
Chumuckla CDP	850	-	-	994	91.1	0.0	3.6	3.6	1.6	13.7	13.9	43.8	42.0	12.0	364	89.8
Cinco Bayou town	383	445	16.2	501	70.9	5.0	1.6	2.0	20.6	13.6	15.0	34.2	27.2	32.7	248	96.0
Citrus Hills CDP	7,470	-	-	7,739	77.5	4.3	9.7	0.9	7.6	8.3	63.0	69.1	30.8	40.1	3,529	96.5
Citrus Park CDP	24,252	-	-	27,026	51.7	10.3	4.1	2.7	31.2	20.7	14.2	40.7	34.4	35.2	10,283	95.3
Citrus Springs CDP	8,622	-	-	8,779	77.2	8.0	0.1	0.3	14.4	22.7	24.1	44.4	49.5	14.6	3,250	93.3
Clarcona CDP	2,990	-	-	3,691	50.7	17.4	7.8	1.5	22.6	22.6	14.8	41.1	38.2	27.6	1,465	85.6
Clearwater city	109,139	116,946	7.2	115,159	66.8	10.3	2.5	3.0	17.5	18.4	22.5	45.4	37.9	30.4	47,593	89.0
Clermont city	28,823	38,654	34.1	35,209	61.2	9.2	4.7	3.5	21.4	19.8	24.8	45.3	32.8	34.1	13,177	96.9
Cleveland CDP	2,990	-	-	3,077	86.1	1.6	1.1	0.0	11.2	9.4	47.0	63.9	43.1	14.0	1,540	88.5
Clewiston city	7,158	8,020	12.0	7,781	32.9	11.5	2.9	0.5	52.3	27.3	11.9	34.0	64.4	11.0	2,480	65.2
Cloud Lake town	135	144	6.7	222	36.0	0.0	0.0	1.4	62.6	15.3	8.1	39.3	44.4	19.9	78	89.7
Cobbtown CDP	67	-	-	77	100.0	0.0	0.0	0.0	0.0	0.0	0.0	27.2	10.4	0.0	40	80.0
Cocoa city	17,167	18,603	8.4	18,285	51.1	27.0	2.8	3.1	16.1	22.5	17.5	40.3	45.1	18.1	6,888	87.7
Cocoa Beach city	11,198	11,705	4.5	11,619	89.3	0.7	1.5	1.6	6.9	11.4	34.3	57.5	23.9	45.0	6,030	92.5
Cocoa West CDP	5,925	-	-	6,595	37.1	39.7	0.8	10.7	11.7	26.7	11.7	32.8	61.8	10.5	2,543	89.0
Coconut Creek city	53,042	61,248	15.5	60,490	55.1	15.8	3.1	3.1	23.0	21.2	17.5	40.2	34.8	34.6	23,277	93.2
Coleman city	703	911	29.6	693	49.1	44.9	0.0	1.3	4.8	22.4	25.8	43.7	56.3	7.3	271	67.5
Combee Settlement CDP	5,577	-	-	6,357	66.7	8.0	0.4	2.0	22.8	24.6	12.6	30.5	70.6	3.4	2,019	81.8
Connerton CDP	2,116	-	-	4,673	64.6	8.4	2.5	6.0	18.5	18.4	2.8	36.2	52.1	19.8	661	100.0
Conway CDP	13,467	-	-	13,528	71.1	2.3	3.7	1.5	21.4	18.1	15.2	43.5	29.4	38.6	5,112	96.8
Cooper City city	28,537	35,800	25.5	35,556	51.9	7.3	7.8	3.4	29.7	25.5	12.8	39.8	25.2	45.9	11,280	97.8
Coral Gables city	46,746	49,700	6.3	50,226	33.5	2.7	2.3	1.2	60.3	19.3	18.0	40.1	15.3	66.7	17,921	97.0
Coral Springs city	122,588	133,759	9.1	132,568	41.0	21.2	5.2	3.1	29.4	26.4	11.5	37.4	29.8	38.6	41,715	97.6
Coral Terrace CDP	24,376	-	-	25,387	9.0	1.2	1.0	0.2	88.6	14.8	23.2	44.9	44.4	28.7	7,468	92.3
Cortez CDP	4,241	-	-	4,377	93.6	0.4	3.2	0.4	2.5	4.7	46.5	62.9	34.8	34.0	1,982	92.1

1 May be of any race.

Table A. All Places — **Population and Housing**

STATE City, town, township, borough, or CDP (county if applicable)	Population				Race and Hispanic or Latino origin (percent)					Age (percent)			Educational attainment of persons age 25 and older		Occupied housing units	
	2010 census total population	2019 estimated population	Percent change 2010-2019	ACS total population estimate 2015-2019	White alone, not Hispanic or Latino	Black alone, not Hispanic or Latino	Asian alone, not Hispanic or Latino	All other races or 2 or more races, not Hispanic or Latino	Hispanic or Latino[1]	Under 18 years old	Age 65 years and older	Median age	Percent High school diploma or less	Percent Bachelor's degree or more	Total	Percent with a computer
	1	2	3	4	5	6	7	8	9	10	11	12	13	14	15	16
FLORIDA—Con.																
Cottondale town	932	895	-4.0	889	67.2	23.7	0.0	4.0	5.1	26.9	15.7	31.5	60.4	10.8	343	70.6
Country Club CDP	47,105	-	-	50,431	5.3	7.4	1.0	0.3	86.0	23.1	11.5	36.9	48.2	23.0	16,710	93.5
Country Walk CDP	15,997	-	-	17,496	16.9	6.0	2.9	1.3	72.9	26.2	10.2	38.9	34.8	32.0	4,729	99.3
Crawfordville CDP	3,702	-	-	5,164	78.4	16.4	1.4	1.5	2.3	26.9	14.1	38.0	44.4	22.6	1,820	93.4
Crescent Beach CDP	931	-	-	1,118	95.0	1.2	1.6	0.9	1.3	10.8	44.8	62.6	26.0	51.7	592	96.8
Crescent City city	1,567	1,535	-2.0	1,646	54.6	19.3	0.3	2.9	22.8	21.4	33.9	51.0	56.8	19.1	746	70.6
Crestview city	21,065	25,274	20.0	24,117	67.4	16.0	1.7	5.9	9.0	26.8	10.5	31.4	39.8	23.2	8,390	91.2
Crooked Lake Park CDP	1,722	-	-	1,592	70.7	5.3	0.0	2.1	21.8	30.0	16.5	33.5	55.3	13.0	579	91.0
Cross City town	1,730	1,713		2,430	69.4	24.4	0.5	3.2	2.5	27.9	13.3	31.4	64.4	10.6	972	74.3
Crystal Lake CDP	5,514	-	-	6,431	47.5	17.9	3.5	4.4	26.6	34.1	10.4	28.5	60.6	15.3	2,019	75.0
Crystal River city	3,103	3,186	2.7	3,129	85.5	8.7	0.5	3.9	1.4	12.0	37.0	56.8	44.2	22.1	1,465	91.1
Crystal Springs CDP	1,327	-	-	841	84.8	0.0	0.4	3.4	11.4	11.2	21.4	55.2	76.0	9.0	368	77.2
Cudjoe Key CDP	1,763	-	-	2,105	91.6	0.2	1.2	0.6	6.4	8.5	33.0	57.6	32.3	41.0	1,054	97.8
Cutler Bay town	40,289	43,718	8.5	44,222	24.6	9.8	1.9	2.6	61.3	24.9	14.0	37.7	37.8	31.8	13,110	94.9
Cypress Gardens CDP	8,917	-	-	10,252	78.2	5.6	4.0	2.5	9.7	20.9	21.9	45.6	35.5	28.0	3,726	91.7
Cypress Lake CDP	11,846	-	-	12,978	88.7	0.6	1.1	2.9	6.8	11.0	41.4	60.5	32.2	33.7	6,458	92.7
Cypress Quarters CDP	1,215	-	-	1,373	39.7	42.8	0.0	0.0	17.6	30.2	13.1	33.7	57.9	30.0	391	82.9
Dade City city	6,449	7,338	13.8	7,121	52.1	25.0	0.2	1.0	21.7	26.3	17.2	35.5	52.3	17.2	2,374	90.5
Dade City North CDP	3,113	-	-	3,335	12.1	16.8	3.4	2.4	65.2	31.5	4.2	26.2	87.0	7.6	810	84.1
Dania Beach city	29,738	32,271	8.5	32,008	42.7	17.8	1.3	3.1	35.1	20.4	15.7	40.1	41.0	28.3	12,237	91.8
Davenport city	2,913	6,005	106.1	4,682	37.8	15.8	0.9	1.2	44.3	27.1	13.0	35.4	52.5	23.1	1,394	93.1
Davie town	91,950	106,306	15.6	104,399	43.4	7.9	5.9	2.9	39.8	21.5	11.6	36.8	33.0	38.7	35,393	95.8
Day CDP	116	-	-	97	100.0	0.0	0.0	0.0	0.0	11.3	37.1	61.4	89.2	0.0	46	100.0
Daytona Beach city	61,591	69,186	12.3	67,604	52.5	32.7	2.4	3.9	8.6	16.2	20.8	40.6	43.0	23.1	29,265	86.3
Daytona Beach Shores city	4,255	4,614	8.4	4,483	91.1	2.7	1.3	1.8	3.1	5.6	50.9	65.3	26.2	43.0	2,547	92.1
DeBary city	19,312	21,305	10.3	20,696	79.8	5.5	1.9	0.9	11.8	18.2	24.2	48.8	38.5	27.5	8,156	94.3
Deerfield Beach city	75,008	81,066	8.1	80,312	49.6	26.8	2.3	3.4	17.9	18.2	21.8	42.9	45.2	26.6	32,105	90.2
DeFuniak Springs city	5,180	6,968	34.5	6,448	72.3	18.3	0.0	5.0	4.3	22.8	16.9	34.3	45.6	17.6	2,662	88.9
DeLand city	26,852	34,851	29.8	32,413	64.9	16.7	1.8	2.0	14.6	18.0	22.9	41.9	36.4	28.8	12,513	90.9
DeLand Southwest CDP	1,052	-	-	923	14.1	43.1	9.1	0.0	33.7	23.2	12.1	40.2	56.3	21.3	419	80.4
De Leon Springs CDP	2,614	-	-	2,840	43.0	3.9	0.7	0.0	52.4	27.1	18.2	40.4	61.5	18.8	853	93.0
Delray Beach city	60,611	69,451	14.6	68,217	56.4	28.9	2.0	2.3	10.4	14.1	26.0	47.7	35.1	38.3	28,582	91.3
Deltona city	85,131	92,757	9.0	90,403	49.0	10.9	1.6	1.8	36.7	23.4	15.6	38.4	46.3	16.2	30,336	94.9
Desoto Lakes CDP	3,646	-	-	4,061	70.8	3.7	0.0	11.6	13.9	9.5	21.0	44.6	40.7	27.7	1,451	98.2
Destin city	12,150	14,247	17.3	13,702	83.0	2.4	1.8	3.3	9.5	19.7	18.7	42.3	25.0	41.6	5,778	96.2
Dickerson City CDP	146	-	-	153	100.0	0.0	0.0	0.0	0.0	0.0	62.1	68.2	65.4	9.2	114	100.0
Dixonville CDP	181	-	-	94	100.0	0.0	0.0	0.0	0.0	0.0	28.7	54.7	54.3	0.0	51	82.4
Doctor Phillips CDP	10,981	-	-	10,488	62.0	5.6	13.6	2.7	16.1	18.5	20.3	46.5	20.1	55.5	4,048	95.4
Doral city	45,712	65,741	43.8	59,972	10.1	1.5	2.9	0.5	85.0	26.5	7.2	35.4	24.1	51.9	17,833	97.4
Dover CDP	3,702	-	-	2,938	32.6	2.7	0.2	1.3	63.2	31.2	6.2	32.6	79.4	4.2	859	93.4
Duck Key CDP	621	-	-	741	83.3	8.1	0.0	0.5	8.1	6.5	34.5	60.7	22.9	44.1	318	95.3
Dundee town	3,702	5,044	36.3	4,512	35.0	25.2	0.4	1.4	38.1	32.3	17.2	29.8	65.0	7.0	1,249	80.7
Dunedin city	35,355	36,537	3.3	36,381	86.2	3.5	2.4	3.2	4.8	13.0	32.6	54.4	35.5	34.7	17,398	89.6
Dunnellon city	1,733	1,840	6.2	2,057	74.0	11.6	1.2	7.2	6.0	17.7	30.8	56.2	43.9	22.7	1,043	83.2
Eagle Lake city	2,265	2,904	28.2	2,621	69.4	9.2	0.6	2.9	17.9	22.6	19.2	40.8	58.2	11.6	794	87.0
East Bronson CDP	1,945	-	-	1,825	79.0	1.9	0.0	1.4	17.7	16.8	27.0	50.0	64.7	10.5	784	90.8
East Lake CDP	30,962	-	-	32,169	85.0	2.1	3.4	3.0	6.5	17.8	28.3	51.8	25.0	45.8	13,112	94.8
East Lake-Orient Park CDP	22,753	-	-	29,346	24.9	41.1	4.0	3.9	26.1	29.2	10.0	31.9	55.0	17.9	10,324	91.5
East Milton CDP	11,074	-	-	13,697	66.6	20.4	0.5	6.5	6.0	15.5	10.5	37.2	61.5	9.8	2,867	92.1
East Palatka CDP	1,654	-	-	1,713	51.3	43.5	1.6	1.6	2.0	21.5	22.0	37.7	58.1	19.3	502	83.1
Eastpoint CDP	2,337	-	-	2,336	92.8	1.2	0.0	2.0	4.1	23.2	20.8	37.0	60.6	10.6	921	82.7
East Williston CDP	694	-	-	697	7.7	90.0	0.0	1.1	1.1	25.1	25.4	40.7	70.9	0.0	308	64.6
Eatonville town	2,118	2,213	4.5	2,321	11.8	73.5	0.3	1.6	12.8	22.9	13.4	35.1	57.5	11.0	722	88.4
Ebro town	271	280	3.3	226	81.9	1.8	2.2	14.2	0.0	16.8	23.0	46.2	80.2	4.3	107	76.6
Edgewater city	21,813	23,918	9.7	23,324	89.1	2.3	0.9	3.7	4.1	16.9	27.7	51.1	49.3	15.4	9,548	93.4
Edgewood city	2,480	3,003	21.1	2,899	59.5	12.0	7.6	5.9	15.0	20.5	15.0	43.2	33.2	38.5	1,061	97.5
Eglin AFB CDP	2,274	-	-	2,152	48.8	8.9	5.5	14.7	22.1	34.2	0.2	22.8	17.8	39.0	651	100.0
Egypt Lake-Leto CDP	35,282	-	-	37,704	21.2	8.9	2.3	3.5	64.1	21.7	12.5	36.8	52.5	21.3	13,838	94.3
Elfers CDP	13,986	-	-	12,600	79.3	1.6	1.3	1.7	16.1	18.9	19.5	43.8	58.5	10.1	5,296	80.9
Ellenton CDP	4,275	-	-	4,192	77.9	6.5	0.6	1.6	13.4	25.2	35.8	50.3	38.8	18.3	1,687	88.9
El Portal village	2,399	2,398	0.0	1,969	25.0	39.7	2.0	3.5	29.8	18.1	20.1	44.0	30.6	44.8	726	91.5
Englewood CDP	14,863	-	-	15,095	92.9	0.0	3.0	1.6	2.3	6.4	51.0	65.3	47.6	24.2	7,486	89.2
Ensley CDP	20,602	-	-	22,194	52.5	30.5	4.8	4.4	7.7	18.9	17.9	40.9	40.5	22.0	9,339	91.7
Estero village	27,991	33,871	21.0	32,815	89.5	1.7	2.8	0.9	5.1	11.7	48.2	64.2	23.4	48.2	15,003	97.2
Esto town	364	356	-2.2	398	86.9	5.8	1.0	1.0	5.3	17.3	17.3	40.9	64.3	6.2	165	83.6
Eustis city	18,460	21,303	15.4	20,700	60.1	21.8	0.5	3.2	14.4	22.5	21.8	40.5	50.9	20.3	7,809	90.9
Everglades city	400	421	5.3	190	91.1	0.0	0.0	0.0	8.9	10.0	30.0	49.9	38.7	38.7	101	91.1
Fairview Shores CDP	10,239	-	-	10,467	51.9	18.2	3.4	4.6	21.9	19.9	13.9	37.6	46.0	25.3	4,276	89.7
Fanning Springs city	979	1,030	5.2	1,182	92.6	2.5	0.3	2.5	2.0	18.1	33.5	52.8	60.4	12.7	462	79.4
Feather Sound CDP	3,420	-	-	3,671	76.5	2.7	9.2	3.3	8.3	15.5	17.6	44.8	11.4	59.6	1,766	97.2
Fellsmere city	5,156	5,695	10.5	5,625	12.7	11.6	0.0	0.0	75.7	33.2	4.0	27.7	73.6	8.3	1,243	68.9
Fernandina Beach city	11,382	13,169	15.7	12,364	79.8	10.0	3.2	0.2	6.7	11.8	34.4	56.9	29.2	40.7	5,631	94.3
Ferndale CDP	472	-	-	462	93.9	0.0	0.0	2.6	3.5	16.7	18.8	43.5	57.1	30.0	180	100.0
Fern Park CDP	7,704	-	-	8,694	61.6	8.7	2.3	0.1	27.3	15.1	18.3	44.6	25.5	38.9	3,492	93.8
Ferry Pass CDP	28,921	-	-	32,376	64.8	15.8	2.9	7.7	8.8	19.9	16.3	32.0	31.9	34.3	12,994	93.4
Fidelis CDP	156	-	-	162	98.1	0.0	0.0	1.9	0.0	14.8	25.9	43.7	47.7	10.8	73	87.7
Fisher Island CDP	132	-	-	383	84.9	0.0	0.0	0.0	15.1	4.2	66.6	71.1	14.7	81.5	197	100.0
Fish Hawk CDP	14,087	-	-	21,929	69.6	5.5	5.6	3.9	15.4	37.4	7.4	35.6	14.7	61.8	6,686	98.0
Five Points CDP	1,265	-	-	1,393	92.5	6.3	0.0	0.6	0.5	19.5	10.3	33.7	81.9	11.4	375	90.1
Flagler Beach city	4,502	5,123	13.8	5,002	89.2	3.8	0.6	1.6	4.8	11.4	38.5	59.6	29.0	35.2	2,512	92.3
Flagler Estates CDP	3,215	-	-	3,707	83.7	4.5	0.0	3.0	8.8	30.9	9.4	35.0	50.9	10.6	1,231	90.2
Fleming Island CDP	27,126	-	-	28,676	80.9	6.4	2.1	3.9	6.7	23.0	18.1	43.1	23.1	44.4	10,428	97.3
Floral City CDP	5,217	-	-	5,395	91.2	1.1	0.3	0.3	7.0	16.3	33.6	56.4	56.1	12.4	2,399	87.8
Florida City city	11,252	11,771	4.6	11,928	1.5	52.6	0.0	0.0	45.9	36.7	7.1	27.4	66.5	7.2	2,860	88.1
Florida Ridge CDP	18,164	-	-	22,372	65.1	10.6	0.3	1.8	22.3	20.5	24.7	44.0	46.2	19.0	6,944	90.1
Floridatown CDP	244	-	-	257	78.6	0.0	0.0	14.4	7.0	30.4	16.7	40.0	24.7	16.0	83	91.6
Forest City CDP	13,854	-	-	14,592	61.2	4.3	4.0	3.8	26.7	21.3	14.8	41.4	31.4	37.8	5,079	94.2
Fort Denaud CDP	1,694	-	-	1,769	80.7	0.0	0.6	1.9	16.8	9.3	29.5	54.7	71.7	9.2	687	86.8
Fort Green CDP	101	-	-	226	84.5	2.7	0.0	4.4	8.4	11.5	8.0	35.9	54.1	24.7	57	100.0
Fort Green Springs CDP	231	-	-	159	100.0	0.0	0.0	0.0	0.0	16.4	3.1	53.8	81.2	3.0	69	27.5

1 May be of any race.

Table A. All Places — **Population and Housing**

STATE City, town, township, borough, or CDP (county if applicable)	Population				Race and Hispanic or Latino origin (percent)					Age (percent)			Educational attainment of persons age 25 and older		Occupied housing units	
	2010 census total population	2019 estimated population	Percent change 2010-2019	ACS total population estimate 2015-2019	White alone, not Hispanic or Latino	Black alone, not Hispanic or Latino	Asian alone, not Hispanic or Latino	All other races or 2 or more races, not Hispanic or Latino	Hispanic or Latino[1]	Under 18 years old	Age 65 years and older	Median age	Percent High school diploma or less	Percent Bachelor's degree or more	Total	Percent with a computer
	1	2	3	4	5	6	7	8	9	10	11	12	13	14	15	16
FLORIDA—Con.																
Fort Lauderdale city	165,754	182,437	10.1	180,124	46.6	31.5	1.6	1.8	18.5	18.3	18.0	42.1	36.7	37.0	74,567	92.2
Fort Meade city	5,627	6,257	11.2	6,104	51.2	20.2	0.1	1.2	27.3	23.0	20.8	39.4	59.8	12.0	2,046	81.3
Fort Myers city	62,305	87,103	39.8	79,927	49.2	21.8	2.7	2.1	24.2	20.7	22.0	40.6	44.2	29.7	30,265	89.2
Fort Myers Beach town	6,275	7,094	13.1	7,048	96.6	0.1	0.8	0.6	1.9	3.7	57.6	67.4	27.7	41.7	3,566	94.5
Fort Myers Shores CDP	5,487	-	-	6,813	75.9	4.3	0.1	1.6	18.2	15.5	17.3	45.2	58.0	11.1	2,241	89.0
Fort Pierce city	41,942	46,103	9.9	45,329	33.5	40.9	0.8	2.0	22.8	23.8	17.9	38.2	57.1	16.1	16,718	85.2
Fort Pierce North CDP	6,474	-	-	6,926	18.6	67.2	0.1	1.2	13.0	21.4	19.0	43.7	62.7	10.9	2,397	74.8
Fort Pierce South CDP	5,062	-	-	4,235	49.4	4.7	2.2	1.9	41.7	20.7	18.3	44.5	63.3	8.7	1,536	90.7
Fort Walton Beach city	19,635	22,521	14.7	22,084	69.5	11.2	4.5	4.8	10.0	17.8	19.3	41.7	34.3	27.1	9,380	88.5
Fort White town	562	600	6.8	695	64.5	27.5	0.0	3.6	4.5	30.8	12.7	38.6	53.3	11.4	232	83.2
Fountainebleau CDP	59,764	-	-	60,547	4.7	0.3	2.0	0.3	92.7	17.2	17.0	41.7	42.5	32.6	20,116	88.7
Four Corners CDP	26,116	-	-	42,346	50.8	8.6	2.0	3.8	34.8	21.6	14.5	36.2	35.5	30.4	14,990	96.8
Franklin Park CDP	860	-	-	1,056	0.9	99.1	0.0	0.0	0.0	33.6	9.5	30.3	52.0	14.7	366	91.3
Freeport city	1,888	2,566	35.9	2,369	81.8	3.7	0.5	5.3	8.7	22.2	19.6	42.5	33.0	27.5	931	94.6
Frostproof city	2,958	3,261	10.2	3,191	73.3	1.9	0.6	2.0	22.2	20.8	33.3	53.4	62.0	14.2	1,221	76.2
Fruit Cove CDP	29,362	-	-	31,314	81.6	4.4	2.7	3.7	7.6	25.3	13.3	41.5	19.4	52.1	10,542	97.7
Fruitland Park city	4,129	10,730	159.9	7,848	85.2	5.0	0.2	3.4	6.2	17.3	26.5	51.7	34.3	30.1	3,245	92.5
Fruitville CDP	13,224	-	-	14,068	84.1	1.4	2.1	1.1	11.3	17.9	23.6	46.4	39.0	33.5	5,574	92.8
Fuller Heights CDP	8,758	-	-	11,143	60.1	10.8	2.4	1.0	25.7	23.9	14.5	33.3	48.5	19.2	3,345	92.7
Fussels Corner CDP	5,561	-	-	4,477	82.7	1.5	0.5	0.6	14.7	13.6	43.4	61.6	51.7	18.2	2,007	86.6
Gainesville city	124,504	133,997	7.6	132,127	56.0	21.5	7.2	3.6	11.9	13.2	10.8	26.3	27.7	45.1	49,143	93.4
Garcon Point CDP	347	-	-	377	78.2	0.0	0.0	0.0	21.8	14.1	27.6	52.3	8.0	31.5	131	100.0
Garden Grove CDP	674	-	-	911	88.4	1.0	5.8	3.1	1.8	17.2	21.7	40.1	60.9	17.7	357	92.4
Gardner CDP	463	-	-	340	99.1	0.0	0.0	0.0	0.9	4.1	74.4	74.9	55.5	10.4	173	49.7
Gateway CDP	8,401	-	-	10,702	76.8	7.6	2.8	1.8	11.0	21.4	17.2	40.0	24.8	48.2	3,345	99.5
Geneva CDP	2,940	-	-	2,496	92.3	0.0	0.0	5.9	1.8	19.3	12.5	48.1	21.6	33.5	949	96.3
Gibsonton CDP	14,234	-	-	18,515	42.8	15.6	2.4	3.7	35.5	31.3	7.7	31.9	51.7	17.8	5,623	92.3
Gifford CDP	9,590	-	-	10,479	46.3	50.2	1.2	0.1	2.3	21.1	32.2	48.6	48.3	29.3	3,853	70.9
Gladeview CDP	11,535	-	-	12,977	0.9	67.2	0.2	0.6	31.1	29.3	10.0	31.1	67.0	9.8	4,013	84.1
Glencoe CDP	2,582	-	-	1,773	95.5	0.0	0.0	0.0	4.5	17.8	15.3	48.8	48.9	18.5	676	97.6
Glen Ridge town	219	243	11.0	195	71.3	1.5	2.6	0.0	24.6	6.2	13.3	50.3	53.9	21.1	71	88.7
Glen St. Mary town	439	460	4.8	703	72.0	12.8	4.3	10.1	0.9	38.5	8.0	27.5	63.5	12.7	206	79.1
Glenvar Heights CDP	16,898	-	-	17,065	22.4	2.5	1.7	1.7	71.7	15.8	17.6	39.3	21.3	51.3	7,273	94.7
Golden Beach town	919	933	1.5	659	61.6	0.0	1.4	0.5	36.6	27.6	14.7	44.6	10.7	76.5	190	91.6
Golden Gate CDP	23,961	-	-	29,552	16.7	13.5	0.1	1.7	68.0	25.0	9.4	34.5	67.8	12.8	7,542	90.9
Golden Glades CDP	33,145	-	-	34,109	6.2	70.2	2.2	2.3	19.1	23.5	13.4	34.9	57.3	16.9	9,547	89.2
Goldenrod CDP	12,039	-	-	12,384	57.6	7.6	3.2	3.6	28.0	16.3	13.6	35.8	34.0	31.5	4,900	93.3
Golf village	235	269	14.5	251	96.0	0.0	0.4	0.0	3.6	1.6	61.8	69.6	10.2	77.0	111	98.2
Gonzalez CDP	13,273	-	-	14,598	76.3	16.0	2.1	1.5	4.1	21.1	17.8	43.2	30.8	34.8	5,499	91.2
Goodland CDP	267	-	-	337	100.0	0.0	0.0	0.0	0.0	26.1	37.4	26.6	23.5	20.4	98	100.0
Gotha CDP	1,915	-	-	2,041	64.2	22.9	12.3	0.6	0.0	37.1	9.1	36.2	13.1	64.6	542	100.0
Goulding CDP	4,102	-	-	4,036	19.9	70.9	0.2	5.5	3.5	26.2	13.9	36.8	66.7	4.3	874	74.5
Goulds CDP	10,103	-	-	11,984	7.5	36.0	0.0	1.3	55.2	27.5	9.0	37.2	63.3	16.0	3,350	89.2
Graceville city	2,279	2,125	-6.8	2,432	68.7	22.9	0.9	0.9	6.7	16.0	23.4	34.3	51.7	20.0	817	85.2
Grand Ridge town	906	872	-3.8	859	78.1	18.3	0.0	1.2	2.4	22.7	24.2	35.7	59.7	9.8	386	82.6
Grant-Valkaria town	3,845	4,286	11.5	4,176	83.1	1.4	0.6	3.1	11.9	21.2	19.8	45.8	34.9	25.4	1,431	96.9
Greenacres city	37,592	41,117	9.4	40,529	31.6	20.3	3.9	2.1	42.0	21.8	16.1	38.4	48.4	22.5	13,986	91.4
Greenbriar CDP	2,502	-	-	3,234	83.2	1.7	0.7	4.7	9.6	14.1	18.3	44.9	38.2	27.7	1,275	98.5
Green Cove Springs city	6,922	8,577	23.9	7,923	64.1	16.3	1.2	3.2	15.1	22.1	18.3	40.9	39.8	26.4	2,803	89.7
Greensboro town	634	615	-3.0	595	21.8	41.2	0.0	0.0	37.0	30.6	21.2	39.7	65.1	11.2	206	66.5
Greenville town	861	824	-4.3	1,062	11.9	84.4	0.0	3.2	0.6	25.8	14.8	29.5	66.1	5.5	329	58.1
Greenwood town	688	662	-3.8	607	55.7	31.3	0.0	4.0	9.1	26.4	14.8	34.4	50.5	25.8	221	81.4
Grenelefe CDP	1,752	-	-	2,220	61.1	6.7	1.3	0.0	30.9	10.5	19.2	47.7	38.6	29.3	942	81.8
Gretna city	1,665	1,436	-13.8	1,025	3.4	84.2	0.0	0.0	12.4	23.7	23.7	42.8	65.4	13.2	465	55.5
Grove City CDP	1,804	-	-	2,253	92.6	0.0	0.0	1.5	5.9	12.6	34.2	56.6	47.7	21.6	967	88.1
Groveland city	8,715	16,423	88.4	13,672	47.4	21.5	5.6	1.5	24.0	26.7	15.4	40.1	43.0	23.3	4,410	93.9
Gulf Breeze city	5,763	6,900	19.7	6,546	91.3	1.8	0.2	2.0	4.7	20.9	24.2	49.0	17.6	56.6	2,804	97.9
Gulf Gate Estates CDP	10,911	-	-	11,118	85.2	2.1	1.2	1.4	10.0	16.6	34.2	54.3	36.1	30.2	5,411	89.3
Gulfport city	12,035	12,342	2.6	12,335	84.5	7.5	2.4	1.7	3.9	9.5	31.6	56.1	30.5	40.4	6,115	93.0
Gulf Stream town	894	985	10.2	1,053	92.8	1.8	0.6	1.1	3.7	20.4	27.3	57.2	6.2	73.9	436	100.0
Gun Club Estates CDP	776	-	-	927	19.0	4.1	2.0	0.0	74.9	24.4	15.2	47.2	61.7	20.7	270	100.0
Haines City city	20,404	26,009	27.5	24,164	26.9	27.5	0.4	1.5	43.8	28.5	13.8	35.0	54.6	15.0	7,064	84.3
Hallandale Beach city	37,113	39,847	7.4	39,656	42.5	18.4	2.1	1.5	35.6	17.1	24.3	44.8	42.0	32.0	17,573	88.0
Hampton city	503	502	-0.2	443	83.1	16.9	0.0	0.0	0.0	13.8	25.1	52.3	69.9	6.8	194	74.7
Harbor Bluffs CDP	2,860	-	-	2,866	89.4	3.7	1.9	1.6	3.4	15.1	25.0	49.6	25.9	36.8	1,125	98.8
Harbour Heights CDP	2,987	-	-	3,752	67.7	14.1	1.3	0.0	16.9	25.3	29.6	48.9	40.2	25.8	1,326	92.8
Harlem CDP	2,658	-	-	2,377	0.0	97.6	0.0	0.0	2.4	30.3	17.2	31.3	60.9	4.6	796	77.8
Harlem Heights CDP	1,975	-	-	1,957	4.9	14.9	0.0	1.7	78.5	34.0	6.7	22.2	60.3	6.5	533	89.7
Harold CDP	823	-	-	1,308	87.5	0.0	0.0	7.0	5.6	20.9	13.8	32.0	35.6	11.6	380	100.0
Hastings CDP	580	-	-	1,464	37.0	58.5	0.0	0.0	4.5	23.8	14.6	40.2	64.0	10.7	492	59.3
Havana town	1,753	1,708	-2.6	1,886	44.6	49.2	0.0	1.3	4.9	13.7	32.7	53.9	45.4	25.2	935	71.3
Haverhill town	1,822	2,143	17.6	2,319	35.8	33.4	0.1	2.7	27.9	25.4	14.6	37.7	47.4	19.6	652	92.9
Hawthorne city	1,414	1,522	7.6	1,669	32.4	58.7	0.0	6.7	2.2	24.9	18.9	39.5	55.9	16.4	560	72.5
Heathrow CDP	5,896	-	-	6,987	64.9	4.2	12.0	2.3	16.6	23.2	18.7	43.0	8.4	64.6	2,812	99.5
Heritage Pines CDP	2,136	-	-	1,945	96.6	0.0	0.0	1.1	2.3	0.0	86.2	72.2	30.4	31.0	1,207	94.6
Hernando CDP	9,054	-	-	9,261	86.3	2.4	5.9	2.4	3.0	14.4	34.0	56.6	55.8	15.6	4,275	85.9
Hernando Beach CDP	2,299	-	-	2,675	87.6	0.0	0.0	2.3	10.2	9.9	33.8	57.6	29.5	27.9	1,163	93.4
Hialeah city	224,704	233,339	3.8	234,539	2.7	0.7	0.6	0.2	95.9	17.4	20.4	44.5	64.0	15.7	74,559	81.8
Hialeah Gardens city	21,740	23,474	8.0	23,709	2.8	0.5	0.1	0.5	96.1	17.9	16.8	42.5	58.4	20.6	6,578	92.9
Highland Beach town	3,631	3,916	7.8	3,885	90.8	0.8	0.9	0.6	6.9	5.0	58.2	67.8	15.6	66.3	2,060	93.0
Highland City CDP	10,834	-	-	10,602	72.1	7.2	2.4	2.7	15.6	23.9	13.2	37.9	40.4	29.2	3,627	94.5
Highland Park village	187	220	17.6	173	89.6	0.0	4.0	0.6	5.8	20.8	34.7	52.3	22.0	46.2	70	100.0
High Point CDP	3,686	-	-	3,974	89.6	3.1	0.2	1.8	5.4	9.1	51.8	65.9	50.3	9.6	2,037	88.1
High Springs city	5,290	6,178	16.8	5,989	70.2	10.6	1.1	4.8	13.3	19.9	17.7	37.4	41.4	26.6	2,173	87.5
Hillcrest Heights town	254	298	17.3	239	92.5	3.8	0.0	3.8	0.0	25.1	23.0	47.1	32.3	39.0	87	95.4
Hilliard town	3,090	3,263	5.6	3,189	83.1	9.5	0.0	2.3	5.1	22.6	15.8	31.9	64.8	9.7	1,166	93.1
Hill 'n Dale CDP	1,934	-	-	3,045	70.9	21.6	0.0	3.8	3.7	25.4	16.8	37.9	66.0	10.8	787	90.0
Hillsboro Beach town	1,875	2,012	7.3	1,752	87.8	0.8	0.9	0.2	10.3	4.3	54.7	66.6	17.9	53.1	999	96.2
Hillsboro Pines CDP	446	-	-	572	50.3	47.9	0.0	0.0	1.7	25.0	6.8	28.9	64.2	23.3	155	100.0
Hobe Sound CDP	11,521	-	-	14,003	81.9	8.1	1.5	2.0	6.5	14.6	32.9	54.9	38.7	32.5	6,079	91.0
Holden Heights CDP	3,679	-	-	3,521	52.4	19.2	2.0	0.8	25.6	12.4	18.2	48.0	48.0	22.5	1,290	91.3
Holiday CDP	22,403	-	-	20,816	78.4	5.5	1.6	1.9	12.6	18.2	21.2	45.4	59.4	12.1	9,351	78.8

1 May be of any race.

Table A. All Places — **Population and Housing**

STATE City, town, township, borough, or CDP (county if applicable)	Population				Race and Hispanic or Latino origin (percent)					Age (percent)			Educational attainment of persons age 25 and older		Occupied housing units	
	2010 census total population	2019 estimated population	Percent change 2010-2019	ACS total population estimate 2015-2019	White alone, not Hispanic or Latino	Black alone, not Hispanic or Latino	Asian alone, not Hispanic or Latino	All other races or 2 or more races, not Hispanic or Latino	Hispanic or Latino[1]	Under 18 years old	Age 65 years and older	Median age	Percent High school diploma or less	Percent Bachelor's degree or more	Total	Percent with a computer
	1	2	3	4	5	6	7	8	9	10	11	12	13	14	15	16
FLORIDA—Con.																
Holley CDP	1,630	-	-	1,720	85.5	6.0	0.5	3.8	4.2	27.3	23.5	39.7	29.6	30.4	698	94.8
Holly Hill city	11,648	12,357	6.1	12,147	68.0	17.2	2.4	3.4	9.0	19.8	22.3	43.6	50.6	17.6	5,210	84.8
Hollywood city	140,709	154,817	10.0	152,511	38.8	17.0	2.2	3.0	38.9	19.8	16.8	41.6	41.9	27.9	56,461	92.3
Holmes Beach city	3,839	4,305	12.1	4,243	96.3	0.0	0.4	0.8	2.6	5.7	47.8	64.1	16.3	48.6	2,309	96.2
Homeland CDP	366	-	-	269	85.1	2.2	0.0	2.6	10.0	40.1	22.3	20.8	29.4	26.6	65	92.3
Homestead city	60,748	69,523	14.4	68,438	11.9	19.1	0.8	1.5	66.6	32.7	7.9	30.6	50.0	22.2	18,938	92.8
Homestead Base CDP	964	-	-	1,054	9.9	37.7	0.0	2.1	50.4	52.9	4.4	16.2	51.3	4.7	143	89.5
Homosassa CDP	2,578	-	-	2,037	93.5	1.2	0.0	0.9	4.4	5.8	54.4	66.1	39.3	27.2	1,093	95.9
Homosassa Springs CDP	13,791	-	-	13,478	93.0	0.8	0.1	4.4	1.7	17.1	30.1	51.8	53.5	9.6	5,726	87.5
Horizon West CDP	14,000	-	-	39,065	63.9	7.3	5.8	3.6	19.5	28.9	6.1	33.5	14.6	56.4	12,562	99.8
Horseshoe Beach town	169	168	-0.6	118	73.7	13.6	2.5	6.8	3.4	9.3	50.8	65.2	68.2	18.7	66	83.3
Hosford CDP	650	-	-	704	95.7	1.1	0.0	3.1	0.0	11.6	26.0	54.5	54.2	19.0	330	88.8
Howey-in-the-Hills town	1,096	1,181	7.8	1,597	84.3	1.5	0.0	0.0	14.2	19.3	29.3	51.5	39.2	26.8	649	95.1
Hudson CDP	12,158	-	-	11,936	90.7	0.8	0.5	2.0	6.1	10.7	40.1	59.1	49.4	20.0	6,017	85.1
Hunters Creek CDP	14,321	-	-	20,817	36.6	7.8	11.5	2.1	42.0	23.1	10.4	37.9	24.5	47.5	7,048	98.7
Hutchinson Island South CDP	5,201	-	-	5,204	91.9	0.0	0.0	0.9	7.2	1.1	65.5	70.4	38.5	33.5	3,036	88.3
Hypoluxo town	2,587	2,839	9.7	2,781	76.5	13.4	0.9	4.2	5.0	9.7	31.9	55.2	26.1	43.1	1,388	98.8
Immokalee CDP	24,154	-	-	26,597	5.0	21.0	0.3	1.5	72.1	32.3	7.5	29.3	84.2	5.2	5,985	76.0
Indialantic town	2,723	2,908	6.8	2,865	89.0	0.6	2.3	1.2	6.9	18.5	22.9	50.9	20.5	42.3	1,161	94.4
Indian Creek village	86	89	3.5	44	63.6	0.0	9.1	2.3	25.0	29.5	20.5	55.3	16.7	60.0	15	100.0
Indian Harbour Beach city	8,166	8,557	4.8	8,470	82.4	0.4	1.1	2.8	13.3	16.4	28.0	53.2	22.8	48.5	3,611	94.3
Indian River Estates CDP	6,220	-	-	6,754	90.8	0.0	3.3	0.0	5.9	13.7	32.1	54.1	44.8	19.8	3,019	89.3
Indian River Shores town	3,870	4,311	11.4	4,206	96.0	0.0	0.8	0.8	2.4	4.9	74.3	72.9	9.5	70.7	2,131	96.9
Indian Rocks Beach city	4,065	4,285	5.4	4,243	95.3	0.2	0.6	0.8	3.2	7.0	33.3	60.3	22.0	46.8	2,228	97.4
Indian Shores town	1,382	1,468	6.2	1,189	93.5	1.7	0.9	0.0	3.9	6.1	42.1	62.4	14.9	51.3	650	93.5
Indiantown village	6,477	7,174	10.8	7,053	17.3	19.3	0.0	1.0	62.4	28.2	14.5	29.9	70.1	6.8	1,841	82.9
Inglis town	1,314	1,347	2.5	1,482	91.8	1.8	0.0	2.5	3.9	9.8	32.8	57.3	59.1	9.9	700	76.7
Interlachen town	1,477	1,471	-0.4	1,526	67.4	11.5	0.0	3.8	17.4	19.3	22.1	43.5	63.1	10.8	575	82.6
Inverness city	7,275	7,414	1.9	7,281	88.8	4.7	0.7	1.1	4.6	16.0	38.1	58.1	52.7	13.9	3,394	79.1
Inverness Highlands North CDP	2,401	-	-	2,587	87.4	3.4	0.0	0.0	9.3	22.0	15.4	39.5	62.4	8.4	894	94.9
Inverness Highlands South CDP	6,542	-	-	6,441	90.6	0.1	2.7	0.2	6.3	13.6	30.4	53.9	50.5	13.5	2,685	91.4
Inwood CDP	6,403	-	-	7,575	49.2	30.2	0.3	3.7	16.6	27.1	12.5	33.5	70.2	6.3	2,354	77.1
Iona CDP	15,369	-	-	14,118	90.5	0.5	1.2	0.9	6.9	5.6	54.4	66.5	34.6	38.7	7,312	93.1
Islamorada, Village of Islands villa	6,119	6,317	3.2	6,433	85.2	0.5	1.1	0.7	12.5	11.7	28.1	54.9	29.9	41.4	2,792	95.4
Island Walk CDP	3,035	-	-	3,112	91.4	0.0	0.0	1.6	7.0	12.2	51.9	68.2	27.8	39.4	1,511	96.3
Istachatta CDP	116	-	-	163	81.6	0.0	0.0	0.0	18.4	31.3	19.6	36.8	65.2	0.0	71	85.9
Ives Estates CDP	19,525	-	-	22,707	16.3	48.1	1.3	1.2	33.1	20.5	12.8	38.5	37.1	30.2	7,859	91.8
Jacksonville city	821,750	911,507	10.9	890,467	51.2	30.5	4.7	3.7	10.0	22.9	13.4	35.9	39.0	28.6	338,991	91.0
Jacksonville Beach city	21,362	23,628	10.6	23,399	87.6	1.2	1.5	3.0	6.7	16.0	18.8	42.3	18.0	57.4	10,912	93.9
Jacob City city	252	246	-2.4	243	3.3	90.9	0.0	4.5	1.2	11.5	20.2	42.6	65.0	2.8	118	82.2
Jan Phyl Village CDP	5,573	-	-	6,346	48.5	19.6	2.2	3.6	26.1	21.1	13.0	37.2	65.2	11.9	2,029	83.6
Jasmine Estates CDP	18,989	-	-	21,865	69.5	3.5	2.6	2.8	21.6	22.4	17.6	40.4	56.3	10.8	8,571	89.7
Jasper city	4,543	4,157	-8.5	4,146	36.2	51.4	0.2	1.8	10.5	9.0	13.7	38.8	77.4	6.4	703	78.9
Jay town	533	634	18.9	423	97.2	0.0	0.0	2.1	0.7	16.8	30.3	51.2	54.8	13.7	187	88.8
Jennings town	870	862	-0.9	690	38.1	17.5	0.0	0.3	44.1	41.9	19.7	27.4	71.3	9.8	225	66.2
Jensen Beach CDP	11,707	-	-	13,479	87.8	3.3	0.6	0.8	7.6	16.4	28.6	52.7	35.2	33.2	5,934	91.6
June Park CDP	4,094	-	-	4,669	88.7	0.7	0.9	1.6	8.0	12.6	17.7	45.2	37.6	25.3	1,771	95.8
Juno Beach town	3,191	3,655	14.5	3,586	94.6	0.4	0.9	0.0	4.2	2.5	52.5	66.4	14.1	61.0	2,190	90.8
Juno Ridge CDP	718	-	-	815	54.5	8.1	0.0	2.2	35.2	24.2	11.7	34.4	49.6	23.1	391	82.9
Jupiter town	55,312	65,791	18.9	64,565	78.3	1.4	2.9	2.6	14.8	19.3	22.5	46.1	23.1	47.8	26,186	95.3
Jupiter Farms CDP	11,994	-	-	12,750	86.8	1.4	1.5	0.4	9.9	19.1	18.1	47.7	30.7	37.1	4,126	98.4
Jupiter Inlet Colony town	400	453	13.3	381	92.7	0.0	2.9	2.1	2.4	14.7	40.4	59.4	15.1	60.5	160	96.3
Jupiter Island town	817	929	13.7	803	78.3	16.8	2.9	0.0	2.0	8.2	47.9	60.9	24.7	56.6	310	92.9
Kathleen CDP	6,332	-	-	6,358	77.4	0.8	1.4	1.6	18.7	23.7	12.8	36.1	63.8	8.2	1,963	92.2
Kendale Lakes CDP	56,148	-	-	56,182	9.1	1.3	1.6	0.3	87.7	17.4	18.1	44.4	45.5	26.8	17,698	93.9
Kendall CDP	75,371	-	-	75,312	22.6	2.9	3.4	1.0	70.1	18.2	18.7	41.9	26.5	45.0	26,874	95.7
Kendall West CDP	36,154	-	-	38,433	4.9	0.7	1.6	0.5	92.4	18.5	15.0	41.0	48.0	31.4	11,474	95.2
Kenneth City town	5,036	5,121	1.7	5,127	65.3	5.7	15.5	3.2	10.3	18.2	24.0	48.0	50.3	16.8	1,811	89.5
Kensington Park CDP	3,901	-	-	4,407	52.8	6.7	0.0	0.2	40.2	21.4	21.7	40.3	44.5	21.1	1,558	93.3
Kenwood Estates CDP	1,283	-	-	1,282	38.5	6.2	0.0	6.2	49.1	17.0	8.4	33.0	72.3	8.9	366	95.1
Key Biscayne village	12,344	12,846	4.1	12,915	29.8	0.0	0.2	0.6	69.4	28.0	16.8	42.4	9.6	73.3	4,422	98.2
Key Colony Beach city	795	803	1.0	534	85.8	4.7	0.0	0.0	9.6	0.0	56.4	65.7	32.0	43.6	320	100.0
Key Largo CDP	10,433	-	-	9,952	72.9	1.1	0.9	1.0	24.1	15.8	26.8	52.9	36.2	31.6	4,326	89.9
Keystone CDP	24,039	-	-	25,493	72.7	3.1	7.7	3.4	13.2	26.3	14.6	43.4	18.2	54.8	8,732	98.1
Keystone Heights city	1,354	1,537	13.5	1,581	92.2	0.8	2.0	1.6	3.4	28.8	14.8	35.5	34.0	25.7	560	96.6
Key Vista CDP	1,757	-	-	1,616	88.9	4.7	2.7	1.6	2.1	17.1	31.3	50.4	28.5	25.2	642	82.7
Key West city	24,635	24,118	-2.1	24,843	59.6	13.4	2.0	1.3	23.7	15.2	17.0	40.9	34.0	35.6	10,501	91.6
Kissimmee city	59,558	72,717	22.1	71,185	18.1	8.3	3.5	1.4	68.7	24.0	12.0	34.5	47.8	18.4	22,210	86.4
LaBelle city	4,851	5,221	7.6	5,106	37.3	7.0	0.2	6.1	49.5	30.7	22.8	32.4	65.8	10.3	1,533	77.4
Lacoochee CDP	1,714	-	-	1,485	32.3	9.8	0.0	6.5	51.4	30.6	4.0	28.3	64.2	12.5	509	92.9
La Crosse town	363	397	9.4	408	52.9	14.0	0.0	3.2	29.9	16.4	22.1	49.7	56.7	10.8	117	76.9
Lady Lake town	14,033	16,020	14.2	15,426	84.0	3.3	1.5	3.6	7.6	11.6	50.8	65.5	46.0	22.7	7,695	91.1
Laguna Beach CDP	3,932	-	-	4,504	92.6	0.5	0.4	0.6	6.0	11.2	29.0	57.3	39.0	26.9	2,159	95.5
Lake Alfred city	4,917	6,257	27.3	5,788	57.2	22.7	7.4	3.3	9.4	25.2	18.8	36.4	48.0	19.8	2,087	90.2
Lake Belvedere Estates CDP	3,334	-	-	4,046	17.1	29.9	5.4	6.7	40.8	31.0	6.6	29.8	58.1	19.9	945	98.1
Lake Buena Vista city	25	27	8.0	4	100.0	0.0	0.0	0.0	0.0	0.0	50.0	66.5	75.0	25.0	3	100.0
Lake Butler CDP	15,400	-	-	19,499	63.6	9.2	6.9	4.0	16.3	30.4	12.1	39.9	13.6	61.8	6,169	100.0
Lake Butler city	1,890	1,804	-4.6	1,778	66.7	26.0	0.0	4.3	3.0	29.8	10.3	26.9	60.9	8.4	808	67.6
Lake City city	11,901	12,352	3.8	12,063	51.7	35.2	2.9	4.0	6.2	27.1	16.5	36.3	45.9	21.6	4,610	89.0
Lake Clarke Shores town	3,396	3,627	6.8	3,600	78.3	0.5	0.0	1.7	19.5	20.3	17.7	49.8	21.9	51.3	1,334	97.5
Lake Hamilton town	1,223	1,496	22.3	1,449	51.8	13.5	0.3	7.7	26.8	21.0	15.3	39.1	67.1	9.2	457	84.9
Lake Harbor CDP	45	-	-	26	100.0	0.0	0.0	0.0	0.0	53.8	0.0	15.9	0.0	100.0	6	100.0
Lake Hart CDP	542	-	-	451	51.0	0.7	11.1	4.7	32.6	12.9	4.7	28.6	18.4	52.5	215	100.0
Lake Helen city	2,627	2,801	6.6	2,760	88.3	4.2	0.2	0.1	7.2	17.0	24.1	48.1	51.7	14.8	1,110	91.0
Lake Kathryn CDP	920	-	-	954	99.1	0.0	0.9	0.0	0.0	12.9	11.2	40.6	64.9	5.0	344	91.0
Lakeland city	97,270	112,136	15.3	107,922	59.7	19.8	2.1	1.9	16.4	19.3	22.2	41.1	45.0	25.9	41,276	85.9
Lakeland Highlands CDP	11,056	-	-	12,332	79.9	2.8	3.6	2.7	10.9	21.4	21.1	46.2	26.2	42.1	4,360	94.6

1 May be of any race.

Table A. All Places — **Population and Housing**

STATE City, town, township, borough, or CDP (county if applicable)	Population: 2010 census total population	Population: 2019 estimated population	Population: Percent change 2010-2019	Population: ACS total population estimate 2015-2019	Race and Hispanic or Latino origin (percent): White alone, not Hispanic or Latino	Race: Black alone, not Hispanic or Latino	Race: Asian alone, not Hispanic or Latino	Race: All other races or 2 or more races, not Hispanic or Latino	Race: Hispanic or Latino[1]	Age (percent): Under 18 years old	Age: Age 65 years and older	Age: Median age	Educational attainment of persons age 25 and older: Percent High school diploma or less	Educational attainment: Percent Bachelor's degree or more	Occupied housing units: Total	Occupied housing units: Percent with a computer
	1	2	3	4	5	6	7	8	9	10	11	12	13	14	15	16
FLORIDA—Con.																
Lake Lindsey CDP	71	-	-	8	100.0	0.0	0.0	0.0	0.0	0.0	0.0	0.0	0.0	100.0	8	100.0
Lake Lorraine CDP	7,010	-	-	7,217	70.1	9.9	4.8	3.9	11.3	19.3	20.9	42.6	28.7	42.4	2,892	91.4
Lake Mack-Forest Hills CDP	1,010	-	-	899	88.9	0.0	0.0	0.0	11.1	17.1	19.9	50.7	60.6	8.9	394	74.6
Lake Magdalene CDP	28,509	-	-	30,805	58.8	8.0	4.0	2.4	26.9	19.3	19.5	43.5	31.1	37.8	12,208	93.5
Lake Mary city	13,803	17,479	26.6	16,698	72.0	4.9	7.8	3.1	12.1	19.7	21.1	45.4	21.9	52.1	6,210	97.6
Lake Mary Jane CDP	1,575	-	-	2,572	79.0	0.0	0.0	0.0	21.0	11.9	22.7	51.9	22.0	35.0	883	96.8
Lake Mystic CDP	500	-	-	547	81.5	0.0	0.0	13.2	5.3	10.2	7.9	45.3	62.7	13.7	211	86.7
Lake Panasoffkee CDP	3,551	-	-	3,197	93.2	0.3	0.6	0.9	4.9	12.6	31.7	57.6	63.3	10.9	1,426	76.6
Lake Park town	8,055	8,556	6.2	8,508	34.4	51.8	1.8	6.3	5.6	23.7	13.2	37.7	42.3	30.1	2,580	87.9
Lake Placid town	2,320	2,479	6.9	1,907	44.4	7.3	0.0	1.4	46.9	28.7	22.9	36.9	66.0	19.6	657	65.0
Lake Sarasota CDP	4,679	-	-	4,749	87.1	2.1	2.5	1.2	7.1	19.1	16.9	39.8	42.2	28.1	1,640	99.1
Lakeside CDP	30,943	-	-	30,458	74.6	9.7	3.4	4.1	8.2	20.9	16.8	40.4	41.7	21.4	11,464	96.5
Lake Wales city	14,154	16,759	18.4	16,035	53.3	25.4	0.3	2.2	18.8	23.6	22.9	40.3	49.4	21.4	5,917	88.5
Lakewood Park CDP	11,323	-	-	14,064	72.7	10.9	3.4	2.0	11.0	15.0	26.4	50.3	53.2	15.8	5,246	87.9
Lake Worth city	34,894	38,526	10.4	38,010	34.9	17.9	0.9	1.8	44.5	22.1	14.4	36.6	55.1	19.1	13,032	91.3
Lamont CDP	178	-	-	50	0.0	100.0	0.0	0.0	0.0	18.0	46.0	56.7	21.2	0.0	13	100.0
Land O' Lakes CDP	31,996	-	-	38,410	69.2	5.6	4.0	3.2	18.0	21.8	16.4	42.3	29.9	37.6	13,526	97.5
Lantana town	10,592	12,581	18.8	11,695	54.4	20.9	0.1	2.8	21.7	16.6	19.3	44.2	47.4	25.1	4,529	86.4
Largo city	79,439	84,948	6.9	84,130	77.7	5.4	2.4	2.9	11.5	15.8	25.9	48.3	42.5	23.1	36,970	86.3
Lauderdale-by-the-Sea town	6,173	6,664	8.0	6,626	80.8	3.2	0.8	3.2	11.9	4.9	47.1	63.6	25.7	49.5	4,003	92.2
Lauderdale Lakes city	32,784	36,194	10.4	35,606	8.2	83.3	1.6	2.6	4.3	23.4	16.6	37.6	62.1	13.4	11,790	87.0
Lauderhill city	66,936	71,868	7.4	71,625	9.1	79.1	0.9	2.8	8.1	26.0	13.9	35.7	52.4	20.2	23,398	89.1
Laurel CDP	8,171	-	-	9,518	84.7	7.6	1.6	3.2	2.9	12.2	39.6	59.1	35.2	32.0	4,609	89.1
Laurel Hill city	535	627	17.2	638	73.0	23.7	0.0	1.4	1.9	30.1	13.9	38.4	60.2	10.0	235	86.4
Lawtey city	728	725	-0.4	988	49.9	46.5	0.0	1.6	2.0	18.6	14.1	37.9	57.0	6.4	347	65.1
Layton city	184	182	-1.1	159	78.0	0.0	0.0	18.2	3.8	8.2	39.6	56.2	43.2	20.5	80	95.0
Lazy Lake village	24	26	8.3	28	100.0	0.0	0.0	0.0	0.0	0.0	14.3	44.5	0.0	39.3	8	100.0
Lealman CDP	19,879	-	-	22,034	65.1	9.2	7.5	7.4	10.8	19.3	17.4	40.7	54.6	14.3	8,554	87.6
Lecanto CDP	5,882	-	-	6,847	87.1	5.8	0.4	1.6	5.0	11.8	21.7	45.7	62.4	11.2	2,252	83.7
Lee town	352	328	-6.8	407	73.5	5.9	0.0	1.2	19.4	30.2	14.5	39.0	67.0	7.8	135	86.7
Leesburg city	20,335	23,671	16.4	22,672	52.6	25.7	1.7	1.7	18.3	23.0	24.6	40.0	53.3	15.4	8,952	85.0
Lehigh Acres CDP	86,784	-	-	123,378	37.1	18.6	1.2	2.7	40.3	27.3	12.5	34.6	56.9	14.6	34,020	93.6
Leisure City CDP	22,655	-	-	26,652	3.4	11.3	0.6	0.6	84.2	28.3	10.4	32.8	66.3	13.2	6,851	90.5
Lely CDP	3,451	-	-	3,675	82.2	1.4	0.0	0.1	16.3	8.0	51.3	65.7	26.8	34.7	1,795	89.9
Lely Resort CDP	4,646	-	-	6,295	67.3	15.7	0.2	1.9	14.9	11.7	37.9	58.5	34.7	40.9	2,993	95.8
Lemon Grove CDP	657	-	-	501	97.6	0.0	0.0	0.0	2.4	17.4	22.4	40.2	76.7	15.2	192	86.5
Lighthouse Point city	10,358	11,270	8.8	11,195	83.5	0.6	0.9	3.7	11.2	14.6	26.5	52.9	23.7	48.4	5,188	93.6
Limestone CDP	132	-	-	217	56.2	43.8	0.0	0.0	0.0	0.0	63.1	67.3	77.9	0.0	41	70.7
Limestone Creek CDP	1,014	-	-	1,285	10.7	58.4	4.6	0.0	26.4	22.8	8.0	38.8	65.2	16.9	362	96.4
Lisbon CDP	260	-	-	406	100.0	0.0	0.0	0.0	0.0	0.0	48.5	62.4	52.0	0.0	119	100.0
Live Oak city	6,859	6,972	1.6	6,890	51.8	26.1	0.1	6.8	15.3	17.8	17.6	42.6	43.9	28.3	2,441	71.2
Lloyd CDP	215	-	-	140	68.6	17.1	0.0	14.3	0.0	0.0	35.7	60.3	86.4	0.0	104	60.6
Lochmoor Waterway Estates CDP	4,204	-	-	4,163	83.4	4.5	1.6	1.3	9.1	17.5	31.3	56.6	37.8	31.8	1,807	87.6
Lockhart CDP	13,060	-	-	14,430	47.2	19.2	4.6	3.7	25.3	21.2	11.1	35.6	44.1	21.8	5,366	92.1
Longboat Key town	6,888	7,296	5.9	7,283	96.0	0.0	1.0	1.0	2.0	1.6	69.7	71.3	14.6	64.5	3,838	96.2
Longwood city	13,651	15,561	14.0	14,930	69.4	7.8	3.6	2.9	16.3	18.8	19.4	42.7	37.7	26.8	5,623	94.4
Loughman CDP	2,680	-	-	5,674	50.0	14.5	2.4	1.7	31.5	14.4	13.7	31.1	38.8	22.9	1,658	93.8
Lower Grand Lagoon CDP	3,881	-	-	4,584	81.2	5.4	2.5	4.5	6.3	11.6	18.4	46.8	33.9	26.0	2,106	93.7
Loxahatchee Groves town	3,190	3,593	12.6	3,520	68.5	2.6	4.6	1.5	22.8	12.4	20.7	45.6	39.0	24.2	1,189	99.7
Lutz CDP	19,344	-	-	22,235	75.3	3.7	4.5	3.7	12.8	22.1	16.8	42.9	24.1	46.0	8,158	96.6
Lynn Haven city	18,727	20,525	9.6	20,948	80.8	9.1	1.4	3.0	5.7	26.5	14.6	35.0	29.9	31.8	7,497	96.1
Macclenny city	6,362	6,940	9.1	6,592	78.9	18.7	0.0	1.8	0.6	24.7	13.8	39.0	45.4	16.8	2,057	81.9
McGregor CDP	7,406	-	-	7,760	88.4	0.4	1.8	0.8	8.6	9.5	38.1	58.9	30.9	43.5	3,470	94.9
McIntosh town	454	496	9.3	357	96.6	0.0	0.0	1.1	2.2	16.0	31.4	55.0	38.9	31.8	167	79.0
Madeira Beach city	4,181	4,301	2.9	4,300	92.4	0.4	0.2	1.1	5.9	7.4	32.0	59.1	30.1	38.8	2,117	93.2
Madison city	3,035	2,763	-9.0	2,793	28.8	65.6	1.0	0.0	4.6	18.2	19.8	41.4	65.0	17.3	976	65.3
Maitland city	15,852	17,652	11.4	17,765	60.0	16.0	4.6	3.4	16.0	19.8	13.7	36.1	15.7	57.5	7,171	96.9
Malabar town	2,757	3,185	15.5	3,061	88.1	3.8	0.3	4.5	3.2	11.3	27.1	55.6	36.0	30.1	1,286	95.2
Malone town	2,088	2,092	0.2	2,013	43.6	39.9	0.3	2.7	13.5	12.3	7.0	35.6	75.2	5.6	272	79.4
Manalapan town	406	466	14.8	303	87.8	5.9	1.7	0.7	4.0	9.6	52.8	65.5	9.2	69.1	158	100.0
Manasota Key CDP	1,229	-	-	1,282	99.4	0.0	0.0	0.0	0.6	0.9	81.8	73.8	39.4	34.6	632	89.9
Manatee Road CDP	2,244	-	-	2,670	96.9	0.4	2.0	0.6	0.0	25.2	30.6	46.0	54.1	10.1	1,136	73.1
Mango CDP	11,313	-	-	11,137	47.1	19.0	0.5	6.2	27.2	27.3	10.9	33.7	53.3	13.2	4,147	88.2
Mangonia Park town	1,888	2,018	6.9	2,333	3.6	82.7	0.4	0.3	13.0	34.4	7.7	28.2	59.9	9.6	689	81.1
Marathon city	8,303	8,581	3.3	8,702	56.0	6.3	0.9	0.2	36.6	16.8	21.4	48.5	39.7	30.7	3,797	92.9
Marco Island city	16,413	17,947	9.3	17,834	87.8	0.1	0.8	0.4	10.9	8.3	50.8	65.3	26.9	44.8	8,379	95.4
Margate city	53,120	58,796	10.7	58,023	35.8	29.5	2.8	2.8	29.0	16.6	22.5	46.4	48.6	20.3	23,306	90.0
Marianna city	7,563	5,803	-23.3	6,923	48.2	47.0	0.3	2.6	1.9	24.4	17.6	39.0	60.4	10.3	3,071	72.5
Marineland town	10	11	10.0	8	75.0	25.0	0.0	0.0	0.0	0.0	0.0	21.5	50.0	50.0	0	0.0
Mary Esther city	3,854	4,434	15.0	4,309	67.7	4.4	6.5	9.3	12.2	21.4	16.7	42.1	34.4	31.2	1,658	93.2
Masaryktown CDP	1,040	-	-	1,006	93.1	0.0	0.0	0.0	6.9	31.5	16.5	38.4	62.9	13.2	365	92.6
Mascotte city	5,089	6,315	24.1	5,743	38.4	11.1	0.3	6.7	43.6	27.5	8.0	31.7	62.1	5.9	1,669	93.8
Matlacha CDP	677	-	-	537	93.9	0.0	1.3	0.0	4.8	0.0	52.7	65.8	27.5	53.2	338	97.0
Matlacha Isles-Matlacha Shores CDP	229	-	-	256	96.1	0.0	0.0	3.9	0.0	34.0	35.9	42.4	22.5	23.1	97	85.6
Mayo town	1,219	1,269	4.1	1,376	30.7	56.9	0.0	3.6	8.8	27.9	13.1	24.9	69.8	4.6	371	75.7
Meadow Oaks CDP	2,442	-	-	2,604	81.8	0.0	1.0	6.5	10.8	14.7	32.2	51.2	54.7	18.4	1,179	91.9
Meadow Woods CDP	25,558	-	-	35,726	16.5	11.8	4.9	4.2	62.5	23.9	9.7	35.3	35.3	32.2	9,855	96.4
Medley town	838	883	5.4	958	3.2	0.0	0.0	0.0	96.8	12.2	32.8	53.9	63.5	12.4	354	66.4
Medulla CDP	8,892	-	-	10,275	63.5	12.1	0.6	3.0	20.8	23.3	12.8	35.9	44.9	22.6	3,513	93.3
Melbourne city	76,217	83,029	8.9	81,468	70.9	9.2	4.2	4.4	11.3	17.4	21.2	42.6	38.6	28.5	32,765	88.4
Melbourne Beach town	3,098	3,298	6.5	3,247	91.0	0.0	0.5	2.3	6.3	18.7	24.0	51.3	23.8	51.1	1,230	90.9
Melbourne Village town	662	694	4.8	814	88.2	0.0	0.6	5.5	5.7	16.0	30.6	55.2	18.8	46.1	307	93.8
Memphis CDP	7,848	-	-	9,647	34.7	37.6	0.2	3.3	24.2	23.5	14.3	39.0	53.6	19.8	2,908	86.6
Merritt Island CDP	34,743	-	-	36,532	83.4	4.5	1.5	2.3	8.3	18.6	23.5	49.4	29.8	35.6	14,727	93.7
Mexico Beach city	1,070	1,114	4.1	1,386	88.2	0.0	2.2	4.0	5.7	5.8	33.5	55.0	25.0	36.0	680	96.8
Miami city	399,481	467,963	17.1	454,279	11.3	14.4	1.0	0.7	72.7	17.5	16.9	40.1	50.5	29.6	176,777	84.9
Miami Beach city	87,380	88,885	1.7	90,108	35.6	3.3	2.3	2.1	56.7	14.8	16.7	41.4	29.7	47.9	43,326	93.1
Miami Gardens city	107,163	110,001	2.6	111,363	3.2	68.6	0.7	1.3	26.2	24.4	13.8	35.5	58.5	14.1	30,485	87.5

1 May be of any race.

Table A. All Places — **Population and Housing**

STATE City, town, township, borough, or CDP (county if applicable)	Population: 2010 census total population	Population: 2019 estimated population	Population: Percent change 2010-2019	Population: ACS total population estimate 2015-2019	Race and Hispanic or Latino origin (percent): White alone, not Hispanic or Latino	Black alone, not Hispanic or Latino	Asian alone, not Hispanic or Latino	All other races or 2 or more races, not Hispanic or Latino	Hispanic or Latino[1]	Age (percent): Under 18 years old	Age 65 years and older	Median age	Educational attainment of persons age 25 and older: Percent High school diploma or less	Percent Bachelor's degree or more	Occupied housing units: Total	Percent with a computer
	1	2	3	4	5	6	7	8	9	10	11	12	13	14	15	16
FLORIDA—Con.																
Miami Lakes town	29,373	31,367	6.8	30,864	10.2	2.5	1.0	0.3	86.1	21.1	16.4	41.3	31.1	38.5	10,570	96.3
Miami Shores village	10,360	10,365	0.0	10,459	39.2	13.0	3.4	4.6	39.8	24.0	12.2	39.8	17.9	55.6	3,221	97.4
Miami Springs city	13,809	13,917	0.8	14,146	20.6	0.9	1.4	0.3	76.7	18.9	19.4	44.6	39.4	35.4	4,879	86.8
Micanopy town	590	635	7.6	542	88.2	8.5	0.4	0.7	2.2	14.8	20.7	38.6	35.6	31.6	229	88.2
Micco CDP	9,052	-	-	9,047	95.8	0.0	0.2	0.5	3.6	4.2	55.2	66.8	50.4	15.3	4,861	80.9
Middleburg CDP	13,008	-	-	14,111	90.7	2.8	0.8	3.9	1.8	23.1	13.3	40.2	55.1	15.0	4,802	94.5
Midway city	3,014	3,000	-0.5	3,221	5.0	87.6	1.0	0.7	5.7	29.9	4.3	35.1	45.0	25.1	1,237	88.1
Midway CDP	16,115	-	-	17,760	87.5	3.1	3.4	2.2	3.7	21.0	16.8	43.7	29.1	35.0	7,325	95.5
Midway CDP	1,705	-	-	1,592	5.5	83.7	0.0	1.6	9.2	20.5	20.9	40.3	62.8	7.3	617	73.4
Milton city	8,814	10,523	19.4	9,995	73.7	7.9	1.7	7.0	9.6	23.3	14.5	37.0	35.9	21.2	3,756	94.8
Mims CDP	7,058	-	-	6,375	85.2	9.9	0.5	2.2	2.2	15.7	24.5	51.7	48.6	16.3	2,493	86.5
Minneola city	9,419	12,595	33.7	11,559	53.5	13.0	4.8	2.4	26.4	29.9	10.5	37.2	33.1	25.1	3,435	99.0
Miramar city	121,958	141,191	15.8	139,468	12.5	43.4	5.7	3.5	34.9	23.1	10.2	37.0	38.2	27.3	41,263	96.3
Miramar Beach CDP	6,146	-	-	8,356	83.5	3.7	4.9	4.3	3.6	14.7	31.0	55.0	16.1	49.9	3,741	96.5
Molino CDP	1,277	-	-	1,202	88.5	4.4	0.0	0.0	7.1	20.0	17.6	37.0	30.9	26.2	457	92.3
Monticello city	2,521	2,409	-4.4	2,248	48.6	48.4	0.0	0.9	2.2	20.7	29.6	53.0	40.6	29.7	1,085	77.5
Montura CDP	3,283	-	-	3,425	28.6	0.0	0.0	0.8	70.6	20.0	17.4	42.6	82.4	2.8	1,213	69.0
Montverde town	1,466	1,705	16.3	1,633	83.0	0.9	0.9	1.2	14.0	23.8	14.8	43.7	26.2	32.1	578	94.3
Moon Lake CDP	4,919	-	-	4,312	89.8	0.9	0.9	4.8	3.6	22.7	13.0	38.9	69.0	3.2	1,685	83.1
Moore Haven city	1,685	1,807	7.2	2,599	33.4	35.1	0.0	0.5	31.0	21.8	13.1	34.9	74.1	6.0	816	72.7
Morriston CDP	164	-	-	126	0.0	0.0	0.0	0.0	100.0	25.4	0.0	28.5	100.0	0.0	38	44.7
Mount Carmel CDP	227	-	-	161	100.0	0.0	0.0	0.0	0.0	12.4	6.8	44.8	22.5	38.0	81	79.0
Mount Dora city	12,135	14,516	19.6	13,897	64.0	17.8	0.6	4.4	13.2	18.4	33.7	50.3	38.6	33.2	5,946	90.4
Mount Plymouth CDP	4,011	-	-	4,757	71.1	18.5	0.0	0.6	9.8	24.8	16.7	40.4	39.4	18.5	1,758	89.2
Mulat CDP	259	-	-	243	96.7	2.1	0.0	0.0	1.2	20.2	16.5	33.0	40.1	24.6	54	74.1
Mulberry city	3,810	4,257	11.7	4,124	71.8	9.9	1.0	0.6	16.6	19.3	29.6	48.7	60.8	9.1	1,506	86.9
Munson CDP	372	-	-	225	88.9	0.0	0.0	5.3	5.8	29.8	10.2	29.6	78.0	7.6	83	81.9
Myrtle Grove CDP	15,870	-	-	16,875	60.2	18.2	6.5	8.2	6.9	20.0	15.4	33.4	37.0	20.0	6,053	91.2
Naples city	19,519	22,088	13.2	21,812	88.8	4.4	0.8	1.1	4.8	8.1	52.5	66.0	20.5	56.7	10,797	92.4
Naples Manor CDP	5,562	-	-	6,507	4.1	25.4	1.9	2.7	65.9	28.8	12.3	27.6	77.8	9.3	1,312	83.2
Naples Park CDP	5,967	-	-	5,733	78.7	1.0	1.8	2.8	15.8	15.7	23.5	45.5	44.3	33.5	2,323	94.5
Naranja CDP	8,303	-	-	11,778	4.9	31.3	2.1	2.9	58.8	37.0	5.9	27.8	54.9	17.9	3,112	95.5
Nassau Village-Ratliff CDP	5,337	-	-	4,801	97.4	0.0	0.0	1.8	0.7	21.1	17.3	41.8	59.6	13.1	1,861	96.2
Navarre CDP	31,378	-	-	37,362	75.6	8.5	2.9	3.4	9.6	24.6	12.6	37.4	30.1	26.8	13,306	97.1
Navarre Beach CDP	638	-	-	1,150	93.7	0.0	0.9	3.4	2.1	13.8	23.7	54.4	13.7	60.8	628	97.8
Neptune Beach city	7,030	7,259	3.3	7,101	88.5	0.6	1.3	4.5	5.1	18.1	14.4	41.2	14.0	56.5	3,048	95.0
Newberry city	5,015	6,231	24.2	5,944	75.8	13.3	0.2	1.4	9.4	31.4	12.4	35.2	34.8	28.9	2,018	88.9
New Port Richey city	14,919	16,737	12.2	16,223	78.9	4.9	0.9	1.4	13.8	14.3	28.3	50.7	51.2	14.2	7,440	84.1
New Port Richey East CDP	10,036	-	-	10,398	82.0	4.8	0.4	1.9	11.0	17.2	25.8	47.1	49.9	15.2	4,832	91.5
New Smyrna Beach city	23,441	27,843	18.8	26,457	90.6	3.7	1.2	2.0	2.6	12.4	38.0	59.3	31.7	34.3	12,529	92.8
Niceville city	12,978	15,972	23.1	15,386	82.5	7.0	2.4	3.8	4.2	24.5	16.9	38.6	22.5	38.5	5,688	95.2
Nobleton CDP	282	-	-	104	86.5	0.0	0.0	0.0	13.5	0.0	27.9	47.8	77.9	13.5	52	44.2
Nocatee CDP	4,524	-	-	14,747	80.3	1.4	7.1	3.1	8.2	29.2	17.4	39.8	13.4	59.2	4,913	98.0
Nokomis CDP	3,167	-	-	3,355	95.6	1.1	0.0	0.7	2.6	11.7	21.4	51.2	56.1	20.1	1,634	91.9
Noma town	209	205	-1.9	251	68.1	29.5	0.0	0.8	1.6	16.3	12.4	50.4	76.0	1.6	106	60.4
North Bay Village city	7,141	8,057	12.8	8,161	26.7	3.5	2.1	1.5	66.3	15.5	11.4	35.3	27.3	46.6	3,398	96.6
North Brooksville CDP	3,544	-	-	3,161	83.3	2.8	0.0	5.8	8.0	16.4	27.9	53.9	56.4	15.4	1,321	89.1
Northdale CDP	22,079	-	-	23,510	56.6	6.7	3.0	1.5	32.2	20.4	14.9	40.2	27.9	39.2	8,728	96.9
North DeLand CDP	1,450	-	-	1,400	84.2	0.0	2.9	3.4	9.6	21.7	22.0	44.7	45.4	15.8	588	91.7
North Fort Myers CDP	39,407	-	-	42,770	85.5	2.4	0.8	1.5	9.8	11.0	46.3	62.5	48.7	19.4	19,600	90.8
North Key Largo CDP	1,244	-	-	886	95.6	0.8	1.1	0.0	2.5	5.5	55.8	69.0	11.8	58.7	404	98.8
North Lauderdale city	41,089	44,262	7.7	44,020	11.1	53.7	3.6	3.2	28.5	26.8	8.9	33.6	54.9	17.4	13,713	94.9
North Miami city	60,134	62,822	4.5	62,489	9.2	58.9	1.2	1.2	29.5	22.3	11.9	36.0	55.3	19.1	19,147	89.4
North Miami Beach city	40,870	43,041	5.3	42,971	16.8	39.7	2.7	2.2	38.6	21.6	13.7	37.3	45.8	22.5	13,676	88.3
North Palm Beach village	12,018	13,127	9.2	13,029	82.4	3.1	2.5	1.0	11.1	12.6	34.0	56.0	26.3	45.2	6,254	95.5
North Port city	57,320	70,724	23.4	66,410	78.8	6.5	1.6	3.1	10.0	20.6	24.2	46.1	45.1	21.8	23,560	93.8
North Redington Beach town	1,421	1,476	3.9	1,242	91.9	0.0	2.2	0.9	5.0	7.7	47.8	63.7	25.8	41.4	653	96.6
North River Shores CDP	3,079	-	-	3,874	87.0	0.4	0.0	1.4	11.3	24.3	24.4	46.7	23.0	41.8	1,553	95.1
North Sarasota CDP	6,982	-	-	8,806	50.4	25.1	0.2	0.5	23.8	21.6	20.9	44.7	59.4	16.3	3,279	84.8
North Weeki Wachee CDP	8,524	-	-	8,238	82.7	3.1	1.0	3.4	9.8	12.0	37.8	58.4	47.8	21.5	3,722	95.9
Oak Hill city	1,938	2,214	14.2	2,082	86.4	9.0	0.9	2.3	1.5	12.2	29.1	56.2	54.3	14.0	850	91.8
Oakland town	2,557	3,123	22.1	3,014	59.3	17.9	4.1	4.8	13.9	23.1	12.4	38.8	30.4	36.2	963	94.0
Oakland Park city	41,299	45,202	9.5	44,699	35.8	26.6	3.8	2.8	31.0	18.6	12.4	41.0	45.4	27.0	16,958	94.8
Oakleaf Plantation CDP	20,315	-	-	28,237	42.4	25.9	6.8	5.8	19.1	29.2	8.1	34.7	28.8	33.4	8,322	98.8
Oak Ridge CDP	22,685	-	-	24,004	8.6	36.5	3.0	2.0	49.9	25.2	9.4	33.3	60.5	13.1	7,069	90.2
Ocala city	56,568	60,786	7.5	59,267	59.4	19.9	2.2	2.8	15.7	22.7	18.1	38.3	44.7	24.2	22,749	85.1
Ocean Breeze town	357	381	6.7	195	100.0	0.0	0.0	0.0	0.0	0.0	61.5	66.8	55.4	11.3	106	77.4
Ocean City CDP	5,550	-	-	6,249	65.0	13.0	1.6	4.8	15.5	19.9	15.1	36.8	34.9	27.0	2,640	88.4
Ocean Ridge town	1,785	1,956	9.6	1,579	86.6	0.0	1.0	0.0	12.4	8.9	42.6	59.9	15.6	58.6	762	96.7
Ocoee city	35,734	48,263	35.1	46,305	43.3	18.8	5.4	4.5	28.0	27.0	9.2	35.0	34.1	34.9	14,591	96.0
Odessa CDP	7,267	-	-	8,036	66.8	10.5	5.5	1.7	15.5	25.4	15.2	40.7	34.4	37.3	2,723	96.7
Ojus CDP	18,036	-	-	16,417	40.1	10.4	1.0	0.9	47.7	19.3	17.5	44.0	32.4	36.0	6,589	91.3
Okahumpka CDP	267	-	-	193	100.0	0.0	0.0	0.0	0.0	0.0	53.9	67.5	86.0	7.3	115	100.0
Okeechobee city	5,664	5,816	2.7	5,724	60.0	10.1	2.3	5.0	22.7	23.4	16.1	36.8	60.3	10.3	1,946	86.3
Oldsmar city	13,730	15,061	9.7	14,657	75.9	3.0	4.7	3.0	13.4	20.9	14.2	39.7	36.5	32.1	5,419	96.9
Olga CDP	1,952	-	-	2,333	87.2	1.0	2.7	1.3	7.8	21.0	20.8	39.1	53.5	18.6	740	88.4
Olympia Heights CDP	13,488	-	-	13,958	9.9	0.4	0.3	0.3	89.1	16.3	22.2	46.1	45.5	27.4	4,049	89.3
Ona CDP	-	-	-	658	24.5	0.0	0.0	0.0	75.5	18.5	14.1	34.7	79.7	0.0	158	17.7
Opa-locka city	15,185	15,887	4.6	16,149	1.2	55.4	0.1	1.2	42.1	29.0	13.5	35.6	71.9	8.5	5,916	75.1
Orange City city	11,324	12,335	8.9	11,990	71.5	7.6	2.0	2.0	16.9	17.8	31.8	49.2	43.1	21.4	5,424	89.3
Orange Park town	8,459	8,824	4.3	8,734	58.3	15.0	3.3	5.1	18.2	17.2	22.3	43.3	32.4	26.9	3,380	93.0
Orangetree CDP	4,406	-	-	4,989	67.4	1.8	0.0	9.3	21.6	32.0	13.7	36.9	29.6	32.9	1,521	100.0
Orchid town	415	454	9.4	516	90.3	3.7	3.3	0.2	2.5	0.6	82.0	71.1	19.5	68.2	243	98.8
Oriole Beach CDP	1,420	-	-	1,815	83.5	0.0	0.8	6.2	9.6	28.2	9.9	33.1	19.5	43.0	575	100.0
Orlando city	238,836	287,442	20.4	280,832	36.5	23.5	4.1	3.3	32.6	21.1	10.2	33.8	32.8	38.1	112,137	94.2
Orlovista CDP	6,123	-	-	6,416	13.8	46.8	11.1	4.2	24.1	20.6	10.2	35.8	54.4	9.3	2,284	92.9
Ormond Beach city	39,429	43,759	11.0	42,545	84.7	4.0	2.4	1.8	7.0	17.2	29.2	50.9	34.2	31.2	18,023	90.2
Ormond-by-the-Sea CDP	7,406	-	-	7,268	91.6	2.5	0.9	1.8	3.2	7.2	37.9	60.1	31.1	31.7	3,857	92.3
Osprey CDP	6,100	-	-	6,931	84.5	1.0	1.1	2.5	10.8	15.7	39.2	58.1	21.9	56.6	2,963	94.6

1 May be of any race.

Table A. All Places — **Population and Housing**

STATE City, town, township, borough, or CDP (county if applicable)	Population				Race and Hispanic or Latino origin (percent)					Age (percent)			Educational attainment of persons age 25 and older		Occupied housing units	
	2010 census total population	2019 estimated population	Percent change 2010-2019	ACS total population estimate 2015-2019	White alone, not Hispanic or Latino	Black alone, not Hispanic or Latino	Asian alone, not Hispanic or Latino	All other races or 2 or more races, not Hispanic or Latino	Hispanic or Latino[1]	Under 18 years old	Age 65 years and older	Median age	Percent High school diploma or less	Percent Bachelor's degree or more	Total	Percent with a computer
	1	2	3	4	5	6	7	8	9	10	11	12	13	14	15	16
FLORIDA—Con.																
Otter Creek town	134	134	0.0	49	79.6	6.1	0.0	14.3	0.0	22.4	26.5	51.4	81.6	0.0	18	66.7
Oviedo city	33,471	41,860	25.1	40,370	64.4	7.4	5.8	2.4	20.0	25.9	10.7	36.9	19.0	49.0	13,137	96.5
Pace CDP	20,039	-	-	22,860	85.2	3.9	2.0	4.8	4.1	24.0	16.3	37.7	34.3	31.0	8,152	93.4
Page Park CDP	514	-	-	490	54.1	15.1	4.9	0.0	25.9	21.6	13.5	45.2	44.7	22.7	202	78.7
Pahokee city	5,695	6,315	10.9	6,269	13.3	62.2	0.0	0.0	24.5	24.3	13.2	35.2	67.5	10.7	1,860	63.1
Paisley CDP	818	-	-	1,479	88.8	0.1	0.0	1.2	9.9	26.3	20.9	37.6	80.8	0.0	470	86.0
Palatka city	10,624	10,451	-1.6	10,363	47.2	41.5	1.0	2.6	7.7	24.1	21.3	35.9	58.5	11.1	4,161	74.7
Palm Bay city	104,006	115,552	11.1	111,997	60.7	16.7	1.5	3.9	17.1	22.4	18.5	40.3	45.5	19.3	38,486	90.9
Palm Beach town	8,161	8,816	8.0	8,723	92.5	0.7	1.5	0.6	4.6	5.0	66.0	70.6	8.0	67.9	4,935	95.1
Palm Beach Gardens city	49,896	57,704	15.6	56,219	78.4	5.7	4.3	2.3	9.4	15.5	29.9	51.1	20.6	52.4	24,191	96.1
Palm Beach Shores town	1,157	1,262	9.1	1,136	94.1	0.7	0.0	3.0	2.2	10.4	36.3	58.4	19.5	49.8	633	90.5
Palm City CDP	23,120	-	-	24,840	88.8	0.9	2.7	1.2	6.3	18.0	29.0	50.6	20.9	46.1	9,892	94.9
Palm Coast city	75,199	89,800	19.4	85,933	71.3	11.4	3.0	2.6	11.8	18.1	28.2	49.4	43.3	22.9	31,683	91.1
Palmetto city	12,641	13,748	8.8	13,611	56.2	13.7	1.0	1.3	27.8	22.4	24.9	42.7	53.2	20.6	4,457	90.0
Palmetto Bay village	23,413	24,523	4.7	24,333	42.1	3.6	4.8	2.9	46.6	25.5	14.8	41.5	17.3	58.5	7,459	97.8
Palmetto Estates CDP	13,535	-	-	15,640	9.3	32.5	3.1	4.3	50.8	22.6	15.0	38.2	53.7	20.9	3,881	93.5
Palm Harbor CDP	57,439	-	-	62,310	84.5	2.2	3.3	2.4	7.6	16.7	28.4	50.4	31.0	34.1	26,306	93.2
Palmona Park CDP	1,146	-	-	1,209	75.9	0.0	0.0	0.0	24.1	30.5	10.0	26.0	77.3	5.1	366	90.2
Palm River-Clair Mel CDP	21,024	-	-	23,844	24.5	27.0	1.4	2.6	44.5	24.5	11.7	35.8	55.5	16.6	8,097	91.3
Palm Shores town	895	1,157	29.3	1,226	77.7	3.8	3.0	2.8	12.7	18.4	13.7	45.0	25.2	26.4	508	90.4
Palm Springs village	23,165	25,216	8.9	24,843	24.1	10.2	1.8	1.7	62.2	24.3	12.3	36.1	57.1	15.9	8,207	91.8
Palm Springs North CDP	5,253	-	-	5,525	18.6	0.1	0.0	0.0	81.3	17.3	20.6	44.0	45.7	25.1	1,478	96.8
Palm Valley CDP	20,019	-	-	21,292	90.6	2.0	1.9	1.7	3.8	20.2	23.3	50.7	14.6	62.8	8,584	97.7
Panacea CDP	816	-	-	910	100.0	0.0	0.0	0.0	0.0	26.0	17.7	46.5	56.1	12.3	390	71.0
Panama City city	34,660	34,667	0.0	36,640	65.7	20.5	2.0	3.7	8.1	21.1	18.9	39.0	42.4	24.2	15,393	90.2
Panama City Beach city	11,549	12,583	9.0	12,751	80.3	6.2	3.3	4.2	6.0	16.7	18.5	42.6	31.6	31.5	5,592	97.0
Paradise Heights CDP	1,215	-	-	609	87.8	12.2	0.0	0.0	0.0	10.8	9.2	54.1	37.3	17.0	263	93.2
Parker city	4,330	4,249	-1.9	4,545	73.8	17.9	1.7	0.7	5.9	20.6	17.5	39.0	45.9	14.6	1,755	90.9
Parkland city	22,513	34,170	51.8	31,454	63.9	7.5	8.2	2.4	18.0	30.7	12.9	41.1	17.9	61.8	9,752	96.0
Pasadena Hills CDP	7,570	-	-	10,530	68.2	13.1	3.2	1.5	14.0	26.2	18.4	39.5	41.0	26.5	3,695	94.3
Patrick AFB CDP	1,222	-	-	1,533	60.7	10.9	5.9	4.4	18.1	28.4	9.1	27.5	20.7	37.8	460	100.0
Paxton town	637	856	34.4	743	85.7	10.8	0.0	1.7	1.7	23.7	17.8	42.3	53.0	8.0	304	76.3
Pea Ridge CDP	3,587	-	-	4,641	92.0	1.7	0.0	2.7	3.6	23.1	11.2	30.6	35.5	20.7	1,626	98.5
Pebble Creek CDP	7,622	-	-	10,249	46.7	13.6	16.3	3.9	19.5	27.9	12.9	38.1	21.8	47.8	3,294	96.3
Pelican Bay CDP	6,346	-	-	6,140	96.9	0.0	1.4	0.0	1.7	0.7	83.1	74.5	10.6	72.9	3,483	96.6
Pembroke Park town	6,194	6,749	9.0	6,677	15.3	44.1	1.4	2.7	36.5	28.8	12.7	32.4	53.3	22.0	2,358	88.8
Pembroke Pines city	154,898	173,591	12.1	170,072	28.5	19.5	4.8	2.8	44.4	20.3	17.4	40.9	34.9	33.9	57,323	94.7
Penney Farms town	751	833	10.9	683	98.5	1.5	0.0	0.0	0.0	11.1	73.8	75.4	30.0	57.7	332	91.9
Pensacola city	52,008	52,975	1.9	52,642	60.0	28.4	1.4	5.0	5.2	24.2	17.3	36.9	29.0	37.2	22,080	90.7
Perry city	7,000	6,879	-1.7	6,896	54.7	35.0	0.0	2.5	7.8	29.4	21.8	40.2	57.2	15.3	2,572	85.2
Pierson town	1,770	1,893	6.9	1,518	55.3	1.1	0.4	0.9	42.4	23.8	16.3	42.4	63.2	8.6	467	86.5
Pine Air CDP	2,024	-	-	2,317	14.2	16.9	4.1	1.4	63.4	24.6	10.7	34.5	57.3	10.4	672	92.1
Pine Castle CDP	10,805	-	-	10,474	23.5	18.4	3.7	2.3	52.1	26.3	11.7	33.5	54.5	17.9	3,681	86.0
Pinecrest village	18,217	19,155	5.1	19,244	43.1	1.7	6.3	3.4	45.5	25.8	15.6	42.3	14.6	66.4	6,033	96.9
Pine Hills CDP	60,076	-	-	78,995	8.3	70.5	2.4	5.0	13.8	28.9	10.9	31.0	54.5	14.3	22,806	91.6
Pine Island CDP	64	-	-	49	100.0	0.0	0.0	0.0	0.0	0.0	67.3	72.5	0.0	67.3	32	100.0
Pine Island Center CDP	1,854	-	-	2,175	78.8	14.9	0.6	1.5	4.2	19.9	37.4	58.9	41.3	21.8	770	87.7
Pine Lakes CDP	862	-	-	540	79.3	0.0	0.0	0.0	20.7	7.4	32.4	52.2	59.0	4.2	231	95.2
Pineland CDP	407	-	-	320	86.9	0.0	0.0	0.0	13.1	0.0	67.8	70.2	23.4	40.9	168	97.0
Pine Level CDP	227	-	-	141	94.3	0.0	0.0	5.7	0.0	24.1	33.3	37.3	26.7	35.6	58	100.0
Pinellas Park city	49,553	53,637	8.2	52,857	70.0	5.9	8.3	3.5	12.4	18.8	21.6	44.2	48.0	21.9	20,636	89.3
Pine Manor CDP	3,428	-	-	4,993	11.8	13.3	0.0	0.0	74.8	50.9	5.3	17.7	78.7	8.7	1,340	91.5
Pine Ridge CDP	9,598	-	-	10,278	83.8	4.6	2.6	3.5	5.5	12.9	47.5	63.8	37.1	26.5	4,866	93.2
Pine Ridge CDP	1,918	-	-	1,662	88.4	1.1	0.0	0.8	9.6	18.4	22.6	50.8	18.0	45.0	663	98.8
Pinewood CDP	16,520	-	-	17,542	0.9	73.7	0.7	0.6	24.1	23.9	14.0	36.3	58.9	13.3	5,133	87.7
Pioneer CDP	697	-	-	420	57.6	0.0	0.0	0.0	42.4	8.6	8.8	54.2	36.1	34.9	280	86.1
Pittman CDP	180	-	-	315	36.8	62.9	0.3	0.0	0.0	26.0	13.0	36.2	67.4	14.9	84	92.9
Plantation city	84,883	94,580	11.4	93,449	43.8	21.3	4.4	3.9	26.5	20.5	16.4	40.2	26.3	43.3	33,788	95.7
Plantation CDP	4,919	-	-	5,026	94.4	1.0	0.5	1.3	2.7	3.3	75.5	72.4	21.5	50.4	2,752	90.7
Plantation Island CDP	163	-	-	14	100.0	0.0	0.0	0.0	0.0	0.0	100.0	0.0	0.0	0.0	14	100.0
Plantation Mobile Home Park CDP	1,260	-	-	1,969	21.1	8.2	0.0	6.4	64.2	17.0	8.6	37.7	70.1	14.2	556	81.7
Plant City city	34,732	39,744	14.4	39,012	50.4	14.2	1.9	1.7	31.8	25.1	13.6	36.8	50.0	22.4	13,966	93.0
Poinciana CDP	53,193	-	-	69,955	17.7	22.2	1.3	3.0	55.7	26.6	17.2	36.5	50.5	18.7	18,982	89.3
Point Baker CDP	2,991	-	-	3,441	82.6	9.6	2.8	3.1	1.9	26.0	13.2	38.8	39.4	11.9	1,154	95.8
Polk City town	1,688	2,724	61.4	2,226	77.0	0.0	0.9	1.8	20.3	16.2	28.5	49.9	55.8	16.9	863	84.8
Pomona Park town	919	920	0.1	1,120	75.1	12.6	0.2	2.7	9.5	27.6	14.1	36.1	58.7	9.0	366	91.3
Pompano Beach city	99,839	112,118	12.3	110,062	42.3	31.6	1.1	2.4	22.5	19.1	19.8	42.8	47.5	25.1	41,727	88.4
Ponce de Leon town	577	567	-1.7	498	98.4	0.0	0.0	1.6	0.0	24.3	10.6	39.7	59.5	11.8	184	89.7
Ponce Inlet town	3,032	3,308	9.1	3,230	93.3	0.0	0.4	2.2	4.1	7.9	41.4	61.8	26.8	48.8	1,528	94.0
Port Charlotte CDP	54,392	-	-	62,327	75.8	9.3	1.3	3.3	10.3	15.2	30.7	53.2	47.2	18.7	24,632	89.6
Port LaBelle CDP	3,530	-	-	5,348	28.8	8.6	0.7	0.2	61.6	34.0	7.3	32.2	58.8	5.9	1,463	77.4
Port Orange city	56,628	64,842	14.5	62,726	81.1	5.6	3.6	2.5	7.2	18.6	24.5	46.2	37.4	25.8	26,185	93.2
Port Richey city	2,678	2,933	9.5	2,831	91.4	2.4	0.5	1.9	3.8	10.8	23.3	52.3	44.5	21.9	1,406	93.3
Port St. Joe city	3,423	3,567	4.2	3,488	58.7	34.2	0.9	1.8	4.4	21.9	19.2	46.2	40.2	21.2	1,449	89.4
Port St. John CDP	12,267	-	-	11,684	80.4	5.1	1.2	7.8	5.6	19.0	16.2	42.5	40.9	19.6	4,544	93.7
Port St. Lucie city	164,203	201,846	22.9	189,396	56.9	17.2	2.5	2.8	20.6	21.9	20.5	42.5	44.7	22.6	65,060	95.4
Port Salerno CDP	10,091	-	-	11,486	68.4	9.2	1.1	1.4	19.9	15.9	29.1	50.9	42.5	25.3	4,358	92.0
Pretty Bayou CDP	3,206	-	-	3,293	84.0	4.7	1.7	3.0	6.6	16.8	26.9	47.5	36.0	30.6	1,318	89.9
Princeton CDP	22,038	-	-	32,299	6.6	19.3	2.0	1.2	70.8	26.9	9.2	34.4	47.6	25.0	8,356	96.4
Progress Village CDP	5,392	-	-	10,020	28.9	36.0	3.5	1.9	29.7	26.3	9.5	32.8	39.1	29.7	3,645	92.0
Punta Gorda city	17,120	20,369	19.0	19,571	90.0	2.7	0.6	1.1	5.7	8.0	54.1	66.5	29.1	38.7	10,066	89.8
Punta Rassa CDP	1,750	-	-	1,697	96.3	0.6	2.8	0.0	0.3	2.8	83.7	80.3	23.5	62.3	984	83.0
Quail Ridge CDP	1,040	-	-	2,267	71.9	4.3	3.3	7.8	12.6	22.7	10.9	36.6	24.5	34.4	763	96.2
Quincy city	8,024	6,827	-14.9	7,334	21.6	59.1	0.0	1.0	18.3	26.4	15.6	36.4	56.7	19.1	2,657	72.1
Raiford town	248	239	-3.6	212	75.5	20.8	1.4	2.4	0.0	23.6	14.6	38.8	59.1	12.1	88	69.3
Raleigh CDP	373	-	-	766	69.6	26.2	0.0	1.3	2.9	35.6	17.4	34.1	67.7	1.9	233	72.1
Reddick town	501	551	10.0	592	44.6	47.0	0.0	2.0	6.4	23.1	15.5	41.5	59.9	10.0	243	77.4
Redington Beach town	1,427	1,471	3.1	1,293	91.2	0.7	1.2	1.2	5.7	9.1	32.5	58.4	21.0	43.1	631	95.4
Redington Shores town	2,155	2,293	6.4	2,176	85.4	0.4	3.6	1.4	9.1	6.5	36.1	58.0	19.5	48.1	1,085	95.3
Richmond Heights CDP	8,541	-	-	10,524	3.7	60.1	1.4	0.2	34.6	18.9	16.1	42.4	55.7	19.4	2,748	94.4
Richmond West CDP	31,973	-	-	37,486	14.1	6.5	1.3	2.1	76.1	22.4	14.0	38.9	41.6	28.1	9,861	98.3

1 May be of any race.

Table A. All Places — **Population and Housing**

STATE City, town, township, borough, or CDP (county if applicable)	Population: 2010 census total population	Population: 2019 estimated population	Population: Percent change 2010-2019	Population: ACS total population estimate 2015-2019	Race and Hispanic or Latino origin (percent): White alone, not Hispanic or Latino	Race: Black alone, not Hispanic or Latino	Race: Asian alone, not Hispanic or Latino	Race: All other races or 2 or more races, not Hispanic or Latino	Race: Hispanic or Latino[1]	Age (percent): Under 18 years old	Age: Age 65 years and older	Age: Median age	Educational attainment of persons age 25 and older: Percent High school diploma or less	Educational attainment: Percent Bachelor's degree or more	Occupied housing units: Total	Occupied housing units: Percent with a computer
	1	2	3	4	5	6	7	8	9	10	11	12	13	14	15	16
FLORIDA—Con.																
Ridgecrest CDP	2,558	-	-	3,602	26.1	59.9	0.9	3.0	10.1	32.4	10.7	30.7	46.0	11.5	946	69.7
Ridge Manor CDP	4,513	-	-	4,820	84.7	2.9	0.4	1.9	10.0	15.0	26.5	48.0	53.3	15.6	2,005	88.2
Ridge Wood Heights CDP	4,795	-	-	4,287	90.7	2.7	1.4	0.4	4.9	13.6	24.6	51.2	39.0	31.2	2,049	93.5
Rio CDP	965	-	-	853	100.0	0.0	0.0	0.0	0.0	5.2	49.7	64.9	43.2	22.3	458	96.5
Rio Pinar CDP	5,211	-	-	5,713	51.8	10.5	9.9	1.9	25.9	19.6	20.1	45.1	26.5	37.7	1,864	95.9
River Park CDP	5,222	-	-	7,071	60.2	15.5	1.0	4.2	19.1	22.2	23.9	45.8	56.1	14.3	2,507	84.2
River Ridge CDP	4,702	-	-	5,157	84.6	6.9	0.0	2.3	6.2	15.5	32.0	51.0	49.2	17.1	1,979	96.2
Riverview CDP	71,050	-	-	95,338	50.0	16.8	2.8	4.0	26.3	26.1	10.3	35.9	35.1	31.3	32,104	97.0
Riviera Beach city	32,540	35,463	9.0	34,702	20.8	69.1	2.2	2.8	5.1	24.3	16.0	36.8	46.5	24.5	11,336	86.4
Rockledge city	24,921	28,227	13.3	27,305	71.8	14.0	2.0	2.3	9.9	19.2	22.8	45.2	32.0	32.5	10,881	95.0
Roeville CDP	608	-	-	568	85.6	6.9	2.1	3.9	1.6	16.7	9.2	40.3	46.7	22.9	191	100.0
Roosevelt Gardens CDP	2,456	-	-	3,034	3.1	86.5	0.0	0.7	9.7	25.2	7.7	37.1	62.5	11.2	964	82.9
Roseland CDP	1,472	-	-	1,514	89.4	4.8	0.0	2.2	3.6	3.6	37.1	61.3	63.2	13.4	762	97.2
Rotonda CDP	8,759	-	-	9,325	94.6	0.6	2.7	0.2	1.9	6.0	54.4	66.9	43.5	24.9	4,617	91.2
Royal Palm Beach village	34,196	40,396	18.1	38,962	43.2	26.2	4.1	2.0	24.6	24.3	13.8	38.9	34.0	36.1	12,090	96.4
Royal Palm Estates CDP	3,025	-	-	3,663	13.1	17.7	2.0	0.8	66.5	35.4	8.7	29.1	71.9	13.5	884	93.8
Ruskin CDP	17,208	-	-	25,530	40.3	15.3	1.5	2.3	40.7	27.8	11.6	34.3	45.0	18.7	7,788	93.1
Safety Harbor city	16,913	18,016	6.5	17,803	82.8	5.1	2.4	2.4	7.3	19.5	21.6	48.0	31.3	40.6	7,039	93.4
St. Augustine city	13,004	15,415	18.5	14,515	78.6	11.6	0.8	2.8	6.2	10.7	22.7	45.0	32.2	40.4	5,852	89.3
St. Augustine Beach city	6,161	7,004	13.7	6,933	93.7	0.1	0.0	0.7	5.6	18.0	24.5	48.0	18.8	52.8	2,582	96.1
St. Augustine Shores CDP	7,359	-	-	9,340	87.1	2.9	2.3	1.4	6.2	14.9	32.2	55.1	32.2	28.5	3,916	92.0
St. Augustine South CDP	4,998	-	-	5,431	89.9	3.2	0.8	0.7	5.4	14.2	22.6	49.1	31.0	31.5	2,004	87.9
St. Cloud city	37,787	54,579	44.4	51,158	46.9	7.5	0.8	3.5	41.3	27.8	13.5	35.6	43.9	18.2	15,080	92.5
St. George Island CDP	-	-	-	863	97.6	0.0	1.3	0.0	1.2	8.5	43.1	62.8	12.9	56.7	435	99.1
St. James City CDP	3,784	-	-	3,489	99.4	0.0	0.4	0.2	0.0	6.1	47.1	63.8	43.0	25.8	1,680	92.9
St. Leo town	1,160	1,370	18.1	1,218	59.4	18.6	4.1	6.1	11.9	3.7	1.6	19.2	8.2	27.6	20	100.0
St. Lucie Village town	591	638	8.0	802	91.9	1.5	1.9	0.0	4.7	20.0	19.2	43.8	31.8	31.3	295	94.2
St. Marks city	293	324	10.6	244	95.5	0.0	0.0	0.4	4.1	12.7	29.5	53.1	42.6	18.3	124	89.5
St. Pete Beach city	9,343	9,587	2.6	9,587	90.2	0.3	3.3	1.5	4.7	7.7	36.1	59.8	21.7	48.0	4,855	95.6
St. Petersburg city	245,177	265,351	8.2	261,338	63.3	21.8	3.4	3.2	8.3	16.9	18.6	42.9	34.1	35.7	109,144	90.9
Samoset CDP	3,854	-	-	4,399	21.8	28.0	0.0	1.0	49.1	20.4	22.1	44.0	76.0	5.5	1,231	85.2
Samsula-Spruce Creek CDP	5,047	-	-	5,637	92.6	0.0	0.4	0.9	6.2	10.8	35.1	58.6	32.5	41.0	2,261	96.9
San Antonio city	1,150	1,475	28.3	1,286	85.0	1.8	1.9	1.3	10.0	22.3	16.6	40.3	34.6	32.1	471	94.9
San Carlos Park CDP	16,824	-	-	17,961	66.5	4.1	0.6	2.3	26.5	20.8	11.5	36.2	42.5	20.5	5,654	96.6
San Castle CDP	3,428	-	-	3,756	29.0	45.0	0.5	1.7	23.7	22.9	11.6	35.9	55.3	17.5	1,089	91.6
Sanford city	53,933	61,448	13.9	59,700	39.0	27.1	4.1	2.9	26.9	24.5	11.8	34.9	42.4	23.0	22,067	90.8
Sanibel city	6,469	7,401	14.4	7,319	96.8	0.4	0.3	1.7	0.8	8.3	56.3	66.9	16.6	61.1	3,684	96.8
Sarasota city	52,107	58,285	11.9	56,919	65.7	13.6	1.7	1.9	17.1	14.1	27.3	49.2	36.6	36.4	24,447	90.7
Sarasota Springs CDP	14,395	-	-	15,854	79.3	1.3	1.6	2.5	15.3	17.5	23.2	46.4	47.7	24.7	6,143	92.6
Satellite Beach city	10,080	11,130	10.4	10,873	83.7	3.7	1.3	3.2	8.2	22.9	20.2	44.3	20.1	49.3	4,077	97.3
Sawgrass CDP	4,880	-	-	4,841	92.4	0.8	1.8	0.0	5.1	14.1	31.8	52.8	15.7	61.1	2,286	94.2
Schall Circle CDP	1,117	-	-	1,284	19.6	32.6	0.0	5.2	42.6	34.1	6.6	26.7	70.0	13.7	367	73.8
Sea Ranch Lakes village	555	619	11.5	574	73.9	0.5	1.4	0.0	24.2	23.5	20.6	51.3	10.7	72.8	206	97.1
Sebastian city	21,935	26,118	19.1	25,107	87.0	4.8	0.3	2.1	5.8	15.9	34.6	55.4	44.4	24.5	9,782	91.1
Sebring city	10,064	10,600	5.3	10,377	54.8	20.5	0.6	3.8	20.2	16.0	26.6	46.4	56.4	16.5	4,113	74.4
Seffner CDP	7,579	-	-	8,362	58.3	11.4	2.5	3.9	24.0	26.8	12.5	39.6	40.2	24.2	2,833	95.5
Seminole city	17,330	18,838	8.7	18,657	86.1	2.2	3.3	2.3	6.2	13.2	33.4	55.9	36.3	31.7	8,648	88.3
Seminole Manor CDP	2,621	-	-	2,688	23.7	29.2	0.4	0.0	46.7	26.0	11.6	36.8	66.7	11.0	794	90.8
Seville CDP	614	-	-	897	27.6	6.8	0.0	0.0	65.6	27.3	16.4	36.0	75.6	12.9	259	75.3
Sewall's Point town	2,003	2,226	11.1	2,099	90.4	0.0	0.3	3.6	5.7	18.9	35.6	58.2	16.5	61.4	863	98.7
Shady Hills CDP	11,523	-	-	12,252	87.3	3.5	1.4	1.2	6.6	18.9	21.7	46.9	57.1	13.1	4,235	88.5
Shalimar town	721	836	16.0	888	71.6	1.5	10.8	5.7	10.4	22.7	18.9	46.2	25.1	49.3	323	94.1
Sharpes CDP	3,411	-	-	3,221	89.9	2.9	0.4	2.5	4.3	14.9	17.4	51.9	36.8	25.7	1,286	90.4
Siesta Key CDP	6,565	-	-	5,573	96.4	0.0	0.7	1.3	1.6	8.4	53.6	67.5	15.1	58.2	2,868	97.0
Silver Lake CDP	1,879	-	-	1,954	87.8	3.9	0.0	0.7	7.6	19.9	28.7	53.9	27.4	36.4	834	95.4
Silver Springs Shores CDP	6,539	-	-	9,031	40.5	28.4	0.3	2.6	28.2	22.7	17.5	36.7	57.9	15.0	3,274	88.6
Sky Lake CDP	6,153	-	-	7,331	20.9	13.2	3.1	0.4	62.4	18.1	9.5	36.7	58.6	16.1	2,113	95.5
Sneads town	1,849	1,779	-3.8	2,016	76.1	18.4	1.7	2.1	1.7	27.4	17.3	38.6	54.9	5.8	866	83.1
Solana CDP	742	-	-	894	87.5	0.0	0.0	2.0	10.5	27.9	26.6	38.2	39.8	40.9	333	98.2
Sopchoppy city	447	492	10.1	480	63.3	31.5	1.5	1.7	2.1	16.5	19.8	53.6	52.4	25.0	232	77.6
Sorrento CDP	861	-	-	366	24.9	0.0	0.0	0.0	75.1	0.0	5.2	36.1	85.2	0.0	150	100.0
South Apopka CDP	5,728	-	-	7,381	14.8	62.1	0.0	0.6	22.5	34.1	12.8	28.5	67.4	9.6	2,125	82.0
South Bay city	4,876	5,200	6.6	5,158	20.4	52.6	1.0	2.2	23.7	8.6	6.8	41.0	80.6	5.3	475	61.7
South Beach CDP	3,501	-	-	3,429	95.4	0.0	0.0	0.9	3.7	10.1	56.9	69.0	9.0	71.3	1,563	95.5
South Bradenton CDP	22,178	-	-	25,227	62.6	9.8	1.1	2.6	24.0	18.3	24.8	44.9	56.9	15.2	10,002	87.0
South Brooksville CDP	4,007	-	-	4,200	76.5	14.9	0.0	3.9	4.6	9.3	35.8	58.2	47.2	23.2	2,030	84.1
Southchase CDP	15,921	-	-	15,314	18.9	12.1	10.8	1.9	56.3	19.6	13.5	36.7	42.2	22.1	4,088	92.3
South Daytona city	12,257	13,080	6.7	12,879	77.7	11.8	1.1	2.0	7.4	16.6	21.1	44.5	46.3	19.1	5,430	90.4
Southeast Arcadia CDP	6,554	-	-	8,272	26.2	3.9	0.1	0.5	69.2	24.5	10.3	31.8	84.7	3.8	2,702	46.2
Southgate CDP	7,173	-	-	7,817	79.4	2.4	4.1	2.8	11.3	16.5	23.6	47.3	32.5	35.7	3,202	91.7
South Gate Ridge CDP	5,688	-	-	6,232	84.9	3.0	1.4	0.9	9.8	17.2	20.3	47.0	37.6	36.7	2,533	92.2
South Highpoint CDP	5,195	-	-	5,435	36.9	17.3	8.3	2.3	35.2	28.0	8.8	31.3	56.9	11.1	1,682	85.9
South Miami city	11,676	11,911	2.0	12,046	25.5	12.3	5.0	2.5	54.7	18.3	14.0	36.9	25.7	57.6	4,431	93.2
South Miami Heights CDP	35,696	-	-	37,119	7.3	14.1	2.3	1.2	75.1	21.3	15.4	40.2	61.9	16.9	10,589	88.0
South Palm Beach town	1,358	1,470	8.2	1,296	86.0	0.5	4.1	0.7	8.7	4.4	49.9	65.0	18.7	61.4	754	94.2
South Pasadena city	4,962	5,095	2.7	5,088	88.9	2.0	0.7	1.2	7.2	4.7	57.0	68.1	38.6	29.2	3,017	80.1
South Patrick Shores CDP	5,875	-	-	6,842	91.6	2.2	0.6	2.9	2.7	16.0	22.0	46.4	26.3	43.4	2,660	95.3
South Sarasota CDP	4,950	-	-	5,283	84.5	0.3	1.8	2.2	11.2	14.1	33.7	54.3	25.7	47.0	2,445	95.3
South Venice CDP	13,949	-	-	13,907	91.4	1.7	1.3	0.3	5.3	13.9	34.0	54.4	42.7	25.6	6,111	94.3
Southwest Ranches town	7,356	7,957	8.2	7,921	50.2	5.5	3.9	1.6	38.8	19.4	17.7	46.7	27.5	44.7	2,235	96.7
Springfield city	8,931	8,577	-4.0	9,319	61.3	23.3	1.6	5.9	7.8	24.4	13.7	35.3	61.5	8.6	3,411	81.2
Spring Hill CDP	98,621	-	-	111,076	72.3	4.9	1.7	3.1	18.1	21.0	22.9	43.5	46.3	17.9	42,099	92.3
Springhill CDP	160	-	-	107	100.0	0.0	0.0	0.0	0.0	0.0	33.6	56.8	42.2	11.8	41	78.0
Spring Lake CDP	458	-	-	554	83.2	0.0	0.0	0.0	16.8	5.4	31.9	55.1	31.3	45.5	210	87.6
Spring Ridge CDP	398	-	-	371	86.3	0.0	0.0	1.3	12.4	13.2	28.8	57.3	39.8	31.1	144	93.1
Stacey Street CDP	858	-	-	568	18.5	70.1	0.0	0.0	11.4	10.0	0.7	39.4	57.4	10.7	164	100.0
Starke city	5,498	5,422	-1.4	5,393	58.4	34.0	0.6	0.9	6.1	21.6	22.9	43.9	58.3	10.4	2,004	76.0
Steinhatchee CDP	1,047	-	-	782	95.4	0.0	4.6	0.0	0.0	2.6	46.3	63.7	74.0	0.0	427	57.4
Stock Island CDP	3,919	-	-	4,416	36.6	9.6	0.5	1.9	51.3	22.0	12.0	37.8	58.5	16.4	1,584	83.3
Stuart city	15,277	16,237	6.3	16,161	71.5	10.5	1.9	1.7	14.3	17.0	28.8	51.1	34.4	27.5	7,263	88.6

1 May be of any race.

Table A. All Places — **Population and Housing**

STATE City, town, township, borough, or CDP (county if applicable)	Population				Race and Hispanic or Latino origin (percent)					Age (percent)			Educational attainment of persons age 25 and older		Occupied housing units	
	2010 census total population	2019 estimated population	Percent change 2010-2019	ACS total population estimate 2015-2019	White alone, not Hispanic or Latino	Black alone, not Hispanic or Latino	Asian alone, not Hispanic or Latino	All other races or 2 or more races, not Hispanic or Latino	Hispanic or Latino[1]	Under 18 years old	Age 65 years and older	Median age	Percent High school diploma or less	Percent Bachelor's degree or more	Total	Percent with a computer
	1	2	3	4	5	6	7	8	9	10	11	12	13	14	15	16
FLORIDA—Con.																
Sugarmill Woods CDP	8,287	-	-	9,082	89.2	1.1	2.2	0.3	7.2	11.9	51.4	65.7	38.3	29.4	4,266	94.5
Sumatra CDP	148	-	-	131	90.8	0.0	0.0	9.2	0.0	16.0	52.7	65.2	74.5	0.0	73	49.3
Sun City Center CDP	19,258	-	-	24,286	87.0	6.1	0.8	0.8	5.3	4.1	71.7	71.5	31.4	33.8	13,759	88.9
Suncoast Estates CDP	4,384	-	-	4,592	82.9	2.1	0.0	2.1	12.8	23.5	13.3	38.2	70.7	6.8	1,481	83.6
Sunny Isles Beach city	20,828	21,804	4.7	21,942	47.5	2.5	2.2	1.8	46.0	14.0	24.1	49.2	20.6	45.5	10,487	91.2
Sunrise city	84,306	95,166	12.9	94,060	27.0	34.4	3.6	3.2	31.8	21.0	17.7	39.5	40.7	26.7	33,250	93.3
Sunset CDP	16,389	-	-	15,871	12.9	0.2	2.8	0.0	84.0	18.9	19.9	43.8	30.6	40.2	4,989	94.7
Surfside town	5,564	5,651	1.6	5,725	54.1	0.0	0.8	0.4	44.7	25.6	23.0	43.4	21.1	65.7	2,328	94.1
Sweetwater city	19,918	20,994	5.4	20,865	2.5	0.8	1.1	0.1	95.5	17.6	18.1	42.8	62.7	21.4	6,075	84.0
Taft CDP	2,205	-	-	1,263	55.6	3.4	6.6	0.0	34.4	16.2	15.8	49.3	70.9	10.8	470	71.1
Tallahassee city	181,050	194,500	7.4	191,279	51.1	34.5	4.5	3.1	6.7	16.7	10.3	26.9	23.5	48.2	75,949	95.2
Tamarac city	60,778	66,721	9.8	65,874	34.9	29.8	3.0	2.4	29.9	17.8	25.6	47.1	41.4	26.1	26,983	90.8
Tamiami CDP	55,271	-	-	56,225	5.4	0.7	0.6	0.0	93.3	16.8	21.1	45.2	49.9	28.9	16,057	91.2
Tampa city	336,150	399,700	18.9	387,916	44.6	22.0	4.2	2.8	26.4	21.4	12.3	35.7	37.7	38.6	152,296	91.9
Tangelo Park CDP	2,231	-	-	2,975	7.4	76.0	0.7	1.0	14.9	26.2	13.5	33.9	53.3	12.1	825	87.5
Tangerine CDP	2,865	-	-	2,722	50.2	18.4	0.5	1.8	29.2	24.0	18.1	41.9	51.4	25.9	991	97.5
Tarpon Springs city	23,526	25,577	8.7	25,176	78.6	7.5	1.5	2.3	10.1	17.2	29.4	52.0	41.1	26.2	9,894	88.7
Tavares city	13,987	17,749	26.9	16,752	70.8	12.3	1.8	2.8	12.3	17.3	33.0	51.2	45.2	20.6	7,129	87.3
Tavernier CDP	2,136	-	-	2,132	59.1	0.1	1.2	0.7	38.9	15.7	16.4	42.2	37.8	34.2	768	94.3
Taylor Creek CDP	4,348	-	-	4,010	83.7	3.0	2.2	5.0	6.1	11.5	37.9	58.3	57.6	10.0	1,890	82.1
Temple Terrace city	24,425	26,639	9.1	26,539	51.7	18.7	4.2	4.5	20.8	19.3	12.8	33.1	25.2	41.3	9,624	96.0
Tequesta village	5,653	6,138	8.6	6,071	86.4	0.3	1.6	3.5	8.2	17.6	29.2	52.7	22.5	47.1	2,684	89.6
The Acreage CDP	38,704	-	-	40,177	61.2	11.1	2.6	3.1	22.0	21.6	11.9	40.4	41.8	23.8	11,734	97.1
The Crossings CDP	22,758	-	-	22,441	23.5	3.2	3.1	1.6	68.6	18.3	18.7	43.6	28.1	37.2	7,485	96.9
The Hammocks CDP	51,003	-	-	61,516	13.9	3.0	2.9	2.0	78.1	21.2	13.6	38.5	32.2	36.4	17,386	97.4
The Meadows CDP	3,994	-	-	4,430	94.1	0.3	0.0	0.0	5.6	7.3	65.4	70.0	23.6	54.5	2,489	93.4
The Villages CDP	51,442	-	-	79,372	96.9	0.3	0.9	0.7	1.2	0.8	81.6	71.7	26.8	42.3	43,870	96.5
Thonotosassa CDP	13,014	-	-	14,460	68.3	14.2	4.2	3.9	9.4	24.4	15.7	40.2	53.9	21.0	4,816	91.4
Three Lakes CDP	15,047	-	-	15,614	23.8	8.6	4.0	2.1	61.5	24.3	8.6	36.3	26.7	40.5	4,830	98.5
Three Oaks CDP	3,592	-	-	4,281	72.3	2.3	3.4	2.8	19.2	25.4	10.0	34.1	27.4	35.1	1,348	97.2
Tice CDP	4,470	-	-	5,092	36.5	2.9	0.1	1.7	58.7	27.5	11.8	34.9	68.3	12.2	1,377	79.2
Tierra Verde CDP	3,721	-	-	3,437	91.8	1.5	0.0	1.1	5.6	8.3	38.1	60.2	17.0	62.9	1,548	97.7
Tiger Point CDP	3,090	-	-	3,360	97.5	0.0	1.2	0.7	0.6	25.9	26.9	44.5	17.6	53.4	1,290	94.9
Tildenville CDP	511	-	-	447	0.0	63.5	0.0	36.5	0.0	38.3	25.3	47.3	100.0	0.0	276	100.0
Timber Pines CDP	5,386	-	-	5,198	98.0	0.0	0.5	0.6	1.0	1.3	78.9	75.6	36.4	30.2	2,952	86.9
Titusville city	43,618	46,580	6.8	45,932	71.7	14.2	2.5	5.7	5.9	19.2	22.5	45.3	41.7	21.9	18,719	93.0
Town 'n' Country CDP	78,442	-	-	87,338	36.1	8.4	4.8	2.7	48.0	21.1	13.2	37.7	43.5	29.0	31,362	94.9
Treasure Island city	6,708	6,921	3.2	6,889	90.0	0.5	0.8	2.2	6.5	5.7	40.6	59.6	23.7	43.5	3,804	94.6
Trenton city	1,994	2,160	8.3	2,151	73.1	13.8	0.0	3.1	9.9	28.5	15.6	33.6	63.5	9.8	661	79.7
Trilby CDP	419	-	-	336	52.7	15.5	25.0	6.8	0.0	26.5	14.6	35.7	56.3	27.9	118	100.0
Trinity CDP	10,907	-	-	11,493	86.8	0.9	2.3	4.4	5.6	21.2	27.4	48.0	27.4	37.9	4,367	97.7
Tyndall AFB CDP	2,994	-	-	2,779	57.5	12.3	6.1	6.4	17.7	38.9	0.7	22.0	13.5	53.0	641	98.6
Umatilla city	3,440	3,861	12.2	3,750	83.0	0.2	0.0	0.0	16.8	15.4	37.0	52.6	43.2	21.4	1,670	87.1
Union Park CDP	9,765	-	-	12,052	32.3	11.7	6.3	4.1	45.6	20.1	13.1	33.1	38.1	28.1	3,938	94.8
University CDP	41,163	-	-	48,436	30.1	25.4	5.4	3.3	35.8	19.5	8.2	27.2	51.3	23.8	19,003	90.5
University CDP	31,084	-	-	35,777	60.3	7.9	5.7	1.8	24.3	7.5	4.7	20.6	36.1	34.2	6,796	95.0
University Park CDP	26,995	-	-	26,620	7.1	4.1	2.9	0.6	85.3	13.6	19.3	41.7	48.1	28.0	7,496	87.5
Upper Grand Lagoon CDP	13,963	-	-	17,550	84.9	3.1	3.9	3.2	5.0	22.1	16.6	39.4	33.6	34.3	7,228	94.9
Valparaiso city	5,013	5,401	7.7	5,145	68.8	9.9	3.8	10.1	7.4	24.1	14.4	30.3	29.4	25.0	1,603	94.0
Valrico CDP	35,545	-	-	37,980	62.1	9.6	4.9	3.3	20.2	21.5	17.0	42.8	34.4	34.3	13,444	96.4
Vamo CDP	4,727	-	-	4,564	91.9	0.2	1.5	0.5	5.9	10.6	36.1	54.9	34.4	36.4	2,362	90.6
Venice city	20,800	23,985	15.3	23,086	92.7	0.6	1.9	2.1	2.7	6.2	62.6	69.1	30.9	41.0	12,228	87.4
Venice Gardens CDP	7,104	-	-	8,171	89.5	0.9	1.6	1.7	6.4	16.5	32.3	54.3	36.9	29.4	3,478	91.3
Vernon city	687	706	2.8	728	84.3	5.4	2.2	4.5	3.6	17.6	18.4	42.5	62.7	13.2	319	91.8
Vero Beach city	15,201	17,503	15.1	16,857	78.7	8.5	1.1	2.6	9.1	14.9	28.0	53.4	38.7	34.3	7,357	87.1
Vero Beach South CDP	23,092	-	-	23,333	78.7	4.8	3.5	3.1	9.9	17.7	26.5	49.9	39.2	25.4	9,022	88.7
Verona Walk CDP	1,782	-	-	2,612	93.1	2.9	0.0	0.5	3.5	1.9	63.8	68.8	29.4	38.3	1,302	95.2
Viera East CDP	10,757	-	-	11,796	75.9	3.9	3.4	5.6	11.2	19.8	29.6	50.9	30.3	37.5	4,836	95.3
Viera West CDP	6,641	-	-	11,369	84.9	1.8	2.4	1.9	9.1	21.1	28.9	47.1	20.0	47.5	4,704	95.0
Villano Beach CDP	2,678	-	-	2,564	95.3	0.0	1.0	0.0	3.7	9.4	28.0	54.5	25.7	42.5	1,089	98.6
Villas CDP	11,569	-	-	13,072	71.7	7.2	1.5	0.6	19.0	11.0	31.2	51.2	39.3	29.7	5,506	92.6
Vineyards CDP	3,375	-	-	3,891	91.8	0.0	2.7	0.0	5.6	3.0	58.3	69.0	19.5	58.6	1,908	99.1
Virginia Gardens village	2,373	2,380	0.3	2,311	15.3	0.3	2.8	0.8	80.8	17.3	15.0	44.0	40.9	31.3	781	87.2
Wabasso CDP	609	-	-	530	93.4	0.0	0.0	0.0	6.6	15.5	28.3	57.9	29.2	39.7	246	61.0
Wabasso Beach CDP	1,853	-	-	1,775	90.8	2.7	0.0	0.0	6.5	0.0	74.4	73.7	8.9	61.6	831	96.3
Wacissa CDP	386	-	-	447	93.3	1.8	0.0	4.9	0.0	27.7	26.2	45.5	48.6	6.3	193	95.9
Wahneta CDP	5,091	-	-	4,862	29.9	0.0	0.0	1.6	68.5	33.1	9.7	31.7	82.4	1.5	1,280	72.6
Waldo city	1,004	1,008	0.4	825	59.3	34.4	0.0	1.1	5.2	24.2	15.8	32.9	60.2	8.9	303	73.9
Wallace CDP	1,785	-	-	2,467	93.2	0.0	1.5	2.4	3.0	19.1	18.2	50.0	30.2	35.7	960	94.6
Warm Mineral Springs CDP	5,061	-	-	5,390	97.0	0.8	0.6	0.4	1.2	3.6	68.6	71.5	47.9	19.4	2,784	82.1
Warrington CDP	14,531	-	-	14,351	67.6	20.5	1.8	4.7	5.4	19.4	17.0	43.1	40.2	20.9	6,445	90.0
Washington Park CDP	1,672	-	-	1,685	1.8	97.0	0.0	1.2	0.0	21.9	10.9	38.6	64.2	5.8	600	86.5
Watergate CDP	2,942	-	-	3,216	57.2	1.1	4.5	1.3	35.8	22.6	10.2	37.4	50.5	17.8	913	95.4
Watertown CDP	2,829	-	-	3,082	56.6	37.6	0.0	1.8	4.0	25.7	18.5	36.3	70.9	4.1	1,283	89.2
Wauchula city	4,903	4,786	-2.4	4,803	49.6	9.8	1.3	1.1	38.2	21.3	13.6	32.8	71.7	12.7	1,742	66.1
Waukeenah CDP	272	-	-	280	91.1	8.9	0.0	0.0	0.0	16.1	12.1	55.2	42.1	23.7	129	100.0
Wausau town	384	399	3.9	447	91.1	6.5	0.4	2.0	0.0	18.1	21.7	44.0	57.1	3.7	191	91.1
Waverly CDP	767	-	-	997	39.4	35.9	0.0	24.7	0.0	31.2	24.2	20.9	74.8	0.0	290	88.3
Webster city	781	1,151	47.4	726	53.4	25.9	0.0	0.8	19.8	13.1	11.7	44.2	59.7	10.1	280	77.5
Wedgefield CDP	6,705	-	-	8,180	56.6	7.9	4.9	4.4	26.2	22.0	13.6	43.0	35.6	31.3	2,672	100.0
Weeki Wachee city	12	13	8.3	2	100.0	0.0	0.0	0.0	0.0	0.0	0.0	0.0	0.0	0.0	2	100.0
Weeki Wachee Gardens CDP	1,146	-	-	1,138	93.1	0.0	0.0	3.0	4.0	9.0	34.3	56.3	55.3	14.3	504	100.0
Wekiwa Springs CDP	21,998	-	-	23,512	77.5	3.5	3.2	1.3	14.5	20.9	20.4	44.8	18.6	50.4	8,888	96.9
Welaka town	712	717	0.7	693	52.4	42.7	0.0	0.7	4.2	22.8	23.7	50.4	61.1	10.9	284	81.0
Wellington village	56,697	65,398	15.3	64,396	58.8	10.8	4.0	1.9	24.5	26.0	16.0	41.2	25.4	45.0	20,844	96.8
Wesley Chapel CDP	44,092	-	-	58,208	57.0	10.2	6.3	3.8	22.7	26.6	11.4	36.9	26.0	41.6	19,358	97.4
West Bradenton CDP	4,192	-	-	4,065	87.5	0.8	1.1	4.0	6.6	18.3	20.5	45.5	35.1	33.3	1,532	94.8
Westchase CDP	21,747	-	-	23,923	64.9	4.1	9.8	2.2	19.0	25.5	11.8	38.1	20.4	57.4	9,265	97.8
Westchester CDP	29,862	-	-	29,778	7.6	0.4	0.7	0.7	90.7	16.1	23.2	45.3	44.6	29.1	8,831	88.6
West DeLand CDP	3,535	-	-	3,970	85.0	9.7	0.0	2.5	2.7	25.6	15.8	41.9	35.3	25.2	1,515	93.9

1 May be of any race.

STATE City, town, township, borough, or CDP (county if applicable)	2010 census total population	2019 estimated population	Percent change 2010-2019	ACS total population estimate 2015-2019	White alone, not Hispanic or Latino	Black alone, not Hispanic or Latino	Asian alone, not Hispanic or Latino	All other races or 2 or more races, not Hispanic or Latino	Hispanic or Latino[1]	Under 18 years old	Age 65 years and older	Median age	Percent High school diploma or less	Percent Bachelor's degree or more	Total	Percent with a computer
	1	2	3	4	5	6	7	8	9	10	11	12	13	14	15	16
FLORIDA—Con.																
Westgate CDP	7,975	-	-	9,783	8.6	36.8	3.0	0.1	51.4	35.2	7.6	29.5	67.3	8.7	2,416	86.3
Westlake city	6	1,447	24016.7	52	3.8	0.0	0.0	0.0	96.2	0.0	0.0	48.1	0.0	50.0	28	100.0
West Lealman CDP	15,651	-	-	14,891	77.8	4.7	4.7	3.8	9.1	14.8	30.3	53.1	51.0	18.4	6,931	90.0
West Little River CDP	34,699	-	-	32,897	3.9	46.3	0.6	0.9	48.3	23.1	15.4	39.2	66.8	10.7	9,543	82.7
West Melbourne city	18,314	24,259	32.5	22,225	73.0	5.1	7.1	4.5	10.3	22.9	20.2	39.8	34.2	33.5	8,134	92.1
West Miami city	5,965	8,767	47.0	7,788	5.8	1.7	0.0	0.2	92.3	17.4	20.0	44.9	43.6	31.1	2,632	90.9
Weston city	65,419	71,166	8.8	70,614	35.7	3.7	6.2	2.2	52.2	29.1	11.2	40.4	16.0	63.0	20,992	98.6
West Palm Beach city	100,665	111,955	11.2	109,767	37.3	33.7	2.0	2.0	25.1	18.4	18.6	39.5	38.8	34.4	41,511	90.6
West Park city	14,064	15,089	7.3	15,012	15.1	51.0	0.7	1.7	31.5	24.5	11.7	34.7	52.0	12.8	4,308	80.6
West Pensacola CDP	21,339	-	-	21,056	51.6	36.4	2.4	5.8	3.8	22.4	17.1	36.8	54.0	11.6	8,790	82.9
West Perrine CDP	9,460	-	-	9,826	4.7	51.3	0.9	3.1	40.0	31.4	12.4	31.6	58.2	19.2	2,890	88.0
West Samoset CDP	5,583	-	-	6,921	20.6	17.0	0.2	1.5	60.7	29.7	11.3	33.0	79.2	4.1	2,001	81.5
West Vero Corridor CDP	7,138	-	-	8,292	88.7	1.1	0.1	0.3	9.8	7.7	53.9	67.6	47.7	23.1	4,034	80.3
Westview CDP	9,650	-	-	11,247	2.9	59.5	0.0	0.2	37.5	27.7	19.4	38.9	58.6	15.1	3,256	86.2
Westville town	287	281	-2.1	323	99.4	0.0	0.0	0.6	0.0	23.5	14.9	37.3	71.8	12.2	131	85.5
Westwood Lakes CDP	11,838	-	-	11,510	9.9	0.3	2.0	0.1	87.7	16.3	19.7	45.1	49.9	27.0	3,192	83.0
Wewahitchka city	1,973	2,133	8.1	1,875	84.4	7.0	1.1	3.3	4.3	21.5	17.1	41.4	53.9	15.2	785	84.2
Whiskey Creek CDP	4,655	-	-	5,022	88.8	2.5	0.8	0.2	7.6	15.1	33.6	54.3	23.4	40.4	2,178	96.4
White City CDP	3,719	-	-	4,464	78.6	6.3	1.3	1.1	12.7	21.6	18.2	44.9	57.8	14.5	1,485	90.3
White Springs town	776	766	-1.3	746	45.8	51.3	0.0	1.2	1.6	11.9	23.9	55.9	67.8	13.3	382	67.8
Whitfield CDP	2,882	-	-	3,743	85.3	1.8	2.3	1.5	9.0	16.5	23.4	50.9	28.4	39.0	1,433	94.3
Whitfield CDP	295	-	-	294	96.6	0.0	0.0	0.0	3.4	4.4	15.3	56.5	45.6	10.7	138	78.3
Wildwood city	5,030	7,276	44.7	6,838	69.6	20.5	4.7	1.5	3.6	18.6	34.0	52.4	48.4	22.4	2,896	81.5
Williamsburg CDP	7,646	-	-	7,823	63.3	4.2	5.5	2.2	24.8	14.6	25.9	43.6	27.5	38.5	3,209	93.1
Williston city	2,766	2,735	-1.1	2,699	70.4	20.0	2.9	1.1	5.7	26.1	17.2	31.8	54.6	12.4	934	83.8
Williston Highlands CDP	2,275	-	-	2,106	72.5	5.6	0.0	1.4	14.8	14.6	21.5	52.6	65.2	12.6	968	83.7
Willow Oak CDP	6,732	-	-	7,236	48.2	6.4	0.0	0.5	44.9	32.5	8.3	32.5	57.0	13.9	2,215	85.2
Wilton Manors city	11,633	12,756	9.7	12,630	73.6	11.7	1.2	1.6	11.9	6.6	25.1	52.8	27.5	44.9	6,577	93.1
Wimauma CDP	6,373	-	-	8,358	20.1	5.0	1.6	0.5	72.8	34.9	8.6	27.8	75.0	9.4	1,967	80.2
Windermere town	2,931	3,544	20.9	3,430	85.0	1.4	2.5	1.1	10.0	18.0	20.7	51.8	8.8	70.6	1,315	98.9
Windsor CDP	256	-	-	218	100.0	0.0	0.0	0.0	0.0	0.0	61.5	72.8	0.0	64.7	127	89.8
Winter Beach CDP	2,067	-	-	2,570	82.6	6.3	0.5	8.1	2.4	9.1	38.9	57.0	30.2	42.4	898	91.8
Winter Garden city	34,754	46,051	32.5	43,648	46.4	15.8	7.2	4.8	25.7	25.0	12.7	38.5	33.5	40.5	14,701	94.9
Winter Haven city	34,624	44,955	29.8	41,248	54.6	24.9	1.8	2.4	16.3	21.4	25.3	44.1	48.5	19.7	15,520	85.9
Winter Park city	27,715	30,825	11.2	30,522	76.7	5.5	3.4	3.3	11.0	17.8	22.4	45.7	17.8	62.6	12,895	92.9
Winter Springs city	33,306	37,312	12.0	36,342	67.1	5.3	4.8	3.1	19.7	19.2	18.8	43.9	22.6	45.2	14,467	94.9
Wiscon CDP	706	-	-	700	98.4	0.0	0.0	0.0	1.6	18.4	21.1	44.9	52.8	11.6	307	97.7
Woodlawn Beach CDP	1,785	-	-	2,977	85.1	1.7	1.0	3.4	8.8	26.7	12.0	35.3	23.6	42.9	1,018	95.4
Woodville CDP	2,978	-	-	2,754	67.2	26.3	0.0	1.2	5.4	22.6	13.7	42.8	41.5	22.3	1,030	93.3
World Golf Village CDP	12,310	-	-	18,327	80.0	4.2	1.8	1.6	12.4	28.9	18.0	37.7	19.3	49.2	6,038	99.3
Worthington Springs town	396	387	-2.3	357	78.4	2.2	0.0	11.5	7.8	27.7	12.3	28.3	76.7	2.1	145	62.1
Wright CDP	23,127	-	-	23,965	61.9	16.7	3.8	3.9	13.7	18.6	14.0	35.1	37.9	24.7	10,475	89.5
Yalaha CDP	1,364	-	-	1,129	75.4	14.1	1.2	1.5	7.9	12.1	43.4	60.5	35.5	16.6	461	93.9
Yankeetown town	522	529	1.3	590	96.1	1.0	0.0	0.8	2.0	22.7	33.2	57.8	45.7	22.2	274	92.0
Yeehaw Junction CDP	240	-	-	203	87.7	3.9	8.4	0.0	0.0	0.0	34.0	47.8	59.6	8.4	70	51.4
Yulee CDP	11,491	-	-	12,754	86.4	7.1	0.1	2.5	4.0	23.8	15.1	38.5	44.0	22.0	4,586	93.4
Zellwood CDP	2,817	-	-	3,166	69.6	4.5	3.0	5.1	17.9	10.1	47.9	63.4	45.2	16.7	1,531	90.5
Zephyrhills city	13,859	16,456	18.7	15,573	73.3	4.6	1.7	2.4	18.0	17.9	33.6	50.3	50.8	13.3	6,775	86.7
Zephyrhills North CDP	2,600	-	-	2,859	91.2	0.1	0.0	1.9	6.8	10.5	45.5	63.4	57.1	10.1	1,437	87.3
Zephyrhills South CDP	5,276	-	-	5,637	86.3	1.0	0.0	1.3	11.4	14.6	41.2	58.3	58.8	8.7	2,670	84.6
Zephyrhills West CDP	5,865	-	-	5,287	88.4	1.3	0.7	0.9	8.7	10.0	56.0	67.3	56.5	14.1	2,795	88.6
Zolfo Springs town	1,806	1,773	-1.8	1,892	21.9	3.9	0.0	0.0	74.2	38.8	8.8	26.1	85.0	2.3	528	65.0
GEORGIA	9,688,729	10,617,423	9.6	10,403,847	52.7	31.2	3.9	2.6	9.5	24.1	13.5	36.7	40.6	31.3	3,758,798	90.2
Abbeville city	2,905	2,684	-7.6	2,793	32.3	61.9	0.0	0.7	5.1	7.3	9.5	40.0	72.7	5.1	338	60.7
Acworth city	20,491	22,818	11.4	22,534	56.7	25.8	2.8	3.2	11.5	25.9	10.4	35.0	30.9	35.6	8,337	96.3
Adairsville city	4,659	4,963	6.5	4,856	76.2	12.9	0.0	1.4	9.5	31.3	9.6	33.0	60.0	12.3	1,830	95.1
Adel city	5,340	5,336	-0.1	5,289	41.6	46.3	2.3	4.2	5.6	21.9	18.4	39.5	50.6	17.2	2,111	84.0
Adrian city	665	668	0.5	650	70.3	26.3	0.0	1.8	1.5	27.5	17.7	33.0	71.4	6.9	261	74.3
Ailey city	550	536	-2.5	624	55.9	32.1	2.6	2.4	7.1	17.8	13.0	22.4	33.6	39.9	143	93.7
Alamo town	2,801	3,317	18.4	3,346	40.2	59.5	0.0	0.0	0.3	15.4	8.8	29.7	53.0	27.0	760	43.9
Alapaha town	668	675	1.0	765	47.3	51.9	0.0	0.0	0.8	15.6	28.4	45.1	64.1	13.4	363	60.3
Albany city	77,436	72,130	-6.9	73,478	21.1	74.2	0.9	1.7	2.2	24.3	14.4	34.3	47.5	20.0	28,156	83.6
Aldora town	103	109	5.8	44	93.2	6.8	0.0	0.0	0.0	29.5	15.9	25.5	54.5	18.2	25	92.0
Allenhurst city	742	716	-3.5	742	23.9	52.8	0.0	10.8	12.5	21.0	15.8	35.3	48.5	22.9	274	86.9
Allentown town	171	154	-9.9	123	74.8	25.2	0.0	0.0	0.0	18.7	31.7	42.9	70.3	18.7	47	59.6
Alma city	3,472	3,380	-2.6	3,437	46.0	45.2	0.0	4.8	4.0	24.6	11.8	32.4	64.8	8.9	1,005	81.8
Alpharetta city	57,383	67,213	17.1	65,590	56.8	11.5	20.1	3.0	8.5	26.6	9.8	39.6	12.1	69.2	24,273	96.7
Alston town	161	159	-1.2	180	72.8	21.1	0.0	0.0	6.1	24.4	32.2	48.8	75.4	11.5	61	59.0
Alto town	1,184	1,198	1.2	1,249	38.7	3.7	7.8	0.7	49.1	33.1	8.2	33.4	77.3	4.9	364	79.4
Ambrose city	375	379	1.1	266	48.9	10.5	0.0	0.0	40.6	28.9	23.3	40.0	83.2	4.6	112	42.0
Americus city	17,116	15,108	-11.7	15,503	28.8	66.8	0.8	1.7	1.9	24.6	13.2	29.9	51.5	18.2	6,162	82.8
Andersonville city	243	221	-9.1	198	47.0	50.5	1.5	1.0	0.0	17.2	22.2	36.0	69.4	6.1	93	77.4
Appling CDP	-	-	-	921	82.0	14.2	0.0	3.8	0.0	27.6	17.5	36.3	55.5	27.4	311	73.0
Arabi town	586	564	-3.8	617	82.0	18.0	0.0	0.0	0.0	17.2	24.0	44.4	65.8	3.8	249	77.5
Aragon city	1,267	1,336	5.4	1,455	89.3	1.0	0.0	3.0	6.7	30.1	13.4	34.6	70.4	5.2	505	82.0
Arcade city	1,800	1,972	9.6	1,515	86.7	3.3	0.5	5.0	4.5	21.8	15.2	41.9	54.9	21.8	548	83.9
Argyle town	212	208	-1.9	163	52.1	47.9	0.0	0.0	0.0	16.6	26.4	57.4	68.2	2.3	71	67.6
Arlington city	1,476	1,326	-10.2	1,405	19.0	77.7	2.6	0.0	0.6	28.9	12.0	36.3	58.9	12.2	511	65.9
Arnoldsville city	356	366	2.8	398	88.9	9.3	0.0	0.3	1.5	15.1	22.9	45.6	55.9	17.8	180	82.2
Ashburn city	4,152	3,704	-10.8	3,684	24.4	73.1	0.0	0.0	2.5	26.2	19.8	41.2	61.6	11.4	1,500	78.1
Athens-Clarke County unified government	116,688	128,331	10.0	126,176	55.0	27.7	3.9	2.6	10.8	17.4	10.6	28.0	31.9	44.0	48,844	91.6
Athens-Clarke County unified government (balance)	115,387	126,913	10.0	124,719	54.8	27.7	3.9	2.6	10.9	17.3	10.5	28.0	31.9	44.0	48,300	91.6
Atlanta city	427,059	506,811	18.7	488,800	38.3	50.5	4.4	2.5	4.3	18.3	11.5	33.3	28.0	51.8	206,229	90.1
Attapulgus city	449	425	-5.3	657	23.0	45.7	0.0	2.9	28.5	28.2	12.8	36.2	76.9	4.5	239	54.8
Auburn city	7,033	7,660	8.9	7,481	73.5	6.1	4.0	1.9	14.5	25.7	9.3	33.9	53.9	13.1	2,436	89.7

1 May be of any race.

Table A. All Places — **Population and Housing**

STATE City, town, township, borough, or CDP (county if applicable)	Population				Race and Hispanic or Latino origin (percent)					Age (percent)			Educational attainment of persons age 25 and older		Occupied housing units	
	2010 census total population	2019 estimated population	Percent change 2010-2019	ACS total population estimate 2015-2019	White alone, not Hispanic or Latino	Black alone, not Hispanic or Latino	Asian alone, not Hispanic or Latino	All other races or 2 or more races, not Hispanic or Latino	Hispanic or Latino[1]	Under 18 years old	Age 65 years and older	Median age	Percent High school diploma or less	Percent Bachelor's degree or more	Total	Percent with a computer
	1	2	3	4	5	6	7	8	9	10	11	12	13	14	15	16
GEORGIA—Con.																
Augusta-Richmond County consolidated government	200,594	202,518	1.0	201,852	34.5	55.6	1.8	3.2	4.9	23.1	13.6	34.1	47.2	21.4	71,400	87.1
Augusta-Richmond County consolidated government (balance)	195,859	197,888	1.0	197,191	33.8	56.3	1.8	3.2	4.9	23.1	13.5	33.9	47.0	21.6	69,754	87.2
Austell city	6,525	7,170	9.9	7,205	31.2	53.3	0.9	2.4	12.2	28.5	8.0	32.9	43.4	27.9	2,691	95.8
Avalon town	217	215	-0.9	204	63.7	10.8	0.0	0.0	25.5	26.5	15.2	38.7	60.3	18.3	64	76.6
Avera city	249	225	-9.6	255	90.2	3.5	0.0	4.7	1.6	20.0	10.6	39.9	55.7	10.9	82	92.7
Avondale Estates city	2,956	3,129	5.9	3,144	84.5	7.5	3.1	3.2	1.7	20.4	23.4	48.5	9.1	74.2	1,422	96.6
Baconton city	914	827	-9.5	1,121	44.5	54.1	0.0	1.3	0.0	36.8	12.0	31.6	54.2	7.1	335	74.9
Bainbridge city	12,798	12,081	-5.6	12,199	35.3	59.3	0.4	2.4	2.6	28.2	14.7	35.1	51.0	13.9	4,471	73.3
Baldwin city	3,279	3,414	4.1	3,517	38.7	0.4	0.9	0.5	59.5	36.8	8.3	27.1	75.9	10.3	984	75.1
Ball Ground city	1,506	2,195	45.8	2,131	94.7	0.1	0.0	0.7	4.6	23.2	10.6	38.2	32.4	24.0	804	98.1
Barnesville city	6,785	6,659	-1.9	6,650	38.8	57.3	0.2	2.1	1.5	17.6	14.5	28.5	53.8	13.3	2,056	81.6
Bartow town	286	250	-12.6	225	48.4	51.1	0.0	0.4	0.0	18.2	24.4	53.4	48.8	15.1	96	62.5
Barwick city	386	372	-3.6	237	58.2	40.9	0.0	0.8	0.0	21.1	13.9	33.5	63.5	8.4	127	69.3
Baxley city	4,682	4,659	-0.5	4,697	48.4	31.4	0.0	1.1	19.1	30.1	13.5	34.2	69.0	6.5	1,436	81.1
Bellville city	123	118	-4.1	102	95.1	0.0	0.0	0.0	4.9	19.6	26.5	52.5	39.1	39.1	43	79.1
Belvedere Park CDP	15,152	-	-	15,441	20.2	72.8	1.3	1.8	3.9	18.0	12.4	40.4	45.4	26.9	6,086	87.7
Berkeley Lake city	1,845	2,147	16.4	1,839	76.0	4.1	12.7	4.0	3.2	18.9	22.6	52.2	9.4	65.7	687	98.3
Berlin city	553	554	0.2	709	49.1	26.9	0.4	2.7	20.9	23.3	14.1	37.5	66.4	5.2	219	85.4
Bethlehem town	613	725	18.3	942	61.7	11.6	0.7	1.0	25.1	37.8	12.6	31.8	54.7	17.6	270	93.3
Between town	296	373	26.0	289	94.1	3.5	0.0	1.0	1.4	26.3	14.9	39.3	27.2	33.7	103	94.2
Bishop town	222	274	23.4	341	78.0	7.6	2.6	2.1	9.7	36.7	7.0	31.6	25.7	51.4	115	96.5
Blackshear city	3,450	3,527	2.2	3,489	68.4	26.7	0.0	3.1	1.8	20.2	20.6	45.9	60.3	11.6	1,355	77.5
Blairsville city	656	643	-2.0	724	77.9	13.4	0.0	3.9	4.8	11.6	17.0	42.4	61.1	8.9	230	76.5
Blakely city	5,074	4,571	-9.9	4,652	25.8	71.5	1.2	1.4	0.1	33.4	12.0	30.5	62.2	12.7	1,584	56.9
Bloomingdale city	2,641	2,686	1.7	2,715	82.3	10.6	0.4	0.9	5.7	18.5	20.0	50.5	56.4	9.7	1,272	90.7
Blue Ridge city	1,356	1,461	7.7	1,157	89.0	3.7	0.0	5.4	1.8	14.1	35.8	52.5	50.8	17.1	476	82.6
Bluffton town	103	92	-10.7	107	75.7	24.3	0.0	0.0	0.0	16.8	29.9	49.3	63.5	14.1	44	70.5
Blythe city	725	711	-1.9	688	76.5	7.6	0.0	5.1	10.9	25.9	14.0	35.5	59.4	11.1	224	81.3
Bogart town	1,142	1,206	5.6	1,440	75.8	13.8	2.9	1.9	5.6	23.3	12.2	36.9	38.3	33.3	574	93.9
Bonanza CDP	3,135	-	-	3,603	13.2	65.9	7.6	2.4	10.9	34.2	9.2	32.2	38.6	23.5	1,220	95.2
Boston city	1,315	1,317	0.2	1,318	40.6	49.8	0.0	0.2	9.5	26.6	18.1	36.9	58.5	15.9	500	77.4
Bostwick city	367	395	7.6	314	86.3	11.5	0.0	0.6	1.6	25.2	10.8	41.4	49.0	26.0	100	91.0
Bowdon city	2,040	2,100	2.9	2,565	68.3	22.0	0.4	4.2	5.0	26.0	15.4	36.1	59.2	14.6	1,028	82.6
Bowersville town	471	485	3.0	559	64.8	18.1	0.0	3.2	14.0	27.2	14.3	38.1	68.9	7.0	224	77.7
Bowman city	862	808	-6.3	866	67.2	27.1	0.0	0.5	5.2	23.1	21.1	44.8	68.9	11.6	359	54.0
Boykin CDP	143	-	-	39	100.0	0.0	0.0	0.0	0.0	0.0	38.5	64.4	30.8	0.0	22	100.0
Braselton town	7,544	12,961	71.8	11,452	77.0	12.3	2.1	3.6	5.0	28.3	13.6	36.9	25.5	51.1	3,779	96.9
Braswell town	375	383	2.1	322	77.3	5.3	10.2	1.6	5.6	21.1	10.9	35.4	55.9	23.9	131	90.8
Bremen city	6,242	6,638	6.3	6,394	85.0	8.9	1.1	2.2	2.7	32.9	9.1	31.0	31.1	29.2	2,180	92.3
Brinson town	215	202	-6.0	177	59.9	31.6	1.1	7.3	0.0	11.3	28.2	54.8	56.4	20.3	69	63.8
Bronwood town	415	367	-11.6	251	24.7	65.3	0.0	0.0	10.0	15.1	21.5	45.8	67.2	6.9	124	68.5
Brookhaven city	49,640	55,554	11.9	53,819	58.0	11.1	5.8	2.7	22.4	22.4	9.9	34.2	21.3	67.4	22,549	93.8
Brooklet city	1,384	1,815	31.1	1,667	89.9	7.4	0.4	1.0	1.3	20.3	16.3	40.6	36.0	31.2	699	92.3
Brooks town	524	559	6.7	527	93.4	1.1	0.2	2.8	2.5	23.1	15.0	48.0	38.4	30.7	198	96.0
Broxton city	1,191	1,196	0.4	1,279	37.1	27.0	0.0	0.0	35.9	21.8	14.5	40.2	69.0	6.0	496	74.2
Brunswick city	15,291	16,256	6.3	16,122	33.1	54.1	2.2	2.2	8.5	23.9	16.5	36.0	47.0	17.9	6,486	79.4
Buchanan city	1,110	1,176	5.9	1,281	83.3	12.2	0.0	3.2	1.3	23.5	13.5	34.8	65.9	5.5	436	81.7
Buckhead town	171	183	7.0	222	82.4	14.0	0.0	0.0	3.6	18.5	14.0	36.3	49.1	22.5	83	94.0
Buena Vista city	2,204	2,053	-6.9	2,113	20.0	65.4	0.0	0.3	14.3	28.8	15.1	37.8	67.5	11.9	722	66.5
Buford city	12,562	15,522	23.6	16,143	53.0	14.1	3.3	2.6	27.0	26.8	12.3	36.4	54.0	25.4	5,003	82.2
Butler city	1,956	1,759	-10.1	1,656	37.9	61.2	0.0	0.4	0.5	18.4	21.0	45.6	68.5	3.4	762	63.1
Byromville town	550	500	-9.1	497	31.8	58.1	0.0	1.0	9.1	15.7	29.4	53.5	71.8	10.3	185	77.3
Byron city	4,532	5,226	15.3	5,149	53.3	39.1	3.8	1.1	2.6	24.1	18.8	40.9	33.1	27.5	2,198	87.6
Cadwell town	528	540	2.3	553	75.2	11.4	1.8	6.7	4.9	21.5	16.1	31.0	56.6	13.8	163	83.4
Cairo city	9,625	9,369	-2.7	9,446	36.5	44.8	0.3	1.6	16.7	24.4	17.4	38.4	63.5	11.7	3,567	73.6
Calhoun city	16,253	17,271	6.3	16,940	61.6	5.3	1.6	2.2	29.3	26.6	13.1	34.1	55.7	17.8	6,088	81.7
Calvary CDP	161	-	-	113	100.0	0.0	0.0	0.0	0.0	29.2	0.0	38.1	20.0	26.3	40	72.5
Camak town	143	126	-11.9	127	19.7	80.3	0.0	0.0	0.0	13.4	13.4	45.3	58.8	5.9	64	70.3
Camilla city	5,313	5,012	-5.7	5,126	26.7	71.6	0.2	1.3	0.2	28.0	16.8	36.2	62.2	9.9	1,926	79.1
Candler-McAfee CDP	23,025	-	-	24,011	8.7	87.7	0.1	2.7	0.7	19.8	19.2	40.3	50.2	22.2	8,685	86.5
Canon city	744	785	5.5	1,003	66.8	18.0	0.0	1.0	14.2	40.2	11.4	33.3	75.0	3.2	325	71.4
Canoochee CDP	71	-	-	48	100.0	0.0	0.0	0.0	0.0	0.0	35.4	52.3	33.3	13.9	21	76.2
Canton city	23,518	30,528	29.8	28,166	59.0	10.6	1.5	1.1	27.7	25.9	12.8	34.1	38.4	29.0	10,233	93.5
Carl town	198	235	18.7	191	86.9	4.7	7.3	0.0	1.0	19.4	15.2	42.8	50.0	17.9	68	95.6
Carlton city	254	260	2.4	440	65.7	24.3	8.0	1.6	0.5	18.6	23.0	53.4	74.2	12.7	184	68.5
Carnesville city	595	601	1.0	755	79.5	16.4	1.3	1.1	1.7	23.7	13.6	37.2	58.3	8.9	247	87.0
Carrollton city	24,380	27,259	11.8	26,570	51.1	32.4	1.1	2.2	13.2	22.6	10.5	26.2	41.9	30.7	9,024	90.9
Cartersville city	19,785	21,760	10.0	20,870	66.0	18.7	0.4	3.9	11.0	26.0	15.5	36.0	43.0	26.0	7,835	92.7
Cave Spring city	1,153	1,070	-7.2	1,143	87.0	8.7	0.0	3.6	0.7	21.3	21.4	49.0	52.4	20.9	459	82.8
Cecil city	284	283	-0.4	300	42.3	56.7	0.0	1.0	0.0	22.3	21.0	44.8	62.7	11.3	128	76.6
Cedar Springs CDP	74	-	-	90	100.0	0.0	0.0	0.0	0.0	0.0	65.6	69.2	90.6	9.4	83	15.7
Cedartown city	9,790	9,997	2.1	9,999	40.5	20.5	0.0	0.7	38.2	27.4	16.6	32.8	64.1	14.0	3,573	76.8
Centerville city	7,178	7,884	9.8	7,751	58.2	29.4	1.8	2.5	8.1	25.9	17.2	36.5	37.3	26.3	2,891	95.2
Centralhatchee town	384	377	-1.8	345	87.0	11.0	0.0	2.0	0.0	22.0	20.0	42.9	71.4	9.9	136	75.7
Chamblee city	26,846	30,307	12.9	29,232	36.0	15.8	7.8	2.9	37.4	23.9	8.0	32.0	39.9	45.1	11,526	89.5
Chatsworth city	4,300	4,290	-0.2	4,261	82.8	3.0	1.0	1.9	11.4	20.5	22.2	38.7	55.2	20.0	1,670	79.6
Chattahoochee Hills city	2,639	3,318	25.7	2,872	71.7	20.2	0.0	0.5	7.6	17.3	21.3	50.7	47.9	30.8	1,106	91.1
Chattanooga Valley CDP	3,846	-	-	3,186	88.3	2.7	0.2	0.3	8.4	15.7	23.8	48.9	53.6	18.4	1,410	90.0
Chauncey city	342	326	-4.7	359	44.8	40.1	0.0	3.9	11.1	30.1	14.2	33.9	66.5	10.8	143	55.2
Cherry Log CDP	119	-	-	40	100.0	0.0	0.0	0.0	0.0	0.0	42.5	46.8	74.2	0.0	22	100.0
Chester town	1,596	1,564	-2.0	2,102	29.9	65.6	0.2	2.0	2.2	8.1	5.8	40.2	82.3	2.2	194	64.9
Chickamauga city	3,226	3,256	0.9	3,249	100.0	0.0	0.0	0.0	0.0	26.5	17.9	35.4	49.3	18.9	1,289	90.1
Clarkesville city	1,720	1,821	5.9	1,754	87.8	7.9	0.3	1.7	2.3	18.4	18.8	37.6	35.2	35.2	709	79.5
Clarkston city	12,103	12,637	4.4	12,750	8.4	59.3	24.6	3.3	4.4	32.4	4.2	27.8	52.5	24.1	3,727	96.7
Claxton city	2,385	2,204	-7.6	2,665	47.4	40.9	0.9	0.8	10.0	35.5	11.2	28.5	52.2	15.3	908	86.1
Clayton city	2,017	2,193	8.7	1,968	88.3	0.7	0.0	2.4	8.6	14.5	28.3	51.2	58.1	22.5	795	78.2
Clermont town	927	1,039	12.1	901	96.0	0.0	0.0	0.9	3.1	21.6	12.5	43.0	46.0	20.3	340	93.8
Cleveland city	3,427	4,165	21.5	3,920	88.6	3.2	0.8	4.2	3.3	24.7	9.5	30.2	42.9	20.5	1,276	77.3

1 May be of any race.

Table A. All Places — **Population and Housing**

STATE City, town, township, borough, or CDP (county if applicable)	Population				Race and Hispanic or Latino origin (percent)					Age (percent)			Educational attainment of persons age 25 and older		Occupied housing units	
	2010 census total population	2019 estimated population	Percent change 2010-2019	ACS total population estimate 2015-2019	White alone, not Hispanic or Latino	Black alone, not Hispanic or Latino	Asian alone, not Hispanic or Latino	All other races or 2 or more races, not Hispanic or Latino	Hispanic or Latino[1]	Under 18 years old	Age 65 years and older	Median age	Percent High school diploma or less	Percent Bachelor's degree or more	Total	Percent with a computer
	1	2	3	4	5	6	7	8	9	10	11	12	13	14	15	16
GEORGIA—Con.																
Climax city	277	262	-5.4	203	58.1	26.1	0.5	1.0	14.3	23.2	22.7	47.8	63.5	10.1	82	73.2
Cobbtown city	364	357	-1.9	383	75.5	9.9	0.0	4.4	10.2	26.1	17.5	44.2	55.6	13.4	180	68.3
Cochran city	5,160	4,993	-3.2	4,921	46.8	45.5	0.5	2.3	5.0	23.6	14.0	22.9	46.9	25.6	1,406	78.5
Cohutta city	633	637	0.6	566	82.5	0.7	1.9	4.2	10.6	22.8	17.5	41.2	46.5	20.3	196	90.3
Colbert city	573	598	4.4	583	87.5	8.2	0.2	0.7	3.4	18.5	17.3	43.0	55.1	12.7	239	91.6
Coleman CDP	127	-	-	22	100.0	0.0	0.0	0.0	0.0	36.4	0.0	45.4	0.0	50.0	7	100.0
College Park city	14,633	15,159	3.6	14,501	13.1	79.7	0.9	2.0	4.2	30.5	9.4	33.7	42.1	24.9	5,861	84.3
Collins city	583	571	-2.1	459	50.1	41.2	0.0	1.3	7.4	29.6	22.4	43.4	56.0	15.7	212	75.0
Colquitt city	1,995	1,834	-8.1	2,274	41.6	55.8	0.0	2.6	0.0	25.6	18.6	35.0	58.7	6.3	854	60.8
Columbus city	190,570	195,769	2.7	195,739	40.3	45.6	2.5	4.0	7.6	24.8	13.0	34.0	39.3	25.8	72,759	87.5
Comer city	1,126	1,178	4.6	1,271	81.0	10.4	3.4	3.8	1.5	24.9	20.8	40.2	45.9	30.0	502	83.3
Commerce city	6,551	7,085	8.2	6,858	67.9	16.9	0.7	3.8	10.6	24.4	17.4	34.6	57.0	17.0	2,547	83.6
Concord city	375	384	2.4	338	74.6	22.5	0.0	0.6	2.4	25.4	19.5	33.8	51.3	14.5	124	83.1
Conley CDP	6,228	-	-	5,783	11.2	51.2	4.2	8.7	24.7	27.0	10.3	37.4	59.4	15.3	2,016	85.5
Conyers city	15,238	16,256	6.7	15,986	19.9	64.9	1.6	0.9	12.7	28.8	11.5	33.6	47.1	27.8	6,300	93.0
Coolidge city	530	529	-0.2	489	40.5	53.4	0.0	1.4	4.7	33.9	9.4	37.4	51.7	7.3	204	78.4
Cordele city	11,186	10,521	-5.9	10,752	25.3	71.6	0.3	0.8	2.0	28.7	14.2	31.5	58.6	10.6	3,874	73.6
Cornelia city	4,196	4,683	11.6	4,375	50.7	7.3	2.5	2.4	37.0	34.2	11.1	30.8	52.6	18.2	1,365	70.5
Country Club Estates CDP	8,545	-	-	8,194	42.2	44.2	0.7	3.4	9.6	23.3	15.0	33.8	44.8	16.4	3,319	85.8
Covington city	13,127	14,206	8.2	13,967	43.6	46.2	0.7	2.6	7.0	27.7	14.6	30.8	49.9	18.3	5,094	89.1
Crawford city	828	836	1.0	947	52.5	43.7	0.6	3.2	0.0	23.0	30.3	46.1	79.0	9.7	396	49.2
Crawfordville city	534	473	-11.4	516	46.9	52.3	0.0	0.8	0.0	18.0	25.6	46.0	74.0	9.3	206	74.3
Crooked Creek CDP	639	-	-	452	72.8	11.3	0.0	5.5	10.4	20.8	22.6	46.6	41.5	10.1	182	95.6
Culloden city	177	186	5.1	239	56.5	43.5	0.0	0.0	0.0	21.3	15.9	39.6	63.6	19.7	75	77.3
Cumming city	5,541	6,547	18.2	6,309	64.2	5.5	6.0	1.8	22.5	18.3	20.0	40.4	45.9	27.5	2,480	84.9
Cusseta-Chattahoochee County unified government	11,263	10,907	-3.2	10,560	57.6	19.9	2.9	3.8	15.9	21.3	3.2	24.5	34.1	29.5	2,570	85.9
Cuthbert city	3,881	3,417	-12.0	3,520	12.2	86.5	0.0	0.0	1.3	27.2	22.1	39.6	68.6	6.7	1,194	82.1
Dacula city	4,446	6,350	42.8	5,919	50.8	28.2	0.4	3.2	17.4	24.9	10.7	35.6	42.9	25.1	1,902	95.4
Dahlonega city	5,264	7,294	38.6	6,773	86.4	7.4	0.9	0.8	4.4	15.8	14.2	22.7	17.9	45.3	1,873	93.0
Daisy city	145	141	-2.8	245	84.9	4.1	0.0	2.9	8.2	49.0	12.2	23.4	59.7	11.8	78	69.2
Dallas city	11,502	13,981	21.6	13,321	57.8	29.5	0.7	7.2	5.0	29.0	14.0	33.0	52.2	13.0	4,944	91.4
Dalton city	33,090	33,665	1.7	33,571	42.9	6.6	2.8	1.4	46.3	27.0	11.8	32.6	57.3	20.1	11,305	84.4
Damascus city	248	224	-9.7	191	20.4	79.6	0.0	0.0	0.0	16.2	24.6	49.9	53.1	9.5	90	45.6
Danielsville city	565	594	5.1	748	90.4	0.5	0.0	6.4	2.7	16.3	9.9	35.6	47.1	22.0	285	86.3
Danville town	238	212	-10.9	251	60.6	39.0	0.4	0.0	0.0	17.5	25.5	46.5	71.2	11.4	76	51.3
Darien city	1,935	1,921	-0.7	2,230	38.5	59.5	0.0	0.8	1.3	20.0	22.9	43.8	56.4	15.2	957	76.5
Dasher town	912	1,015	11.3	937	85.4	6.3	0.2	0.0	8.1	26.4	13.8	35.4	48.5	22.0	315	91.4
Davisboro city	2,006	1,958	-2.4	1,983	26.2	61.6	0.0	1.5	10.6	4.3	6.8	39.1	77.5	3.7	177	79.7
Dawson city	4,618	4,126	-10.7	4,225	17.6	77.7	4.3	0.4	0.0	29.3	15.3	34.8	54.9	10.8	1,577	84.1
Dawsonville city	2,499	3,246	29.9	2,882	87.8	4.6	1.7	1.5	4.4	26.8	13.6	32.6	45.8	23.0	998	95.7
Dearing town	549	532	-3.1	624	77.6	18.1	0.6	2.6	1.1	26.1	15.7	34.5	44.7	20.9	230	75.2
Decatur city	19,630	25,696	30.9	24,002	66.5	20.1	3.5	5.9	4.0	32.2	12.4	36.8	14.0	74.3	8,841	90.7
Deenwood CDP	2,146	-	-	2,579	66.7	18.1	7.1	5.4	2.8	22.4	16.2	37.2	56.2	16.6	1,102	90.0
Deepstep town	131	120	-8.4	105	100.0	0.0	0.0	0.0	0.0	13.3	21.0	45.8	30.2	43.0	50	90.0
Demorest city	1,820	2,125	16.8	1,973	81.4	4.2	1.7	1.3	11.5	16.7	21.0	27.0	43.9	26.0	664	75.0
Denton city	250	248	-0.8	149	75.8	23.5	0.0	0.7	0.0	15.4	26.8	53.8	74.2	4.0	62	59.7
De Soto city	190	173	-8.9	180	8.3	91.7	0.0	0.0	0.0	58.9	12.8	12.7	36.7	5.0	45	64.4
Dewy Rose CDP	154	-	-	185	55.1	0.0	0.0	0.0	44.9	15.7	11.4	46.7	78.8	10.3	78	91.0
Dexter town	575	562	-2.3	832	48.4	51.6	0.0	0.0	0.0	33.7	10.1	30.8	55.0	14.7	271	82.3
Dillard city	370	377	1.9	319	79.9	0.0	18.2	0.0	1.9	7.5	30.7	49.0	36.8	36.4	134	82.1
Dock Junction CDP	7,721	-	-	7,454	60.2	28.3	2.8	4.1	4.6	19.9	17.1	40.8	54.6	13.5	2,976	77.4
Doerun city	774	736	-4.9	818	59.4	38.6	0.0	0.0	2.0	31.7	24.3	33.4	59.9	6.4	341	81.5
Donalsonville city	2,664	2,466	-7.4	2,424	35.1	60.8	0.0	0.9	3.2	30.0	21.7	32.4	62.0	9.7	872	63.2
Dooling town	154	136	-11.7	151	25.2	29.8	0.0	0.0	45.0	41.7	14.6	37.5	66.7	17.9	46	82.6
Doraville city	9,700	10,265	5.8	10,228	21.5	5.2	15.9	2.1	55.4	28.4	8.0	32.6	58.4	26.1	3,231	85.5
Douglas city	11,627	11,695	0.6	11,556	36.9	52.6	0.1	2.0	8.5	32.0	13.1	30.4	59.0	13.0	4,339	74.7
Douglasville city	30,404	33,992	11.8	33,052	26.6	62.0	1.7	3.0	6.6	24.1	10.2	34.9	34.2	35.1	12,675	93.3
Druid Hills CDP	14,568	-	-	8,365	81.3	4.4	9.5	0.8	4.0	16.8	17.8	40.7	4.7	88.0	3,579	99.1
Dublin city	16,184	15,881	-1.9	15,828	32.5	63.5	2.5	0.5	1.0	24.9	16.3	37.2	57.5	18.1	5,520	70.2
Dudley city	575	561	-2.4	720	83.9	13.8	0.0	2.4	0.0	26.3	14.3	38.7	47.1	21.5	273	84.2
Duluth city	26,663	29,609	11.0	29,370	33.9	22.0	25.2	3.4	15.6	22.3	11.6	39.0	24.3	47.6	11,202	94.6
Dunwoody city	46,427	49,356	6.3	49,371	58.4	12.0	18.1	2.6	8.8	26.0	14.2	36.8	12.2	72.2	20,482	96.3
Du Pont town	120	117	-2.5	178	34.3	65.7	0.0	0.0	0.0	33.7	14.0	32.7	78.0	6.4	62	64.5
Dutch Island CDP	1,257	-	-	1,162	88.4	0.0	3.1	7.9	0.6	26.1	27.9	50.5	4.0	75.1	420	100.0
Eagle Grove CDP	164	-	-	-	-	-	-	-	-	-	-	-	-	-	-	-
East Dublin city	2,462	2,398	-2.6	2,708	47.7	47.0	0.0	1.3	4.1	30.7	18.1	30.2	63.3	13.2	982	57.2
East Ellijay city	547	569	4.0	591	69.2	0.0	2.0	5.8	23.0	32.0	17.4	33.1	64.5	12.9	211	82.9
East Griffin CDP	1,451	-	-	1,386	61.3	21.2	0.0	2.4	15.1	26.6	13.3	34.6	75.5	3.8	509	78.0
Eastman city	5,569	5,067	-9.0	5,135	47.6	39.9	1.2	5.6	5.6	21.9	18.5	36.1	53.3	15.0	1,916	83.5
East Newnan CDP	1,321	-	-	810	45.4	34.0	0.0	5.4	15.2	7.9	19.4	47.7	63.2	15.1	365	94.2
East Point city	33,452	34,875	4.3	34,957	11.8	77.5	1.5	1.9	7.3	23.2	11.9	34.7	38.3	31.9	14,216	90.6
Eatonton city	6,488	6,725	3.7	6,603	33.2	57.7	0.2	0.3	8.5	27.2	16.4	38.5	59.6	18.3	2,559	84.8
Echols County consolidated government	4,023	4,006	-0.4	3,981	66.3	2.0	0.0	4.4	27.3	22.1	16.1	40.6	67.8	9.7	1,561	64.6
Edge Hill city	24	23	-4.2	8	100.0	0.0	0.0	0.0	0.0	0.0	37.5	57.5	50.0	0.0	3	66.7
Edison city	1,548	1,396	-9.8	1,327	23.6	71.3	0.0	5.0	0.1	25.7	26.1	39.1	57.8	10.1	528	65.2
Elberton city	4,591	4,329	-5.7	4,343	45.9	44.4	0.0	1.8	7.9	21.5	18.3	42.2	55.9	12.9	1,754	69.2
Ellaville city	1,819	1,867	2.6	1,585	49.5	44.7	0.0	0.3	5.5	32.2	15.5	32.1	52.0	11.5	610	83.3
Ellenton town	281	282	0.4	196	52.0	30.1	12.2	5.1	0.5	21.4	17.9	47.1	71.4	9.7	78	47.4
Ellijay city	1,609	1,714	6.5	2,436	62.2	0.2	1.5	1.2	35.0	22.3	17.4	41.4	66.5	14.3	844	71.1
Emerson city	1,474	1,596	8.3	1,754	76.6	1.9	8.9	3.6	9.0	25.7	15.7	42.2	46.9	27.8	629	88.2
Empire CDP	393	-	-	376	63.0	37.0	0.0	0.0	0.0	5.3	24.7	47.5	72.2	10.3	168	56.0
Enigma town	1,331	1,350	1.4	1,245	76.7	2.5	0.0	2.9	17.9	32.4	15.1	29.7	71.6	3.9	404	68.1
Ephesus city	461	461	0.0	357	98.9	0.0	0.0	1.1	0.0	12.9	26.9	54.1	56.5	14.8	160	81.3
Epworth CDP	480	-	-	195	100.0	0.0	0.0	0.0	0.0	0.0	61.5	66.3	36.4	25.6	102	72.5
Eton city	892	902	1.1	1,221	52.3	2.8	1.0	3.2	40.8	37.1	5.2	29.3	66.5	9.0	354	94.4
Euharlee city	4,145	4,367	5.4	4,309	81.9	11.7	0.0	4.0	2.5	23.9	10.6	39.3	48.0	20.8	1,369	98.0
Evans CDP	29,011	-	-	37,114	74.7	11.7	5.0	3.9	4.8	27.1	14.4	38.5	23.1	48.3	11,171	93.8

1 May be of any race.

Table A. All Places — **Population and Housing**

STATE City, town, township, borough, or CDP (county if applicable)	Population				Race and Hispanic or Latino origin (percent)					Age (percent)			Educational attainment of persons age 25 and older		Occupied housing units	
	2010 census total population	2019 estimated population	Percent change 2010-2019	ACS total population estimate 2015-2019	White alone, not Hispanic or Latino	Black alone, not Hispanic or Latino	Asian alone, not Hispanic or Latino	All other races or 2 or more races, not Hispanic or Latino	Hispanic or Latino[1]	Under 18 years old	Age 65 years and older	Median age	Percent High school diploma or less	Percent Bachelor's degree or more	Total	Percent with a computer
	1	2	3	4	5	6	7	8	9	10	11	12	13	14	15	16
GEORGIA—Con.																
Experiment CDP	2,894	-	-	3,352	48.7	45.2	0.0	4.0	2.1	35.9	18.5	31.7	77.9	9.5	1,092	87.6
Fairburn city	13,100	16,768	28.0	15,295	11.8	71.7	0.2	1.8	14.5	33.3	5.6	28.8	41.5	26.6	5,051	97.5
Fairmount city	721	736	2.1	958	82.2	12.6	0.0	3.3	1.9	29.3	14.5	29.2	54.1	11.7	312	89.1
Fair Oaks CDP	8,225	-	-	9,518	15.0	22.8	0.1	2.3	59.8	30.4	5.4	28.2	66.1	12.4	3,131	92.0
Fairview CDP	6,769	-	-	6,540	94.0	2.9	0.5	1.4	1.3	22.1	19.8	41.1	53.4	15.7	2,439	88.0
Fargo city	321	316	-1.6	256	75.8	22.3	0.0	2.0	0.0	34.0	13.7	36.7	68.6	10.7	89	75.3
Fayetteville city	16,154	17,991	11.4	17,586	41.8	39.7	7.2	5.3	6.0	21.9	19.0	42.0	31.0	38.7	6,833	92.8
Fitzgerald city	9,145	8,662	-5.3	8,812	39.3	57.3	1.3	0.8	1.3	27.9	14.7	35.3	63.7	12.0	3,346	69.5
Flemington city	737	717	-2.7	661	30.4	49.0	8.0	3.6	8.9	28.1	8.3	38.1	36.4	24.5	233	93.1
Flovilla city	645	660	2.3	835	56.3	40.2	1.1	1.8	0.6	20.8	14.6	29.0	81.6	2.9	280	87.5
Flowery Branch city	5,747	8,325	44.9	7,497	76.6	8.1	2.2	4.3	8.7	20.4	12.5	39.3	26.9	39.0	2,976	96.8
Folkston city	4,157	5,037	21.2	4,910	33.0	41.8	0.8	6.1	18.3	20.6	10.6	35.4	73.1	8.4	1,082	67.7
Forest Park city	18,463	20,020	8.4	19,723	17.3	45.4	6.7	3.5	27.1	28.0	10.6	32.7	65.2	8.3	6,618	83.6
Forsyth city	3,850	4,130	7.3	4,077	46.1	49.9	1.4	2.6	0.0	26.7	17.6	39.9	43.9	25.0	1,687	88.6
Fort Gaines city	1,112	963	-13.4	895	15.6	79.1	3.4	1.9	0.0	28.5	15.5	36.3	58.2	9.1	336	81.3
Fort Oglethorpe city	9,295	9,994	7.5	9,954	86.6	3.3	3.3	5.8	1.0	21.1	23.5	40.5	51.1	15.5	3,994	89.6
Fort Stewart CDP	4,924	-	-	9,643	45.3	23.8	1.3	11.2	18.4	35.1	0.0	21.9	29.5	20.6	2,563	96.6
Fort Valley city	9,803	8,962	-8.6	8,742	15.5	78.8	0.5	0.4	4.8	17.7	11.5	26.0	53.7	15.9	3,040	71.2
Franklin city	999	971	-2.8	912	60.1	37.2	0.0	1.1	1.6	17.1	25.7	51.6	62.4	15.3	421	59.4
Franklin Springs city	940	1,192	26.8	783	80.2	12.0	0.3	1.5	6.0	8.0	24.1	25.7	30.6	35.0	230	92.6
Funston city	449	450	0.2	565	71.0	17.5	0.0	0.0	11.5	25.8	11.9	35.2	69.9	9.3	190	86.3
Gainesville city	34,035	43,232	27.0	39,991	39.3	15.3	2.2	2.5	40.7	27.6	14.1	31.5	50.4	27.0	13,314	89.6
Garden City city	8,689	8,713	0.3	8,885	35.4	41.6	1.3	2.0	19.7	24.1	14.3	32.5	51.3	10.2	3,221	88.5
Garfield city	209	201	-3.8	154	44.8	55.2	0.0	0.0	0.0	16.9	21.4	44.5	58.0	11.8	59	78.0
Gay town	89	81	-9.0	92	85.9	0.0	0.0	0.0	14.1	12.0	15.2	51.5	52.6	17.1	43	90.7
Geneva town	106	96	-9.4	144	20.1	79.9	0.0	0.0	0.0	8.3	19.4	59.3	74.8	0.8	62	75.8
Georgetown CDP	11,823	-	-	12,951	49.7	31.8	2.0	5.0	11.5	24.5	9.7	34.1	30.4	33.7	4,971	96.9
Georgetown-Quitman County unified government	2,510	2,299	-8.4	2,289	37.0	51.9	7.3	3.0	0.7	19.8	24.9	47.3	70.8	7.1	842	68.6
Gibson city	663	631	-4.8	869	72.6	26.6	0.0	0.8	0.0	22.1	19.1	42.6	67.5	9.1	278	74.5
Gillsville city	226	240	6.2	270	98.5	0.7	0.7	0.0	0.0	24.1	17.8	39.1	58.8	16.6	90	77.8
Girard town	154	148	-3.9	202	68.3	31.2	0.0	0.0	0.5	37.6	19.3	30.4	68.5	4.0	77	68.8
Glennville city	5,170	5,020	-2.9	5,066	55.3	39.0	0.1	0.9	4.6	24.5	13.0	35.3	58.6	18.3	1,477	86.5
Glenwood city	668	651	-2.5	487	37.2	62.8	0.0	0.0	0.0	27.7	17.9	26.9	74.1	5.5	147	34.0
Good Hope city	267	300	12.4	398	84.4	11.3	0.0	0.0	4.3	17.1	17.8	51.5	39.4	28.4	202	89.6
Gordon city	2,021	1,857	-8.1	1,990	36.6	57.7	0.0	2.0	3.7	33.3	18.4	36.4	59.6	12.9	714	74.4
Graham city	291	290	-0.3	230	73.0	21.3	0.0	3.0	2.6	27.4	16.1	46.0	76.9	8.2	86	77.9
Grantville city	3,053	3,296	8.0	3,236	64.7	30.3	0.6	2.1	2.3	28.1	7.5	32.4	56.3	13.3	1,046	91.2
Gray city	3,291	3,274	-0.5	3,250	75.6	21.3	0.2	2.4	0.5	21.6	18.2	38.1	40.1	26.6	1,219	86.5
Grayson city	2,556	4,452	74.2	3,989	42.1	40.0	5.0	1.1	11.8	25.9	14.6	39.9	24.6	55.0	1,245	96.2
Greensboro city	3,356	3,304	-1.5	3,339	28.8	61.9	0.0	0.1	9.2	23.7	13.4	32.9	63.2	8.3	1,288	71.1
Greenville city	883	845	-4.3	855	17.7	77.1	0.0	4.1	1.2	26.3	15.2	38.1	58.9	6.8	368	66.8
Gresham Park CDP	7,432	-	-	8,877	15.1	80.3	1.0	2.3	1.4	14.2	16.4	39.6	51.0	23.1	3,149	83.5
Griffin city	23,226	22,813	-1.8	22,748	35.7	56.0	1.3	1.6	5.4	25.2	13.0	33.0	56.6	19.5	8,945	81.4
Grovetown city	11,224	15,152	35.0	14,053	47.7	27.7	0.7	7.3	16.6	24.4	8.1	31.4	41.6	23.0	4,028	94.5
Gumbranch city	273	265	-2.9	299	94.0	0.0	0.0	2.7	3.3	37.1	15.4	36.1	72.8	7.1	102	82.4
Gumlog CDP	2,146	-	-	2,287	90.7	5.7	0.0	2.3	1.3	20.1	20.4	47.6	43.9	25.4	951	83.4
Guyton city	1,676	2,226	32.8	2,125	61.1	36.5	0.0	0.5	1.9	29.7	8.0	32.2	53.2	14.1	665	89.2
Hagan city	989	965	-2.4	1,274	59.7	31.2	1.6	0.0	7.5	30.9	11.7	40.4	59.7	23.2	465	91.0
Hahira city	2,747	3,029	10.3	2,950	77.4	8.0	0.0	3.8	10.8	41.3	10.0	24.6	44.1	18.0	869	92.1
Hamilton city	1,016	1,117	9.9	1,867	61.4	28.8	0.3	4.4	5.0	33.4	7.1	30.7	29.9	28.3	514	94.2
Hampton city	6,970	8,073	15.8	7,735	39.4	51.7	0.7	0.0	8.2	22.2	8.3	38.6	50.3	14.1	2,434	91.3
Hannahs Mill CDP	3,298	-	-	3,448	78.7	13.7	1.3	5.0	1.3	24.4	19.6	38.9	67.5	7.4	1,249	79.8
Hapeville city	6,373	6,534	2.5	6,577	22.7	40.4	2.8	10.9	23.2	26.9	8.1	32.5	48.5	26.8	2,780	81.9
Haralson town	163	192	17.8	185	76.2	7.0	1.1	5.9	9.7	21.1	18.9	45.1	48.6	14.5	79	81.0
Hardwick CDP	3,930	-	-	3,329	33.6	59.8	0.2	0.6	5.8	18.6	18.2	37.6	73.8	8.3	1,401	64.2
Harlem city	2,656	3,371	26.9	3,137	75.6	21.5	0.0	1.4	1.4	27.7	15.0	34.8	45.4	14.6	1,021	81.5
Harrison town	489	442	-9.6	492	37.4	61.2	0.2	1.2	0.0	26.2	18.7	38.4	78.6	5.0	176	63.6
Hartwell city	4,365	4,437	1.6	4,356	61.9	25.9	4.1	1.1	7.0	22.8	21.9	39.1	61.1	10.1	1,592	79.8
Hawkinsville city	5,665	5,270	-7.0	5,294	35.1	63.2	0.4	0.5	0.8	16.0	16.7	36.2	58.8	15.3	1,304	77.5
Hazlehurst city	4,234	4,137	-2.3	4,147	49.2	27.3	0.0	1.3	22.2	28.9	12.1	31.3	61.8	7.5	1,494	82.3
Helen city	510	560	9.8	574	94.4	1.0	2.3	2.3	0.0	24.2	25.4	49.9	28.4	35.9	271	87.5
Henderson CDP	1,647	-	-	2,219	60.3	24.0	8.3	1.8	5.5	25.5	12.0	31.3	21.1	55.8	971	100.0
Hephzibah city	4,037	3,944	-2.3	3,977	64.4	26.2	0.5	4.0	4.9	21.8	15.2	42.1	57.4	13.3	1,424	82.8
Heron Bay CDP	3,384	-	-	3,130	53.9	46.0	0.0	0.0	0.1	29.2	8.9	34.5	17.7	60.0	1,046	100.0
Hiawassee city	863	911	5.6	815	92.8	1.7	0.6	0.0	4.9	2.8	62.6	70.0	39.6	32.6	436	77.5
Higgston town	318	312	-1.9	428	52.3	29.2	0.0	3.0	15.4	32.0	17.8	35.7	62.5	17.8	144	67.4
Hilltop CDP	262	-	-	124	0.0	100.0	0.0	0.0	0.0	5.6	56.5	68.7	84.6	0.0	70	81.4
Hiltonia town	342	324	-5.3	323	21.4	78.0	0.0	0.6	0.0	16.4	9.6	39.4	71.6	6.6	94	59.6
Hinesville city	33,347	33,273	-0.2	32,996	31.8	44.7	2.6	6.2	14.6	28.7	7.7	29.0	35.9	19.5	13,332	96.2
Hiram city	3,571	4,223	18.3	4,001	40.1	43.1	0.0	7.7	9.1	21.0	10.7	35.4	40.4	25.1	1,510	91.5
Hoboken city	531	536	0.9	616	70.8	29.2	0.0	0.0	0.0	32.8	15.3	34.9	59.6	16.3	188	84.0
Hogansville city	3,046	3,128	2.7	3,125	57.8	34.8	0.4	2.2	4.8	22.3	14.9	34.2	62.9	9.7	1,056	72.8
Holly Springs city	9,290	15,442	66.2	12,509	80.5	11.8	2.2	0.4	5.1	27.4	11.0	34.7	30.4	41.1	4,145	97.2
Homeland city	921	941	2.2	1,025	86.3	1.2	0.2	3.5	8.8	26.5	11.2	34.5	69.5	4.7	263	92.0
Homer town	1,156	1,220	5.5	1,257	91.2	5.5	0.0	2.5	0.9	22.1	15.6	41.3	59.9	14.7	461	75.9
Homerville city	2,454	2,350	-4.2	2,426	45.9	52.2	0.0	1.5	0.4	30.8	21.0	40.2	74.3	3.7	983	63.0
Hoschton city	1,377	2,180	58.3	1,637	84.4	4.6	2.7	1.8	6.5	25.4	15.6	37.9	44.6	18.7	591	89.5
Howard CDP	110	-	-	-	-	-	-	-	-	-	-	-	-	-	-	-
Hull city	196	201	2.6	187	69.0	8.0	0.0	0.0	23.0	31.0	22.5	38.5	52.8	10.4	73	80.8
Ideal city	500	439	-12.2	312	23.4	76.3	0.0	0.3	0.0	9.0	34.9	59.3	68.4	5.9	124	59.7
Ila city	337	359	6.5	411	100.0	0.0	0.0	0.0	0.0	22.9	12.4	40.1	60.1	10.8	148	79.1
Indian Springs CDP	2,241	-	-	2,509	91.3	0.0	0.0	0.0	8.7	23.9	11.5	31.7	39.5	24.2	868	98.2
Iron City town	311	289	-7.1	242	90.5	1.2	0.8	1.7	5.8	8.3	40.1	60.5	46.3	27.8	110	70.0
Irondale CDP	7,446	-	-	8,224	13.9	61.6	2.9	5.6	15.9	29.3	8.0	31.1	44.9	17.9	2,298	94.8
Irwinton city	589	555	-5.8	552	28.3	63.6	0.0	1.1	7.1	29.2	18.3	31.5	66.7	7.3	166	79.5
Isle of Hope CDP	2,402	-	-	2,487	98.0	0.8	0.0	0.5	0.6	24.8	17.8	41.4	7.9	69.5	997	96.2
Ivey city	986	914	-7.3	1,143	83.5	10.5	0.0	5.9	0.1	31.6	12.8	30.9	58.9	12.6	371	82.7
Jackson city	5,044	5,239	3.9	5,061	51.4	45.2	0.2	1.9	1.4	25.4	14.7	32.6	69.3	12.8	1,799	74.8
Jacksonville city	140	133	-5.0	79	59.5	36.7	0.0	3.8	0.0	15.2	35.4	55.9	71.6	10.4	41	68.3
Jakin city	155	146	-5.8	276	51.8	48.2	0.0	0.0	0.0	28.6	21.7	40.7	51.4	15.5	125	83.2

1 May be of any race.

Table A. All Places — **Population and Housing**

STATE City, town, township, borough, or CDP (county if applicable)	Population: 2010 census total population	Population: 2019 estimated population	Population: Percent change 2010-2019	Population: ACS total population estimate 2015-2019	Race and Hispanic or Latino origin (percent): White alone, not Hispanic or Latino	Race and Hispanic or Latino origin (percent): Black alone, not Hispanic or Latino	Race and Hispanic or Latino origin (percent): Asian alone, not Hispanic or Latino	Race and Hispanic or Latino origin (percent): All other races or 2 or more races, not Hispanic or Latino	Race and Hispanic or Latino origin (percent): Hispanic or Latino[1]	Age (percent): Under 18 years old	Age (percent): Age 65 years and older	Age (percent): Median age	Educational attainment of persons age 25 and older: Percent High school diploma or less	Educational attainment of persons age 25 and older: Percent Bachelor's degree or more	Occupied housing units: Total	Occupied housing units: Percent with a computer
	1	2	3	4	5	6	7	8	9	10	11	12	13	14	15	16
GEORGIA—Con.																
Jasper city	3,671	3,974	8.3	3,850	81.9	4.0	2.8	1.8	9.6	19.7	17.5	42.0	52.6	18.9	1,560	83.7
Jefferson city	9,501	12,032	26.6	11,114	74.7	13.3	1.9	1.5	8.6	30.7	14.7	35.2	42.5	27.6	3,933	87.7
Jeffersonville city	1,033	939	-9.1	1,031	42.0	56.6	0.0	1.2	0.2	21.2	25.6	51.4	66.6	8.9	375	48.0
Jenkinsburg city	369	376	1.9	332	59.0	31.9	0.0	8.1	0.9	27.1	11.7	32.5	66.4	15.0	132	95.5
Jersey city	137	146	6.6	75	100.0	0.0	0.0	0.0	0.0	22.7	25.3	45.2	55.8	11.5	33	93.9
Jesup city	10,209	9,841	-3.6	9,753	49.1	37.6	1.3	0.5	11.5	27.0	17.9	34.8	53.5	16.9	3,754	82.2
Johns Creek city	76,638	84,579	10.4	83,999	51.6	11.7	26.4	3.3	7.0	26.6	10.7	41.1	13.9	67.7	27,941	98.8
Jonesboro city	4,688	4,962	5.8	4,771	22.0	64.0	2.0	4.2	7.8	17.1	8.2	33.0	65.5	10.0	1,195	84.4
Junction City town	177	161	-9.0	183	8.7	90.7	0.0	0.5	0.0	3.8	13.1	52.9	88.2	0.7	84	47.6
Kennesaw city	30,603	34,077	11.4	33,960	52.9	25.0	5.6	4.3	12.3	24.5	10.0	33.3	30.0	39.2	12,803	97.0
Keysville city	344	332	-3.5	206	28.2	70.9	0.0	0.0	1.0	25.7	18.9	32.4	64.2	5.1	88	97.7
Kings Bay Base CDP	1,777	-	-	3,158	67.4	11.1	0.2	6.5	14.9	19.6	0.4	21.4	47.4	22.7	525	97.0
Kingsland city	15,866	17,949	13.1	17,093	61.0	25.3	2.4	2.6	8.7	28.2	9.2	30.1	43.8	23.2	6,118	93.9
Kingston city	640	679	6.1	513	56.9	38.6	0.0	1.0	3.5	24.8	21.1	46.9	76.1	3.7	191	88.0
Kite city	241	227	-5.8	267	74.2	10.5	0.0	0.0	15.4	36.7	13.5	38.3	74.4	0.0	86	94.2
Knoxville CDP	69	-	-	77	81.8	18.2	0.0	0.0	0.0	19.5	24.7	42.4	51.6	0.0	10	100.0
LaFayette city	7,131	7,339	2.9	7,237	80.5	8.5	4.7	4.0	2.4	22.8	19.4	37.6	60.9	10.6	2,847	75.4
LaGrange city	29,338	30,305	3.3	30,400	39.6	51.2	3.0	1.9	4.3	25.8	12.7	33.9	53.0	18.5	11,246	80.3
Lake City city	2,607	2,829	8.5	2,777	11.9	48.8	21.6	1.4	16.3	19.2	12.4	26.0	63.3	11.3	597	86.3
Lakeland city	3,374	3,282	-2.7	3,277	44.9	43.5	0.0	2.0	9.6	27.3	11.3	33.4	70.7	13.4	997	67.7
Lake Park city	734	1,207	64.4	863	71.7	10.5	3.0	2.3	12.4	19.9	17.4	44.1	53.1	19.9	324	78.7
Lakeview CDP	4,839	-	-	5,089	94.3	1.0	1.3	3.3	0.0	21.9	20.5	43.0	61.0	10.3	1,821	80.3
Lakeview Estates CDP	2,695	-	-	2,446	5.9	4.0	0.0	2.0	88.1	36.2	9.1	28.2	92.2	2.5	690	88.0
Lavonia city	2,168	2,200	1.5	2,445	60.3	26.6	0.0	2.5	10.6	23.9	18.8	35.3	63.7	15.2	1,029	82.4
Lawrenceville city	27,219	30,834	13.3	29,719	30.5	33.8	6.1	3.7	25.9	25.1	12.3	33.2	43.4	23.1	10,524	94.1
Leary city	625	559	-10.6	594	19.4	79.1	0.0	0.0	1.5	24.9	34.0	51.3	52.9	11.7	240	70.4
Leesburg city	2,896	3,055	5.5	3,006	62.0	33.2	1.4	1.6	1.8	31.7	9.6	26.9	41.9	18.7	884	92.4
Lenox town	877	850	-3.1	739	58.1	32.2	0.0	1.2	8.5	18.5	21.4	40.8	76.6	9.3	333	54.7
Leslie city	409	371	-9.3	583	32.2	60.4	3.3	0.0	4.1	27.4	15.8	36.7	49.6	15.8	184	89.7
Lexington city	229	228	-0.4	170	91.8	8.2	0.0	0.0	0.0	12.4	24.1	52.8	37.3	34.5	69	79.7
Lilburn city	11,648	12,810	10.0	12,644	29.5	16.0	19.7	2.3	32.5	28.6	11.3	36.2	49.4	29.6	3,807	92.0
Lilly city	221	197	-10.9	192	34.9	52.6	0.0	9.4	3.1	20.8	20.8	39.5	71.7	9.7	68	61.8
Lincoln Park CDP	833	-	-	524	2.9	91.2	0.0	5.9	0.0	11.3	17.0	45.4	66.7	7.5	244	77.0
Lincolnton city	1,562	1,503	-3.8	1,798	48.2	50.0	0.0	0.3	1.4	24.1	14.7	35.8	52.2	18.2	708	64.4
Lindale CDP	4,191	-	-	4,789	78.0	9.9	0.0	4.9	7.2	22.8	14.7	36.9	57.9	15.1	1,680	82.8
Lithia Springs CDP	15,491	-	-	18,054	25.9	52.5	2.2	1.1	18.2	25.9	7.3	32.9	48.2	26.1	6,435	92.4
Lithonia city	1,985	2,331	17.4	2,778	3.7	86.4	1.8	2.1	6.0	42.3	7.3	24.3	54.6	14.0	938	91.3
Locust Grove city	5,789	8,243	42.4	6,954	43.3	45.3	0.2	1.1	10.1	25.8	9.9	36.8	50.5	19.9	2,571	95.8
Loganville city	10,412	12,880	23.7	12,010	52.8	27.1	4.1	6.1	9.9	24.8	15.5	37.4	39.6	24.3	4,101	91.5
Lone Oak town	92	91	-1.1	90	84.4	13.3	0.0	2.2	0.0	0.0	28.9	58.7	61.6	18.6	48	75.0
Lookout Mountain city	1,601	1,574	-1.7	1,727	90.9	2.1	1.9	2.5	2.6	20.8	18.6	44.5	6.7	79.0	612	99.0
Louisville city	2,496	2,215	-11.3	2,605	22.6	71.7	0.1	0.1	5.4	23.1	19.8	35.5	65.3	12.5	897	73.2
Lovejoy city	5,592	6,840	22.3	6,179	13.8	66.8	0.2	4.1	15.1	33.6	4.1	29.4	39.0	21.9	1,756	96.3
Ludowici city	1,701	2,283	34.2	2,379	56.2	36.0	0.4	2.0	5.4	30.4	10.7	32.1	49.6	20.3	763	88.5
Lula city	2,773	2,961	6.8	2,985	74.8	12.0	2.8	3.6	6.9	24.9	8.5	35.8	51.4	16.3	1,012	89.9
Lumber City city	1,325	1,257	-5.1	1,421	40.5	58.8	0.0	0.7	0.0	22.3	24.9	44.5	75.1	16.7	494	27.3
Lumpkin city	1,128	1,266	12.2	942	27.1	69.9	0.0	0.0	3.1	18.4	14.3	33.5	78.8	10.8	424	65.8
Luthersville city	878	831	-5.4	653	40.0	58.0	0.0	2.0	0.0	21.3	15.5	41.9	71.4	7.8	248	78.6
Lyerly town	530	514	-3.0	540	99.1	0.9	0.0	0.0	0.0	19.4	24.6	45.6	73.9	6.0	247	73.7
Lyons city	4,344	4,233	-2.6	4,282	51.6	28.9	0.2	4.3	15.0	33.5	12.1	35.1	59.0	13.4	1,607	71.7
Mableton CDP	37,115	-	-	41,487	30.6	42.7	1.6	3.4	21.7	27.3	9.6	35.3	35.6	38.4	14,465	95.3
McCaysville city	1,102	1,204	9.3	1,388	87.0	0.0	0.0	1.9	11.1	20.8	20.2	44.5	60.3	11.4	605	75.7
McDonough city	22,015	26,768	21.6	24,852	22.3	65.8	1.1	4.5	6.3	26.1	8.0	32.1	37.8	30.3	8,543	95.5
McIntyre town	650	605	-6.9	698	13.3	75.8	0.0	0.0	10.9	19.9	14.6	40.3	74.5	10.7	259	66.8
Macon-Bibb County	155,783	153,159	-1.7	153,200	38.3	54.3	2.0	2.1	3.3	24.6	15.2	36.4	44.5	25.4	58,116	85.3
McRae-Helena city	8,551	8,277	-3.2	8,409	32.4	46.0	0.0	0.5	21.0	15.4	13.6	38.1	81.5	6.3	1,989	51.9
Madison city	3,980	4,210	5.8	4,085	47.4	47.5	0.0	1.4	3.6	25.6	20.7	44.5	47.5	25.7	1,625	84.6
Manassas city	87	85	-2.3	95	70.5	29.5	0.0	0.0	0.0	22.1	13.7	40.6	39.4	33.3	39	82.1
Manchester city	4,264	3,970	-6.9	3,961	45.0	47.9	1.0	2.7	3.4	27.3	15.6	40.0	60.3	7.4	1,494	84.5
Mansfield city	401	442	10.2	454	89.9	3.5	0.0	2.4	4.2	35.0	11.9	32.5	54.1	14.5	150	90.7
Marietta city	56,486	60,867	7.8	60,544	48.1	29.8	2.6	3.7	15.7	22.2	12.9	34.9	31.9	42.0	24,554	94.9
Marshallville city	1,447	1,227	-15.2	1,273	24.5	71.2	0.0	2.1	2.1	21.9	23.6	43.9	58.8	15.7	560	65.7
Martin town	374	383	2.4	347	84.7	2.9	0.0	1.2	11.2	22.2	17.6	37.9	55.8	14.2	139	85.6
Martinez CDP	35,795	-	-	34,844	74.0	14.4	4.9	2.6	4.1	23.5	16.5	40.4	30.6	38.3	11,780	94.6
Matthews CDP	150	-	-	118	100.0	0.0	0.0	0.0	0.0	23.7	11.9	39.7	100.0	0.0	31	100.0
Maxeys town	224	225	0.4	310	91.3	7.4	0.3	0.0	1.0	26.1	16.5	45.8	33.7	24.8	97	80.4
Maysville town	1,836	2,103	14.5	1,941	88.0	10.3	0.3	0.4	1.1	23.1	13.1	40.2	55.7	11.4	645	79.5
Meansville city	210	214	1.9	132	93.2	3.8	0.0	3.0	0.0	12.1	43.9	59.6	51.9	23.1	59	62.7
Meigs city	1,035	1,031	-0.4	1,085	32.7	53.3	0.0	0.0	14.0	29.0	7.6	35.6	61.8	6.8	394	76.6
Mendes CDP	122	-	-	77	59.7	35.1	0.0	0.0	5.2	28.6	11.7	49.3	7.3	20.0	41	78.0
Menlo city	474	456	-3.8	556	96.8	2.0	0.0	1.3	0.0	21.4	20.3	37.9	59.7	7.0	258	77.5
Metter city	4,075	3,942	-3.3	3,960	48.9	35.9	0.5	2.6	12.1	25.3	17.3	37.9	63.5	11.8	1,455	73.3
Midville city	269	254	-5.6	376	49.5	36.4	0.3	5.3	8.5	33.0	21.3	38.4	54.9	10.2	151	82.8
Midway city	2,121	2,061	-2.8	1,763	50.7	36.2	2.4	2.4	8.3	26.3	10.3	32.7	36.2	22.4	615	95.8
Milan city	700	657	-6.1	593	82.0	16.4	0.0	1.7	0.0	16.2	26.3	53.6	70.3	13.1	269	56.9
Milledgeville city	18,428	18,704	1.5	18,738	48.6	45.4	1.8	1.9	2.2	16.5	12.0	26.0	53.4	20.8	5,895	82.6
Millen city	3,120	2,766	-11.3	2,819	40.2	56.2	0.0	0.0	3.7	20.1	21.4	48.9	62.7	10.9	1,113	76.3
Milner city	621	654	5.3	943	75.3	20.8	1.3	1.1	1.6	17.2	15.6	43.2	50.6	20.4	375	95.7
Milton city	32,837	39,587	20.6	38,759	68.0	10.9	12.9	2.3	5.9	28.5	8.3	38.9	11.7	70.9	13,540	98.5
Mineral Bluff CDP	150	-	-	380	88.4	0.0	0.0	11.6	0.0	37.6	5.5	30.8	37.0	24.2	134	100.0
Mitchell town	199	189	-5.0	142	85.2	9.9	0.0	2.1	2.8	23.2	17.6	45.3	57.4	5.6	61	55.7
Molena city	383	400	4.4	467	74.1	22.7	0.0	2.6	0.6	22.9	19.7	44.1	55.5	12.7	158	90.5
Monroe city	12,847	13,673	6.4	13,418	46.3	47.7	1.2	2.1	2.6	31.7	12.2	29.6	65.3	14.0	4,709	83.8
Montezuma city	3,461	2,952	-14.7	3,063	25.6	68.6	0.0	3.2	2.6	19.6	19.8	45.1	49.7	13.3	1,276	74.7
Montgomery CDP	4,523	-	-	4,584	75.3	9.4	2.4	4.2	8.7	25.0	10.9	38.5	40.4	26.3	1,609	95.9
Monticello city	2,688	2,719	1.2	2,670	45.5	48.2	0.0	1.5	4.8	24.0	22.1	47.1	58.5	17.5	1,110	78.4
Montrose town	215	212	-1.4	283	64.3	32.5	0.0	1.8	1.4	35.3	15.9	28.0	59.9	1.8	76	81.6
Moody AFB CDP	886	-	-	1,232	60.5	10.0	10.8	7.5	11.3	11.3	0.0	22.7	25.3	10.3	257	100.0
Moreland town	430	444	3.3	385	86.2	12.2	0.3	1.3	0.0	13.5	21.8	49.1	55.9	14.3	137	83.2
Morgan city	1,861	1,835	-1.4	2,057	24.7	65.2	0.0	2.1	7.9	1.4	5.6	38.8	77.3	3.5	85	70.6
Morganton city	293	323	10.2	295	84.4	0.0	1.0	0.0	14.6	26.4	19.0	38.4	56.9	9.3	94	88.3
Morrow city	5,921	7,192	21.5	6,965	6.5	43.2	39.7	1.1	9.5	23.5	8.7	31.6	58.3	17.7	2,046	92.8

1 May be of any race.

Table A. All Places — **Population and Housing**

STATE City, town, township, borough, or CDP (county if applicable)	Population: 2010 census total population	Population: 2019 estimated population	Population: Percent change 2010-2019	Population: ACS total population estimate 2015-2019	Race and Hispanic or Latino origin (percent): White alone, not Hispanic or Latino	Black alone, not Hispanic or Latino	Asian alone, not Hispanic or Latino	All other races or 2 or more races, not Hispanic or Latino	Hispanic or Latino[1]	Age (percent): Under 18 years old	Age 65 years and older	Median age	Educational attainment of persons age 25 and older: Percent High school diploma or less	Percent Bachelor's degree or more	Occupied housing units: Total	Percent with a computer
	1	2	3	4	5	6	7	8	9	10	11	12	13	14	15	16
GEORGIA—Con.																
Morven city	567	549	-3.2	557	35.5	58.3	0.0	0.2	5.9	25.7	18.1	43.1	73.2	6.2	228	77.6
Moultrie city	14,258	14,211	-0.3	14,069	33.9	45.2	1.7	1.4	17.8	26.9	12.5	35.0	63.9	16.3	4,945	85.1
Mountain City town	1,083	1,108	2.3	1,056	80.2	0.0	11.6	1.2	7.0	17.0	26.1	48.5	55.4	13.6	412	74.5
Mountain Park city	546	568	4.0	649	87.8	2.6	0.2	3.4	6.0	18.5	20.0	48.3	12.3	71.5	273	99.6
Mountain Park CDP	11,554	-	-	13,392	53.3	23.9	13.3	1.4	8.1	25.1	16.8	38.8	24.4	41.7	4,516	94.6
Mount Airy town	1,235	1,265	2.4	1,379	57.3	1.9	4.6	2.5	33.7	35.3	10.4	31.6	63.0	13.9	406	92.1
Mount Vernon city	2,324	2,371	2.0	2,503	39.0	52.7	0.0	5.0	3.4	23.5	18.7	40.8	54.7	12.4	841	86.6
Mount Zion city	1,705	1,813	6.3	2,005	78.0	7.7	0.0	4.2	10.1	30.0	12.7	32.0	52.7	15.2	609	88.2
Nahunta city	1,048	1,141	8.9	893	80.0	16.6	0.0	3.5	0.0	25.9	22.8	36.0	72.0	4.7	332	87.3
Nashville city	4,947	4,851	-1.9	4,830	72.5	20.8	3.6	0.7	2.4	26.4	18.8	37.5	67.6	7.4	2,032	74.4
Nelson city	1,314	1,377	4.8	1,549	89.2	4.6	0.3	3.5	2.5	31.2	11.8	33.6	45.3	21.9	523	92.2
Newborn town	695	783	12.7	724	69.1	25.7	0.0	0.8	4.4	15.6	20.3	45.8	72.0	10.1	253	81.0
Newington town	277	262	-5.4	229	67.2	29.7	0.0	0.4	2.6	24.5	19.2	36.3	52.2	21.0	101	74.3
Newnan city	32,905	41,581	26.4	39,019	50.5	31.4	4.1	2.8	11.1	26.6	11.2	35.1	38.0	31.2	15,135	92.0
Newton city	660	575	-12.9	774	49.4	39.9	5.7	0.0	5.0	26.2	19.9	35.0	60.6	14.6	312	59.3
Nicholls city	2,798	3,333	19.1	3,836	32.2	60.8	0.0	0.9	6.2	6.3	5.0	39.7	76.1	3.1	287	77.0
Nicholson city	1,713	1,869	9.1	1,798	70.0	0.8	0.7	0.7	27.9	27.9	7.6	31.3	57.6	11.3	523	89.3
Norcross city	14,952	16,592	11.0	16,458	19.7	21.9	10.1	2.2	46.2	31.4	5.9	31.1	47.3	28.0	5,087	92.2
Norman Park city	966	962	-0.4	941	56.3	34.8	0.0	0.0	8.9	24.8	15.6	37.4	63.0	9.3	327	86.9
Norristown CDP	59	-	-	8	100.0	0.0	0.0	0.0	0.0	0.0	100.0	0.0	100.0	0.0	8	62.5
North Decatur CDP	16,698	-	-	16,701	67.7	10.9	11.2	5.8	4.4	15.4	17.8	40.9	14.7	70.7	8,169	92.7
North Druid Hills CDP	18,947	-	-	18,002	65.4	14.8	10.1	3.5	6.2	14.8	15.3	33.7	13.6	71.2	8,672	95.2
North High Shoals town	598	721	20.6	531	89.8	4.7	0.0	0.2	5.3	19.4	17.1	45.5	35.5	35.5	148	93.2
Norwood city	245	222	-9.4	284	34.5	65.5	0.0	0.0	0.0	10.6	28.9	49.3	70.7	14.4	128	67.2
Nunez city	147	145	-1.4	151	45.7	50.3	0.0	4.0	0.0	24.5	29.1	47.7	66.7	8.3	63	76.2
Oak Park town	480	470	-2.1	647	84.4	2.9	0.0	0.0	12.7	31.4	10.4	31.4	65.3	6.7	238	83.6
Oakwood city	3,944	4,156	5.4	4,143	51.9	14.1	2.7	6.2	25.1	25.1	8.9	29.0	43.1	17.8	1,445	92.7
Ochlocknee town	676	680	0.6	672	76.8	16.5	3.6	1.2	1.9	25.3	21.0	37.1	66.2	3.5	262	83.2
Ocilla city	3,446	3,732	8.3	3,592	26.9	65.1	0.8	0.0	7.2	23.1	16.4	39.3	65.4	13.4	1,258	60.9
Oconee city	259	243	-6.2	331	85.5	14.5	0.0	0.0	0.0	16.6	28.1	54.8	67.2	6.9	122	82.8
Odum city	504	503	-0.2	418	90.0	4.5	2.6	0.7	2.2	20.8	23.4	46.5	62.1	15.5	165	78.8
Offerman city	438	441	0.7	501	75.4	6.0	0.0	1.2	17.4	37.5	11.0	30.9	68.1	6.0	165	86.7
Oglethorpe city	1,335	1,156	-13.4	1,414	16.0	82.0	0.0	0.8	1.1	27.4	14.9	35.5	61.1	3.6	561	74.5
Oliver city	241	230	-4.6	385	53.0	47.0	0.0	0.0	0.0	30.9	13.8	35.3	79.2	6.4	115	74.8
Omega city	1,218	1,230	1.0	1,216	32.7	10.7	0.2	0.8	55.6	30.8	10.3	35.9	76.5	0.3	440	65.5
Orchard Hill town	214	232	8.4	215	88.4	9.8	0.0	1.9	0.0	23.7	17.2	41.6	64.6	10.2	80	60.0
Oxford city	2,127	2,346	10.3	2,347	53.1	35.1	5.3	1.8	4.7	22.6	14.9	25.6	58.7	22.8	682	89.4
Palmetto city	4,478	4,851	8.3	5,095	28.6	54.2	3.5	1.6	12.1	31.0	15.3	38.4	63.9	12.3	1,950	84.3
Panthersville CDP	9,749	-	-	10,800	1.7	95.3	0.3	1.0	1.6	22.5	16.9	35.2	49.0	15.4	4,036	87.6
Parrott town	158	136	-13.9	131	63.4	35.1	0.0	1.5	0.0	8.4	42.7	62.8	54.9	12.7	63	74.6
Patterson city	730	755	3.4	650	83.7	16.3	0.0	0.0	0.0	18.2	20.2	39.9	45.9	18.0	311	89.4
Pavo city	627	604	-3.7	510	57.3	36.5	0.0	1.0	5.3	19.6	17.8	44.6	64.5	4.1	224	74.6
Peachtree City city	34,366	36,223	5.4	35,443	75.7	7.2	6.3	4.2	6.6	24.9	18.6	43.7	16.3	57.2	13,416	94.1
Peachtree Corners city	38,014	43,905	15.5	43,057	48.9	22.8	10.3	2.9	15.1	23.3	12.5	36.5	24.1	51.7	16,905	97.0
Pearson city	2,113	2,042	-3.4	2,071	27.7	41.7	0.0	0.1	30.5	26.0	12.2	34.9	76.0	5.3	674	72.6
Pelham city	3,894	3,466	-11.0	3,549	36.0	61.6	0.4	0.1	1.9	27.9	14.2	30.7	64.3	9.9	1,325	83.8
Pembroke city	2,143	2,626	22.5	2,481	63.1	28.9	0.5	5.6	1.9	31.0	12.3	30.3	47.2	19.9	887	89.5
Pendergrass town	451	562	24.6	624	81.3	10.9	0.0	2.6	5.3	23.4	13.9	35.8	46.4	16.9	217	86.2
Perkins CDP	91	-	-	129	100.0	0.0	0.0	0.0	0.0	0.0	0.0	51.7	69.1	0.0	56	50.0
Perry city	13,737	17,894	30.3	16,595	56.7	36.0	1.3	1.8	4.3	23.9	14.0	34.6	38.3	24.1	6,242	88.6
Phillipsburg CDP	707	-	-	1,115	0.0	88.7	0.0	11.3	0.0	34.2	10.4	27.4	57.3	0.0	393	46.3
Pinehurst city	455	355	-22.0	405	43.2	47.9	0.5	3.2	5.2	15.3	19.3	44.2	58.7	11.0	149	76.5
Pine Lake city	729	754	3.4	749	72.0	22.6	1.2	0.0	4.3	12.3	16.8	48.4	28.3	47.2	386	95.3
Pine Mountain town	1,298	1,417	9.2	1,279	53.5	40.3	0.5	1.5	4.3	22.0	21.6	33.4	40.2	23.2	516	89.3
Pineview town	526	489	-7.0	653	26.0	64.2	0.0	4.6	5.2	30.6	16.8	31.8	71.2	6.3	205	67.3
Pitts city	315	293	-7.0	343	77.0	21.9	0.0	0.0	1.2	26.2	12.5	38.4	62.9	4.4	117	65.0
Plains city	767	716	-6.6	640	64.1	32.2	0.0	0.8	3.0	17.5	35.5	55.3	59.5	17.4	208	58.7
Plainville city	308	318	3.2	379	91.6	0.3	0.0	5.0	3.2	20.8	11.6	39.5	54.4	10.5	130	80.0
Pooler city	18,489	25,694	39.0	23,858	59.2	26.5	2.3	5.3	6.7	25.5	9.3	36.0	27.8	38.2	8,794	95.3
Portal town	632	692	9.5	676	71.4	20.0	0.0	8.6	0.0	23.1	10.8	37.7	59.7	16.3	260	83.5
Porterdale city	1,429	1,478	3.4	1,748	64.9	28.0	0.2	2.2	4.7	26.3	8.2	36.3	65.9	10.0	667	84.6
Port Wentworth city	5,361	9,641	79.8	8,463	44.6	45.3	0.8	3.8	5.6	28.9	12.2	30.9	35.7	36.3	3,258	93.3
Poulan city	956	870	-9.0	765	63.1	35.9	0.0	0.0	0.9	17.6	21.2	39.6	61.3	3.4	295	82.4
Powder Springs city	13,938	15,758	13.1	15,163	27.8	54.3	1.3	1.4	15.2	24.9	13.3	38.0	33.5	33.8	5,125	93.9
Pulaski town	258	263	1.9	305	63.9	17.7	0.0	3.0	15.4	14.8	32.1	56.6	72.5	16.3	93	80.6
Putney CDP	2,898	-	-	2,549	50.0	35.8	0.0	4.2	9.9	18.9	18.3	50.3	49.9	19.0	977	80.9
Quitman city	3,937	3,652	-7.2	3,744	27.8	71.1	0.0	0.0	1.1	25.9	16.3	39.2	53.6	15.2	1,476	74.5
Ranger town	131	136	3.8	142	100.0	0.0	0.0	0.0	0.0	34.5	10.6	34.8	78.3	6.0	43	62.8
Raoul CDP	2,558	-	-	2,492	70.1	19.2	0.0	0.7	10.0	13.2	3.0	35.5	68.2	5.1	301	87.7
Ray City city	1,100	1,094	-0.5	1,227	73.3	20.2	0.0	1.8	4.7	29.3	7.9	30.3	54.8	15.4	484	89.0
Rayle town	199	185	-7.0	205	36.6	59.0	2.4	0.0	2.0	26.8	18.0	31.3	75.0	10.5	62	48.4
Rebecca town	187	165	-11.8	265	52.5	2.6	9.1	4.5	31.3	26.0	11.3	29.8	68.3	9.1	109	78.9
Redan CDP	33,015	-	-	31,873	2.9	92.8	0.4	1.7	2.2	23.6	11.2	37.1	39.0	25.9	11,471	96.9
Reed Creek CDP	2,604	-	-	2,155	93.5	3.1	0.0	2.6	0.9	6.1	35.3	55.6	40.1	31.1	1,044	85.3
Register town	175	189	8.0	98	84.7	14.3	0.0	1.0	0.0	26.5	21.4	42.7	39.1	30.4	44	79.5
Reidsville city	2,613	2,645	1.2	2,658	51.7	40.6	0.0	2.4	5.3	33.4	23.4	40.8	63.7	11.1	1,189	82.9
Remerton city	1,123	1,079	-3.9	1,112	45.0	47.2	2.5	2.5	2.8	17.4	1.7	23.5	39.4	30.9	500	99.4
Rentz city	295	285	-3.4	234	91.5	4.7	2.1	1.7	0.0	23.9	21.8	41.8	66.7	7.9	100	89.0
Resaca town	768	803	4.6	974	50.3	6.3	1.5	0.8	41.1	25.6	13.2	35.5	67.2	7.4	287	81.5
Rest Haven town	58	63	8.6	70	68.6	0.0	0.0	0.0	31.4	15.7	10.0	27.9	82.9	0.0	29	72.4
Reynolds city	1,073	960	-10.5	1,095	42.8	41.3	0.0	0.0	15.9	25.1	22.4	45.7	48.2	16.5	486	62.3
Rhine town	394	375	-4.8	495	62.4	33.9	0.0	0.0	3.6	23.2	18.4	45.6	66.4	8.0	232	57.3
Riceboro city	799	778	-2.6	701	4.9	90.2	0.0	5.0	0.0	20.4	31.7	46.4	67.1	8.9	310	73.9
Richland city	1,472	1,643	11.6	1,357	31.8	64.6	1.2	2.2	0.2	12.2	29.0	47.9	70.4	11.4	613	71.8
Richmond Hill city	9,376	13,839	47.6	12,720	63.9	16.5	2.7	5.0	11.8	34.4	6.6	32.4	25.2	36.4	4,334	92.4
Riddleville town	96	88	-8.3	60	75.0	16.7	0.0	0.0	8.3	5.0	21.7	54.5	66.7	20.0	31	64.5
Rincon city	8,916	10,361	16.2	10,027	70.1	17.7	1.5	3.4	7.3	30.4	8.3	32.4	39.0	23.8	3,827	92.9
Ringgold city	3,492	3,630	4.0	3,592	86.7	4.9	0.6	4.7	3.1	18.0	17.8	44.3	45.1	18.3	1,565	92.5
Riverdale city	14,276	15,594	9.2	15,291	6.2	83.6	4.0	0.9	5.4	26.9	10.2	34.7	45.0	20.3	5,517	94.8
Roberta city	1,004	973	-3.1	1,031	57.9	36.7	0.0	4.8	0.6	29.9	20.1	41.4	57.5	12.3	354	88.4
Robins AFB CDP	1,170	-	-	1,339	56.6	20.8	4.6	5.5	12.5	29.6	1.9	22.8	16.6	42.1	281	100.0
Rochelle city	1,175	1,103	-6.1	1,060	58.5	41.4	0.0	0.1	0.0	21.9	21.3	37.2	55.9	14.6	417	70.5

1 May be of any race.

Table A. All Places — **Population and Housing**

STATE City, town, township, borough, or CDP (county if applicable)	Population				Race and Hispanic or Latino origin (percent)					Age (percent)			Educational attainment of persons age 25 and older		Occupied housing units	
	2010 census total population	2019 estimated population	Percent change 2010-2019	ACS total population estimate 2015-2019	White alone, not Hispanic or Latino	Black alone, not Hispanic or Latino	Asian alone, not Hispanic or Latino	All other races or 2 or more races, not Hispanic or Latino	Hispanic or Latino[1]	Under 18 years old	Age 65 years and older	Median age	Percent High school diploma or less	Percent Bachelor's degree or more	Total	Percent with a computer
	1	2	3	4	5	6	7	8	9	10	11	12	13	14	15	16
GEORGIA—Con.																
Rockingham CDP	248	-	-	70	82.9	0.0	0.0	17.1	0.0	0.0	67.1	68.7	54.3	18.6	58	62.1
Rockmart city	4,214	4,433	5.2	4,305	65.3	26.6	1.3	6.8	0.0	32.5	14.8	32.7	51.1	13.9	1,557	95.1
Rocky Ford town	144	137	-4.9	189	68.8	22.8	0.0	0.0	8.5	24.9	22.8	40.5	54.3	15.0	72	88.9
Rome city	36,372	36,716	0.9	36,332	49.9	25.6	2.8	3.5	18.2	23.7	15.0	37.2	49.7	25.9	14,169	81.2
Roopville town	218	229	5.0	264	87.1	10.2	0.0	1.5	1.1	23.1	18.2	43.2	54.4	19.2	97	85.6
Rossville city	4,103	4,009	-2.3	4,006	82.7	11.2	0.0	5.6	0.5	26.5	14.9	38.5	59.3	9.0	1,457	81.5
Roswell city	88,332	94,763	7.3	94,498	62.1	13.9	4.3	3.6	16.0	25.1	12.5	38.6	20.2	58.2	34,380	97.3
Royston city	2,575	2,571	-0.2	2,777	76.5	18.0	1.5	2.1	1.9	25.0	21.9	33.7	60.9	13.8	1,133	70.3
Russell CDP	1,203	-	-	1,497	67.6	16.4	5.6	2.5	7.9	37.1	5.9	28.5	73.5	4.1	418	72.2
Rutledge city	781	842	7.8	1,104	59.7	37.2	0.0	2.3	0.8	23.8	16.9	40.8	57.8	18.6	443	74.9
St. Marys city	17,084	18,567	8.7	18,077	74.4	13.4	1.9	3.8	6.5	24.6	14.2	34.5	33.0	26.5	6,966	93.0
St. Simons CDP	12,743	-	-	14,778	93.0	2.6	0.9	1.7	1.9	14.8	35.1	55.4	18.0	56.8	6,836	94.4
Sale City city	380	344	-9.5	439	84.1	12.8	0.0	1.4	1.8	25.3	14.1	35.4	68.4	7.1	173	83.8
Salem CDP	310	-	-	382	2.4	97.6	0.0	0.0	0.0	24.9	16.0	47.2	63.8	5.3	132	84.1
Sandersville city	5,923	5,399	-8.8	5,546	35.8	60.6	0.6	0.9	2.0	22.0	19.9	42.9	61.7	14.2	2,213	73.7
Sandy Springs city	93,826	109,452	16.7	107,072	57.7	18.3	7.3	2.6	14.1	19.8	13.1	36.5	17.4	65.1	47,108	96.8
Santa Claus city	165	159	-3.6	266	94.0	5.6	0.0	0.0	0.4	25.9	24.4	36.6	51.3	20.3	100	64.0
Sardis city	999	960	-3.9	774	48.7	48.8	0.5	1.9	0.0	34.1	13.6	37.6	70.1	14.1	328	67.7
Sasser town	291	255	-12.4	305	45.9	38.4	0.0	0.0	15.7	28.5	18.7	37.4	49.0	13.6	116	85.3
Satilla CDP	421	-	-	356	100.0	0.0	0.0	0.0	0.0	27.5	36.2	44.2	81.0	0.0	151	68.9
Sautee-Nacoochee CDP	363	-	-	279	92.1	4.7	1.1	2.2	0.0	7.2	22.9	48.0	17.8	43.2	168	79.8
Savannah city	136,918	144,464	5.5	145,403	35.4	53.3	2.6	2.9	5.8	20.4	13.1	32.6	39.2	28.2	52,927	89.4
Scotland city	360	337	-6.4	394	70.8	29.2	0.0	0.0	0.0	29.7	13.2	43.2	79.6	1.5	132	38.6
Scottdale CDP	10,631	-	-	11,568	27.7	35.2	16.9	4.7	15.4	23.3	7.5	34.4	38.5	39.4	4,321	93.9
Screven city	766	771	0.7	781	74.6	21.5	0.0	0.3	3.6	22.3	12.2	33.6	67.9	7.5	268	88.8
Senoia city	3,353	4,412	31.6	4,256	84.6	9.0	1.6	2.5	2.4	23.7	13.9	35.1	25.9	44.2	1,387	95.0
Seville CDP	202	-	-	108	100.0	0.0	0.0	0.0	0.0	0.0	61.1	68.8	61.1	19.4	66	62.1
Shady Dale town	249	236	-5.2	359	39.0	7.8	0.0	0.0	53.2	34.5	6.7	29.3	79.9	5.2	101	96.0
Shannon CDP	1,862	-	-	1,870	85.3	0.0	0.7	1.1	12.9	24.4	25.5	44.5	50.6	14.7	784	78.3
Sharon city	140	126	-10.0	149	14.1	85.9	0.0	0.0	0.0	7.4	16.8	44.1	87.7	0.7	61	65.6
Sharpsburg town	353	361	2.3	461	76.6	11.5	0.0	1.5	10.4	23.0	13.2	44.5	45.4	19.5	199	89.4
Shellman city	1,083	933	-13.9	1,013	30.4	58.9	0.0	10.7	0.0	27.9	17.4	38.0	53.0	10.9	374	73.8
Shiloh city	441	486	10.2	376	77.1	21.5	0.0	0.3	1.1	22.6	14.4	43.2	56.1	17.2	155	94.8
Siloam town	281	277	-1.4	334	24.9	72.5	2.7	0.0	0.0	32.9	15.3	37.3	79.9	6.2	137	46.7
Skidaway Island CDP	8,341	-	-	8,986	94.9	2.3	1.5	0.5	0.9	11.1	50.9	65.4	11.7	65.4	4,272	98.6
Sky Valley city	270	273	1.1	355	98.9	0.0	0.0	0.0	1.1	5.4	65.1	69.7	20.8	48.0	194	99.0
Smithville city	601	636	5.8	536	41.8	58.2	0.0	0.0	0.0	17.4	21.8	47.1	67.8	6.9	239	61.9
Smyrna city	51,037	56,666	11.0	56,268	44.2	30.0	7.7	2.9	15.2	22.5	9.8	35.2	22.0	53.5	24,736	96.8
Snellville city	18,259	20,077	10.0	19,778	38.5	44.5	2.8	3.8	10.4	20.9	16.9	39.3	31.2	34.3	6,093	96.9
Social Circle city	4,210	4,544	7.9	4,447	52.3	38.7	0.0	0.8	8.2	24.4	15.1	37.6	57.3	18.0	1,598	86.4
Soperton city	3,113	3,148	1.1	3,076	48.6	50.0	0.0	0.6	0.8	18.4	19.0	42.3	68.3	14.6	1,088	74.9
South Fulton city	85,589	99,155	15.9	96,283	4.7	91.2	0.2	1.6	2.2	24.8	11.3	37.0	30.9	37.4	33,091	94.9
Sparks town	2,044	2,013	-1.5	2,464	31.2	58.3	0.0	2.0	8.5	31.3	13.4	35.8	73.7	8.5	778	71.1
Sparta city	1,400	1,230	-12.1	1,729	9.8	88.5	1.6	0.0	0.0	31.0	27.6	44.6	66.9	10.4	669	66.4
Springfield city	2,794	4,084	46.2	3,786	73.0	22.1	0.0	3.5	1.4	26.5	16.4	31.7	56.0	18.9	1,392	87.9
Stapleton city	438	393	-10.3	418	78.5	11.5	0.0	4.8	5.3	28.7	17.9	34.0	56.9	16.5	143	77.6
Statesboro city	28,365	32,954	16.2	31,495	45.7	43.2	1.6	3.9	5.6	14.5	7.6	22.3	40.0	25.8	10,214	90.0
Statham city	2,489	2,839	14.1	2,696	53.7	26.5	3.1	3.2	13.5	24.2	9.7	35.0	59.0	11.8	895	88.9
Stillmore city	529	518	-2.1	530	33.2	54.2	5.3	4.3	3.0	21.9	22.3	38.2	67.6	4.3	187	72.7
Stockbridge city	26,431	29,904	13.1	29,089	16.2	61.7	10.1	4.5	7.4	26.8	9.8	35.4	35.8	31.4	10,244	93.9
Stonecrest city	50,207	54,903	9.4	54,202	3.1	93.3	0.4	1.6	1.7	26.7	8.1	33.2	35.0	29.3	20,325	94.0
Stone Mountain city	5,836	6,281	7.6	6,285	18.5	77.3	0.7	0.0	3.4	21.8	9.0	34.5	43.6	25.8	2,351	94.2
Sugar Hill city	18,484	24,617	33.2	23,121	56.8	11.7	9.2	2.7	19.6	29.4	7.9	36.6	38.2	39.3	7,195	93.8
Summertown city	160	158	-1.3	168	48.8	51.2	0.0	0.0	0.0	31.0	18.5	46.5	65.5	12.9	56	76.8
Summerville city	4,532	4,243	-6.4	4,320	77.4	19.9	0.0	1.1	1.6	24.3	21.1	44.6	70.8	7.0	1,769	64.6
Sumner town	446	424	-4.9	420	65.7	31.9	0.0	1.7	0.7	21.9	13.3	37.1	69.4	7.0	135	82.2
Sunny Side city	132	140	6.1	155	87.1	12.9	0.0	0.0	0.0	40.0	6.5	20.8	63.6	16.4	51	84.3
Sunnyside CDP	1,303	-	-	968	80.4	14.8	0.0	4.9	0.0	19.3	37.1	44.3	32.5	18.0	408	88.5
Sunset Village CDP	846	-	-	672	98.7	1.3	0.0	0.0	0.0	12.6	21.3	52.6	59.3	17.0	309	92.6
Surrency town	201	202	0.5	336	54.8	36.0	0.0	0.0	9.2	29.8	16.7	29.0	69.3	1.5	114	62.3
Suwanee city	15,343	20,907	36.3	19,743	57.9	12.3	20.7	3.4	5.6	23.8	9.0	37.9	20.2	57.7	7,012	98.8
Swainsboro city	7,243	7,542	4.1	7,396	33.7	63.2	0.0	2.4	0.8	32.5	14.6	31.8	61.9	15.3	2,697	79.8
Sycamore city	714	664	-7.0	1,108	49.8	27.1	3.3	2.0	17.8	28.8	5.5	31.5	75.6	6.5	322	85.1
Sylvania city	2,613	2,463	-5.7	2,949	48.5	46.8	0.9	2.3	1.6	21.7	21.8	38.8	65.1	14.8	1,092	75.5
Sylvester city	6,184	5,776	-6.6	5,865	33.6	62.8	0.3	3.2	0.1	28.3	16.7	34.9	57.7	14.1	2,346	83.4
Talahi Island CDP	1,248	-	-	1,472	87.0	0.0	5.0	1.3	6.7	13.9	33.8	53.7	15.7	50.1	575	97.4
Talbotton city	957	848	-11.4	786	17.0	82.1	0.0	0.3	0.6	17.8	16.8	45.0	72.0	4.1	372	55.6
Talking Rock town	65	71	9.2	109	77.1	0.0	0.0	22.9	0.0	21.1	21.1	45.8	45.3	17.3	42	73.8
Tallapoosa city	3,175	3,185	0.3	3,162	90.4	7.1	0.0	2.5	0.0	21.3	17.9	45.0	54.6	18.4	1,368	78.1
Tallulah Falls town	170	171	0.6	122	73.0	10.7	13.9	0.0	2.5	10.7	19.7	33.6	43.5	15.9	36	97.2
Talmo town	229	257	12.2	273	92.3	0.0	1.5	0.0	6.2	24.2	13.9	37.1	57.4	19.1	96	68.8
Tarrytown town	87	85	-2.3	57	75.4	17.5	0.0	0.0	7.0	12.3	21.1	47.5	52.3	20.5	35	88.6
Tate City CDP	16	-	-	-	-	-	-	-	-	-	-	-	-	-	-	-
Taylorsville town	213	224	5.2	263	99.2	0.0	0.0	0.8	0.0	19.4	31.9	55.3	69.8	12.1	100	82.0
Temple city	4,343	4,795	10.4	4,549	81.8	16.3	0.0	1.5	0.4	25.2	10.2	31.4	44.2	23.3	1,575	92.5
Tennille city	1,543	2,123	37.6	1,617	38.0	53.2	0.4	5.5	2.9	23.2	16.9	40.1	64.7	8.1	695	69.6
The Rock CDP	160	-	-	179	100.0	0.0	0.0	0.0	0.0	30.2	26.8	46.5	23.7	46.5	51	80.4
Thomaston city	9,164	8,752	-4.5	8,774	55.2	36.9	0.2	3.6	4.1	27.1	16.5	34.6	48.2	17.4	3,333	83.5
Thomasville city	18,556	18,518	-0.2	18,539	41.7	52.9	0.1	2.3	2.9	24.5	16.5	36.1	44.0	27.5	7,529	86.5
Thomson city	6,788	6,528	-3.8	6,593	40.4	52.9	0.5	3.6	2.6	25.8	18.0	35.8	60.7	10.2	2,581	76.8
Thunderbolt town	2,524	2,623	3.9	2,651	59.2	34.2	1.6	3.2	1.8	16.1	20.8	41.9	35.3	36.9	1,091	92.4
Tifton city	16,411	16,838	2.6	16,644	52.1	31.7	2.7	1.4	12.1	24.5	12.1	30.2	54.3	16.3	5,906	70.2
Tiger town	403	415	3.0	565	80.5	4.6	0.0	0.9	14.0	19.6	20.4	45.4	56.6	13.3	167	70.1
Tignall town	540	496	-8.1	593	39.5	58.5	0.0	1.0	1.0	14.2	26.5	51.1	67.5	11.7	258	59.7
Toccoa city	8,575	8,336	-2.8	8,308	75.6	18.8	1.6	1.3	2.7	20.8	19.5	42.8	60.1	19.1	3,359	77.9
Toomsboro city	470	486	3.4	436	43.6	48.2	0.0	1.8	6.4	15.4	29.6	50.5	62.0	9.4	135	60.0
Trenton city	2,299	2,151	-6.4	2,455	88.8	0.6	1.5	5.1	4.0	24.3	17.6	42.5	57.0	12.6	1,025	81.5
Trion town	1,829	1,893	3.5	2,481	49.7	4.3	0.1	1.2	44.7	32.6	11.6	30.7	70.0	7.8	837	81.0
Tucker city	33,380	36,395	9.0	35,965	43.7	34.6	6.1	3.4	12.2	18.1	16.8	43.8	27.4	47.6	14,479	94.6
Tunnel Hill city	897	910	1.4	1,435	92.3	2.2	0.0	0.0	5.6	24.2	15.8	36.4	56.9	16.8	478	91.4
Turin town	246	347	41.1	367	84.5	8.7	0.0	0.0	6.8	20.7	19.1	37.8	39.1	32.0	121	96.7
Twin City city	1,747	1,701	-2.6	1,814	35.6	59.5	0.0	3.3	1.6	18.9	16.8	35.5	71.4	4.9	559	76.2

1 May be of any race.

Table A. All Places — **Population and Housing**

STATE City, town, township, borough, or CDP (county if applicable)	Population: 2010 census total population	Population: 2019 estimated population	Population: Percent change 2010-2019	Population: ACS total population estimate 2015-2019	Race and Hispanic or Latino origin (percent): White alone, not Hispanic or Latino	Race: Black alone, not Hispanic or Latino	Race: Asian alone, not Hispanic or Latino	Race: All other races or 2 or more races, not Hispanic or Latino	Race: Hispanic or Latino[1]	Age (percent): Under 18 years old	Age: Age 65 years and older	Age: Median age	Educational attainment of persons age 25 and older: Percent High school diploma or less	Educational attainment: Percent Bachelor's degree or more	Occupied housing units: Total	Occupied housing units: Percent with a computer
	1	2	3	4	5	6	7	8	9	10	11	12	13	14	15	16
GEORGIA—Con.																
Tybee Island city	2,986	3,063	2.6	3,093	95.2	2.4	0.0	2.2	0.2	13.8	28.5	54.6	19.9	54.6	1,305	97.6
Tyrone town	6,882	7,506	9.1	7,295	62.6	25.3	3.2	5.3	3.6	24.3	14.1	40.9	21.1	55.6	2,506	92.5
Ty Ty city	731	737	0.8	774	54.5	31.7	0.0	0.0	13.8	33.5	7.8	30.4	67.7	5.6	260	63.5
Unadilla city	3,794	3,525	-7.1	3,583	36.0	55.0	0.0	0.3	8.6	16.9	13.1	41.7	62.7	8.0	938	77.8
Union City city	19,317	22,399	16.0	21,396	5.7	85.4	0.0	1.4	7.5	32.3	11.3	30.3	41.9	17.5	8,088	87.8
Union Point city	1,618	1,899	17.4	1,841	35.6	56.5	0.3	0.4	7.2	26.8	18.7	33.6	70.8	5.4	694	80.5
Unionville CDP	1,845	-	-	1,904	0.0	100.0	0.0	0.0	0.0	30.4	18.4	32.4	76.6	9.0	651	45.6
Uvalda city	595	582	-2.2	506	56.1	30.6	0.0	1.0	12.3	14.0	26.7	48.1	56.7	14.7	189	83.1
Valdosta city	54,764	56,457	3.1	56,095	38.7	52.7	1.6	1.8	5.3	22.9	11.4	28.5	47.3	25.7	21,153	83.0
Varnell city	2,085	2,139	2.6	2,488	74.5	1.7	0.5	3.3	20.1	24.8	14.4	41.1	47.1	20.6	814	88.9
Vernonburg town	118	124	5.1	113	100.0	0.0	0.0	0.0	0.0	20.4	38.1	59.3	7.8	86.7	45	91.1
Vidalia city	10,424	10,402	-0.2	10,409	46.6	39.1	2.3	1.2	10.9	22.5	17.1	38.3	55.6	18.5	4,042	80.2
Vidette city	112	107	-4.5	203	75.4	19.2	0.0	0.0	5.4	25.6	16.7	35.0	76.5	6.8	67	71.6
Vienna city	4,008	3,549	-11.5	3,664	16.4	78.3	0.0	0.9	4.4	19.5	19.2	38.2	69.1	12.1	1,492	73.6
Villa Rica city	14,046	16,058	14.3	15,392	41.6	41.4	3.8	5.8	7.5	30.5	8.9	32.7	41.0	27.9	5,166	93.3
Vinings CDP	9,734	-	-	12,934	51.6	32.2	6.5	3.2	6.5	13.2	14.8	34.7	11.3	67.8	6,554	97.4
Waco city	517	524	1.4	455	94.3	1.1	1.3	0.7	2.6	14.7	18.2	44.9	57.8	6.5	200	85.0
Wadley city	2,061	1,858	-9.8	1,897	9.6	81.5	0.1	0.0	8.8	26.8	19.5	39.6	75.6	6.7	654	69.7
Waleska city	644	964	49.7	740	53.5	26.4	1.4	13.0	5.8	11.6	7.8	20.5	44.4	18.8	94	84.0
Walnut Grove city	1,291	1,357	5.1	1,471	92.7	6.8	0.0	0.5	0.0	22.2	14.6	35.4	56.3	9.6	515	92.2
Walthourville city	4,203	4,115	-2.1	4,087	28.3	59.4	0.6	4.0	7.8	26.6	7.7	30.7	56.4	11.3	1,652	88.9
Warm Springs city	429	405	-5.6	525	60.6	32.4	2.7	2.9	1.5	23.2	23.2	37.8	58.0	11.5	178	93.8
Warner Robins city	69,596	77,617	11.5	76,115	44.7	39.7	4.8	3.8	7.1	26.0	11.6	33.5	36.0	28.0	30,021	89.9
Warrenton city	1,937	1,720	-11.2	2,052	19.5	78.3	1.6	0.6	0.0	23.9	16.4	37.1	75.8	8.8	840	62.3
Warwick city	417	386	-7.4	520	21.7	74.6	0.6	3.1	0.0	24.4	22.1	41.5	72.1	1.1	215	71.2
Washington city	4,135	3,963	-4.2	3,971	38.9	59.1	0.0	1.8	0.2	23.3	23.2	44.0	60.7	12.0	1,646	60.4
Watkinsville city	2,835	2,936	3.6	2,904	87.5	6.0	1.9	2.1	2.5	25.0	11.9	37.0	23.3	48.2	1,042	94.8
Waverly Hall town	735	807	9.8	932	48.1	48.9	0.3	1.6	1.1	12.6	27.0	51.9	58.4	16.6	331	72.2
Waycross city	14,600	13,480	-7.7	13,692	41.3	54.4	0.3	1.4	2.6	28.3	18.1	36.7	56.3	16.3	5,748	84.9
Waynesboro city	5,893	5,363	-9.0	5,487	23.7	71.5	0.0	2.4	2.4	35.9	13.9	29.8	52.7	20.7	1,991	80.2
Webster County unified government	2,799	2,607	-6.9	2,610	51.8	37.2	0.0	2.2	8.7	24.3	20.0	45.1	61.4	14.7	1,140	81.8
West Point city	3,463	3,737	7.9	3,855	41.0	58.4	0.0	0.5	0.1	25.7	20.8	41.9	42.8	20.2	1,579	77.5
Whigham city	471	464	-1.5	541	64.3	32.0	0.0	0.2	3.5	17.6	26.2	43.1	64.2	19.5	193	75.1
White city	670	725	8.2	820	78.2	0.0	0.5	2.3	19.0	23.7	10.9	32.0	69.2	9.9	297	81.5
Whitemarsh Island CDP	6,792	-	-	6,893	81.0	2.9	7.3	0.9	7.9	24.7	13.7	37.2	16.6	48.7	2,752	97.6
White Plains city	289	342	18.3	236	55.1	37.7	0.4	6.8	0.0	17.4	27.1	52.5	63.4	19.1	98	64.3
Whitesburg city	590	611	3.6	727	84.6	5.4	0.0	2.6	7.4	24.2	10.5	32.8	66.3	9.4	240	85.4
Willacoochee city	1,391	1,354	-2.7	1,422	40.4	19.2	0.0	0.2	40.2	25.4	15.2	38.5	75.9	6.8	529	69.9
Williamson city	489	514	5.1	593	72.2	12.3	0.0	0.8	14.7	24.5	13.8	37.0	53.9	17.4	227	84.6
Wilmington Island CDP	15,138	-	-	15,834	86.6	3.0	2.2	3.8	4.3	21.7	20.7	43.9	24.8	45.0	6,478	94.7
Winder city	14,379	17,937	24.7	16,413	65.6	18.5	2.4	4.1	9.4	24.8	15.1	38.1	49.9	18.8	5,799	86.4
Winterville city	1,135	1,237	9.0	1,202	65.9	25.0	0.0	5.2	4.0	18.5	14.8	42.3	30.0	45.9	449	92.0
Woodbine city	1,414	1,352	-4.4	1,409	46.1	51.0	1.4	0.0	1.5	27.5	12.2	32.3	43.1	15.9	467	91.0
Woodbury city	964	902	-6.4	1,224	22.6	76.9	0.0	0.5	0.0	19.1	14.9	40.7	71.8	7.1	456	67.3
Woodland city	403	353	-12.4	337	35.0	65.0	0.0	0.0	0.0	16.9	27.6	51.9	67.4	4.8	150	71.3
Woodstock city	23,803	33,039	38.8	31,437	70.4	11.9	3.6	3.3	10.7	25.2	13.8	38.0	20.1	46.3	12,878	97.0
Woodville city	321	382	19.0	378	22.0	75.9	0.0	0.0	2.1	10.8	29.1	57.7	74.5	16.8	174	81.0
Woolsey town	158	167	5.7	193	94.3	0.0	1.0	2.6	2.1	17.6	22.8	46.2	36.5	37.3	71	90.1
Wrens city	2,190	1,939	-11.5	2,243	37.1	59.9	1.6	0.0	1.3	28.4	19.5	40.9	60.5	14.3	880	83.0
Wrightsville city	3,754	3,618	-3.6	3,651	41.2	55.5	0.6	1.9	0.9	15.7	17.9	40.2	74.7	6.0	1,148	69.3
Yatesville town	372	360	-3.2	387	80.9	18.3	0.0	0.8	0.0	13.4	27.4	55.6	59.9	7.7	167	88.0
Yonah CDP	507	-	-	496	92.3	0.0	0.0	0.0	7.7	4.4	38.9	50.9	25.7	18.9	264	100.0
Young Harris city	888	1,661	87.0	1,029	79.2	6.5	0.0	5.0	9.3	7.3	4.3	20.8	27.6	27.2	170	88.2
Zebulon city	1,181	1,228	4.0	1,078	66.4	29.8	0.0	2.9	0.9	21.3	16.7	40.1	55.0	14.7	424	85.8
HAWAII	1,360,307	1,415,872	4.1	1,422,094	22.0	1.7	36.9	28.9	10.5	21.4	17.8	39.1	35.4	33.0	459,424	91.2
Ahuimanu CDP	8,810	-	-	8,023	22.3	0.2	33.1	36.4	8.1	20.0	21.3	46.9	23.8	41.2	2,624	97.3
Aiea CDP	9,338	-	-	9,638	13.6	0.2	48.7	24.8	12.7	22.9	18.7	40.1	28.2	36.4	2,713	90.3
Ainaloa CDP	2,965	-	-	3,279	25.0	0.3	8.1	37.7	28.9	28.0	14.2	37.4	49.0	12.3	1,174	85.0
Anahola CDP	2,223	-	-	2,311	11.7	0.0	6.5	72.0	9.8	21.1	17.4	40.9	59.7	12.3	685	79.7
Captain Cook CDP	3,429	-	-	4,171	26.8	0.0	16.4	36.9	20.0	29.0	16.2	34.1	38.5	26.8	1,110	92.6
Discovery Harbour CDP	949	-	-	1,304	48.2	0.2	2.9	37.9	10.8	26.6	19.4	43.5	26.4	30.9	470	94.5
East Honolulu CDP	49,914	-	-	47,540	25.4	0.7	47.8	22.0	4.3	19.5	25.4	48.4	18.2	58.3	16,560	95.0
Eden Roc CDP	942	-	-	764	32.6	1.0	2.5	49.9	14.0	22.3	14.3	44.9	48.0	7.6	303	66.0
Eleele CDP	2,390	-	-	3,145	10.4	0.1	57.6	21.5	10.4	28.6	13.5	35.4	41.2	22.9	819	79.7
Ewa Beach CDP	14,955	-	-	14,479	6.9	0.1	52.4	26.9	13.6	24.7	15.4	36.5	49.4	17.9	3,021	94.2
Ewa Gentry CDP	22,690	-	-	25,641	12.3	3.7	41.0	29.6	13.3	25.9	8.9	34.9	32.5	29.1	7,201	98.4
Ewa Villages CDP	6,108	-	-	6,585	2.8	0.9	62.7	28.0	5.6	25.7	22.2	38.5	51.3	20.5	1,697	79.3
Fern Acres CDP	1,504	-	-	1,997	35.1	1.4	4.8	42.6	16.2	15.6	19.9	41.2	52.8	16.0	655	70.8
Fern Forest CDP	931	-	-	787	38.8	0.3	4.1	36.1	20.8	23.3	19.4	44.1	45.6	16.9	334	72.2
Haena CDP	431	-	-	155	94.2	0.0	3.2	2.6	0.0	18.1	29.7	51.7	17.3	48.8	92	93.5
Haiku-Pauwela CDP	8,118	-	-	8,987	50.4	0.0	11.4	22.9	15.3	22.4	16.0	42.3	37.1	37.5	3,152	91.5
Halaula CDP	469	-	-	640	20.2	0.0	28.1	23.3	28.4	27.2	22.2	35.4	47.1	18.7	178	84.3
Halawa CDP	14,014	-	-	14,453	9.3	2.0	46.8	34.3	7.6	17.1	19.1	39.5	37.3	29.2	4,049	95.2
Haleiwa CDP	3,970	-	-	3,757	31.0	0.3	17.3	36.8	14.6	23.9	17.4	36.4	46.3	20.1	1,030	88.9
Haliimaile CDP	964	-	-	1,196	14.3	0.0	37.2	37.5	11.0	23.7	11.6	32.6	58.6	16.7	342	78.1
Hana CDP	1,235	-	-	782	23.1	0.0	0.4	76.5	0.0	20.6	27.0	42.7	46.1	24.8	223	95.5
Hanalei CDP	450	-	-	299	41.5	0.0	17.1	41.5	0.0	29.8	29.1	48.6	36.7	32.9	131	96.9
Hanamaulu CDP	3,835	-	-	5,150	8.5	0.0	52.5	32.6	6.5	22.2	16.6	37.8	56.5	14.7	1,175	82.8
Hanapepe CDP	2,638	-	-	2,834	14.9	0.2	40.4	34.0	10.6	20.1	20.5	41.3	49.1	19.6	840	87.7
Hauula CDP	4,148	-	-	3,233	22.1	0.0	6.7	62.6	8.5	28.8	13.8	31.6	37.7	31.1	800	91.5
Hawaiian Acres CDP	2,700	-	-	2,976	38.1	0.8	8.3	37.3	15.5	17.0	16.3	42.4	40.8	19.3	1,086	81.9
Hawaiian Beaches CDP	4,280	-	-	5,320	37.7	0.4	8.8	30.8	22.2	24.7	16.3	42.4	33.2	21.8	1,929	89.5
Hawaiian Ocean View CDP	4,437	-	-	5,011	31.9	1.0	1.1	41.8	24.2	42.4	10.3	31.6	55.7	14.7	1,640	77.7
Hawaiian Paradise Park CDP	11,404	-	-	11,202	34.5	0.0	23.7	32.1	9.7	21.9	18.3	44.4	35.3	25.5	3,875	86.3
Hawi CDP	1,081	-	-	1,166	15.5	0.0	32.6	47.0	4.9	14.8	27.0	43.2	48.3	25.9	345	80.0
Heeia CDP	4,963	-	-	4,372	21.8	0.0	44.1	30.6	3.5	13.9	28.8	55.7	26.8	44.3	1,495	97.6
Hickam Housing CDP	6,920	-	-	9,387	53.8	8.3	9.1	6.0	22.7	37.8	0.3	24.1	15.4	43.9	2,716	99.7

1 May be of any race.

Table A. All Places — **Population and Housing**

STATE City, town, township, borough, or CDP (county if applicable)	Population				Race and Hispanic or Latino origin (percent)					Age (percent)			Educational attainment of persons age 25 and older		Occupied housing units	
	2010 census total population	2019 estimated population	Percent change 2010-2019	ACS total population estimate 2015-2019	White alone, not Hispanic or Latino	Black alone, not Hispanic or Latino	Asian alone, not Hispanic or Latino	All other races or 2 or more races, not Hispanic or Latino	Hispanic or Latino[1]	Under 18 years old	Age 65 years and older	Median age	Percent High school diploma or less	Percent Bachelor's degree or more	Total	Percent with a computer
	1	2	3	4	5	6	7	8	9	10	11	12	13	14	15	16
HAWAII—Con.																
Hilo CDP	43,263	-	-	45,056	16.9	0.6	32.1	38.6	11.8	21.0	20.3	40.3	34.2	34.5	16,011	85.0
Holualoa CDP	8,538	-	-	9,688	51.7	3.0	18.7	19.1	7.5	17.3	24.1	49.4	19.0	40.3	3,688	93.5
Honalo CDP	2,423	-	-	2,254	25.6	0.3	23.6	35.9	14.6	27.5	23.5	40.5	49.9	20.9	794	90.3
Honaunau-Napoopoo CDP	2,567	-	-	2,300	56.3	0.0	6.9	32.7	4.1	14.0	24.3	52.1	32.6	37.2	977	84.1
Honokaa CDP	2,258	-	-	2,079	15.2	0.4	30.0	42.9	11.6	18.1	23.1	45.3	50.1	15.5	650	81.5
Honomu CDP	509	-	-	488	35.7	0.8	20.9	28.3	14.3	18.2	18.2	49.2	44.7	30.6	178	90.4
Iroquois Point CDP	3,374	-	-	3,891	41.5	8.7	4.9	22.5	22.5	34.5	5.4	29.6	21.0	31.0	1,094	99.8
Kaaawa CDP	1,379	-	-	1,132	32.1	0.5	8.0	50.1	9.3	26.1	12.9	37.2	24.6	39.9	411	91.7
Kaanapali CDP	1,045	-	-	930	79.4	0.0	6.9	9.4	4.4	8.9	41.9	62.4	17.8	50.4	464	94.4
Kahaluu CDP	4,738	-	-	4,577	20.2	0.3	23.8	40.6	15.2	19.8	23.7	43.9	42.5	29.7	1,292	89.3
Kahaluu-Keauhou CDP	3,549	-	-	5,291	52.6	0.0	34.1	7.4	5.9	15.2	32.6	55.5	30.0	41.2	1,830	94.0
Kahuku CDP	2,614	-	-	2,119	12.3	3.4	17.4	58.7	8.2	30.0	15.0	35.2	46.4	22.6	534	87.8
Kahului CDP	26,337	-	-	31,336	9.3	0.9	52.2	27.5	10.1	23.6	17.0	37.5	50.4	17.5	7,846	88.8
Kailua CDP	11,975	-	-	15,231	29.3	0.3	20.1	36.5	13.7	21.9	17.3	37.5	44.9	25.8	4,813	88.8
Kailua CDP	38,635	-	-	37,586	44.0	1.0	18.9	28.4	7.7	20.0	20.0	42.0	23.9	49.5	12,499	94.7
Kalaeloa CDP	48	-	-	6	66.7	0.0	0.0	33.3	0.0	33.3	0.0	55.5	0.0	100.0	2	100.0
Kalaheo CDP	4,595	-	-	5,487	33.4	0.0	24.1	29.1	13.4	23.2	20.4	43.0	22.9	43.5	1,710	98.1
Kalaoa CDP	9,644	-	-	11,729	39.6	0.6	15.0	37.0	7.9	18.4	17.7	42.4	37.0	33.3	4,091	94.9
Kalihiwai CDP	428	-	-	189	60.8	1.1	6.9	22.2	9.0	7.4	31.2	57.1	26.2	33.5	91	95.6
Kaneohe CDP	34,597	-	-	33,841	19.6	0.8	36.5	35.5	7.6	19.6	20.3	42.4	33.2	37.7	10,543	92.0
Kaneohe Station CDP	9,517	-	-	11,289	62.1	7.5	2.5	6.5	21.4	25.7	0.0	22.4	26.9	30.5	2,617	100.0
Kapaa CDP	10,699	-	-	10,580	38.9	0.3	27.2	26.3	7.2	22.0	16.2	41.5	33.8	35.3	3,623	90.9
Kapaau CDP	1,734	-	-	1,801	21.8	0.8	24.3	34.4	18.7	19.9	22.1	44.7	48.9	21.5	594	90.1
Kapalua CDP	353	-	-	291	72.2	0.0	5.8	17.2	4.8	6.2	38.1	61.9	20.5	51.6	140	100.0
Kapolei CDP	15,186	-	-	21,674	11.6	1.4	30.5	42.7	13.9	30.9	8.5	31.5	32.1	34.0	5,847	98.3
Kaumakani CDP	749	-	-	975	3.1	0.0	64.9	26.1	5.9	22.8	20.1	39.8	64.8	6.4	240	80.0
Kaunakakai CDP	3,425	-	-	3,038	15.6	0.9	24.3	56.4	2.9	25.6	24.6	44.1	47.2	19.9	1,066	77.5
Kawela Bay CDP	330	-	-	225	61.3	0.0	7.1	29.8	1.8	10.7	35.1	55.5	18.6	51.6	114	97.4
Keaau CDP	2,253	-	-	2,613	11.7	0.0	48.6	32.3	7.4	23.8	21.9	43.8	45.9	18.1	815	81.5
Kealakekua CDP	2,019	-	-	1,923	25.3	0.5	35.5	31.4	7.4	18.3	26.3	52.2	38.6	31.1	775	87.9
Kekaha CDP	3,537	-	-	3,442	8.3	0.9	29.7	44.4	16.7	19.8	16.5	39.7	43.3	17.4	1,118	86.5
Keokea CDP	1,612	-	-	2,248	21.1	0.4	9.2	60.0	9.3	24.1	16.9	38.5	37.2	30.1	664	93.2
Kihei CDP	20,881	-	-	22,402	42.6	0.9	23.1	22.3	11.1	20.3	16.9	41.0	33.5	30.1	8,067	95.3
Kilauea CDP	2,803	-	-	2,686	63.4	0.0	22.2	8.9	5.6	24.2	14.0	39.3	29.0	32.3	803	92.7
Koloa CDP	2,144	-	-	2,739	18.8	1.1	25.1	39.4	15.7	31.4	16.1	34.7	48.8	17.8	868	83.8
Ko Olina CDP	1,799	-	-	1,742	63.3	1.8	9.2	17.3	8.3	16.0	19.0	38.5	15.5	56.9	731	98.5
Kualapuu CDP	2,027	-	-	1,693	7.4	0.0	13.1	73.8	5.7	27.5	20.0	38.5	46.4	20.9	543	78.5
Kukuihaele CDP	336	-	-	347	30.0	0.6	8.4	55.6	5.5	20.7	16.4	34.5	43.0	16.1	111	78.4
Kula CDP	6,452	-	-	7,621	50.1	0.0	17.0	25.6	7.3	17.8	23.7	50.6	28.0	34.1	2,874	94.7
Kurtistown CDP	1,298	-	-	1,199	25.1	0.0	30.8	37.7	6.4	15.6	18.8	49.9	38.4	27.7	404	89.1
Lahaina CDP	11,704	-	-	12,776	21.8	0.1	38.0	26.3	13.9	25.1	14.3	36.9	51.4	17.8	3,537	92.1
Laie CDP	6,138	-	-	5,704	32.1	0.4	13.3	47.8	6.4	22.2	5.5	23.1	22.4	39.3	823	98.1
Lanai City CDP	3,102	-	-	2,705	14.0	0.0	53.9	24.8	7.2	16.9	24.7	48.7	49.7	21.0	1,166	70.0
Launiupoko CDP	588	-	-	538	77.3	0.0	3.0	12.1	7.6	16.7	28.1	53.3	23.2	42.2	213	93.9
Laupahoehoe CDP	581	-	-	528	35.6	0.0	19.7	26.9	17.8	15.0	21.4	56.9	35.1	32.2	204	87.3
Lawai CDP	2,363	-	-	2,047	38.4	0.0	19.8	29.8	12.1	22.7	21.7	41.9	24.4	30.3	711	87.9
Leilani Estates CDP	1,560	-	-	1,576	68.4	0.9	2.1	18.6	10.0	12.3	29.1	55.1	27.5	36.0	774	81.0
Lihue CDP	6,455	-	-	7,267	20.4	1.5	43.2	21.6	13.2	22.5	18.5	45.2	40.9	29.6	2,294	90.8
Maalaea CDP	352	-	-	261	81.6	0.0	9.2	6.5	2.7	2.7	44.4	63.0	9.1	53.1	176	98.3
Mahinahina CDP	880	-	-	917	63.7	1.0	13.6	12.2	9.5	22.7	14.0	47.4	21.4	37.1	349	100.0
Maili CDP	9,488	-	-	11,437	10.3	1.3	15.5	53.0	19.9	30.8	11.0	32.6	49.7	17.8	2,681	92.3
Makaha CDP	8,278	-	-	8,404	14.9	3.0	7.0	58.8	16.3	31.5	11.8	35.0	58.7	15.3	2,312	91.2
Makaha Valley CDP	1,341	-	-	1,731	24.9	2.5	5.8	40.3	26.6	32.6	9.1	31.7	40.5	20.9	565	92.9
Makakilo CDP	18,248	-	-	19,775	21.0	5.1	32.4	29.9	11.7	26.1	10.6	34.3	31.3	33.8	5,866	96.4
Makawao CDP	7,184	-	-	7,341	36.7	0.7	16.4	37.7	8.5	20.7	15.2	43.2	36.2	28.9	2,610	91.4
Makena CDP	99	-	-	142	51.4	0.0	16.9	28.9	2.8	20.4	31.7	60.0	20.0	60.9	59	100.0
Manele CDP	29	-	-	25	100.0	0.0	0.0	0.0	0.0	0.0	100.0	70.7	0.0	76.0	15	100.0
Maunaloa CDP	376	-	-	336	9.5	0.9	3.3	74.4	11.9	36.0	11.6	28.9	47.5	14.6	121	75.2
Maunawili CDP	2,040	-	-	1,977	34.7	0.0	28.9	32.1	4.2	19.9	25.7	52.0	9.9	64.9	680	95.7
Mililani Mauka CDP	21,039	-	-	20,090	13.1	2.1	54.5	21.8	8.5	24.8	11.5	39.2	19.1	52.3	6,961	95.4
Mililani Town CDP	27,629	-	-	27,562	14.2	1.8	44.2	29.0	10.8	20.9	21.6	41.4	27.5	35.3	8,749	94.9
Mokuleia CDP	1,811	-	-	1,959	60.6	1.0	6.4	17.0	15.0	20.3	11.9	33.4	19.8	45.4	786	95.3
Mountain View CDP	3,924	-	-	3,381	20.4	0.0	6.2	46.6	26.8	33.9	17.2	37.3	33.9	26.4	1,215	87.7
Naalehu CDP	866	-	-	962	13.5	1.5	49.7	21.5	13.8	19.6	26.7	49.8	48.7	11.2	312	70.5
Nanakuli CDP	12,666	-	-	11,461	3.4	0.3	6.9	75.2	14.2	29.3	11.3	31.5	60.7	11.0	2,649	89.5
Nanawale Estates CDP	1,426	-	-	1,707	31.5	0.0	12.9	34.3	21.4	19.4	16.0	41.7	48.7	16.8	573	83.6
Napili-Honokowai CDP	7,261	-	-	6,739	44.4	0.0	15.6	16.7	23.3	19.5	15.2	40.6	44.4	23.9	2,607	95.7
Ocean Pointe CDP	8,361	-	-	14,989	26.5	3.9	32.9	24.7	12.0	31.2	7.8	33.6	20.9	41.6	4,320	99.6
Olinda CDP	1,084	-	-	1,107	66.0	0.4	5.3	15.6	12.6	16.1	25.9	50.4	26.4	43.1	444	91.4
Olowalu CDP	80	-	-	91	65.9	0.0	9.9	22.0	2.2	3.3	38.5	42.8	21.6	56.8	53	100.0
Omao CDP	1,301	-	-	1,467	38.5	0.0	15.4	25.1	21.0	19.8	18.3	42.6	29.7	28.2	468	93.2
Orchidlands Estates CDP	2,815	-	-	3,139	30.4	0.0	14.7	33.8	21.2	26.9	14.0	37.8	49.1	18.3	1,063	87.2
Paauilo CDP	595	-	-	586	14.5	0.0	33.8	39.2	12.5	14.7	24.1	52.3	62.8	4.7	205	85.4
Pahala CDP	1,356	-	-	1,827	6.1	0.0	30.7	35.5	27.8	29.2	13.8	29.7	58.2	18.9	427	81.3
Pahoa CDP	945	-	-	805	9.3	0.0	30.2	32.5	28.0	18.6	20.9	40.1	49.4	24.0	268	65.7
Paia CDP	2,668	-	-	2,249	45.5	0.0	16.9	23.2	14.5	23.3	12.6	37.3	38.7	31.2	695	90.4
Pakala Village CDP	294	-	-	352	10.8	0.0	30.1	49.4	9.7	15.9	24.7	36.3	73.2	6.4	108	58.3
Papaikou CDP	1,314	-	-	971	20.7	0.0	38.8	11.9	28.5	29.6	19.8	41.5	51.6	25.2	320	83.8
Paukaa CDP	425	-	-	637	41.8	0.0	23.4	23.5	11.3	13.7	34.2	53.5	23.1	45.3	263	85.2
Pearl City CDP	47,698	-	-	45,605	11.7	1.8	51.3	25.7	9.5	19.0	24.2	41.7	33.3	32.8	13,989	91.4
Pepeekeo CDP	1,789	-	-	1,518	15.3	0.0	40.1	37.3	7.3	18.2	24.4	45.5	50.4	14.0	574	65.9
Poipu CDP	979	-	-	993	67.8	0.1	13.5	10.9	7.8	8.5	43.4	62.3	18.1	50.9	471	96.6
Princeville CDP	2,158	-	-	1,669	76.3	0.0	2.2	8.1	13.5	19.4	32.4	54.9	17.8	53.3	726	94.4
Puako CDP	772	-	-	908	70.8	0.0	9.6	11.2	8.4	8.0	42.4	62.3	5.8	63.1	446	98.0
Puhi CDP	2,906	-	-	3,850	14.2	0.6	50.3	26.0	8.9	25.5	18.4	38.9	47.3	17.6	969	91.0
Pukalani CDP	7,574	-	-	7,695	35.8	0.0	26.6	25.0	12.7	17.5	16.3	48.0	36.4	32.5	2,835	88.3
Punaluu CDP	1,164	-	-	1,071	25.9	4.4	12.2	42.0	15.5	24.2	19.5	37.0	35.4	29.9	383	90.6
Pupukea CDP	4,551	-	-	4,443	72.0	0.5	12.4	12.9	2.2	21.7	15.2	37.2	21.2	49.5	1,444	98.3
Royal Kunia CDP	14,525	-	-	14,565	5.9	1.8	62.2	22.9	7.2	19.5	14.4	40.2	36.0	30.0	3,863	96.8
Schofield Barracks CDP	16,370	-	-	19,499	42.3	14.8	3.9	13.1	25.9	33.0	0.5	22.6	26.9	21.5	4,459	99.9
Ualapue CDP	425	-	-	448	14.1	0.0	10.3	70.8	4.9	28.3	20.1	33.0	37.7	24.7	145	86.9

1 May be of any race.

Table A. All Places — **Population and Housing**

STATE City, town, township, borough, or CDP (county if applicable)	Population 2010 census total population	2019 estimated population	Percent change 2010-2019	ACS total population estimate 2015-2019	White alone, not Hispanic or Latino	Black alone, not Hispanic or Latino	Asian alone, not Hispanic or Latino	All other races or 2 or more races, not Hispanic or Latino	Hispanic or Latino[1]	Under 18 years old	Age 65 years and older	Median age	Percent High school diploma or less	Percent Bachelor's degree or more	Occupied housing units Total	Percent with a computer
	1	2	3	4	5	6	7	8	9	10	11	12	13	14	15	16
HAWAII—Con.																
Urban Honolulu CDP	337,721	345,064	2.2	348,985	15.4	2.0	52.3	23.1	7.3	17.1	20.0	41.5	34.4	37.2	129,019	89.4
Volcano CDP	2,575	-	-	3,570	41.0	0.0	8.4	35.6	15.0	14.0	29.1	57.0	34.7	32.3	1,484	92.7
Wahiawa CDP	17,821	-	-	17,122	13.3	1.5	35.1	33.6	16.4	23.9	20.1	38.2	43.5	22.8	5,705	83.8
Waialua CDP	3,860	-	-	3,308	22.9	0.0	35.9	25.9	15.2	22.5	20.0	39.1	44.6	29.4	1,072	87.4
Waianae CDP	13,177	-	-	13,609	7.3	0.7	11.1	60.6	20.2	29.8	13.4	33.1	60.5	11.7	3,239	88.3
Waihee-Waiehu CDP	8,841	-	-	9,319	14.8	0.2	33.6	41.4	10.0	22.5	15.5	39.4	46.3	18.5	2,518	94.4
Waikane CDP	778	-	-	531	24.7	0.0	15.4	56.9	3.0	16.0	24.1	44.3	49.6	21.1	177	88.1
Waikapu CDP	2,965	-	-	3,875	23.1	0.2	34.2	28.3	14.1	34.8	7.5	33.7	30.7	34.0	1,024	94.9
Waikele CDP	7,479	-	-	7,442	19.6	1.4	42.1	25.9	11.1	20.2	13.2	35.5	18.6	41.6	2,765	99.1
Waikoloa Village CDP	6,362	-	-	6,549	44.0	1.9	16.7	23.4	14.0	29.8	15.2	38.5	28.0	34.6	2,494	96.8
Wailea CDP	5,938	-	-	6,218	67.6	0.0	13.1	12.3	7.0	14.1	24.9	53.8	25.1	44.3	2,669	97.6
Wailua CDP	2,254	-	-	2,915	34.9	0.1	24.3	23.8	16.9	25.2	18.9	40.4	33.7	32.0	1,016	92.1
Wailua Homesteads CDP	5,188	-	-	6,117	45.1	0.3	18.1	23.1	13.4	15.5	23.3	48.8	31.1	32.9	1,996	94.4
Wailuku CDP	15,313	-	-	17,708	18.7	0.7	30.0	37.5	13.0	24.6	16.1	39.1	33.8	27.2	6,223	91.8
Waimalu CDP	13,730	-	-	14,043	13.3	4.4	47.9	25.8	8.6	17.9	16.8	36.8	31.3	31.1	5,493	94.9
Waimanalo CDP	5,451	-	-	5,538	9.2	0.0	18.3	59.6	12.9	26.5	16.7	35.6	49.1	20.3	1,197	90.8
Waimanalo Beach CDP	4,481	-	-	4,076	9.7	0.5	5.5	76.8	7.5	21.6	19.8	40.8	49.2	23.1	1,029	90.2
Waimea CDP	9,212	-	-	11,908	23.6	0.0	26.0	45.3	5.0	26.5	17.3	38.9	38.8	31.0	3,345	93.1
Waimea CDP	1,855	-	-	1,865	21.9	0.3	41.4	29.3	7.1	17.0	25.9	44.4	36.2	30.8	691	81.2
Wainaku CDP	1,224	-	-	1,301	17.7	0.0	33.5	38.8	10.0	16.5	23.8	43.8	56.5	24.7	410	89.3
Wainiha CDP	318	-	-	166	44.0	0.0	10.8	42.2	3.0	24.7	30.1	36.2	30.4	33.9	48	100.0
Waiohinu CDP	213	-	-	278	14.4	2.9	20.1	54.0	8.6	21.2	21.9	40.4	50.5	20.1	98	73.5
Waipahu CDP	38,216	-	-	39,469	3.3	0.4	66.0	23.7	6.6	21.5	18.9	39.4	51.2	17.1	8,355	88.7
Waipio CDP	11,674	-	-	11,469	8.7	1.3	55.0	25.7	9.3	19.5	17.1	38.2	30.2	30.7	3,769	97.0
Waipio Acres CDP	5,236	-	-	5,451	12.9	2.1	36.2	35.6	13.2	19.7	12.8	36.3	37.8	26.1	1,827	92.3
West Loch Estate CDP	5,485	-	-	6,139	13.9	0.8	56.0	21.4	7.9	21.5	19.0	40.6	40.7	26.4	1,693	90.4
Wheeler AFB CDP	1,634	-	-	2,331	51.7	15.7	2.4	12.8	17.3	32.6	0.7	24.6	15.5	32.9	838	99.4
Whitmore Village CDP	4,499	-	-	3,965	5.2	0.8	70.4	15.3	8.3	23.5	16.7	39.3	51.9	17.7	985	83.0
IDAHO	1,567,657	1,787,065	14.0	1,717,750	82.0	0.7	1.3	3.5	12.5	25.7	15.4	36.4	36.6	27.6	630,008	91.8
Aberdeen city	1,994	1,977	-0.9	2,088	25.7	0.0	0.0	1.1	73.3	36.9	8.3	21.9	71.6	9.7	535	87.5
Acequia city	130	133	2.3	225	46.7	0.0	0.0	0.0	53.3	25.3	9.3	39.9	49.7	10.5	62	93.5
Albion city	262	276	5.3	414	87.0	0.0	0.0	0.0	13.0	34.1	15.7	31.4	43.0	10.5	138	93.5
American Falls city	4,447	4,315	-3.0	4,322	44.6	0.0	0.0	3.4	52.0	32.6	13.9	34.3	62.7	11.4	1,370	87.3
Ammon city	13,971	17,115	22.5	15,859	87.7	0.0	0.7	3.4	8.1	33.1	11.7	31.6	28.4	35.5	5,307	95.5
Arbon Valley CDP	599	-	-	1,124	67.5	0.5	0.0	10.7	21.3	25.9	16.8	41.9	69.4	6.7	326	90.2
Arco city	986	880	-10.8	777	94.9	0.0	0.0	0.0	5.1	20.1	19.4	40.6	50.2	6.6	295	91.5
Arimo city	350	364	4.0	353	98.9	0.0	0.6	0.0	0.6	34.3	12.2	34.3	27.2	18.4	118	89.0
Ashton city	1,127	1,050	-6.8	833	80.0	0.0	0.0	0.0	20.0	20.4	22.1	45.9	50.3	27.1	333	77.5
Athol city	692	792	14.5	978	97.8	0.0	0.2	1.6	0.4	22.0	18.7	41.6	54.7	5.0	381	92.7
Atomic City city	26	27	3.8	43	95.3	0.0	0.0	4.7	0.0	0.0	37.2	64.1	9.3	0.0	27	70.4
Bancroft city	370	394	6.5	329	92.7	0.0	0.0	0.0	7.3	30.4	11.6	33.4	41.2	13.7	117	96.6
Banks CDP	17	-	-	6	100.0	0.0	0.0	0.0	0.0	0.0	0.0	0.0	0.0	0.0	6	100.0
Basalt city	394	408	3.6	396	91.7	0.0	0.0	1.8	6.6	25.3	20.5	43.0	50.0	10.2	139	92.1
Bellevue city	2,335	2,456	5.2	2,747	71.4	0.0	4.2	1.7	22.8	20.6	12.7	37.8	57.3	19.7	825	96.0
Bennington CDP	190	-	-	130	100.0	0.0	0.0	0.0	0.0	13.1	24.6	56.5	30.9	10.0	81	100.0
Blackfoot city	11,975	12,034	0.5	11,907	75.3	0.8	1.5	5.0	17.4	29.3	12.7	31.8	38.4	22.4	4,236	93.4
Blanchard CDP	261	-	-	201	100.0	0.0	0.0	0.0	0.0	0.0	77.1	70.2	34.8	35.8	128	77.3
Bliss city	316	305	-3.5	243	51.4	0.0	0.0	0.0	48.6	28.4	18.1	30.2	77.7	0.7	103	83.5
Bloomington city	206	209	1.5	206	99.5	0.0	0.0	0.5	0.0	33.0	21.4	38.6	41.7	23.3	75	92.0
Boise City city	209,384	228,959	9.3	226,115	83.2	1.8	2.8	3.3	9.0	21.8	13.9	36.6	26.3	41.6	91,555	93.0
Bonners Ferry city	2,510	2,637	5.1	2,594	88.9	2.2	0.4	2.5	5.9	21.0	20.3	44.8	48.0	19.1	1,172	71.9
Bovill city	254	258	1.6	322	93.5	0.0	0.0	2.2	4.3	22.7	18.9	48.5	54.3	5.7	117	57.3
Buhl city	4,176	4,507	7.9	4,429	74.4	0.0	0.2	1.0	24.4	21.9	21.2	43.4	50.0	9.7	1,801	84.5
Burley city	10,286	10,582	2.9	10,313	58.1	0.2	1.0	2.8	37.8	31.5	12.7	30.1	49.7	16.0	3,534	93.7
Butte City city	74	68	-8.1	80	90.0	3.8	0.0	0.0	6.3	6.3	38.8	59.7	48.0	20.0	43	65.1
Caldwell city	46,346	58,481	26.2	54,887	56.8	0.3	1.0	3.2	38.8	32.6	10.7	29.7	54.3	13.7	16,814	92.8
Cambridge city	328	320	-2.4	248	98.4	0.0	0.0	0.0	1.6	18.1	29.0	50.8	45.3	21.0	129	76.7
Carey city	611	645	5.6	993	83.8	0.0	0.0	0.3	15.9	26.5	19.8	34.1	49.1	17.7	220	83.6
Cascade city	938	1,025	9.3	745	92.3	0.0	0.0	0.9	6.7	25.4	24.7	44.4	41.5	23.6	258	84.5
Castleford city	226	250	10.6	221	61.1	0.0	0.0	0.0	38.9	24.4	17.6	34.8	76.2	4.1	86	64.0
Challis city	1,097	1,091	-0.5	758	86.5	0.0	0.0	3.7	9.8	20.6	17.4	45.1	34.0	27.4	384	92.2
Chubbuck city	13,982	15,588	11.5	14,995	83.4	0.3	1.8	4.1	10.4	33.0	11.9	32.2	29.6	25.9	5,147	92.1
Clark Fork city	530	579	9.2	506	88.1	0.0	0.0	10.7	1.2	14.8	30.4	55.8	59.9	11.5	278	70.5
Clayton city	8	8	0.0	13	100.0	0.0	0.0	0.0	0.0	0.0	100.0	0.0	46.2	0.0	7	0.0
Clifton city	259	304	17.4	337	84.3	0.0	0.0	3.9	11.9	38.0	9.5	22.5	49.1	23.9	106	98.1
Coeur d'Alene city	44,168	52,414	18.7	50,540	88.5	0.3	1.2	4.3	5.7	22.2	16.9	36.8	33.2	27.3	21,283	90.6
Conkling Park CDP	43	-	-	68	100.0	0.0	0.0	0.0	0.0	0.0	38.2	62.5	13.2	39.7	33	90.9
Cottonwood city	901	940	4.3	977	93.8	0.2	1.1	1.7	3.2	28.7	18.2	36.7	42.0	26.5	377	76.7
Council city	839	894	6.6	747	89.8	2.1	0.0	2.3	5.8	18.7	24.9	48.9	53.8	13.6	347	74.1
Craigmont city	505	489	-3.2	510	90.0	0.0	1.4	5.1	3.5	17.3	24.5	50.8	45.5	13.6	236	77.5
Crouch city	162	183	13.0	90	96.7	0.0	0.0	0.0	3.3	0.0	50.0	65.0	32.2	19.5	51	82.4
Culdesac city	380	383	0.8	360	72.5	0.0	0.0	25.3	2.2	23.6	17.5	39.8	56.0	8.6	146	89.0
Dalton Gardens city	2,341	2,410	2.9	2,812	93.4	0.0	0.0	1.5	5.1	22.8	22.1	46.6	25.4	35.8	1,015	96.9
Dayton city	465	494	6.2	561	90.9	0.0	0.0	1.4	7.7	38.9	14.8	25.7	40.6	18.5	169	96.4
Deary city	506	516	2.0	455	99.1	0.0	0.0	0.9	0.0	24.0	25.5	40.9	54.4	13.8	177	81.9
Declo city	349	369	5.7	526	70.5	1.3	2.3	0.0	25.9	34.0	11.6	33.1	45.0	8.3	157	87.9
De Smet CDP	175	-	-	202	13.4	0.0	0.0	52.0	34.7	20.8	8.4	30.1	59.7	6.5	52	75.0
Dietrich city	332	341	2.7	326	90.5	0.0	0.0	0.6	8.9	22.1	13.8	35.7	40.8	8.8	88	93.2
Donnelly city	144	218	51.4	72	76.4	0.0	0.0	0.0	23.6	15.3	33.3	54.5	32.8	24.6	34	91.2
Dover city	544	874	60.7	655	96.8	0.0	0.0	0.9	2.3	23.4	26.7	48.4	24.2	43.9	258	92.2
Downey city	625	633	1.3	775	92.8	0.4	0.0	1.8	5.0	31.4	19.9	35.7	52.8	12.6	283	78.1
Driggs city	1,630	1,817	11.5	1,805	68.9	0.0	0.0	1.6	29.5	27.3	10.5	35.2	25.6	40.3	557	91.0
Drummond city	16	16	0.0	2	100.0	0.0	0.0	0.0	0.0	0.0	100.0	0.0	100.0	0.0	2	0.0
Dubois city	677	584	-13.7	606	40.1	0.0	0.0	1.8	58.1	23.8	16.7	40.5	73.2	11.4	191	75.4
Eagle city	19,982	29,796	49.1	26,514	88.9	0.5	2.2	3.4	5.1	24.2	20.5	47.1	19.9	46.5	9,946	92.5
East Hope city	208	225	8.2	136	97.8	0.0	0.0	2.2	0.0	2.9	52.9	65.3	28.5	40.0	80	97.5
Eden city	403	427	6.0	373	62.2	0.0	0.0	0.0	37.8	32.4	16.6	32.5	63.0	7.0	137	78.8
Elk City CDP	-	-	-	147	100.0	0.0	0.0	0.0	0.0	0.0	39.5	63.4	37.4	12.9	49	100.0
Elk River city	125	122	-2.4	144	100.0	0.0	0.0	0.0	0.0	6.9	42.4	63.0	63.0	14.2	76	84.2
Emmett city	6,554	7,054	7.6	6,770	77.6	0.0	0.1	3.5	18.8	26.6	17.8	36.2	55.4	18.1	2,773	90.3

1 May be of any race.

Table A. All Places — **Population and Housing**

STATE City, town, township, borough, or CDP (county if applicable)	Population				Race and Hispanic or Latino origin (percent)					Age (percent)			Educational attainment of persons age 25 and older		Occupied housing units	
	2010 census total population	2019 estimated population	Percent change 2010-2019	ACS total population estimate 2015-2019	White alone, not Hispanic or Latino	Black alone, not Hispanic or Latino	Asian alone, not Hispanic or Latino	All other races or 2 or more races, not Hispanic or Latino	Hispanic or Latino[1]	Under 18 years old	Age 65 years and older	Median age	Percent High school diploma or less	Percent Bachelor's degree or more	Total	Percent with a computer
	1	2	3	4	5	6	7	8	9	10	11	12	13	14	15	16
IDAHO—Con.																
Fairfield city	416	395	-5.0	519	99.4	0.0	0.0	0.6	0.0	30.3	11.6	33.6	49.5	16.4	168	97.0
Ferdinand city	159	162	1.9	162	97.5	0.0	0.0	2.5	0.0	23.5	11.7	43.3	38.2	11.8	63	95.2
Fernan Lake Village city	169	171	1.2	149	94.6	0.0	0.0	3.4	2.0	20.1	35.6	54.1	11.2	44.8	65	100.0
Filer city	2,511	2,931	16.7	2,804	82.2	0.4	0.0	4.7	12.7	32.2	16.1	30.4	38.0	18.1	1,027	87.7
Firth city	479	499	4.2	526	71.9	0.0	0.2	7.0	20.9	27.9	9.5	34.5	59.1	12.5	182	86.8
Fort Hall CDP	3,201	-	-	2,971	26.8	0.0	0.5	60.6	12.1	27.1	16.0	38.7	51.1	11.1	983	79.8
Franklin city	653	835	27.9	621	89.7	0.0	0.2	0.0	10.1	34.1	11.1	28.8	52.1	11.4	205	92.2
Fruitland city	4,761	5,426	14.0	5,264	75.7	0.0	0.4	4.9	19.0	26.1	19.7	40.4	56.0	12.6	2,189	87.8
Garden City city	10,976	11,969	9.0	11,819	87.2	0.7	0.6	3.1	8.4	17.5	24.9	48.7	29.3	35.0	5,678	85.8
Garden Valley CDP	394	-	-	489	82.0	3.9	1.8	8.4	3.9	26.8	7.6	46.9	13.5	53.4	169	100.0
Genesee city	951	965	1.5	1,051	87.4	0.0	2.1	6.1	4.4	28.6	14.7	37.1	29.1	28.4	404	90.3
Georgetown city	493	494	0.2	566	93.6	3.0	0.9	1.1	1.4	30.4	14.1	37.7	51.9	12.2	200	93.5
Glenns Ferry city	1,323	1,303	-1.5	1,226	74.4	0.0	0.0	5.3	20.3	30.5	23.6	42.9	53.1	11.7	523	75.3
Gooding city	3,602	3,446	-4.3	3,465	70.0	0.0	0.0	2.8	27.2	20.0	17.9	41.4	63.6	8.7	1,406	92.6
Grace city	913	935	2.4	1,244	86.6	0.0	0.2	1.2	12.1	25.6	15.1	35.6	63.0	9.3	439	97.9
Grand View city	449	469	4.5	376	72.6	1.3	0.0	3.5	22.6	27.1	23.7	46.2	49.2	6.7	154	88.3
Grangeville city	3,148	3,237	2.8	3,187	87.8	0.0	0.0	8.6	3.6	26.0	16.2	33.0	47.6	17.7	1,161	86.5
Greenleaf city	837	886	5.9	1,002	66.7	0.0	0.6	1.5	31.2	21.8	15.9	39.3	47.0	19.7	369	92.1
Groveland CDP	877	-	-	624	96.0	0.0	1.9	0.0	2.1	23.4	23.4	43.0	29.4	32.6	212	100.0
Hagerman city	892	893	0.1	1,056	80.9	1.2	0.0	2.7	15.2	26.7	27.4	43.3	53.2	12.2	412	82.8
Hailey city	7,962	8,689	9.1	8,408	66.1	0.0	0.4	1.2	32.3	31.0	10.0	38.9	44.2	28.2	2,662	93.2
Hamer city	89	104	16.9	105	67.6	0.0	0.0	0.0	32.4	48.6	13.3	18.8	40.5	19.0	21	100.0
Hansen city	1,141	1,284	12.5	1,292	67.5	0.0	0.2	3.5	28.8	33.7	15.7	32.6	54.2	8.0	472	85.6
Harrison city	208	216	3.8	231	99.1	0.9	0.0	0.0	0.0	14.3	27.3	55.6	51.3	17.1	105	65.7
Hauser city	674	739	9.6	876	92.9	0.0	0.3	4.2	2.5	20.8	6.8	34.2	41.5	24.3	343	90.7
Hayden city	13,301	15,434	16.0	14,698	94.4	0.2	1.1	2.7	1.6	20.1	24.4	43.2	37.4	26.2	5,889	90.1
Hayden Lake city	587	623	6.1	804	95.9	0.0	0.6	0.0	3.5	25.4	30.7	53.0	8.8	47.6	321	97.5
Hazelton city	805	821	2.0	764	41.6	0.0	0.5	8.5	49.3	31.9	11.6	30.5	57.2	8.9	250	80.4
Heyburn city	3,089	3,447	11.6	3,320	64.5	0.4	0.0	6.8	28.3	35.0	6.7	26.7	52.1	13.1	1,125	93.0
Hidden Springs CDP	2,280	-	-	3,164	94.4	0.0	0.0	2.4	3.2	42.5	8.6	30.5	3.3	65.4	942	100.0
Hollister city	272	309	13.6	232	47.0	0.0	0.4	0.4	52.2	23.3	11.6	46.3	72.4	3.7	92	89.1
Homedale city	2,644	2,720	2.9	2,630	47.1	0.0	0.3	1.7	50.8	24.5	15.6	35.1	68.8	10.1	970	84.2
Hope city	94	102	8.5	98	95.9	0.0	2.0	2.0	0.0	7.1	44.9	59.7	20.8	49.4	49	77.6
Horseshoe Bend city	722	787	9.0	862	84.0	0.0	0.0	4.2	11.8	20.4	25.2	44.5	56.0	13.2	388	82.7
Huetter city	100	112	12.0	141	93.6	2.1	0.0	0.0	4.3	5.0	5.7	34.6	46.8	3.6	63	87.3
Idaho City city	447	467	4.5	520	90.2	0.0	0.0	4.0	5.8	20.6	17.1	39.9	48.1	11.6	219	85.4
Idaho Falls city	57,833	62,888	8.7	61,459	80.4	0.6	1.3	2.9	14.8	28.8	13.7	33.4	33.8	30.7	22,889	93.2
Inkom city	857	902	5.3	820	97.4	0.0	0.0	0.7	1.8	32.8	12.1	34.3	36.7	20.6	304	87.8
Iona city	1,823	2,354	29.1	2,675	94.6	0.0	0.0	0.4	5.0	37.6	7.8	28.5	25.7	29.5	813	95.6
Irwin city	231	247	6.9	245	95.5	0.0	1.2	0.8	2.4	15.5	35.1	59.6	44.5	21.5	121	94.2
Island Park city	277	266	-4.0	185	100.0	0.0	0.0	0.0	0.0	4.9	47.0	62.9	24.6	29.2	94	88.3
Jerome city	10,873	11,994	10.3	11,653	61.1	0.1	0.6	1.7	36.4	33.0	11.6	31.1	57.1	12.6	3,941	85.2
Juliaetta city	579	601	3.8	536	85.4	0.0	0.0	6.9	7.6	22.2	12.1	37.8	51.0	11.1	227	86.3
Kamiah city	1,293	1,244	-3.8	1,256	78.4	0.0	3.4	11.2	6.9	24.1	25.4	48.1	47.5	13.0	553	75.0
Kellogg city	2,149	2,136	-0.6	2,390	89.0	0.0	0.0	7.1	3.9	29.2	13.0	33.1	45.2	13.1	967	94.3
Kendrick city	303	305	0.7	360	91.7	0.0	0.3	5.8	2.2	20.3	23.6	40.4	50.2	8.1	158	84.8
Ketchum city	2,715	2,855	5.2	2,791	86.2	1.0	1.0	0.0	11.8	15.9	19.0	44.6	15.8	59.1	1,110	100.0
Kimberly city	3,294	4,054	23.1	3,859	75.4	0.0	0.0	2.3	22.3	31.6	12.2	33.8	51.5	16.5	1,203	95.0
Kooskia city	649	664	2.3	561	86.3	0.5	0.5	6.6	6.1	19.3	28.2	55.1	57.8	13.5	245	80.8
Kootenai city	744	978	31.5	977	89.5	0.0	0.0	0.0	10.5	31.6	14.6	33.7	49.0	18.3	312	89.1
Kuna city	15,451	22,257	44.0	19,580	84.5	0.0	0.5	4.2	10.9	35.0	6.7	29.1	35.2	24.4	6,233	95.5
Lapwai city	1,128	1,137	0.8	1,229	13.0	0.5	1.2	78.7	6.6	29.2	13.9	32.9	35.2	16.0	365	85.2
Lava Hot Springs city	415	432	4.1	232	91.4	0.0	0.0	8.6	0.0	14.7	19.8	45.3	45.3	25.4	132	84.1
Leadore city	105	106	1.0	93	94.6	0.0	0.0	0.0	5.4	11.8	22.6	55.1	32.4	23.0	36	97.2
Lewiston city	31,891	32,788	2.8	32,664	91.3	0.4	0.8	3.4	4.1	21.3	19.0	39.8	41.0	23.0	13,502	88.9
Lewisville city	451	520	15.3	413	86.0	0.0	0.0	2.4	11.6	20.6	27.6	44.1	35.7	18.8	143	92.3
Lincoln CDP	3,647	-	-	3,817	84.0	0.0	0.0	2.3	13.7	42.9	4.8	26.8	29.7	39.0	1,177	97.2
Lowman CDP	42	-	-	4	100.0	0.0	0.0	0.0	0.0	0.0	0.0	0.0	0.0	0.0	4	100.0
McCall city	2,976	3,597	20.9	3,347	99.2	0.0	0.5	0.1	0.1	15.2	25.4	48.9	30.1	36.3	1,423	95.6
McCammon city	809	831	2.7	814	96.4	0.0	0.0	0.0	3.6	24.4	21.5	41.1	35.1	18.6	296	96.3
Mackay city	512	501	-2.1	467	96.6	0.0	0.0	3.4	0.0	11.1	26.1	42.7	59.8	23.2	175	81.7
Malad City city	2,101	2,137	1.7	2,081	95.8	0.2	0.0	2.2	1.8	24.9	24.1	44.5	43.0	13.1	835	95.2
Malta city	193	205	6.2	136	91.2	0.0	0.0	0.0	8.8	24.3	16.9	43.4	65.9	5.5	46	91.3
Marsing city	1,300	1,318	1.4	1,434	49.0	0.0	0.0	2.1	49.0	35.1	10.3	32.9	65.2	8.2	525	74.3
Melba city	506	558	10.3	576	67.4	0.3	0.0	2.4	29.9	36.6	11.8	31.3	55.9	9.4	177	91.5
Menan city	750	804	7.2	900	83.2	0.0	0.0	3.0	13.8	30.8	21.3	38.9	50.3	19.3	296	90.9
Meridian city	76,986	114,161	48.3	101,905	86.0	1.0	3.1	2.9	7.0	28.0	12.8	36.2	26.1	37.2	36,616	93.0
Middleton city	5,505	8,466	53.8	7,556	89.6	0.0	0.6	2.5	7.4	32.9	11.6	30.6	35.0	24.3	2,547	93.5
Midvale city	163	159	-2.5	249	100.0	0.0	0.0	0.0	0.0	27.7	22.9	36.1	43.9	21.0	92	94.6
Minidoka city	112	113	0.9	120	28.3	0.0	0.0	2.5	69.2	15.0	12.5	34.7	63.2	0.0	39	59.0
Montpelier city	2,596	2,538	-2.2	2,518	91.7	1.2	0.9	0.7	5.5	25.8	16.7	37.7	44.2	21.0	1,034	85.0
Moore city	189	170	-10.1	229	100.0	0.0	0.0	0.0	0.0	31.0	20.5	45.9	36.6	23.5	85	98.8
Moreland CDP	1,278	-	-	1,232	77.3	2.0	0.0	0.0	20.7	32.7	20.5	32.2	51.1	27.9	424	96.5
Moscow city	23,802	25,702	8.0	25,319	86.9	1.5	3.2	3.6	4.7	14.7	9.9	25.0	16.8	55.8	9,885	96.4
Mountain Home city	14,216	14,562	2.4	14,166	74.6	2.8	3.2	6.0	13.4	24.3	12.0	31.8	39.8	16.2	5,811	95.0
Mountain Home AFB CDP	3,238	-	-	3,009	65.6	5.8	6.9	5.2	16.5	29.4	0.1	22.5	23.4	21.2	902	100.0
Moyie Springs city	722	761	5.4	666	94.0	0.0	0.2	3.2	2.7	26.7	22.5	42.8	53.3	10.7	274	85.8
Mud Lake city	358	419	17.0	353	55.2	0.0	0.0	1.4	43.3	32.6	4.0	32.5	59.4	4.2	104	96.2
Mullan city	692	692	0.0	810	90.4	0.4	0.0	3.8	5.4	31.7	20.0	36.0	56.5	11.6	316	82.0
Murphy CDP	97	-	-	63	61.9	6.3	0.0	4.8	27.0	0.0	39.7	50.1	37.0	0.0	14	100.0
Murtaugh city	127	172	35.4	115	85.2	0.0	6.1	3.5	5.2	15.7	13.9	42.0	69.3	5.3	46	91.3
Nampa city	81,879	99,277	21.2	93,952	70.1	0.7	0.9	3.8	24.5	28.1	13.0	32.4	45.9	19.1	32,565	91.1
Newdale city	319	314	-1.6	295	86.4	0.7	0.0	0.0	12.9	23.4	13.2	37.1	41.3	13.3	106	95.3
New Meadows city	493	537	8.9	430	87.9	0.0	0.0	3.3	8.8	32.6	12.3	32.9	50.4	8.7	163	86.5
New Plymouth city	1,506	1,554	3.2	1,493	80.0	0.0	2.1	5.3	12.7	28.8	16.5	37.5	40.0	16.5	575	87.3
Nezperce city	469	458	-2.3	529	82.8	0.6	0.6	11.0	5.1	20.2	22.9	48.4	39.5	24.9	201	93.5
Notus city	592	638	7.8	712	52.4	0.0	0.0	6.3	41.3	30.5	8.0	32.5	52.1	8.2	217	94.9
Oakley city	767	812	5.9	821	79.3	0.0	0.0	1.1	19.6	42.5	14.3	28.5	49.2	16.5	236	91.9
Oldtown city	184	201	9.2	246	87.0	0.0	0.0	3.3	9.8	18.7	12.2	43.4	62.8	13.8	96	61.5
Onaway city	187	188	0.5	155	83.2	0.0	1.3	6.5	9.0	17.4	27.7	51.7	42.1	10.5	67	94.0
Orofino city	3,217	3,099	-3.7	3,109	86.7	0.6	0.4	5.3	6.9	15.5	18.0	40.4	45.0	15.0	954	83.6
Osburn city	1,555	1,556	0.1	1,593	82.1	0.7	0.0	4.5	12.7	21.7	19.6	43.6	52.8	8.4	650	87.7

1 May be of any race.

Table A. All Places — **Population and Housing**

STATE City, town, township, borough, or CDP (county if applicable)	2010 census total population	2019 estimated population	Percent change 2010-2019	ACS total population estimate 2015-2019	White alone, not Hispanic or Latino	Black alone, not Hispanic or Latino	Asian alone, not Hispanic or Latino	All other races or 2 or more races, not Hispanic or Latino	Hispanic or Latino[1]	Under 18 years old	Age 65 years and older	Median age	Percent High school diploma or less	Percent Bachelor's degree or more	Total	Percent with a computer
	1	2	3	4	5	6	7	8	9	10	11	12	13	14	15	16
IDAHO—Con.																
Oxford city	48	52	8.3	60	93.3	0.0	0.0	6.7	0.0	56.7	3.3	14.0	42.3	50.0	18	100.0
Paris city	513	521	1.6	629	84.9	0.0	0.0	3.8	11.3	33.1	18.0	34.7	52.8	10.9	241	84.2
Parker city	305	291	-4.6	243	94.7	0.0	0.0	0.0	5.3	14.0	14.8	40.5	41.7	19.9	93	84.9
Parkline CDP	-	-	-	30	100.0	0.0	0.0	0.0	0.0	0.0	66.7	74.3	13.3	20.0	21	81.0
Parma city	1,972	2,147	8.9	2,057	66.1	0.0	0.7	1.5	31.7	24.8	20.4	38.9	54.3	16.0	814	78.1
Paul city	1,181	1,449	22.7	1,320	62.0	0.0	0.4	4.5	33.2	25.5	21.2	38.1	57.2	19.5	484	86.8
Payette city	7,498	7,727	3.1	7,487	75.3	0.3	0.0	3.5	20.9	22.8	18.5	40.5	51.4	13.8	2,952	89.5
Peck city	191	196	2.6	141	93.6	0.0	0.0	2.8	3.5	17.7	28.4	52.5	44.5	15.5	64	81.3
Pierce city	508	590	16.1	554	94.0	0.0	0.0	2.3	3.6	24.2	29.2	47.9	44.4	15.8	246	87.0
Pinehurst city	1,619	1,626	0.4	1,346	96.4	0.0	0.0	2.7	0.9	20.4	25.6	49.7	54.7	10.7	613	84.5
Placerville city	53	57	7.5	50	84.0	0.0	0.0	0.0	16.0	10.0	36.0	57.7	46.7	17.8	25	100.0
Plummer city	1,044	1,029	-1.4	1,105	44.0	0.4	0.5	42.4	12.8	32.0	11.2	37.9	56.4	10.8	366	84.7
Pocatello city	54,236	56,637	4.4	55,525	83.4	0.9	2.1	4.6	9.0	24.5	13.2	32.5	33.4	30.3	20,747	92.7
Ponderay city	1,044	1,157	10.8	1,098	85.8	3.0	1.0	5.3	4.9	22.8	17.7	38.3	44.5	16.3	482	84.9
Post Falls city	27,787	36,250	30.5	33,225	90.9	0.3	0.8	3.0	5.1	28.8	13.6	33.9	36.1	19.8	12,481	91.2
Potlatch city	806	814	1.0	708	98.6	0.0	0.3	0.0	1.1	25.1	21.3	30.0	42.0	17.1	350	89.7
Preston city	5,264	5,557	5.6	5,376	84.7	0.7	0.0	3.9	10.7	25.5	16.4	35.8	60.7	12.5	1,965	90.6
Priest River city	1,738	1,893	8.9	1,923	94.3	0.0	0.9	1.9	2.9	23.1	22.9	43.8	57.8	10.0	818	83.1
Princeton CDP	148	-	-	115	100.0	0.0	0.0	0.0	0.0	26.1	16.5	46.9	56.5	43.5	56	100.0
Rathdrum city	6,839	9,150	33.8	8,284	90.4	0.1	0.7	4.2	4.6	28.0	15.3	37.7	40.1	13.9	3,052	95.9
Reubens city	65	64	-1.5	69	75.4	0.0	0.0	13.0	11.6	34.8	2.9	33.3	26.2	26.2	29	82.8
Rexburg city	25,490	29,400	15.3	28,414	86.3	0.2	2.1	3.1	8.3	24.4	5.3	23.2	14.0	40.1	8,359	97.4
Richfield city	477	496	4.0	479	79.7	0.0	0.4	7.3	12.5	28.6	13.2	37.8	48.6	9.7	161	87.6
Rigby city	3,944	4,292	8.8	4,117	77.6	0.0	2.1	7.0	13.3	32.8	9.4	27.0	29.9	22.3	1,464	95.2
Riggins city	405	416	2.7	258	96.9	0.0	1.9	1.2	0.0	5.0	45.7	62.6	31.4	21.6	139	56.1
Ririe city	659	681	3.3	505	87.1	0.0	0.0	2.2	10.7	30.9	8.5	25.8	49.4	12.1	178	91.6
Riverside CDP	838	-	-	1,149	90.2	0.0	0.0	0.0	9.8	36.4	17.1	27.9	48.4	18.5	323	94.4
Roberts city	589	637	8.1	530	50.0	0.0	1.3	0.0	48.7	32.8	11.5	35.5	75.7	10.2	184	83.7
Robie Creek CDP	1,162	-	-	1,312	89.2	0.0	2.7	1.9	6.2	12.3	13.8	55.2	36.7	38.9	560	97.3
Rockford CDP	276	-	-	229	68.1	0.0	0.0	0.0	31.9	30.1	28.4	35.3	47.8	24.3	57	100.0
Rockford Bay CDP	184	-	-	328	95.7	0.0	1.8	1.5	0.9	11.0	40.2	59.9	11.9	44.1	150	98.0
Rockland city	292	283	-3.1	246	99.2	0.0	0.0	0.0	0.8	18.3	32.5	57.0	34.2	31.6	101	100.0
Rupert city	5,591	5,893	5.4	5,796	52.7	0.0	0.0	1.9	45.4	28.7	16.4	30.5	58.4	11.2	2,098	88.3
St. Anthony city	3,570	3,553	-0.5	3,519	74.3	0.1	0.7	6.5	18.3	25.2	10.9	33.6	51.5	15.9	1,087	91.7
St. Charles city	142	153	7.7	140	85.7	0.0	8.6	0.0	5.7	30.0	19.3	33.5	36.5	9.5	56	85.7
St. Maries city	2,500	2,448	-2.1	2,924	95.1	0.0	0.0	2.6	2.3	23.8	17.0	38.4	52.5	14.4	1,170	86.1
Salmon city	3,142	3,169	0.9	3,096	93.0	0.0	0.0	2.9	4.1	21.4	24.5	42.5	48.1	18.0	1,351	81.8
Sandpoint city	7,467	8,931	19.6	8,386	90.3	0.2	1.0	2.9	5.5	21.5	18.9	41.5	33.5	31.8	3,378	87.7
Shelley city	4,410	4,466	1.3	4,372	82.9	0.0	0.0	4.6	12.5	35.4	12.5	29.1	42.5	19.4	1,354	94.2
Shoshone city	1,481	1,502	1.4	1,282	69.5	0.0	0.6	4.9	25.0	23.0	24.3	39.8	61.3	9.8	534	79.2
Smelterville city	620	621	0.2	738	89.3	0.0	0.0	4.7	6.0	19.0	21.3	43.9	59.4	4.6	324	87.3
Smiths Ferry CDP	75	-	-	101	100.0	0.0	0.0	0.0	0.0	0.0	57.4	71.3	14.9	15.8	42	100.0
Soda Springs city	3,054	3,023	-	2,966	91.0	0.0	0.1	4.2	4.7	32.0	14.8	34.4	41.7	22.9	1,075	91.0
Spencer city	37	32	-13.5	24	100.0	0.0	0.0	0.0	0.0	0.0	66.7	68.0	50.0	16.7	16	100.0
Spirit Lake city	1,935	2,533	30.9	2,319	92.9	0.0	0.0	3.6	3.5	23.3	15.0	40.2	47.5	14.2	897	93.2
Stanley city	62	69	11.3	69	100.0	0.0	0.0	0.0	0.0	0.0	10.1	27.5	4.6	73.8	17	100.0
Star city	5,841	10,532	80.3	9,115	87.7	0.3	0.6	3.2	8.2	27.6	14.0	36.4	28.8	30.3	3,407	91.1
State Line city	43	49	14.0	7	100.0	0.0	0.0	0.0	0.0	0.0	0.0	23.8	100.0	0.0	4	100.0
Stites city	225	232	3.1	214	96.7	0.0	0.0	3.3	0.0	9.3	24.3	58.1	57.5	8.1	110	75.5
Sugar City city	1,524	1,452	-4.7	1,567	82.7	0.4	0.4	2.6	13.9	39.6	5.9	23.6	31.2	29.3	383	94.3
Sun Valley city	1,410	1,486	5.4	1,353	90.8	1.4	1.1	0.9	5.8	3.9	42.7	61.3	17.2	64.1	550	96.2
Swan Valley city	199	245	23.1	109	100.0	0.0	0.0	0.0	0.0	8.3	26.6	54.3	12.6	42.1	51	100.0
Sweetwater CDP	143	-	-	239	36.4	0.0	0.0	63.6	0.0	41.8	11.3	23.8	26.8	18.8	56	91.1
Tensed city	123	121	-1.6	95	73.7	0.0	0.0	26.3	0.0	20.0	21.1	38.2	53.3	5.0	36	80.6
Teton city	733	740	1.0	1,054	68.7	0.6	0.0	0.0	30.7	36.1	13.1	30.1	53.8	11.0	344	83.7
Tetonia city	264	288	9.1	409	62.3	0.0	0.0	2.0	35.7	28.6	6.4	43.1	63.0	5.0	92	92.4
Troy city	860	895	4.1	739	98.1	0.0	0.0	1.4	0.5	31.1	12.3	34.1	31.4	33.5	275	93.8
Twin Falls city	44,320	50,197	13.3	48,951	77.5	1.3	2.6	2.4	16.2	27.3	13.8	33.3	39.5	20.5	18,438	92.2
Tyhee CDP	-	-	-	1,192	90.2	0.0	0.0	3.7	6.1	28.2	15.4	37.6	41.2	24.6	408	97.8
Ucon city	1,108	1,161	4.8	1,557	89.5	0.3	0.0	0.2	10.1	39.5	8.2	25.0	38.7	20.3	428	97.2
Victor city	1,923	2,503	30.2	2,216	72.3	0.0	0.0	0.0	27.7	27.7	4.6	36.6	25.9	42.9	714	87.4
Wallace city	787	782	-0.6	946	94.8	0.0	1.0	2.0	2.2	22.4	14.6	38.1	32.7	25.2	434	85.3
Wardner city	177	176	-0.6	189	94.7	0.0	0.0	5.3	0.0	22.8	17.5	46.1	45.1	9.7	80	96.3
Warm River city	3	3	-	-	-	-	-	-	-	-	-	-	-	-	-	-
Weippe city	462	444	-3.9	373	100.0	0.0	0.0	0.0	0.0	11.5	34.0	59.3	57.8	13.1	196	65.8
Weiser city	5,499	5,376	-2.2	5,323	66.1	0.0	0.1	3.3	30.5	25.8	20.2	40.2	52.5	13.8	2,101	81.7
Wendell city	2,783	2,714	-2.5	2,703	56.3	0.0	0.0	1.3	42.4	36.2	10.1	31.2	61.8	8.8	839	73.2
Weston city	437	470	7.6	564	98.9	0.0	0.2	0.0	0.9	36.3	11.9	26.8	49.2	13.8	169	96.4
White Bird city	93	95	2.2	53	100.0	0.0	0.0	0.0	0.0	0.0	54.7	67.5	49.1	9.4	45	66.7
Wilder city	1,533	1,823	18.9	1,770	24.3	0.0	1.8	5.5	68.5	32.9	10.9	31.6	75.6	3.3	501	82.2
Winchester city	340	443	30.3	288	89.2	0.7	0.0	5.2	4.9	17.0	30.2	52.8	42.9	16.1	132	84.1
Worley city	257	262	1.9	285	47.4	0.4	0.0	50.2	2.1	25.6	10.5	33.4	47.0	13.0	116	90.5
Yellow Pine CDP	32	-	-	246	100.0	0.0	0.0	0.0	0.0	0.0	34.1	49.6	0.0	13.0	59	100.0
ILLINOIS	12,831,572	12,671,821	-1.2	12,770,631	61.3	14.0	5.4	2.2	17.1	22.6	15.2	38.1	36.7	34.7	4,846,134	89.9
Abingdon city	3,286	3,051	-7.2	3,509	95.1	1.6	0.0	2.8	0.5	21.9	17.1	39.2	60.0	9.2	1,383	84.8
Adair CDP	210	-	-	205	100.0	0.0	0.0	0.0	0.0	8.3	19.0	54.3	71.8	9.0	104	73.1
Addieville village	252	238	-5.6	373	95.4	0.0	0.0	4.6	0.0	20.6	9.4	40.3	42.1	25.1	143	97.2
Addison village	37,084	36,482	-1.6	36,896	44.6	3.8	9.6	1.6	40.4	23.7	14.2	36.2	50.2	23.7	12,567	89.3
Adeline village	85	80	-5.9	105	93.3	1.9	0.0	0.0	4.8	20.0	23.8	54.2	57.9	5.3	43	83.7
Albany village	903	863	-4.4	906	93.2	0.0	0.0	0.4	6.4	20.0	29.8	47.4	50.5	16.1	395	88.1
Albers village	1,182	1,135	-4.0	1,341	84.5	0.0	0.0	7.4	8.1	35.0	12.9	35.1	32.2	39.4	444	86.5
Albion city	2,003	1,899	-5.2	2,113	93.9	1.8	0.6	0.9	2.8	26.9	19.8	39.9	47.1	15.6	954	83.2
Aledo city	3,648	3,432	-5.9	3,494	94.2	1.9	1.0	0.8	2.1	19.3	26.7	47.3	45.3	21.3	1,522	84.0
Alexis village	831	777	-6.5	853	94.3	0.0	0.0	4.3	1.4	26.3	17.1	38.0	42.6	10.1	355	89.6
Algonquin village	30,065	30,897	2.8	30,799	80.7	1.5	7.7	1.8	8.2	23.7	12.0	40.9	23.3	46.2	11,111	96.0
Alhambra village	681	650	-4.6	612	99.7	0.0	0.0	0.0	0.3	17.3	29.4	44.4	50.0	17.0	241	90.0
Allendale village	475	477	0.4	770	91.8	0.0	0.8	0.0	7.4	37.4	10.6	30.4	37.4	20.1	234	93.2
Allenville village	150	141	-6.0	153	81.0	0.0	0.0	1.3	17.6	26.8	17.6	34.6	52.5	6.1	57	86.0
Allerton village	288	266	-7.6	270	91.5	5.2	0.7	0.7	1.9	22.2	15.2	41.3	56.9	12.7	104	95.2
Alma village	321	303	-5.6	349	99.4	0.0	0.0	0.6	0.0	29.2	15.2	36.1	49.5	6.1	151	88.7

1 May be of any race.

Table A. All Places — **Population and Housing**

STATE City, town, township, borough, or CDP (county if applicable)	Population: 2010 census total population	Population: 2019 estimated population	Population: Percent change 2010-2019	Population: ACS total population estimate 2015-2019	Race and Hispanic or Latino origin (percent): White alone, not Hispanic or Latino	Race: Black alone, not Hispanic or Latino	Race: Asian alone, not Hispanic or Latino	Race: All other races or 2 or more races, not Hispanic or Latino	Race: Hispanic or Latino[1]	Age (percent): Under 18 years old	Age: Age 65 years and older	Age: Median age	Educational attainment of persons age 25 and older: Percent High school diploma or less	Educational attainment: Percent Bachelor's degree or more	Occupied housing units: Total	Occupied housing units: Percent with a computer
	1	2	3	4	5	6	7	8	9	10	11	12	13	14	15	16
ILLINOIS—Con.																
Alorton village	2,034	1,901	-6.5	1,847	0.8	97.7	0.2	0.4	0.9	30.9	9.4	28.1	65.9	6.8	638	78.4
Alpha village	669	635	-5.1	578	95.2	0.0	0.0	3.5	1.4	28.4	20.9	37.5	45.2	20.8	243	87.2
Alsey village	227	210	-7.5	143	97.2	2.8	0.0	0.0	0.0	15.4	23.1	52.8	70.4	8.3	74	70.3
Alsip village	19,271	18,709	-2.9	19,022	51.4	22.8	1.4	1.3	23.1	23.9	15.1	36.9	40.9	23.2	7,488	86.3
Altamont city	2,322	2,339	0.7	2,333	99.7	0.3	0.0	0.0	0.0	21.3	23.4	39.8	46.0	12.3	1,038	82.9
Alton city	27,932	26,208	-6.2	26,640	68.7	24.9	0.4	4.4	1.6	23.3	16.2	38.8	42.9	18.6	11,532	84.7
Altona village	529	497	-6.0	628	93.8	5.4	0.5	0.3	0.0	30.9	14.3	32.9	39.2	13.3	233	91.8
Alto Pass village	387	362	-6.5	302	65.2	0.0	0.3	0.0	34.4	17.9	18.9	47.3	47.2	19.7	115	79.1
Alvan village	270	249	-7.8	327	97.9	0.0	0.0	1.8	0.3	24.2	17.4	39.3	57.3	8.7	120	72.5
Amboy city	2,511	2,321	-7.6	2,421	95.1	0.3	0.2	0.9	3.5	26.3	17.2	40.4	47.2	16.0	996	89.5
Anchor village	146	140	-4.1	184	97.3	0.0	0.0	2.7	0.0	33.2	12.5	30.0	62.3	9.6	62	91.9
Andalusia village	1,170	1,148	-1.9	1,174	93.0	1.9	0.4	1.7	3.0	18.4	17.7	47.0	44.3	19.4	516	91.5
Andover village	578	572		534	94.0	0.0	0.0	0.0	6.0	27.0	20.2	43.2	53.3	16.7	202	77.7
Anna city	4,439	4,100	-7.6	4,185	86.9	4.5	0.7	3.7	4.2	22.2	22.7	43.2	50.1	21.9	1,616	73.6
Annapolis CDP	55	-	-	49	100.0	0.0	0.0	0.0	0.0	32.7	0.0	30.6	24.2	30.3	20	100.0
Annawan town	887	853	-3.8	908	89.9	1.7	0.0	2.3	6.2	24.8	18.1	40.1	40.3	24.3	401	85.8
Antioch village	14,475	14,175	-2.1	14,246	83.1	3.5	1.6	3.9	8.0	27.2	12.6	39.6	29.2	37.6	4,993	95.2
Apple Canyon Lake CDP	558	-	-	512	100.0	0.0	0.0	0.0	0.0	11.1	34.4	59.8	28.4	28.2	259	95.8
Apple River village	365	343	-6.0	365	92.1	1.6	1.6	0.0	4.7	29.0	10.7	32.4	54.9	14.0	154	88.3
Arcola city	2,914	2,831	-2.8	2,731	57.2	2.1	0.0	0.8	39.9	26.9	13.5	34.6	56.9	16.0	943	89.9
Arenzville village	409	367	-10.3	465	91.0	0.0	0.0	0.2	8.8	27.5	15.3	38.2	52.6	21.5	180	89.4
Argenta village	939	877	-6.6	1,115	95.3	0.2	0.0	3.7	0.8	29.1	15.6	34.8	41.6	16.9	398	88.7
Arlington village	193	181	-6.2	237	87.8	2.1	0.0	0.0	10.1	17.7	13.5	45.4	57.7	10.4	89	93.3
Arlington Heights village	75,185	74,760	-0.6	75,482	80.4	1.6	10.1	1.6	6.3	21.5	19.8	44.5	19.2	57.9	30,838	93.5
Armington village	347	323	-6.9	380	91.6	0.0	0.8	3.7	3.9	30.3	11.8	35.3	59.1	10.7	153	88.9
Aroma Park village	735	682	-7.2	740	90.4	2.2	0.0	0.4	7.0	15.7	20.1	46.5	54.5	11.5	278	91.4
Arrowsmith village	289	276	-4.5	332	97.6	0.0	0.0	0.6	1.8	27.1	16.9	38.0	46.3	15.8	114	86.8
Arthur village	2,282	2,200	-3.6	2,510	95.6	0.2	0.4	1.3	2.5	23.9	21.7	39.6	50.9	21.1	1,017	89.8
Ashkum village	764	693	-9.3	767	98.7	0.0	0.0	0.4	0.9	27.4	14.7	40.8	48.6	9.2	296	90.2
Ashland village	1,336	1,191	-10.9	1,379	95.6	1.5	0.0	2.0	0.9	20.5	18.5	44.2	53.7	21.0	574	86.2
Ashley city	536	490	-8.6	562	92.2	0.0	0.0	0.0	7.8	27.2	20.1	36.6	63.2	4.3	256	79.7
Ashmore village	785	749	-4.6	782	98.7	0.5	0.0	0.8	0.0	24.6	13.6	37.9	49.6	19.6	349	86.8
Ashton village	972	891	-8.3	948	89.1	1.7	2.3	2.4	4.4	21.0	16.7	43.9	52.3	12.3	415	88.9
Assumption city	1,174	1,066	-9.2	1,106	94.1	0.5	0.0	3.5	1.9	23.3	22.0	40.6	54.5	16.5	495	86.5
Astoria town	1,141	1,036	-9.2	993	97.9	2.1	0.0	0.0	0.0	28.8	17.7	36.8	57.0	9.8	405	73.3
Athens city	1,993	1,908	-4.3	2,120	93.6	0.2	0.2	3.9	2.1	30.8	11.5	35.2	36.0	22.9	825	90.2
Atkinson town	989	964	-2.5	1,248	95.7	0.0	0.3	2.2	1.8	28.4	17.3	38.2	52.2	13.2	472	86.2
Atlanta city	1,694	1,600	-5.5	2,063	98.1	0.1	0.3	1.0	0.5	28.3	16.1	37.7	48.3	14.8	800	91.4
Atwood village	1,221	1,158	-5.2	946	96.8	0.0	0.5	2.1	0.5	23.7	20.8	46.7	61.0	12.4	423	83.0
Auburn city	4,813	4,623	-3.9	4,697	94.2	1.1	0.7	0.8	3.2	22.1	13.9	36.9	48.9	22.3	1,786	89.5
Augusta village	587	543	-7.5	517	92.6	0.0	0.0	3.7	3.7	22.1	17.0	44.4	54.3	15.9	218	82.6
Aurora city	197,975	197,757	-0.1	199,927	35.6	9.9	8.8	2.3	43.4	28.8	9.1	33.9	43.5	31.2	63,568	93.4
Ava city	654	612	-6.4	524	94.7	0.0	0.0	3.6	1.7	21.4	20.2	42.5	55.1	6.7	240	85.8
Aviston village	1,968	2,136	8.5	2,149	97.5	0.4	0.2	0.4	1.5	21.2	14.9	37.9	36.2	28.2	786	92.9
Avon village	799	714	-10.6	614	99.0	0.0	0.0	1.0	0.0	16.3	22.6	47.1	51.6	7.8	304	87.8
Baldwin village	373	340	-8.8	317	98.7	0.0	0.0	1.3	0.0	29.3	12.6	39.1	59.5	6.2	123	82.1
Banner village	189	182	-3.7	221	89.6	0.0	0.0	2.3	8.1	20.4	22.6	41.5	54.0	13.0	97	88.7
Bannockburn village	1,490	1,506	1.1	1,244	66.9	12.6	9.6	2.7	8.1	12.5	11.2	22.8	4.4	78.2	205	100.0
Bardolph village	251	232	-7.6	289	100.0	0.0	0.0	0.0	0.0	19.4	8.0	39.5	61.3	6.5	118	72.0
Barrington village	10,320	10,217		10,290	84.0	1.6	5.2	1.8	7.5	26.0	19.3	41.9	14.0	68.5	3,906	94.9
Barrington Hills village	4,231	4,190		4,070	85.6	0.3	12.0	0.5	1.7	20.2	26.1	52.8	11.8	71.8	1,463	94.5
Barry city	1,318	1,247	-5.4	1,543	97.7	0.3	0.0	1.4	0.6	25.9	19.8	37.7	49.8	14.2	620	82.1
Bartelso village	602	610	1.3	619	99.0	0.0	0.3	0.0	0.6	28.1	12.6	37.7	40.3	30.2	220	87.7
Bartlett village	41,236	40,647	-1.4	41,120	66.8	2.0	15.9	2.5	12.7	23.8	12.8	39.7	27.0	44.2	13,726	94.4
Bartonville village	6,481	6,113	-5.7	6,249	95.1	1.0	0.5	2.4	1.0	21.7	17.0	42.4	47.9	12.8	2,607	90.1
Basco village	98	89	-9.2	90	92.2	2.2	0.0	2.2	3.3	17.8	16.7	54.5	44.6	10.8	46	56.5
Batavia city	26,238	26,420	0.7	26,250	84.2	2.8	1.5	3.4	8.0	24.4	14.7	40.3	20.7	50.5	9,834	92.6
Batchtown village	214	198	-7.5	185	100.0	0.0	0.0	0.0	0.0	23.2	24.9	45.2	56.2	16.8	67	80.6
Bath village	333	308	-7.5	279	95.3	0.0	0.0	4.7	0.0	16.5	24.7	46.3	76.1	0.9	127	86.6
Baylis village	205	196	-4.4	144	91.7	0.0	0.0	8.3	0.0	27.8	19.4	31.8	64.9	3.1	57	68.4
Bay View Gardens village	380	412	8.4	395	92.4	0.0	0.0	2.0	5.6	19.7	14.2	40.2	59.6	9.0	172	88.4
Beach Park village	13,630	13,701	0.5	13,181	45.4	11.2	4.3	3.4	35.8	28.5	12.0	37.4	46.7	21.7	4,527	91.6
Beardstown city	6,165	5,446	-11.7	5,682	54.1	9.0	0.0	0.5	36.3	28.5	13.5	33.6	68.8	10.3	2,173	82.1
Beason CDP	189	-	-	192	99.0	1.0	0.0	0.0	0.0	32.3	1.0	40.2	100.0	0.0	81	91.4
Beaverville village	357	326	-8.7	355	91.3	0.0	0.0	0.6	8.2	23.4	21.4	43.8	62.2	6.9	148	84.5
Beckemeyer village	1,036	1,008	-2.7	1,242	89.1	1.9	0.3	0.3	8.4	23.8	21.1	38.7	51.2	10.9	483	69.4
Bedford Park village	589	604	2.5	614	61.7	0.0	0.0	0.0	38.3	23.5	15.3	37.5	33.2	35.3	208	88.5
Beecher village	4,341	4,427	2.0	4,527	95.3	0.2	0.0	0.7	3.8	22.2	16.0	41.9	41.5	23.9	1,664	95.3
Beecher City village	461	453	-1.7	389	98.7	0.0	0.0	1.0	0.3	26.2	15.2	38.4	59.0	11.6	165	70.3
Belgium village	396	367	-7.3	392	97.2	0.0	1.3	0.3	1.3	19.6	17.3	43.5	54.7	10.0	163	87.1
Belknap village	104	106	1.9	121	99.2	0.0	0.0	0.0	0.8	26.4	9.1	34.8	73.2	8.5	48	52.1
Belle Prairie City town	52	50	-3.8	61	100.0	0.0	0.0	0.0	0.0	29.5	16.4	40.4	39.5	18.6	27	88.9
Belle Rive village	360	350	-2.8	288	97.6	0.0	0.0	1.4	1.0	16.7	25.7	41.5	43.4	15.1	135	91.1
Belleville city	44,301	40,897	-7.7	41,585	66.2	25.2	0.4	5.0	3.2	22.9	14.6	36.9	34.3	24.4	17,570	88.4
Bellevue village	2,002	2,049	2.3	2,008	92.9	2.0	1.1	3.1	0.8	21.5	13.4	39.0	57.9	11.5	741	90.3
Bellflower village	359	344	-4.2	431	99.5	0.0	0.0	0.5	0.0	25.1	17.6	43.1	52.6	15.1	159	86.8
Bellmont village	276	267	-3.3	234	95.3	0.0	0.0	0.4	4.3	30.3	15.0	41.0	45.3	5.3	95	89.5
Bellwood village	19,055	18,672	-2.0	18,996	4.8	74.1	0.9	1.7	18.6	22.2	15.1	36.5	48.7	17.8	6,221	87.6
Belvidere city	25,652	25,143	-2.0	25,027	60.7	1.4	1.0	2.0	34.9	25.7	15.4	35.8	58.8	14.7	8,835	87.2
Bement village	1,728	1,667	-3.5	1,456	94.3	2.5	0.2	1.2	1.7	19.2	16.2	44.6	51.5	14.6	598	84.6
Benld city	1,556	1,422	-8.6	1,507	97.6	0.0	0.3	1.7	0.5	26.1	20.4	39.8	54.5	11.0	585	79.8
Bensenville village	18,348	18,044	-1.7	18,281	42.4	3.1	4.2	1.0	49.3	21.3	14.2	36.1	52.1	21.9	6,559	88.6
Benson village	434	409	-5.8	540	99.8	0.2	0.0	0.0	0.0	24.1	15.2	35.0	45.0	14.8	214	86.9
Bentley town	35	33	-5.7	19	94.7	0.0	0.0	0.0	5.3	21.1	36.8	58.3	23.1	30.8	8	87.5
Benton city	7,079	6,851	-3.2	6,971	93.7	1.0	1.3	1.1	2.9	21.5	20.9	40.0	44.8	20.4	2,816	83.2
Berkeley village	5,207	5,048	-3.1	5,116	29.0	29.2	2.4	1.8	37.5	21.0	15.5	38.7	53.6	19.0	1,781	86.8
Berlin village	176	174	-1.1	183	95.6	2.2	0.0	0.0	2.2	12.6	16.4	50.3	53.9	17.8	85	62.4
Berwyn city	56,653	54,391	-4.0	55,407	25.2	6.4	2.7	1.0	64.7	27.2	10.3	35.1	50.2	22.6	17,869	92.2
Bethalto village	9,516	9,210	-3.2	9,284	94.5	1.7	0.3	1.5	1.9	23.3	19.3	41.4	39.0	23.2	3,862	88.2
Bethany village	1,356	1,239	-8.6	1,251	96.6	0.0	0.0	1.0	2.5	20.3	25.6	50.2	45.1	15.7	607	80.6
Biggsville village	315	278	-11.7	351	98.0	0.0	0.0	2.0	0.0	16.2	26.2	45.4	52.9	19.1	152	88.2
Big Rock village	1,132	1,129	-0.3	1,236	93.7	0.6	0.0	1.6	4.1	20.1	22.6	46.9	34.5	25.2	423	92.4

1 May be of any race.

Table A. All Places — **Population and Housing**

STATE City, town, township, borough, or CDP (county if applicable)	Population				Race and Hispanic or Latino origin (percent)					Age (percent)			Educational attainment of persons age 25 and older		Occupied housing units	
	2010 census total population	2019 estimated population	Percent change 2010-2019	ACS total population estimate 2015-2019	White alone, not Hispanic or Latino	Black alone, not Hispanic or Latino	Asian alone, not Hispanic or Latino	All other races or 2 or more races, not Hispanic or Latino	Hispanic or Latino[1]	Under 18 years old	Age 65 years and older	Median age	Percent High school diploma or less	Percent Bachelor's degree or more	Total	Percent with a computer
	1	2	3	4	5	6	7	8	9	10	11	12	13	14	15	16
ILLINOIS—Con.																
Bingham village	83	80	-3.6	98	100.0	0.0	0.0	0.0	0.0	15.3	25.5	44.8	88.2	3.9	40	72.5
Bishop Hill village	128	122	-4.7	118	100.0	0.0	0.0	0.0	0.0	7.6	33.1	60.6	37.1	21.9	64	75.0
Bismarck village	579	530	-8.5	616	95.5	0.0	1.6	0.3	2.6	26.8	17.7	43.3	37.2	21.8	233	94.0
Blandinsville village	649	595	-8.3	752	93.5	1.9	3.9	0.8	0.0	18.8	17.3	44.3	51.5	10.6	305	86.2
Bloomingdale village	22,059	21,779	-1.3	22,027	69.9	4.5	13.6	1.7	10.4	19.1	20.6	41.8	31.8	37.3	8,525	92.8
Bloomington city	76,724	77,330	0.8	78,015	73.0	10.2	7.9	2.8	6.1	22.8	12.6	35.0	27.0	48.2	31,853	92.9
Blue Island city	23,701	22,899	-3.4	22,611	19.1	31.5	0.2	2.2	47.0	24.3	10.6	35.7	51.0	14.7	7,864	85.3
Blue Mound village	1,156	1,072	-7.3	1,148	89.3	0.3	1.2	8.5	0.6	29.0	18.7	36.1	57.2	14.3	428	86.0
Bluffs village	715	659	-7.8	839	95.7	0.0	0.0	0.0	4.3	28.6	18.4	37.7	58.1	12.8	294	92.5
Bluford village	691	669	-3.2	715	94.8	0.0	0.0	1.0	4.2	28.0	12.7	35.0	44.0	8.7	247	88.3
Bolingbrook village	73,365	74,545	1.6	74,431	41.4	17.8	11.4	4.0	25.4	25.2	9.8	36.2	33.1	38.0	22,921	95.7
Bondville village	440	431	-2.0	451	88.7	1.3	0.7	2.7	6.7	13.5	17.7	48.8	52.5	13.8	212	79.2
Bone Gap village	246	234	-4.9	158	91.8	0.0	0.0	8.2	0.0	28.5	17.7	39.3	31.1	8.7	64	75.0
Bonfield village	382	356	-6.8	437	96.8	0.0	0.0	0.2	3.0	23.6	18.3	42.3	42.1	14.4	161	85.1
Bonnie village	397	381	-4.0	384	92.7	0.5	0.0	4.9	1.8	24.0	21.1	41.3	50.7	16.8	159	83.0
Boody CDP	276	-	-	363	100.0	0.0	0.0	0.0	0.0	31.1	2.5	34.2	37.8	18.2	125	92.8
Boulder Hill CDP	8,108	-	-	10,262	64.0	4.3	0.5	1.4	29.9	27.2	14.8	33.6	46.8	18.0	3,221	95.2
Bourbonnais village	18,690	19,462	4.1	19,653	78.1	9.2	2.1	2.5	8.2	19.3	14.1	34.4	31.8	37.3	6,677	92.0
Bowen village	494	457	-7.5	543	96.9	1.8	1.3	0.0	0.0	31.9	15.3	33.8	52.8	15.5	178	82.6
Braceville village	793	759	-4.3	759	85.4	0.0	0.4	2.6	11.6	27.3	12.5	38.3	54.5	7.8	285	95.1
Bradford village	768	682	-11.2	723	96.7	1.2	0.0	0.0	2.1	24.6	19.4	42.6	52.8	11.3	305	88.2
Bradley village	15,895	15,314	-3.7	15,368	80.5	6.4	0.6	0.4	12.1	24.2	14.9	35.3	47.1	17.5	5,607	90.1
Braidwood city	6,220	6,186	-0.5	6,377	90.4	0.3	0.2	2.8	6.4	23.0	13.3	39.9	46.6	14.5	2,512	93.8
Breese city	4,442	4,483	0.9	4,787	94.9	0.0	1.8	1.5	1.7	21.8	17.0	39.4	29.6	24.1	2,074	86.2
Bridgeport city	1,909	1,705	-10.7	1,740	99.4	0.0	0.0	0.6	0.0	26.5	19.8	38.9	51.4	4.5	762	89.9
Bridgeview village	16,439	16,096	-2.1	16,124	66.5	3.5	5.9	1.3	22.8	23.5	15.3	36.2	53.9	18.8	5,548	84.8
Brighton village	2,253	2,131	-5.4	2,272	97.4	0.5	0.0	0.7	1.4	25.2	16.1	39.1	44.5	15.5	909	87.9
Brimfield village	868	828	-4.6	853	97.4	0.8	0.0	1.8	0.0	25.3	11.1	35.5	37.4	22.3	305	91.1
Broadlands village	349	337	-3.4	362	97.8	0.6	0.0	0.3	1.4	21.8	16.9	42.6	42.6	16.9	128	87.5
Broadview village	7,919	7,618	-3.8	7,755	11.5	76.6	1.3	1.7	8.9	19.3	17.1	41.5	43.5	20.1	2,942	85.3
Broadwell village	145	136	-6.2	175	93.1	0.0	0.0	2.3	4.6	15.4	12.0	45.4	44.5	15.6	74	90.5
Brocton village	322	293	-9.0	340	99.1	0.0	0.0	0.0	0.9	12.6	23.2	50.7	57.6	15.6	153	86.3
Brookfield village	18,974	18,310	-3.5	18,735	68.4	5.2	2.1	1.4	22.9	26.1	13.2	39.4	27.1	44.4	7,038	91.6
Brooklyn village	749	698	-6.8	439	7.3	89.1	0.0	1.8	1.8	16.9	25.7	57.1	54.9	10.2	190	75.8
Brookport city	980	826	-15.7	881	86.8	10.0	0.2	1.6	1.4	15.1	17.9	44.3	59.5	6.6	415	61.0
Broughton village	192	186	-3.1	123	100.0	0.0	0.0	0.0	0.0	18.7	21.1	48.8	61.2	11.8	59	72.9
Browning village	137	123	-10.2	138	89.1	7.2	0.0	3.6	0.0	29.0	25.4	37.2	52.2	13.0	44	95.5
Browns village	134	129	-3.7	146	97.3	0.0	0.0	2.7	0.0	14.4	19.9	51.9	45.3	6.8	69	88.4
Brownstown village	757	727	-4.0	895	99.4	0.0	0.0	0.6	0.0	26.7	16.2	35.1	67.8	10.9	326	72.4
Brussels village	141	131	-7.1	132	98.5	0.0	0.0	0.0	1.5	9.8	19.7	43.6	55.0	11.7	40	75.0
Bryant village	222	213	-4.1	246	94.7	0.0	0.0	5.3	0.0	23.6	14.2	44.5	56.6	10.1	101	92.1
Buckingham village	300	278	-7.3	282	94.7	0.0	1.1	0.0	4.3	25.5	16.3	41.5	49.0	9.7	85	92.9
Buckley village	608	542	-10.9	517	92.1	1.7	0.0	0.0	6.2	18.2	24.0	45.8	57.0	13.0	261	72.4
Buckner village	460	440	-4.3	391	96.2	0.0	0.0	3.1	0.8	16.6	21.7	44.4	48.9	9.4	186	80.1
Buda village	538	501	-6.9	620	92.7	0.0	5.5	0.0	1.8	24.7	12.4	39.5	64.2	8.9	236	78.0
Buffalo village	499	480	-3.8	420	96.9	0.0	1.7	1.2	0.2	24.5	16.7	40.4	52.7	15.1	191	92.1
Buffalo Grove village	41,503	40,494	-2.4	41,062	67.9	1.6	21.0	2.6	6.8	23.0	14.5	41.7	13.4	66.1	15,399	95.6
Bull Valley village	1,111	1,084	-2.4	1,156	84.2	1.6	6.0	2.4	5.9	18.1	25.2	52.3	18.6	55.4	435	97.9
Bulpitt village	222	201	-9.5	214	97.2	0.0	0.0	0.0	2.8	25.2	14.0	37.2	58.8	5.9	75	88.0
Buncombe village	203	203	0.0	242	95.0	0.0	0.4	0.4	4.1	34.7	11.6	26.2	45.9	14.8	83	66.3
Bunker Hill city	1,787	1,687	-5.6	1,711	95.0	0.8	0.1	1.1	3.0	20.9	15.8	42.4	54.2	15.1	719	87.6
Burbank city	28,925	28,289	-2.2	28,729	60.1	2.9	1.6	1.7	33.8	24.0	14.5	37.8	55.3	15.4	9,225	87.0
Bureau Junction village	321	300	-6.5	240	99.2	0.0	0.0	0.4	0.4	25.4	12.1	36.3	73.0	3.3	81	91.4
Burlington village	624	620	-0.6	681	95.0	0.0	0.0	0.6	4.4	17.8	15.0	41.1	37.6	33.0	241	88.8
Burnham village	4,206	4,088	-2.8	4,158	13.0	61.8	0.0	0.5	24.7	25.1	14.4	37.5	43.9	15.8	1,450	89.4
Burnt Prairie village	52	48	-7.7	44	95.5	0.0	0.0	4.5	0.0	29.5	38.6	30.7	75.9	0.0	19	84.2
Burr Ridge village	10,535	10,758	2.1	10,763	75.2	1.0	17.6	2.3	4.0	19.7	26.6	51.5	11.6	70.0	4,244	97.0
Bush village	275	267	-2.9	208	95.7	1.9	0.0	1.4	1.0	11.5	21.2	53.5	49.2	6.8	86	82.6
Bushnell city	3,111	2,866	-7.9	2,775	97.5	1.2	0.0	0.4	0.9	20.8	14.9	41.5	51.6	14.7	1,080	83.0
Butler village	175	165	-5.7	262	100.0	0.0	0.0	0.0	0.0	30.5	17.2	35.9	60.1	4.0	98	83.7
Byron city	3,834	3,668	-4.3	3,611	90.4	0.6	0.8	2.5	5.7	26.3	16.7	35.9	32.9	31.2	1,476	94.1
Cabery village	266	246	-7.5	220	94.5	0.0	0.0	0.9	4.5	26.4	17.7	41.1	53.7	11.4	91	81.3
Cahokia village	15,238	13,880	-8.9	14,162	35.1	58.8	2.9	2.3	0.9	29.2	10.2	33.9	58.7	10.6	4,932	85.3
Cairo city	2,831	2,082	-26.5	2,120	28.6	66.8	0.0	3.7	0.8	24.5	18.3	37.9	54.5	15.0	813	67.7
Caledonia village	199	193	-3.0	206	85.9	0.0	7.8	0.0	6.3	24.3	7.8	39.6	27.1	33.1	80	98.8
Calhoun village	172	166	-3.5	135	100.0	0.0	0.0	0.0	0.0	11.9	19.3	43.8	29.1	9.7	62	93.5
Calumet City city	37,116	35,913	-3.2	36,551	9.5	74.3	0.0	0.5	15.6	23.6	13.1	37.1	44.1	17.9	13,788	84.9
Calumet Park village	7,831	7,602	-2.9	8,208	2.4	86.9	0.0	2.6	8.1	19.1	16.6	42.8	42.1	17.5	3,260	88.5
Camargo village	445	447	0.4	565	99.3	0.0	0.0	0.0	0.7	18.9	22.3	49.8	43.0	20.7	207	87.0
Cambria village	1,229	1,463	19.0	1,239	80.6	3.7	3.3	6.3	6.1	32.3	12.3	33.3	49.3	13.9	479	74.5
Cambridge village	2,163	2,078	-3.9	2,203	92.9	2.4	0.2	3.0	1.5	19.5	18.8	43.0	44.3	18.0	823	89.7
Camden village	86	78	-9.3	86	100.0	0.0	0.0	0.0	0.0	30.2	30.2	46.5	65.0	10.0	37	70.3
Campbell Hill village	336	310	-7.7	374	97.1	0.0	0.0	2.9	0.0	27.0	18.2	38.5	37.3	22.5	154	89.0
Camp Point village	1,136	1,093	-3.8	1,054	98.3	0.0	0.4	1.3	0.0	24.1	19.3	37.9	53.7	13.4	401	86.0
Campton Hills village	11,065	11,091	0.2	11,105	91.6	1.4	2.3	1.9	2.8	28.8	12.9	40.7	11.8	60.5	3,446	98.7
Campus village	166	157	-5.4	151	100.0	0.0	0.0	0.0	0.0	22.5	12.6	42.9	47.8	13.0	61	96.7
Candlewick Lake CDP	-	-	-	4,734	72.6	7.0	0.7	1.6	18.1	27.5	10.9	32.8	49.0	25.2	1,488	98.4
Canton city	14,715	13,506	-8.2	13,682	84.0	8.6	0.1	1.9	5.5	17.6	19.6	40.4	44.2	16.4	5,064	86.3
Cantrall village	139	133	-4.3	128	96.1	0.0	0.0	3.1	0.8	18.0	18.0	49.4	34.8	23.6	55	90.9
Capron village	1,376	1,362		1,578	54.1	0.1	0.0	1.6	44.2	29.6	10.1	33.2	65.0	11.9	480	93.8
Carbon Cliff village	2,079	1,957	-5.9	1,859	77.0	16.1	0.6	0.8	5.5	25.3	17.9	31.6	48.2	12.1	827	82.5
Carbondale city	26,414	25,083	-5.0	25,597	58.2	26.7	5.7	4.0	5.4	13.5	8.9	24.4	20.3	44.5	10,492	92.9
Carbon Hill village	345	335	-2.9	322	90.7	0.0	0.0	0.6	8.7	28.3	15.5	36.8	54.6	14.0	127	93.7
Carlinville city	5,917	5,481	-7.4	5,540	90.3	4.0	0.1	2.4	3.2	22.8	19.0	35.9	47.1	24.1	2,104	90.0
Carlock village	552	557	0.9	579	83.4	10.5	0.2	3.5	2.4	39.4	9.2	30.7	43.4	24.1	198	91.4
Carlyle city	3,299	3,186	-3.4	3,383	93.2	1.5	0.0	2.9	2.5	15.8	17.1	42.4	43.8	28.1	1,370	90.1
Carmi city	5,244	4,811	-8.3	4,808	95.5	1.2	1.4	0.9	1.0	20.9	22.9	42.7	50.2	15.5	2,148	83.0
Carol Stream village	39,541	39,203	-0.9	39,726	57.0	6.8	19.0	1.6	15.5	22.5	13.0	38.4	30.5	39.9	13,974	94.9
Carpentersville village	37,669	37,254	-1.1	37,872	32.4	8.8	7.6	1.4	49.7	31.7	7.4	30.0	51.7	19.5	10,722	95.2
Carrier Mills village	1,653	1,552	-6.1	1,827	82.6	8.7	0.0	4.2	4.5	27.5	20.4	38.4	51.4	10.0	705	78.3
Carrollton city	2,484	2,398	-3.5	2,544	93.6	0.6	0.0	3.1	2.8	19.5	16.2	39.3	47.6	13.4	991	83.2
Carterville city	5,555	5,847	5.3	5,868	85.3	4.9	1.3	2.5	6.1	22.9	16.1	37.3	23.1	48.2	2,502	91.9

1 May be of any race.

Table A. All Places — **Population and Housing**

STATE City, town, township, borough, or CDP (county if applicable)	Population: 2010 census total population	Population: 2019 estimated population	Population: Percent change 2010-2019	Population: ACS total population estimate 2015-2019	Race and Hispanic or Latino origin (percent): White alone, not Hispanic or Latino	Black alone, not Hispanic or Latino	Asian alone, not Hispanic or Latino	All other races or 2 or more races, not Hispanic or Latino	Hispanic or Latino[1]	Age (percent): Under 18 years old	Age 65 years and older	Median age	Educational attainment of persons age 25 and older: Percent High school diploma or less	Percent Bachelor's degree or more	Occupied housing units: Total	Percent with a computer
	1	2	3	4	5	6	7	8	9	10	11	12	13	14	15	16
ILLINOIS—Con.																
Carthage city	2,609	2,457	-5.8	2,363	95.3	0.6	0.5	1.1	2.7	19.6	23.5	44.7	35.6	31.5	1,071	80.2
Cary village	18,341	18,067	-1.5	17,936	83.2	2.0	1.4	2.4	10.9	23.0	12.3	40.5	21.5	45.0	6,424	97.2
Casey city	2,786	2,620	-6.0	2,756	96.2	0.4	0.2	1.3	1.8	22.0	22.8	38.0	53.0	14.6	1,214	86.3
Caseyville village	4,211	4,110	-2.4	4,179	81.3	7.7	0.0	4.1	6.8	29.2	13.1	36.1	49.8	16.0	1,445	90.8
Catlin village	2,044	1,926	-5.8	2,086	96.5	0.0	0.0	0.3	3.3	18.6	22.0	43.0	42.7	24.7	956	86.5
Cave-In-Rock village	318	280	-11.9	273	79.9	0.0	1.5	17.9	0.7	27.8	11.7	34.8	76.9	2.2	66	78.8
Cedar Point village	275	256	-6.9	247	92.7	0.0	0.0	0.0	7.3	21.5	23.9	42.4	63.0	5.8	117	86.3
Cedarville village	742	689	-7.1	652	94.5	0.0	0.0	0.6	4.9	16.3	22.2	48.6	46.7	16.8	296	79.4
Central City village	1,172	1,115	-4.9	1,256	95.5	0.0	0.0	1.0	3.5	26.6	11.9	35.2	45.3	9.4	525	90.3
Centralia city	13,029	12,210	-6.3	12,356	81.4	9.7	1.1	3.9	3.8	24.2	20.9	41.2	44.9	16.0	5,439	83.2
Centreville city	5,327	4,897	-8.1	4,999	4.6	93.2	0.2	2.0	0.0	28.7	20.9	39.3	58.4	7.8	2,150	76.3
Cerro Gordo village	1,430	1,347	-5.8	1,501	98.3	0.1	0.0	1.5	0.1	27.8	17.3	34.6	47.9	20.6	569	84.7
Chadwick village	551	516	-6.4	519	93.4	0.0	0.0	2.3	4.2	18.9	28.7	49.6	49.1	15.4	240	90.0
Champaign city	81,246	88,909	9.4	87,636	59.2	18.4	13.2	2.9	6.3	16.5	9.9	27.4	23.8	49.5	34,636	94.7
Chandlerville village	557	494	-11.3	372	91.1	0.0	0.0	5.9	3.0	22.3	19.6	45.2	56.9	8.7	181	87.8
Channahon village	12,578	13,239	5.3	12,833	87.1	1.0	0.3	1.1	10.6	27.6	13.8	37.8	28.4	28.9	4,279	97.5
Channel Lake CDP	1,664	-	-	1,661	84.3	0.0	1.1	5.8	8.8	22.3	19.6	44.0	45.7	23.0	683	87.6
Chapin village	512	478	-6.6	468	95.3	0.0	0.0	0.0	4.7	23.7	16.9	30.9	48.2	14.2	176	92.6
Charleston city	21,844	20,117	-7.9	20,464	83.5	8.0	2.6	2.1	3.8	14.4	10.4	26.5	32.6	34.7	7,814	91.8
Chatham village	11,732	13,008	10.9	13,072	93.7	1.4	1.1	1.6	2.1	28.0	12.0	35.7	18.7	48.2	4,849	95.9
Chatsworth town	1,212	1,115	-8.0	1,220	83.9	0.0	0.5	3.5	12.0	26.5	15.1	34.9	67.6	10.2	495	85.5
Chebanse village	1,065	971	-8.8	1,291	81.5	6.7	0.0	3.7	8.1	29.1	11.6	34.5	31.6	20.3	501	94.8
Chemung CDP	308	-	-	665	8.0	0.0	0.0	0.0	92.0	45.0	5.6	32.1	97.9	0.0	181	87.8
Chenoa city	1,785	1,723	-3.5	1,997	91.0	1.9	0.7	1.8	4.7	22.9	18.6	41.3	49.5	21.2	790	94.6
Cherry village	486	453	-6.8	403	96.8	0.0	0.0	0.0	3.2	21.1	18.1	43.5	59.7	12.6	171	94.2
Cherry Valley village	2,970	2,877	-3.1	2,614	83.9	1.1	8.1	1.7	5.2	15.1	26.2	53.6	46.8	23.5	1,171	84.6
Chester city	8,586	8,213	-4.3	8,343	67.3	25.4	0.4	0.6	6.2	10.8	15.2	41.0	66.4	9.2	2,172	74.8
Chesterfield village	188	177	-5.9	215	96.3	0.9	0.0	0.0	2.8	30.2	6.5	31.9	49.3	12.3	77	94.8
Chestnut CDP	246	-	-	61	100.0	0.0	0.0	0.0	0.0	19.7	11.5	48.1	41.0	0.0	40	65.0
Chicago city	2,695,652	2,693,976	-0.1	2,709,534	33.3	29.2	6.5	2.2	28.8	20.9	12.4	34.6	37.4	39.5	1,066,829	87.9
Chicago Heights city	30,367	29,322	-3.4	29,856	19.4	38.4	0.1	3.3	38.7	27.3	13.8	33.8	50.1	16.3	9,939	79.1
Chicago Ridge village	14,304	13,928	-2.6	14,153	72.3	11.2	2.5	0.4	13.7	24.7	13.8	34.8	49.6	17.4	5,237	82.3
Chillicothe city	6,095	6,012	-1.4	6,218	86.8	0.8	1.9	5.0	5.5	27.1	19.7	40.0	47.2	20.5	2,496	89.8
Chrisman city	1,383	1,265	-8.5	1,452	99.3	0.3	0.3	0.1	0.0	17.4	27.1	51.6	45.3	18.1	604	83.8
Christopher city	2,847	2,717	-4.6	2,718	97.0	0.6	0.6	0.8	1.0	26.0	18.8	36.4	39.8	14.6	1,140	82.2
Cicero town	84,241	80,796	-4.1	82,330	6.3	3.0	0.6	0.4	89.7	28.8	7.9	30.5	69.5	9.0	22,346	85.9
Cisco village	256	242	-5.5	263	94.3	0.4	0.0	5.3	0.0	18.3	17.1	41.8	57.4	14.2	114	90.4
Cisne village	681	660	-3.1	536	92.2	0.2	0.0	2.2	5.4	11.4	32.1	55.0	50.0	9.3	271	76.0
Cissna Park village	864	779	-9.8	818	92.1	0.0	0.0	5.6	2.3	19.7	35.1	54.3	49.9	22.7	388	78.6
Claremont village	174	170	-2.3	207	99.0	0.0	1.0	0.0	0.0	29.0	13.0	35.0	44.0	8.5	77	85.7
Clarendon Hills village	8,431	8,752	3.8	8,716	79.9	0.7	8.6	2.5	8.4	32.7	12.4	38.3	12.5	76.4	3,231	94.0
Clay City village	964	911	-5.5	865	98.5	1.5	0.0	0.0	0.0	25.7	15.8	31.3	49.8	13.0	372	82.0
Clayton village	707	673	-4.8	582	99.0	0.0	0.0	0.3	0.7	26.1	19.1	40.3	64.2	6.9	281	72.6
Clear Lake village	223	220	-1.3	305	98.4	0.0	0.0	1.6	0.0	17.0	16.1	38.5	54.0	14.6	116	78.4
Cleveland village	190	182	-4.2	285	97.9	0.4	0.7	0.0	1.1	28.4	14.4	39.6	55.1	7.6	100	89.0
Clifton village	1,469	1,321	-10.1	1,326	94.8	0.0	0.8	2.6	1.8	27.5	14.1	39.4	37.4	23.0	508	91.3
Clinton city	7,397	6,857	-7.3	7,062	93.0	1.2	0.1	1.3	4.5	23.4	19.9	39.5	49.4	15.8	2,998	86.9
Coal City village	5,695	5,409	-5.0	5,294	92.1	1.1	0.4	2.3	4.1	26.2	11.6	35.9	38.1	18.6	2,100	93.8
Coalton village	304	286	-5.9	342	97.4	0.0	0.0	2.6	0.0	20.8	16.4	46.3	66.3	9.2	131	84.0
Coal Valley village	3,733	3,723	-0.3	3,714	93.3	0.2	0.6	0.3	5.7	19.7	21.1	48.4	40.6	28.4	1,618	92.9
Coatsburg village	147	142	-3.4	182	100.0	0.0	0.0	0.0	0.0	16.5	19.2	39.0	54.7	8.6	77	87.0
Cobden village	1,145	1,064	-7.1	1,054	65.2	0.0	0.0	1.6	33.2	17.7	16.3	39.3	49.2	20.1	385	63.9
Coffeen city	685	644	-6.0	603	97.5	0.0	0.0	2.5	0.0	20.6	21.6	37.8	59.2	3.8	286	83.2
Colchester city	1,390	1,288	-7.3	1,553	100.0	0.0	0.0	0.0	0.0	18.1	18.7	41.3	54.9	20.3	643	78.4
Coleta village	162	152	-6.2	196	98.5	0.0	0.0	1.5	0.0	29.6	11.7	28.0	48.7	9.4	67	80.6
Colfax village	1,059	1,013	-4.3	1,143	93.7	0.3	0.0	1.8	4.1	27.2	16.7	38.1	48.3	19.5	393	91.1
Collinsville city	25,654	24,395	-4.9	24,626	78.3	13.7	1.6	2.1	4.4	21.6	15.0	38.5	37.0	27.1	10,546	90.6
Colona city	5,153	5,120	-0.6	5,096	84.6	0.2	0.1	2.1	12.9	19.4	14.2	41.5	49.7	21.7	2,122	84.7
Colp village	210	210	0.0	295	44.7	34.9	0.0	7.5	12.9	33.6	5.8	36.1	45.7	5.9	114	86.0
Columbia city	9,698	10,513	8.4	10,752	96.0	0.0	1.9	0.9	1.1	25.9	16.6	40.0	21.4	48.5	4,248	93.6
Columbus village	99	96	-3.0	71	100.0	0.0	0.0	0.0	0.0	19.7	9.9	31.5	48.7	28.2	25	92.0
Como CDP	567	-	-	593	95.1	0.0	0.0	0.0	4.9	19.6	26.1	46.1	44.4	16.3	193	92.7
Compton village	303	283	-6.6	314	86.3	3.8	0.3	5.7	3.8	24.5	13.1	37.3	50.9	10.9	130	91.5
Concord village	167	154	-7.8	172	97.7	0.0	0.0	0.0	2.3	25.0	32.6	36.5	65.8	13.3	74	74.3
Congerville village	477	492	3.1	586	93.0	0.0	3.1	1.0	2.9	27.8	12.6	33.0	39.2	22.3	217	87.6
Cooksville village	189	179	-5.3	164	94.5	0.0	0.0	0.0	5.5	18.3	23.8	50.5	47.0	11.4	76	86.8
Cordova village	676	645	-4.6	752	98.3	1.3	0.4	0.0	0.0	20.2	23.1	45.2	41.3	19.9	327	90.2
Cornell village	486	455	-6.4	487	87.3	0.0	0.0	9.0	3.7	27.3	11.9	28.7	55.8	11.2	185	86.5
Cornland CDP	93	-	-	90	100.0	0.0	0.0	0.0	0.0	0.0	16.7	32.8	64.4	26.7	51	100.0
Cortland town	4,271	4,408	3.2	4,124	74.2	13.5	0.9	0.4	11.0	27.9	5.0	30.7	32.3	36.5	1,354	99.5
Coulterville village	945	895	-5.3	838	90.9	3.2	1.0	4.1	0.8	20.2	31.5	49.8	48.2	7.0	328	75.6
Country Club Hills city	16,783	16,482	-1.8	16,758	3.8	89.8	2.0	0.7	3.7	22.0	17.7	40.3	33.4	30.6	5,882	90.5
Countryside city	5,878	5,933	0.9	5,961	68.4	0.6	1.3	4.4	25.3	20.6	18.2	45.0	40.5	32.0	2,524	86.5
Cowden village	615	579	-5.9	525	92.2	0.4	1.3	1.7	4.4	27.0	18.7	38.7	59.7	11.6	213	88.7
Coyne Center CDP	827	-	-	982	89.3	0.0	0.0	9.1	1.6	18.3	14.0	46.6	53.8	13.2	318	97.5
Crab Orchard CDP	333	-	-	155	97.4	0.0	0.0	2.6	0.0	9.7	9.0	45.9	22.4	18.4	77	80.5
Crainville village	1,264	1,400	10.8	1,457	90.9	3.0	1.4	1.6	3.2	23.5	20.2	41.1	35.7	32.8	613	86.1
Creal Springs city	545	527	-3.3	506	99.6	0.0	0.0	0.4	0.0	21.3	23.5	40.8	52.5	2.3	240	56.3
Crescent City village	615	556	-9.6	555	98.4	0.0	0.0	0.0	1.6	17.7	22.9	45.8	55.1	19.1	247	85.4
Crest Hill city	20,800	20,376	-2.0	20,550	50.1	24.5	3.8	2.6	19.0	16.8	17.0	38.4	48.3	19.6	7,194	90.0
Creston village	667	647	-3.0	641	73.9	1.7	0.0	2.5	21.8	25.0	10.9	34.9	44.5	16.7	256	87.5
Crestwood village	10,948	10,706	-2.2	10,831	80.1	6.6	3.2	0.3	9.8	12.6	27.0	47.9	42.3	21.9	4,882	87.4
Crete village	8,230	8,023	-2.5	8,118	52.6	34.9	0.5	2.8	9.2	18.5	21.4	46.4	32.8	36.9	2,914	93.9
Creve Coeur village	5,481	5,169	-5.7	5,213	95.6	0.6	0.0	2.6	1.2	18.0	11.6	36.2	53.3	6.5	2,027	91.8
Crossville village	750	689	-8.1	802	95.1	0.1	0.0	1.7	3.0	28.7	16.7	35.3	52.8	12.0	348	86.2
Crystal Lake city	40,752	39,829	-2.3	39,974	80.6	1.6	2.5	2.0	13.3	24.0	13.5	39.6	27.6	40.8	14,661	93.7
Crystal Lawns CDP	1,872	-	-	1,815	73.6	3.0	1.4	3.3	18.8	19.7	18.3	40.6	44.6	16.1	646	96.4
Cuba city	1,300	1,170	-10.0	1,133	97.3	1.1	0.0	0.0	1.6	20.9	20.4	47.1	61.6	13.0	424	81.8
Cullom village	566	522	-7.8	580	91.7	0.0	0.0	5.2	3.1	26.2	14.8	33.7	56.3	9.7	245	90.2
Curran village	212	207	-2.4	232	94.4	0.0	4.3	1.3	0.0	22.8	13.4	44.3	51.6	18.0	91	84.6
Cutler village	441	413	-6.3	373	96.5	0.3	0.0	1.6	1.6	22.3	18.8	39.1	60.1	4.8	160	83.1
Cypress village	234	235	0.4	220	99.5	0.0	0.0	0.5	0.0	24.5	17.7	37.8	62.3	8.9	98	72.4

1 May be of any race.

Table A. All Places — **Population and Housing**

STATE City, town, township, borough, or CDP (county if applicable)	Population: 2010 census total population	Population: 2019 estimated population	Population: Percent change 2010-2019	Population: ACS total population estimate 2015-2019	Race and Hispanic or Latino origin (percent): White alone, not Hispanic or Latino	Black alone, not Hispanic or Latino	Asian alone, not Hispanic or Latino	All other races or 2 or more races, not Hispanic or Latino	Hispanic or Latino[1]	Age (percent): Under 18 years old	Age 65 years and older	Median age	Educational attainment of persons age 25 and older: Percent High school diploma or less	Percent Bachelor's degree or more	Occupied housing units: Total	Percent with a computer
	1	2	3	4	5	6	7	8	9	10	11	12	13	14	15	16
ILLINOIS—Con.																
Dahlgren village	525	502	-4.4	607	100.0	0.0	0.0	0.0	0.0	23.2	24.5	46.5	46.3	15.9	257	80.2
Dakota village	507	468	-7.7	562	95.9	0.0	0.0	1.1	3.0	27.6	12.8	35.6	55.3	14.4	211	92.4
Dallas City city	945	872	-7.7	1,049	96.6	0.0	0.0	1.8	1.6	22.4	19.2	44.2	46.5	19.6	436	81.2
Dalton City village	546	501	-8.2	434	97.7	0.0	0.0	0.2	2.1	30.6	9.9	36.5	49.6	18.6	163	95.1
Dalzell village	716	659	-8.0	690	86.7	3.3	3.3	1.3	5.4	13.0	24.8	49.4	41.6	18.8	299	92.0
Damiansville village	486	489	0.6	581	70.7	3.1	2.6	2.6	21.0	22.4	12.6	31.9	44.2	17.5	205	82.4
Dana village	159	150	-5.7	107	86.9	0.0	0.0	0.0	13.1	25.2	12.1	43.8	51.4	10.8	44	93.2
Danforth village	605	552	-8.8	681	93.7	1.2	1.0	1.3	2.8	25.6	28.2	41.6	57.7	14.1	235	88.1
Danvers village	1,154	1,100	-4.7	1,044	97.7	0.5	0.5	0.6	0.8	26.7	14.4	38.6	33.7	31.5	401	94.0
Danville city	33,033	30,479	-7.7	31,246	56.3	32.5	1.4	2.8	7.1	25.5	16.8	36.4	51.9	15.4	12,064	79.5
Darien city	21,951	21,628	-1.5	21,884	74.9	4.0	12.0	3.4	5.7	18.5	21.9	46.4	20.5	50.9	8,857	92.3
Darmstadt CDP	68	-	-	-	-	-	-	-	-	-	-	-	-	-	-	-
Davis village	677	627	-7.4	551	98.9	0.0	0.5	0.5	0.0	23.2	21.2	47.6	48.5	19.2	241	89.6
Davis Junction village	2,362	2,344	-0.8	2,479	81.4	0.1	0.4	1.7	16.4	33.4	4.9	29.9	36.3	20.4	781	96.5
Dawson village	505	482	-4.6	649	91.7	4.6	0.0	0.6	3.1	23.4	11.6	34.2	57.1	13.2	259	84.2
Dayton CDP	537	-	-	566	93.1	0.0	0.0	0.0	6.9	17.0	16.3	50.8	39.3	14.9	251	84.9
Decatur city	76,131	70,746	-7.1	72,359	69.1	20.8	0.7	6.5	2.9	21.3	19.7	40.2	47.3	20.1	31,149	85.2
Deer Creek village	704	663	-5.8	601	99.3	0.0	0.0	0.3	0.3	23.8	16.8	35.8	38.1	17.7	267	89.1
Deerfield village	18,227	18,646	2.3	19,006	89.2	0.8	5.2	1.1	3.7	27.0	15.6	43.9	7.0	79.9	7,058	96.4
Deer Grove village	48	45	-6.3	43	100.0	0.0	0.0	0.0	0.0	4.7	44.2	62.6	43.8	9.4	19	73.7
Deer Park village	3,130	4,225	35.0	3,884	86.6	0.6	10.7	0.9	1.2	23.8	16.5	44.5	15.0	65.1	1,317	98.3
DeKalb city	44,123	42,847	-2.9	42,908	64.7	14.0	4.3	2.8	14.1	17.5	9.1	25.0	28.9	38.9	15,499	93.8
De Land village	446	425	-4.7	524	95.2	0.4	0.0	1.9	2.5	24.6	11.8	32.2	54.3	6.1	186	87.6
Delavan city	1,710	1,616	-5.5	1,751	95.7	0.5	0.5	1.1	2.1	21.1	17.4	43.3	51.5	17.0	730	82.6
De Pue village	1,834	1,683	-8.2	1,802	31.1	2.6	2.0	1.9	62.4	29.6	14.1	35.6	68.2	10.8	608	81.9
De Soto village	1,585	1,502	-5.2	1,697	85.9	0.9	0.6	3.4	9.2	25.0	14.5	36.9	43.2	19.6	662	89.0
Des Plaines city	58,383	58,899	0.9	58,673	63.1	2.0	13.2	2.5	19.2	19.3	19.1	43.3	34.5	38.2	22,327	90.8
Detroit village	83	81	-2.4	28	100.0	0.0	0.0	0.0	0.0	0.0	17.9	54.5	67.9	0.0	14	100.0
De Witt village	184	176	-4.3	215	97.2	0.0	0.0	2.8	0.0	21.4	14.9	49.8	56.8	16.0	98	84.7
Diamond village	2,535	2,506	-1.1	2,697	91.4	1.7	0.0	1.0	5.9	28.3	9.1	35.0	48.5	16.8	1,071	92.3
Dieterich village	617	595	-3.6	594	97.1	0.0	1.7	0.5	0.7	26.1	22.9	39.2	48.1	18.8	233	83.3
Divernon village	1,173	1,105	-5.8	1,153	96.8	0.0	0.8	1.3	1.1	21.7	18.5	39.5	45.8	16.3	498	91.6
Dix village	456	440	-3.5	437	91.5	1.1	0.5	5.0	1.8	19.5	24.7	48.9	54.2	11.1	232	75.9
Dixmoor village	3,584	3,563	-0.6	3,604	5.2	46.0	0.0	0.0	48.8	27.1	10.9	32.0	54.4	12.1	1,191	80.9
Dixon city	15,766	15,115	-4.1	15,433	76.9	11.2	0.5	1.8	9.7	19.0	16.3	40.6	44.4	17.8	5,699	86.4
Dolton village	23,074	22,348	-3.1	22,737	3.8	92.0	0.5	1.9	1.8	25.2	13.0	36.6	38.9	19.2	7,860	90.1
Dongola village	724	678	-6.4	837	94.5	2.9	0.0	1.1	1.6	33.0	13.1	28.2	51.8	8.4	297	52.9
Donnellson village	210	195	-7.1	164	93.3	0.0	4.3	2.4	0.0	16.5	20.1	48.0	65.7	2.2	82	74.4
Donovan village	304	274	-9.9	232	83.6	0.0	0.0	7.8	8.6	27.6	11.6	38.3	53.3	10.2	94	81.9
Dorchester village	151	138	-8.6	111	100.0	0.0	0.0	0.0	0.0	10.8	26.1	54.3	58.2	10.2	55	92.7
Dover village	164	153	-6.7	125	98.4	0.0	0.0	1.6	0.0	29.6	12.0	45.5	47.6	18.3	49	83.7
Dowell village	408	386	-5.4	428	96.5	0.0	0.0	0.9	2.6	17.8	13.8	35.2	65.4	5.5	171	83.0
Downers Grove village	48,882	49,057	0.4	49,470	84.2	4.1	5.6	1.4	4.7	21.8	18.7	42.7	18.0	56.3	20,303	90.2
Downs village	994	951	-4.3	1,010	92.9	0.8	0.4	4.1	1.9	27.2	12.8	34.7	32.1	42.1	356	93.0
Du Bois village	205	189	-7.8	158	93.0	5.7	0.0	0.0	1.3	10.1	27.2	55.2	53.3	5.9	78	80.8
Dunfermline village	313	283	-9.6	303	97.0	0.7	0.0	0.3	2.0	24.1	13.9	38.3	55.1	11.7	116	76.7
Dunlap village	1,500	1,448	-3.5	1,140	80.5	1.8	8.2	8.2	1.3	31.8	8.9	39.6	21.8	49.5	400	94.5
Dupo village	4,179	3,877	-7.2	3,938	91.5	5.1	0.0	0.0	3.4	22.8	18.2	40.1	56.4	13.1	1,739	90.1
Du Quoin city	6,108	5,670	-7.2	5,761	88.2	4.9	1.0	2.6	3.4	19.9	23.4	43.2	53.6	14.5	2,727	80.9
Durand village	1,455	1,394	-4.2	1,360	96.3	0.3	0.4	1.3	1.8	23.8	20.1	40.1	44.7	17.7	530	90.2
Dwight village	4,262	3,984	-6.5	4,096	93.6	0.3	1.3	1.3	3.4	20.1	20.0	43.5	55.1	18.4	1,720	83.3
Eagarville village	127	120	-5.5	175	85.7	5.1	1.1	8.0	0.0	30.3	14.3	32.8	44.1	16.2	63	88.9
Earlville city	1,702	1,587	-6.8	1,928	90.7	0.2	0.0	0.6	8.6	22.6	16.5	41.5	58.6	8.6	787	89.6
East Alton village	6,274	5,954	-5.1	6,061	91.4	4.4	1.8	1.9	0.5	21.2	17.7	39.3	49.3	17.5	2,755	87.4
East Brooklyn village	110	105	-4.5	76	93.4	0.0	0.0	0.0	6.6	2.6	26.3	57.8	49.3	11.6	38	92.1
East Cape Girardeau village	387	286	-26.1	442	89.4	8.8	0.0	1.8	0.0	29.2	16.5	38.8	61.9	16.9	130	53.8
East Carondelet village	504	473	-6.2	414	92.0	6.5	0.0	1.4	0.0	22.2	15.2	38.9	65.2	4.3	145	97.9
East Dubuque city	1,705	1,569	-8.0	1,706	95.9	0.1	1.4	0.7	1.9	21.7	21.3	45.7	49.5	22.7	790	86.2
East Dundee village	2,860	3,216	12.4	3,181	68.1	1.6	6.0	0.0	24.3	13.6	24.1	52.0	34.8	32.3	1,367	93.6
East Galesburg village	816	774	-5.1	615	96.6	0.0	0.2	2.1	1.1	13.7	23.4	50.9	41.5	22.8	305	86.9
East Gillespie village	270	262	-3.0	231	92.2	1.7	0.0	6.1	0.0	10.8	26.4	48.7	41.4	14.5	100	96.0
East Hazel Crest village	1,545	1,497	-3.1	1,586	26.0	53.2	0.6	0.9	19.3	17.1	17.7	45.0	46.2	19.5	584	87.5
East Moline city	21,311	20,645	-3.1	20,916	60.5	13.3	3.8	3.4	19.1	22.7	18.1	38.8	46.8	20.3	7,997	86.1
Easton village	321	287	-10.6	309	98.7	0.0	0.0	0.6	0.6	24.6	20.7	43.4	59.1	8.8	124	85.5
East Peoria city	23,454	22,546	-3.9	22,851	91.1	2.3	2.4	1.5	2.6	18.9	19.8	42.2	39.7	24.8	9,900	87.0
East St. Louis city	26,935	26,047	-3.3	26,543	1.9	96.2	0.3	0.7	1.0	24.3	17.7	37.4	55.0	12.1	10,945	68.9
Eddyville village	103	98	-4.9	98	100.0	0.0	0.0	0.0	0.0	20.4	16.3	40.7	40.8	1.3	54	81.5
Edgewood village	444	430	-3.2	492	98.0	0.0	1.0	1.0	0.0	20.7	17.1	36.7	66.7	4.9	205	84.4
Edinburg village	1,078	1,012	-6.1	1,091	98.4	1.6	0.0	0.0	0.0	23.3	19.3	41.3	45.4	14.6	456	88.4
Edwardsville city	24,410	25,233	3.4	25,171	80.8	11.2	2.6	2.7	2.7	20.3	10.5	28.3	19.4	54.5	8,461	97.2
Effingham city	12,340	12,511	1.4	12,563	91.8	1.0	0.9	1.5	4.8	23.4	17.2	36.7	43.7	22.3	5,336	85.7
Elburn village	5,596	5,997	7.2	5,629	75.9	1.9	4.0	2.5	15.8	32.4	8.5	36.6	20.9	42.3	1,869	96.4
El Dara village	78	76	-2.6	72	100.0	0.0	0.0	0.0	0.0	9.7	37.5	64.2	18.6	23.7	33	93.9
Eldorado city	4,148	3,910	-5.7	4,149	91.3	1.2	0.0	2.8	4.7	19.5	21.3	38.4	47.4	14.5	1,744	80.6
Eldred village	201	186	-7.5	186	85.5	0.0	14.5	0.0	0.0	8.1	43.0	62.5	68.8	9.4	102	47.1
Elgin city	108,219	110,849	2.4	112,653	40.9	5.7	5.7	2.0	45.7	26.5	12.2	35.0	45.4	24.5	36,903	92.9
Elizabeth village	766	722	-5.7	774	95.3	0.9	0.0	2.6	1.2	16.8	27.8	46.1	52.7	21.2	404	83.9
Elizabethtown village	311	273	-12.2	247	87.9	1.2	0.0	3.2	7.7	21.5	24.3	44.3	52.8	12.2	110	59.1
Elk Grove Village village	33,383	32,400	-2.9	32,942	74.6	1.6	9.6	1.9	12.3	18.6	19.1	43.5	30.2	36.0	13,261	91.8
Elkhart village	407	390	-4.2	482	96.3	0.0	1.2	2.5	0.0	29.0	18.5	36.8	28.5	40.1	192	90.1
Elkville village	928	863	-7.0	829	91.0	1.4	0.5	2.2	4.9	26.1	16.0	35.0	47.4	11.6	345	82.9
Elliott village	296	269	-9.1	270	100.0	0.0	0.0	0.0	0.0	17.8	27.8	47.4	53.6	9.3	137	80.3
Ellis Grove village	370	348	-5.9	245	99.6	0.4	0.0	0.0	0.0	23.3	15.9	48.4	55.2	9.2	121	75.2
Ellisville village	96	92	-4.2	105	99.0	0.0	0.0	0.0	1.0	26.7	20.0	42.1	67.2	4.5	40	75.0
Ellsworth village	192	198	3.1	270	98.5	0.7	0.0	0.7	0.0	24.4	15.9	34.4	56.0	11.3	95	85.3
Elmhurst city	44,136	46,746	5.9	46,463	82.7	1.2	6.0	2.1	8.0	26.2	15.2	39.9	18.0	59.9	16,209	93.8
Elmwood city	2,097	2,011	-4.1	2,367	97.7	0.0	0.7	0.9	0.7	26.4	16.1	40.7	39.2	26.2	859	90.3
Elmwood Park village	24,883	24,098	-3.2	24,468	60.4	2.5	4.4	1.4	31.3	21.1	15.8	39.9	40.4	26.9	9,017	90.1
El Paso city	2,813	2,730	-3.0	2,809	96.0	2.0	0.0	1.7	0.2	24.9	16.2	37.4	49.1	20.1	1,025	84.3
Elsah village	673	606	-10.0	697	87.7	5.3	0.7	3.7	2.6	1.7	7.3	20.6	12.0	77.4	71	88.7
Elvaston village	165	154	-6.7	167	92.8	6.0	0.0	0.6	0.6	24.6	18.0	46.5	56.0	1.8	71	85.9

1 May be of any race.

Table A. All Places — **Population and Housing**

STATE City, town, township, borough, or CDP (county if applicable)	Population				Race and Hispanic or Latino origin (percent)					Age (percent)			Educational attainment of persons age 25 and older		Occupied housing units	
	2010 census total population	2019 estimated population	Percent change 2010-2019	ACS total population estimate 2015-2019	White alone, not Hispanic or Latino	Black alone, not Hispanic or Latino	Asian alone, not Hispanic or Latino	All other races or 2 or more races, not Hispanic or Latino	Hispanic or Latino[1]	Under 18 years old	Age 65 years and older	Median age	Percent High school diploma or less	Percent Bachelor's degree or more	Total	Percent with a computer
	1	2	3	4	5	6	7	8	9	10	11	12	13	14	15	16
ILLINOIS—Con.																
Elwood village	2,278	2,226	-2.3	2,367	91.1	0.5	0.6	0.2	7.6	21.0	15.0	40.7	52.0	17.0	890	93.7
Emden village	485	460	-5.2	468	94.0	0.2	0.0	2.1	3.6	32.1	21.2	35.1	42.8	22.4	194	78.9
Emington village	117	108	-7.7	94	100.0	0.0	0.0	0.0	0.0	24.5	9.6	33.4	43.9	15.2	43	83.7
Energy village	1,142	1,109	-2.9	1,016	94.0	1.4	0.0	2.4	2.3	14.4	27.7	50.5	37.9	16.2	481	85.9
Enfield village	596	552	-7.4	521	95.6	2.5	0.0	0.4	1.5	21.5	21.3	44.9	59.2	3.6	206	73.3
Equality village	595	518	-12.9	458	100.0	0.0	0.0	0.0	0.0	12.9	29.7	54.3	61.8	5.0	248	80.2
Erie village	1,603	1,499	-6.5	1,496	94.6	0.0	0.5	1.8	3.1	26.9	16.4	41.4	43.5	21.6	611	89.0
Essex village	802	758	-5.5	907	92.0	1.4	0.4	4.3	1.9	28.1	14.6	37.3	47.5	13.2	290	90.7
Eureka city	5,342	5,283	-1.1	5,731	92.8	1.2	0.2	1.9	4.0	20.3	16.3	34.5	37.1	35.7	2,039	87.7
Evanston city	74,483	73,473	-1.4	74,587	59.2	15.9	9.4	3.9	11.7	20.2	15.6	36.1	18.5	67.1	28,352	94.5
Evansville village	701	647	-7.7	654	98.3	0.0	0.0	0.6	1.1	25.2	18.8	42.1	55.3	8.8	272	75.7
Evergreen Park village	19,848	19,147	-3.5	19,479	57.4	26.3	0.8	1.6	13.9	23.9	13.7	39.9	29.7	34.1	6,981	92.1
Ewing village	307	296	-3.6	279	99.3	0.0	0.0	0.7	0.0	15.1	23.7	50.3	34.0	14.8	124	90.3
Exeter village	65	60	-7.7	99	94.9	0.0	0.0	0.0	5.1	28.3	5.1	38.8	55.9	10.3	33	90.9
Fairbury city	3,813	3,622	-5.0	3,571	89.0	1.9	1.1	0.0	8.1	21.4	23.0	41.2	58.1	12.8	1,582	82.2
Fairfield city	5,150	4,936	-4.2	5,082	92.1	4.4	0.3	2.8	0.3	22.9	21.8	43.1	46.4	17.0	2,431	75.0
Fairmont CDP	2,459	-	-	2,699	28.2	38.9	0.8	2.3	29.7	25.8	10.0	31.3	61.6	11.2	824	87.6
Fairmont City village	2,629	2,453	-6.7	2,298	20.5	0.1	0.3	0.9	78.2	26.3	12.3	30.1	78.9	1.7	705	73.8
Fairmount village	642	596	-7.2	648	98.3	0.8	0.0	0.6	0.3	20.5	20.1	39.4	58.9	8.9	266	91.4
Fairview village	522	471	-9.8	461	93.7	0.0	0.0	0.7	5.6	17.4	25.2	45.8	39.0	21.9	211	83.4
Fairview Heights city	17,078	16,303	-4.5	16,125	56.6	32.7	2.6	5.4	2.8	20.6	15.7	40.0	28.6	34.4	6,926	92.4
Farina village	518	499	-3.7	612	96.6	0.0	0.0	3.4	0.0	27.3	27.5	41.5	62.2	9.7	226	78.3
Farmer City city	2,017	1,936	-4.0	2,185	95.6	0.0	0.0	3.8	0.6	22.7	18.7	44.8	42.3	19.3	922	88.6
Farmersville village	717	671	-6.4	687	91.0	0.3	0.0	0.6	8.2	25.6	16.0	38.3	55.9	16.2	298	91.6
Farmington city	2,442	2,223	-9.0	2,374	93.1	0.0	0.0	3.6	3.3	27.5	15.1	36.6	42.9	20.5	960	87.7
Fayetteville village	366	339	-7.4	379	82.6	0.0	0.0	0.0	17.4	27.7	14.8	36.9	56.3	8.0	148	82.4
Ferris village	156	143	-8.3	150	99.3	0.0	0.0	0.0	0.7	10.0	31.3	57.0	69.2	7.5	57	82.5
Fidelity village	114	112	-1.8	203	84.7	0.0	15.3	0.0	0.0	19.7	23.2	54.5	60.3	10.3	67	68.7
Fieldon village	239	218	-8.8	214	98.6	0.0	0.0	0.0	1.4	16.8	26.2	53.5	74.3	3.6	96	62.5
Fillmore village	330	310	-6.1	300	96.3	0.0	1.3	2.3	0.0	15.7	24.3	51.2	61.2	7.4	141	78.7
Findlay village	684	638	-6.7	702	99.0	0.0	0.0	0.0	1.0	21.4	25.1	47.3	51.4	11.3	323	85.8
Fisher village	1,870	1,937	3.6	2,097	95.8	0.3	0.3	2.2	1.3	28.7	14.9	34.1	41.4	21.0	752	89.8
Fithian village	485	449	-7.4	431	94.0	2.6	0.0	1.2	2.3	14.4	19.7	55.2	49.1	11.0	197	90.9
Flanagan village	1,114	1,064	-4.5	1,011	94.1	0.3	0.0	2.9	2.8	19.2	27.0	48.2	50.3	18.9	390	83.6
Flat Rock village	331	307	-7.3	378	98.9	0.0	0.0	1.1	0.0	23.0	16.9	42.0	45.8	14.2	176	74.4
Flora city	5,065	4,852	-4.2	4,917	92.7	0.6	0.3	6.3	0.1	24.2	19.0	41.9	54.6	15.7	2,093	85.4
Floraville CDP	53	-	-	29	100.0	0.0	0.0	0.0	0.0	0.0	100.0	0.0	48.3	51.7	14	100.0
Florence village	38	37	-2.6	66	100.0	0.0	0.0	0.0	0.0	21.2	4.5	48.2	55.8	9.6	29	65.5
Flossmoor village	9,440	9,155	-3.0	9,472	32.7	60.2	2.2	1.5	3.4	23.2	20.6	44.0	12.2	61.8	3,460	97.7
Foosland village	101	98	-3.0	70	97.1	0.0	0.0	0.0	2.9	27.1	25.7	36.5	70.6	3.9	29	75.9
Ford Heights village	2,772	2,682	-3.2	2,736	1.5	87.9	0.6	6.5	3.5	28.5	14.5	31.9	53.8	7.1	948	80.5
Forest City village	246	225	-8.5	283	99.6	0.0	0.0	0.4	0.0	34.6	12.4	32.0	55.7	13.2	100	93.0
Forest Lake CDP	1,659	-	-	1,327	90.4	0.0	3.7	1.0	4.9	22.5	8.4	42.5	22.0	50.9	541	100.0
Forest Park village	14,167	13,704	-3.3	13,927	53.7	27.9	6.0	3.2	9.2	13.3	15.9	39.5	21.5	50.2	6,996	89.5
Forest View village	698	666	-4.6	943	49.5	0.0	1.4	1.4	47.7	27.1	15.0	40.1	48.9	21.7	305	87.9
Forrest village	1,219	1,135	-6.9	1,058	86.6	0.7	0.0	3.2	9.5	22.8	16.4	38.8	61.2	8.5	451	94.9
Forreston village	1,438	1,341	-6.7	1,549	89.5	1.2	0.4	1.6	7.3	30.1	15.6	35.8	46.2	12.9	634	89.6
Forsyth village	3,487	3,479	-0.2	2,989	81.1	1.6	11.9	2.2	3.1	27.9	20.0	41.6	19.6	53.4	1,124	91.1
Fox Lake village	10,667	10,451	-2.0	10,721	87.1	0.8	1.6	2.0	8.5	18.4	20.8	45.2	43.5	22.4	4,637	89.5
Fox Lake Hills CDP	2,591	-	-	2,204	91.7	1.7	0.5	0.0	6.0	15.5	18.3	45.5	36.1	22.2	931	88.3
Fox River Grove village	4,771	4,573	-4.2	4,676	88.1	0.0	3.6	0.6	7.7	19.7	9.8	37.9	15.9	53.1	1,822	98.0
Frankfort village	17,808	19,373	8.8	18,999	81.8	8.1	3.5	1.3	5.3	28.2	15.1	42.1	18.6	58.6	6,147	96.5
Frankfort Square CDP	9,276	-	-	8,768	87.6	2.0	2.4	1.9	6.1	23.4	9.5	39.8	31.4	33.5	2,990	97.4
Franklin village	638	598	-6.3	565	99.3	0.0	0.7	0.0	0.0	22.1	15.0	39.4	50.1	17.4	236	84.7
Franklin Grove village	1,015	938	-7.6	990	94.8	1.5	0.0	0.7	2.9	23.1	25.1	41.9	48.1	16.7	387	86.8
Franklin Park village	18,311	17,627	-3.7	17,956	47.6	0.3	3.0	1.3	47.8	21.6	14.6	39.1	52.6	18.2	6,072	86.8
Freeburg village	4,400	4,242	-3.6	4,361	95.6	0.3	0.0	2.2	1.9	22.7	17.0	43.3	27.7	34.8	1,701	89.3
Freeman Spur village	289	279	-3.5	303	98.0	2.0	0.0	0.0	0.0	27.4	25.7	36.4	60.5	1.0	113	61.9
Freeport city	25,634	23,775	-7.3	24,119	70.7	17.2	1.4	5.1	5.7	23.2	21.7	41.6	43.1	18.5	10,824	83.8
Fulton city	3,482	3,315	-4.8	3,178	96.8	0.7	0.1	1.1	1.3	22.1	24.4	43.0	42.8	25.4	1,432	86.8
Fults village	26	28	7.7	27	100.0	0.0	0.0	0.0	0.0	18.5	11.1	55.8	50.0	5.0	11	100.0
Gages Lake CDP	10,198	-	-	10,161	76.4	5.7	4.0	2.8	11.0	22.2	12.1	41.6	29.1	39.4	3,746	93.9
Galatia village	933	880	-5.7	883	94.0	0.8	0.0	3.3	1.9	23.7	23.4	41.4	47.2	16.0	366	85.8
Galena city	3,418	3,158	-7.6	3,249	87.0	0.9	0.0	0.0	12.2	18.6	29.6	52.6	44.9	31.7	1,570	87.6
Galesburg city	32,195	30,197	-6.2	30,689	74.9	13.2	1.7	2.0	8.3	18.7	20.2	40.3	50.3	18.3	12,423	78.6
Galva city	2,587	2,478	-4.2	2,541	94.1	0.2	0.4	1.3	4.0	19.6	23.0	47.5	39.9	24.4	1,208	82.1
Garden Prairie CDP	352	-	-	325	89.8	0.0	0.0	0.0	10.2	14.2	21.5	47.6	51.1	0.0	151	78.1
Gardner village	1,463	1,381	-5.6	1,334	91.7	0.5	2.9	0.1	4.7	16.5	14.4	44.6	54.5	12.0	552	92.9
Garrett village	162	158	-2.5	128	93.8	0.0	0.0	3.1	3.1	22.7	14.8	45.0	63.4	0.0	58	86.2
Gays village	281	254	-9.6	227	91.2	0.0	0.0	8.8	0.0	15.9	17.2	46.5	50.0	10.6	101	88.1
Geneseo city	6,623	6,495	-1.9	6,599	97.5	0.8	0.7	0.7	0.3	25.5	23.6	43.0	31.4	32.2	2,739	85.2
Geneva city	21,592	21,809	1.0	21,888	89.7	0.4	2.4	1.7	5.8	23.7	15.7	43.2	20.0	58.6	7,994	96.1
Genoa city	5,178	5,237	1.1	5,220	76.0	0.7	0.1	3.3	20.0	24.1	9.8	36.6	42.5	15.4	1,891	96.6
Georgetown CDP	404	-	-	462	89.2	0.0	8.0	2.8	0.0	23.6	16.7	43.1	11.7	40.2	222	93.2
Georgetown city	3,475	3,185	-8.3	3,271	93.1	4.6	0.0	1.6	0.6	19.7	18.0	44.6	55.1	13.0	1,453	81.5
Germantown village	1,285	1,274	-0.9	1,251	96.6	0.0	0.0	0.5	3.0	20.6	17.3	40.0	39.2	23.5	549	77.6
Germantown Hills village	3,389	3,423	1.0	3,452	95.9	0.0	1.9	0.9	1.2	27.8	11.1	42.2	18.9	50.0	1,207	91.7
German Valley village	457	425	-7.0	553	98.4	0.0	0.9	0.2	0.5	28.2	14.8	37.2	47.3	17.3	224	92.0
Gibson City city	3,411	3,233	-5.2	3,360	96.9	1.0	0.0	1.6	0.5	24.5	18.2	40.5	42.9	25.7	1,555	82.0
Gifford village	978	1,048	7.2	945	96.1	2.3	0.0	0.2	1.4	22.0	25.0	47.9	45.3	18.7	360	89.7
Gilberts village	6,875	8,076	17.5	7,823	62.8	0.0	15.1	3.4	18.7	30.1	7.1	31.8	24.2	43.0	2,555	94.2
Gillespie city	3,322	3,088	-7.0	3,086	94.5	0.0	3.0	1.3	1.3	22.7	16.3	41.8	55.4	12.1	1,378	86.4
Gilman city	1,816	1,652	-9.0	1,832	76.7	1.1	0.3	3.3	18.6	22.2	21.5	41.5	57.4	13.6	706	88.5
Gilson CDP	190	-	-	208	76.4	0.0	0.0	23.6	0.0	18.3	9.6	38.6	64.2	19.0	80	86.3
Girard city	2,103	2,000	-4.9	1,894	96.9	0.1	1.0	0.9	1.1	22.7	25.2	40.4	51.8	14.5	795	87.7
Gladstone village	281	264	-6.0	194	87.1	0.0	0.0	1.5	11.3	19.6	20.1	46.0	67.1	7.7	103	79.6
Glasford village	1,019	957	-6.1	1,186	99.7	0.0	0.0	0.0	0.3	27.6	11.3	36.6	47.6	9.9	460	88.7
Glasgow village	141	132	-6.4	93	92.5	0.0	0.0	7.5	0.0	5.4	33.3	59.4	81.2	1.2	44	63.6
Glen Carbon village	12,917	12,850	-0.5	12,569	88.3	3.6	2.4	1.8	3.8	25.0	18.4	39.0	17.8	55.1	5,027	93.3
Glencoe village	8,721	8,826	1.2	8,888	87.3	2.9	5.2	1.0	3.6	29.3	19.0	45.6	5.1	87.8	3,212	95.0
Glendale Heights village	34,296	33,617	-2.0	34,079	33.5	8.1	21.5	5.0	31.8	24.8	11.3	33.6	41.8	28.2	11,395	96.0
Glen Ellyn village	27,773	27,714	-0.2	27,855	82.3	3.4	7.0	2.4	4.9	26.9	16.4	40.7	14.0	67.6	10,761	92.6

1 May be of any race.

Table A. All Places — **Population and Housing**

STATE City, town, township, borough, or CDP (county if applicable)	Population				Race and Hispanic or Latino origin (percent)					Age (percent)			Educational attainment of persons age 25 and older		Occupied housing units	
	2010 census total population	2019 estimated population	Percent change 2010-2019	ACS total population estimate 2015-2019	White alone, not Hispanic or Latino	Black alone, not Hispanic or Latino	Asian alone, not Hispanic or Latino	All other races or 2 or more races, not Hispanic or Latino	Hispanic or Latino[1]	Under 18 years old	Age 65 years and older	Median age	Percent High school diploma or less	Percent Bachelor's degree or more	Total	Percent with a computer
	1	2	3	4	5	6	7	8	9	10	11	12	13	14	15	16
ILLINOIS—Con.																
Glenview village	44,726	47,308	5.8	47,416	76.1	1.5	14.3	1.9	6.2	25.0	22.1	46.5	16.5	65.5	17,630	91.9
Glenwood village	8,985	8,715	-3.0	8,657	18.7	69.8	0.3	5.0	6.1	26.1	15.1	38.3	31.4	29.8	2,848	94.0
Godfrey village	17,989	17,400	-3.3	17,579	92.4	4.3	0.7	1.1	1.6	18.2	23.8	48.7	29.6	29.4	7,524	87.6
Godley village	601	756	25.8	631	96.7	0.0	0.0	1.7	1.6	19.5	15.7	43.6	62.6	4.9	228	81.6
Golconda city	670	631	-5.8	825	94.3	1.9	0.0	1.5	2.3	11.8	22.3	51.6	63.0	10.5	345	62.3
Golden village	642	617	-3.9	597	94.1	0.0	0.0	5.5	0.3	20.3	24.1	48.1	46.9	16.4	256	80.1
Golden Gate village	68	65	-4.4	95	100.0	0.0	0.0	0.0	0.0	24.2	11.6	34.8	52.9	0.0	36	91.7
Golf village	493	493	0.0	481	85.7	1.7	5.6	0.2	6.9	29.5	15.0	41.4	15.8	71.2	139	100.0
Goodfield village	866	986	13.9	948	99.5	0.3	0.2	0.0	0.0	25.7	15.0	39.5	30.8	39.0	347	96.3
Good Hope village	396	364	-8.1	409	95.1	0.5	0.0	1.5	2.9	27.1	18.6	38.8	43.8	21.3	176	88.1
Goofy Ridge CDP	350	-	-	293	98.6	0.0	0.0	1.4	0.0	26.6	35.8	55.3	77.3	2.8	181	84.0
Goreville village	1,050	1,060	1.0	1,038	99.1	0.0	0.0	0.0	0.9	19.7	26.8	44.6	43.2	17.8	439	78.4
Gorham village	236	219	-7.2	248	90.3	0.0	0.0	0.8	8.9	29.8	11.3	32.5	58.4	8.0	79	78.5
Grafton city	681	640	-6.0	695	96.0	0.0	0.0	2.7	1.3	14.0	39.6	58.3	46.5	23.4	346	86.7
Grand Detour CDP	429	-	-	345	96.2	1.4	0.0	0.0	2.3	22.6	23.8	46.7	9.7	40.8	140	92.9
Grand Ridge village	563	525	-6.7	618	84.3	0.2	1.6	0.6	13.3	26.1	18.9	39.4	38.6	17.4	242	88.0
Grand Tower city	605	564	-6.8	565	97.0	0.0	0.0	0.5	2.5	23.4	16.8	37.0	54.8	4.8	240	80.0
Grandview village	1,444	1,383	-4.2	1,685	80.8	11.6	0.0	4.6	3.0	19.6	16.0	38.7	57.5	10.2	757	83.5
Grandwood Park CDP	5,202	-	-	5,170	62.5	5.6	15.1	4.0	12.8	26.2	8.5	40.0	17.6	53.3	1,803	99.4
Granite City city	29,798	28,158	-5.5	28,612	80.2	9.6	0.6	2.6	7.0	20.9	16.6	41.8	48.3	12.5	12,292	87.8
Grantfork village	351	343	-2.3	331	97.9	0.0	0.3	0.6	1.2	24.2	9.1	37.9	32.6	25.6	135	91.9
Grant Park village	1,342	1,249	-6.9	1,411	90.9	0.0	0.0	3.0	6.1	21.3	18.6	43.8	47.4	15.5	552	89.5
Granville village	1,427	1,308	-8.3	1,344	93.0	0.0	0.0	1.3	5.7	17.9	20.9	44.6	45.6	18.9	595	84.5
Grayslake village	21,053	20,725	-1.6	20,720	73.6	2.8	7.0	4.2	12.4	22.9	10.6	36.7	16.1	54.7	7,777	94.3
Grayville city	1,668	1,565	-6.2	1,609	95.9	0.7	0.1	1.2	2.1	22.2	20.8	42.1	45.5	12.6	699	81.3
Greenfield city	1,071	988	-7.7	1,397	99.0	0.0	0.0	0.7	0.3	24.7	20.6	38.9	58.6	19.8	482	77.0
Green Oaks village	3,868	3,897	0.7	3,846	82.6	3.0	8.2	2.6	3.6	25.4	16.6	47.6	19.5	60.7	1,216	96.1
Greenup village	1,531	1,490	-2.7	1,668	98.5	0.2	0.5	0.8	0.0	25.8	20.0	38.2	54.3	11.2	665	76.8
Green Valley village	686	643	-6.3	652	97.9	0.0	0.0	0.0	2.1	26.2	10.0	35.4	46.1	15.5	253	89.7
Greenview village	778	724	-6.9	852	96.0	0.6	0.0	0.9	2.5	31.0	12.6	36.8	59.5	9.9	334	89.5
Greenville city	7,067	6,417	-9.2	6,665	75.0	16.7	0.6	0.9	6.8	14.3	17.5	39.0	42.0	27.7	2,175	86.9
Greenwood village	235	226	-3.8	192	87.0	0.0	0.0	0.0	13.0	14.1	27.6	53.4	38.6	24.8	72	95.8
Gridley village	1,432	1,398	-2.4	1,590	91.0	3.1	0.0	1.7	4.2	30.6	15.8	36.5	39.0	27.6	582	89.3
Griggsville city	1,226	1,150	-6.2	1,458	92.2	0.0	0.2	1.1	6.4	23.6	18.9	40.0	54.1	11.9	526	82.1
Gulf Port village	54	47	-13.0	28	100.0	0.0	0.0	0.0	0.0	0.0	46.4	59.5	65.4	7.7	13	84.6
Gurnee village	31,238	30,378	-2.8	30,671	62.7	7.7	11.5	3.9	14.3	22.2	12.7	40.3	21.7	50.6	11,577	95.1
Hainesville village	3,658	3,557	-2.8	3,606	75.0	1.9	2.4	3.5	17.1	25.6	5.1	34.0	26.5	41.9	1,361	99.2
Hamburg village	128	119	-7.0	172	100.0	0.0	0.0	0.0	0.0	19.2	19.8	57.3	75.2	16.8	33	60.6
Hamel village	816	810	-0.7	761	96.8	0.0	1.3	1.1	0.8	30.6	14.5	34.4	26.4	30.9	294	94.6
Hamilton city	2,951	2,715	-8.0	2,803	96.7	0.1	1.1	2.1	0.0	21.1	23.9	44.7	39.6	22.8	1,155	86.7
Hammond village	509	479	-5.9	482	95.2	0.0	0.0	2.3	2.5	22.6	25.5	43.5	52.2	10.1	218	86.7
Hampshire village	5,563	6,251	12.4	6,008	92.9	0.0	1.4	0.0	5.7	27.9	8.2	36.5	31.1	32.5	1,946	98.2
Hampton village	1,832	1,742	-4.9	2,118	85.8	3.7	0.0	1.9	8.5	25.9	18.2	40.5	35.7	30.5	870	93.1
Hanaford village	327	322	-1.5	377	93.9	0.0	0.0	3.7	2.4	24.4	14.6	43.1	47.3	4.5	172	86.6
Hanna City village	1,238	1,192	-3.7	1,271	92.7	0.8	1.1	1.1	4.3	18.3	29.1	46.5	43.3	21.0	597	87.6
Hanover village	845	768	-9.1	736	86.0	2.4	0.0	9.8	1.8	16.7	29.1	48.6	57.2	6.6	388	74.7
Hanover Park village	38,092	37,426	-1.7	37,984	33.8	7.9	17.7	2.5	38.1	26.5	10.2	33.8	43.2	27.0	11,301	96.9
Hardin village	962	900	-6.4	857	93.3	1.5	0.0	0.0	5.1	22.5	24.9	48.4	59.7	7.4	271	68.3
Harmon village	119	111	-6.7	128	99.2	0.0	0.0	0.0	0.8	19.5	22.7	43.5	76.2	6.0	54	87.0
Harrisburg city	9,025	8,513	-5.7	8,994	88.1	4.1	1.8	5.1	0.8	24.0	17.7	39.0	39.9	18.4	3,724	84.9
Harrison CDP	970	-	-	805	91.6	0.0	1.6	6.1	0.7	24.8	17.5	38.0	45.6	10.3	378	76.7
Harristown village	1,371	1,292	-5.8	1,268	96.1	0.6	0.6	1.8	0.9	22.4	17.4	46.0	49.8	16.6	528	90.2
Hartford village	1,431	1,341	-6.3	1,826	99.0	0.0	0.0	0.8	0.3	30.7	13.3	33.8	57.3	8.8	677	85.1
Hartsburg village	314	307	-2.2	264	98.1	0.0	0.0	1.1	0.8	15.5	16.3	47.2	52.4	14.8	122	87.7
Harvard city	9,435	9,060	-4.0	9,281	50.5	0.1	0.2	0.9	48.3	32.2	9.4	30.9	64.3	10.7	2,988	95.0
Harvel village	223	211	-5.4	334	76.3	0.0	0.0	1.5	22.2	30.8	9.9	33.0	66.0	5.7	109	76.1
Harvey city	25,265	24,408	-3.4	24,386	4.2	66.4	2.0	2.3	25.1	26.5	13.4	35.2	59.4	9.6	8,271	82.6
Harwood Heights village	8,611	8,333	-3.2	8,487	72.7	0.6	10.5	0.2	15.9	17.0	19.1	43.3	40.7	26.7	3,367	86.5
Havana city	3,301	2,987	-9.5	3,197	97.8	0.9	0.0	1.0	0.3	21.5	23.5	43.1	53.7	17.8	1,377	88.1
Hawthorn Woods village	7,770	8,666	11.5	8,402	81.7	1.9	11.1	1.7	3.5	26.8	11.3	43.3	15.0	69.8	2,670	97.5
Hazel Crest village	14,009	13,565	-3.2	13,549	7.8	86.7	0.2	1.2	4.1	26.4	15.0	38.6	32.3	27.4	4,977	89.5
Hebron village	1,202	1,183	-1.6	1,469	83.7	1.1	0.0	1.0	14.2	25.6	10.1	32.2	45.3	14.5	496	90.1
Hecker village	486	478	-1.6	561	99.5	0.0	0.5	0.0	0.0	27.3	12.3	34.5	29.8	14.8	236	87.7
Henderson village	259	244	-5.8	225	93.8	1.8	0.0	0.4	4.0	14.2	22.2	51.1	41.4	11.2	106	83.0
Hennepin village	759	705	-7.1	750	92.8	0.8	0.5	2.0	3.9	19.2	25.3	47.7	43.5	16.5	345	90.7
Henning village	251	234	-6.8	268	100.0	0.0	0.0	0.0	0.0	33.2	16.0	36.5	63.1	1.7	87	90.8
Henry city	2,464	2,209	-10.3	2,658	94.5	0.0	0.3	5.0	0.2	26.4	21.2	40.8	45.6	23.7	1,065	87.7
Heritage Lake CDP	1,520	-	-	1,690	95.0	0.0	0.0	1.6	3.4	24.4	10.4	40.6	21.8	42.3	590	100.0
Herrick village	436	431	-1.1	328	100.0	0.0	0.0	0.0	0.0	26.5	19.8	34.7	68.4	9.8	147	67.3
Herrin city	12,522	12,687	1.3	12,827	91.0	1.8	3.1	2.1	2.0	23.4	16.2	39.5	38.2	22.4	5,069	83.4
Herscher village	1,596	1,504	-5.8	1,512	93.7	1.1	0.3	2.5	2.3	21.2	22.8	43.0	39.8	29.6	611	79.7
Hettick village	182	171	-6.0	139	97.8	0.0	0.0	2.2	0.0	18.0	18.0	45.3	66.0	12.3	63	90.5
Heyworth village	2,837	2,867	1.1	3,124	92.3	0.6	0.9	2.1	4.1	27.9	11.1	38.3	35.7	33.7	1,100	92.5
Hickory Hills city	14,049	13,710	-2.4	13,816	76.5	4.2	0.5	0.8	17.9	23.5	16.2	38.5	45.0	22.5	4,959	90.7
Hidalgo village	106	105	-0.9	156	98.1	0.0	1.9	0.0	0.0	30.8	12.2	34.2	68.1	1.1	47	80.9
Highland city	9,928	9,834	-0.9	10,012	89.3	1.9	3.4	1.8	3.6	23.7	18.7	38.5	35.0	28.1	4,189	87.9
Highland Park city	29,745	29,515	-0.8	29,628	85.9	0.8	2.9	2.5	7.9	24.4	22.7	47.1	10.8	73.8	11,477	94.9
Highwood city	5,449	5,224	-4.1	5,310	43.0	3.5	1.7	1.1	50.8	27.9	12.3	35.3	45.6	38.8	1,897	88.3
Hillcrest village	1,318	1,225	-7.1	1,240	66.5	0.4	0.0	0.6	32.6	28.9	7.5	35.7	49.9	14.9	435	97.2
Hillsboro city	6,216	5,970	-4.0	6,402	80.2	15.6	0.0	0.7	3.5	15.3	17.2	37.7	50.7	16.1	1,691	86.5
Hillsdale village	517	505	-2.3	448	93.3	0.9	0.0	2.2	3.6	23.4	14.7	38.9	46.5	8.6	173	86.1
Hillside village	8,214	7,933	-3.4	8,080	21.3	40.0	1.0	1.2	36.5	18.3	12.1	37.7	53.1	16.7	2,663	92.1
Hillview village	193	177	-8.3	188	95.7	0.0	0.0	0.0	4.3	26.1	9.6	30.8	81.3	3.7	48	72.9
Hinckley village	2,071	2,050		2,137	92.1	0.0	0.8	2.8	4.3	23.4	14.1	39.4	32.4	29.1	827	95.0
Hindsboro village	311	296	-4.8	413	92.5	0.5	0.0	0.0	7.0	18.4	14.0	38.8	44.7	9.2	157	92.4
Hinsdale village	16,845	17,637	4.7	17,710	81.8	1.4	10.9	2.2	3.8	31.7	13.9	42.1	8.1	80.8	5,819	97.0
Hodgkins village	1,897	1,971	3.9	1,746	51.4	4.3	1.2	0.0	43.1	19.9	18.9	42.0	59.5	11.3	650	72.6
Hoffman village	508	483	-4.9	470	93.4	0.0	0.0	5.3	1.3	22.6	21.9	39.8	43.4	13.2	193	74.6
Hoffman Estates village	51,891	50,932	-1.8	50,841	50.0	4.5	24.2	2.7	18.6	23.4	12.7	38.6	26.7	47.8	17,717	96.6
Holiday Hills village	604	579	-4.1	680	88.5	0.0	2.4	3.1	6.0	16.9	15.7	47.6	55.2	16.8	278	93.9
Holiday Shores CDP	2,882	-	-	2,930	96.9	0.5	0.0	2.3	0.3	22.9	13.8	40.6	30.3	34.0	1,003	100.0
Hollowayville village	92	86	-6.5	57	100.0	0.0	0.0	0.0	0.0	10.5	21.1	45.9	45.0	0.0	27	92.6

1 May be of any race.

Table A. All Places — **Population and Housing**

STATE City, town, township, borough, or CDP (county if applicable)	Population: 2010 census total population	Population: 2019 estimated population	Population: Percent change 2010-2019	Population: ACS total population estimate 2015-2019	Race and Hispanic or Latino origin (percent): White alone, not Hispanic or Latino	Black alone, not Hispanic or Latino	Asian alone, not Hispanic or Latino	All other races or 2 or more races, not Hispanic or Latino	Hispanic or Latino[1]	Age (percent): Under 18 years old	Age 65 years and older	Median age	Educational attainment of persons age 25 and older: Percent High school diploma or less	Percent Bachelor's degree or more	Occupied housing units: Total	Percent with a computer
	1	2	3	4	5	6	7	8	9	10	11	12	13	14	15	16
ILLINOIS—Con.																
Homer village	1,207	1,159	-4.0	1,265	98.3	0.0	0.0	1.4	0.3	28.0	14.1	36.4	47.1	16.3	517	89.7
Homer Glen village	24,210	24,472	1.1	24,592	89.1	0.6	2.1	1.0	7.0	22.5	18.9	43.9	32.1	37.6	8,190	94.3
Hometown city	4,349	4,177	-4.0	4,272	68.7	1.1	0.9	3.1	26.2	21.9	13.7	36.7	49.6	14.0	1,697	88.8
Homewood village	19,307	18,703	-3.1	19,112	44.4	44.4	2.9	2.8	5.5	24.8	16.1	40.5	22.3	43.6	7,394	92.5
Hoopeston city	5,358	5,009	-6.5	5,102	81.7	2.0	2.9	1.5	11.9	23.2	22.7	45.7	66.2	10.3	2,153	86.5
Hooppole village	202	191	-5.4	184	100.0	0.0	0.0	0.0	0.0	33.2	16.8	37.6	56.3	4.2	63	81.0
Hopedale village	869	825	-5.1	887	98.1	0.7	0.0	0.8	0.5	15.0	30.9	54.6	46.1	19.2	372	82.3
Hopewell village	410	398	-2.9	397	99.2	0.0	0.5	0.0	0.3	16.1	22.9	50.1	28.3	29.2	171	95.3
Hopkins Park village	605	598	-1.2	536	3.5	86.4	0.0	5.6	4.5	27.8	15.9	40.2	56.0	15.5	204	68.1
Hoyleton village	531	494	-7.0	598	83.3	3.5	0.8	6.5	5.9	37.8	14.4	28.6	34.7	24.2	188	87.2
Hudson village	1,840	1,813	-1.5	2,136	96.3	0.1	0.4	1.2	1.9	29.7	11.6	35.7	24.9	44.2	695	97.8
Huey village	169	163	-3.6	206	100.0	0.0	0.0	0.0	0.0	20.4	25.7	44.8	56.1	11.5	94	61.7
Hull village	461	433	-6.1	479	89.6	4.0	0.0	2.7	3.8	20.5	14.2	36.6	58.1	9.7	198	80.3
Humboldt village	437	418	-4.3	461	96.7	0.7	0.0	0.7	2.0	23.0	13.0	45.2	49.8	9.0	197	95.4
Hume village	381	347	-8.9	324	95.7	0.6	0.0	0.0	3.7	17.9	25.0	50.0	52.2	6.0	160	85.6
Huntley village	24,312	27,228	12.0	26,966	79.6	2.6	5.9	1.3	10.6	20.4	33.3	49.0	32.8	32.6	11,704	93.3
Hurst city	799	786	-1.6	744	91.0	0.9	0.3	7.1	0.7	21.2	18.5	42.5	53.4	8.6	314	72.3
Hutsonville village	540	522	-3.3	563	97.2	0.0	0.4	0.4	2.1	23.4	13.3	36.2	45.7	18.5	249	83.5
Illiopolis village	891	842	-5.5	822	95.3	0.2	0.0	2.4	2.1	26.5	17.4	40.6	51.0	12.3	316	92.7
Ina village	2,334	2,279	-2.4	2,410	56.4	29.9	0.0	1.5	12.2	3.4	11.5	40.1	76.7	1.9	198	81.8
Indian Creek village	545	535	-1.8	627	63.5	4.5	18.2	1.9	12.0	27.4	13.2	39.5	17.6	68.0	192	97.4
Indian Head Park village	3,816	3,719	-2.5	3,776	83.9	1.3	2.4	2.0	10.4	16.4	36.3	53.7	22.5	51.2	1,681	92.8
Indianola village	276	257	-6.9	220	98.2	0.0	0.0	1.4	0.5	17.7	22.3	48.5	71.9	8.4	85	78.8
Industry village	478	438	-8.4	425	96.7	0.0	0.0	2.1	1.2	14.4	20.5	40.0	46.6	14.4	181	86.2
Ingalls Park CDP	3,314	-	-	3,171	50.0	9.2	0.6	7.2	33.0	22.1	10.2	36.5	56.2	7.4	1,222	90.2
Inverness village	7,400	7,376	-0.3	7,633	80.8	0.9	13.8	3.4	1.1	20.5	26.0	51.9	14.3	66.0	2,716	98.7
Iola village	141	136	-3.5	141	97.9	0.0	0.0	0.7	1.4	28.4	12.1	38.3	60.0	0.0	60	80.0
Ipava village	470	421	-10.4	498	94.6	0.0	0.8	3.6	1.0	22.5	24.5	39.6	55.2	14.2	223	71.7
Iroquois village	154	137	-11.0	182	80.2	10.4	1.1	8.2	0.0	23.6	26.4	46.3	62.3	13.1	77	85.7
Irving village	495	462	-6.7	377	96.6	0.3	0.0	0.0	3.2	21.5	18.6	44.8	61.0	5.6	175	63.4
Irvington village	665	613	-7.8	720	96.3	1.0	0.0	2.8	0.0	21.4	19.6	42.9	42.0	9.4	303	90.1
Irwin village	78	74	-5.1	44	100.0	0.0	0.0	0.0	0.0	20.5	25.0	55.5	48.5	15.2	23	82.6
Island Lake village	8,071	8,020	-0.6	8,035	82.0	0.2	2.8	0.7	14.3	22.5	13.0	42.6	39.3	28.0	3,146	92.5
Itasca village	8,647	9,805	13.4	9,224	76.9	2.6	7.5	1.5	11.6	18.5	18.9	45.4	30.6	39.7	3,740	94.7
Iuka village	486	464	-4.5	498	97.2	0.6	1.4	0.8	0.0	26.3	14.3	37.1	65.0	5.8	199	85.4
Ivesdale village	267	252	-5.6	274	100.0	0.0	0.0	0.0	0.0	23.4	16.1	40.6	51.6	16.1	118	84.7
Jacksonville city	19,444	18,603	-4.3	18,859	81.2	11.6	0.5	2.7	4.0	16.8	18.2	37.3	50.8	16.7	7,248	83.9
Jeffersonville village	367	359	-2.2	379	100.0	0.0	0.0	0.0	0.0	26.9	15.8	37.6	44.2	7.6	159	85.5
Jeisyville village	107	101	-5.6	67	97.0	0.0	0.0	3.0	0.0	19.4	46.3	58.6	69.2	11.5	32	87.5
Jerome village	1,694	1,588	-6.3	2,073	77.5	10.6	2.0	6.1	3.8	19.8	16.5	38.9	29.8	38.1	933	94.4
Jerseyville city	8,464	8,200	-3.1	8,161	95.1	0.2	0.4	2.6	1.7	23.5	18.3	39.2	45.4	22.5	3,254	86.1
Jewett village	223	220	-1.3	266	96.2	0.0	0.0	3.8	0.0	22.6	24.1	43.4	71.2	3.8	98	87.8
Johnsburg village	6,431	6,368		6,384	89.6	0.4	2.3	4.7	3.1	24.4	15.0	41.4	39.1	33.4	2,151	99.7
Johnsonville village	77	77	0.0	60	98.3	0.0	0.0	1.7	0.0	26.7	15.0	51.2	43.2	8.1	23	87.0
Johnston City city	3,557	3,389	-4.7	3,450	96.3	0.0	1.3	0.6	1.9	19.5	19.8	42.6	40.9	14.6	1,392	82.8
Joliet city	147,308	147,344	0.0	147,826	47.8	16.9	2.0	2.2	31.0	27.6	10.0	33.8	46.8	22.1	47,563	91.5
Jonesboro city	1,831	1,700	-7.2	1,855	94.7	0.9	0.3	0.5	3.6	23.3	17.1	39.6	42.5	21.3	713	76.6
Joppa village	338	303	-10.4	274	87.2	9.5	0.0	3.3	0.0	26.3	14.6	31.5	57.5	4.0	109	56.0
Joy village	417	382	-8.4	384	96.6	0.0	0.0	0.8	2.6	16.1	14.6	39.9	55.1	9.1	178	84.8
Junction village	129	111	-14.0	101	88.1	0.0	0.0	0.0	11.9	16.8	19.8	40.7	52.9	14.3	37	83.8
Junction City village	482	466	-3.3	572	91.3	0.2	0.3	7.0	1.2	29.9	17.8	33.5	60.5	5.9	199	89.9
Justice village	12,925	12,608	-2.5	12,800	60.2	20.7	2.2	0.8	16.0	26.9	10.8	32.8	51.5	16.4	4,600	86.7
Kampsville village	328	304	-7.3	379	96.8	0.5	0.3	0.3	2.1	30.9	18.5	39.4	71.2	5.1	143	77.6
Kane village	438	404	-7.8	255	94.9	1.2	0.0	1.2	2.7	18.0	18.8	44.3	55.1	6.1	98	64.3
Kaneville village	482	480	-0.4	434	93.1	1.4	1.2	1.2	3.2	17.1	21.4	49.4	40.1	24.9	176	97.7
Kangley village	251	233	-7.2	240	97.1	0.0	0.0	1.7	1.3	12.9	18.3	53.6	63.5	14.9	103	87.4
Kankakee city	27,540	26,024	-5.5	25,830	38.4	41.3	0.5	1.3	18.5	26.2	14.0	35.4	58.4	13.6	9,047	80.1
Kansas village	787	719	-8.6	689	99.3	0.3	0.0	0.4	0.0	21.0	21.0	42.4	54.7	13.5	332	85.8
Kappa village	227	240	5.7	215	91.2	0.0	0.0	3.7	5.1	23.7	4.2	39.1	46.6	33.1	68	89.7
Karnak village	497	434	-12.7	481	94.8	1.9	0.0	1.5	1.9	21.0	30.1	48.9	58.9	4.4	201	53.2
Kaskaskia village	14	13	-7.1	10	100.0	0.0	0.0	0.0	0.0	0.0	30.0	48.5	57.1	28.6	5	100.0
Keenes village	83	80	-3.6	51	100.0	0.0	0.0	0.0	0.0	7.8	45.1	56.7	83.0	4.3	27	88.9
Keensburg village	210	201	-4.3	82	97.6	0.0	0.0	2.4	0.0	4.9	32.9	59.9	38.2	10.5	44	81.8
Keithsburg city	609	580	-4.8	545	97.8	0.0	1.1	1.1	0.0	16.1	29.0	47.4	71.6	5.9	223	83.0
Kell village	217	207	-4.6	155	91.6	0.0	0.0	0.0	8.4	20.0	18.1	35.7	73.9	1.1	60	86.7
Kempton village	227	206	-9.3	220	97.3	0.0	0.0	2.3	0.5	25.9	11.8	36.3	52.0	9.9	96	93.8
Kenilworth village	2,508	2,475	-1.3	2,460	91.3	0.0	4.7	0.7	3.3	32.2	15.0	42.6	2.6	93.1	777	97.8
Kenney village	327	313	-4.3	391	98.7	0.8	0.0	0.3	0.3	12.8	16.6	44.6	59.3	12.8	169	92.9
Kewanee city	12,919	12,339	-4.5	12,547	80.8	6.0	1.1	1.3	10.7	24.3	19.6	37.8	53.5	14.7	4,897	76.1
Keyesport village	425	405	-4.7	373	99.2	0.0	0.0	0.8	0.0	26.0	24.4	46.6	62.6	7.8	155	65.2
Kilbourne village	302	276	-8.6	274	91.6	0.0	0.0	8.4	0.0	17.9	13.5	49.5	61.9	3.7	139	82.7
Kildeer village	3,907	4,012	2.7	4,024	80.0	0.3	13.8	3.2	2.8	27.2	12.2	44.5	7.4	78.0	1,345	98.2
Kincaid village	1,506	1,372	-8.9	1,533	99.9	0.0	0.0	0.1	0.0	18.5	15.5	41.2	57.2	8.1	638	89.5
Kinderhook village	216	208	-3.7	241	98.8	0.0	0.4	0.8	0.0	23.2	19.5	35.1	49.7	23.0	97	92.8
Kingston village	1,164	1,169	0.4	1,112	82.0	2.2	0.0	2.0	13.8	26.8	12.1	37.1	52.9	15.5	367	91.8
Kingston Mines village	302	282	-6.6	292	97.3	1.4	0.0	0.0	1.4	25.0	13.7	35.4	54.7	10.9	114	91.2
Kinmundy city	795	755	-5.0	881	95.8	0.0	0.0	0.8	3.4	22.8	15.6	40.0	54.0	6.8	383	82.8
Kinsman village	99	97	-2.0	125	92.0	0.0	0.0	0.0	8.0	14.4	18.4	33.5	51.8	8.4	45	88.9
Kirkland village	1,747	1,729		1,845	90.3	0.0	0.4	3.2	6.1	27.0	14.0	33.3	42.7	18.7	685	90.9
Kirkwood village	714	675	-5.5	762	96.5	0.0	0.0	1.3	2.2	25.5	17.3	40.6	51.3	13.9	295	86.4
Knollwood CDP	1,747	-	-	1,665	70.7	0.5	0.4	3.4	25.0	24.6	18.0	38.3	27.9	37.7	552	100.0
Knoxville city	2,907	2,726	-6.2	3,031	94.9	0.2	0.4	2.0	2.5	27.8	21.0	40.1	39.8	22.5	1,093	91.3
Lacon city	1,945	1,739	-10.6	1,759	95.8	0.7	0.4	1.0	2.1	18.8	26.7	50.2	56.0	15.3	741	76.5
Ladd village	1,295	1,195	-7.7	1,211	92.1	0.0	0.0	0.7	7.2	16.4	16.7	44.0	41.9	16.0	528	84.8
La Fayette village	223	200	-10.3	161	97.5	0.0	0.0	0.0	2.5	26.1	16.1	37.3	63.4	6.3	80	73.8
La Grange village	15,554	15,322	-1.5	15,545	84.1	6.0	0.8	2.2	6.9	28.5	16.0	41.7	18.5	63.5	5,352	95.0
La Grange Park village	13,580	13,178	-3.0	13,395	82.9	3.7	2.0	1.0	10.4	26.2	18.4	40.6	16.8	58.2	5,028	90.2
La Harpe city	1,232	1,143	-7.2	1,319	94.3	0.0	0.0	1.3	4.4	19.3	23.6	43.5	53.0	14.1	578	74.2
Lake Barrington village	4,955	4,868	-1.8	5,117	91.6	0.3	3.3	1.2	3.6	16.8	32.4	56.1	13.2	64.6	2,288	97.1
Lake Bluff village	5,688	5,562	-2.2	5,632	90.5	0.0	6.4	0.3	2.7	25.1	15.4	45.0	7.9	77.0	1,955	99.1
Lake Camelot CDP	1,686	-	-	1,755	97.5	0.0	0.0	0.0	2.5	31.2	9.2	37.0	29.9	34.2	600	100.0
Lake Catherine CDP	1,379	-	-	1,454	90.8	0.6	0.0	3.6	5.0	16.1	24.4	47.6	51.8	20.8	612	90.4

1 May be of any race.

STATE City, town, township, borough, or CDP (county if applicable)	Population: 2010 census total population	Population: 2019 estimated population	Population: Percent change 2010-2019	Population: ACS total population estimate 2015-2019	Race and Hispanic or Latino origin (percent): White alone, not Hispanic or Latino	Race and Hispanic or Latino origin (percent): Black alone, not Hispanic or Latino	Race and Hispanic or Latino origin (percent): Asian alone, not Hispanic or Latino	Race and Hispanic or Latino origin (percent): All other races or 2 or more races, not Hispanic or Latino	Race and Hispanic or Latino origin (percent): Hispanic or Latino[1]	Age (percent): Under 18 years old	Age (percent): Age 65 years and older	Age (percent): Median age	Educational attainment of persons age 25 and older: Percent High school diploma or less	Educational attainment of persons age 25 and older: Percent Bachelor's degree or more	Occupied housing units: Total	Occupied housing units: Percent with a computer
	1	2	3	4	5	6	7	8	9	10	11	12	13	14	15	16
ILLINOIS—Con.																
Lake Forest city	19,379	19,446	0.3	19,173	84.3	1.3	8.8	1.4	4.1	22.0	23.6	47.8	6.7	80.5	7,005	96.1
Lake Holiday CDP	4,761	-	-	4,512	91.3	1.2	0.4	1.1	6.0	23.6	10.3	38.9	35.7	24.2	1,552	97.6
Lake in the Hills village	28,948	28,634	-1.1	28,759	77.3	2.2	6.5	1.9	12.1	26.9	8.1	34.9	27.5	38.3	9,679	97.3
Lake Ka-Ho village	236	221	-6.4	234	94.4	0.0	0.0	3.4	2.1	17.1	15.8	43.5	67.4	6.2	115	90.4
Lakemoor village	6,064	5,967	-1.6	5,756	85.1	1.7	1.6	1.1	10.5	23.0	6.6	35.2	32.6	33.8	2,191	98.1
Lake of the Woods CDP	2,912	-	-	2,404	97.8	0.0	0.0	1.4	0.8	30.6	15.6	34.2	32.6	26.4	948	87.2
Lake Petersburg CDP	719	-	-	449	91.1	0.0	4.0	1.1	3.8	2.0	56.3	65.9	26.9	42.1	274	95.6
Lake Summerset CDP	2,048	-	-	2,057	94.9	1.8	1.0	0.0	2.3	16.7	25.0	49.0	34.1	27.2	837	94.9
Lake Villa village	8,631	8,573	-0.7	8,705	77.7	4.4	4.8	1.8	11.3	27.9	11.7	38.1	23.7	47.0	3,064	97.5
Lakewood village	3,811	4,001	5.0	3,780	94.8	1.0	1.2	1.6	1.3	27.1	12.0	40.6	17.9	61.3	1,297	99.2
Lakewood Shores CDP	1,347	-	-	1,459	95.0	2.0	0.0	3.0	0.0	19.9	14.2	44.7	50.6	6.9	563	93.8
Lake Zurich village	19,693	19,877	0.9	19,915	80.6	0.9	8.4	1.8	8.3	24.4	11.8	38.8	20.3	55.5	6,766	96.7
La Moille village	726	679	-6.5	760	88.7	0.8	6.8	3.4	0.3	25.4	19.1	40.0	44.8	14.4	277	92.4
Lanark city	1,461	1,333	-8.8	1,445	92.3	1.0	0.0	2.4	4.3	26.6	20.1	41.8	49.2	17.6	601	86.5
Langleyville CDP	432	-	-	363	100.0	0.0	0.0	0.0	0.0	23.4	22.0	49.9	74.1	0.0	169	100.0
Lansing village	28,353	27,402	-3.4	27,904	37.2	43.1	0.9	2.1	16.7	23.9	15.6	40.4	39.3	24.3	10,873	90.3
LaPlace CDP	259	-	-	144	100.0	0.0	0.0	0.0	0.0	5.6	38.9	57.2	64.8	16.4	82	89.0
La Prairie village	47	45	-4.3	51	94.1	0.0	0.0	5.9	0.0	21.6	21.6	36.6	76.5	0.0	24	75.0
La Rose village	144	130	-9.7	89	91.0	0.0	9.0	0.0	0.0	20.2	31.5	54.3	62.3	7.2	47	78.7
LaSalle city	9,630	8,986	-6.7	9,147	78.8	1.9	1.4	1.1	16.8	23.4	16.7	36.9	49.1	18.4	3,778	87.6
Latham village	388	364	-6.2	409	91.4	0.0	0.0	4.4	4.2	17.8	18.1	37.4	44.5	13.8	187	86.1
Lawrenceville city	4,420	4,399	-0.5	4,165	91.8	1.1	1.4	3.2	2.5	18.9	20.0	42.8	45.9	16.4	1,956	86.1
Leaf River village	443	406	-8.4	422	93.1	2.1	0.2	1.2	3.3	22.3	15.6	39.8	56.7	15.7	196	83.2
Lebanon city	4,452	4,238	-4.8	4,418	79.4	17.3	0.0	2.1	1.2	18.4	20.6	37.5	31.8	34.7	1,722	88.2
Lee village	345	327	-5.2	352	91.2	1.1	0.0	4.3	3.4	28.1	7.7	33.7	43.0	15.2	118	97.5
Leland village	977	914	-6.4	846	94.6	0.0	0.0	2.4	3.1	21.3	13.7	39.1	42.4	20.8	350	92.9
Leland Grove city	1,495	1,464	-2.1	1,406	95.6	0.8	1.2	0.6	1.8	14.4	33.9	55.7	11.0	67.4	660	95.5
Lemont village	16,051	17,291	7.7	17,023	90.6	0.5	2.7	0.8	5.3	23.2	19.2	45.7	32.1	41.6	6,051	92.6
Lena village	2,914	2,719	-6.7	2,879	96.8	0.9	0.4	0.0	1.9	22.0	27.1	49.5	38.3	23.2	1,213	90.5
Lenzburg village	518	487	-6.0	454	93.2	0.0	0.0	0.0	6.8	27.5	15.6	40.6	67.5	8.0	179	91.1
Leonore village	130	123	-5.4	118	100.0	0.0	0.0	0.0	0.0	22.0	17.8	47.1	51.3	3.8	49	87.8
Lerna village	283	273	-3.5	253	98.8	0.0	0.0	1.2	0.0	20.6	23.3	40.8	60.5	9.6	110	92.7
Le Roy city	3,550	3,493	-1.6	3,702	99.5	0.0	0.0	0.5	0.0	23.4	20.9	43.5	42.2	25.6	1,457	86.9
Lewistown city	2,383	2,146	-9.9	2,316	96.2	1.0	0.0	0.3	2.5	21.3	19.7	41.6	54.8	13.1	933	81.7
Lexington city	2,053	2,026	-1.3	1,894	97.2	0.6	0.0	1.0	1.2	22.0	19.0	42.7	37.6	36.3	775	91.9
Liberty village	523	503	-3.8	489	98.0	2.0	0.0	0.0	0.0	30.3	16.4	39.4	52.1	8.6	171	84.2
Libertyville village	20,405	20,205		20,382	85.8	0.9	6.8	1.6	4.9	25.4	16.0	44.2	13.2	70.7	7,435	93.1
Lily Lake village	990	1,023	3.3	1,022	91.2	4.0	0.8	0.6	3.4	22.8	13.5	43.8	19.9	39.1	342	98.0
Lima village	153	148	-3.3	109	95.4	0.0	1.8	0.0	2.8	12.8	13.8	51.2	37.9	25.3	48	91.7
Limestone village	1,599	1,522	-4.8	1,570	96.4	0.6	0.2	0.8	2.1	24.9	20.1	41.2	42.4	15.1	565	86.2
Lincoln city	14,549	13,524	-7.0	13,652	89.3	3.4	1.4	3.4	2.4	19.9	19.6	38.7	48.0	19.8	5,686	84.6
Lincolnshire village	7,308	7,893	8.0	7,572	80.7	0.6	14.6	1.1	3.0	18.8	35.0	53.1	14.7	70.1	3,104	89.2
Lincolnwood village	12,590	12,245	-2.7	12,434	55.3	1.9	28.0	5.2	9.5	21.5	25.2	46.6	27.6	53.6	4,298	84.9
Lindenhurst village	14,577	14,216	-2.5	14,417	82.6	1.6	4.2	1.5	10.1	25.0	12.7	39.5	22.8	47.7	5,039	95.7
Lisbon village	292	308	5.5	347	93.1	0.9	0.0	3.5	2.6	31.4	11.5	29.1	43.3	18.7	107	95.3
Lisle village	22,552	23,270	3.2	23,431	71.3	4.3	14.9	3.1	6.4	19.8	15.3	36.9	15.8	61.8	9,876	93.7
Litchfield city	7,159	6,715	-6.2	6,870	95.7	0.8	0.4	1.5	1.6	22.8	19.4	44.3	45.5	21.6	3,104	83.3
Littleton village	181	160	-11.6	147	99.3	0.0	0.0	0.0	0.7	14.3	21.8	53.1	53.2	16.2	70	80.0
Little York village	331	311	-6.0	317	99.7	0.0	0.0	0.0	0.3	23.0	11.7	34.2	47.6	9.7	140	82.1
Liverpool village	129	123	-4.7	128	100.0	0.0	0.0	0.0	0.0	14.8	22.7	52.2	85.7	5.7	54	90.7
Livingston village	858	804	-6.3	714	95.9	0.0	0.0	2.2	1.8	14.1	25.5	49.9	59.0	12.1	365	74.5
Loami village	743	750	0.9	1,055	91.7	0.8	0.6	0.3	6.7	26.6	7.1	29.4	46.0	16.5	362	89.5
Lockport city	24,819	25,615	3.2	25,307	85.6	2.2	1.4	1.6	9.2	28.5	10.9	36.2	30.4	36.1	8,754	95.3
Loda village	407	398	-2.2	316	91.8	0.6	0.9	1.3	5.4	22.5	12.7	37.0	51.7	7.1	137	89.1
Lomax village	451	401	-11.1	396	94.2	0.0	0.0	0.0	5.8	18.2	27.3	47.7	49.5	12.8	172	86.0
Lombard village	43,466	44,303	1.9	43,998	70.8	4.3	12.5	3.6	8.7	20.3	16.3	37.7	25.4	47.8	17,557	91.6
London Mills village	392	376	-4.1	400	98.5	0.0	0.0	0.0	1.5	24.0	17.8	38.4	56.7	9.7	163	76.7
Long Creek village	1,331	1,273	-4.4	1,459	98.4	0.0	0.0	1.4	0.3	22.4	21.0	47.9	47.2	23.8	527	89.9
Long Grove village	7,921	7,905	-0.2	7,963	72.7	2.5	18.0	1.5	5.3	23.9	17.2	46.6	13.6	70.0	2,369	99.0
Long Lake CDP	3,515	-	-	3,557	72.3	0.0	0.0	0.0	27.7	22.9	14.6	38.1	49.0	20.8	1,184	100.0
Long Point village	226	214	-5.3	285	91.9	0.0	1.8	4.6	1.8	35.4	10.9	33.7	61.8	10.3	93	86.0
Longview village	153	148	-3.3	137	93.4	0.0	0.0	3.6	2.9	22.6	13.9	35.8	61.5	16.7	53	81.1
Loraine village	315	302	-4.1	362	95.0	0.0	0.0	0.6	4.4	28.5	15.7	35.4	52.6	16.2	134	76.1
Lostant village	506	480	-5.1	479	91.9	0.0	0.0	2.5	5.6	21.3	18.6	36.8	50.5	15.6	190	91.1
Lost Nation CDP	708	-	-	639	97.0	0.0	0.0	0.0	3.0	3.8	32.4	62.4	30.7	21.6	313	91.4
Louisville village	1,148	1,095	-4.6	1,049	92.9	5.1	0.2	1.0	0.9	20.0	18.1	37.9	53.2	11.8	462	88.1
Loves Park city	23,994	23,371	-2.6	23,710	80.3	4.6	3.4	3.3	8.3	23.1	15.4	38.2	39.4	25.9	9,738	90.7
Lovington village	1,120	1,026	-8.4	1,202	92.5	1.6	0.0	3.7	2.2	23.2	12.6	36.7	57.2	11.4	558	88.5
Ludlow village	371	356	-4.0	354	87.0	4.5	2.3	1.1	5.1	18.4	9.3	36.7	66.0	6.0	136	86.0
Lyndon village	648	610	-5.9	656	93.3	0.0	0.2	0.0	6.6	23.6	18.1	41.1	64.7	8.6	247	87.0
Lynnville village	119	111	-6.7	79	97.5	0.0	0.0	0.0	2.5	12.7	31.6	59.4	52.3	15.4	38	60.5
Lynwood village	9,026	9,194	1.9	9,279	14.9	70.8	0.2	2.1	12.0	22.4	12.1	38.5	22.1	31.9	3,245	88.5
Lyons village	10,733	10,372	-3.4	10,470	41.7	4.6	0.7	1.2	51.7	25.2	12.9	34.5	51.5	17.3	3,777	85.6
McClure village	402	301	-25.1	364	100.0	0.0	0.0	0.0	0.0	24.2	12.9	44.3	64.8	2.4	115	51.3
McCook village	228	220	-3.5	279	48.7	6.5	0.0	3.2	41.6	22.6	19.4	29.9	51.4	17.5	97	83.5
McCullom Lake village	1,053	1,008	-4.3	1,080	79.9	0.3	2.1	10.3	7.4	30.0	8.5	31.8	52.6	11.6	392	91.8
Macedonia village	63	63	0.0	47	100.0	0.0	0.0	0.0	0.0	25.5	21.3	44.1	54.3	28.6	19	68.4
McHenry city	27,039	27,061	0.1	26,813	81.1	0.5	2.0	1.5	14.9	22.3	14.7	39.8	38.2	27.6	10,184	92.2
Machesney Park village	23,508	22,677	-3.5	22,817	86.4	2.4	1.6	2.6	7.1	22.0	14.9	40.8	48.3	15.4	8,969	91.4
Mackinaw village	1,939	1,884	-2.8	1,949	95.7	1.1	0.0	0.9	2.3	28.4	13.9	38.5	37.5	27.4	783	88.3
McLean village	832	795	-4.4	771	98.7	0.0	0.3	0.6	0.4	18.8	16.0	45.6	60.8	13.9	324	89.8
McLeansboro city	2,884	2,746	-4.8	2,613	98.1	1.1	0.0	0.0	0.8	19.1	24.8	43.1	48.2	18.2	1,206	81.9
McNabb village	285	260	-8.8	271	86.0	0.0	3.7	0.0	10.3	19.6	18.1	44.2	36.3	24.4	118	94.9
Macomb city	19,298	17,413	-9.8	17,857	82.6	7.3	2.5	3.5	4.1	15.0	15.2	25.9	30.4	41.0	6,121	87.7
Macon city	1,151	1,112	-3.4	1,207	94.0	0.7	0.0	5.2	0.0	21.4	18.8	44.5	51.0	14.7	491	87.4
Madison city	3,898	3,758	-3.6	3,338	51.8	43.0	0.0	2.8	2.4	19.6	16.9	39.3	57.0	7.3	1,612	80.2
Maeystown village	159	162	1.9	119	99.2	0.0	0.0	0.0	0.8	32.8	4.2	23.9	6.8	27.1	38	94.7
Magnolia village	260	248	-4.6	302	90.7	2.6	0.0	2.0	4.6	26.5	15.9	36.6	55.8	4.7	123	74.8
Mahomet village	7,290	8,605	18.0	8,392	91.9	0.3	0.5	2.1	5.1	26.3	10.3	37.7	18.7	50.2	2,958	95.2
Makanda village	560	530	-5.4	588	91.0	1.0	4.1	2.2	1.7	27.6	13.1	41.1	17.0	41.4	220	97.3
Malden village	362	341	-5.8	311	96.1	0.0	0.0	0.0	3.9	22.5	16.7	43.6	66.7	7.6	132	83.3
Malta village	1,169	1,158	-0.9	1,190	91.3	0.0	0.5	2.5	5.7	21.8	15.2	39.3	31.4	25.9	446	90.8

1 May be of any race.

Table A. All Places — **Population and Housing**

STATE City, town, township, borough, or CDP (county if applicable)	Population: 2010 census total population	Population: 2019 estimated population	Population: Percent change 2010-2019	Population: ACS total population estimate 2015-2019	Race and Hispanic or Latino origin (percent): White alone, not Hispanic or Latino	Race and Hispanic or Latino origin (percent): Black alone, not Hispanic or Latino	Race and Hispanic or Latino origin (percent): Asian alone, not Hispanic or Latino	Race and Hispanic or Latino origin (percent): All other races or 2 or more races, not Hispanic or Latino	Race and Hispanic or Latino origin (percent): Hispanic or Latino[1]	Age (percent): Under 18 years old	Age (percent): Age 65 years and older	Age (percent): Median age	Educational attainment of persons age 25 and older: Percent High school diploma or less	Educational attainment of persons age 25 and older: Percent Bachelor's degree or more	Occupied housing units: Total	Occupied housing units: Percent with a computer
	1	2	3	4	5	6	7	8	9	10	11	12	13	14	15	16
ILLINOIS—Con.																
Manchester village	292	269	-7.9	258	98.1	0.0	0.0	1.9	0.0	20.9	17.4	49.5	66.3	11.4	92	89.1
Manhattan village	7,051	8,240	16.9	8,164	95.9	0.0	0.3	0.4	3.4	33.1	6.6	30.9	34.4	32.5	2,561	94.1
Manito village	1,647	1,486	-9.8	1,563	94.8	2.4	0.0	1.0	1.8	25.6	20.8	39.3	46.9	17.3	674	86.4
Manlius village	359	334	-7.0	311	97.7	0.0	0.0	0.6	1.6	19.0	23.2	48.1	55.3	7.5	150	86.7
Mansfield village	1,006	948	-5.8	873	91.6	0.0	0.0	1.1	7.2	16.8	17.9	45.9	43.8	16.4	395	86.1
Manteno village	9,208	9,002	-2.2	8,539	87.7	2.2	1.1	2.8	6.2	22.0	20.5	43.4	39.8	23.4	3,405	89.5
Maple Park village	1,308	1,365	4.4	1,650	90.7	0.0	1.0	3.3	5.0	22.9	11.2	38.5	36.2	30.4	560	97.0
Mapleton village	271	269	-0.7	284	98.6	0.0	0.0	0.4	1.1	27.1	12.3	36.0	45.5	18.5	104	92.3
Maquon village	282	260	-7.8	220	99.1	0.0	0.0	0.0	0.9	22.3	27.7	51.5	57.7	8.9	109	69.7
Marengo city	7,665	7,437	-3.0	7,969	79.3	2.2	0.0	1.0	17.5	26.2	13.9	36.7	47.5	21.5	2,978	88.0
Marietta village	113	109	-3.5	93	79.6	18.3	0.0	1.1	1.1	23.7	25.8	50.1	66.2	23.5	41	90.2
Marine village	973	922	-5.2	910	96.7	0.0	1.9	0.2	1.2	21.4	17.6	40.8	41.1	23.1	376	91.2
Marion city	17,227	17,520	1.7	17,595	84.3	8.0	1.1	4.2	2.3	22.8	21.0	39.3	38.7	22.7	7,479	80.1
Marissa village	1,978	1,806	-8.7	1,410	99.5	0.3	0.0	0.2	0.0	17.4	28.9	49.6	47.8	11.0	685	81.6
Mark village	557	539	-3.2	482	84.0	0.0	0.0	0.0	16.0	12.7	15.6	37.9	41.5	13.2	196	87.2
Markham city	12,533	12,314	-1.7	12,493	8.6	79.1	0.8	1.5	9.9	27.6	15.2	37.5	45.4	16.2	4,146	85.7
Maroa city	1,801	1,711	-5.0	1,587	92.1	0.6	0.8	6.5	0.1	25.6	15.6	41.1	42.6	25.4	643	89.0
Marquette Heights city	2,820	2,645	-6.2	2,694	93.5	0.2	0.0	0.6	5.7	25.1	14.4	37.9	43.7	14.8	1,021	92.8
Marseilles city	5,114	4,834	-5.5	5,032	94.3	0.2	0.0	1.3	4.2	26.1	17.3	40.9	49.4	13.0	2,088	88.7
Marshall city	3,950	3,811	-3.5	3,543	98.1	0.2	0.0	0.3	1.4	22.5	22.7	41.7	46.0	22.3	1,569	89.7
Martinsville city	1,166	1,088	-6.7	1,211	97.3	0.0	0.0	2.3	0.4	31.5	16.7	33.1	52.6	15.4	502	89.8
Martinton village	381	343	-10.0	291	82.8	0.0	0.7	0.0	16.5	29.6	13.4	34.8	42.6	7.9	118	92.4
Maryville village	7,558	7,952	5.2	7,953	88.5	4.2	2.4	2.3	2.6	17.9	20.8	45.4	22.7	42.9	3,320	94.8
Mascoutah city	7,509	7,994	6.5	8,245	87.7	4.7	1.4	4.0	2.2	29.6	11.8	36.1	31.6	32.8	2,854	93.4
Mason town	345	336	-2.6	258	94.6	0.0	3.1	2.3	0.0	21.3	17.8	44.5	60.5	5.1	106	83.0
Mason City city	2,343	2,119	-9.6	2,370	97.5	1.4	0.0	0.0	1.2	20.6	24.6	43.5	56.2	13.9	1,058	77.6
Matherville village	720	662	-8.1	857	88.2	0.6	0.7	1.3	9.2	34.3	13.1	34.3	56.1	6.9	313	89.1
Matteson village	19,026	19,448	2.2	19,385	13.1	80.9	1.5	2.3	2.3	20.3	16.2	43.7	26.5	36.2	7,309	93.6
Mattoon city	18,563	17,615	-5.1	17,394	95.2	1.6	0.1	1.2	1.9	21.0	19.2	40.5	44.7	18.2	7,674	86.0
Maunie village	139	130	-6.5	175	100.0	0.0	0.0	0.0	0.0	17.7	14.9	42.1	51.6	2.5	70	70.0
Maywood village	24,100	23,158	-3.9	23,578	4.2	67.4	0.5	1.0	26.9	20.7	14.9	37.9	53.9	13.3	7,795	87.1
Mazon village	1,015	967	-4.7	1,145	89.3	0.0	0.3	0.3	10.1	31.5	11.4	31.1	43.7	15.0	423	88.9
Mechanicsburg village	595	661	11.1	671	97.3	0.4	0.0	1.2	1.0	16.4	19.7	45.1	54.2	17.1	271	83.8
Media village	107	94	-12.1	107	96.3	0.0	0.0	3.7	0.0	32.7	13.1	38.5	52.9	14.3	43	95.3
Medora village	419	392	-6.4	337	100.0	0.0	0.0	0.0	0.0	25.5	15.1	35.9	60.9	9.1	143	77.6
Melrose Park village	25,414	24,703	-2.8	25,605	18.1	5.7	0.7	0.3	75.2	28.9	10.5	33.1	62.7	12.8	7,888	87.2
Melvin village	452	410	-9.3	458	90.0	0.0	1.3	2.2	6.6	31.7	12.9	33.3	51.3	14.9	173	88.4
Mendon village	973	961	-1.2	843	100.0	0.0	0.0	0.0	0.0	22.1	24.0	44.9	47.4	20.0	336	86.6
Mendota city	7,374	6,994	-5.2	7,057	63.1	0.3	1.5	1.4	33.8	24.5	18.5	38.4	54.4	13.3	2,755	85.9
Menominee village	253	240	-5.1	265	85.3	4.5	0.0	2.6	7.5	29.4	13.6	44.8	31.3	26.7	94	93.6
Meredosia village	1,046	972	-7.1	891	100.0	0.0	0.0	0.0	0.0	21.9	26.9	47.6	63.5	6.8	362	81.8
Merrionette Park village	1,900	1,858	-2.2	2,050	70.8	8.5	0.0	1.0	19.7	23.5	13.1	37.7	45.9	14.1	880	81.6
Metamora village	3,673	3,699	0.7	3,773	93.8	0.5	0.5	3.4	1.9	26.8	18.1	38.8	28.4	39.3	1,584	92.6
Metcalf village	188	171	-9.0	186	95.2	0.0	0.0	0.0	4.8	25.8	12.9	42.3	76.5	4.5	79	78.5
Metropolis city	6,580	5,945	-9.7	6,129	85.4	7.2	0.4	2.8	4.1	22.1	23.1	43.7	53.6	13.9	2,718	69.9
Mettawa village	539	543	0.7	556	87.9	1.3	5.0	0.4	5.4	21.2	20.3	49.0	9.0	65.4	203	94.6
Middletown village	322	304	-5.6	290	93.8	0.0	0.0	6.2	0.0	29.7	14.5	35.9	45.5	8.4	115	83.5
Midlothian village	14,817	14,346	-3.2	14,595	58.8	9.9	2.8	3.3	25.2	22.3	12.9	38.8	50.5	14.2	5,403	91.7
Milan village	5,193	4,991	-3.9	5,056	86.6	6.0	0.9	0.9	5.6	19.4	21.6	43.6	48.8	16.2	2,485	88.0
Milford village	1,314	1,171	-10.9	1,345	92.3	0.3	0.0	2.3	5.1	21.7	21.3	46.2	54.0	12.0	608	84.2
Millbrook village	310	328	5.8	412	94.2	0.0	0.0	1.5	4.4	23.1	9.5	36.4	38.0	25.1	137	96.4
Mill Creek village	67	64	-4.5	33	75.8	0.0	0.0	0.0	24.2	12.1	0.0	44.1	47.8	34.8	15	86.7
Milledgeville village	1,036	952	-8.1	996	88.4	0.4	0.0	4.6	6.6	19.3	23.7	42.4	53.9	12.0	481	85.4
Millington village	666	659	-1.1	580	93.3	0.0	0.0	0.0	6.7	23.6	9.8	39.8	47.4	13.8	223	99.1
Mill Shoals village	212	197	-7.1	218	99.5	0.0	0.0	0.0	0.5	30.3	24.3	34.6	36.2	8.0	86	75.6
Millstadt village	4,011	3,857	-3.8	3,892	96.8	0.5	0.0	0.0	2.7	22.5	14.7	37.7	34.1	29.9	1,541	91.4
Milton village	271	266	-1.8	289	91.7	0.0	0.0	6.9	1.4	24.9	24.6	46.0	69.9	6.7	117	77.8
Mineral village	237	222	-6.3	228	95.6	1.3	0.0	3.1	0.0	16.2	18.9	47.5	63.9	9.5	104	70.2
Minier village	1,252	1,190	-5.0	1,172	96.5	0.1	0.0	0.4	3.0	17.8	24.2	45.1	48.0	21.2	481	83.4
Minonk city	2,078	1,974	-5.0	1,979	98.4	0.3	0.3	0.8	0.2	24.4	19.9	41.4	49.4	19.5	794	87.8
Minooka village	10,953	11,397	4.1	11,094	80.3	1.9	1.0	1.4	15.4	30.1	8.0	33.6	29.5	32.6	3,711	94.9
Mitchell CDP	1,356	-	-	1,247	93.4	0.0	0.0	1.3	5.3	16.2	14.1	46.9	58.6	8.9	505	92.5
Modesto village	189	178	-5.8	267	99.3	0.0	0.0	0.0	0.7	22.5	25.8	49.1	68.4	10.9	124	75.0
Mokena village	18,646	20,159	8.1	20,674	89.6	1.2	1.6	1.5	6.1	23.5	13.5	40.4	25.6	47.0	7,190	95.8
Moline city	43,440	41,356	-4.8	41,920	71.3	5.7	2.5	2.9	17.7	22.6	20.1	39.9	35.6	28.2	18,449	90.0
Momence city	3,309	3,094	-6.5	3,143	69.7	7.8	0.3	4.9	17.3	28.6	14.0	35.3	54.7	8.8	1,008	90.1
Monee village	5,113	5,061		5,082	60.6	23.3	5.9	0.4	9.7	18.6	19.1	43.2	39.0	24.1	2,323	92.7
Monmouth city	9,424	8,886	-5.7	8,763	74.3	5.2	4.3	2.4	13.7	20.2	16.8	35.8	50.8	22.9	3,472	88.0
Monroe Center village	471	435	-7.6	399	94.7	0.0	0.0	1.5	3.8	21.8	12.8	40.2	31.6	24.6	161	97.5
Montgomery village	18,307	19,638	7.3	19,213	60.4	5.7	1.5	2.1	30.3	33.8	7.5	31.5	39.1	35.9	5,745	96.4
Monticello city	5,554	5,534	-0.4	5,695	94.3	0.8	1.5	1.8	1.6	24.0	20.8	41.1	31.4	38.1	2,403	89.1
Montrose village	201	195	-3.0	189	92.1	0.0	4.8	0.0	3.2	18.0	15.3	47.2	50.0	12.0	87	74.7
Morris city	13,639	15,053	10.4	14,237	85.9	0.9	0.7	2.9	9.6	23.9	17.4	38.3	40.5	23.2	6,042	87.0
Morrison city	4,191	3,988	-4.8	3,776	96.2	0.6	0.2	0.6	2.3	19.9	23.8	41.9	45.1	23.3	1,613	86.8
Morrisonville village	1,061	998	-5.9	1,250	95.8	0.0	0.0	0.3	3.9	29.0	14.3	34.0	53.2	12.9	470	93.0
Morton village	16,355	16,277	-0.5	16,562	92.6	1.3	2.1	0.6	3.4	23.4	21.8	42.1	25.8	42.1	7,060	91.6
Morton Grove village	23,222	22,796	-1.8	23,089	57.0	2.6	30.5	3.1	6.8	18.5	25.7	47.8	30.6	44.5	8,394	89.5
Mound City city	595	504	-15.3	744	42.5	50.8	0.5	0.8	5.4	22.4	10.5	36.7	52.1	7.5	247	42.1
Mounds city	810	684	-15.6	838	16.7	79.8	0.0	1.8	1.7	32.7	21.1	36.5	49.7	6.9	346	55.2
Mound Station village	122	116	-4.9	139	100.0	0.0	0.0	0.0	0.0	33.8	9.4	31.3	55.3	13.2	57	93.0
Mount Auburn village	482	450	-6.6	592	96.3	0.7	0.3	2.7	0.0	24.3	13.0	36.9	55.4	18.0	250	85.6
Mount Carmel city	7,299	7,001	-4.1	7,019	92.8	1.1	0.9	2.2	3.0	19.2	21.0	45.9	39.0	18.7	3,091	86.3
Mount Carroll city	1,717	1,571	-8.5	1,571	95.0	0.5	0.0	0.0	4.5	20.9	23.6	45.9	44.1	23.8	656	90.9
Mount Clare village	281	263	-6.4	255	97.6	0.0	0.0	2.0	0.4	18.0	30.6	52.8	65.7	7.6	132	85.6
Mount Erie village	85	83	-2.4	91	92.3	0.0	0.0	0.0	7.7	28.6	12.1	28.6	42.9	9.5	40	82.5
Mount Morris village	3,009	2,794	-7.1	3,172	97.7	0.0	0.0	2.3	0.0	21.0	23.2	44.7	47.7	27.4	1,479	80.2
Mount Olive city	2,106	1,939	-7.9	2,062	98.5	0.6	0.8	0.0	0.0	21.2	18.4	40.9	52.0	8.5	847	90.8
Mount Prospect village	55,037	53,719	-2.4	54,604	67.0	3.0	12.1	2.6	15.3	23.6	17.4	40.4	31.1	43.7	20,795	91.1
Mount Pulaski city	1,563	1,464	-6.3	1,590	98.1	0.0	0.0	1.8	0.2	21.1	24.0	47.3	47.8	18.8	665	83.9
Mount Sterling city	2,025	1,909	-5.7	2,189	90.7	0.6	0.0	0.0	8.6	26.5	15.3	34.2	45.7	24.5	911	79.8
Mount Vernon city	15,241	14,723	-3.4	14,742	75.4	15.9	2.1	2.9	3.7	23.4	20.2	38.6	41.3	20.8	6,465	87.4
Mount Zion village	5,842	5,795	-0.8	5,975	84.1	4.5	1.1	9.1	1.2	29.7	14.6	39.1	30.5	35.2	2,094	93.2

1 May be of any race.

Table A. All Places — **Population and Housing**

STATE City, town, township, borough, or CDP (county if applicable)	Population				Race and Hispanic or Latino origin (percent)					Age (percent)			Educational attainment of persons age 25 and older		Occupied housing units	
	2010 census total population	2019 estimated population	Percent change 2010-2019	ACS total population estimate 2015-2019	White alone, not Hispanic or Latino	Black alone, not Hispanic or Latino	Asian alone, not Hispanic or Latino	All other races or 2 or more races, not Hispanic or Latino	Hispanic or Latino[1]	Under 18 years old	Age 65 years and older	Median age	Percent High school diploma or less	Percent Bachelor's degree or more	Total	Percent with a computer
	1	2	3	4	5	6	7	8	9	10	11	12	13	14	15	16
ILLINOIS—Con.																
Moweaqua village	1,829	1,714	-6.3	1,985	97.0	0.7	0.4	1.5	0.5	23.0	24.3	46.6	44.2	19.8	812	91.1
Muddy village	69	63	-8.7	44	77.3	0.0	0.0	0.0	22.7	4.5	11.4	49.3	36.8	5.3	20	95.0
Mulberry Grove village	632	575	-9.0	650	96.5	1.5	0.0	0.6	1.4	23.2	20.9	41.0	68.5	6.3	291	79.4
Mulkeytown CDP	175	-	-	181	100.0	0.0	0.0	0.0	0.0	36.5	22.7	41.9	44.7	6.8	64	59.4
Muncie village	146	138	-5.5	122	100.0	0.0	0.0	0.0	0.0	29.5	7.4	34.0	35.5	11.8	49	85.7
Mundelein village	30,986	31,051	0.2	31,587	51.6	2.0	12.2	2.6	31.6	23.1	13.5	37.2	31.5	43.4	10,819	95.9
Murphysboro city	7,968	7,406	-7.1	7,757	76.3	14.0	0.1	2.7	6.9	26.3	16.9	36.5	48.6	19.2	3,307	81.8
Murrayville village	587	548	-6.6	512	97.7	0.0	0.0	0.6	1.8	18.8	22.3	44.5	58.6	8.1	208	89.4
Naperville city	142,170	148,449	4.4	147,501	67.3	5.0	19.1	2.8	5.8	25.4	12.2	39.1	13.2	68.2	51,940	97.0
Naplate village	496	470	-5.2	480	89.8	0.0	0.0	5.0	5.2	17.9	18.1	48.0	59.4	6.3	235	82.6
Naples town	130	119	-8.5	81	74.1	0.0	0.0	13.6	12.3	13.6	28.4	36.9	66.1	3.2	32	56.3
Nashville city	3,260	3,011	-7.6	3,024	97.2	0.9	0.0	0.0	1.9	21.4	20.5	42.6	38.5	24.4	1,285	87.9
Nason city	236	233	-1.3	231	99.1	0.0	0.0	0.4	0.4	20.3	21.2	44.3	58.2	1.8	103	79.6
Nauvoo city	1,149	1,063	-7.5	990	96.8	0.9	0.6	0.3	1.4	20.5	30.8	45.1	42.7	21.2	356	83.7
Nebo village	340	328	-3.5	330	98.5	0.0	0.3	0.9	0.3	28.2	14.2	35.9	77.0	0.5	123	83.7
Nelson village	170	159	-6.5	136	97.8	0.0	0.0	0.0	2.2	29.4	10.3	38.0	51.2	2.3	60	83.3
Neoga city	1,636	1,602	-2.1	1,719	93.9	0.0	0.0	2.3	3.8	24.8	20.8	38.9	47.0	17.1	634	89.1
Neponset village	473	436	-7.8	454	94.9	0.7	0.4	0.4	3.5	23.6	14.8	39.4	46.8	11.3	188	86.2
Newark village	979	1,028	5.0	1,314	94.0	0.4	0.2	0.3	5.1	26.1	11.2	36.6	44.6	22.6	409	91.7
New Athens village	2,060	1,884	-8.5	2,147	97.5	0.7	0.2	0.8	0.8	27.2	15.7	36.4	46.4	15.2	786	91.6
New Baden village	3,350	3,241	-3.3	3,206	86.8	7.4	0.0	1.0	4.8	24.1	14.0	39.2	35.1	25.6	1,247	85.8
New Bedford village	75	70	-6.7	63	98.4	0.0	0.0	0.0	1.6	7.9	41.3	51.5	80.4	2.0	31	80.6
New Berlin village	1,348	1,333	-1.1	1,478	98.4	0.2	0.0	1.1	0.3	29.8	11.6	36.7	32.1	35.1	570	89.5
New Boston city	687	650	-5.4	566	95.4	0.0	0.2	0.7	3.7	18.7	21.6	47.8	69.2	5.1	247	81.0
New Burnside village	211	214	1.4	134	100.0	0.0	0.0	0.0	0.0	12.7	47.8	60.5	51.3	7.0	67	58.2
New Canton town	359	346	-3.6	328	96.6	0.0	1.2	1.8	0.3	23.8	14.9	45.0	64.6	4.8	143	77.6
New Douglas village	319	307	-3.8	296	87.8	2.0	0.0	1.0	9.1	31.1	8.8	43.0	50.0	13.5	110	90.0
New Grand Chain village	210	182	-13.3	185	76.8	10.8	1.6	5.4	5.4	28.1	28.1	47.2	46.3	22.3	66	74.2
New Haven village	436	382	-12.4	376	93.9	0.0	0.0	4.0	2.1	14.9	18.6	48.8	61.3	7.0	163	77.3
New Holland village	282	268	-5.0	278	97.5	0.0	0.0	1.4	1.1	24.5	14.0	42.6	41.9	16.2	113	89.4
New Lenox village	24,288	26,926	10.9	26,454	91.5	0.7	0.6	1.4	5.8	26.8	10.9	36.9	25.9	40.5	8,796	96.6
Newman city	863	833	-3.5	704	94.2	1.3	0.3	2.1	2.1	17.5	22.2	51.1	54.7	13.8	318	85.2
New Milford village	711	699	-1.7	713	66.1	13.3	3.2	0.3	17.1	20.3	17.5	45.0	57.3	13.1	311	90.4
New Minden village	215	206	-4.2	170	100.0	0.0	0.0	0.0	0.0	15.9	19.4	50.2	44.8	14.0	81	88.9
New Salem village	137	134	-2.2	271	98.2	0.0	0.0	1.8	0.0	24.0	13.3	34.6	36.1	4.7	104	86.5
Newton city	2,894	2,863	-1.1	2,810	96.8	0.8	0.0	1.5	0.9	21.2	23.0	44.3	52.6	17.0	1,265	77.7
Niantic village	707	655	-7.4	574	99.7	0.0	0.0	0.3	0.0	26.7	21.6	42.6	54.1	11.4	228	87.7
Niles village	29,825	28,938	-3.0	29,451	65.7	2.8	19.8	2.7	9.0	16.2	25.1	48.4	38.7	35.9	10,925	84.4
Nilwood town	239	229	-4.2	176	99.4	0.6	0.0	0.0	0.0	12.5	32.4	53.5	76.2	3.3	85	77.6
Noble village	674	641	-4.9	671	94.0	1.3	0.4	1.8	2.4	18.9	20.3	41.5	50.8	13.1	275	85.5
Nokomis city	2,256	2,110	-6.5	2,055	96.8	0.7	0.5	1.5	0.5	25.0	21.2	38.2	56.5	14.7	916	86.2
Nora village	121	116	-4.1	150	93.3	0.0	0.0	6.0	0.7	22.0	12.7	40.7	67.0	17.0	62	82.3
Normal town	52,549	54,469	3.7	54,891	77.7	10.7	4.3	2.1	5.2	17.2	10.0	24.6	23.3	48.5	19,368	95.2
Norridge village	14,574	14,152	-2.9	14,703	85.4	0.6	5.2	0.9	7.9	17.2	23.9	46.8	44.9	27.3	5,477	80.9
Norris village	209	200	-4.3	161	98.1	0.0	1.9	0.0	0.0	20.5	22.4	41.9	55.2	11.2	80	67.5
Norris City village	1,249	1,151	-7.8	1,127	98.2	0.0	0.4	0.9	0.4	27.7	16.3	37.7	43.3	9.9	516	86.2
North Aurora village	16,621	18,057	8.6	17,752	74.3	4.8	4.3	1.3	15.2	22.0	13.6	41.1	29.1	38.8	6,743	95.3
North Barrington village	3,017	2,952	-2.2	2,982	88.1	2.1	4.9	1.9	3.0	22.9	21.0	50.4	10.6	72.2	1,075	96.8
Northbrook village	33,200	32,958	-0.7	33,343	78.3	1.5	17.1	1.1	2.0	21.9	27.1	50.2	13.5	70.4	13,056	95.7
North Chicago city	32,594	29,615	-9.1	29,971	30.7	26.5	5.3	4.4	33.2	17.9	5.7	24.1	48.2	22.0	7,310	90.1
North City village	588	569	-3.2	560	93.9	0.9	0.0	0.5	4.6	13.4	21.8	49.8	42.5	14.4	248	78.2
Northfield village	5,452	5,386	-1.2	5,534	87.0	0.5	7.0	0.4	5.1	23.7	26.7	48.8	7.1	76.9	2,274	96.5
North Henderson village	187	174	-7.0	174	99.4	0.0	0.0	0.6	0.0	19.0	19.0	38.8	48.6	18.8	72	80.6
Northlake city	12,325	12,161	-1.3	12,290	31.0	3.9	1.8	0.6	62.7	26.2	14.1	37.0	59.0	12.4	4,014	87.6
North Pekin village	1,592	1,545	-3.0	1,554	93.9	0.1	0.0	0.2	5.8	24.4	14.5	39.7	57.2	9.3	654	84.7
North Riverside village	6,672	6,429	-3.6	6,646	57.0	7.3	6.3	1.1	28.3	23.5	18.4	41.6	39.3	27.4	2,685	83.8
North Utica village	1,346	1,336	-0.7	1,338	88.8	0.0	1.3	7.2	2.6	24.7	21.4	45.6	38.4	23.2	541	89.5
Norwood village	479	459	-4.2	483	92.8	2.7	0.0	4.6	0.0	21.9	14.7	39.7	47.9	8.6	184	87.0
Oak Brook village	7,888	8,016	1.6	8,075	59.5	2.4	31.8	2.7	3.5	18.6	38.5	56.1	15.5	66.6	3,039	91.5
Oakbrook Terrace city	2,104	2,098	-0.3	2,752	61.3	7.7	17.3	2.2	11.5	15.4	23.9	37.0	26.0	49.4	1,216	88.6
Oakdale village	210	200	-4.8	190	89.5	0.0	0.0	1.1	9.5	26.3	15.8	36.6	35.4	17.3	85	82.4
Oakford village	286	276	-3.5	283	100.0	0.0	0.0	0.0	0.0	23.0	18.4	32.8	52.5	4.9	122	79.5
Oak Forest city	27,966	27,173	-2.8	27,617	71.7	6.4	5.3	1.5	15.1	20.8	14.4	41.8	36.0	31.5	10,275	91.3
Oak Grove village	595	591	-0.7	541	94.5	0.0	0.0	2.4	3.1	32.7	16.3	38.9	57.1	10.1	226	86.7
Oakland city	876	854	-2.5	962	96.3	0.0	0.0	0.0	3.7	26.2	17.3	37.9	46.7	19.3	382	86.6
Oak Lawn village	56,690	55,022	-2.9	55,936	66.2	6.7	3.8	1.3	22.0	21.3	18.5	40.8	36.9	30.0	21,248	86.7
Oak Park village	51,878	52,381	1.0	52,233	63.2	17.9	4.7	5.3	8.9	24.3	14.7	39.8	12.7	70.0	21,603	94.1
Oak Run CDP	547	-	-	556	98.4	0.0	0.0	0.0	1.6	13.3	37.4	58.7	27.7	37.1	252	93.3
Oakwood village	1,595	1,485	-6.9	1,636	96.7	0.0	0.0	0.2	3.1	26.8	14.5	33.8	46.4	11.9	621	89.4
Oakwood Hills village	2,076	2,028	-2.3	2,336	88.6	0.2	1.5	0.8	8.9	25.3	11.2	38.3	27.1	34.8	822	96.2
Oblong village	1,468	1,371	-6.6	1,326	94.2	0.8	0.0	2.6	2.5	22.8	22.8	39.3	52.2	11.9	637	88.2
Oconee village	180	172	-4.4	176	96.6	0.0	0.0	1.1	2.3	26.1	23.3	37.0	47.9	15.4	69	78.3
Odell village	1,039	964	-7.2	1,097	98.7	0.0	0.0	0.8	0.5	32.3	11.9	32.1	48.7	12.4	387	92.0
Odin village	1,076	1,009	-6.2	1,062	98.3	0.0	0.0	1.7	0.0	27.7	23.2	39.4	55.9	5.3	385	84.7
O'Fallon city	28,759	29,583	2.9	29,333	76.4	11.6	2.9	4.1	5.0	27.3	11.8	36.7	18.7	47.8	10,974	95.6
Ogden village	821	800	-2.6	809	99.0	0.0	0.4	0.2	0.4	21.3	17.6	38.8	31.4	26.6	330	90.6
Oglesby city	3,791	3,559	-6.1	3,549	85.7	2.1	0.3	2.2	9.6	25.0	16.6	39.4	42.3	18.8	1,533	83.2
Ohio village	513	480	-6.4	529	97.9	1.5	0.0	0.0	0.6	18.1	21.7	42.5	53.8	10.6	226	82.7
Ohlman village	135	126	-6.7	122	100.0	0.0	0.0	0.0	0.0	15.6	32.8	53.5	63.4	20.8	62	67.7
Okawville village	1,434	1,360	-5.2	1,525	91.8	3.4	0.0	2.0	2.8	25.7	15.9	35.9	30.5	34.7	658	91.3
Old Mill Creek village	173	167	-3.5	194	90.2	0.0	0.0	0.0	9.8	14.9	35.1	61.3	51.9	35.1	84	100.0
Old Ripley village	108	99	-8.3	95	100.0	0.0	0.0	0.0	0.0	15.8	16.8	37.5	68.4	2.6	43	62.8
Old Shawneetown village	192	164	-14.6	81	100.0	0.0	0.0	0.0	0.0	29.6	27.2	49.9	77.8	0.0	45	66.7
Olive Branch CDP	864	-	-	501	100.0	0.0	0.0	0.0	0.0	24.4	30.5	47.2	67.2	4.0	178	74.2
Olivet CDP	428	-	-	355	91.5	0.0	4.8	0.0	3.7	20.8	26.2	35.4	47.0	21.6	169	90.5
Olmsted village	333	294	-11.7	486	89.1	9.3	0.0	1.6	0.0	29.6	20.4	38.2	59.2	10.2	167	62.9
Olney city	9,094	8,674	-4.6	8,723	92.7	1.3	0.8	2.5	2.7	23.7	20.9	41.2	42.1	21.8	3,649	85.8
Olympia Fields village	4,921	4,790	-2.7	4,821	21.8	73.4	1.4	3.4	0.0	19.4	29.8	48.4	20.3	50.9	1,818	90.3
Omaha village	266	228	-14.3	285	97.5	0.0	0.0	2.5	0.0	25.3	20.0	38.1	62.5	9.0	122	82.0
Onarga village	1,377	1,264	-8.2	1,055	46.3	0.6	0.2	0.3	52.7	27.3	13.6	35.7	66.0	8.9	365	82.7
Oneida city	702	662	-5.7	708	94.5	4.8	0.0	0.0	0.7	27.4	14.3	39.5	32.0	29.7	299	83.6
Opdyke CDP	254	-	-	289	98.6	0.0	0.0	0.0	1.4	31.5	9.7	39.0	40.1	1.7	105	88.6

1 May be of any race.

Table A. All Places — **Population and Housing**

STATE City, town, township, borough, or CDP (county if applicable)	Population: 2010 census total population	Population: 2019 estimated population	Population: Percent change 2010-2019	Population: ACS total population estimate 2015-2019	Race and Hispanic or Latino origin (percent): White alone, not Hispanic or Latino	Race: Black alone, not Hispanic or Latino	Race: Asian alone, not Hispanic or Latino	Race: All other races or 2 or more races, not Hispanic or Latino	Race: Hispanic or Latino[1]	Age (percent): Under 18 years old	Age: Age 65 years and older	Age: Median age	Educational attainment of persons age 25 and older: Percent High school diploma or less	Educational attainment: Percent Bachelor's degree or more	Occupied housing units: Total	Occupied housing units: Percent with a computer
	1	2	3	4	5	6	7	8	9	10	11	12	13	14	15	16
ILLINOIS—Con.																
Oquawka village	1,371	1,252	-8.7	1,452	91.9	0.4	2.7	3.1	1.9	18.2	22.2	45.4	56.5	12.4	665	83.5
Orangeville village	807	752	-6.8	752	97.9	0.0	0.1	1.1	0.9	20.7	17.0	41.5	50.2	17.5	379	92.1
Oreana village	878	811	-7.6	755	90.2	0.0	6.0	2.8	1.1	25.6	22.5	42.2	43.6	19.4	292	89.0
Oregon city	3,713	3,470	-6.5	3,819	90.9	0.4	0.2	2.9	5.7	21.0	21.1	46.2	47.0	19.0	1,751	85.7
Orient city	358	343	-4.2	426	93.2	0.0	0.7	1.9	4.2	13.4	20.2	47.9	58.8	7.0	204	74.5
Orion village	1,866	1,798	-3.6	2,006	96.8	0.7	0.0	0.4	2.1	25.0	16.4	38.2	40.1	22.7	752	88.7
Orland Hills village	7,210	7,023	-2.6	7,136	71.0	10.1	5.9	0.4	12.6	26.0	8.8	36.1	31.9	33.3	2,396	95.2
Orland Park village	56,607	57,857	2.2	58,749	82.7	4.3	4.8	1.2	6.9	20.3	21.9	46.0	29.2	44.4	22,218	92.6
Oswego village	30,452	36,252	19.0	34,933	71.7	4.8	4.8	1.6	17.1	29.2	9.6	36.6	23.8	46.0	11,215	97.8
Ottawa city	18,818	18,063	-4.0	18,792	82.2	4.2	0.8	2.9	9.9	22.7	17.9	38.7	47.2	20.0	8,097	87.6
Otterville town	126	118	-6.3	134	93.3	3.7	0.0	3.0	0.0	29.9	38.1	54.5	74.4	2.2	49	73.5
Owaneco village	239	223	-6.7	237	97.9	0.0	0.0	0.8	1.3	20.3	18.6	38.5	50.6	7.2	93	89.2
Paderborn CDP	43	-	-	76	100.0	0.0	0.0	0.0	0.0	0.0	39.5	38.9	100.0	0.0	59	61.0
Palatine village	68,551	67,482	-1.6	68,407	63.2	2.6	11.5	2.2	20.5	23.7	13.6	38.2	25.6	50.0	26,866	94.6
Palestine village	1,368	1,273	-6.9	1,185	98.1	0.2	0.0	1.5	0.3	16.7	29.8	49.9	45.1	7.7	611	86.6
Palmer village	227	205	-9.7	239	100.0	0.0	0.0	0.0	0.0	19.7	19.7	42.4	55.4	15.9	103	74.8
Palmyra village	698	659	-5.6	665	96.8	0.3	0.0	1.4	1.5	23.9	18.2	43.3	60.0	6.0	294	86.1
Palos Heights city	12,515	12,520	0.0	12,480	88.8	2.1	1.8	1.3	5.9	17.9	29.4	52.1	28.7	44.9	4,706	89.2
Palos Hills city	17,480	17,060	-2.4	17,318	80.3	5.3	2.8	1.4	10.2	21.4	20.1	41.8	39.8	28.6	6,725	87.3
Palos Park village	4,849	4,736	-2.3	4,842	88.8	0.9	1.0	2.1	7.2	19.5	31.2	53.6	25.7	43.1	1,955	83.2
Pana city	5,842	5,376	-8.0	5,447	97.9	0.9	0.5	0.3	0.3	22.7	22.8	40.9	62.0	12.7	2,454	83.0
Panama village	343	319	-7.0	296	98.0	0.0	0.0	1.4	0.7	20.3	24.0	35.3	64.1	9.2	135	69.6
Panola village	51	52	2.0	14	100.0	0.0	0.0	0.0	0.0	21.4	35.7	58.0	0.0	54.5	7	71.4
Papineau village	167	149	-10.8	114	83.3	0.0	1.8	14.9	0.0	27.2	15.8	40.3	68.8	1.3	49	93.9
Paris city	8,882	8,285	-6.7	8,372	97.9	0.2	0.0	0.1	1.8	21.0	20.5	42.8	51.6	14.7	3,709	83.5
Park City city	7,569	7,438	-1.7	7,396	12.5	12.8	4.7	0.7	69.4	28.0	5.6	29.0	72.0	10.3	2,347	89.8
Parkersburg village	208	200	-3.8	189	97.4	0.0	0.0	2.6	0.0	21.2	14.8	37.6	54.1	6.6	74	90.5
Park Forest village	21,981	21,210	-3.5	21,563	25.0	66.0	0.5	3.9	4.6	23.8	14.7	39.3	31.3	26.4	8,590	91.6
Park Ridge city	37,479	36,950	-1.4	37,457	86.5	0.8	5.8	2.5	4.3	23.8	20.1	44.9	18.3	60.0	14,197	93.6
Patoka village	578	547	-5.4	576	99.7	0.0	0.3	0.0	0.0	25.3	18.9	41.7	55.2	8.9	233	84.1
Pawnee village	2,749	2,640	-4.0	2,594	98.3	0.0	0.1	1.6	0.0	24.9	14.4	37.6	37.2	23.4	1,001	94.1
Paw Paw village	924	848	-8.2	915	95.5	0.0	0.3	1.1	3.1	21.4	16.7	38.0	49.1	12.8	398	89.7
Paxton city	4,506	4,125	-8.5	4,220	89.0	2.5	1.0	0.9	6.6	26.1	15.9	40.5	42.6	22.2	1,729	84.0
Payson village	1,025	990	-3.4	1,107	99.1	0.0	0.0	0.0	0.9	27.5	8.9	31.9	52.3	18.8	389	94.9
Pearl village	138	132	-4.3	175	100.0	0.0	0.0	0.0	0.0	17.7	20.0	46.2	57.9	13.5	62	77.4
Pearl City village	838	783	-6.6	738	97.2	0.0	0.0	0.5	2.3	28.0	13.7	40.6	32.4	20.5	302	96.0
Pecatonica village	2,203	2,078	-5.7	2,243	90.2	0.0	0.0	7.1	2.7	25.1	17.3	37.5	44.8	16.1	884	91.4
Pekin city	34,018	32,045	-5.8	32,846	93.6	2.0	0.5	2.0	1.9	22.4	18.0	39.7	46.6	18.5	13,559	84.8
Penfield CDP	193	-	-	130	91.5	0.0	0.0	5.4	3.1	9.2	38.5	54.5	72.7	5.5	72	81.9
Peoria city	115,150	110,417	-4.1	113,532	56.6	26.9	6.0	4.3	6.3	24.1	15.3	35.2	34.9	34.9	46,123	86.0
Peoria Heights village	6,079	5,779	-4.9	5,860	88.5	3.8	0.9	4.8	2.0	20.1	14.5	37.9	31.9	25.6	2,763	90.3
Peotone village	4,146	4,105		4,331	91.0	0.3	0.1	3.7	4.9	25.6	12.0	37.5	42.9	23.6	1,501	90.5
Percy village	978	919	-6.0	958	74.5	4.0	0.9	0.0	20.6	32.2	14.3	27.5	70.6	5.5	351	72.4
Perry village	397	382	-3.8	303	94.1	4.3	0.0	0.0	1.7	16.8	33.0	53.2	44.9	14.4	152	75.7
Peru city	10,329	9,730	-5.8	9,798	88.8	0.4	0.7	1.7	8.3	21.1	23.6	46.1	38.7	22.8	4,294	85.9
Pesotum village	551	524	-4.9	508	92.1	0.0	0.0	5.1	2.8	16.1	14.4	44.5	45.6	22.3	209	92.3
Petersburg city	2,331	2,214	-5.0	2,513	92.6	0.7	0.4	5.2	1.2	22.2	15.6	40.5	44.8	22.9	1,116	89.9
Phillipstown village	44	41	-6.8	45	97.8	2.2	0.0	0.0	0.0	15.6	24.4	55.2	55.9	8.8	21	90.5
Philo village	1,468	1,400	-4.6	1,560	100.0	0.0	0.0	0.0	0.0	25.3	17.4	39.7	31.3	31.8	538	96.3
Phoenix village	1,974	1,908	-3.3	1,884	1.9	81.2	0.0	3.4	13.6	27.7	19.5	35.7	58.0	13.1	709	74.3
Pierron village	590	544	-7.8	412	97.8	0.0	0.7	0.0	1.5	18.9	15.0	43.9	48.4	12.7	188	84.6
Pinckneyville city	5,650	5,372	-4.9	5,436	62.8	28.8	1.6	0.6	6.2	15.5	9.6	36.7	63.8	8.1	1,424	87.9
Pingree Grove village	4,518	9,874	118.5	8,107	76.1	2.9	6.5	0.6	13.9	29.9	10.7	37.1	22.0	38.5	2,783	96.0
Piper City village	839	750	-10.6	878	84.7	0.0	0.0	5.6	9.7	18.1	17.8	46.3	65.3	3.8	378	81.5
Pistakee Highlands CDP	3,454	-	-	3,217	95.0	0.0	0.0	1.3	3.7	20.5	16.2	43.1	46.4	15.5	1,295	98.1
Pittsburg village	572	551	-3.7	552	96.9	0.0	0.0	2.2	0.9	20.1	22.3	43.5	54.3	15.3	229	85.6
Pittsfield city	4,596	4,254	-7.4	4,362	95.9	2.5	0.2	0.1	1.3	22.8	21.0	40.3	44.4	22.1	1,732	84.6
Plainfield village	39,884	44,308	11.1	43,110	70.9	7.1	8.5	2.7	10.7	32.0	8.1	35.8	22.3	52.9	12,662	97.6
Plainville village	262	255	-2.7	283	96.8	0.0	0.7	1.8	0.7	24.4	15.9	39.0	60.4	10.4	115	75.7
Plano city	10,850	11,665	7.5	11,752	54.3	10.7	0.8	2.6	31.7	28.2	8.5	32.8	40.6	22.2	3,737	95.0
Plattville village	242	256	5.8	237	94.5	0.4	0.0	0.0	5.1	28.3	15.6	37.7	36.5	17.6	77	98.7
Pleasant Hill village	964	925	-4.0	1,037	99.1	0.0	0.0	0.0	0.9	22.9	14.1	41.4	58.8	20.0	403	83.6
Pleasant Plains village	801	791	-1.2	774	97.7	0.0	1.0	0.5	0.8	26.4	14.9	37.7	41.8	24.0	298	88.6
Plymouth village	505	466	-7.7	445	97.5	2.5	0.0	0.0	0.0	23.1	24.9	46.2	63.5	8.8	190	81.6
Pocahontas village	790	731	-7.5	729	98.4	0.0	0.0	0.0	1.6	20.9	14.1	36.8	49.5	13.2	314	76.1
Polo city	2,347	2,171	-7.5	2,133	90.0	1.9	2.3	0.4	5.3	26.6	18.8	39.9	47.8	15.2	909	84.4
Pontiac city	11,930	11,253	-5.7	11,688	82.3	9.9	1.2	0.7	5.8	21.6	15.6	38.7	56.9	12.6	4,329	87.5
Pontoon Beach village	5,861	5,641	-3.8	5,793	80.0	5.1	1.7	2.0	11.2	25.0	10.8	35.1	49.1	15.1	2,219	96.3
Pontoosuc village	146	136	-6.8	87	97.7	0.0	0.0	2.3	0.0	17.2	20.7	35.5	51.5	7.4	48	60.4
Poplar Grove village	4,922	5,104	3.7	5,270	83.1	5.7	0.0	0.9	10.2	30.9	7.3	34.7	37.0	28.8	1,626	94.5
Port Barrington village	1,513	1,488	-1.7	1,676	86.9	0.6	2.7	1.0	8.8	22.3	7.2	38.8	27.8	44.5	571	97.5
Port Byron village	1,642	1,607	-2.1	2,101	92.7	1.4	0.0	1.6	4.3	29.6	14.5	39.3	31.0	35.2	846	93.3
Posen village	6,047	5,865	-3.0	6,149	22.3	16.3	0.6	3.3	57.5	34.2	7.0	31.1	52.0	19.1	1,973	91.2
Potomac village	749	690	-7.9	804	87.2	4.2	3.4	1.9	3.4	32.6	10.4	32.2	56.2	11.6	311	86.5
Prairie City village	380	351	-7.6	389	82.8	2.8	2.1	8.7	3.6	24.7	28.3	44.9	65.2	12.6	138	72.5
Prairie du Rocher village	604	558	-7.6	475	98.7	0.0	0.0	0.6	0.6	18.9	16.4	42.8	53.0	8.1	210	82.4
Prairie Grove village	1,987	1,931	-2.8	1,805	90.0	3.8	2.0	1.4	2.8	24.7	10.4	42.7	18.2	47.8	643	98.1
Prestbury CDP	1,722	-	-	1,584	96.3	1.0	0.0	0.0	2.7	10.5	37.1	61.1	22.2	56.1	711	95.2
Preston Heights CDP	2,575	-	-	2,651	25.2	37.5	0.3	4.7	32.4	25.0	13.6	34.3	60.2	13.9	891	89.6
Princeton city	7,915	7,468	-5.6	7,603	93.3	0.1	0.0	0.5	6.1	21.3	25.9	46.6	39.2	24.5	3,406	86.6
Princeville village	1,743	1,672	-4.1	1,952	84.9	0.5	0.5	2.2	11.9	27.0	19.1	40.9	43.2	20.6	701	94.3
Prophetstown city	2,078	1,939	-6.7	2,062	95.1	1.8	0.0	1.6	1.5	18.8	24.7	47.4	47.0	22.5	837	86.3
Prospect Heights city	16,258	15,887	-2.3	16,137	52.5	2.2	8.7	0.6	36.1	25.7	15.9	38.2	38.4	35.4	5,694	92.4
Pulaski village	206	175	-15.0	271	16.2	64.6	0.0	17.7	1.5	21.8	19.2	44.5	31.4	6.3	79	25.3
Quincy city	40,709	39,949	-1.9	40,280	88.5	6.3	0.8	2.5	1.8	21.6	20.9	40.7	43.6	23.9	17,254	82.8
Radom village	220	211	-4.1	178	98.9	0.0	0.0	0.0	1.1	14.0	24.2	49.5	54.1	7.4	89	78.7
Raleigh village	350	329	-6.0	302	96.7	0.0	0.0	0.3	3.0	14.9	18.5	49.2	46.4	11.4	135	74.1
Ramsey village	1,042	1,011	-3.0	987	97.7	0.6	0.0	1.7	0.0	25.6	15.9	37.3	67.9	4.1	382	75.7
Rankin village	561	513	-8.6	543	84.3	0.0	0.0	0.7	14.9	29.5	12.9	41.1	62.3	9.2	188	90.4
Ransom village	384	356	-7.3	414	90.1	0.0	0.0	1.2	8.7	25.1	7.2	36.5	54.2	7.9	165	91.5
Rantoul village	12,956	12,493	-3.6	13,218	58.2	24.8	2.1	3.0	11.8	32.6	12.9	30.5	49.4	17.0	4,916	81.8
Rapids City village	961	967	0.6	1,065	95.2	0.0	1.7	1.0	2.1	27.4	22.4	41.9	37.7	29.5	393	91.6

1 May be of any race.

Table A. All Places — **Population and Housing**

STATE City, town, township, borough, or CDP (county if applicable)	Population: 2010 census total population	Population: 2019 estimated population	Population: Percent change 2010-2019	Population: ACS total population estimate 2015-2019	Race and Hispanic or Latino origin (percent): White alone, not Hispanic or Latino	Race and Hispanic or Latino origin (percent): Black alone, not Hispanic or Latino	Race and Hispanic or Latino origin (percent): Asian alone, not Hispanic or Latino	Race and Hispanic or Latino origin (percent): All other races or 2 or more races, not Hispanic or Latino	Race and Hispanic or Latino origin (percent): Hispanic or Latino[1]	Age (percent): Under 18 years old	Age (percent): Age 65 years and older	Age (percent): Median age	Educational attainment of persons age 25 and older: Percent High school diploma or less	Educational attainment of persons age 25 and older: Percent Bachelor's degree or more	Occupied housing units: Total	Occupied housing units: Percent with a computer
	1	2	3	4	5	6	7	8	9	10	11	12	13	14	15	16
ILLINOIS—Con.																
Raritan village	138	122	-11.6	114	92.1	0.0	0.0	7.9	0.0	37.7	18.4	26.8	47.1	12.9	38	100.0
Raymond village	1,004	942	-6.2	968	95.7	0.0	1.5	2.6	0.2	18.0	20.9	47.1	47.9	14.4	434	86.2
Red Bud city	3,697	3,480	-5.9	3,539	97.4	0.0	0.0	0.6	2.0	21.5	20.7	43.1	44.6	14.0	1,471	88.9
Reddick village	166	157	-5.4	216	98.1	0.0	0.0	0.0	1.9	23.6	17.6	34.5	36.0	17.6	84	81.0
Redmon village	173	158	-8.7	129	90.7	0.0	7.0	0.0	2.3	9.3	27.9	55.1	42.7	8.7	73	84.9
Rentchler CDP	34	-	-	6	100.0	0.0	0.0	0.0	0.0	0.0	0.0	0.0	100.0	0.0	6	100.0
Reynolds village	543	507	-6.6	543	96.3	1.5	0.0	0.0	2.2	21.7	15.1	38.0	37.9	30.0	213	93.9
Richmond village	1,865	1,904	2.1	2,061	86.9	1.0	1.1	2.0	8.9	25.7	14.7	39.3	40.5	28.8	852	94.8
Richton Park village	13,670	13,292	-2.8	13,504	9.2	85.5	0.8	1.7	2.8	21.0	11.8	41.4	30.9	25.8	4,837	89.6
Richview village	262	243	-7.3	289	90.3	1.4	0.0	8.3	0.0	28.7	16.6	37.5	57.0	3.9	115	85.2
Ridge Farm village	887	812	-8.5	940	93.7	0.0	0.0	1.3	5.0	21.6	12.9	42.6	59.0	4.3	389	85.3
Ridgway village	869	747	-14.0	788	89.7	0.0	0.8	7.5	2.0	18.3	25.6	43.6	50.3	17.3	371	74.9
Ridott village	161	151	-6.2	164	98.2	0.0	0.0	1.8	0.0	25.0	6.1	38.0	55.8	7.7	67	91.0
Ringwood village	838	813	-3.0	789	90.2	2.4	4.3	0.0	3.0	22.4	15.3	46.1	42.5	28.3	288	94.8
Rio village	220	207	-5.9	182	88.5	4.9	0.5	1.1	4.9	13.2	31.3	49.9	48.6	6.3	80	86.3
Ripley village	86	82	-4.7	53	100.0	0.0	0.0	0.0	0.0	26.4	17.0	44.2	80.6	0.0	27	55.6
Riverdale village	13,549	13,077	-3.5	12,793	4.4	88.6	0.1	2.5	4.4	28.3	8.5	33.6	45.6	13.9	4,868	87.1
River Forest village	11,176	10,816	-3.2	10,970	82.2	5.5	3.6	3.0	5.7	25.6	16.7	41.7	5.2	80.4	3,971	95.6
River Grove village	10,246	9,883	-3.5	10,076	64.0	1.3	1.4	1.6	31.7	22.8	14.5	37.5	50.9	19.5	3,643	86.7
Riverside village	8,875	8,563	-3.5	8,759	78.1	1.2	2.9	1.4	16.4	25.6	14.0	42.5	13.1	65.7	3,163	93.6
Riverton village	3,466	3,434	-0.9	3,474	98.5	0.8	0.0	0.7	0.0	26.9	11.8	37.0	53.5	12.9	1,522	85.8
Riverwoods village	3,671	3,562	-3.0	3,618	90.0	0.6	3.9	3.0	2.5	23.5	26.2	45.8	8.9	77.6	1,199	98.7
Roanoke village	2,077	1,990	-4.2	1,998	93.2	0.3	0.3	0.5	5.7	21.8	24.8	44.2	46.5	18.3	764	84.2
Robbins village	5,337	5,438	1.9	5,037	5.4	83.5	0.4	2.3	8.4	23.4	16.0	35.1	49.0	12.0	1,548	76.9
Roberts village	362	329	-9.1	388	92.8	1.0	0.0	2.1	4.1	30.4	10.3	36.8	60.5	8.6	167	79.6
Robinson city	7,721	7,341	-4.9	7,614	74.8	15.3	0.1	2.8	7.0	15.5	16.4	38.1	46.8	18.1	2,662	82.2
Rochelle city	9,574	9,052	-5.5	9,160	68.8	3.8	0.5	2.2	24.7	24.0	16.6	36.1	49.4	15.8	3,810	86.5
Rochester village	3,695	3,709	0.4	3,801	94.2	2.4	0.2	1.4	1.9	32.4	18.8	38.3	20.4	57.3	1,368	92.3
Rockbridge village	169	157	-7.1	159	100.0	0.0	0.0	0.0	0.0	37.7	17.0	31.4	61.6	19.2	61	68.9
Rock City village	304	283	-6.9	323	91.3	0.0	0.0	8.7	0.0	35.0	13.0	33.3	53.1	15.8	110	90.9
Rockdale village	1,987	1,910	-3.9	1,979	51.5	8.3	0.4	1.7	38.1	21.1	9.1	36.2	58.3	10.4	718	90.1
Rock Falls city	9,406	8,740	-7.1	8,952	80.4	2.7	0.0	0.3	16.7	23.3	17.9	40.5	55.1	10.8	3,728	85.9
Rockford city	153,285	145,609	-5.0	147,070	53.5	21.1	3.4	3.7	18.4	24.9	16.7	37.2	46.7	22.3	59,551	87.3
Rock Island city	38,985	37,176	-4.6	38,111	61.9	19.2	4.1	3.7	11.1	21.8	16.2	36.0	41.1	22.7	15,551	87.9
Rock Island Arsenal CDP	149	-	-	-	-	-	-	-	-	-	-	-	-	-	-	-
Rockton village	7,699	7,441	-3.4	7,638	94.6	0.9	1.0	1.3	2.3	24.9	17.6	41.0	32.6	33.1	2,911	91.7
Rockwood village	42	41	-2.4	27	100.0	0.0	0.0	0.0	0.0	11.1	11.1	56.5	69.6	0.0	10	70.0
Rolling Meadows city	24,091	23,532	-2.3	23,219	58.4	4.1	8.7	2.4	26.5	21.6	15.2	38.1	36.0	37.5	8,702	92.1
Rome CDP	1,738	-	-	1,525	96.4	0.0	0.0	1.8	1.8	20.8	18.8	47.8	41.5	14.0	630	93.5
Romeoville village	39,652	39,746	0.2	39,666	43.9	9.6	6.5	2.9	37.2	25.5	10.2	34.6	45.7	22.7	11,583	94.3
Roodhouse city	1,814	1,677	-7.6	1,757	98.2	0.2	0.0	0.9	0.7	24.8	14.3	35.5	62.3	11.0	676	80.8
Roscoe village	10,847	10,510	-3.1	10,757	89.7	1.5	5.3	1.3	2.2	29.1	11.2	36.5	31.5	35.0	3,822	96.8
Rose Hill village	80	81	1.3	91	93.4	0.0	6.6	0.0	0.0	26.4	9.9	35.9	53.3	13.3	33	87.9
Roselle village	22,724	22,463	-1.1	22,754	75.6	4.0	8.1	2.6	9.7	20.7	13.7	40.4	30.4	40.0	8,511	95.2
Rosemont village	4,206	4,066	-3.3	4,255	50.4	2.5	3.0	1.1	43.0	20.4	12.1	37.1	47.7	24.0	1,574	89.9
Roseville village	949	898	-5.4	879	90.3	3.1	0.0	0.0	6.6	17.5	31.5	49.9	40.2	21.8	380	83.2
Rosewood Heights CDP	4,038	-	-	4,063	96.7	1.5	0.0	0.0	1.8	18.9	24.8	44.0	43.1	22.3	1,712	86.7
Rosiclare city	1,160	1,014	-12.6	694	99.1	0.0	0.0	0.0	0.9	26.4	14.8	45.7	44.3	11.0	281	84.7
Rossville village	1,331	1,217	-8.6	1,320	94.4	0.0	1.4	1.4	2.8	25.5	19.3	36.9	51.6	14.7	494	90.9
Round Lake village	18,342	18,100	-1.3	18,349	50.0	9.0	12.8	3.2	25.1	29.3	8.3	34.6	31.1	36.3	5,748	97.8
Round Lake Beach village	28,093	27,100	-3.5	27,507	40.7	5.1	2.9	2.2	49.1	28.2	9.2	33.0	52.7	17.6	8,334	92.7
Round Lake Heights village	2,741	2,645	-3.5	3,179	45.0	4.2	5.3	1.7	43.9	31.2	5.3	30.9	52.1	22.0	873	97.7
Round Lake Park village	7,458	7,747	3.9	7,817	50.1	5.3	1.5	1.6	41.4	21.5	28.4	42.4	64.0	11.6	3,108	86.3
Roxana village	1,543	1,434	-7.1	1,517	94.8	1.6	0.7	1.5	1.5	21.4	19.2	43.2	40.8	14.5	632	85.4
Royal village	285	277	-2.8	327	99.4	0.0	0.0	0.6	0.0	18.7	26.0	45.4	39.8	28.7	145	94.5
Royal Lakes village	197	185	-6.1	188	34.0	49.5	1.1	15.4	0.0	17.6	26.6	56.8	58.9	6.8	91	83.5
Royalton village	1,151	1,117	-3.0	1,173	91.9	3.8	0.0	1.1	3.2	15.0	25.0	50.4	50.9	15.5	538	81.2
Ruma village	316	304	-3.8	317	97.5	0.6	0.0	1.3	0.6	24.3	19.6	40.8	50.5	18.7	110	93.6
Rushville city	3,199	2,847	-11.0	2,746	89.0	10.1	0.0	0.4	0.6	19.7	23.5	41.3	51.2	23.3	1,350	84.4
Russellville village	94	86	-8.5	95	89.5	0.0	10.5	0.0	0.0	16.8	32.6	44.8	71.4	7.8	58	86.2
Rutland village	318	304	-4.4	263	95.8	0.0	0.0	0.8	3.4	24.0	20.5	49.1	65.1	5.9	126	81.7
Sadorus village	411	390	-5.1	347	97.4	0.3	0.0	1.4	0.9	17.9	26.2	54.5	57.6	12.9	147	73.5
Sailor Springs village	95	93	-2.1	80	97.5	0.0	0.0	1.3	1.3	16.3	22.5	56.4	79.7	0.0	31	80.6
St. Anne village	1,280	1,193	-6.8	1,218	72.9	6.2	0.3	2.7	17.9	25.2	15.8	34.6	57.0	15.0	478	81.0
St. Augustine village	121	112	-7.4	111	99.1	0.0	0.0	0.0	0.9	10.8	27.0	54.9	42.9	11.0	59	69.5
St. Charles city	32,301	32,887	1.8	32,686	82.5	1.8	3.4	1.9	10.3	22.2	17.3	42.8	21.1	48.6	12,642	94.1
St. David village	590	527	-10.7	640	97.5	0.0	0.0	0.8	1.7	22.0	23.0	42.6	52.4	9.0	272	78.7
St. Elmo city	1,461	1,403	-4.0	1,480	99.1	0.2	0.0	0.3	0.3	21.4	17.6	40.8	50.6	10.0	565	82.5
Ste. Marie village	244	238	-2.5	344	97.7	0.3	0.0	0.0	2.0	29.1	11.0	31.8	38.2	13.4	110	92.7
St. Francisville city	697	622	-10.8	566	91.5	0.0	1.8	6.7	0.0	18.2	26.5	52.9	44.9	12.0	278	79.9
St. Jacob village	1,137	1,319	16.0	1,406	96.7	0.0	0.4	1.6	1.3	30.4	11.1	33.4	30.3	33.0	515	94.2
St. Johns village	219	208	-5.0	224	96.4	0.9	0.9	1.8	0.0	21.9	30.4	50.5	54.2	11.4	104	89.4
St. Joseph village	3,985	3,860	-3.1	4,448	96.8	0.0	1.2	0.4	1.6	28.9	12.1	36.6	31.8	33.5	1,499	99.1
St. Libory village	614	603	-1.8	508	94.9	0.0	1.0	2.2	2.0	16.5	23.6	46.7	44.8	16.3	234	92.7
St. Peter village	355	341	-3.9	435	97.7	0.0	2.3	0.0	0.0	32.6	18.4	33.9	49.8	15.9	161	71.4
St. Rose village	403	407	1.0	504	99.2	0.0	0.0	0.8	0.0	26.6	17.5	35.2	44.2	23.7	200	82.0
Salem city	7,446	6,971	-6.4	7,027	93.0	1.8	1.1	2.0	2.0	23.5	17.8	36.6	50.4	13.8	2,974	87.5
Sammons Point village	274	259	-5.5	286	91.3	0.0	1.0	0.0	7.7	30.8	11.9	37.5	52.2	10.0	90	95.6
Sandoval village	1,276	1,214	-4.9	1,207	95.9	0.9	0.0	2.2	1.0	24.4	13.3	36.0	51.1	9.0	530	89.6
Sandwich city	7,420	7,418	0.0	7,297	86.4	0.1	0.0	0.2	13.3	22.8	16.5	37.4	42.9	17.9	2,650	90.5
San Jose village	642	594	-7.5	715	89.2	1.3	0.0	3.1	6.4	22.9	13.4	42.3	60.1	12.8	284	84.9
Sauget village	181	168	-7.2	156	85.3	2.6	0.6	11.5	0.0	16.7	28.2	49.1	56.7	4.2	76	81.6
Sauk Village village	10,553	10,246	-2.9	10,423	17.4	65.9	0.7	3.1	12.9	29.0	10.1	29.1	48.2	13.5	3,270	90.4
Saunemin village	429	404	-5.8	410	91.2	0.0	4.1	1.5	3.2	24.1	13.2	45.3	63.4	8.4	153	96.1
Savanna city	3,062	2,797	-8.7	2,977	90.9	1.4	2.6	0.9	4.1	16.9	27.9	49.7	50.2	17.8	1,557	81.7
Savoy village	7,292	8,401	15.2	8,534	69.8	5.1	19.2	2.9	3.1	20.6	17.5	34.2	14.4	62.4	3,425	92.7
Sawyerville village	279	266	-4.7	247	94.7	0.0	0.4	2.8	2.0	33.6	13.4	32.2	57.0	9.4	91	71.4
Saybrook village	693	668	-3.6	660	94.7	0.0	0.0	0.0	5.3	26.2	19.5	41.8	53.1	18.8	277	84.5
Scales Mound village	386	356	-7.8	454	94.7	0.9	0.4	2.6	1.3	24.0	19.4	40.4	54.6	16.0	190	91.1
Schaumburg village	74,233	72,887	-1.8	74,194	57.0	4.0	25.3	3.1	10.6	22.0	14.9	38.5	24.9	49.4	29,705	95.1
Schiller Park village	11,793	11,403	-3.3	11,621	62.1	1.8	5.4	1.0	29.8	22.7	14.2	41.0	51.0	19.0	4,304	84.3

1 May be of any race.

Table A. All Places — **Population and Housing**

	Population				Race and Hispanic or Latino origin (percent)					Age (percent)			Educational attainment of persons age 25 and older		Occupied housing units	
STATE City, town, township, borough, or CDP (county if applicable)	2010 census total population	2019 estimated population	Percent change 2010-2019	ACS total population estimate 2015-2019	White alone, not Hispanic or Latino	Black alone, not Hispanic or Latino	Asian alone, not Hispanic or Latino	All other races or 2 or more races, not Hispanic or Latino	Hispanic or Latino[1]	Under 18 years old	Age 65 years and older	Median age	Percent High school diploma or less	Percent Bachelor's degree or more	Total	Percent with a computer
	1	2	3	4	5	6	7	8	9	10	11	12	13	14	15	16

ILLINOIS—Con.

	1	2	3	4	5	6	7	8	9	10	11	12	13	14	15	16
Schram City village	588	550	-6.5	674	98.1	0.0	0.0	0.0	1.9	21.1	18.2	37.5	64.3	9.0	315	84.8
Sciota village	61	56	-8.2	81	97.5	0.0	0.0	2.5	0.0	29.6	11.1	37.5	36.4	23.6	33	93.9
Scott AFB CDP	3,612	-	-	2,893	70.5	11.7	2.3	9.4	6.1	42.0	1.2	22.6	13.3	45.6	888	98.5
Scottville village	116	110	-5.2	104	100.0	0.0	0.0	0.0	0.0	14.4	50.0	65.0	69.4	8.2	44	86.4
Seaton village	222	202	-9.0	265	90.2	0.0	0.0	9.8	0.0	29.4	14.3	41.9	47.7	10.2	100	94.0
Seatonville village	314	296	-5.7	333	94.6	0.0	1.8	2.1	1.5	28.5	21.9	38.8	49.8	7.6	134	85.1
Secor village	376	355	-5.6	305	95.1	0.0	1.6	1.6	1.6	22.6	18.0	47.3	52.2	16.4	125	87.2
Seneca village	2,359	2,251	-4.6	2,442	93.9	0.3	0.0	1.3	4.4	28.0	12.8	32.6	39.6	17.7	884	93.9
Sesser city	1,932	1,860	-3.7	1,548	93.9	0.0	0.0	0.9	5.2	22.6	19.0	44.9	49.0	11.2	675	87.4
Seymour CDP	303	-	-	325	100.0	0.0	0.0	0.0	0.0	37.2	3.4	18.8	47.5	14.2	84	100.0
Shabbona village	927	920	-0.8	1,112	95.1	0.4	0.3	1.2	3.0	17.3	22.8	49.4	45.2	15.9	444	86.0
Shannon village	755	688	-8.9	868	91.0	0.0	3.1	0.8	5.1	26.7	18.1	36.7	46.7	17.0	340	82.4
Shawneetown city	1,244	1,077	-13.4	1,249	93.4	0.7	0.0	3.4	2.4	25.5	22.7	39.8	54.4	7.0	532	72.9
Sheffield village	925	863	-6.7	770	94.2	1.7	0.0	1.8	2.3	18.6	25.5	47.7	51.2	11.4	361	87.3
Shelbyville city	4,687	4,495	-4.1	4,312	96.3	3.1	0.0	0.4	0.2	19.6	23.8	45.7	53.0	18.0	2,026	82.3
Sheldon village	1,065	949	-10.9	1,169	95.0	1.5	0.0	2.8	0.7	19.3	16.7	42.5	58.1	9.2	489	85.9
Sheridan village	2,136	2,520	18.0	2,713	46.2	42.0	0.4	1.8	9.6	8.8	3.8	34.0	65.3	2.0	331	85.2
Sherman village	4,148	4,679	12.8	4,549	96.0	0.0	0.0	0.8	3.1	24.7	20.9	44.7	16.6	46.7	1,730	97.2
Sherrard village	640	594	-7.2	691	90.7	3.0	0.4	0.3	5.5	22.3	14.5	39.5	38.7	13.1	282	93.6
Shiloh village	12,557	13,586	8.2	13,482	65.0	20.0	4.3	4.5	6.1	20.0	14.6	40.1	24.1	42.1	5,544	90.8
Shipman town	624	587	-5.9	607	98.2	0.0	0.0	0.8	1.0	19.6	19.4	39.8	61.8	15.0	240	84.6
Shorewood village	15,630	17,509	12.0	17,164	76.7	5.2	2.4	2.0	13.8	24.4	16.5	42.0	30.1	39.8	5,893	93.9
Shumway village	201	195	-3.0	143	100.0	0.0	0.0	0.0	0.0	20.3	13.3	37.4	36.2	16.0	52	92.3
Sibley village	279	252	-9.7	285	97.9	0.0	0.0	1.4	0.7	17.9	17.2	46.1	57.9	7.9	129	86.0
Sidell village	617	563	-8.8	475	97.3	0.0	0.8	0.8	1.1	22.5	20.6	44.9	65.5	10.3	185	80.5
Sidney village	1,245	1,191	-4.3	1,321	95.1	1.1	0.5	1.6	1.7	27.5	12.3	36.5	28.4	24.6	509	96.5
Sigel town	373	355	-4.8	378	98.7	0.0	1.3	0.0	0.0	29.4	16.1	34.0	45.3	19.0	135	82.2
Silvis city	7,514	7,475	-0.5	7,497	66.4	10.4	1.2	5.6	16.4	26.2	16.1	38.4	39.9	16.8	3,359	86.7
Simpson village	60	60	0.0	65	92.3	0.0	0.0	0.0	7.7	43.1	0.0	30.5	22.2	16.7	17	100.0
Sims village	252	240	-4.8	148	93.2	0.0	6.8	0.0	0.0	15.5	20.9	42.9	64.3	3.5	65	69.2
Skokie village	64,845	62,700	-3.3	63,821	48.9	7.7	27.4	4.6	11.5	21.6	20.1	43.7	28.5	47.6	22,366	91.7
Sleepy Hollow village	3,311	3,244	-2.0	3,296	84.4	1.0	1.3	4.2	9.1	18.3	20.6	49.4	24.7	46.9	1,182	93.6
Smithboro village	182	165	-9.3	216	100.0	0.0	0.0	0.0	0.0	33.3	9.3	31.4	53.3	6.6	75	84.0
Smithfield village	230	221	-3.9	189	98.9	0.0	0.0	0.0	1.1	18.0	24.3	50.8	54.1	12.2	89	73.0
Smithton village	3,743	3,816	2.0	3,996	97.7	1.1	0.4	0.3	0.5	23.8	17.2	43.2	29.9	31.5	1,529	87.0
Somonauk village	1,892	1,871	-1.1	2,125	92.8	0.1	0.0	2.6	4.6	24.6	13.5	38.1	42.1	18.8	777	90.0
Sorento village	512	469	-8.4	443	94.4	0.0	3.2	0.9	1.6	18.7	23.5	44.4	68.6	3.4	214	70.1
South Barrington village	4,570	4,996	9.3	4,923	59.3	0.9	34.2	4.6	1.0	28.1	18.6	48.3	10.6	65.8	1,571	93.2
South Beloit city	7,901	7,624	-3.5	7,900	82.3	3.2	0.0	5.4	9.1	28.4	11.2	35.0	50.9	16.2	3,003	92.7
South Chicago Heights village	4,143	4,003	-3.4	4,076	30.0	24.5	0.0	3.2	42.3	29.5	12.8	34.8	62.3	6.8	1,467	72.5
South Elgin village	21,993	24,755	12.6	23,039	69.9	4.2	6.3	2.1	17.5	26.8	10.0	37.5	33.3	36.3	7,476	95.7
Southern View village	1,662	1,570	-5.5	1,671	92.2	3.1	0.4	1.0	3.3	15.6	22.5	45.1	39.6	18.2	785	90.2
South Holland village	21,999	21,296	-3.2	21,677	11.0	83.0	0.4	1.1	4.6	25.2	16.5	39.1	33.2	28.0	7,080	90.0
South Jacksonville village	3,331	3,102	-6.9	3,171	93.9	1.5	0.5	3.1	1.0	20.9	25.3	47.1	43.4	24.5	1,581	88.0
South Pekin village	1,150	1,093	-5.0	1,170	98.6	0.0	0.0	1.3	0.1	26.2	13.6	35.9	61.4	1.8	432	86.1
South Roxana village	2,086	1,991	-4.6	2,073	85.1	9.9	0.0	2.1	2.9	27.2	13.9	31.3	47.8	4.7	796	84.9
South Wilmington village	681	644	-5.4	761	98.2	0.0	0.0	0.8	1.1	20.9	16.4	40.7	52.5	8.7	335	91.0
Sparland village	406	367	-9.6	399	94.2	0.0	0.0	1.3	4.5	20.8	20.8	47.3	60.1	10.1	173	78.0
Sparta city	4,302	4,273	-0.7	4,351	69.2	21.6	3.3	3.2	2.8	20.4	19.0	40.6	45.7	18.9	1,841	90.0
Spaulding village	867	849	-2.1	863	97.1	0.3	0.3	0.8	1.4	20.5	13.1	46.1	31.6	31.4	325	92.0
Spillertown village	203	196	-3.4	292	77.7	12.7	2.1	1.4	6.2	25.3	11.0	34.5	31.3	22.4	118	74.6
Spring Bay village	476	462	-2.9	407	96.1	0.2	0.7	2.5	0.5	15.5	20.4	46.9	53.8	12.2	194	85.6
Springerton village	110	102	-7.3	106	92.5	0.0	0.0	7.5	0.0	12.3	10.4	44.8	46.3	13.8	38	84.2
Springfield city	116,996	114,230	-2.4	115,888	71.1	19.7	3.0	3.3	2.8	21.9	17.6	39.4	34.6	35.8	50,952	88.1
Spring Grove village	5,781	5,706	-1.3	5,614	88.9	0.0	1.3	3.7	6.1	23.4	12.2	44.2	30.7	29.8	1,875	98.5
Spring Valley city	5,548	5,125	-7.6	5,223	76.2	3.9	0.8	1.4	17.7	20.6	21.8	42.7	46.5	19.0	2,229	84.6
Standard village	222	203	-8.6	287	82.2	0.0	0.0	3.8	13.9	24.7	24.0	47.4	53.3	9.0	141	74.5
Standard City village	152	145	-4.6	198	99.0	0.0	0.0	1.0	0.0	22.7	8.1	37.3	57.7	8.9	67	91.0
Stanford village	619	598	-3.4	669	95.5	0.0	0.6	0.6	3.3	25.4	6.4	33.6	56.6	11.7	241	95.4
Staunton city	5,232	4,954	-5.3	5,066	99.9	0.0	0.0	0.1	0.0	20.1	19.3	43.0	48.0	17.0	2,240	86.0
Steeleville village	2,084	1,925	-7.6	2,095	93.2	4.9	0.0	1.2	0.7	23.7	18.9	38.8	39.7	17.3	865	85.5
Steger village	9,550	9,221	-3.4	9,366	60.7	19.6	0.6	2.1	17.0	20.2	13.5	40.7	50.4	15.4	4,127	89.9
Sterling city	15,426	14,463	-6.2	14,782	66.6	2.7	1.4	2.2	27.2	24.0	18.5	41.0	48.2	15.7	6,238	85.1
Steward village	256	241	-5.9	307	95.4	2.3	0.0	1.6	0.7	24.1	12.7	45.3	45.1	18.1	114	94.7
Stewardson village	732	721	-1.5	791	93.9	0.0	5.6	0.0	0.5	24.5	18.8	37.4	49.7	17.3	337	86.9
Stickney village	6,786	6,566	-3.2	6,679	35.3	0.5	0.3	2.5	61.4	27.2	11.5	37.0	52.0	13.2	2,251	89.4
Stillman Valley village	1,120	1,053	-6.0	1,201	94.3	0.0	0.0	0.0	5.7	29.6	14.7	33.0	36.8	25.9	460	94.6
Stockton village	1,869	1,712	-8.4	1,815	97.1	0.1	0.3	0.8	1.7	24.3	26.9	45.2	49.5	13.6	812	84.1
Stonefort village	297	285	-4.0	316	80.4	4.7	0.0	14.9	0.0	29.4	13.0	36.2	53.9	6.3	121	69.4
Stone Park village	4,946	4,826	-2.4	4,894	4.5	2.6	2.2	0.8	89.9	29.2	5.0	32.8	76.0	5.3	1,281	90.1
Stonington village	933	846	-9.3	868	98.2	0.0	0.0	0.0	1.8	20.7	15.0	38.3	48.5	23.1	385	91.2
Stoy village	123	115	-6.5	200	52.0	2.5	0.0	0.0	45.5	30.5	8.5	40.9	52.8	5.7	71	100.0
Strasburg village	467	439	-6.0	536	98.7	0.0	0.0	0.6	0.7	19.6	22.2	47.2	37.4	18.3	235	78.7
Strawn village	99	93	-6.1	79	97.5	0.0	0.0	2.5	0.0	21.5	6.3	36.5	58.3	12.5	33	93.9
Streamwood village	39,839	39,228	-1.5	39,809	43.8	3.9	13.8	2.5	36.1	22.0	12.0	38.7	43.8	28.1	13,125	94.8
Streator city	14,001	13,113	-6.3	12,653	84.6	3.2	0.6	1.7	9.8	20.2	19.8	42.6	55.0	14.0	5,742	79.1
Stronghurst village	883	789	-10.6	950	96.2	0.3	0.0	2.2	1.3	24.0	24.4	41.4	47.1	15.9	375	85.1
Sublette village	449	421	-6.2	415	95.9	0.7	0.5	0.0	2.9	15.4	28.4	48.5	45.6	11.1	203	87.2
Sugar Grove village	9,006	9,888	9.8	9,689	79.6	6.7	5.3	0.4	8.1	22.0	13.7	43.1	30.6	41.0	3,371	97.9
Sullivan city	4,450	4,433	-0.4	4,475	95.8	1.2	0.2	0.6	2.2	22.9	19.2	37.6	41.9	18.9	1,930	88.6
Summerfield village	431	395	-8.4	357	91.9	0.0	0.0	0.0	8.1	27.7	16.2	42.8	51.3	10.3	140	84.3
Summit village	11,054	11,116	0.6	11,260	13.7	7.5	3.3	1.1	74.4	32.1	9.9	32.0	64.7	10.4	3,326	88.8
Sumner city	3,176	2,980	-6.2	3,056	43.7	40.3	0.3	1.9	13.9	7.6	6.2	33.8	74.1	5.0	419	83.1
Sun River Terrace village	528	496	-6.1	445	3.8	86.5	0.0	2.5	7.2	38.7	11.7	30.5	53.3	15.6	159	93.1
Swansea village	13,454	13,350	-0.8	13,851	73.0	18.7	1.5	3.3	3.4	18.7	18.1	43.9	25.9	40.1	5,587	95.0
Sycamore city	17,521	18,322	4.6	17,726	86.5	3.8	2.1	0.8	6.8	25.8	13.8	36.6	24.6	39.6	6,798	94.2
Symerton village	91	91	0.0	101	100.0	0.0	0.0	0.0	0.0	30.7	9.9	29.8	61.3	1.6	33	93.9
Table Grove village	418	383	-8.4	414	98.1	0.0	0.7	0.0	1.2	28.3	12.8	33.1	57.4	11.1	164	81.7
Tallula village	488	474	-2.9	511	98.2	0.0	0.0	0.4	1.4	20.4	20.2	47.1	60.1	11.0	220	86.8
Tamaroa village	638	597	-6.4	650	99.7	0.0	0.0	0.3	0.0	24.0	16.5	41.8	61.9	3.4	290	77.2
Tamms village	1,045	472	-54.8	694	69.9	21.8	0.0	7.2	1.2	22.2	13.7	43.7	50.5	13.8	205	58.5

1 May be of any race.

Table A. All Places — **Population and Housing**

STATE City, town, township, borough, or CDP (county if applicable)	Population				Race and Hispanic or Latino origin (percent)					Age (percent)			Educational attainment of persons age 25 and older		Occupied housing units	
	2010 census total population	2019 estimated population	Percent change 2010-2019	ACS total population estimate 2015-2019	White alone, not Hispanic or Latino	Black alone, not Hispanic or Latino	Asian alone, not Hispanic or Latino	All other races or 2 or more races, not Hispanic or Latino	Hispanic or Latino[1]	Under 18 years old	Age 65 years and older	Median age	Percent High school diploma or less	Percent Bachelor's degree or more	Total	Percent with a computer
	1	2	3	4	5	6	7	8	9	10	11	12	13	14	15	16
ILLINOIS—Con.																
Tampico village	790	729	-7.7	734	93.2	2.2	0.0	0.4	4.2	21.3	19.5	45.2	53.6	10.7	299	79.6
Taylor Springs village	692	659	-4.8	596	99.8	0.0	0.0	0.0	0.2	12.9	27.2	55.3	63.4	6.2	238	79.4
Taylorville city	11,275	10,360	-8.1	10,893	94.7	0.8	0.6	3.0	0.8	19.1	20.9	44.2	50.9	18.5	5,112	81.3
Tennessee village	115	108	-6.1	101	100.0	0.0	0.0	0.0	0.0	7.9	29.7	51.2	58.5	11.0	51	78.4
Teutopolis village	1,537	1,642	6.8	1,730	98.6	0.4	0.3	0.6	0.0	23.8	17.4	36.5	35.8	32.6	699	89.8
Thawville village	241	244	1.2	285	68.1	0.0	0.0	6.3	25.6	38.6	16.8	32.1	58.2	6.3	94	87.2
Thayer village	693	655	-5.5	786	98.1	0.0	0.0	1.9	0.0	23.8	16.2	34.1	44.5	18.5	320	96.3
Thebes village	437	321	-26.5	475	70.1	28.2	0.0	1.7	0.0	44.4	9.3	27.3	59.1	13.5	128	56.3
The Galena Territory CDP	1,058	-	-	1,334	99.0	0.0	0.0	0.0	1.0	8.0	56.1	66.8	17.4	55.2	690	95.2
Third Lake village	1,178	1,146	-2.7	1,079	92.4	0.0	0.6	0.4	6.7	16.5	19.6	51.3	12.5	64.4	408	96.8
Thomasboro village	1,124	1,084	-3.6	997	93.9	2.3	0.0	2.3	1.5	15.2	19.1	45.3	53.0	12.8	455	93.4
Thompsonville village	543	526	-3.1	496	96.4	0.0	0.0	3.6	0.0	27.6	17.3	40.2	55.2	9.1	213	77.9
Thomson village	590	551	-6.6	524	82.1	14.5	0.0	0.0	3.4	10.5	24.0	45.9	59.4	19.9	186	87.1
Thornton village	2,388	2,401	0.5	2,545	65.8	18.1	1.5	0.7	13.9	16.6	18.2	43.5	49.9	18.2	1,078	85.3
Tilden village	934	881	-5.7	895	95.8	1.0	0.0	0.0	3.2	20.7	16.5	39.6	59.8	8.3	344	84.9
Tilton village	2,714	2,686		2,611	92.7	0.4	0.0	1.1	5.8	20.9	21.5	46.9	63.9	7.5	1,199	78.5
Timberlane village	932	946	1.5	1,031	89.6	0.4	1.6	0.2	8.1	29.2	7.1	40.1	23.3	44.9	325	99.4
Time village	23	22	-4.3	18	100.0	0.0	0.0	0.0	0.0	22.2	22.2	41.5	71.4	0.0	8	50.0
Tinley Park village	56,827	55,773	-1.9	56,505	80.4	4.2	4.9	1.2	9.4	22.3	17.0	40.1	31.4	36.6	21,270	93.8
Tiskilwa village	838	766	-8.6	783	93.6	1.3	0.9	2.0	2.2	22.3	18.8	44.1	47.6	15.3	313	86.6
Toledo village	1,225	1,190	-2.9	1,154	94.5	0.4	0.0	4.8	0.3	22.5	16.5	39.8	52.5	12.1	533	81.1
Tolono village	3,460	3,392	-2.0	3,237	88.4	4.7	0.8	3.0	3.0	29.7	7.7	36.4	34.5	29.3	1,175	92.2
Toluca city	1,414	1,269	-10.3	1,219	81.4	1.5	0.6	2.2	14.4	12.1	27.4	51.5	52.5	15.9	566	84.1
Tonica village	768	715	-6.9	797	83.9	0.0	0.0	1.4	14.7	27.0	13.6	38.9	47.3	16.4	329	87.5
Topeka village	76	70	-7.9	94	80.9	0.0	0.0	19.1	0.0	21.3	22.3	55.5	59.4	23.4	41	87.8
Toulon city	1,292	1,161	-10.1	1,165	91.6	3.2	2.1	1.6	1.5	19.3	28.7	47.8	54.1	17.7	486	79.6
Tovey village	512	476	-7.0	454	99.1	0.0	0.0	0.0	0.9	28.9	15.2	41.6	62.7	12.9	180	83.9
Towanda village	483	462	-4.3	436	97.5	0.5	0.0	0.7	1.4	17.2	20.4	47.6	57.5	17.1	187	94.7
Tower Hill village	611	588	-3.8	816	99.4	0.0	0.0	0.6	0.0	29.4	11.0	30.3	72.7	9.7	255	84.3
Tower Lakes village	1,278	1,226	-4.1	1,290	92.9	3.3	0.4	1.9	1.6	28.4	20.0	46.2	11.0	71.4	436	95.9
Tremont village	2,246	2,120	-5.6	2,082	96.7	0.0	0.3	2.5	0.4	25.2	17.9	44.6	34.2	27.8	862	91.4
Trenton city	2,715	2,590	-4.6	2,614	96.9	0.5	0.3	0.3	1.9	22.7	22.1	42.6	33.3	29.8	1,100	82.9
Trout Valley village	531	513	-3.4	411	94.6	0.0	0.2	1.5	3.6	18.7	22.1	52.0	13.8	57.0	142	100.0
Troy city	9,949	10,375	4.3	10,336	91.6	2.0	1.9	1.5	3.1	24.5	11.5	37.6	26.6	33.7	4,051	92.2
Troy Grove village	250	238	-4.8	231	93.5	0.0	0.0	0.0	6.5	24.7	9.1	45.8	47.6	9.0	95	83.2
Tuscola city	4,483	4,363	-2.7	4,564	92.9	0.1	2.0	1.1	3.9	21.5	14.6	39.2	37.2	24.8	2,057	83.2
Twin Grove CDP	1,564	-	-	1,401	96.7	2.5	0.8	0.0	0.0	17.8	22.4	48.3	26.6	55.6	579	99.3
Ullin village	466	400	-14.2	513	68.8	29.6	0.0	1.0	0.6	25.7	19.9	41.2	36.6	22.0	164	68.3
Union village	580	553	-4.7	634	83.9	0.0	6.3	0.0	9.8	29.3	9.1	31.0	39.4	19.0	213	95.3
Union Hill village	60	57	-5.0	78	100.0	0.0	0.0	0.0	0.0	39.7	7.7	24.5	23.7	2.6	22	95.5
University Park village	7,113	6,887	-3.2	6,947	6.8	84.8	0.2	4.4	3.8	29.6	9.8	31.3	26.2	28.0	2,455	89.1
Urbana city	42,136	42,214	0.2	42,718	53.7	16.3	18.9	4.0	7.1	12.9	9.2	25.1	19.8	60.1	16,742	94.1
Ursa village	628	605	-3.7	509	98.2	0.0	0.0	1.0	0.8	23.0	22.4	39.5	36.6	25.7	234	81.6
Valier village	669	637	-4.8	724	94.3	1.0	0.0	1.4	3.3	31.1	22.1	42.3	44.5	12.2	269	78.4
Valley City village	13	13	0.0	22	100.0	0.0	0.0	0.0	0.0	59.1	0.0	15.5	0.0	0.0	4	100.0
Valmeyer village	1,250	1,248	-0.2	1,300	92.4	0.2	0.0	0.6	6.8	25.1	11.7	38.6	36.1	29.1	466	93.6
Vandalia city	7,037	6,684	-5.0	6,909	79.6	14.0	0.1	0.8	5.4	16.2	15.6	38.3	60.0	8.5	2,152	76.8
Varna village	384	347	-9.6	392	96.9	0.0	0.0	1.0	2.0	21.9	22.7	42.1	46.2	12.4	170	81.8
Venedy village	138	133	-3.6	209	77.0	0.0	4.3	17.7	1.0	36.8	10.5	32.1	31.9	9.5	61	90.2
Venetian Village CDP	2,826	-	-	2,934	80.9	0.9	1.0	2.3	14.9	23.9	10.8	36.9	41.3	16.7	1,035	100.0
Venice city	1,891	1,858	-1.7	2,127	5.2	91.5	0.7	1.8	0.8	30.7	16.6	38.4	50.8	9.9	860	75.6
Vergennes village	298	281	-5.7	225	96.9	0.0	0.0	1.3	1.8	23.1	23.6	43.8	38.7	10.3	92	90.2
Vermilion village	223	202	-9.4	231	97.0	0.4	0.0	2.6	0.0	23.8	13.4	49.0	72.6	9.1	96	81.3
Vermont village	667	640	-4.0	818	97.4	0.2	0.5	0.4	1.5	24.1	20.7	41.3	67.8	9.7	345	73.3
Vernon village	123	118	-4.1	92	94.6	0.0	1.1	0.0	4.3	19.6	33.7	58.0	71.2	4.1	49	49.0
Vernon Hills village	25,005	26,521	6.1	26,343	55.7	2.5	23.5	3.3	14.9	26.9	13.0	39.1	17.5	63.2	9,735	94.8
Verona village	215	206	-4.2	226	83.2	0.0	0.0	0.0	16.8	25.7	14.6	38.2	61.1	11.1	91	84.6
Versailles village	478	458	-4.2	513	86.0	0.0	0.0	1.4	12.7	22.4	25.0	47.0	58.3	4.5	235	60.9
Victoria village	314	289	-8.0	274	96.7	0.0	0.0	1.8	1.5	16.8	18.2	49.2	55.4	12.7	117	92.3
Vienna city	1,430	1,440	0.7	1,544	96.5	1.0	0.0	1.1	1.4	24.3	28.3	45.8	47.8	11.8	694	63.3
Villa Grove city	2,537	2,418	-4.7	2,388	94.6	0.6	0.4	3.4	0.9	19.9	19.2	42.1	43.8	18.1	970	86.7
Villa Park village	22,025	21,483	-2.5	21,916	64.1	6.0	4.1	1.7	24.0	23.7	11.8	37.7	34.8	34.9	8,115	92.2
Viola village	955	888	-7.0	966	93.4	0.0	0.0	3.7	2.9	27.0	17.0	36.5	47.1	17.7	380	86.8
Virden city	3,525	3,330	-5.5	3,514	99.0	0.0	0.2	0.0	0.8	25.2	18.5	41.3	46.1	19.7	1,440	85.6
Virgil village	329	327	-0.6	406	77.3	12.3	0.2	0.0	10.1	22.4	11.3	40.6	49.0	19.7	124	99.2
Virginia city	1,615	1,435	-11.1	1,332	97.1	0.4	0.8	0.8	1.1	24.1	19.1	42.2	44.9	17.7	566	88.7
Volo village	2,916	5,813	99.3	5,229	83.4	0.3	1.1	1.3	13.9	34.5	6.6	33.4	24.1	43.1	1,780	99.6
Wadsworth village	3,751	3,651	-2.7	3,563	88.7	3.9	2.0	2.8	2.6	16.7	19.6	51.3	25.4	46.2	1,442	98.4
Waggoner village	266	253	-4.9	192	96.9	3.1	0.0	0.0	0.0	31.8	7.8	27.6	71.8	4.5	80	87.5
Walnut village	1,418	1,306	-7.9	1,370	97.4	0.0	0.0	0.9	1.7	24.6	22.3	40.8	47.5	21.0	550	91.3
Walnut Hill village	108	104	-3.7	132	91.7	0.0	0.0	8.3	0.0	30.3	13.6	41.5	44.0	23.8	46	84.8
Walshville village	64	62	-3.1	176	100.0	0.0	0.0	0.0	0.0	47.7	7.4	31.0	35.9	2.2	50	94.0
Waltonville village	445	432	-2.9	406	98.8	0.5	0.0	0.7	0.0	24.1	20.2	40.8	45.9	10.1	174	92.5
Wamac city	1,182	1,123	-5.0	1,280	85.6	0.2	0.2	4.6	9.4	27.3	9.8	34.0	64.7	6.1	492	73.6
Wapella village	558	522	-6.5	565	92.2	0.0	0.0	7.4	0.4	20.2	17.9	42.0	59.7	14.9	230	90.0
Warren village	1,428	1,304	-8.7	1,237	93.1	1.1	0.7	2.6	2.4	20.4	25.2	49.2	50.2	13.5	585	83.1
Warrensburg village	1,213	1,126	-7.2	1,488	90.4	0.5	0.0	5.6	3.6	29.1	13.5	33.9	36.8	24.5	509	91.0
Warrenville city	13,182	13,174	-0.1	13,158	69.9	5.0	5.5	1.9	17.6	22.3	13.1	37.9	25.6	45.3	4,931	97.6
Warsaw city	1,607	1,480	-7.9	1,690	95.7	0.0	0.0	1.0	3.3	26.7	19.3	41.4	43.7	20.3	678	83.3
Washburn village	1,149	1,082	-5.8	1,148	97.0	0.0	0.0	1.5	1.6	24.3	13.1	33.0	48.3	9.9	450	90.9
Washington city	15,231	16,516	8.4	16,567	93.8	0.4	1.5	1.9	2.4	27.0	16.9	38.8	25.6	39.9	6,589	90.5
Washington Park village	4,196	3,865	-7.9	3,941	2.6	88.8	0.3	2.2	6.1	23.9	13.6	40.3	67.6	9.2	1,501	72.9
Wataga village	845	786	-7.0	820	95.4	2.1	0.6	0.2	1.7	22.6	20.6	40.7	58.2	10.9	357	85.7
Waterloo city	9,982	10,578	6.0	10,367	95.7	0.3	1.4	0.6	1.9	22.5	19.7	40.4	34.9	31.3	4,302	87.5
Waterman village	1,515	1,500		1,426	89.7	1.8	0.1	2.7	5.8	23.6	11.2	38.0	39.0	22.4	524	91.8
Watseka city	5,289	4,767	-9.9	4,954	93.5	0.4	0.9	0.7	4.4	17.7	23.9	44.9	51.9	11.4	2,363	79.6
Watson village	754	732	-2.9	824	99.4	0.4	0.0	0.2	0.0	29.2	11.3	36.7	60.0	6.1	297	87.9
Wauconda village	13,622	13,504	-0.9	13,655	70.2	0.6	4.3	1.8	23.1	22.5	14.4	38.4	34.8	41.3	5,283	91.8
Waukegan city	89,115	86,075	-3.4	87,297	19.2	17.2	5.0	3.0	55.6	28.2	9.5	32.3	56.7	17.4	29,441	91.3
Waverly city	1,297	1,194	-7.9	1,315	94.5	1.0	2.0	1.5	1.0	20.9	21.7	38.9	59.3	18.2	536	84.3
Wayne village	2,441	2,429	-0.5	2,439	86.5	0.0	11.4	0.0	2.1	15.9	23.4	51.1	24.5	44.5	893	94.4
Wayne City village	1,029	993	-3.5	965	96.7	0.0	0.0	2.2	1.1	23.1	29.8	48.4	48.4	15.8	408	85.0

1 May be of any race.

Table A. All Places — **Population and Housing**

STATE City, town, township, borough, or CDP (county if applicable)	Population				Race and Hispanic or Latino origin (percent)					Age (percent)			Educational attainment of persons age 25 and older		Occupied housing units	
	2010 census total population	2019 estimated population	Percent change 2010-2019	ACS total population estimate 2015-2019	White alone, not Hispanic or Latino	Black alone, not Hispanic or Latino	Asian alone, not Hispanic or Latino	All other races or 2 or more races, not Hispanic or Latino	Hispanic or Latino[1]	Under 18 years old	Age 65 years and older	Median age	Percent High school diploma or less	Percent Bachelor's degree or more	Total	Percent with a computer
	1	2	3	4	5	6	7	8	9	10	11	12	13	14	15	16
ILLINOIS—Con.																
Waynesville village	428	410	-4.2	410	100.0	0.0	0.0	0.0	0.0	22.7	18.3	40.1	58.1	9.2	165	82.4
Weldon village	429	412	-4.0	389	94.6	0.0	0.0	5.1	0.3	16.5	27.0	52.8	57.0	8.5	189	78.8
Wellington village	242	216	-10.7	275	90.9	0.0	0.0	0.0	9.1	30.2	22.2	35.6	58.0	8.3	109	81.7
Wenona city	1,056	938	-11.2	1,065	93.6	0.0	0.0	1.8	4.6	25.9	16.6	36.2	47.5	16.5	476	81.5
Wenonah village	37	35	-5.4	38	100.0	0.0	0.0	0.0	0.0	0.0	18.4	46.7	58.6	13.8	13	100.0
West Brooklyn village	142	133	-6.3	146	98.6	0.0	0.0	0.0	1.4	21.9	20.5	48.0	53.5	19.2	58	84.5
Westchester village	16,718	16,117	-3.6	16,440	54.9	18.2	3.6	2.5	20.8	17.6	23.7	46.0	27.7	41.8	6,478	92.9
West Chicago city	27,221	26,816	-1.5	27,180	36.3	1.9	8.1	0.9	52.9	28.2	8.9	34.0	50.5	27.9	7,497	93.1
West City village	661	638	-3.5	772	90.2	0.6	0.0	1.0	8.2	34.6	14.9	33.0	45.9	15.9	275	82.5
West Dundee village	7,294	8,113	11.2	7,644	82.5	2.2	9.3	0.2	5.9	22.8	13.4	42.4	25.1	41.1	3,114	93.8
Western Springs village	12,948	13,359	3.2	13,272	92.4	0.8	1.0	0.9	4.9	32.6	15.9	41.4	8.6	78.0	4,331	95.0
Westervelt CDP	128	-	-	47	100.0	0.0	0.0	0.0	0.0	70.2	0.0	13.4	42.9	0.0	14	100.0
Westfield village	601	558	-7.2	695	98.4	0.0	0.3	0.0	1.3	24.2	18.0	43.0	49.0	7.7	299	85.3
West Frankfort city	8,181	7,823	-4.4	7,715	95.8	1.1	0.4	2.0	0.7	20.4	21.4	43.4	48.8	10.4	3,419	78.2
Westmont village	24,662	24,443	-0.9	24,931	61.3	7.1	14.4	2.5	14.7	20.9	17.6	39.6	27.5	44.0	10,743	85.6
West Peoria city	4,699	4,455	-5.2	4,543	76.7	12.2	0.3	10.5	0.2	21.4	22.1	40.9	40.7	19.7	1,973	89.5
West Point village	178	163	-8.4	195	100.0	0.0	0.0	0.0	0.0	29.7	16.9	45.3	68.7	2.2	66	77.3
West Salem village	897	851	-5.1	903	94.9	1.4	0.0	2.0	1.7	22.0	19.5	40.4	45.8	12.3	357	85.7
West Union CDP	288	-	-	322	87.6	12.4	0.0	0.0	0.0	23.3	24.8	44.1	37.7	15.6	141	86.5
Westville village	3,202	2,945	-8.0	3,219	92.6	1.3	0.5	3.5	2.2	30.2	16.2	36.3	52.5	14.4	1,257	83.9
West York CDP	129	-	-	100	100.0	0.0	0.0	0.0	0.0	31.0	0.0	37.5	39.1	10.1	46	100.0
Wheaton city	53,045	52,745	-0.6	53,270	79.6	4.4	6.3	3.2	6.5	23.2	15.8	37.3	13.8	64.2	19,174	95.3
Wheeler village	147	146	-0.7	171	98.2	0.0	0.0	0.6	1.2	38.6	12.3	33.6	46.9	15.6	62	77.4
Wheeling village	37,644	38,646	2.7	38,499	47.1	2.4	18.4	2.3	29.8	20.6	14.5	37.5	37.2	40.4	14,441	95.0
Whiteash CDP	241	-	-	148	93.2	0.7	0.0	4.7	1.4	19.6	35.1	46.5	46.2	23.1	57	71.9
White City village	232	230	-0.9	218	98.2	0.0	0.0	0.0	1.8	14.2	18.8	46.6	63.8	11.9	103	97.1
White Hall city	2,520	2,329	-7.6	2,332	96.2	1.4	0.0	0.9	1.6	19.5	21.5	47.8	67.7	7.1	991	84.0
White Heath CDP	290	-	-	154	97.4	2.6	0.0	0.0	0.0	0.0	29.9	55.9	63.4	20.7	81	100.0
Williamsfield village	578	545	-5.7	476	99.2	0.4	0.0	0.2	0.2	21.2	21.4	45.0	46.7	18.1	234	81.6
Williamson village	230	215	-6.5	215	97.7	0.0	0.9	1.4	0.0	25.1	20.9	41.2	78.4	5.9	85	87.1
Williamsville village	1,473	1,485	0.8	1,522	97.1	0.0	0.1	1.1	1.7	26.5	9.9	38.7	31.5	35.9	553	92.9
Willisville village	633	587	-7.3	657	99.5	0.2	0.0	0.3	0.0	30.7	5.9	32.6	54.0	9.3	237	84.0
Willowbrook village	8,687	8,579	-1.2	8,673	74.4	2.4	15.8	0.9	6.5	15.5	24.0	48.9	22.0	54.6	3,977	94.5
Willowbrook CDP	2,076	-	-	2,001	40.1	56.1	0.5	0.5	2.7	14.7	24.0	50.1	27.6	36.7	691	95.1
Willow Hill village	230	228	-0.9	176	100.0	0.0	0.0	0.0	0.0	8.0	20.5	49.0	59.1	1.5	73	76.7
Willow Springs village	5,751	5,621	-2.3	5,604	77.7	2.4	4.3	1.6	14.0	18.4	24.1	48.5	33.1	36.7	2,211	92.6
Wilmette village	27,060	27,089	0.1	27,247	80.8	0.7	12.8	3.0	2.7	28.7	19.2	45.5	6.3	83.2	9,717	96.3
Wilmington village	142	132	-7.0	142	95.8	0.0	0.0	0.0	4.2	21.1	19.0	48.5	51.0	21.2	45	84.4
Wilmington city	5,757	5,653	-1.8	6,030	90.3	0.3	0.2	0.5	8.7	20.8	17.6	43.2	50.3	14.7	2,315	87.2
Wilsonville village	586	553	-5.6	634	91.5	1.4	0.0	4.7	2.4	15.3	23.7	47.6	63.9	4.8	281	75.8
Winchester city	1,593	1,467	-7.9	1,856	96.2	0.2	0.0	2.9	0.7	24.4	14.4	39.5	53.0	21.7	698	85.7
Windsor village	748	772	3.2	800	96.5	0.0	0.4	2.6	0.5	23.9	20.1	41.3	51.0	10.5	335	85.4
Windsor city	1,187	1,151	-3.0	1,203	91.4	0.0	0.0	2.3	6.2	27.5	17.8	37.0	48.9	8.6	481	84.2
Winfield village	9,072	9,636	6.2	9,700	89.8	0.8	4.3	1.5	3.6	19.8	18.7	49.7	15.6	63.1	3,946	93.7
Winnebago village	3,136	2,991	-4.6	3,387	96.8	2.3	0.0	0.0	1.0	26.2	13.8	42.0	33.1	27.7	1,295	95.0
Winnetka village	12,192	12,316	1.0	12,428	90.2	0.1	3.9	2.8	2.9	33.1	15.0	40.9	2.5	92.3	4,107	97.9
Winslow village	336	312	-7.1	350	98.0	0.0	0.0	0.0	2.0	21.4	15.7	41.6	57.3	10.7	162	89.5
Winthrop Harbor village	6,867	6,618	-3.6	6,721	86.9	1.5	0.8	0.6	10.2	18.1	16.1	45.9	34.3	28.1	2,530	95.2
Witt city	903	843	-6.6	786	97.7	0.1	0.0	0.0	2.2	18.6	20.4	46.0	62.8	11.0	355	83.4
Wonder Lake village	4,032	3,882	-3.7	4,466	85.5	0.0	2.4	0.4	11.8	28.6	12.4	39.2	36.3	27.4	1,735	94.1
Wood Dale city	13,769	13,607	-1.2	13,796	64.3	1.9	8.8	1.4	23.6	19.3	16.4	41.7	48.2	24.6	5,056	91.4
Woodhull village	817	783	-4.2	740	97.7	0.4	0.0	0.0	1.9	20.9	21.8	42.9	44.1	15.2	330	90.0
Woodland village	323	297	-8.0	246	96.7	0.0	0.0	0.0	3.3	22.8	18.7	46.2	56.0	3.8	99	88.9
Woodlawn village	694	682	-1.7	643	92.4	1.2	0.5	4.0	1.9	31.3	14.3	34.8	39.4	19.4	237	79.7
Woodridge village	32,976	33,432	1.4	33,455	61.8	9.0	12.0	2.5	14.7	21.2	12.0	38.1	20.6	50.8	13,189	94.7
Wood River city	10,633	10,051	-5.5	10,169	91.6	4.4	0.7	2.3	0.9	25.4	15.4	35.0	51.9	14.6	4,241	87.2
Woodson village	513	485	-5.5	433	95.8	0.0	1.8	2.3	0.0	21.9	25.6	45.1	42.8	30.0	182	79.1
Woodstock city	24,794	25,240	1.8	25,348	71.8	2.2	2.3	2.2	21.4	25.8	14.6	36.3	39.1	30.3	9,441	94.7
Worden village	1,070	1,041	-2.7	970	91.3	0.7	0.3	3.3	4.3	25.1	15.7	34.8	49.6	18.2	394	86.3
Worth village	10,789	10,466	-3.0	10,633	81.8	2.9	1.3	1.9	12.1	20.8	14.5	41.8	45.8	16.3	4,026	92.2
Wyanet village	986	923	-6.4	1,052	87.8	0.5	0.5	6.2	5.0	30.0	12.4	37.9	56.4	8.4	382	93.2
Wyoming city	1,429	1,273	-10.9	1,417	96.1	0.0	1.9	1.4	0.6	20.0	23.0	43.4	46.9	15.3	658	85.9
Xenia village	387	368	-4.9	416	96.6	0.0	1.7	1.2	0.5	29.3	17.3	35.8	36.1	21.3	186	84.4
Yale village	86	85	-1.2	113	89.4	0.0	0.0	10.6	0.0	23.0	15.9	40.3	77.1	6.0	37	89.2
Yates City village	691	652	-5.6	832	95.4	0.6	0.6	3.2	0.1	23.2	16.6	38.3	48.5	14.3	359	81.6
Yorkville city	16,950	20,613	21.6	19,352	74.0	9.3	1.4	1.9	13.3	31.9	9.1	33.3	26.8	34.5	6,473	95.9
Zeigler city	1,801	1,712	-4.9	1,801	96.9	0.2	0.0	0.6	2.3	26.0	20.4	37.1	53.6	8.8	633	82.1
Zion city	24,394	23,487	-3.7	23,858	32.5	29.8	4.3	5.0	28.4	28.3	12.2	32.1	49.4	18.2	7,978	90.8
INDIANA	6,484,051	6,732,219	3.8	6,665,703	79.1	9.2	2.3	2.5	6.9	23.6	15.4	37.7	44.6	26.5	2,570,419	88.7
Aberdeen CDP	1,875	-	-	1,591	90.7	4.3	0.8	1.1	3.1	30.0	15.0	37.9	21.7	59.0	663	92.3
Advance town	474	514	8.4	458	96.1	0.0	1.5	0.7	1.7	17.9	15.3	46.8	57.0	18.8	188	83.0
Akron town	1,155	1,105	-4.3	1,206	66.6	0.0	0.0	0.8	32.6	31.5	7.9	31.6	66.1	13.1	357	86.0
Alamo town	64	64	0.0	43	93.0	0.0	0.0	0.0	7.0	37.2	9.3	22.8	63.2	0.0	12	83.3
Albany town	2,264	2,148	-5.1	2,094	95.3	0.5	0.0	2.2	2.0	18.4	21.9	43.6	49.7	16.8	901	90.8
Albion town	2,351	2,373	0.9	2,477	92.2	1.6	0.0	2.2	4.1	25.0	10.6	31.5	60.8	8.2	889	93.5
Alexandria city	5,126	4,968	-3.1	4,988	97.9	0.5	0.0	1.2	0.5	24.4	20.5	35.9	51.3	14.2	1,890	82.1
Alfordsville town	95	100	5.3	49	100.0	0.0	0.0	0.0	0.0	8.2	55.1	66.8	80.0	0.0	26	80.8
Alton town	55	54	-1.8	34	100.0	0.0	0.0	0.0	0.0	0.0	14.7	43.0	44.8	27.6	14	50.0
Altona town	195	197	1.0	358	96.1	0.0	0.3	1.7	2.0	25.7	8.4	39.4	70.3	8.0	112	84.8
Ambia town	227	227	0.0	255	55.7	0.0	0.0	0.0	44.3	35.7	4.3	23.4	69.6	6.1	61	83.6
Amboy town	373	358	-4.0	400	90.5	0.5	0.3	1.5	7.3	23.5	20.3	43.9	49.3	15.8	149	80.5
Americus CDP	423	-	-	292	93.5	0.0	0.0	3.4	3.1	19.2	16.4	59.4	33.5	35.2	132	88.6
Amo town	405	431	6.4	493	98.0	0.2	0.0	1.0	0.8	31.0	13.6	33.9	49.0	18.9	161	94.4
Anderson city	56,082	54,765	-2.3	54,513	74.8	14.5	0.9	4.4	5.5	20.7	18.0	38.3	54.2	16.0	23,067	84.7
Andrews town	1,155	1,137	-1.6	990	95.6	0.0	2.0	2.3	0.1	19.3	17.5	46.3	61.7	5.8	451	88.7
Angola city	8,597	8,732	1.6	8,660	89.5	1.1	0.8	4.0	4.7	19.1	17.5	29.5	46.3	27.0	3,262	86.2
Arcadia town	1,662	1,662	0.0	1,591	98.2	0.9	0.4	0.4	0.0	29.9	12.9	33.8	56.8	15.0	593	91.6
Argos town	1,690	1,626	-3.8	1,802	97.1	0.6	0.0	0.0	2.4	29.0	12.5	32.7	57.5	11.5	661	90.3
Arlington CDP	433	-	-	312	100.0	0.0	0.0	0.0	0.0	11.2	25.3	58.1	77.1	1.2	182	83.0
Ashley town	973	981	0.8	993	90.3	0.1	0.0	4.7	4.8	27.6	12.1	37.1	63.9	8.6	431	82.4

1 May be of any race.

Table A. All Places — **Population and Housing**

STATE City, town, township, borough, or CDP (county if applicable)	Population				Race and Hispanic or Latino origin (percent)					Age (percent)			Educational attainment of persons age 25 and older		Occupied housing units	
	2010 census total population	2019 estimated population	Percent change 2010-2019	ACS total population estimate 2015-2019	White alone, not Hispanic or Latino	Black alone, not Hispanic or Latino	Asian alone, not Hispanic or Latino	All other races or 2 or more races, not Hispanic or Latino	Hispanic or Latino[1]	Under 18 years old	Age 65 years and older	Median age	Percent High school diploma or less	Percent Bachelor's degree or more	Total	Percent with a computer
	1	2	3	4	5	6	7	8	9	10	11	12	13	14	15	16
INDIANA—Con.																
Atlanta town	723	745	3.0	954	93.7	0.4	0.5	0.7	4.6	30.2	11.1	35.1	58.1	5.3	333	97.6
Attica city	3,254	3,241	-0.4	3,174	95.4	0.0	0.0	2.4	2.3	21.0	17.9	43.1	50.0	15.8	1,430	83.4
Auburn city	12,794	13,484	5.4	13,056	96.7	0.8	0.1	0.9	1.6	24.0	17.1	38.1	46.9	20.4	5,666	87.2
Aurora city	3,740	3,676	-1.7	3,995	91.0	0.4	1.7	6.7	0.3	20.9	11.7	33.4	58.8	15.2	1,531	81.5
Austin city	4,290	4,118	-4.0	3,725	97.8	0.0	0.0	1.5	0.8	23.7	16.9	41.9	77.8	3.6	1,411	79.1
Avilla town	2,398	2,454	2.3	2,538	97.0	0.0	0.1	2.0	0.9	22.7	17.5	34.8	48.1	17.0	963	84.6
Avoca CDP	583	-	-	816	100.0	0.0	0.0	0.0	0.0	25.6	21.3	41.4	53.7	14.9	344	72.1
Avon town	13,529	18,706	38.3	17,453	80.9	5.9	3.2	3.1	6.8	27.0	10.3	35.1	26.2	43.8	6,288	95.8
Bainbridge town	746	746	0.0	728	97.8	0.0	0.0	0.0	2.2	22.0	14.4	40.6	65.8	6.6	304	85.5
Bargersville town	6,023	8,076	34.1	7,085	97.5	1.4	1.1	0.0	0.0	28.4	11.3	34.0	30.3	41.7	2,530	94.6
Bass Lake CDP	1,195	-	-	1,510	88.7	0.0	0.0	4.2	7.2	37.5	18.2	37.7	43.2	23.0	520	91.2
Batesville city	6,517	6,686	2.6	6,651	88.4	0.9	3.2	3.6	3.9	23.9	19.8	42.3	40.0	30.9	2,620	82.2
Battle Ground town	1,683	1,975	17.3	1,857	96.0	0.2	0.2	1.6	2.2	24.8	11.0	36.0	19.0	44.3	651	95.2
Bedford city	13,406	13,212	-1.4	13,272	93.3	0.6	1.0	3.0	2.1	20.8	21.5	42.2	51.5	16.3	5,791	83.8
Beech Grove city	14,227	14,937	5.0	14,990	84.9	8.1	1.2	1.3	4.5	24.1	15.2	36.3	50.2	19.2	5,760	87.3
Berne city	4,082	4,247	4.0	4,235	91.7	5.4	0.7	0.7	1.5	25.9	22.7	40.2	50.9	23.2	1,750	84.6
Bethany town	87	89	2.3	62	93.5	3.2	3.2	0.0	0.0	19.4	4.8	41.8	51.1	8.9	24	83.3
Beverly Shores town	594	599	0.8	516	94.0	1.7	0.8	0.0	3.5	6.0	47.3	64.6	10.6	74.0	275	89.5
Bicknell city	2,913	2,840	-2.5	2,978	95.7	0.9	0.0	1.9	1.5	26.2	14.9	36.0	55.5	8.0	1,234	86.9
Birdseye town	414	417	0.7	529	97.9	0.0	0.0	1.1	0.9	29.1	13.0	28.9	69.1	6.7	209	83.3
Blanford CDP	342	-	-	226	100.0	0.0	0.0	0.0	0.0	7.5	25.2	54.8	90.6	0.0	93	86.0
Bloomfield town	2,420	2,300	-5.0	2,463	97.0	0.3	0.2	1.0	1.5	18.8	20.6	42.9	47.5	18.3	1,092	79.9
Bloomingdale town	335	329	-1.8	363	99.4	0.0	0.0	0.6	0.0	30.6	16.0	39.5	48.0	10.7	134	92.5
Bloomington city	80,293	85,755	6.8	84,116	78.3	3.9	10.2	3.2	4.4	11.1	9.5	24.0	22.9	55.9	30,624	94.0
Blountsville town	134	128	-4.5	76	100.0	0.0	0.0	0.0	0.0	14.5	15.8	49.7	68.9	11.5	39	76.9
Bluffton city	9,894	10,147	2.6	9,919	93.3	1.8	0.4	0.9	3.7	25.1	19.2	38.3	49.6	14.4	4,092	88.7
Boonville city	6,469	6,227	-3.7	6,292	92.4	0.6	0.0	1.9	5.2	27.2	17.1	39.9	50.7	18.3	2,621	91.4
Borden town	818	936	14.4	1,244	97.6	0.2	0.0	0.0	2.2	28.8	11.7	29.9	54.9	13.8	446	82.5
Boston town	138	130	-5.8	149	97.3	0.0	0.0	2.7	0.0	18.8	14.8	55.9	58.2	8.2	66	90.9
Boswell town	779	769	-1.3	736	75.0	2.2	1.0	7.5	14.4	26.4	15.5	36.3	68.7	5.4	279	83.2
Bourbon town	1,814	1,754	-3.3	2,023	94.2	0.8	0.2	2.7	2.0	33.6	10.2	32.1	48.9	12.6	706	89.9
Brazil city	8,079	7,993	-1.1	8,380	94.0	1.4	0.0	3.4	1.2	26.5	15.5	34.6	57.6	11.9	3,178	84.9
Bremen town	4,585	4,474	-2.4	4,505	74.9	0.0	0.0	0.0	25.1	24.0	15.1	36.5	55.3	19.8	1,901	78.5
Bright CDP	5,693	-	-	5,816	94.5	0.0	3.4	0.6	1.6	24.7	15.9	41.5	40.7	27.4	2,083	96.4
Bristol town	1,602	1,692	5.6	1,518	91.4	1.8	1.4	1.4	4.0	19.5	23.5	40.7	52.6	17.4	650	89.8
Brook town	1,001	955	-4.6	1,012	80.6	0.2	0.0	1.0	18.2	20.9	16.3	38.7	69.3	8.3	393	88.5
Brooklyn town	1,576	1,597	1.3	1,417	94.2	0.0	2.0	2.3	1.6	21.9	13.2	38.6	54.2	11.1	576	94.3
Brooksburg town	81	79	-2.5	113	100.0	0.0	0.0	0.0	0.0	17.7	9.7	44.6	84.3	0.0	46	78.3
Brookston town	1,576	1,533	-2.7	1,513	95.6	0.0	0.8	0.2	3.4	22.6	14.5	32.5	44.4	20.2	691	90.6
Brookville town	2,590	2,529	-2.4	2,539	94.1	0.0	0.0	2.3	3.7	21.0	20.0	43.5	58.3	21.7	1,137	79.6
Brownsburg town	21,946	27,001	23.0	26,046	86.2	5.6	2.8	1.4	4.0	26.6	12.6	35.5	29.8	39.3	9,093	95.9
Brownstown town	2,957	2,892	-2.2	2,923	97.5	0.0	0.5	0.9	1.1	24.9	18.5	40.4	58.3	14.2	1,097	81.4
Bruceville town	485	475	-2.1	318	100.0	0.0	0.0	0.0	0.0	18.9	23.9	47.5	51.9	5.4	137	89.8
Bryant town	252	245	-2.8	177	96.0	0.0	0.0	4.0	0.0	29.4	18.6	39.6	77.1	4.2	74	75.7
Buck Creek CDP	207	-	-	162	100.0	0.0	0.0	0.0	0.0	0.0	26.5	49.4	78.7	10.7	95	87.4
Buffalo CDP	692	-	-	698	93.7	0.0	0.0	0.0	6.3	11.9	23.1	54.7	65.2	10.0	331	93.4
Bunker Hill town	882	851	-3.5	513	97.1	0.8	0.8	0.8	0.6	23.0	14.2	43.2	53.3	11.5	216	87.0
Burket town	195	195	0.0	113	94.7	0.0	0.0	0.0	5.3	20.4	23.0	52.7	66.3	1.2	52	82.7
Burlington town	601	604	0.5	528	100.0	0.0	0.0	0.0	0.0	16.9	22.9	46.3	41.8	21.9	271	90.4
Burnettsville town	348	339	-2.6	409	96.6	1.2	0.2	2.0	0.0	25.2	13.7	36.2	59.0	13.2	156	83.3
Burns City CDP	117	-	-	90	100.0	0.0	0.0	0.0	0.0	0.0	15.6	55.5	46.7	12.0	39	100.0
Burns Harbor town	1,158	1,828	57.9	1,980	82.7	2.7	0.8	1.8	12.0	25.1	10.4	35.9	46.6	25.9	798	90.4
Butler city	2,676	2,718	1.6	2,715	94.3	0.6	0.0	1.4	3.6	28.6	11.3	32.6	63.7	10.0	934	84.8
Butlerville CDP	282	-	-	181	100.0	0.0	0.0	0.0	0.0	21.0	23.8	34.8	39.9	30.8	90	61.1
Cadiz town	145	136	-6.2	222	98.2	0.0	0.0	1.8	0.0	43.7	4.1	24.7	45.0	6.4	64	96.9
Cambridge City town	1,888	1,750	-7.3	1,744	97.0	0.4	0.0	2.4	0.2	23.8	18.3	41.8	64.5	8.7	732	79.0
Camden town	620	619	-0.2	580	91.7	0.5	0.0	7.8	0.0	21.4	16.9	41.0	50.8	7.9	260	76.5
Campbellsburg town	585	579		676	96.9	0.0	0.0	2.7	0.4	32.7	18.6	33.8	61.9	10.6	253	75.1
Canaan CDP	90	-	-	71	100.0	0.0	0.0	0.0	0.0	14.1	40.8	60.1	45.9	37.7	47	80.9
Cannelburg town	159	164	3.1	119	100.0	0.0	0.0	0.0	0.0	16.0	31.9	55.8	68.1	1.1	51	80.4
Cannelton city	1,563	1,481	-5.2	1,470	94.1	1.7	0.0	3.2	1.0	21.6	17.3	44.2	59.5	7.0	707	79.1
Carbon town	386	377	-2.3	402	99.8	0.0	0.0	0.2	0.0	25.4	9.5	37.7	76.1	4.7	156	82.1
Carlisle town	692	658	-4.9	660	98.0	0.0	0.0	2.0	0.0	23.6	21.2	38.7	54.8	12.6	281	79.7
Carmel city	83,887	101,068	20.5	97,464	80.3	2.7	10.3	3.0	3.7	26.3	13.3	39.4	11.4	70.6	36,954	97.6
Carthage town	932	889	-4.6	998	89.3	0.0	0.0	4.0	6.7	34.1	13.5	34.4	63.2	13.5	378	88.6
Cayuga town	1,159	1,104	-4.7	1,263	97.1	0.0	0.0	2.9	0.0	27.1	15.2	35.0	63.8	10.1	455	81.5
Cedar Grove town	156	152	-2.6	167	98.2	0.0	0.0	0.0	1.8	15.0	22.2	45.2	40.2	21.3	83	89.2
Cedar Lake town	11,579	13,183	13.9	12,491	94.4	0.1	0.3	0.9	4.3	25.5	12.5	35.7	45.6	19.7	4,643	95.6
Center Point town	240	231	-3.8	267	100.0	0.0	0.0	0.0	0.0	25.5	15.7	37.1	50.0	12.0	114	86.8
Centerville town	2,671	2,579	-3.4	2,579	93.4	1.6	0.0	3.8	1.2	26.4	18.7	38.0	47.1	15.0	1,028	90.6
Chalmers town	509	493	-3.1	445	99.1	0.0	0.0	0.9	0.0	30.3	13.9	38.8	50.0	11.5	187	96.3
Chandler town	3,423	3,318	-3.1	3,384	97.4	0.4	0.0	2.0	0.2	25.3	14.5	36.1	57.9	9.2	1,364	92.7
Charlestown city	7,580	8,370	10.4	8,199	89.4	1.5	0.5	4.0	4.5	25.6	12.4	38.6	56.2	13.3	3,178	87.4
Chesterfield town	2,550	2,477	-2.9	2,472	91.7	0.2	0.6	1.4	6.1	19.9	20.4	41.3	58.1	12.7	1,019	85.1
Chesterton town	13,087	14,088	7.6	14,119	85.7	1.5	2.8	2.3	7.7	24.9	15.8	37.6	34.8	32.3	5,474	89.5
Chrisney town	485	472	-2.7	742	95.4	0.0	0.0	2.4	2.2	26.7	16.2	40.9	44.7	15.9	268	88.1
Churubusco town	1,855	1,979	6.7	1,837	95.2	0.0	1.4	1.0	2.4	27.2	18.0	34.8	47.1	10.7	752	88.7
Cicero town	4,815	4,953	2.9	4,891	98.6	0.0	0.3	0.0	1.1	21.8	15.9	42.5	34.6	28.5	2,127	95.0
Clarksburg CDP	149	-	-	46	100.0	0.0	0.0	0.0	0.0	0.0	67.4	65.5	100.0	0.0	31	48.4
Clarks Hill town	614	727	18.4	763	94.8	0.0	0.0	4.1	1.2	29.0	13.5	31.8	59.1	2.6	296	83.8
Clarksville town	21,527	21,558	0.1	21,548	81.3	4.7	1.2	2.8	10.0	20.7	18.5	40.3	50.9	19.0	8,790	83.0
Clay City town	855	827	-3.3	852	97.7	0.0	0.8	1.2	0.4	21.0	18.7	40.2	55.3	13.4	411	78.8
Claypool town	431	434	0.7	534	90.1	0.6	1.5	4.1	3.7	29.4	9.6	34.7	71.1	6.7	193	90.2
Clayton town	967	1,055	9.1	1,110	91.5	3.0	0.0	2.5	3.0	22.3	12.1	40.5	38.8	20.0	425	97.4
Clear Lake town	343	344	0.3	398	99.2	0.0	0.8	0.0	0.0	4.3	60.6	68.0	21.1	52.7	222	97.3
Clermont town	1,374	1,463	6.5	1,421	86.8	4.7	1.4	5.6	1.5	20.6	20.4	44.9	32.9	31.9	548	94.0
Clifford town	228	251	10.1	276	87.7	8.7	1.1	0.0	2.5	13.4	9.4	33.9	42.9	5.4	93	86.0
Clinton city	4,861	4,686	-3.6	4,706	95.4	3.6	0.0	1.0	0.0	22.6	20.0	38.1	53.8	11.8	2,097	89.3
Cloverdale town	2,158	2,145	-0.6	1,799	95.7	0.0	0.0	2.8	1.5	19.0	19.1	42.8	53.2	10.7	761	82.8
Coalmont CDP	402	-	-	304	83.9	0.0	0.0	16.1	0.0	13.8	11.5	54.3	81.4	0.0	177	39.5
Coatesville town	523	564	7.8	555	97.7	0.0	0.0	2.3	0.0	24.1	16.2	37.9	59.6	22.0	189	85.7
Colburn CDP	193	-	-	287	100.0	0.0	0.0	0.0	0.0	7.7	8.4	45.1	74.0	7.2	184	66.8

1 May be of any race.

Table A. All Places — **Population and Housing**

STATE City, town, township, borough, or CDP (county if applicable)	Population: 2010 census total population	Population: 2019 estimated population	Population: Percent change 2010-2019	Population: ACS total population estimate 2015-2019	Race and Hispanic or Latino origin (percent): White alone, not Hispanic or Latino	Black alone, not Hispanic or Latino	Asian alone, not Hispanic or Latino	All other races or 2 or more races, not Hispanic or Latino	Hispanic or Latino[1]	Age (percent): Under 18 years old	Age 65 years and older	Median age	Educational attainment of persons age 25 and older: Percent High school diploma or less	Percent Bachelor's degree or more	Occupied housing units: Total	Percent with a computer
	1	2	3	4	5	6	7	8	9	10	11	12	13	14	15	16
INDIANA—Con.																
Colfax town	689	679	-1.5	787	99.5	0.5	0.0	0.0	0.0	26.6	15.1	36.5	54.6	8.4	275	88.4
Collegeville CDP	330	-	-	547	85.0	2.2	2.7	1.3	8.8	0.0	0.0	20.1	0.0	60.9	9	100.0
Columbia City city	8,781	9,234	5.2	9,116	95.4	0.8	0.0	2.8	0.9	21.8	17.4	37.4	45.8	26.3	4,088	93.0
Columbus city	44,089	48,046	9.0	48,150	75.9	2.2	12.2	3.3	6.4	23.9	15.4	35.3	32.5	41.3	18,832	90.6
Connersville city	13,510	12,796	-5.3	13,165	93.5	3.8	0.0	1.0	1.8	23.2	19.9	41.9	65.7	10.7	5,684	82.1
Converse town	1,285	1,222	-4.9	1,167	87.7	1.1	1.5	3.3	6.5	22.8	22.4	41.1	52.1	14.4	491	87.8
Cordry Sweetwater Lakes CDP	1,128	-	-	1,131	97.3	0.0	0.0	2.7	0.0	16.7	28.9	57.4	30.8	34.1	472	100.0
Corunna town	253	256	1.2	255	87.8	5.9	0.0	5.5	0.8	27.1	14.5	41.1	77.8	13.5	94	91.5
Corydon town	3,145	3,201	1.8	3,162	96.4	1.7	0.0	0.0	1.9	18.1	15.6	38.6	51.2	25.6	1,201	85.4
Country Club Heights town	79	78	-1.3	102	100.0	0.0	0.0	0.0	0.0	15.7	52.9	67.5	17.6	68.2	44	90.9
Country Squire Lakes CDP	3,571	-	-	2,813	88.8	1.2	0.0	0.0	10.0	21.5	11.7	37.1	69.2	4.2	1,097	84.6
Covington city	2,648	2,500	-5.6	2,439	93.4	0.7	2.4	0.6	3.0	21.4	26.5	44.7	52.2	20.6	1,066	88.9
Crandall town	149	151	1.3	139	100.0	0.0	0.0	0.0	0.0	37.4	21.6	29.9	34.5	24.1	50	88.0
Crane town	184	179	-2.7	219	98.2	0.0	0.5	0.5	0.9	31.5	22.8	32.9	52.1	18.1	90	77.8
Crawfordsville city	15,960	16,118	1.0	16,090	86.2	1.5	1.1	2.6	8.5	21.7	17.7	37.5	55.0	18.5	6,642	87.3
Cromwell town	514	509		476	82.8	0.0	1.5	1.7	14.1	30.7	10.5	30.2	64.4	7.5	183	84.7
Crothersville town	1,588	1,546	-2.6	1,788	98.2	0.0	0.0	1.0	0.8	31.7	13.3	33.0	59.1	9.7	613	82.1
Crown Point city	27,870	30,488	9.4	29,850	80.8	5.6	2.2	1.5	10.0	22.6	19.6	41.0	36.0	33.5	11,330	90.1
Crows Nest town	70	75	7.1	116	99.1	0.0	0.0	0.0	0.9	34.5	23.3	38.4	0.0	98.4	30	100.0
Culver town	1,345	1,461	8.6	1,130	97.3	0.0	0.3	0.0	2.5	14.9	34.2	54.8	35.6	36.4	546	79.3
Cumberland town	5,341	6,017	12.7	5,718	82.7	15.7	0.0	1.3	0.4	26.4	12.0	34.9	35.6	27.1	2,139	90.9
Cynthiana town	545	536	-1.7	599	97.0	0.0	0.0	2.2	0.8	24.9	14.0	37.1	62.8	14.0	235	86.0
Dale town	1,593	1,491	-6.4	1,482	75.3	0.0	0.0	0.3	24.4	23.1	22.9	40.8	73.8	7.2	613	74.6
Daleville town	1,659	1,648	-0.7	1,662	94.5	1.6	0.1	1.0	2.8	20.2	16.2	38.8	48.2	17.0	664	91.7
Dana town	608	570	-6.3	586	91.5	0.0	0.0	5.6	2.9	18.9	21.7	45.9	58.1	10.1	252	84.9
Danville town	9,047	10,126	11.9	9,923	87.5	5.9	4.0	0.3	2.2	25.6	12.9	38.2	41.2	29.7	3,542	92.8
Darlington town	865	862	-0.3	857	94.7	0.4	0.0	0.0	4.9	20.4	12.4	37.6	55.6	17.1	356	86.8
Darmstadt town	1,354	1,432	5.8	1,131	98.8	0.2	0.4	0.0	0.6	20.0	25.3	53.9	24.1	40.5	473	93.7
Dayton town	1,420	1,668	17.5	1,578	93.4	0.7	0.0	0.6	5.3	24.7	16.2	39.3	43.8	13.8	608	93.3
Decatur city	9,628	9,858	2.4	9,863	91.1	1.2	0.0	0.4	7.3	23.6	17.9	40.5	53.9	12.9	4,278	85.1
Decker town	248	247	-0.4	241	100.0	0.0	0.0	0.0	0.0	26.6	17.0	34.2	68.9	4.3	84	89.3
Delphi city	2,891	2,909	0.6	2,935	80.8	0.8	0.0	0.9	17.5	22.7	19.8	42.3	58.1	15.3	1,166	90.8
De Motte town	3,815	4,159	9.0	4,054	93.2	0.0	0.0	2.9	3.8	16.8	27.1	46.4	58.3	11.2	1,863	78.7
Denver town	487	467	-4.1	436	91.7	2.3	0.0	6.0	0.0	21.1	18.8	44.2	67.2	7.6	178	87.1
Deputy CDP	86	-	-	47	27.7	0.0	0.0	0.0	72.3	0.0	72.3	78.3	72.3	0.0	30	43.3
Dillsboro town	1,419	1,410	-0.6	1,569	97.6	1.7	0.0	0.0	0.7	28.0	18.0	32.1	74.6	5.0	552	79.0
Dover Hill CDP	114	-	-	26	100.0	0.0	0.0	0.0	0.0	0.0	0.0	56.6	65.4	0.0	17	52.9
Dresser CDP	104	-	-	38	100.0	0.0	0.0	0.0	0.0	13.2	0.0	51.4	38.5	0.0	21	23.8
Dublin town	801	747	-6.7	794	97.9	0.3	0.0	0.0	1.9	23.4	15.7	42.5	56.1	13.1	340	80.6
Dubois CDP	488	-	-	207	68.6	31.4	0.0	0.0	0.0	0.0	36.2	60.6	89.9	10.1	195	63.1
Dugger town	920	872	-5.2	883	90.3	3.6	0.0	3.5	2.6	16.2	20.6	45.3	50.3	10.3	334	89.2
Dune Acres town	182	182	0.0	198	96.0	0.0	1.5	0.0	2.5	7.6	46.0	62.4	7.6	72.4	92	97.8
Dunkirk city	2,367	2,255	-4.7	2,022	96.2	0.1	0.0	0.6	3.0	24.5	18.6	41.4	59.0	8.6	878	77.2
Dunlap CDP	6,235	-	-	6,667	73.4	6.5	0.9	3.4	15.8	22.0	15.5	39.6	52.0	16.1	2,142	93.2
Dunreith town	177	169	-4.5	138	96.4	0.0	0.0	0.0	3.6	22.5	20.3	29.5	54.1	8.2	57	75.4
Dupont town	332	328	-1.2	324	91.7	0.3	0.0	2.5	5.6	24.7	11.7	41.3	65.9	9.4	120	89.2
Dyer town	16,367	15,976	-2.4	15,953	78.9	4.8	3.7	2.9	9.7	19.8	20.7	46.0	36.9	31.4	6,162	94.1
Earl Park town	348	343	-1.4	373	92.0	1.6	0.0	0.5	5.9	15.8	18.2	47.4	56.7	11.6	160	89.4
East Chicago city	29,698	27,817	-6.3	28,201	6.7	34.9	0.1	0.6	57.8	28.4	14.1	33.8	64.9	9.1	10,365	76.8
East Enterprise CDP	148	-	-	219	100.0	0.0	0.0	0.0	0.0	17.8	23.7	46.0	61.3	6.9	99	66.7
East Germantown town	372	351	-5.6	327	98.8	0.0	0.0	1.2	0.0	13.1	23.2	51.9	58.7	5.1	152	83.6
Eaton town	1,813	1,733	-4.4	1,870	97.4	0.6	0.0	1.8	0.2	21.5	18.6	38.4	52.8	9.7	757	82.6
Economy town	185	175	-5.4	135	94.8	0.0	0.0	0.7	4.4	16.3	28.9	46.5	57.4	10.6	57	87.7
Edgewood town	1,910	1,858	-2.7	2,107	89.5	3.7	1.9	0.5	4.5	20.6	22.0	44.5	33.3	32.2	896	94.1
Edinburgh town	4,474	4,590	2.6	4,792	88.6	3.0	0.0	2.0	6.4	21.3	13.5	37.4	64.3	6.8	1,790	83.4
Edwardsport town	304	297	-2.3	340	96.5	0.0	0.0	0.0	3.5	26.2	15.9	32.3	58.9	11.2	126	86.5
Elberfeld town	613	656	7.0	732	98.4	0.0	0.0	1.6	0.0	23.9	10.2	34.4	42.5	21.8	277	98.2
Elizabeth town	203	206	1.5	156	100.0	0.0	0.0	0.0	0.0	21.2	14.7	36.7	56.3	18.4	55	83.6
Elizabethtown town	516	538	4.3	538	94.8	2.2	0.0	0.4	2.6	30.1	5.6	29.4	83.6	1.8	171	87.1
Elkhart city	51,908	52,358	0.9	52,257	55.3	14.6	0.8	3.6	25.8	27.6	13.0	33.5	58.6	15.0	20,070	85.5
Ellettsville town	6,227	6,747	8.4	6,642	96.0	0.9	0.4	2.3	0.4	24.7	13.9	39.2	36.8	29.5	2,770	90.8
Elnora town	645	676	4.8	642	96.7	1.2	0.0	1.2	0.8	18.4	13.2	33.7	58.1	10.7	270	85.2
Elwood city	8,595	8,394	-2.3	8,441	93.3	0.0	0.4	1.1	5.2	22.7	16.4	40.5	62.0	9.6	3,453	82.4
Emison CDP	154	-	-	118	100.0	0.0	0.0	0.0	0.0	0.0	78.0	68.7	83.9	0.0	66	19.7
English town	642	625	-2.6	711	94.4	0.0	0.0	2.5	3.1	26.2	17.6	38.3	77.7	3.9	284	64.4
Etna Green town	586	589	0.5	582	94.3	0.0	0.0	1.2	4.5	20.1	16.8	38.6	56.6	7.4	235	88.5
Evansville city	120,069	117,979	-1.7	118,588	79.0	13.1	1.0	3.8	3.1	21.0	16.1	37.6	47.9	21.5	51,666	87.0
Fairland town	585	579		612	95.4	0.0	0.0	1.0	3.6	20.6	20.8	43.5	57.0	11.7	258	89.9
Fairmount town	2,954	2,768	-6.3	2,773	92.4	0.0	0.0	2.8	4.7	26.4	16.5	37.4	62.1	6.2	1,135	87.7
Fairview Park town	1,377	1,312	-4.7	1,321	97.7	0.0	0.0	0.5	1.9	18.5	18.8	43.6	53.8	16.9	653	91.1
Farmersburg town	1,123	1,070	-4.7	1,180	97.1	0.9	0.0	1.9	0.0	28.3	20.8	36.2	44.9	14.5	510	86.5
Farmland town	1,327	1,251	-5.7	1,416	97.7	0.0	0.2	1.1	1.0	29.2	19.2	38.5	55.0	17.2	566	89.2
Ferdinand town	2,157	2,247	4.2	2,065	96.9	0.3	0.0	0.2	2.6	18.4	28.0	48.2	48.6	28.4	807	83.0
Fillmore town	533	533	0.0	575	96.2	1.4	0.0	2.4	0.0	16.3	18.3	46.4	63.0	6.3	280	86.1
Fishers city	77,293	95,310	23.3	90,332	80.6	6.1	6.9	2.6	3.9	29.6	8.9	35.6	12.7	66.4	32,794	98.0
Fish Lake CDP	1,016	-	-	1,605	83.6	0.0	0.0	1.5	15.0	17.9	20.8	48.4	68.9	11.1	615	83.3
Flora town	2,045	2,002	-2.1	2,013	93.5	5.9	0.0	0.2	0.3	21.7	16.0	35.1	63.2	12.1	772	79.4
Florence CDP	80	-	-	29	100.0	0.0	0.0	0.0	0.0	65.5	0.0	3.6	100.0	0.0	10	100.0
Fontanet CDP	423	-	-	455	100.0	0.0	0.0	0.0	0.0	10.3	21.3	51.9	58.1	30.1	168	82.7
Fort Branch town	2,781	2,766	-0.5	3,040	89.7	0.4	0.3	5.9	3.6	26.1	14.7	34.2	47.5	16.2	1,221	93.4
Fortville town	3,915	4,162	6.3	4,574	93.1	2.0	0.0	4.9	0.0	21.7	13.4	38.6	52.8	20.0	1,852	79.9
Fort Wayne city	253,739	270,402	6.6	265,752	67.0	14.8	4.7	4.3	9.2	25.3	14.0	35.0	39.7	27.8	106,673	91.0
Fountain City town	814	756	-7.1	740	97.6	0.0	0.1	1.5	0.8	22.2	15.0	41.8	57.8	6.4	304	86.5
Fowler town	2,329	2,302	-1.2	2,256	95.7	0.4	0.0	2.5	1.4	22.7	22.7	42.9	54.4	18.7	1,017	90.3
Fowlerton town	261	253	-3.1	262	96.6	0.0	1.5	0.0	1.9	28.6	24.8	47.2	73.5	5.4	94	97.9
Francesville town	882	797	-9.6	908	96.4	0.0	0.0	1.1	2.5	25.2	21.3	42.7	56.1	12.0	376	84.6
Francisco town	555	554	-0.2	639	96.1	0.0	0.0	3.9	0.0	23.6	19.1	41.8	63.2	6.3	273	87.2
Frankfort city	16,420	15,884	-3.3	15,634	69.5	1.0	0.2	1.2	28.1	28.2	14.1	34.6	66.4	12.5	5,899	88.4
Franklin city	23,729	25,608	7.9	25,106	93.4	1.1	0.8	1.9	2.9	23.7	15.9	37.9	46.5	24.3	9,295	88.8

1 May be of any race.

Table A. All Places — **Population and Housing**

STATE City, town, township, borough, or CDP (county if applicable)	Population: 2010 census total population	Population: 2019 estimated population	Population: Percent change 2010-2019	Population: ACS total population estimate 2015-2019	Race and Hispanic or Latino origin (percent): White alone, not Hispanic or Latino	Black alone, not Hispanic or Latino	Asian alone, not Hispanic or Latino	All other races or 2 or more races, not Hispanic or Latino	Hispanic or Latino[1]	Age (percent): Under 18 years old	Age 65 years and older	Median age	Educational attainment of persons age 25 and older: Percent High school diploma or less	Percent Bachelor's degree or more	Occupied housing units: Total	Percent with a computer
	1	2	3	4	5	6	7	8	9	10	11	12	13	14	15	16
INDIANA—Con.																
Frankton town	1,862	1,836	-1.4	2,088	94.8	0.4	0.6	2.8	1.4	29.6	14.9	37.8	55.8	16.0	761	89.6
Fredericksburg CDP	85	-	-	168	100.0	0.0	0.0	0.0	0.0	20.2	8.9	24.4	51.4	0.0	51	43.1
Freelandville CDP	643	-	-	800	96.9	0.0	0.0	3.1	0.0	32.1	26.8	42.9	66.3	11.4	250	90.8
Freetown CDP	385	-	-	337	100.0	0.0	0.0	0.0	0.0	45.1	10.1	32.2	75.3	0.0	102	78.4
Fremont town	2,147	2,190	2.0	2,240	89.0	0.0	1.1	0.8	9.2	19.5	19.1	40.2	66.7	10.3	1,019	75.5
French Lick town	1,793	1,777	-0.9	1,841	74.7	19.0	0.7	3.2	2.3	26.8	17.7	39.8	63.2	9.4	751	77.8
Fulton town	343	327	-4.7	358	94.4	0.8	0.0	3.1	1.7	25.7	14.0	37.8	60.6	7.5	148	81.1
Galena CDP	1,818	-	-	1,780	100.0	0.0	0.0	0.0	0.0	32.1	11.5	38.1	48.5	26.9	572	93.2
Galveston town	1,313	1,259	-4.1	1,226	96.1	1.7	0.0	1.5	0.7	25.4	16.5	38.8	48.7	14.2	525	90.3
Garrett city	6,311	6,413	1.6	6,651	92.7	1.2	0.1	1.6	4.5	24.3	13.9	35.7	59.0	11.8	2,669	87.1
Gary city	80,256	74,879	-6.7	76,010	11.8	78.0	0.2	1.9	8.0	23.9	18.4	39.0	53.3	13.9	31,515	78.3
Gas City city	6,157	5,772	-6.3	5,802	90.3	1.8	2.2	2.2	3.4	27.9	15.5	36.7	52.2	13.5	2,413	89.3
Gaston town	889	873	-1.8	875	94.5	0.0	0.7	2.2	2.6	24.6	15.8	38.4	59.6	15.2	354	82.5
Geneva town	1,304	1,359	4.2	1,312	86.9	0.5	1.6	0.2	10.7	20.8	18.1	46.9	53.5	13.3	526	90.1
Gentryville town	268	265	-1.1	295	96.6	0.0	0.0	0.0	3.4	26.4	12.2	35.4	65.6	7.8	112	75.0
Georgetown town	2,871	3,371	17.4	3,268	93.2	0.0	1.3	3.2	2.3	28.0	11.3	34.3	27.2	36.6	1,138	92.5
Glenwood town	250	236	-5.6	254	100.0	0.0	0.0	0.0	0.0	22.4	14.2	45.2	68.0	1.2	90	85.6
Goodland town	1,043	990	-5.1	1,000	96.3	0.0	0.0	1.1	2.6	21.1	17.9	44.5	59.8	12.4	425	87.8
Goshen city	32,572	34,217	5.1	34,108	66.3	3.5	1.8	2.5	25.9	25.1	17.6	37.6	54.3	23.1	12,432	85.2
Gosport town	837	797	-4.8	834	98.8	0.0	0.5	0.0	0.7	20.7	15.7	42.3	67.8	13.7	340	91.8
Grabill town	1,063	1,152	8.4	1,294	95.9	0.5	0.5	1.4	1.7	28.2	9.4	35.4	39.7	19.4	505	92.3
Grandview town	760	719	-5.4	995	93.8	1.1	0.0	4.2	0.9	23.1	10.7	33.7	63.3	5.5	397	73.3
Granger CDP	30,465	-	-	30,776	83.7	3.1	8.2	2.2	2.8	27.4	16.3	41.7	20.7	54.5	10,749	96.2
Greencastle city	10,311	10,270	-0.4	10,296	87.8	2.2	6.0	0.6	3.4	17.6	16.1	26.7	52.2	20.1	3,746	85.4
Greendale city	4,528	4,341	-4.1	4,279	98.8	0.0	0.0	0.0	1.2	19.6	19.6	43.4	44.4	28.8	1,872	89.7
Greenfield city	20,641	23,006	11.5	22,160	95.5	0.4	0.9	1.3	2.0	22.6	18.9	37.9	48.9	21.9	9,144	90.0
Greensboro town	143	137	-4.2	142	99.3	0.0	0.0	0.7	0.0	42.3	7.7	27.3	60.5	10.5	44	84.1
Greensburg city	11,489	11,891	3.5	11,228	92.4	0.9	3.3	0.8	2.6	22.0	18.2	40.1	50.9	19.8	4,740	89.9
Greens Fork town	417	387	-7.2	430	94.0	0.0	0.0	3.0	3.0	20.2	10.0	39.5	57.2	11.5	158	88.0
Greentown town	2,430	2,374	-2.3	2,187	97.0	0.1	0.0	0.8	2.1	21.4	19.7	44.5	50.9	15.3	934	85.3
Greenville town	650	1,051	61.7	1,117	95.6	2.3	0.2	1.3	0.6	28.1	11.1	37.4	39.2	23.3	359	91.1
Greenwood city	51,116	59,458	16.3	57,764	81.8	4.3	6.1	1.3	6.4	26.4	14.4	35.0	40.7	31.1	22,360	92.6
Griffin town	171	169	-1.2	152	100.0	0.0	0.0	0.0	0.0	26.3	21.1	37.7	57.4	6.9	57	94.7
Griffith town	16,919	16,060	-5.1	16,228	65.7	15.5	1.5	1.8	15.6	19.9	14.2	38.6	43.4	20.7	6,630	91.9
Grissom AFB CDP	5,537	-	-	2,453	80.0	10.0	0.6	1.8	7.6	25.7	8.1	31.2	51.2	10.9	767	92.0
Hagerstown town	1,781	1,673	-6.1	1,934	97.9	0.5	0.0	1.2	0.4	25.0	19.3	37.7	39.0	21.9	730	89.6
Hamilton town	1,561	1,580	1.2	1,500	96.1	0.3	0.2	2.7	0.7	16.9	23.7	47.7	44.5	24.1	676	89.9
Hamlet town	800	761	-4.9	574	93.2	0.0	0.0	2.1	4.7	20.7	14.3	39.7	69.1	12.8	212	85.8
Hammond city	80,825	75,522	-6.6	76,547	36.8	22.0	1.1	2.0	38.1	25.0	12.3	35.7	56.4	14.3	28,620	85.0
Hanna CDP	463	-	-	295	100.0	0.0	0.0	0.0	0.0	22.7	26.8	53.0	43.4	19.3	154	90.3
Hanover town	3,539	3,502		3,427	92.5	3.0	0.3	2.7	1.5	18.1	13.2	25.4	52.2	12.2	1,009	85.6
Hardinsburg town	245	239	-2.4	137	100.0	0.0	0.0	0.0	0.0	12.4	20.4	52.4	63.2	14.9	66	75.8
Harlan CDP	1,634	-	-	1,622	97.5	0.6	0.0	1.4	0.5	34.8	16.6	28.8	46.4	14.6	584	87.5
Harmony town	668	641	-4.0	849	98.0	0.0	0.6	1.1	0.4	20.6	22.3	42.1	55.9	11.9	379	86.5
Harrodsburg CDP	691	-	-	686	93.3	0.0	0.0	6.7	0.0	21.0	13.1	46.8	32.3	34.8	284	86.3
Hartford City city	6,164	5,660	-8.2	5,831	95.7	0.0	0.0	2.0	2.4	24.5	17.0	40.3	62.0	12.1	2,555	84.7
Hartsville town	369	400	8.4	407	100.0	0.0	0.0	0.0	0.0	26.3	11.8	38.1	57.9	12.6	144	90.3
Hatfield CDP	813	-	-	838	99.4	0.0	0.0	0.6	0.0	29.5	9.5	25.1	68.6	2.9	266	85.7
Haubstadt town	1,574	1,697	7.8	1,504	95.9	0.5	0.0	0.9	2.7	25.0	15.0	35.2	40.7	23.4	616	91.2
Hayden CDP	521	-	-	589	88.5	0.0	0.0	4.9	6.6	39.0	4.9	34.8	36.4	14.3	138	100.0
Hazleton town	266	268	0.8	369	88.9	0.5	0.0	6.8	3.8	32.5	15.2	40.1	54.4	15.0	146	89.0
Hebron town	3,711	3,670	-1.1	3,692	88.2	0.0	0.0	0.0	11.8	30.7	10.4	34.2	57.3	12.3	1,311	90.5
Henryville CDP	1,905	-	-	1,878	100.0	0.0	0.0	0.0	0.0	21.2	13.0	37.5	52.9	14.0	722	85.6
Herbst CDP	112	-	-	143	100.0	0.0	0.0	0.0	0.0	22.4	5.6	35.9	36.9	13.5	64	76.6
Heritage Lake CDP	2,880	-	-	2,782	99.3	0.0	0.0	0.7	0.0	18.8	17.4	38.3	25.2	34.1	1,134	91.4
Hidden Valley CDP	5,387	-	-	5,531	95.5	0.0	0.0	1.9	2.5	28.4	16.1	39.1	33.4	41.6	1,790	94.2
Highland town	23,741	22,316	-6.0	22,581	75.1	4.9	2.5	2.0	15.4	20.3	18.6	41.9	38.1	28.7	9,374	90.2
Highland CDP	4,489	-	-	4,609	99.2	0.4	0.4	0.0	0.0	24.1	17.3	40.2	34.8	31.8	1,695	94.1
Hillsboro town	542	501	-7.6	527	90.7	0.0	0.0	1.9	7.4	26.4	17.1	36.3	63.8	9.9	212	91.0
Hoagland CDP	821	-	-	951	95.5	0.0	0.0	0.8	3.7	24.4	19.3	41.1	53.7	20.4	374	77.8
Hobart city	29,336	27,939	-4.8	28,049	74.4	6.3	2.2	3.1	14.1	23.7	16.3	38.2	45.2	23.6	10,831	91.5
Holland town	654	650	-0.6	673	97.8	0.0	0.9	0.0	1.3	29.3	15.8	36.6	54.6	17.1	262	87.4
Holton town	482	450	-6.6	500	96.0	0.0	0.0	1.4	2.6	34.2	9.0	34.1	73.5	6.1	170	89.4
Homecroft town	723	763	5.5	617	93.2	1.8	1.8	2.4	0.8	21.2	15.6	37.8	25.3	43.6	248	96.8
Hope town	2,112	2,228	5.5	2,474	93.7	1.0	0.0	2.9	2.5	29.9	11.6	32.9	56.9	11.8	859	83.5
Howe CDP	807	-	-	270	85.6	0.0	2.2	9.3	3.0	0.0	39.3	47.6	59.6	21.9	102	78.4
Hudson town	514	516	0.4	557	95.7	0.4	0.0	1.6	2.3	29.8	14.4	34.0	58.9	7.9	204	87.3
Hudson Lake CDP	1,297	-	-	1,638	100.0	0.0	0.0	0.0	0.0	29.6	16.8	37.8	59.0	11.6	650	88.3
Huntertown town	6,385	6,824	6.9	6,789	91.5	1.8	0.1	2.5	4.1	34.2	10.4	32.9	29.9	28.7	2,243	94.6
Huntingburg city	6,065	6,170	1.7	6,522	65.9	1.8	2.5	1.1	28.6	31.1	15.3	34.6	60.1	13.3	2,513	86.6
Huntington city	17,524	17,138	-2.2	17,067	93.8	1.2	1.1	1.1	2.8	22.1	15.8	36.9	54.8	16.5	6,789	86.3
Hymera town	793	761	-4.0	776	99.1	0.0	0.0	0.9	0.0	19.7	16.2	44.9	69.4	2.1	329	71.4
Idaville CDP	461	-	-	397	100.0	0.0	0.0	0.0	0.0	30.2	15.9	45.2	65.0	5.8	150	76.0
Indianapolis city (consolidated city)	829,709	886,220	6.8	874,005	54.7	28.1	3.4	3.4	10.4	24.7	12.2	34.2	42.0	30.9	342,052	86.7
Indianapolis city (balance)	820,457	876,384	6.8	864,447	54.5	28.2	3.4	3.4	10.5	24.7	12.2	34.2	42.1	30.9	338,208	86.7
Indian Village town	133	135	1.5	175	64.6	2.9	8.0	24.6	0.0	10.9	18.9	45.1	48.2	23.7	73	94.5
Ingalls town	2,425	2,424	0.0	2,203	92.6	1.6	0.0	3.9	1.9	32.0	10.0	33.5	48.2	15.5	768	96.6
Jalapa CDP	171	-	-	212	100.0	0.0	0.0	0.0	0.0	0.0	0.0	52.5	89.2	0.0	103	100.0
Jamestown town	957	924	-3.4	989	99.0	0.0	0.0	1.0	0.0	25.0	12.9	34.9	39.9	29.2	418	90.4
Jasonville city	2,222	2,122	-4.5	1,966	96.4	0.0	0.0	0.9	2.7	30.4	17.5	32.9	63.1	6.5	722	75.6
Jasper city	15,127	15,724	3.9	15,827	91.3	0.5	0.7	0.4	7.0	22.7	18.2	40.3	45.7	26.8	6,608	87.7
Jeffersonville city	45,026	48,126	6.9	47,673	75.4	12.7	1.7	5.0	5.1	22.7	14.8	37.9	42.3	22.8	18,448	91.7
Jonesboro city	1,760	1,643	-6.6	1,275	92.9	2.2	0.0	2.2	2.7	19.0	21.4	48.5	54.8	14.6	606	89.4
Jonesville town	178	194	9.0	247	85.4	0.0	0.0	0.0	14.6	26.3	14.2	38.3	61.5	11.8	82	89.0
Kempton town	333	309	-7.2	343	90.4	0.0	0.0	9.0	0.6	19.2	18.4	48.2	66.7	8.2	143	93.0
Kendallville city	9,885	9,894	0.1	9,347	90.7	1.5	2.1	2.2	3.5	22.8	19.1	40.4	62.9	10.9	4,028	85.4
Kennard town	471	446	-5.3	540	82.0	2.4	0.0	8.1	7.4	37.8	6.5	27.6	55.7	11.1	155	94.2
Kent CDP	70	-	-	68	100.0	0.0	0.0	0.0	0.0	47.1	0.0	0.0	100.0	0.0	36	100.0
Kentland town	1,749	1,668	-4.6	1,722	88.7	1.7	0.0	0.5	9.2	22.0	17.1	39.0	57.2	11.7	727	87.5
Kewanna town	624	595	-4.6	519	95.6	0.0	0.0	2.9	1.5	20.2	24.1	46.7	63.5	9.7	237	79.7
Kimmell CDP	422	-	-	574	84.0	0.0	0.0	0.0	16.0	27.4	11.8	37.2	67.5	6.8	215	81.9

1 May be of any race.

Table A. All Places — **Population and Housing**

STATE City, town, township, borough, or CDP (county if applicable)	Population: 2010 census total population	Population: 2019 estimated population	Population: Percent change 2010-2019	Population: ACS total population estimate 2015-2019	Race and Hispanic or Latino origin (percent): White alone, not Hispanic or Latino	Race: Black alone, not Hispanic or Latino	Race: Asian alone, not Hispanic or Latino	Race: All other races or 2 or more races, not Hispanic or Latino	Race: Hispanic or Latino[1]	Age (percent): Under 18 years old	Age: Age 65 years and older	Age: Median age	Educational attainment of persons age 25 and older: Percent High school diploma or less	Educational attainment: Percent Bachelor's degree or more	Occupied housing units: Total	Occupied housing units: Percent with a computer
	1	2	3	4	5	6	7	8	9	10	11	12	13	14	15	16
INDIANA—Con.																
Kingman town	490	461	-5.9	433	97.2	0.5	0.0	1.8	0.5	18.0	15.9	39.6	66.0	6.8	194	93.3
Kingsbury town	252	239	-5.2	186	60.2	0.0	0.0	0.0	39.8	14.0	24.7	43.9	74.3	6.6	84	73.8
Kingsford Heights town	1,432	1,386	-3.2	1,216	89.5	4.8	0.9	1.4	3.5	29.4	13.8	37.3	70.7	3.1	445	83.6
Kirklin town	784	772	-1.5	924	90.9	1.4	1.1	0.5	6.1	27.2	8.2	35.6	64.2	11.0	353	91.5
Knightstown town	2,180	2,137	-2.0	2,223	97.0	0.6	0.0	0.9	1.5	29.9	14.3	30.8	56.3	14.3	860	84.4
Knightsville town	793	767	-3.3	707	94.6	3.1	0.6	1.7	0.0	11.5	29.4	53.5	63.3	11.3	293	83.6
Knox city	3,703	3,545	-4.3	3,557	94.2	0.1	0.1	0.0	5.5	21.0	14.9	39.2	65.1	11.4	1,361	87.2
Kokomo city	58,187	58,020	-0.3	58,145	81.1	10.1	1.5	3.2	4.0	21.8	19.0	40.3	49.9	18.4	25,717	87.3
Koontz Lake CDP	1,557	-	-	1,445	90.0	0.0	3.1	1.1	5.7	15.4	24.3	48.8	58.5	15.9	620	91.8
Kouts town	1,878	1,958	4.3	2,018	92.6	0.2	0.0	1.2	5.9	22.7	18.6	40.5	49.1	23.8	848	89.9
Laconia town	50	51	2.0	47	89.4	0.0	0.0	0.0	10.6	4.3	10.6	52.5	78.0	9.8	17	76.5
La Crosse town	540	515	-4.6	549	93.6	1.1	0.0	2.2	3.1	20.6	16.4	37.8	49.2	8.8	228	83.3
Ladoga town	1,003	997	-0.6	1,271	95.6	1.0	0.0	2.0	1.4	33.0	10.9	33.1	59.3	13.6	485	91.5
Lafayette city	68,864	71,721	4.1	72,581	74.4	8.5	1.4	2.3	13.5	22.2	13.2	33.2	42.9	25.5	31,537	92.0
La Fontaine town	871	828	-4.9	992	93.0	2.2	2.6	0.0	2.1	16.4	21.8	49.7	55.1	14.7	405	86.2
Lagrange town	2,605	2,763	6.1	2,789	79.2	0.6	0.1	2.2	17.9	27.0	17.2	34.1	65.8	9.8	1,143	89.4
Lagro town	415	391	-5.8	450	97.1	0.0	0.0	2.4	0.4	29.3	9.8	36.7	67.4	2.9	164	89.6
Lake Dalecarlia CDP	1,355	-	-	1,811	100.0	0.0	0.0	0.0	0.0	24.0	11.5	40.1	45.5	9.9	597	96.6
Lake Holiday CDP	910	-	-	1,323	97.0	0.0	0.0	1.7	1.3	15.3	15.0	48.1	38.4	26.6	573	94.2
Lake Santee CDP	820	-	-	860	100.0	0.0	0.0	0.0	0.0	20.8	21.6	47.9	39.9	27.9	378	96.6
Lakes of the Four Seasons CDP	7,033	-	-	6,809	88.1	1.5	0.0	1.6	8.8	23.0	16.5	41.7	34.7	26.6	2,319	97.7
Lake Station city	12,671	11,845	-6.5	12,002	61.7	5.4	0.4	3.6	29.0	27.8	12.2	35.9	65.9	10.0	4,208	88.0
Laketon CDP	623	-	-	454	93.4	0.0	0.0	5.7	0.9	31.9	16.3	35.5	62.3	17.1	183	100.0
Lake Village CDP	765	-	-	773	100.0	0.0	0.0	0.0	0.0	29.5	11.8	31.8	61.6	15.7	254	100.0
Lakeville town	789	798	1.1	851	88.5	0.6	6.2	2.0	2.7	26.0	14.3	34.7	55.6	9.8	350	84.9
Landess CDP	188	-	-	119	60.5	0.0	0.0	0.0	39.5	26.1	17.6	41.2	37.5	51.1	41	100.0
Lanesville town	553	565	2.2	615	95.4	3.3	0.0	1.3	0.0	20.7	19.8	39.4	44.4	26.1	248	87.9
La Paz town	560	549	-2.0	562	87.9	0.0	0.0	2.7	9.4	33.8	15.7	33.1	62.6	6.1	211	72.5
Lapel town	2,380	2,398	0.8	2,358	98.1	0.4	0.0	0.7	0.7	25.5	16.1	39.9	45.2	25.1	990	91.5
La Porte city	22,063	21,569	-2.2	21,577	81.0	3.4	0.2	2.7	12.7	23.9	16.9	36.8	55.1	16.6	9,253	85.7
Larwill town	284	284	0.0	305	89.2	0.3	0.0	2.3	8.2	28.2	16.1	39.5	65.2	11.1	107	89.7
Laurel town	556	542	-2.5	794	84.4	3.1	0.0	12.5	0.0	33.8	10.6	25.7	83.3	2.1	277	74.4
Lawrence city	45,915	49,462	7.7	48,699	54.6	26.7	1.2	4.6	13.0	25.7	11.6	35.3	39.3	33.5	18,721	85.1
Lawrenceburg city	5,037	5,001	-0.7	4,981	91.4	3.5	0.0	0.8	4.3	23.2	16.2	36.5	60.1	13.6	2,120	81.8
Leavenworth town	238	233	-2.1	328	91.8	3.0	0.0	4.9	0.3	22.3	30.8	44.2	63.7	11.5	101	78.2
Lebanon city	15,739	16,065	2.1	15,932	93.8	0.9	0.4	1.3	3.6	21.5	15.9	39.0	43.6	27.4	6,966	86.2
Leesburg town	553	552	-0.2	776	90.9	0.0	1.9	2.1	5.2	30.2	5.2	34.0	60.1	10.7	229	97.8
Leo-Cedarville town	3,603	3,858	7.1	3,788	95.7	0.0	0.0	0.0	4.3	29.5	15.2	37.7	37.3	28.5	1,301	96.0
Lewisville town	366	350	-4.4	424	96.7	0.0	0.0	0.0	3.3	27.1	10.1	38.3	48.1	18.8	149	89.9
Liberty town	2,133	1,986	-6.9	1,710	93.4	0.2	1.2	3.0	2.3	18.2	20.3	43.6	56.9	17.8	676	89.9
Ligonier city	4,394	4,379	-0.3	4,654	40.7	0.2	0.2	1.8	57.1	28.4	10.7	34.0	77.6	2.1	1,637	90.8
Linden town	769	767	-0.3	690	91.2	1.6	0.0	1.9	5.4	22.2	14.3	40.3	58.1	10.0	298	90.9
Linton city	5,430	5,204	-4.2	5,244	93.1	0.1	0.0	1.8	5.0	21.9	21.0	41.7	56.4	14.4	2,304	79.8
Little York town	192	190		262	100.0	0.0	0.0	0.0	0.0	22.1	16.0	35.9	45.7	10.9	89	85.4
Livonia town	124	123	-0.8	90	90.0	0.0	0.0	0.0	10.0	18.9	14.4	30.3	62.3	9.4	28	82.1
Lizton town	490	489	-0.2	573	97.0	0.0	0.0	3.0	0.0	29.0	4.9	33.1	35.5	32.8	208	88.0
Logansport city	18,271	17,584	-3.8	17,966	66.1	1.4	1.6	3.1	27.8	25.3	15.9	37.8	61.5	10.0	6,842	84.7
Long Beach town	1,168	1,158	-0.9	1,141	98.2	0.0	0.9	0.3	0.7	12.1	41.6	62.0	13.6	66.1	586	96.9
Loogootee city	2,709	2,700	-0.3	2,575	99.0	0.4	0.0	0.3	0.3	15.8	24.8	48.8	52.5	14.7	1,251	80.9
Losantville town	237	224	-5.5	197	100.0	0.0	0.0	0.0	0.0	13.2	22.3	48.5	62.1	8.5	92	82.6
Lowell town	9,298	9,933	6.8	9,659	90.8	0.2	0.1	1.4	7.6	27.7	15.7	35.2	40.4	20.4	3,582	92.9
Lynn town	1,097	1,027	-6.4	1,149	90.2	1.8	1.0	5.0	2.1	19.7	13.6	40.4	53.5	11.3	449	88.6
Lynnville town	888	960	8.1	937	97.7	0.3	0.0	1.8	0.2	21.3	17.7	43.9	49.4	21.2	397	89.2
Lyons town	742	716	-3.5	676	96.6	0.1	1.9	0.0	1.3	20.9	23.8	48.2	73.9	4.1	247	78.1
McCordsville town	5,114	7,479	46.2	6,857	80.6	10.2	0.0	2.7	6.5	30.4	8.3	33.9	15.5	57.2	2,343	100.0
Mackey town	135	132	-2.2	131	98.5	0.0	0.0	1.5	0.0	17.6	5.3	31.2	35.2	14.1	50	86.0
Macy town	209	199	-4.8	250	86.0	0.0	0.4	3.6	10.0	38.4	8.4	28.6	69.1	7.9	75	94.7
Madison city	11,918	11,861	-0.5	11,813	87.3	4.1	1.4	2.1	5.1	17.8	20.1	43.0	48.0	22.0	5,045	85.9
Manilla CDP	267	-	-	401	100.0	0.0	0.0	0.0	0.0	30.2	11.2	37.1	82.5	0.0	170	75.9
Marengo town	825	807	-2.2	656	95.3	0.3	0.0	0.0	4.4	27.7	15.2	37.3	71.0	7.5	254	72.4
Marion city	29,918	27,930	-6.6	27,956	74.9	14.3	1.3	3.5	6.1	19.5	17.9	35.4	56.7	15.0	10,954	83.2
Markle town	1,094	1,093	-0.1	1,435	96.4	0.5	0.1	2.1	1.0	20.3	20.5	37.2	53.0	16.9	558	88.9
Markleville town	528	513	-2.8	463	96.3	1.1	0.0	1.7	0.9	25.9	10.2	41.5	46.8	10.4	171	90.6
Marshall town	324	317	-2.2	293	90.8	0.0	0.0	9.2	0.0	17.4	16.7	49.3	62.8	6.0	104	88.5
Martinsville city	11,753	11,669	-0.7	11,635	93.7	2.1	0.4	2.4	1.5	22.8	15.9	38.3	63.4	9.9	4,289	84.1
Matthews town	591	559	-5.4	622	99.4	0.0	0.0	0.6	0.0	19.9	19.5	47.0	61.7	9.4	272	81.6
Mauckport town	83	85	2.4	46	100.0	0.0	0.0	0.0	0.0	19.6	21.7	44.5	63.3	0.0	21	71.4
Mecca town	328	326	-0.6	365	98.4	0.0	0.0	1.6	0.0	23.6	28.5	46.9	83.9	2.0	129	74.4
Medaryville town	614	565	-8.0	701	90.6	0.0	0.0	0.3	9.1	34.4	18.4	30.4	71.7	2.7	249	75.9
Medora town	710	696	-2.0	618	98.1	0.0	0.0	1.9	0.0	26.2	20.2	37.0	67.9	7.6	242	80.2
Mellott town	209	193	-7.7	140	88.6	0.0	0.0	0.7	10.7	20.0	21.4	40.4	58.3	10.4	60	78.3
Melody Hill CDP	3,628	-	-	3,761	94.7	3.1	1.2	0.8	0.2	27.7	17.0	39.7	34.6	39.1	1,457	94.5
Memphis CDP	695	-	-	891	100.0	0.0	0.0	0.0	0.0	29.0	8.9	33.3	39.7	30.3	296	97.0
Mentone town	997	968	-2.9	1,239	94.5	0.3	0.0	1.5	3.6	27.4	12.8	33.4	64.4	10.6	465	93.5
Meridian Hills town	1,616	1,715	6.1	1,741	92.2	2.9	2.0	1.7	1.2	29.1	18.5	44.7	6.6	80.8	621	95.7
Merom town	228	218	-4.4	193	86.5	0.0	0.0	2.6	10.9	23.3	11.9	33.6	60.5	7.0	78	78.2
Merrillville town	34,969	34,792	-0.5	34,889	36.6	42.0	1.2	3.9	16.4	24.3	15.9	38.2	43.8	24.5	14,050	89.7
Metamora CDP	188	-	-	151	100.0	0.0	0.0	0.0	0.0	10.6	40.4	54.5	82.2	8.1	78	53.8
Mexico CDP	836	-	-	978	95.5	2.8	0.6	0.5	0.6	12.0	16.1	44.3	58.4	6.0	397	91.4
Michiana Shores town	309	297	-3.9	294	99.3	0.0	0.7	0.0	0.0	12.6	36.4	60.5	23.0	53.6	147	97.3
Michigan City city	31,401	31,015	-1.2	31,118	58.9	29.2	0.8	4.8	6.3	23.3	15.2	36.5	52.2	16.0	12,469	87.7
Michigantown town	472	452	-4.2	592	96.6	0.3	0.0	2.4	0.7	28.2	12.3	34.8	59.3	14.1	217	94.0
Middlebury town	3,407	3,613	6.0	3,575	88.6	1.7	0.0	0.5	9.2	26.1	16.8	38.8	39.5	24.5	1,227	96.0
Middletown town	2,326	2,238	-3.8	2,568	96.0	0.1	2.6	0.0	1.3	24.3	13.9	33.8	55.6	15.9	1,057	89.8
Mier CDP	78	-	-	41	100.0	0.0	0.0	0.0	0.0	0.0	34.1	59.5	34.1	65.9	27	100.0
Milan town	1,892	1,848	-2.3	2,040	94.9	0.0	1.5	3.0	0.7	26.3	19.5	37.8	59.4	11.0	739	84.6
Milford town	1,557	1,565	0.5	1,747	73.4	0.2	0.3	5.1	21.0	30.2	14.1	29.9	73.6	7.2	623	80.1
Millersburg town	903	951	5.3	820	93.2	0.4	0.0	2.2	4.3	26.1	9.3	33.6	62.6	9.9	303	93.4
Millhousen town	127	130	2.4	164	97.0	0.0	0.0	3.0	0.0	24.4	6.7	32.7	50.5	12.6	61	91.8
Milltown town	818	810		843	99.2	0.0	0.2	0.4	0.2	20.5	18.5	45.0	58.7	13.7	355	76.3
Milroy CDP	604	-	-	511	95.1	0.0	0.0	0.0	4.9	9.4	23.3	49.1	83.4	3.9	204	87.3

1 May be of any race.

Table A. All Places — **Population and Housing**

STATE City, town, township, borough, or CDP (county if applicable)	Population: 2010 census total population	Population: 2019 estimated population	Population: Percent change 2010-2019	Population: ACS total population estimate 2015-2019	Race and Hispanic or Latino origin (percent): White alone, not Hispanic or Latino	Black alone, not Hispanic or Latino	Asian alone, not Hispanic or Latino	All other races or 2 or more races, not Hispanic or Latino	Hispanic or Latino[1]	Age (percent): Under 18 years old	Age 65 years and older	Median age	Educational attainment of persons age 25 and older: Percent High school diploma or less	Percent Bachelor's degree or more	Occupied housing units: Total	Percent with a computer
	1	2	3	4	5	6	7	8	9	10	11	12	13	14	15	16
INDIANA—Con.																
Milton town	472	446	-5.5	351	97.2	0.0	0.0	2.0	0.9	21.7	14.2	43.8	59.4	11.7	149	92.6
Mishawaka city	48,236	50,363	4.4	49,245	79.6	7.6	2.2	4.8	5.8	21.9	15.5	35.2	45.6	25.0	21,336	85.2
Mitchell city	4,342	4,249	-2.1	4,261	95.0	1.1	0.7	0.0	3.2	23.4	19.2	40.5	65.3	10.6	1,776	78.9
Modoc town	194	181	-6.7	190	83.7	7.4	0.0	8.9	0.0	33.7	8.9	27.0	61.0	1.0	61	75.4
Monon town	1,791	1,745	-2.6	1,833	47.8	0.5	0.0	0.9	50.7	29.3	13.6	34.4	72.5	7.6	648	82.3
Monroe town	844	883	4.6	945	94.0	0.0	0.4	1.3	4.3	35.0	9.8	30.6	39.0	19.9	309	94.5
Monroe City town	538	528	-1.9	715	99.0	0.0	0.0	0.4	0.6	34.5	10.8	31.8	47.2	12.7	258	91.1
Monroeville town	1,261	1,341	6.3	1,229	98.2	0.0	0.2	0.4	1.2	19.4	20.5	45.2	58.0	9.8	502	88.0
Monrovia town	1,066	1,504	41.1	1,610	94.5	0.6	0.3	1.4	3.2	30.3	6.4	29.5	46.6	15.2	527	98.1
Monterey town	218	201	-7.8	350	77.7	0.0	1.7	0.0	20.6	17.4	10.0	40.1	55.1	5.7	120	93.3
Montezuma town	1,022	986	-3.5	887	84.9	2.3	0.0	3.6	9.2	22.7	26.3	40.1	63.0	7.7	357	88.8
Montgomery town	724	759	4.8	814	99.0	0.0	0.0	0.0	1.0	21.1	8.0	37.9	54.0	14.0	273	93.0
Monticello city	5,384	5,243	-2.6	5,262	84.6	0.3	0.0	2.3	12.8	25.2	21.0	36.4	52.8	10.8	2,264	90.0
Montmorenci CDP	243	-	-	348	87.4	0.0	0.0	9.2	3.4	22.1	29.3	46.5	16.2	36.4	113	100.0
Montpelier city	1,802	1,654	-8.2	1,738	88.2	0.0	5.0	5.1	1.7	25.1	16.2	38.1	62.0	6.9	775	84.4
Mooreland town	369	353	-4.3	270	96.3	3.0	0.0	0.4	0.4	25.6	14.8	43.0	68.1	6.6	112	84.8
Moores Hill town	620	618	-0.3	676	98.1	0.0	0.0	1.9	0.0	28.6	9.9	35.2	64.3	6.2	254	87.4
Mooresville town	9,350	9,788	4.7	9,661	96.0	0.0	0.9	1.6	1.6	21.1	19.0	44.0	53.0	15.5	3,852	89.5
Morgantown town	979	984	0.5	1,042	97.1	0.0	0.0	0.0	2.9	22.6	20.6	39.5	65.8	5.9	395	84.6
Morocco town	1,135	1,094	-3.6	1,146	93.6	0.0	0.0	1.4	5.0	24.0	18.2	38.8	59.1	10.5	446	89.0
Morristown town	1,249	1,340	7.3	1,269	97.2	1.6	0.0	1.3	0.0	20.3	16.1	40.9	61.7	10.0	475	85.7
Mount Auburn town	110	104	-5.5	103	100.0	0.0	0.0	0.0	0.0	17.5	18.4	45.5	57.3	16.0	40	92.5
Mount Ayr town	121	117	-3.3	110	100.0	0.0	0.0	0.0	0.0	23.6	18.2	40.7	77.8	1.2	46	89.1
Mount Carmel town	69	68	-1.4	10	100.0	0.0	0.0	0.0	0.0	0.0	40.0	63.0	80.0	10.0	8	100.0
Mount Etna town	105	105	0.0	145	98.6	0.0	0.0	0.0	1.4	16.6	25.5	48.8	58.8	15.7	62	80.6
Mount Summit town	348	331	-4.9	502	96.0	0.0	0.0	0.8	3.2	28.5	18.1	39.4	45.8	15.8	191	95.3
Mount Vernon city	6,800	6,502	-4.4	6,584	89.4	4.1	0.0	2.6	4.0	22.0	18.7	40.4	50.3	18.1	2,799	90.3
Mulberry town	1,244	1,220	-1.9	1,318	94.9	0.9	1.0	0.0	3.2	25.9	29.1	39.0	56.8	13.2	460	86.5
Muncie city	70,206	67,999	-3.1	68,750	80.9	10.8	1.7	3.3	3.4	16.7	13.9	28.6	46.9	23.6	27,363	88.1
Munster town	23,580	22,476	-4.7	22,689	77.7	3.8	3.8	2.0	12.7	20.9	19.2	45.3	28.4	45.4	8,635	90.5
Napoleon town	234	227	-3.0	234	98.7	0.0	0.0	0.0	1.3	23.5	12.8	39.1	76.3	3.6	121	94.2
Nappanee city	6,664	6,843	2.7	7,033	83.8	0.4	2.7	1.1	12.0	27.9	13.1	34.9	52.3	16.3	2,634	88.6
Nashville town	1,113	1,098	-1.3	1,479	92.2	1.6	0.0	2.6	3.7	9.6	35.0	55.7	38.2	25.1	712	92.7
New Albany city	36,374	36,843	1.3	36,647	81.8	9.0	0.8	3.3	5.2	21.1	16.2	38.4	46.7	22.0	14,877	86.5
New Amsterdam town	27	28	3.7	15	100.0	0.0	0.0	0.0	0.0	0.0	60.0	66.4	73.3	0.0	6	100.0
Newberry town	193	185	-4.1	199	89.9	0.0	0.0	10.1	0.0	17.6	29.6	47.9	79.9	5.8	73	71.2
Newburgh town	3,334	3,252	-2.5	3,245	90.5	4.2	5.3	0.0	0.0	18.2	17.1	45.5	37.8	25.5	1,472	86.6
New Carlisle town	1,789	2,095	17.1	1,916	93.6	0.5	2.3	1.4	2.1	27.3	12.0	34.8	39.0	24.1	690	88.0
New Castle city	18,103	17,113	-5.5	17,287	93.8	2.7	0.0	1.5	2.0	23.8	18.1	40.1	58.9	14.0	7,170	80.0
New Chicago town	2,037	1,940	-4.8	1,633	64.0	3.7	0.7	1.3	30.3	22.5	12.0	37.1	63.8	8.2	651	82.0
New Goshen CDP	390	-	-	434	100.0	0.0	0.0	0.0	0.0	12.0	17.7	49.5	43.1	3.0	192	81.3
New Harmony town	792	753	-4.9	719	97.5	0.7	1.5	0.3	0.0	15.6	37.3	55.8	55.1	21.4	301	80.1
New Haven city	14,843	15,922	7.3	16,279	91.8	2.2	0.2	2.2	3.6	25.7	16.9	37.1	46.9	18.6	6,205	89.7
New Market town	624	623	-0.2	599	100.0	0.0	0.0	0.0	0.0	27.4	14.4	37.3	47.8	14.1	237	94.9
New Middletown town	86	87	1.2	113	93.8	6.2	0.0	0.0	0.0	23.9	10.6	34.1	31.3	14.1	31	90.3
New Palestine town	2,106	2,559	21.5	2,365	100.0	0.0	0.0	0.0	0.0	24.9	15.9	41.6	31.9	37.8	902	93.5
New Paris CDP	1,494	-	-	1,503	84.4	0.0	0.7	0.0	14.9	30.4	12.0	34.5	71.0	7.5	519	94.2
New Pekin town	1,406	1,390	-1.1	1,458	91.2	0.0	0.0	4.0	4.8	27.7	13.3	38.2	57.8	10.7	551	80.6
New Point town	331	341	3.0	372	98.7	0.0	0.0	0.0	1.3	25.0	14.0	40.3	77.5	2.9	145	80.0
Newport town	510	482	-5.5	375	88.8	0.0	0.0	7.5	3.7	18.4	22.1	47.8	51.4	16.0	173	90.2
New Richmond town	335	333	-0.6	333	93.4	2.7	3.0	0.0	0.9	26.1	22.8	43.1	63.8	11.7	125	81.6
New Ross town	343	343	0.0	455	97.6	0.0	0.0	0.7	1.8	26.6	10.1	36.3	54.5	15.1	173	93.6
New Salisbury CDP	613	-	-	590	100.0	0.0	0.0	0.0	0.0	14.7	23.2	46.7	58.1	25.4	189	83.1
Newtown town	261	243	-6.9	230	93.5	0.9	0.0	2.2	3.5	23.5	15.7	44.4	55.8	10.9	91	93.4
New Trenton CDP	252	-	-	283	100.0	0.0	0.0	0.0	0.0	5.3	55.1	68.7	92.5	0.0	150	60.0
New Washington CDP	566	-	-	720	97.9	0.0	0.0	0.0	2.1	28.5	18.3	35.2	35.3	22.0	247	96.4
New Whiteland town	5,466	6,241	14.2	6,051	88.4	3.2	0.0	4.3	4.0	25.4	14.7	34.6	49.1	24.8	2,178	91.0
Noblesville city	52,374	64,668	23.5	63,071	86.8	4.7	2.1	2.8	3.6	27.3	11.3	34.3	25.5	47.4	23,161	95.8
North Crows Nest town	45	47	4.4	34	100.0	0.0	0.0	0.0	0.0	17.6	32.4	60.1	7.1	85.7	18	100.0
North Judson town	1,773	1,712	-3.4	2,074	96.7	0.5	0.0	0.7	2.1	29.0	14.8	34.7	54.7	11.4	718	85.4
North Liberty town	1,899	1,915	0.8	1,878	96.2	0.4	0.4	0.0	3.0	31.7	13.5	36.7	42.8	21.8	754	84.5
North Manchester town	6,104	5,747	-5.8	5,710	88.9	1.7	0.0	1.4	8.0	17.7	22.7	35.2	47.6	26.0	2,166	83.1
North Salem town	506	538	6.3	423	97.9	0.0	0.0	0.0	2.1	17.0	21.0	44.5	61.2	12.2	184	81.5
North Terre Haute CDP	4,305	-	-	4,339	95.1	1.7	0.0	2.0	1.1	22.3	17.4	36.9	45.8	20.7	1,779	91.6
North Vernon city	6,970	6,702	-3.8	6,735	89.9	4.0	0.3	1.9	3.9	22.4	16.1	38.4	57.7	12.1	2,677	85.2
North Webster town	1,151	1,168	1.5	1,151	97.7	0.2	0.0	1.4	0.7	18.8	22.6	45.4	53.9	14.4	530	89.8
Norway CDP	386	-	-	355	92.7	0.0	0.0	0.0	7.3	6.8	32.7	58.1	59.3	14.7	186	88.7
Notre Dame CDP	5,973	-	-	6,646	74.3	2.9	9.0	3.9	9.9	0.3	2.0	20.5	9.0	85.1	124	96.0
Oakland City city	2,417	2,404	-0.5	2,576	94.5	1.5	1.0	0.3	2.6	18.5	21.4	44.9	60.8	15.7	1,059	81.8
Oaktown town	608	595	-2.1	614	95.6	0.0	0.3	2.1	2.0	24.6	17.8	41.7	59.6	5.2	225	80.4
Odon town	1,328	1,385	4.3	1,379	93.3	0.4	3.6	2.5	0.2	19.1	29.0	48.2	56.3	14.5	610	76.9
Ogden Dunes town	1,110	1,088	-2.0	1,163	94.2	0.0	1.5	2.5	1.7	12.1	31.3	57.0	10.6	73.1	506	95.1
Oldenburg town	678	663	-2.2	458	97.6	0.0	0.0	0.0	2.4	15.7	42.8	61.2	31.6	47.3	187	86.6
Onward town	100	98	-2.0	100	98.0	0.0	0.0	2.0	0.0	17.0	16.0	46.7	54.9	14.1	47	78.7
Oolitic town	1,167	1,134	-2.8	1,088	94.0	0.0	0.8	2.2	2.9	24.5	19.2	41.8	60.1	10.2	469	83.2
Orestes town	400	404	1.0	566	93.3	0.0	0.0	0.0	6.7	29.0	11.0	37.0	56.9	10.8	201	88.6
Orland town	425	424	-0.2	425	82.6	0.0	0.0	4.5	12.9	21.2	16.0	40.3	70.4	2.8	168	85.1
Orleans town	2,143	2,125	-0.8	2,028	97.5	0.0	0.0	0.0	2.5	22.6	15.8	41.3	70.2	7.6	842	80.5
Osceola town	2,463	2,484	0.9	2,707	83.6	1.7	5.7	3.3	5.8	27.7	16.0	37.0	47.6	22.3	934	90.5
Osgood town	1,624	1,585	-2.4	1,912	94.7	0.3	1.2	1.0	2.8	25.1	14.3	36.4	65.3	10.4	681	86.6
Ossian town	3,298	3,382	2.5	3,350	95.0	0.0	0.4	0.3	4.3	23.9	16.4	34.6	40.6	20.6	1,309	87.2
Otterbein town	1,264	1,265	0.1	953	89.2	0.0	0.0	2.3	8.5	22.6	15.2	38.5	42.4	17.5	430	94.0
Otwell CDP	434	-	-	390	94.1	0.0	0.0	0.0	5.9	7.4	16.9	51.2	50.3	24.6	210	73.3
Owensburg CDP	406	-	-	483	96.5	0.0	0.0	3.5	0.0	21.7	19.0	40.7	44.5	6.1	184	82.1
Owensville town	1,337	1,347	0.7	1,414	97.8	0.4	0.7	0.7	0.4	18.5	21.6	41.2	64.1	11.9	551	90.4
Oxford town	1,158	1,149	-0.8	1,189	95.6	0.0	0.0	0.3	4.0	24.3	21.0	42.2	60.6	8.0	467	87.4
Painted Hills CDP	677	-	-	532	100.0	0.0	0.0	0.0	0.0	18.8	23.1	45.5	40.3	17.6	227	100.0
Palmyra town	936	956	2.1	1,367	96.4	0.4	0.0	2.1	1.0	24.5	25.1	44.9	54.6	12.6	665	70.8
Paoli town	3,691	3,627	-1.7	3,665	97.0	0.6	1.9	0.4	0.1	21.1	17.9	38.8	67.6	8.3	1,434	80.1
Paragon town	664	678	2.1	567	93.5	0.0	0.0	6.5	0.0	21.0	10.1	35.8	74.8	5.3	197	86.8
Parker City town	1,421	1,344	-5.4	1,315	94.3	0.0	1.0	4.1	0.6	23.2	23.2	37.4	59.0	14.0	530	87.0
Parkers Settlement CDP	711	-	-	537	100.0	0.0	0.0	0.0	0.0	17.1	16.4	49.9	51.7	14.0	202	91.1

1 May be of any race.

Table A. All Places — **Population and Housing**

STATE City, town, township, borough, or CDP (county if applicable)	Population				Race and Hispanic or Latino origin (percent)					Age (percent)			Educational attainment of persons age 25 and older		Occupied housing units	
	2010 census total population	2019 estimated population	Percent change 2010-2019	ACS total population estimate 2015-2019	White alone, not Hispanic or Latino	Black alone, not Hispanic or Latino	Asian alone, not Hispanic or Latino	All other races or 2 or more races, not Hispanic or Latino	Hispanic or Latino[1]	Under 18 years old	Age 65 years and older	Median age	Percent High school diploma or less	Percent Bachelor's degree or more	Total	Percent with a computer
	1	2	3	4	5	6	7	8	9	10	11	12	13	14	15	16
INDIANA—Con.																
Patoka town	752	772	2.7	1,210	92.6	0.7	0.0	3.6	3.1	26.6	12.6	32.8	58.6	12.8	490	87.6
Patriot town	205	209	2.0	527	100.0	0.0	0.0	0.0	0.0	45.0	9.7	26.6	85.9	3.0	162	75.9
Pendleton town	4,305	4,371	1.5	4,246	94.8	1.1	0.0	2.0	2.1	25.3	17.7	40.6	34.0	30.6	1,703	89.1
Pennville town	697	675	-3.2	724	96.3	0.3	0.4	1.7	1.4	30.1	12.2	34.2	65.1	9.9	303	88.4
Perrysville town	456	433	-5.0	497	97.2	0.0	0.0	1.6	1.2	25.8	15.5	40.3	54.1	9.5	195	85.1
Peru city	11,588	11,023	-4.9	11,584	84.6	8.5	0.5	2.5	3.9	22.8	17.3	38.7	59.6	11.0	4,851	84.0
Petersburg city	2,380	2,317	-2.6	2,408	95.3	2.2	0.0	2.1	0.4	20.6	21.8	44.1	55.6	14.7	1,002	77.3
Pierceton town	1,019	1,021	0.2	880	89.5	0.0	4.5	0.0	5.9	23.1	18.6	40.6	60.5	17.0	392	85.2
Pine Village town	210	202	-3.8	218	97.2	0.0	0.0	0.9	1.8	21.1	17.0	39.8	61.5	13.5	104	92.3
Pittsboro town	2,933	3,614	23.2	3,396	90.0	3.7	0.0	3.7	2.6	26.1	13.8	36.4	25.5	36.7	1,202	99.2
Plainfield town	27,700	35,287	27.4	32,879	79.5	9.4	4.3	2.7	4.1	23.9	14.0	38.0	38.7	30.8	12,331	93.7
Plainville town	480	498	3.8	341	98.5	1.5	0.0	0.0	0.0	17.6	26.4	51.1	59.6	12.1	169	69.8
Plymouth city	10,138	9,982	-1.5	10,054	70.9	1.7	0.6	2.3	24.5	27.2	15.0	35.7	59.6	17.2	3,749	75.0
Point Isabel CDP	91	-	-	179	100.0	0.0	0.0	0.0	0.0	38.0	18.4	41.4	53.2	20.7	64	100.0
Poneto town	189	193	2.1	175	93.7	0.0	0.6	2.3	3.4	18.9	7.4	37.9	66.2	7.7	67	85.1
Portage city	36,828	36,988	0.4	36,648	68.8	8.0	1.4	2.6	19.2	22.0	15.4	38.4	52.8	16.3	14,764	90.0
Porter town	4,845	4,834	-0.2	4,817	80.3	0.0	1.5	0.7	17.5	23.6	11.2	36.6	37.3	35.0	1,648	96.8
Portland city	6,248	6,002	-3.9	5,886	89.2	0.9	2.2	2.0	5.7	23.9	18.6	38.3	62.6	7.9	2,574	78.7
Poseyville town	1,050	1,036	-1.3	905	98.1	0.0	0.0	1.9	0.0	14.8	31.9	54.3	56.1	13.4	414	87.2
Pottawattamie Park town	235	224	-4.7	266	90.6	3.8	0.8	0.0	4.9	17.3	26.7	49.4	18.4	52.6	107	86.0
Prince's Lakes town	1,310	1,345	2.7	1,681	93.9	0.0	1.5	1.8	2.7	17.1	15.2	44.5	45.4	18.8	685	93.6
Princeton city	8,698	8,733	0.4	8,684	88.2	6.8	0.1	3.2	1.7	23.8	17.8	37.5	54.1	12.5	3,552	85.2
Raglesville CDP	141	-	-	-	-	-	-	-	-	-	-	-	-	-	-	-
Ragsdale CDP	129	-	-	265	100.0	0.0	0.0	0.0	0.0	18.9	22.6	58.8	28.6	11.3	103	89.3
Redkey town	1,335	1,282	-4.0	1,490	94.8	0.0	1.5	0.0	3.7	21.5	17.1	41.2	60.2	8.8	659	83.5
Remington town	1,204	1,155	-4.1	1,300	95.5	0.4	0.5	1.8	1.8	19.5	18.6	45.8	60.0	14.9	581	81.2
Rensselaer city	5,997	5,842	-2.6	6,324	91.2	1.5	0.9	1.5	4.9	28.7	15.1	37.6	56.4	15.7	2,409	86.6
Reynolds town	537	528	-1.7	505	97.4	0.0	0.0	1.2	1.4	17.8	23.2	43.4	54.1	17.9	235	86.0
Richland town	421	391	-7.1	398	99.0	0.8	0.0	0.0	0.3	24.6	13.3	39.3	49.8	14.4	165	83.0
Richmond city	36,779	35,342	-3.9	35,539	80.8	8.3	1.7	4.2	4.9	21.3	18.5	38.9	50.9	19.0	14,523	85.1
Ridgeville town	794	747	-5.9	544	96.5	0.0	0.0	3.1	0.4	23.0	22.1	43.4	67.5	9.7	238	80.3
Riley town	221	216	-2.3	321	98.8	0.0	0.0	1.2	0.0	32.7	22.7	33.3	58.9	10.9	125	88.0
Rising Sun city	2,296	2,139	-6.8	2,099	92.9	1.1	0.1	2.4	3.5	17.0	23.7	50.7	60.1	14.2	1,029	75.3
River Forest town	22	22	0.0	12	100.0	0.0	0.0	0.0	0.0	0.0	16.7	51.5	0.0	58.3	7	100.0
Roachdale town	921	877	-4.8	781	96.5	0.0	0.0	3.1	0.4	21.4	15.6	46.4	57.7	13.1	355	84.5
Roann town	479	451	-5.8	352	96.0	0.0	1.7	1.7	0.6	23.3	21.3	38.7	58.9	5.7	154	80.5
Roanoke town	1,721	1,710	-0.6	1,688	95.9	0.0	0.0	1.4	2.8	24.0	12.9	34.4	33.4	31.5	686	93.9
Rochester city	6,291	5,994	-4.7	6,045	97.7	0.3	0.4	0.6	1.0	22.6	21.9	43.2	50.8	16.6	2,484	87.0
Rockport city	2,279	2,144	-5.9	2,418	88.0	3.8	0.2	3.5	4.5	28.9	13.8	36.1	62.5	11.1	926	84.3
Rockville town	2,609	2,478	-5.0	2,533	97.1	0.0	0.0	2.9	0.0	19.2	19.9	43.0	52.3	11.0	1,103	79.8
Rocky Ripple town	616	652	5.8	647	84.7	5.4	0.0	7.4	2.5	17.5	19.0	37.8	22.6	49.6	290	96.9
Rolling Prairie CDP	582	-	-	463	98.9	1.1	0.0	0.0	0.0	11.9	9.7	54.5	32.9	33.5	175	88.6
Rome City town	1,383	1,397	1.0	1,343	91.7	0.2	0.0	1.4	6.6	17.9	17.2	45.6	51.0	18.3	586	91.3
Rosedale town	717	706	-1.5	845	86.6	0.0	0.0	13.4	0.0	21.8	20.7	46.1	43.0	11.6	342	81.9
Roseland town	634	636	0.3	465	84.5	3.4	3.0	2.6	6.5	16.1	17.4	36.1	49.8	30.2	217	88.0
Roselawn CDP	4,131	-	-	3,954	93.4	0.0	0.0	0.0	6.6	22.7	18.4	43.3	58.1	10.6	1,431	91.8
Rossville town	1,563	1,545	-1.2	1,544	96.4	0.2	0.8	0.7	1.9	29.3	15.7	36.8	46.7	16.2	582	88.3
Royal Center town	865	834	-3.6	833	97.1	0.4	0.0	0.2	2.3	26.9	13.6	34.3	56.7	15.9	329	82.4
Rushville city	6,337	6,008	-5.2	6,050	91.5	4.5	0.0	1.2	2.8	21.9	18.4	41.2	63.1	13.4	2,430	86.4
Russellville town	354	356	0.6	365	92.3	0.0	0.0	0.0	7.7	32.6	11.0	30.3	69.5	9.0	120	86.7
Russiaville town	1,111	1,119	0.7	1,087	94.1	0.3	0.7	1.7	3.1	25.5	19.7	41.1	42.4	17.5	439	92.0
St. Bernice CDP	646	-	-	463	100.0	0.0	0.0	0.0	0.0	21.8	27.4	46.6	74.6	7.4	197	79.7
St. Joe town	462	473	2.4	481	92.7	0.0	0.2	4.2	2.9	29.9	5.4	24.5	70.7	4.3	151	88.1
St. John town	14,831	18,796	26.7	17,426	84.1	2.2	1.8	2.1	9.7	24.5	16.6	43.9	30.1	36.3	6,111	96.3
St. Leon town	673	663	-1.5	872	98.9	0.0	0.0	0.0	1.1	22.8	16.1	36.7	56.7	19.1	307	94.5
St. Mary of the Woods CDP	797	-	-	868	97.0	0.5	1.0	1.0	0.5	7.3	50.7	65.5	46.7	31.3	298	54.0
St. Meinrad CDP	706	-	-	658	96.5	0.0	3.5	0.0	0.0	15.2	28.1	53.4	62.3	18.3	256	77.0
St. Paul town	1,035	1,064	2.8	1,013	94.9	4.8	0.0	0.0	0.3	27.9	14.1	35.8	68.9	8.6	394	83.8
Salamonia town	165	160	-3.0	147	98.0	0.0	0.0	2.0	0.0	22.4	10.9	42.3	76.8	0.0	66	95.5
Salem city	6,323	6,201	-1.9	6,172	96.4	0.4	0.1	2.5	0.6	20.8	20.6	38.3	62.8	13.4	2,761	79.1
Salt Creek Commons CDP	2,117	-	-	2,126	85.7	0.0	1.8	1.7	10.7	34.7	6.0	31.6	55.8	14.1	601	100.0
Saltillo town	90	91	1.1	106	100.0	0.0	0.0	0.0	0.0	21.7	14.2	48.5	78.5	10.1	55	52.7
Sandborn town	414	404	-2.4	317	93.4	0.0	0.9	0.0	5.7	17.4	25.6	50.9	38.2	18.7	148	79.1
San Pierre CDP	144	-	-	86	96.5	0.0	0.0	0.0	3.5	14.0	12.8	28.7	51.8	25.0	38	100.0
Santa Claus town	2,480	2,411	-2.8	2,670	97.2	0.9	0.0	0.6	1.3	25.6	17.3	44.0	37.1	33.5	985	93.1
Saratoga town	252	236	-6.3	288	97.6	0.0	0.0	1.7	0.7	26.7	13.9	34.5	56.2	7.6	113	84.1
Schererville town	29,217	28,527	-2.4	28,590	75.8	4.8	3.4	3.0	13.0	20.2	17.3	44.1	35.2	33.5	11,423	91.6
Schneider town	277	260	-6.1	234	96.6	0.0	0.0	3.0	0.4	26.1	10.3	30.3	58.2	10.4	71	97.2
Scipio CDP	153	-	-	158	100.0	0.0	0.0	0.0	0.0	23.4	10.1	49.9	41.3	38.0	78	89.7
Scotland CDP	134	-	-	192	86.5	0.0	5.7	7.8	0.0	41.7	8.3	29.3	73.2	8.9	60	100.0
Scottsburg city	6,817	6,732	-1.2	6,702	91.7	0.6	0.4	2.0	5.3	21.5	16.3	34.7	54.3	11.4	2,713	81.9
Seelyville town	1,027	1,010	-1.7	864	86.2	0.0	0.0	0.0	13.8	31.7	10.3	32.0	46.4	11.4	313	86.3
Sellersburg town	8,331	8,908	6.9	9,066	84.7	2.9	0.8	5.5	6.1	28.3	13.6	36.3	39.8	20.5	3,157	88.7
Selma town	853	811	-4.9	890	88.1	0.2	0.0	2.8	8.9	25.7	13.6	37.4	58.3	12.1	328	88.4
Seymour city	18,047	19,959	10.6	19,623	78.6	2.0	4.3	2.0	13.0	26.3	14.2	36.4	51.6	20.0	7,866	86.1
Shadeland town	1,608	1,916	19.2	1,913	96.2	0.3	0.7	1.4	1.5	21.2	20.7	43.2	44.7	27.0	736	93.9
Shamrock Lakes town	233	216	-7.3	252	89.7	0.0	0.0	10.3	0.0	16.3	27.4	42.5	36.7	32.2	100	95.0
Sharpsville town	599	567	-5.3	785	90.1	0.0	0.6	2.3	7.0	27.3	12.5	41.4	64.9	14.3	306	91.8
Shelburn town	1,257	1,217	-3.2	1,406	95.3	0.5	0.0	0.0	4.2	25.5	13.2	34.4	58.8	7.9	542	79.0
Shelby CDP	539	-	-	397	91.7	0.0	0.0	0.0	8.3	21.2	36.8	59.2	86.2	10.2	179	74.9
Shelbyville city	19,059	19,407	1.8	18,951	86.6	2.2	1.3	1.2	8.6	25.1	15.3	36.2	59.9	16.1	7,752	84.8
Shepardsville CDP	237	-	-	130	100.0	0.0	0.0	0.0	0.0	22.3	15.4	28.6	25.3	13.9	72	72.2
Sheridan town	2,683	3,048	13.6	2,959	96.3	0.0	0.2	2.8	0.6	26.7	11.4	34.8	54.8	16.2	1,145	87.5
Shipshewana town	678	721	6.3	946	96.9	0.0	0.0	1.0	2.1	29.8	20.3	36.8	65.2	11.8	353	74.2
Shirley town	855	888	3.9	952	89.3	0.0	0.0	9.8	0.9	30.4	8.6	33.9	65.0	5.7	343	93.0
Shoals town	805	789	-2.0	731	97.0	3.0	0.0	0.0	0.0	11.4	37.6	56.3	76.5	6.0	384	68.0
Shorewood Forest CDP	2,708	-	-	2,825	88.6	1.2	4.8	0.0	5.5	21.8	21.1	49.0	22.8	50.1	1,040	97.8
Sidney town	83	81	-2.4	51	96.1	0.0	0.0	0.0	3.9	13.7	45.1	56.5	73.2	4.9	30	60.0
Silver Lake town	918	923	0.5	948	94.1	0.0	0.4	2.4	3.1	23.1	18.7	41.2	63.5	7.0	386	88.1
Simonton Lake CDP	4,678	-	-	5,362	77.9	7.6	4.6	1.5	8.4	28.3	18.0	38.8	45.5	23.7	1,930	90.4

1 May be of any race.

Table A. All Places — **Population and Housing**

STATE City, town, township, borough, or CDP (county if applicable)	Population: 2010 census total population	Population: 2019 estimated population	Population: Percent change 2010-2019	Population: ACS total population estimate 2015-2019	Race and Hispanic or Latino origin (percent): White alone, not Hispanic or Latino	Black alone, not Hispanic or Latino	Asian alone, not Hispanic or Latino	All other races or 2 or more races, not Hispanic or Latino	Hispanic or Latino[1]	Age (percent): Under 18 years old	Age 65 years and older	Median age	Educational attainment of persons age 25 and older: Percent High school diploma or less	Percent Bachelor's degree or more	Occupied housing units: Total	Percent with a computer
	1	2	3	4	5	6	7	8	9	10	11	12	13	14	15	16
INDIANA—Con.																
Sims CDP	156	-	-	106	100.0	0.0	0.0	0.0	0.0	24.5	0.0	50.0	90.4	0.0	39	100.0
Smithville-Sanders CDP	3,184	-	-	3,424	96.0	1.3	0.8	0.8	1.1	24.1	17.7	46.8	25.8	49.2	1,493	92.3
Somerset CDP	401	-	-	420	100.0	0.0	0.0	0.0	0.0	18.6	27.6	55.0	63.7	22.5	202	92.6
Somerville town	292	289	-	343	100.0	0.0	0.0	0.0	0.0	30.0	10.8	46.3	72.3	8.6	125	92.8
South Bend city	101,249	102,026	0.8	102,037	52.4	26.2	1.4	4.2	15.7	27.2	12.8	33.3	46.6	25.7	38,568	83.1
South Haven CDP	5,282	-	-	5,092	80.0	8.7	0.2	1.2	10.0	24.2	16.4	38.2	59.6	9.4	1,890	89.1
Southport city	1,712	1,770	3.4	1,909	69.9	0.6	27.1	1.5	0.9	30.7	14.2	33.4	55.7	18.0	576	91.5
South Whitley town	1,782	1,741	-2.3	1,563	90.3	0.6	0.2	0.6	8.3	23.0	13.9	37.6	60.6	9.3	676	91.7
Speedway town	11,812	12,193	3.2	12,266	55.9	28.0	2.5	4.5	9.0	25.5	12.9	33.8	34.8	31.8	5,249	93.4
Spencer town	2,365	2,256	-4.6	2,335	86.5	1.8	1.9	4.3	5.5	22.9	21.5	40.6	49.5	11.9	1,046	84.7
Spiceland town	984	940	-4.5	825	95.9	1.0	0.7	2.4	0.0	26.1	16.6	40.1	61.6	11.9	308	90.3
Spring Grove town	339	322	-5.0	456	87.5	3.9	1.8	3.3	3.5	14.5	30.7	56.3	50.4	26.1	145	95.2
Spring Hill town	100	106	6.0	69	100.0	0.0	0.0	0.0	0.0	2.9	75.4	71.2	4.5	78.8	41	97.6
Spring Lake town	218	228	4.6	214	98.1	0.0	0.0	1.9	0.0	11.2	22.4	52.3	55.4	14.9	92	95.7
Springport town	146	140	-4.1	156	98.7	1.3	0.0	0.0	0.0	12.2	37.8	54.5	46.3	11.6	73	86.3
Spurgeon town	207	204	-1.4	139	100.0	0.0	0.0	0.0	0.0	8.6	22.3	46.5	58.9	2.8	76	90.8
Star City CDP	344	-	-	171	100.0	0.0	0.0	0.0	0.0	8.8	38.6	36.6	55.8	24.4	87	100.0
State Line City town	143	139	-2.8	173	95.4	0.0	0.0	0.0	4.6	19.1	17.9	49.8	54.4	8.0	72	87.5
Staunton town	521	510	-2.1	384	99.5	0.0	0.0	0.0	0.5	17.4	14.1	40.9	53.9	8.5	153	94.1
Stilesville town	316	337	6.6	235	98.7	0.0	0.0	1.3	0.0	14.9	27.7	54.9	54.1	10.4	116	84.5
Stinesville town	203	218	7.4	213	98.1	0.0	0.0	0.0	1.9	20.2	15.0	45.9	50.0	18.5	88	83.0
Stockwell CDP	545	-	-	435	100.0	0.0	0.0	0.0	0.0	29.2	6.4	35.1	44.5	15.1	201	100.0
Straughn town	222	213	-4.1	260	98.8	0.0	0.0	0.4	0.8	29.2	11.5	32.0	63.9	4.8	86	90.7
Sullivan city	4,236	4,093	-3.4	4,082	97.5	0.0	1.7	0.7	0.0	21.1	18.7	41.7	58.6	8.5	1,823	82.5
Sulphur Springs town	385	371	-3.6	335	99.7	0.0	0.0	0.0	0.3	22.7	13.1	33.5	49.0	17.6	125	88.0
Summitville town	1,006	983	-2.3	947	95.8	1.4	0.0	1.7	1.2	24.0	16.3	42.7	58.2	8.9	363	82.9
Sunman town	1,049	1,033	-1.5	1,184	89.4	0.0	0.0	0.0	10.6	25.9	20.9	36.0	64.7	11.1	439	88.2
Swayzee town	981	911	-7.1	946	92.3	2.0	0.6	3.1	2.0	25.8	20.9	38.3	47.6	20.1	392	89.3
Sweetser town	1,178	1,104	-6.3	1,292	90.6	0.0	0.0	0.0	9.4	23.1	24.2	46.0	57.4	17.0	530	93.2
Switz City town	300	289	-3.7	343	92.1	0.6	0.0	6.1	1.2	27.1	16.3	33.3	56.7	6.3	125	76.0
Syracuse town	2,859	2,882	0.8	2,881	86.8	0.2	0.0	5.9	7.0	22.5	17.2	39.5	52.3	20.9	1,219	88.3
Taylorsville CDP	919	-	-	979	85.9	0.0	0.0	0.0	14.1	35.3	8.2	22.4	60.8	11.1	271	79.0
Tecumseh CDP	658	-	-	799	100.0	0.0	0.0	0.0	0.0	27.0	20.8	42.0	20.2	31.6	307	83.1
Tell City city	7,350	7,211	-1.9	7,256	93.9	2.0	1.2	1.1	1.9	22.5	20.9	40.6	49.4	17.0	3,301	83.3
Tennyson town	276	300	8.7	248	100.0	0.0	0.0	0.0	0.0	19.4	12.1	39.8	68.9	8.7	109	81.7
Terre Haute city	60,785	60,622	-0.3	60,673	80.7	10.6	1.6	4.4	2.8	19.2	15.1	32.5	47.2	22.6	23,249	87.5
Thorntown town	1,520	1,573	3.5	1,231	96.7	0.0	1.7	0.0	1.6	19.2	16.2	40.5	53.1	19.8	533	89.3
Tipton city	5,217	4,970	-4.7	4,969	92.7	0.2	0.0	4.2	2.9	23.2	17.2	43.4	63.4	16.5	2,138	88.8
Toad Hop CDP	108	-	-	216	100.0	0.0	0.0	0.0	0.0	49.1	0.0	30.1	76.4	0.0	63	58.7
Topeka town	1,155	1,225	6.1	933	88.7	0.0	0.0	10.2	1.1	33.0	13.8	30.4	71.1	8.6	332	85.2
Town of Pines town	708	691	-2.4	717	90.4	0.6	0.0	5.9	3.2	16.9	20.9	44.6	58.8	14.2	311	91.3
Trafalgar town	1,098	1,345	22.5	1,148	97.6	0.7	0.0	1.0	0.5	30.5	7.5	32.2	45.5	17.5	432	94.4
Trail Creek town	2,070	1,992	-3.8	1,917	83.9	6.3	1.6	6.7	1.6	22.6	23.2	44.1	40.2	19.5	822	89.3
Tri-Lakes CDP	1,421	-	-	1,750	97.8	0.0	0.0	2.2	0.0	23.7	17.4	46.8	40.4	29.2	665	92.5
Troy town	417	398	-4.6	384	98.4	0.0	0.0	0.5	1.0	13.0	33.6	53.3	64.7	13.3	195	71.3
Ulen town	117	126	7.7	192	97.9	1.0	0.0	0.0	1.0	23.4	25.0	50.1	17.3	51.1	71	94.4
Union City city	3,646	3,440	-5.7	3,291	76.5	0.0	0.0	3.9	19.7	25.2	16.7	39.8	63.6	3.9	1,482	84.2
Uniondale town	308	315	2.3	289	92.4	0.0	0.7	6.9	0.0	26.0	7.3	36.8	55.9	14.7	120	85.0
Universal town	362	344	-5.0	325	97.5	0.0	0.0	0.0	2.5	17.5	18.5	40.4	57.0	10.6	154	82.5
Upland town	3,845	3,726	-3.1	3,733	88.4	2.4	2.8	5.4	1.0	16.5	13.3	22.2	38.4	39.0	958	90.3
Utica town	773	934	20.8	639	71.0	17.7	0.2	5.0	6.1	18.3	16.9	40.9	40.1	19.8	249	85.9
Vallonia CDP	336	-	-	388	100.0	0.0	0.0	0.0	0.0	2.6	18.3	55.8	60.2	20.5	171	77.2
Valparaiso city	31,743	33,897	6.8	33,355	85.8	3.2	2.5	1.5	7.0	19.0	17.0	36.0	31.7	40.7	13,384	91.4
Van Bibber Lake CDP	485	-	-	679	100.0	0.0	0.0	0.0	0.0	16.2	31.2	57.8	81.9	6.2	345	87.2
Van Buren town	866	812	-6.2	889	98.7	0.0	0.0	1.1	0.2	21.3	18.0	42.0	56.4	12.6	373	79.9
Veedersburg town	2,203	2,047	-7.1	2,091	94.2	0.5	0.0	3.3	2.0	19.0	21.6	46.4	65.1	8.4	948	85.0
Vera Cruz town	86	86	0.0	97	100.0	0.0	0.0	0.0	0.0	33.0	6.2	28.6	75.9	6.9	36	86.1
Vernon town	328	317	-3.4	326	95.4	0.0	0.0	0.0	4.6	25.2	21.5	45.9	36.0	19.7	145	81.4
Versailles town	2,134	2,083	-2.4	2,021	95.5	0.9	0.0	3.6	0.0	21.9	16.1	39.7	57.7	16.2	793	85.1
Vevay town	1,657	1,648	-0.5	1,717	95.1	0.0	2.4	1.7	0.8	20.6	18.7	36.9	54.7	12.3	798	77.4
Vincennes city	18,422	16,862	-8.5	17,304	88.3	5.1	1.1	2.4	3.1	18.5	16.8	35.7	50.6	16.2	7,261	85.1
Wabash city	10,665	9,941	-6.8	10,089	95.5	0.5	0.4	1.6	2.0	19.7	20.0	41.3	58.9	13.7	4,574	87.7
Wakarusa town	1,755	1,850	5.4	1,957	90.8	1.3	3.7	1.2	3.1	26.4	18.7	34.9	51.1	27.1	615	88.0
Waldron CDP	804	-	-	647	99.2	0.8	0.0	0.0	0.0	12.7	22.4	47.8	63.4	8.0	274	82.1
Walkerton town	2,145	2,256	5.2	2,174	96.3	0.0	0.2	1.7	1.8	27.6	13.5	37.9	49.1	14.5	866	87.3
Wallace town	89	82	-7.9	74	100.0	0.0	0.0	0.0	0.0	18.9	18.9	36.5	64.6	6.3	38	84.2
Walton town	1,051	1,015	-3.4	1,107	83.4	0.0	2.3	0.8	13.5	23.7	10.3	35.4	52.6	12.8	414	88.2
Wanatah town	1,047	1,004	-4.1	1,235	93.1	0.0	0.0	0.3	6.6	19.9	17.2	41.8	49.9	15.7	478	92.5
Warren town	1,228	1,211	-1.4	1,240	99.5	0.0	0.0	0.0	0.5	17.2	24.1	42.0	59.2	13.4	554	81.0
Warren Park town	1,478	1,572	6.4	1,490	58.3	17.2	0.8	0.8	22.9	15.1	37.1	59.4	53.8	16.2	814	58.6
Warsaw city	13,695	15,150	10.6	15,458	76.8	2.3	4.7	3.7	12.4	26.4	13.3	31.3	42.5	31.3	6,148	90.1
Washington city	11,773	12,528	6.4	12,412	80.6	4.6	0.0	2.0	12.9	25.4	17.2	36.2	58.4	15.4	4,717	80.1
Waterloo town	2,220	2,259	1.8	2,221	92.4	0.0	0.7	1.4	5.5	28.8	11.0	32.1	57.9	12.4	837	87.1
Waveland town	420	418	-0.5	522	83.9	0.0	0.4	9.2	6.5	33.0	12.6	34.2	57.3	16.7	177	81.4
Waynetown town	956	962	0.6	1,134	94.6	0.0	0.0	2.9	2.5	26.9	15.9	38.7	62.0	9.3	431	90.7
West Baden Springs town	574	561	-2.3	511	89.2	4.7	2.3	1.4	2.3	18.4	25.8	43.2	60.3	12.3	260	75.4
West College Corner town	672	626	-6.8	570	91.8	0.0	1.1	0.0	7.2	28.9	14.0	32.5	53.6	23.2	239	83.7
Westfield city	30,133	43,649	44.9	39,610	85.2	3.2	3.7	1.6	6.4	29.9	10.9	35.2	16.5	58.6	14,217	98.1
West Harrison town	284	280	-1.4	274	100.0	0.0	0.0	0.0	0.0	27.4	12.0	28.5	75.8	1.9	118	85.6
West Lafayette city	41,997	50,996	21.4	48,551	65.3	3.5	23.3	3.6	4.3	10.8	6.9	21.7	13.8	71.5	13,956	96.2
West Lebanon town	714	692	-3.1	664	97.6	1.7	0.0	0.0	0.8	21.5	17.9	44.5	53.9	10.9	290	90.0
Westphalia CDP	202	-	-	71	100.0	0.0	0.0	0.0	0.0	26.8	25.4	43.8	32.6	25.6	35	80.0
West Point CDP	594	-	-	465	52.5	0.0	0.0	0.0	47.5	44.7	9.9	32.1	32.7	7.0	126	100.0
Westport town	1,384	1,424	2.9	1,230	95.4	0.0	0.9	1.3	2.4	21.8	20.7	40.7	58.3	12.4	518	85.3
West Terre Haute town	2,236	2,208	-1.3	2,185	91.0	3.1	0.0	2.7	3.2	24.1	14.2	36.7	60.4	3.8	856	82.8
Westville town	6,027	5,866	-2.7	5,848	67.6	24.2	0.4	1.5	6.4	5.9	4.8	36.2	73.3	5.2	655	92.5
Wheatfield town	854	873	2.2	928	88.5	0.0	0.0	4.4	7.1	32.5	10.8	28.9	54.4	9.7	328	88.4
Wheatland town	478	470	-1.7	474	95.8	0.0	1.5	0.4	2.3	28.1	15.2	33.9	57.0	9.6	194	75.3
Wheeler CDP	443	-	-	313	91.4	0.0	0.0	8.6	0.0	6.4	15.0	54.1	83.1	3.9	137	80.3
Whiteland town	4,167	4,532	8.8	4,423	98.8	0.0	1.2	0.0	0.0	18.0	10.4	38.0	44.1	29.4	1,654	95.8
Whitestown town	3,128	9,092	190.7	8,312	76.5	6.0	7.0	2.8	7.7	31.2	6.3	29.9	11.1	61.0	3,164	98.8
Whitewater town	74	70	-5.4	70	100.0	0.0	0.0	0.0	0.0	22.9	30.0	39.5	68.5	1.9	28	75.0

1 May be of any race.

Table A. All Places — **Population and Housing**

STATE City, town, township, borough, or CDP (county if applicable)	Population				Race and Hispanic or Latino origin (percent)					Age (percent)			Educational attainment of persons age 25 and older		Occupied housing units	
	2010 census total population	2019 estimated population	Percent change 2010-2019	ACS total population estimate 2015-2019	White alone, not Hispanic or Latino	Black alone, not Hispanic or Latino	Asian alone, not Hispanic or Latino	All other races or 2 or more races, not Hispanic or Latino	Hispanic or Latino[1]	Under 18 years old	Age 65 years and older	Median age	Percent High school diploma or less	Percent Bachelor's degree or more	Total	Percent with a computer
	1	2	3	4	5	6	7	8	9	10	11	12	13	14	15	16
INDIANA—Con.																
Whiting city	4,996	4,765	-4.6	4,814	53.5	2.1	0.7	2.1	41.6	25.4	12.1	34.4	55.9	17.7	1,740	84.6
Wilkinson town	460	454	-1.3	413	99.8	0.0	0.0	0.2	0.0	22.0	11.1	33.3	47.3	19.1	167	91.0
Williams CDP	286	-	-	235	100.0	0.0	0.0	0.0	0.0	0.0	20.0	50.8	68.3	20.2	141	70.9
Williams Creek town	403	427	6.0	447	90.4	2.7	2.7	2.0	2.2	26.6	21.9	49.4	6.5	79.0	161	99.4
Williamsport town	1,905	1,852	-2.8	2,028	96.5	0.2	0.7	2.2	0.4	20.7	19.5	41.1	55.7	11.1	789	88.1
Winamac town	2,491	2,292	-8.0	2,636	88.8	0.8	2.8	3.0	4.6	24.5	14.2	36.2	49.7	12.0	1,076	89.2
Winchester city	4,953	4,665	-5.8	4,739	91.5	1.7	0.0	5.5	1.3	21.9	20.7	41.9	54.2	15.6	2,009	85.1
Windfall City town	838	782	-6.7	739	88.2	0.0	0.0	1.4	10.4	21.5	18.9	38.1	76.7	7.3	321	75.4
Winfield town	4,536	5,987	32.0	5,705	81.1	4.2	1.0	1.3	12.3	25.7	18.3	41.3	37.9	34.7	1,898	89.9
Wingate town	265	266	0.4	268	100.0	0.0	0.0	0.0	0.0	18.7	18.3	42.3	67.6	8.2	122	77.0
Winona Lake town	4,911	4,902	-0.2	4,910	88.7	1.0	1.0	3.4	5.9	18.0	14.2	33.0	27.9	46.0	1,774	94.9
Winslow town	848	828	-2.4	1,013	91.4	0.0	0.0	3.7	4.9	30.0	10.9	32.8	62.1	6.7	374	88.2
Wolcott town	1,001	969	-3.2	1,103	95.4	0.6	1.3	1.4	1.4	26.7	15.0	33.0	50.6	17.2	405	94.3
Wolcottville town	986	1,044	5.9	974	93.0	0.2	0.0	5.5	1.2	25.2	9.7	35.4	69.7	7.9	373	89.0
Woodburn city	1,526	1,639	7.4	1,710	94.1	0.3	0.0	2.3	3.3	25.7	11.9	34.8	54.7	12.3	629	93.2
Woodlawn Heights town	77	76	-1.3	87	73.6	0.0	0.0	12.6	13.8	29.9	27.6	36.9	30.0	51.7	34	94.1
Worthington town	1,474	1,407	-4.5	1,214	96.3	0.2	0.2	0.0	3.3	19.5	23.5	50.1	55.2	14.6	600	77.2
Wynnedale town	232	248	6.9	177	67.8	18.6	3.4	10.2	0.0	15.8	19.2	52.6	11.9	70.6	69	100.0
Yeoman town	141	141	0.0	134	98.5	0.0	0.0	0.0	1.5	29.1	3.7	32.0	61.2	11.8	52	98.1
Yorktown town	11,301	11,111	-1.7	11,143	95.9	1.3	2.0	0.9	0.0	22.6	19.7	42.2	33.2	28.7	4,464	89.8
Zanesville town	598	621	3.8	715	93.8	0.0	0.0	1.8	4.3	27.0	14.1	37.8	57.3	12.3	265	88.7
Zionsville town	24,392	28,357	16.3	27,463	89.1	1.8	4.6	2.0	2.4	29.6	11.6	39.1	12.1	69.0	9,865	96.5
IOWA	3,046,871	3,155,070	3.6	3,139,508	85.7	3.6	2.4	2.3	6.0	23.2	16.7	38.2	38.9	28.6	1,265,473	89.0
Ackley city	1,591	1,498	-5.8	1,816	83.1	0.0	0.0	0.6	16.3	23.0	20.5	41.0	39.1	25.9	744	81.9
Ackworth city	105	105	0.0	261	54.0	0.0	0.0	46.0	0.0	44.8	11.9	25.1	58.6	17.3	83	97.6
Adair city	781	713	-8.7	750	89.5	2.9	3.6	2.1	1.9	19.3	17.1	39.4	42.6	16.9	340	83.8
Adel city	3,709	5,455	47.1	4,588	96.8	0.6	0.2	1.4	1.1	28.9	15.3	38.2	27.5	37.6	1,828	87.9
Afton city	845	815	-3.6	858	95.0	0.0	0.5	2.2	2.3	21.4	23.9	44.2	43.0	17.2	365	87.1
Agency city	638	643	0.8	648	91.0	0.0	0.0	7.9	1.1	20.5	21.8	43.5	48.9	15.1	294	80.3
Ainsworth city	567	579	2.1	577	67.4	2.3	0.0	0.3	30.0	33.4	13.2	29.4	50.7	13.1	201	89.6
Akron city	1,517	1,463	-3.6	1,588	96.3	0.2	0.0	1.1	2.3	27.3	19.3	39.5	48.6	18.0	653	87.0
Albert City city	699	665	-4.9	564	90.6	0.0	0.4	3.2	5.9	18.3	24.5	49.6	55.5	12.9	269	87.7
Albia city	3,766	3,681	-2.3	3,727	92.6	0.1	0.2	5.1	2.1	22.4	19.8	43.9	51.7	16.0	1,663	87.3
Albion city	505	490	-3.0	570	84.0	0.0	0.0	8.9	7.0	16.7	20.5	45.8	60.2	8.6	243	90.1
Alburnett city	673	699	3.9	697	92.1	0.0	0.0	6.3	1.6	30.1	10.3	32.6	28.6	21.1	244	91.0
Alden city	784	738	-5.9	859	92.3	0.0	0.0	0.6	7.1	23.4	15.0	41.7	48.6	14.2	367	86.4
Alexander city	173	161	-6.9	137	86.9	0.0	0.0	0.0	13.1	25.5	13.9	34.1	41.6	13.5	58	70.7
Algona city	5,558	5,397	-2.9	5,447	95.3	0.8	0.2	0.8	2.9	20.2	26.2	46.6	39.4	19.8	2,588	84.9
Alleman city	432	452	4.6	393	95.9	0.0	1.0	1.0	2.0	13.2	23.2	51.5	25.9	33.6	157	93.6
Allerton city	503	507	0.8	497	88.5	0.0	0.0	10.3	1.2	33.8	14.3	33.7	51.5	11.7	219	87.7
Allison city	1,025	973	-5.1	1,109	96.3	0.4	0.0	1.1	2.3	22.5	22.5	42.3	47.8	14.4	498	76.7
Alta city	1,905	1,903	-0.1	2,039	78.4	2.8	0.3	2.4	16.0	29.9	19.3	35.2	47.0	24.0	772	88.7
Alta Vista city	266	252	-5.3	241	96.7	0.0	0.8	1.2	1.2	10.0	26.1	48.5	72.4	7.5	120	68.3
Alton city	1,226	1,248	1.8	1,336	92.2	0.7	0.9	2.5	3.7	28.5	15.0	32.1	42.3	26.3	506	90.7
Altoona city	14,594	19,221	31.7	18,458	92.2	1.5	0.6	2.3	3.4	29.2	13.0	35.5	34.5	31.2	6,722	93.9
Alvord city	196	201	2.6	220	75.0	0.0	0.5	7.7	16.8	22.3	15.5	30.9	64.4	7.4	93	96.8
Amana CDP	442	-	-	338	100.0	0.0	0.0	0.0	0.0	8.6	21.9	49.7	36.6	19.5	160	93.1
Ames city	59,035	66,258	12.2	66,023	78.7	3.1	11.4	2.9	3.9	12.1	9.8	23.3	14.4	62.7	25,538	95.9
Anamosa city	5,537	5,537	0.0	5,476	85.8	6.2	3.3	0.4	4.4	15.2	19.4	41.9	54.1	16.3	2,117	82.6
Anderson CDP	65	-	-	43	100.0	0.0	0.0	0.0	0.0	30.2	0.0	22.9	81.0	0.0	10	100.0
Andover city	103	98	-4.9	127	97.6	0.0	0.0	0.0	2.4	33.9	9.4	30.9	43.9	23.2	47	85.1
Andrew city	430	408	-5.1	451	96.5	3.5	0.0	0.0	0.0	30.2	11.5	32.5	44.0	12.8	167	86.2
Anita city	979	900	-8.1	1,185	98.5	0.0	0.0	0.0	1.5	19.6	28.2	50.0	49.7	18.1	549	84.3
Ankeny city	45,608	67,355	47.7	61,938	90.6	1.7	2.4	2.5	2.8	27.3	10.0	32.4	19.0	50.8	23,200	96.7
Anthon city	567	561	-1.1	649	97.5	0.0	0.0	0.5	2.0	20.0	22.5	44.7	43.0	19.9	292	77.7
Aplington city	1,128	1,050	-6.9	968	95.9	0.8	0.0	0.0	3.3	19.1	22.4	42.4	45.7	19.4	459	81.9
Arcadia city	484	520	7.4	507	94.3	0.4	0.0	2.4	3.0	27.4	14.2	35.9	48.6	14.3	198	83.3
Archer city	131	124	-5.3	137	100.0	0.0	0.0	0.0	0.0	24.1	23.4	47.5	50.5	4.9	62	88.7
Aredale city	74	69	-6.8	46	100.0	0.0	0.0	0.0	0.0	8.7	37.0	61.4	65.0	10.0	28	71.4
Arion city	108	107	-0.9	105	93.3	0.0	0.0	6.7	0.0	25.7	16.2	45.4	77.0	2.7	44	75.0
Arispe city	100	97	-3.0	124	100.0	0.0	0.0	0.0	0.0	29.0	19.4	30.2	43.8	7.5	49	81.6
Arlington city	429	399	-7.0	454	96.3	0.0	0.7	3.1	0.0	21.1	19.2	40.6	59.0	9.2	194	82.5
Armstrong city	926	840	-9.3	880	97.6	0.0	0.0	0.1	2.3	22.7	38.0	51.3	50.2	11.8	420	78.6
Arnolds Park city	1,125	1,313	16.7	1,009	97.8	0.8	0.0	0.0	1.4	8.0	35.4	58.8	30.2	26.4	567	95.6
Arthur city	206	194	-5.8	282	90.1	0.0	0.0	7.8	2.1	24.8	16.7	37.7	51.8	8.9	123	89.4
Asbury city	4,390	5,747	30.9	5,557	92.9	1.5	2.1	2.2	1.3	32.0	15.2	37.3	25.6	47.2	1,921	97.5
Ashton city	458	420	-8.3	498	92.6	1.4	0.0	3.6	2.4	28.5	14.7	34.8	46.5	11.2	212	90.1
Aspinwall city	40	39	-2.5	20	100.0	0.0	0.0	0.0	0.0	10.0	45.0	62.0	47.1	11.8	9	77.8
Atalissa city	311	308		388	87.9	0.8	0.0	5.2	6.2	27.1	8.5	35.5	57.9	7.5	138	95.7
Athelstan CDP	19	-	-	4	100.0	0.0	0.0	0.0	0.0	0.0	0.0	0.0	100.0	0.0	4	0.0
Atkins city	1,668	1,970	18.1	1,991	96.8	2.0	0.3	0.6	0.3	28.4	12.4	39.6	32.3	31.4	732	93.0
Atlantic city	7,112	6,526	-8.2	6,669	93.7	0.4	0.4	1.8	3.7	20.9	22.1	43.8	51.2	21.5	3,142	84.3
Auburn city	322	305	-5.3	202	98.0	0.0	0.0	1.5	0.5	22.8	18.3	32.8	46.4	10.7	94	85.1
Audubon city	2,176	1,898	-12.8	1,991	94.2	0.1	0.8	5.0	0.0	19.7	25.7	46.2	53.3	13.3	999	84.1
Aurelia city	1,036	958	-7.5	883	94.9	0.0	0.0	0.9	4.2	17.0	21.9	48.0	42.0	21.9	430	89.5
Aurora city	185	161	-13.0	180	93.3	0.0	0.0	6.7	0.0	27.2	28.9	48.3	51.2	19.2	77	70.1
Avoca city	1,505	1,521	1.1	1,413	96.8	0.0	0.0	1.2	2.0	26.5	16.6	35.9	37.8	20.8	600	87.8
Ayrshire city	143	134	-6.3	128	98.4	0.0	0.0	1.6	0.0	25.8	18.0	40.8	34.1	22.0	67	82.1
Badger city	561	532	-5.2	454	94.5	0.0	0.7	2.0	2.9	20.0	24.9	50.3	44.8	17.5	202	87.6
Bagley city	303	286	-5.6	291	91.1	0.0	0.3	1.0	7.6	23.4	28.9	46.3	54.2	15.0	133	83.5
Baldwin city	113	108	-4.4	145	100.0	0.0	0.0	0.0	0.0	20.0	17.9	44.9	70.3	4.0	63	81.0
Balltown city	65	69	6.2	58	70.7	0.0	0.0	3.4	25.9	29.3	29.3	43.5	48.8	22.0	23	78.3
Bancroft city	734	696	-5.2	714	89.4	5.9	0.6	1.5	2.7	25.4	24.6	36.9	45.9	12.7	295	82.4
Bankston city	25	27	8.0	15	100.0	0.0	0.0	0.0	0.0	0.0	20.0	59.1	73.3	13.3	9	77.8
Barnes City city	176	169	-4.0	269	86.6	7.8	0.0	5.6	0.0	26.0	25.7	42.1	52.6	5.3	100	83.0
Barnum city	191	181	-5.2	246	90.2	0.0	0.0	0.4	9.3	30.5	11.4	36.0	48.7	9.9	89	95.5
Bartlett CDP	50	-	-	10	100.0	0.0	0.0	0.0	0.0	0.0	0.0	0.0	100.0	0.0	5	100.0
Bassett city	67	63	-6.0	32	100.0	0.0	0.0	0.0	0.0	0.0	46.9	63.0	65.6	3.1	17	41.2
Batavia city	499	549	10.0	724	99.6	0.0	0.0	0.0	0.4	27.1	13.5	38.3	66.6	5.2	256	83.6
Battle Creek city	713	693	-2.8	748	95.5	0.0	2.1	0.3	2.1	23.0	28.6	48.9	49.0	13.3	321	75.4

1 May be of any race.

Table A. All Places — **Population and Housing**

STATE City, town, township, borough, or CDP (county if applicable)	Population: 2010 census total population	Population: 2019 estimated population	Population: Percent change 2010-2019	Population: ACS total population estimate 2015-2019	Race and Hispanic or Latino origin (percent): White alone, not Hispanic or Latino	Black alone, not Hispanic or Latino	Asian alone, not Hispanic or Latino	All other races, or 2 or more races, not Hispanic or Latino	Hispanic or Latino[1]	Age (percent): Under 18 years old	Age 65 years and older	Median age	Educational attainment of persons age 25 and older: Percent High school diploma or less	Percent Bachelor's degree or more	Occupied housing units: Total	Percent with a computer
	1	2	3	4	5	6	7	8	9	10	11	12	13	14	15	16
IOWA—Con.																
Baxter city	1,101	1,132	2.8	1,004	99.1	0.0	0.7	0.2	0.0	22.4	19.9	43.4	39.1	19.8	439	88.2
Bayard city	472	451	-4.4	399	92.2	0.0	0.0	0.3	7.5	21.8	23.1	41.5	56.8	8.9	186	80.6
Beacon city	494	487	-1.4	639	94.8	1.7	0.8	2.7	0.0	21.8	19.6	45.3	70.2	4.7	253	75.1
Beaconsfield city	15	14	-6.7	18	100.0	0.0	0.0	0.0	0.0	0.0	44.4	64.5	100.0	0.0	10	60.0
Beaman city	191	183	-4.2	204	98.0	0.0	0.0	2.0	0.0	25.0	15.7	40.0	39.1	10.1	84	85.7
Beaver city	48	50	4.2	48	100.0	0.0	0.0	0.0	0.0	27.1	14.6	29.8	45.7	8.6	22	90.9
Beaverdale CDP	952	-	-	1,002	95.2	0.0	0.7	4.1	0.0	19.5	20.0	46.7	51.4	23.2	423	84.9
Bedford city	1,440	1,384	-3.9	1,513	97.6	0.1	0.6	0.0	1.8	21.3	23.7	39.2	49.3	12.1	634	87.5
Belle Plaine city	2,534	2,440	-3.7	2,477	94.3	0.0	0.0	4.7	0.9	23.8	19.8	43.3	49.3	13.0	1,079	84.5
Bellevue city	2,208	2,209	0.0	2,157	97.2	0.0	0.4	0.4	1.9	22.7	24.5	40.2	46.8	25.9	952	84.9
Belmond city	2,376	2,263	-4.8	2,466	86.1	0.4	1.8	1.1	10.5	24.5	23.5	44.8	41.3	17.6	1,152	81.9
Bennett city	394	378	-4.1	393	92.6	0.0	0.5	6.1	0.8	22.6	15.3	43.3	48.0	12.5	167	88.0
Bentley CDP	118	-	-	66	100.0	0.0	0.0	0.0	0.0	37.9	18.2	40.7	41.5	43.9	24	100.0
Benton city	43	41	-4.7	34	100.0	0.0	0.0	0.0	0.0	0.0	73.5	69.5	50.0	35.3	19	68.4
Berkley city	32	33	3.1	12	100.0	0.0	0.0	0.0	0.0	8.3	33.3	48.7	81.8	18.2	6	33.3
Bernard city	114	118	3.5	159	95.6	0.0	0.0	4.4	0.0	18.2	11.9	28.2	41.7	17.6	64	85.9
Bertram city	290	290	0.0	414	93.2	0.0	0.0	2.4	4.3	27.5	20.5	46.9	36.6	30.0	134	94.0
Bettendorf city	33,205	36,543	10.1	35,919	84.7	2.3	6.1	2.7	4.1	25.2	16.0	40.1	21.7	50.6	13,985	92.4
Bevington city	63	69	9.5	40	100.0	0.0	0.0	0.0	0.0	25.0	22.5	35.5	61.9	0.0	13	100.0
Birmingham city	448	421	-6.0	607	92.6	1.2	0.0	1.0	5.3	27.2	14.5	36.0	53.5	12.6	228	83.8
Blairsburg city	215	200	-7.0	168	100.0	0.0	0.0	0.0	0.0	16.1	32.1	53.7	52.0	17.3	75	90.7
Blairstown city	691	659	-4.6	703	91.2	0.0	0.3	2.0	6.5	25.9	20.2	36.5	52.5	9.8	295	86.4
Blakesburg city	296	285	-3.7	248	97.6	0.0	0.4	2.0	0.0	8.9	37.5	57.6	50.5	8.8	153	73.2
Blanchard city	38	36	-5.3	18	100.0	0.0	0.0	0.0	0.0	5.6	5.6	49.0	66.7	0.0	9	100.0
Blencoe city	224	197	-12.1	211	97.6	0.9	0.0	0.0	1.4	23.2	28.9	44.8	39.4	18.7	94	89.4
Blockton city	192	185	-3.6	133	92.5	0.0	0.0	3.0	4.5	12.8	30.8	52.3	46.6	3.9	86	77.9
Bloomfield city	2,639	2,679	1.5	2,658	96.0	0.2	0.7	0.7	2.5	25.5	18.5	38.1	36.9	23.3	1,120	82.6
Blue Grass city	1,452	1,661	14.4	1,568	94.9	2.4	0.0	1.3	1.5	20.8	21.4	42.1	39.0	27.3	626	93.0
Bode city	302	290	-4.0	289	91.0	0.0	0.0	2.4	6.6	15.6	22.1	45.5	54.1	16.7	138	88.4
Bolan CDP	33	-	-	7	100.0	0.0	0.0	0.0	0.0	0.0	100.0	0.0	0.0	0.0	7	100.0
Bonaparte city	433	403	-6.9	459	98.0	0.4	0.0	0.7	0.9	27.2	17.2	35.8	51.8	5.6	183	87.4
Bondurant city	3,865	6,958	80.0	6,191	95.3	1.9	0.0	0.9	1.9	35.9	6.8	31.3	25.0	46.7	2,128	96.2
Boone city	12,671	12,384	-2.3	12,487	91.8	0.7	0.2	3.0	4.3	22.2	16.6	39.2	40.4	21.8	5,291	91.4
Bouton city	127	122	-3.9	122	91.0	0.8	0.0	2.5	5.7	28.7	18.9	38.0	39.5	10.5	48	95.8
Boxholm city	195	186	-4.6	169	100.0	0.0	0.0	0.0	0.0	10.1	21.9	50.0	61.0	12.3	87	87.4
Boyden city	701	679	-3.1	872	90.6	0.2	0.0	0.6	8.6	29.8	9.5	30.5	44.2	18.0	341	94.1
Braddyville city	160	152	-5.0	150	89.3	0.0	0.0	7.3	3.3	16.7	25.3	50.0	41.7	19.1	72	88.9
Bradford CDP	99	-	-	66	100.0	0.0	0.0	0.0	0.0	22.7	24.2	41.5	0.0	0.0	25	100.0
Bradgate city	86	83	-3.5	98	43.9	17.3	0.0	36.7	2.0	36.7	15.3	27.8	69.4	1.6	32	93.8
Brandon city	323	320	-0.9	312	96.2	0.6	0.0	1.0	2.2	30.4	17.0	34.0	53.8	11.3	119	84.0
Brayton city	128	110	-14.1	112	100.0	0.0	0.0	0.0	0.0	16.1	16.1	44.5	58.7	7.6	58	89.7
Breda city	483	476	-1.4	440	100.0	0.0	0.0	0.0	0.0	23.9	17.0	38.3	39.5	19.7	198	90.9
Bridgewater city	176	151	-14.2	121	98.3	0.0	0.0	0.0	1.7	14.0	20.7	53.1	24.7	15.1	63	92.1
Brighton city	655	640	-2.3	723	95.3	2.5	0.0	0.0	2.2	26.3	10.7	37.6	59.0	12.8	279	81.4
Bristow city	160	149	-6.9	153	79.1	5.2	0.0	15.7	0.0	28.1	23.5	42.2	75.8	5.1	73	75.3
Britt city	2,069	1,955	-5.5	1,893	90.7	0.7	1.6	0.0	7.0	22.0	27.8	46.0	57.0	17.4	871	75.3
Bronson city	322	320	-0.6	234	97.0	0.0	0.0	3.0	0.0	22.2	16.7	42.0	53.7	15.2	98	83.7
Brooklyn city	1,475	1,400	-5.1	1,703	95.2	0.2	0.0	0.0	4.6	26.4	12.4	34.4	48.6	19.5	699	89.1
Brunsville city	151	153	1.3	157	90.4	0.0	1.3	1.9	6.4	24.2	17.2	41.0	43.6	16.4	67	95.5
Buckeye city	112	108	-3.6	108	100.0	0.0	0.0	0.0	0.0	25.0	22.2	41.0	54.3	3.7	43	74.4
Buck Grove city	43	41	-4.7	45	100.0	0.0	0.0	0.0	0.0	13.3	13.3	42.1	60.0	4.0	20	90.0
Buffalo city	1,273	1,272	-0.1	1,182	93.3	0.3	1.2	1.2	4.0	18.4	17.3	40.5	67.7	7.8	479	80.0
Buffalo Center city	905	855	-5.5	901	93.2	0.0	0.9	0.4	5.4	26.0	25.4	42.8	44.0	22.9	400	82.5
Burchinal CDP	40	-	-	15	100.0	0.0	0.0	0.0	0.0	26.7	0.0	33.1	36.4	27.3	7	100.0
Burlington city	25,611	24,713	-3.5	24,974	84.0	8.2	0.6	3.3	4.0	22.8	20.3	42.5	43.4	18.9	11,017	85.1
Burr Oak CDP	166	-	-	209	100.0	0.0	0.0	0.0	0.0	18.2	19.1	27.7	50.0	8.5	89	89.9
Burt city	533	498	-6.6	512	93.8	1.4	0.6	3.3	1.0	23.6	25.8	38.2	45.8	9.3	194	86.1
Bussey city	422	413	-2.1	420	98.1	0.0	0.0	0.5	1.4	18.3	19.3	40.5	56.7	10.3	193	74.1
Calamus city	439	401	-8.7	426	97.7	0.0	0.0	0.7	1.6	25.8	23.5	43.0	48.4	9.3	184	86.4
California Junction CDP	85	-	-	55	100.0	0.0	0.0	0.0	0.0	29.1	18.2	44.3	38.5	0.0	20	100.0
Callender city	374	346	-7.5	386	91.2	0.0	0.0	2.1	6.7	26.9	14.5	35.5	47.0	13.4	173	86.1
Calmar city	979	917	-6.3	1,009	93.7	0.0	0.0	0.1	6.2	25.0	8.6	30.0	40.6	21.4	439	94.8
Calumet city	170	157	-7.6	253	89.3	3.6	0.0	0.0	7.1	49.4	9.9	20.3	54.5	14.0	90	90.0
Camanche city	4,448	4,365	-1.9	4,334	95.6	0.0	0.0	2.5	1.9	20.8	21.2	49.3	43.0	12.7	2,040	87.4
Cambridge city	827	796	-3.7	868	94.4	1.6	0.0	1.0	3.0	34.0	10.9	33.5	35.7	25.1	307	95.1
Cantril city	222	207	-6.8	314	100.0	0.0	0.0	0.0	0.0	32.5	15.9	25.9	56.7	16.1	116	78.4
Carbon city	34	30	-11.8	46	97.8	0.0	0.0	0.0	2.2	13.0	60.9	65.5	65.0	30.0	24	83.3
Carlisle city	3,887	4,294	10.5	4,162	94.9	0.0	1.0	2.0	2.1	29.2	14.7	36.3	38.7	29.7	1,543	92.1
Carpenter city	109	106	-2.8	126	100.0	0.0	0.0	0.0	0.0	20.6	6.3	33.5	48.6	5.6	50	98.0
Carroll city	10,128	9,833	-2.9	9,904	95.3	0.2	0.1	0.4	4.0	24.1	19.3	41.6	40.7	25.9	4,424	83.6
Carson city	810	809	-0.1	721	98.8	0.0	0.3	0.3	0.7	22.9	20.9	39.1	36.9	26.6	289	91.0
Carter Lake city	3,785	3,785	0.0	3,796	86.2	1.1	0.4	1.7	10.6	28.6	13.7	36.5	53.6	15.6	1,413	85.7
Cascade city	2,171	2,329	7.3	2,113	93.4	0.6	0.3	0.0	5.7	23.7	24.5	40.9	53.4	15.8	883	80.7
Casey city	426	401	-5.9	385	90.1	0.0	0.0	7.0	2.9	20.5	23.9	50.4	63.5	8.3	171	79.5
Castalia city	173	158	-8.7	163	92.0	0.0	0.0	0.0	8.0	15.3	25.2	56.6	64.1	8.6	85	78.8
Castana city	142	133	-6.3	166	100.0	0.0	0.0	0.0	0.0	33.1	23.5	38.7	54.5	10.9	66	72.7
Cedar Falls city	39,250	40,536	3.3	40,983	89.3	2.5	3.9	1.9	2.4	19.0	14.0	27.2	23.1	47.4	15,255	93.7
Cedar Rapids city	126,580	133,562	5.5	132,301	81.2	7.6	2.9	4.3	4.0	22.6	15.3	36.3	33.3	32.1	55,292	91.0
Center Junction CDP	111	-	-	118	100.0	0.0	0.0	0.0	0.0	10.2	36.4	51.5	59.4	12.3	74	94.6
Center Point city	2,424	2,555	5.4	2,543	97.1	0.4	1.1	1.4	0.0	30.4	10.1	33.3	29.0	26.3	870	93.4
Centerville city	5,644	5,445	-3.5	5,458	94.1	1.3	1.0	1.8	1.8	21.4	19.8	44.1	46.3	16.4	2,460	83.1
Central City city	1,267	1,296	2.3	1,280	95.2	1.5	0.5	1.7	1.1	23.9	14.8	40.9	49.8	9.2	545	86.6
Centralia city	123	128	4.1	123	100.0	0.0	0.0	0.0	0.0	18.7	18.7	40.8	61.4	11.4	48	97.9
Chapin CDP	87	-	-	130	100.0	0.0	0.0	0.0	0.0	5.4	15.4	59.0	55.0	17.1	62	83.9
Chariton city	4,321	4,141	-4.2	4,149	95.9	0.2	0.0	0.3	3.6	22.5	20.9	39.5	50.1	13.6	1,884	87.0
Charles City city	7,652	7,307	-4.5	7,396	85.4	3.2	2.6	3.1	5.6	21.6	23.6	44.1	48.2	20.3	3,442	80.6
Charlotte city	394	361	-8.4	323	90.1	0.6	0.6	1.2	7.4	24.5	18.0	38.5	46.5	17.7	142	81.0
Charter Oak city	502	478	-4.8	624	96.6	0.0	0.8	0.2	2.4	29.5	14.7	39.8	46.1	7.0	251	85.3
Chatsworth city	79	81	2.5	61	100.0	0.0	0.0	0.0	0.0	19.7	8.2	51.5	70.2	4.3	29	86.2
Chelsea city	267	249	-6.7	272	53.3	0.0	0.0	0.4	46.3	29.8	8.1	29.6	75.8	7.5	91	90.1
Cherokee city	5,258	4,869	-7.4	4,920	94.9	1.9	1.8	1.2	0.2	24.3	23.4	44.8	46.0	21.4	2,214	81.9
Chester city	127	120	-5.5	184	92.4	1.6	0.0	0.0	6.0	35.9	15.2	31.0	28.3	7.5	75	84.0

1 May be of any race.

Table A. All Places — **Population and Housing**

STATE City, town, township, borough, or CDP (county if applicable)	Population: 2010 census total population	Population: 2019 estimated population	Population: Percent change 2010-2019	Population: ACS total population estimate 2015-2019	Race and Hispanic or Latino origin (percent): White alone, not Hispanic or Latino	Black alone, not Hispanic or Latino	Asian alone, not Hispanic or Latino	All other races or 2 or more races, not Hispanic or Latino	Hispanic or Latino[1]	Age (percent): Under 18 years old	Age 65 years and older	Median age	Educational attainment of persons age 25 and older: Percent High school diploma or less	Percent Bachelor's degree or more	Occupied housing units: Total	Percent with a computer
	1	2	3	4	5	6	7	8	9	10	11	12	13	14	15	16
IOWA—Con.																
Chillicothe city	97	97	0.0	97	95.9	1.0	0.0	2.1	1.0	19.6	13.4	41.4	53.7	16.4	40	97.5
Churdan city	386	364	-5.7	453	90.3	1.5	1.3	6.2	0.7	27.8	21.4	38.5	45.3	15.2	202	89.1
Cincinnati city	357	344	-3.6	340	96.2	0.0	0.0	3.2	0.6	17.1	27.6	55.2	63.7	14.8	136	75.7
Clare city	146	135	-7.5	184	95.1	0.0	0.0	1.6	3.3	28.8	17.4	38.1	44.9	5.9	66	80.3
Clarence city	974	975	0.1	975	98.2	1.4	0.0	0.0	0.4	19.7	22.9	46.8	39.1	21.0	440	78.6
Clarinda city	5,585	5,366	-3.9	5,388	85.8	4.2	2.2	3.9	3.9	20.5	18.7	41.3	43.7	16.8	1,955	89.1
Clarion city	2,850	2,709	-4.9	2,754	70.5	0.0	0.6	1.6	27.2	26.0	22.6	38.8	49.6	14.2	1,236	70.1
Clarksville city	1,439	1,346	-6.5	1,347	96.7	0.0	0.0	0.5	2.8	23.4	20.3	37.3	54.1	16.8	548	75.2
Clayton city	41	39	-4.9	54	100.0	0.0	0.0	0.0	0.0	0.0	66.7	70.3	29.4	29.4	32	84.4
Clearfield city	363	343	-5.5	383	94.0	0.0	0.0	1.3	4.7	27.9	22.5	37.6	61.1	17.6	131	73.3
Clear Lake city	7,781	7,550	-3.0	7,597	91.2	0.6	3.5	1.5	3.2	18.5	24.6	50.3	35.9	31.7	3,376	84.3
Cleghorn city	237	216	-8.9	212	95.3	2.8	0.0	1.9	0.0	23.1	27.4	45.3	45.4	16.3	94	85.1
Clemons city	148	141	-4.7	140	90.0	0.0	7.1	0.0	2.9	17.9	24.3	47.7	48.1	14.8	61	95.1
Clermont city	623	583	-6.4	566	97.5	0.0	0.0	0.0	2.5	20.3	22.3	49.7	44.2	16.6	258	81.0
Climbing Hill CDP	97	-	-	76	100.0	0.0	0.0	0.0	0.0	0.0	32.9	62.3	60.5	5.3	45	60.0
Clinton city	26,878	25,093	-6.6	25,416	87.6	5.0	0.6	3.4	3.4	21.8	18.7	40.9	51.2	17.5	10,670	81.1
Clio city	80	74	-7.5	66	92.4	0.0	0.0	7.6	0.0	18.2	28.8	58.5	70.6	21.6	28	89.3
Clive city	15,421	17,242	11.8	17,167	82.2	3.7	7.4	2.3	4.4	27.8	15.2	39.5	16.7	56.9	6,597	94.2
Clutier city	213	204	-4.2	171	90.6	0.0	0.0	3.5	5.8	15.2	21.1	43.3	51.5	8.5	84	78.6
Coalville CDP	610	-	-	722	100.0	0.0	0.0	0.0	0.0	26.3	14.4	33.8	31.6	25.5	295	89.8
Coburg city	42	39	-7.1	37	100.0	0.0	0.0	0.0	0.0	29.7	13.5	43.8	60.0	16.0	15	73.3
Coggon city	670	667	-0.4	725	99.6	0.0	0.0	0.0	0.4	28.4	14.6	35.2	44.6	20.7	273	90.5
Coin city	193	174	-9.8	176	100.0	0.0	0.0	0.0	0.0	17.6	30.7	54.6	59.0	9.0	80	83.8
Colesburg city	404	377	-6.7	460	96.1	0.0	0.0	3.9	0.0	17.8	28.0	51.4	59.3	14.2	196	85.2
Colfax city	2,093	2,064	-1.4	1,839	95.6	0.0	0.7	2.1	1.6	21.2	17.7	40.1	44.9	18.1	731	86.6
College Springs city	214	203	-5.1	249	98.0	0.0	0.0	2.0	0.0	31.3	17.3	40.5	48.2	18.3	100	90.0
Collins city	495	467	-5.7	477	93.7	1.3	0.4	4.6	0.0	29.8	19.3	37.5	53.5	11.4	186	83.9
Colo city	876	820	-6.4	984	96.5	0.0	0.1	1.0	2.3	26.9	15.7	39.1	48.7	16.8	378	92.6
Columbus City city	391	372	-4.9	345	39.7	0.0	1.7	3.5	55.1	16.2	26.1	52.3	69.5	10.2	141	90.8
Columbus Junction city	1,896	1,837	-3.1	2,229	41.5	2.2	16.6	0.6	39.1	25.7	18.5	35.1	61.8	18.0	838	70.3
Colwell city	73	70	-4.1	63	98.4	0.0	0.0	0.0	1.6	9.5	14.3	50.9	60.0	2.0	29	79.3
Conesville city	432	427	-1.2	589	26.0	0.5	0.3	1.2	72.0	38.0	11.5	26.0	76.6	2.9	189	77.8
Conrad city	1,105	1,077	-2.5	1,083	98.5	0.0	0.0	1.0	0.5	19.8	33.3	48.5	39.5	27.1	487	77.8
Conroy CDP	259	-	-	268	93.7	0.0	6.3	0.0	0.0	19.0	5.2	43.3	58.0	12.5	147	100.0
Conway city	41	40	-2.4	31	100.0	0.0	0.0	0.0	0.0	6.5	9.7	59.2	43.5	0.0	15	53.3
Coon Rapids city	1,305	1,232	-5.6	1,263	95.1	0.0	0.0	0.2	4.7	27.5	25.5	42.2	44.2	24.1	548	82.8
Coppock city	47	48	2.1	26	100.0	0.0	0.0	0.0	0.0	34.6	7.7	32.0	60.0	0.0	13	84.6
Coralville city	18,910	22,290	17.9	21,103	67.2	13.4	11.1	1.5	6.9	21.8	11.1	32.0	19.7	56.5	8,457	95.6
Corley CDP	26	-	-	27	100.0	0.0	0.0	0.0	0.0	0.0	63.0	65.4	25.9	74.1	17	58.8
Corning city	1,638	1,433	-12.5	1,577	96.9	0.1	0.3	0.6	2.1	22.4	24.2	44.2	43.2	18.3	695	86.0
Correctionville city	821	806	-1.8	807	96.7	0.0	0.0	0.9	2.5	21.9	28.7	49.9	54.8	15.1	348	84.2
Corwith city	309	254	-17.8	222	88.7	0.0	0.0	0.9	10.4	9.9	28.4	53.7	51.5	14.0	137	66.4
Corydon city	1,586	1,600	0.9	1,628	94.7	0.9	0.4	0.3	3.7	25.6	22.9	38.2	50.4	15.4	657	79.6
Cotter city	48	46	-4.2	35	88.6	0.0	0.0	0.0	11.4	8.6	14.3	48.7	71.9	0.0	15	100.0
Coulter city	281	263	-6.4	229	92.6	1.3	0.0	0.9	5.2	24.9	14.4	43.3	45.0	10.6	95	73.7
Council Bluffs city	62,226	62,166	-0.1	62,355	84.1	2.4	1.0	2.2	10.2	22.8	15.9	38.4	46.6	18.9	24,712	87.3
Craig city	91	92	1.1	65	100.0	0.0	0.0	0.0	0.0	32.3	12.3	45.1	52.5	12.5	20	85.0
Crawfordsville city	264	265	0.4	353	93.5	0.0	0.0	2.3	4.2	30.6	13.3	32.6	48.5	17.2	127	92.9
Crescent city	617	616	-0.2	599	99.0	0.0	0.0	1.0	0.0	26.2	19.5	40.1	29.1	23.9	226	89.4
Cresco city	3,866	3,739	-3.3	3,768	95.4	0.7	0.5	2.8	0.7	23.9	19.1	39.9	45.4	17.2	1,648	88.2
Creston city	7,834	7,713	-1.5	7,784	91.4	0.8	2.2	1.4	4.3	21.4	17.9	38.3	47.4	15.8	3,361	87.3
Cromwell city	107	108	0.9	89	97.8	0.0	2.2	0.0	0.0	15.7	37.1	58.3	49.3	18.3	40	85.0
Crystal Lake city	250	232	-7.2	230	96.1	3.0	0.0	0.0	0.9	12.6	22.2	52.6	69.1	6.2	121	86.8
Cumberland city	262	247	-5.7	190	98.4	0.0	0.0	0.0	1.6	22.1	16.8	45.8	62.5	7.6	98	79.6
Cumming city	347	405	16.7	392	95.4	0.0	1.3	0.5	2.8	24.2	16.1	43.4	24.6	47.8	153	98.7
Curlew city	58	55	-5.2	61	100.0	0.0	0.0	0.0	0.0	36.1	8.2	42.3	42.1	2.6	18	100.0
Cushing city	220	217	-1.4	175	90.9	0.0	0.0	5.7	3.4	13.1	28.6	52.8	57.4	17.1	86	82.6
Cylinder city	88	82	-6.8	105	91.4	0.0	0.0	8.6	0.0	34.3	6.7	36.2	46.2	18.5	39	89.7
Dakota City city	843	825	-2.1	846	96.2	0.0	0.0	0.0	3.8	26.0	17.5	38.9	52.7	12.5	367	85.3
Dallas Center city	1,627	1,776	9.2	1,515	96.7	0.8	0.2	0.6	1.7	26.6	19.3	38.8	38.6	30.3	610	89.8
Dana city	71	68	-4.2	29	89.7	0.0	0.0	0.0	10.3	6.9	10.3	49.5	58.3	12.5	14	92.9
Danbury city	349	340	-2.6	376	97.3	0.0	0.0	0.0	2.7	19.4	28.7	45.3	52.3	13.7	171	83.6
Danville city	934	899	-3.7	984	93.6	0.2	0.3	2.2	3.7	29.9	19.6	37.7	40.0	23.7	386	89.9
Davenport city	99,701	101,590	1.9	102,169	74.1	11.2	2.3	3.6	8.7	23.0	15.2	36.7	42.0	25.6	40,295	84.1
Davis City city	202	184	-8.9	235	96.6	0.0	2.6	0.9	0.0	18.7	18.3	51.8	70.9	2.2	109	78.9
Dawson city	131	126	-3.8	130	84.6	0.0	0.0	11.5	3.8	23.8	14.6	28.5	59.1	9.1	50	66.0
Dayton city	837	775	-7.4	767	96.7	0.0	0.0	2.0	1.3	20.1	26.5	49.4	45.2	18.1	310	79.4
Decatur City city	197	184	-6.6	189	98.4	0.0	0.0	1.6	0.0	21.2	16.4	35.8	60.0	4.0	77	87.0
Decorah city	8,142	7,576	-7.0	7,701	92.6	2.9	1.4	0.7	2.4	14.2	18.7	30.5	27.0	46.7	2,725	87.5
Dedham city	266	256	-3.8	261	100.0	0.0	0.0	0.0	0.0	24.9	17.6	33.6	51.5	10.8	98	91.8
Deep River city	279	270	-3.2	236	99.6	0.0	0.0	0.0	0.4	19.5	19.1	45.2	62.2	8.7	114	83.3
Defiance city	284	263	-7.4	204	93.6	0.0	0.0	0.0	6.4	23.5	27.0	53.7	66.7	8.7	97	79.4
Delaware city	159	151	-5.0	144	91.7	0.0	0.0	5.6	2.8	15.3	9.7	48.3	62.0	10.9	80	83.8
Delhi city	460	469	2.0	487	100.0	0.0	0.0	0.0	0.0	17.7	20.3	51.1	53.0	20.3	223	92.8
Delmar city	525	483	-8.0	514	90.7	0.0	2.1	2.3	4.9	25.9	16.0	37.2	39.5	18.5	199	84.4
Deloit city	266	255	-4.1	287	78.4	0.0	0.0	4.5	17.1	26.5	28.2	46.2	60.0	6.3	130	70.8
Delphos city	25	24	-4.0	27	100.0	0.0	0.0	0.0	0.0	33.3	25.9	29.2	66.7	13.3	14	50.0
Delta city	328	318	-3.0	350	99.4	0.0	0.0	0.0	0.6	26.3	16.6	32.9	63.5	5.9	153	79.7
Denison city	8,301	8,244	-0.7	8,337	41.3	5.1	4.0	0.8	48.8	27.5	13.6	33.2	62.4	14.3	2,790	81.3
Denmark CDP	423	-	-	429	99.1	0.0	0.0	0.0	0.9	22.8	19.1	46.3	40.4	20.4	196	91.8
Denver city	1,766	1,856	5.1	1,726	97.2	0.2	1.8	0.8	0.0	25.5	19.2	37.7	33.7	31.5	719	92.2
Derby city	115	112	-2.6	127	96.9	0.0	0.0	3.1	0.0	32.3	14.2	35.4	44.2	1.2	50	82.0
Des Moines city	204,220	214,237	4.9	215,636	65.7	10.9	6.1	3.7	13.6	23.8	12.0	34.2	43.2	26.7	85,833	89.7
De Soto city	1,044	1,025	-1.8	1,025	91.5	0.0	0.2	3.3	5.0	30.0	12.2	34.4	38.9	24.4	401	93.5
DeWitt city	5,319	5,192	-2.4	5,203	93.7	0.1	1.3	0.0	4.9	30.3	17.4	34.8	39.3	28.4	2,056	85.2
Dexter city	603	585	-3.0	606	94.7	0.8	0.2	0.2	4.1	24.9	17.2	36.3	44.3	20.7	246	81.7
Diagonal city	330	317	-3.9	411	98.1	0.0	0.0	0.5	1.5	25.5	28.2	37.6	50.5	18.1	123	80.5
Diamondhead Lake CDP	366	-	-	312	84.0	0.0	5.8	5.4	4.8	11.9	6.1	53.3	47.6	31.3	125	100.0
Dickens city	185	171	-7.6	212	84.9	0.0	0.0	0.0	15.1	36.8	12.3	32.5	54.8	9.5	70	98.6
Dike city	1,209	1,272	5.2	1,294	97.7	1.3	0.0	0.0	1.0	25.7	18.9	39.9	23.5	42.4	543	92.1
Dixon city	243	251	3.3	182	99.5	0.0	0.0	0.5	0.0	15.4	11.0	40.5	53.1	11.7	80	90.0
Dolliver city	66	59	-10.6	60	100.0	0.0	0.0	0.0	0.0	11.7	21.7	54.5	51.0	10.2	33	81.8

1 May be of any race.

Table A. All Places — **Population and Housing**

STATE City, town, township, borough, or CDP (county if applicable)	Population				Race and Hispanic or Latino origin (percent)					Age (percent)			Educational attainment of persons age 25 and older		Occupied housing units	
	2010 census total population	2019 estimated population	Percent change 2010-2019	ACS total population estimate 2015-2019	White alone, not Hispanic or Latino	Black alone, not Hispanic or Latino	Asian alone, not Hispanic or Latino	All other races or 2 or more races, not Hispanic or Latino	Hispanic or Latino[1]	Under 18 years old	Age 65 years and older	Median age	Percent High school diploma or less	Percent Bachelor's degree or more	Total	Percent with a computer
	1	2	3	4	5	6	7	8	9	10	11	12	13	14	15	16
IOWA—Con.																
Donahue city	356	368	3.4	378	97.4	0.0	0.0	2.1	0.5	24.6	15.9	37.4	39.5	32.7	137	92.0
Donnellson city	906	854	-5.7	1,039	97.8	1.3	0.0	0.7	0.2	26.3	19.2	35.9	43.5	23.8	430	90.5
Doon city	582	601	3.3	704	91.3	0.0	0.0	2.6	6.1	29.0	11.8	32.3	58.0	9.8	286	91.6
Douds CDP	152	-	-	81	100.0	0.0	0.0	0.0	0.0	0.0	51.9	66.2	59.3	14.8	59	35.6
Dougherty city	58	57	-1.7	65	100.0	0.0	0.0	0.0	0.0	26.2	20.0	47.5	32.6	23.9	26	92.3
Dow City city	510	497	-2.5	485	91.8	0.0	0.0	2.3	6.0	26.8	17.3	41.4	61.1	7.5	216	80.6
Dows city	542	504	-7.0	580	92.1	3.8	0.0	0.0	4.1	21.6	25.0	37.5	44.6	21.7	291	78.4
Drakesville city	184	190	3.3	180	97.8	0.0	0.0	0.6	1.7	15.6	26.1	51.4	53.1	6.9	89	79.8
Dubuque city	57,605	57,882	0.5	58,196	87.7	5.2	1.3	3.1	2.6	20.6	18.0	37.3	40.2	31.1	23,620	89.0
Dumont city	637	602	-5.5	601	97.2	0.0	0.0	0.5	2.3	22.6	30.3	47.6	62.2	6.4	265	73.2
Duncan CDP	131	-	-	119	90.8	0.0	0.0	0.0	9.2	9.2	16.0	41.5	57.4	18.5	44	56.8
Duncombe city	410	383	-6.6	309	98.1	1.0	0.0	0.0	1.0	14.2	22.7	46.8	47.1	7.6	152	87.5
Dundee city	174	163	-6.3	299	68.9	0.0	0.0	4.0	27.1	36.8	10.0	27.8	70.4	5.0	92	77.2
Dunkerton city	863	849	-1.6	845	98.3	0.0	0.0	0.7	0.9	25.1	14.9	36.9	39.2	20.2	321	92.8
Dunlap city	1,042	973	-6.6	1,059	96.2	0.0	0.8	2.8	0.1	20.7	21.5	44.8	48.7	18.0	483	77.8
Durango city	24	19	-20.8	4	100.0	0.0	0.0	0.0	0.0	0.0	50.0	53.5	100.0	0.0	4	75.0
Durant city	1,867	1,864	-0.2	1,880	95.1	0.0	1.7	2.1	1.1	25.4	17.7	43.4	38.9	25.4	755	84.4
Dyersville city	4,075	4,329	6.2	4,130	94.8	2.3	0.9	0.0	1.9	23.3	20.5	43.1	46.6	24.6	1,810	89.7
Dysart city	1,379	1,313	-4.8	1,391	95.5	1.9	1.4	1.1	0.0	22.8	22.7	48.2	44.8	17.8	558	90.5
Eagle Grove city	3,581	3,406	-4.9	3,429	83.7	0.0	0.0	3.7	12.6	26.1	17.9	39.2	48.8	19.2	1,453	80.3
Earlham city	1,445	1,410	-2.4	1,350	97.8	0.0	0.0	2.2	0.0	27.2	15.1	37.6	36.6	24.2	526	90.3
Earling city	441	409	-7.3	370	95.7	0.0	0.0	4.3	0.0	16.8	33.0	56.0	57.2	18.7	161	76.4
Earlville city	812	772	-4.9	774	93.4	0.6	0.8	1.7	3.5	19.8	18.6	49.1	63.9	8.2	351	82.6
Early city	557	515	-7.5	705	85.0	7.9	0.0	0.6	6.5	28.4	12.1	33.7	38.9	16.1	298	87.9
East Amana CDP	56	-	-	31	100.0	0.0	0.0	0.0	0.0	0.0	22.6	27.2	77.4	0.0	17	58.8
East Peru city	123	131	6.5	134	100.0	0.0	0.0	0.0	0.0	18.7	23.1	34.8	70.5	15.9	54	79.6
Eddyville city	1,024	1,008	-1.6	1,226	92.3	0.4	0.2	1.9	5.3	26.5	18.4	36.5	55.5	10.6	467	89.3
Edgewood city	867	861	-0.7	622	96.3	0.8	2.7	0.2	0.0	13.2	40.4	56.7	58.4	14.3	304	78.6
Elberon city	196	188	-4.1	165	100.0	0.0	0.0	0.0	0.0	22.4	21.2	35.4	62.4	0.8	64	82.8
Eldon city	928	915	-1.4	990	98.2	0.0	0.4	1.3	0.1	19.5	14.0	41.6	61.5	5.8	447	78.3
Eldora city	2,730	2,612	-4.3	2,645	86.5	3.1	0.5	8.2	1.8	24.8	20.5	42.6	52.2	15.6	1,001	78.4
Eldridge city	5,655	6,846	21.1	6,529	87.3	0.6	0.4	3.2	8.4	29.9	15.0	36.4	31.4	29.9	2,392	92.9
Elgin city	682	634	-7.0	628	97.6	1.6	0.0	0.8	0.0	22.8	26.1	40.5	41.5	18.1	278	81.3
Elkader city	1,294	1,217	-6.0	1,376	95.4	1.3	0.2	2.2	0.9	21.7	26.6	46.3	49.1	25.8	644	78.1
Elkhart city	678	918	35.4	688	92.3	1.2	0.7	0.7	5.1	24.7	6.5	39.7	44.1	17.3	278	88.8
Elk Horn city	662	610	-7.9	536	95.7	0.0	0.0	0.0	4.3	20.0	38.6	57.3	43.5	18.6	216	89.4
Elkport city	35	36	2.9	4	100.0	0.0	0.0	0.0	0.0	0.0	25.0	53.0	75.0	0.0	3	33.3
Elk Run Heights city	1,118	1,144	2.3	1,009	93.3	0.2	0.0	3.7	2.9	10.4	25.1	55.0	50.6	15.0	485	87.2
Elliott city	350	318	-9.1	539	93.7	0.0	0.0	0.2	6.1	30.4	8.0	34.2	54.2	7.7	219	95.4
Ellston city	41	39	-4.9	30	100.0	0.0	0.0	0.0	0.0	20.0	20.0	49.5	16.7	58.3	15	93.3
Ellsworth city	531	489	-7.9	510	97.1	0.0	0.0	1.2	1.8	25.7	15.5	31.1	17.6	21.8	200	86.5
Elma city	546	527	-3.5	536	94.8	0.0	0.0	0.0	5.2	22.2	26.3	49.0	63.7	7.9	212	84.0
Ely city	1,781	2,343	31.6	2,227	92.1	0.7	0.7	2.6	3.9	27.8	10.0	36.5	29.0	32.9	769	97.3
Emerson city	438	449	2.5	491	86.8	12.4	0.6	0.2	0.0	26.3	19.3	40.9	42.1	13.7	203	85.7
Emmetsburg city	3,904	3,684	-5.6	3,728	89.8	4.7	0.5	2.2	2.8	22.5	23.2	40.3	35.5	28.2	1,556	86.8
Epworth city	1,866	1,978	6.0	1,967	98.3	0.3	0.2	1.2	0.1	27.0	12.9	35.2	45.1	25.4	736	88.0
Essex city	798	739	-7.4	777	98.7	0.0	0.0	0.0	1.3	18.0	25.9	50.8	55.3	12.7	367	81.7
Estherville city	6,363	5,666	-11.0	5,796	81.8	2.4	0.4	1.4	13.9	20.8	17.5	38.5	40.9	22.5	2,304	87.0
Evansdale city	4,750	4,743	-0.1	4,765	92.3	2.5	0.0	4.2	1.0	23.9	16.6	37.4	58.3	8.9	2,006	89.8
Everly city	591	550	-6.9	632	98.1	0.0	0.0	1.4	0.5	24.2	18.4	36.4	48.1	11.7	282	91.5
Exira city	840	769	-8.5	804	98.9	0.0	0.0	0.2	0.9	19.9	27.9	53.1	58.9	11.7	409	83.9
Exline city	160	154	-3.8	186	97.8	0.0	0.0	2.2	0.0	29.6	30.6	44.7	56.3	2.3	75	70.7
Fairbank city	1,115	1,133	1.6	1,249	98.0	0.0	0.0	2.0	0.0	22.8	17.2	42.8	40.5	15.2	493	86.2
Fairfax city	2,167	2,856	31.8	2,680	94.5	0.0	0.3	0.6	4.6	33.0	12.6	39.8	24.2	35.2	966	95.5
Fairfield city	9,467	10,425	10.1	10,290	70.5	11.9	6.1	8.1	3.4	13.0	20.8	40.7	27.1	40.0	3,829	88.9
Farley city	1,532	1,750	14.2	1,592	98.1	0.0	0.0	1.1	0.9	23.1	14.3	35.6	49.7	20.1	624	91.2
Farmersburg city	302	268	-11.3	307	93.2	0.0	0.0	4.6	2.3	24.1	20.8	41.1	56.4	7.6	141	78.7
Farmington city	664	622	-6.3	675	99.3	0.0	0.0	0.7	0.0	26.1	13.9	46.5	49.2	8.7	310	80.0
Farnhamville city	371	344	-7.3	410	92.2	6.1	0.0	1.2	0.5	26.8	16.3	34.3	37.4	13.0	188	85.6
Farragut city	485	446	-8.0	434	95.2	0.0	0.0	3.0	1.8	17.7	26.0	46.4	39.4	16.6	228	82.5
Fayette city	1,332	1,441	8.2	1,113	81.1	11.8	0.6	1.0	5.5	9.4	19.6	24.9	34.2	29.4	375	80.8
Fenton city	279	233	-16.5	286	96.2	0.0	0.0	3.5	0.3	23.1	18.9	46.3	40.4	9.4	136	77.2
Ferguson city	126	122	-3.2	176	88.1	0.0	0.0	9.1	2.8	13.6	24.4	54.0	66.2	2.0	86	67.4
Fertile city	370	360	-2.7	293	96.9	0.0	0.7	1.7	0.7	11.6	28.7	52.9	46.2	16.9	146	85.6
Floris city	138	143	3.6	193	85.5	0.0	0.0	11.4	3.1	40.4	12.4	29.9	52.3	11.7	62	77.4
Floyd city	335	315	-6.0	335	92.8	0.0	1.5	5.7	0.0	24.2	17.3	41.6	46.6	10.4	135	79.3
Fonda city	631	575	-8.9	578	78.7	0.9	0.0	12.6	7.8	25.6	16.3	43.0	42.0	14.0	247	79.4
Fontanelle city	672	622	-7.4	660	98.8	0.0	0.3	0.6	0.3	21.5	26.8	37.8	61.6	10.5	321	86.6
Forest City city	4,151	4,025	-3.0	3,928	86.5	2.7	3.1	2.1	5.7	21.9	17.4	35.4	42.3	25.7	1,564	86.5
Fort Atkinson city	347	320	-7.8	372	98.4	0.0	0.0	0.0	1.6	14.2	20.7	49.7	40.9	17.8	175	79.4
Fort Dodge city	25,205	23,888	-5.2	24,278	83.3	6.7	1.9	1.9	6.2	21.0	17.2	36.3	45.3	19.9	10,135	81.9
Fort Madison city	11,099	10,321	-7.0	10,513	87.3	3.6	0.0	2.4	6.7	20.5	18.8	42.5	51.2	13.4	4,326	88.7
Fostoria city	243	223	-8.2	211	98.6	0.0	0.0	0.9	0.5	18.5	11.4	41.5	40.9	12.4	81	91.4
Franklin city	145	132	-9.0	161	98.1	0.0	0.0	1.9	0.0	14.3	26.1	46.2	51.9	18.5	76	82.9
Fraser city	98	103	5.1	116	100.0	0.0	0.0	0.0	0.0	25.9	18.1	43.3	48.8	10.7	48	95.8
Fredericksburg city	941	923	-1.9	1,124	93.6	2.7	0.4	2.8	0.4	26.7	20.2	42.4	51.6	21.8	486	82.9
Frederika city	195	203	4.1	346	100.0	0.0	0.0	0.0	0.0	28.6	12.1	30.5	34.2	15.8	140	82.9
Fredonia city	240	235	-2.1	294	55.4	0.0	0.0	0.0	44.6	31.0	7.5	30.7	78.6	1.3	96	82.3
Fremont city	743	721	-3.0	869	89.6	0.8	0.0	2.6	6.9	26.0	11.4	33.4	35.1	13.6	353	94.1
Fruitland city	977	982	0.5	1,036	97.9	0.0	0.0	0.0	2.1	30.5	11.2	36.6	42.6	18.1	346	93.9
Frytown CDP	165	-	-	33	100.0	0.0	0.0	0.0	0.0	0.0	0.0	0.0	51.5	0.0	16	100.0
Galt city	32	31	-3.1	44	20.5	0.0	0.0	0.0	79.5	59.1	9.1	14.5	38.9	11.1	12	83.3
Galva city	434	419	-3.5	491	87.4	0.0	0.0	2.2	10.4	25.5	12.6	29.5	47.7	7.9	214	89.3
Garber city	88	85	-3.4	117	100.0	0.0	0.0	0.0	0.0	20.5	17.1	40.8	72.9	2.9	49	75.5
Garden City CDP	89	-	-	183	100.0	0.0	0.0	0.0	0.0	22.4	32.2	34.9	57.7	0.0	67	100.0
Garden Grove city	209	197	-5.7	176	96.6	0.0	0.0	0.0	3.4	23.9	14.8	44.0	62.2	10.1	73	87.7
Garnavillo city	746	724	-2.9	826	95.5	0.0	0.0	0.0	4.5	18.6	21.3	41.2	53.6	17.3	361	79.8
Garner city	3,129	3,033	-3.1	3,059	93.0	4.2	0.0	0.0	2.7	26.4	22.0	41.4	32.3	34.6	1,253	92.6
Garrison city	375	360	-4.0	368	99.2	0.0	0.3	0.5	0.0	20.7	17.1	37.4	57.1	9.2	155	87.7
Garwin city	527	493	-6.5	530	96.8	0.6	0.0	2.1	0.6	21.9	22.3	46.6	53.6	11.8	247	87.0
Geneva city	165	153	-7.3	103	92.2	0.0	0.0	0.0	7.8	14.6	33.0	53.3	44.7	14.5	45	82.2
George city	1,091	1,042	-4.5	1,188	91.6	0.0	0.0	2.9	5.6	20.8	34.4	50.3	44.2	20.8	504	90.5

1 May be of any race.

Table A. All Places — **Population and Housing**

STATE City, town, township, borough, or CDP (county if applicable)	Population				Race and Hispanic or Latino origin (percent)					Age (percent)			Educational attainment of persons age 25 and older		Occupied housing units	
	2010 census total population	2019 estimated population	Percent change 2010-2019	ACS total population estimate 2015-2019	White alone, not Hispanic or Latino	Black alone, not Hispanic or Latino	Asian alone, not Hispanic or Latino	All other races or 2 or more races, not Hispanic or Latino	Hispanic or Latino[1]	Under 18 years old	Age 65 years and older	Median age	Percent High school diploma or less	Percent Bachelor's degree or more	Total	Percent with a computer
	1	2	3	4	5	6	7	8	9	10	11	12	13	14	15	16
IOWA—Con.																
Gibson city	61	60	-1.6	42	100.0	0.0	0.0	0.0	0.0	11.9	45.2	57.0	61.3	12.9	28	71.4
Gilbert city	1,076	1,147	6.6	1,013	89.5	1.1	1.1	3.5	4.8	32.4	10.3	36.5	24.2	45.0	350	94.0
Gilbertville city	720	728	1.1	859	100.0	0.0	0.0	0.0	0.0	17.0	22.7	44.0	46.4	19.1	373	86.9
Gillett Grove city	49	47	-4.1	30	100.0	0.0	0.0	0.0	0.0	6.7	26.7	59.0	89.3	7.1	22	63.6
Gilman city	509	484	-4.9	509	95.3	0.0	0.4	0.0	4.3	30.5	12.0	36.4	41.8	15.8	207	91.8
Gilmore City city	504	469	-6.9	422	97.6	0.0	0.0	0.0	2.4	20.4	19.9	46.7	55.0	8.0	206	85.0
Gladbrook city	945	858	-9.2	982	97.9	0.0	0.0	1.3	0.8	20.8	24.8	42.4	40.7	17.6	436	90.8
Glenwood city	5,269	5,389	2.3	5,326	94.0	0.6	0.1	1.4	3.9	20.6	19.4	40.0	48.7	21.2	1,924	92.2
Glidden city	1,146	1,106	-3.5	1,131	97.1	0.0	0.8	0.0	2.1	23.7	16.7	41.5	40.8	19.2	475	89.1
Goldfield city	634	593	-6.5	672	94.5	0.0	0.0	0.0	5.5	18.6	18.8	45.2	50.1	11.3	305	79.0
Goodell city	139	128	-7.9	96	97.9	0.0	0.0	0.0	2.1	8.3	19.8	47.5	75.3	2.5	55	90.9
Goose Lake city	240	220	-8.3	207	94.2	0.0	1.0	4.8	0.0	29.5	15.5	40.7	38.2	15.4	83	85.5
Gowrie city	1,037	953	-8.1	923	92.4	3.7	0.0	2.1	1.8	23.2	23.8	48.6	33.8	26.7	425	90.8
Graettinger city	844	795	-5.8	940	95.3	3.5	0.0	0.2	1.0	23.3	16.3	39.4	46.4	13.9	393	88.0
Graf city	79	81	2.5	64	100.0	0.0	0.0	0.0	0.0	26.6	18.8	44.7	56.5	17.4	26	88.5
Grafton city	252	244	-3.2	225	100.0	0.0	0.0	0.0	0.0	15.6	15.6	48.8	43.5	10.6	101	81.2
Grand Junction city	824	773	-6.2	763	97.6	0.0	0.0	2.4	0.0	25.8	13.9	38.5	53.8	9.0	325	86.8
Grand Mound city	642	593	-7.6	628	92.0	0.0	0.0	3.2	4.8	22.5	16.7	37.1	46.5	22.5	225	92.4
Grand River city	236	215	-8.9	219	100.0	0.0	0.0	0.0	0.0	23.7	22.8	36.3	46.2	13.8	102	80.4
Grandview city	557	526	-5.6	430	90.9	3.0	0.0	0.0	6.0	18.8	29.1	47.1	57.9	13.9	205	87.8
Granger city	1,248	1,508	20.8	1,756	95.7	0.3	0.0	0.4	3.6	29.8	11.7	35.9	27.4	38.9	669	92.2
Grant city	92	83	-9.8	91	100.0	0.0	0.0	0.0	0.0	24.2	26.4	47.3	50.7	3.0	44	86.4
Granville city	312	304	-2.6	336	82.1	0.0	0.0	0.9	17.0	25.3	19.3	36.9	50.2	13.7	145	93.8
Gravity city	188	181	-3.7	146	100.0	0.0	0.0	0.0	0.0	15.8	23.3	48.0	64.2	9.2	68	83.8
Gray city	63	57	-9.5	117	100.0	0.0	0.0	0.0	0.0	31.6	10.3	46.3	45.1	42.3	33	75.8
Greeley city	256	242	-5.5	260	98.5	0.0	1.2	0.0	0.4	17.3	16.9	41.5	73.7	3.9	112	81.3
Greene city	1,130	1,063	-5.9	1,026	98.0	0.0	0.0	1.7	0.4	20.2	29.4	50.6	46.6	21.8	486	78.0
Greenfield city	1,988	1,838	-7.5	1,730	97.5	1.0	0.2	0.3	1.0	18.6	27.7	45.8	50.5	14.7	885	80.0
Green Mountain CDP	126	-	-	150	100.0	0.0	0.0	0.0	0.0	25.3	13.3	42.4	67.9	12.5	75	78.7
Greenville city	75	68	-9.3	75	100.0	0.0	0.0	0.0	0.0	20.0	13.3	38.5	51.1	4.3	30	90.0
Grimes city	8,255	14,804	79.3	12,839	90.1	0.0	1.6	1.4	7.0	30.1	9.5	34.1	31.9	38.6	4,780	95.6
Grinnell city	9,221	9,116	-1.1	9,031	87.3	3.7	4.2	1.6	3.3	16.2	20.7	37.1	40.2	33.4	3,719	89.8
Griswold city	1,038	944	-9.1	1,191	90.3	0.0	0.7	5.9	3.2	32.1	18.7	37.8	50.5	13.3	493	85.4
Grundy Center city	2,702	2,670	-1.2	2,675	96.4	1.8	0.9	0.3	0.6	21.9	24.4	45.0	44.0	25.2	1,191	85.4
Gruver city	93	83	-10.8	61	90.2	0.0	0.0	1.6	8.2	4.9	26.2	58.8	58.9	5.4	32	81.3
Guernsey city	63	60	-4.8	46	100.0	0.0	0.0	0.0	0.0	23.9	34.8	49.7	68.6	0.0	25	76.0
Guthrie Center city	1,565	1,494	-4.5	1,678	95.8	0.2	0.2	1.1	2.7	24.4	25.7	38.2	47.4	17.3	735	81.4
Guttenberg city	1,919	1,804	-6.0	1,683	99.6	0.2	0.0	0.1	0.0	10.3	34.3	58.2	53.6	19.1	865	82.0
Halbur city	246	256	4.1	281	100.0	0.0	0.0	0.0	0.0	31.7	8.5	29.1	48.2	15.5	100	91.0
Hamburg city	1,187	1,060	-10.7	1,214	98.2	0.0	0.0	0.0	1.8	23.6	21.8	46.3	50.5	8.7	539	90.7
Hamilton city	130	134	3.1	64	100.0	0.0	0.0	0.0	0.0	35.9	6.3	34.7	66.7	0.0	26	73.1
Hampton city	4,465	4,205	-5.8	4,231	74.5	0.3	0.0	0.0	25.2	26.5	19.1	38.8	53.1	18.0	1,739	75.3
Hancock city	196	196	0.0	202	96.0	0.0	0.0	0.0	4.0	17.8	32.2	55.6	58.3	4.5	94	86.2
Hanlontown city	226	220	-2.7	182	96.2	0.0	0.0	1.1	2.7	20.9	19.2	44.1	37.4	17.3	84	88.1
Hansell city	94	90	-4.3	89	100.0	0.0	0.0	0.0	0.0	22.5	27.0	58.2	60.6	4.5	38	57.9
Harcourt city	303	278	-8.3	308	96.4	0.0	0.0	1.6	1.9	26.9	14.0	43.5	52.0	9.9	122	83.6
Hardy city	47	42	-10.6	67	76.1	0.0	0.0	4.5	19.4	65.7	6.0	14.8	69.6	21.7	20	70.0
Harlan city	5,082	4,766	-6.2	4,845	94.0	1.8	0.4	3.0	0.7	20.3	25.0	47.4	43.0	24.2	2,288	84.8
Harper city	114	110	-3.5	86	84.9	1.2	1.2	12.8	0.0	34.9	14.0	31.3	52.0	24.0	27	92.6
Harpers Ferry city	328	323	-1.5	241	100.0	0.0	0.0	0.0	0.0	6.2	57.3	66.4	56.9	16.5	132	78.8
Harris city	170	157	-7.6	139	87.8	0.0	2.2	2.9	7.2	24.5	21.6	41.5	58.0	6.0	66	84.8
Hartford city	777	777	0.0	775	90.8	0.8	0.0	7.2	1.2	31.9	9.8	33.3	50.1	11.5	284	91.5
Hartley city	1,672	1,574	-5.9	1,695	88.8	1.7	0.4	0.9	8.3	23.2	25.3	47.3	44.8	14.5	776	80.3
Hartwick city	86	80	-7.0	108	89.8	0.0	0.0	10.2	0.0	31.5	15.7	30.0	29.7	27.0	42	92.9
Harvey city	235	244	3.8	151	100.0	0.0	0.0	0.0	0.0	25.8	22.5	41.9	77.4	4.7	64	71.9
Hastings city	152	152	0.0	192	84.9	0.0	0.0	13.5	1.6	32.8	16.1	27.8	55.6	13.0	52	86.5
Havelock city	138	124	-10.1	137	94.2	0.0	0.0	0.0	5.8	29.2	11.7	35.6	52.7	11.0	70	72.9
Haverhill city	173	167	-3.5	179	94.4	0.0	0.6	0.0	5.0	30.7	8.4	36.8	35.3	19.3	67	86.6
Hawarden city	2,532	2,444	-3.5	2,836	62.9	0.4	0.0	1.4	35.4	33.2	17.2	35.0	58.0	13.9	1,041	81.7
Hawkeye city	449	408	-9.1	430	93.5	0.0	0.0	2.8	3.7	23.5	16.3	36.6	52.0	14.8	173	82.1
Hayesville city	50	49	-2.0	40	100.0	0.0	0.0	0.0	0.0	0.0	55.0	71.0	75.0	12.5	26	57.7
Hayfield CDP	43	-	-	90	100.0	0.0	0.0	0.0	0.0	0.0	8.9	45.0	38.3	25.0	34	76.5
Hazleton city	830	833	0.4	775	95.0	0.0	0.0	3.0	2.1	25.9	17.9	38.6	59.2	11.3	307	85.0
Hedrick city	764	754	-1.3	531	100.0	0.0	0.0	0.0	0.0	17.5	25.0	43.5	43.6	15.1	249	81.5
Henderson city	185	185	0.0	272	97.8	0.0	0.0	0.0	2.2	34.9	23.2	36.4	48.0	8.8	86	89.5
Hepburn city	18	17	-5.6	17	100.0	0.0	0.0	0.0	0.0	23.5	11.8	37.3	30.8	0.0	9	77.8
Hiawatha city	7,022	7,420	5.7	7,333	80.8	13.5	1.3	0.9	3.5	23.7	13.7	34.9	39.7	23.9	3,107	91.5
High Amana CDP	115	-	-	81	100.0	0.0	0.0	0.0	0.0	21.0	28.4	42.8	39.1	26.6	43	62.8
Hills city	702	804	14.5	780	92.1	2.3	0.0	3.6	2.1	19.7	22.7	41.5	39.8	23.5	347	88.2
Hillsboro city	180	177	-1.7	202	100.0	0.0	0.0	0.0	0.0	29.7	12.4	33.8	37.6	2.6	77	75.3
Hinton city	953	948	-0.5	813	94.5	1.0	0.4	0.7	3.4	20.5	18.0	40.5	36.4	31.7	331	94.0
Holiday Lake CDP	433	-	-	396	100.0	0.0	0.0	0.0	0.0	5.1	36.9	60.2	50.6	20.7	235	97.0
Holland city	290	277	-4.5	253	100.0	0.0	0.0	0.0	0.0	27.7	15.8	33.7	40.5	19.0	105	87.6
Holstein city	1,397	1,370	-1.9	1,294	87.8	3.2	0.0	4.6	4.5	17.8	25.1	44.9	39.2	28.0	614	86.5
Holy Cross city	374	368	-1.6	361	98.6	0.0	0.0	0.0	1.4	20.8	18.3	35.9	44.6	16.5	155	88.4
Homestead CDP	148	-	-	152	100.0	0.0	0.0	0.0	0.0	38.8	14.5	33.6	8.6	43.0	66	87.9
Hopkinton city	628	597	-4.9	616	89.0	5.0	0.0	3.4	2.6	28.4	20.3	40.6	61.2	8.8	243	79.4
Hornick city	223	218	-2.2	255	98.4	0.0	0.0	0.8	0.8	22.7	12.5	32.5	49.1	12.7	115	95.7
Hospers city	698	696	-0.3	788	97.2	0.0	0.0	0.5	2.3	23.7	18.9	35.8	38.9	19.8	341	89.7
Houghton city	146	136	-6.8	123	100.0	0.0	0.0	0.0	0.0	22.0	25.2	53.1	57.9	18.9	52	75.0
Hubbard city	843	801	-5.0	761	97.8	0.0	0.0	1.8	0.4	19.8	28.9	50.4	45.4	16.8	309	83.8
Hudson city	2,282	2,468	8.2	2,375	96.6	0.0	1.1	0.9	1.4	24.9	12.9	40.6	21.0	38.8	881	96.8
Hull city	2,180	2,299	5.5	2,089	90.7	0.0	0.2	1.0	8.1	23.2	15.4	34.4	38.5	23.5	783	94.4
Humboldt city	4,684	4,587	-2.1	4,583	91.6	0.1	0.3	0.9	7.0	21.1	24.3	45.5	43.2	24.6	2,111	79.2
Humeston city	481	484	0.6	484	88.0	0.0	0.0	6.6	5.4	25.0	27.3	42.4	61.2	7.3	209	83.3
Hutchins CDP	28	-	-	29	100.0	0.0	0.0	0.0	0.0	0.0	0.0	0.0	0.0	0.0	13	100.0
Huxley city	3,321	4,036	21.5	3,769	96.4	0.5	0.8	0.0	2.2	32.2	6.9	33.8	19.7	51.8	1,380	91.6
Ida Grove city	2,142	2,052	-4.2	2,000	98.1	0.1	0.0	0.0	1.9	21.9	24.7	47.2	46.5	19.7	934	89.5
Imogene city	72	70	-2.8	37	100.0	0.0	0.0	0.0	0.0	48.6	10.8	21.5	22.2	16.7	12	91.7
Independence city	5,969	6,124	2.6	6,056	94.1	0.2	0.0	1.5	4.2	24.3	21.9	40.5	43.3	23.6	2,509	85.5
Indianola city	14,780	16,015	8.4	15,802	95.0	0.2	0.9	1.7	2.2	23.4	17.4	35.4	34.7	31.3	6,196	89.4
Inwood city	814	849	4.3	978	88.3	0.0	0.0	5.1	6.5	26.6	21.8	36.3	47.1	16.0	406	88.9

1 May be of any race.

Table A. All Places — **Population and Housing**

STATE City, town, township, borough, or CDP (county if applicable)	Population				Race and Hispanic or Latino origin (percent)					Age (percent)			Educational attainment of persons age 25 and older		Occupied housing units	
	2010 census total population	2019 estimated population	Percent change 2010-2019	ACS total population estimate 2015-2019	White alone, not Hispanic or Latino	Black alone, not Hispanic or Latino	Asian alone, not Hispanic or Latino	All other races or 2 or more races, not Hispanic or Latino	Hispanic or Latino[1]	Under 18 years old	Age 65 years and older	Median age	Percent High school diploma or less	Percent Bachelor's degree or more	Total	Percent with a computer
	1	2	3	4	5	6	7	8	9	10	11	12	13	14	15	16
IOWA—Con.																
Ionia city	290	275	-5.2	269	95.5	0.0	0.0	0.0	4.5	20.4	11.9	41.7	57.7	7.1	124	87.9
Iowa City city	67,961	75,130	10.5	74,950	75.3	8.2	7.3	3.4	5.8	15.2	10.5	26.5	18.3	59.1	30,568	94.6
Iowa Falls city	5,285	5,059	-4.3	5,122	91.3	1.5	0.0	2.1	5.2	18.3	23.3	43.8	41.8	22.5	2,210	82.5
Ireton city	610	599	-1.8	749	83.0	0.0	0.8	15.4	0.8	27.9	15.9	34.7	37.0	28.5	303	85.8
Irvington CDP	38	-	-	16	100.0	0.0	0.0	0.0	0.0	56.3	0.0	0.0	0.0	0.0	7	100.0
Irwin city	341	311	-8.8	344	97.7	0.0	0.0	1.2	1.2	13.7	32.0	52.7	42.8	17.1	159	89.9
Jackson Junction city	58	54	-6.9	62	95.2	0.0	4.8	0.0	0.0	25.8	8.1	43.3	52.6	15.8	23	87.0
Jacksonville CDP	30	-	-	7	100.0	0.0	0.0	0.0	0.0	0.0	100.0	0.0	100.0	0.0	7	100.0
Jamaica city	224	218	-2.7	282	73.8	0.0	0.0	0.4	25.9	23.8	19.9	38.7	49.2	11.0	123	87.0
Janesville city	930	986	6.0	981	97.2	0.0	0.0	0.0	2.8	27.0	20.5	37.7	45.4	22.9	418	86.8
Jefferson city	4,345	4,102	-5.6	4,137	93.5	0.1	0.5	1.1	4.8	23.0	26.3	43.5	46.3	21.2	1,877	87.4
Jesup city	2,522	2,703	7.2	2,806	95.3	0.0	0.0	4.6	0.2	30.5	9.8	32.7	41.1	18.3	994	88.4
Jewell Junction city	1,215	1,139	-6.3	1,187	96.0	0.8	1.8	0.6	0.9	28.2	16.5	41.6	32.8	28.7	470	90.6
Johnston city	17,272	22,582	30.7	21,406	88.2	2.9	4.4	2.3	2.3	25.8	13.8	40.1	18.4	54.5	8,531	95.0
Joice city	217	210	-3.2	249	88.4	0.0	1.2	2.4	8.0	26.9	16.9	40.2	41.3	19.8	116	94.8
Jolley city	39	37	-5.1	19	100.0	0.0	0.0	0.0	0.0	5.3	21.1	57.5	47.1	0.0	9	55.6
Kalona city	2,371	2,537	7.0	2,520	92.6	0.0	0.0	1.2	6.2	24.7	24.9	40.1	45.2	22.2	1,054	87.2
Kamrar city	199	190	-4.5	163	97.5	0.0	2.5	0.0	0.0	14.1	15.3	48.2	63.6	7.4	69	60.9
Kanawha city	652	595	-8.7	845	85.4	0.0	0.4	2.6	11.6	24.3	19.9	33.4	54.0	12.7	365	79.7
Kellerton city	314	297	-5.4	291	90.4	0.0	0.7	4.8	4.1	33.7	15.5	35.7	58.2	6.3	112	90.2
Kelley city	309	300	-2.9	288	84.4	0.0	0.3	1.7	13.5	22.9	8.3	33.4	24.0	31.0	115	97.4
Kellogg city	599	588	-1.8	571	94.4	0.0	0.5	1.2	3.9	18.4	15.6	46.9	47.9	11.4	256	86.7
Kensett city	266	256	-3.8	279	97.8	1.4	0.0	0.0	0.7	14.3	24.0	50.5	58.4	8.2	134	83.6
Kent CDP	61	-	-	22	100.0	0.0	0.0	0.0	0.0	50.0	0.0	30.0	0.0	0.0	5	100.0
Keokuk city	10,776	10,157	-5.7	10,324	87.0	4.6	1.5	3.5	3.4	25.3	20.1	39.0	46.4	16.8	4,431	84.0
Keomah Village city	96	97	1.0	90	100.0	0.0	0.0	0.0	0.0	2.2	46.7	64.4	20.3	50.6	48	100.0
Keosauqua city	1,006	908	-9.7	951	93.1	0.6	0.0	2.5	3.8	14.9	36.1	55.2	47.8	16.2	453	81.0
Keota city	1,011	971	-4.0	958	96.5	1.0	0.6	1.3	0.6	26.7	20.3	38.0	40.9	14.3	426	85.7
Keswick city	246	241	-2.0	241	95.0	0.0	0.0	5.0	0.0	31.5	16.6	30.8	44.7	11.3	94	92.6
Keystone city	622	612	-1.6	590	95.8	0.0	0.0	3.4	0.8	21.9	28.8	44.6	47.7	16.4	249	78.7
Kimballton city	322	280	-13.0	273	90.1	0.0	0.0	4.0	5.9	13.6	27.5	54.5	50.5	13.3	144	82.6
Kingsley city	1,411	1,402	-0.6	1,593	89.7	7.4	0.0	1.8	1.1	26.3	20.8	44.2	34.9	28.3	665	91.4
Kinross city	73	72	-1.4	51	100.0	0.0	0.0	0.0	0.0	21.6	3.9	31.7	70.0	2.5	24	95.8
Kirkman city	64	61	-4.7	68	91.2	0.0	2.9	0.0	5.9	8.8	27.9	51.8	69.1	1.8	31	74.2
Kirkville city	167	175	4.8	199	100.0	0.0	0.0	0.0	0.0	27.1	6.0	35.9	60.7	5.0	77	96.1
Kiron city	279	266	-4.7	295	73.6	0.0	0.0	0.0	26.4	23.4	27.5	43.6	60.8	6.6	134	75.4
Klemme city	507	463	-8.7	702	89.9	0.6	0.0	1.7	7.8	29.3	12.1	31.3	59.0	7.7	309	76.4
Knierim city	60	58	-3.3	45	84.4	0.0	0.0	0.0	15.6	15.6	17.8	41.6	44.4	13.9	21	76.2
Knoxville city	7,313	7,168	-2.0	7,192	94.2	0.6	0.5	1.5	3.1	20.6	19.8	40.9	46.2	14.9	3,320	81.4
Lacona city	353	352	-0.3	318	98.4	0.0	0.0	1.6	0.0	20.1	19.8	44.0	60.8	6.2	156	90.4
Ladora city	283	274	-3.2	255	96.1	0.0	1.2	0.0	2.7	27.1	16.1	36.4	51.2	3.5	107	84.1
Lake City city	1,727	1,642	-4.9	1,764	96.3	2.0	0.7	1.0	0.1	21.7	28.0	50.0	44.1	22.0	749	86.2
Lake Mills city	2,105	1,984	-5.7	2,067	92.9	1.5	0.2	1.3	4.1	23.9	22.0	39.8	45.3	19.3	921	80.0
Lake Panorama CDP	1,309	-	-	860	99.2	0.0	0.0	0.8	0.0	7.8	46.9	61.5	24.9	40.2	411	97.3
Lake Park city	1,105	1,123	1.6	1,230	96.2	0.0	0.7	1.3	1.9	21.8	25.3	43.1	40.4	18.4	563	90.2
Lakeside city	700	689	-1.6	917	63.7	0.8	4.5	0.9	30.2	30.4	13.8	34.7	47.6	26.2	346	95.7
Lake View city	1,142	1,084	-5.1	1,067	98.0	0.7	0.0	0.3	1.0	16.1	34.4	56.9	33.7	25.8	529	85.3
Lakota city	294	279	-5.1	328	90.5	0.0	0.9	0.0	8.5	26.8	22.6	38.4	56.4	6.0	129	92.2
Lambs Grove city	172	169	-1.7	237	99.2	0.0	0.0	0.0	0.8	23.2	25.3	44.2	28.0	25.0	93	96.8
Lamoni city	2,335	2,249	-3.7	2,554	82.7	5.5	1.1	4.0	6.7	14.8	14.8	23.8	32.0	46.6	917	91.1
Lamont city	461	457	-0.9	540	99.6	0.0	0.0	0.0	0.4	28.0	18.7	34.8	64.2	7.0	216	82.4
La Motte city	270	254	-5.9	208	93.8	0.0	0.0	5.3	1.0	16.8	26.9	52.5	60.6	8.1	97	78.4
Lanesboro city	118	109	-7.6	127	100.0	0.0	0.0	0.0	0.0	11.0	26.0	59.6	65.0	7.8	61	68.9
Lansing city	999	935	-6.4	880	95.1	2.4	1.6	0.5	0.5	15.7	31.3	55.0	51.3	19.7	442	76.0
La Porte City city	2,285	2,240	-2.0	2,743	94.0	0.3	0.3	4.7	0.7	28.0	19.6	40.8	39.8	21.1	1,045	90.4
Larchwood city	835	891	6.7	1,027	95.2	0.3	0.4	0.4	3.7	24.5	18.9	40.3	47.3	26.3	411	89.3
Larrabee city	139	131	-5.8	152	94.7	0.0	0.0	5.3	0.0	9.2	25.7	54.5	66.4	6.1	80	86.3
Latimer city	502	470	-6.4	492	71.5	2.2	0.0	1.6	24.6	25.0	16.3	32.9	46.2	14.1	204	76.5
Laurel city	239	231	-3.3	219	94.5	0.5	0.0	5.0	0.0	20.5	17.8	41.9	50.6	16.5	103	82.5
Laurens city	1,259	1,120	-11.0	1,228	89.2	2.4	3.4	0.0	5.0	21.3	23.0	50.0	44.8	12.4	622	87.5
Lawler city	442	419	-5.2	387	98.4	0.0	0.0	0.0	1.6	22.5	22.5	48.5	53.9	17.9	190	74.7
Lawton city	912	980	7.5	1,105	95.9	0.0	0.3	0.8	3.0	28.1	17.1	39.2	33.0	30.2	420	84.0
Leando CDP	115	-	-	38	100.0	0.0	0.0	0.0	0.0	0.0	21.1	0.0	21.1	0.0	38	100.0
Le Claire city	3,747	3,965	5.8	3,971	96.4	0.3	0.0	3.3	0.0	29.1	15.0	39.9	25.8	39.8	1,508	89.5
Ledyard city	130	120	-7.7	77	97.4	0.0	0.0	0.0	2.6	7.8	49.4	64.9	54.9	9.9	50	54.0
Le Grand city	938	914	-2.6	990	94.7	1.5	0.0	1.0	2.7	27.2	18.2	40.6	47.2	13.1	394	86.5
Lehigh city	416	392	-5.8	379	96.6	0.0	0.8	1.1	1.6	16.6	24.8	54.7	47.4	12.6	187	78.6
Leighton city	162	158	-2.5	221	95.5	0.0	0.0	4.5	0.0	21.7	23.1	38.4	44.9	14.0	78	91.0
Leland city	289	271	-6.2	265	83.0	11.7	0.0	0.0	5.3	29.4	15.5	38.9	50.6	12.1	119	83.2
Le Mars city	9,835	10,081	2.5	9,941	91.3	0.3	0.9	1.2	6.4	25.0	18.2	39.0	38.4	24.7	4,222	89.5
Lenox city	1,407	1,389	-1.3	1,437	67.9	0.0	3.8	0.0	28.3	27.1	22.3	40.8	58.6	10.7	602	87.9
Leon city	1,977	1,823	-7.8	1,868	97.0	0.1	0.3	1.2	1.4	29.8	20.8	36.7	55.6	18.9	796	80.0
Le Roy city	15	14	-6.7	3	33.3	0.0	0.0	66.7	0.0	0.0	100.0	0.0	100.0	0.0	1	0.0
Lester city	294	302	2.7	278	96.8	0.0	0.0	0.0	3.2	28.4	22.7	40.5	45.7	16.5	109	92.7
Letts city	384	373	-2.9	375	98.1	0.0	0.0	0.0	1.9	23.5	22.7	41.9	53.6	5.3	146	81.5
Lewis city	433	399	-7.9	420	91.0	0.0	0.0	1.0	8.1	24.0	23.3	51.0	60.5	10.2	187	86.1
Libertyville city	315	341	8.3	433	97.2	0.0	0.9	0.9	0.9	22.4	15.7	41.0	52.0	17.1	163	85.9
Lidderdale city	180	171	-5.0	184	100.0	0.0	0.0	0.0	0.0	26.1	17.4	42.5	72.4	7.1	80	82.5
Lime Springs city	505	474	-6.1	508	97.6	0.0	0.0	0.0	2.4	25.8	20.9	41.1	57.6	13.6	220	74.1
Lincoln city	162	148	-8.6	116	91.4	0.0	0.0	0.0	8.6	22.4	17.2	51.5	62.2	3.7	54	75.9
Linden city	199	208	4.5	176	96.0	0.0	0.0	3.4	0.6	15.9	13.1	45.5	49.3	16.2	78	92.3
Lineville city	217	220	1.4	259	94.2	0.0	0.0	5.8	0.0	16.6	15.8	46.3	61.7	18.2	128	91.4
Linn Grove city	154	146	-5.2	189	69.8	0.0	0.0	0.0	30.2	19.0	27.5	43.9	56.2	21.2	89	85.4
Lisbon city	2,141	2,247	5.0	2,493	92.9	1.9	0.0	2.0	3.2	25.5	12.5	40.5	40.2	28.5	932	96.1
Liscomb city	301	293	-2.7	274	98.5	0.0	0.0	0.0	1.5	22.3	10.2	43.4	55.8	10.2	124	78.2
Little Cedar CDP	60	-	-	42	100.0	0.0	0.0	0.0	0.0	0.0	23.8	62.3	100.0	0.0	25	100.0
Little Rock city	459	433	-5.7	440	95.2	0.0	0.2	0.7	3.9	24.5	20.5	41.3	57.8	9.2	191	87.4
Little Sioux city	170	161	-5.3	144	83.3	4.2	0.0	1.4	11.1	25.0	24.3	49.0	75.0	1.0	65	67.7
Livermore city	384	362	-5.7	381	96.3	2.1	0.0	0.0	1.6	25.2	10.5	36.8	52.5	6.2	154	81.2
Lockridge city	268	290	8.2	442	96.4	0.0	0.0	0.7	2.9	24.9	19.2	36.5	59.5	9.3	142	88.0
Logan city	1,534	1,418	-7.6	1,568	96.8	0.5	0.0	1.6	1.1	28.1	14.7	38.5	44.6	21.2	630	87.5
Lohrville city	368	345	-6.3	365	90.4	0.0	1.9	7.7	0.0	19.2	21.1	48.4	41.8	16.3	187	87.7

1 May be of any race.

Table A. All Places — **Population and Housing**

STATE City, town, township, borough, or CDP (county if applicable)	Population: 2010 census total population	Population: 2019 estimated population	Population: Percent change 2010-2019	Population: ACS total population estimate 2015-2019	Race and Hispanic or Latino origin (percent): White alone, not Hispanic or Latino	Race: Black alone, not Hispanic or Latino	Race: Asian alone, not Hispanic or Latino	Race: All other races or 2 or more races, not Hispanic or Latino	Race: Hispanic or Latino[1]	Age (percent): Under 18 years old	Age: Age 65 years and older	Age: Median age	Educational attainment of persons age 25 and older: Percent High school diploma or less	Educational attainment: Percent Bachelor's degree or more	Occupied housing units: Total	Occupied housing units: Percent with a computer
	1	2	3	4	5	6	7	8	9	10	11	12	13	14	15	16
IOWA—Con.																
Lone Rock city	146	139	-4.8	205	90.2	0.0	1.5	4.4	3.9	19.0	17.6	29.8	42.0	20.2	69	91.3
Lone Tree city	1,302	1,381	6.1	1,312	89.1	0.0	0.2	0.4	10.4	28.7	15.5	38.1	38.3	20.3	513	93.8
Long Grove city	810	872	7.7	994	98.3	0.0	0.0	0.0	1.7	28.1	13.8	40.9	25.8	39.5	353	98.3
Lorimor city	360	343	-4.7	405	98.5	0.0	0.0	0.5	1.0	30.1	13.3	36.0	64.9	3.9	152	82.9
Lost Nation city	446	406	-9.0	461	100.0	0.0	0.0	0.0	0.0	17.1	29.5	48.9	54.7	9.1	227	70.5
Loveland CDP	35	-	-	-	-	-	-	-	-	-	-	-	-	-	-	-
Lovilia city	547	509	-6.9	623	98.6	0.0	0.0	1.4	0.0	25.8	18.3	32.7	60.5	11.1	256	87.9
Lowden city	787	773	-1.8	874	98.3	0.0	0.0	0.5	1.3	24.3	19.1	40.4	46.7	18.3	360	85.8
Low Moor city	273	247	-9.5	284	92.6	0.0	1.4	6.0	0.0	24.3	11.3	44.7	53.7	9.0	105	89.5
Luana city	269	279	3.7	235	98.3	0.0	0.0	0.0	1.7	18.7	18.3	48.1	56.3	16.8	108	78.7
Lucas city	216	209	-3.2	134	98.5	0.0	0.0	0.0	1.5	10.4	31.3	55.2	66.4	0.9	72	80.6
Luther city	122	133	9.0	181	96.1	0.0	0.0	3.9	0.0	22.1	25.4	50.3	41.0	21.6	73	83.6
Lu Verne city	261	249	-4.6	296	92.6	0.0	0.0	7.4	0.0	28.0	16.6	35.6	49.2	9.8	118	83.1
Luxemburg city	242	247	2.1	261	99.2	0.0	0.8	0.0	0.0	22.6	28.7	46.5	60.9	15.1	104	78.8
Luzerne city	96	93	-3.1	148	100.0	0.0	0.0	0.0	0.0	32.4	6.1	47.3	44.8	3.1	48	93.8
Lynnville city	379	393	3.7	471	99.2	0.0	0.0	0.8	0.0	24.2	20.6	36.3	59.6	13.5	198	83.3
Lytton city	316	289	-8.5	275	91.6	2.2	0.0	0.0	6.2	19.3	14.5	45.3	42.6	13.3	143	85.3
McCallsburg city	333	320	-3.9	434	99.3	0.0	0.0	0.7	0.0	34.8	7.6	31.2	30.0	11.5	167	91.0
McCausland city	303	311	2.6	403	96.3	0.0	0.7	2.7	0.2	29.0	15.4	36.6	32.4	26.0	141	96.5
McClelland city	155	155	0.0	177	98.9	0.0	0.0	0.0	1.1	24.3	13.6	42.2	40.7	20.4	66	86.4
Macedonia city	246	243	-1.2	258	95.3	0.0	0.0	1.2	3.5	26.0	16.7	36.5	41.6	19.7	113	92.9
McGregor city	871	838	-3.8	861	95.6	0.5	0.9	3.0	0.0	17.2	26.1	48.6	46.4	20.6	380	87.1
McIntire city	127	125	-1.6	110	97.3	0.0	0.0	2.7	0.0	11.8	22.7	48.5	65.9	0.0	54	70.4
Macksburg city	113	118	4.4	89	97.8	0.0	0.0	1.1	1.1	16.9	28.1	50.5	71.4	1.4	51	82.4
Madrid city	2,565	2,549	-0.6	2,578	97.7	0.1	0.0	1.0	1.2	20.0	20.5	45.6	36.7	25.5	1,082	88.3
Magnolia city	183	176	-3.8	167	97.6	0.0	0.0	2.4	0.0	13.2	22.2	51.9	72.3	2.3	74	85.1
Maharishi Vedic City city	1,294	1,295	0.1	544	55.7	7.5	20.4	7.2	9.2	7.5	32.2	54.6	8.0	66.2	159	100.0
Malcom city	287	272	-5.2	262	93.5	0.0	0.0	1.5	5.0	17.9	16.8	42.5	56.9	12.6	125	80.0
Mallard city	274	258	-5.8	219	94.5	0.0	0.0	0.0	5.5	13.7	35.2	55.8	57.9	9.6	117	78.6
Maloy city	29	28	-3.4	31	100.0	0.0	0.0	0.0	0.0	9.7	12.9	60.6	67.9	3.6	17	94.1
Malvern city	1,148	1,115	-2.9	1,015	96.8	1.2	0.0	0.5	1.5	17.4	25.6	43.8	40.3	22.9	397	89.2
Manchester city	5,180	4,986	-3.7	5,019	96.3	0.0	0.0	2.2	1.5	25.8	23.5	43.9	46.9	18.1	2,124	82.7
Manilla city	776	746	-3.9	895	94.2	0.6	0.0	1.5	3.8	22.6	19.9	38.5	51.4	9.0	359	86.9
Manly city	1,321	1,278	-3.3	1,396	91.5	0.8	0.4	2.4	4.9	22.9	17.0	43.5	42.7	15.9	609	85.7
Manning city	1,516	1,422	-6.2	1,565	98.8	0.0	1.2	0.0	0.0	24.1	23.1	38.6	45.8	19.8	664	83.7
Manson city	1,690	1,566	-7.3	1,867	93.4	0.5	0.3	1.9	3.9	27.1	22.3	39.2	38.2	20.1	837	89.5
Mapleton city	1,224	1,157	-5.5	1,114	98.4	0.0	0.0	0.5	1.1	19.5	30.4	51.8	52.1	19.3	541	80.8
Maquoketa city	6,222	5,990	-3.7	6,010	92.1	0.9	0.3	5.1	1.7	25.8	19.0	40.6	44.6	15.1	2,599	81.8
Marathon city	239	227	-5.0	207	71.5	0.0	0.0	1.9	26.6	17.4	14.5	40.8	57.8	9.1	94	96.8
Marble Rock city	307	287	-6.5	321	95.6	0.0	0.0	2.5	1.9	13.7	29.9	52.6	50.6	13.3	169	84.6
Marcus city	1,117	1,054	-5.6	1,233	81.4	9.2	0.0	6.5	2.9	18.8	25.4	48.1	36.3	26.1	602	80.6
Marengo city	2,528	2,466	-2.5	2,483	93.6	0.2	0.3	0.6	5.4	25.5	21.7	39.8	53.2	10.7	1,085	87.5
Marion city	35,172	40,359	14.7	39,328	92.0	1.5	1.3	2.7	2.5	24.4	16.6	38.7	29.6	36.6	15,909	91.9
Marne city	120	112	-6.7	144	98.6	0.0	0.0	1.4	0.0	23.6	12.5	48.5	49.0	13.5	65	83.1
Marquette city	445	433	-2.7	396	95.2	0.0	0.8	1.8	2.3	12.6	26.8	50.4	55.9	16.5	224	92.9
Marshalltown city	27,557	26,666	-3.2	27,053	59.8	1.5	5.2	2.8	30.7	25.4	18.0	36.7	54.2	18.1	10,273	87.1
Martelle city	254	250	-1.6	232	97.4	0.0	0.0	2.6	0.0	15.9	19.0	37.0	42.6	14.8	106	87.7
Martensdale city	465	461	-0.9	478	95.0	0.0	0.0	0.6	4.4	29.3	8.6	29.7	54.0	14.7	204	96.1
Martinsburg city	112	109	-2.7	89	100.0	0.0	0.0	0.0	0.0	14.6	15.7	45.1	68.4	7.0	45	84.4
Marysville city	66	69	4.5	97	100.0	0.0	0.0	0.0	0.0	34.0	14.4	33.6	71.9	0.0	28	92.9
Mason City city	28,072	26,931	-4.1	27,200	88.6	2.4	0.7	2.0	6.3	20.3	20.9	43.3	39.7	21.2	12,546	85.2
Masonville city	127	120	-5.5	123	100.0	0.0	0.0	0.0	0.0	34.1	12.2	37.3	70.1	3.9	51	98.0
Massena city	352	336	-4.5	314	95.2	0.0	0.0	0.6	4.1	27.4	24.8	38.0	48.2	15.2	138	91.3
Matlock city	87	87	0.0	107	100.0	0.0	0.0	0.0	0.0	20.6	24.3	52.8	54.4	2.5	42	100.0
Maurice city	275	271	-1.5	291	90.7	0.3	0.0	0.3	8.6	28.5	16.8	39.7	54.3	14.4	106	91.5
Maxwell city	922	903	-2.1	784	93.2	0.0	0.5	3.3	2.9	24.4	14.7	36.5	36.1	21.6	334	93.1
Maynard city	518	488	-5.8	543	93.0	0.0	0.0	6.3	0.7	25.8	16.0	37.8	36.6	21.0	221	91.0
Maysville city	184	185	0.5	188	98.9	0.0	1.1	0.0	0.0	24.5	16.0	44.5	60.3	15.6	75	86.7
Mechanicsville city	1,144	1,129	-1.3	1,126	97.9	0.0	0.0	0.0	2.1	20.5	16.7	41.3	51.2	17.0	417	92.1
Mediapolis city	1,560	1,517	-2.8	1,795	96.3	0.0	0.5	1.9	1.2	28.6	17.9	35.2	31.6	26.4	668	87.9
Melbourne city	830	794	-4.3	843	98.0	0.0	0.5	0.0	1.5	27.4	12.9	37.1	36.5	17.7	324	89.5
Melcher-Dallas city	1,288	1,244	-3.4	1,160	98.3	0.0	0.0	1.7	0.0	23.4	22.6	45.3	47.8	9.9	544	81.3
Melrose city	112	104	-7.1	141	94.3	0.0	1.4	4.3	0.0	24.8	32.6	47.3	61.8	6.9	64	87.5
Melvin city	214	198	-7.5	266	82.7	0.0	0.0	0.8	16.5	28.6	17.7	36.6	57.1	16.3	122	83.6
Menlo city	353	347	-1.7	365	94.0	0.0	0.0	3.3	2.7	28.2	15.9	37.6	46.6	13.1	150	77.3
Meriden city	157	148	-5.7	159	95.0	0.0	0.0	3.1	1.9	28.3	15.1	39.1	59.4	14.9	62	82.3
Merrill city	758	731	-3.6	917	85.3	1.7	1.3	1.9	9.8	23.0	14.3	39.6	54.2	11.8	344	84.3
Meservey city	256	238	-7.0	196	98.0	0.0	0.0	2.0	0.0	11.7	26.0	51.6	56.8	4.3	93	87.1
Meyer CDP	31	-	-	9	100.0	0.0	0.0	0.0	0.0	0.0	0.0	0.0	0.0	0.0	5	100.0
Middle Amana CDP	581	-	-	778	93.8	6.2	0.0	0.0	0.0	30.3	18.1	41.0	31.5	29.2	287	93.7
Middletown city	315	335	6.3	397	83.6	3.0	1.3	4.0	8.1	32.0	12.6	30.9	37.9	24.7	140	95.7
Miles city	456	437	-4.2	422	98.1	0.0	0.0	0.9	0.9	22.0	19.0	44.0	49.1	23.9	187	82.9
Milford city	2,903	2,997	3.2	3,004	93.8	1.1	0.0	0.9	4.3	28.4	17.8	35.8	35.0	25.3	1,233	88.0
Miller CDP	60	-	-	30	100.0	0.0	0.0	0.0	0.0	0.0	100.0	0.0	100.0	0.0	14	0.0
Millersburg city	147	142	-3.4	135	83.0	0.0	1.5	2.2	13.3	11.9	19.3	54.3	79.6	3.9	72	87.5
Millerton city	45	42	-6.7	108	100.0	0.0	0.0	0.0	0.0	30.6	4.6	22.6	22.0	39.0	56	98.2
Milo city	771	761	-1.3	856	96.4	0.0	0.0	0.5	3.2	28.7	11.2	33.7	50.0	16.0	337	90.5
Milton city	443	398	-10.2	481	94.2	1.5	0.4	0.0	4.0	36.0	14.1	30.9	59.3	3.0	165	75.2
Minburn city	364	352	-3.3	344	95.9	0.0	0.0	1.7	2.3	29.4	12.8	36.8	44.1	18.1	146	91.8
Minden city	611	598	-2.1	677	98.7	0.0	1.2	0.0	0.1	32.3	16.0	36.5	30.5	19.0	257	91.4
Mineola CDP	166	-	-	224	83.5	0.0	0.0	0.0	16.5	18.8	17.4	55.2	61.9	16.3	81	86.4
Mingo city	302	309	2.3	301	87.4	3.0	2.3	6.0	1.3	31.6	21.6	37.1	46.9	8.9	125	68.8
Missouri Valley city	2,837	2,615	-7.8	2,640	98.0	0.0	0.0	0.0	2.0	23.6	20.3	43.3	54.1	11.4	1,179	78.5
Mitchell city	138	130	-5.8	187	97.9	0.0	0.0	0.0	2.1	30.5	19.8	37.5	44.6	12.3	68	72.1
Mitchellville city	2,254	2,258	0.2	2,365	88.5	4.0	0.0	4.4	3.1	20.5	9.6	34.1	58.0	8.8	609	93.3
Modale city	283	264	-6.7	327	99.4	0.0	0.0	0.6	0.0	22.6	15.0	39.0	55.3	9.3	139	89.2
Mona CDP	34	-	-	144	100.0	0.0	0.0	0.0	0.0	0.0	10.4	55.3	51.6	8.8	50	86.0
Mondamin city	402	374	-7.0	352	95.5	0.0	0.0	2.8	1.7	19.3	19.0	44.0	52.2	16.2	167	93.4
Monmouth city	156	154	-1.3	205	97.1	0.0	2.9	0.0	0.0	18.5	17.6	37.4	70.7	4.1	78	71.8
Monona city	1,549	1,471	-5.0	1,635	96.4	0.0	0.7	0.5	2.4	21.3	18.3	43.7	46.4	18.5	754	76.8
Monroe city	1,830	1,894	3.5	1,733	98.1	0.3	0.3	1.0	0.3	23.2	15.7	38.3	42.5	21.1	749	88.4
Montezuma city	1,454	1,412	-2.9	1,338	95.7	0.5	0.2	0.3	3.2	24.9	16.0	33.3	47.7	17.6	553	84.3

1 May be of any race.

Table A. All Places — **Population and Housing**

STATE City, town, township, borough, or CDP (county if applicable)	Population: 2010 census total population	Population: 2019 estimated population	Population: Percent change 2010-2019	Population: ACS total population estimate 2015-2019	Race and Hispanic or Latino origin (percent): White alone, not Hispanic or Latino	Black alone, not Hispanic or Latino	Asian alone, not Hispanic or Latino	All other races or 2 or more races, not Hispanic or Latino	Hispanic or Latino[1]	Age (percent): Under 18 years old	Age 65 years and older	Median age	Educational attainment of persons age 25 and older: Percent High school diploma or less	Percent Bachelor's degree or more	Occupied housing units: Total	Percent with a computer
	1	2	3	4	5	6	7	8	9	10	11	12	13	14	15	16
IOWA—Con.																
Monticello city	3,773	3,880	2.8	3,837	93.4	0.1	0.0	4.0	2.6	24.0	21.6	39.0	41.8	26.2	1,661	83.3
Montour city	249	243	-2.4	254	86.2	4.3	0.0	3.9	5.5	15.0	19.3	47.0	61.0	9.3	107	87.9
Montrose city	831	778	-6.4	837	99.6	0.0	0.0	0.0	0.4	24.7	26.5	45.5	50.9	11.0	327	85.0
Moorhead city	226	204	-9.7	184	96.2	0.0	0.0	0.5	3.3	19.0	28.8	53.0	51.1	12.8	100	72.0
Moorland city	169	156	-7.7	207	93.7	1.0	0.0	3.4	1.9	27.5	12.1	36.6	56.5	10.7	79	83.5
Moravia city	665	636	-4.4	611	99.3	0.0	0.0	0.7	0.0	22.9	30.4	41.0	50.5	12.8	266	89.5
Morley city	115	113	-1.7	51	100.0	0.0	0.0	0.0	0.0	19.6	15.7	54.5	56.8	5.4	25	84.0
Morning Sun city	836	796	-4.8	783	92.5	0.8	0.0	5.7	1.0	19.8	20.6	44.0	47.7	18.2	280	86.1
Morrison city	94	91	-3.2	154	100.0	0.0	0.0	0.0	0.0	18.8	20.8	54.5	52.9	14.9	66	95.5
Moulton city	605	578	-4.5	613	86.0	0.0	0.0	2.8	11.3	33.8	15.7	33.0	42.3	18.0	235	71.1
Mount Auburn city	150	144	-4.0	129	100.0	0.0	0.0	0.0	0.0	20.2	15.5	36.8	52.6	1.0	57	86.0
Mount Ayr city	1,689	1,619	-4.1	2,056	91.4	0.2	2.3	1.2	5.0	20.2	23.7	48.1	46.3	21.5	857	80.9
Mount Pleasant city	8,666	8,668	0.0	8,581	80.1	4.5	5.0	3.1	7.2	18.4	17.8	36.6	45.1	20.0	3,182	90.3
Mount Sterling CDP	36	-	-	22	100.0	0.0	0.0	0.0	0.0	0.0	100.0	0.0	100.0	0.0	10	0.0
Mount Union CDP	107	-	-	153	98.0	0.0	0.0	0.0	2.0	30.1	5.9	33.1	30.5	4.8	61	77.0
Mount Vernon city	4,493	4,466	-0.6	4,451	92.4	1.3	1.5	2.5	2.3	25.3	9.8	23.0	13.5	60.2	1,285	97.5
Moville city	1,618	1,635	1.1	1,812	90.1	2.8	0.0	3.2	3.9	27.6	14.8	36.7	28.8	30.0	755	94.0
Murray city	756	702	-7.1	733	90.0	0.0	0.0	2.3	7.6	27.0	17.9	36.8	49.5	6.8	306	82.0
Muscatine city	23,777	23,631	-0.6	23,774	72.8	4.1	0.7	2.1	20.3	25.0	15.0	36.1	48.7	20.0	9,478	87.2
Mystic city	425	409	-3.8	364	96.4	0.0	0.0	0.0	3.6	26.1	22.0	48.0	58.7	2.8	166	75.9
Nashua city	1,658	1,589	-4.2	1,506	98.9	0.0	0.0	0.3	0.8	19.4	19.6	44.1	49.7	17.5	687	85.2
Nemaha city	85	81	-4.7	116	75.9	0.0	0.0	1.7	22.4	28.4	12.1	29.3	61.9	9.5	50	94.0
Neola city	846	891	5.3	990	96.8	0.8	0.0	1.0	1.4	29.8	16.4	38.7	40.5	17.1	384	86.7
Nevada city	6,798	6,677	-1.8	6,754	94.3	0.7	0.5	0.7	3.8	26.9	16.5	37.2	31.3	30.3	2,826	92.7
New Albin city	517	499	-3.5	563	98.0	0.0	0.0	0.0	2.0	25.2	18.1	40.5	46.2	10.7	265	59.6
Newell city	876	852	-2.7	909	94.7	0.0	0.3	1.7	3.3	18.4	19.4	41.7	43.8	17.8	401	88.5
Newhall city	896	858	-4.2	1,029	92.0	3.1	0.0	3.4	1.5	23.2	22.8	38.3	36.9	23.3	448	89.1
New Hampton city	3,572	3,406	-4.6	3,421	92.8	1.8	0.2	0.4	4.9	22.9	22.2	44.7	48.6	19.0	1,597	83.9
New Hartford city	516	488	-5.4	703	96.9	1.7	0.0	0.6	0.9	36.1	11.9	33.1	40.6	14.2	246	91.9
New Haven CDP	91	-	-	109	100.0	0.0	0.0	0.0	0.0	44.0	6.4	27.3	73.8	8.2	27	81.5
New Liberty city	139	144	3.6	108	92.6	0.0	2.8	4.6	0.0	19.4	20.4	39.3	59.2	9.2	49	67.3
New London city	1,900	1,839	-3.2	2,128	95.3	0.5	0.4	0.8	2.9	26.3	15.3	38.2	41.4	15.4	865	87.2
New Market city	415	401	-3.4	469	96.6	0.0	0.0	3.2	0.2	17.5	22.4	49.4	38.6	13.0	221	81.0
New Providence city	230	223	-3.0	267	92.5	0.0	0.0	5.6	1.9	28.8	20.2	40.3	46.8	24.7	104	73.1
New Sharon city	1,293	1,293	0.0	1,144	98.8	0.0	0.0	1.2	0.0	17.6	21.2	48.5	42.7	23.5	484	94.0
Newton city	15,254	15,182	-0.5	15,164	91.7	3.2	0.5	1.6	2.9	22.6	21.0	42.4	52.2	15.4	6,464	84.0
New Vienna city	407	411	1.0	402	97.3	0.5	0.7	1.5	0.0	15.9	23.4	47.4	53.9	16.6	175	85.7
New Virginia city	488	491	0.6	465	97.6	0.0	1.3	0.4	0.6	26.7	16.8	37.2	42.2	11.4	196	87.8
Nichols city	374	362	-3.2	374	68.7	0.5	1.6	3.2	25.9	21.7	18.7	45.3	61.1	6.8	135	91.1
Nodaway city	114	103	-9.6	84	97.6	0.0	0.0	2.4	0.0	23.8	25.0	43.5	36.7	18.3	38	78.9
Nora Springs city	1,431	1,354	-5.4	1,535	97.1	0.5	0.0	2.2	0.1	25.4	19.0	38.1	38.1	18.3	626	86.3
Northboro city	58	56	-3.4	73	100.0	0.0	0.0	0.0	0.0	16.4	13.7	45.5	86.2	0.0	39	94.9
North Buena Vista city	121	121	0.0	76	100.0	0.0	0.0	0.0	0.0	9.2	30.3	58.8	73.5	7.4	44	70.5
North English city	1,046	1,007	-3.7	1,087	98.4	0.0	0.0	0.7	0.8	26.7	21.3	38.1	51.6	11.2	437	72.5
North Liberty city	13,393	19,501	45.6	18,829	84.5	5.5	3.8	1.7	4.4	29.2	6.9	30.6	16.8	53.3	7,188	96.9
North Washington city	118	138	16.9	138	98.6	0.0	0.0	0.7	0.7	23.2	8.7	42.2	64.8	5.7	51	90.2
Northwood city	1,989	1,955	-1.7	2,297	92.9	3.3	0.6	0.3	2.9	23.3	21.5	40.4	46.0	20.0	914	83.4
Norwalk city	8,990	11,938	32.8	10,978	94.5	1.0	0.4	1.9	2.2	28.4	12.1	35.6	24.8	42.7	4,239	95.2
Norway city	545	528	-3.1	518	98.8	0.8	0.0	0.4	0.0	23.6	19.5	46.1	51.8	11.5	237	89.5
Numa city	92	89	-3.3	78	100.0	0.0	0.0	0.0	0.0	16.7	33.3	45.6	63.2	5.3	33	84.8
Oakland city	1,527	1,501	-1.7	1,567	86.6	0.4	0.1	2.4	10.5	24.6	15.8	36.0	35.1	22.3	590	92.5
Oakland Acres city	156	159	1.9	138	99.3	0.0	0.7	0.0	0.0	25.4	13.8	46.7	31.4	43.1	56	96.4
Oakville city	173	169	-2.3	210	97.1	1.9	0.0	0.0	1.0	37.6	8.1	30.5	42.2	3.4	75	94.7
Ocheyedan city	490	459	-6.3	514	90.1	0.0	0.0	3.1	6.8	27.2	18.9	37.0	50.3	14.0	223	91.9
Odebolt city	1,014	943	-7.0	915	97.4	0.0	0.7	2.0	0.0	22.0	29.8	50.6	46.2	17.6	394	81.7
Oelwein city	6,416	5,900	-8.0	5,979	91.6	2.9	0.0	2.2	3.3	22.9	22.5	42.5	51.0	16.5	2,588	88.9
Ogden city	2,044	1,979	-3.2	1,875	97.4	0.0	0.0	0.8	1.8	18.6	24.7	46.6	45.1	19.7	856	85.2
Okoboji city	820	792	-3.4	819	88.0	0.2	11.4	0.0	0.4	7.2	38.3	58.8	16.3	50.9	436	97.9
Olds city	229	223	-2.6	200	83.0	8.5	0.0	0.5	8.0	28.5	11.5	37.5	35.3	32.3	86	90.7
Olin city	698	687	-1.6	779	93.3	0.0	1.0	1.8	3.9	27.5	14.5	37.7	59.4	2.9	297	81.5
Ollie city	215	210	-2.3	207	100.0	0.0	0.0	0.0	0.0	22.2	30.0	48.5	51.7	4.1	98	87.8
Onawa city	2,998	2,764	-7.8	2,804	89.2	0.1	0.0	8.0	2.7	15.3	21.9	41.7	47.2	10.9	1,346	86.4
Onslow city	197	193	-2.0	248	94.0	4.8	0.0	0.0	1.2	29.8	14.9	32.3	48.4	5.7	103	77.7
Orange City city	6,060	6,182	2.0	6,127	91.6	0.4	1.5	0.4	6.1	20.2	17.2	34.0	31.0	37.7	2,084	92.0
Orchard city	72	71	-1.4	63	93.7	0.0	6.3	0.0	0.0	6.3	19.0	38.7	58.2	16.4	41	78.0
Orient city	408	377	-7.6	467	97.6	0.0	0.0	1.9	0.4	33.4	10.7	37.1	48.7	6.7	174	83.3
Orleans city	609	587	-3.6	469	97.7	0.0	1.5	0.9	0.0	6.4	44.6	63.8	24.0	42.0	260	91.9
Osage city	3,619	3,555	-1.8	3,568	95.9	0.8	0.6	1.6	1.1	20.9	23.5	45.7	45.9	19.8	1,616	81.4
Osceola city	4,927	5,242	6.4	5,103	70.4	0.0	1.2	3.3	25.1	24.4	17.2	38.6	50.2	15.0	2,168	89.4
Oskaloosa city	11,503	11,506	0.0	11,511	90.9	1.7	2.8	1.7	3.0	24.5	18.7	35.0	46.0	22.5	4,846	86.6
Ossian city	845	778	-7.9	808	96.5	0.0	1.5	0.0	2.0	17.0	28.0	47.2	48.1	21.0	407	89.9
Osterdock city	59	56	-5.1	83	100.0	0.0	0.0	0.0	0.0	14.5	6.0	46.8	64.8	1.9	30	96.7
Otho city	542	507	-6.5	442	96.4	0.2	0.0	2.0	1.4	12.7	16.5	54.1	48.6	15.4	233	82.4
Oto city	110	103	-6.4	129	76.0	0.0	0.0	4.7	19.4	32.6	16.3	40.8	50.0	10.3	54	77.8
Otranto CDP	27	-	-	-	-	-	-	-	-	-	-	-	-	-	-	-
Ottosen city	55	37	-32.7	26	88.5	0.0	0.0	11.5	0.0	11.5	26.9	55.3	73.9	4.3	13	92.3
Ottumwa city	25,021	24,368	-2.6	24,545	76.6	4.7	1.5	2.6	14.6	23.2	15.9	37.3	47.1	17.8	10,169	84.5
Owasa city	43	42	-2.3	22	100.0	0.0	0.0	0.0	0.0	9.1	63.6	68.5	55.0	25.0	16	93.8
Oxford city	803	792	-1.4	812	90.9	0.4	0.7	1.6	6.4	23.3	18.2	37.4	41.8	25.3	332	87.0
Oxford Junction city	495	483	-2.4	442	100.0	0.0	0.0	0.0	0.0	24.0	18.3	40.0	63.8	6.0	179	82.7
Oyens city	101	102	1.0	94	100.0	0.0	0.0	0.0	0.0	23.4	20.2	33.7	32.9	12.9	41	90.2
Pacific Junction city	471	342	-27.4	361	97.5	0.0	0.0	2.5	0.0	23.0	15.2	48.2	56.8	1.1	149	77.9
Packwood city	204	227	11.3	286	95.5	0.3	0.0	4.2	0.0	25.5	17.8	46.3	40.6	16.8	116	84.5
Palmer city	165	149	-9.7	150	94.7	0.0	0.0	0.0	5.3	22.0	16.0	38.3	49.0	9.0	75	88.0
Palo city	944	1,066	12.9	1,044	93.7	0.0	1.1	3.4	1.9	29.8	11.7	31.2	40.5	21.0	392	90.8
Panama city	221	208	-5.9	204	99.0	0.0	0.0	1.0	0.0	28.9	15.7	37.3	38.4	16.7	82	79.3
Panora city	1,121	1,067	-4.8	1,228	91.6	2.5	0.0	2.5	3.3	30.3	19.8	38.6	41.3	18.1	476	89.3
Panorama Park city	129	319	147.3	105	95.2	0.0	1.9	2.9	0.0	17.1	25.7	51.3	47.1	16.1	47	76.6
Parkersburg city	1,870	1,928	3.1	1,940	99.3	0.0	0.0	0.2	0.6	26.5	22.3	42.3	41.7	23.8	831	78.5
Park View CDP	2,389	-	-	2,818	87.5	7.9	0.0	0.3	4.2	30.6	7.6	34.0	51.7	20.8	870	100.0
Parnell city	193	264	36.8	221	96.4	0.0	0.0	3.6	0.0	12.2	7.7	43.9	58.4	3.9	110	90.0
Paton city	236	230	-2.5	178	97.2	0.0	0.0	0.0	2.8	20.8	10.7	37.7	33.8	20.0	82	82.9

1 May be of any race.

Table A. All Places — **Population and Housing**

STATE City, town, township, borough, or CDP (county if applicable)	Population				Race and Hispanic or Latino origin (percent)					Age (percent)			Educational attainment of persons age 25 and older		Occupied housing units	
	2010 census total population	2019 estimated population	Percent change 2010-2019	ACS total population estimate 2015-2019	White alone, not Hispanic or Latino	Black alone, not Hispanic or Latino	Asian alone, not Hispanic or Latino	All other races or 2 or more races, not Hispanic or Latino	Hispanic or Latino[1]	Under 18 years old	Age 65 years and older	Median age	Percent High school diploma or less	Percent Bachelor's degree or more	Total	Percent with a computer
	1	2	3	4	5	6	7	8	9	10	11	12	13	14	15	16
IOWA—Con.																
Patterson city	147	161	9.5	168	98.8	0.0	0.0	0.0	1.2	16.1	18.5	40.5	52.3	7.6	86	89.5
Paullina city	1,051	977	-7.0	953	96.4	0.8	0.0	0.4	2.3	22.4	22.9	41.8	44.4	21.2	446	90.4
Pella city	10,358	10,237	-1.2	10,231	93.2	1.7	3.0	0.7	1.3	18.8	18.1	35.1	36.9	41.7	3,916	91.6
Peosta city	1,393	1,857	33.3	1,910	87.5	7.5	0.5	2.6	1.9	34.6	7.5	35.6	31.4	37.1	665	97.1
Percival CDP	87	-	-	102	56.9	0.0	0.0	0.0	43.1	15.7	21.6	60.3	51.2	10.5	47	68.1
Perry city	7,724	7,676	-0.6	7,599	58.7	4.6	0.2	1.6	34.9	25.9	16.2	35.4	58.7	9.8	3,109	86.3
Persia city	319	287	-10.0	313	96.5	0.0	0.0	0.0	3.5	27.5	18.2	33.4	47.4	16.3	117	88.0
Peterson city	332	309	-6.9	407	95.6	0.2	0.0	2.5	1.7	29.5	13.5	35.0	53.9	17.6	160	88.8
Pierson city	366	354	-3.3	468	85.3	0.0	0.0	10.0	4.7	37.0	10.7	29.6	35.6	10.0	161	85.1
Pilot Mound city	173	168	-2.9	194	100.0	0.0	0.0	0.0	0.0	7.2	42.3	60.6	64.0	4.5	116	87.9
Pioneer city	23	22	-4.3	4	100.0	0.0	0.0	0.0	0.0	0.0	0.0	49.5	66.7	0.0	1	100.0
Pisgah city	251	240	-4.4	261	98.9	0.0	0.0	1.1	0.0	21.8	27.2	52.1	56.2	11.3	127	84.3
Plainfield city	436	414	-5.0	517	99.0	0.0	0.0	1.0	0.0	19.9	13.5	33.7	43.6	11.6	211	82.0
Plano city	70	67	-4.3	64	87.5	0.0	0.0	12.5	0.0	28.1	26.6	38.0	42.2	13.3	27	66.7
Pleasant Hill city	8,799	10,019	13.9	9,871	82.2	2.7	5.3	2.8	6.9	26.9	15.3	38.3	36.2	33.6	3,594	94.0
Pleasanton city	48	44	-8.3	35	100.0	0.0	0.0	0.0	0.0	20.0	8.6	35.8	53.8	23.1	15	86.7
Pleasant Plain city	93	98	5.4	87	100.0	0.0	0.0	0.0	0.0	17.2	32.2	50.2	67.7	10.8	32	84.4
Pleasantville city	1,692	1,696	0.2	1,859	87.1	0.0	0.4	3.5	9.0	30.5	15.2	35.4	40.9	25.8	761	94.0
Plover city	77	69	-10.4	87	100.0	0.0	0.0	0.0	0.0	40.2	13.8	32.3	57.1	2.0	34	58.8
Plymouth city	382	362	-5.2	447	91.9	1.3	0.4	1.3	4.9	31.3	13.2	38.3	33.9	8.4	161	89.4
Pocahontas city	1,789	1,634	-8.7	1,574	96.6	0.3	3.1	0.0	0.0	16.9	26.7	53.7	52.9	11.4	807	86.1
Polk City city	3,418	4,961	45.1	4,625	98.3	0.5	0.0	0.9	0.4	34.6	7.7	33.9	19.8	45.1	1,464	100.0
Pomeroy city	662	613	-7.4	506	97.2	0.0	0.0	1.8	1.0	17.2	36.6	56.3	49.6	15.0	245	86.1
Popejoy city	79	75	-5.1	54	100.0	0.0	0.0	0.0	0.0	25.9	18.5	25.8	51.6	6.5	19	89.5
Portland CDP	35	-	-	30	100.0	0.0	0.0	0.0	0.0	0.0	20.0	64.4	30.0	23.3	15	100.0
Portsmouth city	195	178	-8.7	126	100.0	0.0	0.0	0.0	0.0	19.8	16.7	50.5	52.0	19.4	65	78.5
Postville city	2,225	2,053	-7.7	2,547	46.1	10.7	2.2	3.5	37.6	36.0	12.1	30.7	66.8	9.2	827	76.1
Prairieburg city	178	188	5.6	176	99.4	0.0	0.0	0.6	0.0	17.6	20.5	49.5	52.3	12.1	78	79.5
Prairie City city	1,680	1,718	2.3	2,091	97.4	1.1	0.2	0.1	1.2	32.6	9.4	36.3	36.5	29.3	757	94.5
Prescott city	257	237	-7.8	196	100.0	0.0	0.0	0.0	0.0	21.4	29.1	47.0	43.7	16.7	92	83.7
Preston city	1,010	959	-5.0	1,000	92.4	0.0	0.0	1.3	6.3	23.2	19.2	37.6	52.7	10.8	387	85.8
Primghar city	909	856	-5.8	882	88.2	1.4	2.2	2.2	6.1	23.8	18.8	42.6	44.7	23.3	395	93.7
Princeton city	886	946	6.8	1,102	90.0	0.0	0.0	8.3	1.7	15.9	15.2	44.4	45.6	20.7	425	81.9
Promise City city	109	108	-0.9	78	100.0	0.0	0.0	0.0	0.0	16.7	23.1	55.5	71.4	6.3	47	70.2
Protivin city	283	270	-4.6	391	99.7	0.3	0.0	0.0	0.0	29.2	21.0	40.0	48.7	18.4	173	81.5
Pulaski city	260	289	11.2	364	96.7	0.0	0.0	0.0	3.3	30.2	11.3	31.9	57.7	12.6	130	87.7
Quasqueton city	554	564	1.8	578	98.4	0.3	0.0	0.0	1.2	24.7	13.8	37.6	62.6	9.0	225	87.6
Quimby city	319	292	-8.5	388	89.9	0.0	0.0	0.0	10.1	22.7	16.8	41.6	57.5	6.9	175	86.3
Radcliffe city	545	524	-3.9	633	96.1	0.0	0.0	0.0	3.9	25.9	13.7	43.1	43.7	17.1	254	85.8
Rake city	227	209	-7.9	161	96.3	0.0	0.0	0.0	3.7	16.8	28.6	54.2	62.1	15.2	92	69.6
Ralston city	77	73	-5.2	64	85.9	0.0	0.0	0.0	14.1	25.0	18.8	34.5	61.5	10.3	33	90.9
Randalia city	68	56	-17.6	73	97.3	0.0	0.0	0.0	2.7	26.0	16.4	41.8	73.1	3.8	29	96.6
Randall city	173	163	-5.8	170	81.8	0.0	0.0	2.4	15.9	24.1	14.7	35.0	23.7	25.4	73	86.3
Randolph city	168	155	-7.7	201	77.6	22.4	0.0	0.0	0.0	33.3	14.9	37.7	54.7	12.5	66	90.9
Rathbun city	89	86	-3.4	57	100.0	0.0	0.0	0.0	0.0	0.0	42.1	63.6	36.4	27.3	38	92.1
Raymond city	788	793	0.6	691	100.0	0.0	0.0	0.0	0.0	23.0	19.4	44.8	46.5	19.9	283	87.3
Readlyn city	810	846	4.4	780	94.7	0.0	0.4	0.0	4.9	26.4	22.3	40.3	44.1	21.9	299	90.6
Reasnor city	152	155	2.0	121	100.0	0.0	0.0	0.0	0.0	24.8	28.1	45.7	47.6	17.9	50	82.0
Redding city	82	78	-4.9	76	100.0	0.0	0.0	0.0	0.0	38.2	21.1	30.9	65.9	6.8	26	76.9
Redfield city	831	816	-1.8	622	98.1	0.0	0.0	1.9	0.0	22.7	25.2	45.1	57.8	6.3	260	87.7
Red Oak city	5,742	5,276	-8.1	5,362	90.8	0.0	0.0	3.1	6.1	23.4	20.9	42.3	50.7	17.6	2,469	87.2
Reinbeck city	1,677	1,626	-3.0	1,610	97.8	0.0	0.0	0.8	1.4	20.2	24.2	45.1	38.0	27.9	713	85.7
Rembrandt city	204	194	-4.9	180	84.4	1.7	0.0	0.0	13.9	17.2	20.0	46.7	59.3	6.5	80	82.5
Remsen city	1,663	1,617	-2.8	1,833	91.2	0.0	0.0	3.6	5.2	25.6	18.9	41.4	48.7	18.0	734	83.7
Renwick city	242	262	8.3	274	93.1	3.3	0.0	2.9	0.7	21.2	15.7	36.6	45.5	11.1	123	87.8
Rhodes city	305	297	-2.6	260	96.2	1.2	0.0	0.0	2.7	26.5	11.9	43.5	68.1	7.6	98	89.8
Riceville city	785	764	-2.7	889	85.0	0.0	0.0	6.0	9.0	21.0	21.4	38.1	53.1	18.9	397	81.4
Richland city	584	574	-1.7	595	96.1	0.0	0.0	1.2	2.7	18.8	21.5	46.8	44.0	17.2	264	85.2
Rickardsville city	180	176	-2.2	187	100.0	0.0	0.0	0.0	0.0	21.9	25.1	38.3	43.2	18.9	69	89.9
Ricketts city	145	135	-6.9	118	96.6	0.0	0.0	0.0	3.4	22.9	24.6	56.5	63.4	3.7	47	78.7
Ridgeway city	307	287	-6.5	256	93.4	0.0	2.7	3.1	0.8	21.5	11.7	36.4	44.1	16.4	121	89.3
Rinard city	52	50	-3.8	33	100.0	0.0	0.0	0.0	0.0	12.1	39.4	53.5	55.6	7.4	21	85.7
Ringsted city	426	370	-13.1	499	94.0	0.2	0.0	0.8	5.0	22.8	13.4	41.7	32.4	14.9	236	91.1
Rippey city	292	273	-6.5	233	75.5	11.2	0.0	5.6	7.7	21.5	14.6	33.5	64.7	13.3	102	91.2
Riverdale city	405	435	7.4	477	85.5	0.0	1.3	3.1	10.1	21.4	15.5	41.9	29.9	28.4	172	93.6
Riverside city	993	1,022	2.9	1,115	97.1	0.0	0.0	1.9	1.0	21.9	13.5	41.3	43.6	24.0	503	89.9
River Sioux CDP	59	-	-	48	100.0	0.0	0.0	0.0	0.0	20.8	47.9	59.8	71.1	15.8	27	77.8
Riverton city	304	279	-8.2	261	96.6	0.0	0.0	1.9	1.5	22.2	20.3	40.7	44.2	14.0	115	76.5
Robins city	3,168	3,537	11.6	3,457	93.0	2.8	2.9	0.0	1.3	25.3	13.4	43.7	16.2	55.5	1,215	96.0
Rochester CDP	133	-	-	83	100.0	0.0	0.0	0.0	0.0	0.0	16.9	41.5	15.5	0.0	72	100.0
Rock Falls city	150	143	-4.7	136	95.6	0.0	2.9	0.0	1.5	19.1	19.1	44.0	40.2	12.4	59	88.1
Rockford city	860	822	-4.4	818	96.3	2.2	0.0	0.4	1.1	23.2	21.1	42.7	34.7	23.2	382	79.6
Rock Rapids city	2,547	2,522		2,545	97.5	0.3	0.3	1.1	0.9	26.8	20.9	39.4	39.8	27.7	1,016	88.1
Rock Valley city	3,459	3,854	11.4	3,812	83.8	0.0	0.4	0.4	15.3	32.0	13.1	33.6	50.3	24.1	1,384	87.7
Rockwell city	1,039	990	-4.7	888	99.1	0.7	0.0	0.0	0.2	24.9	22.5	45.7	36.3	17.9	390	84.4
Rockwell City city	2,220	2,082	-6.2	2,258	91.1	3.1	0.4	3.5	1.9	14.8	18.3	40.6	52.8	11.8	800	81.3
Rodman city	43	41	-4.7	22	100.0	0.0	0.0	0.0	0.0	9.1	45.5	60.0	50.0	11.1	12	100.0
Rodney city	60	57	-5.0	45	93.3	0.0	0.0	6.7	0.0	4.4	26.7	63.1	64.9	2.7	27	55.6
Roland city	1,284	1,254	-2.3	1,408	99.2	0.0	0.0	0.8	0.0	30.3	8.5	34.9	26.6	30.2	560	96.4
Rolfe city	584	532	-8.9	572	96.3	0.0	0.0	0.0	3.7	24.3	23.3	42.4	50.5	13.6	244	91.0
Rome city	116	116	0.0	101	100.0	0.0	0.0	0.0	0.0	24.8	12.9	39.1	66.2	4.2	43	81.4
Rose Hill city	166	163	-1.8	126	89.7	0.0	0.0	10.3	0.0	6.3	16.7	51.0	53.2	11.9	62	67.7
Roseville CDP	49	-	-	-	-	-	-	-	-	-	-	-	-	-	-	-
Rossie city	70	68	-2.9	33	100.0	0.0	0.0	0.0	0.0	12.1	18.2	61.5	18.5	11.1	18	38.9
Rowan city	158	150	-5.1	140	93.6	0.0	4.3	0.0	2.1	21.4	32.9	39.8	58.7	13.5	70	94.3
Rowley city	269	270	0.4	272	98.2	0.7	0.0	0.0	1.1	19.1	21.3	45.8	56.1	9.6	107	91.6
Royal city	446	409	-8.3	316	92.4	1.3	0.0	6.3	0.0	15.2	20.3	47.8	41.5	15.7	157	92.4
Rudd city	369	346	-6.2	519	89.2	1.2	0.8	4.8	4.0	21.4	14.5	39.4	45.1	8.4	219	89.0
Runnells city	507	504	-0.6	481	94.6	0.6	0.0	3.3	1.5	28.3	8.9	33.4	38.5	15.1	174	92.0
Russell city	554	536	-3.2	593	100.0	0.0	0.0	0.0	0.0	27.0	18.7	38.6	58.5	10.5	237	87.8
Ruthven city	734	682	-7.1	751	97.3	0.0	0.9	0.7	1.1	28.0	22.9	39.5	46.4	18.3	309	79.6
Rutland city	125	122	-2.4	158	98.1	0.0	0.0	1.9	0.0	15.8	25.9	49.7	60.5	1.7	78	85.9

1 May be of any race.

Table A. All Places — **Population and Housing**

STATE City, town, township, borough, or CDP (county if applicable)	Population: 2010 census total population	Population: 2019 estimated population	Population: Percent change 2010-2019	Population: ACS total population estimate 2015-2019	Race and Hispanic or Latino origin (percent): White alone, not Hispanic or Latino	Race and Hispanic or Latino origin (percent): Black alone, not Hispanic or Latino	Race and Hispanic or Latino origin (percent): Asian alone, not Hispanic or Latino	Race and Hispanic or Latino origin (percent): All other races or 2 or more races, not Hispanic or Latino	Race and Hispanic or Latino origin (percent): Hispanic or Latino[1]	Age (percent): Under 18 years old	Age (percent): Age 65 years and older	Median age	Educational attainment of persons age 25 and older: Percent High school diploma or less	Educational attainment of persons age 25 and older: Percent Bachelor's degree or more	Occupied housing units: Total	Occupied housing units: Percent with a computer
	1	2	3	4	5	6	7	8	9	10	11	12	13	14	15	16
IOWA—Con.																
Ryan city	365	346	-5.2	418	97.1	0.0	0.2	2.6	0.0	22.2	23.2	46.3	60.7	15.2	179	84.9
Sabula city	588	554	-5.8	491	98.4	0.4	1.2	0.0	0.0	17.7	21.0	40.7	57.7	11.7	239	83.3
Sac City city	2,222	2,068	-6.9	2,001	97.5	0.1	0.0	1.1	1.3	22.8	28.0	46.8	47.1	20.8	927	87.3
Sageville city	104	101	-2.9	55	94.5	0.0	0.0	5.5	0.0	12.7	30.9	55.8	52.2	19.6	28	89.3
St. Ansgar city	1,107	1,120	1.2	1,159	97.5	0.0	2.1	0.0	0.4	26.1	22.8	41.4	43.0	24.3	464	90.3
St. Anthony city	102	99	-2.9	36	94.4	0.0	0.0	5.6	0.0	11.1	8.3	45.5	58.6	0.0	25	64.0
St. Benedict CDP	39	-	-	22	100.0	0.0	0.0	0.0	0.0	0.0	13.6	57.5	50.0	36.4	21	90.5
St. Charles city	649	619	-4.6	709	96.8	2.4	0.0	0.3	0.6	24.0	16.4	36.5	44.0	16.5	288	93.4
St. Donatus city	137	129	-5.8	103	99.0	0.0	0.0	1.0	0.0	11.7	30.1	55.7	67.0	11.0	55	78.2
St. Joseph CDP	61	-	-	104	100.0	0.0	0.0	0.0	0.0	49.0	12.5	25.1	45.3	24.5	27	100.0
St. Lucas city	145	136	-6.2	148	99.3	0.0	0.0	0.7	0.0	15.5	21.6	41.9	55.6	25.9	69	73.9
St. Marys city	127	127	0.0	191	86.9	2.1	0.0	9.9	1.0	19.4	17.8	46.2	36.8	17.6	71	93.0
St. Olaf city	108	101	-6.5	160	86.9	4.4	0.0	8.8	0.0	37.5	8.1	30.0	58.1	8.6	50	96.0
St. Paul city	129	124	-3.9	85	100.0	0.0	0.0	0.0	0.0	18.8	14.1	34.7	32.8	11.9	35	94.3
Salem city	387	384	-0.8	494	93.1	0.0	0.8	2.0	4.0	23.9	16.0	40.0	50.6	9.0	192	85.4
Salix city	371	387	4.3	410	97.8	0.0	0.0	1.2	1.0	24.6	16.3	41.9	41.9	14.8	182	90.1
Sanborn city	1,404	1,381	-1.6	1,582	96.1	0.0	0.1	1.8	2.0	29.1	20.4	38.7	55.9	17.2	658	86.0
Sandyville city	51	53	3.9	87	100.0	0.0	0.0	0.0	0.0	27.6	6.9	31.8	69.2	15.4	35	62.9
Saylorville CDP	3,301	-	-	4,009	72.6	16.6	0.7	4.4	5.8	36.5	15.7	38.1	19.5	26.2	1,332	91.4
Scarville city	72	67	-6.9	62	100.0	0.0	0.0	0.0	0.0	14.5	16.1	60.3	47.1	29.4	35	77.1
Schaller city	772	723	-6.3	720	76.1	0.0	0.0	1.1	22.8	22.9	18.6	41.7	54.7	15.4	325	86.8
Schleswig city	882	857	-2.8	857	90.0	0.9	1.6	2.1	5.4	19.1	16.0	43.8	50.5	15.3	390	85.1
Scranton city	557	524	-5.9	558	98.4	0.0	0.0	0.0	1.6	20.1	23.1	48.6	51.2	11.1	273	87.5
Searsboro city	148	147	-0.7	166	99.4	0.0	0.6	0.0	0.0	31.3	9.6	35.8	55.7	7.5	67	80.6
Sergeant Bluff city	4,310	5,127	19.0	4,798	88.3	0.0	0.4	5.0	6.3	33.6	8.3	35.0	23.0	39.2	1,676	97.3
Sexton CDP	37	-	-	-	-	-	-	-	-	-	-	-	-	-	-	-
Seymour city	701	701	0.0	567	95.8	0.7	0.0	1.9	1.6	19.9	29.1	53.7	59.9	12.0	290	77.6
Shambaugh city	189	179	-5.3	142	98.6	0.0	0.0	1.4	0.0	27.5	22.5	40.8	39.0	9.0	61	88.5
Shannon City city	71	69	-2.8	80	96.3	0.0	0.0	0.0	3.8	22.5	13.8	37.5	71.2	5.1	34	88.2
Sharpsburg city	89	85	-4.5	123	91.9	0.0	0.0	1.6	6.5	28.5	8.9	25.3	47.0	4.5	43	88.4
Sheffield city	1,174	1,106	-5.8	1,190	97.7	0.0	0.0	1.2	1.1	22.1	25.2	45.9	38.7	15.1	480	83.5
Shelby city	640	612	-4.4	651	98.0	0.0	0.0	1.2	0.8	18.9	12.4	37.2	47.0	14.6	304	87.5
Sheldahl city	319	321	0.6	334	98.5	0.0	0.0	1.5	0.0	25.7	18.0	40.0	40.4	28.5	138	91.3
Sheldon city	5,196	5,082	-2.2	5,128	87.7	1.2	2.0	0.3	8.7	23.5	16.8	39.7	47.1	20.3	2,232	83.0
Shell Rock city	1,293	1,275	-1.4	1,445	96.5	0.0	0.9	0.0	2.6	23.5	17.7	37.4	41.5	17.8	620	88.7
Shellsburg city	994	972	-2.2	959	93.2	1.8	0.0	2.5	2.5	17.0	17.1	50.5	47.3	16.8	393	91.1
Shenandoah city	5,153	4,820	-6.5	4,897	88.9	1.5	0.2	3.2	6.1	21.4	21.0	41.1	45.9	25.2	2,111	86.0
Sherrill city	179	178	-0.6	223	96.4	1.3	0.0	2.2	0.0	26.5	18.8	43.9	70.3	15.8	82	79.3
Shueyville city	562	655	16.5	772	80.1	0.0	14.5	4.1	1.3	33.8	6.7	38.5	17.0	48.5	249	98.8
Sibley city	2,798	2,574	-8.0	2,611	86.4	1.1	0.2	0.7	11.6	24.0	25.7	41.9	49.9	18.4	1,104	82.7
Sidney city	1,135	1,047	-7.8	1,067	86.2	0.5	0.0	4.2	9.1	24.6	21.1	40.3	52.5	14.5	431	88.2
Sigourney city	2,059	2,017	-2.0	1,867	94.6	0.6	0.2	3.4	1.2	18.9	28.3	50.1	47.9	20.7	865	84.5
Silver City city	245	246	0.4	241	99.6	0.0	0.4	0.0	0.0	26.1	19.9	38.8	48.2	16.5	93	87.1
Sioux Center city	7,036	7,605	8.1	7,534	81.4	0.5	1.3	1.6	15.1	27.4	15.7	30.1	34.9	43.1	2,437	93.1
Sioux City city	82,693	82,651	-0.1	82,531	68.3	3.9	3.4	4.7	19.6	26.4	13.8	34.4	47.4	22.1	31,110	87.8
Sioux Rapids city	775	744	-4.0	833	88.5	1.0	0.0	1.4	9.1	24.7	23.2	37.2	49.3	17.8	350	84.0
Slater city	1,491	1,458	-2.2	1,585	92.2	0.0	0.4	0.9	6.5	30.7	13.8	33.5	24.0	35.6	609	97.0
Sloan city	973	987	1.4	1,215	95.6	0.0	0.0	2.3	2.1	28.5	14.2	36.8	30.3	25.5	464	88.1
Smithland city	224	227	1.3	200	98.5	0.0	1.5	0.0	0.0	24.0	24.0	41.7	68.1	5.8	89	80.9
Soldier city	174	164	-5.7	210	94.8	0.0	0.0	1.4	3.8	20.5	17.1	34.6	38.3	14.8	98	94.9
Solon city	2,085	2,690	29.0	2,615	94.8	0.7	0.0	0.6	4.0	35.3	14.2	33.4	24.5	42.5	886	94.0
Somers city	113	106	-6.2	101	76.2	0.0	2.0	11.9	9.9	27.7	20.8	39.9	34.2	16.4	46	80.4
South Amana CDP	159	-	-	117	100.0	0.0	0.0	0.0	0.0	0.0	5.1	57.3	6.0	41.9	66	100.0
South English city	212	207	-2.4	300	93.0	0.0	0.0	0.0	7.0	24.3	11.0	32.9	59.4	17.8	128	87.5
Spencer city	11,247	10,952	-2.6	11,052	93.1	0.4	0.9	2.7	3.0	23.0	22.1	43.5	41.1	22.3	5,001	89.6
Spillville city	370	344	-7.0	474	94.7	0.0	0.0	0.0	5.3	19.8	29.7	39.3	57.3	18.0	262	67.6
Spirit Lake city	4,863	5,155	6.0	5,069	96.1	0.3	0.6	1.1	2.0	18.9	21.1	42.5	27.4	37.5	2,552	88.8
Spragueville city	80	77	-3.8	135	99.3	0.0	0.0	0.0	0.7	45.2	14.8	25.1	66.2	4.4	40	62.5
Springbrook city	154	146	-5.2	149	100.0	0.0	0.0	0.0	0.0	22.8	16.8	48.9	50.5	10.1	56	83.9
Spring Hill city	63	65	3.2	76	98.7	0.0	0.0	1.3	0.0	15.8	10.5	36.0	67.4	8.7	25	84.0
Springville city	1,068	1,137	6.5	1,092	98.3	0.0	0.6	0.6	0.5	26.3	11.3	36.1	38.5	24.2	417	98.3
Stacyville city	490	463	-5.5	472	98.7	0.6	0.0	0.0	0.6	18.0	33.5	45.6	57.6	8.8	218	76.1
Stanhope city	429	396	-7.7	405	98.3	0.0	0.0	1.2	0.5	18.8	17.8	39.8	46.4	17.0	193	79.3
Stanley city	123	120	-2.4	130	99.2	0.0	0.0	0.0	0.8	25.4	12.3	29.8	57.8	20.5	49	87.8
Stanton city	689	643	-6.7	629	96.3	1.7	0.0	1.0	1.0	21.1	27.3	53.9	31.0	25.7	278	88.8
Stanwood city	684	658	-3.8	655	96.9	1.1	0.0	0.0	2.0	24.0	17.7	39.8	48.1	14.7	243	86.8
State Center city	1,468	1,436	-2.2	1,661	93.5	1.4	0.7	0.5	3.9	33.6	13.6	35.0	39.9	16.0	603	92.9
Steamboat Rock city	310	302	-2.6	283	79.2	1.4	0.0	12.4	7.1	21.2	16.3	48.8	46.9	11.7	136	77.2
Stockport city	296	276	-6.8	393	95.9	0.0	0.0	1.5	2.5	30.8	6.9	27.0	49.8	12.4	120	87.5
Stockton city	197	191	-3.0	160	85.0	0.0	1.9	9.4	3.8	23.8	11.3	37.2	42.5	10.4	69	85.5
Stone City CDP	192	-	-	130	100.0	0.0	0.0	0.0	0.0	11.5	36.9	61.6	63.5	24.3	57	100.0
Storm Lake city	10,641	10,322	-3.0	10,558	37.5	3.9	18.0	3.4	37.1	28.3	10.3	30.2	59.4	16.0	3,626	92.4
Story City city	3,431	3,320	-3.2	3,377	94.4	0.4	1.0	2.5	1.7	20.6	25.5	45.5	28.7	29.5	1,462	87.5
Stout city	218	212	-2.8	187	100.0	0.0	0.0	0.0	0.0	25.7	12.8	42.9	42.0	22.9	70	88.6
Stratford city	743	699	-5.9	616	99.0	0.2	0.0	0.0	0.8	18.8	30.7	50.4	47.7	16.6	261	75.9
Strawberry Point city	1,279	1,218	-4.8	1,462	97.9	0.0	0.8	0.0	1.4	24.5	24.5	39.9	49.7	10.9	620	81.9
Struble city	78	80	2.6	121	96.7	0.0	0.0	3.3	0.0	24.8	4.1	25.8	60.3	4.8	40	95.0
Stuart city	1,648	1,728	4.9	1,573	96.0	0.0	0.6	0.4	3.0	20.9	24.5	45.9	47.6	17.3	692	81.6
Sully city	821	831	1.2	828	96.6	0.0	0.2	3.1	0.0	22.6	19.9	43.0	45.7	22.3	330	91.2
Sumner city	2,028	1,962	-3.3	2,175	97.8	0.2	0.0	1.0	1.0	23.7	22.1	42.5	45.4	22.6	903	81.4
Sun Valley Lake CDP	161	-	-	220	100.0	0.0	0.0	0.0	0.0	3.6	69.1	68.5	29.3	38.9	111	100.0
Superior city	130	119	-8.5	221	87.8	0.0	0.0	1.8	10.4	27.1	13.6	33.1	56.1	1.5	80	91.3
Sutherland city	649	596	-8.2	568	97.2	1.1	0.0	0.5	1.2	16.9	32.6	53.1	53.2	12.8	289	86.9
Swaledale city	166	158	-4.8	105	100.0	0.0	0.0	0.0	0.0	14.3	25.7	49.8	59.5	3.6	58	75.9
Swan city	72	75	4.2	92	60.9	7.6	0.0	0.0	31.5	41.3	2.2	21.4	46.3	9.8	28	75.0
Swea City city	536	507	-5.4	660	81.5	0.0	0.0	9.7	8.8	32.7	15.6	32.6	51.8	17.1	293	85.7
Swisher city	880	953	8.3	887	96.2	0.0	0.0	3.2	0.7	23.9	13.8	40.4	28.0	34.2	362	93.9
Tabor city	1,044	989	-5.3	1,257	94.7	0.0	0.1	4.8	0.4	24.5	19.6	40.3	43.7	18.0	462	88.5
Tama city	2,877	2,732	-5.0	2,769	55.9	2.1	1.1	6.3	34.6	28.0	16.4	35.9	64.5	7.7	1,021	86.9
Templeton city	351	334	-4.8	319	99.7	0.0	0.0	0.3	0.0	14.1	25.1	50.3	46.0	14.5	151	89.4
Tennant city	68	62	-8.8	70	100.0	0.0	0.0	0.0	0.0	22.9	22.9	54.7	59.3	9.3	34	55.9
Terril city	368	336	-8.7	454	89.4	1.5	0.7	5.1	3.3	21.8	12.3	41.9	43.8	17.4	203	93.6

1 May be of any race.

Table A. All Places — **Population and Housing**

STATE City, town, township, borough, or CDP (county if applicable)	Population: 2010 census total population	Population: 2019 estimated population	Population: Percent change 2010-2019	Population: ACS total population estimate 2015-2019	Race and Hispanic or Latino origin (percent): White alone, not Hispanic or Latino	Black alone, not Hispanic or Latino	Asian alone, not Hispanic or Latino	All other races or 2 or more races, not Hispanic or Latino	Hispanic or Latino[1]	Age (percent): Under 18 years old	Age 65 years and older	Median age	Educational attainment of persons age 25 and older: Percent High school diploma or less	Percent Bachelor's degree or more	Occupied housing units: Total	Percent with a computer
	1	2	3	4	5	6	7	8	9	10	11	12	13	14	15	16
IOWA—Con.																
Thayer city	59	55	-6.8	33	100.0	0.0	0.0	0.0	0.0	15.2	3.0	49.3	67.9	0.0	16	87.5
Thompson city	502	469	-6.6	382	86.9	0.0	0.0	0.8	12.3	19.1	30.6	52.4	50.9	11.7	206	73.8
Thor city	186	181	-2.7	208	86.1	0.0	1.9	11.5	0.5	29.3	9.1	37.3	56.2	9.1	74	89.2
Thornburg city	67	62	-7.5	48	85.4	0.0	0.0	0.0	14.6	10.4	16.7	56.0	38.2	35.3	29	89.7
Thornton city	422	402	-4.7	411	92.2	0.7	0.7	1.0	5.4	22.1	19.5	33.9	31.9	19.4	191	85.3
Thurman city	230	214	-7.0	137	98.5	0.0	0.0	0.0	1.5	39.4	8.0	27.8	61.8	5.3	46	89.1
Tiffin city	1,947	4,157	113.5	3,351	83.2	1.9	2.6	4.0	8.3	27.8	10.0	32.7	25.4	34.6	1,307	94.5
Tingley city	184	173	-6.0	117	86.3	0.0	0.0	9.4	4.3	15.4	29.9	56.3	40.4	19.1	55	85.5
Tipton city	3,216	3,223	0.2	3,207	94.4	1.8	0.0	1.2	2.6	21.8	20.4	40.4	50.4	18.0	1,296	87.3
Titonka city	479	443	-7.5	481	95.0	0.0	0.0	0.0	5.0	22.9	24.3	39.0	48.3	11.1	204	89.7
Toeterville CDP	48	-	-	40	100.0	0.0	0.0	0.0	0.0	0.0	60.0	72.2	20.0	20.0	40	40.0
Toledo city	2,341	2,143	-8.5	2,303	75.9	1.2	0.4	8.3	14.2	29.7	20.6	38.6	57.7	12.0	924	88.1
Toronto city	124	117	-5.6	111	98.2	0.0	0.0	0.0	1.8	16.2	25.2	49.7	70.6	2.4	49	85.7
Traer city	1,703	1,596	-6.3	1,547	97.1	0.0	0.0	1.0	1.9	21.0	29.4	47.0	40.2	24.2	669	87.3
Treynor city	923	965	4.6	1,022	97.5	0.0	0.0	0.0	2.5	27.9	13.5	36.2	25.3	39.8	390	90.3
Tripoli city	1,315	1,360	3.4	1,302	95.8	0.0	1.4	0.5	2.3	24.0	18.7	40.4	42.2	21.4	569	85.8
Truesdale city	81	77	-4.9	93	72.0	0.0	0.0	0.0	28.0	25.8	11.8	38.5	53.3	5.0	40	87.5
Truro city	486	491	1.0	483	93.6	2.5	0.0	2.5	1.4	33.5	9.3	27.6	40.2	13.8	167	93.4
Turin city	68	63	-7.4	98	93.9	0.0	0.0	6.1	0.0	41.8	17.3	29.5	64.2	18.9	36	75.0
Twin Lakes CDP	334	-	-	235	100.0	0.0	0.0	0.0	0.0	5.1	32.8	59.0	14.8	39.5	119	100.0
Udell city	47	43	-8.5	54	96.3	0.0	0.0	0.0	3.7	22.2	9.3	40.0	33.3	7.1	25	96.0
Underwood city	938	956	1.9	854	94.4	0.0	0.0	1.6	4.0	27.0	12.6	36.9	24.9	27.4	341	94.1
Union city	399	381	-4.5	380	94.2	0.0	0.0	5.3	0.5	15.5	31.3	57.9	50.5	14.5	178	72.5
Unionville city	99	95	-4.0	86	93.0	0.0	0.0	7.0	0.0	20.9	26.7	48.0	36.7	11.7	44	90.9
University Heights city	1,035	1,026	-0.9	1,159	82.1	5.6	3.7	3.5	5.2	17.6	11.6	28.8	2.0	86.2	531	98.7
University Park city	487	469	-3.7	429	85.8	2.1	0.2	11.9	0.0	36.6	10.7	29.8	40.7	20.7	144	93.8
Urbana city	1,456	1,494	2.6	1,517	98.2	0.0	0.1	0.5	1.3	27.4	9.7	32.9	36.5	26.1	546	94.0
Urbandale city	39,461	44,379	12.5	43,441	86.0	4.0	4.5	1.9	3.7	26.6	14.1	38.3	21.3	48.9	16,733	96.9
Ute city	374	339	-9.4	298	95.3	0.0	0.0	1.3	3.4	13.8	30.2	53.8	55.3	12.3	162	76.5
Vail city	438	417	-4.8	532	60.9	0.9	0.0	1.7	36.5	28.2	15.2	41.5	67.8	7.0	227	76.2
Valeria city	57	59	3.5	39	97.4	0.0	2.6	0.0	0.0	30.8	10.3	44.8	37.5	16.7	15	80.0
Van Horne city	685	656	-4.2	926	97.3	0.0	0.2	2.4	0.1	30.9	7.3	30.8	37.1	22.0	348	94.3
Van Meter city	1,030	1,292	25.4	1,239	93.9	1.5	1.2	2.0	1.4	28.8	9.4	36.0	39.0	25.9	473	94.7
Van Wert city	225	204	-9.3	142	96.5	0.0	0.0	3.5	0.0	9.2	33.1	59.6	56.7	7.5	73	82.2
Varina city	71	65	-8.5	47	78.7	0.0	0.0	0.0	21.3	34.0	29.8	45.5	67.7	9.7	24	83.3
Ventura city	717	713	-0.6	865	96.9	0.0	0.0	0.0	3.1	23.2	14.1	38.9	32.8	31.5	340	92.6
Victor city	893	868	-2.8	796	98.5	0.5	0.0	0.6	0.4	21.4	19.1	46.1	57.0	14.1	369	81.3
Villisca city	1,252	1,142	-8.8	1,243	97.6	0.0	0.0	1.8	0.6	24.0	23.3	44.0	45.2	13.4	567	88.7
Vincent city	174	161	-7.5	141	92.2	0.0	0.0	0.7	7.1	12.8	13.5	43.7	38.5	14.7	66	86.4
Vining city	50	48	-4.0	64	100.0	0.0	0.0	0.0	0.0	15.6	40.6	59.0	59.6	11.5	36	94.4
Vinton city	5,257	5,075	-3.5	5,103	95.4	0.5	0.6	1.2	2.3	21.8	22.3	41.8	48.8	25.8	2,068	87.4
Volga city	208	196	-5.8	193	100.0	0.0	0.0	0.0	0.0	19.7	26.9	51.1	54.0	16.7	89	83.1
Wadena city	262	240	-8.4	248	95.2	0.0	0.0	4.8	0.0	25.0	22.6	46.7	43.5	5.9	106	82.1
Wahpeton city	342	345	0.9	396	99.5	0.0	0.0	0.5	0.0	7.8	50.5	65.3	25.0	45.7	213	88.3
Walcott city	1,619	1,634	0.9	1,672	91.7	0.0	1.2	1.7	5.4	23.1	18.8	39.5	46.5	21.1	667	85.2
Walford city	1,459	1,445		1,385	93.4	0.9	0.1	4.0	1.5	26.5	11.6	42.4	23.5	34.2	516	93.8
Walker city	789	789	0.0	831	99.2	0.0	0.0	0.8	0.0	27.0	13.6	38.4	45.4	17.0	305	85.6
Wallingford city	195	173	-11.3	244	88.5	0.0	0.0	0.0	11.5	26.6	17.2	42.8	49.1	9.2	108	90.7
Wall Lake city	819	769	-6.1	731	99.3	0.0	0.0	0.7	0.0	22.6	29.1	49.6	49.5	12.7	317	82.3
Walnut city	785	769	-2.0	764	97.8	1.2	0.0	0.8	0.3	21.5	29.2	53.0	47.5	15.0	350	82.6
Wapello city	2,068	1,999	-3.3	2,005	83.2	0.7	0.0	2.9	13.2	24.7	17.7	40.6	49.6	12.5	766	89.9
Washburn CDP	876	-	-	643	100.0	0.0	0.0	0.0	0.0	14.3	24.7	46.9	52.8	18.9	307	91.2
Washington city	7,270	7,230	-0.6	7,313	85.3	1.7	1.4	2.3	9.3	23.8	21.5	41.4	51.1	19.5	3,023	88.7
Washta city	246	223	-9.3	164	97.0	0.0	1.2	1.8	0.0	16.5	31.7	51.6	60.7	12.3	84	84.5
Waterloo city	68,496	67,328	-1.7	67,912	70.8	16.6	2.2	3.6	6.9	22.9	16.0	36.8	45.3	23.4	28,311	86.5
Waterville city	145	144	-0.7	97	100.0	0.0	0.0	0.0	0.0	8.2	26.8	52.6	55.4	10.8	48	93.8
Watkins CDP	118	-	-	78	100.0	0.0	0.0	0.0	0.0	5.1	39.7	61.0	60.8	21.6	53	83.0
Waucoma city	261	245	-6.1	223	98.2	0.0	0.0	0.0	1.8	22.4	22.0	44.8	53.8	11.5	96	79.2
Waukee city	13,809	24,089	74.4	20,785	87.4	2.4	3.2	1.6	5.4	30.0	10.3	33.2	16.7	54.4	8,037	94.6
Waukon city	3,904	3,625	-7.1	3,671	96.9	0.0	0.0	0.7	2.4	22.5	25.3	42.7	51.2	20.9	1,709	80.7
Waverly city	9,874	10,198	3.3	10,094	91.4	1.9	2.2	2.7	1.7	20.3	19.8	36.9	30.9	39.6	3,660	89.7
Wayland city	957	943	-1.5	1,066	89.4	0.0	1.5	2.7	6.4	24.2	21.1	38.5	46.0	17.6	410	80.5
Webb city	141	128	-9.2	207	83.6	0.0	0.0	0.0	16.4	24.2	14.0	27.3	57.1	13.4	80	91.3
Webster city	88	71	-19.3	138	97.1	0.0	0.0	0.0	2.9	19.6	12.3	39.3	45.0	10.0	59	93.2
Webster City city	8,072	7,671	-5.0	7,732	81.5	2.5	5.5	0.5	10.0	23.4	20.4	42.0	43.4	23.1	3,404	82.8
Weldon city	125	115	-8.0	142	97.9	0.0	0.0	0.0	2.1	12.0	24.6	57.5	71.2	16.1	77	66.2
Wellman city	1,411	1,395	-1.1	1,321	90.9	1.1	0.0	3.5	4.5	21.5	21.7	45.0	45.8	15.7	541	86.1
Wellsburg city	707	687	-2.8	737	95.1	1.1	0.0	3.3	0.5	23.9	19.1	41.4	39.2	21.3	328	84.8
Welton city	165	148	-10.3	133	97.7	0.0	0.0	0.8	1.5	10.5	26.3	45.3	45.9	6.4	63	87.3
Wesley city	390	365	-6.4	362	91.2	0.6	1.4	5.0	1.9	20.4	19.1	42.0	47.7	8.7	163	85.9
West Amana CDP	135	-	-	109	100.0	0.0	0.0	0.0	0.0	0.0	20.2	45.8	26.4	13.8	60	100.0
West Bend city	787	748	-5.0	659	89.7	0.0	0.0	0.0	10.3	15.5	39.9	56.3	39.5	16.9	304	80.9
West Branch city	2,329	2,492	7.0	2,249	92.8	1.0	1.5	1.9	2.8	23.8	22.5	43.7	32.0	31.1	952	93.4
West Burlington city	3,005	2,890	-3.8	2,927	85.1	5.8	3.7	3.9	1.5	21.1	20.9	39.6	39.9	18.2	1,242	88.3
West Chester city	146	147	0.7	82	92.7	0.0	0.0	7.3	0.0	15.9	24.4	53.0	64.6	9.2	39	84.6
West Des Moines city	56,707	67,899	19.7	65,606	79.8	4.1	7.5	2.6	6.0	22.8	13.7	36.7	18.6	55.4	28,836	96.1
Westfield city	132	128	-3.0	130	76.2	0.0	0.0	1.5	22.3	23.8	10.8	46.6	69.3	2.3	59	89.8
Westgate city	211	198	-6.2	224	98.7	0.0	0.0	0.0	1.3	23.2	9.8	41.5	56.6	5.9	92	89.1
West Liberty city	3,753	3,766	0.3	3,757	41.3	2.0	3.1	3.6	50.0	31.0	11.5	31.4	64.4	12.0	1,156	81.8
West Okoboji city	296	291	-1.7	309	96.1	0.0	2.9	0.0	1.0	8.1	49.2	64.8	26.6	38.8	164	88.4
Weston CDP	92	-	-	54	100.0	0.0	0.0	0.0	0.0	0.0	59.3	66.2	100.0	0.0	32	21.9
Westphalia city	127	118	-7.1	149	100.0	0.0	0.0	0.0	0.0	28.2	14.8	42.8	37.5	4.2	57	86.0
West Point city	973	930	-4.4	892	95.9	0.0	1.2	0.0	2.9	17.8	23.2	44.2	47.6	18.4	414	81.9
Westside city	299	289	-3.3	269	99.3	0.0	0.0	0.0	0.7	16.7	33.5	52.9	53.6	22.0	139	82.0
West Union city	2,477	2,305	-6.9	2,545	90.7	4.5	0.4	0.2	4.2	20.9	20.2	40.0	46.0	23.8	1,094	78.8
Westwood city	112	110	-1.8	97	100.0	0.0	0.0	0.0	0.0	15.5	29.9	58.4	11.3	56.3	44	84.1
What Cheer city	646	624	-3.4	756	90.7	3.2	0.0	0.0	6.1	31.9	19.3	38.3	63.7	7.3	304	79.9
Wheatland city	764	723	-5.4	715	89.5	0.0	0.6	2.0	8.0	32.4	20.6	36.1	51.0	14.9	264	86.7
Whiting city	762	723	-5.1	825	91.8	2.7	0.0	0.6	5.0	25.2	23.5	38.5	49.4	17.0	330	87.0
Whittemore city	504	476	-5.6	497	96.4	2.2	0.0	0.0	1.4	24.3	19.3	37.6	44.9	14.3	238	76.5
Whitten city	147	145	-1.4	190	93.7	0.0	0.0	0.0	6.3	29.5	8.4	47.5	40.8	0.8	73	97.3
Willey city	88	98	11.4	123	100.0	0.0	0.0	0.0	0.0	28.5	10.6	36.6	37.7	11.7	39	100.0

1 May be of any race.

Table A. All Places — **Population and Housing**

STATE City, town, township, borough, or CDP (county if applicable)	Population				Race and Hispanic or Latino origin (percent)					Age (percent)			Educational attainment of persons age 25 and older		Occupied housing units	
	2010 census total population	2019 estimated population	Percent change 2010-2019	ACS total population estimate 2015-2019	White alone, not Hispanic or Latino	Black alone, not Hispanic or Latino	Asian alone, not Hispanic or Latino	All other races or 2 or more races, not Hispanic or Latino	Hispanic or Latino[1]	Under 18 years old	Age 65 years and older	Median age	Percent High school diploma or less	Percent Bachelor's degree or more	Total	Percent with a computer
	1	2	3	4	5	6	7	8	9	10	11	12	13	14	15	16
IOWA—Con.																
Williams city	344	320	-7.0	364	89.8	0.0	0.3	0.8	9.1	20.9	19.2	39.0	44.7	16.0	145	78.6
Williamsburg city	3,065	3,164	3.2	3,152	96.7	0.0	1.0	2.3	0.0	19.9	18.2	39.8	38.1	23.0	1,338	89.9
Williamson city	152	154	1.3	179	98.9	0.0	0.0	0.0	1.1	38.5	7.3	30.3	68.2	0.9	65	87.7
Wilton city	2,788	2,824	1.3	2,843	95.5	0.2	0.0	1.9	2.4	22.1	16.7	40.5	42.3	24.8	1,201	91.2
Windsor Heights city	4,898	4,809	-1.8	4,953	87.7	1.3	3.0	1.0	7.0	19.2	26.2	42.7	27.0	42.7	2,143	90.3
Winfield city	1,134	1,088	-4.1	1,101	93.3	0.0	1.7	1.8	3.2	29.2	18.0	38.5	43.3	17.5	424	83.7
Winterset city	5,195	5,383	3.6	5,260	95.6	0.2	3.5	0.3	0.5	25.2	18.8	38.5	40.5	25.6	2,258	84.3
Winthrop city	850	849	-0.1	926	89.7	0.3	5.8	3.5	0.6	26.5	23.0	44.6	43.2	20.7	363	90.9
Wiota city	116	107	-7.8	58	93.1	0.0	0.0	6.9	0.0	0.0	50.0	65.5	36.2	19.0	35	85.7
Woden city	227	206	-9.3	198	83.3	4.5	0.0	7.1	5.1	26.3	19.7	33.7	58.1	12.5	93	88.2
Woodbine city	1,485	1,385	-6.7	1,488	93.8	0.9	2.4	0.4	2.6	22.2	27.6	46.6	45.1	20.8	638	88.6
Woodburn city	202	194	-4.0	145	93.1	0.0	6.9	0.0	0.0	15.2	11.0	54.2	54.5	7.3	72	75.0
Woodward city	1,474	1,448	-1.8	1,243	93.3	2.0	0.0	3.2	1.4	25.7	12.1	36.2	50.4	9.3	392	93.4
Woolstock city	168	161	-4.2	232	92.2	6.5	0.0	1.3	0.0	21.1	19.0	43.7	35.8	14.2	107	72.0
Worthington city	409	395	-3.4	449	95.1	0.0	0.0	0.0	4.9	25.2	17.8	41.2	60.8	14.4	181	79.0
Wyoming city	515	515	0.0	445	98.4	0.0	1.3	0.2	0.0	27.9	18.0	42.8	45.9	11.5	202	77.7
Yale city	246	239	-2.8	265	97.4	0.0	0.0	2.6	0.0	33.2	20.4	39.6	54.4	15.6	113	81.4
Yetter city	34	32	-5.9	30	100.0	0.0	0.0	0.0	0.0	23.3	23.3	54.5	65.0	0.0	14	71.4
Yorktown city	89	86	-3.4	37	100.0	0.0	0.0	0.0	0.0	0.0	37.8	60.9	68.6	11.4	15	80.0
Zearing city	554	518	-6.5	534	96.4	0.0	1.7	1.7	0.2	21.5	18.4	40.0	38.9	19.1	223	88.3
Zwingle city	90	92	2.2	66	100.0	0.0	0.0	0.0	0.0	10.6	13.6	44.2	58.5	3.8	33	66.7
KANSAS	2,853,123	2,913,314	2.1	2,910,652	75.9	5.7	2.9	3.7	11.9	24.4	15.4	36.7	35.0	33.4	1,129,227	90.0
Abbyville city	89	85	-4.5	72	98.6	0.0	0.0	1.4	0.0	11.1	41.7	60.4	46.7	6.7	35	88.6
Abilene city	6,844	6,201	-9.4	6,362	90.9	1.5	0.0	3.2	4.4	23.4	20.0	40.0	44.4	26.3	2,755	86.9
Ada CDP	100	-	-	160	84.4	0.0	0.0	15.6	0.0	0.0	5.6	42.0	88.9	0.0	56	83.9
Admire city	156	152	-2.6	100	84.0	0.0	0.0	14.0	2.0	20.0	26.0	56.4	27.4	23.3	53	77.4
Agenda city	72	66	-8.3	61	86.9	0.0	0.0	13.1	0.0	16.4	31.1	60.3	44.9	14.3	30	70.0
Agra city	267	241	-9.7	206	97.1	0.0	0.0	1.5	1.5	10.7	29.1	55.9	33.0	10.1	115	93.9
Albert city	175	164	-6.3	185	95.1	0.0	0.0	0.0	4.9	17.8	31.4	47.5	44.7	14.4	73	80.8
Alden city	156	142	-9.0	121	88.4	0.0	2.5	6.6	2.5	33.9	21.5	37.1	39.7	14.1	43	76.7
Alexander city	65	59	-9.2	74	100.0	0.0	0.0	0.0	0.0	24.3	37.8	51.5	33.3	12.5	39	66.7
Allen city	177	172	-2.8	168	83.9	0.0	0.0	10.7	5.4	24.4	23.8	31.5	34.9	16.5	80	80.0
Alma city	832	780	-6.3	899	86.2	0.3	0.3	3.4	9.7	22.0	18.1	44.5	37.3	20.2	401	84.0
Almena city	408	378	-7.4	430	89.8	0.0	0.2	3.3	6.7	25.1	17.7	39.4	48.3	16.7	157	84.7
Altamont city	1,085	1,019	-6.1	1,144	88.8	0.0	0.0	6.5	4.7	30.4	15.5	33.5	44.2	20.5	435	83.7
Alta Vista city	444	424	-4.5	491	85.5	4.5	0.0	6.7	3.3	27.5	21.6	45.0	51.6	17.3	204	81.4
Alton city	103	91	-11.7	88	95.5	0.0	0.0	3.4	1.1	20.5	23.9	46.0	41.3	22.2	44	81.8
Altoona city	413	379	-8.2	253	85.8	0.0	0.0	8.7	5.5	20.6	27.7	48.4	55.3	10.6	121	72.7
Americus city	894	879	-1.7	908	91.4	0.0	0.0	5.0	3.6	24.8	12.9	35.6	51.1	11.6	390	85.4
Andale city	928	987	6.4	934	95.3	0.6	0.0	0.0	4.1	39.5	11.7	28.4	29.3	33.1	279	90.7
Andover city	11,800	13,405	13.6	13,062	81.7	0.7	5.2	3.4	9.0	31.4	12.2	34.8	18.4	52.4	4,576	91.5
Anthony city	2,265	2,070	-8.6	2,193	89.1	0.1	1.0	2.3	7.6	25.9	18.4	37.6	47.3	18.6	840	88.6
Arcadia city	310	309	-0.3	364	95.9	0.0	0.0	3.0	1.1	22.0	15.4	48.7	54.1	11.2	165	73.3
Argonia city	510	471	-7.6	521	87.7	6.1	0.0	3.6	2.5	31.7	13.4	28.5	26.8	27.9	201	90.0
Arkansas City city	12,417	11,669	-6.0	11,868	68.7	4.0	0.5	5.9	21.0	25.8	16.8	34.8	42.6	16.8	4,641	86.7
Arlington city	478	449	-6.1	528	93.9	0.4	0.0	1.7	4.0	18.8	24.1	49.4	46.8	11.6	219	87.7
Arma city	1,487	1,420	-4.5	1,385	92.8	0.0	0.0	4.2	3.0	21.0	23.3	47.9	48.4	16.6	590	79.2
Asherville CDP	28	-	-	-	-	-	-	-	-	-	-	-	-	-	-	-
Ashland city	866	775	-10.5	694	84.4	1.0	0.3	3.6	10.7	18.3	20.9	49.8	36.6	25.0	337	87.5
Assaria city	417	408	-2.2	438	95.4	0.0	0.7	1.6	2.3	24.4	21.5	43.0	40.6	21.9	173	91.9
Atchison city	11,022	10,476	-5.0	10,598	84.9	3.9	0.5	6.7	4.0	23.2	15.2	32.1	43.7	25.6	3,730	79.3
Athol city	44	41	-6.8	34	88.2	0.0	0.0	0.0	11.8	8.8	17.6	54.8	56.7	20.0	18	55.6
Atlanta city	193	181	-6.2	167	92.8	0.0	0.0	0.6	6.6	10.8	36.5	51.3	36.8	14.4	86	91.9
Attica city	626	557	-11.0	682	96.6	0.0	0.0	0.3	3.1	30.4	18.9	36.1	57.7	13.0	270	81.9
Atwood city	1,196	1,217	1.8	1,109	83.9	1.4	0.0	2.6	12.2	21.2	29.0	49.3	36.7	19.2	547	89.2
Auburn city	1,222	1,211	-0.9	1,178	90.3	0.8	4.6	1.4	3.0	29.6	13.9	38.0	43.9	24.3	435	91.5
Augusta city	9,407	9,345	-0.7	9,368	88.3	1.2	0.0	3.8	6.7	29.3	16.8	33.9	35.8	22.5	3,509	87.5
Aurora city	60	56	-6.7	84	100.0	0.0	0.0	0.0	0.0	25.0	22.6	38.0	87.9	0.0	41	75.6
Axtell city	408	403	-1.2	390	92.8	0.0	3.1	1.3	2.8	29.0	17.9	39.0	50.4	19.2	162	80.2
Baileyville CDP	181	-	-	201	97.5	0.0	0.0	0.0	2.5	18.9	37.3	55.8	80.6	0.0	88	85.2
Baldwin City city	4,514	4,700	4.1	4,670	87.9	1.3	0.4	6.2	4.2	20.8	14.8	31.9	31.2	37.3	1,505	94.8
Barnard city	70	63	-10.0	52	100.0	0.0	0.0	0.0	0.0	0.0	38.5	61.5	30.0	32.0	34	85.3
Barnes city	162	152	-6.2	159	78.0	0.0	0.0	0.0	22.0	17.0	25.8	49.3	48.7	6.2	74	81.1
Bartlett city	80	73	-8.8	69	81.2	0.0	0.0	15.9	2.9	27.5	1.4	43.3	77.6	4.1	25	100.0
Basehor city	4,632	6,496	40.2	5,951	92.5	0.5	2.1	3.3	1.6	28.7	14.8	38.0	32.8	35.9	2,037	94.2
Bassett city	23	21	-8.7	13	100.0	0.0	0.0	0.0	0.0	0.0	69.2	67.5	41.7	8.3	7	100.0
Baxter Springs city	4,272	3,948	-7.6	3,983	83.9	0.1	0.4	10.8	4.8	29.5	16.2	36.0	41.5	20.3	1,555	78.0
Bazine city	334	292	-12.6	340	70.3	0.0	0.0	1.5	28.2	30.3	20.3	39.3	53.9	9.6	132	90.2
Beattie city	200	189	-5.5	228	87.3	0.0	0.0	1.8	11.0	18.4	29.4	49.4	57.4	13.6	96	86.5
Bel Aire city	6,769	8,300	22.6	7,858	74.9	8.8	5.6	3.7	6.9	27.5	13.8	37.4	12.5	58.7	2,764	97.0
Belle Plaine city	1,676	1,556	-7.2	1,511	91.1	0.0	0.8	1.9	6.2	21.7	16.7	42.9	44.7	15.2	637	94.3
Belleville city	1,990	1,879	-5.6	1,927	92.0	2.6	0.3	1.5	3.7	23.5	30.0	46.3	40.5	22.9	928	76.8
Beloit city	3,840	3,625	-5.6	3,793	94.7	1.2	0.0	0.4	3.7	21.7	23.9	37.8	33.8	27.7	1,556	88.6
Belpre city	90	82	-8.9	108	65.7	0.0	0.0	0.0	34.3	37.0	11.1	32.8	52.4	9.5	40	77.5
Belvue city	205	200	-2.4	325	84.9	0.0	0.0	1.8	13.2	40.0	4.3	21.2	36.2	9.2	72	98.6
Bendena CDP	117	-	-	134	93.3	0.0	0.0	0.0	6.7	3.7	23.9	50.2	14.3	39.8	73	84.9
Benedict city	73	66	-9.6	102	100.0	0.0	0.0	0.0	0.0	24.5	36.3	48.7	67.1	0.0	42	69.0
Bennington city	660	612	-7.3	833	95.3	0.0	0.0	1.4	3.2	35.1	17.9	34.5	32.0	26.3	331	87.3
Bentley city	530	517	-2.5	487	87.3	0.0	0.0	3.9	8.8	28.3	16.2	36.9	45.4	18.3	186	93.0
Benton city	886	871	-1.7	1,013	85.8	11.9	0.3	2.0	0.0	21.5	11.6	43.6	27.9	32.4	400	92.8
Bern city	166	164	-1.2	170	93.5	0.0	0.0	2.9	3.5	32.4	12.4	31.1	43.7	28.2	61	98.4
Beverly city	159	147	-7.5	125	96.8	0.8	0.0	0.0	2.4	9.6	15.2	46.8	52.6	7.2	56	83.9
Bird City city	447	432	-3.4	536	89.6	0.0	0.0	0.0	10.4	22.0	25.4	43.0	36.8	30.9	258	81.8
Bison city	255	233	-8.6	167	95.2	0.0	0.0	0.0	4.8	19.8	22.2	52.6	43.0	18.2	73	87.7
Blue Mound city	275	270	-1.8	303	100.0	0.0	0.0	0.0	0.0	11.2	15.2	53.7	52.1	4.9	164	59.1
Blue Rapids city	1,019	961	-5.7	1,247	93.3	0.5	0.0	6.3	0.0	25.1	19.2	36.2	55.0	7.9	442	89.1
Bluff City city	65	59	-9.2	111	100.0	0.0	0.0	0.0	0.0	43.2	9.0	31.4	44.3	0.0	25	84.0
Bogue city	143	136	-4.9	250	86.0	3.2	0.0	0.0	10.8	39.6	19.2	30.7	31.6	22.1	101	82.2
Bonner Springs city	7,334	7,906	7.8	7,782	79.3	8.4	0.1	2.6	9.6	29.9	15.8	37.5	48.0	22.8	2,857	93.0
Brewster city	305	292	-4.3	269	88.1	0.0	1.5	0.7	9.7	27.9	16.7	30.2	29.9	30.5	112	97.3

1 May be of any race.

Table A. All Places — **Population and Housing**

STATE City, town, township, borough, or CDP (county if applicable)	Population				Race and Hispanic or Latino origin (percent)					Age (percent)			Educational attainment of persons age 25 and older		Occupied housing units	
	2010 census total population	2019 estimated population	Percent change 2010-2019	ACS total population estimate 2015-2019	White alone, not Hispanic or Latino	Black alone, not Hispanic or Latino	Asian alone, not Hispanic or Latino	All other races or 2 or more races, not Hispanic or Latino	Hispanic or Latino[1]	Under 18 years old	Age 65 years and older	Median age	Percent High school diploma or less	Percent Bachelor's degree or more	Total	Percent with a computer
	1	2	3	4	5	6	7	8	9	10	11	12	13	14	15	16
KANSAS—Con.																
Bronson city	318	305	-4.1	258	86.0	0.0	0.0	4.7	9.3	33.7	19.8	33.6	53.0	9.3	84	83.3
Brookville city	261	253	-3.1	191	94.2	0.0	0.0	4.2	1.6	16.8	17.3	44.3	40.9	13.6	85	85.9
Brownell city	29	26	-10.3	60	100.0	0.0	0.0	0.0	0.0	25.0	30.0	31.8	23.8	21.4	23	87.0
Bucklin city	805	771	-4.2	715	93.3	0.0	0.3	4.3	2.1	22.9	18.6	43.7	25.7	25.9	288	94.4
Bucyrus CDP	193	-	-	322	100.0	0.0	0.0	0.0	0.0	12.7	6.2	29.7	30.2	26.0	141	92.2
Buffalo city	232	209	-9.9	292	99.0	0.0	0.3	0.7	0.0	31.5	18.5	39.1	52.9	8.0	111	89.2
Buhler city	1,333	1,278	-4.1	1,111	95.6	0.0	0.2	1.4	2.8	23.4	27.3	44.9	30.9	30.3	442	93.2
Bunker Hill city	95	94	-1.1	144	93.1	0.0	0.0	6.9	0.0	36.8	24.3	34.5	57.8	19.3	51	74.5
Burden city	537	526	-2.0	666	87.1	0.0	0.0	9.6	3.3	34.1	14.7	30.5	44.0	15.2	234	88.5
Burdett city	247	221	-10.5	503	97.6	0.0	0.0	0.2	2.2	32.0	9.3	35.3	46.6	21.3	124	89.5
Burlingame city	933	901	-3.4	885	99.0	0.0	0.0	0.5	0.6	22.6	21.6	41.0	50.6	14.1	428	86.0
Burlington city	2,670	2,543	-4.8	2,560	92.1	0.7	0.0	6.5	0.7	24.1	21.1	42.2	45.4	20.6	1,082	89.0
Burns city	226	209	-7.5	296	97.0	0.0	0.0	0.3	2.7	37.5	9.8	27.6	62.8	14.0	95	94.7
Burr Oak city	174	161	-7.5	164	90.2	0.0	0.0	7.3	2.4	11.6	32.9	55.3	57.7	10.6	89	78.7
Burrton city	901	860	-4.6	907	92.3	0.2	1.4	5.3	0.8	29.1	12.2	35.1	40.3	21.4	325	87.7
Bushong city	34	33	-2.9	9	66.7	0.0	0.0	33.3	0.0	0.0	66.7	68.5	66.7	0.0	6	66.7
Bushton city	281	255	-9.3	322	76.4	0.0	0.0	16.5	7.1	30.4	16.5	30.3	43.9	15.2	133	88.7
Byers city	35	33	-5.7	15	100.0	0.0	0.0	0.0	0.0	0.0	20.0	56.9	20.0	0.0	10	100.0
Caldwell city	1,069	987	-7.7	1,006	96.1	0.0	0.0	1.3	2.6	17.4	28.1	51.2	49.3	15.3	504	78.6
Cambridge city	84	82	-2.4	151	94.7	2.0	0.0	3.3	0.0	27.2	21.2	44.5	31.7	2.9	53	81.1
Caney city	2,215	1,968	-11.2	1,827	81.5	0.2	2.2	11.2	4.9	24.3	21.7	42.4	47.6	11.1	820	76.0
Canton city	748	695	-7.1	627	97.4	0.6	0.0	1.0	1.0	25.5	15.8	38.8	46.2	19.1	266	83.8
Carbondale city	1,433	1,369	-4.5	1,438	88.8	0.0	0.2	4.7	6.3	24.1	14.5	37.2	53.3	11.1	571	85.1
Carlton city	42	40	-4.8	12	100.0	0.0	0.0	0.0	0.0	16.7	25.0	56.0	80.0	0.0	5	100.0
Cassoday city	129	123	-4.7	149	91.9	0.0	0.0	2.7	5.4	23.5	18.1	44.9	30.3	18.3	74	85.1
Catharine CDP	104	-	-	130	100.0	0.0	0.0	0.0	0.0	35.4	21.5	27.4	10.1	33.3	44	100.0
Cawker City city	469	433	-7.7	581	91.0	0.0	0.5	8.4	0.0	17.6	28.6	48.4	51.3	11.8	277	83.0
Cedar city	14	13	-7.1	25	100.0	0.0	0.0	0.0	0.0	16.0	64.0	69.1	52.4	4.8	12	83.3
Cedar Point city	28	27	-3.6	2	100.0	0.0	0.0	0.0	0.0	0.0	100.0	0.0	100.0	0.0	2	50.0
Cedar Vale city	579	508	-12.3	638	73.2	2.4	0.0	8.5	16.0	32.8	14.9	30.9	40.4	9.4	265	82.6
Centralia city	517	525	1.5	519	97.3	1.2	0.0	1.5	0.0	20.0	25.2	40.2	44.7	24.4	217	85.3
Chanute city	9,125	9,042	-0.9	9,102	89.0	1.9	0.0	3.4	5.7	26.0	19.5	37.9	44.6	15.9	3,771	80.2
Chapman city	1,412	1,340	-5.1	1,213	86.9	2.7	1.0	3.4	6.0	21.4	22.0	43.5	33.5	29.4	535	87.3
Chase city	477	438	-8.2	401	82.3	0.0	0.0	2.2	15.5	28.4	17.2	43.1	47.6	13.9	185	82.7
Chautauqua city	104	91	-12.5	49	81.6	0.0	0.0	18.4	0.0	24.5	30.6	56.1	66.7	8.3	26	46.2
Cheney city	2,099	2,167	3.2	2,014	95.0	0.1	0.0	1.1	3.7	31.0	16.3	36.9	40.9	28.5	704	87.2
Cherokee city	704	708	0.6	849	96.5	0.0	0.0	3.5	0.0	27.8	15.2	34.7	46.1	21.7	312	79.5
Cherryvale city	2,380	2,138	-10.2	2,330	92.1	0.7	0.8	4.1	2.2	29.1	14.0	35.4	45.0	11.7	904	87.2
Chetopa city	1,120	1,018	-9.1	1,238	90.1	0.6	0.0	5.6	3.7	24.9	22.1	43.6	48.3	9.9	522	73.9
Chicopee CDP	408	-	-	565	89.2	0.0	0.0	0.0	10.8	13.6	20.0	49.0	26.3	46.7	278	100.0
Cimarron city	2,184	2,201	0.8	2,293	67.2	0.0	0.0	1.8	31.0	35.5	10.3	33.5	35.5	22.2	797	93.7
Circleville city	170	161	-5.3	186	78.0	0.0	0.0	21.0	1.1	23.7	23.1	33.9	50.0	9.2	92	96.7
Claflin city	645	601	-6.8	406	98.0	0.0	0.0	0.0	2.0	21.2	21.7	46.5	40.1	22.1	200	81.5
Clay Center city	4,348	3,983	-8.4	4,026	97.3	0.9	0.6	0.7	0.4	23.8	26.5	44.9	46.4	24.9	1,890	72.5
Clayton city	59	55	-6.8	61	91.8	0.0	0.0	8.2	0.0	4.9	42.6	60.8	50.0	9.6	24	100.0
Clearwater city	2,488	2,552	2.6	2,520	93.9	0.2	0.0	3.8	2.1	30.0	17.1	36.5	32.9	25.2	875	90.9
Clifton city	554	505	-8.8	367	98.9	0.0	0.0	0.0	1.1	11.4	30.5	55.8	49.2	12.4	181	80.7
Climax city	72	65	-9.7	43	100.0	0.0	0.0	0.0	0.0	34.9	41.9	43.2	60.7	3.6	20	65.0
Clyde city	718	658	-8.4	912	99.1	0.0	0.0	0.3	0.5	27.6	26.4	39.5	38.0	21.6	366	86.1
Coats city	80	76	-5.0	81	74.1	0.0	0.0	4.9	21.0	19.8	28.4	55.8	38.7	3.2	46	54.3
Coffeyville city	10,306	9,275	-10.0	9,457	69.2	8.9	0.8	10.7	10.4	24.8	19.2	36.5	44.2	17.4	3,939	80.5
Colby city	5,398	5,370	-0.5	5,473	89.5	3.1	1.2	0.2	6.0	20.8	14.1	33.3	32.8	19.5	2,389	91.2
Coldwater city	823	736	-10.6	832	95.7	0.0	0.0	0.0	4.3	27.6	21.0	36.9	46.0	10.8	348	82.2
Collyer city	108	100	-7.4	79	96.2	2.5	0.0	0.0	1.3	11.4	20.3	49.6	50.0	10.3	37	78.4
Colony city	410	414	1.0	487	97.1	1.4	0.2	0.8	0.4	24.2	14.4	30.4	38.6	12.6	212	84.0
Columbus city	3,315	3,052	-7.9	3,086	90.7	0.0	0.6	7.8	0.9	21.2	17.5	38.8	47.9	19.8	1,221	88.0
Colwich city	1,327	1,467	10.6	1,270	94.6	0.0	0.2	1.2	4.0	31.4	12.2	30.9	28.0	41.0	479	94.4
Concordia city	5,398	4,987	-7.6	5,070	88.5	3.3	0.2	2.6	5.5	23.6	20.4	37.6	37.0	26.2	2,076	86.8
Conway Springs city	1,276	1,218	-4.5	1,483	95.0	1.7	0.0	0.8	2.5	30.0	14.8	35.3	43.6	22.0	540	90.9
Coolidge city	95	90	-5.3	171	77.8	0.0	0.0	0.0	22.2	25.7	10.5	41.2	72.1	9.0	43	88.4
Copeland city	312	297	-4.8	318	89.9	0.0	0.0	0.0	10.1	17.6	16.7	48.8	51.6	17.1	144	76.4
Corning city	165	164	-0.6	188	95.2	0.0	0.0	4.8	0.0	36.2	13.8	31.6	35.5	30.9	65	89.2
Cottonwood Falls city	904	862	-4.6	785	89.4	4.6	0.0	1.0	5.0	20.6	28.5	48.6	43.0	22.1	313	85.3
Council Grove city	2,203	2,121	-3.7	2,260	90.7	0.0	0.8	1.7	6.7	24.6	22.5	38.8	45.3	17.6	915	86.0
Courtland city	287	264	-8.0	313	95.5	0.0	0.0	0.0	4.5	31.6	24.6	40.2	44.2	23.8	147	74.1
Coyville city	46	42	-8.7	33	100.0	0.0	0.0	0.0	0.0	27.3	18.2	42.8	9.5	0.0	14	92.9
Cuba city	156	144	-7.7	266	97.0	0.0	0.0	0.0	3.0	31.6	19.9	40.4	49.7	13.6	97	81.4
Cullison city	101	97	-4.0	82	100.0	0.0	0.0	0.0	0.0	24.4	13.4	23.3	41.0	17.9	29	89.7
Culver city	123	114	-7.3	111	82.9	0.0	0.0	0.0	17.1	27.9	22.5	50.3	63.2	7.9	49	75.5
Cunningham city	473	438	-7.4	403	96.8	1.0	0.5	0.5	1.2	20.1	29.0	47.3	39.1	23.4	187	88.8
Damar city	132	125	-5.3	153	96.7	0.0	2.6	0.0	0.7	10.5	32.7	53.3	46.4	26.8	90	76.7
Danville city	38	34	-10.5	35	100.0	0.0	0.0	0.0	0.0	28.6	34.3	51.5	48.0	12.0	14	100.0
Dearing city	420	379	-9.8	536	80.0	0.0	0.0	10.6	9.3	20.7	13.8	47.2	58.7	15.5	210	89.5
Deerfield city	700	690	-1.4	769	39.7	0.0	0.0	0.0	60.3	32.0	12.0	23.5	70.9	5.8	213	85.0
Delia city	181	176	-2.8	157	88.5	0.6	0.0	10.2	0.6	22.3	22.3	30.9	46.2	16.3	65	92.3
Delphos city	361	330	-8.6	371	92.5	1.1	0.0	2.7	3.8	21.6	24.8	47.4	70.2	12.8	158	83.5
Denison city	187	177	-5.3	133	100.0	0.0	0.0	0.0	0.0	23.3	18.8	53.8	51.0	6.9	66	83.3
Denton city	148	141	-4.7	164	97.6	0.0	0.0	1.2	1.2	19.5	18.3	48.8	47.7	11.4	73	91.8
Derby city	22,294	24,943	11.9	24,067	85.1	1.9	1.6	4.8	6.5	27.4	14.0	35.5	24.1	40.4	8,926	95.0
De Soto city	5,714	6,512	14.0	6,254	83.1	1.4	0.6	0.4	14.5	31.3	11.9	38.1	32.5	35.4	2,300	88.4
Detroit CDP	114	-	-	178	64.0	0.0	0.0	0.0	36.0	34.3	4.5	23.6	100.0	0.0	56	75.0
Dexter city	278	274	-1.4	275	93.5	0.0	0.0	6.2	0.4	26.2	24.4	40.3	37.6	24.2	97	84.5
Dighton city	1,028	902	-12.3	873	88.4	0.0	2.2	0.1	9.3	25.0	16.8	37.2	40.2	19.2	396	89.9
Dodge City city	27,326	27,104	-0.8	27,555	32.1	2.3	1.7	1.9	62.0	31.2	9.7	29.9	54.4	16.6	8,986	85.3
Dorrance city	185	179	-3.2	220	100.0	0.0	0.0	0.0	0.0	28.6	17.3	29.5	37.5	20.8	77	92.2
Douglass city	1,699	1,658	-2.4	1,780	86.6	0.3	0.6	8.7	3.8	29.7	15.2	36.2	44.2	23.7	653	82.5
Downs city	917	814	-11.2	752	97.2	0.3	0.3	0.9	1.3	12.6	26.9	52.8	44.3	24.0	396	85.6
Dresden city	41	40	-2.4	42	100.0	0.0	0.0	0.0	0.0	19.0	19.0	50.5	63.6	12.1	21	71.4
Dunlap city	30	28	-6.7	23	100.0	0.0	0.0	0.0	0.0	0.0	21.7	54.9	82.6	13.0	10	100.0
Durham city	114	109	-4.4	85	88.2	1.2	2.4	4.7	3.5	5.9	52.9	66.6	73.7	3.9	42	66.7
Dwight city	274	259	-5.5	205	95.1	0.0	1.5	0.5	2.9	13.7	29.8	52.0	64.1	10.9	87	70.1
Earlton city	55	52	-5.5	124	79.0	8.9	0.0	12.1	0.0	41.9	19.4	34.2	40.0	5.7	39	89.7

1 May be of any race.

Table A. All Places — **Population and Housing**

STATE City, town, township, borough, or CDP (county if applicable)	Population: 2010 census total population	Population: 2019 estimated population	Population: Percent change 2010-2019	Population: ACS total population estimate 2015-2019	Race and Hispanic or Latino origin (percent): White alone, not Hispanic or Latino	Race and Hispanic or Latino origin (percent): Black alone, not Hispanic or Latino	Race and Hispanic or Latino origin (percent): Asian alone, not Hispanic or Latino	Race and Hispanic or Latino origin (percent): All other races or 2 or more races, not Hispanic or Latino	Race and Hispanic or Latino origin (percent): Hispanic or Latino[1]	Age (percent): Under 18 years old	Age (percent): Age 65 years and older	Age (percent): Median age	Educational attainment of persons age 25 and older: Percent High school diploma or less	Educational attainment of persons age 25 and older: Percent Bachelor's degree or more	Occupied housing units: Total	Occupied housing units: Percent with a computer
	1	2	3	4	5	6	7	8	9	10	11	12	13	14	15	16
KANSAS—Con.																
Eastborough city	760	732	-3.7	743	93.5	1.7	2.8	1.9	0.0	24.1	17.2	47.7	5.7	71.1	281	97.5
Easton city	254	258	1.6	380	94.2	2.4	0.0	1.1	2.4	14.7	26.3	54.0	56.5	6.2	103	74.8
Edgerton city	1,772	1,784	0.7	1,713	88.7	0.0	0.0	2.1	9.2	29.1	6.3	32.3	41.3	22.6	605	96.9
Edmond city	49	46	-6.1	104	100.0	0.0	0.0	0.0	0.0	9.6	35.6	50.1	73.3	26.7	19	47.4
Edna city	441	402	-8.8	417	88.7	0.0	0.0	8.4	2.9	24.2	18.2	39.1	38.2	26.3	166	91.0
Edwardsville city	4,340	4,495	3.6	4,492	69.1	9.5	0.9	7.5	13.0	28.4	10.9	36.5	38.1	21.7	1,549	94.7
Effingham city	553	522	-5.6	509	97.1	0.0	0.0	0.8	2.2	24.4	29.5	45.9	50.4	13.6	233	72.5
Elbing city	233	226	-3.0	335	96.7	0.6	0.0	1.5	1.2	34.0	11.6	31.3	24.1	29.7	99	90.9
El Dorado city	13,235	12,954	-2.1	12,988	92.0	1.4	0.2	3.0	3.5	23.5	15.9	36.0	36.6	24.7	5,553	86.7
Elgin city	89	79	-11.2	75	80.0	0.0	0.0	5.3	14.7	14.7	18.7	42.9	65.5	0.0	28	82.1
Elk City city	324	292	-9.9	288	82.3	0.0	0.0	6.6	11.1	21.2	18.4	41.6	54.9	11.9	125	82.4
Elk Falls city	107	93	-13.1	86	88.4	0.0	1.2	9.3	1.2	14.0	44.2	62.6	33.8	20.3	46	73.9
Elkhart city	2,205	1,758	-20.3	1,533	77.7	0.1	0.0	2.7	19.4	22.0	22.2	42.8	37.8	18.9	627	87.1
Ellinwood city	2,135	1,943	-9.0	2,063	90.0	0.5	0.0	2.1	7.4	21.6	20.6	42.2	44.4	17.6	834	85.9
Ellis city	2,075	2,011	-3.1	2,047	97.7	0.0	0.0	0.4	1.9	28.2	17.9	38.3	46.5	23.6	845	82.7
Ellsworth city	3,120	2,961	-5.1	3,013	80.4	6.6	1.1	4.5	7.4	16.3	15.9	36.6	47.9	16.7	972	90.2
Elmdale city	55	52	-5.5	28	53.6	28.6	0.0	7.1	10.7	28.6	10.7	41.0	15.8	47.4	11	81.8
Elsmore city	74	67	-9.5	87	100.0	0.0	0.0	0.0	0.0	41.4	11.5	26.3	59.1	6.8	29	75.9
Elwood city	1,227	1,192	-2.9	842	87.8	9.4	0.0	0.7	2.1	19.8	23.5	46.6	70.4	4.3	393	78.4
Emmett city	191	186	-2.6	171	76.6	0.0	0.0	7.6	15.8	26.3	2.3	29.5	73.1	1.9	61	91.8
Emporia city	24,942	24,598	-1.4	24,607	64.0	3.0	2.6	3.2	27.2	22.4	13.2	28.6	41.3	28.2	9,933	91.1
Englewood city	77	69	-10.4	91	94.5	0.0	5.5	0.0	0.0	26.4	33.0	52.5	49.2	0.0	38	81.6
Ensign city	192	183	-4.7	140	65.0	0.0	0.0	2.1	32.9	2.1	37.1	60.2	49.2	8.5	79	81.0
Enterprise city	859	784	-8.7	953	91.5	0.5	0.9	3.3	3.8	19.8	13.1	34.5	45.1	11.7	331	92.1
Erie city	1,157	1,087	-6.1	1,444	88.0	0.4	0.0	3.3	8.2	29.4	17.1	34.9	43.1	12.9	544	87.3
Esbon city	99	92	-7.1	99	85.9	0.0	0.0	12.1	2.0	8.1	26.3	57.5	27.5	15.4	63	92.1
Eskridge city	532	505	-5.1	540	91.7	0.0	0.0	4.3	4.1	17.6	17.6	47.0	62.6	8.3	211	83.4
Eudora city	6,142	6,411	4.4	6,602	82.9	5.1	0.6	3.8	7.6	32.5	7.5	33.1	32.6	33.2	2,114	93.8
Eureka city	2,639	2,346	-11.1	2,262	89.3	0.4	0.5	4.4	5.3	23.3	25.1	43.3	49.4	15.8	1,044	78.7
Everest city	284	274	-3.5	290	88.3	3.4	0.0	3.1	5.2	22.8	24.1	47.0	48.8	17.4	129	79.1
Fairview city	260	248	-4.6	326	81.3	2.8	1.8	2.8	11.3	20.6	17.2	40.5	52.2	10.2	141	88.7
Fairway city	3,872	3,960	2.3	3,960	94.7	0.0	2.2	1.4	1.8	26.1	19.9	39.1	7.9	77.0	1,669	98.4
Fall River city	162	145	-10.5	111	95.5	0.0	0.0	4.5	0.0	9.9	31.5	57.5	39.6	17.6	59	71.2
Falun CDP	87	-	-	84	78.6	0.0	0.0	21.4	0.0	0.0	46.4	64.6	74.2	0.0	29	58.6
Florence city	472	435	-7.8	451	90.5	0.0	0.0	3.5	6.0	20.0	29.9	48.1	50.6	18.3	219	74.4
Fontana city	231	239	3.5	320	91.3	0.9	0.0	3.1	4.7	34.4	10.9	27.7	46.8	10.4	107	97.2
Ford city	216	216	0.0	221	92.8	0.0	0.0	3.2	4.1	28.5	14.9	36.4	55.7	11.4	86	83.7
Formoso city	92	86	-6.5	161	97.5	0.0	0.0	2.5	0.0	21.7	16.8	31.8	57.0	14.9	65	84.6
Fort Dodge CDP	165	-	-	168	92.9	7.1	0.0	0.0	0.0	0.0	64.3	67.7	59.5	30.4	103	70.9
Fort Riley CDP	7,761	-	-	6,368	55.7	14.8	3.0	5.8	20.7	17.7	0.0	22.0	38.4	14.0	1,084	100.0
Fort Scott city	8,082	7,697	-4.8	7,742	87.1	4.3	1.1	4.4	3.0	25.4	19.2	38.4	42.3	17.1	3,080	80.0
Fowler city	591	517	-12.5	509	65.6	0.0	0.0	0.0	34.4	30.1	23.8	36.4	54.8	17.7	223	84.8
Frankfort city	726	695	-4.3	754	96.9	0.0	0.0	0.8	2.3	19.1	30.0	51.0	47.3	18.6	319	84.6
Franklin CDP	375	-	-	590	97.3	2.7	0.0	0.0	0.0	33.2	5.1	36.7	41.9	24.4	185	91.4
Frederick city	18	19	5.6	7	100.0	0.0	0.0	0.0	0.0	0.0	14.3	54.8	100.0	0.0	3	100.0
Fredonia city	2,478	2,225	-10.2	2,141	88.7	0.5	0.0	3.2	7.6	20.0	24.0	48.0	45.4	19.8	957	86.1
Freeport city	5	4	-20.0	-	-	-	-	-	-	-	-	-	-	-	-	-
Frontenac city	3,439	3,388	-1.5	3,400	92.7	1.4	2.9	1.1	1.8	27.6	15.7	36.0	31.5	34.9	1,277	90.1
Fulton city	163	155	-4.9	112	93.8	0.0	1.8	4.5	0.0	30.4	14.3	32.4	45.3	14.7	38	89.5
Galatia city	39	36	-7.7	29	100.0	0.0	0.0	0.0	0.0	3.4	48.3	64.8	35.7	7.1	19	78.9
Galena city	3,114	2,858	-8.2	2,892	86.2	0.0	0.0	9.3	4.5	21.1	17.7	38.9	50.2	12.5	1,122	87.6
Galesburg city	126	119	-5.6	190	52.6	0.0	0.0	0.0	47.4	47.4	10.5	25.2	58.3	21.9	57	82.5
Galva city	872	876	0.5	1,015	96.4	0.6	0.0	1.0	2.1	20.6	15.0	41.2	43.5	25.0	449	87.5
Garden City city	26,727	26,408	-1.2	26,647	38.5	3.7	5.3	1.8	50.7	29.6	11.4	30.8	52.4	16.6	9,296	88.7
Garden Plain city	849	909	7.1	807	98.0	0.4	0.0	1.6	0.0	29.6	14.5	34.3	34.9	35.6	303	82.8
Gardner city	19,134	22,031	15.1	21,528	82.8	3.3	1.5	5.0	7.5	32.6	7.5	32.3	29.2	35.6	7,219	95.6
Garfield city	190	169	-11.1	150	94.7	0.0	2.7	2.7	0.0	22.0	14.0	39.8	53.0	15.7	60	100.0
Garnett city	3,412	3,235	-5.2	3,234	92.2	0.6	0.0	4.9	2.3	24.3	27.0	44.4	53.2	21.2	1,406	81.7
Gas city	558	501	-10.2	510	95.7	0.0	0.6	3.7	0.0	20.4	15.7	43.1	51.1	10.7	215	82.3
Gaylord city	114	105	-7.9	164	92.7	0.0	0.0	7.3	0.0	30.5	28.7	37.5	52.0	22.5	87	75.9
Gem city	88	85	-3.4	142	99.3	0.0	0.0	0.7	0.0	38.0	6.3	18.9	40.7	18.6	51	94.1
Geneseo city	267	257	-3.7	264	89.4	0.4	0.0	0.0	10.2	12.9	25.4	48.5	53.2	15.6	141	66.0
Geuda Springs city	187	176	-5.9	120	81.7	0.0	0.0	13.3	5.0	6.7	28.3	51.8	52.5	8.9	62	74.2
Girard city	2,780	2,671	-3.9	2,707	92.0	0.9	0.0	4.6	2.5	26.0	17.0	35.6	42.8	24.4	1,044	87.4
Glade city	98	90	-8.2	30	96.7	0.0	0.0	3.3	0.0	0.0	53.3	66.5	60.0	16.7	19	100.0
Glasco city	498	455	-8.6	489	99.2	0.0	0.0	0.6	0.2	19.2	24.1	46.1	49.7	15.6	203	85.2
Glen Elder city	445	423	-4.9	438	98.2	0.0	0.0	0.0	1.8	23.7	17.4	40.5	31.2	16.1	189	84.1
Goddard city	4,381	4,796	9.5	4,330	89.6	0.1	0.6	3.3	6.4	33.4	10.0	33.6	35.2	27.7	1,335	90.0
Goessel city	539	501	-7.1	639	99.1	0.0	0.0	0.9	0.0	22.4	24.6	45.1	42.3	22.3	251	86.9
Goff city	121	118	-2.5	100	95.0	0.0	5.0	0.0	0.0	26.0	15.0	36.5	42.2	15.6	43	88.4
Goodland city	4,486	4,406	-1.8	4,315	80.8	1.0	0.9	3.0	14.3	22.6	16.4	38.1	34.6	23.4	1,895	90.9
Gorham city	341	337	-1.2	365	87.1	0.0	0.0	5.2	7.7	23.3	17.5	31.1	38.3	18.2	161	82.6
Gove City city	78	70	-10.3	86	100.0	0.0	0.0	0.0	0.0	19.8	15.1	28.5	45.1	17.6	34	91.2
Grainfield city	274	244	-10.9	328	97.6	0.0	0.0	1.2	1.2	25.0	18.9	45.0	41.6	17.2	146	89.0
Grandview Plaza city	1,637	1,528	-6.7	1,191	50.7	16.5	2.7	9.0	21.1	21.4	7.2	25.4	46.1	14.8	520	93.3
Grantville CDP	180	-	-	201	94.5	0.0	0.0	5.5	0.0	17.4	0.0	36.9	23.3	27.1	68	100.0
Great Bend city	16,005	14,974	-6.4	15,358	73.6	1.2	0.2	2.7	22.3	25.6	16.7	36.8	44.5	19.6	6,142	87.8
Greeley city	302	296	-2.0	324	95.4	0.0	0.0	1.2	3.4	29.3	14.5	32.3	57.2	8.8	135	81.5
Greeley County unified government	1,180	1,166	-1.2	1,105	75.3	0.0	0.0	0.2	24.5	25.0	21.2	43.1	37.1	28.6	492	86.2
Greeley County unified government (balance)	433	421	-2.8	301	87.4	0.0	0.0	0.0	12.6	23.6	20.3	44.9	31.1	32.5	136	81.6
Green city	128	121	-5.5	173	97.7	0.0	0.0	2.3	0.0	30.6	8.1	37.1	36.0	20.7	58	86.2
Greenleaf city	331	305	-7.9	400	83.5	0.0	0.0	0.5	16.0	27.5	15.8	37.1	64.5	7.2	172	71.5
Greensburg city	774	778	0.5	863	85.3	0.2	1.0	2.7	10.8	25.3	24.0	45.6	40.0	24.0	385	83.1
Grenola city	216	188	-13.0	170	88.2	0.0	0.0	10.0	1.8	24.1	35.9	55.8	51.2	16.3	79	87.3
Gridley city	341	324	-5.0	352	94.0	0.0	0.3	0.6	5.1	29.0	19.6	32.7	51.4	11.6	157	87.9
Grinnell city	259	230	-11.2	269	91.4	0.0	0.0	3.3	5.2	13.8	33.8	53.9	45.2	18.0	154	87.0
Gypsum city	405	391	-3.5	464	81.3	2.4	1.3	11.6	3.4	25.9	19.6	39.1	42.9	13.6	176	80.7
Haddam city	104	96	-7.7	88	97.7	0.0	0.0	0.0	2.3	23.9	28.4	39.4	49.2	25.4	35	71.4
Halstead city	2,083	2,041	-2.0	2,277	89.4	1.4	0.4	1.2	7.7	28.6	15.4	35.6	41.1	21.3	853	84.2
Hamilton city	270	242	-10.4	259	88.8	0.0	0.0	6.2	5.0	25.1	23.9	38.3	44.2	10.4	115	80.0

1 May be of any race.

Table A. All Places — **Population and Housing**

STATE City, town, township, borough, or CDP (county if applicable)	Population: 2010 census total population	Population: 2019 estimated population	Population: Percent change 2010-2019	Population: ACS total population estimate 2015-2019	Race and Hispanic or Latino origin (percent): White alone, not Hispanic or Latino	Black alone, not Hispanic or Latino	Asian alone, not Hispanic or Latino	All other races or 2 or more races, not Hispanic or Latino	Hispanic or Latino[1]	Age (percent): Under 18 years old	Age 65 years and older	Median age	Educational attainment of persons age 25 and older: Percent High school diploma or less	Percent Bachelor's degree or more	Occupied housing units: Total	Percent with a computer
	1	2	3	4	5	6	7	8	9	10	11	12	13	14	15	16
KANSAS—Con.																
Hamlin city	37	36	-2.7	79	67.1	0.0	0.0	27.8	5.1	48.1	1.3	18.4	46.2	34.6	20	100.0
Hanover city	684	648	-5.3	674	98.4	0.9	0.7	0.0	0.0	23.9	22.4	44.8	45.6	29.3	270	80.0
Hanston city	216	201	-6.9	300	82.3	0.0	0.0	2.0	15.7	31.3	16.0	33.3	33.3	29.2	104	79.8
Hardtner city	172	158	-8.1	220	96.8	0.0	0.0	2.3	0.9	16.4	20.0	52.4	44.4	11.8	97	73.2
Harper city	1,473	1,317	-10.6	1,360	80.1	0.4	0.1	8.0	11.4	25.5	20.1	39.9	55.4	10.8	536	85.1
Harris CDP	51	-	-	8	100.0	0.0	0.0	0.0	0.0	0.0	100.0	0.0	50.0	0.0	4	100.0
Hartford city	375	371	-1.1	369	95.4	0.0	0.5	1.6	2.4	25.7	14.4	32.6	54.2	15.0	154	92.9
Harveyville city	246	248	0.8	307	91.5	0.0	7.8	0.0	0.7	14.3	11.7	42.0	49.7	23.2	117	98.3
Havana city	118	105	-11.0	85	92.9	0.0	0.0	7.1	0.0	5.9	10.6	50.9	78.6	4.3	39	79.5
Haven city	1,245	1,188	-4.6	1,166	92.7	0.8	0.9	4.6	1.0	29.6	19.0	36.0	34.9	18.8	424	92.0
Havensville city	133	155	16.5	125	88.0	0.0	0.0	4.0	8.0	20.0	14.4	44.5	62.0	14.0	46	91.3
Haviland city	701	672	-4.1	750	83.2	1.9	0.5	8.0	6.4	19.9	18.1	30.1	32.6	36.5	223	87.9
Hays city	20,539	20,744	1.0	20,899	87.9	1.1	1.5	3.0	6.6	20.5	14.5	31.0	30.5	39.9	8,370	89.6
Haysville city	10,830	11,338	4.7	11,132	86.1	0.2	0.4	6.8	6.4	30.2	12.9	34.0	46.1	16.1	4,202	89.4
Hazelton city	93	86	-7.5	117	65.8	0.0	0.0	25.6	8.5	33.3	27.4	48.9	56.4	5.1	47	97.9
Healy CDP	234	-	-	223	83.9	0.0	0.0	6.7	9.4	22.0	18.8	35.4	38.9	21.5	111	86.5
Hepler city	132	131	-0.8	158	90.5	0.0	0.0	4.4	5.1	29.1	7.0	27.7	38.7	8.6	57	84.2
Herington city	2,529	2,268	-10.3	2,147	75.3	3.9	3.5	5.5	11.7	22.5	22.1	43.1	44.9	15.7	991	87.7
Herndon city	131	130	-0.8	139	97.1	0.0	0.0	0.0	2.9	18.0	28.1	41.5	55.7	7.2	63	88.9
Hesston city	3,711	3,742	0.8	3,803	86.2	0.2	0.4	1.7	11.5	22.3	26.1	40.0	15.3	58.5	1,483	83.7
Hiawatha city	3,261	3,118	-4.4	3,147	88.3	0.9	0.0	6.8	4.0	21.1	22.3	44.3	42.8	21.2	1,377	85.8
Highland city	1,017	995	-2.2	1,152	62.2	31.4	0.3	2.0	4.0	9.1	11.4	19.9	34.5	34.8	205	85.4
Hill City city	1,468	1,410	-4.0	1,629	87.9	5.5	2.7	2.5	1.4	21.8	24.1	43.2	39.3	23.4	734	84.2
Hillsboro city	2,996	2,816	-6.0	2,839	88.2	1.5	1.1	4.2	5.0	14.5	23.0	37.5	34.3	27.2	1,125	86.0
Hillsdale CDP	229	-	-	311	69.8	0.0	0.0	0.0	30.2	8.4	14.8	53.6	13.4	23.6	122	100.0
Hoisington city	2,701	2,470	-8.6	2,840	88.8	3.1	0.0	3.6	4.4	26.3	16.4	34.4	40.8	21.2	1,079	85.4
Holcomb city	2,089	2,073	-0.8	2,188	57.2	0.0	0.5	6.8	35.5	32.9	7.4	31.7	43.6	20.3	671	94.8
Hollenberg city	21	20	-4.8	22	81.8	0.0	0.0	9.1	9.1	0.0	31.8	63.5	72.7	0.0	17	35.3
Holton city	3,323	3,208	-3.5	3,237	88.0	0.1	1.1	3.6	7.2	20.9	18.5	37.9	41.4	23.3	1,477	87.5
Holyrood city	447	415	-7.2	506	89.5	0.0	2.8	5.3	2.4	22.5	22.1	44.6	43.8	14.4	218	83.0
Home CDP	160	-	-	128	88.3	0.0	0.0	11.7	0.0	13.3	32.0	46.8	32.4	33.3	63	82.5
Hope city	364	329	-9.6	400	95.0	0.0	0.8	2.5	1.8	22.5	18.8	43.5	57.1	15.0	173	78.6
Horace city	68	66	-2.9	80	63.8	0.0	0.0	8.8	27.5	41.3	11.3	31.2	85.1	4.3	27	59.3
Horton city	1,769	1,685	-4.7	1,750	82.4	0.5	1.5	8.1	7.5	25.1	17.7	39.1	53.3	13.7	700	82.1
Howard city	687	606	-11.8	602	86.0	1.7	1.8	3.7	6.8	24.4	34.7	49.4	51.4	21.5	289	75.4
Hoxie city	1,203	1,193	-0.8	1,197	90.6	0.8	0.0	1.4	7.3	20.5	27.5	45.9	39.1	23.6	585	86.8
Hoyt city	661	630	-4.7	555	82.7	0.5	1.4	8.1	7.2	19.3	14.8	42.6	43.9	17.4	244	94.3
Hudson city	129	124	-3.9	99	99.0	0.0	0.0	1.0	0.0	7.1	38.4	58.7	51.3	24.4	52	69.2
Hugoton city	3,921	3,745	-4.5	4,226	54.5	0.0	0.4	2.0	42.9	31.3	14.0	34.3	49.8	10.2	1,323	89.8
Humboldt city	1,944	1,769	-9.0	1,880	89.9	1.2	1.1	4.0	3.7	25.4	23.9	44.6	37.3	14.6	777	84.6
Hunnewell city	67	64	-4.5	87	94.3	0.0	0.0	2.3	3.4	25.3	8.0	32.3	43.5	15.2	28	92.9
Hunter city	59	54	-8.5	53	92.5	0.0	7.5	0.0	0.0	11.3	41.5	62.4	44.7	12.8	29	82.8
Huron city	75	73	-2.7	77	96.1	2.6	0.0	1.3	0.0	28.6	23.4	48.2	66.0	9.4	30	40.0
Hutchinson city	42,180	40,383	-4.3	40,914	79.0	3.9	0.7	3.5	13.0	22.5	18.7	38.6	39.4	21.2	16,416	87.2
Independence city	9,481	8,505	-10.3	8,698	76.9	6.2	1.9	5.9	9.1	22.3	19.7	39.4	38.5	20.1	3,847	86.1
Ingalls city	298	289	-3.0	259	56.8	0.0	0.0	13.9	29.3	30.1	10.8	40.1	42.2	22.7	95	100.0
Inman city	1,386	1,334	-3.8	1,406	90.8	0.3	0.0	5.2	3.8	27.7	23.8	40.7	38.2	26.6	557	85.3
Iola city	5,697	5,266	-7.6	5,351	86.2	1.8	1.1	6.0	4.9	20.8	19.5	37.4	41.6	22.7	2,416	83.5
Isabel city	90	81	-10.0	115	96.5	0.0	0.0	0.0	3.5	20.9	27.8	41.5	71.3	2.5	43	83.7
Iuka city	163	156	-4.3	188	99.5	0.0	0.0	0.5	0.0	23.9	21.3	35.5	38.1	21.6	87	90.8
Jamestown city	286	263	-8.0	289	99.3	0.0	0.0	0.7	0.0	21.1	15.9	40.2	39.4	23.2	106	92.5
Jennings city	96	92	-4.2	84	100.0	0.0	0.0	0.0	0.0	13.1	33.3	56.3	68.1	11.6	46	82.6
Jetmore city	867	813	-6.2	962	86.8	0.1	3.7	2.9	6.4	20.7	22.5	44.2	32.9	28.4	386	89.6
Jewell city	432	402	-6.9	397	90.9	0.0	0.0	1.0	8.1	16.4	30.7	50.9	52.3	20.3	207	80.7
Johnson City city	1,495	1,343	-10.2	1,142	53.7	0.0	0.0	1.1	45.2	24.1	19.8	38.1	57.4	11.3	470	78.1
Junction City city	23,361	21,482	-8.0	23,104	53.9	20.6	3.3	7.9	14.3	28.1	10.2	28.1	32.5	22.1	9,163	92.0
Kanopolis city	492	452	-8.1	574	89.2	0.0	0.0	0.2	10.6	23.9	24.4	50.4	55.2	13.3	264	87.9
Kanorado city	153	154	0.7	224	50.4	0.0	0.0	8.0	41.5	21.0	21.9	50.7	74.9	4.8	93	77.4
Kansas City city	145,783	152,960	4.9	152,522	38.1	22.8	4.9	3.9	30.4	27.8	11.9	33.5	53.9	17.8	55,690	87.4
Kechi city	1,912	2,005	4.9	2,745	84.2	4.2	1.3	3.6	6.6	21.2	12.0	40.7	27.9	39.3	964	95.6
Kensington city	473	437	-7.6	488	94.7	1.0	1.0	1.2	2.0	23.2	36.5	54.2	46.8	20.1	205	83.9
Kickapoo Site 1 CDP	101	-	-	68	0.0	4.4	0.0	80.9	14.7	51.5	0.0	17.9	50.0	0.0	18	77.8
Kickapoo Site 2 CDP	34	-	-	70	0.0	0.0	0.0	100.0	0.0	50.0	0.0	19.5	44.4	0.0	14	100.0
Kickapoo Site 5 CDP	66	-	-	44	6.8	0.0	52.3	40.9	0.0	13.6	18.2	45.5	78.8	6.1	13	76.9
Kickapoo Site 6 CDP	15	-	-	35	11.4	0.0	0.0	25.7	62.9	80.0	11.4	11.0	100.0	0.0	5	100.0
Kickapoo Site 7 CDP	66	-	-	43	0.0	0.0	0.0	97.7	2.3	20.9	9.3	26.5	64.0	0.0	25	80.0
Kickapoo Tribal Center CDP	194	-	-	158	7.0	0.0	0.0	88.0	5.1	21.5	19.6	48.5	38.2	15.5	60	58.3
Kincaid city	120	116	-3.3	108	100.0	0.0	0.0	0.0	0.0	25.9	10.2	31.5	44.2	2.6	50	78.0
Kingman city	3,178	2,842	-10.6	2,928	89.7	0.8	0.0	2.3	7.2	21.6	22.5	44.9	46.6	17.7	1,325	84.4
Kinsley city	1,464	1,353	-7.6	1,515	71.0	0.7	1.2	2.4	24.8	21.3	20.2	45.0	48.6	18.1	706	82.9
Kiowa city	1,029	931	-9.5	840	87.9	3.0	0.0	7.6	1.5	23.1	26.7	47.3	40.8	22.6	349	85.7
Kipp CDP	59	-	-	-	-	-	-	-	-	-	-	-	-	-	-	-
Kirwin city	171	156	-8.8	166	98.8	0.0	0.0	1.2	0.0	28.3	17.5	34.5	59.3	18.6	65	80.0
Kismet city	461	435	-5.6	367	56.4	0.0	4.4	1.4	37.9	24.3	13.9	35.5	48.4	24.2	141	92.2
Labette city	72	66	-8.3	57	98.2	0.0	0.0	1.8	0.0	14.0	45.6	64.4	60.4	8.3	23	56.5
La Crosse city	1,342	1,232	-8.2	1,232	87.7	0.5	0.3	5.0	6.5	24.6	25.5	45.2	36.0	26.7	566	89.6
La Cygne city	1,152	1,119	-2.9	1,186	90.2	1.7	0.0	7.1	1.0	25.0	21.2	42.1	55.5	6.3	521	83.9
La Harpe city	572	530	-7.3	506	87.9	0.0	2.4	5.5	4.2	21.3	17.6	45.9	52.6	9.8	214	83.6
Lake Quivira city	901	933	3.6	920	96.6	0.2	0.2	1.8	1.1	25.2	23.0	48.7	5.7	81.1	338	100.0
Lakin city	2,224	2,141	-3.7	1,780	58.3	0.8	0.0	1.5	39.4	25.2	13.5	34.8	68.5	10.8	578	87.9
Lancaster city	298	283	-5.0	245	99.6	0.0	0.0	0.4	0.0	17.6	15.5	46.8	47.0	10.4	97	87.6
Lane city	225	225	0.0	179	94.4	0.0	1.1	3.4	1.1	11.7	27.9	42.8	53.7	16.2	100	81.0
Langdon city	42	41	-2.4	34	100.0	0.0	0.0	0.0	0.0	0.0	17.6	29.8	67.7	25.8	14	78.6
Lansing city	11,261	11,949	6.1	11,900	68.3	11.4	3.2	7.5	9.6	19.1	12.7	38.0	34.5	35.2	3,317	95.0
Larned city	4,038	3,671	-9.1	3,813	85.8	1.2	0.0	4.1	8.9	21.7	23.8	48.4	36.1	23.8	1,822	89.2
Latham city	139	138	-0.7	125	92.8	0.8	0.0	6.4	0.0	28.0	24.0	50.4	51.7	3.4	57	36.8
Latimer city	20	19	-5.0	31	45.2	0.0	0.0	54.8	0.0	48.4	3.2	34.3	37.5	25.0	8	100.0
Lawrence city	87,918	98,193	11.7	96,369	75.5	4.6	6.4	6.6	6.9	17.0	11.0	28.2	20.5	53.3	38,395	95.9
Leavenworth city	35,245	35,957	2.0	36,064	70.2	14.1	1.5	4.8	9.4	24.5	12.1	35.1	36.6	31.2	12,388	91.9
Leawood city	31,888	34,727	8.9	34,670	91.0	0.7	4.1	1.3	2.8	25.0	19.3	45.9	6.3	76.9	12,905	97.6
Lebanon city	216	198	-8.3	252	84.5	0.0	0.4	9.1	6.0	21.4	23.0	51.2	56.9	17.0	121	87.6

1 May be of any race.

Table A. All Places — **Population and Housing**

STATE City, town, township, borough, or CDP (county if applicable)	Population: 2010 census total population	Population: 2019 estimated population	Population: Percent change 2010-2019	Population: ACS total population estimate 2015-2019	Race and Hispanic or Latino origin (percent): White alone, not Hispanic or Latino	Black alone, not Hispanic or Latino	Asian alone, not Hispanic or Latino	All other races or 2 or more races, not Hispanic or Latino	Hispanic or Latino[1]	Age (percent): Under 18 years old	Age 65 years and older	Median age	Educational attainment of persons age 25 and older: Percent High school diploma or less	Percent Bachelor's degree or more	Occupied housing units: Total	Percent with a computer
	1	2	3	4	5	6	7	8	9	10	11	12	13	14	15	16
KANSAS—Con.																
Lebo city	940	887	-5.6	804	89.9	2.9	0.9	1.5	4.9	17.7	23.0	42.7	39.0	22.9	364	87.4
Lecompton city	633	654	3.3	749	82.5	0.0	0.5	13.5	3.5	28.3	13.2	29.6	51.5	19.6	260	94.6
Lehigh city	177	169	-4.5	255	96.1	1.2	0.0	0.0	2.7	31.8	17.3	33.6	45.9	15.5	86	97.7
Lenexa city	48,216	55,625	15.4	54,011	79.0	6.4	4.4	2.7	7.5	21.7	14.7	37.8	18.5	55.5	21,683	96.0
Lenora city	250	230	-8.0	345	79.7	0.0	0.0	0.3	20.0	30.1	18.0	39.8	50.0	19.7	126	71.4
Leon city	739	733	-0.8	614	92.8	3.3	1.1	0.3	2.4	25.1	15.0	38.0	47.2	10.6	243	87.7
Leona city	53	50	-5.7	48	100.0	0.0	0.0	0.0	0.0	22.9	6.3	28.5	88.9	5.6	15	100.0
Leonardville city	450	431	-4.2	464	96.3	0.0	0.4	1.7	1.5	19.2	36.6	53.0	44.0	16.8	173	80.9
Leoti city	1,526	1,448	-5.1	1,582	51.8	0.3	0.0	1.6	46.3	26.5	21.2	41.2	46.2	17.1	661	87.6
LeRoy city	563	538	-4.4	617	97.9	0.0	0.0	1.3	0.8	20.4	16.4	33.2	47.3	12.1	285	89.5
Levant CDP	61	-	-	11	100.0	0.0	0.0	0.0	0.0	0.0	45.5	0.0	54.5	0.0	5	100.0
Lewis city	451	416	-7.8	393	71.5	0.0	0.0	0.0	28.5	21.1	25.7	49.5	43.0	13.0	189	91.0
Liberal city	20,531	19,174	-6.6	19,731	27.7	5.1	2.9	1.7	62.6	31.1	8.9	29.4	63.7	9.9	6,569	88.6
Liberty city	123	111	-9.8	87	78.2	0.0	0.0	21.8	0.0	18.4	14.9	33.5	56.9	3.1	51	90.2
Liebenthal city	103	94	-8.7	164	100.0	0.0	0.0	0.0	0.0	22.6	17.7	31.8	55.9	17.1	69	89.9
Lincoln Center city	1,291	1,181	-8.5	1,266	91.9	0.2	0.0	1.3	6.6	18.8	25.1	44.6	45.7	13.8	561	76.5
Lincolnville city	203	193	-4.9	189	89.9	0.0	0.0	4.2	5.8	11.1	20.1	54.3	62.2	12.8	101	85.1
Lindsborg city	3,459	3,290	-4.9	3,301	89.7	3.2	0.7	0.8	5.6	21.6	21.5	34.7	28.1	40.5	1,316	91.9
Linn city	410	382	-6.8	354	85.3	0.0	0.0	1.7	13.0	15.3	32.2	50.3	59.9	12.0	154	70.1
Linn Valley city	810	868	7.2	746	96.8	0.9	0.5	0.4	1.3	20.6	21.8	52.0	43.9	23.6	373	91.4
Linwood city	384	419	9.1	484	93.2	0.0	0.0	2.7	4.1	22.9	12.4	38.3	60.8	11.0	174	88.5
Little River city	550	522	-5.1	446	94.6	0.0	1.3	3.1	0.9	19.1	21.5	39.1	44.0	18.7	202	90.1
Logan city	589	534	-9.3	602	95.0	0.5	0.0	0.3	4.2	23.8	28.9	46.0	34.1	25.1	278	87.8
Lone Elm city	24	23	-4.2	10	100.0	0.0	0.0	0.0	0.0	0.0	20.0	56.5	60.0	10.0	7	100.0
Longford city	79	72	-8.9	138	86.2	0.0	0.0	13.8	0.0	33.3	5.8	31.6	34.7	20.0	50	88.0
Long Island city	134	121	-9.7	154	100.0	0.0	0.0	0.0	0.0	30.5	7.8	34.2	36.7	21.1	56	89.3
Longton city	348	308	-11.5	340	89.4	0.0	0.0	7.4	3.2	21.2	19.7	44.7	48.5	12.4	160	86.9
Lorraine city	138	127	-8.0	139	74.1	0.0	0.0	15.8	10.1	23.7	17.3	30.8	40.8	16.3	60	90.0
Lost Springs city	70	67	-4.3	115	51.3	0.0	0.0	0.0	48.7	27.0	22.6	51.0	78.5	2.5	40	57.5
Louisburg city	4,307	4,562	5.9	4,443	92.2	0.7	0.2	1.7	5.1	30.0	12.5	37.5	30.3	27.7	1,648	93.9
Louisville city	188	225	19.7	174	71.3	0.0	0.0	20.1	8.6	16.7	14.9	42.1	75.2	9.0	82	75.6
Lowell CDP	283	-	-	349	100.0	0.0	0.0	0.0	0.0	37.2	30.9	41.2	25.6	23.3	92	90.2
Lucas city	396	391	-1.3	370	98.9	0.0	0.0	1.1	0.0	14.1	27.0	45.8	44.0	15.6	187	83.4
Luray city	189	184	-2.6	212	95.3	0.0	0.0	4.7	0.0	25.0	25.0	45.5	53.6	13.7	86	86.0
Lyndon city	1,056	1,021	-3.3	1,058	93.5	0.0	0.5	3.6	2.5	29.3	13.3	35.9	31.4	30.8	390	86.7
Lyons city	3,734	3,504	-6.2	3,564	78.9	1.2	0.5	2.2	17.2	23.1	21.6	40.2	41.7	15.5	1,490	85.6
McConnell AFB CDP	1,777	-	-	1,532	55.2	17.8	0.0	11.2	15.9	24.0	0.3	25.2	15.9	35.3	403	95.8
McCracken city	192	176	-8.3	141	82.3	0.0	0.0	17.7	0.0	24.8	25.5	42.8	46.6	14.6	68	85.3
McCune city	408	412	1.0	406	92.9	0.7	0.0	3.4	3.0	28.6	17.0	36.7	36.0	25.1	170	83.5
McDonald city	160	157	-1.9	176	76.1	0.6	0.0	1.7	21.6	12.5	22.2	43.0	49.2	12.7	80	81.3
McFarland city	256	248	-3.1	332	81.9	0.0	0.0	8.1	9.9	19.6	13.9	42.6	53.6	14.9	128	87.5
Macksville city	549	530	-3.5	500	41.6	0.0	0.0	3.8	54.6	33.8	9.4	34.2	54.1	19.4	181	95.0
McLouth city	888	849	-4.4	1,237	89.8	0.4	0.0	3.5	6.3	27.9	12.5	32.2	50.5	18.9	454	85.9
McPherson city	13,161	13,061	-0.8	13,054	88.9	1.4	1.3	2.8	5.6	22.9	16.4	37.6	32.7	28.9	5,687	92.2
Madison city	697	618	-11.3	851	91.2	0.0	0.0	1.4	7.4	24.1	18.9	38.6	53.0	15.7	371	81.9
Mahaska city	83	76	-8.4	56	96.4	0.0	0.0	3.6	0.0	8.9	26.8	51.6	68.6	13.7	31	67.7
Maize city	3,442	4,934	43.3	4,579	90.0	0.6	0.0	8.1	1.4	29.4	13.5	30.6	36.3	33.8	1,618	89.1
Manchester city	97	96		130	92.3	0.0	0.0	7.7	0.0	23.1	7.7	41.3	67.5	19.3	47	93.6
Manhattan city	52,158	54,604	4.7	55,290	76.9	5.8	5.8	4.5	7.1	15.4	8.6	24.5	19.5	51.9	20,252	95.2
Mankato city	871	816	-6.3	829	95.4	1.2	0.0	1.1	2.3	25.9	28.3	50.6	45.5	20.5	376	78.5
Manter city	171	154	-9.9	220	64.5	0.0	0.0	7.3	28.2	20.0	21.4	35.9	47.2	12.8	62	95.2
Maple Hill city	620	606	-2.3	592	89.9	0.0	1.0	1.7	7.4	30.6	10.8	40.1	50.1	23.0	204	90.2
Mapleton city	84	81	-3.6	116	96.6	0.0	0.9	2.6	0.0	22.4	27.6	32.0	59.7	4.8	39	66.7
Marienthal CDP	71	-	-	52	73.1	0.0	26.9	0.0	0.0	0.0	63.5	68.1	1.9	63.5	42	83.3
Marion city	1,926	1,775	-7.8	2,046	92.0	0.7	0.0	3.1	4.2	25.4	24.3	43.3	35.4	26.6	895	77.9
Marquette city	650	599	-7.8	801	94.1	0.0	0.0	0.2	5.6	21.7	23.1	46.7	45.1	17.6	376	93.1
Marysville city	3,308	3,269	-1.2	3,281	94.0	0.7	0.0	1.3	4.1	26.3	17.3	38.8	49.2	20.9	1,476	88.4
Matfield Green city	45	43	-4.4	52	100.0	0.0	0.0	0.0	0.0	34.6	26.9	49.2	41.2	32.4	23	100.0
Mayetta city	361	346	-4.2	315	73.3	1.6	5.4	16.2	3.5	24.1	14.6	35.4	53.1	8.9	146	81.5
Mayfield city	113	107	-5.3	91	97.8	0.0	0.0	0.0	2.2	18.7	27.5	50.6	63.2	16.2	45	88.9
Meade city	1,721	1,523	-11.5	1,466	88.4	0.9	1.6	4.0	5.0	18.5	19.7	45.1	43.7	22.0	608	83.6
Medicine Lodge city	2,020	1,835	-9.2	1,725	92.7	0.7	4.1	0.0	2.5	17.4	19.3	47.3	47.3	15.4	776	86.5
Melvern city	387	374	-3.4	400	97.5	0.0	0.0	2.5	0.0	27.0	16.5	45.3	58.2	13.4	156	91.0
Menlo city	61	59	-3.3	49	100.0	0.0	0.0	0.0	0.0	42.9	0.0	30.5	53.6	7.1	14	92.9
Meriden city	814	780	-4.2	792	90.7	0.0	0.0	8.6	0.8	27.0	11.7	33.0	40.7	13.8	303	91.7
Merriam city	11,017	11,081	0.6	11,185	78.8	5.9	2.6	2.9	9.9	17.0	17.7	39.4	29.8	34.7	5,132	91.4
Milan city	82	78	-4.9	73	91.8	0.0	0.0	6.8	1.4	13.7	26.0	58.1	60.7	4.9	35	80.0
Mildred city	24	23	-4.2	15	100.0	0.0	0.0	0.0	0.0	46.7	0.0	27.5	62.5	0.0	4	75.0
Milford city	530	511	-3.6	283	89.4	2.5	0.7	3.5	3.9	32.2	19.4	31.6	38.0	28.2	116	94.8
Milton CDP	155	-	-	184	100.0	0.0	0.0	0.0	0.0	14.7	14.7	47.1	64.1	0.0	74	100.0
Miltonvale city	536	487	-9.1	586	97.6	0.0	0.0	2.4	0.0	24.9	18.4	36.2	54.1	23.1	242	78.5
Minneapolis city	2,038	1,900	-6.8	1,795	94.8	0.9	0.0	1.2	3.1	21.8	21.7	47.8	38.0	23.2	838	78.5
Minneola city	748	679	-9.2	788	94.0	0.0	2.0	2.0	1.9	27.8	26.5	41.3	31.9	27.6	311	83.0
Mission city	9,317	9,911	6.4	9,523	78.2	7.1	5.0	2.7	7.0	14.6	13.7	34.9	18.9	52.3	4,730	95.2
Mission Hills city	3,471	3,547	2.2	3,574	89.9	0.0	7.2	0.6	2.3	26.8	20.9	46.0	2.6	90.2	1,218	96.7
Mission Woods city	178	193	8.4	186	93.5	0.0	2.7	2.7	1.1	18.8	28.0	46.8	4.9	86.0	76	100.0
Moline city	371	323	-12.9	399	98.2	0.0	0.0	1.0	0.8	26.8	26.1	46.7	49.8	9.7	161	88.8
Montezuma city	961	964	0.3	885	92.5	0.0	0.0	0.0	7.5	19.0	33.1	49.6	57.8	14.3	384	77.1
Moran city	563	510	-9.4	394	89.1	1.0	0.0	5.8	4.1	20.8	30.5	52.1	56.5	16.4	178	74.2
Morganville city	196	190	-3.1	177	100.0	0.0	0.0	0.0	0.0	27.7	21.5	43.6	49.2	7.3	70	72.9
Morland city	154	146	-5.2	177	98.3	0.0	0.0	1.7	0.0	23.7	11.9	44.4	25.2	26.7	86	90.7
Morrill city	237	227	-4.2	208	67.8	0.0	0.0	32.2	0.0	32.2	7.7	35.4	51.5	14.0	79	75.9
Morrowville city	157	147	-6.4	145	100.0	0.0	0.0	0.0	0.0	24.8	15.2	43.4	68.1	7.7	57	82.5
Moscow city	318	299	-6.0	245	53.9	0.0	0.0	9.4	36.7	30.2	10.6	34.3	67.9	10.7	66	92.4
Mound City city	695	678	-2.4	1,088	94.1	2.4	0.0	3.2	0.3	20.5	16.5	38.3	39.3	22.3	501	81.0
Moundridge city	1,871	1,869	-0.1	2,222	92.1	0.0	0.0	3.5	4.4	23.5	27.9	43.7	50.5	23.5	985	84.5
Mound Valley city	407	372	-8.6	337	92.9	0.0	0.0	2.7	4.5	16.9	15.7	47.1	45.4	7.7	158	82.9
Mount Hope city	813	801	-1.5	749	89.1	0.0	0.0	1.7	9.2	23.5	23.0	41.4	38.9	18.4	272	91.5
Mulberry city	519	521	0.4	378	92.1	0.0	0.0	7.9	0.0	17.2	19.3	48.1	60.2	13.1	165	67.3
Mullinville city	255	241	-5.5	253	91.7	0.0	0.0	1.6	6.7	22.9	23.7	40.8	38.6	9.7	111	86.5
Mulvane city	6,147	6,489	5.6	6,045	93.1	0.0	0.0	5.6	1.3	26.5	16.9	38.9	26.0	32.1	2,310	92.9
Munden city	100	93	-7.0	109	94.5	0.0	5.5	0.0	0.0	13.8	27.5	51.9	24.7	27.3	56	75.0

1 May be of any race.

Table A. All Places — **Population and Housing**

STATE City, town, township, borough, or CDP (county if applicable)	Population: 2010 census total population	Population: 2019 estimated population	Population: Percent change 2010-2019	Population: ACS total population estimate 2015-2019	Race and Hispanic or Latino origin (percent): White alone, not Hispanic or Latino	Black alone, not Hispanic or Latino	Asian alone, not Hispanic or Latino	All other races or 2 or more races, not Hispanic or Latino	Hispanic or Latino[1]	Age (percent): Under 18 years old	Age 65 years and older	Median age	Educational attainment of persons age 25 and older: Percent High school diploma or less	Percent Bachelor's degree or more	Occupied housing units: Total	Percent with a computer
	1	2	3	4	5	6	7	8	9	10	11	12	13	14	15	16
KANSAS—Con.																
Munjor CDP	213	-	-	193	100.0	0.0	0.0	0.0	0.0	31.6	14.0	47.2	65.9	5.3	78	88.5
Muscotah city	176	167	-5.1	155	94.2	0.0	0.0	0.0	5.8	25.8	20.6	42.3	55.4	7.9	72	69.4
Narka city	94	86	-8.5	109	100.0	0.0	0.0	0.0	0.0	26.6	3.7	35.3	59.1	16.7	55	94.5
Nashville city	62	57	-8.1	41	100.0	0.0	0.0	0.0	0.0	2.4	53.7	67.3	42.5	15.0	24	83.3
Natoma city	335	295	-11.9	273	96.7	2.6	0.0	0.0	0.7	16.5	27.1	50.4	44.1	20.9	132	85.6
Neodesha city	2,490	2,262	-9.2	2,083	91.9	0.3	0.0	5.0	2.7	24.8	19.9	40.4	43.3	16.9	907	83.6
Neosho Falls city	141	137	-2.8	104	89.4	0.0	0.0	8.7	1.9	23.1	14.4	46.1	70.0	3.8	52	61.5
Neosho Rapids city	265	262	-1.1	280	89.3	0.4	0.0	10.0	0.4	21.4	20.0	42.8	46.0	18.0	121	79.3
Ness City city	1,468	1,303	-11.2	1,571	84.9	1.0	0.0	1.7	12.4	25.5	21.5	41.1	37.8	25.2	649	83.1
Netawaka city	143	137	-4.2	164	84.8	0.0	0.0	14.6	0.6	21.3	16.5	48.0	52.1	14.3	65	86.2
New Albany city	56	51	-8.9	40	80.0	0.0	0.0	20.0	0.0	20.0	27.5	39.8	48.3	6.9	18	44.4
New Cambria city	126	126	0.0	74	93.2	0.0	0.0	0.0	6.8	5.4	12.2	50.7	69.1	5.9	34	67.6
New Strawn city	391	380	-2.8	408	93.9	0.0	0.0	3.4	2.7	22.5	19.9	40.8	30.3	33.1	166	99.4
Newton city	19,116	18,861	-1.3	18,877	76.8	2.2	0.7	4.0	16.3	25.5	17.8	38.3	37.1	28.8	7,470	87.0
Nickerson city	1,063	998	-6.1	1,015	93.1	2.1	0.0	0.6	4.2	25.3	13.4	42.6	42.7	15.3	393	90.6
Niotaze city	82	73	-11.0	65	100.0	0.0	0.0	0.0	0.0	9.2	49.2	61.5	52.6	3.5	24	95.8
Norcatur city	151	144	-4.6	323	95.7	0.0	0.0	3.4	0.9	27.9	16.4	28.6	42.5	9.4	159	93.7
North Newton city	1,766	1,762	-0.2	1,778	91.3	3.2	0.3	1.7	3.5	11.8	30.5	45.9	20.3	55.4	677	91.4
Norton city	2,888	2,722	-5.7	2,766	97.0	0.1	0.5	1.5	0.8	23.7	24.0	45.3	42.0	19.6	1,053	82.8
Nortonville city	637	610	-4.2	696	92.8	0.0	0.0	5.5	1.7	27.6	19.5	38.4	49.7	15.7	266	85.7
Norwich city	491	440	-10.4	511	95.3	1.2	0.0	0.6	2.9	33.5	12.3	32.9	25.0	33.0	193	90.2
Oak Hill city	24	23	-4.2	59	88.1	0.0	0.0	11.9	0.0	23.7	1.7	35.5	37.5	0.0	24	58.3
Oaklawn-Sunview CDP	3,276	-	-	3,441	55.1	1.7	11.7	11.0	20.4	24.4	11.6	36.5	74.9	5.4	1,361	84.9
Oakley city	2,043	2,075	1.6	2,090	88.9	0.1	0.0	3.6	7.4	23.8	22.9	39.8	39.2	15.5	893	84.4
Oberlin city	1,788	1,700	-4.9	1,622	93.8	0.1	0.3	0.8	5.1	20.1	29.7	47.3	42.5	16.8	820	88.9
Odin CDP	101	-	-	124	100.0	0.0	0.0	0.0	0.0	28.2	14.5	39.8	31.5	18.0	61	86.9
Offerle city	199	183	-8.0	283	74.9	0.0	1.4	7.8	15.9	29.0	11.7	33.3	32.1	24.6	102	87.3
Ogden city	2,080	1,958	-5.9	1,600	76.2	6.4	2.7	7.4	7.3	23.4	10.0	29.2	39.1	12.5	707	92.4
Oketo city	66	63	-4.5	75	100.0	0.0	0.0	0.0	0.0	20.0	24.0	42.4	61.7	28.3	32	78.1
Olathe city	125,922	140,545	11.6	137,618	75.1	6.1	4.1	3.0	11.7	28.5	11.0	35.4	22.6	49.7	48,227	95.9
Olivet city	67	67	0.0	50	98.0	0.0	0.0	2.0	0.0	8.0	60.0	69.0	65.2	2.2	30	73.3
Olmitz city	114	105	-7.9	71	100.0	0.0	0.0	0.0	0.0	22.5	12.7	43.8	40.0	12.7	39	71.8
Olpe city	547	535	-2.2	577	89.6	0.0	0.0	9.9	0.5	29.6	17.9	37.9	55.9	17.4	229	87.8
Olsburg city	219	218	-0.5	239	93.7	0.0	0.0	1.7	4.6	32.6	15.1	35.8	54.2	19.4	89	86.5
Onaga city	700	682	-2.6	751	94.4	0.9	0.1	4.3	0.3	16.6	41.1	57.6	56.2	20.8	337	75.1
Oneida city	72	72	0.0	167	98.8	1.2	0.0	0.0	0.0	31.7	4.2	20.6	76.3	7.9	67	97.0
Osage City city	2,943	2,809	-4.6	2,808	92.6	1.4	0.0	1.6	4.4	26.7	21.4	37.6	54.0	16.1	1,181	80.5
Osawatomie city	4,438	4,284	-3.5	4,293	86.8	2.1	1.3	3.1	6.7	26.5	13.6	34.9	53.1	16.1	1,593	80.9
Osborne city	1,436	1,272	-11.4	1,575	90.8	0.5	0.0	4.8	3.9	25.1	22.5	37.1	44.8	19.0	711	79.2
Oskaloosa city	1,107	1,057	-4.5	1,344	92.0	0.0	0.0	4.1	3.9	24.3	17.6	38.3	46.6	25.1	548	83.6
Oswego city	1,849	1,680	-9.1	1,676	91.9	1.2	0.0	5.5	1.3	18.2	21.7	44.4	41.4	15.6	728	83.9
Otis city	283	260	-8.1	218	95.4	0.0	0.0	0.0	4.6	12.8	28.9	57.7	55.7	9.7	116	77.6
Ottawa city	12,652	12,254	-3.1	12,260	88.2	1.4	0.6	4.3	5.5	24.0	15.3	35.5	41.6	22.6	5,028	85.7
Overbrook city	1,056	1,023	-3.1	800	95.9	0.0	0.3	0.8	3.1	18.4	27.0	49.7	46.4	21.0	344	82.6
Overland Park city	173,329	195,494	12.8	191,011	77.5	4.6	8.5	2.7	6.7	22.9	14.9	37.7	15.1	61.6	78,001	95.7
Oxford city	1,049	999	-4.8	1,078	81.1	0.0	0.0	4.3	14.7	29.0	21.0	42.7	42.7	20.5	425	80.9
Ozawkie city	647	620	-4.2	759	91.2	2.6	0.4	1.2	4.6	27.0	17.1	36.1	30.8	31.4	288	92.7
Palco city	281	267	-5.0	157	93.0	5.7	0.0	0.0	1.3	17.2	32.5	45.5	42.3	23.1	85	85.9
Palmer city	111	104	-6.3	146	97.3	0.0	0.0	0.0	2.7	19.9	21.9	49.3	30.8	22.2	68	83.8
Paola city	5,609	5,719	2.0	5,611	87.6	4.0	1.9	3.5	3.0	25.8	21.1	41.1	40.9	22.6	2,348	87.1
Paradise city	49	48	-2.0	29	100.0	0.0	0.0	0.0	0.0	0.0	20.7	57.6	22.2	14.8	14	78.6
Park city	126	113	-10.3	129	83.7	0.0	0.0	11.6	4.7	21.7	17.8	26.9	58.0	14.8	72	80.6
Park City city	7,284	7,764	6.6	8,138	71.2	7.3	6.5	4.7	10.3	30.1	11.0	34.2	34.1	28.7	2,906	94.5
Parker city	275	266	-3.3	503	99.2	0.0	0.0	0.0	0.8	38.2	8.0	25.7	42.2	12.9	174	86.2
Parkerfield city	422	415	-1.7	389	86.6	0.0	0.0	1.8	11.6	12.6	30.8	55.5	32.9	24.7	153	95.4
Parkerville city	63	61	-3.2	64	100.0	0.0	0.0	0.0	0.0	39.1	6.3	24.5	58.1	12.9	17	64.7
Parsons city	10,499	9,477	-9.7	9,736	79.4	9.2	0.2	4.3	6.9	24.3	17.0	37.3	43.1	19.1	4,078	88.5
Partridge city	248	240	-3.2	188	85.1	0.0	0.0	0.5	14.4	25.0	19.7	43.4	54.8	8.7	80	82.5
Pawnee Rock city	253	231	-8.7	310	92.3	0.3	0.0	2.6	4.8	23.2	13.9	36.8	57.7	6.1	133	78.9
Paxico city	225	215	-4.4	280	90.4	0.0	0.0	4.6	5.0	35.4	15.0	37.0	32.9	27.6	110	74.5
Peabody city	1,202	1,101	-8.4	1,083	94.5	1.8	0.0	2.0	1.7	18.3	28.1	47.9	48.1	12.5	416	89.4
Penalosa city	19	17	-10.5	2	100.0	0.0	0.0	0.0	0.0	0.0	50.0	0.0	0.0	0.0	1	100.0
Perry city	926	910	-1.7	949	94.1	1.3	0.0	1.5	3.2	25.0	19.6	36.0	49.8	11.2	394	88.6
Peru city	140	124	-11.4	203	92.1	0.0	0.0	7.9	0.0	14.3	35.5	59.8	72.4	9.0	87	59.8
Phillipsburg city	2,574	2,445	-5.0	2,583	90.8	1.2	0.4	2.1	5.5	22.3	20.4	41.6	44.4	18.4	1,115	90.0
Piqua CDP	107	-	-	81	100.0	0.0	0.0	0.0	0.0	27.2	25.9	56.3	33.9	23.7	28	78.6
Pittsburg city	20,237	20,050	-0.9	20,171	79.3	3.7	3.1	4.5	9.5	20.2	12.9	25.9	37.7	31.2	7,888	87.8
Plains city	1,146	1,021	-10.9	1,161	47.7	1.1	0.0	1.5	49.7	33.2	11.3	31.4	46.1	21.0	438	87.9
Plainville city	1,901	1,804	-5.1	1,987	97.0	0.0	0.0	0.7	2.3	27.8	19.5	36.1	40.3	24.6	809	91.7
Pleasanton city	1,209	1,162	-3.9	1,409	97.7	0.0	0.3	1.8	0.3	28.4	13.8	36.9	53.5	12.8	663	83.6
Plevna city	101	98	-3.0	113	95.6	0.0	0.0	2.7	1.8	20.4	35.4	60.2	42.9	8.3	51	76.5
Pomona city	844	820	-2.8	1,232	91.9	0.0	0.0	5.7	2.4	24.5	15.7	35.8	63.0	9.0	466	83.9
Portis city	103	91	-11.7	144	100.0	0.0	0.0	0.0	0.0	27.1	11.8	40.0	45.5	13.1	46	91.3
Potwin city	453	437	-3.5	466	82.0	0.9	0.0	7.5	9.7	27.5	9.0	32.8	55.7	9.5	169	88.8
Powhattan city	75	72	-4.0	74	91.9	0.0	0.0	8.1	0.0	31.1	17.6	31.8	45.5	6.8	31	83.9
Prairie View city	132	119	-9.8	109	99.1	0.0	0.0	0.9	0.0	12.8	26.6	49.8	38.6	27.7	52	94.2
Prairie Village city	21,447	22,295	4.0	22,170	93.2	1.0	1.1	1.4	3.4	21.3	20.5	39.1	8.0	73.4	9,813	95.3
Pratt city	6,844	6,496	-5.1	6,703	87.1	3.6	0.1	1.2	8.0	25.9	17.5	35.0	35.7	28.6	2,606	89.7
Prescott city	264	268	1.5	261	94.3	0.0	0.0	3.8	1.9	13.8	36.0	58.8	57.8	15.7	121	76.0
Preston city	153	146	-4.6	163	87.1	0.0	0.0	8.0	4.9	21.5	16.0	40.6	36.0	16.2	68	82.4
Pretty Prairie city	672	649	-3.4	514	98.6	1.0	0.0	0.4	0.0	25.5	23.2	44.6	36.5	27.0	197	91.9
Princeton city	278	269	-3.2	237	94.9	0.0	2.5	1.7	0.8	27.8	17.7	36.3	51.6	12.4	90	81.1
Protection city	514	463	-9.9	340	92.6	0.0	0.0	0.9	6.5	12.1	36.5	55.3	44.7	18.3	154	91.6
Quenemo city	388	377	-2.8	382	83.8	0.0	0.0	5.5	10.7	22.3	10.7	37.7	82.1	2.2	153	80.4
Quinter city	926	1,057	14.1	917	91.1	0.3	0.9	5.5	2.3	24.3	25.7	44.0	44.5	20.8	398	86.4
Radium city	25	24	-4.0	20	100.0	0.0	0.0	0.0	0.0	15.0	15.0	27.8	70.6	29.4	10	80.0
Ramona city	187	177	-5.3	82	97.6	0.0	0.0	0.0	2.4	26.8	14.6	41.0	40.4	8.8	34	82.4
Randall city	67	62	-7.5	123	89.4	0.0	4.1	6.5	0.0	29.3	13.0	30.4	37.5	3.8	54	87.0
Randolph city	163	156	-4.3	173	96.0	0.0	1.7	2.3	0.0	16.8	17.3	40.4	37.4	24.4	67	92.5
Ransom city	294	260	-11.6	329	92.1	0.0	3.0	4.0	0.9	15.2	33.4	56.6	38.3	12.3	161	77.6
Rantoul city	184	186	1.1	185	93.5	0.0	0.0	2.2	4.3	33.0	20.0	38.1	73.4	7.3	64	79.7
Raymond city	79	76	-3.8	86	93.0	0.0	7.0	0.0	0.0	7.0	22.1	44.8	49.1	1.8	49	87.8

1 May be of any race.

Table A. All Places — **Population and Housing**

STATE City, town, township, borough, or CDP (county if applicable)	Population				Race and Hispanic or Latino origin (percent)					Age (percent)			Educational attainment of persons age 25 and older		Occupied housing units	
	2010 census total population	2019 estimated population	Percent change 2010-2019	ACS total population estimate 2015-2019	White alone, not Hispanic or Latino	Black alone, not Hispanic or Latino	Asian alone, not Hispanic or Latino	All other races or 2 or more races, not Hispanic or Latino	Hispanic or Latino[1]	Under 18 years old	Age 65 years and older	Median age	Percent High school diploma or less	Percent Bachelor's degree or more	Total	Percent with a computer
	1	2	3	4	5	6	7	8	9	10	11	12	13	14	15	16
KANSAS—Con.																
Reading city	233	227	-2.6	219	90.9	0.0	1.4	4.6	3.2	26.0	7.8	32.6	46.3	12.2	83	96.4
Redfield city	148	143	-3.4	124	96.0	0.0	0.0	3.2	0.8	23.4	12.9	38.8	71.9	0.0	49	85.7
Republic city	117	107	-8.5	101	95.0	0.0	0.0	3.0	2.0	9.9	23.8	59.4	33.3	11.1	55	81.8
Reserve city	84	81	-3.6	50	74.0	6.0	0.0	20.0	0.0	10.0	52.0	66.0	74.4	4.7	30	60.0
Rexford city	234	225	-3.8	154	64.9	0.0	0.0	1.9	33.1	31.8	18.8	41.8	34.3	22.2	66	65.2
Richfield city	43	36	-16.3	30	100.0	0.0	0.0	0.0	0.0	6.7	40.0	53.5	41.7	8.3	11	100.0
Richmond city	464	456	-1.7	596	90.6	0.0	0.2	4.2	5.0	28.5	17.3	38.0	56.8	9.7	195	90.3
Riley city	961	952	-0.9	1,421	94.3	0.0	0.0	2.5	3.2	24.8	12.8	35.9	28.3	27.4	555	93.5
Riverton CDP	929	-	-	741	92.6	0.0	0.0	4.2	3.2	21.6	26.3	34.1	53.7	19.1	302	87.4
Robinson city	237	225	-5.1	202	91.6	0.0	0.0	1.0	7.4	26.7	25.2	46.0	57.0	9.6	80	66.3
Roeland Park city	6,729	6,688	-0.6	6,769	80.4	3.1	1.4	4.6	10.5	17.1	9.7	33.8	16.7	55.0	3,010	94.2
Rolla city	442	356	-19.5	622	51.9	3.2	0.8	4.5	39.5	36.7	18.0	33.8	53.4	15.3	213	90.6
Rosalia CDP	171	-	-	108	97.2	0.0	0.0	2.8	0.0	16.7	21.3	53.4	60.0	14.4	62	83.9
Rose Hill city	3,934	3,968	0.9	4,038	92.3	0.8	1.3	0.0	5.5	27.5	12.7	37.8	28.4	28.9	1,421	100.0
Roseland city	73	67	-8.2	84	89.3	6.0	0.0	4.8	0.0	16.7	7.1	29.3	50.0	23.2	26	92.3
Rossville city	1,163	1,124	-3.4	1,248	88.4	0.7	0.0	5.3	5.6	27.3	16.3	37.2	44.0	19.0	408	90.7
Roxbury CDP	104	-	-	16	100.0	0.0	0.0	0.0	0.0	0.0	100.0	0.0	100.0	0.0	16	0.0
Rozel city	156	140	-10.3	119	100.0	0.0	0.0	0.0	0.0	17.6	12.6	35.9	41.3	2.7	48	89.6
Rush Center city	170	157	-7.6	227	95.6	0.0	4.4	0.0	0.0	20.7	22.0	49.0	40.5	16.8	103	81.6
Russell city	4,506	4,423	-1.8	4,525	90.2	3.5	0.0	1.8	4.5	19.7	23.7	49.5	41.7	20.2	1,973	78.6
Russell Springs city	24	24	0.0	21	71.4	0.0	0.0	28.6	0.0	23.8	14.3	59.8	75.0	6.3	12	100.0
Sabetha city	2,562	2,583	0.8	2,552	93.9	0.8	0.0	1.9	3.4	23.9	23.2	41.8	47.7	27.1	1,079	84.8
St. Francis city	1,329	1,292	-2.8	1,421	91.9	0.0	0.0	0.2	7.9	22.9	28.1	44.4	35.8	27.3	641	83.9
St. George city	638	998	56.4	914	91.5	2.3	0.8	1.6	3.8	35.6	4.5	32.6	23.0	41.9	302	96.0
St. John city	1,295	1,176	-9.2	1,390	78.5	0.5	0.0	4.1	16.9	22.3	19.6	39.2	34.3	24.8	548	85.8
St. Marys city	2,676	2,658	-0.7	2,714	88.3	1.3	0.5	2.2	7.7	34.9	15.7	26.3	41.5	21.5	807	95.3
St. Paul city	629	597	-5.1	575	91.0	0.0	0.7	1.9	6.4	25.0	23.0	43.1	43.1	20.2	202	77.7
Salina city	47,777	46,550	-2.6	46,998	78.1	3.1	2.6	3.8	12.5	23.5	16.9	37.6	38.6	27.3	19,120	87.7
Satanta city	1,197	1,130	-5.6	1,078	56.3	0.0	0.0	0.5	43.2	30.8	16.8	37.7	44.4	17.6	327	92.7
Savonburg city	109	103	-5.5	69	91.3	0.0	0.0	0.0	8.7	30.4	24.6	45.2	50.0	17.4	25	72.0
Sawyer city	137	131	-4.4	157	91.7	0.0	0.0	1.3	7.0	23.6	8.9	33.1	50.0	7.0	68	92.6
Scammon city	482	444	-7.9	574	93.9	0.0	1.9	2.4	1.7	22.1	14.6	40.0	42.2	13.7	224	89.3
Scandia city	368	342	-7.1	454	99.6	0.4	0.0	0.0	0.0	22.5	22.2	42.1	36.4	19.9	206	77.7
Schoenchen city	207	205		170	95.3	0.0	0.0	1.8	2.9	13.5	19.4	41.0	43.9	19.5	65	90.8
Scott City city	3,820	3,748	-1.9	3,970	78.5	0.0	0.5	2.2	18.8	26.5	19.5	38.5	46.2	21.7	1,589	88.7
Scottsville city	25	23	-8.0	31	100.0	0.0	0.0	0.0	0.0	6.5	41.9	55.8	51.7	10.3	17	70.6
Scranton city	708	682	-3.7	585	89.7	0.0	0.0	6.5	3.8	20.5	14.5	41.6	50.4	15.6	236	82.6
Sedan city	1,126	998	-11.4	859	93.8	0.3	0.0	4.8	1.0	20.0	30.3	45.3	55.5	13.4	407	73.5
Sedgwick city	1,687	1,658	-1.7	1,467	82.8	0.0	0.0	5.5	11.7	28.9	19.7	38.1	32.5	25.9	590	89.3
Selden city	215	211	-1.9	272	93.0	0.0	0.0	0.4	6.6	18.0	25.4	49.5	37.4	24.7	131	93.1
Seneca city	2,004	2,075	3.5	2,084	92.1	1.2	0.0	3.2	3.5	19.0	27.9	47.4	51.3	19.2	960	81.7
Severance city	94	90	-4.3	116	100.0	0.0	0.0	0.0	0.0	34.5	19.0	38.8	56.3	1.4	44	59.1
Severy city	257	231	-10.1	223	94.6	0.0	0.0	4.0	1.3	19.7	18.8	52.1	52.6	13.3	120	82.5
Seward city	64	62	-3.1	47	100.0	0.0	0.0	0.0	0.0	12.8	29.8	36.3	78.6	0.0	22	72.7
Sharon city	158	144	-8.9	147	93.9	0.0	2.7	3.4	0.0	15.6	32.0	48.8	62.8	4.4	73	86.3
Sharon Springs city	747	760	1.7	882	91.5	0.1	0.7	3.4	4.3	27.3	24.7	42.2	33.8	25.1	359	77.2
Shawnee city	62,203	65,807	5.8	65,540	81.6	5.0	3.4	3.6	6.5	25.3	13.5	38.4	23.6	48.3	24,516	95.0
Silver Lake city	1,439	1,406	-2.3	1,395	97.1	0.0	0.2	0.9	1.8	32.3	19.6	36.5	30.9	33.8	524	89.9
Simpson city	86	79	-8.1	58	94.8	0.0	0.0	0.0	5.2	10.3	27.6	55.0	52.1	0.0	31	67.7
Smith Center city	1,666	1,570	-5.8	1,477	95.9	0.3	1.4	1.9	0.5	18.9	28.6	49.6	40.9	23.8	722	88.5
Smolan city	217	204	-6.0	197	97.0	1.0	0.0	0.0	2.0	10.2	19.8	52.5	43.1	15.3	88	90.9
Soldier city	136	132	-2.9	83	84.3	0.0	0.0	8.4	7.2	21.7	25.3	35.1	38.6	8.8	44	81.8
Solomon city	1,095	1,000	-8.7	1,166	93.7	0.0	0.0	3.6	2.7	31.3	12.9	31.1	50.9	14.3	401	88.0
South Haven city	365	346	-5.2	388	93.0	4.4	0.0	1.8	0.8	23.2	10.6	36.5	41.0	22.3	157	87.9
South Hutchinson city	2,452	2,488	1.5	2,499	93.4	2.2	1.0	0.9	2.5	16.1	30.9	54.5	47.6	10.4	1,238	84.8
Spearville city	774	784	1.3	925	90.9	0.0	0.0	3.0	6.1	30.2	16.6	36.6	25.2	42.9	331	82.2
Speed city	37	34	-8.1	41	100.0	0.0	0.0	0.0	0.0	4.9	12.2	60.5	79.5	2.6	28	57.1
Spivey city	85	78	-8.2	31	80.6	0.0	0.0	3.2	16.1	0.0	41.9	57.5	38.5	7.7	18	66.7
Spring Hill city	5,428	7,326	35.0	6,626	87.5	2.5	0.0	3.1	6.9	31.1	9.5	31.9	32.7	27.8	2,158	95.2
Stafford city	1,044	949	-9.1	939	92.3	0.5	0.4	1.4	5.3	22.7	30.2	49.6	42.2	21.3	433	82.9
Stark city	71	67	-5.6	74	98.6	0.0	0.0	1.4	0.0	24.3	20.3	39.5	31.5	1.9	33	93.9
Sterling city	2,337	2,209	-5.5	2,596	85.6	3.9	0.4	2.9	7.2	22.3	15.1	28.2	32.7	33.0	895	84.9
Stockton city	1,325	1,257	-5.1	1,525	90.2	2.2	0.0	3.5	4.1	22.6	22.5	43.1	43.2	20.3	637	77.2
Strong City city	485	455	-6.2	480	88.3	0.0	0.0	9.6	2.1	18.3	22.9	43.2	40.4	18.4	202	77.7
Sublette city	1,451	1,339	-7.7	1,420	67.7	0.1	0.4	6.5	25.3	23.2	18.0	38.9	35.2	23.7	544	87.1
Summerfield city	156	147	-5.8	113	89.4	1.8	6.2	2.7	0.0	15.9	31.9	57.5	75.0	7.6	58	81.0
Sun City city	53	48	-9.4	40	82.5	0.0	0.0	2.5	15.0	17.5	10.0	48.5	51.5	3.0	19	84.2
Susank city	34	31	-8.8	30	96.7	0.0	0.0	3.3	0.0	13.3	53.3	66.5	38.5	15.4	13	100.0
Sylvan Grove city	295	266	-9.8	296	98.6	0.3	0.0	0.0	1.0	22.6	23.3	48.0	35.8	26.1	140	89.3
Sylvia city	214	205	-4.2	115	90.4	0.0	0.0	1.7	7.8	22.6	32.2	58.4	56.2	7.9	57	70.2
Syracuse city	1,809	1,706	-5.7	1,833	61.3	0.0	0.0	0.6	38.1	28.9	10.8	33.4	60.0	18.9	649	82.1
Talmage CDP	99	-	-	112	100.0	0.0	0.0	0.0	0.0	29.5	29.5	58.1	40.5	0.0	40	100.0
Tampa city	112	102	-8.9	146	84.9	0.0	0.0	0.7	14.4	22.6	23.3	31.3	51.1	22.2	68	72.1
Tescott city	319	291	-8.8	293	99.0	0.0	0.0	0.7	0.3	19.8	20.5	42.8	50.3	18.4	137	86.9
Thayer city	497	470	-5.4	391	86.2	0.5	0.5	3.8	9.0	18.7	20.7	40.3	48.5	16.1	185	75.1
The Highlands city	328	314	-4.3	380	100.0	0.0	0.0	0.0	0.0	16.8	30.8	54.4	21.5	44.3	187	96.3
Timken city	70	65	-7.1	79	72.2	0.0	0.0	27.8	0.0	38.0	15.2	39.2	27.7	17.0	30	96.7
Tipton city	210	193	-8.1	212	86.3	0.0	4.7	9.0	0.0	25.9	27.4	51.1	39.7	27.6	89	93.3
Tonganoxie city	5,003	5,583	11.6	5,359	94.5	0.4	0.0	2.2	2.9	28.8	14.1	34.0	35.0	29.4	1,979	91.1
Topeka city	127,630	125,310	-1.8	126,397	67.9	10.2	1.8	4.7	15.4	22.9	17.4	37.7	41.8	28.6	53,757	85.3
Toronto city	283	263	-7.1	246	94.3	3.3	0.0	2.4	0.0	22.0	29.7	46.8	46.1	11.1	122	77.9
Towanda city	1,489	1,454	-2.4	1,311	96.8	0.0	0.0	1.7	1.5	30.7	13.3	34.1	30.9	15.0	483	88.6
Tribune city	747	745	-0.3	804	70.8	0.0	0.0	0.2	29.0	25.5	21.5	42.9	39.3	27.1	356	87.9
Troy city	1,011	960	-5.0	892	85.5	0.1	0.1	1.0	13.2	20.7	16.3	40.7	50.6	15.9	382	81.7
Turon city	387	371	-4.1	311	92.6	1.6	0.0	1.0	4.8	22.8	26.0	39.8	36.3	16.7	130	92.3
Tyro city	219	197	-10.0	163	91.4	0.0	0.0	4.3	4.3	30.7	25.8	39.1	59.6	13.5	68	80.9
Udall city	753	707	-6.1	695	91.9	0.0	0.0	8.1	0.0	27.9	16.7	42.2	42.9	10.4	280	91.8
Ulysses city	6,152	5,604	-8.9	5,712	49.2	0.1	0.0	0.4	50.4	31.7	12.3	31.5	47.4	12.9	2,000	88.9
Uniontown city	272	264	-2.9	261	90.8	0.0	0.0	8.4	0.8	36.0	14.9	31.6	26.8	25.5	109	89.0
Utica city	158	141	-10.8	104	100.0	0.0	0.0	0.0	0.0	3.8	24.0	56.3	30.0	6.7	72	90.3
Valley Center city	6,814	7,325	7.5	7,176	89.7	1.0	0.7	4.9	3.7	33.0	13.9	33.5	26.6	39.2	2,540	93.7
Valley Falls city	1,186	1,153	-2.8	1,039	93.6	0.6	0.0	0.8	5.0	20.6	24.4	47.5	54.9	17.4	397	85.4

1 May be of any race.

Table A. All Places — **Population and Housing**

STATE City, town, township, borough, or CDP (county if applicable)	2010 census total population	2019 estimated population	Percent change 2010–2019	ACS total population estimate 2015–2019	White alone, not Hispanic or Latino	Black alone, not Hispanic or Latino	Asian alone, not Hispanic or Latino	All other races or 2 or more races, not Hispanic or Latino	Hispanic or Latino[1]	Under 18 years old	Age 65 years and older	Median age	Percent High school diploma or less	Percent Bachelor's degree or more	Total	Percent with a computer
	1	2	3	4	5	6	7	8	9	10	11	12	13	14	15	16
KANSAS—Con.																
Vassar CDP	530	-	-	799	96.7	0.0	0.0	0.0	3.3	16.4	24.9	51.5	49.0	20.5	352	92.0
Vermillion city	109	102	-6.4	73	91.8	0.0	0.0	4.1	4.1	28.8	28.8	42.3	52.0	20.0	34	64.7
Victoria city	1,218	1,212	-0.5	1,019	91.7	0.0	0.9	2.5	5.0	23.2	19.4	37.1	40.0	29.9	450	87.8
Vining city	44	42	-4.5	73	90.4	0.0	2.7	6.8	0.0	32.9	9.6	29.0	67.3	10.2	31	35.5
Viola city	130	128	-1.5	96	99.0	0.0	0.0	1.0	0.0	20.8	26.0	50.5	55.7	20.0	40	90.0
Virgil city	71	63	-11.3	43	100.0	0.0	0.0	0.0	0.0	0.0	58.1	65.9	74.3	11.4	31	67.7
Wakarusa CDP	260	-	-	226	93.8	0.0	0.0	4.0	2.2	31.0	27.0	31.5	58.3	17.4	81	93.8
WaKeeney city	1,886	1,764	-6.5	1,949	93.4	0.1	2.5	1.4	2.7	17.3	24.6	49.5	38.7	19.4	973	90.2
Wakefield city	975	920	-5.6	956	87.1	0.0	2.1	7.9	2.8	23.4	13.8	34.4	32.3	25.3	372	96.8
Waldo city	30	30	0.0	53	96.2	0.0	0.0	3.8	0.0	24.5	49.1	48.5	62.5	10.0	22	95.5
Waldron city	11	10	-9.1	28	100.0	0.0	0.0	0.0	0.0	0.0	71.4	81.5	76.9	7.7	14	28.6
Wallace city	58	60	3.4	54	100.0	0.0	0.0	0.0	0.0	7.4	24.1	53.0	48.8	22.0	28	78.6
Walnut city	227	227	0.0	183	88.5	0.0	0.0	11.5	0.0	33.3	10.4	30.9	52.8	1.9	68	75.0
Walton city	238	233	-2.1	315	84.4	0.0	2.9	4.8	7.9	22.2	11.1	37.1	54.3	12.4	108	85.2
Wamego city	4,390	4,732	7.8	4,876	90.0	2.9	1.4	2.0	3.7	28.3	12.0	33.9	33.2	33.1	1,908	96.9
Washington city	1,135	1,060	-6.6	1,069	97.9	0.0	0.3	0.0	1.8	21.8	26.1	44.9	49.4	18.1	489	82.6
Waterville city	681	636	-6.6	635	88.7	0.0	0.9	4.4	6.0	27.7	24.6	43.2	37.3	26.3	255	84.7
Wathena city	1,357	1,294	-4.6	1,547	97.3	0.6	0.0	1.0	1.0	23.8	19.5	42.9	45.2	24.6	682	83.0
Waverly city	592	545	-7.9	650	96.3	0.0	0.0	0.0	3.7	28.9	25.8	41.7	43.6	24.6	240	80.8
Webber city	25	24	-4.0	25	100.0	0.0	0.0	0.0	0.0	0.0	48.0	64.8	44.0	0.0	16	62.5
Weir city	686	636	-7.3	659	97.0	0.0	0.0	2.3	0.8	19.4	17.1	36.6	56.6	14.4	288	74.7
Welda CDP	129	-	-	61	100.0	0.0	0.0	0.0	0.0	45.9	58.9	59.0	100.0	0.0	46	78.3
Wellington city	8,171	7,662	-6.2	7,788	84.4	1.7	0.0	5.4	8.6	26.0	18.3	37.8	45.2	20.3	3,172	88.4
Wellsville city	1,854	1,781	-3.9	2,026	89.8	0.9	0.3	1.6	7.4	25.9	14.3	35.3	46.8	15.8	765	90.3
Weskan CDP	161	-	-	138	94.2	1.4	0.0	2.9	1.4	31.9	10.9	28.3	19.8	44.2	52	96.2
West Mineral city	185	171	-7.6	129	86.0	0.0	0.0	13.2	0.8	27.9	20.9	37.8	51.2	13.1	52	69.2
Westmoreland city	765	742	-3.0	763	89.0	1.6	0.0	4.5	5.0	22.1	20.6	39.0	48.6	19.7	301	80.4
Westphalia city	165	162	-1.8	143	90.9	0.0	0.0	7.7	1.4	25.2	14.0	33.6	57.8	24.4	49	87.8
Westwood city	1,506	1,641	9.0	1,657	82.1	1.3	5.2	2.7	8.8	22.6	15.4	36.7	11.5	67.3	707	95.3
Westwood Hills city	359	391	8.9	463	84.4	0.6	1.3	5.6	8.0	28.5	12.5	36.8	4.4	88.1	186	100.0
Wetmore city	368	366	-0.5	303	89.1	1.0	1.0	6.9	2.0	28.4	23.1	41.3	43.4	17.0	120	80.0
Wheaton city	95	113	18.9	84	90.5	0.0	0.0	0.0	9.5	33.3	3.6	29.8	41.1	17.9	26	96.2
White City city	618	581	-6.0	621	95.8	0.0	0.3	1.4	2.4	21.4	18.5	38.4	55.0	8.1	232	84.1
White Cloud city	176	168	-4.5	116	86.2	0.0	0.0	13.8	0.0	16.4	18.1	47.7	46.8	15.6	58	77.6
Whitewater city	739	721	-2.4	778	92.4	0.8	0.4	4.2	2.2	25.4	15.2	34.2	35.6	28.3	257	91.4
Whiting city	187	183	-2.1	207	92.8	1.0	0.0	5.3	1.0	28.0	16.9	43.3	53.2	15.8	87	92.0
Wichita city	382,437	389,938	2.0	389,877	62.8	10.6	5.0	4.4	17.2	25.2	14.0	35.0	38.1	30.1	153,279	88.6
Willard city	92	90	-2.2	81	100.0	0.0	0.0	0.0	0.0	22.2	19.8	36.3	50.0	0.0	39	79.5
Williamsburg city	402	391	-2.7	388	94.1	0.0	0.0	5.9	0.0	28.9	25.0	45.0	68.2	9.7	153	73.9
Willis city	39	38	-2.6	28	89.3	0.0	0.0	10.7	0.0	0.0	39.3	59.5	70.8	16.7	17	94.1
Willowbrook city	87	85	-2.3	81	97.5	0.0	0.0	2.5	0.0	21.0	34.6	56.8	9.7	69.4	34	100.0
Wilmore city	53	48	-9.4	40	100.0	0.0	0.0	0.0	0.0	12.5	27.5	60.7	48.5	0.0	21	100.0
Wilroads Gardens CDP	609	-	-	446	29.1	0.0	2.0	0.0	68.8	19.1	11.4	45.5	68.0	2.1	183	83.6
Wilsey city	153	143	-6.5	166	91.6	0.0	0.0	2.4	6.0	15.1	24.1	44.7	48.0	18.1	78	78.2
Wilson city	777	724	-6.8	708	93.9	0.0	1.8	2.0	2.3	22.2	29.9	51.3	36.2	22.9	291	85.9
Winchester city	550	526	-4.4	578	93.6	0.9	0.0	3.8	1.7	20.4	19.4	45.3	51.5	20.2	271	74.5
Windom city	130	124	-4.6	89	92.1	0.0	0.0	0.0	7.9	34.8	16.9	31.3	48.2	14.3	38	94.7
Winfield city	12,332	11,943	-3.2	12,085	79.0	4.0	4.0	4.9	8.0	23.0	17.0	35.7	41.8	25.5	4,260	88.1
Winona city	160	159	-0.6	237	92.4	0.0	0.0	7.6	0.0	37.6	9.3	33.4	30.9	15.8	86	93.0
Woodbine city	169	165	-2.4	209	90.9	0.0	0.0	1.0	8.1	15.8	12.9	51.8	51.3	18.2	90	83.3
Woodston city	136	129	-5.1	108	100.0	0.0	0.0	0.0	0.0	27.8	3.7	37.8	73.8	7.7	44	77.3
Wright CDP	163	-	-	97	59.8	0.0	0.0	0.0	40.2	33.0	14.4	52.7	21.5	32.3	49	100.0
Yates Center city	1,420	1,321	-7.0	1,381	88.7	0.4	0.0	10.1	0.7	21.7	22.2	44.6	45.9	16.3	642	79.9
Yoder CDP	194	-	-	179	100.0	0.0	0.0	0.0	0.0	0.0	42.5	53.6	19.6	33.5	106	100.0
Zenda city	85	78	-8.2	70	100.0	0.0	0.0	0.0	0.0	18.6	42.9	54.5	40.4	22.8	38	63.2
Zurich city	99	93	-6.1	85	100.0	0.0	0.0	0.0	0.0	24.7	16.5	47.9	50.0	15.6	43	83.7
KENTUCKY	4,339,333	4,467,673	3.0	4,449,052	84.6	8.0	1.5	2.4	3.7	22.7	16.0	38.9	46.6	24.2	1,734,618	86.4
Adairville city	902	885	-1.9	1,006	80.0	13.1	1.8	3.8	1.3	26.6	23.1	41.8	66.8	13.4	394	57.9
Ages CDP	-	-	-	367	83.9	4.1	0.0	0.0	12.0	29.4	22.6	35.7	60.2	0.0	126	79.4
Albany city	2,031	2,002	-1.4	2,272	88.9	0.2	1.3	5.9	3.7	16.5	25.8	47.4	63.3	11.3	1,018	52.9
Alexandria city	8,474	9,715	14.6	9,425	97.1	0.0	0.3	1.2	1.5	24.9	13.3	40.2	36.2	33.6	3,401	93.6
Allen city	193	172	-10.9	201	98.0	0.0	0.0	2.0	0.0	37.8	10.9	29.5	67.0	2.6	85	82.4
Allensville CDP	157	-	-	155	63.2	36.8	0.0	0.0	0.0	14.2	32.3	60.8	78.2	6.0	80	52.5
Anchorage city	2,346	2,423	3.3	2,376	91.8	1.1	3.6	3.0	0.5	34.0	16.7	41.4	4.3	82.1	771	97.9
Annville CDP	1,095	-	-	893	94.1	1.0	0.0	4.8	0.1	18.5	31.9	50.0	76.0	8.9	393	82.2
Anthoston CDP	-	-	-	278	94.2	0.0	0.0	5.8	0.0	33.1	5.8	34.1	66.1	19.9	97	100.0
Arjay CDP	-	-	-	440	90.5	0.0	0.0	9.5	0.0	27.0	11.6	32.6	95.4	0.0	185	85.9
Arlington city	324	301	-7.1	305	84.9	4.9	1.3	6.2	2.6	11.8	30.2	51.6	63.2	7.9	180	68.3
Artemus CDP	590	-	-	615	94.5	5.5	0.0	0.0	0.0	29.9	13.2	37.5	71.4	1.7	198	88.4
Ashland city	21,691	20,146	-7.1	20,626	92.5	1.9	0.7	3.5	1.4	23.7	18.3	39.3	42.1	23.6	8,294	85.3
Auburn city	1,348	1,380	2.4	1,240	83.2	7.7	0.0	0.0	9.0	19.0	23.1	42.2	53.6	18.7	539	74.8
Audubon Park city	1,468	1,489	1.4	1,298	96.1	0.3	1.4	0.8	1.5	18.2	23.5	48.4	20.2	54.5	564	95.0
Augusta city	1,190	1,148	-3.5	1,204	99.1	0.0	0.0	0.2	0.7	24.2	16.3	42.2	63.1	14.2	462	85.7
Auxier CDP	669	-	-	1,045	96.8	0.0	0.0	3.2	0.0	25.9	2.8	35.2	67.4	21.2	353	91.8
Bancroft city	494	512	3.6	475	89.9	3.4	2.1	0.8	3.8	19.8	27.4	51.7	14.0	63.8	198	97.0
Bandana CDP	203	-	-	376	100.0	0.0	0.0	0.0	0.0	31.4	18.9	36.3	3.5	41.5	132	100.0
Barbourmeade city	1,214	1,250	3.0	1,393	92.9	2.2	0.7	1.7	2.6	26.9	24.5	46.1	8.4	61.2	531	96.2
Barbourville city	3,165	3,033	-4.2	3,072	94.5	3.1	0.2	1.3	0.9	13.4	16.7	37.1	49.3	26.8	991	84.3
Bardstown city	12,527	13,253	5.8	13,094	80.9	12.6	0.3	3.3	2.9	25.7	14.6	33.3	45.2	18.3	5,277	87.6
Bardwell city	723	673	-6.9	662	98.3	0.0	0.3	0.9	0.5	20.2	25.8	46.9	48.6	11.7	252	87.3
Barlow city	675	644	-4.6	577	93.1	4.0	0.0	1.4	1.6	25.8	20.6	35.6	55.0	11.8	254	77.6
Beattyville city	1,302	1,221	-6.2	1,375	89.5	3.6	0.0	4.7	2.2	19.6	15.2	40.2	63.9	12.6	597	71.4
Beaver Dam city	3,506	3,571	1.9	3,562	85.1	0.8	0.8	2.3	10.9	32.7	19.6	39.2	48.6	17.8	1,366	69.0
Bedford city	610	576	-5.6	622	91.2	0.0	0.0	5.3	3.5	32.8	14.1	34.6	62.9	11.4	255	80.8
Beech Grove CDP	243	-	-	404	94.1	5.9	0.0	0.0	0.0	20.3	5.7	39.5	61.7	10.7	161	52.8
Beechmont CDP	689	-	-	559	93.9	0.0	0.0	6.1	0.0	7.9	26.1	48.7	72.0	1.9	238	64.7
Beechwood Village city	1,322	1,350	2.1	1,306	95.0	0.5	2.1	1.3	1.1	21.1	17.7	41.1	13.5	60.5	601	91.2
Belfry CDP	-	-	-	358	80.7	0.0	19.3	0.0	0.0	13.7	21.8	46.6	67.0	13.9	165	69.1
Bellefonte city	882	822	-6.8	870	94.9	1.0	2.4	1.6	0.0	18.9	26.8	50.2	17.5	48.1	345	95.9
Bellemeade city	865	886	2.4	916	89.4	4.7	0.8	2.1	3.1	14.1	32.9	57.2	15.9	54.2	436	93.1

1 May be of any race.

Table A. All Places — **Population and Housing**

STATE City, town, township, borough, or CDP (county if applicable)	Population: 2010 census total population	Population: 2019 estimated population	Population: Percent change 2010–2019	Population: ACS total population estimate 2015–2019	Race and Hispanic or Latino origin (percent): White alone, not Hispanic or Latino	Black alone, not Hispanic or Latino	Asian alone, not Hispanic or Latino	All other races or 2 or more races, not Hispanic or Latino	Hispanic or Latino[1]	Age (percent): Under 18 years old	Age 65 years and older	Median age	Educational attainment of persons age 25 and older: Percent High school diploma or less	Percent Bachelor's degree or more	Occupied housing units: Total	Percent with a computer
	1	2	3	4	5	6	7	8	9	10	11	12	13	14	15	16
KENTUCKY—Con.																
Belleview CDP	343	-	-	336	100.0	0.0	0.0	0.0	0.0	37.2	17.0	34.2	43.1	19.0	116	70.7
Bellevue city	5,957	5,721	-4.0	5,804	94.1	2.0	0.3	3.0	0.6	19.8	12.6	36.9	36.4	41.3	2,518	92.5
Bellewood city	321	327	1.9	260	95.8	0.0	1.2	0.4	2.7	22.3	24.6	42.0	7.5	74.9	107	94.4
Benham city	505	425	-15.8	570	94.4	0.0	0.0	5.6	0.0	17.5	25.3	41.8	41.5	16.8	226	88.9
Benton city	4,531	4,463	-1.5	4,477	92.4	3.0	0.0	2.1	2.5	20.9	22.9	41.2	45.8	22.1	1,945	80.1
Berea city	13,558	16,026	18.2	15,474	87.7	3.9	0.5	3.0	4.9	24.2	13.2	30.7	42.4	29.4	5,508	90.3
Berry city	264	260	-1.5	267	95.9	0.0	0.0	4.1	0.0	29.2	14.6	38.4	63.4	13.4	103	71.8
Betsy Layne CDP	688	-	-	345	100.0	0.0	0.0	0.0	0.0	7.2	22.6	56.6	63.2	20.7	194	86.6
Big Clifty CDP	-	-	-	343	99.1	0.0	0.0	0.9	0.0	29.2	8.5	26.9	72.7	10.9	131	60.3
Blackey city	120	143	19.2	104	97.1	0.0	0.0	1.0	1.9	20.2	26.0	40.7	65.8	21.1	55	72.7
Blaine city	47	46	-2.1	61	95.1	4.9	0.0	0.0	0.0	6.6	14.8	56.1	96.5	0.0	30	16.7
Blandville city	90	87	-3.3	68	100.0	0.0	0.0	0.0	0.0	0.0	73.5	65.7	100.0	0.0	14	0.0
Bloomfield city	1,015	1,066	5.0	808	83.7	9.8	0.2	4.0	2.4	21.5	21.9	42.7	64.0	10.3	349	77.1
Blue Ridge Manor city	745	777	4.3	833	76.6	8.0	0.0	8.9	6.5	11.4	22.6	40.3	15.2	61.8	450	93.3
Bonnieville city	255	264	3.5	197	93.4	2.5	0.0	0.0	4.1	21.3	21.8	48.5	74.1	7.7	99	73.7
Booneville city	175	158	-9.7	147	95.2	0.0	4.8	0.0	0.0	30.6	19.7	34.4	36.3	44.1	52	78.8
Boston CDP	266	-	-	131	100.0	0.0	0.0	0.0	0.0	0.0	0.0	51.4	60.0	0.0	71	100.0
Bowling Green city	59,407	70,543	18.7	67,600	70.4	12.7	4.9	4.2	7.8	20.7	11.0	27.0	37.2	32.6	25,305	90.2
Bradfordsville city	294	297	1.0	293	91.8	0.0	0.0	6.5	1.7	18.4	15.7	47.9	78.3	4.9	136	80.9
Brandenburg city	2,683	2,877	7.2	2,842	87.8	4.4	2.5	4.6	0.7	20.4	17.5	33.1	53.8	21.0	1,084	86.5
Breckinridge Center CDP	2,080	-	-	2,109	36.2	47.4	2.1	7.9	6.4	15.0	2.6	22.0	66.9	1.3	223	100.0
Bremen city	195	190	-2.6	292	97.9	0.0	0.3	0.0	1.7	26.7	14.7	37.4	84.3	4.3	104	80.8
Briarwood city	432	445	3.0	527	84.3	5.3	0.6	5.7	4.2	17.8	18.6	37.6	24.6	45.8	253	98.0
Brodhead city	1,211	1,180	-2.6	1,500	97.1	0.0	0.0	1.4	1.5	23.5	17.1	35.4	67.6	8.7	482	81.1
Broeck Pointe city	272	282	3.7	268	90.7	9.0	0.0	0.0	0.4	29.9	20.5	43.2	15.5	62.4	100	96.0
Bromley city	802	797	-0.6	925	89.2	3.0	0.0	2.9	4.9	31.2	7.2	34.6	51.9	12.7	339	88.8
Brooks CDP	2,401	-	-	2,481	86.6	0.4	0.0	2.5	10.5	19.6	18.3	44.8	60.7	6.5	942	94.8
Brooksville city	648	631	-2.6	739	92.8	0.0	3.9	1.1	2.2	25.2	23.4	34.9	63.8	14.7	337	62.6
Brownsboro Farm city	650	672	3.4	649	94.8	0.6	2.3	0.3	2.0	23.7	24.5	43.8	14.8	62.2	235	99.6
Brownsboro Village city	319	326	2.2	347	97.7	0.6	0.9	0.3	0.6	13.8	28.2	42.7	6.9	72.0	179	93.3
Brownsville city	838	826	-1.4	854	97.8	0.0	0.0	1.4	0.8	15.5	35.8	47.0	58.4	12.5	350	86.0
Buckhorn city	155	139	-10.3	110	80.9	11.8	0.0	0.0	7.3	42.7	11.8	25.5	64.3	19.6	31	80.6
Buckner CDP	5,837	-	-	5,545	85.9	8.9	0.0	2.4	2.9	19.4	10.6	38.3	39.5	27.5	1,032	98.7
Buffalo CDP	498	-	-	334	76.9	0.0	4.5	12.3	6.3	21.6	12.6	34.7	63.7	4.2	194	85.6
Burgin city	961	992	3.2	1,032	90.4	6.7	0.5	2.4	0.0	21.1	15.6	39.3	54.0	14.0	429	83.2
Burkesville city	1,535	1,464	-4.6	1,789	86.4	7.8	0.0	2.0	3.8	18.2	25.1	46.9	68.9	12.2	702	72.6
Burlington CDP	15,926	-	-	17,401	84.1	5.1	0.8	4.9	5.1	26.1	10.8	34.5	40.0	27.3	6,049	95.6
Burna CDP	257	-	-	224	100.0	0.0	0.0	0.0	0.0	30.8	6.3	29.1	85.5	5.6	52	73.1
Burnside city	833	843	1.2	843	95.1	0.0	0.0	3.0	1.9	17.0	27.5	53.1	57.9	20.1	376	79.3
Butler city	614	583	-5.0	751	81.4	12.8	0.0	5.9	0.0	27.4	28.5	37.6	63.1	6.3	262	77.5
Cadiz city	2,605	2,671	2.5	2,639	79.3	16.3	0.0	3.3	1.0	18.4	24.6	44.5	49.6	14.5	1,298	82.0
Calhoun city	763	734	-3.8	826	96.7	0.5	0.5	0.5	1.8	24.2	25.7	41.1	55.4	9.9	317	81.4
California city	92	98	6.5	91	98.9	0.0	1.1	0.0	0.0	23.1	7.7	45.8	50.0	16.7	39	92.3
Calvert City city	2,582	2,505	-3.0	2,513	95.1	0.0	0.0	0.6	4.3	21.0	24.8	46.0	49.2	16.0	1,040	82.3
Camargo city	1,077	1,144	6.2	1,389	92.4	0.0	0.2	1.9	5.5	26.9	16.2	36.3	60.2	12.0	487	83.6
Cambridge city	175	180	2.9	147	89.1	0.0	0.0	6.8	4.1	12.9	18.4	37.4	16.1	46.6	77	93.5
Campbellsburg city	766	789	3.0	970	95.5	0.4	2.0	1.2	0.9	26.7	13.2	33.3	50.4	10.8	366	87.4
Campbellsville city	10,676	11,482	7.5	11,419	83.3	7.7	1.8	5.0	2.2	21.4	17.0	32.1	52.1	22.2	4,594	76.9
Campton city	436	422	-3.2	461	98.9	0.0	1.1	0.0	0.0	27.8	24.7	36.9	67.0	16.2	221	62.9
Caneyville city	609	607	-0.3	698	94.6	0.0	0.0	5.0	0.4	24.5	11.2	36.5	61.6	10.3	225	86.2
Cannonsburg CDP	856	-	-	639	100.0	0.0	0.0	0.0	0.0	28.5	12.1	23.7	19.1	45.5	259	94.6
Carlisle city	2,002	1,986	-0.8	2,554	96.7	1.6	0.0	1.1	0.5	25.6	15.8	40.0	65.6	10.7	1,022	82.0
Carrollton city	3,939	3,780	-4.0	3,811	85.8	5.6	0.0	1.2	7.5	27.1	13.5	36.7	57.4	5.3	1,537	82.2
Carrsville city	50	48	-4.0	51	98.0	0.0	0.0	2.0	0.0	15.7	39.2	62.5	59.0	5.1	19	78.9
Catlettsburg city	1,863	1,747	-6.2	1,895	90.2	4.8	0.0	4.0	1.0	15.5	22.3	43.3	58.1	10.6	700	75.4
Cave City city	2,318	2,426	4.7	2,566	88.9	5.3	1.3	1.1	3.4	22.8	13.4	34.2	61.6	7.4	1,002	78.4
Cawood CDP	731	-	-	501	89.4	10.6	0.0	0.0	0.0	27.1	20.2	35.6	76.1	10.3	207	84.5
Cayce CDP	123	-	-	90	78.9	0.0	0.0	21.1	0.0	23.3	8.9	45.9	5.4	30.4	32	100.0
Cecilia CDP	572	-	-	618	100.0	0.0	0.0	0.0	0.0	35.6	5.3	25.9	63.7	15.3	191	100.0
Centertown city	437	430	-1.6	507	96.3	0.0	2.6	1.2	0.0	28.4	15.2	41.1	68.1	6.3	173	83.2
Central City city	5,978	5,730	-4.1	5,808	85.8	8.1	1.2	2.0	2.9	23.3	18.9	37.6	61.9	16.7	2,057	80.7
Cerulean CDP	314	-	-	357	27.5	64.1	3.9	4.5	0.0	23.0	20.4	48.1	44.3	4.9	125	82.4
Chaplin CDP	418	-	-	606	95.9	0.0	0.0	0.0	4.1	25.6	12.9	43.5	81.5	2.0	187	75.4
Clarkson city	874	886	1.4	1,104	86.4	1.4	0.0	1.4	10.7	29.5	13.4	33.6	60.9	9.4	442	83.3
Claryville CDP	2,355	-	-	2,432	95.3	1.1	0.3	0.7	2.5	25.1	15.7	35.9	37.6	31.0	881	89.3
Clay city	1,181	1,096	-7.2	966	99.2	0.0	0.0	0.8	0.0	21.3	18.2	45.8	65.8	3.5	456	74.8
Clay City city	1,129	1,094	-3.1	1,124	96.6	0.0	0.0	0.0	3.4	22.4	15.4	36.0	69.2	4.1	538	67.3
Cleaton CDP	-	-	-	175	93.1	0.0	0.0	6.9	0.0	6.3	20.0	53.1	78.5	0.0	112	52.7
Clinton city	1,388	1,251	-9.9	1,294	68.0	22.5	1.2	7.9	0.4	26.1	23.2	46.4	65.0	8.2	461	75.5
Cloverport city	1,152	1,152	0.0	1,006	95.4	2.5	0.0	1.1	1.0	19.3	20.0	46.3	65.2	6.8	448	75.9
Coal Run Village city	1,703	1,520	-10.7	1,405	92.1	0.0	2.0	2.1	3.8	16.9	20.6	42.0	49.3	19.4	694	82.3
Coldiron CDP	223	-	-	232	100.0	0.0	0.0	0.0	0.0	35.8	0.0	29.5	86.0	8.5	61	100.0
Cold Spring city	5,927	6,571	10.9	6,401	97.6	0.3	0.7	1.1	0.2	19.0	22.8	48.8	33.2	45.3	2,655	96.6
Coldstream city	1,114	1,161	4.2	1,311	59.3	29.2	4.0	5.7	1.7	30.4	7.6	32.5	23.1	38.7	460	96.7
Columbia city	4,452	4,604	3.4	4,653	85.9	8.3	0.4	1.5	3.8	17.8	17.9	34.9	57.7	15.1	1,605	71.5
Columbus city	170	153	-10.0	232	84.5	6.9	0.4	7.3	0.9	22.8	13.4	29.1	70.9	3.0	82	76.8
Combs CDP	-	-	-	164	100.0	0.0	0.0	0.0	0.0	0.0	76.2	70.5	48.2	0.0	89	51.7
Concord city	35	33	-5.7	20	100.0	0.0	0.0	0.0	0.0	0.0	60.0	77.2	60.0	25.0	12	75.0
Corbin city	7,315	7,202	-1.5	7,325	94.4	0.2	0.0	2.7	2.6	27.1	19.0	37.6	47.1	20.0	2,766	75.6
Corinth city	229	226	-1.3	274	100.0	0.0	0.0	0.0	0.0	22.6	22.3	35.9	82.4	1.1	107	65.4
Corydon city	717	692	-3.5	839	77.4	12.4	0.0	2.9	7.4	30.9	12.5	35.1	61.9	11.1	297	79.5
Covington city	40,506	40,341	-0.4	40,548	78.3	11.4	0.7	3.7	6.0	22.6	12.4	36.0	47.5	25.1	16,951	85.6
Coxton CDP	-	-	-	165	95.2	4.8	0.0	0.0	0.0	13.3	6.7	41.0	79.0	0.0	75	81.3
Crab Orchard city	841	825	-1.9	813	94.8	2.8	0.0	0.0	2.3	20.8	22.6	39.9	69.7	6.3	386	64.8
Crayne CDP	173	-	-	266	85.0	0.0	0.0	3.4	11.7	32.7	17.7	29.5	50.6	12.7	117	90.6
Creekside city	309	320	3.6	266	95.9	0.8	1.5	1.9	0.0	16.5	26.3	49.3	19.9	54.1	107	97.2
Crescent Springs city	3,940	4,058	3.0	4,036	90.7	3.7	1.7	0.5	3.3	31.0	9.6	29.9	30.7	39.3	1,526	96.9
Crestview city	470	494	5.1	426	95.1	1.4	0.0	2.6	0.9	24.9	12.9	33.2	34.6	36.3	151	95.4
Crestview Hills city	3,111	3,343	7.5	3,300	93.8	2.7	1.1	1.4	1.0	11.6	25.5	48.8	28.5	43.9	1,362	94.2
Crestwood city	4,542	5,081	11.9	4,973	79.5	1.2	1.4	1.0	17.0	32.5	8.8	34.6	27.8	48.8	1,580	93.4
Crittenden city	3,815	3,876	1.6	3,857	95.9	2.1	0.0	2.0	0.0	27.6	13.6	37.5	57.4	11.5	1,471	83.4
Crofton city	768	707	-7.9	450	86.9	7.3	0.0	5.3	0.4	18.7	19.6	46.9	67.0	6.4	224	76.3

1 May be of any race.

Table A. All Places — **Population and Housing**

STATE City, town, township, borough, or CDP (county if applicable)	Population				Race and Hispanic or Latino origin (percent)					Age (percent)			Educational attainment of persons age 25 and older		Occupied housing units	
	2010 census total population	2019 estimated population	Percent change 2010–2019	ACS total population estimate 2015–2019	White alone, not Hispanic or Latino	Black alone, not Hispanic or Latino	Asian alone, not Hispanic or Latino	All other races or 2 or more races, not Hispanic or Latino	Hispanic or Latino[1]	Under 18 years old	Age 65 years and older	Median age	Percent High school diploma or less	Percent Bachelor's degree or more	Total	Percent with a computer
	1	2	3	4	5	6	7	8	9	10	11	12	13	14	15	16
KENTUCKY—Con.																
Crossgate city	224	230	2.7	285	98.2	0.0	0.7	0.0	1.1	22.1	22.1	42.6	5.1	74.1	106	100.0
Cumberland city	2,237	1,931	-13.7	1,724	95.2	0.5	0.3	2.1	1.9	24.3	24.4	42.6	58.6	12.1	825	70.4
Cunningham CDP	-	-	-	247	100.0	0.0	0.0	0.0	0.0	15.8	34.4	52.2	46.4	30.4	124	91.1
Cynthiana city	6,422	6,337	-1.3	6,312	87.2	5.1	0.0	4.3	3.4	22.2	20.4	42.4	61.8	11.9	2,535	73.1
Danville city	16,206	16,769	3.5	16,730	79.1	11.7	1.4	3.0	4.8	18.9	18.7	36.6	45.7	24.3	6,252	84.6
Dawson Springs city	2,764	2,631	-4.8	2,672	93.7	1.7	0.4	3.7	0.4	22.9	22.0	43.5	68.6	9.3	1,224	71.5
Dayton city	5,341	5,609	5.0	5,496	92.8	3.1	0.2	2.4	1.4	20.4	12.8	37.3	47.7	23.6	2,151	85.3
Dexter CDP	277	-	-	289	97.6	0.0	0.0	0.0	2.4	22.8	19.7	42.5	66.4	17.9	113	75.2
Diablock CDP	453	-	-	595	100.0	0.0	0.0	0.0	0.0	17.8	11.4	39.7	45.7	11.7	276	100.0
Dixon city	920	881	-4.2	1,081	90.3	6.4	0.4	2.0	0.9	19.1	12.0	37.5	59.3	9.5	316	83.9
Doe Valley CDP	1,931	-	-	1,847	99.0	0.0	0.0	1.0	0.0	20.5	22.4	51.2	29.9	35.1	751	93.9
Douglass Hills city	5,495	5,707	3.9	5,710	78.1	13.6	2.3	5.3	0.6	24.4	16.0	37.7	18.3	45.2	2,276	91.8
Dover city	252	248	-1.6	266	100.0	0.0	0.0	0.0	0.0	25.6	15.4	38.3	72.6	8.1	102	77.5
Drakesboro city	515	498	-3.3	584	77.6	22.4	0.0	0.0	0.0	15.4	10.4	46.8	75.9	4.9	168	86.9
Druid Hills city	308	313	1.6	291	97.9	0.0	0.0	1.7	0.3	25.1	20.3	43.1	3.3	83.0	132	91.7
Dry Ridge city	2,209	2,205	-0.2	2,161	96.3	0.0	0.0	2.4	1.3	34.0	12.4	30.7	61.0	12.9	818	82.3
Dunmor CDP	-	-	-	213	100.0	0.0	0.0	0.0	0.0	18.3	30.0	48.2	60.2	10.6	84	100.0
Dwale CDP	329	-	-	107	100.0	0.0	0.0	0.0	0.0	12.1	35.5	54.1	27.2	19.8	53	100.0
Earlington city	1,413	1,332	-5.7	1,427	84.0	9.5	0.0	3.3	3.3	27.7	13.6	36.8	55.7	9.6	542	83.9
East Bernstadt CDP	716	-	-	906	94.5	1.7	0.0	1.7	2.2	25.9	13.6	38.7	56.5	16.2	342	79.5
Eddyville city	2,554	2,545	-0.4	2,548	86.4	8.0	0.7	1.3	3.6	15.5	10.9	38.5	58.4	13.5	860	74.8
Edgewood city	8,605	8,759	1.8	8,745	94.8	1.6	1.3	2.1	0.2	24.5	21.9	44.6	21.4	52.6	3,324	93.6
Edmonton city	1,612	1,595	-1.1	1,665	90.1	5.1	1.3	3.0	0.5	16.6	24.9	48.8	63.3	9.9	707	77.9
Ekron city	156	150	-3.8	258	96.1	0.0	2.3	1.6	0.0	21.7	6.2	34.3	62.0	2.9	91	89.0
Elizabethtown city	28,055	30,289	8.0	29,620	73.1	11.2	3.8	6.3	5.5	23.5	13.7	36.6	35.3	28.6	12,553	86.8
Elizaville CDP	181	-	-	142	100.0	0.0	0.0	0.0	0.0	0.0	21.8	57.5	64.8	28.2	73	100.0
Elk Creek CDP	-	-	-	1,654	92.9	1.2	3.1	0.0	2.8	23.0	16.7	42.0	36.1	30.9	622	100.0
Elkhorn City city	1,001	890	-11.1	1,097	93.7	5.3	0.0	0.6	0.4	21.7	29.4	38.3	68.6	15.0	430	84.7
Elkton city	2,154	2,129	-1.2	2,292	81.5	11.0	0.3	0.4	6.7	23.3	13.1	35.3	58.8	11.5	856	71.6
Elsmere city	8,379	8,595	2.6	8,567	85.6	6.1	0.0	3.2	5.1	29.9	9.0	32.2	47.5	18.4	2,939	91.9
Eminence city	2,499	2,581	3.3	2,553	66.6	12.5	3.2	6.5	11.2	25.9	13.1	35.1	57.3	13.4	967	82.2
Emlyn CDP	427	-	-	558	100.0	0.0	0.0	0.0	0.0	20.4	19.7	47.3	54.2	40.2	185	51.9
Erlanger city	18,138	19,246	6.1	18,967	87.9	3.2	2.3	4.0	2.7	22.9	14.5	38.2	42.9	29.7	7,203	90.4
Eubank city	319	330	3.4	409	97.6	1.0	0.0	0.5	1.0	30.6	13.0	30.8	54.9	8.4	149	83.2
Evarts city	884	803	-9.2	686	93.6	2.2	0.0	3.5	0.7	9.9	11.2	37.7	74.3	5.5	198	69.7
Ewing city	247	245	-0.8	283	95.4	4.6	0.0	0.0	0.0	24.4	15.2	45.2	64.3	8.0	117	78.6
Ezel CDP	235	-	-	140	100.0	0.0	0.0	0.0	0.0	16.4	13.6	43.1	73.1	0.0	70	82.9
Fairfield city	113	118	4.4	89	95.5	0.0	0.0	4.5	0.0	6.7	36.0	55.9	73.6	11.1	40	95.0
Fairview CDP	286	-	-	253	100.0	0.0	0.0	0.0	0.0	64.8	0.0	11.0	53.3	0.0	39	0.0
Fairview city	143	144	0.7	129	100.0	0.0	0.0	0.0	0.0	12.4	20.9	52.9	68.5	18.5	59	83.1
Falmouth city	2,209	2,103	-4.8	2,577	96.8	0.5	0.3	1.7	0.7	25.7	14.7	35.9	73.8	8.7	1,005	85.0
Fancy Farm CDP	458	-	-	588	99.8	0.2	0.0	0.0	0.0	30.4	23.1	36.1	55.4	26.4	201	90.5
Farley CDP	4,701	-	-	4,245	88.9	3.4	0.0	3.5	4.2	27.2	17.3	38.2	62.0	9.3	1,727	85.9
Farmers CDP	284	-	-	25	100.0	0.0	0.0	0.0	0.0	0.0	0.0	0.0	0.0	0.0	10	100.0
Farmington CDP	245	-	-	153	78.4	21.6	0.0	0.0	0.0	15.7	11.1	33.3	41.9	16.2	74	86.5
Ferguson city	932	947	1.6	985	97.9	1.4	0.0	0.3	0.4	21.4	21.7	43.2	50.5	14.3	382	82.5
Fincastle city	814	844	3.7	737	47.2	38.3	3.4	6.6	4.5	17.8	17.5	43.0	27.0	30.4	270	97.0
Flat Lick CDP	960	-	-	1,072	100.0	0.0	0.0	0.0	0.0	33.4	11.7	35.5	80.1	3.4	354	54.8
Flatwoods city	7,439	7,079	-4.8	7,160	94.7	2.4	0.8	2.1	0.0	19.5	19.9	43.3	43.8	14.4	2,998	87.9
Fleming-Neon city	770	677	-12.1	537	95.7	2.0	0.0	0.0	2.2	13.4	18.8	46.4	56.5	19.3	253	77.1
Flemingsburg city	2,839	2,805	-1.2	2,820	85.4	8.9	0.0	1.5	4.3	29.1	18.3	37.5	59.4	16.3	1,183	77.3
Florence city	29,531	33,004	11.8	32,369	85.5	5.7	2.6	2.1	4.2	23.7	16.2	38.1	37.8	24.9	13,154	92.1
Fordsville city	524	530	1.1	552	96.7	0.7	0.0	0.0	2.5	20.5	21.4	50.3	62.0	2.8	205	74.1
Forest Hills city	447	458	2.5	432	90.5	5.6	0.5	2.1	1.4	26.2	16.0	38.1	24.7	39.3	148	94.6
Fort Campbell North CDP	13,685	-	-	13,735	53.3	15.9	3.9	6.6	20.2	28.7	0.0	22.0	25.6	19.6	2,910	98.1
Fort Knox CDP	10,124	-	-	8,695	58.1	13.3	2.2	5.6	20.9	28.2	1.3	26.9	16.6	34.4	2,473	98.4
Fort Mitchell city	8,164	8,241	0.9	8,257	89.2	1.3	3.8	1.9	3.8	27.3	13.6	36.0	28.5	47.2	3,313	93.1
Fort Thomas city	16,165	16,263	0.6	16,308	93.2	1.6	1.2	2.2	1.7	25.4	16.1	39.4	20.4	53.4	6,441	92.6
Fort Wright city	5,675	5,745	1.2	5,745	92.1	1.7	2.5	1.4	2.3	19.7	15.5	38.4	20.0	53.0	2,516	97.3
Fountain Run city	217	209	-3.7	218	99.1	0.9	0.0	0.0	0.0	18.8	25.2	42.0	69.9	9.2	105	67.6
Fox Chase city	447	487	8.9	572	95.5	0.5	0.0	3.3	0.7	12.6	33.4	56.7	45.2	23.9	219	89.0
Francisville CDP	7,944	-	-	9,387	90.2	1.7	3.5	2.1	2.5	30.6	8.2	37.4	21.5	47.8	2,888	99.0
Frankfort city	27,269	27,755	1.8	27,680	74.1	13.2	2.6	4.8	5.2	19.8	16.1	38.3	41.0	30.2	12,434	88.9
Franklin city	8,472	9,010	6.4	8,835	77.1	16.8	1.2	2.1	2.8	26.2	15.1	35.4	60.1	13.9	3,413	78.6
Fredonia city	401	396	-1.2	646	94.4	4.3	0.0	1.2	0.0	33.9	14.2	32.0	60.0	8.9	188	87.2
Freeburn CDP	399	-	-	354	75.7	0.0	0.0	0.0	24.3	29.4	4.8	32.8	87.4	0.0	158	61.4
Frenchburg city	531	545	2.6	798	89.8	0.0	0.0	1.4	8.8	24.1	17.3	38.5	65.5	12.5	319	83.1
Fulton city	2,446	2,120	-13.3	2,592	62.0	29.8	0.2	5.0	3.0	27.6	17.2	37.4	55.9	14.4	1,004	85.8
Gamaliel city	376	358	-4.8	323	95.0	0.0	0.0	2.8	2.2	17.3	25.1	40.4	66.8	11.5	152	72.4
Garrison CDP	866	-	-	776	100.0	0.0	0.0	0.0	0.0	33.0	19.2	36.4	60.4	12.3	255	92.9
Georgetown city	29,138	34,992	20.1	33,605	84.1	6.1	1.5	4.4	3.9	25.8	9.9	33.4	38.1	27.5	12,915	92.4
Germantown city	154	149	-3.2	62	100.0	0.0	0.0	0.0	0.0	11.3	22.6	47.7	52.0	6.0	32	65.6
Ghent city	323	305	-5.6	407	91.6	0.5	2.2	4.2	1.5	25.3	9.3	38.4	56.0	6.4	148	87.2
Gilbertsville CDP	458	-	-	569	100.0	0.0	0.0	0.0	0.0	16.3	18.1	52.6	67.9	8.4	241	78.4
Glasgow city	14,050	14,485	3.1	14,393	81.2	8.8	0.4	4.3	5.2	22.1	20.9	42.6	59.7	17.8	5,867	79.8
Glencoe city	359	366	1.9	360	97.8	0.0	0.0	0.0	2.2	29.4	17.8	38.5	84.7	1.7	120	78.3
Glenview city	528	543	2.8	569	90.9	0.0	6.3	1.4	1.4	18.5	32.2	57.4	3.8	82.5	237	99.2
Glenview Hills city	319	330	3.4	442	97.1	0.0	0.0	0.5	2.5	32.4	19.9	43.3	5.5	75.6	155	99.4
Glenview Manor city	192	196	2.1	266	98.9	0.0	0.8	0.4	0.0	29.3	19.9	43.8	12.4	68.4	102	84.3
Goose Creek city	294	303	3.1	304	93.1	2.3	0.7	1.3	2.6	15.8	29.9	53.7	23.7	45.7	120	93.3
Goshen city	909	1,010	11.1	976	92.2	3.1	1.4	3.1	0.2	28.4	8.5	33.6	19.6	49.0	306	97.7
Gracey CDP	138	-	-	71	71.8	0.0	0.0	0.0	28.2	0.0	0.0	40.3	67.5	0.0	30	43.3
Grand Rivers city	382	367	-3.9	298	95.6	0.0	0.0	4.4	0.0	8.4	39.9	62.7	49.8	24.5	163	88.3
Gratz city	78	77	-1.3	79	100.0	0.0	0.0	0.0	0.0	39.2	3.8	29.1	88.1	2.4	14	78.6
Graymoor-Devondale city	2,871	2,948	2.7	2,943	86.4	2.3	1.5	1.9	7.9	19.2	26.7	42.3	20.4	53.4	1,183	92.5
Grayson city	4,111	3,894	-5.3	3,976	85.5	3.0	0.0	4.7	6.8	16.4	18.8	34.9	57.6	9.8	1,347	72.8
Greensburg city	2,163	2,066	-4.5	2,243	89.0	3.7	0.0	3.1	4.2	19.9	25.6	48.5	62.8	14.3	916	81.4
Green Spring city	717	747	4.2	735	88.7	5.7	2.0	1.4	2.2	23.9	28.0	50.3	7.2	67.9	276	98.2
Greenup city	1,190	1,113	-6.5	1,307	82.6	8.8	0.0	2.7	6.0	17.1	21.3	43.8	48.2	12.1	523	85.7
Greenville city	4,487	4,204	-6.3	4,281	89.0	9.0	0.2	1.2	0.6	20.6	17.2	36.4	55.6	18.3	1,541	80.2
Guthrie city	1,420	1,409	-0.8	1,291	45.5	46.7	0.0	4.9	2.9	30.4	12.9	38.6	71.5	3.2	606	57.1
Hanson city	739	710	-3.9	792	92.4	1.0	0.0	1.9	4.7	18.8	26.8	45.0	50.4	14.9	285	77.5

1 May be of any race.

Table A. All Places — Population and Housing

STATE City, town, township, borough, or CDP (county if applicable)	2010 census total population	2019 estimated population	Percent change 2010–2019	ACS total population estimate 2015–2019	White alone, not Hispanic or Latino	Black alone, not Hispanic or Latino	Asian alone, not Hispanic or Latino	All other races or 2 or more races, not Hispanic or Latino	Hispanic or Latino[1]	Under 18 years old	Age 65 years and older	Median age	Percent High school diploma or less	Percent Bachelor's degree or more	Occupied housing units Total	Percent with a computer
	1	2	3	4	5	6	7	8	9	10	11	12	13	14	15	16
KENTUCKY—Con.																
Hardin city	615	604	-1.8	517	93.2	0.4	4.1	2.3	0.0	27.3	13.5	36.0	67.0	8.0	233	74.7
Hardinsburg city	2,339	2,338	0.0	2,487	94.6	2.6	0.0	2.5	0.3	19.7	23.5	45.6	56.2	12.9	989	81.9
Hardyville CDP	156	-	-	362	100.0	0.0	0.0	0.0	0.0	47.0	6.1	26.0	57.1	30.2	135	71.9
Harlan city	1,745	1,504	-13.8	1,447	91.2	6.5	2.0	0.3	0.0	18.2	21.4	43.9	56.8	18.0	736	74.2
Harrodsburg city	8,362	8,533	2.0	8,418	85.4	7.4	0.9	3.1	3.2	22.2	18.3	38.6	57.0	16.5	3,569	76.8
Hartford city	2,669	2,726	2.1	2,730	94.1	1.1	0.3	0.3	4.2	21.1	19.5	41.6	50.5	16.9	1,098	82.1
Hawesville city	984	990	0.6	872	96.7	1.9	0.9	0.5	0.0	23.2	16.2	39.8	61.0	11.0	385	80.0
Hazard city	5,482	4,860	-11.3	5,046	90.0	2.7	4.4	1.4	1.5	20.5	22.1	48.0	42.1	30.0	2,074	81.2
Hazel city	407	403	-	457	78.6	12.0	0.0	6.8	2.6	28.0	16.4	40.9	60.7	19.3	182	84.6
Hazel Green CDP	228	-	-	57	100.0	0.0	0.0	0.0	0.0	0.0	43.9	58.9	73.7	14.0	33	75.8
Hebron CDP	5,929	-	-	6,461	81.4	2.4	0.4	6.1	9.8	32.8	5.2	31.8	32.7	25.5	1,868	96.5
Hebron Estates city	1,078	1,177	9.2	1,187	92.0	0.0	0.0	6.7	1.3	12.7	27.5	55.7	48.3	13.7	522	91.8
Henderson city	28,924	28,207	-2.5	28,625	81.6	10.3	0.6	4.1	3.4	23.1	17.6	39.7	50.2	17.6	12,039	80.9
Hendron CDP	4,687	-	-	5,228	91.5	5.3	0.5	1.6	1.0	23.3	21.2	41.9	34.3	28.9	2,231	85.5
Heritage Creek city	1,076	1,133	5.3	1,000	86.4	7.9	0.0	2.4	3.3	14.9	20.6	46.8	53.6	10.5	442	87.6
Hickman city	2,395	2,108	-12.0	2,079	62.8	33.1	0.1	1.9	2.1	21.2	17.1	39.2	64.1	7.0	752	73.4
Hickory CDP	-	-	-	277	80.5	7.9	10.1	0.0	1.4	6.9	9.0	28.5	72.3	4.2	92	100.0
Hickory Hill city	114	118	3.5	121	77.7	7.4	14.0	0.8	0.0	11.6	31.4	56.7	31.7	44.6	49	100.0
High Bridge CDP	242	-	-	263	95.4	0.0	0.0	4.6	0.0	0.0	6.1	50.5	75.8	0.0	132	53.0
Highland Heights city	6,933	7,065	1.9	7,149	88.4	6.0	3.0	0.8	1.8	9.5	15.3	25.0	37.5	33.5	2,528	85.5
Hills and Dales city	142	146	2.8	179	98.9	1.1	0.0	0.0	0.0	21.2	31.8	54.9	11.5	64.9	68	94.1
Hillview city	8,464	9,225	9.0	9,071	90.8	4.7	1.7	1.9	0.8	23.7	13.7	38.6	63.7	8.6	3,072	89.7
Hindman city	777	678	-12.7	635	93.2	2.2	1.7	1.3	1.6	22.0	15.9	34.7	44.8	37.3	241	79.3
Hiseville CDP	240	-	-	204	100.0	0.0	0.0	0.0	0.0	20.1	10.8	52.5	96.3	0.0	117	84.6
Hodgenville city	3,234	3,249	0.5	3,212	85.5	4.4	0.0	1.5	8.7	31.4	18.7	35.5	49.2	11.2	1,142	83.0
Hollow Creek city	779	806	3.5	845	84.6	7.6	2.2	1.2	4.4	19.5	26.7	51.0	36.2	35.2	316	93.7
Hollyvilla city	540	555	2.8	435	92.4	2.3	0.5	2.5	2.3	24.6	14.7	37.8	59.1	8.1	193	86.0
Hopkinsville city	31,988	30,680	-4.1	31,056	60.9	31.2	1.5	2.7	3.6	25.9	16.4	36.3	46.7	19.6	12,671	85.2
Horse Cave city	2,350	2,425	3.2	2,613	75.5	12.4	0.5	5.5	6.0	25.5	19.1	42.0	59.8	12.1	1,144	80.2
Houston Acres city	490	504	2.9	539	90.2	8.7	1.1	0.0	0.0	23.0	28.0	48.4	22.3	46.8	237	84.0
Hunters Hollow city	330	358	8.5	270	96.3	0.0	0.0	1.5	2.2	21.9	10.7	39.8	47.6	4.2	100	96.0
Hurstbourne city	4,221	4,388	4.0	4,394	78.8	3.1	16.4	1.4	0.3	20.6	25.6	45.4	11.6	69.5	1,748	91.8
Hurstbourne Acres city	1,811	1,890	4.4	2,027	44.0	5.7	38.0	7.4	4.9	16.3	10.4	30.7	15.8	62.5	1,019	95.4
Hustonville city	376	369	-1.9	561	98.4	0.0	1.1	0.5	0.0	35.5	20.1	41.2	60.4	8.8	220	73.2
Hyden city	370	332	-10.3	398	90.7	1.3	6.3	0.5	1.3	8.5	37.7	54.8	51.5	25.4	131	83.2
Independence city	24,759	28,521	15.2	27,683	93.4	2.6	1.5	1.2	1.2	26.7	10.4	35.3	38.6	28.5	9,434	96.2
Indian Hills city	2,878	2,968	3.1	2,961	91.5	0.9	4.8	1.8	1.0	24.4	27.3	47.4	6.2	81.5	1,107	99.5
Inez city	716	620	-13.4	998	99.6	0.0	0.0	0.4	0.0	19.9	21.9	32.9	58.6	17.4	370	81.1
Ironville CDP	-	-	-	984	100.0	0.0	0.0	0.0	0.0	29.0	13.8	37.4	49.5	11.2	361	100.0
Irvine city	2,475	2,298	-7.2	2,439	98.8	0.5	0.0	0.7	0.0	22.2	20.8	43.2	58.0	13.2	1,075	74.0
Irvington city	1,174	1,189	1.3	1,213	83.9	11.7	0.0	4.0	0.3	20.4	23.2	44.6	72.6	5.9	511	70.3
Island city	458	451	-1.5	462	82.9	0.0	0.2	2.8	14.1	26.4	16.2	35.7	63.1	6.0	194	79.9
Jackson city	2,191	1,939	-11.5	2,106	98.8	0.0	0.9	0.3	0.0	18.9	18.7	43.3	52.4	20.7	847	80.6
Jamestown city	1,795	1,791	-0.2	2,187	92.0	2.1	2.4	3.1	0.3	25.8	20.4	40.2	55.9	10.1	808	73.6
Jeff CDP	323	-	-	198	100.0	0.0	0.0	0.0	0.0	18.2	15.2	53.3	81.5	13.6	89	100.0
Jeffersontown city	27,813	27,715	-0.4	28,035	72.7	12.6	6.0	3.3	5.3	24.3	16.5	38.5	31.7	37.8	11,057	92.3
Jeffersonville city	1,638	1,753	7.0	1,973	97.2	0.1	0.0	1.5	1.2	25.1	15.1	38.9	61.9	9.2	719	86.0
Jenkins city	2,224	1,929	-13.3	2,245	94.5	1.1	0.1	2.7	1.6	23.1	17.1	33.2	64.4	12.0	938	87.0
Junction City city	2,245	2,306	2.7	2,015	91.3	3.3	0.0	1.6	3.8	21.7	14.6	45.3	65.5	6.3	849	82.6
Keene city	77	88	14.3	-	-	-	-	-	-	-	-	-	-	-	-	-
Kenton Vale city	110	108	-1.8	121	92.6	0.0	0.0	0.0	7.4	11.6	11.6	41.3	52.6	8.2	56	76.8
Kenvir CDP	297	-	-	472	100.0	0.0	0.0	0.0	0.0	26.7	19.5	31.2	50.5	9.1	195	90.8
Kevil city	620	584	-5.8	685	93.4	0.7	0.0	2.9	2.9	21.2	30.7	47.3	46.2	15.7	303	74.6
Kingsley city	385	390	1.3	436	98.2	0.0	0.0	1.1	0.7	19.0	19.5	42.5	12.2	61.8	190	98.4
Kuttawa city	660	670	1.5	582	74.9	13.2	2.1	5.7	4.1	20.6	32.5	54.9	52.5	20.3	194	82.0
La Center city	1,009	959	-5.0	925	82.7	14.1	1.3	1.9	0.0	15.6	22.7	48.6	58.0	12.0	336	83.9
LaFayette city	172	160	-7.0	135	94.1	2.2	0.0	1.5	2.2	20.7	13.3	34.3	56.8	11.6	66	86.4
La Grange city	8,083	9,031	11.7	8,854	82.0	5.8	1.5	4.2	6.6	26.6	13.5	35.4	39.1	27.2	3,289	90.0
Lakeside Park city	2,722	2,762	1.5	2,762	92.2	0.0	3.6	2.3	1.8	17.5	15.4	49.2	20.1	47.7	1,238	95.2
Lakeview Heights city	229	224	-2.2	267	98.5	0.7	0.0	0.0	0.7	21.3	27.0	51.0	19.3	57.8	106	96.2
Lancaster city	3,804	3,867	1.7	3,842	87.9	7.8	0.7	1.9	1.7	25.6	16.7	34.9	64.3	10.1	1,463	78.9
Langdon Place city	878	915	4.2	807	78.8	10.2	6.8	2.4	1.9	23.3	21.2	39.6	18.0	55.1	324	97.5
Lawrenceburg city	11,018	11,509	4.5	11,350	92.3	4.7	0.0	1.4	1.6	25.6	12.9	36.0	46.9	17.6	4,490	88.4
Lebanon city	5,558	5,708	2.7	5,644	72.6	18.0	0.1	2.8	6.4	21.0	21.5	46.0	65.0	14.0	2,688	74.8
Lebanon Junction city	1,813	1,962	8.2	1,931	98.8	0.9	0.0	0.0	0.3	18.1	19.6	43.5	67.0	8.0	732	85.9
Ledbetter CDP	1,683	-	-	1,860	91.3	1.7	0.0	0.0	7.0	28.2	8.5	40.4	46.4	12.0	720	97.8
Leitchfield city	6,648	6,858	3.2	6,807	91.7	3.7	0.0	3.9	0.6	26.6	18.2	38.2	63.6	10.8	2,689	80.5
Lewisburg city	810	804	-0.7	756	90.1	0.9	0.9	2.8	5.3	25.9	24.1	38.7	63.2	12.3	339	66.4
Lewisport city	1,678	1,690	0.7	1,898	91.6	3.2	1.6	1.1	2.5	26.0	14.9	36.8	57.8	15.2	763	89.1
Lexington-Fayette urban county	295,870	323,152	9.2	320,601	71.0	14.5	3.7	3.6	7.2	20.9	13.0	34.6	28.4	43.6	129,784	93.6
Liberty city	2,168	2,130	-1.8	2,341	90.9	1.5	0.0	1.4	6.2	18.5	24.9	42.5	65.5	13.3	897	73.4
Lincolnshire city	148	150	1.4	168	78.0	19.6	0.0	2.4	0.0	21.4	23.8	40.6	25.6	51.9	65	92.3
Livermore city	1,365	1,289	-5.6	1,172	95.0	0.0	0.0	5.0	0.0	21.7	21.8	50.9	62.1	7.4	530	85.1
Livingston city	225	215	-4.4	123	97.6	0.0	0.0	2.4	0.0	9.8	31.7	45.2	74.4	2.4	56	71.4
London city	7,985	8,068	1.0	8,059	92.4	1.7	2.0	2.9	1.0	18.4	17.6	43.4	58.3	13.8	3,435	83.6
Loretto city	695	693	-0.3	771	91.2	1.4	0.3	6.6	0.5	29.2	14.7	36.8	71.5	7.6	289	82.7
Louisa city	2,456	2,327	-5.3	2,703	95.7	0.5	0.0	0.5	3.3	27.3	18.4	42.5	61.7	14.7	969	75.2
Louisville/Jefferson County metro government	741,075	766,757	3.5	767,419	67.4	21.5	2.9	2.7	5.4	22.3	15.7	38.3	36.1	33.4	312,679	89.4
Louisville/Jefferson County metro government (balance)	595,710	617,638	3.7	617,790	65.6	23.3	2.7	2.8	5.6	22.5	14.9	37.6	39.1	29.9	248,404	88.8
Lovelaceville CDP	148	-	-	19	100.0	0.0	0.0	0.0	0.0	0.0	0.0	0.0	100.0	0.0	19	100.0
Lowes CDP	98	-	-	78	70.5	0.0	17.9	11.5	0.0	11.5	0.0	54.9	79.7	0.0	55	67.3
Loyall city	688	601	-12.6	654	96.6	1.8	0.0	0.0	1.5	23.1	16.7	42.3	64.2	10.8	285	67.0
Ludlow city	4,546	4,504	-0.9	4,530	89.3	1.8	0.0	3.0	5.8	20.9	13.8	38.0	42.7	23.0	1,821	89.4
Lynch city	747	644	-13.8	553	81.9	14.8	0.0	2.2	1.1	13.9	28.9	57.5	42.0	15.1	268	75.7
Lyndon city	11,002	11,423	3.8	11,431	74.4	12.6	1.6	2.2	9.1	17.5	16.4	35.1	24.8	43.8	5,686	92.9
Lynnview city	914	933	2.1	1,038	79.6	2.1	1.3	2.3	14.6	24.6	14.1	40.3	51.1	16.9	418	87.3
McCarr CDP	164	-	-	83	100.0	0.0	0.0	0.0	0.0	10.8	31.3	50.5	62.2	13.5	39	100.0

1 May be of any race.

Table A. All Places — **Population and Housing**

STATE City, town, township, borough, or CDP (county if applicable)	Population: 2010 census total population	Population: 2019 estimated population	Population: Percent change 2010–2019	Population: ACS total population estimate 2015–2019	Race and Hispanic or Latino origin (percent): White alone, not Hispanic or Latino	Black alone, not Hispanic or Latino	Asian alone, not Hispanic or Latino	All other races or 2 or more races, not Hispanic or Latino	Hispanic or Latino[1]	Age (percent): Under 18 years old	Age 65 years and older	Median age	Educational attainment of persons age 25 and older: Percent High school diploma or less	Percent Bachelor's degree or more	Occupied housing units: Total	Percent with a computer
	1	2	3	4	5	6	7	8	9	10	11	12	13	14	15	16
KENTUCKY—Con.																
McDowell CDP	-	-	-	656	97.7	0.0	0.0	0.0	2.3	11.3	43.8	61.0	66.8	11.8	319	68.3
Maceo CDP	413	-	-	407	100.0	0.0	0.0	0.0	0.0	11.1	14.3	47.1	68.1	5.0	196	95.9
McHenry city	388	388	0.0	309	99.4	0.0	0.0	0.0	0.6	24.3	15.2	39.9	77.4	5.5	123	78.9
McKee city	805	779	-3.2	851	96.4	1.8	0.0	0.8	1.1	25.4	20.7	40.9	80.5	2.5	419	58.2
McKinney CDP	-	-	-	115	100.0	0.0	0.0	0.0	0.0	11.3	0.0	56.2	40.2	0.0	57	66.7
Mackville city	222	223	0.5	245	93.5	0.0	0.0	6.5	0.0	43.3	17.1	34.5	58.8	20.6	78	87.2
McRoberts CDP	784	-	-	898	95.8	4.2	0.0	0.0	0.0	16.5	20.7	45.0	69.2	11.4	358	84.1
Madisonville city	19,841	18,621	-6.1	18,936	80.1	11.8	1.3	3.5	3.3	25.7	17.4	36.3	49.1	20.8	7,584	82.9
Magnolia CDP	524	-	-	616	100.0	0.0	0.0	0.0	0.0	26.8	11.9	27.0	51.0	15.3	255	81.6
Manchester city	1,447	1,290	-10.9	1,779	82.8	13.9	0.0	2.9	0.3	16.2	20.2	41.1	63.6	11.3	761	85.9
Manitou CDP	181	-	-	434	100.0	0.0	0.0	0.0	0.0	47.2	1.6	19.4	20.4	32.0	109	100.0
Manor Creek city	226	233	3.1	287	90.6	3.1	0.0	2.1	4.2	32.8	18.5	36.7	11.5	71.0	100	98.0
Marion city	3,039	2,841	-6.5	2,912	92.4	2.4	0.0	3.4	1.8	20.3	19.1	44.0	58.6	12.2	1,155	85.3
Marrowbone CDP	217	-	-	103	100.0	0.0	0.0	0.0	0.0	16.5	33.0	48.6	91.9	0.0	57	40.4
Martin city	625	554	-11.4	446	99.1	0.0	0.9	0.0	0.0	15.2	17.9	38.3	61.6	6.2	224	74.6
Maryhill Estates city	179	184	2.8	204	99.5	0.0	0.0	0.0	0.5	33.3	15.7	43.4	6.9	81.7	71	93.0
Masonville CDP	1,014	-	-	1,381	98.6	0.0	0.0	0.0	1.4	29.5	11.9	34.4	36.3	25.8	461	89.8
Massac CDP	4,505	-	-	5,064	79.1	9.6	0.6	8.5	2.3	26.1	18.1	29.8	34.9	29.3	2,188	90.7
Mayfield city	10,033	9,817	-2.2	9,867	70.2	12.0	0.8	2.2	14.8	28.8	16.3	32.9	50.3	17.8	3,734	81.3
Mayking CDP	487	-	-	488	100.0	0.0	0.0	0.0	0.0	30.1	10.9	33.3	56.7	12.8	212	75.9
Mays Lick CDP	242	-	-	293	93.2	6.8	0.0	0.0	0.0	11.9	17.4	46.6	42.3	11.6	124	87.1
Maysville city	9,025	8,728	-3.3	8,782	82.9	9.1	1.6	3.3	3.2	22.6	19.8	42.1	44.4	19.5	3,572	78.0
Maytown CDP	-	-	-	92	100.0	0.0	0.0	0.0	0.0	0.0	43.5	62.9	58.7	9.8	43	100.0
Meadowbrook Farm city	136	142	4.4	123	94.3	1.6	1.6	2.4	0.0	23.6	21.1	47.5	23.3	51.1	43	100.0
Meadow Vale city	736	759	3.1	745	82.3	11.8	0.3	3.5	2.1	22.8	25.6	43.0	19.6	49.9	294	96.3
Meadowview Estates city	161	167	3.7	104	97.1	0.0	0.0	2.9	0.0	2.9	42.3	64.0	30.0	37.8	66	87.9
Melbourne city	461	482	4.6	511	95.3	0.0	1.2	0.4	3.1	18.0	26.6	52.9	49.1	29.0	169	85.2
Mentor city	209	223	6.7	300	100.0	0.0	0.0	0.0	0.0	25.0	13.3	40.0	48.1	24.3	97	91.8
Middlesborough city	10,190	9,084	-10.9	9,395	89.2	5.8	0.5	2.4	2.2	25.0	17.4	40.0	68.5	9.1	3,662	74.7
Middletown city	7,572	7,877	4.0	7,891	76.3	10.4	1.7	5.1	6.4	20.9	19.5	45.0	17.5	45.1	3,601	91.6
Midway city	1,640	1,893	15.4	1,807	84.8	6.4	0.6	2.2	6.0	15.7	17.9	38.8	27.4	46.8	675	89.5
Millersburg city	790	780	-1.3	761	96.5	1.2	0.0	0.0	2.4	19.4	20.9	52.4	63.6	11.8	349	69.9
Millstone CDP	117	-	-	172	100.0	0.0	0.0	0.0	0.0	0.0	61.6	81.1	100.0	0.0	62	22.6
Milton city	629	601	-4.5	652	87.3	0.0	0.0	8.7	4.0	19.9	20.4	46.1	53.9	15.7	315	90.2
Mockingbird Valley city	160	164	2.5	159	98.1	0.0	1.9	0.0	0.0	24.5	34.0	50.5	5.1	83.1	69	91.3
Monterey city	138	133	-3.6	118	100.0	0.0	0.0	0.0	0.0	16.1	11.0	51.2	58.3	5.2	72	91.7
Monticello city	6,182	5,988	-3.1	6,070	83.1	4.4	0.0	2.0	10.4	24.5	19.6	36.0	62.4	14.6	2,341	68.3
Moorland city	434	445	2.5	466	96.1	0.9	0.0	1.3	1.7	16.3	13.5	38.8	37.7	29.2	213	92.0
Morehead city	6,840	7,562	10.6	7,653	89.7	3.2	1.7	2.3	3.0	10.2	10.7	22.6	34.4	32.6	2,193	85.3
Morganfield city	3,216	3,366	4.7	3,422	78.6	16.9	0.0	3.0	1.5	20.4	19.9	41.0	60.3	10.6	1,444	83.2
Morgantown city	2,445	2,431	-0.6	2,650	83.2	0.3	0.0	1.9	14.6	25.0	18.0	37.9	66.4	12.3	1,078	74.7
Mortons Gap city	863	826	-4.3	1,001	92.4	5.6	0.0	2.0	0.0	22.7	13.9	43.4	66.2	6.4	391	74.9
Mount Olivet city	368	336	-8.7	343	90.1	9.9	0.0	0.0	0.0	26.5	10.2	32.5	56.5	17.9	135	49.6
Mount Sterling city	6,899	7,231	4.8	7,166	89.7	5.4	0.0	2.4	2.5	26.5	13.8	37.2	50.3	19.8	2,714	88.8
Mount Vernon city	2,508	2,415	-3.7	2,701	92.4	0.7	0.0	6.9	0.0	21.3	19.1	38.9	55.4	18.3	1,038	79.1
Mount Washington city	13,521	14,817	9.6	14,567	94.1	0.4	0.4	2.7	2.5	26.3	13.2	36.6	43.3	19.2	5,278	92.9
Muldraugh city	947	986	4.1	1,040	84.5	8.2	0.0	4.6	2.7	20.9	8.9	36.6	61.4	10.2	427	78.5
Munfordville city	1,613	1,659	2.9	1,615	88.0	8.6	0.9	2.0	0.4	15.7	18.7	47.0	70.6	8.4	686	66.8
Murray city	17,735	19,327	9.0	19,171	85.3	6.0	2.2	3.6	2.9	14.5	12.6	26.5	37.9	33.7	7,265	90.6
Murray Hill city	582	605	4.0	568	92.4	3.3	2.5	0.4	1.4	13.2	45.8	59.8	17.3	59.3	305	80.7
Nebo city	236	226	-4.2	226	89.8	4.0	0.0	6.2	0.0	19.5	13.3	44.4	53.2	13.9	90	91.1
New Castle city	912	939	3.0	1,021	90.0	3.9	0.0	4.9	1.2	19.9	29.9	49.5	66.4	13.1	410	70.2
New Haven city	852	894	4.9	676	97.5	0.4	0.0	1.3	0.7	22.9	14.8	40.9	61.3	7.0	308	80.5
New Hope CDP	129	-	-	103	100.0	0.0	0.0	0.0	0.0	17.5	26.2	37.7	90.6	0.0	52	88.5
Newport city	15,440	14,932	-3.3	15,123	82.2	11.1	0.2	1.4	5.1	18.6	13.8	37.1	51.0	28.8	6,402	84.3
Nicholasville city	28,021	30,865	10.1	30,301	87.0	6.4	1.5	1.3	3.8	25.3	13.2	35.9	51.6	19.9	11,169	88.4
Norbourne Estates city	443	449	1.4	466	98.9	0.0	0.0	0.0	1.1	20.2	25.8	52.4	7.5	80.5	183	97.3
North Corbin CDP	1,773	-	-	2,035	100.0	0.0	0.0	0.0	0.0	29.2	12.9	34.5	65.6	14.1	747	76.7
Northfield city	1,020	1,051	3.0	1,181	92.8	1.5	3.0	0.5	2.1	25.2	23.4	43.9	11.9	65.9	438	94.3
North Middletown city	654	646	-1.2	657	92.2	0.0	0.0	1.7	6.1	27.7	16.1	37.7	72.8	7.5	257	87.5
Nortonville city	1,204	1,150	-4.5	943	94.0	1.9	0.0	3.8	0.3	17.8	24.5	45.6	62.8	9.2	440	77.3
Norwood city	370	382	3.2	450	94.4	1.1	1.8	1.8	0.9	22.2	16.7	41.3	19.9	61.3	190	92.6
Oakbrook CDP	9,036	-	-	9,023	90.3	1.1	4.9	2.8	0.9	19.6	17.9	43.2	30.0	32.6	3,628	95.4
Oak Grove city	7,489	7,320	-2.3	7,338	55.0	24.1	1.0	4.5	15.3	27.4	2.0	24.6	34.4	15.5	2,774	98.4
Oakland city	221	218	-1.4	232	91.8	6.5	0.0	1.7	0.0	12.9	29.3	57.7	55.0	16.9	112	77.7
Old Brownsboro Place city	353	366	3.7	380	88.2	5.0	4.7	1.1	1.1	20.0	25.5	49.1	11.2	71.3	145	97.2
Olive Hill city	1,633	1,556	-4.7	1,352	99.6	0.0	0.0	0.4	0.0	23.5	24.5	47.2	59.3	15.4	612	72.2
Oneida CDP	410	-	-	427	89.7	2.6	0.0	6.6	1.2	30.0	8.2	27.4	58.1	22.7	173	78.6
Onton CDP	141	-	-	40	100.0	0.0	0.0	0.0	0.0	0.0	50.0	61.0	72.5	15.0	27	66.7
Orchard Grass Hills city	1,595	1,775	11.3	1,781	85.5	2.2	0.7	4.0	7.6	34.1	5.8	29.9	26.8	38.3	532	99.4
Owensboro city	57,482	60,131	4.6	59,536	83.2	6.2	2.3	3.8	4.5	24.3	17.5	38.0	44.7	23.0	25,339	86.8
Owenton city	1,526	1,533	0.5	1,686	95.1	2.7	0.0	1.4	0.8	19.7	23.5	44.4	73.6	6.5	679	72.2
Owingsville city	1,510	1,573	4.2	2,129	94.3	2.2	0.9	1.3	1.4	26.7	17.6	38.0	57.3	17.8	864	77.3
Paducah city	25,027	24,865	-0.6	24,894	71.4	21.8	0.8	2.9	3.1	20.5	19.5	42.0	42.7	25.1	11,330	82.2
Paintsville city	4,228	3,990	-5.6	4,090	94.3	1.5	2.3	0.6	1.3	21.6	21.4	41.6	54.0	18.3	1,575	84.6
Paris city	9,837	9,671	-1.7	9,817	83.3	13.1	1.3	0.1	2.2	23.8	17.1	37.2	50.3	16.8	3,987	83.1
Park City city	537	559	4.1	641	86.1	3.6	0.0	10.3	0.0	24.8	11.9	35.1	58.0	9.5	237	78.9
Park Hills city	2,989	2,984	-0.2	2,987	83.3	4.0	2.5	8.0	2.2	21.8	17.5	34.6	22.6	41.8	1,314	98.2
Parkway Village city	650	660	1.5	646	87.2	7.9	1.4	3.6	0.0	17.0	13.2	36.6	29.8	42.9	320	91.3
Pathfork CDP	379	-	-	464	100.0	0.0	0.0	0.0	0.0	29.3	12.5	39.8	64.0	11.1	190	64.7
Payne Gap CDP	329	-	-	282	100.0	0.0	0.0	0.0	0.0	9.2	12.8	52.0	68.6	1.8	128	100.0
Pembroke city	869	889	2.3	862	80.7	12.1	2.3	2.7	2.2	23.3	20.9	35.4	40.9	17.7	329	92.7
Perryville city	741	749	1.1	839	92.7	6.4	0.0	0.2	0.6	15.4	21.5	46.4	62.1	14.2	359	86.9
Petersburg CDP	620	-	-	579	100.0	0.0	0.0	0.0	0.0	21.1	21.8	49.0	65.4	21.0	173	95.4
Pewee Valley city	1,435	1,569	9.3	1,592	92.7	1.8	1.8	2.0	1.8	20.8	24.3	49.3	23.4	46.1	520	94.6
Phelps CDP	893	-	-	771	100.0	0.0	0.0	0.0	0.0	11.7	13.1	48.7	74.9	4.0	356	78.4
Pikeville city	6,913	6,551	-5.2	6,810	91.7	2.8	1.3	2.0	2.2	18.8	12.8	32.5	41.2	33.7	2,749	87.6
Pine Knot CDP	1,621	-	-	1,486	79.9	10.0	2.4	6.5	1.3	18.0	14.0	43.4	61.8	16.0	539	64.4
Pineville city	1,936	1,730	-10.6	1,831	94.9	1.0	0.0	3.9	0.2	17.0	22.9	44.8	65.2	12.0	878	67.4
Pioneer Village city	2,711	2,941	8.5	2,889	96.2	1.2	0.0	0.8	1.8	16.6	22.3	49.2	54.7	15.7	1,200	93.4
Pippa Passes city	533	659	23.6	657	88.0	3.3	1.4	3.0	4.3	3.7	1.5	20.2	2.0	74.5	55	98.2
Plano CDP	1,117	-	-	1,348	95.9	2.2	0.0	1.9	0.0	35.5	3.2	35.1	26.3	41.6	440	95.2

1 May be of any race.

Table A. All Places — **Population and Housing**

STATE City, town, township, borough, or CDP (county if applicable)	Population: 2010 census total population	Population: 2019 estimated population	Population: Percent change 2010–2019	Population: ACS total population estimate 2015–2019	Race and Hispanic or Latino origin (percent): White alone, not Hispanic or Latino	Race: Black alone, not Hispanic or Latino	Race: Asian alone, not Hispanic or Latino	Race: All other races or 2 or more races, not Hispanic or Latino	Race: Hispanic or Latino[1]	Age (percent): Under 18 years old	Age: Age 65 years and older	Age: Median age	Educational attainment of persons age 25 and older: Percent High school diploma or less	Educational attainment: Percent Bachelor's degree or more	Occupied housing units: Total	Occupied housing units: Percent with a computer
	1	2	3	4	5	6	7	8	9	10	11	12	13	14	15	16
KENTUCKY—Con.																
Plantation city	832	854	2.6	864	85.3	7.4	1.5	2.1	3.7	30.6	8.6	32.7	20.5	45.0	331	92.1
Pleasant View CDP	350	-	-	483	100.0	0.0	0.0	0.0	0.0	26.9	4.6	39.4	75.6	15.0	164	60.4
Pleasureville city	829	883	6.5	1,117	95.6	4.1	0.0	0.0	0.3	24.5	9.6	30.8	71.9	5.6	400	84.0
Plum Springs city	464	528	13.8	463	75.4	13.4	0.0	1.5	9.7	26.3	13.0	36.6	50.8	21.2	175	92.0
Poole CDP	-	-	-	95	100.0	0.0	0.0	0.0	0.0	11.6	18.9	49.0	76.2	0.0	50	64.0
Poplar Hills city	408	423	3.7	439	13.2	37.6	0.0	0.0	49.2	30.5	3.9	27.9	64.7	7.2	223	82.5
Powderly city	743	736	-0.9	873	98.3	0.0	0.0	1.0	0.7	15.5	24.1	47.3	65.1	8.4	335	80.3
Prestonsburg city	3,730	3,532	-5.3	3,591	89.6	6.4	1.0	1.7	1.4	20.0	19.4	33.6	56.1	17.6	1,349	85.5
Prestonville city	161	159	-1.2	113	88.5	0.0	0.0	2.7	8.8	27.4	23.9	44.4	63.4	0.0	51	64.7
Princeton city	6,334	6,115	-3.5	6,116	82.8	11.9	0.0	0.1	5.2	29.0	18.1	35.5	56.7	20.2	2,372	85.6
Prospect city	4,689	4,905	4.6	4,896	88.0	3.9	5.7	0.4	2.0	20.1	30.1	54.8	8.3	75.0	2,030	95.5
Providence city	3,193	2,999	-6.1	3,027	82.2	11.7	0.0	6.0	0.2	24.5	19.8	38.5	66.7	13.0	1,200	74.8
Pryorsburg CDP	311	-	-	272	75.0	1.5	0.0	15.1	8.5	27.9	22.8	26.9	57.3	7.0	95	74.7
Rabbit Hash CDP	315	-	-	233	97.0	0.0	0.0	3.0	0.0	12.4	16.3	58.1	27.0	22.1	115	100.0
Raceland city	2,407	2,355	-2.2	2,511	98.8	0.0	0.0	1.2	0.0	20.4	20.0	43.8	49.5	20.4	1,005	90.6
Radcliff city	22,309	22,914	2.7	22,639	54.9	28.2	3.0	5.8	8.1	24.2	13.0	34.7	41.0	17.5	9,192	91.6
Ravenna city	605	559	-7.6	530	94.7	0.6	0.4	2.1	2.3	20.9	24.2	45.4	63.1	14.1	204	81.4
Raywick city	134	135	0.7	158	100.0	0.0	0.0	0.0	0.0	15.8	11.4	37.8	68.9	2.8	71	64.8
Reidland CDP	4,491	-	-	4,265	97.5	1.5	0.0	1.0	0.0	23.5	19.6	45.3	36.1	21.6	1,765	89.1
Richlawn city	405	412	1.7	403	97.8	0.7	0.0	0.0	1.5	14.9	23.3	44.1	9.2	67.2	192	97.9
Richmond city	31,321	36,157	15.4	35,133	85.6	7.2	1.3	3.6	2.3	17.8	10.2	26.1	37.3	31.1	13,317	89.9
Rineyville CDP	-	-	-	3,565	88.7	0.5	0.9	1.5	8.4	31.3	5.0	30.9	40.7	22.6	1,156	96.5
River Bluff city	398	442	11.1	567	78.3	4.1	0.7	2.3	14.6	21.2	15.2	36.5	19.4	49.7	169	96.4
Riverwood city	450	466	3.6	488	96.1	0.0	1.2	0.0	2.7	25.8	19.5	44.8	3.9	82.4	181	97.2
Robards city	515	502	-2.5	507	94.9	3.2	0.2	1.8	0.0	20.3	14.8	41.6	47.8	12.1	195	88.7
Rochester city	152	151	-0.7	280	95.7	0.0	0.0	4.3	0.0	32.1	23.6	32.8	64.5	11.5	89	96.6
Rockholds CDP	390	-	-	297	100.0	0.0	0.0	0.0	0.0	11.8	29.3	46.1	86.4	13.6	105	73.3
Rockport city	266	265	-0.4	253	94.9	0.0	0.0	0.0	5.1	20.9	18.2	39.7	76.1	4.9	95	82.1
Rolling Fields city	646	661	2.3	616	99.5	0.0	0.0	0.5	0.0	26.8	23.1	46.3	1.4	89.3	236	98.3
Rolling Hills city	957	989	3.3	898	69.2	14.7	4.7	2.9	8.6	20.0	16.8	41.2	30.9	35.0	368	92.4
Rosine CDP	113	-	-	176	100.0	0.0	0.0	0.0	0.0	9.7	27.8	59.2	78.3	7.9	78	100.0
Russell city	3,452	3,231	-6.4	3,287	92.9	0.5	2.9	1.5	2.3	21.3	21.6	44.7	29.1	35.2	1,383	90.1
Russell Springs city	2,437	2,638	8.2	2,565	78.8	0.3	0.0	6.7	14.2	24.9	17.7	37.5	68.0	13.6	892	75.1
Russellville city	6,958	7,109	2.2	7,039	77.8	19.1	0.4	1.3	1.3	23.6	22.8	40.7	62.4	14.5	3,021	63.6
Ryland Heights city	1,022	1,077	5.4	1,086	96.5	0.0	0.0	0.0	3.5	25.7	15.4	40.0	54.6	11.4	353	87.5
Sacramento city	460	440	-4.3	463	89.4	8.6	0.4	1.5	0.0	20.7	24.6	42.6	66.7	12.3	218	79.4
Sadieville city	301	362	20.3	344	100.0	0.0	0.0	0.0	0.0	27.6	5.5	38.6	43.5	17.2	133	94.7
St. Charles city	275	269	-2.2	336	97.6	0.0	0.0	1.8	0.6	36.0	13.7	35.5	76.6	3.9	124	73.4
St. Mary city	129	128	-0.8	183	100.0	0.0	0.0	0.0	0.0	14.2	6.6	28.4	74.8	11.8	89	82.0
St. Matthews city	17,577	18,105	3.0	18,161	82.0	7.8	2.1	2.3	5.9	16.2	19.4	38.7	18.1	53.2	9,070	91.1
St. Regis Park city	1,457	1,497	2.7	1,410	95.2	2.1	0.6	0.9	1.3	18.1	23.3	49.5	20.0	55.3	596	97.5
Salem city	752	723	-3.9	704	93.5	1.4	0.4	3.1	1.6	16.8	33.1	56.3	58.2	12.8	298	76.5
Salt Lick city	303	327	7.9	300	94.7	0.0	4.0	1.0	0.3	20.3	8.7	45.2	44.8	29.9	133	82.0
Salvisa CDP	420	-	-	121	100.0	0.0	0.0	0.0	0.0	21.5	9.1	31.3	51.9	14.3	44	86.4
Salyersville city	1,875	1,657	-11.6	2,033	97.0	0.0	0.6	0.2	2.1	28.9	18.4	38.0	64.5	14.6	720	83.2
Sanders city	238	235	-1.3	191	84.8	10.5	0.0	4.7	0.0	13.1	31.4	55.8	80.7	3.0	64	71.9
Sandy Hook city	644	609	-5.4	790	96.5	1.3	0.0	1.5	0.8	23.2	26.8	44.3	66.1	11.3	341	65.1
Sardis city	103	101	-1.9	75	97.3	0.0	0.0	2.7	0.0	9.3	18.7	54.4	73.5	5.9	44	63.6
Science Hill city	693	696	0.4	665	95.3	1.2	0.0	2.9	0.6	22.1	19.5	35.4	50.1	13.8	286	83.2
Scottsville city	4,226	4,541	7.5	4,444	95.9	2.5	0.0	1.6	0.0	20.5	19.0	43.9	53.2	11.5	1,701	86.5
Sebree city	1,603	1,530	-4.6	1,475	57.6	0.0	0.0	6.8	35.6	32.0	16.3	38.7	71.6	7.5	488	65.6
Sedalia CDP	295	-	-	433	71.6	0.0	0.0	19.4	9.0	16.6	25.4	48.5	60.4	6.5	138	94.9
Seneca Gardens city	700	709	1.3	658	98.6	0.5	0.0	0.9	0.0	20.7	24.3	52.3	1.6	85.9	292	94.9
Sharpsburg city	323	338	4.6	430	80.2	11.9	0.0	1.2	6.7	24.0	17.7	51.1	64.2	11.0	204	75.5
Shelbyville city	14,195	16,585	16.8	16,009	68.0	12.6	1.5	1.7	16.3	23.9	11.8	36.6	48.4	21.2	5,845	87.6
Shepherdsville city	11,343	12,442	9.7	12,218	92.1	0.9	0.9	3.1	3.0	25.0	10.3	33.2	54.4	15.7	4,645	86.1
Shively city	15,262	15,689	2.8	15,726	37.7	54.6	0.4	2.7	4.6	22.9	16.8	40.8	53.7	12.1	6,666	83.0
Silver Grove city	1,102	1,186	7.6	1,499	91.8	0.5	0.4	0.0	7.3	24.5	14.0	41.3	50.3	20.8	532	89.1
Simpsonville city	2,487	2,923	17.5	2,815	76.6	5.0	1.8	6.3	10.2	31.8	8.7	31.0	31.6	40.5	1,010	93.7
Slaughters city	216	205	-5.1	282	95.4	0.0	1.1	1.4	2.1	19.9	12.8	39.8	67.8	2.9	100	70.0
Smithfield city	106	114	7.5	157	77.7	1.3	0.0	0.0	21.0	23.6	10.8	33.5	76.3	4.1	63	85.7
Smithland city	301	288	-4.3	308	89.9	0.0	0.3	3.6	6.2	25.6	29.9	40.5	52.5	19.6	129	91.5
Smiths Grove city	718	798	11.1	763	79.2	15.6	0.9	3.8	0.5	20.2	23.7	48.1	56.8	16.4	334	87.4
Somerset city	11,234	11,585	3.1	11,447	88.1	2.5	0.6	2.6	6.2	22.5	19.1	40.4	55.2	14.7	4,384	86.1
Sonora city	514	520	1.2	705	97.2	1.0	0.6	0.4	0.9	34.6	13.2	32.1	55.3	7.0	254	92.1
South Carrollton city	184	180	-2.2	231	91.8	0.0	0.0	8.2	0.0	23.8	23.8	50.3	82.4	1.8	92	46.7
Southgate city	3,779	4,013	6.2	3,920	87.6	3.8	2.8	1.5	4.3	22.9	12.0	33.2	34.9	30.0	1,828	93.1
South Park View city	7	7	0.0	3	100.0	0.0	0.0	0.0	0.0	0.0	0.0	0.0	100.0	0.0	1	100.0
South Shore city	1,126	1,057	-6.1	1,009	90.7	0.6	0.0	5.0	3.8	16.4	27.2	39.7	70.1	8.5	413	84.7
South Wallins CDP	859	-	-	849	100.0	0.0	0.0	0.0	0.0	24.7	21.1	42.9	63.8	9.8	332	74.1
South Williamson CDP	602	-	-	569	85.8	0.0	7.9	6.3	0.0	8.8	45.9	61.2	69.9	24.2	279	78.1
Sparta city	268	277	3.4	295	88.8	2.4	0.0	4.4	4.4	27.1	16.9	35.3	67.6	8.9	93	79.6
Spottsville CDP	325	-	-	442	89.1	0.0	0.0	10.9	0.0	15.2	11.1	51.6	30.8	57.0	193	82.4
Springfield city	2,835	2,961	4.4	2,980	69.5	16.9	0.7	2.8	10.1	23.9	18.3	31.1	55.6	18.9	1,200	82.0
Spring Mill city	287	296	3.1	332	88.6	4.5	0.0	3.3	3.6	25.3	18.7	40.2	22.4	46.6	109	91.7
Spring Valley city	658	683	3.8	770	92.7	2.3	1.6	1.7	1.7	27.3	16.8	42.1	6.9	68.4	259	97.7
Stamping Ground city	659	802	21.7	794	93.8	5.4	0.0	0.0	0.8	27.6	14.9	34.4	52.9	11.8	339	78.8
Stanford city	3,746	3,662	-2.2	3,677	87.6	4.8	0.9	1.8	4.8	18.9	19.9	43.7	58.3	15.4	1,352	80.7
Stanton city	2,818	2,713	-3.7	2,710	91.6	1.6	2.7	2.5	1.5	22.8	15.1	36.8	65.2	12.9	919	82.7
Stearns CDP	1,416	-	-	1,190	99.3	0.0	0.0	0.7	0.0	26.1	17.6	39.6	45.5	10.8	438	73.3
Strathmoor Manor city	337	341	1.2	351	96.0	1.1	0.6	2.3	0.0	25.9	13.4	42.5	5.2	76.7	131	99.2
Strathmoor Village city	651	660	1.4	669	94.3	1.8	1.3	0.7	1.8	23.3	16.6	38.8	15.5	67.7	258	95.3
Sturgis city	1,893	1,781	-5.9	1,903	94.6	5.4	0.0	0.0	0.0	22.1	18.9	38.6	61.8	7.5	773	87.5
Summer Shade CDP	307	-	-	233	100.0	0.0	0.0	0.0	0.0	34.3	9.0	29.9	39.3	6.9	101	92.1
Summersville CDP	568	-	-	457	100.0	0.0	0.0	0.0	0.0	30.2	23.4	31.7	55.2	8.8	222	83.3
Sycamore city	160	165	3.1	188	76.6	12.2	0.0	0.0	11.2	15.4	26.6	57.0	29.4	38.6	97	96.9
Symsonia CDP	615	-	-	522	100.0	0.0	0.0	0.0	0.0	19.3	15.7	36.4	38.4	15.7	221	87.8
Taylor Mill city	6,648	6,802	2.3	6,763	91.8	3.3	0.2	0.9	3.8	26.4	13.4	39.9	36.7	31.4	2,649	91.7
Taylorsville city	1,187	1,308	10.2	1,618	72.9	13.4	0.0	6.9	6.8	17.7	25.5	43.7	63.6	8.0	640	76.4
Ten Broeck city	103	105	1.9	99	96.0	0.0	2.0	2.0	0.0	13.1	16.2	48.3	12.0	57.3	42	97.6
Thornhill city	180	187	3.9	269	95.2	3.0	0.0	1.5	0.4	42.0	14.1	39.2	2.0	76.5	86	97.7
Tolu CDP	88	-	-	42	100.0	0.0	0.0	0.0	0.0	21.4	42.9	49.5	53.6	0.0	23	43.5

1 May be of any race.

Table A. All Places — **Population and Housing**

STATE City, town, township, borough, or CDP (county if applicable)	Population				Race and Hispanic or Latino origin (percent)					Age (percent)			Educational attainment of persons age 25 and older		Occupied housing units	
	2010 census total population	2019 estimated population	Percent change 2010–2019	ACS total population estimate 2015–2019	White alone, not Hispanic or Latino	Black alone, not Hispanic or Latino	Asian alone, not Hispanic or Latino	All other races or 2 or more races, not Hispanic or Latino	Hispanic or Latino[1]	Under 18 years old	Age 65 years and older	Median age	Percent High school diploma or less	Percent Bachelor's degree or more	Total	Percent with a computer
	1	2	3	4	5	6	7	8	9	10	11	12	13	14	15	16
KENTUCKY—Con.																
Tompkinsville city	2,348	2,252	-4.1	2,966	86.3	8.0	0.0	1.1	4.6	25.4	16.0	37.6	61.2	12.6	1,222	83.0
Trenton city	384	375	-2.3	420	83.8	8.6	0.0	7.6	0.0	25.5	12.4	38.6	38.2	18.6	182	79.7
Union city	5,350	6,034	12.8	5,910	89.6	0.5	5.5	3.6	0.8	28.7	13.7	38.9	21.9	52.1	1,929	99.0
Uniontown city	1,002	930	-7.2	802	95.5	3.1	0.0	1.4	0.0	22.1	14.2	44.0	65.1	0.0	336	78.6
Upton city	690	698	1.2	700	90.4	7.1	0.0	2.4	0.0	21.4	15.3	40.4	58.8	14.3	269	82.2
Utica CDP	-	-	-	512	100.0	0.0	0.0	0.0	0.0	50.6	0.0	17.7	42.1	8.3	123	92.7
Vanceburg city	1,474	1,400	-5.0	1,462	96.8	0.6	0.0	2.6	0.0	22.2	24.0	43.2	78.0	3.7	610	60.5
Verona CDP	1,455	-	-	1,414	100.0	0.0	0.0	0.0	0.0	22.0	17.8	48.4	57.6	19.7	506	93.1
Versailles city	8,784	9,318	6.1	9,215	77.6	7.9	0.6	2.6	11.3	24.2	14.0	37.7	46.6	24.9	3,702	88.5
Vicco city	337	301	-10.7	317	96.2	0.0	0.0	3.8	0.0	29.0	10.7	32.4	73.6	11.4	112	85.7
Villa Hills city	7,307	7,461	2.1	7,449	97.5	0.2	0.3	0.7	1.3	20.9	22.2	47.0	20.4	46.2	2,812	98.0
Vine Grove city	5,093	6,439	26.4	6,106	73.3	14.1	1.6	9.3	1.7	32.0	10.2	34.0	36.4	21.3	2,230	94.8
Virgie CDP	279	-	-	215	100.0	0.0	0.0	0.0	0.0	12.1	14.9	47.4	74.5	6.9	89	88.8
Wallins Creek CDP	156	-	-	343	92.4	0.0	7.6	0.0	0.0	13.4	7.9	34.0	62.8	0.9	129	61.2
Walton city	3,636	4,058	11.6	4,268	97.1	0.5	0.6	1.5	0.3	33.1	9.9	31.2	36.6	20.4	1,429	94.6
Warfield city	269	231	-14.1	205	100.0	0.0	0.0	0.0	0.0	22.0	13.7	36.4	72.7	4.9	83	88.0
Warsaw city	1,681	1,703	1.3	1,884	72.1	7.5	0.3	0.8	19.2	20.0	16.9	43.0	69.1	8.7	787	81.1
Water Valley CDP	279	-	-	187	88.2	0.0	7.0	4.3	0.5	11.2	30.5	54.3	73.2	10.2	85	82.4
Watterson Park city	976	1,020	4.5	1,074	53.7	26.7	0.0	2.6	16.9	19.4	14.6	39.7	54.5	20.9	542	81.0
Waverly city	308	291	-5.5	349	98.9	0.0	0.0	1.1	0.0	25.2	17.5	39.0	49.3	6.6	140	79.3
Wayland city	426	381	-10.6	352	95.5	0.9	0.0	3.1	0.6	24.4	13.9	34.5	65.2	9.8	137	74.5
Wellington city	565	574	1.6	470	95.3	0.0	1.5	0.9	2.3	14.0	23.6	46.3	9.9	68.5	243	92.2
West Buechel city	1,230	1,272	3.4	1,486	31.3	47.2	12.0	2.4	7.1	25.9	8.8	33.6	47.6	24.3	585	86.3
West Liberty city	3,481	3,520	1.1	3,388	81.9	11.5	2.3	3.7	0.6	11.9	12.1	37.5	61.6	12.5	808	81.9
West Point city	921	876	-4.9	1,010	97.0	0.0	0.0	1.3	1.7	28.3	12.7	34.5	59.5	12.7	355	86.5
Westport CDP	268	-	-	261	100.0	0.0	0.0	0.0	0.0	11.9	17.2	48.8	52.5	11.4	107	94.4
Westwood CDP	4,746	-	-	4,706	92.7	0.7	0.0	1.5	5.1	18.9	22.2	47.1	52.5	15.7	1,972	83.9
Westwood city	636	657	3.3	564	91.1	2.7	0.4	2.3	3.5	28.4	22.3	41.4	10.8	61.5	193	99.0
Wheatcroft city	160	153	-4.4	156	100.0	0.0	0.0	0.0	0.0	10.9	25.0	45.9	88.5	0.0	54	87.0
Wheelwright city	784	503	-35.8	696	95.5	4.5	0.0	0.0	0.0	15.7	12.5	38.0	61.2	2.8	224	77.2
White Plains city	923	897	-2.8	938	97.3	0.6	0.5	0.9	0.6	19.5	19.4	41.9	64.0	13.0	415	82.9
Whitesburg city	2,132	1,843	-13.6	2,382	96.1	0.4	1.2	2.3	0.0	20.6	18.1	40.5	40.5	26.1	961	86.9
Whitesville city	552	555	0.5	522	91.4	0.0	0.0	7.1	1.5	27.6	19.5	37.5	55.7	12.6	213	75.6
Whitley City CDP	1,170	-	-	1,400	92.1	4.3	3.1	0.0	0.6	22.1	14.2	31.2	66.4	10.9	546	78.4
Wickliffe city	688	649	-5.7	845	82.1	7.3	0.7	5.6	4.3	23.1	19.8	43.3	60.3	7.4	350	81.7
Wilder city	3,035	3,056	0.7	3,088	92.0	2.1	4.4	0.9	0.5	12.7	17.6	42.9	33.6	47.1	1,446	92.2
Wildwood city	261	269	3.1	259	97.3	0.8	0.0	0.4	1.5	25.1	23.6	42.8	20.3	54.4	110	94.5
Williamsburg city	5,090	5,274	3.6	5,260	89.8	4.1	1.3	1.0	3.7	22.1	8.8	22.4	44.6	32.5	1,320	82.0
Williamstown city	3,927	3,909	-0.5	3,905	93.3	1.2	0.0	5.5	0.0	29.7	12.6	31.5	58.3	12.4	1,354	90.2
Willisburg city	283	285	0.7	383	100.0	0.0	0.0	0.0	0.0	17.0	13.1	35.7	60.5	16.1	115	87.8
Wilmore city	5,914	6,435	8.8	6,335	84.5	4.9	2.9	5.4	2.3	23.7	13.8	26.5	21.9	56.3	1,792	94.5
Winchester city	18,359	18,548	1.0	18,429	86.2	7.6	1.0	2.0	3.2	22.9	16.7	39.3	51.4	17.5	7,713	83.9
Windy Hills city	2,384	2,459	3.1	2,433	92.5	2.5	1.8	1.3	1.9	17.1	32.7	55.7	12.7	66.8	1,142	95.9
Wingo city	632	631	-0.2	818	91.2	2.0	2.0	1.3	3.5	19.6	16.3	32.8	63.0	15.6	305	90.2
Woodburn city	325	365	12.3	377	99.2	0.8	0.0	0.0	0.0	17.8	28.6	52.0	56.8	11.6	117	88.9
Woodbury city	90	90	0.0	51	100.0	0.0	0.0	0.0	0.0	15.7	25.5	56.5	50.0	26.2	25	88.0
Woodland Hills city	719	738	2.6	634	85.8	6.0	0.9	4.3	3.0	24.8	15.8	36.5	18.9	48.0	254	95.3
Woodlawn city	228	238	4.4	206	91.7	3.4	2.4	0.5	1.9	14.1	11.7	35.6	38.2	43.9	88	95.5
Woodlawn Park city	944	967	2.4	882	90.1	4.1	1.0	3.6	1.1	14.7	20.5	48.3	23.9	52.2	423	93.4
Worthington city	1,607	1,505	-6.3	1,549	97.4	0.8	0.0	0.3	1.5	18.7	23.8	45.5	45.9	12.7	620	91.1
Worthington Hills city	1,485	1,550	4.4	1,487	54.5	22.4	8.1	3.8	11.2	26.8	7.8	33.9	28.1	40.3	608	97.0
Worthville city	189	186	-1.6	184	100.0	0.0	0.0	0.0	0.0	26.6	9.8	43.1	72.1	1.6	64	79.7
Wurtland city	993	1,026	3.3	1,271	97.3	0.0	0.0	0.4	2.3	18.6	29.0	48.0	54.3	10.2	474	74.7
LOUISIANA	4,533,487	4,648,794	2.5	4,664,362	58.7	32.0	1.7	2.5	5.1	23.7	15.0	36.9	48.7	24.1	1,739,497	85.6
Abbeville city	12,227	12,038	-1.5	12,236	47.0	42.8	4.8	2.4	3.0	24.2	17.5	39.4	65.8	12.7	4,761	77.8
Abita Springs town	2,360	2,614	10.8	2,532	90.0	0.4	0.0	0.5	9.1	22.3	15.8	37.0	25.6	37.6	1,010	92.4
Addis town	3,593	6,221	73.1	5,274	48.2	44.8	0.3	2.3	4.4	33.3	7.5	29.4	48.1	23.8	1,694	93.8
Albany town	1,133	1,159	2.3	1,141	99.7	0.0	0.0	0.0	0.3	23.0	16.2	38.8	46.7	25.3	452	82.1
Alexandria city	47,918	46,180	-3.6	47,012	38.3	55.1	2.1	2.2	2.4	22.6	16.3	38.6	48.9	24.3	17,920	83.3
Ama CDP	1,316	-	-	1,172	50.0	48.9	0.0	0.0	1.1	21.4	15.8	40.0	57.3	12.6	484	91.9
Amelia CDP	2,459	-	-	2,215	25.2	12.7	12.3	4.1	45.7	24.8	10.8	31.2	88.7	4.2	904	69.8
Amite City town	4,141	4,436	7.1	4,401	40.4	55.3	2.2	1.4	0.7	11.7	15.2	43.3	61.3	12.5	1,468	91.5
Anacoco village	869	783	-9.9	1,015	77.9	7.3	1.8	7.4	5.6	24.2	15.4	34.7	61.2	13.4	329	86.3
Angie village	249	249	0.0	299	71.2	21.7	5.0	1.3	0.7	30.8	20.4	34.2	58.5	22.8	114	92.1
Arabi CDP	3,635	-	-	4,387	72.8	13.1	3.2	3.0	7.9	21.2	14.4	39.6	45.8	15.8	1,683	85.8
Arcadia town	2,993	2,700	-9.8	2,774	21.6	73.2	0.0	4.8	0.4	18.5	19.4	41.5	60.1	17.5	1,127	69.6
Arnaudville town	1,044	1,046	0.2	1,392	71.3	18.0	0.0	7.9	2.8	27.8	11.9	30.3	70.3	11.3	498	83.1
Ashland village	269	263	-2.2	214	62.1	13.1	0.0	24.8	0.0	24.8	13.6	49.0	47.5	12.7	77	74.0
Athens village	305	269	-11.8	338	77.8	21.0	0.0	1.2	0.0	22.5	26.0	42.6	59.1	9.4	152	69.7
Atlanta village	163	146	-10.4	142	70.4	25.4	0.0	4.2	0.0	27.5	14.1	36.0	68.1	5.5	63	68.3
Avondale CDP	4,954	-	-	5,321	40.3	34.8	15.9	0.1	9.0	29.9	14.1	36.7	70.0	8.7	1,729	86.1
Baker city	13,854	13,194	-4.8	13,437	13.6	84.6	0.3	1.0	0.5	23.5	12.2	34.8	48.0	16.9	4,693	91.1
Baldwin town	2,434	2,219	-8.8	2,272	29.1	65.4	0.0	4.0	1.4	15.8	12.6	41.9	78.8	6.5	804	75.7
Ball town	3,993	3,935	-1.5	3,971	91.1	4.4	1.1	1.2	2.1	21.8	14.1	29.9	46.3	20.7	1,332	89.6
Banks Springs CDP	1,192	-	-	1,142	35.9	41.8	0.0	1.1	21.2	40.2	12.3	24.7	66.9	9.7	353	74.5
Barataria CDP	1,109	-	-	1,200	80.7	7.8	0.0	11.6	0.0	16.9	16.6	45.5	67.0	13.4	428	89.0
Basile town	1,821	1,783	-2.1	1,987	59.8	29.9	1.6	2.4	6.3	33.9	10.6	29.9	82.3	2.5	570	78.6
Baskin village	250	244	-2.4	239	87.9	12.1	0.0	0.0	0.0	22.2	16.7	44.4	76.6	7.4	90	90.0
Bastrop city	11,361	10,023	-11.8	10,311	18.1	80.5	0.5	0.8	0.1	29.7	12.9	32.8	64.6	7.3	3,834	54.0
Baton Rouge city	229,423	220,236	-4.0	224,149	36.6	54.6	3.5	1.6	3.7	21.6	13.8	31.5	39.8	33.2	83,733	87.7
Bawcomville CDP	3,588	-	-	2,696	82.6	11.4	0.5	0.8	4.7	15.2	21.0	52.1	76.2	5.8	1,270	69.5
Bayou Blue CDP	12,352	-	-	11,401	79.3	6.1	0.3	6.2	8.1	25.0	12.6	36.0	65.4	8.5	3,891	90.1
Bayou Cane CDP	19,355	-	-	20,093	68.6	17.8	2.3	7.4	3.9	25.3	14.6	33.7	54.9	16.8	7,500	88.3
Bayou Corne CDP	-	-	-	41	0.0	0.0	0.0	0.0	100.0	0.0	100.0	0.0	100.0	0.0	20	0.0
Bayou Country Club CDP	1,396	-	-	1,146	95.8	1.6	0.0	1.3	1.3	14.3	29.7	56.3	28.8	43.4	481	90.6
Bayou Gauche CDP	2,071	-	-	1,819	96.1	0.0	0.0	0.0	3.9	27.2	15.7	38.9	49.3	27.9	642	96.6
Bayou Goula CDP	612	-	-	531	3.0	97.0	0.0	0.0	0.0	37.1	22.4	25.1	65.9	7.4	186	91.4
Bayou L'Ourse CDP	1,978	-	-	1,892	84.9	3.3	0.9	6.0	5.0	30.2	12.2	31.5	74.3	3.3	585	83.4
Bayou Vista CDP	4,652	-	-	4,316	82.9	6.8	0.9	4.4	5.1	26.5	17.4	36.6	74.4	7.6	1,859	81.7
Belcher village	263	248	-5.7	278	80.9	14.4	0.0	0.0	4.7	21.9	17.3	39.5	48.2	31.4	100	77.0

1 May be of any race.

Table A. All Places — **Population and Housing**

STATE City, town, township, borough, or CDP (county if applicable)	Population				Race and Hispanic or Latino origin (percent)					Age (percent)			Educational attainment of persons age 25 and older		Occupied housing units	
	2010 census total population	2019 estimated population	Percent change 2010–2019	ACS total population estimate 2015–2019	White alone, not Hispanic or Latino	Black alone, not Hispanic or Latino	Asian alone, not Hispanic or Latino	All other races or 2 or more races, not Hispanic or Latino	Hispanic or Latino[1]	Under 18 years old	Age 65 years and older	Median age	Percent High school diploma or less	Percent Bachelor's degree or more	Total	Percent with a computer
	1	2	3	4	5	6	7	8	9	10	11	12	13	14	15	16
LOUISIANA—Con.																
Belle Chasse CDP	12,679	-	-	14,024	73.3	11.0	2.4	2.8	10.5	29.3	10.7	35.0	42.1	25.5	5,099	93.4
Belle Rose CDP	1,902	-	-	2,338	36.2	60.1	0.0	0.8	3.0	21.7	18.1	39.0	54.0	9.0	851	87.1
Belmont CDP	361	-	-	304	80.3	0.0	0.0	19.7	0.0	36.8	19.7	36.9	49.5	5.2	107	69.2
Benton town	1,961	2,079	6.0	2,165	53.4	39.6	1.1	3.8	2.1	21.5	11.1	39.3	47.3	15.9	850	80.6
Bernice town	1,689	1,594	-5.6	1,538	30.2	60.3	0.0	0.3	9.2	26.1	15.8	40.8	72.4	10.5	571	49.7
Berwick town	4,946	4,419	-10.7	4,584	82.2	11.6	0.0	2.0	4.2	27.2	12.2	38.2	60.5	13.7	1,665	79.8
Bienville village	218	198	-9.2	186	78.0	22.0	0.0	0.0	0.0	16.1	21.0	52.1	74.8	8.2	85	75.3
Blanchard town	2,900	3,140	8.3	3,112	74.2	18.2	0.0	2.3	5.3	20.7	14.2	44.1	34.5	24.7	1,277	95.4
Bogalusa city	12,251	11,504	-6.1	11,673	46.6	47.9	0.0	1.9	3.6	25.7	16.7	36.2	64.3	10.5	4,874	78.9
Bonita village	282	246	-12.8	248	18.5	76.6	0.0	4.8	0.0	11.7	24.2	44.6	72.8	9.3	92	57.6
Boothville CDP	854	-	-	594	57.6	22.1	0.0	12.5	7.9	18.0	20.4	48.5	81.9	0.0	268	77.2
Bordelonville CDP	525	-	-	377	84.4	15.6	0.0	0.0	0.0	20.4	5.8	49.2	69.5	11.3	192	90.1
Bossier City city	61,768	68,159	10.3	68,248	58.5	27.8	2.4	2.6	8.6	24.2	13.8	34.0	41.8	22.9	26,927	88.5
Bourg CDP	2,579	-	-	2,479	98.5	0.0	0.0	1.5	0.0	27.5	20.7	41.3	54.4	13.0	842	95.0
Boutte CDP	3,075	-	-	3,030	30.1	62.2	0.0	1.6	6.1	28.7	13.3	34.1	49.8	18.7	1,080	81.1
Boyce town	1,004	980	-2.4	1,041	23.8	71.2	0.4	2.2	2.4	28.6	10.7	30.9	68.2	6.8	352	77.0
Branch CDP	388	-	-	231	88.3	5.2	0.0	6.5	0.0	43.3	3.9	21.6	85.4	0.0	54	83.3
Breaux Bridge city	8,135	8,148	0.2	8,262	56.5	39.1	0.2	3.7	0.5	25.2	15.1	37.7	59.4	18.2	2,944	84.5
Bridge City CDP	7,706	-	-	6,602	32.6	46.0	3.1	2.4	15.9	29.3	13.9	33.6	66.0	6.3	2,499	82.5
Broussard city	8,377	12,700	51.6	11,913	78.4	14.7	1.3	1.0	4.7	25.2	9.9	35.1	38.3	37.3	4,370	93.2
Brownfields CDP	5,401	-	-	5,772	19.7	77.1	2.3	0.5	0.5	19.6	16.7	39.9	53.8	15.5	2,027	90.5
Brownsville CDP	4,317	-	-	3,756	61.2	34.3	0.2	2.7	1.6	19.8	16.6	40.2	63.0	6.1	1,667	68.8
Brusly town	2,589	2,617	1.1	2,741	73.8	24.8	0.0	0.0	1.4	27.8	14.0	35.9	48.0	29.3	1,033	90.6
Bryceland village	106	99	-6.6	88	75.0	12.5	0.0	0.0	12.5	4.5	25.0	52.0	62.8	24.4	43	81.4
Bunkie city	4,174	3,858	-7.6	3,943	40.8	55.3	0.0	2.9	1.0	24.2	25.3	43.3	52.5	12.6	1,702	78.5
Buras CDP	945	-	-	789	65.0	0.0	33.5	1.5	0.0	32.1	11.9	37.0	69.6	3.2	342	83.9
Cade CDP	1,723	-	-	1,655	68.2	24.8	1.0	6.0	0.0	29.3	16.8	38.2	56.8	13.8	665	82.7
Calhoun CDP	679	-	-	385	52.7	47.3	0.0	0.0	0.0	35.6	3.9	33.8	23.4	45.2	135	100.0
Calvin village	238	219	-8.0	289	84.1	15.9	0.0	0.0	0.0	34.3	11.1	35.8	47.1	14.4	96	92.7
Cameron CDP	406	-	-	203	100.0	0.0	0.0	0.0	0.0	16.3	16.7	46.1	68.6	19.5	82	62.2
Campti town	1,056	1,047	-0.9	1,045	18.0	74.4	2.8	4.9	0.0	27.4	10.7	32.4	71.2	7.2	427	49.2
Cankton village	484	505	4.3	651	82.0	9.2	0.0	1.5	7.2	33.5	8.4	33.2	67.0	11.5	223	85.2
Carencro city	7,640	9,449	23.7	8,984	50.4	46.0	0.3	0.8	2.4	26.5	12.2	33.0	54.5	19.2	3,533	82.6
Carlyss CDP	4,670	-	-	5,248	84.7	7.2	2.6	0.9	4.6	32.9	10.5	33.9	50.2	19.0	1,773	91.4
Castor village	258	242	-6.2	327	83.8	13.5	0.0	2.1	0.6	33.6	14.1	27.8	63.7	15.4	126	81.0
Catahoula CDP	1,094	-	-	1,054	99.1	0.0	0.9	0.0	0.0	26.7	12.8	38.4	60.3	23.2	393	86.0
Cecilia CDP	1,980	-	-	1,917	61.1	38.9	0.0	0.0	0.0	31.8	14.2	34.2	68.1	15.2	700	83.9
Center Point CDP	492	-	-	486	97.1	1.6	0.0	0.0	1.2	28.8	24.1	43.6	55.2	28.6	156	100.0
Central city	27,211	29,357	7.9	29,107	86.9	8.5	0.8	1.2	2.7	24.9	16.9	39.5	45.5	25.7	10,233	92.0
Chackbay CDP	5,177	-	-	5,368	96.8	0.7	0.0	0.7	1.8	27.3	12.4	37.7	55.4	18.9	2,003	89.1
Chalmette CDP	16,751	-	-	23,851	61.2	21.8	3.4	3.1	10.6	28.1	9.1	32.8	50.4	11.5	7,544	89.4
Charenton CDP	1,903	-	-	1,500	41.3	28.7	0.5	28.7	0.9	22.5	17.7	40.7	75.7	5.0	665	84.8
Chataignier village	364	360	-1.1	306	41.5	51.6	0.0	0.0	6.9	20.9	25.2	50.3	66.7	15.1	142	81.0
Chatham town	557	550	-1.3	780	64.9	30.6	0.0	4.5	0.0	32.9	16.0	31.4	76.8	5.1	316	71.5
Chauvin CDP	2,912	-	-	2,408	89.5	1.5	0.0	5.5	3.6	23.6	16.9	45.5	80.0	2.8	862	87.6
Cheneyville town	627	584	-6.9	629	39.4	51.4	0.0	7.5	1.7	22.6	28.8	49.6	64.1	12.1	275	71.3
Choctaw CDP	879	-	-	1,060	95.9	0.0	0.0	1.5	2.5	20.1	20.9	46.5	85.4	7.1	366	79.8
Choudrant village	856	981	14.6	1,001	86.2	11.4	0.4	0.6	1.4	28.8	13.9	34.5	32.7	41.3	382	95.3
Church Point town	4,592	4,361	-5.0	4,443	58.2	28.8	0.0	2.9	10.1	23.4	18.3	36.4	67.7	9.6	1,823	80.6
Claiborne CDP	11,507	-	-	11,602	91.4	3.8	1.5	1.4	1.9	23.3	15.1	36.6	35.4	33.6	4,532	84.2
Clarence village	499	484	-3.0	278	27.3	72.7	0.0	0.0	0.0	25.2	25.5	49.4	56.1	6.4	131	30.5
Clarks village	1,019	1,000	-1.9	847	53.1	46.9	0.0	0.0	0.0	7.6	15.0	37.9	83.8	2.8	214	62.1
Clayton town	706	640	-9.3	458	34.3	65.7	0.0	0.0	0.0	27.7	20.1	31.8	70.5	4.8	189	52.4
Clinton town	1,651	1,502	-9.0	1,708	43.9	51.8	2.9	1.4	0.0	26.2	20.8	38.4	53.0	25.6	737	83.2
Colfax town	1,552	1,464	-5.7	2,492	36.0	57.1	0.0	4.2	2.7	30.8	14.6	29.7	56.5	11.2	686	74.9
Collinston village	285	251	-11.9	239	65.3	34.7	0.0	0.0	0.0	25.9	24.7	39.5	63.3	3.2	109	55.0
Columbia town	390	366	-6.2	423	58.4	37.6	0.0	2.4	1.7	15.6	19.4	42.1	70.4	17.5	152	64.5
Convent CDP	711	-	-	446	28.3	71.7	0.0	0.0	0.0	27.6	8.5	29.6	72.1	15.6	157	77.1
Converse village	440	433	-1.6	321	71.0	5.3	4.0	12.1	7.5	19.3	18.4	41.5	63.3	9.3	125	64.0
Cottonport town	2,009	1,900	-5.4	1,760	42.5	56.6	0.0	0.7	0.2	33.4	14.3	33.1	61.0	12.5	711	71.4
Cotton Valley town	1,009	936	-7.2	1,060	31.0	68.3	0.0	0.5	0.2	34.8	9.2	31.5	70.6	5.5	444	53.6
Coushatta town	1,964	1,787	-9.0	2,525	28.1	66.5	0.0	1.5	3.8	31.7	15.3	31.3	69.3	9.4	856	72.5
Covington city	8,850	10,564	19.4	10,372	74.6	18.8	0.3	2.2	4.0	21.6	18.6	38.6	33.5	40.3	3,710	90.7
Creola village	213	227	6.6	256	93.0	0.0	0.0	7.0	0.0	58.6	0.8	15.9	72.4	0.0	47	83.0
Crescent CDP	959	-	-	878	76.2	17.1	0.0	0.0	6.7	23.9	8.1	42.6	68.6	4.9	287	88.9
Crowley city	13,265	12,588	-5.1	12,796	58.5	34.8	0.0	2.3	4.4	27.6	17.2	37.7	65.9	14.5	4,807	78.4
Cullen town	1,163	1,066	-8.3	1,131	5.3	94.4	0.0	0.3	0.0	24.8	17.0	37.3	72.6	5.3	552	43.3
Cut Off CDP	5,976	-	-	5,985	75.6	1.7	0.9	10.9	10.8	22.2	16.8	41.2	71.9	12.0	2,375	86.0
Delcambre town	1,862	1,849	-0.7	2,020	79.8	13.3	0.0	5.3	1.6	29.0	21.5	35.7	63.4	14.8	748	84.4
Delhi town	2,939	2,795	-4.9	2,846	33.1	60.2	0.0	0.7	6.0	25.0	17.2	41.1	61.0	16.3	1,082	70.1
Delta village	284	252	-11.3	275	95.6	1.8	0.0	2.5	0.0	39.3	10.9	24.9	59.6	7.4	104	76.9
Denham Springs city	10,370	9,753	-5.9	9,937	81.6	13.9	0.0	0.9	3.6	24.2	17.1	36.5	45.3	22.8	3,615	90.5
DeQuincy city	3,235	3,086	-4.6	3,143	78.9	9.3	0.0	10.9	0.9	22.8	16.1	35.3	65.6	12.6	972	82.2
DeRidder city	10,577	10,588	0.1	10,861	52.3	35.5	0.9	3.7	7.6	22.8	14.9	34.7	48.0	22.5	3,838	87.8
Des Allemands CDP	2,505	-	-	1,690	81.5	8.8	0.0	7.0	2.7	20.8	27.6	38.3	59.8	11.1	670	82.4
Destrehan CDP	11,535	-	-	11,398	74.6	15.9	0.0	0.5	9.0	22.0	14.2	40.6	35.4	36.0	4,257	94.9
Deville CDP	1,764	-	-	1,314	100.0	0.0	0.0	0.0	0.0	27.2	18.9	36.9	51.8	6.3	602	83.7
Dixie Inn village	283	263	-7.1	249	37.8	53.4	0.0	0.8	8.0	14.9	16.5	40.2	65.9	6.1	125	72.8
Dodson village	334	300	-10.2	323	89.2	4.6	0.0	2.5	3.7	29.4	10.2	23.8	64.3	12.1	123	87.8
Donaldsonville city	7,436	8,441	13.5	8,237	21.1	75.1	0.0	2.1	1.6	26.8	18.6	39.8	62.3	16.1	3,031	79.0
Downsville village	141	130	-7.8	109	95.4	0.0	0.9	0.9	2.8	7.3	25.7	49.9	24.5	33.7	49	71.4
Doyline village	818	782	-4.4	734	86.4	11.6	0.3	0.0	1.8	26.0	23.7	39.2	59.0	11.6	330	75.2
Dry Prong village	440	438	-0.5	501	91.8	5.6	0.4	1.8	0.4	25.7	16.4	37.8	50.5	15.1	183	79.8
Dubach town	956	907	-5.1	976	64.4	29.5	4.5	1.5	0.0	17.7	17.2	31.9	67.4	15.8	387	78.0
Dubberly village	271	257	-5.2	233	80.3	16.3	0.4	3.0	0.0	13.7	21.0	52.9	51.9	18.8	105	76.2
Dulac CDP	1,463	-	-	1,154	42.4	0.0	0.0	56.1	1.6	16.7	34.3	52.6	78.8	0.0	521	78.5
Duson town	1,740	1,768	1.6	1,712	56.7	38.0	0.0	1.4	3.9	30.5	11.9	31.2	80.8	1.0	586	72.5
East Hodge village	289	275	-4.8	323	0.0	98.1	0.0	1.9	0.0	21.1	28.2	43.8	60.7	14.5	147	63.9
Eastwood CDP	4,093	-	-	4,548	87.5	9.7	0.0	1.0	1.8	35.7	16.5	36.4	30.7	32.1	1,673	93.1
Eden Isle CDP	7,041	-	-	7,365	82.8	8.9	2.3	4.3	1.6	14.2	24.8	52.8	35.3	31.4	3,225	95.8
Edgard CDP	2,441	-	-	1,785	6.3	91.9	0.0	1.8	0.0	18.3	16.1	36.7	53.4	18.4	571	79.9
Edgefield village	218	192	-11.9	313	73.2	24.3	0.0	0.6	1.9	28.4	17.9	38.9	45.1	14.1	124	85.5

1 May be of any race.

Table A. All Places — **Population and Housing**

STATE City, town, township, borough, or CDP (county if applicable)	Population: 2010 census total population	Population: 2019 estimated population	Population: Percent change 2010–2019	Population: ACS total population estimate 2015–2019	Race and Hispanic or Latino origin (percent): White alone, not Hispanic or Latino	Black alone, not Hispanic or Latino	Asian alone, not Hispanic or Latino	All other races or 2 or more races, not Hispanic or Latino	Hispanic or Latino[1]	Age (percent): Under 18 years old	Age 65 years and older	Median age	Educational attainment of persons age 25 and older: Percent High school diploma or less	Percent Bachelor's degree or more	Occupied housing units: Total	Percent with a computer
	1	2	3	4	5	6	7	8	9	10	11	12	13	14	15	16
LOUISIANA—Con.																
Egan CDP	631	-	-	616	100.0	0.0	0.0	0.0	0.0	6.0	35.1	51.3	66.0	10.9	269	66.2
Elizabeth town	531	537	1.1	501	96.8	1.8	0.0	1.4	0.0	31.7	8.0	31.7	55.5	23.7	159	86.8
Elmwood CDP	4,635	-	-	5,698	52.4	28.0	6.0	1.8	11.8	18.9	6.8	31.6	14.4	59.2	2,995	95.7
Elton town	1,128	1,141	1.2	1,309	53.1	31.5	4.5	5.2	5.7	28.7	19.1	33.2	67.4	16.7	504	66.1
Empire CDP	993	-	-	1,222	45.6	20.0	14.6	14.1	5.7	22.9	12.1	34.1	68.0	10.0	584	86.6
Epps village	854	813	-4.8	914	38.2	54.7	0.0	2.3	4.8	13.6	11.2	33.3	80.0	3.9	211	56.4
Erath town	2,114	2,039	-3.5	2,326	83.0	4.0	6.4	0.0	6.6	28.5	14.4	36.4	64.0	15.1	934	84.6
Eros town	155	151	-2.6	213	93.0	0.0	1.4	0.9	4.7	23.0	12.2	36.3	79.3	2.1	82	82.9
Erwinville CDP	2,192	-	-	2,180	69.0	29.3	0.0	1.4	0.2	15.1	20.7	44.3	57.6	8.9	918	89.4
Estelle CDP	16,377	-	-	17,968	50.5	26.6	6.2	4.3	12.3	24.2	11.8	37.6	54.9	17.5	5,700	92.4
Estherwood village	889	1,074	20.8	930	98.0	0.0	0.0	1.8	0.2	32.0	8.7	30.8	60.1	9.5	285	81.1
Eunice city	10,398	9,814	-5.6	10,140	57.6	33.6	0.0	2.6	6.3	27.2	15.1	34.5	67.6	11.1	3,642	81.8
Evergreen town	310	288	-7.1	324	71.6	26.5	0.0	0.0	1.9	10.8	23.8	54.3	68.1	4.6	157	59.9
Farmerville town	3,921	3,717	-5.2	3,787	35.7	57.6	0.0	4.4	2.3	26.1	19.4	37.7	63.6	11.8	954	61.4
Fenton village	383	359	-6.3	280	32.5	64.3	3.2	0.0	0.0	23.6	17.9	39.6	62.5	8.3	130	66.2
Ferriday town	3,511	3,204	-8.7	3,312	8.9	91.1	0.0	0.0	0.0	27.0	18.7	41.3	51.0	24.8	1,354	72.7
Fifth Ward CDP	800	-	-	809	87.6	0.0	0.0	12.4	0.0	27.4	12.9	30.8	65.3	5.9	338	78.4
Fisher village	230	219	-4.8	355	55.5	40.3	0.0	3.1	1.1	30.4	10.7	32.9	57.9	8.8	98	74.5
Florien village	627	599	-4.5	642	78.8	19.2	0.6	0.0	1.4	26.8	20.4	30.7	64.3	11.6	257	70.4
Folsom village	718	862	20.1	981	60.0	21.0	0.0	0.0	19.0	32.7	8.9	30.0	50.9	20.9	302	93.4
Fordoche town	928	913	-1.6	1,074	90.2	5.6	0.0	3.3	0.9	27.2	21.9	40.6	75.7	6.3	401	76.3
Forest village	355	337	-5.1	295	85.8	2.4	0.0	4.1	7.8	19.7	13.6	43.8	49.6	7.3	113	76.1
Forest Hill village	816	843	3.3	782	43.5	0.0	0.0	1.0	55.5	28.3	9.7	33.7	69.3	12.1	315	93.0
Fort Jesup CDP	509	-	-	413	100.0	0.0	0.0	0.0	0.0	25.9	28.6	29.5	82.0	12.8	159	78.0
Fort Polk North CDP	2,864	-	-	2,263	47.5	20.9	3.7	5.7	22.2	23.4	0.0	23.7	36.3	31.6	1,015	95.7
Fort Polk South CDP	9,038	-	-	9,048	52.0	20.5	2.1	4.4	21.0	32.5	0.1	22.5	31.2	21.0	2,531	95.3
Franklin city	7,660	6,709	-12.4	6,960	36.6	58.2	0.0	2.9	2.3	24.7	19.3	40.0	69.3	9.7	2,743	78.3
Franklinton town	3,853	3,745	-2.8	3,782	46.5	50.6	0.0	2.0	0.8	18.7	22.3	49.5	58.6	16.6	1,739	76.4
French Settlement village	1,109	1,192	7.5	934	98.6	0.0	0.0	1.0	0.4	27.5	11.9	33.4	53.0	21.0	348	87.4
Frierson CDP	143	-	-	205	51.2	38.0	0.0	0.0	10.7	61.0	5.9	11.9	37.5	0.0	62	100.0
Galliano CDP	7,676	-	-	6,987	75.7	3.2	0.0	9.0	12.1	22.7	17.5	44.3	75.2	9.5	2,841	80.7
Gardere CDP	10,580	-	-	11,394	25.6	55.7	1.4	3.2	14.0	25.7	4.1	26.8	40.9	29.6	4,332	89.7
Garyville CDP	2,811	-	-	2,155	44.9	54.3	0.0	0.0	0.8	20.7	19.7	42.6	57.1	11.5	822	87.3
Georgetown village	327	320	-2.1	459	98.5	0.0	0.2	0.9	0.4	43.6	6.1	21.5	67.5	15.2	120	90.0
Gibsland town	979	878	-10.3	563	21.1	78.5	0.0	0.4	0.0	15.3	14.6	44.9	62.9	7.8	261	83.5
Gilbert village	577	553	-4.2	464	63.8	36.2	0.0	0.0	0.0	11.2	26.7	55.5	67.7	11.0	223	51.1
Gilliam village	164	152	-7.3	112	77.7	17.9	0.0	0.0	4.5	7.1	43.8	57.5	51.1	28.3	49	67.3
Gillis CDP	657	-	-	569	90.2	0.0	0.0	0.0	9.8	19.9	14.2	40.2	54.4	12.7	234	100.0
Glencoe CDP	211	-	-	261	2.7	97.3	0.0	0.0	0.0	10.3	21.1	59.1	75.6	0.0	94	47.9
Glenmora town	1,344	1,312	-2.4	1,299	40.3	38.7	0.2	1.0	19.7	29.9	9.2	26.5	61.7	13.6	463	79.9
Gloster CDP	94	-	-	321	100.0	0.0	0.0	0.0	0.0	24.9	11.2	32.7	26.6	63.1	124	100.0
Golden Meadow town	2,112	1,960	-7.2	1,964	83.5	5.0	2.2	5.1	4.2	22.8	18.3	39.1	75.0	8.4	754	80.2
Goldonna village	432	423	-2.1	435	96.1	0.0	1.1	0.7	2.1	27.4	24.4	45.3	66.4	11.4	146	69.9
Gonzales city	9,783	10,957	12.0	10,789	34.1	51.2	2.1	2.6	10.0	26.0	15.0	34.7	46.4	19.0	4,159	88.7
Grambling city	4,996	5,150	3.1	5,185	5.9	90.0	0.2	0.4	3.6	19.1	9.7	24.1	25.1	39.6	1,812	90.0
Gramercy town	3,488	3,281	-5.9	3,306	46.8	52.1	1.1	0.0	0.0	25.5	14.6	38.1	56.7	10.7	1,177	86.9
Grand Cane village	242	240	-0.8	211	83.4	15.2	0.0	1.4	0.0	12.8	20.4	47.9	34.6	49.0	98	88.8
Grand Coteau town	928	905	-2.5	821	32.2	67.0	0.0	0.0	0.9	22.5	20.1	36.9	71.9	14.0	296	65.5
Grand Isle town	1,296	1,438	11.0	740	94.9	0.8	0.0	2.0	2.3	18.6	21.2	51.9	71.8	10.2	330	72.1
Grand Point CDP	2,473	-	-	3,275	64.8	35.2	0.0	0.0	0.0	27.2	9.9	33.6	45.8	12.8	1,031	89.6
Gray CDP	5,584	-	-	5,944	56.6	32.9	0.0	5.5	5.0	29.0	8.2	31.5	52.7	15.6	2,094	93.1
Grayson village	528	513	-2.8	568	77.3	22.7	0.0	0.0	0.0	32.6	10.0	32.9	54.8	15.2	233	74.7
Greensburg town	721	652	-9.6	799	39.9	53.3	2.5	1.5	2.8	16.1	13.8	37.3	65.5	14.2	232	85.8
Greenwood town	3,217	3,128	-2.8	3,181	57.7	34.5	0.0	4.5	3.3	13.9	16.1	44.9	44.1	19.0	1,322	93.6
Gretna city	17,745	17,647	-0.6	17,774	44.9	35.5	1.9	1.8	16.0	17.9	15.6	39.6	51.0	20.3	7,156	81.6
Grosse Tete village	649	629	-3.1	731	54.2	43.4	0.0	2.5	0.0	26.7	16.8	34.2	61.9	8.7	265	91.3
Gueydan town	1,398	1,348	-3.6	1,249	81.6	14.7	0.0	1.6	2.2	20.1	25.0	44.4	73.0	13.0	518	80.9
Hackberry CDP	1,261	-	-	1,384	96.1	0.0	0.0	0.0	3.9	33.1	16.0	37.9	49.8	11.2	531	88.5
Hahnville CDP	3,344	-	-	3,269	46.1	49.2	0.0	0.9	3.9	17.8	15.6	45.6	53.8	18.7	1,354	84.6
Hall Summit village	300	287	-4.3	415	66.5	23.4	0.0	0.7	9.4	26.0	14.5	37.6	58.6	10.9	144	96.5
Hammond city	20,007	21,437	7.1	20,668	45.3	47.8	1.4	1.1	4.4	21.9	12.3	28.7	43.7	29.5	6,871	90.0
Harahan city	9,259	9,250	-0.1	9,304	83.9	4.8	1.1	0.1	10.0	17.8	20.6	44.2	32.5	34.4	3,733	88.3
Harrisonburg village	348	317	-8.9	297	75.1	23.2	0.0	0.0	1.7	29.0	14.1	38.9	63.8	20.2	111	80.2
Harvey CDP	20,348	-	-	21,054	34.2	50.6	4.9	0.8	9.5	23.6	13.2	36.4	54.0	16.7	8,119	82.9
Haughton town	3,461	3,296	-4.8	3,340	83.6	13.9	0.7	0.1	1.6	30.1	8.2	34.1	40.3	18.3	1,139	89.6
Hayes CDP	780	-	-	1,182	100.0	0.0	0.0	0.0	0.0	33.2	2.3	30.5	71.2	28.8	341	61.9
Haynesville town	2,324	2,019	-13.1	2,575	26.4	70.1	0.0	3.1	0.4	22.3	19.1	39.7	63.1	11.6	1,081	76.4
Heflin village	240	221	-7.9	237	81.9	4.2	1.7	2.5	9.7	27.8	21.5	35.1	48.7	14.9	92	91.3
Henderson town	1,689	1,795	6.3	1,990	46.1	13.7	10.8	2.1	27.3	22.5	13.1	32.9	84.0	3.2	628	71.2
Hessmer village	796	750	-5.8	892	64.0	27.8	0.0	0.0	8.2	20.3	9.5	33.8	59.8	11.0	400	85.3
Hester CDP	498	-	-	327	100.0	0.0	0.0	0.0	0.0	29.7	8.6	49.9	50.0	17.3	123	89.4
Hodge village	470	436	-7.2	528	67.4	29.9	0.0	0.0	2.7	23.1	27.7	44.8	55.2	14.6	214	77.1
Homer town	3,237	2,834	-12.4	2,911	24.9	72.3	0.6	1.8	0.4	26.5	14.2	36.2	68.8	9.4	1,268	66.4
Hornbeck town	480	437	-9.0	604	97.0	0.8	0.0	0.5	1.7	21.5	8.4	38.3	63.2	9.8	201	90.5
Hosston village	315	299	-5.1	316	76.9	14.6	0.0	2.5	6.0	25.0	18.7	36.8	78.8	7.5	129	82.9
Houma city	33,664	32,696	-2.9	33,334	62.1	23.3	0.3	9.9	4.3	24.1	14.6	36.8	54.1	19.3	12,612	83.5
Ida village	220	208	-5.5	256	95.3	2.7	1.2	0.0	0.8	9.4	33.2	55.5	62.0	13.2	139	71.9
Independence town	1,762	1,893	7.4	1,971	49.3	40.6	0.0	1.7	8.4	30.4	17.5	34.6	70.1	10.6	711	84.5
Inniswold CDP	6,180	-	-	5,963	74.8	20.2	2.3	0.0	2.8	23.9	14.2	37.7	23.7	45.9	2,230	98.3
Iota town	1,500	1,433	-4.5	1,824	84.6	3.8	0.9	4.9	5.8	31.0	10.3	30.9	56.5	9.9	648	73.6
Iowa town	2,998	3,164	5.5	3,225	63.2	31.7	1.5	2.4	1.3	35.1	12.4	33.0	48.2	15.6	1,211	88.9
Jackson town	3,840	3,728	-2.9	5,041	34.0	59.6	0.0	1.9	4.5	10.0	7.8	38.7	80.2	5.5	750	70.1
Jamestown village	139	126	-9.4	153	100.0	0.0	0.0	0.0	0.0	17.0	19.0	50.6	63.1	21.3	74	87.8
Jeanerette city	5,533	5,218	-5.7	5,385	21.1	77.2	0.0	0.0	1.7	26.6	13.1	35.4	69.0	9.5	1,956	67.9
Jean Lafitte town	1,903	2,000	5.1	1,818	92.4	0.1	0.0	4.1	3.5	23.4	16.4	39.7	62.1	13.5	604	85.9
Jefferson CDP	11,193	-	-	10,501	62.0	23.5	1.1	2.6	10.8	14.2	20.4	46.6	45.6	27.1	5,138	85.0
Jena town	3,398	3,397	0.0	3,409	81.0	7.7	5.0	0.2	6.1	23.6	13.4	34.1	56.2	22.5	1,169	79.6
Jennings city	10,383	9,800	-5.6	9,980	68.7	28.1	0.0	2.9	0.3	26.1	17.8	37.2	62.2	15.3	3,862	76.7
Jonesboro town	4,704	4,473	-4.9	4,529	44.8	53.5	0.0	0.3	1.5	21.0	14.0	34.7	73.1	6.9	1,374	69.9
Jonesville town	2,265	2,000	-11.7	1,691	20.9	77.6	0.0	1.5	0.0	24.8	17.9	40.2	67.4	16.0	703	55.3
Jordan Hill CDP	211	-	-	65	100.0	0.0	0.0	0.0	0.0	36.9	9.2	42.8	85.4	0.0	26	100.0
Joyce CDP	384	-	-	138	100.0	0.0	0.0	0.0	0.0	0.0	53.6	65.4	95.7	2.6	59	100.0

1 May be of any race.

Table A. All Places — **Population and Housing**

STATE City, town, township, borough, or CDP (county if applicable)	Population				Race and Hispanic or Latino origin (percent)					Age (percent)			Educational attainment of persons age 25 and older		Occupied housing units	
	2010 census total population	2019 estimated population	Percent change 2010–2019	ACS total population estimate 2015–2019	White alone, not Hispanic or Latino	Black alone, not Hispanic or Latino	Asian alone, not Hispanic or Latino	All other races or 2 or more races, not Hispanic or Latino	Hispanic or Latino[1]	Under 18 years old	Age 65 years and older	Median age	Percent High school diploma or less	Percent Bachelor's degree or more	Total	Percent with a computer
	1	2	3	4	5	6	7	8	9	10	11	12	13	14	15	16
LOUISIANA—Con.																
Junction City village	584	554	-5.1	686	35.7	58.3	0.0	0.9	5.1	43.9	13.7	26.4	70.9	20.2	251	45.4
Kaplan city	4,608	4,422	-4.0	4,522	84.1	14.8	0.5	0.6	0.0	24.8	17.5	39.5	68.5	9.0	1,638	79.7
Keachi town	289	303	4.8	238	81.5	7.6	0.0	0.8	10.1	27.3	13.4	44.8	64.7	16.5	101	66.3
Kenner city	66,631	66,340	-0.4	66,777	45.4	23.4	3.7	1.9	25.6	24.2	15.5	37.0	46.5	25.1	24,891	84.8
Kentwood town	2,198	2,436	10.8	2,112	24.0	73.3	2.2	0.0	0.5	28.4	19.5	38.0	76.3	5.3	771	64.7
Kilbourne village	416	383	-7.9	270	87.8	12.2	0.0	0.0	0.0	8.1	35.6	58.8	68.9	12.9	147	50.3
Killian town	1,201	1,322	10.1	1,350	85.1	10.9	0.0	0.9	3.1	19.8	20.6	51.6	50.1	18.4	576	94.3
Killona CDP	793	-	-	816	0.0	94.4	0.0	0.0	5.6	36.6	8.8	35.0	74.0	2.1	252	79.0
Kinder town	2,477	2,368	-4.4	2,751	80.6	12.8	0.2	4.9	1.5	35.1	11.1	26.5	59.7	16.7	973	89.9
Kraemer CDP	934	-	-	767	100.0	0.0	0.0	0.0	0.0	13.2	15.4	51.9	87.6	2.8	349	79.9
Krotz Springs town	1,198	1,176	-1.8	961	100.0	0.0	0.0	0.0	0.0	27.8	13.5	36.4	78.1	4.6	373	76.7
Labadieville CDP	1,854	-	-	1,698	84.2	12.1	0.0	0.4	3.4	12.5	17.7	47.0	64.0	16.7	738	91.5
Lacassine CDP	480	-	-	278	29.9	70.1	0.0	0.0	0.0	14.0	19.8	19.9	65.7	7.5	109	89.0
Lacombe CDP	8,679	-	-	8,960	67.5	25.0	0.3	3.7	3.6	19.4	21.8	49.5	42.8	24.7	3,456	90.1
Lafayette city	121,667	126,185	3.7	126,666	61.3	30.8	2.2	2.2	3.6	21.0	14.9	35.8	37.5	38.2	50,827	89.6
Lafitte CDP	972	-	-	816	89.0	0.0	0.0	11.0	0.0	17.2	11.2	46.8	69.2	8.0	316	81.3
Lafourche Crossing CDP	2,002	-	-	2,142	84.7	9.5	3.0	0.0	2.8	21.3	17.7	42.8	55.4	22.7	724	88.1
Lake Arthur town	2,738	2,748	0.4	2,746	82.2	11.9	0.0	1.8	4.1	28.0	13.0	31.5	73.5	10.3	982	83.0
Lake Charles city	72,398	78,396	8.3	77,283	44.4	47.5	1.9	3.0	3.2	22.1	16.4	36.2	42.7	27.5	32,710	84.0
Lake Providence town	3,973	3,429	-13.7	2,753	21.9	78.1	0.0	0.0	0.0	32.3	17.4	35.4	62.3	13.6	1,221	45.7
Lakeshore CDP	1,930	-	-	2,170	41.0	57.0	0.6	0.5	0.9	21.4	14.0	38.4	45.7	17.3	842	88.0
Lakeview CDP	948	-	-	1,312	75.5	22.0	0.2	0.7	1.5	31.0	11.9	40.1	46.8	23.4	472	82.2
Laplace CDP	29,872	-	-	29,108	37.0	51.6	1.6	3.1	6.8	25.6	12.5	36.3	49.2	17.9	10,142	90.8
Larose CDP	7,400	-	-	7,151	82.2	3.7	2.1	6.1	5.8	23.6	13.7	40.1	67.9	13.9	2,671	81.2
Lawtell CDP	1,198	-	-	1,252	31.1	68.9	0.0	0.0	0.0	36.7	22.9	34.6	67.6	5.8	418	67.9
Lecompte town	1,227	1,160	-5.5	961	39.5	53.6	0.0	6.0	0.8	17.5	15.1	49.9	50.9	12.3	416	78.1
Leesville city	6,508	5,598	-14.0	5,891	50.0	34.6	2.3	3.4	9.6	23.6	15.3	35.2	54.2	14.8	2,415	81.9
Lemannville CDP	860	-	-	1,118	20.8	71.0	0.0	3.4	4.7	15.2	4.7	30.4	72.6	9.9	198	83.8
Leonville town	1,086	1,102	1.5	1,029	48.1	35.5	0.3	0.9	15.3	30.7	11.5	36.0	86.8	4.7	340	66.2
Lillie village	118	120	1.7	201	74.6	25.4	0.0	0.0	0.0	23.4	21.9	41.6	42.6	14.9	67	53.7
Lisbon village	185	167	-9.7	169	48.5	50.3	0.0	0.0	1.2	6.5	17.8	45.1	69.1	18.4	65	69.2
Livingston town	1,766	1,974	11.8	1,844	93.9	5.0	0.0	0.2	0.9	28.4	13.0	34.6	53.9	19.6	679	91.0
Livonia town	1,451	1,400	-3.5	1,398	84.3	15.7	0.0	0.0	0.0	20.3	16.8	43.9	66.1	11.1	572	78.0
Lockport town	2,582	2,404	-6.9	2,784	86.8	1.6	0.0	4.0	7.7	25.8	14.4	37.1	76.1	6.3	983	81.4
Lockport Heights CDP	1,286	-	-	1,588	93.8	1.4	0.0	4.8	0.0	31.3	10.8	35.2	61.6	15.4	549	85.6
Logansport town	1,549	1,537	-0.8	1,854	52.5	33.7	0.0	7.3	6.5	30.9	11.1	32.1	60.9	9.7	684	83.3
Longstreet village	157	162	3.2	190	87.4	4.2	0.0	1.1	7.4	8.9	22.6	43.5	63.0	2.7	72	95.8
Longville CDP	635	-	-	261	100.0	0.0	0.0	0.0	0.0	0.0	26.8	57.8	94.3	0.0	118	100.0
Loreauville village	884	840	-5.0	885	69.7	25.3	0.0	3.8	1.1	33.3	13.3	30.7	78.4	9.5	296	74.0
Lucky village	272	256	-5.9	218	33.5	65.6	0.9	0.0	0.0	22.9	21.1	42.6	76.7	13.3	109	59.6
Luling CDP	12,119	-	-	14,049	74.8	14.9	2.2	2.4	5.6	28.3	10.7	35.9	38.1	29.7	4,713	93.7
Lutcher town	3,557	3,183	-10.5	3,262	51.9	46.4	0.0	0.0	1.7	17.5	26.6	48.9	60.7	18.3	1,321	81.3
Lydia CDP	952	-	-	1,061	59.7	8.8	3.3	0.0	28.3	30.3	6.3	36.8	75.3	2.9	459	81.3
McNary village	207	210	1.4	170	88.8	7.6	0.0	3.5	0.0	11.8	22.9	43.8	54.3	19.7	69	87.0
Madisonville town	748	848	13.4	849	87.8	10.1	0.0	0.2	1.9	23.1	16.7	39.4	21.3	50.5	333	96.4
Mamou town	3,276	3,118	-4.8	3,156	48.1	48.2	0.0	2.4	1.3	27.3	14.0	35.5	78.5	4.2	1,128	67.1
Mandeville city	12,058	12,475	3.5	12,448	90.2	2.8	2.8	0.5	3.6	23.0	18.3	43.7	22.7	53.6	4,718	89.6
Mangham town	670	631	-5.8	631	54.0	44.1	0.0	1.7	0.2	31.1	18.1	32.5	64.3	16.8	236	75.8
Mansfield city	4,982	4,624	-7.2	4,736	20.8	76.5	0.0	1.7	1.0	21.9	14.8	36.2	68.4	11.3	1,916	75.9
Mansura town	1,459	1,352	-7.3	1,477	33.4	53.8	0.3	12.4	0.1	23.3	29.8	44.7	65.9	6.1	623	62.9
Many town	2,853	2,690	-5.7	2,729	46.8	47.8	0.7	3.0	1.8	24.5	19.1	35.2	59.9	17.7	898	72.4
Maringouin town	1,101	994	-9.7	985	12.8	87.2	0.0	0.0	0.0	10.6	15.5	50.0	58.0	17.4	393	79.4
Marion town	765	738	-3.5	956	39.5	59.4	0.0	0.5	0.5	16.4	20.2	41.9	51.7	18.9	294	65.0
Marksville city	5,697	5,338	-6.3	5,432	51.7	33.2	0.6	12.2	2.3	26.0	17.1	33.8	58.5	13.1	2,145	84.0
Marrero CDP	33,141	-	-	30,894	37.2	50.1	5.2	2.6	4.9	22.8	17.7	41.8	58.3	12.3	11,660	84.2
Martin village	594	554	-6.7	707	98.6	0.0	0.0	1.4	0.0	26.2	14.1	37.4	57.4	17.7	232	87.9
Mathews CDP	2,209	-	-	2,551	94.0	1.4	2.4	2.2	0.0	23.0	17.0	41.7	63.0	13.6	1,067	78.7
Maurice village	1,058	1,609	52.1	1,711	89.6	5.9	1.5	0.8	2.2	28.3	19.4	34.5	51.9	20.4	628	92.7
Melville town	1,039	1,029		1,164	34.5	44.1	0.0	5.2	16.3	31.3	17.5	28.3	87.4	7.6	422	62.3
Meraux CDP	5,816	-	-	7,007	75.0	11.5	3.0	1.0	9.5	27.5	9.8	34.6	49.1	13.9	2,184	92.4
Mermentau village	661	629	-4.8	671	78.4	18.5	0.0	2.2	0.9	23.5	13.9	38.2	69.8	6.8	253	83.0
Mer Rouge village	622	549	-11.7	546	56.6	43.4	0.0	0.0	0.0	20.0	28.8	54.0	59.3	18.8	177	66.7
Merrydale CDP	9,772	-	-	8,903	2.1	94.4	0.0	0.6	3.0	27.1	12.6	34.2	50.5	16.8	2,901	94.1
Merryville town	1,103	1,108	0.5	1,196	71.9	24.8	0.0	2.8	0.5	26.2	15.0	37.3	69.9	7.3	440	80.9
Metairie CDP	138,481	-	-	142,135	69.2	9.7	3.9	1.6	15.5	19.2	19.8	41.6	36.7	36.9	59,854	88.0
Midway CDP	1,291	-	-	1,155	47.4	52.6	0.0	0.0	0.0	31.5	18.0	24.5	83.4	6.0	424	68.4
Milton CDP	3,030	-	-	2,299	95.7	4.3	0.0	0.0	0.0	17.3	8.2	45.1	31.2	38.7	858	96.2
Minden city	13,087	11,840	-9.5	12,274	44.3	51.4	0.6	2.9	0.8	22.5	19.7	39.3	54.9	18.9	5,189	75.7
Minorca CDP	2,317	-	-	1,691	77.9	22.1	0.0	0.0	0.0	19.3	14.5	43.7	71.9	7.0	667	71.5
Monroe city	48,878	47,294	-3.2	48,241	32.7	62.0	0.8	2.1	2.3	27.1	14.4	32.7	48.3	25.9	17,327	77.2
Montegut CDP	1,540	-	-	2,133	81.9	0.0	0.0	18.1	0.0	32.6	5.4	29.4	80.8	11.2	594	84.3
Monterey CDP	439	-	-	481	100.0	0.0	0.0	0.0	0.0	21.0	20.8	47.3	68.0	19.6	203	75.9
Montgomery town	721	734	1.8	573	80.5	11.7	0.9	6.5	0.5	23.4	23.6	43.7	53.0	10.0	261	61.7
Monticello CDP	5,172	-	-	4,774	9.4	87.1	0.9	0.7	1.9	24.8	13.1	37.0	43.8	28.6	1,747	93.4
Montpelier village	266	241	-9.4	367	35.7	56.7	0.0	1.1	6.5	25.9	17.2	40.4	58.8	20.4	135	77.8
Montz CDP	1,918	-	-	2,111	92.7	5.8	0.0	0.8	0.8	23.3	7.9	35.3	44.4	26.9	746	93.3
Moonshine CDP	194	-	-	160	0.0	100.0	0.0	0.0	0.0	7.5	50.0	64.5	79.7	10.5	87	62.1
Mooringsport town	798	750	-6.0	593	85.7	9.9	0.3	3.5	0.5	25.6	15.3	39.1	60.9	9.2	257	77.0
Moreauville village	928	857	-7.7	912	57.8	29.7	0.4	12.1	0.0	19.4	13.6	44.7	52.1	12.3	416	79.6
Morgan City city	12,404	10,742	-13.4	11,206	61.0	22.6	0.6	4.2	11.6	23.4	16.5	39.5	66.2	10.6	4,732	80.7
Morganza village	610	575	-5.7	839	57.8	34.8	0.0	0.5	6.9	22.4	16.7	36.7	68.1	11.8	290	84.1
Morse village	812	802	-1.2	1,059	95.4	0.8	0.0	3.9	0.0	26.3	8.5	33.6	76.1	4.8	324	71.3
Moss Bluff CDP	11,557	-	-	11,055	86.8	7.9	0.3	1.7	3.4	25.5	13.7	38.3	44.0	19.2	4,163	95.0
Mound village	19	16	-15.8	3	100.0	0.0	0.0	0.0	0.0	0.0	100.0	71.3	0.0	66.7	2	100.0
Mount Lebanon town	80	70	-12.5	72	33.3	66.7	0.0	0.0	0.0	27.8	4.2	28.4	73.5	8.2	29	82.8
Napoleonville village	660	590	-10.6	700	28.7	71.3	0.0	0.0	0.0	26.7	15.9	32.7	65.5	5.0	229	65.5
Natalbany CDP	2,984	-	-	2,908	41.1	44.2	0.0	8.9	5.8	22.1	7.4	28.2	55.4	18.3	1,130	90.2
Natchez village	594	601	1.2	586	10.2	89.8	0.0	0.0	0.0	25.4	18.6	32.8	54.5	3.9	253	60.1
Natchitoches city	18,545	17,485	-5.7	17,898	37.4	57.0	0.4	2.2	3.1	22.6	12.0	25.6	46.1	22.6	6,222	68.9
Newellton town	1,187	963	-18.9	1,190	32.5	66.6	0.0	0.0	0.8	26.0	16.6	36.7	80.7	5.2	403	53.6
New Iberia city	30,617	28,454	-7.1	29,456	51.6	40.7	1.4	2.4	3.8	26.0	15.8	36.2	62.8	16.9	11,030	82.6
New Llano town	2,598	2,212	-14.9	2,439	36.3	44.2	4.7	6.8	8.1	26.0	10.6	31.2	54.6	17.2	934	83.7

1 May be of any race.

Table A. All Places — **Population and Housing**

STATE City, town, township, borough, or CDP (county if applicable)	Population				Race and Hispanic or Latino origin (percent)					Age (percent)			Educational attainment of persons age 25 and older		Occupied housing units	
	2010 census total population	2019 estimated population	Percent change 2010–2019	ACS total population estimate 2015–2019	White alone, not Hispanic or Latino	Black alone, not Hispanic or Latino	Asian alone, not Hispanic or Latino	All other races or 2 or more races, not Hispanic or Latino	Hispanic or Latino[1]	Under 18 years old	Age 65 years and older	Median age	Percent High school diploma or less	Percent Bachelor's degree or more	Total	Percent with a computer
	1	2	3	4	5	6	7	8	9	10	11	12	13	14	15	16
LOUISIANA—Con.																
New Orleans city	343,828	390,144	13.5	390,845	30.7	58.9	2.9	2.1	5.5	20.1	14.1	36.8	36.3	37.6	153,819	85.1
New Roads city	4,827	4,480	-7.2	4,570	37.1	61.5	0.7	0.4	0.3	24.7	22.5	39.1	57.7	19.2	1,692	78.6
New Sarpy CDP	1,464	-	-	1,389	33.8	58.5	6.6	1.1	0.0	34.1	13.0	32.1	70.8	11.1	441	76.9
Noble village	252	244	-3.2	264	55.3	0.0	3.4	31.1	10.2	15.2	15.9	43.3	68.9	9.3	96	82.3
Norco CDP	3,074	-	-	2,850	95.1	2.6	0.7	1.6	0.0	20.3	14.3	39.3	45.9	17.3	1,201	90.0
North Hodge village	388	376	-3.1	445	69.2	24.7	4.5	1.6	0.0	33.9	13.0	32.7	61.6	6.1	147	83.7
North Vacherie CDP	2,346	-	-	1,857	32.3	58.4	0.0	0.0	9.3	24.7	12.0	35.7	49.0	22.3	680	75.1
Norwood village	322	291	-9.6	251	90.0	8.8	0.0	0.0	1.2	19.1	23.9	52.4	50.0	26.6	127	78.7
Oakdale city	7,784	7,561	-2.9	7,607	52.2	28.1	1.8	1.8	16.1	14.6	19.8	43.7	64.5	9.9	2,112	75.3
Oak Grove town	1,727	1,553	-10.1	1,649	63.1	35.4	0.0	1.0	0.5	21.6	21.5	45.0	70.6	9.2	652	52.1
Oak Hills Place CDP	8,195	-	-	8,326	79.0	11.0	3.9	3.9	2.3	18.8	23.3	45.1	13.3	63.3	3,818	93.1
Oak Ridge village	144	123	-14.6	100	83.0	17.0	0.0	0.0	0.0	19.0	29.0	49.0	42.0	35.8	58	50.0
Oberlin town	1,770	1,730	-2.3	1,577	56.2	33.4	0.0	9.8	0.6	36.1	11.2	31.6	66.5	10.9	496	85.9
Oil City town	1,006	970	-3.6	998	53.0	36.0	0.0	0.4	10.6	20.8	15.2	44.8	66.2	8.4	406	67.7
Old Jefferson CDP	6,980	-	-	7,659	68.4	20.6	5.5	3.4	2.2	25.5	9.7	33.9	27.4	38.3	2,772	96.3
Olla town	1,389	1,375	-	1,754	93.6	2.3	0.0	3.4	0.8	25.9	17.9	36.3	53.4	16.1	581	88.6
Opelousas city	16,758	15,911	-5.1	16,234	22.6	74.7	0.1	1.3	1.3	27.0	16.9	35.9	65.0	13.4	6,248	62.1
Oretta CDP	418	-	-	306	100.0	0.0	0.0	0.0	0.0	10.1	21.2	54.7	58.0	20.8	152	85.5
Ossun CDP	2,144	-	-	1,993	55.0	44.4	0.0	0.0	0.6	28.5	7.1	29.8	46.2	16.2	609	88.5
Paincourtville CDP	911	-	-	1,205	53.1	39.0	0.0	0.6	7.3	29.5	8.5	36.7	67.0	11.5	386	100.0
Palmetto village	164	160	-2.4	148	33.8	61.5	0.0	3.4	1.4	29.7	23.0	42.6	64.1	10.7	63	55.6
Paradis CDP	1,298	-	-	1,586	90.5	0.0	0.0	5.9	3.7	20.7	10.2	43.7	69.3	12.8	527	78.9
Parks village	665	699	5.1	672	56.3	42.1	0.0	0.9	0.7	23.7	13.1	40.4	46.9	21.9	265	89.4
Patterson city	6,112	5,792	-5.2	5,953	53.2	33.7	2.8	6.8	3.5	23.6	14.9	37.1	70.7	9.6	2,217	79.7
Paulina CDP	1,178	-	-	1,280	85.2	14.8	0.0	0.0	0.0	34.2	15.3	34.8	34.1	39.8	433	85.7
Pearl River town	2,412	2,610	8.2	2,579	89.1	3.8	0.0	3.8	3.4	26.8	13.3	36.7	54.3	13.5	902	89.5
Pierre Part CDP	3,169	-	-	2,179	100.0	0.0	0.0	0.0	0.0	12.9	23.2	52.6	75.3	4.2	1,099	75.8
Pine Prairie village	1,475	1,454	-1.4	1,331	62.1	11.6	3.2	6.3	16.8	16.7	13.1	34.9	69.3	8.8	310	81.3
Pineville city	14,511	14,122	-2.7	14,237	57.8	34.9	0.3	4.4	2.6	24.5	13.0	32.0	47.1	23.3	5,065	84.4
Pioneer village	156	147	-5.8	181	82.3	14.9	0.0	2.8	0.0	17.7	7.7	42.6	49.2	23.4	71	66.2
Pitkin CDP	576	-	-	588	79.6	0.0	0.0	13.3	7.1	25.2	11.2	32.9	54.0	30.3	177	100.0
Plain Dealing town	1,017	944	-7.2	958	50.3	42.6	0.0	3.4	3.7	13.5	25.8	54.5	57.5	12.0	424	73.3
Plaquemine city	7,119	6,539	-8.1	6,680	38.6	54.9	0.0	0.1	6.4	30.0	15.6	33.9	57.7	19.5	2,578	82.6
Plaucheville village	248	229	-7.7	217	98.2	1.4	0.0	0.0	0.5	18.0	15.7	44.9	47.5	15.4	104	81.7
Pleasant Hill village	723	688	-4.8	586	53.9	37.5	0.0	6.8	1.7	24.9	24.6	47.6	60.3	11.6	273	64.1
Pleasure Bend CDP	250	-	-	287	100.0	0.0	0.0	0.0	0.0	26.8	20.9	50.6	80.5	0.0	101	44.6
Pointe a la Hache CDP	187	-	-	134	0.0	100.0	0.0	0.0	0.0	0.0	4.5	39.1	81.9	6.4	45	84.4
Point Place CDP	400	-	-	446	42.8	29.1	0.0	19.7	8.3	32.3	30.7	36.1	31.7	17.7	221	53.4
Pollock town	483	479	-0.8	554	96.8	1.3	0.2	0.0	1.8	33.6	13.9	27.1	58.1	9.8	178	79.8
Ponchatoula city	6,547	7,369	12.6	7,195	63.9	30.4	0.6	3.3	1.9	23.3	17.1	34.4	54.3	20.0	2,863	83.0
Port Allen city	5,180	4,743	-8.4	4,958	39.5	58.9	0.0	0.0	1.6	18.9	19.7	42.9	50.0	19.3	2,097	91.4
Port Barre town	2,093	2,111	0.9	1,780	79.2	18.0	0.0	0.6	2.2	32.3	14.5	34.6	78.1	4.3	680	69.6
Port Sulphur CDP	1,760	-	-	1,789	8.0	75.0	0.8	16.1	0.0	24.6	11.2	32.4	71.0	2.9	553	71.4
Port Vincent village	733	755	3.0	619	96.3	0.3	0.0	2.3	1.1	10.3	10.0	47.2	48.4	17.3	250	93.6
Powhatan village	135	128	-5.2	268	4.5	94.4	1.1	0.0	0.0	53.4	7.5	15.5	87.7	6.6	72	33.3
Poydras CDP	2,351	-	-	2,790	78.6	8.2	0.0	3.2	10.0	27.2	16.6	33.7	74.1	8.4	944	81.4
Prairieville CDP	26,895	-	-	31,974	76.5	10.0	2.1	4.8	6.6	28.3	10.3	35.0	34.2	37.1	10,928	95.0
Presquille CDP	1,807	-	-	1,424	100.0	0.0	0.0	0.0	0.0	24.6	17.1	40.1	55.3	27.1	553	100.0
Prien CDP	7,810	-	-	8,437	79.7	8.5	6.5	2.4	2.8	30.9	12.3	36.2	32.2	37.5	2,999	86.2
Prospect CDP	476	-	-	417	100.0	0.0	0.0	0.0	0.0	11.8	19.4	47.4	44.6	27.0	204	100.0
Provencal village	611	607	-0.7	366	97.0	3.0	0.0	0.0	0.0	25.1	29.5	42.9	51.6	12.0	167	50.3
Quitman village	181	174	-3.9	265	90.9	3.4	0.8	4.9	0.0	32.8	11.3	34.3	41.7	6.7	99	84.8
Raceland CDP	10,193	-	-	10,698	63.1	32.6	0.0	1.6	2.7	22.0	17.1	42.0	68.1	13.3	3,971	83.1
Rayne city	7,945	7,992	0.6	8,041	58.0	37.6	0.0	3.3	1.1	24.0	16.6	40.2	61.6	8.7	2,834	82.3
Rayville town	3,695	3,474	-6.0	3,556	20.9	73.5	2.2	1.4	1.9	32.2	11.9	31.3	65.8	5.4	1,248	63.0
Red Chute CDP	6,261	-	-	7,335	82.4	3.2	1.5	1.6	11.4	27.7	10.4	34.7	36.9	23.0	2,841	92.2
Reddell CDP	733	-	-	895	84.5	14.2	0.0	0.0	1.3	27.7	14.5	23.8	74.0	5.6	431	89.1
Reeves village	232	244	5.2	216	100.0	0.0	0.0	0.0	0.0	25.5	17.6	41.0	53.3	6.7	97	73.2
Reserve CDP	9,766	-	-	8,611	30.9	60.6	0.2	0.9	7.4	24.5	16.1	37.0	62.4	11.2	3,232	78.9
Richmond village	577	544	-5.7	541	74.3	23.7	0.0	1.1	0.9	20.0	29.0	52.5	50.4	22.1	171	81.3
Richwood town	3,363	3,399	1.1	4,495	25.6	72.1	0.2	0.0	2.0	12.5	4.3	33.5	75.8	4.4	607	78.3
Ridgecrest town	680	603	-11.3	847	78.4	17.7	0.0	3.9	0.0	34.9	11.8	25.9	67.4	5.4	298	68.5
Ringgold town	1,495	1,370	-8.4	1,632	32.1	62.9	0.0	1.3	3.7	31.9	14.8	30.5	67.3	8.0	605	79.7
River Ridge CDP	13,494	-	-	13,337	81.7	10.5	1.1	1.8	4.9	18.6	22.7	48.5	34.3	35.7	5,546	89.1
Roanoke CDP	546	-	-	440	79.5	20.5	0.0	0.0	0.0	14.8	25.0	50.8	52.0	14.4	181	66.3
Robeline village	174	166	-4.6	107	86.9	8.4	0.0	4.7	0.0	23.4	14.0	47.1	53.7	9.8	41	70.7
Rock Hill CDP	274	-	-	134	100.0	0.0	0.0	0.0	0.0	10.4	16.4	34.8	65.8	0.0	46	100.0
Rodessa village	269	261	-3.0	146	77.4	11.0	0.0	1.4	10.3	23.3	21.9	35.2	54.5	7.9	59	62.7
Romeville CDP	130	-	-	139	10.8	89.2	0.0	0.0	0.0	21.6	2.9	23.8	44.4	22.2	37	100.0
Rosedale village	791	743	-6.1	835	78.2	21.8	0.0	0.0	0.0	23.0	17.5	33.5	56.2	17.4	338	84.9
Roseland town	1,121	1,262	12.6	1,099	28.5	66.6	0.5	3.0	1.5	26.8	18.3	36.3	67.3	6.9	366	81.4
Rosepine town	1,692	1,539	-9.0	1,846	76.1	7.9	1.0	3.4	11.8	20.6	18.4	35.5	52.5	19.1	697	91.2
Ruston city	21,887	21,854	-0.2	21,976	45.6	47.9	2.7	1.6	2.2	18.0	10.4	23.7	32.9	41.7	7,970	91.0
St. Francisville town	1,761	1,625	-7.7	1,964	69.6	27.0	0.0	1.7	1.7	19.0	16.5	41.9	41.1	22.6	762	81.6
St. Gabriel city	6,677	7,460	11.7	7,282	29.7	67.0	0.1	1.3	1.9	11.8	10.8	37.7	64.3	11.5	1,635	82.1
St. James CDP	828	-	-	734	8.2	91.8	0.0	0.0	0.0	12.1	27.9	51.0	64.3	12.8	289	67.5
St. Joseph town	1,176	973	-17.3	915	25.7	73.9	0.0	0.2	0.2	29.5	20.2	39.6	70.8	9.2	377	61.3
St. Martinville city	6,102	5,820	-4.6	5,945	32.8	63.0	0.4	2.3	1.5	20.4	22.4	47.5	66.6	8.4	2,567	75.8
St. Maurice CDP	323	-	-	368	2.4	97.6	0.0	0.0	0.0	34.2	12.8	25.9	57.8	23.5	161	61.5
St. Rose CDP	8,122	-	-	7,352	36.9	49.6	1.4	0.7	11.4	25.2	12.9	36.4	42.4	20.6	2,914	86.9
Saline village	277	277	0.0	482	78.2	20.1	0.6	1.0	0.0	29.9	10.8	32.2	55.7	29.5	178	82.0
Sarepta town	899	826	-8.1	857	96.7	0.2	0.0	0.5	2.6	27.1	11.3	36.7	50.5	9.6	332	84.0
Schriever CDP	6,853	-	-	6,500	58.0	27.3	2.3	5.4	7.0	24.1	14.1	31.0	65.4	13.5	2,584	91.7
Scott city	8,477	8,675	2.3	8,729	68.1	11.7	5.3	3.3	11.6	23.9	11.1	37.9	46.9	23.5	3,391	89.1
Shenandoah CDP	18,399	-	-	20,252	67.3	19.7	5.7	2.6	4.7	24.6	15.1	39.8	20.0	48.4	7,346	98.0
Shongaloo village	182	168	-7.7	139	100.0	0.0	0.0	0.0	0.0	22.3	26.6	54.4	59.8	18.7	62	62.9
Shreveport city	200,976	187,112	-6.9	192,035	36.8	56.9	1.7	2.0	2.6	24.4	15.5	35.7	45.4	24.7	75,620	83.7
Sibley town	1,220	1,160	-4.9	1,323	71.4	23.8	0.4	0.9	3.5	21.3	21.4	44.7	54.1	15.5	554	78.7
Sicily Island village	523	465	-11.1	482	26.6	73.4	0.0	0.0	0.0	26.1	16.0	40.1	82.0	10.2	178	52.2
Sikes village	120	121	0.8	166	92.2	0.0	0.0	3.0	4.8	31.3	13.3	32.5	72.2	10.0	67	73.1
Simmesport town	2,161	2,060	-4.7	1,622	30.4	69.2	0.0	0.2	0.2	34.8	12.8	29.0	77.2	5.2	627	69.2
Simpson village	638	586	-8.2	531	95.7	0.0	1.1	3.2	0.0	25.6	10.9	33.4	60.9	12.0	175	79.4

1 May be of any race.

Table A. All Places — **Population and Housing**

STATE City, town, township, borough, or CDP (county if applicable)	Population				Race and Hispanic or Latino origin (percent)					Age (percent)			Educational attainment of persons age 25 and older		Occupied housing units	
	2010 census total population	2019 estimated population	Percent change 2010–2019	ACS total population estimate 2015–2019	White alone, not Hispanic or Latino	Black alone, not Hispanic or Latino	Asian alone, not Hispanic or Latino	All other races or 2 or more races, not Hispanic or Latino	Hispanic or Latino[1]	Under 18 years old	Age 65 years and older	Median age	Percent High school diploma or less	Percent Bachelor's degree or more	Total	Percent with a computer
	1	2	3	4	5	6	7	8	9	10	11	12	13	14	15	16
LOUISIANA—Con.																
Simsboro village	841	835	-0.7	969	52.1	42.5	1.4	3.3	0.6	22.7	12.3	38.1	47.5	13.8	352	89.2
Singer CDP	287	-	-	314	100.0	0.0	0.0	0.0	0.0	35.7	11.8	41.4	63.1	19.0	124	82.3
Siracusaville CDP	422	-	-	532	0.0	71.2	7.3	21.4	0.0	34.0	17.3	31.7	64.1	0.0	191	48.7
Slaughter town	997	906	-9.1	980	87.6	8.0	0.0	1.4	3.1	18.4	20.7	48.1	52.2	15.4	435	86.2
Slidell city	27,265	27,633	1.3	27,822	71.8	16.9	1.3	2.9	7.1	26.8	15.9	36.7	42.8	25.1	9,818	92.1
Sorrel CDP	766	-	-	504	55.2	44.8	0.0	0.0	0.0	16.9	19.6	52.3	85.6	0.0	200	79.5
Sorrento town	1,418	1,704	20.2	1,681	72.9	18.6	0.2	4.9	3.4	23.7	10.9	33.1	56.4	11.2	634	84.7
South Mansfield village	349	357	2.3	348	14.4	84.2	0.0	1.4	0.0	11.8	27.3	39.0	74.0	13.7	167	75.4
South Vacherie CDP	3,642	-	-	3,392	62.4	35.4	0.0	1.6	0.6	16.6	20.1	49.2	60.6	16.0	1,261	78.2
Spearsville village	137	127	-7.3	164	87.2	10.4	0.0	0.0	2.4	20.7	23.8	39.4	42.1	11.1	63	65.1
Spokane CDP	442	-	-	360	100.0	0.0	0.0	0.0	0.0	10.0	31.4	58.8	19.7	25.1	203	85.2
Springfield town	478	526	10.0	469	84.9	6.8	3.2	4.7	0.4	22.6	19.8	41.3	58.0	18.6	184	87.0
Springhill city	5,267	4,772	-9.4	4,943	57.5	36.5	0.0	0.8	5.1	25.2	22.7	46.9	63.5	13.3	2,270	66.7
Stanley village	107	110	2.8	134	88.8	0.0	0.0	4.5	6.7	29.9	17.2	35.4	60.9	13.8	46	93.5
Starks CDP	664	-	-	303	100.0	0.0	0.0	0.0	0.0	4.0	32.3	52.2	68.4	8.2	166	79.5
Start CDP	905	-	-	1,067	97.3	0.0	0.0	1.2	1.5	23.0	16.0	35.8	62.6	14.5	443	66.6
Sterlington town	1,609	2,931	82.2	2,643	67.9	25.4	0.9	0.7	5.1	33.6	13.7	30.6	49.0	18.1	926	80.8
Stonewall town	1,846	2,465	33.5	3,123	89.6	7.2	0.4	0.6	2.2	29.6	10.7	35.5	43.8	27.9	1,127	90.9
Sugartown CDP	54	-	-	196	100.0	0.0	0.0	0.0	0.0	62.2	0.0	12.3	100.0	0.0	35	100.0
Sulphur city	20,390	20,065	-1.6	20,113	83.9	6.8	0.5	2.5	6.3	26.0	15.7	36.7	50.6	16.9	8,033	86.0
Sun village	464	489	5.4	419	76.6	17.7	1.2	3.8	0.7	20.3	17.9	47.2	60.6	4.5	158	80.4
Sunset town	2,888	2,861	-0.9	2,920	51.7	44.9	0.4	0.9	2.2	28.6	13.0	32.6	61.1	15.6	1,063	83.3
Supreme CDP	1,052	-	-	839	11.4	85.6	0.0	3.0	0.0	40.5	10.6	18.8	66.1	9.1	197	76.1
Swartz CDP	4,536	-	-	4,629	68.3	17.5	2.1	8.6	3.6	23.3	16.4	39.4	40.5	18.7	1,523	89.6
Taft CDP	63	-	-	59	100.0	0.0	0.0	0.0	0.0	0.0	0.0	0.0	100.0	0.0	32	100.0
Tallulah city	7,335	6,666	-9.1	6,851	19.6	79.6	0.0	0.0	0.8	27.3	14.5	34.1	62.0	12.4	2,561	63.9
Tangipahoa village	755	853	13.0	635	3.5	96.5	0.0	0.0	0.0	29.9	6.1	32.9	69.9	11.5	190	80.0
Terrytown CDP	23,319	-	-	24,953	32.1	35.9	2.9	5.3	23.8	28.2	11.1	33.1	54.0	18.8	8,609	91.3
Thibodaux city	14,502	14,425	-0.5	14,494	58.2	35.2	0.8	3.0	2.8	22.7	15.4	30.6	47.1	29.7	5,548	86.5
Tickfaw village	694	764	10.1	806	75.8	8.8	0.7	2.1	12.5	27.5	14.0	30.1	65.9	9.6	257	86.4
Timberlane CDP	10,243	-	-	9,950	37.4	40.8	7.2	4.0	10.6	26.4	14.4	37.2	48.3	16.3	3,441	94.3
Triumph CDP	216	-	-	500	70.8	4.4	20.2	4.6	0.0	41.6	8.2	23.7	74.0	12.6	156	85.9
Tullos town	385	391	1.6	419	80.0	6.9	2.1	11.0	0.0	30.1	11.7	43.0	79.6	5.7	164	65.2
Turkey Creek village	441	464	5.2	458	99.8	0.0	0.0	0.0	0.2	20.1	17.0	39.8	78.9	1.6	167	77.2
Union CDP	892	-	-	518	31.5	68.5	0.0	0.0	0.0	13.3	18.0	51.6	77.2	3.7	199	83.4
Urania town	1,313	1,301	-0.9	1,321	59.1	35.9	0.0	3.6	1.4	9.4	9.6	39.7	80.2	6.0	217	71.9
Varnado village	334	335	0.3	431	85.6	11.4	0.0	2.1	0.9	26.5	13.2	41.3	60.7	18.2	170	74.1
Venice CDP	202	-	-	232	79.7	2.6	0.0	3.4	14.2	25.0	13.4	34.1	75.6	20.5	73	100.0
Ventress CDP	890	-	-	864	93.6	0.7	0.0	0.0	5.7	5.9	32.2	59.4	61.2	11.6	463	72.8
Vidalia town	4,299	3,815	-11.3	3,968	65.7	31.0	0.0	0.0	3.3	30.7	16.9	29.9	51.6	18.3	1,480	79.3
Vienna town	384	374	-2.6	520	92.1	1.5	1.0	2.7	2.7	22.5	21.3	40.0	35.3	39.4	201	90.5
Vienna Bend CDP	1,251	-	-	1,230	28.8	59.1	1.1	11.0	0.0	27.9	14.0	38.9	30.3	13.1	472	73.5
Village St. George CDP	7,104	-	-	7,334	57.5	26.7	6.7	2.6	6.5	21.2	17.4	40.9	24.7	47.6	2,635	93.9
Ville Platte city	7,431	7,033	-5.4	7,159	37.3	61.6	0.0	1.2	0.0	25.9	18.0	34.2	75.5	8.2	3,007	67.7
Vinton town	3,387	3,234	-4.5	3,298	84.3	9.3	2.3	1.9	2.2	24.9	13.3	33.9	60.3	14.7	1,152	87.8
Violet CDP	4,973	-	-	5,755	28.7	63.0	0.0	0.7	7.6	26.2	13.3	37.7	58.8	7.3	1,816	84.5
Vivian town	3,674	3,482	-5.2	3,563	57.8	37.2	0.0	1.7	3.2	26.4	15.5	38.9	65.5	7.6	1,395	72.3
Waggaman CDP	10,015	-	-	10,017	24.8	65.6	0.0	3.4	6.3	25.0	14.0	37.5	60.4	12.8	3,495	85.1
Walker town	6,100	6,248	2.4	6,261	77.8	12.2	3.7	0.3	6.0	28.5	15.4	36.7	52.0	20.9	2,449	88.1
Wallace CDP	671	-	-	1,263	1.6	97.5	0.0	0.0	0.9	23.8	11.5	40.6	55.0	9.9	382	85.3
Wallace Ridge CDP	710	-	-	936	88.2	11.8	0.0	0.0	0.0	19.8	15.3	46.0	45.1	22.9	342	88.9
Washington town	960	914	-4.8	1,020	42.3	54.2	0.0	0.0	3.5	30.1	12.0	33.3	76.0	15.3	382	62.8
Waterproof town	682	555	-18.6	775	10.2	89.2	0.6	0.0	0.0	28.8	15.2	36.2	69.8	8.4	287	57.5
Watson CDP	1,047	-	-	1,252	88.9	0.0	0.0	0.0	11.1	26.4	15.3	42.8	42.3	19.2	512	96.9
Welcome CDP	800	-	-	884	0.0	96.8	0.0	3.2	0.0	32.8	13.8	34.4	40.8	29.0	334	79.9
Welsh town	3,226	3,227	0.0	3,227	76.0	12.4	0.0	3.5	8.1	29.8	15.9	35.8	56.3	15.8	1,128	76.5
Westlake city	4,570	4,951	8.3	4,727	76.6	18.3	0.5	4.0	0.6	29.2	12.5	29.9	59.0	12.1	1,935	81.2
Westminster CDP	3,008	-	-	2,760	80.5	4.5	10.5	4.5	0.0	18.2	22.1	42.5	15.4	58.0	1,240	94.0
West Monroe city	13,080	12,227	-6.5	12,583	59.2	35.2	1.4	1.2	3.1	18.6	18.0	38.5	48.3	21.1	5,616	74.5
Westwego city	8,535	8,326	-2.4	8,438	58.4	26.7	4.4	3.1	7.4	23.5	17.1	38.9	67.9	8.8	3,265	74.1
White Castle town	1,883	1,691	-10.2	1,833	14.2	82.7	0.0	2.3	0.7	22.4	14.6	36.9	72.2	10.4	672	78.7
Wilson village	596	567	-4.9	443	19.0	70.4	1.8	8.8	0.0	30.0	16.0	35.3	57.4	21.1	202	74.8
Winnfield city	4,841	4,260	-12.0	4,420	46.2	51.9	0.0	0.4	1.6	25.7	17.8	39.5	63.6	15.4	1,967	78.3
Winnsboro city	4,910	4,550	-7.3	4,640	23.4	75.4	0.0	0.3	0.8	36.9	13.0	29.7	64.0	9.7	1,504	79.3
Wisner town	964	900	-6.6	820	48.2	48.8	0.0	2.7	0.4	18.8	27.2	47.7	64.8	11.5	345	61.4
Woodmere CDP	12,080	-	-	10,173	10.7	78.8	4.0	3.1	3.5	26.3	12.3	39.3	46.5	15.4	3,536	94.0
Woodworth town	1,129	1,142	1.2	1,557	91.5	4.2	0.0	1.0	3.3	26.1	11.4	39.7	38.1	33.1	628	90.4
Youngsville city	8,308	14,704	77.0	13,407	79.6	12.3	2.4	2.8	2.9	31.7	8.4	33.1	29.0	44.4	4,396	95.5
Zachary city	15,146	17,949	18.5	17,283	48.7	47.6	1.2	2.0	0.5	30.6	11.0	35.1	32.1	39.7	5,790	92.0
Zwolle town	1,982	1,937	-2.3	1,980	32.9	43.6	0.2	16.5	6.9	30.7	15.3	32.0	69.2	10.0	696	68.2
MAINE	1,328,358	1,344,212	1.2	1,335,492	93.2	1.3	1.1	2.7	1.7	18.9	20.0	44.7	38.9	31.8	559,921	89.7
Abbot town (Piscataquis)	714	677	-5.2	752	92.3	0.3	0.0	7.4	0.0	15.3	21.3	48.4	57.4	12.1	279	93.9
Acton town (York)	2,445	2,621	7.2	2,593	99.0	0.0	0.0	0.7	0.3	13.9	22.4	49.3	37.4	23.6	1,047	93.4
Addison town (Washington)	1,266	1,254	-0.9	1,200	95.8	0.0	0.3	3.9	0.0	17.2	27.6	50.7	46.8	20.3	494	89.7
Albion town (Kennebec)	2,041	2,094	2.6	2,217	96.3	0.3	0.0	3.4	0.0	21.0	18.2	40.7	49.5	16.5	838	85.2
Alexander town (Washington)	501	480	-4.2	508	97.2	0.0	2.2	0.6	0.0	16.5	19.1	51.0	57.4	18.2	227	91.6
Alfred CDP	-	-	-	1,106	99.1	0.0	0.0	0.0	0.9	22.8	24.9	40.7	52.1	22.8	450	91.1
Alfred town (York)	3,023	3,163	4.6	3,115	96.6	0.6	0.7	1.3	0.7	17.4	22.4	49.8	54.5	18.0	1,230	92.9
Allagash town (Aroostook)	239	217	-9.2	220	95.0	0.0	0.0	0.0	5.0	18.6	36.4	51.7	58.8	12.1	109	78.9
Alna town (Lincoln)	709	734	3.5	874	79.5	0.0	3.5	4.2	12.7	24.4	18.4	42.7	29.7	42.7	348	94.0
Alton town (Penobscot)	890	858	-3.6	888	95.6	1.1	0.9	1.5	0.9	20.3	18.5	48.4	50.9	17.8	357	91.0
Amherst town (Hancock)	265	257	-3.0	316	82.6	0.0	0.0	16.1	1.3	23.4	23.7	48.8	42.1	26.9	123	84.6
Amity town (Aroostook)	238	217	-8.8	189	90.5	1.1	0.0	1.1	7.4	12.7	22.8	53.3	50.3	14.1	102	90.2
Andover town (Oxford)	823	831	1.0	652	97.5	0.0	0.0	2.1	0.3	13.5	42.2	60.0	53.8	12.0	274	81.4
Anson CDP	752	-	-	1,075	93.6	0.0	0.0	6.4	0.0	26.5	14.9	35.1	67.1	9.0	416	72.6
Anson town (Somerset)	2,511	2,384	-5.1	2,633	96.1	0.0	0.0	3.9	0.0	20.6	14.8	44.3	63.8	12.1	1,053	80.2
Appleton town (Knox)	1,316	1,368	4.0	1,603	94.1	0.5	0.2	2.6	2.7	25.1	15.5	40.1	39.0	29.2	593	91.6
Argyle UT (Penobscot)	277	265	-4.3	155	91.6	0.0	0.0	8.4	0.0	6.5	23.9	57.8	64.1	13.7	88	94.3

1 May be of any race.

Table A. All Places — **Population and Housing**

STATE City, town, township, borough, or CDP (county if applicable)	2010 census total population	2019 estimated population	Percent change 2010–2019	ACS total population estimate 2015–2019	White alone, not Hispanic or Latino	Black alone, not Hispanic or Latino	Asian alone, not Hispanic or Latino	All other races or 2 or more races, not Hispanic or Latino	Hispanic or Latino[1]	Under 18 years old	Age 65 years and older	Median age	Percent High school diploma or less	Percent Bachelor's degree or more	Total	Percent with a computer
	1	2	3	4	5	6	7	8	9	10	11	12	13	14	15	16
MAINE—Con.																
Arrowsic town (Sagadahoc)	427	461	8.0	387	96.4	0.0	0.0	2.8	0.8	13.7	38.5	61.0	30.2	48.8	192	92.2
Arundel town (York)	4,026	4,394	9.1	4,277	97.0	0.2	1.5	0.6	0.7	22.0	19.5	45.5	37.5	37.0	1,730	89.8
Ashland CDP	709	-	-	573	97.7	0.0	0.0	0.3	1.9	21.8	27.7	46.0	47.3	20.6	287	77.4
Ashland town (Aroostook) ..	1,302	1,217	-6.5	1,274	98.6	0.0	0.0	0.5	0.9	19.6	25.3	46.5	53.4	13.7	587	78.5
Athens town (Somerset) ...	1,019	979	-3.9	985	98.1	0.1	0.8	0.1	0.9	21.5	19.1	46.7	56.1	16.5	379	76.8
Atkinson town (Piscataquis)	326	306	-6.1	303	100.0	0.0	0.0	0.0	0.0	15.8	26.1	51.5	52.0	14.5	124	75.8
Auburn city & MCD (Androscoggin)	23,057	23,414	1.5	23,187	90.3	1.2	1.2	5.3	2.0	21.3	18.3	40.0	39.7	28.5	10,442	89.3
Augusta city & MCD (Kennebec)	19,132	18,697	-2.3	18,605	92.9	0.8	1.3	3.0	1.9	15.4	23.8	46.1	46.3	26.3	9,040	85.3
Aurora town (Hancock)	114	111	-2.6	96	97.9	0.0	0.0	2.1	0.0	12.5	27.1	51.7	40.0	37.3	46	69.6
Avon town (Franklin)	461	438	-5.0	646	93.7	1.4	0.0	0.0	5.0	23.8	16.3	41.6	56.6	19.3	251	90.8
Baileyville town (Washington)	1,523	1,447	-5.0	1,433	88.0	0.0	0.0	8.8	3.2	20.9	18.6	42.7	44.2	15.1	609	92.6
Baldwin town (Cumberland)	1,524	1,622	6.4	1,506	99.4	0.3	0.0	0.0	0.3	17.3	18.4	47.8	56.7	15.0	551	90.9
Bancroft town (Aroostook)	72	65	-9.7	52	100.0	0.0	0.0	0.0	0.0	21.2	32.7	61.5	64.7	32.4	19	78.9
Bangor city & MCD (Penobscot)	33,031	32,262	-2.3	32,095	89.5	1.8	2.5	4.2	2.0	17.5	16.6	37.9	34.5	35.8	13,805	89.4
Bar Harbor CDP	2,552	-	-	2,292	78.9	6.9	9.4	1.4	3.4	10.8	13.6	41.2	20.5	42.0	990	92.2
Bar Harbor town (Hancock)	5,234	5,559	6.2	5,470	88.2	2.9	4.5	1.2	3.2	16.3	18.7	45.2	22.5	50.4	2,336	91.8
Baring plantation (Washington)	251	237	-5.6	220	91.8	1.4	0.0	6.8	0.0	18.6	21.8	47.9	50.9	14.7	95	83.2
Bath city & MCD (Sagadahoc)	8,513	8,338	-2.1	8,319	95.1	0.7	0.0	2.6	1.6	21.6	20.4	41.4	34.6	35.6	3,928	88.2
Beals town (Washington)..	508	498	-2.0	384	96.9	1.0	0.5	0.8	0.8	12.5	28.1	51.4	56.4	27.7	180	76.1
Beaver Cove town (Piscataquis)	122	116	-4.9	154	87.0	0.0	0.0	0.0	13.0	0.0	61.7	67.2	37.7	23.8	65	86.2
Beddington town (Washington)	50	48	-4.0	36	100.0	0.0	0.0	0.0	0.0	0.0	16.7	46.5	54.5	21.2	18	55.6
Belfast city & MCD (Waldo)	6,668	6,679	0.2	6,688	92.8	1.1	0.0	4.3	1.8	17.9	26.2	46.9	25.8	47.4	3,018	89.4
Belgrade town (Kennebec)	3,189	3,149	-1.3	3,150	97.5	0.0	0.9	1.6	0.0	19.6	19.6	46.4	30.9	34.4	1,232	95.6
Belmont town (Waldo)	942	913	-3.1	923	98.7	0.0	0.0	0.7	0.7	21.5	18.2	44.5	44.2	25.1	409	90.5
Benton town (Kennebec) ..	2,731	2,713	-0.7	2,709	99.2	0.0	0.0	0.8	0.0	18.2	20.3	46.0	43.7	20.0	1,072	92.8
Berwick CDP	2,187	-	-	2,354	93.5	0.0	0.0	5.8	0.6	28.3	14.2	39.6	39.3	39.5	911	81.0
Berwick town (York)	7,241	7,872	8.7	7,683	95.6	0.0	0.2	2.9	1.3	23.3	17.8	41.5	37.4	34.7	3,185	86.7
Bethel town (Oxford)........	2,600	2,738	5.3	2,690	96.4	0.0	0.3	1.0	2.3	13.5	24.7	48.2	40.5	29.1	1,157	90.0
Biddeford city & MCD (York)	21,276	21,504	1.1	21,462	89.6	3.0	3.3	1.8	2.3	16.1	16.9	38.1	46.2	27.7	9,029	85.6
Bingham CDP	758	-	-	784	96.0	1.4	0.4	1.1	1.0	20.2	22.1	48.7	50.9	15.2	368	84.0
Bingham town (Somerset)	913	900	-1.4	841	96.3	1.3	0.4	1.1	1.0	18.8	22.7	49.5	49.1	17.5	394	84.0
Blaine CDP	301	-	-	244	98.4	0.0	1.2	0.4	0.0	9.0	34.8	64.3	51.2	13.9	120	63.3
Blaine town (Aroostook) ...	726	671	-7.6	678	95.0	2.1	0.4	2.5	0.0	17.3	28.2	51.8	50.8	13.4	295	78.3
Blanchard UT (Piscataquis)	98	92	-6.1	65	100.0	0.0	0.0	0.0	0.0	3.1	49.2	63.8	55.6	14.3	28	82.1
Blue Hill CDP	943	-	-	901	92.0	0.0	0.0	2.0	6.0	24.2	32.9	52.5	26.6	47.7	427	86.4
Blue Hill town (Hancock)..	2,686	2,652	-1.3	2,660	96.8	0.0	0.0	1.2	2.0	18.5	22.3	50.3	28.1	40.5	1,173	91.6
Boothbay town (Lincoln) ...	3,122	3,173	1.6	3,123	98.1	0.1	0.0	1.8	0.0	10.8	35.1	57.3	33.3	36.8	1,483	97.6
Boothbay Harbor CDP	1,086	-	-	1,152	92.4	2.0	0.0	0.3	5.3	12.6	31.1	56.0	42.0	36.3	574	88.0
Boothbay Harbor town (Lincoln)	2,163	2,213	2.3	1,984	95.5	1.2	0.0	0.2	3.1	9.7	42.7	61.7	40.2	41.3	990	86.4
Bowdoin town (Sagadahoc)	3,053	3,211	5.2	3,158	98.5	1.1	0.0	0.4	0.0	21.6	16.7	48.9	40.6	30.2	1,331	82.9
Bowdoinham CDP	722	-	-	788	80.6	7.1	1.9	4.3	6.1	17.8	27.8	51.8	36.1	33.0	320	83.8
Bowdoinham town (Sagadahoc)	2,889	3,056	5.8	2,979	94.0	1.9	0.5	2.0	1.6	19.5	20.8	44.7	39.7	31.9	1,326	90.3
Bowerbank town (Piscataquis)	116	112	-3.4	122	100.0	0.0	0.0	0.0	0.0	4.9	45.1	63.8	39.7	32.8	65	87.7
Bradford town (Penobscot)	1,284	1,228	-4.4	1,154	92.6	0.0	0.0	2.9	4.5	18.2	16.5	47.2	52.7	19.4	461	84.2
Bradley town (Penobscot).	1,489	1,488	-0.1	1,715	94.6	0.0	0.3	4.8	0.2	19.8	16.9	42.5	46.7	24.4	678	91.3
Bremen town (Lincoln)......	803	807	0.5	788	99.4	0.0	0.0	0.6	0.0	21.3	26.6	48.3	37.6	44.0	324	91.4
Brewer city & MCD (Penobscot)	9,485	9,035	-4.7	9,090	96.8	0.7	0.0	2.0	0.5	20.7	17.9	40.9	33.2	29.4	3,770	87.2
Bridgewater town (Aroostook)	610	562	-7.9	586	91.1	6.1	0.0	0.9	1.9	24.7	17.6	42.7	52.1	11.3	253	77.1
Bridgton CDP	2,071	-	-	2,542	96.5	0.4	0.0	2.4	0.7	13.1	20.8	37.7	47.5	30.3	1,112	85.6
Bridgton town (Cumberland)	5,214	5,434	4.2	5,382	96.7	0.2	0.0	1.5	1.7	9.8	23.9	47.2	44.0	33.7	2,449	88.0
Brighton plantation (Somerset)	70	67	-4.3	45	80.0	0.0	0.0	20.0	0.0	0.0	33.3	61.8	45.0	12.5	25	72.0
Bristol town (Lincoln)	2,755	2,787	1.2	2,747	98.8	0.0	0.0	0.9	0.2	14.0	32.4	55.7	38.1	36.6	1,241	91.2
Brooklin town (Hancock)....	824	812	-1.5	684	95.5	0.0	2.9	0.0	1.6	12.0	36.5	56.9	26.2	46.3	319	84.0
Brooks town (Waldo)	1,075	1,133	5.4	985	91.2	2.1	0.7	3.8	2.2	22.8	19.9	44.1	46.9	18.1	416	88.2
Brooksville town (Hancock)..................	934	913	-2.2	936	92.3	0.6	5.8	0.6	0.6	18.4	34.7	55.1	25.2	47.3	400	82.3
Brownfield town (Oxford) ..	1,596	1,643	2.9	1,401	99.9	0.0	0.1	0.0	0.0	20.7	21.6	50.8	56.2	18.3	596	91.9
Brownville town (Piscataquis)	1,246	1,187	-4.7	1,198	96.9	0.0	0.0	0.7	2.4	17.4	25.6	46.5	55.1	10.2	476	89.7
Brunswick CDP..............	15,175	-	-	14,994	86.9	2.5	3.2	3.9	3.5	15.2	22.4	43.9	29.9	47.8	6,256	89.4
Brunswick town (Cumberland)	20,281	20,535	1.3	20,517	88.0	1.9	2.6	4.1	3.4	16.6	21.4	44.4	28.8	48.0	8,455	91.1
Brunswick Station CDP.....	578	-	-	806	75.7	0.9	2.4	9.8	11.3	28.5	6.2	28.2	32.2	28.7	301	95.3
Buckfield town (Oxford)	2,009	2,041	1.6	2,221	94.1	3.5	0.0	2.4	0.0	16.6	15.7	42.5	58.8	11.8	789	92.1
Bucksport CDP	2,885	-	-	2,624	98.3	0.0	0.0	0.4	1.3	16.2	33.2	53.7	45.5	17.9	1,197	79.2
Bucksport town (Hancock)	4,910	4,925	0.3	4,916	97.1	1.2	0.0	0.8	0.9	24.4	24.6	41.2	39.9	20.9	2,093	83.9
Burlington town (Penobscot)	363	457	25.9	371	99.5	0.0	0.0	0.5	0.0	13.2	28.0	56.6	63.3	9.8	179	87.7
Burnham town (Waldo)......	1,166	1,231	5.6	1,081	92.7	0.0	0.0	6.4	0.9	17.2	28.2	50.5	58.9	15.9	498	76.3

1 May be of any race.

Table A. All Places — **Population and Housing**

STATE City, town, township, borough, or CDP (county if applicable)	Population — 2010 census total population	Population — 2019 estimated population	Population — Percent change 2010–2019	Population — ACS total population estimate 2015–2019	Race and Hispanic or Latino origin (percent) — White alone, not Hispanic or Latino	Black alone, not Hispanic or Latino	Asian alone, not Hispanic or Latino	All other races or 2 or more races, not Hispanic or Latino	Hispanic or Latino[1]	Age (percent) — Under 18 years old	Age 65 years and older	Median age	Educational attainment of persons age 25 and older — Percent High school diploma or less	Percent Bachelor's degree or more	Occupied housing units — Total	Percent with a computer
	1	2	3	4	5	6	7	8	9	10	11	12	13	14	15	16
MAINE—Con.																
Buxton town (York)	8,032	8,327	3.7	8,243	95.1	0.4	0.2	1.6	2.8	21.7	16.2	42.6	36.4	23.7	3,131	89.2
Byron town (Oxford)..........	145	149	2.8	100	100.0	0.0	0.0	0.0	0.0	19.0	40.0	59.5	56.4	11.5	37	83.8
Calais city & MCD (Washington)................	3,123	3,005	-3.8	2,993	98.2	0.2	0.0	1.5	0.0	17.8	25.1	50.3	44.4	20.4	1,539	77.7
Cambridge town (Somerset)	462	452	-2.2	482	93.4	0.6	1.7	4.4	0.0	23.0	31.5	49.3	66.4	15.3	200	85.0
Camden CDP....................	3,570	-	-	3,468	93.2	1.5	0.3	4.3	0.7	15.7	36.1	55.0	23.5	53.3	1,819	89.4
Camden town (Knox)	4,847	4,783	-1.3	4,817	95.1	1.1	0.2	3.1	0.5	15.3	36.6	55.2	22.4	53.7	2,431	92.1
Canaan town (Somerset)..	2,275	2,170	-4.6	2,418	98.4	1.0	0.0	0.4	0.2	28.0	13.1	35.0	51.2	17.4	873	89.5
Canton town (Oxford)	988	1,098	11.1	819	93.2	0.0	2.6	1.8	2.4	17.9	18.8	47.5	46.5	23.7	282	82.3
Cape Elizabeth town (Cumberland)	8,995	9,304	3.4	9,275	96.7	0.0	1.1	1.7	0.5	22.2	22.3	49.8	7.7	72.7	3,750	95.0
Cape Neddick CDP	2,568	-	-	2,217	97.6	0.0	0.6	1.8	0.0	10.5	36.4	59.6	16.6	50.9	1,194	93.6
Caratunk town (Somerset)	69	65	-5.8	68	94.1	0.0	0.0	5.9	0.0	0.0	48.5	61.8	33.3	41.3	31	100.0
Caribou city & MCD (Aroostook)	8,189	7,593	-7.3	7,710	94.0	1.5	0.1	2.4	2.1	18.9	21.9	47.9	49.6	19.6	3,426	79.1
Carmel town (Penobscot) .	2,796	2,845	1.8	2,799	98.5	0.0	0.0	1.0	0.5	20.8	16.1	40.1	39.4	23.3	1,080	92.2
Carrabassett Valley town (Franklin)	778	787	1.2	465	99.6	0.0	0.4	0.0	0.0	4.7	42.6	60.4	18.7	54.1	249	96.0
Carroll plantation (Penobscot)	153	146	-4.6	134	90.3	0.0	0.0	9.7	0.0	17.9	20.1	56.3	53.7	14.8	53	69.8
Carthage town (Franklin) ..	560	542	-3.2	501	99.0	0.0	0.0	1.0	0.0	15.0	15.4	49.4	55.9	11.6	174	81.6
Cary plantation (Aroostook)	218	201	-7.8	291	100.0	0.0	0.0	0.0	0.0	22.0	24.1	50.7	55.9	6.2	138	90.6
Casco CDP......................	587	-	-	653	99.8	0.0	0.0	0.2	0.0	7.8	28.3	52.7	53.5	22.1	282	86.9
Casco town (Cumberland)	3,746	3,928	4.9	3,920	98.1	0.2	0.0	1.7	0.0	18.4	21.0	44.3	51.1	25.7	1,616	87.1
Castine CDP....................	1,029	-	-	806	95.7	0.0	0.0	3.0	1.4	3.3	11.8	20.5	0.0	59.1	106	100.0
Castine town (Hancock)....	1,366	992	-27.4	1,117	95.8	0.0	0.3	2.2	1.7	7.1	14.9	21.0	16.0	52.5	225	100.0
Castle Hill town (Aroostook)	425	393	-7.5	349	95.4	0.0	0.9	0.0	3.7	16.3	27.5	48.8	35.6	27.7	148	78.4
Caswell town (Aroostook) .	304	282	-7.2	231	97.4	0.0	0.0	2.6	0.0	15.2	26.8	47.8	45.6	6.4	122	84.4
Central Aroostook UT (Aroostook)	185	171	-7.6	98	100.0	0.0	0.0	0.0	0.0	7.1	13.3	61.3	59.1	12.1	49	89.8
Central Hancock UT (Hancock)...................	117	115	-1.7	200	95.0	0.0	0.0	5.0	0.0	27.5	16.0	44.5	62.0	7.0	81	82.7
Central Somerset UT (Somerset)	338	323	-4.4	340	90.9	7.9	0.0	1.2	0.0	28.8	27.4	41.2	50.9	16.7	133	78.2
Chapman town (Aroostook)	468	445	-4.9	445	95.1	0.0	0.0	4.9	0.0	17.5	21.1	44.5	46.7	13.7	171	91.2
Charleston town (Penobscot)	1,415	1,717	21.3	1,514	95.4	0.9	0.3	3.1	0.3	24.0	9.0	42.4	51.8	15.1	482	83.6
Charlotte town (Washington)................	332	317	-4.5	396	89.6	0.0	1.0	9.3	0.0	21.2	19.7	45.0	56.9	14.5	156	81.4
Chebeague Island town (Cumberland)	341	346	1.5	449	95.5	0.0	0.0	4.5	0.0	12.0	42.1	60.4	28.1	50.9	232	81.0
Chelsea town (Kennebec)	2,721	2,750	1.1	2,727	95.4	1.3	0.3	2.2	0.8	18.6	23.4	48.3	52.2	20.8	1,004	88.1
Cherryfield town (Washington)................	1,232	1,161	-5.8	916	88.8	0.0	1.9	6.1	3.3	11.2	28.9	53.8	44.3	24.6	482	73.0
Chester town (Penobscot)	546	525	-3.8	516	99.4	0.0	0.0	0.0	0.6	21.3	15.5	43.0	60.9	8.2	210	88.1
Chesterville town (Franklin)	1,355	1,350	-0.4	1,258	98.4	0.0	0.2	1.4	0.0	18.2	20.8	50.2	53.0	17.9	549	85.6
China town (Kennebec)	4,314	4,302	-0.3	4,261	97.2	1.7	0.0	0.1	1.0	22.7	15.7	40.8	37.7	33.6	1,781	93.4
Chisholm CDP..................	1,380	-	-	1,513	96.5	0.0	0.7	2.8	0.0	22.3	19.5	38.0	54.3	21.6	638	85.3
Clifton town (Penobscot)...	921	905	-1.7	844	91.4	0.0	0.4	3.6	4.7	22.0	16.7	40.9	41.2	27.6	308	92.2
Clinton CDP.....................	1,419	-	-	953	98.1	1.9	0.0	0.0	0.0	9.2	22.2	48.6	50.1	27.9	418	80.1
Clinton town (Kennebec) ..	3,486	3,354	-3.8	3,367	91.5	0.5	0.0	3.2	4.8	14.6	19.5	47.4	55.3	17.5	1,471	85.2
Codyville plantation (Washington)................	24	23	-4.2	14	100.0	0.0	0.0	0.0	0.0	14.3	0.0	21.8	83.3	16.7	5	100.0
Columbia town (Washington)................	491	464	-5.5	435	86.7	0.0	0.0	0.9	12.4	29.2	10.1	37.5	59.1	11.2	161	87.0
Columbia Falls town (Washington)................	555	531	-4.3	435	89.0	0.0	0.5	2.3	8.3	16.6	18.6	46.5	49.3	23.0	215	90.7
Connor UT (Aroostook)	459	424	-7.6	398	90.2	0.0	0.0	6.8	3.0	21.4	12.6	43.6	55.9	13.2	156	86.5
Cooper town (Washington)	154	145	-5.8	149	100.0	0.0	0.0	0.0	0.0	10.7	38.9	59.6	42.7	22.9	78	82.1
Coplin plantation (Franklin)	166	159	-4.2	196	99.5	0.0	0.0	0.5	0.0	17.3	18.4	49.0	31.5	27.2	89	84.3
Corinna town (Penobscot)	2,203	2,141	-2.8	2,052	98.2	0.7	0.0	1.1	0.0	16.0	24.1	48.6	53.0	12.3	878	87.4
Corinth town (Penobscot) .	2,877	2,804	-2.5	2,803	95.2	0.2	0.0	3.2	1.4	22.5	20.3	44.0	43.5	18.8	1,013	91.6
Cornish town (York)	1,406	1,421	1.1	1,369	99.0	0.6	0.1	0.4	0.0	18.7	25.6	48.5	39.3	24.3	619	88.9
Cornville town (Somerset)	1,307	1,380	5.6	1,510	93.5	2.8	0.0	2.6	1.1	22.8	20.5	44.8	43.4	25.3	596	89.8
Cousins Island CDP	490	-	-	451	98.0	0.0	2.0	0.0	0.0	13.7	17.5	54.0	15.7	70.0	194	87.6
Cranberry Isles town (Hancock)...................	141	138	-2.1	134	100.0	0.0	0.0	0.0	0.0	10.4	32.1	61.8	24.6	60.5	77	90.9
Crawford town (Washington)................	101	96	-5.0	65	89.2	0.0	0.0	10.8	0.0	3.1	36.9	63.6	25.0	31.7	39	82.1
Criehaven UT (Knox)	1	1	0.0	-	-	-	-	-	-	-	-	-	-	-	-	-
Crystal town (Aroostook) ..	269	248	-7.8	277	95.7	0.0	0.7	3.6	0.0	17.7	24.2	47.8	45.4	19.0	113	80.5
Cumberland town (Cumberland)	7,217	8,208	13.7	7,998	91.5	0.6	1.4	1.2	5.3	25.9	17.5	43.4	15.6	69.2	2,878	96.0
Cumberland Center CDP..	2,499	-	-	2,926	92.4	0.0	1.5	1.8	4.2	26.1	17.3	44.5	17.4	71.4	1,072	95.0
Cushing town (Knox)	1,534	1,495	-2.5	1,512	98.1	0.0	0.0	0.8	1.1	20.4	27.1	50.6	44.4	26.4	627	86.9
Cutler town (Washington) .	507	511	0.8	508	92.3	0.0	0.0	7.1	0.6	25.2	20.5	45.3	49.3	18.6	214	88.8
Cyr plantation (Aroostook)	103	94	-8.7	98	68.4	0.0	0.0	0.0	31.6	13.3	28.6	52.5	40.0	41.2	28	82.1
Dallas plantation (Franklin)	309	296	-4.2	215	97.2	0.0	0.0	2.8	0.0	4.7	34.4	59.3	33.7	26.8	119	89.9
Damariscotta CDP............	1,142	-	-	1,269	91.2	3.1	1.6	2.0	2.1	16.5	35.4	48.5	34.7	40.6	560	88.8
Damariscotta town (Lincoln)	2,218	2,151	-3.0	2,037	92.0	1.9	2.3	2.2	1.5	18.4	29.6	46.4	33.0	38.0	895	91.8
Danforth town (Washington)................	588	577	-1.9	667	92.7	0.0	0.0	6.6	0.7	18.1	38.2	53.6	65.0	6.4	264	75.4
Dayton town (York)	1,959	2,082	6.3	2,186	95.6	0.0	1.1	1.4	1.9	25.3	12.9	42.6	47.6	25.0	781	94.4

1 May be of any race.

Table A. All Places — **Population and Housing**

STATE City, town, township, borough, or CDP (county if applicable)	Population				Race and Hispanic or Latino origin (percent)					Age (percent)			Educational attainment of persons age 25 and older		Occupied housing units	
	2010 census total population	2019 estimated population	Percent change 2010–2019	ACS total population estimate 2015–2019	White alone, not Hispanic or Latino	Black alone, not Hispanic or Latino	Asian alone, not Hispanic or Latino	All other races or 2 or more races, not Hispanic or Latino	Hispanic or Latino[1]	Under 18 years old	Age 65 years and older	Median age	Percent High school diploma or less	Percent Bachelor's degree or more	Total	Percent with a computer
	1	2	3	4	5	6	7	8	9	10	11	12	13	14	15	16
MAINE—Con.																
Deblois town (Washington)	57	54	-5.3	30	100.0	0.0	0.0	0.0	0.0	40.0	16.7	37.3	56.3	6.3	13	61.5
Dedham town (Hancock)	1,681	1,670	-0.7	1,713	96.2	0.2	0.0	1.3	2.2	16.3	14.2	49.9	28.5	42.6	714	96.9
Deer Isle town (Hancock)	1,975	1,906	-3.5	1,967	92.4	0.7	0.8	2.8	3.3	18.1	37.9	56.3	38.5	40.6	853	87.8
Denmark town (Oxford)	1,148	1,151	0.3	1,282	98.7	0.0	0.5	0.8	0.0	20.9	18.5	47.1	38.3	30.8	445	95.3
Dennistown plantation (Somerset)	33	31	-6.1	43	76.7	0.0	0.0	23.3	0.0	20.9	39.5	46.9	61.8	32.4	17	100.0
Dennysville town (Washington)	342	328	-4.1	275	97.8	0.0	0.0	1.5	0.7	16.0	14.5	51.6	48.4	23.7	129	85.3
Detroit town (Somerset)	852	827	-2.9	871	99.2	0.0	0.0	0.0	0.8	25.1	13.7	44.3	58.4	9.7	338	81.1
Dexter CDP	2,158	-	-	2,124	95.5	0.0	0.7	2.1	1.7	17.1	31.3	52.2	60.2	14.4	970	87.1
Dexter town (Penobscot)	3,886	3,706	-4.6	3,725	97.4	0.0	0.4	1.2	1.0	15.8	25.0	50.0	63.1	16.4	1,650	82.8
Dixfield CDP	1,076	-	-	1,345	92.5	0.0	1.6	5.9	0.0	20.8	16.4	41.2	56.4	8.2	532	84.8
Dixfield town (Oxford)	2,550	2,486	-2.5	1,991	90.5	0.7	1.2	7.6	0.0	18.9	17.7	42.5	63.2	8.4	796	82.4
Dixmont town (Penobscot)	1,181	1,126	-4.7	1,282	97.7	0.0	0.0	2.0	0.4	16.3	18.6	49.0	41.5	30.2	530	88.7
Dover-Foxcroft town (Piscataquis)	4,211	4,037	-4.1	4,057	90.1	1.1	1.7	5.3	1.8	20.8	26.4	52.1	43.2	27.0	1,702	91.3
Dover-Foxcroft CDP	2,528	-	-	2,740	87.5	1.6	2.5	7.0	1.5	23.1	23.9	47.8	42.5	29.5	1,202	90.5
Dresden town (Lincoln)	1,672	1,678	0.4	1,673	98.5	0.0	0.4	1.0	0.1	17.8	19.2	47.8	41.4	27.7	717	92.3
Drew plantation (Penobscot)	39	37	-5.1	30	86.7	0.0	0.0	13.3	0.0	30.0	0.0	40.4	82.4	17.6	9	100.0
Durham town (Androscoggin)	3,850	3,993	3.7	3,944	96.0	0.1	0.0	3.2	0.7	24.5	12.6	42.3	32.0	41.4	1,647	94.1
Dyer Brook town (Aroostook)	206	194	-5.8	245	97.1	0.0	0.0	2.9	0.0	20.4	16.7	45.4	40.2	16.1	93	88.2
Eagle Lake CDP	625	-	-	465	98.3	0.0	0.0	1.7	0.0	7.7	44.7	62.0	65.3	12.6	170	84.1
Eagle Lake town (Aroostook)	867	803	-7.4	624	98.7	0.0	0.0	1.3	0.0	9.3	42.5	61.8	58.0	19.2	242	83.5
Eastbrook town (Hancock)	423	417	-1.4	398	84.9	2.8	0.0	12.3	0.0	15.3	16.1	51.0	55.6	10.6	168	79.8
East Central Franklin UT (Franklin)	808	775	-4.1	775	95.2	0.0	0.8	0.0	4.0	18.6	23.7	48.6	53.1	16.0	316	84.5
East Central Penobscot UT (Penobscot)	343	329	-4.1	354	97.5	0.0	1.7	0.8	0.0	22.3	27.4	48.5	57.6	13.3	125	78.4
East Central Washington UT (Washington)	726	689	-5.1	769	96.7	0.0	0.9	2.3	0.0	26.1	10.4	33.2	35.3	28.3	277	96.4
East Hancock UT (Hancock)	92	90	-2.2	49	100.0	0.0	0.0	0.0	0.0	14.3	4.1	53.5	80.6	0.0	21	100.0
East Machias town (Washington)	1,365	1,298	-4.9	1,376	98.7	0.3	0.5	0.5	0.0	20.9	12.1	43.6	47.3	21.5	564	86.0
East Millinocket town (Penobscot)	1,720	1,627	-5.4	1,682	95.1	0.1	1.2	1.7	1.9	16.5	25.4	50.8	42.0	15.8	813	86.0
East Millinocket CDP	1,567	-	-	1,601	94.8	0.1	1.2	1.8	2.0	17.4	23.4	48.7	42.2	15.8	758	85.0
Easton town (Aroostook)	1,287	1,181	-8.2	1,261	95.3	1.2	0.0	3.5	0.0	16.2	26.7	45.7	46.0	19.4	571	76.4
Eastport city & MCD (Washington)	1,331	1,265	-5.0	1,326	87.3	2.1	0.0	8.7	2.0	15.2	34.0	56.5	43.4	25.5	629	87.3
Eddington town (Penobscot)	2,221	2,208	-0.6	2,306	94.9	0.5	0.0	3.8	0.8	20.9	20.6	45.6	46.6	22.7	897	88.7
Edgecomb town (Lincoln)	1,249	1,262	1.0	1,111	96.8	0.0	1.1	0.3	1.9	13.5	31.1	55.6	34.4	39.1	561	95.0
Edinburg town (Penobscot)	131	125	-4.6	111	97.3	0.0	0.0	2.7	0.0	20.7	32.4	50.3	53.4	26.1	54	83.3
Eliot town (York)	6,214	6,908	11.2	6,589	94.8	0.3	0.5	1.6	2.8	20.2	19.6	48.6	27.7	40.4	2,676	96.0
Ellsworth city & MCD (Hancock)	7,741	8,180	5.7	7,991	94.8	0.3	1.4	2.3	1.2	18.2	18.6	45.2	35.9	30.0	3,585	91.4
Embden town (Somerset)	936	950	1.5	738	99.7	0.0	0.0	0.1	0.1	11.0	24.7	56.4	52.2	19.5	333	84.1
Enfield town (Penobscot)	1,609	1,536	-4.5	1,442	97.1	0.0	1.0	1.5	0.3	17.9	21.7	46.9	54.3	16.1	630	89.2
Etna town (Penobscot)	1,260	1,199	-4.8	1,051	94.6	0.7	0.0	4.0	0.8	16.8	22.9	49.1	51.3	22.1	402	95.5
Eustis town (Franklin)	618	618	0.0	517	98.5	0.0	0.0	1.5	0.0	31.3	23.6	37.7	52.8	16.7	238	71.0
Exeter town (Penobscot)	1,092	1,096	0.4	1,093	91.6	0.0	0.0	0.3	8.1	22.8	17.8	46.5	58.1	14.6	428	85.0
Fairfield CDP	2,638	-	-	3,027	99.2	0.4	0.0	0.0	0.4	20.1	15.2	43.6	57.3	6.8	1,354	79.5
Fairfield town (Somerset)	6,740	6,552	-2.8	6,557	97.8	0.8	0.0	0.5	0.9	20.0	14.0	43.4	51.2	11.1	2,793	83.3
Falmouth CDP	1,855	-	-	1,949	91.0	0.0	3.8	3.2	1.9	18.1	25.7	52.5	17.7	62.4	948	96.0
Falmouth town (Cumberland)	11,176	12,312	10.2	12,141	95.7	0.0	2.9	0.6	0.8	24.9	18.7	46.7	14.4	67.0	4,727	95.6
Falmouth Foreside CDP	1,511	-	-	1,611	99.3	0.0	0.5	0.2	0.0	22.7	24.5	48.7	7.5	75.6	599	98.7
Farmingdale CDP	1,970	-	-	2,312	97.8	0.0	0.0	2.2	0.0	21.8	13.5	40.0	22.7	41.5	1,101	94.5
Farmingdale town (Kennebec)	2,968	2,925	-1.4	2,921	97.6	0.0	0.0	2.4	0.0	23.1	14.9	40.8	22.5	41.4	1,357	93.4
Farmington CDP	4,288	-	-	4,143	91.5	0.9	0.3	5.3	2.0	10.7	25.6	25.6	33.8	42.5	1,329	98.1
Farmington town (Franklin)	7,760	7,762	0.0	7,597	93.5	0.7	0.1	4.6	1.1	14.2	21.8	39.0	36.1	37.8	2,715	92.0
Fayette town (Kennebec)	1,140	1,163	2.0	1,080	96.0	0.3	0.6	1.5	1.6	13.6	23.4	51.2	28.7	35.6	480	94.6
Fort Fairfield CDP	1,825	-	-	1,808	97.6	0.0	0.0	1.1	1.3	16.8	21.2	49.7	44.5	22.1	845	78.6
Fort Fairfield town (Aroostook)	3,496	3,285	-6.0	3,320	97.0	0.0	0.5	1.7	0.7	22.4	22.0	47.3	36.8	24.5	1,452	82.5
Fort Kent CDP	2,488	-	-	2,238	90.3	3.4	0.4	3.5	2.3	12.8	27.7	51.4	45.8	29.7	978	77.5
Fort Kent town (Aroostook)	4,097	3,856	-5.9	3,893	93.0	2.0	0.3	2.7	2.1	17.2	20.8	42.9	45.3	28.6	1,594	83.1
Frankfort town (Waldo)	1,124	1,189	5.8	1,045	97.2	0.0	0.0	2.8	0.0	19.6	15.8	39.8	58.7	20.7	466	86.3
Franklin town (Hancock)	1,481	1,559	5.3	1,397	97.1	0.0	1.1	1.8	0.0	15.5	27.9	48.3	44.7	23.8	607	91.9
Freedom town (Waldo)	721	724	0.4	786	96.2	0.3	0.0	1.5	2.0	23.7	15.0	41.8	43.6	24.3	306	94.1
Freeport CDP	1,485	-	-	1,537	86.3	0.0	4.4	9.1	0.2	23.3	16.7	42.7	23.4	55.4	693	95.8
Freeport town (Cumberland)	7,878	8,558	8.6	8,439	90.8	0.4	1.4	4.7	2.8	21.4	18.2	47.7	25.2	55.2	3,447	94.9
Frenchboro town (Hancock)	61	59	-3.3	13	100.0	0.0	0.0	0.0	0.0	15.4	23.1	20.8	33.3	33.3	6	100.0
Frenchville town (Aroostook)	1,087	1,037	-4.6	902	98.6	0.0	1.4	0.0	0.0	16.2	21.4	54.3	60.8	13.7	418	87.8
Friendship town (Knox)	1,152	1,134	-1.6	1,118	100.0	0.0	0.0	0.0	0.0	21.1	24.5	45.1	46.1	31.4	436	89.4
Fryeburg CDP	1,631	-	-	1,542	97.4	0.1	1.0	1.0	0.5	18.4	21.9	49.1	53.1	22.2	542	89.1
Fryeburg town (Oxford)	3,448	3,451	0.1	3,421	93.8	0.0	0.5	5.4	0.2	22.6	17.4	41.8	45.9	20.7	1,053	91.1
Frye Island town (Cumberland)	13	13	0.0	41	95.1	4.9	0.0	0.0	0.0	0.0	65.9	67.9	26.8	53.7	20	100.0

1 May be of any race.

Table A. All Places — **Population and Housing**

STATE City, town, township, borough, or CDP (county if applicable)	2010 census total population	2019 estimated population	Percent change 2010–2019	ACS total population estimate 2015–2019	White alone, not Hispanic or Latino	Black alone, not Hispanic or Latino	Asian alone, not Hispanic or Latino	All other races or 2 or more races, not Hispanic or Latino	Hispanic or Latino[1]	Under 18 years old	Age 65 years and older	Median age	Percent High school diploma or less	Percent Bachelor's degree or more	Total	Percent with a computer
	1	2	3	4	5	6	7	8	9	10	11	12	13	14	15	16
MAINE—Con.																
Gardiner city & MCD (Kennebec)..............	5,790	5,653	-2.4	5,657	95.2	0.7	0.1	2.1	1.9	24.2	17.4	40.4	37.5	24.2	2,401	85.8
Garfield plantation (Aroostook)	81	74	-8.6	93	100.0	0.0	0.0	0.0	0.0	12.9	14.0	43.9	46.7	6.7	52	78.8
Garland town (Penobscot)	1,110	1,052	-5.2	1,022	97.7	0.8	0.0	0.5	1.0	14.6	26.3	52.9	56.2	20.5	464	88.6
Georgetown town (Sagadahoc)........	1,042	1,069	2.6	954	97.8	0.0	0.0	1.5	0.7	12.5	39.7	60.2	26.3	45.1	458	96.7
Gilead town (Oxford).........	212	204	-3.8	127	99.2	0.0	0.0	0.8	0.0	19.7	19.7	50.9	41.6	28.7	50	92.0
Glenburn town (Penobscot)...........	4,603	4,563	-0.9	4,566	98.2	0.0	0.0	1.8	0.0	22.1	12.5	39.6	36.8	28.8	1,871	95.9
Glenwood plantation (Aroostook)	3	3	0.0	3	100.0	0.0	0.0	0.0	0.0	0.0	0.0	0.0	100.0	0.0	2	100.0
Gorham CDP...................	6,882	-	-	6,759	92.4	1.7	0.5	2.5	2.9	14.6	16.7	35.9	27.3	45.4	2,425	89.7
Gorham town (Cumberland)	16,368	17,978	9.8	17,582	95.3	0.7	0.5	1.5	2.0	22.7	13.9	35.8	29.7	43.6	6,012	92.1
Gouldsboro town (Hancock)............	1,737	1,741	0.2	1,544	99.7	0.3	0.0	0.0	0.0	15.7	33.1	52.0	49.5	28.6	680	89.7
Grand Isle town (Aroostook)	467	430	-7.9	382	96.9	0.0	1.0	2.1	0.0	14.1	33.8	57.6	68.3	8.5	203	74.4
Grand Lake Stream plantation (Washington)	109	104	-4.6	132	93.2	0.0	0.0	6.8	0.0	1.5	61.4	68.6	43.8	30.0	77	79.2
Gray CDP.......................	884	-	-	949	90.8	2.6	5.2	1.4	0.0	17.1	27.9	40.9	25.5	40.4	425	94.8
Gray town (Cumberland) ..	7,757	8,223	6.0	8,117	92.7	0.5	1.9	4.0	0.9	19.3	18.7	41.5	30.5	40.8	3,476	92.8
Great Pond town (Hancock)............	58	56	-3.4	65	95.4	0.0	0.0	4.6	0.0	21.5	29.2	55.8	25.5	29.4	32	100.0
Greenbush town (Penobscot)...........	1,491	1,513	1.5	1,421	89.4	2.0	0.0	8.6	0.0	21.9	15.1	44.1	67.4	9.5	573	84.8
Greene town (Androscoggin)	4,351	4,339	-0.3	4,342	94.4	0.1	0.3	2.3	2.9	25.0	13.0	40.4	38.3	24.4	1,592	92.6
Greenville CDP................	1,257	-	-	1,029	98.6	0.0	0.0	0.8	0.6	15.8	26.4	55.3	49.8	16.0	454	77.1
Greenville town (Piscataquis)	1,646	1,604	-2.6	1,428	98.2	0.0	0.0	0.6	1.2	15.3	33.7	56.9	39.4	19.5	641	78.6
Greenwood town (Oxford)	830	807	-2.8	555	96.2	1.1	0.0	0.0	2.7	14.4	24.3	50.6	35.6	34.5	243	88.1
Guilford CDP..................	903	-	-	591	93.4	0.0	6.6	0.0	0.0	21.5	27.6	53.6	65.9	8.2	280	78.2
Guilford town (Piscataquis)	1,523	1,448	-4.9	1,192	96.7	0.0	3.3	0.0	0.0	17.1	25.7	54.1	61.1	10.8	531	79.8
Hallowell city & MCD (Kennebec)..............	2,375	2,381	0.3	2,445	96.9	0.4	1.6	0.4	0.6	22.2	23.5	37.2	23.2	48.4	1,104	90.8
Hamlin town (Aroostook) ..	219	203	-7.3	163	100.0	0.0	0.0	0.0	0.0	11.7	48.5	62.8	43.2	14.4	64	79.7
Hammond town (Aroostook)	118	110	-6.8	171	95.9	0.0	0.0	4.1	0.0	33.3	7.6	36.1	56.9	5.9	65	89.2
Hampden CDP...............	4,343	-	-	4,122	98.4	0.5	0.0	0.6	0.5	15.8	17.2	45.8	26.5	50.5	1,639	98.2
Hampden town (Penobscot).............	7,273	7,412	1.9	7,352	97.6	1.4	0.0	0.6	0.3	20.3	16.8	43.0	25.4	49.1	2,950	96.7
Hancock town (Hancock)..	2,393	2,431	1.6	2,432	94.0	4.6	0.0	0.5	0.9	15.1	22.7	46.8	50.3	22.9	1,135	91.7
Hanover town (Oxford)	238	262	10.1	174	100.0	0.0	0.0	0.0	0.0	3.4	24.1	55.9	27.7	21.9	89	91.0
Harmony town (Somerset)	939	898	-4.4	891	97.9	0.0	0.0	0.0	2.1	12.0	28.7	54.8	53.0	11.3	432	82.2
Harpswell town (Cumberland)	4,740	4,918	3.8	4,898	97.9	0.0	0.3	1.3	0.5	14.1	34.8	57.0	27.5	50.1	2,253	94.6
Harrington town (Washington).............	1,004	964	-4.0	1,012	95.8	0.0	1.5	1.8	1.0	22.8	25.6	45.7	55.0	21.5	388	86.9
Harrison town (Cumberland)	2,732	2,800	2.5	2,795	96.3	0.3	2.3	0.4	0.6	14.2	24.4	52.4	47.2	23.6	1,243	86.6
Hartford town (Oxford)......	1,184	1,214	2.5	1,161	94.7	0.0	0.0	3.8	1.6	14.8	17.4	46.0	52.1	22.8	402	89.1
Hartland CDP.................	813	-	-	666	100.0	0.0	0.0	0.0	0.0	19.7	17.4	44.0	60.2	14.2	299	84.3
Hartland town (Somerset)	1,782	1,724	-3.3	1,649	99.0	0.0	0.0	0.8	0.2	17.1	21.7	49.7	55.8	18.2	743	84.0
Haynesville town (Aroostook)	121	112	-7.4	82	91.5	0.0	0.0	8.5	0.0	2.4	29.3	61.1	53.8	18.8	52	67.3
Hebron town (Oxford)	1,416	1,419	0.2	1,784	92.2	0.6	0.4	3.0	3.8	27.8	8.0	35.2	50.0	20.1	476	94.1
Hermon town (Penobscot)	5,400	6,033	11.7	5,896	93.9	0.5	0.0	4.9	0.7	23.2	11.2	39.6	27.1	32.8	2,265	97.0
Hersey town (Aroostook)..	83	75	-9.6	78	92.3	0.0	0.0	7.7	0.0	11.5	9.0	39.5	55.6	20.4	30	86.7
Hibberts gore (Lincoln)	1	1	0.0	-	-	-	-	-	-	-	-	-	-	-	-	-
Highland plantation (Somerset)	73	70	-4.1	29	96.6	0.0	0.0	0.0	3.4	0.0	44.8	64.3	50.0	29.2	19	89.5
Hiram town (Oxford)	1,620	1,642	1.4	1,747	92.2	0.0	0.0	6.6	1.3	19.1	20.4	41.9	54.9	17.0	621	87.1
Hodgdon town (Aroostook)	1,309	1,267	-3.2	1,495	97.5	0.0	0.0	2.2	0.3	24.5	14.6	40.5	50.2	19.9	549	87.2
Holden town (Penobscot) .	3,085	3,104	0.6	3,082	94.3	0.0	0.6	2.1	3.0	18.2	17.2	46.6	41.0	25.6	1,301	93.0
Hollis town (York)............	4,285	4,747	10.8	4,607	96.8	0.3	0.2	2.5	0.3	14.8	18.6	47.9	39.2	23.4	2,082	93.9
Hope town (Knox)............	1,538	1,687	9.7	1,619	99.0	0.0	0.2	0.5	0.2	24.5	17.2	43.2	33.8	39.4	634	93.7
Houlton CDP...................	4,856	-	-	4,603	93.5	2.5	0.6	1.7	1.7	19.6	24.8	46.8	51.8	17.6	1,986	81.8
Houlton town (Aroostook) .	6,123	5,752	-6.1	5,829	89.3	2.1	0.6	6.4	1.5	20.6	24.1	46.1	52.0	16.7	2,499	83.4
Howland town (Penobscot).............	1,243	1,203	-3.2	1,191	99.0	0.0	0.0	1.0	0.0	17.0	25.5	44.8	60.1	12.8	475	85.3
Howland CDP.................	1,096	-	-	1,066	100.0	0.0	0.0	0.0	0.0	17.4	23.5	43.5	63.1	10.7	415	83.1
Hudson town (Penobscot)	1,531	1,513	-1.2	1,410	94.3	0.0	0.4	4.8	0.6	17.1	16.7	44.3	51.1	18.9	562	94.7
Industry town (Franklin)	924	931	0.8	880	99.3	0.3	0.3	0.0	0.0	17.5	18.6	47.3	45.6	27.3	340	89.7
Island Falls town (Aroostook)	844	778	-7.8	882	85.5	0.8	0.0	10.8	2.9	18.7	37.5	55.3	45.3	22.5	373	85.8
Isle au Haut town (Knox) ..	69	67	-2.9	20	90.0	0.0	0.0	10.0	0.0	10.0	10.0	27.8	61.1	11.1	14	78.6
Islesboro town (Waldo).....	566	561	-0.9	659	99.2	0.2	0.6	0.0	0.0	20.9	37.9	52.3	21.7	50.4	293	89.8
Jackman town (Somerset)	865	815	-5.8	707	97.3	1.6	0.3	0.8	0.0	12.0	29.7	50.9	52.9	13.5	334	85.3
Jackson town (Waldo).......	552	585	6.0	534	99.6	0.0	0.0	0.4	0.0	16.7	23.4	50.1	41.3	22.1	250	86.0
Jay town (Franklin)...........	4,848	4,623	-4.6	4,638	94.6	0.0	1.1	3.2	1.1	22.5	16.6	41.1	56.3	15.1	1,880	88.7
Jefferson town (Lincoln).....	2,425	2,455	1.2	2,626	97.2	0.1	0.9	0.8	1.0	24.0	23.5	42.9	45.2	25.9	1,022	90.7
Jonesboro town (Washington)	583	587	0.7	745	100.0	0.0	0.0	0.0	0.0	31.5	11.7	34.7	48.0	26.1	277	86.6
Jonesport town (Washington).............	1,370	1,317	-3.9	1,270	95.9	0.1	0.9	1.3	1.8	17.1	27.9	48.4	60.8	17.3	578	81.7
Kenduskeag town (Penobscot).............	1,358	1,365	0.5	1,231	99.0	0.0	0.0	0.5	0.5	18.8	12.0	48.1	47.2	16.4	506	92.9
Kennebunk CDP..............	5,214	-	-	5,872	96.3	0.2	0.3	0.3	3.0	15.4	35.7	53.0	25.6	49.8	2,768	89.5

1 May be of any race.

Table A. All Places — **Population and Housing**

STATE City, town, township, borough, or CDP (county if applicable)	Population				Race and Hispanic or Latino origin (percent)					Age (percent)			Educational attainment of persons age 25 and older		Occupied housing units	
	2010 census total population	2019 estimated population	Percent change 2010–2019	ACS total population estimate 2015–2019	White alone, not Hispanic or Latino	Black alone, not Hispanic or Latino	Asian alone, not Hispanic or Latino	All other races or 2 or more races, not Hispanic or Latino	Hispanic or Latino[1]	Under 18 years old	Age 65 years and older	Median age	Percent High school diploma or less	Percent Bachelor's degree or more	Total	Percent with a computer
	1	2	3	4	5	6	7	8	9	10	11	12	13	14	15	16
MAINE—Con.																
Kennebunk town (York).....	10,793	11,625	7.7	11,424	95.5	0.1	2.0	0.8	1.6	16.5	30.9	51.9	26.1	48.8	4,983	91.4
Kennebunkport CDP........	1,238	-	-	1,098	96.6	0.0	0.0	2.5	0.9	13.8	28.1	54.7	10.1	57.5	535	98.7
Kennebunkport town (York)..............	3,474	3,651	5.1	3,596	99.0	0.0	0.0	0.8	0.3	17.2	25.8	53.4	17.7	54.8	1,607	96.4
Kingfield town (Franklin) ...	997	974	-2.3	797	96.9	0.0	1.0	1.0	1.1	16.2	27.0	53.8	30.7	35.8	364	89.3
Kingman UT (Penobscot) .	180	171	-5.0	129	100.0	0.0	0.0	0.0	0.0	5.4	32.6	60.4	66.4	0.0	75	72.0
Kingsbury plantation (Piscataquis)	28	27	-3.6	3	100.0	0.0	0.0	0.0	0.0	0.0	100.0	70.0	100.0	0.0	3	0.0
Kittery CDP..................	4,562	-	-	4,829	84.3	1.0	4.3	5.6	4.7	15.5	20.2	38.4	23.9	43.5	2,282	94.9
Kittery town (York)...........	9,494	9,819	3.4	9,731	89.8	1.2	2.2	3.1	3.7	13.8	23.2	47.7	26.8	43.2	4,516	93.0
Kittery Point CDP............	1,012	-	-	985	100.0	0.0	0.0	0.0	0.0	5.9	28.8	59.5	35.3	47.2	512	89.6
Knox town (Waldo)	803	789	-1.7	852	97.3	0.0	0.0	2.7	0.0	22.9	13.5	43.5	49.2	24.5	317	89.6
Lagrange town (Penobscot)	708	679	-4.1	683	99.6	0.0	0.0	0.0	0.4	12.2	24.6	49.8	70.3	10.5	307	78.2
Lake Arrowhead CDP.......	3,071	-	-	3,067	92.4	1.1	0.0	5.5	0.9	26.3	5.1	37.5	43.5	14.7	950	99.4
Lake View plantation (Piscataquis)	89	85	-4.5	140	100.0	0.0	0.0	0.0	0.0	24.3	17.1	54.0	26.9	36.5	51	90.2
Lakeville town (Penobscot)	105	101	-3.8	87	93.1	0.0	0.0	6.9	0.0	4.6	65.5	70.5	39.8	26.5	49	85.7
Lamoine town (Hancock)..	1,601	1,703	6.4	1,680	95.2	0.0	0.7	0.9	3.2	12.6	26.2	52.6	30.1	38.3	754	91.2
Lebanon town (York)........	6,031	6,391	6.0	6,270	94.7	0.0	0.7	2.5	2.1	22.1	14.3	39.3	52.3	12.4	2,142	94.2
Lee town (Penobscot).......	922	874	-5.2	736	99.0	1.0	0.0	0.0	0.0	20.8	27.0	51.1	51.8	13.4	266	86.8
Leeds town (Androscoggin)..............	2,325	2,314	-0.5	2,215	96.1	0.1	0.4	1.8	1.6	25.5	18.2	43.9	50.5	21.0	835	92.3
Levant town (Penobscot)...	2,857	2,981	4.3	2,974	96.1	0.0	0.6	2.8	0.6	23.3	15.5	38.4	41.4	22.2	1,074	96.6
Lewiston city & MCD (Androscoggin)..............	36,592	36,225	-1.0	36,095	85.8	5.3	1.1	5.5	2.2	19.2	18.5	39.7	49.9	20.3	15,617	87.5
Liberty town (Waldo)........	913	968	6.0	896	97.3	0.1	0.0	1.2	1.3	22.5	19.8	48.1	40.0	31.9	387	78.8
Limerick town (York)........	2,892	3,022	4.5	2,959	94.8	2.1	0.6	1.5	1.1	22.6	16.0	40.5	43.2	22.5	1,154	90.0
Limestone CDP	1,075	-	-	1,504	91.2	0.0	1.1	6.8	0.9	30.5	14.0	31.3	46.6	18.8	456	88.6
Limestone town (Aroostook)..................	2,314	2,173	-6.1	2,009	90.3	0.7	1.0	5.1	2.9	27.2	13.8	33.4	45.7	17.2	645	89.5
Limington town (York).......	3,713	3,918	5.5	3,815	97.1	0.0	0.0	1.8	1.1	22.3	18.1	43.3	51.5	20.6	1,388	94.4
Lincoln plantation (Oxford)	45	44	-2.2	43	100.0	0.0	0.0	0.0	0.0	0.0	44.2	61.8	74.4	9.3	21	100.0
Lincoln CDP..................	2,884	-	-	2,677	99.4	0.0	0.0	0.0	0.6	11.1	29.6	56.8	72.9	13.5	1,288	89.3
Lincoln town (Penobscot)..	5,083	4,862	-4.3	4,919	98.5	0.8	0.0	0.0	0.7	16.5	23.9	51.3	63.7	14.8	2,106	92.7
Lincolnville town (Waldo)..	2,164	2,226	2.9	2,027	96.2	0.0	1.7	0.4	1.7	15.3	28.6	54.6	25.3	46.1	947	94.0
Linneus town (Aroostook).	984	910	-7.5	706	98.7	0.0	0.0	1.3	0.0	16.0	19.0	47.3	46.1	24.7	304	92.8
Lisbon town (Androscoggin)..............	9,021	9,005	-0.2	8,906	95.0	0.1	0.5	3.9	0.6	24.1	14.4	38.9	45.1	15.9	3,728	92.5
Lisbon Falls CDP............	4,100	-	-	4,019	95.5	0.0	1.0	3.4	0.0	25.3	14.0	38.2	41.3	21.2	1,555	94.4
Litchfield town (Kennebec)	3,623	3,658	1.0	3,626	97.9	0.1	0.9	1.2	0.0	17.8	19.8	48.8	43.4	25.6	1,521	92.1
Little Falls CDP.............	708	-	-	958	97.2	0.0	0.0	0.1	2.7	16.9	11.5	33.1	43.1	27.1	345	88.7
Littlejohn Island CDP.......	118	-	-	52	100.0	0.0	0.0	0.0	0.0	0.0	73.1	66.5	32.7	42.3	29	100.0
Littleton town (Aroostook).	1,068	989	-7.4	1,015	94.7	0.0	0.0	4.9	0.4	22.1	21.4	45.6	47.1	15.2	423	86.8
Livermore town (Androscoggin)..............	2,095	2,119	1.1	2,066	95.2	0.3	0.0	4.4	0.1	23.1	16.7	42.7	43.7	16.9	837	90.8
Livermore Falls CDP........	1,594	-	-	1,586	94.8	0.3	0.0	4.0	1.0	23.9	12.2	40.4	53.1	14.7	788	81.7
Livermore Falls town (Androscoggin)...	3,187	3,157	-0.9	3,156	93.8	0.1	0.0	3.5	2.6	25.0	19.1	39.9	51.9	15.6	1,500	86.1
Long Island town (Cumberland)..............	230	238	3.5	314	89.8	0.0	4.5	5.7	0.0	21.3	28.3	57.7	25.6	53.4	140	94.3
Louds Island UT (Lincoln).	-	-	-	-	-	-	-	-	-	-	-	-	-	-	-	-
Lovell town (Oxford)........	1,135	1,134	-0.1	999	96.0	0.0	0.0	1.4	2.6	12.4	24.4	52.3	38.3	30.9	406	88.4
Lowell town (Penobscot)...	358	362	1.1	396	100.0	0.0	0.0	0.0	0.0	17.9	26.3	50.6	53.0	15.1	145	92.4
Lubec CDP..................	349	-	-	314	87.9	6.4	0.0	0.0	5.7	8.9	46.2	64.1	55.2	25.5	191	74.3
Lubec town (Washington).	1,359	1,258	-7.4	1,319	95.1	1.5	0.0	0.8	2.7	12.2	36.8	60.8	54.2	22.6	699	78.5
Ludlow town (Aroostook)..	404	368	-8.9	504	90.5	0.6	0.0	7.5	1.4	19.4	22.0	44.8	41.1	23.7	210	86.2
Lyman town (York)...........	4,351	4,517	3.8	4,443	99.6	0.0	0.4	0.0	0.0	17.2	18.4	46.9	46.9	18.7	1,659	96.4
Machias CDP................	1,274	-	-	1,157	92.0	0.8	0.0	3.9	3.4	14.7	27.6	47.9	52.1	18.0	554	78.2
Machias town (Washington)..............	2,217	2,027	-8.6	2,033	92.5	0.7	0.9	3.7	2.2	17.7	23.8	44.5	47.3	23.9	864	83.8
Machiasport town (Washington)..............	1,119	947	-15.4	956	91.7	0.7	0.9	3.5	3.1	17.2	23.3	35.4	58.2	25.1	339	91.2
Macwahoc plantation (Aroostook)..................	81	74	-8.6	97	96.9	0.0	3.1	0.0	0.0	14.4	14.4	50.8	83.1	7.8	41	90.2
Madawaska CDP............	2,967	-	-	2,769	99.7	0.0	0.0	0.3	0.0	10.5	40.3	56.0	60.2	15.0	1,385	83.0
Madawaska town (Aroostook)..................	4,035	3,735	-7.4	3,774	99.4	0.0	0.0	0.6	0.0	11.7	34.7	54.7	55.4	19.7	1,905	79.5
Madison CDP................	2,630	-	-	2,433	96.7	0.0	0.0	2.8	0.5	12.2	24.1	52.7	52.4	12.0	1,060	92.8
Madison town (Somerset).	4,849	4,620	-4.7	4,651	94.2	0.3	0.1	4.5	1.0	13.4	22.8	50.6	48.2	16.9	1,900	94.0
Magalloway plantation (Oxford)......................	46	45	-2.2	24	100.0	0.0	0.0	0.0	0.0	29.2	41.7	53.5	41.2	11.8	10	100.0
Manchester town (Kennebec)..................	2,566	2,556	-0.4	2,543	95.2	0.0	0.9	1.2	2.7	18.6	18.2	46.8	26.0	40.2	1,069	93.9
Mapleton CDP	683	-	-	756	97.8	0.3	0.8	1.1	0.1	23.7	11.0	34.9	32.1	24.8	321	90.3
Mapleton town (Aroostook)..................	1,948	1,834	-5.9	1,983	98.3	0.6	0.3	0.4	0.4	21.9	15.9	41.2	30.8	28.5	891	91.4
Mariaville town (Hancock)	513	538	4.9	472	94.7	1.5	0.6	1.3	1.9	17.2	19.1	47.7	41.5	20.3	203	87.7
Marshall Island UT (Hancock)............	-	-	-	-	-	-	-	-	-	-	-	-	-	-	-	-
Marshfield town (Washington)..............	525	512	-2.5	511	97.3	0.0	0.0	1.2	1.6	23.1	20.0	37.3	41.2	24.3	200	87.0
Mars Hill CDP...............	980	-	-	990	98.7	0.1	0.0	1.2	0.0	19.9	17.8	41.5	59.1	10.1	372	80.4
Mars Hill town (Aroostook)	1,493	1,469	-1.6	1,405	98.2	0.1	0.0	1.7	0.0	19.6	19.8	42.1	53.1	12.6	549	81.1
Masardis town (Aroostook)..................	249	227	-8.8	229	98.7	0.0	0.0	1.3	0.0	17.5	30.6	50.2	69.0	8.0	100	69.0
Matinicus Isle plantation (Knox)......................	74	72	-2.7	91	97.8	0.0	0.0	2.2	0.0	7.7	35.2	54.4	34.5	40.5	42	95.2
Mattawamkeag town (Penobscot)..............	683	651	-4.7	820	95.4	1.0	0.0	3.7	0.0	19.4	20.7	50.7	58.8	13.5	377	67.4
Maxfield town (Penobscot)	95	98	3.2	134	100.0	0.0	0.0	0.0	0.0	24.6	11.2	40.2	77.6	1.0	53	81.1

1 May be of any race.

Table A. All Places — **Population and Housing**

STATE City, town, township, borough, or CDP (county if applicable)	2010 census total population	2019 estimated population	Percent change 2010–2019	ACS total population estimate 2015–2019	White alone, not Hispanic or Latino	Black alone, not Hispanic or Latino	Asian alone, not Hispanic or Latino	All other races or 2 or more races, not Hispanic or Latino	Hispanic or Latino[1]	Under 18 years old	Age 65 years and older	Median age	Percent High school diploma or less	Percent Bachelor's degree or more	Total	Percent with a computer
	1	2	3	4	5	6	7	8	9	10	11	12	13	14	15	16

<!-- Spanning headers: cols 1-4 Population; cols 5-9 Race and Hispanic or Latino origin (percent); cols 10-12 Age (percent); cols 13-14 Educational attainment of persons age 25 and older; cols 15-16 Occupied housing units -->

MAINE—Con.

STATE City, town, township, borough, or CDP (county if applicable)	1	2	3	4	5	6	7	8	9	10	11	12	13	14	15	16
Mechanic Falls town (Androscoggin)..............	3,031	2,979	-1.7	2,980	92.2	1.2	1.6	4.9	0.0	26.7	18.2	40.9	48.7	14.5	1,213	84.3
Mechanic Falls CDP	2,237	-	-	2,112	90.9	1.7	1.1	6.3	0.0	29.5	14.5	40.4	47.5	14.0	885	83.5
Meddybemps town (Washington)................	157	147	-6.4	129	87.6	4.7	0.0	7.8	0.0	8.5	27.9	59.3	39.8	22.1	57	91.2
Medford town (Piscataquis)................	254	241	-5.1	248	97.2	0.8	0.4	1.6	0.0	9.3	10.1	45.8	58.9	12.7	101	82.2
Medway town (Penobscot)	1,352	1,310	-3.1	1,241	97.6	0.3	0.0	0.3	1.8	18.0	20.9	49.7	55.5	13.0	535	89.0
Mercer town (Somerset) ...	665	637	-4.2	773	96.5	0.0	0.0	3.1	0.4	20.3	26.0	54.5	52.9	17.6	304	91.8
Merrill town (Aroostook)....	273	250	-8.4	262	98.5	0.0	0.0	0.0	1.5	20.2	22.9	52.9	51.5	19.8	123	80.5
Mexico CDP.....................	1,743	-	-	1,701	88.9	0.0	1.1	2.8	7.2	12.6	29.9	55.9	50.9	16.3	658	73.9
Mexico town (Oxford)........	2,680	2,629	-1.9	2,628	92.8	0.0	0.7	1.8	4.7	13.7	28.4	55.3	51.9	17.2	1,051	79.3
Milbridge town (Washington)................	1,353	1,294	-4.4	1,560	79.9	0.3	0.6	2.2	17.0	18.8	23.7	44.2	49.9	27.3	607	87.6
Milford CDP....................	2,233	-	-	2,272	94.7	0.0	0.0	3.1	2.2	18.2	15.1	36.9	54.9	20.0	985	97.0
Milford town (Penobscot) ..	3,068	2,980	-2.9	2,991	96.0	0.0	0.0	2.4	1.6	19.0	12.6	36.3	46.6	20.9	1,277	97.7
Millinocket town (Penobscot)................	4,506	4,252	-5.6	4,287	93.1	0.0	0.0	1.6	5.2	12.6	33.8	57.4	57.9	12.8	2,287	80.8
Millinocket CDP...............	4,466	-	-	4,287	93.1	0.0	0.0	1.6	5.2	12.6	33.8	57.4	57.9	12.8	2,287	80.8
Milo CDP........................	1,847	-	-	2,134	96.9	1.1	0.5	1.2	0.2	19.8	18.2	44.7	46.0	14.3	854	84.0
Milo town (Piscataquis).....	2,340	2,285	-2.4	2,602	96.6	0.9	0.4	1.0	1.0	20.8	17.7	43.6	48.0	13.0	1,028	85.0
Milton UT (Oxford)............	143	141	-1.4	189	100.0	0.0	0.0	0.0	0.0	25.9	17.5	43.5	64.3	10.7	70	80.0
Minot town (Androscoggin)................	2,604	2,586	-0.7	2,587	96.3	0.3	0.3	2.8	0.3	27.5	15.1	42.5	40.7	22.3	932	95.5
Monhegan plantation (Lincoln).....................	69	68	-1.4	54	100.0	0.0	0.0	0.0	0.0	5.6	27.8	53.7	8.2	63.3	29	100.0
Monmouth town (Kennebec)..................	4,096	4,136	1.0	4,100	94.0	0.5	0.3	4.7	0.5	19.2	16.1	47.5	43.6	19.6	1,716	92.0
Monroe town (Waldo)	890	943	6.0	1,068	93.4	0.0	1.1	2.2	3.4	22.7	13.9	46.8	44.7	28.0	468	88.7
Monson town (Piscataquis)................	686	655	-4.5	505	97.8	2.2	0.0	0.0	0.0	19.2	30.7	57.0	46.7	25.9	245	82.0
Monticello town (Aroostook).................	790	741	-6.2	650	94.2	0.0	1.8	4.0	0.0	9.1	29.8	56.2	62.3	9.9	317	79.2
Montville town (Waldo)	1,030	1,087	5.5	1,013	96.9	0.0	1.3	1.0	0.8	16.9	27.2	51.4	44.7	29.6	419	88.8
Moose River town (Somerset).................	215	206	-4.2	248	94.8	0.0	0.0	5.2	0.0	21.4	23.8	42.3	68.8	15.1	105	80.0
Moro plantation (Aroostook).................	38	35	-7.9	26	100.0	0.0	0.0	0.0	0.0	0.0	84.6	69.5	65.4	0.0	13	30.8
Morrill town (Waldo)..........	884	889	0.6	1,056	98.9	0.0	0.5	0.7	0.0	19.3	19.9	43.0	42.9	26.0	442	93.4
Moscow town (Somerset) .	519	505	-2.7	546	95.1	0.0	0.0	4.9	0.0	17.8	16.7	48.8	64.9	9.7	249	75.1
Mount Chase town (Penobscot)................	201	193	-4.0	170	100.0	0.0	0.0	0.0	0.0	27.1	34.7	52.5	62.9	16.9	81	74.1
Mount Desert town (Hancock)...................	2,060	2,113	2.6	1,754	97.9	0.7	0.1	1.2	0.1	15.4	30.0	54.4	26.5	49.5	799	90.5
Mount Vernon town (Kennebec)..................	1,640	1,691	3.1	1,464	97.3	0.0	0.0	1.9	0.8	19.5	20.4	47.9	41.3	34.7	623	92.9
Muscle Ridge Islands UT (Knox)......................	6	6	0.0	10	100.0	0.0	0.0	0.0	0.0	0.0	0.0	0.0	50.0	50.0	5	100.0
Naples CDP.....................	428	-	-	496	99.6	0.0	0.0	0.4	0.0	18.5	24.8	48.6	27.4	34.2	212	100.0
Naples town (Cumberland)................	3,872	3,969	2.5	3,957	98.1	0.1	0.4	1.1	0.4	20.5	20.9	46.3	37.1	25.5	1,737	96.1
Nashville plantation (Aroostook).................	46	42	-8.7	14	71.4	0.0	28.6	0.0	0.0	0.0	14.3	49.5	64.3	28.6	7	100.0
Newburgh town (Penobscot)................	1,549	1,519	-1.9	1,584	97.3	0.0	1.3	1.1	0.3	22.4	18.2	44.8	37.2	21.3	649	83.8
New Canada town (Aroostook).................	321	302	-5.9	304	93.1	0.0	0.0	1.0	5.9	16.1	18.8	56.1	60.6	14.1	129	81.4
Newcastle CDP	667	-	-	512	93.0	3.9	0.0	0.6	2.5	14.8	40.8	61.2	27.2	56.0	265	91.3
Newcastle town (Lincoln)..	1,752	1,767	0.9	1,750	95.0	1.1	0.9	0.2	2.7	19.5	21.4	46.6	31.2	47.7	796	94.0
Newfield town (York)........	1,522	1,585	4.1	1,391	98.2	0.0	0.5	0.0	1.3	18.7	20.8	51.1	48.8	16.7	593	88.4
New Gloucester town (Cumberland)................	5,542	5,812	4.9	5,738	95.9	0.1	1.7	2.2	0.1	23.3	11.1	39.9	37.7	30.5	2,049	98.0
New Limerick town (Aroostook).................	510	475	-6.9	565	81.1	2.3	0.0	12.9	3.7	25.1	13.5	40.8	37.9	28.2	214	93.5
Newport town (Penobscot)	3,281	3,273	-0.2	3,257	96.5	0.4	0.4	1.7	1.0	20.3	23.0	47.7	45.0	17.9	1,424	87.4
Newport CDP..................	1,776	-	-	1,766	94.3	0.8	0.8	2.3	1.8	20.7	17.0	47.6	46.3	18.1	835	79.5
New Portland town (Somerset).................	721	688	-4.6	627	93.9	0.0	0.8	5.3	0.0	10.7	34.4	58.6	49.4	25.9	325	80.0
Newry town (Oxford)........	329	353	7.3	295	98.3	0.0	0.0	1.7	0.0	20.3	19.0	53.1	27.4	34.1	126	78.6
New Sharon town (Franklin)..................	1,407	1,415	0.6	1,684	95.0	0.0	0.3	3.9	0.8	24.1	17.4	39.8	43.0	26.4	629	91.4
New Sweden town (Aroostook).................	602	569	-5.5	527	92.8	0.0	0.0	7.2	0.0	20.5	24.9	51.6	37.4	29.3	224	76.3
New Vineyard town (Franklin)..................	761	779	2.4	975	91.7	0.5	0.2	2.5	5.1	17.1	17.1	48.0	53.2	22.7	344	89.0
Nobleboro town (Lincoln)..	1,643	1,653	0.6	1,713	89.0	1.0	8.2	1.0	0.9	18.7	24.8	50.0	32.2	32.9	761	93.0
Norridgewock CDP	1,438	-	-	1,428	93.2	4.5	0.0	2.3	0.0	15.8	19.5	48.2	68.6	19.1	580	78.6
Norridgewock town (Somerset).................	3,377	3,222	-4.6	3,244	97.0	2.0	0.0	1.0	0.0	18.5	15.5	43.3	54.9	15.9	1,278	84.6
North Berwick CDP..........	1,615	-	-	1,439	91.9	1.3	1.4	0.0	5.4	23.5	23.6	44.3	50.9	15.0	581	92.8
North Berwick town (York)	4,581	4,728	3.2	4,697	95.8	0.8	0.7	0.8	1.8	18.1	22.2	47.4	41.4	22.9	1,860	90.4
Northeast Piscataquis UT (Piscataquis)................	277	264	-4.7	366	97.5	0.0	0.0	0.0	2.5	11.7	35.2	57.4	38.9	31.7	168	83.3
Northeast Somerset UT (Somerset).................	390	375	-3.8	396	100.0	0.0	0.0	0.0	0.0	5.1	46.0	64.6	49.4	25.4	202	98.5
Northfield town (Washington)................	148	140	-5.4	266	89.5	0.0	0.0	7.9	2.6	30.8	8.6	30.8	29.1	31.1	101	88.1
North Franklin UT (Franklin)..................	61	59	-3.3	22	100.0	0.0	0.0	0.0	0.0	0.0	54.5	80.2	54.5	45.5	12	41.7
North Haven town (Knox) .	355	355	0.0	455	95.2	0.0	0.0	1.5	3.3	15.8	28.8	47.6	27.2	36.3	209	91.4
North Oxford UT (Oxford).	24	23	-4.2	5	100.0	0.0	0.0	0.0	0.0	0.0	0.0	0.0	100.0	0.0	2	100.0

1   May be of any race.

Table A. All Places — **Population and Housing**

STATE City, town, township, borough, or CDP (county if applicable)	Population				Race and Hispanic or Latino origin (percent)					Age (percent)			Educational attainment of persons age 25 and older		Occupied housing units	
	2010 census total population	2019 estimated population	Percent change 2010–2019	ACS total population estimate 2015–2019	White alone, not Hispanic or Latino	Black alone, not Hispanic or Latino	Asian alone, not Hispanic or Latino	All other races or 2 or more races, not Hispanic or Latino	Hispanic or Latino[1]	Under 18 years old	Age 65 years and older	Median age	Percent High school diploma or less	Percent Bachelor's degree or more	Total	Percent with a computer
	1	2	3	4	5	6	7	8	9	10	11	12	13	14	15	16
MAINE—Con.																
North Penobscot UT (Penobscot)	461	441	-4.3	387	100.0	0.0	0.0	0.0	0.0	3.4	29.7	59.4	39.4	23.5	223	78.5
Northport town (Waldo)	1,518	1,581	4.2	1,862	94.9	0.0	0.7	1.7	2.7	18.6	22.6	47.2	29.6	39.5	776	92.4
North Washington UT (Washington)	499	473	-5.2	434	93.5	0.0	0.0	6.5	0.0	7.8	37.1	60.9	54.2	18.3	206	75.7
Northwest Aroostook UT (Aroostook)	10	9	-10.0	4	100.0	0.0	0.0	0.0	0.0	0.0	0.0	0.0	0.0	100.0	4	100.0
Northwest Hancock UT (Hancock)	2	2	0.0	2	100.0	0.0	0.0	0.0	0.0	0.0	100.0	0.0	0.0	0.0	2	0.0
Northwest Piscataquis UT (Piscataquis)	149	142	-4.7	39	100.0	0.0	0.0	0.0	0.0	0.0	100.0	67.1	35.9	30.8	21	100.0
Northwest Somerset UT (Somerset)	62	60	-3.2	-	-	-	-	-	-	-	-	-	-	-	-	-
North Windham CDP	4,904	-	-	6,131	91.5	2.2	2.3	3.9	0.1	23.9	15.3	41.2	26.6	31.7	2,240	97.1
North Yarmouth town (Cumberland)	3,583	3,864	7.8	3,779	94.9	0.0	0.8	0.8	3.5	24.4	11.9	42.4	20.1	58.5	1,397	95.4
Norway CDP	2,748	-	-	2,641	96.9	0.7	0.0	0.7	1.7	23.5	21.7	37.7	52.5	16.3	975	88.0
Norway town (Oxford)	5,018	4,991	-0.5	4,955	95.3	0.4	0.0	3.1	1.2	25.6	22.0	41.2	45.9	23.2	1,732	89.3
Oakfield town (Aroostook)	737	678	-8.0	722	93.9	0.0	1.0	3.0	2.1	17.9	24.0	47.6	58.5	10.7	305	74.8
Oakland CDP	2,602	-	-	2,389	93.7	0.0	0.0	6.3	0.0	17.2	19.5	50.8	33.2	22.3	1,012	85.6
Oakland town (Kennebec)	6,243	6,309	1.1	6,274	95.9	0.0	0.5	3.6	0.0	18.3	19.6	49.7	32.7	28.8	2,692	88.5
Ogunquit town (York)	899	929	3.3	1,030	97.2	0.0	0.3	1.9	0.6	9.8	40.4	59.5	18.7	53.6	544	91.7
Old Orchard Beach town & CDP (York)	8,613	9,015	4.7	8,862	94.2	0.3	0.4	4.2	0.9	8.1	25.4	53.4	34.2	33.4	4,788	91.6
Old Town city & MCD (Penobscot)	7,846	7,431	-5.3	7,474	92.3	0.7	1.0	6.1	0.0	18.3	17.1	36.3	37.2	31.1	3,213	92.3
Orient town (Aroostook)	147	140	-4.8	143	97.2	0.0	2.8	0.0	0.0	14.0	35.7	60.8	49.6	26.0	69	91.3
Orland town (Hancock)	2,225	2,181	-2.0	2,059	98.3	1.0	0.0	0.2	0.5	12.9	29.8	55.1	47.7	25.4	935	95.1
Orono town (Penobscot)	10,359	10,799	4.2	10,776	87.8	2.1	3.7	3.0	3.5	8.4	11.2	21.9	17.9	60.7	3,149	91.0
Orono CDP	9,474	-	-	9,541	86.4	2.4	4.2	3.2	3.9	7.5	10.9	21.6	15.6	61.6	2,643	90.6
Orrington town (Penobscot)	3,730	3,688	-1.1	3,671	96.7	0.2	0.7	2.0	0.4	20.9	20.8	48.7	40.7	31.4	1,466	91.5
Osborn town (Hancock)	67	66	-1.5	51	90.2	0.0	0.0	0.0	9.8	11.8	31.4	57.8	22.0	34.1	24	62.5
Otis town (Hancock)	670	659	-1.6	876	94.6	0.0	0.5	4.1	0.8	13.9	21.8	49.9	47.1	23.4	347	91.6
Otisfield town (Oxford)	1,770	1,806	2.0	2,299	97.5	0.1	0.6	0.7	1.2	24.1	19.1	43.9	50.9	21.5	721	93.8
Owls Head town (Knox)	1,578	1,603	1.6	1,524	99.0	0.2	0.0	0.5	0.4	16.1	28.8	52.1	47.7	27.1	700	88.9
Oxford CDP	1,263	-	-	1,026	100.0	0.0	0.0	0.0	0.0	37.2	14.8	30.2	45.0	22.3	384	70.8
Oxford town (Oxford)	4,110	4,096	-0.3	4,051	98.3	0.0	0.0	1.7	0.0	24.5	18.8	40.4	55.2	17.7	1,496	84.7
Palermo town (Waldo)	1,535	1,521	-0.9	1,455	98.1	0.0	0.9	0.2	0.8	18.1	19.2	48.6	46.8	27.4	620	90.3
Palmyra town (Somerset)	1,986	1,975	-0.6	2,071	96.6	0.0	0.0	2.7	0.7	19.0	20.1	46.5	56.5	16.2	881	86.4
Paris town (Oxford)	5,181	5,152	-0.6	5,111	93.0	0.0	0.0	3.4	3.6	20.5	24.6	46.5	47.5	18.9	1,932	86.6
Parkman town (Piscataquis)	841	795	-5.5	896	94.0	0.0	0.2	2.3	3.5	18.5	16.4	48.3	56.6	12.9	333	77.8
Parsonsfield town (York)	1,895	1,962	3.5	1,926	97.7	1.2	0.0	1.0	0.2	16.8	18.3	46.4	47.3	23.3	826	89.2
Passadumkeag town (Penobscot)	374	358	-4.3	534	95.3	0.0	0.0	4.7	0.0	18.5	20.8	47.7	67.4	7.5	213	85.4
Passamaquoddy Indian Township Reservation (Washington)	718	683	-4.9	773	12.4	0.0	1.0	86.3	0.3	35.1	9.2	27.3	47.8	11.2	270	86.7
Passamaquoddy Pleasant Point Reservation (Washington)	749	713	-4.8	683	10.4	0.0	0.1	84.8	4.7	33.7	9.7	35.7	48.5	18.3	258	78.3
Patten town (Penobscot)	1,017	970	-4.6	808	98.4	0.1	0.0	1.5	0.0	17.1	31.9	53.5	67.6	15.6	373	73.2
Pembroke town (Washington)	840	788	-6.2	866	90.3	0.0	0.2	8.8	0.7	17.9	30.4	53.4	44.2	23.8	404	86.4
Penobscot town (Hancock)	1,263	1,222	-3.2	1,225	89.9	0.0	1.0	8.7	0.5	17.4	32.4	51.7	38.4	36.7	575	86.4
Penobscot Indian Island Reservation (Aroostook)	-	-	-	-	-	-	-	-	-	-	-	-	-	-	-	-
Penobscot Indian Island Reservation (Penobscot)	610	585	-4.1	758	13.7	0.0	1.1	81.4	3.8	24.5	19.7	39.8	38.3	24.0	328	90.5
Perham town (Aroostook)	386	365	-5.4	394	92.9	0.5	0.0	5.6	1.0	18.3	23.4	48.3	51.0	18.5	163	82.2
Perkins UT (Sagadahoc)	-	-	-	-	-	-	-	-	-	-	-	-	-	-	-	-
Perry town (Washington)	889	927	4.3	708	85.5	0.0	1.3	8.6	4.7	19.8	27.5	50.0	41.6	29.8	315	84.1
Peru town (Oxford)	1,543	1,511	-2.1	1,386	98.8	0.0	0.9	0.3	0.0	13.1	18.8	51.0	44.3	17.5	560	91.8
Phillips town (Franklin)	1,028	1,022	-0.6	1,035	96.5	0.0	0.0	2.3	1.2	18.0	29.9	54.1	54.6	16.3	445	84.0
Phippsburg town (Sagadahoc)	2,216	2,268	2.3	2,101	97.2	0.0	0.0	1.9	0.9	15.3	29.2	55.9	38.6	34.0	990	89.8
Pittsfield CDP	3,150	-	-	2,958	90.2	1.0	0.0	1.3	7.5	23.1	20.4	40.1	47.2	19.5	1,245	87.2
Pittsfield town (Somerset)	4,215	3,994	-5.2	4,006	91.2	0.9	0.0	2.4	5.5	21.7	19.7	44.3	49.8	19.0	1,610	89.1
Pittston town (Kennebec)	2,672	2,735	2.4	2,671	98.1	0.1	0.2	0.5	1.2	22.6	13.3	44.4	46.7	17.3	1,103	84.7
Pleasant Ridge plantation (Somerset)	93	89	-4.3	72	100.0	0.0	0.0	0.0	0.0	2.8	62.5	74.2	69.4	6.5	40	67.5
Plymouth town (Penobscot)	1,359	1,350	-0.7	1,219	94.3	0.0	0.7	4.6	0.4	23.7	19.4	44.8	45.8	13.1	483	87.4
Poland town (Androscoggin)	5,376	5,647	5.0	5,588	95.5	0.0	0.0	4.3	0.2	20.9	15.1	44.7	46.8	20.5	2,234	91.1
Portage Lake town (Aroostook)	391	372	-4.9	376	94.9	0.5	0.0	2.9	1.6	16.0	38.3	61.3	49.4	17.7	192	88.0
Porter town (Oxford)	1,498	1,520	1.5	1,427	94.5	0.0	0.2	4.4	0.8	12.5	21.7	52.3	62.5	9.0	556	84.4
Portland city & MCD (Cumberland)	66,191	66,215	0.0	66,595	82.3	8.3	3.5	3.0	3.0	15.6	14.8	36.8	23.0	52.6	30,422	91.9
Pownal town (Cumberland)	1,462	1,549	6.0	1,635	91.3	0.0	0.4	7.0	1.3	17.6	19.8	46.2	29.1	44.1	590	96.9
Prentiss UT (Penobscot)	214	205	-4.2	265	98.1	0.0	0.0	0.0	1.9	26.0	7.5	37.8	53.6	10.8	104	82.7
Presque Isle city & MCD (Aroostook)	9,692	9,007	-7.1	9,116	91.9	0.7	1.3	4.8	1.3	19.9	19.2	41.6	39.2	25.4	4,058	83.1
Princeton town (Washington)	832	792	-4.8	622	93.9	0.0	0.0	5.1	1.0	19.3	17.4	48.6	57.1	13.6	296	84.1
Prospect town (Waldo)	706	746	5.7	739	95.5	0.4	0.0	3.5	0.5	14.7	15.7	49.4	56.4	20.6	351	93.4

1 May be of any race.

Table A. All Places — **Population and Housing**

STATE City, town, township, borough, or CDP (county if applicable)	Population				Race and Hispanic or Latino origin (percent)					Age (percent)			Educational attainment of persons age 25 and older		Occupied housing units	
	2010 census total population	2019 estimated population	Percent change 2010–2019	ACS total population estimate 2015–2019	White alone, not Hispanic or Latino	Black alone, not Hispanic or Latino	Asian alone, not Hispanic or Latino	All other races or 2 or more races, not Hispanic or Latino	Hispanic or Latino[1]	Under 18 years old	Age 65 years and older	Median age	Percent High school diploma or less	Percent Bachelor's degree or more	Total	Percent with a computer
	1	2	3	4	5	6	7	8	9	10	11	12	13	14	15	16
MAINE—Con.																
Randolph town & CDP (Kennebec)..............	1,772	1,709	-3.6	1,921	94.5	0.5	3.0	0.7	1.4	18.4	20.2	44.2	55.7	16.7	858	88.0
Rangeley town (Franklin)..	1,171	1,155	-1.4	1,047	100.0	0.0	0.0	0.0	0.0	18.3	18.0	54.8	42.9	24.1	452	89.6
Rangeley plantation (Franklin).................	189	181	-4.2	145	100.0	0.0	0.0	0.0	0.0	7.6	58.6	68.2	25.4	41.0	73	67.1
Raymond town (Cumberland)................	4,429	4,523	2.1	4,500	97.0	0.2	0.0	0.0	2.8	17.6	19.1	47.7	23.0	43.5	1,874	93.8
Readfield town (Kennebec).................	2,594	2,571	-0.9	2,556	96.4	0.4	0.0	1.2	2.0	21.3	15.6	46.5	38.1	40.4	1,010	93.3
Reed plantation (Aroostook)................	157	144	-8.3	116	100.0	0.0	0.0	0.0	0.0	12.1	26.7	56.5	67.7	3.0	66	83.3
Richmond CDP................	1,760	-		1,671	91.1	0.0	0.0	4.2	4.7	18.7	19.3	47.3	31.8	32.2	842	88.6
Richmond town (Sagadahoc)................	3,411	3,470	1.7	3,423	93.7	0.0	0.0	4.0	2.3	18.8	17.4	45.9	42.1	25.5	1,640	91.1
Ripley town (Somerset)	488	471	-3.5	467	100.0	0.0	0.0	0.0	0.0	14.1	26.6	53.7	55.6	22.4	210	79.5
Robbinston town (Washington)...............	574	559	-2.6	571	99.1	0.0	0.0	0.9	0.0	11.7	31.0	55.3	45.9	27.2	237	86.5
Rockland city & MCD (Knox)...................	7,301	7,165	-1.9	7,178	95.6	0.0	1.1	1.9	1.4	18.3	23.1	45.2	42.6	33.1	3,486	88.4
Rockport town (Knox).......	3,329	3,363	1.0	3,372	94.9	0.4	1.3	0.8	2.6	18.1	26.5	49.2	28.5	51.0	1,356	97.6
Rome town (Kennebec)....	1,006	1,007	0.1	990	96.7	0.6	0.0	1.1	1.6	23.3	21.3	45.0	36.9	36.5	407	88.9
Roque Bluffs town (Washington)...............	307	296	-3.6	384	87.2	5.2	0.0	1.0	6.5	15.6	25.5	52.3	41.9	33.5	154	86.4
Roxbury town (Oxford)......	370	361	-2.4	337	100.0	0.0	0.0	0.0	0.0	9.8	34.1	59.2	58.8	9.0	150	92.0
Rumford CDP................	4,218	-		3,672	95.3	0.5	1.3	1.9	1.0	10.4	23.6	55.1	50.9	17.9	1,644	82.2
Rumford town (Oxford)	5,839	5,744	-1.6	5,719	95.9	0.9	1.0	1.5	0.8	9.1	22.9	54.5	47.7	19.1	2,389	83.4
Sabattus town (Androscoggin)............	4,878	5,036	3.2	5,000	94.9	0.7	0.0	4.4	0.0	20.4	21.3	46.6	51.5	19.6	2,153	93.8
Saco city & MCD (York)....	18,495	19,964	7.9	19,497	94.8	0.8	0.7	2.3	1.5	20.2	17.1	41.6	32.3	39.4	7,953	92.7
St. Agatha town (Aroostook)................	747	713	-4.6	764	98.6	0.0	0.0	0.4	1.0	14.1	30.6	56.9	57.8	17.6	359	83.6
St. Albans town (Somerset)................	2,009	1,961	-2.4	1,934	98.7	0.0	1.0	0.2	0.2	21.9	19.0	44.8	48.3	13.5	766	93.1
St. Francis town (Aroostook)................	485	442	-8.9	368	98.6	0.0	0.0	1.4	0.0	17.9	24.5	49.4	62.7	9.7	186	83.3
St. George town (Knox)	2,588	2,574	-0.5	2,581	97.3	0.0	0.0	2.7	0.0	16.0	38.8	60.9	34.4	33.3	1,182	89.3
St. John plantation (Aroostook)................	267	249	-6.7	263	87.8	0.0	0.4	11.8	0.0	12.9	31.6	55.1	59.5	9.3	142	71.8
Sandy River plantation (Franklin).................	133	128	-3.8	179	90.5	0.0	0.0	0.0	9.5	17.3	30.2	58.1	27.7	40.5	71	100.0
Sanford city & MCD (York)	20,793	21,223	2.1	21,073	91.7	1.0	2.5	3.1	1.8	22.4	16.9	40.5	48.6	19.4	8,908	88.2
Sangerville town (Piscataquis)............	1,343	1,269	-5.5	1,423	98.0	0.0	0.0	0.0	2.0	13.1	26.7	53.8	67.1	17.1	585	81.9
Scarborough CDP	4,403	-	-	4,603	86.9	0.3	9.9	1.3	1.6	21.3	27.3	47.5	32.9	49.8	2,026	89.7
Scarborough town (Cumberland)................	18,919	20,991	11.0	20,146	90.8	0.2	4.8	2.4	1.8	21.1	22.1	48.1	25.0	54.5	8,101	93.9
Searsmont town (Waldo)..	1,390	1,417	1.9	1,323	95.5	0.9	1.1	0.7	1.7	19.9	25.2	47.6	48.9	25.2	532	89.8
Searsport CDP	992	-		1,185	93.1	0.0	0.0	1.9	5.1	18.2	35.1	53.2	38.8	18.6	669	79.7
Searsport town (Waldo)....	2,616	2,634	0.7	2,645	94.5	0.0	0.0	0.8	4.7	17.4	25.2	49.8	36.7	15.5	1,377	77.1
Sebago town (Cumberland)................	1,720	1,829	6.3	1,600	96.9	0.2	0.0	1.9	1.1	16.8	25.9	49.1	41.4	27.3	699	92.1
Sebec town (Piscataquis).	630	592	-6.0	615	89.6	0.0	1.1	7.5	1.8	17.1	21.5	49.1	49.5	18.2	236	85.6
Seboeis plantation (Penobscot)................	35	34	-2.9	69	100.0	0.0	0.0	0.0	0.0	20.3	13.0	36.3	44.4	13.0	21	100.0
Seboomook Lake UT (Somerset)................	43	41	-4.7	26	100.0	0.0	0.0	0.0	0.0	0.0	0.0	50.0	0.0	13	100.0
Sedgwick town (Hancock)	1,196	1,176	-1.7	1,281	95.6	0.3	1.2	1.5	1.4	16.5	21.5	47.5	41.9	37.3	525	86.3
Shapleigh town (York).......	2,667	2,754	3.3	2,726	98.5	0.4	0.2	1.0	0.0	21.3	16.7	45.0	41.9	15.6	1,072	94.5
Sherman town (Aroostook)	846	778	-8.0	920	93.0	2.7	0.0	3.3	1.0	16.3	23.6	50.3	48.1	18.3	359	82.2
Shirley town (Piscataquis)	233	225	-3.4	169	98.8	0.0	0.0	1.2	0.0	10.1	37.9	54.7	46.7	24.4	81	65.4
Sidney town (Kennebec)...	4,228	4,468	5.7	4,360	98.1	0.6	0.0	0.4	0.9	22.4	13.9	39.6	39.1	28.4	1,655	95.3
Skowhegan CDP	6,297	-		6,313	92.1	0.1	1.3	4.6	1.8	21.3	26.8	46.5	53.2	14.4	2,799	82.0
Skowhegan town (Somerset)................	8,584	8,239	-4.0	8,260	92.9	0.1	1.6	3.9	1.5	20.8	25.2	46.3	50.4	17.2	3,674	83.7
Smithfield town (Somerset)................	1,030	1,009	-2.0	942	96.1	0.0	0.0	2.8	1.2	16.3	23.6	50.3	39.4	32.5	415	88.9
Smyrna town (Aroostook).	442	418	-5.4	539	89.8	0.0	0.0	6.9	3.3	30.8	17.3	37.3	58.1	15.0	183	65.0
Solon town (Somerset)......	1,058	1,076	1.7	857	98.5	0.0	0.0	1.2	0.4	19.3	23.5	52.3	44.9	15.6	374	93.3
Somerville town (Lincoln) .	548	565	3.1	543	89.3	1.7	2.0	4.1	2.9	20.3	16.2	46.2	44.9	25.5	226	88.1
Sorrento town (Hancock)..	274	268	-2.2	246	93.5	0.0	0.8	5.7	0.0	19.1	37.8	58.8	31.2	43.7	112	90.2
South Aroostook UT (Aroostook)................	386	356	-7.8	438	95.2	4.8	0.0	0.0	0.0	13.9	34.5	58.1	63.1	4.8	208	90.9
South Berwick town (York)	7,213	7,565	4.9	7,470	89.5	0.6	1.9	4.9	3.1	26.3	13.0	40.3	25.5	44.1	2,785	98.5
South Bristol town (Lincoln).................	894	878	-1.8	909	97.5	0.0	0.0	1.1	1.4	11.4	37.3	57.0	37.2	45.4	436	92.4
Southeast Piscataquis UT (Piscataquis)............	253	240	-5.1	275	94.9	0.0	1.1	4.0	0.0	5.5	41.8	59.4	72.7	6.9	125	63.2
South Eliot CDP..............	3,550	-	-	3,160	94.3	0.5	0.0	0.0	5.2	18.8	22.8	47.8	22.4	43.3	1,436	93.5
South Franklin UT (Franklin).................	69	66	-4.3	36	100.0	0.0	0.0	0.0	0.0	36.1	11.1	42.0	21.7	21.7	12	75.0
South Oxford UT (Oxford).	580	569	-1.9	585	96.4	0.7	0.0	1.9	1.0	26.0	16.6	47.5	70.8	13.0	218	62.8
South Paris CDP	2,267	-		2,319	91.3	0.0	0.0	0.8	7.9	24.6	22.7	43.4	49.8	10.8	997	77.9
Southport town (Lincoln) ..	606	600		514	97.5	0.0	0.0	1.9	0.6	7.8	52.5	65.4	25.9	52.7	278	85.6
South Portland city & MCD (Cumberland).......	25,022	25,532	2.0	25,548	88.2	4.1	1.6	3.2	2.8	17.9	16.7	41.9	26.1	45.7	10,856	93.4
South Thomaston town (Knox)...................	1,563	1,614	3.3	1,248	96.7	0.0	0.0	2.2	1.0	17.2	27.6	50.7	37.3	30.4	562	88.8
Southwest Harbor CDP	720	-		647	99.7	0.0	0.0	0.0	0.3	19.0	31.2	53.9	27.3	51.6	324	77.2
Southwest Harbor town (Hancock)................	1,769	1,792	1.3	1,491	99.1	0.0	0.0	0.5	0.4	15.7	34.2	58.3	32.6	45.9	673	86.3
South Windham CDP........	1,374	-	-	1,119	74.1	5.2	1.2	16.3	3.3	9.6	11.9	34.5	61.1	9.4	216	95.4

1 May be of any race.

Table A. All Places — **Population and Housing**

STATE City, town, township, borough, or CDP (county if applicable)	2010 census total population	2019 estimated population	Percent change 2010–2019	ACS total population estimate 2015–2019	White alone, not Hispanic or Latino	Black alone, not Hispanic or Latino	Asian alone, not Hispanic or Latino	All other races or 2 or more races, not Hispanic or Latino	Hispanic or Latino[1]	Under 18 years old	Age 65 years and older	Median age	Percent High school diploma or less	Percent Bachelor's degree or more	Total	Percent with a computer
	1	2	3	4	5	6	7	8	9	10	11	12	13	14	15	16
MAINE—Con.																
Springfield town (Penobscot)..................	409	425	3.9	320	97.2	0.0	0.0	0.0	2.8	12.5	29.7	56.4	58.6	5.7	145	75.9
Square Lake UT (Aroostook)	591	545	-7.8	501	91.6	0.0	0.0	7.4	1.0	6.0	47.7	62.5	39.8	32.0	255	89.0
Stacyville town (Penobscot)	395	383	-3.0	436	98.6	0.0	0.0	1.4	0.0	25.5	13.8	41.9	43.0	5.7	170	77.1
Standish CDP..............	469	-	-	219	100.0	0.0	0.0	0.0	0.0	0.0	79.0	71.9	20.5	37.0	172	74.4
Standish town (Cumberland)..............	9,872	10,099	2.3	10,078	97.4	0.6	0.3	0.8	0.9	19.8	15.0	35.9	31.4	30.7	3,402	94.3
Starks town (Somerset)....	637	636	-0.2	542	95.4	0.0	0.0	4.6	0.0	15.9	19.9	47.6	53.8	17.9	251	80.5
Steep Falls CDP..........	1,139	-	-	1,683	99.9	0.0	0.0	0.1	0.0	26.0	3.4	31.6	24.8	24.9	483	96.7
Stetson town (Penobscot).	1,200	1,190	-0.8	1,559	99.1	0.3	0.0	0.3	0.3	24.4	15.1	42.5	53.2	21.1	555	89.2
Steuben town (Washington)..............	1,131	1,132	0.1	1,227	96.8	0.6	0.7	1.1	0.9	22.0	24.1	48.0	47.0	30.1	558	85.5
Stockholm town (Aroostook)	253	232	-8.3	256	85.9	5.9	0.0	8.2	0.0	22.7	16.8	44.1	37.9	21.9	101	89.1
Stockton Springs town (Waldo)	1,594	1,626	2.0	1,730	96.6	0.3	1.0	1.8	0.3	8.7	37.0	59.3	33.8	40.6	827	93.2
Stoneham town (Oxford)...	239	248	3.8	272	98.5	0.0	0.0	1.5	0.0	16.2	27.6	50.8	49.1	22.7	111	88.3
Stonington town (Hancock)..................	1,043	1,032	-1.1	1,063	95.4	0.5	0.0	2.1	2.1	17.9	26.4	53.4	51.1	17.8	481	87.5
Stow town (Oxford)..........	385	456	18.4	448	90.2	2.5	0.0	4.5	2.9	18.8	20.5	46.6	50.5	22.7	142	83.8
Strong town (Franklin)......	1,213	1,160	-4.4	1,346	98.7	0.0	0.0	0.5	0.7	27.4	16.8	43.5	48.2	13.5	471	83.7
Sullivan town (Hancock)....	1,236	1,266	2.4	1,317	94.3	0.0	0.0	4.6	1.1	22.3	18.7	46.0	43.7	26.8	489	90.8
Sumner town (Oxford)	939	919	-2.1	1,106	93.4	0.0	0.6	4.2	1.8	23.9	19.2	40.6	51.2	16.3	354	91.0
Surry town (Hancock).......	1,471	1,502	2.1	1,712	97.1	0.2	0.5	0.6	1.6	15.1	27.0	52.1	28.2	44.2	771	94.3
Swans Island town (Hancock).................	330	324	-1.8	449	95.8	0.2	3.1	0.7	0.2	21.8	24.3	52.6	40.7	39.8	189	88.9
Swanville town (Waldo).....	1,383	1,351	-2.3	1,269	94.2	2.0	0.0	2.8	1.0	22.4	16.1	41.6	53.7	20.4	561	93.4
Sweden town (Oxford)......	398	410	3.0	453	94.3	0.0	2.0	1.3	2.4	19.4	21.0	48.6	37.7	35.0	183	86.9
Talmadge town (Washington)..................	64	61	-4.7	70	100.0	0.0	0.0	0.0	0.0	27.1	28.6	44.3	55.1	6.1	26	80.8
Temple town (Franklin)	528	517	-2.1	584	82.5	0.0	3.6	0.0	13.9	18.2	22.3	45.9	42.9	22.9	237	74.3
The Forks plantation (Somerset)	37	35	-5.4	23	100.0	0.0	0.0	0.0	0.0	13.0	39.1	49.8	47.1	17.6	13	100.0
Thomaston CDP..............	1,875	-	-	1,967	89.8	1.4	0.0	4.0	4.7	22.7	26.5	39.4	35.9	27.5	887	95.2
Thomaston town (Knox)....	2,781	2,745	-1.3	2,760	90.9	1.0	0.0	2.9	5.3	18.2	23.1	44.8	38.9	25.7	1,252	92.1
Thorndike town (Waldo)....	889	893	0.4	805	97.0	0.2	0.0	2.0	0.7	21.2	14.0	41.6	47.7	25.0	326	90.8
Topsfield town (Washington)..................	237	225	-5.1	236	95.3	0.0	0.0	4.7	0.0	12.7	21.2	52.5	61.9	15.3	98	98.0
Topsham CDP	5,931	-	-	6,222	93.3	0.0	2.0	1.5	3.3	16.9	27.1	48.0	31.4	43.3	2,782	92.9
Topsham town (Sagadahoc)	8,785	8,878	1.1	8,810	91.6	0.7	1.9	2.9	2.9	16.8	24.2	47.9	31.4	43.5	3,870	91.8
Tremont town (Hancock)...	1,563	1,599	2.3	1,565	95.6	0.0	0.0	1.0	3.4	18.0	23.5	49.9	41.3	34.2	711	87.2
Trenton town (Hancock)....	1,483	1,558	5.1	1,863	91.8	1.0	4.6	2.4	0.2	17.1	19.2	45.6	35.7	33.3	792	96.0
Troy town (Waldo)	1,024	1,047	2.2	960	95.1	0.1	0.0	4.2	0.6	23.1	15.7	43.1	40.2	29.8	404	88.1
Turner town (Androscoggin)	5,735	5,846	1.9	5,784	91.2	0.1	0.6	2.4	5.8	22.6	16.0	45.7	41.7	27.5	2,308	89.8
Twombly Ridge UT (Penobscot).................	-	-	-	-	-	-	-	-	-	-	-	-	-	-	-	-
Union town (Knox)	2,259	2,255	-0.2	2,741	94.2	0.5	0.6	3.3	1.4	22.2	18.2	42.1	45.5	24.5	966	87.7
Unity UT (Kennebec)........	43	42	-2.3	48	100.0	0.0	0.0	0.0	0.0	31.3	16.7	39.5	48.5	51.5	19	94.7
Unity CDP....................	469	-	-	377	92.6	2.1	0.0	5.3	0.0	22.0	20.2	42.9	55.8	24.7	205	87.8
Unity town (Waldo)	2,105	2,133	1.3	2,325	93.0	1.4	1.0	2.5	2.1	19.1	13.8	28.2	51.0	24.1	842	84.1
Upton town (Oxford)	113	110	-2.7	48	95.8	0.0	0.0	4.2	0.0	0.0	52.1	65.3	52.1	31.3	28	85.7
Van Buren CDP	1,937	-	-	1,683	95.2	2.7	1.0	0.4	0.7	9.5	27.9	55.3	59.8	9.5	773	77.2
Van Buren town (Aroostook)	2,171	1,999	-7.9	1,926	95.8	2.4	0.8	0.4	0.6	9.8	29.2	54.3	57.7	8.6	872	77.9
Vanceboro town (Washington)..................	140	133	-5.0	144	94.4	5.6	0.0	0.0	0.0	9.0	26.4	58.5	73.0	3.3	72	81.9
Vassalboro town (Kennebec).................	4,356	4,368	0.3	4,341	94.2	0.0	0.3	3.4	2.1	19.1	17.3	44.9	41.0	21.0	1,866	88.7
Veazie town (Penobscot)..	1,919	1,832	-4.5	1,999	95.7	0.3	0.1	3.6	0.5	21.0	19.0	44.7	27.1	45.0	846	92.9
Verona Island town (Hancock).................	545	553	1.5	625	94.9	0.0	0.0	2.9	2.2	23.4	22.1	48.1	53.2	19.2	249	93.6
Vienna town (Kennebec)..	570	573	0.5	482	88.2	0.0	0.4	1.9	9.5	19.1	24.3	47.4	37.6	42.3	207	92.8
Vinalhaven town (Knox)....	1,165	1,127	-3.3	905	98.0	0.0	0.0	0.2	1.8	7.4	27.5	54.8	39.6	30.6	438	88.4
Wade town (Aroostook)	283	263	-7.1	348	91.1	0.0	3.2	4.0	1.7	20.7	24.4	47.8	42.2	11.4	142	71.8
Waite town (Washington)..	101	95	-5.9	53	100.0	0.0	0.0	0.0	0.0	22.6	18.9	54.2	34.1	31.7	24	91.7
Waldo town (Waldo).........	770	864	12.2	882	93.2	0.2	0.0	2.9	3.6	23.4	17.2	42.1	43.5	22.5	358	90.8
Waldoboro CDP...............	1,233	-	-	1,295	100.0	0.0	0.0	0.0	0.0	18.0	38.2	60.3	63.3	19.6	742	82.3
Waldoboro town (Lincoln).	5,075	5,069	-0.1	5,009	98.6	0.0	0.0	1.4	0.0	16.5	27.6	52.4	53.0	28.2	2,401	89.9
Wales town (Androscoggin)..............	1,607	1,617	0.6	1,752	90.8	0.0	0.0	6.0	3.2	30.8	11.4	37.5	48.7	19.2	592	98.0
Wallagrass town (Aroostook)	547	525	-4.0	589	94.4	2.5	0.0	2.4	0.7	20.2	20.4	39.4	53.7	19.8	240	86.7
Waltham town (Hancock)..	353	339	-4.0	369	98.9	0.0	0.0	1.1	0.0	17.9	25.5	49.7	60.8	16.0	146	81.5
Warren town (Knox)	4,751	4,844	2.0	4,751	91.3	1.4	0.4	5.3	1.7	16.3	11.1	42.7	54.1	18.5	1,491	97.9
Washburn CDP................	997	-	-	1,058	97.4	0.0	0.0	2.6	0.0	14.7	26.9	49.8	60.9	8.0	461	85.9
Washburn town (Aroostook)	1,687	1,541	-8.7	1,585	98.3	0.0	0.0	1.7	0.0	16.6	24.4	49.7	58.5	10.9	676	82.1
Washington town (Knox)....	1,527	1,514	-0.9	1,454	95.3	0.0	1.8	1.9	1.1	18.8	17.7	47.1	51.3	23.4	596	90.6
Waterboro town (York).....	7,692	7,969	3.6	7,846	95.3	0.6	0.0	2.7	1.4	24.1	10.7	38.0	41.8	19.4	2,687	97.0
Waterford town (Oxford) ...	1,549	1,590	2.6	1,518	97.3	0.5	0.3	1.7	0.2	14.1	26.9	49.5	47.0	16.7	605	90.1
Waterville city & MCD (Kennebec).................	15,719	16,558	5.3	16,577	92.1	0.8	2.6	2.1	2.4	19.9	19.7	39.7	37.3	31.1	6,953	81.4
Wayne town (Kennebec)...	1,189	1,156	-2.8	1,104	98.7	0.0	0.4	0.5	0.4	20.5	25.7	50.2	21.2	43.7	473	90.7
Webster plantation (Penobscot).................	85	81	-4.7	63	98.4	1.6	0.0	0.0	0.0	0.0	22.2	52.5	73.0	3.2	29	65.5
Weld town (Franklin)........	419	417	-0.5	383	99.0	0.0	0.0	1.0	0.0	8.6	36.8	58.4	37.0	25.2	179	82.1
Wellington town (Piscataquis)	260	245	-5.8	183	100.0	0.0	0.0	0.0	0.0	18.6	31.7	55.5	66.4	11.6	85	78.8

1 May be of any race.

Table A. All Places — **Population and Housing**

STATE City, town, township, borough, or CDP (county if applicable)	Population				Race and Hispanic or Latino origin (percent)					Age (percent)			Educational attainment of persons age 25 and older		Occupied housing units	
	2010 census total population	2019 estimated population	Percent change 2010–2019	ACS total population estimate 2015–2019	White alone, not Hispanic or Latino	Black alone, not Hispanic or Latino	Asian alone, not Hispanic or Latino	All other races or 2 or more races, not Hispanic or Latino	Hispanic or Latino[1]	Under 18 years old	Age 65 years and older	Median age	Percent High school diploma or less	Percent Bachelor's degree or more	Total	Percent with a computer
	1	2	3	4	5	6	7	8	9	10	11	12	13	14	15	16
MAINE—Con.																
Wells town (York)	9,589	10,675	11.3	10,366	93.2	1.0	1.8	0.8	3.2	17.1	26.7	51.7	32.9	37.7	4,593	88.8
Wesley town (Washington)	98	93	-5.1	130	100.0	0.0	0.0	0.0	0.0	11.5	28.5	51.3	57.0	17.0	59	81.4
West Bath town (Sagadahoc)	1,879	1,924	2.4	2,216	92.4	3.1	1.2	0.7	2.6	21.3	18.8	46.9	35.1	44.9	966	91.2
Westbrook city & MCD (Cumberland)	17,520	19,074	8.9	18,633	88.6	4.9	2.0	3.0	1.5	17.8	17.0	38.8	37.8	32.3	8,073	90.6
West Central Franklin UT (Franklin)	-	-	-	-	-	-	-	-	-	-	-	-	-	-	-	-
Westfield town (Aroostook)	549	509	-7.3	660	97.6	0.5	0.0	2.0	0.0	7.7	23.8	56.7	59.3	8.7	217	88.5
West Forks plantation (Somerset)	60	58	-3.3	28	100.0	0.0	0.0	0.0	0.0	10.7	28.6	32.7	72.0	16.0	18	55.6
West Gardiner town (Kennebec)	3,481	3,364	-3.4	3,380	90.5	0.4	1.1	2.6	5.4	23.4	13.4	40.2	47.4	28.1	1,222	96.4
West Kennebunk CDP	1,176	-	-	993	87.1	0.0	12.0	0.9	0.0	16.9	14.2	46.4	32.0	42.0	379	100.0
Westmanland town (Aroostook)	62	57	-8.1	59	100.0	0.0	0.0	0.0	0.0	6.8	54.2	66.2	27.3	23.6	29	86.2
Weston town (Aroostook)	229	210	-8.3	190	100.0	0.0	0.0	0.0	0.0	14.2	37.9	59.3	54.2	20.9	90	83.3
West Paris town (Oxford)	1,811	1,691	-6.6	2,339	94.8	0.2	0.0	4.1	0.9	22.9	19.4	41.1	63.8	8.5	708	85.5
Westport Island town (Lincoln)	715	730	2.1	660	96.8	0.6	0.0	0.6	2.0	14.5	29.4	55.8	33.0	42.6	302	95.0
Whitefield town (Lincoln)	2,294	2,280	-0.6	2,389	94.3	0.4	2.1	2.9	0.3	22.5	13.8	41.8	44.5	24.2	959	89.4
Whiting town (Washington)	489	480	-1.8	378	95.2	0.0	0.0	4.8	0.0	14.3	26.5	51.3	30.9	38.9	172	89.5
Whitney UT (Penobscot)	5	5	-	-	-	-	-	-	-	-	-	-	-	-	-	-
Whitneyville town (Washington)	216	204	-5.6	144	100.0	0.0	0.0	0.0	0.0	11.8	22.2	56.0	45.2	17.7	67	86.6
Willimantic town (Piscataquis)	150	141	-6.0	101	100.0	0.0	0.0	0.0	0.0	3.0	39.6	57.9	46.8	25.5	52	71.2
Wilton CDP	2,198	-	-	1,950	96.6	0.0	0.0	3.4	0.0	18.1	18.9	47.1	59.2	15.4	844	71.6
Wilton town (Franklin)	4,116	3,960	-3.8	3,959	98.3	0.0	0.0	1.7	0.0	16.9	23.6	49.3	49.2	19.8	1,612	83.6
Windham town (Cumberland)	16,997	18,540	9.1	18,195	93.3	1.3	1.0	3.7	0.7	19.5	15.4	41.8	32.7	33.8	6,786	94.1
Windsor town (Kennebec)	2,575	2,609	1.3	2,592	92.3	0.6	0.0	6.4	0.7	17.6	17.4	43.5	52.4	15.9	1,052	91.4
Winn town (Penobscot)	411	406	-1.2	442	89.1	0.9	1.1	8.8	0.0	23.3	15.6	45.9	60.1	11.7	185	94.1
Winslow CDP	7,794	-	-	4,928	95.4	1.1	0.4	0.8	2.4	19.9	20.9	42.6	41.1	22.7	2,230	89.0
Winslow town (Kennebec)	7,801	7,618	-2.3	7,602	94.6	0.7	1.6	1.3	1.8	21.5	18.2	43.7	41.2	24.3	3,227	88.8
Winter Harbor CDP	426	-	-	286	98.3	0.0	0.0	0.0	1.7	17.1	43.4	61.1	49.8	23.8	160	90.0
Winter Harbor town (Hancock)	511	511	0.0	403	96.8	0.0	0.0	0.0	1.2	12.2	38.0	60.2	49.8	25.4	210	89.0
Winterport CDP	1,340	-	-	1,242	94.8	0.8	0.0	4.3	0.0	16.5	26.6	45.8	38.4	40.4	546	95.1
Winterport town (Waldo)	3,759	3,985	6.0	3,931	96.0	0.3	0.6	3.1	0.0	19.1	16.1	45.5	48.3	28.5	1,626	91.5
Winterville plantation (Aroostook)	224	207	-7.6	145	100.0	0.0	0.0	0.0	0.0	11.0	38.6	59.8	52.0	16.3	74	78.4
Winthrop CDP	2,650	-	-	2,467	96.4	0.0	0.0	3.6	0.0	15.5	28.5	51.9	27.4	29.1	1,158	95.2
Winthrop town (Kennebec)	6,093	5,993	-1.6	5,983	92.4	4.8	0.2	1.8	0.7	18.0	23.1	51.0	30.1	36.3	2,652	93.1
Wiscasset CDP	1,097	-	-	1,220	98.5	0.0	0.0	1.5	0.0	10.2	28.0	47.2	60.4	24.9	617	86.9
Wiscasset town (Lincoln)	3,732	3,763	0.8	3,697	96.1	0.1	0.0	2.5	1.4	16.0	20.4	45.9	55.8	21.1	1,567	88.3
Woodland town (Aroostook)	1,213	1,143	-5.8	998	90.9	1.1	1.2	4.8	2.0	16.6	23.2	49.7	50.9	17.8	456	81.6
Woodland CDP	952	-	-	990	87.5	0.0	0.0	12.0	0.5	20.0	21.4	45.2	45.4	15.0	416	93.0
Woodstock town (Oxford)	1,278	1,296	1.4	1,188	97.6	0.0	0.0	0.3	2.0	17.5	20.7	48.7	46.5	22.0	457	87.5
Woodville town (Penobscot)	248	236	-4.8	209	96.7	0.0	0.0	3.3	0.0	20.6	9.6	43.6	49.0	13.1	81	91.4
Woolwich town (Sagadahoc)	3,072	3,181	3.5	3,105	97.2	0.0	2.1	0.5	0.3	19.2	19.2	45.7	40.9	30.4	1,279	92.4
Wyman UT (Franklin)	88	85	-3.4	102	94.1	0.0	0.0	5.9	0.0	3.9	29.4	58.3	6.1	38.8	27	100.0
Yarmouth CDP	5,869	-	-	5,681	91.3	0.8	4.8	2.3	0.9	20.8	23.5	47.8	20.8	64.8	2,319	90.3
Yarmouth town (Cumberland)	8,349	8,589	2.9	8,529	93.2	0.7	3.5	1.5	1.1	22.3	22.1	48.3	18.4	67.3	3,409	91.0
York town (York)	12,517	13,290	6.2	13,070	97.7	0.3	0.5	0.7	0.7	18.4	27.1	52.2	19.3	52.2	5,746	94.2
York Harbor CDP	3,033	-	-	2,522	94.5	0.0	1.9	2.2	1.5	14.7	37.5	56.3	21.4	51.6	1,230	80.5
MARYLAND	5,773,794	6,045,680	4.7	6,018,848	50.9	29.4	6.2	3.4	10.1	22.3	15.0	38.7	34.4	40.2	2,205,204	92.4
Aberdeen city	14,982	16,019	6.9	15,848	55.8	24.1	5.4	6.1	8.6	20.6	15.6	40.5	43.1	24.8	6,489	87.4
Aberdeen Proving Ground CDP	2,093	-	-	2,872	47.0	32.1	3.1	4.9	12.8	30.8	1.2	23.9	25.8	43.1	750	97.9
Accident town	325	312	-4.0	335	90.7	0.3	0.6	1.8	6.6	26.3	14.3	33.7	43.2	23.6	142	82.4
Accokeek CDP	10,573	-	-	11,647	21.0	61.5	7.4	6.1	4.0	20.1	14.0	45.0	28.7	41.3	4,154	96.0
Adamstown CDP	2,372	-	-	2,512	84.2	8.4	2.9	2.2	2.2	31.3	4.6	38.3	21.0	49.7	787	100.0
Adelphi CDP	15,086	-	-	16,377	11.3	34.5	6.0	1.4	46.8	23.2	10.5	33.7	48.6	29.3	4,933	95.9
Algonquin CDP	1,241	-	-	1,237	85.4	3.3	0.0	4.1	7.1	14.6	33.5	53.3	42.4	28.1	548	86.5
Allen CDP	210	-	-	453	100.0	0.0	0.0	0.0	0.0	0.0	14.1	56.5	0.0	48.3	129	100.0
Andrews AFB CDP	2,973	-	-	3,079	52.4	15.0	2.3	10.3	20.0	37.3	0.5	23.8	15.8	38.6	829	100.0
Annapolis city	38,335	39,223	2.3	39,278	51.9	21.2	1.8	2.3	22.7	21.7	15.5	37.3	31.8	47.2	15,775	91.3
Annapolis Neck CDP	10,950	-	-	12,551	83.5	9.0	0.7	3.2	3.5	20.4	22.2	49.5	11.8	68.8	5,096	98.4
Antietam CDP	89	-	-	77	100.0	0.0	0.0	0.0	0.0	0.0	0.0	58.5	64.9	13.0	42	100.0
Aquasco CDP	981	-	-	957	29.6	43.3	0.5	26.6	0.0	22.2	19.6	45.7	44.4	24.4	303	84.8
Arbutus CDP	20,483	-	-	19,292	77.2	6.7	9.7	3.7	2.7	20.1	13.5	36.8	42.4	28.0	7,400	93.9
Arden on the Severn CDP	1,953	-	-	1,880	72.2	10.2	0.0	6.5	11.2	21.2	18.1	48.6	29.1	46.4	698	98.0
Arnold CDP	23,106	-	-	23,406	86.0	3.8	3.1	3.2	3.9	26.6	15.6	40.6	18.2	55.6	8,397	97.7
Ashton-Sandy Spring CDP	5,628	-	-	5,997	60.3	18.1	9.6	3.7	8.3	25.2	19.6	43.5	20.1	54.8	1,948	92.7
Aspen Hill CDP	48,759	-	-	53,049	33.1	17.9	11.0	4.6	33.4	24.6	13.3	37.5	35.3	42.9	16,790	94.9
Baden CDP	2,128	-	-	1,743	43.1	35.4	0.0	6.5	14.9	16.2	16.8	46.5	47.2	27.8	652	89.7
Bagtown CDP	333	-	-	386	97.2	0.0	0.0	2.8	0.0	7.8	18.7	47.1	45.5	11.1	156	94.2
Bakersville CDP	30	-	-	53	100.0	0.0	0.0	0.0	0.0	41.5	0.0	31.6	77.4	0.0	7	100.0
Ballenger Creek CDP	18,274	-	-	21,080	57.5	15.8	7.3	4.3	15.0	24.3	9.2	35.9	28.3	40.2	8,024	95.4
Baltimore city	620,770	593,490	-4.4	609,032	27.5	61.8	2.6	2.9	5.3	20.7	13.6	35.4	43.9	31.9	239,116	85.7
Baltimore Highlands CDP	7,019	-	-	7,944	49.6	22.4	5.1	2.1	20.8	25.4	8.7	31.6	67.1	16.1	2,513	89.4
Barclay town	174	165	-5.2	275	26.2	26.9	0.0	0.0	46.9	19.6	4.4	25.3	82.4	11.3	64	79.7

1 May be of any race.

Table A. All Places — **Population and Housing**

STATE City, town, township, borough, or CDP (county if applicable)	Population: 2010 census total population	Population: 2019 estimated population	Population: Percent change 2010–2019	Population: ACS total population estimate 2015–2019	Race and Hispanic or Latino origin (percent): White alone, not Hispanic or Latino	Black alone, not Hispanic or Latino	Asian alone, not Hispanic or Latino	All other races or 2 or more races, not Hispanic or Latino	Hispanic or Latino[1]	Age (percent): Under 18 years old	Age 65 years and older	Median age	Educational attainment of persons age 25 and older: Percent High school diploma or less	Percent Bachelor's degree or more	Occupied housing units: Total	Percent with a computer
	1	2	3	4	5	6	7	8	9	10	11	12	13	14	15	16
MARYLAND—Con.																
Barnesville town	170	179	5.3	125	92.0	0.0	1.6	0.0	6.4	16.8	29.6	57.3	15.3	63.3	52	98.1
Barrelville CDP	73	-	-	83	100.0	0.0	0.0	0.0	0.0	0.0	14.5	30.9	73.0	0.0	20	100.0
Barton town	454	423	-6.8	441	96.4	0.0	0.0	3.6	0.0	21.3	20.9	37.0	61.5	4.5	186	83.3
Bartonsville CDP	1,451	-	-	1,707	80.0	6.3	4.6	1.8	7.4	26.0	14.9	41.7	30.6	44.2	541	95.0
Beaver Creek CDP	251	-	-	304	85.5	0.0	0.0	8.9	5.6	35.2	17.8	40.9	5.6	74.1	93	100.0
Bel Air CDP	1,258	-	-	1,579	93.9	0.6	0.0	5.4	0.0	30.1	16.1	32.7	43.9	40.4	620	80.6
Bel Air town	10,100	10,119	0.2	10,071	86.1	3.6	3.2	1.9	5.2	19.6	20.6	41.7	32.2	38.2	4,490	88.2
Bel Air North CDP	30,568	-	-	31,941	89.1	4.4	1.7	2.4	2.5	23.6	14.2	40.2	27.0	43.5	11,174	94.7
Bel Air South CDP	47,709	-	-	48,425	80.2	8.4	3.9	3.5	4.0	23.8	15.4	39.3	28.3	43.4	18,878	93.6
Beltsville CDP	16,772	-	-	17,812	23.0	31.3	9.9	2.2	33.7	25.3	15.6	36.0	38.2	36.4	5,683	92.0
Benedict CDP	261	-	-	203	76.4	0.0	0.0	23.6	0.0	0.0	100.0	82.9	63.5	0.0	138	55.1
Bensville CDP	-	-	-	13,227	34.5	52.3	5.2	3.8	4.2	22.4	11.1	41.1	28.2	40.0	4,418	98.8
Berlin town	4,452	4,866	9.3	4,657	78.9	15.6	2.5	0.8	2.2	27.9	18.1	42.3	37.7	30.2	1,830	87.4
Berwyn Heights town	3,123	3,255	4.2	3,273	40.9	11.8	10.7	4.2	32.3	17.5	14.3	40.6	37.4	37.4	992	97.7
Bethesda CDP	60,858	-	-	63,195	74.2	4.0	9.8	3.2	8.8	22.4	19.0	43.4	6.3	85.9	25,835	97.5
Betterton town	338	316	-6.5	431	77.5	9.0	0.0	12.3	1.2	28.3	19.5	38.4	41.0	39.7	183	89.1
Bier CDP	173	-	-	214	100.0	0.0	0.0	0.0	0.0	11.2	33.2	30.0	48.4	7.4	112	100.0
Big Pool CDP	82	-	-	88	100.0	0.0	0.0	0.0	0.0	20.5	20.5	55.5	38.6	61.4	35	74.3
Big Spring CDP	84	-	-	63	100.0	0.0	0.0	0.0	0.0	12.7	0.0	51.5	14.3	57.1	27	100.0
Bishopville CDP	531	-	-	774	97.7	2.3	0.0	0.0	0.0	25.1	16.9	45.3	55.7	15.9	249	92.8
Bivalve CDP	201	-	-	109	51.4	0.0	48.6	0.0	0.0	0.0	45.0	60.7	51.4	0.0	67	79.1
Bladensburg town	8,971	9,408	4.9	9,402	4.5	67.7	1.2	1.0	25.6	29.0	15.8	33.4	51.0	16.3	3,768	87.5
Bloomington CDP	305	-	-	192	80.7	0.0	12.0	7.3	0.0	14.6	18.2	53.1	58.5	26.8	91	92.3
Boonsboro town	3,458	3,655	5.7	3,556	84.7	5.4	2.2	4.4	3.3	27.2	17.3	40.1	34.2	31.7	1,432	80.8
Bowie city	55,296	58,643	6.1	58,481	31.1	52.1	5.1	4.5	7.2	21.8	14.8	42.7	25.1	48.2	20,983	96.1
Bowleys Quarters CDP	6,755	-	-	6,412	80.3	13.0	1.9	3.8	1.1	18.7	13.5	43.8	38.5	25.8	2,570	92.0
Bowling Green CDP	1,077	-	-	1,217	94.2	0.0	0.4	1.6	3.9	13.0	22.7	45.4	44.9	14.7	526	91.8
Bowmans Addition CDP	627	-	-	571	98.1	0.0	0.0	1.9	0.0	26.4	18.9	42.4	53.4	13.2	249	83.1
Braddock Heights CDP	2,608	-	-	2,910	84.1	1.8	4.8	0.0	9.3	20.9	23.9	46.6	22.8	51.0	1,099	95.2
Brandywine CDP	6,719	-	-	9,849	10.8	77.5	2.8	3.9	5.0	23.6	9.7	40.1	34.7	35.0	3,067	97.4
Breathedsville CDP	254	-	-	298	29.9	70.1	0.0	0.0	0.0	40.9	8.7	32.6	29.5	0.0	101	100.0
Brentwood town	3,341	3,471	3.9	3,476	13.4	24.3	3.0	1.2	58.2	27.5	10.1	32.4	56.8	26.0	1,018	92.5
Brock Hall CDP	9,552	-	-	12,117	4.3	86.9	2.1	3.4	3.2	23.7	9.1	39.6	19.5	53.2	4,211	97.9
Brookeville town	134	144	7.5	155	99.4	0.0	0.6	0.0	0.0	12.9	27.7	52.8	21.9	55.5	54	98.1
Brooklyn Park CDP	14,373	-	-	14,850	58.8	18.1	2.5	5.9	14.7	21.5	16.6	39.3	57.7	13.1	5,341	88.6
Brookmont CDP	3,468	-	-	3,921	77.3	0.0	6.5	6.5	9.6	29.0	16.0	45.8	5.0	90.7	1,359	98.9
Brookview town	60	58	-3.3	51	90.2	7.8	0.0	2.0	0.0	21.6	27.5	40.3	63.2	28.9	21	66.7
Broomes Island CDP	405	-	-	421	100.0	0.0	0.0	0.0	0.0	0.0	15.0	48.9	41.3	18.8	198	93.4
Brownsville CDP	89	-	-	31	100.0	0.0	0.0	0.0	0.0	35.5	32.3	59.5	50.0	0.0	10	100.0
Brunswick city	5,870	6,491	10.6	6,258	79.5	7.2	1.7	7.0	4.7	26.4	10.3	35.4	36.7	33.2	2,203	91.4
Bryans Road CDP	7,244	-	-	7,847	21.9	61.2	4.3	5.5	7.2	20.8	13.5	42.6	45.5	27.4	2,912	87.7
Bryantown CDP	655	-	-	637	85.4	10.7	0.0	0.0	3.9	19.9	38.1	52.4	37.3	39.8	231	89.2
Buckeystown CDP	1,019	-	-	1,286	84.6	0.9	1.4	5.2	7.9	9.1	54.4	68.3	23.8	49.5	607	82.2
Burkittsville town	151	165	9.3	151	94.0	0.0	0.0	3.3	2.6	19.9	17.9	45.9	25.5	51.9	69	85.5
Burtonsville CDP	8,323	-	-	9,823	21.5	45.4	19.2	4.2	9.7	22.9	10.6	38.9	25.0	51.6	2,860	98.6
Butlertown CDP	505	-	-	302	88.1	11.9	0.0	0.0	0.0	16.6	15.9	39.5	33.9	24.6	97	80.4
Cabin John CDP	2,280	-	-	2,121	70.8	4.3	13.2	2.6	9.1	25.9	20.6	48.6	0.0	91.2	857	98.4
California CDP	11,857	-	-	14,815	63.7	20.1	3.0	4.2	9.0	24.7	9.5	34.8	32.3	37.3	5,550	96.3
Calvert Beach CDP	808	-	-	960	90.8	1.8	1.7	4.7	1.0	27.6	16.0	34.2	46.2	20.3	321	97.2
Calverton CDP	17,724	-	-	16,888	22.6	46.9	14.8	2.8	12.8	18.3	24.1	45.8	27.7	49.3	6,319	93.2
Cambridge city	12,416	12,260	-1.3	12,375	39.8	44.0	1.9	7.0	7.3	24.9	16.8	37.3	51.3	20.3	5,047	83.6
Camp Springs CDP	19,096	-	-	21,841	8.9	75.8	1.5	2.3	11.4	20.0	15.6	40.1	37.1	29.4	7,590	94.6
Cape St. Claire CDP	8,747	-	-	8,729	89.3	1.7	2.0	4.0	3.0	23.2	15.0	41.3	16.9	51.2	3,251	96.6
Capitol Heights town	4,302	4,514	4.9	4,528	2.0	82.6	0.0	2.1	13.3	24.8	13.5	38.7	53.0	16.7	1,510	90.7
Carlos CDP	153	-	-	83	100.0	0.0	0.0	0.0	0.0	0.0	0.0	41.5	68.6	0.0	39	100.0
Carney CDP	29,941	-	-	30,289	64.3	19.3	10.4	2.4	3.7	21.6	22.7	39.5	31.5	37.7	12,948	90.1
Catonsville CDP	41,567	-	-	41,547	72.7	15.2	6.5	3.0	2.7	20.0	18.3	40.0	25.2	50.6	15,142	91.0
Cavetown CDP	1,473	-	-	1,129	93.8	2.0	1.1	0.6	2.5	19.4	27.6	47.1	44.2	19.1	448	88.2
Cearfoss CDP	178	-	-	89	69.7	0.0	30.3	0.0	0.0	0.0	15.7	53.1	100.0	0.0	58	75.9
Cecilton town	663	670	1.1	880	83.3	7.6	0.0	2.5	6.6	19.0	11.8	44.2	70.8	14.5	386	68.4
Cedarville CDP	717	-	-	539	51.8	35.3	1.7	9.6	1.7	7.6	36.0	57.4	51.8	18.8	219	69.4
Centreville town	4,254	4,944	16.2	4,761	83.5	10.7	2.7	0.0	3.0	19.8	22.4	45.5	32.3	32.9	1,671	94.0
Chance CDP	353	-	-	470	73.8	25.3	0.0	0.0	0.9	23.0	18.1	46.5	51.7	10.7	190	72.1
Charlestown town	1,177	1,196	1.6	1,518	83.8	3.5	0.4	10.9	1.4	27.0	12.7	40.3	35.1	28.4	557	93.0
Charlotte Hall CDP	1,420	-	-	1,865	81.8	12.8	1.4	4.0	0.0	32.4	30.7	39.5	54.4	15.6	391	77.7
Charlton CDP	171	-	-	288	100.0	0.0	0.0	0.0	0.0	20.8	7.6	47.8	63.7	4.2	92	100.0
Chesapeake Beach town	5,767	6,030	4.6	5,960	82.2	6.4	1.7	8.7	0.9	27.0	13.1	37.0	27.0	40.2	2,300	92.7
Chesapeake City town	689	691	0.3	705	89.4	0.6	1.0	2.4	6.7	12.6	21.6	50.0	32.0	35.3	347	91.1
Chesapeake Ranch Estates CDP	10,519	-	-	9,702	78.5	13.1	1.1	5.0	2.3	28.7	6.9	34.9	42.5	24.5	3,352	97.1
Chester CDP	4,167	-	-	4,658	88.0	6.2	0.9	2.1	2.8	18.4	21.1	47.0	31.5	37.4	2,077	93.5
Chestertown town	5,271	5,051	-4.2	5,088	75.0	16.7	3.5	1.4	3.5	9.1	26.7	39.4	36.1	43.3	2,067	81.5
Cheverly town	6,170	6,428	4.2	6,435	36.9	46.0	5.1	4.8	7.2	24.2	15.9	37.7	24.6	50.4	2,422	92.0
Chevy Chase town	2,824	2,984	5.7	2,973	86.9	1.2	3.8	3.8	4.1	28.1	18.9	47.4	3.4	93.2	998	99.5
Chevy Chase CDP	9,545	-	-	9,622	81.6	5.9	3.3	3.3	6.0	24.0	23.0	48.4	5.4	86.1	3,696	96.5
Chevy Chase Section Five village	667	702	5.2	638	88.9	0.5	2.0	1.3	7.4	32.0	17.2	45.9	2.0	92.8	213	99.1
Chevy Chase Section Three village	756	794	5.0	732	89.1	1.2	4.9	3.7	1.1	26.2	25.1	48.5	3.4	90.7	252	97.2
Chevy Chase View town	925	980	5.9	1,017	88.5	1.9	1.7	0.2	7.8	30.0	18.2	43.8	3.7	89.1	322	97.2
Chevy Chase Village town	1,951	2,056	5.4	1,937	89.8	0.9	1.4	2.7	5.2	25.8	24.2	49.4	3.3	92.8	655	98.3
Chewsville CDP	238	-	-	335	100.0	0.0	0.0	0.0	0.0	24.8	20.9	46.2	49.1	19.0	113	95.6
Chillum CDP	33,513	-	-	35,557	3.8	42.6	2.9	2.3	48.5	23.9	11.2	34.8	58.5	20.4	10,434	90.3
Choptank CDP	129	-	-	183	100.0	0.0	0.0	0.0	0.0	15.3	12.6	46.3	35.3	17.6	69	100.0
Church Creek town	125	121	-3.2	80	98.8	0.0	0.0	1.3	0.0	16.3	17.5	42.4	50.8	20.6	39	87.2
Church Hill town	745	753	1.1	797	67.5	17.1	0.3	2.9	12.3	30.0	13.7	32.5	43.6	28.6	284	94.4
Clarksburg CDP	13,766	-	-	24,767	28.3	18.3	38.4	4.7	10.3	35.0	7.0	34.6	13.8	69.4	7,272	99.6
Clarysville CDP	73	-	-	32	100.0	0.0	0.0	0.0	0.0	0.0	100.0	0.0	100.0	0.0	14	0.0
Clear Spring town	364	362	-0.5	479	76.8	1.0	9.6	3.8	8.8	18.4	14.2	41.9	64.2	12.3	190	86.3
Clinton CDP	35,970	-	-	39,018	7.5	80.8	2.7	2.2	6.8	20.6	16.0	42.7	36.1	28.9	12,464	95.8
Cloverly CDP	15,126	-	-	15,464	39.9	25.4	14.6	4.2	15.8	21.1	17.6	42.4	22.7	58.5	4,771	98.1
Cobb Island CDP	1,166	-	-	846	89.6	6.1	0.0	4.3	0.0	24.9	10.2	40.3	60.6	13.1	299	77.6

1 May be of any race.

Table A. All Places — **Population and Housing**

STATE City, town, township, borough, or CDP (county if applicable)	Population: 2010 census total population	Population: 2019 estimated population	Population: Percent change 2010–2019	Population: ACS total population estimate 2015–2019	Race and Hispanic or Latino origin (percent): White alone, not Hispanic or Latino	Black alone, not Hispanic or Latino	Asian alone, not Hispanic or Latino	All other races or 2 or more races, not Hispanic or Latino	Hispanic or Latino[1]	Age (percent): Under 18 years old	Age 65 years and older	Median age	Educational attainment of persons age 25 and older: Percent High school diploma or less	Percent Bachelor's degree or more	Occupied housing units: Total	Percent with a computer
	1	2	3	4	5	6	7	8	9	10	11	12	13	14	15	16
MARYLAND—Con.																
Cockeysville CDP	20,776	-	-	21,038	51.0	19.6	11.7	2.6	15.1	21.0	12.8	34.3	26.1	47.9	9,233	92.2
Colesville CDP	14,647	-	-	13,992	32.7	29.1	19.5	5.0	13.7	17.8	23.8	50.5	22.5	55.5	4,751	96.0
College Park city	30,397	32,163	5.8	32,159	47.2	18.8	14.4	4.1	15.5	10.1	6.7	21.6	30.2	49.3	7,407	96.3
Colmar Manor town	1,404	1,454	3.6	1,191	14.3	31.6	9.1	2.9	42.1	26.2	15.4	37.4	52.0	23.5	376	94.9
Columbia CDP	99,615	-	-	103,991	46.6	26.2	12.7	5.2	9.4	22.1	14.9	38.4	17.2	62.7	40,396	96.6
Coral Hills CDP	9,895	-	-	8,685	2.9	86.3	0.3	1.9	8.6	20.2	13.0	38.5	57.9	15.5	3,322	91.6
Cordova CDP	562	-	-	612	87.9	12.1	0.0	0.0	0.0	25.2	23.7	30.3	70.3	14.1	244	90.2
Corriganville CDP	455	-	-	559	84.1	6.8	0.0	9.1	0.0	14.0	32.4	48.7	63.6	10.1	205	79.5
Cottage City town	1,305	1,356	3.9	1,326	10.0	35.7	5.4	5.2	43.7	22.0	14.3	45.3	52.7	19.4	471	85.8
Crellin CDP	264	-	-	84	100.0	0.0	0.0	0.0	0.0	0.0	70.2	67.3	84.5	0.0	61	80.3
Cresaptown CDP	4,592	-	-	5,916	52.6	40.5	0.9	2.5	3.5	7.7	12.5	42.7	66.5	9.6	1,177	81.1
Crisfield city	2,722	2,564	-5.8	2,601	57.9	36.2	0.2	1.8	4.0	23.7	23.3	44.1	70.3	10.1	1,121	72.3
Crofton CDP	27,348	-	-	29,136	66.4	16.9	5.6	5.1	6.0	26.6	11.0	36.0	17.5	58.8	10,434	98.7
Croom CDP	2,631	-	-	2,174	58.2	31.8	0.0	8.0	2.0	10.8	23.7	51.0	30.4	41.8	927	92.6
Crownsville CDP	1,757	-	-	1,530	90.5	8.1	0.4	0.0	1.0	13.2	28.2	55.8	29.9	43.5	600	88.3
Cumberland city	20,824	19,284	-7.4	19,650	88.8	5.7	0.5	3.5	1.5	21.4	20.2	39.7	48.7	19.4	8,374	79.3
Damascus CDP	15,257	-	-	15,250	64.3	10.4	8.3	3.6	13.4	23.6	11.1	39.7	25.7	46.0	4,945	97.1
Dames Quarter CDP	167	-	-	50	100.0	0.0	0.0	0.0	0.0	0.0	68.0	72.0	54.0	22.0	37	83.8
Danville CDP	271	-	-	201	100.0	0.0	0.0	0.0	0.0	31.8	16.4	32.6	70.8	0.0	78	100.0
Dargan CDP	165	-	-	166	100.0	0.0	0.0	0.0	0.0	9.0	0.0	42.1	0.0	19.0	50	100.0
Darlington CDP	409	-	-	499	92.8	0.0	0.0	6.2	1.0	9.6	29.5	53.3	30.5	55.4	219	84.5
Darnestown CDP	6,802	-	-	6,462	69.3	5.5	16.7	1.0	7.4	22.8	17.7	47.3	11.2	72.5	2,182	99.0
Dawson CDP	103	-	-	82	100.0	0.0	0.0	0.0	0.0	0.0	23.2	56.4	75.6	11.0	49	61.2
Deale CDP	4,945	-	-	4,706	84.3	7.3	2.3	3.3	2.8	20.7	17.7	47.4	30.9	39.2	1,800	92.5
Deal Island CDP	471	-	-	351	87.5	2.6	0.0	10.0	0.0	8.0	51.0	65.1	52.4	21.6	192	80.7
Deer Park town	383	368	-3.9	429	99.1	0.0	0.7	0.2	0.0	19.6	16.6	46.3	56.2	7.4	166	90.4
Delmar town	3,092	3,354	8.5	3,214	51.8	29.8	7.5	5.4	5.5	26.7	11.5	41.9	46.4	29.4	1,340	92.9
Denton town	4,403	4,512	2.5	4,429	65.9	24.2	0.7	2.8	6.3	25.0	12.2	34.5	52.2	20.7	1,567	92.9
Derwood CDP	2,381	-	-	1,890	48.9	1.2	27.8	9.8	12.3	19.2	23.8	51.0	13.4	70.7	775	97.3
Detmold CDP	71	-	-	109	100.0	0.0	0.0	0.0	0.0	38.5	17.4	35.0	37.3	43.3	40	52.5
District Heights city	5,742	5,984	4.2	6,000	1.2	89.4	0.4	1.7	7.4	28.3	12.5	33.3	52.9	16.6	1,892	97.6
Downsville CDP	355	-	-	318	100.0	0.0	0.0	0.0	0.0	11.9	19.8	52.3	85.7	0.0	194	83.0
Drum Point CDP	2,731	-	-	2,227	90.4	0.0	2.0	2.4	5.2	23.8	26.1	45.9	33.4	33.7	825	98.1
Dundalk CDP	63,597	-	-	63,015	72.7	12.2	2.9	3.9	8.3	23.2	15.4	38.6	60.2	12.9	23,296	84.3
Dunkirk CDP	-	-	-	2,638	90.8	2.7	1.3	1.8	3.4	19.1	16.4	43.3	27.0	41.7	836	95.5
Eagle Harbor town	66	69	4.5	16	25.0	62.5	0.0	0.0	12.5	6.3	50.0	63.0	53.3	13.3	11	90.9
Eakles Mill CDP	27	-	-	-	-	-	-	-	-	-	-	-	-	-	-	-
East New Market town	390	377	-3.3	457	55.8	28.0	0.0	11.2	5.0	21.7	22.1	36.4	40.4	23.5	183	77.6
Easton town	16,210	16,671	2.8	16,591	69.7	10.9	2.1	6.5	10.8	22.5	23.4	41.6	36.0	36.6	7,525	90.1
East Riverdale CDP	15,509	-	-	16,416	7.5	26.3	2.2	3.7	60.4	31.6	6.7	31.5	70.2	14.2	4,187	92.9
Eckhart Mines CDP	932	-	-	665	93.4	0.0	0.0	0.8	5.9	15.2	18.3	36.7	66.7	8.2	272	100.0
Eden CDP	823	-	-	765	40.0	49.0	0.0	6.9	4.1	24.8	11.9	33.3	68.0	13.2	353	79.9
Edesville CDP	169	-	-	238	13.0	65.5	0.0	21.4	0.0	16.4	16.0	51.1	100.0	0.0	109	60.6
Edgemere CDP	8,669	-	-	8,526	91.0	5.3	0.6	1.9	1.2	18.7	22.0	47.0	48.2	18.9	3,305	86.7
Edgemont CDP	231	-	-	244	100.0	0.0	0.0	0.0	0.0	10.2	25.0	55.9	34.4	18.2	86	100.0
Edgewater CDP	9,023	-	-	9,112	83.6	4.2	1.2	1.7	9.2	17.3	18.3	43.2	37.8	34.1	3,753	94.8
Edgewood CDP	25,562	-	-	25,574	37.7	47.9	1.4	5.0	7.9	26.1	11.6	34.8	40.7	22.8	9,061	93.2
Edmonston town	1,428	1,490	4.3	1,436	9.1	29.5	1.5	5.2	54.7	27.4	7.7	31.2	60.0	12.7	421	96.2
Eldersburg CDP	30,531	-	-	31,108	87.4	3.4	3.6	2.1	3.5	22.6	14.4	42.3	26.0	47.8	10,951	95.2
Eldorado town	59	57	-3.4	76	89.5	10.5	0.0	0.0	0.0	22.4	13.2	50.5	74.5	3.6	27	88.9
Elkridge CDP	15,593	-	-	21,458	48.5	23.4	15.5	4.1	8.5	27.6	6.7	33.9	22.7	55.3	7,956	98.1
Elkton town	15,482	15,622	0.9	15,644	67.3	15.9	3.1	4.3	9.4	23.7	11.3	34.9	50.0	22.5	5,545	88.0
Ellerslie CDP	572	-	-	390	97.7	0.0	0.0	0.0	2.3	20.8	22.8	51.5	71.7	9.1	174	91.4
Ellicott City CDP	65,834	-	-	72,665	54.4	8.7	29.8	3.8	3.3	25.0	15.8	41.4	16.1	67.3	25,860	95.6
Elliott CDP	52	-	-	38	100.0	0.0	0.0	0.0	0.0	0.0	60.5	67.8	50.0	28.9	22	68.2
Emmitsburg town	2,807	3,198	13.9	3,098	82.1	8.2	1.2	2.5	6.0	20.9	16.5	42.4	44.3	27.5	1,152	87.0
Ernstville CDP	56	-	-	45	100.0	0.0	0.0	0.0	0.0	0.0	31.1	64.4	64.4	35.6	23	34.8
Essex CDP	39,262	-	-	39,437	59.0	31.3	1.5	2.7	5.6	23.7	15.3	37.6	53.4	15.8	14,951	86.4
Fairland CDP	23,681	-	-	25,220	15.5	56.7	13.3	3.0	11.4	26.2	10.5	34.9	25.1	44.5	9,023	97.5
Fairlee CDP	490	-	-	591	48.6	38.9	0.0	10.5	2.0	33.7	17.8	22.9	64.2	20.6	211	79.6
Fairmount CDP	457	-	-	367	74.4	25.6	0.0	0.0	0.0	12.8	1.9	42.2	46.1	31.5	169	95.9
Fairmount Heights town	1,451	1,522	4.9	1,579	1.6	76.7	2.5	2.3	17.0	17.9	21.7	43.9	59.2	11.2	504	89.7
Fairplay CDP	580	-	-	435	100.0	0.0	0.0	0.0	0.0	10.8	28.5	52.1	39.4	23.7	176	84.1
Fairview CDP	76	-	-	27	100.0	0.0	0.0	0.0	0.0	0.0	100.0	0.0	100.0	0.0	14	0.0
Fairwood CDP	5,031	-	-	6,261	8.8	78.7	7.8	2.7	2.0	26.4	9.8	39.2	8.2	71.4	2,098	100.0
Fallston CDP	8,958	-	-	8,972	94.6	1.5	0.7	0.8	2.3	23.1	21.0	45.1	32.3	43.8	3,130	94.3
Federalsburg town	2,738	2,661	-2.8	2,665	40.6	42.6	0.1	7.3	9.3	33.2	14.9	33.0	64.9	9.4	960	74.8
Ferndale CDP	16,746	-	-	17,208	62.5	21.5	2.6	5.6	7.7	24.1	12.7	35.8	47.5	18.5	6,289	90.5
Finzel CDP	547	-	-	767	100.0	0.0	0.0	0.0	0.0	26.7	9.0	41.0	62.5	14.6	271	96.3
Fishing Creek CDP	163	-	-	197	100.0	0.0	0.0	0.0	0.0	6.6	38.1	62.8	58.2	17.7	92	100.0
Flintstone CDP	177	-	-	238	100.0	0.0	0.0	0.0	0.0	41.6	17.2	18.8	64.6	0.0	86	76.7
Forest Glen CDP	6,582	-	-	6,469	48.2	21.2	9.1	2.9	18.5	23.6	20.1	43.7	18.3	65.8	2,430	92.3
Forest Heights town	2,469	2,564	3.8	2,565	3.5	66.7	1.4	3.0	25.5	26.6	16.5	35.6	47.4	18.3	748	92.2
Forestville CDP	12,353	-	-	12,342	3.3	89.1	1.0	0.8	5.8	24.9	15.0	35.7	49.1	19.3	4,302	92.8
Fort Meade CDP	9,327	-	-	10,873	54.0	18.1	5.8	9.6	12.4	32.4	0.7	25.3	17.1	42.6	2,875	99.5
Fort Ritchie CDP	314	-	-	73	100.0	0.0	0.0	0.0	0.0	39.7	0.0	35.3	86.4	13.6	27	100.0
Fort Washington CDP	23,717	-	-	24,237	8.5	65.4	11.0	2.8	12.3	19.1	20.9	46.9	28.9	41.9	7,978	94.8
Fountainhead-Orchard Hills CDP	5,666	-	-	5,774	82.5	7.5	4.6	3.0	2.3	23.3	22.4	41.9	27.7	40.4	2,388	89.3
Four Corners CDP	7,945	-	-	8,246	60.8	12.2	6.6	3.6	16.8	26.2	15.2	40.0	17.5	65.5	2,811	94.7
Franklin CDP	290	-	-	186	97.3	2.7	0.0	0.0	0.0	0.0	83.9	76.3	79.0	5.9	86	19.8
Frederick city	65,289	72,244	10.7	70,887	55.0	18.9	6.1	3.1	16.8	22.3	13.0	35.9	33.7	40.2	27,752	91.1
Frenchtown-Rumbly CDP	100	-	-	109	59.6	16.5	0.0	23.9	0.0	23.9	41.3	27.8	75.9	0.0	21	76.2
Friendly CDP	9,250	-	-	10,051	4.9	67.6	2.9	7.9	16.7	19.8	15.7	42.4	37.0	28.9	3,068	97.1
Friendship CDP	447	-	-	294	84.7	15.3	0.0	0.0	0.0	30.6	20.7	47.2	33.8	37.7	98	100.0
Friendship Heights Village CDP	4,698	-	-	5,396	70.0	3.4	11.0	3.9	11.9	13.5	29.6	46.7	5.6	88.1	2,957	93.1
Friendsville town	503	479	-4.8	564	97.5	0.0	0.0	2.3	0.2	26.4	14.7	38.4	63.3	11.9	253	83.0
Frostburg city	8,983	8,505	-5.3	8,591	77.9	12.7	2.4	3.7	3.3	14.4	15.4	24.0	43.7	29.3	2,819	89.7
Fruitland city	4,826	5,309	10.0	5,244	49.6	32.0	4.5	3.5	10.3	19.3	10.2	28.5	42.2	35.4	1,924	95.5
Fulton CDP	2,049	-	-	4,326	53.2	13.0	19.7	8.3	5.8	34.4	9.1	38.4	9.3	78.3	1,395	100.0
Funkstown town	882	871	-1.2	959	94.5	0.0	1.1	0.0	4.4	10.9	19.8	50.6	53.2	14.3	499	80.6

1 May be of any race.

Table A. All Places — **Population and Housing**

STATE City, town, township, borough, or CDP (county if applicable)	Population: 2010 census total population	Population: 2019 estimated population	Population: Percent change 2010–2019	Population: ACS total population estimate 2015–2019	Race and Hispanic or Latino origin (percent): White alone, not Hispanic or Latino	Black alone, not Hispanic or Latino	Asian alone, not Hispanic or Latino	All other races or 2 or more races, not Hispanic or Latino	Hispanic or Latino[1]	Age (percent): Under 18 years old	Age 65 years and older	Median age	Educational attainment of persons age 25 and older: Percent High school diploma or less	Percent Bachelor's degree or more	Occupied housing units: Total	Percent with a computer
	1	2	3	4	5	6	7	8	9	10	11	12	13	14	15	16
MARYLAND—Con.																
Gaithersburg city	59,899	67,985	13.5	67,742	34.4	17.4	18.9	4.2	25.0	22.9	11.5	36.5	26.4	54.0	24,799	95.3
Galena town	610	582	-4.6	654	90.4	3.7	0.5	1.2	4.3	19.1	20.3	34.0	39.9	27.8	283	80.2
Galestown town	138	133	-3.6	75	100.0	0.0	0.0	0.0	0.0	8.0	36.0	59.7	30.4	24.6	33	84.8
Galesville CDP	684	-	-	645	68.4	30.4	0.0	1.2	0.0	17.2	27.8	56.3	43.3	28.4	246	93.1
Gambrills CDP	2,800	-	-	2,837	79.9	5.3	3.4	5.2	6.2	22.2	15.2	43.3	31.4	41.7	979	91.7
Gapland CDP	109	-	-	78	100.0	0.0	0.0	0.0	0.0	20.5	19.2	35.3	24.2	75.8	30	100.0
Garrett Park town	992	1,049	5.7	873	88.0	1.1	2.6	0.3	7.9	21.6	28.8	51.4	3.5	84.4	342	99.4
Garretts Mill CDP	234	-	-	319	81.8	3.8	3.4	11.0	0.0	26.3	36.4	46.7	30.2	48.5	153	90.8
Garrison CDP	8,823	-	-	8,309	51.2	36.7	3.1	2.5	6.5	21.9	16.8	37.2	22.7	52.4	3,549	92.9
Georgetown CDP	143	-	-	88	35.2	64.8	0.0	0.0	0.0	14.8	9.1	44.6	100.0	0.0	38	100.0
Germantown CDP	86,395	-	-	90,582	30.6	24.1	19.3	3.6	22.3	25.8	8.8	35.2	24.5	50.0	30,799	98.2
Gilmore CDP	127	-	-	222	100.0	0.0	0.0	0.0	0.0	40.5	3.6	23.6	71.7	8.5	53	75.5
Girdletree CDP	149	-	-	106	85.8	0.0	14.2	0.0	0.0	7.5	39.6	57.7	76.5	0.0	63	33.3
Glassmanor CDP	17,295	-	-	16,935	2.4	73.7	1.3	3.5	19.1	24.0	9.2	34.2	56.1	13.7	6,404	91.4
Glenarden city	5,827	6,143	5.4	6,140	2.4	83.3	0.2	2.2	11.8	25.3	17.7	40.1	37.8	33.7	2,071	94.3
Glen Burnie CDP	67,639	-	-	69,872	59.1	22.6	4.3	4.4	9.7	22.2	13.7	36.9	44.7	25.1	27,035	91.8
Glen Echo town	255	270	5.9	309	89.6	5.2	0.3	4.5	0.3	32.7	14.6	39.6	4.7	91.6	101	100.0
Glenmont CDP	13,529	-	-	16,659	24.6	21.4	14.6	3.6	35.8	23.3	13.4	37.2	38.9	39.1	5,134	95.8
Glenn Dale CDP	13,466	-	-	13,361	17.4	62.8	6.2	5.3	8.2	20.8	15.0	40.8	24.6	48.2	4,143	98.9
Golden Beach CDP	3,796	-	-	3,060	89.7	2.9	1.3	1.5	4.5	20.8	19.5	40.9	49.2	18.7	1,228	92.0
Goldsboro town	241	230	-4.6	262	63.7	4.6	0.0	4.2	27.5	35.9	6.5	28.3	87.4	6.3	79	87.3
Gorman CDP	106	-	-	91	100.0	0.0	0.0	0.0	0.0	28.6	0.0	38.1	100.0	0.0	16	100.0
Grahamtown CDP	364	-	-	305	100.0	0.0	0.0	0.0	0.0	0.0	15.1	58.0	38.8	52.1	170	80.6
Grantsville town	890	865	-2.8	638	95.9	0.3	0.6	1.7	1.4	11.8	41.7	58.0	59.5	13.2	290	81.0
Grasonville CDP	3,425	-	-	3,495	80.1	13.6	1.3	3.1	1.9	28.3	11.4	36.5	43.0	31.6	1,268	95.8
Greenbelt city	22,128	23,224	5.0	23,219	24.7	45.9	9.5	3.5	16.5	24.5	9.7	35.5	27.3	46.6	9,350	95.3
Greensboro town	1,911	1,877	-1.8	2,837	69.2	10.4	0.1	4.6	15.7	39.9	7.1	29.0	60.7	11.3	869	84.2
Greensburg CDP	229	-	-	253	94.1	0.0	0.0	0.0	5.9	17.4	35.2	57.5	69.4	14.8	105	82.9
Hagerstown city	39,752	40,100	0.9	40,152	64.7	16.6	2.8	6.8	9.1	26.2	13.9	35.2	54.6	16.3	16,353	85.6
Halfway CDP	10,701	-	-	10,898	85.4	5.2	0.7	5.3	3.3	20.0	20.6	44.3	46.9	24.2	4,483	86.3
Hampstead town	6,318	6,401	1.3	6,362	90.0	2.4	2.7	2.5	2.4	22.9	12.3	36.6	38.5	37.3	2,488	93.6
Hampton CDP	5,052	-	-	4,624	86.7	1.3	5.7	2.1	4.2	21.3	23.6	50.4	12.4	70.5	1,713	96.8
Hancock town	1,558	1,529	-1.9	1,587	97.3	0.7	0.5	1.5	0.0	22.3	22.3	42.4	63.1	8.3	696	79.7
Havre de Grace city	13,003	14,018	7.8	13,652	72.8	15.3	2.2	3.5	6.1	18.6	19.7	45.1	33.3	40.2	5,724	90.8
Hebron town	1,080	1,096	1.5	1,110	81.3	9.9	0.3	2.5	6.0	24.1	11.2	36.2	44.9	21.6	409	86.3
Henderson town	146	143	-2.1	139	38.8	3.6	0.0	0.0	57.6	38.8	7.2	28.4	84.6	0.0	32	68.8
Herald Harbor CDP	2,603	-	-	2,747	79.8	9.7	1.5	4.0	5.0	19.6	17.8	46.2	17.5	51.7	1,082	100.0
Highfield-Cascade CDP	1,112	-	-	809	94.1	1.4	0.0	2.0	2.6	19.4	19.8	48.7	57.1	14.6	348	90.8
Highland CDP	1,034	-	-	1,206	67.2	3.5	25.2	2.5	1.6	26.0	18.7	48.5	6.2	77.1	399	100.0
Highland Beach town	103	110	6.8	91	38.5	52.7	0.0	8.8	0.0	14.3	36.3	57.1	9.7	66.7	41	100.0
Hillandale CDP	6,043	-	-	6,487	31.1	24.1	10.7	4.3	29.9	19.1	21.1	44.5	33.5	48.5	1,944	94.0
Hillcrest Heights CDP	16,469	-	-	16,388	2.6	89.4	0.0	2.0	6.0	20.6	15.2	37.2	46.1	18.3	6,676	92.0
Hillsboro town	161	156	-3.1	114	100.0	0.0	0.0	0.0	0.0	21.9	17.5	39.0	52.3	19.8	40	87.5
Hughesville CDP	2,197	-	-	2,279	69.2	24.2	4.4	2.2	0.0	16.3	15.2	49.5	30.9	30.4	831	97.4
Huntingtown CDP	-	-	-	3,486	83.8	6.8	4.3	3.8	1.3	23.2	9.5	40.5	28.8	39.2	1,010	97.0
Hurlock town	2,105	2,024	-3.8	2,042	56.9	25.1	3.4	3.9	10.8	21.2	25.9	44.4	52.2	16.3	866	85.6
Hutton CDP	86	-	-	72	100.0	0.0	0.0	0.0	0.0	0.0	15.3	60.3	100.0	0.0	30	100.0
Hyattsville city	17,535	18,230	4.0	18,242	25.4	29.4	4.5	3.8	36.9	23.5	9.9	34.9	38.5	35.7	6,592	94.7
Ilchester CDP	23,476	-	-	26,974	55.6	12.2	17.9	4.6	9.6	27.0	8.3	34.9	16.3	64.9	9,229	98.6
Indian Head town	3,850	3,802	-1.2	3,822	20.2	59.7	7.7	6.1	6.2	28.6	7.1	33.4	42.5	26.4	1,377	95.4
Indian Springs CDP	64	-	-	19	100.0	0.0	0.0	0.0	0.0	0.0	100.0	0.0	47.4	0.0	10	100.0
Jarrettsville CDP	2,916	-	-	3,023	93.3	1.4	0.3	2.5	2.5	21.1	19.3	45.1	30.4	39.2	1,016	92.6
Jefferson CDP	2,111	-	-	2,235	86.0	3.6	2.5	2.1	5.7	23.7	13.4	41.6	28.4	43.4	801	97.0
Jennings CDP	113	-	-	232	100.0	0.0	0.0	0.0	0.0	34.1	6.5	32.5	71.2	9.8	71	88.7
Jessup CDP	7,137	-	-	9,509	36.4	51.6	0.7	2.5	8.9	4.8	4.6	36.7	64.9	11.3	1,083	100.0
Jesterville CDP	188	-	-	214	100.0	0.0	0.0	0.0	0.0	14.0	0.0	45.1	23.0	32.4	68	100.0
Joppatowne CDP	12,616	-	-	12,304	73.9	16.1	2.2	2.5	5.3	20.4	14.0	38.8	34.4	33.7	4,730	94.5
Jugtown CDP	204	-	-	284	85.2	0.0	0.0	14.8	0.0	24.6	17.6	42.5	35.1	45.0	66	100.0
Keedysville town	1,149	1,221	6.3	1,070	90.9	3.5	0.4	1.3	3.9	25.7	12.5	43.7	28.3	35.8	374	97.3
Kemp Mill CDP	12,564	-	-	14,733	50.2	22.5	7.4	2.5	17.5	25.9	17.9	39.1	22.1	55.3	4,615	98.2
Kemps Mill CDP	126	-	-	31	100.0	0.0	0.0	0.0	0.0	0.0	48.4	0.0	100.0	0.0	15	0.0
Kennedyville CDP	199	-	-	436	100.0	0.0	0.0	0.0	0.0	16.5	27.3	49.5	56.8	31.9	153	66.0
Kensington town	2,199	2,329	5.9	2,098	71.7	4.7	5.2	2.0	16.3	26.5	13.7	43.2	15.1	73.2	798	97.4
Kent Narrows CDP	567	-	-	511	100.0	0.0	0.0	0.0	0.0	1.8	55.2	66.6	21.3	56.8	295	100.0
Kettering CDP	12,790	-	-	13,527	2.6	90.2	2.6	2.6	2.0	16.4	22.8	48.3	26.2	41.7	5,672	95.7
Kingstown CDP	1,733	-	-	1,917	94.5	5.3	0.0	0.0	0.2	14.3	29.2	50.6	34.3	37.6	828	89.7
Kingsville CDP	4,318	-	-	4,385	97.6	0.2	0.3	0.9	1.1	17.7	22.5	49.9	29.1	46.4	1,506	96.0
Kitzmiller town	321	303	-5.6	234	98.7	0.0	0.9	0.4	0.0	9.4	25.6	51.8	71.8	6.6	108	71.3
Klondike CDP	118	-	-	134	100.0	0.0	0.0	0.0	0.0	26.9	15.7	35.9	35.0	38.8	54	63.0
Konterra CDP	2,527	-	-	2,536	19.4	48.4	19.8	3.8	8.6	11.9	35.1	58.4	19.1	52.2	1,138	93.1
Lake Arbor CDP	9,776	-	-	9,973	3.2	91.4	1.2	3.1	1.0	18.5	14.1	39.0	22.4	49.1	4,315	92.5
Lake Shore CDP	19,477	-	-	19,791	87.3	3.8	2.3	3.4	3.3	22.6	14.8	40.7	33.4	32.9	6,990	95.2
Landover CDP	23,078	-	-	22,553	3.9	70.4	1.6	2.4	21.7	25.7	10.9	34.8	56.3	17.0	7,809	92.2
Landover Hills town	1,575	1,636	3.9	1,894	10.5	33.3	0.2	7.4	48.6	30.9	8.7	33.3	54.4	18.6	483	94.2
Langley Park CDP	18,755	-	-	19,520	2.3	10.9	1.8	1.0	84.0	31.8	4.8	29.9	82.3	8.9	4,694	90.6
Lanham CDP	10,157	-	-	11,120	10.4	55.3	4.0	2.2	28.1	25.7	13.6	37.4	47.3	25.6	3,064	95.4
Lansdowne CDP	8,409	-	-	8,477	56.8	21.5	2.5	5.0	14.2	29.8	12.8	32.6	60.7	14.4	3,032	84.4
La Plata town	8,793	9,631	9.5	9,376	56.0	29.4	4.8	5.8	3.9	20.7	17.2	40.5	37.7	28.4	3,188	85.3
Largo CDP	10,709	-	-	10,961	5.6	82.9	2.3	3.2	5.9	20.0	12.8	40.1	28.3	39.7	3,989	96.6
Laurel city	24,901	25,631	2.9	25,767	21.2	52.6	7.1	3.5	15.6	23.8	9.5	35.4	30.4	44.2	9,740	96.2
La Vale CDP	3,551	-	-	3,429	92.0	0.4	2.8	2.3	2.6	14.3	24.7	49.3	32.5	31.2	1,635	84.5
Layhill CDP	5,169	-	-	5,216	23.3	40.4	18.8	4.5	13.0	19.6	20.0	47.8	31.7	48.9	1,639	98.2
Laytonsville town	356	381	7.0	456	54.4	12.3	9.6	3.5	20.2	25.2	12.7	46.2	28.4	55.9	152	96.1
Leisure World CDP	8,749	-	-	9,040	63.1	18.3	8.4	1.5	8.7	3.2	74.3	75.9	24.5	45.2	5,881	86.4
Leitersburg CDP	573	-	-	460	97.4	0.9	0.0	1.7	0.0	10.0	14.1	48.1	46.0	16.9	200	84.0
Leonardtown town	2,967	3,824	28.9	3,749	69.6	14.1	9.1	4.3	2.9	30.0	17.6	36.8	41.0	37.2	1,287	79.2
Lexington Park CDP	11,626	-	-	11,082	49.3	35.1	5.0	3.5	7.0	23.2	7.0	32.1	38.2	25.0	4,449	92.9
Libertytown CDP	950	-	-	993	95.0	0.0	4.0	0.0	1.0	19.9	27.0	32.9	55.5	24.2	385	94.8
Linganore CDP	8,543	-	-	9,112	85.5	5.2	1.8	4.2	3.2	28.3	11.6	40.8	13.6	60.2	3,313	98.8
Linthicum CDP	10,324	-	-	10,442	88.2	3.1	2.4	4.1	2.2	19.1	19.5	42.6	38.0	35.7	3,992	94.5
Little Orleans CDP	42	-	-	35	100.0	0.0	0.0	0.0	0.0	0.0	0.0	0.0	100.0	0.0	35	37.1
Lochearn CDP	25,333	-	-	25,771	12.1	78.9	1.4	1.9	5.7	20.3	20.1	42.8	37.2	32.3	9,927	90.9

1 May be of any race.

Table A. All Places — **Population and Housing**

STATE City, town, township, borough, or CDP (county if applicable)	Population: 2010 census total population	Population: 2019 estimated population	Population: Percent change 2010–2019	Population: ACS total population estimate 2015–2019	Race and Hispanic or Latino origin (percent): White alone, not Hispanic or Latino	Race: Black alone, not Hispanic or Latino	Race: Asian alone, not Hispanic or Latino	Race: All other races or 2 or more races, not Hispanic or Latino	Race: Hispanic or Latino[1]	Age (percent): Under 18 years old	Age: Age 65 years and older	Age: Median age	Educational attainment of persons age 25 and older: Percent High school diploma or less	Educational attainment: Percent Bachelor's degree or more	Occupied housing units: Total	Occupied housing units: Percent with a computer
	1	2	3	4	5	6	7	8	9	10	11	12	13	14	15	16
MARYLAND—Con.																
Loch Lynn Heights town	549	530	-3.5	494	98.4	0.0	0.0	1.0	0.6	18.4	15.0	44.0	69.1	13.7	201	75.6
Lonaconing town	1,190	1,107	-7.0	1,278	98.9	0.0	0.0	0.3	0.8	26.9	20.7	37.0	55.3	18.4	444	84.9
Long Beach CDP	1,821	-	-	2,143	81.7	5.9	0.0	3.1	9.3	15.6	11.2	37.4	40.9	25.1	810	99.1
Luke town	65	60	-7.7	102	97.1	0.0	0.0	0.0	2.9	28.4	11.8	29.9	52.3	7.7	38	89.5
Lusby CDP	1,835	-	-	1,824	63.3	28.0	0.0	4.2	4.6	14.3	22.3	49.6	40.2	23.2	798	73.9
Lutherville CDP	6,504	-	-	6,856	80.6	3.6	10.6	3.5	1.8	23.2	18.0	41.5	18.2	62.1	2,606	91.7
McCoole CDP	511	-	-	692	100.0	0.0	0.0	0.0	0.0	18.5	21.1	42.7	56.8	3.5	269	61.3
Madison CDP	204	-	-	204	90.2	4.4	0.0	0.0	5.4	9.8	58.3	70.0	40.3	27.8	97	83.5
Manchester town	4,813	4,851	0.8	4,832	89.8	3.7	1.9	2.1	2.4	24.8	13.2	36.9	35.6	30.2	1,618	91.5
Mapleville CDP	238	-	-	300	95.0	0.0	0.0	5.0	0.0	34.7	14.0	43.5	55.6	11.2	108	100.0
Mardela Springs town	346	351	1.4	463	77.1	14.5	0.0	3.0	5.4	27.2	12.7	38.3	50.5	16.4	164	93.9
Marlboro Meadows CDP	3,672	-	-	3,468	5.1	82.3	1.4	2.3	8.9	17.0	16.4	45.3	35.7	30.4	1,259	96.3
Marlboro Village CDP	9,438	-	-	9,325	4.9	88.7	0.2	3.9	2.2	17.7	7.1	36.7	34.3	34.9	3,353	98.9
Marlow Heights CDP	5,618	-	-	5,872	3.2	87.0	0.6	2.4	6.7	19.3	18.2	40.1	41.9	15.5	2,287	88.4
Marlton CDP	9,031	-	-	9,071	9.1	80.4	2.4	4.5	3.7	22.1	11.7	39.9	28.0	40.8	3,393	97.3
Martin's Additions village	941	993	5.5	1,043	94.2	1.0	1.9	0.3	2.7	29.4	18.8	42.7	2.3	87.5	336	99.4
Marydel town	142	139	-2.1	328	26.8	3.0	0.6	4.6	64.9	23.8	7.6	32.1	83.5	5.4	68	79.4
Maryland City CDP	16,093	-	-	17,513	32.4	46.7	6.9	2.6	11.4	25.0	7.2	34.6	30.7	44.8	6,748	97.0
Maugansville CDP	3,071	-	-	2,543	78.2	6.2	0.4	0.9	14.3	25.5	23.1	49.0	54.4	22.6	1,005	73.4
Mayo CDP	8,298	-	-	8,031	94.2	1.8	1.2	0.8	1.9	22.1	15.1	42.1	33.6	41.8	3,003	96.2
Mays Chapel CDP	11,420	-	-	12,253	79.2	1.5	14.9	1.8	2.7	22.1	19.8	43.6	12.9	69.7	4,792	95.4
Mechanicsville CDP	1,508	-	-	1,765	88.3	7.5	0.0	0.6	3.6	27.5	8.6	37.2	52.5	32.0	578	91.0
Melwood CDP	-	-	-	4,289	14.8	57.4	1.5	5.3	21.0	21.4	18.5	41.7	35.0	32.5	1,637	84.7
Mercersville CDP	130	-	-	89	100.0	0.0	0.0	0.0	0.0	28.1	43.8	51.7	0.0	50.0	56	100.0
Middleburg CDP	70	-	-	18	100.0	0.0	0.0	0.0	0.0	0.0	0.0	0.0	0.0	0.0	18	100.0
Middle River CDP	25,191	-	-	25,129	56.4	32.4	3.6	2.2	5.4	24.5	15.2	37.2	53.7	18.3	9,324	89.6
Middletown town	4,288	4,792	11.8	4,609	87.7	1.2	4.0	5.1	2.0	28.9	15.3	37.6	15.7	61.0	1,567	97.8
Midland town	450	414	-8.0	701	95.4	0.0	0.4	4.1	0.0	28.5	15.1	34.6	51.3	14.8	259	77.6
Midlothian CDP	320	-	-	388	100.0	0.0	0.0	0.0	0.0	8.2	33.5	50.2	65.0	9.0	173	78.0
Milford Mill CDP	29,042	-	-	29,926	9.9	80.6	5.5	1.1	3.0	23.0	13.0	35.6	39.0	29.9	11,464	94.1
Millington town	646	604	-6.5	695	60.0	20.9	3.6	0.4	15.1	25.2	8.9	38.3	59.6	14.9	241	92.5
Mitchellville CDP	10,967	-	-	11,547	5.8	84.0	1.8	3.7	4.7	19.8	16.9	43.1	26.4	43.3	3,680	96.9
Monrovia CDP	416	-	-	903	71.0	21.3	4.1	3.7	0.0	26.7	9.9	34.5	8.3	53.7	285	100.0
Montgomery Village CDP	32,032	-	-	34,332	27.4	20.4	10.8	3.2	38.2	24.8	11.7	35.9	32.8	42.2	11,583	97.0
Morningside town	1,219	1,279	4.9	1,246	30.4	49.8	0.7	7.1	11.9	21.2	19.1	41.3	61.3	15.2	400	82.0
Moscow CDP	240	-	-	253	100.0	0.0	0.0	0.0	0.0	13.4	33.6	55.0	71.8	0.0	133	94.0
Mount Aetna CDP	561	-	-	689	89.7	0.7	8.3	1.3	0.0	22.1	18.9	46.7	29.0	45.4	214	100.0
Mountain Lake Park town	2,161	2,074	-4.0	2,184	97.3	0.5	1.4	0.9	0.0	18.4	23.4	45.6	57.2	21.6	922	89.2
Mount Airy town	9,281	9,458	1.9	9,397	83.7	4.1	1.5	4.6	6.1	26.8	10.9	36.9	25.1	44.6	3,135	95.3
Mount Briar CDP	160	-	-	171	100.0	0.0	0.0	0.0	0.0	19.3	15.8	41.0	44.9	9.4	76	80.3
Mount Lena CDP	515	-	-	451	85.8	0.0	0.0	12.4	1.8	30.2	13.1	35.0	57.5	10.5	155	94.8
Mount Rainier city	7,789	8,093	3.9	8,107	17.2	42.8	2.6	3.2	34.3	18.9	9.1	38.1	47.1	30.0	3,581	92.1
Mount Savage CDP	873	-	-	747	97.7	0.0	0.0	1.2	1.1	14.5	11.1	46.1	57.5	5.3	324	70.1
Mount Vernon CDP	779	-	-	966	72.9	13.8	11.9	1.4	0.0	19.3	20.6	46.8	52.3	11.0	345	96.8
Myersville town	1,640	1,838	12.1	1,924	87.8	3.1	3.2	3.2	2.7	28.2	10.8	36.6	25.5	48.9	603	96.8
Nanticoke CDP	225	-	-	330	67.3	32.7	0.0	0.0	0.0	0.0	48.5	61.7	35.7	27.8	116	83.6
Nanticoke Acres CDP	103	-	-	34	100.0	0.0	0.0	0.0	0.0	0.0	100.0	68.3	0.0	0.0	24	100.0
National CDP	56	-	-	146	100.0	0.0	0.0	0.0	0.0	50.0	6.8	20.5	34.2	47.9	43	100.0
National Harbor CDP	3,788	-	-	4,296	17.6	58.4	9.2	2.8	12.1	16.1	13.9	44.5	29.8	42.1	2,031	93.6
Naval Academy CDP	4,802	-	-	5,970	65.2	8.9	5.7	6.8	13.4	2.7	0.2	20.9	33.7	25.3	109	82.6
Newark CDP	336	-	-	572	76.0	5.2	0.0	18.7	0.0	9.8	21.3	50.9	53.7	7.7	194	94.8
New Carrollton city	12,348	12,928	4.7	12,935	7.2	62.3	2.7	3.2	24.6	23.1	10.9	36.6	41.7	28.7	4,284	93.0
New Market town	664	738	11.1	1,551	80.5	2.1	1.2	2.9	13.3	36.2	4.6	34.2	17.1	56.1	463	97.0
New Windsor town	1,393	1,398	0.4	1,298	88.5	1.2	1.9	2.9	5.4	25.3	8.9	36.2	50.9	25.1	457	90.4
Nikep CDP	116	-	-	-	-	-	-	-	-	-	-	-	-	-	-	-
North Beach town	1,975	2,039	3.2	2,609	71.5	10.8	5.8	3.4	8.4	25.1	14.4	37.1	30.0	30.7	1,144	91.7
North Bethesda CDP	43,828	-	-	49,872	54.0	9.7	14.3	5.8	16.2	19.7	16.7	39.8	14.3	70.9	21,372	96.4
North Brentwood town	529	551	4.2	756	2.6	49.2	0.9	1.6	45.6	25.8	10.8	37.5	66.9	16.5	217	92.2
North Chevy Chase village	559	595	6.4	591	67.2	3.6	14.4	6.3	8.6	28.1	19.1	44.2	4.9	84.4	203	99.0
North East town	3,585	3,642	1.6	3,620	79.0	11.8	0.4	3.9	4.9	28.1	10.6	30.9	51.5	17.7	1,482	87.8
North Kensington CDP	9,514	-	-	9,036	49.1	12.8	8.5	6.9	22.7	22.8	15.0	39.3	20.4	56.8	3,414	94.1
North Laurel CDP	4,474	-	-	24,873	31.8	38.7	15.6	4.5	9.4	29.6	6.8	33.4	22.2	54.2	8,233	96.2
North Potomac CDP	24,410	-	-	23,914	47.8	7.1	35.4	3.5	6.3	25.0	14.9	43.7	9.7	78.0	7,935	98.7
Oakland town	1,896	1,815	-4.3	1,745	95.4	2.5	0.2	0.2	1.8	11.6	24.8	49.9	54.1	21.7	800	77.1
Ocean CDP	32	-	-	-	-	-	-	-	-	-	-	-	-	-	-	-
Ocean City town	7,101	6,944	-2.2	6,972	88.9	1.6	0.1	3.1	6.3	6.8	33.9	56.4	37.5	32.2	3,621	89.7
Ocean Pines CDP	11,710	-	-	12,499	88.5	2.6	2.6	3.1	3.2	14.1	39.3	59.3	31.3	35.3	5,579	93.0
Odenton CDP	37,132	-	-	41,846	57.1	22.2	6.5	5.6	8.5	23.5	12.3	36.3	26.0	47.3	16,705	95.7
Oldtown CDP	86	-	-	52	100.0	0.0	0.0	0.0	0.0	0.0	0.0	57.3	25.0	15.4	21	100.0
Olney CDP	33,844	-	-	35,191	63.2	12.3	10.7	5.0	8.9	22.8	16.2	42.3	16.7	61.8	11,762	97.1
Overlea CDP	12,275	-	-	12,195	61.8	22.9	4.7	3.9	6.7	19.8	16.8	42.0	42.3	27.0	5,000	87.8
Owings CDP	2,149	-	-	2,528	92.3	1.3	0.0	3.7	2.8	29.1	13.1	40.2	21.0	44.7	790	98.4
Owings Mills CDP	30,622	-	-	35,081	23.7	54.7	8.1	4.4	9.0	22.5	11.3	34.4	26.2	47.4	13,369	95.7
Oxford town	651	606	-6.9	580	92.4	4.7	1.7	0.0	1.2	7.2	45.0	63.3	8.5	62.4	325	98.8
Oxon Hill CDP	17,722	-	-	18,080	4.4	74.1	4.1	3.1	14.4	17.5	16.0	40.9	43.3	26.9	6,726	94.5
Paramount-Long Meadow CDP	2,571	-	-	3,062	88.0	3.3	0.0	3.1	5.6	28.9	21.7	42.3	27.2	41.6	961	97.8
Parkville CDP	30,734	-	-	31,451	55.9	34.1	2.6	2.4	5.0	22.8	13.8	35.3	39.6	29.3	12,194	90.8
Parole CDP	15,922	-	-	17,074	86.5	6.1	1.6	2.3	3.5	12.2	32.1	53.7	17.9	58.7	8,492	94.0
Parsonsburg CDP	339	-	-	420	84.5	12.6	0.0	2.9	0.0	44.0	6.0	30.3	52.3	0.0	127	87.4
Pasadena CDP	24,287	-	-	29,918	76.1	10.6	2.9	4.7	5.6	21.2	10.9	34.9	37.0	31.7	10,961	95.9
Pecktonville CDP	167	-	-	244	93.4	0.0	0.0	0.0	6.6	27.5	23.0	39.3	84.8	7.3	51	100.0
Peppermill Village CDP	4,895	-	-	4,575	3.0	85.6	2.1	3.1	6.3	20.4	18.1	40.2	44.7	29.4	1,724	91.7
Perry Hall CDP	28,474	-	-	28,266	71.0	14.1	10.7	2.1	2.1	20.3	16.1	39.2	33.0	42.6	10,942	94.2
Perryman CDP	2,342	-	-	2,412	57.2	29.6	0.5	5.4	7.2	23.3	18.5	40.7	52.7	14.5	1,011	90.3
Perryville town	4,337	4,419	1.9	4,404	78.0	10.6	3.7	2.2	5.5	23.5	17.4	44.9	40.1	30.4	1,818	88.8
Pikesville CDP	30,764	-	-	33,486	71.4	18.3	4.6	1.8	4.0	22.5	24.9	44.3	17.8	64.9	13,851	90.9
Pinesburg CDP	449	-	-	247	100.0	0.0	0.0	0.0	0.0	15.8	24.7	56.4	66.8	6.7	92	100.0
Piney Point CDP	864	-	-	794	74.1	11.8	2.1	1.0	11.0	9.7	26.4	51.1	44.0	35.2	356	73.6
Pittsville town	1,425	1,474	3.4	1,547	91.9	2.3	1.6	3.5	0.7	18.7	15.8	38.8	58.9	9.1	622	89.4
Pleasant Grove CDP	353	-	-	476	100.0	0.0	0.0	0.0	0.0	29.0	14.3	39.0	41.1	23.4	170	90.6

1 May be of any race.

Table A. All Places — **Population and Housing**

STATE City, town, township, borough, or CDP (county if applicable)	Population				Race and Hispanic or Latino origin (percent)					Age (percent)			Educational attainment of persons age 25 and older		Occupied housing units	
	2010 census total population	2019 estimated population	Percent change 2010–2019	ACS total population estimate 2015–2019	White alone, not Hispanic or Latino	Black alone, not Hispanic or Latino	Asian alone, not Hispanic or Latino	All other races or 2 or more races, not Hispanic or Latino	Hispanic or Latino[1]	Under 18 years old	Age 65 years and older	Median age	Percent High school diploma or less	Percent Bachelor's degree or more	Total	Percent with a computer
	1	2	3	4	5	6	7	8	9	10	11	12	13	14	15	16
MARYLAND—Con.																
Pleasant Hills CDP	3,379	-	-	3,821	89.6	3.5	4.3	1.4	1.2	21.2	20.6	47.4	34.2	48.0	1,334	97.9
Pocomoke City city	4,181	4,088	-2.2	4,075	46.2	46.8	1.8	2.1	3.1	24.9	18.7	39.2	50.2	23.0	1,692	77.9
Point of Rocks CDP	1,466	-	-	1,857	77.8	5.0	5.7	4.4	7.2	32.6	7.2	37.0	28.9	51.6	594	97.8
Pomfret CDP	517	-	-	519	28.3	29.7	5.6	36.4	0.0	19.3	6.7	40.9	46.4	17.9	197	82.2
Pondsville CDP	158	-	-	50	100.0	0.0	0.0	0.0	0.0	40.0	22.0	28.6	36.7	33.3	20	45.0
Poolesville town	4,856	5,244	8.0	5,191	77.4	3.5	5.1	3.4	10.6	25.5	10.1	39.6	16.6	58.2	1,495	98.1
Port Deposit town	759	763	0.5	614	71.2	15.0	0.5	8.0	5.4	22.1	12.7	40.1	47.5	27.5	227	90.3
Port Tobacco Village town	13	15	15.4	6	100.0	0.0	0.0	0.0	0.0	0.0	100.0	74.7	0.0	100.0	2	100.0
Potomac CDP	44,965	-	-	45,940	61.8	5.2	21.5	3.2	8.3	24.3	23.0	47.4	8.5	80.6	16,193	98.1
Potomac Heights CDP	1,117	-	-	1,289	90.7	4.9	0.6	2.8	1.0	17.7	18.5	41.6	63.4	8.0	560	81.3
Potomac Park CDP	2,530	-	-	818	92.5	0.5	0.0	3.8	3.2	20.0	17.8	37.8	34.2	18.8	378	84.9
Powellville CDP	189	-	-	52	100.0	0.0	0.0	0.0	0.0	17.3	17.3	36.5	75.7	0.0	28	67.9
Preston town	722	703	-2.6	735	83.3	10.9	0.0	0.0	5.9	29.7	13.3	37.0	40.7	24.6	280	93.2
Prince Frederick CDP	2,538	-	-	2,928	55.0	25.0	6.4	4.9	8.8	19.3	21.8	39.3	47.8	19.7	1,185	84.1
Princess Anne town	3,300	3,513	6.5	3,487	19.8	70.4	0.3	0.3	9.2	33.3	6.7	25.0	37.3	17.9	1,359	90.7
Pylesville CDP	693	-	-	1,084	100.0	0.0	0.0	0.0	0.0	43.4	8.9	21.8	38.4	36.9	274	100.0
Quantico CDP	133	-	-	278	100.0	0.0	0.0	0.0	0.0	20.1	5.4	30.2	20.7	68.3	72	100.0
Queen Anne CDP	1,280	-	-	1,049	47.0	44.6	0.0	0.7	7.7	11.9	19.4	53.6	27.5	38.2	386	100.0
Queen Anne town	222	213	-4.1	271	82.3	8.5	4.8	1.1	3.3	19.2	14.8	35.4	39.0	13.0	100	96.0
Queensland CDP	-	-	-	1,918	12.7	73.2	0.4	6.7	7.0	17.8	9.0	47.5	23.8	51.7	638	100.0
Queenstown town	669	695	3.9	816	63.2	0.9	0.0	0.7	35.2	26.3	16.4	34.7	49.2	31.0	287	89.5
Randallstown CDP	32,430	-	-	35,528	12.2	81.5	2.1	2.8	1.4	20.7	17.5	42.0	32.3	35.8	12,513	94.5
Rawlings CDP	693	-	-	469	100.0	0.0	0.0	0.0	0.0	13.2	25.8	49.3	50.7	9.5	190	93.7
Redland CDP	17,242	-	-	17,414	39.8	10.3	15.7	3.4	30.9	21.5	13.4	40.1	31.2	49.1	5,361	96.8
Reid CDP	54	-	-	36	100.0	0.0	0.0	0.0	0.0	47.2	0.0	36.1	52.6	47.4	9	100.0
Reisterstown CDP	25,968	-	-	27,007	43.5	35.4	5.8	4.1	11.3	24.0	13.9	39.8	32.8	37.5	10,124	93.1
Ridgely town	1,640	1,657	1.0	1,721	71.2	10.7	1.3	5.1	11.6	29.0	13.1	35.8	54.1	15.6	665	84.8
Ringgold CDP	166	-	-	138	100.0	0.0	0.0	0.0	0.0	21.0	6.5	55.5	58.7	17.4	62	71.0
Rising Sun town	2,791	2,781	-0.4	2,791	91.6	1.4	0.0	3.3	3.8	32.0	10.2	33.1	48.1	19.3	993	88.1
Riva CDP	4,076	-	-	4,130	92.2	1.5	0.5	0.0	5.8	24.6	16.7	44.4	20.0	57.1	1,502	99.3
Riverdale Park town	6,927	7,200	3.9	7,198	17.6	22.1	2.2	1.8	56.3	25.6	8.3	35.4	58.5	28.2	2,066	94.6
Riverside CDP	6,425	-	-	6,038	57.2	26.8	3.6	5.0	7.4	22.9	10.3	33.0	26.1	35.0	2,459	98.7
Riviera Beach CDP	12,677	-	-	12,658	87.9	7.0	0.7	1.5	2.9	21.5	13.6	37.9	44.6	21.4	4,605	93.1
Robinwood CDP	6,918	-	-	7,684	71.8	9.5	5.6	5.2	7.8	22.8	17.3	38.2	34.1	36.3	3,017	84.9
Rock Hall town	1,307	1,274	-2.5	1,340	82.5	12.6	0.6	3.3	1.0	23.4	34.3	53.4	47.5	28.0	592	78.7
Rock Point CDP	107	-	-	85	87.1	12.9	0.0	0.0	0.0	0.0	36.5	62.0	38.9	29.2	40	82.5
Rockville city	61,242	68,079	11.2	67,542	47.8	10.6	20.9	6.0	14.8	21.1	16.0	38.7	17.8	64.9	25,562	96.3
Rohrersville CDP	175	-	-	117	100.0	0.0	0.0	0.0	0.0	13.7	26.5	32.0	55.4	29.7	58	100.0
Rosaryville CDP	10,697	-	-	10,501	9.2	82.2	2.2	3.6	2.9	18.2	15.3	46.2	32.9	38.4	3,486	99.3
Rosedale CDP	19,257	-	-	19,842	48.3	39.8	3.9	1.8	6.1	23.5	16.3	37.7	43.4	25.2	7,041	88.8
Rosemont village	294	322	9.5	305	96.7	1.6	0.0	0.7	1.0	22.6	26.9	49.5	46.4	34.8	124	91.1
Rossville CDP	15,147	-	-	15,127	38.9	32.9	11.1	2.8	14.4	20.6	12.8	37.4	37.5	34.9	6,009	91.0
Sabillasville CDP	354	-	-	354	75.4	13.8	0.0	0.0	10.7	21.5	32.5	50.6	63.5	5.5	144	69.4
St. George Island CDP	257	-	-	357	78.2	0.0	0.0	21.8	0.0	30.0	10.4	37.8	80.8	9.2	74	100.0
St. James CDP	2,953	-	-	3,860	75.0	13.8	4.0	4.4	2.9	24.5	9.1	36.0	36.2	37.1	1,173	95.2
St. Leonard CDP	742	-	-	494	89.7	2.0	0.0	0.0	8.3	17.0	13.0	43.9	32.6	41.4	184	100.0
St. Michaels town	1,030	1,040	1.0	1,108	66.0	29.8	2.3	0.5	1.5	11.7	30.3	56.2	27.6	42.1	587	89.1
Salisbury city	30,264	32,935	8.8	32,693	46.7	40.3	4.3	3.5	5.1	22.9	11.5	28.7	43.4	28.2	12,542	87.4
Sandy Hook CDP	188	-	-	234	100.0	0.0	0.0	0.0	0.0	0.0	41.5	22.8	76.1	0.0	141	60.3
San Mar CDP	384	-	-	333	92.8	3.9	0.0	0.0	3.3	3.9	44.7	62.2	60.4	20.7	113	65.5
Savage CDP	7,054	-	-	6,428	51.7	30.8	4.6	1.9	11.1	18.7	16.1	38.9	29.3	43.3	2,556	91.9
Scaggsville CDP	-	-	-	9,751	54.2	11.4	26.2	4.1	4.1	23.0	14.8	43.2	17.2	61.8	3,148	99.1
Seabrook CDP	17,287	-	-	18,616	6.1	66.3	5.4	2.0	20.2	25.2	11.8	35.9	37.8	32.4	5,715	92.9
Seat Pleasant city	4,523	4,738	4.8	4,739	1.1	85.1	0.2	0.2	13.4	24.8	16.3	45.0	51.2	9.2	1,842	88.8
Secretary town	528	500	-5.3	445	81.1	1.1	0.7	7.2	9.9	22.7	20.4	42.4	59.8	18.9	190	94.2
Severn CDP	44,231	-	-	50,496	43.7	35.1	9.1	4.3	7.7	23.4	10.5	36.1	27.2	43.5	18,480	96.6
Severna Park CDP	37,634	-	-	38,188	86.8	2.8	3.4	3.5	3.5	26.9	15.9	42.5	17.1	61.8	13,021	95.0
Shady Side CDP	5,803	-	-	5,423	86.4	7.5	1.1	2.7	2.3	20.8	15.9	42.5	42.1	33.8	2,046	97.2
Shaft CDP	235	-	-	351	100.0	0.0	0.0	0.0	0.0	21.9	11.7	38.2	45.9	30.7	108	85.2
Sharpsburg town	662	647	-2.3	784	99.5	0.0	0.1	0.4	0.0	21.8	18.5	42.8	48.8	17.2	327	89.3
Sharptown town	655	658	0.5	689	96.4	0.9	0.0	2.0	0.7	26.1	17.0	41.9	60.8	15.5	253	91.3
Silver Hill CDP	5,950	-	-	5,120	1.5	92.3	2.4	0.0	3.8	22.0	10.8	36.3	44.4	23.2	2,341	95.5
Silver Spring CDP	71,452	-	-	81,773	33.3	28.0	7.1	3.7	28.0	22.4	10.4	34.5	29.2	54.9	31,827	94.9
Smith Island CDP	276	-	-	149	100.0	0.0	0.0	0.0	0.0	22.1	35.6	54.7	69.8	13.8	66	77.3
Smithsburg town	2,989	2,974	-0.5	2,967	89.0	5.9	1.2	1.9	2.0	31.2	9.3	35.3	34.1	26.4	1,039	93.6
Snow Hill town	2,111	2,050	-2.9	2,150	57.0	34.5	0.0	8.0	0.6	23.3	22.4	41.2	52.7	21.4	848	78.9
Solomons CDP	2,368	-	-	2,132	98.0	1.5	0.0	0.1	0.4	11.1	54.7	67.9	31.6	43.3	977	93.8
Somerset town	1,202	1,273	5.9	1,090	87.1	0.4	3.1	1.7	7.8	31.6	19.5	45.9	1.1	94.1	369	94.3
South Kensington CDP	8,462	-	-	8,763	80.4	2.9	4.2	4.7	7.9	27.2	19.9	44.4	9.7	78.7	2,984	97.8
South Laurel CDP	26,112	-	-	28,683	13.8	62.7	6.1	2.4	15.0	26.1	9.8	34.1	29.9	43.0	10,119	95.2
Spencerville CDP	1,594	-	-	2,079	31.6	26.3	13.3	4.5	24.3	24.2	14.1	38.7	24.5	47.9	595	100.0
Springdale CDP	2,994	-	-	3,199	0.0	90.7	0.7	0.6	7.9	18.1	19.5	44.8	41.2	29.8	1,013	97.8
Spring Gap CDP	55	-	-	57	100.0	0.0	0.0	0.0	0.0	22.8	15.8	49.3	100.0	0.0	19	52.6
Spring Ridge CDP	5,795	-	-	5,876	82.1	5.5	2.2	1.7	8.5	25.4	12.4	39.1	19.5	60.8	2,135	96.0
Stevensville CDP	6,803	-	-	7,267	82.0	8.1	1.0	3.6	5.3	27.3	10.8	38.9	31.9	39.6	2,622	97.1
Stockton CDP	92	-	-	86	62.8	19.8	0.0	17.4	0.0	29.1	0.0	49.9	19.7	44.3	39	100.0
Sudlersville town	483	474	-1.9	435	84.6	9.7	0.0	4.4	1.4	21.4	28.0	40.6	63.0	22.0	222	70.3
Suitland CDP	25,825	-	-	24,522	1.8	88.2	0.9	1.1	8.0	24.1	10.2	33.6	49.2	15.7	9,688	92.0
Summerfield CDP	10,898	-	-	14,343	2.3	90.3	0.3	1.5	5.5	25.0	11.7	35.0	38.9	30.3	5,389	96.5
Swanton CDP	58	-	-	-	-	-	-	-	-	-	-	-	-	-	-	-
Sykesville town	3,942	3,958	0.4	3,939	89.3	2.5	2.3	1.7	4.1	26.6	11.7	35.7	25.1	50.8	1,444	95.9
Takoma Park city	16,739	17,725	5.9	17,672	46.3	32.2	5.3	4.6	11.6	24.8	11.8	38.7	26.6	59.4	6,567	93.8
Tall Timbers CDP	462	-	-	602	84.6	8.5	7.0	0.0	0.0	12.8	39.0	58.9	2.3	71.5	237	82.3
Taneytown city	6,747	6,817	1.0	6,787	91.3	3.8	1.0	1.6	2.2	24.0	19.7	43.2	54.2	23.6	2,601	92.0
Taylors Island CDP	173	-	-	221	94.6	5.4	0.0	0.0	0.0	29.9	24.0	52.0	25.8	43.9	86	86.0
Temple Hills CDP	7,852	-	-	7,926	2.5	82.9	0.6	2.1	11.8	23.9	10.8	35.9	46.3	20.0	3,051	94.8
Templeville town	115	117	1.7	237	21.5	0.0	0.0	2.5	75.9	47.7	3.0	21.5	96.1	3.9	48	83.3
Thurmont town	6,180	6,895	11.6	6,638	94.5	0.9	0.4	1.8	2.4	25.4	18.0	40.9	42.6	25.3	2,546	87.4
Tilghman Island CDP	784	-	-	1,005	92.3	0.0	0.0	0.4	7.3	16.7	32.4	57.0	51.9	22.9	421	93.1
Tilghmanton CDP	465	-	-	868	100.0	0.0	0.0	0.0	0.0	17.3	9.6	27.9	85.0	7.8	225	46.2
Timonium CDP	9,925	-	-	10,557	81.8	4.7	10.3	1.4	1.8	20.3	27.8	48.9	20.1	58.0	4,016	92.9
Tolchester CDP	329	-	-	350	67.1	25.4	0.0	3.7	3.7	15.7	22.9	42.2	37.0	28.8	130	100.0

1 May be of any race.

Table A. All Places — **Population and Housing**

STATE City, town, township, borough, or CDP (county if applicable)	Population — 2010 census total population	2019 estimated population	Percent change 2010–2019	ACS total population estimate 2015–2019	Race and Hispanic or Latino origin (percent) — White alone, not Hispanic or Latino	Black alone, not Hispanic or Latino	Asian alone, not Hispanic or Latino	All other races or 2 or more races, not Hispanic or Latino	Hispanic or Latino[1]	Age (percent) — Under 18 years old	Age 65 years and older	Median age	Educational attainment of persons age 25 and older — Percent High school diploma or less	Percent Bachelor's degree or more	Occupied housing units — Total	Percent with a computer
	1	2	3	4	5	6	7	8	9	10	11	12	13	14	15	16
MARYLAND—Con.																
Towson CDP	55,197	-	-	57,817	71.4	15.6	5.0	3.4	4.6	17.6	16.8	33.3	16.2	65.1	21,099	94.3
Trappe town	1,067	1,000	-6.3	1,200	58.8	20.3	1.3	4.7	15.0	21.9	18.9	37.6	51.8	23.6	485	89.3
Travilah CDP	12,159	-	-	11,301	51.4	4.8	35.5	5.2	3.1	22.9	18.9	48.4	10.0	82.2	3,602	98.4
Trego-Rohrersville Station CDP	172	-	-	119	100.0	0.0	0.0	0.0	0.0	0.0	23.5	54.4	52.8	0.0	44	100.0
Tyaskin CDP	236	-	-	148	100.0	0.0	0.0	0.0	0.0	10.1	0.0	37.1	34.5	18.2	52	100.0
Union Bridge town	975	963	-1.2	872	92.3	2.2	0.3	1.6	3.6	18.3	16.9	38.8	56.5	17.4	375	82.4
University Park town	2,553	2,631	3.1	2,651	66.3	11.7	5.8	3.7	12.4	18.4	16.8	43.0	14.7	74.8	914	98.5
Upper Marlboro town	635	673	6.0	771	34.1	64.6	0.0	1.3	0.0	25.2	9.3	38.1	30.7	41.7	314	90.4
Urbana CDP	9,175	-	-	12,587	54.6	9.6	19.8	6.3	9.7	35.6	4.6	35.0	16.6	67.6	3,864	99.6
Vale Summit CDP	139	-	-	92	100.0	0.0	0.0	0.0	0.0	15.2	0.0	41.3	79.7	0.0	33	100.0
Vienna town	278	265	-4.7	371	85.7	7.8	0.0	6.2	0.3	19.4	14.6	40.3	35.6	20.8	152	92.8
Waldorf CDP	67,752	-	-	75,489	24.0	59.7	3.3	5.5	7.5	25.8	9.2	35.2	35.2	29.5	27,760	94.2
Walker Mill CDP	11,302	-	-	10,904	2.3	86.9	0.9	3.4	6.6	19.7	17.8	40.1	46.2	23.9	4,446	89.5
Walkersville town	5,815	6,415	10.3	6,179	79.2	9.1	3.4	2.3	6.1	23.1	17.0	40.1	30.4	35.1	2,328	93.6
Washington Grove town	529	561	6.0	694	74.2	16.3	2.4	1.7	5.3	17.3	20.7	52.1	22.2	65.6	281	98.6
Waterview CDP	40	-	-	19	100.0	0.0	0.0	0.0	0.0	0.0	100.0	0.0	52.6	0.0	9	100.0
West Denton CDP	52	-	-	16	100.0	0.0	0.0	0.0	0.0	0.0	0.0	23.2	100.0	0.0	9	100.0
Westernport town	1,882	1,726	-8.3	2,156	98.9	0.1	0.0	0.6	0.3	26.1	14.4	30.8	54.9	12.6	819	77.8
West Laurel CDP	4,230	-	-	4,383	53.1	15.8	6.1	8.7	16.2	23.8	16.8	39.0	29.1	44.8	1,422	96.6
Westminster city	18,496	18,640	0.8	18,552	76.0	9.8	3.4	4.3	6.5	19.0	16.4	35.8	41.3	32.7	7,228	85.6
West Ocean City CDP	4,375	-	-	4,310	85.8	7.9	0.9	2.7	2.7	18.2	22.7	45.7	41.6	30.9	1,814	91.3
Westphalia CDP	7,266	-	-	9,944	4.6	84.2	1.6	1.6	8.0	24.6	11.3	39.3	25.4	46.1	3,548	96.0
West Pocomoke CDP	454	-	-	323	54.5	45.5	0.0	0.0	0.0	6.5	41.2	61.5	51.4	30.5	186	83.3
Whaleyville CDP	149	-	-	55	100.0	0.0	0.0	0.0	0.0	32.7	0.0	56.6	100.0	0.0	17	100.0
Wheaton CDP	48,284	-	-	50,229	23.2	14.9	13.3	4.6	44.1	24.6	11.1	36.2	43.4	35.6	15,281	93.9
Whitehaven CDP	43	-	-	64	0.0	43.8	0.0	56.3	0.0	56.3	20.3	13.8	0.0	46.4	13	100.0
White Marsh CDP	9,513	-	-	9,216	69.7	13.2	11.8	2.0	3.3	21.6	14.2	39.5	26.6	44.0	3,475	95.4
White Oak CDP	17,403	-	-	19,020	14.7	51.8	8.2	4.1	21.3	26.6	11.0	35.3	33.8	41.7	6,610	95.2
Willards town	963	1,009	4.8	886	77.0	6.1	0.3	3.4	13.2	26.4	11.3	34.1	58.4	12.1	350	87.4
Williamsport town	2,087	2,089	0.1	1,996	85.9	5.8	0.4	5.2	2.8	23.1	21.8	42.3	55.7	15.0	927	80.0
Williston CDP	155	-	-	96	100.0	0.0	0.0	0.0	0.0	0.0	44.8	62.4	24.0	26.0	41	100.0
Wilson-Conococheague CDP	2,282	-	-	2,263	88.7	5.3	0.0	5.6	0.4	19.4	17.6	40.5	68.4	9.1	961	85.1
Woodland CDP	113	-	-	37	100.0	0.0	0.0	0.0	0.0	0.0	64.9	67.6	100.0	0.0	30	30.0
Woodlawn CDP	37,879	-	-	40,469	18.3	56.7	14.9	2.9	7.2	20.7	13.5	37.9	39.9	32.7	14,438	93.7
Woodlawn CDP	6,334	-	-	6,692	4.8	35.7	0.7	2.4	56.4	28.8	12.0	34.5	63.7	13.6	1,768	92.1
Woodmore CDP	3,936	-	-	4,608	8.4	81.1	3.0	4.4	3.3	18.4	14.7	47.5	13.7	64.8	1,552	100.0
Woodsboro town	1,141	1,269	11.2	1,131	85.2	3.8	1.5	1.3	8.1	20.9	17.9	46.6	37.9	32.8	444	83.6
Worton CDP	249	-	-	79	100.0	0.0	0.0	0.0	0.0	22.8	15.2	58.1	59.0	0.0	46	73.9
Yarrowsburg CDP	133	-	-	275	100.0	0.0	0.0	0.0	0.0	0.0	0.0	57.2	58.5	19.2	90	100.0
Zihlman CDP	362	-	-	369	91.3	0.0	0.0	1.9	6.8	13.8	21.1	43.8	45.1	18.3	143	78.3
MASSACHUSETTS	6,547,785	6,892,503	5.3	6,850,553	71.6	6.9	6.6	3.1	11.8	20.0	16.2	39.5	33.3	43.7	2,617,497	91.4
Abington town & CDP (Plymouth)	16,026	16,668	4.0	16,436	88.2	2.0	3.6	3.5	2.6	19.3	14.9	42.2	32.9	39.1	6,396	95.9
Acton town (Middlesex)	21,912	23,662	8.0	23,627	66.1	1.4	26.0	3.0	3.5	24.6	15.4	43.7	11.3	74.9	8,795	94.6
Acushnet town (Bristol)	10,304	10,625	3.1	10,529	88.8	0.1	2.0	5.7	3.4	16.2	20.1	47.1	52.4	22.2	4,094	87.6
Acushnet Center CDP	3,073	-	-	3,177	83.6	0.2	0.6	6.4	9.2	20.8	14.4	45.2	55.0	16.3	1,300	89.3
Adams town (Berkshire)	8,486	8,010	-5.6	8,125	95.4	0.9	0.8	1.4	1.5	17.2	19.1	44.5	49.7	24.8	3,749	87.9
Adams CDP	5,515	-	-	5,335	95.1	1.3	0.2	1.8	1.6	16.2	19.5	43.5	51.0	22.9	2,629	86.7
Agawam Town city & MCD (Hampden)	28,438	28,613	0.6	28,696	88.9	2.1	1.6	2.0	5.4	18.9	21.4	46.4	37.1	33.2	11,829	89.7
Alford town (Berkshire)	498	488	-2.0	431	91.0	0.0	1.9	2.1	5.1	14.8	45.7	63.1	23.2	52.2	198	93.9
Amesbury Town city & MCD (Essex)	16,286	17,532	7.7	17,434	93.8	0.6	1.1	2.0	2.5	19.7	16.8	43.9	31.8	41.1	7,215	92.8
Amherst town (Hampshire)	37,819	39,924	5.6	39,814	69.4	5.0	13.5	4.7	7.5	9.2	9.1	21.3	18.2	65.7	9,162	96.6
Amherst Center CDP	19,065	-	-	20,409	71.1	4.1	13.8	3.9	7.2	4.7	6.0	20.4	20.7	62.9	3,077	94.7
Andover CDP	8,762	-	-	8,914	84.7	2.6	7.8	2.4	2.5	16.6	19.4	42.8	13.6	70.0	3,472	91.8
Andover town (Essex)	33,071	36,356	9.9	35,816	75.8	2.6	14.7	2.0	4.9	24.2	14.8	42.4	11.6	74.5	12,801	96.9
Aquinnah town (Dukes)	305	320	4.9	531	55.6	0.0	0.4	32.8	11.3	29.6	19.4	41.6	23.6	49.9	176	93.2
Arlington town & CDP (Middlesex)	42,823	45,531	6.3	45,304	75.8	3.1	12.3	3.9	4.9	21.3	16.7	40.7	15.7	70.9	19,065	93.0
Ashburnham town (Worcester)	6,076	6,348	4.5	6,281	95.9	1.1	0.3	0.9	1.7	24.5	13.2	39.1	26.9	39.8	2,031	96.9
Ashby town (Middlesex)	3,077	3,219	4.6	3,220	95.3	0.2	0.7	1.3	2.5	19.4	15.7	45.9	39.5	33.2	1,167	95.4
Ashfield town (Franklin)	1,739	1,717	-1.3	1,449	94.0	0.1	0.5	2.8	2.7	11.5	25.0	54.8	28.0	48.9	660	90.9
Ashland town (Middlesex)	16,615	17,807	7.2	17,710	77.9	2.1	11.3	1.7	7.0	22.1	16.0	42.0	24.0	58.5	6,796	95.5
Athol town (Worcester)	11,579	11,732	1.3	11,713	90.1	0.6	0.4	3.4	5.4	19.9	17.1	43.7	47.4	19.4	4,639	88.3
Athol CDP	8,265	-	-	8,617	88.8	0.7	0.3	3.8	6.5	21.6	13.6	39.3	52.3	17.0	3,354	85.7
Attleboro city & MCD (Bristol)	43,568	45,237	3.8	44,789	83.2	4.0	4.2	2.0	6.6	21.4	16.9	41.5	38.3	31.6	17,632	90.9
Auburn town (Worcester)	16,219	16,766	3.4	16,684	91.5	0.8	1.9	1.2	4.6	20.1	19.0	45.1	33.3	40.4	6,672	88.6
Avon town (Norfolk)	4,354	4,549	4.5	4,500	71.6	18.2	2.7	3.2	4.2	18.8	14.3	40.0	49.4	26.9	1,574	89.9
Ayer town (Middlesex)	7,425	8,196	10.4	8,106	82.4	4.3	3.5	4.0	5.7	18.9	14.9	41.0	28.0	48.7	3,552	90.3
Ayer CDP	2,868	-	-	2,910	82.2	4.2	0.6	5.6	7.4	21.5	16.8	43.2	30.8	47.9	1,421	83.0
Baldinville CDP	2,028	-	-	1,736	87.6	0.0	2.4	0.0	10.0	19.2	28.3	48.3	45.4	22.4	721	83.8
Barnstable Town city & MCD (Barnstable)	45,188	44,477	-1.6	44,406	84.3	5.6	0.9	3.2	5.9	17.4	23.3	48.3	32.9	38.6	18,796	95.0
Barre CDP	1,009	-	-	986	100.0	0.0	0.0	0.0	0.0	8.4	25.6	55.8	38.9	34.5	514	70.2
Barre town (Worcester)	5,398	5,578	3.3	5,539	93.8	2.2	0.6	1.0	2.4	19.8	14.6	47.9	42.5	32.3	2,039	87.8
Becket town (Berkshire)	1,782	1,716	-3.7	1,941	92.4	1.4	0.0	2.3	3.9	17.2	21.5	50.8	37.2	31.0	825	92.4
Bedford town (Middlesex)	13,316	14,123	6.1	14,142	74.2	4.0	15.0	3.0	3.8	25.0	17.3	42.2	12.0	71.8	5,312	95.8
Belchertown CDP	2,899	-	-	2,874	84.1	0.5	6.6	3.5	5.2	21.1	16.2	42.0	30.1	40.5	1,137	90.3
Belchertown town (Hampshire)	14,649	15,098	3.1	15,005	91.9	0.6	4.4	1.7	1.4	22.7	14.8	42.3	27.9	48.6	5,563	95.8
Bellingham town (Norfolk)	16,411	17,270	5.2	17,108	91.4	1.7	1.4	1.4	4.0	22.0	14.0	40.7	32.8	35.8	6,526	94.7
Bellingham CDP	4,854	-	-	4,383	90.7	2.4	1.1	2.6	3.3	20.3	20.7	46.5	29.6	35.2	1,960	89.3
Belmont town & CDP (Middlesex)	24,650	26,116	5.9	26,113	73.2	1.4	17.2	3.9	4.3	25.3	16.5	41.1	12.1	75.4	9,819	95.1

1 May be of any race.

Table A. All Places — **Population and Housing**

STATE City, town, township, borough, or CDP (county if applicable)	2010 census total population	2019 estimated population	Percent change 2010–2019	ACS total population estimate 2015–2019	White alone, not Hispanic or Latino	Black alone, not Hispanic or Latino	Asian alone, not Hispanic or Latino	All other races or 2 or more races, not Hispanic or Latino	Hispanic or Latino[1]	Under 18 years old	Age 65 years and older	Median age	Percent High school diploma or less	Percent Bachelor's degree or more	Total	Percent with a computer
	1	2	3	4	5	6	7	8	9	10	11	12	13	14	15	16
MASSACHUSETTS—Con.																
Berkley town (Bristol)........	6,408	6,851	6.9	6,730	96.8	0.1	0.0	3.0	0.1	23.5	14.0	43.2	34.6	35.7	2,384	94.5
Berlin town (Worcester)	2,868	3,240	13.0	3,182	97.0	0.4	0.9	1.5	0.2	17.5	25.5	49.7	30.1	50.5	1,179	90.2
Bernardston town (Franklin).................	2,126	2,090	-1.7	2,064	99.0	0.0	0.0	0.6	0.4	21.7	22.0	50.4	47.2	25.8	891	84.7
Beverly city & MCD (Essex).....................	39,504	42,174	6.8	41,885	88.5	1.6	2.1	2.6	5.1	18.1	16.8	40.4	27.4	50.6	16,443	91.0
Billerica town (Middlesex).	40,235	43,367	7.8	43,200	81.8	4.7	7.1	1.9	4.5	19.2	15.2	41.4	38.3	36.1	14,935	95.7
Blackstone town (Worcester)..................	9,011	9,288	3.1	9,263	93.5	1.2	0.8	2.2	2.4	22.2	14.5	41.7	36.3	35.4	3,526	94.6
Blandford CDP.................	393	-	-	278	98.6	0.0	0.0	1.4	0.0	11.5	18.7	54.7	47.8	31.7	130	86.2
Blandford town (Hampden).................	1,227	1,252	2.0	1,105	97.2	0.0	0.0	1.2	1.6	10.9	24.7	54.5	43.3	34.1	481	87.9
Bliss Corner CDP	5,280	-	-	5,150	91.4	0.0	1.8	0.7	6.1	14.2	28.1	50.1	48.8	32.3	2,240	84.7
Bolton town (Worcester) ...	4,899	5,426	10.8	5,299	92.5	0.2	4.2	1.7	1.4	28.5	13.0	43.0	12.7	68.9	1,739	96.8
Boston city & MCD (Suffolk)...................	617,792	692,600	12.1	684,379	44.5	22.7	9.6	3.4	19.8	15.9	11.5	32.2	32.5	49.7	269,522	91.0
Bourne CDP	1,418	-	-	1,408	99.0	0.0	0.0	0.0	1.0	17.4	48.3	63.2	22.4	53.0	781	92.6
Bourne town (Barnstable).	19,748	19,762	0.1	19,831	90.9	0.9	1.0	3.3	3.9	16.4	25.7	49.0	31.4	37.4	8,611	92.7
Boxborough town (Middlesex).................	5,012	5,793	15.6	5,561	73.4	0.7	18.0	2.8	5.1	22.2	11.7	43.2	13.5	66.2	2,266	97.7
Boxford CDP....................	2,339	-	-	2,585	91.9	0.0	2.9	3.7	1.5	27.3	10.9	46.7	14.7	61.0	795	97.7
Boxford town (Essex).......	7,959	8,332	4.7	8,282	93.5	0.0	2.0	2.1	2.4	25.1	16.1	46.6	11.8	68.1	2,839	98.2
Boylston town (Worcester)	4,355	4,712	8.2	4,623	92.6	0.2	2.6	0.4	4.1	22.0	17.3	45.2	17.0	57.5	1,799	95.1
Braintree Town city & MCD (Norfolk)...........	35,726	37,190	4.1	37,220	79.4	2.7	13.8	2.0	2.1	22.6	17.0	41.5	31.6	43.4	14,016	93.6
Brewster CDP..................	2,000	-	-	1,637	92.3	4.1	0.0	3.3	0.3	10.0	44.4	63.4	20.3	54.0	815	96.9
Brewster town (Barnstable).................	9,825	9,775	-0.5	9,837	94.7	0.9	0.6	1.6	2.2	16.3	32.1	54.3	24.0	49.0	4,198	96.3
Bridgewater Town city & MCD (Plymouth)	26,569	27,619	4.0	27,436	83.5	8.0	2.1	2.5	3.9	18.2	13.8	34.5	34.1	35.8	8,133	96.0
Brimfield town (Hampden)	3,611	3,680	1.9	3,658	92.0	3.9	0.5	1.5	2.2	20.9	20.1	46.8	34.2	36.4	1,447	89.7
Brockton city & MCD (Plymouth).................	93,767	95,708	2.1	95,594	30.8	44.1	2.0	12.1	11.1	25.0	13.1	35.7	53.1	18.6	31,817	88.8
Brookfield CDP................	833	-	-	690	91.0	1.4	4.1	3.5	0.0	13.3	14.8	34.3	43.6	22.8	320	85.6
Brookfield town (Worcester)..................	3,379	3,452	2.2	3,441	95.9	0.3	1.4	2.4	0.0	20.8	19.3	44.0	45.5	28.7	1,404	84.9
Brookline town & CDP (Norfolk)...................	58,613	59,121	0.9	59,180	68.0	3.0	17.3	4.9	6.8	18.6	16.0	33.7	8.3	83.5	24,436	96.6
Buckland town (Franklin) ..	1,897	1,850	-2.5	1,950	90.2	2.2	4.9	2.4	0.4	19.0	21.7	48.9	34.2	42.5	876	90.1
Burlington town & CDP (Middlesex).................	24,492	28,627	16.9	27,650	71.5	4.5	16.8	4.1	3.1	20.5	19.2	41.1	24.7	56.9	10,001	94.3
Buzzards Bay CDP	3,859	-	-	3,528	93.5	0.6	0.6	2.4	2.9	15.3	22.4	47.0	35.7	36.2	1,450	94.8
Cambridge city & MCD (Middlesex).................	105,148	118,927	13.1	116,632	59.8	9.9	16.6	4.2	9.5	12.2	11.1	30.5	12.3	79.0	46,835	94.2
Canton town (Norfolk).....	21,581	23,805	10.3	23,369	80.9	5.2	7.1	2.6	4.1	21.7	18.7	42.6	21.7	55.1	9,064	93.0
Carlisle town (Middlesex).	4,852	5,252	8.2	5,224	85.9	0.0	11.4	1.9	0.8	22.3	19.4	50.7	5.8	82.2	1,876	99.3
Carver town (Plymouth)...	11,490	11,767	2.4	11,720	92.5	0.5	1.2	3.4	2.4	21.2	19.8	45.2	47.1	21.8	4,489	91.4
Charlemont town (Franklin).................	1,266	1,233	-2.6	1,086	91.7	0.0	0.9	4.9	2.5	18.2	23.8	50.4	46.8	31.2	442	86.4
Charlton town (Worcester)	12,986	13,713	5.6	13,550	90.5	0.9	0.6	1.8	6.1	22.0	14.8	43.3	34.6	37.2	5,064	92.5
Chatham CDP	1,421	-	-	1,428	99.0	0.0	0.0	1.0	0.0	3.7	55.0	67.4	15.1	65.8	840	89.8
Chatham town (Barnstable).................	6,124	5,982	-2.3	6,019	94.6	1.8	0.3	1.0	2.3	9.6	44.8	61.8	18.1	58.8	2,894	92.7
Chelmsford town (Middlesex).................	33,792	35,391	4.7	35,126	85.2	0.9	9.1	1.5	3.3	20.7	18.8	44.5	22.2	56.5	13,564	93.8
Chelsea city & MCD (Suffolk)...................	35,181	39,690	12.8	39,992	20.6	5.4	3.7	3.3	67.0	26.0	9.5	33.3	63.0	18.5	13,268	87.8
Cheshire CDP.................	514	-	-	539	98.5	0.0	0.0	1.5	0.0	13.0	13.0	51.8	24.0	37.6	216	94.4
Cheshire town (Berkshire)	3,235	3,129	-3.3	3,159	96.3	0.6	0.0	0.7	2.4	12.3	23.0	51.3	36.8	27.1	1,473	89.5
Chester CDP	627	-	-	787	98.2	0.5	0.0	0.8	0.5	20.2	16.8	43.6	54.9	15.6	295	86.1
Chester town (Hampden) .	1,337	1,369	2.4	1,470	99.0	0.3	0.0	0.4	0.3	16.8	19.7	45.8	49.4	22.4	583	89.7
Chesterfield town (Hampshire)................	1,222	1,249	2.2	1,234	96.7	0.0	0.0	0.7	2.6	16.0	22.7	46.9	41.7	30.1	537	89.2
Chicopee city & MCD (Hampden).................	55,307	55,126	-0.3	55,421	71.2	4.1	2.4	1.3	21.0	20.0	18.4	39.7	48.5	20.0	23,090	87.4
Chilmark town (Dukes)	870	922	6.0	1,222	93.5	0.9	0.2	0.6	4.7	12.8	28.3	51.2	9.0	66.4	456	96.7
Clarksburg town (Berkshire).................	1,707	1,638	-4.0	1,777	96.1	1.1	0.0	0.7	2.1	19.6	22.3	45.0	44.5	27.7	709	89.7
Clinton town (Worcester) .	13,600	14,000	2.9	13,935	77.8	1.1	1.8	2.0	17.3	20.6	13.0	37.2	39.5	29.4	5,594	91.2
Clinton CDP....................	7,389	-	-	7,154	72.4	1.9	0.1	2.6	22.9	20.0	11.6	36.2	43.2	25.6	2,895	87.5
Cochituate CDP...............	6,569	-	-	7,226	80.3	0.1	10.8	2.9	5.9	26.1	15.9	42.7	10.6	76.4	2,427	96.5
Cohasset town (Norfolk)...	7,540	8,548	13.4	8,484	95.4	0.6	1.0	1.6	1.4	28.8	17.0	44.0	13.2	70.8	3,087	94.1
Colrain town (Franklin).....	1,669	1,661	-0.5	1,771	97.0	0.5	0.0	0.9	1.6	16.4	25.1	52.7	39.0	33.0	751	88.1
Concord town (Middlesex)	17,680	18,918	7.0	19,116	79.4	4.0	7.4	1.9	7.2	24.1	20.8	45.8	16.6	74.2	6,635	95.8
Conway town (Franklin)	1,900	1,873	-1.4	1,968	96.8	0.0	0.2	0.4	2.6	20.5	24.4	51.2	17.3	62.5	800	94.4
Cordaville CDP................	2,650	-	-	3,039	80.7	0.6	15.5	2.8	0.4	31.4	6.1	39.7	14.0	67.2	971	99.1
Cummington town (Hampshire)................	868	874	0.7	845	96.4	0.0	0.6	1.3	1.7	17.8	25.6	52.4	33.4	41.1	422	84.4
Dalton town (Berkshire)	6,751	6,525	-3.3	6,610	95.4	0.1	1.6	0.7	2.1	16.5	21.6	50.7	32.0	35.4	3,034	91.8
Danvers town & CDP (Essex).....................	26,500	27,549	4.0	27,586	87.6	2.3	2.6	2.4	5.1	19.0	20.9	44.6	29.4	43.2	10,689	90.9
Dartmouth town (Bristol)...	34,033	34,188	0.5	34,204	89.1	2.9	2.5	2.4	3.1	15.3	20.3	41.0	42.5	34.6	11,563	88.3
Dedham town & CDP (Norfolk)...................	24,723	25,219	2.0	25,283	78.8	6.8	2.7	2.9	8.7	19.1	19.3	42.9	25.3	53.3	10,035	92.5
Deerfield CDP..................	643	-	-	621	59.9	20.3	0.6	9.7	9.5	18.5	14.0	40.0	10.0	74.6	155	80.0
Deerfield town (Franklin)...	5,122	4,991	-2.6	5,017	90.3	2.8	0.4	2.7	3.9	19.2	20.8	50.2	20.3	49.4	1,960	89.8
Dennis CDP....................	2,407	-	-	2,307	95.8	0.0	0.8	3.1	0.3	5.8	51.1	65.9	27.7	51.0	1,165	90.2
Dennis town (Barnstable) .	14,221	13,871	-2.5	13,939	90.8	4.0	1.0	2.2	2.1	12.3	37.4	57.9	30.1	41.3	6,862	90.9
Dennis Port CDP	3,162	-	-	3,428	81.7	11.2	0.4	2.3	4.4	19.3	22.3	47.9	34.1	33.0	1,609	89.4
Devens CDP....................	1,840	-	-	1,969	55.8	17.3	10.9	2.0	14.0	12.7	13.0	43.1	32.6	30.9	239	100.0
Dighton town (Bristol)	7,104	7,967	12.1	7,730	92.0	2.9	0.0	4.6	0.4	19.5	13.9	43.1	39.0	29.6	2,835	89.9
Douglas town (Worcester)	8,468	9,038	6.7	8,859	91.1	0.3	1.8	1.1	5.7	23.6	12.1	44.1	28.2	39.5	3,234	91.2

1 May be of any race.

Table A. All Places — **Population and Housing**

STATE City, town, township, borough, or CDP (county if applicable)	Population 2010 census total population	Population 2019 estimated population	Population Percent change 2010–2019	ACS total population estimate 2015–2019	White alone, not Hispanic or Latino	Black alone, not Hispanic or Latino	Asian alone, not Hispanic or Latino	All other races or 2 or more races, not Hispanic or Latino	Hispanic or Latino[1]	Under 18 years old	Age 65 years and older	Median age	Percent High school diploma or less	Percent Bachelor's degree or more	Occupied housing units Total	Percent with a computer
	1	2	3	4	5	6	7	8	9	10	11	12	13	14	15	16
MASSACHUSETTS—Con.																
Dover CDP......................	2,265	-	-	2,539	85.4	0.0	10.5	3.6	0.4	29.4	16.4	43.9	8.3	80.8	853	99.1
Dover town (Norfolk).........	5,591	6,127	9.6	6,044	84.8	0.0	10.1	2.0	3.1	27.7	15.5	45.2	6.8	84.8	2,031	99.2
Dracut town (Middlesex)...	29,407	31,634	7.6	31,373	83.4	3.9	4.0	2.1	6.6	21.8	15.3	40.1	41.0	31.1	11,501	92.2
Dudley town (Worcester) ..	11,375	11,773	3.5	11,723	88.4	1.9	3.3	2.8	3.6	20.7	14.4	38.4	37.9	32.0	3,905	94.0
Dunstable town (Middlesex)	3,179	3,403	7.0	3,366	92.6	0.0	4.0	1.3	2.0	21.4	14.8	45.2	19.2	54.8	1,178	96.8
Duxbury CDP..................	1,802	-	-	1,567	97.4	0.0	1.5	0.0	1.1	18.1	24.4	53.2	4.6	78.6	628	95.2
Duxbury town (Plymouth) .	15,060	15,921	5.7	15,812	95.5	0.8	1.9	1.0	0.9	25.3	21.4	46.5	11.2	72.5	5,714	95.6
East Bridgewater town (Plymouth)	13,796	14,526	5.3	14,466	88.0	3.9	1.5	4.4	2.1	25.5	15.4	37.8	35.5	30.5	4,828	95.9
East Brookfield town (Worcester)	2,188	2,210	1.0	2,040	95.6	1.1	0.0	0.4	2.8	21.7	15.7	37.8	35.9	36.6	795	89.1
East Brookfield CDP.........	1,323	-	-	1,037	95.9	0.0	0.0	0.9	3.3	17.6	16.0	35.5	39.2	30.1	428	87.9
East Dennis CDP..............	2,753	-	-	2,575	91.4	1.3	1.2	3.3	2.8	9.0	53.2	65.7	23.8	50.0	1,348	85.3
East Douglas CDP............	2,557	-	-	2,592	85.4	0.0	5.4	2.2	7.1	20.1	15.1	48.4	34.8	36.7	1,056	83.2
East Falmouth CDP...........	6,038	-	-	6,441	89.3	3.5	0.8	4.5	2.0	17.4	30.3	53.3	37.6	33.1	2,786	93.0
Eastham town (Barnstable)	4,956	4,906		4,901	91.5	1.7	3.1	2.8	0.9	11.2	38.4	60.1	23.4	50.6	2,396	93.2
Easthampton Town city & MCD (Hampshi........	16,049	15,829	-1.4	15,960	89.2	1.9	1.5	2.8	4.5	15.2	19.1	44.6	31.1	39.1	7,209	92.5
East Harwich CDP............	4,872	-	-	4,796	95.6	1.5	0.3	1.7	0.9	12.0	31.3	56.4	23.5	44.8	2,086	97.9
East Longmeadow town (Hampden)	15,767	16,192	2.7	16,242	85.3	4.7	4.4	1.8	3.9	21.7	21.7	45.5	28.5	42.6	5,958	85.4
Easton town (Bristol)	23,116	25,105	8.6	24,621	88.1	4.2	2.5	2.3	3.0	20.6	15.1	41.3	25.0	49.1	8,477	95.5
East Pepperell CDP..........	2,059	-	-	1,811	93.3	1.9	0.6	0.6	3.6	17.1	21.5	49.6	34.6	31.6	799	94.0
East Sandwich CDP	3,940	-	-	3,473	98.2	0.0	1.5	0.0	0.3	16.8	31.5	54.6	13.6	63.4	1,383	95.3
Edgartown CDP................	-	-	-	508	95.7	3.7	0.0	0.0	0.6	0.0	36.2	61.0	22.4	44.2	226	73.0
Edgartown town (Dukes) ..	4,067	4,348	6.9	4,320	80.7	1.2	0.7	10.4	6.9	18.1	19.9	47.3	31.0	40.8	1,453	87.5
Egremont town (Berkshire)	1,223	1,205	-1.5	1,402	90.2	1.1	1.4	1.6	5.8	17.0	27.9	51.5	20.7	52.5	614	95.9
Erving town (Franklin).......	1,800	1,750	-2.8	1,740	92.8	1.4	0.0	2.9	2.9	22.2	19.0	44.0	52.1	16.1	670	86.7
Essex CDP.....................	1,471	-	-	1,393	100.0	0.0	0.0	0.0	0.0	19.5	21.0	47.3	17.6	58.1	601	98.3
Essex town (Essex).........	3,504	3,799	8.4	3,745	99.0	0.0	0.0	0.7	0.3	24.6	18.4	46.1	17.5	58.3	1,457	98.7
Everett city & MCD (Middlesex)	41,553	46,451	11.8	46,118	43.6	16.5	8.1	3.4	28.3	22.4	11.2	35.9	54.0	20.0	16,021	89.1
Fairhaven town (Bristol)....	15,873	16,078	1.3	16,045	90.6	0.7	3.6	3.1	2.0	18.2	22.7	46.4	43.9	25.5	6,392	87.8
Fall River city & MCD (Bristol)...................	88,865	89,541	0.8	89,388	77.2	5.3	1.9	5.1	10.5	20.7	16.6	39.6	59.3	15.4	38,456	81.9
Falmouth CDP	3,799	-	-	3,540	85.2	2.6	1.6	7.5	3.1	9.0	42.0	62.2	30.8	44.7	2,010	79.3
Falmouth town (Barnstable)	31,532	30,993	-1.7	31,124	88.8	2.0	1.8	4.8	2.5	15.1	31.9	55.0	28.6	44.8	13,821	92.6
Fiskdale CDP...................	2,583	-	-	3,087	93.6	0.0	3.7	0.0	2.7	24.7	17.8	38.1	36.5	42.4	1,192	84.1
Fitchburg city & MCD (Worcester)	40,325	40,638	0.8	40,702	62.3	3.6	2.3	2.9	28.8	22.6	13.5	35.5	49.8	21.0	14,965	89.8
Florida town (Berkshire) ...	760	715	-5.9	808	95.3	0.0	0.0	3.0	1.7	20.5	19.4	45.8	59.6	18.7	314	88.2
Forestdale CDP...............	4,099	-	-	3,791	98.4	0.0	0.4	0.5	0.7	16.6	18.0	49.4	27.4	30.0	1,434	95.7
Foxborough town (Norfolk)	16,872	18,399	9.1	17,727	83.8	5.7	3.5	1.7	5.3	21.9	17.8	42.4	23.8	52.8	6,805	94.9
Foxborough CDP..............	5,625	-	-	6,296	79.1	10.7	3.4	0.3	6.5	19.3	24.2	45.1	30.7	45.3	2,728	89.5
Framingham city & MCD (Middlesex)	68,323	74,416	8.9	72,308	63.0	6.2	7.8	6.9	16.1	19.6	15.7	38.9	33.2	47.6	28,222	93.2
Franklin Town city & MCD (Norfolk)..............	31,633	34,087	7.8	33,256	89.2	0.9	5.8	2.5	1.6	23.9	12.8	41.1	22.1	55.7	11,941	95.7
Freetown town (Bristol).....	8,872	9,394	5.9	9,299	93.1	0.5	0.7	2.7	3.0	20.7	17.9	44.9	39.5	32.4	3,262	93.8
Gardner city & MCD (Worcester)	20,233	20,683	2.2	20,610	81.2	2.3	3.2	4.0	9.3	19.7	15.4	41.0	46.0	18.3	8,228	86.2
Georgetown town (Essex)	8,203	8,768	6.9	8,695	93.2	0.5	1.2	1.6	3.5	22.5	15.8	43.4	21.7	53.4	3,295	95.4
Gill town (Franklin)...........	1,469	1,465	-0.3	1,596	89.8	5.5	3.0	1.0	0.6	13.8	19.5	48.8	27.4	49.5	579	95.2
Gloucester city & MCD (Essex)....................	28,789	30,430	5.7	30,162	91.9	1.4	1.9	2.3	2.4	16.5	23.0	50.9	33.8	39.9	13,110	91.0
Goshen town (Hampshire)	1,056	1,059	0.3	913	94.3	0.0	0.0	0.0	5.7	12.4	16.8	53.7	31.2	40.9	413	96.6
Gosnold town (Dukes)......	75	75	0.0	49	100.0	0.0	0.0	0.0	0.0	0.0	36.7	63.3	28.6	63.3	26	92.3
Grafton town (Worcester) .	17,763	18,883	6.3	18,743	78.9	2.8	8.1	3.9	6.3	24.1	13.1	41.2	26.4	50.4	7,034	95.2
Granby CDP....................	1,368	-	-	1,272	85.8	0.0	0.0	1.4	12.7	7.2	25.1	50.2	33.4	47.2	605	82.8
Granby town (Hampshire)	6,240	6,291	0.8	6,322	92.2	1.0	0.8	2.0	3.9	16.8	18.7	47.5	29.7	43.6	2,603	88.1
Granville town (Hampden)	1,566	1,611	2.9	1,691	95.5	0.0	0.2	0.7	3.6	21.5	16.7	42.4	41.7	31.4	622	95.8
Great Barrington CDP	2,231	-	-	2,070	87.2	2.4	0.0	1.5	8.9	13.8	22.1	49.3	38.9	44.1	1,055	95.5
Great Barrington town (Berkshire)	7,104	6,945	-2.2	6,901	85.8	3.7	2.8	1.4	6.3	21.1	22.9	46.5	36.1	41.2	2,813	90.9
Greenfield Town city & MCD (Franklin).............	17,450	17,258	-1.1	17,375	86.9	1.9	1.3	2.3	7.7	17.5	21.2	43.7	36.2	34.7	8,063	90.3
Green Harbor-Cedar Crest CDP...................	2,609	-	-	2,703	100.0	0.0	0.0	0.0	0.0	14.6	29.1	53.3	29.0	38.6	974	96.5
Groton CDP.....................	1,124	-	-	1,345	80.3	0.0	8.4	9.2	2.1	27.6	13.8	41.3	22.7	45.3	516	90.9
Groton town (Middlesex)...	10,643	11,325	6.4	11,313	91.0	0.2	3.6	3.9	1.4	23.3	14.9	45.6	16.9	64.2	4,071	95.4
Groveland town (Essex)....	6,450	6,849	6.2	6,780	95.9	0.0	0.7	0.3	3.2	20.3	17.8	45.8	24.3	48.7	2,448	97.8
Hadley town (Hampshire) .	5,249	5,342	1.8	5,319	84.6	7.9	3.4	1.8	2.3	16.1	23.7	48.9	24.5	54.7	2,294	91.6
Halifax town (Plymouth)....	7,515	7,896	5.1	7,842	96.2	2.3	0.4	0.5	0.7	21.2	15.2	41.7	44.2	30.6	2,904	90.7
Hamilton town (Essex)......	7,764	8,051	3.7	8,031	91.0	0.3	6.0	1.3	1.5	25.8	14.1	41.1	13.4	69.3	2,719	95.7
Hampden town (Hampden)..................	5,137	5,177	0.8	5,178	93.9	0.2	0.7	1.5	3.7	16.5	24.9	51.5	35.5	35.3	2,000	95.1
Hancock town (Berkshire)	719	696	-3.2	599	93.5	1.2	4.2	0.3	0.8	14.5	23.2	54.4	41.0	35.2	242	88.8
Hanover town (Plymouth) .	13,873	14,570	5.0	14,459	96.5	1.0	0.4	1.5	0.6	26.0	16.7	41.9	26.1	48.7	4,913	93.5
Hanscom AFB CDP...........	-	-	-	2,045	68.1	2.4	11.5	4.3	13.7	43.0	0.2	24.4	10.4	57.3	554	100.0
Hanson CDP....................	2,118	-	-	1,769	96.6	0.0	0.6	1.3	1.5	17.0	18.2	44.6	41.2	30.8	620	96.0
Hanson town (Plymouth) ..	10,203	10,914	7.0	10,777	93.3	0.3	3.1	2.4	0.9	19.3	17.5	44.8	36.0	32.5	3,907	93.3
Hardwick town (Worcester)	3,002	3,057	1.8	3,048	93.9	0.6	0.1	0.5	4.9	20.1	20.2	44.3	38.7	31.3	1,216	89.4
Harvard town (Worcester)	6,521	6,620	1.5	6,569	81.5	5.2	5.2	2.0	6.1	22.0	17.0	45.8	18.2	63.6	1,864	99.4
Harwich town (Barnstable)	12,223	12,142	-0.7	12,147	91.8	3.1	0.4	2.5	2.2	13.9	34.6	57.6	25.3	47.6	5,433	95.4
Harwich Center CDP	1,798	-	-	1,406	83.9	14.9	0.0	0.0	1.2	18.3	34.4	49.9	27.1	55.3	608	93.1
Harwich Port CDP	1,644	-	-	1,809	95.5	1.7	0.0	0.5	2.3	10.2	51.9	65.6	16.5	57.3	962	91.6
Hatfield CDP....................	1,318	-	-	1,305	92.0	1.0	0.0	0.7	6.4	13.9	25.7	54.0	36.7	33.4	631	82.3

1 May be of any race.

Table A. All Places — **Population and Housing**

STATE City, town, township, borough, or CDP (county if applicable)	Population				Race and Hispanic or Latino origin (percent)					Age (percent)			Educational attainment of persons age 25 and older		Occupied housing units	
	2010 census total population	2019 estimated population	Percent change 2010–2019	ACS total population estimate 2015–2019	White alone, not Hispanic or Latino	Black alone, not Hispanic or Latino	Asian alone, not Hispanic or Latino	All other races or 2 or more races, not Hispanic or Latino	Hispanic or Latino[1]	Under 18 years old	Age 65 years and older	Median age	Percent High school diploma or less	Percent Bachelor's degree or more	Total	Percent with a computer
	1	2	3	4	5	6	7	8	9	10	11	12	13	14	15	16
MASSACHUSETTS—Con.																
Hatfield town (Hampshire)	3,259	3,251	-0.2	3,274	95.4	0.4	0.3	0.7	3.2	16.3	22.1	49.5	30.5	42.1	1,493	83.3
Haverhill city & MCD (Essex)	60,878	64,014	5.2	63,533	69.7	3.1	1.3	2.7	23.2	23.1	12.7	36.8	39.9	29.8	24,256	92.9
Hawley town (Franklin)	337	334	-0.9	370	91.6	1.6	3.0	0.0	3.8	15.1	25.7	53.9	35.8	41.1	136	83.1
Heath town (Franklin)	706	695	-1.6	746	95.4	0.0	0.0	2.1	2.4	25.1	27.7	42.7	33.1	28.4	262	85.1
Hingham CDP	5,650	-	-	6,461	98.5	0.7	0.3	0.0	0.5	28.9	13.9	43.1	7.7	76.9	2,225	94.4
Hingham town (Plymouth)	22,155	24,679	11.4	23,652	95.2	0.5	1.6	1.4	1.1	26.1	20.7	45.6	13.3	71.1	8,873	91.5
Hinsdale town (Berkshire)	2,025	1,911	-5.6	1,837	97.8	0.0	0.0	1.1	1.1	15.1	24.6	51.7	42.3	33.8	798	92.6
Holbrook town & CDP (Norfolk)	10,806	11,033	2.1	11,045	72.1	15.7	3.5	2.2	6.6	18.0	17.6	44.2	33.3	28.2	4,174	90.6
Holden town (Worcester)	17,464	19,303	10.5	19,051	91.5	0.7	2.0	1.5	4.3	23.5	17.4	43.3	18.9	57.7	7,046	95.9
Holland CDP	1,464	-	-	1,547	97.4	0.3	0.0	0.6	1.7	22.4	19.5	42.4	35.5	25.6	619	93.2
Holland town (Hampden)	2,478	2,482	0.2	2,630	95.9	0.8	0.0	0.8	2.5	22.3	17.6	45.5	33.2	27.9	1,006	93.9
Holliston town (Middlesex)	13,546	14,912	10.1	14,724	87.4	0.9	5.5	2.4	3.9	25.4	14.4	42.2	14.1	66.2	5,270	94.3
Holyoke city & MCD (Hampden)	39,881	40,117	0.6	40,241	41.3	2.9	0.6	1.2	53.9	23.8	14.2	35.2	53.9	21.5	15,278	85.6
Hopedale town (Worcester)	5,905	5,951	0.8	5,947	96.1	0.3	0.5	2.2	1.0	24.3	17.1	45.0	27.8	43.3	2,181	90.6
Hopedale CDP	3,753	-	-	3,363	96.6	0.6	0.8	1.7	0.4	20.5	13.6	47.8	26.0	40.3	1,319	91.9
Hopkinton CDP	2,550	-	-	3,098	88.2	0.8	2.8	3.5	4.7	25.8	16.9	40.6	26.1	57.6	1,127	88.6
Hopkinton town (Middlesex)	14,909	18,470	23.9	17,598	81.6	1.8	11.4	2.0	3.2	26.5	14.1	40.6	14.6	71.9	6,304	96.4
Housatonic CDP	1,109	-	-	753	79.9	0.0	0.0	0.0	20.1	13.7	26.4	57.6	48.5	25.2	443	90.7
Hubbardston town (Worcester)	4,382	4,829	10.2	4,708	88.5	0.8	3.5	1.5	5.8	19.0	18.6	46.1	30.8	31.6	1,697	94.4
Hudson town (Middlesex)	19,075	19,864	4.1	19,887	89.2	1.2	2.7	1.0	5.8	19.4	17.8	44.0	33.4	44.4	7,877	91.3
Hudson CDP	14,907	-	-	15,346	88.0	1.3	2.9	0.7	7.0	19.0	18.6	43.9	37.9	40.4	6,213	90.1
Hull town & CDP (Plymouth)	10,293	10,475	1.8	10,455	94.6	0.5	1.0	2.2	1.7	13.0	24.0	53.5	28.0	45.8	4,765	91.4
Huntington CDP	936	-	-	634	95.1	0.0	0.0	2.8	2.1	10.6	15.5	40.9	44.5	11.6	326	92.3
Huntington town (Hampshire)	2,182	2,169	-0.6	2,058	95.7	0.8	0.0	2.6	1.0	16.0	18.0	47.7	38.6	28.8	921	96.0
Ipswich CDP	4,222	-	-	4,699	89.1	4.2	1.8	1.3	3.6	20.0	17.8	44.4	30.5	47.1	2,112	86.8
Ipswich town (Essex)	13,176	14,074	6.8	13,963	92.0	2.0	0.9	0.9	4.2	20.6	22.4	48.4	22.2	54.1	5,761	90.6
Kingston CDP	5,591	-	-	6,278	91.9	0.0	0.0	2.8	5.3	23.1	16.1	41.9	34.2	39.7	2,439	97.5
Kingston town (Plymouth)	12,628	13,863	9.8	13,566	93.7	0.1	0.4	2.3	3.6	23.0	19.2	44.0	31.7	43.5	4,949	94.4
Lakeville town (Plymouth)	10,610	11,561	9.0	11,372	92.4	2.0	0.8	2.0	2.8	21.0	15.7	44.2	31.2	39.2	4,083	95.5
Lancaster town (Worcester)	8,069	8,082	0.2	8,044	81.4	6.9	2.0	2.3	7.3	19.0	16.9	40.7	38.8	39.5	2,530	91.5
Lanesborough town (Berkshire)	3,090	2,940	-4.9	2,973	96.4	1.8	1.1	0.6	0.0	19.5	24.7	52.3	27.9	41.8	1,255	95.1
Lawrence city & MCD (Essex)	76,343	80,028	4.8	79,942	14.8	2.2	1.7	0.7	80.6	26.3	10.4	32.3	64.5	10.8	25,959	83.9
Lee CDP	2,051	-	-	1,717	85.7	0.9	0.2	11.1	2.2	15.7	25.0	44.1	35.0	28.4	762	96.6
Lee town (Berkshire)	5,948	5,664	-4.8	5,742	89.6	1.9	3.2	3.9	1.4	19.7	24.9	44.7	34.7	32.7	2,243	93.6
Leicester town (Worcester)	10,892	11,341	4.1	11,306	91.0	3.0	0.5	1.7	3.8	18.2	14.4	42.5	36.8	28.7	4,070	90.7
Lenox CDP	1,675	-	-	1,899	91.3	1.6	0.0	0.9	6.2	8.8	45.9	61.5	31.3	46.9	1,020	75.2
Lenox town (Berkshire)	5,072	4,944	-2.5	4,963	89.3	2.8	0.6	1.1	6.1	13.0	38.4	55.4	26.1	51.8	2,278	87.0
Leominster city & MCD (Worcester)	40,760	41,716	2.3	41,606	69.3	5.8	2.9	3.6	18.4	21.7	15.9	40.5	41.0	29.2	16,830	91.4
Leverett town (Franklin)	1,842	1,837	-0.3	2,001	94.6	0.3	2.1	1.8	1.2	20.7	25.9	47.5	19.5	65.1	766	96.1
Lexington town & CDP (Middlesex)	31,406	33,132	5.5	33,340	62.7	1.2	30.1	4.0	2.1	27.1	19.6	45.7	7.7	84.7	11,811	96.0
Leyden town (Franklin)	718	715	-0.4	710	99.2	0.0	0.0	0.0	0.8	15.8	21.0	51.7	28.3	37.3	283	92.9
Lincoln town (Middlesex)	6,371	7,052	10.7	6,830	81.4	0.8	6.3	2.8	8.6	27.3	19.8	43.5	6.2	74.8	2,709	95.6
Littleton town (Middlesex)	8,910	10,227	14.8	10,071	89.0	0.6	5.9	3.2	1.3	23.2	15.4	44.7	21.0	56.0	3,657	95.3
Littleton Common CDP	2,789	-	-	3,293	90.3	0.1	4.1	3.9	1.6	21.7	14.3	45.3	25.1	49.7	1,306	97.7
Longmeadow town & CDP (Hampden)	15,783	15,705	-0.5	15,791	84.4	0.9	5.9	1.9	6.8	23.6	20.8	45.0	17.7	65.1	5,609	94.9
Lowell city & MCD (Middlesex)	106,525	110,997	4.2	111,306	48.7	7.2	23.0	3.0	18.1	21.2	11.0	33.5	52.6	24.1	39,421	83.4
Ludlow town (Hampden)	21,099	21,233	0.6	21,291	87.3	1.1	1.0	2.0	8.6	19.0	18.7	44.1	51.3	22.9	7,925	85.9
Lunenburg CDP	1,760	-	-	1,778	94.8	0.1	0.4	4.5	0.2	17.4	16.5	44.4	29.8	37.3	684	98.7
Lunenburg town (Worcester)	10,076	11,736	16.5	11,402	88.4	1.3	1.4	3.0	5.9	23.0	16.9	44.3	33.1	37.1	4,310	93.5
Lynn city & MCD (Essex)	90,324	94,299	4.4	93,743	35.9	10.8	7.2	3.3	42.8	24.5	11.7	34.5	56.1	18.5	32,599	87.1
Lynnfield town & CDP (Essex)	11,593	12,999	12.1	12,894	90.7	0.6	4.4	1.9	2.4	24.8	19.7	43.6	21.9	55.1	4,590	92.4
Madaket CDP	236	-	-	274	100.0	0.0	0.0	0.0	0.0	5.5	30.7	51.3	25.5	53.7	113	100.0
Malden city & MCD (Middlesex)	59,536	60,470	1.6	60,984	47.0	17.8	22.5	4.3	8.5	19.4	12.7	34.6	39.3	39.0	23,025	91.0
Manchester-by-the-Sea town (Essex)	5,136	5,434	5.8	5,383	97.1	0.0	0.7	0.6	1.5	22.6	23.6	48.9	15.5	70.8	2,075	94.6
Mansfield town (Bristol)	23,183	24,470	5.6	23,947	86.4	1.9	6.0	1.6	4.1	22.5	10.9	39.3	21.7	54.8	8,650	96.4
Mansfield Center CDP	7,360	-	-	7,905	84.8	1.9	3.7	3.1	6.6	19.4	12.9	39.6	24.8	49.5	3,196	95.2
Marblehead town & CDP (Essex)	19,808	20,555	3.8	20,500	91.1	1.4	1.4	1.1	5.0	23.2	21.8	47.9	11.2	71.3	8,122	97.2
Marion town (Plymouth)	4,907	5,188	5.7	5,132	84.7	1.4	1.6	7.9	4.4	22.2	27.0	50.2	30.5	51.4	1,942	90.4
Marion Center CDP	1,111	-	-	1,076	87.7	3.3	5.5	3.3	0.2	18.2	38.2	54.8	18.3	60.2	411	92.7
Marlborough city & MCD (Middlesex)	38,501	39,597	2.8	39,736	69.2	3.8	5.5	6.5	15.1	20.5	14.2	39.8	36.1	39.0	15,730	94.6
Marshfield CDP	4,335	-	-	4,928	94.0	0.0	0.7	1.8	3.5	26.4	16.4	41.5	18.8	53.2	1,912	88.2
Marshfield town (Plymouth)	25,125	25,967	3.4	25,838	96.3	0.2	0.5	0.8	2.1	21.2	18.3	45.0	21.8	48.0	9,649	94.1
Marshfield Hills CDP	2,356	-	-	2,315	99.5	0.0	0.5	0.0	0.0	26.0	12.5	43.7	8.5	64.5	844	94.7
Mashpee town (Barnstable)	14,004	14,229	1.6	14,148	85.7	3.2	2.2	8.2	0.6	15.9	29.0	52.7	24.6	41.4	6,360	94.2
Mashpee Neck CDP	1,000	-	-	1,386	87.3	0.4	7.6	2.5	2.1	22.2	16.1	45.8	13.2	56.6	517	93.2
Mattapoisett town (Plymouth)	6,045	6,401	5.9	6,336	95.2	0.0	0.0	2.3	2.4	14.7	25.3	53.4	25.3	48.7	2,648	94.1
Mattapoisett Center CDP	2,915	-	-	3,354	95.5	0.0	0.0	1.6	2.9	14.0	23.2	52.1	24.9	50.0	1,391	93.4

1 May be of any race.

Table A. All Places — **Population and Housing**

STATE City, town, township, borough, or CDP (county if applicable)	Population				Race and Hispanic or Latino origin (percent)					Age (percent)			Educational attainment of persons age 25 and older		Occupied housing units	
	2010 census total population	2019 estimated population	Percent change 2010–2019	ACS total population estimate 2015–2019	White alone, not Hispanic or Latino	Black alone, not Hispanic or Latino	Asian alone, not Hispanic or Latino	All other races or 2 or more races, not Hispanic or Latino	Hispanic or Latino[1]	Under 18 years old	Age 65 years and older	Median age	Percent High school diploma or less	Percent Bachelor's degree or more	Total	Percent with a computer
	1	2	3	4	5	6	7	8	9	10	11	12	13	14	15	16
MASSACHUSETTS—Con.																
Maynard town & CDP (Middlesex)	10,112	11,336	12.1	10,754	91.9	1.3	1.7	1.7	3.4	21.6	15.2	41.7	23.0	51.1	4,262	97.3
Medfield CDP	6,483	-	-	6,966	90.5	1.6	5.4	1.3	1.2	26.8	16.1	43.5	12.6	69.8	2,525	95.9
Medfield town (Norfolk)	12,027	12,955	7.7	12,841	91.1	0.9	4.8	1.3	2.0	29.9	13.4	41.8	9.9	73.7	4,245	97.4
Medford city & MCD (Middlesex)	56,280	57,341	1.9	57,637	71.1	9.1	9.8	3.5	6.5	14.7	14.8	35.3	27.5	53.8	22,917	93.4
Medway town (Norfolk)	12,754	13,479	5.7	13,325	90.0	2.7	2.4	2.3	2.6	24.6	13.4	41.6	20.0	59.0	4,735	96.5
Melrose city & MCD (Middlesex)	26,967	28,016	3.9	28,113	85.7	2.9	6.2	2.1	3.2	20.1	17.2	41.3	18.9	61.6	11,329	91.5
Mendon town (Worcester)	5,853	6,223	6.3	6,115	92.3	0.1	1.6	3.7	2.3	23.9	16.1	43.7	28.5	46.2	2,059	96.5
Merrimac town (Essex)	6,338	6,960	9.8	6,890	95.6	0.2	1.0	0.7	2.4	19.5	19.1	47.7	29.0	43.7	2,710	92.7
Methuen Town city & MCD (Essex)	47,328	50,706	7.1	50,282	60.9	3.2	4.1	2.4	29.5	20.9	16.0	40.7	41.9	28.1	17,907	92.3
Middleborough town (Plymouth)	23,114	25,463	10.2	24,850	92.6	1.6	0.9	2.4	2.4	19.1	18.9	44.9	41.4	26.2	9,283	93.6
Middleborough Center CDP	7,319	-	-	7,343	92.2	1.8	0.0	3.0	3.0	21.1	13.8	35.0	44.7	25.2	2,785	91.3
Middlefield town (Hampshire)	519	534	2.9	408	94.4	0.0	1.2	4.4	0.0	3.9	21.3	59.0	39.1	23.3	199	95.5
Middleton town (Essex)	8,987	10,110	12.5	9,872	90.3	0.8	1.2	1.5	6.2	18.9	18.4	42.9	37.6	39.3	2,999	93.6
Milford town (Worcester)	27,989	29,101	4.0	28,883	73.8	2.3	2.8	7.1	14.0	23.1	15.2	39.4	38.1	36.3	11,046	91.9
Milford CDP	25,055	-	-	26,084	72.8	1.5	2.8	7.3	15.5	24.0	14.5	38.2	40.7	34.3	9,986	91.4
Millbury town (Worcester)	13,261	13,947	5.2	13,732	91.1	1.4	2.4	3.8	1.2	20.1	17.7	44.9	38.1	32.5	5,275	94.9
Millers Falls CDP	1,139	-	-	1,284	97.8	0.2	0.0	1.5	0.5	19.4	16.4	40.1	50.0	17.1	488	85.9
Millis town (Norfolk)	7,900	8,310	5.2	8,233	92.9	2.3	1.5	1.0	2.3	21.9	17.9	45.4	25.2	52.4	3,161	94.6
Millis-Clicquot CDP	4,403	-	-	4,658	91.6	4.0	1.5	1.7	1.1	23.4	15.6	43.6	29.9	47.5	1,929	92.5
Millville town (Worcester)	3,189	3,257	2.1	3,256	96.3	0.5	0.0	2.2	0.9	24.3	12.2	41.3	38.5	27.9	1,241	92.9
Milton town & CDP (Norfolk)	27,007	27,593	2.2	27,572	71.7	14.9	6.5	3.6	3.2	24.6	16.9	39.5	19.4	61.0	8,875	94.3
Monomoscoy Island CDP	147	-	-	100	100.0	0.0	0.0	0.0	0.0	0.0	31.0	60.0	43.0	31.0	60	100.0
Monroe town (Franklin)	120	115	-4.2	87	100.0	0.0	0.0	0.0	0.0	20.7	20.7	57.1	52.2	10.4	49	77.6
Monson town (Hampden)	8,563	8,787	2.6	8,779	95.9	1.1	0.5	1.0	1.5	18.0	19.9	48.0	42.3	26.7	3,472	90.7
Monson Center CDP	2,107	-	-	1,881	95.9	2.5	0.0	1.0	0.6	14.0	18.8	44.0	43.3	23.9	839	92.8
Montague town (Franklin)	8,463	8,212	-3.0	8,279	88.9	1.9	0.2	4.7	4.2	15.5	20.5	44.9	41.7	27.2	3,804	84.3
Monterey town (Berkshire)	956	924	-3.3	774	96.9	0.4	0.4	1.4	0.9	14.1	36.4	58.5	27.0	54.6	362	97.0
Montgomery town (Hampden)	843	866	2.7	798	94.6	0.5	1.3	2.3	1.4	17.4	18.4	49.9	32.2	36.0	330	90.9
Monument Beach CDP	2,790	-	-	2,807	83.8	0.0	0.0	7.0	9.2	13.5	32.0	54.1	38.8	30.1	1,258	91.3
Mount Washington town (Berkshire)	167	157	-6.0	148	93.2	0.0	1.4	4.1	1.4	0.7	32.4	54.8	27.7	53.2	86	84.9
Nahant town & CDP (Essex)	3,410	3,513	3.0	3,502	95.4	0.0	2.2	0.9	1.5	13.6	24.4	52.3	21.9	57.2	1,602	95.8
Nantucket CDP	7,446	-	-	7,984	87.4	3.7	0.7	3.1	5.1	20.8	12.7	39.4	25.2	51.4	2,612	96.1
Nantucket town (Nantucket)	10,172	11,399	12.1	11,168	85.2	6.6	0.6	3.4	4.2	20.7	14.6	40.3	24.2	52.8	3,713	96.6
Natick town (Middlesex)	33,012	36,050	9.2	36,128	78.9	1.8	12.8	2.4	4.1	24.0	15.4	41.0	15.4	68.8	14,537	94.3
Needham town & CDP (Norfolk)	28,973	31,388	8.3	30,970	82.6	2.8	8.8	2.4	3.2	26.9	18.9	43.5	12.3	76.0	10,801	96.2
New Ashford town (Berkshire)	228	223	-2.2	299	94.6	0.0	0.0	0.0	5.4	12.0	27.4	51.7	51.1	31.9	121	87.6
New Bedford city & MCD (Bristol)	95,071	95,363	0.3	95,239	60.5	6.4	1.5	10.8	20.8	22.9	15.1	36.6	58.5	17.0	38,888	82.5
New Braintree town (Worcester)	999	1,024	2.5	1,211	98.2	0.0	0.3	0.9	0.6	21.1	14.4	48.8	40.6	29.7	460	92.8
Newbury town (Essex)	6,671	7,148	7.2	7,060	92.1	0.3	1.6	3.1	3.0	25.1	22.6	48.3	21.4	53.1	2,577	97.2
Newburyport city & MCD (Essex)	17,410	18,289	5.0	18,077	92.4	1.6	2.2	0.9	2.8	20.6	21.0	48.9	17.6	62.4	7,836	94.0
New Marlborough town (Berkshire)	1,513	1,458	-3.6	1,544	93.3	1.4	0.3	0.6	4.4	17.6	28.2	53.9	33.4	41.6	683	89.0
New Salem town (Franklin)	994	1,021	2.7	1,009	92.1	0.0	0.3	7.2	0.4	16.9	23.8	55.6	32.7	41.6	441	91.8
New Seabury CDP	717	-	-	710	98.6	0.0	0.0	0.0	1.4	2.8	62.4	69.2	13.2	63.7	422	95.5
Newton city & MCD (Middlesex)	85,089	88,414	3.9	88,593	73.7	2.8	14.8	3.7	4.9	21.7	18.0	41.0	10.8	79.2	30,657	95.2
Norfolk town (Norfolk)	11,215	12,003	7.0	11,786	83.2	6.2	1.2	1.7	7.6	21.7	13.5	41.8	29.9	50.5	3,186	96.8
North Adams city & MCD (Berkshire)	13,693	12,730	-7.0	12,959	86.0	1.6	1.0	4.8	6.6	17.9	19.1	42.4	51.8	23.0	5,568	83.0
North Amherst CDP	6,819	-	-	6,907	71.6	2.1	16.1	3.1	7.0	8.2	8.4	21.7	13.0	72.5	1,841	99.1
Northampton city & MCD (Hampshire)	28,560	28,451	-0.4	28,516	82.2	2.1	3.3	3.7	8.7	15.6	18.0	40.0	22.0	60.1	11,292	92.3
North Andover town (Essex)	28,358	31,188	10.0	30,842	81.1	3.1	6.1	2.2	7.6	24.2	15.9	38.9	19.6	59.7	11,112	93.7
North Attleborough town (Bristol)	28,699	29,364	2.3	29,180	84.2	2.0	6.1	2.1	5.6	23.9	12.6	39.5	30.5	41.8	11,071	94.9
Northborough CDP	6,167	-	-	6,298	85.7	1.6	6.9	2.7	3.2	21.2	18.4	44.6	20.8	58.7	2,267	95.2
Northborough town (Worcester)	14,199	15,109	6.4	15,056	82.7	3.2	9.2	2.2	2.7	23.7	15.8	43.4	17.1	64.1	5,399	97.0
Northbridge town (Worcester)	15,701	16,679	6.2	16,582	87.4	1.9	1.1	3.4	6.2	22.8	17.1	40.8	37.6	36.1	6,166	91.6
North Brookfield CDP	2,265	-	-	2,466	94.8	1.5	0.7	0.9	2.1	18.5	14.5	36.9	49.7	26.6	965	90.1
North Brookfield town (Worcester)	4,676	4,792	2.5	4,774	96.4	1.0	0.6	0.4	1.6	19.2	16.1	44.2	43.9	28.6	1,841	89.6
North Eastham CDP	1,806	-	-	1,612	94.5	0.0	1.7	2.3	1.4	10.2	43.6	62.8	19.8	55.3	896	90.2
North Falmouth CDP	3,084	-	-	2,516	99.2	0.2	0.0	0.6	0.0	11.2	40.3	60.7	21.5	59.5	1,188	97.8
Northfield CDP	1,089	-	-	1,032	100.0	0.0	0.0	0.0	0.0	13.5	30.1	51.6	32.6	45.3	478	91.2
Northfield town (Franklin)	3,031	2,958	-2.4	2,981	94.6	0.3	0.2	0.8	4.1	19.3	19.8	48.3	37.6	38.3	1,225	90.9
North Lakeville CDP	2,630	-	-	3,114	85.3	6.5	0.6	3.7	3.9	21.8	17.9	42.9	35.7	36.7	1,262	94.2
North Pembroke CDP	3,292	-	-	3,458	87.9	1.9	0.7	8.0	1.5	23.1	18.6	46.0	29.4	47.8	1,341	90.5
North Plymouth CDP	3,600	-	-	4,091	88.7	5.6	0.0	2.4	3.3	19.8	15.1	41.6	44.7	26.1	1,581	91.4
North Reading town (Middlesex)	14,891	15,865	6.5	15,581	89.3	1.2	4.6	2.8	2.0	21.8	14.4	43.8	26.7	51.0	5,543	95.7
North Scituate CDP	5,077	-	-	5,044	98.1	0.1	0.8	1.0	0.0	25.3	20.9	46.2	9.2	72.2	1,930	95.2

1 May be of any race.

Table A. All Places — **Population and Housing**

STATE City, town, township, borough, or CDP (county if applicable)	Population 2010 census total population	2019 estimated population	Percent change 2010–2019	ACS total population estimate 2015–2019	Race and Hispanic or Latino origin (percent) White alone, not Hispanic or Latino	Black alone, not Hispanic or Latino	Asian alone, not Hispanic or Latino	All other races or 2 or more races, not Hispanic or Latino	Hispanic or Latino[1]	Age (percent) Under 18 years old	Age 65 years and older	Median age	Educational attainment of persons age 25 and older Percent High school diploma or less	Percent Bachelor's degree or more	Occupied housing units Total	Percent with a computer
	1	2	3	4	5	6	7	8	9	10	11	12	13	14	15	16
MASSACHUSETTS—Con.																
North Seekonk CDP........	2,643	-	-	2,398	86.6	0.0	0.0	2.9	10.5	19.8	18.4	48.1	36.4	31.4	994	89.5
Northwest Harwich CDP...	3,929	-	-	4,136	88.2	1.6	0.9	5.1	4.1	16.2	30.9	56.4	30.8	43.5	1,777	95.3
North Westport CDP........	4,571	-	-	4,510	98.0	0.0	0.0	0.3	1.7	19.2	27.8	49.5	45.3	29.5	1,927	83.4
Norton town (Bristol)........	19,025	19,948	4.9	19,745	90.3	3.8	1.5	1.6	2.7	17.6	13.8	41.2	30.4	40.8	6,570	94.7
Norton Center CDP.........	2,671	-	-	2,774	81.8	7.5	3.7	2.5	4.5	6.2	5.7	21.4	27.7	49.3	437	98.4
Norwell town (Plymouth)...	10,514	11,153	6.1	11,054	94.5	0.3	1.9	1.1	2.3	27.4	17.5	42.2	17.1	65.4	3,666	95.8
Norwood town & CDP (Norfolk)	28,609	29,725	3.9	29,306	80.4	5.7	5.4	1.7	6.8	19.8	18.0	40.8	27.8	47.4	11,971	91.9
Oak Bluffs town (Dukes)...	4,524	4,667	3.2	4,665	87.5	4.7	0.0	5.8	2.1	24.4	22.7	40.8	29.5	42.2	1,750	96.3
Oakham town (Worcester)	1,905	1,957	2.7	1,833	96.6	0.3	0.2	0.8	2.1	17.2	16.5	49.3	33.3	36.7	688	95.6
Ocean Bluff-Brant Rock CDP	4,970	-	-	5,199	96.9	0.8	0.0	0.9	1.4	17.4	20.1	47.9	23.4	41.2	1,983	92.3
Ocean Grove CDP..........	2,811	-	-	3,092	94.6	0.0	2.4	2.0	1.0	14.5	17.3	45.7	48.7	16.9	1,309	94.8
Onset CDP....................	1,573	-	-	754	60.2	12.5	0.0	27.3	0.0	4.0	39.5	58.3	34.7	19.0	492	92.9
Orange CDP..................	4,018	-	-	3,772	92.4	0.4	1.7	2.4	3.0	19.4	14.5	43.1	51.3	16.1	1,550	89.7
Orange town (Franklin)....	7,839	7,582	-3.3	7,644	94.7	0.6	0.9	1.4	2.5	19.4	18.2	45.4	50.6	19.2	3,102	87.2
Orleans CDP..................	1,621	-	-	1,798	85.0	11.5	0.0	0.0	3.5	9.0	40.5	61.9	29.2	40.4	902	93.2
Orleans town (Barnstable)	5,889	5,788	-1.7	5,808	93.4	3.6	1.1	0.0	1.9	15.0	39.7	60.1	17.9	58.4	2,718	92.5
Otis town (Berkshire)........	1,612	1,539	-4.5	1,393	97.1	0.0	0.0	1.4	1.5	9.4	28.1	54.5	37.4	37.7	691	90.0
Oxford CDP...................	6,103	-	-	5,595	91.6	0.4	1.5	1.9	4.7	20.5	17.2	41.3	45.4	25.7	2,222	91.2
Oxford town (Worcester)..	13,711	14,009	2.2	13,974	87.9	1.5	2.5	2.4	5.6	21.7	13.5	39.5	41.7	29.1	5,200	92.1
Palmer Town city & MCD (Hampden)	12,138	12,232	0.8	12,237	87.4	2.1	2.0	4.0	4.5	18.5	16.0	42.6	43.1	24.9	4,884	87.5
Paxton town (Worcester)..	4,797	4,963	3.5	4,900	85.3	8.2	1.6	0.9	4.0	18.5	16.3	37.5	20.0	56.3	1,499	91.3
Peabody city & MCD (Essex)	51,266	53,070	3.5	52,906	82.7	3.3	1.1	3.0	9.9	17.1	22.5	45.8	40.6	34.0	21,713	86.5
Pelham town (Hampshire)	1,323	1,313	-0.8	1,283	89.5	4.4	0.9	1.9	3.3	17.1	26.0	48.1	15.5	66.8	571	94.9
Pembroke town (Plymouth)	17,844	18,509	3.7	18,380	93.5	0.6	1.3	3.1	1.5	21.3	15.2	43.8	33.1	38.8	6,563	94.3
Pepperell CDP................	2,504	-	-	2,826	88.7	2.2	0.9	4.5	3.7	18.9	13.9	40.2	40.5	28.8	1,087	86.0
Pepperell town (Middlesex)	11,498	12,114	5.4	12,105	93.0	0.8	2.3	1.9	2.0	21.2	15.5	44.0	29.8	41.1	4,444	92.8
Peru town (Berkshire).......	847	834	-1.5	823	96.0	0.2	0.0	1.1	2.7	18.1	12.2	49.0	44.0	21.0	349	92.8
Petersham CDP..............	243	-	-	259	91.5	0.0	0.0	0.0	8.5	12.7	32.0	51.4	31.7	45.5	101	90.1
Petersham town (Worcester)	1,238	1,250	1.0	1,188	94.7	0.0	1.0	0.9	3.4	14.2	25.4	51.9	33.6	36.4	473	85.2
Phillipston town (Worcester)	1,687	1,746	3.5	1,784	92.5	1.5	0.7	4.0	1.3	20.2	14.1	44.7	45.1	22.5	643	90.4
Pinehurst CDP................	7,152	-	-	7,283	84.6	2.4	8.8	2.5	1.8	21.7	16.9	42.3	38.9	33.0	2,435	95.8
Pittsfield city & MCD (Berkshire)	44,743	42,142	-5.8	42,766	83.3	4.1	2.0	3.9	6.8	18.3	20.3	44.4	38.8	28.5	19,318	87.2
Plainfield town (Hampshire)	648	661	2.0	661	92.1	0.3	2.3	1.4	3.9	13.5	29.3	51.9	29.6	45.5	302	91.1
Plainville town (Norfolk)...	8,273	9,293	12.3	9,183	87.9	1.2	4.1	2.3	4.5	22.1	14.7	42.0	26.6	43.6	3,666	96.3
Plymouth CDP...............	7,494	-	-	7,081	91.1	1.5	0.8	4.4	2.1	16.7	21.0	44.3	41.9	32.3	3,310	90.3
Plymouth town (Plymouth)	56,468	61,528	9.0	60,024	91.6	1.7	1.5	2.8	2.4	18.1	21.8	47.1	33.0	38.4	23,345	93.9
Plympton town (Plymouth)	2,839	2,987	5.2	2,954	93.9	2.8	0.0	0.7	2.5	19.6	18.0	46.0	41.0	33.3	1,010	93.5
Pocasset CDP................	2,851	-	-	2,893	98.8	0.3	0.0	0.0	0.9	10.4	37.9	60.0	26.4	41.6	1,496	84.4
Popponesset CDP...........	220	-	-	150	100.0	0.0	0.0	0.0	0.0	6.0	22.0	62.3	8.0	68.8	70	87.1
Popponesset Island CDP..	26	-	-	34	100.0	0.0	0.0	0.0	0.0	0.0	100.0	81.1	0.0	76.5	17	100.0
Princeton town (Worcester)	3,415	3,488	2.1	3,455	95.0	0.3	0.2	3.0	1.5	19.9	22.4	49.7	15.1	61.5	1,271	95.2
Provincetown town (Barnstable)	2,942	2,961	0.6	2,973	89.5	1.9	1.2	3.2	4.2	5.1	27.6	56.8	20.7	54.8	1,702	91.4
Provincetown CDP	2,642	-	-	2,730	88.6	2.1	1.3	3.5	4.5	5.5	27.9	57.0	19.3	55.4	1,570	91.2
Quincy city & MCD (Norfolk)	92,262	94,470	2.4	94,207	59.0	5.0	30.3	2.7	3.1	14.6	16.7	39.7	34.5	45.1	41,187	90.2
Randolph Town city & MCD (Norfolk)	32,100	34,362	7.0	34,064	29.4	43.7	13.1	5.0	8.8	19.8	15.6	40.7	44.2	28.1	11,832	93.4
Raynham town (Bristol)	13,425	14,470	7.8	14,196	93.3	1.7	0.9	2.1	2.0	21.1	18.8	42.4	34.5	40.9	5,225	93.6
Raynham Center CDP.......	4,100	-	-	4,923	93.5	3.3	0.8	1.2	1.3	24.2	11.9	36.8	30.9	41.4	1,771	96.5
Reading town & CDP (Middlesex)	23,987	25,400	5.9	25,132	91.1	0.4	4.4	1.0	3.0	24.2	17.5	43.2	17.0	64.4	9,191	95.6
Rehoboth town (Bristol)....	11,606	12,385	6.7	12,173	92.4	0.5	1.4	2.9	2.8	21.3	13.1	43.7	23.5	45.9	4,160	95.2
Revere city & MCD (Suffolk)	51,713	53,073	2.6	53,692	53.3	5.0	4.8	3.3	33.6	20.1	14.4	39.2	57.4	22.9	19,223	87.9
Richmond town (Berkshire)	1,482	1,416	-4.5	1,489	95.6	0.6	1.4	1.9	0.5	15.3	30.0	56.9	28.2	49.8	679	95.7
Rochester town (Plymouth)	5,230	5,687	8.7	5,580	97.4	0.6	0.9	0.5	0.6	24.7	15.4	44.3	31.5	47.9	1,928	94.7
Rockland town (Plymouth)	17,478	17,986	2.9	17,953	91.5	2.6	0.6	2.2	3.1	22.1	15.8	40.1	36.4	33.7	6,959	91.8
Rockport CDP................	4,966	-	-	5,260	97.6	0.1	0.1	1.2	1.0	14.2	33.4	56.7	20.8	58.1	2,402	89.5
Rockport town (Essex)	6,952	7,282	4.7	7,231	96.5	0.1	0.1	2.6	0.7	14.7	33.7	56.1	20.5	56.9	3,324	91.3
Rowe town (Franklin)........	398	389	-2.3	441	96.8	1.1	0.0	0.0	2.0	15.4	27.2	50.6	42.7	34.8	191	86.4
Rowley CDP..................	1,416	-	-	1,629	92.2	0.0	4.1	0.6	3.1	16.8	18.5	50.7	33.3	45.3	589	90.2
Rowley town (Essex)	5,853	6,473	10.6	6,372	95.4	1.2	1.1	1.6	0.8	21.8	16.9	45.8	27.8	44.5	2,210	94.1
Royalston town (Worcester)	1,258	1,277	1.5	1,366	98.9	0.0	0.7	0.4	0.0	17.4	22.8	50.8	48.6	19.9	570	86.7
Russell CDP..................	786	-	-	526	80.0	3.2	0.0	5.9	10.8	20.5	15.8	45.3	46.6	20.7	247	95.5
Russell town (Hampden) ..	1,781	1,792	0.6	1,470	89.5	2.9	0.0	3.4	4.2	22.2	15.4	40.4	47.0	26.3	568	97.0
Rutland CDP..................	2,111	-	-	2,360	95.0	0.0	2.3	0.0	2.7	23.2	13.9	41.1	36.8	34.4	834	95.6
Rutland town (Worcester).	7,979	8,938	12.0	8,685	92.1	0.0	4.1	0.4	3.3	26.8	11.4	39.2	29.4	46.3	2,885	96.7
Sagamore CDP...............	3,623	-	-	3,675	87.9	1.6	2.2	5.6	2.7	18.4	19.6	46.0	24.9	36.5	1,497	95.1
Salem city & MCD (Essex)	41,312	43,226	4.6	43,252	71.8	4.7	2.5	3.1	17.8	16.2	16.2	37.1	34.0	43.0	18,437	91.6
Salisbury CDP................	4,869	-	-	5,131	94.3	0.0	0.0	1.7	4.0	14.4	27.6	48.0	32.9	42.6	2,375	93.6
Salisbury town (Essex)	8,290	9,534	15.0	9,360	92.8	0.7	1.1	1.8	3.6	17.3	20.7	46.8	36.3	35.8	3,891	93.2
Sandisfield town (Berkshire)	917	891	-2.8	891	94.8	0.9	0.3	1.8	2.1	19.9	25.9	48.6	41.0	32.8	353	89.2
Sandwich CDP................	2,962	-	-	3,002	91.4	0.0	1.7	0.0	6.9	12.7	25.7	51.7	18.1	55.4	1,302	97.6
Sandwich town (Barnstable)	20,676	20,169	-2.5	20,286	93.0	1.0	1.6	2.3	2.1	17.9	22.9	50.2	22.5	47.3	7,818	96.3

1 May be of any race.

Table A. All Places — **Population and Housing**

STATE City, town, township, borough, or CDP (county if applicable)	Population 2010 census total population	Population 2019 estimated population	Population Percent change 2010–2019	Population ACS total population estimate 2015–2019	White alone, not Hispanic or Latino	Black alone, not Hispanic or Latino	Asian alone, not Hispanic or Latino	All other races or 2 or more races, not Hispanic or Latino	Hispanic or Latino[1]	Under 18 years old	Age 65 years and older	Median age	Percent High school diploma or less	Percent Bachelor's degree or more	Occupied housing units Total	Occupied housing units Percent with a computer
	1	2	3	4	5	6	7	8	9	10	11	12	13	14	15	16
MASSACHUSETTS—Con.																
Saugus town & CDP (Essex)	26,634	28,361	6.5	28,215	83.3	2.0	3.8	2.2	8.6	17.2	20.2	47.1	44.9	28.8	10,424	91.3
Savoy town (Berkshire)	690	675	-2.2	680	86.0	8.4	0.0	2.4	3.2	15.0	20.7	52.3	53.0	19.5	293	86.0
Scituate CDP	5,245	-	-	5,558	96.2	0.0	0.0	3.1	0.7	20.9	25.5	51.2	22.6	45.2	2,212	93.0
Scituate town (Plymouth)	18,135	18,924	4.4	18,720	95.3	0.7	0.3	2.8	1.0	21.8	22.6	49.9	16.1	60.2	7,234	95.9
Seabrook CDP	455	-	-	517	100.0	0.0	0.0	0.0	0.0	9.5	34.8	62.1	20.7	60.0	240	100.0
Seconset Island CDP	100	-	-	40	100.0	0.0	0.0	0.0	0.0	0.0	47.5	37.9	0.0	22.5	19	100.0
Seekonk town (Bristol)	13,722	15,770	14.9	15,441	92.3	0.7	1.3	3.3	2.5	21.5	18.0	45.0	29.0	40.8	6,052	92.6
Sharon town (Norfolk)	17,554	18,895	7.6	18,526	73.1	2.6	16.7	2.1	5.4	27.1	16.2	42.8	9.5	73.0	6,344	95.1
Sharon CDP	5,658	-	-	5,914	85.0	0.7	9.4	2.1	2.8	29.3	13.3	40.7	9.0	72.9	2,072	96.4
Sheffield town (Berkshire)	3,257	3,129	-3.9	3,160	97.3	0.0	0.0	0.4	2.2	12.9	27.7	52.3	45.0	30.5	1,384	82.8
Shelburne town (Franklin)	1,900	1,837	-3.3	1,649	95.6	0.6	2.9	0.4	0.5	10.9	30.7	57.1	22.5	47.0	829	93.1
Shelburne Falls CDP	1,731	-	-	1,806	88.5	2.9	6.7	1.0	0.9	15.9	23.8	52.7	31.8	37.2	929	89.5
Sherborn town (Middlesex)	4,119	4,335	5.2	4,316	87.6	0.6	6.2	3.4	2.2	27.5	16.8	46.6	5.8	83.6	1,525	95.7
Shirley CDP	1,441	-	-	1,861	92.7	1.3	0.8	5.2	0.0	8.3	23.8	58.1	56.8	15.6	941	90.6
Shirley town (Middlesex)	7,211	7,636	5.9	7,633	74.9	8.4	4.0	2.8	9.8	12.0	13.9	47.2	47.2	24.4	2,449	92.6
Shrewsbury town (Worcester)	35,561	38,526	8.3	37,416	69.9	3.0	19.1	3.3	4.8	23.3	16.7	41.5	22.2	58.5	13,561	94.7
Shutesbury town (Franklin)	1,776	1,754	-1.2	1,755	88.0	0.7	1.2	5.6	4.4	17.2	18.7	47.7	13.9	69.8	740	90.7
Siasconset CDP	205	-	-	81	87.7	11.1	1.2	0.0	0.0	11.1	77.8	78.0	23.9	55.2	39	100.0
Smith Mills CDP	4,760	-	-	4,678	95.4	1.4	0.6	2.5	0.1	19.9	24.3	46.2	48.8	28.8	2,004	86.5
Somerset town & CDP (Bristol)	18,153	18,129	-0.1	18,165	97.5	0.5	0.3	0.8	0.9	18.8	23.6	47.1	40.2	27.5	6,956	89.8
Somerville city & MCD (Middlesex)	75,701	81,360	7.5	80,906	68.2	5.6	10.2	3.6	12.4	11.7	9.0	31.3	23.2	64.4	32,802	91.8
South Amherst CDP	4,994	-	-	5,106	56.6	9.8	13.7	10.0	9.9	14.6	9.9	24.0	20.2	61.5	1,418	99.0
Southampton town (Hampshire)	5,792	6,171	6.5	6,144	95.6	0.4	2.3	1.6	0.0	17.0	19.5	47.9	33.8	41.6	2,406	95.7
South Ashburnham CDP	1,062	-	-	924	96.5	0.0	0.0	0.0	3.5	21.9	16.5	44.4	23.3	23.7	330	89.1
Southborough town (Worcester)	9,767	10,208	4.5	10,121	79.2	0.6	14.4	1.9	3.9	26.2	14.7	43.1	16.8	66.5	3,542	97.2
Southbridge Town city & MCD (Worcester)	16,709	16,878	1.0	16,887	62.9	1.9	0.4	1.9	32.9	22.5	15.0	39.3	52.8	17.2	6,813	86.5
South Deerfield CDP	1,880	-	-	2,041	94.1	0.0	0.7	2.2	3.0	25.7	20.0	43.8	19.2	50.1	830	91.9
South Dennis CDP	3,643	-	-	3,393	96.6	0.4	1.8	1.1	0.1	14.8	30.7	54.5	34.0	31.5	1,567	94.3
South Duxbury CDP	3,360	-	-	3,629	97.1	0.0	1.7	0.3	0.9	28.9	18.3	45.7	9.5	78.0	1,270	95.8
South Hadley town (Hampshire)	17,522	17,625	0.6	17,703	84.8	1.8	4.3	2.7	6.4	13.9	19.3	39.1	28.9	42.6	6,616	93.1
South Lancaster CDP	1,894	-	-	1,630	78.1	1.1	6.3	1.0	13.6	16.0	36.5	56.6	33.1	47.5	764	78.8
Southwick town (Hampden)	9,498	9,740	2.5	9,720	92.8	0.1	1.7	1.9	3.5	19.8	21.7	47.3	32.3	35.8	3,804	85.6
South Yarmouth CDP	11,092	-	-	11,091	89.3	2.9	2.7	2.8	2.2	13.1	29.7	52.4	40.5	28.8	4,869	93.3
Spencer CDP	5,700	-	-	5,792	85.3	1.8	6.4	2.8	3.7	14.4	16.7	44.8	53.8	9.6	2,481	81.9
Spencer town (Worcester)	11,708	11,935	1.9	11,928	90.0	1.0	3.5	2.3	3.3	16.0	18.2	45.7	47.4	19.4	4,883	89.5
Springfield city & MCD (Hampden)	153,132	153,606	0.3	154,139	31.2	18.5	2.5	2.7	45.0	24.8	12.6	33.4	53.9	18.5	56,358	81.8
Sterling town (Worcester)	7,796	8,174	4.8	8,091	92.4	1.1	0.4	1.0	5.1	23.2	18.9	46.8	23.5	52.8	2,777	95.9
Stockbridge town (Berkshire)	1,943	1,890	-2.7	1,795	87.8	4.8	2.2	2.5	2.7	8.7	36.9	60.2	28.9	46.4	847	87.4
Stoneham town & CDP (Middlesex)	21,286	24,126	13.3	23,223	87.7	2.8	4.5	1.7	3.3	17.1	20.2	43.8	30.0	46.3	9,666	90.3
Stoughton town (Norfolk)	26,995	28,915	7.1	28,639	71.5	14.8	5.0	4.9	3.8	19.2	18.5	44.8	35.1	37.6	10,900	92.1
Stow town (Middlesex)	6,584	7,234	9.9	7,133	88.4	0.0	3.5	5.2	2.9	26.1	16.3	42.0	11.9	73.6	2,558	95.5
Sturbridge CDP	2,253	-	-	2,243	91.5	1.8	4.1	0.8	1.8	24.1	13.2	45.0	20.6	47.8	878	89.1
Sturbridge town (Worcester)	9,240	9,597	3.9	9,539	92.2	0.8	3.1	0.9	3.0	25.2	17.8	42.3	29.7	45.1	3,619	90.6
Sudbury town (Middlesex)	17,675	19,655	11.2	19,122	82.5	1.7	10.1	3.1	2.5	28.2	15.8	44.2	10.4	80.5	6,386	97.9
Sunderland town (Franklin)	3,690	3,629	-1.7	3,647	79.5	1.2	6.9	7.5	4.9	13.5	15.7	34.1	28.0	48.0	1,677	96.1
Sutton town (Worcester)	8,974	9,582	6.8	9,444	92.3	2.1	2.1	1.9	1.6	23.7	15.3	43.9	33.9	41.0	3,426	94.1
Swampscott town & CDP (Essex)	13,790	15,298	10.9	15,002	91.7	1.5	2.2	2.1	2.5	22.2	18.8	44.8	20.4	57.3	5,780	90.7
Swansea town (Bristol)	15,858	16,834	6.2	16,567	96.4	0.1	1.1	2.0	0.5	18.0	20.1	45.8	45.0	23.9	6,361	92.8
Taunton city & MCD (Bristol)	55,826	57,464	2.9	57,124	75.0	8.4	1.8	5.8	9.0	22.6	15.1	39.6	47.9	22.6	22,359	88.2
Teaticket CDP	1,692	-	-	1,697	88.7	2.9	0.0	2.9	5.4	13.7	38.3	56.9	23.6	47.9	849	96.3
Templeton town (Worcester)	7,982	8,138	2.0	8,130	94.6	0.0	2.2	0.3	2.9	19.9	17.4	44.2	38.1	21.9	3,317	92.5
Tewksbury town (Middlesex)	29,069	31,178	7.3	31,098	90.1	2.1	3.5	2.1	2.2	19.4	18.1	44.7	33.9	38.3	11,822	92.1
The Pinehills CDP	955	-	-	1,419	94.5	0.0	5.5	0.0	0.0	2.0	67.4	68.9	10.0	69.8	825	96.1
Tisbury town (Dukes)	3,949	4,096	3.7	4,107	85.4	10.3	0.0	3.0	1.3	15.9	21.0	46.1	38.6	38.7	1,836	85.7
Tolland town (Hampden)	490	508	3.7	530	94.5	0.0	0.0	5.1	0.4	10.9	28.5	57.8	34.0	35.8	242	90.1
Topsfield CDP	2,717	-	-	3,216	95.8	0.0	0.2	1.5	2.5	30.2	21.1	43.2	16.4	68.0	1,058	93.2
Topsfield town (Essex)	6,086	6,641	9.1	6,568	94.8	0.1	2.6	0.7	1.7	26.2	23.0	44.6	15.7	64.4	2,206	93.5
Townsend CDP	1,128	-	-	1,310	89.0	1.6	2.9	0.0	6.5	24.6	9.0	39.3	33.6	21.3	546	94.0
Townsend town (Middlesex)	8,926	9,506	6.5	9,473	94.4	0.5	1.3	0.6	3.2	21.2	14.8	43.2	32.5	34.3	3,520	94.7
Truro town (Barnstable)	2,005	2,008	0.1	1,122	95.0	3.4	0.0	0.1	1.5	9.0	38.4	61.0	28.8	48.5	601	85.9
Turners Falls CDP	4,470	-	-	4,010	83.6	2.5	0.0	5.7	8.3	16.2	22.6	46.3	45.2	25.7	2,015	79.3
Tyngsborough town (Middlesex)	11,314	12,527	10.7	12,364	83.6	0.9	8.4	2.7	4.5	19.6	11.9	42.7	26.3	48.7	4,408	96.0
Tyringham town (Berkshire)	324	312	-3.7	474	92.4	0.4	0.6	0.0	6.5	13.3	33.5	53.3	26.7	50.5	190	85.3
Upton CDP	3,013	-	-	2,292	90.0	2.1	0.0	0.0	7.9	19.1	20.7	47.9	24.3	50.7	959	92.0
Upton town (Worcester)	7,540	8,065	7.0	7,894	80.2	7.6	2.9	5.7	3.6	24.8	14.3	42.4	16.9	60.1	2,716	96.1
Uxbridge town (Worcester)	13,455	14,195	5.5	13,993	94.9	1.9	0.5	1.1	1.7	21.7	14.2	42.3	38.1	34.9	5,024	93.6
Vineyard Haven CDP	2,114	-	-	2,123	86.9	9.8	0.0	3.1	0.1	17.6	24.3	43.5	44.0	38.1	955	89.6

1 May be of any race.

Table A. All Places — **Population and Housing**

STATE City, town, township, borough, or CDP (county if applicable)	Population 2010 census total population	2019 estimated population	Percent change 2010–2019	ACS total population estimate 2015–2019	Race and Hispanic or Latino origin (percent) White alone, not Hispanic or Latino	Black alone, not Hispanic or Latino	Asian alone, not Hispanic or Latino	All other races or 2 or more races, not Hispanic or Latino	Hispanic or Latino[1]	Age (percent) Under 18 years old	Age 65 years and older	Median age	Educational attainment of persons age 25 and older Percent High school diploma or less	Percent Bachelor's degree or more	Occupied housing units Total	Percent with a computer
	1	2	3	4	5	6	7	8	9	10	11	12	13	14	15	16
MASSACHUSETTS—Con.																
Wakefield town & CDP (Middlesex)	25,101	27,045	7.7	26,993	91.0	1.7	2.4	1.5	3.5	19.2	18.6	43.9	26.4	51.2	10,723	93.7
Wales town (Hampden)	1,839	1,874	1.9	2,088	93.3	0.3	0.0	0.9	5.5	24.5	15.3	41.4	41.9	23.6	844	94.4
Walpole CDP	5,918	-	-	6,197	82.6	1.2	5.4	0.3	10.5	25.3	18.4	41.2	26.5	46.9	2,582	89.3
Walpole town (Norfolk)	24,069	25,200	4.7	25,129	82.8	2.0	5.0	2.3	7.9	25.7	16.3	40.8	24.2	53.1	8,746	93.3
Waltham city & MCD (Middlesex)	60,638	62,495	3.1	62,777	65.9	6.7	11.6	2.2	13.6	13.7	13.8	34.3	27.2	54.2	23,690	93.8
Ware CDP	6,170	-	-	5,888	86.6	1.5	0.0	1.2	10.7	21.3	19.9	40.2	51.5	22.0	2,671	84.8
Ware town (Hampshire)....	9,862	9,711	-1.5	9,801	89.3	1.3	0.2	1.5	7.7	20.1	20.9	44.0	45.3	25.3	4,351	87.7
Wareham town (Plymouth)	21,836	22,745	4.2	22,641	84.5	2.2	0.6	9.1	3.6	18.0	21.2	47.4	44.4	24.1	9,497	91.3
Wareham Center CDP.......	2,896	-	-	3,205	78.1	5.1	0.0	12.4	4.4	29.4	18.5	37.1	34.8	17.8	1,306	92.1
Warren CDP	1,405	-	-	510	100.0	0.0	0.0	0.0	0.0	14.7	25.5	42.0	65.7	16.3	298	56.4
Warren town (Worcester)..	5,135	5,222	1.7	5,213	95.6	0.6	2.5	0.0	1.2	22.6	12.9	38.9	47.2	31.0	1,859	86.8
Warwick town (Franklin)....	780	769	-1.4	796	95.1	0.0	0.5	2.4	2.0	16.2	20.0	54.9	37.4	32.6	348	89.9
Washington town (Berkshire)	542	541	-0.2	502	90.0	4.6	1.6	2.8	1.0	13.5	32.5	56.5	34.9	35.2	242	91.3
Watertown Town city & MCD (Middlesex)	31,986	35,939	12.4	35,401	76.4	1.5	9.9	2.9	9.2	15.4	16.2	38.2	19.7	65.9	15,620	93.4
Wayland town (Middlesex)	12,940	13,835	6.9	13,802	79.6	0.7	11.5	3.4	4.8	26.5	18.3	44.0	8.3	80.7	4,786	96.4
Webster town (Worcester)	16,772	16,949	1.1	16,973	80.0	4.6	1.3	2.0	12.1	20.3	18.0	42.2	46.1	25.0	6,946	89.5
Webster CDP....................	11,412	-	-	11,943	76.0	4.2	1.2	2.9	15.7	20.5	15.7	40.6	51.6	19.0	4,873	88.6
Wellesley town & CDP (Norfolk)	27,898	28,670	2.8	28,747	76.6	2.3	12.4	3.6	5.1	25.0	14.8	35.6	7.4	83.8	8,449	95.8
Wellfleet town (Barnstable)	2,750	2,724	-0.9	3,617	89.2	1.9	3.3	4.3	1.2	13.1	32.6	57.2	24.5	53.6	1,598	88.7
Wendell town (Franklin)....	844	878	4.0	862	88.2	4.4	0.8	5.3	1.3	16.8	22.7	50.2	27.9	47.2	383	85.6
Wenham town (Essex)......	4,875	5,278	8.3	5,240	87.8	2.4	3.1	1.2	5.4	15.7	15.5	28.3	14.4	67.6	1,418	93.4
Westborough town (Worcester)	18,278	19,144	4.7	19,037	65.0	1.8	24.9	2.1	6.2	25.7	13.7	38.8	19.0	66.7	7,069	95.2
Westborough CDP...........	4,045	-	-	3,957	85.8	0.9	5.2	2.1	5.9	20.9	12.8	41.5	27.1	55.2	1,729	93.5
West Boylston town (Worcester)	7,673	8,077	5.3	7,966	79.4	5.4	1.4	1.4	12.3	13.8	19.1	42.6	41.3	33.2	2,336	89.0
West Bridgewater town (Plymouth)	6,927	7,281	5.1	7,198	92.8	1.8	1.0	1.3	3.1	21.0	18.7	43.9	35.0	35.4	2,499	95.3
West Brookfield CDP.........	1,413	-	-	1,479	96.2	0.0	0.0	2.3	1.5	12.6	28.1	54.1	56.5	28.0	613	85.3
West Brookfield town (Worcester)	3,649	3,727	2.1	3,728	94.3	0.2	0.0	2.1	3.4	18.2	22.9	46.2	44.8	29.1	1,510	89.5
West Chatham CDP	1,410	-	-	1,154	96.5	1.3	0.0	2.2	0.0	11.8	44.0	61.6	21.6	56.9	559	91.8
West Concord CDP	6,028	-	-	7,394	70.3	8.9	3.7	2.2	15.0	20.2	19.9	41.9	24.7	63.3	2,605	94.8
West Dennis CDP.............	2,242	-	-	2,236	90.1	5.5	0.4	1.3	2.8	8.4	38.6	58.3	29.0	45.8	1,173	95.5
West Falmouth CDP.........	1,738	-	-	1,971	94.5	0.0	1.5	4.0	0.0	19.7	30.5	54.8	4.8	70.0	744	98.7
Westfield city & MCD (Hampden)..................	41,090	41,204	0.3	41,449	85.0	1.4	2.8	1.2	9.5	18.0	17.3	39.6	40.1	32.2	15,271	90.9
Westford town (Middlesex)	21,962	24,817	13.0	24,342	76.1	0.8	19.8	1.8	1.5	26.3	13.0	43.2	15.3	67.4	8,571	95.6
Westhampton town (Hampshire)	1,603	1,637	2.1	1,858	97.2	0.0	0.4	0.5	1.8	17.4	18.2	47.9	31.8	41.2	719	94.4
Westminster town (Worcester)	7,271	7,997	10.0	7,766	96.2	0.0	0.2	0.2	3.3	21.3	17.5	44.3	30.9	40.4	2,870	94.0
West Newbury town (Essex)	4,234	4,714	11.3	4,631	96.2	0.0	1.0	0.2	2.6	20.8	21.1	49.7	16.9	62.3	1,678	97.7
Weston town (Middlesex) .	11,260	12,124	7.7	12,112	76.4	1.7	12.9	5.2	3.8	25.5	21.0	45.1	10.7	82.8	3,787	94.3
Westport town (Bristol)	15,531	16,034	3.2	15,925	97.0	0.1	0.2	1.0	1.7	17.3	25.4	48.9	36.7	36.6	6,525	91.5
West Springfield Town city & MCD (Hampden)	28,391	28,517	0.4	28,609	79.6	2.8	4.0	2.9	10.6	20.4	15.9	41.0	36.2	33.7	12,605	86.7
West Stockbridge town (Berkshire)	1,298	1,257	-3.2	1,084	88.7	4.7	1.6	1.6	3.5	16.7	26.3	52.1	26.2	58.0	461	97.6
West Tisbury town (Dukes)	2,745	2,904	5.8	2,418	93.1	1.0	1.0	2.4	2.6	13.2	32.4	54.9	18.9	54.3	1,068	95.6
West Wareham CDP.........	2,064	-	-	2,259	85.3	1.3	0.0	8.9	4.5	15.9	35.3	56.5	55.3	13.9	1,071	86.4
Westwood town (Norfolk)..	14,625	16,400	12.1	16,136	84.8	0.7	8.8	2.6	3.0	25.5	18.5	44.6	12.6	71.5	5,532	94.8
West Yarmouth CDP.........	6,012	-	-	5,741	81.9	3.7	4.1	5.1	5.1	16.8	26.3	48.8	34.8	34.7	2,543	89.5
Weweantic CDP	2,105	-	-	1,797	86.9	2.9	1.3	8.8	0.0	22.7	24.6	43.2	49.8	25.6	710	90.6
Weymouth Town city & MCD (Norfolk)	53,762	57,746	7.4	56,734	81.6	5.5	6.7	2.4	3.8	17.9	17.9	42.4	33.5	39.2	23,723	93.2
Whately town (Franklin)....	1,505	1,567	4.1	1,584	95.3	0.0	0.6	0.6	3.5	16.2	21.0	45.8	31.7	42.8	641	90.3
White Island Shores CDP.	2,106	-	-	2,634	71.6	0.0	3.3	18.7	6.5	17.2	4.9	39.7	58.6	12.3	909	98.6
Whitinsville CDP	6,704	-	-	7,220	82.1	3.5	2.0	6.7	5.7	27.7	17.2	36.3	35.5	31.5	2,554	91.8
Whitman town (Plymouth)	14,485	15,216	5.0	15,056	91.7	1.6	0.8	3.3	2.5	22.9	12.8	38.0	39.3	29.0	5,466	93.4
Wilbraham CDP	3,915	-	-	3,466	90.8	1.5	0.3	0.6	6.8	24.7	28.4	46.7	27.5	50.6	1,188	96.8
Wilbraham town (Hampden)..................	14,219	14,689	3.3	14,638	85.3	2.8	0.9	1.4	9.7	21.0	21.2	46.3	28.6	47.4	5,217	92.1
Williamsburg town (Hampshire)	2,484	2,466	-0.7	2,576	97.1	0.9	0.0	0.0	2.0	15.8	23.5	50.5	23.8	53.3	1,161	95.1
Williamstown CDP	4,325	-	-	4,506	74.5	5.7	8.3	2.4	9.1	12.8	13.0	21.4	17.0	69.4	1,057	90.7
Williamstown town (Berkshire)	7,763	7,434	-4.2	7,514	79.1	5.0	6.2	3.6	6.1	14.5	19.6	29.0	20.1	62.7	2,275	91.3
Wilmington town & CDP (Middlesex)	22,341	23,445	4.9	23,377	87.0	4.1	6.2	1.8	1.0	21.5	16.4	42.1	31.7	43.5	7,957	94.9
Winchendon CDP.............	4,213	-	-	3,999	86.9	1.1	5.8	2.1	4.1	18.2	17.6	40.5	47.4	25.3	1,575	86.5
Winchendon town (Worcester)	10,332	10,905	5.5	10,841	90.8	1.1	2.6	2.3	3.2	23.2	14.1	37.9	43.9	22.7	3,781	86.9
Winchester town & CDP (Middlesex)	21,389	22,799	6.6	22,738	79.5	0.3	14.6	3.6	2.1	28.6	17.7	42.8	12.2	77.3	7,884	95.1
Windsor town (Berkshire) .	899	866	-3.7	862	95.1	0.0	1.4	2.4	1.0	13.9	21.1	51.9	31.1	40.8	366	88.5
Winthrop Town city & MCD (Suffolk).....................	17,497	18,544	6.0	18,542	86.5	1.6	1.0	1.4	9.5	18.5	18.0	44.9	35.6	38.3	7,831	91.1
Woburn city & MCD (Middlesex)	38,882	40,228	3.5	40,304	77.4	5.4	8.8	3.8	4.6	19.6	16.3	40.0	30.8	45.4	15,935	92.2
Woods Hole CDP	781	-	-	816	95.7	0.0	0.0	4.3	0.0	9.2	45.3	61.8	9.7	81.2	443	100.0
Worcester city & MCD (Worcester)	180,891	185,428	2.5	185,143	55.2	12.2	7.4	3.4	21.9	18.8	13.6	34.7	44.5	30.2	71,595	87.4

1 May be of any race.

Table A. All Places — **Population and Housing**

STATE City, town, township, borough, or CDP (county if applicable)	Population				Race and Hispanic or Latino origin (percent)					Age (percent)			Educational attainment of persons age 25 and older		Occupied housing units	
	2010 census total population	2019 estimated population	Percent change 2010–2019	ACS total population estimate 2015–2019	White alone, not Hispanic or Latino	Black alone, not Hispanic or Latino	Asian alone, not Hispanic or Latino	All other races or 2 or more races, not Hispanic or Latino	Hispanic or Latino[1]	Under 18 years old	Age 65 years and older	Median age	Percent High school diploma or less	Percent Bachelor's degree or more	Total	Percent with a computer
	1	2	3	4	5	6	7	8	9	10	11	12	13	14	15	16
MASSACHUSETTS—Con.																
Worthington town (Hampshire)	1,157	1,175	1.6	1,338	98.2	0.3	0.0	0.7	0.7	17.0	24.1	49.9	34.4	34.7	604	90.6
Wrentham town (Norfolk)..	11,037	12,023	8.9	11,823	92.7	2.9	1.0	0.6	2.9	24.0	14.2	43.4	23.3	51.4	4,258	95.8
Yarmouth town (Barnstable)	23,797	23,203	-2.5	23,338	89.2	2.4	2.9	2.8	2.7	14.1	32.5	53.8	34.0	36.8	10,515	91.5
Yarmouth Port CDP	5,320	-	-	5,242	97.4	0.2	0.0	0.6	1.8	11.4	45.7	63.3	20.1	53.0	2,622	90.1
MICHIGAN	9,884,116	9,986,857	1.0	9,965,265	75.0	13.6	3.1	3.1	5.1	21.9	16.7	39.7	38.1	29.1	3,935,041	89.6
Acme township (Grand Traverse)	4,375	4,736	8.3	4,694	94.2	1.6	0.0	2.6	1.6	14.8	25.0	49.6	18.9	48.5	2,039	89.7
Ada township (Kent)	13,123	14,832	13.0	14,558	88.9	2.0	4.9	1.6	2.6	27.8	15.1	42.1	13.2	64.3	4,963	97.2
Adams township (Arenac)	563	527	-6.4	560	99.1	0.0	0.0	0.0	0.9	20.9	12.3	43.8	65.5	11.4	237	81.4
Adams township (Hillsdale)	2,493	2,445	-1.9	2,380	97.8	0.0	0.2	0.7	1.3	21.3	23.5	48.1	55.6	11.9	1,010	80.0
Adams township (Houghton)	2,600	2,503	-3.7	2,526	96.7	0.1	0.2	2.7	0.2	28.6	12.5	32.5	49.9	16.7	852	86.5
Addison village	605	583	-3.6	700	99.0	0.3	0.4	0.3	0.0	28.3	14.4	36.0	50.9	13.7	287	96.5
Addison township (Oakland)	6,343	6,608	4.2	6,568	97.0	0.4	0.7	0.7	1.2	18.9	16.9	46.7	29.9	37.2	2,290	91.9
Adrian city & MCD (Lenawee)	21,189	20,600	-2.8	20,572	72.9	4.1	0.1	3.8	19.2	20.8	17.3	34.6	53.8	17.7	7,807	85.3
Adrian township (Lenawee)	5,982	6,212	3.8	6,222	92.4	0.4	0.4	1.6	5.2	22.9	22.0	44.8	38.1	30.2	2,621	93.9
Advance CDP	328	-	-	391	99.0	0.0	0.0	1.0	0.0	5.4	38.4	60.4	16.2	45.1	196	93.4
Aetna township (Mecosta)	2,299	2,330	1.3	2,317	97.3	0.3	0.2	0.9	1.3	22.1	15.8	42.7	69.0	5.2	797	85.3
Aetna township (Missaukee)	413	419	1.5	495	94.7	0.8	0.0	3.6	0.8	28.3	15.8	37.4	57.9	13.8	200	88.0
Ahmeek village	146	144	-1.4	90	95.6	0.0	0.0	0.0	4.4	18.9	33.3	53.0	50.7	17.4	50	86.0
Akron village	402	375	-6.7	424	84.9	0.5	0.0	3.8	10.8	22.6	11.3	40.0	56.7	4.0	165	83.0
Akron township (Tuscola) .	1,503	1,399	-6.9	1,447	91.8	0.0	0.5	3.2	4.6	21.6	18.2	44.0	52.2	15.0	592	86.5
Alabaster township (Iosco)	477	461	-3.4	431	99.3	0.0	0.0	0.0	0.7	15.3	41.5	60.7	37.5	34.9	214	90.7
Alaiedon township (Ingham)	2,885	2,968	2.9	2,957	88.2	0.7	2.5	2.1	6.6	20.5	21.7	46.7	25.5	45.5	1,075	95.6
Alamo township (Kalamazoo)	3,759	3,948	5.0	3,923	96.7	0.7	0.4	1.4	0.7	20.2	22.8	46.7	36.4	26.4	1,500	91.9
Alanson village	738	764	3.5	909	89.7	0.2	0.0	6.1	4.1	28.8	12.7	35.5	54.6	11.4	358	90.8
Alba CDP	295	-	-	342	98.2	0.0	0.0	0.0	1.8	31.6	20.8	32.9	64.1	1.3	127	97.6
Albee township (Saginaw)	2,160	2,021	-6.4	1,872	90.8	3.2	0.0	1.2	4.9	21.2	20.6	45.3	57.3	13.4	740	89.2
Albert township (Montmorency)	2,526	2,399	-5.0	2,384	97.7	0.0	0.0	1.3	1.0	14.1	29.8	55.9	57.6	12.5	1,193	83.7
Albion city & MCD (Calhoun)	8,613	8,402	-2.4	8,336	57.2	30.4	0.4	4.8	7.2	23.4	13.8	30.8	54.6	18.2	2,812	79.6
Albion township (Calhoun)	1,121	1,108	-1.2	1,120	97.8	0.4	0.0	1.1	0.7	21.3	23.1	46.2	50.8	18.8	440	85.2
Alcona township (Alcona) .	965	910	-5.7	1,022	98.8	0.0	0.0	0.6	0.6	7.7	46.7	62.9	43.7	27.9	534	85.2
Alden CDP	125	-	-	125	100.0	0.0	0.0	0.0	0.0	14.4	32.8	55.0	40.2	48.5	58	89.7
Algansee township (Branch)	1,978	1,958	-	1,648	98.6	0.1	0.0	0.7	0.6	21.1	21.8	44.4	50.0	21.1	690	83.5
Algoma township (Kent)....	9,939	12,752	28.3	11,983	94.4	0.7	1.4	1.7	1.8	25.5	13.3	39.7	33.5	33.9	4,140	95.6
Algonac city & MCD (St. Clair)	4,105	4,037	-1.7	4,028	95.8	0.3	0.0	2.2	1.8	20.0	17.3	42.8	46.4	15.2	1,762	87.6
Allegan city & MCD (Allegan)	4,997	5,020	0.5	5,036	77.4	7.4	2.1	3.8	9.3	25.8	11.3	31.2	47.3	14.5	1,713	82.6
Allegan township (Allegan)	4,410	4,698	6.5	4,605	95.0	1.4	0.4	0.9	2.4	19.8	23.8	45.4	49.2	15.6	1,772	77.7
Allen village	196	190	-3.1	289	95.2	1.0	2.4	0.3	1.0	21.8	23.5	43.3	58.3	12.7	118	82.2
Allen township (Hillsdale) .	1,657	1,616	-2.5	1,446	93.4	1.5	0.5	1.3	3.3	20.0	20.5	47.9	60.1	11.6	609	76.2
Allendale CDP	17,579	-	-	21,672	85.5	3.9	1.6	3.8	5.3	18.5	5.8	21.3	32.2	35.7	5,866	95.7
Allendale charter township (Ottawa)	20,708	26,709	29.0	25,481	86.3	3.5	1.5	3.6	5.1	18.9	5.6	21.3	32.4	34.8	7,035	95.9
Allen Park city & MCD (Wayne)	28,212	26,940	-4.5	27,216	84.4	2.4	0.9	2.3	10.0	20.6	17.3	42.5	37.0	25.7	10,964	91.5
Allis township (Presque Isle)	948	895	-5.6	970	96.7	0.6	0.4	0.9	1.3	19.2	24.7	49.0	59.9	7.9	384	85.7
Allouez township (Keweenaw)	1,571	1,542	-1.8	1,474	98.6	0.2	0.0	0.8	0.3	19.1	25.8	49.8	47.4	26.0	721	84.0
Alma city & MCD (Gratiot)	9,374	8,890	-5.2	8,976	87.4	1.9	0.6	1.0	9.1	18.2	17.1	30.8	42.3	21.4	3,519	85.6
Almena township (Van Buren)	4,992	5,181	3.8	5,090	87.2	1.1	0.9	4.9	5.9	27.5	14.5	38.1	28.6	34.3	1,759	98.4
Almer township (Tuscola) .	2,082	1,969	-5.4	2,097	90.7	1.6	0.0	4.2	3.5	18.3	24.9	46.1	43.9	17.3	927	88.5
Almira township (Benzie)..	3,647	3,700	1.5	3,665	95.9	0.0	0.0	2.6	1.5	24.3	17.5	37.9	28.8	35.1	1,286	96.1
Almont village	2,673	2,795	4.6	2,778	88.7	0.0	2.1	0.3	9.0	20.6	15.7	38.1	49.9	16.8	1,118	91.8
Almont township (Lapeer).	6,583	6,905	4.9	6,838	94.6	0.0	0.8	0.4	4.2	20.8	15.8	42.7	41.8	21.0	2,582	94.8
Aloha township (Cheboygan)	944	916	-3.0	1,093	94.1	1.0	0.0	4.7	0.2	22.1	24.2	48.0	41.8	28.1	428	90.9
Alpena city & MCD (Alpena)	10,505	9,956	-5.2	10,034	94.8	1.1	0.3	1.3	2.4	20.0	21.2	42.4	39.4	18.2	4,512	85.7
Alpena township (Alpena).	9,041	8,747	-3.3	8,773	96.1	0.3	1.2	1.5	0.8	15.8	25.1	52.3	40.2	21.1	4,152	83.0
Alpha village	145	134	-7.6	175	98.3	0.0	0.6	1.1	0.0	15.4	20.0	52.8	68.8	19.4	91	71.4
Alpine township (Kent)......	13,318	13,941	4.7	13,947	77.3	5.9	2.2	4.2	10.5	23.7	12.8	35.1	39.6	24.3	5,519	93.1
Amasa CDP	283	-	-	200	95.5	0.0	0.0	3.5	1.0	17.5	41.5	56.3	45.6	11.4	121	65.3
Amber township (Mason)..	2,535	2,599	2.5	2,582	95.5	0.2	1.1	0.7	2.4	19.1	23.8	47.5	44.7	22.7	1,081	93.5
Amboy township (Hillsdale)	1,173	1,154	-1.6	1,065	97.8	0.0	0.0	0.8	1.4	16.3	26.0	55.6	49.9	13.5	461	77.4
Ann Arbor city & MCD (Washtenaw)	113,988	119,980	5.3	120,735	67.5	6.6	16.8	4.2	4.8	12.8	11.7	27.5	9.8	76.0	47,765	95.9
Ann Arbor charter township (Washtenaw)..	4,349	4,520	3.9	4,544	70.0	2.1	22.0	1.7	4.3	18.6	21.1	47.9	6.6	83.6	1,894	97.0
Antioch township (Wexford)	815	831	2.0	788	94.2	0.0	2.9	1.6	1.3	29.3	21.1	39.7	52.3	14.0	293	91.5
Antrim township (Shiawassee)	2,163	2,098	-3.0	2,250	93.6	0.0	0.6	1.8	4.0	18.5	11.7	45.0	47.2	17.1	847	85.6

1 May be of any race.

Table A. All Places — **Population and Housing**

STATE City, town, township, borough, or CDP (county if applicable)	2010 census total population	2019 estimated population	Percent change 2010–2019	ACS total population estimate 2015–2019	White alone, not Hispanic or Latino	Black alone, not Hispanic or Latino	Asian alone, not Hispanic or Latino	All other races or 2 or more races, not Hispanic or Latino	Hispanic or Latino[1]	Under 18 years old	Age 65 years and older	Median age	Percent High school diploma or less	Percent Bachelor's degree or more	Total	Percent with a computer
	1	2	3	4	5	6	7	8	9	10	11	12	13	14	15	16
MICHIGAN—Con.																
Antwerp township (Van Buren)	12,182	12,308	1.0	12,170	89.0	0.9	0.8	3.3	5.9	25.0	13.8	38.6	32.7	29.0	4,514	92.0
Applegate village	248	232	-6.5	265	96.6	0.8	0.4	0.0	2.3	21.1	15.1	36.1	61.8	11.2	109	93.6
Arbela township (Tuscola)	3,070	2,921	-4.9	2,957	92.7	0.4	0.2	4.4	2.3	23.0	19.5	41.0	57.2	12.1	1,100	85.9
Arcada township (Gratiot)	1,680	1,616	-3.8	1,730	93.8	0.0	0.2	1.2	4.9	20.3	19.6	43.8	44.0	22.6	747	84.3
Arcadia township (Lapeer)	3,113	3,093	-0.6	3,104	98.3	0.2	0.0	1.2	0.3	21.1	19.0	47.7	39.1	20.9	1,264	87.0
Arcadia CDP	291	-	-	255	95.7	3.1	0.0	0.8	0.4	10.2	41.6	62.5	30.8	29.0	116	90.5
Arcadia township (Manistee)	639	631	-1.3	639	95.3	2.8	0.0	0.8	1.1	15.2	37.7	58.0	37.6	31.8	265	84.5
Arenac township (Arenac)	903	839	-7.1	917	95.6	1.6	0.0	0.9	1.9	21.7	16.2	44.1	60.6	8.6	355	77.2
Argentine CDP	2,525	-	-	2,558	96.1	0.2	0.8	2.4	0.5	21.0	18.2	46.7	42.3	27.0	995	92.1
Argentine township (Genesee)	6,907	6,514	-5.7	6,563	96.8	0.1	0.4	1.1	1.5	20.6	15.8	45.0	42.0	23.7	2,465	91.2
Argyle township (Sanilac)	759	714	-5.9	626	99.7	0.0	0.0	0.0	0.3	22.0	21.6	50.3	67.3	5.9	254	83.5
Arlington township (Van Buren)	2,066	2,046		2,015	79.5	1.3	0.1	4.6	14.6	25.6	15.6	43.2	56.2	12.1	771	86.0
Armada village	1,725	1,715	-0.6	1,799	95.8	0.9	0.2	2.1	0.9	23.9	19.1	40.9	45.2	21.2	676	82.2
Armada township (Macomb)	5,379	5,532	2.8	5,509	94.7	0.8	0.2	1.8	2.5	19.0	18.3	46.2	39.2	18.2	2,057	91.5
Arthur township (Clare)	647	649	0.3	724	96.3	0.0	0.0	3.5	0.3	30.2	14.0	37.7	47.3	15.9	229	78.6
Arvon township (Baraga)	450	428	-4.9	429	91.8	0.5	0.0	6.8	0.9	15.2	44.8	64.0	44.2	22.8	196	86.2
Ash township (Monroe)	7,786	7,748	-0.5	7,719	94.0	0.4	0.1	1.9	3.7	20.9	19.9	45.5	48.5	17.1	3,065	89.7
Ashland township (Newaygo)	2,772	2,769	-0.1	2,733	87.6	0.5	0.6	0.7	10.5	25.4	10.3	38.1	45.3	21.3	964	91.5
Ashley village	563	545	-3.2	525	95.8	3.0	0.6	0.6	0.0	16.8	26.5	52.1	60.3	8.4	220	79.5
Assyria township (Barry)	1,986	2,067	4.1	2,150	97.6	0.0	0.2	0.9	1.2	23.0	19.0	43.0	53.3	15.5	858	82.2
Athens village	1,024	996	-2.7	977	96.0	0.6	0.0	2.9	0.5	29.2	10.4	35.0	43.1	11.1	345	93.3
Athens township (Calhoun)	2,554	2,517	-1.4	2,513	91.9	2.1	0.1	3.7	2.1	25.9	19.9	39.3	49.5	12.6	908	89.8
Atlanta CDP	827	-	-	703	96.4	0.9	0.0	2.7	0.0	12.1	26.2	53.5	55.7	12.0	367	80.4
Atlas township (Genesee)	7,993	7,856	-1.7	7,821	97.0	1.0	0.2	0.9	0.8	24.6	16.1	45.6	29.7	38.7	2,807	97.9
Attica CDP	994	-	-	828	100.0	0.0	0.0	0.0	0.0	11.2	23.3	47.1	63.5	11.6	338	87.9
Attica township (Lapeer)	4,754	4,713	-0.9	4,744	94.1	0.0	0.0	0.8	5.1	21.4	17.3	43.0	49.0	11.7	1,703	87.7
Auburn city & MCD (Bay)	2,088	2,083	-0.2	2,109	96.9	0.0	0.6	0.8	1.7	17.7	22.0	45.3	33.8	26.3	1,055	88.9
Auburn Hills city & MCD (Oakland)	21,414	24,748	15.6	23,572	56.2	16.7	17.4	4.1	5.6	15.3	11.5	32.5	26.9	45.4	9,541	94.5
Au Gres city & MCD (Arenac)	889	829	-6.7	808	91.2	1.2	0.6	6.7	0.2	15.7	30.8	55.2	54.3	11.9	418	70.8
Au Gres township (Arenac)	951	882	-7.3	885	97.2	0.0	1.0	1.8	0.0	16.4	30.5	53.4	43.3	12.2	417	85.9
Augusta village	885	899	1.6	971	91.9	0.3	0.0	2.5	5.4	24.0	7.0	37.9	41.3	16.1	362	89.8
Augusta charter township (Washtenaw)	6,741	7,276	7.9	7,174	84.9	5.4	0.4	6.9	2.4	23.3	15.1	40.1	35.9	28.3	2,518	94.1
Aurelius township (Ingham)	3,534	4,371	23.7	4,343	91.7	1.3	3.0	0.8	3.2	25.7	13.4	38.7	31.8	29.2	1,518	96.8
Au Sable CDP	1,404	-	-	1,488	92.7	0.3	2.6	4.0	0.4	21.2	21.4	44.5	56.4	11.2	623	86.5
Au Sable charter township (Iosco)	2,039	1,976	-3.1	2,074	92.2	2.2	2.1	3.0	0.5	18.0	25.4	47.2	53.8	15.1	931	86.3
Au Sable township (Roscommon)	255	252	-1.2	254	97.6	0.0	0.0	2.0	0.4	19.3	25.6	50.8	51.5	14.9	107	90.7
Austin township (Mecosta)	1,563	1,581	1.2	1,977	97.0	0.5	0.0	0.7	1.9	28.4	14.7	38.5	53.7	12.0	620	83.9
Austin township (Sanilac)	665	629	-5.4	560	97.1	0.0	0.0	0.0	2.9	18.0	24.1	47.8	62.7	9.3	239	78.2
Au Train township (Alger)	1,138	1,074	-5.6	1,167	81.7	0.4	0.3	16.7	0.9	11.8	29.0	56.5	43.9	24.4	459	88.7
Avery township (Montmorency)	646	624	-3.4	654	90.4	0.0	0.0	0.8	8.9	15.0	32.3	56.3	62.3	9.4	306	79.4
Backus township (Roscommon)	330	328	-0.6	269	94.4	0.0	1.5	1.5	2.6	16.0	17.5	49.9	39.0	15.2	120	85.0
Bad Axe city & MCD (Huron)	3,112	2,914	-6.4	2,948	91.7	0.5	2.0	0.9	5.0	21.9	25.4	41.0	51.2	13.6	1,228	73.6
Bagley township (Otsego)	5,883	6,012	2.2	5,954	93.8	0.2	0.2	3.8	1.9	23.3	19.0	42.5	38.1	23.6	2,382	91.4
Bainbridge township (Berrien)	2,850	2,803	-1.6	2,812	85.8	0.5	0.0	2.6	11.1	20.2	23.0	45.5	37.8	16.1	1,132	85.6
Baldwin township (Delta)	759	743	-2.1	678	93.8	0.0	0.0	6.2	0.0	19.0	23.6	51.6	55.0	13.6	299	77.6
Baldwin township (Iosco)	1,697	1,641	-3.3	1,644	95.3	1.0	0.2	1.3	2.3	19.8	26.8	48.8	41.3	25.1	685	88.8
Baldwin village	1,200	1,079	-10.1	1,149	56.6	31.0	0.0	8.0	4.4	15.1	20.7	38.1	64.8	3.5	408	74.5
Baltimore township (Barry)	1,866	1,957	4.9	1,996	93.9	0.5	0.8	1.9	3.0	22.8	18.8	41.3	49.7	16.1	815	82.9
Bancroft village	525	497	-5.3	477	90.4	0.0	0.6	3.6	5.5	28.3	15.5	35.8	38.9	14.6	172	88.4
Bangor charter township (Bay)	14,642	13,946	-4.8	14,082	91.6	2.1	0.4	4.0	2.0	20.3	23.4	46.1	48.0	17.2	6,083	88.0
Bangor city & MCD (Van Buren)	1,892	1,833	-3.1	1,860	59.8	6.7	0.9	7.6	25.0	26.9	13.4	33.3	56.3	11.8	682	88.4
Bangor township (Van Buren)	2,145	2,106	-1.8	2,187	73.1	5.3	0.4	2.9	18.3	23.0	15.3	39.5	56.9	12.9	768	82.8
Banks township (Antrim)	1,609	1,592	-1.1	1,604	93.9	1.5	0.6	3.6	0.4	18.7	21.7	48.4	40.5	26.7	679	86.7
Baraga village	2,053	1,946	-5.2	2,142	41.4	33.4	1.0	22.3	2.0	15.1	11.8	34.4	70.8	7.3	494	78.3
Baraga township (Baraga)	3,815	3,546	-7.1	3,635	58.0	19.8	0.7	20.2	1.3	15.3	14.6	38.7	58.2	12.1	1,080	78.3
Bark River township (Delta)	1,578	1,528	-3.2	1,649	92.3	0.3	0.5	5.1	1.8	24.0	14.6	40.8	43.1	20.5	654	91.3
Barnes Lake-Millers Lake CDP	1,093	-	-	1,142	94.0	0.0	0.0	4.4	1.6	17.2	26.1	51.3	44.8	9.6	458	93.4
Baroda village	876	882	0.7	790	95.7	0.5	0.6	0.8	2.4	18.7	18.9	47.5	41.2	19.6	378	88.9
Baroda township (Berrien)	2,801	2,746	-2.0	2,757	93.4	0.9	0.2	1.1	4.5	19.8	18.9	45.9	37.8	22.6	1,178	90.7
Barry township (Barry)	3,375	3,515	4.1	3,459	96.0	0.5	0.0	2.6	0.9	19.4	20.6	46.7	40.3	22.8	1,598	84.3
Barryton village	355	353	-0.6	398	93.5	0.8	1.3	4.3	0.3	24.4	23.4	43.3	56.1	10.7	173	75.1
Barton township (Newaygo)	716	815	13.8	710	98.3	0.0	0.0	1.1	0.6	20.1	14.8	40.1	54.8	12.7	295	86.1
Barton Hills village	297	307	3.4	342	84.2	2.9	4.7	5.3	2.9	18.1	35.4	55.0	5.7	84.5	144	96.5
Batavia township (Branch)	1,330	1,328	-0.2	1,409	86.4	2.3	0.0	4.6	6.7	23.8	17.0	41.8	51.8	9.5	561	86.6
Bates township (Iron)	922	865	-6.2	909	87.0	0.0	2.3	10.7	0.0	18.2	36.0	57.0	47.0	15.3	406	86.2
Bath CDP	2,083	-	-	2,319	90.4	0.7	0.0	6.6	2.3	24.0	15.1	40.2	29.2	32.4	962	86.7
Bath charter township (Clinton)	11,616	13,004	11.9	12,745	86.6	2.6	3.5	4.0	3.3	20.5	13.8	37.0	24.6	43.8	4,944	92.8

1 May be of any race.

Table A. All Places — **Population and Housing**

STATE City, town, township, borough, or CDP (county if applicable)	Population				Race and Hispanic or Latino origin (percent)					Age (percent)			Educational attainment of persons age 25 and older		Occupied housing units	
	2010 census total population	2019 estimated population	Percent change 2010–2019	ACS total population estimate 2015–2019	White alone, not Hispanic or Latino	Black alone, not Hispanic or Latino	Asian alone, not Hispanic or Latino	All other races or 2 or more races, not Hispanic or Latino	Hispanic or Latino[1]	Under 18 years old	Age 65 years and older	Median age	Percent High school diploma or less	Percent Bachelor's degree or more	Total	Percent with a computer
	1	2	3	4	5	6	7	8	9	10	11	12	13	14	15	16
MICHIGAN—Con.																
Battle Creek city & MCD (Calhoun)	52,401	51,093	-2.5	51,316	65.3	17.6	3.6	6.1	7.5	25.4	15.1	36.3	45.4	21.9	20,813	86.3
Bay township (Charlevoix)	1,122	1,125	0.3	1,165	96.5	0.0	0.0	2.1	1.4	16.7	21.7	53.3	29.7	41.2	510	90.0
Bay City city & MCD (Bay)	34,929	32,717	-6.3	33,167	83.3	3.1	0.6	3.4	9.6	23.2	13.9	37.5	46.1	16.2	13,958	85.8
Bay de Noc township (Delta)	307	297	-3.3	339	98.8	0.0	0.0	1.2	0.0	4.4	41.6	63.0	42.2	35.9	189	73.0
Bay Mills township (Chippewa)	1,477	1,447	-2.0	1,748	39.2	1.1	2.6	55.1	2.0	18.9	17.8	40.4	33.8	23.1	644	91.5
Bay Port CDP	477	-	-	520	95.0	0.0	2.1	0.0	2.9	16.2	25.0	50.1	61.0	17.3	252	79.4
Bay Shore CDP	-	-	-	703	93.6	0.0	0.9	5.5	0.0	24.5	14.2	36.7	24.0	28.3	278	93.5
Bay View CDP	133	-	-	256	100.0	0.0	0.0	0.0	0.0	0.0	55.5	70.2	10.6	62.0	138	90.6
Beal City CDP	357	-	-	336	100.0	0.0	0.0	0.0	0.0	24.7	14.3	37.4	40.1	32.7	129	86.8
Bear Creek township (Emmet)	6,202	6,352	2.4	6,285	92.2	1.0	0.5	4.7	1.5	18.2	19.8	41.9	26.0	34.5	2,829	90.4
Bearinger township (Presque Isle)	369	347	-6.0	336	97.6	0.0	0.0	2.4	0.0	7.1	47.6	64.3	44.2	21.3	173	89.6
Bear Lake CDP	327	-	-	368	97.6	0.0	0.0	1.6	0.8	9.2	35.3	61.1	55.3	14.5	177	88.7
Bear Lake township (Kalkaska)	661	695	5.1	623	97.6	0.0	0.0	1.9	0.5	10.8	34.7	59.7	51.6	16.3	303	85.8
Bear Lake village	292	286	-2.1	203	83.7	0.0	0.0	9.9	6.4	21.7	28.1	49.1	48.3	11.6	80	90.0
Bear Lake township (Manistee)	1,751	1,724	-1.5	1,799	89.3	0.3	0.1	3.2	7.1	21.0	25.5	49.9	44.2	26.7	611	88.5
Beaugrand township (Cheboygan)	1,168	1,138	-2.6	1,279	89.4	0.0	1.0	8.4	1.2	14.2	31.7	57.1	43.8	20.2	570	83.9
Beaver township (Bay)	2,885	2,785	-3.5	2,800	97.3	0.0	0.1	0.2	2.5	22.9	14.8	42.2	47.8	20.3	1,022	86.4
Beaver township (Newaygo)	509	510	0.2	439	92.0	1.6	0.0	4.6	1.8	19.1	21.2	50.5	69.4	5.7	184	79.3
Beaver Creek township (Crawford)	1,733	1,721	-0.7	1,608	95.1	0.0	0.8	2.5	1.6	13.9	27.3	53.3	44.6	18.5	760	88.4
Beaverton city & MCD (Gladwin)	1,197	1,179	-1.5	1,380	94.3	0.1	0.0	3.3	2.4	23.3	15.7	38.1	55.4	9.4	621	75.8
Beaverton township (Gladwin)	1,835	1,832	-0.2	1,795	96.3	0.1	0.0	2.8	0.8	22.5	17.7	45.6	55.9	7.3	724	75.7
Bedford charter township (Calhoun)	9,349	9,501	1.6	9,480	85.8	8.8	0.1	2.2	3.2	19.7	17.8	44.6	49.7	14.0	3,747	90.5
Bedford township (Monroe)	31,091	32,083	3.2	31,383	92.5	1.0	1.0	1.8	3.8	22.2	19.0	44.4	37.8	27.1	12,504	89.9
Beecher CDP	10,232	-	-	9,041	27.8	57.4	0.3	11.7	2.8	27.2	12.2	31.2	53.8	8.1	3,457	80.9
Beechwood CDP	3,015	-	-	3,109	74.7	1.6	0.6	2.0	21.1	28.4	12.0	33.9	41.9	30.2	1,110	96.5
Belding city & MCD (Ionia)	5,740	5,740	0.0	5,718	94.1	0.1	0.0	3.4	2.4	28.6	13.4	34.1	54.1	11.8	2,223	89.7
Belknap township (Presque Isle)	753	706	-6.2	690	97.4	1.0	0.0	0.7	0.9	19.4	30.0	55.1	66.4	6.5	285	75.8
Bellaire village	1,086	1,066	-1.8	1,015	96.6	0.4	0.0	2.4	0.7	17.1	23.2	44.5	37.9	29.8	454	84.6
Belleville city & MCD (Wayne)	3,989	3,896	-2.3	3,889	79.2	14.2	0.5	4.2	2.0	19.4	19.1	44.6	31.5	33.8	1,805	90.3
Bellevue village	1,282	1,303	1.6	1,247	91.9	0.0	0.0	3.0	5.1	25.3	13.6	35.4	32.8	16.4	477	91.6
Bellevue township (Eaton)	3,150	3,207	1.8	3,187	86.4	3.0	0.1	3.8	6.7	28.4	17.0	38.1	39.3	15.9	1,136	92.6
Belvidere township (Montcalm)	2,209	2,235	1.2	2,131	93.7	0.9	0.0	3.9	1.5	18.2	17.7	45.2	54.9	9.9	875	81.1
Bendon CDP	208	-	-	181	96.1	0.0	0.0	3.9	0.0	24.3	7.2	32.8	52.4	27.4	81	66.7
Bengal township (Clinton)	1,188	1,203	1.3	1,106	93.4	0.1	0.0	2.3	4.2	20.8	18.5	50.6	34.9	20.2	428	86.2
Bennington township (Shiawassee)	3,168	3,065	-3.3	3,069	96.1	0.7	0.2	0.5	2.5	21.9	16.6	45.1	34.7	30.5	1,181	93.5
Benona township (Oceana)	1,441	1,434	-0.5	1,382	88.4	0.2	0.0	0.0	11.4	13.8	31.0	54.1	36.5	32.3	624	84.8
Bentley township (Gladwin)	844	837	-0.8	860	95.1	0.0	0.0	3.1	1.7	19.3	17.4	44.3	52.6	11.0	365	84.4
Benton charter township (Berrien)	14,757	14,300	-3.1	14,406	38.7	48.5	0.3	3.8	8.7	28.6	15.3	33.9	51.4	14.7	5,802	81.9
Benton township (Cheboygan)	3,206	3,100	-3.3	3,119	90.4	1.1	1.4	5.7	1.4	11.0	29.1	55.1	45.9	17.8	1,449	87.0
Benton township (Eaton)	2,777	2,846	2.5	2,832	89.5	0.8	0.0	2.2	7.5	18.6	18.8	46.3	35.3	21.2	1,072	95.1
Benton Harbor city & MCD (Berrien)	10,030	9,741	-2.9	9,843	9.5	83.6	0.0	1.5	5.4	27.9	12.0	33.7	60.5	8.1	4,143	74.6
Benton Heights CDP	4,084	-	-	4,121	21.5	61.9	0.0	3.0	13.5	35.1	9.8	27.8	59.6	10.9	1,404	83.3
Benzonia village	502	506	0.8	503	87.7	0.0	0.0	11.1	1.2	20.7	17.9	41.3	53.7	24.6	193	90.7
Benzonia township (Benzie)	2,727	2,748	0.8	2,735	89.3	0.7	1.8	7.2	1.1	19.0	30.3	55.2	37.0	36.0	1,049	94.0
Bergland township (Ontonagon)	467	397	-15.0	310	100.0	0.0	0.0	0.0	0.0	4.2	56.8	66.0	50.3	18.2	164	78.0
Berkley city & MCD (Oakland)	14,970	15,366	2.6	15,372	89.2	3.0	1.2	3.1	3.5	20.3	12.6	37.2	18.4	53.4	6,683	94.9
Berlin township (Ionia)	2,113	2,153	1.9	2,616	94.7	0.6	0.0	1.1	3.6	24.9	18.5	39.1	40.1	18.8	895	86.8
Berlin charter township (Monroe)	9,306	9,474	1.8	9,347	90.3	1.3	1.1	3.0	4.3	21.3	13.4	39.0	47.0	17.7	3,551	93.3
Berlin township (St. Clair)	3,285	3,203	-2.5	3,224	97.7	0.0	0.0	1.3	1.0	20.0	16.5	43.9	42.8	15.1	1,236	89.6
Berrien township (Berrien)	5,084	5,018	-1.3	5,043	75.5	5.8	1.2	4.3	13.2	21.6	18.6	43.2	37.4	29.5	1,861	91.9
Berrien Springs village	1,800	1,727	-4.1	1,608	59.0	17.9	7.4	5.2	10.6	20.7	16.3	36.3	32.6	35.6	657	94.8
Bertrand township (Berrien)	2,657	2,602	-2.1	2,613	92.5	0.8	0.4	5.0	1.3	18.5	22.0	49.0	40.9	24.6	1,087	93.4
Bessemer city & MCD (Gogebic)	1,908	1,707	-10.5	1,812	96.7	0.8	1.0	0.2	1.3	20.8	24.3	48.8	44.3	17.9	848	77.7
Bessemer township (Gogebic)	1,171	1,084	-7.4	1,194	96.8	1.9	0.0	0.9	0.3	18.8	22.3	49.4	40.5	21.0	530	83.8
Bethany township (Gratiot)	1,414	1,348	-4.7	1,249	88.4	0.0	0.6	1.4	9.7	25.8	22.5	42.1	43.3	18.4	521	86.6
Bethel township (Branch)	1,436	1,426	-0.7	1,340	82.7	0.5	1.2	4.7	10.9	26.6	12.0	36.8	61.6	9.3	480	90.2
Beulah village	343	345	0.6	203	91.6	5.4	0.0	2.0	1.0	3.9	35.0	56.8	36.8	29.5	75	85.3
Beverly Hills village	10,251	10,352	1.0	10,387	83.7	9.0	2.3	2.8	2.1	22.4	21.6	47.9	9.6	71.8	4,156	95.6
Big Bay CDP	319	-	-	189	95.8	0.0	0.0	4.2	0.0	2.1	19.6	61.2	18.9	45.1	118	88.1
Big Creek township (Oscoda)	2,861	2,733	-4.5	2,734	94.7	1.0	0.0	2.6	1.8	13.1	27.0	53.3	60.6	7.7	1,374	77.9

1 May be of any race.

Table A. All Places — **Population and Housing**

STATE City, town, township, borough, or CDP (county if applicable)	Population 2010 census total population	Population 2019 estimated population	Population Percent change 2010–2019	Population ACS total population estimate 2015–2019	White alone, not Hispanic or Latino	Black alone, not Hispanic or Latino	Asian alone, not Hispanic or Latino	All other races or 2 or more races, not Hispanic or Latino	Hispanic or Latino[1]	Under 18 years old	Age 65 years and older	Median age	Percent High school diploma or less	Percent Bachelor's degree or more	Occupied housing units Total	Occupied housing units Percent with a computer
	1	2	3	4	5	6	7	8	9	10	11	12	13	14	15	16
MICHIGAN—Con.																
Big Prairie township (Newaygo)	2,574	2,645	2.8	2,609	92.6	1.2	0.0	4.6	1.6	15.9	21.7	49.8	63.4	10.0	1,129	81.3
Big Rapids city & MCD (Mecosta)	10,433	10,363	-0.7	10,355	84.4	7.1	1.6	2.6	4.3	13.5	8.1	21.9	35.3	31.1	3,157	86.3
Big Rapids charter township (Mecosta)	4,376	4,847	10.8	4,744	86.8	4.7	2.2	5.2	1.1	17.7	12.2	28.1	33.4	37.4	1,638	95.5
Billings township (Gladwin)	2,412	2,386	-1.1	2,045	95.3	0.0	0.0	1.8	3.0	10.2	33.4	58.2	49.9	14.4	1,004	77.6
Bingham township (Clinton)	2,861	2,951	3.1	2,922	94.6	0.2	0.0	2.9	2.4	25.1	15.8	40.6	32.9	24.2	1,095	88.0
Bingham township (Huron)	1,709	1,600	-6.4	1,687	98.3	0.4	0.0	0.2	1.1	20.2	18.1	46.7	54.3	13.0	724	85.5
Bingham township (Leelanau)	2,497	2,502	0.2	2,496	89.1	0.0	0.2	5.0	5.8	16.0	26.7	51.2	24.2	43.4	1,078	91.1
Bingham Farms village	1,131	1,148	1.5	1,129	81.8	9.8	1.4	5.0	1.9	14.4	48.0	64.5	8.9	70.3	522	88.9
Birch Run village	1,555	1,476	-5.1	1,499	92.3	2.4	0.2	1.3	3.8	20.1	15.8	41.2	45.6	15.0	704	88.1
Birch Run township (Saginaw)	6,033	5,721	-5.2	5,734	95.2	0.7	0.1	0.3	3.7	20.4	18.9	46.0	40.2	20.1	2,376	88.6
Birmingham city & MCD (Oakland)	20,107	21,389	6.4	21,201	87.8	3.4	3.8	2.5	2.5	25.1	16.4	42.4	8.5	76.8	9,131	96.5
Bismarck township (Presque Isle)	386	364	-5.7	391	88.5	0.8	2.8	2.0	5.9	13.8	32.7	57.3	42.5	13.3	176	77.3
Blackman charter township (Jackson)	23,987	23,470	-2.2	23,471	74.8	14.5	1.6	6.0	3.1	14.1	14.5	38.4	48.9	15.7	7,667	86.6
Blaine township (Benzie)	553	559	1.1	493	99.2	0.0	0.0	0.8	0.0	14.0	35.7	58.6	28.1	38.4	225	93.3
Blair township (Grand Traverse)	8,212	9,092	10.7	8,933	85.9	0.2	2.3	3.8	7.8	26.1	10.4	34.4	45.4	17.3	3,204	93.4
Blendon township (Ottawa)	5,772	6,802	17.8	6,519	94.4	0.7	1.6	0.6	2.7	24.9	14.3	38.3	38.4	30.2	2,214	94.0
Bliss township (Emmet)	618	636	2.9	579	92.1	0.3	0.9	6.6	0.2	18.3	24.9	52.8	47.6	23.4	268	90.7
Blissfield village	3,336	3,266	-2.1	3,276	94.3	1.1	0.0	2.5	2.1	23.8	17.5	38.0	39.9	18.5	1,370	91.8
Blissfield township (Lenawee)	3,973	3,880	-2.3	3,876	93.8	0.9	0.0	2.1	3.1	24.4	16.4	38.0	37.3	22.6	1,573	92.4
Bloomer township (Montcalm)	3,881	3,782	-2.6	3,659	62.8	27.2	0.2	4.3	5.4	12.3	8.0	40.2	64.9	6.6	560	76.6
Bloomfield township (Huron)	455	423	-7.0	403	87.8	0.0	1.2	5.0	6.0	18.6	25.8	46.6	62.7	9.9	160	83.8
Bloomfield township (Missaukee)	531	549	3.4	578	93.8	0.5	0.0	3.6	2.1	27.5	16.4	38.5	49.2	11.6	229	79.0
Bloomfield charter township (Oakland)	40,875	41,945	2.6	42,054	79.1	7.2	7.5	3.1	3.0	22.6	24.6	48.7	10.4	72.6	16,381	96.1
Bloomfield Hills city & MCD (Oakland)	3,863	3,997	3.5	4,004	82.9	3.6	7.0	5.7	0.8	20.4	32.8	51.0	16.1	67.9	1,325	94.6
Bloomingdale village	454	439	-3.3	551	83.5	3.3	0.0	5.4	7.8	26.0	14.7	38.2	63.6	11.8	219	84.0
Bloomingdale township (Van Buren)	3,097	3,031	-2.1	3,025	92.8	1.7	0.0	3.1	2.4	18.5	23.3	51.0	51.6	22.1	1,371	90.4
Blue Lake township (Kalkaska)	387	402	3.9	460	98.0	0.0	0.0	0.0	2.0	4.3	47.2	63.8	35.5	34.3	226	87.6
Blue Lake township (Muskegon)	2,395	2,459	2.7	2,377	81.6	4.2	0.0	11.1	3.1	30.8	12.7	36.6	39.8	22.1	786	93.8
Blumfield township (Saginaw)	1,960	1,834	-6.4	1,842	95.4	0.9	0.0	0.3	3.4	20.7	22.2	47.8	40.1	24.3	734	91.0
Boardman township (Kalkaska)	1,530	1,622	6.0	1,550	92.4	3.7	0.3	3.4	0.2	21.7	16.6	40.3	48.7	12.5	556	84.9
Bohemia township (Ontonagon)	82	69	-15.9	79	100.0	0.0	0.0	0.0	0.0	20.3	36.7	61.2	49.2	14.3	44	86.4
Bois Blanc township (Mackinac)	95	91	-4.2	76	100.0	0.0	0.0	0.0	0.0	2.6	56.6	67.0	48.6	18.9	44	79.5
Boon CDP	167	-	-	240	97.5	0.0	0.0	1.7	0.8	39.2	6.3	33.3	50.7	13.0	73	94.5
Boon township (Wexford)	687	703	2.3	744	98.7	0.0	0.0	0.5	0.8	23.7	14.8	45.6	50.9	14.7	268	89.2
Boston township (Ionia)	5,704	5,810	1.9	5,765	95.2	0.2	0.4	0.3	3.9	24.6	14.4	39.9	36.9	26.0	2,193	90.8
Bourret township (Gladwin)	461	459	-0.4	355	99.4	0.0	0.0	0.0	0.6	7.9	38.3	58.8	62.5	10.9	194	64.9
Bowne township (Kent)	3,082	3,468	12.5	3,408	95.2	0.0	0.0	1.4	3.4	27.2	14.6	40.8	29.2	32.2	1,139	94.7
Boyne City city & MCD (Charlevoix)	3,735	3,729	-0.2	3,729	94.9	0.2	1.0	3.4	0.6	22.5	21.5	42.7	33.0	34.4	1,702	92.7
Boyne Falls village	294	297	1.0	404	93.1	2.2	0.0	4.0	0.7	24.8	15.6	35.5	46.5	18.5	168	92.9
Boyne Valley township (Charlevoix)	1,197	1,199	0.2	1,314	90.4	0.7	0.0	7.9	1.0	20.8	22.2	47.8	44.3	22.8	563	92.7
Brady township (Kalamazoo)	4,261	4,554	6.9	4,491	97.5	0.3	0.4	1.3	0.4	22.8	16.1	42.5	35.3	33.6	1,673	88.0
Brady township (Saginaw)	2,218	2,121	-4.4	2,129	95.4	0.4	0.1	1.2	2.9	23.5	20.4	43.4	57.4	8.0	858	81.9
Brampton township (Delta)	1,063	1,029	-3.2	984	94.3	0.0	0.0	5.7	0.0	17.1	36.8	58.5	38.6	21.0	441	77.6
Branch township (Mason)	1,328	1,355	2.0	1,254	95.2	0.5	0.0	3.8	0.5	28.5	19.4	39.9	46.7	15.2	533	86.9
Brandon charter township (Oakland)	15,184	16,061	5.8	15,898	94.3	0.7	0.4	1.8	2.4	22.3	14.4	42.9	34.1	28.2	5,775	94.9
Brant township (Saginaw)	2,012	1,921	-4.5	1,892	95.2	0.6	0.0	1.8	2.3	21.1	18.3	46.7	52.0	12.9	775	87.6
Breckenridge village	1,331	1,273	-4.4	1,206	94.9	0.0	0.0	2.5	2.7	24.4	13.1	36.0	51.0	16.4	536	91.0
Breedsville village	199	191	-4.0	243	60.9	0.0	0.0	21.4	17.7	20.6	25.5	51.5	60.3	4.9	115	67.0
Breen township (Dickinson)	499	486	-2.6	454	99.1	0.0	0.7	0.2	0.0	20.0	24.9	48.8	47.2	8.6	194	77.8
Breitung charter township (Dickinson)	5,839	5,671	-2.9	5,716	98.7	0.1	0.0	0.2	1.0	16.3	22.7	53.3	33.7	29.2	2,548	87.1
Brethren CDP	410	-	-	429	98.4	0.0	0.0	1.6	0.0	23.3	15.9	43.7	65.2	13.4	149	85.2
Brevort township (Mackinac)	594	570	-4.0	554	64.6	0.0	0.0	28.7	6.7	14.8	27.1	54.6	59.6	16.3	248	87.5
Bridgehampton township (Sanilac)	853	804	-5.7	848	96.6	0.0	0.0	0.5	2.9	23.6	18.6	41.2	63.5	10.5	334	85.6
Bridgeport CDP	6,950	-	-	6,425	49.9	34.8	0.5	1.1	13.6	21.7	20.7	40.8	55.8	13.1	2,634	82.2
Bridgeport charter township (Saginaw)	10,514	9,809	-6.7	9,958	61.7	24.6	0.3	1.5	11.9	19.6	21.3	44.5	51.9	13.3	4,078	84.6
Bridgeton township (Newaygo)	2,141	2,166	1.2	1,929	90.1	0.0	0.4	3.2	6.3	24.4	14.3	41.2	57.2	11.2	776	83.6

1 May be of any race.

Table A. All Places — **Population and Housing**

STATE City, town, township, borough, or CDP (county if applicable)	Population 2010 census total population	2019 estimated population	Percent change 2010–2019	ACS total population estimate 2015–2019	Race and Hispanic or Latino origin (percent) White alone, not Hispanic or Latino	Black alone, not Hispanic or Latino	Asian alone, not Hispanic or Latino	All other races or 2 or more races, not Hispanic or Latino	Hispanic or Latino[1]	Age (percent) Under 18 years old	Age 65 years and older	Median age	Educational attainment of persons age 25 and older Percent High school diploma or less	Percent Bachelor's degree or more	Occupied housing units Total	Percent with a computer
	1	2	3	4	5	6	7	8	9	10	11	12	13	14	15	16
MICHIGAN—Con.																
Bridgewater township (Washtenaw)	1,675	1,731	3.3	1,444	93.9	1.0	0.0	0.8	4.3	15.9	19.9	49.1	32.1	31.7	572	89.2
Bridgman city & MCD (Berrien)	2,289	2,212	-3.4	2,559	92.1	2.1	0.0	1.7	4.2	21.7	21.6	44.5	34.2	27.1	1,043	88.8
Brighton city & MCD (Livingston)	7,453	7,656	2.7	7,649	92.6	1.1	2.0	0.9	3.4	14.9	23.4	45.2	32.0	37.3	3,651	90.6
Brighton township (Livingston)	17,789	18,865	6.0	18,667	94.8	1.4	0.4	1.0	2.5	22.3	16.5	44.3	23.5	47.3	6,705	96.5
Briley township (Montmorency)	1,860	1,773	-4.7	1,888	95.5	0.3	0.0	3.9	0.3	15.6	27.6	54.5	58.4	10.3	878	86.9
Britton village	586	563	-3.9	641	93.3	0.0	0.0	4.2	2.5	22.0	10.6	39.6	51.8	11.4	242	93.8
Brockway township (St. Clair)	2,026	1,973	-2.6	1,901	96.3	0.0	0.0	2.7	1.0	23.3	14.6	45.1	51.8	11.0	706	89.2
Bronson city & MCD (Branch)	2,354	2,303	-2.2	2,177	89.1	0.4	0.0	3.2	7.4	24.9	11.3	34.3	58.0	7.2	924	86.1
Bronson township (Branch)	1,349	1,338	-0.8	1,390	94.5	0.0	0.8	1.4	3.3	29.1	15.5	40.5	52.6	9.1	535	92.5
Brookfield township (Eaton)	1,537	1,568	2.0	1,511	94.1	0.4	0.0	1.9	3.6	23.9	13.3	42.8	52.1	13.5	560	96.3
Brookfield township (Huron)	760	706	-7.1	790	91.3	0.1	1.4	4.1	3.2	25.7	14.7	38.9	53.7	10.6	302	94.4
Brooklyn village	1,204	1,176	-2.3	1,211	90.6	1.4	0.2	4.1	3.7	22.9	25.4	46.8	47.9	21.8	574	82.1
Brooks township (Newaygo)	3,506	3,536	0.9	3,496	91.0	0.0	0.0	0.8	8.1	20.0	20.5	46.6	49.7	21.0	1,501	81.5
Broomfield township (Isabella)	1,849	1,855	0.3	2,002	92.5	0.4	0.0	5.6	1.4	23.7	19.7	41.1	35.7	25.9	731	91.1
Brown township (Manistee)	749	739	-1.3	643	89.1	4.8	0.0	6.1	0.0	14.0	25.8	53.6	53.7	13.3	231	83.1
Brown City city	1,327	1,250	-5.8	1,201	89.8	0.4	0.0	0.8	8.9	23.1	14.2	36.7	58.7	11.3	553	85.2
Brown City city (Lapeer)	7	7	0.0	13	100.0	0.0	0.0	0.0	0.0	30.8	0.0	23.6	60.0	0.0	7	100.0
Brown City city (Sanilac)	1,320	1,243	-5.8	1,188	89.7	0.4	0.0	0.8	9.0	23.0	14.4	37.1	58.7	11.4	546	85.0
Brownlee Park CDP	2,108	-		1,686	86.1	7.1	0.0	2.9	3.9	21.6	20.6	40.0	74.9	6.6	686	86.7
Brownstown charter township (Wayne)	30,623	32,081	4.8	31,588	76.5	9.6	5.6	2.2	6.0	23.3	15.9	42.5	40.8	24.3	11,909	91.5
Bruce township (Chippewa)	2,128	2,074	-2.5	2,099	77.9	1.1	2.7	17.0	1.3	17.7	18.9	46.8	39.6	27.2	804	91.5
Bruce township (Macomb)	8,702	9,337	7.3	9,211	88.6	1.8	1.5	1.4	6.8	20.2	18.6	46.8	36.5	30.8	3,467	93.6
Brutus CDP	218	-		89	97.8	0.0	0.0	2.2	0.0	24.7	14.6	40.4	46.8	27.4	35	100.0
Buchanan city & MCD (Berrien)	4,458	4,263	-4.4	4,304	81.4	11.1	0.5	6.6	0.5	27.3	15.8	35.3	41.1	23.7	1,720	82.0
Buchanan township (Berrien)	3,521	3,516	-0.1	3,506	89.9	3.9	0.0	5.7	0.5	25.3	20.4	45.3	45.1	14.1	1,338	95.7
Buckeye township (Gladwin)	1,298	1,292	-0.5	1,311	96.5	0.0	0.0	1.5	2.0	20.2	22.1	46.2	62.2	7.8	539	80.1
Buckley village	704	718	2.0	759	92.9	0.5	1.6	3.4	1.6	32.0	10.0	32.8	52.3	11.7	240	88.8
Buel township (Sanilac)	1,265	1,215	-4.0	1,451	89.1	0.1	0.1	1.8	8.8	20.7	19.9	40.6	63.2	7.6	553	83.7
Buena Vista CDP	6,816	-		6,234	9.7	79.2	0.0	2.5	8.5	24.4	18.3	41.0	57.1	5.9	2,951	75.3
Buena Vista charter township (Saginaw)	8,674	8,106	-6.5	8,190	27.2	63.0	0.0	2.4	7.4	24.4	18.9	41.9	56.5	7.1	3,720	78.1
Bunker Hill township (Ingham)	2,115	2,180	3.1	1,895	93.7	0.0	0.0	1.3	5.0	19.2	16.7	44.7	41.9	17.5	763	89.5
Burdell township (Osceola)	1,331	1,329	-0.2	1,186	95.8	0.6	0.5	3.1	0.0	22.1	20.4	43.9	47.2	21.6	471	84.1
Burleigh township (Iosco)	785	774	-1.4	638	98.1	0.0	0.0	0.6	1.3	18.3	23.8	51.3	61.7	18.7	286	82.5
Burlington village	280	278	-0.7	355	96.3	0.6	0.0	3.1	0.0	29.0	13.8	37.8	61.4	12.9	126	90.5
Burlington township (Calhoun)	1,939	1,924	-0.8	1,824	95.9	0.4	0.0	2.9	0.8	26.2	16.3	41.9	53.8	12.3	669	87.9
Burlington township (Lapeer)	1,479	1,464		1,447	97.0	0.0	0.0	0.2	2.8	28.7	15.6	40.0	58.3	6.0	549	88.5
Burns township (Shiawassee)	3,458	3,341	-3.4	3,345	96.1	0.0	0.0	2.7	1.2	24.0	16.7	41.4	49.5	16.9	1,259	83.8
Burnside township (Lapeer)	1,868	1,853	-0.8	2,026	93.6	0.0	0.0	3.1	3.3	24.6	17.0	44.1	62.2	7.5	710	83.1
Burr Oak village	828	806	-2.7	763	86.5	0.3	0.0	4.7	8.5	27.0	11.5	37.4	64.7	4.8	278	86.0
Burr Oak township (St. Joseph)	2,627	2,642	0.6	2,623	93.9	0.3	0.0	2.0	3.7	28.8	17.8	38.7	52.2	12.3	965	79.9
Burt township (Alger)	522	491	-5.9	410	94.1	2.7	0.5	1.2	1.5	8.5	54.6	69.2	50.1	32.5	179	86.0
Burt township (Cheboygan)	680	654	-3.8	777	94.3	1.3	0.0	1.0	3.3	12.5	48.8	64.1	30.3	41.3	347	93.9
Burt CDP	1,228	-		1,106	93.7	0.0	0.0	4.2	2.1	24.7	20.3	36.8	46.7	19.0	412	83.7
Burtchville township (St. Clair)	3,994	3,936	-1.5	3,925	88.2	0.4	0.8	4.2	6.4	24.1	18.5	42.8	40.7	21.7	1,637	91.8
Burton city & MCD (Genesee)	29,999	28,574	-4.8	28,654	85.6	7.5	1.3	3.1	2.6	23.5	15.4	39.2	46.2	16.4	11,428	86.7
Bushnell township (Montcalm)	1,604	1,637	2.1	1,569	96.9	0.0	0.1	1.1	1.8	23.1	17.1	43.4	60.9	5.3	540	88.9
Butler township (Branch)	1,465	1,445	-1.4	1,329	99.0	0.0	0.0	0.0	1.0	26.2	17.3	36.0	57.3	13.5	476	75.8
Butman township (Gladwin)	1,999	1,978	-1.1	1,927	97.9	0.2	0.0	0.4	1.6	9.4	51.8	65.5	43.7	26.4	960	81.5
Butterfield township (Missaukee)	489	501	2.5	449	96.7	0.0	0.0	1.8	1.6	14.5	22.7	50.5	56.9	6.3	200	91.5
Byron township (Kent)	20,324	24,913	22.6	23,818	81.7	4.3	3.3	3.9	6.8	28.2	15.5	37.9	36.4	32.4	8,664	91.9
Byron village	581	549	-5.5	494	89.7	0.0	0.0	8.1	2.2	21.7	15.0	37.6	50.3	16.7	193	89.1
Byron Center CDP	5,822	-		7,089	88.8	2.0	2.2	1.9	5.2	33.9	15.8	37.8	30.5	39.9	2,336	92.8
Caberfae CDP	64	-		57	100.0	0.0	0.0	0.0	0.0	14.0	26.3	49.5	31.4	54.3	21	90.5
Cadillac city & MCD (Wexford)	10,354	10,497	1.4	10,419	94.3	1.1	0.0	2.6	2.0	23.1	18.6	38.2	44.4	17.0	4,433	83.1
Caldwell township (Missaukee)	1,319	1,349	2.3	1,439	91.9	0.6	0.8	1.6	5.1	20.8	18.6	45.0	58.5	9.9	565	86.2
Caledonia township (Alcona)	1,169	1,110	-5.0	1,041	97.1	0.0	0.2	2.0	0.7	11.0	40.0	60.9	44.4	21.1	514	89.5
Caledonia village	1,511	1,636	8.3	1,544	93.2	0.9	1.7	2.1	2.1	30.5	8.5	35.7	25.0	37.4	562	90.2

1 May be of any race.

Table A. All Places — **Population and Housing**

STATE City, town, township, borough, or CDP (county if applicable)	2010 census total population	2019 estimated population	Percent change 2010–2019	ACS total population estimate 2015–2019	White alone, not Hispanic or Latino	Black alone, not Hispanic or Latino	Asian alone, not Hispanic or Latino	All other races or 2 or more races, not Hispanic or Latino	Hispanic or Latino[1]	Under 18 years old	Age 65 years and older	Median age	Percent High school diploma or less	Percent Bachelor's degree or more	Total	Percent with a computer
	1	2	3	4	5	6	7	8	9	10	11	12	13	14	15	16
MICHIGAN—Con.																
Caledonia township (Kent)	12,340	14,890	20.7	14,417	94.2	0.9	1.1	2.6	1.2	27.2	12.3	37.6	21.6	44.7	4,898	95.1
Caledonia charter township (Shiawassee)	4,465	4,297	-3.8	4,324	91.4	0.0	0.9	1.5	6.2	21.9	22.8	48.7	40.3	17.9	1,837	81.5
California township (Branch)	1,040	1,028	-1.2	1,445	99.4	0.0	0.4	0.2	0.0	52.7	6.7	16.8	69.6	5.1	329	65.0
Calumet village	726	687	-5.4	744	87.2	0.9	0.0	5.5	6.3	21.9	15.2	31.5	39.0	23.8	358	77.7
Calumet charter township (Houghton)	6,489	6,212	-4.3	6,288	93.9	0.3	0.2	3.4	2.2	22.0	20.1	42.5	45.9	21.2	2,641	81.1
Calvin township (Cass)	2,036	2,062	1.3	1,793	80.3	14.3	0.2	4.8	0.3	19.8	18.6	47.6	46.9	17.0	714	90.9
Cambria township (Hillsdale)	2,533	2,482	-2.0	2,390	91.5	0.0	1.8	2.9	3.8	23.9	22.3	43.2	55.3	15.4	963	80.4
Cambridge township (Lenawee)	5,739	5,684		5,652	88.9	0.9	0.6	3.9	5.8	17.4	21.4	51.6	35.1	24.9	2,496	95.3
Camden village	511	501	-2.0	675	96.9	0.0	0.0	1.2	1.9	37.3	10.5	30.0	71.4	5.5	199	78.9
Camden township (Hillsdale)	2,047	2,009	-1.9	2,138	97.6	0.0	0.1	1.0	1.3	29.8	17.5	38.5	67.4	8.1	747	73.0
Campbell township (Ionia)	2,393	2,431	1.6	2,271	92.4	0.0	0.9	3.1	3.6	23.1	16.2	40.6	43.7	25.8	868	90.1
Canada Creek Ranch CDP	304	-	-	248	100.0	0.0	0.0	0.0	0.0	4.4	65.7	69.8	39.7	28.7	138	86.2
Canadian Lakes CDP	2,756	-	-	2,574	97.4	0.0	0.0	0.0	2.6	13.8	49.3	64.6	29.9	34.9	1,200	94.4
Cannon township (Kent)	13,334	15,167	13.7	14,792	94.8	0.4	1.9	2.1	0.9	24.9	13.3	41.4	19.5	51.5	5,150	97.4
Canton charter township (Wayne)	90,176	93,704	3.9	91,920	65.4	9.2	19.0	3.6	2.8	24.4	14.1	39.8	20.7	52.4	33,671	97.0
Capac village	1,890	1,837	-2.8	1,821	78.5	0.5	0.0	2.6	18.3	21.3	15.1	41.3	58.0	7.1	764	91.6
Carleton village	2,345	2,354	0.4	2,432	93.7	0.3	0.2	3.7	2.2	26.2	13.8	37.8	54.2	13.1	925	89.9
Carlton township (Barry)	2,392	2,489	4.1	2,170	94.1	0.0	0.0	1.4	4.5	21.0	15.4	47.1	45.2	18.3	859	89.1
Carmel township (Eaton)	2,855	2,903	1.7	2,895	93.2	1.7	0.0	2.5	2.6	20.1	21.2	46.1	37.6	26.0	1,065	91.3
Carney village	192	182	-5.2	216	88.0	6.0	0.0	2.8	3.2	15.3	23.1	51.5	52.9	13.4	87	82.8
Caro city & MCD (Tuscola)	4,261	3,988	-6.4	4,054	93.9	0.9	0.0	1.2	4.0	19.5	23.0	45.5	54.6	12.5	1,812	79.0
Carp Lake CDP	357	-	-	368	98.6	1.1	0.0	0.3	0.0	13.3	38.9	60.7	50.2	21.7	183	78.7
Carp Lake township (Emmet)	766	786	2.6	673	92.6	0.6	0.0	6.8	0.0	13.2	31.1	56.8	53.0	20.2	317	81.1
Carp Lake township (Ontonagon)	722	610	-15.5	661	93.5	0.0	2.0	1.5	3.0	13.9	35.4	58.8	44.2	17.1	304	87.8
Carrollton township (Saginaw)	6,103	5,646	-7.5	5,732	66.6	18.1	0.0	1.0	14.2	23.5	14.4	37.3	42.4	15.9	2,277	84.1
Carson City city & MCD (Montcalm)	1,116	1,111	-0.4	993	89.7	1.4	0.4	1.0	7.5	22.9	22.2	38.7	41.3	13.8	414	84.1
Carsonville village	527	495	-6.1	504	93.5	0.0	0.6	1.4	4.6	26.6	12.1	36.3	57.2	10.6	197	91.9
Cascade charter township (Kent)	17,157	19,406	13.1	19,028	88.5	2.3	4.1	1.4	3.7	25.6	17.5	42.5	11.4	66.6	7,247	93.7
Casco township (Allegan)	2,820	3,084	9.4	3,013	84.7	1.6	0.6	4.1	9.0	17.8	25.5	50.2	41.9	29.7	1,226	84.7
Casco township (St. Clair)	4,105	4,056	-1.2	4,036	92.6	0.2	1.6	1.1	4.6	21.9	18.6	42.5	44.2	18.7	1,481	90.1
Case township (Presque Isle)	903	853	-5.5	756	89.6	1.7	1.6	2.5	4.6	19.8	24.9	51.0	51.0	14.2	344	85.5
Caseville city & MCD (Huron)	781	735	-5.9	591	97.8	1.7	0.0	0.5	0.0	7.6	44.2	62.5	54.0	13.4	372	80.1
Caseville township (Huron)	1,789	1,673	-6.5	1,745	93.3	0.0	1.5	1.3	3.9	14.1	42.7	58.7	48.1	22.2	812	89.5
Casnovia village	317	321	1.3	323	83.9	0.0	1.5	3.4	11.1	24.1	9.0	36.8	43.0	13.6	121	89.3
Casnovia township (Muskegon)	2,801	2,907	3.8	2,873	94.0	2.2	0.3	0.7	2.8	23.5	16.3	42.7	48.6	15.2	977	88.2
Caspian city & MCD (Iron)	906	845	-6.7	477	85.3	1.5	1.9	2.3	9.0	15.1	30.2	52.6	59.3	8.5	277	76.9
Cass City village	2,426	2,276	-6.2	2,353	95.5	0.5	0.7	0.7	2.5	16.5	26.9	47.3	45.5	19.7	953	81.7
Cassopolis village	1,769	1,699	-4.0	1,692	53.9	34.8	2.1	8.2	1.0	25.8	16.8	33.9	58.4	11.2	724	75.8
Castleton township (Barry)	3,477	3,646	4.9	3,572	93.3	0.0	0.1	2.1	4.6	22.5	20.4	42.0	53.2	8.1	1,413	82.7
Cato township (Montcalm)	2,735	2,757	0.8	2,750	93.9	0.8	0.4	1.2	3.8	24.4	18.5	39.6	49.4	15.0	1,029	83.4
Cedar CDP	93	-	-	106	97.2	0.0	0.0	0.0	2.8	10.4	15.1	24.9	19.2	61.5	36	100.0
Cedar township (Osceola)	455	455	0.0	409	99.3	0.0	0.0	0.0	0.7	15.2	34.5	59.6	55.2	11.6	179	82.1
Cedar Creek township (Muskegon)	3,186	3,321	4.2	3,249	92.0	2.6	0.7	3.1	1.6	20.5	17.5	47.0	49.0	9.3	1,254	93.7
Cedar Creek township (Wexford)	1,758	1,811	3.0	1,811	95.7	0.6	0.0	3.1	0.6	26.1	12.0	36.7	55.8	10.4	628	83.3
Cedar Springs city & MCD (Kent)	3,487	3,711	6.4	3,666	86.9	2.6	0.2	3.5	6.8	25.9	10.2	34.3	53.3	17.3	1,351	91.6
Cedarville township (Menominee)	253	243	-4.0	256	93.4	0.0	0.4	6.3	0.0	18.8	39.5	59.8	38.8	24.5	123	88.6
Cement City village	440	427	-3.0	482	93.4	0.0	0.2	3.3	1.5	19.9	13.7	38.7	63.8	10.4	191	88.0
Center township (Emmet)	568	584	2.8	636	84.7	0.0	1.9	11.8	1.6	21.7	15.3	42.8	48.7	13.2	268	81.7
Center Line city & MCD (Macomb)	8,255	8,171		8,260	66.3	21.9	3.9	3.6	4.3	22.7	15.9	38.3	48.0	14.1	3,462	86.9
Centerville township (Leelanau)	1,274	1,277	0.2	1,449	93.6	0.4	0.0	0.9	5.1	16.7	24.5	48.0	28.9	40.5	587	89.8
Central Lake village	952	939	-1.4	953	95.9	0.1	0.7	3.1	0.1	20.0	20.7	47.1	45.5	20.4	420	88.1
Central Lake township (Antrim)	2,198	2,169	-1.3	1,976	98.0	0.1	0.4	1.5	0.1	15.5	29.7	54.7	37.9	23.2	913	91.2
Centreville village	1,421	1,406	-1.1	1,278	88.6	6.7	0.0	2.6	2.1	18.6	16.7	43.9	53.7	11.1	442	85.3
Champion township (Marquette)	297	297	0.0	278	98.2	0.0	0.0	1.8	0.0	18.3	12.2	36.8	49.5	13.3	105	97.1
Chandler township (Charlevoix)	259	259	0.0	264	90.2	0.8	0.0	7.6	1.5	27.7	21.6	37.0	52.8	8.9	97	79.4
Chandler township (Huron)	472	436	-7.6	543	91.3	0.0	0.0	3.3	5.3	30.4	13.4	37.0	46.9	18.0	187	93.6
Chapin township (Saginaw)	1,060	1,005	-5.2	1,023	97.2	0.2	0.2	1.3	1.2	23.6	16.8	43.9	61.6	9.7	395	79.2
Charleston township (Kalamazoo)	1,965	2,078	5.8	1,965	95.1	0.2	0.1	1.1	3.5	21.6	19.2	43.1	30.7	28.2	730	93.8
Charlevoix city & MCD (Charlevoix)	2,512	2,488		2,338	90.0	2.4	0.0	3.6	4.0	14.2	24.2	47.5	27.5	32.0	1,294	84.9
Charlevoix township (Charlevoix)	1,642	1,656	0.9	1,752	89.4	0.2	0.9	4.9	4.6	18.8	30.7	53.9	28.8	41.4	768	90.1

1 May be of any race.

Table A. All Places — **Population and Housing**

STATE City, town, township, borough, or CDP (county if applicable)	Population				Race and Hispanic or Latino origin (percent)					Age (percent)			Educational attainment of persons age 25 and older		Occupied housing units	
	2010 census total population	2019 estimated population	Percent change 2010–2019	ACS total population estimate 2015–2019	White alone, not Hispanic or Latino	Black alone, not Hispanic or Latino	Asian alone, not Hispanic or Latino	All other races or 2 or more races, not Hispanic or Latino	Hispanic or Latino[1]	Under 18 years old	Age 65 years and older	Median age	Percent High school diploma or less	Percent Bachelor's degree or more	Total	Percent with a computer
	1	2	3	4	5	6	7	8	9	10	11	12	13	14	15	16
MICHIGAN—Con.																
Charlotte city & MCD (Eaton)	9,091	9,090	0.0	9,082	92.2	0.6	0.4	1.0	5.8	23.2	15.2	37.3	45.2	14.5	3,477	90.6
Charlton township (Otsego)	1,358	1,391	2.4	1,282	93.9	0.0	1.0	1.6	3.5	16.1	29.3	52.6	45.7	21.8	545	93.6
Chase township (Lake)	1,138	1,186	4.2	1,427	93.9	0.4	0.0	2.8	2.9	28.2	18.5	40.1	57.4	15.9	445	81.3
Chassell township (Houghton)	1,812	1,750	-3.4	1,825	96.7	0.0	0.7	1.9	0.7	27.5	17.8	38.7	37.5	37.6	674	90.7
Chatham village	220	205	-6.8	192	99.0	0.0	0.0	1.0	0.0	21.9	26.0	49.0	58.3	15.8	90	60.0
Cheboygan city & MCD (Cheboygan)	4,865	4,686	-3.7	4,719	87.5	2.8	0.5	5.0	4.3	20.7	22.9	39.9	55.9	14.6	2,026	83.0
Chelsea city & MCD (Washtenaw)	4,936	5,416	9.7	5,331	94.5	0.9	0.3	2.3	1.9	21.4	25.0	44.5	19.8	53.3	2,189	91.4
Cherry Grove township (Wexford)	2,377	2,412	1.5	2,433	96.0	0.6	0.6	1.9	0.9	19.1	23.6	47.5	34.3	28.8	948	90.9
Cherry Valley township (Lake)	396	416	5.1	391	88.0	3.6	0.0	8.2	0.3	14.1	35.8	57.7	73.8	5.2	162	78.4
Chesaning village	2,404	2,238	-6.9	2,339	87.6	0.8	0.0	0.9	10.8	24.2	19.1	38.3	45.3	20.0	990	84.7
Chesaning township (Saginaw)	4,659	4,380	-6.0	4,421	89.5	0.4	0.4	0.8	8.8	20.7	21.1	43.8	47.2	20.7	1,859	85.7
Cheshire township (Allegan)	2,197	2,293	4.4	2,208	92.3	2.5	0.5	2.9	1.9	18.1	15.4	40.5	61.5	15.0	889	79.5
Chester township (Eaton)	1,747	1,778	1.8	1,776	95.5	0.9	0.4	1.7	1.5	22.4	19.5	45.6	41.5	18.7	696	89.4
Chester township (Otsego)	1,290	1,317	2.1	1,227	96.6	0.7	2.3	0.0	0.5	16.4	17.0	47.7	40.6	20.1	508	93.1
Chester township (Ottawa)	2,017	2,057	2.0	2,126	91.3	0.1	0.9	1.6	6.2	22.2	14.5	40.2	44.6	25.3	767	90.1
Chesterfield township (Macomb)	43,387	46,680	7.6	45,660	86.2	6.0	1.1	3.0	3.7	22.9	13.8	40.6	34.9	25.5	17,749	93.5
Chestonia township (Antrim)	511	509	-0.4	433	92.8	2.1	0.9	2.1	2.1	18.7	23.8	54.8	66.8	10.6	201	94.0
Chikaming township (Berrien)	3,100	3,080	-0.6	3,091	96.6	1.7	0.0	0.0	1.7	10.9	36.7	59.0	34.2	39.8	1,480	92.8
China township (St. Clair)	3,551	3,450	-2.8	3,447	96.5	0.0	1.1	2.1	0.2	20.0	18.9	48.4	39.0	23.1	1,281	94.8
Chippewa township (Chippewa)	213	209	-1.9	206	90.3	0.5	0.0	9.2	0.0	27.7	19.9	42.5	58.1	3.4	78	82.1
Chippewa township (Isabella)	4,654	4,705	1.1	4,688	66.1	1.0	0.7	27.5	4.6	22.0	15.6	40.4	59.5	13.7	1,719	90.5
Chippewa township (Mecosta)	1,212	1,212	0.0	1,257	99.1	0.0	0.0	0.7	0.2	18.3	29.5	45.4	60.5	8.6	514	82.1
Chocolay charter township (Marquette)	5,903	5,917	0.2	5,941	93.0	0.5	0.9	4.8	0.8	20.2	21.8	45.0	29.3	44.0	2,374	94.4
Chums Corner CDP	946	-	-	984	98.4	0.0	0.0	0.0	1.6	23.5	25.8	45.5	36.1	47.8	387	90.2
Churchill township (Ogemaw)	1,702	1,649	-3.1	1,576	93.1	0.0	0.0	2.5	4.3	17.2	25.4	49.8	54.3	11.9	688	87.4
Clam Lake township (Wexford)	2,146	2,196	2.3	2,427	89.2	0.0	0.9	2.5	7.3	23.9	20.2	46.6	41.8	25.9	868	91.9
Clam Union township (Missaukee)	882	890	0.9	902	91.1	0.0	0.0	0.3	8.5	29.0	14.5	32.2	52.6	9.9	351	92.0
Clare city	3,118	3,077	-1.3	3,042	95.9	0.8	0.0	1.2	2.2	21.4	20.9	41.6	38.3	27.6	1,309	87.7
Clare city (Clare)	3,052	3,012	-1.3	2,995	95.8	0.8	0.0	1.2	2.2	21.6	21.3	41.7	38.2	28.0	1,298	87.6
Clare city (Isabella)	66	65	-1.5	47	100.0	0.0	0.0	0.0	0.0	10.6	0.0	28.9	45.2	9.5	11	100.0
Clarence township (Calhoun)	1,985	1,960	-1.3	2,006	92.5	1.5	0.2	1.6	4.1	16.6	22.1	46.3	45.1	20.9	805	85.7
Clarendon township (Calhoun)	1,147	1,162	1.3	1,077	96.3	0.0	0.0	0.2	3.5	21.1	18.5	43.9	53.7	13.0	426	78.4
Clark township (Mackinac)	2,057	1,976	-3.9	1,718	83.5	0.0	0.9	15.2	0.5	17.5	29.5	53.9	33.7	30.5	845	95.3
Clarksville village	394	396	0.5	357	97.2	0.0	0.3	1.1	1.4	21.0	19.3	36.6	37.4	24.9	165	86.1
Clawson city & MCD (Oakland)	11,833	11,845	0.1	11,971	91.3	1.2	1.9	2.5	3.2	15.6	18.0	40.6	28.3	41.0	5,739	91.1
Clay township (St. Clair)	9,071	8,902	-1.9	8,874	97.2	0.0	0.8	1.4	0.6	14.4	27.6	53.2	41.5	17.4	4,129	91.2
Claybanks township (Oceana)	777	776	-0.1	1,017	95.1	0.0	0.3	1.5	3.1	16.6	27.2	50.0	29.9	28.8	407	91.4
Clayton township (Arenac)	1,097	1,044	-4.8	1,038	97.3	0.0	0.0	2.7	0.0	19.7	20.7	45.1	66.3	5.3	383	81.2
Clayton charter township (Genesee)	7,581	7,174	-5.4	7,235	89.6	5.4	1.2	1.6	2.2	22.0	20.0	43.5	28.0	28.7	2,770	94.0
Clayton village	344	330	-4.1	334	86.2	0.0	0.0	1.8	12.0	31.7	13.5	38.5	67.9	4.2	116	82.8
Clearwater township (Kalkaska)	2,444	2,557	4.6	2,493	94.1	1.9	0.2	2.3	1.4	21.0	20.0	46.1	54.5	14.7	985	92.9
Clement township (Gladwin)	905	898	-0.8	932	94.8	0.0	0.0	1.5	3.6	10.8	40.0	59.2	59.9	9.9	481	80.7
Cleon township (Manistee)	957	954	-0.3	788	95.1	0.0	0.0	1.5	3.4	15.2	23.2	53.8	56.2	14.2	315	80.3
Cleveland township (Leelanau)	1,031	1,033	0.2	1,197	96.8	0.6	0.0	1.2	1.4	15.0	32.2	55.8	34.5	39.6	513	91.6
Clifford village	325	319	-1.8	286	99.0	0.0	0.0	0.3	0.7	24.8	20.6	45.5	70.1	1.5	112	83.9
Climax village	767	783	2.1	762	95.8	1.0	0.0	2.8	0.4	24.9	15.4	40.1	36.0	28.0	295	93.6
Climax township (Kalamazoo)	2,465	2,539	3.0	2,542	94.8	0.6	1.2	2.4	1.0	24.7	20.4	42.0	36.2	21.8	960	91.8
Clinton village	2,334	2,290	-1.9	2,775	95.5	0.4	1.2	1.6	1.3	23.7	13.8	35.2	29.7	30.4	1,051	96.2
Clinton township (Lenawee)	3,603	3,554	-1.4	3,541	96.5	0.3	1.0	1.3	1.0	20.2	17.8	42.9	31.6	27.7	1,413	96.3
Clinton charter township (Macomb)	96,798	100,471	3.8	100,406	73.6	18.6	2.0	3.4	2.3	20.1	17.8	40.9	41.6	21.4	43,892	90.2
Clinton township (Oscoda)	439	416	-5.2	535	97.2	0.0	0.0	1.5	1.3	16.1	28.8	59.4	46.2	13.5	260	79.2
Clio city & MCD (Genesee)	2,646	2,497	-5.6	2,421	86.5	0.9	0.0	3.5	9.1	18.8	26.4	44.1	48.8	17.5	1,277	78.6
Clyde township (Allegan)	2,084	2,148	3.1	2,171	66.6	0.7	0.0	2.2	30.5	22.5	13.9	43.0	69.8	11.5	802	82.8
Clyde township (St. Clair)	5,579	5,436	-2.6	5,451	97.6	0.3	0.0	1.1	1.0	19.1	20.4	47.3	38.8	22.4	2,204	91.7
Coe township (Isabella)	3,079	3,049		3,071	87.7	0.7	0.0	2.9	8.7	27.9	12.2	38.6	47.7	21.4	1,154	88.9
Cohoctah township (Livingston)	3,316	3,341	0.8	3,336	95.3	0.1	0.8	2.5	1.3	20.6	16.9	47.3	38.3	15.6	1,281	91.5
Coldsprings township (Kalkaska)	1,464	1,542	5.3	1,475	97.0	0.7	0.0	1.5	0.7	17.6	23.8	52.1	64.6	11.8	639	86.7

1 May be of any race.

Table A. All Places — **Population and Housing**

STATE City, town, township, borough, or CDP (county if applicable)	Population 2010 census total population	2019 estimated population	Percent change 2010–2019	ACS total population estimate 2015–2019	Race and Hispanic or Latino origin (percent) White alone, not Hispanic or Latino	Black alone, not Hispanic or Latino	Asian alone, not Hispanic or Latino	All other races or 2 or more races, not Hispanic or Latino	Hispanic or Latino[1]	Age (percent) Under 18 years old	Age 65 years and older	Median age	Educational attainment of persons age 25 and older Percent High school diploma or less	Percent Bachelor's degree or more	Occupied housing units Total	Percent with a computer
	1	2	3	4	5	6	7	8	9	10	11	12	13	14	15	16
MICHIGAN—Con.																
Coldwater city & MCD (Branch)	13,612	12,215	-10.3	12,241	81.4	7.4	1.6	2.3	7.3	21.8	17.3	38.5	53.6	12.7	4,196	87.9
Coldwater township (Branch)	3,445	3,430	-0.4	3,428	87.2	0.8	0.8	1.0	10.2	20.5	20.7	44.3	49.5	17.5	1,388	91.1
Coldwater township (Isabella)	777	779	0.3	731	83.7	0.0	0.3	13.1	2.9	14.0	23.4	49.8	49.8	17.3	307	78.5
Coleman city & MCD (Midland)	1,243	1,203	-3.2	1,324	96.0	0.0	1.2	0.9	1.9	22.8	19.6	35.6	53.9	14.0	582	75.8
Colfax township (Benzie)	659	674	2.3	663	79.6	0.0	0.0	9.8	10.6	18.1	21.0	50.3	50.5	9.0	248	83.1
Colfax township (Huron)	1,904	1,806	-5.1	1,728	93.3	0.0	0.3	0.8	5.5	20.9	21.9	48.4	55.9	19.3	713	85.3
Colfax township (Mecosta)	1,933	1,934	0.1	1,923	93.0	0.7	1.3	4.0	1.0	18.9	22.9	46.4	34.1	33.9	727	87.8
Colfax township (Oceana)	462	462	0.0	587	75.5	0.2	0.3	4.4	19.6	25.6	13.8	35.2	62.4	17.7	194	85.1
Colfax township (Wexford)	840	855	1.8	1,071	97.7	1.0	0.0	1.0	0.3	29.1	17.4	35.1	52.2	18.3	349	84.8
Coloma city & MCD (Berrien)	1,481	1,411	-4.7	1,594	91.1	2.7	0.0	2.9	3.3	24.7	18.1	34.4	49.9	16.9	618	82.2
Coloma charter township (Berrien)	5,030	4,926	-2.1	4,956	91.8	1.2	0.4	4.0	2.6	23.2	18.3	45.4	40.9	21.9	2,087	84.3
Colon village	1,181	1,158	-1.9	1,133	96.8	0.0	0.3	2.9	0.0	23.9	20.6	36.0	51.9	15.5	506	79.6
Colon township (St. Joseph)	3,335	3,324	-0.3	3,312	98.0	0.4	0.3	1.0	0.3	24.1	22.1	43.2	57.4	18.1	1,386	74.0
Columbia township (Jackson)	7,415	7,356	-0.8	7,376	91.1	3.8	1.1	2.2	1.8	20.5	23.2	48.2	36.4	26.5	3,109	91.3
Columbia township (Tuscola)	1,284	1,193	-7.1	1,167	94.1	0.0	0.4	0.6	4.9	19.7	20.0	43.7	50.6	12.1	476	86.3
Columbia township (Van Buren)	2,591	2,572	-0.7	2,559	70.2	7.2	0.3	6.7	15.6	23.8	13.5	41.6	52.0	18.6	919	83.5
Columbiaville village	787	763	-3.0	910	94.1	0.0	0.0	3.4	2.5	28.5	13.3	33.9	47.8	11.1	340	90.3
Columbus township (Luce)	201	187	-7.0	148	93.9	0.0	0.0	6.1	0.0	8.1	34.5	59.0	52.7	16.8	76	77.6
Columbus township (St. Clair)	4,070	4,029		4,013	93.9	2.6	0.0	1.9	1.6	22.8	17.2	44.1	42.0	19.8	1,557	95.0
Comins township (Oscoda)	1,923	1,839	-4.4	1,693	96.4	0.5	0.0	2.5	0.6	24.4	25.4	45.8	51.2	13.8	725	76.8
Commerce charter township (Oakland)	40,106	44,065	9.9	43,289	86.3	2.4	4.5	2.6	4.2	23.5	14.7	41.6	24.7	45.3	16,216	95.4
Comstock charter township (Kalamazoo)	14,851	15,594	5.0	15,531	81.1	7.9	3.1	4.8	3.1	21.1	14.4	35.8	30.6	36.8	6,200	93.4
Comstock Northwest CDP	5,455	-	-	6,318	70.0	15.0	8.1	4.4	2.6	20.8	13.7	32.1	27.2	37.6	2,762	93.0
Comstock Park CDP	10,088	-	-	10,306	74.1	6.6	2.7	4.4	12.2	23.3	13.4	35.1	36.6	25.7	4,433	92.2
Concord village	1,048	1,040	-0.8	1,299	82.8	8.8	1.8	2.2	4.5	32.4	10.5	31.9	40.0	21.8	468	87.2
Concord township (Jackson)	2,725	2,703	-0.8	2,710	90.8	4.2	0.8	1.2	2.9	27.2	11.7	41.9	36.5	27.7	1,009	89.6
Constantine village	2,117	2,111	-0.3	2,099	87.9	0.0	0.6	3.0	8.4	28.6	12.4	36.3	62.6	8.7	840	87.1
Constantine township (St. Joseph)	4,217	4,194	-0.5	4,188	89.6	0.0	0.7	3.7	6.0	23.0	17.2	40.9	58.0	13.3	1,690	84.7
Convis township (Calhoun)	1,634	1,642	0.5	1,699	96.2	0.4	0.0	1.6	1.7	22.8	16.0	43.5	45.6	18.8	642	89.3
Conway CDP	204	-	-	170	98.2	0.0	0.0	1.8	0.0	21.8	24.1	36.9	38.4	8.9	72	90.3
Conway township (Livingston)	3,546	3,610	1.8	3,588	94.4	0.0	0.0	5.0	0.6	27.4	9.4	35.3	45.3	22.8	1,190	98.0
Cooper charter township (Kalamazoo)	10,117	11,067	9.4	10,861	87.6	3.9	0.7	2.7	5.0	28.0	14.9	36.6	34.4	34.0	4,044	93.3
Coopersville city & MCD (Ottawa)	4,278	4,387	2.5	4,396	88.5	0.0	0.2	6.6	4.7	30.4	12.1	30.5	44.4	18.7	1,568	85.0
Copemish village	194	193	-0.5	143	86.7	0.0	0.0	2.1	11.2	11.2	24.5	53.6	57.7	15.4	58	74.1
Copper City village	190	182	-4.2	197	97.0	0.0	1.0	2.0	0.0	18.8	19.8	45.4	55.8	12.3	82	79.3
Copper Harbor CDP	108	-	-	85	100.0	0.0	0.0	0.0	0.0	3.5	44.7	62.5	16.0	40.7	52	78.8
Cornell township (Delta)	593	576	-2.9	605	98.8	0.0	0.0	1.2	0.0	18.7	21.2	47.2	41.6	20.4	250	82.8
Corunna city & MCD (Shiawassee)	3,500	3,344	-4.5	3,371	86.7	3.2	0.0	1.8	8.3	22.8	19.0	38.8	47.8	17.0	1,370	89.7
Corwith township (Otsego)	1,748	1,788	2.3	1,636	96.9	0.0	0.2	1.9	1.0	18.5	19.2	46.0	53.4	13.0	685	85.3
Cottrellville township (St. Clair)	3,559	3,450	-3.1	3,471	100.0	0.0	0.0	0.0	0.0	21.0	19.7	45.3	55.4	16.7	1,447	83.2
Courtland township (Kent)	7,703	8,850	14.9	8,667	94.6	0.2	0.4	3.1	1.6	30.0	11.4	37.3	23.1	43.6	2,864	95.9
Covert township (Van Buren)	2,894	2,891	-0.1	2,869	48.2	19.4	0.2	4.2	28.0	20.5	18.9	42.0	54.1	13.9	1,149	78.1
Covington township (Baraga)	476	435	-8.6	449	96.0	0.0	0.0	3.3	0.7	10.0	37.2	57.9	68.5	14.9	200	86.0
Crockery township (Ottawa)	3,960	4,611	16.4	4,477	93.5	0.9	0.3	1.1	4.2	24.7	13.5	39.5	41.1	33.1	1,730	91.4
Cross Village CDP	93	-	-	62	88.7	0.0	0.0	9.7	1.6	1.6	59.7	68.5	41.4	20.7	31	87.1
Cross Village township (Emmet)	281	287	2.1	227	84.6	0.0	0.0	15.0	0.4	17.2	44.9	61.3	40.3	30.4	111	81.1
Croswell city & MCD (Sanilac)	2,453	2,286	-6.8	2,466	83.9	0.6	0.0	5.4	10.1	24.8	17.6	39.7	56.2	11.8	1,124	84.3
Croton township (Newaygo)	3,227	3,289	1.9	3,237	93.6	0.0	0.5	1.9	4.0	19.7	24.3	50.6	62.4	14.5	1,403	80.2
Crystal township (Montcalm)	2,689	2,721	1.2	2,701	96.5	0.0	0.5	0.5	2.4	23.5	19.9	44.6	49.5	13.6	1,094	82.0
Crystal township (Oceana)	835	850	1.8	751	71.4	4.7	0.0	4.9	19.0	21.4	15.3	42.4	61.4	9.9	270	80.4
Crystal Downs Country Club CDP	47	-	-	77	100.0	0.0	0.0	0.0	0.0	0.0	75.3	73.6	0.0	90.9	42	100.0
Crystal Falls city & MCD (Iron)	1,464	1,364	-6.8	1,716	94.8	0.6	1.0	1.3	2.4	23.2	20.3	41.8	49.6	16.3	697	82.4
Crystal Falls township (Iron)	1,748	1,653	-5.4	1,488	95.0	0.1	0.4	1.0	3.5	8.8	38.0	60.9	48.4	19.5	664	85.7
Crystal Lake township (Benzie)	958	965	0.7	1,162	99.7	0.2	0.2	0.0	0.0	10.7	40.4	59.5	35.1	47.9	460	90.2
Crystal Mountain CDP	54	-	-	48	56.3	0.0	0.0	43.8	0.0	0.0	47.9	61.5	4.2	43.8	18	100.0
Cumming township (Ogemaw)	698	674	-3.4	645	90.9	0.0	1.9	4.7	2.6	21.4	19.5	49.1	48.9	9.8	268	85.1
Curtis township (Alcona)	1,232	1,180	-4.2	1,241	93.7	0.0	0.5	2.6	3.2	13.2	35.5	57.7	53.5	12.1	607	82.0
Custer township (Antrim)	1,136	1,123	-1.1	949	97.6	0.0	0.0	0.7	1.7	19.7	30.8	48.9	37.4	29.1	406	91.9

1 May be of any race.

Table A. All Places — **Population and Housing**

STATE City, town, township, borough, or CDP (county if applicable)	2010 census total population	2019 estimated population	Percent change 2010–2019	ACS total population estimate 2015–2019	White alone, not Hispanic or Latino	Black alone, not Hispanic or Latino	Asian alone, not Hispanic or Latino	All other races or 2 or more races, not Hispanic or Latino	Hispanic or Latino[1]	Under 18 years old	Age 65 years and older	Median age	Percent High school diploma or less	Percent Bachelor's degree or more	Total occupied housing units	Percent with a computer
	1	2	3	4	5	6	7	8	9	10	11	12	13	14	15	16
MICHIGAN—Con.																
Custer village................	283	285	0.7	289	98.6	0.0	0.0	0.7	0.7	29.8	11.1	33.3	47.2	10.6	106	85.8
Custer township (Mason)..	1,259	1,271	1.0	1,354	90.2	3.2	0.2	1.0	5.4	24.0	17.4	41.7	45.6	17.4	500	86.4
Custer township (Sanilac).	1,004	961	-4.3	860	98.4	0.0	0.1	0.7	0.8	22.3	26.4	51.0	47.3	17.4	420	77.4
Cutlerville CDP..............	14,370	-	-	16,895	69.1	8.6	4.9	6.2	11.2	25.5	12.2	32.9	47.9	20.9	6,185	93.0
Dafter township (Chippewa).................	1,261	1,246	-1.2	1,398	86.2	0.1	0.9	11.8	1.0	22.3	16.4	41.8	44.9	18.0	475	83.4
Daggett village..............	258	244	-5.4	190	94.7	0.0	0.0	0.0	5.3	21.1	20.5	47.8	44.3	13.6	80	83.8
Daggett township (Menominee)...............	715	684	-4.3	635	95.1	0.0	0.0	2.2	2.7	19.8	19.8	49.1	49.3	18.3	278	82.0
Dallas township (Clinton)..	2,369	2,393	1.0	2,579	86.2	0.4	0.1	2.4	10.9	25.9	13.0	37.3	46.8	19.9	879	92.3
Dalton township (Muskegon).................	9,281	9,377	1.0	9,343	90.2	0.6	0.4	2.6	6.2	24.3	15.9	41.2	41.1	18.4	3,495	93.0
Danby township (Ionia).....	2,988	3,046	1.9	3,026	97.7	0.4	0.3	1.1	0.6	21.1	18.7	42.8	39.6	25.7	1,140	92.8
Dansville village............	563	569	1.1	630	84.6	0.0	1.6	7.3	6.5	31.1	9.5	34.9	38.8	21.9	221	95.0
Davison city & MCD (Genesee).................	5,201	4,881	-6.2	4,937	94.4	0.0	0.6	1.6	3.4	23.2	18.9	42.8	37.1	23.6	2,371	83.3
Davison township (Genesee).................	19,547	19,231	-1.6	19,173	87.3	3.3	2.1	2.6	4.7	21.3	18.6	40.1	35.6	22.0	8,712	91.3
Day township (Montcalm).	1,172	1,188	1.4	1,286	88.3	0.0	0.0	4.6	7.2	25.6	15.9	37.9	46.1	14.2	493	86.2
Dayton township (Newaygo).................	1,955	1,954	-0.1	1,949	92.4	2.3	0.5	1.6	3.2	27.2	17.5	38.5	39.4	27.1	683	90.8
Dayton township (Tuscola)	1,869	1,754	-6.2	1,866	90.6	5.6	0.2	1.0	2.6	19.6	23.4	48.2	61.7	15.0	794	81.9
Dearborn city & MCD (Wayne)...................	98,146	93,932	-4.3	94,701	88.2	3.0	2.4	3.4	2.9	29.3	12.2	31.6	41.7	29.8	30,596	90.8
Dearborn Heights city & MCD (Wayne)..............	57,774	55,353	-4.2	55,857	83.5	7.7	1.7	2.7	4.5	24.5	16.0	36.9	47.3	21.5	20,205	89.2
Decatur village..............	1,812	1,732	-4.4	1,913	75.8	3.9	0.6	10.1	9.6	24.7	15.2	37.6	52.9	11.6	781	86.3
Decatur township (Van Buren)...................	3,729	3,613	-3.1	3,635	78.0	2.1	1.0	5.9	13.0	25.0	16.4	42.1	54.1	13.5	1,531	87.5
Deckerville village...........	830	781	-5.9	830	91.2	0.7	0.2	1.4	6.4	21.9	21.9	47.5	61.6	11.1	332	80.4
Deep River township (Arenac)...................	2,149	2,031	-5.5	1,988	94.2	0.6	0.0	1.3	3.9	24.0	22.3	47.3	51.1	13.4	795	82.0
Deerfield township (Isabella).................	3,188	3,186	-0.1	3,187	92.1	0.0	1.0	3.3	3.6	21.8	16.3	42.7	30.5	40.8	1,123	93.7
Deerfield township (Lapeer)...................	5,695	5,680	-0.3	5,695	98.6	0.0	0.0	1.1	0.3	23.1	16.2	41.7	48.5	12.8	2,044	93.6
Deerfield village.............	896	857	-4.4	1,052	96.7	0.3	0.0	1.0	2.1	25.3	11.8	36.6	50.0	13.4	373	92.5
Deerfield township (Lenawee)..................	1,568	1,512	-3.6	1,759	94.2	0.7	0.3	1.0	3.8	21.4	16.1	40.7	51.4	14.4	662	91.7
Deerfield township (Livingston)................	4,177	4,278	2.4	4,244	99.2	0.4	0.0	0.1	0.2	22.7	15.8	43.8	34.3	25.3	1,450	92.0
Deerfield township (Mecosta).................	1,816	1,833	0.9	1,631	92.2	0.1	1.3	3.6	2.8	25.4	17.7	42.0	56.4	15.4	590	84.9
Delaware township (Sanilac).................	856	805	-6.0	809	93.0	0.0	0.2	5.3	1.5	20.9	20.9	46.2	49.2	12.6	350	88.6
Delhi charter township (Ingham)...................	25,873	28,082	8.5	27,528	79.3	6.8	4.6	4.5	4.8	24.4	14.8	39.0	26.5	37.8	10,832	92.1
Delta charter township (Eaton)...................	32,393	33,408	3.1	33,124	71.4	11.8	5.6	3.7	7.5	17.8	19.0	40.8	23.9	40.6	14,738	93.0
Delton CDP..................	872	-	-	879	87.6	0.0	0.0	10.1	2.3	13.9	24.2	57.1	38.0	23.9	473	84.1
Denmark township (Tuscola).................	3,068	2,879	-6.2	2,923	91.9	0.2	0.1	1.3	6.5	19.1	19.6	44.4	46.8	19.4	1,284	89.0
Denton township (Roscommon)..............	5,557	5,434	-2.2	5,391	94.4	0.0	0.9	1.9	2.9	13.4	34.9	56.3	47.9	14.8	2,758	82.5
Denver township (Isabella)	1,148	1,154	0.5	1,302	84.9	0.4	0.0	11.1	3.6	25.9	11.1	36.0	56.1	15.1	439	88.4
Denver township (Newaygo).................	1,928	1,964	1.9	2,166	85.9	0.0	0.0	2.8	11.3	23.8	17.1	45.1	64.5	5.8	866	75.6
Detour township (Chippewa).................	807	790	-2.1	714	78.7	0.0	0.6	20.7	0.0	15.4	39.5	60.8	39.6	16.3	303	84.2
De Tour Village village	325	317	-2.5	264	78.0	0.0	1.5	20.5	0.0	10.2	49.2	64.3	41.3	15.7	122	77.9
Detroit city & MCD (Wayne)...................	713,898	670,031	-6.1	674,841	10.5	78.0	1.7	2.1	7.7	25.0	13.6	34.7	51.6	15.3	263,688	82.2
Detroit Beach CDP..........	2,087	-	-	1,742	88.9	0.0	0.0	2.9	8.2	13.9	11.1	44.6	55.6	12.1	765	94.0
DeWitt city & MCD (Clinton)..................	4,492	4,808	7.0	4,691	91.2	1.8	0.9	2.2	3.9	25.9	14.0	39.2	19.8	48.4	1,785	94.5
DeWitt charter township (Clinton)..................	14,342	15,608	8.8	15,111	86.0	2.8	1.7	1.9	7.6	22.0	18.1	44.5	30.5	34.1	6,017	92.5
Dexter city & MCD (Washtenaw)...............	4,070	4,715	15.8	4,644	87.4	0.0	2.4	3.2	7.0	29.4	16.3	37.8	19.5	62.5	1,725	95.1
Dexter township (Washtenaw)...............	6,031	6,554	8.7	6,511	93.8	0.3	1.5	2.7	1.6	24.0	19.3	44.2	15.8	54.0	2,333	96.5
Dickson township (Manistee).................	991	985	-0.6	899	96.2	0.0	0.0	1.2	2.6	18.8	23.9	52.2	55.2	13.0	363	78.5
Dimondale village...........	1,238	1,257	1.5	1,370	87.9	1.4	0.9	4.5	5.4	22.5	14.3	40.3	17.8	31.6	532	94.5
Dollar Bay CDP..............	1,082	-	-	853	97.9	0.5	0.0	0.0	1.6	28.6	17.8	34.9	47.6	19.0	315	91.7
Dorr township (Allegan)....	7,440	7,897	6.1	7,764	94.5	0.3	0.2	2.4	2.6	26.1	11.2	36.5	48.6	17.6	2,720	94.6
Douglas city & MCD (Allegan).................	1,232	1,345	9.2	936	87.1	0.0	1.6	0.3	11.0	18.1	25.7	55.1	36.0	45.9	475	84.0
Douglass township (Montcalm)................	2,180	2,205	1.1	2,094	94.5	0.0	0.0	1.9	3.7	21.7	19.6	46.2	40.4	10.4	930	86.3
Dover township (Lake)......	394	411	4.3	502	92.8	0.0	0.0	6.6	0.6	25.5	17.9	45.3	56.2	17.2	157	80.3
Dover township (Lenawee)	1,836	1,813	-1.3	1,716	93.4	0.4	0.0	5.7	0.4	23.0	20.5	47.6	57.1	12.3	682	84.2
Dover township (Otsego)..	561	569	1.4	587	90.6	0.0	0.5	0.0	8.9	15.8	22.7	47.5	46.3	20.7	229	92.1
Dowagiac city & MCD (Cass)....................	5,874	5,669	-3.5	5,743	66.8	13.3	0.9	10.1	9.0	26.6	14.9	34.0	48.3	8.7	2,518	84.0
Dowling CDP.................	374	-	-	411	89.5	0.0	0.0	0.0	10.5	33.6	21.4	34.3	52.8	3.8	164	78.0
Doyle township (Schoolcraft)...............	624	596	-4.5	468	87.2	0.0	0.2	8.8	3.8	13.5	29.9	58.0	45.4	26.3	211	87.7
Drummond township (Chippewa).................	1,058	1,039	-1.8	1,051	89.6	0.0	0.4	8.8	1.2	10.8	39.1	58.2	42.5	21.5	507	83.2
Dryden village...............	951	938	-1.4	1,212	96.2	0.0	0.4	0.2	3.2	28.3	13.9	36.5	45.8	13.2	419	95.2
Dryden township (Lapeer)	4,768	4,728	-0.8	4,763	96.5	0.2	1.2	0.7	1.4	18.8	16.7	46.2	34.1	23.1	1,787	94.1

1 May be of any race.

Table A. All Places — **Population and Housing**

	Population				Race and Hispanic or Latino origin (percent)					Age (percent)			Educational attainment of persons age 25 and older		Occupied housing units	
STATE City, town, township, borough, or CDP (county if applicable)	2010 census total population	2019 estimated population	Percent change 2010–2019	ACS total population estimate 2015–2019	White alone, not Hispanic or Latino	Black alone, not Hispanic or Latino	Asian alone, not Hispanic or Latino	All other races or 2 or more races, not Hispanic or Latino	Hispanic or Latino[1]	Under 18 years old	Age 65 years and older	Median age	Percent High school diploma or less	Percent Bachelor's degree or more	Total	Percent with a computer
	1	2	3	4	5	6	7	8	9	10	11	12	13	14	15	16

MICHIGAN—Con.

	1	2	3	4	5	6	7	8	9	10	11	12	13	14	15	16
Duncan township (Houghton)	236	229	-3.0	220	99.5	0.0	0.5	0.0	0.0	15.0	35.0	59.5	73.8	8.6	97	70.1
Dundee village	3,957	4,601	16.3	4,252	95.2	1.4	0.7	1.6	1.0	22.0	10.6	36.4	33.9	25.9	1,928	88.1
Dundee township (Monroe)	6,759	7,344	8.7	7,020	96.7	0.9	0.4	1.2	0.9	19.5	16.0	41.0	36.2	25.4	2,988	90.0
Duplain township (Clinton)	2,363	2,394	1.3	2,466	84.2	1.4	0.2	7.3	6.9	23.2	18.5	40.0	53.4	15.0	911	87.5
Durand city & MCD (Shiawassee)	3,462	3,290	-5.0	3,316	93.0	0.0	0.4	4.9	1.7	17.9	21.1	43.9	54.1	9.1	1,473	86.4
Dwight township (Huron)	758	706	-6.9	693	100.0	0.0	0.0	0.0	0.0	20.9	15.3	48.5	58.1	9.4	300	84.7
Eagle village	119	120	0.8	133	100.0	0.0	0.0	0.0	0.0	27.1	3.8	30.7	21.3	7.5	47	100.0
Eagle township (Clinton)	2,673	2,730	2.1	2,713	87.2	3.6	0.0	1.0	8.1	19.9	18.2	47.5	27.4	30.9	968	92.9
Eagle Harbor CDP	76	-	-	95	95.8	0.0	0.0	4.2	0.0	9.5	64.2	71.4	12.9	64.7	52	96.2
Eagle Harbor township (Keweenaw)	217	213	-1.8	264	88.3	5.3	1.5	2.7	2.3	3.4	64.0	68.5	18.3	50.0	149	91.9
Eagle River CDP	71	-	-	112	88.4	1.8	0.0	4.5	5.4	2.7	62.5	67.6	26.4	37.7	61	90.2
East Bay township (Grand Traverse)	10,688	11,621	8.7	11,492	93.7	1.1	0.2	2.1	2.9	19.0	18.9	45.6	27.7	37.3	4,575	96.0
East China township (St. Clair)	3,782	3,722	-1.6	3,723	95.4	1.6	0.0	1.8	1.2	16.4	31.4	53.0	38.3	24.5	1,685	83.7
East Grand Rapids city & MCD (Kent)	10,687	11,956	11.9	11,759	93.1	0.9	1.0	2.9	2.1	31.5	12.1	38.2	5.7	79.6	4,071	98.6
East Jordan city & MCD (Charlevoix)	2,348	2,348	0.0	2,261	90.4	0.7	0.8	4.2	3.9	21.8	18.8	43.6	58.5	11.7	1,032	84.9
Eastlake village	512	507	-1.0	463	85.3	0.6	0.0	10.8	3.2	16.6	34.1	53.3	57.5	18.8	194	73.7
East Lansing city	48,561	48,145	-0.9	48,729	72.3	6.6	12.5	3.6	5.0	7.8	7.3	21.4	10.3	72.0	13,519	95.6
East Lansing city (Clinton)	1,947	1,969	1.1	2,187	69.8	8.5	12.5	6.7	2.5	23.9	7.2	28.0	12.0	65.1	821	100.0
East Lansing city (Ingham)	46,614	46,176	-0.9	46,542	72.4	6.5	12.5	3.5	5.2	7.1	7.3	21.3	10.1	72.5	12,698	95.3
Easton township (Ionia)	3,075	3,185	3.6	3,141	94.4	0.0	0.3	2.4	3.0	11.6	15.9	48.5	47.5	10.5	1,326	93.4
Eastpointe city & MCD (Macomb)	32,403	32,081	-	32,443	44.4	47.4	0.8	5.3	2.0	23.5	11.3	37.3	47.5	15.4	12,676	90.2
Eastport CDP	218	-	-	245	82.9	0.0	0.0	7.3	9.8	13.1	37.1	52.4	25.5	35.1	103	100.0
East Tawas city & MCD (Iosco)	2,813	2,723	-3.2	2,733	93.7	0.4	1.6	3.0	1.4	11.4	33.9	57.1	43.8	21.3	1,440	82.8
Eastwood CDP	6,340	-	-	5,656	55.7	30.9	0.0	9.4	3.9	21.0	8.4	33.2	33.0	21.5	2,252	91.3
Eaton township (Eaton)	4,061	4,142	2.0	4,116	91.9	0.3	0.0	3.9	3.9	24.9	18.2	43.5	35.3	22.5	1,511	95.6
Eaton Rapids city & MCD (Eaton)	5,219	5,245	0.5	5,231	94.4	0.2	0.0	0.9	4.5	24.5	16.9	37.3	40.1	17.5	2,170	86.6
Eaton Rapids township (Eaton)	4,105	4,215	2.7	4,183	93.9	1.4	0.1	1.4	3.2	18.9	18.9	47.3	35.6	27.1	1,588	89.4
Eau Claire village	625	597	-4.5	740	73.5	5.5	0.0	7.8	13.1	33.4	10.4	33.4	37.6	28.7	235	95.3
Echo township (Antrim)	872	861	-1.3	846	98.9	0.0	0.0	0.0	1.1	21.4	22.7	50.9	45.8	17.9	349	82.2
Eckford township (Calhoun)	1,300	1,264	-2.8	1,410	97.9	0.0	0.0	1.0	1.1	23.6	19.7	44.6	41.5	23.5	540	87.6
Ecorse city & MCD (Wayne)	9,552	9,570	0.2	9,432	31.4	40.9	0.0	9.0	18.7	24.1	21.2	42.4	58.9	10.7	3,703	74.1
Eden township (Lake)	489	512	4.7	638	95.8	0.0	0.0	3.9	0.3	8.5	32.3	54.8	58.9	6.6	250	75.2
Eden township (Mason)	582	595	2.2	509	89.4	7.3	0.0	2.2	1.2	16.9	19.1	46.6	45.6	15.0	183	87.4
Edenville township (Midland)	2,551	2,541	-0.4	2,533	98.2	0.0	0.0	1.4	0.4	18.6	20.6	48.7	45.2	20.4	1,050	88.9
Edgemont Park CDP	2,358	-	-	2,329	71.3	13.2	0.0	5.2	10.3	16.7	17.0	41.7	30.5	21.4	1,139	86.2
Edmore village	1,192	1,192	0.0	1,273	91.4	0.0	0.0	0.9	7.7	23.9	18.7	44.2	63.2	8.6	527	75.1
Edwards township (Ogemaw)	1,408	1,359	-3.5	1,385	98.0	0.1	0.0	1.0	0.9	19.8	21.8	50.3	49.9	15.5	552	87.0
Edwardsburg village	1,262	1,238	-1.9	1,255	92.0	0.3	0.5	3.5	3.7	25.1	11.5	35.0	50.0	14.3	508	91.5
Egelston township (Muskegon)	9,910	10,325	4.2	10,131	89.7	3.7	0.4	2.6	3.6	26.8	13.3	35.7	57.5	10.2	3,539	86.9
Elba township (Gratiot)	1,396	1,341	-3.9	1,245	91.8	1.3	3.3	3.0	0.6	22.0	24.5	46.5	52.8	12.9	497	85.3
Elba township (Lapeer)	5,252	5,202	-	5,222	94.7	0.3	0.0	1.3	3.7	21.6	19.8	46.7	40.2	21.7	2,013	88.9
Elberta village	370	371	0.3	165	88.5	0.0	0.0	3.0	8.5	26.1	12.7	44.6	60.4	23.6	69	85.5
Elbridge township (Oceana)	979	980	0.1	954	76.3	6.8	0.0	3.4	13.5	24.9	18.0	37.0	55.0	9.4	316	83.5
Elk township (Lake)	987	1,022	3.5	1,050	96.0	0.0	1.0	1.9	1.1	4.1	42.0	61.2	46.9	19.6	470	73.6
Elk township (Sanilac)	1,526	1,434	-6.0	1,357	95.6	1.8	0.1	1.5	1.1	22.0	19.7	47.1	48.8	9.8	573	85.7
Elkland township (Tuscola)	3,529	3,304	-6.4	3,351	94.5	1.1	0.6	0.5	3.3	20.4	22.0	43.6	44.1	19.6	1,301	83.6
Elk Rapids village	1,642	1,615	-1.6	1,494	96.9	0.0	0.0	1.7	1.4	16.9	38.4	56.6	30.0	37.0	716	91.5
Elk Rapids township (Antrim)	2,631	2,592	-1.5	2,575	97.9	0.0	0.0	1.3	0.8	17.8	33.4	53.7	26.9	37.2	1,142	92.6
Elkton village	808	749	-7.3	771	97.9	0.9	0.0	0.0	1.2	23.7	15.2	40.0	50.0	13.8	359	87.2
Ellington township (Tuscola)	1,332	1,259	-5.5	1,207	96.4	0.0	0.0	1.6	2.1	17.2	23.4	52.5	51.2	16.1	488	89.5
Ellis township (Cheboygan)	596	579	-2.9	568	86.1	0.0	0.0	13.9	0.0	20.6	21.1	45.4	58.6	8.4	233	81.5
Ellsworth village	352	347	-1.4	339	93.8	2.9	1.5	1.8	0.0	18.9	14.7	46.1	44.2	14.6	143	88.8
Ellsworth township (Lake)	820	855	4.3	808	97.6	0.0	0.0	0.6	1.7	24.8	22.4	45.5	66.9	6.5	310	71.6
Elmer township (Oscoda)	1,163	1,115	-4.1	1,184	95.2	0.1	0.0	2.0	2.7	31.6	18.9	37.3	54.7	6.9	403	67.7
Elmer township (Sanilac)	806	757	-6.1	704	97.6	0.0	0.0	0.0	2.4	17.2	20.0	43.4	64.3	9.3	295	85.4
Elmira township (Otsego)	1,684	1,721	2.2	2,003	95.2	0.3	1.6	1.9	0.9	23.9	18.6	43.2	45.9	26.7	718	93.6
Elm River township (Houghton)	177	171	-3.4	475	98.5	0.0	0.0	0.0	1.5	41.9	11.2	18.8	59.4	17.4	125	92.8
Elmwood charter township (Leelanau)	4,509	4,518	0.2	4,497	95.1	0.0	1.7	2.8	0.4	18.2	27.4	51.4	23.9	48.0	1,839	91.5
Elmwood township (Tuscola)	1,207	1,136	-5.9	1,109	95.0	0.3	0.0	2.2	2.5	19.1	21.0	45.8	56.6	12.0	515	83.5
Elsie village	966	978	1.2	1,059	89.3	3.2	0.0	3.2	4.2	26.6	18.9	36.9	57.0	9.9	415	84.6
Ely township (Marquette)	1,952	1,962	0.5	2,086	97.2	0.4	0.0	1.8	0.6	23.8	16.6	42.7	48.8	16.9	748	88.8
Emerson township (Gratiot)	952	904	-5.0	916	91.7	0.4	0.2	2.0	5.7	25.1	16.8	44.9	40.4	15.2	376	81.6
Emmett charter township (Calhoun)	11,791	11,627	-1.4	11,637	83.0	4.5	3.5	4.2	4.9	20.5	18.0	43.5	40.0	23.4	4,705	91.9
Emmett village	269	260	-3.3	227	96.9	0.0	0.0	3.1	0.0	20.7	16.7	40.9	56.1	10.3	93	90.3

1 May be of any race.

Table A. All Places — **Population and Housing**

STATE City, town, township, borough, or CDP (county if applicable)	Population				Race and Hispanic or Latino origin (percent)					Age (percent)			Educational attainment of persons age 25 and older		Occupied housing units	
	2010 census total population	2019 estimated population	Percent change 2010–2019	ACS total population estimate 2015–2019	White alone, not Hispanic or Latino	Black alone, not Hispanic or Latino	Asian alone, not Hispanic or Latino	All other races or 2 or more races, not Hispanic or Latino	Hispanic or Latino[1]	Under 18 years old	Age 65 years and older	Median age	Percent High school diploma or less	Percent Bachelor's degree or more	Total	Percent with a computer
	1	2	3	4	5	6	7	8	9	10	11	12	13	14	15	16
MICHIGAN—Con.																
Emmett township (St. Clair)	2,656	2,610	-1.7	2,605	95.0	0.0	0.0	1.1	3.9	21.7	14.7	44.1	53.9	12.0	961	89.1
Empire village	377	376	-0.3	263	96.2	1.9	0.8	1.1	0.0	8.7	42.2	62.3	20.4	48.4	141	92.2
Empire township (Leelanau)	1,184	1,185	0.1	1,161	97.0	0.4	1.3	1.3	0.0	9.1	38.5	62.1	17.0	49.2	572	95.3
Ensign township (Delta)	747	723	-3.2	756	93.1	0.0	0.4	4.9	1.6	14.0	25.1	51.9	40.2	22.6	345	81.2
Ensley township (Newaygo)	2,635	2,718	3.1	2,661	95.4	0.0	0.5	1.6	2.6	24.6	11.4	38.1	41.1	18.3	905	91.9
Enterprise township (Missaukee)	194	197	1.5	164	100.0	0.0	0.0	0.0	0.0	15.9	17.1	49.5	51.1	6.0	69	98.6
Erie township (Monroe)	4,517	4,328	-4.2	4,347	90.8	2.5	0.0	3.0	3.8	22.1	17.2	41.6	48.4	14.6	1,730	89.8
Erwin township (Gogebic)	322	293	-9.0	348	89.7	0.0	2.0	6.9	1.4	19.8	22.4	54.0	43.5	13.0	150	83.3
Escanaba city & MCD (Delta)	12,615	12,160	-3.6	12,251	90.8	0.9	0.6	6.7	1.0	20.0	23.1	43.4	35.6	21.5	5,893	82.3
Escanaba township (Delta)	3,475	3,385	-2.6	3,399	92.6	0.0	0.5	3.8	3.1	22.3	22.5	50.4	35.4	26.0	1,390	87.0
Essex township (Clinton)	1,910	1,939	1.5	1,890	97.5	0.0	0.0	0.3	2.3	21.5	16.6	40.1	39.6	17.9	709	88.4
Essexville city & MCD (Bay)	3,478	3,278	-5.8	3,325	93.6	1.1	0.0	1.1	4.6	21.7	17.8	40.7	38.7	23.5	1,389	87.3
Estral Beach village	416	397	-4.6	342	93.6	1.5	0.0	2.9	2.0	13.5	27.2	49.5	38.9	18.4	158	93.0
Eureka township (Montcalm)	3,969	4,026	1.4	4,009	90.7	0.0	0.0	1.7	7.6	22.1	14.8	38.8	48.1	24.4	1,509	85.6
Evangeline township (Charlevoix)	712	713	0.1	773	97.0	0.4	0.3	1.2	1.2	16.4	32.2	55.3	32.0	40.8	335	93.7
Evart city & MCD (Osceola)	1,913	1,882	-1.6	1,793	92.4	0.0	0.7	3.4	3.5	28.8	12.8	34.7	65.6	11.6	732	82.2
Evart township (Osceola)	1,493	1,485	-0.5	1,561	89.8	1.7	0.0	5.6	2.9	20.4	24.6	48.9	56.6	8.6	598	88.8
Eveline township (Charlevoix)	1,485	1,480	-0.3	1,670	95.3	0.0	0.5	2.2	2.0	13.5	31.0	56.9	28.4	41.9	737	92.5
Everett township (Newaygo)	1,860	1,855	-0.3	2,219	93.6	1.9	0.0	2.7	1.8	24.7	14.8	38.6	58.8	8.7	843	86.8
Evergreen township (Montcalm)	2,858	2,901	1.5	2,879	92.8	0.0	0.2	1.6	5.4	24.9	17.5	39.7	53.4	12.8	1,018	83.0
Evergreen township (Sanilac)	931	880	-5.5	997	90.4	0.0	0.0	0.8	8.8	29.6	18.3	34.1	69.3	6.2	357	73.4
Ewing township (Marquette)	160	160	0.0	123	94.3	0.0	4.9	0.8	0.0	5.7	54.5	67.3	43.1	19.0	70	71.4
Excelsior township (Kalkaska)	953	1,006	5.6	918	98.5	0.0	0.0	1.5	0.0	28.0	14.7	35.3	48.2	12.1	344	94.5
Exeter township (Monroe)	3,977	3,823	-3.9	3,849	89.5	5.5	0.9	1.3	2.7	21.3	14.4	45.2	53.8	15.2	1,297	93.9
Fabius township (St. Joseph)	3,249	3,242	-0.2	3,228	89.7	1.6	1.0	6.8	0.9	21.0	22.5	47.1	32.1	23.4	1,351	93.2
Fairbanks township (Delta)	281	274	-2.5	394	70.3	0.5	0.3	28.4	0.5	27.7	29.9	52.7	49.2	15.6	166	76.5
Fairfield township (Lenawee)	1,764	1,729	-2.0	1,683	89.1	3.0	0.0	0.7	7.2	23.4	20.0	41.8	51.4	8.8	652	89.3
Fairfield township (Shiawassee)	759	730	-3.8	679	93.7	0.0	0.6	3.8	1.9	15.9	17.8	45.5	41.6	13.3	287	86.1
Fairgrove village	563	525	-6.7	511	90.6	4.9	0.0	0.0	4.5	24.7	11.9	39.7	50.6	9.5	202	95.0
Fairgrove township (Tuscola)	1,579	1,475	-6.6	1,633	93.7	2.1	0.0	1.3	2.9	24.1	14.9	40.4	50.9	14.0	654	90.8
Fairhaven township (Huron)	1,107	1,045	-5.6	1,291	96.4	0.0	0.9	0.0	2.7	15.9	19.8	46.9	63.5	13.9	586	82.1
Fair Plain CDP	7,631	-	-	7,076	45.8	43.0	0.8	4.9	5.4	21.0	19.7	42.2	43.6	16.1	3,193	84.3
Fairplain township (Montcalm)	1,836	1,866	1.6	2,062	92.0	2.4	0.5	0.0	5.1	21.0	14.5	44.2	54.2	12.0	765	87.5
Faithorn township (Menominee)	243	231	-4.9	217	96.8	0.9	0.0	2.3	0.0	12.0	33.2	57.9	42.5	22.3	119	88.2
Farmington city & MCD (Oakland)	10,381	10,491	1.1	10,563	67.4	10.6	14.9	5.0	2.1	18.9	16.3	37.9	16.3	55.3	4,658	92.5
Farmington Hills city & MCD (Oakland)	79,725	80,612	1.1	81,214	60.9	19.9	14.1	2.8	2.3	19.0	19.5	42.9	19.5	54.5	33,972	93.6
Farwell village	873	871	-0.2	980	93.4	0.0	0.0	4.1	2.6	22.8	12.9	29.5	60.6	9.5	336	82.7
Fawn River township (St. Joseph)	1,348	1,343	-0.4	1,236	85.0	0.0	0.1	1.5	13.4	19.0	25.3	48.2	49.4	14.4	479	79.3
Fayette township (Hillsdale)	1,072	1,051	-2.0	1,090	96.0	0.0	0.6	1.6	1.8	21.3	22.4	45.9	44.1	18.5	422	84.6
Felch township (Dickinson)	752	730	-2.9	773	96.8	0.0	0.3	2.5	0.5	21.6	17.7	43.2	39.7	17.2	303	85.8
Fennville city & MCD (Allegan)	1,394	1,429	2.5	1,876	56.9	0.4	0.9	0.7	41.1	31.6	9.8	30.7	58.1	8.7	670	80.1
Fenton city	11,740	11,403	-2.9	11,375	92.4	1.0	0.0	3.0	3.6	21.8	17.5	38.9	32.3	27.0	5,051	91.1
Fenton city (Genesee)	11,738	11,401	-2.9	11,351	92.4	1.0	0.0	3.0	3.6	21.8	17.5	38.9	32.4	26.9	5,039	91.1
Fenton city (Livingston)	-	-	-	-	-	-	-	-	-	-	-	-	-	-	-	-
Fenton city (Oakland)	2	2	0.0	24	100.0	0.0	0.0	0.0	0.0	0.0	0.0	0.0	0.0	50.0	12	100.0
Fenton charter township (Genesee)	15,572	15,688	0.7	15,452	93.5	1.2	1.1	2.3	1.8	22.5	21.2	46.6	27.7	41.0	6,051	94.8
Ferndale city & MCD (Oakland)	19,891	20,033	0.7	20,137	85.6	6.2	1.3	4.4	2.6	10.9	9.9	35.0	20.1	48.3	10,225	94.9
Ferris township (Montcalm)	1,422	1,446	1.7	1,342	94.6	1.0	0.5	1.4	2.5	19.1	15.2	46.4	61.6	7.9	524	84.4
Ferry township (Oceana)	1,292	1,295	0.2	1,126	86.4	0.0	0.5	2.8	10.2	19.6	25.7	50.6	52.0	21.0	474	79.1
Ferrysburg city & MCD (Ottawa)	2,884	3,028	5.0	3,013	93.9	0.8	0.0	2.3	3.1	16.8	28.0	50.8	28.7	35.1	1,359	93.7
Fife Lake village	441	480	8.8	382	90.3	0.0	0.8	7.3	1.6	19.6	16.0	47.5	48.8	14.9	161	91.3
Fife Lake township (Grand Traverse)	2,791	1,555	-44.3	1,978	83.4	6.7	0.5	6.6	2.8	14.7	16.3	46.6	54.6	12.2	618	91.1
Filer charter township (Manistee)	2,323	2,289	-1.5	2,641	95.0	0.2	0.8	2.4	1.7	19.1	26.4	49.7	43.0	19.6	1,043	81.7
Filer City CDP	116	-	-	57	100.0	0.0	0.0	0.0	0.0	0.0	29.8	57.5	68.4	0.0	17	70.6
Fillmore township (Allegan)	2,683	2,769	3.2	2,746	93.6	0.3	0.3	1.6	4.2	25.9	17.0	40.4	56.9	16.6	1,003	84.6

1 May be of any race.

Table A. All Places — **Population and Housing**

STATE City, town, township, borough, or CDP (county if applicable)	2010 census total population	2019 estimated population	Percent change 2010–2019	ACS total population estimate 2015–2019	White alone, not Hispanic or Latino	Black alone, not Hispanic or Latino	Asian alone, not Hispanic or Latino	All other races or 2 or more races, not Hispanic or Latino	Hispanic or Latino[1]	Under 18 years old	Age 65 years and older	Median age	Percent High school diploma or less	Percent Bachelor's degree or more	Occupied housing units Total	Percent with a computer
	1	2	3	4	5	6	7	8	9	10	11	12	13	14	15	16
MICHIGAN—Con.																
Flat Rock city	9,878	10,004	1.3	9,967	83.9	5.6	0.2	1.4	8.9	28.6	11.5	37.7	46.2	17.1	3,629	94.4
Flat Rock city (Monroe)	-	-	-	-	-	-	-	-	-	-	-	-	-	-	-	-
Flat Rock city (Wayne)	9,878	10,004	1.3	9,967	83.9	5.6	0.2	1.4	8.9	28.6	11.5	37.7	46.2	17.1	3,629	94.4
Flint city & MCD (Genesee)	102,266	95,538	-6.6	96,559	36.9	53.2	0.5	5.0	4.5	24.9	13.5	35.5	50.6	12.2	40,362	76.6
Flint charter township (Genesee)	32,085	30,357	-5.4	30,614	63.3	27.3	1.6	5.3	2.4	21.3	17.6	42.0	42.6	18.7	12,924	85.3
Florence township (St. Joseph)	1,238	1,243	0.4	1,236	89.5	1.5	0.0	1.4	7.7	21.0	23.1	49.6	57.9	9.5	522	82.2
Flowerfield township (St. Joseph)	1,559	1,601	2.7	1,562	93.1	0.2	1.3	0.8	4.5	21.8	24.0	50.1	50.3	18.1	638	87.6
Flushing city & MCD (Genesee)	8,390	7,880	-6.1	7,968	92.1	1.4	0.0	3.3	3.3	20.4	24.4	46.9	34.0	29.6	3,406	86.7
Flushing charter township (Genesee)	10,639	10,181	-4.3	10,237	88.0	2.5	0.1	3.3	6.1	22.3	18.6	43.8	32.4	30.3	3,805	93.8
Flynn township (Sanilac)	1,045	991	-5.2	1,146	93.5	0.0	0.0	0.8	5.8	29.0	14.0	31.5	55.6	15.8	396	78.8
Ford River township (Delta)	2,046	2,002	-2.2	2,063	97.3	0.0	0.5	2.2	0.0	15.3	24.6	52.7	41.7	26.4	1,022	88.1
Forest township (Cheboygan)	1,045	1,015	-2.9	961	99.5	0.0	0.2	0.3	0.0	20.0	23.9	50.3	53.8	11.7	419	86.9
Forest township (Genesee)	4,699	4,476	-4.7	4,492	95.1	0.1	2.2	1.3	1.3	19.4	20.1	48.4	45.6	15.8	1,770	90.7
Forest township (Missaukee)	1,159	1,199	3.5	1,124	95.3	0.2	0.0	2.0	2.6	23.8	19.3	41.4	62.5	11.5	489	80.6
Forester township (Sanilac)	1,011	957	-5.3	895	96.3	0.0	0.0	0.0	3.7	15.6	36.0	57.0	42.2	24.1	413	86.2
Forest Hills CDP	25,867	-	-	27,830	89.0	1.7	4.6	1.8	2.9	26.5	16.1	42.5	11.0	67.9	9,957	96.5
Forest Home township (Antrim)	1,720	1,695	-1.5	1,594	100.0	0.0	0.0	0.0	0.0	11.5	39.0	58.8	28.3	47.0	765	89.4
Forestville village	136	127	-6.6	106	92.5	0.0	1.9	0.0	5.7	13.2	39.6	59.5	55.7	13.6	50	88.0
Fork township (Mecosta)	1,604	1,626	1.4	1,566	92.5	0.9	0.3	5.7	0.6	17.9	25.5	49.3	57.4	12.0	714	83.3
Forsyth township (Marquette)	6,162	6,180	0.3	6,196	91.0	0.3	0.9	5.3	2.4	23.3	18.3	41.7	46.1	18.5	2,519	88.8
Fort Gratiot charter township (St. Clair)	11,108	10,991	-1.1	11,007	94.9	1.1	0.4	1.9	1.7	20.8	22.8	47.1	37.0	23.6	4,412	85.9
Foster township (Ogemaw)	842	815	-3.2	795	95.7	0.0	0.0	1.5	2.8	11.6	31.1	59.2	50.8	12.7	378	76.7
Fostoria CDP	694	-	-	563	97.5	0.0	0.0	0.7	1.8	22.0	16.5	45.2	49.0	5.7	238	89.5
Fountain village	193	198	2.6	202	84.2	0.0	0.0	5.4	10.4	33.7	16.3	31.7	59.3	3.3	67	79.1
Fowler village	1,207	1,222	1.2	1,369	86.9	0.7	0.2	3.6	8.6	27.3	16.5	36.5	46.4	22.0	478	91.6
Fowlerville village	2,883	2,893	0.3	2,881	96.5	0.4	0.3	2.6	0.2	26.3	13.6	35.6	48.7	15.6	1,245	84.8
Frankenlust township (Bay)	3,560	3,499	-1.7	3,507	90.0	1.9	3.9	1.1	3.1	13.5	25.7	47.6	30.1	39.5	1,545	84.6
Frankenmuth city & MCD (Saginaw)	4,983	5,529	11.0	5,274	95.5	0.3	0.3	0.2	3.7	18.7	29.6	47.7	31.2	44.0	2,403	89.9
Frankenmuth township (Saginaw)	1,920	1,880	-2.1	1,859	96.6	0.0	0.0	0.0	3.4	20.9	26.8	48.8	30.6	39.1	735	85.3
Frankfort city & MCD (Benzie)	1,284	1,290	0.5	1,059	94.1	0.6	0.0	1.0	4.2	7.6	46.2	63.5	40.7	35.2	468	82.1
Franklin township (Clare)	823	832	1.1	902	91.0	0.6	0.0	6.3	2.1	20.4	28.4	50.9	59.7	10.4	359	79.7
Franklin township (Houghton)	1,455	1,399	-3.8	1,610	92.9	0.0	0.7	3.6	2.7	38.5	9.3	27.0	44.2	25.2	507	91.7
Franklin township (Lenawee)	3,172	3,193	0.7	3,181	93.5	0.3	0.5	4.2	1.5	17.8	20.4	48.4	45.8	20.0	1,281	91.6
Franklin village	3,150	3,246	3.0	3,310	73.4	11.1	6.7	5.5	3.4	27.1	21.1	45.7	8.2	75.9	1,138	99.1
Fraser township (Bay)	3,192	3,032	-5.0	3,070	98.7	0.0	0.0	0.0	1.3	10.0	25.9	56.9	59.6	12.6	1,547	86.3
Fraser city & MCD (Macomb)	14,480	14,480	0.0	14,580	87.4	5.0	2.1	2.8	2.8	19.9	18.7	42.9	37.0	24.1	6,018	91.3
Frederic township (Crawford)	1,347	1,385	2.8	1,142	97.5	0.0	0.0	2.5	0.0	13.1	26.4	54.5	42.6	18.4	548	93.8
Fredonia township (Calhoun)	1,626	1,611	-0.9	1,670	97.3	0.1	0.3	1.6	0.8	22.5	21.1	47.5	37.1	21.0	703	88.3
Freedom township (Washtenaw)	1,428	1,489	4.3	1,493	92.8	4.1	0.2	0.9	2.0	18.1	21.8	52.0	25.6	42.0	582	90.7
Freeland CDP	6,969	-	-	6,898	81.2	7.6	1.6	4.5	5.0	20.5	10.7	36.6	36.0	26.9	2,154	96.3
Freeman township (Clare)	1,159	1,157	-0.2	951	95.3	0.0	0.0	3.4	1.4	8.9	36.7	58.5	58.5	8.4	429	82.5
Freeport village	483	500	3.5	547	93.6	0.0	0.0	0.7	5.7	30.0	10.4	30.9	50.3	9.9	207	92.8
Free Soil village	144	144	0.0	103	94.2	0.0	0.0	5.8	0.0	13.6	26.2	47.6	46.2	2.6	50	74.0
Free Soil township (Mason)	806	818	1.5	775	92.0	2.1	0.0	2.6	3.4	14.7	22.8	53.1	42.2	10.5	331	85.8
Fremont township (Isabella)	1,455	1,447	-0.5	1,675	95.9	0.0	0.0	1.9	2.1	23.8	14.0	40.6	56.4	18.5	573	83.4
Fremont city & MCD (Newaygo)	4,115	4,080	-0.9	4,055	86.6	1.5	0.7	3.3	7.9	28.7	22.2	37.0	45.3	23.4	1,690	88.0
Fremont township (Saginaw)	2,096	2,019	-3.7	1,982	93.1	0.0	0.8	2.9	3.1	21.5	19.2	45.9	42.1	16.3	783	85.1
Fremont township (Sanilac)	1,043	983	-5.8	901	97.2	0.0	0.0	0.2	2.6	24.2	15.9	44.5	50.1	14.9	351	89.2
Fremont township (Tuscola)	3,309	3,106	-6.1	3,154	94.8	0.8	1.3	0.2	2.9	20.2	21.9	48.1	62.4	13.9	1,321	84.8
Frenchtown township (Monroe)	20,511	19,980	-2.6	19,989	89.2	4.6	0.1	1.7	4.4	20.8	17.7	43.4	48.1	16.9	8,304	88.6
Friendship township (Emmet)	889	910	2.4	837	93.3	0.4	1.4	3.7	1.2	21.1	21.7	48.9	31.9	38.0	352	86.6
Frost township (Clare)	1,053	1,055	0.2	1,208	87.8	0.3	2.0	8.7	1.2	11.2	25.5	53.5	50.5	13.2	552	81.0
Fruitland township (Muskegon)	5,566	5,738	3.1	5,666	93.5	0.5	0.2	2.0	3.8	21.3	20.4	45.0	33.4	30.6	2,214	94.4
Fruitport village	1,091	1,149	5.3	1,212	97.4	1.7	0.0	0.6	0.3	22.5	18.2	41.1	33.1	26.9	474	87.6
Fruitport charter township (Muskegon)	13,604	14,386	5.7	14,132	91.5	1.6	0.3	1.7	4.9	23.0	15.9	43.4	36.6	22.0	5,222	92.1
Fulton township (Gratiot)	2,521	2,414	-4.2	2,549	95.9	0.4	0.0	2.6	1.2	26.2	16.4	44.4	49.8	16.5	1,008	79.8
Gaastra city & MCD (Iron)	347	325	-6.3	323	98.8	0.0	0.3	0.6	0.3	17.0	27.6	55.4	56.7	18.4	146	81.5

1 May be of any race.

Table A. All Places — **Population and Housing**

STATE City, town, township, borough, or CDP (county if applicable)	Population				Race and Hispanic or Latino origin (percent)					Age (percent)			Educational attainment of persons age 25 and older		Occupied housing units	
	2010 census total population	2019 estimated population	Percent change 2010–2019	ACS total population estimate 2015–2019	White alone, not Hispanic or Latino	Black alone, not Hispanic or Latino	Asian alone, not Hispanic or Latino	All other races or 2 or more races, not Hispanic or Latino	Hispanic or Latino[1]	Under 18 years old	Age 65 years and older	Median age	Percent High school diploma or less	Percent Bachelor's degree or more	Total	Percent with a computer
	1	2	3	4	5	6	7	8	9	10	11	12	13	14	15	16
MICHIGAN—Con.																
Gagetown village............	388	363	-6.4	260	93.8	1.2	0.0	1.9	3.1	18.5	26.5	47.0	64.8	8.5	140	87.1
Gaines village.................	380	358	-5.8	346	97.7	0.3	0.0	0.0	2.0	23.4	20.5	46.6	51.0	9.5	144	79.9
Gaines township (Genesee)......................	6,820	6,493	-4.8	6,525	94.7	1.9	0.4	1.1	2.0	21.1	18.7	46.3	35.9	23.4	2,560	93.4
Gaines charter township (Kent)...........................	25,145	27,345	8.7	26,906	75.0	9.1	6.1	3.7	6.2	26.7	11.7	34.0	36.2	31.1	9,484	96.2
Galesburg city & MCD (Kalamazoo).................	2,011	2,081	3.5	2,150	87.3	3.3	0.0	6.7	2.6	28.7	13.8	33.2	54.7	9.1	836	92.7
Galien village.................	549	529	-3.6	473	93.7	1.3	0.0	3.0	2.1	18.6	11.2	33.1	48.2	11.9	223	90.6
Galien township (Berrien).	1,452	1,410	-2.9	1,454	95.8	0.7	0.5	2.2	0.8	20.8	19.5	42.6	50.3	15.7	595	86.9
Ganges township (Allegan).......................	2,530	2,669	5.5	2,634	80.5	0.3	0.6	1.6	17.0	14.9	24.8	52.0	37.6	35.6	1,080	88.8
Garden village................	219	211	-3.7	171	81.9	0.0	0.6	9.9	7.6	25.1	26.9	44.1	42.9	24.1	70	80.0
Garden township (Delta)...	752	729	-3.1	768	84.8	0.0	0.5	11.8	2.9	16.3	35.4	61.7	43.8	20.6	349	80.2
Garden City city & MCD (Wayne)......................	27,636	26,408	-4.4	26,683	88.4	3.4	1.7	2.6	3.9	19.7	15.6	41.4	49.9	12.1	10,749	89.8
Garfield township (Bay).....	1,743	1,688	-3.2	1,804	95.2	0.0	0.0	3.2	1.6	17.7	20.7	47.3	57.9	9.8	736	85.3
Garfield township (Clare)..	1,882	1,894	0.6	1,922	96.9	0.0	0.0	0.0	3.1	19.5	28.6	49.3	51.6	9.5	799	82.5
Garfield charter township (Grand Traverse)	16,217	17,740	9.4	17,319	93.5	0.7	0.1	3.0	2.7	20.6	22.3	40.4	31.6	32.8	7,666	89.5
Garfield township (Kalkaska)......................	804	845	5.1	721	98.3	0.0	0.4	0.3	1.0	14.6	29.3	55.6	61.6	8.8	345	82.9
Garfield township (Mackinac).....................	1,146	1,115	-2.7	1,243	86.2	0.0	0.2	12.6	1.0	21.3	26.1	51.7	39.8	18.7	548	79.7
Garfield township (Newaygo)......................	2,525	2,584	2.3	2,539	91.3	1.1	0.0	0.4	7.2	18.2	30.1	53.7	54.3	20.3	940	88.0
Gaylord city & MCD (Otsego)......................	3,630	3,685	1.5	3,663	92.1	1.9	0.0	2.3	3.7	22.2	23.2	38.2	38.9	18.9	1,792	87.6
Genesee charter township (Genesee)......................	21,559	20,440	-5.2	20,574	85.4	5.9	0.3	3.6	4.7	21.4	16.3	42.5	52.4	10.3	8,403	85.3
Geneva township (Midland)......................	1,056	1,020	-3.4	932	94.8	0.0	0.0	1.0	4.2	18.9	25.2	50.7	53.8	18.9	436	74.3
Geneva township (Van Buren)......................	3,576	3,539		3,528	82.8	2.7	5.7	2.1	6.7	22.1	21.0	44.2	45.0	14.7	1,408	86.5
Genoa township (Livingston)..................	19,790	20,690	4.5	20,316	94.6	0.5	0.9	1.6	2.5	19.6	20.8	46.2	26.8	41.2	8,191	93.4
Georgetown charter township (Ottawa).........	46,985	52,637	12.0	51,716	91.3	1.0	1.1	2.8	3.8	25.8	15.6	35.6	29.4	37.4	18,488	94.3
Germfask township (Schoolcraft)..................	486	469	-3.5	564	84.6	1.8	0.0	13.7	0.0	27.3	19.5	41.2	62.8	5.6	217	79.3
Gerrish township (Roscommon)	2,994	2,951	-1.4	2,931	98.2	0.0	0.0	0.5	1.3	10.3	40.3	61.9	37.6	25.4	1,393	94.0
Gibraltar city & MCD (Wayne)......................	4,656	4,519	-2.9	4,535	86.1	2.1	0.6	3.1	8.1	21.4	18.8	42.4	41.0	17.1	1,777	92.0
Gibson township (Bay).....	1,212	1,174	-3.1	1,125	96.3	0.0	0.4	1.4	1.9	19.5	21.4	47.6	56.1	10.8	457	74.2
Gilead township (Branch) .	661	654	-1.1	714	97.5	0.0	0.0	0.7	1.8	20.6	16.2	42.0	49.5	19.1	295	85.1
Gilford township (Tuscola)	741	689	-7.0	783	95.9	0.0	0.0	2.4	1.7	23.9	20.4	44.8	49.5	14.2	291	87.3
Gilmore township (Benzie)	819	827	1.0	690	94.3	0.0	0.0	1.4	4.2	22.2	21.2	46.0	40.8	24.8	285	88.1
Gilmore township (Isabella).......................	1,461	1,458	-0.2	1,208	94.0	0.4	0.0	1.5	4.1	20.0	25.2	50.1	58.7	11.5	503	86.5
Girard township (Branch)..	1,780	1,761	-1.1	1,671	89.2	0.0	2.6	1.2	7.1	22.1	21.1	47.5	45.0	22.8	695	94.7
Gladstone city & MCD (Delta)........................	4,965	4,698	-5.4	4,753	94.8	0.2	0.0	3.5	1.5	25.1	19.2	41.7	43.5	18.4	2,005	85.6
Gladwin city & MCD (Gladwin).....................	2,944	2,893	-1.7	2,884	92.4	1.3	1.7	2.2	2.4	27.5	17.7	38.5	45.9	14.6	1,218	81.4
Gladwin township (Gladwin).....................	1,118	1,112	-0.5	1,152	98.6	0.0	0.1	0.7	0.6	28.6	17.5	32.8	58.0	13.3	370	64.9
Glen Arbor CDP..............	229	-	-	129	100.0	0.0	0.0	0.0	0.0	7.0	58.9	68.1	5.0	64.2	70	100.0
Glen Arbor township (Leelanau)...................	859	859	0.0	668	92.4	3.4	0.6	0.0	3.6	8.4	51.5	65.5	12.0	67.8	323	95.7
Gobles city & MCD (Van Buren)......................	831	798	-4.0	840	86.9	0.1	0.7	3.1	9.2	25.0	13.7	39.1	49.5	12.1	330	85.5
Golden township (Oceana).......................	1,735	1,752	1.0	1,639	85.4	0.1	0.0	4.9	9.6	15.4	33.1	54.3	46.3	19.8	725	90.3
Goodar township (Ogemaw).....................	398	384	-3.5	312	97.8	0.0	0.0	1.9	0.3	7.4	45.2	63.1	61.0	9.2	182	81.9
Goodland township (Lapeer).......................	1,828	1,808	-1.1	1,831	88.6	0.0	0.0	0.2	11.1	20.6	16.9	44.0	56.7	12.3	667	86.8
Goodrich village.............	1,860	1,884	1.3	1,847	95.0	1.7	0.0	0.3	3.0	29.0	15.3	41.8	29.4	35.6	634	97.6
Goodwell township (Newaygo)......................	547	551	0.7	478	98.5	0.0	0.0	0.2	1.3	20.1	17.6	43.7	51.7	13.4	199	86.4
Gore township (Huron)	144	138	-4.2	114	99.1	0.0	0.0	0.9	0.0	6.1	48.2	64.3	51.0	19.0	58	74.1
Gourley township (Menominee).................	420	402	-4.3	464	90.7	0.0	0.0	3.9	5.4	28.0	14.4	41.6	44.0	16.2	174	81.6
Grand Beach village.........	270	281	4.1	314	96.5	0.0	0.0	3.5	0.0	10.5	51.9	65.5	7.6	75.5	163	92.0
Grand Blanc city & MCD (Genesee)......................	8,246	7,870	-4.6	7,905	79.9	14.6	2.3	0.7	2.5	22.1	20.6	42.7	20.3	45.4	3,435	94.6
Grand Blanc charter township (Genesee)......	37,528	36,593	-2.5	36,646	81.0	10.2	3.3	2.5	2.9	22.6	16.1	39.5	24.0	39.6	14,924	93.9
Grand Haven city & MCD (Ottawa)......................	10,363	11,047	6.6	10,994	95.4	0.3	0.4	1.9	2.0	17.2	23.5	47.4	32.6	35.9	4,901	87.1
Grand Haven charter township (Ottawa)	15,227	17,614	15.7	16,909	92.4	0.1	1.3	1.6	4.6	22.7	15.4	41.2	25.2	41.4	6,466	95.6
Grand Island township (Alger)........................	47	44	-6.4	33	100.0	0.0	0.0	0.0	0.0	0.0	33.3	45.9	48.5	51.5	12	100.0
Grand Ledge city............	7,794	7,896	1.3	7,842	92.4	0.6	0.4	2.4	4.2	22.0	17.0	39.1	28.6	31.3	3,634	89.1
Grand Ledge city (Clinton)	-	-	-	-											-	
Grand Ledge city (Eaton) .	7,794	7,896	1.3	7,842	92.4	0.6	0.4	2.4	4.2	22.0	17.0	39.1	28.6	31.3	3,634	89.1
Grand Rapids city & MCD (Kent)...........................	188,036	201,013	6.9	198,401	59.0	17.9	2.4	4.5	16.1	22.2	12.1	31.4	35.2	36.4	75,422	89.5
Grand Rapids charter township (Kent)	16,662	18,722	12.4	18,384	87.5	0.8	6.8	2.3	2.7	26.8	18.8	42.0	14.5	61.4	6,616	92.2

1 May be of any race.

STATE City, town, township, borough, or CDP (county if applicable)	Population				Race and Hispanic or Latino origin (percent)					Age (percent)			Educational attainment of persons age 25 and older		Occupied housing units	
	2010 census total population	2019 estimated population	Percent change 2010–2019	ACS total population estimate 2015–2019	White alone, not Hispanic or Latino	Black alone, not Hispanic or Latino	Asian alone, not Hispanic or Latino	All other races or 2 or more races, not Hispanic or Latino	Hispanic or Latino[1]	Under 18 years old	Age 65 years and older	Median age	Percent High school diploma or less	Percent Bachelor's degree or more	Total	Percent with a computer
	1	2	3	4	5	6	7	8	9	10	11	12	13	14	15	16

MICHIGAN—Con.

STATE City, town, township, borough, or CDP (county if applicable)	1	2	3	4	5	6	7	8	9	10	11	12	13	14	15	16
Grandville city & MCD (Kent)	15,372	15,858	3.2	15,942	85.2	1.2	1.4	4.1	8.1	23.4	18.7	35.2	31.4	31.9	6,250	88.1
Grant township (Cheboygan)	846	818	-3.3	856	97.3	0.0	0.2	2.2	0.2	14.0	35.9	57.7	46.1	25.1	385	86.5
Grant township (Clare)	3,284	3,339	1.7	3,287	95.8	0.3	0.0	0.0	3.9	24.6	23.0	44.5	40.5	19.7	1,243	87.6
Grant township (Grand Traverse)	1,061	1,139	7.4	1,216	92.9	0.0	1.5	5.6	0.0	26.0	18.1	40.5	36.0	19.6	451	95.6
Grant township (Huron)	913	861	-5.7	996	96.6	0.0	0.0	0.6	2.8	25.4	15.2	42.0	58.7	11.0	343	80.5
Grant township (Iosco)	1,526	1,482	-2.9	1,403	96.7	0.1	0.0	1.0	2.1	13.1	27.8	56.1	55.6	12.3	695	87.5
Grant township (Keweenaw)	219	214	-2.3	201	98.0	0.0	0.0	2.0	0.0	6.0	47.3	64.3	19.8	47.6	115	87.0
Grant township (Mason)	911	926	1.6	912	95.0	0.0	0.0	1.5	3.5	14.5	24.2	56.3	40.8	22.2	416	82.9
Grant township (Mecosta)	686	695	1.3	691	93.3	0.4	0.9	3.8	1.6	19.5	22.0	52.3	44.8	17.2	265	88.7
Grant city & MCD (Newaygo)	895	884	-1.2	960	77.2	0.0	0.0	2.5	20.3	29.5	28.2	39.0	58.3	13.0	388	80.2
Grant township (Newaygo)	3,294	3,319	0.8	3,289	85.7	0.4	1.1	2.1	10.7	24.8	14.8	38.9	47.7	15.3	1,174	87.9
Grant township (Oceana)	2,974	2,974	0.0	2,950	83.9	0.9	0.4	2.1	12.7	23.9	13.5	39.3	52.1	13.7	1,044	88.8
Grant township (St. Clair)	1,891	1,838	-2.8	1,664	93.5	0.0	1.4	2.8	2.3	17.7	16.6	48.8	40.1	15.6	657	90.6
Grass Lake village	1,172	1,145	-2.3	1,230	93.3	0.0	0.0	0.7	6.1	24.6	17.5	37.1	36.4	24.7	482	97.1
Grass Lake charter township (Jackson)	5,697	6,109	7.2	5,983	95.6	0.2	1.8	0.7	1.6	21.9	16.8	44.7	25.0	36.6	2,308	96.1
Grattan township (Kent)	3,625	3,949	8.9	3,905	96.3	0.2	0.1	0.8	2.6	20.8	18.3	48.2	31.8	33.8	1,452	93.4
Grawn CDP	772	-	-	912	78.4	0.0	15.2	0.0	6.4	31.6	4.9	33.3	63.6	8.9	270	95.6
Grayling city & MCD (Crawford)	1,885	1,851	-1.8	1,981	83.0	5.1	1.0	2.7	8.2	25.9	19.3	37.4	56.2	10.8	821	84.3
Grayling charter township (Crawford)	5,826	5,800	-0.4	5,739	98.1	0.0	1.5	0.3	0.1	19.5	24.3	49.9	36.7	23.2	2,430	89.5
Green township (Alpena)	1,236	1,195	-3.3	1,167	98.1	0.2	0.0	0.0	1.7	20.9	23.1	48.8	49.1	18.2	481	89.2
Green charter township (Mecosta)	3,292	3,331	1.2	3,314	90.9	4.1	0.0	2.9	2.2	20.2	20.9	43.1	40.6	23.5	1,485	87.2
Greenbush township (Alcona)	1,413	1,335	-5.5	1,201	97.8	0.5	0.0	1.2	0.5	10.9	38.3	59.8	44.8	17.6	607	85.0
Greenbush township (Clinton)	2,197	2,232	1.6	2,054	96.1	0.1	0.2	0.8	2.8	20.4	19.1	46.2	38.2	16.2	777	87.9
Greendale township (Midland)	1,751	1,772	1.2	1,648	95.0	0.1	0.3	3.3	1.3	18.7	16.1	43.6	58.4	14.5	692	84.5
Green Lake township (Grand Traverse)	5,788	6,288	8.6	6,213	95.5	0.8	0.0	0.4	3.3	16.4	17.9	47.4	29.5	30.9	2,525	95.4
Greenland township (Ontonagon)	790	654	-17.2	776	93.3	1.4	0.0	2.7	2.6	21.3	31.3	53.5	56.5	10.6	326	79.8
Greenleaf township (Sanilac)	780	734	-5.9	782	94.1	0.0	0.0	0.0	5.9	27.5	16.6	39.5	59.9	10.7	295	74.6
Green Oak township (Livingston)	17,471	18,976	8.6	18,807	92.3	0.7	1.8	2.1	3.2	19.9	16.2	44.8	28.5	39.6	7,076	96.0
Greenville city & MCD (Montcalm)	8,471	8,420	-0.6	8,396	91.0	0.9	0.0	4.1	4.0	24.9	19.6	36.3	48.7	12.5	3,648	78.1
Greenwood township (Clare)	1,039	1,043	0.4	1,176	99.8	0.0	0.0	0.0	0.2	19.6	19.3	49.0	65.8	3.3	410	79.3
Greenwood township (Oceana)	1,183	1,184	0.1	1,178	87.4	0.0	1.4	1.3	9.9	30.2	12.6	36.6	57.9	9.8	391	84.1
Greenwood township (Oscoda)	1,119	1,069	-4.5	1,133	95.9	0.5	0.0	2.1	1.5	14.7	36.2	59.1	55.0	11.4	565	81.2
Greenwood township (St. Clair)	1,544	1,545	0.1	1,578	96.3	1.1	0.4	1.5	0.8	30.1	12.9	40.8	45.5	14.9	529	83.6
Greenwood township (Wexford)	587	600	2.2	620	94.4	0.5	0.0	3.7	1.5	18.7	14.2	46.0	49.3	22.2	207	92.8
Greilickville CDP	1,530	-	-	1,647	94.3	0.0	0.7	3.9	1.1	20.6	36.9	54.7	24.0	54.6	743	82.4
Grim township (Gladwin)	136	136	0.0	130	100.0	0.0	0.0	0.0	0.0	25.4	20.8	40.0	67.0	8.5	63	88.9
Grosse Ile township (Wayne)	10,371	10,137	-2.3	10,159	94.0	0.6	2.5	0.7	2.0	19.7	26.2	52.9	18.1	48.3	4,146	93.8
Grosse Pointe city & MCD (Wayne)	5,421	5,154	-4.9	5,206	89.7	3.4	0.4	3.6	2.9	24.4	21.2	47.0	8.6	71.2	2,152	94.3
Grosse Pointe Farms city & MCD (Wayne)	9,479	9,114	-3.9	9,168	93.3	1.8	1.1	1.0	2.7	26.7	22.5	44.7	8.2	74.7	3,361	95.5
Grosse Pointe Park city & MCD (Wayne)	11,553	11,050	-4.4	11,153	85.2	8.0	2.5	3.3	1.0	22.4	16.3	43.0	9.3	67.0	4,325	94.2
Grosse Pointe Woods city & MCD (Wayne)	15,947	15,332	-3.9	15,498	88.3	6.0	2.0	1.8	2.0	22.8	20.5	45.6	13.7	61.0	6,016	93.6
Grout township (Gladwin)	1,955	1,937	-0.9	2,222	93.1	0.0	3.6	2.7	0.6	30.9	17.9	35.7	57.5	10.6	731	79.3
Groveland township (Oakland)	5,476	5,668	3.5	5,644	94.7	1.1	0.5	0.7	3.0	21.3	16.7	44.2	36.2	27.9	1,917	97.8
Gun Plain township (Allegan)	5,893	6,131	4.0	6,058	94.9	0.0	0.0	2.9	2.2	27.8	15.3	40.8	36.0	33.4	2,207	87.6
Gustin township (Alcona)	806	771	-4.3	720	94.3	0.7	0.4	2.8	1.8	19.6	27.4	49.1	58.6	10.8	345	77.7
Gwinn CDP	1,917	-	-	2,033	93.2	0.0	1.5	3.9	1.4	21.0	17.5	49.3	49.0	20.4	803	87.8
Hadley township (Lapeer)	4,519	4,473		4,499	93.6	0.6	2.2	1.9	1.6	19.6	19.6	46.3	35.1	29.1	1,724	97.8
Hagar township (Berrien)	3,663	3,545	-3.2	3,575	94.7	1.1	0.2	1.1	2.8	19.5	20.3	46.6	40.9	25.0	1,566	89.7
Haight township (Ontonagon)	214	181	-15.4	167	95.8	0.0	2.4	0.0	1.8	9.6	33.5	57.2	43.7	27.2	83	74.7
Hamburg township (Livingston)	21,161	21,794	3.0	21,661	96.4	0.4	0.6	1.2	1.3	20.1	17.9	46.6	24.9	42.0	8,474	98.1
Hamilton township (Clare)	1,823	1,814	-0.5	1,874	94.6	0.0	0.0	1.9	3.5	12.7	28.0	55.5	55.2	6.6	860	85.9
Hamilton township (Gratiot)	465	446	-4.1	443	94.4	0.0	1.1	3.4	1.1	17.6	24.6	52.8	58.5	11.3	194	76.8
Hamilton township (Van Buren)	1,486	1,465	-1.4	1,252	81.6	1.0	0.0	3.3	14.1	21.4	19.9	47.4	53.6	14.8	498	90.8
Hamlin township (Eaton)	3,343	3,429	2.6	3,392	94.3	0.9	1.8	2.0	1.1	21.0	16.8	47.1	40.5	19.2	1,276	88.7
Hamlin township (Mason)	3,408	3,486	2.3	3,458	94.8	0.0	1.1	2.8	1.3	15.8	31.7	56.7	33.8	28.6	1,655	91.1
Hampton charter township (Bay)	9,659	9,383	-2.9	9,445	89.2	2.6	1.0	2.7	4.4	17.4	23.3	47.7	41.1	20.1	4,339	87.2
Hamtramck city & MCD (Wayne)	22,448	21,599	-3.8	21,822	53.7	11.5	26.0	7.5	1.3	31.9	8.0	27.9	65.7	12.3	6,069	82.9

1 May be of any race.

Table A. All Places — **Population and Housing**

STATE City, town, township, borough, or CDP (county if applicable)	Population				Race and Hispanic or Latino origin (percent)					Age (percent)			Educational attainment of persons age 25 and older		Occupied housing units	
	2010 census total population	2019 estimated population	Percent change 2010–2019	ACS total population estimate 2015–2019	White alone, not Hispanic or Latino	Black alone, not Hispanic or Latino	Asian alone, not Hispanic or Latino	All other races or 2 or more races, not Hispanic or Latino	Hispanic or Latino[1]	Under 18 years old	Age 65 years and older	Median age	Percent High school diploma or less	Percent Bachelor's degree or more	Total	Percent with a computer
	1	2	3	4	5	6	7	8	9	10	11	12	13	14	15	16
MICHIGAN—Con.																
Hancock city & MCD (Houghton)	4,668	4,506	-3.5	4,554	91.6	0.0	1.8	3.0	3.6	11.9	24.7	40.9	39.5	38.6	1,873	86.7
Hancock township (Houghton)	461	447	-3.0	508	95.7	1.6	0.6	2.2	0.0	39.6	20.7	39.2	41.6	36.2	165	89.7
Handy township (Livingston)	8,010	8,482	5.9	8,355	94.1	0.2	0.5	2.6	2.5	26.4	11.0	35.9	46.5	20.0	3,112	87.8
Hanover village	441	427	-3.2	476	91.2	2.7	0.0	4.0	2.1	33.2	10.7	30.2	41.6	11.5	172	88.4
Hanover township (Jackson)	3,704	3,698	-0.2	3,691	97.6	0.4	0.4	0.5	1.1	23.8	17.4	43.6	34.3	26.0	1,434	93.3
Hanover township (Wexford)	1,560	1,601	2.6	1,592	95.7	0.3	0.8	1.6	1.7	27.1	14.1	36.1	51.7	11.3	584	92.6
Harbor Beach city & MCD (Huron)	1,703	1,587	-6.8	1,936	93.3	1.3	1.5	2.0	1.9	22.7	22.0	48.0	55.7	18.1	863	74.9
Harbor Springs city & MCD (Emmet)	1,188	1,205	1.4	1,158	90.8	0.3	1.2	7.0	0.6	12.1	43.6	61.6	22.1	40.7	565	89.2
Hardwood Acres CDP	432	-	-	517	100.0	0.0	0.0	0.0	0.0	34.2	0.0	27.8	32.8	42.4	132	100.0
Haring CDP	328	-	-	484	96.7	0.0	0.0	3.3	0.0	31.4	2.9	43.0	71.4	0.0	129	100.0
Haring charter township (Wexford)	3,495	3,549	1.5	3,530	95.5	0.0	0.7	1.8	2.0	24.3	20.4	43.9	41.6	23.5	1,237	87.7
Harper Woods city & MCD (Wayne)	14,396	13,746	-4.5	13,895	32.3	59.8	2.2	4.8	0.8	25.4	13.8	36.0	40.7	22.8	5,328	87.7
Harrietta village	143	146	2.1	154	98.1	0.0	0.0	0.0	1.9	20.1	16.9	45.5	66.3	7.9	65	84.6
Harris township (Menominee)	1,966	1,878	-4.5	1,927	68.7	0.0	1.6	28.2	1.5	24.7	14.6	37.3	50.8	14.0	696	85.8
Harrison city & MCD (Clare)	2,099	2,073	-1.2	1,973	91.9	3.9	0.0	2.0	2.2	13.4	22.3	45.9	51.1	12.1	869	82.2
Harrison charter township (Macomb)	24,589	24,977	1.6	24,979	85.3	9.2	1.1	2.0	2.4	17.3	17.6	45.9	33.2	24.7	11,625	89.3
Harrisville city & MCD (Alcona)	493	467	-5.3	425	89.2	2.8	0.5	3.5	4.0	12.7	37.6	55.8	52.6	19.2	212	74.5
Harrisville township (Alcona)	1,349	1,283	-4.9	1,399	94.1	0.4	0.5	3.9	1.0	15.2	35.5	56.4	48.4	16.9	606	84.8
Hart city & MCD (Oceana)	2,112	2,068	-2.1	2,106	67.1	1.8	0.0	1.9	29.2	26.9	17.2	37.4	58.0	11.2	763	88.3
Hart township (Oceana)	1,867	1,849		1,652	81.5	2.2	0.4	2.4	13.5	18.5	22.8	49.3	45.8	28.5	708	89.3
Hartford city & MCD (Van Buren)	2,685	2,592	-3.5	2,595	58.0	0.7	0.3	4.5	36.5	30.6	13.3	31.0	68.4	3.7	893	78.1
Hartford township (Van Buren)	3,275	3,200	-2.3	3,203	74.7	1.0	0.2	1.0	23.0	30.2	13.8	35.0	59.6	9.9	1,105	85.2
Hartland township (Livingston)	14,665	15,170	3.4	15,001	93.8	0.5	0.7	1.6	3.5	25.9	14.8	41.7	29.1	37.5	5,326	93.3
Hartwick township (Osceola)	567	561	-1.1	546	95.4	0.0	0.9	3.1	0.5	14.1	33.9	55.6	60.7	16.0	247	77.7
Harvey CDP	1,393	-	-	1,534	93.4	1.8	0.0	2.7	2.1	22.2	14.2	36.5	36.5	41.0	575	92.2
Haslett CDP	19,220	-	-	19,565	77.4	3.4	10.2	3.8	5.3	19.9	19.6	40.1	16.5	59.0	8,910	94.4
Hastings city & MCD (Barry)	7,350	7,310	-0.5	7,311	90.6	0.1	2.5	1.9	5.0	23.0	16.1	35.4	42.5	24.2	3,015	89.2
Hastings charter township (Barry)	2,938	3,061	4.2	3,015	98.4	0.0	0.1	0.5	1.0	16.7	23.4	52.8	53.1	15.0	1,113	91.3
Hatton township (Clare)	933	941	0.9	949	97.9	0.6	0.0	1.5	0.0	19.0	20.4	44.4	55.3	13.1	339	85.0
Hawes township (Alcona)	1,100	1,043	-5.2	1,023	94.8	0.3	0.0	1.6	3.3	9.7	38.6	60.4	55.8	12.3	488	84.2
Hay township (Gladwin)	1,362	1,357	-0.4	1,328	95.4	0.0	0.1	2.3	2.2	13.5	23.3	52.9	59.2	10.3	638	75.7
Hayes township (Charlevoix)	1,919	1,925	0.3	1,884	93.5	0.0	0.3	5.3	0.9	15.6	26.5	52.3	29.0	33.4	792	94.1
Hayes township (Clare)	4,680	4,665	-0.3	4,620	96.4	0.1	0.0	2.1	1.4	20.7	21.1	47.3	55.7	7.4	1,708	85.1
Hayes township (Otsego)	2,623	2,693	2.7	2,680	96.6	0.6	0.0	2.1	0.6	20.4	19.0	45.4	44.8	23.3	1,010	97.4
Haynes township (Alcona)	716	680	-5.0	691	99.1	0.0	0.0	0.3	0.6	17.5	31.0	52.6	42.5	22.8	293	85.3
Hazel Park city & MCD (Oakland)	16,422	16,347	-0.5	16,525	78.2	13.3	1.4	5.7	1.5	19.9	12.9	36.8	51.4	15.0	7,088	85.3
Hazelton township (Shiawassee)	2,071	1,994	-3.7	2,208	95.3	1.9	0.1	1.5	1.1	22.7	18.6	41.3	38.9	17.9	832	90.7
Heath township (Allegan)	3,325	3,686	10.9	3,565	94.2	0.3	0.2	2.4	2.9	26.2	12.3	37.3	49.2	23.1	1,173	93.4
Hebron township (Cheboygan)	269	260	-3.3	283	93.6	0.0	0.0	6.4	0.0	18.4	10.2	45.4	48.2	17.1	106	87.7
Helena township (Antrim)	1,001	986	-1.5	1,024	96.3	0.0	0.4	3.3	0.0	10.9	39.1	60.9	28.0	42.4	493	87.6
Hematite township (Iron)	338	318	-5.9	219	95.9	0.0	0.0	3.2	0.9	16.0	43.4	59.3	46.9	11.9	134	64.9
Hemlock CDP	1,466	-	-	1,261	99.2	0.0	0.0	0.0	0.8	19.7	14.8	42.6	54.6	9.7	573	88.3
Henderson CDP	399	-	-	370	94.6	0.0	0.0	1.6	3.8	20.5	20.8	51.3	37.0	17.4	139	96.4
Henderson township (Wexford)	163	168	3.1	180	99.4	0.0	0.0	0.6	0.0	10.0	25.0	55.0	58.3	5.3	87	83.9
Hendricks township (Mackinac)	153	230	50.3	101	81.2	0.0	1.0	17.8	0.0	2.0	35.6	60.9	51.0	10.4	54	64.8
Henrietta township (Jackson)	4,705	4,784	1.7	4,740	97.0	0.8	0.0	0.8	1.5	20.4	17.5	46.6	39.4	18.4	1,944	89.8
Hersey village	346	346	0.0	315	94.6	0.0	0.0	3.8	1.6	24.1	20.0	46.6	51.8	18.6	127	84.3
Hersey township (Osceola)	1,950	1,951	0.1	1,698	95.1	0.4	0.0	2.7	1.9	19.7	24.7	46.6	52.2	11.8	683	84.8
Hesperia village	950	929	-2.2	951	94.6	0.0	0.3	3.7	1.4	25.7	17.0	36.3	49.9	9.0	391	82.6
Hiawatha township (Schoolcraft)	1,301	1,240	-4.7	1,264	85.6	0.0	0.8	11.8	1.8	16.9	29.5	56.7	44.5	21.3	576	86.8
Hickory Corners CDP	322	-	-	159	100.0	0.0	0.0	0.0	0.0	0.0	0.0	55.9	89.9	0.0	78	100.0
Higgins township (Roscommon)	1,930	1,892	-2.0	2,043	85.6	1.1	0.0	11.5	1.8	25.7	18.7	41.4	38.2	20.0	805	91.9
Highland charter township (Oakland)	19,208	20,172	5.0	20,031	95.4	0.5	0.5	1.7	1.9	21.0	17.7	47.0	32.2	31.2	7,533	94.6
Highland township (Osceola)	1,250	1,247	-0.2	1,161	99.4	0.0	0.0	0.0	0.6	27.8	20.7	39.5	60.1	14.3	428	84.8
Highland Park city & MCD (Wayne)	11,776	10,775	-8.5	10,867	5.3	91.4	0.1	1.7	1.6	24.7	19.2	39.6	60.2	10.6	4,583	63.6
Hill township (Ogemaw)	1,355	1,304	-3.8	1,367	98.0	0.0	0.0	1.6	0.4	13.5	38.4	62.3	44.3	17.4	668	84.6
Hillman village	698	669	-4.2	638	97.8	0.0	0.0	0.5	1.7	13.0	35.4	58.3	63.8	9.1	291	82.5
Hillman township (Montmorency)	2,168	2,086	-3.8	2,076	97.5	0.8	0.0	1.0	0.7	14.7	31.5	55.8	55.2	12.9	1,016	83.3

1 May be of any race.

Table A. All Places — **Population and Housing**

	Population				Race and Hispanic or Latino origin (percent)					Age (percent)			Educational attainment of persons age 25 and older		Occupied housing units	
STATE City, town, township, borough, or CDP (county if applicable)	2010 census total population	2019 estimated population	Percent change 2010–2019	ACS total population estimate 2015–2019	White alone, not Hispanic or Latino	Black alone, not Hispanic or Latino	Asian alone, not Hispanic or Latino	All other races or 2 or more races, not Hispanic or Latino	Hispanic or Latino[1]	Under 18 years old	Age 65 years and older	Median age	Percent High school diploma or less	Percent Bachelor's degree or more	Total	Percent with a computer
	1	2	3	4	5	6	7	8	9	10	11	12	13	14	15	16

MICHIGAN—Con.

	1	2	3	4	5	6	7	8	9	10	11	12	13	14	15	16
Hillsdale city & MCD (Hillsdale)	8,294	8,003	-3.5	8,097	91.6	1.8	0.9	2.3	3.5	20.1	15.3	28.2	47.8	25.6	2,955	79.1
Hillsdale township (Hillsdale)	2,036	1,994	-2.1	2,093	98.5	0.1	0.5	0.3	0.5	21.5	21.2	46.0	39.1	26.2	825	91.0
Hinton township (Mecosta)	1,126	1,126	0.0	1,052	96.3	1.7	0.0	0.3	1.7	20.8	15.3	45.3	54.2	18.3	386	80.3
Holland township (Missaukee)	248	255	2.8	173	94.8	0.0	0.0	0.0	5.2	11.6	30.6	56.3	56.9	18.2	82	76.8
Holland city	33,101	33,216	0.3	33,402	66.9	4.2	2.1	2.5	24.3	21.0	15.9	32.5	39.1	32.6	12,027	88.0
Holland city (Allegan)	6,997	7,088	1.3	7,077	71.1	4.2	0.1	1.4	23.1	25.1	19.4	38.3	42.6	26.9	2,810	87.4
Holland city (Ottawa)	26,104	26,128	0.1	26,325	65.8	4.1	2.6	2.8	24.7	20.0	15.0	30.3	37.9	34.4	9,217	88.2
Holland charter township (Ottawa)	35,569	38,690	8.8	38,118	57.9	2.3	9.9	2.2	27.7	27.3	10.7	33.1	46.8	24.3	13,723	94.1
Holly village	6,073	6,149	1.3	6,174	92.8	1.6	0.4	1.9	3.3	19.4	15.0	42.1	37.7	21.8	2,773	89.7
Holly township (Oakland)	11,360	11,687	2.9	11,622	91.4	3.2	0.7	1.8	2.9	22.5	15.9	42.7	33.7	26.2	4,644	92.1
Holmes township (Menominee)	337	324	-3.9	345	97.4	0.0	0.3	1.2	0.9	13.6	16.8	53.2	52.3	9.2	177	89.8
Holt CDP	23,973	-	-	26,065	78.5	7.0	4.7	4.7	5.1	25.0	14.4	38.5	26.5	38.3	10,238	92.4
Holton township (Muskegon)	2,515	2,614	3.9	2,570	83.4	0.0	0.0	7.7	8.9	24.6	15.8	40.3	49.4	13.7	982	89.5
Home township (Montcalm)	2,542	2,560	0.7	2,553	94.4	0.0	0.0	1.1	4.3	23.6	15.0	43.7	55.3	12.1	1,027	81.8
Home township (Newaygo)	232	232	0.0	191	92.7	1.6	0.0	1.6	4.2	7.9	31.9	57.4	65.3	9.0	80	88.8
Homer village	1,668	1,645	-1.4	1,648	89.5	0.0	0.0	6.9	3.6	27.5	13.7	34.9	53.0	14.7	661	91.4
Homer township (Calhoun)	3,013	3,004	-0.3	2,977	91.9	0.0	0.0	4.0	4.1	24.4	15.2	36.4	52.8	12.9	1,170	85.5
Homer township (Midland)	4,007	3,996	-0.3	3,990	96.6	0.0	0.5	2.9	0.0	21.6	23.7	45.4	40.1	26.9	1,643	89.7
Homestead township (Benzie)	2,356	2,404	2.0	2,084	95.3	0.0	0.2	3.4	1.1	18.2	23.7	49.9	50.4	14.1	786	83.6
Honor village	328	331	0.9	222	83.8	0.0	0.5	11.3	4.5	18.9	25.7	44.1	47.9	24.5	93	82.8
Hope township (Barry)	3,242	3,306	2.0	3,277	93.5	3.1	0.0	3.4	0.0	10.3	25.0	50.9	54.8	17.3	1,583	86.4
Hope township (Midland)	1,346	1,362	1.2	1,442	95.9	0.0	1.5	2.6	0.0	19.1	18.2	48.5	43.2	21.2	579	87.6
Hopkins village	610	607	-0.5	885	94.6	1.4	0.0	3.3	0.8	36.3	8.1	25.8	44.3	21.4	258	93.0
Hopkins township (Allegan)	2,601	2,714	4.3	2,705	96.0	0.9	0.0	2.7	0.4	27.5	14.7	35.0	55.3	14.3	924	87.1
Horton township (Ogemaw)	939	911	-3.0	820	93.3	0.0	2.8	2.6	1.3	17.0	26.2	51.5	51.2	9.5	372	74.5
Horton Bay CDP	512	-	-	510	98.6	0.0	0.0	0.0	1.4	12.2	27.1	57.0	29.5	41.2	246	87.0
Houghton city & MCD (Houghton)	7,684	7,754	0.9	7,870	81.3	2.5	10.4	3.9	2.0	11.4	8.1	22.1	27.1	52.0	2,533	86.1
Houghton township (Keweenaw)	82	81	-1.2	114	88.6	1.8	0.0	4.4	5.3	2.6	61.4	67.8	28.7	27.8	63	87.3
Houghton Lake CDP	3,427	-	-	3,350	96.0	0.0	0.0	1.9	2.1	17.3	29.3	55.7	54.2	9.4	1,572	83.2
Howard township (Cass)	6,207	6,103	-1.7	6,091	91.4	5.2	0.7	1.3	1.4	20.2	21.7	45.5	43.9	18.0	2,562	92.1
Howard City village	1,803	1,830	1.5	1,589	92.5	0.4	0.2	5.0	2.0	30.3	13.8	34.8	59.2	11.2	580	84.8
Howell city & MCD (Livingston)	9,475	9,604	1.4	9,580	89.2	1.2	2.0	3.4	4.2	19.7	15.0	39.5	36.7	23.2	4,307	85.0
Howell township (Livingston)	6,680	7,230	8.2	7,107	93.0	0.5	0.8	2.2	3.5	21.2	15.7	38.7	40.1	24.4	2,570	90.6
Hubbard Lake CDP	1,002	-	-	894	95.7	0.3	0.2	3.2	0.4	7.0	53.9	66.7	39.3	30.6	457	90.4
Hubbardston village	395	400	1.3	341	90.0	1.8	0.0	6.2	2.1	18.2	18.5	48.4	60.7	7.0	133	85.7
Hubbell CDP	946	-	-	925	98.7	0.0	0.0	0.6	0.0	25.1	11.9	38.2	45.8	22.2	354	98.0
Hudson township (Charlevoix)	679	681	0.3	700	94.9	1.0	0.0	3.6	0.6	18.4	22.9	45.6	47.4	19.9	288	87.2
Hudson city & MCD (Lenawee)	2,304	2,210	-4.1	2,536	89.9	0.2	0.0	0.9	8.9	28.1	11.8	33.5	56.0	12.6	891	90.5
Hudson township (Lenawee)	1,497	1,524	1.8	1,399	93.4	0.0	0.0	3.4	3.1	14.1	27.2	54.1	52.1	14.3	667	87.0
Hudson township (Mackinac)	181	186	2.8	254	66.5	1.6	0.0	31.9	0.0	21.7	29.5	53.0	46.8	10.8	124	83.9
Hudsonville city & MCD (Ottawa)	7,116	7,348	3.3	7,366	91.5	1.1	1.1	2.9	3.4	28.1	14.4	31.6	36.5	32.9	2,551	90.3
Hulbert township (Chippewa)	168	164	-2.4	171	90.6	7.0	0.0	2.3	0.0	14.6	31.0	58.5	53.4	11.6	86	80.2
Humboldt township (Marquette)	461	460	-0.2	467	94.6	0.0	0.0	4.5	0.9	20.8	35.3	44.3	63.0	14.4	200	86.5
Hume township (Huron)	749	703	-6.1	717	98.6	0.0	0.0	0.7	0.7	15.5	31.5	58.0	42.2	17.9	361	83.7
Huntington Woods city & MCD (Oakland)	6,238	6,265	0.4	6,322	92.2	1.4	2.1	2.4	1.9	28.5	16.9	43.4	6.4	77.1	2,351	97.7
Huron township (Huron)	437	412	-5.7	317	98.1	0.0	0.0	1.9	0.0	11.0	41.0	61.5	52.2	14.5	168	85.7
Huron charter township (Wayne)	15,879	16,247	2.3	15,967	90.5	3.5	0.7	2.0	3.3	23.2	15.0	43.1	45.5	23.9	5,897	90.3
Ida township (Monroe)	4,963	4,824	-2.8	4,835	97.4	0.0	0.0	1.1	1.4	19.4	16.6	47.0	37.7	22.7	1,875	94.1
Imlay township (Lapeer)	3,128	3,086	-1.3	3,121	77.5	0.0	0.8	4.7	17.0	25.3	13.2	40.0	50.3	15.2	1,048	85.9
Imlay City city & MCD (Lapeer)	3,597	3,569	-0.8	3,568	69.5	0.3	0.0	1.0	29.2	26.3	14.2	35.4	58.5	11.6	1,474	90.6
Independence charter township (Oakland)	34,626	37,026	6.9	36,745	88.9	3.3	2.4	1.7	3.7	23.5	14.8	40.6	22.5	44.9	13,561	96.1
Indianfields township (Tuscola)	2,803	2,519	-10.1	2,539	92.3	2.6	0.2	0.3	4.6	21.4	20.6	44.8	48.6	17.5	908	89.6
Indian River CDP	1,959	-	-	1,883	97.3	0.0	0.0	1.3	1.4	8.6	33.7	56.5	43.0	30.2	995	82.4
Ingallston township (Menominee)	935	893	-4.5	834	96.5	0.0	0.0	3.5	0.0	13.5	28.2	56.6	37.8	26.4	402	85.1
Ingersoll township (Midland)	2,744	2,658	-3.1	2,681	95.4	0.3	0.6	0.4	3.2	18.0	19.5	45.7	43.8	24.1	1,055	89.9
Ingham township (Ingham)	2,452	2,508	2.3	2,496	93.0	0.0	0.8	3.2	3.0	21.2	17.2	45.2	37.8	24.5	898	93.0
Inkster city & MCD (Wayne)	25,366	24,284	-4.3	24,520	17.1	73.3	0.5	5.4	3.6	30.3	12.0	31.0	54.2	11.1	9,002	87.6
Inland township (Benzie)	2,071	2,109	1.8	2,374	95.6	0.0	0.8	1.3	2.3	21.7	13.6	41.0	37.2	21.6	880	90.7
Interior township (Ontonagon)	336	281	-16.4	325	92.9	0.0	2.5	3.4	1.2	16.3	28.3	57.6	50.4	16.1	146	77.4
Interlochen CDP	583	-	-	268	85.4	0.7	0.0	7.8	6.0	4.9	35.4	63.1	56.5	8.6	125	76.0

1 May be of any race.

Table A. All Places — **Population and Housing**

STATE City, town, township, borough, or CDP (county if applicable)	2010 census total population	2019 estimated population	Percent change 2010–2019	ACS total population estimate 2015–2019	White alone, not Hispanic or Latino	Black alone, not Hispanic or Latino	Asian alone, not Hispanic or Latino	All other races or 2 or more races, not Hispanic or Latino	Hispanic or Latino[1]	Under 18 years old	Age 65 years and older	Median age	Percent High school diploma or less	Percent Bachelor's degree or more	Total occupied housing units	Percent with a computer
	1	2	3	4	5	6	7	8	9	10	11	12	13	14	15	16
MICHIGAN—Con.																
Inverness township (Cheboygan)	2,261	2,191	-3.1	2,176	91.3	0.0	0.3	8.0	0.4	18.8	25.5	50.3	46.7	23.4	937	83.1
Inwood township (Schoolcraft)	733	701	-4.4	704	85.2	0.0	0.6	10.9	3.3	17.2	31.1	55.5	55.6	13.3	299	85.3
Ionia city & MCD (Ionia)....	11,326	11,168	-1.4	11,147	65.1	21.7	0.3	3.0	9.8	17.6	9.1	36.6	59.0	12.2	2,924	92.3
Ionia township (Ionia)	3,834	3,908	1.9	3,880	93.1	1.7	0.1	1.3	3.8	23.4	19.0	40.3	54.3	12.2	1,500	85.9
Iosco township (Livingston)	3,801	3,860	1.6	3,850	96.8	0.0	0.9	1.8	0.5	23.7	13.5	42.6	44.7	20.3	1,354	95.1
Ira township (St. Clair)	5,192	5,105	-1.7	5,094	98.4	1.0	0.0	0.1	0.5	23.9	16.8	44.8	40.3	21.2	1,994	92.0
Iron Mountain city & MCD (Dickinson)	7,634	7,309	-4.3	7,369	96.2	1.2	0.7	0.5	1.4	23.8	17.2	40.0	36.0	27.4	2,952	85.9
Iron River city & MCD (Iron)	3,033	2,829	-6.7	2,854	95.5	0.6	0.0	1.3	2.7	18.4	23.6	47.4	57.6	17.5	1,413	80.0
Iron River township (Iron) .	1,026	960	-6.4	1,185	97.4	0.0	0.3	2.3	0.0	17.8	30.5	52.9	48.5	18.4	545	78.2
Ironton CDP	140	-	-	114	100.0	0.0	0.0	0.0	0.0	7.9	46.5	61.7	42.2	18.9	53	73.6
Ironwood city & MCD (Gogebic)	5,391	4,870	-9.7	4,955	94.1	3.0	0.2	1.2	1.5	12.3	26.8	51.2	45.0	18.9	2,574	76.0
Ironwood charter township (Gogebic)	2,333	2,170	-7.0	2,329	95.2	1.6	0.0	2.8	0.3	22.1	22.4	44.7	28.9	30.7	967	85.5
Irving township (Barry)	3,250	3,398	4.6	3,348	95.5	0.4	0.4	1.7	2.0	29.2	16.0	35.6	45.9	20.8	1,220	86.5
Isabella township (Isabella)	2,253	2,253	0.0	1,962	90.0	0.6	0.7	4.1	4.6	20.6	13.8	43.3	47.5	18.1	755	88.7
Ishpeming city & MCD (Marquette)	6,474	6,416	-0.9	6,464	94.7	1.3	0.7	2.7	0.7	18.8	21.1	42.9	46.4	24.6	2,832	86.3
Ishpeming township (Marquette)	3,515	3,513	-0.1	3,526	93.6	0.2	1.6	4.5	0.0	21.3	25.6	50.5	41.0	32.4	1,341	83.4
Ithaca city & MCD (Gratiot)	2,924	2,766	-5.4	2,797	91.2	0.1	0.0	0.9	7.7	28.3	16.0	34.6	39.5	20.9	1,094	85.8
Jackson city & MCD (Jackson)......................	33,477	32,440	-3.1	32,673	66.6	20.3	0.9	5.3	6.9	26.2	10.7	33.8	49.0	17.2	13,244	86.2
James township (Saginaw).....................	2,023	1,881	-7.0	1,965	92.5	0.0	0.0	1.3	6.3	18.9	19.4	47.4	45.3	15.9	801	90.8
Jamestown charter township (Ottawa)	7,034	8,901	26.5	8,370	93.7	0.0	0.1	0.6	5.6	31.1	11.8	32.8	35.2	33.3	2,695	96.5
Jasper CDP	412	-	-	383	92.4	0.0	0.0	0.0	7.6	22.2	18.3	38.9	52.5	1.7	129	88.4
Jasper township (Midland)	1,180	1,138	-3.6	1,007	92.9	0.0	0.0	1.7	5.5	19.9	16.5	45.2	59.4	14.4	401	76.1
Jefferson township (Cass)	2,550	2,559	0.4	2,530	86.3	5.2	0.7	4.1	3.6	21.7	16.6	44.7	44.9	19.0	964	91.4
Jefferson township (Hillsdale)....................	3,063	3,001	-2.0	3,004	95.4	1.0	0.0	0.6	3.0	17.0	21.7	48.9	57.1	8.3	1,282	80.4
Jenison CDP	16,538	-	-	17,431	91.1	1.1	0.4	2.5	4.9	24.4	20.7	39.5	35.0	28.4	6,719	91.7
Jennings CDP	264	-	-	266	100.0	0.0	0.0	0.0	0.0	21.4	14.7	41.4	79.5	1.7	108	89.8
Jerome township (Midland)	4,796	4,679	-2.4	4,693	97.0	0.7	0.0	2.0	0.4	18.3	21.1	47.6	37.5	26.7	1,949	82.8
Johnstown township (Barry)	3,014	3,134	4.0	3,086	94.4	1.6	0.0	2.4	1.6	22.7	23.9	47.5	45.4	14.5	1,296	82.7
Jonesfield township (Saginaw).....................	1,667	1,561	-6.4	1,599	93.4	0.3	0.0	1.3	5.1	25.0	17.8	42.0	50.6	16.1	643	84.9
Jonesville city & MCD (Hillsdale)....................	2,262	2,215	-2.1	2,409	89.8	2.6	0.8	5.8	1.0	26.0	17.5	36.2	51.3	14.8	1,008	85.5
Jordan township (Antrim)..	987	985	-0.2	929	93.0	0.0	1.0	3.3	2.7	23.4	18.0	45.3	48.6	20.3	367	83.1
Joyfield township (Benzie)	799	817	2.3	836	94.1	0.0	0.0	0.6	5.3	22.5	22.7	45.8	53.9	13.2	305	79.0
Juniata township (Tuscola)	1,567	1,479	-5.6	1,511	93.8	0.9	0.5	2.8	2.1	22.4	19.1	47.6	52.6	12.1	635	83.9
Kalamazoo city & MCD (Kalamazoo).................	74,263	76,200	2.6	76,019	63.3	21.2	2.0	6.0	7.6	18.8	10.4	26.5	31.4	33.8	29,007	91.3
Kalamazoo charter township (Kalamazoo) ..	21,913	22,651	3.4	22,608	68.4	16.2	3.3	5.2	6.8	21.0	13.6	34.3	30.0	35.2	9,025	92.7
Kalamo township (Eaton) .	1,842	1,879	2.0	1,966	96.2	0.0	0.0	1.3	2.5	28.3	17.5	40.5	51.8	10.9	668	83.1
Kaleva village.................	470	460	-2.1	436	78.7	2.3	0.0	6.0	13.1	18.8	19.0	36.3	50.0	14.8	170	91.2
Kalkaska village...............	2,018	2,094	3.8	2,076	93.2	0.8	0.6	4.2	1.2	21.9	19.7	41.9	61.5	6.6	916	79.0
Kalkaska township (Kalkaska)	4,722	4,944	4.7	4,833	89.6	0.5	1.2	4.0	4.7	24.1	18.2	40.3	53.7	8.7	1,996	84.3
Kasson township (Leelanau)	1,605	1,613	0.5	1,457	93.6	0.0	0.4	2.9	3.1	16.3	23.1	48.0	34.3	33.4	593	89.0
Kawkawlin township (Bay)	4,850	4,660	-3.9	4,695	97.3	0.0	0.0	0.5	2.2	17.6	23.9	49.8	44.3	19.7	2,001	88.3
Kearney township (Antrim)	1,765	1,741	-1.4	1,882	92.2	0.9	0.9	2.6	3.5	14.9	28.2	52.5	41.6	26.5	754	89.8
Keego Harbor city & MCD (Oakland)	2,979	3,381	13.5	3,252	87.1	1.4	2.3	0.2	9.0	19.6	11.0	37.1	30.5	36.6	1,491	93.2
Keeler township (Van Buren)	2,176	2,159	-0.8	2,341	76.0	1.8	0.0	3.0	19.2	19.9	18.6	43.2	43.5	23.6	932	88.7
Keene township (Ionia)	1,829	1,869	2.2	1,843	93.2	0.4	0.0	1.7	4.7	26.6	13.5	37.5	46.3	17.8	615	91.4
Kenockee township (St. Clair)	2,470	2,432	-1.5	2,480	95.1	0.0	0.2	3.3	1.3	20.9	13.9	42.2	49.8	15.6	930	93.1
Kent City village.............	1,054	1,187	12.6	1,083	74.6	2.7	0.0	4.5	18.2	29.9	8.7	31.4	57.2	10.8	355	83.9
Kentwood city & MCD (Kent)	48,701	51,898	6.6	51,693	56.8	21.3	8.7	3.1	10.2	24.4	13.4	34.4	37.2	31.9	20,339	92.5
Kimball township (St. Clair)	9,356	9,264		9,172	92.3	0.1	0.4	2.9	4.3	21.3	17.8	44.7	44.5	14.5	3,494	93.4
Kinde village..................	448	414	-7.6	500	94.0	0.0	1.2	4.8	0.0	34.0	13.8	32.5	54.1	9.8	187	90.4
Kinderhook township (Branch)	1,496	1,493	-0.2	1,456	96.4	0.3	0.0	3.2	0.1	14.1	26.0	54.6	46.7	21.6	701	86.6
Kingsford city & MCD (Dickinson)	5,133	4,951	-3.5	4,992	88.1	1.1	1.5	6.7	2.6	20.7	26.1	43.7	42.9	23.1	2,360	81.0
Kingsley village..............	1,472	1,625	10.4	1,352	93.4	0.0	0.4	4.1	2.0	26.8	13.5	36.5	31.6	28.6	525	91.8
Kingston village	440	409	-7.0	439	97.3	0.0	0.0	0.5	2.3	26.0	14.8	33.8	52.7	11.8	175	89.7
Kingston township (Tuscola)	1,575	1,474	-6.4	1,358	94.6	0.0	0.0	3.2	2.1	23.1	18.7	44.3	55.9	9.9	557	87.3
Kinross charter township (Chippewa).................	7,714	7,454	-3.4	7,435	51.7	23.0	1.3	21.5	2.6	17.8	7.4	36.6	63.2	9.0	1,619	90.4
K. I. Sawyer CDP	2,624	-	-	3,005	84.7	0.8	0.5	9.7	4.3	31.0	9.6	29.9	42.6	14.8	1,068	89.9
Klacking township (Ogemaw)	614	594	-3.3	594	95.1	0.0	0.0	3.4	1.5	17.5	32.5	56.6	50.4	14.0	278	78.8

1 May be of any race.

STATE City, town, township, borough, or CDP (county if applicable)	Population 2010 census total population	2019 estimated population	Percent change 2010–2019	ACS total population estimate 2015–2019	Race and Hispanic or Latino origin (percent) White alone, not Hispanic or Latino	Black alone, not Hispanic or Latino	Asian alone, not Hispanic or Latino	All other races or 2 or more races, not Hispanic or Latino	Hispanic or Latino[1]	Age (percent) Under 18 years old	Age 65 years and older	Median age	Educational attainment of persons age 25 and older Percent High school diploma or less	Percent Bachelor's degree or more	Occupied housing units Total	Percent with a computer
	1	2	3	4	5	6	7	8	9	10	11	12	13	14	15	16
MICHIGAN—Con.																
Kochville township (Saginaw)	5,074	4,699	-7.4	4,854	85.6	5.4	2.9	2.5	3.6	7.4	9.5	21.1	33.6	25.1	1,103	89.4
Koehler township (Cheboygan)	1,283	1,250	-2.6	1,042	95.4	1.4	0.0	3.2	0.0	22.1	20.6	45.8	56.1	17.4	446	89.5
Koylton township (Tuscola)	1,565	1,484	-5.2	1,439	96.3	0.0	0.0	1.5	2.2	21.6	16.1	44.8	53.1	9.8	567	90.8
Krakow township (Presque Isle)	701	661	-5.7	676	98.8	0.0	0.0	1.2	0.0	9.3	35.1	58.8	47.2	19.7	339	82.0
Lafayette township (Gratiot)	591	562	-4.9	514	93.0	0.0	0.0	0.0	7.0	22.6	20.0	45.1	42.0	17.9	207	89.9
LaGrange township (Cass)	3,497	3,385	-3.2	3,391	71.0	20.1	1.2	6.1	1.7	18.9	19.7	40.7	56.9	13.6	1,319	82.8
Laingsburg city & MCD (Shiawassee)	1,283	1,285	0.2	1,264	91.3	3.8	0.9	1.0	3.0	29.0	13.6	33.5	38.9	20.4	486	94.0
Laird township (Houghton)	553	539	-2.5	362	98.1	0.0	0.0	1.9	0.0	22.1	21.3	48.1	52.0	15.6	154	85.7
Lake township (Benzie)	759	766	0.9	844	98.7	0.0	0.0	0.7	0.6	1.2	52.3	65.8	16.9	56.1	404	96.3
Lake charter township (Berrien)	2,974	3,004	1.0	2,977	95.9	0.0	1.2	2.8	0.1	9.0	31.1	55.6	37.7	28.5	1,478	90.7
Lake township (Huron)	855	800	-6.4	539	99.3	0.0	0.7	0.0	0.0	10.8	51.4	65.6	48.5	19.7	292	85.6
Lake township (Lake)	860	891	3.6	830	90.6	0.4	0.7	3.5	4.8	12.3	30.4	56.5	52.3	18.5	314	91.7
Lake township (Menominee)	559	537	-3.9	543	95.9	2.2	0.0	1.8	0.0	15.1	26.3	55.4	53.2	17.5	242	80.6
Lake township (Missaukee)	2,798	2,836	1.4	2,822	95.4	0.7	0.4	2.9	0.6	16.4	29.3	51.0	41.6	20.0	1,251	87.3
Lake township (Roscommon)	1,215	1,201	-1.2	1,171	97.4	0.0	0.0	2.2	0.4	11.9	42.9	61.5	52.9	17.8	553	84.3
Lake Angelus city & MCD (Oakland)	300	307	2.3	274	88.0	0.0	2.9	0.7	8.4	11.3	24.5	58.3	17.7	70.7	119	99.2
Lake Ann village (Benzie)	268	271	1.1	196	98.0	0.0	0.0	2.0	0.0	6.1	26.0	59.2	45.5	20.2	85	96.5
Lake City city & MCD (Missaukee)	836	837	0.1	771	87.5	3.4	0.4	6.5	2.2	31.5	18.5	37.9	41.7	20.5	278	85.6
Lake Fenton CDP	5,559	-	-	5,284	98.2	0.0	0.4	0.7	0.7	21.3	24.8	46.9	28.0	44.8	2,196	93.9
Lakefield township (Luce)	1,064	989	-7.0	938	95.7	0.0	0.0	2.5	1.8	11.8	42.8	62.1	41.1	21.1	441	71.4
Lakefield township (Saginaw)	1,029	1,001	-2.7	1,060	93.6	0.0	0.0	2.1	4.3	23.9	22.7	42.6	47.3	18.1	409	79.5
Lake Isabella village	1,674	1,676	0.1	2,063	97.1	0.1	0.0	1.5	1.4	22.8	19.5	39.2	31.5	31.5	740	94.3
Lake Leelanau CDP	253	-	-	160	100.0	0.0	0.0	0.0	0.0	34.4	13.8	42.8	31.4	50.5	60	100.0
Lake Linden village	983	946	-3.8	1,113	95.6	0.3	0.0	3.1	1.1	20.6	21.3	39.7	44.4	22.7	459	80.6
Lake Michigan Beach CDP	1,216	-	-	1,190	99.5	0.0	0.0	0.5	0.0	21.8	19.6	45.4	33.6	28.5	520	95.2
Lake Odessa village	2,018	2,040	1.1	2,079	85.8	2.0	0.0	2.0	10.2	25.4	18.4	38.4	53.0	13.5	867	87.8
Lake Orion village	3,038	3,189	5.0	3,141	92.8	0.3	3.0	0.1	3.8	20.7	18.9	41.7	24.3	40.7	1,365	93.5
Lakes of the North CDP	-	-	-	805	95.5	0.0	0.7	3.7	0.0	4.7	36.6	57.4	48.9	18.9	397	84.1
Laketon township (Muskegon)	7,569	7,661	1.2	7,612	92.8	1.9	0.9	1.7	2.6	20.1	19.3	47.3	28.0	32.1	2,972	92.4
Laketown township (Allegan)	5,561	5,950	7.0	5,834	90.7	0.3	3.2	1.7	4.0	18.6	22.5	50.5	30.5	43.9	2,402	96.5
Lake Victoria CDP	930	-	-	841	97.4	1.0	0.2	0.0	1.4	13.3	19.4	51.0	19.3	47.0	346	100.0
Lakeview village	1,002	1,002	0.0	1,012	96.0	0.0	0.0	1.7	2.3	21.4	19.9	37.5	56.9	9.3	413	78.9
Lakewood Club village	1,297	1,292	-0.4	1,212	86.6	0.0	0.0	6.6	6.8	24.2	12.6	39.2	46.4	9.7	471	94.1
Lambertville CDP	9,953	-	-	9,524	92.3	1.2	0.4	3.4	2.6	23.5	18.9	42.3	32.3	33.0	3,762	89.3
Lamotte township (Sanilac)	919	865	-5.9	792	98.1	1.3	0.0	0.3	0.4	22.6	21.5	42.8	60.3	11.5	336	84.8
L'Anse village	2,017	1,842	-8.7	2,063	86.0	2.5	0.2	10.1	1.2	23.8	23.1	45.6	42.6	16.1	866	84.2
L'Anse township (Baraga)	3,843	3,529	-8.2	3,667	80.4	1.6	0.2	15.6	2.2	22.4	23.4	47.3	43.7	18.3	1,529	84.2
Lansing city	114,265	118,210	3.5	117,159	54.1	22.2	4.4	6.8	12.4	22.6	11.9	32.6	37.2	26.2	49,034	89.9
Lansing city (Clinton)	-	-	-	-	-	-	-	-	-	-	-	-	-	-	-	-
Lansing city (Eaton)	4,749	4,882	2.8	4,831	29.8	50.5	5.2	7.0	7.6	24.3	12.0	32.3	44.7	17.5	1,997	91.4
Lansing city (Ingham)	109,516	113,328	3.5	112,328	55.2	21.0	4.4	6.8	12.6	22.5	11.9	32.6	36.9	26.5	47,037	89.8
Lansing charter township (Ingham)	8,178	8,247	0.8	8,262	63.5	15.8	4.1	4.2	12.4	15.6	15.5	35.9	33.5	30.4	3,985	93.1
Lapeer city & MCD (Lapeer)	8,826	8,535	-3.3	8,676	82.1	10.7	0.6	2.3	4.2	17.7	15.5	40.6	51.6	13.9	3,495	84.7
Lapeer township (Lapeer)	5,056	5,020	-0.7	5,045	95.8	0.3	1.7	0.3	1.8	18.2	19.3	49.3	42.8	21.0	1,861	92.6
Larkin charter township (Midland)	5,147	5,406	5.0	5,368	95.0	0.8	2.9	0.7	0.6	27.0	16.1	43.5	19.3	53.0	1,993	94.3
La Salle township (Monroe)	4,897	4,692	-4.2	4,727	93.9	0.1	0.2	1.0	4.8	19.1	20.4	47.3	43.5	17.0	1,866	91.0
Lathrup Village city & MCD (Oakland)	4,095	4,091	-0.1	4,128	31.4	61.1	0.2	4.4	2.9	17.2	18.0	44.8	18.9	51.6	1,523	99.5
Laurium village	1,979	1,898	-4.1	2,073	97.5	0.3	0.0	1.4	0.8	23.2	20.7	38.7	37.0	25.8	829	81.5
Lawrence village	996	976	-2.0	1,029	71.0	1.0	0.0	2.5	25.5	33.7	9.9	32.5	59.3	16.7	355	87.0
Lawrence township (Van Buren)	3,261	3,244	-0.5	3,241	77.4	0.6	0.0	1.4	20.6	24.7	15.4	40.4	51.6	18.7	1,145	87.9
Lawton village	1,855	1,805	-2.7	1,570	83.6	0.3	0.2	4.8	11.1	25.1	16.4	40.4	44.5	16.8	666	88.1
Leavitt township (Oceana)	891	887	-0.4	942	80.5	0.0	0.0	5.9	13.6	31.3	14.8	35.5	59.4	7.8	335	85.1
Lebanon township (Clinton)	605	611	1.0	553	99.1	0.0	0.7	0.2	0.0	23.0	19.7	47.1	46.8	22.8	219	81.7
Lee township (Allegan)	4,012	4,123	2.8	4,081	63.1	1.4	0.0	0.5	35.0	36.2	12.1	32.3	65.0	6.8	1,224	75.8
Lee township (Calhoun)	1,219	1,210	-0.7	1,029	90.7	0.0	0.0	2.1	7.2	21.1	23.8	50.5	51.0	13.6	414	86.5
Lee township (Midland)	4,315	4,250	-1.5	4,255	92.6	3.5	0.0	0.9	3.0	21.2	14.5	40.1	55.9	15.8	1,595	86.3
Leelanau township (Leelanau)	2,027	2,029	0.1	2,007	89.3	1.1	0.0	5.3	4.2	10.9	41.4	59.6	22.8	51.3	938	91.3
Leighton township (Allegan)	4,930	5,966	21.0	5,692	92.8	0.4	2.9	1.0	2.9	30.3	9.2	33.6	36.4	29.8	1,933	92.8
Leland CDP	377	-	-	226	92.5	0.0	1.8	0.0	5.8	6.2	39.4	64.3	2.5	59.8	134	100.0
Leland township (Leelanau)	2,043	2,041	-0.1	1,756	91.3	0.6	0.2	2.1	5.8	17.8	32.2	55.9	15.1	54.2	756	90.1
Lennon village	511	482	-5.7	520	93.3	0.2	0.8	5.2	0.6	27.9	16.0	31.5	46.2	14.7	174	86.8
Lenox township (Macomb)	10,457	10,953	4.7	10,784	81.4	11.7	0.0	4.2	2.7	24.7	9.8	37.0	48.8	13.6	3,225	92.8
Leonard village	403	409	1.5	359	97.5	0.0	0.0	0.8	1.7	23.1	19.5	40.7	36.1	32.5	141	91.5
Leoni township (Jackson)	13,785	13,637	-1.1	13,660	93.7	0.6	0.4	2.0	3.2	23.0	19.5	42.9	41.9	17.6	5,678	89.0

1 May be of any race.

Table A. All Places — **Population and Housing**

STATE City, town, township, borough, or CDP (county if applicable)	Population				Race and Hispanic or Latino origin (percent)					Age (percent)			Educational attainment of persons age 25 and older		Occupied housing units	
	2010 census total population	2019 estimated population	Percent change 2010–2019	ACS total population estimate 2015–2019	White alone, not Hispanic or Latino	Black alone, not Hispanic or Latino	Asian alone, not Hispanic or Latino	All other races or 2 or more races, not Hispanic or Latino	Hispanic or Latino[1]	Under 18 years old	Age 65 years and older	Median age	Percent High school diploma or less	Percent Bachelor's degree or more	Total	Percent with a computer
	1	2	3	4	5	6	7	8	9	10	11	12	13	14	15	16
MICHIGAN—Con.																
Leonidas township (St. Joseph)	1,185	1,190	0.4	1,023	95.3	0.9	0.6	1.7	1.6	23.5	23.5	47.3	60.2	9.5	399	81.5
Leroy township (Calhoun).	3,711	3,742	0.8	3,709	87.6	1.4	1.1	6.3	3.6	22.4	22.5	45.3	35.6	27.2	1,429	89.3
Leroy township (Ingham)..	3,530	3,674	4.1	3,642	95.3	0.0	0.0	2.5	2.2	24.8	12.1	39.7	42.4	24.9	1,353	88.8
Le Roy village	256	252	-1.6	305	95.7	1.0	0.0	1.6	1.6	26.2	20.0	36.8	56.2	13.5	101	92.1
Le Roy township (Osceola)	1,210	1,212	0.2	1,551	97.5	1.0	0.0	0.8	0.7	29.0	14.4	36.9	55.8	15.2	499	87.2
Leslie city & MCD (Ingham)	1,849	1,898	2.7	2,028	91.4	0.1	0.0	3.6	4.9	30.2	12.3	33.7	44.0	14.9	707	87.1
Leslie township (Ingham)..	2,391	2,440	2.0	2,494	91.1	1.6	0.0	2.5	4.9	21.3	17.4	45.6	38.9	18.7	903	88.6
Level Park-Oak Park CDP	3,409	-	-	3,833	89.5	7.0	0.0	1.6	1.8	19.4	14.4	43.2	40.8	13.3	1,608	94.3
Levering CDP	215	-	-	126	81.7	0.0	0.0	18.3	0.0	13.5	28.6	51.0	62.6	9.1	72	94.4
Lewiston CDP	1,392	-	-	1,289	97.6	0.0	0.0	2.4	0.0	12.0	32.4	58.4	62.6	11.7	653	79.6
Lexington village	1,160	1,118	-3.6	1,011	98.3	0.0	0.0	0.6	1.1	9.7	40.2	61.9	38.7	30.7	644	83.1
Lexington township (Sanilac)	3,678	3,483	-5.3	3,478	94.0	0.2	0.4	2.4	3.1	17.9	24.2	54.2	41.0	25.3	1,652	86.1
Liberty township (Jackson)	2,959	2,965	0.2	2,954	94.5	0.6	0.0	1.2	3.7	17.9	22.8	51.9	36.6	26.5	1,220	90.0
Liberty township (Wexford)	861	882	2.4	935	98.8	0.2	0.0	0.4	0.5	21.0	14.5	40.6	58.4	13.6	356	79.8
Lilley township (Newaygo)	797	813	2.0	705	91.8	2.3	0.0	4.8	1.1	14.9	29.9	56.3	57.8	10.1	345	80.6
Lima township (Washtenaw)	3,317	3,958	19.3	3,880	92.3	0.4	2.2	2.0	3.1	24.4	16.5	41.9	25.3	44.6	1,451	97.8
Limestone township (Alger)	438	414	-5.5	472	97.9	0.0	0.0	1.7	0.4	20.8	27.5	59.7	56.3	16.6	176	80.7
Lincoln village	332	314	-5.4	350	93.1	0.9	0.0	4.3	1.7	16.0	23.4	48.4	60.8	8.4	166	75.3
Lincoln township (Arenac)	946	888	-6.1	970	95.6	0.0	0.0	0.9	3.5	27.8	16.5	38.8	55.6	11.9	382	79.1
Lincoln charter township (Berrien)	14,691	14,597	-0.6	14,562	89.1	2.5	3.3	1.9	3.2	22.7	20.9	43.6	26.0	43.2	6,057	91.7
Lincoln township (Clare)...	1,816	1,805	-0.6	1,771	90.9	0.7	0.7	5.8	2.0	13.0	33.2	55.0	53.1	15.5	789	75.8
Lincoln township (Huron)..	807	754	-6.6	704	95.7	0.0	0.9	3.4	0.0	26.7	19.6	41.6	58.6	11.0	291	83.5
Lincoln township (Isabella)	2,115	2,112	-0.1	2,100	93.7	1.0	0.3	2.5	2.6	22.4	13.9	39.8	42.7	22.7	762	90.7
Lincoln township (Midland)	2,474	2,480	0.2	2,550	93.8	0.8	0.0	2.9	2.5	18.7	24.3	47.1	42.7	26.3	1,057	85.7
Lincoln township (Newaygo)	1,275	1,263	-0.9	1,158	92.7	0.5	0.0	3.9	2.9	18.9	20.6	49.0	52.5	14.0	511	73.0
Lincoln township (Osceola)	1,498	1,506	0.5	1,478	96.4	0.4	0.0	1.8	1.4	22.0	20.6	42.4	59.8	12.2	606	82.2
Lincoln Park city & MCD (Wayne)	38,085	36,321	-4.6	36,697	66.4	8.2	0.5	3.2	21.6	25.1	12.0	36.1	58.9	9.4	14,244	86.6
Linden city & MCD (Genesee)	3,991	3,939	-1.3	3,895	94.4	2.8	0.3	1.9	0.7	27.0	22.2	42.8	38.7	31.5	1,551	92.5
Litchfield city & MCD (Hillsdale)	1,369	1,331	-2.8	1,208	96.7	0.0	0.0	2.9	0.4	23.3	17.0	38.0	48.2	14.3	530	92.1
Litchfield township (Hillsdale)	1,003	985	-1.8	1,019	93.9	0.6	0.0	3.3	2.2	23.4	21.4	47.1	65.2	8.6	428	80.6
Littlefield township (Emmet)	2,985	3,054	2.3	3,022	82.5	0.1	0.0	14.0	3.5	20.5	14.7	36.4	44.4	13.9	1,217	90.1
Little Traverse township (Emmet)	2,375	2,421	1.9	2,585	95.8	0.9	0.3	2.1	1.0	20.2	19.8	45.5	29.2	36.6	1,109	93.6
Livingston township (Otsego)	2,542	2,588	1.8	2,572	92.1	0.4	1.7	5.1	0.7	20.1	18.9	42.5	37.9	27.9	960	91.1
Livonia city & MCD (Wayne)	96,857	93,665	-3.3	94,249	87.8	4.3	3.2	2.2	2.5	18.6	19.9	45.5	27.7	37.4	37,271	92.6
Locke township (Ingham)..	1,791	1,858	3.7	1,726	95.0	0.0	0.4	1.1	3.5	21.3	16.2	44.7	36.3	29.3	652	92.3
Lockport township (St. Joseph)	3,813	3,792	-0.6	3,786	88.2	3.8	1.5	4.4	2.2	22.8	13.5	41.1	41.5	25.1	1,467	88.6
Lodi township (Washtenaw)	6,041	6,579	8.9	6,501	86.7	3.8	2.6	5.9	1.0	23.3	15.2	42.3	12.3	66.1	2,210	95.6
Logan township (Mason) ..	312	322	3.2	245	98.0	0.0	1.2	0.8	0.0	8.2	44.5	62.7	45.2	15.5	123	83.7
Logan township (Ogemaw)	552	533	-3.4	675	93.5	0.0	0.0	6.5	0.0	18.4	22.5	50.4	47.5	10.9	306	70.6
London township (Monroe)	3,043	2,935	-3.5	2,946	83.0	7.9	0.6	2.2	6.3	20.8	14.7	44.7	43.5	14.6	1,094	89.9
Long Lake township (Grand Traverse)	8,659	9,417	8.8	9,321	96.1	0.0	0.1	1.3	2.5	22.6	15.0	43.8	24.6	37.4	3,589	95.2
Long Rapids township (Alpena)	1,000	980	-2.0	951	99.3	0.0	0.0	0.3	0.4	15.0	22.5	52.8	45.5	18.6	456	89.9
Loomis CDP	213	-	-	163	100.0	0.0	0.0	0.0	0.0	9.2	23.3	47.5	71.3	6.2	77	87.0
Lost Lake Woods CDP	312	-	-	340	99.7	0.0	0.0	0.0	0.3	11.2	59.7	68.4	29.2	34.2	182	86.3
Loud township (Montmorency)	293	281	-4.1	271	95.9	0.0	0.0	3.7	0.4	13.3	29.5	58.2	50.7	18.5	136	75.0
Lovells township (Crawford)	628	621	-1.1	727	96.7	0.0	1.4	1.5	0.4	10.0	32.9	60.0	40.1	28.9	356	89.9
Lowell city & MCD (Kent)..	3,788	4,171	10.1	4,096	88.4	0.5	0.6	2.8	7.7	24.9	14.9	37.8	39.0	24.4	1,579	94.6
Lowell charter township (Kent)	5,947	6,765	13.8	6,612	92.9	1.4	0.5	2.8	2.5	17.6	15.0	41.6	37.1	25.4	2,560	90.8
Ludington city & MCD (Mason)	8,074	8,108	0.4	8,069	90.5	1.2	0.2	2.4	5.8	21.0	24.0	43.9	45.1	24.0	3,603	80.5
Luna Pier city & MCD (Monroe)	1,436	1,396	-2.8	1,217	93.3	0.0	0.0	3.2	3.5	20.5	24.2	48.2	47.8	17.9	603	85.9
Lupton CDP	348	-	-	293	86.0	0.0	0.0	3.1	10.9	20.8	19.1	49.8	51.6	5.6	144	81.3
Luther village	318	324	1.9	306	93.5	0.0	2.0	0.0	4.6	25.2	16.7	38.9	71.2	2.0	103	84.5
Lyndon township (Washtenaw)	2,723	2,785	2.3	2,782	95.5	2.5	0.0	0.6	1.4	19.3	18.3	47.8	25.4	47.7	960	90.6
Lynn township (St. Clair)...	1,230	1,222	-0.7	1,035	93.7	0.6	0.0	2.1	3.6	18.6	18.0	47.3	44.9	13.6	400	87.3
Lyon charter township (Oakland)	14,557	20,975	44.1	19,744	89.0	1.3	4.4	2.4	2.8	30.1	11.3	36.9	18.2	53.4	6,744	94.5
Lyon township (Roscommon)	1,370	1,355	-1.1	1,244	95.0	1.3	0.0	3.5	0.2	12.9	33.2	60.8	32.2	30.9	631	90.2
Lyons village	792	807	1.9	935	88.9	0.9	0.0	6.7	3.5	27.3	7.5	30.0	58.7	7.2	328	90.2
Lyons township (Ionia)	3,468	3,537	2.0	3,518	93.0	0.3	0.3	4.0	2.4	27.9	15.3	37.8	58.9	13.9	1,265	85.1
McBain city & MCD (Missaukee)	666	668	0.3	659	92.0	2.6	0.0	5.5	0.0	15.8	31.9	51.6	56.4	13.6	273	82.8
McBride village	205	205	0.0	220	96.4	0.0	0.0	3.6	0.0	27.7	13.2	37.3	67.1	7.4	88	77.3

1 May be of any race.

Table A. All Places — Population and Housing

STATE City, town, township, borough, or CDP (county if applicable)	Population 2010 census total population	2019 estimated population	Percent change 2010–2019	ACS total population estimate 2015–2019	Race and Hispanic or Latino origin (percent) White alone, not Hispanic or Latino	Black alone, not Hispanic or Latino	Asian alone, not Hispanic or Latino	All other races or 2 or more races, not Hispanic or Latino	Hispanic or Latino[1]	Age (percent) Under 18 years old	Age 65 years and older	Median age	Educational attainment of persons age 25 and older Percent High school diploma or less	Percent Bachelor's degree or more	Occupied housing units Total	Percent with a computer
	1	2	3	4	5	6	7	8	9	10	11	12	13	14	15	16
MICHIGAN—Con.																
Mackinac Island city & MCD (Mackinac)	492	471	-4.3	1,072	66.9	16.9	1.4	12.5	2.3	10.6	21.5	45.6	32.0	35.8	514	87.5
Mackinaw township (Cheboygan)	539	519	-3.7	487	83.0	0.2	0.0	16.4	0.4	11.1	35.5	56.2	35.5	31.3	238	82.8
Mackinaw City village	802	795	-0.9	805	79.6	9.1	0.7	9.3	1.2	15.5	27.7	52.6	39.6	22.9	384	82.6
McKinley township (Emmet)	1,297	1,335	2.9	1,318	87.2	0.4	0.0	11.5	1.0	24.4	19.0	39.0	49.2	10.9	548	92.5
McKinley township (Huron) .	445	414	-7.0	389	94.3	0.0	0.0	2.1	3.6	13.4	25.2	55.1	52.2	12.3	179	87.2
McMillan township (Luce) .	2,692	2,488	-7.6	2,666	81.8	0.6	0.2	14.0	3.5	22.2	20.2	41.8	46.7	21.4	1,064	78.9
McMillan township (Ontonagon)	479	404	-15.7	523	97.3	0.0	0.0	2.7	0.0	15.3	25.6	53.8	48.6	22.1	232	86.2
Macomb township (Macomb)	79,574	91,574	15.1	89,230	87.4	5.3	3.0	1.7	2.6	26.0	12.8	39.6	29.6	34.4	30,210	96.4
Macon township (Lenawee)	1,482	1,448	-2.3	1,436	90.5	2.1	0.1	5.4	1.9	24.5	18.2	47.8	37.2	24.7	526	92.8
Madison charter township (Lenawee)	8,621	8,255	-4.2	8,403	69.6	12.3	0.4	4.4	13.4	20.1	15.9	38.7	55.1	13.9	2,360	90.4
Madison Heights city & MCD (Oakland)	29,694	29,886	0.6	30,120	79.7	8.4	5.8	3.0	3.1	17.6	13.9	38.5	44.0	24.0	13,186	91.6
Mancelona village	1,391	1,366	-1.8	1,574	87.0	2.7	1.4	6.4	2.6	35.6	8.9	28.7	62.3	9.3	547	89.9
Mancelona township (Antrim)	4,401	4,371	-0.7	4,350	92.7	1.0	0.5	4.0	1.8	24.6	15.1	38.5	61.3	10.7	1,637	85.4
Manchester village	2,088	2,154	3.2	1,993	95.7	0.7	0.0	2.2	1.5	19.1	25.7	47.0	26.6	39.1	1,033	88.5
Manchester township (Washtenaw)	4,567	4,741	3.8	4,732	93.2	1.2	0.4	1.5	3.7	18.4	21.3	48.9	28.1	36.2	2,047	87.3
Manistee city & MCD (Manistee)	6,226	6,114	-1.8	6,083	87.8	0.0	0.5	7.4	4.2	21.6	21.1	43.9	37.1	24.2	2,575	88.8
Manistee township (Manistee)	4,084	4,078	-0.1	4,076	75.0	14.1	0.4	6.8	3.7	10.7	26.4	47.2	52.3	16.1	1,283	83.8
Manistee Lake CDP	456	-	-	489	99.2	0.0	0.0	0.0	0.8	21.7	21.7	39.0	57.1	10.5	208	87.0
Manistique city & MCD (Schoolcraft)	3,094	2,939	-5.0	2,919	86.7	0.9	0.0	12.1	0.0	17.7	22.8	49.2	57.9	10.8	1,277	82.4
Manistique township (Schoolcraft)	1,099	1,052	-4.3	1,081	77.0	0.0	0.0	21.9	1.1	17.9	23.2	49.7	55.1	17.0	426	89.7
Manitou Beach-Devils Lake CDP	2,019	-	-	1,724	100.0	0.0	0.0	0.0	0.0	11.1	31.3	55.4	34.7	38.6	852	87.2
Manlius township (Allegan)	3,021	3,215	6.4	3,141	88.6	0.3	0.0	0.2	11.0	28.7	12.1	37.2	51.5	25.9	1,048	91.3
Mansfield township (Iron) .	241	226	-6.2	230	97.4	0.0	0.4	1.7	0.4	8.3	42.2	62.6	36.0	22.5	108	81.5
Manton city & MCD (Wexford)	1,286	1,555	20.9	1,123	92.4	0.0	1.0	4.0	2.6	22.9	13.2	35.3	60.9	10.3	470	78.9
Maple City CDP	207	-	-	113	80.5	0.0	0.0	2.7	16.8	8.8	9.7	47.4	22.8	26.1	56	78.6
Maple Forest township (Crawford)	653	653	0.0	799	92.0	0.0	0.0	4.0	4.0	18.8	19.0	48.7	52.6	9.1	317	93.7
Maple Grove township (Barry)	1,591	1,657	4.1	1,371	97.3	0.0	0.0	1.8	0.9	21.2	15.6	45.9	50.4	16.2	538	91.6
Maple Grove CDP	132	-	-	180	100.0	0.0	0.0	0.0	0.0	0.0	39.4	50.1	24.5	59.1	66	72.7
Maple Grove township (Manistee)	1,316	1,301	-1.1	1,342	87.3	3.6	0.0	3.8	5.3	17.5	21.1	46.5	54.1	13.2	488	84.6
Maple Grove township (Saginaw)	2,668	2,522	-5.5	2,543	94.8	0.5	0.0	2.2	2.5	21.8	18.4	46.3	40.8	16.1	966	89.6
Maple Rapids village	672	681	1.3	541	99.3	0.0	0.0	0.0	0.7	16.8	14.2	44.2	52.8	6.6	225	83.1
Maple Ridge township (Alpena)	1,687	1,645	-2.5	1,598	93.4	0.3	0.4	5.2	0.6	21.5	22.3	44.4	41.4	13.3	624	89.4
Maple Ridge township (Delta)	766	746	-2.6	683	93.9	0.0	0.0	4.0	2.2	16.1	23.6	46.4	44.9	17.4	320	90.3
Maple River township (Emmet)	1,348	1,383	2.6	1,394	95.6	0.9	0.4	3.2	0.0	24.0	14.6	43.4	40.5	20.1	485	91.5
Maple Valley township (Montcalm)	1,944	1,952	0.4	1,958	93.3	1.1	0.4	3.4	1.8	22.8	19.2	43.5	55.4	11.7	749	86.6
Maple Valley township (Sanilac)	1,217	1,144	-6.0	1,450	98.5	0.0	0.7	0.5	0.3	38.5	12.6	29.8	59.6	8.0	452	79.2
Marathon township (Lapeer)	4,574	4,470	-2.3	4,508	93.7	0.4	0.0	3.8	2.1	19.8	18.0	45.5	48.2	14.5	1,721	89.3
Marcellus village	1,203	1,139	-5.3	1,297	93.4	1.3	0.5	1.6	3.1	28.8	14.2	34.2	48.2	15.8	463	88.6
Marcellus township (Cass)	2,534	2,457	-3.0	2,629	94.1	0.6	0.6	2.9	1.7	22.5	15.6	42.4	47.8	18.3	998	87.7
Marengo township (Calhoun)	2,215	2,232	0.8	2,366	96.1	0.8	0.1	0.5	2.5	22.9	16.6	45.2	46.4	25.9	845	93.1
Marenisco CDP	254	-	-	134	90.3	0.0	0.0	7.5	2.2	13.4	40.3	60.5	57.4	13.0	64	76.6
Marenisco township (Gogebic)	1,724	530	-69.3	1,277	59.4	26.7	0.2	6.3	7.3	5.2	12.4	39.8	63.2	5.3	188	84.6
Marilla township (Manistee)	393	391	-0.5	336	97.6	0.0	0.3	2.1	0.0	14.6	25.9	47.4	58.4	9.3	128	88.3
Marine City city & MCD (St. Clair)	4,254	4,058	-4.6	4,102	96.3	0.0	0.0	2.3	1.3	18.4	17.5	46.1	47.3	11.3	1,801	90.6
Marion township (Charlevoix)	1,718	1,903	10.8	1,646	94.9	0.2	0.3	1.5	3.1	23.8	20.9	45.6	35.8	30.6	655	91.8
Marion township (Livingston)	10,020	11,165	11.4	10,972	95.5	0.0	1.1	1.0	2.3	22.3	15.0	42.3	30.6	32.2	3,779	95.1
Marion village	867	856	-1.3	896	96.4	0.6	1.2	0.7	1.1	22.5	19.6	37.5	56.7	13.8	362	83.7
Marion township (Osceola)	1,692	1,677	-0.9	1,678	94.0	0.3	0.7	3.9	1.1	21.5	17.5	42.7	57.1	14.9	670	84.0
Marion township (Saginaw)	923	883	-4.3	849	91.9	0.0	0.0	5.2	2.9	20.3	16.3	44.1	61.4	5.0	329	76.6
Marion township (Sanilac)	1,662	1,566	-5.8	1,589	93.0	0.4	0.2	0.8	5.7	20.8	23.0	46.2	57.8	8.7	649	84.1
Markey township (Roscommon)	2,360	2,318	-1.8	2,418	96.0	0.0	0.4	1.7	1.9	16.8	33.9	56.5	47.7	15.9	1,131	84.9
Marlette city & MCD (Sanilac)	1,877	1,767	-5.9	2,030	90.9	2.3	0.0	2.5	4.2	27.7	17.4	34.5	57.5	11.2	847	85.2
Marlette township (Sanilac)	1,761	1,652	-6.2	1,681	96.5	0.0	1.3	1.0	1.2	22.8	18.3	44.1	44.3	15.0	661	87.9

1 May be of any race.

Table A. All Places — **Population and Housing**

STATE City, town, township, borough, or CDP (county if applicable)	Population: 2010 census total population	2019 estimated population	Percent change 2010–2019	ACS total population estimate 2015–2019	Race and Hispanic or Latino origin (percent): White alone, not Hispanic or Latino	Black alone, not Hispanic or Latino	Asian alone, not Hispanic or Latino	All other races or 2 or more races, not Hispanic or Latino	Hispanic or Latino[1]	Age (percent): Under 18 years old	Age 65 years and older	Median age	Educational attainment of persons age 25 and older: Percent High school diploma or less	Percent Bachelor's degree or more	Occupied housing units: Total	Percent with a computer
	1	2	3	4	5	6	7	8	9	10	11	12	13	14	15	16
MICHIGAN—Con.																
Marquette township (Mackinac)	603	585	-3.0	660	81.1	0.3	0.2	15.9	2.6	20.3	23.6	49.1	46.5	24.2	304	91.8
Marquette city & MCD (Marquette)	21,366	20,995	-1.7	20,822	89.6	3.9	0.4	3.3	2.8	11.7	14.8	28.6	27.4	44.1	7,911	92.4
Marquette charter township (Marquett	3,895	3,896	0.0	3,917	86.8	0.9	7.1	5.2	0.0	17.5	20.8	41.7	33.1	36.3	1,588	89.8
Marshall city & MCD (Calhoun)	7,070	6,964	-1.5	6,998	94.0	0.3	1.5	0.5	3.7	21.7	23.9	42.9	33.0	35.0	3,276	86.4
Marshall township (Calhoun)	3,129	3,121	-0.3	3,123	95.6	0.4	0.0	3.2	0.8	19.7	17.8	43.8	39.4	33.0	1,257	90.6
Martin village	410	409	-0.2	435	97.0	0.0	0.0	0.5	2.5	19.8	14.3	41.8	51.5	23.1	195	84.1
Martin township (Allegan).	2,632	2,750	4.5	2,701	95.9	0.8	0.0	1.4	1.9	24.7	17.0	40.5	55.5	17.0	1,097	79.9
Martiny township (Mecosta)	1,625	1,638	0.8	1,661	95.5	0.4	0.0	1.9	2.2	17.5	25.6	56.6	50.3	16.1	652	82.4
Marysville city & MCD (St. Clair)	9,959	9,672	-2.9	9,693	93.6	0.5	0.0	1.5	4.4	22.3	20.6	43.6	35.1	26.9	4,236	89.1
Mason township (Arenac) .	863	809	-6.3	847	90.2	0.0	0.0	6.8	3.0	18.1	19.8	49.0	67.2	4.2	357	74.2
Mason township (Cass)	2,943	3,011	2.3	2,944	88.6	1.2	3.3	5.5	1.4	22.3	15.0	41.1	46.1	15.3	1,145	93.3
Mason city & MCD (Ingham)	8,254	8,458	2.5	8,487	87.1	4.2	2.5	1.7	4.5	23.1	15.7	39.0	31.5	33.2	3,436	92.9
Masonville township (Delta)	1,733	1,680	-3.1	1,493	89.6	0.0	0.2	6.4	3.8	18.8	23.8	47.6	39.9	12.7	682	87.0
Mastodon township (Iron) .	656	614	-6.4	682	96.9	0.0	0.7	0.7	1.6	10.6	38.6	60.0	54.7	20.4	348	75.3
Matchwood township (Ontonagon)	94	78	-17.0	83	84.3	3.6	0.0	0.0	12.0	0.0	41.0	62.6	63.4	13.4	46	63.0
Mathias township (Alger) ..	554	519	-6.3	345	95.4	0.0	0.0	4.6	0.0	12.8	38.6	57.8	58.2	16.4	144	84.7
Mattawan village	1,991	1,982	-0.5	2,333	87.3	0.0	0.7	5.7	6.3	29.5	13.3	36.5	36.6	20.5	906	87.9
Matteson township (Branch)	1,218	1,196	-1.8	1,078	96.7	0.0	0.0	3.3	0.0	18.6	21.0	47.9	56.6	8.5	455	89.2
Maybee village	562	532	-5.3	683	91.9	0.0	2.3	1.3	4.4	34.1	5.3	32.9	39.5	19.6	229	90.8
Mayfield township (Grand Traverse)	1,550	1,685	8.7	1,612	92.1	0.0	1.4	4.0	2.6	25.6	14.6	36.9	38.4	21.7	565	91.9
Mayfield township (Lapeer)	7,966	7,877	-1.1	7,909	92.4	0.4	0.8	2.8	3.6	20.4	22.8	46.2	41.8	17.6	3,190	92.2
Mayville village ..	950	885	-6.8	905	90.6	2.7	0.3	0.7	5.7	19.4	25.6	43.7	54.6	12.4	411	78.1
Meade township (Huron) ..	717	672	-6.3	622	100.0	0.0	0.0	0.0	0.0	17.5	21.9	51.3	58.2	8.7	283	89.0
Meade township (Mason) .	179	182	1.7	228	80.7	0.0	0.0	16.2	3.1	22.8	17.1	41.3	47.2	25.4	84	84.5
Mecosta village	457	454	-0.7	404	89.4	3.7	0.0	5.4	1.5	17.8	18.1	39.5	74.7	8.2	147	76.2
Mecosta township (Mecosta)	2,613	2,664	2.0	2,660	94.2	1.8	0.2	2.3	1.5	21.1	19.5	41.3	50.4	21.1	995	90.5
Medina township (Lenawee)	1,090	1,094	0.4	985	96.0	1.5	0.0	0.8	1.6	22.3	18.3	45.4	49.1	15.6	382	89.3
Mellen township (Menominee)	1,151	1,095	-4.9	1,007	96.7	0.1	0.4	0.2	2.6	15.8	27.6	53.5	50.5	15.0	464	85.3
Melrose township (Charlevoix)	1,403	1,407	0.3	1,356	96.8	0.4	0.2	1.5	1.1	21.3	17.0	44.6	35.3	32.2	592	88.2
Melvin village	180	168	-6.7	184	96.7	0.0	0.0	0.0	3.3	21.7	9.8	37.0	68.5	4.7	71	85.9
Melvindale city & MCD (Wayne)	10,727	10,248	-4.5	10,348	55.9	15.0	1.6	3.6	23.8	31.0	9.8	31.5	61.8	12.5	3,724	82.3
Memphis city	1,203	1,177	-2.2	1,236	98.9	0.0	0.0	0.7	0.3	20.6	11.0	44.1	48.8	12.9	509	84.5
Memphis city (Macomb) ...	841	832	-1.1	747	98.9	0.0	0.0	0.5	0.5	15.0	13.1	46.8	53.6	8.3	351	84.6
Memphis city (St. Clair).....	362	345	-4.7	489	99.0	0.0	0.0	1.0	0.0	29.0	7.8	36.3	38.5	22.6	158	84.2
Mendon village	876	851	-2.9	939	94.8	0.0	0.2	0.5	4.5	31.9	9.3	32.6	39.0	16.6	330	97.3
Mendon township (St. Joseph)	2,717	2,692	-0.9	2,684	94.8	0.4	0.1	0.9	3.9	25.8	18.3	41.1	43.7	15.4	1,040	91.1
Menominee city & MCD (Menominee)	8,593	8,029	-6.6	8,150	94.1	0.5	0.1	2.8	2.5	19.4	21.0	43.5	48.9	16.3	4,018	80.5
Menominee township (Menominee)	3,491	3,339	-4.4	3,365	95.5	0.0	1.0	2.4	1.1	13.1	28.4	55.1	50.0	19.4	1,635	85.1
Mentor township (Cheboygan)	818	790	-3.4	743	93.1	0.0	0.4	6.1	0.4	14.5	26.0	51.5	41.2	20.4	342	84.2
Mentor township (Oscoda)	1,133	1,069	-5.6	969	95.5	0.0	1.2	1.4	1.9	18.8	28.0	49.0	41.9	15.1	479	76.8
Meridian charter township (Ingham)......................	39,690	43,196	8.8	42,824	71.5	4.3	15.4	4.5	4.3	21.3	16.5	36.7	12.7	67.1	18,210	95.4
Merrill township (Newaygo)	667	672	0.7	562	86.1	11.7	0.0	1.2	0.9	17.4	26.2	50.7	68.6	8.1	286	70.3
Merrill village	777	723	-6.9	761	88.3	0.5	0.0	2.4	8.8	27.2	14.5	37.4	52.3	16.0	304	80.6
Merritt township (Bay).......	1,441	1,369	-5.0	1,322	96.6	0.2	0.8	1.4	1.1	15.5	23.2	51.8	52.1	18.1	554	87.5
Mesick village	394	405	2.8	366	88.8	0.0	0.5	8.7	1.9	19.4	17.8	45.8	62.6	9.7	142	79.6
Metamora village	565	563	-0.4	534	91.2	0.0	1.1	0.2	7.5	21.5	12.5	41.2	32.4	22.5	226	97.3
Metamora township (Lapeer)	4,249	4,279	0.7	4,264	93.8	0.0	1.2	2.1	2.8	20.8	17.3	48.7	32.3	27.7	1,660	92.8
Metz township (Presque Isle)	302	286	-5.3	234	93.6	0.0	0.0	3.8	2.6	9.4	40.2	62.2	72.1	7.8	129	62.8
Meyer township (Menominee)	1,004	955	-4.9	1,042	90.8	0.0	0.4	6.4	2.4	20.6	23.8	45.4	56.7	11.0	445	85.4
Michiana village	182	181	-0.5	200	92.0	0.0	5.0	0.0	3.0	8.0	53.0	65.9	5.0	80.0	110	91.8
Michigamme CDP.............	271	-	-	236	99.2	0.0	0.0	0.0	0.8	12.7	35.2	58.8	26.0	28.2	116	81.0
Michigamme township (Marquette)	343	342	-0.3	295	98.0	0.0	0.0	1.0	1.0	10.8	37.3	59.7	29.0	30.3	146	82.2
Michigan Center CDP.......	4,672	-	-	4,797	95.8	1.1	0.0	0.8	2.4	19.5	20.5	43.5	37.1	17.9	2,145	88.7
Middle Branch township (Osceola)	843	855	1.4	769	97.7	0.7	0.0	1.4	0.3	11.8	21.5	52.0	55.1	10.8	372	75.5
Middlebury township (Shiawassee)	1,515	1,469	-3.0	1,626	91.9	0.4	2.6	0.8	4.3	20.7	17.3	42.3	43.3	17.7	625	86.7
Middletown CDP..............	897	-	-	834	90.6	0.0	1.3	1.9	6.1	23.3	16.9	51.4	41.2	7.4	371	93.0
Middleville village	3,323	3,475	4.6	3,412	92.8	0.6	0.6	1.0	5.0	33.4	6.9	28.2	46.3	20.6	1,239	87.0
Midland city	41,866	41,701	-0.4	41,920	87.6	2.0	4.0	2.6	3.8	21.7	17.1	38.7	27.1	44.9	17,665	91.5
Midland city (Bay)........	149	155	4.0	206	93.2	0.0	0.0	0.0	6.8	30.6	0.0	31.8	29.4	18.2	56	100.0
Midland city (Midland) ...	41,717	41,546	-0.4	41,714	87.6	2.0	4.0	2.6	3.8	21.6	17.2	38.8	27.1	45.0	17,609	91.4
Midland charter township (Midland)	2,281	2,217	-2.8	2,355	94.0	0.0	0.0	0.2	5.9	23.8	15.5	42.1	35.0	29.7	944	93.2

1 May be of any race.

Table A. All Places — **Population and Housing**

STATE City, town, township, borough, or CDP (county if applicable)	Population				Race and Hispanic or Latino origin (percent)					Age (percent)			Educational attainment of persons age 25 and older		Occupied housing units	
	2010 census total population	2019 estimated population	Percent change 2010–2019	ACS total population estimate 2015–2019	White alone, not Hispanic or Latino	Black alone, not Hispanic or Latino	Asian alone, not Hispanic or Latino	All other races or 2 or more races, not Hispanic or Latino	Hispanic or Latino[1]	Under 18 years old	Age 65 years and older	Median age	Percent High school diploma or less	Percent Bachelor's degree or more	Total	Percent with a computer
	1	2	3	4	5	6	7	8	9	10	11	12	13	14	15	16
MICHIGAN—Con.																
Mikado township (Alcona)	947	902	-4.8	946	94.7	1.0	0.0	2.9	1.5	18.5	19.7	46.7	55.7	10.4	413	83.5
Milan township (Monroe)	1,599	1,520	-4.9	1,555	94.9	0.3	0.0	3.4	1.4	15.9	15.6	48.5	48.6	18.8	629	88.1
Milan city	5,838	6,042	3.5	6,107	91.6	1.9	0.0	1.7	4.7	30.6	13.1	36.9	30.9	28.5	2,288	92.4
Milan city (Monroe)	2,069	2,088	0.9	2,170	91.1	1.8	0.0	2.4	4.7	29.7	17.2	39.5	35.1	17.6	847	92.3
Milan city (Washtenaw)	3,769	3,954	4.9	3,937	91.9	2.1	0.0	1.3	4.7	31.1	10.8	36.1	28.5	34.7	1,441	92.5
Milford village	6,175	6,515	5.5	6,499	94.9	0.8	0.5	2.4	1.4	24.7	17.4	43.8	21.5	46.8	2,673	97.6
Milford charter township (Oakland)	15,739	16,905	7.4	16,756	93.7	1.0	1.3	2.0	2.0	22.5	19.5	46.8	24.8	43.3	6,535	94.3
Millbrook township (Mecosta)	1,113	1,116	0.3	1,147	99.0	0.0	0.0	0.0	1.0	33.0	17.3	39.9	58.9	14.6	392	82.1
Millen township (Alcona)	403	388	-3.7	382	97.4	0.0	0.0	2.6	0.0	9.9	38.5	61.5	56.3	14.0	222	68.9
Millersburg village	206	194	-5.8	215	82.3	1.9	0.0	7.4	8.4	26.5	15.8	36.3	44.4	16.1	75	81.3
Millington village	1,072	997	-7.0	1,120	92.9	1.2	4.2	0.2	1.5	27.2	14.4	36.4	42.7	15.3	466	89.1
Millington township (Tuscola)	4,354	4,066	-6.6	4,131	96.1	0.3	1.1	0.7	1.8	17.8	18.9	47.5	48.8	15.7	1,677	91.3
Mills township (Midland)	1,939	1,921	-0.9	1,970	96.9	0.0	0.2	0.7	2.2	18.2	16.6	45.4	45.2	16.8	776	88.3
Mills township (Ogemaw)	4,286	4,172	-2.7	4,145	94.8	0.1	0.0	3.2	1.9	21.0	21.7	46.5	58.0	7.0	1,838	83.2
Milton township (Antrim)	2,204	2,181		2,545	88.6	0.1	0.0	1.6	9.7	18.4	26.9	52.5	27.8	43.4	1,068	91.7
Milton township (Cass)	3,886	3,928	1.1	3,885	88.9	1.1	0.6	1.8	7.7	21.3	19.4	47.6	39.7	26.7	1,500	92.5
Minden township (Sanilac)	545	515	-5.5	590	93.2	0.0	0.0	0.8	5.9	28.0	13.7	40.2	60.2	6.0	234	88.5
Minden City village	197	184	-6.6	150	100.0	0.0	0.0	0.0	0.0	22.7	26.0	50.8	59.3	7.1	69	76.8
Mio CDP	1,826	-	-	1,743	94.3	0.7	0.3	2.8	1.9	21.3	18.7	41.4	49.8	14.9	815	75.1
Mitchell township (Alcona)	350	336	-4.0	262	98.9	0.0	0.0	1.1	0.0	5.3	46.2	63.9	55.7	14.3	147	83.7
Moffatt township (Arenac)	1,182	1,105	-6.5	1,144	91.0	1.0	2.0	0.4	5.6	15.3	30.2	55.2	47.8	17.7	538	86.6
Moltke township (Presque Isle)	296	280	-5.4	263	94.3	0.0	0.8	4.9	0.0	8.0	36.9	57.9	55.8	12.5	121	78.5
Monitor charter township (Bay)	10,735	10,456	-2.6	10,503	93.4	0.0	0.3	0.9	5.4	19.5	26.4	49.2	33.2	26.5	4,459	89.2
Monroe city & MCD (Monroe)	20,676	19,552	-5.4	19,775	86.1	5.0	0.7	4.1	4.1	23.2	14.9	37.6	43.2	20.9	8,219	88.2
Monroe charter township (Monroe)	14,534	14,183	-2.4	14,196	92.6	2.2	0.8	1.9	2.5	22.0	18.8	41.7	48.1	19.4	5,855	87.9
Monroe township (Newaygo)	320	323	0.9	368	91.8	2.2	0.5	0.5	4.9	21.2	18.8	50.5	62.5	13.2	150	83.3
Montague city & MCD (Muskegon)	2,361	2,361	0.0	2,636	85.2	0.3	0.0	1.3	13.1	27.2	17.1	38.9	38.5	21.6	1,083	85.7
Montague township (Muskegon)	1,608	1,631	1.4	1,469	87.9	2.1	0.0	1.4	8.6	18.0	23.4	47.0	43.8	15.3	563	88.6
Montcalm township (Montcalm)	3,350	3,408	1.7	3,378	94.9	0.0	1.9	2.0	1.2	17.5	21.0	48.4	46.8	13.2	1,437	80.0
Monterey township (Allegan)	2,345	2,458	4.8	2,633	88.0	1.7	0.0	1.2	9.2	26.7	11.6	37.0	58.0	10.1	931	84.7
Montgomery village	339	331	-2.4	393	96.4	0.0	0.0	1.3	2.3	28.5	12.2	36.9	64.1	8.0	138	71.0
Montmorency township (Montmorency)	1,121	1,068	-4.7	977	95.7	0.0	1.4	1.9	0.9	11.9	45.8	62.6	45.7	22.7	476	83.0
Montrose city & MCD (Genesee)	1,657	1,549	-6.5	1,660	88.4	2.3	0.4	2.3	6.7	25.2	16.1	41.2	44.8	15.7	672	86.8
Montrose charter township (Genesee)	6,223	5,924	-4.8	5,953	93.3	1.1	0.1	4.0	1.5	19.2	21.3	48.5	52.3	12.4	2,162	92.0
Moore township (Sanilac)	1,203	1,129	-6.2	1,150	98.8	0.4	0.2	0.0	0.6	26.3	20.5	44.7	65.5	11.2	444	84.0
Moorland township (Muskegon)	1,579	1,694	7.3	1,554	91.3	0.3	1.1	1.9	5.3	23.5	12.6	41.7	49.7	7.7	554	90.3
Moran township (Mackinac)	1,013	974	-3.8	799	71.2	0.3	0.0	25.0	3.5	18.0	27.0	57.2	31.1	29.1	370	92.7
Morenci city & MCD (Lenawee)	2,220	2,147	-3.3	2,298	92.3	0.0	0.7	3.9	3.1	27.1	18.0	36.7	56.0	12.6	922	91.5
Morley village	493	493	0.0	529	89.4	1.1	0.2	3.4	5.9	19.8	17.0	44.9	66.6	9.2	193	78.2
Morrice village	927	910	-1.8	1,119	91.1	0.0	0.5	2.5	5.9	30.7	11.6	37.0	42.9	17.6	394	94.7
Morton township (Mecosta)	4,311	4,333	0.5	4,335	96.3	0.4	0.0	1.6	1.7	15.8	37.3	57.8	36.2	29.9	1,861	90.0
Moscow township (Hillsdale)	1,472	1,445	-1.8	1,567	93.9	0.0	0.0	1.1	5.0	25.5	17.4	39.8	49.5	11.1	592	90.0
Mottville township (St. Joseph)	1,437	1,430	-0.5	1,504	86.6	0.4	1.4	3.9	7.7	20.3	14.6	40.7	64.9	6.8	607	87.6
Mount Clemens city & MCD (Macomb)	16,312	16,163	-0.9	16,315	68.4	24.6	0.1	4.4	2.5	19.7	15.0	39.9	48.7	16.4	6,853	82.3
Mount Forest township (Bay)	1,390	1,369	-1.5	1,308	97.2	0.0	0.0	1.9	0.8	20.6	17.8	46.6	57.3	9.2	542	79.7
Mount Haley township (Midland)	1,678	1,652	-1.5	1,853	94.8	0.4	0.2	3.2	1.5	26.2	15.2	38.2	39.4	24.9	677	85.2
Mount Morris city & MCD (Genesee)	3,041	2,842	-6.5	2,881	77.3	16.6	1.1	1.6	3.4	23.2	10.8	33.0	50.6	8.0	1,270	87.3
Mount Morris township (Genesee)	21,580	20,336	-5.8	20,528	52.5	35.5	0.2	7.6	4.3	24.9	15.4	36.1	51.0	11.2	8,247	86.5
Mount Pleasant city & MCD (Isabella)	26,032	24,797	-4.7	25,629	82.6	4.0	3.3	5.5	4.7	11.6	9.0	22.5	28.5	44.5	7,963	93.8
Mueller township (Schoolcraft)	234	223	-4.7	212	97.2	0.0	0.5	2.4	0.0	6.6	49.5	64.5	51.3	21.0	99	82.8
Muir village	604	611	1.2	733	85.7	0.8	0.3	6.7	6.5	33.4	12.4	32.1	55.1	5.3	256	82.0
Mullett township (Cheboygan)	1,312	1,265	-3.6	1,178	94.0	0.0	0.0	5.8	0.3	18.2	29.1	52.2	39.5	29.6	493	90.3
Mulliken village	553	561	1.4	519	92.9	0.2	0.6	5.0	1.3	17.0	17.9	48.0	44.1	14.6	211	96.7
Mundy township (Genesee)	15,092	14,473	-4.1	14,522	87.0	6.9	1.9	2.2	2.0	21.5	20.1	46.2	35.4	23.7	6,102	92.2
Munising city & MCD (Alger)	2,346	2,203	-6.1	2,200	89.1	0.6	0.0	8.6	1.6	20.4	23.3	45.7	42.4	20.0	799	80.2
Munising township (Alger)	2,992	2,895	-3.2	2,908	67.8	23.0	0.2	6.4	2.6	11.1	16.3	38.7	73.8	8.0	603	84.9
Munro township (Cheboygan)	571	550	-3.7	579	93.8	0.0	0.0	5.5	0.7	6.7	36.8	59.2	37.2	34.3	309	84.8
Muskegon city & MCD (Muskegon)	38,399	36,565	-4.8	37,633	51.6	31.9	0.2	6.6	9.7	21.8	13.8	35.8	50.6	13.0	13,952	82.7

1 May be of any race.

Table A. All Places — **Population and Housing**

STATE City, town, township, borough, or CDP (county if applicable)	Population				Race and Hispanic or Latino origin (percent)					Age (percent)			Educational attainment of persons age 25 and older		Occupied housing units	
	2010 census total population	2019 estimated population	Percent change 2010–2019	ACS total population estimate 2015–2019	White alone, not Hispanic or Latino	Black alone, not Hispanic or Latino	Asian alone, not Hispanic or Latino	All other races or 2 or more races, not Hispanic or Latino	Hispanic or Latino[1]	Under 18 years old	Age 65 years and older	Median age	Percent High school diploma or less	Percent Bachelor's degree or more	Total	Percent with a computer
	1	2	3	4	5	6	7	8	9	10	11	12	13	14	15	16
MICHIGAN—Con.																
Muskegon charter township (Muskegon)....	17,820	18,000	1.0	17,878	85.9	4.1	0.2	4.4	5.4	23.1	17.4	38.3	48.7	12.9	6,785	84.8
Muskegon Heights city & MCD (Muskegon)...........	10,852	10,736	-1.1	10,748	16.2	75.4	0.1	5.1	3.2	28.7	11.5	30.6	58.9	7.2	4,040	76.8
Mussey township (St. Clair).................	4,206	4,092	-2.7	4,098	84.2	0.2	0.0	3.9	11.7	22.6	13.5	40.9	54.4	11.9	1,581	93.0
Nadeau township (Menominee)................	1,160	1,109	-4.4	1,088	97.0	1.2	0.0	1.2	0.6	14.2	31.0	52.4	52.1	16.8	514	80.0
Nahma township (Delta)...	493	478	-3.0	452	95.6	0.0	0.0	4.4	0.0	8.4	39.2	59.8	49.6	17.1	252	67.9
Napoleon CDP................	1,258	-	-	975	97.2	0.0	0.0	1.5	1.2	24.6	12.0	39.5	55.5	11.3	397	88.4
Napoleon township (Jackson).................	6,779	6,767	-0.2	6,758	94.2	2.1	0.0	1.4	2.3	21.5	19.9	47.9	39.8	26.8	2,879	88.9
Nashville village.............	1,623	1,684	3.8	1,585	92.4	0.0	0.2	4.7	2.6	24.2	16.7	38.2	58.7	11.9	670	87.5
Negaunee city & MCD (Marquette)...............	4,568	4,525	-0.9	4,547	96.2	0.4	0.1	3.1	0.2	25.8	17.6	36.1	34.7	31.4	1,890	84.6
Negaunee township (Marquette)...............	3,088	3,113	0.8	3,115	94.1	0.0	0.0	3.8	2.1	26.3	13.5	39.0	28.2	33.9	1,089	94.5
Nelson township (Kent)....	4,774	5,135	7.6	5,076	93.9	1.1	0.0	1.9	3.2	24.1	10.0	39.5	44.8	18.4	1,836	94.9
Nessen City CDP............	97	-	-	103	85.4	0.0	0.0	14.6	0.0	14.6	29.1	48.8	43.2	6.8	40	85.0
Nester township (Roscommon)...............	293	297	1.4	176	98.3	0.0	0.0	0.0	1.7	4.5	47.2	63.8	55.8	10.9	91	73.6
Newark township (Gratiot)	1,093	1,047	-4.2	1,137	86.5	3.7	0.0	5.5	4.4	24.6	12.8	36.8	59.4	9.2	412	89.1
Newaygo city & MCD (Newaygo).................	1,988	2,067	4.0	2,063	93.7	1.5	0.0	1.7	3.1	25.5	11.6	34.7	46.1	14.8	879	84.0
New Baltimore city & MCD (Macomb).................	12,084	12,347	2.2	12,358	92.2	3.2	0.4	1.9	2.3	25.2	14.1	40.3	32.3	28.3	4,672	93.3
Newberg township (Cass)	1,631	1,633	0.1	1,468	97.0	0.7	0.3	1.4	0.6	14.9	23.8	52.3	55.2	11.8	646	86.7
Newberry village.............	1,519	1,397	-8.0	1,368	85.2	0.8	0.4	10.1	3.6	22.1	22.6	40.2	45.1	16.6	596	78.2
New Buffalo city & MCD (Berrien).................	1,885	1,868	-0.9	1,714	86.5	0.0	4.3	0.2	9.0	18.3	22.8	50.8	36.9	30.1	829	88.5
New Buffalo township (Berrien).................	2,384	2,435	2.1	2,318	91.8	1.7	1.0	0.6	4.8	14.5	37.0	58.6	19.4	54.4	1,089	90.4
New Era village................	451	440	-2.4	472	92.4	0.0	0.0	1.3	6.4	23.9	23.7	43.1	29.1	38.7	175	92.0
Newfield township (Oceana)..................	2,401	2,377		2,175	97.8	0.4	0.1	0.0	1.4	21.6	18.7	46.6	57.5	9.7	855	86.5
New Haven township (Gratiot).................	1,009	976	-3.3	1,011	97.4	0.5	0.0	1.5	0.6	24.5	19.3	46.8	50.8	13.7	412	78.9
New Haven village..........	4,645	4,907	5.6	4,785	86.0	8.1	0.0	4.7	1.2	33.4	5.2	31.5	40.8	17.5	1,532	93.9
New Haven township (Shiawassee)...............	1,329	1,283	-3.5	1,137	95.4	0.0	0.3	2.1	2.2	17.3	20.6	50.8	37.6	17.8	472	93.4
Newkirk township (Lake)...	630	654	3.8	736	91.2	0.0	0.8	0.0	8.0	15.9	18.9	48.6	65.7	7.7	292	78.1
New Lothrop village..........	581	554	-4.6	628	87.3	6.8	0.5	3.8	1.6	27.2	14.8	33.5	33.3	17.3	245	87.3
Newton township (Calhoun).................	2,548	2,567	0.7	2,555	96.2	0.0	1.4	1.2	1.1	17.9	20.5	49.9	36.3	24.4	1,036	91.9
Newton township (Mackinac)................	427	416	-2.6	411	81.3	6.8	0.0	11.9	0.0	15.1	35.0	54.6	50.8	21.9	204	85.8
New Troy CDP.................	497	-	-	487	95.7	0.0	0.0	2.9	1.4	23.2	9.0	44.4	53.1	18.2	214	88.3
Niles city & MCD (Berrien)	11,596	11,149	-3.9	11,211	79.9	8.8	0.9	4.7	5.7	24.8	15.0	36.1	50.0	14.4	4,811	83.3
Niles city (Cass).............	-	-	-	-	-	-	-	-	-	-	-	-	-	-	-	-
Niles township (Berrien) ...	14,160	13,801	-2.5	13,880	83.9	6.6	0.4	3.6	5.5	22.4	18.8	41.4	43.2	17.8	5,758	91.0
Noble township (Branch) ..	518	512	-1.2	457	92.6	0.0	3.1	0.2	4.2	18.4	23.0	43.9	51.3	18.4	182	85.7
Norman township (Manistee).................	1,547	1,541	-0.4	1,390	96.3	0.1	0.0	2.5	1.1	14.1	28.0	51.5	55.9	12.1	561	84.1
North Adams village	477	461	-3.4	566	96.5	0.2	0.0	2.8	0.5	27.2	11.3	34.8	56.5	13.5	208	78.8
North Allis township (Presque Isle)................	521	490	-6.0	338	92.3	0.0	0.0	6.2	1.5	14.5	29.9	55.5	55.4	11.2	170	75.9
North Branch village.........	1,033	1,006	-2.6	1,038	91.2	0.2	0.0	5.1	3.5	23.8	19.4	39.9	53.2	9.9	475	85.5
North Branch township (Lapeer)..................	3,644	3,535	-3.0	3,575	93.3	1.0	0.0	1.7	4.1	21.4	18.2	40.3	49.6	20.0	1,493	89.0
Northfield township (Washtenaw)...............	8,245	8,673	5.2	8,636	92.2	0.3	0.8	2.9	3.8	20.1	14.7	40.2	32.3	35.4	3,395	92.1
North Muskegon city & MCD (Muskegon)..........	3,801	3,793	-0.2	3,790	90.4	1.8	0.4	2.2	5.2	23.4	21.3	44.6	16.4	46.8	1,592	92.1
North Plains township (Ionia)..................	1,279	1,307	2.2	1,290	96.2	0.5	0.0	1.6	1.7	24.4	13.9	39.1	53.3	9.8	457	84.0
Northport village	526	525	-0.2	457	87.1	0.0	0.0	3.3	9.6	9.6	50.5	65.1	20.1	50.8	247	86.6
North Shade township (Gratiot).................	665	634	-4.7	586	95.2	0.0	0.0	0.0	4.8	16.4	17.1	45.3	46.4	15.6	257	89.1
North Star township (Gratiot).................	874	837	-4.2	854	95.8	0.0	0.2	1.3	2.7	21.0	18.7	43.5	55.3	13.2	364	87.1
Northview CDP................	14,541	-	-	15,394	87.6	4.6	1.4	3.3	3.0	21.2	16.5	40.6	30.8	35.6	6,451	92.0
Northville city.................	5,979	5,958	-0.4	6,007	89.5	0.1	5.0	2.7	2.7	22.4	18.5	46.7	16.1	65.9	2,528	95.1
Northville city (Oakland) ...	3,240	3,281	1.3	3,313	88.7	0.0	7.2	0.0	4.1	22.2	15.3	45.1	13.7	66.7	1,370	98.0
Northville city (Wayne)......	2,739	2,677	-2.3	2,694	90.5	0.3	2.2	6.1	1.0	22.7	22.5	48.7	19.1	64.9	1,158	91.7
Northville township (Wayne)..................	28,571	29,342	2.7	29,069	75.7	2.3	15.3	3.5	3.2	24.4	18.2	44.2	13.0	66.6	11,302	95.7
Norton Shores city & MCD (Muskegon)................	23,998	24,664	2.8	24,467	88.7	3.4	0.9	3.5	3.5	22.4	20.3	42.1	30.6	32.0	9,901	90.7
Norvell township (Jackson).................	2,961	2,954	-0.2	2,961	98.8	0.1	0.0	0.4	0.7	16.3	27.6	54.0	49.5	15.0	1,295	95.3
Norway city & MCD (Dickinson)................	2,859	2,748	-3.9	2,774	94.9	0.1	1.1	2.3	1.5	15.5	25.9	52.3	33.9	27.0	1,462	84.3
Norway township (Dickinson)................	1,475	1,425	-3.4	1,527	94.9	0.0	0.3	2.6	2.3	16.7	22.7	46.6	43.3	27.1	639	88.1
Norwich township (Missaukee)................	611	627	2.6	621	95.2	0.0	0.0	4.8	0.0	18.2	22.5	47.8	57.8	4.4	254	79.9
Norwich township (Newaygo).................	607	606	-0.2	497	90.5	4.2	1.0	3.8	0.4	20.1	16.9	47.9	41.1	29.0	205	87.3
Norwood CDP................	142	-	-	195	84.1	0.0	0.0	3.1	12.8	14.4	31.3	50.3	38.8	40.1	85	100.0
Norwood township (Charlevoix)................	723	724	0.1	707	93.6	0.1	0.0	2.4	3.8	12.7	31.8	54.7	30.1	40.2	341	89.1

1 May be of any race.

Table A. All Places — **Population and Housing**

STATE City, town, township, borough, or CDP (county if applicable)	Population				Race and Hispanic or Latino origin (percent)					Age (percent)			Educational attainment of persons age 25 and older		Occupied housing units	
	2010 census total population	2019 estimated population	Percent change 2010–2019	ACS total population estimate 2015–2019	White alone, not Hispanic or Latino	Black alone, not Hispanic or Latino	Asian alone, not Hispanic or Latino	All other races or 2 or more races, not Hispanic or Latino	Hispanic or Latino[1]	Under 18 years old	Age 65 years and older	Median age	Percent High school diploma or less	Percent Bachelor's degree or more	Total	Percent with a computer
	1	2	3	4	5	6	7	8	9	10	11	12	13	14	15	16
MICHIGAN—Con.																
Nottawa township (Isabella)	2,282	2,266	-0.7	2,236	95.7	0.0	0.0	4.2	0.2	21.9	16.6	42.9	54.0	16.3	856	87.6
Nottawa township (St. Joseph)	3,854	3,884	0.8	3,878	96.2	2.2	0.0	0.9	0.7	25.5	17.0	41.6	41.7	21.4	1,397	83.0
Novesta township (Tuscola)	1,482	1,393	-6.0	1,322	97.4	0.0	0.0	0.5	2.1	16.9	23.8	48.5	59.7	6.6	589	81.7
Novi city & MCD (Oakland)	55,232	60,896	10.3	60,014	61.7	7.6	23.8	2.8	4.2	24.2	13.5	38.6	16.9	60.6	23,471	96.2
Novi township (Oakland)	150	151	0.7	158	74.7	0.0	2.5	10.8	12.0	14.6	22.8	54.2	10.1	65.5	61	98.4
Nunda township (Cheboygan)	1,042	1,018	-2.3	1,056	92.0	0.0	1.2	6.3	0.6	17.5	18.6	47.3	61.1	11.7	415	84.1
Oakfield township (Kent)	5,781	6,399	10.7	6,277	92.5	3.2	0.0	0.4	4.0	22.3	15.2	43.9	36.9	22.0	2,327	95.1
Oak Hill CDP	569	-	-	617	100.0	0.0	0.0	0.0	0.0	25.4	20.6	39.6	49.0	12.6	218	80.7
Oakland charter township (Oakland)	16,779	19,547	16.5	19,115	85.3	1.3	7.2	2.2	4.0	27.3	14.4	42.8	15.8	62.4	6,387	97.3
Oakley village	292	274	-6.2	329	88.1	0.6	0.6	0.0	10.6	31.0	19.8	37.3	53.5	11.3	135	84.4
Oak Park city & MCD (Oakland)	29,408	29,431	0.1	29,726	36.6	55.5	1.6	4.2	2.0	20.3	15.7	37.8	29.7	32.0	12,107	90.1
Oceola township (Livingston)	11,973	14,812	23.7	14,358	94.8	0.4	1.0	1.8	2.0	25.7	15.5	40.4	27.5	39.0	5,026	97.4
Ocqueoc township (Presque Isle)	655	620	-5.3	622	96.0	0.0	0.0	1.3	2.7	14.1	39.4	59.5	50.3	22.8	303	76.6
Oden CDP	363	-	-	424	97.4	0.0	0.0	0.0	2.6	23.3	3.8	26.3	38.9	4.2	202	95.0
Odessa township (Ionia)	3,782	3,827	1.2	3,812	87.4	4.0	0.9	1.6	6.1	26.5	17.5	39.3	45.0	14.3	1,502	87.5
Ogden township (Lenawee)	973	944	-3.0	900	97.1	0.0	0.0	0.8	2.1	21.6	17.9	44.3	47.2	21.3	368	88.9
Ogemaw township (Ogemaw)	1,220	1,177	-3.5	1,219	96.8	0.0	0.5	1.8	0.9	20.3	22.6	43.6	39.3	19.1	463	91.8
Okemos CDP	21,369	-	-	24,141	67.5	4.9	19.2	5.1	3.3	22.5	14.3	34.5	8.7	74.9	9,633	96.6
Olive township (Clinton)	2,476	2,516	1.6	2,509	90.2	0.4	0.0	0.2	9.2	22.7	17.9	42.2	32.4	26.5	890	88.2
Olive township (Ottawa)	4,726	5,305	12.3	5,172	77.2	1.8	2.9	1.6	16.6	23.1	12.1	37.2	59.8	13.4	1,758	95.6
Oliver township (Huron)	1,483	1,385	-6.6	1,422	96.0	0.8	0.0	1.5	1.7	20.6	18.7	43.8	52.5	13.2	618	86.1
Oliver township (Kalkaska)	281	295	5.0	305	99.0	0.0	0.0	1.0	0.0	17.0	24.3	45.9	53.2	9.3	127	82.7
Olivet city & MCD (Eaton)	1,596	1,762	10.4	1,643	85.6	9.2	0.2	2.2	2.7	19.3	7.1	20.4	36.8	24.8	371	89.8
Omena CDP	267	-	-	144	97.9	0.0	0.0	2.1	0.0	6.9	31.9	55.7	21.3	66.1	58	100.0
Omer city & MCD (Arenac)	313	289	-7.7	259	91.9	1.9	0.0	5.0	1.2	25.1	20.1	41.5	58.3	4.3	111	82.9
Onaway city & MCD (Presque Isle)	880	828	-5.9	807	91.8	1.4	0.0	5.0	1.9	16.2	17.0	41.3	58.6	5.8	375	78.1
Oneida charter township (Eaton)	3,857	3,919	1.6	3,895	93.6	0.7	0.1	0.8	4.8	21.2	21.6	49.2	32.8	32.2	1,521	97.0
Onekama village	411	404	-1.7	461	85.9	0.0	0.0	14.1	0.0	29.7	16.7	39.3	24.4	33.0	148	87.2
Onekama township (Manistee)	1,329	1,307	-1.7	1,320	94.6	0.0	0.2	4.9	0.3	17.8	29.8	52.8	19.4	42.5	518	91.9
Onondaga township (Ingham)	3,158	3,252	3.0	3,236	93.1	1.5	0.0	1.9	3.5	27.6	14.7	40.6	43.8	16.2	1,145	94.1
Onota township (Alger)	352	331	-6.0	363	91.7	0.0	0.0	7.4	0.8	12.9	38.6	61.5	30.8	34.6	153	82.4
Onsted village	963	950	-1.3	1,132	89.8	4.3	0.6	4.0	1.3	23.1	18.7	43.4	33.0	22.4	479	89.6
Ontonagon village	1,484	1,250	-15.8	1,450	94.3	1.0	0.0	4.3	0.3	10.4	38.1	59.9	50.6	17.5	733	76.8
Ontonagon township (Ontonagon)	2,579	2,190	-15.1	2,099	95.5	0.7	0.0	3.0	0.8	9.5	37.7	59.6	44.4	20.6	1,040	81.3
Ontwa township (Cass)	6,549	6,596	0.7	6,524	95.1	0.2	0.7	2.3	1.7	21.3	18.6	44.2	38.1	26.5	2,660	92.2
Orange township (Ionia)	985	1,004	1.9	906	93.6	1.2	1.5	1.0	2.6	19.9	19.1	43.6	45.6	15.6	354	90.1
Orange township (Kalkaska)	1,233	1,312	6.4	1,395	97.6	0.2	0.0	1.3	0.9	25.4	11.9	34.0	59.7	9.0	482	87.8
Orangeville township (Barry)	3,310	3,469	4.8	3,401	90.0	1.1	0.0	1.7	7.2	18.0	17.3	49.5	57.2	18.6	1,456	86.7
Orchard Lake Village city & MCD (Oakland)	2,386	2,473	3.6	2,505	79.0	9.4	9.0	0.6	1.9	18.0	23.0	50.5	14.5	63.6	888	98.1
Oregon township (Lapeer)	5,786	5,722	-1.1	5,762	94.8	0.1	0.0	2.6	2.6	19.6	16.7	47.5	42.2	21.4	2,167	92.9
Orient township (Osceola)	773	777	0.5	840	95.7	0.7	0.0	1.5	2.0	22.7	23.1	41.4	53.2	9.8	319	90.3
Orion charter township (Oakland)	35,406	39,816	12.5	38,999	85.3	2.8	3.4	2.4	6.2	23.7	12.8	40.3	22.2	47.8	14,523	96.6
Orleans township (Ionia)	2,746	2,827	2.9	2,790	89.3	0.5	0.3	0.5	9.4	20.6	15.4	44.3	59.3	9.1	1,023	85.0
Oronoko charter township (Berrien)	9,191	8,923	-2.9	8,988	52.6	18.1	7.7	5.8	15.9	15.0	16.5	35.3	24.6	46.8	2,812	92.2
Ortonville village	1,439	1,443	0.3	1,650	92.0	0.4	0.0	3.8	3.8	29.0	12.4	35.8	37.8	20.1	532	96.2
Osceola township (Houghton)	1,885	1,820	-3.4	1,419	94.9	1.2	0.0	3.2	0.6	23.1	19.9	43.1	49.6	20.0	581	91.4
Osceola township (Osceola)	1,076	1,075	-0.1	1,132	90.9	2.1	1.1	0.7	5.2	21.7	15.8	40.6	56.3	17.5	404	80.0
Oscoda CDP	903	-	-	743	85.3	2.4	5.1	4.3	2.8	11.0	29.5	49.9	43.0	22.5	366	92.1
Oscoda charter township (Iosco)	6,998	6,765	-3.3	6,803	90.1	0.7	1.1	2.8	5.3	17.6	28.0	49.5	44.3	15.2	3,267	89.6
Oshtemo charter township (Kalamazoo)	21,704	23,190	6.8	22,961	74.2	11.8	3.2	6.9	3.8	18.7	19.5	37.0	22.8	47.3	10,273	90.2
Ossineke CDP	938	-	-	899	96.8	1.9	0.6	0.0	0.8	17.8	20.6	52.1	45.2	18.5	409	86.6
Ossineke township (Alpena)	1,672	1,599	-4.4	1,870	97.4	0.1	0.4	1.7	0.4	22.0	27.3	47.2	52.2	10.7	752	73.5
Otisco township (Ionia)	2,295	2,343	2.1	1,952	94.8	0.0	0.3	2.3	2.6	19.0	15.8	45.9	46.2	17.8	756	93.9
Otisville village	864	835	-3.4	968	93.6	0.4	0.4	3.6	2.0	23.2	11.6	44.7	52.5	13.3	405	91.9
Otsego city & MCD (Allegan)	3,965	3,994	0.7	3,985	95.7	0.9	1.3	2.0	0.0	20.4	14.8	43.5	49.8	13.5	1,724	86.1
Otsego township (Allegan)	5,585	5,856	4.9	5,785	90.6	0.6	0.0	6.2	2.6	24.3	17.0	39.3	54.5	16.8	2,030	87.6
Otsego Lake township (Otsego)	2,848	2,904	2.0	2,886	97.7	0.0	0.0	2.3	0.0	21.1	24.0	44.9	35.5	32.4	1,115	86.5
Otter Lake village	389	378	-2.8	396	95.2	0.3	1.0	1.0	2.5	22.2	16.2	39.4	49.2	14.0	147	89.1
Otto township (Oceana)	827	845	2.2	947	88.0	0.8	0.3	1.5	9.4	24.3	9.7	36.8	47.7	11.1	337	90.5
Overisel township (Allegan)	2,868	3,022	5.4	2,969	98.3	0.0	0.0	0.2	1.5	27.8	13.1	36.6	46.2	20.7	1,013	89.6
Ovid township (Branch)	2,322	2,302	-0.9	2,485	98.4	0.0	0.0	0.3	1.2	18.2	28.3	51.7	38.7	23.9	1,111	88.6
Ovid city	1,586	1,613	1.7	1,698	90.4	0.0	0.0	1.4	8.2	27.7	16.6	36.7	48.6	9.2	631	82.1

1 May be of any race.

Table A. All Places — **Population and Housing**

STATE City, town, township, borough, or CDP (county if applicable)	2010 census total population	2019 estimated population	Percent change 2010–2019	ACS total population estimate 2015–2019	White alone, not Hispanic or Latino	Black alone, not Hispanic or Latino	Asian alone, not Hispanic or Latino	All other races or 2 or more races, not Hispanic or Latino	Hispanic or Latino[1]	Under 18 years old	Age 65 years and older	Median age	Percent High school diploma or less	Percent Bachelor's degree or more	Total	Percent with a computer
	1	2	3	4	5	6	7	8	9	10	11	12	13	14	15	16
MICHIGAN—Con.																
Ovid city (Clinton)	1,580	1,607	1.7	1,670	90.2	0.0	0.0	1.4	8.3	27.7	16.9	36.7	47.7	9.3	620	81.8
Ovid city (Shiawassee)	6	6	0.0	28	100.0	0.0	0.0	0.0	0.0	28.6	0.0	35.8	100.0	0.0	11	100.0
Ovid township (Clinton)	2,194	2,227	1.5	2,049	97.2	1.4	0.0	0.2	1.2	20.8	16.7	44.8	37.9	16.3	766	93.2
Owendale village	241	224	-7.1	274	86.5	0.0	0.0	10.9	2.6	32.5	14.6	31.3	55.7	6.6	93	94.6
Owosso city & MCD (Shiawassee)	15,180	14,441	-4.9	14,536	93.0	1.4	0.1	2.4	3.2	23.4	13.9	34.8	52.3	12.1	6,033	88.1
Owosso charter township (Shiawassee)	4,846	4,742	-2.1	4,741	95.7	0.0	0.0	2.2	2.1	17.5	23.5	47.8	46.0	20.9	2,087	85.5
Oxford village	3,434	3,556	3.6	3,542	90.1	0.3	1.2	1.8	6.6	22.5	11.4	41.3	27.6	38.7	1,470	90.0
Oxford charter township (Oakland)	20,532	22,886	11.5	22,316	92.0	0.5	1.9	1.6	4.0	26.2	13.2	39.7	23.9	41.2	8,143	95.4
Palmer CDP	418	-	-	423	98.6	0.0	0.0	1.4	0.0	21.3	10.2	40.3	48.6	6.0	155	81.9
Palmyra township (Lenawee)	2,082	2,001	-3.9	1,966	87.1	1.3	0.5	3.7	7.4	17.7	20.1	46.4	52.7	16.6	780	90.4
Paradise township (Grand Traverse)	4,713	5,178	9.9	5,085	95.2	0.2	0.7	2.2	1.6	27.1	10.5	37.7	33.2	19.8	1,632	94.0
Parchment city & MCD (Kalamazoo)	1,800	1,828	1.6	1,953	76.8	8.7	1.4	8.7	4.5	23.2	12.4	34.1	33.5	26.9	816	91.9
Paris township (Huron)	481	447	-7.1	454	94.7	1.8	0.0	0.9	2.6	25.3	18.5	38.6	61.1	11.1	177	76.3
Park township (Ottawa)	17,801	18,905	6.2	18,752	86.1	0.7	2.5	1.4	9.2	23.3	18.3	44.6	25.4	46.9	6,984	95.8
Park township (St. Joseph)	2,602	2,574	-1.1	2,558	95.1	2.0	0.2	0.6	2.2	16.0	24.5	48.3	39.3	23.0	1,097	93.2
Parkdale CDP	704	-	-	740	93.1	2.3	0.0	0.7	3.9	14.5	37.6	60.2	56.6	9.9	258	81.0
Parma village	763	744	-2.5	600	94.3	1.5	0.5	1.0	2.7	26.5	19.5	40.1	48.5	18.0	206	91.7
Parma township (Jackson)	2,726	2,697	-1.1	2,705	91.8	3.0	0.1	3.5	1.6	19.3	18.6	45.9	53.4	15.3	1,081	89.8
Pavilion township (Kalamazoo)	6,193	6,438	4.0	6,419	91.2	1.8	2.1	4.0	1.0	16.9	17.6	44.6	37.0	21.3	2,550	90.9
Paw Paw village	3,514	3,366	-4.2	3,390	86.8	1.2	0.0	5.6	6.4	25.7	16.8	36.5	47.6	8.3	1,375	89.0
Paw Paw township (Van Buren)	7,043	6,821	-3.2	6,850	90.2	1.0	0.0	3.8	4.9	22.5	20.0	40.2	42.0	20.2	2,805	89.6
Paw Paw Lake CDP	3,511	-	-	3,520	92.5	0.2	0.0	4.5	2.8	23.9	21.9	48.3	35.3	24.2	1,523	75.6
Peacock township (Lake)..	494	514	4.0	372	96.8	0.0	0.0	1.1	2.2	4.6	40.9	62.7	59.8	11.0	159	78.6
Peaine township (Charlevoix)	292	292	0.0	266	96.6	0.0	0.0	1.5	1.9	9.0	51.1	65.2	26.6	51.1	133	97.0
Pearl Beach CDP	2,829	-	-	2,872	98.9	0.0	0.7	0.0	0.3	10.9	33.7	58.7	40.3	20.4	1,441	93.8
Peck village	635	595	-6.3	571	96.8	0.0	0.0	2.8	0.4	24.7	21.0	42.4	44.3	11.3	251	83.3
Pellston village	822	843	2.6	932	84.2	1.3	0.0	13.4	1.1	30.2	13.5	35.4	49.6	13.6	360	95.0
Peninsula township (Grand Traverse)	5,387	5,840	8.4	5,776	93.3	0.3	0.6	4.5	1.2	17.8	32.2	55.2	10.2	65.3	2,554	96.6
Penn township (Cass).......	1,772	1,719	-3.0	1,859	82.3	5.5	2.9	4.9	4.3	18.9	24.0	49.5	43.2	23.5	751	85.2
Pennfield charter township (Calhoun)	8,934	8,764	-1.9	8,782	89.1	2.9	0.2	5.1	2.8	18.6	20.4	48.1	46.1	18.7	3,705	90.6
Pentland township (Luce) .	2,674	2,565	-4.1	2,586	65.9	15.4	1.0	13.3	4.3	12.8	14.1	40.1	52.4	14.8	650	90.9
Pentwater village	862	848	-1.6	717	91.9	0.0	0.0	0.8	7.3	11.2	54.7	66.1	26.2	48.8	377	89.9
Pentwater township (Oceana)	1,515	1,487	-1.8	1,622	95.3	0.0	0.0	0.8	3.9	13.3	44.8	63.0	26.4	47.0	786	93.4
Pere Marquette charter township (Mason)	2,365	2,440	3.2	2,360	94.7	0.5	2.2	1.1	1.5	20.2	22.7	45.9	27.2	37.0	949	94.9
Perrinton village	406	392	-3.4	526	97.3	0.0	0.0	2.1	0.6	27.2	13.9	35.8	57.8	7.9	220	80.0
Perry city & MCD (Shiawassee)	2,165	2,092	-3.4	2,173	97.3	1.0	0.0	0.7	1.0	24.7	12.8	35.7	42.5	16.0	927	91.4
Perry township (Shiawassee)	4,348	4,210	-3.2	4,212	96.7	0.1	0.1	1.2	1.8	26.0	14.7	39.3	42.8	15.8	1,383	93.1
Petersburg city & MCD (Monroe)	1,145	1,128	-1.5	1,200	92.1	1.0	0.3	3.7	2.9	24.4	14.3	39.6	43.6	18.8	475	85.7
Petoskey city & MCD (Emmet)	5,670	5,756	1.5	5,724	89.1	0.8	0.3	6.1	3.7	19.7	18.8	41.8	25.2	39.0	2,790	87.9
Pewamo village	481	484	0.6	466	99.1	0.0	0.0	0.2	0.6	23.8	18.0	37.2	57.2	12.6	181	85.6
Pickford township (Chippewa)	1,598	1,573	-1.6	1,460	91.0	0.0	0.0	8.4	0.5	18.2	24.0	47.6	41.4	20.8	644	83.1
Pierson village	172	175	1.7	173	85.5	0.0	1.2	10.4	2.9	24.3	8.1	24.8	79.8	3.6	63	81.0
Pierson township (Montcalm)	3,216	3,271	1.7	3,247	89.3	0.9	0.7	3.8	5.2	22.4	15.8	43.3	55.8	14.4	1,227	91.2
Pigeon village	1,204	1,120	-7.0	1,259	91.3	2.5	0.0	2.3	3.8	20.5	23.0	45.3	46.0	20.4	623	83.5
Pilgrim CDP	11	-	-	20	100.0	0.0	0.0	0.0	0.0	0.0	100.0	75.8	0.0	100.0	10	100.0
Pinckney village	2,430	2,420	-0.4	2,317	94.6	0.1	1.0	1.3	3.1	23.9	9.1	38.0	28.7	25.9	909	96.6
Pinconning city & MCD (Bay)	1,307	1,230	-5.9	1,296	93.4	2.7	0.0	0.3	3.5	27.7	16.7	39.2	57.5	9.5	564	85.8
Pinconning township (Bay)	2,431	2,351	-3.3	2,336	94.5	0.4	0.0	2.2	2.9	20.7	20.1	43.6	45.8	12.5	949	88.7
Pine township (Montcalm)	1,834	1,857	1.3	2,181	97.3	0.1	0.6	0.0	2.1	27.6	17.5	35.7	46.0	14.9	742	74.4
Pine Grove township (Van Buren)	2,947	2,948	0.0	2,936	97.4	0.1	0.2	1.7	0.5	25.8	15.9	37.6	44.3	20.4	1,093	89.1
Pine River township (Gratiot)	2,287	2,212	-3.3	2,241	92.5	1.1	0.4	1.6	4.4	19.6	22.6	47.9	40.6	21.9	940	81.9
Pinora township (Lake)	717	752	4.9	828	96.1	0.0	0.0	1.9	1.9	22.9	19.4	45.6	66.9	7.9	293	81.9
Pioneer township (Missaukee)	451	461	2.2	516	94.8	0.0	0.6	2.3	2.3	23.3	22.7	45.6	60.2	7.7	191	86.9
Pipestone township (Berrien)	2,312	2,230	-3.5	2,246	81.8	4.7	0.7	2.5	10.2	20.3	17.1	46.6	46.3	21.5	835	85.6
Pittsfield charter township (Washtenaw)	34,789	38,921	11.9	38,567	62.9	11.7	14.2	5.3	5.9	20.4	12.0	35.4	18.3	57.6	14,736	95.9
Pittsford township (Hillsdale)	1,603	1,564	-2.4	1,516	93.9	0.7	0.0	4.1	1.4	25.2	22.1	43.9	49.2	17.6	575	85.2
Plainfield township (Iosco)	3,825	3,716	-2.8	3,711	96.4	0.0	0.0	3.4	0.2	14.3	36.7	58.6	54.0	10.0	1,776	80.5
Plainfield charter township (Kent)	30,970	34,147	10.3	33,711	90.7	2.1	1.2	2.4	3.5	23.7	16.1	40.7	27.5	37.8	13,223	93.4
Plainwell city & MCD (Allegan)	3,803	3,777	-0.7	3,785	92.7	1.3	0.0	1.3	4.7	21.2	19.3	42.1	38.6	21.5	1,543	90.8
Platte township (Benzie)...	354	358	1.1	380	77.6	1.3	0.0	3.4	17.6	18.2	22.1	55.4	44.4	31.6	146	89.7
Pleasanton township (Manistee)	820	814	-0.7	727	88.2	0.0	0.0	6.5	5.4	15.5	31.1	54.7	45.2	23.0	329	85.7

1 May be of any race.

Table A. All Places — **Population and Housing**

STATE City, town, township, borough, or CDP (county if applicable)	2010 census total population	2019 estimated population	Percent change 2010–2019	ACS total population estimate 2015–2019	White alone, not Hispanic or Latino	Black alone, not Hispanic or Latino	Asian alone, not Hispanic or Latino	All other races or 2 or more races, not Hispanic or Latino	Hispanic or Latino[1]	Under 18 years old	Age 65 years and older	Median age	Percent High school diploma or less	Percent Bachelor's degree or more	Total	Percent with a computer
	1	2	3	4	5	6	7	8	9	10	11	12	13	14	15	16
MICHIGAN—Con.																
Pleasant Plains township (Lake)	1,585	1,625	2.5	1,444	70.6	13.1	0.0	14.6	1.7	13.2	28.8	55.0	56.2	10.7	623	77.2
Pleasant Ridge city & MCD (Oakland)	2,446	2,425	-0.9	2,431	89.3	2.1	2.3	4.1	2.2	19.9	18.3	46.5	5.6	75.8	1,071	96.6
Pleasantview township (Emmet)	823	840	2.1	940	96.8	0.0	1.0	1.9	0.3	19.8	23.4	48.5	26.8	42.6	423	90.5
Plymouth city & MCD (Wayne)	9,135	9,154	0.2	9,124	93.6	1.5	0.9	2.8	1.2	19.0	16.2	41.6	16.4	56.5	4,326	91.0
Plymouth charter township (Wayne)	27,521	27,035	-1.8	27,065	89.7	1.4	4.6	1.3	2.9	18.6	23.3	47.8	22.4	51.6	11,240	93.9
Pointe Aux Barques township (Huron)	10	9	-10.0	18	100.0	0.0	0.0	0.0	0.0	0.0	50.0	66.0	0.0	56.3	11	81.8
Pokagon township (Cass)	2,035	1,975	-2.9	2,153	82.9	7.8	0.5	2.8	5.9	20.7	21.1	45.3	51.1	16.9	881	88.0
Polkton charter township (Ottawa)	2,420	2,612	7.9	2,521	97.6	0.2	0.8	0.2	1.2	24.9	17.3	41.3	44.6	28.4	895	85.6
Ponshewaing CDP	69	-	-	45	100.0	0.0	0.0	0.0	0.0	0.0	37.8	36.5	64.4	17.8	28	100.0
Pontiac city & MCD (Oakland)	59,695	59,438	-0.4	59,955	23.5	50.2	1.8	5.6	18.9	26.7	10.0	31.9	52.8	13.2	22,975	83.0
Portage charter township (Houghton)	3,217	3,123	-2.9	3,150	94.9	0.4	1.7	2.3	0.7	20.0	16.9	37.5	33.9	46.1	1,214	96.1
Portage city & MCD (Kalamazoo)	46,304	49,445	6.8	48,774	82.8	5.0	2.9	4.6	4.7	22.9	16.0	37.5	24.0	45.5	19,984	91.6
Portage township (Mackinac)	981	960	-2.1	738	90.7	0.4	0.0	4.9	4.1	11.8	34.7	57.6	47.8	19.4	378	83.6
Port Austin village	664	622	-6.3	704	92.6	0.0	0.0	2.6	4.8	12.6	34.5	56.0	39.5	21.5	367	90.2
Port Austin township (Huron)	1,424	1,335	-6.3	1,279	95.5	0.0	0.0	1.4	3.0	9.8	36.7	60.6	43.2	22.8	692	88.4
Porter township (Cass)	3,795	3,837	1.1	3,787	95.5	0.2	0.6	2.4	1.3	19.8	27.2	53.0	43.7	24.1	1,510	91.1
Porter township (Midland)	1,277	1,264		1,236	95.3	0.0	0.4	3.1	1.2	26.4	17.0	37.0	50.5	14.7	457	91.7
Porter township (Van Buren)	2,466	2,460	-0.2	2,343	91.0	0.0	0.4	4.1	4.5	16.6	21.0	49.7	35.7	26.1	967	90.3
Port Hope village	267	249	-6.7	253	94.1	0.0	0.0	4.3	1.6	17.0	39.1	60.2	54.5	12.9	120	81.7
Port Huron city & MCD (St. Clair)	30,199	28,749	-4.8	29,025	78.3	7.8	1.6	6.0	6.2	22.7	15.0	37.0	47.3	15.6	12,298	86.5
Port Huron charter township (St. Clair)	10,639	10,356	-2.7	10,380	83.9	6.6	0.4	3.3	5.7	20.7	15.7	40.6	46.1	17.1	4,116	89.3
Portland city & MCD (Ionia)	3,895	3,948	1.4	3,923	90.6	2.0	2.2	2.8	2.4	27.3	11.4	33.4	33.7	21.6	1,534	90.6
Portland township (Ionia)	3,390	3,462	2.1	3,441	95.6	2.2	0.0	0.0	2.2	28.2	17.6	39.1	33.2	28.6	1,224	96.7
Port Sanilac village	620	581	-6.3	592	97.6	0.0	0.5	0.0	1.9	15.2	32.6	57.7	45.4	24.0	267	92.9
Port Sheldon township (Ottawa)	4,247	4,713	11.0	4,598	87.8	0.0	0.4	1.9	10.0	24.8	18.9	46.7	39.8	34.2	1,762	95.1
Portsmouth charter township (Bay)	3,303	3,155	-4.5	3,175	91.8	0.7	0.0	0.8	6.7	22.6	22.2	42.3	40.2	17.6	1,274	87.8
Posen village	233	218	-6.4	185	98.4	0.0	0.0	0.5	1.1	16.8	25.9	50.8	60.7	6.2	100	53.0
Posen township (Presque Isle)	850	796	-6.4	845	95.4	2.6	0.0	0.8	1.2	19.5	22.4	50.6	53.9	8.1	360	76.1
Potterville city & MCD (Eaton)	2,636	2,752	4.4	2,713	85.6	4.1	0.0	4.2	6.1	27.3	9.5	30.6	30.0	19.3	1,056	96.7
Powell township (Marquette)	813	816	0.4	547	96.9	0.4	0.0	2.7	0.0	15.0	19.2	52.8	29.5	34.9	281	79.7
Powers village	417	405	-2.9	453	97.6	0.0	0.0	1.3	1.1	14.1	48.1	63.5	59.0	9.3	133	80.5
Prairie Ronde township (Kalamazoo)	2,264	2,418	6.8	2,386	93.8	1.5	0.4	1.5	2.9	23.6	15.3	42.5	28.3	38.0	853	96.8
Prairieville township (Barry)	3,403	3,520	3.4	3,480	95.4	1.1	0.2	1.4	1.9	17.1	22.7	43.6	32.2	31.7	1,383	95.4
Prescott village	266	254	-4.5	246	95.5	0.0	0.0	0.8	3.7	19.9	19.1	51.0	73.8	7.5	106	79.2
Presque Isle township (Presque Isle)	1,660	1,562	-5.9	1,709	98.3	0.0	0.9	0.1	0.7	13.6	35.2	58.8	30.5	35.8	808	93.9
Presque Isle Harbor CDP	600	-	-	579	99.1	0.0	0.0	0.0	0.9	3.8	47.3	64.4	26.8	33.9	314	94.9
Prudenville CDP	1,682	-	-	1,942	93.4	0.0	0.0	4.3	2.4	16.3	33.5	48.9	35.0	20.0	885	87.2
Pulaski township (Jackson)	2,070	2,109	1.9	2,087	97.7	0.1	0.2	1.1	0.8	19.3	22.2	47.3	42.6	18.1	830	86.5
Pulawski township (Presque Isle)	345	324	-6.1	336	99.7	0.0	0.0	0.3	0.0	19.9	32.4	49.5	66.4	4.4	145	67.6
Putnam township (Livingston)	8,252	8,443	2.3	8,419	95.7	0.5	1.3	0.9	1.6	19.7	15.4	45.9	32.5	28.9	3,297	94.5
Quincy village	1,652	1,617	-2.1	1,476	95.5	0.1	0.3	2.8	1.2	23.2	14.0	38.5	52.9	8.9	621	86.5
Quincy township (Branch)	4,282	4,220	-1.4	4,232	97.7	0.2	0.1	1.0	1.0	23.3	16.7	41.6	50.7	16.8	1,649	88.5
Quincy township (Houghton)	247	237	-4.0	306	96.4	1.3	0.0	2.0	0.3	34.3	17.6	37.9	36.0	41.5	93	94.6
Quinnesec CDP	1,191	-	-	1,177	98.8	0.0	0.0	0.0	1.2	9.7	18.4	49.7	31.9	30.8	504	84.7
Raber township (Chippewa)	643	635	-1.2	577	89.6	0.0	1.0	9.4	0.0	11.1	37.1	59.9	44.0	16.9	301	74.1
Raisin township (Lenawee)	7,578	7,762	2.4	7,661	90.5	0.0	1.0	3.4	5.2	24.8	12.8	39.6	40.7	24.8	2,666	94.4
Raisinville township (Monroe)	5,816	5,792	-0.4	5,789	93.3	1.3	0.0	2.7	2.6	21.8	19.4	43.8	46.6	14.0	2,127	92.1
Ransom township (Hillsdale)	932	913	-2.0	947	96.9	0.0	0.0	2.0	1.1	24.7	12.0	41.8	56.2	12.1	349	78.8
Rapid City CDP	1,352	-	-	1,493	92.2	1.6	0.4	3.3	2.4	23.5	16.6	43.6	53.4	13.1	604	95.2
Rapid River township (Kalkaska)	1,145	1,210	5.7	1,370	94.4	0.0	1.4	1.4	2.8	20.8	16.4	40.8	56.5	10.0	558	87.1
Ravenna village	1,261	1,274	1.0	1,258	96.7	0.0	0.0	0.5	2.8	27.6	11.1	34.3	47.6	15.8	481	84.4
Ravenna township (Muskegon)	2,905	2,981	2.6	2,952	89.9	0.5	0.2	1.6	7.9	27.7	12.7	36.3	43.8	19.5	1,060	89.2
Ray township (Macomb)	3,739	4,059	8.6	4,010	99.6	0.1	0.0	0.0	0.2	18.9	20.2	48.7	39.7	23.2	1,642	83.1
Reading city & MCD (Hillsdale)	1,078	1,044	-3.2	998	96.6	0.0	0.1	0.0	2.5	28.1	12.7	33.1	51.8	11.6	359	86.9
Reading township (Hillsdale)	1,765	1,723	-2.4	1,833	97.5	0.4	0.0	0.8	1.3	20.1	23.5	50.9	46.2	18.5	752	82.6

1 May be of any race.

Table A. All Places — **Population and Housing**

STATE City, town, township, borough, or CDP (county if applicable)	2010 census total population	2019 estimated population	Percent change 2010–2019	ACS total population estimate 2015–2019	White alone, not Hispanic or Latino	Black alone, not Hispanic or Latino	Asian alone, not Hispanic or Latino	All other races or 2 or more races, not Hispanic or Latino	Hispanic or Latino[1]	Under 18 years old	Age 65 years and older	Median age	Percent High school diploma or less	Percent Bachelor's degree or more	Total	Percent with a computer
	1	2	3	4	5	6	7	8	9	10	11	12	13	14	15	16
MICHIGAN—Con.																
Readmond township (Emmet)	581	594	2.2	559	89.3	0.0	0.5	7.2	3.0	9.7	32.9	56.7	37.7	33.3	278	87.1
Redding township (Clare)	532	536	0.8	344	98.5	0.0	0.0	0.0	1.5	16.0	21.2	52.2	63.2	10.5	144	85.4
Redford charter township (Wayne)	48,289	46,674	-3.3	47,078	49.9	43.3	0.4	2.7	3.6	22.0	12.8	40.4	43.9	20.4	18,294	90.8
Reed City city & MCD (Osceola)	2,419	2,391	-1.2	2,472	90.0	5.0	0.7	1.7	2.6	23.3	20.3	41.8	55.0	17.4	1,080	84.8
Reeder township (Missaukee)	1,128	1,152	2.1	1,120	98.3	0.7	0.0	1.0	0.0	21.7	20.7	44.3	54.5	12.7	475	92.6
Reese village	1,450	1,364	-5.9	1,397	90.4	0.4	0.2	2.7	6.3	20.3	17.3	41.2	44.5	15.4	630	89.0
Reno township (Iosco)	590	579	-1.9	579	99.0	0.0	0.0	0.5	0.5	21.9	24.0	47.1	63.2	5.0	232	78.9
Republic CDP	570	-		520	97.9	0.0	0.0	1.0	1.2	18.7	23.8	52.6	59.0	11.6	275	74.9
Republic township (Marquette)	1,063	1,062	-0.1	975	98.1	0.0	0.0	1.3	0.6	15.0	31.4	55.8	49.9	18.4	501	79.4
Resort township (Emmet)	2,697	2,765	2.5	2,746	94.4	0.1	1.9	3.6	0.0	22.8	22.1	46.2	24.6	45.0	1,021	92.6
Reynolds township (Montcalm)	5,310	5,420	2.1	5,355	97.0	0.1	0.1	2.2	0.6	27.1	13.7	37.3	58.5	11.8	1,874	87.9
Rich township (Lapeer)	1,624	1,588	-2.2	1,428	92.4	0.3	0.0	1.1	6.2	23.7	20.2	44.7	55.4	16.7	541	82.3
Richfield township (Genesee)	8,730	8,333	-4.5	8,375	92.5	1.6	0.1	2.1	3.7	23.5	17.9	40.4	41.2	21.7	3,119	90.8
Richfield township (Roscommon)	3,733	3,661	-1.9	3,648	95.7	0.0	0.2	3.0	1.0	12.2	30.6	55.4	63.3	5.7	1,668	78.2
Richland village	743	831	11.8	772	97.0	0.0	0.8	0.4	1.8	18.3	29.3	48.3	15.2	46.4	349	92.8
Richland township (Kalamazoo)	7,578	8,375	10.5	8,220	90.2	4.6	1.8	1.1	2.2	26.0	19.2	40.3	21.1	50.4	3,179	93.1
Richland township (Missaukee)	1,481	1,497	1.1	1,540	96.8	0.0	0.0	0.8	2.4	33.0	8.8	31.8	49.2	17.7	517	93.2
Richland township (Montcalm)	2,778	2,831	1.9	2,817	96.8	0.1	0.3	2.5	0.2	21.3	23.3	44.6	49.5	17.8	1,138	86.4
Richland township (Ogemaw)	914	883	-3.4	843	96.4	0.0	0.0	1.7	1.9	18.6	25.7	52.2	69.0	7.7	364	83.8
Richland township (Saginaw)	4,144	3,927	-5.2	3,955	97.5	0.0	0.3	0.0	2.2	22.6	21.5	44.9	40.5	25.2	1,636	85.6
Richmond city	5,785	5,849	1.1	5,869	86.9	1.6	0.0	6.5	5.0	26.1	19.0	37.8	47.3	18.4	2,186	92.8
Richmond city (Macomb)	5,783	5,847	1.1	5,869	86.9	1.6	0.0	6.5	5.0	26.1	19.0	37.8	47.3	18.4	2,186	92.8
Richmond city (St. Clair)	2	2	0.0	-	-	-	-	-	-	-	-	-	-	-	-	-
Richmond township (Macomb)	3,606	3,622	0.4	3,767	92.4	0.0	0.0	2.6	5.0	27.0	13.1	41.0	37.5	22.5	1,212	95.9
Richmond township (Marquette)	884	878	-0.7	950	97.5	0.0	0.0	2.4	0.1	18.6	20.3	47.8	48.5	8.5	392	85.2
Richmond township (Osceola)	1,562	1,548	-0.9	1,712	97.9	0.0	0.0	1.3	0.8	20.3	22.3	44.8	48.6	16.3	642	87.5
Ridgeway township (Lenawee)	1,546	1,484	-4.0	1,591	94.0	0.0	0.3	4.2	1.5	22.9	10.4	39.9	46.0	19.2	608	96.5
Riga township (Lenawee)	1,406	1,348	-4.1	1,131	93.9	0.0	0.0	0.8	5.3	14.4	19.1	49.5	48.5	17.1	475	88.2
Riley township (Clinton)	2,024	2,060	1.8	1,919	97.6	0.0	0.7	0.6	1.1	21.4	16.6	46.4	36.0	27.7	685	94.2
Riley township (St. Clair)	3,351	3,275	-2.3	3,268	96.8	0.1	0.0	1.2	1.9	18.1	16.8	45.5	43.3	18.1	1,239	92.9
River Rouge city & MCD (Wayne)	7,903	7,419	-6.1	7,502	32.4	48.9	0.0	0.9	17.8	25.2	12.4	34.4	62.1	9.3	3,055	77.8
Riverside township (Missaukee)	1,179	1,204	2.1	1,185	90.4	0.0	0.0	0.2	9.5	30.7	13.1	33.9	58.7	14.8	417	75.8
Riverton township (Mason)	1,153	1,165	1.0	1,448	83.1	2.8	0.8	3.1	10.1	27.4	16.0	38.1	43.7	18.5	475	92.2
Riverview city & MCD (Wayne)	12,486	12,032	-3.6	12,137	89.6	3.1	0.2	1.3	5.7	18.0	25.6	45.9	43.0	19.7	5,136	88.6
Rives township (Jackson)	4,683	4,708	0.5	4,690	90.8	1.2	0.0	3.6	4.4	21.6	19.1	42.9	47.0	16.8	1,762	89.4
Robin Glen-Indiantown CDP	722	-	-	752	89.8	2.3	0.0	1.6	6.4	31.0	18.0	34.7	63.9	4.8	273	92.3
Robinson township (Ottawa)	6,086	6,523	7.2	6,454	89.3	0.4	0.3	1.3	8.7	27.3	13.2	38.7	40.6	26.3	2,135	95.1
Rochester city & MCD (Oakland)	12,714	13,296	4.6	13,162	88.6	2.6	4.7	1.9	2.3	22.6	14.6	40.7	15.1	59.7	5,564	93.1
Rochester Hills city & MCD (Oakland)	70,987	74,516	5.0	74,206	76.3	4.0	12.5	2.0	5.2	21.8	18.2	42.2	19.0	57.4	28,888	94.8
Rockford city & MCD (Kent)	5,699	6,391	12.1	6,254	92.0	1.7	0.2	0.6	5.4	25.7	12.1	35.4	23.1	42.5	2,327	94.8
Rockland township (Ontonagon)	227	191	-15.9	202	93.1	0.0	0.0	6.9	0.0	11.9	31.2	60.8	62.8	8.1	93	78.5
Rock River township (Alger)	1,212	1,137	-6.2	1,253	97.4	0.3	0.0	1.3	1.0	20.1	23.5	50.9	56.0	14.9	482	74.1
Rockwood city & MCD (Wayne)	3,289	3,158	-4.0	3,186	94.8	0.2	2.1	1.7	1.2	19.1	16.9	45.9	40.8	18.2	1,392	84.0
Rogers township (Presque Isle)	984	927	-5.8	1,056	95.5	0.0	0.0	1.8	2.7	19.4	32.2	55.0	49.5	19.9	455	83.5
Rogers City city & MCD (Presque Isle)	2,827	2,653	-6.2	2,685	95.8	0.4	1.0	2.5	0.2	17.3	30.5	51.6	43.4	20.6	1,230	84.2
Rolland township (Isabella)	1,305	1,312	0.5	1,430	93.3	2.0	0.0	3.4	1.4	28.0	14.4	35.0	51.3	13.3	464	75.2
Rollin township (Lenawee)	3,272	3,260	-0.4	3,251	99.2	0.0	0.1	0.6	0.2	16.3	25.1	51.0	39.9	25.8	1,441	84.2
Rome township (Lenawee)	1,791	1,773		1,643	97.1	0.7	0.0	1.3	0.9	20.3	18.3	47.7	53.4	18.2	645	89.3
Romeo village	3,598	3,606	0.2	3,836	81.2	7.0	0.0	0.6	11.2	18.6	16.7	41.2	37.5	30.9	1,713	87.2
Romulus city & MCD (Wayne)	23,989	23,573	-1.7	23,527	52.0	40.7	1.5	3.5	2.4	26.4	12.5	35.5	47.9	17.2	8,513	90.7
Ronald township (Ionia)	1,892	1,944	2.7	1,953	86.6	1.5	0.4	1.2	10.3	22.8	15.7	38.5	54.2	13.2	737	87.7
Roosevelt Park city & MCD (Muskegon)	3,831	3,796	-0.9	3,789	72.8	11.6	5.4	4.6	5.6	20.8	15.7	34.7	34.2	29.7	1,683	89.5
Roscommon village	1,079	1,050	-2.7	1,050	80.5	2.1	0.0	15.1	2.3	29.5	16.8	39.2	36.1	12.8	405	92.3
Roscommon township (Roscommon)	4,411	4,330	-1.8	4,306	95.4	0.0	0.0	1.9	2.8	19.9	26.2	52.3	52.5	10.6	1,882	86.7
Rose township (Oakland)	6,255	6,452	3.1	6,448	91.1	1.2	0.2	2.0	5.5	20.8	19.3	48.5	34.6	29.0	2,450	97.4
Rose township (Ogemaw)	1,364	1,326	-2.8	1,178	96.0	0.0	0.0	1.3	2.7	12.2	27.2	57.5	55.3	9.2	588	83.0

1 May be of any race.

Table A. All Places — **Population and Housing**

STATE City, town, township, borough, or CDP (county if applicable)	Population				Race and Hispanic or Latino origin (percent)					Age (percent)			Educational attainment of persons age 25 and older		Occupied housing units	
	2010 census total population	2019 estimated population	Percent change 2010–2019	ACS total population estimate 2015–2019	White alone, not Hispanic or Latino	Black alone, not Hispanic or Latino	Asian alone, not Hispanic or Latino	All other races or 2 or more races, not Hispanic or Latino	Hispanic or Latino[1]	Under 18 years old	Age 65 years and older	Median age	Percent High school diploma or less	Percent Bachelor's degree or more	Total	Percent with a computer
	1	2	3	4	5	6	7	8	9	10	11	12	13	14	15	16
MICHIGAN—Con.																
Rosebush village	368	362	-1.6	343	79.6	0.6	0.9	9.3	9.6	17.8	21.3	47.4	52.5	16.6	158	84.2
Rose City city & MCD (Ogemaw)	653	632	-3.2	656	95.4	1.4	0.0	1.4	1.8	25.6	26.1	39.2	55.4	5.2	240	75.8
Rose Lake township (Osceola)	1,373	1,392	1.4	1,405	95.9	0.0	0.0	0.8	3.3	22.6	23.4	44.0	50.9	17.5	549	79.6
Roseville city & MCD (Macomb)	47,324	47,018	-0.6	47,400	72.5	20.1	1.6	3.4	2.4	20.9	14.0	38.4	48.6	12.9	20,135	88.0
Ross township (Kalamazoo)	4,669	4,960	6.2	4,909	93.3	0.9	0.3	1.9	3.6	21.5	20.7	44.3	23.6	43.2	1,995	94.8
Rothbury village	448	448	0.0	446	79.4	0.0	0.0	3.1	17.5	30.7	13.5	33.3	54.1	14.6	149	89.9
Roxand township (Eaton) .	1,848	1,882	1.8	1,705	95.4	0.1	0.2	2.6	1.8	20.5	18.8	44.1	39.9	15.2	694	91.6
Royal Oak city & MCD (Oakland)	57,232	59,277	3.6	59,195	87.1	3.7	4.1	1.8	3.4	15.3	14.2	35.8	18.5	57.9	28,728	95.3
Royal Oak charter township (Oakland)	2,419	2,418	0.0	2,411	5.1	83.9	0.0	9.4	1.5	25.2	18.7	36.0	50.8	10.7	1,072	84.8
Royalton township (Berrien)	4,766	4,781	0.3	4,766	89.6	0.7	5.1	2.6	2.0	26.4	18.7	42.6	21.3	46.4	1,663	91.6
Rubicon township (Huron)	732	686	-6.3	688	94.2	0.0	0.0	3.1	2.8	15.4	32.1	56.2	50.8	12.2	321	83.2
Rudyard township (Chippewa)	1,370	1,341	-2.1	1,193	80.5	1.6	0.6	14.2	3.2	23.6	14.2	41.1	45.3	19.3	416	80.8
Rush township (Shiawassee)	1,291	1,244	-3.6	1,095	95.6	0.4	0.0	1.2	2.8	17.0	20.4	51.6	39.3	18.0	444	92.3
Rust township (Montmorency)	561	536	-4.5	470	93.0	0.0	0.0	5.3	1.7	20.4	28.1	54.4	54.3	18.8	214	75.2
Rutland charter township (Barry)	3,987	4,044	1.4	4,023	93.4	0.0	1.2	3.2	2.1	27.5	17.2	39.0	42.1	24.3	1,383	93.9
Sage township (Gladwin)..	2,457	2,427	-1.2	2,341	96.1	0.8	0.0	2.6	0.4	19.6	25.0	48.9	46.3	13.7	981	85.1
Saginaw city & MCD (Saginaw)	51,469	48,115	-6.5	48,650	37.5	42.7	0.3	4.7	14.8	26.2	13.0	35.0	55.2	10.9	19,689	80.0
Saginaw charter township (Saginaw)	40,855	39,150	-4.2	39,383	74.5	10.5	4.1	3.5	7.4	17.9	23.3	44.7	31.2	33.0	18,007	88.0
Sagola township (Dickinson)	1,106	1,076	-2.7	979	94.6	0.0	0.0	4.3	1.1	18.4	24.1	51.9	58.5	13.3	426	72.5
St. Charles village	2,049	1,896	-7.5	2,121	83.0	0.6	0.0	1.6	14.9	24.4	17.2	36.7	45.3	15.1	879	81.1
St. Charles township (Saginaw)	3,330	3,107	-6.7	3,157	87.0	0.7	0.0	1.3	11.0	24.1	16.8	39.3	47.3	14.2	1,313	84.7
St. Clair city & MCD (St. Clair)	5,479	5,279	-3.7	5,327	92.7	0.8	1.6	2.0	3.0	21.1	17.5	41.5	31.6	28.7	2,234	84.8
St. Clair township (St. Clair)	6,825	7,042	3.2	6,861	95.6	0.1	1.2	1.3	1.8	22.4	17.6	44.3	37.5	24.7	2,621	96.1
St. Clair Shores city & MCD (Macomb)	59,765	58,984	-1.3	59,528	89.9	5.2	0.6	1.8	2.4	17.5	20.4	44.9	36.3	25.3	26,990	89.4
St. Helen CDP	2,668	-	-	2,671	94.5	0.0	0.3	3.7	1.4	13.6	27.3	54.3	64.4	5.3	1,204	74.8
St. Ignace city & MCD (Mackinac)	2,433	2,323	-4.5	2,239	63.0	4.6	1.7	29.4	1.4	13.7	24.8	51.7	49.3	21.4	1,209	86.5
St. Ignace township (Mackinac)	939	902	-3.9	915	50.2	3.0	0.2	46.4	0.2	15.0	27.8	49.5	54.1	12.0	427	84.8
St. James CDP	205	-	-	171	98.8	0.0	0.0	1.2	0.0	12.9	39.2	60.4	33.3	35.4	97	82.5
St. James township (Charlevoix)	365	364	-0.3	311	92.6	0.0	0.0	3.5	3.9	12.2	35.7	59.6	33.5	39.2	161	89.4
St. Johns city & MCD (Clinton)	7,863	7,945	1.0	7,898	95.2	1.6	0.5	1.3	1.4	22.8	16.8	40.1	38.9	26.4	3,087	90.6
St. Joseph city & MCD (Berrien)	8,365	8,317	-0.6	8,316	82.5	4.9	6.4	3.9	2.3	16.7	19.6	40.8	21.8	49.2	4,059	90.1
St. Joseph charter township (Berrien)	10,028	9,676	-3.5	9,786	78.5	11.0	4.3	2.0	4.2	19.7	22.6	45.9	23.3	41.0	4,046	92.6
St. Louis city & MCD (Gratiot)	7,477	7,265	-2.8	7,189	62.4	25.6	0.8	3.3	7.9	12.5	11.5	37.5	58.7	8.3	1,336	85.2
Salem township (Allegan).	4,446	5,023	13.0	4,858	93.7	0.1	0.7	3.3	2.3	27.6	11.5	37.9	53.7	16.2	1,688	87.7
Salem township (Washtenaw)	5,729	6,293	9.8	6,193	92.3	2.6	0.4	1.6	3.1	18.8	16.8	45.2	31.2	40.8	2,143	95.6
Saline city & MCD (Washtenaw)	8,829	9,343	5.8	9,251	88.7	1.3	3.7	2.4	3.9	21.7	19.5	43.2	19.3	51.7	3,780	93.5
Saline township (Washtenaw)	1,897	2,248	18.5	2,274	91.0	0.7	1.3	1.9	5.1	21.5	22.5	44.9	34.9	28.9	878	88.0
Sanborn township (Alpena)	2,116	2,025	-4.3	2,031	95.0	0.8	0.9	2.7	0.5	24.3	17.1	42.8	42.5	15.3	801	87.6
Sand Beach township (Huron)	1,221	1,135	-7.0	1,079	96.5	0.6	0.2	2.7	0.0	19.6	23.7	51.5	48.8	18.9	436	89.2
Sand Lake CDP	1,412	-	-	1,407	97.3	0.1	0.1	0.4	2.1	14.6	33.9	58.2	53.3	10.6	692	87.4
Sand Lake village	500	538	7.6	538	93.7	0.4	0.0	1.7	4.3	32.0	16.0	36.1	56.4	16.0	201	82.6
Sands township (Marquette)	2,285	2,318	1.4	2,472	90.3	2.3	0.3	4.5	2.6	21.0	16.5	44.8	25.9	37.9	937	95.9
Sandstone township (Jackson)	3,984	3,974	-0.3	3,976	97.7	0.3	0.0	1.5	0.5	25.2	15.7	38.6	39.9	15.5	1,505	89.0
Sandusky city & MCD (Sanilac)	2,678	2,520	-5.9	2,534	90.6	2.2	1.5	2.0	3.6	18.6	22.6	42.6	52.7	14.7	1,056	81.8
Sanford village	864	844	-2.3	791	98.4	1.0	0.0	0.3	0.4	15.0	23.9	44.6	33.9	32.4	387	85.3
Sanilac township (Sanilac)	2,431	2,303	-5.3	2,296	96.7	0.0	0.1	0.7	2.4	17.1	29.1	54.2	50.3	18.5	1,026	88.2
Saranac village	1,321	1,328	0.5	1,409	97.4	0.6	0.0	1.2	0.7	23.3	17.0	40.1	48.5	15.7	580	82.6
Sauble township (Lake)	333	346	3.9	320	95.3	0.0	0.0	4.1	0.6	7.2	42.8	61.9	42.5	18.4	172	86.0
Saugatuck city & MCD (Allegan)	925	960	3.8	850	91.6	0.0	0.0	1.3	7.1	19.4	29.9	53.2	25.6	56.6	411	91.2
Saugatuck township (Allegan)	2,949	3,360	13.9	3,256	91.7	0.0	0.4	2.5	5.3	16.0	25.0	53.1	27.7	51.1	1,397	84.6
Sault Ste. Marie city & MCD (Chippewa)	14,144	13,420	-5.1	13,591	74.8	2.2	0.4	20.5	2.0	18.9	16.5	33.4	38.3	26.0	5,674	85.5
Schoolcraft township (Houghton)	1,839	1,776	-3.4	1,759	96.8	0.2	0.0	2.0	1.0	22.2	22.3	42.2	40.0	26.2	710	83.5
Schoolcraft village	1,525	1,551	1.7	1,332	95.9	0.0	0.5	3.5	0.0	22.4	15.5	41.0	37.7	24.4	570	88.4
Schoolcraft township (Kalamazoo)	8,212	9,091	10.7	8,898	94.9	0.1	0.2	2.1	2.8	25.3	16.7	38.1	34.3	30.3	3,461	88.4

1 May be of any race.

Table A. All Places — **Population and Housing**

	Population				Race and Hispanic or Latino origin (percent)					Age (percent)			Educational attainment of persons age 25 and older		Occupied housing units	
STATE City, town, township, borough, or CDP (county if applicable)	2010 census total population	2019 estimated population	Percent change 2010–2019	ACS total population estimate 2015–2019	White alone, not Hispanic or Latino	Black alone, not Hispanic or Latino	Asian alone, not Hispanic or Latino	All other races or 2 or more races, not Hispanic or Latino	Hispanic or Latino[1]	Under 18 years old	Age 65 years and older	Median age	Percent High school diploma or less	Percent Bachelor's degree or more	Total	Percent with a computer
	1	2	3	4	5	6	7	8	9	10	11	12	13	14	15	16
MICHIGAN—Con.																
Scio township (Washtenaw)	16,442	17,921	9.0	17,624	75.3	3.5	14.3	4.3	2.6	24.1	17.1	42.2	10.7	70.3	6,563	97.7
Sciota township (Shiawassee)	1,840	1,779	-3.3	1,533	95.6	0.3	0.5	1.9	1.8	17.6	18.7	48.0	32.9	25.1	661	89.0
Scipio township (Hillsdale)	1,889	1,869	-1.1	1,782	96.4	0.0	0.0	3.1	0.5	21.3	16.0	43.0	50.6	13.7	666	81.4
Scottville city & MCD (Mason)	1,209	1,211	0.2	1,194	83.7	0.0	1.2	4.4	10.7	21.6	13.6	36.5	49.1	15.2	478	87.7
Sebewa township (Ionia)	1,167	1,188	1.8	1,308	95.5	0.0	0.0	1.8	2.7	24.6	11.9	32.6	53.4	8.0	428	88.3
Sebewaing village	1,759	1,631	-7.3	1,601	96.3	2.1	0.2	1.0	0.4	14.2	23.6	51.6	46.9	17.6	760	86.1
Sebewaing township (Huron)	2,724	2,526	-7.3	2,564	97.7	1.3	0.2	0.6	0.2	18.6	22.3	48.4	47.3	17.2	1,145	88.4
Secord township (Gladwin)	1,155	1,141	-1.2	1,107	99.2	0.0	0.0	0.5	0.3	10.5	47.1	64.1	52.4	15.0	588	76.2
Selma township (Wexford)	2,093	2,142	2.3	2,202	91.9	0.2	1.6	4.7	1.6	21.9	23.6	47.6	44.5	23.6	884	83.0
Seneca township (Lenawee)	1,230	1,190	-3.3	1,127	94.1	0.0	0.3	1.1	4.6	21.6	19.9	45.5	59.2	8.6	475	82.3
Seney township (Schoolcraft)	119	115	-3.4	101	80.2	1.0	0.0	18.8	0.0	1.0	39.6	60.3	81.3	3.3	37	54.1
Seville township (Gratiot)	2,173	2,086	-4.0	2,155	90.4	0.0	0.0	2.9	6.7	19.1	20.4	43.9	48.7	12.7	884	88.3
Sharon township (Washtenaw)	1,737	1,797	3.5	2,015	95.8	0.7	0.1	1.2	2.1	17.4	19.4	46.6	26.2	44.4	672	93.8
Shelby charter township (Macomb)	73,832	80,628	9.2	79,165	88.2	2.4	4.8	2.3	2.4	21.0	19.1	42.9	31.6	34.5	31,080	94.0
Shelby village	2,058	2,012	-2.2	2,427	50.8	1.3	0.2	1.7	45.9	36.1	10.2	30.3	62.1	11.3	792	86.7
Shelby township (Oceana)	4,069	4,028	-1.0	4,023	66.2	0.9	0.1	1.5	31.3	30.8	14.9	35.9	52.3	21.0	1,460	87.5
Shepherd village	1,508	1,486	-1.5	1,495	91.7	0.9	0.0	4.5	2.8	23.7	14.6	40.3	39.1	26.0	595	89.9
Sheridan township (Calhoun)	1,941	1,913	-1.4	1,901	85.3	3.8	0.3	4.5	6.2	28.9	20.7	43.2	59.5	14.4	745	85.2
Sheridan township (Clare)	1,575	1,598	1.5	1,653	97.8	0.0	0.0	2.0	0.2	30.7	14.4	35.5	54.9	8.9	510	64.7
Sheridan township (Huron)	712	671	-5.8	594	99.0	0.0	0.0	1.0	0.0	23.2	20.0	40.8	60.9	12.4	249	82.7
Sheridan township (Mason)	1,072	1,095	2.1	990	89.9	0.3	0.3	3.3	6.2	23.1	22.7	46.5	46.5	20.6	406	78.3
Sheridan township (Mecosta)	1,393	1,414	1.5	1,253	91.7	0.5	1.0	4.4	2.5	21.9	18.6	44.6	56.7	12.7	463	83.4
Sheridan village	649	650	0.2	622	95.2	0.0	1.1	2.7	1.0	20.7	19.8	43.5	52.0	17.0	244	85.7
Sheridan charter township (Newaygo)	2,470	2,454	-0.6	2,767	90.6	0.3	0.8	1.4	7.0	22.0	19.0	41.8	36.5	28.6	1,053	91.4
Sherman township (Gladwin)	1,043	1,027	-1.5	969	97.9	1.0	0.0	0.5	0.5	20.8	30.2	51.9	60.5	12.3	419	69.5
Sherman township (Huron)	1,083	1,011	-6.6	932	95.7	0.0	0.8	0.2	3.3	15.6	31.4	54.1	64.1	10.5	432	76.2
Sherman township (Iosco)	448	441	-1.6	453	94.5	1.8	0.0	3.1	0.7	19.0	28.9	51.5	63.2	13.0	206	74.3
Sherman township (Isabella)	2,991	3,000	0.3	2,995	94.2	0.1	0.0	3.6	2.1	21.8	18.8	40.6	46.6	17.3	1,131	88.9
Sherman township (Keweenaw)	67	66	-1.5	58	100.0	0.0	0.0	0.0	0.0	10.3	46.6	64.0	51.9	25.0	33	87.9
Sherman township (Mason)	1,186	1,214	2.4	1,099	93.9	0.3	0.0	1.9	3.9	23.8	16.8	40.9	58.0	13.0	418	84.7
Sherman township (Newaygo)	2,113	2,121	0.4	2,127	96.4	0.8	0.2	1.6	1.0	20.9	22.8	44.2	49.3	19.1	806	87.3
Sherman township (Osceola)	1,042	1,036	-0.6	1,033	98.5	0.2	0.0	1.3	0.1	27.7	16.7	41.3	47.5	12.6	384	89.8
Sherman township (St. Joseph)	3,207	3,297	2.8	3,268	97.4	0.1	0.2	2.1	0.2	19.6	21.3	50.2	43.7	22.8	1,503	81.9
Sherwood village	309	307	-0.6	353	92.1	0.0	0.0	7.1	0.8	28.0	9.3	39.1	61.4	4.0	135	79.3
Sherwood township (Branch)	2,088	2,089	0.0	2,189	95.9	0.0	0.0	2.1	1.9	24.5	19.5	45.1	67.7	7.4	797	83.2
Shiawassee township (Shiawassee)	2,840	2,739	-3.6	2,760	95.7	0.0	0.1	2.8	1.4	20.0	17.9	47.0	43.3	12.7	1,098	89.3
Shields CDP	6,587	-		5,945	95.3	0.4	1.0	0.6	2.8	19.4	27.8	50.8	32.3	24.1	2,589	87.4
Shoreham village	858	832	-3.0	846	77.2	4.7	4.6	8.6	4.8	15.7	26.7	50.9	15.1	51.0	382	94.5
Shorewood-Tower Hills-Harbert CDP	1,344	-	-	1,455	99.2	0.0	0.0	0.0	0.8	4.5	47.5	63.4	28.7	44.2	762	92.9
Sidney township (Montcalm)	2,574	2,606	1.2	2,591	96.2	0.0	1.6	1.2	1.0	18.4	21.7	50.0	48.8	15.8	1,089	85.0
Sigel township (Huron)	465	434	-6.7	494	99.6	0.0	0.0	0.4	0.0	28.1	17.6	39.3	56.5	18.0	176	84.1
Silver Creek township (Cass)	3,207	3,156	-1.6	3,142	88.3	0.7	0.0	3.7	7.3	18.0	30.4	50.9	42.2	26.3	1,395	88.1
Sims township (Arenac)	1,100	1,034	-6.0	1,052	98.1	0.0	0.0	1.4	0.5	10.6	43.6	62.7	42.3	19.5	539	88.1
Skandia township (Marquette)	826	832	0.7	878	91.5	0.0	1.9	6.4	0.2	12.2	22.2	54.3	46.3	21.2	387	86.0
Skidway Lake CDP	3,392	-		3,369	93.7	0.1	0.0	3.9	2.3	24.0	19.8	43.6	59.5	6.2	1,462	83.7
Slagle township (Wexford)	503	520	3.4	515	93.4	0.8	0.0	0.6	5.2	17.9	27.2	51.4	55.8	9.1	232	82.3
Snover CDP	448	-		368	97.6	0.0	0.5	0.0	1.9	25.8	19.6	45.3	60.7	8.8	149	85.9
Sodus township (Berrien)	1,932	1,951	1.0	1,933	82.9	3.9	0.0	1.6	11.5	19.2	28.0	49.7	46.6	23.1	803	84.7
Solon township (Kent)	5,984	6,851	14.5	6,734	96.0	0.0	1.1	1.9	1.1	26.5	13.1	37.7	41.3	24.4	2,564	91.5
Solon township (Leelanau)	1,509	1,517	0.5	1,747	96.2	0.0	0.4	1.5	1.9	19.6	23.0	51.2	34.5	39.8	676	92.3
Somerset township (Hillsdale)	4,621	4,530	-2.0	4,543	94.9	0.6	0.2	1.2	3.1	15.6	24.2	51.1	36.1	32.6	2,057	91.3
Soo township (Chippewa)	3,143	3,071	-2.3	3,105	62.9	4.6	2.1	29.0	1.4	17.6	20.4	46.7	33.8	32.9	1,256	90.3
South Arm township (Charlevoix)	1,881	1,880	-0.1	2,054	98.2	0.0	0.2	1.0	0.6	19.9	22.9	46.5	40.4	24.1	760	90.8
South Boardman CDP	536	-		535	97.0	0.0	0.0	3.0	0.0	21.9	14.2	38.8	50.8	9.1	175	88.0
South Branch township (Crawford)	2,009	1,998	-0.5	1,896	93.6	0.0	0.0	3.6	2.8	14.8	29.3	53.8	47.2	17.0	909	90.9
South Branch township (Wexford)	383	393	2.6	300	97.7	0.0	1.0	1.3	0.0	13.3	23.7	53.0	45.9	22.9	133	82.0
Southfield city & MCD (Oakland)	71,715	72,689	1.4	73,174	22.4	69.1	2.3	4.4	1.8	18.4	20.4	42.9	27.6	37.7	32,345	89.5
Southfield township (Oakland)	14,545	14,759	1.5	14,826	81.3	9.5	3.2	3.5	2.4	22.8	23.5	48.4	9.3	72.5	5,816	95.7

1 May be of any race.

Table A. All Places — **Population and Housing**

STATE City, town, township, borough, or CDP (county if applicable)	Population 2010 census total population	Population 2019 estimated population	Population Percent change 2010–2019	Population ACS total population estimate 2015–2019	Race and Hispanic or Latino origin (percent) White alone, not Hispanic or Latino	Black alone, not Hispanic or Latino	Asian alone, not Hispanic or Latino	All other races or 2 or more races, not Hispanic or Latino	Hispanic or Latino[1]	Age (percent) Under 18 years old	Age 65 years and older	Median age	Educational attainment of persons age 25 and older Percent High school diploma or less	Percent Bachelor's degree or more	Occupied housing units Total	Percent with a computer
	1	2	3	4	5	6	7	8	9	10	11	12	13	14	15	16
MICHIGAN—Con.																
Southgate city & MCD (Wayne)	30,047	28,959	-3.6	29,165	79.2	6.1	4.0	2.4	8.4	17.5	19.6	43.6	45.3	19.2	12,696	86.3
South Gull Lake CDP	1,182	-	-	1,236	99.0	0.5	0.0	0.5	0.0	21.4	30.6	53.8	10.1	62.7	540	95.4
South Haven city	4,416	4,348	-1.5	4,354	79.2	14.5	1.0	2.7	2.7	13.2	32.7	57.8	30.2	41.3	2,168	83.6
South Haven city (Allegan)	3	3	0.0	-	-	-	-	-	-	-	-	-	-	-	-	-
South Haven city (Van Buren)	4,413	4,345	-1.5	4,354	79.2	14.5	1.0	2.7	2.7	13.2	32.7	57.8	30.2	41.3	2,168	83.6
South Haven charter township (Van Buren)	3,966	3,993	0.7	3,941	72.7	3.9	0.0	1.4	21.9	27.7	18.5	39.7	42.0	21.7	1,554	87.1
South Lyon city & MCD (Oakland)	11,315	11,821	4.5	11,788	91.0	0.9	1.9	2.1	4.1	21.9	16.6	42.0	28.4	42.0	4,963	93.7
South Monroe CDP	6,433	-	-	5,977	90.1	4.1	1.1	2.5	2.2	19.6	24.5	43.7	52.6	16.8	2,764	83.5
South Range village	758	729	-3.8	685	99.0	0.3	0.0	0.7	0.0	17.7	17.8	39.4	49.1	16.5	284	80.3
South Rockwood village	1,674	1,657		1,770	87.1	4.1	2.3	1.0	5.6	15.7	14.6	44.4	43.1	22.7	780	93.2
Spalding township (Menominee)	1,673	1,602	-4.2	1,666	98.4	0.0	0.2	1.1	0.3	18.4	27.8	50.9	54.8	12.3	680	83.8
Sparta village	4,138	4,399	6.3	4,354	91.1	0.6	0.6	2.4	5.4	24.9	13.1	34.0	49.5	16.0	1,628	83.4
Sparta township (Kent)	9,111	9,703	6.5	9,616	91.8	0.5	0.3	1.2	6.3	25.6	13.2	36.8	51.3	17.9	3,351	87.5
Spaulding township (Saginaw)	2,162	2,000	-7.5	2,137	67.4	13.5	0.0	4.9	14.2	23.5	23.0	42.5	55.8	11.7	866	84.2
Speaker township (Sanilac)	1,483	1,406	-5.2	1,277	93.0	0.9	0.2	2.7	3.2	20.2	15.7	47.6	49.9	13.7	551	88.2
Spencer township (Kent)	3,961	4,314	8.9	4,236	94.1	0.1	0.4	1.2	4.2	21.9	16.0	44.8	46.7	14.1	1,567	87.0
Spring Arbor CDP	2,881	-	-	2,402	84.5	3.5	0.5	3.2	8.3	10.5	19.3	22.6	25.4	44.0	543	84.7
Spring Arbor township (Jackson)	8,265	7,879	-4.7	8,016	92.3	1.0	0.8	3.2	2.6	22.9	18.3	32.5	28.7	36.2	2,563	92.6
Springdale township (Manistee)	779	855	9.8	949	98.5	0.4	0.0	0.7	0.3	24.2	18.8	44.6	59.8	16.5	336	85.1
Springfield city & MCD (Calhoun)	5,262	5,198	-1.2	5,193	62.0	9.2	14.2	7.0	7.6	23.2	14.3	33.6	62.9	12.4	2,276	84.7
Springfield township (Kalkaska)	1,523	1,608	5.6	1,442	96.1	0.3	0.3	3.0	0.3	18.0	17.2	46.8	58.8	11.6	584	89.4
Springfield charter township (Oakland)	13,940	14,489	3.9	14,431	89.3	2.7	1.2	2.8	3.9	23.4	15.4	44.3	28.3	40.3	5,300	96.2
Spring Lake village	2,321	2,485	7.1	2,390	96.1	0.2	0.8	0.4	2.6	21.3	27.8	46.7	22.3	40.0	1,107	93.0
Spring Lake township (Ottawa)	14,303	15,100	5.6	15,020	93.7	0.6	1.5	2.1	2.2	24.1	21.0	43.1	25.8	42.7	6,085	92.2
Springport village	800	787	-1.6	852	88.3	0.8	0.0	8.7	2.2	29.7	14.4	35.8	62.9	8.0	311	91.0
Springport township (Jackson)	2,159	2,156	-0.1	2,163	94.4	0.6	0.0	3.7	1.3	26.1	16.1	41.6	53.6	8.8	812	89.8
Springvale township (Emmet)	2,140	2,193	2.5	2,121	96.3	0.0	0.3	2.5	0.9	21.7	15.2	44.1	35.3	29.1	807	90.2
Springville township (Wexford)	1,751	1,811	3.4	1,583	94.9	0.0	0.4	3.8	0.9	26.0	16.9	40.3	61.6	8.5	618	83.5
Spurr township (Baraga)	282	271	-3.9	241	97.5	1.2	0.0	1.2	0.0	7.9	33.2	59.4	40.3	22.8	102	87.3
Stambaugh township (Iron)	1,136	1,067	-6.1	1,069	93.1	2.5	0.1	3.6	0.7	9.9	35.4	59.6	42.3	28.0	487	92.2
Standish city & MCD (Arenac)	1,498	1,382	-7.7	1,421	92.6	0.6	0.7	4.4	1.7	18.1	16.1	43.1	50.2	12.0	625	85.3
Standish township (Arenac)	1,907	1,778	-6.8	1,792	94.7	0.0	0.3	3.6	1.4	13.6	23.4	52.1	53.7	10.4	760	81.1
Stannard township (Ontonagon)	790	665	-15.8	652	94.0	0.2	0.0	3.5	2.3	10.3	35.3	57.2	71.4	4.7	315	72.1
Stanton township (Houghton)	1,419	1,388	-2.2	1,454	99.6	0.1	0.0	0.3	0.0	25.4	24.6	47.3	44.4	29.3	496	81.0
Stanton city & MCD (Montcalm)	1,417	1,422	0.4	1,355	86.3	3.3	0.0	1.3	9.0	22.9	15.6	37.0	47.9	12.1	497	78.7
Stanwood village	211	212	0.5	257	93.8	0.4	0.0	0.8	5.1	29.6	13.2	35.8	61.1	11.1	91	82.4
Star township (Antrim)	926	922	-0.4	929	94.9	0.6	0.6	1.0	2.8	18.5	22.5	45.9	54.9	13.3	397	95.0
Stephenson city & MCD (Menominee)	862	826	-4.2	937	95.0	0.0	0.4	0.3	4.3	26.0	25.5	38.9	55.9	11.1	387	74.9
Stephenson township (Menominee)	667	633	-5.1	598	98.2	0.0	0.5	0.5	0.8	18.2	23.9	52.6	52.2	10.6	273	75.8
Sterling village	530	499	-5.8	538	93.1	0.0	0.0	2.8	4.1	23.8	22.7	39.9	53.8	8.2	182	84.1
Sterling Heights city & MCD (Macomb)	129,675	132,438	2.1	132,476	81.7	5.8	7.7	2.6	2.2	20.2	18.0	40.6	41.9	28.4	50,082	91.8
Stevensville village	1,142	1,129	-1.1	1,059	91.9	2.4	0.5	0.6	4.7	12.7	29.9	53.7	34.8	24.1	539	88.3
Stockbridge village	1,218	1,250	2.6	1,365	92.8	0.9	0.0	1.5	4.8	20.8	15.5	39.4	36.4	27.1	586	83.3
Stockbridge township (Ingham)	3,896	4,020	3.2	3,978	92.7	0.8	1.2	1.7	3.6	19.9	18.4	41.2	37.7	20.8	1,481	91.5
Stony Point CDP	1,724	-	-	1,762	91.5	3.6	0.0	0.0	4.9	26.2	9.4	42.5	29.4	14.4	687	96.2
Stronach CDP	162	-	-	187	93.0	0.0	2.7	1.6	2.7	16.0	17.6	47.6	55.8	6.5	74	90.5
Stronach township (Manistee)	843	835	-0.9	825	95.8	0.0	0.8	2.8	0.6	12.5	28.5	55.5	53.6	11.6	380	83.2
Sturgis city & MCD (St. Joseph)	11,139	10,861	-2.5	10,905	71.2	0.9	0.0	3.1	24.9	27.5	12.7	34.4	56.2	9.6	4,251	83.3
Sturgis township (St. Joseph)	2,229	2,208	-0.9	2,397	87.8	0.2	0.0	1.5	10.5	31.7	14.0	31.6	52.5	11.6	805	90.2
Sugar Island township (Chippewa)	652	639	-2.0	704	64.2	0.0	0.7	33.0	2.1	8.5	33.5	58.4	46.6	18.4	288	79.9
Sullivan township (Muskegon)	2,441	2,574	5.4	2,536	93.6	0.0	0.0	0.8	5.6	20.7	19.7	47.4	56.1	10.0	947	87.3
Summerfield township (Clare)	466	463	-0.6	309	98.1	0.0	0.0	1.9	0.0	6.8	34.6	57.2	51.7	3.3	156	81.4
Summerfield township (Monroe)	3,310	3,189	-3.7	3,205	92.0	0.7	0.5	2.1	4.7	25.0	16.6	41.9	47.7	19.8	1,124	92.3
Summit township (Jackson)	22,626	22,518	-0.5	22,474	86.8	5.3	1.2	3.0	3.7	22.6	22.5	45.6	32.8	33.3	9,186	91.8
Summit township (Mason)	927	945	1.9	1,066	81.0	0.0	0.2	5.6	13.2	18.0	25.3	49.3	34.4	34.6	425	91.8
Sumner township (Gratiot)	1,925	1,868	-3.0	1,753	95.6	0.0	0.0	2.7	1.7	18.6	17.3	45.8	60.8	10.0	751	86.3
Sumpter township (Wayne)	9,549	9,365	-1.9	9,354	85.6	9.5	0.2	3.8	1.0	22.4	18.8	44.5	52.3	11.5	3,592	94.8

1 May be of any race.

Table A. All Places — **Population and Housing**

STATE City, town, township, borough, or CDP (county if applicable)	2010 census total population	2019 estimated population	Percent change 2010–2019	ACS total population estimate 2015–2019	White alone, not Hispanic or Latino	Black alone, not Hispanic or Latino	Asian alone, not Hispanic or Latino	All other races or 2 or more races, not Hispanic or Latino	Hispanic or Latino[1]	Under 18 years old	Age 65 years and older	Median age	Percent High school diploma or less	Percent Bachelor's degree or more	Total	Percent with a computer
	1	2	3	4	5	6	7	8	9	10	11	12	13	14	15	16
MICHIGAN—Con.																
Sunfield village	578	589	1.9	504	91.3	0.2	0.0	0.6	7.9	25.0	17.1	33.3	50.5	8.3	202	87.6
Sunfield township (Eaton).	1,997	2,035	1.9	2,126	94.5	0.0	0.2	1.7	3.4	25.3	18.7	39.6	42.4	12.0	799	89.2
Superior township (Chippewa)	1,337	1,308	-2.2	1,474	67.3	0.1	0.7	28.9	2.9	22.5	18.2	42.0	37.8	21.1	593	83.1
Superior charter township (Washtenaw)	13,060	14,287	9.4	13,977	56.4	29.7	5.4	4.3	4.2	27.0	15.3	38.7	25.8	48.7	5,357	95.6
Surrey township (Clare)	3,602	3,614	0.3	3,564	92.2	1.4	0.0	3.8	2.6	24.2	19.7	40.0	57.7	11.5	1,315	86.8
Suttons Bay village	620	619	-0.2	544	93.6	1.8	1.3	1.3	2.0	10.7	61.0	68.1	18.7	50.8	239	90.8
Suttons Bay township (Leelanau)	2,982	2,996	0.5	2,985	69.0	0.6	0.5	16.3	13.5	18.0	31.1	55.1	34.3	32.7	1,180	89.9
Swan Creek township (Saginaw)	2,456	2,374	-3.3	2,247	97.0	0.1	0.0	0.6	2.3	15.3	22.7	52.3	45.8	16.4	953	90.0
Swartz Creek city & MCD (Genesee)	5,758	5,501	-4.5	5,535	87.0	4.3	1.6	2.2	4.8	20.4	23.6	40.4	37.5	14.9	2,487	86.7
Sweetwater township (Lake)	245	258	5.3	244	81.6	13.9	0.4	2.0	2.0	15.6	30.7	58.3	50.3	17.9	102	81.4
Sylvan township (Osceola)	1,079	1,081	0.2	866	87.6	3.6	0.0	3.5	5.3	23.0	25.4	49.7	54.3	10.5	318	82.7
Sylvan township (Washtenaw)	2,835	2,992	5.5	2,983	91.6	0.7	1.8	2.9	3.0	20.9	21.3	47.8	19.6	45.0	1,145	95.5
Sylvan Lake city & MCD (Oakland)	1,763	1,858	5.4	1,818	89.5	8.5	0.0	1.0	0.9	17.5	15.7	46.7	12.2	56.7	874	98.5
Tallmadge charter township (Ottawa)	7,575	8,332	10.0	8,232	95.9	0.3	2.3	1.3	0.3	23.7	14.2	35.9	33.6	33.5	2,986	92.4
Tawas township (Iosco)	1,747	1,696	-2.9	1,752	97.5	0.2	0.1	1.8	0.5	17.4	25.2	53.4	52.3	17.1	713	88.2
Tawas City city & MCD (Iosco)	1,832	1,783	-2.7	1,881	90.0	2.8	1.0	3.6	2.7	19.1	23.8	45.3	47.8	19.6	713	89.8
Taylor city & MCD (Wayne)	63,131	60,922	-3.5	61,379	71.2	18.9	1.5	3.0	5.4	21.8	14.9	38.0	56.0	11.6	24,030	89.6
Taymouth township (Saginaw)	4,520	4,284	-5.2	4,319	94.1	1.1	0.0	1.1	3.7	21.8	19.5	45.6	48.0	17.3	1,665	86.8
Tecumseh city & MCD (Lenawee)	8,475	8,398	-0.9	8,356	92.4	0.6	0.3	2.1	4.6	20.8	20.8	42.9	37.5	30.2	3,708	92.4
Tecumseh township (Lenawee)	1,996	1,971	-1.3	2,032	91.9	0.7	0.2	1.0	6.1	24.3	20.2	44.5	33.5	35.1	720	89.9
Tekonsha village	728	725	-0.4	653	95.9	0.8	0.0	2.5	0.9	18.8	18.2	39.2	56.3	8.0	278	81.7
Tekonsha township (Calhoun)	1,648	1,633	-0.9	1,491	94.8	0.3	0.3	3.8	0.8	20.1	22.1	43.8	56.3	14.1	628	81.7
Temperance CDP	8,517	-	-	8,201	91.3	2.1	1.0	1.5	4.1	18.8	20.8	48.3	39.1	28.3	3,577	90.2
Texas charter township (Kalamazoo)	14,694	17,250	17.4	16,871	86.8	2.1	4.6	3.7	2.7	29.3	13.9	39.9	17.3	57.0	5,879	99.7
Thetford township (Genesee)	7,044	6,646	-5.7	6,698	92.0	3.0	0.4	2.7	1.9	20.4	17.4	43.0	50.5	10.1	2,594	90.4
Thomas township (Saginaw)	11,985	11,465	-4.3	11,539	94.8	0.7	1.2	0.8	2.5	19.4	25.8	50.4	36.1	28.7	4,877	90.2
Thompson township (Schoolcraft)	795	759	-4.5	735	92.2	0.0	0.4	5.6	1.8	15.1	31.2	57.0	44.5	23.0	326	81.6
Thompsonville village	443	453	2.3	481	90.2	0.0	0.4	5.4	4.0	27.0	10.6	37.9	63.6	2.7	189	79.9
Thornapple township (Barry)	7,880	8,391	6.5	8,161	94.2	0.4	0.2	1.3	3.8	28.0	11.2	37.4	38.7	28.4	2,935	89.3
Three Oaks village...........	1,618	1,545	-4.5	1,354	90.7	0.7	0.0	3.4	5.2	19.9	20.2	44.3	43.2	20.1	631	91.0
Three Oaks township (Berrien)	2,574	2,466	-4.2	2,427	94.3	0.4	0.0	2.4	2.9	20.1	19.6	45.5	45.1	18.6	1,059	89.1
Three Rivers city & MCD (St. Joseph)	7,792	7,623	-2.2	7,659	75.3	11.0	1.5	5.8	6.4	30.2	12.3	29.8	49.1	15.5	2,936	88.6
Tilden township (Marquette)	1,009	1,007	-0.2	1,047	93.3	0.0	0.0	6.5	0.2	17.4	18.9	40.7	43.1	23.7	406	89.2
Tittabawassee township (Saginaw)	9,747	9,984	2.4	9,877	86.5	5.3	1.1	3.2	3.9	22.4	11.8	37.3	35.4	27.5	3,239	95.2
Tobacco township (Gladwin)	2,577	2,558	-0.7	2,541	97.0	0.0	0.0	0.0	3.0	14.8	25.3	52.7	47.4	14.9	1,151	90.9
Tompkins township (Jackson)	2,670	2,687	0.6	2,679	97.2	0.0	0.0	1.1	1.7	17.9	20.5	49.2	48.5	13.0	1,110	83.2
Torch Lake township (Antrim)	1,194	1,179	-1.3	1,208	94.2	0.0	0.0	2.5	3.3	11.3	40.9	60.4	23.2	48.7	584	98.3
Torch Lake township (Houghton)	1,883	1,830	-2.8	1,744	98.9	0.0	0.0	0.6	0.5	16.4	21.4	48.0	32.8	35.1	671	88.5
Traverse City city	14,731	15,738	6.8	15,570	90.5	1.5	1.0	4.5	2.4	18.0	21.3	41.4	23.8	46.2	6,781	88.6
Traverse City city (Grand Traverse)	14,540	15,547	6.9	15,338	90.4	1.5	1.0	4.6	2.5	17.7	21.5	41.2	24.1	45.6	6,697	88.5
Traverse City city (Leelanau)	191	191	0.0	232	100.0	0.0	0.0	0.0	0.0	36.2	5.2	44.7	0.0	89.2	84	100.0
Trenton city & MCD (Wayne)	18,853	18,157	-3.7	18,295	92.2	1.0	0.8	1.5	4.5	19.2	21.8	47.2	38.1	25.6	7,777	90.0
Trout Lake township (Chippewa)	384	375	-2.3	211	84.4	0.0	0.0	15.6	0.0	8.1	44.5	63.3	43.3	16.0	106	68.9
Trowbridge township (Allegan)	2,502	2,570	2.7	2,539	92.8	0.9	2.7	2.0	1.6	17.4	18.7	47.5	59.9	11.6	1,025	82.6
Trowbridge Park CDP	2,176	-	-	2,278	80.7	1.6	12.2	5.5	0.0	14.0	16.5	37.2	34.9	31.9	918	88.3
Troy township (Newaygo)..	283	286	1.1	216	85.2	1.4	6.9	6.0	0.5	23.1	15.7	42.0	48.6	18.9	91	65.9
Troy city & MCD (Oakland)	80,972	84,092	3.9	83,989	65.8	3.6	25.6	2.6	2.4	21.5	17.2	42.2	17.7	60.8	31,760	96.1
Turin township (Marquette)	153	154	0.7	169	98.2	0.6	0.0	1.2	0.0	26.6	24.3	41.9	69.9	5.3	68	70.6
Turner village	108	102	-5.6	156	84.6	0.0	1.3	14.1	0.0	24.4	10.3	32.5	77.6	6.5	52	71.2
Turner township (Arenac) .	540	506	-6.3	527	92.8	0.0	0.4	5.3	1.5	15.7	18.8	53.3	59.7	7.9	219	81.7
Tuscarora township (Cheboygan)	3,038	2,916	-4.0	2,937	95.1	0.0	0.0	3.8	1.2	12.6	28.8	53.7	42.2	27.4	1,421	83.6
Tuscola township (Tuscola)	2,082	1,935	-7.1	1,975	98.0	0.0	0.0	2.0	0.0	17.5	20.3	44.4	47.0	14.3	840	88.3
Tustin village	221	217	-1.8	215	96.7	0.0	2.8	0.5	0.0	24.2	18.6	35.4	62.3	15.1	79	84.8
Twining village	181	168	-7.2	136	100.0	0.0	0.0	0.0	0.0	23.5	13.2	37.7	62.8	5.3	58	74.1
Twin Lake CDP	1,720	-	-	1,513	96.6	0.0	0.8	0.0	2.6	11.8	26.8	55.5	35.8	20.7	627	90.1
Tyrone township (Kent).....	4,729	5,129	8.5	5,051	83.4	2.0	0.0	1.7	12.9	28.9	12.5	33.8	50.3	15.0	1,544	85.9

1 May be of any race.

Table A. All Places — **Population and Housing**

STATE City, town, township, borough, or CDP (county if applicable)	Population				Race and Hispanic or Latino origin (percent)					Age (percent)			Educational attainment of persons age 25 and older		Occupied housing units	
	2010 census total population	2019 estimated population	Percent change 2010–2019	ACS total population estimate 2015–2019	White alone, not Hispanic or Latino	Black alone, not Hispanic or Latino	Asian alone, not Hispanic or Latino	All other races or 2 or more races, not Hispanic or Latino	Hispanic or Latino[1]	Under 18 years old	Age 65 years and older	Median age	Percent High school diploma or less	Percent Bachelor's degree or more	Total	Percent with a computer
	1	2	3	4	5	6	7	8	9	10	11	12	13	14	15	16

MICHIGAN—Con.

STATE City, town, township, borough, or CDP (county if applicable)	1	2	3	4	5	6	7	8	9	10	11	12	13	14	15	16
Tyrone township (Livingston)	10,019	10,562	5.4	10,432	93.5	0.5	0.3	2.6	3.0	23.6	15.4	43.2	28.3	34.6	3,737	94.5
Ubly village	842	785	-6.8	785	96.8	0.9	0.0	0.0	2.3	22.0	18.7	42.1	52.8	14.8	365	85.5
Unadilla township (Livingston)	3,366	3,457	2.7	3,412	96.8	0.6	0.1	1.6	1.0	14.9	22.9	47.8	45.0	20.9	1,474	94.2
Union township (Branch)	2,868	2,819	-1.7	2,824	95.2	0.1	0.8	0.5	3.3	21.0	18.2	43.0	48.1	13.3	1,186	85.8
Union township (Grand Traverse)	403	439	8.9	411	98.3	0.0	0.0	1.0	0.7	13.6	17.3	52.7	33.5	26.9	175	94.3
Union charter township (Isabella)	12,911	13,701	6.1	13,702	83.3	5.0	2.3	5.4	4.0	15.4	9.0	23.4	31.9	33.9	5,249	93.7
Union City village	1,594	1,564	-1.9	1,665	97.1	0.2	0.4	1.7	0.7	25.0	15.6	36.6	51.3	16.3	703	88.9
Unionville village	508	471	-7.3	533	92.1	0.0	0.0	0.9	6.9	22.3	19.3	41.2	51.5	11.0	216	83.8
Utica city & MCD (Macomb)	4,753	5,107	7.4	5,006	86.6	2.2	5.4	1.5	4.2	15.6	20.3	44.2	35.3	25.3	2,267	85.9
Valley township (Allegan)	2,022	2,227	10.1	1,927	93.4	0.6	0.6	3.0	2.4	19.3	16.8	46.8	45.6	22.9	774	90.2
Van Buren charter township (Wayne)	28,823	28,396	-1.5	28,335	62.4	27.3	1.4	5.1	3.9	20.0	12.7	38.8	37.6	27.5	11,811	94.1
Vandalia village	295	282	-4.4	381	48.0	19.4	12.3	14.4	5.8	30.7	10.2	28.6	68.9	3.5	122	79.5
Vanderbilt village	559	565	1.1	561	94.1	0.0	0.7	2.9	2.3	16.6	15.9	39.0	76.7	4.0	226	85.4
Vandercook Lake CDP	4,721	-	-	4,615	90.2	1.2	0.0	1.2	7.4	29.5	15.7	39.4	40.7	18.4	1,799	91.1
Vassar city & MCD (Tuscola)	2,703	2,542	-6.0	2,576	78.4	3.8	0.5	8.3	9.0	29.1	15.3	33.5	55.3	14.0	1,059	84.6
Vassar township (Tuscola)	4,087	3,885	-4.9	3,910	97.1	0.0	0.0	0.2	2.7	23.3	16.0	41.7	60.4	5.8	1,595	82.5
Venice township (Shiawassee)	2,574	2,507	-2.6	2,500	96.8	0.0	0.2	2.4	0.6	22.1	18.7	45.4	52.5	12.9	917	79.3
Vergennes township (Kent)	4,184	4,743	13.4	4,666	98.6	0.9	0.0	0.2	0.3	23.2	14.0	42.9	19.4	37.8	1,661	98.1
Vermontville village	759	771	1.6	731	89.9	0.0	0.0	4.5	5.6	28.6	10.4	32.1	50.5	9.2	268	94.8
Vermontville township (Eaton)	2,053	2,094	2.0	1,966	92.3	0.0	0.2	3.9	3.6	22.4	17.5	41.1	53.7	10.8	746	88.6
Vernon township (Isabella)	1,350	1,348	-0.1	1,420	98.5	0.0	0.5	0.5	0.5	24.6	16.9	40.8	43.7	23.4	506	88.7
Vernon village	815	772	-5.3	679	100.0	0.0	0.0	0.0	0.0	23.3	9.0	38.5	41.9	10.8	270	89.6
Vernon township (Shiawassee)	4,601	4,466	-2.9	4,467	92.7	0.0	0.7	1.5	5.0	17.1	22.1	48.6	49.0	10.6	1,887	87.2
Verona township (Huron)	1,259	1,187	-5.7	1,263	91.8	0.0	2.3	1.9	4.0	20.8	17.7	45.2	52.4	18.8	504	85.7
Vevay township (Ingham)	3,535	3,738	5.7	3,684	97.0	0.0	0.0	1.2	1.8	19.8	19.7	43.5	41.0	26.5	1,416	94.8
Vicksburg village	2,899	3,483	20.1	3,291	97.2	0.0	0.0	1.5	1.2	25.6	13.5	35.2	40.4	20.5	1,266	90.0
Victor township (Clinton)	3,465	3,521	1.6	3,509	97.5	1.1	0.1	0.5	0.9	19.9	20.1	45.2	32.1	34.0	1,320	94.1
Victory township (Mason)	1,383	1,412	2.1	1,411	95.0	0.0	0.0	2.3	2.7	20.9	21.6	44.7	48.1	15.0	526	81.9
Vienna charter township (Genesee)	13,255	12,626	-4.7	12,701	91.8	1.8	0.3	2.8	3.4	19.0	21.3	44.9	41.5	16.1	5,189	91.2
Vienna township (Montmorency)	585	561	-4.1	545	91.9	0.0	0.0	7.7	0.4	18.0	27.7	53.3	60.4	14.3	233	83.3
Village of Clarkston city & MCD (Oak...	918	921	0.3	988	91.6	5.5	0.0	2.6	0.3	23.7	22.2	43.7	11.3	53.7	424	93.6
Village of Grosse Pointe Shores city	2,875	2,794	-2.8	2,767	85.5	3.3	6.6	1.9	2.7	19.5	28.9	53.5	12.4	65.3	1,082	93.0
Village of Grosse Pointe Shores city (Macomb)	77	77	0.0	32	100.0	0.0	0.0	0.0	0.0	18.8	50.0	57.5	0.0	46.2	19	36.8
Village of Grosse Pointe Shores city (Wayne)	2,798	2,717	-2.9	2,735	85.4	3.3	6.7	1.9	2.7	19.5	28.7	53.5	12.5	65.6	1,063	94.0
Vineyard Lake CDP	980	-	-	642	97.0	0.5	2.5	0.0	0.0	7.2	28.7	55.0	50.4	15.1	343	91.3
Volinia township (Cass)	1,117	1,088	-2.6	992	91.1	3.0	0.0	3.3	2.5	16.8	19.6	46.6	40.4	20.2	410	88.5
Wacousta CDP	1,440	-	-	1,571	95.9	0.0	1.2	1.8	1.0	19.4	20.8	49.0	26.4	40.5	570	93.3
Wakefield city & MCD (Gogebic)	1,832	1,668	-9.0	1,529	96.7	0.4	1.0	1.5	0.3	13.7	28.6	53.8	41.4	16.4	712	84.3
Wakefield township (Gogebic)	324	296	-8.6	346	98.0	0.0	0.0	1.4	0.6	16.5	23.7	50.1	43.4	17.2	165	81.2
Wakeshma township (Kalamazoo)	1,304	1,359	4.2	1,264	95.0	0.2	0.0	2.5	2.3	21.0	19.4	45.4	49.2	11.0	480	86.5
Waldron village	538	523	-2.8	489	97.5	0.0	0.0	2.2	0.2	23.1	14.5	43.8	67.8	7.8	198	73.2
Wales township (St. Clair)	3,248	3,187	-1.9	3,194	97.9	0.0	0.0	1.4	0.7	19.7	16.9	48.0	48.9	13.0	1,232	90.8
Walker township (Cheboygan)	327	320	-2.1	329	91.8	0.0	0.9	7.0	0.3	22.2	17.9	41.8	67.2	9.7	117	81.2
Walker city & MCD (Kent)	23,545	24,869	5.6	24,816	87.3	2.9	2.4	3.1	4.3	22.8	15.0	35.4	31.3	31.0	9,865	93.1
Walkerville village	262	260	-0.8	224	80.8	0.0	0.0	4.9	14.3	34.4	14.3	34.0	43.5	4.6	71	80.3
Walled Lake city & MCD (Oakland)	7,059	7,134	1.1	7,173	82.3	8.2	1.6	4.0	3.9	17.5	13.7	42.2	33.8	30.2	3,526	91.9
Walloon Lake CDP	290	-	-	224	96.4	0.4	0.0	0.9	2.2	11.2	21.9	56.9	16.1	53.8	126	92.1
Walton township (Eaton)	2,273	2,319	2.0	2,483	93.4	0.7	1.7	1.3	2.9	27.0	15.1	39.0	47.5	21.1	840	90.2
Warner township (Antrim)	419	418	-0.2	362	97.5	0.0	0.0	2.5	0.0	24.6	12.4	43.5	49.8	12.9	144	86.1
Warren city & MCD (Macomb)	134,070	133,943	-0.1	134,797	65.9	19.3	9.3	2.8	2.7	21.3	16.2	39.4	47.7	18.5	53,652	85.8
Warren township (Midland)	2,119	2,051	-3.2	1,804	96.2	0.1	0.0	3.0	0.7	23.8	20.2	40.0	46.6	16.3	704	85.2
Washington township (Gratiot)	872	835	-4.2	882	84.2	13.8	0.3	0.7	0.9	21.0	17.5	41.9	49.4	13.6	365	89.9
Washington township (Macomb)	25,154	28,651	13.9	27,793	91.8	1.9	1.5	1.8	3.0	21.4	20.0	45.5	31.0	36.2	10,880	93.9
Washington township (Sanilac)	1,653	2,090	26.4	1,492	94.1	0.5	0.3	3.4	1.7	22.1	16.6	41.8	52.1	12.2	599	87.3
Waterford charter township (Oakland)	71,688	72,631	1.3	72,976	82.2	5.3	1.9	3.5	7.1	19.3	15.9	41.9	36.4	27.7	30,708	92.9
Waterloo township (Jackson)	2,856	2,899	1.5	2,869	95.9	0.2	0.0	1.0	3.0	22.0	17.0	45.7	45.6	23.2	1,169	89.5
Watersmeet CDP	428	-	-	400	75.0	0.0	2.3	21.5	1.3	22.5	26.0	46.7	56.1	11.0	176	75.0
Watersmeet township (Gogebic)	1,419	1,357	-4.4	1,271	70.3	0.6	2.0	26.5	0.5	17.7	42.3	60.6	45.0	25.7	610	82.8
Watertown charter township (Clinton)	4,836	5,482	13.4	5,321	90.2	0.7	1.4	3.2	4.5	23.6	17.5	43.8	28.4	36.6	1,940	94.8
Watertown township (Sanilac)	1,323	1,245	-5.9	1,244	94.3	0.0	0.1	1.0	4.6	16.7	18.3	46.9	56.3	14.1	554	84.7

1 May be of any race.

STATE City, town, township, borough, or CDP (county if applicable)	Population				Race and Hispanic or Latino origin (percent)					Age (percent)			Educational attainment of persons age 25 and older		Occupied housing units	
	2010 census total population	2019 estimated population	Percent change 2010–2019	ACS total population estimate 2015–2019	White alone, not Hispanic or Latino	Black alone, not Hispanic or Latino	Asian alone, not Hispanic or Latino	All other races or 2 or more races, not Hispanic or Latino	Hispanic or Latino[1]	Under 18 years old	Age 65 years and older	Median age	Percent High school diploma or less	Percent Bachelor's degree or more	Total	Percent with a computer
	1	2	3	4	5	6	7	8	9	10	11	12	13	14	15	16
MICHIGAN—Con.																
Watertown township (Tuscola)	2,202	2,061	-6.4	2,105	94.4	0.4	0.5	3.1	1.5	20.8	16.3	43.8	54.4	8.9	816	91.1
Watervliet city & MCD (Berrien)	1,715	1,646	-4.0	1,544	90.1	0.6	0.6	6.6	2.1	27.5	16.6	39.4	51.9	12.0	686	85.3
Watervliet township (Berrien)	3,126	3,090	-1.2	3,098	83.0	8.6	0.6	4.5	3.3	23.4	21.3	39.7	49.8	18.1	1,191	84.2
Watson township (Allegan)	2,063	2,190	6.2	2,185	98.1	0.5	0.0	1.0	0.3	20.4	13.8	43.9	53.5	13.6	812	88.5
Waucedah township (Dickinson)	804	778	-3.2	838	95.8	0.0	0.4	2.1	1.7	24.7	20.8	49.6	38.5	25.8	339	87.0
Waverly township (Cheboygan)	457	440	-3.7	410	96.3	0.0	0.2	1.5	2.0	18.0	27.1	52.2	46.9	16.7	183	88.5
Waverly CDP	23,925	-	-	24,201	66.4	14.7	6.7	3.5	8.7	15.6	19.8	40.2	25.0	38.9	11,161	92.2
Waverly township (Van Buren)	2,556	2,532	-0.9	2,524	96.7	0.3	0.4	1.3	1.3	18.5	17.8	47.4	47.3	19.0	1,049	90.6
Wawatam township (Emmet)	656	668	1.8	649	76.7	11.9	0.9	6.9	3.5	21.9	25.3	48.2	41.7	19.0	293	85.0
Wayland city & MCD (Allegan)	4,079	4,225	3.6	4,197	91.5	2.0	0.0	3.2	3.3	24.2	14.2	33.3	45.9	20.1	1,715	81.2
Wayland township (Allegan)	3,086	3,441	11.5	3,331	89.3	2.0	1.1	6.6	1.0	27.4	16.2	42.7	46.8	16.7	1,185	83.5
Wayne township (Cass)	2,656	2,609	-1.8	2,592	83.6	2.3	0.0	5.1	9.0	19.4	23.4	46.4	53.1	13.2	1,046	80.7
Wayne city & MCD (Wayne)	17,593	16,814	-4.4	16,976	73.5	18.2	0.8	3.6	3.9	23.6	14.0	38.9	50.2	13.1	6,605	90.9
Weare township (Oceana)	1,210	1,219	0.7	1,365	82.3	1.5	0.0	2.8	13.4	22.3	16.7	39.2	48.2	12.9	467	91.9
Webber township (Lake)	1,695	1,621	-4.4	1,670	60.6	31.8	0.1	2.9	4.6	16.8	27.5	47.9	60.1	8.8	603	78.9
Webberville village	1,268	1,310	3.3	1,322	98.0	0.0	0.0	0.4	1.7	25.5	11.3	36.8	48.7	18.1	506	89.1
Webster township (Washtenaw)	6,324	6,809	7.7	6,727	93.4	0.0	2.6	2.0	2.0	21.0	18.8	48.9	11.6	64.6	2,499	96.2
Wedgewood CDP	237	-	-	279	100.0	0.0	0.0	0.0	0.0	21.9	30.1	53.4	11.3	52.2	98	95.9
Weesaw township (Berrien)	1,936	1,894	-2.2	1,854	90.5	0.6	0.8	1.7	6.4	16.6	19.3	48.7	54.3	13.3	839	88.0
Weidman CDP	959	-	-	817	96.0	0.0	0.0	2.0	2.1	18.1	26.3	40.3	53.5	8.5	357	88.8
Weldon township (Benzie)	540	549	1.7	630	90.2	0.0	0.3	6.5	3.0	20.8	19.5	45.8	55.4	12.4	250	85.6
Wellington township (Alpena)	308	297	-3.6	317	99.7	0.0	0.0	0.3	0.0	10.7	24.6	49.8	50.8	16.3	153	80.4
Wells township (Delta)	4,896	4,736	-3.3	4,759	96.7	0.0	0.6	1.4	1.3	18.8	22.9	51.9	41.8	19.3	1,977	84.7
Wells township (Marquette)	231	231	0.0	255	99.6	0.0	0.0	0.4	0.0	20.0	26.7	55.1	61.5	13.8	119	86.6
Wells township (Tuscola)	1,778	1,688	-5.1	1,685	93.1	0.4	0.0	2.1	4.5	19.3	19.4	47.7	53.3	11.5	672	87.4
Wellston CDP	311	-	-	246	94.7	0.0	0.0	3.7	1.6	20.7	27.2	44.6	68.8	2.3	108	70.4
West Bloomfield charter township (Oakland)	64,676	65,610	1.4	65,928	73.6	12.6	9.2	3.0	1.6	21.0	22.2	46.3	18.2	60.4	24,577	95.9
West Branch township (Dickinson)	67	65	-3.0	17	100.0	0.0	0.0	0.0	0.0	23.5	11.8	35.8	60.0	0.0	8	75.0
West Branch township (Marquette)	1,623	1,625	0.1	1,616	90.8	2.0	0.7	4.6	1.9	18.8	15.2	40.1	36.4	27.8	648	91.8
West Branch township (Missaukee)	466	477	2.4	470	88.5	0.0	0.4	4.5	6.6	17.7	26.8	50.7	56.2	15.0	214	81.3
West Branch city & MCD (Ogemaw)	2,136	2,050	-4.0	2,177	92.4	1.7	3.9	0.3	1.7	18.0	29.6	45.4	54.3	14.5	990	81.3
West Branch township (Ogemaw)	2,607	2,534	-2.8	2,511	92.0	0.6	0.4	2.3	4.7	21.4	17.8	43.8	46.9	16.5	1,009	93.6
West Ishpeming CDP	2,662	-	-	2,739	91.8	0.3	2.1	5.8	0.0	21.4	26.0	48.8	43.5	29.6	1,028	81.0
Westland city & MCD (Wayne)	84,150	81,511	-3.1	81,938	71.5	17.2	4.6	2.5	4.1	20.6	16.5	40.2	42.4	22.1	35,183	90.3
West Monroe CDP	3,503	-	-	3,488	94.7	0.0	0.0	2.8	2.5	27.4	10.9	31.7	58.4	12.8	1,359	87.5
Westphalia village	921	933	1.3	989	93.9	0.0	0.0	0.6	5.5	27.3	26.3	40.2	51.1	20.2	359	76.3
Westphalia township (Clinton)	2,363	2,395	1.4	2,497	97.0	0.0	0.1	0.2	2.7	27.8	18.5	36.6	39.6	27.8	867	81.3
West Traverse township (Emmet)	1,610	1,646	2.2	1,651	95.0	0.0	0.3	4.2	0.4	13.5	43.9	62.0	13.0	56.2	782	95.9
Westwood CDP	8,653	-	-	9,271	73.9	10.5	6.0	3.9	5.6	16.2	16.1	32.4	19.9	49.3	4,086	94.8
Wexford township (Wexford)	1,076	1,105	2.7	983	94.4	0.4	0.5	4.7	0.0	21.3	16.2	44.4	49.6	14.3	368	90.8
Wheatfield township (Ingham)	1,623	1,661	2.3	1,846	90.0	0.9	2.1	1.9	5.1	25.2	18.6	45.9	31.0	43.2	654	89.6
Wheatland township (Hillsdale)	1,349	1,328	-1.6	1,154	91.9	0.0	0.3	4.9	3.0	17.5	16.4	47.4	46.1	11.2	483	85.3
Wheatland township (Mecosta)	1,403	1,410	0.5	1,368	88.7	2.9	0.0	4.0	4.3	18.0	18.6	48.0	50.6	20.5	552	84.1
Wheatland township (Sanilac)	487	460	-5.5	441	91.8	0.0	0.0	2.3	5.9	25.6	18.1	37.6	62.8	10.0	192	73.4
Wheeler township (Gratiot)	2,786	2,664	-4.4	2,689	92.2	0.0	0.0	1.1	6.7	23.2	19.1	42.4	52.7	12.6	1,151	89.6
White Cloud city & MCD (Newaygo)	1,410	1,387	-1.6	1,205	85.1	9.3	0.4	1.9	3.3	22.6	14.5	34.7	64.4	9.1	376	77.9
Whitefish township (Chippewa)	575	564	-1.9	492	87.6	0.2	0.0	10.8	1.4	20.3	33.7	55.5	35.9	28.0	205	88.8
Whiteford township (Monroe)	4,596	4,421	-3.8	4,458	93.7	1.3	1.7	0.7	2.6	18.4	21.2	46.3	43.5	23.6	1,776	91.1
Whitehall city & MCD (Muskegon)	2,711	2,832	4.5	2,749	88.2	1.3	3.1	3.6	3.8	23.0	22.8	44.4	36.6	25.4	1,150	88.3
Whitehall township (Muskegon)	1,734	1,760	1.5	1,899	92.2	1.9	1.1	1.8	3.0	26.3	16.5	40.5	31.7	26.3	690	94.1
White Lake charter township (Oakland)	30,019	31,356	4.5	31,208	94.1	0.9	1.1	1.2	2.8	21.5	16.1	42.8	30.9	31.8	11,669	93.8
White Oak township (Ingham)	1,173	1,202	2.5	1,201	94.2	0.0	0.0	4.2	1.6	19.1	16.2	46.3	49.0	16.9	451	93.6
White Pigeon village	1,535	1,527	-0.5	1,613	90.8	0.0	0.0	2.3	6.9	24.9	13.6	31.9	53.6	10.6	655	88.5
White Pigeon township (St. Joseph)	3,755	3,824	1.8	3,789	92.7	0.0	0.0	1.0	6.3	20.2	22.1	44.5	50.1	16.9	1,617	90.0

1 May be of any race.

Table A. All Places — Population and Housing

STATE City, town, township, borough, or CDP (county if applicable)	2010 census total population	2019 estimated population	Percent change 2010–2019	ACS total population estimate 2015–2019	White alone, not Hispanic or Latino	Black alone, not Hispanic or Latino	Asian alone, not Hispanic or Latino	All other races or 2 or more races, not Hispanic or Latino	Hispanic or Latino[1]	Under 18 years old	Age 65 years and older	Median age	Percent High school diploma or less	Percent Bachelor's degree or more	Total	Percent with a computer
	1	2	3	4	5	6	7	8	9	10	11	12	13	14	15	16
MICHIGAN—Con.																
White Pine CDP.............	474	-	-	455	91.2	0.0	2.9	2.2	3.7	16.7	37.1	57.4	43.3	16.3	201	88.6
White River township (Muskegon).................	1,327	1,391	4.8	1,244	97.6	0.4	0.0	1.4	0.6	20.4	30.8	51.3	30.1	35.1	498	91.6
Whitewater township (Grand Traverse).........	2,599	2,811	8.2	2,793	94.7	0.2	0.0	5.1	0.0	23.5	18.4	46.5	26.3	34.4	1,029	94.6
Whitmore Lake CDP........	6,423	-	-	6,618	92.6	0.3	1.1	2.0	3.9	19.8	15.0	36.6	36.2	29.3	2,797	92.8
Whitney township (Arenac).................	1,002	940	-6.2	862	98.4	0.0	0.0	0.0	1.6	10.9	38.9	59.6	46.5	26.8	435	81.1
Whittemore city & MCD (Iosco).................	386	375	-2.8	432	97.7	0.0	0.0	1.4	0.9	22.2	19.2	45.5	61.7	7.9	193	79.8
Wilber township (Iosco)....	730	715	-2.1	663	98.0	0.0	0.6	0.2	1.2	11.8	29.9	56.2	53.9	9.7	318	81.8
Wilcox township (Newaygo).................	1,098	1,117	1.7	1,038	89.5	0.8	1.0	3.2	5.6	20.4	16.1	47.4	64.7	8.2	439	82.7
Williams charter township (Bay).................	4,779	4,796	0.4	4,829	92.8	0.0	1.4	1.9	3.9	22.3	14.3	38.7	40.7	26.3	1,809	96.7
Williamston city & MCD (Ingham).................	3,864	3,965	2.6	3,959	92.6	0.0	0.4	2.6	4.4	26.4	16.8	37.5	18.7	51.6	1,685	94.4
Williamstown township (Ingham).................	4,970	5,184	4.3	5,131	94.9	1.4	1.8	1.2	0.6	19.7	20.5	49.9	17.4	51.9	1,941	95.6
Wilmot township (Cheboygan).................	878	851	-3.1	826	98.7	0.0	0.0	0.7	0.6	21.8	21.1	45.7	60.5	8.1	331	85.8
Wilson township (Alpena).	2,029	1,961	-3.4	1,779	95.7	0.0	0.0	2.9	1.4	16.0	21.5	52.0	43.4	14.8	821	87.3
Wilson township (Charlevoix).................	1,963	1,970	0.4	1,998	94.1	0.0	1.5	3.4	1.1	25.2	16.5	43.9	36.4	24.8	743	92.2
Windsor charter township (Eaton).................	6,838	7,017	2.6	6,957	86.2	1.9	2.9	4.0	5.0	16.3	25.6	51.4	24.7	31.0	2,865	88.0
Winfield township (Montcalm).................	2,235	2,266	1.4	2,107	95.0	1.0	0.0	2.3	1.7	25.6	10.7	35.9	41.8	20.8	734	92.4
Winsor township (Huron)..	1,907	1,770	-7.2	1,809	93.7	1.8	0.0	1.9	2.7	20.4	23.2	46.4	45.3	20.7	864	85.2
Winterfield township (Clare).................	459	460	0.2	429	93.5	0.0	0.0	6.1	0.5	17.7	22.8	48.2	50.6	9.8	190	83.7
Wise township (Isabella)...	1,397	1,385	-0.9	1,303	97.5	0.0	0.0	1.0	1.5	21.5	20.0	43.7	57.4	10.4	493	84.6
Wisner township (Tuscola)	690	647	-6.2	640	80.0	0.0	0.0	8.6	11.4	13.0	22.0	53.6	58.6	6.8	307	75.2
Wixom city & MCD (Oakland).................	13,505	14,049	4.0	13,902	70.7	16.5	7.4	2.6	2.8	21.1	11.3	37.1	24.0	43.5	6,285	96.0
Wolf Lake CDP..............	4,104	-	-	3,884	94.3	0.5	0.7	3.2	1.2	17.9	12.3	38.3	57.0	8.3	1,515	86.5
Wolverine village...........	244	234	-4.1	253	99.6	0.0	0.0	0.4	0.0	28.5	14.6	37.2	65.4	6.3	91	93.4
Wolverine Lake village......	4,338	4,783	10.3	4,648	91.5	0.0	0.4	2.3	5.8	19.6	16.8	43.6	30.4	37.1	1,967	93.4
Woodbridge township (Hillsdale).................	1,325	1,294	-2.3	1,347	99.4	0.0	0.0	0.2	0.4	38.0	10.7	32.6	66.0	9.4	403	70.2
Woodhaven city & MCD (Wayne).................	12,879	12,469	-3.2	12,518	82.4	5.9	3.1	1.6	6.9	18.9	19.9	45.4	38.8	24.0	5,225	94.4
Woodhull township (Shiawassee).................	3,804	3,700	-2.7	3,706	97.8	0.2	0.0	1.2	0.8	18.4	21.3	48.9	29.1	34.3	1,476	97.1
Woodland village	427	446	4.4	550	87.3	0.0	0.2	0.2	12.4	22.5	17.5	33.6	52.8	13.1	216	86.6
Woodland township (Barry).................	2,047	2,129	4.0	2,426	94.8	0.0	0.0	0.7	4.4	24.6	16.5	41.7	45.5	16.3	958	91.2
Woodland Beach CDP......	2,049	-	-	2,294	95.8	0.0	0.0	4.2	0.0	32.2	13.3	34.1	46.0	12.9	851	95.5
Woodstock township (Lenawee).................	3,510	3,465	-1.3	3,464	97.2	0.1	0.0	1.8	0.9	19.6	21.4	48.0	48.2	18.7	1,524	88.5
Worth township (Sanilac)..	3,872	3,632	-6.2	3,661	97.7	0.7	0.0	0.7	1.0	12.6	29.5	54.6	42.3	17.8	1,746	83.2
Wright township (Hillsdale)	1,655	1,609	-2.8	1,731	95.4	0.0	0.0	2.0	2.6	25.2	15.0	41.0	62.0	8.7	631	79.4
Wright township (Ottawa) .	3,147	3,281	4.3	3,267	94.3	0.0	0.0	2.5	3.2	24.0	16.7	40.9	45.2	19.1	1,167	89.8
Wyandotte city & MCD (Wayne).................	25,883	24,859	-4.0	25,044	92.5	0.9	0.6	1.3	4.7	20.1	16.3	41.9	42.6	18.5	11,070	88.1
Wyoming city & MCD (Kent).................	72,117	75,667	4.9	75,702	62.1	7.0	3.2	4.9	22.9	25.5	10.5	33.5	46.6	20.7	27,773	92.1
Yale city & MCD (St. Clair)	1,953	1,870	-4.2	2,082	94.8	0.2	0.6	2.8	1.6	24.2	18.9	40.2	53.6	10.9	832	79.6
Yankee Springs township (Barry).................	4,069	4,457	9.5	4,294	95.2	0.0	1.6	1.5	1.8	21.1	18.3	45.6	36.3	27.6	1,873	92.7
Yates township (Lake).......	761	790	3.8	592	67.4	27.5	0.0	4.1	1.0	18.4	29.4	55.2	61.3	6.4	279	69.9
York charter township (Washtenaw).................	8,710	9,232	6.0	9,128	69.8	9.1	4.4	8.5	8.2	20.8	14.9	43.3	27.8	40.7	2,525	94.9
Ypsilanti city & MCD (Washtenaw).................	19,569	20,171	3.1	20,828	61.8	28.0	2.4	3.2	4.6	14.6	7.6	24.2	21.7	43.3	7,743	93.5
Ypsilanti charter township (Washtenaw).................	53,362	55,216	3.5	55,089	52.9	32.3	2.2	5.9	6.7	23.0	10.9	34.1	30.9	33.2	22,122	93.0
Zeba CDP.................	480	-	-	389	40.9	0.5	1.0	54.2	3.3	24.2	15.9	43.4	45.0	10.8	148	85.8
Zeeland city & MCD (Ottawa).................	5,502	5,536	0.6	5,572	88.9	1.3	2.0	1.5	6.3	21.9	25.4	39.2	40.3	28.2	2,421	85.3
Zeeland charter township (Ottawa).................	9,971	11,564	16.0	11,160	86.0	0.3	3.8	2.3	7.6	30.1	12.9	37.7	41.0	34.7	3,703	91.8
Zilwaukee city & MCD (Saginaw).................	1,658	1,529	-7.8	1,668	83.1	0.9	1.2	3.9	10.9	21.9	13.5	36.3	44.8	14.0	668	92.5
Zilwaukee township (Saginaw).................	67	65	-3.0	111	89.2	0.0	0.0	3.6	7.2	38.7	2.7	28.5	25.0	40.0	36	97.2
MINNESOTA...................	5,303,927	5,639,632	6.3	5,563,378	79.8	6.3	4.8	3.7	5.4	23.3	15.4	38.0	31.5	36.1	2,185,603	91.6
Aastad township (Otter Tail).................	213	213	0.0	182	100.0	0.0	0.0	0.0	0.0	15.4	15.9	46.8	38.1	18.3	77	76.6
Acoma township (McLeod)	1,149	1,128	-1.8	1,165	98.9	0.0	0.5	0.0	0.6	23.3	17.3	44.8	27.2	27.6	426	97.9
Acton township (Meeker)..	374	377	0.8	427	97.4	0.5	0.7	0.0	1.4	25.3	14.5	35.8	31.5	28.3	156	94.2
Ada city & MCD (Norman)	1,705	1,563	-8.3	1,763	86.3	0.4	0.0	5.3	7.9	28.1	19.6	39.3	44.0	21.8	706	85.0
Adams city & MCD (Mower).................	786	790	0.5	755	98.3	0.0	0.4	0.0	1.3	14.4	31.8	53.8	47.2	20.7	314	81.8
Adams township (Mower) .	453	473	4.4	461	93.9	0.0	0.0	0.0	6.1	26.9	17.1	37.7	31.0	28.5	175	94.9
Adrian city & MCD (Nobles).................	1,221	1,218	-0.2	1,178	90.1	0.0	2.4	2.5	5.1	21.3	18.8	40.6	45.4	16.6	504	86.1
Adrian township (Watonwan).................	138	136	-1.4	76	100.0	0.0	0.0	0.0	0.0	28.9	25.0	39.3	41.2	15.7	34	85.3

1 May be of any race.

Table A. All Places — **Population and Housing**

STATE City, town, township, borough, or CDP (county if applicable)	Population				Race and Hispanic or Latino origin (percent)					Age (percent)			Educational attainment of persons age 25 and older		Occupied housing units	
	2010 census total population	2019 estimated population	Percent change 2010–2019	ACS total population estimate 2015–2019	White alone, not Hispanic or Latino	Black alone, not Hispanic or Latino	Asian alone, not Hispanic or Latino	All other races or 2 or more races, not Hispanic or Latino	Hispanic or Latino[1]	Under 18 years old	Age 65 years and older	Median age	Percent High school diploma or less	Percent Bachelor's degree or more	Total	Percent with a computer
	1	2	3	4	5	6	7	8	9	10	11	12	13	14	15	16

MINNESOTA—Con.

STATE	1	2	3	4	5	6	7	8	9	10	11	12	13	14	15	16
Aetna township (Pipestone)	194	189	-2.6	217	100.0	0.0	0.0	0.0	0.0	29.5	14.7	41.3	42.0	18.9	86	88.4
Afton city & MCD (Washington)	2,878	3,028	5.2	2,999	94.7	1.6	2.5	1.3	0.0	21.1	23.0	48.4	17.7	56.1	1,095	97.5
Agassiz township (Lac qui Parle)	103	95	-7.8	64	100.0	0.0	0.0	0.0	0.0	18.8	17.2	49.7	28.6	34.7	28	89.3
Agder township (Marshall)	109	110	0.9	160	100.0	0.0	0.0	0.0	0.0	26.9	13.1	40.6	48.1	20.2	58	100.0
Agram township (Morrison)	572	587	2.6	502	97.0	0.0	1.6	0.6	0.8	20.3	18.5	46.2	42.9	17.9	213	87.8
Aitkin city & MCD (Aitkin)	2,132	1,985	-6.9	2,330	92.0	0.7	0.6	3.8	3.0	22.6	30.1	43.8	50.4	20.4	1,082	75.0
Aitkin township (Aitkin)	888	883	-0.6	954	95.1	1.3	0.0	3.4	0.3	19.6	20.2	46.8	40.1	22.1	405	90.9
Akeley city & MCD (Hubbard)	434	443	2.1	394	95.7	0.5	0.0	3.8	0.0	19.5	25.9	49.0	63.8	9.5	186	74.7
Akeley township (Hubbard)	549	575	4.7	520	95.6	0.0	0.0	2.1	2.3	11.7	31.3	55.1	44.9	20.0	249	83.5
Akron township (Big Stone)	168	163	-3.0	169	92.3	0.0	0.0	0.0	7.7	18.9	17.8	56.4	42.6	20.9	68	82.4
Akron township (Wilkin)	133	127	-4.5	123	92.7	0.0	0.0	7.3	0.0	23.6	22.0	51.9	35.9	18.5	47	93.6
Alango township (St. Louis)	258	260	0.8	176	97.2	0.0	0.0	2.8	0.0	15.9	32.4	56.3	32.9	22.6	90	82.2
Alaska township (Beltrami)	217	215	-0.9	199	97.5	0.0	0.0	2.5	0.0	21.1	19.6	47.8	39.7	33.8	79	91.1
Alba township (Jackson)	170	164	-3.5	156	85.3	0.0	0.0	0.0	14.7	25.0	20.5	45.3	51.4	14.7	55	96.4
Albany city & MCD (Stearns)	2,585	2,766	7.0	2,729	92.0	3.4	0.3	2.1	2.2	27.9	21.6	35.9	51.5	21.3	1,020	85.2
Albany township (Stearns)	956	1,038	8.6	1,020	95.6	0.0	1.9	2.5	0.0	27.6	11.8	41.2	44.1	15.4	347	87.3
Alberta township (Benton)	826	862	4.4	799	99.2	0.0	0.0	0.8	0.0	28.3	15.1	43.2	58.2	13.4	296	84.5
Alberta city & MCD (Stevens)	103	99	-3.9	126	100.0	0.0	0.0	0.0	0.0	17.5	19.8	49.6	42.0	18.0	51	74.5
Albert Lea city & MCD (Freeborn)	18,203	17,656	-3.0	17,773	78.9	1.5	3.4	1.9	14.4	22.4	23.3	42.6	48.6	16.4	7,752	85.5
Albert Lea township (Freeborn)	584	566	-3.1	633	85.8	0.0	0.8	0.6	12.8	26.5	21.2	44.0	28.9	27.8	241	95.9
Albertville city & MCD (Wright)	7,063	7,539	6.7	7,436	92.8	3.2	0.9	3.1	0.0	28.7	9.4	35.8	33.4	29.3	2,872	93.2
Albin township (Brown)	348	340	-2.3	265	97.7	0.8	0.0	0.0	1.5	24.5	29.4	47.3	51.5	16.8	107	84.1
Albion township (Wright)	1,249	1,326	6.2	1,225	99.3	0.0	0.0	0.7	0.0	23.1	18.0	43.6	41.8	22.0	436	93.6
Alborn township (St. Louis)	460	463	0.7	472	96.0	0.0	0.0	4.0	0.0	18.2	20.3	44.8	33.9	16.1	205	91.2
Alden city & MCD (Freeborn)	660	639	-3.2	658	90.9	0.0	0.0	1.1	8.1	21.9	17.5	43.6	44.1	16.1	283	85.9
Alden township (Freeborn)	306	296	-3.3	217	100.0	0.0	0.0	0.0	0.0	17.5	25.3	55.1	43.6	15.7	94	93.6
Alden township (St. Louis)	213	213	0.0	186	89.8	0.0	5.4	4.8	0.0	26.3	10.8	48.3	28.2	35.1	79	89.9
Aldrich city & MCD (Wadena)	48	45	-6.3	51	100.0	0.0	0.0	0.0	0.0	15.7	23.5	47.3	55.8	11.6	26	96.2
Aldrich township (Wadena)	427	419	-1.9	425	92.9	0.0	0.5	0.7	5.9	22.1	18.1	42.9	38.5	11.5	182	90.1
Alexandria city & MCD (Douglas)	12,508	13,822	10.5	13,554	92.4	0.7	0.7	3.2	3.0	19.0	22.1	37.5	37.3	24.7	6,646	87.0
Alexandria township (Douglas)	2,704	2,877	6.4	2,799	96.7	0.6	0.0	1.4	1.3	30.8	16.0	38.4	28.5	35.2	1,026	95.9
Alfsborg township (Sibley)	316	311	-1.6	321	96.6	0.0	0.3	3.1	0.0	26.2	20.6	46.8	43.5	20.2	124	93.5
Alliance township (Clay)	235	246	4.7	252	100.0	0.0	0.0	0.0	0.0	25.4	15.5	38.6	32.4	15.6	104	92.3
Alma township (Marshall)	88	87	-1.1	62	100.0	0.0	0.0	0.0	0.0	21.0	19.4	39.0	18.2	29.5	23	87.0
Almond township (Big Stone)	102	100	-2.0	123	100.0	0.0	0.0	0.0	0.0	25.2	26.0	44.1	44.3	35.2	45	100.0
Alpha city & MCD (Jackson)	128	119	-7.0	118	98.3	0.0	0.0	0.0	1.7	24.6	16.9	38.8	52.8	12.4	61	77.0
Alta Vista township (Lincoln)	175	171	-2.3	151	100.0	0.0	0.0	0.0	0.0	12.6	21.2	56.5	23.0	19.8	69	85.5
Alton township (Waseca)	434	437	0.7	440	99.5	0.0	0.0	0.5	0.0	27.7	11.4	38.7	39.9	26.3	161	89.4
Altona township (Pipestone)	153	150	-2.0	111	100.0	0.0	0.0	0.0	0.0	17.1	18.9	56.1	48.9	22.7	52	96.2
Altura city & MCD (Winona)	493	476	-3.4	474	81.0	1.1	0.0	2.7	15.2	33.1	12.0	33.7	41.3	17.3	178	87.6
Alvarado city & MCD (Marshall)	363	362	-0.3	386	82.6	0.8	0.0	2.6	14.0	27.2	18.1	37.3	53.4	17.6	169	84.0
Alvwood township (Itasca)	42	42	0.0	33	100.0	0.0	0.0	0.0	0.0	36.4	33.3	28.3	52.6	10.5	13	84.6
Amador township (Chisago)	885	934	5.5	823	96.7	0.2	1.0	1.5	0.6	20.4	17.7	48.6	34.6	22.5	315	89.2
Amboy city & MCD (Blue Earth)	535	507	-5.2	651	89.7	0.0	0.0	2.3	8.0	26.3	17.5	38.0	50.3	15.3	265	83.8
Amboy township (Cottonwood)	164	160	-2.4	115	100.0	0.0	0.0	0.0	0.0	20.9	39.1	58.3	33.3	14.3	51	82.4
Amherst township (Fillmore)	378	396	4.8	340	100.0	0.0	0.0	0.0	0.0	32.4	19.4	34.0	61.6	13.2	119	68.9
Amiret township (Lyon)	245	242	-1.2	202	99.5	0.5	0.0	0.0	0.0	20.3	28.2	55.4	32.1	26.9	91	91.2
Amo township (Cottonwood)	132	128	-3.0	88	100.0	0.0	0.0	0.0	0.0	26.1	21.6	34.5	16.7	45.8	38	94.7
Amor township (Otter Tail)	495	493	-0.4	485	96.5	1.0	0.0	2.3	0.2	15.1	30.1	54.8	31.8	28.4	203	91.1
Andover city & MCD (Anoka)	30,588	33,140	8.3	32,733	88.3	3.6	2.0	1.9	4.2	26.6	11.6	39.9	24.0	37.6	10,850	96.2
Andover township (Polk)	119	119	0.0	84	100.0	0.0	0.0	0.0	0.0	13.1	4.8	55.8	26.6	40.6	35	100.0
Andrea township (Wilkin)	65	62	-4.6	36	100.0	0.0	0.0	0.0	0.0	19.4	22.2	55.2	86.2	6.9	15	66.7
Angle Inlet CDP	60	-	-	-	-	-	-	-	-	-	-	-	-	-	-	-
Angora township (St. Louis)	244	246	0.8	229	90.0	2.2	0.0	6.6	1.3	17.0	21.4	52.8	52.1	11.2	118	75.4
Angus township (Polk)	76	77	1.3	76	100.0	0.0	0.0	0.0	0.0	26.3	23.7	43.5	29.6	37.0	30	100.0
Ann township (Cottonwood)	179	173	-3.4	119	98.3	0.0	0.0	0.0	1.7	14.3	39.5	57.6	25.3	27.3	55	98.2
Annandale city & MCD (Wright)	3,227	3,517	9.0	3,387	90.1	1.4	0.0	0.0	8.6	22.6	22.6	42.2	45.5	26.0	1,490	84.2

1 May be of any race.

Table A. All Places — Population and Housing

STATE City, town, township, borough, or CDP (county if applicable)	Population 2010 census total population	2019 estimated population	Percent change 2010–2019	ACS total population estimate 2015–2019	Race and Hispanic or Latino origin (percent) White alone, not Hispanic or Latino	Black alone, not Hispanic or Latino	Asian alone, not Hispanic or Latino	All other races or 2 or more races, not Hispanic or Latino	Hispanic or Latino[1]	Age (percent) Under 18 years old	Age 65 years and older	Median age	Educational attainment of persons age 25 and older Percent High school diploma or less	Percent Bachelor's degree or more	Occupied housing units Total	Percent with a computer
	1	2	3	4	5	6	7	8	9	10	11	12	13	14	15	16
MINNESOTA—Con.																
Ann Lake township (Kanabec)	454	448	-1.3	421	93.8	0.5	0.0	4.8	1.0	15.4	22.1	50.3	56.3	11.3	197	79.2
Anoka city & MCD (Anoka)	17,149	17,549	2.3	17,471	83.0	7.2	1.4	4.3	4.1	21.7	18.2	38.4	37.8	25.2	6,959	90.2
Ansel township (Cass)	97	102	5.2	86	100.0	0.0	0.0	0.0	0.0	7.0	24.4	57.8	48.6	13.9	42	83.3
Anthony township (Norman)	62	59	-4.8	54	90.7	0.0	0.0	0.0	9.3	29.6	11.1	30.0	25.0	18.8	17	100.0
Antrim township (Watonwan)	240	237	-1.3	242	85.5	0.0	0.8	0.0	13.6	28.1	13.2	33.9	45.8	16.1	92	82.6
Appleton city & MCD (Swift)	1,417	1,325	-6.5	1,412	83.8	2.8	0.0	6.4	7.1	21.0	24.9	44.2	54.8	18.7	717	72.1
Appleton township (Swift) ..	196	189	-3.6	222	100.0	0.0	0.0	0.0	0.0	15.8	37.4	60.0	45.4	18.0	106	87.7
Apple Valley city & MCD (Dakota)	49,092	55,135	12.3	52,889	75.3	8.6	6.0	3.7	6.4	24.6	14.3	38.2	24.6	45.0	19,976	94.6
Arago township (Hubbard)	607	624	2.8	621	98.7	0.3	0.0	0.3	0.6	17.1	37.4	59.3	27.0	28.1	292	93.8
Arbo township (Itasca)	867	863	-0.5	977	93.1	0.9	0.0	5.9	0.0	22.4	19.2	39.4	38.8	22.1	395	91.1
Arco city & MCD (Lincoln)	75	69	-8.0	84	100.0	0.0	0.0	0.0	0.0	31.0	11.9	37.8	59.3	7.4	39	76.9
Arctander township (Kandiyohi)	381	392	2.9	346	97.1	0.0	0.0	0.3	2.6	22.5	17.9	46.3	33.1	19.5	140	90.0
Arden Hills city & MCD (Ramsey)	9,552	10,281	7.6	10,293	84.6	1.2	6.5	3.7	4.0	19.3	19.7	35.9	19.7	60.3	3,123	92.3
Ardenhurst township (Itasca)	164	164	0.0	122	97.5	0.0	1.6	0.0	0.8	9.8	43.4	62.9	44.9	17.8	68	89.7
Arena township (Lac qui Parle)	122	113	-7.4	101	100.0	0.0	0.0	0.0	0.0	11.9	35.6	50.5	37.6	15.3	50	100.0
Arendahl township (Fillmore)	337	352	4.5	341	96.2	0.6	0.0	1.5	1.8	30.8	14.1	46.4	30.6	35.6	121	91.7
Argyle city & MCD (Marshall)	639	642	0.5	679	87.9	0.0	0.0	2.2	9.9	22.5	19.4	48.0	52.2	19.8	287	89.5
Arlington city & MCD (Sibley)	2,236	2,146	-4.0	2,463	74.4	0.7	0.3	1.1	23.5	26.8	17.3	35.2	56.6	13.1	945	84.3
Arlington township (Sibley)	540	532	-1.5	500	95.0	0.0	1.6	2.0	1.4	14.6	20.8	48.1	41.4	15.7	198	88.4
Arlone township (Pine)	359	353	-1.7	431	89.8	1.4	5.1	3.2	0.5	21.6	20.6	47.3	64.2	16.1	169	88.2
Arna township (Pine)	112	124	10.7	71	91.5	0.0	0.0	8.5	0.0	11.3	43.7	62.2	50.8	27.1	34	73.5
Arrowhead township (St. Louis)	223	224	0.4	282	89.0	0.0	1.1	9.9	0.0	17.0	14.9	29.0	52.8	9.2	71	88.7
Arthur township (Kanabec)	1,859	1,854	-0.3	1,753	96.1	0.2	0.7	2.1	1.0	19.5	20.1	45.0	47.4	19.8	693	87.0
Arthur township (Traverse)	81	77	-4.9	45	100.0	0.0	0.0	0.0	0.0	20.0	4.4	41.5	30.6	19.4	24	91.7
Artichoke township (Big Stone)	79	77	-2.5	45	100.0	0.0	0.0	0.0	0.0	22.2	26.7	48.2	22.9	28.6	19	100.0
Arveson township (Kittson)	97	93	-4.1	54	100.0	0.0	0.0	0.0	0.0	20.4	11.1	45.4	41.5	19.5	25	100.0
Ashby city & MCD (Grant)	445	441	-0.9	474	93.9	0.4	0.4	0.8	4.4	26.8	27.0	40.7	40.1	16.0	224	83.5
Ash Lake township (Lincoln)	151	148	-2.0	124	100.0	0.0	0.0	0.0	0.0	21.8	40.3	54.5	54.4	15.6	47	66.0
Ashland township (Dodge)	319	328	2.8	341	99.4	0.0	0.0	0.6	0.0	25.2	15.8	42.1	36.5	29.2	117	94.0
Ashley township (Stearns)	262	277	5.7	239	97.5	0.0	0.0	0.4	2.1	25.9	15.9	36.8	48.4	23.6	94	84.0
Askov city & MCD (Pine) ..	364	353	-3.0	359	96.7	0.0	0.0	1.9	1.4	23.7	21.4	47.5	45.3	18.6	169	82.2
Athens township (Isanti)	2,175	2,233	2.7	2,003	93.4	0.0	2.5	3.5	0.5	18.0	15.6	45.0	49.7	16.2	803	94.4
Atherton township (Wilkin)	145	140	-3.4	97	92.8	0.0	0.0	7.2	0.0	21.6	26.8	48.5	32.0	14.7	38	81.6
Atkinson township (Carlton)	414	429	3.6	431	96.3	0.0	0.5	1.2	2.1	21.6	14.4	48.2	37.6	30.5	173	89.0
Atlanta township (Becker)	119	126	5.9	84	86.9	0.0	0.0	4.8	8.3	28.6	11.9	38.3	33.3	29.6	28	85.7
Atwater city & MCD (Kandiyohi)	1,135	1,119	-1.4	1,014	97.3	0.0	0.4	0.4	1.9	25.3	11.3	38.0	38.0	13.4	415	97.1
Audubon city & MCD (Becker)	519	520	0.2	625	88.5	0.0	0.0	9.6	1.9	23.4	15.8	34.4	44.2	14.1	275	92.0
Audubon township (Becker)	541	576	6.5	556	95.5	0.4	0.0	3.8	0.4	23.2	19.1	47.8	38.6	28.1	211	94.3
Augsburg township (Marshall)	74	73	-1.4	54	100.0	0.0	0.0	0.0	0.0	20.4	16.7	38.3	37.2	51.2	26	84.6
Augusta township (Lac qui Parle)	112	103	-8.0	93	100.0	0.0	0.0	0.0	0.0	15.1	32.3	53.8	36.0	13.3	46	82.6
Ault township (St. Louis) ...	106	107	0.9	98	96.9	0.0	0.0	0.0	3.1	4.1	40.8	63.4	42.9	27.5	61	68.9
Aurdal township (Otter Tail)	1,451	1,483	2.2	1,592	96.7	1.4	0.0	0.9	1.1	26.4	11.7	43.6	23.8	36.4	582	96.4
Aurora city	1,682	1,626	-3.3	1,775	96.7	0.0	3.2	0.1	0.0	23.5	24.3	43.4	46.1	18.2	763	80.6
Aurora township (Steele) ..	574	577	0.5	499	99.6	0.0	0.0	0.4	0.0	20.0	18.0	45.5	56.9	15.0	197	85.3
Austin city & MCD (Mower)	24,909	25,233	1.3	25,114	69.7	6.1	5.1	2.8	16.3	25.3	17.7	37.3	46.5	23.1	9,953	88.0
Austin township (Mower) ..	819	852	4.0	817	95.8	0.5	0.4	1.2	2.1	16.6	27.4	51.5	32.7	22.8	322	92.9
Automba township (Carlton)	140	145	3.6	114	95.6	0.0	0.0	4.4	0.0	19.3	25.4	41.8	57.5	10.3	54	85.2
Avoca city & MCD (Murray)	147	135	-8.2	98	98.0	0.0	0.0	0.0	2.0	13.3	32.7	57.3	63.9	7.2	53	84.9
Avon city & MCD (Stearns)	1,398	1,590	13.7	1,670	99.0	0.0	0.0	0.4	0.7	28.2	13.2	34.1	30.2	26.9	662	92.3
Avon township (Stearns)...	2,290	2,479	8.3	2,315	98.7	0.2	0.5	0.0	0.5	21.3	17.8	45.0	36.7	25.3	864	89.9
Babbitt city & MCD (St. Louis)	1,475	1,484	0.6	1,419	94.8	0.1	0.6	4.1	0.4	15.9	28.1	52.9	41.5	14.7	729	79.4
Backus city & MCD (Cass)	250	252	0.8	322	92.9	0.0	0.0	5.0	2.2	24.5	30.5	42.9	66.2	8.3	143	88.8
Badger township (Polk)	117	120	2.6	108	100.0	0.0	0.0	0.0	0.0	25.9	12.0	36.4	66.3	12.5	50	92.0
Badger city & MCD (Roseau)	375	355	-5.3	429	91.8	0.2	1.6	5.6	0.7	31.2	16.6	35.2	50.4	16.2	186	90.9
Badoura township (Hubbard)	128	130	1.6	96	94.8	0.0	2.1	3.1	0.0	2.1	46.9	63.0	34.0	33.0	47	76.6
Bagley city & MCD (Clearwater)	1,380	1,406	1.9	1,398	85.9	0.9	0.4	12.7	0.1	22.7	27.7	40.3	56.6	14.3	576	75.5
Baker CDP	55	-	-	37	100.0	0.0	0.0	0.0	0.0	16.2	21.6	48.8	30.0	23.3	18	83.3
Baker township (Stevens).	114	115	0.9	80	82.5	0.0	0.0	0.0	17.5	20.0	35.0	52.7	53.3	15.0	30	80.0
Balaton city & MCD (Lyon)	641	624	-2.7	600	97.2	0.0	0.0	1.3	1.5	19.3	24.2	40.0	48.0	14.5	253	92.5

1 May be of any race.

Table A. All Places — **Population and Housing**

STATE City, town, township, borough, or CDP (county if applicable)	2010 census total population	2019 estimated population	Percent change 2010–2019	ACS total population estimate 2015–2019	White alone, not Hispanic or Latino	Black alone, not Hispanic or Latino	Asian alone, not Hispanic or Latino	All other races or 2 or more races, not Hispanic or Latino	Hispanic or Latino[1]	Under 18 years old	Age 65 years and older	Median age	Percent High school diploma or less	Percent Bachelor's degree or more	Total	Percent with a computer
															Occupied housing units	
	1	2	3	4	5	6	7	8	9	10	11	12	13	14	15	16
MINNESOTA—Con.																
Baldwin township (Sherburne)	6,737	7,346	9.0	7,146	98.4	0.0	1.2	0.4	0.1	29.5	8.0	38.0	38.3	22.4	2,295	97.8
Balkan township (St. Louis)	825	828	0.4	923	97.5	0.0	0.3	1.0	1.2	22.8	16.0	43.5	30.8	22.8	376	88.8
Ball Bluff township (Aitkin)	278	276	-0.7	296	96.3	0.0	0.0	1.7	2.0	6.8	43.2	60.9	46.8	15.8	147	85.0
Ball Club CDP	342	-	-	165	38.8	0.0	0.0	57.0	4.2	31.5	11.5	37.2	43.4	13.3	57	78.9
Balsam township (Aitkin)	42	42	0.0	46	100.0	0.0	0.0	0.0	0.0	8.7	41.3	63.8	45.2	19.0	24	79.2
Balsam township (Itasca)	553	551	-0.4	589	92.7	1.7	0.0	3.2	2.4	9.2	30.9	56.4	36.1	23.7	276	88.0
Bancroft township (Freeborn)	848	820	-3.3	808	94.1	0.0	0.4	2.1	3.5	21.2	25.7	52.7	37.8	24.3	321	90.7
Bandon township (Renville)	175	164	-6.3	155	87.7	0.0	0.0	1.3	11.0	23.2	16.1	47.6	46.7	16.2	58	91.4
Bangor township (Pope)	185	194	4.9	175	100.0	0.0	0.0	0.0	0.0	27.4	13.1	43.9	38.3	13.3	63	96.8
Barber township (Faribault)	248	236	-4.8	254	98.8	0.0	0.0	0.4	0.8	19.7	22.0	43.6	38.4	36.2	99	89.9
Barclay township (Cass)	564	590	4.6	559	99.3	0.0	0.0	0.7	0.0	17.2	24.2	50.3	35.0	17.9	257	89.1
Barnesville city & MCD (Clay)	2,564	2,602	1.5	2,582	90.2	1.5	0.3	3.9	4.1	30.7	13.3	35.6	34.0	27.9	992	85.7
Barnesville township (Clay)	153	161	5.2	174	97.7	0.0	0.0	0.0	2.3	21.8	12.1	36.7	33.3	28.1	68	97.1
Barnett township (Roseau)	139	130	-6.5	163	98.2	0.0	0.6	1.2	0.0	19.6	20.9	51.1	33.9	24.3	60	78.3
Barnum city & MCD (Carlton)	618	600	-2.9	649	96.0	0.2	0.5	3.4	0.0	29.0	11.6	35.1	44.2	14.1	266	88.0
Barnum township (Carlton)	1,055	1,095	3.8	978	97.2	0.0	0.0	0.5	2.2	21.6	27.5	49.3	36.4	25.8	406	88.7
Barrett city & MCD (Grant)	413	407	-1.5	410	92.2	0.0	0.0	0.0	7.8	18.3	24.4	44.8	51.7	13.4	178	83.7
Barry city & MCD (Big Stone)	16	15	-6.3	10	100.0	0.0	0.0	0.0	0.0	50.0	0.0	19.0	20.0	40.0	2	100.0
Barry township (Pine)	582	569	-2.2	530	59.2	1.5	0.2	19.8	19.2	21.3	21.5	46.5	55.5	9.3	194	87.6
Barsness township (Pope)	142	150	5.6	88	97.7	0.0	0.0	2.3	0.0	15.9	25.0	56.5	46.4	11.6	31	93.5
Bartlett township (Todd)	445	447	0.4	454	99.6	0.0	0.0	0.4	0.0	32.2	19.8	40.3	43.5	10.0	140	80.7
Barto township (Roseau)	138	131	-5.1	106	97.2	0.0	0.0	0.0	2.8	15.1	12.3	48.0	60.0	10.0	46	89.1
Bashaw township (Brown)	243	236	-2.9	216	100.0	0.0	0.0	0.0	0.0	20.8	22.2	61.2	46.7	14.4	97	85.6
Bassett township (St. Louis)	41	41	0.0	38	89.5	0.0	0.0	10.5	0.0	7.9	26.3	58.0	63.6	15.2	21	81.0
Bath township (Freeborn)	437	424	-3.0	455	97.8	0.0	0.4	0.0	1.8	24.6	18.2	47.2	24.5	29.4	185	93.0
Battle township (Beltrami)	50	50	0.0	89	69.7	1.1	0.0	29.2	0.0	28.1	5.6	36.8	65.6	4.9	29	79.3
Battle Lake city & MCD (Otter Tail)	875	929	6.2	670	95.5	1.5	0.0	2.5	0.4	14.2	42.5	58.4	39.5	23.0	324	88.0
Battle Plain township (Rock)	199	194	-2.5	223	99.1	0.0	0.0	0.0	0.9	28.7	15.7	39.4	35.4	24.3	77	94.8
Baudette city	1,106	1,020	-7.8	1,030	87.0	0.1	0.3	12.4	0.2	28.3	22.3	37.7	47.4	16.9	424	81.8
Baxter city & MCD (Crow Wing)	7,623	8,364	9.7	8,202	92.8	0.7	1.2	4.0	1.4	26.6	19.1	40.4	25.1	33.2	3,215	91.4
Baxter township (Lac qui Parle)	200	184	-8.0	131	100.0	0.0	0.0	0.0	0.0	16.8	29.8	57.7	29.6	29.6	59	89.8
Bay Lake township (Crow Wing)	929	978	5.3	920	96.8	0.5	0.0	1.6	1.0	7.2	43.7	62.2	39.5	28.2	469	87.6
Bayport city & MCD (Washington)	3,471	3,765	8.5	3,723	77.9	12.5	0.6	5.9	3.1	17.7	15.2	37.8	37.8	30.7	1,139	89.7
Baytown township (Washington)	1,625	1,992	22.6	1,940	95.2	0.1	2.4	1.2	1.1	25.3	12.7	45.0	13.1	62.8	689	95.9
Bear Creek township (Clearwater)	111	114	2.7	145	95.2	0.0	0.0	0.0	4.8	9.7	33.1	58.5	50.9	18.1	66	86.4
Beardsley city & MCD (Big Stone)	233	212	-9.0	181	98.9	0.0	0.0	0.0	1.1	16.6	26.0	49.9	43.8	14.6	94	78.7
Bear Park township (Norman)	192	182	-5.2	230	95.2	0.0	2.2	2.6	0.0	44.3	18.7	34.2	42.9	27.0	71	84.5
Bearville township (Itasca)	203	202	-0.5	173	100.0	0.0	0.0	0.0	0.0	15.6	49.1	64.9	42.3	27.0	86	83.7
Beatty township (St. Louis)	372	373	0.3	442	98.2	0.0	0.0	1.4	0.5	8.8	44.6	62.7	26.8	39.0	213	90.6
Beauford township (Blue Earth)	406	404	-0.5	455	91.0	0.4	1.5	3.5	3.5	24.4	12.7	41.3	40.3	21.3	177	95.5
Beaulieu CDP	48	-	-	33	51.5	0.0	0.0	48.5	0.0	12.1	36.4	48.8	84.0	8.0	15	73.3
Beaulieu township (Mahnomen)	108	111	2.8	77	39.0	0.0	0.0	61.0	0.0	31.2	14.3	31.1	46.8	14.9	27	81.5
Beaver township (Aitkin)	53	53	0.0	44	100.0	0.0	0.0	0.0	0.0	4.5	61.4	66.5	34.1	9.8	25	68.0
Beaver township (Fillmore)	242	253	4.5	203	90.6	0.0	0.0	0.0	9.4	24.6	22.7	49.7	49.3	9.4	81	88.9
Beaver township (Roseau)	105	99	-5.7	87	96.6	3.4	0.0	0.0	0.0	16.1	25.3	53.2	46.5	18.3	43	81.4
Beaver Bay city & MCD (Lake)	180	171	-5.0	98	73.5	0.0	0.0	26.5	0.0	2.0	28.6	57.3	16.0	44.7	65	92.3
Beaver Bay township (Lake)	483	495	2.5	347	94.2	0.0	0.0	1.2	4.6	1.2	47.6	63.7	39.3	28.1	193	87.6
Beaver Creek city & MCD (Rock)	297	280	-5.7	417	92.3	6.7	0.0	1.0	0.0	23.3	9.4	29.2	34.3	24.5	176	97.2
Beaver Creek township (Rock)	386	376	-2.6	443	85.8	2.5	0.7	5.4	5.6	32.7	16.0	40.8	18.6	29.4	155	88.4
Beaver Falls township (Renville)	197	186	-5.6	234	85.5	0.0	0.0	12.0	2.6	28.2	17.1	35.2	43.5	15.0	102	85.3
Becker township (Cass)	517	543	5.0	475	99.2	0.0	0.0	0.8	0.0	21.3	21.9	44.1	31.8	13.3	214	84.1
Becker city & MCD (Sherburne)	4,565	4,954	8.5	4,844	93.6	0.7	0.0	4.9	0.8	27.0	8.9	33.3	33.2	26.0	1,719	94.6
Becker township (Sherburne)	4,815	5,478	13.8	5,321	97.2	0.0	0.6	1.8	0.4	38.3	7.6	32.9	33.4	29.6	1,563	97.4
Bejou city & MCD (Mahnomen)	89	91	2.2	63	87.3	4.8	0.0	7.9	0.0	12.7	23.8	53.3	69.1	1.8	30	70.0
Bejou township (Mahnomen)	79	79	0.0	74	89.2	0.0	2.7	0.0	8.1	20.3	25.7	50.5	42.6	37.0	32	78.1
Belfast township (Murray)	192	185	-3.6	192	98.4	0.0	0.0	1.6	0.0	9.4	24.0	50.5	52.1	18.8	80	90.0
Belgium township (Polk)	81	83	2.5	61	96.7	0.0	0.0	0.0	3.3	4.9	27.9	61.1	41.3	8.7	25	80.0
Belgrade township (Nicollet)	1,035	1,052	1.6	1,071	98.2	0.0	0.4	0.0	1.4	21.2	13.3	44.5	24.7	33.4	399	94.0

1 May be of any race.

Table A. All Places — **Population and Housing**

STATE City, town, township, borough, or CDP (county if applicable)	Population 2010 census total population	2019 estimated population	Percent change 2010– 2019	ACS total population estimate 2015–2019	Race and Hispanic or Latino origin (percent) White alone, not Hispanic or Latino	Black alone, not Hispanic or Latino	Asian alone, not Hispanic or Latino	All other races or 2 or more races, not Hispanic or Latino	Hispanic or Latino[1]	Age (percent) Under 18 years old	Age 65 years and older	Median age	Educational attainment of persons age 25 and older Percent High school diploma or less	Percent Bachelor's degree or more	Occupied housing units Total	Percent with a computer
	1	2	3	4	5	6	7	8	9	10	11	12	13	14	15	16
MINNESOTA—Con.																
Belgrade city & MCD (Stearns)	740	779	5.3	1,048	87.3	0.0	1.2	0.1	11.4	25.6	21.9	37.8	51.0	14.5	389	86.1
Bellechester city	175	174	-0.6	165	84.8	0.0	1.8	9.7	3.6	13.9	17.0	43.5	66.9	13.2	89	88.8
Bellechester city (Goodhue)	133	133	0.0	125	80.0	0.0	2.4	12.8	4.8	10.4	12.0	43.3	64.8	12.1	71	93.0
Bellechester city (Wabasha)	42	41	-2.4	40	100.0	0.0	0.0	0.0	0.0	25.0	32.5	43.7	73.3	16.7	18	72.2
Belle Creek township (Goodhue)	503	500	-0.6	537	98.7	0.0	0.0	0.0	1.3	27.7	9.9	37.1	33.7	25.9	206	84.5
Belle Plaine city & MCD (Scott)	6,665	7,185	7.8	7,093	90.7	1.8	3.0	0.4	4.2	29.2	15.5	34.7	38.1	23.6	2,277	91.8
Belle Plaine township (Scott)	874	947	8.4	903	94.4	2.7	0.2	1.1	1.7	21.6	14.0	43.8	41.7	24.3	309	92.2
Belle Prairie township (Morrison)	625	637	1.9	650	96.5	0.0	0.0	0.0	3.5	20.9	17.2	44.9	38.0	16.2	261	87.0
Belle River township (Douglas)	345	357	3.5	321	96.9	0.0	0.0	0.6	2.5	24.3	23.4	47.2	41.5	9.0	131	87.0
Bellevue township (Morrison)	1,105	1,132	2.4	1,094	97.1	0.6	0.0	1.4	0.9	26.3	13.3	39.4	36.8	15.0	411	85.6
Bellingham city & MCD (Lac qui Parle)	168	150	-10.7	233	87.6	0.0	0.0	0.0	12.4	20.2	20.6	40.1	65.0	12.1	97	82.5
Belmont township (Jackson)	218	212	-2.8	199	93.5	0.0	0.0	6.5	0.0	20.1	32.7	48.9	40.0	16.6	91	83.5
Beltrami city & MCD (Polk)	107	101	-5.6	178	98.3	0.0	0.0	1.7	0.0	33.7	13.5	39.9	43.5	21.7	63	88.9
Belvidere township (Goodhue)	462	459	-0.6	456	98.2	0.0	0.0	0.0	1.8	24.6	9.2	37.3	43.4	26.6	172	95.3
Belview city & MCD (Redwood)	384	354	-7.8	360	95.6	0.0	0.6	0.6	3.3	13.6	35.3	55.5	52.3	9.3	176	68.8
Bemidji city & MCD (Beltrami)	14,248	15,434	8.3	15,132	78.4	1.1	0.7	16.6	3.2	19.5	16.7	27.9	33.5	27.7	6,139	85.4
Bemidji township (Beltrami)	3,027	4,165	37.6	3,831	84.5	2.5	0.2	8.6	4.2	22.3	14.9	41.5	29.0	38.5	1,504	93.9
Bena city & MCD (Cass)	119	123	3.4	128	21.9	2.3	0.0	75.8	0.0	35.9	11.7	39.1	49.3	4.0	50	62.0
Bennington township (Mower)	169	175	3.6	166	100.0	0.0	0.0	0.0	0.0	19.9	15.1	39.0	46.1	14.8	63	93.7
Benson city & MCD (Swift)	3,245	3,043	-6.2	3,078	90.2	5.0	0.6	0.8	3.4	24.2	23.3	44.3	36.1	21.0	1,469	82.4
Benson township (Swift)	334	323	-3.3	292	98.3	0.0	0.0	0.3	1.4	21.6	19.5	43.1	38.1	26.2	126	89.7
Benton township (Carver)	802	822	2.5	764	95.2	0.0	0.8	1.3	2.7	17.9	16.9	46.5	44.0	23.3	280	93.6
Benville township (Beltrami)	86	85	-1.2	111	98.2	0.0	1.8	0.0	0.0	31.5	10.8	35.9	64.6	12.3	38	100.0
Ben Wade township (Pope)	250	265	6.0	264	97.7	1.5	0.0	0.8	0.0	25.8	17.8	42.5	37.0	14.1	110	89.1
Bergen township (McLeod)	971	952	-2.0	868	94.0	0.0	0.2	0.0	5.8	21.2	13.8	44.2	44.5	18.7	313	89.1
Berlin township (Steele)	515	520	1.0	432	98.8	0.0	0.0	1.2	0.0	18.5	21.5	51.8	44.8	30.7	178	92.1
Bernadotte township (Nicollet)	280	285	1.8	248	96.0	0.0	0.0	0.0	4.0	26.6	12.9	41.3	36.5	17.4	89	97.8
Bertha city & MCD (Todd)	497	482	-3.0	635	93.1	1.3	0.0	5.7	0.0	36.1	12.8	28.9	43.8	19.5	231	84.0
Bertha township (Todd)	408	402	-1.5	358	94.1	5.9	0.0	0.0	0.0	15.9	26.0	51.7	48.9	14.7	152	80.3
Beseman township (Carlton)	137	142	3.6	132	91.7	0.0	0.0	3.0	5.3	18.9	26.5	49.6	44.8	16.7	53	90.6
Bethel city & MCD (Anoka)	494	501	1.4	500	90.2	0.0	1.6	2.2	6.0	30.8	4.4	34.6	45.4	8.9	161	99.4
Beulah township (Cass)	64	67	4.7	78	94.9	0.0	0.0	5.1	0.0	9.0	38.5	59.3	46.0	11.1	42	90.5
Big Bend township (Chippewa)	242	232	-4.1	263	97.3	0.0	0.0	0.8	1.9	23.2	19.0	52.4	28.8	22.2	114	99.1
Bigelow city & MCD (Nobles)	235	231	-1.7	218	57.3	1.8	0.0	2.8	38.1	33.0	14.2	34.0	56.3	12.6	71	81.7
Bigelow township (Nobles)	373	373	0.0	414	93.2	0.0	0.0	0.5	6.3	32.9	11.6	35.4	30.4	27.5	128	94.5
Big Falls city	229	208	-9.2	199	95.5	0.0	0.0	4.5	0.0	15.1	28.6	54.4	50.0	7.6	111	84.7
Bigfork city & MCD (Itasca)	448	442	-1.3	405	91.6	0.5	0.0	1.7	6.2	16.3	53.6	66.5	53.1	11.9	193	60.1
Bigfork township (Itasca)	306	303		253	86.6	5.1	0.0	5.5	2.8	20.9	31.2	50.5	53.0	14.6	116	87.1
Big Lake CDP	443	-	-	378	55.3	0.8	0.0	42.3	1.6	19.6	22.5	50.5	27.5	29.4	162	79.0
Big Lake city & MCD (Sherburne)	10,085	11,226	11.3	10,856	86.5	2.3	0.3	2.7	8.2	30.7	5.9	30.9	36.0	27.7	3,560	94.7
Big Lake township (Sherburne)	7,366	8,013	8.8	7,794	95.9	0.2	1.0	1.9	1.0	18.6	12.2	44.2	32.8	24.9	2,854	99.2
Big Stone township (Big Stone)	273	268	-1.8	312	92.9	0.0	0.0	6.7	0.3	22.8	28.5	55.0	36.2	35.3	132	98.5
Big Woods township (Marshall)	53	52	-1.9	52	92.3	0.0	3.8	3.8	0.0	42.3	5.8	35.5	27.6	44.8	16	100.0
Bingham Lake city & MCD (Cottonwood)	126	124	-1.6	171	79.5	17.0	3.5	0.0	0.0	29.8	9.9	26.1	41.3	14.4	72	97.2
Birch township (Beltrami)	118	117	-0.8	64	81.3	0.0	0.0	18.8	0.0	18.8	29.7	57.4	50.0	23.1	30	76.7
Birch Cooley township (Renville)	243	227	-6.6	167	89.2	0.0	0.0	10.8	0.0	18.6	16.8	55.3	49.6	13.7	67	85.1
Birch Creek township (Pine)	233	228	-2.1	247	98.8	0.0	0.0	0.8	0.4	24.7	16.2	38.8	56.3	10.2	103	86.4
Birchdale township (Todd)	856	861	0.6	826	98.4	0.0	0.0	0.0	1.6	19.5	20.2	48.8	42.7	16.7	345	92.5
Birch Lake township (Cass)	524	550	5.0	517	96.7	0.0	1.7	0.4	1.2	16.2	42.2	58.8	43.5	19.8	241	91.7
Birch Lake UT (St. Louis)	505	509	0.8	498	100.0	0.0	0.0	0.0	0.0	15.5	31.9	59.3	31.4	27.6	256	80.1
Birchwood Village city & MCD (Washington)	879	882	0.3	957	95.2	3.0	1.3	0.3	0.2	20.7	19.2	45.8	10.6	65.6	357	96.1
Bird Island city & MCD (Renville)	1,042	959	-8.0	858	98.6	0.0	0.0	1.4	0.0	14.8	23.8	52.4	48.1	14.3	420	81.0
Bird Island township (Renville)	196	183	-6.6	213	95.8	0.0	0.0	4.2	0.0	23.0	10.3	43.3	35.0	22.1	79	97.5
Biscay city & MCD (McLeod)	117	110	-6.0	135	92.6	0.0	0.0	0.0	7.4	20.0	10.4	36.5	51.5	2.1	53	88.7

1 May be of any race.

Table A. All Places — **Population and Housing**

STATE City, town, township, borough, or CDP (county if applicable)	2010 census total population	2019 estimated population	Percent change 2010–2019	ACS total population estimate 2015–2019	White alone, not Hispanic or Latino	Black alone, not Hispanic or Latino	Asian alone, not Hispanic or Latino	All other races or 2 or more races, not Hispanic or Latino	Hispanic or Latino[1]	Under 18 years old	Age 65 years and older	Median age	Percent High school diploma or less	Percent Bachelor's degree or more	Total	Percent with a computer
	1	2	3	4	5	6	7	8	9	10	11	12	13	14	15	16
MINNESOTA—Con.																
Bismarck township (Sibley)	316	313	-0.9	352	94.9	0.0	5.1	0.0	0.0	23.6	10.2	38.7	37.8	28.1	104	90.4
Biwabik city & MCD (St. Louis)	962	969	0.7	598	94.5	0.0	0.0	4.0	1.5	14.4	21.4	45.5	34.2	18.0	323	74.3
Biwabik township (St. Louis)	808	816	1.0	905	97.8	0.0	0.2	0.9	1.1	14.9	29.4	56.5	31.3	26.0	407	88.5
Blackberry township (Itasca)	880	881	0.1	763	92.9	0.0	0.0	1.2	5.9	19.3	16.1	49.3	32.0	15.7	312	86.9
Blackduck city & MCD (Beltrami)	784	833	6.3	884	87.4	1.8	0.0	9.6	1.1	27.4	20.8	37.7	50.7	10.3	352	78.1
Black Hammer township (Houston)	243	241	-0.8	246	100.0	0.0	0.0	0.0	0.0	24.0	25.6	40.5	29.7	33.0	106	93.4
Blackhoof township (Carlton)	888	924	4.1	1,036	91.5	0.0	4.5	1.1	2.9	20.8	14.1	44.2	39.6	26.6	399	90.7
Black River township (Pennington)	82	79	-3.7	36	100.0	0.0	0.0	0.0	0.0	8.3	8.3	54.0	54.5	30.3	19	84.2
Blaine city & MCD (Anoka)	57,179	65,607	14.7	64,114	77.0	5.8	8.6	3.6	5.1	26.6	12.0	37.7	32.1	34.9	23,123	94.0
Blaine city (Ramsey)	-	-	-	-	-	-	-	-	-	-	-	-	-	-	-	-
Blakeley township (Scott)	418	451	7.9	475	97.3	0.0	0.8	1.9	0.0	24.4	15.6	41.8	42.3	28.5	170	93.5
Blind Lake township (Cass)	82	86	4.9	98	100.0	0.0	0.0	0.0	0.0	27.6	6.1	47.5	38.2	17.6	37	94.6
Blomkest city & MCD (Kandiyohi)	157	158	0.6	144	75.0	0.0	0.0	7.6	17.4	10.4	33.3	54.0	56.0	5.2	72	76.4
Bloom township (Nobles)	158	157	-0.6	121	100.0	0.0	0.0	0.0	0.0	11.6	14.9	51.9	38.6	15.9	50	98.0
Bloomer township (Marshall)	89	88	-1.1	86	90.7	0.0	0.0	0.0	9.3	36.0	1.2	29.5	24.5	30.2	28	100.0
Bloomfield township (Fillmore)	353	370	4.8	286	97.9	0.0	0.3	0.7	1.0	24.1	22.7	46.4	34.2	11.4	119	89.9
Blooming Grove township (Waseca)	525	532	1.3	517	96.7	0.0	0.0	2.5	0.8	26.9	21.3	47.3	32.9	26.7	202	87.6
Blooming Prairie city	1,996	1,936	-3.0	1,916	90.9	0.3	0.0	0.4	8.4	26.2	24.1	36.4	47.5	16.4	760	79.5
Blooming Prairie city (Dodge)	-	-	-	-	-	-	-	-	-	-	-	-	-	-	-	-
Blooming Prairie city (Steele)	1,996	1,936	-3.0	1,916	90.9	0.3	0.0	0.4	8.4	26.2	24.1	36.4	47.5	16.4	760	79.5
Blooming Prairie township (Steele)	430	432	0.5	387	96.4	0.0	0.3	0.0	3.4	24.0	14.5	44.3	40.0	17.4	144	88.9
Bloomington city	82,893	84,943	2.5	85,332	72.1	9.4	5.3	4.2	8.9	20.0	19.4	41.6	27.1	41.9	35,494	93.8
Blowers township (Otter Tail)	321	320	-0.3	438	99.8	0.0	0.0	0.0	0.2	37.0	9.1	35.1	45.3	13.1	129	75.2
Blueberry township (Wadena)	721	713	-1.1	863	93.4	0.2	1.5	4.9	0.0	32.7	18.5	37.3	45.5	24.1	311	89.4
Blue Earth city & MCD (Faribault)	3,318	3,108	-6.3	3,138	87.7	0.7	0.2	0.7	10.6	18.3	29.5	51.3	47.4	16.6	1,546	80.1
Blue Earth City township (Faribault)	422	404	-4.3	388	97.2	0.0	0.0	0.3	2.6	20.9	21.1	52.8	35.8	22.3	157	92.4
Blue Hill township (Sherburne)	2,176	2,371	9.0	2,228	97.0	0.0	0.3	0.9	1.8	29.1	9.1	34.5	41.3	21.6	713	97.3
Blue Mounds township (Pope)	186	197	5.9	171	89.5	0.0	2.9	7.6	0.0	25.1	26.9	54.2	34.6	19.7	73	83.6
Bluffton city & MCD (Otter Tail)	207	214	3.4	241	99.2	0.0	0.0	0.8	0.0	31.1	19.1	32.8	57.6	4.9	96	80.2
Bluffton township (Otter Tail)	479	478	-0.2	507	92.1	0.0	0.0	0.2	7.7	25.6	16.2	39.8	49.4	9.0	188	85.1
Bock city & MCD (Mille Lacs)	106	107	0.9	104	98.1	0.0	0.0	1.9	0.0	22.1	10.6	48.5	41.8	7.5	37	83.8
Bogus Brook township (Mille Lacs)	1,421	1,440	1.3	1,574	92.9	0.2	0.0	1.2	5.7	28.1	11.0	38.7	35.2	20.6	529	92.2
Bondin township (Murray)	268	258	-3.7	232	96.6	0.0	0.0	0.0	3.4	22.4	24.6	50.6	38.5	26.6	95	87.4
Boon Lake township (Renville)	378	355	-6.1	339	99.1	0.0	0.0	0.6	0.3	20.6	21.2	52.5	45.0	9.6	135	96.3
Borgholm township (Mille Lacs)	1,718	1,746	1.6	1,907	95.8	0.4	2.6	0.7	0.5	29.5	12.1	37.7	43.4	16.5	652	91.7
Borup city & MCD (Norman)	110	103	-6.4	102	63.7	0.0	2.9	3.9	29.4	21.6	17.6	40.2	52.3	10.8	36	77.8
Bovey city & MCD (Itasca)	804	784	-2.5	755	72.7	0.5	0.7	9.8	16.3	27.5	11.9	35.4	43.6	6.4	318	88.4
Bowlus city & MCD (Morrison)	290	279	-3.8	285	98.6	0.0	0.0	0.7	0.7	27.0	15.8	34.6	59.6	8.8	128	82.0
Bowstring township (Itasca)	230	228	-0.9	191	94.8	0.0	0.0	5.2	0.0	8.9	39.3	62.9	47.6	21.2	92	80.4
Bowstring Lake UT (Itasca)	1,172	1,166	-0.5	870	50.1	1.0	0.0	47.7	1.1	23.0	20.1	48.1	47.6	16.4	327	85.3
Boxville township (Marshall)	39	38	-2.6	24	91.7	8.3	0.0	0.0	0.0	20.8	29.2	46.5	26.3	26.3	11	81.8
Boyd city & MCD (Lac qui Parle)	177	157	-11.3	111	93.7	0.0	3.6	2.7	0.0	0.9	31.5	60.4	64.1	3.9	61	68.9
Boy Lake township (Cass)	256	268	4.7	301	46.2	0.0	0.0	53.2	0.7	34.2	16.3	33.2	49.4	18.2	113	82.3
Boy River city & MCD (Cass)	47	51	8.5	35	100.0	0.0	0.0	0.0	0.0	25.7	17.1	41.3	76.0	0.0	17	35.3
Boy River township (Cass)	86	90	4.7	45	93.3	0.0	0.0	6.7	0.0	24.4	31.1	44.5	55.9	23.5	22	90.9
Bradbury township (Mille Lacs)	266	271	1.9	195	98.5	0.0	0.0	1.5	0.0	21.5	14.9	43.9	41.7	16.5	77	83.1
Bradford township (Isanti)	3,380	3,522	4.2	3,463	96.0	1.0	0.3	2.3	0.3	21.0	12.0	43.7	35.6	18.8	1,249	97.1
Bradford township (Wilkin)	91	88	-3.3	41	100.0	0.0	0.0	0.0	0.0	0.0	12.2	54.1	54.5	9.1	14	100.0
Braham city & MCD (Isanti)	1,793	1,816	1.3	1,820	87.1	0.9	0.5	6.0	5.5	27.0	12.2	33.8	49.8	14.4	783	87.6
Braham city (Kanabec)	-	-	-	-	-	-	-	-	-	-	-	-	-	-	-	-
Brainerd city & MCD (Crow Wing)	13,587	13,434	-1.1	13,373	91.0	2.7	0.7	4.2	1.4	23.3	16.2	35.0	42.1	15.4	6,018	86.9
Brandon city & MCD (Douglas)	487	485	-0.4	610	96.4	1.6	0.0	2.0	0.0	26.1	20.2	35.8	47.8	21.3	260	95.4

1 May be of any race.

Table A. All Places — Population and Housing

STATE City, town, township, borough, or CDP (county if applicable)	Population				Race and Hispanic or Latino origin (percent)					Age (percent)			Educational attainment of persons age 25 and older		Occupied housing units	
	2010 census total population	2019 estimated population	Percent change 2010–2019	ACS total population estimate 2015–2019	White alone, not Hispanic or Latino	Black alone, not Hispanic or Latino	Asian alone, not Hispanic or Latino	All other races or 2 or more races, not Hispanic or Latino	Hispanic or Latino[1]	Under 18 years old	Age 65 years and older	Median age	Percent High school diploma or less	Percent Bachelor's degree or more	Total	Percent with a computer
	1	2	3	4	5	6	7	8	9	10	11	12	13	14	15	16
MINNESOTA—Con.																
Brandon township (Douglas)	715	743	3.9	642	97.4	0.0	0.5	2.0	0.2	23.5	27.4	49.7	39.1	17.7	270	91.5
Brandrup township (Wilkin)	161	155	-3.7	84	100.0	0.0	0.0	0.0	0.0	10.7	21.4	55.8	38.0	2.8	36	83.3
Brandsvold township (Polk)	243	248	2.1	322	97.8	0.0	0.0	1.2	0.9	25.5	12.4	24.8	31.6	38.1	116	94.0
Brandt township (Polk)	50	51	2.0	87	92.0	0.0	0.0	0.0	8.0	14.9	33.3	46.8	27.7	23.1	42	88.1
Bray township (Pennington)	64	61	-4.7	34	100.0	0.0	0.0	0.0	0.0	26.5	47.1	58.0	52.0	20.0	12	100.0
Breckenridge city & MCD (Wilkin)	3,390	3,172	-6.4	3,205	98.1	0.7	0.0	1.0	0.2	23.1	21.2	43.0	30.4	29.2	1,555	83.0
Breckenridge township (Wilkin)	253	245	-3.2	271	97.4	0.7	0.0	1.8	0.0	19.9	14.4	46.4	26.7	24.6	100	96.0
Breezy Point city & MCD (Crow Wing)	2,316	2,413	4.2	2,319	99.3	0.0	0.2	0.2	0.3	25.8	21.4	43.8	21.5	37.4	907	95.4
Breitung township (St. Louis)	609	611	0.3	486	99.2	0.0	0.0	0.8	0.0	14.4	28.4	56.8	28.3	26.6	243	82.7
Bremen township (Pine)	240	239	-0.4	196	98.0	0.0	0.0	1.5	0.5	9.7	33.7	61.1	52.6	11.6	92	87.0
Brevator township (St. Louis)	1,270	1,279	0.7	1,304	73.7	0.2	0.0	25.7	0.4	25.4	13.5	40.1	39.7	19.9	469	87.0
Brewster city & MCD (Nobles)	473	467	-1.3	453	84.5	3.3	1.3	1.5	9.3	22.1	17.9	36.3	42.5	10.2	189	87.8
Bricelyn city & MCD (Faribault)	365	337	-7.7	283	81.6	0.4	1.4	4.6	12.0	20.5	23.3	48.5	50.2	14.4	135	79.3
Bridgewater township (Rice)	1,767	1,823	3.2	1,835	96.8	0.0	0.2	0.9	2.1	21.7	19.9	49.0	24.3	45.2	690	88.8
Brighton township (Nicollet)	149	152	2.0	145	94.5	0.0	0.0	0.0	5.5	22.1	19.3	42.8	58.4	10.6	55	100.0
Brislet township (Polk)	53	53	0.0	50	100.0	0.0	0.0	0.0	0.0	40.0	10.0	26.8	30.0	33.3	15	100.0
Bristol township (Fillmore)	396	416	5.1	452	93.1	0.0	0.7	6.2	0.0	44.9	7.3	27.6	46.6	21.0	120	70.8
Brockway township (Stearns)	2,695	2,927	8.6	2,861	97.3	0.0	1.3	0.8	0.5	24.8	13.7	41.2	32.4	29.9	1,059	88.6
Brookfield township (Renville)	156	146	-6.4	162	96.9	0.0	0.0	0.0	3.1	25.3	19.1	40.7	47.2	9.3	55	83.6
Brook Lake UT (Beltrami)	231	228	-1.3	177	42.9	0.0	5.1	48.6	3.4	19.2	17.5	51.4	54.5	0.0	87	77.0
Brooklyn Center city	30,180	30,690	1.7	30,849	38.3	28.9	16.2	3.2	13.5	28.9	10.8	31.9	45.0	20.3	10,394	90.9
Brooklyn Park city	75,776	80,389	6.1	80,068	42.5	28.4	18.5	4.6	5.9	28.1	10.7	35.0	33.7	30.3	27,275	94.8
Brook Park city & MCD (Pine)	139	133	-4.3	141	92.9	0.0	0.0	0.0	7.1	16.3	10.6	37.3	81.5	2.2	46	78.3
Brook Park township (Pine)	522	516	-1.1	540	96.7	0.0	0.0	1.5	1.9	21.1	16.1	42.7	58.5	7.2	183	77.6
Brooks city & MCD (Red Lake)	138	137	-0.7	143	93.0	0.0	0.0	2.8	4.2	16.8	30.8	56.3	51.9	13.9	67	79.1
Brookston city & MCD (St. Louis)	141	141	0.0	103	78.6	0.0	0.0	21.4	0.0	16.5	21.4	42.3	63.5	10.8	39	97.4
Brookville township (Redwood)	224	214	-4.5	150	100.0	0.0	0.0	0.0	0.0	20.0	23.3	57.4	29.7	14.4	68	69.1
Brooten city	745	750	0.7	702	82.2	7.1	0.0	6.3	4.4	24.5	22.1	41.1	45.0	23.2	284	77.5
Brooten city (Pope)	-	-	-	-					-							
Brooten city (Stearns)	745	750	0.7	702	82.2	7.1	0.0	6.3	4.4	24.5	22.1	41.1	45.0	23.2	284	77.5
Browerville city & MCD (Todd)	781	743	-4.9	901	85.5	2.3	2.4	5.4	4.3	27.7	16.8	39.2	51.1	17.1	336	71.7
Browns Creek township (Red Lake)	48	48	0.0	26	88.5	3.8	0.0	0.0	7.7	19.2	38.5	59.5	42.9	14.3	12	91.7
Brownsdale city & MCD (Mower)	685	691	0.9	596	91.8	0.0	1.5	0.3	6.4	17.4	20.8	42.4	42.7	17.7	263	84.4
Browns Valley township (Big Stone)	125	122	-2.4	80	100.0	0.0	0.0	0.0	0.0	20.0	22.5	56.8	42.2	14.1	36	91.7
Browns Valley city & MCD (Traverse)	589	528	-10.4	566	60.6	0.0	0.0	36.4	3.0	25.4	25.6	49.6	54.9	3.4	244	80.7
Brownsville city & MCD (Houston)	491	505	2.9	568	98.2	0.0	0.0	1.6	0.2	20.6	19.4	45.6	48.4	18.2	258	89.9
Brownsville township (Houston)	418	415	-0.7	388	98.2	1.5	0.0	0.0	0.3	14.7	38.1	58.3	34.4	18.8	202	68.3
Brownton city & MCD (McLeod)	762	720	-5.5	706	89.1	7.5	0.0	1.1	2.3	19.5	25.4	44.5	52.9	8.5	303	85.8
Bruce township (Todd)	585	582	-0.5	514	99.6	0.0	0.4	0.0	0.0	15.6	23.5	50.2	43.8	15.9	220	86.4
Bruno city & MCD (Pine)	102	99	-2.9	79	91.1	0.0	0.0	8.9	0.0	43.0	17.7	36.2	82.2	4.4	30	83.3
Bruno township (Pine)	184	179	-2.7	190	84.2	0.0	1.6	0.0	14.2	22.6	19.5	50.5	53.2	8.6	72	73.6
Brunswick township (Kanabec)	1,333	1,337	0.3	1,405	93.8	0.0	0.0	1.6	4.6	20.6	16.5	40.7	46.0	13.5	544	93.6
Brush Creek township (Faribault)	225	214	-4.9	189	87.3	0.0	0.0	4.2	8.5	28.0	14.3	44.8	34.2	23.3	67	80.6
Buckman city & MCD (Morrison)	270	276	2.2	260	99.6	0.0	0.4	0.0	0.0	26.2	5.4	27.0	42.1	22.1	93	90.3
Buckman township (Morrison)	733	749	2.2	771	96.9	0.0	0.0	0.0	3.1	33.7	8.4	33.0	44.8	9.9	253	82.6
Buffalo city & MCD (Wright)	15,471	16,442	6.3	16,210	96.6	0.6	0.8	0.9	1.1	26.3	14.2	36.5	33.9	30.9	6,163	90.3
Buffalo township (Wright)	1,787	1,900	6.3	1,866	98.6	0.1	0.5	0.9	0.0	20.9	15.1	45.2	37.5	26.0	678	94.2
Buffalo Lake city & MCD (Renville)	745	686	-7.9	621	84.7	1.9	0.0	5.3	8.1	20.6	31.1	50.7	47.5	9.9	275	74.5
Buh township (Morrison)	528	536	1.5	463	99.4	0.0	0.0	0.0	0.6	23.3	19.9	40.9	49.1	14.7	174	77.6
Buhl city & MCD (St. Louis)	1,000	973	-2.7	963	91.5	2.3	1.2	5.0	0.0	14.3	22.7	48.9	46.0	17.4	455	81.5
Bullard township (Wadena)	219	218	-0.5	138	100.0	0.0	0.0	0.0	0.0	9.4	23.9	51.5	57.9	6.5	67	77.6
Bull Moose township (Cass)	133	140	5.3	110	90.0	0.0	0.0	0.0	10.0	20.9	11.8	38.6	25.9	40.7	44	93.2
Bungo township (Cass)	188	197	4.8	133	100.0	0.0	0.0	0.0	0.0	24.1	16.5	36.2	46.5	12.8	51	78.4
Burbank township (Kandiyohi)	566	582	2.8	486	99.4	0.0	0.0	0.6	0.0	23.9	13.4	46.2	32.2	24.9	177	93.2

1 May be of any race.

Table A. All Places — **Population and Housing**

STATE City, town, township, borough, or CDP (county if applicable)	Population				Race and Hispanic or Latino origin (percent)					Age (percent)			Educational attainment of persons age 25 and older		Occupied housing units	
	2010 census total population	2019 estimated population	Percent change 2010–2019	ACS total population estimate 2015–2019	White alone, not Hispanic or Latino	Black alone, not Hispanic or Latino	Asian alone, not Hispanic or Latino	All other races or 2 or more races, not Hispanic or Latino	Hispanic or Latino[1]	Under 18 years old	Age 65 years and older	Median age	Percent High school diploma or less	Percent Bachelor's degree or more	Total	Percent with a computer
	1	2	3	4	5	6	7	8	9	10	11	12	13	14	15	16

MINNESOTA—Con.

STATE City, town, township, borough, or CDP (county if applicable)	1	2	3	4	5	6	7	8	9	10	11	12	13	14	15	16
Burke township (Pipestone)	209	205	-1.9	250	99.2	0.0	0.0	0.0	0.8	30.4	12.8	35.7	39.1	28.8	82	96.3
Burleene township (Todd)	345	348	0.9	409	96.1	0.0	1.5	0.0	2.4	22.5	13.9	42.7	54.1	6.3	146	78.8
Burlington township (Becker)	1,545	1,643	6.3	1,771	93.1	0.2	0.7	1.9	4.2	27.1	13.8	38.4	37.9	22.9	610	95.9
Burnhamville township (Todd)	755	762	0.9	705	96.5	0.0	0.3	1.3	2.0	19.1	26.2	50.1	45.4	20.0	299	90.3
Burnstown township (Brown)	275	269	-2.2	293	100.0	0.0	0.0	0.0	0.0	20.1	15.7	35.1	37.3	14.1	110	92.7
Burnsville city & MCD (Dakota)	60,286	61,339	1.7	61,311	69.2	13.5	4.7	4.5	8.0	22.8	15.4	36.8	28.3	39.0	24,702	94.8
Burton township (Yellow Medicine)	148	139	-6.1	77	96.1	0.0	0.0	0.0	3.9	24.7	19.5	42.8	39.6	34.0	33	81.8
Burtrum city & MCD (Todd)	144	136	-5.6	103	100.0	0.0	0.0	0.0	0.0	26.2	18.4	46.8	67.6	4.2	48	70.8
Buse township (Otter Tail)	447	453	1.3	488	96.3	2.3	0.0	0.0	1.4	26.4	13.7	43.5	22.1	32.7	177	94.4
Butler township (Otter Tail)	279	279	0.0	193	97.9	0.0	0.0	2.1	0.0	8.8	11.4	50.3	43.1	14.4	84	94.0
Butterfield city & MCD (Watonwan)	584	589	0.9	501	55.5	0.0	18.6	1.0	25.0	24.8	23.0	38.8	72.8	13.9	187	78.1
Butterfield township (Watonwan)	215	215	0.0	151	94.0	0.0	6.0	0.0	0.0	23.2	17.2	49.5	43.6	14.5	57	98.2
Butternut Valley township (Blue Eart)	325	324	-0.3	274	98.2	0.0	0.0	1.5	0.4	18.2	24.8	49.7	49.8	24.9	116	82.8
Buzzle township (Beltrami)	310	307	-1.0	216	94.4	0.9	0.0	4.6	0.0	18.5	21.3	52.2	42.4	25.0	94	86.2
Bygland township (Polk)	272	276	1.5	294	98.0	0.0	0.0	2.0	0.0	22.8	23.5	42.8	35.9	25.7	122	76.2
Byron township (Cass)	144	152	5.6	139	100.0	0.0	0.0	0.0	0.0	15.1	20.9	44.6	57.0	9.7	61	83.6
Byron city & MCD (Olmsted)	4,922	5,639	14.6	5,462	94.5	0.0	2.4	1.2	2.0	31.8	8.3	34.3	19.0	46.1	2,046	97.0
Byron township (Waseca)	228	229	0.4	196	100.0	0.0	0.0	0.0	0.0	15.8	13.8	47.7	36.0	22.3	84	89.3
Cairo township (Renville)	230	214	-7.0	196	90.3	0.0	3.6	2.6	3.6	9.2	35.7	59.5	59.8	13.6	100	79.0
Caledonia city & MCD (Houston)	2,868	2,753	-4.0	2,756	95.0	4.0	0.0	0.8	0.3	21.6	21.6	42.3	48.7	19.1	1,261	86.7
Caledonia township (Houston)	643	637	-0.9	696	98.7	1.3	0.0	0.0	0.0	28.0	17.4	39.4	37.9	25.3	256	91.8
Callaway city & MCD (Becker)	234	230	-1.7	165	40.6	0.0	0.0	58.2	1.2	18.2	20.6	49.1	58.7	7.9	76	82.9
Callaway township (Becker)	287	305	6.3	317	55.2	0.3	1.9	31.9	10.7	28.1	14.2	37.4	52.5	13.1	106	84.0
Calumet city	367	351	-4.4	413	95.6	0.0	0.0	2.4	1.9	22.0	14.0	41.9	47.9	6.7	199	80.4
Cambria township (Blue Earth)	260	260	0.0	250	98.4	0.0	0.0	1.6	0.0	13.2	20.4	53.8	42.1	20.8	122	85.2
Cambridge city & MCD (Isanti)	8,098	9,176	13.3	8,774	91.0	1.0	3.7	2.8	1.6	24.5	19.4	37.9	44.0	18.9	3,426	83.5
Cambridge township (Isanti)	2,377	2,466	3.7	2,456	97.1	0.0	0.9	1.9	0.0	23.2	19.9	45.5	40.7	23.5	882	86.6
Camden township (Carver)	921	954	3.6	847	98.0	0.0	1.1	0.5	0.5	22.8	19.1	45.7	48.5	20.7	318	85.8
Cameron township (Murray)	137	132	-3.6	100	100.0	0.0	0.0	0.0	0.0	21.0	16.0	37.3	50.8	8.2	39	89.7
Camp Release township (Renville)	186	175	-5.9	178	86.5	0.0	2.8	1.1	9.6	25.3	14.0	45.6	37.4	17.4	66	87.9
Camp 5 township (St. Louis)	35	35	0.0	32	100.0	0.0	0.0	0.0	0.0	0.0	56.3	67.5	0.0	20.0	20	75.0
Campbell city & MCD (Wilkin)	158	151	-4.4	171	94.7	0.0	0.0	5.3	0.0	22.8	14.6	37.1	43.5	16.7	72	87.5
Campbell township (Wilkin)	62	60	-3.2	77	97.4	0.0	0.0	0.0	2.6	23.4	6.5	39.4	27.1	10.2	41	100.0
Camp Lake township (Swift)	213	205	-3.8	125	100.0	0.0	0.0	0.0	0.0	12.8	37.6	60.4	50.5	22.0	63	98.4
Camp Release township (Lac qui Parle)	315	292	-7.3	219	95.0	0.0	0.0	0.0	5.0	26.0	7.3	47.2	28.4	35.2	106	93.4
Canby city & MCD (Yellow Medicine)	1,795	1,671	-6.9	1,605	98.4	0.0	0.4	1.2	0.0	20.2	28.0	51.4	51.4	15.0	733	80.1
Candor township (Otter Tail)	559	559	0.0	616	93.7	0.0	0.0	4.5	1.8	19.3	25.5	47.9	36.5	26.6	265	93.6
Canisteo township (Dodge)	659	683	3.6	583	97.4	0.0	0.2	0.2	2.2	20.4	22.3	49.6	17.1	36.0	235	91.9
Cannon township (Kittson)	20	19	-5.0	-	-	-	-	-	-	-	-	-	-	-	-	-
Cannon City township (Rice)	1,222	1,284	5.1	1,092	98.0	0.3	0.0	1.5	0.3	21.2	18.8	46.9	40.6	27.8	423	85.8
Cannon Falls city & MCD (Goodhue)	4,082	4,050	-0.8	4,054	96.4	0.0	0.3	1.9	1.4	21.9	15.7	37.8	37.9	24.5	1,691	89.8
Cannon Falls township (Goodhue)	1,092	1,089	-0.3	932	95.0	0.0	2.3	2.1	0.6	19.6	19.3	51.7	38.1	25.7	346	94.5
Canosia township (St. Louis)	2,167	2,217	2.3	2,341	97.7	1.1	0.0	0.2	1.0	20.0	17.1	46.0	32.7	29.3	916	93.4
Canton city & MCD (Fillmore)	346	344	-0.6	387	89.9	10.1	0.0	0.0	0.0	23.5	11.4	44.4	48.9	19.7	172	87.2
Canton township (Fillmore)	724	761	5.1	726	93.3	0.0	0.0	0.0	6.7	43.9	7.9	24.7	71.4	5.6	225	46.7
Caribou township (Kittson)	48	45	-6.3	39	100.0	0.0	0.0	0.0	0.0	15.4	38.5	64.4	69.7	6.1	17	64.7
Carimona township (Fillmore)	296	309	4.4	360	97.8	0.0	0.0	2.2	0.0	24.7	20.8	40.5	27.8	32.1	143	93.0
Carlisle township (Otter Tail)	156	154	-1.3	102	100.0	0.0	0.0	0.0	0.0	14.7	35.3	63.2	35.3	24.7	51	96.1
Carlos city & MCD (Douglas)	502	491	-2.2	458	92.6	0.0	0.0	0.0	7.4	27.9	9.6	32.2	35.4	10.5	188	92.6
Carlos township (Douglas)	2,033	2,117	4.1	1,837	98.9	0.0	0.4	0.0	0.7	20.0	27.3	54.2	22.5	36.8	817	93.0
Carlston township (Freeborn)	306	298	-2.6	265	100.0	0.0	0.0	0.0	0.0	17.7	21.5	53.3	41.5	23.1	108	86.1
Carlton city & MCD (Carlton)	1,020	1,033	1.3	1,098	89.8	0.1	0.0	5.5	4.6	20.4	26.6	50.0	43.6	13.5	464	83.2

1   May be of any race.

Table A. All Places — **Population and Housing**

STATE City, town, township, borough, or CDP (county if applicable)	2010 census total population	2019 estimated population	Percent change 2010–2019	ACS total population estimate 2015–2019	White alone, not Hispanic or Latino	Black alone, not Hispanic or Latino	Asian alone, not Hispanic or Latino	All other races or 2 or more races, not Hispanic or Latino	Hispanic or Latino[1]	Under 18 years old	Age 65 years and older	Median age	Percent High school diploma or less	Percent Bachelor's degree or more	Total	Percent with a computer
	1	2	3	4	5	6	7	8	9	10	11	12	13	14	15	16
MINNESOTA—Con.																
Carpenter township (Itasca)	179	178	-0.6	172	97.7	0.0	0.0	1.2	1.2	10.5	37.2	61.6	38.4	17.9	100	73.0
Carrolton township (Fillmore)	314	329	4.8	280	100.0	0.0	0.0	0.0	0.0	20.0	12.1	40.5	39.4	30.0	100	92.0
Carson township (Cottonwood)	280	271	-3.2	255	99.6	0.0	0.0	0.4	0.0	28.2	22.4	43.8	40.1	22.0	99	77.8
Carsonville township (Becker)	220	233	5.9	168	93.5	0.0	0.0	5.4	1.2	18.5	23.8	50.5	32.0	19.5	77	89.6
Carver city & MCD (Carver)	3,728	5,046	35.4	4,771	90.9	0.0	1.9	4.0	3.2	30.6	5.3	36.1	14.8	53.8	1,478	100.0
Cascade township (Olmsted)	2,820	2,846	0.9	2,872	92.9	0.2	4.5	0.4	2.0	20.4	17.0	51.2	18.5	58.9	1,161	95.1
Cashel township (Swift)	174	167	-4.0	151	90.7	0.0	0.0	2.0	7.3	25.8	25.8	44.6	40.2	21.6	51	82.4
Cass Lake city & MCD (Cass)	765	756	-1.2	633	17.4	0.2	2.1	72.7	7.7	34.8	10.6	31.4	45.5	11.2	285	84.6
Castle Rock township (Dakota)	1,322	1,360	2.9	1,481	97.0	0.2	0.0	0.7	2.0	22.3	16.3	43.0	38.5	24.4	495	91.1
Cedar township (Marshall)	86	85	-1.2	79	100.0	0.0	0.0	0.0	0.0	30.4	29.1	38.6	54.5	14.5	31	48.4
Cedar township (Martin)	223	213	-4.5	224	97.3	0.0	0.0	2.7	0.0	26.8	23.2	42.4	32.1	23.1	94	90.4
Cedarbend township (Roseau)	221	211	-4.5	182	83.5	0.0	2.2	14.3	0.0	14.3	22.5	51.9	66.4	19.7	73	93.2
Cedar Lake township (Scott)	2,779	3,034	9.2	2,988	95.9	0.4	1.1	1.5	1.1	24.0	12.1	44.2	27.6	43.4	992	96.2
Cedar Mills city & MCD (Meeker)	45	47	4.4	53	100.0	0.0	0.0	0.0	0.0	22.6	18.9	35.8	51.2	24.4	27	66.7
Cedar Mills township (Meeker)	460	462	0.4	391	96.9	0.0	0.0	0.8	2.3	16.9	18.4	49.9	48.0	10.0	165	87.9
Cedar Valley township (St. Louis)	195	197	1.0	262	96.6	0.0	1.5	1.9	0.0	24.0	13.7	43.7	31.9	25.3	104	83.7
Center township (Crow Wing)	910	957	5.2	953	96.6	1.4	0.0	1.4	0.6	22.1	22.4	46.8	30.4	24.6	401	91.0
Center City city & MCD (Chisago)	632	664	5.1	672	98.2	1.2	0.0	0.0	0.6	15.3	19.5	48.6	38.9	27.8	288	93.1
Center Creek township (Martin)	217	208	-4.1	227	100.0	0.0	0.0	0.0	0.0	30.8	19.4	38.7	41.7	22.5	80	96.3
Centerville city & MCD (Anoka)	3,789	4,002	5.6	3,985	91.6	0.0	2.2	5.0	1.3	29.1	10.5	38.6	27.3	39.5	1,396	94.2
Ceresco township (Blue Earth)	239	237	-0.8	166	98.8	1.2	0.0	0.0	0.0	22.3	21.7	50.3	37.0	23.6	63	90.5
Cerro Gordo township (Lac qui Parle)	197	181	-8.1	123	91.1	0.0	6.5	2.4	0.0	20.3	15.4	52.9	28.3	38.0	45	95.6
Ceylon city & MCD (Martin)	366	339	-7.4	332	96.1	0.0	0.0	1.5	2.4	19.0	19.9	40.8	61.7	6.7	150	82.7
Champion township (Wilkin)	53	52	-1.9	46	100.0	0.0	0.0	0.0	0.0	6.5	37.0	59.0	39.5	18.6	22	72.7
Champlin city	23,097	25,268	9.4	24,755	83.6	10.6	1.7	1.4	2.6	25.5	11.1	39.6	23.9	39.4	9,167	95.9
Chanarambie township (Murray)	208	200	-3.8	250	84.0	4.4	1.6	5.2	4.8	24.0	18.8	36.3	39.2	20.3	77	81.8
Chandler city & MCD (Murray)	270	246	-8.9	320	55.9	0.0	7.8	0.0	36.3	19.7	16.9	36.3	65.3	18.0	145	81.4
Chanhassen city & MCD (Carver)	22,929	26,389	15.1	25,657	87.3	1.6	5.9	2.0	3.1	25.6	11.2	39.8	11.5	64.7	9,419	98.4
Charlestown township (Redwood)	208	198	-4.8	188	98.9	0.0	1.1	0.0	0.0	21.3	17.6	42.5	35.7	28.6	69	91.3
Chaska city & MCD (Carver)	23,865	26,989	13.1	26,371	80.6	3.1	3.4	3.6	9.2	27.7	9.8	36.2	24.6	46.1	9,857	94.0
Chatfield city	2,777	2,829	1.9	2,990	96.2	1.3	0.4	1.7	0.4	25.1	15.8	38.1	35.7	33.5	1,210	86.8
Chatfield city (Fillmore)	1,570	1,593	1.5	1,895	96.8	2.0	0.4	0.7	0.0	25.3	16.2	37.3	35.9	34.9	771	86.4
Chatfield city (Olmsted)	1,207	1,236	2.4	1,095	95.0	0.0	0.5	3.5	1.1	24.7	15.1	43.3	35.3	31.2	439	87.5
Chatfield township (Fillmore)	533	561	5.3	559	98.4	0.0	0.0	0.0	1.6	25.6	19.9	47.0	38.8	29.0	212	94.8
Chatham township (Wright)	1,299	1,383	6.5	1,392	98.9	0.0	0.4	0.6	0.1	24.6	12.4	46.6	28.8	35.8	451	96.5
Chengwatana township (Pine)	988	993	0.5	996	96.4	0.0	1.0	2.6	0.0	28.8	13.9	40.2	36.9	25.9	322	90.7
Cherry township (St. Louis)	863	869	0.7	910	92.9	0.5	0.0	5.8	0.8	25.8	17.1	43.8	34.2	22.3	353	83.9
Cherry Grove township (Goodhue)	397	393		350	100.0	0.0	0.0	0.0	0.0	20.3	26.3	50.7	40.2	27.4	139	84.2
Chester township (Polk)	75	76	1.3	73	100.0	0.0	0.0	0.0	0.0	38.4	6.8	33.3	44.4	0.0	24	87.5
Chester township (Wabasha)	452	453	0.2	511	98.6	0.0	0.0	0.0	1.4	21.7	11.9	37.8	60.5	16.7	167	88.6
Chickamaw Beach city & MCD (Cass)	114	111	-2.6	110	90.9	0.0	0.0	7.3	1.8	19.1	38.2	58.7	25.8	24.7	53	90.6
Chief township (Mahnomen)	96	98	2.1	63	57.1	0.0	0.0	42.9	0.0	12.7	27.0	54.4	49.1	18.9	33	75.8
Chippewa Falls township (Pope)	228	239	4.8	307	98.4	0.0	0.0	0.0	1.6	13.4	25.7	48.6	43.8	16.5	136	91.2
Chisago City city & MCD (Chisago)	4,946	5,224	5.6	5,090	95.1	0.4	0.6	3.4	0.5	23.7	23.1	45.6	34.7	25.6	1,960	87.9
Chisago Lake township (Chisago)	4,605	4,871	5.8	4,759	96.0	0.0	0.5	0.4	3.0	23.6	15.3	45.4	29.7	32.0	1,750	95.0
Chisholm city & MCD (St. Louis)	4,983	4,849	-2.7	4,914	96.1	0.7	0.0	3.0	0.2	24.1	19.8	41.8	37.5	15.5	2,188	90.0
Chokio city & MCD (Stevens)	400	386	-3.5	422	96.0	0.0	4.0	0.0	0.0	16.1	26.8	47.6	47.6	21.1	187	88.2
Christiania township (Jackson)	249	242	-2.8	317	94.6	0.0	0.0	0.0	5.4	27.1	12.6	39.1	32.5	23.4	123	97.6
Circle Pines city & MCD (Anoka)	4,912	4,938	0.5	4,950	88.5	2.1	1.4	6.2	1.8	23.2	13.4	39.8	29.4	34.5	1,891	93.9
Clara City city & MCD (Chippewa)	1,360	1,276	-6.2	1,402	88.9	0.0	0.0	1.4	9.7	25.3	30.0	40.4	51.3	17.5	584	82.4

1 May be of any race.

Table A. All Places — **Population and Housing**

STATE City, town, township, borough, or CDP (county if applicable)	Population				Race and Hispanic or Latino origin (percent)					Age (percent)			Educational attainment of persons age 25 and older		Occupied housing units	
	2010 census total population	2019 estimated population	Percent change 2010–2019	ACS total population estimate 2015–2019	White alone, not Hispanic or Latino	Black alone, not Hispanic or Latino	Asian alone, not Hispanic or Latino	All other races or 2 or more races, not Hispanic or Latino	Hispanic or Latino[1]	Under 18 years old	Age 65 years and older	Median age	Percent High school diploma or less	Percent Bachelor's degree or more	Total	Percent with a computer
	1	2	3	4	5	6	7	8	9	10	11	12	13	14	15	16

MINNESOTA—Con.

STATE City, town, township, borough, or CDP (county if applicable)	1	2	3	4	5	6	7	8	9	10	11	12	13	14	15	16
Claremont city & MCD (Dodge)	550	537	-2.4	779	72.8	1.8	0.0	4.9	20.5	27.0	10.1	33.9	72.7	5.5	262	84.7
Claremont township (Dodge)	459	475	3.5	493	96.1	0.0	0.0	2.6	1.2	20.5	16.0	46.1	45.1	23.4	167	91.0
Clarissa city & MCD (Todd)	685	653	-4.7	694	94.4	0.4	0.7	2.6	1.9	19.6	25.6	44.3	54.0	14.8	282	77.7
Clark township (Aitkin)	172	171	-0.6	123	95.9	0.0	0.0	4.1	0.0	16.3	19.5	55.8	40.6	25.7	62	96.8
Clark township (Faribault)	256	246	-3.9	317	99.4	0.0	0.0	0.0	0.6	27.8	14.8	41.4	36.5	20.4	120	88.3
Clarkfield city & MCD (Yellow Medici)	861	787	-8.6	903	95.0	0.0	1.2	2.2	1.6	29.2	23.6	36.1	40.6	20.1	378	78.8
Clarks Grove city & MCD (Freeborn)	719	687	-4.5	693	79.2	0.9	15.2	0.3	4.5	20.5	12.4	40.9	44.5	10.4	299	90.6
Clay township (Hubbard)	73	75	2.7	85	100.0	0.0	0.0	0.0	0.0	7.1	55.3	66.1	35.1	41.9	41	100.0
Clayton township (Mower)	158	163	3.2	156	98.7	0.0	1.3	0.0	0.0	24.4	26.9	39.2	51.4	22.0	58	82.8
Clearbrook city & MCD (Clearwater)	516	521	1.0	483	89.4	0.0	0.0	6.8	3.7	19.7	27.3	50.4	44.4	20.4	214	81.8
Clear Creek UT (Carlton)	160	168	5.0	104	94.2	1.9	0.0	3.8	0.0	7.7	24.0	52.6	38.5	16.7	60	85.0
Clear Lake city & MCD (Sherburne)	545	707	29.7	573	95.1	0.3	0.5	3.3	0.7	29.1	7.3	31.3	34.9	25.1	206	98.5
Clear Lake township (Sherburne)	1,539	1,663	8.1	1,659	98.6	0.2	0.5	0.2	0.5	25.0	21.3	46.2	26.6	34.7	600	94.5
Clearwater city	1,735	1,818	4.8	1,859	92.4	1.0	1.3	0.5	4.8	27.5	10.1	31.3	39.6	22.9	743	92.5
Clearwater city (Stearns)	-	-	-	-	-	-	-	-	-	-	-	-	-	-	-	-
Clearwater city (Wright)	1,735	1,818	4.8	1,859	92.4	1.0	1.3	0.5	4.8	27.5	10.1	31.3	39.6	22.9	743	92.5
Clearwater township (Wright)	1,306	1,390	6.4	1,358	98.3	0.0	0.5	1.2	0.0	20.6	13.0	44.7	38.6	25.0	480	88.8
Clements city & MCD (Redwood)	153	141	-7.8	177	81.4	0.0	0.0	5.1	13.6	33.9	14.1	30.7	69.4	2.8	67	85.1
Cleveland city & MCD (Le Sueur)	724	738	1.9	797	98.6	0.0	0.4	0.0	1.0	32.5	14.6	32.3	39.6	16.7	273	93.8
Cleveland township (Le Sueur)	660	697	5.6	641	98.4	0.0	1.1	0.0	0.5	21.7	23.4	48.3	30.5	31.3	257	93.8
Clifton township (Lyon)	249	246	-1.2	202	94.6	0.0	5.4	0.0	0.0	17.3	17.8	47.8	30.6	30.6	80	91.3
Clifton township (Traverse)	75	70	-6.7	71	100.0	0.0	0.0	0.0	0.0	19.7	19.7	50.3	28.1	36.8	31	83.9
Climax city & MCD (Polk)	260	263	1.2	248	88.7	0.0	1.6	3.6	6.0	26.6	13.7	36.2	41.8	26.1	106	79.2
Clinton city & MCD (Big Stone)	452	413	-8.6	394	96.4	0.0	0.0	3.6	0.0	19.8	20.8	53.3	53.4	11.6	209	79.4
Clinton township (Rock)	276	270	-2.2	191	99.5	0.0	0.0	0.5	0.0	17.3	25.1	51.3	40.9	17.5	100	89.0
Clinton township (St. Louis)	1,013	1,022	0.9	994	93.7	2.4	0.0	2.8	1.1	16.5	23.2	49.9	39.6	15.0	438	85.2
Clinton Falls township (Steele)	360	362	0.6	426	92.7	0.0	2.1	0.0	5.2	18.3	27.2	49.8	42.8	24.8	175	87.4
Clitherall city & MCD (Otter Tail)	105	106	1.0	92	95.7	0.0	0.0	2.2	2.2	19.6	35.9	53.4	67.6	7.0	48	58.3
Clitherall township (Otter Tail)	455	469	3.1	511	98.0	0.0	0.0	1.4	0.6	12.7	35.8	59.3	27.1	38.4	240	94.2
Clontarf city & MCD (Swift)	164	157	-4.3	141	100.0	0.0	0.0	0.0	0.0	23.4	11.3	38.7	42.4	8.1	64	92.2
Clontarf township (Swift)	86	83	-3.5	67	98.5	0.0	0.0	0.0	1.5	19.4	13.4	46.8	40.7	31.5	32	87.5
Cloquet city & MCD (Carlton)	12,130	12,009		12,005	85.1	1.5	0.8	10.9	1.8	26.2	15.1	35.6	36.1	21.2	4,750	87.7
Clover township (Clearwater)	113	114	0.9	65	96.9	0.0	0.0	3.1	0.0	13.8	29.2	58.9	35.7	17.9	32	84.4
Clover township (Hubbard)	154	160	3.9	156	100.0	0.0	0.0	0.0	0.0	18.6	35.3	61.4	41.0	23.0	64	75.0
Clover township (Mahnomen)	121	124	2.5	166	44.0	0.0	0.0	53.6	2.4	38.0	16.3	31.5	57.3	15.7	44	75.0
Clover township (Pine)	405	402	-0.7	387	91.7	0.8	0.0	4.7	2.8	19.6	30.0	53.1	46.8	12.9	169	78.1
Cloverleaf township (Pennington)	84	81	-3.6	49	100.0	0.0	0.0	0.0	0.0	26.5	10.2	36.4	50.0	25.0	16	93.8
Clow township (Kittson)	46	43	-6.5	49	100.0	0.0	0.0	0.0	0.0	44.9	10.2	42.1	14.8	48.1	15	100.0
Coates city & MCD (Dakota)	157	156	-0.6	152	94.1	0.0	0.0	0.0	5.9	19.7	17.1	39.5	60.9	11.3	59	88.1
Cobden city & MCD (Brown)	36	35	-2.8	20	100.0	0.0	0.0	0.0	0.0	20.0	35.0	54.0	56.3	0.0	9	88.9
Cohasset city & MCD (Itasca)	2,692	2,725	1.2	2,729	89.7	0.9	0.7	6.2	2.5	23.8	17.9	42.6	25.8	33.3	1,079	90.1
Cokato city & MCD (Wright)	2,690	2,747	2.1	2,738	85.0	0.6	1.2	4.4	8.8	29.3	16.6	36.0	46.5	17.6	1,007	88.1
Cokato township (Wright)	1,315	1,393	5.9	1,305	97.9	0.0	0.0	0.2	1.8	29.3	12.3	37.9	42.3	20.1	404	88.1
Cold Spring city & MCD (Stearns)	4,019	4,284	6.6	4,189	93.6	0.0	0.0	0.0	6.4	26.1	22.5	36.8	42.6	25.2	1,668	86.6
Coleraine city & MCD (Itasca)	1,972	1,972	0.0	1,665	92.6	0.2	0.4	6.8	0.0	22.1	18.7	39.0	32.9	24.2	731	84.5
Colfax township (Kandiyohi)	545	563	3.3	571	96.7	0.7	0.0	1.9	0.7	19.4	21.9	46.2	44.5	14.7	224	82.1
Collegeville township (Stearns)	3,340	3,459	3.6	3,485	88.3	2.6	3.0	2.7	3.6	9.8	15.3	21.7	25.6	43.1	767	94.4
Collins township (McLeod)	473	463	-2.1	414	98.6	0.0	0.0	0.5	1.0	22.7	21.3	50.0	41.2	15.3	172	91.9
Collinwood township (Meeker)	1,113	1,120	0.6	1,163	97.9	0.0	0.3	0.0	1.8	24.8	18.7	44.6	31.6	26.6	420	92.9
Cologne city & MCD (Carver)	1,503	1,797	19.6	1,981	82.8	9.0	0.9	3.8	3.5	34.4	7.6	32.6	31.1	30.2	675	93.5
Columbia township (Polk)	466	474	1.7	428	95.1	0.7	0.0	3.3	0.9	21.5	14.5	50.3	40.9	13.0	166	90.4
Columbia Heights city & MCD (Anoka)	19,480	20,427	4.9	20,118	59.4	17.9	6.5	5.6	10.5	21.3	16.3	36.6	41.8	26.9	8,062	85.9
Columbus city & MCD (Anoka)	3,911	4,130	5.6	4,055	87.0	0.0	5.8	5.1	2.1	20.1	15.4	48.2	32.4	26.5	1,524	92.8
Colvin township (St. Louis)	317	318	0.3	275	96.0	0.7	0.0	3.3	0.0	16.0	27.3	57.2	30.7	23.6	141	84.4
Comfort township (Kanabec)	1,078	1,112	3.2	1,064	97.7	0.0	0.8	0.5	1.1	27.9	15.7	45.4	45.2	18.6	385	79.2
Comfrey city	382	354	-7.3	375	97.3	0.0	0.5	0.0	2.1	26.7	24.0	40.8	45.3	20.1	169	85.2
Comfrey city (Brown)	366	339	-7.4	340	97.1	0.0	0.6	0.0	2.4	26.5	22.1	40.8	43.7	21.0	156	85.9

1 May be of any race.

Table A. All Places — **Population and Housing**

STATE City, town, township, borough, or CDP (county if applicable)	Population 2010 census total population	2019 estimated population	Percent change 2010– 2019	ACS total population estimate 2015–2019	Race and Hispanic or Latino origin (percent) White alone, not Hispanic or Latino	Black alone, not Hispanic or Latino	Asian alone, not Hispanic or Latino	All other races or 2 or more races, not Hispanic or Latino	Hispanic or Latino[1]	Age (percent) Under 18 years old	Age 65 years and older	Median age	Educational attainment of persons age 25 and older Percent High school diploma or less	Percent Bachelor's degree or more	Occupied housing units Total	Percent with a computer
	1	2	3	4	5	6	7	8	9	10	11	12	13	14	15	16
MINNESOTA—Con.																
Comfrey city (Cottonwood)	16	15	-6.3	35	100.0	0.0	0.0	0.0	0.0	28.6	42.9	45.5	60.0	12.0	13	76.9
Como township (Marshall)	39	38	-2.6	30	100.0	0.0	0.0	0.0	0.0	0.0	33.3	61.7	56.7	10.0	16	75.0
Compton township (Otter Tail)	798	829	3.9	827	95.8	0.0	0.0	2.9	1.3	28.7	15.7	35.1	42.4	19.5	270	85.2
Comstock city & MCD (Clay)	104	108	3.8	78	94.9	0.0	5.1	0.0	0.0	17.9	19.2	49.5	18.6	44.1	35	82.9
Comstock township (Marshall)	105	104		80	100.0	0.0	0.0	0.0	0.0	16.3	40.0	61.5	48.4	8.1	39	92.3
Concord township (Dodge)	574	594	3.5	540	97.6	0.0	0.0	0.2	2.2	21.5	18.9	46.2	44.8	17.8	228	92.5
Conger city & MCD (Freeborn)	150	144	-4.0	140	100.0	0.0	0.0	0.0	0.0	24.3	10.0	35.0	47.3	9.9	58	93.1
Connelly township (Wilkin)	120	115	-4.2	109	98.2	0.0	0.0	1.8	0.0	8.3	16.5	54.8	47.9	14.9	51	88.2
Cook city & MCD (St. Louis)	567	562	-0.9	515	93.0	1.2	0.4	3.3	2.1	15.5	36.5	54.4	49.5	15.3	251	75.3
Coon Creek township (Lyon)	235	233	-0.9	222	96.4	0.9	0.9	0.9	0.9	18.5	14.4	40.5	36.3	17.5	90	94.4
Coon Rapids city & MCD (Anoka)	61,485	62,998	2.5	62,517	81.6	8.0	3.5	3.8	3.1	21.6	16.2	39.4	37.5	25.7	24,328	93.0
Copley township (Clearwater)	881	910	3.3	862	86.0	0.0	0.8	13.2	0.0	26.7	15.2	41.6	44.2	19.9	304	95.1
Corcoran city	5,395	6,250	15.8	5,911	88.1	0.3	5.5	1.4	4.8	25.1	13.0	43.0	29.5	38.5	2,138	97.2
Cordova township (Le Sueur)	465	495	6.5	468	96.8	0.0	1.9	1.3	0.0	15.0	15.8	53.6	52.5	18.8	184	90.2
Corinna township (Wright)	2,321	2,466	6.2	2,630	99.0	0.0	0.0	0.0	1.0	21.1	18.7	48.8	29.8	30.3	1,044	91.6
Corliss township (Otter Tail)	497	495	-0.4	542	95.6	0.0	0.4	2.8	1.3	24.5	21.0	41.3	38.6	23.9	207	94.7
Cormant township (Beltrami)	158	158	0.0	179	87.7	0.0	0.0	5.6	6.7	26.3	12.3	44.8	48.8	10.7	60	86.7
Cormorant township (Becker)	1,039	1,104	6.3	1,116	96.4	0.0	0.4	0.8	2.4	16.2	31.7	59.6	29.7	37.6	497	94.8
Cornish township (Aitkin)	28	28	0.0	36	100.0	0.0	0.0	0.0	0.0	8.3	16.7	57.5	37.9	24.1	24	70.8
Cornish township (Sibley)	241	238	-1.2	177	94.9	0.0	0.0	2.8	2.3	18.6	19.8	53.9	35.5	16.7	81	82.7
Correll city & MCD (Big Stone)	34	32	-5.9	45	100.0	0.0	0.0	0.0	0.0	31.1	13.3	34.4	51.6	0.0	19	94.7
Cosmos city & MCD (Meeker)	473	449	-5.1	508	97.0	0.0	0.0	1.8	1.2	18.7	18.9	44.4	45.8	7.5	241	88.8
Cosmos township (Meeker)	228	229	0.4	243	93.0	0.0	0.0	0.0	7.0	17.7	16.5	46.5	44.9	12.4	98	88.8
Cottage Grove city & MCD (Washington)	34,601	37,604	8.7	36,602	80.9	4.8	6.8	2.9	4.5	28.1	11.3	36.8	26.3	36.3	12,162	95.5
Cotton township (St. Louis)	445	449	0.9	424	95.5	0.5	0.0	1.7	2.4	6.4	29.2	57.7	35.6	25.7	238	82.4
Cottonwood township (Brown)	840	827	-1.5	896	99.6	0.0	0.0	0.0	0.4	21.2	20.5	53.5	46.9	16.1	396	89.9
Cottonwood city & MCD (Lyon)	1,231	1,236	0.4	1,332	91.4	0.0	0.7	0.0	7.9	30.0	12.2	35.9	40.1	26.0	522	93.5
Courtland city & MCD (Nicollet)	611	696	13.9	726	96.7	0.0	0.0	1.1	2.2	24.2	17.8	38.8	29.1	27.1	290	95.5
Courtland township (Nicollet)	630	638	1.3	529	94.5	0.0	0.9	1.7	2.8	24.8	18.3	49.4	29.7	29.7	215	87.4
Crane Lake township (St. Louis)	82	82	0.0	100	94.0	0.0	0.0	3.0	3.0	13.0	25.0	57.5	26.2	35.7	56	96.4
Crate township (Chippewa)	211	202	-4.3	226	98.2	0.0	0.0	0.0	1.8	37.6	9.3	34.0	30.4	17.8	79	92.4
Credit River township (Scott)	5,085	5,625	10.6	5,548	95.2	0.0	2.6	1.1	1.1	29.7	10.8	40.9	20.1	48.4	1,779	95.8
Croke township (Traverse)	75	71	-5.3	82	100.0	0.0	0.0	0.0	0.0	13.4	1.2	38.9	24.6	40.6	33	100.0
Cromwell city & MCD (Carlton)	236	232	-1.7	272	99.6	0.0	0.0	0.4	0.0	19.5	33.8	53.5	58.2	7.0	121	59.5
Cromwell township (Clay)	345	362	4.9	398	99.0	0.0	0.5	0.5	0.0	30.2	10.1	38.9	28.1	36.5	136	94.1
Crooked Creek township (Houston)	287	284		265	89.4	0.0	10.6	0.0	0.0	21.9	20.4	50.5	37.3	23.3	101	92.1
Crooked Lake township (Cass)	560	586	4.6	474	95.8	0.0	0.2	3.4	0.6	5.9	58.2	66.7	44.7	23.3	264	91.7
Crooks township (Renville)	191	179	-6.3	165	100.0	0.0	0.0	0.0	0.0	25.5	20.0	41.8	30.6	15.3	66	86.4
Crookston city & MCD (Polk)	7,891	7,764	-1.6	7,756	80.0	2.6	2.8	2.7	12.0	23.8	16.1	35.4	40.2	26.8	2,989	87.2
Crookston township (Polk)	413	420	1.7	476	96.0	0.0	0.0	1.5	2.5	20.0	15.5	48.0	40.5	27.9	195	90.8
Crosby city & MCD (Crow Wing)	2,386	2,323	-2.6	2,749	89.1	0.0	0.2	5.7	5.1	17.5	27.6	48.0	48.1	15.0	1,169	79.1
Crosby township (Pine)	93	91	-2.2	104	100.0	0.0	0.0	0.0	0.0	38.5	16.3	32.8	64.9	14.0	33	78.8
Crosslake city & MCD (Crow Wing)	2,148	2,354	9.6	2,204	99.2	0.0	0.0	0.2	0.6	10.9	43.1	61.6	35.0	32.6	1,056	92.7
Crow Lake township (Stearns)	317	343	8.2	413	98.3	0.7	0.0	1.0	0.0	24.0	24.0	46.3	51.6	11.1	158	84.8
Crow River township (Stearns)	327	352	7.6	322	99.4	0.0	0.0	0.0	0.6	26.4	21.1	44.0	49.1	17.0	124	83.9
Crow Wing township (Crow Wing)	1,972	2,083	5.6	2,102	97.0	0.0	0.8	0.6	1.7	21.4	13.8	41.6	38.8	20.1	788	92.6
Crow Wing Lake township (Hubbard)	332	340	2.4	377	100.0	0.0	0.0	0.0	0.0	11.7	43.2	63.1	19.9	39.9	181	95.0
Crystal city	22,103	22,899	3.6	22,975	71.4	16.8	3.4	2.4	6.1	20.5	13.0	37.3	33.9	33.0	9,245	92.2
Crystal Bay township (Lake)	472	485	2.8	479	92.9	1.5	0.0	3.5	2.1	15.4	20.3	51.9	49.9	12.0	250	86.8
Cuba township (Becker)	277	292	5.4	298	100.0	0.0	0.0	0.0	0.0	28.5	11.4	34.8	31.9	39.3	99	89.9
Culdrum township (Morrison)	487	496	1.8	622	86.7	0.0	0.0	1.3	12.1	24.1	12.5	38.6	54.1	11.5	233	86.7
Culver township (St. Louis)	294	297	1.0	312	90.1	0.0	0.0	9.9	0.0	24.0	21.8	42.0	41.1	18.2	122	78.7

1 May be of any race.

Table A. All Places — **Population and Housing**

STATE City, town, township, borough, or CDP (county if applicable)	Population				Race and Hispanic or Latino origin (percent)					Age (percent)			Educational attainment of persons age 25 and older		Occupied housing units	
	2010 census total population	2019 estimated population	Percent change 2010–2019	ACS total population estimate 2015–2019	White alone, not Hispanic or Latino	Black alone, not Hispanic or Latino	Asian alone, not Hispanic or Latino	All other races or 2 or more races, not Hispanic or Latino	Hispanic or Latino[1]	Under 18 years old	Age 65 years and older	Median age	Percent High school diploma or less	Percent Bachelor's degree or more	Total	Percent with a computer
	1	2	3	4	5	6	7	8	9	10	11	12	13	14	15	16
MINNESOTA—Con.																
Currie city & MCD (Murray)	233	216	-7.3	200	99.5	0.0	0.0	0.0	0.5	13.5	40.5	58.4	62.3	11.3	108	79.6
Cushing township (Morrison)	724	739	2.1	728	96.6	0.3	0.0	2.7	0.4	21.4	16.5	41.9	48.6	14.9	278	87.8
Custer township (Lyon)	203	201		164	100.0	0.0	0.0	0.0	0.0	6.7	33.5	59.5	62.9	15.7	85	83.5
Cuyuna city & MCD (Crow Wing)	319	360	12.9	271	99.6	0.0	0.0	0.4	0.0	22.1	20.7	46.3	49.3	6.0	112	86.6
Cyrus city & MCD (Pope)	287	276	-3.8	311	88.7	0.0	0.0	6.8	4.5	21.5	18.0	29.0	53.6	9.9	151	78.8
Daggett Brook township (Crow Wing)	526	552	4.9	678	100.0	0.0	0.0	0.0	0.0	27.7	14.6	37.8	43.3	18.8	253	82.2
Dahlgren township (Carver)	1,323	1,360	2.8	1,280	91.6	3.6	0.3	2.7	1.8	17.9	16.7	49.9	39.7	25.4	497	92.8
Dailey township (Mille Lacs)	234	236	0.9	198	100.0	0.0	0.0	0.0	0.0	13.1	19.7	51.7	54.9	13.6	91	86.8
Dakota city & MCD (Winona)	319	306	-4.1	287	100.0	0.0	0.0	0.0	0.0	10.8	27.2	52.3	37.3	22.0	144	89.6
Dalbo township (Isanti)	743	772	3.9	860	95.9	0.5	1.9	1.3	0.5	28.3	11.9	37.9	54.1	9.5	294	89.1
Dale township (Cottonwood)	145	142	-2.1	128	100.0	0.0	0.0	0.0	0.0	25.0	22.7	55.1	38.5	28.1	50	82.0
Dalton city & MCD (Otter Tail)	253	249	-1.6	308	97.1	1.3	0.0	1.0	0.6	26.6	13.3	35.7	48.8	13.5	129	88.4
Dane Prairie township (Otter Tail)	883	878	-0.6	845	97.9	0.4	0.2	1.1	0.5	19.1	26.0	50.7	33.3	24.5	323	91.6
Danforth township (Pine)	78	76	-2.6	74	93.2	0.0	0.0	6.8	0.0	6.8	21.6	56.5	27.5	30.4	31	90.3
Danielson township (Meeker)	295	296	0.3	301	98.3	0.0	0.7	1.0	0.0	19.3	21.9	48.6	38.9	15.7	128	82.8
Danube city & MCD (Renville)	505	458	-9.3	522	89.7	0.0	0.0	0.0	10.3	38.9	14.4	33.5	52.1	12.6	181	87.8
Danvers city & MCD (Swift)	97	90	-7.2	152	100.0	0.0	0.0	0.0	0.0	28.9	9.2	30.0	29.3	29.3	60	100.0
Danville township (Blue Earth)	238	235	-1.3	196	100.0	0.0	0.0	0.0	0.0	5.1	37.8	61.5	31.2	25.4	100	90.0
Darfur city & MCD (Watonwan)	108	103	-4.6	74	90.5	0.0	0.0	6.8	2.7	28.4	28.4	40.3	76.5	2.0	36	72.2
Darling township (Morrison)	529	539	1.9	460	99.3	0.0	0.2	0.4	0.0	17.2	25.7	50.9	48.0	6.3	206	83.5
Darnen township (Stevens)	292	300	2.7	227	83.3	0.9	0.0	0.0	15.9	21.1	12.8	30.8	37.1	28.8	65	89.2
Darwin city & MCD (Meeker)	350	353	0.9	339	89.4	0.0	0.0	0.0	10.6	28.6	18.6	41.1	50.5	11.8	126	88.9
Darwin township (Meeker)	681	683	0.3	619	99.0	0.0	0.0	0.5	0.5	16.8	19.7	52.7	32.6	25.7	253	94.5
Dassel city & MCD (Meeker)	1,460	1,449	-0.8	1,506	93.9	0.0	1.6	4.1	0.5	24.7	21.6	39.7	48.5	21.4	583	84.0
Dassel township (Meeker)	1,535	1,547	0.8	1,451	96.7	0.0	0.0	2.1	1.2	29.4	17.0	43.8	38.9	28.6	511	93.9
Davidson UT (Aitkin)	42	41	-2.4	71	100.0	0.0	0.0	0.0	0.0	19.7	25.4	56.9	31.6	31.6	26	100.0
Davis township (Kittson)	30	28	-6.7	11	100.0	0.0	0.0	0.0	0.0	0.0	54.5	68.3	9.1	27.3	5	100.0
Dawson city & MCD (Lac qui Parle)	1,547	1,400	-9.5	1,620	93.1	2.5	0.0	0.9	3.6	20.3	29.9	48.4	47.7	16.3	742	83.3
Dayton city	4,671	6,686	43.1	5,817	75.7	2.8	6.9	1.2	13.4	26.9	12.2	39.2	36.5	39.1	2,018	93.4
Dayton city (Wright)	54	75	38.9	-	-	-	-	-	-	-	-	-	-	-	-	-
Dead Lake township (Otter Tail)	494	496	0.4	566	99.1	0.0	0.0	0.0	0.9	21.0	22.6	47.6	30.3	31.3	229	94.8
Decoria township (Blue Earth)	1,104	1,106	0.2	1,207	98.1	0.0	0.4	0.0	1.5	24.1	16.6	43.0	27.4	34.5	473	92.0
Deephaven city	3,623	3,928	8.4	3,879	96.3	0.1	1.6	0.2	1.8	27.9	17.2	43.7	8.7	72.0	1,457	95.8
Deer township (Roseau)	105	99	-5.7	128	100.0	0.0	0.0	0.0	0.0	28.9	17.2	39.8	57.3	14.6	48	83.3
Deer Creek city & MCD (Otter Tail)	322	321	-0.3	227	84.1	0.0	0.0	15.9	0.0	21.1	22.9	47.3	43.3	12.8	104	78.8
Deer Creek township (Otter Tail)	344	341	-0.9	433	100.0	0.0	0.0	0.0	0.0	36.0	5.5	33.7	48.3	14.2	134	91.8
Deerfield township (Cass)	118	124	5.1	113	94.7	0.0	2.7	0.0	2.7	8.8	24.8	53.4	57.8	15.7	57	94.7
Deerfield township (Steele)	517	519	0.4	502	94.2	0.4	0.2	0.4	4.8	28.7	17.7	39.3	34.6	18.4	160	91.9
Deerhorn township (Wilkin)	97	93	-4.1	76	100.0	0.0	0.0	0.0	0.0	15.8	19.7	45.0	29.1	7.3	25	96.0
Deer Lake UT (Itasca)	3,494	3,479	-0.4	3,488	96.6	0.3	0.0	3.2	0.0	22.8	24.5	46.9	29.7	30.7	1,488	83.5
Deer Park township (Pennington)	126	121	-4.0	170	100.0	0.0	0.0	0.0	0.0	40.6	10.6	29.0	40.0	14.0	53	100.0
Deer River city & MCD (Itasca)	942	930	-1.3	951	70.6	0.5	0.0	28.5	0.4	28.1	20.9	42.6	53.2	16.2	386	73.8
Deer River township (Itasca)	707	704	-0.4	529	93.6	0.0	0.0	2.5	4.0	14.4	32.5	55.2	40.2	26.5	248	83.1
Deerwood city & MCD (Crow Wing)	529	532	0.6	553	86.8	0.0	0.0	1.1	12.1	30.7	17.2	34.6	44.1	19.4	229	84.3
Deerwood township (Crow Wing)	1,320	1,386	5.0	1,331	94.1	1.4	0.5	3.2	0.8	20.1	31.2	55.8	26.1	35.2	549	95.8
Deerwood township (Kittson)	153	144	-5.9	150	100.0	0.0	0.0	0.0	0.0	7.3	32.0	48.7	50.0	17.3	83	79.5
De Graff city & MCD (Swift)	115	123	7.0	126	100.0	0.0	0.0	0.0	0.0	7.9	18.3	54.0	44.1	16.7	66	90.9
Delafield township (Jackson)	226	219	-3.1	293	98.0	0.0	0.0	2.0	0.0	25.3	26.6	48.4	26.9	28.2	117	87.2
Delano city & MCD (Wright)	5,476	6,302	15.1	6,085	89.6	0.0	0.3	6.2	3.9	29.4	11.1	36.3	28.3	42.9	2,153	90.9
Delavan city & MCD (Faribault)	178	166	-6.7	238	98.7	0.0	0.4	0.0	0.8	18.1	13.9	39.5	54.5	17.0	114	81.6
Delavan township (Faribault)	229	219	-4.4	184	100.0	0.0	0.0	0.0	0.0	17.4	26.6	49.5	24.6	26.9	79	91.1
Delaware township (Grant)	102	102	0.0	50	92.0	8.0	0.0	0.0	0.0	16.0	40.0	59.5	51.3	15.4	23	100.0
Delhi city & MCD (Redwood)	70	64	-8.6	37	100.0	0.0	0.0	0.0	0.0	0.0	45.9	59.9	70.3	2.7	25	84.0

1 May be of any race.

STATE City, town, township, borough, or CDP (county if applicable)	2010 census total population	2019 estimated population	Percent change 2010–2019	ACS total population estimate 2015–2019	White alone, not Hispanic or Latino	Black alone, not Hispanic or Latino	Asian alone, not Hispanic or Latino	All other races or 2 or more races, not Hispanic or Latino	Hispanic or Latino[1]	Under 18 years old	Age 65 years and older	Median age	Percent High school diploma or less	Percent Bachelor's degree or more	Total	Percent with a computer
	1	2	3	4	5	6	7	8	9	10	11	12	13	14	15	16
MINNESOTA—Con.																
Delhi township (Redwood)	292	279	-4.5	280	91.8	1.1	1.1	2.9	3.2	16.8	20.7	47.0	38.3	25.0	102	89.2
Dell Grove township (Pine)	697	698	0.1	614	94.8	0.8	1.6	1.6	1.1	12.2	31.8	54.3	48.8	18.5	287	77.0
Dellwood city & MCD (Washington)	1,090	1,126	3.3	1,298	93.3	3.5	1.0	0.2	2.0	29.1	14.8	41.8	7.2	76.7	402	99.0
Delton township (Cottonwood)	123	119	-3.3	86	100.0	0.0	0.0	0.0	0.0	17.4	11.6	49.7	36.1	19.7	34	88.2
Denham city & MCD (Pine)	35	34	-2.9	27	100.0	0.0	0.0	0.0	0.0	18.5	18.5	58.4	68.2	13.6	13	61.5
Denmark township (Washington)	1,744	1,898	8.8	1,660	96.9	0.4	0.4	0.9	1.4	18.4	22.2	50.9	28.3	45.6	638	94.2
Dennison city	217	214	-1.4	202	98.5	0.0	0.0	0.0	1.5	30.7	9.4	36.9	35.8	16.4	68	94.1
Dennison city (Goodhue)..	199	196	-1.5	175	98.3	0.0	0.0	0.0	1.7	32.0	10.3	36.2	40.7	18.6	58	93.1
Dennison city (Rice)	18	18	0.0	27	100.0	0.0	0.0	0.0	0.0	22.2	3.7	49.2	9.5	4.8	10	100.0
Dent city & MCD (Otter Tail)	188	186	-1.1	190	96.3	0.0	0.5	3.2	0.0	31.1	12.1	29.5	36.1	18.5	80	86.3
Denver township (Rock) ...	173	169	-2.3	142	100.0	0.0	0.0	0.0	0.0	12.0	14.8	42.0	60.2	15.0	67	82.1
Derrynane township (Le Sueur)	508	534	5.1	411	100.0	0.0	0.0	0.0	0.0	23.4	12.2	41.9	29.9	17.9	167	92.2
Des Moines township (Jackson)	236	228	-3.4	209	99.5	0.5	0.0	0.0	0.0	28.2	16.7	44.4	37.8	28.4	87	74.7
Des Moines River township (Murray)	133	129	-3.0	100	100.0	0.0	0.0	0.0	0.0	19.0	26.0	36.3	43.7	14.1	46	89.1
Detroit township (Becker) .	1,917	2,040	6.4	2,195	83.8	0.1	0.7	12.2	3.2	23.9	19.4	42.8	37.1	29.4	860	92.4
Detroit Lakes city & MCD (Becker)...........	8,710	9,288	6.6	9,197	89.8	1.0	1.3	6.9	1.0	22.1	21.6	40.3	33.8	30.2	4,075	88.8
Dewald township (Nobles)	254	252	-0.8	219	88.6	0.0	0.0	1.8	9.6	18.7	17.4	48.3	45.3	6.8	93	90.3
Dewey township (Roseau)	122	113	-7.4	147	90.5	0.0	0.0	0.0	9.5	33.3	10.9	34.1	39.8	42.0	37	91.9
Dexter city & MCD (Mower).......................	341	347	1.8	322	99.1	0.0	0.6	0.3	0.0	10.9	29.2	54.6	53.5	10.1	146	87.7
Dexter township (Mower)..	310	323	4.2	261	98.9	0.0	0.0	0.0	1.1	22.6	26.1	46.4	32.3	23.7	90	82.2
Diamond Lake township (Lincoln)	207	203	-1.9	183	98.4	0.0	0.0	0.0	1.6	29.5	9.8	37.5	48.2	18.4	62	85.5
Dieter township (Roseau).	148	140	-5.4	133	91.7	2.3	0.8	1.5	3.8	21.1	18.0	45.5	52.6	6.2	55	98.2
Dilworth city & MCD (Clay)	4,019	4,422	10.0	4,410	89.0	1.0	0.9	2.0	7.1	26.4	14.9	37.4	26.9	29.4	1,718	92.7
Dodge Center city & MCD (Dodge)	2,685	2,768	3.1	2,737	84.9	0.0	1.2	1.0	12.9	27.5	15.9	37.5	43.4	19.0	1,067	87.3
Dollymount township (Traverse)	77	72	-6.5	38	97.4	0.0	0.0	0.0	2.6	7.9	28.9	60.4	5.9	11.8	19	100.0
Donaldson city & MCD (Kittson)...................	42	40	-4.8	4	100.0	0.0	0.0	0.0	0.0	0.0	0.0	0.0	100.0	0.0	4	100.0
Donnelly township (Marshall)	19	19	0.0	7	100.0	0.0	0.0	0.0	0.0	0.0	14.3	28.9	71.4	28.6	5	100.0
Donnelly city & MCD (Stevens)...................	243	234	-3.7	244	92.6	0.0	1.6	5.7	0.0	16.8	19.3	43.8	61.9	13.1	120	84.2
Donnelly township (Stevens)..................	98	100	2.0	52	96.2	0.0	0.0	0.0	3.8	17.3	13.5	44.5	35.5	12.9	25	92.0
Dora township (Otter Tail)	725	725	0.0	697	99.1	0.0	0.0	0.1	0.7	13.3	38.7	58.0	37.2	33.7	334	89.5
Doran city & MCD (Wilkin)	52	50	-3.8	22	100.0	0.0	0.0	0.0	0.0	4.5	22.7	58.5	66.7	9.5	14	85.7
Douglas township (Dakota)	726	752	3.6	853	96.1	2.0	0.5	0.9	0.5	27.2	15.4	44.2	45.7	24.2	293	94.9
Dover city & MCD (Olmsted)	735	770	4.8	763	93.7	0.5	0.0	0.5	5.2	28.7	8.4	33.8	36.6	24.6	295	90.8
Dover township (Olmsted)	389	398	2.3	415	95.2	0.7	0.0	0.2	3.9	23.9	18.8	41.3	36.4	26.8	151	88.1
Dovray city & MCD (Murray)...................	57	51	-10.5	49	100.0	0.0	0.0	0.0	0.0	0.0	36.7	60.3	51.0	6.1	27	77.8
Dovray township (Murray).	152	147	-3.3	149	100.0	0.0	0.0	0.0	0.0	24.8	22.8	41.7	49.0	18.4	62	90.3
Dovre township (Kandiyohi).................	2,119	2,191	3.4	2,123	96.6	0.0	0.3	1.4	1.7	25.9	16.0	42.1	24.4	39.7	761	95.1
Drammen township (Lincoln)	118	115	-2.5	109	100.0	0.0	0.0	0.0	0.0	22.0	10.1	32.6	23.0	24.3	40	95.0
Dresbach township (Winona)	456	456	0.0	383	94.8	0.0	1.6	1.3	2.3	16.4	20.6	52.7	21.3	47.3	163	94.5
Dryden township (Sibley)..	287	283	-1.4	402	86.8	0.0	0.2	1.2	11.7	29.1	7.5	34.3	37.0	10.9	138	94.9
Dublin township (Swift).....	152	146	-3.9	148	83.1	0.0	0.0	0.0	16.9	14.2	17.6	44.5	59.6	14.7	49	98.0
Dudley township (Clearwater)	396	403	1.8	442	95.0	0.0	0.5	2.0	2.5	23.8	16.3	46.0	48.2	17.5	170	81.2
Duluth city & MCD (St. Louis).....................	86,266	85,618	-0.8	85,915	88.3	2.2	1.6	5.5	2.3	17.8	15.7	34.1	28.9	37.9	36,182	89.1
Duluth township (St. Louis)....................	1,948	2,114	8.5	1,949	96.5	1.0	0.3	0.8	1.4	22.6	21.6	47.5	27.3	40.2	751	95.5
Dumont city & MCD (Traverse)	100	88	-12.0	98	100.0	0.0	0.0	0.0	0.0	16.3	13.3	29.5	38.8	20.9	46	93.5
Dunbar township (Faribault)................	283	271	-4.2	322	97.8	0.0	1.2	0.9	0.0	35.1	16.5	35.0	49.0	20.2	117	88.9
Dundas city & MCD (Rice)	1,364	1,646	20.7	1,579	91.3	1.1	2.4	2.0	3.2	31.3	9.0	34.8	28.4	33.3	554	96.8
Dundee city & MCD (Nobles)	68	67	-1.5	103	100.0	0.0	0.0	0.0	0.0	29.1	23.3	39.3	75.4	9.2	43	81.4
Dunn township (Otter Tail)	905	901	-0.4	907	95.4	2.4	0.2	1.2	0.8	12.5	40.1	60.3	22.4	42.6	412	94.7
Dunnell city & MCD (Martin)	158	146	-7.6	168	94.0	0.0	0.0	1.2	4.8	22.6	25.0	58.3	55.4	12.4	87	58.6
Durand township (Beltrami)	211	209	-0.9	219	90.0	0.0	0.0	10.0	0.0	21.0	21.0	51.1	31.0	31.5	83	92.8
Eagan city & MCD (Dakota)	64,150	66,372	3.5	66,379	73.3	9.9	8.4	3.2	5.3	22.8	12.1	38.2	18.2	51.8	26,211	96.7
Eagle township (Carlton) ..	578	598	3.5	534	99.3	0.0	0.0	0.7	0.0	13.5	26.0	51.5	40.2	20.3	242	83.5
Eagle Bend city & MCD (Todd)...................	537	519	-3.4	519	98.5	0.0	0.0	1.5	0.0	18.1	26.4	44.0	51.1	8.1	269	84.0
Eagle Lake city & MCD (Blue Earth).................	2,421	3,087	27.5	3,007	85.6	2.6	0.5	7.3	4.0	30.2	7.3	31.4	28.1	33.0	1,074	97.6

1 May be of any race.

Table A. All Places — **Population and Housing**

STATE City, town, township, borough, or CDP (county if applicable)	Population				Race and Hispanic or Latino origin (percent)					Age (percent)			Educational attainment of persons age 25 and older		Occupied housing units	
	2010 census total population	2019 estimated population	Percent change 2010–2019	ACS total population estimate 2015–2019	White alone, not Hispanic or Latino	Black alone, not Hispanic or Latino	Asian alone, not Hispanic or Latino	All other races or 2 or more races, not Hispanic or Latino	Hispanic or Latino[1]	Under 18 years old	Age 65 years and older	Median age	Percent High school diploma or less	Percent Bachelor's degree or more	Total	Percent with a computer
	1	2	3	4	5	6	7	8	9	10	11	12	13	14	15	16
MINNESOTA—Con.																
Eagle Lake township (Otter Tail)	378	376	-0.5	379	93.4	0.0	0.3	5.8	0.5	20.1	31.1	53.1	33.9	22.6	166	92.2
Eagle Point township (Marshall)	17	17	0.0	3	100.0	0.0	0.0	0.0	0.0	0.0	0.0	0.0	0.0	0.0	3	100.0
Eagles Nest township (St. Louis)	242	244	0.8	196	96.4	0.0	1.0	1.5	1.0	5.1	46.9	63.9	27.0	41.6	102	99.0
Eagle Valley township (Todd)	535	536	0.2	466	91.2	0.0	0.0	8.6	0.2	29.6	21.2	39.1	44.3	15.5	174	82.8
Eagle View township (Becker)	131	139	6.1	122	50.8	0.0	0.0	47.5	1.6	14.8	43.4	64.0	48.0	23.5	57	71.9
East Bethel city & MCD (Anoka)	11,591	12,038	3.9	11,870	94.1	0.5	1.4	2.7	1.3	21.0	11.5	40.1	35.7	23.8	4,285	96.6
East Cass UT (Cass)	62	66	6.5	37	48.6	0.0	0.0	51.4	0.0	0.0	13.5	49.7	22.2	59.3	16	100.0
East Chain township (Martin)	296	282	-4.7	246	96.7	0.0	0.0	2.4	0.8	20.3	19.9	51.3	28.7	32.0	103	96.1
East Cook UT (Cook)	775	832	7.4	726	90.5	0.0	0.0	7.9	1.7	10.6	32.2	59.9	28.0	40.2	375	93.3
Eastern township (Otter Tail)	230	228	-0.9	220	99.5	0.0	0.0	0.0	0.5	22.7	14.5	48.2	40.8	8.3	91	90.1
East Grand Forks city & MCD (Polk)	8,608	8,535	-0.8	8,604	83.0	4.4	0.4	5.8	6.4	27.2	14.5	34.5	34.6	30.4	3,558	84.9
East Gull Lake city & MCD (Cass)	1,004	1,039	3.5	995	98.5	0.0	0.1	0.0	1.4	18.1	26.6	48.6	18.2	44.1	455	94.9
East Lake Lillian township (Kandiyoh)	199	204	2.5	176	100.0	0.0	0.0	0.0	0.0	15.3	30.1	51.5	50.0	16.9	92	79.3
Easton city & MCD (Faribault)	199	184	-7.5	189	98.4	0.0	0.0	0.0	1.6	18.0	18.5	48.6	43.7	12.7	82	89.0
East Park township (Marshall)	23	23	0.0	9	100.0	0.0	0.0	0.0	0.0	0.0	49.3	42.9	0.0	0.0	5	100.0
East Side township (Mille Lacs)	620	629	1.5	575	97.9	0.0	0.0	0.5	1.6	8.0	36.5	59.5	55.0	15.6	299	82.3
East Valley township (Marshall)	43	42	-2.3	14	100.0	0.0	0.0	0.0	0.0	0.0	42.9	64.5	85.7	0.0	9	100.0
Ebro CDP	64	-	-	84	7.1	0.0	0.0	91.7	1.2	36.9	7.1	24.5	40.0	2.5	27	51.9
Echo city & MCD (Yellow Medicine)	278	254	-8.6	288	89.2	3.1	0.7	6.9	0.0	19.1	16.3	43.6	46.6	9.4	128	85.2
Echo township (Yellow Medicine)	145	136	-6.2	73	100.0	0.0	0.0	0.0	0.0	20.5	28.8	50.5	48.3	3.4	36	80.6
Eckles township (Beltrami)	1,514	1,515	0.1	1,855	77.1	0.6	0.8	18.9	2.6	24.3	9.8	34.2	37.5	27.9	641	90.6
Eckvoll township (Marshall)	77	76	-1.3	78	100.0	0.0	0.0	0.0	0.0	12.8	16.7	40.7	46.4	17.9	33	84.8
Eddy township (Clearwater)	346	349	0.9	307	94.5	0.0	3.6	2.0	0.0	17.3	19.9	48.2	32.9	23.1	140	82.9
Eden township (Brown)	254	248	-2.4	218	100.0	0.0	0.0	0.0	0.0	22.0	20.2	52.3	31.3	9.4	95	82.1
Eden township (Pipestone)	274	270	-1.5	247	93.9	0.0	0.0	0.0	6.1	32.4	19.0	40.3	33.3	38.9	82	95.1
Eden township (Polk)	168	172	2.4	227	57.7	0.0	5.7	23.3	13.2	39.2	14.1	36.4	38.5	29.2	86	82.6
Eden Lake township (Stearns)	1,542	1,676	8.7	1,409	98.6	0.2	0.1	0.9	0.1	19.7	20.1	50.0	46.2	19.6	543	90.1
Eden Prairie city	60,797	64,893	6.7	64,179	72.5	8.0	11.6	3.3	4.6	24.7	12.9	39.4	14.1	63.7	24,790	96.6
Eden Valley city	1,042	1,039	-0.3	1,019	94.0	1.7	0.0	2.5	1.9	24.9	15.7	35.0	54.8	10.0	467	79.7
Eden Valley city (Meeker) .	553	535	-3.3	604	93.4	0.7	0.0	4.1	1.8	29.8	13.2	33.5	53.2	10.2	253	78.7
Eden Valley city (Stearns).	489	504	3.1	415	94.9	3.1	0.0	0.0	1.9	17.8	19.3	41.7	56.8	9.7	214	80.8
Edgerton city & MCD (Pipestone)	1,189	1,125	-5.4	1,244	91.2	0.0	0.3	1.6	6.8	26.4	28.7	42.1	45.9	29.0	524	84.2
Edina city	47,980	52,857	10.2	51,746	84.2	2.6	7.6	3.0	2.6	23.5	21.3	44.2	11.2	69.8	21,816	93.6
Edison township (Swift)	106	102	-3.8	80	100.0	0.0	0.0	0.0	0.0	23.8	38.8	49.5	32.8	21.3	36	83.3
Edna township (Otter Tail)	901	903	0.2	874	97.3	0.3	0.3	0.8	1.3	21.7	28.4	51.5	20.4	39.5	349	89.7
Edwards township (Kandiyohi)	243	249	2.5	241	95.4	1.7	0.0	0.8	2.1	23.2	18.7	39.7	44.6	12.7	92	93.5
Effie city & MCD (Itasca) ..	123	118	-4.1	87	97.7	0.0	2.3	0.0	0.0	16.1	20.7	48.5	43.5	14.5	41	82.9
Effie UT (Itasca)...............	218	218	0.0	209	88.5	0.0	0.0	6.7	4.8	19.6	31.1	58.1	42.7	13.4	113	87.6
Effington township (Otter Tail)	264	262	-0.8	188	100.0	0.0	0.0	0.0	0.0	7.4	27.1	56.5	62.5	8.8	90	94.4
Eglon township (Clay).......	508	535	5.3	844	99.6	0.0	0.4	0.0	0.0	38.6	12.8	34.5	39.1	25.7	269	94.8
Eidsvold township (Lyon)..	236	234	-0.8	249	98.4	0.0	0.0	0.0	1.6	32.5	10.8	35.8	43.2	26.7	81	92.6
Eitzen city & MCD (Houston)	243	249	2.5	252	96.0	0.0	0.0	0.0	4.0	20.2	24.6	40.6	48.4	23.9	118	88.1
Elba city & MCD (Winona)	152	156	2.6	76	98.7	0.0	0.0	0.0	1.3	11.8	18.4	56.0	65.2	3.0	34	91.2
Elba township (Winona)....	315	316	0.3	342	98.2	0.6	0.0	0.6	0.6	35.1	11.7	38.9	29.9	36.0	104	88.5
Elbow Lake CDP	95	-	-	79	13.9	0.0	0.0	83.5	2.5	31.6	24.1	34.5	67.3	0.0	32	65.6
Elbow Lake city & MCD (Grant)....................	1,176	1,153	-2.0	1,267	90.8	0.2	0.0	8.9	0.0	22.2	18.9	39.8	39.7	18.9	589	93.0
Elbow Lake township (Grant)....................	141	139	-1.4	137	100.0	0.0	0.0	0.0	0.0	19.7	17.5	51.6	36.6	21.8	56	98.2
Eldorado township (Stevens)..................	94	96	2.1	90	100.0	0.0	0.0	0.0	0.0	25.6	4.4	35.5	14.6	18.8	25	100.0
Elgin city & MCD (Wabasha)	1,102	1,079	-2.1	1,268	97.3	0.0	0.0	1.7	0.9	28.3	8.8	32.0	34.4	22.7	499	92.0
Elgin township (Wabasha)	727	732	0.7	701	93.9	0.0	2.4	0.3	3.4	22.5	19.0	41.7	37.7	28.8	254	96.9
Elizabeth city & MCD (Otter Tail)	173	171	-1.2	141	99.3	0.0	0.0	0.0	0.7	19.1	13.5	40.1	38.8	7.8	64	98.4
Elizabeth township (Otter Tail)	819	823	0.5	955	91.1	0.8	1.3	6.1	0.7	29.7	14.5	41.4	17.8	35.9	342	95.3
Elk township (Nobles)	253	251	-0.8	325	96.0	0.0	0.0	0.0	4.0	20.0	19.1	45.3	35.3	25.7	123	94.3
Elk Lake township (Grant)	283	283	0.0	340	100.0	0.0	0.0	0.0	0.0	21.2	20.3	50.4	43.8	13.8	122	95.1
Elko New Market city & MCD (Scott)	4,092	4,774	16.7	4,657	93.6	2.7	2.0	0.7	1.1	35.6	3.3	31.3	20.9	48.0	1,364	100.0
Elk River city & MCD (Sherburne)	22,960	25,213	9.8	24,522	89.9	3.7	1.3	1.9	3.2	26.8	12.0	36.3	31.6	27.9	8,503	93.1
Elkton township (Clay).....	308	324	5.2	394	96.4	0.0	0.0	2.3	1.3	29.7	11.7	40.9	29.8	30.2	149	92.6
Elkton city & MCD (Mower)	141	148	5.0	134	100.0	0.0	0.0	0.0	0.0	26.1	11.2	37.3	39.1	16.1	55	98.2

1 May be of any race.

Table A. All Places — **Population and Housing**

STATE City, town, township, borough, or CDP (county if applicable)	Population				Race and Hispanic or Latino origin (percent)					Age (percent)			Educational attainment of persons age 25 and older		Occupied housing units	
	2010 census total population	2019 estimated population	Percent change 2010–2019	ACS total population estimate 2015–2019	White alone, not Hispanic or Latino	Black alone, not Hispanic or Latino	Asian alone, not Hispanic or Latino	All other races or 2 or more races, not Hispanic or Latino	Hispanic or Latino[1]	Under 18 years old	Age 65 years and older	Median age	Percent High school diploma or less	Percent Bachelor's degree or more	Total	Percent with a computer
	1	2	3	4	5	6	7	8	9	10	11	12	13	14	15	16
MINNESOTA—Con.																
Ellendale city & MCD (Steele)..............	690	672	-2.6	739	92.3	3.8	0.9	1.5	1.5	24.9	20.7	39.1	54.8	14.4	306	80.1
Ellington township (Dodge)................	261	268	2.7	254	94.5	0.0	0.0	2.0	3.5	15.0	21.7	41.3	42.5	17.6	104	79.8
Ellsborough township (Murray)...............	145	139	-4.1	146	100.0	0.0	0.0	0.0	0.0	24.7	19.9	43.5	51.7	24.7	61	82.0
Ellsburg township (St. Louis)................	216	218	0.9	179	99.4	0.0	0.0	0.6	0.0	12.8	29.6	57.6	33.8	33.1	81	84.0
Ellsworth township (Meeker)...............	848	856	0.9	752	96.9	0.0	1.3	1.5	0.3	18.8	28.1	55.0	33.6	24.0	318	89.6
Ellsworth city & MCD (Nobles)...............	463	456	-1.5	494	94.9	0.6	0.0	0.0	4.5	19.4	26.9	47.8	45.2	20.6	225	81.8
Elm Creek township (Martin)................	188	180	-4.3	214	91.1	0.0	0.0	8.9	0.0	25.7	18.2	44.4	41.4	17.1	74	85.1
Elmdale city & MCD (Morrison).............	116	117	0.9	81	95.1	0.0	0.0	4.9	0.0	8.6	21.0	49.8	46.7	11.7	38	84.2
Elmdale township (Morrison).............	1,007	1,027	2.0	983	98.1	0.0	0.0	0.0	1.9	29.3	13.2	42.1	44.8	15.4	363	86.8
Elmer township (Pipestone).............	232	228	-1.7	178	100.0	0.0	0.0	0.0	0.0	25.8	6.7	39.5	33.6	17.2	82	86.6
Elmer township (St. Louis)......	151	153	1.3	127	100.0	0.0	0.0	0.0	0.0	11.8	33.9	55.5	39.4	16.5	59	88.1
Elmira township (Olmsted)	354	377	6.5	364	99.2	0.0	0.5	0.0	0.3	17.9	26.6	48.0	38.0	21.4	144	91.7
Elmo township (Otter Tail).	331	330	-0.3	385	99.2	0.0	0.0	0.8	0.0	24.9	19.5	41.5	51.6	14.0	149	78.5
Elmore city & MCD (Faribault)............	663	616	-7.1	480	83.5	0.0	0.0	2.5	14.0	20.2	21.0	44.1	58.9	10.4	230	82.2
Elmore township (Faribault)............	181	174	-3.9	181	93.4	0.0	0.0	1.1	5.5	26.5	35.9	56.5	47.7	17.4	81	72.8
Elmwood township (Clay) .	415	436	5.1	383	97.7	0.5	0.0	1.3	0.5	15.4	26.6	50.4	36.6	22.6	162	93.2
Elrosa city & MCD (Stearns)...............	211	228	8.1	219	99.1	0.5	0.0	0.5	0.0	23.7	31.5	46.3	50.9	11.0	99	77.8
Ely city & MCD (St. Louis)......	3,455	3,355	-2.9	3,390	96.9	0.9	0.1	1.8	0.2	14.5	20.4	48.2	24.7	32.9	1,616	87.3
Elysian city....................	690	765	10.9	650	99.5	0.0	0.0	0.5	0.0	12.2	30.5	52.8	43.7	25.1	295	91.9
Elysian city (Le Sueur)..	688	763	10.9	645	99.5	0.0	0.0	0.5	0.0	12.2	29.9	52.4	43.1	25.4	292	92.8
Elysian city (Waseca)	2	2	0.0	5	100.0	0.0	0.0	0.0	0.0	0.0	100.0	0.0	100.0	0.0	3	0.0
Elysian township (Le Sueur)................	1,011	1,066	5.4	1,069	96.1	0.0	0.3	1.5	2.2	17.5	24.9	50.2	39.0	31.0	445	89.9
Emardville township (Red Lake)................	196	194		217	94.0	0.0	0.0	0.0	6.0	18.0	26.7	48.2	56.3	12.6	80	81.3
Embarrass township (St. Louis)................	610	613	0.5	665	97.0	0.3	0.6	2.1	0.0	17.0	24.4	50.4	42.4	14.0	322	75.8
Emerald township (Faribault)............	222	211	-5.0	183	98.4	0.0	0.0	1.6	0.0	15.8	18.6	47.5	20.3	33.8	81	98.8
Emily city & MCD (Crow Wing)...................	811	840	3.6	593	99.0	0.0	0.0	1.0	0.0	7.9	51.4	65.2	36.3	25.5	334	88.3
Emmet township (Renville)...............	218	203	-6.9	190	100.0	0.0	0.0	0.0	0.0	28.4	6.3	37.1	36.5	15.9	70	92.9
Emmons city & MCD (Freeborn).............	391	379	-3.1	356	99.2	0.0	0.0	0.0	0.8	14.9	32.9	53.7	49.1	13.0	173	83.8
Empire township (Dakota)	2,461	3,084	25.3	2,983	92.7	3.2	1.5	1.3	1.3	30.4	7.4	35.4	26.9	30.8	988	97.9
Enstrom township (Roseau)...............	455	435	-4.4	385	94.0	0.0	0.8	3.9	1.3	26.8	13.5	35.8	40.2	19.5	150	91.3
Enterprise township (Jackson)................	187	181	-3.2	162	100.0	0.0	0.0	0.0	0.0	25.9	6.8	32.5	43.2	32.2	73	89.0
Equality township (Red Lake)................	131	130	-0.8	157	98.7	0.0	0.0	0.0	1.3	27.4	18.5	40.1	43.5	10.2	59	84.7
Erdahl township (Grant)....	351	349	-0.6	388	95.9	0.0	0.0	0.0	4.1	24.5	21.9	46.5	25.4	30.3	158	91.8
Erhard city & MCD (Otter Tail)...................	148	146	-1.4	102	97.1	0.0	0.0	2.9	0.0	15.7	34.3	57.5	63.0	8.6	46	82.6
Erhards Grove township (Otter Tail)	442	441	-0.2	439	94.1	1.4	0.2	1.8	2.5	20.0	16.9	49.0	40.1	18.5	178	89.9
Ericson township (Renville)...............	206	192	-6.8	259	89.2	0.0	7.7	0.8	2.3	21.6	24.3	48.5	30.5	21.6	95	94.7
Erie township (Becker)......	1,642	1,747	6.4	1,841	95.1	0.2	0.2	4.3	0.3	24.0	15.6	46.7	36.2	22.6	695	93.8
Erin township (Rice)	859	902	5.0	966	93.0	0.5	0.3	0.5	5.7	25.4	13.7	44.5	42.7	20.7	370	92.2
Erskine city & MCD (Polk)	500	475	-5.0	478	87.4	0.0	0.0	4.6	7.9	25.3	21.3	37.6	56.7	10.5	224	70.1
Esko CDP......................	1,869	-		2,042	96.9	0.2	0.0	1.5	1.4	23.1	13.1	43.4	20.1	33.3	844	91.0
Espelie township (Marshall)...............	39	38	-2.6	29	100.0	0.0	0.0	0.0	0.0	31.0	10.3	35.1	80.0	10.0	15	86.7
Esther township (Polk)......	165	166	0.6	236	75.8	0.0	0.8	3.4	19.9	29.2	15.7	38.3	21.6	19.4	79	87.3
Euclid township (Polk)......	151	154	2.0	149	94.6	2.0	0.0	0.0	3.4	18.1	30.2	49.4	54.7	19.8	59	72.9
Eureka township (Dakota)	1,427	1,474	3.3	1,447	95.7	0.0	0.0	1.4	2.9	18.4	20.0	49.3	34.1	32.3	519	95.8
Evan city & MCD (Brown) .	86	84	-2.3	77	90.9	0.0	0.0	6.5	2.6	18.2	15.6	52.9	54.8	16.1	41	80.5
Evansville city & MCD (Douglas)...............	612	598	-2.3	608	98.4	0.0	0.0	1.6	0.0	15.5	30.1	46.8	34.1	16.9	295	81.4
Evansville township (Douglas)...............	242	250	3.3	243	100.0	0.0	0.0	0.0	0.0	21.4	25.9	57.3	37.9	14.7	98	92.9
Eveleth city & MCD (St. Louis)................	3,718	3,569	-4.0	3,609	97.9	0.1	0.0	1.6	0.3	19.6	18.3	36.2	35.9	23.3	1,683	84.1
Everglade township (Stevens)...............	108	110	1.9	166	100.0	0.0	0.0	0.0	0.0	21.7	13.9	23.3	17.9	20.9	47	85.1
Evergreen township (Becker).................	340	361	6.2	347	95.7	0.0	0.0	1.4	2.9	30.3	18.2	44.4	46.8	15.0	121	76.9
Everts township (Otter Tail)	658	649	-1.4	884	96.5	0.0	0.0	2.8	0.7	18.9	36.5	58.1	22.0	47.9	389	96.1
Ewington township (Jackson)................	244	237	-2.9	199	97.0	0.0	0.0	0.0	3.0	10.6	25.6	54.4	49.3	11.5	99	91.9
Excel township (Marshall).	300	296	-1.3	322	98.1	0.0	0.0	1.9	0.0	24.2	23.9	48.0	32.1	28.3	137	85.4
Excelsior city..................	2,211	2,340	5.8	2,434	85.3	0.7	1.0	2.0	11.0	18.9	17.5	41.8	19.7	50.9	1,124	91.2
Eyota city & MCD (Olmsted)...............	1,977	2,001	1.2	2,035	93.6	1.7	0.8	0.8	3.0	30.7	10.6	35.5	31.5	26.2	813	90.2
Eyota township (Olmsted)	466	477	2.4	425	95.1	0.7	0.5	0.0	3.8	16.2	23.1	48.4	26.8	31.5	180	90.6

1 May be of any race.

Table A. All Places — **Population and Housing**

STATE City, town, township, borough, or CDP (county if applicable)	Population				Race and Hispanic or Latino origin (percent)					Age (percent)			Educational attainment of persons age 25 and older		Occupied housing units	
	2010 census total population	2019 estimated population	Percent change 2010–2019	ACS total population estimate 2015–2019	White alone, not Hispanic or Latino	Black alone, not Hispanic or Latino	Asian alone, not Hispanic or Latino	All other races or 2 or more races, not Hispanic or Latino	Hispanic or Latino[1]	Under 18 years old	Age 65 years and older	Median age	Percent High school diploma or less	Percent Bachelor's degree or more	Total	Percent with a computer
	1	2	3	4	5	6	7	8	9	10	11	12	13	14	15	16
MINNESOTA—Con.																
Fahlun township (Kandiyohi)	335	345	3.0	505	100.0	0.0	0.0	0.0	0.0	24.6	17.2	44.3	25.5	27.1	198	95.5
Fairbanks township (St. Louis)	63	63	0.0	54	96.3	0.0	0.0	3.7	0.0	5.6	24.1	60.4	39.2	31.4	39	94.9
Fairfax township (Polk)	198	203	2.5	176	94.3	2.8	0.0	0.0	2.8	15.9	15.3	50.6	34.1	17.0	78	89.7
Fairfax city & MCD (Renville)	1,235	1,131	-8.4	1,149	79.4	0.0	1.9	1.0	17.7	26.0	21.0	37.5	49.0	9.1	453	86.1
Fairfield township (Crow Wing)	345	362	4.9	324	100.0	0.0	0.0	0.0	0.0	27.2	28.7	46.6	42.0	26.1	124	88.7
Fairfield township (Swift)	128	123	-3.9	110	98.2	0.0	0.0	0.0	1.8	20.0	6.4	51.7	25.0	35.2	52	100.0
Fairhaven CDP	358	-	-	416	99.8	0.0	0.0	0.2	0.0	28.4	15.4	37.8	40.8	10.9	159	96.2
Fair Haven township (Stearns)	1,509	1,612	6.8	1,466	99.9	0.0	0.0	0.1	0.0	20.5	15.6	45.8	39.7	18.9	607	92.9
Fairmont city & MCD (Martin)	10,669	10,030	-6.0	10,127	89.1	0.6	1.0	1.6	7.8	22.2	23.6	44.0	45.2	23.0	4,578	83.9
Fairmont township (Martin)	313	301	-3.8	362	98.1	0.0	0.0	0.0	1.9	27.9	18.5	42.7	34.4	37.8	129	93.8
Fairview township (Cass)	818	857	4.8	906	97.9	0.0	0.3	1.2	0.6	20.4	19.4	47.0	19.2	41.7	380	95.0
Fairview township (Lyon)	393	391	-0.5	360	90.8	1.1	1.1	1.9	5.0	25.8	12.8	38.8	28.3	25.2	137	97.1
Falcon Heights city & MCD (Ramsey)	5,323	5,528	3.9	5,571	70.4	8.9	15.4	3.6	1.8	18.1	16.4	33.4	13.3	74.2	2,188	96.7
Falk township (Clearwater)	284	289	1.8	345	59.7	1.2	0.0	36.5	2.6	33.9	7.2	32.1	60.5	7.6	121	81.8
Fall Lake township (Lake)	549	562	2.4	753	98.9	0.1	0.0	0.9	0.0	10.1	49.1	64.9	20.2	50.5	368	91.3
Falun township (Roseau)	253	241	-4.7	231	99.1	0.0	0.0	0.9	0.0	35.9	16.0	29.9	48.9	16.8	79	84.8
Fanny township (Polk)	100	101	1.0	89	93.3	0.0	2.2	4.5	0.0	14.6	34.8	61.3	38.4	32.9	40	90.0
Farden township (Hubbard)	1,137	1,172	3.1	1,074	83.8	0.3	1.3	11.3	3.4	25.6	19.8	41.8	30.1	34.5	423	87.5
Faribault city & MCD (Rice)	23,344	23,897	2.4	23,800	69.2	13.7	2.1	1.7	13.3	23.5	15.8	37.9	53.5	17.2	8,513	83.1
Farley township (Polk)	45	45	0.0	32	100.0	0.0	0.0	0.0	0.0	15.6	21.9	39.3	27.3	36.4	16	100.0
Farming township (Stearns)	987	1,075	8.9	959	98.6	0.0	0.0	0.4	0.9	26.8	10.9	39.1	40.9	18.1	322	91.3
Farmington city & MCD (Dakota)	21,084	23,091	9.5	22,869	88.0	1.6	1.6	5.1	3.7	32.4	7.9	33.7	24.9	34.6	7,790	96.8
Farmington township (Olmsted)	444	435	-2.0	382	97.4	0.0	1.8	0.0	0.8	16.8	26.2	54.3	39.2	28.5	177	89.8
Farm Island township (Aitkin)	1,106	1,101	-0.5	984	99.3	0.0	0.0	0.3	0.4	14.6	39.5	60.5	40.1	24.1	467	95.3
Farwell city & MCD (Pope)	51	52	2.0	31	100.0	0.0	0.0	0.0	0.0	22.6	22.6	49.8	52.2	21.7	16	87.5
Fawn Lake township (Todd)	557	563	1.1	391	98.2	0.0	0.0	1.8	0.0	22.5	15.3	43.9	33.1	13.3	158	89.2
Faxon township (Sibley)	703	697	-0.9	578	97.6	0.0	0.2	0.0	2.2	20.2	16.8	46.8	39.2	22.1	243	91.8
Fayal township (St. Louis)	1,813	1,823	0.6	1,846	98.9	0.1	0.2	0.5	0.3	19.0	22.0	49.3	22.1	37.9	736	95.0
Featherstone township (Goodhue)	777	771	-0.8	651	98.6	0.9	0.0	0.5	0.0	25.8	21.4	41.7	39.8	31.0	252	89.3
Federal Dam city & MCD (Cass)	110	110	0.0	98	65.3	0.0	2.0	32.7	0.0	22.4	37.8	59.0	46.1	14.5	41	90.2
Feeley township (Itasca)	306	304	-0.7	296	89.5	0.0	5.1	4.1	1.4	16.9	32.1	57.5	44.3	17.9	142	81.0
Felton city & MCD (Clay)	177	172	-2.8	135	100.0	0.0	0.0	0.0	0.0	23.7	11.9	44.3	46.9	10.2	63	90.5
Felton township (Clay)	84	89	6.0	88	100.0	0.0	0.0	0.0	0.0	20.5	23.9	46.0	58.1	8.1	37	73.0
Fenton township (Murray)	177	170	-4.0	123	96.7	0.0	0.0	0.0	3.3	13.8	24.4	54.1	43.4	15.2	63	85.7
Fergus Falls city & MCD (Otter Tail)	13,450	13,794	2.6	13,707	91.5	2.0	0.8	2.3	3.3	20.9	24.1	42.9	34.8	27.0	6,285	82.3
Fergus Falls township (Otter Tail)	741	769	3.8	818	99.4	0.0	0.0	0.0	0.6	26.8	11.1	38.7	40.0	20.6	281	88.6
Fern township (Hubbard)	273	281	2.9	239	92.9	0.0	0.8	6.3	0.0	19.7	16.7	43.9	36.5	18.5	104	92.3
Fertile city & MCD (Polk)	842	818	-2.9	966	94.5	0.2	0.0	2.7	2.6	22.0	24.0	46.2	46.5	16.5	422	77.7
Field township (St. Louis)	385	389	1.0	349	97.7	0.0	0.0	0.0	2.3	12.9	28.4	54.1	48.1	21.5	167	82.0
Fieldon township (Watonwan)	209	205	-1.9	271	100.0	0.0	0.0	0.0	0.0	40.2	14.4	36.7	38.3	26.5	89	97.8
Fifty Lakes city & MCD (Crow Wing)	387	404	4.4	340	96.5	0.0	0.0	0.3	3.2	12.4	37.1	61.0	33.1	29.9	174	92.0
Fillmore township (Fillmore)	457	480	5.0	501	99.4	0.0	0.0	0.6	0.0	22.0	16.6	49.4	47.6	19.7	213	94.8
Fine Lakes township (St. Louis)	134	135	0.7	131	98.5	0.0	0.0	0.8	0.8	13.7	29.0	55.9	44.3	13.2	52	96.2
Finland CDP	195	-	-	179	91.1	0.0	0.0	6.1	2.8	15.1	21.2	48.7	49.7	7.0	94	95.7
Finlayson city & MCD (Pine)	315	307	-2.5	321	98.1	0.0	0.0	0.0	1.9	24.0	16.8	39.3	53.3	10.7	136	73.5
Finlayson township (Pine)	456	451	-1.1	435	94.0	3.4	0.0	2.1	0.5	29.0	18.4	40.1	54.7	16.8	164	82.3
First Assessment UT (Crow Wing)	5,416	5,710	5.4	5,647	98.2	0.0	0.2	0.7	0.9	21.8	19.0	46.5	32.4	26.6	2,199	96.7
Fisher city & MCD (Polk)	435	419	-3.7	503	92.4	0.4	0.0	0.8	6.4	23.9	13.1	29.2	29.9	32.4	193	91.7
Fisher township (Polk)	200	201	0.5	106	96.2	0.0	0.0	0.0	3.8	17.0	6.6	51.8	20.7	30.5	43	93.0
Fish Lake CDP	51	-	-	104	100.0	0.0	0.0	0.0	0.0	27.9	24.0	41.6	25.3	37.3	37	94.6
Fish Lake township (Chisago)	2,019	2,136	5.8	2,215	96.9	0.5	0.1	1.9	0.7	24.8	12.7	41.4	32.0	21.5	782	93.2
Fleming township (Aitkin)	312	309	-1.0	262	92.0	3.1	0.0	5.0	0.0	6.5	47.3	64.7	40.0	19.2	147	89.8
Fleming township (Pine)	141	138	-2.1	126	87.3	4.8	0.0	2.4	5.6	15.9	26.2	51.8	52.1	23.4	50	86.0
Flensburg city & MCD (Morrison)	225	227	0.9	207	93.7	0.0	0.5	5.8	0.0	12.6	18.8	47.9	55.8	3.9	97	79.4
Flom township (Norman)	218	205	-6.0	189	88.4	0.0	0.0	11.6	0.0	25.9	21.2	47.3	47.7	25.8	74	82.4
Floodwood city & MCD (St. Louis)	533	522	-2.1	449	96.0	0.0	0.0	1.8	2.2	19.6	22.7	45.3	50.3	5.3	241	80.5
Floodwood township (St. Louis)	276	278	0.7	256	96.5	1.2	0.0	2.3	0.0	13.3	25.4	57.2	51.1	13.7	115	78.3
Flora township (Renville)	188	175	-6.9	177	94.4	0.0	0.0	2.3	3.4	20.9	33.9	54.6	50.8	17.4	71	78.9
Florence township (Goodhue)	1,581	1,588	0.4	1,514	96.4	0.0	0.6	2.3	0.7	18.1	24.2	53.3	35.7	32.6	664	90.2
Florence city & MCD (Lyon)	37	36	-2.7	28	71.4	0.0	0.0	0.0	28.6	46.4	17.9	34.5	60.0	13.3	11	100.0

1 May be of any race.

Table A. All Places — Population and Housing

STATE City, town, township, borough, or CDP (county if applicable)	2010 census total population	2019 estimated population	Percent change 2010–2019	ACS total population estimate 2015–2019	White alone, not Hispanic or Latino	Black alone, not Hispanic or Latino	Asian alone, not Hispanic or Latino	All other races or 2 or more races, not Hispanic or Latino	Hispanic or Latino[1]	Under 18 years old	Age 65 years and older	Median age	Percent High school diploma or less	Percent Bachelor's degree or more	Total	Percent with a computer
	1	2	3	4	5	6	7	8	9	10	11	12	13	14	15	16
MINNESOTA—Con.																
Florida township (Yellow Medicine)	129	122	-5.4	141	100.0	0.0	0.0	0.0	0.0	17.7	38.3	60.9	52.6	12.9	66	65.2
Flowing township (Clay)	79	84	6.3	73	100.0	0.0	0.0	0.0	0.0	12.3	26.0	47.7	38.3	16.7	33	78.8
Foldahl township (Marshall)	64	63	-1.6	69	100.0	0.0	0.0	0.0	0.0	8.7	5.8	24.6	50.0	25.0	27	88.9
Folden township (Otter Tail)	299	300	0.3	243	97.1	0.0	0.0	2.9	0.0	22.2	32.1	52.0	53.0	14.1	95	86.3
Foley city & MCD (Benton)	2,630	2,673	1.6	2,647	93.5	1.1	1.1	1.9	2.4	29.9	12.6	32.4	47.6	20.0	954	84.9
Folsom township (Traverse)	128	120	-6.3	99	93.9	0.0	6.1	0.0	0.0	13.1	29.3	59.1	48.1	9.9	48	87.5
Forada city & MCD (Douglas)	185	190	2.7	157	96.2	1.3	0.0	2.5	0.0	17.2	21.7	49.3	39.0	26.0	73	90.4
Ford township (Kanabec)	195	191	-2.1	144	93.8	0.0	2.8	3.5	0.0	10.4	25.0	53.6	55.1	14.4	70	80.0
Forest township (Becker)	77	82	6.5	106	95.3	0.0	0.0	0.9	3.8	0.9	67.0	71.1	17.1	61.0	56	92.9
Forest township (Rice)	1,233	1,297	5.2	1,190	96.8	0.0	0.4	0.2	2.6	21.2	17.1	50.3	30.0	37.0	465	95.7
Forest City township (Meeker)	653	656	0.5	668	96.6	0.0	0.0	1.9	1.5	26.9	16.9	41.7	41.6	17.3	253	90.1
Forest Lake city & MCD (Washington)	18,405	20,933	13.7	20,004	86.5	1.7	4.1	3.1	4.6	22.8	15.1	39.1	34.2	32.0	7,588	92.8
Foreston city & MCD (Mille Lacs)	533	533	0.0	471	98.1	0.0	0.0	0.6	1.3	30.4	8.7	32.1	45.4	10.3	182	97.3
Forest Prairie township (Meeker)	972	980	0.8	928	98.0	0.0	0.6	1.1	0.3	24.4	18.8	43.9	47.8	18.0	331	90.6
Forestville township (Fillmore)	356	371	4.2	291	96.6	0.0	0.0	0.0	3.4	12.0	31.3	54.8	49.8	20.1	126	86.5
Fork township (Marshall)	10	10	0.0	12	100.0	0.0	0.0	0.0	0.0	0.0	75.0	75.6	83.3	0.0	7	28.6
Fortier township (Yellow Medicine)	99	94	-5.1	67	100.0	0.0	0.0	0.0	0.0	34.3	6.0	31.1	46.5	7.0	23	100.0
Fort Ripley city & MCD (Crow Wing)	70	67	-4.3	45	88.9	0.0	2.2	0.0	8.9	22.2	35.6	52.8	42.9	25.7	21	95.2
Fort Ripley township (Crow Wing)	884	930	5.2	1,110	97.7	0.0	0.0	1.3	1.0	31.2	12.9	36.0	36.2	24.1	376	89.9
Fosston city & MCD (Polk)	1,532	1,464	-4.4	1,571	89.4	0.7	0.6	3.6	5.7	20.8	29.3	45.0	42.3	26.3	685	81.0
Fossum township (Norman)	156	149	-4.5	141	88.7	0.0	0.0	11.3	0.0	14.2	26.2	49.8	47.8	18.3	66	89.4
Foster township (Big Stone)	112	110	-1.8	111	100.0	0.0	0.0	0.0	0.0	12.6	31.5	55.5	49.5	7.5	50	90.0
Foster township (Faribault)	239	227	-5.0	220	99.5	0.0	0.0	0.5	0.0	26.4	14.1	41.0	27.8	22.5	86	90.7
Fountain city & MCD (Fillmore)	406	399	-1.7	345	98.8	0.0	0.6	0.6	0.0	17.1	19.7	44.5	40.0	22.4	151	95.4
Fountain township (Fillmore)	315	331	5.1	360	98.6	0.6	0.8	0.0	0.0	27.8	16.4	43.7	37.4	22.3	143	86.7
Fountain Prairie township (Pipestone)	188	187	-0.5	209	100.0	0.0	0.0	0.0	0.0	41.6	14.4	31.8	56.1	19.3	57	89.5
Foxhome city & MCD (Wilkin)	116	111	-4.3	106	100.0	0.0	0.0	0.0	0.0	27.4	20.8	39.3	64.9	9.5	44	84.1
Foxhome township (Wilkin)	103	99	-3.9	85	97.6	0.0	0.0	0.0	2.4	18.8	22.4	56.4	51.5	4.5	38	65.8
Fox Lake township (Martin)	256	247	-3.5	236	100.0	0.0	0.0	0.0	0.0	11.4	28.4	56.8	41.9	22.2	106	97.2
Framnas township (Stevens)	305	313	2.6	356	99.7	0.0	0.0	0.3	0.0	29.5	16.6	35.8	32.5	27.7	121	94.2
Franconia township (Chisago)	1,805	1,896	5.0	1,759	93.9	0.3	0.2	2.3	3.2	13.8	15.5	48.4	31.1	32.8	603	95.5
Frankford township (Mower)	355	372	4.8	417	100.0	0.0	0.0	0.0	0.0	27.3	13.9	39.6	45.6	19.9	142	95.1
Franklin city & MCD (Renville)	512	469	-8.4	553	70.2	4.9	0.0	22.6	2.4	22.2	19.0	38.6	61.3	9.3	223	81.6
Franklin township (Wright)	2,748	2,922	6.3	2,866	98.4	0.0	0.6	0.9	0.2	29.9	18.2	42.8	38.5	33.8	1,035	89.8
Fraser township (Martin)	304	293	-3.6	233	98.3	0.0	0.0	1.7	0.0	26.6	18.5	47.3	46.3	12.3	90	87.8
Frazee city & MCD (Becker)	1,350	1,391	3.0	1,341	87.1	1.6	0.7	7.3	3.4	25.3	19.7	35.0	51.7	12.0	519	78.4
Fredenberg township (St. Louis)	1,331	1,342	0.8	1,417	96.7	1.2	0.3	0.0	1.8	20.7	22.9	51.4	28.5	35.5	579	93.6
Freeborn city & MCD (Freeborn)	284	274	-3.5	276	94.2	0.0	0.0	2.2	3.6	23.9	9.1	37.6	43.6	11.2	109	93.6
Freeborn township (Freeborn)	280	271	-3.2	173	98.8	0.0	0.0	1.2	0.0	11.0	22.0	56.1	46.3	12.5	79	75.9
Freedom township (Waseca)	326	328	0.6	362	96.7	0.0	0.0	0.0	3.3	17.4	23.5	53.2	40.1	13.5	154	77.9
Freeland township (Lac qui Parle)	102	94	-7.8	115	93.0	0.0	0.0	7.0	0.0	28.7	7.0	45.2	28.6	16.9	44	88.6
Freeman township (Freeborn)	496	478	-3.6	503	92.2	2.2	0.0	2.4	3.2	22.1	15.5	45.4	52.1	14.8	180	90.0
Freeport city & MCD (Stearns)	635	669	5.4	841	87.9	0.0	0.0	3.0	9.2	32.3	15.6	30.6	45.6	22.6	316	77.8
Fremont township (Winona)	355	355	0.0	300	80.0	0.0	0.7	0.7	18.7	28.3	16.3	36.2	51.8	19.1	102	88.2
French township (St. Louis)	570	572	0.4	562	98.2	0.0	0.7	1.1	0.0	14.1	31.1	60.6	27.1	30.5	255	90.2
French Lake township (Wright)	1,174	1,249	6.4	1,171	98.0	0.0	0.4	0.9	0.6	24.2	20.5	44.2	40.0	20.8	456	87.3
Friberg township (Otter Tail)	809	808	-0.1	931	98.8	0.6	0.0	0.0	0.5	18.4	21.6	51.3	38.8	23.2	367	86.9
Fridley city & MCD (Anoka)	27,222	27,826	2.2	27,668	62.5	15.7	5.6	4.3	11.9	22.5	15.0	35.5	39.2	31.1	10,932	93.5
Friendship township (Yellow Medicine)	194	184	-5.2	202	95.5	0.0	0.0	4.5	0.0	24.8	18.3	45.4	31.4	21.4	74	93.2
Frohn township (Beltrami)	1,431	1,528	6.8	1,548	84.6	0.1	1.0	12.3	1.9	22.5	18.9	44.8	33.3	31.7	587	91.7
Frontenac CDP	282	-	-	227	84.6	0.0	0.0	11.9	3.5	11.9	15.0	48.9	48.5	23.7	110	86.4
Frost city & MCD (Faribault)	198	182	-8.1	212	91.5	0.9	0.0	0.9	6.6	25.9	17.5	35.5	40.7	13.0	87	86.2

1 May be of any race.

STATE City, town, township, borough, or CDP (county if applicable)	2010 census total population	2019 estimated population	Percent change 2010–2019	ACS total population estimate 2015–2019	White alone, not Hispanic or Latino	Black alone, not Hispanic or Latino	Asian alone, not Hispanic or Latino	All other races or 2 or more races, not Hispanic or Latino	Hispanic or Latino[1]	Under 18 years old	Age 65 years and older	Median age	Percent High school diploma or less	Percent Bachelor's degree or more	Total	Percent with a computer
	1	2	3	4	5	6	7	8	9	10	11	12	13	14	15	16
MINNESOTA—Con.																
Fulda city & MCD (Murray)	1,318	1,208	-8.3	1,366	81.8	0.0	7.1	3.4	7.8	25.0	25.6	44.4	52.1	16.3	565	83.4
Funkley city & MCD (Beltrami)	8	8	0.0	15	100.0	0.0	0.0	0.0	0.0	20.0	0.0	40.3	60.0	0.0	7	100.0
Gail Lake township (Crow Wing)	97	102	5.2	93	87.1	0.0	1.1	5.4	6.5	19.4	25.8	56.5	61.6	9.6	42	90.5
Galena township (Martin)	246	233	-5.3	194	92.3	0.0	0.0	0.0	7.7	21.1	27.3	47.0	40.7	26.9	89	97.8
Gales township (Redwood)	137	133	-2.9	158	95.6	0.0	4.4	0.0	0.0	38.6	13.9	26.3	38.3	22.2	50	84.0
Garden township (Polk)	212	213	0.5	245	100.0	0.0	0.0	0.0	0.0	16.3	20.0	49.1	26.1	24.1	96	91.7
Garden City CDP	255	-	-	317	96.2	0.0	0.0	2.2	1.6	19.2	7.9	34.3	51.8	14.2	126	91.3
Garden City township (Blue Earth)	689	689	0.0	779	97.6	0.0	0.0	1.0	1.4	19.9	10.3	43.2	42.3	29.9	300	90.0
Garfield city & MCD (Douglas)	355	350	-1.4	399	97.5	0.8	0.0	0.5	1.3	32.6	7.8	41.0	23.5	23.1	157	90.4
Garfield township (Lac qui Parle)	145	133	-8.3	113	100.0	0.0	0.0	0.0	0.0	23.9	15.0	47.9	29.3	25.6	44	100.0
Garfield township (Polk)	461	468	1.5	599	99.0	0.0	0.0	0.5	0.5	41.7	13.5	32.9	31.0	22.3	178	90.4
Garnes township (Red Lake)	190	188	-1.1	248	96.4	0.0	0.0	3.6	0.0	27.4	12.9	37.2	40.4	15.2	70	97.1
Garrison city & MCD (Crow Wing)	203	207	2.0	171	94.2	0.0	0.0	3.5	2.3	7.6	42.1	58.4	55.3	10.0	90	70.0
Garrison township (Crow Wing)	775	818	5.5	836	98.3	0.0	0.0	0.5	1.2	14.1	33.4	59.9	52.7	14.3	364	94.8
Garvin city & MCD (Lyon)	135	131	-3.0	121	96.7	0.0	1.7	0.8	0.8	14.9	8.3	42.7	65.2	10.1	59	98.3
Gary city & MCD (Norman)	214	202	-5.6	321	85.7	6.2	2.5	5.6	0.0	25.9	13.1	29.5	41.9	11.2	129	86.8
Gaylord city & MCD (Sibley)	2,305	2,207	-4.3	1,769	76.2	2.6	3.4	0.0	17.8	18.4	25.1	48.9	58.0	15.3	849	81.4
Gem Lake city & MCD (Ramsey)	393	500	27.2	567	96.3	0.4	2.1	0.9	0.4	31.0	15.2	36.6	25.5	45.0	181	94.5
Geneva city & MCD (Freeborn)	553	537	-2.9	349	94.6	0.0	0.0	5.4	0.0	13.2	26.4	55.7	37.3	23.2	166	82.5
Geneva township (Freeborn)	420	407	-3.1	356	98.9	0.0	0.0	0.6	0.6	23.0	15.7	48.3	33.8	22.9	141	92.9
Gennessee township (Kandiyohi)	411	423	2.9	448	98.2	0.0	0.0	0.4	1.3	24.3	17.6	44.5	38.1	18.1	170	94.7
Genola city & MCD (Morrison)	71	67	-5.6	71	100.0	0.0	0.0	0.0	0.0	43.7	9.9	24.7	50.0	2.9	24	66.7
Gentilly township (Polk)	280	281	0.4	238	83.6	0.0	0.0	3.4	13.0	18.1	18.5	53.6	53.3	11.5	91	95.6
Georgetown city & MCD (Clay)	129	126	-2.3	76	84.2	0.0	0.0	7.9	7.9	27.6	15.8	43.6	54.5	10.9	37	94.6
Georgetown township (Clay)	156	164	5.1	140	95.0	0.0	0.0	0.0	5.0	27.1	10.7	41.5	32.7	38.8	51	96.1
Germania township (Todd)	500	502	0.4	535	100.0	0.0	0.0	0.0	0.0	30.8	21.3	31.1	56.1	13.7	174	72.4
Germantown township (Cottonwood)	207	202	-2.4	222	90.5	0.0	0.0	0.0	9.5	29.7	23.4	46.8	42.9	23.1	86	93.0
Gervais township (Red Lake)	224	220	-1.8	186	99.5	0.0	0.0	0.0	0.5	33.3	20.4	41.0	42.2	22.4	66	90.9
Getty township (Stearns)	376	404	7.4	373	98.7	0.0	0.0	0.8	0.5	31.1	13.9	38.2	55.6	11.5	118	87.3
Gheen UT (St. Louis)	19	19	0.0	-	-	-	-	-	-	-	-	-	-	-	-	-
Ghent city & MCD (Lyon)	377	366	-2.9	407	82.8	2.0	0.2	0.0	15.0	27.0	15.2	36.4	40.0	19.3	154	98.7
Gibbon city & MCD (Sibley)	790	755	-4.4	749	86.2	3.1	0.0	0.3	10.4	24.4	16.7	39.4	49.4	10.2	338	89.1
Gilbert city & MCD (St. Louis)	1,793	1,780	-0.7	1,850	97.2	0.1	0.2	2.5	0.0	20.9	20.4	45.9	39.4	11.8	836	83.0
Gilchrist township (Pope)	194	205	5.7	230	90.0	3.9	0.0	3.9	2.2	18.3	23.0	49.5	29.5	25.3	109	81.7
Gillford township (Wabasha)	575	578	0.5	526	98.9	0.4	0.4	0.2	0.2	28.5	16.5	39.7	51.4	21.4	203	91.1
Gilman city & MCD (Benton)	223	219	-1.8	235	95.7	0.0	0.0	0.4	3.8	30.6	15.7	32.0	45.6	15.4	97	77.3
Gilmanton township (Benton)	807	839	4.0	897	92.1	0.0	0.0	1.1	6.8	31.8	12.4	35.0	46.3	19.6	295	90.8
Girard township (Otter Tail)	736	734	-0.3	660	98.5	1.1	0.0	0.0	0.5	9.5	45.6	63.2	28.1	35.1	323	92.9
Glasgow township (Wabasha)	249	250	0.4	239	100.0	0.0	0.0	0.0	0.0	22.6	15.1	45.7	48.2	21.8	90	88.9
Glen township (Aitkin)	446	443	-0.7	422	99.3	0.0	0.0	0.7	0.0	4.5	48.3	63.9	49.4	12.3	253	79.8
Glencoe city & MCD (McLeod)	5,630	5,544	-1.5	5,495	79.3	0.7	0.0	4.1	15.8	26.2	19.3	38.3	56.8	12.4	2,077	87.9
Glencoe township (McLeod)	492	480	-2.4	436	98.6	0.0	0.0	0.0	1.4	22.0	18.1	45.6	51.6	7.8	177	89.8
Glendorado township (Benton)	762	793	4.1	795	96.0	0.3	0.8	1.3	1.8	23.9	10.3	41.2	35.9	21.4	296	92.6
Glenville city & MCD (Freeborn)	642	622	-3.1	625	94.1	0.0	0.0	0.6	5.3	17.4	25.8	53.3	56.2	14.3	279	86.4
Glenwood city & MCD (Pope)	2,567	2,611	1.7	2,567	98.3	0.6	0.0	0.3	0.8	18.5	27.3	44.3	35.7	27.4	1,308	84.4
Glenwood township (Pope)	1,058	1,069	1.0	1,234	94.2	0.3	1.5	1.9	2.2	22.0	25.0	50.8	25.2	33.5	506	93.5
Glyndon city & MCD (Clay)	1,392	1,373	-1.4	1,299	79.3	0.8	0.0	7.2	12.6	30.7	7.9	31.3	35.6	28.3	461	90.0
Glyndon township (Clay)	280	294	5.0	222	92.8	0.0	1.4	0.5	5.4	31.1	15.3	35.8	37.0	32.6	82	96.3
Gnesen township (St. Louis)	1,683	1,748	3.9	2,033	93.6	0.1	1.0	2.5	2.8	19.1	18.9	46.5	29.4	36.6	822	98.5
Godfrey township (Polk)	313	317	1.3	289	98.6	0.0	0.0	1.4	0.0	13.5	23.9	54.9	36.5	24.6	140	95.7
Golden Valley city	20,357	21,886	7.5	21,566	85.3	4.3	3.0	4.9	2.6	17.7	21.7	45.9	13.9	60.1	9,596	93.0
Golden Valley township (Roseau)	189	179	-5.3	204	88.7	0.0	7.8	1.5	2.0	24.0	12.3	41.5	57.0	11.9	73	95.9
Gonvick city & MCD (Clearwater)	279	279	0.0	260	77.7	0.0	3.5	17.7	1.2	27.7	24.2	40.3	56.4	16.2	120	70.0
Good Hope township (Itasca)	99	98	-	98	100.0	0.0	0.0	0.0	0.0	6.1	36.7	59.4	61.4	18.1	52	84.6

1 May be of any race.

Table A. All Places — Population and Housing

STATE City, town, township, borough, or CDP (county if applicable)	2010 census total population	2019 estimated population	Percent change 2010–2019	ACS total population estimate 2015–2019	White alone, not Hispanic or Latino	Black alone, not Hispanic or Latino	Asian alone, not Hispanic or Latino	All other races or 2 or more races, not Hispanic or Latino	Hispanic or Latino[1]	Under 18 years old	Age 65 years and older	Median age	Percent High school diploma or less	Percent Bachelor's degree or more	Total	Percent with a computer
	1	2	3	4	5	6	7	8	9	10	11	12	13	14	15	16
MINNESOTA—Con.																
Good Hope township (Norman)	43	40	-7.0	36	75.0	0.0	0.0	2.8	22.2	16.7	38.9	61.5	42.3	15.4	18	66.7
Goodhue city & MCD (Goodhue)	1,176	1,177	0.1	1,261	86.8	0.2	0.0	1.2	11.9	29.7	9.5	31.7	45.9	18.3	484	96.1
Goodhue township (Goodhue)	528	527	-0.2	503	97.6	0.0	0.0	0.6	1.8	28.2	18.7	39.2	44.1	18.6	187	91.4
Goodland township (Itasca)	466	463	-0.6	486	90.5	0.0	0.0	9.5	0.0	12.6	30.9	57.8	31.2	29.1	229	83.0
Goodridge city & MCD (Pennington)	132	129	-2.3	138	90.6	0.0	0.0	3.6	5.8	23.2	9.4	38.0	50.0	3.8	62	88.7
Goodridge township (Pennington)	79	76	-3.8	114	100.0	0.0	0.0	0.0	0.0	33.3	6.1	22.6	53.8	5.8	30	93.3
Good Thunder city & MCD (Blue Earth)	585	565	-3.4	564	93.8	0.0	0.0	4.8	1.4	27.5	12.8	37.0	43.9	16.3	220	86.4
Goodview city & MCD (Winona)	4,011	4,109	2.4	4,124	85.9	0.2	1.9	6.5	5.5	16.7	14.4	40.3	34.8	24.1	1,727	91.5
Goose Prairie township (Clay)	175	183	4.6	165	95.2	0.0	0.0	1.8	3.0	26.7	12.7	38.4	28.6	21.9	58	96.6
Gordon township (Todd)	657	667	1.5	558	99.5	0.0	0.0	0.0	0.5	20.8	24.2	52.1	42.7	15.7	244	88.1
Gorman township (Otter Tail)	465	463	-0.4	410	98.0	0.2	0.0	1.5	0.2	22.2	21.2	50.6	39.5	20.7	170	94.7
Gorton township (Grant)	49	49	0.0	86	100.0	0.0	0.0	0.0	0.0	17.4	24.4	45.7	17.9	33.9	30	86.7
Gould township (Cass)	224	234	4.5	254	37.4	1.2	2.4	59.1	0.0	26.8	24.8	49.5	43.8	18.2	104	76.9
Grace township (Chippewa)	95	92	-3.2	99	98.0	0.0	0.0	2.0	0.0	14.1	16.2	40.9	41.2	17.6	41	95.1
Graceville city & MCD (Big Stone)	589	560	-4.9	670	98.8	0.4	0.0	0.0	0.7	22.2	37.8	57.2	58.0	15.2	291	72.2
Graceville township (Big Stone)	185	181	-2.2	81	97.5	0.0	0.0	1.2	1.2	8.6	17.3	55.7	68.6	7.1	35	57.1
Grafton township (Sibley)	238	233	-2.1	188	100.0	0.0	0.0	0.0	0.0	17.0	25.5	51.7	41.7	19.4	79	93.7
Graham township (Benton)	582	606	4.1	609	91.6	0.8	0.0	1.0	6.6	35.6	12.2	32.7	43.6	17.6	186	91.9
Graham Lakes township (Nobles)	218	219	0.5	255	100.0	0.0	0.0	0.0	0.0	18.4	14.5	50.7	51.4	12.0	90	91.1
Granada city & MCD (Martin)	305	285	-6.6	257	95.3	0.0	0.0	1.9	2.7	22.6	17.9	41.8	57.4	7.7	115	84.3
Granby township (Nicollet)	246	250	1.6	220	100.0	0.0	0.0	0.0	0.0	17.3	31.4	52.5	55.7	10.3	93	86.0
Grand Forks township (Polk)	179	182	1.7	110	100.0	0.0	0.0	0.0	0.0	8.2	23.6	53.0	25.5	10.6	41	92.7
Grand Lake township (St. Louis)	2,775	2,797	0.8	2,787	91.9	1.7	0.0	5.2	1.2	21.8	14.0	41.9	34.1	28.0	1,071	92.6
Grand Marais city & MCD (Cook)	1,348	1,357	0.7	1,332	91.6	0.1	0.0	3.8	4.5	15.8	25.9	45.1	32.3	39.8	699	86.4
Grand Meadow city & MCD (Mower)	1,153	1,192	3.4	1,125	93.7	1.8	0.4	1.9	2.3	28.5	15.7	36.5	38.2	19.2	454	89.0
Grand Meadow township (Mower)	308	321	4.2	320	93.1	0.0	0.9	5.9	0.0	21.3	11.3	43.0	35.7	20.9	120	92.5
Grand Plain township (Marshall)	55	54	-1.8	24	100.0	0.0	0.0	0.0	0.0	12.5	20.8	50.5	33.3	52.4	12	75.0
Grand Portage UT (Cook)	565	608	7.6	684	22.7	0.4	6.0	69.2	1.8	20.3	15.6	43.1	46.4	19.8	345	88.1
Grand Prairie township (Nobles)	206	204		237	98.7	0.0	0.0	1.3	0.0	29.5	14.8	42.8	53.2	5.1	80	88.8
Grand Rapids city & MCD (Itasca)	10,869	11,214	3.2	11,165	95.1	0.3	0.8	2.7	1.0	22.6	23.3	41.3	33.7	26.2	4,907	87.6
Grandview township (Lyon)	281	280	-0.4	263	97.3	0.8	0.4	0.8	0.8	28.9	13.7	44.6	34.9	30.9	95	88.4
Grange township (Pipestone)	204	201	-1.5	192	98.4	0.0	0.0	0.5	1.0	27.6	16.1	42.5	45.0	14.5	65	93.8
Granite township (Morrison)	481	489	1.7	542	98.3	0.0	0.0	1.3	0.4	28.2	14.2	39.3	51.4	16.2	170	89.4
Granite Falls township (Chippewa)	249	241	-3.2	225	81.8	0.0	0.0	17.8	0.4	31.1	23.6	45.5	48.6	13.0	83	88.0
Granite Falls city	2,901	2,698	-7.0	2,660	85.4	1.0	0.0	8.3	5.2	19.4	22.3	42.6	44.0	17.6	1,160	92.5
Granite Falls city (Chippewa)	857	810	-5.5	802	84.4	0.0	0.0	11.7	3.9	17.1	21.6	45.5	49.3	18.6	383	90.1
Granite Falls city (Yellow Medicine)	2,044	1,888	-7.6	1,858	85.8	1.5	0.0	6.9	5.8	20.3	22.6	42.1	41.6	17.1	777	93.7
Granite Ledge township (Benton)	743	773	4.0	799	95.5	0.0	1.0	0.9	2.6	29.2	15.9	38.3	42.5	13.7	291	84.9
Granite Rock township (Redwood)	225	215	-4.4	168	100.0	0.0	0.0	0.0	0.0	22.6	18.5	49.7	31.7	15.9	63	93.7
Grant city & MCD (Washington)	4,047	4,116	1.7	4,100	95.0	1.9	1.3	0.0	1.8	20.0	24.3	51.3	22.3	45.6	1,561	96.3
Grant Valley township (Beltrami)	2,019	2,006	-0.6	2,091	80.9	0.9	1.8	12.2	4.2	32.3	12.3	34.4	28.7	39.5	712	95.4
Granville township (Kittson)	78	75	-3.8	34	100.0	0.0	0.0	0.0	0.0	11.8	20.6	58.5	33.3	16.7	18	94.4
Grass Lake township (Kanabec)	1,038	1,056	1.7	1,063	95.4	0.2	0.0	1.6	2.8	21.8	16.8	41.4	57.7	7.3	431	86.8
Grasston city & MCD (Kanabec)	158	153	-3.2	188	100.0	0.0	0.0	0.0	0.0	29.3	5.9	37.0	61.5	3.3	67	95.5
Grattan township (Itasca)	44	44	0.0	35	82.9	0.0	0.0	17.1	0.0	14.3	11.4	56.8	46.7	13.3	17	64.7
Gray township (Pipestone)	220	218	-0.9	194	97.4	0.0	0.0	2.6	0.0	23.2	19.1	50.9	42.0	21.7	80	91.3
Great Bend township (Cottonwood)	305	297	-2.6	423	97.9	0.0	0.0	2.1	0.0	31.2	17.3	37.8	32.0	13.9	150	95.3
Great Scott township (St. Louis)	427	431	0.9	456	94.3	0.0	0.4	3.1	2.2	15.6	23.5	53.6	36.2	19.4	197	84.3
Greenbush township (Mille Lacs)	1,293	1,301	0.6	1,368	90.4	0.0	1.9	7.4	0.4	29.2	15.4	38.4	50.7	15.3	458	89.3
Greenbush city & MCD (Roseau)	719	698	-2.9	782	85.8	9.2	0.0	5.0	0.0	26.5	20.6	41.6	44.0	19.1	295	86.4
Greenfield city	2,771	3,038	9.6	2,986	96.8	0.3	1.1	1.9	0.0	28.0	12.6	43.0	21.9	44.5	1,029	95.7

1 May be of any race.

Table A. All Places — Population and Housing

STATE City, town, township, borough, or CDP (county if applicable)	Population				Race and Hispanic or Latino origin (percent)					Age (percent)			Educational attainment of persons age 25 and older		Occupied housing units	
	2010 census total population	2019 estimated population	Percent change 2010–2019	ACS total population estimate 2015–2019	White alone, not Hispanic or Latino	Black alone, not Hispanic or Latino	Asian alone, not Hispanic or Latino	All other races or 2 or more races, not Hispanic or Latino	Hispanic or Latino[1]	Under 18 years old	Age 65 years and older	Median age	Percent High school diploma or less	Percent Bachelor's degree or more	Total	Percent with a computer
	1	2	3	4	5	6	7	8	9	10	11	12	13	14	15	16
MINNESOTA—Con.																
Greenfield township (Wabasha)................	1,330	1,334	0.3	1,096	98.4	0.0	0.4	1.2	0.0	19.4	27.2	51.2	37.3	20.9	455	96.0
Green Isle city & MCD (Sibley).....................	569	558	-1.9	617	86.5	0.3	0.0	3.2	9.9	32.4	13.0	33.9	56.1	16.1	215	87.4
Green Isle township (Sibley).....................	521	514	-1.3	595	91.3	6.2	0.0	0.0	2.5	26.4	13.4	41.5	46.6	19.7	205	87.3
Green Lake township (Kandiyohi)................	1,575	1,626	3.2	1,679	91.8	1.4	0.4	6.4	0.0	20.5	24.4	51.1	20.2	36.7	702	93.6
Greenleaf township (Meeker)...................	676	680	0.6	631	98.7	0.0	0.6	0.0	0.6	21.2	19.3	49.4	30.8	25.1	255	89.8
Green Meadow township (Norman)...................	108	102	-5.6	71	100.0	0.0	0.0	0.0	0.0	26.8	25.4	45.1	34.6	11.5	25	92.0
Green Prairie township (Morrison).................	752	767	2.0	654	98.6	0.0	1.1	0.3	0.0	16.7	16.8	51.7	41.2	17.4	274	87.6
Greenvale township (Dakota)....................	803	840	4.6	791	96.6	0.4	0.0	1.3	1.8	26.8	16.4	45.0	36.6	28.0	277	93.5
Green Valley township (Becker)....................	376	401	6.6	312	97.4	0.3	0.0	2.2	0.0	24.7	17.0	47.0	46.8	9.6	119	88.2
Greenwald city & MCD (Stearns).................	222	222	0.0	238	100.0	0.0	0.0	0.0	0.0	30.3	14.7	32.0	60.7	7.3	89	86.5
Greenway township (Itasca)....................	1,939	1,884	-2.8	2,101	91.9	0.2	0.0	6.3	1.6	24.1	16.4	42.2	48.4	13.9	906	82.8
Greenwood township (Clearwater)..............	83	84	1.2	64	79.7	0.0	3.1	17.2	0.0	18.8	26.6	53.5	48.1	19.2	25	96.0
Greenwood city...............	696	752	8.0	694	96.3	0.6	0.7	1.3	1.2	13.5	20.7	57.1	9.3	67.8	309	97.4
Greenwood township (St. Louis)......................	937	951	1.5	1,200	55.3	0.0	0.5	43.0	1.2	15.2	35.8	56.0	28.3	28.9	515	91.8
Gregory township (Mahnomen)...............	74	76	2.7	51	96.1	0.0	0.0	3.9	0.0	9.8	33.3	54.5	63.0	4.3	25	76.0
Grey Cloud Island township (Washington)..	295	300	1.7	369	91.6	0.0	0.8	5.7	1.9	18.7	18.4	43.8	25.0	36.8	144	93.1
Grey Eagle city & MCD (Todd).....................	348	329	-5.5	307	97.7	0.0	0.0	0.7	1.6	18.6	34.2	54.0	64.4	12.8	144	77.8
Grey Eagle township (Todd).....................	638	637	-0.2	488	98.4	0.0	0.0	1.6	0.0	6.1	38.3	59.9	45.4	25.2	232	86.6
Grimstad township (Roseau)...................	146	138	-5.5	110	100.0	0.0	0.0	0.0	0.0	9.1	20.9	49.3	34.1	7.1	44	93.2
Grove township (Stearns).	495	535	8.1	588	96.4	0.0	1.5	0.0	2.0	31.5	16.0	36.3	50.3	14.3	196	88.8
Grove City city & MCD (Meeker)..................	636	619	-2.7	615	91.2	0.0	0.5	4.9	3.4	34.3	15.4	29.6	53.9	12.4	237	79.3
Grove Lake township (Pope)......................	255	269	5.5	276	81.5	0.0	0.0	0.0	18.5	30.4	19.9	40.0	43.9	9.4	126	74.6
Grove Park-Tilden township (Polk).............	282	287	1.8	243	91.8	0.0	2.9	5.3	0.0	16.5	27.2	54.9	33.5	16.5	114	89.5
Grygla city & MCD (Marshall).................	217	211	-2.8	185	98.9	0.0	0.0	1.1	0.0	22.7	18.9	46.1	51.1	16.0	88	80.7
Gully city & MCD (Polk)	66	66	0.0	70	94.3	0.0	0.0	5.7	0.0	17.1	32.9	49.2	64.3	5.4	38	60.5
Gully township (Polk)	136	139	2.2	200	85.0	15.0	0.0	0.0	0.0	32.0	19.5	45.2	43.9	27.2	61	78.7
Guthrie township (Hubbard).................	555	571	2.9	537	98.0	0.0	0.6	0.4	1.1	26.1	14.0	41.5	37.6	24.2	216	96.8
Hackensack city & MCD (Cass).....................	311	310	-0.3	290	89.3	0.0	0.0	10.7	0.0	13.4	18.6	47.7	32.4	20.0	167	91.0
Hadley city & MCD (Murray)..................	61	57	-6.6	56	100.0	0.0	0.0	0.0	0.0	16.1	30.4	59.0	57.4	12.8	29	86.2
Hagali township (Beltrami)	370	369	-0.3	338	91.4	0.3	5.3	2.1	0.9	21.3	20.4	44.7	32.7	30.3	133	91.0
Hagen township (Clay)	154	164	6.5	163	93.9	0.0	0.0	1.2	4.9	19.6	22.1	51.6	55.2	16.0	67	77.6
Halden township (St. Louis)......................	129	130	0.8	114	96.5	0.0	0.0	3.5	0.0	16.7	21.9	48.5	51.7	11.2	49	85.7
Hale township (McLeod)...	922	906	-1.7	914	99.6	0.4	0.0	0.0	0.0	22.2	17.1	46.3	46.5	14.7	337	84.0
Hallock city & MCD (Kittson)...................	984	921	-6.4	1,059	95.3	0.8	1.1	0.6	2.2	22.0	20.4	48.9	38.2	34.4	452	86.9
Hallock township (Kittson)	101	98	-3.0	96	92.7	0.0	2.1	5.2	0.0	45.8	6.3	33.3	17.6	54.9	25	92.0
Halma city & MCD (Kittson)...................	63	61	-3.2	31	100.0	0.0	0.0	0.0	0.0	32.3	29.0	51.5	100.0	0.0	19	36.8
Halstad city & MCD (Norman)...................	597	554	-7.2	581	80.7	4.1	0.0	5.2	10.0	18.2	22.7	50.1	45.0	16.5	266	76.7
Halstad township (Norman)...................	108	101	-6.5	99	100.0	0.0	0.0	0.0	0.0	19.2	24.2	43.8	27.8	5.6	40	85.0
Hamburg city & MCD (Carver)....................	519	517	-0.4	571	95.6	0.0	0.4	0.5	3.5	16.5	17.7	42.9	45.5	15.7	234	92.3
Hamden township (Becker)....................	206	217	5.3	195	95.9	0.0	0.0	1.0	3.1	28.7	14.9	40.0	30.7	19.7	70	94.3
Ham Lake city & MCD (Anoka)	15,296	16,783	9.7	16,434	90.3	0.9	5.2	2.8	0.7	23.2	15.6	43.6	32.1	32.4	5,805	95.7
Hamlin township (Lac qui Parle)	165	152	-7.9	122	100.0	0.0	0.0	0.0	0.0	4.1	19.7	56.5	32.7	22.7	58	86.2
Hammer township (Yellow Medicine).................	194	182	-6.2	175	78.3	0.0	0.0	2.3	19.4	19.4	25.7	53.5	49.6	31.5	70	92.9
Hammond township (Polk)	44	45	2.3	21	100.0	0.0	0.0	0.0	0.0	4.8	57.1	71.8	15.8	10.5	12	100.0
Hammond city & MCD (Wabasha).................	134	134	0.0	91	86.8	0.0	0.0	0.0	13.2	13.2	9.9	43.5	60.0	10.0	42	90.5
Hampden township (Kittson)...................	38	36	-5.3	20	100.0	0.0	0.0	0.0	0.0	0.0	75.0	76.7	15.0	15.0	15	53.3
Hampton city & MCD (Dakota)....................	684	697	1.9	689	94.9	0.0	1.5	2.0	1.6	31.5	4.4	29.7	31.9	23.6	248	91.5
Hampton township (Dakota)....................	903	923	2.2	832	98.6	0.0	0.0	0.2	1.2	19.0	18.0	49.9	50.5	20.3	310	89.7
Hamre township (Beltrami)	13	13	0.0	8	100.0	0.0	0.0	0.0	0.0	25.0	12.5	48.0	33.3	16.7	4	75.0
Hancock township (Carver)....................	345	353	2.3	266	89.5	2.6	2.3	0.8	4.9	19.2	24.1	49.3	46.4	18.9	109	84.4
Hancock city & MCD (Stevens).................	764	745	-2.5	795	83.1	0.0	6.9	6.4	3.5	25.3	9.3	31.4	34.2	22.4	263	92.4

1 May be of any race.

Table A. All Places — **Population and Housing**

STATE City, town, township, borough, or CDP (county if applicable)	2010 census total population	2019 estimated population	Percent change 2010–2019	ACS total population estimate 2015–2019	White alone, not Hispanic or Latino	Black alone, not Hispanic or Latino	Asian alone, not Hispanic or Latino	All other races or 2 or more races, not Hispanic or Latino	Hispanic or Latino[1]	Under 18 years old	Age 65 years and older	Median age	Percent High school diploma or less	Percent Bachelor's degree or more	Total	Percent with a computer
	Population				Race and Hispanic or Latino origin (percent)					Age (percent)			Educational attainment of persons age 25 and older		Occupied housing units	
	1	2	3	4	5	6	7	8	9	10	11	12	13	14	15	16
MINNESOTA—Con.																
Hangaard township (Clearwater)	5	5	0.0	-	-	-	-	-	-	-	-	-	-	-	-	-
Hanley Falls city & MCD (Yellow Medicine)	304	277	-8.9	497	50.3	0.4	0.0	2.0	47.3	34.4	6.6	26.8	55.6	11.6	164	89.0
Hanover city	2,938	3,507	19.4	3,298	97.4	0.1	1.4	0.0	1.2	34.1	6.8	34.7	23.6	41.3	1,081	98.4
Hanover city (Wright)	2,329	2,776	19.2	2,704	97.2	0.0	1.7	0.0	1.2	34.8	6.5	34.3	24.2	39.2	888	99.1
Hanska city & MCD (Brown)	402	375	-6.7	415	97.6	0.0	0.0	0.0	2.4	27.2	12.3	35.8	57.2	7.4	181	89.0
Hansonville township (Lincoln)	90	88	-2.2	51	100.0	0.0	0.0	0.0	0.0	11.8	21.6	48.3	40.0	26.7	25	84.0
Hantho township (Lac qui Parle)	105	97	-7.6	92	91.3	0.0	0.0	8.7	0.0	28.3	14.1	38.5	16.9	35.4	38	92.1
Harding city & MCD (Morrison)	125	123	-1.6	141	97.2	0.0	0.7	2.1	0.0	22.0	21.3	49.1	63.0	17.0	48	83.3
Hardwick city & MCD (Rock)	198	183	-7.6	188	98.4	0.0	0.0	0.0	1.6	15.4	16.0	42.5	43.0	18.0	91	86.8
Harmony city & MCD (Fillmore)	1,018	987	-3.0	976	98.0	0.6	0.0	0.6	0.8	13.3	39.2	59.7	43.6	23.5	481	77.8
Harmony township (Fillmore)	389	406	4.4	428	99.8	0.0	0.0	0.2	0.0	44.4	13.3	28.3	44.3	24.4	120	79.2
Harris city & MCD (Chisago)	1,132	1,186	4.8	1,065	92.9	2.0	2.3	1.8	1.1	16.3	15.0	44.3	48.4	11.7	418	95.2
Harris township (Itasca)	3,257	3,239	-0.6	3,242	92.7	0.1	0.4	6.0	0.9	18.1	23.5	50.5	23.1	31.8	1,383	95.1
Harrison township (Kandiyohi)	576	593	3.0	564	99.5	0.5	0.0	0.0	0.0	16.1	20.7	52.7	30.9	27.7	259	93.8
Hart township (Winona)	361	359	-0.6	322	91.6	0.0	2.5	5.9	0.0	21.7	20.5	48.8	45.0	17.5	108	79.6
Hartford township (Todd) ..	671	673	0.3	592	96.5	0.0	0.0	2.7	0.8	23.8	16.2	41.5	48.9	13.1	222	82.4
Hart Lake township (Hubbard)	509	525	3.1	504	80.0	0.0	0.0	18.8	1.2	23.8	17.7	41.0	38.0	24.0	192	95.3
Hartland city & MCD (Freeborn)	317	306	-3.5	331	90.6	2.4	2.4	0.0	4.5	19.0	19.6	44.5	49.4	23.9	163	93.3
Hartland township (Freeborn)	254	246	-3.1	275	100.0	0.0	0.0	0.0	0.0	17.1	19.3	45.7	25.4	32.3	116	87.9
Harvey township (Meeker)	374	376	0.5	379	93.1	0.0	0.8	0.0	6.1	22.4	17.2	45.3	44.4	19.8	151	86.1
Hassan Valley township (McLeod)	689	675	-2.0	629	100.0	0.0	0.0	0.0	0.0	20.2	23.1	48.1	44.4	16.5	242	88.4
Hastings city & MCD (Dakota)	22,220	22,884	3.0	22,738	90.6	1.4	0.5	3.6	3.9	21.3	17.0	39.8	37.3	27.5	9,049	90.4
Hastings city (Washington)	-	2	-	-	-	-	-	-	-	-	-	-	-	-	-	-
Hatfield city & MCD (Pipestone)	55	52	-5.5	30	100.0	0.0	0.0	0.0	0.0	13.3	0.0	50.8	76.9	0.0	14	100.0
Haugen township (Aitkin)..	177	176	-0.6	169	99.4	0.0	0.0	0.6	0.0	2.4	45.6	61.9	45.9	12.1	94	91.5
Havana township (Steele).	570	572	0.4	581	90.9	0.0	7.6	0.0	1.5	16.9	20.8	47.3	46.5	20.0	231	88.7
Havelock township (Chippewa)	181	174	-3.9	142	98.6	0.0	0.0	1.4	0.0	19.7	26.1	46.2	49.5	22.6	55	92.7
Haven township (Sherburne)	1,986	2,157	8.6	2,128	94.9	0.8	0.3	3.0	1.1	23.3	15.5	46.3	30.6	26.6	775	93.5
Haverhill township (Olmsted)	1,411	1,444	2.3	1,301	93.8	1.1	2.7	1.5	0.9	21.2	21.2	49.8	15.1	59.8	506	96.0
Hawk Creek township (Renville)	201	187	-7.0	171	94.2	0.0	0.0	5.8	0.0	28.1	23.4	51.5	33.9	15.7	66	95.5
Hawley city & MCD (Clay)	2,069	2,198	6.2	2,143	88.2	0.8	0.0	7.4	3.5	32.2	9.0	31.3	31.1	28.6	849	88.7
Hawley township (Clay)	472	498	5.5	523	99.2	0.0	0.0	0.6	0.2	24.5	14.1	37.9	36.4	25.0	222	73.9
Hay Brook township (Kanabec)	252	258	2.4	249	100.0	0.0	0.0	0.0	0.0	17.7	18.1	46.8	55.1	10.2	105	81.9
Hay Creek township (Goodhue)	887	883	-0.5	762	96.1	0.4	0.0	3.5	0.0	22.2	12.7	47.3	39.0	30.7	294	96.9
Hayes township (Swift)	199	190	-4.5	228	100.0	0.0	0.0	0.0	0.0	25.0	20.6	39.6	41.8	18.4	96	85.4
Hayfield city & MCD (Dodge)	1,340	1,337	-0.2	1,431	93.9	2.2	0.3	0.8	2.9	22.7	20.6	39.0	49.4	20.8	630	85.9
Hayfield township (Dodge)	465	480	3.2	440	99.1	0.0	0.2	0.0	0.7	19.5	9.3	38.6	23.2	35.6	150	95.3
Hay Lake UT (St. Louis)....	83	83	0.0	101	100.0	0.0	0.0	0.0	0.0	30.7	0.0	52.5	34.3	0.0	45	66.7
Hayland township (Mille Lacs)	501	509	1.6	570	96.7	0.0	0.7	2.6	0.0	25.3	14.0	41.4	62.5	8.8	209	88.5
Hayward city & MCD (Freeborn)	250	242	-3.2	218	99.1	0.0	0.0	0.0	0.9	18.3	25.2	47.0	48.1	3.1	105	74.3
Hayward township (Freeborn)	381	370	-2.9	333	98.5	0.9	0.0	0.6	0.0	16.8	19.2	55.5	50.0	13.1	138	89.1
Hazel Run city & MCD (Yellow Medicine)	63	56	-11.1	64	78.1	0.0	0.0	0.0	21.9	25.0	23.4	48.7	41.9	25.6	30	76.7
Hazel Run township (Yellow Medicine)	193	181	-6.2	187	94.1	0.0	0.0	5.9	0.0	28.9	7.5	38.7	38.5	23.8	75	98.7
Hazelton township (Aitkin)	832	825	-0.8	720	96.8	0.0	0.0	1.9	1.3	9.4	43.8	63.0	45.9	25.2	374	88.5
Hazelton township (Kittson).....................	104	98	-5.8	103	97.1	1.0	0.0	1.9	0.0	35.0	10.7	36.1	48.4	10.9	36	88.9
Hector city & MCD (Renville)	1,155	1,050	-9.1	972	86.0	0.2	0.0	0.6	13.2	22.6	22.2	46.5	41.7	18.0	433	86.6
Hector township (Renville)	222	209	-5.9	190	97.9	0.0	0.0	2.1	0.0	16.8	16.8	51.3	36.1	22.2	89	92.1
Hegbert township (Swift) ..	95	91	-4.2	98	100.0	0.0	0.0	0.0	0.0	2.0	50.0	65.0	71.0	15.1	49	71.4
Hegne township (Norman)	40	38	-5.0	38	92.1	0.0	0.0	5.3	2.6	28.9	21.1	44.5	29.6	51.9	15	100.0
Heidelberg city & MCD (Le Sueur)	123	124	0.8	104	100.0	0.0	0.0	0.0	0.0	10.6	16.3	51.2	52.9	14.1	46	80.4
Heier township (Mahnomen).................	143	146	2.1	130	90.0	0.0	0.0	6.9	3.1	13.8	23.1	50.3	41.9	18.1	44	93.2
Height of Land township (Becker)......................	673	717	6.5	569	94.7	0.7	0.0	2.5	2.1	12.1	29.2	54.9	47.7	17.1	259	80.7
Helen township (McLeod).	863	845	-2.1	838	97.5	0.0	0.0	0.1	2.4	24.0	18.6	44.1	40.1	19.3	296	90.9
Helena township (Scott) ...	1,650	1,796	8.8	2,026	97.9	0.0	0.1	0.5	1.4	30.7	8.0	39.4	33.6	37.0	595	94.8
Helga township (Hubbard)	1,400	1,646	17.6	1,733	89.4	0.2	5.3	3.9	1.2	25.4	13.2	42.1	32.1	33.8	583	95.0
Helgeland township (Polk)	54	54	0.0	31	100.0	0.0	0.0	0.0	0.0	25.8	32.3	57.5	19.0	28.6	10	100.0
Henderson city & MCD (Sibley)	897	930	3.7	888	97.9	0.2	0.0	0.0	1.9	25.9	15.7	40.3	49.7	15.4	361	90.3

1 May be of any race.

STATE City, town, township, borough, or CDP (county if applicable)	2010 census total population	2019 estimated population	Percent change 2010–2019	ACS total population estimate 2015–2019	White alone, not Hispanic or Latino	Black alone, not Hispanic or Latino	Asian alone, not Hispanic or Latino	All other races or 2 or more races, not Hispanic or Latino	Hispanic or Latino[1]	Under 18 years old	Age 65 years and older	Median age	Percent High school diploma or less	Percent Bachelor's degree or more	Total	Percent with a computer
	1	2	3	4	5	6	7	8	9	10	11	12	13	14	15	16
MINNESOTA—Con.																
Henderson township (Sibley)	717	709	-1.1	744	99.5	0.0	0.1	0.4	0.0	31.6	12.1	34.4	43.1	21.1	245	92.7
Hendricks city & MCD (Lincoln)	713	675	-5.3	770	87.3	2.1	0.0	4.7	6.0	14.0	33.6	52.8	49.5	15.9	399	77.9
Hendricks township (Lincoln)	201	197	-2.0	174	100.0	0.0	0.0	0.0	0.0	32.8	23.6	39.8	36.8	21.4	66	89.4
Hendrickson township (Hubbard)	314	323	2.9	238	97.1	0.4	1.3	1.3	0.0	28.6	18.9	36.7	45.3	23.9	91	85.7
Hendrum city & MCD (Norman)	307	281	-8.5	311	96.5	0.0	0.0	0.6	2.9	29.3	12.5	38.8	55.3	22.3	125	88.8
Hendrum township (Norman)	95	89	-6.3	97	87.6	0.0	0.0	11.3	1.0	27.8	20.6	44.3	20.0	11.4	41	85.4
Henning city & MCD (Otter Tail)	802	808	0.7	853	92.7	0.9	0.7	3.5	2.1	19.7	33.8	44.5	44.6	14.6	385	83.9
Henning township (Otter Tail)	378	375	-0.8	294	99.3	0.0	0.0	0.0	0.7	15.6	33.0	54.5	40.2	27.6	130	93.1
Henrietta township (Hubbard)	1,479	1,511	2.2	1,574	97.1	0.0	0.0	2.6	0.3	21.3	27.9	52.5	39.7	30.1	652	93.6
Henriette city & MCD (Pine)	71	69	-2.8	82	96.3	0.0	0.0	3.7	0.0	14.6	18.3	48.0	84.3	0.0	37	40.5
Henryville township (Renville)	208	194	-6.7	147	100.0	0.0	0.0	0.0	0.0	31.3	13.6	31.9	40.4	21.3	54	88.9
Hereim township (Roseau)	228	216	-5.3	205	97.6	1.5	0.0	1.0	0.0	25.9	25.9	46.2	57.2	15.2	85	91.8
Herman city & MCD (Grant)	437	440	0.7	429	98.1	1.9	0.0	0.0	0.0	19.3	32.2	55.3	42.9	13.7	216	80.1
Hermantown city & MCD (St. Louis)	9,413	9,637	2.4	9,604	91.8	3.4	0.5	2.2	2.2	22.3	18.7	41.5	29.7	34.4	3,660	90.1
Heron Lake city & MCD (Jackson)	698	648	-7.2	750	89.2	0.0	0.0	2.8	8.0	25.6	16.7	35.5	42.3	21.2	324	88.9
Heron Lake township (Jackson)	313	303	-3.2	236	100.0	0.0	0.0	0.0	0.0	15.7	19.1	51.0	53.7	21.6	96	91.7
Hersey township (Nobles)	219	217	-0.9	217	99.5	0.0	0.0	0.0	0.5	19.8	17.5	46.4	35.5	19.1	81	85.2
Hewitt city & MCD (Todd)	266	256	-3.8	223	96.4	0.0	0.0	2.2	1.3	19.3	19.3	49.4	45.7	9.8	100	84.0
Hibbing city & MCD (St. Louis)	16,358	15,855	-3.1	16,014	90.9	2.6	1.9	2.6	2.1	25.5	18.4	41.3	31.2	19.5	6,755	86.3
Hickory township (Pennington)	80	77	-3.8	79	100.0	0.0	0.0	0.0	0.0	8.9	49.4	64.9	58.0	4.3	37	86.5
Higdem township (Polk)	84	85	1.2	54	100.0	0.0	0.0	0.0	0.0	35.2	9.3	25.5	55.6	25.9	22	77.3
High Forest township (Olmsted)	973	981	0.8	1,239	97.7	0.0	0.5	0.3	1.5	29.5	18.0	43.1	35.5	31.9	416	90.9
Highland township (Wabasha)	462	462	0.0	500	94.4	0.0	0.6	0.0	5.0	17.0	12.2	47.6	53.3	15.8	199	85.9
Highland Grove township (Clay)	288	304	5.6	354	98.6	0.0	0.6	0.8	0.0	25.7	17.5	42.5	34.4	33.2	145	89.7
Highlanding township (Pennington)	194	184	-5.2	180	92.8	0.0	0.0	3.9	3.3	40.0	7.2	25.2	35.2	20.9	49	89.8
Highwater township (Cottonwood)	166	162	-2.4	150	100.0	0.0	0.0	0.0	0.0	24.0	33.3	52.5	13.0	36.1	57	98.2
Hill township (Kittson)	15	14	-6.7	30	100.0	0.0	0.0	0.0	0.0	23.3	23.3	42.5	60.9	8.7	13	100.0
Hill City city & MCD (Aitkin)	627	585	-6.7	654	86.9	1.1	0.2	11.9	0.0	29.7	19.4	34.0	43.9	6.1	324	85.5
Hill Lake township (Aitkin)	436	434	-0.5	456	91.9	0.0	0.0	4.8	3.3	24.6	27.2	44.3	32.9	19.2	199	89.9
Hillman township (Kanabec)	438	434	-0.9	408	95.3	1.2	0.0	2.9	0.5	18.9	22.5	47.6	53.2	8.9	174	79.3
Hillman city & MCD (Morrison)	38	37	-2.6	35	91.4	0.0	0.0	8.6	0.0	37.1	2.9	37.9	45.5	18.2	12	83.3
Hillman township (Morrison)	197	202	2.5	163	99.4	0.0	0.6	0.0	0.0	19.6	18.4	50.4	55.9	8.5	75	82.7
Hill River township (Polk)	157	159	1.3	103	93.2	0.0	0.0	0.0	6.8	22.3	18.4	40.8	46.2	21.8	50	94.0
Hills city & MCD (Rock)	684	651	-4.8	719	95.7	1.1	0.0	2.6	0.6	20.2	25.9	46.7	46.0	14.8	303	86.5
Hillsdale township (Winona)	921	931	1.1	847	87.8	0.0	4.6	2.7	4.8	11.7	13.9	42.4	49.2	17.3	295	88.5
Hilltop city & MCD (Anoka)	744	757	1.7	1,049	23.5	11.4	2.6	11.0	51.5	27.6	7.7	32.9	66.7	11.8	438	88.8
Hinckley city & MCD (Pine)	1,803	1,928	6.9	1,606	73.3	1.0	0.4	21.9	3.4	25.9	17.5	36.8	55.9	10.8	693	79.5
Hinckley township (Pine)	806	816	1.2	821	91.0	0.0	0.0	6.0	3.0	16.3	17.8	47.3	60.0	9.6	317	83.6
Hines township (Beltrami)	689	683	-0.9	474	94.5	0.0	0.0	1.3	4.2	17.5	26.2	53.8	43.6	16.3	205	89.3
Hiram township (Cass)	316	330	4.4	308	98.1	0.3	0.6	0.3	0.6	6.8	52.3	65.9	41.8	37.5	160	91.9
Hitterdal city & MCD (Clay)	201	211	5.0	206	88.8	0.0	0.0	0.0	11.2	16.5	35.4	52.6	68.9	10.4	101	83.2
Hobart township (Otter Tail)	778	777	-0.1	825	96.8	0.5	0.1	2.3	0.2	20.2	26.8	52.1	25.6	41.3	355	93.0
Hodges township (Stevens)	277	306	10.5	299	84.9	0.0	0.0	0.0	15.1	23.4	13.0	41.3	33.5	30.1	93	98.9
Hoff township (Pope)	152	161	5.9	161	98.1	1.9	0.0	0.0	0.0	29.2	18.6	37.5	27.4	23.9	63	95.2
Hoffman city & MCD (Grant)	681	682	0.1	608	98.4	0.0	0.0	1.3	0.3	27.3	20.7	36.3	48.4	13.6	289	83.7
Hokah city & MCD (Houston)	580	547	-5.7	649	87.8	8.5	0.0	2.0	1.7	25.3	11.6	35.7	51.9	13.1	275	87.6
Hokah township (Houston)	497	493	-0.8	462	99.1	0.0	0.0	0.0	0.9	21.4	20.3	47.9	24.7	30.7	194	92.8
Holden township (Goodhue)	454	452	-0.4	375	98.9	0.0	0.5	0.0	0.0	20.0	22.4	50.4	34.1	36.3	149	91.3
Holding township (Stearns)	1,143	1,236	8.1	1,358	99.8	0.0	0.0	0.0	0.2	26.7	12.5	38.6	50.8	11.7	477	86.0
Holdingford city & MCD (Stearns)	704	721	2.4	660	99.2	0.0	0.5	0.0	0.3	25.6	14.4	38.9	46.5	16.6	318	83.3
Holland township (Kandiyohi)	338	347	2.7	350	96.6	0.0	0.0	2.0	1.4	30.3	12.6	39.5	34.3	29.6	123	94.3
Holland city & MCD (Pipestone)	186	173	-7.0	151	80.8	0.0	3.3	7.3	8.6	7.9	16.6	50.4	54.5	7.4	89	84.3

1 May be of any race.

Table A. All Places — **Population and Housing**

STATE City, town, township, borough, or CDP (county if applicable)	Population				Race and Hispanic or Latino origin (percent)					Age (percent)			Educational attainment of persons age 25 and older		Occupied housing units	
	2010 census total population	2019 estimated population	Percent change 2010–2019	ACS total population estimate 2015–2019	White alone, not Hispanic or Latino	Black alone, not Hispanic or Latino	Asian alone, not Hispanic or Latino	All other races or 2 or more races, not Hispanic or Latino	Hispanic or Latino[1]	Under 18 years old	Age 65 years and older	Median age	Percent High school diploma or less	Percent Bachelor's degree or more	Total	Percent with a computer
	1	2	3	4	5	6	7	8	9	10	11	12	13	14	15	16
MINNESOTA—Con.																
Hollandale city & MCD (Freeborn)	308	299	-2.9	410	91.2	0.0	0.0	5.6	3.2	28.0	18.0	41.6	47.0	17.9	160	88.8
Holloway city & MCD (Swift)	92	85	-7.6	97	100.0	0.0	0.0	0.0	0.0	15.5	29.9	60.8	32.9	30.5	59	64.4
Holly township (Murray)	127	122	-3.9	92	100.0	0.0	0.0	0.0	0.0	14.1	16.3	46.5	40.3	22.6	43	86.0
Hollywood township (Carver)	1,044	1,067	2.2	963	94.3	0.0	0.7	2.0	3.0	22.8	15.0	44.8	46.9	18.3	363	89.8
Holmes City township (Douglas)	804	835	3.9	927	99.6	0.0	0.0	0.4	0.0	21.8	25.4	49.5	27.9	26.0	364	89.3
Holmesville township (Becker)	505	538	6.5	658	76.0	1.2	1.1	15.3	6.4	31.8	18.4	37.4	27.3	24.7	217	90.8
Holst township (Clearwater)	364	365	0.3	343	95.6	0.0	0.9	3.5	0.0	21.3	16.9	43.1	52.1	18.2	123	84.6
Holt township (Fillmore)	271	283	4.4	240	99.2	0.0	0.0	0.0	0.8	15.8	30.4	55.0	24.0	28.1	106	83.0
Holt city & MCD (Marshall)	88	87	-1.1	92	90.2	0.0	1.1	6.5	2.2	21.7	12.0	35.0	62.1	5.2	29	86.2
Holt township (Marshall)	132	130	-1.5	172	90.1	0.0	0.0	9.9	0.0	29.1	22.1	45.3	44.3	17.2	77	74.0
Holy Cross township (Clay)	129	136	5.4	132	100.0	0.0	0.0	0.0	0.0	13.6	18.9	53.0	37.9	26.2	55	96.4
Holyoke township (Carlton)	182	189	3.8	221	92.8	0.0	0.0	5.9	1.4	15.8	19.0	50.3	32.0	20.9	94	93.6
Home township (Brown)	542	530	-2.2	478	100.0	0.0	0.0	0.0	0.0	20.9	24.9	52.9	40.2	19.1	207	89.9
Home Brook township (Cass)	257	271	5.4	216	98.6	0.0	1.4	0.0	0.0	20.8	31.0	50.5	40.0	15.0	84	89.3
Home Lake township (Norman)	148	141	-4.7	121	100.0	0.0	0.0	0.0	0.0	24.8	13.2	28.8	29.6	29.6	41	75.6
Homer CDP	181	-	-	193	97.9	0.0	0.0	2.1	0.0	13.0	40.9	59.1	18.1	41.9	88	92.0
Homer township (Winona)	1,347	1,347	0.0	1,457	99.4	0.0	0.0	0.3	0.3	17.2	23.9	50.3	25.7	39.2	595	90.8
Homestead township (Otter Tail)	362	361	-0.3	387	97.4	0.0	0.0	2.3	0.3	32.6	13.7	41.8	47.5	16.3	139	88.5
Honner township (Redwood)	69	67	-2.9	95	96.8	0.0	0.0	0.0	3.2	28.4	18.9	41.3	47.5	29.5	34	100.0
Hope township (Lincoln)	272	265	-2.6	286	98.3	0.0	0.3	1.4	0.0	33.6	18.5	34.8	33.2	35.3	108	87.0
Hopkins city	17,584	18,468	5.0	18,382	58.9	19.1	8.0	3.3	10.7	19.8	13.5	34.2	25.8	46.2	8,886	90.4
Hornet township (Beltrami)	229	231	0.9	196	94.4	0.0	0.0	5.6	0.0	15.3	21.4	52.0	50.6	12.5	78	76.9
Horton township (Stevens)	174	178	2.3	144	96.5	3.5	0.0	0.0	0.0	43.8	2.1	23.7	25.7	30.0	40	97.5
Houston city & MCD (Houston)	987	965	-2.2	1,033	97.5	0.1	0.0	2.4	0.0	23.9	21.4	41.6	44.2	15.6	479	87.3
Houston township (Houston)	388	383	-1.3	354	97.7	0.0	0.0	2.3	0.0	27.4	13.8	43.0	29.5	29.5	131	88.5
Howard Lake city & MCD (Wright)	1,969	2,136	8.5	1,881	92.2	2.6	0.4	1.6	3.3	24.5	17.5	40.1	47.7	14.1	827	85.7
Hoyt Lakes city & MCD (St. Louis)	2,019	1,946	-3.6	2,074	97.3	0.0	0.0	1.4	1.3	16.8	27.3	51.8	40.4	13.5	961	88.6
Hubbard township (Hubbard)	784	803	2.4	765	97.8	1.2	0.0	0.3	0.8	19.5	30.8	58.0	34.4	28.2	329	92.1
Hubbard township (Polk)	78	80	2.6	85	94.1	0.0	0.0	5.9	0.0	12.9	55.3	67.8	58.8	5.9	38	94.7
Hudson township (Douglas)	876	913	4.2	984	98.1	0.1	0.0	0.7	1.1	20.9	24.1	46.7	33.8	27.3	403	92.3
Hugo city & MCD (Washington)	13,332	15,267	14.5	14,767	92.3	1.0	2.4	1.3	2.9	25.9	11.6	35.7	26.8	37.5	5,512	96.0
Humboldt township (Clay)	268	284	6.0	258	95.3	0.0	0.8	3.9	0.0	25.6	22.9	43.3	28.7	35.4	97	82.5
Humboldt city & MCD (Kittson)	45	42	-6.7	41	80.5	0.0	0.0	19.5	0.0	24.4	4.9	54.6	48.4	3.2	19	57.9
Hunter township (Jackson)	224	217	-3.1	192	94.3	0.0	0.0	5.7	0.0	19.8	13.5	38.2	35.0	37.1	90	95.6
Huntersville township (Wadena)	119	118	-0.8	103	91.3	1.0	0.0	3.9	3.9	20.4	19.4	48.8	42.1	14.5	45	100.0
Huntly township (Marshall)	77	75	-2.6	54	100.0	0.0	0.0	0.0	0.0	7.4	35.2	53.6	60.5	16.3	23	100.0
Huntsville township (Polk)	464	470	1.3	525	88.6	0.4	0.6	0.0	10.5	19.4	14.1	40.7	23.9	24.7	203	89.7
Huss township (Roseau)	120	114	-5.0	73	100.0	0.0	0.0	0.0	0.0	30.1	20.5	35.7	56.8	9.1	23	69.6
Hutchinson city & MCD (McLeod)	14,173	13,983	-1.3	13,914	91.8	0.6	1.2	1.4	4.9	20.4	19.1	38.9	39.0	20.0	6,215	89.8
Hutchinson township (McLeod)	1,231	1,212	-1.5	1,177	97.4	0.0	0.8	0.8	0.9	21.7	22.2	48.4	31.5	26.5	460	93.7
Hyde Park township (Wabasha)	283	283	0.0	282	100.0	0.0	0.0	0.0	0.0	28.7	23.4	35.8	42.4	27.2	102	89.2
Ida township (Douglas)	1,229	1,283	4.4	1,376	98.7	0.0	0.0	0.0	1.3	19.0	30.8	54.0	31.6	30.6	612	91.2
Ideal township (Crow Wing)	1,084	1,139	5.1	1,210	98.3	0.2	0.0	0.9	0.7	12.1	33.1	57.2	25.1	42.6	571	92.6
Idun township (Aitkin)	256	255	-0.4	296	100.0	0.0	0.0	0.0	0.0	31.1	22.0	40.8	47.5	11.0	113	84.1
Ihlen city & MCD (Pipestone)	67	66	-1.5	38	86.8	0.0	7.9	0.0	5.3	7.9	26.3	56.7	82.9	11.4	20	80.0
Independence city	3,518	3,803	8.1	3,776	94.1	2.5	0.0	0.5	2.9	25.8	15.7	44.8	20.8	50.4	1,153	96.4
Indian Lake township (Nobles)	232	230	-0.9	205	99.0	0.0	0.0	1.0	0.0	17.1	22.9	50.1	36.2	30.3	86	89.5
Industrial township (St. Louis)	799	807	1.0	702	95.3	0.3	0.0	2.4	2.0	21.8	15.0	46.1	37.0	22.0	289	87.5
Inger CDP	212	-	-	193	0.0	0.0	0.0	100.0	0.0	31.1	6.2	30.0	55.4	0.0	63	79.4
Inguadona township (Cass)	190	199	4.7	170	89.4	1.8	1.2	5.9	1.8	8.8	38.8	63.0	53.6	17.6	90	84.4
Inman township (Otter Tail)	290	290	0.0	311	92.6	0.0	0.0	0.3	7.1	30.2	15.1	36.6	61.8	4.5	110	85.5
International Falls city	6,424	5,811	-9.5	5,981	93.1	1.2	0.4	4.8	0.5	19.9	23.2	46.5	44.6	15.7	2,658	84.0
Inver Grove Heights city & MCD (Dakota)	33,986	35,672	5.0	35,320	76.2	3.5	4.3	2.8	13.1	22.2	15.7	39.7	30.0	36.2	14,086	93.9
Iona city & MCD (Murray)	137	131	-4.4	129	97.7	0.0	0.0	0.0	2.3	23.3	17.1	44.9	39.8	9.7	60	93.3
Iona township (Murray)	163	156	-4.3	131	100.0	0.0	0.0	0.0	0.0	24.4	11.5	38.9	38.2	29.2	54	85.2
Iona township (Todd)	490	490	0.0	657	99.7	0.0	0.2	0.2	0.0	44.1	10.8	21.8	70.6	5.4	163	63.8
Iosco township (Waseca)	550	557	1.3	574	97.6	0.0	0.0	0.3	2.1	17.9	24.6	53.1	38.9	27.7	235	88.1
Irondale township (Crow Wing)	1,134	1,118	-1.4	1,402	92.7	0.9	0.0	6.0	0.5	25.2	19.6	44.4	33.5	24.7	524	94.8
Iron Junction city & MCD (St. Louis)	86	86	0.0	110	100.0	0.0	0.0	0.0	0.0	21.8	27.3	53.5	47.6	16.7	43	90.7

1 May be of any race.

Table A. All Places — **Population and Housing**

STATE City, town, township, borough, or CDP (county if applicable)	Population				Race and Hispanic or Latino origin (percent)					Age (percent)			Educational attainment of persons age 25 and older		Occupied housing units	
	2010 census total population	2019 estimated population	Percent change 2010–2019	ACS total population estimate 2015–2019	White alone, not Hispanic or Latino	Black alone, not Hispanic or Latino	Asian alone, not Hispanic or Latino	All other races or 2 or more races, not Hispanic or Latino	Hispanic or Latino[1]	Under 18 years old	Age 65 years and older	Median age	Percent High school diploma or less	Percent Bachelor's degree or more	Total	Percent with a computer
	1	2	3	4	5	6	7	8	9	10	11	12	13	14	15	16
MINNESOTA—Con.																
Ironton city & MCD (Crow Wing)	572	556	-2.8	552	97.8	0.0	1.1	0.0	1.1	20.3	25.0	40.2	60.7	13.2	266	78.6
Irving township (Kandiyohi)	906	935	3.2	1,008	97.7	0.0	0.0	0.1	2.2	20.6	25.7	50.5	29.2	38.0	413	93.2
Isanti city & MCD (Isanti)	5,294	6,120	15.6	5,749	93.2	0.0	0.0	2.5	4.3	30.4	7.2	30.1	40.4	14.0	2,081	94.6
Isanti township (Isanti)	2,290	2,387	4.2	2,522	98.2	0.0	0.6	1.2	0.0	22.6	14.3	45.0	37.8	23.9	942	95.1
Island Lake township (Lyon)	175	174	-0.6	176	98.9	0.0	0.0	1.1	0.0	28.4	21.6	41.0	27.4	23.4	68	88.2
Island Lake township (Mahnomen)	233	239	2.6	336	68.5	5.7	0.0	14.3	11.6	31.3	22.6	40.7	45.8	16.4	109	79.8
Isle city & MCD (Mille Lacs)	770	798	3.6	718	73.8	0.0	0.0	23.4	2.8	21.0	30.5	52.0	47.7	16.0	368	81.0
Isle Harbor township (Mille Lacs)	576	587	1.9	498	92.4	0.6	0.0	5.2	1.8	18.9	25.9	52.5	44.8	17.3	213	91.1
Itasca township (Clearwater)	132	132	0.0	130	80.0	0.0	0.0	20.0	0.0	20.0	18.5	49.8	26.9	21.5	49	89.8
Ivanhoe city & MCD (Lincoln)	570	531	-6.8	599	97.7	0.7	0.0	0.5	1.2	13.7	25.4	49.8	46.3	16.0	304	84.9
Jackson city & MCD (Jackson)	3,295	3,179	-3.5	3,219	88.9	0.2	5.4	1.7	3.8	17.1	23.6	48.8	38.7	23.7	1,523	86.1
Jackson township (Scott)	1,473	1,632	10.8	1,557	63.5	0.0	2.6	3.5	30.3	27.7	8.9	35.5	52.4	21.3	499	92.2
Jadis township (Roseau)	578	563	-2.6	698	96.3	1.1	0.9	1.1	0.6	24.6	19.8	42.6	34.8	20.8	238	94.5
Jamestown township (Blue Earth)	695	696	0.1	753	99.7	0.0	0.0	0.3	0.0	17.0	16.1	44.4	30.1	42.8	305	97.4
Janesville city & MCD (Waseca)	2,256	2,252	-0.2	2,507	91.3	3.5	0.5	1.3	3.5	28.4	14.8	32.9	39.6	26.8	908	91.1
Janesville township (Waseca)	513	520	1.4	566	99.1	0.4	0.0	0.0	0.5	27.4	15.2	40.1	37.1	23.9	194	89.2
Janette Lake UT (St. Louis)	295	297	0.7	273	100.0	0.0	0.0	0.0	0.0	8.4	24.5	55.2	44.0	18.5	141	84.4
Jasper city	643	603	-6.2	672	85.6	0.4	0.4	5.8	7.7	25.0	23.8	43.8	58.0	11.9	308	71.4
Jasper city (Pipestone)	573	537	-6.3	622	84.4	0.5	0.5	6.3	8.4	26.4	24.1	42.2	56.7	12.1	281	72.6
Jasper city (Rock)	70	66	-5.7	50	100.0	0.0	0.0	0.0	0.0	8.0	20.0	55.5	69.6	10.9	27	59.3
Jay township (Martin)	237	226	-4.6	220	100.0	0.0	0.0	0.0	0.0	16.4	17.7	47.8	27.3	16.1	93	94.6
Jeffers city & MCD (Cottonwood)	369	346	-6.2	358	85.5	0.0	0.0	0.0	14.5	22.1	21.2	48.5	56.6	8.8	178	70.8
Jefferson township (Houston)	129	127	-1.6	90	100.0	0.0	0.0	0.0	0.0	7.8	35.6	59.0	60.3	12.8	47	91.5
Jenkins city & MCD (Crow Wing)	436	469	7.6	417	98.6	0.0	0.0	0.0	1.4	33.3	7.0	32.3	43.7	12.3	157	93.0
Jenkins township (Crow Wing)	352	370	5.1	372	97.6	0.0	0.0	2.4	0.0	12.1	41.9	61.0	38.4	26.7	175	92.0
Jessenland township (Sibley)	444	439	-1.1	435	98.9	0.2	0.0	0.9	0.0	17.7	15.9	49.9	41.1	17.7	177	89.3
Jevne township (Aitkin)	322	320	-0.6	361	91.7	0.0	4.7	3.0	0.6	18.3	21.6	53.6	40.1	9.7	160	85.6
Jewett UT (Aitkin)	47	47	0.0	67	100.0	0.0	0.0	0.0	0.0	19.4	0.0	48.1	0.0	0.0	21	100.0
Jo Daviess township (Faribault)	245	235	-4.1	217	98.6	0.0	0.0	0.9	0.5	19.8	12.4	47.8	45.3	17.6	94	90.4
Johnson city & MCD (Big Stone)	29	27	-6.9	12	100.0	0.0	0.0	0.0	0.0	33.3	16.7	34.5	25.0	0.0	4	100.0
Johnson township (Polk)	51	51	0.0	50	98.0	0.0	2.0	0.0	0.0	12.0	16.0	45.8	37.8	0.0	18	94.4
Johnsonville township (Redwood)	152	144	-5.3	98	100.0	0.0	0.0	0.0	0.0	10.2	19.4	50.5	39.2	18.9	39	94.9
Jones township (Beltrami)	277	275	-0.7	254	99.2	0.0	0.0	0.8	0.0	20.1	17.7	47.9	33.2	26.9	97	89.7
Jordan township (Fillmore)	352	368	4.5	328	100.0	0.0	0.0	0.0	0.0	29.0	6.7	40.1	27.2	22.6	117	95.7
Jordan city & MCD (Scott)	5,464	6,402	17.2	6,230	79.3	3.0	1.6	1.4	14.6	33.2	6.4	31.6	39.9	23.6	2,124	90.1
Judson township (Blue Earth)	566	564	-0.4	636	97.0	2.4	0.0	0.6	0.0	20.3	19.5	42.8	33.0	29.2	257	96.1
Jupiter township (Kittson)	111	106	-4.5	100	100.0	0.0	0.0	0.0	0.0	32.0	21.0	44.6	27.7	23.1	36	94.4
Kabetogama township (St. Louis)	135	135	0.0	104	100.0	0.0	0.0	0.0	0.0	6.7	64.4	68.1	43.3	23.7	65	76.9
Kalevala township (Carlton)	327	341	4.3	285	98.2	0.4	0.0	0.0	1.4	17.9	16.1	47.8	37.2	11.5	133	85.7
Kalmar township (Olmsted)	1,038	1,066	2.7	1,113	89.1	0.0	1.5	0.0	9.3	22.3	23.4	51.1	28.3	36.2	429	93.9
Kanabec township (Kanabec)	928	926	-0.2	873	95.3	0.0	1.3	2.2	1.3	20.4	15.7	45.2	55.6	8.6	333	80.5
Kanaranzi township (Rock)	247	242	-2.0	279	98.2	0.0	0.7	0.0	1.1	25.1	7.5	39.1	58.0	8.0	115	90.4
Kandiyohi city & MCD (Kandiyohi)	490	481	-1.8	554	94.9	2.3	0.0	0.0	2.7	32.7	12.6	29.9	34.1	19.9	202	93.6
Kandiyohi township (Kandiyohi)	637	658	3.3	581	99.0	0.0	0.0	0.0	1.0	19.4	22.7	45.3	34.9	26.0	239	84.5
Kandota township (Todd)	729	733	0.5	754	98.4	1.1	0.0	0.5	0.0	19.6	24.0	48.7	37.5	23.1	309	88.7
Karlstad city & MCD (Kittson)	759	719	-5.3	795	90.3	4.4	0.6	4.7	0.0	23.3	25.2	47.4	48.7	26.2	341	83.9
Kasota city & MCD (Le Sueur)	675	672	-0.4	803	86.7	9.7	0.0	2.7	0.9	28.8	14.4	36.0	54.6	15.1	323	89.2
Kasota township (Le Sueur)	1,585	1,670	5.4	1,501	98.9	0.0	0.0	0.2	0.9	17.5	19.0	51.4	33.2	32.6	597	93.6
Kasson city & MCD (Dodge)	5,983	6,493	8.5	6,350	94.7	0.0	2.0	2.0	1.3	28.6	12.2	34.6	35.4	27.4	2,360	96.7
Kathio township (Mille Lacs)	1,627	1,657	1.8	1,456	32.1	0.7	1.2	60.9	5.1	31.2	14.9	35.2	49.1	14.2	512	84.4
Keene township (Clay)	155	163	5.2	231	95.2	0.0	0.0	0.0	4.8	22.9	20.3	45.9	46.8	9.7	78	94.9
Keewatin city & MCD (Itasca)	1,056	1,013	-4.1	1,114	92.2	0.9	0.0	3.4	3.5	20.6	20.6	46.7	46.3	13.1	519	87.7
Kego township (Cass)	513	539	5.1	513	88.7	0.0	0.4	10.1	0.8	13.3	33.1	57.8	46.3	20.9	269	87.0
Kelliher city & MCD (Beltrami)	272	267	-1.8	291	87.6	1.7	0.0	9.6	1.0	25.4	12.0	40.3	62.0	17.1	111	87.4
Kelliher township (Beltrami)	130	129	-0.8	83	81.9	0.0	0.0	18.1	0.0	6.0	30.1	56.3	57.4	16.4	33	75.8

1 May be of any race.

Table A. All Places — Population and Housing

STATE City, town, township, borough, or CDP (county if applicable)	2010 census total population	2019 estimated population	Percent change 2010–2019	ACS total population estimate 2015–2019	White alone, not Hispanic or Latino	Black alone, not Hispanic or Latino	Asian alone, not Hispanic or Latino	All other races or 2 or more races, not Hispanic or Latino	Hispanic or Latino[1]	Under 18 years old	Age 65 years and older	Median age	Percent High school diploma or less	Percent Bachelor's degree or more	Occupied housing units Total	Percent with a computer
	1	2	3	4	5	6	7	8	9	10	11	12	13	14	15	16
MINNESOTA—Con.																
Kellogg city & MCD (Wabasha)	475	453	-4.6	464	90.7	0.0	1.1	4.3	3.9	21.3	20.9	40.7	44.6	11.9	194	87.1
Kelsey township (St. Louis)	140	141	0.7	136	98.5	0.0	0.0	1.5	0.0	21.3	19.1	57.5	55.9	14.7	58	82.8
Kelso township (Sibley)	292	287	-1.7	247	96.8	0.0	0.4	1.6	1.2	15.4	19.0	49.4	38.9	20.7	112	93.8
Kennedy city & MCD (Kittson)	193	180	-6.7	215	97.7	1.9	0.0	0.5	0.0	17.2	22.3	44.8	38.3	17.3	119	88.2
Kenneth city & MCD (Rock)	68	66	-2.9	62	100.0	0.0	0.0	0.0	0.0	4.8	35.5	53.6	54.2	3.4	32	100.0
Kensington city & MCD (Douglas)	292	303	3.8	246	99.2	0.0	0.8	0.0	0.0	20.7	14.2	43.3	54.2	9.6	115	80.9
Kent city & MCD (Wilkin)	81	74	-8.6	57	100.0	0.0	0.0	0.0	0.0	12.3	19.3	44.9	37.0	19.6	31	74.2
Kenyon city & MCD (Goodhue)	1,815	1,801	-0.8	1,960	90.3	1.9	1.0	1.5	5.3	23.7	17.9	37.8	46.1	19.6	796	87.1
Kenyon township (Goodhue)	393	391	-0.5	413	99.8	0.2	0.0	0.0	0.0	17.2	15.5	44.2	41.6	19.9	158	89.9
Kerkhoven city & MCD (Swift)	758	706	-6.9	691	77.7	0.0	0.0	0.6	21.7	32.7	16.5	33.3	38.2	18.8	296	80.1
Kerkhoven township (Swift)	236	227	-3.8	241	98.8	0.0	0.0	1.2	0.0	16.2	29.9	52.1	58.7	20.1	103	73.8
Kerrick city & MCD (Pine)	65	63	-3.1	74	100.0	0.0	0.0	0.0	0.0	23.0	5.4	26.1	41.5	34.0	28	96.4
Kerrick township (Pine)	325	332	2.2	298	95.3	0.0	1.3	2.7	0.7	25.8	26.2	49.0	43.3	20.9	107	83.2
Kertsonville township (Polk)	94	95	1.1	68	97.1	0.0	0.0	2.9	0.0	19.1	38.2	56.6	34.0	47.2	27	92.6
Kettle River city & MCD (Carlton)	178	172	-3.4	182	87.4	0.0	0.0	12.6	0.0	23.1	11.0	40.0	38.8	14.9	81	88.9
Kettle River township (Pine)	504	518	2.8	610	95.2	0.0	0.0	3.4	1.3	23.8	12.6	39.2	46.2	12.7	204	85.3
Keystone township (Polk)	91	93	2.2	77	100.0	0.0	0.0	0.0	0.0	26.0	18.2	50.6	37.7	26.4	29	93.1
Kiester city & MCD (Faribault)	501	462	-7.8	549	85.2	0.0	0.0	4.4	10.4	28.4	18.6	41.6	42.0	21.5	234	83.3
Kiester township (Faribault)	260	247	-5.0	194	100.0	0.0	0.0	0.0	0.0	15.5	20.6	53.6	45.3	22.0	87	85.1
Kildare township (Swift)	151	145	-4.0	136	100.0	0.0	0.0	0.0	0.0	19.9	22.8	54.5	49.5	17.1	57	91.2
Kilkenny city & MCD (Le Sueur)	143	144	0.7	168	98.2	0.0	0.0	0.0	1.8	26.2	9.5	27.0	48.5	13.9	67	85.1
Kilkenny township (Le Sueur)	395	416	5.3	425	97.2	0.0	0.0	1.6	1.2	14.6	23.3	52.6	49.4	22.5	178	89.9
Kimball township (Jackson)	129	126	-2.3	92	100.0	0.0	0.0	0.0	0.0	29.3	20.7	46.0	37.5	25.0	36	91.7
Kimball city & MCD (Stearns)	760	798	5.0	925	90.7	0.1	0.5	7.9	0.8	32.9	10.9	31.3	37.2	14.2	341	92.1
Kimberly township (Aitkin)	199	197	-1.0	191	82.7	0.0	0.0	0.0	17.3	6.8	31.9	59.6	32.3	21.5	85	89.4
Kinbrae city & MCD (Nobles)	12	12	0.0	8	100.0	0.0	0.0	0.0	0.0	25.0	25.0	44.5	66.7	0.0	3	100.0
King township (Polk)	219	220	0.5	199	98.0	0.0	0.0	0.0	2.0	28.1	12.1	37.3	56.4	15.7	80	85.0
Kinghurst township (Itasca)	106	106	0.0	88	100.0	0.0	0.0	0.0	0.0	1.1	33.0	60.8	45.8	20.5	47	80.9
Kingman township (Renville)	201	188	-6.5	223	93.7	0.0	0.0	0.0	6.3	15.7	17.0	50.4	47.7	12.1	94	87.2
Kingston city & MCD (Meeker)	161	162	0.6	209	91.9	0.0	0.0	1.4	6.7	32.1	11.5	29.1	31.4	14.9	76	84.2
Kingston township (Meeker)	1,256	1,262	0.5	1,337	99.6	0.0	0.4	0.0	0.0	25.3	12.7	37.6	39.8	17.8	460	92.2
Kinney city & MCD (St. Louis)	141	143	1.4	192	64.1	17.7	0.0	13.0	5.2	38.0	13.0	32.0	48.3	7.8	72	86.1
Kintire township (Redwood)	182	174	-4.4	212	85.4	0.0	0.0	0.0	14.6	37.3	9.4	32.4	32.5	30.1	76	85.5
Klondike UT (Kittson)	-	-	-	-	-	-	-	-	-	-	-	-	-	-	-	-
Knife Lake township (Kanabec)	1,156	1,164	0.7	1,127	96.1	0.0	2.4	0.9	0.6	26.8	17.7	46.3	38.4	22.7	448	86.2
Knute township (Polk)	522	530	1.5	550	98.9	0.0	0.0	1.1	0.0	22.7	35.8	54.4	40.7	23.5	185	89.7
Kragero township (Chippewa)	125	120	-4.0	83	100.0	0.0	0.0	0.0	0.0	20.5	28.9	56.3	20.6	38.1	37	89.2
Kragnes township (Clay)	293	306	4.4	212	100.0	0.0	0.0	0.0	0.0	16.5	19.3	49.7	32.8	31.6	99	84.8
Krain township (Stearns)	982	1,061	8.0	1,101	98.5	0.0	0.0	0.2	1.4	29.1	16.0	35.6	60.7	13.4	365	84.9
Kratka township (Pennington)	131	126	-3.8	130	96.2	0.0	1.5	0.0	2.3	36.9	15.4	38.5	30.6	25.0	41	80.5
Kroschel township (Kanabec)	216	224	3.7	208	98.1	0.0	0.0	1.4	0.5	15.4	36.1	57.5	54.4	13.6	89	78.7
Kugler township (St. Louis)	175	177	1.1	116	99.1	0.0	0.0	0.0	0.9	6.9	25.0	59.0	42.9	9.5	66	93.9
Kurtz township (Clay)	293	309	5.5	225	88.0	0.0	0.0	11.6	0.4	25.8	15.6	43.1	21.8	50.3	75	96.0
Lac qui Parle township (Lac qui Parle)	178	163	-8.4	196	100.0	0.0	0.0	0.0	0.0	38.3	16.8	31.5	37.5	30.4	63	93.7
La Crescent city	5,147	5,029	-2.3	5,138	92.7	1.2	0.8	2.6	2.7	21.2	19.5	42.2	30.9	35.3	2,352	92.5
La Crescent city (Houston)	5,147	5,029	-2.3	5,058	93.9	0.7	0.8	1.8	2.8	20.7	19.8	42.9	31.2	34.6	2,339	92.5
La Crescent city (Winona)	-	-	-	80	16.3	31.3	0.0	52.5	0.0	52.5	0.0	7.9	0.0	100.0	13	100.0
La Crescent township (Houston)	1,129	1,097	-2.8	1,302	97.7	0.8	0.0	0.3	1.2	18.0	18.0	48.8	26.9	30.3	519	95.2
La Crosse township (Jackson)	156	151	-3.2	128	100.0	0.0	0.0	0.0	0.0	25.0	41.4	57.5	40.0	20.0	57	93.0
Lafayette city & MCD (Nicollet)	504	493	-2.2	565	95.9	0.0	0.0	4.1	0.0	26.0	11.3	34.2	44.3	19.1	212	90.1
Lafayette township (Nicollet)	694	702	1.2	675	99.1	0.0	0.0	0.9	0.0	22.8	21.5	47.1	27.1	25.5	247	97.6
La Garde township (Mahnomen)	157	158	0.6	139	44.6	0.0	1.4	50.4	3.6	33.8	7.9	35.1	56.5	13.0	36	86.1
La Grand township (Douglas)	4,179	4,347	4.0	4,272	97.6	0.3	0.0	0.9	1.2	23.0	19.6	47.9	23.3	35.3	1,736	94.4
Lake township (Roseau)	2,066	2,017	-2.4	1,784	82.7	0.0	11.7	3.6	2.0	23.7	13.7	44.1	39.7	19.1	707	93.9
Lake township (Wabasha)	446	450	0.9	528	93.8	1.1	0.0	5.1	0.0	21.0	23.5	50.2	32.3	31.5	211	82.9

1 May be of any race.

204 MN(Kellogg city & MCD (Wabasha))—MN(Lake township (Wabasha))   Items 1–16

Table A. All Places — Population and Housing

STATE City, town, township, borough, or CDP (county if applicable)	2010 census total population	2019 estimated population	Percent change 2010–2019	ACS total population estimate 2015–2019	White alone, not Hispanic or Latino	Black alone, not Hispanic or Latino	Asian alone, not Hispanic or Latino	All other races or 2 or more races, not Hispanic or Latino	Hispanic or Latino[1]	Under 18 years old	Age 65 years and older	Median age	Percent High school diploma or less	Percent Bachelor's degree or more	Total	Percent with a computer
	1	2	3	4	5	6	7	8	9	10	11	12	13	14	15	16
MINNESOTA—Con.																
Lake Alice township (Hubbard)	93	95	2.2	66	100.0	0.0	0.0	0.0	0.0	22.7	13.6	53.0	43.1	11.8	27	100.0
Lake Andrew township (Kandiyohi)	984	1,016	3.3	1,031	95.6	1.2	0.0	0.3	2.9	16.4	30.1	55.8	30.2	31.7	454	97.4
Lake Belt township (Martin)	192	183	-4.7	141	96.5	0.0	0.0	3.5	0.0	12.8	22.0	56.8	38.3	14.8	75	89.3
Lake Benton city & MCD (Lincoln)	684	635	-7.2	668	96.3	0.0	0.0	1.3	2.4	21.6	25.1	45.9	50.0	14.0	330	79.7
Lake Benton township (Lincoln)	240	237	-1.3	172	99.4	0.0	0.0	0.6	0.0	18.6	22.7	53.8	37.0	21.0	92	80.4
Lake Bronson city & MCD (Kittson)	221	205	-7.2	167	98.8	0.6	0.0	0.6	0.0	10.2	25.1	57.8	62.6	6.5	101	63.4
Lake City city (Goodhue)	5,063	5,122	1.2	5,261	91.8	1.7	1.6	0.6	4.3	17.4	28.2	50.4	36.9	27.9	2,406	86.7
Lake City city (Goodhue)	746	765	2.5	927	95.7	0.2	3.6	0.0	0.5	12.2	46.0	61.4	37.4	29.8	432	84.0
Lake City city (Wabasha)	4,317	4,357	0.9	4,334	90.9	2.1	1.2	0.8	5.1	18.6	24.4	48.4	36.8	27.5	1,974	87.3
Lake Crystal city & MCD (Blue Earth)	2,536	2,487	-1.9	2,625	98.1	0.0	0.3	0.2	1.4	25.2	16.5	37.8	43.6	22.7	1,120	83.7
Lake Edward township (Crow Wing)	2,108	2,215	5.1	2,020	97.5	0.0	0.0	1.6	0.9	14.0	31.8	56.5	35.5	25.3	871	91.5
Lake Elizabeth township (Kandiyohi)	233	241	3.4	151	95.4	0.0	0.0	3.3	1.3	11.9	22.5	55.3	41.3	9.9	72	81.9
Lake Elmo city & MCD (Washington)	8,051	9,210	14.4	8,969	87.4	2.0	1.5	2.0	7.2	26.4	13.3	40.6	23.3	50.1	3,158	95.9
Lake Emma township (Hubbard)	985	1,008	2.3	1,094	97.0	0.5	0.2	1.8	0.5	15.6	37.2	60.0	26.1	38.3	501	92.0
Lake Eunice township (Becker)	1,545	1,643	6.3	1,521	92.4	0.9	0.2	5.1	1.4	18.5	26.8	52.6	31.6	29.2	665	90.8
Lakefield city & MCD (Jackson)	1,714	1,615	-5.8	1,763	92.2	1.9	0.9	2.2	2.9	25.7	19.9	36.4	44.6	13.9	778	92.0
Lake Fremont township (Martin)	171	162	-5.3	196	77.6	13.8	0.0	7.1	1.5	40.3	21.4	31.5	28.4	24.5	64	93.8
Lake George CDP	230	-	-	277	93.5	0.0	0.0	5.4	1.1	9.7	33.2	53.3	43.6	28.4	110	98.2
Lake George township (Hubbard)	378	387	2.4	462	92.6	0.0	0.0	4.1	3.2	11.9	26.2	52.6	45.6	21.9	184	96.2
Lake George township (Stearns)	335	362	8.1	257	100.0	0.0	0.0	0.0	0.0	19.1	14.4	49.3	43.9	11.2	94	91.5
Lake Grove township (Mahnomen)	189	193	2.1	196	66.3	0.0	0.0	27.0	6.6	32.1	19.9	38.2	37.8	10.9	67	80.6
Lake Hanska township (Brown)	339	332	-2.1	304	95.7	0.0	0.3	3.6	0.3	22.4	19.4	47.7	38.2	27.3	122	93.4
Lake Hattie township (Hubbard)	202	207	2.5	143	90.9	1.4	0.0	7.7	0.0	21.7	18.9	42.1	39.8	13.6	59	88.1
Lake Henry city & MCD (Stearns)	103	111	7.8	52	100.0	0.0	0.0	0.0	0.0	11.5	17.3	54.0	47.7	11.4	26	92.3
Lake Henry township (Stearns)	278	299	7.6	228	96.1	0.0	1.8	0.0	2.2	24.1	21.1	47.7	68.6	5.0	90	66.7
Lake Ida township (Norman)	160	152	-5.0	112	94.6	0.0	0.0	5.4	0.0	19.6	33.9	57.3	45.2	17.9	48	81.3
Lake Jessie township (Itasca)	303	300		214	99.5	0.0	0.0	0.5	0.0	7.5	30.4	55.0	39.9	9.8	113	85.0
Lake Johanna township (Pope)	139	146	5.0	86	89.5	0.0	10.5	0.0	0.0	11.6	26.7	55.0	48.6	26.4	35	74.3
Lakeland city & MCD (Washington)	1,796	1,819	1.3	1,799	96.6	0.0	2.0	0.7	0.7	20.0	18.5	47.6	29.8	38.4	731	95.6
Lakeland Shores city & MCD (Washington)	309	312	1.0	347	99.1	0.0	0.0	0.3	0.6	25.4	17.0	41.3	18.2	41.9	120	98.3
Lake Lillian city & MCD (Kandiyohi)	238	235	-1.3	304	96.7	0.0	1.0	0.3	2.0	18.4	28.0	35.0	44.8	7.5	132	84.1
Lake Lillian township (Kandiyohi)	190	195	2.6	173	96.5	0.0	1.2	0.0	2.3	10.4	23.7	53.5	25.6	17.6	71	94.4
Lake Marshall township (Lyon)	559	557	-0.4	552	92.8	2.0	0.2	1.1	4.0	27.4	16.3	45.3	24.2	39.1	201	97.5
Lake Mary township (Douglas)	1,100	1,148	4.4	1,256	99.6	0.0	0.0	0.0	0.4	21.3	22.1	45.9	35.8	22.9	501	92.0
Lake No. 1 UT (Lake)	154	157	1.9	109	100.0	0.0	0.0	0.0	0.0	0.0	11.9	60.2	56.0	44.0	65	67.7
Lake No. 2 UT (Lake)	2,094	2,141	2.2	1,973	95.6	0.0	0.0	2.7	1.6	19.6	20.3	48.8	27.1	31.1	931	91.9
Lake Park city & MCD (Becker)	781	793	1.5	732	88.8	0.0	0.8	4.5	5.9	30.6	13.1	33.2	52.1	9.0	297	87.5
Lake Park township (Becker)	483	509	5.4	467	95.5	0.0	0.0	2.8	1.3	23.1	25.5	48.9	38.9	26.0	153	91.5
Lake Pleasant township (Red Lake)	103	102		85	100.0	0.0	0.0	0.0	0.0	34.1	15.3	39.8	27.8	24.1	29	89.7
Lakeport township (Hubbard)	844	865	2.5	866	93.3	0.0	0.1	6.2	0.3	19.7	26.1	53.3	37.6	31.4	370	91.4
Lake Prairie township (Nicollet)	682	692	1.5	704	88.1	0.0	0.0	2.3	9.7	26.8	15.2	38.9	24.4	38.1	226	96.0
Lake St. Croix Beach city & MCD (Washington)	1,060	1,076	1.5	1,058	95.7	0.8	0.0	3.6	0.0	16.6	14.7	43.9	33.1	30.5	458	91.5
Lake Sarah township (Murray)	393	380	-3.3	355	98.3	0.8	0.0	0.0	0.8	16.9	34.9	57.9	35.6	32.7	155	89.0
Lake Shore city & MCD (Cass)	1,002	1,058	5.6	1,019	93.1	0.0	0.0	1.7	5.2	16.8	24.8	51.5	20.6	43.4	470	94.9
Lake Shore township (Lac qui Parle)	191	175	-8.4	162	87.7	0.0	0.0	12.3	0.0	9.9	21.6	55.0	33.6	16.1	79	96.2
Lakeside township (Aitkin)	463	460	-0.6	448	97.3	0.0	0.0	1.1	1.6	18.1	39.3	58.7	45.6	14.4	233	79.0
Lakeside township (Cottonwood)	237	230	-3.0	248	94.8	0.0	1.6	0.0	3.6	16.9	16.5	53.1	28.6	22.0	96	97.9
Lake Stay township (Lincoln)	156	154	-1.3	88	100.0	0.0	0.0	0.0	0.0	25.0	26.1	46.5	46.0	22.2	31	90.3
Laketown township (Carver)	2,126	2,220	4.4	2,042	91.2	1.9	3.0	1.9	2.1	13.5	13.5	31.7	28.2	45.5	592	92.6

1 May be of any race.

Table A. All Places — **Population and Housing**

STATE City, town, township, borough, or CDP (county if applicable)	Population 2010 census total population	Population 2019 estimated population	Population Percent change 2010–2019	Population ACS total population estimate 2015–2019	Race White alone, not Hispanic or Latino	Race Black alone, not Hispanic or Latino	Race Asian alone, not Hispanic or Latino	Race All other races or 2 or more races, not Hispanic or Latino	Race Hispanic or Latino[1]	Age Under 18 years old	Age 65 years and older	Age Median age	Educational Percent High school diploma or less	Educational Percent Bachelor's degree or more	Occupied housing units Total	Occupied housing units Percent with a computer
	1	2	3	4	5	6	7	8	9	10	11	12	13	14	15	16
MINNESOTA—Con.																
Lake Valley township (Traverse)	237	223	-5.9	178	98.3	1.1	0.0	0.6	0.0	15.2	16.9	55.2	43.0	9.4	87	92.0
Lake View township (Becker)	1,662	1,760	5.9	1,853	91.4	0.4	0.1	5.1	2.9	21.2	22.9	49.8	25.5	37.3	774	93.0
Lakeview township (Carlton)	184	192	4.3	206	98.5	0.0	0.0	0.5	1.0	32.5	20.4	37.4	32.1	19.0	78	88.5
Lakeville city & MCD (Dakota)	56,001	67,317	20.2	63,915	83.4	2.4	5.7	3.5	5.0	28.7	9.5	36.6	18.7	50.6	22,246	96.7
Lake Wilson city & MCD (Murray)	249	227	-8.8	222	98.2	0.0	0.0	0.0	1.8	9.9	34.2	58.3	46.6	5.7	130	80.0
Lakewood township (St. Louis)	2,184	2,257	3.3	2,275	93.4	0.0	0.4	2.4	3.8	26.2	13.9	41.5	26.3	42.9	803	94.8
Lakin township (Morrison)	450	460	2.2	395	95.9	0.8	0.3	1.8	1.3	27.6	13.7	37.6	54.8	5.6	137	86.9
Lambert township (Red Lake)	129	128	-0.8	155	89.0	0.0	0.0	0.0	11.0	24.5	16.8	41.6	65.5	5.5	56	92.9
Lamberton city & MCD (Redwood)	824	768	-6.8	766	94.1	0.0	1.3	2.3	2.2	19.8	30.3	48.2	56.5	14.5	346	81.5
Lamberton township (Redwood)	193	184	-4.7	205	95.6	0.0	0.0	0.0	4.4	19.5	22.0	52.6	41.9	20.3	87	86.2
Lammers township (Beltrami)	592	587	-0.8	581	91.9	0.0	0.3	6.2	1.5	24.1	13.3	38.5	48.4	15.1	231	88.7
Lancaster city & MCD (Kittson)	351	334	-4.8	385	94.8	0.0	0.0	0.8	4.4	22.3	21.6	39.6	47.1	19.6	170	87.6
Land township (Grant)	261	261	0.0	297	99.3	0.0	0.0	0.0	0.7	26.3	10.8	34.9	25.7	40.2	110	93.6
Landfall city & MCD (Washington)	707	728	3.0	854	41.9	4.4	1.4	1.6	50.6	29.2	10.5	30.0	74.2	6.7	318	89.0
Lanesboro city & MCD (Fillmore)	754	725	-3.8	673	96.6	0.0	0.0	0.4	3.0	18.3	30.5	54.2	27.8	35.6	318	89.6
Lanesburgh township (Le Sueur)	2,041	2,152	5.4	2,115	97.1	0.0	0.9	1.7	0.4	24.3	11.8	43.6	41.6	21.6	721	94.3
Langhei township (Pope)	177	185	4.5	171	100.0	0.0	0.0	0.0	0.0	26.3	18.7	39.6	37.0	25.0	74	79.7
Langola township (Benton)	907	950	4.7	956	96.0	0.0	0.4	1.9	1.7	24.0	17.3	43.4	37.1	22.3	353	93.8
Langor township (Beltrami)	213	213	0.0	138	97.8	0.0	0.0	2.2	0.0	11.6	19.6	52.7	62.9	7.6	61	77.0
Lansing CDP	181	-	-	133	76.7	0.0	0.0	0.0	23.3	15.0	36.1	50.4	60.4	13.9	64	64.1
Lansing township (Mower)	935	976	4.4	1,088	83.8	0.0	10.6	0.6	5.0	26.6	16.9	40.4	39.2	23.9	403	84.6
Laona township (Roseau)	543	518	-4.6	390	92.6	0.0	1.0	2.1	4.4	22.3	14.9	46.5	54.7	17.4	158	88.0
Laporte city & MCD (Hubbard)	111	116	4.5	152	100.0	0.0	0.0	0.0	0.0	8.6	25.7	52.5	74.2	8.3	81	85.2
La Prairie township (Clearwater)	362	365	0.8	454	19.8	0.0	0.4	75.6	4.2	39.6	12.6	29.0	59.6	12.0	120	75.0
La Prairie city & MCD (Itasca)	665	660	-0.8	920	94.7	0.0	0.0	3.6	1.7	30.9	15.0	35.0	39.8	21.2	355	89.9
Larkin township (Nobles)	188	187	-0.5	162	92.0	2.5	0.0	1.9	3.7	21.6	17.9	50.0	42.2	14.7	64	82.8
La Salle city & MCD (Watonwan)	88	85	-3.4	87	100.0	0.0	0.0	0.0	0.0	21.8	10.3	35.3	46.8	14.5	40	97.5
Lastrup city & MCD (Morrison)	104	99	-4.8	182	97.3	0.0	0.0	2.7	0.0	27.5	19.8	38.4	61.8	13.0	65	78.5
Lauderdale city & MCD (Ramsey)	2,379	2,521	6.0	2,514	69.0	8.4	15.4	5.0	2.2	12.6	17.8	34.9	12.7	64.1	1,284	93.4
Lavell township (St. Louis)	301	303	0.7	274	95.6	0.0	0.0	4.4	0.0	18.6	26.6	54.1	32.4	12.6	121	81.8
Lawrence township (Grant)	84	82	-2.4	40	87.5	0.0	0.0	0.0	12.5	15.0	22.5	47.3	28.6	32.1	18	88.9
Lawrence township (Itasca)	435	433	-0.5	386	94.6	0.0	0.0	4.9	0.5	22.3	17.9	47.9	33.3	17.4	174	84.5
Leaf Lake township (Otter Tail)	560	559	-0.2	607	99.2	0.8	0.0	0.0	0.0	26.4	21.7	48.2	42.7	21.1	242	91.7
Leaf Mountain township (Otter Tail)	326	325	-0.3	281	100.0	0.0	0.0	0.0	0.0	17.1	27.0	54.1	46.8	15.1	130	76.9
Leaf River township (Wadena)	527	519	-1.5	531	85.5	7.0	0.0	5.1	2.4	13.7	22.6	53.4	57.7	9.7	190	79.5
Leaf Valley township (Douglas)	457	476	4.2	442	98.2	0.2	0.0	0.7	0.9	16.7	30.1	55.1	23.7	30.9	208	88.0
Leavenworth township (Brown)	287	280	-2.4	395	100.0	0.0	0.0	0.0	0.0	33.9	16.5	36.3	48.8	17.1	144	85.4
Le Center city & MCD (Le Sueur)	2,501	2,516	0.6	2,475	76.6	0.0	0.2	0.5	22.7	28.0	14.3	34.0	48.4	19.3	923	84.9
Lee township (Aitkin)	50	50	0.0	39	92.3	0.0	0.0	0.0	7.7	10.3	38.5	60.3	41.4	24.1	19	68.4
Lee township (Beltrami)	51	51	0.0	19	68.4	0.0	10.5	21.1	0.0	15.8	10.5	55.3	13.3	13.3	8	87.5
Lee township (Norman)	128	120	-6.3	99	96.0	0.0	0.0	2.0	2.0	5.1	26.3	57.5	41.2	34.1	55	85.5
Leech Lake township (Cass)	436	459	5.3	436	73.4	0.0	0.5	23.4	2.8	17.9	32.3	56.2	41.3	25.3	196	89.8
Leeds township (Murray)	210	202	-3.8	234	82.5	0.0	0.0	4.7	12.8	23.9	18.8	45.7	45.2	25.8	94	86.2
Leenthrop township (Chippewa)	243	233	-4.1	237	98.3	0.0	0.0	1.7	0.0	24.9	17.3	47.3	34.2	22.4	84	90.5
Leiding township (St. Louis)	402	404	0.5	410	70.7	0.5	0.0	28.8	0.0	19.8	29.8	53.2	43.6	15.3	173	87.3
Leigh township (Morrison)	212	220	3.8	216	89.8	0.0	0.0	10.2	0.0	15.7	14.8	45.3	66.9	6.6	94	70.2
Lemond township (Steele)	501	501	0.0	558	94.6	0.0	2.9	0.4	2.2	24.0	15.1	45.3	38.2	25.7	202	85.6
Lengby city & MCD (Polk)	86	87	1.2	47	93.6	0.0	0.0	6.4	0.0	6.4	44.7	53.8	54.8	21.4	26	80.8
Lent township (Chisago)	3,091	3,116	0.8	3,084	95.2	0.0	1.1	3.2	0.5	20.1	13.2	47.9	36.1	21.2	1,171	92.1
Leon township (Clearwater)	350	353	0.9	358	97.5	0.0	0.0	0.0	2.5	28.2	12.6	42.6	36.2	26.3	132	89.4
Leon township (Goodhue)	885	880	-0.6	906	97.8	0.0	0.6	1.7	0.0	19.3	19.3	51.2	37.4	25.0	370	94.6
Leonard city & MCD (Clearwater)	43	43	0.0	40	100.0	0.0	0.0	0.0	0.0	22.5	7.5	33.0	69.0	10.3	13	92.3
Leonardsville township (Traverse)	107	100	-6.5	110	100.0	0.0	0.0	0.0	0.0	30.9	21.8	37.5	18.1	19.4	39	94.9
Leonidas city & MCD (St. Louis)	52	53	1.9	51	100.0	0.0	0.0	0.0	0.0	7.8	33.3	58.9	63.8	6.4	31	67.7
Leota CDP	209	-	-	192	96.4	0.0	2.1	0.0	1.6	19.3	31.8	46.0	41.7	2.2	94	90.4

1 May be of any race.

Table A. All Places — Population and Housing

STATE City, town, township, borough, or CDP (county if applicable)	Population 2010 census total population	2019 estimated population	Percent change 2010–2019	ACS total population estimate 2015–2019	Race and Hispanic or Latino origin (percent) White alone, not Hispanic or Latino	Black alone, not Hispanic or Latino	Asian alone, not Hispanic or Latino	All other races or 2 or more races, not Hispanic or Latino	Hispanic or Latino[1]	Age (percent) Under 18 years old	Age 65 years and older	Median age	Educational attainment of persons age 25 and older Percent High school diploma or less	Percent Bachelor's degree or more	Occupied housing units Total	Percent with a computer
	1	2	3	4	5	6	7	8	9	10	11	12	13	14	15	16
MINNESOTA—Con.																
Leota township (Nobles)...	390	389	-0.3	361	97.8	0.0	1.1	0.0	1.1	19.1	25.5	45.9	43.4	9.7	169	92.3
Le Ray township (Blue Earth)...............	738	737	-0.1	753	94.3	0.3	1.6	3.3	0.5	21.4	19.5	50.3	34.6	29.4	306	88.6
Le Roy city & MCD (Mower).............	923	932	1.0	1,079	92.4	0.0	0.6	4.0	3.1	26.7	26.8	43.6	43.2	21.3	450	80.4
Le Roy township (Mower).	360	374	3.9	326	92.0	0.0	1.5	1.8	4.6	25.2	16.6	45.4	45.8	17.3	121	87.6
Le Sauk township (Stearns).............	1,552	1,671	7.7	1,704	92.3	3.5	3.3	1.0	0.0	17.8	19.3	46.4	27.0	36.2	715	95.4
Leslie township (Todd)......	642	647	0.8	641	96.6	0.8	0.0	0.5	2.2	17.6	28.2	54.0	49.2	15.2	275	80.7
Lessor township (Polk)	175	177	1.1	154	94.8	0.0	0.0	0.0	5.2	9.7	11.7	49.8	29.0	16.8	61	91.8
Lester Prairie city & MCD (McLeod).............	1,765	1,728	-2.1	1,981	85.1	0.3	0.0	1.5	13.2	32.7	13.7	34.7	40.9	16.9	745	87.7
Le Sueur city & MCD (Le Sueur).............	4,043	4,057	0.3	4,018	77.2	2.1	0.8	2.0	18.0	23.9	17.7	36.0	41.4	18.9	1,617	87.0
Le Sueur city (Sibley)........	-	-	-	-	-	-	-	-	-	-	-	-	-	-	-	-
Leven township (Pope)	499	495	-0.8	426	100.0	0.0	0.0	0.0	0.0	19.2	25.8	53.0	29.6	32.3	204	76.0
Lewis township (Mille Lacs)...............	52	52	0.0	43	95.3	0.0	0.0	4.7	0.0	16.3	18.6	44.5	43.8	25.0	18	94.4
Lewiston city & MCD (Winona)..............	1,619	1,547	-4.4	1,802	89.5	1.3	0.4	4.1	4.7	26.6	14.9	39.4	37.5	21.4	629	85.7
Lewisville city & MCD (Watonwan).............	250	247	-1.2	237	83.1	0.0	0.8	0.0	16.0	14.3	29.1	49.9	54.1	7.2	112	74.1
Lexington city & MCD (Anoka).............	2,057	2,652	28.9	2,144	80.2	3.7	8.9	2.9	4.3	20.9	9.2	38.0	50.0	16.7	823	94.7
Lexington township (Le Sueur).............	706	743	5.2	843	97.6	0.0	0.0	0.2	2.1	28.6	15.2	42.2	51.8	14.7	291	93.1
Libby township (Aitkin)......	45	45	0.0	47	93.6	0.0	0.0	6.4	0.0	4.3	59.6	69.3	44.4	33.3	26	100.0
Liberty township (Beltrami)	730	728	-0.3	593	93.1	0.5	0.7	5.2	0.5	21.6	19.6	42.0	31.1	29.0	230	93.0
Liberty UT (Itasca)......	62	62	0.0	70	100.0	0.0	0.0	0.0	0.0	7.1	41.4	56.5	25.8	37.1	34	94.1
Liberty township (Polk)	108	108	0.0	52	96.2	0.0	0.0	0.0	3.8	28.8	23.1	52.5	45.9	10.8	18	94.4
Lida township (Otter Tail) ..	757	758	0.1	778	98.1	0.0	0.6	0.4	0.9	10.2	31.2	58.7	32.1	34.1	345	93.3
Lien township (Grant)	111	109	-1.8	91	95.6	0.0	0.0	0.0	4.4	22.0	27.5	46.9	35.9	17.2	35	100.0
Lilydale city & MCD (Dakota).............	614	846	37.8	917	96.0	0.3	1.7	1.6	0.3	4.7	64.9	70.9	18.7	55.4	601	82.2
Lima township (Cass).......	105	111	5.7	118	93.2	0.0	0.0	6.8	0.0	25.4	18.6	46.5	57.7	9.9	49	91.8
Lime township (Blue Earth)...............	1,031	1,043	1.2	1,043	95.0	0.9	0.0	2.8	1.3	23.0	11.5	39.7	30.2	33.7	381	96.1
Lime Lake township (Murray)..............	181	174	-3.9	224	98.2	0.0	0.0	0.0	1.8	32.1	8.5	33.6	45.4	16.3	71	95.8
Limestone township (Lincoln)..............	136	135	-0.7	87	100.0	0.0	0.0	0.0	0.0	36.8	20.7	26.6	10.9	32.6	27	96.3
Lincoln township (Blue Earth)...............	200	199	-0.5	215	94.9	0.0	0.9	1.4	2.8	20.5	18.1	45.1	31.1	26.3	87	89.7
Lincoln township (Marshall)..............	117	115	-1.7	69	95.7	0.0	0.0	0.0	4.3	27.5	29.0	51.8	34.0	40.4	26	84.6
Lind township (Roseau)......	56	53	-5.4	38	100.0	0.0	0.0	0.0	0.0	13.2	15.8	31.5	27.3	0.0	16	93.8
Linden township (Brown) ..	295	288	-2.4	270	96.3	0.0	0.0	0.0	3.7	28.5	16.3	44.3	51.7	12.8	115	79.1
Linden Grove township (St. Louis)..............	145	146	0.7	119	98.3	0.0	0.0	1.7	0.0	17.6	21.0	51.5	47.8	18.9	48	83.3
Lindstrom city & MCD (Chisago)	4,507	4,720	4.7	4,614	91.0	0.0	3.6	2.0	3.4	24.9	14.5	38.5	30.8	32.8	1,919	91.0
Lino Lakes city & MCD (Anoka).............	20,219	22,119	9.4	21,404	90.0	2.0	2.8	3.3	1.8	24.7	8.4	39.6	24.5	44.9	6,903	96.1
Linsell township (Marshall)	29	29	0.0	28	100.0	0.0	0.0	0.0	0.0	32.1	10.7	28.0	71.4	0.0	14	71.4
Linwood township (Anoka)	5,123	5,442	6.2	5,104	95.9	0.5	0.0	3.2	0.4	21.0	15.1	45.4	37.9	21.3	1,877	95.7
Lisbon township (Yellow Medicine)	201	189	-6.0	191	100.0	0.0	0.0	0.0	0.0	22.0	12.0	43.8	43.2	12.9	73	95.9
Lismore city & MCD (Nobles).............	227	221	-2.6	227	81.5	0.0	0.0	0.0	18.5	22.9	19.4	39.2	46.2	12.4	88	92.0
Lismore township (Nobles)	175	174	-0.6	185	80.5	0.0	0.0	0.0	19.5	34.6	9.7	38.3	46.8	17.4	58	91.4
Litchfield city & MCD (Meeker).............	6,725	6,650	-1.1	6,631	89.2	1.1	0.0	0.5	9.1	22.9	22.9	42.9	45.2	19.7	2,803	86.1
Litchfield township (Meeker).............	831	838	0.8	869	92.8	0.0	0.0	6.1	1.2	25.2	20.9	43.8	31.1	24.2	355	92.4
Little Canada city & MCD (Ramsey)	9,777	10,501	7.4	10,451	63.5	12.2	16.3	2.7	5.3	16.6	16.5	44.4	35.3	32.4	4,695	89.6
Little Elbow township (Mahnomen).............	259	268	3.5	269	21.6	0.0	0.0	78.4	0.0	32.3	26.8	44.5	49.1	13.0	101	76.2
Little Elk township (Todd)..	289	290	0.3	198	100.0	0.0	0.0	0.0	0.0	18.7	29.8	55.0	50.0	16.5	99	79.8
Little Falls city & MCD (Morrison)..............	8,807	8,696	-1.3	8,664	93.8	1.8	0.9	1.8	1.7	21.8	21.6	41.2	48.8	19.7	3,740	82.8
Little Falls township (Morrison)..............	1,691	1,726	2.1	1,785	98.7	0.0	0.4	0.9	0.0	24.5	16.1	43.8	33.4	33.5	706	90.8
Littlefork city.............	648	592	-8.6	701	96.6	0.0	0.1	0.0	3.3	18.5	25.5	54.9	46.2	9.3	299	83.9
Little Pine township (Crow Wing)...............	86	90	4.7	70	100.0	0.0	0.0	0.0	0.0	8.6	15.7	52.3	57.1	3.6	37	94.6
Little Rock CDP	1,208	-	-	1,170	0.5	0.0	0.0	99.5	0.0	45.5	7.0	20.0	53.7	11.2	297	77.4
Little Rock township (Nobles).............	211	209	-0.9	187	95.7	0.0	0.0	0.0	4.3	31.6	11.2	36.3	42.7	20.5	65	72.3
Little Sand Lake UT (Itasca).............	349	345	-1.1	295	98.0	0.0	0.0	2.0	0.0	15.3	9.8	42.7	40.8	14.4	108	90.7
Little Sauk township (Todd)...............	829	833	0.5	819	100.0	0.0	0.0	0.0	0.0	19.7	15.4	39.6	54.3	12.3	308	84.1
Livonia township (Sherburne)..................	5,943	6,477	9.0	6,302	95.1	0.5	2.0	1.9	0.5	30.0	6.6	37.9	23.2	33.0	1,984	99.2
Lockhart township (Norman).............	50	47	-6.0	55	100.0	0.0	0.0	0.0	0.0	14.5	14.5	56.8	43.2	31.8	27	88.9
Lodi township (Mower)......	268	279	4.1	211	96.2	0.0	0.0	1.4	2.4	26.1	15.2	42.7	46.5	13.9	81	80.2
Logan township (Aitkin)	179	177	-1.1	192	99.5	0.0	0.0	0.5	0.0	17.2	20.8	47.1	47.9	9.7	93	94.6
Logan township (Grant)	93	93	0.0	97	100.0	0.0	0.0	0.0	0.0	25.8	16.5	50.3	47.1	19.1	42	78.6

1 May be of any race.

Table A. All Places — Population and Housing

STATE City, town, township, borough, or CDP (county if applicable)	Population				Race and Hispanic or Latino origin (percent)					Age (percent)			Educational attainment of persons age 25 and older		Occupied housing units	
	2010 census total population	2019 estimated population	Percent change 2010–2019	ACS total population estimate 2015–2019	White alone, not Hispanic or Latino	Black alone, not Hispanic or Latino	Asian alone, not Hispanic or Latino	All other races or 2 or more races, not Hispanic or Latino	Hispanic or Latino[1]	Under 18 years old	Age 65 years and older	Median age	Percent High school diploma or less	Percent Bachelor's degree or more	Total	Percent with a computer
	1	2	3	4	5	6	7	8	9	10	11	12	13	14	15	16
MINNESOTA—Con.																
London township (Freeborn)	317	306	-3.5	229	97.4	0.0	2.6	0.0	0.0	11.4	15.7	34.3	59.1	14.4	101	88.1
Lone Pine township (Itasca)	410	405	-1.2	474	96.6	0.0	1.1	1.5	0.8	16.5	21.9	54.1	18.8	30.8	208	96.2
Lone Tree township (Chippewa)	199	191	-4.0	204	96.1	0.0	0.0	0.0	3.9	42.6	7.8	27.0	17.1	18.0	59	89.8
Long Beach city & MCD (Pope)	334	415	24.3	296	100.0	0.0	0.0	0.0	0.0	20.3	28.7	57.2	18.9	38.8	130	94.6
Long Lake township (Crow Wing)	1,069	1,121	4.9	1,125	99.4	0.0	0.0	0.6	0.0	18.8	22.4	50.5	28.3	26.9	481	91.1
Long Lake city	1,775	1,816	2.3	1,789	91.5	2.6	0.6	3.4	2.0	22.9	16.7	45.0	26.5	44.9	774	87.0
Long Lake township (Watonwan)	338	335	-0.9	325	99.1	0.0	0.0	0.9	0.0	17.2	36.3	60.3	34.5	27.7	144	97.9
Long Lost Lake township (Clearwater)	39	39	0.0	54	83.3	0.0	0.0	16.7	0.0	9.3	83.3	70.0	24.5	38.8	29	82.8
Long Prairie city & MCD (Todd)	3,461	3,301	-4.6	3,311	62.1	2.0	3.4	0.5	32.0	27.2	21.7	43.2	62.7	16.8	1,330	82.5
Long Prairie township (Todd)	842	849	0.8	1,043	91.9	0.0	0.0	1.2	6.9	24.8	19.4	44.9	45.0	16.7	393	86.3
Longville city & MCD (Cass)	148	150	1.4	174	97.7	0.0	0.0	2.3	0.0	2.9	67.2	70.5	31.6	39.9	118	93.2
Lonsdale city & MCD (Rice)	3,669	4,207	14.7	4,010	94.8	1.0	1.9	0.3	2.0	32.7	7.1	29.2	33.9	27.4	1,374	94.8
Loon Lake township (Cass)	540	566	4.8	593	100.0	0.0	0.0	0.0	0.0	25.3	13.3	42.6	33.7	20.8	239	90.4
Lorain township (Nobles)	297	295	-0.7	320	87.2	0.0	0.0	0.6	12.2	25.3	16.9	44.2	45.1	23.0	120	90.0
Loretto city	647	664	2.6	762	99.1	0.0	0.0	0.0	0.9	31.1	11.2	38.9	29.7	38.8	295	89.8
Louisburg city & MCD (Lac qui Parle)	47	44	-6.4	32	100.0	0.0	0.0	0.0	0.0	3.1	25.0	54.8	54.8	22.6	21	100.0
Louisville township (Red Lake)	190	188	-1.1	119	100.0	0.0	0.0	0.0	0.0	15.1	16.0	52.6	51.0	14.6	58	82.8
Louisville township (Scott)	1,262	1,371	8.6	1,354	89.7	0.0	4.9	0.7	4.7	27.3	10.2	42.5	28.3	37.3	444	94.1
Louriston township (Chippewa)	165	159	-3.6	143	92.3	0.0	0.0	0.0	7.7	22.4	14.7	41.1	29.4	17.6	52	84.6
Lowell township (Polk)	298	299	0.3	316	63.3	6.0	0.0	19.3	11.4	14.6	3.8	32.9	52.6	13.1	44	93.2
Lower Red Lake UT (Beltrami)	5,786	5,749	-0.6	5,762	2.0	0.4	0.1	96.0	1.4	43.8	5.3	21.7	59.5	6.9	1,366	75.5
Lowry city & MCD (Pope)	299	300	0.3	392	93.9	0.0	4.1	1.3	0.8	26.8	18.9	38.5	37.5	18.8	166	84.9
Lowville township (Murray)	169	162	-4.1	174	99.4	0.0	0.0	0.0	0.6	25.9	19.5	41.0	23.3	29.3	67	88.1
Lucan city & MCD (Redwood)	191	175	-8.4	168	90.5	0.0	0.0	7.1	2.4	26.2	25.0	41.3	35.1	17.5	70	78.6
Lucas township (Lyon)	227	225	-0.9	197	100.0	0.0	0.0	0.0	0.0	31.5	8.6	42.8	31.7	28.5	71	91.5
Lund township (Douglas)	325	338	4.0	316	99.1	0.0	0.0	0.9	0.0	21.8	20.3	46.1	34.4	17.9	132	87.9
Lura township (Faribault)	163	155	-4.9	145	100.0	0.0	0.0	0.0	0.0	16.6	35.9	54.3	41.4	16.2	64	82.8
Lutsen CDP	190	-	-	213	92.0	0.0	0.0	0.0	8.0	8.5	16.9	39.4	31.1	33.8	118	94.1
Lutsen township (Cook)	429	460	7.2	447	96.2	0.0	0.0	0.0	3.8	10.5	23.5	46.0	25.2	39.5	231	96.1
Luverne city & MCD (Rock)	4,729	4,531	-4.2	4,564	91.5	0.6	1.5	1.4	5.1	27.6	21.4	37.1	38.8	27.8	1,904	87.1
Luverne township (Rock)	491	480	-2.2	444	99.8	0.0	0.2	0.0	0.0	28.4	19.1	41.5	35.7	18.9	163	92.6
Luxemburg township (Stearns)	637	688	8.0	690	96.7	0.6	0.0	0.0	2.8	22.3	15.9	46.7	54.6	14.0	250	91.2
Lyle city & MCD (Mower)	551	554	0.5	502	84.7	3.2	0.2	8.8	3.2	24.7	20.5	42.8	47.6	10.4	207	84.5
Lyle township (Mower)	356	370	3.9	382	99.0	0.5	0.0	0.5	0.0	25.4	22.0	48.5	49.1	18.6	146	91.8
Lynd city & MCD (Lyon)	453	466	2.9	400	72.0	1.3	4.0	2.5	20.3	29.8	6.8	35.1	44.5	25.7	159	91.8
Lynd township (Lyon)	417	416	-0.2	435	97.2	0.0	0.7	1.6	0.5	21.6	24.1	51.9	29.0	39.9	170	93.5
Lynden township (Stearns)	1,938	2,076	7.1	1,806	96.7	0.1	0.8	1.0	1.4	19.7	21.2	49.7	39.9	21.2	685	92.6
Lynn township (McLeod)	544	535	-1.7	515	96.7	0.0	0.4	1.6	1.4	21.2	19.4	45.8	45.0	20.3	205	89.3
Lyons township (Lyon)	201	200	-0.5	167	100.0	0.0	0.0	0.0	0.0	22.8	15.6	48.1	28.1	35.5	70	95.7
Lyons township (Wadena)	192	191	-0.5	173	87.9	0.0	0.0	8.1	4.0	16.2	38.7	57.5	50.4	16.3	86	80.2
Lyra township (Blue Earth)	325	322	-0.9	294	97.3	0.0	0.0	1.7	1.0	20.7	18.4	46.7	38.5	24.4	125	80.8
Mabel city & MCD (Fillmore)	780	749	-4.0	823	97.7	0.0	1.0	0.0	1.3	15.3	31.2	55.8	61.6	8.9	365	79.7
McCauleyville township (Wilkin)	55	53	-3.6	35	100.0	0.0	0.0	0.0	0.0	22.9	20.0	46.9	51.9	7.4	17	94.1
McCormack UT (St. Louis)	209	209	0.0	171	100.0	0.0	0.0	0.0	0.0	21.1	29.2	56.1	13.3	44.4	67	100.0
McCrea township (Marshall)	239	234	-2.1	300	97.7	0.0	0.0	1.0	1.3	47.0	10.3	31.6	27.7	20.1	85	92.9
McDavitt township (St. Louis)	461	464	0.7	480	94.2	0.0	0.0	3.3	2.5	17.7	25.6	52.6	45.0	14.8	192	82.3
McDonaldsville township (Norman)	177	168	-5.1	142	100.0	0.0	0.0	0.0	0.0	13.4	28.2	54.8	32.1	26.8	66	84.8
McGrath city & MCD (Aitkin)	80	74	-7.5	32	100.0	0.0	0.0	0.0	0.0	0.0	18.8	56.3	45.2	0.0	17	94.1
McGregor city & MCD (Aitkin)	390	363	-6.9	392	91.1	0.5	0.0	8.4	0.0	15.8	17.6	37.0	62.0	10.6	188	85.6
McGregor township (Aitkin)	106	107	0.9	117	99.1	0.0	0.0	0.9	0.0	9.4	29.9	52.1	52.5	15.2	57	89.5
McIntosh city & MCD (Polk)	627	605	-3.5	612	88.6	0.5	2.1	6.0	2.8	19.0	30.9	47.4	53.9	11.5	276	74.3
McKinley township (Cass)	133	141	6.0	118	92.4	0.0	0.0	7.6	0.0	28.0	17.8	39.3	48.8	11.9	47	76.6
McKinley UT (Kittson)	38	37	-2.6	21	100.0	0.0	0.0	0.0	0.0	23.8	47.6	60.8	75.0	25.0	10	60.0
McKinley city & MCD (St. Louis)	128	123	-3.9	134	98.5	0.0	1.5	0.0	0.0	25.4	18.7	38.3	35.3	9.4	58	86.2
McPherson township (Blue Earth)	466	463	-0.6	422	99.1	0.9	0.0	0.0	0.0	22.3	8.5	39.7	35.4	31.9	163	96.3
Macsville township (Grant)	114	112	-1.8	82	100.0	0.0	0.0	0.0	0.0	3.7	23.2	55.5	25.4	11.9	32	96.9
Macville township (Aitkin)	206	205	-0.5	146	89.0	0.0	0.0	7.5	3.4	5.5	32.2	58.6	54.7	12.0	75	77.3
Madelia city & MCD (Watonwan)	2,325	2,254	-3.1	2,628	66.6	3.2	0.8	2.5	26.9	25.0	18.7	35.4	55.9	16.7	952	88.6
Madelia township (Watonwan)	334	329	-1.5	305	96.7	0.0	0.0	0.0	3.3	27.9	12.1	45.1	32.3	26.4	114	86.8

1 May be of any race.

Table A. All Places — **Population and Housing**

STATE City, town, township, borough, or CDP (county if applicable)	Population				Race and Hispanic or Latino origin (percent)					Age (percent)			Educational attainment of persons age 25 and older		Occupied housing units	
	2010 census total population	2019 estimated population	Percent change 2010–2019	ACS total population estimate 2015–2019	White alone, not Hispanic or Latino	Black alone, not Hispanic or Latino	Asian alone, not Hispanic or Latino	All other races or 2 or more races, not Hispanic or Latino	Hispanic or Latino[1]	Under 18 years old	Age 65 years and older	Median age	Percent High school diploma or less	Percent Bachelor's degree or more	Total	Percent with a computer
	1	2	3	4	5	6	7	8	9	10	11	12	13	14	15	16
MINNESOTA—Con.																
Madison city & MCD (Lac qui Parle)	1,551	1,400	-9.7	1,617	94.7	0.8	2.2	1.7	0.7	17.4	31.9	52.2	46.2	16.2	820	81.1
Madison township (Lac qui Parle)	216	200	-7.4	143	100.0	0.0	0.0	0.0	0.0	29.4	18.2	39.3	32.7	12.9	55	90.9
Madison Lake city & MCD (Blue Earth)	1,024	1,174	14.6	976	93.3	2.3	0.4	2.8	1.2	22.1	13.1	40.1	27.5	32.5	429	92.8
Magnolia city & MCD (Rock)	222	209	-5.9	201	71.6	1.5	10.0	4.5	12.4	23.9	20.4	47.3	58.8	13.0	83	92.8
Magnolia township (Rock)	212	208	-1.9	245	100.0	0.0	0.0	0.0	0.0	15.5	35.1	55.8	25.4	31.2	115	97.4
Mahnomen city & MCD (Mahnomen)	1,212	1,231	1.6	1,288	41.9	0.0	0.5	50.4	7.1	27.3	23.2	39.1	54.7	7.2	514	77.4
Mahnomen CDP	239	-	-	225	3.6	1.3	0.0	95.1	0.0	41.3	3.1	26.5	63.2	0.0	73	80.8
Mahtomedi city & MCD (Washington)	7,703	8,294	7.7	8,164	90.7	4.7	1.5	1.5	1.6	26.3	18.0	46.3	19.6	53.9	3,141	89.9
Mahtowa CDP	370	-	-	358	96.6	0.0	1.7	0.0	1.7	23.7	17.6	39.3	50.0	16.1	154	85.7
Mahtowa township (Carlton)	605	626	3.5	609	97.0	0.0	1.6	0.3	1.0	23.5	16.3	42.3	44.0	19.3	242	88.4
Maine township (Otter Tail)	653	655	0.3	602	93.5	0.8	0.0	5.0	0.7	20.8	36.5	57.6	31.0	27.2	261	90.4
Maine Prairie township (Stearns)	1,889	2,009	6.4	2,143	98.4	0.4	0.0	0.2	1.0	22.0	15.5	44.8	41.9	23.0	781	91.4
Makinen UT (St. Louis)	1,309	1,317	0.6	1,440	98.4	0.0	0.0	1.6	0.0	11.5	27.1	53.3	36.4	21.7	680	86.3
Malmo township (Aitkin)	338	336	-0.6	362	93.4	1.1	3.9	1.7	0.0	7.7	42.5	57.7	52.1	17.7	200	84.0
Malta township (Big Stone)	98	96	-2.0	69	100.0	0.0	0.0	0.0	0.0	39.1	5.8	36.7	68.3	7.3	24	100.0
Malung township (Roseau)	438	412	-5.9	388	99.0	0.0	0.5	0.5	0.0	24.0	19.3	47.6	38.9	18.9	155	81.3
Mamre township (Kandiyohi)	385	393	2.1	530	97.2	0.4	0.0	0.4	2.1	34.0	15.3	37.4	23.4	18.2	171	92.4
Manannah township (Meeker)	604	605	0.2	578	97.8	0.0	1.0	0.7	0.5	27.3	13.1	42.6	45.8	13.9	216	85.2
Manchester city & MCD (Freeborn)	57	55	-3.5	91	52.7	0.0	0.0	47.3	0.0	39.6	6.6	32.5	64.7	3.9	28	85.7
Manchester township (Freeborn)	424	411	-3.1	500	88.6	2.6	0.4	4.8	3.6	28.8	17.2	38.1	43.8	17.1	166	94.0
Mandt township (Chippewa)	152	146	-3.9	134	100.0	0.0	0.0	0.0	0.0	28.4	23.9	37.8	35.5	19.4	62	95.2
Manfred township (Lac qui Parle)	99	92	-7.1	74	100.0	0.0	0.0	0.0	0.0	27.0	40.5	59.5	65.3	20.4	26	65.4
Manhattan Beach city & MCD (Crow Wing)	59	66	11.9	73	100.0	0.0	0.0	0.0	0.0	26.0	17.8	41.3	57.4	9.3	29	93.1
Mankato city	39,847	42,931	7.7	42,093	84.0	5.6	3.2	2.7	4.6	17.4	11.6	25.8	28.9	39.3	16,414	93.2
Mankato city (Blue Earth)	39,843	42,927	7.7	42,093	84.0	5.6	3.2	2.7	4.6	17.4	11.6	25.8	28.9	39.3	16,414	93.2
Mankato city (Le Sueur)	-	-	-	-	-	-	-	-	-	-	-	-	-	-	-	-
Mankato city (Nicollet)	4	4	0.0	-	-	-	-	-	-	-	-	-	-	-	-	-
Mankato township (Blue Earth)	1,783	1,776	-0.4	1,699	96.9	0.4	1.9	0.8	0.0	21.7	21.3	50.0	21.1	45.3	630	97.5
Mansfield township (Freeborn)	237	229	-3.4	179	97.2	0.0	1.1	1.7	0.0	20.1	30.7	58.8	48.3	21.0	92	78.3
Manston township (Wilkin)	48	46	-4.2	42	92.9	0.0	0.0	0.0	7.1	4.8	23.8	52.5	63.6	12.1	25	80.0
Mantorville city & MCD (Dodge)	1,195	1,210	1.3	1,015	92.1	1.6	0.0	3.4	2.9	23.9	14.0	41.5	27.7	26.5	386	93.3
Mantorville township (Dodge)	1,871	1,946	4.0	1,817	97.5	0.0	0.0	1.6	0.9	24.5	11.7	44.9	25.2	45.2	632	96.4
Mantrap township (Hubbard)	519	555	6.9	518	100.0	0.0	0.0	0.0	0.0	12.0	39.2	59.3	25.7	40.9	228	93.0
Manyaska township (Martin)	308	295	-4.2	394	100.0	0.0	0.0	0.0	0.0	22.6	20.6	51.1	44.7	25.1	161	93.2
Maple township (Cass)	377	405	7.4	485	98.1	0.8	0.0	0.0	1.0	29.5	14.0	35.6	42.9	17.5	195	90.3
Maple Grove township (Becker)	455	485	6.6	449	33.6	0.4	1.1	63.5	1.3	31.8	22.5	40.9	52.2	14.9	158	84.2
Maple Grove township (Crow Wing)	770	810	5.2	640	98.4	0.0	0.0	1.6	0.0	16.4	20.5	51.7	34.4	16.9	260	93.5
Maple Grove city	61,548	72,622	18.0	70,627	82.7	5.6	6.5	3.2	2.1	25.1	12.7	40.0	17.0	54.0	27,332	97.7
Maple Lake city & MCD (Wright)	2,063	2,148	4.1	2,315	93.5	0.1	0.0	5.2	1.3	29.9	9.6	35.2	40.9	13.6	842	90.6
Maple Lake township (Wright)	2,050	2,179	6.3	1,955	97.7	0.2	0.3	1.5	0.3	20.1	18.7	49.6	43.2	23.3	777	92.4
Maple Plain city	1,760	2,114	20.1	1,861	76.2	9.7	1.0	5.7	7.3	27.2	16.4	40.2	28.6	36.1	753	93.8
Maple Ridge township (Beltrami)	104	103	-	120	83.3	0.0	0.0	16.7	0.0	16.7	20.0	37.5	29.6	33.3	45	84.4
Maple Ridge township (Isanti)	761	788	3.5	794	87.4	0.0	0.5	2.5	9.6	23.4	20.2	47.9	44.0	19.9	314	87.6
Mapleton city & MCD (Blue Earth)	1,756	1,692	-3.6	1,716	93.6	1.3	0.2	1.5	3.3	24.9	18.9	38.3	39.0	22.3	681	92.1
Mapleton township (Blue Earth)	310	308	-0.6	320	88.1	0.0	0.0	0.0	11.9	31.9	20.0	38.5	51.0	26.2	105	82.9
Mapleview city & MCD (Mower)	176	175	-0.6	133	76.7	0.0	0.8	0.0	22.6	27.8	28.6	47.8	62.1	0.0	64	92.2
Maplewood township (Otter Tail)	318	318	0.0	308	98.4	0.0	0.6	0.0	1.0	16.2	16.9	52.2	40.6	25.9	131	82.4
Maplewood city & MCD (Ramsey)	38,016	40,885	7.5	40,545	62.5	9.7	14.5	4.5	8.8	22.1	16.8	38.3	36.4	31.9	15,086	91.5
Marble city & MCD (Itasca)	701	671	-4.3	614	83.1	0.7	0.0	14.3	2.0	25.4	14.2	39.5	51.0	10.9	279	84.9
Marble township (Lincoln)	161	157	-2.5	147	99.3	0.0	0.0	0.7	0.0	25.9	15.6	49.8	44.7	23.3	58	89.7
Marcell township (Itasca)	467	464	-0.6	453	99.6	0.0	0.0	0.4	0.0	20.1	38.4	56.9	46.9	25.2	196	92.9
Marietta city & MCD (Lac qui Parle)	159	141	-11.3	144	98.6	0.0	0.7	0.7	0.0	12.5	39.6	54.8	63.6	13.2	83	71.1
Marine on St. Croix city & MCD (Washington)	688	712	3.5	733	87.6	0.0	0.5	10.5	1.4	21.4	21.0	51.2	9.8	59.8	304	95.7
Marion township (Olmsted)	3,672	3,780	2.9	3,803	97.7	0.0	0.8	0.2	1.4	23.1	17.1	46.3	32.8	27.4	1,368	93.8

1 May be of any race.

Table A. All Places — Population and Housing

STATE City, town, township, borough, or CDP (county if applicable)	Population				Race and Hispanic or Latino origin (percent)					Age (percent)			Educational attainment of persons age 25 and older		Occupied housing units	
	2010 census total population	2019 estimated population	Percent change 2010–2019	ACS total population estimate 2015–2019	White alone, not Hispanic or Latino	Black alone, not Hispanic or Latino	Asian alone, not Hispanic or Latino	All other races or 2 or more races, not Hispanic or Latino	Hispanic or Latino[1]	Under 18 years old	Age 65 years and older	Median age	Percent High school diploma or less	Percent Bachelor's degree or more	Total	Percent with a computer
	1	2	3	4	5	6	7	8	9	10	11	12	13	14	15	16

MINNESOTA—Con.

STATE City, town, township, borough, or CDP (county if applicable)	1	2	3	4	5	6	7	8	9	10	11	12	13	14	15	16
Marshall city & MCD (Lyon)	13,691	13,487	-1.5	13,651	77.0	6.0	6.1	1.8	9.1	25.5	13.6	31.8	38.9	29.2	5,211	91.2
Marshall township (Mower)	361	376	4.2	372	96.8	0.3	2.7	0.3	0.0	30.4	13.7	35.5	29.3	28.8	115	95.7
Marshan township (Dakota)	1,106	1,135	2.6	1,231	94.2	0.3	0.2	0.8	4.5	18.0	24.0	49.6	39.2	26.2	470	88.1
Marsh Creek township (Mahnomen)	152	156	2.6	156	78.2	0.0	0.0	21.8	0.0	43.6	8.3	27.1	12.8	44.2	49	95.9
Marshfield township (Lincoln)	242	238	-1.7	223	92.4	0.0	0.0	0.0	7.6	36.3	9.0	38.1	43.4	31.0	73	97.3
Marsh Grove township (Marshall)	143	139	-2.8	122	100.0	0.0	0.0	0.0	0.0	11.5	17.2	39.4	25.0	10.0	47	87.2
Martin township (Rock)	384	376	-2.1	370	95.7	3.0	1.4	0.0	0.0	30.0	14.1	38.5	32.6	32.6	132	93.9
Martin Lake CDP	933	-		806	99.1	0.0	0.0	0.9	0.0	13.4	19.2	51.9	38.0	14.6	381	89.8
Martinsburg township (Renville)	197	184	-6.6	161	98.1	0.0	0.0	1.9	0.0	13.0	33.5	55.1	44.8	17.6	72	91.7
Mary township (Norman)	76	72	-5.3	85	96.5	0.0	0.0	3.5	0.0	18.8	18.8	47.1	20.0	26.7	37	100.0
Marysland township (Swift)	96	93	-3.1	69	100.0	0.0	0.0	0.0	0.0	4.3	29.0	59.2	65.2	3.0	37	78.4
Marysville township (Wright)	2,138	2,285	6.9	2,386	94.0	0.4	0.4	2.8	2.4	26.9	13.3	37.3	44.2	20.8	799	90.9
Mason township (Murray)	299	289	-3.3	315	99.4	0.0	0.0	0.6	0.0	16.8	33.0	56.6	32.1	33.7	147	87.8
Max township (Itasca)	141	140	-0.7	128	73.4	0.0	0.0	26.6	0.0	18.0	23.4	58.0	56.3	15.6	61	93.4
Maxwell township (Lac qui Parle)	179	165	-7.8	110	100.0	0.0	0.0	0.0	0.0	19.1	16.4	32.0	24.1	24.1	52	88.5
May township (Cass)	848	893	5.3	783	96.9	0.4	0.0	2.2	0.5	19.7	20.1	50.2	46.0	15.6	350	91.7
May township (Washington)	2,785	2,917	4.7	2,896	94.6	0.1	2.0	1.0	2.2	17.4	22.4	53.0	17.4	50.8	1,113	98.5
Mayer city & MCD (Carver)	1,744	2,266	29.9	1,955	94.6	0.5	0.7	3.2	1.1	29.7	7.6	33.2	24.4	37.0	659	97.4
Mayfield township (Pennington)	51	49	-3.9	54	94.4	0.0	0.0	5.6	0.0	11.1	33.3	59.5	54.3	10.9	23	78.3
Mayhew Lake township (Benton)	827	857	3.6	728	99.6	0.0	0.0	0.4	0.0	22.3	15.7	45.2	37.4	18.0	282	87.6
Maynard city & MCD (Chippewa)	366	345	-5.7	394	92.1	0.0	0.0	1.8	6.1	26.6	20.3	41.5	53.8	11.4	173	78.6
Mayville township (Houston)	409	407	-0.5	308	99.4	0.0	0.0	0.6	0.0	24.4	28.2	49.0	52.3	8.7	120	87.5
Maywood township (Benton)	954	991	3.9	957	95.0	0.0	0.2	2.5	2.3	31.9	15.3	40.1	44.6	14.2	338	89.3
Mazeppa city & MCD (Wabasha)	840	845	0.6	829	98.3	0.0	0.0	0.0	1.7	22.9	17.6	44.5	44.3	20.1	353	83.3
Mazeppa township (Wabasha)	707	709	0.3	629	96.5	0.8	0.6	2.1	0.0	10.5	22.6	54.0	25.5	34.3	268	85.4
Meadow township (Wadena)	217	215	-0.9	205	100.0	0.0	0.0	0.0	0.0	17.6	26.3	49.5	44.2	14.3	97	81.4
Meadow Brook township (Cass)	226	239	5.8	247	83.0	0.0	2.0	9.7	5.3	27.5	25.9	45.8	54.9	8.7	100	64.0
Meadowlands city & MCD (St. Louis)	132	127	-3.8	136	85.3	11.8	0.7	2.2	0.0	14.0	17.6	56.5	60.6	6.7	69	65.2
Meadowlands township (St. Louis)	306	307	0.3	309	97.4	0.0	0.0	2.6	0.0	23.3	28.2	52.3	50.4	16.4	132	84.8
Meadows township (Wilkin)	38	36	-5.3	30	100.0	0.0	0.0	0.0	0.0	43.3	0.0	31.0	23.5	5.9	13	92.3
Medford city & MCD (Steele)	1,240	1,256	1.3	1,404	78.4	0.0	0.6	0.6	20.4	35.9	7.8	31.6	40.2	21.9	471	92.4
Medford township (Steele)	812	830	2.2	785	65.5	2.7	0.6	0.5	30.7	32.5	11.1	35.9	57.0	16.7	275	86.9
Medicine Lake city	355	374	5.4	436	92.0	0.7	2.3	5.0	0.0	23.9	15.1	42.6	16.0	65.9	177	96.0
Medina city	4,893	6,712	37.2	6,380	86.5	1.1	8.8	3.7	0.0	30.1	11.7	40.5	11.3	64.2	2,260	97.4
Medo township (Blue Earth)	361	359	-0.6	329	98.8	0.3	0.0	0.3	0.6	23.7	18.8	42.2	36.5	30.4	126	83.3
Mehurin township (Lac qui Parle)	77	71	-7.8	82	100.0	0.0	0.0	0.0	0.0	9.8	56.1	65.4	54.1	6.8	45	86.7
Meire Grove city & MCD (Stearns)	182	197	8.2	191	97.9	0.0	0.0	0.0	2.1	26.2	12.6	31.8	54.5	15.4	82	92.7
Melrose city & MCD (Stearns)	3,595	3,656	1.7	3,647	79.8	0.7	0.0	1.7	17.7	27.0	18.1	39.6	53.8	12.9	1,398	80.1
Melrose township (Stearns)	758	816	7.7	773	99.2	0.0	0.0	0.0	0.8	18.5	22.5	50.1	45.7	15.6	297	91.2
Melville township (Renville)	225	212	-5.8	181	98.9	0.0	0.0	0.0	1.1	16.6	11.0	47.8	31.0	28.4	72	93.1
Menahga city & MCD (Wadena)	1,306	1,302	-0.3	1,068	97.4	0.3	1.4	0.9	0.0	22.8	25.6	49.4	54.1	10.4	485	79.4
Mendota city & MCD (Dakota)	206	217	5.3	157	89.8	0.0	0.6	4.5	5.1	16.6	15.3	43.6	39.5	37.0	75	89.3
Mendota Heights city & MCD (Dakota)	11,072	11,343	2.4	11,289	91.9	1.2	1.5	2.2	3.2	19.7	26.0	51.2	13.9	63.7	4,764	94.5
Mentor city & MCD (Polk)	153	147	-3.9	229	98.3	0.0	0.0	0.4	1.3	30.6	14.4	31.6	76.7	5.3	87	80.5
Meriden township (Steele)	621	623	0.3	562	96.6	0.0	0.2	2.0	1.2	25.8	15.7	42.1	48.3	13.3	207	80.7
Merrifield CDP	140	-		73	100.0	0.0	0.0	0.0	0.0	0.0	72.6	69.4	80.8	19.2	38	63.2
Merton township (Steele)	348	349	0.3	393	98.7	0.0	0.0	0.8	0.5	26.5	14.2	39.9	46.0	14.4	142	85.2
Mickinock township (Roseau)	303	289	-4.6	270	99.3	0.0	0.0	0.0	0.7	30.0	15.9	36.7	53.2	11.1	101	92.1
Middle River city & MCD (Marshall)	303	301	-0.7	268	100.0	0.0	0.0	0.0	0.0	16.4	30.6	49.2	60.7	12.0	152	81.6
Middle River township (Marshall)	78	77	-1.3	100	100.0	0.0	0.0	0.0	0.0	27.0	16.0	36.7	26.0	35.6	27	77.8
Middletown township (Jackson)	227	220	-3.1	208	97.6	0.0	0.0	0.0	2.4	15.9	16.3	47.2	23.1	60.4	95	94.7
Middleville township (Wright)	928	986	6.3	962	90.6	3.8	2.3	0.2	3.0	23.7	12.5	43.6	43.1	25.7	364	92.0

1 May be of any race.

Table A. All Places — Population and Housing

STATE City, town, township, borough, or CDP (county if applicable)	Population				Race and Hispanic or Latino origin (percent)					Age (percent)			Educational attainment of persons age 25 and older		Occupied housing units	
	2010 census total population	2019 estimated population	Percent change 2010–2019	ACS total population estimate 2015–2019	White alone, not Hispanic or Latino	Black alone, not Hispanic or Latino	Asian alone, not Hispanic or Latino	All other races or 2 or more races, not Hispanic or Latino	Hispanic or Latino[1]	Under 18 years old	Age 65 years and older	Median age	Percent High school diploma or less	Percent Bachelor's degree or more	Total	Percent with a computer
	1	2	3	4	5	6	7	8	9	10	11	12	13	14	15	16
MINNESOTA—Con.																
Midway township (Cottonwood)	220	214	-2.7	209	94.7	0.0	4.3	0.0	1.0	24.4	22.0	48.8	29.1	29.1	83	91.6
Midway CDP	26	-	-	37	13.5	0.0	0.0	86.5	0.0	48.6	0.0	25.2	68.4	10.5	7	100.0
Midway township (St. Louis)	1,396	1,421	1.8	1,373	95.8	0.0	0.0	4.2	0.0	19.2	20.0	44.0	36.0	26.7	590	87.5
Miesville city & MCD (Dakota)	119	122	2.5	119	100.0	0.0	0.0	0.0	0.0	16.8	22.7	34.0	44.4	13.3	53	94.3
Milaca city & MCD (Mille Lacs)	2,959	2,930		2,901	92.0	0.7	0.0	5.4	1.9	21.3	23.1	41.5	54.7	15.1	1,313	82.3
Milaca township (Mille Lacs)	1,614	1,631	1.1	1,580	92.8	0.0	0.6	2.6	4.1	26.6	14.2	39.9	47.0	14.0	541	92.6
Milan city & MCD (Chippewa)	369	354	-4.1	308	44.8	0.0	0.3	45.1	9.7	21.4	20.8	32.5	57.3	20.6	126	73.8
Milford township (Brown) ..	692	679	-1.9	805	98.6	0.0	0.4	0.0	1.0	28.1	15.3	43.9	36.9	25.1	292	94.5
Millerville city & MCD (Douglas)	106	104	-1.9	106	100.0	0.0	0.0	0.0	0.0	34.0	14.2	33.1	54.7	10.9	47	87.2
Millerville township (Douglas)	338	351	3.8	368	97.0	0.0	0.0	3.0	0.0	33.7	19.3	37.2	44.1	14.3	128	92.2
Millville city & MCD (Wabasha)	186	178	-4.3	171	90.6	0.0	1.8	0.0	7.6	9.9	20.5	49.2	50.8	12.3	80	75.0
Millward township (Aitkin) .	72	71	-1.4	90	91.1	6.7	0.0	2.2	0.0	20.0	27.8	44.4	61.0	6.8	38	81.6
Millwood township (Stearns)	966	1,045	8.2	1,022	99.5	0.0	0.0	0.5	0.0	22.4	19.0	48.2	44.1	15.9	387	92.0
Milo township (Mille Lacs)	1,385	1,409	1.7	1,442	94.8	0.2	0.3	0.5	4.2	23.0	13.8	42.2	40.3	14.9	538	92.2
Milroy city & MCD (Redwood)	252	237	-6.0	222	93.7	0.0	0.0	0.0	6.3	25.2	19.8	40.4	40.0	14.0	105	83.8
Milton township (Dodge)...	734	759	3.4	801	89.6	0.0	1.1	1.9	7.4	25.2	15.9	43.3	37.6	30.0	306	94.8
Miltona city & MCD (Douglas)	424	424	0.0	364	99.2	0.0	0.0	0.8	0.0	24.7	15.4	39.6	39.8	17.8	163	86.5
Miltona township (Douglas)	810	845	4.3	886	100.0	0.0	0.0	0.0	0.0	11.1	36.8	58.9	40.5	24.3	430	90.7
Minden township (Benton)	1,654	1,723	4.2	1,529	99.1	0.0	0.0	0.4	0.5	19.9	17.9	43.5	34.7	27.2	646	90.1
Minerva township (Clearwater)	259	261	0.8	232	90.1	0.0	0.0	8.6	1.3	30.6	10.8	45.8	51.6	14.8	93	88.2
Minneapolis city	382,603	429,606	12.3	420,324	60.0	18.9	5.9	5.6	9.6	19.8	10.0	32.3	25.2	50.4	176,974	92.8
Minneiska city	112	108	-3.6	106	99.1	0.0	0.0	0.9	0.0	13.2	29.2	57.0	27.2	23.9	51	96.1
Minneiska city (Wabasha)	61	59	-3.3	57	98.2	0.0	0.0	1.8	0.0	12.3	31.6	61.3	26.0	18.0	28	96.4
Minneiska city (Winona) ...	51	49	-3.9	49	100.0	0.0	0.0	0.0	0.0	14.3	26.5	54.1	28.6	31.0	23	95.7
Minneiska township (Wabasha)	185	185		150	98.0	0.0	0.0	0.0	2.0	13.3	44.0	62.0	46.9	26.6	68	89.7
Minneola township (Goodhue)	619	616	-0.5	625	97.4	0.6	0.5	1.3	0.2	23.2	13.4	44.7	30.9	35.5	252	93.3
Minneota township (Jackson)	259	251	-3.1	269	97.8	0.0	2.2	0.0	0.0	14.9	34.9	58.3	34.9	24.5	126	87.3
Minneota city & MCD (Lyon)	1,392	1,356	-2.6	1,282	92.9	0.9	1.1	0.2	4.9	20.5	25.7	47.4	43.0	20.9	538	88.5
Minnesota City city & MCD (Winona)	198	187	-5.6	166	80.1	0.0	0.0	1.8	18.1	24.7	14.5	36.0	40.0	10.0	65	100.0
Minnesota Falls township (Yellow Medicine)	429	404	-5.8	364	49.5	0.0	0.8	47.3	2.5	22.8	14.8	48.8	36.7	28.8	167	98.2
Minnesota Lake city	689	644	-6.5	642	96.7	0.0	0.0	1.7	1.6	20.6	17.3	45.3	37.9	19.1	280	90.7
Minnesota Lake city (Blue Earth)	6	6	0.0	15	100.0	0.0	0.0	0.0	0.0	0.0	0.0	55.5	33.3	33.3	8	100.0
Minnesota Lake city (Faribault)	683	638	-6.6	627	96.7	0.0	0.0	1.8	1.6	21.1	17.7	45.1	38.1	18.6	272	90.4
Minnesota Lake township (Faribault)	190	181	-4.7	176	100.0	0.0	0.0	0.0	0.0	29.5	16.5	43.5	37.1	26.7	68	94.1
Minnetonka city	49,735	54,064	8.7	53,025	84.8	5.2	5.8	2.5	1.6	20.2	20.7	44.4	15.6	60.2	23,065	93.9
Minnetonka Beach city	534	581	8.8	611	91.3	0.3	1.8	4.6	2.0	27.2	16.2	45.8	10.1	72.1	229	99.1
Minnetrista city	6,314	8,130	28.8	7,621	97.7	0.0	1.7	0.3	0.4	27.5	11.6	44.4	13.9	62.5	2,596	98.2
Minnewaska township (Pope)	495	499	0.8	405	99.5	0.0	0.0	0.5	0.0	18.8	27.7	52.2	26.1	28.8	186	93.5
Minnie township (Beltrami)	26	26	0.0	38	100.0	0.0	0.0	0.0	0.0	7.9	42.1	59.7	73.5	11.8	20	75.0
Mission township (Crow Wing)	815	858	5.3	797	99.5	0.0	0.0	0.0	0.5	16.4	27.0	54.2	35.4	27.2	338	88.8
Mission Creek township (Pine)	635	634	-0.2	724	88.8	0.7	0.0	5.9	4.6	27.8	12.0	39.6	55.8	2.9	218	84.4
Mitchell township (Wilkin) .	85	80	-5.9	73	100.0	0.0	0.0	0.0	0.0	26.0	19.2	48.5	9.8	41.2	28	96.4
Mizpah city	56	52	-7.1	76	76.3	0.0	0.0	23.7	0.0	27.6	17.1	38.0	62.0	6.0	24	79.2
Moe township (Douglas)...	784	816	4.1	697	98.0	0.0	0.6	1.0	0.4	18.8	28.3	50.8	25.2	31.4	310	95.2
Moland township (Clay)....	299	313	4.7	249	92.4	0.0	0.0	2.0	5.6	10.8	16.5	51.5	35.9	29.8	107	91.6
Moltke township (Sibley)...	279	274	-1.8	263	98.5	0.0	0.0	1.5	0.0	20.9	23.2	49.6	39.2	19.1	114	82.5
Money Creek township (Houston)	590	589	-0.2	522	99.0	0.0	0.0	1.0	0.0	19.5	19.2	48.5	38.9	17.6	234	89.7
Monroe township (Lyon) ...	204	202		209	88.5	0.0	1.4	0.0	10.0	25.8	20.6	41.2	50.0	19.7	93	81.7
Monson township (Traverse)	133	125	-6.0	63	100.0	0.0	0.0	0.0	0.0	22.2	34.9	45.9	44.7	25.5	31	67.7
Montevideo city & MCD (Chippewa)	5,361	5,043	-5.9	5,108	83.1	1.6	2.0	2.3	11.0	21.5	20.9	41.0	48.2	18.0	2,426	78.6
Montgomery city & MCD (Le Sueur)	2,948	3,050	3.5	2,977	87.1	2.0	0.0	4.9	5.9	26.2	13.8	38.7	43.7	13.3	1,177	91.2
Montgomery township (Le Sueur)	667	699	4.8	758	98.3	0.0	0.0	0.0	1.7	26.4	13.7	41.8	49.4	19.2	299	80.6
Monticello city & MCD (Wright)	12,793	13,824	8.1	13,583	86.1	1.2	1.2	3.3	8.2	27.7	11.7	33.7	44.0	19.3	5,092	92.0
Monticello township (Wright)	3,147	3,347	6.4	3,280	96.2	0.9	0.2	1.2	1.4	27.4	12.5	41.3	42.0	21.2	1,091	97.3
Montrose city & MCD (Wright)	2,837	3,317	16.9	3,182	87.7	1.6	0.9	5.8	3.9	34.1	7.4	32.4	39.2	20.7	1,081	95.2
Moonshine township (Big Stone)	102	100	-2.0	165	100.0	0.0	0.0	0.0	0.0	44.8	10.9	34.6	42.2	18.9	47	100.0
Moore township (Stevens)	244	250	2.5	322	67.1	0.0	0.0	0.0	32.9	38.2	5.6	30.6	54.5	27.2	65	95.4

1 May be of any race.

Table A. All Places — Population and Housing

STATE City, town, township, borough, or CDP (county if applicable)	2010 census total population	2019 estimated population	Percent change 2010–2019	ACS total population estimate 2015–2019	White alone, not Hispanic or Latino	Black alone, not Hispanic or Latino	Asian alone, not Hispanic or Latino	All other races or 2 or more races, not Hispanic or Latino	Hispanic or Latino[1]	Under 18 years old	Age 65 years and older	Median age	Percent High school diploma or less	Percent Bachelor's degree or more	Total	Percent with a computer
	1	2	3	4	5	6	7	8	9	10	11	12	13	14	15	16
MINNESOTA—Con.																
Moorhead city & MCD (Clay)	39,437	43,652	10.7	42,939	85.1	5.1	1.7	3.6	4.5	22.9	12.1	30.4	26.2	37.7	16,495	90.3
Moorhead township (Clay)	186	194	4.3	231	73.2	0.0	1.3	0.9	24.7	29.4	20.8	41.5	34.2	36.8	76	96.1
Moose township (Roseau)	114	108	-5.3	113	100.0	0.0	0.0	0.0	0.0	23.9	21.2	44.9	54.2	15.3	42	88.1
Moose Creek township (Clearwater)	230	232	0.9	232	94.4	0.0	0.0	5.6	0.0	21.6	31.0	53.5	41.7	25.0	94	89.4
Moose Lake township (Beltrami)	228	227	-0.4	238	90.3	0.0	0.0	7.1	2.5	21.4	26.1	49.0	36.5	26.4	94	80.9
Moose Lake city & MCD (Carlton)	2,812	2,815	0.1	2,812	69.8	15.0	0.6	12.1	2.6	7.2	18.6	43.9	59.6	9.4	530	75.7
Moose Lake township (Carlton)	1,012	1,046	3.4	958	96.7	0.0	0.3	2.5	0.5	20.9	24.3	51.7	37.0	23.9	416	87.0
Moose Lake township (Cass)	111	116	4.5	105	100.0	0.0	0.0	0.0	0.0	21.0	21.9	48.7	55.3	15.8	49	71.4
Moose Park township (Itasca)	68	67	-1.5	53	90.6	0.0	0.0	9.4	0.0	11.3	34.0	52.5	66.0	19.1	27	85.2
Moose River township (Marshall)	25	25	0.0	25	76.0	0.0	0.0	24.0	0.0	24.0	12.0	51.8	47.4	21.1	13	100.0
Mora city & MCD (Kanabec)	3,560	3,554	-0.2	3,490	94.5	0.0	0.0	4.6	1.0	21.9	25.8	41.0	48.9	15.9	1,417	86.7
Moran township (Todd)	506	509	0.6	429	91.6	3.0	0.0	5.4	0.0	20.3	24.9	48.7	40.5	15.1	182	80.8
Moranville township (Roseau)	887	837	-5.6	849	87.2	0.0	0.6	11.4	0.8	32.2	14.5	35.1	45.6	15.4	259	86.1
Morcom township (St. Louis)	92	93	1.1	71	98.6	0.0	0.0	1.4	0.0	14.1	28.2	49.9	52.6	19.3	35	65.7
Morgan city & MCD (Redwood)	896	840	-6.3	872	91.4	1.4	0.0	3.4	3.8	28.2	18.8	36.2	45.1	24.5	352	79.3
Morgan township (Redwood)	257	247	-3.9	232	98.3	0.0	0.0	1.7	0.0	20.3	17.2	42.0	35.8	20.5	86	96.5
Morken township (Clay)	156	164	5.1	85	94.1	0.0	0.0	0.0	5.9	10.6	24.7	48.8	25.8	37.1	35	94.3
Morrill township (Morrison)	696	714	2.6	786	95.2	0.0	0.0	3.8	1.0	26.3	15.0	36.4	61.3	12.8	296	82.8
Morris city & MCD (Stevens)	5,288	5,333	0.9	5,334	87.1	2.3	2.9	2.9	4.9	18.0	18.3	31.4	35.9	35.9	2,125	85.9
Morris township (Stevens)	394	403	2.3	365	94.8	0.0	0.0	5.2	0.0	39.5	11.8	23.8	29.8	20.2	121	96.7
Morrison township (Aitkin)	200	198		186	94.6	3.8	0.0	1.6	0.0	18.3	23.7	51.2	66.4	4.9	95	74.7
Morristown city & MCD (Rice)	982	995	1.3	985	99.0	0.6	0.0	0.4	0.0	20.1	20.0	41.7	54.3	15.2	392	87.8
Morristown township (Rice)	702	742	5.7	740	96.2	0.0	0.4	0.0	3.4	22.6	12.7	43.5	44.3	19.8	281	87.5
Morse township (Itasca)	603	603	0.0	671	79.1	0.0	0.0	20.3	0.6	24.9	14.0	39.7	49.7	8.9	240	85.8
Morse township (St. Louis)	1,221	1,228	0.6	1,264	98.4	0.0	0.5	0.4	0.7	11.1	41.1	61.0	25.9	37.9	655	86.4
Morton city & MCD (Renville)	411	374	-9.0	368	88.9	0.0	3.5	7.1	0.5	21.7	17.7	41.8	59.5	6.9	170	80.6
Moscow township (Freeborn)	538	520	-3.3	574	97.2	0.0	0.0	0.0	2.8	15.0	23.7	51.5	45.7	20.8	261	84.3
Motley city	675	660	-2.2	610	95.9	0.0	0.0	1.6	2.5	17.0	24.8	46.4	53.5	7.7	302	81.8
Motley city (Cass)	15	15	0.0	33	100.0	0.0	0.0	0.0	0.0	54.5	12.1	17.8	60.0	13.3	11	100.0
Motley city (Morrison)	660	645	-2.3	577	95.7	0.0	0.0	1.7	2.6	14.9	25.5	47.5	53.3	7.5	291	81.1
Motley township (Morrison)	202	207	2.5	231	100.0	0.0	0.0	0.0	0.0	25.1	17.3	41.8	47.3	19.4	98	93.9
Moulton township (Murray)	206	198	-3.9	167	100.0	0.0	0.0	0.0	0.0	35.3	11.4	39.1	45.0	21.0	53	94.3
Mound city	9,059	9,509	5.0	9,480	93.3	0.6	2.0	3.5	0.7	19.1	14.1	43.5	20.8	42.8	4,118	96.5
Mound township (Rock)	256	251	-2.0	218	99.1	0.0	0.0	0.9	0.0	26.1	11.9	40.2	36.9	33.8	85	95.3
Mound Prairie township (Houston)	606	603	-0.5	607	98.4	0.0	0.0	1.6	0.0	22.7	19.3	51.1	35.1	33.3	267	85.8
Mounds View city & MCD (Ramsey)	12,155	13,324	9.6	13,094	69.3	6.0	8.7	8.4	7.6	25.5	14.6	34.8	33.0	30.8	4,868	88.6
Mountain Iron city & MCD (St. Louis)	2,864	2,834		2,853	95.2	0.2	2.3	2.2	0.0	19.6	20.3	46.6	37.2	21.3	1,338	84.8
Mountain Lake city & MCD (Cottonwood)	2,106	2,037	-3.3	2,092	69.7	1.5	14.2	4.7	9.8	28.0	21.7	37.8	54.5	11.8	899	85.3
Mountain Lake township (Cottonwood)	381	370	-2.9	315	92.1	0.0	0.0	0.0	7.9	24.8	13.7	34.6	43.4	23.2	114	94.7
Mount Morris township (Morrison)	93	94	1.1	58	93.1	0.0	0.0	6.9	0.0	5.2	29.3	53.0	75.6	4.4	26	65.4
Mount Pleasant township (Wabasha)	443	444	0.2	453	99.8	0.0	0.0	0.0	0.2	26.9	13.7	39.8	41.3	19.4	154	91.6
Mount Vernon township (Winona)	272	272	0.0	197	98.0	0.0	1.0	0.0	1.0	19.8	18.8	48.3	32.6	24.3	80	90.0
Moyer township (Swift)	88	83	-5.7	82	98.8	0.0	0.0	1.2	0.0	20.7	19.5	38.3	33.3	24.1	32	100.0
Moylan township (Marshall)	98	97		93	90.3	9.7	0.0	0.0	0.0	9.7	25.8	40.2	54.1	16.4	43	93.0
Mudgett township (Mille Lacs)	84	84	0.0	68	95.6	0.0	0.0	0.0	4.4	16.2	23.5	53.7	57.9	21.1	31	71.0
Mud Lake UT (Marshall)	-	-		-	-	-	-	-	-	-	-	-	-	-	-	-
Mulligan township (Brown)	218	212	-2.8	163	97.5	1.2	0.0	1.2	0.0	18.4	28.2	57.1	65.6	11.7	66	83.3
Munch township (Pine)	301	312	3.7	323	95.4	1.5	0.0	3.1	0.0	8.7	25.7	53.1	51.2	7.0	112	91.1
Munson township (Stearns)	1,469	1,578	7.4	1,632	97.9	0.0	0.4	1.3	0.3	21.1	23.0	47.2	39.4	20.8	599	94.3
Murdock city & MCD (Swift)	278	263	-5.4	280	91.1	0.0	0.0	0.7	8.2	29.6	6.4	28.1	42.5	9.8	107	90.7
Murray township (Murray)	177	171	-3.4	171	97.7	0.0	0.0	2.3	0.0	18.1	28.7	56.5	40.0	21.5	70	92.9
Myrtle city & MCD (Freeborn)	46	45	-2.2	69	100.0	0.0	0.0	0.0	0.0	18.8	29.0	48.3	81.3	6.3	26	46.2
Nashua city & MCD (Wilkin)	68	64	-5.9	79	100.0	0.0	0.0	0.0	0.0	74.7	6.3	13.5	50.0	0.0	10	90.0
Nashville township (Martin)	195	187	-4.1	198	99.5	0.0	0.0	0.5	0.0	12.1	26.8	50.4	42.5	11.8	89	89.9
Nashwauk city	990	952	-3.8	1,151	88.2	1.6	1.1	4.7	4.4	18.2	18.7	40.1	42.5	13.7	541	81.0
Nashwauk township (Itasca)	1,684	1,641	-2.6	1,861	92.5	1.0	0.7	3.1	2.7	19.0	18.0	42.1	40.9	14.7	829	84.3

1 May be of any race.

Table A. All Places — Population and Housing

STATE City, town, township, borough, or CDP (county if applicable)	Population				Race and Hispanic or Latino origin (percent)					Age (percent)			Educational attainment of persons age 25 and older		Occupied housing units	
	2010 census total population	2019 estimated population	Percent change 2010–2019	ACS total population estimate 2015–2019	White alone, not Hispanic or Latino	Black alone, not Hispanic or Latino	Asian alone, not Hispanic or Latino	All other races or 2 or more races, not Hispanic or Latino	Hispanic or Latino[1]	Under 18 years old	Age 65 years and older	Median age	Percent High school diploma or less	Percent Bachelor's degree or more	Total	Percent with a computer
	1	2	3	4	5	6	7	8	9	10	11	12	13	14	15	16
MINNESOTA—Con.																
Nassau city & MCD (Lac qui Parle)	72	67	-6.9	71	100.0	0.0	0.0	0.0	0.0	18.3	21.1	53.6	68.5	3.7	34	82.4
Naytahwaush CDP	578	-	-	463	3.5	0.0	0.0	87.7	8.9	41.3	11.2	24.3	55.6	8.9	151	72.8
Nebish township (Beltrami)	288	287	-0.3	227	96.0	0.0	0.0	4.0	0.0	15.4	18.5	49.8	40.6	28.0	92	83.7
Nelson city & MCD (Douglas)	186	194	4.3	151	96.0	0.0	0.0	1.3	2.6	10.6	17.9	56.4	53.5	11.8	82	85.4
Nelson township (Watonwan)	291	287	-1.4	310	96.5	0.0	0.0	0.0	3.5	23.5	26.1	42.9	42.5	16.8	117	97.4
Nelson Park township (Marshall)	125	123	-1.6	118	100.0	0.0	0.0	0.0	0.0	15.3	29.7	60.0	37.9	3.2	52	92.3
Nereson township (Roseau)	58	55	-5.2	40	100.0	0.0	0.0	0.0	0.0	2.5	10.0	55.3	71.1	10.5	21	85.7
Nerstrand city & MCD (Rice)	295	294	-0.3	329	97.6	0.0	0.0	0.6	1.8	27.4	13.1	35.3	40.6	20.1	123	91.1
Nesbit township (Polk)	99	99	0.0	130	88.5	6.9	0.0	4.6	0.0	36.2	3.1	22.0	11.3	50.0	37	100.0
Ness township (St. Louis)	62	62	0.0	83	97.6	0.0	0.0	1.2	1.2	38.6	12.0	45.9	35.3	11.8	31	96.8
Nessel township (Chisago)	1,944	2,054	5.7	1,758	95.5	1.0	0.3	1.5	1.6	17.3	22.2	52.0	43.1	18.5	701	92.9
Nett Lake CDP	284	-	-	326	4.3	2.1	0.0	92.9	0.6	40.5	10.4	25.6	49.1	6.0	94	67.0
Nett Lake UT (St. Louis)	311	313	0.6	305	3.3	2.3	0.0	92.1	2.3	38.0	8.9	27.3	56.2	2.6	93	73.1
Nevada township (Mower)	338	351	3.8	331	97.9	0.0	0.0	0.0	2.1	16.3	26.9	53.2	38.2	16.9	134	87.3
Nevis city & MCD (Hubbard)	390	414	6.2	403	94.8	0.0	0.0	3.2	2.0	24.3	24.3	44.1	47.1	12.8	190	88.9
Nevis township (Hubbard)	1,009	1,037	2.8	993	97.7	2.0	0.0	0.0	0.3	21.3	27.3	53.0	27.4	29.6	381	90.6
New Auburn city & MCD (Sibley)	456	437	-4.2	531	93.8	0.0	0.0	0.0	6.2	20.0	16.6	33.9	63.1	6.5	224	88.4
New Auburn township (Sibley)	417	411	-1.4	391	99.7	0.0	0.3	0.0	0.0	25.3	16.4	49.3	42.5	20.4	161	85.1
New Avon township (Redwood)	191	182	-4.7	166	100.0	0.0	0.0	0.0	0.0	20.5	15.7	50.0	32.3	17.7	67	89.6
New Brighton city & MCD (Ramsey)	21,390	22,753	6.4	22,556	74.2	11.9	4.9	2.2	6.8	23.7	17.2	37.5	24.7	48.3	8,859	93.3
Newburg township (Fillmore)	379	398	5.0	394	99.7	0.0	0.3	0.0	0.0	23.1	14.7	36.9	45.6	25.9	144	86.1
New Dosey township (Pine)	74	78	5.4	63	98.4	0.0	0.0	1.6	0.0	20.6	25.4	57.4	42.0	12.0	31	83.9
Newfolden city & MCD (Marshall)	368	363	-1.4	438	97.5	0.0	0.0	1.4	1.1	23.1	18.0	34.3	40.6	18.4	179	86.6
New Folden township (Marshall)	230	227	-1.3	238	99.2	0.0	0.0	0.8	0.0	16.0	21.8	54.5	57.7	12.4	104	92.3
New Germany city & MCD (Carver)	373	419	12.3	466	98.5	0.0	0.4	0.9	0.2	30.3	7.9	31.7	48.2	15.8	177	91.5
New Hartford township (Winona)	894	892	-0.2	806	95.8	0.9	1.4	0.5	1.5	28.3	13.9	38.4	34.9	26.6	293	92.8
New Haven township (Olmsted)	1,183	1,231	4.1	1,249	96.5	0.0	0.8	1.8	1.0	20.1	19.1	52.6	28.8	38.3	501	94.4
New Hope city	20,329	20,907	2.8	20,925	63.4	22.3	3.4	4.6	6.3	23.1	19.2	39.4	35.3	31.6	8,294	88.4
New Independence township (St. Louis)	301	303	0.7	318	96.5	0.0	0.0	2.2	1.3	17.9	11.3	46.5	37.1	19.6	139	93.5
New London city & MCD (Kandiyohi)	1,271	1,420	11.7	1,197	92.7	0.0	0.2	2.8	4.3	22.2	29.6	42.7	40.4	21.2	513	81.5
New London township (Kandiyohi)	2,925	3,017	3.1	2,994	98.6	0.0	1.1	0.0	0.3	21.4	20.3	47.9	23.6	31.3	1,219	90.4
New Maine township (Marshall)	199	196	-1.5	279	99.3	0.0	0.0	0.0	0.7	24.4	17.6	35.5	39.8	21.8	104	100.0
New Market township (Scott)	3,449	3,752	8.8	3,706	97.0	0.1	0.5	2.3	0.1	22.4	13.0	45.4	23.5	44.9	1,276	96.8
New Munich city & MCD (Stearns)	321	324	0.9	305	98.0	0.0	0.0	2.0	0.0	24.6	20.0	35.9	54.8	12.4	124	89.5
Newport city & MCD (Washington)	3,430	3,588	4.6	3,532	78.7	8.4	5.0	2.7	5.2	22.4	14.2	41.1	41.6	19.7	1,422	94.0
New Prague city	7,319	8,263	12.9	7,899	89.4	0.0	2.7	3.8	4.1	28.1	16.1	35.0	38.1	29.6	2,882	88.5
New Prague city (Le Sueur)	3,039	3,397	11.8	3,229	95.0	0.0	0.7	1.3	3.1	31.6	14.5	34.0	36.9	31.0	1,092	95.2
New Prague city (Scott)	4,280	4,866	13.7	4,670	85.5	0.0	4.2	5.5	4.9	25.7	17.3	35.9	39.0	28.7	1,790	84.5
New Prairie township (Pope)	198	207	4.5	209	93.3	0.0	0.0	0.0	6.7	12.4	27.3	49.4	40.2	20.1	89	87.6
New Richland city & MCD (Waseca)	1,212	1,182	-2.5	1,136	95.2	0.0	0.7	0.2	4.0	24.3	21.6	39.0	48.0	13.5	472	87.5
New Richland township (Waseca)	434	439	1.2	444	96.6	0.0	0.0	1.6	1.8	20.9	18.9	50.6	38.2	24.2	179	92.2
Newry township (Freeborn)	450	436	-3.1	548	90.9	0.0	0.0	0.4	8.8	29.6	13.5	36.1	34.2	23.6	206	95.1
New Solum township (Marshall)	325	323	-0.6	316	93.7	0.0	2.2	2.2	1.9	20.3	11.1	41.4	47.5	10.6	127	93.7
New Sweden township (Nicollet)	295	298	1.0	249	96.8	0.0	0.8	0.0	2.4	12.9	25.7	57.8	36.1	28.3	100	92.0
Newton township (Otter Tail)	748	747	-0.1	743	100.0	0.0	0.0	0.0	0.0	24.4	20.2	43.7	41.0	15.5	277	83.4
New Trier city & MCD (Dakota)	108	106	-1.9	93	100.0	0.0	0.0	0.0	0.0	17.2	11.8	39.6	35.4	27.7	32	93.8
New Ulm city & MCD (Brown)	13,524	13,212	-2.3	13,242	91.9	1.2	1.1	1.2	4.6	19.5	20.8	40.4	38.9	25.8	5,716	90.1
New York Mills city & MCD (Otter Tail)	1,197	1,223	2.2	1,307	97.0	0.4	0.1	1.8	0.8	28.0	17.8	37.8	44.1	14.5	525	79.6
Nickerson township (Pine)	167	171	2.4	169	97.6	0.0	0.0	2.4	0.0	24.9	20.1	49.8	41.8	13.1	65	89.2
Nicollet city & MCD (Nicollet)	1,090	1,169	7.2	1,250	87.4	0.0	0.0	0.0	12.6	26.8	9.9	31.2	35.9	19.6	466	94.8
Nicollet township (Nicollet)	530	535	0.9	537	99.8	0.0	0.0	0.0	0.2	18.8	20.7	46.8	39.7	28.2	207	90.8
Nidaros township (Otter Tail)	323	319	-1.2	268	93.3	0.0	0.0	3.7	3.0	10.8	37.7	61.1	27.2	23.4	133	92.5

1 May be of any race.

Table A. All Places — **Population and Housing**

STATE City, town, township, borough, or CDP (county if applicable)	2010 census total population	2019 estimated population	Percent change 2010–2019	ACS total population estimate 2015–2019	White alone, not Hispanic or Latino	Black alone, not Hispanic or Latino	Asian alone, not Hispanic or Latino	All other races or 2 or more races, not Hispanic or Latino	Hispanic or Latino[1]	Under 18 years old	Age 65 years and older	Median age	Percent High school diploma or less	Percent Bachelor's degree or more	Total	Percent with a computer
	1	2	3	4	5	6	7	8	9	10	11	12	13	14	15	16
Nielsville city & MCD (Polk)	87	82	-5.7	115	69.6	0.0	0.0	0.0	30.4	29.6	8.7	30.8	58.6	10.0	39	94.9
Nilsen township (Wilkin) ...	60	59	-1.7	63	100.0	0.0	0.0	0.0	0.0	34.9	0.0	21.6	30.0	14.8	23	100.0
Nimrod city & MCD (Wadena)	69	64	-7.2	102	100.0	0.0	0.0	0.0	0.0	28.4	20.6	37.5	37.5	4.2	42	81.0
Nininger township (Dakota)	898	925	3.0	887	98.4	0.0	0.1	0.8	0.7	21.5	18.7	48.4	33.2	29.1	338	94.4
Nisswa city & MCD (Crow Wing)	1,959	2,096	7.0	1,817	95.4	0.0	0.8	1.8	1.9	20.3	27.1	48.9	20.9	44.2	748	92.6
Nokay Lake township (Crow Wing)	826	871	5.4	869	95.7	0.0	0.0	1.0	3.2	27.8	19.9	40.9	42.3	22.5	321	95.0
Nora township (Clearwater)	442	447	1.1	570	85.4	0.0	0.0	4.4	10.2	27.9	15.4	40.9	48.5	15.5	197	91.9
Nora township (Pope)	205	215	4.9	180	98.9	1.1	0.0	0.0	0.0	25.6	13.3	47.4	30.5	25.8	76	86.8
Norcross city & MCD (Grant)	70	70	0.0	46	91.3	0.0	0.0	8.7	0.0	8.7	28.3	37.0	32.5	2.5	28	85.7
Norden township (Pennington)	379	373	-1.6	492	100.0	0.0	0.0	0.0	0.0	19.3	13.4	46.4	34.9	15.1	175	94.3
Nordick township (Wilkin) .	87	84	-3.4	35	100.0	0.0	0.0	0.0	0.0	20.0	25.7	57.5	30.8	38.5	17	82.4
Nordland township (Aitkin)	970	964	-0.6	942	98.6	0.2	0.0	0.2	1.0	14.2	37.8	60.0	42.9	18.1	449	92.7
Nordland township (Lyon).	213	212	-0.5	216	93.5	0.0	0.5	6.0	0.0	21.3	12.0	45.5	38.1	23.1	80	97.5
Nore township (Itasca)	64	64	0.0	104	62.5	0.0	0.0	37.5	0.0	26.9	12.5	30.4	35.0	8.3	33	93.9
Norfolk township (Renville)	161	151	-6.2	118	92.4	0.0	1.7	1.7	4.2	19.5	11.9	45.0	40.7	27.2	49	87.8
Norman township (Pine)...	248	262	5.6	326	91.7	0.0	0.0	8.3	0.0	34.4	18.4	33.2	50.0	16.3	97	95.9
Norman township (Yellow Medicine)	266	251	-5.6	205	100.0	0.0	0.0	0.0	0.0	29.3	14.6	42.3	43.9	24.2	70	87.1
Normania township (Yellow Medicine)	191	181	-5.2	270	95.2	0.0	0.0	0.0	4.8	21.9	11.5	27.9	39.6	22.5	102	93.1
Normanna township (St. Louis)	788	795	0.9	910	94.6	1.9	0.3	1.9	1.3	32.7	12.0	38.0	23.2	40.0	309	92.6
North township (Pennington)	673	688	2.2	714	97.5	0.0	0.3	2.2	0.0	25.8	14.1	37.0	30.4	24.5	243	93.4
North Beltrami UT (Beltrami)	34	34	0.0	61	95.1	0.0	4.9	0.0	0.0	9.8	8.2	52.4	41.8	18.2	28	100.0
North Branch city & MCD (Chisago)	10,125	10,767	6.3	10,454	93.3	0.5	1.8	1.5	2.9	23.6	12.6	38.1	41.3	18.5	3,775	89.2
North Branch township (Isanti)	1,779	1,849	3.9	1,706	92.7	0.1	1.3	3.3	2.5	19.0	16.4	46.3	39.6	18.7	663	91.0
North Carlton UT (Carlton)	983	1,017	3.5	951	80.4	1.1	0.0	18.2	0.3	23.2	17.2	46.3	49.7	19.1	371	86.0
North Cass UT (Cass)	261	273	4.6	151	55.0	0.0	0.0	45.0	0.0	14.6	37.1	49.6	43.4	37.2	89	75.3
North Central Cass UT (Cass)	28	29	3.6	-	-	-	-	-	-	-	-	-	-	-	-	-
North Clearwater UT (Clearwater)	87	88	1.1	39	0.0	0.0	0.0	74.4	25.6	0.0	28.2	64.2	100.0	0.0	29	37.9
Northeast Aitkin UT (Aitkin)	11	11	0.0	7	100.0	0.0	0.0	0.0	0.0	0.0	0.0	0.0	0.0	0.0	4	100.0
Northeast Itasca UT (Itasca)	1,181	1,173	-0.7	1,275	93.2	2.2	0.6	2.6	1.4	13.5	31.5	56.6	34.6	11.3	574	91.1
Northeast St. Louis UT (St. Louis)	252	255	1.2	232	100.0	0.0	0.0	0.0	0.0	0.0	36.2	60.9	38.9	28.1	142	94.4
Northern township (Beltrami)	3,954	4,126	4.4	4,104	81.3	1.9	2.3	12.2	2.3	28.1	15.0	35.3	22.0	50.9	1,658	90.5
Northfield city	20,017	20,742	3.6	20,347	82.3	2.0	3.8	2.9	8.9	17.4	14.8	27.2	23.4	47.4	6,321	93.4
Northfield city (Dakota)	1,147	1,206	5.1	991	90.0	0.8	3.1	6.1	0.0	21.4	29.4	50.9	16.6	60.9	374	97.3
Northfield city (Rice)	18,870	19,536	3.5	19,356	81.9	2.0	3.9	2.8	9.4	17.2	14.1	24.7	23.9	46.3	5,947	93.2
Northfield township (Rice)	832	876	5.3	853	96.7	0.0	0.1	0.9	2.2	19.8	18.5	49.3	25.8	42.7	330	94.8
North Fork township (Stearns)	246	266	8.1	305	100.0	0.0	0.0	0.0	0.0	32.5	10.5	29.3	39.4	16.3	99	82.8
North Germany township (Wadena)	313	309	-1.3	262	93.5	0.0	0.0	4.2	2.3	27.1	25.2	44.0	48.9	10.6	118	85.6
North Hero township (Redwood)	161	154	-4.3	168	89.9	0.0	10.1	0.0	0.0	20.2	22.0	46.6	44.5	25.2	69	89.9
Northland township (Polk)	160	163	1.9	246	94.7	0.0	0.0	0.8	4.5	25.2	17.5	43.5	30.7	19.0	94	84.0
Northland township (St. Louis)	167	168	0.6	196	89.3	0.0	1.5	9.2	0.0	17.3	9.7	49.3	43.8	20.1	71	98.6
North Mankato city	13,403	13,948	4.1	13,778	88.5	4.1	1.2	3.5	2.7	25.1	15.3	37.5	25.6	40.3	5,827	91.2
North Mankato city (Blue Earth)	-	-	-	-	-	-	-	-	-	-	-	-	-	-	-	-
North Mankato city (Nicollet)	13,403	13,948	4.1	13,778	88.5	4.1	1.2	3.5	2.7	25.1	15.3	37.5	25.6	40.3	5,827	91.2
North Oaks city & MCD (Ramsey)	4,469	5,351	19.7	5,177	89.8	0.8	7.0	1.0	1.4	17.5	33.6	55.9	9.8	74.5	2,100	88.2
Northome city	205	188	-8.3	218	97.2	0.0	0.5	0.5	1.8	21.1	31.7	53.8	54.2	10.8	97	71.1
North Ottawa township (Grant)	50	50	0.0	31	100.0	0.0	0.0	0.0	0.0	22.6	38.7	50.5	12.5	41.7	15	86.7
North Red River UT (Kittson)	-	-	-	-	-	-	-	-	-	-	-	-	-	-	-	-
Northrop city & MCD (Martin)	227	213	-6.2	179	98.3	0.0	0.0	0.0	1.7	14.0	31.8	55.9	49.3	14.6	100	92.0
North Roseau UT (Roseau)	139	134	-3.6	155	100.0	0.0	0.0	0.0	0.0	54.2	13.5	15.5	0.0	0.0	43	100.0
North St. Paul city & MCD (Ramsey)	11,460	12,506	9.1	12,406	66.8	8.6	12.5	6.1	6.0	22.7	14.3	34.9	40.1	27.3	4,808	93.7
North Star township (Brown)	282	276	-2.1	237	99.2	0.0	0.0	0.0	0.8	24.9	15.2	42.4	35.6	19.5	99	89.9
North Star township (St. Louis)	192	194	1.0	222	91.9	0.0	0.9	4.1	3.2	17.1	23.0	52.5	22.1	35.5	93	93.5
Northwest Aitkin UT (Aitkin)	342	338	-1.2	265	97.0	0.0	0.0	3.0	0.0	10.6	46.8	62.9	45.1	10.1	149	67.8
Northwest Roseau UT (Roseau)	25	24	-4.0	67	100.0	0.0	0.0	0.0	0.0	50.7	9.0	4.0	100.0	0.0	21	71.4

1   May be of any race.

Table A. All Places — **Population and Housing**

STATE City, town, township, borough, or CDP (county if applicable)	Population				Race and Hispanic or Latino origin (percent)					Age (percent)			Educational attainment of persons age 25 and older		Occupied housing units	
	2010 census total population	2019 estimated population	Percent change 2010–2019	ACS total population estimate 2015–2019	White alone, not Hispanic or Latino	Black alone, not Hispanic or Latino	Asian alone, not Hispanic or Latino	All other races or 2 or more races, not Hispanic or Latino	Hispanic or Latino[1]	Under 18 years old	Age 65 years and older	Median age	Percent High school diploma or less	Percent Bachelor's degree or more	Total	Percent with a computer
	1	2	3	4	5	6	7	8	9	10	11	12	13	14	15	16
MINNESOTA—Con.																
Northwest St. Louis UT (St. Louis)	304	306	0.7	276	100.0	0.0	0.0	0.0	0.0	17.8	12.3	50.5	60.5	8.8	104	83.7
Norton township (Winona)	486	483	-0.6	449	97.6	0.2	0.4	1.8	0.0	23.2	19.6	46.3	44.3	28.8	182	88.5
Norway township (Fillmore)	343	358	4.4	313	84.0	0.0	0.0	0.0	16.0	30.7	11.5	35.1	54.5	18.0	112	85.7
Norway township (Kittson)	89	85	-4.5	83	92.8	4.8	0.0	2.4	0.0	18.1	37.3	44.8	52.4	9.5	40	65.0
Norway Lake township (Kandiyohi)	274	281	2.6	226	100.0	0.0	0.0	0.0	0.0	15.9	24.8	54.2	34.4	18.3	99	86.9
Norwegian Grove township (Otter Tail)	300	300	0.0	239	98.3	0.0	0.4	1.3	0.0	22.2	13.0	45.8	26.9	25.7	98	89.8
Norwood Young America city & MCD (Carver)	3,569	3,769	5.6	3,725	92.2	3.6	0.0	3.4	0.8	23.4	13.1	35.3	38.2	26.7	1,450	88.8
Nowthen city & MCD (Anoka)	4,442	4,741	6.7	4,682	89.3	0.7	2.0	4.7	3.3	25.9	10.8	38.7	30.8	29.4	1,442	96.3
Numedal township (Pennington)	90	89	-1.1	109	98.2	0.0	0.0	0.0	1.8	41.3	11.9	24.9	18.5	42.6	39	84.6
Nunda township (Freeborn)	320	309	-3.4	382	91.4	0.0	3.4	1.8	3.4	19.6	23.6	49.6	45.7	15.5	145	92.4
Oak township (Stearns)	595	625	5.0	662	94.6	0.0	0.0	0.6	4.8	31.9	12.1	35.2	55.0	17.8	216	87.5
Oakdale city & MCD (Washington)	27,364	27,933	2.1	27,963	72.9	9.4	9.2	3.9	4.6	20.5	16.3	39.6	34.7	31.7	11,299	91.4
Oak Grove city & MCD (Anoka)	8,046	8,917	10.8	8,682	90.4	0.8	5.0	2.3	1.5	23.8	12.6	40.9	33.5	28.8	2,987	95.4
Oakland township (Freeborn)	396	382	-3.5	347	96.3	0.0	0.9	0.9	2.0	26.5	19.0	40.3	31.8	21.3	131	91.6
Oakland township (Mahnomen)	295	302	2.4	294	66.3	0.0	0.7	33.0	0.0	25.9	17.3	48.2	49.2	19.1	110	80.0
Oak Lawn township (Crow Wing)	1,781	1,871	5.1	1,949	95.4	0.0	0.6	0.5	3.5	24.9	14.1	37.9	41.5	18.5	717	96.7
Oak Park township (Marshall)	131	129	-1.5	114	100.0	0.0	0.0	0.0	0.0	20.2	4.4	31.5	51.1	20.5	52	96.2
Oak Park Heights city & MCD (Washington)	4,431	5,003	12.9	4,889	84.4	5.3	1.8	6.2	2.3	12.0	27.2	46.1	39.4	28.9	2,027	86.0
Oakport township (Clay)	413	438	6.1	592	99.5	0.0	0.0	0.0	0.5	34.0	7.6	37.4	26.4	31.9	200	96.5
Oak Valley township (Otter Tail)	355	354	-0.3	379	99.5	0.0	0.0	0.0	0.5	32.7	12.4	37.3	53.5	7.5	146	85.6
Oakwood township (Wabasha)	394	394	0.0	358	98.3	0.0	0.0	0.0	1.7	21.5	16.5	49.5	46.4	16.0	146	94.5
O'Brien township (Beltrami)	58	57	-1.7	22	100.0	0.0	0.0	0.0	0.0	0.0	4.5	59.3	77.3	9.1	12	100.0
Odessa city & MCD (Big Stone)	135	131	-3.0	115	100.0	0.0	0.0	0.0	0.0	12.2	30.4	50.2	50.5	14.0	62	79.0
Odessa township (Big Stone)	132	130	-1.5	104	100.0	0.0	0.0	0.0	0.0	22.1	26.9	53.0	45.7	19.8	45	84.4
Odin city & MCD (Watonwan)	106	105	-0.9	128	93.0	0.0	0.0	0.0	7.0	34.4	21.9	32.7	42.9	6.0	53	96.2
Odin township (Watonwan)	170	167	-1.8	123	100.0	0.0	0.0	0.0	0.0	13.0	37.4	49.9	42.9	24.8	57	91.2
Ogema city & MCD (Becker)	184	185	0.5	214	37.4	0.0	1.9	55.6	5.1	39.7	5.1	26.3	46.1	16.5	73	84.9
Ogema township (Pine)	356	351	-1.4	296	46.6	0.0	0.0	51.7	1.7	22.6	16.9	44.0	61.5	5.0	107	70.1
Ogilvie city & MCD (Kanabec)	377	374	-0.8	492	92.1	2.4	0.6	2.8	2.0	33.5	14.4	30.7	53.2	11.3	179	83.2
Okabena city & MCD (Jackson)	211	195	-7.6	240	90.0	0.0	5.4	0.0	4.6	22.9	18.3	43.8	41.2	26.6	102	90.2
Oklee city & MCD (Red Lake)	435	429	-1.4	464	88.8	0.0	0.0	11.2	0.0	29.1	19.2	39.0	51.7	13.3	186	83.3
Olivia city & MCD (Renville)	2,516	2,335	-7.2	2,471	86.3	0.4	0.6	0.6	12.1	23.5	20.6	39.4	45.3	17.6	1,025	85.4
Olney township (Nobles)	193	194	0.5	184	98.4	1.6	0.0	0.0	0.0	33.7	19.6	32.5	32.4	18.5	63	92.1
Omro township (Yellow Medicine)	161	152	-5.6	66	100.0	0.0	0.0	0.0	0.0	16.7	7.6	44.7	30.0	14.0	30	83.3
Onamia city & MCD (Mille Lacs)	878	864	-1.6	946	70.7	4.8	0.0	20.0	4.5	28.1	23.6	42.1	52.4	19.4	353	78.5
Onamia township (Mille Lacs)	567	580	2.3	511	96.7	0.0	0.0	2.9	0.4	16.2	18.0	46.5	56.0	10.8	204	83.8
Onstad township (Polk)	71	71	0.0	53	100.0	0.0	0.0	0.0	0.0	20.8	32.1	47.8	31.0	28.6	20	95.0
Orange township (Douglas)	313	326	4.2	382	96.1	0.0	0.0	3.4	0.5	22.0	17.0	42.0	40.4	9.6	147	81.0
Orion township (Olmsted)	592	605	2.2	664	99.5	0.0	0.0	0.5	0.0	22.3	20.5	42.9	39.8	27.2	266	85.7
Ormsby city	131	122	-6.9	133	98.5	0.0	0.0	0.0	1.5	19.5	35.3	37.5	70.7	3.7	51	68.6
Ormsby city (Martin)	56	51	-8.9	23	100.0	0.0	0.0	0.0	0.0	13.0	78.3	70.8	85.0	0.0	14	71.4
Ormsby city (Watonwan)	75	71	-5.3	110	98.2	0.0	0.0	0.0	1.8	20.9	26.4	32.0	66.1	4.8	37	67.6
Orono city	7,423	8,339	12.3	8,113	96.7	0.0	1.7	1.0	0.6	23.6	18.7	48.2	14.5	65.3	3,089	98.2
Oronoco city & MCD (Olmsted)	1,301	1,525	17.2	1,577	94.4	0.0	3.2	0.5	1.8	35.3	9.3	36.7	19.3	51.0	529	96.6
Oronoco township (Olmsted)	2,232	2,301	3.1	2,162	95.0	0.5	2.3	1.4	0.7	22.8	16.9	51.6	23.1	44.8	865	90.9
Orr city & MCD (St. Louis)	267	334	25.1	241	73.4	0.0	0.0	25.3	1.2	19.5	16.6	49.8	48.1	16.0	118	80.5
Orrock township (Sherburne)	3,451	3,763	9.0	3,652	93.8	0.7	2.8	1.3	1.4	24.1	12.2	39.7	34.7	25.9	1,284	95.6
Orton township (Wadena)	204	203	-0.5	176	96.6	0.0	0.0	0.0	3.4	17.6	31.8	56.5	54.3	10.9	92	76.1
Ortonville city & MCD (Big Stone)	1,921	1,782	-7.2	1,984	93.1	0.0	0.0	3.4	3.5	17.8	26.2	45.0	57.3	11.8	983	84.3
Ortonville township (Big Stone)	94	92	-2.1	74	100.0	0.0	0.0	0.0	0.0	40.5	12.2	41.5	34.1	31.8	27	96.3
Orwell township (Otter Tail)	170	180	5.9	88	85.2	0.0	0.0	13.6	1.1	20.5	8.0	41.5	37.3	15.3	30	93.3
Osage CDP	323	-		317	98.1	0.0	0.0	0.0	1.9	21.1	24.0	42.4	42.4	18.2	121	88.4
Osage township (Becker)	895	952	6.4	863	95.5	0.0	0.0	2.1	2.4	27.3	18.1	38.9	40.5	18.9	318	89.9
Osakis city	1,742	1,744	0.1	1,745	97.0	0.0	0.0	1.4	1.5	22.7	25.8	46.9	40.2	22.5	798	87.3
Osakis city (Douglas)	1,591	1,596	0.3	1,601	96.8	0.0	0.0	1.6	1.7	24.1	25.1	46.1	42.7	21.7	723	86.4

1 May be of any race.

Table A. All Places — **Population and Housing**

STATE City, town, township, borough, or CDP (county if applicable)	2010 census total population	2019 estimated population	Percent change 2010–2019	ACS total population estimate 2015–2019	White alone, not Hispanic or Latino	Black alone, not Hispanic or Latino	Asian alone, not Hispanic or Latino	All other races or 2 or more races, not Hispanic or Latino	Hispanic or Latino[1]	Under 18 years old	Age 65 years and older	Median age	Percent High school diploma or less	Percent Bachelor's degree or more	Total	Percent with a computer
	1	2	3	4	5	6	7	8	9	10	11	12	13	14	15	16
MINNESOTA—Con.																
Osakis city (Todd)	151	148	-2.0	144	100.0	0.0	0.0	0.0	0.0	6.9	33.3	60.7	18.7	29.9	75	96.0
Osakis township (Douglas)	596	617	3.5	591	99.0	0.0	0.0	1.0	0.0	24.0	24.0	47.8	44.9	16.9	243	82.3
Osborne township (Pipestone)	286	282	-1.4	301	99.0	0.0	0.0	0.0	1.0	35.9	17.9	40.1	38.8	21.3	100	90.0
Oscar township (Otter Tail)	207	207	0.0	148	91.2	0.0	0.0	0.0	8.8	24.3	18.2	44.3	29.0	35.5	55	89.1
Osceola township (Renville)	158	148	-6.3	117	100.0	0.0	0.0	0.0	0.0	17.1	23.1	54.2	49.5	12.6	56	87.5
Oshawa township (Nicollet)	513	521	1.6	636	90.4	0.0	0.2	0.8	8.6	29.6	10.1	37.2	29.2	45.8	196	94.4
Oshkosh township (Yellow Medicine)	210	197	-6.2	169	92.3	0.0	0.0	7.7	0.0	24.9	35.5	59.8	70.4	8.8	72	76.4
Oslo city & MCD (Marshall)	330	322	-2.4	259	66.8	1.9	0.0	0.0	31.3	19.7	23.6	41.6	48.6	13.3	118	90.7
Osseo city	2,430	2,738	12.7	2,753	83.6	5.0	6.8	2.5	2.1	15.4	27.2	45.8	36.5	23.7	1,273	85.5
Ostrander city & MCD (Fillmore)	254	248	-2.4	282	91.5	0.0	0.0	2.1	6.4	22.0	31.9	41.9	58.7	3.9	115	80.0
Oteneagen township (Itasca)	310	308	-0.6	392	86.7	1.0	0.0	11.7	0.5	31.4	12.8	35.4	39.6	12.8	135	88.1
Otisco township (Waseca)	599	605	1.0	525	91.2	0.8	0.8	0.6	6.7	20.2	21.5	47.2	45.0	15.9	226	80.1
Otrey township (Big Stone)	87	85	-2.3	51	100.0	0.0	0.0	0.0	0.0	13.7	7.8	55.8	27.9	32.6	26	100.0
Otsego city & MCD (Wright)	13,571	18,113	33.5	16,763	90.8	1.9	2.0	3.7	1.5	30.4	9.1	34.3	25.3	36.3	5,669	95.4
Ottawa township (Le Sueur)	286	301	5.2	337	99.4	0.0	0.6	0.0	0.0	24.9	14.5	39.8	26.9	38.4	129	95.3
Ottertail city & MCD (Otter Tail)	577	648	12.3	575	91.8	0.0	0.0	0.2	8.0	19.1	19.7	49.5	41.4	23.4	249	94.8
Otter Tail township (Otter Tail)	486	485	-0.2	495	99.4	0.0	0.2	0.0	0.4	10.7	40.2	61.0	23.1	34.1	249	90.0
Otter Tail Peninsula township (Cass)	54	57	5.6	74	98.6	0.0	0.0	1.4	0.0	2.7	43.2	63.5	43.3	35.8	38	100.0
Otto township (Otter Tail)	554	553	-0.2	485	96.3	0.0	0.0	0.6	3.1	22.9	24.9	47.5	41.3	21.5	209	87.6
Owatonna city & MCD (Steele)	25,622	25,704	0.3	25,685	84.9	4.2	1.3	1.6	7.9	25.0	16.9	38.5	38.5	29.3	10,524	90.5
Owatonna township (Steele)	582	587	0.9	592	95.6	0.0	0.8	0.0	3.5	14.0	17.4	49.8	53.4	16.3	243	84.4
Owens township (St. Louis)	276	276	0.0	231	99.1	0.0	0.0	0.9	0.0	16.5	25.1	51.8	39.9	19.1	100	85.0
Oxford township (Isanti)	888	925	4.2	919	85.6	0.0	7.0	5.8	1.6	19.6	14.8	45.3	38.0	24.5	336	94.3
Paddock township (Otter Tail)	346	348	0.6	407	98.8	0.2	0.0	1.0	0.0	28.7	17.0	38.9	55.3	12.5	147	81.0
Page township (Mille Lacs)	743	754	1.5	715	94.3	0.0	0.0	3.8	2.0	22.2	12.3	40.1	50.7	9.3	257	90.7
Palisade city & MCD (Aitkin)	172	169	-1.7	228	66.7	0.0	0.0	33.3	0.0	28.5	18.4	49.5	57.0	10.1	110	72.7
Palmer township (Sherburne)	2,354	2,554	8.5	2,495	98.1	0.8	0.6	0.0	0.5	19.6	17.2	47.0	36.8	29.8	945	92.1
Palmville township (Roseau)	39	37	-5.1	28	100.0	0.0	0.0	0.0	0.0	7.1	60.7	68.6	34.6	23.1	14	100.0
Palmyra township (Renville)	179	167	-6.7	170	97.1	0.0	1.2	1.8	0.0	19.4	24.1	49.7	31.3	17.9	71	87.3
Park township (Pine)	37	37	0.0	16	100.0	0.0	0.0	0.0	0.0	18.8	31.3	56.0	38.5	23.1	6	100.0
Parke township (Clay)	485	512	5.6	492	92.5	0.0	0.0	2.4	5.1	20.1	19.3	51.9	34.5	27.5	221	92.8
Parker township (Marshall)	35	35	0.0	31	100.0	0.0	0.0	0.0	0.0	16.1	22.6	56.8	33.3	33.3	11	81.8
Parker township (Morrison)	470	480	2.1	478	99.6	0.0	0.0	0.2	0.2	29.1	12.3	35.0	45.9	13.0	188	85.1
Parkers Prairie city & MCD (Otter Tail)	1,011	997	-1.4	1,086	98.8	0.0	0.1	0.7	0.4	23.7	23.7	37.8	48.7	9.7	410	79.3
Parkers Prairie township (Otter Tail)	348	347	-0.3	416	100.0	0.0	0.0	0.0	0.0	26.2	12.3	40.7	24.2	22.3	152	94.7
Park Rapids city & MCD (Hubbard)	3,856	4,235	9.8	4,054	84.8	1.7	0.4	6.6	6.5	24.1	21.4	36.0	46.7	21.8	1,701	81.1
Parnell township (Polk)	64	64	0.0	31	100.0	0.0	0.0	0.0	0.0	9.7	0.0	45.2	77.3	4.5	15	100.0
Parnell township (Traverse)	60	56	-6.7	36	100.0	0.0	0.0	0.0	0.0	27.8	0.0	28.6	15.4	42.3	17	94.1
Partridge township (Pine)	639	635	-0.6	583	94.2	0.5	0.0	1.0	4.3	18.9	27.3	53.0	52.1	20.8	254	83.5
Paxton township (Redwood)	555	536	-3.4	640	48.3	0.0	1.6	38.9	11.3	28.3	14.8	40.8	29.0	26.8	256	93.8
Paynesville city & MCD (Stearns)	2,427	2,519	3.8	2,503	87.7	0.3	1.4	2.2	8.3	24.9	23.6	43.7	45.8	17.7	1,069	81.0
Paynesville township (Stearns)	1,426	1,509	5.8	1,449	98.0	0.0	0.8	1.2	0.0	19.6	22.4	48.6	38.2	28.7	562	90.6
Peace township (Kanabec)	937	978	4.4	1,050	90.4	0.3	0.0	4.5	4.9	17.5	18.2	48.2	49.1	11.8	433	86.8
Pease city & MCD (Mille Lacs)	232	229	-1.3	248	99.2	0.0	0.0	0.8	0.0	27.0	10.1	32.4	42.1	13.8	91	98.9
Peatland UT (Kittson)	9	8	-11.1	4	100.0	0.0	0.0	0.0	0.0	0.0	0.0	0.0	50.0	0.0	2	100.0
Pelan township (Kittson)	45	42	-6.7	49	93.9	0.0	0.0	6.1	0.0	16.3	26.5	38.9	21.6	16.2	21	100.0
Pelican township (Crow Wing)	455	478	5.1	477	97.3	0.0	0.0	1.5	1.3	16.6	33.3	54.9	25.8	32.1	192	92.2
Pelican township (Otter Tail)	628	631	0.5	506	96.6	0.0	0.4	1.0	2.0	14.2	21.3	53.1	33.4	24.4	222	93.7
Pelican Lake township (Grant)	451	451	0.0	521	94.6	0.0	0.0	0.0	5.4	27.4	29.9	50.8	44.2	19.7	196	96.4
Pelican Rapids city & MCD (Otter Tai	2,461	2,552	3.7	2,487	45.5	11.5	6.2	3.0	33.9	29.9	12.6	35.7	62.7	12.8	902	76.4
Pemberton city & MCD (Blue Earth)	250	241	-3.6	240	96.7	0.0	0.0	0.0	3.3	27.9	12.9	40.4	50.3	12.9	97	82.5
Pembina township (Mahnomen)	709	725	2.3	753	42.0	0.0	0.1	55.8	2.1	33.6	9.4	28.4	54.8	7.7	245	75.9
Penn township (McLeod)	316	308	-2.5	381	87.4	0.0	0.3	7.6	4.7	28.3	18.6	40.6	49.8	16.0	134	84.3

1 May be of any race.

Table A. All Places — **Population and Housing**

STATE City, town, township, borough, or CDP (county if applicable)	Population				Race and Hispanic or Latino origin (percent)					Age (percent)			Educational attainment of persons age 25 and older		Occupied housing units	
	2010 census total population	2019 estimated population	Percent change 2010–2019	ACS total population estimate 2015–2019	White alone, not Hispanic or Latino	Black alone, not Hispanic or Latino	Asian alone, not Hispanic or Latino	All other races or 2 or more races, not Hispanic or Latino	Hispanic or Latino[1]	Under 18 years old	Age 65 years and older	Median age	Percent High school diploma or less	Percent Bachelor's degree or more	Total	Percent with a computer
	1	2	3	4	5	6	7	8	9	10	11	12	13	14	15	16
MINNESOTA—Con.																
Pennock city & MCD (Kandiyohi)	508	513	1.0	557	74.3	0.0	0.0	1.6	24.1	23.9	5.7	30.7	41.9	5.0	190	96.8
Pepin township (Wabasha)	378	379	0.3	342	98.8	0.0	0.0	0.3	0.9	8.8	30.4	59.4	36.6	28.2	159	96.2
Pepperton township (Stevens)	134	135	0.7	120	89.2	0.0	2.5	8.3	0.0	11.7	28.3	52.6	47.5	20.0	41	90.2
Pequaywan township (St. Louis)	130	130	0.0	121	100.0	0.0	0.0	0.0	0.0	2.5	47.1	64.3	26.7	25.9	67	97.0
Pequot Lakes city & MCD (Crow Wing)	2,162	2,299	6.3	2,179	97.4	1.2	0.2	0.0	1.1	23.8	15.8	36.3	32.8	32.4	875	88.3
Perch Lake township (Carlton)	1,043	1,077	3.3	1,009	63.2	0.3	0.3	34.2	2.0	19.6	16.6	44.7	36.5	18.1	410	82.0
Percy township (Kittson)	39	37	-5.1	140	85.7	7.1	7.1	0.0	0.0	2.1	60.0	72.9	15.3	71.5	12	83.3
Perham city & MCD (Otter Tail)	3,006	3,645	21.3	3,432	87.2	1.4	0.6	1.7	9.0	22.9	23.8	40.9	47.5	25.2	1,646	79.0
Perham township (Otter Tail)	806	890	10.4	785	97.5	0.6	0.0	1.7	0.3	23.9	20.1	45.4	33.3	26.5	322	92.5
Perley city & MCD (Norman)	92	83	-9.8	76	92.1	0.0	0.0	7.9	0.0	10.5	11.8	47.5	45.5	10.6	40	95.0
Perry township (Lac qui Parle)	101	93	-7.9	68	86.8	0.0	13.2	0.0	0.0	17.6	14.7	55.5	55.4	8.9	34	97.1
Perry Lake township (Crow Wing)	302	318	5.3	348	91.1	3.4	0.0	1.7	3.7	17.0	23.9	53.7	48.7	19.3	126	90.5
Petersburg township (Jackson)	232	224	-3.4	218	98.6	0.0	0.0	0.0	1.4	18.8	15.6	51.5	23.8	22.5	102	78.4
Peterson city & MCD (Fillmore)	198	198	0.0	188	100.0	0.0	0.0	0.0	0.0	11.7	37.2	58.2	52.3	18.1	99	88.9
Pickerel Lake township (Freeborn)	669	648	-3.1	610	98.9	0.0	0.8	0.0	0.3	23.9	19.2	46.8	37.3	24.5	240	93.8
Pierz city & MCD (Morrison)	1,387	1,365	-1.6	1,697	96.7	0.0	0.2	1.9	1.1	28.8	21.9	36.2	49.4	16.0	625	79.5
Pierz township (Morrison)	537	547	1.9	566	98.8	0.7	0.4	0.2	0.0	33.7	11.0	34.6	54.5	14.0	174	89.1
Pike township (St. Louis)	416	418	0.5	445	91.9	0.0	0.0	8.1	0.0	18.7	33.7	58.0	34.4	25.0	207	83.1
Pike Bay township (Cass)	1,615	1,697	5.1	1,802	20.3	0.2	0.6	70.6	8.3	39.0	10.1	26.0	51.4	11.1	604	83.9
Pike Creek township (Morrison)	956	974	1.9	997	93.9	0.0	0.2	3.7	2.2	22.8	20.7	49.0	53.1	12.4	380	85.8
Pillager city & MCD (Cass)	465	483	3.9	419	97.4	1.4	0.0	0.0	1.2	25.8	15.5	30.6	38.1	9.2	191	83.2
Pillsbury township (Swift)	255	246	-3.5	300	99.3	0.0	0.0	0.7	0.0	21.3	15.3	38.5	27.7	16.9	123	95.1
Pilot Grove township (Faribault)	156	149	-4.5	136	100.0	0.0	0.0	0.0	0.0	24.3	12.5	50.0	38.9	21.1	60	90.0
Pilot Mound township (Fillmore)	338	356	5.3	322	99.4	0.0	0.6	0.0	0.0	21.7	14.6	47.7	29.3	36.0	130	94.6
Pine Bend CDP	28	-	-	56	12.5	33.9	0.0	53.6	0.0	25.0	25.0	37.5	69.7	0.0	15	53.3
Pine City city & MCD (Pine)	3,132	3,146	0.4	3,100	94.4	1.6	0.9	2.0	1.1	17.0	26.4	43.9	40.7	19.4	1,369	86.0
Pine City township (Pine)	1,394	1,369	-1.8	1,393	91.7	0.8	0.0	3.2	4.2	22.9	15.1	44.2	47.9	14.7	480	92.1
Pine Island city	3,265	3,475	6.4	3,600	96.3	1.8	0.4	1.1	0.5	29.6	14.3	35.0	29.3	37.5	1,406	92.6
Pine Island city (Goodhue)	2,562	2,724	6.3	2,644	95.6	2.5	0.5	1.4	0.0	24.4	17.3	35.8	37.0	29.1	1,137	90.9
Pine Island city (Olmsted)	703	751	6.8	956	98.2	0.0	0.0	0.0	1.8	43.8	6.1	31.8	4.3	65.2	269	100.0
Pine Island township (Goodhue)	538	533	-0.9	624	96.8	1.4	1.4	0.3	0.0	26.4	15.5	39.0	28.1	29.5	233	88.4
Pine Lake township (Cass)	207	217	4.8	218	95.0	0.0	1.4	3.7	0.0	12.8	45.9	63.7	24.9	37.0	116	89.7
Pine Lake township (Clearwater)	414	420	1.4	418	91.9	0.0	0.0	6.9	1.2	29.9	16.5	35.8	45.4	15.8	133	82.0
Pine Lake township (Otter Tail)	639	641	0.3	619	99.2	0.2	0.0	0.0	0.6	19.2	21.6	52.6	24.7	32.8	265	94.0
Pine Lake township (Pine)	583	568	-2.6	619	89.7	0.3	0.2	8.2	1.6	17.1	27.8	53.3	54.9	12.3	236	84.7
Pine Point CDP	338	-	-	373	2.1	0.0	0.8	90.9	6.2	38.3	4.0	23.0	59.0	19.7	95	90.5
Pine Point township (Becker)	403	427	6.0	417	12.5	0.0	0.7	81.3	5.5	35.5	7.9	31.5	57.3	16.4	118	85.6
Pine River city & MCD (Cass)	945	927	-1.9	911	87.2	1.2	6.5	2.9	2.3	21.1	23.3	40.2	63.8	14.3	428	76.9
Pine River township (Cass)	1,161	1,225	5.5	1,284	95.6	1.2	1.2	0.6	1.3	24.2	20.2	44.3	47.7	16.0	544	90.3
Pine Springs city & MCD (Washington)	388	391	0.8	444	93.9	1.6	0.7	0.5	3.4	17.3	23.9	45.8	14.0	57.0	164	99.4
Pipestone city & MCD (Pipestone)	4,325	4,046	-6.5	4,092	81.5	0.9	0.0	7.0	10.6	23.7	22.1	41.2	45.2	21.7	1,899	85.6
Plainview city & MCD (Wabasha)	3,340	3,298	-1.3	3,277	92.2	0.3	0.0	0.5	7.0	28.8	15.6	36.8	36.1	23.4	1,281	87.4
Plainview township (Wabasha)	443	445	0.5	457	100.0	0.0	0.0	0.0	0.0	17.9	21.0	55.2	46.4	17.2	214	72.0
Plato city & MCD (McLeod)	320	304	-5.0	252	100.0	0.0	0.0	0.0	0.0	19.8	19.8	40.5	40.5	16.8	113	84.1
Platte township (Morrison)	357	364	2.0	319	98.1	0.0	0.9	0.0	0.9	18.8	25.4	49.3	54.7	9.1	133	84.2
Platte Lake township (Crow Wing)	414	438	5.8	493	99.8	0.0	0.0	0.2	0.0	33.1	13.0	34.7	58.4	10.3	178	84.8
Pleasant Grove township (Olmsted)	805	804	-0.1	680	98.4	0.0	0.4	0.4	0.7	15.6	23.8	53.0	40.8	34.0	308	85.4
Pleasant Hill township (Winona)	531	529	-0.4	491	99.4	0.0	0.0	0.0	0.6	24.2	15.7	39.6	36.5	13.5	187	86.6
Pleasant Mound township (Blue Earth)	214	212	-0.9	258	99.2	0.0	0.0	0.0	0.8	21.3	16.7	39.5	52.8	17.2	105	83.8
Pleasant Prairie township (Martin)	244	233	-4.5	210	100.0	0.0	0.0	0.0	0.0	26.7	8.1	38.7	50.7	19.6	89	92.1
Pleasant Valley township (Mower)	304	317	4.3	290	97.6	0.0	0.0	1.7	0.7	27.2	14.5	40.0	38.8	25.0	104	89.4
Pleasant View township (Norman)	108	102	-5.6	98	85.7	0.0	0.0	8.2	6.1	10.2	35.7	55.0	51.3	27.5	48	77.1
Pliny township (Aitkin)	109	109	0.0	110	100.0	0.0	0.0	0.0	0.0	18.2	13.6	31.5	72.7	2.6	54	75.9

1 May be of any race.

Table A. All Places — **Population and Housing**

	Population				Race and Hispanic or Latino origin (percent)					Age (percent)			Educational attainment of persons age 25 and older		Occupied housing units	
STATE City, town, township, borough, or CDP (county if applicable)	2010 census total population	2019 estimated population	Percent change 2010–2019	ACS total population estimate 2015–2019	White alone, not Hispanic or Latino	Black alone, not Hispanic or Latino	Asian alone, not Hispanic or Latino	All other races or 2 or more races, not Hispanic or Latino	Hispanic or Latino[1]	Under 18 years old	Age 65 years and older	Median age	Percent High school diploma or less	Percent Bachelor's degree or more	Total	Percent with a computer
	1	2	3	4	5	6	7	8	9	10	11	12	13	14	15	16
MINNESOTA—Con.																
Plummer city & MCD (Red Lake)	291	291	0.0	333	82.3	5.1	0.0	3.9	8.7	31.8	12.9	36.1	40.8	11.8	129	88.4
Plymouth city	70,591	79,768	13.0	78,134	76.3	5.7	9.6	3.3	5.1	23.3	15.3	39.9	14.9	59.5	31,218	96.0
Pohlitz township (Roseau)	34	32	-5.9	36	100.0	0.0	0.0	0.0	0.0	41.7	0.0	32.3	42.9	33.3	13	100.0
Pokegama township (Pine)	2,734	2,654	-2.9	2,647	97.8	0.1	0.3	1.6	0.2	15.9	23.2	52.4	48.1	15.0	1,028	89.3
Polk Centre township (Pennington)	87	190	118.4	48	100.0	0.0	0.0	0.0	0.0	20.8	29.2	49.3	59.4	28.1	17	100.0
Polonia township (Roseau)	34	32	-5.9	17	100.0	0.0	0.0	0.0	0.0	0.0	41.2	57.8	64.7	23.5	10	100.0
Pomme de Terre township (Grant)	133	133	0.0	94	98.9	0.0	0.0	1.1	0.0	13.8	41.5	60.8	64.9	16.9	47	89.4
Pomroy township (Itasca)	39	39	0.0	30	100.0	0.0	0.0	0.0	0.0	43.3	16.7	32.0	20.0	40.0	10	100.0
Pomroy township (Kanabec)	425	426	0.2	415	98.6	0.2	0.0	0.2	1.0	20.0	26.7	52.1	54.4	10.4	174	76.4
Ponemah CDP	724	-	-	742	1.9	0.0	0.8	97.3	0.0	48.4	6.1	20.4	79.2	2.5	176	69.9
Ponto Lake township (Cass)	482	504	4.6	655	98.0	0.8	0.0	0.5	0.8	13.0	40.9	60.2	39.9	25.7	332	85.2
Poplar township (Cass)	170	178	4.7	196	99.0	0.0	0.0	1.0	0.0	17.3	27.0	45.5	63.4	7.0	99	73.7
Poplar Grove township (Roseau)	82	78	-4.9	66	100.0	0.0	0.0	0.0	0.0	36.4	13.6	23.5	51.6	22.6	19	94.7
Poplar River township (Red Lake)	110	107	-2.7	60	100.0	0.0	0.0	0.0	0.0	25.0	33.3	51.5	33.3	44.4	26	76.9
Popple township (Clearwater)	529	537	1.5	488	92.8	0.0	0.0	4.5	2.7	25.8	16.6	41.7	41.9	19.6	188	89.9
Popple Grove township (Mahnomen)	139	142	2.2	120	65.8	0.0	2.5	31.7	0.0	34.2	9.2	36.7	42.3	21.8	44	97.7
Poppleton township (Kittson)	114	107	-6.1	63	100.0	0.0	0.0	0.0	0.0	31.7	22.2	31.5	27.9	11.6	22	100.0
Portage township (St. Louis)	166	167	0.6	193	94.3	0.0	0.0	5.7	0.0	11.9	32.6	56.6	48.3	17.4	93	83.9
Porter city & MCD (Yellow Medicine)	183	171	-6.6	181	93.9	0.0	0.0	0.0	6.1	10.5	32.0	53.8	44.1	10.3	94	81.9
Port Hope township (Beltrami)	669	665	-0.6	590	94.1	0.0	2.0	3.6	0.3	19.8	23.4	53.0	27.1	30.1	247	93.1
Posen township (Yellow Medicine)	219	205	-6.4	167	100.0	0.0	0.0	0.0	0.0	29.3	19.2	35.9	38.3	22.6	60	90.0
Potshot Lake UT (St. Louis)	76	77	1.3	29	100.0	0.0	0.0	0.0	0.0	0.0	41.4	64.2	31.0	13.8	20	85.0
Powers township (Cass)	712	746	4.8	753	95.8	1.2	0.0	3.1	0.0	12.6	33.6	59.1	46.1	16.3	387	88.1
Prairie Lake township (St. Louis)	50	51	2.0	29	100.0	0.0	0.0	0.0	0.0	3.4	37.9	58.5	59.3	7.4	14	78.6
Prairie View township (Wilkin)	196	187	-4.6	303	100.0	0.0	0.0	0.0	0.0	28.1	9.6	37.3	24.0	29.5	109	100.0
Prairieville township (Brown)	255	249	-2.4	273	100.0	0.0	0.0	0.0	0.0	23.1	16.5	45.9	46.0	7.6	113	86.7
Preble township (Fillmore)	209	218	4.3	165	98.2	0.0	0.0	0.0	1.8	15.8	23.6	51.8	37.8	20.5	74	91.9
Prescott township (Faribault)	163	157	-3.7	174	98.3	0.0	0.0	0.0	1.7	20.7	23.6	52.0	34.8	21.2	82	90.2
Preston city & MCD (Fillmore)	1,325	1,289	-2.7	1,408	96.1	0.1	0.2	0.7	2.8	26.2	19.0	36.9	36.7	27.6	632	90.2
Preston township (Fillmore)	359	376	4.7	338	100.0	0.0	0.0	0.0	0.0	31.1	18.3	42.8	44.7	24.4	117	76.1
Preston Lake township (Renville)	259	243	-6.2	213	100.0	0.0	0.0	0.0	0.0	16.4	23.5	49.8	45.5	18.8	111	75.7
Princeton city (Mille Lacs)	4,742	4,729	-0.3	4,709	93.5	0.4	0.0	3.5	2.6	25.9	20.9	32.8	55.4	10.0	1,969	81.0
Princeton city (Mille Lacs)	4,690	4,676	-0.3	4,618	93.4	0.4	0.0	3.6	2.6	26.4	19.4	32.0	54.1	10.3	1,907	82.8
Princeton city (Sherburne)	52	53	1.9	91	100.0	0.0	0.0	0.0	0.0	0.0	100.0	88.0	100.0	0.0	62	24.2
Princeton township (Mille Lacs)	2,214	2,217	0.1	2,128	97.6	0.4	0.8	0.5	0.8	16.5	16.9	48.1	42.3	19.6	898	93.7
Prinsburg city & MCD (Kandiyohi)	497	498	0.2	532	96.2	1.1	0.6	0.4	1.7	29.1	29.1	36.2	29.3	35.1	189	83.1
Prior township (Big Stone)	249	244	-2.0	174	100.0	0.0	0.0	0.0	0.0	20.1	24.7	55.5	62.4	10.4	68	60.3
Prior Lake city & MCD (Scott)	22,997	27,241	18.5	26,365	87.7	0.8	4.5	4.1	2.9	27.4	12.9	39.5	20.0	46.2	9,640	95.4
Proctor city & MCD (St. Louis)	3,055	3,028	-0.9	3,040	91.5	0.2	1.6	2.3	4.3	20.6	22.9	45.8	43.1	21.2	1,274	83.0
Providence township (Lac qui Parle)	169	158	-6.5	180	100.0	0.0	0.0	0.0	0.0	32.2	17.2	43.3	33.3	15.0	65	100.0
Pulaski township (Morrison)	300	305	1.7	289	99.3	0.0	0.3	0.3	0.0	27.7	22.5	41.4	55.6	14.8	114	71.9
Quamba city & MCD (Kanabec)	123	127	3.3	97	91.8	1.0	0.0	7.2	0.0	18.6	19.6	47.6	61.8	10.3	35	91.4
Queen township (Polk)	214	217	1.4	243	96.3	0.0	0.8	0.0	2.9	23.9	25.5	51.6	43.2	19.7	94	90.4
Quincy township (Olmsted)	339	347	2.4	405	99.0	0.0	0.5	0.0	0.5	38.5	14.1	35.0	38.6	32.5	121	95.0
Quiring township (Beltrami)	70	69	-1.4	83	81.9	18.1	0.0	0.0	0.0	25.3	8.4	44.4	41.7	6.3	24	91.7
Rabbit Lake township (Crow Wing)	319	336	5.3	372	95.4	0.0	0.5	4.0	0.0	25.8	17.5	34.0	29.3	19.5	145	93.8
Racine city & MCD (Mower)	445	593	33.3	494	97.4	0.4	0.0	0.2	2.0	34.2	12.1	34.6	36.0	17.3	165	95.2
Racine township (Mower)	452	468	3.5	546	99.6	0.0	0.0	0.0	0.4	28.6	18.9	41.3	39.7	23.9	177	87.0
Ramsey city & MCD (Anoka)	23,683	27,721	17.1	26,638	88.8	2.7	3.8	1.7	3.0	26.1	11.7	35.8	31.1	29.1	9,141	96.9
Randall city & MCD (Morrison)	650	624	-4.0	625	100.0	0.0	0.0	0.0	0.0	30.2	17.3	33.9	47.6	15.8	250	85.2
Randolph city & MCD (Dakota)	436	446	2.3	481	99.2	0.0	0.0	0.0	0.8	27.7	11.4	36.1	48.6	15.1	167	91.6
Randolph township (Dakota)	659	748	13.5	733	97.0	0.0	0.5	0.5	1.9	22.6	19.8	47.4	29.6	30.2	274	98.5
Ranier city	612	556	-9.2	626	88.2	0.0	0.0	10.4	1.4	13.7	35.3	55.3	41.8	13.5	257	86.8

1 May be of any race.

Table A. All Places — **Population and Housing**

STATE City, town, township, borough, or CDP (county if applicable)	Population				Race and Hispanic or Latino origin (percent)					Age (percent)			Educational attainment of persons age 25 and older		Occupied housing units	
	2010 census total population	2019 estimated population	Percent change 2010–2019	ACS total population estimate 2015–2019	White alone, not Hispanic or Latino	Black alone, not Hispanic or Latino	Asian alone, not Hispanic or Latino	All other races or 2 or more races, not Hispanic or Latino	Hispanic or Latino[1]	Under 18 years old	Age 65 years and older	Median age	Percent High school diploma or less	Percent Bachelor's degree or more	Total	Percent with a computer
	1	2	3	4	5	6	7	8	9	10	11	12	13	14	15	16

MINNESOTA—Con.

STATE City, town, township, borough, or CDP (county if applicable)	1	2	3	4	5	6	7	8	9	10	11	12	13	14	15	16
Ransom township (Nobles)	230	228	-0.9	178	94.4	0.0	0.0	5.6	0.0	22.5	24.7	49.5	51.1	12.2	67	82.1
Rapidan township (Blue Earth)	1,101	1,098	-0.3	1,094	95.7	0.0	0.1	1.4	2.8	22.3	26.3	49.3	33.1	32.9	416	92.8
Ravenna township (Dakota)	2,334	2,432	4.2	2,331	94.3	1.9	1.2	1.6	1.0	22.2	14.2	45.1	33.1	25.9	824	97.0
Raymond city	763	756	-0.9	816	85.4	0.4	0.4	5.8	8.1	28.2	16.4	38.0	42.2	14.9	318	85.8
Raymond city (Chippewa)	-	-	-	-	-	-	-	-	-	-	-	-	-	-	-	-
Raymond city (Kandiyohi)	763	756	-0.9	816	85.4	0.4	0.4	5.8	8.1	28.2	16.4	38.0	42.2	14.9	318	85.8
Raymond township (Stearns)	259	279	7.7	213	100.0	0.0	0.0	0.0	0.0	37.1	17.8	26.4	67.9	3.6	61	86.9
Redby CDP	1,334	-	-	1,143	0.6	1.1	0.0	96.5	1.7	42.0	6.0	21.3	51.3	4.6	270	80.4
Red Eye township (Wadena)	490	480	-2.0	506	94.5	1.0	0.0	0.8	3.8	31.0	13.0	39.3	49.8	14.5	177	90.4
Red Lake CDP	1,731	-	-	1,787	4.1	0.6	0.0	91.8	3.5	44.7	2.2	21.0	56.9	10.1	462	75.1
Red Lake Falls city & MCD (Red Lake)	1,423	1,418	-0.4	1,372	90.5	0.0	0.0	4.5	5.0	22.2	21.3	46.1	42.8	17.3	652	81.6
Red Lake Falls township (Red Lake)	204	202	-	228	91.7	0.0	0.0	1.3	7.0	17.5	18.4	47.2	42.8	22.8	95	90.5
Redpath township (Traverse)	48	45	-6.3	68	100.0	0.0	0.0	0.0	0.0	35.3	11.8	31.0	47.1	38.2	28	100.0
Red Rock township (Mower)	738	768	4.1	700	98.4	0.0	0.0	1.6	0.0	25.0	15.9	47.0	30.7	26.5	275	93.5
Red Wing city & MCD (Goodhue)	16,457	16,320	-0.8	16,338	86.3	2.8	0.7	4.3	5.9	21.8	20.8	42.7	39.7	25.8	7,222	89.6
Redwood Falls city & MCD (Redwood)	5,265	4,963	-5.7	4,989	88.7	0.9	0.8	5.8	3.9	25.7	21.2	39.1	50.4	19.4	2,028	86.9
Redwood Falls city (Renville)	-	-	-	-	-	-	-	-	-	-	-	-	-	-	-	-
Redwood Falls township (Redwood)	180	172	-4.4	154	100.0	0.0	0.0	0.0	0.0	13.0	32.5	58.0	34.4	32.8	69	89.9
Regal city & MCD (Kandiyohi)	34	35	2.9	56	100.0	0.0	0.0	0.0	0.0	30.4	16.1	34.5	51.4	5.7	22	95.5
Reine township (Roseau)	94	90	-4.3	115	100.0	0.0	0.0	0.0	0.0	9.6	17.4	54.6	76.8	3.2	51	86.3
Reiner township (Pennington)	87	84	-3.4	118	88.1	0.0	5.1	5.1	1.7	26.3	5.9	39.8	56.8	13.6	33	100.0
Reis township (Polk)	79	80	1.3	80	97.5	0.0	0.0	0.0	2.5	10.0	42.5	62.8	34.7	2.8	34	82.4
Remer city & MCD (Cass)	370	398	7.6	354	92.4	0.0	0.0	7.6	0.0	18.9	21.8	44.8	46.6	9.7	182	72.5
Remer township (Cass)	185	194	4.9	206	92.7	7.3	0.0	0.0	0.0	31.6	22.3	39.3	48.1	18.0	64	78.1
Rendsville township (Stevens)	161	166	3.1	120	100.0	0.0	0.0	0.0	0.0	20.0	21.7	40.0	40.0	21.4	47	85.1
Reno township (Pope)	395	407	3.0	407	96.8	2.0	0.0	1.2	0.0	22.6	21.6	52.9	38.3	16.3	167	91.6
Renville city & MCD (Renville)	1,295	1,189	-8.2	1,235	70.7	0.1	0.6	1.1	27.6	24.7	23.3	42.3	54.6	15.5	481	80.5
Revere city & MCD (Redwood)	95	88	-7.4	77	89.6	0.0	10.4	0.0	0.0	13.0	24.7	43.8	78.5	3.1	30	73.3
Reynolds township (Todd)	661	664	0.5	743	99.2	0.0	0.0	0.0	0.8	29.2	14.5	33.3	57.5	16.7	258	68.6
Rheiderland township (Chippewa)	269	258	-4.1	292	90.1	0.0	0.0	1.0	8.9	24.0	19.9	45.8	26.0	34.0	118	88.1
Rhinehart township (Polk)	132	133	0.8	176	97.7	0.0	0.0	0.0	2.3	33.5	5.1	26.7	10.8	34.2	61	98.4
Rice city & MCD (Benton)	1,275	1,391	9.1	1,633	94.2	1.5	0.0	3.4	0.9	33.7	5.6	30.3	32.7	22.2	569	96.7
Rice township (Clearwater)	158	158	0.0	120	71.7	0.0	0.0	20.0	8.3	26.7	23.3	46.5	55.8	15.1	49	69.4
Rice Lake CDP	235	-	-	284	7.7	0.0	0.0	90.8	1.4	46.8	6.7	21.5	63.2	5.3	67	65.7
Rice Lake city & MCD (St. Louis)	4,099	4,139	1.0	4,149	95.7	0.0	0.4	3.6	0.3	19.8	20.6	44.1	37.9	25.6	1,736	93.1
Riceland township (Freeborn)	432	417	-3.5	485	98.8	0.0	0.0	0.2	1.0	24.1	20.4	43.5	37.7	10.7	172	89.5
Rice River township (Aitkin)	136	136	0.0	106	100.0	0.0	0.0	0.0	0.0	6.6	24.5	56.4	38.1	8.2	63	87.3
Riceville township (Becker)	83	87	4.8	107	95.3	0.0	0.0	1.9	2.8	15.0	17.8	45.2	63.3	12.7	41	90.2
Richardson township (Morrison)	536	545	1.7	502	91.2	0.0	0.0	8.8	0.0	17.3	28.9	57.4	57.1	13.3	243	87.7
Richardville township (Kittson)	102	96	-5.9	61	100.0	0.0	0.0	0.0	0.0	24.6	21.3	48.3	26.1	13.0	25	88.0
Richfield city	35,094	36,354	3.6	36,063	60.7	10.8	6.9	4.1	17.5	21.5	15.5	35.7	29.4	42.4	15,180	91.6
Richland township (Rice)	417	438	5.0	397	96.0	0.0	0.0	0.0	4.0	20.7	19.6	44.5	44.7	26.0	145	82.1
Richmond city & MCD (Stearns)	1,418	1,470	3.7	1,582	93.6	0.0	0.7	0.0	5.8	25.9	23.1	39.0	50.9	12.6	652	83.3
Richmond township (Winona)	699	699	0.0	598	98.8	0.0	0.0	0.0	1.2	13.0	24.4	53.0	31.7	27.6	274	93.1
Rich Valley township (McLeod)	698	683	-2.1	709	92.0	1.8	1.8	2.3	2.1	21.0	17.2	50.6	42.7	22.1	278	89.6
Richville city & MCD (Otter Tail)	96	98	2.1	89	100.0	0.0	0.0	0.0	0.0	20.2	10.1	37.3	60.0	5.5	34	79.4
Richwood township (Becker)	662	702	6.0	578	92.6	0.0	0.0	7.4	0.0	22.5	20.9	45.9	26.9	30.8	242	92.1
Ridgely township (Nicollet)	117	118	0.9	115	100.0	0.0	0.0	0.0	0.0	32.2	17.0	39.8	33.3	21.8	41	87.8
Ripley township (Dodge)	195	202	3.6	170	81.8	0.0	0.0	0.0	18.2	28.8	17.1	37.2	50.0	12.2	61	82.0
Ripley township (Morrison)	729	746	2.3	708	83.6	0.0	0.3	0.0	16.1	20.1	20.5	46.5	40.5	18.1	278	94.2
River township (Red Lake)	65	65	0.0	34	100.0	0.0	0.0	0.0	0.0	2.9	32.4	60.0	39.4	21.2	18	83.3
Riverdale township (Watonwan)	293	291	-0.7	248	100.0	0.0	0.0	0.0	0.0	25.4	27.4	55.5	36.9	25.7	108	88.0
River Falls township (Pennington)	178	171	-3.9	221	97.3	0.0	0.5	1.8	0.5	15.4	12.7	35.2	41.5	5.1	91	93.4
Riverland CDP	276	-	-	323	1.5	0.0	0.3	94.1	4.0	48.3	1.2	19.5	64.4	1.5	87	63.2
Riverside township (Lac qui Parle)	303	282	-6.9	294	94.6	0.0	0.0	4.4	1.0	18.7	36.1	56.5	40.6	26.1	114	95.6
Riverton township (Clay)	446	470	5.4	519	90.0	0.0	0.6	2.7	6.7	35.8	7.9	39.6	25.1	25.1	182	87.4
Riverton city & MCD (Crow Wing)	117	113	-3.4	178	96.1	0.0	0.0	3.9	0.0	29.2	14.6	31.2	51.0	13.7	58	94.8

1   May be of any race.

Table A. All Places — **Population and Housing**

STATE City, town, township, borough, or CDP (county if applicable)	Population				Race and Hispanic or Latino origin (percent)					Age (percent)			Educational attainment of persons age 25 and older		Occupied housing units	
	2010 census total population	2019 estimated population	Percent change 2010–2019	ACS total population estimate 2015–2019	White alone, not Hispanic or Latino	Black alone, not Hispanic or Latino	Asian alone, not Hispanic or Latino	All other races or 2 or more races, not Hispanic or Latino	Hispanic or Latino[1]	Under 18 years old	Age 65 years and older	Median age	Percent High school diploma or less	Percent Bachelor's degree or more	Total	Percent with a computer
	1	2	3	4	5	6	7	8	9	10	11	12	13	14	15	16
MINNESOTA—Con.																
Robbinsdale city	13,953	14,389	3.1	14,468	68.9	10.9	3.1	6.3	10.8	21.6	14.7	36.2	28.6	38.0	6,288	90.9
Roberts township (Wilkin).	110	105	-4.5	153	99.3	0.0	0.7	0.0	0.0	10.5	3.9	24.7	20.0	11.4	61	98.4
Rochester city & MCD (Olmsted)	106,823	118,935	11.3	115,557	75.0	7.9	7.2	3.9	5.9	24.0	14.9	35.7	24.6	46.7	47,097	93.5
Rochester township (Olmsted)	1,641	1,903	16.0	1,689	84.0	1.8	5.0	4.5	4.8	20.5	24.5	54.6	7.6	71.6	657	97.7
Rock township (Pipestone)...................	182	180	-1.1	171	100.0	0.0	0.0	0.0	0.0	33.9	10.5	28.8	36.8	23.2	75	92.0
Rock Creek city & MCD (Pine)	1,625	1,652	1.7	1,620	96.6	0.0	0.6	1.9	0.9	21.2	17.5	45.5	46.7	18.2	570	89.8
Rock Dell township (Olmsted)	645	656	1.7	701	98.4	0.9	0.0	0.0	0.7	21.5	24.0	50.5	40.6	29.9	269	92.9
Rockford city	4,356	4,515	3.7	4,551	86.8	0.3	0.0	1.1	11.9	23.7	9.6	39.2	28.7	28.2	1,684	93.4
Rockford city (Wright)	3,930	4,076	3.7	4,030	86.2	0.3	0.0	1.1	13.4	23.3	10.0	38.7	26.7	30.7	1,476	93.1
Rockford township (Wright)	3,156	3,357	6.4	3,311	97.1	1.0	0.0	1.1	0.8	28.0	15.5	40.1	37.3	26.1	1,065	95.5
Rock Lake township (Lyon)	267	265	-0.7	324	97.5	0.0	0.0	0.0	2.5	25.9	23.1	44.2	35.0	30.0	130	88.5
Rocksbury township (Pennington).................	1,202	1,164	-3.2	1,085	90.9	0.0	3.9	4.9	0.4	24.1	15.1	44.4	27.4	24.1	402	94.0
Rockville city & MCD (Stearns)	2,435	2,585	6.2	2,551	88.5	0.5	0.0	0.1	10.9	22.2	13.2	43.6	37.5	27.0	993	90.9
Rockwell township (Norman)	61	58	-4.9	58	100.0	0.0	0.0	0.0	0.0	27.6	22.4	39.5	33.3	14.3	26	76.9
Rockwood township (Hubbard)	427	437	2.3	424	95.5	0.5	0.0	3.8	0.2	15.8	23.3	48.9	33.1	33.4	157	91.1
Rockwood township (Wadena)	394	387	-1.8	390	95.4	0.3	0.8	1.8	1.8	25.9	14.9	43.1	49.4	10.1	137	88.3
Rogers township (Cass) ...	63	66	4.8	102	80.4	0.0	1.0	18.6	0.0	19.6	50.0	65.0	53.1	23.5	50	72.0
Rogers city	11,197	13,490	20.5	12,971	90.9	0.1	7.2	0.5	1.4	29.7	10.9	38.8	27.1	46.9	4,283	96.4
Rolling Forks township (Pope)	151	153	1.3	144	100.0	0.0	0.0	0.0	0.0	17.4	21.5	52.5	46.9	14.2	62	85.5
Rolling Green township (Martin)	266	254	-4.5	254	89.8	0.0	0.0	10.2	0.0	18.1	28.7	55.1	34.6	20.1	111	90.1
Rollingstone city & MCD (Winona)	633	639	0.9	644	98.0	0.0	0.3	1.1	0.6	23.8	13.7	40.3	26.0	31.3	253	96.0
Rollingstone township (Winona)	755	759	0.5	798	96.6	1.0	0.0	0.8	1.6	18.7	20.4	47.1	50.1	20.6	305	85.9
Rollis township (Marshall).	115	114	-0.9	112	100.0	0.0	0.0	0.0	0.0	25.9	34.8	50.7	54.9	11.0	42	81.0
Rome township (Faribault)	143	137	-4.2	145	100.0	0.0	0.0	0.0	0.0	22.1	31.7	40.8	42.3	22.1	65	87.7
Ronneby CDP	67	-	-	37	100.0	0.0	0.0	0.0	0.0	43.2	5.4	26.5	36.8	31.6	11	100.0
Roome township (Polk).....	177	178	0.6	117	93.2	0.0	0.0	6.8	0.0	9.4	34.2	56.3	44.6	22.8	48	100.0
Roosevelt township (Beltrami)	225	223	-0.9	193	96.4	0.0	0.0	3.6	0.0	11.9	22.3	49.8	42.7	22.0	95	86.3
Roosevelt township (Crow Wing)..................	601	632	5.2	508	91.3	0.0	0.0	7.7	1.0	14.8	32.1	56.0	41.1	15.3	255	82.0
Roosevelt city (Roseau)	146	138	-5.5	139	96.4	0.0	0.0	0.7	2.9	30.2	7.2	32.6	42.9	19.0	55	92.7
Roosevelt city (Roseau)....	144	136	-5.6	139	96.4	0.0	0.0	0.7	2.9	30.2	7.2	32.6	42.9	19.0	55	92.7
Roscoe township (Goodhue)	732	730	-0.3	863	96.1	1.9	0.0	2.1	0.0	20.9	9.3	39.0	33.9	32.7	292	96.2
Roscoe city & MCD (Stearns)	104	113	8.7	132	96.2	0.0	0.0	0.0	3.8	28.8	16.7	30.6	69.2	2.6	46	69.6
Roseau city & MCD (Roseau)	2,642	2,672	1.1	2,697	95.3	0.3	0.6	1.4	2.3	18.8	21.4	44.8	37.7	30.1	1,210	81.2
Rosebud township (Polk)..	350	356	1.7	293	98.6	0.0	0.0	1.4	0.0	12.6	20.1	53.5	31.9	26.0	133	86.5
Rose Creek city & MCD (Mower)	416	424	1.9	469	87.8	0.0	0.2	2.3	9.6	26.9	24.1	38.7	52.2	18.2	192	79.2
Rosedale township (Mahnomen)	135	138	2.2	164	73.2	0.0	0.6	26.2	0.0	30.5	12.8	41.3	35.8	16.8	57	87.7
Rose Dell township (Rock)	206	201	-2.4	87	98.9	0.0	0.0	0.0	1.1	1.1	26.4	55.3	39.5	13.2	51	88.2
Rose Hill township (Cottonwood)	166	160	-3.6	104	100.0	0.0	0.0	0.0	0.0	28.8	18.3	41.5	39.7	9.6	37	97.3
Roseland township (Kandiyohi)..................	371	381	2.7	331	100.0	0.0	0.0	0.0	0.0	15.1	18.4	49.1	37.5	13.7	149	89.3
Rosemount city & MCD (Dakota)	21,881	25,207	15.2	24,292	84.9	3.8	5.0	3.1	3.2	29.0	10.1	37.2	19.8	47.4	8,563	96.7
Rosendale township (Watonwan)	303	298	-1.7	328	99.1	0.0	0.9	0.0	0.0	10.4	18.6	56.3	58.3	6.7	144	93.8
Roseville township (Grant)	124	121	-2.4	94	100.0	0.0	0.0	0.0	0.0	3.2	35.1	56.7	37.1	17.1	50	88.0
Roseville township (Kandiyohi)..................	622	645	3.7	646	95.4	0.0	0.0	1.4	3.3	23.4	14.2	48.0	45.1	21.3	249	93.2
Roseville city & MCD (Ramsey)	33,661	36,457	8.3	36,026	74.5	8.3	8.5	5.0	3.8	19.1	21.2	40.9	23.3	51.5	15,362	90.5
Rosewood township (Chippewa)	348	335	-3.7	351	100.0	0.0	0.0	0.0	0.0	29.3	12.8	41.9	40.5	22.5	116	93.1
Rosing township (Morrison)	146	149	2.1	158	98.1	0.0	0.0	0.6	1.3	20.9	18.4	50.6	46.7	20.0	70	88.6
Ross township (Roseau) ..	429	415	-3.3	388	99.0	0.0	0.5	0.0	0.5	25.8	14.2	44.3	45.2	10.3	160	88.8
Ross Lake township (Crow Wing)	165	174	5.5	174	98.9	0.0	0.0	1.1	0.0	6.3	55.7	66.3	47.5	22.5	97	88.7
Rost township (Jackson)...	211	203	-3.8	194	100.0	0.0	0.0	0.0	0.0	41.8	8.8	31.3	38.5	24.8	60	88.3
Rothsay city	493	471	-4.5	605	97.9	1.5	0.0	0.7	0.0	25.0	18.5	41.6	44.1	21.5	253	86.2
Rothsay city (Otter Tail).....	219	219	0.0	211	95.7	4.3	0.0	0.0	0.0	24.6	9.5	42.1	36.1	23.1	86	90.7
Rothsay city (Wilkin)	274	252	-8.0	394	99.0	0.0	0.0	1.0	0.0	25.1	23.4	41.3	48.7	20.5	167	83.8
Round Grove township (McLeod)...................	251	245	-2.4	247	98.0	0.0	0.0	1.6	0.4	25.9	14.2	40.8	27.2	20.7	95	87.4
Round Lake township (Becker)	180	192	6.7	168	54.2	0.0	0.0	45.8	0.0	27.4	31.0	58.0	34.2	25.6	73	80.8
Round Lake township (Jackson)	166	161	-3.0	151	93.4	0.0	0.0	0.0	6.6	16.6	29.1	49.4	36.1	28.7	65	96.9
Round Lake city & MCD (Nobles)	376	368	-2.1	380	93.2	0.0	0.8	3.9	2.1	17.4	23.2	49.4	59.3	8.1	186	79.6

1 May be of any race.

Table A. All Places — Population and Housing

STATE City, town, township, borough, or CDP (county if applicable)	2010 census total population	2019 estimated population	Percent change 2010–2019	ACS total population estimate 2015–2019	White alone, not Hispanic or Latino	Black alone, not Hispanic or Latino	Asian alone, not Hispanic or Latino	All other races or 2 or more races, not Hispanic or Latino	Hispanic or Latino[1]	Under 18 years old	Age 65 years and older	Median age	Percent High school diploma or less	Percent Bachelor's degree or more	Total	Percent with a computer
	1	2	3	4	5	6	7	8	9	10	11	12	13	14	15	16
MINNESOTA—Con.																
Round Prairie township (Todd)	706	714	1.1	870	93.8	0.0	0.0	2.3	3.9	37.6	13.2	30.0	54.9	10.2	250	87.6
Royal township (Lincoln)	178	175	-1.7	183	100.0	0.0	0.0	0.0	0.0	44.8	14.8	39.0	27.1	22.9	50	84.0
Royalton city (Benton)	1,229	1,233	0.3	1,239	97.3	0.0	0.4	2.3	0.0	23.1	15.7	37.0	42.4	21.0	506	91.5
Royalton city (Benton)	2	2	0.0	18	100.0	0.0	0.0	0.0	0.0	0.0	0.0	0.0	0.0	55.6	10	100.0
Royalton city (Morrison)	1,227	1,231	0.3	1,221	97.3	0.0	0.4	2.3	0.0	23.4	16.0	37.6	43.3	20.3	496	91.3
Royalton township (Pine)	1,163	1,158	-0.4	1,164	91.5	1.2	0.0	0.3	7.0	19.1	16.9	39.7	43.9	23.1	377	86.7
Roy Lake CDP	12	-	-	23	82.6	0.0	8.7	8.7	0.0	21.7	17.4	47.5	61.1	27.8	10	80.0
Runeberg township (Becker)	486	516	6.2	594	96.8	0.0	0.0	2.2	1.0	41.2	14.6	33.5	52.0	9.6	183	85.2
Rush City city & MCD (Chisago)	3,091	3,218	4.1	3,170	75.8	15.0	1.5	4.9	2.7	18.0	10.5	33.0	66.2	8.7	879	88.2
Rushford city & MCD (Fillmore)	1,723	1,695	-1.6	1,744	95.6	0.2	0.2	0.9	3.0	24.4	24.9	43.9	44.3	21.8	720	87.1
Rushford Village city & MCD (Fillmore)	823	836	1.6	843	100.0	0.0	0.0	0.0	0.0	24.8	22.7	43.4	31.3	28.4	325	87.4
Rush Lake township (Otter Tail)	970	978	0.8	917	96.7	0.0	1.9	1.4	0.0	17.2	28.4	54.8	36.9	26.8	386	91.5
Rushmore city & MCD (Nobles)	342	335	-2.0	354	85.0	0.0	0.3	2.0	12.7	28.5	20.3	33.0	55.6	13.3	142	78.9
Rushseba township (Chisago)	795	838	5.4	734	90.2	1.9	3.4	3.1	1.4	20.4	13.1	46.2	42.2	16.7	295	92.9
Russell city & MCD (Lyon)	345	342	-0.9	296	89.5	0.7	6.4	2.7	0.7	23.0	17.6	39.8	52.8	13.7	131	90.1
Russia township (Polk)	27	28	3.7	23	100.0	0.0	0.0	0.0	0.0	17.4	21.7	48.6	31.3	12.5	11	90.9
Ruthton city & MCD (Pipestone)	241	221	-8.3	241	83.4	0.0	0.0	6.2	10.4	23.2	19.5	36.8	47.5	13.1	108	91.7
Rutland township (Martin)	437	416	-4.8	457	98.2	0.7	0.0	0.4	0.7	20.8	19.0	50.0	38.5	20.6	171	85.4
Rutledge city & MCD (Pine)	229	221	-3.5	217	97.2	0.0	0.5	0.0	2.3	17.1	26.7	51.5	59.3	3.0	87	81.6
Sabin city & MCD (Clay)	522	558	6.9	622	94.9	0.0	0.0	2.3	2.9	33.3	9.6	31.7	35.6	20.5	205	99.5
Sacred Heart city & MCD (Renville)	550	502	-8.7	608	88.2	0.0	0.0	0.0	11.8	32.6	14.1	38.0	52.8	10.3	257	81.7
Sacred Heart township (Renville)	268	252	-6.0	263	97.3	0.0	1.5	1.1	0.0	21.7	13.7	44.4	29.8	23.4	108	95.4
Sago township (Itasca)	176	177	0.6	169	97.0	0.0	0.0	1.2	1.8	18.3	22.5	51.9	45.5	16.4	74	94.6
St. Anthony city	8,226	9,013	9.6	9,038	79.1	7.6	4.6	5.5	3.2	22.2	24.8	42.2	26.4	48.2	3,946	87.1
St. Anthony city (Ramsey)	3,070	3,437	12.0	3,428	69.4	17.2	7.0	3.1	3.3	19.3	24.5	39.3	32.2	41.1	1,680	87.3
St. Anthony city & MCD (Stearns)	89	91	2.2	89	100.0	0.0	0.0	0.0	0.0	28.1	10.1	32.5	50.0	32.6	31	77.4
St. Augusta city & MCD (Stearns)	3,315	3,835	15.7	3,720	96.3	0.1	1.2	1.7	0.8	20.7	11.4	38.9	30.3	22.4	1,316	96.7
St. Bonifacius city	2,307	2,374	2.9	2,078	89.7	0.3	5.4	1.2	3.4	21.6	12.5	45.5	25.9	35.2	893	95.1
St. Charles city & MCD (Winona)	3,737	3,758	0.6	3,728	84.7	0.0	10.4	2.5	2.4	24.4	15.6	34.4	29.2	32.0	1,394	93.2
St. Charles township (Winona)	627	627	0.0	732	99.0	0.0	1.0	0.0	0.0	35.7	12.6	31.5	40.2	24.0	196	80.6
St. Clair city & MCD (Blue Earth)	868	824	-5.1	762	91.1	3.4	0.9	0.5	4.1	26.9	7.3	31.5	33.1	34.0	301	90.4
St. Cloud city	65,905	68,462	3.9	68,000	74.9	14.6	3.4	4.0	3.2	20.2	12.7	30.9	34.7	30.7	26,374	92.5
St. Cloud city (Benton)	6,410	6,576	2.6	6,550	69.9	20.6	1.1	5.0	3.4	19.5	9.7	34.5	43.4	24.0	3,183	92.4
St. Cloud city (Sherburne)	6,785	7,203	6.2	7,118	70.2	14.0	4.9	7.3	3.7	16.8	17.8	31.9	40.0	27.5	2,553	85.6
St. Cloud city (Stearns)	52,710	54,683	3.7	54,333	76.2	13.9	3.4	3.4	3.1	20.8	12.4	30.1	32.7	32.2	20,638	93.4
St. Francis city & MCD (Anoka)	7,214	7,916	9.7	7,652	90.3	1.4	0.2	4.3	3.8	28.9	8.9	33.5	42.4	16.5	2,566	96.1
St. Francis city (Isanti)	-	-	-	-	-	-	-	-	-	-	-	-	-	-	-	-
St. George township (Benton)	1,153	1,199	4.0	1,194	92.5	0.4	0.0	6.4	0.7	35.5	14.2	34.5	39.4	19.0	391	89.0
St. Hilaire city & MCD (Pennington)	279	264	-5.4	220	96.8	0.0	0.9	0.9	1.4	24.1	17.3	46.0	55.1	5.8	97	82.5
St. James city & MCD (Watonwan)	4,594	4,400	-4.2	4,444	58.0	0.1	0.0	0.1	41.9	26.0	17.6	37.1	67.0	11.7	1,763	80.4
St. James township (Watonwan)	268	264	-1.5	206	100.0	0.0	0.0	0.0	0.0	13.6	36.9	56.8	37.1	28.1	94	90.4
St. Johns township (Kandiyohi)	411	414	0.7	427	82.9	0.0	6.6	1.2	9.4	29.0	15.0	42.9	32.9	25.1	153	90.2
St. Joseph township (Kittson)	56	53	-5.4	69	100.0	0.0	0.0	0.0	0.0	37.7	24.6	22.5	45.5	30.3	22	86.4
St. Joseph city & MCD (Stearns)	6,499	7,351	13.1	7,030	90.6	4.6	1.2	2.7	1.0	22.7	11.1	22.8	21.5	36.8	1,916	98.7
St. Joseph township (Stearns)	1,261	1,340	6.3	1,464	98.2	0.0	0.0	0.6	1.2	23.9	14.8	40.1	32.3	27.4	556	93.3
St. Lawrence township (Scott)	496	536	8.1	374	97.3	0.0	0.0	1.1	1.6	19.5	16.6	48.5	29.8	30.2	136	95.6
St. Leo city & MCD (Yellow Medicine)	100	91	-9.0	112	84.8	9.8	0.0	5.4	0.0	6.3	25.9	53.5	64.1	2.2	63	68.3
St. Louis Park city	45,205	48,662	7.6	48,677	81.0	6.7	4.5	3.6	4.2	17.5	14.7	35.3	16.0	59.2	23,256	94.1
St. Martin city & MCD (Stearns)	340	348	2.4	340	96.5	0.0	0.0	0.3	3.2	26.8	14.1	35.4	47.6	13.2	132	87.9
St. Martin township (Stearns)	515	555	7.8	601	100.0	0.0	0.0	0.0	0.0	26.6	8.3	40.2	57.2	10.0	190	87.4
St. Mary township (Waseca)	457	461	0.9	394	95.9	1.0	1.3	0.0	1.8	23.1	15.5	44.0	33.5	25.1	153	92.8
St. Marys Point city & MCD (Washington)	370	392	5.9	321	97.2	0.0	2.2	0.6	0.0	19.0	24.9	50.1	24.4	36.3	131	96.9
St. Mathias township (Crow Wing)	613	645	5.2	750	89.9	0.0	0.3	3.9	6.0	33.5	14.5	36.1	40.0	18.7	240	94.6
St. Michael city & MCD (Wright)	16,380	18,204	11.1	17,586	89.5	4.0	3.0	1.1	2.4	34.3	7.7	33.8	24.5	42.2	5,447	92.6
St. Olaf township (Otter Tail)	352	350	-0.6	385	93.0	0.0	0.0	7.0	0.0	24.9	20.8	39.5	36.6	17.0	135	90.4
St. Paul city & MCD (Ramsey)	285,112	308,096	8.1	304,547	51.4	15.8	18.6	4.9	9.2	25.0	10.5	32.0	34.0	40.8	113,154	91.6

1 May be of any race.

Table A. All Places — **Population and Housing**

STATE City, town, township, borough, or CDP (county if applicable)	Population				Race and Hispanic or Latino origin (percent)					Age (percent)			Educational attainment of persons age 25 and older		Occupied housing units	
	2010 census total population	2019 estimated population	Percent change 2010–2019	ACS total population estimate 2015–2019	White alone, not Hispanic or Latino	Black alone, not Hispanic or Latino	Asian alone, not Hispanic or Latino	All other races or 2 or more races, not Hispanic or Latino	Hispanic or Latino[1]	Under 18 years old	Age 65 years and older	Median age	Percent High school diploma or less	Percent Bachelor's degree or more	Total	Percent with a computer
	1	2	3	4	5	6	7	8	9	10	11	12	13	14	15	16
MINNESOTA—Con.																
St. Paul Park city & MCD (Washington)	5,244	5,362	2.3	5,356	78.2	0.9	9.3	5.0	6.6	21.8	11.5	35.1	37.1	20.1	1,935	94.2
St. Peter city & MCD (Nicollet)	11,188	11,953	6.8	11,854	84.6	3.2	3.3	2.0	7.0	17.4	15.4	31.3	36.1	31.1	3,913	90.4
St. Rosa city & MCD (Stearns)	65	71	9.2	44	100.0	0.0	0.0	0.0	0.0	13.6	15.9	45.3	52.8	16.7	23	91.3
St. Stephen city & MCD (Stearns)	858	865	0.8	963	94.2	0.3	1.9	0.4	3.2	25.9	10.0	36.1	40.1	16.9	343	93.3
St. Vincent city & MCD (Kittson)	64	62	-3.1	36	100.0	0.0	0.0	0.0	0.0	5.6	36.1	58.7	58.8	2.9	21	71.4
St. Vincent township (Kittson)	58	55	-5.2	25	100.0	0.0	0.0	0.0	0.0	0.0	60.0	67.4	44.0	36.0	15	100.0
St. Wendel township (Stearns)	2,150	2,329	8.3	2,074	97.6	0.0	0.8	0.9	0.8	18.5	18.4	50.3	36.0	28.5	821	91.5
Salem township (Cass)	95	100	5.3	112	88.4	0.0	8.0	3.6	0.0	19.6	26.8	59.2	48.3	9.0	53	94.3
Salem township (Olmsted)	1,086	1,104	1.7	1,189	96.0	1.0	0.0	0.3	2.7	25.0	22.0	44.3	28.5	35.5	452	95.1
Salo township (Aitkin)	102	101	0.0	79	96.2	0.0	0.0	3.8	0.0	7.6	44.3	61.3	62.7	17.9	42	81.0
Sanborn city & MCD (Redwood)	339	310	-8.6	361	93.9	1.9	0.0	0.8	3.3	14.1	26.0	51.9	54.2	8.0	179	81.0
Sand Creek township (Scott)	1,514	1,634	7.9	1,563	96.0	0.0	0.6	1.7	1.7	24.1	18.2	39.2	40.6	30.5	524	89.5
Sanders township (Pennington)	298	305	2.3	353	99.2	0.0	0.0	0.0	0.8	33.4	8.5	37.1	34.7	21.1	110	90.9
Sand Lake township (Itasca)	141	141	0.0	192	80.2	0.0	0.0	19.8	0.0	8.3	39.1	59.0	42.1	23.2	102	89.2
Sand Lake UT (St. Louis)	1,071	1,075	0.4	1,094	99.9	0.1	0.0	0.0	0.0	16.5	24.9	55.3	32.9	25.8	535	93.8
Sandnes township (Yellow Medicine)	199	187	-6.0	183	97.8	0.0	0.0	0.0	2.2	25.1	13.7	34.2	30.6	29.0	72	93.1
Sandstone city & MCD (Pine)	2,841	2,639	-7.1	2,670	70.1	12.7	1.6	7.1	8.5	13.4	11.8	39.5	58.9	7.9	531	78.9
Sandstone township (Pine)	832	812	-2.4	954	80.2	3.7	0.5	13.3	2.3	27.4	13.7	38.0	54.2	14.6	324	82.4
Sandsville township (Polk)	67	69	3.0	32	93.8	0.0	0.0	0.0	6.3	6.3	9.4	54.7	36.7	20.0	16	100.0
Sandy township (St. Louis)	356	358	0.6	354	98.9	0.6	0.0	0.0	0.6	13.6	22.6	53.8	36.8	25.8	184	80.4
Sanford township (Grant)	149	149	0.0	132	100.0	0.0	0.0	0.0	0.0	32.6	17.4	36.9	30.3	27.0	50	96.0
San Francisco township (Carver)	832	855	2.8	979	94.8	2.7	0.0	1.2	1.3	21.0	13.8	41.7	36.9	27.9	326	96.6
Santiago township (Sherburne)	1,895	2,065	9.0	2,077	97.6	0.2	0.6	1.5	0.0	32.8	6.0	33.0	38.8	24.4	628	91.9
Saratoga township (Winona)	618	608	-1.6	761	97.1	0.0	0.5	0.7	1.7	43.5	9.1	21.8	40.7	17.9	190	76.3
Sargeant city & MCD (Mower)	61	60	-1.6	47	100.0	0.0	0.0	0.0	0.0	8.5	21.3	44.3	59.5	8.1	22	90.9
Sargeant township (Mower)	310	324	4.5	367	97.8	0.0	1.9	0.3	0.0	18.0	18.5	42.4	48.8	29.1	112	84.8
Sartell city	16,075	18,926	17.7	18,005	90.6	2.2	3.3	1.6	2.2	28.7	11.4	33.7	20.1	42.4	6,975	92.1
Sartell city (Benton)	2,240	2,510	12.1	2,412	92.9	4.8	0.2	1.0	1.1	19.2	30.1	47.8	40.5	24.7	1,213	76.9
Sartell city (Stearns)	13,835	16,416	18.7	15,593	90.3	1.8	3.8	1.7	2.4	30.2	8.5	32.2	16.3	45.8	5,762	95.3
Sauk Centre city & MCD (Stearns)	4,304	4,505	4.7	4,426	89.0	1.6	0.3	2.6	6.5	25.8	20.2	35.4	50.0	15.5	1,844	83.3
Sauk Centre township (Stearns)	1,101	1,164	5.7	1,110	98.0	0.0	0.0	0.6	1.4	27.5	16.0	41.1	44.0	15.4	409	89.0
Sauk Rapids city & MCD (Benton)	12,840	14,146	10.2	13,703	91.8	0.5	1.9	2.9	2.9	25.9	13.2	33.5	30.8	27.4	5,703	93.1
Sauk Rapids township (Benton)	523	544	4.0	469	93.2	0.6	1.7	0.0	4.5	19.2	21.7	53.1	27.0	29.3	204	91.2
Savage city & MCD (Scott)	26,911	32,362	20.3	31,254	77.3	7.7	8.5	2.4	4.2	28.5	8.5	35.8	20.1	49.6	10,447	98.0
Savannah township (Becker)	163	174	6.7	165	97.6	0.0	0.0	2.4	0.0	13.9	32.1	60.3	42.9	28.6	73	69.9
Scambler township (Otter Tail)	476	477	0.2	417	98.1	0.0	0.0	0.7	1.2	10.6	28.1	58.3	29.8	26.5	205	96.1
Scandia township (Polk)	74	74	0.0	59	78.0	0.0	0.0	0.0	22.0	37.3	16.9	31.3	11.8	35.3	16	100.0
Scandia city & MCD (Washington)	3,928	4,176	6.3	4,112	99.0	0.4	0.0	0.7	0.0	21.5	21.0	50.6	27.5	33.2	1,502	92.8
Scandia Valley township (Morrison)	1,191	1,212	1.8	1,037	99.6	0.0	0.0	0.4	0.0	14.3	34.9	60.2	34.6	32.0	495	89.5
Scanlon city & MCD (Carlton)	991	959	-3.2	1,181	83.0	1.1	0.0	5.9	10.0	27.7	21.3	34.9	31.7	23.0	469	80.6
Schoolcraft township (Hubbard)	103	105	1.9	115	90.4	0.0	0.9	8.7	0.0	16.5	18.3	42.7	41.3	23.9	42	92.9
Schroeder township (Cook)	203	217	6.9	178	93.8	0.0	0.0	6.2	0.0	5.1	34.3	59.6	39.2	28.9	109	89.9
Sciota township (Dakota)	423	469	10.9	514	98.8	0.0	0.2	1.0	0.0	27.8	14.4	38.8	31.4	20.1	162	94.4
Scott township (Stevens)	144	149	3.5	141	82.3	0.0	0.0	0.0	17.7	22.7	24.8	50.5	64.6	12.1	52	76.9
Seaforth city & MCD (Redwood)	86	82	-4.7	85	100.0	0.0	0.0	0.0	0.0	32.9	10.6	38.8	43.4	9.4	40	67.5
Searles CDP	171	-	-	270	98.5	0.0	0.0	0.0	1.5	18.5	28.5	61.3	57.3	9.2	129	89.9
Seavey township (Aitkin)	64	63	-1.6	55	100.0	0.0	0.0	0.0	0.0	14.5	40.0	49.2	45.2	19.0	28	75.0
Sebeka city & MCD (Wadena)	711	666	-6.3	778	96.9	0.0	0.3	2.8	0.0	27.1	18.6	37.6	45.6	14.3	329	87.8
Second Assessment UT (Crow Wing)	117	123	5.1	73	100.0	0.0	0.0	0.0	0.0	0.0	15.1	49.3	50.7	9.6	34	100.0
Sedan city & MCD (Pope)	45	47	4.4	47	100.0	0.0	0.0	0.0	0.0	12.8	10.6	49.3	51.2	9.8	27	77.8
Seely township (Faribault)	193	184	-4.7	133	100.0	0.0	0.0	0.0	0.0	11.3	42.1	60.5	35.2	32.4	73	76.7
Selma township (Cottonwood)	193	188	-2.6	140	100.0	0.0	0.0	0.0	0.0	23.6	14.3	42.0	37.1	39.2	58	77.6
Severance township (Sibley)	235	231	-1.7	288	88.9	0.0	0.0	3.5	7.6	33.7	16.3	35.8	41.0	23.0	97	79.4
Seward township (Nobles)	208	206	-	176	90.3	1.7	0.0	5.1	2.8	14.8	17.6	50.4	27.5	32.1	71	84.5
Shafer city & MCD (Chisago)	1,045	1,117	6.9	1,171	94.4	0.0	0.0	2.7	2.9	32.8	5.6	29.1	40.9	16.9	409	93.4

1 May be of any race.

Table A. All Places — **Population and Housing**

STATE City, town, township, borough, or CDP (county if applicable)	Population				Race and Hispanic or Latino origin (percent)					Age (percent)			Educational attainment of persons age 25 and older		Occupied housing units	
	2010 census total population	2019 estimated population	Percent change 2010–2019	ACS total population estimate 2015–2019	White alone, not Hispanic or Latino	Black alone, not Hispanic or Latino	Asian alone, not Hispanic or Latino	All other races or 2 or more races, not Hispanic or Latino	Hispanic or Latino[1]	Under 18 years old	Age 65 years and older	Median age	Percent High school diploma or less	Percent Bachelor's degree or more	Total	Percent with a computer
	1	2	3	4	5	6	7	8	9	10	11	12	13	14	15	16
MINNESOTA—Con.																
Shafer township (Chisago)	1,048	1,107	5.6	1,006	98.0	0.3	0.2	1.5	0.0	25.5	12.2	42.1	34.6	22.1	351	93.4
Shakopee city & MCD (Scott)	36,988	41,570	12.4	40,731	68.9	7.6	10.0	5.7	7.9	27.7	8.7	34.6	33.3	34.1	13,694	95.1
Shamrock township (Aitkin)	1,271	1,261	-0.8	1,308	96.8	0.0	0.0	2.0	1.2	16.9	38.7	59.1	40.7	26.1	676	84.6
Shaokatan township (Lincoln)	178	174	-2.2	159	100.0	0.0	0.0	0.0	0.0	23.9	20.1	45.5	40.4	19.3	67	86.6
Sharon township (Le Sueur)	636	670	5.3	584	99.3	0.0	0.0	0.7	0.0	12.3	20.7	54.7	41.4	27.2	248	92.7
Shelburne township (Lyon)	180	179	-0.6	229	99.1	0.0	0.0	0.0	0.9	37.1	4.4	37.6	40.3	27.8	81	100.0
Shelby township (Blue Earth)	264	263	-0.4	268	97.4	0.0	0.0	0.0	2.6	19.8	23.5	52.2	44.7	17.6	122	84.4
Sheldon township (Houston)	266	265	-0.4	257	99.2	0.0	0.0	0.0	0.8	19.8	13.6	50.8	46.1	19.7	115	73.9
Shell Lake township (Becker)	293	311	6.1	283	95.1	0.0	0.0	4.9	0.0	10.6	34.6	59.9	40.0	8.8	135	88.1
Shell River township (Wadena)	233	231	-0.9	294	92.5	0.0	5.4	2.0	0.0	24.1	13.6	38.6	45.3	14.4	112	91.1
Shell Rock township (Freeborn)	428	414	-3.3	452	97.8	0.0	0.0	0.0	2.2	19.5	22.1	53.3	50.7	9.0	214	85.5
Shelly city & MCD (Norman)	192	179	-6.8	133	69.2	0.0	0.0	9.0	21.8	19.5	24.8	43.5	47.9	21.3	56	87.5
Shelly township (Norman)	114	107	-6.1	108	84.3	0.0	0.0	0.0	15.7	11.1	44.4	64.5	60.4	14.3	65	92.3
Sherburn city & MCD (Martin)	1,137	1,087	-4.4	1,033	96.6	0.0	0.3	1.7	1.4	21.6	21.6	42.7	47.4	13.2	466	79.6
Sheridan township (Redwood)	197	188	-4.6	217	100.0	0.0	0.0	0.0	0.0	27.6	22.1	43.6	40.7	21.5	88	85.2
Sherman township (Redwood)	371	360	-3.0	419	33.7	0.7	0.0	52.3	13.4	27.9	12.2	35.1	53.9	10.4	172	89.5
Shetek township (Murray)	296	288	-2.7	299	97.7	0.0	0.0	1.0	1.3	14.4	36.8	60.9	38.4	19.0	137	83.9
Shevlin city & MCD (Clearwater)	176	175	-0.6	153	97.4	0.0	0.0	2.6	0.0	16.3	20.3	43.0	58.9	0.0	63	90.5
Shevlin township (Clearwater)	452	462	2.2	545	97.4	0.0	0.0	1.1	1.5	25.1	16.7	34.7	53.7	12.4	203	85.7
Shible township (Swift)	124	119	-4.0	134	97.0	0.0	3.0	0.0	0.0	27.6	26.9	42.5	46.2	12.1	64	87.5
Shieldsville township (Rice)	1,137	1,197	5.3	1,000	99.3	0.0	0.0	0.7	0.0	21.1	22.2	50.7	34.2	27.3	403	89.8
Shingobee township (Cass)	1,513	1,583	4.6	1,565	73.4	0.3	0.4	25.3	0.6	22.8	28.2	53.8	31.6	34.6	666	86.3
Shooks township (Beltrami)	179	177	-1.1	216	90.7	0.0	0.0	9.3	0.0	34.7	12.0	31.7	55.0	7.0	67	86.6
Shoreview city & MCD (Ramsey)	25,043	27,130	8.3	26,791	83.1	2.3	9.2	2.4	3.0	21.8	19.7	45.4	16.2	56.2	11,070	94.5
Shorewood city	7,297	8,084	10.8	7,867	93.4	0.2	1.2	2.1	3.2	26.7	17.5	46.2	11.2	69.4	2,783	99.0
Shotley township (Beltrami)	35	35	0.0	53	100.0	0.0	0.0	0.0	0.0	0.0	88.7	78.2	73.6	13.2	31	67.7
Shotley Brook UT (Beltrami)	25	25	0.0	13	100.0	0.0	0.0	0.0	0.0	0.0	38.5	62.8	0.0	0.0	9	100.0
Sibley township (Sibley)	255	251	-1.6	295	98.6	0.0	0.0	1.4	0.0	20.7	19.3	48.5	46.0	16.4	134	88.8
Sigel township (Brown)	344	337	-2.0	334	99.7	0.0	0.3	0.0	0.0	18.6	16.2	49.2	56.3	10.6	145	82.8
Silver township (Carlton)	456	471	3.3	434	93.5	2.3	0.0	2.8	1.4	20.5	16.6	45.9	40.7	13.9	166	89.2
Silver Bay city & MCD (Lake)	1,877	1,762	-6.1	1,722	94.1	0.5	0.6	3.0	1.9	16.8	25.7	51.6	38.3	27.4	850	89.9
Silver Brook township (Carlton)	648	672	3.7	634	94.3	0.2	0.0	5.2	0.3	14.2	21.6	54.1	45.3	15.9	279	88.2
Silver Creek township (Lake)	1,135	1,164	2.6	1,332	97.1	0.0	0.3	2.6	0.0	16.1	25.4	54.6	37.6	27.7	649	87.5
Silver Creek CDP	256	-	-	272	100.0	0.0	0.0	0.0	0.0	7.7	33.5	55.7	42.8	12.6	111	86.5
Silver Creek township (Wright)	2,335	2,484	6.4	2,815	95.3	0.6	0.2	2.8	1.1	23.0	18.0	46.5	32.3	28.9	1,032	93.2
Silver Lake city & MCD (McLeod)	857	814	-5.0	945	91.6	0.0	0.0	4.6	3.8	31.3	12.2	36.4	47.6	10.8	387	84.0
Silver Lake township (Martin)	521	500	-4.0	458	100.0	0.0	0.0	0.0	0.0	18.1	26.9	53.9	45.8	27.4	207	94.2
Silver Leaf township (Becker)	534	567	6.2	423	91.0	0.0	0.0	2.4	6.6	25.3	14.9	37.3	59.0	14.2	154	83.8
Silverton township (Pennington)	187	180	-3.7	178	100.0	0.0	0.0	0.0	0.0	12.4	15.7	45.4	35.5	18.5	65	90.8
Sinclair township (Clearwater)	164	165	0.6	179	96.1	0.0	0.0	0.0	3.9	17.3	40.2	56.8	43.4	20.0	77	83.1
Sinnott township (Marshall)	24	24	0.0	23	100.0	0.0	0.0	0.0	0.0	0.0	39.1	62.5	26.1	47.8	13	84.6
Sioux Agency township (Yellow Medicine)	226	212	-6.2	193	93.3	0.5	4.7	1.6	0.0	23.8	9.3	42.9	51.2	13.8	71	94.4
Sioux Valley township (Jackson)	192	187	-2.6	158	91.1	0.0	0.0	0.0	8.9	20.9	20.9	50.5	49.1	24.1	65	75.4
Six Mile Grove township (Swift)	171	164	-4.1	139	100.0	0.0	0.0	0.0	0.0	30.2	17.3	43.3	31.9	13.2	50	86.0
Skagen township (Roseau)	235	222	-5.5	255	98.4	0.0	1.2	0.0	0.4	22.7	20.0	47.1	46.0	8.0	97	96.9
Skandia township (Murray)	172	165	-4.1	121	100.0	0.0	0.0	0.0	0.0	39.7	12.4	34.5	28.6	34.3	42	95.2
Skane township (Kittson)	46	43	-6.5	64	100.0	0.0	0.0	0.0	0.0	42.2	6.3	19.7	33.3	13.3	13	100.0
Skelton township (Carlton)	414	431	4.1	415	98.3	0.0	0.0	1.7	0.0	19.8	19.0	49.7	41.4	21.7	161	88.8
Skree township (Clay)	159	167	5.0	137	100.0	0.0	0.0	0.0	0.0	18.2	35.8	54.8	26.9	42.6	56	83.9
Skyline city & MCD (Blue Earth)	302	300	-0.7	277	96.0	0.0	1.1	0.4	2.5	20.9	22.4	51.5	13.1	60.6	115	93.0
Slater township (Cass)	215	225	4.7	226	93.4	0.0	0.9	2.7	3.1	19.9	27.9	57.7	44.1	27.1	102	80.4
Slayton city & MCD (Murray)	2,155	1,974	-8.4	2,002	97.2	0.8	0.1	0.0	1.8	22.2	26.5	46.0	47.5	22.3	962	83.4
Slayton township (Murray)	293	282	-3.8	279	100.0	0.0	0.0	0.0	0.0	21.5	32.3	50.5	38.6	30.0	110	84.5

1 May be of any race.

Table A. All Places — Population and Housing

STATE City, town, township, borough, or CDP (county if applicable)	Population				Race and Hispanic or Latino origin (percent)					Age (percent)			Educational attainment of persons age 25 and older		Occupied housing units	
	2010 census total population	2019 estimated population	Percent change 2010–2019	ACS total population estimate 2015–2019	White alone, not Hispanic or Latino	Black alone, not Hispanic or Latino	Asian alone, not Hispanic or Latino	All other races or 2 or more races, not Hispanic or Latino	Hispanic or Latino[1]	Under 18 years old	Age 65 years and older	Median age	Percent High school diploma or less	Percent Bachelor's degree or more	Total	Percent with a computer
	1	2	3	4	5	6	7	8	9	10	11	12	13	14	15	16
MINNESOTA—Con.																
Sleepy Eye city & MCD (Brown)	3,602	3,356	-6.8	3,401	87.9	0.4	0.0	0.2	11.4	23.0	20.9	41.0	48.2	21.8	1,486	83.8
Sletten township (Polk)	177	178	0.6	176	98.3	0.0	1.7	0.0	0.0	42.0	15.9	36.8	32.7	39.6	55	92.7
Smiley township (Pennington)	580	559	-3.6	728	90.0	0.0	2.5	5.5	2.1	30.2	11.8	37.9	41.1	20.5	254	97.6
Smoky Hollow township (Cass)	70	73	4.3	67	100.0	0.0	0.0	0.0	0.0	13.4	31.3	58.5	57.9	8.8	35	68.6
Sobieski city & MCD (Morrison)	197	201	2.0	194	96.9	0.0	0.0	3.1	0.0	21.1	18.6	38.4	56.3	5.6	81	79.0
Sodus township (Lyon)	283	282	-0.4	331	99.1	0.0	0.3	0.0	0.6	26.3	12.1	39.9	32.1	27.2	117	90.6
Solem township (Douglas)	233	242	3.9	233	99.1	0.0	0.0	0.9	0.0	22.7	25.8	53.5	26.9	16.4	104	91.3
Soler township (Roseau)	95	90	-5.3	105	97.1	2.9	0.0	0.0	0.0	30.5	17.1	32.9	37.7	4.3	33	93.9
Solway city & MCD (Beltrami)	96	95		83	94.0	0.0	0.0	2.4	3.6	19.3	26.5	43.8	31.7	19.0	36	100.0
Solway township (St. Louis)	1,942	1,957	0.8	2,048	95.3	0.0	0.0	4.6	0.1	20.5	17.4	44.9	38.5	20.2	842	88.2
Somerset township (Steele)	732	736	0.5	798	97.2	0.8	0.0	0.8	1.3	22.1	18.0	44.7	55.5	11.1	316	82.3
Soudan CDP	446	-	-	378	98.9	0.0	0.0	1.1	0.0	16.4	19.3	51.9	28.4	17.8	178	88.8
South Bend township (Blue Earth)	1,682	1,679	-0.2	1,628	94.0	1.9	0.4	2.6	1.0	21.3	23.6	45.3	46.6	21.7	554	91.9
South Branch township (Watonwan)	282	279	-1.1	178	100.0	0.0	0.0	0.0	0.0	9.0	23.6	54.6	34.0	34.7	80	81.3
Southbrook township (Cottonwood)	79	77	-2.5	32	90.6	0.0	0.0	9.4	0.0	12.5	50.0	64.0	42.9	14.3	18	72.2
South Clearwater UT (Clearwater)	10	10	0.0	-	-	-	-	-	-	-	-	-	-	-	-	-
Southeast Roseau UT (Roseau)	231	221	-4.3	245	100.0	0.0	0.0	0.0	0.0	29.0	12.2	37.8	40.8	8.0	102	92.2
South End CDP	-	-	-	49	0.0	0.0	0.0	69.4	30.6	40.8	6.1	28.5	58.6	0.0	7	100.0
South Fork township (Kanabec)	789	800	1.4	820	88.8	0.0	2.0	8.9	0.4	22.2	19.6	44.1	43.7	14.3	314	91.7
South Harbor township (Mille Lacs)	808	818	1.2	775	80.1	0.4	0.5	13.9	5.0	17.3	26.8	53.0	45.7	15.2	345	86.7
South Haven city & MCD (Wright)	187	193	3.2	179	97.2	0.0	0.0	1.7	1.1	23.5	16.8	42.3	66.7	4.9	75	82.7
South Red River township (Kittson)	19	18	-5.3	13	100.0	0.0	0.0	0.0	0.0	46.2	7.7	45.3	0.0	14.3	4	100.0
South St. Paul city & MCD (Dakota)	20,118	20,060	-0.3	20,194	75.0	3.1	2.0	5.8	14.2	24.3	13.0	35.1	36.8	27.2	8,053	91.3
Southside township (Wright)	1,521	1,618	6.4	1,581	97.8	0.0	0.4	1.4	0.4	20.0	19.4	49.7	35.6	29.9	664	94.0
Spalding township (Aitkin)	329	327	-0.6	264	48.9	0.0	0.0	42.8	8.3	28.0	17.4	31.5	50.0	14.9	108	95.4
Spang township (Itasca)	264	263	-0.4	246	97.6	0.0	1.2	1.2	0.0	18.3	19.1	53.0	36.1	21.5	108	92.6
Sparta township (Chippewa)	770	744	-3.4	757	98.5	0.0	0.0	0.8	0.7	21.8	21.1	47.1	38.0	24.2	313	90.4
Spencer township (Aitkin)	518	515	-0.6	445	95.3	0.0	2.0	0.0	2.7	17.5	21.1	49.9	31.5	27.0	196	91.3
Spencer Brook township (Isanti)	1,589	1,647	3.7	1,642	96.5	0.4	0.0	0.5	2.6	22.6	17.2	43.9	40.3	18.9	570	92.6
Spicer city & MCD (Kandiyohi)	1,172	1,222	4.3	1,188	94.9	0.0	0.0	1.3	3.8	19.4	19.5	47.3	34.1	29.9	544	91.2
Splithand township (Itasca)	250	250	0.0	225	93.3	0.0	0.0	2.2	4.4	19.1	25.3	51.9	49.7	20.5	95	78.9
Split Rock township (Carlton)	166	173	4.2	192	98.4	0.0	0.0	0.0	1.6	22.4	17.2	47.5	51.4	19.7	75	68.0
Spring Brook township (Kittson)	52	49	-5.8	37	100.0	0.0	0.0	0.0	0.0	16.2	43.2	53.8	78.6	21.4	19	47.4
Spring Creek township (Becker)	114	122	7.0	120	67.5	0.0	0.0	32.5	0.0	39.2	18.3	30.0	21.2	21.2	38	92.1
Spring Creek township (Norman)	81	77	-4.9	41	95.1	0.0	4.9	0.0	0.0	4.9	36.6	58.3	54.1	13.5	16	68.8
Springdale township (Redwood)	217	209	-3.7	206	96.6	1.5	1.9	0.0	0.0	23.8	18.4	44.8	33.6	35.7	82	87.8
Springfield city & MCD (Brown)	2,150	2,004	-6.8	2,030	95.4	0.0	0.3	1.5	2.8	25.7	26.5	45.1	46.2	19.4	879	87.6
Springfield township (Cottonwood)	120	116	-3.3	101	100.0	0.0	0.0	0.0	0.0	28.7	19.8	44.1	42.9	21.4	43	86.0
Spring Grove city & MCD (Houston)	1,336	1,266	-5.2	1,320	98.4	1.1	0.0	0.3	0.2	24.6	28.6	45.8	51.4	16.7	575	79.3
Spring Grove township (Houston)	396	392		358	98.0	0.0	0.0	0.8	1.1	16.5	23.5	52.2	46.4	12.9	162	77.2
Spring Hill city & MCD (Stearns)	85	91	7.1	55	100.0	0.0	0.0	0.0	0.0	10.9	58.2	65.8	61.2	12.2	36	61.1
Spring Hill township (Stearns)	368	395	7.3	365	100.0	0.0	0.0	0.0	0.0	29.0	12.1	35.5	62.6	9.7	124	86.3
Spring Lake township (Scott)	3,511	3,835	9.2	3,781	98.8	0.0	0.2	1.0	0.0	18.5	17.6	50.5	27.4	34.7	1,419	96.2
Spring Lake Park city	6,412	6,919	7.9	6,535	74.4	7.8	5.4	6.5	5.9	20.4	20.1	43.2	36.7	20.8	2,746	90.2
Spring Lake Park city (Anoka)	6,234	6,717	7.7	6,483	74.4	7.9	5.4	6.4	5.9	20.6	19.9	43.1	36.4	20.8	2,705	90.0
Spring Lake Park city (Ramsey)	178	202	13.5	52	78.8	0.0	0.0	21.2	0.0	0.0	42.3	59.6	61.5	17.3	41	100.0
Spring Park city	1,674	1,784	6.6	1,906	90.4	3.1	1.8	4.2	0.5	9.3	34.9	57.6	37.2	29.6	1,098	83.8
Spring Prairie township (Clay)	368	389	5.7	409	97.3	0.0	0.5	2.2	0.0	29.3	10.8	34.1	41.5	31.5	123	87.8
Springvale township (Isanti)	1,444	1,501	3.9	1,627	95.0	0.0	1.8	0.9	2.4	25.1	14.6	43.1	37.0	20.2	578	93.6
Spring Valley city & MCD (Fillmore)	2,480	2,410	-2.8	2,481	92.4	0.0	0.0	4.9	0.2	22.5	19.8	41.2	47.9	16.2	1,108	84.0
Spring Valley township (Fillmore)	517	543	5.0	579	99.0	0.0	0.0	0.5	0.5	25.2	19.3	45.0	46.2	13.4	228	90.4

1 May be of any race.

Table A. All Places — **Population and Housing**

STATE City, town, township, borough, or CDP (county if applicable)	Population				Race and Hispanic or Latino origin (percent)					Age (percent)			Educational attainment of persons age 25 and older		Occupied housing units	
	2010 census total population	2019 estimated population	Percent change 2010–2019	ACS total population estimate 2015–2019	White alone, not Hispanic or Latino	Black alone, not Hispanic or Latino	Asian alone, not Hispanic or Latino	All other races or 2 or more races, not Hispanic or Latino	Hispanic or Latino[1]	Under 18 years old	Age 65 years and older	Median age	Percent High school diploma or less	Percent Bachelor's degree or more	Total	Percent with a computer
	1	2	3	4	5	6	7	8	9	10	11	12	13	14	15	16

MINNESOTA—Con.

STATE City, town, township, borough, or CDP (county if applicable)	1	2	3	4	5	6	7	8	9	10	11	12	13	14	15	16
Springwater township (Rock)	252	246	-2.4	237	97.9	0.0	0.0	0.0	2.1	29.5	11.0	43.3	41.2	21.2	87	87.4
Spruce township (Roseau)	552	523	-5.3	713	89.5	4.5	0.4	2.8	2.8	25.8	11.2	40.3	32.6	29.8	221	97.3
Spruce Grove township (Becker)	405	430	6.2	458	98.5	0.0	0.7	0.9	0.0	42.4	10.3	22.0	50.9	12.7	137	82.5
Spruce Grove township (Beltrami)	55	56	1.8	65	100.0	0.0	0.0	0.0	0.0	21.5	20.0	49.2	38.0	30.0	25	92.0
Spruce Hill township (Douglas)	437	451	3.2	455	97.8	0.0	0.0	2.2	0.0	28.4	15.2	41.3	37.6	11.4	151	84.8
Spruce Valley township (Marshall)	242	241	-0.4	268	98.5	0.0	0.0	1.5	0.0	23.9	23.9	48.1	54.4	16.4	116	85.3
Squaw Lake city & MCD (Itasca)	107	106	-0.9	95	46.3	0.0	0.0	53.7	0.0	26.3	18.9	45.2	52.3	7.7	32	71.9
Stacy city & MCD (Chisago)	1,439	1,518	5.5	1,987	88.9	1.7	2.2	4.6	2.6	32.3	6.9	30.5	48.5	16.8	661	93.2
Stafford township (Roseau)	284	267	-6.0	255	98.4	0.8	0.8	0.0	0.0	20.8	22.4	46.5	35.8	18.1	102	90.2
Stanchfield township (Isanti)	1,209	1,251	3.5	958	98.2	0.6	0.0	0.0	1.1	21.7	23.3	45.7	49.9	9.7	404	82.7
Stanchfield CDP	118	-	-	68	100.0	0.0	0.0	0.0	0.0	14.7	19.1	46.5	50.9	5.5	32	68.8
Stanford township (Isanti)	2,261	2,348	3.8	2,241	97.2	0.4	0.0	0.4	1.9	20.6	20.3	47.4	45.2	19.1	820	91.5
Stanley township (Lyon)	238	236	-0.8	202	94.6	0.0	0.5	4.0	1.0	30.2	7.9	41.8	28.6	28.6	71	90.1
Stanton township (Goodhue)	1,121	1,117	-0.4	1,095	96.9	0.0	0.5	1.9	0.6	22.5	14.5	43.2	34.5	24.7	445	90.8
Staples city	3,017	3,000	-0.6	3,093	90.8	0.6	0.0	2.9	5.8	24.8	19.3	42.3	45.0	16.8	1,228	83.6
Staples city (Todd)	2,115	2,099	-0.8	2,210	88.3	0.8	0.0	2.8	8.1	24.9	15.7	42.1	47.1	16.3	952	81.6
Staples city (Wadena)	902	901	-0.1	883	96.8	0.0	0.0	3.2	0.0	24.6	28.3	42.3	38.9	18.3	276	90.6
Staples township (Todd)	624	628	0.6	547	100.0	0.0	0.0	0.0	0.0	13.7	27.6	54.9	43.0	13.6	273	84.2
Star township (Pennington)	120	115	-4.2	72	98.6	0.0	0.0	1.4	0.0	4.2	37.5	61.8	46.4	2.9	39	84.6
Starbuck city & MCD (Pope)	1,304	1,270	-2.6	1,383	92.8	0.0	1.1	4.6	1.5	23.6	23.4	37.8	44.2	14.5	591	85.4
Stark township (Brown)	348	339	-2.6	383	99.0	0.0	0.3	0.0	0.8	27.4	16.2	44.2	55.6	11.3	143	83.2
Star Lake township (Otter Tail)	415	414	-0.2	409	95.1	0.7	0.0	4.2	0.0	17.8	33.5	58.4	50.0	19.8	183	85.8
Stately township (Brown)	165	161	-2.4	108	96.3	0.0	0.0	3.7	0.0	21.3	38.9	58.5	48.8	8.5	45	86.7
Steamboat River township (Hubbard)	127	130	2.4	115	93.0	0.0	0.0	7.0	0.0	13.9	46.1	62.1	39.8	35.5	56	91.1
Steen city & MCD (Rock)	180	165	-8.3	193	99.5	0.0	0.0	0.5	0.0	32.1	13.5	33.8	53.2	10.3	88	85.2
Steenerson township (Beltrami)	23	23	0.0	21	100.0	0.0	0.0	0.0	0.0	0.0	61.9	65.3	78.9	10.5	9	77.8
Stephen city & MCD (Marshall)	652	645	-1.1	681	80.5	0.0	2.5	0.6	16.4	26.3	26.0	42.9	52.9	27.0	275	84.0
Sterling township (Blue Earth)	296	296	0.0	282	96.8	0.4	2.1	0.0	0.7	26.6	23.0	48.8	33.0	37.9	102	85.3
Stevens township (Stevens)	73	74	1.4	41	100.0	0.0	0.0	0.0	0.0	24.4	19.5	48.3	48.4	16.1	15	100.0
Stewart city & MCD (McLeod)	571	539	-5.6	490	90.2	0.0	0.8	1.2	7.8	22.0	15.9	45.3	42.0	5.8	229	90.0
Stewartville city & MCD (Olmsted)	5,921	6,094	2.9	6,120	96.7	0.0	0.4	1.6	1.2	30.5	13.9	35.5	36.8	27.7	2,412	88.6
Stillwater city & MCD (Washington)	18,620	19,627	5.4	19,341	89.0	2.6	1.0	3.0	4.5	24.1	16.5	41.6	23.1	48.3	7,491	93.8
Stillwater township (Washington)	1,957	2,028	3.6	1,890	98.0	0.0	0.3	0.8	0.8	18.1	23.6	54.4	17.7	55.5	702	95.6
Stockholm township (Wright)	959	1,001	4.4	876	95.7	2.9	0.0	0.7	0.8	25.0	13.0	38.7	46.1	11.9	302	90.4
Stockton city & MCD (Winona)	700	737	5.3	835	95.2	0.0	0.4	4.1	0.4	29.0	9.0	36.3	38.5	17.4	286	97.6
Stokes township (Itasca)	230	228	-0.9	181	96.7	0.0	0.6	0.0	2.8	10.5	35.9	60.2	32.9	21.9	88	89.8
Stokes township (Roseau)	215	204	-5.1	231	99.1	0.0	0.9	0.0	0.0	24.7	16.9	33.7	57.0	5.6	92	90.2
Stoneham township (Chippewa)	241	234	-2.9	187	94.7	0.0	0.0	0.0	5.3	13.4	21.4	52.1	30.3	15.5	76	92.1
Stoney Brook township (St. Louis)	336	340	1.2	362	61.9	0.0	1.4	34.5	2.2	26.5	13.5	40.8	45.1	11.5	142	83.8
Stony Brook township (Grant)	133	133	0.0	106	87.7	0.0	0.0	0.0	12.3	18.9	17.9	50.5	29.2	7.7	46	89.1
Stony River township (Lake)	171	175	2.3	238	86.1	0.0	0.0	8.0	5.9	9.7	41.6	61.7	35.4	44.7	109	92.7
Stony Run township (Yellow Medicine)	432	407	-5.8	429	96.7	0.7	0.0	2.6	0.0	23.8	17.7	49.5	35.1	23.5	159	95.0
Storden city & MCD (Cottonwood)	219	204	-6.8	302	91.7	0.0	0.0	5.3	3.0	37.4	15.9	36.3	46.1	12.0	101	91.1
Storden township (Cottonwood)	165	161	-2.4	111	98.2	0.0	0.0	0.0	1.8	27.0	23.4	51.5	32.1	14.8	46	89.1
Stowe Prairie township (Todd)	454	452	-0.4	445	99.6	0.0	0.0	0.4	0.0	23.1	11.2	41.4	33.3	9.2	171	84.8
Straight River township (Hubbard)	726	745	2.6	901	97.8	0.0	0.0	0.6	1.7	26.9	15.0	42.4	38.8	22.7	321	89.4
Strand township (Norman)	99	93	-6.1	75	92.0	0.0	0.0	8.0	0.0	20.0	29.3	52.3	50.0	5.0	39	74.4
Strandquist city & MCD (Marshall)	69	68	-1.4	65	100.0	0.0	0.0	0.0	0.0	7.7	15.4	51.8	54.7	17.0	44	84.1
Strathcona city & MCD (Roseau)	44	42	-4.5	33	97.0	3.0	0.0	0.0	0.0	15.2	6.1	55.8	57.1	10.7	13	100.0
Sturgeon township (St. Louis)	140	140	0.0	149	94.6	0.0	3.4	2.0	0.0	14.8	19.5	46.8	49.2	21.2	65	80.0
Sturgeon Lake city & MCD (Pine)	421	429	1.9	438	93.2	2.3	0.0	2.1	2.5	23.7	13.0	38.2	58.6	6.1	154	88.3
Sturgeon Lake township (Pine)	508	517	1.8	501	80.8	11.6	0.0	7.2	0.4	14.0	21.4	46.4	58.9	5.7	138	81.2
Sugar Bush township (Becker)	504	540	7.1	540	68.9	0.0	0.0	31.1	0.0	23.1	20.2	44.0	52.5	16.4	213	82.6

1 May be of any race.

Table A. All Places — Population and Housing

STATE City, town, township, borough, or CDP (county if applicable)	2010 census total population	2019 estimated population	Percent change 2010–2019	ACS total population estimate 2015–2019	White alone, not Hispanic or Latino	Black alone, not Hispanic or Latino	Asian alone, not Hispanic or Latino	All other races or 2 or more races, not Hispanic or Latino	Hispanic or Latino[1]	Under 18 years old	Age 65 years and older	Median age	Percent High school diploma or less	Percent Bachelor's degree or more	Total	Percent with a computer
	1	2	3	4	5	6	7	8	9	10	11	12	13	14	15	16
MINNESOTA—Con.																
Sugar Bush township (Beltrami)	243	243	0.0	250	78.0	0.0	0.8	21.2	0.0	23.2	15.6	47.5	30.7	35.2	101	88.1
Sullivan township (Polk)....	173	174	0.6	135	100.0	0.0	0.0	0.0	0.0	13.3	12.6	51.3	31.4	30.5	51	96.1
Summit township (Beltrami)	252	248	-1.6	299	100.0	0.0	0.0	0.0	0.0	33.1	20.4	35.5	49.7	29.0	101	83.2
Summit township (Steele).	471	473	0.4	424	99.1	0.0	0.0	0.9	0.0	23.3	16.7	46.8	39.8	25.5	161	85.7
Summit Lake township (Nobles)	323	320	-0.9	372	92.7	0.0	0.0	4.8	2.4	29.0	16.9	44.0	40.0	14.0	139	88.5
Sumner township (Fillmore).................	458	480	4.8	364	99.2	0.0	0.0	0.0	0.8	22.3	10.4	42.3	44.4	11.7	150	88.7
Sumter township (McLeod).................	535	525	-1.9	481	95.4	0.0	0.0	1.9	2.7	22.9	17.3	43.5	39.1	20.4	187	90.4
Sunburg city & MCD (Kandiyohi)................	100	99		75	100.0	0.0	0.0	0.0	0.0	10.7	33.3	55.2	66.2	9.2	48	50.0
Sundal township (Norman)................	157	149	-5.1	123	98.4	0.0	1.6	0.0	0.0	19.5	17.9	45.1	50.5	22.0	62	66.1
Sundown township (Redwood)	185	177	-4.3	209	97.6	0.0	1.4	1.0	0.0	22.0	18.2	43.5	37.2	16.8	81	91.4
Sunfish Lake city & MCD (Dakota)	521	544	4.4	542	93.9	1.3	1.8	1.1	1.8	23.4	19.7	47.5	8.7	72.9	178	99.4
Sunnyside township (Wilkin).................	136	132	-2.9	119	96.6	0.0	0.0	0.0	3.4	19.3	21.0	46.8	34.5	17.9	48	91.7
Sunrise township (Chisago)	1,997	2,113	5.8	1,950	93.0	3.0	0.9	1.0	2.1	25.6	14.3	40.2	35.5	15.6	683	91.7
Svea township (Kittson)....	49	46	-6.1	17	100.0	0.0	0.0	0.0	0.0	5.9	23.5	56.5	25.0	25.0	8	100.0
Sverdrup township (Otter Tail)	621	624	0.5	646	86.7	5.3	0.2	2.0	5.9	20.3	23.5	50.7	41.3	23.2	273	96.0
Swan Lake township (Stevens).................	194	192		145	98.6	1.4	0.0	0.0	0.0	17.9	31.0	52.3	22.9	41.7	63	90.5
Swan River township (Morrison)................	741	756	2.0	629	94.0	2.5	0.0	1.3	2.2	20.8	22.3	50.2	51.6	16.6	257	73.2
Swanville city	346	342	-1.2	293	95.9	0.0	0.0	0.0	4.1	22.5	17.1	42.5	50.5	13.3	124	87.9
Swanville city (Morrison).	344	340	-1.2	293	95.9	0.0	0.0	0.0	4.1	22.5	17.1	42.5	50.5	13.3	124	87.9
Swanville city (Todd)........	2	2	0.0	-	-	-	-	-	-	-	-	-	-	-	-	-
Swanville township (Morrison)................	521	533	2.3	484	99.2	0.0	0.8	0.0	0.0	19.6	17.6	46.4	44.8	14.2	187	90.4
Swede Grove township (Meeker)	400	401	0.3	329	93.3	0.0	0.0	0.6	6.1	25.8	12.5	41.8	48.6	7.9	127	85.8
Swede Prairie township (Yellow Medicine)	170	160	-5.9	185	98.4	0.0	0.0	0.0	1.6	42.2	5.4	37.5	14.3	19.0	56	87.5
Swedes Forest township (Redwood)	121	115	-5.0	102	93.1	0.0	0.0	6.9	0.0	16.7	38.2	55.0	35.1	24.7	49	93.9
Sweet township (Pipestone)	320	315	-1.6	272	97.4	1.1	0.0	1.5	0.0	24.6	11.8	47.2	39.8	20.4	105	91.4
Swenoda township (Swift)	140	135	-3.6	113	98.2	0.0	0.0	0.9	0.9	22.1	14.2	50.5	31.4	14.0	52	86.5
Sylvan township (Cass)	2,707	2,846	5.1	2,793	92.2	0.1	0.0	1.5	6.2	24.0	16.1	44.3	41.1	18.9	1,141	89.7
Synnes township (Stevens).................	118	121	2.5	200	40.0	0.0	0.0	2.5	57.5	18.5	5.5	29.9	27.7	53.5	28	92.9
Tabor township (Polk)	113	113	0.0	64	100.0	0.0	0.0	0.0	0.0	9.4	43.8	60.5	34.5	31.0	32	71.9
Taconite city & MCD (Itasca)..................	649	633	-2.5	770	94.4	1.3	0.0	4.3	0.0	26.4	17.5	40.4	42.9	13.0	325	85.2
Tamarac township (Marshall)................	77	76	-1.3	56	100.0	0.0	0.0	0.0	0.0	23.2	17.9	47.5	35.7	31.0	20	95.0
Tamarack city & MCD (Aitkin)...................	92	94	2.2	115	93.9	6.1	0.0	0.0	0.0	21.7	10.4	39.2	74.2	0.0	51	86.3
Tanberg township (Wilkin)	69	65	-5.8	52	100.0	0.0	0.0	0.0	0.0	13.5	11.5	53.5	45.0	17.5	20	90.0
Tansem township (Clay) ...	259	274	5.8	260	91.2	0.0	0.0	3.1	5.8	18.8	21.2	53.5	34.1	33.7	99	98.0
Taopi city & MCD (Mower)	64	65	1.6	51	100.0	0.0	0.0	0.0	0.0	19.6	19.6	45.5	64.9	8.1	25	84.0
Tara township (Swift)	88	83	-5.7	105	96.2	0.0	0.0	0.0	3.8	38.1	19.0	37.9	52.3	29.2	31	100.0
Tara township (Traverse)...	92	87	-5.4	61	100.0	0.0	0.0	0.0	0.0	18.0	39.3	60.1	46.0	16.0	25	92.0
Taunton city & MCD (Lyon)....................	139	133	-4.3	153	100.0	0.0	0.0	0.0	0.0	25.5	10.5	40.5	57.3	17.7	74	82.4
Taylor township (Beltrami)	107	107	0.0	134	96.3	0.0	0.0	3.7	0.0	20.9	15.7	39.7	37.5	26.1	50	96.0
Taylor township (Traverse)	105	99	-5.7	79	100.0	0.0	0.0	0.0	0.0	13.9	35.4	55.7	50.8	10.8	36	88.9
Taylors Falls city & MCD (Chisago)	976	1,034	5.9	1,090	96.4	0.4	0.0	2.5	0.7	21.2	21.7	42.4	40.5	22.7	443	93.5
Tegner township (Kittson).	48	45	-6.3	27	100.0	0.0	0.0	0.0	0.0	14.8	48.1	63.8	39.1	39.1	15	100.0
Teien township (Kittson) ...	73	69	-5.5	19	100.0	0.0	0.0	0.0	0.0	26.3	36.8	60.3	21.4	64.3	8	75.0
Tenhassen township (Martin)..................	260	248	-4.6	279	100.0	0.0	0.0	0.0	0.0	25.4	21.1	49.1	36.5	19.8	124	96.8
Ten Lake township (Beltrami)	1,027	1,110	8.1	1,032	29.6	2.1	0.0	64.9	3.4	32.9	16.1	31.4	33.6	24.9	349	87.4
Ten Mile Lake township (Lac qui Parle)..............	151	139	-7.9	150	100.0	0.0	0.0	0.0	0.0	14.0	25.3	45.0	29.6	21.7	64	93.8
Tenstrike city & MCD (Beltrami)	203	200	-1.5	329	98.8	0.9	0.0	0.3	0.0	29.8	9.1	35.5	63.6	13.3	121	88.4
Terrebonne township (Red Lake)...................	147	144	-2.0	117	97.4	0.0	0.0	2.6	0.0	31.6	14.5	39.6	23.4	23.4	44	95.5
The Lakes CDP	667	-	-	631	97.0	0.5	0.0	1.4	1.1	7.9	46.4	64.3	35.3	30.1	308	89.3
The Ranch CDP	9	-	-	2	0.0	0.0	100.0	0.0	0.0	0.0	0.0	0.0	100.0	0.0	2	0.0
Thief Lake township (Marshall)................	37	37	0.0	28	96.4	3.6	0.0	0.0	0.0	3.6	96.4	73.5	88.9	3.7	17	94.1
Thief River Falls city & MCD (Pennington)	8,617	8,828	2.4	8,790	87.9	1.6	1.0	3.9	5.6	22.0	20.1	39.1	41.4	19.7	4,050	86.1
Third River township (Itasca)..................	50	50	0.0	69	95.7	0.0	0.0	0.0	4.3	10.1	31.9	61.6	58.1	12.9	31	93.5
Thomastown township (Wadena)	788	777	-1.4	689	94.0	0.0	0.0	3.6	2.3	22.4	23.9	48.2	34.9	23.3	278	85.3
Thompson township (Kittson).................	152	145	-4.6	200	100.0	0.0	0.0	0.0	0.0	17.0	15.0	48.2	31.3	18.7	90	93.3
Thomson township (Carlton)..................	5,000	5,178	3.6	5,119	97.9	0.2	0.0	1.3	0.7	24.8	12.9	41.3	23.6	37.6	1,964	92.9

1 May be of any race.

Table A. All Places — Population and Housing

STATE City, town, township, borough, or CDP (county if applicable)	Population				Race and Hispanic or Latino origin (percent)					Age (percent)			Educational attainment of persons age 25 and older		Occupied housing units	
	2010 census total population	2019 estimated population	Percent change 2010–2019	ACS total population estimate 2015–2019	White alone, not Hispanic or Latino	Black alone, not Hispanic or Latino	Asian alone, not Hispanic or Latino	All other races or 2 or more races, not Hispanic or Latino	Hispanic or Latino[1]	Under 18 years old	Age 65 years and older	Median age	Percent High school diploma or less	Percent Bachelor's degree or more	Total	Percent with a computer
	1	2	3	4	5	6	7	8	9	10	11	12	13	14	15	16

MINNESOTA—Con.

STATE City, town, township, borough, or CDP (county if applicable)	1	2	3	4	5	6	7	8	9	10	11	12	13	14	15	16
Thorpe township (Hubbard)	45	47	4.4	27	100.0	0.0	0.0	0.0	0.0	11.1	40.7	64.2	29.2	54.2	13	69.2
Three Lakes township (Redwood)	194	186	-4.1	166	100.0	0.0	0.0	0.0	0.0	30.7	15.1	41.0	41.8	15.5	64	85.9
Thunder Lake township (Cass)	272	284	4.4	257	98.1	0.0	0.4	1.6	0.0	5.1	44.7	63.2	30.9	31.8	149	88.6
Timothy township (Crow Wing)	164	171	4.3	153	100.0	0.0	0.0	0.0	0.0	13.7	32.7	53.5	46.7	17.5	62	87.1
Tintah city & MCD (Traverse)	63	55	-12.7	44	95.5	0.0	0.0	4.5	0.0	43.2	20.5	30.0	69.6	4.3	16	93.8
Tintah township (Traverse)	33	31	-6.1	32	100.0	0.0	0.0	0.0	0.0	6.3	34.4	28.8	43.3	23.3	19	100.0
Toad Lake township (Becker)	539	571	5.9	607	99.3	0.0	0.0	0.7	0.0	33.3	17.6	33.8	51.0	17.2	223	74.9
Todd township (Hubbard)	1,409	1,443	2.4	1,296	97.1	0.0	0.0	0.2	2.7	22.3	24.8	47.8	45.1	24.9	534	85.4
Tofte township (Cook)	251	270	7.6	224	85.7	0.0	4.0	0.0	10.3	9.8	29.9	53.9	30.7	36.2	121	95.0
Toivola township (St. Louis)	170	171	0.6	193	94.8	0.0	4.7	0.5	0.0	17.6	23.3	48.9	49.3	4.1	93	84.9
Tonka Bay city	1,475	1,568	6.3	1,570	89.7	2.7	0.5	2.0	5.1	18.9	23.9	51.1	16.9	62.1	638	97.5
Toqua township (Big Stone)	53	51	-3.8	27	100.0	0.0	0.0	0.0	0.0	29.6	3.7	31.4	21.1	5.3	12	66.7
Tordenskjold township (Otter Tail)	551	554	0.5	532	94.7	0.0	0.0	5.3	0.0	17.5	25.2	52.8	28.2	22.4	224	82.1
Torning township (Swift)	435	418	-3.9	409	92.7	0.0	1.0	1.2	5.1	14.9	13.9	45.8	39.9	16.8	163	92.0
Torrey township (Cass)	155	162	4.5	168	98.2	0.0	0.0	1.8	0.0	13.1	40.5	63.6	53.1	11.9	86	74.4
Tower city & MCD (St. Louis)	500	486	-2.8	470	84.3	5.1	0.2	8.5	1.9	20.9	23.6	41.5	36.6	22.4	251	71.3
Tracy city & MCD (Lyon)	2,162	2,077	-3.9	2,323	82.3	0.0	8.5	4.6	4.6	27.7	19.2	35.2	46.4	16.5	898	89.8
Trail city & MCD (Polk)	46	47	2.2	61	85.2	0.0	0.0	14.8	0.0	29.5	24.6	39.4	61.1	0.0	26	46.2
Transit township (Sibley)	275	270	-1.8	227	99.1	0.0	0.4	0.0	0.4	19.8	24.2	46.8	52.8	15.0	96	84.4
Traverse township (Nicollet)	335	340	1.5	287	96.2	0.0	0.7	2.4	0.7	8.0	31.7	54.6	46.2	16.2	148	98.6
Trelipe township (Cass)	149	156	4.7	156	92.3	0.0	0.0	1.9	5.8	3.8	58.3	66.1	52.1	19.0	76	90.8
Trimont city & MCD (Martin)	749	700	-6.5	779	95.6	0.3	0.0	2.8	1.3	22.6	18.6	38.5	48.0	18.4	317	89.6
Trommald city & MCD (Crow Wing)	98	100	2.0	63	96.8	0.0	0.0	3.2	0.0	7.9	14.3	54.5	71.1	13.3	37	89.2
Trondhjem township (Otter Tail)	192	190		150	96.7	0.0	0.0	0.7	2.7	22.7	20.0	39.8	35.5	17.8	62	85.5
Trosky city & MCD (Pipestone)	86	79	-8.1	83	97.6	0.0	0.0	2.4	0.0	26.5	12.0	38.8	56.4	1.8	32	84.4
Trout Lake township (Itasca)	1,085	1,081	-0.4	1,222	96.3	1.8	0.0	1.6	0.2	17.1	18.9	48.0	30.6	25.2	491	89.0
Troy township (Pipestone)	289	284	-1.7	260	91.9	0.0	0.0	8.1	0.0	24.2	16.9	45.5	46.3	19.7	101	94.1
Troy township (Renville)	261	245	-6.1	238	99.2	0.0	0.8	0.0	0.0	22.3	17.2	46.6	30.1	25.4	95	85.3
Truman city & MCD (Martin)	1,116	1,042	-6.6	1,068	98.8	0.0	0.0	1.2	0.0	16.9	29.5	51.9	51.6	11.1	482	83.6
Tumuli township (Otter Tail)	449	448	-0.2	456	99.3	0.0	0.0	0.4	0.2	23.2	19.3	45.2	30.3	28.1	171	95.3
Tunsberg township (Chippewa)	210	204	-2.9	195	99.0	0.0	0.5	0.5	0.0	29.7	16.4	44.3	41.7	22.7	68	89.7
Turner township (Aitkin)	208	207	-0.5	148	86.5	0.0	0.0	13.5	0.0	15.5	36.5	60.1	48.4	25.8	82	79.3
Turtle Creek township (Todd)	295	297	0.7	261	100.0	0.0	0.0	0.0	0.0	13.8	35.6	55.5	49.7	13.1	119	78.2
Turtle Lake township (Beltrami)	1,195	1,188	-0.6	1,271	93.4	0.1	0.5	4.4	1.7	22.7	24.0	45.6	17.6	50.3	486	96.7
Turtle Lake township (Cass)	679	714	5.2	711	65.1	0.0	0.4	32.3	2.1	20.7	25.3	49.2	32.8	23.5	334	90.7
Turtle River city & MCD (Beltrami)	81	80	-1.2	98	98.0	0.0	2.0	0.0	0.0	13.3	17.3	53.4	27.1	16.5	54	90.7
Turtle River township (Beltrami)	1,091	1,132	3.8	1,160	89.4	0.0	0.4	9.3	0.9	21.3	26.2	47.7	21.4	43.8	460	95.4
Twin Lakes township (Carlton)	2,106	2,188	3.9	1,904	93.5	0.8	0.9	4.1	0.6	20.2	17.8	44.4	32.9	25.4	727	92.0
Twin Lakes city & MCD (Freeborn)	151	148	-2.0	150	97.3	0.0	0.0	2.7	0.0	15.3	32.7	56.8	63.4	9.8	77	79.2
Twin Lakes CDP	149	-	-	235	30.2	0.0	0.0	63.8	6.0	31.5	26.8	42.6	38.9	25.0	82	84.1
Twin Lakes township (Mahnomen)	823	845	2.7	729	9.5	0.0	0.0	83.0	7.5	41.3	12.1	25.5	51.9	14.5	228	75.0
Twin Valley city & MCD (Norman)	820	755	-7.9	765	94.1	1.0	0.8	1.2	2.9	25.9	23.0	38.9	50.9	16.6	305	80.7
Two Harbors city & MCD (Lake)	3,747	3,529	-5.8	3,509	96.4	1.5	0.0	0.9	1.3	22.3	21.8	39.6	42.4	22.5	1,712	88.3
Two Inlets township (Becker)	213	224	5.2	211	98.6	0.0	0.0	1.4	0.0	13.3	36.0	57.4	38.2	26.1	93	95.7
Two Rivers township (Morrison)	689	703	2.0	764	94.4	0.0	1.7	3.4	0.5	31.2	15.7	38.1	49.4	16.0	262	83.2
Tyler city & MCD (Lincoln)	1,142	1,069	-6.4	1,316	95.5	0.4	0.6	1.4	2.1	25.9	27.9	45.0	55.2	20.0	533	75.2
Tynsid township (Polk)	64	64	0.0	71	95.8	0.0	0.0	0.0	4.2	32.4	7.0	40.8	31.8	25.0	24	100.0
Tyro township (Yellow Medicine)	181	170	-6.1	119	100.0	0.0	0.0	0.0	0.0	10.9	26.1	52.6	36.3	15.7	56	92.9
Tyrone township (Le Sueur)	564	592	5.0	545	98.0	0.0	0.0	1.5	0.6	21.8	22.2	50.7	37.0	26.8	219	87.2
Udolpho township (Mower)	448	464	3.6	461	99.8	0.0	0.0	0.0	0.2	26.2	16.9	40.2	40.4	22.0	169	81.1
Ulen city & MCD (Clay)	545	544	-0.2	500	93.0	0.0	0.0	3.2	3.8	20.6	42.2	60.5	52.2	15.7	217	76.0
Ulen township (Clay)	176	184	4.5	160	100.0	0.0	0.0	0.0	0.0	21.9	16.9	46.3	53.0	6.8	69	73.9
Underwood city & MCD (Otter Tail)	341	365	7.0	380	88.4	2.6	0.0	8.4	0.5	24.2	23.7	44.2	39.7	18.8	173	87.3
Underwood township (Redwood)	206	197	-4.4	164	78.0	17.7	0.0	1.2	3.0	32.3	18.3	43.3	36.6	14.0	45	84.4
Union township (Houston)	370	367	-0.8	326	99.7	0.0	0.0	0.0	0.3	23.0	14.4	47.9	34.7	24.7	131	88.5

1 May be of any race.

Table A. All Places — **Population and Housing**

STATE City, town, township, borough, or CDP (county if applicable)	Population				Race and Hispanic or Latino origin (percent)					Age (percent)			Educational attainment of persons age 25 and older		Occupied housing units	
	2010 census total population	2019 estimated population	Percent change 2010–2019	ACS total population estimate 2015–2019	White alone, not Hispanic or Latino	Black alone, not Hispanic or Latino	Asian alone, not Hispanic or Latino	All other races or 2 or more races, not Hispanic or Latino	Hispanic or Latino[1]	Under 18 years old	Age 65 years and older	Median age	Percent High school diploma or less	Percent Bachelor's degree or more	Total	Percent with a computer
	1	2	3	4	5	6	7	8	9	10	11	12	13	14	15	16
MINNESOTA—Con.																
Union Grove township (Meeker)	633	637	0.6	630	96.2	2.7	0.0	0.0	1.1	24.1	19.8	43.2	40.2	21.4	248	90.3
Upper Red Lake UT (Beltrami)	14	14	0.0	14	0.0	0.0	0.0	100.0	0.0	0.0	0.0	0.0	0.0	0.0	14	0.0
Upsala city & MCD (Morrison)	430	424	-1.4	497	89.9	0.0	0.0	0.0	10.1	22.7	16.9	36.6	61.0	10.5	210	85.7
Urbank city & MCD (Otter Tail)	54	52	-3.7	80	100.0	0.0	0.0	0.0	0.0	33.8	7.5	35.3	34.0	28.3	28	85.7
Urness township (Douglas)	243	252	3.7	232	98.7	0.0	1.3	0.0	0.0	14.2	28.4	55.0	44.0	17.1	103	89.3
Utica city & MCD (Winona)	291	276	-5.2	276	90.2	0.0	0.0	9.8	0.0	29.0	10.1	30.0	33.5	17.4	98	95.9
Utica township (Winona)...	640	640	0.0	536	98.3	0.0	0.0	1.7	0.0	34.0	14.4	33.2	43.6	23.7	168	81.0
Vadnais Heights city & MCD (Ramsey)	12,298	13,607	10.6	13,444	78.6	6.7	7.9	3.7	3.1	23.6	18.0	43.3	24.6	44.0	5,458	96.0
Vail township (Redwood)..	229	221	-3.5	208	100.0	0.0	0.0	0.0	0.0	27.4	15.4	47.7	40.7	26.9	77	93.5
Vallers township (Lyon)	214	212	-0.9	228	98.2	0.4	0.0	0.4	0.9	22.4	19.3	50.0	40.2	13.6	96	95.8
Valley township (Marshall)	153	151	-1.3	95	100.0	0.0	0.0	0.0	0.0	37.9	11.6	37.8	35.6	33.9	33	100.0
Van Buren township (St. Louis)	186	188	1.1	173	100.0	0.0	0.0	0.0	0.0	27.7	16.2	40.9	37.6	21.4	68	85.3
Vasa township (Goodhue)	896	891	-0.6	993	97.6	0.0	0.3	1.7	0.4	22.2	12.9	43.3	38.6	20.9	366	92.9
Vega township (Marshall) .	125	123	-1.6	146	100.0	0.0	0.0	0.0	0.0	17.8	24.0	54.0	37.3	30.4	67	97.0
Veldt township (Marshall)..	30	30	0.0	31	100.0	0.0	0.0	0.0	0.0	19.4	38.7	37.3	76.5	0.0	13	84.6
Verdi township (Lincoln)..	206	203	-1.5	103	99.0	0.0	0.0	0.0	1.0	10.7	42.7	61.3	63.7	6.6	48	77.1
Verdon township (Aitkin)...	45	44	-2.2	31	100.0	0.0	0.0	0.0	0.0	0.0	19.4	58.4	41.9	29.0	18	55.6
Vergas city & MCD (Otter Tail)	331	352	6.3	358	92.2	0.0	0.8	6.4	0.6	17.3	24.6	48.4	36.8	19.8	173	78.6
Vermilion Lake township (St. Louis)	278	280	0.7	228	99.1	0.0	0.0	0.0	0.9	6.6	38.2	61.9	26.1	27.5	123	90.2
Vermillion city & MCD (Dakota)	419	419	0.0	506	93.3	0.0	2.2	0.8	3.8	19.6	15.6	44.5	42.2	21.0	189	88.4
Vermillion township (Dakota)	1,193	1,238	3.8	1,235	94.4	0.0	4.6	0.5	0.5	23.1	13.4	43.1	41.7	20.0	458	93.0
Verndale city & MCD (Wadena)	602	570	-5.3	555	93.0	0.4	0.0	6.1	0.5	30.5	16.2	33.8	46.2	18.3	238	87.0
Vernon township (Dodge).	665	691	3.9	751	99.6	0.1	0.0	0.3	0.0	29.2	14.8	38.5	36.8	30.2	255	86.3
Vernon Center city & MCD (Blue Earth)	332	313	-5.7	366	96.4	0.0	0.0	0.5	3.0	28.7	10.1	37.6	48.9	19.1	152	91.4
Vernon Center township (Blue Earth)	262	260	-0.8	182	96.7	2.7	0.0	0.5	0.0	21.4	23.1	46.3	34.1	17.8	80	81.3
Verona township (Faribault)	364	349	-4.1	354	98.6	0.6	0.0	0.0	0.8	19.2	25.4	49.3	35.0	24.6	158	93.7
Vesta city & MCD (Redwood)	319	296	-7.2	288	99.0	0.0	0.0	0.0	1.0	26.7	16.7	36.0	51.6	18.1	122	73.8
Vesta township (Redwood)	192	184	-4.2	221	100.0	0.0	0.0	0.0	0.0	32.1	10.0	42.9	49.2	22.7	69	88.4
Victor township (Wright) ...	1,034	1,096	6.0	1,066	99.8	0.0	0.0	0.2	0.0	20.3	20.7	49.0	47.0	21.7	419	91.6
Victoria city & MCD (Carver)	7,399	10,206	37.9	9,383	95.1	0.0	0.7	2.7	1.5	29.7	11.5	39.5	12.5	62.9	3,145	99.0
Viding township (Clay)	103	109	5.8	91	78.0	0.0	0.0	22.0	0.0	25.3	20.9	44.2	25.8	36.4	36	100.0
Vienna township (Rock)....	156	151	-3.2	129	100.0	0.0	0.0	0.0	0.0	12.4	33.3	59.3	46.8	9.9	63	85.7
Viking city & MCD (Marshall)	102	101		104	87.5	0.0	0.0	5.8	6.7	20.2	20.2	52.8	55.0	15.0	48	81.3
Viking township (Marshall)	158	156	-1.3	124	93.5	0.0	0.0	6.5	0.0	10.5	23.4	53.5	50.0	10.9	67	86.6
Villard city & MCD (Pope).	254	253	-0.4	274	97.4	0.0	0.0	2.6	0.0	22.6	19.3	33.3	37.5	9.9	126	83.3
Villard township (Todd)	656	664	1.2	682	95.6	0.9	0.4	2.2	0.9	15.7	23.9	52.3	49.9	12.5	289	79.2
Vineland CDP	1,001	-	-	861	5.7	1.2	0.0	90.5	2.7	40.7	8.6	24.9	54.9	7.9	254	84.3
Vineland township (Polk) ..	94	95	1.1	139	100.0	0.0	0.0	0.0	0.0	34.5	20.1	39.7	33.7	51.7	44	95.5
Vining city & MCD (Otter Tail)	78	78	0.0	39	100.0	0.0	0.0	0.0	0.0	20.5	30.8	56.5	48.4	12.9	19	73.7
Viola township (Olmsted)..	589	587	-0.3	591	94.6	2.0	1.5	1.9	0.0	17.4	18.8	51.2	29.0	32.2	237	94.9
Virginia city & MCD (St. Louis)	8,716	8,373	-3.9	8,484	91.3	0.7	0.2	5.8	2.0	15.9	22.7	44.3	41.9	18.1	4,305	81.8
Vivian township (Waseca)	261	264	1.1	196	99.0	0.0	1.0	0.0	0.0	14.8	24.0	54.3	41.7	17.2	92	81.5
Waasa township (St. Louis)	249	251	0.8	261	98.5	0.0	0.0	1.5	0.0	19.5	28.7	52.5	39.0	12.7	116	81.0
Wabana township (Itasca)	537	534	-0.6	499	98.0	0.0	0.0	1.6	0.4	17.4	26.9	54.3	29.8	39.6	229	87.3
Wabasha city & MCD (Wabasha)	2,521	2,473	-1.9	2,673	96.9	0.0	0.3	1.6	1.2	18.7	32.7	51.4	37.1	26.9	1,216	87.8
Wabasso city & MCD (Redwood)	695	659	-5.2	765	87.6	2.1	2.5	4.2	3.7	21.0	24.4	49.5	43.7	22.9	309	82.5
Wabedo township (Cass)..	342	358	4.7	356	99.2	0.0	0.0	0.8	0.0	4.2	57.3	67.1	29.3	35.2	197	89.8
Waconia city & MCD (Carver)	10,778	12,370	14.8	12,131	95.0	0.7	0.6	0.9	2.9	30.3	13.2	37.5	21.1	51.3	4,323	92.9
Waconia township (Carver)	1,151	1,186	3.0	1,055	98.2	1.0	0.0	0.6	0.2	24.8	23.7	47.6	32.8	39.4	387	90.2
Wacouta township (Goodhue)	386	385	-0.3	389	93.8	1.5	0.8	3.3	0.5	15.7	28.8	52.9	27.1	41.9	175	89.7
Wadena city (Wadena)	4,085	4,105	0.5	4,158	94.6	0.7	0.0	3.4	1.4	25.0	22.0	38.1	48.4	12.9	1,904	81.3
Wadena city (Otter Tail)	69	74	7.2	154	100.0	0.0	0.0	0.0	0.0	11.7	42.2	61.8	52.6	13.2	88	93.2
Wadena city (Wadena)	4,016	4,031	0.4	4,004	94.4	0.7	0.0	3.5	1.4	25.5	21.2	36.6	48.2	12.9	1,816	80.7
Wadena township (Wadena)	877	862	-1.7	978	89.2	0.2	0.0	0.0	10.6	32.2	15.0	36.5	41.1	7.3	351	85.8
Wagner township (Aitkin)..	332	330	-0.6	299	97.7	0.0	0.0	1.7	0.7	14.7	39.8	60.8	52.7	12.2	145	73.8
Wahkon city & MCD (Mille Lacs)	206	219	6.3	256	87.1	0.0	0.8	11.7	0.4	13.3	28.9	55.0	56.5	12.6	126	93.7
Wahnena UT (Cass)	180	190	5.6	149	97.3	0.0	0.0	2.7	0.0	27.5	6.7	44.3	33.3	25.0	77	87.0
Waite Park city & MCD (Stearns)	7,384	7,768	5.2	7,692	64.2	20.2	4.2	3.1	8.4	21.0	17.8	31.1	47.8	16.6	3,499	91.5
Wakefield township (Stearns)	2,768	2,927	5.7	2,893	98.8	0.0	0.0	0.0	1.2	23.4	17.3	46.9	33.8	27.3	1,051	94.8
Walcott township (Rice)....	953	1,004	5.4	989	99.7	0.0	0.0	0.0	0.0	19.7	17.2	47.8	42.5	20.6	390	94.4

1 May be of any race.

Table A. All Places — **Population and Housing**

STATE City, town, township, borough, or CDP (county if applicable)	Population				Race and Hispanic or Latino origin (percent)					Age (percent)			Educational attainment of persons age 25 and older		Occupied housing units	
	2010 census total population	2019 estimated population	Percent change 2010–2019	ACS total population estimate 2015–2019	White alone, not Hispanic or Latino	Black alone, not Hispanic or Latino	Asian alone, not Hispanic or Latino	All other races or 2 or more races, not Hispanic or Latino	Hispanic or Latino[1]	Under 18 years old	Age 65 years and older	Median age	Percent High school diploma or less	Percent Bachelor's degree or more	Total	Percent with a computer
	1	2	3	4	5	6	7	8	9	10	11	12	13	14	15	16

MINNESOTA—Con.

STATE City, town, township, borough, or CDP (county if applicable)	1	2	3	4	5	6	7	8	9	10	11	12	13	14	15	16
Walden township (Cass)...	500	528	5.6	491	95.9	0.0	0.0	0.6	3.5	21.4	17.5	42.0	47.6	19.0	233	91.8
Walden township (Pope)...	169	175	3.6	163	98.2	0.6	0.0	1.2	0.0	25.2	21.5	37.8	57.6	10.1	68	89.7
Waldorf city & MCD (Waseca)..................	229	226	-1.3	226	95.6	0.0	1.8	1.8	0.9	31.9	18.1	39.5	58.8	16.9	93	98.9
Walker city & MCD (Cass)	946	934	-1.3	938	72.9	1.6	0.6	23.9	1.0	20.8	31.2	43.8	36.5	32.7	444	83.1
Walls township (Traverse).	65	61	-6.2	30	100.0	0.0	0.0	0.0	0.0	13.3	40.0	62.3	30.8	0.0	14	100.0
Walnut Grove city & MCD (Redwood)	871	806	-7.5	687	57.1	0.0	39.4	3.5	0.0	24.9	21.1	34.4	52.5	14.2	282	80.9
Walnut Lake township (Faribault)	214	204	-4.7	175	100.0	0.0	0.0	0.0	0.0	11.4	21.1	53.8	49.3	17.4	79	88.6
Walter township (Lac qui Parle)	148	136	-8.1	126	100.0	0.0	0.0	0.0	0.0	15.1	22.2	48.5	56.2	19.1	58	82.8
Walters city & MCD (Faribault)	73	67	-8.2	68	97.1	0.0	0.0	0.0	2.9	14.7	27.9	52.0	79.3	5.2	38	71.1
Waltham city & MCD (Mower)	151	150	-0.7	151	94.7	0.0	0.0	0.0	5.3	28.5	10.6	36.1	43.2	10.5	64	87.5
Waltham township (Mower)	339	352	3.8	411	97.6	0.0	1.5	1.0	0.0	14.8	20.9	49.6	34.6	20.8	157	82.8
Walworth township (Becker)	87	91	4.6	88	94.3	0.0	1.1	4.5	0.0	35.2	31.8	42.5	49.1	12.3	32	68.8
Wanamingo city & MCD (Goodhue)	1,086	1,078	-0.7	1,140	92.5	0.0	1.8	1.3	4.5	23.8	18.4	40.7	44.6	18.2	499	89.4
Wanamingo township (Goodhue)	456	451	-1.1	368	98.4	0.0	0.8	0.8	0.0	19.3	17.7	51.5	46.2	20.1	160	90.0
Wanda city & MCD (Redwood)	84	80	-4.8	55	87.3	0.0	0.0	7.3	5.5	14.5	50.9	65.3	57.8	6.7	29	72.4
Wang township (Renville).	249	234	-6.0	261	97.3	0.0	0.4	2.3	0.0	21.1	13.8	42.5	31.2	23.7	96	91.7
Wanger township (Marshall)	75	74	-1.3	75	100.0	0.0	0.0	0.0	0.0	29.3	13.3	34.9	50.0	18.0	32	81.3
Warba city & MCD (Itasca)	181	182	0.6	184	95.7	0.0	0.0	4.3	0.0	22.8	15.8	39.2	32.0	13.3	83	88.0
Ward township (Todd).......	447	447	0.0	449	99.6	0.0	0.0	0.0	0.4	20.9	27.2	54.4	48.4	13.9	199	83.9
Warren city & MCD (Marshall)	1,565	1,552	-0.8	1,700	92.6	0.8	0.2	2.4	4.1	21.5	23.7	44.0	45.1	17.0	743	84.9
Warren township (Winona)	647	646	-0.2	685	88.5	0.0	7.9	2.5	1.2	20.9	16.4	46.2	31.0	34.8	237	95.8
Warrenton township (Marshall)	101	100		61	100.0	0.0	0.0	0.0	0.0	23.0	9.8	32.5	32.4	27.0	24	95.8
Warroad city & MCD (Roseau)	1,805	1,795	-0.6	1,881	85.4	0.0	6.4	7.5	0.7	23.9	12.6	35.9	35.6	24.6	730	83.8
Warsaw township (Goodhue)	607	604	-0.5	581	90.9	0.0	0.0	2.6	6.5	22.0	18.1	48.4	25.7	32.4	237	92.8
Warsaw CDP	627	-	-	774	94.6	0.0	0.0	3.6	1.8	25.1	15.9	40.9	38.3	28.7	281	99.3
Warsaw township (Rice)...	1,320	1,389	5.2	1,548	97.0	0.0	0.2	1.9	0.9	22.3	16.7	41.0	38.8	26.1	581	93.1
Waseca city & MCD (Waseca)	9,421	8,865	-5.9	8,988	83.0	3.7	0.7	2.9	9.7	22.5	17.0	39.2	47.6	18.6	3,631	85.3
Washington township (Le Sueur)	709	749	5.6	767	96.2	0.4	1.2	0.7	1.6	15.4	30.0	55.6	25.5	45.0	322	95.7
Washington Lake township (Sibley)..........	498	492	-1.2	491	99.2	0.0	0.2	0.6	0.0	16.3	19.6	51.6	47.3	13.0	200	91.5
Wasioja township (Dodge)	899	930	3.4	994	84.3	0.6	1.3	0.8	13.0	29.5	15.1	37.5	37.9	21.9	340	94.4
Waskish township (Beltrami)	118	117	-0.8	88	95.5	0.0	4.5	0.0	0.0	3.4	43.2	62.3	46.3	21.3	47	63.8
Watab township (Benton) .	3,093	3,235	4.6	3,199	97.2	0.0	0.4	1.5	0.9	24.5	12.7	41.0	44.8	20.4	1,145	94.3
Waterbury township (Redwood)	196	189	-3.6	128	98.4	0.0	0.0	0.0	1.6	14.1	34.4	54.7	42.2	23.9	60	75.0
Waterford township (Dakota)	493	501	1.6	513	90.6	1.2	0.0	3.9	4.3	19.9	18.1	45.7	41.0	29.3	189	95.8
Watertown city & MCD (Carver)	4,215	4,529	7.4	4,408	95.8	0.0	0.0	1.3	2.8	29.1	10.7	36.5	31.8	23.1	1,608	94.4
Watertown township (Carver)	1,231	1,268	3.0	1,480	97.9	0.2	0.0	1.9	0.0	20.9	17.6	45.1	40.4	24.3	536	85.1
Waterville city & MCD (Le Sueur)	1,871	1,892	1.1	1,872	94.4	0.8	0.3	1.5	2.9	19.7	20.6	45.6	49.7	20.5	826	86.6
Waterville township (Le Sueur)	713	750	5.2	690	97.1	0.0	0.0	0.0	2.9	26.2	17.0	44.3	44.8	24.3	246	91.9
Watkins city & MCD (Meeker)	962	953	-0.9	944	91.1	0.0	0.0	1.8	7.1	27.8	17.8	32.8	56.8	8.7	418	81.6
Watopa township (Wabasha)	247	246	-0.4	249	98.8	0.0	0.0	1.2	0.0	9.2	28.9	54.3	60.6	11.9	104	85.6
Watson city & MCD (Chippewa)	203	189	-6.9	193	97.9	0.0	0.5	1.6	0.0	24.9	12.4	40.8	39.0	5.9	87	83.9
Waubun city & MCD (Mahnomen)..................	400	405	1.3	433	34.2	1.6	0.2	62.8	1.2	36.0	17.6	30.1	45.6	15.2	151	82.8
Waukenabo township (Aitkin)	316	315	-0.3	279	98.2	0.0	0.0	1.8	0.0	10.4	46.2	63.0	47.5	12.4	148	84.5
Waukon township (Norman)	114	107	-6.1	109	89.9	0.0	0.0	10.1	0.0	15.6	15.6	47.8	52.9	12.6	55	80.0
Waverly township (Martin)	208	199	-4.3	162	100.0	0.0	0.0	0.0	0.0	17.9	20.4	48.9	34.9	14.0	75	92.0
Waverly city & MCD (Wright)	1,358	1,603	18.0	1,410	90.3	0.4	0.7	4.9	3.8	26.8	7.2	33.2	42.1	21.5	534	93.1
Wawina township (Itasca)	77	77	0.0	77	93.5	0.0	0.0	6.5	0.0	2.6	26.0	54.4	38.4	9.6	38	86.8
Wayzata city	3,684	4,657	26.4	4,561	91.7	5.6	1.3	1.2	0.2	17.8	33.3	52.2	15.1	60.1	2,200	91.0
Wealthwood township (Aitkin)	267	265	-0.7	255	96.9	0.0	0.0	3.1	0.0	5.9	55.7	66.8	56.0	18.1	139	79.9
Webster township (Rice)...	1,770	1,863	5.3	2,057	95.1	0.6	0.3	3.1	0.9	24.7	16.4	41.7	35.3	33.3	694	93.4
Weimer township (Jackson)..................	142	138	-2.8	179	90.5	0.0	0.0	0.0	9.5	19.6	34.1	53.3	52.6	11.3	69	81.2
Welch township (Goodhue)	755	754	-0.1	634	87.2	0.2	1.9	7.4	3.3	17.5	16.9	47.8	34.3	24.4	271	86.3
Welcome city & MCD (Martin)	684	649	-5.1	696	95.5	0.0	0.0	2.3	2.2	25.6	17.0	40.2	48.0	12.5	295	89.8
Wellington township (Renville)..................	185	173	-6.5	209	98.1	0.0	0.0	0.0	1.9	12.9	27.8	55.7	51.2	9.1	94	93.6

1 May be of any race.

Table A. All Places — **Population and Housing**

STATE City, town, township, borough, or CDP (county if applicable)	2010 census total population	2019 estimated population	Percent change 2010–2019	ACS total population estimate 2015–2019	White alone, not Hispanic or Latino	Black alone, not Hispanic or Latino	Asian alone, not Hispanic or Latino	All other races or 2 or more races, not Hispanic or Latino	Hispanic or Latino[1]	Under 18 years old	Age 65 years and older	Median age	Percent High school diploma or less	Percent Bachelor's degree or more	Total	Percent with a computer
	1	2	3	4	5	6	7	8	9	10	11	12	13	14	15	16
MINNESOTA—Con.																
Wells city & MCD (Faribault)	2,341	2,169	-7.3	2,336	84.2	0.4	1.5	4.6	9.3	25.8	22.0	44.1	46.4	18.9	997	85.3
Wells township (Rice)	1,598	1,682	5.3	1,483	97.3	1.0	0.4	0.7	0.6	14.8	26.3	51.2	36.0	29.6	651	90.2
Wendell city & MCD (Grant)	167	163	-2.4	115	85.2	0.0	0.0	2.6	12.2	13.0	31.3	55.4	58.2	5.1	58	89.7
Wergeland township (Yellow Medicine)	153	144	-5.9	137	100.0	0.0	0.0	0.0	0.0	15.3	16.8	54.0	47.3	10.0	63	95.2
West Albany township (Wabasha)	396	399	0.8	341	100.0	0.0	0.0	0.0	0.0	19.1	23.5	43.6	53.2	15.9	148	80.4
West Bank township (Swift)	148	142	-4.1	133	84.2	0.0	0.0	0.8	15.0	14.3	22.6	50.0	44.1	20.4	53	90.6
Westbrook city & MCD (Cottonwood)	738	704	-4.6	790	99.2	0.0	0.0	0.4	0.4	21.1	30.5	46.5	49.1	17.2	369	79.9
Westbrook township (Cottonwood)	217	210	-3.2	277	98.6	0.0	0.0	1.4	0.0	22.4	30.3	57.8	47.3	20.3	100	84.0
West Concord city & MCD (Dodge)	782	768	-1.8	721	88.1	0.0	0.0	2.4	9.6	29.1	14.8	34.7	49.7	13.2	283	83.0
West Cook UT (Cook)	1,605	1,719	7.1	1,785	99.5	0.0	0.0	0.5	0.0	17.8	30.6	54.6	14.5	50.1	811	91.7
Westerheim township (Lyon)	235	233	-0.9	237	100.0	0.0	0.0	0.0	0.0	19.0	21.1	54.5	42.1	20.5	101	95.0
Western township (Otter Tail)	129	134	3.9	69	98.6	0.0	0.0	1.4	0.0	21.7	37.7	50.5	46.3	5.6	28	75.0
Westfield township (Dodge)	451	465	3.1	452	95.4	0.0	0.4	0.0	4.2	25.9	13.3	40.1	48.7	18.4	173	90.8
Westford township (Martin)	294	281	-4.4	285	98.6	0.4	0.0	0.0	1.1	16.1	27.7	52.3	31.8	20.6	131	91.6
West Heron Lake township (Jackson)	158	154	-2.5	84	100.0	0.0	0.0	0.0	0.0	22.6	25.0	52.5	22.2	31.7	35	91.4
West Lakeland township (Washington)	4,052	4,215	4.0	4,182	94.4	1.9	2.5	0.4	0.9	24.1	12.9	48.8	18.9	56.0	1,363	100.0
Westline township (Redwood)	178	170	-4.5	202	92.1	1.5	5.9	0.5	0.0	25.2	13.4	45.1	45.1	18.0	81	93.8
West Newton township (Nicollet)	423	428	1.2	365	98.1	0.0	1.6	0.3	0.0	18.1	28.2	57.1	51.5	19.4	161	84.5
Westport city & MCD (Pope)	57	61	7.0	42	69.0	0.0	0.0	0.0	31.0	11.9	4.8	45.5	54.1	8.1	27	48.1
Westport township (Pope)	278	278	0.0	179	100.0	0.0	0.0	0.0	0.0	24.0	15.1	40.1	42.9	23.0	73	89.0
West Roy Lake CDP	74	-	-	42	11.9	0.0	0.0	88.1	0.0	28.6	2.4	35.8	32.1	25.0	13	84.6
West St. Paul city & MCD (Dakota)	19,541	19,961	2.1	19,779	65.1	4.6	4.8	3.4	22.2	20.5	17.4	37.3	34.5	31.3	8,475	88.5
Westside township (Nobles)	218	219	0.5	234	94.4	0.0	0.0	5.6	0.0	28.2	15.8	43.1	49.0	12.7	81	82.7
West Union city & MCD (Todd)	111	124	11.7	113	100.0	0.0	0.0	0.0	0.0	36.3	0.0	30.1	23.5	0.0	39	100.0
West Union township (Todd)	268	269	0.4	271	98.5	0.0	0.7	0.7	0.0	23.2	28.4	49.1	54.2	10.3	108	89.8
West Valley township (Marshall)	132	130	-1.5	135	94.8	0.0	2.2	0.0	3.0	29.6	14.1	29.8	34.7	37.5	47	93.6
Whalan city & MCD (Fillmore)	63	66	4.8	37	91.9	8.1	0.0	0.0	0.0	16.2	40.5	62.6	22.6	41.9	22	63.6
Wheatland township (Rice)	1,240	1,303	5.1	1,344	93.5	0.0	0.0	5.4	1.1	25.8	14.4	39.8	52.5	15.1	465	91.8
Wheaton city & MCD (Traverse)	1,424	1,288	-9.6	1,500	91.3	1.0	0.0	2.6	5.1	17.6	28.7	46.3	42.0	20.3	810	86.4
Wheeling township (Rice)	551	579	5.1	605	98.5	0.0	0.5	0.2	0.8	23.0	9.9	34.8	38.4	30.2	204	93.6
Whipholt CDP	99	-	-	95	100.0	0.0	0.0	0.0	0.0	26.3	27.4	52.5	18.6	37.1	45	95.6
White township (St. Louis)	3,234	3,192	-1.3	3,218	95.5	0.1	2.0	2.5	0.0	22.6	21.3	44.9	42.4	16.7	1,340	80.5
White Bear township (Ramsey)	10,908	11,774	7.9	11,702	92.6	0.2	2.5	0.9	3.8	19.9	20.1	50.6	22.4	45.5	4,644	97.8
White Bear Lake township (Pope)	439	455	3.6	429	99.5	0.0	0.0	0.5	0.0	14.5	25.4	55.6	39.1	22.9	188	95.7
White Bear Lake city	23,849	25,875	8.5	25,673	86.7	2.6	2.7	2.4	5.5	21.5	19.4	42.4	27.9	34.0	10,664	92.6
White Bear Lake city (Ramsey)	23,455	25,468	8.6	25,278	86.5	2.6	2.8	2.5	5.6	21.6	19.1	42.2	28.2	33.5	10,442	93.2
White Bear Lake city (Washington)	394	407	3.3	395	100.0	0.0	0.0	0.0	0.0	18.7	34.2	55.3	11.5	64.5	222	62.6
Whited township (Kanabec)	928	921	-0.8	822	97.4	0.7	0.5	0.7	0.6	17.2	21.7	51.7	47.8	17.4	351	87.2
White Earth CDP	580	-	-	567	3.4	0.0	1.8	88.2	6.7	35.1	14.6	27.6	70.3	4.8	184	61.4
White Earth township (Becker)	828	880	6.3	909	27.4	0.0	1.1	66.9	4.6	33.7	12.2	27.7	60.6	13.8	298	73.8
Whiteface Reservoir UT (St. Louis)	478	484	1.3	418	100.0	0.0	0.0	0.0	0.0	4.5	26.8	56.5	38.6	19.9	206	86.9
Whitefield township (Kandiyohi)	525	540	2.9	536	92.7	0.9	0.4	2.1	3.9	22.0	13.2	44.2	23.6	21.3	202	89.6
Whiteford township (Marshall)	46	45	-2.2	50	100.0	0.0	0.0	0.0	0.0	18.0	36.0	53.5	66.7	12.8	18	88.9
White Oak township (Hubbard)	475	486	2.3	477	98.5	0.0	0.0	0.8	0.6	20.8	29.6	54.3	36.9	26.5	193	91.7
White Pine township (Aitkin)	32	32	0.0	16	100.0	0.0	0.0	0.0	0.0	0.0	37.5	54.5	75.0	0.0	9	100.0
Whitewater township (Winona)	198	198	0.0	194	99.5	0.0	0.0	0.5	0.0	29.4	11.9	34.6	32.3	23.3	71	94.4
Wilder city & MCD (Jackson)	60	57	-5.0	37	45.9	0.0	0.0	0.0	54.1	37.8	13.5	28.4	59.1	0.0	13	100.0
Wild Rice township (Norman)	257	244	-5.1	240	97.5	0.0	0.0	0.8	1.7	13.3	27.9	54.5	51.8	10.1	111	84.7
Wildwood township (Itasca)	193	193	0.0	110	94.5	0.0	5.5	0.0	0.0	15.5	32.7	55.3	38.6	35.2	54	92.6
Wilkinson township (Cass)	401	425	6.0	560	39.1	1.1	0.7	56.1	3.0	36.1	17.0	34.5	51.0	15.2	200	82.0
Willernie city & MCD (Washington)	502	509	1.4	368	91.8	0.0	0.0	0.8	7.3	15.2	22.6	48.2	53.2	13.8	177	80.8

1 May be of any race.

Table A. All Places — **Population and Housing**

STATE City, town, township, borough, or CDP (county if applicable)	Population				Race and Hispanic or Latino origin (percent)					Age (percent)			Educational attainment of persons age 25 and older		Occupied housing units	
	2010 census total population	2019 estimated population	Percent change 2010–2019	ACS total population estimate 2015–2019	White alone, not Hispanic or Latino	Black alone, not Hispanic or Latino	Asian alone, not Hispanic or Latino	All other races or 2 or more races, not Hispanic or Latino	Hispanic or Latino[1]	Under 18 years old	Age 65 years and older	Median age	Percent High school diploma or less	Percent Bachelor's degree or more	Total	Percent with a computer
	1	2	3	4	5	6	7	8	9	10	11	12	13	14	15	16
MINNESOTA—Con.																
Williams township (Aitkin).	144	142	-1.4	112	100.0	0.0	0.0	0.0	0.0	20.5	27.7	45.3	66.7	6.7	41	82.9
Williams city	191	174	-8.9	102	96.1	0.0	0.0	3.9	0.0	3.9	16.7	45.9	53.6	17.9	52	82.7
Willmar city & MCD (Kandiyohi)	19,578	19,869	1.5	19,712	62.6	11.1	1.6	1.6	23.0	26.3	16.5	33.7	43.5	19.3	7,585	88.7
Willmar township (Kandiyohi)	545	563	3.3	569	80.5	4.2	1.2	6.3	7.7	30.9	20.4	43.4	36.4	25.7	230	86.5
Willow Lake township (Redwood)	222	212	-4.5	196	94.4	0.0	0.0	3.6	2.0	17.3	28.6	51.0	50.6	10.4	98	81.6
Willow River city & MCD (Pine)	415	400	-3.6	457	93.4	0.0	0.0	1.1	5.5	26.5	16.2	38.9	47.9	17.0	190	83.7
Willow Valley township (St. Louis)	126	126	0.0	78	87.2	0.0	0.0	12.8	0.0	5.1	23.1	59.6	45.9	28.4	49	89.8
Wilma township (Pine)	65	63	-3.1	69	71.0	23.2	0.0	5.8	0.0	4.3	33.3	61.3	37.9	21.2	35	91.4
Wilmington township (Houston)	434	428	-1.4	327	93.0	0.0	0.0	3.7	3.4	22.3	20.8	50.6	43.5	16.1	137	89.8
Wilmont city & MCD (Nobles)	333	326	-2.1	336	91.7	0.0	4.2	0.9	3.3	19.6	19.9	44.8	46.9	12.4	140	92.9
Wilmont township (Nobles)	190	189	-0.5	197	100.0	0.0	0.0	0.0	0.0	27.9	10.2	40.1	40.6	16.5	69	91.3
Wilson township (Cass)	638	672	5.3	637	89.3	0.0	0.0	9.9	0.8	20.7	16.0	39.9	41.0	17.0	274	85.0
Wilson township (Winona)	1,164	1,171	0.6	1,157	92.0	0.0	0.3	3.0	4.8	15.2	28.3	52.6	37.9	32.7	425	94.1
Wilton city & MCD (Beltrami)	206	296	43.7	156	86.5	0.0	0.0	13.5	0.0	10.9	19.2	35.8	40.9	13.0	67	86.6
Wilton township (Waseca)	365	367	0.5	338	93.2	0.0	0.0	0.3	6.5	19.2	18.0	48.4	43.2	24.1	127	96.1
Winchester township (Norman)	56	53	-5.4	47	100.0	0.0	0.0	0.0	0.0	21.3	19.1	46.5	37.8	5.4	20	85.0
Windemere township (Pine)	1,729	1,762	1.9	1,515	95.8	0.0	0.7	2.4	1.2	15.6	32.8	55.8	41.6	25.0	668	86.4
Windom city & MCD (Cottonwood)	4,634	4,386	-5.4	4,428	83.4	0.9	2.5	1.0	12.2	21.7	23.0	42.0	50.0	23.6	1,999	85.3
Windom township (Mower)	584	610	4.5	752	78.2	0.0	0.0	0.0	21.8	36.6	9.0	31.6	35.2	23.7	227	96.9
Windsor township (Traverse)	66	63	-4.5	111	92.8	0.0	0.0	0.0	7.2	19.8	8.1	45.8	31.5	27.0	41	95.1
Winfield township (Renville)	224	209	-6.7	198	85.9	0.0	0.0	14.1	0.0	25.3	15.7	38.0	40.2	17.4	76	92.1
Winger city & MCD (Polk)	220	222	0.9	192	97.4	0.0	0.0	2.6	0.0	29.2	15.1	45.8	42.4	13.6	89	78.7
Winger township (Polk)	206	208	1.0	146	98.6	0.0	0.0	1.4	0.0	27.4	30.8	44.5	51.9	21.2	51	88.2
Wing River township (Wadena)	468	461	-1.5	480	95.8	0.0	1.3	2.9	0.0	22.9	19.4	39.6	38.8	13.9	211	83.4
Winnebago city & MCD (Faribault)	1,445	1,340	-7.3	1,417	87.0	0.0	0.0	1.2	11.8	24.5	19.0	36.1	55.6	12.9	609	77.5
Winnebago township (Houston)	240	238	-0.8	242	98.3	0.0	1.2	0.4	0.0	27.7	12.4	43.7	39.3	23.9	99	86.9
Winnebago City township (Faribault)	193	184	-4.7	177	100.0	0.0	0.0	0.0	0.0	12.4	23.2	50.9	44.8	21.6	76	88.2
Winona city & MCD (Winona)	27,610	26,594	-3.7	26,854	91.2	2.1	2.7	1.2	2.8	13.9	16.5	29.7	32.2	33.5	10,509	90.0
Winsor township (Clearwater)	90	92	2.2	95	83.2	0.0	0.0	16.8	0.0	17.9	34.7	52.9	24.0	29.3	45	91.1
Winsted city & MCD (McLeod)	2,342	2,240	-4.4	2,180	92.5	0.6	0.0	0.0	6.9	26.3	15.0	36.4	42.8	13.6	884	89.1
Winsted township (McLeod)	974	954	-2.1	960	96.6	0.0	0.0	2.9	0.5	23.0	18.5	47.6	43.8	19.0	386	92.0
Winthrop city & MCD (Sibley)	1,407	1,347	-4.3	1,381	85.8	2.1	0.3	1.7	10.1	24.7	22.2	38.9	43.4	19.1	591	83.2
Winton city & MCD (St. Louis)	171	167	-2.3	116	100.0	0.0	0.0	0.0	0.0	12.9	20.7	52.8	43.7	16.1	58	91.4
Wirt township (Itasca)	106	106	0.0	76	97.4	0.0	0.0	2.6	0.0	15.8	40.8	60.0	46.8	25.8	39	74.4
Wisconsin township (Jackson)	221	215	-2.7	183	96.7	0.0	0.0	3.3	0.0	28.4	29.5	45.9	47.6	24.6	77	74.0
Wiscoy township (Winona)	361	362	0.3	275	93.8	0.0	0.0	0.4	5.8	15.3	19.3	48.2	32.3	32.8	114	95.6
Wolf Lake city & MCD (Becker)	56	56	0.0	31	100.0	0.0	0.0	0.0	0.0	22.6	0.0	27.6	61.1	16.7	13	92.3
Wolf Lake township (Becker)	243	256	5.3	230	93.9	3.5	0.0	1.7	0.9	30.9	20.0	43.0	43.3	10.7	86	88.4
Wolford township (Crow Wing)	381	402	5.5	322	96.9	0.9	0.0	2.2	0.0	16.5	34.8	57.4	33.6	26.5	136	93.4
Wolverton city & MCD (Wilkin)	144	130	-9.7	160	96.9	0.0	0.0	0.0	3.1	22.5	11.3	44.3	25.7	25.7	76	96.1
Wolverton township (Wilkin)	126	120	-4.8	147	100.0	0.0	0.0	0.0	0.0	25.2	13.6	38.9	37.1	16.2	61	91.8
Woodbury city & MCD (Washington)	61,963	72,828	17.5	69,906	76.5	6.0	9.7	3.1	4.7	27.7	11.7	37.1	15.8	59.1	25,366	97.1
Wood Lake city & MCD (Yellow Medicine)	439	401	-8.7	423	83.7	3.5	6.9	2.6	3.3	19.1	13.2	41.2	44.5	11.3	197	87.8
Wood Lake township (Yellow Medicine)	231	216	-6.5	283	97.9	0.0	0.0	1.1	1.1	26.1	17.7	35.7	46.0	14.4	95	84.2
Woodland city	432	486	12.5	439	98.4	0.0	0.0	0.0	1.6	20.7	23.9	56.6	3.6	78.3	167	98.8
Woodland township (Wright)	1,097	1,165	6.2	1,045	97.6	1.5	0.4	0.2	0.3	25.3	15.1	44.2	38.9	22.1	386	89.1
Woodrow township (Beltrami)	73	72	-1.4	98	100.0	0.0	0.0	0.0	0.0	32.7	21.4	35.8	47.5	22.0	31	100.0
Woodrow township (Cass)	611	639	4.6	703	93.7	1.4	1.1	3.6	0.1	5.1	50.6	65.3	26.5	37.2	390	90.0
Woods township (Chippewa)	227	218	-4.0	208	70.2	9.1	0.5	11.5	8.7	33.2	11.1	30.2	33.6	23.0	73	82.2
Woodside township (Otter Tail)	277	278	0.4	197	82.7	0.0	0.0	16.8	0.5	27.9	21.8	44.9	56.8	12.8	83	79.5
Woodside township (Polk)	505	513	1.6	394	100.0	0.0	0.0	0.0	0.0	7.4	32.7	59.3	35.4	31.6	188	90.4
Woodstock city & MCD (Pipestone)	124	118	-4.8	88	92.0	0.0	0.0	4.5	3.4	21.6	10.2	47.8	52.3	13.8	39	89.7
Woodville township (Waseca)	1,326	1,346	1.5	1,326	95.5	1.1	1.4	0.8	1.4	22.4	15.7	45.7	31.5	33.8	511	94.5

1 May be of any race.

Table A. All Places — **Population and Housing**

STATE City, town, township, borough, or CDP (county if applicable)	2010 census total population	2019 estimated population	Percent change 2010–2019	ACS total population estimate 2015–2019	White alone, not Hispanic or Latino	Black alone, not Hispanic or Latino	Asian alone, not Hispanic or Latino	All other races or 2 or more races, not Hispanic or Latino	Hispanic or Latino[1]	Under 18 years old	Age 65 years and older	Median age	Percent High school diploma or less	Percent Bachelor's degree or more	Total	Percent with a computer
	1	2	3	4	5	6	7	8	9	10	11	12	13	14	15	16
MINNESOTA—Con.																
Workman township (Aitkin)	208	206		237	94.5	0.0	0.0	3.8	1.7	21.5	25.3	48.3	45.0	16.1	96	97.9
Worthington city & MCD (Nobles)	12,776	13,099	2.5	13,105	38.3	6.4	10.6	2.4	42.4	29.7	14.3	32.1	62.8	14.4	4,618	88.0
Worthington township (Nobles)	316	316	0.0	329	93.6	0.0	2.4	0.0	4.0	17.9	27.1	51.1	31.5	27.9	127	80.3
Wrenshall city & MCD (Carlton)	399	424	6.3	510	91.8	0.0	0.0	7.8	0.4	22.7	19.4	37.0	37.6	15.3	181	94.5
Wrenshall township (Carlton)	382	398	4.2	529	83.7	0.0	0.4	14.0	1.9	33.8	12.1	38.3	34.2	32.7	187	84.5
Wright city & MCD (Carlton)	122	127	4.1	129	93.8	0.0	0.0	6.2	0.0	36.4	9.3	28.6	57.3	9.8	61	90.2
Wright township (Marshall)	116	114	-1.7	58	98.3	0.0	0.0	1.7	0.0	24.1	13.8	54.0	56.8	13.6	24	100.0
Wuori township (St. Louis)	571	575	0.7	572	97.9	0.0	0.0	1.9	0.2	18.9	17.3	49.5	28.5	25.8	220	90.5
Wyandotte township (Pennington)	130	126	-3.1	71	100.0	0.0	0.0	0.0	0.0	5.6	31.0	52.3	47.4	15.8	38	89.5
Wyanett township (Isanti)	1,729	1,795	3.8	1,896	97.0	0.7	0.5	0.7	1.1	21.4	17.2	47.9	38.9	22.5	758	92.2
Wykeham township (Todd)	407	406	-0.2	229	96.5	0.0	0.0	3.1	0.4	11.4	36.2	55.7	48.4	8.2	111	73.9
Wykoff city & MCD (Fillmore)	444	430	-3.2	418	90.4	0.7	0.0	1.0	7.9	23.2	23.2	37.8	47.2	12.6	174	87.9
Wylie township (Red Lake)	65	64	-1.5	71	100.0	0.0	0.0	0.0	0.0	29.6	26.8	35.3	50.0	4.0	22	90.9
Wyoming city & MCD (Chisago)	7,808	8,066	3.3	7,914	96.6	0.0	0.0	0.8	2.6	23.4	16.6	42.4	40.5	17.3	2,839	92.0
Yellow Bank township (Lac qui Parle)	159	146	-8.2	133	85.0	0.0	0.0	0.0	15.0	25.6	10.5	50.2	52.5	30.3	59	88.1
York township (Fillmore)	368	383	4.1	279	97.1	2.9	0.0	0.0	0.0	12.9	23.7	55.0	44.6	16.0	143	90.9
Young America township (Carver)	689	707	2.6	854	94.8	0.0	2.9	1.4	0.8	19.1	25.5	55.1	48.9	20.0	321	91.0
Yucatan township (Houston)	323	320	-0.9	262	94.7	0.0	0.0	5.0	0.4	16.8	24.4	52.5	38.8	26.2	127	92.1
Zemple city & MCD (Itasca)	93	90	-3.2	114	83.3	3.5	0.0	13.2	0.0	25.4	14.0	31.7	63.1	9.2	36	97.2
Zimmerman city & MCD (Sherburne)	5,238	5,995	14.5	5,657	90.6	0.5	0.7	4.6	3.5	26.5	10.7	33.6	36.4	17.1	1,962	95.6
Zion township (Stearns)	333	358	7.5	268	98.9	0.0	0.0	0.0	1.1	20.5	16.8	52.2	46.9	17.2	121	87.6
Zumbro township (Wabasha)	725	728	0.4	706	96.5	0.0	0.7	2.5	0.3	19.8	17.4	50.1	44.2	18.8	296	89.9
Zumbro Falls city & MCD (Wabasha)	205	239	16.6	265	62.6	2.3	0.0	31.3	3.8	36.6	6.4	32.3	33.8	14.9	97	97.9
Zumbrota city & MCD (Goodhue)	3,273	3,501	7.0	3,426	94.9	0.0	2.5	0.0	2.6	26.4	20.5	39.9	34.8	26.6	1,445	89.4
Zumbrota township (Goodhue)	586	581	-0.9	625	99.5	0.0	0.3	0.0	0.2	23.4	19.8	46.9	37.9	25.1	249	89.6
MISSISSIPPI	2,968,130	2,976,149	0.3	2,984,418	56.6	37.6	1.0	1.8	3.1	23.9	15.4	37.5	45.9	22.0	1,104,394	83.8
Abbeville town	412	423	2.7	407	68.8	23.6	0.0	2.0	5.7	24.6	18.4	40.7	59.2	12.7	138	93.5
Aberdeen city	5,612	5,205	-7.3	5,326	26.0	72.2	0.0	0.5	1.2	22.3	19.2	40.0	56.6	15.3	2,016	74.4
Ackerman town	1,532	1,448	-5.5	1,503	56.4	42.2	0.1	0.1	1.1	22.9	22.8	46.2	51.0	19.5	611	81.0
Alcorn State University CDP	1,017	-	-	974	2.7	96.2	0.3	0.4	0.4	11.1	7.7	19.9	0.0	86.3	139	92.8
Algoma town	634	689	8.7	896	79.1	9.0	0.0	6.5	5.4	43.1	9.0	28.1	46.8	12.9	265	91.7
Alligator town	208	187	-10.1	195	12.8	87.2	0.0	0.0	0.0	33.8	3.6	28.4	78.5	0.0	70	51.4
Amory city	7,316	6,794	-7.1	6,932	66.6	31.2	0.1	1.5	0.5	20.8	22.4	41.6	52.1	21.1	2,900	81.0
Anguilla town	712	625	-12.2	612	12.7	87.3	0.0	0.0	0.0	24.2	18.8	43.5	48.1	15.4	254	66.1
Arcola town	364	321	-11.8	329	9.7	90.3	0.0	0.0	0.0	33.1	15.8	35.8	58.6	6.3	95	69.5
Arnold Line CDP	1,719	-	-	2,113	50.8	37.7	10.7	0.0	0.8	19.1	11.3	30.9	43.1	24.8	699	95.6
Artesia town	441	425	-3.6	348	7.8	88.5	0.0	3.7	0.0	18.4	15.8	42.3	67.2	3.8	138	72.5
Ashland town	569	519	-8.8	619	83.8	11.3	0.0	1.9	2.9	21.0	27.8	47.9	52.6	10.0	224	74.6
Baldwyn city	3,297	3,268	-0.9	2,674	45.6	51.6	0.0	2.4	0.4	13.4	25.9	47.5	61.2	11.4	1,162	77.4
Bassfield town	244	212	-13.1	276	40.6	59.4	0.0	0.0	0.0	34.1	22.5	35.4	60.7	9.6	104	71.2
Batesville city	7,465	7,218	-3.3	7,245	45.9	47.4	0.0	5.9	0.8	30.0	11.3	31.0	38.4	29.2	2,429	86.4
Bay St. Louis city	9,262	14,034	51.5	13,018	73.8	15.8	0.8	3.1	6.5	20.9	21.2	45.1	36.6	27.2	5,995	87.9
Bay Springs city	1,787	1,658	-7.2	1,632	36.9	61.1	0.0	2.0	0.0	27.3	21.1	35.7	49.3	20.3	641	79.1
Beaumont town	951	914	-3.9	887	62.3	35.7	0.0	1.9	0.0	17.1	28.1	49.9	63.7	9.3	381	77.2
Beauregard village	326	324	-0.6	488	43.0	47.5	0.0	0.0	9.4	31.4	5.9	30.6	47.5	10.8	134	93.3
Beechwood CDP	3,426	-	-	3,047	56.2	38.4	4.4	0.0	1.0	23.7	17.3	39.5	43.3	27.4	1,151	88.3
Belmont town	2,029	1,988	-2.0	2,290	96.6	0.0	0.0	1.0	2.4	26.7	15.5	30.7	45.9	21.6	862	81.9
Belzoni city	2,245	1,915	-14.7	2,157	17.2	77.9	0.0	0.0	5.0	24.1	14.4	42.3	61.8	19.3	809	73.8
Benoit town	480	423	-11.9	492	19.7	80.3	0.0	0.0	0.0	29.7	17.9	33.0	54.6	14.6	169	72.8
Bentonia town	440	419	-4.8	479	49.5	50.5	0.0	0.0	0.0	17.5	31.1	54.6	56.9	16.9	198	70.7
Beulah town	348	325	-6.6	500	1.4	96.0	0.0	0.0	2.6	30.8	15.0	36.5	50.5	15.5	174	82.8
Big Creek village	154	147	-4.5	296	75.7	3.0	0.0	21.3	0.0	36.5	9.5	38.6	79.5	3.5	63	66.7
Big Point CDP	611	-	-	925	100.0	0.0	0.0	0.0	0.0	4.1	4.0	38.2	42.2	6.2	248	100.0
Biloxi city	44,250	46,212	4.4	45,906	63.1	20.1	5.1	3.3	8.5	21.6	15.2	35.7	39.6	25.8	17,923	85.7
Blue Mountain town	917	948	3.4	1,107	68.4	25.6	1.4	0.9	3.8	20.8	10.0	25.9	58.3	13.4	359	80.5
Blue Springs village	228	241	5.7	384	58.1	29.4	0.0	9.4	3.1	27.1	5.5	25.1	64.8	18.1	107	94.4
Bogue Chitto CDP	887	-	-	553	0.0	10.7	0.0	89.3	0.0	36.9	0.0	27.2	14.3	5.7	188	91.5
Bogue Chitto CDP	522	-	-	326	85.0	15.0	0.0	0.0	0.0	29.4	23.9	25.7	65.2	4.8	119	19.3
Bolton town	567	531	-6.3	878	20.2	79.3	0.6	0.0	0.0	18.5	12.2	35.6	58.8	11.2	271	82.3
Booneville city	8,742	8,497	-2.8	8,637	75.9	15.1	0.1	6.9	2.0	21.7	19.0	35.8	54.1	16.8	2,877	79.6
Boyle town	650	588	-9.5	842	59.1	40.3	0.6	0.0	0.0	26.5	9.3	34.7	47.9	17.7	329	88.4
Brandon city	22,062	24,289	10.1	23,930	76.5	19.0	0.4	0.6	3.5	24.7	17.4	39.6	25.2	40.6	8,780	93.6
Braxton village	183	179	-2.2	251	97.2	0.0	0.0	0.8	2.0	19.1	17.9	42.7	72.0	4.0	76	98.7
Bridgetown CDP	1,742	-	-	2,325	88.7	4.0	0.0	5.8	1.5	27.5	11.9	35.3	43.2	17.2	696	98.3
Brookhaven city	12,510	11,947	-4.5	12,115	37.5	60.6	1.4	0.0	0.5	24.3	16.5	37.5	46.7	19.4	4,346	76.9
Brooksville town	1,225	1,083	-11.6	1,244	16.6	78.3	0.4	4.7	0.0	28.1	14.5	34.5	59.2	14.3	448	76.3
Bruce town	1,939	1,818	-6.2	1,506	49.9	44.8	2.3	3.1	0.0	20.8	18.6	44.8	62.7	14.1	714	65.3
Buckatunna CDP	516	-	-	490	59.6	40.4	0.0	0.0	0.0	39.2	14.7	41.5	57.4	11.7	168	63.1
Bude town	1,062	1,000	-5.8	750	41.5	53.7	0.0	4.8	0.0	26.0	15.2	39.7	62.0	2.9	359	79.1
Burnsville town	934	934	0.0	862	86.5	0.7	0.0	0.8	11.9	25.1	8.1	36.3	65.4	1.5	353	79.3

1 May be of any race.

Table A. All Places — **Population and Housing**

STATE City, town, township, borough, or CDP (county if applicable)	Population				Race and Hispanic or Latino origin (percent)					Age (percent)			Educational attainment of persons age 25 and older		Occupied housing units	
	2010 census total population	2019 estimated population	Percent change 2010–2019	ACS total population estimate 2015–2019	White alone, not Hispanic or Latino	Black alone, not Hispanic or Latino	Asian alone, not Hispanic or Latino	All other races or 2 or more races, not Hispanic or Latino	Hispanic or Latino[1]	Under 18 years old	Age 65 years and older	Median age	Percent High school diploma or less	Percent Bachelor's degree or more	Total	Percent with a computer
	1	2	3	4	5	6	7	8	9	10	11	12	13	14	15	16
MISSISSIPPI—Con.																
Byhalia town	1,298	1,210	-6.8	1,660	29.9	54.2	0.0	0.2	15.7	35.5	19.1	38.2	63.2	11.0	637	85.1
Byram city	11,487	11,428	-0.5	11,578	28.8	69.5	0.7	0.8	0.2	24.9	8.5	33.6	27.6	34.8	4,491	95.9
Caledonia town	1,041	1,058	1.6	1,301	89.8	1.5	1.8	1.3	5.7	33.4	12.0	35.3	43.3	21.7	456	94.3
Calhoun City town	1,774	1,668	-6.0	1,862	51.8	45.5	0.0	1.0	1.7	29.4	19.5	36.7	53.0	19.7	709	77.3
Canton city	12,012	12,094	0.7	12,222	16.4	72.7	1.6	1.2	8.1	26.2	15.6	33.7	53.2	18.0	4,774	84.4
Carrollton town	197	176	-10.7	181	92.8	7.2	0.0	0.0	0.0	19.3	22.1	42.6	37.5	27.8	73	80.8
Carthage city	5,068	4,782	-5.6	4,830	34.6	46.8	1.6	1.5	15.5	32.9	12.1	31.0	55.5	16.0	1,359	92.9
Cary town	313	272	-13.1	396	21.2	77.5	0.0	0.0	1.3	21.2	13.4	38.5	54.8	18.3	135	74.8
Centreville town	1,681	1,424	-15.3	1,739	24.6	72.9	0.5	1.7	0.3	28.0	12.7	37.6	65.0	12.8	724	75.3
Charleston city	2,185	1,867	-14.6	2,402	33.1	65.4	0.0	1.5	0.0	28.1	17.7	38.5	59.1	9.9	792	83.6
Chunky town	322	315	-2.2	344	86.6	0.9	0.0	1.5	11.0	20.1	16.9	36.0	60.9	8.9	145	91.7
Clara CDP	410	-	-	436	100.0	0.0	0.0	0.0	0.0	8.7	41.5	54.0	24.7	57.1	139	55.4
Clarksdale city	17,962	14,894	-17.1	15,734	16.6	81.8	0.7	0.5	0.2	28.4	15.0	33.1	43.6	17.9	5,847	77.0
Cleary CDP	1,544	-	-	1,271	100.0	0.0	0.0	0.0	0.0	20.7	25.4	53.3	38.7	13.8	526	84.4
Cleveland city	12,341	11,073	-10.3	11,627	44.6	50.3	2.2	1.0	1.9	22.1	15.1	34.2	39.2	33.3	4,266	82.5
Clinton city	25,226	24,440	-3.1	25,131	51.7	37.7	4.7	1.8	4.0	26.4	15.9	34.7	24.3	43.2	9,047	90.7
Cloverdale CDP	645	-	-	666	31.1	66.7	0.0	2.3	0.0	9.0	18.0	52.8	53.9	8.1	237	79.7
Coahoma town	377	320	-15.1	322	0.3	99.1	0.0	0.0	0.6	36.6	5.9	24.2	74.5	3.2	110	61.8
Coffeeville town	904	826	-8.6	1,086	36.9	60.5	1.7	0.6	0.2	33.3	13.5	32.5	54.3	16.6	457	79.9
Coldwater town	1,667	1,533	-8.0	1,812	17.3	78.9	0.0	1.2	2.5	19.0	17.3	42.1	61.5	10.8	711	75.0
Collins city	2,579	2,425	-6.0	3,006	40.9	51.7	0.0	0.0	7.4	26.0	19.6	32.4	59.2	21.5	905	77.2
Collinsville CDP	1,948	-	-	1,506	75.6	23.6	0.8	0.0	0.0	11.5	36.7	58.3	35.7	26.3	672	83.2
Columbia city	6,582	5,837	-11.3	5,992	48.0	48.7	0.5	1.8	1.0	22.3	20.0	37.0	57.1	15.9	2,080	73.2
Columbus city	25,183	23,573	-6.4	24,083	33.0	63.1	0.6	1.6	1.6	22.2	18.6	38.0	47.6	22.5	9,572	81.1
Columbus AFB CDP	1,373	-	-	1,667	62.9	6.7	3.4	9.9	17.1	34.4	0.1	23.1	9.7	53.7	517	100.0
Como town	1,275	1,188	-6.8	1,390	30.7	68.8	0.0	0.0	0.5	25.0	21.2	31.6	61.0	12.9	590	67.5
Conehatta CDP	1,342	-	-	1,158	6.0	0.9	0.0	87.8	5.4	40.6	0.9	24.6	59.7	18.8	364	66.8
Corinth city	14,565	14,472	-0.6	14,562	68.3	24.2	0.0	3.3	4.2	21.4	20.4	38.8	48.2	23.1	6,087	75.3
Courtland town	511	511	0.0	565	44.4	51.9	0.9	1.4	1.4	34.0	9.0	28.0	63.2	17.1	179	68.2
Crawford town	641	650	1.4	489	8.0	91.6	0.0	0.4	0.0	21.1	18.8	46.5	72.8	11.3	229	60.7
Crenshaw town	888	845	-4.8	1,093	19.5	77.9	0.0	1.2	1.5	37.9	10.8	26.1	56.3	8.5	351	76.1
Crosby town	320	276	-13.8	218	16.1	81.7	2.3	0.0	0.0	31.7	22.5	39.5	75.4	12.3	99	66.7
Crowder town	713	639	-10.4	837	45.6	54.4	0.0	0.0	0.0	30.1	14.8	30.6	73.0	8.5	331	81.3
Cruger town	387	336	-13.2	374	19.8	80.2	0.0	0.0	0.0	13.4	19.8	45.6	69.6	17.4	138	58.0
Crystal Springs city	5,031	4,715	-6.3	4,794	26.2	70.4	0.0	0.8	2.6	22.6	16.7	44.1	58.9	13.1	1,418	69.8
Darling CDP	226	-	-	230	24.3	75.7	0.0	0.0	0.0	6.1	26.5	29.6	73.0	0.0	109	70.6
Decatur town	1,843	1,705	-7.5	1,897	47.7	47.6	0.0	2.1	2.6	16.8	9.9	22.5	39.0	17.8	614	79.2
De Kalb town	1,139	1,007	-11.6	1,268	24.0	75.6	0.0	0.4	0.0	21.8	28.3	44.7	60.5	11.6	480	69.8
DeLisle CDP	1,147	-	-	1,208	52.5	46.3	0.0	1.2	0.0	23.2	23.6	35.4	48.2	24.6	440	90.5
Derma town	1,022	974	-4.7	1,130	37.5	50.3	0.0	12.2	0.0	29.8	13.4	34.5	72.5	7.4	465	72.9
Diamondhead city	8,378	8,048	-3.9	8,103	91.9	1.2	0.0	2.2	4.6	16.1	27.6	52.7	27.9	34.0	3,767	94.3
D'Iberville city	11,567	14,012	21.1	13,673	55.2	26.6	9.7	6.0	2.5	27.2	11.7	32.3	39.2	22.8	4,979	93.6
D'Lo town	452	437	-3.3	599	73.3	26.7	0.0	0.0	0.0	29.4	20.9	38.4	48.7	16.5	205	81.0
Doddsville town	98	88	-10.2	290	3.1	96.9	0.0	0.0	0.0	42.8	6.9	23.8	51.4	11.8	85	70.6
Drew city	1,932	1,608	-16.8	2,068	12.6	86.7	0.0	0.3	0.4	32.6	9.6	29.7	49.3	13.4	729	79.1
Duck Hill town	730	1,646	125.5	1,102	28.9	69.7	0.0	0.5	1.0	26.7	15.7	35.6	59.3	16.6	495	78.0
Dumas town	463	456	-1.5	512	96.3	0.0	0.4	2.3	1.0	21.7	11.1	40.8	50.6	11.8	198	85.4
Duncan town	423	380	-10.2	302	23.2	75.2	1.7	0.0	0.0	11.9	17.9	49.3	56.6	14.8	91	67.0
Durant city	2,677	2,262	-15.5	2,726	12.7	86.6	0.0	0.0	0.7	32.4	13.9	33.5	63.3	6.4	886	71.6
Ecru town	897	1,037	15.6	1,531	66.6	20.2	0.0	1.4	11.8	36.1	6.2	30.7	49.8	18.7	481	87.5
Eden village	122	121	-0.8	227	38.8	55.5	0.0	0.0	5.7	30.4	9.7	34.9	85.5	0.0	81	58.0
Edwards town	1,052	1,005	-4.5	756	7.8	90.3	0.0	0.0	1.9	14.3	26.6	56.6	48.8	19.3	404	67.6
Elliott CDP	990	-	-	934	82.1	11.1	0.0	6.7	0.0	22.7	9.4	45.3	67.3	10.9	410	89.8
Ellisville city	4,441	4,559	2.7	4,714	43.9	49.7	0.1	1.1	5.2	23.4	15.9	32.5	49.2	20.4	1,264	80.7
Enterprise town	530	475	-10.4	615	86.7	13.3	0.0	0.0	0.0	19.2	19.5	44.0	46.6	10.5	212	94.3
Escatawpa CDP	3,722	-	-	2,257	79.9	18.9	0.0	1.2	0.0	7.9	30.7	55.6	69.7	6.9	1,199	72.6
Ethel town	418	385	-7.9	642	41.6	54.2	1.4	2.8	0.0	26.5	12.0	37.3	67.3	5.3	211	81.0
Eupora city	2,192	2,005	-8.5	2,327	51.1	47.7	0.8	0.0	0.4	32.8	13.9	35.3	55.9	18.6	816	76.5
Falcon town	167	143	-14.4	161	0.0	100.0	0.0	0.0	0.0	23.0	9.3	30.0	53.1	7.1	56	64.3
Falkner town	498	489	-1.8	758	86.1	7.8	0.0	4.9	1.2	25.1	9.0	34.5	49.8	16.9	257	86.4
Farmington town	2,179	2,155	-1.1	2,382	94.4	3.9	0.2	0.0	1.5	27.0	16.0	35.7	45.5	18.0	855	93.1
Farrell CDP	218	-	-	191	4.7	95.3	0.0	0.0	0.0	20.9	15.7	48.2	69.5	3.3	110	68.2
Fayette city	1,590	1,436	-9.7	1,388	0.0	99.2	0.0	0.8	0.0	34.9	13.4	24.4	52.0	25.2	510	66.1
Flora town	1,891	1,862	-1.5	1,832	48.9	45.9	0.0	3.3	1.9	26.2	13.5	30.1	46.2	25.5	652	85.9
Florence city	4,121	4,494	9.1	4,413	94.9	4.8	0.0	0.0	0.3	27.7	12.3	34.3	30.1	25.6	1,583	91.2
Flowood city	7,828	9,380	19.8	9,030	59.1	31.2	4.8	3.3	1.6	21.3	9.8	34.5	25.3	46.1	3,626	96.6
Forest city	5,687	5,536	-2.7	5,629	25.4	42.4	0.8	0.0	31.4	24.5	14.0	36.0	69.0	7.4	1,987	77.1
Foxworth CDP	603	-	-	469	78.0	22.0	0.0	0.0	0.0	27.9	21.1	48.6	63.4	4.8	213	92.0
French Camp town	173	165	-4.6	327	93.9	5.5	0.0	0.0	0.6	33.0	7.6	22.4	12.8	38.3	66	92.4
Friars Point town	1,200	1,015	-15.4	1,395	3.2	96.8	0.0	0.0	0.0	33.8	9.7	32.2	48.8	7.9	528	72.0
Fulton city	3,943	3,980	0.9	4,016	77.8	18.6	0.1	2.9	0.6	21.1	14.5	32.1	48.9	18.4	1,255	83.7
Gattman village	90	88	-2.2	91	100.0	0.0	0.0	0.0	0.0	13.2	23.1	53.0	63.1	9.2	45	66.7
Gautier city	18,572	18,490	-0.4	18,496	55.4	29.9	3.0	0.8	11.0	21.8	17.1	40.0	37.5	20.5	7,013	85.0
Georgetown town	282	268	-5.0	283	58.0	31.1	0.0	0.0	11.0	11.0	17.0	46.0	67.4	8.4	140	61.4
Glen town	414	414	0.0	418	95.9	0.0	0.2	1.2	2.6	29.2	16.0	37.5	36.7	11.2	156	87.8
Glendale CDP	1,657	-	-	2,155	43.2	55.5	0.0	1.4	0.0	31.2	4.2	32.4	50.2	18.5	740	87.4
Glendora village	151	132	-12.6	72	0.0	100.0	0.0	0.0	0.0	23.6	9.7	27.5	62.5	5.0	33	57.6
Gloster town	953	869	-8.8	1,081	18.9	81.1	0.0	0.0	0.0	31.5	6.6	33.5	71.5	4.4	402	56.0
Golden town	191	188	-1.6	186	89.2	0.0	0.0	1.1	9.7	26.3	19.4	35.8	51.5	20.8	90	74.4
Goodman town	1,386	1,164	-16.0	1,252	28.8	70.8	0.0	0.0	0.4	21.6	7.0	20.2	63.5	6.9	271	73.1
Greenville city	34,403	29,085	-15.5	30,588	16.0	81.6	0.8	1.0	0.6	26.2	15.5	36.9	52.0	18.8	12,142	77.2
Greenwood city	16,152	13,561	-16.0	14,040	25.0	73.1	0.8	0.2	1.0	29.0	13.0	34.8	56.2	22.0	4,924	62.8
Grenada city	13,083	12,219	-6.6	12,475	42.5	56.5	0.2	0.3	0.5	23.4	16.4	37.9	47.4	22.0	5,100	81.4
Gulf Hills CDP	7,144	-	-	8,352	62.9	22.1	8.0	2.2	4.8	22.7	15.8	35.5	41.1	30.2	3,072	94.8
Gulf Park Estates CDP	5,719	-	-	7,053	86.4	4.1	3.4	1.3	4.7	28.7	9.5	30.8	30.0	32.5	2,145	93.5
Gulfport city	67,785	71,705	5.8	71,676	52.3	37.5	1.3	2.9	6.0	24.5	13.5	34.8	42.0	22.2	27,918	85.0
Gunnison town	452	408	-9.7	445	6.3	90.6	0.0	3.1	0.0	27.2	14.4	36.5	63.9	6.9	168	78.0
Guntown town	2,083	2,792	34.0	2,725	79.0	16.8	0.7	2.6	0.9	34.8	7.3	31.0	35.8	19.2	880	93.1
Hamilton CDP	457	-	-	375	92.5	7.5	0.0	0.0	0.0	15.5	28.5	50.5	54.5	5.6	182	72.5
Hatley town	482	460	-4.6	628	89.5	3.3	0.0	0.0	7.2	26.4	26.0	37.5	47.9	23.4	223	79.4
Hattiesburg city	45,758	45,863	0.2	46,098	40.6	53.0	1.1	2.2	3.2	20.1	11.4	29.0	35.6	32.6	17,778	86.7
Hazlehurst city	4,029	3,730	-7.4	3,834	15.2	77.9	2.5	0.4	4.0	26.6	14.7	38.0	60.1	14.5	1,108	67.1

1 May be of any race.

Table A. All Places — **Population and Housing**

STATE City, town, township, borough, or CDP (county if applicable)	Population: 2010 census total population	Population: 2019 estimated population	Population: Percent change 2010–2019	Population: ACS total population estimate 2015–2019	Race and Hispanic or Latino origin (percent): White alone, not Hispanic or Latino	Black alone, not Hispanic or Latino	Asian alone, not Hispanic or Latino	All other races or 2 or more races, not Hispanic or Latino	Hispanic or Latino[1]	Age (percent): Under 18 years old	Age 65 years and older	Median age	Educational attainment of persons age 25 and older: Percent High school diploma or less	Percent Bachelor's degree or more	Occupied housing units: Total	Percent with a computer
	1	2	3	4	5	6	7	8	9	10	11	12	13	14	15	16
MISSISSIPPI—Con.																
Heidelberg town	704	659	-6.4	716	15.1	84.8	0.0	0.1	0.0	19.0	26.7	53.0	54.5	9.3	269	84.0
Helena CDP	1,184	-	-	1,190	100.0	0.0	0.0	0.0	0.0	20.4	21.3	46.4	69.5	0.0	570	76.7
Henderson Point CDP	170	-	-	155	77.4	0.0	0.0	0.0	22.6	3.9	34.8	61.6	65.1	9.4	91	89.0
Hernando city	14,046	16,399	16.8	15,942	81.7	13.4	0.1	1.4	3.5	27.8	17.2	37.0	30.6	33.4	5,770	93.2
Hickory town	530	529	-0.2	632	34.2	64.9	0.2	0.6	0.2	36.4	9.7	33.5	42.5	6.9	207	93.2
Hickory Flat town	601	550	-8.5	654	77.8	15.0	0.0	0.3	6.9	31.8	13.5	30.5	49.8	18.5	207	86.5
Hide-A-Way Lake CDP	1,859	-	-	2,392	98.5	0.0	0.7	0.8	0.0	20.4	28.1	51.6	22.2	34.9	908	94.8
Hillsboro CDP	1,130	-	-	1,255	31.6	45.6	2.1	6.4	14.4	38.3	6.1	30.4	69.2	8.4	398	78.6
Holcomb CDP	600	-	-	368	79.9	20.1	0.0	0.0	0.0	29.6	13.3	42.1	37.1	27.0	159	79.2
Hollandale city	2,704	2,304	-14.8	2,077	15.9	83.7	0.0	0.1	0.2	23.6	13.5	42.2	58.6	13.7	802	72.3
Holly Springs city	7,821	7,798	-0.3	7,737	17.4	80.6	0.0	1.0	0.9	19.7	11.6	35.2	58.6	11.9	2,369	80.5
Horn Lake city	26,068	27,272	4.6	27,080	45.5	44.7	1.0	1.6	7.3	27.5	8.2	33.2	48.0	15.8	9,620	92.0
Houston city	3,623	3,427	-5.4	3,478	41.6	49.0	0.6	0.6	8.2	26.2	19.5	38.1	54.1	14.5	1,404	85.5
Hurley CDP	1,551	-	-	1,292	99.2	0.8	0.0	0.0	0.0	27.1	12.0	36.9	47.8	20.4	507	100.0
Indianola city	10,618	9,037	-14.9	9,450	16.6	81.7	0.1	0.7	0.9	25.4	16.1	34.2	53.5	21.2	3,483	79.5
Inverness town	1,019	866	-15.0	931	43.5	56.0	0.0	0.5	0.0	26.5	15.9	37.6	39.4	23.0	355	86.5
Isola town	713	611	-14.3	761	18.9	79.4	0.0	0.0	1.7	26.1	14.1	37.7	55.6	11.2	302	84.8
Itta Bena city	2,048	1,809	-11.7	1,544	7.6	90.2	0.0	1.1	1.1	23.3	20.9	37.8	67.6	13.3	605	52.9
Iuka city	3,034	2,937	-3.2	2,956	93.4	6.0	0.0	0.5	0.1	16.7	26.7	45.5	68.4	8.6	1,244	68.9
Jackson city	173,551	160,628	-7.4	166,383	15.6	82.0	0.3	0.7	1.4	25.1	12.4	33.0	39.8	27.2	62,108	85.9
Jonestown town	1,300	1,100	-15.4	1,047	0.0	100.0	0.0	0.0	0.0	24.0	7.8	36.4	46.9	8.8	434	56.9
Jumpertown town	482	488	1.2	620	85.8	0.3	2.3	5.6	6.0	23.2	14.8	30.2	53.3	9.9	206	77.2
Kearney Park CDP	1,054	-	-	1,776	4.3	95.7	0.0	0.0	0.0	41.5	3.8	20.9	52.1	9.4	405	92.8
Kilmichael town	699	557	-20.3	829	37.4	61.4	0.0	1.2	0.0	23.6	24.7	45.1	74.8	11.5	315	73.0
Kiln CDP	2,238	-	-	2,319	87.2	0.1	0.0	5.8	6.9	13.7	27.5	44.2	42.0	9.4	1,023	92.1
Kosciusko city	7,399	6,720	-9.2	6,855	43.8	53.9	0.0	2.1	0.2	27.3	16.9	36.1	53.7	15.7	2,645	82.3
Kossuth village	209	208	-0.5	229	99.6	0.0	0.0	0.4	0.0	19.2	17.9	46.1	46.5	16.5	93	91.4
Lake town	335	324	-3.3	439	38.3	61.7	0.0	0.0	0.0	31.0	21.0	28.7	60.5	3.1	158	79.1
Lambert town	1,638	1,343	-18.0	1,296	4.6	93.8	0.0	1.7	0.0	27.6	13.6	38.3	64.9	6.6	584	63.4
Latimer CDP	6,079	-	-	6,895	78.2	6.3	3.4	2.8	9.4	22.8	13.7	36.6	51.2	14.4	2,561	87.2
Lauderdale CDP	442	-	-	446	67.0	19.5	0.0	13.5	0.0	46.2	2.7	31.2	87.1	6.7	177	61.0
Laurel city	18,529	18,338		18,508	28.9	64.1	0.2	1.2	5.6	24.6	16.6	37.2	48.7	22.0	6,825	82.5
Leakesville town	955	894	-6.4	989	76.9	19.4	0.0	1.2	2.4	34.7	23.8	32.5	44.3	20.1	340	77.4
Learned town	94	88	-6.4	86	86.0	14.0	0.0	0.0	0.0	12.8	33.7	47.2	11.8	57.4	32	90.6
Leland city	4,479	3,766	-15.9	3,965	25.3	70.9	0.5	0.1	3.2	27.2	15.3	37.2	48.0	24.7	1,642	71.9
Lena town	148	136	-8.1	151	94.0	6.0	0.0	0.0	0.0	15.9	29.1	50.1	40.2	29.5	63	84.1
Lexington city	1,731	1,453	-16.1	1,784	15.3	84.6	0.0	0.1	0.0	30.5	13.3	30.6	58.3	16.4	545	77.2
Liberty town	726	667	-8.1	765	61.2	36.2	0.0	2.6	0.0	20.1	30.2	51.0	62.0	12.9	282	84.8
Long Beach city	14,814	16,023	8.2	15,698	81.0	7.8	3.1	2.2	6.0	22.0	20.1	43.7	40.0	20.9	6,545	90.5
Louin town	277	259	-6.5	378	55.0	44.4	0.0	0.5	0.0	32.3	21.7	32.3	35.6	32.0	138	87.0
Louise town	199	169	-15.1	193	29.0	65.3	3.6	2.1	0.0	15.5	6.7	37.1	62.0	12.0	81	91.4
Louisville city	6,622	5,983	-9.6	6,124	31.5	62.7	0.1	2.7	2.9	27.0	19.9	39.0	51.2	17.2	2,309	77.9
Lucedale city	2,926	3,153	7.8	3,070	72.7	24.2	1.3	0.0	1.9	20.0	16.0	36.7	60.4	13.1	975	75.5
Lula town	298	249	-16.4	245	5.3	93.9	0.0	0.0	0.8	16.7	19.6	44.9	57.0	10.9	103	42.7
Lumberton city	2,045	2,218	8.5	1,882	42.7	54.5	0.0	2.8	0.0	31.0	13.2	33.0	45.0	9.1	725	83.9
Lyman CDP	1,277	-	-	2,347	93.7	1.2	0.0	0.0	5.0	27.7	6.7	33.9	40.0	18.8	835	98.1
Lynchburg CDP	2,437	-	-	2,533	75.7	18.2	1.2	2.1	2.9	22.6	9.1	34.4	42.9	17.4	847	95.0
Lyon town	350	288	-17.7	400	54.3	42.3	0.0	2.8	0.8	21.0	14.5	44.5	23.6	38.7	203	91.6
Maben town	873	840	-3.8	675	31.7	68.1	0.0	0.1	0.0	32.0	13.0	34.6	68.3	6.6	258	67.1
McComb city	12,764	13,013	2.0	12,725	22.0	77.5	0.2	0.0	0.3	32.9	13.6	32.9	55.5	15.3	4,478	74.8
McCool town	135	124	-8.1	91	89.0	11.0	0.0	0.0	0.0	22.0	15.4	46.4	53.0	21.2	37	81.1
McLain town	441	436	-1.1	311	70.7	28.9	0.0	0.3	0.0	24.8	17.7	43.6	64.1	6.8	148	83.1
Macon city	2,746	2,421	-11.8	3,038	21.0	77.3	0.0	0.0	1.7	31.6	13.0	30.4	54.7	19.6	1,110	80.4
Madison city	24,086	25,661	6.5	25,592	81.0	10.7	5.0	1.6	1.7	27.7	13.7	40.6	10.7	68.5	8,972	97.5
Magee city	4,424	4,097	-7.4	4,206	50.8	47.8	0.1	0.5	0.8	26.0	18.5	40.6	57.1	11.3	1,465	72.0
Magnolia city	2,419	2,212	-8.6	2,260	34.3	63.8	0.4	0.3	1.2	14.7	20.9	46.1	60.9	16.1	825	70.5
Mantachie town	1,144	1,111	-2.9	1,414	97.9	0.7	0.0	0.9	0.4	24.3	14.6	39.2	60.5	9.0	532	84.0
Mantee village	232	214	-7.8	247	95.1	2.0	0.0	0.8	2.0	21.1	22.7	48.8	53.8	20.4	116	92.2
Marietta town	256	255	-0.4	202	100.0	0.0	0.0	0.0	0.0	15.8	33.7	51.5	44.4	16.9	86	79.1
Marion town	1,483	1,495	0.8	1,683	38.4	57.2	0.0	0.0	4.5	29.9	11.4	34.7	37.3	25.5	667	92.1
Marks city	1,735	1,419	-18.2	1,754	22.5	76.5	0.0	0.8	0.2	17.2	18.9	44.0	53.9	13.5	699	74.0
Mathiston town	688	664	-3.5	596	70.8	23.3	2.3	2.9	0.7	22.1	31.2	44.8	56.8	20.6	250	76.8
Mayersville town	547	591	8.0	609	19.9	78.8	0.0	0.0	1.3	12.2	7.2	33.8	71.0	1.6	155	44.5
Meadville town	449	421	-6.2	604	80.0	17.9	0.7	1.0	0.5	23.0	29.3	44.5	40.2	29.5	230	73.9
Mendenhall city	2,504	2,387	-4.7	2,924	45.2	54.7	0.0	0.1	0.0	32.5	14.9	33.5	46.8	21.0	1,024	73.5
Meridian city	41,130	36,347	-11.6	37,848	33.3	62.8	0.8	0.8	2.4	24.2	16.2	36.5	43.4	20.2	15,947	82.3
Meridian Station CDP	1,090	-	-	660	57.0	24.8	11.2	3.2	3.8	9.5	0.0	21.8	9.0	33.5	158	100.0
Merigold town	439	377	-14.1	429	43.8	55.5	0.7	0.0	0.0	23.3	13.3	40.3	44.3	25.7	172	93.0
Metcalfe town	1,067	965	-9.6	744	0.0	100.0	0.0	0.0	0.0	25.4	9.1	37.2	63.4	13.0	351	60.1
Mississippi State CDP	4,005	-	-	3,542	70.6	22.7	1.3	1.5	3.8	1.5	0.0	19.5	0.0	85.3	101	100.0
Mize town	340	323	-5.0	270	75.6	0.0	1.9	16.3	6.3	34.8	12.2	28.8	53.7	19.5	88	84.1
Monticello town	1,570	1,472	-6.2	1,369	68.3	28.1	1.5	2.1	0.0	28.0	19.4	35.3	40.5	30.7	640	76.9
Montrose town	140	135	-3.6	123	70.7	12.2	0.0	17.1	0.0	27.6	12.2	32.9	38.6	26.1	55	83.6
Mooreville CDP	650	-	-	1,076	95.3	3.9	0.0	0.0	0.8	27.2	11.7	37.9	36.1	36.6	402	89.3
Moorhead city	2,402	2,063	-14.1	1,520	7.6	91.8	0.0	0.5	0.0	30.3	12.4	22.2	62.2	7.5	522	61.7
Morgan City town	255	238	-6.7	241	0.0	100.0	0.0	0.0	0.0	39.0	8.7	34.0	85.7	9.8	78	43.6
Morgantown CDP	1,412	-	-	1,774	17.5	62.2	0.0	0.0	20.3	21.2	14.9	37.5	65.4	15.5	685	88.6
Morton city	3,690	3,527	-4.4	3,589	32.3	38.9	0.0	2.5	26.3	36.5	11.8	27.8	69.9	7.7	1,006	78.9
Moss Point city	13,704	13,350	-2.6	13,451	24.7	69.6	0.3	3.1	2.3	18.6	18.7	42.3	44.1	16.4	5,102	83.4
Mound Bayou city	1,539	1,370	-11.0	1,714	0.0	100.0	0.0	0.0	0.0	29.0	12.3	29.1	43.5	21.7	641	81.1
Mount Olive town	984	912	-7.3	1,204	32.2	65.1	0.0	0.5	2.2	27.6	11.0	31.7	45.8	18.8	424	85.1
Myrtle town	490	498	1.6	540	78.9	15.6	0.0	3.9	1.7	24.1	7.6	39.8	56.7	9.7	205	86.8
Natchez city	15,750	14,615	-7.2	14,981	33.5	63.5	0.8	1.4	0.9	25.0	21.2	42.2	50.2	21.7	6,026	76.4
Nellieburg CDP	1,414	-	-	1,519	72.9	27.1	0.0	0.0	0.0	20.4	14.2	40.8	54.0	12.4	527	90.9
Nettleton city	1,989	1,919	-3.5	2,293	51.7	37.8	0.0	0.0	10.6	27.9	14.3	34.7	67.1	5.8	808	84.7
New Albany city	8,034	8,753	8.9	8,705	55.5	32.9	0.1	0.6	10.9	27.0	16.3	36.1	53.0	16.7	2,971	82.3
New Augusta town	642	601	-6.4	657	59.1	37.1	1.2	2.4	0.2	26.5	15.7	34.6	63.6	10.2	238	77.3
New Hamilton CDP	553	-	-	573	100.0	0.0	0.0	0.0	0.0	16.1	21.5	37.5	41.2	35.4	255	93.3
New Hebron town	447	421	-5.8	543	79.6	17.7	0.0	1.1	1.7	34.8	14.7	32.1	40.3	24.2	189	85.2
New Hope CDP	3,193	-	-	3,908	64.1	32.2	0.0	0.7	3.0	26.2	14.2	36.0	33.8	26.5	1,247	96.3
New Houlka town	626	607	-3.0	647	61.4	22.6	1.7	0.0	14.4	37.6	13.9	24.3	58.0	9.8	205	74.6
Newton city	3,371	3,155	-6.4	3,220	23.9	73.0	0.2	0.3	2.5	26.9	12.8	37.5	45.7	15.9	1,305	83.8

1 May be of any race.

Table A. All Places — **Population and Housing**

STATE City, town, township, borough, or CDP (county if applicable)	Population				Race and Hispanic or Latino origin (percent)					Age (percent)			Educational attainment of persons age 25 and older		Occupied housing units	
	2010 census total population	2019 estimated population	Percent change 2010–2019	ACS total population estimate 2015–2019	White alone, not Hispanic or Latino	Black alone, not Hispanic or Latino	Asian alone, not Hispanic or Latino	All other races or 2 or more races, not Hispanic or Latino	Hispanic or Latino[1]	Under 18 years old	Age 65 years and older	Median age	Percent High school diploma or less	Percent Bachelor's degree or more	Total	Percent with a computer
	1	2	3	4	5	6	7	8	9	10	11	12	13	14	15	16
MISSISSIPPI—Con.																
Nicholson CDP	3,092	-	-	2,534	88.2	7.5	0.0	0.0	4.2	23.8	13.3	39.7	57.7	13.1	1,139	86.1
North Carrollton town	472	429	-9.1	333	52.6	42.6	0.0	4.8	0.0	27.3	18.3	39.7	73.9	3.5	170	75.9
North Tunica CDP	1,035	-	-	886	2.0	98.0	0.0	0.0	0.0	38.0	9.7	33.5	51.0	12.7	281	91.8
Noxapater town	471	438	-7.0	506	44.5	51.8	0.0	0.6	3.2	17.6	23.3	49.7	57.4	11.0	218	77.1
Oakland town	527	501	-4.9	477	11.5	86.2	0.0	2.3	0.0	18.9	15.7	40.4	67.9	4.1	237	57.4
Ocean Springs city	17,442	17,862	2.4	17,729	78.7	6.7	3.7	3.2	7.7	24.9	18.9	42.2	29.3	37.7	6,639	88.7
Okolona city	2,712	2,591	-4.5	2,605	22.6	77.0	0.0	0.4	0.0	25.1	22.0	39.7	64.5	13.0	1,164	68.1
Olive Branch city	33,487	38,924	16.2	37,461	59.6	30.3	1.7	3.1	5.3	24.5	13.3	38.1	37.7	27.3	13,252	93.7
Osyka town	440	411	-6.6	480	45.4	48.1	0.0	3.5	2.9	42.7	13.8	20.8	62.4	13.3	154	81.8
Oxford city	22,136	28,122	27.0	26,962	68.9	24.4	3.4	1.3	2.1	17.7	11.7	28.0	20.2	56.3	10,351	94.8
Pace town	274	240	-12.4	206	13.1	80.6	6.3	0.0	0.0	15.5	26.2	56.0	47.0	18.5	99	70.7
Pachuta town	261	233	-10.7	143	62.2	37.8	0.0	0.0	0.0	11.9	33.6	56.3	48.8	17.4	73	80.8
Paden village	116	113	-2.6	141	100.0	0.0	0.0	0.0	0.0	22.0	9.2	43.1	57.8	5.6	50	92.0
Pascagoula city	22,392	21,699	-3.1	21,809	49.5	34.9	0.5	2.1	13.0	23.9	14.3	36.6	45.4	16.9	8,415	86.6
Pass Christian city	4,612	6,307	36.8	5,877	61.7	23.9	4.9	4.7	4.7	27.7	19.3	37.9	26.9	35.7	2,163	89.4
Pearl city	25,688	26,510	3.2	26,461	67.8	26.3	0.7	2.1	3.1	24.9	15.3	35.1	45.6	18.1	10,463	90.1
Pearlington CDP	1,332	-	-	911	85.1	9.5	0.0	3.4	2.0	13.3	20.9	48.6	54.8	11.5	371	75.7
Pearl River CDP	3,601	-	-	4,100	9.6	1.7	1.8	86.1	0.7	34.4	9.1	29.3	58.0	7.1	1,082	86.4
Pelahatchie town	1,336	1,382	3.4	1,693	66.4	31.8	0.4	0.7	0.7	27.8	23.6	38.8	64.4	9.0	613	81.6
Petal city	10,434	10,632	1.9	10,584	78.0	13.1	0.9	1.9	6.1	29.7	14.3	35.4	37.0	31.0	3,655	92.1
Philadelphia city	7,477	7,078	-5.3	7,218	42.3	47.5	0.6	3.6	5.9	26.0	17.3	38.8	58.2	16.3	2,836	82.1
Picayune city	11,626	10,904	-6.2	11,040	54.6	39.1	0.6	2.3	3.4	25.4	16.1	35.1	47.8	14.2	4,457	81.8
Pickens town	1,157	995	-14.0	1,083	1.0	99.0	0.0	0.0	0.0	33.2	16.7	32.3	56.3	24.8	392	70.2
Pittsboro village	202	192	-5.0	209	50.7	49.3	0.0	0.0	0.0	26.3	7.7	34.6	43.3	18.1	54	92.6
Plantersville town	1,155	1,137	-1.6	927	19.4	75.4	0.0	5.2	0.0	21.4	16.4	37.4	54.4	18.9	390	71.8
Polkville town	833	821	-1.4	813	96.4	3.6	0.0	0.0	0.0	26.1	15.9	31.9	73.2	5.3	257	79.0
Pontotoc city	5,581	6,169	10.5	6,015	59.0	24.5	0.2	0.8	15.5	25.8	16.1	38.0	53.3	16.3	1,906	75.5
Pope village	258	248	-3.9	409	69.7	26.9	0.0	0.5	2.9	26.9	17.6	39.0	36.7	26.6	150	94.7
Poplarville city	2,891	2,899	0.3	2,931	64.6	31.3	0.0	3.3	0.8	23.9	10.7	22.1	38.5	24.4	733	85.8
Port Gibson city	1,567	1,312	-16.3	1,487	11.2	88.4	0.0	0.1	0.3	22.7	21.3	35.6	43.0	34.7	554	63.7
Potts Camp town	523	467	-10.7	609	50.9	39.1	0.0	0.3	9.7	27.9	20.4	40.3	63.7	11.4	257	84.0
Prentiss town	1,085	933	-14.0	1,159	55.9	44.1	0.0	0.0	0.0	19.3	28.0	48.9	54.5	17.3	429	73.4
Puckett village	315	348	10.5	291	100.0	0.0	0.0	0.0	0.0	19.6	19.6	49.2	37.0	13.0	125	89.6
Purvis city	2,173	2,392	10.1	2,406	62.9	28.7	0.0	7.4	1.0	25.3	19.9	35.5	50.8	12.5	821	82.1
Quitman city	2,323	2,111	-9.1	1,974	55.4	40.2	0.0	1.5	2.8	19.6	24.4	50.8	41.4	27.4	897	80.4
Raleigh town	1,451	1,411	-2.8	1,152	50.3	49.0	0.0	0.0	0.6	17.5	25.4	47.3	61.9	11.9	435	78.9
Rawls Springs CDP	1,254	-	-	1,047	53.3	44.4	2.3	0.0	0.0	17.4	13.4	47.3	53.6	18.9	437	86.0
Raymond city	1,936	2,115	9.2	1,986	36.2	60.7	0.0	1.6	1.5	4.7	9.2	20.5	29.9	35.9	361	78.9
Redwater CDP	633	-	-	642	4.4	17.9	0.0	73.1	4.7	23.8	17.6	39.1	51.0	30.5	219	83.6
Renova town	668	747	11.8	868	0.6	98.2	0.0	0.0	1.3	31.9	12.4	30.6	56.1	15.1	337	74.5
Richland city	6,908	7,241	4.8	7,175	64.8	21.6	0.3	2.2	11.1	25.1	13.1	35.1	43.6	18.6	2,645	91.8
Richton town	1,068	1,008	-5.6	978	60.3	36.5	0.0	0.0	3.2	25.2	21.6	40.6	52.8	17.3	345	76.5
Ridgeland city	24,300	24,104	-0.8	24,269	52.5	37.1	3.5	1.6	5.2	21.5	12.1	36.1	22.6	51.6	10,632	95.7
Rienzi town	317	308	-2.8	276	75.0	21.0	0.0	2.9	1.1	18.1	33.0	53.8	63.8	4.3	124	69.4
Ripley city	5,414	5,273	-2.6	5,290	45.2	33.4	0.2	2.8	18.4	29.4	16.6	36.8	56.5	18.1	1,735	80.9
Robinhood CDP	1,605	-	-	1,332	92.2	3.7	0.4	0.4	3.4	18.1	18.2	45.4	62.8	11.7	553	84.6
Rolling Fork city	2,143	1,929	-10.0	2,103	21.5	78.0	0.0	0.5	0.0	21.7	18.9	42.9	49.5	21.4	857	75.4
Rosedale city	1,874	1,588	-15.3	1,627	6.9	93.1	0.0	0.0	0.0	30.9	13.2	33.0	66.3	6.1	642	66.5
Roxie town	497	466	-6.2	429	35.7	64.3	0.0	0.0	0.0	22.4	10.0	33.4	58.2	10.9	136	91.2
Ruleville city	3,007	2,557	-15.0	2,668	22.8	76.5	0.0	0.1	0.6	21.3	14.8	36.9	50.7	17.1	986	77.3
St. Martin CDP	7,730	-	-	7,963	74.9	15.2	5.6	2.5	1.7	22.5	13.2	36.3	48.7	13.4	2,977	87.2
Sallis town	140	128	-8.6	236	64.4	22.5	6.8	0.0	6.4	30.5	17.4	43.3	34.0	18.5	88	97.7
Saltillo city	4,752	5,062	6.5	5,009	83.3	10.0	2.4	0.9	3.4	27.6	11.2	35.0	39.2	26.8	1,839	87.5
Sandersville town	731	728	-0.4	752	97.9	1.9	0.0	0.0	0.3	26.7	17.2	29.8	53.7	17.1	280	91.4
Sardis town	1,702	1,581	-7.1	1,870	29.8	66.7	0.0	1.3	2.1	17.9	24.9	40.0	52.2	15.2	776	75.1
Satartia village	55	50	-9.1	26	61.5	38.5	0.0	0.0	0.0	11.5	23.1	57.0	43.5	21.7	17	100.0
Saucier CDP	1,342	-	-	1,185	100.0	0.0	0.0	0.0	0.0	16.7	14.1	43.7	40.9	26.7	429	96.7
Schlater town	310	287	-7.4	215	20.0	76.7	0.0	3.3	0.0	17.7	19.1	45.1	68.4	5.7	87	49.4
Scooba town	732	686	-6.3	878	28.1	70.2	0.8	0.0	0.9	17.4	9.6	19.9	45.7	13.5	191	77.5
Sebastopol town	279	276	-1.1	359	82.7	16.4	0.0	0.0	0.8	26.2	16.2	30.9	38.5	24.0	128	93.8
Seminary town	312	284	-9.0	279	96.1	0.0	0.0	0.7	3.2	24.7	19.7	38.9	49.0	16.0	115	73.9
Senatobia city	8,157	7,610	-6.7	7,840	56.2	40.1	0.4	0.8	2.6	18.5	13.6	28.5	41.9	21.2	2,470	83.5
Shannon town	1,753	1,763	0.6	1,850	35.2	61.4	0.0	0.0	3.4	30.2	11.9	31.7	56.7	11.4	700	79.9
Sharon CDP	1,406	-	-	1,313	81.8	14.2	0.0	3.0	1.1	26.1	16.6	37.4	24.8	18.6	461	88.7
Shaw city	1,947	1,685	-13.5	2,004	5.3	94.7	0.0	0.0	0.0	32.0	13.2	31.8	56.0	17.9	737	69.5
Shelby city	2,229	1,949	-12.6	1,688	3.8	95.9	0.0	0.3	0.0	24.9	14.8	39.2	45.4	14.2	649	72.7
Sherman town	647	704	8.8	806	65.0	33.0	0.0	1.4	0.6	29.4	21.6	38.2	52.9	11.8	289	76.5
Shubuta town	441	406	-7.9	337	19.3	80.7	0.0	0.0	0.0	24.0	15.4	43.0	79.4	4.5	151	80.1
Shuqualak town	501	436	-13.0	546	4.9	95.1	0.0	0.0	0.0	16.5	14.3	39.4	65.1	7.3	199	70.9
Sidon town	509	464	-8.8	390	1.3	98.7	0.0	0.0	0.0	33.8	8.5	33.0	82.6	4.3	95	54.7
Silver City town	336	288	-14.3	370	18.4	81.6	0.0	0.0	0.0	34.1	11.9	33.2	69.2	18.3	142	69.0
Silver Creek town	208	198	-4.8	197	82.2	16.2	0.0	1.5	0.0	26.4	23.4	40.8	71.0	2.3	70	54.3
Slate Springs village	110	104	-5.5	106	99.1	0.9	0.0	0.0	0.0	10.4	15.1	48.7	55.2	11.5	44	90.9
Sledge town	545	476	-12.7	457	10.5	89.5	0.0	0.0	0.0	18.2	17.7	44.2	63.3	7.5	205	62.9
Smithville town	942	737	-21.8	638	96.2	1.7	0.0	2.0	0.0	13.3	24.3	46.3	56.6	9.0	257	75.9
Snow Lake Shores town	315	289	-8.3	312	94.9	0.0	0.0	0.3	4.8	5.4	44.9	63.2	37.6	24.0	181	89.5
Soso town	398	394		582	65.6	32.0	0.5	0.7	1.2	25.6	17.2	37.6	52.6	9.5	192	76.6
Southaven city	48,979	55,780	13.9	54,152	62.3	27.9	2.0	2.4	5.4	26.6	13.6	36.0	38.4	25.2	19,735	92.3
Standing Pine CDP	504	-	-	554	17.5	0.0	0.0	82.5	0.0	33.2	2.9	28.9	54.7	9.7	156	75.0
Starkville city	23,874	25,653	7.5	25,387	57.3	34.8	4.1	2.1	1.8	19.1	10.7	27.2	28.8	47.3	10,092	90.2
State Line town	565	556	-1.6	601	35.6	64.4	0.0	0.0	0.0	29.6	7.8	33.4	69.6	3.8	224	85.3
Stonewall town	1,092	975	-10.7	933	80.0	20.0	0.0	0.0	0.0	14.5	28.7	51.8	62.5	11.1	363	61.2
Sturgis town	265	263	-0.8	166	88.6	11.4	0.0	0.0	0.0	15.7	27.1	48.5	46.2	30.8	80	80.0
Summit town	1,712	1,570	-8.3	2,146	17.6	82.1	0.0	0.0	0.4	26.9	14.1	30.4	52.3	21.3	770	71.0
Sumner town	318	267	-16.0	303	55.8	38.6	5.0	0.7	0.0	16.5	24.1	52.3	44.2	23.5	140	78.6
Sumrall town	1,425	1,867	31.0	1,920	75.2	22.9	0.4	1.1	0.4	31.9	9.2	33.9	32.9	34.2	618	92.9
Sunflower town	1,159	978	-15.6	1,123	21.5	77.8	0.0	0.7	0.0	32.2	8.7	32.4	52.3	16.7	424	80.7
Sylvarena village	109	104	-4.6	147	92.5	7.5	0.0	0.0	0.0	24.5	29.3	40.8	49.5	8.2	45	100.0
Taylor village	319	444	39.2	282	64.9	30.1	0.0	3.9	1.1	24.8	20.6	43.8	31.6	35.4	134	85.8
Taylorsville town	1,349	1,245	-7.7	2,080	65.6	30.4	0.0	1.1	2.9	28.8	15.2	33.7	55.0	13.1	654	87.5
Tchula town	2,096	1,929	-8.0	1,924	1.8	98.1	0.0	0.2	0.0	26.8	12.2	30.7	77.5	4.1	735	55.6
Terry town	1,063	1,227	15.4	1,286	28.9	71.1	0.0	0.0	0.0	26.3	13.6	37.7	32.0	37.1	449	84.4

1 May be of any race.

Table A. All Places — **Population and Housing**

STATE City, town, township, borough, or CDP (county if applicable)	Population				Race and Hispanic or Latino origin (percent)					Age (percent)			Educational attainment of persons age 25 and older		Occupied housing units	
	2010 census total population	2019 estimated population	Percent change 2010–2019	ACS total population estimate 2015–2019	White alone, not Hispanic or Latino	Black alone, not Hispanic or Latino	Asian alone, not Hispanic or Latino	All other races or 2 or more races, not Hispanic or Latino	Hispanic or Latino[1]	Under 18 years old	Age 65 years and older	Median age	Percent High school diploma or less	Percent Bachelor's degree or more	Total	Percent with a computer
	1	2	3	4	5	6	7	8	9	10	11	12	13	14	15	16
MISSISSIPPI—Con.																
Thaxton town	643	686	6.7	749	87.9	3.2	0.0	4.9	4.0	30.7	11.5	33.0	38.8	25.6	251	93.6
Tishomingo town	365	356	-2.5	413	89.1	8.7	0.0	2.2	0.0	20.8	21.5	38.9	55.0	13.3	176	76.7
Toccopola town	246	258	4.9	278	96.4	0.0	0.0	0.7	2.9	27.3	10.4	39.1	50.0	13.5	91	97.8
Toomsuba CDP	773	-	-	928	43.2	56.8	0.0	0.0	0.0	13.0	15.1	31.5	48.4	0.0	324	69.8
Tremont town	463	463	0.0	463	99.6	0.0	0.0	0.2	0.2	31.1	14.3	37.7	49.8	18.8	175	78.9
Tucker CDP	662	-	-	731	0.0	0.0	0.0	94.4	5.6	52.5	0.0	15.9	66.2	0.0	147	66.0
Tunica town	1,033	864	-16.4	1,155	58.1	35.1	0.6	2.2	4.1	22.3	22.5	45.1	38.5	27.0	501	76.8
Tunica Resorts CDP	1,910	-	-	2,260	22.9	71.2	5.9	0.0	0.0	27.2	7.0	31.9	30.8	26.9	1,041	95.6
Tupelo city	37,673	38,312	1.7	38,271	54.7	38.9	0.7	1.6	4.1	26.6	14.9	35.5	35.7	31.8	14,751	86.7
Tutwiler town	3,553	3,416	-3.9	3,448	10.8	45.7	4.4	0.8	38.3	8.3	7.9	30.6	75.4	3.4	323	71.8
Tylertown town	1,609	1,428	-11.2	1,845	45.6	48.5	0.8	0.8	4.3	21.0	22.0	43.2	49.7	18.0	618	76.7
Union town	1,988	1,897	-4.6	2,349	49.9	49.0	0.1	1.0	0.0	30.4	17.2	37.8	56.8	15.7	838	76.8
University CDP	4,202	-	-	4,067	83.5	10.9	1.9	1.9	1.8	0.2	0.0	19.3	100.0	0.0	0	0.0
Utica town	820	883	7.7	820	17.9	72.3	0.0	4.5	5.2	22.2	14.3	39.6	46.4	12.6	337	86.1
Vaiden town	960	957	-0.3	592	37.8	60.6	0.0	0.0	1.5	17.6	15.5	43.4	71.4	19.3	217	71.9
Vancleave CDP	5,886	-	-	4,939	93.4	3.9	0.5	2.2	0.0	26.7	18.1	37.6	40.7	17.4	1,785	82.1
Vardaman town	1,316	1,279	-2.8	1,420	44.2	24.1	0.0	0.6	31.1	33.5	7.9	31.0	72.6	6.8	440	80.2
Verona city	2,988	3,232	8.2	3,141	22.5	70.5	0.0	3.9	3.1	23.8	11.1	34.1	63.6	6.3	1,282	73.5
Vicksburg city	23,856	21,653	-9.2	22,332	28.1	67.5	0.6	1.0	2.8	27.7	14.4	35.5	44.3	22.1	8,969	82.9
Wade CDP	1,074	-	-	1,336	87.4	12.6	0.0	0.0	0.0	19.1	13.4	29.5	57.4	15.4	483	92.8
Walls town	1,125	1,420	26.2	1,312	31.9	65.3	2.1	0.5	0.2	30.3	3.7	28.1	39.9	18.4	445	92.1
Walnut town	771	754	-2.2	1,152	80.3	18.6	0.9	0.3	0.0	33.7	11.1	29.0	51.9	18.6	345	85.8
Walnut Grove town	1,906	1,673	-12.2	901	22.2	75.8	0.0	0.0	2.0	27.1	9.1	31.4	57.1	10.1	242	80.2
Walthall village	146	138	-5.5	120	89.2	9.2	0.8	0.8	0.0	14.2	25.0	36.5	33.0	43.3	54	81.5
Water Valley city	3,392	3,255	-4.0	3,323	46.6	52.5	0.0	0.9	0.0	23.9	22.1	38.8	60.2	15.2	1,336	65.5
Waveland city	6,433	6,302	-2.0	6,336	80.9	13.3	0.6	2.5	2.6	25.6	15.3	39.8	43.9	25.6	2,642	84.4
Waynesboro city	5,043	4,805	-4.7	4,863	31.0	63.0	0.0	3.3	2.7	28.6	16.1	36.0	70.2	11.5	1,786	82.8
Webb town	565	478	-15.4	434	11.3	85.5	3.2	0.0	0.0	32.5	15.4	34.5	62.8	13.5	151	58.9
Weir town	459	427	-7.0	811	23.7	75.5	0.0	0.2	0.6	30.0	9.5	28.9	65.6	10.7	262	78.6
Wesson town	1,917	1,722	-10.2	2,204	77.4	17.2	0.0	3.9	1.5	19.6	9.6	23.6	41.5	20.3	609	90.8
West town	185	149	-19.5	119	61.3	37.0	0.0	1.7	0.0	14.3	31.9	51.9	38.0	33.0	53	77.4
West Hattiesburg CDP	5,909	-	-	6,352	45.8	37.1	1.9	4.2	11.0	28.6	13.8	34.8	36.9	34.5	2,387	84.7
West Point city	11,309	10,404	-8.0	10,626	37.3	62.1	0.5	0.0	0.0	24.6	17.5	37.0	51.6	19.4	4,211	82.9
White Oak CDP	692	-	-	275	0.0	100.0	0.0	0.0	0.0	27.6	40.0	28.9	94.6	0.0	141	53.2
Wiggins city	4,390	4,541	3.4	4,506	66.2	27.9	0.0	2.4	3.5	24.1	15.4	35.5	55.9	13.2	1,348	70.5
Winona city	5,042	3,964	-21.4	4,227	41.3	54.2	0.7	3.8	0.0	28.3	14.9	33.1	53.6	19.6	1,696	80.8
Winstonville town	191	167	-12.6	120	0.0	100.0	0.0	0.0	0.0	20.0	21.7	49.3	54.3	17.0	52	59.6
Woodland village	125	129	3.2	174	50.6	45.4	0.0	0.0	4.0	30.5	10.3	26.6	57.4	2.1	75	73.3
Woodville town	1,074	919	-14.4	1,064	36.0	63.3	0.7	0.0	0.0	25.9	18.2	33.3	46.5	15.9	386	59.8
Yazoo City city	11,394	10,869	-4.6	11,063	11.6	85.3	0.1	1.5	1.4	29.7	11.5	31.4	64.1	10.9	3,670	75.3
MISSOURI	5,988,950	6,137,428	2.5	6,104,910	79.4	11.4	2.0	3.0	4.2	22.6	16.5	38.6	40.7	29.2	2,414,521	89.0
Adrian city	1,685	1,597	-5.2	1,861	94.2	2.8	0.2	1.8	0.9	23.3	20.7	39.1	52.5	17.6	735	89.3
Advance city	1,347	1,336	-0.8	1,363	96.4	0.2	0.0	2.1	1.3	15.0	27.6	53.1	53.1	11.5	679	74.5
Affton CDP	20,307	-	-	20,148	86.4	4.4	3.1	2.9	3.1	17.7	18.1	41.8	34.6	31.7	8,958	89.6
Agency village	683	660	-3.4	733	88.3	3.0	0.1	5.0	3.5	26.9	12.3	37.5	46.7	18.6	248	94.0
Airport Drive village	698	868	24.4	744	93.4	0.0	0.4	4.8	1.3	18.3	15.2	33.5	27.7	35.9	318	95.9
Alba city	549	542	-1.3	681	95.2	0.0	0.0	2.1	2.8	30.4	9.3	32.0	47.6	16.4	269	84.4
Albany city	1,731	1,675	-3.2	2,010	93.5	0.9	0.6	1.3	3.5	23.2	18.8	41.1	52.2	18.0	821	80.4
Aldrich village	80	81	1.3	68	97.1	0.0	0.0	2.9	0.0	29.4	33.8	42.3	33.3	40.5	26	80.8
Alexandria city	159	150	-5.7	93	94.6	0.0	0.0	5.4	0.0	8.6	35.5	52.7	77.0	0.0	40	65.0
Allendale village	53	51	-3.8	67	97.0	0.0	0.0	3.0	0.0	16.4	35.8	53.5	37.5	19.6	34	91.2
Allenville village	120	122	1.7	95	91.6	0.0	0.0	4.2	4.2	17.9	14.7	46.8	72.4	13.2	36	83.3
Alma city	401	383	-4.5	467	96.4	0.4	0.0	2.4	0.9	28.3	22.1	37.5	54.0	22.8	181	89.0
Altamont village	204	201	-1.5	201	98.0	0.0	0.0	2.0	0.0	32.3	10.9	28.6	53.6	12.8	66	86.4
Altenburg city	349	333	-4.6	381	98.7	0.0	0.5	0.8	0.0	21.3	16.0	44.6	47.2	27.9	157	86.0
Alton city	873	834	-4.5	628	95.2	2.5	0.0	2.2	0.0	22.5	28.7	50.1	58.9	17.7	304	78.6
Amazonia village	314	321	2.2	267	94.0	0.0	0.0	6.0	0.0	18.7	33.7	44.3	87.5	1.0	116	58.6
Amity town	55	53	-3.6	24	100.0	0.0	0.0	0.0	0.0	0.0	58.3	65.7	43.5	13.0	20	45.0
Amoret city	190	180	-5.3	178	97.2	0.0	0.0	0.0	2.8	15.7	14.6	45.0	75.0	3.9	65	89.2
Amsterdam city	242	229	-5.4	178	95.5	0.0	0.0	2.2	2.2	13.5	25.8	47.9	69.2	6.3	81	79.0
Anderson city	1,933	1,919	-0.7	2,069	67.5	2.8	0.2	11.3	18.2	27.9	13.0	34.1	63.2	13.7	696	87.1
Annada village	29	28	-3.4	52	100.0	0.0	0.0	0.0	0.0	19.2	11.5	52.3	91.7	0.0	32	56.3
Annapolis city	362	343	-5.2	387	90.4	1.6	0.0	3.6	4.4	17.6	15.5	41.5	63.7	13.5	149	79.9
Anniston town	232	208	-10.3	155	92.9	1.3	0.0	1.3	4.5	24.5	30.3	48.3	83.3	0.0	67	58.2
Appleton City city	1,131	1,080	-4.5	1,163	92.5	0.7	0.0	5.3	1.5	21.7	28.0	44.4	63.8	13.5	489	82.8
Arbela town	41	42	2.4	25	100.0	0.0	0.0	0.0	0.0	20.0	24.0	53.1	70.6	0.0	14	85.7
Arbyrd city	509	462	-9.2	444	76.1	0.0	0.0	6.8	17.1	24.8	18.5	36.2	77.9	4.4	194	82.0
Arcadia city	594	559	-5.9	702	94.4	1.4	0.0	2.8	1.3	23.9	23.8	46.0	58.6	13.5	359	61.3
Archie city	1,170	1,202	2.7	1,199	95.8	0.0	0.0	2.3	1.9	32.7	13.3	27.8	47.5	20.9	450	94.7
Arcola village	55	53	-3.6	87	100.0	0.0	0.0	0.0	0.0	11.5	26.4	47.5	50.8	15.4	37	94.6
Argyle town	165	160	-3.0	166	95.8	0.0	0.0	4.2	0.0	21.1	16.3	36.5	51.7	14.7	72	79.2
Arkoe town	70	64	-8.6	37	100.0	0.0	0.0	0.0	0.0	16.2	8.1	47.5	68.0	12.0	19	84.2
Armstrong city	283	276	-2.5	198	86.4	1.0	0.0	1.0	11.6	30.8	12.1	39.0	69.9	13.5	66	68.2
Arnold city	20,839	21,091	1.2	21,146	96.3	0.4	0.2	1.4	1.7	22.0	18.1	41.0	46.9	19.6	8,278	90.9
Arrow Point village	86	87	1.2	97	100.0	0.0	0.0	0.0	0.0	20.6	28.9	54.8	72.7	18.2	53	69.8
Arrow Rock town	52	52	0.0	36	100.0	0.0	0.0	0.0	0.0	22.2	41.7	60.5	7.1	64.3	21	90.5
Asbury city	207	215	3.9	279	96.4	0.0	0.0	0.4	3.2	25.4	21.5	42.3	59.3	16.9	116	92.2
Ash Grove city	1,474	1,444	-2.0	1,546	95.6	0.0	0.0	2.3	2.1	23.8	22.3	43.0	51.0	14.2	651	74.3
Ashland city	3,716	3,968	6.8	3,907	95.0	0.4	0.4	3.4	0.8	29.3	14.1	36.9	32.6	31.3	1,554	94.7
Ashley CDP	90	-	-	78	100.0	0.0	0.0	0.0	0.0	0.0	0.0	51.0	87.2	12.8	39	25.6
Atlanta city	390	380	-2.6	696	92.2	1.4	0.0	2.7	3.6	31.8	7.3	33.2	56.6	10.1	199	88.4
Augusta town	267	267	0.0	290	99.3	0.0	0.0	0.7	0.0	22.1	21.4	47.7	32.3	30.0	130	88.5
Aullville village	102	101		93	100.0	0.0	0.0	0.0	0.0	30.1	7.5	34.4	75.8	4.8	26	92.3
Aurora city	7,513	7,447	-0.9	7,438	87.0	0.1	0.0	5.5	7.4	20.3	17.7	40.6	52.0	12.6	3,302	88.6
Auxvasse city	985	978	-0.7	1,078	81.4	0.7	0.3	3.9	13.7	26.0	17.9	39.3	57.0	14.7	480	77.7
Ava city	2,990	2,865	-4.2	2,889	99.1	0.9	0.0	0.0	0.0	29.6	22.1	36.7	55.8	15.0	1,175	82.0
Avilla town	125	129	3.2	46	100.0	0.0	0.0	0.0	0.0	21.7	30.4	51.0	80.0	2.9	21	47.6
Avondale city	433	451	4.2	507	80.7	1.8	3.6	9.1	4.9	23.7	18.5	40.6	50.8	17.1	230	87.0
Bagnell town	93	95	2.2	44	86.4	0.0	0.0	11.4	2.3	6.8	27.3	56.8	87.8	7.3	27	55.6
Bakersfield village	241	227	-5.8	269	92.2	0.0	0.0	5.9	1.9	35.3	15.6	28.2	69.2	4.1	105	63.8

1 May be of any race.

Table A. All Places — **Population and Housing**

STATE City, town, township, borough, or CDP (county if applicable)	Population				Race and Hispanic or Latino origin (percent)					Age (percent)			Educational attainment of persons age 25 and older		Occupied housing units	
	2010 census total population	2019 estimated population	Percent change 2010–2019	ACS total population estimate 2015–2019	White alone, not Hispanic or Latino	Black alone, not Hispanic or Latino	Asian alone, not Hispanic or Latino	All other races or 2 or more races, not Hispanic or Latino	Hispanic or Latino[1]	Under 18 years old	Age 65 years and older	Median age	Percent High school diploma or less	Percent Bachelor's degree or more	Total	Percent with a computer
	1	2	3	4	5	6	7	8	9	10	11	12	13	14	15	16
MISSOURI—Con.																
Baldwin Park village	92	96	4.3	91	95.6	0.0	0.0	0.0	4.4	26.4	7.7	44.2	76.9	1.5	41	80.5
Ballwin city	30,417	30,082	-1.1	30,252	88.2	1.4	5.9	1.9	2.7	23.1	18.0	42.1	17.7	56.4	11,922	95.7
Baring city	132	127	-3.8	104	97.1	0.0	0.0	0.0	2.9	19.2	11.5	38.7	71.6	6.0	37	70.3
Barnard city	221	198	-10.4	227	95.2	0.0	2.6	0.0	2.2	22.0	11.9	34.8	60.6	9.7	79	88.6
Barnett city	203	201		225	91.6	3.6	0.0	2.2	2.7	21.3	23.1	51.4	70.9	2.4	79	79.7
Barnhart CDP	5,682	-	-	5,948	98.7	0.2	0.0	0.0	1.1	24.5	9.7	31.6	38.2	25.6	2,075	97.8
Bates City city	223	218	-2.2	203	98.0	0.0	1.0	1.0	0.0	22.2	27.1	47.1	48.3	12.6	82	85.4
Battlefield city	5,654	6,622	17.1	6,240	85.6	1.6	3.2	2.9	6.7	31.8	10.8	36.5	31.4	35.7	2,403	91.1
Bella Villa city	737	724	-1.8	815	87.7	2.3	3.7	2.3	3.9	17.2	12.9	45.1	44.4	25.4	358	88.0
Bell City city	443	422	-4.7	489	98.0	0.8	0.0	1.2	0.0	30.5	11.9	36.1	67.1	11.8	182	79.7
Belle city	1,545	1,479	-4.3	1,437	95.1	0.0	3.9	0.3	0.7	14.5	18.2	46.8	55.7	12.9	718	76.7
Bellefontaine Neighbors city	10,780	10,397	-3.6	10,517	19.4	77.4	0.0	1.7	1.5	21.2	18.3	40.9	42.2	14.5	4,093	86.9
Bellerive Acres city	188	181	-3.7	178	56.7	41.0	0.0	1.1	1.1	0.6	37.6	59.0	15.8	60.5	77	97.4
Bellflower city	389	366	-5.9	329	89.4	0.6	1.5	8.5	0.0	26.1	15.2	33.4	77.9	1.4	132	81.8
Bel-Nor village	1,449	1,397	-3.6	1,471	47.4	38.7	8.4	4.1	1.4	13.3	21.5	43.6	17.4	55.4	641	93.6
Bel-Ridge village	2,759	2,675	-3.0	2,703	6.7	87.6	0.0	2.1	3.6	33.0	11.6	30.3	49.5	9.9	1,009	82.5
Belton city	23,099	23,642	2.4	23,425	83.2	3.4	0.8	3.4	9.1	26.5	13.9	35.5	48.3	18.9	8,716	94.0
Bennett Springs CDP	130	-	-	179	100.0	0.0	0.0	0.0	0.0	0.0	30.2	51.5	73.2	8.9	98	100.0
Benton city	865	873	0.9	900	91.2	5.7	0.6	0.8	1.8	21.8	13.0	38.2	44.7	25.2	332	85.2
Benton City village	104	102	-1.9	133	100.0	0.0	0.0	0.0	0.0	17.3	23.3	50.8	71.3	0.0	66	78.8
Berger city	221	221	0.0	176	98.9	0.0	0.0	1.1	0.0	27.8	13.6	40.0	58.6	12.1	72	86.1
Berkeley city	9,138	8,841	-3.3	8,927	13.4	84.1	0.0	1.2	1.4	28.1	14.8	36.5	45.0	12.9	3,534	82.8
Bernie city	1,958	1,880	-4.0	1,848	90.2	6.6	0.0	3.0	0.2	24.2	18.5	40.1	64.4	8.3	743	83.3
Bertrand city	826	743	-10.0	838	94.5	3.2	0.0	1.4	0.8	15.5	27.7	52.9	77.2	5.0	383	83.6
Bethany city	3,292	3,062	-7.0	3,119	92.6	0.7	0.5	1.5	4.7	22.7	26.2	45.3	55.6	16.0	1,336	82.0
Bethel village	122	112	-8.2	116	96.6	0.0	2.6	0.9	0.0	11.2	37.9	61.4	52.5	15.8	62	95.2
Beverly Hills city	574	554	-3.5	417	1.9	96.6	0.7	0.0	0.7	16.8	22.1	46.2	57.0	10.8	225	77.3
Bevier city	716	691	-3.5	702	92.9	2.0	0.0	5.1	0.0	19.1	20.1	49.1	69.2	5.5	290	82.4
Biehle CDP	48	-	-	25	100.0	0.0	0.0	0.0	0.0	36.0	0.0	43.5	0.0	0.0	7	100.0
Bigelow village	27	24	-11.1	7	100.0	0.0	0.0	0.0	0.0	0.0	28.6	62.8	100.0	0.0	5	80.0
Big Lake village	159	145	-8.8	95	97.9	0.0	2.1	0.0	0.0	0.0	33.7	62.7	46.3	24.2	56	80.4
Big Spring CDP	167	-	-	265	75.5	6.0	0.0	18.5	0.0	59.2	0.0	12.4	5.7	19.3	64	92.2
Billings city	1,035	1,111	7.3	944	98.8	0.0	0.0	0.0	1.2	20.6	23.8	45.1	50.9	11.2	416	92.8
Birch Tree city	679	649	-4.4	667	97.3	1.8	0.0	0.9	0.0	20.8	14.7	46.1	77.5	9.7	295	60.0
Birmingham village	183	205	12.0	217	88.9	0.0	0.0	0.0	11.1	20.7	13.4	39.0	55.5	8.9	85	89.4
Bismarck city	1,543	1,478	-4.2	1,453	93.7	4.0	0.0	2.3	0.0	22.6	15.1	39.2	58.2	10.4	608	74.8
Blackburn city	248	237	-4.4	210	98.6	1.4	0.0	0.0	0.0	15.2	27.1	52.5	48.8	14.8	100	75.0
Black Jack city	6,925	6,918	-0.1	6,932	16.8	80.9	0.0	2.1	0.2	28.8	14.7	32.5	29.7	20.7	2,441	94.4
Blackwater city	153	150	-2.0	171	96.5	0.0	0.0	0.0	3.5	36.3	11.7	35.3	55.1	13.1	60	91.7
Blairstown city	97	94	-3.1	74	100.0	0.0	0.0	0.0	0.0	14.9	18.9	36.9	70.0	5.0	32	96.9
Blanchard CDP	22	-	-	-	-	-	-	-	-	-	-	-	-	-	-	-
Bland city	547	528	-3.5	481	97.7	0.0	0.0	2.3	0.0	18.1	31.0	51.1	64.6	12.1	254	69.7
Blodgett village	213	204	-4.2	174	100.0	0.0	0.0	0.0	0.0	35.1	10.3	25.0	86.2	6.9	54	88.9
Bloomfield city	1,934	1,833	-5.2	2,191	98.6	0.9	0.0	0.1	0.3	25.0	19.9	39.3	57.9	17.8	806	90.6
Bloomsdale city	523	555	6.1	713	98.5	0.0	0.0	1.5	0.0	24.0	17.8	38.3	45.7	19.0	290	93.8
Blue Eye town	162	161	-0.6	284	84.2	0.0	2.8	8.1	4.9	12.0	33.8	53.2	50.0	17.6	134	83.6
Blue Springs city	52,593	55,829	6.2	54,850	81.4	7.2	1.6	3.9	5.9	28.7	13.4	35.4	30.6	34.6	19,814	95.8
Blythedale village	199	185	-7.0	202	97.5	1.5	0.0	0.0	1.0	29.2	20.3	35.8	65.4	9.2	82	79.3
Bogard city	164	154	-6.1	126	94.4	0.0	0.0	5.6	0.0	7.1	35.7	55.8	65.4	1.9	70	75.7
Bolckow city	187	189	1.1	193	100.0	0.0	0.0	0.0	0.0	15.5	21.8	51.3	62.4	11.4	100	83.0
Bolivar city	10,334	11,067	7.1	10,880	89.7	2.3	0.1	2.5	5.3	24.0	16.6	28.5	47.1	23.7	3,989	88.1
Bonne Terre city	6,910	7,118	3.0	7,165	77.1	17.7	0.0	3.7	1.6	15.6	9.3	34.1	68.1	6.1	1,638	97.3
Boonville city	8,352	8,439	1.0	8,418	78.9	11.1	0.6	6.4	3.0	17.7	17.0	38.0	47.5	20.8	3,013	87.7
Bosworth city	305	290	-4.9	174	94.3	0.0	0.0	3.4	2.3	14.4	17.2	50.8	85.9	1.5	72	87.5
Bourbon city	1,616	1,582	-2.1	1,946	94.2	0.0	1.2	2.0	2.6	25.3	18.6	40.4	68.6	8.1	794	78.8
Bowling Green city	5,315	5,585	5.1	5,516	76.1	17.3	0.8	3.3	2.5	16.6	11.0	34.7	70.1	11.4	1,441	88.8
Bragg City town	149	131	-12.1	142	70.4	0.0	0.0	0.0	29.6	37.3	9.2	20.8	75.0	7.4	36	91.7
Brandsville city	156	152	-2.6	111	97.3	0.0	0.0	0.0	2.7	17.1	29.7	58.4	78.6	4.8	50	68.0
Branson city	10,543	11,630	10.3	11,416	79.6	4.2	3.0	1.3	11.8	19.4	25.0	40.6	40.3	22.7	4,915	86.2
Branson West city	472	446	-5.5	607	84.2	0.5	0.0	8.4	6.9	9.9	26.5	51.4	51.5	15.1	226	82.3
Brashear city	273	259	-5.1	152	97.4	0.0	0.0	0.7	2.0	21.1	9.2	41.5	53.9	7.8	75	82.7
Braymer city	878	846	-3.6	660	94.1	0.0	0.0	5.9	0.0	13.3	25.3	48.1	43.0	14.8	354	80.5
Breckenridge city	383	353	-7.8	313	86.9	1.9	1.0	8.6	1.6	18.5	19.5	45.7	65.2	8.1	140	74.3
Breckenridge Hills city	4,731	4,566	-3.5	4,616	41.7	34.4	0.4	4.2	19.3	19.3	8.9	35.0	59.2	7.3	1,888	86.8
Brentwood city	8,052	7,966	-1.1	8,005	83.0	4.1	8.4	1.3	3.2	17.2	11.8	34.1	8.5	71.6	4,117	95.1
Brewer CDP	374	-	-	409	100.0	0.0	0.0	0.0	0.0	20.3	11.5	42.6	44.1	19.3	131	85.5
Bridgeton city	11,516	11,520	0.0	11,606	62.8	24.5	1.9	2.3	8.5	22.5	20.0	39.8	40.1	27.8	4,288	90.4
Brimson village	63	61	-3.2	40	87.5	0.0	0.0	0.0	12.5	20.0	50.0	65.0	93.5	0.0	26	38.5
Bronaugh city	247	235	-4.9	199	96.5	0.0	1.5	0.0	2.0	23.1	5.0	37.9	65.0	6.6	73	86.3
Brookfield city	4,538	4,213	-7.2	4,403	93.6	1.1	0.6	1.4	3.4	26.0	19.5	37.1	60.6	11.3	1,831	84.2
Brooklyn Heights town	100	106	6.0	97	90.7	3.1	0.0	6.2	0.0	14.4	30.9	53.5	57.7	11.3	53	77.4
Browning city	265	245	-7.5	224	96.4	0.0	0.0	0.0	3.6	22.8	10.7	43.3	54.2	10.5	85	83.5
Brownington town	105	104		162	85.2	0.0	0.0	14.8	0.0	22.2	7.4	33.7	62.6	6.5	67	80.6
Brumley town	92	94	2.2	85	91.8	0.0	0.0	0.0	8.2	17.6	11.8	36.9	59.3	25.9	38	86.8
Brunswick city	858	814	-5.1	1,025	84.5	7.9	0.0	7.6	0.0	23.9	26.4	47.3	60.9	17.9	391	65.0
Bucklin city	467	436	-6.6	394	94.9	0.0	0.0	2.3	2.8	14.0	34.5	53.9	66.0	12.6	217	73.7
Buckner city	3,075	3,022	-1.7	3,045	94.9	0.2	1.3	1.2	2.4	26.5	12.8	36.0	57.6	13.0	1,195	93.7
Buffalo city	3,091	3,091	0.0	3,047	86.2	0.1	1.3	7.4	5.0	24.0	26.2	39.9	68.5	7.8	1,215	72.8
Bull Creek village	603	635	5.3	496	86.9	2.4	1.0	3.6	6.0	38.9	6.5	29.1	66.7	4.6	177	92.1
Bunceton city	357	358	0.3	359	98.3	0.6	0.0	0.8	0.3	27.3	10.3	34.5	62.9	8.6	132	80.3
Bunker city	395	379	-4.1	294	92.9	0.0	0.0	4.1	3.1	9.9	27.9	47.3	81.8	0.0	152	61.8
Burgess CDP	57	-	-	33	72.7	0.0	0.0	27.3	0.0	30.3	18.2	45.5	81.8	4.5	16	68.8
Burlington Junction city	537	481	-10.4	547	98.7	0.0	0.0	0.7	0.5	33.1	12.6	27.7	63.9	6.2	196	86.2
Butler city	4,221	3,999	-5.3	4,130	91.7	3.4	0.0	2.3	2.6	27.7	18.8	36.6	54.5	14.8	1,707	78.3
Butterfield city	464	475	2.4	525	51.6	0.0	0.0	1.0	47.4	29.5	13.3	32.4	79.1	7.3	159	86.8
Byrnes Mill city	2,780	3,002	8.0	2,970	94.2	0.0	0.7	1.8	3.3	20.7	17.2	41.8	39.5	26.7	1,157	96.8
Cabool city	2,138	2,080	-2.7	2,426	83.1	0.7	0.0	11.5	4.8	25.3	22.4	41.7	48.6	15.5	1,015	81.9
Cainsville city	293	273	-6.8	248	92.7	0.0	0.8	5.2	1.2	25.8	25.8	41.5	67.2	5.2	117	81.2
Cairo village	288	279	-3.1	242	96.3	0.0	0.0	2.1	1.7	19.0	29.3	46.0	47.6	12.4	105	82.9
Caledonia village	130	127	-2.3	196	100.0	0.0	0.0	0.0	0.0	15.3	24.0	42.5	66.4	16.8	73	82.2
Calhoun city	469	453	-3.4	322	91.3	0.0	0.6	7.5	0.6	20.2	21.7	41.5	67.7	7.2	145	91.7

1 May be of any race.

Table A. All Places — **Population and Housing**

STATE City, town, township, borough, or CDP (county if applicable)	Population				Race and Hispanic or Latino origin (percent)					Age (percent)			Educational attainment of persons age 25 and older		Occupied housing units	
	2010 census total population	2019 estimated population	Percent change 2010–2019	ACS total population estimate 2015–2019	White alone, not Hispanic or Latino	Black alone, not Hispanic or Latino	Asian alone, not Hispanic or Latino	All other races or 2 or more races, not Hispanic or Latino	Hispanic or Latino[1]	Under 18 years old	Age 65 years and older	Median age	Percent High school diploma or less	Percent Bachelor's degree or more	Total	Percent with a computer
	1	2	3	4	5	6	7	8	9	10	11	12	13	14	15	16
MISSOURI—Con.																
California city	4,299	4,416	2.7	4,405	84.5	1.3	0.2	0.9	13.1	25.3	17.4	35.1	48.6	23.0	1,685	85.7
Callao city	307	293	-4.6	290	100.0	0.0	0.0	0.0	0.0	21.0	17.9	47.0	66.8	4.3	123	78.9
Calverton Park city	1,287	1,268	-1.5	1,321	52.2	45.0	0.0	2.5	0.3	23.2	17.6	42.9	46.0	24.8	517	91.3
Camden city	191	188	-1.6	269	99.3	0.0	0.0	0.0	0.7	23.8	39.4	46.9	80.4	3.1	112	45.5
Camden Point city	474	548	15.6	491	93.9	0.0	0.0	5.3	0.8	25.5	14.3	34.5	44.0	24.5	172	93.0
Camdenton city	3,726	4,145	11.2	4,038	88.5	2.0	0.0	6.7	2.8	26.1	22.8	36.8	49.0	16.4	1,190	87.6
Cameron city	9,929	9,649	-2.8	9,665	78.5	11.7	0.8	5.3	3.7	16.1	14.6	37.5	60.3	11.5	2,609	82.1
Campbell city	1,992	1,807	-9.3	1,851	96.0	0.6	0.0	2.5	0.9	26.7	19.8	43.1	65.3	5.5	741	83.1
Canalou city	338	301	-10.9	217	97.2	0.0	0.0	0.0	2.8	34.1	14.3	36.1	78.6	2.3	70	84.3
Canton city	2,377	2,302	-3.2	2,463	85.5	6.1	0.0	7.1	1.3	21.3	13.6	28.1	50.4	20.5	903	86.2
Cape Girardeau city	37,973	40,559	6.8	39,566	78.8	12.8	2.8	2.6	3.1	18.9	16.3	33.3	35.2	35.0	15,260	89.5
Cardwell city	713	639	-10.4	769	79.6	0.0	0.9	4.0	15.5	24.2	13.7	37.2	76.4	4.7	324	84.3
Carl Junction city	7,469	8,274	10.8	8,072	91.9	0.6	0.8	5.5	1.2	34.6	13.3	34.3	33.7	35.6	2,777	93.9
Carrollton city	3,781	3,476	-8.1	3,637	91.7	2.1	1.2	2.5	2.6	24.2	21.9	42.5	62.7	14.6	1,445	79.5
Carterville city	1,891	1,968	4.1	2,253	88.2	1.7	0.2	5.5	4.4	30.8	8.7	31.7	63.8	8.7	742	86.5
Carthage city	14,378	14,746	2.6	14,708	60.5	1.4	0.7	5.3	32.2	29.4	13.0	32.5	56.4	17.7	5,034	85.4
Caruthersville city	6,135	5,348	-12.8	5,616	57.6	38.9	0.0	0.4	3.2	21.9	15.8	39.1	62.4	16.3	2,360	72.5
Carytown city	271	283	4.4	232	98.7	0.0	0.0	1.3	0.0	19.8	22.4	51.9	56.0	19.6	98	80.6
Cassville city	3,271	3,290	0.6	3,267	87.3	1.7	0.0	2.4	8.6	23.4	20.3	36.9	66.3	10.9	1,158	86.1
Castle Point CDP	3,962	-	-	2,820	5.1	90.6	0.0	2.6	1.6	32.3	13.0	30.9	49.0	14.7	1,057	90.5
Catron town	67	60	-10.4	38	71.1	28.9	0.0	0.0	0.0	5.3	47.4	64.0	70.6	20.6	23	47.8
Cave town	5	5	0.0	3	100.0	0.0	0.0	0.0	0.0	0.0	100.0	0.0	0.0	0.0	1	0.0
Cedar Hill CDP	1,721	-	-	1,834	96.8	0.0	0.4	0.8	2.0	25.1	8.1	33.0	36.9	17.3	697	95.7
Cedar Hill Lakes village	236	227	-3.8	255	96.1	0.0	1.6	2.0	0.4	10.2	22.0	54.1	56.9	19.1	119	87.4
Center city	508	506	-0.4	521	96.7	2.3	0.0	1.0	0.0	19.6	29.9	45.9	77.0	9.0	217	73.3
Centertown town	278	287	3.2	318	98.1	0.0	0.0	1.6	0.3	22.0	15.1	33.0	60.4	17.6	141	89.4
Centerview city	275	273	-0.7	189	97.4	0.0	0.0	1.6	1.1	27.5	18.5	44.8	63.6	6.2	85	80.0
Centerville city	194	181	-6.7	198	79.8	7.1	0.0	0.0	13.1	28.8	14.6	38.5	68.6	5.8	60	81.7
Centralia city	4,026	4,271	6.1	4,213	99.5	0.0	0.0	0.0	0.5	27.2	18.7	36.6	44.7	25.1	1,860	82.2
Chaffee city	2,961	2,898	-2.1	2,919	95.5	4.3	0.0	0.1	0.0	24.2	14.6	39.3	49.2	9.4	1,071	89.2
Chain of Rocks village	93	100	7.5	114	100.0	0.0	0.0	0.0	0.0	30.7	6.1	32.0	46.4	15.9	29	82.8
Chain-O-Lakes village	128	128	0.0	86	100.0	0.0	0.0	0.0	0.0	14.0	40.7	52.0	33.8	29.7	41	100.0
Chamois city	394	379	-3.8	495	99.0	0.0	0.0	0.6	0.4	17.8	21.6	35.8	53.4	18.9	184	84.8
Champ village	13	13	0.0	2	100.0	0.0	0.0	0.0	0.0	0.0	100.0	0.0	0.0	0.0	1	100.0
Charlack city	1,365	1,354	-0.8	1,651	47.8	42.1	0.8	1.6	7.6	25.8	8.2	29.4	50.8	16.1	648	90.7
Charleston city	5,947	5,468	-8.1	5,614	41.3	53.6	0.0	2.9	2.2	17.5	14.9	39.3	65.3	11.5	1,683	74.1
Charmwood town	32	31	-3.1	38	92.1	0.0	0.0	7.9	0.0	23.7	5.3	45.5	73.1	0.0	17	100.0
Cherokee Pass CDP	235	-	-	288	100.0	0.0	0.0	0.0	0.0	21.9	16.0	41.7	67.7	19.4	115	100.0
Chesapeake CDP	49	-	-	32	100.0	0.0	0.0	0.0	0.0	34.4	0.0	38.5	0.0	47.6	11	100.0
Chesterfield city	47,483	47,538	0.1	47,605	79.6	3.8	11.5	2.3	2.8	21.0	24.2	46.5	12.7	69.2	19,209	95.4
Chilhowee town	325	323	-0.6	425	94.1	0.0	0.9	3.5	1.4	36.0	8.9	31.4	73.3	12.1	138	86.2
Chillicothe city	9,517	9,705	2.0	9,162	89.4	4.0	0.8	3.6	2.2	22.0	18.9	37.2	54.4	18.2	3,499	82.4
Chula city	210	205	-2.4	198	93.9	2.0	1.0	0.5	2.5	22.2	17.7	46.7	60.0	2.3	81	84.0
Clarence city	813	750	-7.7	1,004	92.7	0.0	0.0	0.3	7.0	26.7	20.1	37.5	62.6	7.8	361	82.5
Clark city	301	290	-3.7	285	87.4	1.1	0.0	11.6	0.0	26.3	12.3	36.6	66.7	5.8	98	75.5
Clarksburg city	334	350	4.8	190	91.1	2.6	0.0	0.5	5.8	14.7	16.3	47.0	67.6	11.7	93	93.5
Clarksdale city	265	255	-3.8	237	96.6	0.0	0.0	2.5	0.8	20.3	24.9	50.3	71.7	6.4	110	83.6
Clarkson Valley city	2,636	2,606	-1.1	2,614	87.5	0.0	8.1	0.8	3.5	21.1	26.8	52.2	8.5	77.9	931	94.4
Clarksville city	449	431	-4.0	432	93.8	5.1	0.0	1.2	0.0	14.1	29.6	51.7	51.6	23.9	213	81.2
Clarkton city	1,285	1,152	-10.4	1,290	71.0	5.3	0.0	4.7	18.9	32.2	12.0	29.1	69.5	4.4	529	80.5
Claycomo village	1,402	1,514	8.0	1,586	84.4	5.2	0.6	5.4	4.4	12.0	18.5	47.5	53.9	10.3	713	90.6
Clayton city	15,977	16,747	4.8	16,588	73.5	6.9	12.7	3.0	3.9	15.7	14.1	30.0	10.6	77.7	5,646	96.2
Clearmont city	171	155	-9.4	142	98.6	0.0	0.0	0.0	1.4	23.2	26.1	51.0	58.7	21.1	64	79.7
Cleveland city	661	661	0.0	570	91.8	0.0	0.0	3.0	5.3	18.1	20.4	48.8	40.3	24.8	233	93.6
Clever city	2,161	2,770	28.2	2,667	97.2	0.4	0.4	0.5	1.5	31.8	13.4	30.7	39.5	17.0	993	94.2
Cliff Village village	40	39	-2.5	17	100.0	0.0	0.0	0.0	0.0	0.0	23.5	45.9	100.0	0.0	9	77.8
Clifton Hill city	115	109	-5.2	51	100.0	0.0	0.0	0.0	0.0	29.4	29.4	39.5	52.8	11.1	21	71.4
Climax Springs CDP	124	-	-	277	83.8	0.7	0.0	15.5	0.0	30.0	0.7	42.0	75.7	3.3	72	83.3
Clinton city	9,009	8,945	-0.7	9,118	90.0	2.7	0.9	2.6	3.8	23.5	20.1	39.8	51.3	19.7	3,955	87.1
Clyde village	87	79	-9.2	63	100.0	0.0	0.0	0.0	0.0	25.4	25.4	36.3	63.2	10.5	27	81.5
Cobalt village	227	224	-1.3	256	97.7	0.0	0.0	2.3	0.0	14.5	20.3	47.0	65.0	2.5	130	73.1
Coffey city	166	164	-1.2	207	99.5	0.0	0.0	0.5	0.0	34.3	11.6	27.4	57.5	0.8	69	87.0
Cole Camp city	1,120	1,134	1.3	1,230	98.5	0.0	0.0	0.0	1.5	18.9	27.6	50.4	52.6	11.5	467	88.2
Collins village	159	152	-4.4	192	91.7	0.0	0.0	6.3	2.1	22.4	21.4	46.4	59.6	5.9	74	86.5
Columbia city	109,044	123,195	13.0	121,230	74.5	10.9	6.2	4.7	3.6	18.3	10.6	28.5	22.9	52.2	48,189	94.2
Commerce village	67	66	-1.5	134	100.0	0.0	0.0	0.0	0.0	20.9	16.4	28.6	84.6	7.7	34	88.2
Conception CDP	210	-	-	289	81.0	0.0	10.4	1.0	7.6	0.3	14.9	22.1	15.4	35.4	25	88.0
Conception Junction town	203	182	-10.3	197	97.0	0.0	0.0	3.0	0.0	28.9	18.3	39.3	67.2	19.2	77	85.7
Concord CDP	16,421	-	-	17,912	95.0	0.5	1.6	1.7	1.2	21.2	22.7	44.3	28.2	40.3	7,449	89.9
Concordia city	2,454	2,366	-3.6	2,902	95.7	0.3	0.0	2.9	1.2	25.7	18.4	37.0	51.5	21.5	1,089	87.7
Coney Island village	75	75	0.0	48	89.6	0.0	0.0	0.0	10.4	6.3	56.3	67.5	75.0	10.0	20	75.0
Conway city	789	776	-1.6	713	95.7	0.0	0.0	2.2	2.1	31.0	14.6	35.7	63.8	8.0	302	66.2
Cool Valley city	1,169	1,130	-3.3	1,152	19.9	76.5	1.6	1.8	0.3	20.2	18.2	40.7	50.9	15.1	433	85.5
Cooter city	469	404	-13.9	348	96.6	0.0	0.0	0.3	3.2	25.3	14.7	34.6	61.1	14.7	149	83.9
Corder city	408	401	-1.7	469	89.1	3.4	0.0	6.6	0.9	26.7	19.0	43.2	61.8	16.0	164	90.9
Corning town	15	14	-6.7	5	100.0	0.0	0.0	0.0	0.0	0.0	100.0	75.8	100.0	0.0	4	100.0
Cosby village	124	125	0.8	213	89.2	5.6	0.9	4.2	0.0	28.6	5.6	28.0	26.8	17.1	70	94.3
Cottleville city	3,054	5,608	83.6	5,200	90.8	0.7	1.6	1.4	5.6	24.0	9.9	36.6	22.8	56.9	1,890	99.6
Country Club village	2,452	2,497	1.8	2,729	84.0	7.1	0.3	4.0	4.6	26.0	14.5	37.5	36.4	38.0	965	93.8
Country Club Hills city	1,267	1,246	-1.7	1,415	3.6	91.6	0.0	4.8	0.0	30.7	8.3	29.6	56.6	7.2	544	91.2
Country Life Acres village	74	73	-1.4	75	88.0	0.0	9.3	1.3	1.3	12.0	32.0	55.3	4.7	54.7	31	100.0
Cowgill city	188	182	-3.2	221	88.2	0.0	0.0	10.4	1.4	28.5	13.1	31.3	69.5	5.3	84	86.9
Craig city	248	223	-10.1	172	91.9	0.0	8.1	0.0	0.0	33.7	18.0	33.5	73.8	7.8	60	81.7
Crane city	1,439	1,357	-5.7	1,413	94.3	0.6	0.0	4.4	0.8	24.6	25.9	42.6	54.4	10.1	566	82.7
Creighton city	349	342	-2.0	354	89.5	2.5	0.0	3.7	4.2	20.9	14.7	35.2	71.7	7.7	139	91.4
Crestwood city	11,885	11,834	-0.4	11,865	92.0	1.2	1.4	1.9	3.6	22.0	19.9	42.7	18.6	53.4	4,855	91.5
Creve Coeur city	17,811	18,622	4.6	18,538	74.2	8.6	10.9	2.4	3.9	17.3	26.1	48.8	12.8	68.0	8,340	94.0
Crocker city	1,110	1,039	-6.4	1,103	82.9	0.4	1.4	14.5	0.9	26.9	19.0	34.6	48.4	17.1	414	87.7
Cross Timbers city	216	211	-2.3	239	100.0	0.0	0.0	0.0	0.0	28.0	24.3	34.2	72.1	7.0	101	91.1
Crystal City city	4,838	4,700	-2.9	4,740	93.4	3.4	0.1	2.5	0.5	20.1	18.2	39.6	40.2	19.7	1,998	92.0
Crystal Lake Park city	470	486	3.4	395	87.6	1.3	5.3	0.8	5.1	18.5	35.9	56.3	5.1	79.4	179	97.8
Crystal Lakes city	364	355	-2.5	346	92.8	0.6	0.9	2.0	3.8	19.7	15.3	46.8	58.8	9.2	128	96.1

1 May be of any race.

Table A. All Places — **Population and Housing**

STATE City, town, township, borough, or CDP (county if applicable)	Population				Race and Hispanic or Latino origin (percent)					Age (percent)			Educational attainment of persons age 25 and older		Occupied housing units	
	2010 census total population	2019 estimated population	Percent change 2010–2019	ACS total population estimate 2015–2019	White alone, not Hispanic or Latino	Black alone, not Hispanic or Latino	Asian alone, not Hispanic or Latino	All other races or 2 or more races, not Hispanic or Latino	Hispanic or Latino[1]	Under 18 years old	Age 65 years and older	Median age	Percent High school diploma or less	Percent Bachelor's degree or more	Total	Percent with a computer
	1	2	3	4	5	6	7	8	9	10	11	12	13	14	15	16
MISSOURI—Con.																
Cuba city	3,364	3,292	-2.1	3,314	86.8	1.3	0.0	2.1	9.8	27.2	15.6	35.1	63.3	10.4	1,437	80.1
Curryville city	225	223	-0.9	237	95.4	1.3	0.4	3.0	0.0	32.5	17.3	33.5	72.3	5.7	91	86.8
Dadeville village	233	224	-3.9	245	91.4	0.0	0.0	7.3	1.2	21.2	20.8	39.3	42.6	22.5	87	88.5
Dalton town	17	16	-5.9	24	4.2	95.8	0.0	0.0	0.0	0.0	54.2	69.3	25.0	0.0	5	60.0
Danville CDP	34	-	-	27	100.0	0.0	0.0	0.0	0.0	37.0	37.0	33.5	100.0	0.0	10	0.0
Dardenne Prairie city	11,633	13,348	14.7	13,293	89.7	3.1	2.8	3.2	1.2	26.7	12.5	42.2	20.1	50.9	4,401	96.7
Darlington village	121	118	-2.5	64	100.0	0.0	0.0	0.0	0.0	14.1	32.8	56.7	71.7	13.2	43	51.2
Dawn CDP	128	-	-	154	91.6	0.0	0.0	8.4	0.0	26.6	24.0	41.2	67.0	5.2	76	59.2
Dearborn city	496	523	5.4	517	93.4	0.0	0.0	3.3	3.3	23.0	18.8	39.9	53.1	19.0	226	81.4
Deepwater city	431	413	-4.2	412	88.8	1.0	0.0	9.0	1.2	23.8	19.2	42.3	58.2	13.9	196	80.6
Deerfield village	81	78	-3.7	48	100.0	0.0	0.0	0.0	0.0	18.8	35.4	59.8	56.4	12.8	26	53.8
Defiance CDP	155	-	-	93	100.0	0.0	0.0	0.0	0.0	0.0	49.5	61.0	77.4	11.8	63	76.2
De Kalb town	220	222	0.9	260	95.0	0.0	0.0	5.0	0.0	26.5	9.6	35.7	59.6	14.6	95	91.6
Dellwood city	5,060	4,997	-1.2	5,013	12.7	85.3	0.0	2.0	0.0	26.1	9.3	35.0	44.3	14.2	2,029	94.2
Delta city	438	425	-3.0	352	96.0	0.0	0.0	4.0	0.0	21.3	26.7	44.2	71.7	11.4	142	81.7
Dennis Acres village	71	70	-1.4	41	73.2	0.0	0.0	0.0	26.8	9.8	14.6	37.2	47.1	8.8	18	100.0
Denver village	39	36	-7.7	25	100.0	0.0	0.0	0.0	0.0	20.0	24.0	61.3	42.1	15.8	12	83.3
Des Arc village	170	162	-4.7	200	100.0	0.0	0.0	0.0	0.0	31.0	13.5	27.5	68.2	0.0	70	68.6
Desloge city	5,072	4,882	-3.7	4,886	95.8	1.0	0.2	0.8	2.3	20.5	16.7	39.3	53.3	10.8	2,183	80.0
De Soto city	6,376	6,345	-0.5	6,380	95.8	1.5	0.3	2.4	0.0	24.5	17.3	37.5	48.5	15.7	2,664	89.6
Des Peres city	8,382	8,697	3.8	8,619	93.4	0.9	2.5	2.3	0.9	27.6	22.6	43.8	10.2	74.3	2,984	96.6
De Witt city	124	117	-5.6	104	80.8	11.5	0.0	7.7	0.0	20.2	26.9	53.0	84.4	0.0	41	75.6
Dexter city	7,868	7,815	-0.7	7,862	95.3	1.0	0.0	1.8	2.0	23.9	21.4	40.5	60.9	12.0	3,193	84.0
Diamond town	888	910	2.5	874	95.3	0.0	0.0	3.5	1.1	24.4	16.9	35.1	54.8	11.6	365	80.8
Diehlstadt village	161	151	-6.2	159	100.0	0.0	0.0	0.0	0.0	22.0	23.9	39.5	72.5	6.4	52	88.5
Diggins village	304	323	6.3	268	97.4	0.0	0.0	1.5	1.1	20.5	23.9	52.3	65.9	12.2	105	89.5
Dixon city	1,547	1,450	-6.3	1,130	94.2	0.1	0.0	2.4	3.4	22.5	17.8	34.6	54.4	9.1	422	76.1
Doe Run CDP	915	-	-	994	89.2	0.0	0.0	0.0	10.8	19.1	12.6	42.7	61.9	4.1	387	60.7
Doniphan city	2,001	1,916	-4.2	2,062	97.3	0.1	0.4	2.1	0.0	18.7	23.9	44.5	56.1	12.4	835	72.5
Doolittle city	636	601	-5.5	670	94.6	3.3	0.6	0.0	1.5	25.5	17.9	42.0	43.1	11.8	287	87.8
Dover town	103	102		81	96.3	0.0	0.0	0.0	3.7	14.8	23.5	55.6	70.1	3.0	39	82.1
Downing city	335	351	4.8	413	99.8	0.0	0.0	0.2	0.0	26.4	14.0	42.3	76.9	3.6	143	67.1
Drexel city	965	944	-2.2	942	97.8	0.8	0.0	1.4	0.0	19.7	25.8	45.4	56.7	12.9	421	83.4
Dudley city	232	222	-4.3	194	90.2	0.0	1.5	7.7	0.5	14.4	8.2	43.7	64.2	15.9	73	90.4
Duenweg city	1,364	1,379	1.1	1,384	88.5	0.3	0.4	0.7	10.0	21.9	13.4	38.1	54.0	18.2	569	88.6
Duquesne village	1,763	1,639	-7.0	1,918	83.5	1.5	2.8	8.3	3.9	17.0	15.7	40.3	44.2	23.2	849	91.6
Dutchtown CDP	94	-	-	124	100.0	0.0	0.0	0.0	0.0	9.7	8.9	47.7	75.6	9.3	56	100.0
Eagle Rock CDP	199	-	-	170	100.0	0.0	0.0	0.0	0.0	17.1	8.8	56.5	40.0	25.8	80	100.0
Eagleville town	322	300	-6.8	284	97.2	0.0	0.0	2.8	0.0	22.9	19.0	42.0	65.4	5.8	132	78.0
East Lynne city	299	305	2.0	242	97.9	0.0	0.0	2.1	0.0	21.9	9.1	31.4	61.4	9.8	105	83.8
Easton city	236	233	-1.3	203	85.7	0.0	0.0	11.3	3.0	10.8	25.1	55.5	51.4	6.2	104	79.8
East Prairie city	3,121	2,941	-5.8	3,006	94.4	4.5	0.0	1.1	0.0	20.4	17.5	44.2	73.0	4.3	1,388	71.5
Edgar Springs city	210	195	-7.1	181	94.5	0.0	0.0	0.0	5.5	32.6	14.4	34.9	53.3	14.8	79	91.1
Edgerton city	546	616	12.8	580	86.4	0.2	0.0	8.3	5.2	29.0	16.7	29.5	54.5	21.4	215	84.7
Edina city	1,177	1,124	-4.5	1,236	97.0	0.4	0.2	1.8	0.6	26.9	19.6	38.9	49.6	20.5	490	79.0
Edinburg CDP	92	-	-	103	100.0	0.0	0.0	0.0	0.0	2.9	11.7	48.8	47.8	10.9	50	100.0
Edmundson city	834	829	-0.6	1,202	54.0	30.4	1.1	7.3	7.2	39.1	5.8	27.9	41.6	13.7	397	88.9
Eldon city	4,577	4,706	2.8	4,636	93.3	0.1	0.0	4.7	1.9	24.7	19.6	36.1	58.0	15.6	2,023	81.1
El Dorado Springs city	3,578	3,612	1.0	3,534	92.1	0.0	0.0	5.9	2.0	25.2	19.2	36.8	44.9	14.3	1,562	83.7
Ellington city	987	928	-6.0	1,182	95.4	0.1	0.3	3.8	0.3	28.5	17.1	36.8	64.1	8.7	472	75.8
Ellisville city	9,301	9,862	6.0	9,661	80.6	1.6	4.7	5.9	7.2	22.4	22.8	44.6	23.1	50.1	3,820	91.6
Ellsinore city	448	429	-4.2	545	96.5	0.0	0.0	2.8	0.7	35.2	13.6	29.3	52.5	8.2	214	74.8
Elmer city	80	77	-3.8	65	100.0	0.0	0.0	0.0	0.0	18.5	36.9	59.9	83.0	0.0	26	53.8
Elmira village	50	50	0.0	34	100.0	0.0	0.0	0.0	0.0	17.6	23.5	40.0	70.4	14.8	13	84.6
Elmo city	168	150	-10.7	110	100.0	0.0	0.0	0.0	0.0	9.1	23.6	49.6	65.5	14.3	65	67.7
Elsberry city	1,934	2,077	7.4	2,303	90.1	4.6	0.1	4.5	0.7	29.3	15.3	36.6	61.0	15.2	875	75.5
Emerald Beach village	228	244	7.0	151	98.7	0.0	0.0	0.0	1.3	0.7	51.0	65.3	55.0	14.8	89	89.9
Eminence city	599	578	-3.5	767	94.1	0.3	0.0	3.0	2.6	22.0	17.7	46.6	51.1	26.3	275	78.9
Emma city	236	229	-3.0	219	96.3	0.0	0.0	3.7	0.0	15.5	34.2	54.5	49.7	22.6	98	75.5
Eolia village	522	509	-2.5	421	94.8	2.4	0.0	1.4	1.4	23.3	20.4	41.6	64.2	18.8	168	88.1
Essex city	470	448	-4.7	524	98.7	1.3	0.0	0.0	0.0	21.9	18.3	40.9	67.6	6.0	200	79.5
Ethel town	62	60	-3.2	29	100.0	0.0	0.0	0.0	0.0	0.0	55.2	70.2	44.8	34.5	16	87.5
Eugene CDP	-	-	-	246	96.3	0.0	0.0	3.7	0.0	20.7	25.2	49.4	46.5	29.1	87	54.0
Eureka city	10,179	10,946	7.5	10,666	89.5	3.2	2.8	1.8	2.7	26.7	13.7	39.7	25.1	47.4	3,523	93.6
Evergreen village	28	28	0.0	20	80.0	0.0	5.0	15.0	0.0	5.0	20.0	59.3	56.3	25.0	8	100.0
Everton city	313	299	-4.5	321	92.5	0.0	0.0	7.5	0.0	26.2	23.4	39.1	58.4	6.8	112	85.7
Ewing city	454	430	-5.3	393	96.9	2.3	0.0	0.8	0.0	18.6	21.4	53.2	67.9	5.0	180	85.0
Excello CDP	49	-	-	12	100.0	0.0	0.0	0.0	0.0	0.0	100.0	0.0	0.0	0.0	12	100.0
Excelsior Estates village	147	148	0.7	228	72.8	0.0	0.0	14.0	13.2	30.7	8.8	31.3	79.9	2.2	74	90.5
Excelsior Springs city	11,081	11,731	5.9	11,640	89.6	4.7	0.8	2.4	2.4	24.5	16.5	35.7	56.3	16.2	4,365	90.4
Exeter city	773	769	-0.5	818	96.6	0.0	0.0	1.0	2.4	26.0	16.6	41.7	60.9	10.9	324	79.3
Fairdealing CDP	676	-	-	731	84.0	0.0	0.0	0.0	16.0	20.7	2.3	37.3	61.4	18.4	256	80.1
Fairfax city	638	574	-10.0	673	96.4	1.2	0.0	1.5	0.9	20.5	25.0	44.9	57.0	16.0	335	78.2
Fair Grove city	1,395	1,529	9.6	1,432	95.7	0.0	0.3	0.8	3.2	30.5	16.9	35.8	41.8	24.6	554	85.9
Fair Play city	475	483	1.7	425	96.2	0.0	0.0	1.9	1.9	19.5	19.5	47.7	65.6	6.7	159	73.6
Fairview town	382	377	-1.3	424	76.7	0.0	16.0	5.7	1.7	23.6	18.6	39.5	69.3	8.8	150	84.7
Farber city	322	313	-2.8	333	93.1	4.5	0.0	1.5	0.9	12.0	29.7	47.4	68.1	10.0	165	86.1
Farley village	269	301	11.9	276	94.9	0.0	2.2	1.8	1.1	23.6	22.8	50.5	45.5	25.1	105	82.9
Farmington city	16,293	19,113	17.3	18,515	88.5	6.3	1.6	1.7	1.9	19.1	16.1	38.2	47.5	19.5	6,563	87.6
Fayette city	2,690	2,689	0.0	2,693	80.5	15.4	0.3	2.6	1.3	15.1	16.2	27.6	50.6	29.9	771	80.3
Fenton city	4,023	4,026	0.1	4,025	96.0	2.3	0.5	0.8	0.4	21.7	20.6	45.9	23.5	45.2	1,589	93.2
Ferguson city	21,190	20,525	-3.1	20,738	24.4	67.5	0.9	5.6	1.6	27.7	11.8	34.5	43.8	20.1	8,198	89.8
Ferrelview village	451	798	76.9	659	72.2	8.8	0.5	13.4	5.2	9.6	10.0	42.7	50.3	16.3	307	90.6
Festus city	11,587	12,036	3.9	11,982	94.0	2.0	0.5	1.0	2.4	22.8	16.5	37.6	42.4	20.0	4,614	89.6
Fidelity town	257	268	4.3	269	98.9	0.0	0.0	1.1	0.0	20.8	18.2	38.9	53.3	10.8	112	83.9
Fillmore city	184	188	2.2	194	99.0	1.0	0.0	0.0	0.0	12.4	13.4	43.6	71.5	5.8	93	64.5
Fisk city	342	334	-2.3	321	98.4	0.0	0.0	1.6	0.0	25.2	22.1	44.8	54.2	7.0	133	76.7
Fleming city	132	129	-2.3	71	100.0	0.0	0.0	0.0	0.0	18.3	15.5	45.8	80.8	1.9	25	88.0
Flemington village	148	148	0.0	74	98.6	0.0	0.0	1.4	0.0	9.5	29.7	58.4	49.2	0.0	39	74.4
Flint Hill city	704	777	10.4	946	98.1	0.0	0.0	0.7	1.2	16.1	19.8	49.2	42.1	22.5	388	83.2
Flordell Hills city	829	802	-3.3	861	1.9	97.0	0.0	0.9	0.2	31.1	6.5	26.7	56.8	9.3	323	89.2
Florissant city	52,260	50,952	-2.5	51,455	50.5	40.1	0.7	5.6	3.1	25.4	13.7	35.9	39.8	23.9	19,710	91.5

1 May be of any race.

Table A. All Places — **Population and Housing**

STATE City, town, township, borough, or CDP (county if applicable)	Population				Race and Hispanic or Latino origin (percent)					Age (percent)			Educational attainment of persons age 25 and older		Occupied housing units	
	2010 census total population	2019 estimated population	Percent change 2010–2019	ACS total population estimate 2015–2019	White alone, not Hispanic or Latino	Black alone, not Hispanic or Latino	Asian alone, not Hispanic or Latino	All other races or 2 or more races, not Hispanic or Latino	Hispanic or Latino[1]	Under 18 years old	Age 65 years and older	Median age	Percent High school diploma or less	Percent Bachelor's degree or more	Total	Percent with a computer
	1	2	3	4	5	6	7	8	9	10	11	12	13	14	15	16
MISSOURI—Con.																
Foley city	161	173	7.5	128	96.9	0.0	0.0	1.6	1.6	16.4	3.9	38.5	69.3	3.4	49	89.8
Fordland city	795	846	6.4	933	91.6	0.0	0.0	7.7	0.6	29.7	18.1	37.7	54.9	9.3	372	89.0
Forest City city	275	246	-10.5	263	94.7	0.0	0.0	3.4	1.9	20.2	27.4	43.5	57.8	12.0	128	66.4
Foristell city	538	606	12.6	783	95.9	0.0	0.6	0.6	2.8	27.3	19.4	48.0	37.5	31.2	281	97.5
Forsyth city	2,465	2,560	3.9	2,549	88.3	1.9	1.8	3.6	4.4	19.4	30.5	47.0	53.7	15.2	978	87.5
Fortescue town	32	29	-9.4	47	100.0	0.0	0.0	0.0	0.0	66.0	0.0	11.9	75.0	0.0	12	83.3
Fort Leonard Wood CDP	15,061	-	-	16,026	51.8	17.6	4.0	5.9	20.8	18.3	0.1	20.8	19.8	39.6	2,220	99.5
Foster village	117	111	-5.1	165	99.4	0.0	0.0	0.0	0.6	7.9	14.5	52.0	54.7	28.0	75	96.0
Fountain N' Lakes village	165	182	10.3	165	85.5	1.2	0.0	4.8	8.5	24.8	6.1	44.6	74.4	1.7	58	91.4
Frankclay CDP	221	-	-	132	100.0	0.0	0.0	0.0	0.0	17.4	0.0	52.5	63.3	0.0	78	84.6
Frankford city	327	314	-4.0	406	97.3	1.7	0.5	0.5	0.0	27.3	19.7	37.8	69.6	11.7	180	81.1
Franklin city	95	93	-2.1	106	82.1	0.0	0.0	17.9	0.0	27.4	34.9	49.7	86.5	1.4	41	80.5
Fredericktown city	3,988	3,984	-0.1	3,999	91.8	0.6	1.4	1.9	4.3	19.8	16.7	34.4	44.7	20.9	1,768	81.8
Freeburg village	440	423	-3.9	487	100.0	0.0	0.0	0.0	0.0	32.0	20.5	33.5	69.2	4.7	188	83.0
Freeman city	478	485	1.5	517	94.8	0.4	0.0	2.7	2.1	23.6	16.8	32.4	53.0	11.1	205	92.2
Freistatt village	163	161	-1.2	180	78.3	0.0	0.0	0.0	21.7	21.7	17.8	43.3	58.3	11.4	92	73.9
Fremont CDP	129	-	-	33	57.6	0.0	0.0	0.0	42.4	42.4	0.0	0.0	0.0	0.0	19	100.0
Fremont Hills city	826	922	11.6	1,042	97.1	0.3	1.5	0.8	0.3	24.8	24.7	47.1	16.1	61.3	400	96.5
Frohna city	254	245	-3.5	320	100.0	0.0	0.0	0.0	0.0	19.7	10.9	34.2	53.3	12.8	134	91.8
Frontenac city	3,412	3,543	3.8	3,513	81.2	2.1	12.0	0.1	4.6	23.0	20.7	50.2	7.7	82.8	1,305	98.9
Fulton city	12,793	12,596	-1.5	12,779	84.3	10.4	0.7	2.2	2.4	17.5	11.8	33.4	59.1	17.2	3,614	83.1
Gainesville city	765	723	-5.5	608	98.4	1.0	0.0	0.5	0.2	21.5	20.7	47.9	72.1	4.9	311	58.8
Galena city	440	437	-0.7	733	95.8	0.0	0.0	3.8	0.4	29.5	11.7	31.8	57.9	3.8	216	85.2
Gallatin city	1,786	1,749	-2.1	1,597	95.2	0.0	0.2	1.9	2.7	22.8	21.2	41.2	51.4	20.8	674	85.8
Galt city	259	247	-4.6	175	97.7	0.0	2.3	0.0	0.0	8.6	29.7	57.2	68.1	3.8	91	73.6
Garden City city	1,646	1,638	-0.5	1,345	91.5	0.0	0.7	4.5	3.3	20.1	13.6	36.0	61.9	10.0	576	88.4
Gasconade city	223	215	-3.6	334	91.3	0.0	0.0	8.7	0.0	38.9	9.9	36.4	70.0	2.6	115	84.3
Gentry village	72	70	-2.8	60	93.3	0.0	0.0	0.0	6.7	30.0	21.7	34.3	76.2	0.0	20	90.0
Gerald city	1,352	1,313	-2.9	1,280	92.3	0.1	0.0	6.3	1.3	29.1	16.8	31.9	51.2	13.1	496	90.5
Gerster town	25	24	-4.0	20	100.0	0.0	0.0	0.0	0.0	5.0	25.0	57.5	78.9	0.0	11	45.5
Gibbs village	107	102	-4.7	87	100.0	0.0	0.0	0.0	0.0	33.3	13.8	22.1	71.8	0.0	20	90.0
Gideon city	1,093	972	-11.1	935	95.3	1.2	0.0	2.2	1.3	21.3	23.1	47.0	80.5	7.9	345	76.2
Gilliam city	197	190	-3.6	222	93.7	0.5	0.0	0.0	5.9	24.3	11.7	40.5	60.7	10.3	82	80.5
Gilman City city	385	357	-7.3	386	97.7	0.8	0.0	1.6	0.0	26.2	19.2	36.5	62.7	6.3	165	81.2
Ginger Blue village	55	54	-1.8	33	100.0	0.0	0.0	0.0	0.0	0.0	6.1	56.8	54.5	15.2	21	100.0
Gladstone city	25,439	27,489	8.1	27,126	78.3	6.0	0.8	6.6	8.3	19.4	18.0	40.2	37.6	30.2	11,258	92.4
Glasgow city	1,103	1,084	-1.7	1,038	87.7	7.3	0.0	1.3	3.7	20.4	26.0	46.5	49.7	24.3	433	82.4
Glasgow Village CDP	5,429	-	-	4,918	6.2	91.1	0.0	2.7	0.0	43.5	5.9	20.8	51.1	7.9	1,384	92.1
Glenaire city	537	577	7.4	489	93.9	0.0	0.4	3.5	2.2	19.6	27.6	48.5	44.3	23.9	208	88.0
Glen Allen town	85	82	-3.5	169	92.3	0.0	0.0	7.7	0.0	34.3	14.8	21.9	64.3	13.1	38	100.0
Glendale city	5,930	5,866	-1.1	5,891	94.4	1.7	2.0	0.0	1.9	28.5	16.6	43.3	5.1	74.1	2,237	96.9
Glen Echo Park village	172	170	-1.2	109	10.1	89.9	0.0	0.0	0.0	25.7	16.5	43.3	23.5	30.9	47	89.4
Glenwood village	196	206	5.1	233	100.0	0.0	0.0	0.0	0.0	40.3	10.7	26.6	32.0	4.1	69	92.8
Golden CDP	280	-	-	415	97.1	0.0	0.0	2.9	0.0	1.9	37.3	62.3	27.5	46.2	250	90.4
Golden City city	763	719	-5.8	703	83.8	1.3	0.0	14.5	0.4	20.5	27.0	49.2	62.3	9.7	354	73.7
Goodman city	1,254	1,249	-0.4	1,381	87.9	0.9	0.0	6.3	4.9	27.1	12.4	34.1	69.2	9.4	494	77.1
Goodnight village	18	18	0.0	22	100.0	0.0	0.0	0.0	0.0	18.2	31.8	64.2	44.4	11.1	10	90.0
Gordonville village	380	371	-2.4	478	98.1	0.6	0.0	0.2	1.0	13.8	19.2	45.5	41.3	35.7	186	86.6
Gower city	1,523	1,454	-4.5	1,617	97.2	0.2	0.0	0.4	2.2	24.5	20.4	39.9	46.7	19.3	652	81.3
Graham town	171	155	-9.4	164	100.0	0.0	0.0	0.0	0.0	33.5	18.3	29.8	64.9	14.4	72	81.9
Grain Valley city	12,855	14,526	13.0	13,966	87.2	0.9	0.3	5.9	5.7	30.4	9.4	33.9	38.3	25.4	5,126	95.6
Granby city	2,134	2,085	-2.3	2,047	88.8	0.2	0.2	9.4	1.3	27.4	19.3	38.2	58.9	7.7	784	76.7
Grand Falls Plaza town	114	112	-1.8	146	69.9	19.2	0.0	9.6	1.4	19.2	21.2	35.0	34.0	32.1	56	87.5
Grandin city	243	229	-5.8	278	100.0	0.0	0.0	0.0	0.0	32.7	14.0	30.6	65.0	8.1	106	83.0
Grand Pass village	66	64	-3.0	62	100.0	0.0	0.0	0.0	0.0	32.3	9.7	33.8	82.9	0.0	19	84.2
Grandview city	24,455	24,856	1.6	25,069	46.1	35.5	1.8	6.5	10.0	24.6	12.5	34.3	45.0	19.4	10,071	93.7
Granger village	34	34	0.0	25	100.0	0.0	0.0	0.0	0.0	16.0	32.0	53.1	61.9	19.0	9	55.6
Grant City town	857	791	-7.7	930	98.0	1.2	0.0	0.3	0.5	18.3	25.5	47.7	56.9	21.1	403	81.1
Grantwood Village town	859	856	-0.3	907	94.0	1.5	1.5	1.8	1.1	22.4	22.5	51.1	15.6	58.0	351	92.0
Gravois Mills town	148	148	0.0	153	100.0	0.0	0.0	0.0	0.0	30.1	4.6	31.4	64.6	0.0	38	94.7
Grayhawk CDP	525	-	-	562	100.0	0.0	0.0	0.0	0.0	12.5	13.0	48.8	34.3	29.9	214	100.0
Grayridge CDP	127	-	-	183	91.3	0.0	0.0	0.0	8.7	35.5	15.3	33.3	44.2	7.7	47	93.6
Gray Summit CDP	2,701	-	-	2,699	92.2	2.7	0.0	2.4	2.7	24.2	10.6	34.1	44.4	23.1	995	94.5
Greencastle city	272	246	-9.6	205	87.8	0.0	0.0	7.8	4.4	21.5	20.5	46.1	64.3	21.4	70	74.3
Green City city	657	589	-10.4	494	97.4	0.0	0.0	0.0	2.6	22.1	23.5	48.0	62.0	16.8	228	72.4
Greendale city	664	654	-1.5	817	18.7	72.1	3.3	0.7	5.1	19.7	17.6	48.1	22.7	36.9	404	84.9
Greenfield city	1,376	1,313	-4.6	1,530	87.8	0.6	0.0	4.9	6.7	23.3	23.7	41.5	60.6	8.7	634	79.8
Green Park city	2,626	2,618	-0.3	2,631	93.2	3.4	1.3	1.1	1.1	19.7	23.3	46.5	35.4	26.5	993	93.6
Green Ridge city	476	495	4.0	431	91.4	4.9	0.0	1.9	1.9	26.5	16.5	37.9	48.4	15.5	158	95.6
Greentop city	442	459	3.8	589	99.5	0.2	0.0	0.3	0.0	20.4	27.3	50.0	63.4	11.9	241	77.6
Greenville city	490	463	-5.5	526	91.3	2.1	0.0	0.8	5.9	28.3	16.5	36.0	52.0	7.9	190	83.2
Greenwood city	5,223	5,833	11.7	6,247	89.7	2.3	1.0	2.0	5.0	31.3	8.1	34.3	26.5	36.6	2,179	97.1
Guilford town	81	73	-9.9	69	95.7	4.3	0.0	0.0	0.0	23.2	5.8	35.7	71.2	11.5	32	87.5
Gunn City village	118	120	1.7	132	58.3	0.0	0.0	31.1	10.6	32.6	8.3	28.6	46.4	11.6	41	97.6
Hale city	419	397	-5.3	425	95.8	0.0	0.0	0.0	4.2	26.6	15.8	41.2	63.6	13.6	175	81.7
Halfway village	175	177	1.1	119	84.9	0.0	0.0	5.9	9.2	22.7	24.4	53.4	63.6	9.1	63	87.3
Hallsville city	1,476	1,577	6.8	1,771	93.3	1.1	0.4	1.5	3.7	31.1	10.7	35.0	40.7	26.9	683	92.4
Halltown village	171	171	0.0	153	100.0	0.0	0.0	0.0	0.0	41.8	7.2	31.8	56.1	4.9	51	90.2
Hamilton city	1,809	1,684	-6.9	1,893	93.0	1.0	1.3	3.3	1.4	28.7	18.1	38.7	58.2	16.7	752	80.1
Hanley Hills village	2,125	2,101	-1.1	1,863	14.4	81.5	0.0	4.1	0.0	18.7	13.6	38.3	46.9	14.1	767	88.3
Hannibal city	17,784	17,346	-2.5	17,320	87.7	5.5	0.7	3.7	2.5	23.8	16.9	36.6	50.7	21.0	6,947	85.1
Hardin city	570	537	-5.8	609	93.8	0.0	0.0	3.3	3.0	28.7	10.2	34.3	62.4	14.6	220	84.5
Harris town	61	56	-8.2	38	100.0	0.0	0.0	0.0	0.0	39.5	7.9	23.5	52.9	0.0	16	87.5
Harrisburg town	265	286	7.9	410	95.4	0.0	3.4	0.0	1.2	40.0	7.6	29.0	41.0	26.4	148	90.5
Harrisonville city	10,019	10,078	0.6	10,043	90.3	1.5	0.4	5.2	2.6	25.3	15.6	34.6	55.7	16.4	3,982	86.8
Hartsburg town	103	110	6.8	86	98.8	0.0	0.0	0.0	1.2	10.5	24.4	50.3	37.7	28.6	54	87.0
Hartville city	629	607	-3.5	547	96.0	2.2	0.0	0.4	1.5	15.2	28.5	48.4	72.1	5.4	246	62.6
Hartwell CDP	16	-	-	79	100.0	0.0	0.0	0.0	0.0	10.1	0.0	48.9	100.0	0.0	22	100.0
Harviell CDP	106	-	-	-	-	-	-	-	-	-	-	-	-	-	-	-
Harwood village	47	45	-4.3	19	100.0	0.0	0.0	0.0	0.0	52.6	0.0	8.8	100.0	0.0	5	0.0
Hawk Point city	661	712	7.7	630	90.0	1.1	7.5	0.8	0.6	23.2	14.8	38.8	67.7	6.5	229	76.0
Hayti city	2,933	2,501	-14.7	2,652	56.3	37.6	0.0	3.4	2.8	32.5	17.3	34.6	71.6	5.0	1,133	81.3

1 May be of any race.

Table A. All Places — **Population and Housing**

STATE City, town, township, borough, or CDP (county if applicable)	Population				Race and Hispanic or Latino origin (percent)					Age (percent)			Educational attainment of persons age 25 and older		Occupied housing units	
	2010 census total population	2019 estimated population	Percent change 2010–2019	ACS total population estimate 2015–2019	White alone, not Hispanic or Latino	Black alone, not Hispanic or Latino	Asian alone, not Hispanic or Latino	All other races or 2 or more races, not Hispanic or Latino	Hispanic or Latino[1]	Under 18 years old	Age 65 years and older	Median age	Percent High school diploma or less	Percent Bachelor's degree or more	Total	Percent with a computer
	1	2	3	4	5	6	7	8	9	10	11	12	13	14	15	16
MISSOURI—Con.																
Hayti Heights city	640	547	-14.5	537	0.4	99.6	0.0	0.0	0.0	47.1	9.1	18.7	64.9	3.3	177	87.0
Hayward CDP	131	-	-	96	83.3	10.4	0.0	0.0	6.3	14.6	20.8	44.6	76.8	5.8	39	84.6
Haywood City village	206	202	-1.9	122	3.3	96.7	0.0	0.0	0.0	17.2	23.0	54.5	75.3	2.4	55	58.2
Hazelwood city	25,726	25,117	-2.4	25,319	51.3	37.7	3.3	3.7	3.9	21.8	14.7	38.2	35.9	28.5	10,955	94.4
Henrietta city	369	357	-3.3	350	90.9	2.0	0.0	4.3	2.9	22.0	15.7	37.7	79.6	5.4	116	92.2
Herculaneum city	3,471	4,138	19.2	4,025	99.7	0.0	0.2	0.2	0.0	27.1	18.2	37.5	38.3	21.4	1,428	87.3
Hermann city	2,436	2,342	-3.9	2,438	96.3	1.0	0.0	1.9	0.8	22.4	23.7	45.1	46.3	25.4	1,039	84.0
Hermitage city	469	464	-1.1	760	95.1	0.3	0.0	2.2	2.4	14.9	26.8	46.1	57.9	17.4	282	70.9
Higbee city	567	550	-3.0	456	95.8	0.4	0.0	0.4	3.3	16.9	19.5	47.2	66.6	7.5	197	81.7
Higginsville city	4,795	4,609	-3.9	4,619	85.5	4.2	0.0	2.1	8.3	29.1	17.0	33.1	44.3	23.3	1,754	87.9
High Hill city	192	177	-7.8	206	100.0	0.0	0.0	0.0	0.0	29.1	15.5	39.8	56.4	20.7	86	84.9
Highlandville city	918	1,051	14.5	936	96.9	0.0	0.0	2.6	0.5	14.4	19.8	46.7	47.3	13.4	372	91.4
High Ridge CDP	4,305	-	-	4,459	96.9	0.2	1.0	1.6	0.3	18.5	15.5	41.6	46.2	20.2	1,740	94.9
Hillsboro city	2,871	3,292	14.7	3,185	92.0	3.0	0.9	1.9	2.2	26.4	8.9	29.4	41.8	23.6	947	90.5
Hillsdale village	1,477	1,542	4.4	1,288	2.6	94.3	0.0	2.3	0.8	36.0	6.8	27.4	60.5	10.1	439	85.9
Hoberg village	58	57	-1.7	58	100.0	0.0	0.0	0.0	0.0	20.7	39.7	47.8	51.1	6.7	23	78.3
Holcomb city	637	576	-9.6	594	87.2	0.0	3.0	3.0	6.7	30.0	15.2	34.3	64.9	3.6	253	90.1
Holden city	2,248	2,236	-0.5	2,398	94.1	0.8	0.0	3.3	1.8	26.9	13.8	38.5	55.9	18.7	950	85.6
Holland town	229	197	-14.0	147	73.5	0.0	0.0	0.0	26.5	6.8	26.5	50.5	69.8	3.4	75	85.3
Holliday village	135	132	-2.2	116	100.0	0.0	0.0	0.0	0.0	17.2	32.8	59.0	84.6	6.6	69	68.1
Hollister city	4,418	4,592	3.9	4,532	90.0	0.0	0.3	6.3	3.4	23.7	18.5	37.4	48.6	17.3	1,854	88.9
Holt city	486	502	3.3	414	87.7	0.0	0.0	3.4	8.9	32.1	14.5	33.8	62.9	12.0	154	81.8
Holts Summit city	3,623	4,391	21.2	4,193	85.1	4.1	1.6	8.2	1.0	25.5	18.7	33.7	42.0	31.4	1,829	89.1
Homestead village	185	185	0.0	145	89.7	0.0	0.0	4.1	6.2	22.1	15.2	45.1	69.6	9.8	54	81.5
Homestown city	151	130	-13.9	123	0.0	100.0	0.0	0.0	0.0	28.5	19.5	34.9	62.2	24.4	58	81.0
Hopkins city	532	476	-10.5	369	96.2	0.0	0.0	1.1	2.7	17.3	16.0	41.8	60.6	11.4	172	90.7
Horine CDP	821	-	-	1,133	83.8	10.7	0.0	5.5	0.0	33.5	11.3	29.8	48.3	0.0	326	100.0
Hornersville city	663	594	-10.4	562	87.0	7.5	0.0	0.7	4.8	24.2	20.8	45.0	67.4	6.5	259	71.4
Houston city	2,084	2,082	-0.1	2,592	82.6	1.2	1.3	7.3	7.7	21.0	20.4	40.8	54.0	14.0	969	88.5
Houstonia city	220	219	-0.5	124	97.6	0.0	0.0	2.4	0.0	15.3	21.8	48.4	54.4	13.6	54	88.9
Houston Lake city	235	247	5.1	337	88.1	2.4	0.0	5.6	3.9	11.9	16.6	45.8	35.7	21.3	126	92.9
Howardville city	382	338	-11.5	270	2.2	95.2	0.0	0.4	2.2	28.9	10.0	33.1	70.2	10.1	131	76.3
Hughesville village	188	189	0.5	203	93.6	0.0	0.0	3.0	3.4	25.1	9.4	31.5	43.4	7.0	77	87.0
Humansville city	1,053	1,059	0.6	1,023	91.3	0.2	2.8	3.9	1.8	15.9	30.8	54.0	76.3	6.5	370	81.4
Hume town	336	314	-6.5	376	97.3	0.0	0.0	1.1	1.6	27.1	9.0	29.5	67.9	8.0	128	91.4
Humphreys village	118	107	-9.3	69	100.0	0.0	0.0	0.0	0.0	7.2	18.8	47.6	72.1	4.7	32	84.4
Hunnewell city	184	173	-6.0	161	99.4	0.6	0.0	0.0	0.0	18.6	13.7	45.7	72.7	15.6	80	72.5
Hunter CDP	168	-	-	134	100.0	0.0	0.0	0.0	0.0	14.9	0.0	54.0	58.8	41.2	41	100.0
Huntleigh city	389	388	-0.3	525	93.9	1.3	3.0	1.0	0.8	30.7	13.9	46.7	6.6	77.4	167	98.8
Huntsdale town	31	32	3.2	21	57.1	0.0	0.0	0.0	42.9	0.0	19.0	53.5	47.6	33.3	13	46.2
Huntsville city	1,566	1,507	-3.8	1,664	93.8	3.4	0.0	2.9	0.0	23.1	19.0	40.9	54.0	7.8	603	82.6
Hurdland city	163	157	-3.7	153	97.4	2.6	0.0	0.0	0.0	13.7	15.0	38.5	71.2	9.6	70	52.9
Hurley city	178	177	-0.6	228	84.6	0.0	0.0	15.4	0.0	23.7	10.1	36.0	58.4	2.9	77	83.1
Iatan village	45	55	22.2	45	100.0	0.0	0.0	0.0	0.0	8.9	6.7	48.8	84.8	12.1	15	86.7
Iberia city	733	749	2.2	727	93.8	0.0	1.7	1.2	3.3	26.4	14.6	28.4	64.7	10.8	279	84.2
Imperial CDP	4,709	-	-	4,260	92.3	0.5	1.8	2.2	3.1	24.9	16.5	42.8	47.4	19.4	1,647	95.4
Independence city	116,812	116,672	-0.1	117,084	75.9	7.9	1.4	5.4	9.4	23.0	17.8	40.1	47.2	19.6	48,087	87.6
Indian Point village	532	523	-1.7	440	100.0	0.0	0.0	0.0	0.0	8.4	36.8	59.3	36.9	31.0	213	100.0
Innsbrook village	544	588	8.1	595	96.1	0.7	0.0	0.0	3.2	10.8	55.3	67.0	25.0	51.4	271	98.2
Ionia town	88	87	-1.1	80	100.0	0.0	0.0	0.0	0.0	18.8	38.8	58.7	55.4	6.2	38	86.8
Irena village	18	17	-5.6	20	95.0	0.0	0.0	5.0	0.0	15.0	25.0	45.5	26.7	26.7	8	100.0
Irondale city	442	440	-0.5	456	94.1	0.0	2.4	3.5	0.0	34.9	14.7	34.3	55.1	7.3	159	84.9
Iron Mountain Lake city	740	746	0.8	704	93.0	0.0	0.0	1.3	5.7	19.5	15.2	44.4	62.7	5.8	293	73.4
Ironton city	1,469	1,389	-5.4	1,528	95.9	0.5	0.0	0.7	3.0	24.3	26.7	40.7	52.8	16.1	592	79.1
Irwin CDP	69	-	-	53	71.7	0.0	0.0	28.3	0.0	0.0	0.0	56.2	71.7	0.0	47	31.9
Jackson city	13,754	14,836	7.9	14,872	93.6	2.3	0.3	2.1	1.7	25.3	15.6	35.5	39.8	30.8	5,525	93.4
Jacksonville village	150	145	-3.3	127	92.9	0.0	0.0	7.1	0.0	18.1	17.3	40.4	80.5	2.6	30	100.0
Jameson town	131	127	-3.1	95	100.0	0.0	0.0	0.0	0.0	28.4	35.8	54.8	84.8	3.0	42	88.1
Jamesport city	524	515	-1.7	486	95.9	0.2	0.6	1.4	1.9	20.8	16.7	37.8	70.6	6.2	203	77.8
Jamestown town	386	398	3.1	443	92.3	0.0	0.0	2.3	5.4	27.3	16.0	38.6	60.6	20.4	175	77.7
Jane town	314	312	-0.6	546	79.7	2.7	0.0	9.7	7.9	29.5	12.5	36.0	58.8	8.2	171	87.1
Jasper city	931	972	4.4	920	92.8	0.0	0.0	5.4	1.7	24.6	17.6	40.9	59.4	14.6	389	86.4
Jefferson City city	43,124	42,708		42,919	72.5	18.7	2.5	2.6	3.7	20.0	16.0	37.9	36.2	32.6	17,084	89.0
Jennings city	14,776	14,575	-1.4	14,712	7.2	87.5	0.0	3.4	1.9	21.9	13.3	36.6	59.9	7.6	6,527	83.9
Jerico Springs village	228	231	1.3	236	100.0	0.0	0.0	0.0	0.0	30.1	13.6	36.9	54.8	6.2	100	91.0
Jonesburg city	768	714	-7.0	717	95.0	1.3	0.0	0.0	3.8	23.3	22.9	43.8	70.6	8.2	275	83.3
Joplin city	50,798	50,925	0.3	50,386	83.4	3.2	2.3	6.1	5.1	22.4	16.5	36.7	40.9	26.5	20,369	88.6
Josephville village	421	476	13.1	472	96.6	0.0	0.2	0.4	2.8	14.4	23.7	55.0	57.9	25.3	171	90.1
Junction City village	323	319	-1.2	268	97.8	0.0	0.7	1.5	0.0	23.9	17.9	38.5	46.4	7.7	138	71.0
Kahoka city	2,082	2,028	-2.6	2,160	95.5	0.1	1.4	1.1	1.9	26.0	21.7	40.4	55.8	10.8	827	83.6
Kansas City city	459,902	495,327	7.7	486,404	55.2	27.9	2.7	3.6	10.6	23.1	12.9	35.1	35.3	35.2	203,356	89.8
Kearney city	8,376	10,858	29.6	10,095	91.1	0.3	0.2	1.5	6.9	28.3	13.6	35.2	35.7	27.8	3,335	91.5
Kelso village	580	587	1.2	592	93.4	0.3	0.0	0.0	6.3	24.8	22.5	35.9	49.9	25.3	239	90.4
Kennett city	10,934	10,094	-7.7	10,062	73.7	17.1	0.4	3.1	5.8	22.7	18.9	41.6	57.4	19.2	4,342	81.6
Keytesville city	469	447	-4.7	347	95.7	2.9	0.0	1.2	0.3	17.0	22.5	51.6	65.9	10.0	169	65.1
Kidder city	323	317	-1.9	215	100.0	0.0	0.0	0.0	0.0	17.2	30.7	50.5	61.2	12.2	91	72.5
Kimberling City city	2,436	2,300	-5.6	2,665	94.7	0.0	0.3	2.0	3.0	14.1	36.0	53.7	30.5	29.4	1,099	89.9
Kimmswick city	148	143	-3.4	111	100.0	0.0	0.0	0.0	0.0	27.0	18.0	38.1	57.5	6.3	49	79.6
King City city	1,015	992	-2.3	943	94.4	0.0	1.0	2.8	1.9	22.2	25.8	41.9	56.0	17.6	376	85.1
Kingdom City village	129	130	0.8	168	97.6	2.4	0.0	0.0	0.0	19.0	14.9	36.3	70.6	15.1	60	96.7
Kingston city	348	332	-4.6	297	78.1	7.1	0.0	0.0	14.8	12.8	14.1	36.4	64.9	6.1	96	77.1
Kingsville city	266	259	-2.6	277	96.8	0.7	0.0	2.5	0.0	30.3	13.4	31.7	60.2	6.3	94	86.2
Kinloch city	298	290	-2.7	327	22.9	66.7	0.0	0.6	9.8	22.3	9.2	24.7	71.7	9.4	137	78.8
Kirbyville village	207	228	10.1	161	80.1	19.9	0.0	0.0	0.0	23.0	13.0	46.1	67.5	7.9	67	91.0
Kirksville city	17,505	17,602	0.6	17,554	88.4	3.7	3.3	2.9	1.6	16.1	12.8	23.6	42.7	32.1	6,413	87.9
Kirkwood city	27,567	27,807	0.9	27,708	88.2	5.6	1.5	2.0	2.7	24.0	21.1	43.0	14.1	64.3	11,734	94.0
Kissee Mills CDP	1,109	-	-	1,036	93.1	0.0	0.0	6.2	0.7	16.6	36.1	59.8	70.8	10.3	503	84.5
Knob Noster city	2,719	2,785	2.4	2,767	77.1	5.0	4.0	4.2	9.8	25.4	6.1	27.6	38.2	17.3	1,214	94.2
Knox City city	216	206	-4.6	266	99.2	0.8	0.0	0.0	0.0	37.6	15.4	27.0	73.9	4.5	90	85.6
Koshkonong town	209	200	-4.3	195	86.7	0.0	2.1	11.3	0.0	31.3	9.7	33.9	65.3	6.5	66	60.6
LaBarque Creek CDP	1,558	-	-	1,499	87.3	0.5	0.0	5.7	6.5	12.0	13.7	40.8	34.6	37.9	614	92.2
La Belle city	659	625	-5.2	723	88.7	8.4	0.0	2.9	0.0	23.2	24.1	44.0	59.0	10.8	296	81.8

1 May be of any race.

Table A. All Places — **Population and Housing**

STATE City, town, township, borough, or CDP (county if applicable)	Population				Race and Hispanic or Latino origin (percent)					Age (percent)			Educational attainment of persons age 25 and older		Occupied housing units	
	2010 census total population	2019 estimated population	Percent change 2010–2019	ACS total population estimate 2015–2019	White alone, not Hispanic or Latino	Black alone, not Hispanic or Latino	Asian alone, not Hispanic or Latino	All other races or 2 or more races, not Hispanic or Latino	Hispanic or Latino[1]	Under 18 years old	Age 65 years and older	Median age	Percent High school diploma or less	Percent Bachelor's degree or more	Total	Percent with a computer
	1	2	3	4	5	6	7	8	9	10	11	12	13	14	15	16
MISSOURI—Con.																
Laclede city	345	322	-6.7	378	93.1	0.0	0.5	2.1	4.2	14.3	29.9	53.0	62.7	8.7	185	80.5
Laddonia city	513	498	-2.9	599	97.5	2.5	0.0	0.0	0.0	23.9	17.5	45.6	70.6	11.0	261	80.1
Ladue city	8,516	8,616	1.2	8,601	87.6	1.6	5.8	4.2	0.8	24.6	21.3	47.2	4.1	82.4	3,159	96.5
La Grange city	926	892	-3.7	957	81.3	16.0	0.0	2.7	0.0	16.5	20.4	45.8	73.0	10.0	403	82.4
Lake Annette city	100	100	0.0	95	88.4	0.0	0.0	11.6	0.0	0.0	13.7	49.9	55.6	16.0	60	90.0
Lake Lafayette city	325	336	3.4	255	89.4	6.3	0.0	0.4	3.9	18.8	22.7	41.9	76.0	4.4	104	65.4
Lake Lotawana city	1,937	2,109	8.9	2,120	91.6	0.5	0.4	1.1	6.4	20.0	18.4	49.3	23.6	50.5	862	95.8
Lake Ozark city	1,598	1,828	14.4	1,858	93.4	1.2	0.0	4.4	1.1	18.8	29.8	53.0	28.7	38.2	886	98.3
Lake St. Louis city	14,558	16,864	15.8	15,989	89.3	1.9	1.6	1.8	5.3	20.2	21.5	45.4	23.5	45.1	6,258	96.8
Lakeshire city	1,432	1,389	-3.0	1,543	94.9	1.2	1.2	1.0	1.7	19.6	19.2	40.5	26.9	32.9	743	85.5
Lake Tapawingo city	729	719	-1.4	825	95.5	0.2	1.0	1.3	1.9	13.3	35.3	59.1	24.1	36.1	387	95.1
Lake Tekakwitha village	253	259	2.4	229	96.5	0.0	2.2	0.4	0.9	10.9	13.1	45.5	42.4	21.5	105	85.7
Lake Viking CDP	483	-	-	434	99.3	0.7	0.0	0.0	0.0	11.3	44.5	62.6	39.7	30.6	231	84.4
Lake Waukomis city	816	873	7.0	817	95.2	0.0	0.0	2.0	2.8	13.8	30.5	52.5	20.7	46.0	378	95.8
Lake Winnebago city	1,131	1,269	12.2	1,113	92.5	5.3	0.2	0.6	1.3	20.9	27.0	51.4	16.3	64.6	465	97.0
Lamar city	4,537	4,294	-5.4	4,303	94.4	0.6	0.0	2.8	2.3	21.8	19.4	41.6	56.7	16.7	1,902	83.2
Lamar Heights city	185	175	-5.4	179	93.9	0.0	0.0	4.5	1.7	34.1	14.5	34.5	49.5	29.7	68	92.6
La Monte city	1,140	1,135	-0.4	1,178	42.7	0.0	0.0	1.3	56.0	34.9	9.8	25.8	70.8	9.8	401	85.5
Lanagan town	412	405	-1.7	438	66.9	0.0	0.0	13.5	19.6	20.5	10.0	40.3	86.8	3.3	165	71.5
Lancaster city	730	765	4.8	810	94.6	1.2	0.0	3.6	0.6	24.3	20.2	42.5	51.0	17.9	242	83.5
La Plata city	1,365	1,308	-4.2	1,258	96.3	0.2	0.2	1.3	2.1	24.6	24.8	43.0	52.3	17.0	485	79.0
Laredo city	198	190	-4.0	171	100.0	0.0	0.0	0.0	0.0	16.4	21.1	50.3	77.7	4.6	84	69.0
La Russell city	114	118	3.5	130	98.5	0.0	0.0	0.0	1.5	31.5	5.4	33.2	75.9	2.5	46	78.3
Lathrop city	2,092	2,010	-3.9	2,184	91.0	1.5	0.9	3.1	3.5	28.0	15.9	35.1	46.8	19.2	835	87.9
La Tour CDP	62	-	-	167	100.0	0.0	0.0	0.0	0.0	15.0	10.8	23.5	78.3	0.0	58	100.0
Laurie city	953	967	1.5	949	94.9	2.0	2.0	1.1	0.0	13.4	44.3	59.0	51.2	19.3	422	79.4
Lawson city	2,479	2,414	-2.6	2,145	93.5	1.0	0.0	3.3	2.1	27.3	16.5	39.7	57.6	17.4	811	88.2
Leadington city	426	598	40.4	621	96.5	0.8	0.0	1.8	1.0	28.7	14.8	34.0	48.8	11.2	253	85.4
Leadwood city	1,234	1,165	-5.6	1,443	98.9	0.0	0.0	0.8	0.3	24.4	10.3	34.9	61.0	6.9	546	88.1
Leasburg village	338	325	-3.8	366	98.1	0.0	0.0	0.0	1.9	32.5	10.7	25.1	75.0	4.3	134	76.1
Leawood village	683	675	-1.2	646	92.4	0.8	1.1	4.6	1.1	23.1	22.8	49.2	22.2	43.9	254	98.4
Lebanon city	14,471	14,798	2.3	14,652	88.8	1.3	0.6	5.1	4.1	25.6	14.7	35.0	52.6	12.9	6,132	86.7
Lee's Summit city	91,368	99,357	8.7	97,275	81.9	8.5	2.0	3.6	3.9	26.5	15.3	38.7	21.6	48.0	36,809	95.1
Leeton city	566	556	-1.8	425	93.2	0.0	0.0	4.0	2.8	17.2	17.9	46.9	39.4	12.2	195	89.2
Leisure Lake CDP	160	-	-	102	87.3	0.0	0.0	12.7	0.0	11.8	29.4	58.2	73.3	11.1	62	74.2
Lemay CDP	16,645	-	-	16,918	88.9	2.8	1.6	4.1	2.6	21.2	14.9	38.8	51.6	19.9	6,899	86.1
Leonard village	61	57	-6.6	70	100.0	0.0	0.0	0.0	0.0	21.4	18.6	41.0	50.0	24.0	25	88.0
Leslie village	170	170	0.0	108	95.4	0.0	0.0	4.6	0.0	41.7	2.8	27.5	34.5	7.3	34	97.1
Levasy city	83	82	-1.2	80	82.5	0.0	2.5	15.0	0.0	20.0	6.3	41.6	61.3	17.7	33	100.0
Lewis and Clark Village town	132	128	-3.0	130	87.7	0.0	0.0	12.3	0.0	17.7	16.9	42.9	56.3	2.1	50	86.0
Lewistown town	538	512	-4.8	675	95.3	2.4	0.0	2.1	0.3	24.4	16.6	34.6	60.0	13.7	270	75.2
Lexington city	4,724	4,534	-4.0	4,555	87.1	5.3	1.0	4.3	2.3	20.3	19.6	42.4	53.4	22.5	1,953	90.7
Liberal city	759	721	-5.0	612	87.7	0.0	0.0	10.9	1.3	25.5	16.8	41.9	57.8	14.1	284	76.1
Liberty city	29,244	32,100	9.8	31,328	86.9	3.9	0.8	2.6	5.8	24.0	14.1	38.0	31.7	38.6	11,228	93.6
Licking city	3,124	3,075	-1.6	2,705	74.8	17.3	0.0	4.3	3.6	12.7	18.8	42.3	69.7	3.9	695	80.6
Lilbourn city	1,191	1,057	-11.3	1,137	73.6	24.8	0.0	1.1	0.4	19.6	15.0	38.0	80.5	8.4	470	78.1
Lincoln city	1,192	1,194	0.2	948	93.6	0.6	1.2	0.9	3.7	21.3	20.7	39.4	49.2	14.2	412	80.6
Linn city	1,455	1,593	9.5	1,492	97.4	0.0	0.3	0.6	1.7	23.9	12.9	27.4	47.0	19.5	577	87.0
Linn Creek city	243	253	4.1	321	99.7	0.0	0.0	0.3	0.0	19.3	28.0	48.1	52.2	27.9	131	78.6
Linneus city	278	259	-6.8	252	92.1	0.8	0.0	3.6	3.6	19.0	21.0	49.0	67.5	13.9	109	75.2
Lithium CDP	89	-	-	102	100.0	0.0	0.0	0.0	0.0	8.8	18.6	47.3	81.5	0.0	39	74.4
Livonia village	74	71	-4.1	94	39.4	0.0	0.0	47.9	12.8	47.9	4.3	19.3	61.5	7.7	17	58.8
Loch Lloyd village	610	811	33.0	706	91.1	2.3	2.0	3.8	0.8	11.6	39.0	59.5	10.0	68.5	321	100.0
Lock Springs village	57	56	-1.8	44	90.9	0.0	0.0	9.1	0.0	29.5	13.6	37.5	86.2	0.0	16	81.3
Lockwood city	944	899	-4.8	1,166	93.1	0.0	0.3	4.0	2.5	18.9	22.6	46.6	63.5	12.5	461	85.5
Lohman city	163	166	1.8	195	100.0	0.0	0.0	0.0	0.0	26.2	26.2	33.9	45.2	31.7	77	85.7
Loma Linda town	725	776	7.0	723	80.1	5.7	0.8	6.9	6.5	11.1	29.0	57.5	24.6	36.9	334	95.2
Lone Jack city	1,049	1,323	26.1	1,371	88.8	5.4	0.2	4.0	1.6	29.2	10.1	32.3	30.6	34.9	466	95.7
Longtown town	100	100	0.0	129	81.4	0.0	0.0	0.0	18.6	21.7	8.5	28.6	74.6	11.3	46	95.7
Louisburg village	117	116	-0.9	75	100.0	0.0	0.0	0.0	0.0	20.0	21.3	53.5	70.7	13.8	32	84.4
Louisiana city	3,365	3,207	-4.7	3,264	82.8	7.2	0.5	3.3	6.1	21.4	17.9	39.5	66.4	13.1	1,399	85.8
Lowry City city	640	613	-4.2	709	94.9	0.4	0.0	3.9	0.7	17.5	28.6	53.3	59.7	11.0	303	79.2
Lucerne village	85	79	-7.1	46	100.0	0.0	0.0	0.0	0.0	15.2	28.3	47.3	30.0	30.0	25	96.0
Ludlow town	137	127	-7.3	126	97.6	0.0	0.0	0.0	2.4	19.0	15.9	41.5	73.2	12.4	48	72.9
Lupus town	33	34	3.0	25	100.0	0.0	0.0	0.0	0.0	0.0	28.0	59.8	16.0	44.0	16	93.8
Luray village	99	93	-6.1	73	100.0	0.0	0.0	0.0	0.0	38.4	4.1	27.5	81.4	11.6	28	78.6
McBaine town	10	11	10.0	10	100.0	0.0	0.0	0.0	0.0	20.0	0.0	48.5	75.0	0.0	6	33.3
McCord Bend village	297	299	0.7	371	93.3	0.0	0.0	5.1	1.6	30.7	17.8	43.2	72.1	3.2	135	80.0
McFall city	95	91	-4.2	123	99.2	0.0	0.0	0.8	0.0	37.4	5.7	22.8	84.5	0.0	39	71.8
McKittrick town	62	58	-6.5	58	100.0	0.0	0.0	0.0	0.0	24.1	24.1	53.5	48.8	16.3	30	66.7
Macks Creek CDP	244	-	-	376	83.8	0.0	0.0	7.2	9.0	22.1	19.7	36.5	79.1	13.0	117	46.2
Macon city	5,471	5,341	-2.4	5,358	86.5	4.5	1.3	5.0	2.6	26.0	25.6	38.3	54.7	20.1	2,137	81.3
Madison city	554	541	-2.3	496	98.4	0.0	0.0	1.6	0.0	24.2	13.3	39.0	62.9	6.9	207	76.8
Maitland city	344	308	-10.5	256	96.9	0.0	0.0	1.2	2.0	23.4	14.5	42.5	69.2	7.0	121	88.4
Malden city	4,348	3,898	-10.3	4,165	70.7	28.0	0.0	0.3	1.0	29.6	17.2	36.6	65.6	12.7	1,648	78.2
Malta Bend town	250	239	-4.4	221	100.0	0.0	0.0	0.0	0.0	25.8	8.6	34.8	47.2	19.2	79	81.0
Manchester city	18,081	18,073	0.0	18,110	82.1	3.4	6.6	2.0	5.9	21.9	17.3	41.2	17.2	55.1	7,466	95.9
Mansfield city	1,291	1,245	-3.6	1,275	94.4	0.0	0.0	4.4	1.3	24.2	16.4	40.4	54.5	10.4	574	78.0
Maplewood city	8,069	8,092	0.3	8,051	72.9	17.1	3.3	3.7	3.0	20.7	9.7	34.0	25.3	48.3	4,151	90.1
Marble Hill city	1,492	1,464	-1.9	1,780	86.3	2.1	1.2	6.0	4.4	27.8	18.7	35.8	64.5	8.3	664	81.9
Marceline city	2,233	2,085	-6.6	2,002	91.1	0.2	0.7	4.9	3.0	28.9	17.2	35.0	58.3	13.7	828	80.0
Marionville city	2,238	2,181	-2.5	2,416	92.3	0.0	0.0	2.1	5.7	30.9	18.6	32.0	63.3	9.9	908	87.0
Marlborough village	2,156	2,147	-0.4	2,567	81.4	5.6	3.5	2.5	6.9	8.6	11.9	29.2	26.5	38.2	1,649	93.7
Marquand city	202	197	-2.5	260	96.9	0.0	0.0	2.3	0.8	18.1	9.2	43.8	68.4	10.0	118	81.4
Marshall city	13,036	12,841	-1.5	12,949	70.3	7.3	0.9	4.4	17.1	24.3	16.4	34.7	52.9	21.1	4,422	86.0
Marshfield city	6,671	7,562	13.4	7,318	91.7	1.3	0.3	5.2	1.6	29.6	16.4	32.0	49.0	16.8	2,624	83.4
Marston city	503	446	-11.3	472	69.7	26.1	0.0	4.2	0.0	32.6	9.5	35.4	90.6	0.7	181	77.3
Marthasville city	1,136	1,201	5.7	1,357	94.2	0.4	0.4	0.4	4.6	28.7	8.6	34.0	40.8	17.4	453	93.8
Martinsburg town	304	295	-3.0	286	88.5	7.0	0.0	3.8	0.7	12.2	29.7	51.0	59.3	19.5	134	86.6
Maryland Heights city	27,471	26,956	-1.9	27,080	64.2	13.2	16.1	3.3	3.2	18.3	14.5	36.9	25.6	46.4	11,991	95.5
Maryville city	12,034	11,599	-3.6	11,696	89.7	4.0	2.1	2.1	2.0	12.2	13.1	23.5	38.3	37.5	4,412	91.7

1 May be of any race.

Table A. All Places — **Population and Housing**

STATE City, town, township, borough, or CDP (county if applicable)	Population: 2010 census total population	Population: 2019 estimated population	Population: Percent change 2010–2019	Population: ACS total population estimate 2015–2019	Race and Hispanic or Latino origin (percent): White alone, not Hispanic or Latino	Race and Hispanic or Latino origin (percent): Black alone, not Hispanic or Latino	Race and Hispanic or Latino origin (percent): Asian alone, not Hispanic or Latino	Race and Hispanic or Latino origin (percent): All other races or 2 or more races, not Hispanic or Latino	Race and Hispanic or Latino origin (percent): Hispanic or Latino[1]	Age (percent): Under 18 years old	Age (percent): Age 65 years and older	Age (percent): Median age	Educational attainment of persons age 25 and older: Percent High school diploma or less	Educational attainment of persons age 25 and older: Percent Bachelor's degree or more	Occupied housing units: Total	Occupied housing units: Percent with a computer
	1	2	3	4	5	6	7	8	9	10	11	12	13	14	15	16
MISSOURI—Con.																
Matthews city	628	595	-5.3	640	94.7	2.8	0.0	0.0	2.5	19.7	17.7	44.9	77.0	6.2	253	83.0
Maysville city	1,118	1,081	-3.3	1,241	90.4	0.7	0.3	3.9	4.6	29.6	16.6	37.2	49.4	15.6	445	89.2
Mayview city	212	212	0.0	261	62.8	23.4	8.8	1.1	3.8	19.5	27.2	48.2	69.7	4.3	100	81.0
Meadville city	464	436	-6.0	476	96.0	0.0	0.0	3.4	0.6	27.5	17.2	34.3	55.5	17.2	198	90.9
Mehlville CDP	28,380	-	-	27,971	87.4	6.2	3.5	1.4	1.5	15.3	19.7	42.4	37.0	31.8	13,145	90.3
Memphis city	1,822	1,833	0.6	1,706	98.3	0.0	0.0	1.7	0.0	20.3	23.3	45.2	51.9	17.7	794	85.3
Mendon city	171	161	-5.8	232	92.2	7.8	0.0	0.0	0.0	13.8	18.1	42.1	61.4	9.1	83	85.5
Mercer town	315	301	-4.4	279	96.8	0.0	0.0	0.0	3.2	16.8	34.8	57.6	73.0	11.7	143	51.0
Merriam Woods village	1,753	1,847	5.4	2,210	74.7	0.0	0.5	4.0	20.9	32.6	10.0	30.7	60.5	9.3	779	91.7
Merwin village	60	57	-5.0	32	100.0	0.0	0.0	0.0	0.0	0.0	15.6	54.5	88.9	0.0	26	88.5
Meta city	229	220	-3.9	204	97.5	2.5	0.0	0.0	0.0	22.5	16.2	39.9	67.1	6.6	74	83.8
Metz town	49	47	-4.1	30	60.0	0.0	0.0	40.0	0.0	33.3	30.0	33.5	95.0	0.0	14	35.7
Mexico city	11,554	11,517	-0.3	11,543	84.4	5.7	0.0	4.7	5.1	25.1	17.8	36.7	59.3	14.3	4,566	82.1
Miami city	175	169	-3.4	103	98.1	0.0	0.0	0.0	1.9	26.2	20.4	40.3	38.2	9.2	41	75.6
Middletown town	169	154	-8.9	270	89.3	4.8	0.0	5.9	0.0	26.3	15.6	36.3	67.1	5.5	115	82.6
Milan city	1,960	1,775	-9.4	2,463	52.1	5.3	0.2	1.8	40.6	24.2	14.9	38.5	71.2	6.1	741	80.0
Milford village	25	24	-4.0	16	100.0	0.0	0.0	0.0	0.0	0.0	50.0	64.5	37.5	0.0	5	100.0
Millard village	89	85	-4.5	74	91.9	5.4	0.0	2.7	0.0	18.9	32.4	51.8	63.2	1.8	27	96.3
Miller city	699	681	-2.6	762	86.1	6.2	0.0	7.7	0.0	31.6	20.9	36.3	59.5	13.3	318	84.9
Mill Spring village	186	176	-5.4	182	54.9	0.0	0.0	40.1	4.9	36.3	10.4	31.3	79.8	3.2	63	69.8
Milo village	90	87	-3.3	64	100.0	0.0	0.0	0.0	0.0	0.0	17.2	50.5	78.0	2.4	24	33.3
Mindenmines city	365	346	-5.2	331	56.8	0.0	0.0	28.4	14.8	23.6	14.8	43.0	57.7	9.5	142	79.6
Mine La Motte CDP	348	-	-	295	94.2	0.0	0.0	5.8	0.0	26.1	29.2	46.8	38.2	0.0	131	58.8
Miner city	974	934	-4.1	1,039	69.9	12.9	0.7	13.2	3.4	16.4	19.7	45.9	65.7	5.6	438	84.0
Mineral Point town	364	355	-2.5	378	94.2	1.6	0.0	4.2	0.0	35.4	8.5	30.5	78.0	1.0	124	71.0
Miramiguoa Park village	120	121	0.8	111	94.6	0.0	1.8	2.7	0.9	23.4	9.0	42.5	50.0	7.3	45	93.3
Missouri City city	271	296	9.2	569	93.7	1.4	0.9	2.8	1.2	13.2	41.7	53.9	78.8	5.6	253	71.9
Moberly city	13,984	13,615	-2.6	13,707	82.3	10.0	1.1	3.9	2.6	22.4	14.5	35.9	48.3	16.6	4,601	81.9
Mokane city	185	181	-2.2	267	99.3	0.0	0.0	0.0	0.7	30.0	13.1	29.4	59.1	8.5	79	86.1
Moline Acres city	2,422	2,346	-3.1	2,407	10.3	88.0	0.0	1.7	0.0	25.6	16.6	39.2	53.2	14.2	959	77.6
Monett city	8,896	9,124	2.6	8,984	67.2	0.0	1.0	4.4	27.4	29.2	13.7	33.9	54.1	18.3	3,103	88.0
Monroe City city	2,531	2,438	-3.7	2,402	87.4	5.5	1.3	4.3	1.5	21.5	20.8	44.4	61.4	15.3	1,085	82.5
Montgomery City city	2,847	2,678	-5.9	2,677	92.0	2.4	0.3	3.3	2.0	24.1	17.1	42.3	55.2	14.1	1,247	84.1
Monticello village	98	92	-6.1	100	82.0	10.0	0.0	8.0	0.0	16.0	9.0	40.5	42.7	17.3	45	86.7
Montier CDP	98	-	-	19	100.0	0.0	0.0	0.0	0.0	0.0	57.9	0.0	100.0	0.0	11	100.0
Montreal CDP	-	-	-	122	100.0	0.0	0.0	0.0	0.0	32.0	0.0	23.4	100.0	0.0	27	100.0
Montrose city	389	378	-2.8	388	94.3	1.5	0.0	0.3	3.9	19.1	15.2	51.6	62.4	13.7	177	80.8
Mooresville village	91	90	-1.1	159	100.0	0.0	0.0	0.0	0.0	32.7	11.9	28.8	61.7	12.1	54	81.5
Morehouse city	975	865	-11.3	1,001	97.1	0.0	0.0	0.3	2.6	19.8	13.7	44.3	69.5	4.9	447	77.9
Morley city	701	671	-4.3	762	85.3	9.1	0.0	2.9	2.8	16.4	22.4	43.9	69.9	5.8	303	78.2
Morrison city	136	130	-4.4	85	100.0	0.0	0.0	0.0	0.0	23.5	16.5	53.2	72.3	13.8	40	80.0
Morrisville town	388	392	1.0	474	92.6	1.9	0.0	4.4	1.1	19.2	23.0	42.3	55.3	6.8	195	78.5
Mosby city	191	200	4.7	169	92.3	0.0	0.0	4.7	3.0	24.9	10.1	45.0	77.1	0.0	64	93.8
Moscow Mills city	2,544	3,496	37.4	3,034	92.8	1.5	0.0	4.1	1.7	31.9	11.2	29.5	58.7	7.8	966	88.9
Mound City city	1,159	1,039	-10.4	1,040	93.7	3.8	0.0	0.4	2.2	20.3	24.5	49.0	49.5	22.3	474	77.0
Moundville town	123	120	-2.4	119	98.3	0.0	0.0	1.7	0.0	19.3	18.5	44.8	51.1	5.6	56	69.6
Mountain Grove city	4,779	4,690	-1.9	4,683	97.8	1.4	0.0	0.5	0.3	24.8	21.4	41.9	67.2	8.6	2,126	84.3
Mountain View city	2,711	2,649	-2.3	2,656	96.2	0.0	1.1	1.8	0.9	20.9	22.1	41.3	60.8	12.7	1,066	82.3
Mount Leonard town	88	85	-3.4	29	96.6	0.0	3.4	0.0	0.0	0.0	20.7	56.3	72.4	3.4	16	81.3
Mount Moriah town	87	80	-8.0	67	83.6	11.9	0.0	0.0	4.5	28.4	17.9	36.8	73.7	15.8	26	57.7
Mount Vernon city	4,573	4,508	-1.4	4,505	95.6	0.6	0.2	1.7	1.8	22.5	27.2	45.2	49.6	14.6	1,869	86.6
Murphy CDP	8,690	-	-	7,961	88.1	1.6	1.1	3.1	6.1	21.6	12.5	38.7	48.3	14.0	3,328	88.9
Napoleon city	222	213	-4.1	189	95.8	0.0	0.0	2.1	2.1	22.8	33.9	50.5	70.4	9.2	85	68.2
Naylor city	623	583	-6.4	801	95.3	0.0	0.0	4.7	0.0	27.2	16.5	36.0	56.9	6.3	275	79.6
Neck City city	186	195	4.8	161	94.4	0.0	0.0	4.3	1.2	26.7	15.5	40.7	63.9	6.5	64	95.3
Neelyville city	478	474	-0.8	329	79.0	9.1	0.0	5.8	6.1	26.4	10.9	43.4	68.1	6.9	116	59.5
Nelson city	190	183	-3.7	152	81.6	13.8	3.3	0.0	1.3	22.4	19.1	41.3	61.5	7.3	57	75.4
Neosho city	11,830	12,054	1.9	11,990	76.4	1.9	0.9	6.5	14.2	27.8	14.9	32.0	47.6	19.6	4,372	81.9
Nevada city	8,399	8,261	-1.6	8,317	91.6	1.1	1.5	4.2	1.6	23.7	20.3	39.8	46.7	21.4	3,587	90.0
Newark village	94	90	-4.3	77	96.1	3.9	0.0	0.0	0.0	29.9	16.9	45.2	51.9	7.4	36	80.6
New Bloomfield city	674	673	-0.1	536	86.9	3.4	0.4	7.5	1.9	24.4	13.1	36.4	51.8	15.5	248	85.9
Newburg city	468	436	-6.8	479	94.2	0.0	1.0	4.8	0.0	19.0	24.6	39.2	66.3	2.9	224	69.6
New Cambria city	195	187	-4.1	132	91.7	0.0	0.0	6.1	2.3	12.9	11.4	46.4	54.1	9.2	59	81.4
New Florence city	769	718	-6.6	771	88.6	0.6	0.9	1.2	8.7	21.0	23.5	41.5	77.1	4.7	302	69.2
New Franklin city	1,089	1,057	-2.9	1,191	94.8	3.0	0.2	0.7	1.3	25.8	19.5	36.7	54.1	15.8	431	80.0
New Hampton city	291	271	-6.9	280	97.1	0.0	0.0	0.0	2.9	37.1	13.6	31.6	61.6	8.5	88	75.0
New Haven city	2,087	2,072	-0.7	2,038	88.6	1.1	0.5	7.2	2.6	25.6	17.1	33.5	41.6	14.5	767	84.1
New London city	982	987	0.5	852	86.5	7.9	0.8	3.8	1.1	23.4	16.2	33.6	69.8	8.4	332	87.3
New Madrid city	3,129	2,818	-9.9	2,898	62.6	30.7	0.0	5.3	1.4	23.9	18.9	39.9	58.4	12.9	1,264	83.3
New Melle city	498	508	2.0	508	96.1	0.0	0.2	0.0	3.7	17.9	30.7	55.5	39.2	30.4	197	92.9
Newtonia town	199	195	-2.0	227	81.9	0.0	0.0	3.1	15.0	15.0	30.4	50.6	59.2	10.3	78	84.6
Newtown town	186	168	-9.7	195	88.2	0.0	0.0	1.5	10.3	27.7	17.4	41.3	68.0	14.8	50	92.0
Niangua city	400	426	6.5	436	92.2	0.0	0.2	4.6	3.0	28.7	21.6	37.3	64.2	2.5	175	76.0
Nixa city	19,055	22,515	18.2	21,544	90.6	0.6	1.0	3.4	4.4	26.7	15.3	35.6	33.7	31.2	8,167	92.2
Noel city	1,833	1,807	-1.4	2,141	41.4	12.6	0.4	7.4	38.2	26.7	7.1	30.8	77.4	5.7	734	66.8
Norborne city	708	647	-8.6	858	95.9	3.6	0.0	0.0	0.5	20.4	22.1	42.5	56.5	11.6	358	86.9
Normandy city	4,987	4,838	-3.0	4,883	18.9	70.2	1.7	8.1	1.0	15.2	16.3	33.7	47.2	18.4	2,271	89.0
North Kansas City city	4,183	4,571	9.3	4,477	76.3	3.5	5.2	4.7	10.3	12.6	18.5	36.8	43.7	21.4	2,422	89.5
North Lilbourn village	49	44	-10.2	14	0.0	100.0	0.0	0.0	0.0	0.0	28.6	51.8	100.0	0.0	9	100.0
Northmoor city	344	365	6.1	360	84.7	5.8	0.6	5.0	3.9	19.7	14.4	40.8	54.5	14.8	119	93.3
Northwoods city	4,217	4,076	-3.3	4,121	3.9	96.1	0.0	0.0	0.0	16.8	32.3	53.7	57.7	16.3	1,725	79.4
Norwood city	665	647	-2.7	765	90.7	1.0	0.0	4.8	3.4	35.4	11.5	33.3	65.6	7.8	243	80.7
Norwood Court town	959	955	-0.4	973	3.9	94.0	0.0	1.0	1.0	23.4	7.8	32.4	47.5	7.8	506	88.1
Novelty village	139	132	-5.0	150	95.3	0.0	0.0	0.0	4.7	17.3	15.3	47.9	71.6	14.7	49	77.6
Novinger city	456	433	-5.0	377	91.5	0.0	1.1	4.0	3.4	23.1	12.2	32.3	65.2	9.4	133	82.0
Oak Grove city	7,883	8,258	4.8	8,217	92.5	0.9	0.5	1.6	4.5	31.7	13.1	33.8	42.1	18.6	2,865	95.1
Oak Grove Village village	493	472	-4.3	495	93.7	1.6	0.0	1.0	3.6	22.0	19.8	37.9	69.5	9.8	169	85.2
Oakland city	1,378	1,367	-0.8	1,713	90.1	5.7	0.6	1.9	1.7	16.5	34.9	51.1	20.4	56.8	594	94.8
Oak Ridge town	239	233	-2.5	255	99.2	0.0	0.8	0.0	0.0	30.6	14.1	35.3	65.3	9.5	76	90.8
Oaks village	129	134	3.9	149	67.8	0.0	1.3	2.7	28.2	20.1	12.1	47.3	10.7	50.5	53	88.7
Oakview village	375	390	4.0	446	80.5	0.0	0.7	11.0	7.8	26.7	9.4	37.7	30.7	36.0	170	92.9
Oakville CDP	36,143	-	-	36,407	94.8	1.4	1.7	0.8	1.3	19.7	20.4	45.4	26.5	41.4	14,263	94.1

1 May be of any race.

Table A. All Places — **Population and Housing**

STATE City, town, township, borough, or CDP (county if applicable)	Population				Race and Hispanic or Latino origin (percent)					Age (percent)			Educational attainment of persons age 25 and older		Occupied housing units	
	2010 census total population	2019 estimated population	Percent change 2010–2019	ACS total population estimate 2015–2019	White alone, not Hispanic or Latino	Black alone, not Hispanic or Latino	Asian alone, not Hispanic or Latino	All other races or 2 or more races, not Hispanic or Latino	Hispanic or Latino[1]	Under 18 years old	Age 65 years and older	Median age	Percent High school diploma or less	Percent Bachelor's degree or more	Total	Percent with a computer
	1	2	3	4	5	6	7	8	9	10	11	12	13	14	15	16
MISSOURI—Con.																
Oakwood village	187	198	5.9	169	92.3	0.0	0.0	4.7	3.0	20.7	31.4	55.6	20.0	52.8	68	98.5
Oakwood Park village	188	197	4.8	331	65.6	6.3	5.7	2.7	19.6	24.5	9.4	37.4	35.4	39.5	111	93.7
Odessa city	5,313	5,246	-1.3	5,210	93.9	1.6	1.2	0.7	2.5	21.5	14.8	38.7	59.6	17.3	2,155	83.5
O'Fallon city	79,597	88,673	11.4	87,242	86.4	4.6	3.4	2.6	3.1	27.1	12.0	37.0	27.8	41.6	30,978	95.9
Old Appleton town	85	83	-2.4	74	100.0	0.0	0.0	0.0	0.0	24.3	8.1	28.5	69.2	10.3	20	100.0
Old Jamestown CDP	19,184	-	-	19,777	30.4	62.2	0.8	5.1	1.5	22.6	19.7	44.7	27.1	37.2	7,117	97.8
Old Monroe city	265	287	8.3	216	100.0	0.0	0.0	0.0	0.0	17.1	16.2	48.4	65.4	11.7	100	86.0
Olean town	118	121	2.5	94	81.9	0.0	0.0	18.1	0.0	18.1	12.8	41.3	77.9	5.9	44	59.1
Olivette city	7,755	7,822	0.9	7,849	52.0	25.4	14.6	4.2	3.7	29.4	13.9	38.1	11.7	61.7	2,926	96.5
Olympian Village city	774	752	-2.8	710	98.3	0.0	0.3	1.4	0.0	32.3	9.9	31.7	50.2	10.1	229	97.4
Oran city	1,272	1,215	-4.5	1,512	87.9	0.9	0.0	4.4	6.8	22.1	14.7	38.2	61.1	13.9	593	85.2
Oregon city	850	765	-10.0	968	94.6	0.8	0.2	3.4	0.9	22.7	19.6	41.1	52.1	15.6	403	84.1
Oronogo city	2,381	2,667	12.0	2,609	91.5	1.1	0.3	4.6	2.5	36.3	5.7	30.7	31.5	33.3	848	98.1
Orrick city	839	804	-4.2	746	96.1	0.0	1.2	1.2	1.5	22.8	16.5	39.9	60.2	13.8	284	93.3
Osage Beach city	4,402	4,666	6.0	5,080	86.9	1.9	0.0	4.7	6.5	25.4	26.8	48.3	50.2	22.2	1,731	93.4
Osborn city	419	407	-2.9	380	93.9	0.0	0.0	3.4	2.6	22.4	17.4	42.5	59.9	10.7	175	85.1
Osceola city	949	908	-4.3	1,032	82.2	4.5	2.4	8.3	2.6	16.3	22.7	44.0	66.1	7.4	435	80.7
Osgood village	48	44	-8.3	99	53.5	0.0	0.0	0.0	46.5	31.3	5.1	22.2	55.6	0.0	26	80.8
Otterville city	454	453	-0.2	375	94.4	0.8	0.0	4.0	0.8	29.1	19.2	37.0	55.6	9.5	155	84.5
Overland city	16,055	15,551	-3.1	15,715	58.6	21.1	3.1	4.6	12.5	23.2	14.0	36.0	44.4	20.4	6,559	89.1
Owensville city	2,676	2,590	-3.2	2,599	94.7	0.0	0.6	0.9	3.8	24.2	21.9	37.9	48.9	22.6	1,038	86.3
Oxly CDP	200	-	-	131	100.0	0.0	0.0	0.0	0.0	26.7	53.4	66.3	85.4	0.0	64	67.2
Ozark city	17,811	20,482	15.0	19,767	93.7	1.5	0.4	2.2	2.2	29.7	11.4	32.3	32.0	33.9	7,433	93.7
Ozora CDP	183	-	-	151	99.3	0.0	0.0	0.7	0.0	0.0	31.1	60.6	54.3	12.1	64	70.3
Pacific city	7,006	7,229	3.2	6,339	91.2	4.6	0.0	1.5	2.7	19.7	16.0	39.4	50.2	16.2	2,642	88.2
Pagedale city	3,317	3,291	-0.8	3,306	2.7	96.3	0.0	1.0	0.0	24.7	18.6	41.0	55.1	8.0	1,427	83.7
Palmyra city	3,615	3,599	-0.4	3,612	91.1	1.6	1.0	5.6	0.8	28.2	17.1	35.3	50.8	18.8	1,441	87.6
Paris city	1,224	1,167	-4.7	1,390	89.2	9.4	0.0	1.4	0.0	23.5	23.7	44.2	54.6	16.4	587	82.1
Parkdale village	172	166	-3.5	189	93.7	2.1	1.1	3.2	0.0	16.4	31.7	53.5	56.0	13.3	75	92.0
Park Hills city	8,746	8,529	-2.5	8,544	92.9	2.6	0.0	3.5	0.9	29.9	11.0	33.3	52.7	11.9	3,304	84.8
Parkville city	5,519	7,162	29.8	6,724	90.6	3.7	2.8	2.2	0.7	24.7	12.4	41.9	14.0	68.3	2,454	94.8
Parkway village	484	509	5.2	644	97.4	0.0	0.6	1.4	0.6	21.7	17.9	37.6	50.3	6.9	240	90.0
Parma city	701	619	-11.7	608	61.7	9.5	0.0	5.3	23.5	37.2	14.5	31.6	69.0	8.4	222	80.6
Parnell city	189	171	-9.5	193	92.2	1.0	0.0	1.6	5.2	30.6	14.0	31.1	72.8	8.8	77	67.5
Pasadena Hills city	926	891	-3.8	954	31.0	66.0	0.3	1.4	1.3	18.0	23.6	50.6	12.1	54.0	436	97.0
Pasadena Park village	473	456	-3.6	368	38.0	53.8	4.6	3.5	0.0	18.2	25.0	47.8	22.2	48.6	190	86.3
Pascola village	108	93	-13.9	79	100.0	0.0	0.0	0.0	0.0	20.3	7.6	48.8	88.5	0.0	31	90.3
Passaic town	34	32	-5.9	21	66.7	0.0	0.0	23.8	9.5	0.0	28.6	59.1	71.4	0.0	12	100.0
Pattonsburg city	348	345	-0.9	318	80.2	11.6	0.0	4.1	4.1	11.9	11.9	39.0	65.5	6.0	63	79.4
Paynesville village	78	75	-3.8	41	80.5	19.5	0.0	0.0	0.0	9.8	39.0	56.7	54.1	5.4	21	76.2
Peaceful Village village	65	65	0.0	61	95.1	0.0	0.0	0.0	4.9	1.6	9.8	55.6	54.2	10.2	24	100.0
Peculiar city	4,611	5,478	18.8	5,139	91.8	0.3	0.5	1.0	6.3	23.7	9.3	38.8	47.3	23.8	2,071	91.9
Pendleton village	43	46	7.0	29	100.0	0.0	0.0	0.0	0.0	10.3	34.5	58.8	79.2	0.0	13	92.3
Penermon village	64	61	-4.7	77	0.0	100.0	0.0	0.0	0.0	10.4	26.0	52.5	83.0	0.0	35	51.4
Perry city	689	695	0.9	614	98.9	0.0	1.0	0.2	0.0	15.8	36.3	59.6	62.5	11.7	308	79.9
Perryville city	8,238	8,496	3.1	8,451	92.2	1.1	2.4	1.4	2.8	25.4	19.5	38.1	57.2	16.9	3,407	84.4
Pevely city	5,588	5,978	7.0	5,893	87.8	3.8	0.0	3.3	5.1	29.3	12.9	34.4	42.4	15.2	2,238	94.5
Phelps City CDP	24	-	-	-	-	-	-	-	-	-	-	-	-	-	-	-
Phillipsburg village	202	199	-1.5	158	98.7	0.0	0.0	0.0	1.3	15.8	21.5	46.5	61.7	0.0	78	93.6
Pickering town	158	142	-10.1	153	100.0	0.0	0.0	0.0	0.0	22.2	17.0	24.4	56.9	16.7	62	82.3
Piedmont city	1,989	1,889	-5.0	2,697	95.8	1.2	0.6	1.3	1.1	26.0	16.3	40.6	61.1	11.4	1,010	78.5
Pierce City city	1,293	1,309	1.2	1,271	89.3	0.2	0.3	7.7	2.5	30.4	13.7	37.2	57.7	14.7	508	80.5
Pierpont village	70	75	7.1	56	100.0	0.0	0.0	0.0	0.0	8.9	50.0	63.5	32.0	52.0	28	85.7
Pilot Grove city	768	761	-0.9	655	94.4	3.5	0.0	2.1	0.0	21.1	30.7	45.7	62.6	10.0	280	78.9
Pilot Knob city	745	715	-4.0	828	86.1	0.0	1.1	6.5	6.3	25.0	10.4	30.0	63.7	8.8	310	78.4
Pine Lawn city	3,319	3,593	8.3	3,579	0.7	98.9	0.0	0.0	0.4	33.2	11.1	30.4	69.5	4.4	1,181	86.2
Pineville city	802	807	0.6	817	88.0	1.8	0.0	9.2	1.0	23.5	14.8	39.8	59.5	11.6	338	88.2
Plato village	109	106	-2.8	73	93.2	0.0	0.0	5.5	1.4	30.1	20.5	30.1	27.3	43.2	29	79.3
Platte City city	4,664	4,955	6.2	4,901	88.6	3.8	0.6	2.3	4.7	27.5	9.2	30.8	36.6	29.4	1,895	96.6
Platte Woods city	385	405	5.2	485	84.3	1.6	7.2	0.8	6.0	14.2	24.5	51.5	30.4	44.6	183	98.4
Plattsburg city	2,319	2,238	-3.5	2,236	88.2	7.0	2.0	2.5	0.3	22.2	17.5	41.7	45.8	22.0	951	83.8
Pleasant Hill city	8,133	8,683	6.8	8,510	88.8	6.0	0.0	2.1	3.1	32.3	13.3	32.9	50.0	20.8	2,923	91.4
Pleasant Hope city	597	604	1.2	662	93.5	0.0	0.0	6.5	0.0	27.3	8.8	33.7	44.8	15.9	275	94.2
Pleasant Valley city	2,878	3,026	5.1	3,003	82.1	2.0	0.3	3.8	11.9	18.8	16.1	41.1	47.7	14.2	1,159	94.7
Plevna CDP	21	-	-	5	100.0	0.0	0.0	0.0	0.0	0.0	100.0	0.0	100.0	0.0	5	100.0
Pocahontas town	110	105	-4.5	54	98.1	0.0	0.0	0.0	1.9	13.0	16.7	47.3	37.8	35.1	26	92.3
Pollock village	89	79	-11.2	52	92.3	0.0	0.0	7.7	0.0	23.1	21.2	47.0	75.0	0.0	21	85.7
Polo city	575	528	-8.2	489	91.2	0.0	0.0	2.2	6.5	23.3	13.7	38.8	66.5	5.9	228	79.8
Pomona CDP	511	-	-	369	100.0	0.0	0.0	0.0	0.0	12.7	5.1	50.3	64.2	0.0	126	77.0
Pontiac CDP	175	-	-	232	39.2	0.0	0.0	12.5	48.3	37.5	4.7	54.7	55.9	40.0	81	100.0
Poplar Bluff city	17,035	16,937	-0.6	17,023	80.5	10.9	1.4	3.3	3.9	25.8	16.2	35.6	55.1	10.9	6,604	80.5
Portage Des Sioux city	331	328	-0.9	381	95.0	0.0	0.0	1.0	3.9	23.4	13.1	40.9	57.4	9.9	134	91.8
Portageville city	3,202	2,943	-8.1	3,011	72.8	22.9	0.0	4.3	0.0	25.0	18.0	39.8	71.5	11.4	1,294	82.4
Potosi city	2,661	2,577	-3.2	2,608	94.0	1.6	1.2	1.9	1.3	20.9	18.6	41.5	56.0	15.9	1,079	78.2
Powersville village	58	54	-6.9	28	100.0	0.0	0.0	0.0	0.0	25.0	35.7	39.8	71.4	0.0	10	60.0
Prairie Home city	280	280	0.0	237	95.8	0.0	0.0	1.7	2.5	20.7	20.3	45.9	50.3	19.6	100	84.0
Prathersville village	124	134	8.1	145	96.6	0.0	0.7	2.1	0.7	16.6	11.7	40.4	40.0	16.2	54	100.0
Preston village	223	219	-1.8	370	89.5	0.0	0.0	1.6	8.9	35.4	17.0	29.7	61.2	6.2	131	96.2
Princeton city	1,158	1,099	-5.1	1,142	90.6	1.0	1.5	2.5	4.5	31.5	18.7	38.1	59.2	11.2	412	71.1
Purcell city	408	428	4.9	423	93.1	0.0	0.0	6.9	0.0	29.8	11.8	35.5	58.9	7.5	137	86.1
Purdin city	190	177	-6.8	105	99.0	0.0	0.0	0.0	1.0	19.0	12.4	38.4	74.3	0.0	47	68.1
Purdy city	1,131	1,128	-0.3	1,276	46.9	0.0	0.9	6.7	45.5	28.8	15.8	34.6	74.3	8.0	472	82.0
Puxico city	886	846	-4.5	986	98.4	0.1	0.0	0.7	0.8	26.0	15.8	36.3	57.3	15.2	362	82.6
Queen City city	596	625	4.9	697	96.8	1.4	1.7	0.0	0.0	31.6	22.2	35.4	58.3	6.2	202	87.1
Quitman CDP	45	-	-	15	100.0	0.0	0.0	0.0	0.0	6.7	26.7	62.5	61.5	0.0	10	60.0
Qulin city	459	456	-0.7	734	91.6	1.8	0.0	2.0	4.6	32.3	17.0	37.2	63.3	8.4	238	76.9
Randolph village	52	55	5.8	24	91.7	8.3	0.0	0.0	0.0	0.0	8.3	47.8	68.2	13.6	10	100.0
Ravanna CDP	98	-	-	100	100.0	0.0	0.0	0.0	0.0	19.0	22.0	50.1	69.7	0.0	34	85.3
Ravenwood town	445	401	-9.9	423	91.5	1.2	0.9	1.7	4.7	24.1	15.6	31.4	51.1	18.6	177	93.2
Raymondville town	363	352	-3.0	612	97.5	0.0	0.0	1.8	0.7	33.5	11.1	31.5	62.2	7.3	201	88.1
Raymore city	19,210	22,194	15.5	21,196	80.8	10.3	1.6	2.5	4.7	23.8	18.3	41.7	27.9	37.5	8,450	95.7
Raytown city	29,611	28,991	-2.1	29,264	55.8	32.4	1.0	4.3	6.5	21.3	18.3	40.5	41.8	23.0	12,390	90.2

1 May be of any race.

Table A. All Places — **Population and Housing**

STATE City, town, township, borough, or CDP (county if applicable)	Population				Race and Hispanic or Latino origin (percent)					Age (percent)			Educational attainment of persons age 25 and older		Occupied housing units	
	2010 census total population	2019 estimated population	Percent change 2010–2019	ACS total population estimate 2015–2019	White alone, not Hispanic or Latino	Black alone, not Hispanic or Latino	Asian alone, not Hispanic or Latino	All other races or 2 or more races, not Hispanic or Latino	Hispanic or Latino[1]	Under 18 years old	Age 65 years and older	Median age	Percent High school diploma or less	Percent Bachelor's degree or more	Total	Percent with a computer
	1	2	3	4	5	6	7	8	9	10	11	12	13	14	15	16
MISSOURI—Con.																
Rayville CDP	223	-	-	282	100.0	0.0	0.0	0.0	0.0	27.0	0.0	39.8	84.0	0.0	72	100.0
Rea city	47	48	2.1	39	100.0	0.0	0.0	0.0	0.0	5.1	30.8	60.5	83.8	5.4	23	47.8
Redings Mill village	155	150	-3.2	120	93.3	0.8	0.0	0.0	5.8	15.0	36.7	59.4	34.8	27.2	58	89.7
Reeds town	95	100	5.3	99	97.0	0.0	0.0	3.0	0.0	21.2	30.3	48.7	74.3	2.7	36	83.3
Reeds Spring city	905	867	-4.2	1,266	89.7	0.0	0.6	5.8	3.9	26.7	22.3	33.2	58.4	12.3	417	85.4
Renick village	172	169	-1.7	164	94.5	0.6	0.0	0.0	4.9	7.3	25.0	53.9	61.0	10.3	86	81.4
Rensselaer village	227	230	1.3	278	98.2	0.0	0.0	0.0	1.8	13.3	26.3	47.2	46.9	21.2	117	97.4
Republic city	14,920	16,938	13.5	16,247	91.8	1.0	2.4	2.9	2.0	29.8	12.3	32.1	41.1	23.8	6,327	95.4
Revere town	79	75	-5.1	53	100.0	0.0	0.0	0.0	0.0	47.2	18.9	25.3	74.1	0.0	19	89.5
Rhineland town	142	131	-7.7	135	100.0	0.0	0.0	0.0	0.0	28.9	14.1	34.1	52.6	22.1	59	96.6
Richards town	97	95	-2.1	151	100.0	0.0	0.0	0.0	0.0	39.7	3.3	23.8	73.2	9.9	29	100.0
Rich Hill city	1,393	1,317	-5.5	1,500	92.7	1.0	0.8	4.7	0.7	27.5	18.7	36.2	66.8	12.4	616	78.7
Richland city	1,870	1,795	-4.0	1,797	85.5	0.9	0.4	2.9	10.2	25.3	14.1	41.2	48.3	9.4	640	82.3
Richmond city	5,801	5,653	-2.6	5,628	89.6	3.4	0.0	2.3	4.7	22.1	18.2	37.9	58.9	10.1	2,367	85.2
Richmond Heights city	8,551	8,801	2.9	8,500	78.1	10.3	6.4	1.5	3.7	16.8	15.6	38.3	8.7	72.1	4,149	93.7
Ridgely village	99	106	7.1	103	99.0	0.0	0.0	0.0	1.0	17.5	10.7	27.8	66.1	17.9	24	100.0
Ridgeway city	464	432	-6.9	398	97.5	0.0	0.0	2.3	0.3	21.1	24.4	44.0	69.8	12.5	157	75.8
Risco city	346	310	-10.4	392	98.0	2.0	0.0	0.0	0.0	25.5	18.1	35.3	70.9	4.6	172	70.3
Ritchey town	82	80	-2.4	45	91.1	0.0	0.0	0.0	8.9	8.9	40.0	61.3	44.7	13.2	23	78.3
River Bend village	10	10	0.0	10	50.0	0.0	0.0	30.0	20.0	0.0	0.0	25.2	16.7	50.0	3	100.0
Riverside city	2,928	3,505	19.7	3,342	72.1	14.0	4.2	3.3	6.4	21.2	15.3	35.8	40.7	27.6	1,462	87.6
Riverview village	2,940	2,832	-3.7	2,863	23.3	69.9	1.5	4.7	0.7	24.4	10.0	34.6	51.6	8.7	1,159	89.3
Riverview Estates village	82	84	2.4	71	93.0	0.0	0.0	4.2	2.8	16.9	21.1	50.5	41.1	30.4	28	82.1
Rives town	63	59	-6.3	74	91.9	0.0	0.0	0.0	8.1	29.7	18.9	39.7	75.0	0.0	29	93.1
Rocheport city	239	254	6.3	244	98.0	0.8	0.4	0.0	0.8	26.2	23.0	50.5	32.1	25.5	107	93.5
Rockaway Beach city	850	869	2.2	872	86.8	0.0	2.1	9.2	1.9	22.9	16.2	44.3	36.9	19.9	416	94.0
Rock Hill city	4,669	4,620		4,634	69.3	25.5	1.0	0.0	4.2	20.0	14.0	40.1	18.7	62.2	1,975	97.2
Rock Port city	1,316	1,191	-9.5	1,440	94.0	0.3	0.8	2.1	2.7	18.4	27.4	49.7	44.8	25.2	713	82.9
Rockville city	166	157	-5.4	147	94.6	0.0	0.0	0.0	5.4	37.4	23.1	36.9	66.3	6.7	53	94.3
Rogersville city	3,087	3,863	25.1	3,697	90.9	0.0	0.1	3.0	6.0	29.5	7.9	30.5	39.6	24.3	1,341	87.5
Rolla city	19,540	20,431	4.6	20,169	84.7	3.6	6.5	2.7	2.6	19.2	11.7	26.0	35.4	35.8	8,029	88.1
Roscoe village	124	117	-5.6	99	100.0	0.0	0.0	0.0	0.0	18.2	29.3	60.4	51.9	0.0	47	87.2
Rosebud city	405	405	0.0	519	96.7	0.0	0.0	1.5	1.7	32.8	10.8	31.5	62.9	11.2	179	81.0
Rosendale city	143	146	2.1	111	100.0	0.0	0.0	0.0	0.0	32.4	9.9	36.3	67.6	4.4	38	84.2
Rothville village	97	92	-5.2	93	92.5	0.0	0.0	0.0	7.5	38.7	11.8	20.4	51.2	27.9	25	96.0
Rush Hill village	146	143	-2.1	184	100.0	0.0	0.0	0.0	0.0	27.2	16.3	38.1	80.3	1.6	58	81.0
Rushville village	293	280	-4.4	283	93.6	0.0	1.4	1.8	3.2	33.9	10.2	42.3	53.1	19.8	111	84.7
Russellville city	804	822	2.2	793	96.1	0.0	1.4	1.8	0.8	24.0	12.9	33.6	47.1	20.0	327	90.8
Rutledge town	109	110	0.9	53	96.2	0.0	0.0	3.8	0.0	37.7	35.8	30.3	81.8	12.1	20	35.0
Saddlebrooke village	202	244	20.8	254	87.4	0.0	4.7	0.0	7.9	12.2	33.1	62.0	22.3	36.4	103	100.0
Saginaw village	297	302	1.7	367	85.8	0.5	1.1	8.4	4.1	27.0	16.1	35.8	33.5	21.5	148	87.8
St. Ann city	13,031	12,629	-3.1	12,744	57.9	31.0	3.6	2.6	4.9	24.8	11.5	34.6	46.7	19.3	5,500	86.3
St. Charles city	66,218	71,028	7.3	70,171	81.2	6.6	3.2	3.7	5.3	17.5	16.4	36.9	31.2	37.2	28,343	93.4
St. Clair city	4,729	4,712	-0.4	4,718	94.5	0.6	0.2	3.7	1.0	24.8	17.1	31.9	55.6	11.0	2,030	84.0
St. Clement CDP	78	-	-	150	100.0	0.0	0.0	0.0	0.0	80.0	0.0	12.3	26.7	73.3	18	55.6
St. Cloud village	41	39	-4.9	48	100.0	0.0	0.0	0.0	0.0	16.7	16.7	34.0	36.4	18.2	18	66.7
Ste. Genevieve city	4,416	4,416	0.0	4,418	87.1	7.9	1.9	2.3	0.8	20.8	21.2	41.2	48.1	22.6	1,890	80.3
St. Elizabeth village	338	346	2.4	378	91.5	1.6	0.5	3.4	2.9	27.0	22.2	36.0	43.7	31.7	128	91.4
St. Francisville CDP	179	-	-	274	84.3	0.0	13.9	1.8	0.0	23.7	4.4	36.9	83.2	9.8	88	93.2
St. George CDP	1,337	-	-	2,058	96.7	0.0	0.0	0.0	3.3	19.2	14.2	35.6	47.7	23.9	928	98.3
St. James city	4,218	4,034	-4.4	4,076	90.7	0.6	1.0	2.6	5.1	23.9	18.1	36.1	48.6	22.9	1,670	88.2
St. John city	6,528	6,338	-2.9	6,396	62.2	24.7	4.0	2.5	6.6	21.1	10.6	36.4	49.4	15.1	2,586	86.3
St. Joseph city	76,783	74,875	-2.5	75,913	81.6	5.9	1.2	4.0	7.3	22.7	15.5	36.8	50.1	20.5	28,686	84.7
St. Louis city	319,289	300,576	-5.9	308,174	43.6	46.2	3.3	2.8	4.0	19.4	13.1	35.8	36.2	36.3	141,952	85.1
St. Martins city	1,155	1,195	3.5	1,159	95.9	0.0	0.0	3.1	1.0	19.8	17.4	43.9	41.4	28.0	484	91.1
St. Mary city	362	346	-4.4	370	94.1	0.0	4.9	0.0	1.1	26.2	19.7	41.3	63.1	12.4	130	74.6
St. Paul city	1,933	2,574	33.2	2,295	95.8	1.4	1.2	0.9	0.7	19.3	17.6	46.7	37.3	37.9	826	95.5
St. Peters city	52,595	58,212	10.7	57,273	86.6	5.4	2.7	2.3	3.0	22.1	15.5	39.5	28.3	38.9	22,490	94.0
St. Robert city	4,626	6,275	35.6	6,122	57.0	16.6	3.2	9.7	13.5	30.0	5.9	31.2	26.3	32.6	2,333	97.9
St. Thomas town	264	271	2.7	243	91.4	0.4	7.4	0.8	0.0	26.7	14.0	33.4	44.8	35.7	95	82.1
Salem city	4,945	4,919	-0.5	4,935	94.2	0.5	0.0	4.1	1.1	20.3	24.9	46.6	63.7	13.7	2,402	80.3
Salisbury city	1,613	1,523	-5.6	1,754	93.0	2.3	0.0	3.5	1.1	25.3	23.7	39.8	53.3	15.0	641	80.3
Sappington CDP	7,580	-	-	7,484	91.7	1.1	2.5	1.6	3.1	21.2	25.5	47.2	29.0	41.3	3,400	89.0
Sarcoxie city	1,576	1,551	-1.6	1,682	95.6	1.0	0.0	2.8	0.7	24.8	12.4	40.8	59.5	9.3	590	78.3
Savannah city	5,054	5,223	3.3	5,159	99.5	0.3	0.0	0.2	0.0	25.3	17.7	38.3	45.8	24.2	2,033	85.1
Schell City city	249	238	-4.4	227	100.0	0.0	0.0	0.0	0.0	14.1	27.3	40.8	72.7	11.0	103	87.4
Scotsdale town	210	216	2.9	144	95.8	0.0	0.0	2.1	2.1	20.1	13.9	42.3	43.1	25.5	51	100.0
Scott City city	4,558	4,468	-2.0	4,498	94.0	0.3	0.0	2.0	3.7	27.9	15.0	35.9	57.7	10.5	1,674	87.2
Sedalia city	21,514	21,629	0.5	21,633	79.9	5.9	0.7	1.8	11.7	23.3	16.3	36.1	50.4	15.8	8,743	86.9
Sedgewickville village	173	167	-3.5	160	100.0	0.0	0.0	0.0	0.0	37.5	9.4	29.0	58.9	21.1	46	87.0
Seligman city	843	841	-0.2	881	95.6	0.0	0.0	1.5	3.0	31.6	9.2	33.7	78.3	3.4	343	72.3
Senath city	1,768	1,611	-8.9	1,767	64.7	0.5	0.0	0.0	34.8	24.1	16.2	36.1	68.0	11.2	649	83.5
Seneca city	2,338	2,387	2.1	2,490	87.7	0.0	1.2	9.1	2.0	28.1	19.6	33.7	50.6	17.2	881	81.2
Seymour city	1,910	2,010	5.2	2,022	88.9	2.9	0.0	4.5	3.7	23.8	20.6	37.4	60.1	9.3	823	88.7
Shelbina city	1,704	1,589	-6.7	1,635	97.2	0.2	0.0	2.0	0.6	24.5	24.7	43.3	57.0	12.6	650	85.1
Shelbyville city	552	513	-7.1	461	97.4	2.0	0.0	0.7	0.0	16.1	29.1	51.8	46.4	25.2	231	79.7
Sheldon city	543	520	-4.2	444	99.1	0.0	0.0	0.9	0.0	26.8	16.2	36.5	65.2	13.0	158	82.3
Shell Knob CDP	1,379	-	-	1,091	98.1	0.0	0.0	1.0	0.9	8.0	42.2	62.5	31.0	27.3	523	96.7
Sheridan town	193	179	-7.3	212	79.2	0.0	1.4	10.4	9.0	21.2	26.9	50.6	57.1	13.5	99	83.8
Shoal Creek Drive village	337	326	-3.3	384	85.7	0.0	1.6	6.8	6.0	28.4	13.5	34.0	35.3	28.6	138	92.8
Shoal Creek Estates village	96	94	-2.1	84	89.3	2.4	0.0	4.8	3.6	17.9	35.7	53.0	17.9	46.3	34	100.0
Shrewsbury city	6,248	6,091	-2.5	6,150	89.6	4.3	2.1	3.8	0.2	16.5	28.5	46.9	16.1	58.4	3,221	86.1
Sibley village	354	366	3.4	363	99.2	0.0	0.0	0.8	0.0	22.6	15.7	44.4	63.2	10.0	151	75.5
Sikeston city	16,334	16,023	-1.9	16,200	69.1	25.0	0.9	2.5	2.6	24.5	19.8	39.9	53.6	21.8	6,882	79.2
Silex village	187	292	56.1	68	95.6	0.0	0.0	0.0	4.4	4.4	30.9	55.5	86.2	3.1	7	85.7
Skidmore city	285	257	-9.8	189	96.8	1.1	0.0	1.1	1.1	19.0	25.4	50.5	59.7	10.1	91	82.4
Slater city	1,856	1,762	-5.1	2,057	82.8	5.3	0.3	9.5	2.0	21.2	21.9	40.0	56.3	13.5	876	82.0
Smithton city	573	571	-0.3	508	90.4	2.8	0.0	0.6	6.3	26.6	10.6	37.6	45.3	6.1	188	95.2
Smithville city	8,384	10,795	28.8	9,884	89.9	0.4	2.8	5.9	1.1	27.8	12.2	35.4	32.6	30.4	3,530	95.4
South Fork CDP	241	-	-	51	100.0	0.0	0.0	0.0	0.0	0.0	13.7	52.7	56.9	0.0	28	85.7
South Gifford village	50	48	-4.0	65	86.2	0.0	0.0	1.5	12.3	26.2	10.8	27.9	79.5	0.0	19	63.2

1 May be of any race.

Table A. All Places — **Population and Housing**

STATE City, town, township, borough, or CDP (county if applicable)	Population: 2010 census total population	Population: 2019 estimated population	Population: Percent change 2010–2019	Population: ACS total population estimate 2015–2019	Race and Hispanic or Latino origin (percent): White alone, not Hispanic or Latino	Black alone, not Hispanic or Latino	Asian alone, not Hispanic or Latino	All other races or 2 or more races, not Hispanic or Latino	Hispanic or Latino[1]	Age (percent): Under 18 years old	Age 65 years and older	Median age	Educational attainment of persons age 25 and older: Percent High school diploma or less	Percent Bachelor's degree or more	Occupied housing units: Total	Percent with a computer
	1	2	3	4	5	6	7	8	9	10	11	12	13	14	15	16
MISSOURI—Con.																
South Gorin town	91	92	1.1	68	100.0	0.0	0.0	0.0	0.0	50.0	7.4	26.0	44.1	5.9	20	90.0
South Greenfield village	90	85	-5.6	74	98.6	0.0	0.0	1.4	0.0	31.1	24.3	37.0	68.6	7.8	32	84.4
South Lineville town	28	27	-3.6	5	100.0	0.0	0.0	0.0	0.0	20.0	0.0	24.5	50.0	0.0	3	100.0
Southwest City town	973	956	-1.7	1,056	35.6	0.0	0.0	8.0	56.3	35.0	11.7	31.6	68.5	7.4	317	66.9
Spanish Lake CDP	19,650	-	-	17,485	16.6	78.9	0.0	3.2	1.2	27.4	13.5	30.7	40.9	15.5	6,918	89.9
Sparta city	1,746	1,946	11.5	1,612	94.9	0.0	0.0	0.8	4.3	22.5	16.1	36.3	53.9	8.6	655	89.0
Spickard city	254	243	-4.3	238	88.2	0.0	0.0	11.8	0.0	26.1	24.8	35.8	63.0	9.7	112	69.6
Spokane CDP	177	-	-	33	100.0	0.0	0.0	0.0	0.0	0.0	100.0	0.0	51.5	0.0	16	100.0
Springfield city	159,341	167,882	5.4	167,051	85.3	4.3	2.1	4.0	4.3	17.9	15.7	33.1	38.3	27.4	75,948	86.5
Stanberry city	1,185	1,175	-0.8	1,239	98.0	0.0	0.6	0.3	1.1	27.0	22.1	35.7	55.5	17.7	478	77.8
Stark City town	139	136	-2.2	119	66.4	0.0	0.0	9.2	24.4	28.6	18.5	38.8	61.3	11.3	43	93.0
Steele city	2,169	1,889	-12.9	1,976	66.9	27.7	0.0	5.1	0.3	29.6	11.7	34.1	66.7	13.8	672	89.3
Steelville city	1,640	1,650	0.6	1,728	92.6	1.6	0.2	2.3	3.3	23.4	19.9	39.3	62.4	9.1	629	69.5
Stella town	158	153	-3.2	153	87.6	0.0	0.0	11.1	1.3	25.5	15.7	29.3	73.8	10.7	57	73.7
Stewartsville city	750	733	-2.3	733	95.4	2.2	0.0	1.5	1.0	24.7	12.7	33.8	59.1	19.1	310	86.1
Stockton city	1,815	1,934	6.6	1,836	97.0	0.2	0.0	1.1	1.7	20.9	27.5	45.5	56.9	16.2	834	81.8
Stotesbury town	18	17	-5.6	8	100.0	0.0	0.0	0.0	0.0	25.0	62.5	66.5	83.3	0.0	5	60.0
Stotts City city	220	217	-1.4	137	91.2	0.0	0.0	8.8	0.0	38.7	9.5	30.9	62.5	0.0	41	95.1
Stoutland city	196	201	2.6	234	90.2	0.9	0.0	4.3	4.7	17.9	20.5	54.7	75.8	8.4	77	79.2
Stoutsville village	40	40	0.0	33	100.0	0.0	0.0	0.0	0.0	30.3	27.3	43.5	47.8	17.4	14	92.9
Stover city	1,096	1,094	-0.2	1,176	95.7	0.2	0.0	3.1	1.0	29.3	20.7	39.5	62.9	12.5	455	63.3
Strafford city	2,348	2,460	4.8	2,100	89.0	0.4	0.4	8.6	1.6	27.0	15.9	36.5	45.8	17.0	845	86.2
Strasburg city	141	142	0.7	144	100.0	0.0	0.0	0.0	0.0	23.6	4.2	43.5	52.6	12.4	56	82.1
Sturgeon city	893	947	6.0	990	97.8	0.4	0.0	1.7	0.1	25.8	19.9	34.2	45.5	18.1	388	83.8
Sugar Creek city	3,338	3,260	-2.3	3,290	90.1	0.6	0.0	4.8	4.5	23.3	14.4	40.7	62.7	9.1	1,405	86.4
Sullivan city	7,120	7,127	0.1	6,564	92.8	0.9	0.2	1.3	4.8	23.4	18.7	38.2	51.6	18.7	2,991	86.1
Summersville city	503	490	-2.6	515	90.7	8.0	1.4	0.0	0.0	24.7	18.8	35.7	49.9	16.9	219	73.1
Sumner town	102	97	-4.9	131	98.5	0.0	0.0	1.5	0.0	36.6	13.7	30.9	62.7	25.3	38	92.1
Sundown CDP	48	-	-	48	100.0	0.0	0.0	0.0	0.0	0.0	64.6	73.2	25.0	64.6	24	100.0
Sunrise Beach village	475	542	14.1	487	84.6	1.6	0.8	0.0	12.9	12.3	19.3	41.4	49.5	13.3	187	86.1
Sunset Hills city	8,460	8,447	-0.2	8,472	94.1	1.0	2.2	0.6	2.1	20.4	29.2	50.5	26.2	50.5	3,456	90.0
Sweet Springs city	1,483	1,412	-4.8	1,399	93.6	0.4	0.2	4.4	1.3	24.4	18.4	40.0	63.0	8.1	507	89.5
Sycamore Hills village	660	653	-1.1	728	57.8	33.1	1.6	7.4	0.0	23.4	13.3	35.5	27.0	32.3	291	91.4
Syracuse city	174	171	-1.7	123	97.6	0.0	2.4	0.0	0.0	25.2	18.7	46.3	82.1	2.4	50	78.0
Tallapoosa city	168	149	-11.3	96	95.8	0.0	0.0	0.0	4.2	18.8	11.5	45.3	90.3	0.0	40	100.0
Taneyville village	351	362	3.1	292	94.2	0.0	0.0	5.8	0.0	23.3	20.5	45.0	51.3	13.6	120	84.2
Taos city	1,114	1,153	3.5	1,349	97.3	1.0	0.4	0.7	0.5	32.0	11.0	36.8	40.4	34.7	455	94.1
Tarkio city	1,584	1,432	-9.6	1,508	96.3	0.7	0.7	0.7	1.6	19.5	26.0	43.1	52.9	19.9	756	85.4
Terre du Lac CDP	-	-	-	2,662	97.6	0.0	0.0	0.4	2.0	17.2	27.2	47.7	39.7	13.2	1,065	88.2
Thayer city	2,216	2,131	-3.8	2,355	92.8	0.0	0.5	4.8	1.8	25.1	24.6	37.2	54.1	14.8	993	77.7
Theodosia village	244	267	9.4	164	98.8	0.0	0.0	1.2	0.0	7.9	56.7	67.2	56.3	7.3	99	78.8
Thomasville CDP	68	-	-	-	-	-	-	-	-	-	-	-	-	-	-	-
Three Creeks village	6	6	0.0	4	100.0	0.0	0.0	0.0	0.0	0.0	100.0	0.0	100.0	0.0	2	100.0
Tightwad village	62	60	-3.2	74	100.0	0.0	0.0	0.0	0.0	5.4	29.7	60.9	61.4	15.7	37	94.6
Tina village	157	148	-5.7	303	100.0	0.0	0.0	0.0	0.0	13.9	17.5	38.4	87.6	3.6	90	87.8
Tindall town	79	76	-3.8	61	100.0	0.0	0.0	0.0	0.0	23.0	23.0	50.3	34.1	17.1	30	100.0
Tipton city	3,262	3,389	3.9	3,372	84.3	10.7	0.0	1.0	4.0	14.1	15.3	40.4	67.2	10.5	897	76.7
Town and Country city	10,820	11,109	2.7	11,077	83.7	1.3	12.9	0.6	1.6	19.2	29.5	52.4	11.0	75.5	4,085	96.1
Tracy city	230	337	46.5	235	94.0	1.3	0.0	1.7	3.0	23.4	21.7	42.5	56.3	17.6	77	98.7
Trenton city	6,001	5,763	-4.0	5,770	92.4	0.5	0.9	2.7	3.6	21.2	22.8	38.1	51.1	17.2	2,315	82.7
Trimble city	646	613	-5.1	616	95.9	0.0	0.0	1.8	2.3	24.7	14.1	36.1	60.4	10.9	252	90.1
Triplett city	41	39	-4.9	9	100.0	0.0	0.0	0.0	0.0	0.0	55.6	72.3	55.6	11.1	6	66.7
Troy city	10,599	12,820	21.0	12,079	89.5	2.3	0.5	2.5	5.2	28.7	11.1	31.4	50.1	16.4	3,977	91.4
Truesdale city	732	886	21.0	735	81.0	5.0	1.2	4.5	8.3	33.2	9.7	30.7	63.2	11.1	271	84.9
Truxton village	91	103	13.2	141	100.0	0.0	0.0	0.0	0.0	21.3	4.3	36.1	79.8	2.8	40	100.0
Turney village	148	148	0.0	255	90.2	0.8	0.4	3.9	4.7	25.1	3.5	38.7	60.6	10.3	91	96.7
Tuscumbia town	201	203	1.0	168	73.8	17.9	4.2	0.0	4.2	19.6	10.1	33.0	75.9	7.4	36	88.9
Twin Oaks village	398	396	-0.5	374	98.9	0.0	0.0	1.1	0.0	11.8	31.3	55.5	17.9	46.6	175	97.7
Umber View Heights village	48	49	2.1	55	89.1	0.0	0.0	10.9	0.0	5.5	23.6	53.9	34.0	32.0	25	96.0
Union city	10,288	11,990	16.5	11,475	95.4	0.7	0.5	1.6	1.8	26.3	13.5	33.9	48.0	18.4	4,441	88.7
Union Star town	437	417	-4.6	448	94.6	0.0	0.0	0.9	4.5	26.3	14.3	37.0	65.2	9.8	180	75.6
Unionville city	1,864	1,742	-6.5	1,813	98.3	0.3	0.2	0.6	0.6	21.8	20.6	37.5	46.6	11.5	697	79.6
Unity Village village	75	73	-2.7	90	81.1	11.1	3.3	0.0	4.4	0.0	11.1	48.5	11.3	58.1	49	100.0
University City city	35,292	34,165	-3.2	34,498	53.4	35.6	5.4	3.0	2.7	17.4	17.8	35.2	21.1	57.7	15,580	89.7
Uplands Park village	430	424	-1.4	386	2.6	94.6	1.0	1.8	0.0	31.9	20.7	39.6	57.4	10.4	148	83.8
Urbana city	414	415	0.2	361	90.9	0.0	0.0	8.0	1.1	19.1	23.3	47.6	62.2	8.0	185	85.9
Urich city	501	484	-3.4	573	93.5	0.0	0.0	5.2	1.2	18.5	16.6	34.9	68.7	8.3	263	88.2
Utica village	269	251	-6.7	164	92.7	0.0	0.0	0.0	7.3	3.0	19.5	54.7	71.1	8.7	84	82.1
Valley Park city	6,873	6,796	-1.1	6,799	89.0	3.6	4.0	1.3	2.1	19.8	16.6	38.1	29.4	40.9	2,982	91.5
Van Buren town	824	798	-3.2	897	100.0	0.0	0.0	0.0	0.0	19.6	22.2	38.3	49.1	13.0	376	79.5
Vandalia city	3,896	4,030	3.4	4,149	80.3	12.5	0.7	5.5	1.0	14.9	11.8	35.7	68.0	8.0	1,073	75.0
Vandiver village	71	69	-2.8	85	98.8	0.0	0.0	1.2	0.0	20.0	37.6	57.1	53.0	21.2	40	80.0
Vanduser village	267	261	-2.2	168	84.5	8.9	0.0	6.5	0.0	3.6	35.7	55.5	83.6	7.3	62	67.7
Velda City city	1,410	1,360	-3.5	1,404	4.1	94.2	0.0	0.3	1.4	27.7	17.3	35.7	46.9	9.4	578	86.5
Velda Village Hills city	1,051	1,029	-2.1	876	0.0	99.2	0.0	0.3	0.5	14.7	28.1	45.3	59.3	10.1	361	78.7
Verona town	616	601	-2.4	647	80.7	0.0	0.0	2.0	17.3	47.3	11.7	20.0	79.2	1.0	220	61.8
Versailles city	2,481	2,477	-0.2	2,961	82.2	2.8	0.0	4.1	10.9	26.8	15.8	34.6	56.6	13.6	1,005	76.1
Viburnum city	683	651	-4.7	762	95.5	0.0	0.0	4.5	0.0	30.1	11.2	32.3	54.5	16.0	275	91.3
Vienna city	625	594	-5.0	738	96.5	3.5	0.0	0.0	0.0	19.5	23.0	38.1	52.6	16.1	273	74.7
Village of Four Seasons village	2,213	2,294	3.7	2,371	98.7	0.3	0.0	0.8	0.3	26.8	29.9	49.5	29.8	35.0	840	98.6
Villa Ridge CDP	2,636	-	-	2,603	97.2	2.1	0.0	0.7	0.0	15.3	20.5	53.3	48.8	20.0	1,097	93.1
Vinita Park city	2,151	2,116	-1.6	1,619	35.3	59.1	0.9	3.2	1.5	15.4	20.2	41.5	52.2	19.8	709	85.0
Vista village	48	46	-4.2	47	100.0	0.0	0.0	0.0	0.0	40.4	4.3	18.9	52.4	9.5	12	91.7
Waco city	87	91	4.6	67	94.0	0.0	0.0	6.0	0.0	14.9	16.4	55.6	50.9	24.5	30	83.3
Walker city	266	256	-3.8	282	90.4	0.0	0.0	1.1	8.5	28.4	19.5	42.4	73.1	2.1	128	74.2
Walnut Grove city	668	781	16.9	615	96.4	0.0	0.0	2.1	1.5	21.6	16.7	41.8	66.5	8.1	274	74.1
Wardell town	421	359	-14.7	295	98.3	1.4	0.0	0.3	0.0	16.3	17.6	45.4	71.9	7.1	137	80.3
Wardsville village	1,503	1,560	3.8	1,878	97.4	0.0	0.7	0.7	1.1	29.2	12.6	38.6	33.4	39.2	697	93.5
Warrensburg city	18,866	20,418	8.2	20,139	81.1	6.8	2.0	5.5	4.8	17.3	10.2	25.1	29.1	40.7	7,273	95.4
Warrenton city	7,910	8,396	6.1	8,226	91.5	0.9	0.2	3.0	4.4	28.9	15.1	34.3	46.5	16.3	3,064	85.8

1 May be of any race.

Table A. All Places — **Population and Housing**

	Population				Race and Hispanic or Latino origin (percent)					Age (percent)			Educational attainment of persons age 25 and older		Occupied housing units	
STATE City, town, township, borough, or CDP (county if applicable)	2010 census total population	2019 estimated population	Percent change 2010–2019	ACS total population estimate 2015–2019	White alone, not Hispanic or Latino	Black alone, not Hispanic or Latino	Asian alone, not Hispanic or Latino	All other races or 2 or more races, not Hispanic or Latino	Hispanic or Latino[1]	Under 18 years old	Age 65 years and older	Median age	Percent High school diploma or less	Percent Bachelor's degree or more	Total	Percent with a computer
	1	2	3	4	5	6	7	8	9	10	11	12	13	14	15	16
MISSOURI—Con.																
Warsaw city	2,123	2,204	3.8	2,683	89.1	0.9	0.0	6.6	3.4	25.6	22.2	37.6	61.7	11.4	972	78.9
Warson Woods city	1,945	1,897	-2.5	2,046	94.6	0.7	2.2	2.0	0.5	28.3	21.3	42.1	5.4	82.0	776	94.7
Washburn city	433	432	-0.2	456	88.4	0.4	0.0	5.9	5.3	20.8	20.4	35.9	61.4	9.7	188	84.6
Washington city	13,999	14,081	0.6	14,014	94.9	0.1	2.5	1.8	0.6	22.9	18.9	40.9	40.8	26.2	5,751	89.2
Wasola CDP	113	-	-	177	100.0	0.0	0.0	0.0	0.0	7.3	55.9	80.2	31.1	14.6	86	100.0
Watson village	100	90	-10.0	46	100.0	0.0	0.0	0.0	0.0	23.9	15.2	30.0	79.3	0.0	22	59.1
Waverly city	849	838	-1.3	823	88.5	1.6	0.0	0.6	9.4	26.1	20.4	39.3	62.1	14.7	324	79.0
Wayland city	531	501	-5.6	595	96.8	3.2	0.0	0.0	0.0	20.8	16.0	39.7	67.3	3.1	203	64.5
Waynesville city	4,826	5,295	9.7	5,257	74.3	11.9	1.6	6.7	5.5	28.6	11.8	34.8	29.8	34.8	2,042	89.6
Weatherby town	107	103	-3.7	71	91.5	0.0	0.0	8.5	0.0	11.3	28.2	52.8	81.0	0.0	28	82.1
Weatherby Lake city	1,727	2,073	20.0	2,088	91.7	0.8	1.6	2.2	3.7	20.3	26.7	50.5	12.9	58.0	797	98.4
Weaubleau city	418	410	-1.9	596	88.9	0.0	0.0	8.4	2.7	35.4	14.8	34.6	68.9	7.1	193	77.2
Webb City city	10,999	12,134	10.3	11,721	87.9	2.3	1.5	4.1	4.3	26.6	15.0	34.6	47.1	24.9	4,569	86.7
Webster Groves city	23,019	22,819	-0.9	22,951	90.7	4.1	1.3	1.6	2.4	24.6	18.3	39.5	12.8	67.7	8,897	92.8
Weingarten CDP	133	-	-	89	100.0	0.0	0.0	0.0	0.0	34.8	10.1	35.6	86.2	0.0	41	53.7
Weldon Spring city	5,413	5,533	2.2	5,531	93.8	3.0	1.1	0.8	1.3	15.6	27.1	55.8	21.0	50.3	2,313	96.8
Weldon Spring Heights town	91	90	-1.1	99	94.9	0.0	1.0	3.0	1.0	13.1	24.2	58.1	28.6	41.6	38	94.7
Wellington city	812	805	-0.9	774	85.7	3.6	0.0	1.3	9.4	29.6	15.6	36.6	59.8	12.1	317	85.2
Wellston city	2,319	2,285	-1.5	1,932	3.3	93.6	0.0	2.7	0.3	38.8	10.7	27.5	54.7	5.1	705	71.1
Wellsville city	1,220	1,159	-5.0	1,186	91.3	2.2	0.0	1.6	4.9	22.2	19.1	43.4	63.9	7.9	457	82.3
Wentworth village	147	144	-2.0	134	100.0	0.0	0.0	0.0	0.0	15.7	11.2	38.8	67.4	20.2	43	93.0
Wentzville city	29,144	41,784	43.4	38,841	89.8	4.7	2.0	1.3	2.0	32.4	10.0	33.1	29.5	35.3	12,969	96.3
West Alton city	522	527	1.0	388	97.7	0.0	0.0	2.3	0.0	12.6	17.0	43.3	54.7	13.8	178	87.6
Westboro city	141	127	-9.9	103	99.0	0.0	1.0	0.0	0.0	20.4	17.5	49.4	70.4	4.9	47	89.4
West Line village	97	101	4.1	130	73.1	0.0	0.0	26.9	0.0	11.5	9.2	39.5	55.8	29.5	49	81.6
Weston city	1,641	1,815	10.6	1,728	94.3	1.6	0.2	2.2	1.7	22.9	21.6	42.8	31.4	36.6	716	93.2
Westphalia city	392	379	-3.3	345	98.3	1.2	0.0	0.0	0.6	13.3	38.6	55.2	71.6	13.1	156	66.0
West Plains city	12,009	12,304	2.5	12,233	95.3	0.2	0.3	2.6	1.6	24.3	19.8	36.1	42.2	26.3	5,041	83.1
West Sullivan town	116	113	-2.6	226	90.3	0.0	0.0	3.5	6.2	42.0	1.3	24.4	71.6	5.9	78	91.0
Westwood village	283	281	-0.7	310	77.7	7.7	5.8	0.0	8.7	21.9	23.2	49.3	12.4	78.8	116	99.1
Wheatland city	373	366	-1.9	341	91.5	0.0	2.3	6.2	0.0	15.5	29.9	43.6	49.4	7.2	171	70.8
Wheaton city	696	688	-1.1	581	96.4	0.0	0.0	3.6	0.0	20.0	18.8	46.7	64.5	1.3	237	75.1
Wheeling city	271	263	-3.0	273	96.3	0.0	1.1	0.0	2.6	21.6	19.4	46.9	64.2	6.7	111	72.1
Whiteman AFB CDP	2,556	-	-	4,169	75.6	10.1	2.1	2.5	9.7	25.7	0.0	22.2	21.8	33.4	979	99.7
Whiteside village	75	81	8.0	70	92.9	0.0	0.0	7.1	0.0	7.1	28.6	58.8	73.8	0.0	42	76.2
Whitewater town	125	122	-2.4	107	86.9	0.9	3.7	8.4	0.0	14.0	31.8	46.4	59.2	15.5	45	73.3
Wilbur Park village	473	466	-1.5	482	98.8	0.0	0.6	0.0	0.6	15.6	9.3	45.5	28.2	29.5	232	97.8
Wildwood city	35,305	35,432	0.4	35,459	87.7	2.0	5.4	2.4	2.4	25.8	14.0	44.4	10.9	63.5	12,438	98.7
Willard city	5,306	5,632	6.1	5,519	93.0	1.4	0.0	1.9	3.7	30.7	10.2	34.7	37.5	28.1	1,967	96.4
Williamsville city	350	332	-5.1	445	93.9	0.2	0.0	2.9	2.9	16.6	20.2	44.1	69.0	2.8	170	69.4
Willow Springs city	2,178	2,099	-3.6	2,225	95.7	0.0	0.5	2.8	1.0	23.1	17.0	38.0	53.4	13.3	933	83.5
Wilson City village	115	112	-2.6	33	6.1	93.9	0.0	0.0	0.0	6.1	18.2	59.5	64.5	3.2	22	36.4
Winchester city	1,553	1,513	-2.6	1,368	87.9	2.1	3.1	3.6	3.2	15.9	17.9	43.1	37.8	26.0	546	94.0
Windsor city	2,905	2,784	-4.2	2,937	91.7	0.7	0.0	6.8	0.8	24.4	18.8	37.7	54.1	6.9	1,080	86.6
Windsor Place village	330	333	0.9	339	92.0	1.8	0.3	2.7	3.2	29.2	10.6	33.5	30.5	35.5	117	91.5
Winfield city	1,404	1,499	6.8	1,288	86.3	0.5	0.5	4.0	8.6	27.5	15.1	37.3	57.8	14.5	455	87.9
Winigan CDP	44	-	-	30	60.0	0.0	0.0	40.0	0.0	40.0	23.3	44.5	83.3	0.0	9	33.3
Winona city	1,331	1,293	-2.9	1,284	88.2	0.0	0.0	9.4	2.3	22.8	15.9	36.3	67.6	10.7	509	75.6
Winston village	259	253	-2.3	214	94.9	0.5	0.0	2.8	1.9	16.4	26.6	49.6	61.5	7.4	90	84.4
Wood Heights city	730	698	-4.4	672	94.6	1.9	0.6	2.2	0.6	19.8	15.3	44.3	45.1	15.8	252	90.9
Woodson Terrace city	4,087	4,037	-1.2	4,052	47.5	32.8	0.0	4.6	15.1	24.0	11.1	37.4	57.2	12.0	1,498	91.7
Wooldridge village	58	58	0.0	27	96.3	0.0	0.0	3.7	0.0	0.0	33.3	61.9	59.3	3.7	14	100.0
Worth village	63	59	-6.3	64	100.0	0.0	0.0	0.0	0.0	25.0	10.9	30.0	68.9	11.1	25	72.0
Wortham CDP	275	-	-	246	100.0	0.0	0.0	0.0	0.0	18.7	29.7	36.9	55.8	0.0	87	78.2
Worthington village	87	82	-5.7	183	100.0	0.0	0.0	0.0	0.0	62.8	1.1	12.8	100.0	0.0	34	97.1
Wright City city	3,164	4,309	36.2	3,810	73.4	6.1	0.0	6.3	14.3	31.0	12.5	30.7	54.2	16.4	1,308	93.3
Wyaconda city	227	211	-7.0	139	100.0	0.0	0.0	0.0	0.0	26.6	28.1	41.3	70.5	8.0	67	67.2
Wyatt city	319	283	-11.3	301	94.0	6.0	0.0	0.0	0.0	23.6	22.3	41.8	70.0	8.4	137	73.7
Zalma CDP	122	-	-	93	79.6	0.0	0.0	20.4	0.0	12.9	20.4	60.1	88.9	8.6	53	28.3
MONTANA	989,407	1,068,778	8.0	1,050,649	86.1	0.4	0.8	8.9	3.8	21.7	18.2	39.9	35.3	32.0	427,871	88.9
Absarokee CDP	1,150	-	-	1,061	91.8	0.0	0.0	5.7	2.5	19.8	27.3	46.6	38.2	21.6	470	87.4
Alberton town	417	446	7.0	555	85.9	0.0	3.2	6.7	4.1	31.7	14.2	33.7	45.9	18.8	188	89.9
Alder CDP	103	-	-	109	100.0	0.0	0.0	0.0	0.0	12.8	37.6	58.3	37.9	25.3	47	85.1
Alzada CDP	29	-	-	23	100.0	0.0	0.0	0.0	0.0	0.0	52.2	68.5	77.3	9.1	14	50.0
Amsterdam CDP	180	-	-	173	75.7	0.0	0.0	6.9	3.5	21.4	19.7	40.5	43.2	19.7	61	85.2
Anaconda-Deer Lodge County	9,294	9,140	-1.7	9,106	90.1	0.7	0.8	4.9	3.5	15.9	22.8	48.6	47.0	20.4	3,903	83.7
Antelope CDP	51	-	-	68	100.0	0.0	0.0	0.0	0.0	57.4	0.0	11.8	17.2	37.9	14	100.0
Arlee CDP	636	-	-	641	49.3	0.0	0.0	46.8	3.9	24.6	12.9	36.2	35.9	23.3	251	78.9
Ashland CDP	824	-	-	957	25.5	1.0	0.2	72.4	0.8	35.8	10.8	25.2	27.9	25.0	295	67.1
Augusta CDP	309	-	-	318	100.0	0.0	0.0	0.0	0.0	25.2	23.3	47.2	34.8	33.5	142	93.7
Avon CDP	111	-	-	156	100.0	0.0	0.0	0.0	0.0	17.9	11.5	27.5	72.5	6.9	58	91.4
Azure CDP	286	-	-	400	0.0	0.0	0.0	100.0	0.0	41.8	6.3	21.5	56.0	8.8	94	76.6
Babb CDP	174	-	-	72	11.1	0.0	0.0	88.9	0.0	0.0	38.9	59.2	69.4	0.0	29	31.0
Bainville town	208	316	51.9	215	80.0	0.0	0.0	17.2	2.8	27.4	7.0	35.4	64.2	18.2	85	97.6
Baker city	1,776	1,893	6.6	1,756	91.5	0.1	2.9	3.1	2.4	25.2	15.8	38.8	43.8	17.4	798	87.7
Ballantine CDP	320	-	-	225	51.6	0.0	0.0	48.4	0.0	15.1	21.8	43.9	41.4	9.9	133	100.0
Basin CDP	212	-	-	232	97.4	1.3	0.0	0.9	0.4	19.4	24.1	51.3	38.4	21.5	104	92.3
Batavia CDP	385	-	-	436	84.4	0.0	0.0	8.9	6.7	31.7	17.7	31.4	50.4	24.5	142	87.3
Bearcreek town	77	82	6.5	117	91.5	0.0	0.0	8.5	0.0	21.4	32.5	47.1	31.5	26.1	41	100.0
Bear Dance CDP	275	-	-	282	92.6	0.0	0.0	0.0	7.4	0.0	46.5	61.5	14.7	53.5	147	100.0
Beaver Creek CDP	271	-	-	428	78.0	0.0	0.0	22.0	0.0	24.8	4.0	41.7	54.4	6.8	128	91.4
Belfry CDP	218	-	-	305	97.4	0.0	0.0	2.0	0.7	25.6	19.0	40.5	47.5	13.7	126	82.5
Belgrade city	7,458	9,503	27.4	8,685	93.5	0.0	0.1	1.7	4.7	26.0	8.5	31.8	33.9	33.6	3,492	86.0
Belknap CDP	158	-	-	227	100.0	0.0	0.0	0.0	0.0	55.9	0.0	15.7	59.0	0.0	41	100.0
Belt town	576	564	-2.1	514	93.2	0.0	0.0	2.3	4.5	19.1	32.7	54.4	60.5	8.4	276	72.8
Biddle CDP	41	-	-	48	100.0	0.0	0.0	0.0	0.0	31.3	12.5	47.5	42.4	15.2	17	100.0
Big Arm CDP	177	-	-	169	89.9	0.0	0.0	10.1	0.0	9.5	38.5	53.9	22.9	45.8	86	100.0
Bigfork CDP	4,270	-	-	4,668	90.6	0.6	0.3	4.3	4.2	16.0	32.8	54.7	26.5	38.1	2,064	90.2

1 May be of any race.

Table A. All Places — **Population and Housing**

STATE City, town, township, borough, or CDP (county if applicable)	Population: 2010 census total population	Population: 2019 estimated population	Population: Percent change 2010–2019	Population: ACS total population estimate 2015–2019	Race and Hispanic or Latino origin (percent): White alone, not Hispanic or Latino	Race and Hispanic or Latino origin (percent): Black alone, not Hispanic or Latino	Race and Hispanic or Latino origin (percent): Asian alone, not Hispanic or Latino	Race and Hispanic or Latino origin (percent): All other races or 2 or more races, not Hispanic or Latino	Race and Hispanic or Latino origin (percent): Hispanic or Latino[1]	Age (percent): Under 18 years old	Age (percent): Age 65 years and older	Age (percent): Median age	Educational attainment of persons age 25 and older: Percent High school diploma or less	Educational attainment of persons age 25 and older: Percent Bachelor's degree or more	Occupied housing units: Total	Occupied housing units: Percent with a computer
	1	2	3	4	5	6	7	8	9	10	11	12	13	14	15	16
MONTANA—Con.																
Big Sandy town	595	562	-5.5	560	83.4	1.8	3.0	11.8	0.0	25.0	19.6	42.0	48.1	27.8	220	81.4
Big Sky CDP	2,308	-	-	3,058	88.8	0.0	0.6	2.3	8.3	17.7	9.1	33.3	16.3	60.7	1,181	99.2
Big Timber city	1,657	1,701	2.7	1,639	91.7	0.0	0.0	3.6	4.7	23.6	24.8	46.1	45.2	22.9	722	82.1
Billings city	104,284	109,577	5.1	109,595	85.1	0.6	0.8	7.1	6.3	23.0	16.6	36.9	34.0	35.0	46,818	91.7
Birney CDP	137	-	-	110	0.0	0.0	0.0	100.0	0.0	32.7	21.8	29.5	37.8	12.2	33	100.0
Black Eagle CDP	904	-	-	923	86.2	0.0	0.0	13.8	0.0	23.3	20.6	50.1	50.4	23.5	429	73.0
Boneau CDP	380	-	-	354	0.0	1.1	0.0	91.2	7.6	26.8	6.5	25.5	69.4	4.6	106	44.3
Bonner-West Riverside CDP	1,663	-	-	1,486	96.1	0.0	0.4	0.3	3.2	20.5	13.9	33.1	50.0	15.6	675	86.7
Boulder city	1,179	1,276	8.2	869	85.6	0.0	0.0	6.9	7.5	16.1	20.7	49.0	59.5	17.4	331	91.8
Box Elder CDP	87	-	-	47	70.2	0.0	0.0	14.9	14.9	2.1	14.9	48.8	68.2	2.3	28	46.4
Boyd CDP	35	-	-	61	96.7	0.0	0.0	0.0	3.3	3.3	19.7	31.9	18.6	71.2	25	100.0
Bozeman city	37,273	49,831	33.7	46,746	89.6	0.7	2.2	3.7	3.8	14.9	9.2	27.8	14.2	58.7	19,505	96.2
Brady CDP	140	-	-	149	100.0	0.0	0.0	0.0	0.0	24.2	18.8	39.7	38.1	37.2	54	100.0
Bridger town	708	755	6.6	775	94.7	0.0	0.0	3.7	1.5	19.1	30.2	48.3	46.5	15.2	311	87.1
Bridger CDP	30	-	-	103	88.3	0.0	0.0	11.7	0.0	28.2	0.0	29.3	0.0	62.7	39	100.0
Broadus town	475	462	-2.7	518	94.8	0.0	0.0	3.9	1.4	17.0	23.7	39.4	44.4	21.1	206	91.7
Broadview town	192	183	-4.7	150	95.3	0.0	0.0	3.3	1.3	15.3	25.3	46.8	41.7	13.9	66	77.3
Brockton CDP	255	-	-	319	3.8	0.0	0.0	95.6	0.6	34.8	4.1	25.6	49.1	14.1	79	53.2
Browning town	982	1,014	3.3	940	4.0	0.0	0.0	96.0	0.0	28.6	9.9	31.7	50.5	12.9	322	66.1
Busby CDP	745	-	-	647	1.9	0.0	0.0	89.2	9.0	41.9	4.3	23.7	42.1	12.6	123	83.7
Butte-Silver Bow (consolidated city)	34,209	34,915	2.1	34,770	90.4	0.5	0.7	3.7	4.6	20.2	18.7	40.0	39.5	27.2	14,960	84.1
Butte-Silver Bow (balance)	33,505	34,207	2.1	33,964	90.3	0.6	0.8	3.8	4.6	20.1	18.7	40.0	39.3	27.4	14,605	84.1
Bynum CDP	31	-	-	25	80.0	0.0	0.0	0.0	20.0	0.0	72.0	71.8	52.2	4.3	15	73.3
Camas CDP	58	-	-	73	57.5	0.0	0.0	19.2	23.3	26.0	24.7	57.1	57.4	7.4	30	73.3
Camp Three CDP	173	-	-	134	96.3	0.0	1.5	2.2	0.0	30.6	17.2	45.6	43.5	27.1	67	79.1
Cardwell CDP	50	-	-	104	98.1	0.0	0.0	1.9	0.0	40.4	16.3	28.4	62.7	20.3	25	80.0
Carlton CDP	694	-	-	750	90.0	0.0	5.2	2.7	2.1	14.4	31.2	53.9	53.7	33.5	347	86.2
Carter CDP	58	-	-	87	100.0	0.0	0.0	0.0	0.0	18.4	6.9	25.9	73.1	11.5	21	66.7
Cascade town	686	679		712	89.6	0.0	1.3	6.5	2.7	25.3	29.2	47.0	51.1	18.2	292	72.9
Charlo CDP	379	-	-	286	79.4	4.9	0.0	14.3	1.4	22.7	8.4	39.2	45.6	23.6	132	88.6
Charlos Heights CDP	120	-	-	17	100.0	0.0	0.0	0.0	0.0	0.0	0.0	0.0	0.0	0.0	17	100.0
Chester town	850	853	0.4	1,099	97.5	0.0	0.0	1.0	1.5	24.3	31.9	52.7	40.7	20.6	477	87.4
Chinook city	1,205	1,254	4.1	1,057	87.3	1.8	0.0	9.3	1.6	20.2	22.6	47.2	38.7	26.7	588	77.6
Choteau city	1,673	1,710	2.2	1,829	91.9	1.5	0.0	4.2	2.5	19.8	26.5	49.1	46.0	23.4	820	85.6
Churchill CDP	902	-	-	1,035	95.6	0.0	1.4	0.0	3.1	31.0	19.8	41.8	34.7	41.7	390	88.5
Circle town	623	605	-2.9	481	97.1	0.0	0.0	2.9	0.0	16.4	35.3	38.2	49.7	13.0	234	76.5
Clancy CDP	1,661	-	-	2,052	89.0	0.0	0.0	10.3	0.6	20.6	21.8	45.9	29.9	33.6	746	94.6
Clinton CDP	1,052	-	-	757	76.8	0.0	2.9	8.9	11.5	20.2	13.1	41.7	46.7	19.8	279	91.4
Clyde Park town	299	311	4.0	276	99.3	0.0	0.0	0.7	0.0	25.0	19.6	51.0	40.4	17.2	135	84.4
Colstrip city	2,216	2,246	1.4	2,448	69.0	0.0	1.5	14.6	14.9	32.3	6.1	42.1	35.9	19.0	842	95.2
Columbia Falls city	4,717	5,876	24.6	5,429	95.5	0.0	0.2	2.3	2.0	21.6	15.6	44.1	35.2	26.8	2,368	88.4
Columbus town	1,888	2,079	10.1	2,194	93.3	0.0	1.3	2.3	3.1	31.6	14.7	36.6	40.9	26.2	794	88.3
Condon CDP	343	-	-	247	96.4	0.0	0.0	0.0	3.6	3.6	43.7	64.0	47.3	31.3	147	92.5
Conner CDP	216	-	-	98	95.9	0.0	0.0	0.0	4.1	14.3	9.2	53.8	61.9	11.9	46	89.1
Conrad city	2,574	2,470	-4.0	2,633	96.4	0.2	0.0	2.3	1.1	24.1	21.3	43.8	39.6	19.8	1,058	82.4
Cooke City CDP	75	-	-	63	93.7	0.0	0.0	0.0	6.3	1.6	6.3	51.5	12.7	50.9	41	97.6
Coram CDP	539	-	-	434	89.2	0.0	0.0	10.8	0.0	20.0	17.1	51.4	39.9	17.8	186	82.8
Corvallis CDP	976	-	-	976	96.8	0.0	0.0	0.0	3.2	32.9	15.4	38.9	45.5	10.1	382	93.2
Corwin Springs CDP	109	-	-	87	78.2	0.0	0.0	10.3	11.5	16.1	39.1	56.0	27.4	47.9	44	100.0
Craig CDP	43	-	-	16	100.0	0.0	0.0	0.0	0.0	0.0	25.0	56.3	50.0	25.0	13	69.2
Crane CDP	102	-	-	186	100.0	0.0	0.0	0.0	0.0	17.7	11.3	53.7	20.0	45.9	79	100.0
Crow Agency CDP	1,616	-	-	2,010	1.0	0.0	0.0	94.5	4.5	40.1	8.6	23.7	50.2	10.0	406	73.2
Culbertson town	720	795	10.4	690	84.6	0.7	0.0	13.8	0.9	27.8	20.6	38.7	38.9	25.2	242	90.9
Custer CDP	159	-	-	120	90.8	0.0	0.0	0.8	8.3	20.0	37.5	56.5	62.8	14.9	70	75.7
Cut Bank city	2,929	3,061	4.5	3,058	65.2	0.5	0.1	26.1	8.1	32.4	15.5	34.3	44.3	20.4	1,204	81.6
Darby town	720	798	10.8	745	89.9	0.0	1.3	7.4	1.3	14.1	21.6	49.4	56.2	10.3	350	83.4
Dayton CDP	84	-	-	97	94.8	0.0	0.0	5.2	0.0	8.2	45.4	64.1	40.0	35.3	48	85.4
De Borgia CDP	78	-	-	86	100.0	0.0	0.0	0.0	0.0	0.0	59.3	65.7	86.0	0.0	42	100.0
Deer Lodge city	3,162	2,853	-9.8	2,934	95.3	0.6	0.0	3.9	0.2	15.6	29.2	53.5	39.4	24.8	1,447	87.6
Denton town	246	233	-5.3	296	89.2	0.0	0.0	9.5	1.4	23.0	17.2	48.2	9.8	28.4	131	90.8
Dillon city	4,142	4,301	3.8	4,261	91.1	0.1	0.3	2.8	5.8	16.7	18.0	31.5	31.0	34.3	1,766	92.6
Dixon CDP	203	-	-	216	72.2	0.0	0.0	21.8	6.0	28.7	25.5	47.0	45.5	29.7	86	91.9
Dodson town	126	117	-7.1	94	33.0	0.0	0.0	53.2	13.8	38.3	28.7	21.9	61.0	4.9	33	72.7
Drummond town	307	335	9.1	271	91.1	1.1	0.0	7.7	0.0	26.9	12.2	39.5	50.0	20.1	118	72.9
Dupuyer CDP	86	-	-	118	89.8	0.0	0.0	10.2	0.0	0.0	58.5	69.2	50.9	14.3	48	77.1
Dutton town	316	319	0.9	270	95.2	0.0	0.0	3.3	1.5	13.7	23.0	52.6	44.3	19.2	135	81.5
East Glacier Park Village CDP	363	-	-	388	47.4	0.0	0.8	51.8	0.0	29.4	13.7	37.0	22.9	46.2	140	90.7
East Helena city	2,011	2,103	4.6	1,514	87.1	0.0	0.3	10.4	2.2	16.4	22.9	46.4	37.3	21.0	759	89.2
East Missoula CDP	2,157	-	-	2,111	94.3	0.0	0.3	3.6	1.8	19.2	15.3	39.6	30.0	33.3	909	83.5
Edgar CDP	114	-	-	135	90.4	0.0	0.0	9.6	0.0	17.8	27.4	54.1	69.2	3.8	66	59.1
Ekalaka town	329	372	13.1	363	96.1	0.0	0.0	3.9	0.0	7.7	32.5	57.2	44.6	17.3	218	84.9
Elkhorn CDP	10	-	-	-	-	-	-	-	-	-	-	-	-	-	-	-
Elliston CDP	219	-	-	207	98.6	0.0	0.0	1.4	0.0	18.4	25.1	46.7	45.8	23.2	101	92.1
Elmo CDP	180	-	-	165	33.9	0.0	0.0	66.1	0.0	35.8	10.9	29.1	49.1	16.0	73	76.7
Emigrant CDP	488	-	-	271	100.0	0.0	0.0	0.0	0.0	0.0	45.4	56.0	23.0	45.9	169	85.2
Ennis town	838	993	18.5	849	93.8	0.2	0.0	4.9	1.1	10.5	28.3	48.4	35.8	20.0	407	85.3
Eureka town	1,403	1,406	0.2	1,645	90.6	0.0	0.0	5.1	4.3	16.4	27.2	51.7	62.2	14.2	653	79.5
Evaro CDP	322	-	-	343	71.4	1.5	0.0	27.1	0.0	23.6	16.9	39.9	47.2	12.6	124	73.4
Evergreen CDP	7,616	-	-	8,002	86.3	0.0	0.6	2.0	11.1	25.6	13.5	41.3	52.1	14.3	2,912	90.2
Fairfield town	694	723	4.2	607	93.7	0.8	2.0	3.5	0.0	26.7	20.1	38.9	36.3	28.7	261	84.3
Fairview town	837	864	3.2	919	92.7	0.0	0.0	2.7	4.6	26.6	18.0	36.5	46.9	14.9	334	77.5
Fallon CDP	164	-	-	107	87.9	0.0	9.3	0.0	2.8	43.9	0.0	37.2	60.0	5.0	30	100.0
Finley Point CDP	480	-	-	413	89.3	0.0	0.0	7.5	3.1	6.5	39.2	60.3	52.5	20.3	258	84.9
Flaxville town	71	67	-5.6	17	82.4	0.0	0.0	0.0	17.6	0.0	5.9	54.3	12.5	43.8	9	100.0
Florence CDP	765	-	-	643	88.5	0.0	0.0	3.9	7.6	33.3	12.3	31.2	29.1	31.0	263	100.0
Forest Hill Village CDP	206	-	-	117	100.0	0.0	0.0	0.0	0.0	0.0	13.7	54.7	41.0	0.0	117	86.3
Forsyth city	1,860	1,770	-4.8	1,495	97.2	0.0	0.1	2.2	0.5	14.1	31.2	51.2	57.5	12.4	720	75.0
Fort Belknap Agency CDP	1,293	-	-	1,542	3.0	0.5	0.0	90.4	6.1	41.6	6.9	23.9	36.8	15.3	425	74.6
Fort Benton city	1,466	1,432	-2.3	1,523	96.5	0.0	1.0	0.6	1.9	21.7	25.3	45.0	40.1	30.7	666	81.1

1 May be of any race.

STATE City, town, township, borough, or CDP (county if applicable)	Population				Race and Hispanic or Latino origin (percent)					Age (percent)			Educational attainment of persons age 25 and older		Occupied housing units	
	2010 census total population	2019 estimated population	Percent change 2010–2019	ACS total population estimate 2015–2019	White alone, not Hispanic or Latino	Black alone, not Hispanic or Latino	Asian alone, not Hispanic or Latino	All other races or 2 or more races, not Hispanic or Latino	Hispanic or Latino[1]	Under 18 years old	Age 65 years and older	Median age	Percent High school diploma or less	Percent Bachelor's degree or more	Total	Percent with a computer
	1	2	3	4	5	6	7	8	9	10	11	12	13	14	15	16
MONTANA—Con.																
Fortine CDP	325	-	-	421	91.2	0.0	1.2	0.0	7.6	32.5	11.4	27.9	52.2	19.2	134	90.3
Fort Peck town	233	239	2.6	246	74.8	0.0	0.0	25.2	0.0	16.3	26.4	47.5	25.1	23.6	128	91.4
Fort Shaw CDP	280	-	-	116	93.1	0.0	0.0	6.9	0.0	14.7	46.6	63.2	39.4	11.1	52	69.2
Fort Smith CDP	161	-	-	119	100.0	0.0	0.0	0.0	0.0	12.6	31.1	61.2	29.8	29.8	53	100.0
Four Corners CDP	3,146	-	-	5,084	95.1	0.5	0.0	0.8	3.5	29.8	11.5	36.7	16.1	52.1	1,908	98.8
Fox Lake CDP	158	-	-	100	100.0	0.0	0.0	0.0	0.0	21.0	13.0	42.1	27.7	35.4	41	97.6
Frazer CDP	362	-	-	344	2.0	0.0	0.0	95.1	2.9	40.4	2.0	24.5	54.8	10.1	95	62.1
Frenchtown CDP	1,825	-	-	1,949	95.7	1.2	0.9	2.2	0.0	27.0	12.0	42.5	36.0	21.5	709	80.4
Froid town	194	203	4.6	235	73.6	0.0	0.0	1.7	24.7	25.5	17.4	42.2	41.7	28.5	76	94.7
Fromberg town	439	464	5.7	418	96.7	0.0	0.0	0.0	3.3	23.0	35.2	54.1	52.9	19.6	191	77.5
Gallatin Gateway CDP	856	-	-	884	91.5	0.0	0.5	7.7	0.3	24.5	11.9	42.4	29.6	42.0	361	90.0
Gallatin River Ranch CDP	69	-	-	146	96.6	0.0	0.0	3.4	0.0	31.5	19.9	45.1	38.0	47.0	51	100.0
Gardiner CDP	875	-	-	879	88.5	0.0	0.0	7.2	4.3	8.8	8.8	43.2	30.2	44.9	492	83.5
Garrison CDP	96	-	-	80	100.0	0.0	0.0	0.0	0.0	35.0	33.8	38.5	43.1	3.9	31	54.8
Geraldine town	255	249	-2.4	179	96.1	0.0	0.0	0.0	3.9	10.6	36.9	58.7	36.5	21.6	96	75.0
Geyser CDP	87	-	-	129	73.6	0.0	0.0	0.0	26.4	21.7	17.8	55.2	43.3	17.5	66	78.8
Gibson Flats CDP	199	-	-	200	62.5	0.0	0.0	37.5	0.0	26.0	17.5	58.0	37.2	31.8	82	85.4
Gildford CDP	179	-	-	171	98.8	0.0	0.0	1.2	0.0	40.9	20.5	32.5	26.7	34.4	58	82.8
Glasgow city	3,284	3,322	1.2	3,344	91.5	0.7	0.0	5.1	2.7	21.3	19.7	40.1	40.4	26.9	1,528	89.2
Glendive city	4,939	4,910	-0.6	5,126	93.2	1.4	0.0	3.0	2.4	21.5	18.5	39.3	41.1	23.9	2,126	83.9
Grass Range town	110	105	-4.5	120	95.0	0.0	0.0	0.0	5.0	12.5	37.5	59.6	43.3	14.4	71	74.6
Great Falls city	59,121	58,434	-1.2	58,835	84.3	0.8	0.6	9.4	4.8	21.8	18.4	38.6	40.9	25.4	25,659	84.0
Greycliff CDP	112	-	-	83	73.5	0.0	7.2	12.0	7.2	14.5	9.6	43.3	54.4	7.4	39	94.9
Hamilton city	4,273	4,898	14.6	4,723	90.8	0.0	0.6	3.3	5.3	17.9	25.2	40.0	39.5	32.3	2,181	86.8
Happys Inn CDP	164	-	-	68	100.0	0.0	0.0	0.0	0.0	0.0	14.7	59.4	16.2	22.1	50	80.0
Hardin city	3,662	3,788	3.4	3,808	39.5	0.0	0.3	47.5	12.6	38.0	10.6	26.8	50.8	24.6	1,162	84.9
Harlem city	806	835	3.6	820	37.9	0.0	0.9	54.8	6.5	23.8	12.1	33.7	36.9	24.0	288	84.7
Harlowton city	999	987	-1.2	1,170	93.6	0.0	0.0	1.1	5.3	21.1	21.5	41.9	53.5	17.4	465	89.0
Harrison CDP	137	-	-	103	100.0	0.0	0.0	0.0	0.0	24.3	14.6	54.1	81.3	0.0	37	78.4
Havre city	9,497	9,791	3.1	9,786	79.6	0.3	0.6	14.8	4.7	25.3	15.0	34.1	37.5	26.4	4,160	89.3
Havre North CDP	716	-	-	614	85.0	0.0	0.0	15.0	0.0	12.5	27.0	45.9	38.9	31.8	278	83.8
Hays CDP	843	-	-	930	5.6	0.0	0.0	92.9	1.5	34.5	11.1	26.1	40.6	15.4	259	71.4
Heart Butte CDP	582	-	-	600	0.7	0.0	0.8	96.3	2.2	34.5	7.0	26.4	40.6	8.7	106	76.4
Hebgen Lake Estates CDP	70	-	-	81	80.2	0.0	19.8	0.0	0.0	46.9	60.8	19.8	19.8		41	100.0
Helena city	28,809	33,124	15.0	32,024	90.6	0.5	0.9	3.8	4.3	19.2	19.3	40.1	23.9	47.9	14,052	89.4
Helena Flats CDP	1,043	-	-	1,148	86.1	0.0	0.7	10.8	2.4	23.8	15.4	38.6	43.0	21.1	405	79.5
Helena Valley Northeast CDP	2,995	-	-	3,557	94.8	0.2	0.0	4.6	0.4	16.8	28.7	52.4	30.6	37.7	1,227	93.2
Helena Valley Northwest CDP	3,482	-	-	4,465	94.2	0.0	0.6	2.1	3.2	30.3	9.1	32.6	25.7	35.5	1,523	94.8
Helena Valley Southeast CDP	8,227	-	-	8,448	95.3	0.0	0.2	4.0	0.5	30.0	8.7	31.0	39.0	22.0	3,086	95.1
Helena Valley West Central CDP	7,883	-	-	8,082	89.7	0.1	1.1	6.7	2.4	25.8	17.7	42.0	29.5	33.8	2,964	93.0
Helena West Side CDP	1,637	-	-	1,039	83.0	0.4	0.0	6.8	9.8	16.9	12.1	41.4	30.0	35.3	482	72.2
Heron CDP	282	-	-	141	95.0	0.0	0.0	0.0	5.0	7.8	40.4	61.9	61.5	24.6	97	88.7
Herron CDP	116	-	-	189	31.7	0.0	0.0	6.9	61.4	20.6	24.3	30.7	31.0	50.0	44	88.6
Highwood CDP	176	-	-	201	91.0	0.0	0.0	7.0	2.0	24.9	14.9	47.3	41.9	26.5	80	78.8
Hingham town	118	119	0.8	125	93.6	0.0	0.0	3.2	3.2	13.6	37.6	58.2	50.9	19.8	68	86.8
Hinsdale CDP	217	-	-	242	92.6	0.0	0.0	7.4	0.0	14.9	27.7	49.4	39.4	25.7	127	92.1
Hobson city	225	231	2.7	234	86.8	0.0	0.0	12.4	0.9	25.2	34.6	59.8	50.9	20.2	108	84.3
Hot Springs town	541	582	7.6	558	91.0	0.0	0.0	5.9	3.0	8.6	38.0	59.6	53.2	18.9	288	61.8
Hungry Horse CDP	826	-	-	634	92.3	0.0	0.0	7.7	0.0	28.4	21.6	38.7	26.4	25.2	272	87.5
Huntley CDP	446	-	-	414	95.2	0.0	0.0	0.0	4.8	17.4	8.5	44.6	30.5	22.2	184	85.3
Huson CDP	210	-	-	56	100.0	0.0	0.0	0.0	0.0	0.0	0.0	61.5	100.0	0.0	37	100.0
Hysham town	312	304	-2.6	269	88.8	0.0	7.4	2.2	1.5	11.9	32.7	60.2	55.2	16.5	157	89.8
Indian Springs CDP	31	-	-	-	-	-	-	-	-	-	-	-	-	-	-	-
Inverness CDP	55	-	-	45	100.0	0.0	0.0	0.0	0.0	35.6	40.0	47.3	62.1	17.2	17	35.3
Ismay town	19	19	0.0	-	-	-	-	-	-	-	-	-	-	-	-	-
Jardine CDP	57	-	-	38	71.1	0.0	0.0	0.0	28.9	7.9	0.0	37.7	20.0	22.9	24	79.2
Jefferson City CDP	472	-	-	581	95.9	0.0	0.0	2.2	1.9	23.8	12.9	47.4	32.9	22.9	215	97.2
Jette CDP	253	-	-	143	77.6	0.0	0.0	22.4	0.0	7.7	62.9	75.0	20.5	9.1	76	100.0
Joliet town	581	655	12.7	513	97.7	0.0	0.0	2.3	0.0	22.6	22.2	39.7	43.7	16.5	183	88.5
Joplin CDP	157	-	-	218	100.0	0.0	0.0	0.0	0.0	29.4	16.1	35.1	21.1	24.8	83	95.2
Jordan town	352	386	9.7	442	98.4	1.6	0.0	0.0	0.0	15.2	28.7	51.2	51.6	11.9	207	84.5
Judith Gap city	126	125	-0.8	80	100.0	0.0	0.0	0.0	0.0	17.5	35.0	62.0	42.4	13.6	40	82.5
Kalispell city	20,042	24,565	22.6	23,241	92.2	0.7	1.4	2.8	2.9	23.3	17.1	36.8	35.5	30.0	9,318	89.8
Kerr CDP	251	-	-	73	100.0	0.0	0.0	0.0	0.0	0.0	100.0	77.6	35.6	43.8	42	100.0
Kevin town	154	136	-11.7	139	92.8	0.0	0.0	7.2	0.0	22.3	18.7	44.3	69.7	1.0	73	90.4
Kicking Horse CDP	286	-	-	45	82.2	0.0	0.0	17.8	0.0	0.0	82.2	75.4	17.8	44.4	28	100.0
Kila CDP	392	-	-	385	80.5	0.0	0.0	19.5	0.0	26.5	24.4	44.7	43.8	25.2	147	89.8
King Arthur Park CDP	738	-	-	1,686	94.1	0.0	0.0	3.3	2.6	19.2	2.0	29.4	20.0	44.5	663	94.9
Kings Point CDP	151	-	-	229	49.8	0.0	0.0	50.2	0.0	27.9	19.2	48.9	8.5	34.5	106	100.0
Klein CDP	168	-	-	53	100.0	0.0	0.0	0.0	0.0	24.5	0.0	58.3	52.5	25.0	30	66.7
Kremlin CDP	98	-	-	66	100.0	0.0	0.0	0.0	0.0	13.6	13.6	54.3	61.1	24.1	44	86.4
Lake Mary Ronan CDP	65	-	-	47	100.0	0.0	0.0	0.0	0.0	0.0	68.1	67.9	25.5	25.5	30	90.0
Lakeside CDP	2,669	-	-	2,249	97.9	0.0	0.2	1.0	1.0	11.5	40.6	62.6	30.0	38.8	1,079	86.4
Lame Deer CDP	2,052	-	-	2,086	2.9	0.3	0.0	94.0	2.8	37.7	7.4	25.8	37.9	14.2	515	66.0
Laurel city	6,752	6,735	-0.3	6,834	94.6	0.0	0.2	1.7	3.6	22.5	19.3	40.9	47.8	18.6	3,005	82.3
Lavina town	183	167	-8.7	180	86.1	0.0	0.0	13.9	0.0	12.2	20.0	55.0	55.1	21.7	89	89.9
Lewistown city	6,066	5,801	-4.4	5,885	91.8	0.1	0.7	5.8	1.5	23.4	20.3	38.4	41.7	27.1	2,726	87.4
Lewistown Heights CDP	407	-	-	266	100.0	0.0	0.0	0.0	0.0	8.6	26.7	56.2	51.7	13.5	105	86.7
Libby city	2,602	2,779	6.8	2,703	87.6	1.2	0.0	4.0	7.2	19.8	22.5	46.2	54.3	15.7	1,108	76.5
Lima town	221	227	2.7	180	94.4	0.0	0.0	5.6	0.0	9.4	43.9	59.5	44.4	9.2	109	64.2
Lincoln CDP	1,013	-	-	857	82.0	0.0	0.0	11.1	6.9	18.4	25.2	48.5	40.2	16.5	437	73.0
Lindisfarne CDP	284	-	-	409	100.0	0.0	0.0	0.0	0.0	11.2	12.2	41.8	15.7	33.6	143	100.0
Little Bitterroot Lake CDP	194	-	-	154	100.0	0.0	0.0	0.0	0.0	10.4	58.4	68.4	14.5	39.1	81	79.0
Little Browning CDP	206	-	-	210	26.2	0.0	0.0	73.8	0.0	50.5	0.0	17.9	69.6	8.7	49	100.0
Livingston city	7,043	7,801	10.8	7,575	92.0	1.0	0.0	3.0	4.0	19.4	20.2	40.6	39.7	28.8	3,711	87.0
Lockwood CDP	6,797	-	-	8,066	84.0	0.0	0.0	10.5	5.4	25.5	12.2	34.5	51.3	18.8	3,117	92.3
Lodge Grass town	428	447	4.4	456	3.9	0.0	0.0	94.5	1.5	36.4	9.0	25.5	52.1	5.1	104	41.3

1 May be of any race.

Table A. All Places — **Population and Housing**

STATE City, town, township, borough, or CDP (county if applicable)	Population				Race and Hispanic or Latino origin (percent)					Age (percent)			Educational attainment of persons age 25 and older		Occupied housing units	
	2010 census total population	2019 estimated population	Percent change 2010–2019	ACS total population estimate 2015–2019	White alone, not Hispanic or Latino	Black alone, not Hispanic or Latino	Asian alone, not Hispanic or Latino	All other races or 2 or more races, not Hispanic or Latino	Hispanic or Latino[1]	Under 18 years old	Age 65 years and older	Median age	Percent High school diploma or less	Percent Bachelor's degree or more	Total	Percent with a computer
	1	2	3	4	5	6	7	8	9	10	11	12	13	14	15	16
MONTANA—Con.																
Lodge Pole CDP	265	-	-	308	0.0	0.0	0.0	92.5	7.5	34.1	11.7	27.1	38.2	9.1	89	79.8
Logan CDP	99	-	-	20	100.0	0.0	0.0	0.0	0.0	0.0	50.0	0.0	100.0	0.0	20	100.0
Lolo CDP	3,892	-	-	3,961	91.9	0.4	2.5	2.8	2.4	27.9	10.7	33.7	34.2	34.6	1,447	95.4
Loma CDP	85	-	-	86	100.0	0.0	0.0	0.0	0.0	0.0	22.1	63.6	75.6	0.0	50	100.0
Lonepine CDP	162	-	-	160	83.8	0.0	0.0	13.8	2.5	18.8	34.4	52.3	41.0	15.4	81	71.6
Malmstrom AFB CDP	3,472	-	-	4,179	69.1	10.9	1.4	3.3	15.3	31.8	0.0	23.0	18.4	35.2	1,174	98.0
Malta city	1,994	1,861	-6.7	2,090	83.8	0.0	0.6	11.0	4.7	21.4	27.6	51.4	53.6	18.6	912	75.7
Manhattan town	1,517	1,906	25.6	1,549	90.6	0.0	0.0	7.5	1.9	26.4	19.1	40.3	26.3	35.6	649	83.4
Marion CDP	886	-	-	966	93.9	0.0	1.9	2.4	1.9	28.1	14.1	36.8	44.0	14.9	319	88.4
Martin City CDP	500	-	-	384	85.2	0.0	0.0	14.8	0.0	14.6	26.3	44.9	56.7	19.8	197	82.2
Martinsdale CDP	64	-	-	27	100.0	0.0	0.0	0.0	0.0	0.0	85.2	69.8	18.5	66.7	15	60.0
Marysville CDP	80	-	-	43	100.0	0.0	0.0	0.0	0.0	0.0	32.6	56.6	46.5	34.9	29	65.5
Maxville CDP	130	-	-	157	100.0	0.0	0.0	0.0	0.0	0.0	33.8	63.0	17.2	30.6	72	80.6
Medicine Lake town	225	223	-0.9	242	98.3	0.0	0.0	1.7	0.0	19.4	24.8	41.5	36.7	35.6	135	92.6
Melstone town	110	110	0.0	128	76.6	0.0	0.0	19.5	3.9	29.7	22.7	50.8	40.0	6.7	69	65.2
Miles City city	8,399	8,264	-1.6	8,487	92.2	0.8	0.1	3.4	3.4	21.3	19.1	40.0	36.8	24.4	3,650	85.0
Missoula city	67,358	75,516	12.1	73,710	88.5	0.8	2.1	4.9	3.7	17.8	12.8	32.8	22.3	47.9	32,313	93.6
Montana City CDP	2,715	-	-	2,872	98.2	0.4	0.2	1.0	0.2	23.8	15.3	47.1	24.0	47.4	997	96.9
Moore town	186	177	-4.8	181	99.4	0.0	0.0	0.6	0.0	21.0	31.5	55.1	49.3	19.9	80	82.5
Muddy CDP	617	-	-	617	4.5	0.0	0.0	88.8	6.6	42.5	4.5	22.5	38.9	4.3	141	73.8
Musselshell CDP	60	-	-	44	100.0	0.0	0.0	0.0	0.0	9.1	45.5	60.5	75.0	25.0	27	74.1
Nashua town	288	287	-0.3	331	89.1	0.3	0.0	7.9	2.7	21.5	18.7	44.1	56.4	12.7	159	76.1
Neihart town	51	49	-3.9	37	100.0	0.0	0.0	0.0	0.0	13.5	24.3	60.4	28.1	40.6	20	90.0
Niarada CDP	27	-	-	7	100.0	0.0	0.0	0.0	0.0	0.0	57.1	0.0	57.1	0.0	7	100.0
North Browning CDP	2,408	-	-	2,861	4.0	0.0	0.0	92.7	3.3	36.9	10.5	28.6	52.5	20.9	730	57.9
Noxon CDP	218	-	-	223	97.8	0.0	0.0	2.2	0.0	15.7	28.7	45.5	56.9	15.4	109	72.5
Old Agency CDP	107	-	-	74	9.5	5.4	0.0	85.1	0.0	29.7	9.5	43.5	68.8	16.7	35	62.9
Olney CDP	191	-	-	146	100.0	0.0	0.0	0.0	0.0	17.8	18.5	39.2	57.0	3.5	65	86.2
Opheim town	83	83	0.0	96	66.7	0.0	0.0	2.1	31.3	0.0	29.2	55.0	32.6	12.0	75	93.3
Orchard Homes CDP	5,197	-	-	5,847	92.1	0.0	0.1	6.3	1.5	19.0	21.5	40.9	25.1	41.9	2,215	93.5
Outlook town	47	47	0.0	82	92.7	0.0	0.0	0.0	7.3	36.6	18.3	34.0	28.8	25.0	27	70.4
Ovando CDP	81	-	-	64	100.0	0.0	0.0	0.0	0.0	18.8	21.9	49.5	72.7	2.3	22	68.2
Pablo CDP	2,254	-	-	2,274	28.4	0.9	0.0	63.6	7.1	36.8	7.9	26.9	47.3	15.8	721	84.5
Paradise CDP	163	-	-	158	98.1	0.0	0.0	0.0	1.9	25.9	32.3	48.2	57.0	9.3	57	57.9
Park City CDP	983	-	-	813	100.0	0.0	0.0	0.0	0.0	25.5	20.0	40.5	48.1	15.8	310	93.9
Parker School CDP	340	-	-	625	1.1	0.0	0.0	98.9	0.0	48.3	4.8	19.5	48.1	7.6	114	86.0
Philipsburg town	843	923	9.5	768	97.3	0.0	0.0	1.3	1.4	16.8	25.9	42.9	48.4	23.6	261	78.2
Piltzville CDP	395	-	-	593	99.2	0.0	0.0	0.0	0.8	9.9	15.3	52.6	39.1	19.9	227	95.6
Pinesdale town	938	1,011	7.8	955	96.6	0.0	0.0	1.0	2.3	42.7	5.9	20.2	68.3	5.8	191	97.4
Pioneer Junction CDP	959	-	-	813	95.3	0.0	0.0	4.7	0.0	19.1	42.1	63.0	59.6	17.0	377	85.9
Plains town	1,049	1,139	8.6	1,049	95.0	0.7	0.0	2.9	1.4	15.8	27.9	49.7	62.2	18.2	444	63.1
Plentywood city	1,740	1,732	-0.5	1,825	88.1	0.0	0.5	4.6	6.8	17.8	25.9	47.3	42.2	21.2	889	89.4
Plevna town	162	147	-9.3	334	95.5	0.0	0.0	0.0	4.5	48.2	6.0	26.3	33.1	25.4	95	92.6
Polson city	4,586	5,060	10.3	4,918	64.6	0.6	0.6	29.5	4.7	23.4	20.6	36.5	36.5	31.5	2,060	85.3
Ponderosa Pines CDP	336	-	-	488	78.9	0.0	0.0	21.1	0.0	25.4	16.6	39.5	22.4	18.7	198	95.5
Pony CDP	118	-	-	141	95.7	0.0	0.7	0.7	2.8	32.6	25.5	38.7	38.9	35.6	54	83.3
Poplar city	804	840	4.5	852	23.4	0.5	0.0	71.9	4.2	30.2	8.2	28.9	38.3	22.0	255	80.8
Power CDP	179	-	-	177	90.4	0.0	0.0	9.6	0.0	25.4	28.8	49.6	34.2	18.3	79	77.2
Pray CDP	681	-	-	749	96.4	0.0	0.0	2.3	1.3	14.8	20.0	57.6	39.7	24.1	370	95.9
Pryor CDP	618	-	-	539	16.0	0.0	0.0	77.6	6.5	31.9	11.1	35.9	49.7	12.7	144	77.8
Rader Creek CDP	363	-	-	282	93.3	0.0	0.0	0.0	6.7	11.0	14.2	56.1	33.1	27.9	164	93.3
Radersburg CDP	66	-	-	61	100.0	0.0	0.0	0.0	0.0	0.0	86.9	77.5	68.9	18.0	61	31.1
Ravalli CDP	76	-	-	90	85.6	0.0	0.0	14.4	0.0	0.0	54.4	66.4	23.3	24.4	59	64.4
Red Lodge city	2,119	2,303	8.7	2,212	89.6	0.9	0.6	1.2	7.8	15.1	23.1	49.3	31.5	38.5	1,028	90.4
Reed Point CDP	193	-	-	307	94.8	0.0	0.0	5.2	0.0	22.1	22.1	39.7	41.0	17.0	129	68.2
Reserve CDP	23	-	-	35	97.1	0.0	0.0	2.9	0.0	11.4	17.1	59.4	32.1	17.9	21	85.7
Rexford town	105	158	50.5	123	61.0	0.0	0.0	0.0	39.0	13.0	25.2	53.3	83.2	0.0	51	90.2
Richey town	177	171	-3.4	186	89.8	0.0	1.6	3.2	5.4	19.9	17.7	45.0	35.3	25.0	96	82.3
Riverbend CDP	484	-	-	272	94.5	0.0	5.5	0.0	0.0	12.5	29.4	54.3	34.2	16.0	129	90.7
Roberts CDP	361	-	-	299	100.0	0.0	0.0	0.0	0.0	25.4	20.1	45.7	32.7	36.4	129	82.2
Rocky Boy's Agency CDP	355	-	-	402	2.7	0.0	0.0	97.3	0.0	36.6	17.4	28.9	60.8	20.7	105	61.9
Rocky Boy West CDP	890	-	-	852	2.5	0.0	0.0	87.6	10.0	34.9	5.9	25.9	51.4	7.9	257	43.2
Rocky Point CDP	97	-	-	30	100.0	0.0	0.0	0.0	0.0	0.0	100.0	0.0	46.7	0.0	16	0.0
Rollins CDP	209	-	-	201	88.1	0.0	0.0	3.5	8.5	17.9	34.3	52.8	19.1	53.9	98	98.0
Ronan city	1,894	2,116	11.7	1,955	52.7	0.5	1.7	36.8	8.2	26.9	18.5	36.1	44.4	17.6	797	82.6
Roscoe CDP	15	-	-	49	100.0	0.0	0.0	0.0	0.0	0.0	20.4	55.1	24.5	10.2	18	100.0
Rosebud CDP	111	-	-	72	100.0	0.0	0.0	0.0	0.0	11.1	4.2	56.7	29.7	37.5	41	70.7
Roundup city	1,774	1,850	4.3	1,790	90.4	0.0	2.3	3.6	3.7	20.0	24.3	46.1	63.8	14.6	854	75.4
Roy CDP	108	-	-	138	93.5	2.9	0.0	3.6	0.0	26.1	21.7	48.7	39.8	11.2	64	87.5
Rudyard CDP	258	-	-	183	100.0	0.0	0.0	0.0	0.0	39.3	9.3	35.4	46.8	28.8	75	89.3
Ryegate town	247	234	-5.3	202	86.1	0.0	0.0	0.0	13.9	17.8	32.7	60.4	50.6	17.5	92	77.2
Saco town	199	187	-6.0	244	91.4	0.0	0.0	8.6	0.0	13.9	16.8	49.0	53.8	7.7	110	86.4
Saddle Butte CDP	128	-	-	65	92.3	0.0	0.0	7.7	0.0	10.8	21.5	53.3	56.1	15.8	41	87.8
St. Ignatius town	799	828	3.6	839	49.8	0.0	0.0	47.8	2.4	31.5	16.7	35.3	50.7	16.1	314	81.8
St. Marie CDP	264	-	-	470	60.6	0.0	0.0	35.5	3.8	21.5	23.6	46.4	56.9	3.8	232	89.2
St. Pierre CDP	350	-	-	343	0.0	0.0	0.0	100.0	0.0	42.6	7.9	20.4	43.5	14.3	79	68.4
St. Regis CDP	319	-	-	210	98.6	0.0	0.0	1.4	0.0	33.3	27.1	40.5	45.2	31.9	88	71.6
St. Xavier CDP	83	-	-	136	3.7	0.0	0.0	96.3	0.0	35.3	15.4	30.5	12.5	41.3	31	77.4
Sand Coulee CDP	212	-	-	210	100.0	0.0	0.0	0.0	0.0	11.9	24.3	52.4	36.4	35.8	90	90.0
Sangrey CDP	306	-	-	351	0.0	0.0	0.0	97.2	2.8	43.6	6.8	22.7	52.1	2.5	81	49.4
Santa Rita CDP	113	-	-	250	90.0	0.0	0.0	7.6	2.4	41.2	3.2	20.6	41.0	10.5	107	91.6
Savage CDP	-	-	-	268	84.7	0.0	0.0	15.3	0.0	15.7	25.7	51.8	50.5	13.4	122	78.7
Scobey city	1,019	997	-2.2	1,155	92.6	0.0	0.6	3.0	3.7	20.6	29.4	51.5	49.4	17.4	599	75.8
Sedan CDP	99	-	-	77	94.8	0.0	0.0	5.2	0.0	0.0	53.2	65.6	14.3	26.0	57	94.7
Seeley Lake CDP	1,659	-	-	1,286	91.6	0.0	3.0	1.6	3.8	8.9	32.5	52.7	42.4	21.1	614	90.2
Shawmut CDP	42	-	-	51	100.0	0.0	0.0	0.0	0.0	0.0	62.7	66.3	66.7	15.7	29	69.0
Shelby city	3,394	3,023	-10.9	3,078	82.9	0.7	0.6	10.4	5.3	17.3	18.2	44.0	55.1	13.5	1,123	85.8
Shepherd CDP	516	-	-	895	90.8	0.0	0.0	9.2	0.0	38.5	5.5	24.9	34.2	31.9	261	100.0
Sheridan town	658	742	12.8	843	90.0	0.0	0.0	6.6	3.3	16.3	32.3	57.2	33.7	29.0	346	86.7
Sidney city	5,324	6,173	15.9	6,416	85.1	0.0	0.0	7.6	7.3	26.5	13.6	35.3	42.5	18.4	2,610	83.9
Silesia CDP	96	-	-	21	100.0	0.0	0.0	0.0	0.0	0.0	0.0	61.1	23.8	23.8	16	68.8
Silver Gate CDP	20	-	-	29	100.0	0.0	0.0	0.0	0.0	13.8	37.9	63.5	12.0	52.0	13	84.6

1 May be of any race.

Table A. All Places — **Population and Housing**

STATE City, town, township, borough, or CDP (county if applicable)	Population 2010 census total population	2019 estimated population	Percent change 2010–2019	ACS total population estimate 2015–2019	Race and Hispanic or Latino origin (percent) White alone, not Hispanic or Latino	Black alone, not Hispanic or Latino	Asian alone, not Hispanic or Latino	All other races or 2 or more races, not Hispanic or Latino	Hispanic or Latino[1]	Age (percent) Under 18 years old	Age 65 years and older	Median age	Educational attainment of persons age 25 and older Percent High school diploma or less	Percent Bachelor's degree or more	Occupied housing units Total	Percent with a computer
	1	2	3	4	5	6	7	8	9	10	11	12	13	14	15	16
MONTANA—Con.																
Simms CDP	354	-	-	342	96.5	0.0	0.0	3.5	0.0	39.2	20.8	39.1	34.6	18.3	119	95.8
Somers CDP	1,109	-	-	1,095	99.5	0.0	0.0	0.5	0.1	12.3	22.6	55.2	40.7	27.1	449	78.0
South Browning CDP	1,785	-	-	1,600	3.4	0.0	0.0	95.6	1.0	45.8	9.2	24.4	53.0	18.6	471	53.3
South Glastonbury CDP	-	-	-	345	91.3	0.0	4.1	4.6	0.0	11.6	16.2	59.0	31.1	22.0	198	97.5
South Hills CDP	517	-	-	671	94.5	0.0	0.0	4.8	0.7	35.3	8.3	36.6	3.4	76.3	187	100.0
Spokane Creek CDP	355	-	-	467	100.0	0.0	0.0	0.0	0.0	2.6	19.9	56.1	31.4	31.4	183	94.5
Springdale CDP	42	-	-	19	100.0	0.0	0.0	0.0	0.0	5.3	21.1	59.8	50.0	0.0	9	100.0
Springhill CDP	130	-	-	126	100.0	0.0	0.0	0.0	0.0	17.5	17.5	49.1	20.2	41.5	39	100.0
Stanford town	404	391	-3.2	347	88.2	0.0	0.0	6.6	5.2	13.5	21.0	53.6	41.1	19.9	206	81.1
Starr School CDP	252	-	-	329	0.0	0.0	0.0	100.0	0.0	23.4	13.7	44.3	83.3	7.1	93	23.7
Stevensville town	1,822	2,072	13.7	2,182	93.0	0.3	0.0	4.5	2.2	26.9	18.4	36.0	39.7	27.1	931	89.5
Stockett CDP	169	-	-	180	82.8	0.0	0.0	17.2	0.0	27.8	15.0	37.0	48.8	15.7	72	83.3
Stryker CDP	26	-	-	19	100.0	0.0	0.0	0.0	0.0	42.1	0.0	37.4	100.0	0.0	6	100.0
Sula CDP	37	-	-	122	100.0	0.0	0.0	0.0	0.0	35.2	9.8	38.3	0.0	22.8	48	100.0
Sunburst town	375	332	-11.5	360	95.6	0.0	0.0	2.2	2.2	23.6	15.6	39.9	34.9	22.8	141	92.9
Sun Prairie CDP	1,630	-	-	1,717	93.1	0.8	0.0	6.1	0.0	27.8	23.0	39.1	52.9	16.0	649	86.7
Sun River CDP	124	-	-	56	100.0	0.0	0.0	0.0	0.0	37.5	8.9	18.9	18.5	37.0	27	100.0
Superior town	809	867	7.2	703	90.6	0.4	0.4	4.7	3.8	10.8	29.3	55.2	59.5	12.4	340	64.7
Swan Lake CDP	113	-	-	168	91.7	0.0	0.0	0.0	8.3	8.3	25.6	54.2	38.8	21.1	73	91.8
Sweet Grass CDP	58	-	-	58	100.0	0.0	0.0	0.0	0.0	22.4	10.3	37.6	11.1	46.7	26	100.0
Sylvanite CDP	103	-	-	78	94.9	0.0	5.1	0.0	0.0	7.7	30.8	55.5	23.6	33.3	37	75.7
Terry town	605	556	-8.1	694	97.8	0.0	0.0	0.3	1.9	26.5	32.9	48.1	46.6	24.0	290	81.7
The Silos CDP	506	-	-	507	100.0	0.0	0.0	0.0	0.0	21.5	28.0	47.0	15.5	44.7	175	100.0
Thompson Falls city	1,315	1,427	8.5	1,460	92.7	0.0	0.0	2.4	4.9	29.1	13.6	39.0	58.3	15.5	553	82.1
Three Forks city	1,865	2,055	10.2	1,729	94.4	0.0	0.6	0.5	4.5	20.1	20.9	45.1	46.3	20.5	728	85.9
Toston CDP	108	-	-	73	83.6	0.0	0.0	0.0	16.4	0.0	58.9	70.5	86.3	13.7	59	16.9
Townsend city	1,889	2,152	13.9	2,104	92.6	0.2	0.0	1.4	5.8	21.9	28.8	48.8	46.5	22.8	808	86.6
Trego CDP	541	-	-	569	96.8	0.4	0.0	0.4	2.5	9.3	30.4	60.5	45.8	26.1	249	89.6
Trout Creek CDP	242	-	-	178	88.2	8.4	3.4	0.0	0.0	11.2	48.3	60.5	43.0	19.0	90	100.0
Troy city	944	964	2.1	732	94.9	0.0	0.0	4.9	0.1	6.1	45.2	63.5	50.8	12.4	374	71.9
Turah CDP	306	-	-	366	92.9	0.0	3.8	3.3	0.0	20.8	19.7	45.1	27.8	45.2	128	100.0
Turner CDP	61	-	-	85	100.0	0.0	0.0	0.0	0.0	27.1	21.2	43.6	48.2	25.0	33	93.9
Turtle Lake CDP	209	-	-	318	10.1	0.0	0.0	89.9	0.0	61.9	7.5	9.8	66.9	0.0	62	71.0
Twin Bridges town	364	417	14.6	235	97.4	0.0	0.0	1.7	0.9	14.5	33.2	55.8	49.7	18.8	130	80.0
Ulm CDP	738	-	-	591	97.5	0.0	0.0	2.2	0.3	16.2	33.2	51.3	48.6	19.0	252	85.7
Valier town	509	486	-4.5	551	84.0	0.0	0.0	16.0	0.0	23.4	27.4	41.5	50.8	15.6	218	86.2
Vaughn CDP	658	-	-	807	85.0	0.0	0.0	13.8	1.2	25.2	14.0	39.6	58.1	14.4	321	85.7
Victor CDP	745	-	-	704	92.6	0.0	0.0	7.4	0.0	23.3	37.2	56.0	57.2	8.9	348	80.7
Virginia City town	192	216	12.5	207	91.8	0.0	1.0	2.9	4.3	8.7	33.3	60.4	33.3	25.4	95	88.4
Walkerville town	704	708	0.6	806	95.9	0.0	0.0	2.0	2.1	23.3	21.0	45.0	48.4	20.0	355	83.7
Weeksville CDP	83	-	-	65	100.0	0.0	0.0	0.0	0.0	21.5	0.0	41.2	11.8	0.0	24	100.0
Westby town	163	154	-5.5	134	95.5	0.0	0.0	4.5	0.0	17.9	31.3	52.8	31.4	28.6	65	87.7
West Glacier CDP	227	-	-	166	100.0	0.0	0.0	0.0	0.0	16.3	28.3	35.9	13.3	54.0	75	74.7
West Glendive CDP	1,948	-	-	1,620	93.8	0.0	0.1	5.1	1.0	19.6	19.6	45.9	40.4	15.5	780	92.3
West Havre CDP	316	-	-	222	83.8	0.0	0.0	16.2	0.0	28.8	34.2	37.9	18.1	45.8	95	100.0
West Kootenai CDP	365	-	-	58	100.0	0.0	0.0	0.0	0.0	0.0	100.0	69.9	51.7	25.9	43	65.1
West Yellowstone town	1,270	1,376	8.3	936	98.3	0.0	1.7	0.0	0.0	16.7	15.0	39.8	33.3	35.4	470	74.9
Wheatland CDP	568	-	-	545	100.0	0.0	0.0	0.0	0.0	27.5	13.4	36.4	35.9	28.9	206	94.2
Whitefish city	6,512	8,295	27.4	7,714	96.6	0.0	0.3	0.9	2.2	17.4	16.7	40.3	19.6	54.3	3,342	92.0
Whitehall town	1,044	1,150	10.2	921	91.5	0.0	0.0	2.1	6.4	16.3	25.2	50.9	37.4	27.0	425	80.5
White Haven CDP	577	-	-	475	90.9	0.0	0.0	4.6	4.4	6.1	22.7	45.9	71.0	12.9	217	80.2
White Sulphur Springs city	937	931	-0.6	1,012	96.1	0.1	0.3	3.4	0.1	19.5	24.9	43.9	53.4	18.6	431	78.4
Whitewater CDP	64	-	-	127	64.6	0.0	0.0	35.4	0.0	39.4	8.7	21.2	29.5	37.7	44	84.1
Wibaux town	590	592	0.3	600	92.7	0.0	1.3	2.2	3.8	20.5	28.3	56.0	50.8	21.7	294	82.7
Willow Creek CDP	210	-	-	258	100.0	0.0	0.0	0.0	0.0	22.9	23.3	50.6	43.8	23.4	136	86.8
Wilsall CDP	178	-	-	337	93.5	0.0	0.0	0.0	6.5	22.8	27.0	51.4	33.1	40.8	152	90.8
Wineglass CDP	256	-	-	339	100.0	0.0	0.0	0.0	0.0	16.5	21.8	44.9	37.7	12.5	142	100.0
Winifred town	206	195	-5.3	111	100.0	0.0	0.0	0.0	0.0	4.5	34.2	52.5	33.0	36.8	59	94.9
Winnett town	177	185	4.5	198	87.4	0.0	12.6	0.0	0.0	22.2	29.8	48.9	47.9	26.1	98	86.7
Winston CDP	147	-	-	269	77.7	0.0	0.0	22.3	0.0	10.0	0.0	60.5	36.0	44.6	95	100.0
Wisdom CDP	98	-	-	91	84.6	0.0	0.0	5.5	9.9	9.9	51.6	65.5	43.9	11.0	55	81.8
Wolf Point city	2,606	2,730	4.8	2,774	45.7	0.5	2.4	49.2	2.2	31.1	14.2	31.0	37.8	21.5	817	86.2
Woods Bay CDP	661	-	-	810	100.0	0.0	0.0	0.0	0.0	14.6	21.7	52.6	24.9	42.8	335	100.0
Worden CDP	577	-	-	780	97.8	0.0	0.0	2.2	0.0	35.9	9.5	38.3	40.3	17.6	281	92.5
Wye CDP	511	-	-	788	90.6	4.7	0.0	4.7	0.0	35.3	5.6	32.5	49.5	20.2	248	92.3
Wyola CDP	215	-	-	220	14.5	0.0	0.0	83.6	1.8	27.7	10.0	30.5	52.3	16.7	66	51.5
Yaak CDP	248	-	-	300	100.0	0.0	0.0	0.0	0.0	13.3	33.7	58.6	40.8	21.0	128	87.5
Zortman CDP	69	-	-	26	69.2	0.0	0.0	30.8	0.0	0.0	100.0	67.7	30.8	42.3	26	26.9
NEBRASKA	1,826,305	1,934,408	5.9	1,914,571	79.0	4.7	2.4	3.1	10.9	24.8	15.4	36.5	34.7	31.9	759,176	90.0
Abie village	69	65	-5.8	59	100.0	0.0	0.0	0.0	0.0	22.0	13.6	39.9	60.9	6.5	24	95.8
Adams village	583	617	5.8	508	98.4	0.4	0.0	1.2	0.0	22.0	22.4	45.1	44.4	24.3	225	89.3
Ainsworth city	1,728	1,620	-6.3	1,688	92.3	0.1	0.8	3.7	3.1	20.3	24.9	47.5	41.7	21.5	847	88.3
Albion city	1,664	1,585	-4.7	1,501	96.2	0.0	0.0	0.5	3.3	22.4	27.4	48.0	37.3	22.7	707	86.6
Alda village	646	662	2.5	665	80.0	0.0	0.3	1.1	18.6	28.9	12.3	34.5	63.3	6.4	243	86.8
Alexandria village	177	171	-3.4	144	96.5	0.0	0.0	3.5	0.0	7.6	24.3	45.0	48.6	17.1	72	86.1
Allen village	377	349	-7.4	356	96.6	0.0	0.6	1.7	1.1	23.3	19.4	42.0	50.2	16.2	151	92.1
Alliance city	8,502	8,092	-4.8	8,235	77.4	1.8	1.3	4.3	15.1	27.1	15.7	38.1	42.8	16.9	3,543	88.4
Alma city	1,156	1,141	-1.3	1,293	98.6	0.2	0.2	0.0	0.9	18.6	28.5	50.1	29.6	24.3	591	88.0
Alvo village	132	137	3.8	130	96.2	0.0	0.0	1.5	2.3	33.8	22.3	34.0	46.8	17.7	50	88.0
Ames CDP	24	-	-	-	-	-	-	-	-	-	-	-	-	-	-	-
Amherst village	248	253	2.0	136	99.3	0.0	0.0	0.0	0.7	25.0	19.1	43.0	33.7	35.7	65	89.2
Anoka village	6	5	-16.7	26	100.0	0.0	0.0	0.0	0.0	34.6	26.9	36.8	82.4	0.0	7	100.0
Anselmo village	145	138	-4.8	164	100.0	0.0	0.0	0.0	0.0	11.0	40.9	59.5	46.1	12.8	80	78.8
Ansley village	441	425	-3.6	471	90.4	0.0	0.0	0.8	8.7	24.2	20.4	36.0	45.5	20.0	224	85.7
Arapahoe city	1,026	976	-4.9	1,333	92.3	0.0	0.5	1.4	5.9	33.2	14.8	36.1	43.3	11.9	483	84.5
Arcadia village	311	305	-1.9	271	88.2	2.6	0.0	3.3	5.9	22.9	24.7	38.5	45.8	28.4	137	86.1
Archer CDP	81	-	-	51	100.0	0.0	0.0	0.0	0.0	11.8	35.3	50.4	33.3	28.9	21	81.0
Arlington village	1,243	1,315	5.8	1,513	92.0	0.0	0.0	2.4	5.6	36.8	11.8	34.2	36.7	30.2	512	95.9
Arnold village	597	568	-4.9	802	97.8	0.0	0.0	0.0	2.2	28.3	19.1	39.1	31.6	32.8	327	88.7
Arthur village	117	118	0.9	136	98.5	0.0	0.0	1.5	0.0	21.3	31.6	48.3	45.2	16.1	75	78.7

1 May be of any race.

Table A. All Places — **Population and Housing**

STATE City, town, township, borough, or CDP (county if applicable)	Population				Race and Hispanic or Latino origin (percent)					Age (percent)			Educational attainment of persons age 25 and older		Occupied housing units	
	2010 census total population	2019 estimated population	Percent change 2010–2019	ACS total population estimate 2015–2019	White alone, not Hispanic or Latino	Black alone, not Hispanic or Latino	Asian alone, not Hispanic or Latino	All other races or 2 or more races, not Hispanic or Latino	Hispanic or Latino[1]	Under 18 years old	Age 65 years and older	Median age	Percent High school diploma or less	Percent Bachelor's degree or more	Total	Percent with a computer
	1	2	3	4	5	6	7	8	9	10	11	12	13	14	15	16
NEBRASKA—Con.																
Ashland city	2,453	2,644	7.8	2,523	93.0	0.3	1.1	1.2	4.3	23.3	20.7	38.7	46.4	23.7	1,055	86.5
Ashton village	194	185	-4.6	190	98.4	0.0	0.0	0.0	1.6	25.3	19.5	39.3	63.8	9.4	86	93.0
Aten CDP	112	-	-	28	100.0	0.0	0.0	0.0	0.0	17.9	0.0	54.7	39.1	0.0	13	100.0
Atkinson city	1,245	1,229	-1.3	1,462	97.5	0.0	0.0	1.0	1.4	29.4	22.7	39.6	39.1	27.2	610	90.2
Atlanta village	131	132	0.8	70	98.6	0.0	0.0	0.0	1.4	8.6	15.7	56.3	79.7	8.5	35	88.6
Auburn city	3,460	3,324	-3.9	3,311	96.6	0.2	1.6	0.8	0.9	24.1	19.2	37.5	38.2	27.6	1,482	89.9
Aurora city	4,476	4,547	1.6	4,497	98.0	0.1	0.0	0.0	1.9	25.3	20.8	40.4	33.0	23.0	1,870	90.1
Avoca village	242	252	4.1	281	96.4	0.7	0.0	1.1	1.8	24.6	18.1	31.3	58.1	0.6	92	89.1
Axtell village	730	751	2.9	818	97.7	0.5	0.0	0.0	1.8	29.1	15.8	36.6	34.4	28.9	309	90.0
Ayr village	110	122	10.9	92	93.5	6.5	0.0	0.0	0.0	42.4	21.7	27.5	40.0	44.0	35	71.4
Bancroft village	490	466	-4.9	458	98.9	0.0	0.0	0.7	0.4	22.3	20.7	45.5	30.8	18.0	201	85.1
Barada village	24	22	-8.3	33	100.0	0.0	0.0	0.0	0.0	18.2	9.1	51.9	66.7	3.7	13	100.0
Barneston village	116	111	-4.3	107	97.2	0.0	0.0	1.9	0.9	14.0	13.1	36.9	40.0	10.7	51	88.2
Bartlett village	117	114	-2.6	111	98.2	0.0	0.0	1.8	0.0	3.6	32.4	56.5	43.1	26.5	73	80.8
Bartley village	283	269	-4.9	384	97.4	0.0	0.0	0.5	2.1	29.4	22.4	46.3	46.1	14.2	146	95.2
Bassett city	619	540	-12.8	728	94.1	2.1	0.0	1.5	2.3	15.1	27.6	46.7	40.4	22.5	334	85.6
Battle Creek city	1,207	1,187	-1.7	1,215	89.2	0.3	0.9	2.4	7.2	28.1	20.2	38.1	34.4	23.0	473	89.2
Bayard city	1,209	1,084	-10.3	1,067	80.6	0.0	1.7	1.0	16.7	24.1	22.8	40.1	49.8	9.9	440	84.3
Bazile Mills village	29	29	0.0	24	100.0	0.0	0.0	0.0	0.0	12.5	12.5	50.3	29.4	41.2	9	77.8
Beatrice city	12,686	12,279	-3.2	12,300	93.6	0.9	1.1	1.8	2.6	21.0	22.8	44.1	48.4	18.9	5,395	84.0
Beaver City city	609	575	-5.6	489	92.0	0.2	0.0	4.3	3.5	20.7	32.9	47.8	46.2	17.9	245	82.4
Beaver Crossing village	403	416	3.2	390	94.6	0.0	2.3	1.8	1.3	23.6	16.4	42.8	48.4	13.8	179	84.4
Bee village	191	184	-3.7	208	99.0	0.0	0.0	1.0	0.0	30.8	8.7	40.3	23.6	10.7	102	88.2
Beemer village	678	655	-3.4	610	92.5	0.5	0.5	6.1	0.5	17.9	40.0	56.9	53.3	14.8	294	61.9
Belden village	115	109	-5.2	127	100.0	0.0	0.0	0.0	0.0	26.8	18.1	40.1	38.4	12.8	52	82.7
Belgrade village	126	114	-9.5	163	77.3	0.0	0.0	0.0	22.7	16.6	29.4	53.8	58.7	7.1	86	74.4
Bellevue city	51,520	53,544	3.9	53,324	70.4	6.0	2.9	4.0	16.8	24.4	13.8	33.8	34.4	28.5	20,406	93.6
Bellwood village	435	420	-3.4	416	96.2	0.0	0.0	1.2	2.6	22.8	16.3	40.7	49.4	14.6	165	77.0
Belmar CDP	216	-	-	104	100.0	0.0	0.0	0.0	0.0	0.0	91.3	72.8	25.0	17.3	59	100.0
Belvidere village	48	46	-4.2	45	100.0	0.0	0.0	0.0	0.0	0.0	48.9	64.5	75.0	0.0	23	65.2
Benedict village	234	228	-2.6	301	87.0	0.0	13.0	0.0	0.0	15.9	15.0	32.6	40.1	31.8	122	91.8
Benkelman city	953	790	-17.1	978	98.6	0.2	0.0	0.0	1.2	22.4	27.7	47.8	37.6	22.9	462	82.0
Bennet village	724	977	34.9	1,103	95.8	0.2	0.0	3.5	0.5	33.9	11.0	34.0	28.3	29.8	392	94.1
Bennington city	1,460	1,521	4.2	1,931	95.2	0.0	1.0	1.0	2.8	26.3	16.7	38.8	28.9	36.1	759	87.0
Berea CDP	41	-	-	22	100.0	0.0	0.0	0.0	0.0	0.0	27.3	62.4	63.6	0.0	16	100.0
Bertrand village	750	709	-5.5	787	90.1	2.0	0.0	1.1	6.7	20.7	20.3	42.4	49.9	21.0	354	94.4
Berwyn village	83	80	-3.6	93	82.8	0.0	0.0	12.9	4.3	18.3	24.7	49.2	51.4	8.6	44	100.0
Big Springs village	400	377	-5.8	476	84.9	0.6	0.8	3.2	10.5	19.7	20.2	50.0	51.7	13.8	230	89.1
Bladen village	238	219	-8.0	175	80.6	0.0	0.0	4.6	14.9	21.1	21.1	39.9	58.5	17.8	77	77.9
Blair city	7,990	7,892	-1.2	7,781	93.7	1.0	0.1	1.0	4.1	27.3	18.5	40.3	38.2	28.8	3,238	92.5
Bloomfield city	1,028	940	-8.6	885	93.9	1.5	0.6	1.0	3.1	15.0	40.5	59.6	48.0	17.6	481	86.7
Bloomington village	103	97	-5.8	121	93.4	0.0	0.0	0.0	6.6	27.3	22.3	48.1	69.0	7.1	55	76.4
Blue Hill city	940	866	-7.9	983	92.6	0.0	0.0	2.4	5.0	26.6	18.0	43.3	38.3	24.7	388	91.2
Blue Springs city	331	319	-3.6	274	96.4	0.0	0.0	2.6	1.1	18.6	21.5	43.5	67.0	10.3	106	81.1
Bow Valley CDP	116	-	-	77	100.0	0.0	0.0	0.0	0.0	24.7	18.2	45.6	36.2	12.1	36	86.1
Boys Town village	745	562	-24.6	864	66.1	21.1	0.0	3.1	9.7	77.7	12.8	16.8	2.5	4.1	13	100.0
Bradshaw village	273	268	-1.8	331	94.3	0.0	0.0	1.5	4.2	30.5	16.9	35.6	45.8	25.9	134	94.8
Brady village	428	420	-1.9	405	97.3	0.2	0.0	0.0	2.5	29.9	19.8	37.0	32.7	28.4	165	98.2
Brainard village	330	314	-4.8	420	95.7	0.0	0.0	2.6	1.7	20.7	17.4	35.2	30.6	24.4	194	80.4
Brewster village	17	17	0.0	13	100.0	0.0	0.0	0.0	0.0	0.0	76.9	68.3	15.4	0.0	8	100.0
Bridgeport city	1,545	1,472	-4.7	1,686	78.6	1.7	0.3	2.4	17.0	24.8	14.6	37.9	39.6	21.5	651	94.2
Bristow village	65	59	-9.2	99	100.0	0.0	0.0	0.0	0.0	30.3	33.3	39.9	56.1	7.6	40	67.5
Broadwater village	128	117	-8.6	180	70.0	0.0	0.0	2.2	27.8	11.7	17.8	44.2	75.5	11.9	85	82.4
Brock village	112	106	-5.4	115	100.0	0.0	0.0	0.0	0.0	17.4	27.0	39.9	41.8	15.4	59	84.7
Broken Bow city	3,558	3,497	-1.7	3,517	91.0	0.1	2.3	2.0	4.6	25.1	20.4	39.8	40.0	21.3	1,656	80.7
Brownlee CDP	15	-	-	6	100.0	0.0	0.0	0.0	0.0	0.0	100.0	0.0	100.0	0.0	3	0.0
Brownville village	132	128	-3.0	127	94.5	0.0	0.0	4.7	0.8	18.1	38.6	56.9	44.6	17.8	62	77.4
Brule village	326	305	-6.4	311	79.1	2.3	1.0	1.6	16.1	22.2	25.7	47.8	43.7	15.6	148	84.5
Bruning village	279	269	-3.6	288	94.4	0.0	0.0	4.5	1.0	28.1	26.4	40.6	40.7	19.1	136	72.1
Bruno village	99	92	-7.1	129	100.0	0.0	0.0	0.0	0.0	35.7	16.3	34.9	63.8	15.0	50	78.0
Brunswick village	138	132	-4.3	220	90.0	0.0	0.0	0.0	10.0	15.5	31.8	51.6	50.9	18.9	98	79.6
Burchard village	82	74	-9.8	40	100.0	0.0	0.0	0.0	0.0	10.0	45.0	58.0	78.6	10.7	24	83.3
Burr village	57	59	3.5	32	100.0	0.0	0.0	0.0	0.0	9.4	40.6	59.0	45.8	0.0	23	82.6
Burton village	10	10	0.0	-	-	-	-	-	-	-	-	-	-	-	-	-
Burwell city	1,209	1,161	-4.0	1,244	96.5	0.6	0.0	0.0	3.0	20.3	30.4	50.3	35.0	25.1	548	77.0
Bushnell village	124	116	-6.5	195	88.7	0.0	0.0	3.6	7.7	13.8	30.8	55.9	59.9	4.9	74	86.5
Butte village	326	303	-7.1	337	96.7	0.0	0.0	2.4	0.9	15.4	33.2	54.8	42.5	11.8	152	81.6
Byron village	83	80	-3.6	94	100.0	0.0	0.0	0.0	0.0	30.9	34.0	43.8	31.7	9.5	37	81.1
Cairo village	785	792	0.9	916	93.1	0.0	0.2	0.0	6.7	29.0	10.7	31.2	42.7	17.2	359	92.2
Callaway village	539	536	-0.6	646	91.3	0.8	0.0	1.7	6.2	29.6	21.7	42.7	44.8	17.8	280	79.3
Cambridge city	1,062	1,002	-5.6	1,143	94.4	0.2	0.0	2.7	2.7	17.6	26.7	49.2	39.3	23.9	528	87.1
Campbell village	347	301	-13.3	332	96.4	0.0	0.3	0.3	3.0	12.3	38.0	59.8	59.6	8.4	147	72.8
Carleton village	91	87	-4.4	54	96.3	3.7	0.0	0.0	0.0	27.8	31.5	42.8	35.9	25.6	19	100.0
Carroll village	229	213	-7.0	237	100.0	0.0	0.0	0.0	0.0	25.3	19.8	34.5	44.8	14.5	98	87.8
Cedar Bluffs village	610	583	-4.4	631	86.5	0.0	0.0	5.9	7.6	26.8	16.2	36.4	43.9	13.7	237	86.1
Cedar Creek village	390	410	5.1	416	98.1	0.0	0.5	0.7	0.7	17.5	27.4	48.5	39.0	21.4	181	89.0
Cedar Rapids village	382	360	-5.8	467	94.6	2.4	0.0	1.9	1.1	23.1	14.3	39.7	33.7	25.2	193	85.5
Center village	94	87	-7.4	82	87.8	7.3	0.0	1.2	3.7	14.6	6.1	38.0	55.9	3.4	27	88.9
Central City city	2,934	2,874	-2.0	2,903	88.8	1.2	0.0	4.2	5.8	24.1	25.5	43.1	40.8	19.8	1,231	81.3
Ceresco village	889	899	1.1	1,238	91.4	0.8	0.8	2.8	4.1	26.3	13.8	34.9	34.2	21.6	477	90.1
Chadron city	5,851	5,412	-7.5	5,591	81.6	6.2	0.8	6.3	5.2	17.6	13.6	28.3	23.6	42.9	2,218	93.1
Chalco CDP	10,994	-	-	10,952	85.4	2.3	1.6	5.7	4.9	26.0	6.7	34.8	28.2	34.9	4,250	95.3
Chambers village	268	256	-4.5	348	100.0	0.0	0.0	0.0	0.0	26.7	34.2	44.5	47.3	19.2	168	77.4
Champion CDP	103	-	-	42	100.0	0.0	0.0	0.0	0.0	0.0	47.6	54.9	33.3	0.0	25	100.0
Chapman village	287	287	0.0	254	90.9	0.0	0.0	3.5	5.5	17.7	10.6	43.5	50.8	12.3	118	94.9
Chappell city	929	849	-8.6	871	92.0	0.0	0.3	2.0	5.7	17.8	30.0	50.7	44.7	18.0	389	84.8
Chester village	232	222	-4.3	289	95.5	0.0	0.0	2.4	2.1	28.0	17.0	42.5	43.7	13.7	130	80.8
Clarks village	369	344	-6.8	374	81.8	0.0	0.0	0.0	18.2	26.7	13.4	32.9	48.2	10.4	162	90.7
Clarkson city	657	633	-3.7	631	91.0	0.0	0.0	3.0	6.0	17.3	26.9	49.5	35.2	22.9	309	79.9
Clatonia village	231	220	-4.8	462	89.0	0.0	0.0	1.1	10.0	35.7	7.6	34.0	36.8	19.1	158	88.6
Clay Center city	760	724	-4.7	801	94.5	1.1	0.0	2.6	1.7	20.8	19.9	41.3	36.8	20.7	363	85.7
Clearwater village	419	400	-4.5	361	88.9	0.0	0.0	0.0	11.1	32.7	17.7	35.2	41.6	13.2	144	87.5

1 May be of any race.

Table A. All Places — **Population and Housing**

STATE City, town, township, borough, or CDP (county if applicable)	Population: 2010 census total population	Population: 2019 estimated population	Population: Percent change 2010–2019	Population: ACS total population estimate 2015–2019	Race and Hispanic or Latino origin (percent): White alone, not Hispanic or Latino	Black alone, not Hispanic or Latino	Asian alone, not Hispanic or Latino	All other races or 2 or more races, not Hispanic or Latino	Hispanic or Latino[1]	Age (percent): Under 18 years old	Age 65 years and older	Median age	Educational attainment of persons age 25 and older: Percent High school diploma or less	Percent Bachelor's degree or more	Occupied housing units: Total	Percent with a computer
	1	2	3	4	5	6	7	8	9	10	11	12	13	14	15	16
NEBRASKA—Con.																
Clinton village	41	39	-4.9	49	79.6	0.0	0.0	20.4	0.0	18.4	14.3	55.8	35.0	22.5	21	100.0
Cody village	154	153	-0.6	205	94.6	0.0	0.0	5.4	0.0	22.0	19.0	48.8	35.3	30.0	100	89.0
Coleridge village	473	450	-4.9	554	96.8	1.3	0.0	2.0	0.0	25.5	23.5	47.4	42.6	10.5	239	82.0
Colon village	110	106	-3.6	129	100.0	0.0	0.0	0.0	0.0	17.8	27.9	48.5	32.2	32.2	54	98.1
Columbus city	22,286	23,468	5.3	23,195	74.3	0.5	0.6	1.5	23.1	25.9	16.7	36.5	40.7	21.5	9,269	86.9
Comstock village	93	88	-5.4	105	99.0	0.0	0.0	0.0	1.0	8.6	25.7	48.9	61.7	13.8	60	80.0
Concord village	166	152	-8.4	162	100.0	0.0	0.0	0.0	0.0	26.5	24.1	39.5	43.9	28.1	76	89.5
Cook village	322	302	-6.2	410	94.6	0.5	2.4	0.2	2.2	27.3	14.6	36.1	51.7	22.4	180	88.3
Cordova village	137	132	-3.6	95	98.9	0.0	0.0	0.0	1.1	36.8	9.5	35.5	41.7	11.7	37	91.9
Cornlea village	36	36	0.0	10	100.0	0.0	0.0	0.0	0.0	0.0	20.0	58.0	80.0	0.0	6	50.0
Cortland village	482	472	-2.1	497	96.6	0.4	2.0	1.0	0.0	29.6	13.9	42.6	36.4	18.8	189	87.3
Cotesfield village	46	47	2.2	36	100.0	0.0	0.0	0.0	0.0	11.1	19.4	62.5	70.0	13.3	18	83.3
Cowles village	30	27	-10.0	11	72.7	0.0	0.0	27.3	0.0	36.4	18.2	36.5	28.6	14.3	3	33.3
Cozad city	3,977	3,735	-6.1	3,787	82.0	1.9	0.8	1.1	14.2	22.5	22.7	44.2	51.0	16.1	1,594	87.9
Crab Orchard village	38	36	-5.3	46	93.5	0.0	0.0	0.0	6.5	21.7	15.2	55.1	75.0	5.6	22	77.3
Craig village	199	187	-6.0	166	85.5	0.0	0.0	10.2	4.2	17.5	18.1	50.6	62.8	11.6	70	92.9
Crawford city	999	930	-6.9	1,114	78.5	0.4	1.2	5.8	14.1	24.2	22.6	44.4	37.5	24.3	460	81.3
Creighton city	1,154	1,086	-5.9	1,225	97.6	0.7	0.7	1.1	0.0	21.8	26.2	52.8	41.1	26.2	567	83.4
Creston village	203	203	0.0	206	94.7	0.0	0.0	0.0	5.3	26.7	20.4	42.0	37.0	17.8	88	78.4
Crete city	6,960	7,007	0.7	7,043	48.2	2.8	2.6	1.3	45.2	25.9	8.8	27.7	56.3	15.4	2,197	83.2
Crofton city	726	663	-8.7	868	85.4	0.5	0.0	9.3	4.8	27.5	23.7	37.6	42.1	20.9	374	82.6
Crookston village	69	69	0.0	72	97.2	0.0	0.0	2.8	0.0	36.1	18.1	27.0	36.1	13.9	26	100.0
Culbertson village	594	559	-5.9	587	100.0	0.0	0.0	0.0	0.0	29.8	20.4	38.9	44.6	17.1	253	88.9
Curtis city	939	889	-5.3	811	92.0	1.6	0.0	2.6	3.8	20.1	17.6	32.8	30.4	21.3	325	81.8
Cushing village	32	33	3.1	43	95.3	0.0	0.0	0.0	4.7	39.5	14.0	30.3	61.5	0.0	20	60.0
Dakota City city	1,919	1,859	-3.1	2,032	58.7	1.0	0.9	2.0	37.4	30.0	10.2	31.4	55.7	16.2	711	91.7
Dalton village	319	278	-12.9	330	93.0	0.0	0.0	0.0	7.0	24.5	26.7	44.5	31.1	29.4	151	87.4
Danbury village	101	95	-5.9	69	95.7	0.0	0.0	4.3	0.0	13.0	33.3	56.3	43.3	8.3	37	83.8
Dannebrog village	303	305	0.7	298	96.6	0.0	0.3	0.7	2.3	22.5	19.1	43.4	38.2	12.4	123	81.3
Davenport village	294	283	-3.7	397	91.2	0.0	0.0	1.5	7.3	34.5	22.4	40.1	61.5	17.5	147	78.9
Davey village	154	154	0.0	160	95.6	0.0	0.0	1.9	2.5	24.4	15.0	46.5	40.7	23.9	71	85.9
David City city	2,920	2,852	-2.3	2,841	92.9	0.4	0.0	0.5	6.2	22.2	22.9	42.7	47.1	21.9	1,222	82.7
Dawson village	146	135	-7.5	168	100.0	0.0	0.0	0.0	0.0	18.5	19.0	51.5	63.1	9.8	84	100.0
Daykin village	166	159	-4.2	186	100.0	0.0	0.0	0.0	0.0	31.7	26.9	40.5	39.8	31.7	86	75.6
Decatur village	481	463	-3.7	377	89.7	0.0	4.2	1.9	4.2	9.5	40.6	61.4	55.8	9.7	215	67.9
Denton village	190	206	8.4	197	95.9	0.0	2.5	0.0	1.5	18.8	25.4	46.8	32.2	9.8	88	96.6
Deshler city	747	737	-1.3	817	95.0	0.0	0.0	0.4	4.7	27.5	29.0	38.1	48.0	16.1	321	76.6
Deweese village	67	65	-3.0	59	100.0	0.0	0.0	0.0	0.0	23.7	16.9	31.8	78.4	0.0	24	79.2
De Witt village	513	498	-2.9	653	93.9	0.0	0.0	2.6	3.5	27.4	11.8	39.0	42.1	15.2	241	94.6
Diller village	260	254	-2.3	281	89.3	0.0	0.0	3.2	7.5	21.7	21.4	40.7	47.3	13.8	136	78.7
Dix village	255	242	-5.1	308	88.0	0.0	1.0	3.9	7.1	19.5	15.6	43.0	36.8	4.9	121	93.4
Dixon village	87	81	-6.9	125	98.4	0.0	0.0	0.8	0.8	21.6	32.8	47.8	44.8	8.0	59	88.1
Dodge village	612	593	-3.1	550	97.5	0.0	0.0	0.0	2.5	19.8	33.6	52.2	50.1	10.8	254	82.3
Doniphan village	822	830	1.0	958	96.6	0.0	0.0	0.9	2.5	30.2	13.6	36.9	48.9	19.5	353	89.2
Dorchester village	586	574	-2.0	620	84.0	0.0	0.0	0.0	16.0	23.9	13.7	39.2	55.8	11.5	244	89.3
Douglas village	173	179	3.5	151	96.0	0.0	0.7	3.3	0.0	21.9	15.2	39.8	35.5	30.0	68	95.6
Du Bois village	147	137	-6.8	97	89.7	4.1	0.0	4.1	2.1	2.1	42.3	61.9	67.4	10.5	58	86.2
Dunbar village	187	193	3.2	176	73.9	1.1	0.0	2.8	22.2	11.9	23.3	52.4	58.9	7.3	87	80.5
Duncan village	349	369	5.7	547	92.3	1.3	0.0	1.5	4.9	21.2	32.2	48.7	55.5	12.9	231	64.5
Dunning village	103	99	-3.9	102	100.0	0.0	0.0	0.0	0.0	24.5	19.6	33.5	39.4	25.4	44	86.4
Dwight village	204	191	-6.4	206	100.0	0.0	0.0	0.0	0.0	22.8	18.4	46.2	54.9	11.3	100	84.0
Eagle village	1,024	1,096	7.0	900	93.9	0.0	0.0	2.2	3.9	24.8	9.7	35.7	25.9	22.3	344	99.4
Eddyville village	97	94	-3.1	93	80.6	8.6	0.0	0.0	10.8	16.1	35.5	54.3	67.1	14.5	43	90.7
Edgar city	498	450	-9.6	456	97.6	0.0	0.0	1.5	0.9	25.9	20.8	40.0	41.1	14.8	200	93.0
Edison village	133	123	-7.5	156	94.9	1.9	0.0	0.0	3.2	26.9	19.9	51.4	65.2	3.6	73	84.9
Elba village	215	225	4.7	334	94.3	0.3	0.0	2.4	3.0	22.2	14.1	34.0	48.2	14.5	148	84.5
Elgin city	659	617	-6.4	720	99.7	0.0	0.0	0.0	0.3	21.8	33.2	58.4	35.8	21.7	354	75.4
Elk Creek village	98	94	-4.1	80	91.3	0.0	0.0	5.0	3.8	16.3	18.8	40.0	59.6	9.6	51	84.3
Elm Creek village	901	949	5.3	1,134	96.6	0.0	0.0	0.4	3.1	29.5	10.8	30.3	37.0	22.3	427	91.1
Elmwood village	634	661	4.3	720	92.8	0.0	0.0	2.6	4.6	23.3	16.3	34.6	33.9	15.6	296	94.9
Elsie village	106	105	-0.9	142	98.6	0.0	0.0	0.0	1.4	17.6	12.0	39.8	49.5	23.8	69	87.0
Elwood village	707	683	-3.4	829	88.1	0.6	0.2	2.2	8.9	18.0	29.4	49.8	42.0	23.3	401	84.5
Elyria village	51	51	0.0	64	100.0	0.0	0.0	0.0	0.0	17.2	14.1	45.3	46.9	6.1	27	81.5
Emerson village	840	792	-5.7	902	82.8	1.4	1.0	8.1	6.7	31.9	19.8	37.4	47.6	12.4	343	88.9
Emmet village	48	46	-4.2	28	100.0	0.0	0.0	0.0	0.0	21.4	10.7	38.8	50.0	18.2	16	93.8
Enders CDP	42	-	-	8	100.0	0.0	0.0	0.0	0.0	0.0	100.0	0.0	0.0	100.0	8	0.0
Endicott village	132	125	-5.3	161	100.0	0.0	0.0	0.0	0.0	24.2	19.9	46.8	60.7	10.3	73	90.4
Ericson village	93	90	-3.2	140	96.4	0.0	1.4	0.0	2.1	27.9	30.7	47.5	29.7	17.8	58	86.2
Eustis village	401	373	-7.0	520	98.3	0.4	0.4	1.0	0.0	22.1	20.8	41.5	34.8	23.6	224	83.9
Ewing village	387	372	-3.9	395	99.5	0.0	0.0	0.5	0.0	28.9	16.7	41.1	48.3	11.5	182	89.0
Exeter village	591	522	-11.7	558	99.6	0.0	0.0	0.4	0.0	16.1	23.8	48.8	36.6	20.5	272	86.0
Fairbury city	3,942	3,626	-8.0	3,686	90.5	1.2	0.4	2.0	5.9	25.8	18.0	39.2	48.1	16.3	1,690	86.1
Fairfield city	387	369	-4.7	374	97.6	0.0	0.0	2.1	0.3	20.1	20.3	47.0	48.0	14.8	178	86.0
Fairmont village	560	515	-8.0	700	94.3	0.0	0.6	2.0	3.1	21.0	23.7	44.5	51.7	20.0	283	77.4
Falls City city	4,325	4,117	-4.8	4,156	89.5	0.3	0.0	7.6	2.6	24.2	21.0	40.5	44.1	18.3	1,960	79.7
Farnam village	171	165	-3.5	216	84.7	0.0	0.0	2.8	12.5	16.7	35.2	46.9	53.2	17.7	97	88.7
Farwell village	122	117	-4.1	118	99.2	0.0	0.0	0.0	0.8	16.9	12.7	49.5	45.6	6.7	52	82.7
Filley village	132	126	-4.5	105	100.0	0.0	0.0	0.0	0.0	17.1	17.1	53.3	38.4	16.3	55	80.0
Firth village	590	627	6.3	435	93.8	0.0	0.7	1.4	4.1	26.2	16.1	37.8	40.4	24.2	180	90.0
Fontanelle CDP	54	-	-	29	100.0	0.0	0.0	0.0	0.0	0.0	24.1	60.3	100.0	0.0	18	61.1
Fordyce village	139	131	-5.8	154	89.6	0.0	0.0	0.0	10.4	20.8	18.8	40.0	58.5	5.7	70	87.1
Fort Calhoun city	922	980	6.3	882	89.5	0.6	0.0	2.5	7.5	20.0	18.0	40.9	44.6	23.5	398	84.7
Foster village	51	51	0.0	50	90.0	0.0	10.0	0.0	0.0	28.0	16.0	32.0	34.4	12.5	21	85.7
Franklin city	1,000	910	-9.0	1,031	97.6	0.7	0.2	0.5	1.1	20.4	26.6	47.8	43.0	18.3	466	84.5
Fremont city	26,413	26,383	-0.1	26,437	81.0	0.9	0.4	2.6	15.2	24.0	17.8	37.4	47.5	18.3	10,990	88.0
Friend city	1,027	965	-6.0	1,176	83.3	9.0	1.3	4.8	1.5	24.5	23.5	40.9	42.7	20.3	418	86.4
Fullerton city	1,307	1,222	-6.5	1,446	96.3	0.5	0.0	0.9	2.3	27.6	21.6	37.7	43.9	19.2	618	84.1
Funk village	194	183	-5.7	192	89.1	0.0	1.0	2.6	7.3	22.9	21.4	50.0	46.4	19.2	72	72.2
Gandy village	32	31	-3.1	57	100.0	0.0	0.0	0.0	0.0	29.8	36.8	58.1	12.5	12.5	25	88.0
Garland village	216	213	-1.4	247	98.8	1.2	0.0	0.0	0.0	22.7	23.5	40.9	53.4	15.3	103	82.5
Garrison village	54	51	-5.6	49	98.0	0.0	0.0	0.0	2.0	32.7	12.2	29.5	66.7	13.3	16	93.8
Geneva city	2,217	2,086	-5.9	2,071	91.0	0.7	1.3	2.9	4.1	21.9	27.0	46.6	39.1	23.5	915	88.5

1 May be of any race.

Table A. All Places — **Population and Housing**

STATE City, town, township, borough, or CDP (county if applicable)	Population: 2010 census total population	Population: 2019 estimated population	Population: Percent change 2010–2019	Population: ACS total population estimate 2015–2019	Race and Hispanic or Latino origin (percent): White alone, not Hispanic or Latino	Race: Black alone, not Hispanic or Latino	Race: Asian alone, not Hispanic or Latino	Race: All other races or 2 or more races, not Hispanic or Latino	Race: Hispanic or Latino[1]	Age (percent): Under 18 years old	Age: Age 65 years and older	Age: Median age	Educational attainment of persons age 25 and older: Percent High school diploma or less	Educational attainment: Percent Bachelor's degree or more	Occupied housing units: Total	Occupied housing units: Percent with a computer
	1	2	3	4	5	6	7	8	9	10	11	12	13	14	15	16
NEBRASKA—Con.																
Genoa city	1,003	948	-5.5	1,065	97.3	0.0	0.0	0.0	2.7	21.9	17.7	40.8	50.0	16.6	463	84.0
Gering city	8,500	8,128	-4.4	8,254	75.1	0.8	0.2	1.5	22.3	25.7	20.0	38.1	38.2	24.6	3,165	86.5
Gibbon city	1,833	1,869	2.0	2,080	64.4	0.0	0.0	1.0	34.7	31.2	13.2	34.3	53.2	14.4	719	85.4
Gilead village	39	38	-2.6	38	100.0	0.0	0.0	0.0	0.0	0.0	15.8	40.5	21.1	26.3	25	96.0
Giltner village	352	367	4.3	295	93.6	0.0	0.0	1.0	5.4	24.1	17.3	43.5	44.0	17.7	122	91.0
Glenvil village	307	292	-4.9	374	89.6	0.0	1.3	0.0	9.1	27.8	15.8	39.0	45.5	5.5	154	87.7
Glenwood CDP	466	-	-	549	100.0	0.0	0.0	0.0	0.0	41.2	5.5	33.8	18.6	59.4	191	100.0
Goehner village	154	158	2.6	117	95.7	0.0	0.0	0.9	3.4	21.4	29.9	46.8	61.2	14.1	50	86.0
Gordon city	1,612	1,521	-5.6	1,733	72.5	4.5	0.8	19.0	3.2	25.7	21.4	42.1	43.7	23.2	762	84.5
Gothenburg city	3,598	3,448	-4.2	3,489	97.9	0.0	0.0	1.2	0.9	30.5	17.0	35.3	39.7	18.8	1,339	86.1
Grafton village	126	118	-6.3	142	93.7	4.2	0.0	0.0	2.1	24.6	21.8	43.5	49.0	11.0	68	79.4
Grand Island city	48,655	51,267	5.4	51,147	62.0	2.9	1.3	2.2	31.6	28.0	14.0	34.9	47.7	20.6	19,243	87.8
Grant city	1,169	1,115	-4.6	1,345	92.3	0.3	0.0	1.0	6.5	24.9	24.6	42.9	38.8	21.4	578	85.8
Greeley Center village	466	428	-8.2	353	96.9	1.4	0.0	1.7	0.0	14.7	38.2	58.9	40.7	22.5	181	76.8
Greenwood village	568	595	4.8	529	94.3	0.0	2.5	0.8	2.5	19.7	21.7	47.2	49.5	12.8	207	89.4
Gresham village	223	212	-4.9	231	94.8	0.0	0.0	2.2	3.0	15.2	11.7	35.5	52.3	6.8	110	85.5
Gretna city	4,925	5,058	2.7	5,037	96.0	0.4	0.1	0.2	3.3	27.5	12.7	35.8	25.6	43.4	1,954	94.0
Gross village	2	2	0.0	-	-	-	-	-	-	-	-	-	-	-	-	-
Guide Rock village	225	202	-10.2	204	94.1	0.0	0.0	0.0	5.9	26.0	26.0	40.3	43.1	9.5	89	75.3
Gurley village	214	187	-12.6	211	86.3	0.0	2.8	3.8	7.1	24.6	17.5	41.5	39.2	19.6	94	80.9
Hadar village	293	305	4.1	268	90.3	2.2	0.0	0.0	7.5	23.5	11.2	39.0	29.2	15.1	113	88.5
Haigler village	162	140	-13.6	182	76.4	0.0	0.0	1.1	22.5	24.7	15.4	39.8	58.2	9.8	80	78.8
Hallam village	213	266	24.9	204	96.6	0.0	0.0	0.5	2.9	29.4	9.3	35.6	36.7	15.8	73	93.2
Halsey village	74	81	9.5	64	100.0	0.0	0.0	0.0	0.0	25.0	23.4	55.3	28.9	6.7	28	100.0
Hamlet village	57	56	-1.8	44	100.0	0.0	0.0	0.0	0.0	13.6	38.6	63.3	44.7	13.2	29	100.0
Hampton village	423	433	2.4	471	82.2	0.0	1.1	5.9	10.8	25.9	20.8	35.9	35.4	24.5	191	87.4
Harbine village	49	46	-6.1	79	100.0	0.0	0.0	0.0	0.0	26.6	19.0	55.3	53.4	13.8	31	77.4
Hardy village	159	146	-8.2	235	100.0	0.0	0.0	0.0	0.0	37.0	17.9	25.1	58.5	5.9	72	83.3
Harrisburg CDP	100	-	-	88	100.0	0.0	0.0	0.0	0.0	12.5	30.7	45.7	57.8	15.6	39	92.3
Harrison village	251	223	-11.2	297	99.3	0.0	0.0	0.3	0.3	26.6	25.6	38.7	39.8	25.5	132	78.8
Hartington city	1,554	1,464	-5.8	1,645	98.4	0.1	0.1	0.5	0.9	25.7	27.7	42.5	48.3	20.3	727	84.9
Harvard city	1,013	964	-4.8	1,086	75.1	0.4	0.0	0.0	24.5	23.5	23.0	41.3	55.5	17.4	396	87.1
Hastings city	25,234	24,692	-2.1	24,906	83.1	0.7	1.1	2.3	12.9	23.4	17.4	36.1	39.7	24.5	10,124	86.3
Hayes Center village	214	203	-5.1	288	85.1	0.0	0.0	0.0	14.9	13.9	20.8	56.3	41.0	13.7	132	81.1
Hay Springs village	570	540	-5.3	596	85.7	2.7	0.7	8.1	2.9	11.4	39.6	59.9	39.0	25.8	260	81.2
Hazard village	70	66	-5.7	58	93.1	0.0	0.0	1.7	5.2	8.6	29.3	35.5	32.1	34.0	39	66.7
Heartwell village	71	69	-2.8	83	75.9	0.0	2.4	0.0	21.7	31.3	25.3	37.9	70.2	10.5	37	100.0
Hebron city	1,579	1,472	-6.8	1,630	92.8	1.4	0.0	4.2	1.6	17.9	30.8	53.6	42.4	18.9	770	82.3
Hemingford village	803	773	-3.7	909	90.4	0.0	0.0	2.6	6.9	22.0	14.0	39.6	39.9	23.1	384	85.2
Henderson city	1,005	985	-2.0	1,006	85.7	1.0	0.0	4.6	8.7	25.3	32.0	46.6	32.1	24.0	452	83.2
Hendley village	24	23	-4.2	12	100.0	0.0	0.0	0.0	0.0	0.0	50.0	76.5	33.3	0.0	11	45.5
Henry village	106	100	-5.7	91	93.4	0.0	0.0	1.1	5.5	31.9	8.8	31.9	44.3	9.8	40	85.0
Herman village	268	271	1.1	324	88.9	0.6	1.5	6.2	2.8	30.6	13.9	33.4	42.5	11.9	128	91.4
Hershey village	665	656	-1.4	606	87.8	0.3	0.0	0.5	11.4	25.1	27.6	45.0	42.8	12.6	261	85.4
Hickman city	1,659	2,371	42.9	2,447	98.0	0.3	0.0	0.9	0.8	40.1	7.4	31.4	21.7	44.1	760	94.2
Hildreth village	378	352	-6.9	413	95.6	1.9	0.0	1.5	1.0	22.8	29.3	43.5	31.6	25.7	185	84.3
Holbrook village	207	194	-6.3	255	93.3	0.0	1.6	1.6	3.5	21.6	22.7	48.2	58.8	9.9	109	92.7
Holdrege city	5,495	5,408	-1.6	5,455	90.5	0.2	0.2	2.3	6.8	22.3	19.9	40.8	35.6	22.9	2,454	89.5
Holmesville CDP	51	-	-	18	100.0	0.0	0.0	0.0	0.0	27.8	22.2	49.5	69.2	0.0	8	100.0
Holstein village	220	238	8.2	263	96.6	0.0	2.7	0.0	0.8	21.3	16.7	43.1	57.3	8.6	106	87.7
Homer village	549	521	-5.1	502	87.6	0.0	0.0	10.2	2.2	16.9	20.1	48.0	51.5	14.9	233	80.3
Hooper city	832	838	0.7	775	93.0	0.8	1.9	3.0	1.3	20.6	22.8	46.6	38.8	17.8	368	87.5
Hordville village	144	148	2.8	87	100.0	0.0	0.0	0.0	0.0	11.5	33.3	55.8	52.1	5.5	52	82.7
Hoskins village	285	299	4.9	281	99.6	0.0	0.4	0.0	0.0	22.1	17.1	36.9	42.7	10.8	116	83.6
Howard City (Boelus) village	189	187	-1.1	170	93.5	0.0	0.0	2.9	3.5	11.8	31.8	56.2	54.2	9.2	89	70.8
Howells village	561	564	0.5	657	86.6	5.2	0.0	0.9	7.3	23.4	25.9	42.2	49.7	24.2	276	77.2
Hubbard village	236	224	-5.1	181	74.6	0.0	0.0	23.2	2.2	24.3	15.5	35.6	53.0	14.2	80	85.0
Hubbell village	68	65	-4.4	71	87.3	0.0	0.0	0.0	12.7	15.5	26.8	51.3	50.0	0.0	32	68.8
Humboldt city	877	810	-7.6	863	96.5	0.0	0.0	2.4	1.0	15.4	30.0	56.1	51.6	14.5	403	82.1
Humphrey city	760	817	7.5	896	99.8	0.1	0.0	0.0	0.1	25.7	25.4	40.4	43.1	18.3	376	79.3
Huntley village	44	43	-2.3	56	75.0	0.0	0.0	25.0	0.0	35.7	0.0	22.7	28.0	0.0	16	100.0
Hyannis village	182	184	1.1	168	97.0	0.0	0.0	0.0	3.0	6.5	38.1	61.3	45.3	22.3	95	76.8
Imperial city	2,071	2,055	-0.8	2,008	81.5	0.1	0.5	0.6	17.2	26.2	21.6	40.8	36.4	22.9	872	91.9
Inavale CDP	117	-	-	65	100.0	0.0	0.0	0.0	0.0	0.0	38.5	61.6	50.8	16.9	35	91.4
Indianola city	584	550	-5.8	559	94.1	0.0	0.0	0.0	5.9	17.7	19.1	48.3	52.6	13.4	240	86.3
Inglewood village	325	320	-1.5	401	66.8	5.5	0.0	2.2	25.4	33.9	9.0	34.6	57.2	8.6	140	85.0
Inland CDP	-	-	-	7	100.0	0.0	0.0	0.0	0.0	0.0	100.0	0.0	0.0	0.0	7	0.0
Inman village	129	122	-5.4	99	96.0	0.0	0.0	4.0	0.0	7.1	31.3	56.1	56.0	17.9	50	92.0
Ithaca village	148	148	0.0	122	88.5	0.0	0.0	5.7	5.7	14.8	13.1	44.8	50.0	19.6	51	82.4
Jackson village	223	203	-9.0	140	95.7	0.0	0.0	0.0	4.3	13.6	17.9	43.8	46.8	21.3	67	89.6
Jansen village	118	112	-5.1	106	100.0	0.0	0.0	0.0	0.0	11.3	26.4	48.5	55.1	11.2	55	81.8
Johnson village	328	326	-0.6	272	94.1	2.6	0.0	0.7	2.6	19.9	29.4	58.2	41.8	23.0	139	85.6
Johnstown village	64	61	-4.7	46	100.0	0.0	0.0	0.0	0.0	15.2	28.3	55.0	62.9	20.0	26	57.7
Julian village	59	55	-6.8	56	76.8	0.0	0.0	0.0	23.2	14.3	23.2	55.7	70.8	25.0	33	84.8
Juniata village	754	823	9.2	714	96.5	0.0	0.0	2.1	1.4	24.2	22.3	40.6	41.4	19.1	281	92.5
Kearney city	30,952	33,867	9.4	33,464	85.7	1.1	1.7	2.1	9.3	21.5	13.5	31.7	30.6	37.9	12,987	92.4
Kenesaw village	895	962	7.5	1,111	98.1	0.0	0.3	1.0	0.6	29.7	19.8	38.9	39.5	17.0	393	89.1
Kennard village	361	366	1.4	364	98.6	0.0	0.0	0.0	1.4	25.3	13.5	34.0	44.2	14.6	156	91.7
Keystone CDP	59	-	-	62	100.0	0.0	0.0	0.0	0.0	0.0	24.2	61.1	46.3	22.2	31	83.9
Kilgore village	77	79	2.6	57	57.9	0.0	0.0	42.1	0.0	33.3	7.0	37.5	36.1	25.0	20	95.0
Kimball city	2,496	2,373	-4.9	2,578	83.0	0.1	0.3	4.5	12.0	26.1	20.9	41.2	49.0	15.7	1,100	86.5
King Lake CDP	280	-	-	79	100.0	0.0	0.0	0.0	0.0	0.0	45.6	63.0	35.4	0.0	59	81.4
Lakeview CDP	317	-	-	370	84.9	0.0	11.1	0.0	4.1	19.7	38.6	58.0	33.7	33.7	146	100.0
Lamar village	23	22	-4.3	17	100.0	0.0	0.0	0.0	0.0	0.0	0.0	55.6	52.9	0.0	8	100.0
La Platte CDP	114	-	-	158	41.8	0.0	0.0	0.0	58.2	39.9	0.0	26.1	71.3	28.8	58	100.0
Laurel city	964	916	-5.0	1,111	96.3	0.5	0.0	2.3	0.9	24.5	20.2	33.5	33.5	28.8	469	92.1
La Vista city	16,610	17,170	3.4	17,078	83.4	1.3	2.1	2.6	10.6	24.5	12.8	36.1	31.0	30.8	6,990	94.8
Lawrence village	304	281	-7.6	391	84.4	0.0	0.5	3.3	11.8	22.8	23.8	50.4	45.1	16.9	158	81.0
Lebanon village	80	77	-3.8	77	100.0	0.0	0.0	0.0	0.0	16.9	15.6	46.5	22.4	22.4	34	85.3
Leigh village	403	417	3.5	396	92.7	0.0	1.0	3.0	3.3	18.9	14.4	44.4	36.1	26.0	213	86.9
Lemoyne CDP	82	-	-	102	100.0	0.0	0.0	0.0	0.0	6.9	6.9	60.1	63.2	17.9	42	83.3

1 May be of any race.

Table A. All Places — **Population and Housing**

STATE City, town, township, borough, or CDP (county if applicable)	Population				Race and Hispanic or Latino origin (percent)					Age (percent)			Educational attainment of persons age 25 and older		Occupied housing units	
	2010 census total population	2019 estimated population	Percent change 2010–2019	ACS total population estimate 2015–2019	White alone, not Hispanic or Latino	Black alone, not Hispanic or Latino	Asian alone, not Hispanic or Latino	All other races or 2 or more races, not Hispanic or Latino	Hispanic or Latino[1]	Under 18 years old	Age 65 years and older	Median age	Percent High school diploma or less	Percent Bachelor's degree or more	Total	Percent with a computer
	1	2	3	4	5	6	7	8	9	10	11	12	13	14	15	16
NEBRASKA—Con.																
Leshara village	112	119	6.3	73	100.0	0.0	0.0	0.0	0.0	8.2	32.9	55.3	65.1	6.3	41	70.7
Lewellen village	224	199	-11.2	192	97.4	0.0	0.0	0.5	2.1	18.8	27.1	55.0	48.4	9.2	95	86.3
Lewiston village	68	63	-7.4	63	98.4	0.0	0.0	0.0	1.6	17.5	22.2	28.4	24.2	12.1	38	86.8
Lexington city	10,230	10,115	-1.1	10,097	25.0	13.2	1.1	1.0	59.6	29.9	10.3	30.8	64.6	11.7	3,494	85.7
Liberty village	76	73	-3.9	67	100.0	0.0	0.0	0.0	0.0	40.3	9.0	41.3	40.0	5.0	28	64.3
Lincoln city	258,794	289,102	11.7	283,839	79.6	4.2	4.6	4.0	7.6	22.5	13.0	32.7	28.0	39.6	113,551	93.5
Lindsay village	262	262	0.0	276	98.2	0.0	0.0	1.8	0.0	13.8	24.3	50.3	48.8	20.3	136	80.1
Lindy CDP	13	-	-	20	100.0	0.0	0.0	0.0	0.0	0.0	75.0	72.7	50.0	15.0	10	70.0
Linwood village	88	82	-6.8	153	70.6	0.0	0.0	29.4	0.0	36.6	2.0	28.5	26.7	26.7	46	100.0
Lisco CDP	64	-	-	30	100.0	0.0	0.0	0.0	0.0	0.0	70.0	80.5	60.0	0.0	16	75.0
Litchfield village	262	249	-5.0	300	96.3	0.0	0.0	0.0	3.7	19.7	19.0	42.0	39.4	10.4	136	82.4
Lodgepole village	318	275	-13.5	325	94.8	0.0	1.5	0.0	3.7	19.1	23.4	48.0	35.7	11.9	166	88.0
Long Pine city	307	288	-6.2	275	98.5	0.0	0.4	0.7	0.4	11.3	37.8	61.1	52.1	19.3	137	76.6
Loomis village	382	376	-1.6	408	93.1	0.0	0.0	0.0	6.9	25.2	19.9	46.5	43.5	14.1	175	93.1
Lorenzo CDP	58	-	-	23	100.0	0.0	0.0	0.0	0.0	0.0	0.0	50.3	0.0	0.0	8	100.0
Loretto CDP	42	-	-	109	100.0	0.0	0.0	0.0	0.0	42.2	0.0	39.4	44.4	0.0	40	100.0
Lorton village	41	43	4.9	24	100.0	0.0	0.0	0.0	0.0	29.2	0.0	35.0	76.5	5.9	9	100.0
Louisville city	1,106	1,306	18.1	1,184	96.8	0.4	0.3	2.5	0.0	29.7	15.5	36.4	31.7	28.1	455	84.2
Loup City city	1,028	973	-5.4	975	93.6	0.0	0.8	0.3	5.2	12.5	41.6	58.1	42.6	21.3	499	80.6
Lushton village	30	29	-3.3	14	100.0	0.0	0.0	0.0	0.0	0.0	64.3	73.0	21.4	21.4	9	77.8
Lyman village	341	323	-5.3	379	48.5	0.0	0.0	1.8	49.6	24.5	15.8	39.9	68.1	1.6	134	85.8
Lynch village	245	220	-10.2	206	90.3	0.0	0.0	9.7	0.0	14.6	41.3	63.4	56.1	14.5	128	57.8
Lyons city	851	799	-6.1	818	91.2	0.7	0.0	1.2	6.8	17.4	28.5	50.2	46.9	15.6	385	83.6
McCook city	7,715	7,560	-2.0	7,587	91.1	0.5	0.1	3.2	5.1	24.0	19.9	38.2	37.8	20.5	3,286	87.9
McCool Junction village	409	429	4.9	389	89.2	5.7	0.0	4.6	0.5	31.6	12.9	37.0	40.3	14.8	153	94.8
McGrew village	105	101	-3.8	102	77.5	0.0	0.0	9.8	12.7	28.4	17.6	48.3	60.3	17.6	42	95.2
McLean village	36	36	0.0	25	84.0	0.0	0.0	16.0	0.0	0.0	40.0	64.2	28.6	19.0	17	82.4
Macy CDP	1,023	-	-	988	0.6	0.0	1.0	97.3	1.1	46.8	5.6	19.1	48.5	5.8	228	70.6
Madison city	2,402	2,392	-0.4	2,561	33.1	0.5	2.7	0.8	62.9	30.0	12.1	33.2	59.3	9.5	783	76.9
Madrid village	234	231	-1.3	197	90.4	0.0	0.0	0.0	9.6	23.4	28.9	47.8	52.6	5.1	89	83.1
Magnet village	57	54	-5.3	54	100.0	0.0	0.0	0.0	0.0	11.1	35.2	58.0	91.7	0.0	28	71.4
Malcolm village	382	406	6.3	483	98.1	0.0	0.0	1.4	0.4	33.1	7.0	31.4	29.8	28.0	179	92.7
Malmo village	120	114	-5.0	162	84.6	4.9	0.0	0.0	10.5	23.5	8.0	39.5	51.4	13.1	59	86.4
Manley village	164	172	4.9	163	99.4	0.0	0.0	0.6	0.0	11.7	23.3	47.8	64.1	9.2	73	84.9
Marquette village	233	239	2.6	243	94.2	0.0	0.0	4.1	1.6	22.6	23.5	37.1	68.3	1.2	98	87.8
Martin CDP	92	-	-	51	100.0	0.0	0.0	0.0	0.0	0.0	100.0	74.0	52.9	0.0	34	100.0
Martinsburg village	94	88	-6.4	81	100.0	0.0	0.0	0.0	0.0	17.3	9.9	53.4	42.9	14.3	52	84.6
Maskell village	76	71	-6.6	61	100.0	0.0	0.0	0.0	0.0	19.7	26.2	43.4	53.3	0.0	26	92.3
Mason City village	171	169	-1.2	198	95.5	4.5	0.0	0.0	0.0	25.8	25.8	43.5	46.0	30.7	93	66.7
Max CDP	57	-	-	84	100.0	0.0	0.0	0.0	0.0	28.6	9.5	44.9	22.6	37.7	33	63.6
Maxwell village	310	295	-4.8	230	91.3	2.2	0.0	1.3	5.2	21.3	19.1	44.5	48.5	10.4	104	83.7
Maywood village	261	249	-4.6	350	92.0	0.0	0.0	7.7	0.3	19.7	21.4	44.3	39.5	16.3	153	94.8
Mead village	569	567	-0.4	608	88.7	0.0	0.0	1.6	9.7	30.1	10.7	31.3	38.8	16.3	247	93.1
Meadow Grove village	301	289	-4.0	249	91.2	0.0	0.0	0.8	8.0	14.9	19.3	34.9	42.8	17.5	120	83.3
Melbeta village	112	108	-3.6	144	79.9	1.4	0.0	0.0	18.8	15.3	6.3	31.5	34.4	3.3	59	98.3
Memphis village	114	110	-3.5	74	77.0	0.0	0.0	23.0	0.0	16.2	23.0	46.5	65.4	3.8	28	75.0
Merna village	363	363	0.0	353	87.0	0.0	0.0	5.9	7.1	23.5	15.9	37.6	51.5	13.5	156	84.6
Merriman village	128	129	0.8	154	86.4	0.0	3.2	10.4	0.0	31.8	27.9	43.5	48.5	9.7	68	66.2
Milford city	2,090	2,090	0.0	2,363	92.3	0.4	1.2	2.1	4.0	26.2	15.4	28.3	41.0	20.6	841	90.0
Miller village	136	131	-3.7	153	97.4	2.6	0.0	0.0	0.0	21.6	24.2	56.5	61.8	5.5	61	65.6
Milligan village	285	266	-6.7	278	97.5	0.0	0.0	0.7	1.8	21.6	13.7	48.3	43.8	15.3	137	73.7
Minatare city	816	789	-3.3	896	51.1	0.0	0.0	3.7	45.2	29.9	11.3	36.8	61.0	8.7	327	82.0
Minden city	2,918	2,950	1.1	2,808	87.4	0.1	0.0	0.1	12.4	25.7	22.5	39.3	38.5	20.7	1,192	86.3
Mitchell city	1,702	1,623	-4.6	1,795	72.9	0.3	0.2	1.2	25.4	21.0	20.7	41.4	45.0	15.9	783	86.3
Monowi village	1	1	0.0	-	-	-	-	-	-	-	-	-	-	-	-	-
Monroe village	284	282	-0.7	388	91.0	1.3	1.0	4.4	2.3	28.6	18.8	38.4	45.8	11.5	160	90.6
Moorefield village	32	30	-6.3	19	94.7	0.0	0.0	0.0	5.3	0.0	21.1	56.3	22.2	11.1	6	100.0
Morrill village	920	889	-3.4	758	79.0	1.5	0.4	2.0	17.2	17.2	19.7	50.3	43.2	24.5	391	82.4
Morse Bluff village	135	142	5.2	128	100.0	0.0	0.0	0.0	0.0	18.0	18.8	51.5	36.5	12.5	59	84.7
Mullen village	509	463	-9.0	351	98.6	0.0	0.0	0.0	1.4	14.8	32.2	55.5	38.5	19.5	179	76.0
Murdock village	236	247	4.7	185	99.5	0.0	0.0	0.0	0.5	14.6	37.3	56.1	43.9	19.7	98	80.6
Murray village	463	485	4.8	505	89.5	0.0	0.2	3.8	6.5	20.6	21.4	41.8	44.3	19.5	206	88.3
Naper village	84	76	-9.5	94	87.2	0.0	12.8	0.0	0.0	1.1	59.6	68.0	68.5	16.9	63	65.1
Naponee village	106	100	-5.7	116	100.0	0.0	0.0	0.0	0.0	6.9	37.1	51.0	44.4	15.6	66	93.9
Nebraska City city	7,293	7,292	0.0	7,273	79.7	0.8	0.7	3.4	15.5	24.8	19.3	38.3	50.2	19.6	3,050	89.0
Nehawka village	204	212	3.9	186	97.3	0.0	1.1	1.1	0.5	31.2	23.1	37.7	54.3	16.4	72	84.7
Neligh city	1,625	1,501	-7.6	1,622	95.4	0.6	0.1	0.7	3.2	26.6	23.4	44.9	38.3	19.5	674	84.6
Nelson city	488	445	-8.8	467	91.2	1.3	0.0	0.0	7.5	18.6	26.1	44.3	43.5	12.0	207	85.0
Nemaha village	149	142	-4.7	112	100.0	0.0	0.0	0.0	0.0	17.9	22.3	47.4	56.4	23.1	62	83.9
Nenzel village	20	19	-5.0	30	100.0	0.0	0.0	0.0	0.0	0.0	10.0	63.1	30.0	6.7	13	100.0
Newcastle village	325	346	6.5	314	98.4	0.0	0.6	0.0	1.0	22.9	27.7	47.5	44.0	19.3	140	77.9
Newman Grove city	721	703	-2.5	723	88.0	0.0	1.2	0.1	10.7	23.4	22.7	43.3	42.3	17.8	322	87.0
Newport village	97	87	-10.3	64	100.0	0.0	0.0	0.0	0.0	6.3	31.3	55.5	31.5	3.7	37	94.6
Nickerson village	369	369	0.0	334	73.4	0.0	0.0	0.3	26.3	33.2	10.8	39.6	69.7	8.2	127	88.2
Niobrara village	369	338	-8.4	293	89.8	0.0	0.0	10.2	0.0	15.4	35.8	59.5	37.9	28.1	156	78.8
Nora village	21	20	-4.8	6	100.0	0.0	0.0	0.0	0.0	0.0	33.3	55.5	50.0	0.0	3	100.0
Norfolk city	24,231	24,449	0.9	24,424	80.3	1.6	1.8	2.8	13.5	24.6	15.1	35.7	39.4	24.5	10,290	87.4
Norman village	43	44	2.3	47	100.0	0.0	0.0	0.0	0.0	10.6	17.0	46.7	37.8	13.5	18	83.3
North Bend city	1,215	1,269	4.4	1,340	97.1	0.0	1.3	0.5	1.1	29.6	16.3	36.6	43.8	24.1	480	94.2
North Loup village	297	293	-1.3	281	81.1	0.0	0.0	1.4	17.4	13.5	37.4	58.4	57.7	12.3	168	77.4
North Platte city	24,738	23,639	-4.4	23,892	84.9	1.7	1.2	1.3	10.9	23.6	17.6	38.8	36.6	21.4	10,309	87.7
Oak village	66	61	-7.6	32	100.0	0.0	0.0	0.0	0.0	0.0	15.6	49.4	75.9	6.9	27	96.3
Oakdale village	322	293	-9.0	366	91.0	5.5	0.0	0.8	2.7	18.9	17.5	48.2	58.3	4.5	158	83.5
Oakland city	1,248	1,179	-5.5	1,556	89.8	0.8	0.0	6.4	3.0	24.6	23.9	41.4	44.4	23.5	644	84.3
Obert village	23	22	-4.3	18	100.0	0.0	0.0	0.0	0.0	0.0	55.6	68.5	77.8	0.0	10	60.0
Oconto village	151	144	-4.6	143	94.4	0.0	0.0	2.8	2.8	9.1	25.9	53.3	44.2	7.8	83	79.5
Octavia village	127	120	-5.5	151	75.5	0.0	0.0	0.0	24.5	23.2	12.6	45.3	56.6	15.0	62	95.2
Odell village	307	291	-5.2	396	99.2	0.0	0.5	0.3	0.0	27.3	13.6	31.5	47.3	15.2	156	93.6
Odessa CDP	130	-	-	81	100.0	0.0	0.0	0.0	0.0	8.6	44.4	53.8	39.2	16.2	37	100.0
Offutt AFB CDP	4,644	-	-	5,048	67.4	8.1	2.7	8.9	12.8	33.2	0.3	23.9	18.7	27.4	1,705	99.3
Ogallala city	4,740	4,497	-5.1	4,536	87.6	0.9	1.0	1.5	9.0	21.8	22.4	42.4	40.6	19.4	2,284	85.9
Ohiowa village	115	106	-7.8	136	57.4	0.0	0.0	2.2	40.4	24.3	9.6	35.5	62.1	4.2	57	91.2

1 May be of any race.

Table A. All Places — **Population and Housing**

STATE City, town, township, borough, or CDP (county if applicable)	Population: 2010 census total population	Population: 2019 estimated population	Population: Percent change 2010–2019	Population: ACS total population estimate 2015–2019	Race and Hispanic or Latino origin (percent): White alone, not Hispanic or Latino	Black alone, not Hispanic or Latino	Asian alone, not Hispanic or Latino	All other races or 2 or more races, not Hispanic or Latino	Hispanic or Latino[1]	Age (percent): Under 18 years old	Age 65 years and older	Median age	Educational attainment of persons age 25 and older: Percent High school diploma or less	Percent Bachelor's degree or more	Occupied housing units: Total	Percent with a computer
	1	2	3	4	5	6	7	8	9	10	11	12	13	14	15	16
NEBRASKA—Con.																
Omaha city	458,989	478,192	4.2	475,862	66.6	12.2	3.8	3.5	13.9	25.1	12.8	34.5	32.8	37.7	186,883	89.9
O'Neill city	3,705	3,579	-3.4	3,615	89.6	0.4	0.0	1.8	8.3	23.5	23.3	45.2	40.9	22.7	1,601	85.7
Ong village	63	59	-6.3	71	94.4	0.0	0.0	0.0	5.6	11.3	29.6	53.5	46.7	23.3	39	61.5
Orchard village	379	345	-9.0	524	89.9	0.2	0.0	0.6	9.4	23.1	20.2	37.9	50.8	15.6	216	88.9
Ord city	2,140	2,076	-3.0	2,310	94.1	0.6	0.0	1.9	3.4	18.7	26.9	48.3	41.2	24.8	1,067	81.4
Orleans village	386	371	-3.9	442	96.4	0.0	0.0	3.2	0.5	20.4	24.7	45.2	51.0	17.0	230	82.2
Osceola city	880	843	-4.2	924	93.7	0.0	0.0	6.2	0.1	27.6	21.0	41.6	37.4	19.6	364	89.3
Oshkosh city	883	777	-12.0	861	88.9	0.3	0.3	0.9	9.5	25.7	26.8	40.0	38.6	24.1	378	93.1
Osmond city	783	749	-4.3	873	99.2	0.8	0.0	0.0	0.0	28.4	24.2	41.4	43.7	14.6	363	78.2
Otoe village	171	178	4.1	288	96.5	0.0	0.0	0.3	3.1	34.4	11.5	31.4	50.8	13.6	102	89.2
Overland CDP	153	-	-	100	100.0	0.0	0.0	0.0	0.0	0.0	52.0	67.2	30.0	33.0	48	100.0
Overton village	594	567	-4.5	586	79.7	0.0	0.0	11.9	8.4	35.5	9.6	35.2	56.4	10.8	227	86.8
Oxford village	776	733	-5.5	783	84.8	0.0	0.0	1.7	13.5	19.7	19.4	44.0	50.8	15.4	382	79.1
Page village	166	158	-4.8	186	100.0	0.0	0.0	0.0	0.0	22.0	23.1	46.8	31.2	22.5	87	89.7
Palisade village	351	330	-6.0	328	97.9	0.0	0.0	0.9	1.2	14.9	27.4	47.5	41.9	16.2	169	82.8
Palmer village	472	467	-1.1	524	96.9	0.0	0.0	1.5	1.5	21.9	15.6	34.9	43.2	21.2	205	88.8
Palmyra village	545	565	3.7	571	93.5	0.0	0.7	1.9	3.9	29.9	12.4	38.1	36.6	13.3	221	97.3
Panama village	256	274	7.0	236	96.6	1.7	0.0	0.4	1.3	25.4	13.1	42.1	29.0	23.9	81	95.1
Papillion city	20,067	20,471	2.0	20,423	85.2	3.3	2.6	3.1	5.8	24.6	14.4	37.6	27.4	37.2	7,707	93.4
Parks CDP	23	-	-	12	100.0	0.0	0.0	0.0	0.0	0.0	66.7	0.0	0.0	33.3	8	100.0
Pawnee City city	878	832	-5.2	1,077	93.4	0.0	0.0	2.7	3.9	26.5	22.9	47.6	55.1	15.2	478	78.0
Paxton village	523	490	-6.3	532	83.8	3.2	0.0	2.1	10.9	27.8	22.0	48.0	36.0	22.3	224	80.4
Pender village	1,002	1,108	10.6	1,204	90.8	0.2	0.0	2.7	6.4	21.4	23.2	42.5	44.2	25.6	490	85.9
Peru city	773	755	-2.3	908	79.7	8.1	0.0	2.6	9.5	10.4	4.0	22.3	37.6	28.9	261	95.4
Petersburg village	333	312	-6.3	408	89.7	0.7	0.0	0.7	8.8	25.0	20.1	47.3	52.6	9.2	177	80.8
Phillips village	287	298	3.8	299	87.6	0.0	0.0	9.0	3.3	19.7	17.1	47.1	45.9	4.1	108	92.6
Pickrell village	199	191	-4.0	247	91.5	0.0	0.0	2.4	6.1	27.9	12.6	39.6	50.3	16.0	88	96.6
Pierce city	1,767	1,728	-2.2	2,013	94.8	0.1	0.0	3.4	1.7	27.8	17.0	35.3	33.7	23.9	823	88.3
Pilger village	352	358	1.7	305	83.9	10.8	1.6	0.0	3.6	13.4	14.8	44.3	46.7	12.5	148	86.5
Plainview city	1,246	1,192	-4.3	1,398	93.1	0.0	2.8	2.4	1.6	25.0	23.6	40.1	46.8	19.0	631	86.2
Platte Center village	336	336	0.0	384	99.5	0.0	0.0	0.0	0.5	24.5	15.9	43.2	58.6	9.2	158	87.3
Plattsmouth city	6,504	6,441		6,448	94.0	0.4	0.0	2.5	3.1	25.1	15.5	35.3	44.3	12.8	2,624	90.4
Pleasant Dale village	205	208	1.5	260	99.6	0.0	0.0	0.4	0.0	26.2	15.4	31.8	37.5	20.8	105	81.0
Pleasanton village	341	359	5.3	391	97.2	0.0	2.8	0.0	0.0	28.9	17.6	35.6	27.9	24.3	159	86.2
Plymouth village	409	377	-7.8	452	92.5	0.0	0.0	0.0	7.5	24.1	19.7	42.1	49.1	14.2	188	75.5
Polk village	322	305	-5.3	309	83.8	0.6	0.0	0.0	15.5	20.4	22.0	44.3	43.6	13.2	152	83.6
Ponca city	961	912	-5.1	915	91.4	0.3	0.0	1.9	6.4	20.2	28.6	45.7	44.6	25.9	445	82.9
Poole CDP	19	-	-	50	90.0	0.0	0.0	0.0	10.0	32.0	10.0	37.4	14.7	52.9	10	100.0
Potter village	337	292	-13.4	328	96.3	0.9	0.0	1.2	1.5	20.4	19.8	48.3	29.4	22.2	158	86.7
Prague village	311	309	-0.6	345	94.8	0.0	0.0	1.4	3.8	21.7	19.7	42.4	61.3	5.2	132	72.7
Preston village	28	26	-7.1	33	63.6	0.0	0.0	15.2	21.2	15.2	36.4	57.4	78.6	7.1	15	46.7
Primrose village	61	58	-4.9	68	97.1	0.0	0.0	0.0	2.9	13.2	26.5	45.5	48.0	6.0	33	93.9
Prosser village	66	72	9.1	97	100.0	0.0	0.0	0.0	0.0	23.7	25.8	55.4	39.7	41.1	37	94.6
Raeville CDP	22	-	-	-	-	-	-	-	-	-	-	-	-	-	-	-
Ragan village	38	38	0.0	21	100.0	0.0	0.0	0.0	0.0	23.8	14.3	43.9	60.0	13.3	9	88.9
Ralston city	5,943	7,273	22.4	7,321	76.3	5.6	1.9	4.4	11.9	22.1	16.9	36.5	35.3	30.2	3,020	92.5
Randolph city	944	890	-5.7	1,010	92.8	0.0	0.0	0.4	6.8	24.3	25.6	43.1	46.2	18.1	422	83.4
Ravenna city	1,365	1,358	-0.5	1,439	92.7	0.0	0.0	1.4	5.9	23.9	19.9	37.0	51.0	18.9	606	82.5
Raymond village	167	185	10.8	181	100.0	0.0	0.0	0.0	0.0	11.6	8.8	50.6	43.8	14.6	78	93.6
Red Cloud city	1,020	916	-10.2	1,095	84.3	0.9	0.0	6.8	8.0	22.1	25.8	45.4	46.2	20.3	489	85.1
Republican City village	150	154	2.7	162	99.4	0.0	0.0	0.6	0.0	15.4	43.2	63.5	42.3	13.9	90	86.7
Reynolds village	69	66	-4.3	63	100.0	0.0	0.0	0.0	0.0	4.8	27.0	47.3	77.1	0.0	36	58.3
Richfield CDP	43	-	-	21	100.0	0.0	0.0	0.0	0.0	0.0	33.3	64.4	0.0	0.0	6	100.0
Richland village	73	72	-1.4	134	68.7	0.0	0.0	7.5	23.9	38.8	11.2	24.5	30.3	34.8	52	90.4
Rising City village	374	352	-5.9	428	96.5	0.0	0.7	1.2	1.6	23.4	18.7	40.4	52.9	10.8	169	84.6
Riverdale village	182	179	-1.6	302	91.7	0.0	0.0	0.0	8.3	37.1	12.6	26.9	24.0	28.0	95	98.9
Riverton village	89	84	-5.6	40	92.5	0.0	7.5	0.0	0.0	5.0	60.0	73.3	71.1	21.1	30	73.3
Roca village	212	350	65.1	181	98.3	1.7	0.0	0.0	0.0	21.5	13.8	40.7	36.4	13.6	80	91.3
Rockville village	106	100	-5.7	143	99.3	0.0	0.7	0.0	0.0	28.7	11.2	30.4	39.1	9.2	52	80.8
Rogers village	95	94	-1.1	124	81.5	0.0	0.0	1.6	16.9	23.4	8.1	37.1	83.3	0.0	43	97.7
Rosalie village	157	162	3.2	161	56.5	0.0	0.6	37.3	5.6	35.4	11.8	34.3	44.9	10.2	61	86.9
Roscoe CDP	63	-	-	109	89.0	0.0	0.0	0.0	11.0	59.6	0.0	17.0	41.7	0.0	18	100.0
Roseland village	245	267	9.0	233	94.0	0.0	0.0	0.0	6.0	34.3	16.7	37.3	37.4	25.2	90	87.8
Royal village	63	58	-7.9	71	100.0	0.0	0.0	0.0	0.0	26.8	8.5	26.1	35.6	22.2	33	81.8
Rulo village	172	160	-7.0	120	59.2	1.7	0.0	39.2	0.0	10.8	33.3	54.5	52.5	14.1	69	89.9
Rushville city	890	879	-1.2	807	65.1	0.2	0.4	9.9	24.4	27.4	26.8	43.3	52.0	16.4	351	77.5
Ruskin village	123	113	-8.1	100	93.0	0.0	0.0	0.0	7.0	15.0	13.0	56.3	43.8	18.8	39	97.4
St. Edward city	705	659	-6.5	744	95.8	0.4	0.4	0.9	2.4	17.7	28.9	44.3	42.5	16.6	340	79.1
St. Helena village	96	91	-5.2	78	98.7	0.0	0.0	1.3	0.0	28.2	19.2	47.8	61.1	18.5	32	93.8
St. Libory CDP	264	-	-	166	97.0	0.0	0.0	3.0	0.0	6.0	40.4	57.3	49.6	17.7	80	87.5
St. Paul city	2,309	2,333	1.0	2,362	91.6	0.3	0.1	3.3	4.7	27.2	21.6	39.9	37.8	24.6	1,032	86.5
Salem village	112	104	-7.1	103	94.2	0.0	0.0	2.9	2.9	16.5	20.4	58.1	57.7	15.5	53	92.5
Santee village	336	340	1.2	389	3.6	0.5	0.5	88.4	6.9	42.7	5.9	24.0	52.4	5.3	112	75.0
Sarben CDP	31	-	-	105	70.5	29.5	0.0	0.0	0.0	45.7	5.7	44.2	85.2	14.8	28	100.0
Sargent city	530	506	-4.5	501	94.0	0.0	0.0	0.0	6.0	20.8	28.3	55.7	53.7	15.9	256	81.3
Saronville village	47	45	-4.3	72	69.4	0.0	0.0	0.0	30.6	44.4	2.8	20.8	48.6	31.4	22	90.9
Schuyler city	6,212	6,303	1.5	6,284	20.8	5.3	0.0	0.7	73.2	35.2	8.0	30.1	77.1	9.8	1,805	84.2
Scotia village	318	289	-9.1	329	95.4	1.5	0.0	3.0	0.0	29.8	20.7	36.4	47.0	16.3	125	84.8
Scottsbluff city	15,047	14,556	-3.3	14,737	64.1	1.0	0.8	4.0	30.2	25.8	17.2	35.3	39.6	24.7	6,139	88.5
Scribner city	857	799	-6.8	754	92.3	0.7	0.5	4.6	1.9	21.9	28.4	52.5	48.1	17.0	351	83.2
Seneca CDP	33	-	-	35	82.9	0.0	0.0	17.1	0.0	0.0	62.9	66.3	54.3	11.4	22	45.5
Seward city	6,965	7,216	3.6	7,176	94.0	0.7	0.6	1.6	3.1	22.1	14.6	32.8	31.2	38.1	2,625	91.1
Shelby village	714	701	-1.8	752	72.1	0.0	0.0	2.7	25.3	25.0	19.3	39.6	46.9	20.6	297	89.6
Shelton village	1,059	1,055	-0.4	1,107	89.8	1.1	0.0	0.0	9.1	28.7	15.0	33.3	33.2	20.7	429	85.5
Shickley village	343	319	-7.0	260	83.8	0.0	0.0	0.0	16.2	17.7	18.8	52.5	34.9	24.0	125	88.8
Sholes village	21	20	-4.8	31	100.0	0.0	0.0	0.0	0.0	19.4	35.5	35.9	60.0	40.0	15	46.7
Shubert village	150	138	-8.0	176	96.6	0.0	0.0	0.0	3.4	17.0	25.0	55.0	51.1	14.2	82	89.0
Sidney city	6,776	6,115	-9.8	6,572	87.8	1.2	0.8	1.4	8.9	24.5	17.1	37.9	34.1	28.3	3,051	89.0
Silver Creek village	359	357	-0.6	409	98.0	0.0	0.0	0.0	2.0	25.4	16.9	37.6	42.4	10.4	187	74.3
Smithfield village	54	53	-1.9	65	100.0	0.0	0.0	0.0	0.0	20.0	30.8	41.5	65.4	3.8	30	96.7
Snyder village	300	289	-3.7	327	88.7	1.2	0.0	0.6	9.5	27.5	15.0	44.9	42.5	12.3	135	88.1
South Bend village	99	104	5.1	94	96.8	0.0	0.0	0.0	3.2	10.6	35.1	57.0	59.5	12.7	40	82.5

1 May be of any race.

Table A. All Places — **Population and Housing**

STATE City, town, township, borough, or CDP (county if applicable)	Population: 2010 census total population	Population: 2019 estimated population	Population: Percent change 2010–2019	Population: ACS total population estimate 2015–2019	Race and Hispanic or Latino origin (percent): White alone, not Hispanic or Latino	Race and Hispanic or Latino origin (percent): Black alone, not Hispanic or Latino	Race and Hispanic or Latino origin (percent): Asian alone, not Hispanic or Latino	Race and Hispanic or Latino origin (percent): All other races or 2 or more races, not Hispanic or Latino	Race and Hispanic or Latino origin (percent): Hispanic or Latino[1]	Age (percent): Under 18 years old	Age (percent): Age 65 years and older	Age (percent): Median age	Educational attainment of persons age 25 and older: Percent High school diploma or less	Educational attainment of persons age 25 and older: Percent Bachelor's degree or more	Occupied housing units: Total	Occupied housing units: Percent with a computer
	1	2	3	4	5	6	7	8	9	10	11	12	13	14	15	16
NEBRASKA—Con.																
South Sioux City city	13,365	12,809	-4.2	12,896	37.0	7.6	3.6	3.6	48.1	29.0	13.1	31.9	62.2	10.6	4,721	87.4
Spalding village	487	440	-9.7	492	91.1	0.0	0.8	0.0	8.1	16.5	28.9	45.8	41.8	12.8	226	87.2
Spencer village	455	416	-8.6	368	97.6	1.9	0.0	0.5	0.0	15.8	34.5	58.3	39.4	24.6	199	80.9
Sprague village	142	151	6.3	91	97.8	0.0	0.0	1.1	1.1	17.6	39.6	59.5	61.3	17.3	46	87.0
Springfield city	1,552	1,624	4.6	1,466	95.0	0.5	0.3	0.2	3.9	22.9	17.7	42.9	34.2	35.6	623	90.2
Springview village	242	236	-2.5	202	96.5	0.0	0.0	0.5	3.0	23.3	28.2	46.5	42.2	22.4	99	87.9
Stamford village	183	175	-4.4	211	77.3	0.0	1.9	6.6	14.2	52.6	7.6	17.7	26.0	21.0	70	90.0
Stanton city	1,577	1,502	-4.8	1,632	93.4	0.3	0.9	0.6	4.8	27.7	23.5	40.3	39.2	13.2	675	83.6
Staplehurst village	242	232	-4.1	260	93.1	0.0	0.4	5.8	0.8	28.8	14.6	37.6	34.7	18.8	112	85.7
Stapleton village	305	299	-2.0	357	86.8	0.0	0.0	2.2	10.9	18.2	26.9	44.9	52.3	17.7	155	83.9
Steele City village	61	58	-4.9	76	100.0	0.0	0.0	0.0	0.0	27.6	22.4	41.6	39.2	3.9	39	79.5
Steinauer village	75	70	-6.7	100	97.0	0.0	0.0	0.0	3.0	23.0	32.0	40.6	51.4	5.7	50	90.0
Stella village	152	143	-5.9	230	93.9	0.0	0.0	4.3	1.7	22.6	44.8	60.6	50.9	30.6	105	73.3
Sterling village	476	459	-3.6	456	96.1	0.4	0.0	0.4	3.1	26.8	25.0	42.8	40.7	26.4	193	94.3
Stockham village	44	45	2.3	20	100.0	0.0	0.0	0.0	0.0	25.0	40.0	64.0	46.7	20.0	9	100.0
Stockville village	25	25	0.0	13	100.0	0.0	0.0	0.0	0.0	0.0	92.3	72.4	38.5	0.0	7	71.4
Strang village	29	27	-6.9	31	100.0	0.0	0.0	0.0	0.0	29.0	19.4	39.5	50.0	27.3	14	92.9
Stratton village	343	324	-5.5	347	99.1	0.0	0.0	0.9	0.0	21.0	30.0	55.3	46.1	19.9	159	88.1
Stromsburg city	1,171	1,139	-2.7	1,082	99.2	0.0	0.0	0.4	0.5	20.3	30.2	50.2	43.8	24.4	447	86.8
Stuart village	594	584	-1.7	667	99.1	0.0	0.3	0.0	0.6	18.6	15.7	40.2	38.1	15.3	306	87.6
Sumner village	236	219	-7.2	214	83.2	0.0	0.0	0.0	16.8	29.0	13.6	36.7	54.5	20.0	85	94.1
Sunol CDP	73	-	-	64	100.0	0.0	0.0	0.0	0.0	17.2	9.4	40.3	47.2	7.5	30	90.0
Superior city	1,957	1,807	-7.7	1,979	94.7	0.0	3.7	0.8	0.8	20.4	27.8	46.7	46.8	21.5	904	79.2
Surprise village	43	41	-4.7	56	82.1	0.0	0.0	0.0	17.9	16.1	28.6	48.0	47.7	2.3	25	92.0
Sutherland village	1,370	1,320	-3.6	1,607	94.9	0.3	0.7	1.0	3.1	27.2	19.2	41.6	36.1	18.3	617	89.3
Sutton city	1,502	1,434	-4.5	1,503	87.1	0.0	0.0	2.1	10.8	29.3	20.2	38.3	40.8	20.9	601	87.0
Swanton village	94	91	-3.2	81	91.4	0.0	0.0	0.0	8.6	16.0	19.8	48.1	46.6	20.7	38	94.7
Syracuse city	1,942	1,960	0.9	2,076	97.3	0.1	0.0	2.3	0.3	24.9	25.1	41.3	36.0	26.0	913	82.0
Table Rock village	269	253	-5.9	366	99.7	0.0	0.0	0.3	0.0	28.4	19.7	42.8	61.7	15.6	168	82.7
Talmage village	233	241	3.4	247	96.0	0.0	0.0	0.0	4.0	17.8	24.3	44.3	60.1	15.6	87	88.5
Tamora CDP	58	-	-	9	100.0	0.0	0.0	0.0	0.0	0.0	100.0	0.0	0.0	0.0	9	100.0
Tarnov village	46	46	0.0	15	100.0	0.0	0.0	0.0	0.0	13.3	0.0	50.8	80.0	0.0	5	80.0
Taylor village	190	200	5.3	146	91.1	0.0	0.0	1.4	7.5	4.8	24.0	55.0	35.8	17.0	94	76.6
Tecumseh city	1,676	1,586	-5.4	1,682	73.4	0.2	3.7	1.4	21.3	22.7	24.0	45.1	54.3	22.2	722	81.9
Tekamah city	1,825	1,708	-6.4	1,802	95.7	0.7	0.8	0.0	2.8	26.6	21.8	43.7	46.0	19.5	777	83.7
Terrytown city	1,197	1,169	-2.3	1,195	50.8	0.6	0.3	6.7	41.6	31.4	13.7	32.3	69.2	6.8	482	80.3
Thayer village	62	58	-6.5	78	100.0	0.0	0.0	0.0	0.0	44.9	9.0	41.1	30.2	14.0	23	100.0
Thedford village	196	219	11.7	190	86.3	0.0	0.0	13.7	0.0	11.6	19.5	33.8	34.4	27.9	100	94.0
Thurston village	132	136	3.0	125	93.6	0.0	0.0	6.4	0.0	20.0	21.6	36.5	68.2	2.3	52	84.6
Tilden city	959	930	-3.0	1,105	92.3	2.8	0.5	0.5	3.9	28.7	24.5	39.7	45.2	16.1	417	85.6
Tobias village	106	105	-0.9	112	80.4	0.0	8.0	4.5	7.1	25.0	23.2	46.0	47.6	13.1	50	80.0
Trenton village	558	535	-4.1	514	97.3	0.4	0.0	0.2	2.1	24.1	30.2	47.0	56.2	11.0	214	66.8
Trumbull village	205	196	-4.4	251	94.8	0.0	0.0	5.2	0.0	29.9	8.0	31.3	38.5	7.0	80	95.0
Tryon CDP	157	-	-	92	100.0	0.0	0.0	0.0	0.0	13.0	33.7	58.9	46.3	12.5	61	68.9
Uehling village	230	222	-3.5	271	79.3	0.0	0.0	14.8	5.9	24.0	22.5	46.7	52.9	18.5	114	88.6
Ulysses village	171	159	-7.0	203	97.5	0.0	0.0	0.0	2.5	9.4	19.7	47.3	50.0	21.3	107	88.8
Unadilla village	311	322	3.5	289	99.0	0.0	0.0	1.0	0.0	18.3	20.4	49.9	49.3	29.8	134	82.8
Union village	233	243	4.3	142	98.6	0.0	0.0	0.0	1.4	16.2	23.2	52.3	61.3	0.9	64	84.4
Upland village	143	134	-6.3	196	78.1	0.0	0.0	3.6	18.4	23.5	9.2	39.9	50.0	18.6	82	100.0
Utica village	861	831	-3.5	922	96.4	1.1	0.3	0.5	1.6	29.7	21.0	37.4	37.6	27.2	352	92.9
Valentine city	2,737	2,706	-1.1	2,760	80.5	0.0	0.5	14.9	4.1	27.4	18.2	35.0	39.2	24.9	1,293	80.4
Valley city	2,408	2,890	20.0	2,773	92.9	1.0	0.0	2.6	3.5	20.2	18.4	48.1	27.0	41.3	1,260	85.4
Valparaiso village	570	543	-4.7	605	99.7	0.0	0.0	0.0	0.3	25.5	20.8	41.2	47.0	16.8	257	87.2
Venango village	167	160	-4.2	186	91.9	0.0	0.0	0.5	7.5	17.7	19.9	49.2	37.7	23.8	89	95.5
Venice CDP	75	-	-	50	86.0	0.0	0.0	14.0	0.0	0.0	70.0	68.6	74.3	0.0	36	100.0
Verdel village	30	30	0.0	26	76.9	0.0	0.0	23.1	0.0	7.7	46.2	64.7	41.7	37.5	15	86.7
Verdigre village	575	527	-8.3	555	83.8	0.0	0.0	16.2	0.0	18.7	36.6	56.1	41.4	22.6	255	80.0
Verdon village	172	158	-8.1	207	95.7	0.0	0.0	4.3	0.0	21.3	20.8	50.9	60.3	3.5	96	84.4
Virginia village	60	57	-5.0	71	94.4	0.0	0.0	2.8	2.8	29.6	19.7	50.4	75.0	12.5	33	69.7
Waco village	236	236	0.0	272	93.8	0.0	2.2	1.8	2.2	14.3	31.6	52.6	30.3	26.6	138	92.0
Wahoo city	4,513	4,548	0.8	4,502	94.7	1.4	0.0	1.1	2.8	28.3	17.7	37.7	42.0	20.4	1,786	81.6
Wakefield city	1,460	1,363	-6.6	1,545	52.6	1.2	0.0	0.6	45.6	30.5	14.2	33.2	54.7	21.9	537	87.5
Wallace village	366	344	-6.0	274	82.1	0.0	1.5	2.2	14.2	21.5	24.5	43.3	33.7	25.5	119	88.2
Walthill village	785	798	1.7	792	9.6	0.6	0.4	74.6	14.8	39.3	10.5	24.5	41.6	9.0	187	83.4
Walton CDP	306	-	-	179	93.9	6.1	0.0	0.0	0.0	2.8	59.2	65.9	15.4	64.5	84	94.0
Wann CDP	86	-	-	103	100.0	0.0	0.0	0.0	0.0	22.3	0.0	38.5	70.1	11.9	28	100.0
Washington village	150	157	4.7	85	96.5	0.0	0.0	3.5	0.0	21.2	18.8	50.2	44.6	15.4	38	94.7
Waterbury village	73	67	-8.2	77	92.2	0.0	0.0	7.8	0.0	10.4	0.0	47.5	75.0	11.5	45	75.6
Waterloo village	848	915	7.9	966	88.8	0.0	0.0	1.0	10.1	30.1	13.5	36.6	39.5	17.4	358	93.0
Wauneta village	577	556	-3.6	733	93.2	0.0	0.0	0.0	6.8	28.8	25.6	39.8	41.2	16.2	316	82.3
Wausa village	634	559	-11.8	562	93.1	0.0	0.9	2.1	3.9	18.3	30.8	53.2	35.4	21.4	223	94.6
Waverly city	3,277	4,075	24.4	3,873	95.7	0.1	0.0	1.1	3.2	31.6	14.9	35.8	24.6	37.3	1,363	95.0
Wayne city	5,668	5,660	-0.1	5,557	85.5	2.4	0.6	2.9	8.6	16.7	13.0	22.8	29.5	39.6	2,143	93.6
Weeping Water city	1,050	1,095	4.3	910	96.3	0.7	0.0	1.5	1.5	17.0	27.6	49.6	52.4	15.4	437	85.6
Wellfleet village	78	78	0.0	52	80.8	0.0	0.0	0.0	19.2	28.8	19.2	33.5	26.5	23.5	22	63.6
Western village	235	232	-1.3	252	98.0	0.0	0.0	0.4	1.6	13.1	27.4	53.3	57.4	9.2	128	85.2
Westerville CDP	39	-	-	-	-	-	-	-	-	-	-	-	-	-	-	-
Weston village	324	330	1.9	283	99.3	0.0	0.0	0.0	0.7	14.8	18.7	56.2	64.7	4.5	139	91.4
West Point city	3,368	3,283	-2.5	3,301	76.8	0.0	0.4	1.4	21.4	23.8	20.1	42.3	50.7	22.1	1,345	85.4
White Clay CDP	10	-	-	-	-	-	-	-	-	-	-	-	-	-	-	-
Whitney village	77	72	-6.5	116	100.0	0.0	0.0	0.0	0.0	16.4	19.0	44.5	72.2	7.2	64	81.3
Wilber city	1,855	1,850	-0.3	1,880	85.7	0.1	3.9	1.7	8.6	26.6	17.0	39.5	47.7	16.3	750	84.4
Wilcox village	358	345	-3.6	408	83.1	0.0	0.7	15.9	0.2	28.2	9.8	35.4	45.7	20.3	143	92.3
Willow Island CDP	26	-	-	9	100.0	0.0	0.0	0.0	0.0	0.0	0.0	0.0	0.0	0.0	5	100.0
Wilsonville village	93	87	-6.5	45	80.0	0.0	8.9	8.9	2.2	6.7	60.0	69.1	59.5	11.9	32	65.6
Winnebago village	774	787	1.7	759	4.5	0.0	0.5	90.1	4.9	39.1	8.7	23.2	45.9	9.9	215	75.3
Winnetoon village	68	66	-2.9	75	100.0	0.0	0.0	0.0	0.0	24.0	30.7	55.8	63.2	5.3	32	78.1
Winside village	427	401	-6.1	574	93.9	0.7	0.0	3.8	1.6	25.3	13.1	31.5	33.4	20.1	261	91.2
Winslow village	105	101	-3.8	83	94.0	0.0	0.0	3.6	2.4	22.9	12.0	39.7	40.7	0.0	36	97.2
Wisner city	1,193	1,170	-1.9	1,257	94.4	0.0	0.0	1.2	4.4	25.2	23.2	34.6	50.9	18.1	530	84.7
Wolbach village	283	254	-10.2	255	92.5	0.0	0.0	3.5	3.9	26.7	22.0	44.2	47.6	22.2	124	81.5
Wood Lake village	63	63	0.0	32	100.0	0.0	0.0	0.0	0.0	18.8	18.8	38.3	34.6	30.8	18	83.3

1 May be of any race.

Table A. All Places — **Population and Housing**

STATE City, town, township, borough, or CDP (county if applicable)	2010 census total population	2019 estimated population	Percent change 2010–2019	ACS total population estimate 2015–2019	White alone, not Hispanic or Latino	Black alone, not Hispanic or Latino	Asian alone, not Hispanic or Latino	All other races or 2 or more races, not Hispanic or Latino	Hispanic or Latino[1]	Under 18 years old	Age 65 years and older	Median age	Percent High school diploma or less	Percent Bachelor's degree or more	Total	Percent with a computer
	1	2	3	4	5	6	7	8	9	10	11	12	13	14	15	16
NEBRASKA—Con.																
Woodland Hills CDP	215	-	-	232	100.0	0.0	0.0	0.0	0.0	12.9	15.9	53.5	15.2	47.2	87	100.0
Woodland Park CDP	1,866	-	-	1,588	82.2	1.0	0.0	2.0	14.7	26.0	12.0	34.1	39.5	23.1	644	93.9
Wood River city	1,329	1,340	0.8	1,420	67.3	0.0	0.5	2.1	30.1	27.8	17.8	36.7	49.4	16.3	489	88.8
Wymore city	1,457	1,336	-8.3	1,531	92.6	0.7	0.0	2.6	4.1	24.2	22.1	43.4	52.8	9.7	597	81.7
Wynot village	166	183	10.2	200	99.5	0.0	0.0	0.5	0.0	26.0	24.5	39.0	55.5	10.2	81	86.4
Yankee Hill CDP	292	-	-	286	100.0	0.0	0.0	0.0	0.0	31.5	8.0	29.9	22.3	38.6	115	100.0
York city	7,773	7,846	0.9	7,841	90.8	1.2	0.1	1.6	6.2	24.2	19.5	37.8	32.0	32.3	3,323	85.5
Yutan city	1,187	1,310	10.4	992	91.4	0.0	0.6	3.9	4.0	20.6	14.1	37.4	36.4	19.4	424	92.2
NEVADA	2,700,677	3,080,156	14.1	2,972,382	49.2	8.7	8.0	5.3	28.7	22.9	15.4	38.0	41.4	24.7	1,098,602	92.5
Alamo CDP	1,080			1,128	99.2	0.0	0.0	0.8	0.0	22.9	28.2	37.4	46.1	24.2	463	87.7
Austin CDP	192			113	100.0	0.0	0.0	0.0	0.0	10.6	0.0	51.6	54.5	0.0	65	70.8
Baker CDP	68			58	100.0	0.0	0.0	0.0	0.0	0.0	37.9	64.3	17.2	17.2	28	64.3
Battle Mountain CDP	3,635	-	-	3,698	53.3	0.0	0.1	4.0	42.6	26.1	14.9	38.7	47.8	15.7	1,465	92.0
Beatty CDP	1,010	-	-	804	89.2	3.6	0.0	0.9	6.3	11.1	30.1	55.4	62.9	18.0	455	78.9
Beaverdam CDP	44	-	-	25	100.0	0.0	0.0	0.0	0.0	48.0	57.9	52.0	52.0	0.0	18	100.0
Bennett Springs CDP	132	-	-	46	100.0	0.0	0.0	0.0	0.0	0.0	89.1	73.2	34.8	0.0	41	100.0
Blue Diamond CDP	290	-	-	326	98.2	0.0	0.0	0.0	1.8	17.5	25.8	54.4	45.2	42.3	129	83.7
Boulder City city	15,020	16,207	7.9	15,840	84.4	1.2	1.6	3.9	8.9	16.7	30.2	53.5	35.4	29.8	6,615	87.4
Bunkerville CDP	1,303	-	-	1,479	78.4	0.0	0.0	2.1	19.5	39.5	12.1	28.8	61.8	10.2	337	77.7
Caliente city	1,156	1,076	-6.9	888	92.9	3.8	0.0	0.0	3.3	18.6	18.8	44.6	46.1	19.3	388	87.9
Cal-Nev-Ari CDP	244	-	-	111	100.0	0.0	0.0	0.0	0.0	0.0	72.1	69.9	45.0	10.8	82	85.4
Carlin city	2,366	2,277	-3.8	2,025	79.7	2.4	0.4	5.8	11.7	18.1	11.8	44.1	57.3	3.7	700	95.6
Carson City	55,269	55,916	1.2	54,773	67.0	2.0	2.6	4.3	24.1	20.5	19.8	42.4	39.0	22.2	22,755	90.1
Carter Springs CDP	553	-	-	446	72.6	0.7	0.4	6.7	19.5	21.5	25.6	48.8	35.1	16.1	207	94.7
Cold Springs CDP	8,544	-	-	9,633	77.1	1.7	2.2	2.7	16.2	27.2	10.2	35.9	37.9	18.5	3,351	97.3
Crescent Valley CDP	392	-	-	462	76.6	0.0	0.0	16.7	6.7	9.5	21.2	48.9	43.7	6.1	244	93.0
Crystal Bay CDP	305	-	-	184	100.0	0.0	0.0	0.0	0.0	0.0	86.4	70.3	4.3	91.3	96	100.0
Dayton CDP	8,964	-	-	9,363	75.4	0.1	2.0	5.8	16.6	20.7	18.2	42.2	46.7	14.3	3,571	96.2
Denio CDP	47	-	-	-	-	-	-	-	-	-	-	-	-	-	-	-
Double Spring CDP	158	-	-	275	96.7	0.0	1.1	0.7	1.5	18.5	26.9	54.8	40.2	17.8	97	95.9
Dry Valley CDP	78	-	-	-	-	-	-	-	-	-	-	-	-	-	-	-
Dyer CDP	259	-	-	324	64.5	0.0	0.0	2.5	33.0	25.0	24.4	40.7	50.2	23.4	134	82.1
East Valley CDP	1,474	-	-	1,543	89.3	0.0	0.6	2.9	7.3	12.5	42.3	62.7	20.1	40.9	656	88.0
Elko city	18,341	20,452	11.5	20,304	65.8	0.7	2.0	4.2	27.2	25.9	10.0	32.6	43.7	18.9	7,232	92.2
Ely city	4,259	3,993	-6.2	4,035	73.9	0.4	1.2	7.0	17.4	27.2	16.2	39.0	51.2	15.1	1,703	87.1
Empire CDP	217	-	-	134	100.0	0.0	0.0	0.0	0.0	41.8	0.0	19.6	24.1	0.0	44	68.2
Enterprise CDP	108,481	-	-	171,108	42.4	9.6	22.3	6.8	18.9	24.5	9.4	35.0	30.6	31.6	58,158	98.0
Eureka CDP	610	-	-	462	93.9	0.2	2.8	0.0	3.0	13.9	20.3	56.0	62.3	7.0	249	79.1
Fallon city	8,641	8,645	0.0	8,430	72.7	3.7	5.6	6.9	11.2	23.4	12.7	34.4	42.9	17.0	3,697	94.9
Fallon Station CDP	705	-	-	438	52.5	38.1	0.0	0.0	9.4	32.9	0.0	24.7	25.2	15.0	149	100.0
Fernley city	19,368	21,476	10.9	20,068	71.8	1.6	1.6	6.0	19.0	24.2	16.8	38.4	48.6	13.2	7,419	92.6
Fish Springs CDP	648	-	-	564	92.4	0.7	0.2	0.0	6.7	18.1	31.9	56.0	39.2	31.8	220	94.5
Fort McDermitt CDP	341	-	-	344	2.0	0.0	0.3	93.9	3.8	33.7	16.9	36.2	74.2	4.5	120	36.7
Gabbs CDP	269	-	-	105	100.0	0.0	0.0	0.0	0.0	22.9	57.4	58.7	56.2	0.0	62	75.8
Gardnerville CDP	5,656	-	-	6,121	75.6	1.9	2.2	3.9	16.4	20.5	20.9	43.9	36.0	25.7	2,728	89.1
Gardnerville Ranchos CDP	11,312	-	-	11,380	84.3	0.0	1.5	2.8	11.5	18.0	22.3	45.1	44.0	18.2	4,528	91.8
Genoa CDP	939	-	-	659	95.8	0.0	2.9	1.4	0.0	16.1	41.7	61.7	17.5	52.8	293	100.0
Gerlach CDP	206	-	-	34	100.0	0.0	0.0	0.0	0.0	0.0	0.0	0.0	0.0	100.0	17	100.0
Glenbrook CDP	215	-	-	258	62.0	0.0	38.0	0.0	0.0	7.0	39.5	58.7	15.5	74.9	99	100.0
Golconda CDP	214	-	-	74	100.0	0.0	0.0	0.0	0.0	0.0	20.3	55.2	41.9	24.3	38	100.0
Golden Valley CDP	1,556	-	-	1,295	66.6	0.0	3.0	9.4	21.0	17.1	39.2	60.2	32.0	15.1	536	96.5
Goldfield CDP	268	-	-	298	94.6	0.0	0.0	3.0	2.3	16.1	37.2	56.1	43.0	16.9	146	89.0
Goodsprings CDP	229	-	-	-	-	-	-	-	-	-	-	-	-	-	-	-
Grass Valley CDP	1,161	-	-	760	77.5	0.0	0.0	2.0	20.5	16.2	22.0	47.0	45.3	15.4	253	90.9
Hawthorne CDP	3,269	-	-	2,686	78.8	3.9	1.4	2.0	13.9	15.7	35.4	55.8	44.3	19.1	1,325	78.2
Henderson city	257,001	320,189	24.6	300,116	64.6	5.7	8.1	4.8	16.8	21.4	19.4	42.2	31.9	33.4	116,123	93.8
Hiko CDP	119	-	-	62	100.0	0.0	0.0	0.0	0.0	0.0	46.8	0.0	0.0	0.0	29	100.0
Humboldt River Ranch CDP	119	-	-	158	81.6	0.0	3.8	14.6	0.0	0.0	90.5	68.2	0.0	27.2	80	96.3
Imlay CDP	171	-	-	218	100.0	0.0	0.0	0.0	0.0	51.4	7.8	11.9	87.7	0.0	55	69.1
Incline Village CDP	8,777	-	-	8,669	76.6	0.5	2.1	2.7	18.0	14.9	24.1	50.7	16.2	56.6	3,793	98.2
Indian Hills CDP	5,627	-	-	6,104	76.2	0.4	0.9	4.8	17.7	21.1	23.1	47.9	36.2	25.3	2,486	94.2
Indian Springs CDP	991	-	-	881	68.7	9.9	0.0	2.0	19.4	23.7	15.1	40.1	54.7	10.2	321	80.4
Jackpot CDP	1,195	-	-	1,244	24.3	0.0	0.0	1.3	74.4	23.3	21.5	41.1	64.8	8.6	434	71.7
Johnson Lane CDP	6,490	-	-	5,957	84.3	1.2	0.9	2.4	11.3	14.1	36.5	59.0	21.2	32.0	2,693	94.8
Kingsbury CDP	2,152	-	-	2,144	83.6	1.6	0.0	1.8	12.9	12.7	25.2	54.2	14.4	51.1	1,030	98.4
Kingston CDP	113	-	-	94	100.0	0.0	0.0	0.0	0.0	0.0	27.7	53.7	72.3	0.0	58	100.0
Lakeridge CDP	371	-	-	367	93.2	0.0	3.5	0.0	3.3	3.3	41.7	63.6	9.3	73.0	199	95.0
Lamoille CDP	105	-	-	276	100.0	0.0	0.0	0.0	0.0	18.8	60.5	66.6	12.1	51.3	139	100.0
Las Vegas city	584,489	651,319	11.4	634,773	43.5	11.6	6.7	5.1	33.1	23.8	14.9	37.8	42.8	24.6	231,915	91.8
Laughlin CDP	7,323	-	-	7,965	74.0	6.8	2.0	1.7	15.4	7.7	42.8	61.1	50.3	13.4	4,094	81.9
Lemmon Valley CDP	5,040	-	-	5,383	78.3	0.5	0.0	1.4	19.9	19.4	12.8	40.6	50.5	12.7	2,035	96.7
Logan Creek CDP	26	-	-	37	100.0	0.0	0.0	0.0	0.0	0.0	100.0	67.3	73.0	27.0	23	100.0
Lovelock city	1,891	1,828	-3.3	1,959	72.4	0.5	0.5	5.2	21.4	25.7	16.4	39.8	64.0	12.2	919	81.5
Lund CDP	282	-	-	105	100.0	0.0	0.0	0.0	0.0	30.5	44.8	64.8	53.4	0.0	38	100.0
McDermitt CDP	172	-	-	126	51.6	0.0	0.0	0.0	48.4	0.0	74.6	67.3	100.0	0.0	93	100.0
McGill CDP	1,148	-	-	905	79.6	0.0	0.0	5.2	15.2	20.4	22.8	43.0	49.3	13.2	411	79.3
Mesquite city	15,276	19,726	29.1	18,446	71.1	1.1	2.8	2.5	22.5	15.7	41.0	60.2	40.4	23.3	8,042	89.9
Mina CDP	155	-	-	182	100.0	0.0	0.0	0.0	0.0	2.2	47.3	62.7	66.7	8.3	125	60.0
Minden CDP	3,001	-	-	3,151	82.9	0.2	1.4	6.4	9.1	16.5	33.0	53.6	22.9	33.4	1,409	96.2
Moapa Town CDP	1,025	-	-	710	45.8	0.0	0.0	8.3	45.9	22.4	17.0	30.5	62.1	7.3	227	94.7
Moapa Valley CDP	6,924	-	-	7,213	86.3	0.0	0.5	3.1	10.1	32.6	16.7	36.7	41.2	17.6	2,337	96.1
Mogul CDP	1,290	-	-	1,334	95.1	0.0	1.2	0.0	3.7	15.4	23.5	47.1	16.0	41.7	515	90.1
Montello CDP	84	-	-	59	100.0	0.0	0.0	0.0	0.0	0.0	59.3	72.2	0.0	18.6	46	100.0
Mount Charleston CDP	357	-	-	369	80.2	0.8	13.0	1.9	4.1	5.1	30.1	52.7	35.2	39.2	169	97.6
Mount Wilson CDP	33	-	-	-	-	-	-	-	-	-	-	-	-	-	-	-
Nellis AFB CDP	3,187	-	-	3,501	61.4	15.0	3.3	7.5	12.8	38.4	0.3	21.8	14.8	33.6	900	100.0
Nelson CDP	37	-	-	34	100.0	0.0	0.0	0.0	0.0	58.8	14.7	8.7	100.0	0.0	14	0.0
Nixon CDP	374	-	-	231	6.1	0.0	2.2	86.1	5.6	18.2	16.9	35.4	66.3	9.9	112	64.3

1 May be of any race.

Table A. All Places — **Population and Housing**

STATE City, town, township, borough, or CDP (county if applicable)	Population				Race and Hispanic or Latino origin (percent)					Age (percent)			Educational attainment of persons age 25 and older		Occupied housing units	
	2010 census total population	2019 estimated population	Percent change 2010–2019	ACS total population estimate 2015–2019	White alone, not Hispanic or Latino	Black alone, not Hispanic or Latino	Asian alone, not Hispanic or Latino	All other races or 2 or more races, not Hispanic or Latino	Hispanic or Latino[1]	Under 18 years old	Age 65 years and older	Median age	Percent High school diploma or less	Percent Bachelor's degree or more	Total	Percent with a computer
	1	2	3	4	5	6	7	8	9	10	11	12	13	14	15	16
NEVADA—Con.																
North Las Vegas city........	216,667	251,974	16.3	241,369	26.6	20.4	6.2	5.7	41.2	28.7	10.5	32.8	50.5	16.8	73,347	94.2
Oasis CDP.....................	29	-	-	38	100.0	0.0	0.0	0.0	0.0	0.0	0.0	0.0	52.6	0.0	18	100.0
Orovada CDP	155	-	-	64	100.0	0.0	0.0	0.0	0.0	0.0	21.9	63.3	57.8	0.0	41	65.9
Osino CDP.....................	709	-	-	519	93.6	0.0	0.0	0.0	6.4	35.1	11.4	46.2	49.3	0.0	183	100.0
Owyhee CDP	953	-	-	1,135	2.7	0.2	0.0	95.2	1.9	31.2	13.6	34.7	50.1	13.5	423	72.8
Pahrump CDP	36,441	-	-	37,298	78.9	1.6	1.9	5.2	12.4	16.8	31.9	54.8	52.0	10.7	15,804	87.7
Panaca CDP	963	-	-	1,157	93.9	0.0	0.0	2.1	4.1	31.2	14.5	35.5	46.5	20.1	398	88.2
Paradise CDP	223,167	-	-	235,087	39.0	10.1	10.5	5.7	34.7	20.2	13.5	36.8	45.2	22.4	90,933	90.3
Paradise Valley CDP........	109	-	-	51	58.8	0.0	0.0	0.0	41.2	2.0	96.1	69.4	42.0	0.0	35	100.0
Pioche CDP	1,002	-	-	1,354	69.7	11.9	1.3	1.0	16.0	7.2	21.0	45.1	59.3	16.3	441	61.5
Preston CDP...................	78	-	-	16	100.0	0.0	0.0	0.0	0.0	0.0	0.0	0.0	0.0	0.0	16	100.0
Rachel CDP....................	54	-	-	70	100.0	0.0	0.0	0.0	0.0	0.0	0.0	0.0	0.0	52.9	33	100.0
Reno city.......................	225,317	255,601	13.4	246,500	61.0	2.6	6.5	5.2	24.7	21.2	14.8	35.8	33.2	33.5	102,283	92.5
Round Hill Village CDP.....	759	-	-	993	88.0	0.9	6.2	3.5	1.3	16.2	26.9	53.3	21.0	47.0	429	94.4
Ruhenstroth CDP	1,293	-	-	1,318	87.6	0.0	0.0	1.8	10.5	22.5	29.6	51.1	21.9	21.9	546	94.1
Ruth CDP	440	-	-	132	100.0	0.0	0.0	0.0	0.0	0.0	33.3	59.4	17.4	11.4	80	86.3
Sandy Valley CDP	2,051	-	-	1,727	76.5	0.9	0.0	0.0	22.6	26.5	18.9	44.8	58.2	10.1	577	87.3
Schurz CDP....................	658	-	-	1,026	7.9	11.0	0.0	74.7	6.4	29.9	14.0	30.3	53.6	5.8	352	79.5
Searchlight CDP	539	-	-	318	93.4	0.0	0.0	0.0	6.6	2.2	58.8	68.2	67.8	6.8	205	63.4
Silver City CDP	-	-	-	158	89.2	0.0	0.0	0.0	10.8	16.5	46.8	60.0	12.8	40.8	88	58.0
Silver Peak CDP	107	-	-	142	97.9	0.0	0.0	0.0	2.1	3.5	14.1	51.6	59.9	2.9	87	89.7
Silver Springs CDP	5,296	-	-	5,073	88.1	0.0	1.0	6.6	4.3	15.2	27.1	51.2	47.7	12.5	2,059	87.6
Skyland CDP	376	-	-	321	72.6	0.0	13.7	9.0	4.7	15.9	24.0	54.4	6.3	58.1	161	95.0
Smith Valley CDP	1,603	-	-	1,627	83.1	0.0	0.0	2.2	14.7	19.2	38.5	59.9	26.4	23.3	662	95.3
Spanish Springs CDP.......	15,064	-	-	15,938	82.8	2.1	1.7	3.4	10.0	24.0	18.2	45.6	29.7	28.1	5,918	97.3
Sparks city.....................	91,117	105,006	15.2	100,589	57.7	2.0	5.6	4.6	30.1	23.5	15.6	38.3	41.2	23.3	38,850	93.2
Spring Creek CDP	12,361	-	-	13,671	89.1	0.0	0.8	2.1	8.0	29.2	8.6	33.5	39.6	20.5	4,559	97.2
Spring Valley CDP	178,395	-	-	207,127	38.5	12.1	18.5	6.3	24.5	20.3	13.7	37.3	41.0	25.2	76,949	94.6
Stagecoach CDP	1,874	-	-	1,920	89.3	0.0	0.0	3.1	7.6	16.4	22.3	50.5	41.5	15.1	716	89.8
Stateline CDP	842	-	-	950	33.3	6.5	2.6	3.1	54.5	19.9	3.6	34.5	43.6	18.3	400	96.5
Summerlin South CDP	24,085	-	-	27,908	68.0	4.5	12.6	4.4	10.5	20.2	24.1	46.8	21.5	48.8	11,786	96.8
Sunrise Manor CDP..........	189,372	-	-	193,781	23.5	13.1	5.6	3.9	53.9	27.4	10.9	33.1	60.6	10.6	62,650	89.0
Sun Valley CDP	19,299	-	-	21,159	44.4	1.9	1.7	6.2	45.8	27.0	11.2	34.2	58.4	8.2	6,596	91.6
Sutcliffe CDP	253	-	-	293	21.2	0.0	0.0	77.5	1.4	8.2	23.2	55.4	55.8	2.7	114	78.9
Tonopah CDP	2,478	-	-	2,009	73.6	8.9	0.3	3.6	13.6	8.8	22.3	46.2	57.0	4.2	1,086	76.6
Topaz Lake CDP.............	157	-	-	207	79.7	0.0	0.0	1.4	18.8	2.4	50.2	65.5	41.0	11.0	107	87.9
Topaz Ranch Estates CDP	1,501	-	-	1,630	78.6	1.9	0.5	5.9	13.1	13.2	31.9	56.7	47.3	10.7	769	92.7
Unionville CDP	-	-	-	-	-	-	-	-	-	-	-	-	-	-	-	-
Ursine CDP....................	91	-	-	-	-	-	-	-	-	-	-	-	-	-	-	-
Valmy CDP	37	-	-	91	100.0	0.0	0.0	0.0	0.0	20.9	30.8	55.1	22.7	30.3	43	53.5
Verdi CDP	1,415	-	-	1,287	94.2	0.3	0.5	3.3	1.7	12.4	23.5	57.5	23.1	41.4	561	90.0
Virginia City CDP	855	-	-	779	98.5	1.2	0.0	0.4	0.0	20.5	28.9	48.4	21.2	51.4	254	74.0
Wadsworth CDP	834	-	-	792	33.7	0.6	0.9	56.1	8.7	21.6	14.4	40.6	53.3	6.9	314	88.2
Walker Lake CDP	-	-	-	310	74.8	0.0	6.5	17.7	1.0	14.2	47.4	64.1	31.1	10.9	158	76.6
Washoe Valley CDP.........	3,019	-	-	2,670	90.0	0.9	2.2	1.2	5.7	7.6	33.0	58.4	30.4	24.1	1,343	96.5
Wells city	1,274	1,252	-1.7	1,022	61.8	0.0	0.3	13.7	24.2	20.6	23.1	50.5	46.9	7.4	463	91.6
West Wendover city	4,410	4,273	-3.1	4,285	41.4	0.0	0.0	0.0	58.6	36.9	7.5	32.0	79.9	6.0	1,232	100.0
Whitney CDP	38,585	-	-	42,973	32.0	10.5	12.5	7.4	37.5	23.8	13.7	35.6	45.6	19.8	14,960	93.9
Winchester CDP	27,978	-	-	28,231	32.1	10.5	5.6	3.3	48.5	19.8	14.5	38.2	53.7	19.9	11,394	85.0
Winnemucca city	7,444	7,754	4.2	7,762	59.2	0.8	0.0	4.4	35.6	27.1	12.8	33.7	51.4	19.4	3,115	84.8
Yerington city	3,108	3,241	4.3	3,137	69.0	1.7	0.0	5.7	23.7	26.8	26.2	41.7	45.7	16.7	1,456	86.5
Zephyr Cove CDP............	565	-	-	434	100.0	0.0	0.0	0.0	0.0	0.0	45.2	63.6	12.5	66.9	255	85.1
NEW HAMPSHIRE...............	1,316,462	1,359,711	3.3	1,348,124	90.1	1.4	2.7	2.1	3.7	19.3	17.5	42.9	34.3	37.0	532,037	93.0
Acworth town (Sullivan)....	893	895	0.2	906	95.0	0.0	0.9	2.5	1.5	10.5	31.1	57.1	41.7	32.4	370	91.6
Albany town (Carroll)	745	751	0.8	703	95.3	0.0	0.6	4.1	0.0	15.6	21.3	50.4	24.7	42.5	307	91.9
Alexandria town (Grafton).	1,621	1,618	-0.2	2,006	95.1	0.0	1.7	1.2	1.9	15.9	19.0	48.4	49.8	19.9	715	88.3
Allenstown town (Merrimack)...................	4,322	4,447	2.9	4,390	93.3	0.8	1.1	4.3	0.5	18.6	15.8	42.2	51.2	16.0	1,788	86.0
Alstead town (Cheshire) ...	1,941	1,938	-0.2	1,744	95.9	0.0	0.5	1.5	2.1	18.3	24.7	48.7	47.5	28.8	749	87.3
Alton CDP......................	501	-	-	252	81.0	0.0	0.0	1.6	17.5	27.0	33.3	47.3	39.4	36.1	102	100.0
Alton town (Belknap)	5,244	5,328	1.6	5,303	97.5	0.0	0.6	0.3	1.6	21.3	27.9	49.6	28.6	34.1	2,075	96.2
Amherst CDP..................	613	-	-	754	100.0	0.0	0.0	0.0	0.0	36.3	15.9	45.2	1.5	73.5	258	100.0
Amherst town (Hillsborough)...............	11,196	11,393	1.8	11,333	94.0	0.1	1.8	1.5	2.6	24.0	17.5	45.8	13.4	62.8	4,129	97.7
Andover town (Merrimack)	2,354	2,373	0.8	2,782	97.5	0.0	1.4	0.6	0.5	21.4	17.0	42.2	30.9	41.2	1,054	96.1
Antrim CDP.....................	1,397	-	-	1,388	94.3	1.2	0.0	3.5	1.1	20.5	18.4	41.0	39.0	26.9	522	88.3
Antrim town (Hillsborough)	2,628	2,690	2.4	2,680	96.8	0.9	0.0	1.8	0.6	21.2	16.6	42.0	40.2	28.3	993	91.9
Ashland CDP...................	1,244	-	-	1,363	95.5	1.3	0.0	2.1	1.1	24.0	23.2	37.8	41.1	25.7	594	75.3
Ashland town (Grafton).....	2,077	2,055	-1.1	2,017	91.9	0.9	0.0	6.4	0.7	22.8	20.6	37.6	42.0	29.1	842	81.1
Atkinson town (Rockingham)................	6,768	7,145	5.6	6,952	95.3	0.0	1.6	1.0	2.1	19.9	19.8	48.6	21.9	49.0	2,745	97.4
Atkinson and Gilmanton Academy grant (Coos)..	-	-	-	-	-	-	-	-	-	-	-	-	-	-	-	-
Auburn town (Rockingham)................	4,955	5,582	12.7	5,446	96.9	0.0	0.8	0.4	2.0	20.4	13.9	44.4	26.0	45.5	1,973	97.9
Barnstead town (Belknap)	4,638	4,744	2.3	4,680	91.9	0.0	1.3	4.5	2.2	19.8	12.5	42.9	45.0	21.6	1,753	96.1
Barrington town (Strafford)	8,536	9,264	8.5	9,063	95.5	0.0	2.8	0.8	0.9	23.7	8.8	39.6	28.4	43.0	3,183	93.3
Bartlett CDP	373	-	-	201	96.5	2.0	0.0	0.5	1.0	0.0	62.2	65.7	73.2	2.1	130	68.5
Bartlett town (Carroll)	2,776	2,804	1.0	2,774	99.2	0.1	0.0	0.0	0.6	11.0	30.9	54.2	37.7	29.6	1,466	89.7
Bath town (Grafton)	1,079	1,093	1.3	922	97.1	0.0	0.0	2.9	0.0	18.9	25.3	51.3	43.5	31.6	380	89.2
Beans grant (Coos)	-	-	-	-	-	-	-	-	-	-	-	-	-	-	-	-
Beans purchase (Coos)....	-	-	-	-	-	-	-	-	-	-	-	-	-	-	-	-
Bedford town (Hillsborough)...............	21,222	22,628	6.6	22,535	90.1	0.9	3.7	2.4	2.8	25.7	16.6	43.9	15.6	63.4	7,813	96.1
Belmont CDP..................	1,301	-	-	1,546	96.6	0.0	0.0	0.0	3.4	12.0	13.1	37.9	51.2	9.5	700	95.9
Belmont town (Belknap) ...	7,335	7,333	0.0	7,311	94.9	0.0	2.0	1.1	2.0	19.8	15.7	44.4	42.4	27.1	2,998	93.5
Bennington CDP	381	-	-	321	93.5	0.0	0.9	3.7	1.9	22.4	20.2	36.5	26.9	47.1	132	97.7
Bennington town (Hillsborough)...............	1,497	1,516	1.3	1,513	93.3	1.4	0.2	3.4	1.7	21.3	13.1	36.0	42.1	34.1	640	91.9

1 May be of any race.

Table A. All Places — **Population and Housing**

STATE City, town, township, borough, or CDP (county if applicable)	Population				Race and Hispanic or Latino origin (percent)					Age (percent)			Educational attainment of persons age 25 and older		Occupied housing units	
	2010 census total population	2019 estimated population	Percent change 2010–2019	ACS total population estimate 2015–2019	White alone, not Hispanic or Latino	Black alone, not Hispanic or Latino	Asian alone, not Hispanic or Latino	All other races or 2 or more races, not Hispanic or Latino	Hispanic or Latino[1]	Under 18 years old	Age 65 years and older	Median age	Percent High school diploma or less	Percent Bachelor's degree or more	Total	Percent with a computer
	1	2	3	4	5	6	7	8	9	10	11	12	13	14	15	16
NEW HAMPSHIRE—Con.																
Benton town (Grafton)	364	371	1.9	457	94.1	2.4	0.0	1.5	2.0	8.5	39.2	60.7	58.9	19.1	124	80.6
Berlin city & MCD (Coos)	10,051	10,122	0.7	10,221	85.6	6.2	0.5	2.1	5.7	15.5	18.7	42.3	60.3	12.4	3,977	85.5
Bethlehem CDP	972	-	-	1,057	98.3	0.0	0.0	1.7	0.0	14.9	17.0	50.4	23.6	34.3	456	98.0
Bethlehem town (Grafton)	2,532	2,574	1.7	2,569	96.4	0.0	0.4	1.4	1.7	13.5	20.7	52.3	30.4	31.5	1,082	94.6
Blodgett Landing CDP	101	-	-	105	100.0	0.0	0.0	0.0	0.0	34.3	11.4	42.4	15.9	69.6	34	100.0
Boscawen town (Merrimack)	3,976	4,026	1.3	4,004	98.0	0.2	0.5	0.5	0.8	18.9	21.3	44.7	52.9	18.6	1,374	95.3
Bow town (Merrimack)	7,533	7,980	5.9	7,862	95.1	0.2	1.4	0.5	2.8	26.2	16.9	44.0	19.9	55.4	2,715	96.4
Bradford CDP	356	-	-	273	98.9	0.0	0.0	0.0	1.1	22.7	16.1	35.8	43.2	24.3	124	85.5
Bradford town (Merrimack)	1,650	1,707	3.5	1,587	98.1	0.1	0.3	0.9	0.5	21.6	22.6	48.3	30.6	40.3	647	89.8
Brentwood town (Rockingham)	4,495	4,518	0.5	4,612	95.1	0.8	1.8	1.4	1.0	24.3	14.8	44.5	24.7	48.7	1,533	95.1
Bridgewater town (Grafton)	1,073	1,071	-0.2	1,188	97.6	0.0	0.0	1.6	0.8	16.9	32.4	55.8	30.1	41.5	516	95.3
Bristol CDP	1,688	-	-	1,870	85.9	0.0	3.4	9.9	0.8	16.4	15.6	40.8	47.8	17.7	752	83.0
Bristol town (Grafton)	3,041	3,096	1.8	3,079	88.5	0.1	2.8	7.7	0.9	14.9	19.4	44.1	41.6	22.6	1,249	86.3
Brookfield town (Carroll)	695	688	-	803	95.8	0.0	0.0	0.2	4.0	16.8	18.9	46.8	27.5	40.4	303	98.7
Brookline town (Hillsborough)	4,989	5,453	9.3	5,348	93.3	1.0	0.6	3.1	2.1	28.0	10.3	39.9	20.9	55.6	1,736	97.3
Cambridge township (Coos)	8	7	-12.5	-	-	-	-	-	-	-	-	-	-	-	-	-
Campton town (Grafton)	3,335	3,300	-	3,291	98.5	0.1	0.0	0.8	0.5	15.3	19.0	47.3	39.7	41.2	1,342	85.2
Canaan CDP	524	-	-	342	93.9	0.0	0.0	0.0	6.1	9.1	18.4	54.3	32.6	27.0	203	100.0
Canaan town (Grafton)	3,945	3,899	-1.2	3,920	91.1	0.6	3.4	3.0	1.8	17.9	14.3	44.2	42.2	28.0	1,487	95.7
Candia town (Rockingham)	3,906	3,959	1.4	3,936	91.7	0.7	0.4	3.8	3.4	16.5	17.6	50.5	36.2	30.7	1,537	92.1
Canterbury town (Merrimack)	2,364	2,464	4.2	2,357	91.6	1.3	0.8	0.6	5.6	15.3	18.0	47.6	19.9	51.7	970	91.5
Carroll town (Coos)	763	747	-2.1	772	95.1	3.6	0.0	1.3	0.0	18.1	25.1	54.3	39.6	28.0	324	96.0
Center Harbor town (Belknap)	1,091	1,097	0.5	1,056	97.1	2.9	0.0	0.0	0.0	13.9	30.3	53.3	30.6	42.6	419	94.5
Center Ossipee CDP	561	-	-	522	100.0	0.0	0.0	0.0	0.0	17.6	28.7	49.5	80.0	5.3	263	96.6
Center Sandwich CDP	123	-	-	154	100.0	0.0	0.0	0.0	0.0	24.7	19.5	49.8	10.3	57.0	57	96.5
Chandlers purchase (Coos)	-	-	-	-	-	-	-	-	-	-	-	-	-	-	-	-
Charlestown CDP	1,152	-	-	1,065	99.2	0.0	0.0	0.0	0.8	28.8	16.1	32.0	58.7	13.9	443	74.7
Charlestown town (Sullivan)	5,118	5,021	-1.9	5,019	94.2	0.0	1.8	2.6	1.4	19.5	21.5	47.9	57.5	16.5	2,086	75.0
Chatham town (Carroll)	339	364	7.4	372	95.2	0.0	0.8	3.0	1.1	17.7	24.2	50.6	42.1	26.9	143	90.9
Chester town (Rockingham)	4,775	5,270	10.4	5,129	94.0	0.4	2.1	1.1	2.3	21.3	12.4	42.5	26.2	44.1	1,687	97.4
Chesterfield town (Cheshire)	3,604	3,627	0.6	3,585	98.7	1.0	0.0	0.3	0.0	23.8	21.6	46.1	31.9	35.1	1,348	98.8
Chichester town (Merrimack)	2,527	2,706	7.1	2,662	92.4	0.0	2.3	3.6	1.8	22.2	15.2	44.2	39.0	28.5	969	97.6
Claremont city & MCD (Sullivan)	13,351	12,932	-3.1	12,977	94.3	1.6	0.4	1.4	2.3	20.7	18.2	41.7	52.7	20.5	5,231	91.2
Clarksville town (Coos)	273	251	-8.1	324	90.7	0.0	0.0	9.3	0.0	9.6	22.5	56.3	58.0	19.7	141	95.7
Colebrook CDP	1,394	-	-	998	97.3	0.0	0.0	2.2	0.5	11.1	27.3	55.8	54.0	12.0	550	79.8
Colebrook town (Coos)	2,303	2,138	-7.2	1,908	98.1	0.0	0.0	1.2	0.7	15.8	25.9	52.3	49.4	15.6	954	80.9
Columbia town (Coos)	755	735	-2.6	633	98.6	0.0	0.0	0.5	0.9	12.5	24.6	52.9	50.6	12.4	316	80.1
Concord city & MCD (Merrimack)	42,686	43,627	2.2	43,244	86.1	3.4	4.7	2.9	3.0	18.4	16.4	40.2	32.6	37.9	17,530	90.1
Contoocook CDP	1,444	-	-	1,528	96.3	0.0	0.0	2.0	1.7	22.2	26.6	53.2	21.8	47.0	569	90.7
Conway CDP	1,823	-	-	3,924	97.0	0.0	0.3	0.7	2.0	26.2	17.7	37.4	43.9	19.7	1,764	90.8
Conway town (Carroll)	10,102	10,252	1.5	10,127	96.2	0.0	0.3	1.2	2.3	21.3	21.9	44.8	29.5	36.3	4,632	92.9
Cornish town (Sullivan)	1,640	1,617	-1.4	1,783	96.5	0.8	0.4	1.9	0.3	19.6	28.8	54.1	34.1	41.9	741	90.3
Crawfords purchase (Coos)	-	-	-	-	-	-	-	-	-	-	-	-	-	-	-	-
Croydon town (Sullivan)	766	765	-0.1	863	98.3	1.2	0.0	0.3	0.2	16.7	16.3	45.8	51.6	19.9	293	82.3
Cutts grant (Coos)	-	-	-	-	-	-	-	-	-	-	-	-	-	-	-	-
Dalton town (Coos)	966	885	-8.4	906	87.3	1.9	1.2	4.0	5.6	14.6	17.9	53.3	38.4	21.4	424	93.6
Danbury town (Merrimack)	1,170	1,226	4.8	1,129	96.8	0.6	0.4	1.5	0.6	21.9	14.1	46.7	47.0	19.9	481	91.5
Danville town (Rockingham)	4,378	4,556	4.1	4,515	91.3	0.6	0.9	4.0	3.3	21.0	12.2	44.1	41.5	26.7	1,685	93.0
Deerfield town (Rockingham)	4,280	4,541	6.1	4,476	96.9	1.4	0.4	0.9	0.4	19.8	15.1	45.2	32.2	42.8	1,653	92.1
Deering town (Hillsborough)	1,925	1,973	2.5	1,917	95.1	0.0	0.3	4.3	0.3	18.4	17.6	50.7	43.0	24.7	756	89.0
Derry CDP	22,015	-	-	21,817	92.0	1.1	1.2	1.4	4.3	20.9	12.6	39.6	40.7	26.1	8,895	93.0
Derry town (Rockingham)	33,219	33,485	0.8	33,448	92.5	0.8	1.2	1.3	4.2	21.2	12.1	40.1	39.2	28.9	12,741	94.8
Dixs grant (Coos)	1	1	0.0	-	-	-	-	-	-	-	-	-	-	-	-	-
Dixville township (Coos)	12	11	-8.3	11	90.9	0.0	0.0	0.0	9.1	18.2	18.2	23.5	60.0	40.0	1	100.0
Dorchester town (Grafton)	355	356	0.3	401	94.5	0.0	1.0	1.0	3.5	19.5	25.4	45.1	49.7	26.3	144	88.9
Dover city & MCD (Strafford)	29,986	32,191	7.4	31,577	88.1	1.1	4.1	3.1	3.7	19.1	16.0	36.1	27.2	46.5	13,489	93.0
Dublin town (Cheshire)	1,589	1,543	-2.9	1,458	92.9	0.3	0.4	1.6	4.9	15.5	23.8	52.6	24.7	55.4	581	97.9
Dummer town (Coos)	304	284	-6.6	306	98.7	0.0	0.0	1.3	0.0	20.6	28.4	52.6	50.9	20.8	127	81.1
Dunbarton town (Merrimack)	2,748	2,879	4.8	2,827	95.0	0.9	1.0	0.4	2.7	25.9	11.7	42.5	29.9	38.2	938	97.7
Durham CDP	10,345	-	-	11,159	87.5	1.0	6.1	3.0	2.4	6.4	4.9	20.2	6.7	77.5	1,687	96.8
Durham town (Strafford)	14,638	16,293	11.3	16,481	89.7	0.8	4.9	2.7	2.0	8.2	7.5	20.8	7.6	75.0	3,187	97.7
East Kingston town (Rockingham)	2,352	2,418	2.8	2,442	97.5	0.0	0.0	0.6	1.9	21.6	18.6	47.3	26.1	37.3	888	97.5
East Merrimack CDP	4,197	-	-	4,449	92.2	0.0	0.6	6.6	0.5	22.2	21.3	41.9	31.0	34.4	2,026	88.5
Easton town (Grafton)	254	263	3.5	288	95.1	0.0	1.0	2.8	1.0	5.9	34.7	60.7	21.4	62.2	135	95.6
Eaton town (Carroll)	382	400	4.7	265	98.9	0.0	1.1	0.0	0.0	8.7	36.2	58.5	19.0	60.2	135	96.3
Effingham town (Carroll)	1,465	1,478	0.9	1,630	92.6	0.0	0.8	5.1	1.5	22.0	16.8	41.0	47.3	24.6	594	90.6
Ellsworth town (Grafton)	83	88	6.0	74	100.0	0.0	0.0	0.0	0.0	13.5	48.6	62.7	57.8	29.7	35	88.6
Enfield CDP	1,540	-	-	1,830	100.0	0.0	0.0	0.0	0.0	23.1	13.0	40.5	36.6	25.6	761	89.1
Enfield town (Grafton)	4,577	4,531	-	4,545	99.6	0.1	0.0	0.4	0.0	14.7	20.6	45.1	29.8	39.4	2,027	92.5
Epping CDP	1,681	-	-	1,889	95.8	0.0	0.0	2.9	1.3	20.0	26.7	42.9	47.9	22.9	763	82.7

1 May be of any race.

Table A. All Places — **Population and Housing**

STATE City, town, township, borough, or CDP (county if applicable)	Population 2010 census total population (1)	2019 estimated population (2)	Percent change 2010–2019 (3)	ACS total population estimate 2015–2019 (4)	White alone, not Hispanic or Latino (5)	Black alone, not Hispanic or Latino (6)	Asian alone, not Hispanic or Latino (7)	All other races or 2 or more races, not Hispanic or Latino (8)	Hispanic or Latino[1] (9)	Under 18 years old (10)	Age 65 years and older (11)	Median age (12)	Percent High school diploma or less (13)	Percent Bachelor's degree or more (14)	Occupied housing units Total (15)	Percent with a computer (16)
NEW HAMPSHIRE—Con.																
Epping town (Rockingham)	6,404	7,036	9.9	6,966	94.4	0.3	0.5	3.1	1.7	19.6	18.3	42.2	41.4	28.1	2,680	94.5
Epsom town (Merrimack)	4,590	4,767	3.9	4,722	94.6	0.0	0.7	3.1	1.5	20.4	19.4	44.9	40.7	32.5	1,787	93.3
Errol town (Coos)	291	265	-8.9	205	99.5	0.0	0.0	0.5	0.0	13.2	32.2	56.6	50.0	12.9	113	69.9
Ervings location (Coos)	-	-	-	-	-	-	-	-	-	-	-	-	-	-	-	-
Exeter CDP	9,242	-	-	9,244	92.2	1.2	2.1	2.0	2.6	16.0	20.3	47.7	34.0	38.0	4,187	91.9
Exeter town (Rockingham)	14,301	15,313	7.1	15,077	92.5	1.6	2.3	1.3	2.3	18.9	22.9	47.3	27.3	48.3	6,542	92.1
Farmington CDP	3,885	-	-	4,477	95.2	0.0	0.0	2.9	2.0	23.9	11.9	38.0	50.8	11.2	1,756	90.3
Farmington town (Strafford)	6,775	6,973	2.9	6,930	95.9	0.0	1.0	1.8	1.3	20.5	15.5	44.0	47.1	14.9	2,868	93.4
Fitzwilliam town (Cheshire)	2,408	2,371	-1.5	2,312	99.7	0.0	0.2	0.2	0.0	18.1	21.5	50.2	44.2	28.7	1,008	88.3
Francestown town (Hillsborough)	1,548	1,583	2.3	1,549	95.4	1.4	0.0	1.9	1.3	18.4	22.0	50.5	26.6	45.5	624	91.8
Franconia town (Grafton)	1,103	1,105	0.2	1,075	94.0	0.0	1.6	0.4	4.0	9.4	32.7	58.0	19.6	51.7	434	91.9
Franklin city & MCD (Merrimack)	8,478	8,686	2.5	8,623	94.8	0.1	0.8	1.6	2.6	16.6	21.7	48.1	50.8	17.6	3,909	86.3
Freedom town (Carroll)	1,492	1,583	6.1	1,349	98.7	0.0	0.4	0.9	0.0	12.5	38.8	61.3	32.3	38.1	611	92.5
Fremont town (Rockingham)	4,287	4,710	9.9	4,677	97.4	0.0	1.7	0.2	0.7	19.4	17.3	46.1	29.5	36.1	1,764	96.8
Gilford town (Belknap)	7,087	7,233	2.1	7,153	96.3	0.0	0.7	1.8	1.2	19.5	23.1	47.8	26.5	42.0	3,032	95.9
Gilmanton town (Belknap)	3,751	3,773	0.6	3,738	94.9	0.5	1.0	1.6	1.9	21.0	20.0	44.8	33.3	36.5	1,515	93.0
Gilsum town (Cheshire)	809	804	-0.6	798	91.5	0.8	0.4	2.0	5.4	19.7	21.9	46.9	44.0	22.9	291	91.8
Goffstown CDP	3,196	-	-	2,541	98.3	0.0	1.7	0.0	0.0	12.5	20.3	47.2	24.2	32.5	1,240	89.4
Goffstown town (Hillsborough)	17,632	18,053	2.4	18,061	94.0	0.4	0.7	2.1	2.8	19.4	16.4	38.8	34.2	29.0	6,115	94.7
Gorham CDP	1,600	-	-	1,489	96.2	0.0	0.0	2.8	0.9	13.1	24.1	55.4	37.0	29.7	719	90.8
Gorham town (Coos)	2,849	2,611	-8.4	2,623	92.1	0.4	1.1	2.9	3.6	15.6	25.2	54.2	38.7	26.7	1,243	91.7
Goshen town (Sullivan)	810	810	0.0	702	91.7	0.0	0.0	2.1	6.1	19.5	23.9	46.5	55.4	18.1	277	90.3
Grafton town (Grafton)	1,340	1,329	-0.8	1,362	95.7	0.0	0.5	2.8	1.0	19.3	19.8	46.7	44.8	27.4	540	91.7
Grantham town (Sullivan)	2,976	2,945	-	2,945	97.8	0.0	0.0	1.4	0.8	17.7	22.2	50.5	13.8	66.1	1,222	100.0
Greenfield town (Hillsborough)	1,747	1,847	5.7	1,906	97.7	0.1	0.6	0.8	0.8	20.0	21.7	47.4	42.2	26.0	696	88.5
Greenland town (Rockingham)	3,541	4,120	16.4	4,009	88.7	1.7	4.5	2.7	2.4	23.4	18.1	45.2	18.9	54.6	1,516	97.1
Greens grant (Coos)	1	1	0.0	13	76.9	23.1	0.0	0.0	0.0	0.0	0.0	38.8	30.0	40.0	0	
Greenville CDP	1,108	-	-	992	76.4	10.2	0.0	0.9	12.5	19.5	17.1	40.9	35.6	28.3	395	82.0
Greenville town (Hillsborough)	2,098	2,110	0.6	2,061	87.2	4.9	0.0	1.8	6.0	18.0	17.1	45.7	46.6	21.1	872	84.2
Groton town (Grafton)	593	595	0.3	464	100.0	0.0	0.0	0.0	0.0	9.9	22.0	56.5	63.9	12.5	200	76.0
Groveton CDP	1,118	-	-	1,221	90.7	0.0	2.4	4.7	2.3	22.4	14.1	39.4	68.5	5.3	523	82.4
Hadleys purchase (Coos)	-	-	-	-	-	-	-	-	-	-	-	-	-	-	-	-
Hale's location (Carroll)	120	129	7.5	183	96.7	0.0	3.3	0.0	0.0	1.6	73.8	71.2	19.7	48.6	89	91.0
Hampstead town (Rockingham)	8,512	8,632	1.4	8,621	93.8	0.6	1.6	1.3	2.7	21.3	19.5	45.2	25.4	42.6	3,573	95.4
Hampton CDP	9,656	-	-	9,166	95.7	0.2	0.9	2.7	0.6	18.3	19.6	48.2	21.9	50.8	3,953	95.6
Hampton town (Rockingham)	14,987	15,495	3.4	15,467	95.2	0.3	1.0	2.4	1.2	15.6	24.3	51.4	25.1	48.2	7,088	94.1
Hampton Beach CDP	2,275	-	-	2,685	93.3	1.1	1.2	1.4	3.1	13.6	21.7	54.2	33.1	38.0	1,350	88.1
Hampton Falls town (Rockingham)	2,240	2,414	7.8	2,383	97.6	0.3	1.3	0.4	0.4	18.3	15.6	47.4	21.7	54.3	909	98.1
Hancock CDP	204	-	-	280	94.6	0.0	0.0	0.0	5.4	0.0	36.8	61.5	7.4	71.5	150	96.7
Hancock town (Hillsborough)	1,649	1,656	0.4	1,747	94.6	0.3	0.3	1.8	3.0	15.2	31.6	56.5	22.1	56.7	781	95.5
Hanover CDP	8,636	-	-	8,508	76.3	3.1	11.7	4.0	4.9	9.9	12.0	21.9	9.7	83.4	1,859	98.5
Hanover town (Grafton)	11,260	11,473	1.9	11,467	78.0	2.9	11.2	4.2	3.7	14.0	13.3	24.5	9.3	82.7	2,839	98.7
Harrisville town (Cheshire)	969	951	-1.9	927	89.3	2.2	0.6	2.6	5.3	11.2	30.6	57.7	28.0	46.6	419	92.6
Hart's Location town (Carroll)	41	45	9.8	42	100.0	0.0	0.0	0.0	0.0	0.0	26.2	58.3	40.5	23.8	24	66.7
Haverhill town (Grafton)	4,697	4,565	-2.8	4,601	95.2	0.2	0.1	2.3	2.2	19.7	20.2	47.4	49.1	23.2	1,754	89.1
Hebron town (Grafton)	615	627	2.0	537	95.3	0.0	0.0	1.5	3.2	6.1	51.0	65.3	16.2	65.0	263	93.5
Henniker CDP	1,747	-	-	1,756	90.7	4.4	1.8	1.7	1.4	9.8	11.7	22.7	19.3	46.4	568	94.9
Henniker town (Merrimack)	4,836	5,018	3.8	4,962	94.6	1.6	0.6	1.2	2.0	18.6	15.5	36.2	25.0	45.2	1,805	93.6
Hill town (Merrimack)	1,082	1,108	2.4	920	98.5	0.0	0.0	0.0	1.5	17.5	18.5	50.1	44.2	25.8	373	90.1
Hillsborough CDP	1,976	-	-	1,716	93.3	0.0	0.0	6.7	0.0	19.1	24.6	49.1	53.0	12.9	779	96.8
Hillsborough town (Hillsborough)	6,007	6,002	-0.1	5,995	94.3	0.6	0.0	5.1	0.0	24.0	15.7	42.8	39.9	27.2	2,324	96.4
Hinsdale CDP	1,548	-	-	1,380	92.8	0.0	0.0	7.2	0.0	21.4		44.1	60.3	17.8	584	87.5
Hinsdale town (Cheshire)	4,037	3,907	-3.2	3,911	93.7	0.6	0.0	2.9	2.9	18.8	17.3	47.1	57.2	15.9	1,643	91.1
Holderness town (Grafton)	2,115	2,107	-0.4	2,206	95.8	0.6	1.9	0.7	1.0	19.4	22.9	47.3	33.1	30.9	796	93.6
Hollis town (Hillsborough)	7,699	8,006	4.0	7,918	91.2	0.2	2.3	4.2	2.1	21.7	16.3	49.6	16.1	63.4	2,968	96.2
Hooksett CDP	4,147	-	-	5,355	92.5	1.3	2.5	2.6	1.1	18.6	17.3	38.4	30.4	39.9	2,242	96.6
Hooksett town (Merrimack)	13,465	14,542	8.0	14,289	92.1	1.4	1.9	1.8	2.8	18.8	15.4	39.4	31.4	38.5	5,252	95.6
Hopkinton town (Merrimack)	5,582	5,761	3.2	5,691	97.7	0.3	0.0	1.5	0.5	20.9	19.0	49.1	23.0	50.8	2,193	94.3
Hudson CDP	7,336	-	-	7,486	92.2	0.7	1.1	2.0	4.0	19.5	19.1	44.4	40.3	26.6	3,008	95.4
Hudson town (Hillsborough)	24,471	25,619	4.7	25,356	93.1	0.5	2.5	1.6	2.3	20.1	15.8	43.8	33.5	35.9	9,214	98.0
Jackson town (Carroll)	835	860	3.0	891	99.7	0.0	0.0	0.0	0.3	16.7	34.6	58.9	17.7	56.4	416	96.2
Jaffrey CDP	2,757	-	-	2,765	96.6	0.0	0.5	2.9	0.0	18.2	17.6	42.2	46.9	18.3	1,191	83.9
Jaffrey town (Cheshire)	5,462	5,277	-3.4	5,283	95.5	0.0	1.5	1.6	1.4	19.7	19.0	44.2	42.0	27.8	2,107	86.6
Jefferson town (Coos)	1,107	1,047	-5.4	850	96.2	0.0	1.6	0.7	1.4	14.4	23.5	54.8	34.2	35.6	396	90.4
Keene city & MCD (Cheshire)	23,563	22,786	-3.3	22,953	91.0	1.2	2.5	2.6	2.7	15.4	18.2	36.4	30.9	41.8	9,192	89.3
Kensington town (Rockingham)	2,112	2,106	-0.3	2,291	95.6	0.0	1.0	2.9	0.5	20.6	19.7	48.2	22.9	49.9	845	96.3
Kilkenny township (Coos)	-	-	-	-	-	-	-	-	-	-	-	-	-	-	-	-
Kingston town (Rockingham)	6,035	6,446	6.8	6,260	96.6	0.0	0.9	2.2	0.3	18.6	17.2	45.5	33.8	35.6	2,411	96.6

1 May be of any race.

Table A. All Places — **Population and Housing**

STATE City, town, township, borough, or CDP (county if applicable)	Population				Race and Hispanic or Latino origin (percent)					Age (percent)			Educational attainment of persons age 25 and older		Occupied housing units	
	2010 census total population	2019 estimated population	Percent change 2010–2019	ACS total population estimate 2015–2019	White alone, not Hispanic or Latino	Black alone, not Hispanic or Latino	Asian alone, not Hispanic or Latino	All other races or 2 or more races, not Hispanic or Latino	Hispanic or Latino[1]	Under 18 years old	Age 65 years and older	Median age	Percent High school diploma or less	Percent Bachelor's degree or more	Total	Percent with a computer
	1	2	3	4	5	6	7	8	9	10	11	12	13	14	15	16
NEW HAMPSHIRE—Con.																
Laconia city & MCD (Belknap)	15,974	16,581	3.8	16,476	94.1	1.3	0.7	1.9	2.0	17.9	22.1	46.4	41.6	28.4	6,933	93.2
Lancaster CDP	1,725	-	-	1,797	96.3	1.3	0.8	0.7	0.9	19.0	23.7	44.1	47.6	22.7	745	87.2
Lancaster town (Coos)	3,507	3,255	-7.2	3,275	97.1	0.7	0.5	1.1	0.7	20.8	22.5	44.5	43.5	23.1	1,366	88.9
Landaff town (Grafton)	413	439	6.3	496	97.0	1.8	0.8	0.4	0.0	15.5	24.2	53.0	45.8	33.1	210	87.1
Langdon town (Sullivan)	688	684	-0.6	712	93.0	0.8	1.3	3.7	1.3	23.7	14.6	44.4	37.1	30.6	257	91.8
Lebanon city & MCD (Grafton)	13,147	13,651	3.8	13,623	85.1	2.0	6.6	1.1	5.2	16.4	20.1	38.7	27.7	53.5	6,083	89.6
Lee town (Strafford)	4,335	4,569	5.4	4,485	84.7	0.0	8.7	2.6	3.9	18.5	16.4	47.8	21.0	56.3	1,876	95.8
Lempster town (Sullivan)	1,154	1,168	1.2	923	94.9	0.0	3.5	1.6	0.0	24.2	18.6	47.5	50.4	22.2	393	93.1
Lincoln CDP	993	-	-	712	93.1	0.0	4.9	1.1	0.8	12.9	26.8	46.8	39.0	30.6	319	93.4
Lincoln town (Grafton)	1,662	1,760	5.9	945	94.0	0.0	3.7	1.3	1.1	11.1	30.8	55.5	35.5	29.6	448	90.8
Lisbon CDP	980	-	-	964	96.1	0.0	0.0	1.7	2.3	22.0	15.7	36.8	48.8	23.4	388	95.4
Lisbon town (Grafton)	1,595	1,579	-	1,752	94.7	0.0	0.2	3.5	1.5	20.8	16.1	41.8	54.9	20.9	647	91.3
Litchfield town (Hillsborough)	8,267	8,641	4.5	8,566	97.2	0.0	0.8	1.4	0.6	22.3	13.9	42.5	27.9	41.5	3,060	98.2
Littleton CDP	4,412	-	-	4,680	94.4	0.0	1.0	2.5	2.2	18.6	18.1	45.1	35.7	26.4	2,257	86.2
Littleton town (Grafton)	5,922	5,870	-0.9	5,915	95.5	0.0	0.8	2.0	1.7	16.4	20.9	49.9	33.4	27.2	2,891	89.2
Livermore town (Grafton)	-	-	-	-	-	-	-	-	-	-	-	-	-	-	-	-
Londonderry CDP	11,037	-	-	11,841	93.9	1.6	0.6	1.1	2.8	21.9	14.8	42.7	27.2	40.4	4,427	96.0
Londonderry town (Rockingham)	24,023	26,490	10.3	25,927	92.6	1.1	1.7	1.5	3.2	22.7	14.1	42.1	26.5	43.3	9,338	96.1
Loudon CDP	559	-	-	770	100.0	0.0	0.0	0.0	0.0	11.0	41.7	62.4	72.0	8.6	315	82.2
Loudon town (Merrimack)	5,280	5,634	6.7	5,534	99.1	0.0	0.0	0.9	0.0	16.6	20.9	49.7	39.7	19.7	2,050	95.3
Low and Burbanks grant (Coos)	-	-	-	-	-	-	-	-	-	-	-	-	-	-	-	-
Lyman town (Grafton)	533	526	-1.3	653	96.9	0.0	1.4	1.4	0.3	11.3	21.1	53.4	38.0	42.7	283	89.0
Lyme town (Grafton)	1,716	1,675	-2.4	1,852	91.0	0.6	1.0	0.9	6.5	24.5	24.5	46.7	23.3	66.4	684	96.5
Lyndeborough town (Hillsborough)	1,680	1,732	3.1	1,701	97.6	1.2	0.0	0.2	0.9	14.7	18.3	52.2	29.2	39.6	687	96.8
Madbury town (Strafford)	1,778	1,883	5.9	1,901	93.6	0.0	3.9	2.0	0.5	26.5	10.5	41.2	20.8	55.0	615	96.3
Madison town (Carroll)	2,497	2,606	4.4	2,553	92.6	2.2	1.3	3.0	0.9	19.5	24.6	51.7	38.4	30.4	977	96.9
Manchester city & MCD (Hillsborough)	109,549	112,673	2.9	112,109	76.9	5.1	5.1	2.5	10.4	19.5	13.2	36.0	41.8	30.1	46,188	92.1
Marlborough CDP	1,094	-	-	1,164	93.8	0.0	3.5	2.7	0.0	17.8	19.8	43.8	46.2	27.5	495	84.8
Marlborough town (Cheshire)	2,063	2,076	0.6	2,397	93.4	0.0	2.2	3.4	1.0	19.1	20.7	44.2	40.1	34.6	920	87.6
Marlow town (Cheshire)	742	730	-1.6	829	95.4	0.0	0.8	1.3	2.4	26.1	18.9	43.4	39.6	25.1	327	92.7
Martins location (Coos)	-	-	-	-	-	-	-	-	-	-	-	-	-	-	-	-
Mason town (Hillsborough)	1,384	1,433	3.5	1,532	92.4	0.0	1.2	0.2	6.3	21.1	14.9	42.9	31.7	36.2	599	96.8
Melvin Village CDP	241	-	-	151	100.0	0.0	0.0	0.0	0.0	0.0	72.2	68.8	10.6	52.3	73	76.7
Meredith CDP	1,718	-	-	1,495	94.8	1.0	0.0	2.7	1.5	29.9	20.3	31.8	41.6	27.9	648	84.7
Meredith town (Belknap)	6,264	6,456	3.1	6,391	95.9	0.2	0.0	1.8	2.1	18.4	24.1	50.6	29.4	43.8	2,861	91.1
Merrimack town (Hillsborough)	25,485	26,490	3.9	25,987	90.7	1.0	2.0	2.6	3.7	21.6	15.1	43.0	24.9	46.6	9,993	94.0
Middleton town (Strafford)	1,793	1,838	2.5	1,783	94.3	1.7	0.3	2.1	1.5	20.2	12.3	42.4	48.0	18.1	658	90.6
Milan town (Coos)	1,337	1,235	-7.6	1,332	94.6	0.0	0.4	0.2	4.8	16.5	18.9	48.4	47.7	22.5	589	90.6
Milford CDP	8,835	-	-	8,892	90.5	1.7	3.5	0.8	3.5	20.8	19.0	43.1	37.4	34.2	3,838	93.7
Milford town (Hillsborough)	15,116	16,411	8.6	15,732	91.1	1.7	2.9	1.5	2.8	22.8	15.7	41.8	34.4	36.1	6,316	94.5
Millsfield township (Coos)	23	21	-8.7	8	100.0	0.0	0.0	0.0	0.0	0.0	50.0	0.0	100.0	0.0	4	100.0
Milton CDP	575	-	-	400	100.0	0.0	0.0	0.0	0.0	2.5	23.0	54.5	47.0	14.8	198	70.7
Milton town (Strafford)	4,591	4,624	0.7	4,620	97.7	0.0	0.3	1.8	0.2	19.0	18.5	46.8	44.4	24.9	1,811	92.5
Milton Mills CDP	299	-	-	206	100.0	0.0	0.0	0.0	0.0	4.4	40.3	55.0	75.8	20.3	74	100.0
Monroe town (Grafton)	788	802	1.8	966	100.0	0.0	0.0	0.0	0.0	22.6	22.8	46.3	40.7	31.1	357	82.6
Mont Vernon town (Hillsborough)	2,428	2,659	9.5	2,576	98.2	0.0	0.0	1.6	0.2	21.2	14.6	46.0	24.8	49.4	909	98.3
Moultonborough town (Carroll)	4,059	4,184	3.1	4,099	95.1	0.0	1.2	2.4	1.3	15.4	29.3	54.3	26.6	45.9	1,765	96.1
Mountain Lakes CDP	488	-	-	662	90.6	0.0	0.0	6.8	2.6	15.9	14.5	48.1	22.2	17.3	241	100.0
Nashua city & MCD (Hillsborough)	86,475	89,355	3.3	88,815	73.2	2.9	8.4	2.9	12.7	19.5	15.7	39.6	35.4	36.2	36,534	93.6
Nelson town (Cheshire)	729	734	0.7	613	88.7	0.0	0.0	0.3	10.9	15.2	21.9	48.4	24.8	54.7	245	94.7
New Boston town (Hillsborough)	5,317	5,899	10.9	5,711	97.7	0.0	0.2	1.0	1.1	25.5	11.3	40.0	27.9	43.8	1,964	95.0
Newbury town (Merrimack)	2,072	2,228	7.5	2,096	96.2	0.0	1.7	1.4	0.7	14.7	26.6	53.7	16.1	59.6	910	97.9
New Castle town (Rockingham)	968	979	1.1	835	100.0	0.0	0.0	0.0	0.0	15.3	39.4	61.6	8.9	65.2	436	94.5
New Durham town (Strafford)	2,652	2,706	2.0	2,697	96.1	0.0	0.0	3.4	0.5	22.1	16.6	45.7	33.4	31.2	953	97.5
Newfields CDP	301	-	-	314	93.9	3.2	0.0	2.9	0.0	24.2	10.5	47.1	25.0	41.4	114	95.6
Newfields town (Rockingham)	1,680	1,736	3.3	1,757	95.3	1.0	1.7	1.9	0.1	24.4	13.6	46.8	20.2	53.9	600	96.8
New Hampton CDP	351	-	-	354	72.9	5.9	8.5	10.7	2.0	27.4	7.6	26.8	28.1	43.2	95	90.5
New Hampton town (Belknap)	2,160	2,221	2.8	2,245	93.3	1.8	1.8	2.6	0.5	14.8	24.1	49.8	34.4	39.4	913	91.9
Newington town (Rockingham)	753	813	8.0	713	95.8	1.5	2.1	0.3	0.3	12.3	25.9	55.7	20.0	51.5	307	96.1
New Ipswich town (Hillsborough)	5,105	5,393	5.6	5,320	95.7	0.0	1.0	2.9	0.4	25.3	13.2	37.3	38.2	26.3	1,858	97.0
New London CDP	1,415	-	-	1,415	87.3	3.3	4.7	0.4	4.4	9.0	10.8	20.9	15.5	49.2	216	81.9
New London town (Merrimack)	4,392	4,308	-1.9	4,390	94.9	1.1	1.9	0.5	1.7	14.3	29.5	42.0	13.3	62.3	1,551	94.2
Newmarket CDP	5,297	-	-	5,660	91.4	1.1	5.9	0.7	1.0	15.4	10.0	34.1	25.0	47.0	2,640	97.3
Newmarket town (Rockingham)	8,936	9,156	2.5	9,063	92.9	0.9	3.7	1.7	0.8	17.2	14.5	36.3	26.4	47.4	4,035	94.3
Newport CDP	4,769	-	-	5,240	92.4	0.0	0.5	4.6	2.4	21.1	16.1	41.0	49.7	20.8	2,097	89.1
Newport town (Sullivan)	6,507	6,358	-2.3	6,374	92.6	0.2	0.4	4.7	2.0	19.1	18.5	44.1	49.5	21.2	2,600	87.5
Newton town (Rockingham)	4,613	4,928	6.8	4,920	96.2	0.0	1.1	0.3	2.4	18.4	15.4	43.7	38.6	32.7	1,853	95.3
North Conway CDP	2,349	-	-	2,179	94.6	0.0	1.0	2.5	1.9	19.8	24.4	48.8	14.9	53.6	1,077	91.7

1 May be of any race.

Table A. All Places — **Population and Housing**

STATE City, town, township, borough, or CDP (county if applicable)	Population				Race and Hispanic or Latino origin (percent)					Age (percent)			Educational attainment of persons age 25 and older		Occupied housing units	
	2010 census total population	2019 estimated population	Percent change 2010–2019	ACS total population estimate 2015–2019	White alone, not Hispanic or Latino	Black alone, not Hispanic or Latino	Asian alone, not Hispanic or Latino	All other races or 2 or more races, not Hispanic or Latino	Hispanic or Latino[1]	Under 18 years old	Age 65 years and older	Median age	Percent High school diploma or less	Percent Bachelor's degree or more	Total	Percent with a computer
	1	2	3	4	5	6	7	8	9	10	11	12	13	14	15	16
NEW HAMPSHIRE—Con.																
Northfield town (Merrimack)	4,824	4,942	2.4	4,881	92.5	0.8	2.4	2.7	1.6	21.7	10.8	37.5	45.8	20.4	1,860	96.6
North Hampton town (Rockingham)	4,293	4,486	4.5	4,457	89.7	1.5	3.1	2.1	3.6	17.9	24.3	51.8	21.9	51.0	1,820	97.7
North Haverhill CDP	-	-	-	905	87.8	0.9	0.0	8.3	3.0	9.0	30.4	53.4	52.9	24.3	263	96.6
Northumberland town (Coos)	2,293	2,139	-6.7	2,322	94.1	0.2	1.2	3.2	1.2	22.5	17.5	45.5	62.2	8.9	984	85.6
North Walpole CDP	828	-	-	832	100.0	0.0	0.0	0.0	0.0	26.6	9.6	35.6	21.6	38.4	325	76.0
Northwood town (Rockingham)	4,239	4,309	1.7	4,299	93.5	1.2	0.5	1.0	3.8	17.3	17.3	44.2	40.4	33.9	1,611	95.0
North Woodstock CDP	528	-	-	378	95.5	0.0	0.0	4.5	0.0	6.1	31.5	59.5	38.3	27.8	229	91.7
Nottingham town (Rockingham)	4,781	5,136	7.4	5,058	96.5	0.3	1.0	0.3	1.8	22.0	16.4	44.4	31.9	41.1	1,900	95.5
Odell township (Coos)	4	4	0.0	-	-	-	-	-	-	-	-	-	-	-	-	-
Orange town (Grafton)	310	309	-0.3	264	94.7	0.0	1.1	4.2	0.0	9.8	28.4	53.9	38.3	40.7	110	93.6
Orford town (Grafton)	1,237	1,301	5.2	1,444	71.7	4.7	18.1	0.3	5.1	14.1	19.4	44.0	43.8	28.5	484	95.7
Ossipee town (Carroll)	4,342	4,384	1.0	4,334	89.9	2.8	0.0	5.2	2.1	15.2	25.7	51.2	54.4	19.9	2,011	88.1
Pelham town (Hillsborough)	12,906	14,220	10.2	13,798	91.9	0.9	1.7	2.8	2.8	21.7	16.1	45.0	39.8	35.3	4,832	95.7
Pembroke town (Merrimack)	7,108	7,203	1.3	7,187	94.6	0.2	0.3	2.7	2.2	21.2	15.3	40.3	37.8	27.6	2,690	92.6
Peterborough CDP	3,103	-	-	2,971	97.7	0.0	0.0	0.0	2.3	12.2	35.3	55.9	23.2	53.3	1,577	90.9
Peterborough town (Hillsborough)	6,272	6,688	6.6	6,604	96.0	0.0	0.3	0.0	3.7	15.7	26.9	52.3	23.6	51.0	3,019	92.9
Piermont town (Grafton)	790	808	2.3	868	96.8	0.0	1.6	0.0	1.6	18.9	19.7	44.6	31.1	40.3	332	94.3
Pinardville CDP	4,780	-	-	5,208	89.9	0.1	0.6	4.7	4.7	20.5	16.6	42.4	45.9	19.0	2,025	94.5
Pinkhams grant (Coos)	9	9	0.0	10	50.0	0.0	0.0	50.0	0.0	0.0	0.0	0.0	100.0	0.0	0	0.0
Pittsburg town (Coos)	869	820	-5.6	740	97.2	0.0	0.0	1.2	1.6	7.7	34.2	59.0	44.2	14.7	423	81.1
Pittsfield CDP	1,576	-	-	1,615	96.0	0.0	1.9	0.9	1.2	13.3	13.7	46.7	53.2	19.1	778	79.4
Pittsfield town (Merrimack)	4,122	4,125	0.1	4,117	96.3	0.0	0.7	0.4	2.6	23.9	15.1	44.0	56.4	18.0	1,675	88.5
Plainfield CDP	205	-	-	249	73.5	0.0	26.5	0.0	0.0	11.6	9.6	43.1	41.9	38.6	128	100.0
Plainfield town (Sullivan)	2,364	2,400	1.5	2,555	94.9	0.6	3.2	0.7	0.5	19.5	18.6	45.2	31.0	45.6	915	95.2
Plaistow town (Rockingham)	7,605	7,716	1.5	7,689	93.6	0.4	0.7	2.3	3.0	18.1	16.5	42.1	40.2	24.9	3,119	94.8
Plymouth CDP	4,456	-	-	3,438	85.3	2.9	7.4	3.0	1.4	15.6	8.2	20.7	29.5	51.2	755	97.5
Plymouth town (Grafton)	6,997	6,862	-1.9	6,755	91.4	1.6	3.7	2.5	0.7	16.2	17.8	34.2	36.9	38.0	2,147	88.5
Portsmouth city & MCD (Rockingham)	21,233	21,927	3.3	21,775	87.7	2.1	4.8	2.2	3.2	15.3	17.4	39.8	20.5	58.6	10,063	95.0
Randolph town (Coos)	310	286	-7.7	365	98.4	0.0	0.0	0.3	1.4	6.3	34.2	60.3	16.1	56.8	196	96.4
Raymond CDP	2,855	-	-	2,977	93.6	0.0	1.0	5.1	0.3	19.2	14.8	37.9	33.8	30.5	1,321	92.1
Raymond town (Rockingham)	10,150	10,529	3.7	10,428	96.0	0.0	0.3	1.5	2.1	22.0	13.6	42.1	44.1	23.0	4,112	95.8
Richmond town (Cheshire)	1,142	1,124	-1.6	1,121	99.4	0.0	0.1	0.4	0.1	18.7	15.6	48.8	41.3	21.5	421	93.1
Rindge town (Cheshire)	6,009	6,090	1.3	6,054	92.4	1.3	0.4	2.0	4.0	20.3	14.3	31.0	39.1	30.4	1,762	93.4
Rochester city & MCD (Strafford)	29,787	31,526	5.8	30,955	92.3	0.7	1.8	2.5	2.7	20.0	18.0	41.8	45.8	21.7	12,780	89.6
Rollinsford town (Strafford)	2,527	2,586	2.3	2,567	93.4	2.5	0.0	2.3	1.9	18.7	16.2	45.6	31.8	37.0	1,040	93.8
Roxbury town (Cheshire)	229	220	-3.9	180	100.0	0.0	0.0	0.0	0.0	15.0	11.7	46.4	35.3	33.8	74	87.8
Rumney town (Grafton)	1,480	1,567	5.9	1,510	96.0	0.1	0.3	3.0	0.7	18.6	19.9	46.9	40.1	27.1	599	87.0
Rye town (Rockingham)	5,306	5,470	3.1	5,466	98.2	0.0	0.7	1.2	0.0	14.3	28.4	55.4	17.0	62.1	2,364	96.0
Salem town (Rockingham)	28,753	29,791	3.6	29,234	85.1	0.5	3.7	2.1	8.6	17.5	18.7	44.0	37.0	36.2	11,536	92.7
Salisbury town (Merrimack)	1,387	1,446	4.3	1,422	98.7	0.0	0.4	0.9	0.0	17.8	21.0	51.1	44.2	28.1	554	92.2
Sanbornton town (Belknap)	2,977	2,994	0.6	2,983	95.8	0.4	1.8	1.6	0.3	18.1	17.3	48.8	28.9	35.5	1,119	89.6
Sanbornville CDP	1,056	-	-	555	100.0	0.0	0.0	0.0	0.0	10.1	52.4	66.5	37.9	17.8	297	100.0
Sandown town (Rockingham)	5,985	6,547	9.4	6,389	94.5	0.4	0.6	1.8	2.7	21.8	12.3	41.7	34.1	29.7	2,229	96.5
Sandwich town (Carroll)	1,327	1,358	2.3	1,440	94.5	2.7	1.3	0.8	0.8	11.5	36.0	59.8	27.3	49.3	643	89.0
Sargents purchase (Coos)	-	-	-	11	100.0	0.0	0.0	0.0	0.0	0.0	0.0	0.0	0.0	0.0	0	0.0
Seabrook town (Rockingham)	8,675	8,842	1.9	8,830	94.6	1.3	1.3	1.6	1.3	14.7	25.9	50.3	52.8	18.2	3,824	92.4
Seabrook Beach CDP	992	-	-	1,015	98.9	0.0	0.0	1.1	0.0	8.2	38.9	58.8	26.3	54.9	499	94.2
Second College grant (Coos)	-	-	-	-	-	-	-	-	-	-	-	-	-	-	-	-
Sharon town (Hillsborough)	351	369	5.1	408	100.0	0.0	0.0	0.0	0.0	16.9	28.7	50.3	11.4	63.4	184	96.7
Shelburne town (Coos)	371	345	-7.0	408	99.5	0.0	0.0	0.5	0.0	13.0	31.9	58.0	36.7	31.2	200	93.5
Somersworth city & MCD (Strafford)	11,765	11,968	1.7	11,925	83.0	3.2	6.6	4.8	2.4	20.5	13.2	36.9	43.1	25.8	5,127	90.9
South Hampton town (Rockingham)	816	827	1.3	775	93.0	0.0	2.6	2.1	2.3	17.2	24.4	47.4	23.1	39.9	302	93.0
South Hooksett CDP	5,418	-	-	5,831	89.4	1.0	2.4	1.4	5.9	18.1	13.5	37.2	34.2	37.0	1,813	95.8
Springfield town (Sullivan)	1,317	1,341	1.8	1,084	99.2	0.0	0.0	0.8	0.0	14.4	29.7	50.6	42.5	39.3	442	92.3
Stark town (Coos)	548	498	-9.1	606	96.9	1.5	0.0	1.7	0.0	23.9	25.9	51.0	57.7	11.0	233	85.4
Stewartstown town (Coos)	996	918	-7.8	976	96.8	0.3	0.0	1.5	1.3	14.3	40.5	59.1	57.7	14.8	418	74.6
Stoddard town (Cheshire)	1,232	1,240	0.6	1,255	96.7	0.2	0.0	2.2	1.0	18.7	23.0	48.5	37.0	26.5	473	91.3
Strafford town (Strafford)	3,988	4,212	5.6	4,140	94.6	0.9	0.1	0.2	4.2	22.4	15.7	43.7	25.6	42.5	1,395	97.2
Stratford town (Coos)	746	684	-8.3	630	97.8	0.2	0.0	0.8	1.3	17.8	20.6	48.0	63.9	5.5	277	72.9
Stratham town (Rockingham)	7,270	7,488	3.0	7,427	91.9	0.0	6.1	1.3	0.7	22.3	16.4	46.9	16.0	58.6	2,817	96.1
Success township (Coos)	-	-	-	-	-	-	-	-	-	-	-	-	-	-	-	-
Sugar Hill town (Grafton)	564	577	2.3	681	90.5	0.0	0.7	4.0	4.8	18.4	24.5	58.4	17.2	55.7	285	92.6
Suissevale CDP	249	-	-	295	85.8	0.0	7.1	7.1	0.0	17.6	19.7	55.4	74.1	7.4	136	100.0
Sullivan town (Cheshire)	677	675	-0.3	792	98.7	0.0	0.4	0.4	0.5	25.0	15.0	43.5	41.7	26.0	290	89.3
Sunapee town (Sullivan)	3,363	3,487	3.7	3,449	98.8	0.2	0.9	0.0	0.1	20.1	20.5	44.6	32.3	41.8	1,393	93.6
Suncook CDP	5,379	-	-	4,888	94.5	0.3	0.5	3.7	1.1	16.0	17.8	42.8	44.4	20.7	2,218	86.2
Surry town (Cheshire)	743	744	0.1	841	98.6	0.2	0.0	1.2	0.0	20.3	23.3	46.2	33.4	38.6	353	94.1
Sutton town (Merrimack)	1,844	1,922	4.2	1,905	94.9	0.2	1.5	2.5	0.9	23.9	20.3	45.9	21.6	45.9	769	95.2
Swanzey town (Cheshire)	7,214	7,220	0.1	7,199	95.1	0.1	1.7	3.1	0.0	14.8	21.8	50.0	40.2	27.3	3,089	89.2
Tamworth town (Carroll)	2,864	3,077	7.4	2,994	95.9	0.0	1.2	1.7	1.2	19.6	17.4	50.7	44.4	26.4	1,300	96.0

1 May be of any race.

Table A. All Places — **Population and Housing**

STATE City, town, township, borough, or CDP (county if applicable)	2010 census total population	2019 estimated population	Percent change 2010–2019	ACS total population estimate 2015–2019	White alone, not Hispanic or Latino	Black alone, not Hispanic or Latino	Asian alone, not Hispanic or Latino	All other races or 2 or more races, not Hispanic or Latino	Hispanic or Latino[1]	Under 18 years old	Age 65 years and older	Median age	Percent High school diploma or less	Percent Bachelor's degree or more	Total	Percent with a computer
	1	2	3	4	5	6	7	8	9	10	11	12	13	14	15	16
NEW HAMPSHIRE—Con.																
Temple town (Hillsborough)	1,367	1,422	4.0	1,268	96.4	0.0	0.2	1.3	2.1	13.2	20.7	49.5	33.7	39.7	491	96.7
Thompson and Meserves purchase (Coos)	3	3	0.0	-	-	-	-	-	-	-	-	-	-	-	-	-
Thornton town (Grafton)	2,490	2,536	1.8	2,504	92.6	0.7	0.9	2.4	3.4	18.7	20.8	44.1	32.8	35.3	966	93.3
Tilton town (Belknap)	3,554	3,543	-0.3	3,551	95.5	1.0	0.9	1.2	1.4	16.4	24.4	48.6	44.9	20.5	1,434	90.4
Tilton Northfield CDP	3,075	-	-	2,812	93.6	1.3	2.5	0.8	1.8	14.9	22.0	50.1	48.6	16.6	1,083	92.5
Troy CDP	1,221	-	-	918	89.4	0.0	1.0	8.5	1.1	18.4	13.0	43.7	54.7	21.4	402	93.5
Troy town (Cheshire)	2,150	2,105	-2.1	2,002	93.3	0.0	0.7	5.0	1.0	21.0	13.7	43.2	46.8	24.6	837	90.1
Tuftonboro town (Carroll)	2,367	2,419	2.2	2,213	94.2	0.0	0.0	0.8	5.1	13.4	37.8	59.3	29.6	38.2	923	91.4
Union CDP	204	-	-	193	100.0	0.0	0.0	0.0	0.0	0.0	0.0	34.0	74.7	8.9	70	80.0
Unity town (Sullivan)	1,669	1,620	-2.9	1,613	96.0	0.7	0.0	0.9	2.4	9.4	29.6	56.1	54.8	16.0	571	92.5
Wakefield town (Carroll)	5,092	5,110	0.4	5,046	99.3	0.0	0.0	0.0	0.7	13.2	19.5	51.8	39.0	20.3	2,117	96.6
Walpole CDP	605	-	-	537	100.0	0.0	0.0	0.0	0.0	9.7	39.1	63.1	23.5	62.3	331	84.0
Walpole town (Cheshire)	3,734	4,009	7.4	3,936	97.0	1.8	0.0	0.9	0.3	18.3	21.1	46.7	25.7	44.0	1,677	88.2
Warner CDP	444	-	-	542	84.1	4.1	0.0	2.6	9.2	18.6	21.0	34.3	49.4	16.2	240	92.9
Warner town (Merrimack)	2,826	2,920	3.3	2,910	93.4	1.6	0.4	1.5	3.0	20.4	19.5	42.1	32.9	35.0	1,144	95.2
Warren town (Grafton)	904	936	3.5	874	96.6	0.0	0.0	0.5	3.0	13.8	25.7	52.4	47.2	14.8	348	90.5
Washington town (Sullivan)	1,123	1,103	-1.8	1,199	94.2	0.0	0.0	3.3	2.6	11.6	26.3	52.2	35.6	21.4	537	94.4
Waterville Valley town (Grafton)	247	241	-2.4	186	98.4	0.0	0.0	1.6	0.0	17.7	30.1	53.9	8.5	68.8	92	100.0
Weare town (Hillsborough)	8,789	9,091	3.4	9,031	95.4	0.0	0.2	2.5	1.9	23.6	10.7	41.6	30.1	37.0	3,129	98.9
Webster town (Merrimack)	1,881	1,954	3.9	1,781	98.2	0.0	0.0	1.3	0.5	14.8	17.5	49.3	37.5	29.5	760	89.6
Wentworth town (Grafton)	911	966	6.0	894	94.7	1.7	2.5	1.1	0.0	12.8	25.5	52.8	39.1	33.0	358	90.5
Wentworth location (Coos)	33	30	-9.1	26	100.0	0.0	0.0	0.0	0.0	0.0	73.1	70.0	80.8	0.0	16	75.0
Westmoreland town (Cheshire)	1,730	1,688	-2.4	1,612	97.6	0.0	0.4	1.6	0.4	12.4	27.0	54.4	26.2	46.0	676	93.5
West Stewartstown CDP	386	-	-	314	91.1	0.0	0.0	4.8	4.1	15.9	44.6	59.6	69.4	8.2	95	49.5
West Swanzey CDP	1,308	-	-	896	91.5	0.0	5.6	2.9	0.0	26.0	24.6	40.8	48.4	36.3	378	78.8
Whitefield CDP	1,142	-	-	1,058	90.9	3.3	0.0	5.8	0.0	15.0	33.6	52.5	52.6	22.9	537	82.1
Whitefield town (Coos)	2,319	2,211	-4.7	2,260	92.4	1.8	0.6	4.2	1.0	17.9	31.2	51.5	44.9	26.3	1,046	85.5
Wilmot town (Merrimack)	1,352	1,392	3.0	1,643	96.8	0.0	1.5	1.3	0.4	16.1	22.4	51.5	20.1	57.6	704	95.9
Wilton CDP	1,163	-	-	1,267	100.0	0.0	0.0	0.0	0.0	14.0	9.8	35.7	55.4	26.9	628	82.3
Wilton town (Hillsborough)	3,683	3,789	2.9	3,751	94.6	0.0	1.8	2.6	1.0	15.6	20.9	47.2	37.0	39.1	1,586	87.8
Winchester CDP	1,733	-	-	2,261	99.6	0.0	0.0	0.4	0.0	36.3	9.7	30.4	61.6	7.2	764	87.4
Winchester town (Cheshire)	4,346	4,226	-2.8	4,240	97.5	0.6	1.3	0.7	0.0	24.7	18.6	40.3	59.5	11.7	1,659	87.7
Windham town (Rockingham)	13,578	14,853	9.4	14,610	90.6	0.9	3.4	1.9	3.3	27.0	14.9	44.0	14.9	57.9	5,009	96.4
Windsor town (Hillsborough)	224	231	3.1	207	97.1	1.0	0.0	1.9	0.0	14.5	11.6	47.8	46.9	18.6	76	98.7
Wolfeboro CDP	2,838	-	-	2,845	99.6	0.0	0.0	0.3	0.1	9.5	42.8	61.0	33.8	40.8	1,457	87.1
Wolfeboro town (Carroll)	6,283	6,418	2.1	6,320	97.3	0.0	2.0	0.1	0.6	12.5	37.4	58.5	35.2	41.1	3,000	84.0
Woodstock town (Grafton)	1,374	1,365	-0.7	1,126	91.3	0.0	6.0	1.5	1.2	21.0	20.2	42.2	31.4	38.9	499	87.0
Woodsville CDP	1,126	-	-	851	97.5	0.0	0.0	0.0	2.5	32.3	8.3	32.2	72.3	10.7	276	92.4
NEW JERSEY	8,791,978	8,882,190	1.0	8,878,503	55.4	12.7	9.4	2.3	20.2	22.1	15.9	39.9	37.4	39.7	3,231,874	91.4
Aberdeen township (Monmouth)	18,142	19,332	6.6	18,540	74.1	7.8	3.8	2.3	12.1	19.7	12.7	40.0	29.6	42.4	7,387	96.7
Absecon city & MCD (Atlantic)	8,498	8,818	3.8	8,362	71.2	10.1	5.5	1.0	12.2	18.8	22.8	45.9	43.8	28.0	3,177	92.7
Alexandria township (Hunterdon)	4,902	4,754	-3.0	4,785	96.5	0.3	2.3	0.6	0.3	19.1	20.5	48.3	21.6	51.1	1,716	98.4
Allamuchy CDP	78	-	-	87	100.0	0.0	0.0	0.0	0.0	39.1	0.0	18.8	24.4	48.8	31	100.0
Allamuchy township (Warren)	4,314	4,666	8.2	4,597	85.8	2.3	3.5	0.5	7.8	15.8	22.3	49.5	26.2	51.1	2,196	93.7
Allendale borough & MCD (Bergen)	6,505	6,734	3.5	6,765	82.9	0.7	11.0	2.8	2.6	30.0	14.2	45.1	8.8	73.7	2,210	93.0
Allenhurst borough & MCD (Monmouth)	495	483	-2.4	475	92.4	1.1	0.2	4.2	2.1	15.6	23.2	50.7	19.5	55.7	185	97.8
Allentown borough & MCD (Monmouth)	1,824	1,775	-2.7	1,892	86.4	6.7	0.8	2.5	3.6	23.4	12.9	40.0	23.0	50.2	709	96.1
Allenwood CDP	925	-	-	883	96.9	1.2	1.8	0.0	0.0	23.3	22.8	47.0	13.0	60.3	305	89.8
Alloway CDP	1,402	-	-	1,342	91.3	1.6	0.0	4.5	2.5	25.6	15.3	44.4	37.5	24.1	487	83.4
Alloway township (Salem)	3,494	3,359	-3.9	3,357	87.9	3.9	1.0	4.6	2.7	24.2	17.6	44.1	39.1	26.2	1,208	87.7
Alpha borough & MCD (Warren)	2,368	2,255	-4.8	2,082	90.6	0.5	0.0	2.8	6.1	16.3	20.9	46.8	49.6	20.7	917	86.8
Alpine borough & MCD (Bergen)	1,818	1,844	1.4	1,547	52.6	5.8	30.9	1.9	8.8	22.4	28.8	49.8	18.3	72.9	564	97.2
Anderson CDP	342	-	-	351	53.8	10.3	2.6	9.4	23.9	30.5	23.9	40.4	32.6	43.1	110	90.0
Andover borough & MCD (Sussex)	604	563	-6.8	589	90.0	1.4	1.4	6.6	0.7	18.0	12.1	40.9	36.1	31.5	245	93.9
Andover township (Sussex)	6,290	5,870	-6.7	5,949	90.1	2.2	4.3	0.7	2.7	16.9	23.7	47.9	36.9	38.8	2,024	93.3
Annandale CDP	1,695	-	-	1,646	81.4	3.0	4.5	3.9	7.2	19.5	11.1	39.4	21.0	58.1	574	94.3
Asbury CDP	273	-	-	225	96.0	4.0	0.0	0.0	0.0	8.0	36.4	56.9	56.2	33.0	101	95.0
Asbury Park city & MCD (Monmouth)	16,114	15,408	-4.4	15,597	31.1	41.5	0.9	3.1	23.4	20.7	12.0	36.8	45.7	30.5	7,033	87.1
Ashland CDP	8,302	-	-	8,405	69.8	9.1	11.2	2.3	7.6	20.5	20.5	42.8	26.2	50.4	3,036	97.5
Atlantic City city & MCD (Atlantic)	39,552	37,743	-4.6	37,999	15.6	33.7	16.5	3.2	31.1	24.5	15.0	36.4	60.9	16.2	15,504	77.7
Atlantic Highlands borough & MCD (Monmouth)	4,381	4,351	-0.7	4,309	93.8	0.0	0.4	0.3	5.4	18.4	18.7	47.4	23.9	49.8	1,761	92.0
Audubon borough & MCD (Camden)	8,819	8,637	-2.1	8,661	89.4	5.9	0.2	1.2	3.3	20.3	15.0	39.7	35.3	37.3	3,337	92.7
Audubon Park borough & MCD (Camden)	1,023	1,002	-2.1	854	98.1	0.0	0.0	0.9	0.9	8.7	27.5	54.3	55.8	16.1	456	85.7
Avalon borough & MCD (Cape May)	1,334	1,236	-7.3	1,406	98.5	0.1	0.1	0.0	1.3	7.3	51.9	66.0	18.3	60.6	726	92.7

1 May be of any race.

Table A. All Places — **Population and Housing**

STATE City, town, township, borough, or CDP (county if applicable)	Population				Race and Hispanic or Latino origin (percent)					Age (percent)			Educational attainment of persons age 25 and older		Occupied housing units	
	2010 census total population	2019 estimated population	Percent change 2010–2019	ACS total population estimate 2015–2019	White alone, not Hispanic or Latino	Black alone, not Hispanic or Latino	Asian alone, not Hispanic or Latino	All other races or 2 or more races, not Hispanic or Latino	Hispanic or Latino[1]	Under 18 years old	Age 65 years and older	Median age	Percent High school diploma or less	Percent Bachelor's degree or more	Total	Percent with a computer
	1	2	3	4	5	6	7	8	9	10	11	12	13	14	15	16
NEW JERSEY—Con.																
Avenel CDP	17,011	-	-	18,592	34.8	21.9	19.6	3.1	20.6	20.1	11.0	39.0	56.7	24.8	5,222	91.7
Avon-by-the-Sea borough & MCD (Monmouth)......	1,900	1,783	-6.2	1,789	89.7	0.5	1.3	0.5	7.9	14.0	27.8	54.2	16.6	63.8	897	92.0
Barclay CDP	4,428	-	-	4,248	88.7	0.5	3.8	1.2	5.8	23.2	19.3	45.1	13.9	71.1	1,505	97.5
Barnegat CDP	2,817	-	-	2,988	80.2	3.3	0.0	4.1	12.4	22.1	10.4	41.7	39.4	25.8	1,075	91.3
Barnegat township (Ocean)	20,930	23,655	13.0	22,754	85.2	5.8	0.5	1.2	7.3	21.3	28.2	46.8	45.4	24.6	8,731	92.3
Barnegat Light borough & MCD (Ocean)	586	587	0.2	369	95.4	0.0	0.8	1.9	1.9	2.2	60.4	68.3	24.4	52.9	202	93.6
Barrington borough & MCD (Camden)............	6,965	6,642	-4.6	6,716	88.1	3.0	1.3	2.7	5.0	19.7	15.3	41.4	34.6	37.0	2,874	90.6
Bass River township (Burlington)	1,445	1,416	-2.0	1,319	91.7	0.4	0.9	0.5	6.5	18.6	14.8	45.6	53.4	20.4	520	88.5
Bay Head borough & MCD (Ocean)	971	977	0.6	1,048	91.2	0.0	2.5	3.2	3.1	17.5	37.0	58.0	13.5	63.9	470	93.4
Bayonne city & MCD (Hudson)	63,015	64,897	3.0	65,091	44.3	9.3	9.8	3.1	33.5	23.5	14.2	38.0	42.5	37.2	24,967	89.0
Beach Haven borough & MCD (Ocean)	1,175	1,205	2.6	1,090	96.4	0.0	1.6	0.9	1.1	11.1	33.9	58.6	16.8	60.3	527	89.0
Beach Haven West CDP...	3,896	-	-	3,682	93.8	0.0	0.7	0.0	5.5	6.8	37.9	59.9	35.3	41.7	1,845	94.4
Beachwood borough & MCD (Ocean)	11,042	11,312	2.4	11,226	85.2	3.2	0.1	2.6	8.9	24.6	11.6	35.8	44.2	22.7	3,740	94.5
Beattystown CDP	4,554	-	-	4,575	66.0	11.6	7.8	2.1	12.5	21.8	10.2	41.2	37.1	36.5	1,881	88.3
Beckett CDP	4,847	-	-	4,947	76.8	13.3	1.0	3.0	5.9	27.9	10.2	37.2	26.5	43.5	1,680	99.3
Bedminster township (Somerset)	8,158	7,968	-2.3	8,045	76.0	1.1	8.0	2.1	12.8	14.3	20.5	46.4	14.4	65.6	4,003	97.2
Belford CDP	1,768	-	-	2,129	85.2	0.0	2.7	1.5	10.6	24.7	11.6	33.1	33.1	37.9	660	96.8
Belle Mead CDP	216	-	-	203	100.0	0.0	0.0	0.0	0.0	16.3	9.9	37.6	5.5	40.7	81	100.0
Belleplain CDP	597	-	-	555	96.8	0.0	0.0	0.0	3.2	28.1	15.3	41.2	67.3	7.5	218	80.3
Belleville township (Essex)	35,854	36,497	1.8	36,181	29.0	8.7	10.1	3.9	48.3	21.6	13.3	38.5	46.5	26.3	12,257	91.9
Bellmawr borough & MCD (Camden)	11,614	11,359	-2.2	11,398	75.0	2.0	11.4	1.3	10.4	20.1	18.9	41.7	51.9	19.8	4,392	85.7
Belmar borough & MCD (Monmouth)...........	5,786	5,545	-4.2	5,624	81.7	3.6	0.5	0.2	14.0	13.8	16.8	44.3	27.4	49.5	2,472	93.4
Belvidere town & MCD (Warren)	2,686	2,561	-4.7	2,590	89.8	0.3	1.4	2.6	5.8	23.8	13.3	40.0	39.5	27.4	981	93.9
Bergenfield borough & MCD (Bergen)	26,839	27,327	1.8	27,373	35.8	8.2	25.3	1.5	29.2	22.5	15.3	39.6	32.4	44.3	8,946	93.1
Berkeley township (Ocean)	41,377	42,036	1.6	41,815	85.9	2.0	2.0	1.3	8.8	12.6	40.0	59.8	54.3	19.7	19,575	83.7
Berkeley Heights township (Union)	13,134	13,363	1.7	13,310	76.6	1.7	13.4	2.1	6.2	24.3	18.6	44.2	16.8	67.8	4,462	95.5
Berlin borough & MCD (Camden)	7,598	7,536	-0.8	7,539	86.5	3.6	1.9	3.6	4.4	23.7	20.3	42.9	36.8	36.1	2,902	84.1
Berlin township (Camden)	5,364	5,691	6.1	5,553	64.5	11.8	8.0	1.3	14.4	19.8	18.6	42.2	49.9	24.3	1,957	83.5
Bernards township (Somerset)	26,690	27,038	1.3	27,082	68.4	2.5	20.7	2.3	6.1	25.0	15.6	45.3	13.1	75.1	9,696	96.2
Bernardsville borough & MCD (Somerset)..........	7,737	7,594	-1.8	7,678	82.4	0.1	4.3	0.4	12.8	24.5	12.3	41.8	16.8	69.7	2,627	97.2
Bethlehem township (Hunterdon)	4,013	3,854	-4.0	3,881	92.7	0.0	2.3	1.4	3.6	22.0	14.6	49.5	17.3	56.8	1,526	95.4
Beverly city & MCD (Burlington)	2,546	2,479	-2.6	2,267	61.1	16.0	0.5	7.4	15.0	21.1	14.2	47.1	54.3	19.0	913	84.8
Blackwells Mills CDP	803	-	-	684	55.8	7.2	17.3	0.0	19.7	23.1	5.1	52.5	4.5	93.0	212	100.0
Blackwood CDP	4,545	-	-	4,929	78.8	6.9	3.8	1.2	9.3	20.6	15.2	37.4	48.5	19.2	1,850	91.7
Blairstown CDP	515	-	-	343	85.4	8.7	0.0	0.0	5.8	9.3	10.8	43.7	75.2	12.9	122	100.0
Blairstown township (Warren)	5,944	5,691	-4.3	5,732	88.6	1.2	1.3	2.8	6.1	18.8	23.1	50.9	37.5	39.9	2,159	93.2
Blawenburg CDP	280	-	-	115	27.8	0.0	72.2	0.0	0.0	6.1	7.8	48.3	0.0	90.0	40	100.0
Bloomfield township (Essex)	47,366	49,973	5.5	49,260	41.1	18.5	8.6	2.4	29.4	20.7	13.4	37.7	35.4	41.5	18,577	93.4
Bloomingdale borough & MCD (Passaic).............	7,662	8,061	5.2	8,088	66.9	3.4	4.8	1.7	23.2	21.2	13.0	41.5	32.9	44.2	2,980	91.8
Bloomsbury borough & MCD (Hunterdon).........	874	839	-4.0	729	93.4	2.7	1.6	1.0	1.2	17.0	11.5	46.8	35.0	41.4	296	93.9
Bogota borough & MCD (Bergen)	8,176	8,335	1.9	8,360	36.3	10.7	7.9	1.1	44.0	21.6	13.2	38.9	38.7	35.0	2,792	94.5
Boonton town & MCD (Morris)	8,338	8,919	7.0	8,398	69.5	4.8	10.3	1.7	13.6	20.7	14.1	40.0	32.0	46.4	3,184	92.3
Boonton township (Morris)	4,271	4,237	-0.8	4,292	83.2	0.9	11.3	1.2	3.4	22.0	17.9	49.0	15.8	66.9	1,481	97.4
Bordentown city & MCD (Burlington)	3,917	3,792	-3.2	3,823	75.9	12.5	4.4	2.5	4.7	14.6	18.4	39.1	30.1	41.8	1,707	89.2
Bordentown township (Burlington)	11,380	11,914	4.7	11,967	71.5	9.4	9.0	1.9	8.3	22.2	14.0	42.6	30.8	40.8	4,566	94.2
Bound Brook borough & MCD (Somerset)	10,421	10,180	-2.3	10,288	37.0	4.7	3.7	2.3	52.3	24.8	10.2	34.1	55.5	21.2	3,504	94.6
Bradley Beach borough & MCD (Monmout..	4,299	4,148	-3.5	4,193	79.5	5.2	1.1	2.7	11.5	12.7	20.1	42.4	23.6	55.3	2,152	91.2
Bradley Gardens CDP	14,206	-	-	14,400	53.4	1.3	38.0	0.9	6.4	23.2	12.2	42.5	20.8	61.3	4,850	96.1
Brainards CDP	202	-	-	236	76.7	0.0	0.0	0.0	23.3	33.1	11.4	37.0	49.7	21.9	71	70.4
Branchburg township (Somerset)	14,456	14,499	0.3	14,480	83.1	3.0	8.3	0.8	4.9	21.6	14.6	45.6	18.2	60.9	5,363	96.3
Branchville borough & MCD (Sussex).............	837	779	-6.9	786	90.8	2.9	0.9	0.5	4.8	20.0	20.9	44.1	46.6	21.4	300	93.0
Brass Castle CDP	1,555	-	-	1,834	88.1	8.3	0.0	0.0	3.5	20.8	13.2	39.5	38.2	20.1	644	91.5
Brick township (Ocean)	75,049	76,100	1.4	75,342	84.3	2.1	1.8	1.5	10.2	19.8	20.0	44.7	39.7	29.9	30,122	91.3
Bridgeton city & MCD (Cumberland)	25,404	24,160	-4.9	24,540	15.5	32.3	0.6	2.2	49.4	29.6	7.1	30.6	73.7	5.9	6,299	78.7
Bridgeville CDP	106	-	-	112	100.0	0.0	0.0	0.0	0.0	32.1	0.0	29.5	25.0	51.3	39	100.0
Bridgewater township (Somerset)	44,420	43,968	-	44,467	64.2	2.1	24.0	1.0	8.6	22.6	16.6	43.2	22.3	58.9	15,401	94.9

1 May be of any race.

Table A. All Places — **Population and Housing**

STATE City, town, township, borough, or CDP (county if applicable)	2010 census total population	2019 estimated population	Percent change 2010–2019	ACS total population estimate 2015–2019	White alone, not Hispanic or Latino	Black alone, not Hispanic or Latino	Asian alone, not Hispanic or Latino	All other races or 2 or more races, not Hispanic or Latino	Hispanic or Latino[1]	Under 18 years old	Age 65 years and older	Median age	Percent High school diploma or less	Percent Bachelor's degree or more	Total occupied housing units	Percent with a computer
	1	2	3	4	5	6	7	8	9	10	11	12	13	14	15	16
Brielle borough & MCD (Monmouth)	4,755	4,666	-1.9	4,697	95.0	1.3	0.3	0.6	2.8	23.1	20.4	47.5	17.5	65.3	1,745	95.7
Brigantine city & MCD (Atlantic)	9,450	8,650	-8.5	8,832	87.4	0.3	5.4	0.9	6.1	11.7	30.6	56.0	32.7	36.7	4,052	92.8
Broadway CDP	244	-	-	186	100.0	0.0	0.0	0.0	0.0	0.0	56.2	65.6	2.2		110	93.6
Brookdale CDP	9,239	-	-	9,801	62.9	5.9	11.8	2.8	16.6	23.9	16.5	40.2	25.2	55.7	3,450	93.9
Brookfield CDP	675	-	-	822	98.3	0.0	1.7	0.0	0.0	0.0	87.8	78.7	34.4	24.8	558	84.9
Brooklawn borough & MCD (Camden)	1,938	1,898	-2.1	2,004	78.5	5.8	5.9	1.4	8.3	20.4	7.6	36.9	59.9	17.5	676	90.4
Browns Mills CDP	11,223	-	-	10,998	54.6	23.1	3.2	9.4	9.8	23.9	12.9	35.9	47.3	13.1	3,921	93.2
Brownville CDP	2,383	-	-	2,554	66.7	1.6	10.3	0.0	21.5	23.9	15.2	42.2	32.3	43.4	1,040	97.4
Budd Lake CDP	8,968	-	-	9,743	69.7	6.3	6.5	1.6	15.9	27.4	9.1	37.2	34.2	43.6	3,379	98.0
Buena borough & MCD (Atlantic)	4,605	4,284	-7.0	4,356	60.7	8.2	2.9	2.4	25.8	24.6	17.1	36.6	50.7	19.2	1,750	83.0
Buena Vista township (Atlantic)	7,560	7,215	-4.6	7,295	72.5	10.0	0.6	3.6	13.3	21.6	18.9	40.2	59.8	13.3	2,558	93.5
Burleigh CDP	725	-	-	534	74.2	25.8	0.0	0.0	0.0	8.4	27.5	57.6	56.9	26.7	277	79.1
Burlington city & MCD (Burlington)	9,937	9,858	-0.8	9,815	53.6	27.5	3.4	4.5	11.1	22.0	18.7	42.2	47.5	22.2	3,960	85.7
Burlington township (Burlington)	22,569	22,594	0.1	22,586	43.7	31.5	9.9	4.5	10.4	24.3	13.7	38.6	35.7	33.0	7,888	94.1
Butler borough & MCD (Morris)	7,650	7,654	0.1	7,679	74.9	0.6	5.2	0.8	18.5	17.4	16.9	42.8	38.3	38.3	3,093	95.1
Buttzville CDP	146	-	-	-											-	-
Byram township (Sussex)	8,421	7,932	-5.8	7,974	87.4	0.9	2.0	1.8	7.8	19.1	13.8	44.5	24.3	43.6	2,988	96.6
Byram Center CDP	90	-	-	39	0.0	100.0	0.0	0.0	0.0	0.0	0.0	39.6	48.1	0.0	14	100.0
Caldwell borough & MCD (Essex)	7,887	7,941	0.7	7,969	78.8	3.6	5.6	1.5	10.5	16.6	16.3	40.9	23.2	58.5	3,239	96.5
Califon borough & MCD (Hunterdon)	1,063	1,046	-1.6	1,139	95.6	0.0	1.5	1.6	1.3	27.0	11.2	39.8	19.4	56.9	439	94.1
Camden city & MCD (Camden)	76,866	73,562	-4.3	74,002	5.8	39.1	2.4	1.7	51.0	30.8	9.6	30.8	66.3	9.8	24,652	79.5
Cape May city & MCD (Cape May)	3,617	3,422	-5.4	3,463	78.7	2.8	0.1	1.8	16.7	12.9	26.3	33.4	23.7	47.1	1,354	90.5
Cape May Court House CDP	5,338	-	-	4,617	82.7	5.9	0.6	3.7	7.0	14.4	27.4	50.7	35.1	34.3	2,069	89.5
Cape May Point borough & MCD (Cape May)	291	275	-5.5	176	98.9	1.1	0.0	0.0	0.0	1.1	72.7	71.3	12.7	79.8	92	96.7
Carlstadt borough & MCD (Bergen)	6,125	6,132	0.1	6,178	63.3	0.4	10.7	1.3	24.4	16.5	21.1	41.7	41.1	37.3	2,414	91.8
Carneys Point CDP	7,382	-	-	7,076	64.7	17.1	0.6	1.6	16.2	18.8	20.4	42.0	55.7	13.0	2,734	88.7
Carneys Point township (Salem)	8,079	7,674	-5.0	7,734	64.9	16.0	0.5	1.6	17.0	18.3	20.4	42.4	55.7	12.6	2,989	89.2
Carteret borough & MCD (Middlesex)	22,851	23,408	2.4	23,589	26.5	12.0	20.2	1.5	39.8	23.7	12.0	37.1	49.3	24.3	7,925	85.5
Cedar Glen Lakes CDP	1,421	-	-	1,549	92.3	0.0	2.5	0.6	4.6	0.0	79.4	71.5	61.4	19.5	1,077	70.8
Cedar Glen West CDP	1,267	-	-	1,300	86.8	8.3	2.2	2.7	0.0	4.2	48.2	63.8	60.0	18.1	814	78.6
Cedar Grove township (Essex)	12,420	12,489	0.6	12,516	80.8	3.4	8.3	1.4	6.0	17.7	26.5	48.1	29.0	53.1	4,530	94.5
Cedarville CDP	776	-	-	1,101	61.0	2.5	0.0	3.0	33.5	39.5	11.4	27.6	72.2	2.2	264	95.8
Chatham borough & MCD (Morris)	8,987	8,635	-3.9	8,816	81.1	0.9	9.3	1.7	6.9	32.4	11.4	41.8	10.4	77.7	2,932	96.8
Chatham township (Morris)	10,412	10,117	-2.8	10,299	79.5	1.7	13.2	1.9	3.7	28.9	16.0	42.6	11.4	79.4	3,637	96.7
Cherry Hill township (Camden)	70,811	71,245	0.6	70,965	70.6	6.3	13.6	2.8	6.7	21.3	20.0	43.2	23.0	54.6	26,689	93.8
Cherry Hill Mall CDP	14,171	-	-	14,068	64.1	7.9	15.8	2.1	10.0	19.4	17.7	41.0	26.1	40.6	5,313	92.2
Chesilhurst borough & MCD (Camden)	1,628	1,618	-0.6	1,489	49.2	31.1	0.0	4.0	15.7	14.2	24.7	53.7	58.6	10.7	544	81.4
Chester borough & MCD (Morris)	1,649	1,624	-1.5	1,653	82.5	1.3	1.6	0.7	13.9	23.2	21.9	45.1	26.9	55.4	618	90.0
Chester township (Morris)	7,839	7,670	-2.2	7,783	86.6	1.5	4.3	3.0	4.7	24.0	15.9	48.5	11.0	74.5	2,872	94.9
Chesterfield township (Burlington)	7,653	7,573		7,506	55.1	19.2	14.9	1.3	9.4	23.2	8.3	29.4	34.5	44.4	1,738	97.0
Cinnaminson township (Burlington)	15,562	16,342	5.0	16,416	86.9	5.0	1.0	2.0	5.0	19.8	18.2	43.1	29.3	41.2	5,878	94.3
City of Orange township (Essex)	30,347	30,551	0.7	30,484	2.9	68.2	1.6	2.3	25.0	24.8	13.7	35.2	52.3	20.4	11,742	83.8
Clark township (Union)	14,742	15,911	7.9	15,748	82.9	1.6	4.1	0.2	11.3	17.9	19.7	44.6	35.3	43.2	5,945	92.1
Clayton borough & MCD (Gloucester)	8,184	8,738	6.8	8,626	72.1	15.6	1.7	2.8	7.9	21.6	17.2	42.2	44.2	27.0	3,029	88.5
Clearbrook Park CDP	2,667	-	-	2,813	87.7	5.1	0.0	1.1	6.1	0.0	70.2	71.1	58.2	24.4	1,883	83.4
Clementon borough & MCD (Camden)	4,983	4,957	-0.5	4,918	45.8	35.4	2.0	2.9	13.9	25.8	11.9	34.9	47.7	19.5	1,831	86.6
Cliffside Park borough & MCD (Bergen)	23,565	26,133	10.9	25,126	45.5	3.1	16.5	3.6	31.2	16.1	21.0	43.0	37.7	42.9	10,512	89.5
Cliffwood Beach CDP	3,194	-	-	2,892	68.2	11.0	2.1	3.3	15.4	17.4	13.4	43.9	39.3	21.0	1,155	96.4
Clifton city & MCD (Passaic)	84,117	85,052	1.1	85,204	45.3	4.9	9.5	2.0	38.2	20.0	16.3	39.5	45.1	32.7	29,256	87.7
Clinton town & MCD (Hunterdon)	2,719	2,687	-1.2	2,686	78.4	1.8	12.2	0.8	6.7	22.2	13.6	42.0	20.5	55.2	1,082	92.6
Clinton township (Hunterdon)	13,510	12,565	-7.0	12,787	75.5	10.1	5.5	1.6	7.2	21.2	13.7	38.1	21.1	60.3	4,028	93.3
Closter borough & MCD (Bergen)	8,415	8,511	1.1	8,565	50.6	0.8	41.4	1.9	5.2	23.5	14.9	44.9	22.7	64.9	2,778	96.4
Clyde CDP	213	-	-	233	57.5	42.5	0.0	0.0	0.0	0.9	14.2	54.7	49.5	26.6	96	92.7
Collings Lakes CDP	1,706	-	-	1,539	88.2	2.0	0.0	0.0	9.8	28.7	10.5	35.5	63.3	4.3	488	97.3
Collingswood borough & MCD (Camden)	13,939	13,884	-0.4	13,912	78.2	10.5	1.7	2.1	7.5	19.3	16.4	41.1	27.9	47.1	6,075	94.1
Colonia CDP	17,795	-	-	17,801	64.3	6.0	15.8	1.8	12.0	19.4	18.1	42.7	35.6	40.6	6,036	93.6
Colts Neck township (Monmouth)	10,138	9,822	-3.1	9,895	90.8	1.1	1.8	1.0	5.2	25.7	13.7	45.3	13.9	63.9	3,226	96.5

1 May be of any race.

Table A. All Places — **Population and Housing**

STATE City, town, township, borough, or CDP (county if applicable)	Population 2010 census total population	2019 estimated population	Percent change 2010–2019	ACS total population estimate 2015–2019	White alone, not Hispanic or Latino	Black alone, not Hispanic or Latino	Asian alone, not Hispanic or Latino	All other races or 2 or more races, not Hispanic or Latino	Hispanic or Latino[1]	Under 18 years old	Age 65 years and older	Median age	Percent High school diploma or less	Percent Bachelor's degree or more	Occupied housing units Total	Percent with a computer
	1	2	3	4	5	6	7	8	9	10	11	12	13	14	15	16
NEW JERSEY—Con.																
Columbia CDP..................	229	-	-	182	98.9	1.1	0.0	0.0	0.0	0.0	17.0	57.0	39.8	40.9	73	100.0
Commercial township (Cumberland)..............	5,178	4,916	-5.1	4,979	80.7	5.0	1.3	4.9	8.1	25.4	14.8	38.3	60.0	11.9	1,932	87.2
Concordia CDP..............	3,092	-	-	3,401	82.2	3.4	8.0	0.5	5.9	0.9	76.3	73.0	35.3	39.7	2,196	85.6
Corbin City city & MCD (Atlantic)..............	498	491	-1.4	537	96.8	0.4	0.4	1.5	0.9	18.1	12.1	44.4	43.2	31.9	182	98.9
Country Lake Estates CDP	3,943	-	-	3,766	59.5	10.7	4.9	4.9	20.1	23.2	14.1	40.3	57.5	12.1	1,271	88.8
Cranbury CDP	2,181	-	-	1,919	77.1	2.9	16.5	1.9	1.6	21.7	20.2	48.0	15.4	73.0	692	97.3
Cranbury township (Middlesex)	3,861	4,067	5.3	3,649	74.7	4.7	12.8	1.9	6.0	20.9	21.2	48.8	16.0	70.8	1,299	97.8
Crandon Lakes CDP........	1,178	-	-	1,252	100.0	0.0	0.0	0.0	0.0	17.3	16.6	42.4	39.6	29.4	484	84.5
Cranford township (Union)	22,635	24,054	6.3	24,014	82.0	2.0	3.3	3.5	9.2	23.3	19.2	42.9	22.4	57.1	8,894	92.4
Cresskill borough & MCD (Bergen)	8,534	8,668	1.6	8,699	61.9	0.2	30.8	0.5	6.6	27.5	15.6	41.2	19.4	64.0	2,812	95.4
Crestwood Village CDP	7,907	-	-	8,155	91.2	3.3	0.8	0.4	4.3	0.4	73.8	73.0	58.5	15.3	5,613	65.1
Dayton CDP..................	7,063	-	-	7,576	20.7	10.6	56.4	2.5	9.8	26.9	7.8	38.9	19.3	65.2	2,482	98.8
Deal borough & MCD (Monmouth)..................	750	719	-4.1	519	80.3	0.2	0.6	0.0	18.9	16.8	36.4	54.7	39.5	28.9	235	87.7
Deerfield township (Cumberland)...............	3,129	3,012	-3.7	3,053	65.7	19.3	1.1	3.7	10.3	21.9	20.1	42.7	61.4	17.2	1,060	90.0
Delanco township (Burlington)..............	4,268	4,430	3.8	4,469	74.3	14.7	1.4	3.5	6.1	18.5	21.6	47.0	42.4	30.7	1,991	91.6
Delaware township (Hunterdon)..............	4,567	4,425	-3.1	4,455	90.3	0.0	0.6	1.7	7.3	16.3	24.6	53.7	27.6	52.0	1,736	96.7
Delaware CDP..............	150	-	-	107	100.0	0.0	0.0	0.0	0.0	0.0	29.0	60.5	66.4	17.8	56	100.0
Delaware Park CDP.........	700	-	-	300	80.3	0.0	0.0	3.7	16.0	5.0	31.3	51.9	24.2	53.3	152	91.4
Delran township (Burlington)..............	16,925	16,492	-2.6	16,548	81.4	9.5	3.7	2.6	2.7	21.5	14.7	39.9	33.3	41.3	5,991	95.0
Demarest borough & MCD (Bergen)..............	4,895	4,894	0.0	4,942	59.2	0.1	28.7	2.1	9.9	28.7	15.9	43.5	12.1	70.8	1,680	94.7
Dennis township (Cape May)........................	6,443	6,144	-4.6	6,204	91.4	0.3	1.0	0.3	7.0	22.5	19.8	44.0	44.9	27.2	2,305	93.9
Denville township (Morris)	16,679	16,446	-1.4	16,606	82.5	2.2	7.6	1.8	6.0	21.4	19.1	45.1	20.8	57.8	6,368	93.2
Deptford township (Gloucester)	30,619	30,349	-0.9	30,448	73.1	11.8	6.2	2.6	6.4	19.5	17.5	42.0	47.9	25.1	11,737	92.6
Diamond Beach CDP	136	-	-	189	100.0	0.0	0.0	0.0	0.0	0.0	79.9	70.6	43.4	30.7	96	100.0
Dover town & MCD (Morris).............:..	18,158	17,725	-2.4	17,977	19.7	8.3	1.9	1.9	68.3	22.2	11.1	37.5	53.0	18.7	5,548	90.6
Dover Beaches North CDP	1,239	-	-	1,756	94.4	0.3	0.6	0.8	3.9	6.5	42.6	61.8	31.7	47.1	916	83.7
Dover Beaches South CDP	1,209	-	-	1,243	96.1	0.0	1.6	0.0	2.3	6.2	36.7	60.0	28.0	54.0	658	87.5
Downe township (Cumberland)..............	1,598	1,447	-9.4	1,107	88.1	1.6	0.3	7.4	2.6	22.5	22.7	48.6	63.8	14.0	452	78.1
Dumont borough & MCD (Bergen)..............	17,392	17,516	0.7	17,624	59.7	3.0	16.5	1.8	19.1	19.1	18.2	44.4	35.0	43.6	6,370	89.6
Dunellen borough & MCD (Middlesex)	7,223	7,202	-0.3	7,252	47.5	12.2	7.2	0.7	32.4	27.5	11.2	36.9	40.9	33.4	2,460	90.9
Eagleswood township (Ocean)	1,602	1,603	0.1	1,583	94.6	0.0	0.3	3.9	1.1	19.0	20.8	48.6	47.2	22.5	595	91.3
Eastampton township (Burlington)..............	6,072	6,144	1.2	5,989	58.4	20.2	7.0	4.2	10.3	22.6	8.9	35.2	29.2	43.5	2,138	97.1
East Amwell township (Hunterdon)..............	3,987	3,858	-3.2	3,890	91.1	1.5	0.8	0.8	5.7	13.3	22.5	50.3	38.6	36.2	1,468	89.6
East Brunswick township (Middlesex)...............	47,465	47,611	0.3	47,819	59.5	3.2	25.7	2.0	9.6	21.0	17.5	45.0	25.1	56.0	16,840	93.1
East Franklin CDP...........	8,669	-	-	7,649	9.1	45.9	5.9	6.1	33.0	24.3	10.6	35.1	52.0	24.3	2,566	91.5
East Freehold CDP...........	4,894	-	-	4,880	79.4	4.3	6.8	5.1	4.5	17.8	14.3	46.8	26.5	44.3	1,599	94.6
East Greenwich township (Gloucester)	9,508	10,719	12.7	10,488	80.1	8.8	5.6	2.6	2.9	26.7	14.8	39.9	29.9	44.3	3,387	97.6
East Hanover township (Morris)..................	11,155	10,921	-2.1	11,072	71.8	1.1	11.3	1.5	14.3	18.4	20.6	47.0	35.4	45.2	3,771	93.1
East Millstone CDP..........	579	-	-	471	79.4	0.0	20.6	0.0	0.0	14.4	16.1	42.5	18.2	67.4	158	91.1
East Newark borough & MCD (Hudson).............	2,449	2,600	6.2	2,644	20.0	0.0	4.6	1.4	74.1	24.5	14.4	35.3	58.3	18.6	779	91.0
East Orange city & MCD (Essex).............	64,169	64,367	0.3	64,374	2.1	82.7	1.8	2.2	11.2	24.1	12.3	35.1	49.1	19.7	23,521	89.6
East Rocky Hill CDP.........	469	-	-	338	88.8	0.3	0.0	0.0	10.9	0.0	29.9	52.2	18.3	52.9	169	88.8
East Rutherford borough & MCD (Bergen)	8,913	9,687	8.7	9,584	51.3	5.8	17.5	3.6	21.7	18.3	17.5	35.7	33.4	41.7	3,966	90.4
East Windsor township (Mercer)..............	27,179	27,288	0.4	27,245	47.5	7.8	20.0	1.2	23.5	24.1	15.1	39.2	30.0	50.9	9,711	93.6
Eatontown borough & MCD (Monmouth)	12,685	12,157	-4.2	12,214	63.2	9.1	7.9	5.2	14.7	19.4	14.9	42.8	41.7	37.3	5,260	90.9
Echelon CDP..................	10,743	-	-	11,957	43.6	17.7	24.2	6.3	8.1	19.7	14.6	36.1	30.4	46.5	5,051	89.7
Edgewater borough & MCD (Bergen)..............	11,516	13,364	16.0	12,403	40.8	4.5	38.0	3.5	13.1	18.6	11.8	36.7	16.1	73.5	5,751	94.5
Edgewater Park township (Burlington)..............	8,911	8,647	-3.0	8,692	49.2	26.1	1.2	3.8	19.7	19.0	17.2	41.5	50.4	22.6	3,414	90.8
Edison township (Middlesex)	100,323	99,758	-0.6	100,447	30.7	7.8	48.6	3.0	9.9	22.8	14.8	39.6	27.3	55.5	34,571	94.4
Egg Harbor township (Atlantic)..............	43,420	42,249	-2.7	42,714	59.7	6.3	11.5	4.3	18.3	24.6	14.0	39.2	42.8	31.6	14,245	96.1
Egg Harbor City city & MCD (Atlantic)..............	4,247	4,052	-4.6	4,100	41.1	24.3	6.8	0.9	27.0	26.8	16.0	33.5	55.1	16.2	1,454	88.4
Elizabeth city & MCD (Union)	124,973	129,216	3.4	128,333	12.2	17.6	1.8	3.4	65.0	26.9	10.3	34.5	64.4	13.5	40,785	84.3
Elk township (Gloucester).	4,167	4,173	0.1	4,135	81.0	12.2	0.6	1.8	4.4	18.3	16.2	44.3	40.8	25.4	1,320	90.1
Ellisburg CDP	4,413	-	-	4,254	71.5	5.0	14.5	4.9	4.1	19.3	27.0	46.2	31.7	45.5	1,910	88.3
Elmer borough & MCD (Salem)	1,402	1,308	-6.7	1,436	91.4	1.2	1.7	2.6	3.1	21.7	14.3	37.4	45.9	26.2	495	89.3

1 May be of any race.

Table A. All Places — **Population and Housing**

STATE City, town, township, borough, or CDP (county if applicable)	2010 census total population	2019 estimated population	Percent change 2010–2019	ACS total population estimate 2015–2019	White alone, not Hispanic or Latino	Black alone, not Hispanic or Latino	Asian alone, not Hispanic or Latino	All other races or 2 or more races, not Hispanic or Latino	Hispanic or Latino[1]	Under 18 years old	Age 65 years and older	Median age	Percent High school diploma or less	Percent Bachelor's degree or more	Occupied housing units Total	Percent with a computer
	1	2	3	4	5	6	7	8	9	10	11	12	13	14	15	16
NEW JERSEY—Con.																
Elmwood Park borough & MCD (Bergen)	19,488	19,966	2.5	20,059	54.3	6.2	8.4	3.3	27.8	22.2	15.1	38.6	46.1	29.7	6,738	89.0
Elsinboro township (Salem)	1,036	968	-6.6	1,052	81.3	11.8	1.3	0.5	5.1	19.7	23.3	45.2	47.6	21.5	424	89.9
Elwood CDP	1,437	-	-	1,041	60.7	23.2	0.0	0.0	16.1	13.8	19.1	50.3	52.5	15.8	401	88.8
Emerson borough & MCD (Bergen)	7,386	7,596	2.8	7,596	73.5	0.9	12.2	0.0	13.4	21.9	18.9	45.8	27.2	46.3	2,541	95.3
Englewood city & MCD (Bergen)	27,116	28,402	4.7	28,353	32.5	25.4	9.7	3.5	28.8	20.0	16.4	43.5	36.0	43.7	11,114	94.7
Englewood Cliffs borough & MCD (Bergen)	5,310	5,354	0.8	5,371	43.8	1.3	42.8	2.3	9.7	22.4	25.3	49.0	19.0	67.8	1,816	97.7
Englishtown borough & MCD (Monmouth)	1,827	1,912	4.7	2,119	73.9	5.5	7.8	2.0	10.7	22.8	15.4	40.7	37.0	28.6	754	86.9
Erma CDP	2,134	-	-	1,876	91.5	0.1	2.6	4.5	1.4	17.0	19.5	46.9	43.7	20.4	820	94.1
Essex Fells borough & MCD (Essex)	2,116	2,088	-1.3	2,110	87.0	0.0	3.0	1.8	8.2	25.3	19.6	45.7	8.6	80.1	768	96.6
Estell Manor city & MCD (Atlantic)	1,753	1,729	-1.4	1,728	94.6	1.6	0.5	0.4	3.0	18.0	11.5	44.3	44.7	28.8	587	95.1
Evesham township (Burlington)	45,534	45,188	-0.8	45,135	81.2	5.5	6.0	2.1	5.1	21.1	16.7	42.2	25.8	47.9	17,624	95.0
Ewing township (Mercer)	35,729	36,303	1.6	36,037	55.1	29.3	4.6	2.3	8.7	15.6	16.7	37.8	38.6	37.5	12,748	91.5
Fairfield township (Cumberland)	6,269	5,911	-5.7	6,090	28.6	48.3	0.5	8.7	13.9	20.1	15.6	39.6	64.4	12.3	1,741	82.5
Fairfield township (Essex)	7,454	7,474	0.3	7,486	84.6	0.0	3.6	0.9	10.9	20.3	28.4	51.8	33.2	46.9	2,641	92.2
Fair Haven borough & MCD (Monmouth)	6,112	5,736	-6.2	5,873	93.1	3.3	0.8	0.4	2.3	34.6	11.3	40.8	11.7	71.2	1,822	97.4
Fair Lawn borough & MCD (Bergen)	32,385	32,896	1.6	33,017	70.5	1.9	12.0	1.3	14.2	22.2	17.5	43.3	22.2	56.5	11,387	94.1
Fairton CDP	1,264	-	-	980	54.2	19.3	0.8	13.9	11.8	23.5	20.5	43.0	71.3	11.0	384	84.4
Fairview borough & MCD (Bergen)	13,835	14,189	2.6	14,258	28.3	1.5	7.0	1.7	61.5	17.1	12.9	37.6	60.5	24.0	5,236	85.9
Fairview CDP	3,806	-	-	3,742	94.2	0.0	1.5	0.3	4.0	23.5	16.3	42.7	24.8	49.5	1,228	95.7
Fanwood borough & MCD (Union)	7,307	7,697	5.3	7,660	78.5	3.7	6.3	2.8	8.7	27.7	14.6	40.1	19.7	66.7	2,506	95.0
Far Hills borough & MCD (Somerset)	921	903	-2.0	860	80.2	0.2	3.3	2.6	13.7	20.6	19.4	48.9	17.1	66.5	325	93.5
Farmingdale borough & MCD (Monmouth)	1,324	1,354	2.3	1,299	78.4	0.9	2.9	2.2	15.5	23.2	12.2	39.8	39.9	29.0	551	88.9
Fieldsboro borough & MCD (Burlington)	545	552	1.3	752	58.2	6.3	5.7	16.1	13.7	18.9	8.8	39.1	35.2	29.3	287	90.9
Finderne CDP	5,600	-	-	5,919	47.9	4.5	22.1	1.4	24.1	21.4	14.0	37.5	37.2	37.2	2,109	91.2
Finesville CDP	175	-	-	280	100.0	0.0	0.0	0.0	0.0	29.6	16.4	40.2	36.5	34.0	104	100.0
Flemington borough & MCD (Hunterdon)	4,586	4,577	-0.2	4,608	50.8	3.5	9.2	3.5	33.0	24.6	9.2	33.3	47.2	31.4	1,652	93.0
Florence CDP	-	-	-	4,455	70.5	9.8	3.4	10.1	6.2	19.6	16.9	38.9	45.9	19.8	1,899	82.7
Florence township (Burlington)	12,122	12,486	3.0	12,552	71.7	9.1	6.1	5.0	8.1	20.7	17.1	42.1	37.2	32.1	4,941	88.9
Florham Park borough & MCD (Morris)	11,736	11,496	-2.0	11,623	77.1	4.0	9.0	1.5	8.4	16.2	19.4	40.2	16.0	67.7	4,026	94.2
Folsom borough & MCD (Atlantic)	1,887	1,775	-5.9	1,697	86.2	2.8	1.1	4.4	5.5	19.4	19.0	43.8	47.8	22.7	588	90.3
Fords CDP	15,187	-	-	15,250	45.4	9.8	20.0	1.6	23.3	21.4	13.8	37.1	39.2	35.4	5,248	90.8
Forked River CDP	5,244	-	-	4,761	90.0	0.0	2.4	0.5	7.1	20.6	19.2	46.9	41.1	26.3	1,935	91.2
Fort Dix CDP	7,716	-	-	7,668	38.4	29.8	1.8	6.9	23.1	13.1	2.5	33.9	50.1	16.7	903	99.4
Fort Lee borough & MCD (Bergen)	35,433	38,605	9.0	37,430	40.7	1.9	42.4	1.9	13.1	15.6	24.9	46.6	23.0	59.6	17,479	92.1
Frankford township (Sussex)	5,547	5,301	-4.4	5,340	91.1	0.1	2.0	0.8	5.9	18.3	22.2	51.6	37.6	34.5	1,957	95.4
Franklin township (Gloucester)	16,778	16,300	-2.8	16,440	85.3	6.5	1.3	1.2	5.8	20.8	13.5	41.8	51.2	20.2	5,804	92.1
Franklin township (Hunterdon)	3,205	3,518	9.8	3,348	95.2	0.3	0.5	0.8	3.2	16.5	23.4	50.1	28.8	48.5	1,269	92.7
Franklin township (Somerset)	62,337	65,642	5.3	65,554	33.8	27.9	20.7	3.0	14.5	18.9	17.8	41.3	27.2	51.7	25,098	95.6
Franklin borough & MCD (Sussex)	5,067	4,721	-6.8	4,778	89.1	3.9	0.8	0.2	6.0	19.4	15.9	44.0	51.8	19.6	1,983	88.3
Franklin township (Warren)	3,156	3,024	-4.2	3,050	93.8	1.2	2.1	0.7	2.2	21.1	16.0	47.0	35.9	34.8	1,089	94.0
Franklin Center CDP	4,460	-	-	5,860	53.5	8.4	24.7	2.0	11.4	11.5	40.3	58.6	22.1	57.3	2,675	97.6
Franklin Lakes borough & MCD (Bergen)	10,579	11,119	5.1	10,946	81.2	2.6	6.1	1.7	8.3	21.7	21.2	48.3	13.9	69.1	3,845	96.8
Franklin Park CDP	13,295	-	-	13,977	26.5	33.4	27.7	2.1	10.2	20.2	11.5	38.4	24.0	55.9	5,611	96.7
Fredon township (Sussex)	3,382	3,160	-6.6	3,197	92.6	0.2	0.7	1.6	4.9	23.7	18.4	45.4	25.5	45.5	1,044	95.3
Freehold borough & MCD (Monmouth)	12,045	11,682	-3.0	11,797	39.6	8.8	1.4	1.6	48.6	25.1	12.1	35.9	58.4	20.6	4,134	85.4
Freehold township (Monmouth)	36,206	34,624	-4.4	34,945	74.9	5.2	7.3	2.4	10.2	21.1	16.7	43.0	29.2	46.1	12,446	93.5
Frelinghuysen township (Warren)	2,246	2,173	-3.3	2,344	89.6	1.5	0.4	1.5	7.0	21.5	20.2	45.7	34.3	38.2	764	92.5
Frenchtown borough & MCD (Hunterdon)	1,394	1,351	-3.1	1,464	88.9	1.1	5.3	0.4	4.3	26.8	15.4	40.6	31.7	49.9	620	89.5
Galloway township (Atlantic)	37,241	35,618	-4.4	36,094	65.1	11.5	8.2	4.3	11.0	16.9	17.3	41.1	38.3	31.0	12,840	94.5
Garfield city & MCD (Bergen)	30,494	31,802	4.3	31,645	53.2	3.7	2.2	1.8	39.0	22.3	11.8	36.6	55.1	20.1	11,547	90.5
Garwood borough & MCD (Union)	4,231	4,352	2.9	4,338	78.9	1.2	4.2	2.1	13.6	18.0	14.7	38.7	34.0	41.3	1,725	95.4
Gibbsboro borough & MCD (Camden)	2,276	2,218	-2.5	2,169	87.9	1.4	2.2	1.6	7.0	21.3	19.8	45.0	39.3	31.0	763	92.5
Gibbstown CDP	3,739	-	-	3,778	92.4	3.7	2.3	0.0	1.5	22.0	20.3	45.8	55.5	18.5	1,500	87.4
Glassboro borough & MCD (Gloucester)	18,578	20,288	9.2	19,826	63.4	17.0	4.0	4.2	11.3	17.2	12.1	28.2	36.9	36.8	6,068	92.8

1 May be of any race.

Table A. All Places — **Population and Housing**

	Population				Race and Hispanic or Latino origin (percent)					Age (percent)			Educational attainment of persons age 25 and older		Occupied housing units	
STATE City, town, township, borough, or CDP (county if applicable)	2010 census total population	2019 estimated population	Percent change 2010–2019	ACS total population estimate 2015–2019	White alone, not Hispanic or Latino	Black alone, not Hispanic or Latino	Asian alone, not Hispanic or Latino	All other races or 2 or more races, not Hispanic or Latino	Hispanic or Latino[1]	Under 18 years old	Age 65 years and older	Median age	Percent High school diploma or less	Percent Bachelor's degree or more	Total	Percent with a computer
	1	2	3	4	5	6	7	8	9	10	11	12	13	14	15	16
NEW JERSEY—Con.																
Glendora CDP	4,750	-	-	4,851	83.8	2.3	0.5	4.1	9.3	15.7	18.2	42.8	57.0	15.5	1,962	86.2
Glen Gardner borough & MCD (Hunterdon)	1,975	1,911	-3.2	1,488	83.9	2.4	0.8	1.6	11.2	15.3	13.9	48.1	28.7	42.4	767	93.7
Glen Ridge borough & MCD (Essex)	7,507	7,574	0.9	7,584	76.4	3.8	6.8	5.9	7.2	32.5	9.3	40.0	10.1	78.8	2,452	99.2
Glen Rock borough & MCD (Bergen)	11,581	11,707	1.1	11,780	75.3	1.7	11.7	3.6	7.7	29.3	14.2	40.6	10.7	74.4	3,776	95.5
Gloucester township (Camden)	64,660	63,903	-1.2	63,705	68.6	17.0	3.3	3.1	8.0	21.2	14.9	39.3	41.5	27.7	23,248	92.9
Gloucester City city & MCD (Camden)	11,453	11,219	-2.0	11,248	76.7	4.2	5.8	2.0	11.5	26.3	11.1	35.2	53.9	17.3	3,947	88.5
Golden Triangle CDP	4,145	-	-	4,185	70.1	4.4	6.9	9.1	9.5	21.4	23.0	44.1	38.7	28.1	1,600	88.4
Great Meadows CDP	303	-	-	32	93.8	0.0	3.1	3.1	0.0	0.0	9.4	55.5	51.6	3.2	14	100.0
Green township (Sussex)	3,615	3,471	-4.0	3,484	83.3	3.4	0.1	1.6	11.5	25.8	16.5	43.3	20.9	55.9	1,233	99.6
Green Brook township (Somerset)	7,164	7,007	-2.2	7,114	56.2	5.2	23.2	0.7	14.8	22.8	14.5	42.3	27.5	52.4	2,174	95.9
Green Knoll CDP	6,200	-	-	6,631	62.2	2.7	23.5	1.9	9.8	21.1	22.6	44.9	26.0	55.9	2,383	92.4
Greentree CDP	11,367	-	-	11,262	70.4	2.5	18.7	2.6	5.9	22.2	19.3	44.3	15.1	68.7	4,071	97.5
Greenwich township (Cumberland)	799	758	-5.1	599	89.1	0.3	5.2	5.3	0.0	20.7	21.5	44.9	34.1	31.3	231	89.2
Greenwich township (Gloucester)	4,907	4,795	-2.3	4,831	91.6	3.7	1.9	1.1	1.7	22.2	20.3	44.7	50.6	21.7	1,926	87.3
Greenwich CDP	2,755	-	-	2,731	60.5	14.1	11.9	3.9	9.6	30.9	6.0	38.7	14.9	58.7	818	100.0
Greenwich township (Warren)	5,704	5,442	-4.6	5,480	76.2	7.7	6.1	2.4	7.6	24.8	11.2	42.5	19.8	50.0	1,893	94.9
Griggstown CDP	819	-	-	611	99.7	0.3	0.0	0.0	0.0	8.2	50.7	66.2	51.5	38.5	325	94.2
Groveville CDP	2,945	-	-	1,961	80.9	11.5	2.5	0.0	5.2	24.6	13.5	45.8	36.8	36.5	825	92.8
Guttenberg town & MCD (Hudson)	11,157	11,121	-0.3	11,317	22.9	1.8	8.4	0.8	66.0	18.3	13.2	36.8	46.9	36.3	4,506	94.3
Hackensack city & MCD (Bergen)	43,024	44,188	2.7	44,339	24.9	22.5	11.2	1.7	39.7	17.7	14.3	38.1	39.4	39.4	19,080	91.1
Hackettstown town & MCD (Warren)	9,718	9,356	-3.7	9,485	70.6	2.1	4.5	1.5	21.3	20.2	17.1	37.7	38.1	35.5	3,445	89.8
Haddon township (Camden)	14,688	14,541		14,539	89.9	2.9	0.4	1.6	5.2	19.3	20.8	44.1	26.2	48.5	6,001	93.2
Haddonfield borough & MCD (Camden)	11,610	11,317	-2.5	11,345	92.6	1.0	1.9	1.3	3.3	29.2	16.8	41.9	9.6	77.2	4,117	96.5
Haddon Heights borough & MCD (Camden)	7,467	7,529	0.8	7,514	93.8	1.2	1.5	1.3	2.3	21.3	20.7	43.2	24.8	53.2	2,941	91.4
Hainesburg CDP	91	-	-	61	82.0	0.0	0.0	18.0	0.0	6.6	11.5	52.4	26.3	8.8	26	73.1
Hainesport township (Burlington)	6,129	5,976	-2.5	6,010	85.4	4.0	3.4	3.3	4.0	18.2	19.0	47.1	38.0	34.9	2,305	92.0
Haledon borough & MCD (Passaic)	8,322	8,293	-0.3	8,325	32.7	11.1	1.5	2.9	51.8	21.5	13.0	34.8	53.0	24.7	2,714	91.9
Hamburg borough & MCD (Sussex)	3,323	3,131	-5.8	3,148	91.8	0.6	2.1	0.0	5.4	20.9	15.2	42.8	35.2	30.8	1,325	92.7
Hamilton township (Atlantic)	26,498	25,746	-2.8	25,973	56.2	15.3	9.1	3.9	15.5	23.0	13.4	38.5	37.1	33.9	9,776	95.1
Hamilton township (Mercer)	88,442	87,065	-1.6	87,424	63.7	14.4	4.4	1.7	15.8	18.9	18.0	41.6	41.0	30.6	32,936	91.8
Hamilton Square CDP	12,784	-	-	11,989	86.6	2.3	5.1	1.2	4.9	18.3	21.4	46.2	30.1	42.8	4,225	94.9
Hammonton town & MCD (Atlantic)	14,771	13,934	-5.7	14,139	73.1	2.8	1.2	0.5	22.5	23.6	18.1	42.0	43.2	27.2	4,992	91.1
Hampton borough & MCD (Hunterdon)	1,375	1,318	-4.1	1,309	85.1	3.2	0.9	0.9	9.9	18.3	19.8	43.8	32.6	37.1	577	85.8
Hampton township (Sussex)	5,186	4,842	-6.6	4,879	92.3	1.9	1.5	0.0	4.4	16.7	20.0	47.1	33.5	34.2	2,009	90.5
Hancocks Bridge CDP	254	-	-	198	94.4	2.0	0.0	0.0	3.5	31.3	5.1	38.2	39.4	7.1	75	96.0
Hanover township (Morris)	13,718	14,252	3.9	14,399	76.9	2.0	14.4	1.0	5.7	20.4	19.8	44.7	25.5	56.3	5,650	93.3
Harding township (Morris)	3,799	3,760		3,806	93.0	1.6	1.7	0.9	2.9	19.2	27.7	52.2	14.4	71.0	1,608	96.4
Hardwick township (Warren)	1,673	1,619	-3.2	1,547	92.7	1.4	0.6	1.7	3.6	19.1	17.9	48.3	32.1	36.2	575	93.4
Hardyston township (Sussex)	8,174	7,786	-4.7	7,849	86.4	3.9	2.0	1.3	6.4	21.0	19.7	45.1	32.2	39.3	3,113	95.3
Harlingen CDP	297	-	-	416	64.4	0.0	22.1	0.0	13.5	25.0	8.4	39.2	6.6	87.1	128	100.0
Harmony CDP	441	-	-	453	98.7	1.3	0.0	0.0	0.0	9.9	19.2	48.4	51.3	19.2	184	79.9
Harmony township (Warren)	2,634	2,466	-6.4	2,737	93.1	0.2	3.7	0.0	3.0	16.9	17.0	47.1	49.1	23.0	996	88.7
Harrington Park borough & MCD (Bergen)	4,668	4,730	1.3	4,753	71.2	0.0	19.2	2.7	6.8	26.7	18.3	44.7	14.8	63.3	1,626	95.8
Harrison township (Gloucester)	12,384	13,116	5.9	12,995	92.5	2.0	0.9	0.1	4.5	28.9	10.3	40.1	21.7	56.1	4,264	97.2
Harrison town & MCD (Hudson)	13,537	20,061	48.2	17,213	27.1	2.1	21.1	1.7	48.0	20.9	8.9	33.3	41.8	41.5	6,474	93.2
Harvey Cedars borough & MCD (Ocean)	341	345	1.2	475	96.6	0.0	0.6	2.3	0.4	8.4	48.6	64.4	14.9	69.3	250	96.0
Hasbrouck Heights borough & MCD (Bergen)	11,887	11,992	0.9	12,082	61.2	5.2	14.4	1.1	18.0	19.5	17.4	43.4	31.7	43.1	4,224	92.9
Haworth borough & MCD (Bergen)	3,374	3,393	0.6	3,418	77.5	1.4	15.7	1.9	3.5	26.9	18.8	46.2	13.6	71.1	1,113	97.5
Hawthorne borough & MCD (Passaic)	18,786	18,753	-0.2	18,784	68.8	5.9	0.7	0.9	23.8	19.7	16.6	40.5	37.8	37.3	7,118	90.6
Hazlet township (Monmouth)	20,321	19,664	-3.2	19,844	83.4	2.3	3.8	1.5	9.0	20.8	18.6	43.5	42.4	34.0	6,965	91.6
Heathcote CDP	5,821	-	-	6,507	32.4	8.6	49.2	6.9	3.0	23.3	20.2	44.1	12.8	72.6	2,699	92.4
Helmetta borough & MCD (Middlesex)	2,172	2,155	-0.8	2,475	77.0	4.2	3.2	0.4	15.2	20.0	12.0	41.6	41.1	33.5	956	96.7
High Bridge borough & MCD (Hunterdon)	3,645	3,410	-6.4	3,500	81.8	3.8	1.9	1.2	11.3	20.1	13.1	44.7	31.0	49.3	1,495	89.8
Highland Lakes CDP	-	-		5,098	86.3	0.3	0.2	1.0	12.1	20.7	13.2	40.6	35.6	35.6	1,867	97.4

1 May be of any race.

Table A. All Places — Population and Housing

STATE City, town, township, borough, or CDP (county if applicable)	2010 census total population	2019 estimated population	Percent change 2010–2019	ACS total population estimate 2015–2019	White alone, not Hispanic or Latino	Black alone, not Hispanic or Latino	Asian alone, not Hispanic or Latino	All other races or 2 or more races, not Hispanic or Latino	Hispanic or Latino[1]	Under 18 years old	Age 65 years and older	Median age	Percent High school diploma or less	Percent Bachelor's degree or more	Occupied housing units Total	Percent with a computer
	1	2	3	4	5	6	7	8	9	10	11	12	13	14	15	16
NEW JERSEY—Con.																
Highland Park borough & MCD (Middlesex)	13,982	13,711	-1.9	13,883	56.9	11.3	13.9	3.1	14.7	20.9	12.8	35.3	15.4	71.2	5,735	95.0
Highlands borough & MCD (Monmouth)	5,021	4,714	-6.1	4,768	85.0	2.6	5.1	4.6	2.7	11.3	18.8	52.5	31.7	32.9	2,628	91.5
Hightstown borough & MCD (Mercer)	5,523	5,304	-4.0	5,375	53.0	12.1	4.5	1.1	29.2	19.3	18.0	38.4	34.9	41.0	1,867	91.0
Hillsborough township (Somerset)	38,316	39,950	4.3	39,542	67.0	3.7	18.5	3.2	7.6	22.7	13.3	41.3	21.7	59.3	13,794	95.8
Hillsdale borough & MCD (Bergen)	10,184	10,307	1.2	10,346	79.2	2.3	8.9	2.3	7.3	24.9	16.3	43.5	22.8	54.6	3,490	96.8
Hillside township (Union) ..	21,463	21,967	2.3	21,928	19.2	51.4	3.2	7.8	18.4	21.3	13.0	37.0	45.2	25.8	7,342	93.8
Hi-Nella borough & MCD (Camden)	870	858	-1.4	988	66.1	10.5	6.6	7.2	9.6	21.3	11.1	33.6	46.4	21.8	414	96.6
Hoboken city & MCD (Hudson)	50,020	52,677	5.3	53,193	69.4	2.6	9.6	2.4	16.0	13.9	6.2	31.7	12.3	80.5	25,182	95.6
Ho-Ho-Kus borough & MCD (Bergen)	4,084	4,065	-0.5	4,094	80.9	0.3	12.4	1.5	4.9	30.5	14.3	42.1	7.1	84.0	1,438	97.9
Holiday City-Berkeley CDP	12,831	-	-	12,040	93.5	0.9	1.2	0.0	4.4	0.3	69.4	70.8	61.8	13.1	7,354	78.7
Holiday City South CDP ...	3,689	-	-	4,464	76.3	10.9	3.6	2.1	7.2	4.3	58.2	67.6	58.4	18.9	2,385	78.9
Holiday Heights CDP	2,099	-	-	1,903	97.7	0.0	0.7	0.6	1.0	0.0	76.1	78.0	60.3	18.0	1,165	67.0
Holland township (Hunterdon)	5,313	5,097	-4.1	5,133	97.0	0.5	0.0	0.0	2.6	21.3	19.9	46.3	37.5	40.9	1,914	91.3
Holmdel township (Monmouth)	16,785	16,731	-0.3	16,609	72.7	0.9	19.3	1.8	5.3	21.8	22.3	49.7	19.6	63.8	5,800	94.7
Hopatcong borough & MCD (Sussex)	15,136	14,186	-6.3	14,281	75.1	2.8	4.5	0.7	16.9	17.5	13.9	42.0	40.6	29.4	5,570	95.7
Hope CDP	195	-	-	125	72.8	0.0	0.0	0.0	27.2	16.0	34.4	48.6	49.5	16.2	46	100.0
Hope township (Warren)...	1,935	1,857	-4.0	1,737	92.0	0.1	0.9	0.6	6.4	16.6	21.9	49.4	39.0	34.1	690	91.0
Hopewell township (Cumberland)	4,607	4,350	-5.6	4,386	78.7	7.2	2.4	3.9	7.8	20.1	23.5	46.6	49.3	25.6	1,680	88.0
Hopewell borough & MCD (Mercer)	1,928	1,906	-1.1	1,915	92.5	0.2	1.0	1.6	4.7	26.4	13.9	43.0	15.7	67.3	742	96.9
Hopewell township (Mercer)	18,304	17,725	-3.2	18,067	78.7	4.4	10.5	1.6	4.8	20.9	16.8	46.1	20.1	64.4	6,325	96.9
Howell township (Monmouth)	51,088	51,952	1.7	51,959	77.2	4.1	6.0	1.6	11.1	22.8	13.8	40.3	32.4	40.0	17,910	95.6
Hutchinson CDP	135	-	-	78	82.1	0.0	0.0	0.0	17.9	12.8	16.7	55.1	34.5	46.6	28	57.1
Independence township (Warren)	5,650	5,411	-4.2	5,450	80.6	4.5	0.8	1.7	12.4	20.2	15.7	41.8	33.8	40.5	2,112	95.4
Interlaken borough & MCD (Monmouth)	820	789	-3.8	749	94.0	0.0	1.2	1.7	3.1	15.4	32.2	57.4	12.3	68.8	343	93.9
Irvington township (Essex)	53,838	54,312	0.9	54,079	2.2	85.7	0.9	1.4	10.0	25.3	12.0	34.5	53.4	18.9	20,024	81.6
Iselin CDP	18,695	-	-	18,175	27.6	6.8	53.9	5.0	6.7	19.0	19.2	43.7	36.7	44.6	6,579	93.0
Island Heights borough & MCD (Ocean)	1,644	1,679	2.1	1,497	86.0	0.8	0.4	9.4	3.5	18.5	27.2	50.1	27.0	45.3	635	94.0
Jackson township (Ocean)	54,890	57,731	5.2	56,968	80.7	5.3	3.2	1.3	9.6	22.7	17.4	42.2	35.6	33.3	20,498	95.0
Jamesburg borough & MCD (Middlesex)	5,889	5,885	-0.1	5,921	65.3	1.0	7.3	4.1	22.3	30.1	12.3	37.3	43.0	33.7	2,051	97.1
Jefferson township (Morris)	21,289	20,716	-2.7	21,035	85.7	3.0	4.3	2.2	4.8	19.7	15.2	45.6	33.4	40.7	8,115	93.2
Jersey City city & MCD (Hudson)	247,608	262,075	5.8	261,940	21.9	21.1	24.9	3.6	28.5	20.6	11.1	34.3	35.1	47.5	103,225	91.4
Johnsonburg CDP	101	-	-	98	67.3	0.0	0.0	0.0	32.7	43.9	5.1	34.5	29.1	60.0	25	100.0
Juliustown CDP	429	-	-	308	100.0	0.0	0.0	0.0	0.0	26.3	18.2	45.6	26.7	30.1	110	95.5
Keansburg borough & MCD (Monmouth)	10,097	9,632	-4.6	9,735	68.7	11.9	3.3	2.8	13.2	22.9	11.9	40.2	56.8	17.4	3,704	88.4
Kearny town & MCD (Hudson)	40,714	41,058	0.8	41,412	36.0	4.3	4.9	2.2	52.6	21.8	13.3	38.0	53.0	25.7	13,364	92.3
Kendall Park CDP...........	9,339	-	-	9,234	48.0	7.2	32.4	2.4	10.0	24.1	14.2	43.6	19.9	58.2	3,150	94.4
Kenilworth borough & MCD (Union)	7,914	8,191	3.5	8,161	59.5	2.5	2.8	7.2	28.0	24.3	13.6	38.2	42.4	28.9	2,733	94.0
Kenvil CDP	3,009	-	-	3,013	86.3	2.8	2.0	1.3	7.7	22.2	23.2	46.1	42.3	27.3	1,129	90.1
Keyport borough & MCD (Monmouth)	7,220	6,977	-3.4	7,034	70.2	7.3	4.5	2.9	15.2	16.0	20.4	44.3	46.2	22.7	3,169	86.6
Kingston CDP	1,493	-	-	1,184	60.6	0.0	36.5	1.0	1.9	14.1	17.7	49.9	10.2	68.7	534	100.0
Kingston Estates CDP	5,685	-	-	6,407	65.7	12.7	16.4	0.4	4.8	23.7	19.7	36.2	25.8	52.5	2,449	90.1
Kingwood township (Hunterdon)	3,826	3,741	-2.2	3,752	95.2	2.3	0.0	0.8	1.7	15.9	22.1	51.1	32.3	42.9	1,497	87.4
Kinnelon borough & MCD (Morris)	10,125	9,896	-2.3	10,054	81.3	0.1	6.5	2.3	9.9	25.3	17.2	44.5	19.1	64.5	3,358	96.9
Knowlton township (Warren)	3,060	2,928	-4.3	2,946	92.2	1.1	2.4	2.3	2.0	18.1	18.3	45.7	41.8	33.4	1,054	95.4
Lacey township (Ocean)...	27,642	29,295	6.0	28,804	93.5	0.8	1.0	0.3	4.4	20.1	19.1	43.8	39.7	28.8	10,991	93.9
Lafayette township (Sussex)	2,517	2,363	-6.1	2,328	91.8	0.8	0.6	1.3	5.4	19.7	20.2	47.2	36.2	36.7	810	96.4
Lake Como borough & MCD (Monmouth)	1,763	1,682	-4.6	1,740	74.8	2.7	0.7	1.3	20.4	20.1	12.2	37.0	24.2	49.4	741	94.2
Lakehurst borough & MCD (Ocean)	2,654	2,708	2.0	2,684	73.6	4.7	5.9	1.1	14.6	25.9	8.8	37.4	51.3	18.9	919	89.8
Lake Mohawk CDP..........	9,916	-	-	8,999	90.9	0.2	2.0	1.1	5.9	21.9	18.3	45.5	20.9	53.7	3,610	97.3
Lake Telemark CDP.........	1,255	-	-	1,197	97.2	0.0	0.0	0.0	2.8	18.5	12.6	38.8	25.9	52.9	464	92.9
Lakewood township (Ocean)	92,799	106,300	14.5	102,466	83.0	2.7	1.1	0.5	12.7	48.3	10.3	19.3	42.7	30.5	23,781	80.9
Lakewood CDP...............	53,805	-	-	56,072	85.9	1.4	0.6	0.3	11.8	52.0	4.3	16.9	43.8	31.5	10,298	78.6
Lambertville city & MCD (Hunterdon)	3,922	3,801	-3.1	3,822	87.5	0.0	1.8	0.7	10.1	15.6	21.9	48.8	26.6	51.6	1,863	97.6
Laurel Lake CDP	2,989	-	-	3,325	80.7	2.1	1.3	5.1	10.9	29.7	9.4	36.0	66.5	7.9	1,205	88.0
Laurel Springs borough & MCD (Camden)	1,905	1,866	-2.0	1,959	89.3	2.8	1.9	3.1	2.9	20.0	14.4	41.1	33.8	37.4	696	92.0
Laurence Harbor CDP	6,536	-	-	6,534	62.6	6.2	8.2	0.0	23.0	23.7	12.7	39.7	45.9	29.0	2,315	93.5

1 May be of any race.

Table A. All Places — **Population and Housing**

STATE City, town, township, borough, or CDP (county if applicable)	Population				Race and Hispanic or Latino origin (percent)					Age (percent)			Educational attainment of persons age 25 and older		Occupied housing units	
	2010 census total population	2019 estimated population	Percent change 2010–2019	ACS total population estimate 2015–2019	White alone, not Hispanic or Latino	Black alone, not Hispanic or Latino	Asian alone, not Hispanic or Latino	All other races or 2 or more races, not Hispanic or Latino	Hispanic or Latino[1]	Under 18 years old	Age 65 years and older	Median age	Percent High school diploma or less	Percent Bachelor's degree or more	Total	Percent with a computer
	1	2	3	4	5	6	7	8	9	10	11	12	13	14	15	16
NEW JERSEY—Con.																
Lavallette borough & MCD (Ocean)	1,875	1,866	-0.5	2,155	94.2	0.0	0.3	1.6	3.9	8.0	48.5	64.2	24.0	49.7	1,110	93.1
Lawnside borough & MCD (Camden)	2,948	2,882	-2.2	2,885	5.5	80.4	0.5	4.7	8.9	16.3	24.9	46.5	51.8	27.0	1,159	84.0
Lawrence township (Cumberland)	3,286	3,060	-6.9	3,123	65.8	11.8	0.0	4.5	17.9	26.9	12.6	34.6	62.0	12.4	977	90.8
Lawrence township (Mercer)	33,483	32,435	-3.1	32,614	63.4	10.6	15.3	1.8	9.0	17.4	16.5	41.1	24.5	55.4	12,067	93.7
Lawrenceville CDP	3,887	-	-	3,949	85.9	1.0	8.3	1.3	3.4	14.5	19.2	50.3	15.3	63.4	1,835	99.1
Lebanon borough & MCD (Hunterdon)	1,358	1,644	21.1	1,856	86.2	1.0	5.2	1.1	6.6	18.8	14.7	40.9	30.4	45.8	780	95.8
Lebanon township (Hunterdon)	6,331	6,081	-3.9	6,124	90.6	0.9	1.1	2.3	5.0	17.9	17.1	48.0	25.3	51.5	2,313	95.6
Leisure Knoll CDP	2,490	-	-	2,537	91.1	3.6	2.0	0.0	3.3	0.0	79.4	74.5	50.9	19.2	1,582	79.3
Leisuretowne CDP	3,582	-	-	3,262	92.0	3.2	0.0	2.2	2.6	4.1	69.0	72.0	53.8	21.9	2,060	79.5
Leisure Village CDP	4,400	-	-	4,547	64.9	10.2	0.8	0.0	24.1	5.2	48.1	63.0	46.9	17.5	2,410	73.5
Leisure Village East CDP	4,217	-	-	3,687	91.5	1.5	0.3	1.7	5.0	0.0	74.0	75.8	44.6	30.5	2,503	72.9
Leisure Village West CDP	-	-	-	3,412	93.5	2.3	1.9	0.5	1.8	0.0	76.3	73.0	46.1	27.3	2,292	79.2
Leonardo CDP	2,757	-	-	2,568	91.9	0.0	3.2	0.0	4.9	19.8	12.5	41.9	36.5	32.1	972	91.6
Leonia borough & MCD (Bergen)	8,944	9,035	1.0	9,086	38.0	1.9	39.7	1.5	18.9	21.6	19.1	44.6	23.5	54.6	3,355	91.5
Liberty township (Warren)	2,943	2,802	-4.8	2,829	93.2	1.1	1.6	0.6	3.5	20.4	12.9	43.4	33.8	40.7	1,068	96.7
Lincoln Park borough & MCD (Morris)	10,539	10,111	-4.1	10,262	79.5	2.0	5.2	1.3	12.0	18.7	17.2	45.1	34.8	38.0	3,669	95.2
Lincroft CDP	6,135	-	-	6,405	88.5	0.0	7.9	0.5	3.1	24.4	19.0	44.3	22.1	55.6	2,089	89.3
Linden city & MCD (Union)	40,533	42,361	4.5	42,222	31.6	29.5	3.7	3.0	32.3	21.0	14.3	39.6	47.4	22.7	14,647	89.2
Lindenwold borough & MCD (Camden)	17,620	17,263	-2.0	17,320	35.1	34.5	1.8	4.7	24.0	22.6	13.0	35.2	51.4	17.1	7,590	87.2
Linwood city & MCD (Atlantic)	7,091	6,658	-6.1	6,742	82.9	1.5	6.2	1.2	8.3	21.8	20.3	47.8	25.1	51.4	2,509	92.9
Little Egg Harbor township (Ocean)	20,053	21,712	8.3	21,127	90.4	0.1	1.5	2.0	6.0	17.2	28.3	51.2	43.2	27.3	9,228	90.7
Little Falls township (Passaic)	14,423	14,474	0.4	14,483	79.3	3.5	4.6	2.2	10.3	16.6	17.1	41.1	33.2	43.7	5,223	93.5
Little Ferry borough & MCD (Bergen)	10,638	10,739	0.9	10,782	44.1	1.5	25.8	1.0	27.5	15.8	13.9	39.9	35.5	37.0	4,096	94.5
Little Silver borough & MCD (Monmouth)	5,952	5,782	-2.9	5,844	94.4	0.0	0.9	0.7	3.9	27.2	19.5	46.3	7.6	72.9	2,043	98.4
Livingston township (Essex)	29,382	30,303	3.1	29,846	66.2	1.7	26.2	2.5	3.4	25.4	19.4	45.5	16.0	72.1	10,225	94.6
Loch Arbour village & MCD (Monmouth)	195	180	-7.7	230	93.5	0.9	1.7	3.5	0.4	18.3	23.0	48.5	7.6	73.2	88	96.6
Lodi borough & MCD (Bergen)	24,091	24,347	1.1	24,430	44.3	6.2	9.7	1.8	37.9	21.2	14.1	37.3	48.7	25.1	8,805	92.5
Logan township (Gloucester)	6,045	5,874	-2.8	5,924	79.2	12.0	0.8	3.0	5.1	23.9	10.9	39.2	36.3	35.6	2,056	98.1
Long Beach township (Ocean)	3,069	3,071	0.1	3,056	98.2	0.0	0.2	1.1	0.5	4.9	52.0	65.5	22.3	60.4	1,574	92.1
Long Branch city & MCD (Monmouth)	30,717	30,241	-1.5	30,516	52.0	13.3	1.5	2.9	30.3	22.0	14.8	36.9	48.1	28.4	12,032	91.1
Long Hill township (Morris)	8,719	8,430	-3.3	8,590	88.4	0.2	5.6	0.8	5.0	21.6	17.8	44.1	19.3	62.2	3,131	96.0
Longport borough & MCD (Atlantic)	895	851	-4.9	869	97.5	0.0	0.8	1.0	0.7	12.0	41.7	61.2	20.5	56.9	420	91.9
Long Valley CDP	1,879	-	-	2,201	77.7	0.0	3.6	3.4	15.3	32.8	11.4	38.2	26.2	46.9	700	95.4
Lopatcong township (Warren)	8,055	8,387	4.1	8,295	82.1	5.2	4.3	0.8	7.6	19.1	22.2	48.4	35.9	39.7	3,476	88.8
Lopatcong Overlook CDP	734	-	-	763	91.0	5.8	0.0	0.0	3.3	25.6	11.3	42.3	33.6	47.9	361	100.0
Lower township (Cape May)	22,874	21,339	-6.7	21,653	89.0	1.5	0.9	2.1	6.5	17.7	23.6	49.3	45.8	24.4	9,431	91.1
Lower Alloways Creek township (Salem)	1,784	1,672	-6.3	1,719	93.0	4.2	0.0	1.0	1.8	19.7	21.7	45.6	50.2	15.6	646	88.9
Lumberton township (Burlington)	12,544	12,192	-2.8	12,232	64.3	18.5	6.8	3.7	6.7	22.4	15.9	43.0	30.7	40.5	4,626	93.3
Lyndhurst township (Bergen)	20,554	22,918	11.5	22,298	66.6	1.9	6.2	2.1	23.2	18.0	16.3	41.6	42.1	34.9	8,738	88.5
McGuire AFB CDP	3,710	-	-	5,113	58.6	9.0	2.6	5.2	24.5	38.5	0.0	23.1	11.7	36.9	1,394	99.6
Madison borough & MCD (Morris)	15,813	17,654	11.6	16,377	77.9	3.3	6.6	2.6	9.6	22.6	14.3	40.4	17.4	67.2	5,579	93.6
Madison Park CDP	7,144	-	-	7,834	34.6	17.2	21.8	2.2	24.2	26.5	11.9	36.5	37.1	33.3	2,809	94.5
Magnolia borough & MCD (Camden)	4,353	4,273	-1.8	4,272	66.3	16.9	4.3	1.2	11.3	19.5	13.7	36.5	43.5	26.5	1,680	95.1
Mahwah township (Bergen)	25,883	26,200	1.2	26,275	72.3	2.8	12.2	1.2	11.5	18.6	19.1	42.9	23.2	57.3	9,778	95.1
Manahawkin CDP	2,303	-	-	2,094	83.5	0.0	2.2	0.5	13.8	19.1	17.8	47.1	36.6	38.8	968	90.5
Manalapan township (Monmouth)	38,975	39,325	0.9	39,702	83.3	1.9	7.1	1.3	6.4	22.0	16.2	44.3	25.0	52.3	14,060	94.2
Manasquan borough & MCD (Monmouth)	5,902	5,806	-1.6	5,829	92.3	0.0	4.0	0.5	3.2	19.8	19.6	47.3	18.7	62.9	2,296	95.2
Manchester township (Ocean)	43,057	43,723	1.5	43,503	85.7	4.0	2.2	2.0	6.1	9.9	49.4	64.6	53.3	22.0	23,268	79.0
Mannington township (Salem)	1,789	1,716	-4.1	1,748	71.4	14.0	1.4	1.5	11.7	14.8	20.1	43.5	56.4	20.9	466	85.4
Mansfield township (Burlington)	8,577	8,533	-0.5	8,533	74.6	9.6	9.5	1.2	5.1	15.2	31.1	52.2	34.0	42.1	3,577	89.6
Mansfield township (Warren)	7,708	7,361	-4.5	7,397	76.1	7.7	4.9	1.8	9.5	21.5	15.0	42.7	38.4	33.3	2,935	88.8
Mantoloking borough & MCD (Ocean)	294	249	-15.3	396	93.4	1.5	0.5	0.0	4.5	14.4	61.1	69.3	5.9	80.1	181	98.3
Mantua township (Gloucester)	15,286	14,840	-2.9	14,941	90.5	3.3	2.2	1.3	2.8	22.4	15.5	40.6	37.9	35.4	5,580	94.8

1 May be of any race.

Table A. All Places — **Population and Housing**

STATE City, town, township, borough, or CDP (county if applicable)	2010 census total population	2019 estimated population	Percent change 2010–2019	ACS total population estimate 2015–2019	White alone, not Hispanic or Latino	Black alone, not Hispanic or Latino	Asian alone, not Hispanic or Latino	All other races or 2 or more races, not Hispanic or Latino	Hispanic or Latino[1]	Under 18 years old	Age 65 years and older	Median age	Percent High school diploma or less	Percent Bachelor's degree or more	Total	Percent with a computer
	1	2	3	4	5	6	7	8	9	10	11	12	13	14	15	16
NEW JERSEY—Con.																
Manville borough & MCD (Somerset)	10,344	10,121	-2.2	10,230	63.3	8.7	3.3	2.0	22.6	24.7	15.5	37.3	56.6	18.1	3,761	85.9
Maple Shade township (Burlington)	19,147	18,476	-3.5	18,642	72.0	10.2	8.2	2.0	7.6	18.7	16.3	38.8	42.5	27.9	8,285	91.5
Maplewood township (Essex)	23,841	25,380	6.5	24,784	48.6	37.5	2.7	3.4	7.8	28.4	11.8	39.6	18.6	61.2	7,959	93.2
Margate City city & MCD (Atlantic)	6,354	5,865	-7.7	5,997	93.5	2.0	1.0	2.2	1.3	11.9	37.4	58.3	24.4	52.4	2,933	91.9
Marksboro CDP	82	-	-	136	100.0	0.0	0.0	0.0	0.0	47.1	3.7	18.3	44.4	17.8	22	100.0
Marlboro township (Monmouth)	40,061	39,640	-1.1	39,982	70.6	2.5	19.7	1.7	5.5	25.7	13.8	42.6	18.6	63.3	12,751	97.4
Marlton CDP	10,133	-	-	9,672	83.0	3.4	5.8	1.4	6.4	18.3	16.8	42.0	34.8	39.7	4,016	94.8
Martinsville CDP	11,980	-	-	11,586	80.1	1.7	14.2	0.8	3.3	22.5	18.6	45.7	15.3	65.4	4,006	97.3
Matawan borough & MCD (Monmouth)	8,840	8,640	-2.3	8,747	69.4	9.1	6.7	3.1	11.7	22.4	14.0	38.5	28.0	45.1	3,379	93.5
Maurice River township (Cumberland)	7,652	5,949	-22.3	7,484	43.8	37.1	0.5	3.6	15.0	6.6	7.7	39.7	71.7	6.3	963	86.5
Mays Landing CDP	2,135	-	-	2,524	79.2	2.7	1.2	0.3	16.5	21.4	12.2	38.5	33.7	34.3	1,068	97.3
Maywood borough & MCD (Bergen)	9,549	9,614	0.7	9,661	55.0	4.1	16.9	2.2	21.8	19.2	18.8	44.3	38.0	37.4	3,511	88.5
Medford township (Burlington)	23,004	23,394	1.7	23,312	91.2	1.0	2.9	2.0	2.9	22.1	20.8	46.5	19.3	58.9	8,535	97.6
Medford Lakes borough & MCD (Burlington)	4,152	3,914	-5.7	3,984	95.8	0.2	0.0	0.5	3.4	24.4	20.2	44.2	17.4	55.9	1,465	98.0
Mendham borough & MCD (Morris)	4,991	4,847	-2.9	4,917	90.8	1.1	1.5	1.7	4.9	25.1	25.3	49.8	13.7	68.4	1,787	93.8
Mendham township (Morris)	5,874	5,662	-3.6	5,755	86.3	1.0	3.7	2.8	6.2	25.4	14.0	44.7	11.9	74.6	1,920	94.1
Mercerville CDP	13,230	-	-	12,730	78.1	5.6	2.3	2.1	11.9	17.8	19.2	44.9	35.5	35.0	4,638	91.5
Merchantville borough & MCD (Camden)	3,780	3,700	-2.1	3,719	64.1	12.4	5.5	0.2	17.8	22.7	19.1	40.4	37.7	33.8	1,413	91.0
Metuchen borough & MCD (Middlesex)	13,581	14,543	7.1	14,048	66.2	5.9	16.9	3.6	7.4	23.5	15.3	41.0	17.5	62.5	5,273	93.0
Middle township (Cape May)	18,933	18,175	-4.0	18,365	75.1	12.3	1.0	1.7	9.9	19.3	21.5	43.0	43.9	23.9	7,327	90.5
Middlebush CDP	2,326	-	-	2,647	49.9	10.5	23.0	2.8	13.9	23.3	15.2	44.4	32.5	35.7	796	82.2
Middlesex borough & MCD (Middlesex)	13,635	13,679	0.3	13,662	56.5	6.9	6.3	1.6	28.7	23.1	15.1	40.7	44.7	25.7	4,868	93.4
Middletown township (Monmouth)	66,507	65,305	-1.8	65,336	88.0	0.9	3.4	1.3	6.4	21.9	17.9	44.2	28.0	47.0	23,805	93.8
Midland Park borough & MCD (Bergen)	7,154	7,216	0.9	7,244	82.8	1.2	2.4	3.7	9.9	22.3	19.2	43.1	32.7	45.5	2,669	93.8
Milford borough & MCD (Hunterdon)	1,232	1,181	-4.1	1,298	95.3	0.0	0.5	1.2	3.0	15.8	20.0	46.1	32.1	37.2	520	92.3
Millburn township (Essex)	20,141	20,080	-0.3	20,148	62.7	2.7	25.1	4.4	5.1	31.5	13.0	41.0	8.9	82.9	6,662	98.3
Millstone township (Monmouth)	10,666	10,397	-2.5	10,443	82.3	1.7	5.8	1.2	9.0	21.0	12.4	45.2	23.5	52.9	3,394	97.4
Millstone borough & MCD (Somerset)	417	408	-2.2	498	83.3	1.6	3.6	3.4	8.0	28.5	16.3	40.8	32.5	50.6	154	93.5
Milltown borough & MCD (Middlesex)	6,896	6,967	1.0	6,998	76.0	2.7	3.9	1.0	16.4	23.5	13.6	40.7	30.9	38.0	2,352	93.1
Millville city & MCD (Cumberland)	28,417	27,391	-3.6	27,721	61.2	15.2	2.7	2.7	18.3	24.3	16.5	40.5	55.7	17.8	10,949	87.1
Mine Hill township (Morris)	3,648	3,478	-4.7	3,530	53.8	2.3	9.5	2.1	32.3	21.7	16.0	42.2	32.1	42.9	1,257	90.5
Monmouth Beach borough & MCD (Monmouth)	3,286	3,239	-1.4	3,212	94.8	0.0	0.5	1.5	3.2	16.6	27.4	53.8	11.7	70.6	1,423	95.9
Monmouth Junction CDP	2,887	-	-	2,906	40.5	2.4	45.4	4.5	7.2	29.9	8.7	39.3	10.1	77.7	912	100.0
Monroe township (Gloucester)	36,119	36,865	2.1	36,789	74.4	13.8	2.0	2.7	7.1	24.1	16.0	40.9	42.6	26.6	13,357	91.3
Monroe township (Middlesex)	39,176	45,030	14.9	44,306	71.0	2.8	19.4	2.2	4.6	17.3	37.9	56.5	32.3	46.9	18,837	90.3
Montague township (Sussex)	3,868	3,648	-5.7	3,681	93.3	1.3	2.4	1.3	1.6	20.4	19.0	43.7	47.1	26.1	1,525	89.8
Montclair township (Essex)	37,671	38,564	2.4	38,427	60.4	21.3	3.7	4.3	10.4	25.0	13.0	40.7	15.2	69.6	14,593	95.4
Montgomery township (Somerset)	22,255	23,124	3.9	23,045	54.6	3.5	35.9	2.0	4.0	25.9	13.4	42.3	13.3	75.0	7,657	96.3
Montvale borough & MCD (Bergen)	7,844	8,570	9.3	8,489	73.3	3.3	14.4	0.7	8.3	23.4	19.1	45.3	20.7	59.8	2,975	92.8
Montville township (Morris)	21,505	21,058	-2.1	21,371	71.0	0.5	20.1	1.8	6.6	23.5	17.3	44.6	19.7	63.4	7,526	96.9
Moonachie borough & MCD (Bergen)	2,690	2,702	0.4	2,716	47.9	0.6	6.3	5.0	40.3	22.2	18.2	42.0	46.9	26.4	937	96.4
Moorestown township (Burlington)	20,741	20,516	-1.1	20,449	81.1	6.2	7.1	2.2	3.4	24.8	16.0	43.5	17.4	64.6	7,145	93.9
Moorestown-Lenola CDP	14,217	-	-	13,806	83.4	7.9	2.0	2.2	4.6	23.7	15.9	43.6	19.0	59.3	5,109	92.5
Morganville CDP	5,040	-	-	5,088	64.0	1.0	24.7	2.4	7.9	27.8	15.7	42.2	17.9	62.9	1,762	96.2
Morris township (Morris)	22,413	22,156	-1.1	22,268	76.7	5.2	4.9	2.0	11.2	20.1	21.4	46.2	17.4	68.3	8,417	95.2
Morris Plains borough & MCD (Morris)	5,532	6,255	13.1	5,748	81.5	1.9	4.7	2.9	8.9	18.8	17.4	44.1	20.7	62.0	2,178	95.5
Morristown town & MCD (Morris)	18,352	19,261	5.0	18,909	54.0	8.5	5.8	2.8	28.9	14.5	13.6	34.4	28.3	58.3	8,448	94.1
Mountain Lake CDP	575	-	-	471	97.9	0.0	1.3	0.0	0.8	11.0	17.6	47.7	44.9	30.0	252	94.0
Mountain Lakes borough & MCD (Morris)	4,167	4,223	1.3	4,270	81.1	0.0	14.0	0.7	4.2	30.8	11.0	42.9	5.7	85.8	1,342	99.2
Mountainside borough & MCD (Union)	6,656	6,885	3.4	6,826	80.5	1.9	6.4	0.9	10.3	23.6	26.9	48.7	25.4	53.8	2,504	93.2
Mount Arlington borough & MCD (Morris)	5,038	5,852	16.2	5,637	67.6	6.3	1.5	0.6	24.1	20.2	18.5	45.0	32.9	37.4	2,203	95.2
Mount Ephraim borough & MCD (Camden)	4,674	4,587	-1.9	4,582	94.4	2.3	0.0	0.3	2.9	18.4	13.6	37.5	45.3	22.6	1,761	92.3
Mount Hermon CDP	141	-	-	120	100.0	0.0	0.0	0.0	0.0	30.0	28.3	40.5	27.5	40.0	42	85.7

1 May be of any race.

Table A. All Places — **Population and Housing**

STATE City, town, township, borough, or CDP (county if applicable)	Population				Race and Hispanic or Latino origin (percent)					Age (percent)			Educational attainment of persons age 25 and older		Occupied housing units	
	2010 census total population	2019 estimated population	Percent change 2010–2019	ACS total population estimate 2015–2019	White alone, not Hispanic or Latino	Black alone, not Hispanic or Latino	Asian alone, not Hispanic or Latino	All other races or 2 or more races, not Hispanic or Latino	Hispanic or Latino[1]	Under 18 years old	Age 65 years and older	Median age	Percent High school diploma or less	Percent Bachelor's degree or more	Total	Percent with a computer
	1	2	3	4	5	6	7	8	9	10	11	12	13	14	15	16

NEW JERSEY—Con.

STATE City, town, township, borough, or CDP (county if applicable)	1	2	3	4	5	6	7	8	9	10	11	12	13	14	15	16
Mount Holly township (Burlington)	9,551	9,547	0.0	9,563	54.7	22.1	1.6	4.6	17.0	20.3	12.1	37.3	43.4	27.1	3,554	90.7
Mount Laurel township (Burlington)	41,860	41,250	-1.5	41,422	70.6	11.0	9.7	3.4	5.3	20.5	18.8	43.8	24.5	53.0	17,302	94.4
Mount Olive township (Morris)	28,181	28,926	2.6	28,915	69.7	6.0	8.1	1.6	14.7	23.8	11.9	38.6	31.1	41.9	10,856	93.7
Mullica township (Atlantic)	6,147	5,856	-4.7	5,925	91.6	4.1	0.0	0.6	3.7	21.8	17.9	45.8	44.4	22.7	2,282	94.5
Mullica Hill CDP	3,982	-	-	3,662	93.7	3.7	0.9	0.3	1.5	20.7	19.1	44.8	23.6	52.1	1,514	93.3
Mystic Island CDP	8,493	-	-	8,484	87.9	0.2	0.2	2.6	9.2	15.8	30.1	55.0	52.5	20.1	3,864	87.6
National Park borough & MCD (Gloucester)	3,035	2,943	-3.0	2,959	89.2	2.7	0.4	2.9	4.8	21.2	13.7	39.7	53.3	14.8	1,087	89.4
Navesink CDP	2,020	-	-	1,470	87.2	9.3	3.5	0.0	0.0	21.6	22.1	47.3	18.3	50.2	558	97.1
Neptune township (Monmouth)	27,991	27,384	-2.2	27,563	49.2	33.9	2.4	3.9	10.6	16.9	19.7	44.9	35.6	34.9	11,402	89.3
Neptune City borough & MCD (Monmouth)	4,812	4,596	-4.5	4,672	75.7	7.6	2.7	0.6	13.4	20.7	14.2	41.9	41.5	30.1	2,075	89.5
Netcong borough & MCD (Morris)	3,232	3,131	-3.1	3,177	76.0	7.1	1.7	1.4	13.8	16.2	15.1	44.5	46.3	29.0	1,418	88.9
Newark city & MCD (Essex)	277,135	282,011	1.8	281,054	11.0	48.3	1.8	2.6	36.3	24.6	10.5	34.4	60.3	15.3	100,262	84.9
New Brunswick city & MCD (Middlesex)	54,500	55,676	2.2	55,960	26.7	15.3	9.7	1.5	46.8	22.8	5.9	23.6	59.9	22.6	15,328	87.9
New Egypt CDP	2,512	-	-	2,460	96.3	2.2	0.0	0.0	1.5	20.3	17.1	39.3	60.6	17.5	1,000	79.1
Newfield borough & MCD (Gloucester)	1,589	1,543	-2.9	1,521	85.3	2.0	0.0	1.1	11.6	21.3	17.9	43.6	47.4	29.3	585	89.2
New Hanover township (Burlington)	7,385	7,808	5.7	7,548	42.1	29.1	1.9	3.7	23.2	9.3	3.9	35.7	53.8	16.6	674	94.1
New Milford borough & MCD (Bergen)	16,347	16,429	0.5	16,545	58.3	3.7	16.9	2.2	18.9	21.4	16.4	40.9	31.2	44.3	5,859	93.8
New Providence borough & MCD (Union)	12,207	13,595	11.4	13,049	72.9	0.7	14.5	3.7	8.3	26.6	15.4	40.0	15.8	68.9	4,515	95.7
Newton town & MCD (Sussex)	8,126	8,019	-1.3	7,910	76.6	4.7	2.9	1.7	14.0	15.9	18.3	44.7	38.5	27.6	3,372	88.4
New Village CDP	421	-	-	439	93.8	1.6	0.0	4.6	0.0	15.5	26.4	51.3	51.1	12.5	180	77.8
North Arlington borough & MCD (Bergen)	15,392	15,683	1.9	15,677	59.5	2.4	6.3	0.9	30.9	17.5	18.2	41.7	41.8	33.8	6,384	90.9
North Beach Haven CDP	2,235	-	-	2,128	97.4	0.0	0.3	1.6	0.7	3.3	49.5	64.9	26.2	55.0	1,107	90.0
North Bergen township (Hudson)	60,790	60,666	-0.2	61,619	19.7	3.0	7.3	1.7	68.2	20.7	14.5	38.5	48.3	28.4	21,794	90.7
North Brunswick township (Middlesex)	41,423	41,431	0.0	41,760	34.6	19.6	24.7	2.0	19.1	21.9	11.9	36.1	31.7	49.8	14,243	93.0
North Caldwell borough & MCD (Essex)	6,175	6,621	7.2	6,615	84.2	0.7	9.3	2.0	3.9	25.0	20.5	46.8	10.2	73.3	2,399	98.8
North Cape May CDP	3,226	-	-	3,107	84.7	6.7	0.0	0.0	8.7	18.5	24.9	51.3	49.6	21.2	1,365	92.8
Northfield city & MCD (Atlantic)	8,524	8,031	-5.8	8,153	77.7	2.5	5.3	1.3	13.3	21.2	17.5	44.5	38.7	36.6	2,863	94.6
North Haledon borough & MCD (Passaic)	8,422	8,395	-0.3	8,437	84.2	1.2	2.4	0.9	11.3	16.8	23.3	48.5	37.5	38.4	3,194	89.2
North Hanover township (Burlington)	7,707	7,470	-3.1	7,526	67.2	6.1	1.6	6.6	18.4	32.5	7.3	30.1	28.8	33.0	2,565	97.1
North Middletown CDP	3,295	-	-	3,179	79.4	0.0	0.0	1.2	19.4	23.0	11.3	36.4	40.9	32.3	1,154	95.5
North Plainfield borough & MCD (Somerset)	21,774	21,289	-2.2	21,501	26.8	17.3	3.6	2.8	49.4	24.2	10.2	36.6	43.3	26.0	7,296	94.3
Northvale borough & MCD (Bergen)	4,623	4,927	6.6	4,862	57.0	1.7	27.5	1.0	12.7	22.2	15.4	43.8	29.4	51.7	1,641	93.4
North Wildwood city & MCD (Cape May)	4,038	3,760	-6.9	3,812	94.5	3.0	0.0	0.4	2.1	9.5	37.5	57.8	40.3	25.5	1,974	92.2
Norwood borough & MCD (Bergen)	5,730	5,793	1.1	5,812	62.9	0.5	28.4	2.3	5.8	21.1	21.6	47.4	26.8	55.2	2,160	92.9
Nutley township (Essex)	28,376	28,434	0.2	28,478	66.6	2.3	10.6	2.6	17.9	20.5	16.6	40.9	31.2	47.8	11,054	93.7
Oakhurst CDP	3,995	-	-	3,804	88.0	6.0	1.4	1.7	2.8	25.8	20.4	45.5	29.4	43.9	1,401	93.4
Oakland borough & MCD (Bergen)	12,753	12,926	1.4	12,972	85.9	0.4	5.9	0.6	7.2	24.6	16.3	43.5	27.1	50.4	4,237	97.9
Oaklyn borough & MCD (Camden)	4,038	3,955	-2.1	3,964	85.8	3.8	2.0	2.7	5.7	18.3	13.2	41.1	29.8	36.3	1,674	93.3
Oak Valley CDP	3,483	-	-	3,345	88.1	1.2	0.3	3.3	7.1	18.5	15.4	38.1	61.6	13.0	1,131	92.6
Ocean township (Monmouth)	27,293	26,542	-2.8	26,709	75.7	8.8	4.1	1.2	10.2	20.2	20.6	45.8	28.3	45.6	10,845	95.4
Ocean township (Ocean)	8,332	9,088	9.1	9,003	94.1	0.8	0.0	2.1	2.9	13.6	35.4	57.2	44.0	27.5	4,071	88.6
Ocean Acres CDP	16,142	-	-	17,333	86.4	3.9	0.5	3.1	6.1	24.2	15.2	37.5	40.7	30.7	6,035	95.2
Ocean City city & MCD (Cape May)	11,702	10,971	-6.2	11,132	86.9	3.2	1.4	2.3	6.2	16.9	35.0	56.9	27.7	51.4	5,253	87.9
Ocean Gate borough & MCD (Ocean)	2,003	2,035	1.6	1,601	89.6	0.9	0.3	0.8	8.4	16.2	20.5	43.5	50.3	27.2	691	93.2
Ocean Grove CDP	3,342	-	-	3,047	92.0	2.3	0.6	0.3	4.9	2.2	32.4	60.1	16.8	61.1	1,937	87.0
Oceanport borough & MCD (Monmouth)	5,832	5,722	-1.9	5,725	88.0	0.7	2.4	2.3	6.6	17.6	21.4	51.1	25.2	51.2	2,290	90.3
Ogdensburg borough & MCD (Sussex)	2,426	2,255	-7.0	2,317	81.1	0.0	2.7	0.0	16.3	18.0	16.3	42.5	43.4	24.7	822	92.8
Old Bridge CDP	23,753	-	-	23,545	71.3	3.6	10.2	1.0	14.0	20.5	15.0	43.5	33.4	39.8	8,015	93.0
Old Bridge township (Middlesex)	65,406	65,590	0.3	65,782	63.3	6.0	13.8	1.7	15.2	21.1	14.9	42.1	33.9	39.9	24,163	94.3
Oldmans township (Salem)	1,781	1,788	0.4	1,760	84.0	5.3	0.5	4.0	6.3	24.4	19.7	40.4	48.0	25.5	638	93.6
Old Tappan borough & MCD (Bergen)	5,744	5,894	2.6	5,914	68.8	0.8	21.7	3.8	5.0	24.0	19.8	46.3	19.8	65.7	2,045	96.5
Olivet CDP	1,408	-	-	1,394	97.7	0.0	0.0	0.0	2.3	20.2	18.2	45.5	31.6	41.8	534	90.8
Oradell borough & MCD (Bergen)	7,978	8,131	1.9	8,141	70.8	1.3	16.8	3.0	8.1	25.1	18.9	45.5	17.9	59.6	2,788	98.5
Oxford CDP	1,090	-	-	1,182	89.4	3.3	0.0	1.8	5.5	18.0	17.5	43.9	63.8	18.9	481	79.4
Oxford township (Warren)	2,519	2,422	-3.9	2,431	86.9	1.9	0.2	2.8	8.1	20.7	14.6	43.8	51.5	24.4	970	84.4

1 May be of any race.

Table A. All Places — **Population and Housing**

STATE City, town, township, borough, or CDP (county if applicable)	Population				Race and Hispanic or Latino origin (percent)					Age (percent)			Educational attainment of persons age 25 and older		Occupied housing units	
	2010 census total population	2019 estimated population	Percent change 2010–2019	ACS total population estimate 2015–2019	White alone, not Hispanic or Latino	Black alone, not Hispanic or Latino	Asian alone, not Hispanic or Latino	All other races or 2 or more races, not Hispanic or Latino	Hispanic or Latino[1]	Under 18 years old	Age 65 years and older	Median age	Percent High school diploma or less	Percent Bachelor's degree or more	Total	Percent with a computer
	1	2	3	4	5	6	7	8	9	10	11	12	13	14	15	16
NEW JERSEY—Con.																
Palisades Park borough & MCD (Bergen)	19,589	20,715	5.7	20,604	18.1	0.8	58.2	1.3	21.6	15.5	14.3	39.5	36.7	45.8	7,403	90.2
Palmyra borough & MCD (Burlington)	7,378	7,140	-3.2	7,189	68.6	18.8	2.8	2.3	7.6	19.1	13.8	39.9	38.5	28.1	2,825	91.6
Panther Valley CDP	3,327	-	-	3,815	84.8	2.5	4.2	0.6	8.0	14.2	24.6	50.6	25.5	52.3	1,925	93.2
Paramus borough & MCD (Bergen)	26,342	26,264	-0.3	26,503	56.6	2.8	28.1	1.3	11.3	19.1	23.4	47.5	29.6	48.8	8,232	92.1
Park Ridge borough & MCD (Bergen)	8,656	8,694	0.4	8,766	78.5	0.7	4.1	0.7	16.1	22.7	21.7	46.0	20.6	59.2	3,244	91.4
Parsippany-Troy Hills township (Morris)	53,185	51,561	-3.1	52,407	50.1	3.5	34.1	2.5	9.8	19.0	16.7	41.4	25.2	56.7	19,553	95.9
Passaic city & MCD (Passaic)	69,811	69,703	-0.2	70,019	15.4	6.4	2.7	0.7	74.8	32.2	8.9	30.1	68.7	15.7	19,827	80.9
Paterson city & MCD (Passaic)	146,181	145,233	-0.6	145,710	8.5	24.8	4.5	1.4	60.8	27.3	11.3	33.5	68.5	11.1	45,046	81.3
Paulsboro borough & MCD (Gloucester)	6,094	5,854	-3.9	5,904	61.1	27.5	0.0	4.1	7.3	17.8	13.5	42.4	54.6	16.2	2,475	87.7
Peapack and Gladstone borough & MCD (Somerset)	2,565	2,597	1.2	2,575	79.5	4.8	1.1	1.7	12.9	30.7	16.3	40.9	20.7	55.5	807	96.8
Pedricktown CDP	524	-	-	360	84.4	0.0	0.0	2.5	13.1	23.9	16.1	46.2	58.4	10.5	163	95.1
Pemberton borough & MCD (Burlington)	1,404	1,324	-5.7	1,499	59.2	10.5	3.4	6.9	20.0	19.2	22.1	44.8	43.9	25.0	605	82.5
Pemberton township (Burlington)	27,913	26,979	-3.3	27,169	56.7	19.9	2.9	8.1	12.4	22.8	14.8	36.4	47.6	16.9	9,991	91.1
Pemberton Heights CDP	2,423	-	-	2,878	33.9	39.1	2.0	15.2	9.8	21.4	16.0	34.3	48.7	22.9	1,245	87.2
Pennington borough & MCD (Mercer)	2,553	2,576	0.9	2,531	88.6	4.4	2.9	1.5	2.6	22.7	23.7	47.8	11.4	75.4	988	87.1
Pennsauken township (Camden)	36,015	35,761	-0.7	35,660	33.0	21.5	7.8	2.2	35.5	23.7	13.5	38.1	51.2	19.9	12,276	91.1
Penns Grove borough & MCD (Salem)	5,106	4,757	-6.8	4,816	25.9	31.1	1.1	5.2	36.8	27.1	10.0	30.6	57.6	10.7	1,755	83.7
Pennsville CDP	11,888	-	-	11,164	89.8	3.1	1.9	1.8	3.4	21.2	20.3	44.6	51.8	16.0	4,500	84.2
Pennsville township (Salem)	13,422	12,418	-7.5	12,571	88.5	4.0	1.9	2.5	3.1	20.3	20.1	45.0	52.0	17.1	5,119	84.4
Pequannock township (Morris)	15,538	14,965	-3.7	15,191	86.4	0.2	2.5	1.5	9.4	19.8	27.1	48.4	28.9	44.5	6,171	85.7
Perth Amboy city & MCD (Middlesex)	50,827	51,390	1.1	51,678	13.9	6.4	1.1	0.6	78.0	27.1	11.2	33.3	65.6	15.3	15,980	85.9
Phillipsburg town & MCD (Warren)	14,950	14,212	-4.9	14,344	68.5	10.1	2.0	5.0	14.5	23.8	13.4	39.0	53.7	19.0	5,746	89.3
Pilesgrove township (Salem)	4,026	3,981	-1.1	4,011	90.7	4.6	2.8	0.0	1.9	19.5	21.7	50.6	32.3	40.6	1,619	90.8
Pine Beach borough & MCD (Ocean)	2,135	2,184	2.3	2,278	87.1	1.3	0.2	0.1	11.3	19.6	21.7	50.8	27.0	42.8	871	94.7
Pine Hill borough & MCD (Camden)	10,230	10,417	1.8	10,442	56.4	28.9	2.0	4.5	8.2	22.2	12.2	38.1	46.9	22.1	4,429	86.5
Pine Lake Park CDP	8,707	-	-	8,427	74.8	4.4	2.6	5.5	12.7	25.6	13.6	39.4	52.3	24.5	2,841	94.0
Pine Ridge at Crestwood CDP	2,369	-	-	2,293	90.5	1.6	2.0	0.0	5.8	0.0	60.4	68.7	62.7	12.4	1,502	79.9
Pine Valley borough & MCD (Camden)	12	11	-8.3	5	100.0	0.0	0.0	0.0	0.0	0.0	100.0	68.3	0.0	100.0	3	100.0
Piscataway township (Middlesex)	55,984	56,837	1.5	56,884	26.7	19.0	37.0	3.2	14.1	16.4	11.8	32.5	28.6	50.1	16,160	95.7
Pitman borough & MCD (Gloucester)	9,009	8,741	-3.0	8,805	89.1	3.5	0.7	3.4	3.3	20.9	18.9	42.0	31.9	32.9	3,366	91.7
Pittsgrove township (Salem)	9,383	8,799	-6.2	8,898	85.1	7.1	0.6	2.9	4.3	18.7	17.5	46.4	47.1	28.1	3,393	88.5
Plainfield city & MCD (Union)	49,595	50,317	1.5	50,362	8.9	39.0	1.0	5.0	46.1	26.0	12.0	34.6	59.0	19.5	15,701	83.6
Plainsboro township (Middlesex)	22,995	22,884	-0.5	23,028	29.7	5.9	58.9	2.8	2.7	24.6	10.0	37.4	11.1	79.0	9,251	98.1
Plainsboro Center CDP	2,712	-	-	2,771	26.2	5.3	65.6	1.2	1.8	26.1	9.3	35.3	5.1	88.6	1,166	96.7
Pleasant Plains CDP	922	-	-	540	38.9	21.1	40.0	0.0	0.0	23.1	17.2	51.2	10.5	71.4	149	100.0
Pleasantville city & MCD (Atlantic)	20,272	20,149	-0.6	20,301	10.3	37.8	1.7	2.9	47.3	24.9	12.0	35.1	60.8	13.2	6,774	87.5
Plumsted township (Ocean)	8,432	8,571	1.6	8,513	87.4	2.2	0.5	0.5	9.4	21.6	15.6	41.5	48.8	26.5	3,272	89.0
Pohatcong township (Warren)	3,340	3,175	-4.9	3,208	91.2	1.1	0.0	2.1	5.6	19.6	16.0	42.1	38.1	30.7	1,308	91.4
Point Pleasant borough & MCD (Ocean)	18,373	18,772	2.2	18,598	89.8	0.2	0.1	0.5	9.4	20.8	16.5	42.3	29.3	42.2	7,349	95.4
Point Pleasant Beach borough & MCD (Ocean)	4,686	4,551	-2.9	4,537	91.2	0.5	0.6	2.0	5.8	15.1	20.8	48.9	22.8	58.5	1,875	95.4
Pomona CDP	7,124	-	-	7,363	44.1	16.4	19.5	4.2	15.8	19.1	19.0	41.9	42.8	22.0	2,244	92.2
Pompton Lakes borough & MCD (Passaic)	11,097	10,986	-	11,029	69.4	1.5	6.1	3.4	19.6	18.7	13.6	40.4	43.9	38.0	4,004	93.0
Port Colden CDP	122	-	-	75	100.0	0.0	0.0	0.0	0.0	0.0	0.0	0.0	0.0	0.0	37	100.0
Port Monmouth CDP	3,818	-	-	3,360	82.6	1.9	2.4	2.6	10.4	23.1	13.1	42.4	44.5	25.8	1,197	95.5
Port Murray CDP	129	-	-	28	100.0	0.0	0.0	0.0	0.0	0.0	100.0	0.0	100.0	0.0	14	0.0
Port Norris CDP	1,377	-	-	1,037	78.9	16.2	0.8	0.0	4.1	17.7	19.6	42.9	56.1	10.4	450	86.9
Port Reading CDP	3,728	-	-	3,864	45.1	14.8	14.5	0.4	25.3	21.4	16.0	44.3	49.1	25.3	1,316	92.6
Port Republic city & MCD (Atlantic)	1,119	1,052	-6.0	1,121	96.9	0.7	1.1	1.2	0.2	17.3	24.3	47.5	28.4	42.2	413	92.5
Presidential Lakes Estates CDP	2,365	-	-	1,830	76.2	16.0	3.1	2.3	2.3	24.8	17.1	42.5	39.9	15.9	722	98.3
Princeton & MCD (Mercer)	28,584	31,187	9.1	31,000	67.2	5.4	16.9	3.1	7.5	18.3	16.8	33.8	11.2	81.0	9,959	96.9
Princeton Junction CDP	2,465	-	-	2,336	69.3	2.0	24.4	3.4	0.9	19.0	19.3	47.5	9.4	85.3	954	96.4
Princeton Meadows CDP	13,834	-	-	13,717	25.2	8.6	59.5	2.9	3.8	25.7	4.8	34.1	11.4	78.6	5,648	98.5
Prospect Park borough & MCD (Passaic)	5,865	5,843	-0.4	5,865	21.0	22.6	0.8	2.5	53.1	28.7	9.8	31.0	57.9	17.2	1,633	92.8

1 May be of any race.

Table A. All Places — **Population and Housing**

STATE City, town, township, borough, or CDP (county if applicable)	Population				Race and Hispanic or Latino origin (percent)					Age (percent)			Educational attainment of persons age 25 and older		Occupied housing units	
	2010 census total population	2019 estimated population	Percent change 2010–2019	ACS total population estimate 2015–2019	White alone, not Hispanic or Latino	Black alone, not Hispanic or Latino	Asian alone, not Hispanic or Latino	All other races or 2 or more races, not Hispanic or Latino	Hispanic or Latino[1]	Under 18 years old	Age 65 years and older	Median age	Percent High school diploma or less	Percent Bachelor's degree or more	Total	Percent with a computer
	1	2	3	4	5	6	7	8	9	10	11	12	13	14	15	16
NEW JERSEY—Con.																
Quinton CDP	588	-	-	514	72.4	14.6	0.0	1.0	12.1	26.8	11.1	38.9	54.5	19.1	210	91.0
Quinton township (Salem)	2,621	2,448	-6.6	2,278	77.3	16.2	0.0	0.4	6.1	20.8	19.2	44.1	50.1	18.0	940	90.9
Rahway city & MCD (Union)	27,324	29,895	9.4	29,543	33.5	26.5	4.5	3.9	31.6	19.7	13.5	39.0	44.9	30.3	11,304	90.9
Ramblewood CDP	5,907	-	-	5,812	77.3	8.3	6.4	1.5	6.6	21.3	18.3	41.9	25.5	50.2	2,236	97.6
Ramsey borough & MCD (Bergen)	14,521	14,884	2.5	14,940	85.6	0.5	7.8	0.8	5.3	24.9	16.9	46.1	15.1	69.1	5,524	95.2
Ramtown CDP	6,242	-	-	6,393	82.8	2.2	3.2	0.9	10.8	25.9	7.9	36.5	31.1	39.8	2,033	97.0
Randolph township (Morris)	25,701	25,378	-1.3	25,549	71.7	3.6	12.2	1.7	10.8	23.6	12.9	41.9	17.4	62.5	9,130	96.2
Raritan township (Hunterdon)	22,196	22,382	0.8	22,129	82.7	2.6	7.3	1.5	6.0	21.6	16.7	45.5	21.5	60.8	8,154	95.6
Raritan borough & MCD (Somerset)	6,882	7,765	12.8	7,865	62.9	0.9	16.0	2.8	17.4	17.3	14.5	43.9	41.6	36.2	2,995	88.5
Readington township (Hunterdon)	16,120	15,843	-1.7	15,897	87.0	0.2	4.2	1.3	7.3	18.9	20.8	49.7	24.7	55.3	6,244	94.5
Red Bank borough & MCD (Monmouth)	12,227	11,966	-2.1	12,072	54.6	8.9	2.6	0.9	33.1	22.2	14.5	35.6	34.8	44.2	5,255	93.2
Richwood CDP	3,459	-	-	3,925	95.7	1.6	0.4	0.2	2.1	31.5	9.1	39.7	21.2	55.9	1,139	100.0
Ridgefield borough & MCD (Bergen)	11,041	11,171	1.2	11,227	39.1	1.0	29.9	1.4	28.6	17.6	10.6	40.6	36.9	39.1	3,827	94.0
Ridgefield Park village & MCD (Bergen)	12,722	12,901	1.4	12,922	38.3	2.8	12.4	2.5	44.0	20.7	14.0	37.7	33.8	41.7	4,720	94.9
Ridgewood village & MCD (Bergen)	24,951	25,056	0.4	25,179	72.3	1.2	15.5	3.0	7.9	30.2	14.1	41.2	13.1	76.0	8,300	96.8
Ringwood borough & MCD (Passaic)	12,261	12,198	-0.5	12,251	83.8	1.3	2.9	2.4	9.5	22.2	17.0	42.8	32.4	44.8	4,138	97.2
Rio Grande CDP	2,670	-	-	2,834	67.1	0.9	1.1	0.2	30.7	21.5	25.9	41.9	52.5	13.2	1,168	89.0
Riverdale borough & MCD (Morris)	3,574	4,135	15.7	4,197	79.4	0.7	4.5	1.1	14.3	19.3	16.7	40.9	29.3	48.2	1,817	96.8
River Edge borough & MCD (Bergen)	11,340	11,435	0.8	11,500	62.0	2.9	24.0	1.7	9.3	25.7	12.7	39.2	17.7	63.2	3,867	96.6
Riverside township (Burlington)	8,066	7,816	-3.1	7,857	71.4	9.3	2.0	1.0	16.3	20.0	13.0	38.7	56.4	17.1	3,047	89.3
Riverton borough & MCD (Burlington)	2,770	2,685	-3.1	2,705	90.3	3.0	0.5	2.7	3.6	21.4	20.1	45.7	25.7	52.6	1,020	96.7
River Vale township (Bergen)	9,658	9,984	3.4	9,995	83.0	0.6	8.5	3.4	4.5	24.5	19.8	46.7	15.9	58.9	3,608	95.4
Robbinsville CDP	3,041	-	-	2,836	51.4	3.6	31.3	3.2	10.4	22.3	11.4	41.0	17.7	66.7	1,101	85.4
Robbinsville township (Mercer)	13,648	14,543	6.6	14,365	66.2	5.0	21.5	2.2	5.1	24.3	10.8	41.9	18.1	64.2	5,094	95.2
Robertsville CDP	11,297	-	-	11,874	73.3	1.9	14.9	1.8	8.1	24.7	13.1	39.5	19.4	60.7	3,649	98.4
Rochelle Park township (Bergen)	5,526	5,569	0.8	5,597	56.7	2.2	13.4	2.3	25.3	16.8	24.1	45.0	42.6	34.3	2,001	87.3
Rockaway borough & MCD (Morris)	6,438	6,276	-2.5	6,384	67.6	0.7	9.9	3.2	18.7	21.4	19.6	43.3	30.6	41.0	2,413	94.2
Rockaway township (Morris)	24,136	25,876	7.2	25,069	77.5	3.3	5.8	1.9	11.5	20.0	18.1	44.7	26.6	52.3	9,674	95.0
Rockleigh borough & MCD (Bergen)	531	529	-0.4	625	79.2	3.2	5.1	0.3	12.2	22.6	50.9	67.2	37.7	38.7	72	97.2
Rocky Hill borough & MCD (Somerset)	682	669	-1.9	636	86.6	3.9	0.0	1.3	8.2	21.7	23.9	47.4	13.3	74.0	243	96.7
Roebling CDP	3,715	-	-	3,909	77.6	6.2	3.1	3.1	10.0	22.4	13.2	38.2	39.3	27.9	1,443	90.8
Roosevelt borough & MCD (Monmouth)	867	836	-3.6	854	87.2	4.1	1.9	2.5	4.3	22.1	20.0	42.5	27.8	50.6	295	95.6
Roseland borough & MCD (Essex)	5,836	5,835	0.0	5,834	84.2	0.0	7.2	2.4	6.3	19.3	26.3	47.7	21.7	60.5	2,349	89.3
Roselle borough & MCD (Union)	21,067	21,811	3.5	21,637	13.0	48.1	1.4	6.0	31.6	21.3	14.2	39.0	46.0	22.1	7,402	88.6
Roselle Park borough & MCD (Union)	13,290	13,588	2.2	13,581	45.0	7.7	8.7	7.1	31.4	21.4	12.1	37.3	35.7	40.0	4,948	91.6
Rosenhayn CDP..............	1,098	-	-	1,351	66.8	26.9	0.8	1.0	4.5	23.5	20.4	37.2	66.9	16.4	470	90.0
Ross Corner CDP	13	-	-	60	0.0	0.0	100.0	0.0	0.0	0.0	51.7	0.0	0.0	100.0	31	100.0
Rossmoor CDP	2,666	-	-	2,643	87.8	3.7	4.7	0.0	3.8	0.0	78.1	70.1	42.3	30.8	1,860	76.4
Roxbury township (Morris)	23,308	22,551	-3.2	22,956	79.2	5.5	4.9	1.8	8.6	21.2	18.0	44.2	29.6	42.2	8,175	94.4
Rumson borough & MCD (Monmouth)..................	7,065	6,714	-5.0	6,792	91.9	0.7	1.3	1.2	4.8	32.5	12.1	43.9	11.6	72.7	2,180	96.8
Runnemede borough & MCD (Camden)............	8,465	8,300	-1.9	8,327	73.6	9.3	4.4	0.5	12.2	20.4	14.9	36.4	47.1	25.4	3,158	92.6
Rutherford borough & MCD (Bergen)	18,061	18,303	1.3	18,398	57.6	2.5	17.3	3.0	19.6	21.2	13.9	40.0	26.5	53.0	6,977	93.3
Saddle Brook township (Bergen)	13,658	13,562	-0.7	13,845	69.2	3.4	8.0	1.1	18.3	17.6	18.4	43.7	38.9	35.7	5,328	88.9
Saddle River borough & MCD (Bergen)	3,151	3,173	0.7	3,192	63.2	4.2	21.8	4.3	6.5	16.4	30.3	55.7	18.8	66.6	1,232	88.2
Salem city & MCD (Salem)	5,151	4,706	-8.6	4,781	23.6	58.9	0.3	4.8	12.5	32.4	15.5	33.2	65.3	7.2	1,864	75.9
Sandyston township (Sussex)	1,973	1,823	-7.6	1,999	90.4	0.3	0.4	2.4	6.6	20.2	17.9	46.3	46.0	32.1	758	92.7
Sayreville borough & MCD (Middlesex)	42,770	44,173	3.3	44,292	53.7	11.2	15.1	2.6	17.5	21.8	13.7	39.2	40.0	34.4	16,298	93.5
Scotch Plains township (Union)	23,646	24,274	2.7	24,205	71.2	9.5	7.9	2.4	8.9	22.1	17.0	43.8	21.8	60.9	8,761	94.9
Sea Bright borough & MCD (Monmouth)	1,465	1,338	-8.7	1,337	91.1	1.3	1.6	2.6	3.4	9.7	22.5	53.0	12.3	66.9	745	94.0
Seabrook Farms CDP	1,484	-	-	2,033	24.8	26.7	0.0	15.7	32.8	35.3	5.5	27.5	45.5	16.0	645	100.0
Sea Girt borough & MCD (Monmouth).................	1,828	1,765	-3.4	1,655	97.5	0.1	0.0	0.0	2.4	14.5	35.4	58.1	10.0	77.2	737	98.2
Sea Isle City city & MCD (Cape May)	2,114	2,029	-4.0	2,147	98.0	0.0	0.7	0.0	1.3	8.8	44.8	62.9	30.4	46.7	1,111	96.2
Seaside Heights borough & MCD (Ocean)	2,887	2,910	0.8	2,892	63.5	4.5	0.0	3.8	28.1	23.9	10.6	37.8	49.1	21.0	1,259	95.9

1 May be of any race.

Table A. All Places — **Population and Housing**

NEW JERSEY—Con.

STATE City, town, township, borough, or CDP (county if applicable)	Population 2010 census total population	2019 estimated population	Percent change 2010–2019	ACS total population estimate 2015–2019	White alone, not Hispanic or Latino	Black alone, not Hispanic or Latino	Asian alone, not Hispanic or Latino	All other races or 2 or more races, not Hispanic or Latino	Hispanic or Latino[1]	Under 18 years old	Age 65 years and older	Median age	Percent High school diploma or less	Percent Bachelor's degree or more	Occupied housing units Total	Percent with a computer
	1	2	3	4	5	6	7	8	9	10	11	12	13	14	15	16
Seaside Park borough & MCD (Ocean)	1,577	1,543	-2.2	1,628	98.3	0.3	0.2	0.6	0.6	10.9	37.5	58.8	21.2	50.8	879	91.7
Secaucus town & MCD (Hudson)	16,264	21,893	34.6	20,125	45.7	3.9	25.3	3.3	21.7	19.3	17.5	40.6	32.0	49.9	7,557	92.8
Sewaren CDP	2,756	-	-	2,627	55.0	9.8	2.9	0.4	32.0	19.5	13.7	39.2	38.8	36.6	970	93.3
Shamong township (Burlington)	6,525	6,367	-2.4	6,396	90.2	1.7	0.4	4.9	2.8	27.5	13.7	39.6	24.7	51.9	2,135	93.8
Shark River Hills CDP	3,697	-	-	3,299	93.5	1.6	1.2	1.0	2.7	17.8	18.7	50.6	27.0	41.7	1,342	93.6
Shiloh borough & MCD (Cumberland)	516	487	-5.6	399	84.2	0.5	2.0	6.8	6.5	22.3	16.8	40.8	59.6	15.4	152	92.8
Ship Bottom borough & MCD (Ocean)	1,147	1,153	0.5	1,049	97.3	0.0	0.5	0.7	1.5	8.8	41.8	61.6	25.1	50.1	495	91.5
Short Hills CDP	13,165	-	-	13,428	64.4	0.9	26.9	4.5	3.3	33.6	12.7	41.0	6.1	87.8	4,153	99.1
Shrewsbury borough & MCD (Monmouth)	3,807	4,053	6.5	4,086	93.6	0.6	3.5	1.4	0.9	26.8	22.4	46.1	18.7	63.1	1,434	92.5
Shrewsbury township (Monmouth)	1,036	993	-4.2	1,032	45.0	27.0	12.8	5.2	10.0	14.5	12.0	42.6	34.4	31.5	488	90.0
Silver Lake CDP	4,243	-	-	4,197	17.7	18.0	20.0	4.3	40.0	23.0	15.0	35.5	50.4	23.0	1,432	92.3
Silver Lake CDP	368	-	-	299	97.3	0.0	1.7	0.0	1.0	10.7	22.7	47.9	40.0	25.1	132	95.5
Silver Ridge CDP	1,133	-	-	948	97.5	0.8	0.0	0.8	0.8	0.0	69.3	70.8	62.3	6.9	673	79.2
Singac CDP	3,618	-	-	4,215	79.9	3.7	0.0	0.0	16.4	15.6	20.3	49.0	47.0	32.5	1,595	93.1
Six Mile Run CDP	3,184	-	-	2,898	21.5	38.8	33.0	2.8	3.8	26.8	8.4	36.7	25.1	62.7	1,112	98.7
Skillman CDP	242	-	-	401	63.1	2.5	16.2	3.5	14.7	23.7	28.4	36.9	16.2	58.5	151	94.0
Smithville CDP	7,242	-	-	7,365	69.5	18.4	3.5	4.2	4.4	15.1	29.6	52.7	34.2	33.3	3,504	95.0
Society Hill CDP	3,829	-	-	3,640	28.5	12.7	44.1	1.3	13.4	17.4	12.4	33.3	22.4	57.1	1,092	96.9
Somerdale borough & MCD (Camden)	5,132	5,477	6.7	5,448	56.7	24.8	2.2	4.0	12.3	16.6	16.5	43.3	40.7	25.5	2,236	95.4
Somerset CDP	22,083	-	-	24,509	35.4	28.3	18.2	3.1	15.1	18.0	16.1	39.0	24.5	53.6	9,075	96.4
Somers Point city & MCD (Atlantic)	10,795	10,174	-5.8	10,321	70.5	11.4	5.6	1.2	11.3	22.7	17.8	42.4	46.8	26.8	4,371	91.6
Somerville borough & MCD (Somerset)	12,093	12,063	-0.2	12,085	52.0	10.4	12.4	2.3	22.9	21.0	12.8	35.0	34.0	43.2	4,487	92.0
South Amboy city & MCD (Middlesex)	8,577	9,176	7.0	8,772	67.0	6.1	3.4	1.0	22.5	19.6	17.6	42.6	40.4	28.2	3,320	89.1
Southampton township (Burlington)	10,440	10,095	-3.3	10,154	89.9	2.5	0.5	2.2	4.9	15.7	33.6	55.3	46.6	27.8	4,579	87.7
South Bound Brook borough & MCD (Somerset)	4,528	4,518	-0.2	4,534	41.6	12.8	12.1	3.2	30.2	24.1	10.7	36.6	43.1	28.4	1,590	89.2
South Brunswick township (Middlesex)	43,419	45,685	5.2	45,400	36.1	9.0	45.1	3.2	6.6	24.8	12.7	40.8	16.8	66.9	16,009	95.2
South Hackensack township (Bergen)	2,380	2,435	2.3	2,625	43.5	0.2	1.1	0.7	54.5	21.4	14.9	37.6	60.3	21.4	810	92.8
South Harrison township (Gloucester)	3,200	3,123	-2.4	3,148	90.5	1.1	0.5	0.8	7.1	29.3	12.9	36.4	26.3	51.2	987	95.8
South Orange Village township (Essex)	16,175	16,691	3.2	16,521	59.9	24.7	4.9	4.3	6.3	19.3	12.3	34.3	14.3	71.4	5,137	94.0
South Plainfield borough & MCD (Middlesex)	23,392	24,052	2.8	23,956	51.7	11.7	14.6	3.2	18.8	21.9	15.5	40.4	39.6	34.9	7,924	93.3
South River borough & MCD (Middlesex)	16,050	15,779	-1.7	16,001	61.5	6.1	4.2	2.8	25.3	22.4	13.6	37.4	50.0	25.4	5,770	89.1
South Toms River borough & MCD (Ocean)	3,584	3,685	2.8	3,648	56.6	12.1	0.9	7.6	22.9	30.3	7.8	29.8	61.4	10.8	1,037	93.9
Sparta township (Sussex)	19,581	18,575	-5.1	18,720	86.5	1.7	3.4	1.4	7.0	25.0	14.6	43.1	20.0	57.2	6,666	97.0
Spotswood borough & MCD (Middlesex)	8,256	8,228	-0.3	8,269	76.4	3.7	5.1	1.7	13.1	21.1	21.0	44.3	45.3	25.2	3,207	90.5
Springdale CDP	14,518	-	-	13,878	75.0	4.1	14.2	3.1	3.6	22.3	22.8	47.0	15.9	69.5	5,123	94.7
Springfield township (Burlington)	3,403	3,257	-4.3	3,275	87.2	5.1	0.7	1.8	5.2	23.8	14.3	44.8	33.8	36.3	1,110	93.8
Springfield township (Union)	15,799	17,464	10.5	17,406	65.7	7.8	11.3	3.5	11.6	21.1	17.7	42.7	23.6	61.8	6,901	95.1
Spring Lake borough & MCD (Monmouth)	2,993	2,904	-3.0	2,927	96.4	0.0	3.3	0.0	0.3	16.4	42.1	60.0	17.5	68.8	1,344	95.2
Spring Lake Heights borough & MCD (Monmouth)	4,695	4,521	-3.7	4,564	92.4	0.8	4.1	0.6	2.2	13.5	27.7	51.7	16.1	54.0	2,272	91.5
Stafford township (Ocean)	26,541	27,845	4.9	27,347	87.5	1.9	1.3	2.2	7.0	20.4	20.6	45.4	39.3	34.4	10,785	92.0
Stanhope borough & MCD (Sussex)	3,602	3,306	-8.2	3,346	82.6	1.3	1.5	2.1	12.6	24.3	14.1	43.8	34.7	44.2	1,314	97.1
Stewartsville CDP	349	-	-	439	80.9	0.0	0.0	6.2	13.0	28.2	12.8	28.7	39.0	16.8	192	82.3
Stillwater township (Sussex)	4,151	3,870	-6.8	3,911	96.7	0.0	0.0	1.2	2.1	18.4	22.2	47.1	43.0	30.8	1,398	95.4
Stockton borough & MCD (Hunterdon)	537	512	-4.7	614	93.8	0.0	0.0	0.0	6.2	20.7	31.4	54.9	33.0	47.4	266	94.4
Stone Harbor borough & MCD (Cape May)	866	810	-6.5	885	98.9	0.1	0.3	0.0	0.7	5.4	51.2	65.9	20.1	61.3	476	93.7
Stow Creek township (Cumberland)	1,432	1,370	-4.3	1,012	86.1	5.7	0.2	3.8	4.2	19.3	22.1	46.5	50.7	20.4	407	87.5
Stratford borough & MCD (Camden)	7,054	6,955	-1.4	6,971	75.2	10.7	6.1	1.4	6.6	19.9	14.3	39.5	41.3	35.4	2,551	92.5
Strathmere CDP	158	-	-	171	100.0	0.0	0.0	0.0	0.0	12.9	25.1	62.0	38.7	61.3	55	100.0
Strathmore CDP	7,258	-	-	7,816	83.3	1.5	2.8	2.6	9.8	24.3	14.4	38.8	21.5	56.4	2,725	97.5
Succasunna CDP	9,152	-	-	8,514	84.4	3.7	5.5	0.9	5.6	20.2	19.6	47.8	22.5	49.0	3,038	95.7
Summit city & MCD (Union)	21,460	21,897	2.0	21,913	68.9	5.5	9.0	3.1	13.5	28.3	13.2	40.1	18.7	71.0	7,677	95.1
Surf City borough & MCD (Ocean)	1,180	1,199	1.6	1,271	98.1	0.0	0.6	0.4	0.9	6.6	49.7	64.9	24.0	52.9	639	94.7
Sussex borough & MCD (Sussex)	2,129	1,985	-6.8	1,870	87.6	2.5	1.8	2.5	5.6	15.1	13.3	40.5	60.6	16.5	776	83.4
Swedesboro borough & MCD (Gloucester)	2,584	2,568	-0.6	2,579	58.9	10.5	1.7	4.4	24.4	30.2	7.4	35.5	38.2	31.5	852	92.6

1 May be of any race.

Table A. All Places — **Population and Housing**

STATE City, town, township, borough, or CDP (county if applicable)	Population 2010 census total population	2019 estimated population	Percent change 2010–2019	ACS total population estimate 2015–2019	Race and Hispanic or Latino origin (percent) White alone, not Hispanic or Latino	Black alone, not Hispanic or Latino	Asian alone, not Hispanic or Latino	All other races or 2 or more races, not Hispanic or Latino	Hispanic or Latino[1]	Age (percent) Under 18 years old	Age 65 years and older	Median age	Educational attainment of persons age 25 and older Percent High school diploma or less	Percent Bachelor's degree or more	Occupied housing units Total	Percent with a computer
	1	2	3	4	5	6	7	8	9	10	11	12	13	14	15	16
NEW JERSEY—Con.																
Tabernacle township (Burlington)	6,962	6,794	-2.4	6,851	96.3	0.5	1.1	1.5	0.6	20.2	18.4	46.6	39.9	30.2	2,465	93.0
Tavistock borough & MCD (Camden)	5	5	0.0	2	100.0	0.0	0.0	0.0	0.0	0.0	100.0	0.0	0.0	100.0	1	100.0
Teaneck township (Bergen)	39,760	40,284	1.3	40,458	45.6	25.2	8.7	2.4	18.1	24.0	16.5	38.1	24.7	55.5	13,072	92.3
Tenafly borough & MCD (Bergen)	14,513	14,453	-0.4	14,632	59.4	2.2	27.8	2.2	8.5	31.4	13.3	42.5	10.0	81.7	4,690	98.5
Ten Mile Run CDP	1,959	-	-	1,423	19.8	15.5	55.2	5.6	3.9	18.9	6.0	47.9	3.5	88.5	546	100.0
Teterboro borough & MCD (Bergen)	67	68	1.5	102	62.7	2.9	0.0	0.0	34.3	18.6	10.8	37.5	71.2	2.7	40	85.0
Tewksbury township (Hunterdon)	5,974	5,776	-3.3	5,812	93.5	0.0	4.1	1.2	1.1	22.8	21.1	49.3	15.6	65.8	2,123	96.6
Tinton Falls borough & MCD (Monmouth)	18,032	17,451	-3.2	17,632	73.8	8.3	8.3	2.6	7.1	17.4	26.6	48.1	23.2	52.0	8,048	84.4
Toms River CDP	88,791	-	-	89,254	79.9	3.3	3.7	2.6	10.5	22.0	18.8	42.7	40.6	31.6	33,456	92.5
Toms River township (Ocean)	91,261	94,108	3.1	92,325	80.4	3.2	3.6	2.5	10.2	21.5	19.5	43.5	40.2	32.4	35,079	92.2
Totowa borough & MCD (Passaic)	10,807	10,792	-0.1	10,828	69.8	4.7	6.0	1.7	17.8	16.7	19.7	44.3	44.5	30.7	3,595	92.6
Trenton city & MCD (Mercer)	84,959	83,203	-2.1	83,412	12.1	47.4	1.3	1.1	38.1	26.4	10.1	34.0	63.5	12.2	27,561	83.2
Tuckerton borough & MCD (Ocean)	3,358	3,388	0.9	3,367	92.6	0.8	2.6	1.1	2.9	18.9	19.3	44.8	44.5	28.4	1,461	89.9
Turnersville CDP	3,742	-	-	3,731	83.9	5.7	5.1	1.8	3.5	24.2	19.8	42.5	28.5	50.1	1,208	97.4
Twin Rivers CDP	7,443	-	-	6,870	41.8	10.6	7.2	0.2	40.2	25.1	11.7	35.7	41.2	41.9	2,284	99.5
Union township (Hunterdon)	5,892	5,461	-7.3	5,560	80.5	6.6	5.9	2.5	4.4	19.1	15.1	42.7	25.9	52.3	1,749	94.3
Union township (Union)	56,717	58,488	3.1	58,297	37.0	31.6	9.6	4.1	17.6	17.5	17.2	42.4	41.8	35.3	20,300	91.3
Union Beach borough & MCD (Monmouth)	6,273	5,305	-15.4	5,390	77.9	6.3	2.7	1.1	12.0	21.9	12.7	44.4	47.9	21.0	1,890	94.6
Union City city & MCD (Hudson)	66,467	67,982	2.3	68,226	16.7	2.3	3.6	1.3	76.1	22.5	10.9	36.2	61.3	21.6	24,499	88.7
Upper township (Cape May)	12,379	11,917	-3.7	11,886	96.3	0.1	0.5	0.9	2.2	21.8	18.6	42.5	27.0	45.9	4,842	93.0
Upper Deerfield township (Cumberland)	7,606	7,277	-4.3	7,379	61.7	11.9	2.5	7.2	16.7	24.3	18.7	37.2	52.2	20.2	2,805	88.4
Upper Freehold township (Monmouth)	6,907	7,077	2.5	6,940	82.6	3.1	7.4	1.4	5.6	22.2	22.4	46.8	20.8	55.4	2,552	96.0
Upper Montclair CDP	11,565	-	-	11,589	82.4	3.9	3.5	3.1	7.0	29.7	13.3	42.8	6.1	84.5	3,960	98.5
Upper Pittsgrove township (Salem)	3,490	3,355	-3.9	3,373	88.6	1.7	1.5	3.2	5.0	21.4	20.3	42.2	48.3	24.7	1,122	94.3
Upper Pohatcong CDP	1,781	-	-	1,830	87.9	0.6	0.0	2.5	9.1	19.6	13.8	41.5	37.9	30.0	709	89.7
Upper Saddle River borough & MCD (Bergen)	8,163	8,205	0.5	8,227	69.8	4.3	11.3	5.7	8.9	28.0	14.9	44.0	15.1	65.2	2,615	98.5
Upper Stewartsville CDP	212	-	-	216	88.4	0.0	0.0	0.0	11.6	25.9	13.4	36.5	48.6	20.1	78	89.7
Ventnor City city & MCD (Atlantic)	10,650	9,895	-7.1	10,095	67.0	5.0	9.8	1.3	16.9	13.8	27.0	53.3	44.4	33.6	4,366	90.5
Vernon township (Sussex)	23,605	21,989	-6.8	22,216	85.2	3.2	0.2	2.0	9.3	19.7	14.2	42.9	38.8	32.9	8,241	96.5
Vernon Center CDP	1,713	-	-	1,371	88.0	3.0	0.0	0.8	8.2	10.9	15.1	41.8	30.3	29.7	815	89.9
Vernon Valley CDP	1,626	-	-	1,448	93.7	0.0	0.0	0.0	6.3	17.4	11.6	49.1	44.4	25.5	540	98.3
Verona township (Essex)	13,343	13,390	0.4	13,437	84.6	1.8	5.4	1.2	6.9	22.3	19.5	45.0	17.3	63.6	5,181	94.3
Victory Gardens borough & MCD (Morris)	1,516	1,470	-3.0	1,505	26.8	8.7	2.2	3.4	58.9	22.9	7.8	37.8	61.6	14.9	568	96.0
Victory Lakes CDP	2,111	-	-	1,899	90.7	4.4	1.0	0.0	3.9	17.9	18.2	45.7	48.6	19.9	747	92.6
Vienna CDP	981	-	-	1,174	73.9	0.0	3.7	1.1	21.3	16.0	11.0	38.5	34.2	28.8	326	95.1
Villas CDP	9,483	-	-	8,769	84.9	0.5	0.1	3.5	11.0	19.2	19.1	44.3	53.2	18.1	3,828	89.9
Vineland city & MCD (Cumberland)	60,734	59,439	-2.1	60,034	43.2	11.9	1.0	3.0	40.9	23.9	16.7	38.1	56.6	18.8	21,081	85.9
Vista Center CDP	2,095	-	-	2,241	88.2	0.0	0.0	2.3	9.5	15.7	42.5	62.7	29.4	35.6	914	100.0
Voorhees township (Camden)	29,310	29,175	-0.5	29,212	61.6	9.7	19.5	4.4	4.8	20.1	20.1	44.3	26.4	54.6	11,014	92.4
Voorhees CDP	976	-	-	1,708	6.4	44.9	14.2	6.6	28.0	32.2	6.6	28.0	31.4	32.6	520	97.3
Waldwick borough & MCD (Bergen)	9,573	10,108	5.6	9,986	80.4	0.6	6.5	2.0	10.6	24.2	18.0	41.2	22.6	53.1	3,566	94.4
Wall township (Monmouth)	26,156	25,554	-2.3	25,745	90.5	3.3	1.3	0.8	4.1	20.8	22.2	47.9	26.8	49.9	9,725	93.5
Wallington borough & MCD (Bergen)	11,335	11,495	1.4	11,540	73.9	3.9	6.4	0.8	15.0	16.6	15.0	39.8	45.2	32.1	4,683	90.0
Walpack township (Sussex)	12	11	-8.3	6	100.0	0.0	0.0	0.0	0.0	0.0	100.0	67.5	33.3	0.0	4	100.0
Wanamassa CDP	4,532	-	-	4,630	78.8	0.4	5.5	0.2	15.2	17.7	15.2	43.6	33.7	40.7	1,616	96.5
Wanaque borough & MCD (Passaic)	11,072	11,762	6.2	11,709	78.6	2.9	3.9	2.2	12.4	19.1	21.6	46.4	43.0	32.5	4,196	97.2
Wantage township (Sussex)	11,364	10,902	-4.1	10,925	91.4	0.4	1.7	1.6	5.0	21.2	18.1	45.7	42.6	26.9	3,845	94.4
Waretown CDP	1,569	-	-	1,964	96.3	1.7	0.0	0.0	1.9	14.6	27.1	47.1	56.6	15.3	901	78.7
Warren township (Somerset)	15,320	15,625	2.0	15,720	72.1	0.8	18.8	2.8	5.5	22.5	18.2	47.2	20.0	65.2	5,199	96.1
Washington township (Bergen)	9,127	9,176	0.5	9,237	83.1	0.3	5.4	0.7	10.5	21.3	22.1	46.0	21.5	56.5	3,330	94.3
Washington township (Burlington)	687	711	3.5	774	89.4	0.0	0.4	0.1	10.1	16.8	19.5	51.4	51.3	23.2	333	87.4
Washington township (Gloucester)	49,035	47,753	-2.6	47,833	82.7	5.7	4.9	2.3	4.3	21.1	17.1	42.6	33.8	38.7	17,209	94.3
Washington township (Morris)	18,542	18,152	-2.1	18,429	86.8	0.1	4.7	0.9	7.4	25.0	15.9	43.5	18.7	60.3	6,079	98.8
Washington borough & MCD (Warren)	6,502	6,450	-0.8	6,490	74.5	9.0	3.2	2.2	11.1	19.8	12.6	41.4	47.1	22.7	2,689	91.7
Washington township (Warren)	6,646	6,353	-4.4	6,395	90.8	3.0	1.6	1.0	3.7	19.7	15.9	47.1	32.8	33.2	2,451	95.8

1 May be of any race.

Table A. All Places — **Population and Housing**

	Population				Race and Hispanic or Latino origin (percent)					Age (percent)			Educational attainment of persons age 25 and older		Occupied housing units	
STATE City, town, township, borough, or CDP (county if applicable)	2010 census total population	2019 estimated population	Percent change 2010–2019	ACS total population estimate 2015–2019	White alone, not Hispanic or Latino	Black alone, not Hispanic or Latino	Asian alone, not Hispanic or Latino	All other races or 2 or more races, not Hispanic or Latino	Hispanic or Latino[1]	Under 18 years old	Age 65 years and older	Median age	Percent High school diploma or less	Percent Bachelor's degree or more	Total	Percent with a computer
	1	2	3	4	5	6	7	8	9	10	11	12	13	14	15	16

NEW JERSEY—Con.

Watchung borough & MCD (Somerset)...........	5,999	6,006	0.1	6,039	76.8	0.7	15.3	0.3	6.9	21.4	23.1	45.5	21.6	58.5	2,019	90.8
Waterford township (Camden).....................	10,662	10,684	0.2	10,702	86.4	4.8	1.3	1.7	5.8	19.1	17.1	42.7	45.0	23.2	3,537	95.2
Wayne township (Passaic)	54,713	53,369	-2.5	53,954	75.4	1.9	7.8	1.3	13.6	20.9	19.2	42.9	28.4	53.0	18,350	94.3
Weehawken township (Hudson)....................	12,553	14,638	16.6	14,604	47.2	2.6	11.6	3.6	35.0	16.7	11.7	37.1	27.8	58.1	6,633	93.8
Wenonah borough & MCD (Gloucester)................	2,278	2,212	-2.9	2,259	91.9	0.9	1.9	3.4	1.9	24.9	14.5	42.8	21.5	56.2	766	97.9
Westampton township (Burlington)	8,800	8,649	-1.7	8,672	53.4	23.3	6.4	5.9	11.0	21.4	10.7	41.8	26.9	40.0	3,169	98.0
West Amwell township (Hunterdon)	2,845	2,739	-3.7	2,757	90.7	0.0	3.9	2.7	2.7	20.4	20.6	47.0	27.9	48.4	1,081	93.6
West Belmar CDP	2,493	-	-	2,325	89.1	0.0	0.0	2.8	8.1	12.1	19.1	50.2	32.9	47.4	926	98.4
West Caldwell township (Essex)	10,694	10,837	1.3	10,858	86.1	1.6	4.1	1.1	7.1	21.0	21.1	45.5	26.4	54.5	3,915	89.2
West Cape May borough & MCD (Cape May).......	1,012	1,001	-1.1	1,093	83.3	5.5	2.0	8.1	1.1	18.8	32.0	54.0	22.3	47.8	495	94.3
West Deptford township (Gloucester)................	21,656	20,980	-3.1	21,149	83.2	6.8	2.5	2.2	5.2	20.4	18.1	42.1	39.0	33.7	8,405	91.9
Westfield town & MCD (Union)....................	30,300	29,512	-2.6	29,877	78.6	3.3	7.0	2.9	8.1	28.8	14.9	42.2	13.3	74.1	10,290	93.7
West Freehold CDP.........	13,613	-	-	13,680	73.4	4.0	5.9	2.4	14.2	22.9	16.1	40.0	26.4	50.0	5,036	94.0
West Long Branch borough & MCD (Monmouth).................	8,084	7,881	-2.5	7,908	85.8	4.3	0.6	2.5	6.9	21.0	14.4	33.1	32.4	44.1	2,485	92.9
West Milford township (Passaic)...................	26,242	26,331	0.3	26,404	84.5	1.4	2.0	2.9	9.3	21.4	15.1	44.6	35.9	35.6	9,622	94.9
West New York town & MCD (Hudson)............	49,710	52,723	6.1	52,662	13.9	2.0	5.7	1.1	77.3	21.0	12.6	36.2	53.5	30.2	19,611	89.1
Weston CDP...................	1,235	-	-	1,783	84.1	2.2	13.7	0.0	0.0	0.0	80.0	72.4	28.9	51.3	987	92.2
West Orange township (Essex)	46,164	47,563	3.0	47,359	42.1	27.3	7.3	3.5	19.9	20.7	18.4	43.2	26.3	53.9	16,421	92.5
Westville borough & MCD (Gloucester)................	4,287	4,144	-3.3	4,169	80.1	8.7	4.1	2.3	4.8	24.1	12.9	38.6	53.9	16.6	1,646	86.8
West Wildwood borough & MCD (Cape May).........	603	550	-8.8	385	94.5	2.3	0.0	2.9	0.3	12.2	42.9	60.7	64.1	18.0	217	90.3
West Windsor township (Mercer).....................	27,153	27,895	2.7	27,937	43.7	3.0	47.1	3.3	2.9	25.7	13.1	40.7	7.7	82.7	9,938	98.5
Westwood borough & MCD (Bergen)..............	10,928	11,078	1.4	11,115	66.8	2.5	9.7	2.5	18.5	21.9	19.6	41.8	27.2	51.7	4,381	94.3
Weymouth township (Atlantic)...................	2,698	2,835	5.1	2,755	83.8	8.8	0.2	5.0	2.1	18.1	35.6	57.8	48.8	20.1	1,214	88.7
Wharton borough & MCD (Morris)....................	6,534	6,369	-2.5	6,474	37.7	0.8	8.2	1.9	51.4	23.6	13.5	36.9	45.3	26.4	2,312	88.7
White township (Warren)..	4,891	4,656	-4.8	4,696	87.8	2.2	1.7	1.0	7.2	10.1	39.1	60.0	38.6	26.7	2,073	86.3
White Horse CDP	9,494	-	-	8,576	74.9	10.3	2.7	2.3	9.8	15.6	18.6	44.1	40.2	27.9	3,392	92.3
White House Station CDP	2,089	-	-	2,508	88.1	0.0	0.8	1.0	10.1	14.0	26.9	50.3	38.1	45.6	1,155	89.0
White Meadow Lake CDP	8,836	-	-	9,548	77.9	4.8	3.7	2.3	11.4	22.4	13.9	42.9	21.0	56.5	3,326	95.2
Whitesboro CDP.............	-	-	-	2,837	38.2	44.9	3.7	2.3	11.0	33.4	13.1	27.7	55.3	15.1	961	94.4
Whittingham CDP	2,476	-	-	2,631	87.8	4.8	2.5	0.7	4.2	1.5	81.9	76.8	33.9	41.3	1,500	93.4
Wildwood city & MCD (Cape May)	5,325	4,948	-7.1	5,042	69.7	6.9	2.5	3.0	17.9	17.8	20.1	47.8	58.2	15.6	2,304	88.4
Wildwood Crest borough & MCD (Cape May).......	3,256	3,048	-6.4	3,096	90.0	0.0	0.0	1.7	8.4	11.7	35.4	60.1	36.9	37.2	1,460	89.7
Williamstown CDP	15,567	-	-	14,641	77.7	11.3	2.4	3.0	5.6	23.0	18.2	41.6	40.4	25.3	5,610	90.2
Willingboro township (Burlington)	31,615	32,005	1.2	31,662	14.2	67.7	1.8	4.9	11.5	19.7	18.0	41.8	43.5	24.1	10,701	95.7
Winfield township (Union).	1,471	1,503	2.2	1,623	77.7	1.7	0.6	4.1	15.9	16.9	16.8	42.9	49.8	23.6	759	96.8
Winslow township (Camden)....................	39,784	38,629	-2.9	38,829	46.4	35.4	2.6	3.8	11.8	22.0	13.3	38.8	39.4	27.2	13,571	93.1
Woodbine borough & MCD (Cape May)	2,470	2,414	-2.3	2,341	46.4	22.0	1.5	1.9	28.3	20.9	18.0	43.5	75.5	6.6	804	85.0
Woodbridge CDP............	19,265	-	-	18,768	37.7	9.3	22.2	2.0	28.7	21.9	14.0	38.2	36.2	37.8	7,058	91.1
Woodbridge township (Middlesex).................	99,385	100,145	0.8	100,089	41.5	10.7	24.2	2.6	20.9	20.3	14.9	40.0	41.7	35.8	34,185	92.2
Woodbury city & MCD (Gloucester)................	10,138	9,794	-3.4	9,861	53.3	24.7	1.5	5.8	14.7	20.3	16.3	40.3	42.0	27.7	4,016	83.6
Woodbury Heights borough & MCD (Gloucester)................	3,062	2,964	-3.2	2,986	90.1	0.6	1.4	1.1	6.7	21.0	14.0	41.0	37.2	27.2	1,052	95.4
Woodcliff Lake borough & MCD (Bergen)..............	5,720	5,839	2.1	5,832	88.6	3.1	3.5	1.4	3.3	23.5	16.5	45.4	14.6	75.2	1,963	95.5
Woodland township (Burlington)	1,780	1,768	-0.7	1,741	83.2	3.2	0.5	6.4	6.7	21.3	16.9	45.6	61.2	15.0	498	94.2
Woodland Park borough & MCD (Passaic)............	11,819	12,581	6.4	12,547	61.8	6.9	5.4	2.4	23.6	22.1	20.1	40.1	43.1	38.4	4,533	92.8
Woodlynne borough & MCD (Camden)............	2,976	2,915	-2.0	2,920	12.3	35.3	9.1	1.3	41.9	30.9	10.3	28.9	65.8	9.3	818	92.4
Wood-Ridge borough & MCD (Bergen)..............	7,628	9,294	21.8	8,769	66.7	2.3	13.2	3.0	14.7	18.4	13.7	38.8	28.0	47.8	3,315	94.7
Woodstown borough & MCD (Salem)	3,508	3,436	-2.1	3,456	82.5	3.7	0.2	4.9	8.7	23.8	15.8	42.7	33.5	35.2	1,255	94.2
Woolwich township (Gloucester)................	10,214	12,960	26.9	12,549	75.5	12.4	4.8	0.8	6.5	28.6	10.6	38.1	23.5	54.4	3,934	96.7
Wrightstown borough & MCD (Burlington)	804	776	-3.5	701	41.2	27.0	8.0	2.7	21.1	20.8	12.8	39.9	47.4	10.8	324	88.9
Wyckoff township (Bergen)....................	16,731	16,947	1.3	17,017	89.1	0.8	4.9	0.6	4.6	25.8	20.4	45.3	19.3	62.6	5,833	93.7
Yardville CDP.................	7,186	-	-	6,801	84.3	2.4	4.8	0.5	8.0	15.7	17.0	45.9	38.5	29.7	2,365	96.8
Yorketown CDP..............	6,535	-	-	6,459	88.2	1.6	2.5	2.0	5.7	24.7	10.3	40.8	23.1	50.8	2,009	99.6
Zarephath CDP..............	37	-	-	26	100.0	0.0	0.0	0.0	0.0	0.0	65.4	65.5	30.8	34.6	17	100.0

1 May be of any race.

Table A. All Places — **Population and Housing**

STATE City, town, township, borough, or CDP (county if applicable)	Population: 2010 census total population	Population: 2019 estimated population	Population: Percent change 2010–2019	Population: ACS total population estimate 2015–2019	Race and Hispanic or Latino origin (percent): White alone, not Hispanic or Latino	Black alone, not Hispanic or Latino	Asian alone, not Hispanic or Latino	All other races or 2 or more races, not Hispanic or Latino	Hispanic or Latino[1]	Age (percent): Under 18 years old	Age 65 years and older	Median age	Educational attainment of persons age 25 and older: Percent High school diploma or less	Percent Bachelor's degree or more	Occupied housing units: Total	Percent with a computer
	1	2	3	4	5	6	7	8	9	10	11	12	13	14	15	16
NEW MEXICO	2,059,199	2,096,829	1.8	2,092,454	37.4	1.8	1.5	10.6	48.8	23.3	16.9	37.8	40.9	27.3	780,249	85.9
Abeytas CDP	56	-	-	293	0.0	0.0	0.0	0.0	100.0	13.3	10.6	19.0	0.0	100.0	31	100.0
Abiquiu CDP	231	-	-	151	49.0	0.0	0.0	0.0	51.0	0.0	25.2	64.0	25.2	49.0	77	0.0
Acomita Lake CDP	416	-	-	574	3.5	0.0	0.0	94.3	2.3	28.2	8.0	31.0	58.9	12.9	108	78.7
Adelino CDP	823	-	-	919	39.3	0.0	0.0	3.2	57.6	1.4	42.0	57.1	40.6	12.9	469	68.4
Agua Fria CDP	2,800	-	-	2,734	16.9	0.4	1.1	3.1	78.5	17.5	14.4	45.8	67.4	14.0	1,180	75.7
Alamillo CDP	102	-	-	143	82.5	0.0	0.0	0.0	17.5	0.0	18.2	59.2	88.1	7.7	31	64.5
Alamo CDP	1,085	-	-	851	1.5	0.0	0.0	98.1	0.4	20.1	12.1	44.6	84.5	3.1	180	26.1
Alamogordo city	30,409	31,980	5.2	31,384	55.6	3.8	1.7	4.0	34.8	22.3	16.9	36.3	40.0	19.5	12,813	89.2
Albuquerque city	546,153	560,513	2.6	559,374	38.9	2.8	2.8	6.3	49.2	22.4	15.1	36.6	32.9	35.2	224,166	90.7
Alcalde CDP	285	-	-	159	0.0	0.0	0.0	0.0	100.0	41.5	15.7	30.0	45.1	5.5	60	63.3
Algodones CDP	814	-	-	704	25.4	0.0	0.0	12.4	62.2	16.2	23.0	48.4	55.3	23.3	302	75.2
Angel Fire village	1,216	1,070	-12.0	773	75.2	1.6	0.0	3.2	20.1	16.3	30.4	53.1	14.7	49.7	389	100.0
Animas CDP	237	-	-	114	65.8	0.0	0.0	17.5	16.7	12.3	11.4	49.8	22.4	22.4	44	90.9
Anthony city	9,467	9,239	-2.4	9,310	1.0	0.0	0.5	0.0	98.5	34.6	8.3	25.9	72.4	8.8	2,715	73.5
Anton Chico CDP	188	-	-	124	0.0	0.0	0.0	0.0	100.0	0.0	51.6	65.1	70.2	4.0	92	14.1
Anzac Village CDP	54	-	-	36	0.0	0.0	0.0	100.0	0.0	0.0	69.4	80.1	0.0	19.4	18	0.0
Apache Creek CDP	67	-	-	93	100.0	0.0	0.0	0.0	0.0	0.0	51.6	66.1	75.3	16.1	34	100.0
Aragon CDP	94	-	-	93	38.7	0.0	0.0	0.0	61.3	0.0	69.9	70.9	100.0	0.0	33	54.5
Arenas Valley CDP	1,522	-	-	1,813	34.6	0.0	0.0	4.5	60.9	28.7	20.4	40.7	35.9	21.6	594	94.8
Arrey CDP	232	-	-	25	0.0	0.0	0.0	0.0	100.0	0.0	100.0	0.0	100.0	0.0	25	0.0
Arroyo Hondo CDP	474	-	-	176	48.9	0.0	0.0	6.3	44.9	0.0	40.3	52.5	35.8	50.6	89	73.0
Arroyo Seco CDP	1,785	-	-	1,794	25.4	0.0	0.0	0.0	74.6	19.7	23.6	44.0	59.7	28.1	365	94.5
Artesia city	11,513	12,356	7.3	12,262	42.8	1.5	0.1	2.8	52.9	32.1	15.8	33.3	57.9	15.5	4,762	89.7
Atoka CDP	1,077	-	-	1,193	51.4	0.8	0.0	0.0	47.9	27.7	16.8	38.7	68.4	11.6	431	69.1
Aztec city	6,736	6,369	-5.4	6,530	56.6	0.2	0.3	18.7	24.2	27.3	16.4	32.6	45.6	16.4	2,496	87.9
Bayard city	2,334	2,123	-9.0	2,442	17.7	0.7	0.0	1.4	80.1	28.1	21.6	38.1	50.0	17.2	928	76.3
Beclabito CDP	317	-	-	295	2.4	0.0	0.0	97.6	0.0	17.6	15.9	38.6	49.5	8.6	87	64.4
Belen city	7,586	7,416	-2.2	7,403	30.2	0.4	0.8	12.0	56.7	20.7	20.1	38.4	50.7	18.2	2,860	80.7
Bent CDP	119	-	-	62	100.0	0.0	0.0	0.0	0.0	0.0	0.0	0.0	100.0	0.0	17	100.0
Berino CDP	1,441	-	-	1,877	2.6	0.0	0.0	0.0	97.4	29.8	10.7	30.8	73.5	6.8	538	73.2
Bernalillo town	8,293	10,477	26.3	9,669	24.5	0.8	0.3	9.8	64.7	18.1	20.2	42.4	54.9	18.2	3,624	85.9
Bibo CDP	140	-	-	55	0.0	0.0	0.0	0.0	100.0	20.0	60.0	72.2	0.0	100.0	44	100.0
Black Rock CDP	1,323	-	-	1,656	2.8	0.0	4.8	86.5	6.0	37.0	2.8	24.4	45.1	15.6	344	86.0
Blanco CDP	388	-	-	159	30.2	0.0	0.0	7.5	62.3	0.0	23.9	43.7	86.8	0.0	62	80.6
Bloomfield city	8,158	7,685	-5.8	7,846	41.6	0.5	0.4	19.8	37.7	32.5	15.3	32.2	44.4	13.2	2,642	84.6
Bluewater Acres CDP	206	-	-	202	49.5	0.0	0.0	0.0	50.5	8.4	40.1	48.9	35.3	6.6	130	100.0
Bluewater Village CDP	628	-	-	82	46.3	0.0	0.0	0.0	53.7	0.0	0.0	52.8	46.3	18.3	53	100.0
Boles Acres CDP	1,638	-	-	2,173	66.5	7.6	4.7	4.3	16.8	17.2	30.0	51.1	42.3	14.4	786	84.7
Bosque Farms village	3,977	3,888	-2.2	3,876	48.4	0.2	2.0	8.1	41.3	23.7	23.5	45.4	40.3	28.6	1,524	84.3
Brazos CDP	44	-	-	88	0.0	0.0	0.0	0.0	100.0	0.0	84.1	79.5	100.0	0.0	45	0.0
Brimhall Nizhoni CDP	199	-	-	345	2.3	0.0	0.0	87.5	10.1	24.6	12.8	32.1	51.4	6.7	84	53.6
Buckhorn CDP	200	-	-	150	100.0	0.0	0.0	0.0	0.0	0.0	74.0	74.5	62.7	24.0	68	100.0
Caballo CDP	112	-	-	45	91.1	0.0	0.0	0.0	8.9	0.0	91.1	0.0	8.9	91.1	45	100.0
Cañada de los Alamos CDP	434	-	-	511	13.5	0.0	0.0	0.0	86.5	31.9	11.0	30.3	50.9	18.7	165	70.3
Canjilon CDP	256	-	-	337	0.0	0.0	0.0	0.0	100.0	11.9	3.0	44.1	58.0	28.5	113	52.2
Cannon AFB CDP	2,245	-	-	2,475	59.8	9.4	3.5	9.3	18.0	32.7	0.0	21.9	5.5	28.6	630	100.0
Cañon CDP	327	-	-	198	44.9	0.0	0.0	7.6	47.5	28.3	28.8	27.3	61.9	38.1	55	100.0
Cañones CDP	118	-	-	92	59.8	0.0	0.0	8.7	31.5	0.0	3.3	46.3	100.0	0.0	36	77.8
Canova CDP	118	-	-	102	0.0	0.0	0.0	0.0	100.0	0.0	0.0	53.5	100.0	0.0	78	100.0
Capitan village	1,491	1,431	-4.0	1,518	53.4	0.2	0.0	0.9	45.5	25.9	24.4	40.7	44.4	14.7	569	83.8
Capulin CDP	66	-	-	34	8.8	0.0	2.9	0.0	88.2	32.4	11.8	22.7	71.4	0.0	7	100.0
Carlsbad city	26,251	29,810	13.6	29,158	44.5	1.8	0.8	1.9	51.1	24.5	13.5	34.9	50.1	17.8	10,611	90.8
Carnuel CDP	1,232	-	-	1,305	44.3	0.0	0.0	0.7	55.0	12.9	30.8	56.3	36.6	27.5	535	84.9
Carrizozo town	996	935	-6.1	760	38.4	0.8	0.0	8.0	52.8	14.2	20.7	44.5	49.8	16.5	297	66.3
Casa Colorada CDP	272	-	-	125	60.0	0.0	0.0	0.0	40.0	24.0	16.8	49.4	34.4	24.4	58	67.2
Causey village	107	98	-8.4	131	26.7	0.0	0.0	1.5	71.8	25.2	18.3	34.9	48.8	17.5	43	97.7
Cedar Crest CDP	958	-	-	691	72.6	1.3	0.0	2.0	24.0	9.6	43.7	60.0	10.0	37.2	402	100.0
Cedar Grove CDP	747	-	-	535	90.1	0.0	0.0	0.0	9.9	10.7	35.3	60.5	27.3	41.3	247	83.8
Cedar Hill CDP	847	-	-	773	85.5	0.0	0.0	0.0	14.5	16.8	24.3	55.1	36.4	23.5	366	87.4
Cedro CDP	430	-	-	402	74.4	0.0	0.0	15.7	10.0	11.7	25.4	57.1	19.0	34.2	203	95.1
Chama village	1,024	992	-3.1	1,026	10.8	0.0	0.0	6.5	82.7	16.3	20.3	48.5	53.9	12.9	384	62.8
Chamberino CDP	919	-	-	625	0.0	0.0	0.0	0.0	100.0	25.0	16.5	37.9	59.9	25.2	231	54.1
Chamisal CDP	310	-	-	348	3.4	0.0	0.0	0.9	95.7	13.5	24.7	50.4	55.1	13.3	120	55.0
Chamita CDP	870	-	-	899	8.8	1.1	0.1	7.3	82.6	19.7	22.1	53.2	63.0	6.9	374	40.9
Chamizal CDP	101	-	-	76	0.0	0.0	0.0	0.0	100.0	0.0	100.0	0.0	10.5	89.5	8	0.0
Chaparral CDP	14,631	-	-	14,437	12.0	1.1	0.0	1.2	85.7	30.2	10.3	31.6	61.6	11.3	4,331	79.3
Chical CDP	107	-	-	108	0.0	0.0	0.0	100.0	0.0	21.3	8.3	30.9	79.5	10.3	37	64.9
Chili CDP	654	-	-	549	13.1	0.0	0.0	0.0	86.9	4.6	34.4	61.6	18.9	17.0	201	100.0
Chilili CDP	137	-	-	54	13.0	0.0	0.0	0.0	87.0	0.0	46.3	61.7	87.0	0.0	47	53.2
Chimayo CDP	3,177	-	-	2,641	7.6	0.0	0.0	6.2	86.3	19.6	13.2	41.0	35.5	17.7	1,059	60.9
Chupadero CDP	362	-	-	204	73.5	4.9	0.0	5.4	16.2	17.2	22.1	53.5	4.2	83.2	91	100.0
Church Rock CDP	1,128	-	-	887	0.6	1.6	0.8	92.9	4.2	28.0	11.0	34.3	56.5	5.9	254	50.8
Cimarron village	1,018	881	-13.5	930	22.4	1.4	0.0	5.2	71.1	24.7	16.1	48.2	39.7	22.6	459	85.0
City of the Sun CDP	31	-	-	46	100.0	0.0	0.0	0.0	0.0	0.0	100.0	0.0	0.0	0.0	46	100.0
Clayton town	2,977	2,681	-9.9	3,184	41.2	1.9	0.0	6.2	50.7	19.2	18.2	38.6	69.1	10.2	948	67.8
Cliff CDP	293	-	-	135	70.4	0.0	0.0	0.0	29.6	14.1	34.8	55.4	69.8	9.5	67	92.5
Cloudcroft village	672	701	4.3	654	71.3	0.0	0.0	3.7	25.1	21.3	33.9	53.7	23.5	30.0	254	85.8
Clovis city	37,794	38,319	1.4	38,891	43.0	5.5	1.4	3.9	46.2	27.1	11.8	31.3	45.9	19.0	14,744	87.2
Cobre CDP	39	-	-	23	0.0	0.0	0.0	0.0	100.0	0.0	100.0	0.0	0.0	100.0	23	0.0
Cochiti CDP	528	-	-	445	0.0	0.0	0.0	92.8	7.2	28.1	18.2	34.8	45.6	12.8	134	51.5
Cochiti Lake CDP	569	-	-	487	59.8	3.9	1.4	27.3	7.6	11.5	40.2	61.6	16.0	51.9	263	90.9
Columbus village	1,690	1,617	-4.3	1,118	12.9	0.0	0.0	0.0	87.1	28.2	16.5	31.9	84.1	6.2	390	66.2
Conchas Dam CDP	186	-	-	13	100.0	0.0	0.0	0.0	0.0	0.0	0.0	0.0	100.0	0.0	13	100.0
Cordova CDP	414	-	-	704	0.0	0.0	0.0	0.0	100.0	18.3	26.7	42.8	67.5	9.9	199	69.3
Corona village	174	163	-6.3	121	73.6	0.0	0.0	0.0	26.4	2.5	23.1	61.0	63.9	25.9	58	96.6
Corrales village	8,340	8,696	4.3	8,588	69.0	1.5	1.4	2.6	25.6	15.5	29.4	55.0	16.2	61.4	3,699	96.6
Costilla CDP	205	-	-	92	0.0	0.0	0.0	0.0	100.0	0.0	0.0	0.0	100.0	0.0	35	100.0
Cotton City CDP	388	-	-	333	43.2	0.0	0.0	6.0	50.8	22.2	11.1	39.5	61.7	6.0	106	86.8
Coyote CDP	128	-	-	72	0.0	0.0	0.0	0.0	100.0	0.0	52.8	66.2	54.2	0.0	45	44.4

1 May be of any race.

Table A. All Places — Population and Housing

STATE City, town, township, borough, or CDP (county if applicable)	2010 census total population	2019 estimated population	Percent change 2010–2019	ACS total population estimate 2015–2019	White alone, not Hispanic or Latino	Black alone, not Hispanic or Latino	Asian alone, not Hispanic or Latino	All other races or 2 or more races, not Hispanic or Latino	Hispanic or Latino[1]	Under 18 years old	Age 65 years and older	Median age	Percent High school diploma or less	Percent Bachelor's degree or more	Total	Percent with a computer
	1	2	3	4	5	6	7	8	9	10	11	12	13	14	15	16
NEW MEXICO—Con.																
Crownpoint CDP	2,278	-	-	2,419	5.7	0.7	1.1	91.2	1.3	23.0	11.5	31.4	40.8	18.4	695	76.5
Cruzville CDP	72	-	-	249	46.6	0.0	0.0	0.0	53.4	6.0	3.2	43.1	46.9	0.0	75	60.0
Crystal CDP	311	-	-	345	1.4	0.0	0.0	97.4	1.2	27.0	15.7	46.0	43.2	22.0	103	36.9
Cuartelez CDP	469	-	-	21	0.0	0.0	0.0	0.0	100.0	0.0	0.0	0.0	100.0	0.0	21	100.0
Cuba village	729	757	3.8	678	7.7	0.0	0.0	36.3	56.0	27.1	15.6	37.1	71.9	11.3	252	63.5
Cubero CDP	289	-	-	331	0.0	0.0	0.0	22.4	77.6	30.2	25.4	54.8	27.9	6.8	139	76.3
Cundiyo CDP	72	-	-	34	41.2	0.0	0.0	0.0	58.8	0.0	100.0	77.7	58.8	41.2	24	58.3
Cuyamungue CDP	479	-	-	431	19.3	0.0	0.0	2.1	78.7	24.8	20.2	42.4	41.7	25.0	174	77.0
Cuyamungue Grant CDP	226	-	-	217	30.0	0.0	0.0	0.9	69.1	23.0	11.1	45.6	56.0	32.7	89	95.5
Datil CDP	54	-	-	24	100.0	0.0	0.0	0.0	0.0	0.0	100.0	0.0	0.0	62.5	15	100.0
Deming city	14,821	13,880	-6.3	14,139	24.2	1.9	1.2	0.7	72.0	29.9	19.3	35.1	64.7	13.5	5,332	73.3
Des Moines village	140	122	-12.9	115	78.3	0.0	0.0	0.0	21.7	30.4	15.7	15.9	38.6	14.0	37	59.5
Dexter town	1,264	1,243	-1.7	1,121	12.3	0.0	0.0	0.0	87.7	31.6	19.3	33.3	73.7	8.9	363	82.9
Dixon CDP	926	-	-	386	23.6	0.0	0.0	1.6	74.9	12.2	67.4	73.9	40.7	48.1	245	35.5
Do??a Ana CDP	1,211	-	-	1,158	14.9	0.0	0.0	0.0	85.1	20.7	24.1	53.1	53.9	1.8	565	52.7
Dora village	133	121	-9.0	110	70.0	0.0	0.0	15.5	14.5	17.3	18.2	44.7	59.7	2.6	52	76.9
Dulce CDP	2,743	-	-	2,750	2.0	0.1	0.0	81.4	16.5	33.9	9.8	28.8	50.4	12.0	651	66.2
Duran CDP	35	-	-	37	73.0	0.0	0.0	0.0	27.0	24.3	24.3	63.1	67.9	7.1	17	76.5
Eagle Nest village	290	251	-13.4	271	56.5	0.0	0.0	5.2	38.4	14.8	17.7	54.5	23.0	43.2	156	91.0
East Pecos CDP	757	-	-	646	7.7	10.4	0.0	32.5	49.4	32.5	18.1	38.6	52.3	24.8	285	100.0
Edgewood town	5,888	6,107	3.7	6,071	69.9	0.2	0.1	1.4	28.4	23.0	14.9	43.3	31.3	27.5	2,311	98.2
Edith Endave CDP	211	-	-	336	38.7	0.0	1.8	7.1	52.4	16.4	16.4	47.5	52.2	24.1	107	69.2
El Cerro CDP	2,953	-	-	3,202	33.4	0.0	0.0	2.4	64.2	21.7	15.3	36.9	34.9	30.2	1,132	88.0
El Cerro Mission CDP	4,657	-	-	4,170	23.1	0.0	0.0	4.5	72.4	24.4	9.8	35.5	64.2	11.8	1,380	81.4
Eldorado at Santa Fe CDP	6,130	-	-	5,823	79.5	1.1	1.4	2.9	15.2	8.4	43.2	62.8	9.0	68.6	2,879	97.8
El Duende CDP	707	-	-	743	0.4	0.0	0.0	0.0	99.6	52.9	6.3	14.9	56.6	0.6	209	100.0
Elephant Butte city	1,431	1,310	-8.5	1,352	89.0	0.0	0.0	0.0	11.0	4.3	66.5	70.3	39.8	20.7	740	74.5
Elida town	197	176	-10.7	178	81.5	0.0	0.0	0.0	18.5	28.7	25.8	41.2	42.3	29.7	83	92.8
El Rancho CDP	1,199	-	-	1,183	16.6	0.9	0.0	11.6	70.9	22.7	20.4	44.2	37.9	23.9	459	76.0
El Rito CDP	808	-	-	808	2.4	0.0	0.0	0.0	97.6	12.7	25.4	45.1	30.2	35.5	184	50.5
El Valle de Arroyo Seco CDP	1,440	-	-	2,009	16.9	0.0	0.0	0.0	83.1	31.8	7.1	34.4	61.3	15.0	669	53.8
Encinal CDP	210	-	-	284	0.0	0.0	0.0	95.8	4.2	21.1	9.9	30.4	72.6	4.6	73	75.3
Encino village	82	78	-4.9	74	10.8	0.0	0.0	0.0	89.2	10.8	27.0	59.5	56.1	12.1	43	58.1
Ensenada CDP	107	-	-	24	0.0	0.0	0.0	0.0	100.0	0.0	100.0	0.0	0.0	0.0	24	100.0
Escondida CDP	47	-	-	24	100.0	0.0	0.0	0.0	0.0	0.0	54.2	0.0	0.0	0.0	11	100.0
Escudilla Bonita CDP	119	-	-	72	100.0	0.0	0.0	0.0	0.0	0.0	47.2	64.9	51.4	29.2	46	69.6
Espa±ola city	10,267	10,044	-2.2	10,102	10.7	1.0	1.1	2.2	85.0	26.6	17.1	36.7	53.7	15.4	3,615	67.7
Estancia town	1,635	1,571	-3.9	1,478	28.6	1.5	0.0	2.6	67.3	13.6	18.3	35.6	60.5	14.9	473	77.8
Eunice city	2,916	3,038	4.2	3,037	45.6	0.0	0.0	0.0	54.4	34.9	11.6	31.6	57.0	10.6	997	88.4
Fairacres CDP	824	-	-	1,294	25.7	0.0	0.0	4.6	69.6	17.1	11.1	43.0	48.6	16.7	400	96.3
Farmington city	45,954	44,372	-3.4	45,258	43.8	1.3	1.1	30.3	23.5	28.2	12.8	33.8	38.5	21.4	16,060	91.0
Faywood CDP	33	-	-	46	0.0	0.0	0.0	0.0	100.0	0.0	21.7	53.9	65.2	15.2	17	0.0
Fence Lake CDP	42	-	-	113	100.0	0.0	0.0	0.0	0.0	17.7	73.5	73.5	66.7	0.0	41	0.0
Flora Vista CDP	2,191	-	-	1,688	79.1	0.3	0.0	0.9	19.7	8.1	31.9	56.4	42.5	5.9	808	83.5
Floyd village	121	110	-9.1	108	84.3	0.0	0.0	0.0	15.7	38.0	18.5	39.7	44.8	24.1	38	71.1
Folsom village	66	57	-13.6	43	95.3	0.0	0.0	0.0	4.7	39.5	14.0	21.9	28.6	19.0	12	83.3
Fort Sumner village	1,036	897	-13.4	1,209	34.6	2.0	0.0	0.9	62.5	34.9	21.2	34.2	62.6	7.9	364	81.0
Galisteo CDP	253	-	-	234	74.4	0.0	0.0	10.7	15.0	21.8	42.7	51.0	18.0	53.0	133	80.5
Gallina CDP	-	-	-	120	0.0	0.0	17.5	0.0	82.5	18.3	7.5	46.6	52.9	7.4	43	18.6
Gallup city	21,758	21,493	-1.2	21,854	20.0	1.5	2.6	42.7	33.2	31.4	12.5	32.7	45.4	22.4	7,294	77.0
Garfield CDP	137	-	-	-	-	-	-	-	-	-	-	-	-	-	-	-
Gila CDP	314	-	-	226	87.6	0.0	0.0	0.0	12.4	19.5	4.0	55.8	17.0	28.0	105	100.0
Glen Acres CDP	208	-	-	171	38.0	0.0	0.0	0.0	62.0	11.7	22.2	55.8	41.1	14.6	84	66.7
Glenwood CDP	143	-	-	34	79.4	0.0	0.0	0.0	20.6	0.0	52.9	79.1	20.6	0.0	25	28.0
Glorieta CDP	430	-	-	618	51.0	0.0	0.0	0.0	49.0	11.3	19.6	55.1	37.4	29.4	252	74.2
Golden CDP	37	-	-	-	-	-	-	-	-	-	-	-	-	-	-	-
Grady village	107	103	-3.7	151	74.2	0.0	0.0	1.3	24.5	25.8	20.5	42.8	56.5	15.7	53	75.5
Grants city	9,199	8,942	-2.8	9,036	28.0	1.0	0.3	21.9	48.8	22.6	18.7	37.3	48.4	15.4	3,149	81.4
Grenville village	32	29	-9.4	19	100.0	0.0	0.0	0.0	0.0	10.5	15.8	54.7	0.0	52.9	10	70.0
Hachita CDP	49	-	-	38	100.0	0.0	0.0	0.0	0.0	0.0	57.9	66.2	34.2	65.8	22	100.0
Hagerman town	1,245	1,220	-2.0	790	24.3	0.3	1.3	1.6	72.5	19.6	15.7	42.1	64.9	9.5	287	80.8
Hanover CDP	167	-	-	205	3.4	0.0	0.0	0.0	96.6	25.4	32.7	57.8	33.6	19.0	87	35.6
Happy Valley CDP	519	-	-	774	70.2	0.0	0.0	7.8	22.1	26.1	9.4	38.1	67.6	4.4	229	86.0
Hatch village	1,649	1,650	0.1	1,955	12.3	0.4	0.0	0.4	86.9	40.7	10.1	24.9	62.7	22.9	590	75.3
Hernandez CDP	946	-	-	751	12.5	1.5	0.0	2.3	83.8	24.1	22.0	44.4	54.0	13.4	252	76.6
Highland Meadows CDP	624	-	-	451	33.9	0.0	0.0	8.4	57.6	9.8	13.1	34.5	43.2	13.3	175	69.1
High Rolls CDP	834	-	-	910	70.5	0.0	0.0	8.5	21.0	30.2	33.3	46.4	16.5	41.8	360	91.7
Hillsboro CDP	124	-	-	154	93.5	0.0	0.0	6.5	0.0	10.4	74.0	75.2	32.6	33.3	103	53.4
Hobbs city	34,167	39,141	14.6	38,375	30.9	5.4	1.0	2.6	60.1	30.8	9.7	30.6	55.1	15.5	12,028	87.3
Holloman AFB CDP	3,054	-	-	4,096	62.7	14.3	1.8	9.3	11.9	36.4	0.6	22.3	19.6	23.5	1,096	100.0
Homestead CDP	47	-	-	32	100.0	0.0	0.0	0.0	0.0	0.0	0.0	0.0	0.0	0.0	13	100.0
Hope village	105	106	1.0	110	24.5	0.0	0.0	0.0	75.5	30.0	28.2	52.1	55.8	7.8	38	84.2
Hot Springs Landing CDP	110	-	-	-	-	-	-	-	-	-	-	-	-	-	-	-
House village	68	62	-8.8	66	98.5	0.0	0.0	0.0	1.5	4.5	30.3	53.6	49.2	14.3	29	100.0
Hurley town	1,297	1,176	-9.3	1,384	19.1	0.0	0.0	6.4	74.4	29.3	21.5	37.1	52.1	13.2	516	80.4
Indian Hills CDP	892	-	-	1,075	65.3	0.6	0.0	0.0	34.1	20.4	15.3	47.3	45.0	11.7	340	77.9
Isleta Village Proper CDP	491	-	-	402	0.0	0.0	0.0	95.8	4.2	16.7	24.6	43.8	47.8	14.2	154	44.8
Jacona CDP	412	-	-	387	37.7	0.3	0.0	1.3	60.7	17.1	25.6	52.1	38.9	28.3	171	75.4
Jaconita CDP	332	-	-	323	39.6	0.6	0.0	2.5	57.3	5.6	37.5	59.5	50.0	26.7	161	64.6
Jal city	2,052	2,117	3.2	1,896	40.7	1.1	0.0	0.6	57.6	24.0	18.7	40.1	69.2	5.3	710	77.2
Jarales CDP	2,475	-	-	2,026	29.4	2.0	0.0	2.6	66.0	19.1	20.2	48.4	49.9	13.1	813	63.6
Jemez Pueblo CDP	1,788	-	-	2,018	0.2	0.0	0.0	98.8	0.9	32.3	11.9	31.3	57.3	4.2	433	42.7
Jemez Springs village	262	267	1.9	285	78.2	0.0	0.0	2.5	19.3	3.5	40.0	60.5	15.4	65.1	122	93.4
Keeler Farm CDP	1,305	-	-	1,706	29.2	0.0	0.0	0.5	70.2	27.0	17.7	41.1	78.3	7.2	478	81.6
Kingston CDP	32	-	-	21	61.9	0.0	0.0	38.1	0.0	0.0	0.0	0.0	38.1	0.0	13	100.0
Kirtland town	647	601	-7.1	917	45.7	0.0	0.2	33.3	20.8	20.9	13.6	43.3	17.6	23.1	342	83.9
La Cienega CDP	3,819	-	-	3,732	21.5	0.0	0.3	3.0	75.2	23.0	12.0	39.0	55.6	18.8	1,196	92.1
La Cueva CDP	168	-	-	137	66.4	0.0	9.5	0.0	24.1	0.0	46.0	63.5	35.8	35.8	87	85.1

1 May be of any race.

Table A. All Places — **Population and Housing**

STATE City, town, township, borough, or CDP (county if applicable)	Population				Race and Hispanic or Latino origin (percent)					Age (percent)			Educational attainment of persons age 25 and older		Occupied housing units	
	2010 census total population	2019 estimated population	Percent change 2010–2019	ACS total population estimate 2015–2019	White alone, not Hispanic or Latino	Black alone, not Hispanic or Latino	Asian alone, not Hispanic or Latino	All other races or 2 or more races, not Hispanic or Latino	Hispanic or Latino[1]	Under 18 years old	Age 65 years and older	Median age	Percent High school diploma or less	Percent Bachelor's degree or more	Total	Percent with a computer
	1	2	3	4	5	6	7	8	9	10	11	12	13	14	15	16
NEW MEXICO—Con.																
Laguna CDP	1,241	-	-	1,075	2.0	0.0	0.8	95.2	2.0	29.4	15.3	38.7	41.2	8.8	287	65.9
La Hacienda CDP	725	-	-	587	13.6	0.0	0.0	0.0	86.4	15.7	25.7	39.6	72.8	11.8	240	81.3
La Huerta CDP	1,246	-	-	1,608	67.2	0.0	1.7	0.0	31.2	25.2	20.6	44.1	39.2	16.8	541	96.9
La Jara CDP	207	-	-	325	12.0	0.0	0.0	11.7	76.3	23.7	38.5	36.4	53.2	31.6	149	57.7
La Joya CDP	82	-	-	14	64.3	0.0	0.0	0.0	35.7	0.0	0.0	0.0	0.0	0.0	5	100.0
Lake Arthur town	424	420	-0.9	479	40.5	0.0	0.0	0.0	59.5	24.4	12.1	34.8	57.9	10.1	152	81.6
Lake Roberts CDP	53	-	-	33	42.4	0.0	0.0	0.0	57.6	33.3	0.0	52.7	0.0	100.0	14	100.0
Lake Roberts Heights CDP	32	-	-	50	100.0	0.0	0.0	0.0	0.0	0.0	70.0	65.3	0.0	56.0	37	100.0
Lake Sumner CDP	143	-	-	142	23.9	0.0	0.0	0.0	76.1	30.3	4.2	18.8	21.2	24.2	43	100.0
Lake Valley CDP	64	-	-	96	0.0	0.0	0.0	37.5	62.5	8.3	2.1	39.5	47.7	44.3	40	90.0
La Luz CDP	1,697	-	-	1,222	74.4	0.0	0.0	8.3	17.3	14.0	27.3	55.2	41.3	15.5	544	87.1
La Madera CDP	154	-	-	25	0.0	0.0	0.0	0.0	100.0	0.0	0.0	0.0	100.0	0.0	25	0.0
La Mesa CDP	728	-	-	638	11.4	0.0	0.0	4.1	84.5	19.1	46.1	63.6	68.4	5.9	301	60.8
La Mesilla CDP	1,772	-	-	2,314	29.0	0.1	0.0	2.2	68.7	18.4	20.1	46.7	31.2	28.4	814	89.3
Lamy CDP	218	-	-	159	68.6	0.0	0.0	0.0	31.4	17.6	30.2	42.6	39.7	51.9	67	83.6
La Plata CDP	612	-	-	503	73.2	0.0	0.0	8.0	18.9	22.9	22.3	40.9	38.7	24.7	200	91.5
La Puebla CDP	1,186	-	-	952	22.5	0.0	0.0	15.7	61.9	24.5	15.7	35.7	44.3	32.4	361	100.0
Las Cruces city	97,706	103,432	5.9	102,102	32.5	2.5	1.8	2.7	60.5	23.1	15.6	32.3	34.9	32.2	39,925	89.6
Las Maravillas CDP	1,628	-	-	1,723	31.7	5.6	0.3	2.8	59.5	27.9	18.2	34.6	37.4	16.2	578	87.2
Las Nutrias CDP	149	-	-	124	15.3	0.0	0.0	0.0	84.7	20.2	27.4	54.8	87.9	0.0	61	68.9
Las Palomas CDP	173	-	-	319	50.5	0.0	0.0	0.0	49.5	25.7	20.7	57.3	24.5	27.0	151	100.0
Las Vegas city	14,043	12,919	-8.0	13,176	15.3	1.2	0.8	2.5	80.3	17.7	18.8	40.8	48.7	23.8	5,395	72.1
La Union CDP	1,106	-	-	994	1.6	0.0	0.0	0.0	98.4	12.3	14.8	50.7	66.2	15.6	349	69.6
La Villita CDP	957	-	-	573	0.0	0.0	0.0	0.0	100.0	14.5	20.4	50.4	47.2	26.5	271	48.0
Lee Acres CDP	5,858	-	-	5,735	35.2	1.2	0.0	25.5	38.1	23.8	15.8	39.0	50.0	14.4	2,013	78.5
Lemitar CDP	330	-	-	653	15.3	0.0	0.0	0.0	84.7	26.6	3.4	47.1	89.1	10.9	163	32.5
Livingston Wheeler CDP	609	-	-	706	96.3	0.0	0.0	0.0	3.7	34.8	23.4	42.8	38.4	13.3	293	91.1
Llano del Medio CDP	118	-	-	134	0.0	0.0	0.0	0.0	100.0	0.0	13.4	43.6	69.4	0.0	18	0.0
Loco Hills CDP	126	-	-	24	0.0	0.0	0.0	0.0	100.0	0.0	0.0	0.0	100.0	0.0	12	100.0
Logan village	1,041	979	-6.0	620	79.0	0.0	2.4	0.6	17.9	17.1	42.1	58.7	52.4	22.2	294	89.8
Lordsburg city	2,809	2,398	-14.6	2,408	15.7	1.5	0.0	0.7	82.1	25.2	20.6	36.3	65.6	7.9	929	73.1
Los Alamos CDP	12,019	-	-	12,666	69.6	0.7	6.6	4.4	18.8	22.0	16.4	40.9	12.2	68.3	5,558	92.5
Los Cerrillos CDP	321	-	-	182	43.4	0.0	0.0	0.0	56.6	0.0	23.6	61.4	51.5	22.0	62	75.8
Los Chaves CDP	5,446	-	-	6,109	35.4	0.0	0.0	6.1	58.4	26.7	19.5	39.7	48.3	23.5	1,993	78.3
Los Luceros CDP	906	-	-	604	10.3	5.5	0.0	0.5	83.8	26.5	25.3	27.4	55.4	8.5	180	75.0
Los Lunas village	15,030	16,061	6.9	15,589	34.7	2.6	0.2	4.1	58.4	26.0	16.5	36.8	42.6	23.9	5,699	87.5
Los Ojos CDP	125	-	-	52	0.0	0.0	0.0	0.0	100.0	0.0	51.9	0.0	48.1	51.9	27	100.0
Los Ranchos de Albuquerque village	6,068	6,108	0.7	6,114	53.1	0.6	0.2	2.7	43.4	19.9	30.4	53.9	23.8	44.1	2,498	93.9
Loving village	1,380	1,393	0.9	1,241	16.5	0.0	0.0	9.9	73.6	25.4	18.5	38.0	64.1	2.4	480	75.2
Lovington city	11,058	11,489	3.9	11,491	24.8	2.3	0.0	0.8	72.2	31.3	12.8	30.7	63.2	7.7	3,534	89.4
Lower Frisco CDP	31	-	-	-	-	-	-	-	-	-	-	-	-	-	-	-
Luis Lopez CDP	107	-	-	83	100.0	0.0	0.0	0.0	0.0	0.0	63.9	74.3	0.0	63.9	47	100.0
Lumberton CDP	73	-	-	116	3.4	1.7	0.0	0.0	94.8	79.3	1.7	4.6	75.0	16.7	7	100.0
Luna CDP	158	-	-	27	100.0	0.0	0.0	0.0	0.0	0.0	66.7	0.0	0.0	0.0	9	100.0
Lyden CDP	245	-	-	199	0.0	0.0	0.0	0.0	100.0	33.7	49.2	27.9	89.4	0.0	60	23.3
McCartys Village CDP	48	-	-	103	6.8	0.0	0.0	82.5	10.7	33.0	29.1	37.1	31.9	26.1	19	100.0
McIntosh CDP	1,484	-	-	939	63.2	0.0	0.0	0.0	36.8	12.0	31.1	50.5	40.8	10.4	413	77.0
Madrid CDP	204	-	-	218	100.0	0.0	0.0	0.0	0.0	15.1	48.2	53.9	18.9	39.5	109	89.0
Madrone CDP	707	-	-	590	34.2	0.0	0.0	0.0	65.8	23.9	14.9	48.9	71.1	4.4	231	76.2
Magdalena village	940	878	-6.6	653	48.9	0.0	0.0	6.0	45.2	26.3	18.2	47.0	42.7	27.2	194	60.3
Malaga CDP	147	-	-	114	0.0	0.0	0.0	0.0	100.0	12.3	0.0	47.1	75.0	0.0	42	100.0
Manzano CDP	29	-	-	-	-	-	-	-	-	-	-	-	-	-	-	-
Manzano Springs CDP	137	-	-	311	60.5	0.0	0.0	0.0	39.5	42.1	5.8	32.3	19.4	29.4	95	100.0
Maxwell village	243	212	-12.8	312	22.8	0.0	0.0	4.2	73.1	38.1	13.1	28.5	37.4	24.5	111	73.0
Mayhill CDP	75	-	-	56	92.9	0.0	0.0	0.0	7.1	0.0	0.0	42.5	92.5	3.8	25	100.0
Meadow Lake CDP	4,708	-	-	3,832	19.8	0.0	0.0	2.9	77.3	28.5	10.9	37.4	61.5	6.4	1,317	75.2
Melrose village	653	629	-3.7	600	87.2	0.0	0.0	0.7	12.2	17.7	24.8	52.9	47.1	9.7	277	87.7
Mescalero CDP	1,338	-	-	1,244	2.8	0.1	0.0	88.8	8.3	22.7	12.1	35.5	52.1	10.0	394	72.1
Mesilla town	1,904	1,828	-4.0	2,280	33.4	0.0	0.2	1.7	64.7	17.0	20.9	42.4	38.2	44.7	967	84.3
Mesita CDP	804	-	-	825	1.3	0.0	0.0	94.5	4.1	24.0	12.6	33.3	39.5	6.0	193	70.5
Mesquite CDP	1,112	-	-	408	21.6	0.0	0.0	16.9	61.5	31.9	40.7	42.5	57.2	36.0	160	56.3
Middle Frisco CDP	77	-	-	27	0.0	0.0	0.0	0.3	100.0	0.0	100.0	72.3	100.0	0.0	18	0.0
Midway CDP	971	-	-	861	31.8	0.0	0.0	0.3	67.8	23.6	16.0	38.9	57.2	6.5	291	85.9
Milan village	3,616	3,669	1.5	3,660	18.4	0.5	0.0	12.7	68.5	26.1	6.2	33.4	48.2	16.0	1,233	92.1
Mimbres CDP	667	-	-	572	74.7	0.0	0.0	1.6	23.8	0.0	62.6	67.3	37.9	30.4	328	81.1
Monterey Park CDP	1,567	-	-	1,600	0.0	0.0	0.0	1.4	98.6	38.9	4.6	24.1	86.9	0.0	340	50.9
Monument CDP	206	-	-	134	73.9	0.0	0.0	0.0	26.1	23.9	9.0	39.0	50.0	17.9	45	100.0
Moquino CDP	37	-	-	58	0.0	0.0	0.0	0.0	100.0	0.0	100.0	0.0	100.0	0.0	33	100.0
Mora CDP	656	-	-	807	1.9	0.0	0.0	15.4	82.8	9.5	9.4	25.9	27.2	0.0	178	60.1
Moriarty city	1,985	1,860	-6.3	2,223	33.9	0.4	0.0	3.1	62.6	24.1	16.5	35.2	64.8	8.7	823	91.3
Morningside CDP	367	-	-	787	3.8	0.0	0.0	0.0	96.2	51.5	0.0	17.6	37.2	15.2	195	82.1
Mosquero village	93	85	-8.6	55	67.3	0.0	0.0	0.0	32.7	30.9	32.7	51.8	52.6	15.8	24	54.2
Mountainair town	938	873	-6.9	852	56.6	0.0	1.1	0.0	42.4	15.0	27.6	49.0	43.7	22.4	353	75.4
Mountain View CDP	122	-	-	125	64.0	0.0	0.0	0.0	36.0	0.0	48.0	60.9	90.4	0.0	64	78.1
Nadine CDP	376	-	-	294	49.0	0.0	0.0	0.0	51.0	11.9	21.1	48.0	49.6	12.6	131	96.2
Nageezi CDP	286	-	-	183	1.6	0.0	0.0	90.7	7.7	29.0	21.3	36.6	63.0	0.0	65	58.5
Nakaibito CDP	466	-	-	297	0.0	0.0	0.0	100.0	0.0	22.6	13.8	41.5	60.1	3.8	103	48.5
Nambe CDP	1,818	-	-	1,820	17.4	0.2	0.0	25.2	57.1	18.6	21.9	47.7	40.7	24.3	751	69.8
Napi Headquarters CDP	727	-	-	728	0.4	1.0	0.0	98.6	0.0	29.0	8.0	26.8	61.9	2.3	160	71.3
Nara Visa CDP	95	-	-	44	100.0	0.0	0.0	0.0	0.0	0.0	31.8	62.7	31.8	0.0	32	56.3
Naschitti CDP	301	-	-	383	1.3	0.0	0.0	96.1	2.6	18.5	19.8	43.3	50.8	14.4	91	44.0
Navajo CDP	1,645	-	-	1,450	0.9	0.1	0.2	95.7	3.1	43.2	5.6	21.7	61.0	3.8	402	46.3
Navajo Dam CDP	281	-	-	266	62.8	0.0	0.0	8.3	28.9	12.4	22.6	52.3	22.2	40.7	112	100.0
Nenahnezad CDP	688	-	-	644	0.6	1.2	0.0	91.6	6.5	31.4	12.3	32.0	54.3	8.4	157	66.2
Newcomb CDP	339	-	-	359	5.8	0.0	7.5	79.7	7.0	24.8	13.1	37.2	44.3	23.3	128	46.9
Newkirk CDP	7	-	-	-	-	-	-	-	-	-	-	-	-	-	-	-
Nogal CDP	96	-	-	140	75.7	0.0	0.0	22.1	2.1	15.0	23.6	56.2	38.8	14.3	52	61.5
North Acomita Village CDP	303	-	-	273	2.6	17.2	0.0	78.8	1.5	22.3	15.0	43.1	45.1	8.7	87	56.3
North Hobbs CDP	5,391	-	-	6,301	54.2	0.2	0.5	1.2	43.9	25.3	11.5	37.5	54.0	17.2	2,302	90.7

1 May be of any race.

NM(Laguna CDP)—NM(North Hobbs CDP) 281

STATE City, town, township, borough, or CDP (county if applicable)	Population: 2010 census total population	Population: 2019 estimated population	Population: Percent change 2010–2019	Population: ACS total population estimate 2015–2019	Race and Hispanic or Latino origin (percent): White alone, not Hispanic or Latino	Race and Hispanic or Latino origin (percent): Black alone, not Hispanic or Latino	Race and Hispanic or Latino origin (percent): Asian alone, not Hispanic or Latino	Race and Hispanic or Latino origin (percent): All other races or 2 or more races, not Hispanic or Latino	Race and Hispanic or Latino origin (percent): Hispanic or Latino[1]	Age (percent): Under 18 years old	Age (percent): Age 65 years and older	Age (percent): Median age	Educational attainment of persons age 25 and older: Percent High school diploma or less	Educational attainment of persons age 25 and older: Percent Bachelor's degree or more	Occupied housing units: Total	Occupied housing units: Percent with a computer
	1	2	3	4	5	6	7	8	9	10	11	12	13	14	15	16
NEW MEXICO—Con.																
North Hurley CDP	300	-	-	98	51.0	0.0	0.0	0.0	49.0	9.2	9.2	57.1	6.7	28.1	50	60.0
North Light Plant CDP	414	-	-	296	68.6	0.0	0.0	0.0	31.4	26.0	0.0	35.4	58.9	10.5	113	82.3
North San Ysidro CDP	159	-	-	51	100.0	0.0	0.0	0.0	0.0	0.0	0.0	0.0	0.0	100.0	24	100.0
North Valley CDP	11,333	-	-	13,449	32.7	2.1	0.6	1.0	63.6	16.9	19.7	45.2	44.0	27.8	4,969	82.7
Oasis CDP	149	-	-	67	67.2	0.0	0.0	32.8	0.0	10.4	10.4	62.3	68.3	31.7	56	32.1
Ohkay Owingeh CDP	1,143	-	-	1,256	2.4	1.1	0.2	69.7	26.7	21.3	13.1	38.3	45.8	12.2	292	55.1
Ojo Amarillo CDP	766	-	-	637	0.0	0.0	0.0	93.7	6.3	35.0	10.2	28.0	49.4	7.2	182	70.3
Organ CDP	323	-	-	210	89.0	0.0	0.0	0.0	11.0	0.0	3.8	34.4	0.0	15.6	119	80.7
Orogrande CDP	52	-	-	41	100.0	0.0	0.0	0.0	0.0	0.0	85.4	68.8	85.4	0.0	24	0.0
Paguate CDP	421	-	-	379	0.0	0.0	0.0	97.9	2.1	12.9	17.7	52.1	49.5	16.6	117	56.4
Pajarito Mesa CDP	579	-	-	266	0.0	0.0	0.0	0.0	100.0	30.1	7.5	22.7	79.0	0.0	74	100.0
Paradise Hills CDP	4,256	-	-	4,656	54.0	0.7	1.2	3.5	40.6	23.3	19.1	42.4	28.4	33.7	1,905	93.0
Paraje CDP	777	-	-	903	3.5	0.0	0.0	95.6	0.9	18.1	21.9	43.3	51.9	13.8	233	77.7
Pastura CDP	23	-	-	5	0.0	0.0	0.0	0.0	100.0	0.0	100.0	0.0	100.0	0.0	2	0.0
Peak Place CDP	377	-	-	409	4.4	0.0	0.7	10.3	84.6	35.9	5.6	26.7	69.5	7.3	127	63.0
Pecan Park CDP	75	-	-	-	-	-	-	-	-	-	-	-	-	-	-	-
Pecos village	1,398	1,320	-5.6	1,468	8.5	0.0	0.0	0.5	90.9	19.2	16.6	45.5	63.7	4.5	699	56.7
Peña Blanca CDP	709	-	-	731	21.5	0.0	0.0	21.3	57.2	34.7	6.6	29.4	58.1	7.4	223	68.6
Peñasco CDP	589	-	-	667	8.5	0.0	0.1	3.7	87.6	22.9	19.3	40.7	51.5	16.1	226	73.9
Peralta town	3,652	3,584	-1.9	3,576	40.0	0.0	3.2	0.0	56.8	19.2	16.9	45.0	45.3	17.9	1,261	87.7
Picuris Pueblo CDP	68	-	-	113	0.0	0.0	0.0	100.0	0.0	14.2	30.1	51.3	47.4	18.6	37	45.9
Pie Town CDP	186	-	-	111	100.0	0.0	0.0	0.0	0.0	7.2	28.8	57.1	9.7	35.0	50	84.0
Pinehill CDP	88	-	-	69	0.0	0.0	0.0	95.7	4.3	10.1	37.7	56.8	53.4	0.0	26	57.7
Pinon CDP	25	-	-	-	-	-	-	-	-	-	-	-	-	-	-	-
Pinos Altos CDP	198	-	-	372	95.2	0.0	0.0	0.0	4.8	25.3	20.2	45.4	15.1	50.0	253	71.5
Placitas CDP	576	-	-	364	0.0	0.0	0.0	0.0	100.0	10.4	23.9	28.7	67.9	0.0	222	59.5
Placitas CDP	4,977	-	-	4,686	73.4	0.0	1.0	3.4	22.2	7.2	35.7	61.8	18.4	55.2	2,305	98.1
Playas CDP	74	-	-	54	59.3	14.8	0.0	0.0	25.9	0.0	0.0	21.0	0.0	0.0	0	0.0
Pleasanton CDP	106	-	-	450	96.9	0.0	0.0	0.0	3.1	22.7	24.7	36.9	46.0	18.4	148	91.9
Pojoaque CDP	1,907	-	-	2,027	13.7	0.3	0.4	22.6	63.0	23.8	12.6	37.0	44.4	21.2	816	69.5
Polvadera CDP	269	-	-	126	59.5	0.0	0.0	0.0	40.5	0.0	40.5	60.2	54.8	19.0	62	85.5
Ponderosa CDP	387	-	-	255	42.0	0.0	3.9	7.1	47.1	11.4	20.8	46.3	41.8	22.8	97	89.7
Ponderosa Pine CDP	1,195	-	-	1,159	65.6	0.0	9.2	7.5	17.7	7.9	18.1	58.9	9.3	58.0	539	98.5
Portales city	12,306	11,610	-5.7	11,854	45.8	3.6	0.6	3.8	46.2	24.8	12.6	26.3	44.9	26.8	4,115	87.7
Pueblito CDP	91	-	-	106	0.0	0.0	0.0	25.5	74.5	15.1	18.9	34.7	83.3	9.5	18	66.7
Pueblitos CDP	794	-	-	314	27.4	0.0	0.0	4.5	68.2	23.6	47.8	61.7	58.3	18.3	147	61.2
Pueblo CDP	-	-	-	-	-	-	-	-	-	-	-	-	-	-	-	-
Pueblo of Sandia Village CDP	369	-	-	422	0.9	0.0	0.0	86.3	12.8	27.3	12.1	32.7	45.3	10.6	133	74.4
Pueblo Pintado CDP	192	-	-	388	0.5	0.0	0.0	94.1	5.4	31.2	5.7	25.5	43.6	3.3	72	68.1
Puerto de Luna CDP	141	-	-	62	16.1	0.0	0.0	0.0	83.9	0.0	58.1	65.5	59.7	0.0	31	67.7
Pulpotio Bareas CDP	120	-	-	320	24.1	0.0	0.0	0.0	75.9	15.9	8.1	42.0	0.0	0.0	66	100.0
Quemado CDP	228	-	-	177	100.0	0.0	0.0	0.0	0.0	36.2	0.0	37.1	70.8	0.0	66	100.0
Questa village	1,775	1,755	-1.1	1,997	12.9	0.0	0.0	0.2	86.9	27.8	17.1	34.9	46.2	9.4	719	67.3
Radium Springs CDP	1,699	-	-	1,467	50.4	3.2	0.0	1.0	45.4	14.4	17.9	37.2	48.1	29.4	548	88.0
Ramah CDP	370	-	-	427	54.8	0.0	0.0	39.3	5.9	18.7	19.0	42.2	27.4	16.0	160	100.0
Rancho Grande CDP	142	-	-	-	-	-	-	-	-	-	-	-	-	-	-	-
Ranchos de Taos CDP	2,518	-	-	2,178	22.4	0.0	0.0	0.0	77.6	21.4	22.9	41.4	43.3	26.9	742	72.5
Raton city	6,876	5,938	-13.6	6,047	42.6	0.0	0.2	1.5	55.6	20.1	28.1	44.8	51.4	14.2	3,090	71.2
Red River town	477	463	-2.9	465	95.1	0.0	0.0	0.0	4.9	17.6	20.4	39.1	15.6	43.8	187	92.5
Regina CDP	105	-	-	69	27.5	0.0	0.0	36.2	36.2	15.9	18.8	40.9	81.0	0.0	20	60.0
Reserve village	292	277	-5.1	537	45.6	0.0	0.0	0.4	54.0	29.6	20.3	37.6	66.2	8.2	136	44.9
Ribera CDP	416	-	-	552	18.3	0.0	0.0	1.6	80.1	11.4	20.1	42.8	30.6	2.0	279	73.5
Rincon CDP	271	-	-	365	0.0	0.0	0.0	0.0	100.0	54.0	0.0	17.6	100.0	0.0	36	100.0
Rio Communities city	4,729	4,552	-3.7	4,568	48.0	2.2	0.6	2.6	46.6	22.1	26.1	47.8	44.0	13.8	1,904	80.4
Rio en Medio CDP	143	-	-	89	25.8	0.0	0.0	0.0	74.2	9.0	15.7	56.3	82.3	15.2	45	42.2
Rio Lucio CDP	389	-	-	424	5.4	0.0	0.0	0.0	94.6	15.8	21.9	50.0	61.9	10.9	123	57.7
Rio Rancho city	87,387	99,178	13.5	96,210	49.1	2.8	1.5	5.1	41.5	24.4	15.4	38.4	31.6	30.5	34,576	94.0
Rivers CDP	28	-	-	-	-	-	-	-	-	-	-	-	-	-	-	-
Rock Springs CDP	567	-	-	506	0.0	0.0	0.0	100.0	0.0	46.2	2.6	21.3	64.7	0.8	129	64.3
Rodeo CDP	101	-	-	71	60.6	0.0	0.0	0.0	39.4	0.0	76.1	76.1	59.2	15.5	45	100.0
Rodey CDP	388	-	-	594	30.3	0.0	0.0	0.0	69.7	32.8	11.6	37.1	82.0	0.0	141	50.4
Rosedale CDP	394	-	-	122	48.4	0.0	0.0	0.0	51.6	0.0	35.2	64.4	73.8	13.1	109	86.2
Roswell city	48,417	47,551	-1.8	47,941	36.5	1.6	1.2	2.4	58.3	26.5	15.6	34.9	48.0	18.8	17,506	81.5
Rowe CDP	415	-	-	319	12.2	0.0	0.0	0.0	87.8	5.3	57.1	65.3	64.2	8.3	142	48.6
Roy village	234	211	-9.8	188	29.8	0.0	0.0	0.0	70.2	6.9	38.3	57.0	53.3	9.2	95	40.0
Ruidoso village	8,043	7,901	-1.8	7,791	59.8	0.5	0.2	0.9	38.6	17.1	27.2	50.9	39.3	27.9	3,087	91.2
Ruidoso Downs city	2,776	2,574	-7.3	2,573	53.1	1.4	0.0	0.0	45.5	24.2	22.7	40.1	55.0	6.7	752	71.3
Sacramento CDP	58	-	-	86	86.0	0.0	4.7	0.0	9.3	27.9	0.0	28.3	34.0	66.0	30	100.0
Salem CDP	942	-	-	311	0.0	0.0	0.0	0.0	100.0	21.5	10.0	41.8	100.0	0.0	158	80.4
San Acacia CDP	44	-	-	72	100.0	0.0	0.0	0.0	0.0	0.0	15.3	61.4	75.0	4.2	16	100.0
San Antonio CDP	165	-	-	11	0.0	0.0	0.0	0.0	100.0	0.0	100.0	0.0	100.0	0.0	11	100.0
San Antonito CDP	985	-	-	1,150	84.5	0.0	0.0	0.0	15.5	33.6	27.9	39.0	6.2	73.0	469	96.6
San Antonito CDP	94	-	-	-	-	-	-	-	-	-	-	-	-	-	-	-
San Cristobal CDP	273	-	-	184	19.0	0.0	0.0	21.2	59.8	0.0	67.9	66.6	23.8	21.3	90	100.0
Sandia Heights CDP	3,193	-	-	3,571	77.3	3.7	2.9	4.8	11.2	13.1	44.0	62.6	5.0	79.5	1,593	98.7
Sandia Knolls CDP	1,208	-	-	1,475	80.3	0.0	0.0	2.6	17.1	21.6	17.2	46.1	29.7	37.9	525	97.9
Sandia Park CDP	237	-	-	236	87.3	0.0	8.5	0.0	4.2	6.4	27.1	60.9	3.2	54.3	109	100.0
San Felipe Pueblo CDP	2,404	-	-	2,217	0.3	0.0	0.0	95.4	4.4	33.2	8.6	30.5	68.9	7.0	419	43.7
San Fidel CDP	138	-	-	473	1.1	0.0	0.0	0.0	98.9	39.1	10.4	22.7	48.5	1.8	135	65.2
San Ildefonso Pueblo CDP	524	-	-	803	8.7	0.0	0.7	74.1	16.4	17.9	14.9	35.0	40.5	19.8	261	73.9
San Jon village	223	202	-9.4	263	55.5	0.0	0.0	18.6	25.9	27.4	17.9	43.0	52.0	14.3	79	58.2
San Jose CDP	695	-	-	680	16.3	0.0	0.0	0.0	83.7	22.9	18.5	37.5	48.4	4.7	221	76.0
San Jose CDP	137	-	-	172	37.8	0.0	0.0	0.0	62.2	18.6	20.3	48.2	40.7	59.3	64	100.0
San Lorenzo CDP	97	-	-	166	14.5	0.0	0.0	0.0	85.5	0.0	33.1	47.2	63.3	14.5	46	100.0
San Luis CDP	59	-	-	212	3.8	0.0	0.0	70.3	25.9	26.4	15.1	32.5	90.3	4.8	59	11.9
San Mateo CDP	161	-	-	346	61.3	0.0	0.0	0.0	38.7	27.7	26.0	43.9	43.7	36.9	73	60.3
San Miguel CDP	1,153	-	-	978	4.7	0.0	1.4	0.0	93.9	17.3	15.1	46.1	45.5	19.8	365	78.6
Sanostee CDP	371	-	-	500	0.0	0.0	0.0	100.0	0.0	25.4	11.6	30.5	68.4	4.4	143	45.5
San Pablo CDP	806	-	-	1,019	26.5	0.0	0.0	0.0	73.5	27.1	9.5	28.0	30.6	30.3	280	90.7
San Pedro CDP	184	-	-	137	100.0	0.0	0.0	0.0	0.0	17.5	51.8	65.4	0.0	46.9	71	100.0

1 May be of any race.

Table A. All Places — **Population and Housing**

STATE City, town, township, borough, or CDP (county if applicable)	Population				Race and Hispanic or Latino origin (percent)					Age (percent)			Educational attainment of persons age 25 and older		Occupied housing units	
	2010 census total population	2019 estimated population	Percent change 2010–2019	ACS total population estimate 2015–2019	White alone, not Hispanic or Latino	Black alone, not Hispanic or Latino	Asian alone, not Hispanic or Latino	All other races or 2 or more races, not Hispanic or Latino	Hispanic or Latino[1]	Under 18 years old	Age 65 years and older	Median age	Percent High school diploma or less	Percent Bachelor's degree or more	Total	Percent with a computer
	1	2	3	4	5	6	7	8	9	10	11	12	13	14	15	16
NEW MEXICO—Con.																
San Rafael CDP	933	-	-	1,413	11.8	0.0	0.0	0.0	88.2	19.8	4.7	35.3	65.0	7.9	367	100.0
Santa Ana Pueblo CDP	610	-	-	682	0.1	0.0	0.0	95.3	4.5	24.6	14.7	34.2	49.0	9.8	177	80.8
Santa Clara village	1,908	1,761	-7.7	1,766	21.8	7.1	0.0	1.6	69.5	23.0	32.4	46.7	61.8	11.7	585	62.2
Santa Clara Pueblo CDP	1,018	-	-	820	1.6	0.0	0.0	81.0	17.4	26.8	16.6	36.0	34.6	19.7	225	69.3
Santa Cruz CDP	368	-	-	249	7.2	0.0	0.0	1.2	91.6	20.1	15.3	28.5	67.0	1.6	113	62.8
Santa Fe city	80,871	84,683	4.7	83,922	40.0	1.1	1.1	2.6	55.2	18.9	22.6	44.1	33.8	41.7	35,327	89.0
Santa Rosa city	2,848	2,636	-7.4	3,379	21.7	0.7	0.3	7.6	69.6	20.9	17.2	37.8	63.2	7.2	871	60.5
Santa Teresa CDP	4,258	-	-	5,515	20.4	0.9	0.0	0.7	78.1	28.0	13.1	33.5	28.5	38.9	1,857	94.5
Santo Domingo Pueblo CDP	2,456	-	-	2,292	0.0	0.0	0.0	90.1	9.9	30.3	11.3	30.8	67.1	4.8	436	42.9
San Ysidro CDP	2,090	-	-	2,060	45.9	0.0	0.4	0.0	53.7	25.0	15.0	37.8	25.8	39.6	711	90.7
San Ysidro village	193	201	4.1	254	12.2	0.0	0.0	46.1	41.7	9.4	18.9	43.6	59.9	3.7	130	74.6
Sausal CDP	1,056	-	-	1,566	20.4	0.0	0.0	0.0	79.6	38.8	14.6	30.1	34.5	26.6	442	86.7
Seama CDP	465	-	-	368	0.0	0.0	0.0	100.0	0.0	30.7	16.0	36.2	49.6	0.0	107	73.8
Seboyeta CDP	179	-	-	169	0.0	0.0	0.0	17.2	82.8	0.0	28.4	57.3	77.5	22.5	102	36.3
Sedillo CDP	802	-	-	986	80.9	0.0	1.0	0.8	17.2	10.8	24.2	54.8	16.2	58.3	473	79.5
Sena CDP	129	-	-	-	-	-	-	-	-	-	-	-	-	-	-	-
Sheep Springs CDP	245	-	-	250	0.0	0.0	0.0	100.0	0.0	23.6	8.4	28.8	60.8	8.2	61	37.7
Shiprock CDP	8,295	-	-	9,020	1.7	0.2	0.8	94.5	2.8	28.1	10.6	33.0	47.1	11.9	2,351	66.3
Silver City town	10,301	9,386	-8.9	9,627	44.2	0.5	1.4	1.3	52.7	20.2	20.9	38.4	34.8	34.3	4,218	84.9
Skyline-Ganipa CDP	1,224	-	-	1,055	0.0	0.0	0.0	91.7	8.3	28.2	9.8	35.9	49.5	11.0	261	75.9
Socorro city	9,049	8,348	-7.7	8,460	33.7	1.1	6.3	7.4	51.4	24.8	14.9	30.1	42.4	28.4	2,512	73.4
Soham CDP	210	-	-	167	13.8	0.0	0.0	0.0	86.2	40.1	13.8	40.2	0.0	23.0	100	100.0
Sombrillo CDP	351	-	-	83	14.5	0.0	2.4	0.0	83.1	6.0	54.2	65.5	43.8	11.0	42	85.7
South Acomita Village CDP	105	-	-	37	0.0	0.0	0.0	100.0	0.0	0.0	37.8	60.9	59.5	13.5	22	22.7
South Valley CDP	40,976	-	-	40,080	16.6	0.7	0.4	2.3	80.0	22.4	17.6	40.9	59.2	14.0	14,256	81.8
Spencerville CDP	1,258	-	-	1,609	70.8	0.0	0.0	7.6	21.6	21.8	12.4	36.5	41.7	15.0	534	92.3
Springer town	1,043	906	-13.1	782	23.5	2.9	5.1	1.7	66.8	7.5	38.0	60.9	44.8	18.8	452	75.2
Sunland Park city	14,260	17,978	26.1	17,081	4.4	0.2	0.3	0.1	95.0	31.7	12.8	30.9	63.1	12.4	5,524	81.7
Sunshine CDP	420	-	-	328	74.1	16.5	0.0	0.0	9.5	24.7	27.1	49.0	36.8	18.8	143	83.2
Tajique CDP	130	-	-	266	29.7	0.0	0.0	0.0	70.3	49.2	17.3	23.1	24.4	29.1	56	100.0
Talpa CDP	778	-	-	934	19.5	0.0	0.0	0.0	80.5	9.1	24.6	53.9	36.3	34.2	419	83.5
Taos town	6,050	5,929	-2.0	5,967	51.4	0.2	0.3	8.9	39.2	17.2	29.6	50.8	29.7	35.4	2,693	85.2
Taos Pueblo CDP	1,135	-	-	1,425	6.4	1.5	0.0	82.8	9.3	15.8	17.3	44.8	43.5	9.1	405	62.5
Taos Ski Valley village	71	71	0.0	56	100.0	0.0	0.0	0.0	0.0	0.0	46.4	61.0	7.1	48.2	24	100.0
Tatum town	795	829	4.3	726	57.2	0.8	0.0	0.7	41.3	27.7	11.2	34.3	54.4	10.3	270	98.5
Tecolote CDP	298	-	-	149	24.2	0.0	0.0	0.0	75.8	35.6	24.8	39.1	47.9	8.3	47	63.8
Tecolotito CDP	232	-	-	254	0.0	0.0	0.0	2.0	98.0	36.6	24.2	60.0	61.2	15.7	101	70.3
Tesuque CDP	925	-	-	1,008	61.6	0.0	3.5	3.0	31.9	11.9	36.6	60.8	19.0	56.4	551	85.3
Tesuque Pueblo CDP	233	-	-	318	0.9	0.0	0.0	96.2	2.8	23.9	14.2	38.6	40.1	13.0	95	46.3
Texico city	1,109	1,067	-3.8	1,033	26.4	4.0	0.0	2.1	67.5	33.1	12.4	29.6	64.3	10.5	334	89.2
Thoreau CDP	1,865	-	-	1,641	5.9	0.4	0.1	57.0	36.7	39.4	10.7	25.9	60.4	4.3	513	60.4
Tierra Amarilla CDP	382	-	-	784	10.5	0.0	0.0	1.0	88.5	29.1	2.6	36.5	32.9	10.6	233	56.7
Tijeras village	529	535	1.1	610	43.4	0.0	0.0	2.1	54.4	20.0	14.3	44.5	36.1	25.1	253	98.8
Timberon CDP	348	-	-	275	88.7	0.0	0.0	0.0	11.3	0.0	78.2	71.0	21.5	21.1	197	57.9
Tohatchi CDP	808	-	-	741	4.9	0.9	1.5	89.9	2.8	32.5	17.0	36.1	45.0	15.3	221	65.2
Tome CDP	1,867	-	-	1,988	25.3	0.0	0.0	1.0	73.7	28.5	19.4	38.4	52.2	16.2	664	75.3
Torreon CDP	326	-	-	243	11.5	0.0	0.0	86.8	1.6	35.0	7.4	35.1	59.6	10.6	61	32.8
Torreon CDP	237	-	-	200	25.0	0.0	0.0	0.0	75.0	0.0	25.0	34.8	18.5	0.0	91	100.0
Trout Valley CDP	16	-	-	-	-	-	-	-	-	-	-	-	-	-	-	-
Truchas CDP	560	-	-	176	27.3	0.0	0.6	4.5	67.6	20.5	23.9	46.5	21.0	72.5	103	100.0
Truth or Consequences city	6,471	5,753	-11.1	5,894	63.5	0.7	1.4	5.1	29.4	17.5	29.5	51.5	47.0	19.8	2,949	77.1
Tse Bonito CDP	299	-	-	186	25.3	0.0	0.0	74.7	0.0	0.0	25.8	52.8	100.0	0.0	83	100.0
Tucumcari city	5,371	4,867	-9.4	4,919	28.6	2.7	0.6	2.4	65.7	25.7	20.8	38.0	60.1	11.7	1,654	66.3
Tularosa village	2,844	3,006	5.7	2,944	51.7	1.1	2.6	0.0	44.6	12.8	31.9	56.8	41.8	18.8	1,210	76.5
Twin Forks CDP	196	-	-	185	79.5	0.0	0.0	7.6	13.0	16.8	27.6	56.9	11.7	52.6	83	83.1
Twin Lakes CDP	1,052	-	-	1,117	1.4	0.0	0.0	97.4	1.2	24.6	12.9	38.6	67.4	7.3	284	53.2
Tyrone CDP	637	-	-	680	54.9	0.0	0.0	0.0	45.1	34.0	7.1	30.4	21.5	37.9	276	87.7
University Park CDP	4,192	-	-	2,945	36.3	3.5	1.6	6.8	51.8	4.8	0.0	19.6	0.0	30.9	311	100.0
Upper Fruitland CDP	1,662	-	-	1,686	1.7	0.0	0.0	97.2	1.1	21.4	17.7	39.0	65.5	5.7	503	63.6
Ute Park CDP	71	-	-	205	69.8	0.0	0.0	0.0	30.2	0.0	0.0	42.0	63.4	0.0	57	100.0
Vadito CDP	270	-	-	315	4.1	0.0	0.0	1.0	94.9	21.0	20.0	40.5	57.6	6.9	101	73.3
Vado CDP	3,194	-	-	3,099	0.0	0.0	0.0	1.4	98.6	33.2	8.1	29.8	78.1	6.1	846	74.5
Valencia CDP	2,192	-	-	2,018	40.3	0.0	0.0	2.8	56.9	15.7	15.8	52.7	41.5	24.8	885	86.1
Vaughn town	446	397	-11.0	300	21.3	0.0	0.0	0.0	78.7	23.0	39.3	57.1	81.2	6.7	138	54.3
Veguita CDP	232	-	-	73	19.2	0.0	0.0	0.0	80.8	0.0	80.8	65.8	38.4	0.0	42	33.3
Velarde CDP	502	-	-	302	0.0	0.0	0.0	0.0	100.0	17.5	0.0	35.5	27.7	40.6	131	68.7
Ventura CDP	468	-	-	714	22.7	0.0	0.0	11.8	65.5	23.1	6.9	41.6	68.6	16.1	320	59.4
Villanueva CDP	229	-	-	309	0.0	0.0	0.0	0.0	100.0	23.0	32.4	31.5	62.2	21.4	77	50.6
Virden village	149	129	-13.4	127	81.9	7.1	0.0	0.0	11.0	28.3	29.9	49.1	13.2	35.2	54	85.2
Wagon Mound village	311	287	-7.7	268	9.7	0.0	0.0	0.0	90.3	16.4	26.9	53.5	52.6	18.0	100	59.0
Waterflow CDP	1,670	-	-	1,623	38.0	3.3	0.0	50.4	8.3	25.0	12.1	36.8	37.1	15.5	514	94.7
Watrous CDP	135	-	-	123	0.0	0.0	0.0	0.0	100.0	35.8	30.9	51.4	20.3	0.0	28	0.0
Weed CDP	63	-	-	31	100.0	0.0	0.0	0.0	0.0	0.0	0.0	100.0	100.0	0.0	16	0.0
West Hammond CDP	2,790	-	-	2,777	53.1	0.0	0.1	6.7	40.1	24.4	13.4	41.1	58.5	9.0	1,024	90.5
White Rock CDP	5,725	-	-	5,751	76.1	0.4	1.6	5.4	16.4	24.8	20.0	46.1	9.0	66.0	2,247	95.8
White Sands CDP	1,651	-	-	1,246	48.5	22.6	4.3	1.9	22.7	31.4	1.9	23.9	18.7	34.6	276	100.0
Whites City CDP	7	-	-	85	100.0	0.0	0.0	0.0	0.0	0.0	0.0	100.0	100.0	0.0	38	100.0
White Signal CDP	181	-	-	244	70.9	0.0	0.0	0.0	29.1	17.6	24.2	56.2	17.9	47.4	118	89.8
Willard village	256	242	-5.5	225	20.0	0.0	0.0	0.0	80.0	23.1	12.9	29.0	79.1	6.5	46	76.1
Williamsburg village	450	408	-9.3	465	66.7	1.1	0.0	1.3	31.0	12.0	24.7	50.4	48.6	10.9	191	70.7
Windmill CDP	43	-	-	93	91.4	0.0	0.0	0.0	8.6	30.1	12.9	50.2	46.2	10.8	45	100.0
Winston CDP	61	-	-	72	100.0	0.0	0.0	0.0	0.0	0.0	100.0	67.8	75.0	0.0	46	34.8
Yah-ta-hey CDP	590	-	-	548	4.9	0.0	0.0	95.1	0.0	22.1	12.2	22.5	43.6	10.2	149	76.5
Young Place CDP	187	-	-	240	76.7	0.0	0.0	0.0	23.3	39.2	12.5	34.4	78.8	0.0	107	43.0
Youngsville CDP	56	-	-	44	40.9	0.0	0.0	0.0	59.1	0.0	15.9	57.3	59.1	0.0	24	37.5
Zia Pueblo CDP	737	-	-	939	0.2	0.0	0.0	95.3	4.5	39.4	6.9	27.7	54.8	6.2	222	63.5
Zuni Pueblo CDP	6,302	-	-	7,001	0.4	0.0	0.1	98.3	1.2	27.1	11.2	35.1	61.8	4.6	1,472	66.8

1 May be of any race.

Table A. All Places — **Population and Housing**

STATE City, town, township, borough, or CDP (county if applicable)	Population: 2010 census total population	Population: 2019 estimated population	Population: Percent change 2010–2019	Population: ACS total population estimate 2015–2019	Race and Hispanic or Latino origin (percent): White alone, not Hispanic or Latino	Black alone, not Hispanic or Latino	Asian alone, not Hispanic or Latino	All other races or 2 or more races, not Hispanic or Latino	Hispanic or Latino[1]	Age (percent): Under 18 years old	Age 65 years and older	Median age	Educational attainment of persons age 25 and older: Percent High school diploma or less	Percent Bachelor's degree or more	Occupied housing units: Total	Percent with a computer
	1	2	3	4	5	6	7	8	9	10	11	12	13	14	15	16
NEW YORK	19,378,144	19,453,561	0.4	19,572,319	55.6	14.3	8.3	2.8	19.0	21.0	16.1	38.8	39.2	36.6	7,343,234	89.6
Accord CDP	562	-	-	560	85.5	3.2	10.9	0.2	0.2	15.2	22.3	48.3	53.2	33.4	214	93.5
Adams village	1,785	1,714	-4.0	1,966	90.5	0.0	0.5	3.4	5.6	35.4	12.1	31.8	40.6	25.9	718	91.2
Adams town (Jefferson)	5,145	4,928	-4.2	5,068	95.6	0.0	0.2	1.7	2.5	28.5	16.5	36.7	42.2	24.2	1,992	93.5
Adams Center CDP	1,568	-	-	1,385	97.8	0.1	0.0	0.9	1.1	23.6	23.3	38.9	46.8	20.0	564	97.9
Addison village	1,763	1,652	-6.3	1,823	96.2	1.1	0.2	0.7	1.9	28.4	12.5	33.9	46.0	15.7	669	88.2
Addison town (Steuben)	2,605	2,472	-5.1	2,617	97.1	0.8	0.1	0.5	1.6	25.9	16.4	36.7	51.3	16.3	997	85.4
Afton village	835	799	-4.3	933	93.5	0.6	0.6	1.9	3.3	20.4	25.1	46.3	53.5	15.4	434	80.2
Afton town (Chenango)	2,852	2,718	-4.7	2,737	96.7	1.3	0.2	0.7	1.1	13.6	24.7	50.9	59.3	14.0	1,260	90.4
Airmont village	8,625	8,786	1.9	8,770	77.6	2.9	4.7	1.5	13.4	30.1	17.9	33.8	37.2	38.3	2,551	95.6
Akron village	2,894	2,856	-1.3	2,871	95.8	0.0	0.6	2.0	1.7	24.3	19.6	38.9	35.0	28.4	1,231	88.3
Alabama town (Genesee)	1,860	1,736	-6.7	1,864	95.0	1.6	0.0	2.1	1.3	18.2	11.3	41.7	52.8	10.7	708	90.5
Albany city & MCD (Albany)	97,845	96,460	-1.4	97,478	50.3	26.9	6.9	5.8	10.1	17.7	12.9	30.9	35.1	39.6	41,255	88.4
Albertson CDP	5,182	-	-	5,225	64.3	0.0	23.4	3.3	9.0	20.7	21.7	45.6	27.1	55.4	1,813	92.2
Albion village	6,077	5,735	-5.6	5,479	78.3	11.7	0.0	5.4	4.6	23.9	19.3	39.1	60.0	10.4	2,440	82.3
Albion town (Orleans)	8,476	7,982	-5.8	8,200	73.0	16.9	0.3	3.7	6.1	16.1	14.3	37.7	60.2	11.6	2,625	82.1
Albion town (Oswego)	2,081	2,287	9.9	2,300	96.2	0.2	0.3	2.2	1.2	27.9	11.6	36.4	62.5	9.4	815	90.8
Alden village	2,605	2,569	-1.4	2,577	95.9	1.0	0.0	2.2	0.9	19.9	17.5	42.5	38.2	25.8	1,163	88.9
Alden town (Erie)	10,875	9,918	-8.8	9,995	84.7	10.8	0.7	1.2	2.7	18.8	17.0	41.1	44.2	23.7	3,293	90.8
Alexander village	509	493	-3.1	524	95.0	0.8	0.0	2.7	1.5	28.8	14.7	38.6	37.8	25.0	195	86.7
Alexander town (Genesee)	2,541	2,428	-4.4	2,474	98.1	0.2	0.0	1.3	0.5	22.6	17.5	43.1	49.6	17.9	971	89.6
Alexandria town (Jefferson)	4,060	3,896	-4.0	3,982	97.6	1.2	0.2	0.3	0.7	24.3	18.4	43.6	45.6	23.3	1,578	87.6
Alexandria Bay village	1,075	1,028	-4.4	927	94.0	4.0	0.9	0.5	0.6	14.0	24.4	52.2	42.9	24.7	490	85.3
Alfred village	4,182	3,991	-4.6	4,293	76.4	8.1	5.6	2.1	7.8	2.7	2.4	20.1	6.0	72.9	385	94.0
Alfred town (Allegany)	5,238	4,985	-4.8	5,035	79.7	6.9	4.8	1.8	6.7	6.0	4.5	20.3	18.8	56.5	693	92.6
Allegany village	1,805	1,696	-6.0	1,865	91.6	1.8	1.6	2.0	2.9	18.8	16.6	37.5	29.5	41.8	798	93.1
Allegany town (Cattaraugus)	7,994	7,547	-5.6	7,612	90.9	2.1	2.1	2.3	2.6	15.3	20.1	39.2	35.7	29.4	2,769	90.3
Allegany Reservation (Cattaraugus)	1,002	1,023	2.1	823	27.6	2.4	2.2	67.8	0.0	23.2	15.1	41.1	69.6	7.1	331	77.9
Allen town (Allegany)	446	428	-4.0	490	92.9	0.0	1.8	2.9	2.4	21.8	15.1	46.6	50.1	12.6	202	81.2
Alma town (Allegany)	835	830	-0.6	619	96.3	0.0	0.8	2.9	0.0	17.9	19.5	48.8	43.8	15.7	281	85.1
Almond village	463	430	-7.1	433	93.1	0.2	4.4	2.3	0.0	26.1	18.9	43.3	31.2	28.1	170	91.2
Almond town (Allegany)	1,631	1,529	-6.3	1,601	94.7	0.2	3.2	1.4	0.5	24.4	16.6	42.8	33.8	31.1	657	92.8
Altamont village	1,718	1,669	-2.9	1,665	89.0	0.8	4.8	1.7	3.7	22.8	21.9	44.4	25.3	53.6	683	87.8
Altmar CDP	407	-	-	406	97.5	0.2	0.2	0.0	2.0	37.9	8.1	27.9	81.0	5.6	129	90.7
Altona CDP	730	-	-	729	46.4	30.6	1.6	2.3	19.1	5.3	1.1	37.9	74.3	4.8	101	65.3
Altona town (Clinton)	2,890	2,926	1.2	2,910	82.0	7.7	0.7	3.8	5.7	21.1	12.5	40.8	61.8	13.7	929	78.8
Amagansett CDP	1,165	-	-	739	90.0	0.0	0.0	0.4	9.6	7.3	43.6	60.9	33.9	46.8	359	79.4
Amboy town (Oswego)	1,264	1,311	3.7	1,110	97.7	0.2	0.3	1.9	0.0	15.0	21.0	48.7	70.2	6.7	472	80.9
Amenia CDP	955	-	-	1,074	74.5	4.5	0.0	5.3	15.7	26.4	21.4	43.3	57.6	19.2	390	83.1
Amenia town (Dutchess)	4,452	4,399	-1.2	4,303	76.0	2.9	0.9	2.1	18.2	23.0	19.1	40.8	57.9	22.0	1,593	85.5
Ames village	145	139	-4.1	185	95.1	0.0	0.0	2.2	2.7	20.0	14.1	35.6	40.9	19.7	68	91.2
Amherst town (Erie)	122,376	126,082	3.0	125,509	78.0	6.2	9.2	2.7	3.9	19.4	20.3	40.5	19.9	55.8	50,842	91.1
Amity town (Allegany)	2,308	2,132	-7.6	2,127	89.0	5.6	1.1	1.8	2.4	20.1	19.7	42.3	53.0	19.3	888	84.3
Amityville village	9,500	9,399	-1.1	9,443	70.6	14.1	0.9	0.5	13.9	20.7	19.9	46.9	33.2	36.2	3,413	94.0
Amsterdam city & MCD (Montgomery)	18,606	17,766	-4.5	17,836	61.5	4.2	0.8	2.3	31.1	24.0	17.3	36.9	49.3	16.4	7,367	82.9
Amsterdam town (Montgomery)	5,567	5,997	7.7	5,990	94.3	1.1	0.0	0.3	4.3	13.5	27.7	52.8	38.9	24.9	2,797	87.6
Ancram town (Columbia)	1,589	1,491	-6.2	1,250	89.0	1.8	1.1	2.0	6.1	14.8	25.6	53.5	45.8	36.2	566	91.2
Andes CDP	252	-	-	243	99.2	0.0	0.0	0.8	0.0	8.2	29.6	49.5	25.1	39.6	106	80.2
Andes town (Delaware)	1,301	1,193	-8.3	1,042	93.3	0.0	1.0	3.6	2.2	8.9	39.3	59.8	35.3	35.4	525	78.5
Andover village	1,041	977	-6.1	854	99.6	0.0	0.0	0.0	0.4	24.2	16.3	42.8	44.5	16.7	376	85.9
Andover town (Allegany)	1,832	1,721	-6.1	1,639	99.7	0.0	0.0	0.0	0.3	21.2	18.7	47.9	46.2	17.8	729	83.8
Angelica village	869	818	-5.9	751	97.3	0.5	0.0	0.8	1.3	22.6	24.5	43.7	51.0	18.2	325	88.3
Angelica town (Allegany)	1,401	1,339	-4.4	1,236	96.6	0.3	1.8	0.5	0.8	24.0	23.0	45.7	50.9	19.1	519	89.2
Angola village	2,136	2,101	-1.6	2,373	89.0	1.9	0.0	3.9	5.1	26.2	16.4	34.8	41.7	25.0	906	84.8
Angola on the Lake CDP	1,675	-	-	1,692	93.0	0.2	0.0	5.4	1.4	16.5	27.4	50.1	43.0	18.4	719	89.6
Annsville town (Oneida)	3,014	2,940	-2.5	2,954	95.8	0.6	0.6	1.9	1.1	25.8	13.9	38.2	56.5	10.4	1,086	83.1
Antwerp village	680	653	-4.0	580	95.9	0.3	0.0	0.9	2.9	30.2	14.5	39.7	45.6	9.7	214	90.7
Antwerp town (Jefferson)	1,839	1,768	-3.9	1,805	94.4	0.1	0.0	3.0	2.4	28.9	13.6	37.4	53.7	10.1	640	90.2
Apalachin CDP	1,131	-	-	1,037	99.8	0.2	0.0	0.0	0.0	12.4	23.6	49.4	50.6	23.5	495	87.3
Aquebogue CDP	2,438	-	-	2,042	82.9	6.4	0.0	0.0	10.7	22.3	16.0	45.8	36.3	37.5	829	98.1
Arcade village	2,068	1,933	-6.5	2,170	94.3	0.0	2.4	1.7	1.6	25.4	18.0	39.3	50.7	18.4	981	85.8
Arcade town (Wyoming)	4,210	4,097	-2.7	4,118	91.7	1.9	1.3	0.9	4.2	22.9	17.9	41.7	51.7	16.7	1,834	84.0
Arcadia town (Wayne)	14,252	13,536	-5.0	13,649	85.4	4.0	1.2	3.6	5.8	20.7	21.5	45.2	45.9	19.5	5,752	85.1
Ardsley village	4,379	4,502	2.8	4,512	69.7	3.2	13.1	5.4	8.6	23.4	21.9	47.4	20.6	65.7	1,601	89.8
Argyle village	302	292	-3.3	469	89.8	1.7	0.0	6.2	2.3	22.4	23.9	42.1	51.5	26.1	190	73.2
Argyle town (Washington)	3,776	3,664	-3.0	3,688	97.5	0.2	0.2	1.2	0.8	16.3	23.2	49.3	47.2	19.0	1,480	81.6
Arietta town (Hamilton)	304	274	-9.9	146	98.6	0.0	0.0	1.4	0.0	13.0	24.0	51.3	34.2	31.5	55	98.2
Arkport village	845	791	-6.4	867	96.2	0.2	0.5	3.1	0.0	26.6	12.3	34.6	30.8	31.3	364	89.3
Arkwright town (Chautauqua)	1,058	1,036	-2.1	1,082	90.6	0.0	0.8	1.0	7.6	18.1	16.8	46.6	45.3	32.4	448	89.5
Arlington CDP	4,061	-	-	3,674	46.5	20.4	7.5	7.8	17.7	16.3	9.5	25.3	35.3	39.4	1,153	90.5
Armonk CDP	4,330	-	-	4,438	81.0	0.0	5.5	2.4	11.1	27.1	13.6	44.1	8.4	80.1	1,492	94.5
Asharoken village	657	646	-1.7	440	92.5	0.7	1.8	1.6	3.4	14.1	32.7	57.6	10.6	68.3	187	94.7
Ashford town (Cattaraugus)	2,138	2,031	-5.0	2,192	90.3	0.7	0.0	6.9	2.1	21.0	22.4	39.7	43.7	20.4	869	92.4
Ashland town (Chemung)	1,689	1,582	-6.3	1,472	96.7	0.6	0.0	1.6	1.1	21.0	23.6	46.1	57.2	12.1	580	83.1
Ashland town (Greene)	779	745	-4.4	752	94.3	0.5	2.8	0.0	2.4	13.4	29.0	50.4	42.4	28.3	296	81.8
Athens village	1,675	1,598	-4.6	1,604	88.2	2.7	7.0	1.1	1.1	10.4	22.6	50.4	39.4	22.7	696	89.7
Athens town (Greene)	4,094	3,941	-3.7	3,949	88.4	1.4	3.1	0.6	6.5	14.4	25.7	50.5	47.1	20.2	1,585	87.3
Atlantic Beach village	1,888	1,902	0.7	1,317	88.7	2.0	1.6	3.3	4.4	18.1	29.8	55.0	19.5	54.9	567	98.1
Attica village	2,537	2,404	-5.2	3,196	93.6	0.0	0.0	3.4	3.0	23.2	13.1	34.8	38.2	21.8	1,332	92.2
Attica town (Wyoming)	7,713	6,886	-10.7	7,117	71.8	16.8	0.1	2.0	9.1	15.6	10.7	37.2	54.0	14.4	1,891	90.3
Auburn city & MCD (Cayuga)	27,690	26,173	-5.5	26,601	81.5	9.0	0.8	4.3	4.3	18.9	17.8	39.0	44.3	20.7	11,508	85.6

1 May be of any race.

Table A. All Places — **Population and Housing**

STATE City, town, township, borough, or CDP (county if applicable)	Population: 2010 census total population	Population: 2019 estimated population	Population: Percent change 2010–2019	Population: ACS total population estimate 2015–2019	Race and Hispanic or Latino origin (percent): White alone, not Hispanic or Latino	Black alone, not Hispanic or Latino	Asian alone, not Hispanic or Latino	All other races or 2 or more races, not Hispanic or Latino	Hispanic or Latino[1]	Age (percent): Under 18 years old	Age 65 years and older	Median age	Educational attainment of persons age 25 and older: Percent High school diploma or less	Percent Bachelor's degree or more	Occupied housing units: Total	Percent with a computer
	1	2	3	4	5	6	7	8	9	10	11	12	13	14	15	16
NEW YORK—Con.																
Augusta town (Oneida)	2,010	2,039	1.4	2,546	94.9	2.7	0.7	0.8	0.9	25.0	19.0	41.6	48.5	19.9	939	83.5
Aurelius town (Cayuga)	2,792	2,649	-5.1	2,681	97.1	0.4	0.6	0.6	1.3	19.8	22.6	46.0	43.8	21.2	1,085	89.0
Aurora village	724	672	-7.2	661	74.9	3.2	2.0	3.6	16.3	4.5	14.7	21.6	18.9	59.4	128	89.8
Aurora town (Erie)	13,783	13,753	-0.2	13,783	97.1	0.6	0.5	1.2	0.6	19.9	20.5	47.4	23.6	47.1	5,466	93.2
Au Sable town (Clinton)	3,146	3,043	-3.3	3,060	95.2	0.9	0.0	1.4	2.5	24.4	16.0	40.8	51.0	14.2	1,192	83.6
Au Sable Forks CDP	559	-	-	424	100.0	0.0	0.0	0.0	0.0	21.0	24.5	48.0	67.4	5.9	179	81.6
Austerlitz town (Columbia)	1,663	1,581	-4.9	1,495	95.3	0.0	1.1	0.5	3.1	15.3	34.3	55.1	27.5	48.3	662	89.3
Ava town (Oneida)	676	708	4.7	683	90.2	0.6	2.9	3.5	2.8	23.6	17.1	41.5	53.9	14.9	259	79.9
Averill Park CDP	1,693	-	-	1,228	92.1	0.0	0.0	0.0	7.9	12.5	21.8	53.0	21.8	35.8	618	100.0
Avoca village	946	894	-5.5	951	96.2	0.6	0.0	2.3	0.8	20.5	19.8	43.3	51.6	19.2	351	89.7
Avoca town (Steuben)	2,263	2,143	-5.3	1,860	96.6	0.8	0.0	2.2	0.4	18.5	20.6	49.4	52.8	17.0	778	87.1
Avon village	3,380	3,282	-2.9	3,260	93.0	0.2	0.0	4.0	2.8	20.0	19.9	42.3	30.9	40.2	1,397	90.8
Avon town (Livingston)	7,141	6,860	-3.9	6,897	94.7	0.1	1.8	1.9	1.4	20.1	20.5	45.5	31.5	37.6	3,032	93.6
Babylon village	12,157	11,992	-1.4	12,056	88.9	0.6	2.2	1.7	6.6	19.3	15.8	41.3	22.3	53.7	4,395	92.5
Babylon town (Suffolk)	213,580	210,141	-1.6	211,207	55.3	16.3	3.6	2.6	22.2	21.3	15.0	40.0	43.7	28.2	65,994	93.2
Bainbridge village	1,368	1,303	-4.8	1,340	95.1	0.4	0.1	1.6	2.8	30.7	16.8	36.3	39.1	34.8	580	85.5
Bainbridge town (Chenango)	3,320	3,158	-4.9	3,176	95.5	0.2	0.1	1.8	2.5	28.7	21.7	39.3	48.2	25.5	1,302	87.4
Baiting Hollow CDP	1,642	-	-	1,731	88.0	1.1	1.0	2.5	7.3	18.8	31.2	56.1	26.2	47.8	684	96.3
Baldwin town (Chemung)	834	805	-3.5	850	98.9	0.0	0.0	0.7	0.4	18.8	26.8	51.8	62.5	9.2	377	78.2
Baldwin CDP	24,033	-	-	24,727	35.0	35.4	3.9	2.4	23.2	22.1	14.3	41.5	31.5	40.4	7,916	91.9
Baldwin Harbor CDP	8,102	-	-	7,623	41.6	29.3	4.3	4.4	20.4	17.9	14.6	44.5	24.5	45.2	2,512	95.7
Baldwinsville village	7,191	7,822	8.8	7,645	93.8	1.2	0.4	2.3	2.3	20.5	22.0	45.4	31.1	32.7	3,264	89.1
Ballston town (Saratoga)	9,757	11,464	17.5	10,975	90.9	0.1	3.2	1.7	4.0	22.5	18.7	44.6	28.5	46.9	4,252	93.7
Ballston Spa village	5,427	5,226	-3.7	5,399	93.0	0.1	2.3	1.3	3.3	20.8	20.2	39.7	33.5	33.4	2,265	88.3
Balmville CDP	3,178	-	-	3,476	55.8	20.9	0.5	0.8	22.0	20.7	14.9	43.3	40.7	27.5	1,321	90.1
Bangor town (Franklin)	2,221	2,260	1.8	2,238	91.8	0.0	0.3	4.4	3.5	24.0	14.0	38.4	53.9	15.8	843	89.4
Bardonia CDP	4,108	-	-	3,966	77.7	1.8	13.3	2.0	5.2	17.2	24.8	49.2	20.3	59.9	1,400	93.9
Barker town (Broome)	2,729	2,584	-5.3	2,631	95.5	0.8	0.5	2.9	0.2	20.2	17.8	48.7	55.4	16.7	1,024	89.8
Barker village	534	507	-5.1	582	94.8	0.0	0.0	1.7	3.4	28.7	17.0	37.0	50.5	16.1	224	87.5
Barneveld CDP	284	-	-	245	97.1	0.0	0.0	0.0	2.9	17.6	20.0	41.9	24.9	43.8	123	92.7
Barnum Island CDP	2,414	-	-	2,416	78.7	3.9	4.2	2.6	10.6	17.0	22.5	48.5	41.3	32.7	892	85.4
Barre town (Orleans)	2,018	1,875	-7.1	1,770	94.5	2.0	0.3	1.9	1.2	16.2	18.9	51.0	53.7	16.3	744	89.5
Barrington town (Yates)	1,661	1,663	0.1	1,749	99.1	0.3	0.2	0.3	0.0	25.9	29.4	47.5	58.8	23.2	644	77.2
Barton town (Tioga)	8,866	8,360	-5.7	8,455	95.5	0.9	0.5	1.6	1.5	24.4	17.5	40.2	54.6	15.6	3,346	88.5
Batavia city & MCD (Genesee)	15,390	14,379	-6.6	14,578	84.5	4.7	0.8	5.4	4.6	21.0	18.9	39.9	43.6	23.8	6,187	85.5
Batavia town (Genesee)	6,791	6,869	1.1	6,889	94.1	0.2	2.8	0.7	2.2	17.1	19.0	48.2	38.4	22.6	3,016	87.9
Bath village	5,789	5,472	-5.5	5,543	91.2	5.8	1.1	1.3	0.6	18.7	21.1	48.1	57.8	15.4	2,692	78.0
Bath town (Steuben)	12,378	11,929	-3.6	12,029	91.0	4.2	0.9	1.4	2.4	19.2	20.6	46.5	56.5	15.6	5,192	80.7
Baxter Estates village	1,047	1,049	0.2	1,031	75.3	1.2	7.1	1.1	15.4	21.6	21.2	45.4	19.1	66.5	432	97.2
Bay Park CDP	2,212	-	-	1,550	88.0	0.0	10.5	0.0	1.5	15.9	21.2	42.3	54.8	25.3	624	85.4
Bayport CDP	8,896	-	-	8,402	86.5	2.1	1.5	2.1	7.9	20.5	16.9	42.1	23.2	45.0	3,099	94.7
Bay Shore CDP	26,337	-	-	29,799	34.7	20.2	4.1	2.2	38.9	26.9	11.2	35.7	42.0	31.3	8,915	89.4
Bayville village	6,668	6,732	1.0	6,735	92.4	0.3	1.3	2.4	3.7	18.5	21.3	49.1	25.6	48.2	2,551	98.1
Baywood CDP	7,350	-	-	7,275	46.0	10.6	2.6	2.2	38.6	20.1	11.6	41.7	49.9	20.4	2,133	93.7
Beacon city & MCD (Dutchess)	13,806	13,968	1.2	13,634	62.2	13.2	2.1	3.8	18.7	20.3	13.6	40.5	35.1	33.5	5,259	92.3
Beaver Dam Lake CDP	-	-	-	1,827	86.5	8.0	0.0	3.7	1.8	13.4	21.7	51.8	24.1	47.5	661	97.3
Bedford CDP	1,834	-	-	1,705	91.3	0.5	4.6	0.6	3.0	18.5	20.3	45.5	13.4	76.8	581	100.0
Bedford town (Westchester)	17,436	17,651	1.2	17,803	73.1	4.0	3.3	2.4	17.1	22.8	14.6	41.1	23.0	62.4	5,878	94.0
Bedford Hills CDP	3,001	-	-	3,225	47.5	0.0	3.1	1.1	48.3	21.4	11.3	38.1	41.3	47.7	1,252	91.1
Beekman town (Dutchess)	14,743	14,387	-2.4	14,443	72.7	14.0	1.8	1.1	10.4	21.0	12.0	43.1	38.5	32.5	4,273	96.7
Beekmantown town (Clinton)	5,546	5,476	-1.3	5,475	96.9	0.4	0.6	0.1	2.1	20.0	17.6	43.3	41.2	29.0	2,336	92.0
Belfast CDP	837	-	-	771	97.3	0.3	0.0	2.5	0.0	28.1	13.9	36.7	51.1	21.1	309	86.4
Belfast town (Allegany)	1,665	1,575	-5.4	1,798	97.6	0.1	0.4	1.4	0.6	31.2	13.2	32.5	54.8	16.7	675	76.4
Bellerose village	1,166	1,162	-0.3	1,243	82.5	0.7	3.5	1.3	11.9	26.0	22.8	44.6	15.5	65.5	423	92.4
Bellerose Terrace CDP	2,198	-	-	2,056	22.3	1.4	43.0	9.2	24.1	22.1	8.5	42.2	48.0	34.0	533	97.6
Belle Terre village	790	786	-0.5	697	85.8	3.2	4.6	1.3	5.2	22.1	26.5	52.0	10.9	73.8	267	97.8
Belleville CDP	226	-	-	287	92.3	0.0	0.0	0.0	7.7	40.1	24.0	40.2	36.5	37.7	118	68.6
Bellmont town (Franklin)	1,431	1,409	-1.5	1,332	93.0	0.5	0.0	4.0	2.6	17.9	23.3	50.3	55.7	19.4	605	87.9
Bellmore CDP	16,218	-	-	15,368	86.8	1.3	3.3	1.4	7.3	20.3	18.3	45.5	25.0	53.9	5,331	94.7
Bellport village	2,085	2,047	-1.8	2,041	92.5	1.0	2.1	2.5	1.9	14.7	29.1	54.1	15.1	55.4	857	94.2
Belmont village	969	902	-6.9	813	97.8	1.6	0.0	0.0	0.6	24.7	17.5	40.1	44.9	26.2	366	84.7
Bemus Point village	367	347	-5.4	256	98.8	1.2	0.0	0.0	0.0	7.0	32.8	58.0	13.1	41.0	160	75.6
Bennington town (Wyoming)	3,357	3,221	-4.1	3,243	99.7	0.0	0.0	0.0	0.3	17.1	22.9	45.7	46.6	19.8	1,344	86.5
Benson town (Hamilton)	192	174	-9.4	361	96.7	0.0	0.0	0.0	3.3	26.9	24.9	40.7	30.6	38.7	88	83.0
Benton town (Yates)	2,827	2,750	-2.7	2,776	91.5	1.8	0.4	1.3	5.0	22.3	20.6	40.0	54.7	18.7	844	73.1
Bergen village	1,160	1,083	-6.6	1,135	90.6	1.5	1.7	1.9	4.3	21.6	14.3	36.1	34.3	31.7	432	89.8
Bergen town (Genesee)	3,104	2,938	-5.3	2,965	93.2	0.6	0.6	3.9	1.7	21.8	15.8	44.5	41.9	23.3	1,180	89.7
Berkshire town (Tioga)	1,412	1,351	-4.3	1,182	98.8	0.0	0.4	0.5	0.3	24.2	21.1	45.0	56.1	15.8	456	85.3
Berlin town (Rensselaer)	1,818	1,803	-0.8	1,622	98.1	0.0	0.4	0.1	1.4	16.0	19.1	50.3	50.6	26.2	705	87.0
Berne town (Albany)	2,800	2,764	-1.3	2,797	95.1	0.4	1.3	1.9	1.2	20.3	17.7	46.8	36.8	32.8	1,171	90.8
Bethany town (Genesee)	1,767	1,693	-4.2	1,899	86.2	1.8	0.0	1.6	10.3	24.5	14.4	40.4	50.0	21.2	752	87.2
Bethel town (Sullivan)	4,258	4,155	-2.4	4,136	89.2	1.0	0.4	1.2	8.2	16.4	24.3	50.8	46.8	24.8	1,674	88.2
Bethlehem town (Albany)	33,634	34,895	3.7	34,946	89.1	2.4	4.4	1.5	2.5	20.7	18.9	43.5	18.4	58.8	14,283	93.8
Bethpage CDP	16,429	-	-	17,627	79.0	1.0	8.2	1.2	10.6	19.3	20.1	45.2	33.2	44.3	6,033	92.0
Big Flats CDP	5,277	-	-	5,215	97.3	0.7	1.5	0.0	0.5	20.5	21.8	44.0	20.8	41.3	2,162	98.3
Big Flats town (Chemung)	7,747	7,528	-2.8	7,641	97.6	0.7	1.1	0.0	0.7	22.0	20.0	43.8	25.0	41.9	3,086	94.8
Billington Heights CDP	1,685	-	-	1,452	97.5	0.9	0.0	1.6	0.0	18.5	32.6	58.0	25.8	55.5	747	84.1
Binghamton city & MCD (Broome)	47,404	44,399	-6.3	45,140	70.7	11.0	4.9	6.2	7.1	19.3	16.1	35.8	44.4	25.8	19,691	85.3
Binghamton town (Broome)	4,952	4,713	-4.8	4,767	92.6	0.4	2.1	2.7	2.2	18.6	19.2	48.9	34.4	34.4	1,865	94.6
Binghamton University CDP	6,177	-	-	6,130	67.4	5.2	16.8	2.5	8.1	1.7	0.2	19.5	0.0	18.5	8	100.0
Birdsall town (Allegany)	223	225	0.9	189	97.4	0.0	0.0	1.6	1.1	15.3	31.7	56.4	58.6	10.2	90	67.8
Black Brook town (Clinton)	1,504	1,471	-2.2	1,404	100.0	0.0	0.0	0.0	0.0	16.7	26.5	51.1	58.7	13.2	609	77.0
Black River village	1,350	1,241	-8.1	1,246	86.8	0.8	6.4	3.6	2.4	21.8	14.9	38.0	34.7	30.0	547	89.8

1 May be of any race.

Table A. All Places — **Population and Housing**

STATE City, town, township, borough, or CDP (county if applicable)	Population: 2010 census total population	Population: 2019 estimated population	Population: Percent change 2010–2019	Population: ACS total population estimate 2015–2019	Race and Hispanic or Latino origin (percent): White alone, not Hispanic or Latino	Race and Hispanic or Latino origin (percent): Black alone, not Hispanic or Latino	Race and Hispanic or Latino origin (percent): Asian alone, not Hispanic or Latino	Race and Hispanic or Latino origin (percent): All other races or 2 or more races, not Hispanic or Latino	Race and Hispanic or Latino origin (percent): Hispanic or Latino[1]	Age (percent): Under 18 years old	Age (percent): Age 65 years and older	Age (percent): Median age	Educational attainment of persons age 25 and older: Percent High school diploma or less	Educational attainment of persons age 25 and older: Percent Bachelor's degree or more	Occupied housing units: Total	Occupied housing units: Percent with a computer
	1	2	3	4	5	6	7	8	9	10	11	12	13	14	15	16
NEW YORK—Con.																
Blasdell village	2,583	2,662	3.1	2,645	94.4	0.1	0.0	2.8	2.8	18.4	17.4	40.5	47.4	18.2	1,254	78.8
Blauvelt CDP	5,689	-	-	5,152	82.6	1.2	7.6	3.2	5.4	21.9	16.6	39.6	23.4	57.8	1,516	97.4
Bleecker town (Fulton)	530	500	-5.7	582	99.8	0.0	0.2	0.0	0.0	14.6	29.0	54.7	53.7	22.1	279	84.6
Blenheim town (Schoharie)	383	367	-4.2	325	97.5	0.6	0.3	0.0	1.5	20.9	24.0	45.7	50.8	20.2	121	88.4
Bliss CDP	527	-	-	477	98.5	0.0	1.0	0.0	0.4	14.5	15.1	46.3	55.1	16.3	189	85.7
Blodgett Mills CDP	303	-	-	199	91.5	0.0	0.0	0.0	8.5	0.0	12.1	56.3	52.3	43.0	101	100.0
Bloomfield village	1,365	1,307	-4.2	1,431	94.5	1.6	0.0	1.3	2.5	21.3	15.7	43.8	30.2	31.1	592	90.5
Bloomingburg village	425	412	-3.1	383	94.8	1.0	0.0	0.0	4.2	30.5	19.8	28.9	67.4	5.0	142	62.7
Blooming Grove town (Orange)	18,026	17,623	-2.2	17,606	73.5	7.5	1.7	1.2	16.1	23.8	12.2	40.5	34.8	30.8	6,063	94.7
Bloomville CDP	213	-	-	158	98.1	0.0	1.9	0.0	0.0	7.0	24.7	48.8	33.8	39.2	75	92.0
Blue Point CDP	4,773	-	-	4,942	89.3	0.3	0.2	0.3	10.0	21.8	19.0	45.7	29.6	47.7	1,766	96.5
Bohemia CDP	10,180	-	-	9,262	84.9	2.6	1.8	0.3	10.4	21.6	14.2	41.5	37.4	32.6	3,395	96.6
Bolivar village	1,047	976	-6.8	874	97.1	0.2	0.8	1.8	0.0	21.7	23.7	41.3	48.3	19.7	421	82.7
Bolivar town (Allegany)	2,195	2,042	-7.0	2,194	96.0	0.1	0.3	1.6	1.9	28.4	18.8	38.8	49.6	13.2	878	84.6
Bolton town (Warren)	2,326	2,247	-3.4	2,135	93.0	3.4	0.0	0.5	3.1	9.5	28.0	55.2	33.4	35.8	1,012	91.3
Bolton Landing CDP	513	-	-	580	84.7	9.8	0.0	0.0	5.5	11.9	36.0	55.0	44.8	20.8	295	81.7
Bombay town (Franklin)	1,357	1,286	-5.2	1,099	86.4	0.1	0.4	13.1	0.0	28.2	19.6	38.6	62.1	9.9	416	77.9
Boonville village	2,053	1,981	-3.5	2,120	96.6	0.7	0.2	1.7	0.8	21.1	22.8	45.1	54.4	13.2	838	80.7
Boonville town (Oneida)	4,548	4,477	-1.6	4,494	95.2	0.4	0.1	2.2	2.0	23.3	19.6	42.7	47.3	21.1	1,728	86.3
Boston town (Erie)	8,005	8,077	0.9	8,042	98.9	0.0	0.0	0.7	0.4	18.5	21.3	50.3	30.1	30.0	3,547	88.8
Bovina town (Delaware)	633	572	-9.6	593	89.5	1.2	2.7	4.4	2.2	17.0	24.5	52.8	27.2	38.6	277	92.1
Boylston town (Oswego)	551	554	0.5	516	96.3	0.0	1.0	1.6	1.2	20.7	17.4	46.1	53.7	14.5	222	86.9
Bradford town (Steuben)	856	809	-5.5	724	97.7	0.0	0.0	1.9	0.4	19.5	16.9	41.9	53.8	12.9	292	74.7
Brandon town (Franklin)	580	562	-3.1	517	99.8	0.0	0.0	0.2	0.0	19.5	12.2	39.2	56.1	18.5	226	78.3
Brant town (Erie)	2,066	2,057	-0.4	2,000	91.5	2.1	0.1	5.0	1.4	17.8	20.4	49.3	43.6	21.5	868	83.8
Brasher town (St. Lawrence)	2,511	2,361	-6.0	2,855	97.0	0.4	0.1	1.9	0.7	28.7	12.9	36.3	66.0	12.4	1,125	83.6
Brasher Falls CDP	669	-	-	796	99.2	0.4	0.4	0.0	0.0	31.0	19.3	29.0	68.9	17.3	336	82.7
Breesport CDP	626	-	-	773	84.2	0.0	3.5	0.0	12.3	17.3	36.5	59.0	40.7	9.0	272	94.1
Brentwood CDP	60,664	-	-	63,399	15.4	12.2	1.9	1.5	69.0	25.3	9.3	34.1	64.1	13.9	13,769	90.7
Brewerton CDP	4,029	-	-	4,074	94.2	0.0	1.5	1.1	3.3	25.7	13.4	35.2	37.3	23.6	1,692	95.1
Brewster village	2,410	2,337	-3.0	2,228	26.0	4.6	2.1	2.2	65.1	21.9	6.1	33.9	56.4	22.1	809	87.5
Brewster Hill CDP	2,089	-	-	2,196	75.8	0.0	8.0	2.3	13.9	13.6	22.6	49.2	36.9	30.4	848	100.0
Briarcliff Manor village	7,850	8,094	3.1	7,616	81.9	1.9	5.1	2.9	8.1	22.0	20.2	48.8	14.2	73.3	2,717	92.0
Bridgehampton CDP	1,756	-	-	1,323	63.3	18.9	2.0	1.1	14.7	17.8	33.7	49.7	28.8	52.5	551	53.9
Bridgeport CDP	1,490	-	-	1,330	89.2	0.2	3.6	6.8	0.1	22.0	18.3	50.3	52.4	17.3	559	81.4
Bridgewater CDP	470	-	-	415	98.3	0.0	0.0	0.0	1.7	27.7	12.5	30.6	60.9	10.5	151	72.2
Bridgewater town (Oneida)	1,522	1,471	-3.4	1,385	98.7	0.0	0.0	0.1	1.2	21.6	14.3	44.6	58.7	15.2	546	86.1
Brighton town (Franklin)	1,432	1,418		1,349	88.7	4.9	2.4	1.6	2.4	4.9	11.3	21.6	22.3	49.3	352	96.0
Brighton town (Monroe)	36,592	35,928	-1.8	36,272	75.8	5.9	10.1	3.1	5.1	17.8	20.2	38.6	15.9	66.3	15,459	92.6
Brightwaters village	3,118	3,059	-1.9	3,075	87.6	1.9	0.3	3.2	7.0	23.9	15.7	42.9	15.3	60.6	1,082	95.1
Brinckerhoff CDP	2,900	-	-	2,267	77.0	6.2	7.1	1.2	8.5	16.5	25.6	47.7	29.9	39.8	932	90.0
Bristol town (Ontario)	2,321	2,218	-4.4	2,136	97.7	0.3	0.2	0.8	0.9	16.3	22.8	53.0	32.2	30.5	921	96.4
Broadalbin village	1,355	1,275	-5.9	1,397	96.3	0.4	0.0	0.0	3.2	20.7	16.6	38.6	34.7	20.7	594	91.2
Broadalbin town (Fulton)	5,261	5,169	-1.7	5,168	96.4	0.8	1.2	0.1	1.5	18.5	17.3	44.8	39.7	19.4	2,208	90.0
Brockport village	8,355	8,163	-2.3	8,292	83.0	5.0	2.9	3.1	5.9	12.4	12.2	22.0	33.4	41.4	2,344	91.9
Brocton village	1,483	1,395	-5.9	1,336	92.8	0.9	0.7	4.1	1.4	19.6	22.7	45.8	48.7	21.2	647	81.9
Bronxville village	6,272	6,408	2.2	6,409	82.4	1.1	7.1	2.0	7.3	26.1	15.2	41.1	8.5	79.9	2,212	93.7
Brookfield town (Madison)	2,544	2,405	-5.5	2,347	99.1	0.0	0.0	0.9	0.0	18.2	19.2	44.7	53.3	17.8	886	79.9
Brookhaven CDP	3,451	-	-	3,455	77.7	7.3	0.2	2.6	12.1	23.7	16.0	46.3	38.3	35.7	1,171	89.8
Brookhaven town (Suffolk)	486,336	480,763	-1.1	483,546	72.1	5.5	4.5	1.9	16.0	21.3	15.6	40.2	38.0	32.6	161,215	92.8
Brookville village	3,479	3,605	3.6	3,586	67.8	5.1	12.9	2.6	11.5	17.1	14.1	24.7	9.1	77.2	869	100.0
Broome town (Schoharie)	973	998	2.6	808	91.8	0.2	0.4	1.1	6.4	12.9	28.7	57.3	59.5	14.4	390	79.7
Brownville village	1,125	1,081	-3.9	849	97.6	0.4	0.0	0.0	2.0	23.1	23.2	49.0	46.2	27.4	350	74.9
Brownville town (Jefferson)	6,239	5,972	-4.3	6,129	96.3	0.8	0.0	0.7	2.3	23.3	16.0	42.0	43.5	19.4	2,328	90.7
Brunswick town (Rensselaer)	11,952	13,046	9.2	12,796	94.5	0.7	1.5	1.0	2.3	15.6	18.9	45.9	28.1	44.1	5,295	90.7
Brushton village	458	432	-5.7	423	100.0	0.0	0.0	0.0	0.0	12.1	12.5	47.3	53.4	19.4	198	84.3
Brutus town (Cayuga)	4,464	4,239	-5.0	4,294	96.0	0.6	0.9	1.1	1.4	22.1	14.9	44.5	43.7	24.8	1,794	89.5
Buchanan village	2,217	2,232	0.7	2,140	75.4	6.7	0.4	2.5	15.0	19.9	14.5	39.9	33.4	33.4	728	93.8
Buffalo city & MCD (Erie)	261,346	255,284	-2.3	256,480	43.1	35.5	5.8	3.3	12.3	22.6	12.4	33.1	43.3	27.6	110,427	85.7
Burdett village	340	316	-7.1	394	93.4	0.0	2.3	0.0	4.3	13.7	27.4	49.8	31.8	31.5	179	89.9
Burke village	207	200	-3.4	262	78.2	5.3	0.4	0.0	16.0	34.0	15.3	34.0	44.7	24.1	95	78.9
Burke town (Franklin)	1,461	1,469	0.5	1,413	91.6	3.4	0.1	0.8	4.0	24.1	16.2	43.8	55.8	13.8	531	74.2
Burlington town (Otsego)	1,142	1,080	-5.4	1,133	96.6	0.0	1.4	1.3	0.7	21.2	18.8	44.8	50.6	20.5	410	86.8
Burns town (Allegany)	1,181	1,102	-6.7	965	97.6	0.0	0.9	0.0	1.5	16.4	23.3	50.7	50.6	17.0	414	84.1
Busti CDP	391	-	-	275	100.0	0.0	0.0	0.0	0.0	8.0	9.1	33.6	40.0	8.5	126	92.9
Busti town (Chautauqua)	7,351	7,146	-2.8	7,248	95.3	0.1	0.6	1.6	2.3	16.1	27.8	48.9	35.4	32.7	3,341	89.6
Butler town (Wayne)	2,058	1,899	-7.7	1,864	92.8	1.5	0.2	2.3	3.2	21.9	14.9	38.5	59.6	7.0	715	83.9
Butternuts town (Otsego)	1,786	1,679	-6.0	1,753	94.6	0.0	1.1	4.1	0.2	13.4	24.7	50.7	41.5	31.8	766	82.0
Byersville CDP	47	-	-	43	95.3	0.0	0.0	4.7	0.0	4.7	30.2	53.5	48.6	20.0	25	84.0
Byron town (Genesee)	2,373	2,238	-5.7	2,035	95.4	1.1	1.0	1.2	1.3	16.9	19.5	46.4	49.2	19.5	861	90.7
Cairo CDP	1,402	-	-	955	86.5	0.0	2.3	3.7	7.5	17.9	22.6	51.2	36.0	11.0	451	70.5
Cairo town (Greene)	6,663	6,415	-3.7	6,423	88.7	0.4	0.7	2.2	8.1	15.0	18.0	45.6	51.1	20.0	2,249	84.4
Calcium CDP	3,491	-	-	3,405	40.7	21.6	13.6	4.6	19.6	27.0	2.5	25.9	43.6	31.5	1,370	96.3
Caledonia village	2,201	2,094	-4.9	2,078	93.7	2.6	1.0	2.1	0.6	17.7	16.2	40.5	38.9	22.7	886	88.8
Caledonia town (Livingston)	4,255	4,102	-3.6	4,138	91.9	2.2	2.1	1.2	2.6	18.9	16.6	42.0	43.6	23.1	1,653	91.3
Callicoon CDP	167	-	-	273	66.7	19.8	2.9	7.7	2.9	8.4	24.5	44.2	32.1	23.5	168	95.2
Callicoon town (Sullivan)	3,056	2,917	-4.5	2,925	89.0	1.3	0.9	3.0	5.8	15.0	30.1	53.5	44.4	26.7	1,319	87.5
Calverton CDP	6,510	-	-	6,987	75.8	7.5	2.6	2.6	11.5	13.2	30.3	53.2	48.6	15.5	3,231	90.2
Cambria town (Niagara)	5,847	5,745	-1.7	5,773	98.7	0.3	1.0	0.0	0.0	18.7	21.8	46.0	38.3	26.6	2,387	87.1
Cambridge village	1,870	1,810	-3.2	1,976	94.3	0.0	2.1	2.0	1.6	24.2	22.5	43.0	42.6	36.3	885	85.6
Cambridge town (Washington)	2,013	1,930	-4.1	1,961	92.9	0.1	3.9	1.7	1.5	25.1	19.8	43.4	32.1	42.8	772	93.8
Camden village	2,234	2,159	-3.4	2,534	96.2	0.1	0.0	2.2	1.5	22.9	23.4	42.9	51.0	19.7	1,158	82.0
Camden town (Oneida)	4,939	4,844	-1.9	4,878	97.3	0.6	0.0	1.1	1.0	17.5	27.5	50.8	53.4	21.2	2,198	82.9
Cameron town (Steuben)	945	915	-3.2	871	97.7	0.0	0.0	2.3	0.0	24.2	18.6	40.9	64.4	7.0	342	73.1

1 May be of any race.

Table A. All Places — **Population and Housing**

STATE City, town, township, borough, or CDP (county if applicable)	2010 census total population	2019 estimated population	Percent change 2010–2019	ACS total population estimate 2015–2019	White alone, not Hispanic or Latino	Black alone, not Hispanic or Latino	Asian alone, not Hispanic or Latino	All other races or 2 or more races, not Hispanic or Latino	Hispanic or Latino[1]	Under 18 years old	Age 65 years and older	Median age	Percent High school diploma or less	Percent Bachelor's degree or more	Occupied housing units Total	Percent with a computer
	1	2	3	4	5	6	7	8	9	10	11	12	13	14	15	16
NEW YORK—Con.																
Camillus village...............	1,263	1,195	-5.4	1,156	91.3	3.1	0.5	4.6	0.5	20.1	17.0	38.0	39.3	26.3	561	89.1
Camillus town (Onondaga)	24,145	24,105	-0.2	24,262	91.6	1.4	2.7	1.6	2.6	21.9	19.2	42.8	28.0	39.4	9,843	91.1
Campbell CDP..................	713	-	-	713	98.6	1.0	0.0	0.0	0.4	21.6	9.8	42.9	39.6	23.7	260	91.9
Campbell town (Steuben).	3,402	3,232	-5.0	3,272	96.3	0.2	0.2	1.1	2.2	16.6	22.5	50.6	48.4	18.2	1,343	87.4
Canaan town (Columbia)..	1,712	1,604	-6.3	1,785	93.2	1.5	0.0	0.7	4.5	17.7	27.2	53.0	31.4	40.7	729	95.9
Canadice town (Ontario)...	1,756	1,645	-6.3	1,648	94.4	0.0	0.0	1.4	4.2	17.9	21.6	53.1	46.1	23.1	701	91.6
Canajoharie village..........	2,234	2,133	-4.5	1,905	88.5	0.0	1.2	6.5	3.9	18.0	18.2	41.2	53.4	17.5	884	86.5
Canajoharie town (Montgomery)	3,733	3,584	-4.0	3,595	93.0	0.1	0.6	4.0	2.2	22.2	16.9	40.2	54.1	18.3	1,464	87.4
Canandaigua city & MCD (Ontario)......................	10,591	10,156	-4.1	10,287	93.9	1.2	0.6	1.5	2.7	18.9	23.0	44.1	29.0	39.7	4,932	87.2
Canandaigua town (Ontario)......................	9,962	11,302	13.5	11,082	93.9	1.0	0.5	2.1	2.5	18.4	22.4	47.0	23.5	48.6	4,644	92.0
Canaseraga village..........	546	509	-6.8	457	98.2	0.0	0.9	0.0	0.9	19.7	18.8	43.5	51.1	11.0	186	87.1
Canastota village............	4,791	4,544	-5.2	4,586	95.3	0.4	0.0	4.3	0.0	24.4	13.3	34.1	51.5	17.8	1,758	82.9
Candor village.................	852	790	-7.3	697	97.7	0.0	0.0	0.3	2.0	27.7	13.6	36.3	40.7	23.7	289	88.9
Candor town (Tioga)........	5,356	4,981	-7.0	5,057	97.6	0.0	0.0	0.4	2.0	23.3	16.7	42.4	48.4	20.2	1,958	95.7
Caneadea town (Allegany)	2,538	2,246	-11.5	2,307	86.6	3.7	4.3	2.0	3.4	15.3	15.4	22.2	33.2	48.3	565	90.1
Canisteo village...............	2,272	2,135	-6.0	2,341	98.3	0.5	0.3	0.6	0.2	26.1	21.8	42.8	49.2	22.0	925	87.9
Canisteo town (Steuben)..	3,388	3,202	-5.5	3,251	97.2	0.4	0.4	1.1	0.9	22.0	22.5	44.5	54.1	17.8	1,359	84.5
Canton village.................	6,331	6,496	2.6	6,505	85.5	6.0	2.3	2.2	4.0	8.9	13.7	21.7	25.8	54.5	1,612	90.9
Canton town (St. Lawrence).....................	10,993	11,041	0.4	11,095	88.9	3.6	2.1	2.3	3.1	13.8	15.9	28.6	33.8	38.8	3,469	89.6
Cape Vincent village.........	723	692	-4.3	573	93.2	0.5	0.7	0.3	5.2	25.3	18.2	45.1	38.4	35.4	253	92.1
Cape Vincent town (Jefferson)......................	2,777	2,684	-3.3	2,773	72.5	12.1	1.0	3.7	10.7	13.2	18.9	44.7	51.7	20.2	872	91.6
Carle Place CDP	4,981	-	-	5,131	67.0	2.6	8.8	5.8	15.7	18.6	18.5	43.1	40.8	36.1	1,824	95.2
Carlisle town (Schoharie) .	1,955	1,854	-5.2	1,616	92.5	1.7	0.5	1.3	4.0	17.2	20.1	46.2	43.6	26.8	660	85.0
Carlton town (Orleans).....	2,990	2,850	-4.7	2,870	92.3	4.0	0.0	2.2	1.5	17.5	21.0	47.6	48.8	18.4	1,192	92.3
Carmel town (Putnam)......	34,229	34,106	-0.4	34,210	84.6	1.0	1.6	1.1	11.7	21.3	17.1	43.5	33.2	37.0	12,102	94.2
Carmel Hamlet CDP..........	6,817	-	-	6,345	81.7	3.0	0.1	0.8	14.4	19.7	25.0	48.0	35.8	39.8	2,489	89.5
Caroga town (Fulton)........	1,221	1,165	-4.6	1,238	85.1	0.0	7.8	7.0	0.0	15.9	28.4	55.0	46.0	23.5	584	86.3
Caroga Lake CDP	518	-	-	516	87.8	0.0	0.0	12.2	0.0	13.8	32.9	60.3	36.0	31.3	251	83.7
Caroline town (Tompkins).	3,287	3,296	0.3	3,362	78.1	4.2	1.9	10.4	5.3	28.9	12.0	33.5	24.3	52.0	1,319	92.5
Carroll town (Chautauqua)	3,524	3,329	-5.5	3,361	99.0	1.0	0.0	0.0	0.0	16.5	20.9	52.4	51.0	17.7	1,484	81.5
Carrollton town (Cattaraugus).................	1,292	1,204	-6.8	1,307	95.0	1.5	0.0	2.9	0.6	20.7	18.9	47.3	57.2	15.8	581	84.0
Carthage village...............	3,651	3,289	-9.9	3,405	87.8	1.9	0.0	6.0	4.3	28.8	16.3	30.3	49.5	14.1	1,275	93.5
Cassadaga village	639	593	-7.2	608	94.9	0.0	2.8	0.0	2.3	16.6	24.8	49.6	44.8	17.8	271	89.3
Castile village	1,020	979	-4.0	1,026	90.9	0.0	0.0	9.1	0.0	24.3	17.6	40.2	47.7	18.2	444	92.8
Castile town (Wyoming)....	2,902	2,778	-4.3	2,796	90.8	0.3	0.0	4.2	4.7	21.3	21.6	47.1	45.5	25.0	1,215	92.2
Castleton-on-Hudson village.......................	1,481	1,462	-1.3	1,365	91.9	0.5	0.0	1.5	6.0	23.1	19.3	43.0	36.3	41.4	535	95.1
Castorland village............	351	343	-2.3	360	75.0	0.8	0.0	2.8	21.4	35.8	17.8	31.5	54.2	14.8	109	87.2
Catharine town (Schuyler)	1,763	1,668	-5.4	1,571	98.1	0.3	0.0	1.7	0.0	18.2	23.8	50.0	48.0	22.8	647	88.1
Catlin town (Chemung).....	2,637	2,484	-5.8	3,001	91.1	0.3	1.3	2.3	5.0	28.4	11.2	37.4	44.3	18.5	1,127	94.5
Cato village.....................	532	498	-6.4	521	100.0	0.0	0.0	0.0	0.0	32.8	9.6	31.4	44.4	16.8	207	93.7
Cato town (Cayuga).........	2,534	2,425	-4.3	2,478	98.0	0.3	0.4	1.3	0.0	22.7	14.9	42.2	52.1	22.5	938	90.6
Caton town (Steuben)......	2,174	2,113	-2.8	2,083	97.6	0.0	0.4	1.3	0.7	22.9	17.5	44.8	38.9	29.8	801	89.8
Catskill village.................	4,081	3,814	-6.5	3,846	67.5	22.4	2.0	5.6	2.5	10.5	18.5	41.1	60.9	21.3	1,413	85.4
Catskill town (Greene)......	11,785	11,334	-3.8	11,360	79.4	8.7	1.2	5.5	5.2	17.0	22.0	44.2	53.1	25.3	4,558	78.7
Cattaraugus village..........	969	904	-6.7	1,042	92.3	1.0	0.0	1.2	5.5	24.9	22.3	40.9	51.8	20.6	426	68.5
Cattaraugus Reservation (Cattaraugus).................	314	323	2.9	316	2.5	0.0	2.2	90.8	4.4	33.2	11.7	34.3	39.9	28.0	100	90.0
Cattaraugus Reservation (Chautauqua)................	38	40	5.3	-	-	-	-	-	-	-	-	-	-	-	-	-
Cattaraugus Reservation (Erie)............................	1,872	1,994	6.5	2,045	6.9	0.9	2.2	88.9	1.1	28.9	12.0	34.3	59.1	18.8	782	74.0
Cayuga village	549	519	-5.5	454	94.9	0.9	1.5	1.8	0.9	20.0	21.8	49.4	42.6	20.8	208	88.5
Cayuga Heights village.....	3,736	3,604	-3.5	3,689	76.6	0.9	12.9	3.6	6.0	10.7	24.3	41.7	8.0	83.7	1,480	95.1
Cayuta town (Schuyler) ...	552	514	-6.9	427	91.3	5.4	0.0	1.6	1.6	14.8	17.8	46.8	72.2	9.9	201	73.1
Cazenovia village	2,836	2,849	0.5	2,846	84.4	6.9	1.5	1.7	5.6	12.6	17.5	22.0	26.1	48.6	902	83.1
Cazenovia town (Madison)	7,082	6,990	-1.3	7,001	92.4	2.8	1.1	1.0	2.7	17.4	20.1	44.3	23.0	49.4	2,371	89.5
Cedarhurst village............	6,572	6,633	0.9	6,642	89.3	1.6	2.0	0.4	6.7	32.9	16.5	29.5	26.4	56.5	2,078	89.6
Celoron village.................	1,101	1,027	-6.7	1,001	93.8	0.0	1.7	1.7	2.8	16.2	29.0	50.9	60.4	14.7	457	84.2
Centereach CDP...............	31,578	-	-	31,493	72.2	4.1	4.9	2.1	16.7	22.2	14.6	37.9	39.8	29.7	9,675	94.6
Center Moriches CDP.......	7,580	-	-	8,147	79.4	3.4	0.9	1.1	15.1	23.4	15.4	41.4	34.3	29.6	2,858	97.7
Centerport CDP................	5,508	-	-	5,394	89.3	0.2	5.7	0.9	3.9	21.6	19.7	48.3	15.7	63.3	1,975	96.9
Centerville town (Allegany)	820	812		958	96.5	0.0	1.4	1.6	0.6	41.1	11.0	28.5	58.0	14.4	290	71.7
Central Bridge CDP..........	593	-	-	360	87.5	0.0	0.0	12.5	0.0	30.8	3.6	36.2	34.7	0.0	148	100.0
Central Islip CDP	34,450	-	-	31,205	22.9	23.6	3.6	2.3	47.5	23.5	10.1	36.0	56.2	18.0	9,145	89.1
Central Square village.......	1,842	1,750	-5.0	1,933	98.6	0.5	0.0	0.9	0.1	20.1	22.1	46.5	44.1	23.1	943	80.3
Centre Island village........	410	409	-0.2	446	89.7	0.7	5.4	1.3	2.9	16.1	27.6	54.4	11.3	70.7	174	99.4
Chadwicks CDP................	1,506	-	-	1,059	100.0	0.0	0.0	0.0	0.0	5.2	17.2	43.1	28.4	20.1	518	96.1
Champion town (Jefferson)......................	4,494	4,308	-4.1	4,420	86.9	5.0	1.7	1.9	4.5	25.6	16.1	35.0	44.5	23.3	1,811	86.1
Champlain village.............	1,098	1,050	-4.4	1,002	94.9	0.0	1.2	1.6	2.3	24.9	12.3	34.0	53.2	23.3	451	94.7
Champlain town (Clinton) .	5,754	5,614	-2.4	5,639	97.4	0.1	0.7	1.2	0.6	22.9	17.4	38.5	48.3	15.8	2,416	88.3
Chappaqua CDP	1,436	-	-	1,434	74.8	0.0	22.6	1.3	1.3	18.4	10.0	39.8	6.6	83.6	533	96.2
Charleston town (Montgomery)	1,371	1,320	-3.7	1,320	98.1	0.0	0.2	0.1	1.6	26.2	12.2	37.1	41.7	24.4	502	90.2
Charlotte town (Chautauqua).................	1,719	1,676	-2.5	1,627	96.6	0.0	0.2	1.5	1.7	22.7	15.0	42.7	60.9	14.6	657	86.9
Charlton town (Saratoga) .	4,140	4,178	0.9	4,180	95.3	2.6	0.0	0.1	1.9	20.8	27.5	49.3	26.9	41.7	1,631	92.5
Chateaugay village...........	838	798	-4.8	745	95.4	1.6	0.7	0.7	1.6	25.4	15.4	40.0	49.4	15.9	295	81.0
Chateaugay town (Franklin)	2,156	1,871	-13.2	1,595	96.2	1.2	0.3	1.1	1.3	23.1	16.6	46.6	46.6	17.0	677	81.8
Chatham village...............	1,777	1,622	-8.7	1,625	86.7	6.5	0.9	1.8	4.1	11.8	19.4	46.9	24.3	34.5	751	93.1
Chatham town (Columbia)	4,131	3,819	-7.6	3,905	86.8	6.0	0.4	5.6	1.1	19.2	26.6	47.6	27.2	42.9	1,638	95.7
Chaumont village..............	626	578	-7.7	753	85.9	1.9	0.4	7.7	4.1	31.5	15.1	36.6	48.5	19.7	247	93.1
Chautauqua CDP	191	-	-	323	66.6	17.6	2.5	7.7	5.6	1.5	12.7	19.8	4.8	77.8	31	100.0

1 May be of any race.

Table A. All Places — Population and Housing

STATE City, town, township, borough, or CDP (county if applicable)	Population				Race and Hispanic or Latino origin (percent)					Age (percent)			Educational attainment of persons age 25 and older		Occupied housing units	
	2010 census total population	2019 estimated population	Percent change 2010–2019	ACS total population estimate 2015–2019	White alone, not Hispanic or Latino	Black alone, not Hispanic or Latino	Asian alone, not Hispanic or Latino	All other races or 2 or more races, not Hispanic or Latino	Hispanic or Latino[1]	Under 18 years old	Age 65 years and older	Median age	Percent High school diploma or less	Percent Bachelor's degree or more	Total	Percent with a computer
	1	2	3	4	5	6	7	8	9	10	11	12	13	14	15	16
NEW YORK—Con.																
Chautauqua town (Chautauqua)	4,470	4,212	-5.8	4,286	93.2	3.0	0.2	1.3	2.2	19.8	23.4	43.6	38.4	28.6	1,683	79.7
Chautauqua Lake UT (Chautauqua)	-	-	-	-	-	-	-	-	-	-	-	-	-	-	-	-
Chazy CDP	565	-	-	727	97.0	0.0	0.0	3.0	0.0	25.3	12.4	34.7	55.8	20.0	258	97.3
Chazy town (Clinton)	4,271	4,160	-2.6	4,165	94.2	0.3	0.8	3.5	1.2	22.2	14.5	39.6	51.8	21.8	1,581	93.0
Cheektowaga CDP	75,178	-	-	73,740	79.8	12.9	2.0	2.5	2.8	17.4	19.4	41.2	42.7	23.6	33,085	84.7
Cheektowaga town (Erie)	88,170	85,884	-2.6	86,477	81.5	11.5	1.9	2.4	2.7	17.6	19.5	41.4	43.0	23.0	38,628	85.1
Chemung town (Chemung)	2,563	2,428	-5.3	2,165	95.7	0.1	0.3	0.6	3.3	19.3	19.7	49.4	53.4	16.3	863	88.9
Chenango town (Broome)	11,212	10,505	-6.3	10,701	94.1	1.1	0.9	3.6	0.4	20.7	19.8	44.4	35.0	31.8	4,205	92.8
Chenango Bridge CDP	2,883	-	-	2,856	95.2	0.0	1.5	3.3	0.0	20.1	20.8	44.2	30.8	41.1	1,085	94.2
Cherry Creek village	461	431	-6.5	478	99.0	0.0	0.4	0.0	0.6	26.8	12.3	34.5	45.8	15.2	172	84.9
Cherry Creek town (Chautauqua)	1,119	1,046	-6.5	1,048	98.2	0.2	0.2	0.6	0.9	27.1	15.8	37.3	52.4	15.2	381	80.8
Cherry Valley village	517	489	-5.4	486	96.3	0.4	0.0	0.0	3.3	18.1	23.7	44.7	33.7	38.3	201	86.6
Cherry Valley town (Otsego)	1,219	1,151	-5.6	1,096	98.4	0.2	0.0	0.0	1.5	19.7	19.8	46.6	33.2	37.5	441	91.2
Chester village	3,935	4,091	4.0	4,011	47.1	12.5	4.5	2.2	33.7	16.3	14.8	40.1	43.3	25.8	1,569	93.5
Chester town (Orange)	12,003	12,185	1.5	12,023	65.9	7.0	3.6	2.2	21.3	20.3	13.5	39.0	32.1	35.2	4,011	96.5
Chester town (Warren)	3,351	3,249	-3.0	3,268	95.9	2.1	0.7	0.0	1.3	19.9	23.7	50.1	42.4	36.7	1,480	86.9
Chesterfield town (Essex)	2,445	2,340	-4.3	2,311	97.0	0.2	0.1	1.4	1.3	15.4	22.0	50.3	37.3	28.6	1,069	92.0
Chestertown CDP	677	-	-	430	98.6	0.7	0.0	0.0	0.7	11.9	12.3	53.7	52.1	19.6	217	53.0
Chestnut Ridge village	7,920	8,020	1.3	8,057	66.5	15.4	4.8	4.0	9.3	32.5	16.6	32.4	30.9	43.0	2,246	87.7
Chili town (Monroe)	28,629	28,527	-0.4	28,564	83.4	9.5	1.7	2.7	2.7	20.6	17.6	42.2	30.2	38.2	11,111	92.9
Chittenango village	5,070	4,850	-4.3	4,880	96.2	0.4	0.1	0.8	2.5	22.9	16.1	40.6	34.5	27.3	1,746	93.6
Churchville village	1,976	2,110	6.8	2,112	95.4	0.9	0.0	1.7	2.0	19.7	20.5	48.3	26.7	41.8	896	93.6
Cicero town (Onondaga)	31,566	30,721	-2.7	30,868	93.6	1.6	1.6	1.6	1.5	22.2	16.1	42.8	33.0	31.8	12,299	91.1
Cincinnatus town (Cortland)	1,056	1,006	-4.7	828	94.9	0.0	0.0	1.0	4.1	19.6	24.6	50.3	59.3	12.3	381	84.0
Clare town (St. Lawrence)	105	101	-3.8	76	97.4	0.0	2.6	0.0	0.0	22.4	14.5	48.0	65.4	7.7	29	100.0
Clarence CDP	2,646	-	-	2,650	95.9	1.5	1.3	0.4	0.9	20.5	31.6	49.2	34.3	42.3	1,076	86.6
Clarence town (Erie)	30,654	32,906	7.3	32,440	93.6	0.7	3.0	1.3	1.4	23.2	18.9	45.8	21.1	54.2	12,388	93.2
Clarence Center CDP	2,257	-	-	2,970	97.4	0.0	0.6	2.0	0.0	29.8	10.4	37.1	11.3	68.9	979	95.0
Clarendon town (Orleans)	3,646	3,471	-4.8	3,508	95.4	0.8	0.9	2.5	0.5	16.6	20.0	50.0	54.4	14.9	1,511	89.9
Clark Mills CDP	1,905	-	-	1,585	94.1	0.0	4.4	0.0	1.6	17.2	21.8	46.5	37.9	34.5	791	89.1
Clarkson CDP	4,358	-	-	4,749	88.4	4.5	1.9	0.3	4.9	25.6	14.7	39.2	24.6	47.2	1,876	94.7
Clarkson town (Monroe)	6,723	7,080	5.3	7,084	90.5	3.1	1.3	0.4	4.7	21.8	17.4	44.3	29.2	40.0	2,672	92.9
Clarkstown town (Rockland)	84,536	86,237	2.0	86,488	62.3	10.3	10.1	2.6	14.7	20.5	20.0	45.0	25.4	51.5	29,692	92.8
Clarksville town (Allegany)	1,161	1,083	-6.7	909	99.3	0.2	0.0	0.4	0.0	20.0	28.8	51.4	56.4	17.3	408	83.6
Claverack town (Columbia)	6,012	5,630	-6.4	5,708	89.5	2.6	2.1	4.4	1.3	20.3	22.8	49.7	38.1	28.0	2,483	87.7
Claverack-Red Mills CDP	913	-	-	552	100.0	0.0	0.0	0.0	0.0	18.3	24.6	50.7	26.6	34.8	248	93.1
Clay town (Onondaga)	58,320	59,250	1.6	59,364	85.9	5.2	2.3	3.4	3.1	21.5	15.5	40.1	31.9	36.8	24,225	93.7
Clayton village	2,002	1,834	-8.4	2,029	95.4	2.8	0.0	0.9	0.8	20.9	22.1	40.9	36.2	24.5	891	86.5
Clayton town (Jefferson)	5,159	4,735	-8.2	4,892	95.7	1.2	0.0	1.6	1.5	18.8	22.4	46.6	39.0	23.6	2,044	86.3
Clayville village	353	339	-4.0	190	93.7	0.5	0.0	0.0	5.8	18.4	13.7	47.9	40.1	31.4	80	85.0
Clermont town (Columbia)	1,951	1,864	-4.5	2,052	91.3	0.8	1.5	1.1	5.2	19.0	19.0	47.3	35.2	37.1	731	93.4
Cleveland village	755	716	-5.2	632	98.3	0.0	0.2	1.6	0.0	19.6	13.0	45.3	51.8	14.3	263	96.2
Clifton town (St. Lawrence)	751	723	-3.7	578	95.3	0.0	0.0	4.3	0.3	12.3	29.2	59.0	54.3	20.6	290	94.1
Clifton Park town (Saratoga)	36,733	36,366		36,663	83.0	3.1	5.8	3.5	4.6	23.5	17.9	42.3	16.4	58.0	14,097	95.9
Clifton Springs village	2,106	2,004	-4.8	2,173	91.8	0.9	0.1	1.8	5.4	17.3	23.8	47.9	44.8	19.5	926	79.3
Clinton town (Clinton)	731	705	-3.6	634	97.5	0.8	0.5	1.3	0.0	17.8	18.9	50.1	60.6	17.6	273	80.2
Clinton town (Dutchess)	4,301	4,236	-1.5	4,215	91.9	1.9	0.4	0.7	5.3	18.8	21.7	49.1	28.5	43.8	1,534	93.4
Clinton village	1,787	1,707	-4.5	1,830	91.2	0.5	0.9	3.4	4.0	20.5	17.8	42.0	18.4	61.3	785	97.3
Clintondale CDP	1,452	-	-	1,414	72.7	2.6	6.2	3.6	14.9	21.5	11.0	48.6	30.0	41.4	604	88.4
Clyde village	2,095	1,961	-6.4	2,075	84.6	2.6	0.0	2.8	9.9	29.2	14.3	37.0	58.5	9.6	779	87.7
Clymer town (Chautauqua)	1,698	1,650	-2.8	1,759	99.4	0.0	0.3	0.2	0.0	33.7	9.3	29.0	57.5	13.9	543	69.8
Cobleskill village	4,672	4,356	-6.8	4,581	87.2	4.2	0.5	2.2	5.8	12.0	17.4	25.9	39.8	30.1	1,475	84.5
Cobleskill town (Schoharie)	6,643	6,221	-6.4	6,313	89.9	3.1	0.4	2.2	4.4	13.3	21.8	33.4	40.1	27.1	2,215	83.7
Cochecton town (Sullivan)	1,364	1,299	-4.8	1,430	87.1	5.8	0.2	0.1	6.9	20.4	16.4	44.9	38.5	30.3	597	87.8
Coeymans town (Albany)	7,402	7,262	-1.9	7,329	95.9	1.9	0.0	1.2	1.0	20.7	18.8	41.8	48.1	21.9	3,094	86.4
Cohocton village	838	791	-5.6	826	90.6	0.6	0.0	8.6	0.2	25.8	12.2	35.1	45.2	18.8	304	94.7
Cohocton town (Steuben)	2,567	2,448	-4.6	2,457	91.8	0.6	0.0	3.4	4.2	23.2	17.4	43.3	51.9	15.8	958	90.2
Cohoes city & MCD (Albany)	16,177	16,687	3.2	16,684	80.3	6.1	0.7	7.2	5.8	18.8	19.0	37.5	44.7	26.1	7,390	89.9
Colchester town (Delaware)	2,077	1,960	-5.6	2,016	91.0	2.5	0.0	1.6	5.0	15.6	26.7	52.9	56.9	18.0	818	82.4
Cold Brook village	328	306	-6.7	289	98.3	0.0	0.0	1.4	0.3	34.9	14.5	30.4	61.4	12.9	104	79.8
Colden town (Erie)	3,273	3,352	2.4	3,328	96.1	0.0	0.5	0.0	3.4	19.6	19.0	47.8	40.5	28.1	1,374	91.6
Coldspring town (Cattaraugus)	666	644	-3.3	653	98.3	0.0	0.0	0.9	0.8	19.0	15.9	40.5	61.4	10.9	282	81.9
Cold Spring village	2,009	1,947	-3.1	1,775	91.4	0.6	1.8	1.9	4.3	21.6	19.1	47.1	18.2	59.5	834	92.8
Cold Spring Harbor CDP	5,070	-	-	4,932	85.1	0.2	6.1	2.4	6.2	22.4	17.1	46.8	15.3	70.0	1,671	97.8
Colesville town (Broome)	5,242	4,947	-5.6	5,039	93.9	0.5	0.4	4.6	0.7	23.5	22.1	47.9	52.7	16.6	2,089	87.0
Collins town (Erie)	6,568	6,260	-4.7	6,461	70.6	16.1	0.3	3.6	9.4	11.2	12.4	42.1	60.0	11.9	1,650	77.5
Colonie village	7,793	7,618	-2.2	7,737	79.3	3.9	11.2	3.3	2.4	15.4	19.3	42.9	34.9	33.8	3,004	91.3
Colonie town (Albany)	81,588	82,798	1.5	82,849	77.0	5.6	9.6	3.1	4.7	18.8	17.9	40.2	28.4	42.0	32,341	91.3
Colton CDP	345	-	-	357	99.2	0.0	0.0	0.0	0.8	20.7	17.9	43.5	39.9	28.6	151	88.7
Colton town (St. Lawrence)	1,451	1,410	-2.8	1,389	99.7	0.0	0.0	0.0	0.3	15.8	26.6	51.1	31.8	39.8	623	89.2
Columbia town (Herkimer)	1,572	1,510	-3.9	1,584	98.7	0.0	0.0	0.0	1.3	19.8	19.0	45.7	51.7	17.5	623	84.1
Columbus town (Chenango)	975	924	-5.2	961	95.7	0.7	0.0	0.8	2.7	18.1	17.6	46.5	61.8	14.0	396	84.1
Commack CDP	36,124	-	-	36,953	86.6	1.3	4.4	1.4	6.3	20.8	18.6	46.6	24.5	51.0	11,981	94.4
Concord town (Erie)	8,495	8,472	-0.3	8,484	96.3	0.4	0.3	1.5	1.6	21.5	18.7	45.8	46.8	23.6	3,580	86.6
Conesus town (Livingston)	2,473	2,361	-4.5	2,325	95.7	1.7	0.0	1.2	1.4	12.4	20.3	51.9	35.0	28.2	1,014	90.1

1 May be of any race.

Table A. All Places — **Population and Housing**

STATE City, town, township, borough, or CDP (county if applicable)	Population 2010 census total population	2019 estimated population	Percent change 2010–2019	ACS total population estimate 2015–2019	Race and Hispanic or Latino origin (percent) White alone, not Hispanic or Latino	Black alone, not Hispanic or Latino	Asian alone, not Hispanic or Latino	All other races or 2 or more races, not Hispanic or Latino	Hispanic or Latino[1]	Age (percent) Under 18 years old	Age 65 years and older	Median age	Educational attainment of persons age 25 and older Percent High school diploma or less	Percent Bachelor's degree or more	Occupied housing units Total	Percent with a computer
	1	2	3	4	5	6	7	8	9	10	11	12	13	14	15	16
NEW YORK—Con.																
Conesus Hamlet CDP	308	-	-	354	96.6	0.0	0.0	0.0	3.4	11.3	13.8	41.4	15.8	39.2	144	86.8
Conesus Lake CDP	2,584	-	-	2,105	89.0	0.0	2.1	7.4	1.5	11.2	30.5	58.0	25.5	37.2	1,045	94.5
Conesville town (Schoharie)	734	688	-6.3	697	85.5	0.0	1.4	1.7	11.3	8.9	30.0	56.4	52.4	20.3	339	82.3
Conewango town (Cattaraugus)	1,882	1,792	-4.8	1,642	99.9	0.0	0.0	0.1	0.0	40.1	14.6	27.2	62.6	17.5	519	60.5
Congers CDP	8,363	-	-	8,406	69.1	3.7	9.3	3.9	14.0	20.0	18.9	45.5	29.4	45.6	2,769	93.4
Conklin town (Broome)..	5,436	5,102	-6.1	5,179	91.6	0.7	0.0	0.0	7.7	20.5	18.5	44.0	49.1	15.2	2,128	91.0
Conquest town (Cayuga)..	1,819	1,730	-4.9	1,899	97.1	0.0	0.0	2.1	0.8	20.6	15.3	45.1	65.0	14.1	756	87.4
Constable town (Franklin).	1,570	1,574	0.3	1,649	93.1	2.2	0.0	2.1	2.6	23.2	14.3	39.0	58.2	10.7	672	86.2
Constableville village	242	236	-2.5	330	97.9	0.0	0.0	0.0	2.1	32.4	14.2	31.7	52.3	14.0	113	93.8
Constantia CDP	1,182	-	-	1,133	95.2	0.0	0.0	4.8	0.0	11.2	26.3	54.3	49.1	11.8	556	83.8
Constantia town (Oswego)	4,973	4,827	-2.9	4,857	98.0	0.0	0.0	2.0	0.0	19.8	20.7	47.4	47.1	13.3	2,013	91.8
Coopers Plains CDP........	598	-	-	472	95.3	0.0	0.0	4.7	0.0	28.6	21.6	41.7	34.4	18.7	209	72.7
Cooperstown village	1,853	1,754	-5.3	1,926	81.8	4.7	8.3	2.7	2.5	13.1	25.3	49.6	14.4	61.2	905	95.6
Copake town (Columbia)..	3,618	3,394	-6.2	3,451	91.2	0.0	1.5	3.8	3.5	16.0	25.1	49.3	52.0	27.6	1,268	93.3
Copake Falls CDP	-	-	-	290	78.6	0.0	0.0	21.4	0.0	18.6	10.7	28.6	87.5	0.0	130	76.2
Copake Hamlet CDP	-	-	-	257	90.7	0.0	9.3	0.0	0.0	9.3	33.1	55.3	31.8	51.5	110	91.8
Copake Lake CDP	823	-	-	688	92.3	0.0	1.3	1.9	4.5	12.1	34.3	54.5	53.6	34.0	268	100.0
Copenhagen village	798	772	-3.3	833	90.8	1.3	2.4	2.8	2.8	26.5	10.3	33.1	47.0	16.9	345	84.1
Copiague CDP...............	22,993	-	-	23,561	47.7	7.8	2.1	3.9	38.5	20.7	14.1	39.7	51.9	21.2	7,068	92.6
Coram CDP	39,113	-	-	40,311	64.4	11.3	4.4	1.8	18.1	21.7	15.0	40.7	36.8	31.3	14,798	92.9
Corfu village..................	702	701	-0.1	739	90.9	6.1	0.5	0.7	1.8	12.7	23.0	45.2	44.0	21.2	305	85.6
Corinth village................	2,567	2,445	-4.8	2,589	95.4	0.0	0.0	2.5	2.0	24.6	13.5	39.7	61.3	12.4	1,006	88.6
Corinth town (Saratoga) ...	6,529	6,393	-2.1	6,429	96.5	0.6	0.0	1.4	1.4	24.5	16.6	42.4	58.7	15.9	2,423	90.2
Corning city & MCD (Steuben)	11,184	10,538	-5.8	10,696	92.3	2.2	1.7	1.5	2.3	20.2	15.8	37.7	31.2	38.8	5,026	88.9
Corning town (Steuben)...	6,241	6,175	-1.1	6,262	93.6	3.9	0.3	1.6	0.6	20.2	17.6	44.4	36.5	32.1	2,574	87.8
Cornwall town (Orange)...	12,596	12,465		12,445	83.1	1.4	3.4	1.1	11.0	23.1	16.1	42.6	24.1	50.7	4,601	92.5
Cornwall-on-Hudson village..................	2,980	2,918	-2.1	2,915	89.3	0.4	2.2	0.7	7.5	23.4	15.0	41.7	19.0	50.4	1,030	90.6
Cortland city & MCD (Cortland)	19,184	18,670	-2.7	18,739	90.5	3.7	0.5	2.0	3.3	15.4	12.8	27.5	40.4	27.6	6,657	87.2
Cortlandt town (Westchester)................	41,585	42,294	1.7	42,426	70.0	5.0	3.1	2.9	19.0	22.0	16.5	44.1	27.1	48.7	14,914	94.2
Cortlandville town (Cortland)...................	8,487	8,120	-4.3	8,180	89.2	1.2	0.9	3.8	4.9	18.2	17.1	40.5	38.1	34.4	3,164	89.3
Cortland West CDP	1,356	-	-	1,248	88.9	3.5	3.1	4.4	0.0	17.7	24.9	58.2	33.6	42.7	498	97.2
Country Knolls CDP	2,224	-	-	2,119	90.3	1.8	6.3	1.7	0.0	26.3	20.2	41.6	10.2	69.3	760	97.4
Cove Neck village.............	294	301	2.4	268	91.4	0.0	4.5	0.0	4.1	23.1	22.8	50.3	7.4	66.3	98	96.9
Coventry town (Chenango)	1,654	1,565	-5.4	1,569	97.9	0.3	0.0	1.1	0.8	21.9	15.5	44.5	49.5	17.7	663	85.2
Covert town (Seneca).......	2,150	2,092	-2.7	2,086	92.6	0.4	1.0	3.3	2.8	19.1	29.9	49.5	39.0	34.3	923	81.4
Covington town (Wyoming)	1,255	1,204	-4.1	1,086	96.1	0.0	0.0	3.2	0.6	24.7	17.6	41.3	54.3	19.1	448	84.2
Coxsackie village	2,816	2,670	-5.2	2,687	95.8	0.1	0.9	0.3	2.9	21.9	25.6	44.3	52.1	18.0	1,115	78.5
Coxsackie town (Greene).	8,941	8,321	-6.9	8,485	70.8	15.9	0.8	0.3	12.2	15.8	15.3	40.4	66.0	13.6	2,220	84.0
Cragsmoor CDP	449	-	-	263	100.0	0.0	0.0	0.0	0.0	0.0	18.3	38.8	26.7	49.4	119	100.0
Cranberry Lake CDP	200	-	-	155	100.0	0.0	0.0	0.0	0.0	5.8	45.2	62.5	31.5	53.4	83	95.2
Crawford town (Orange) ...	9,326	9,223	-1.1	9,202	80.2	4.1	0.7	1.7	13.3	23.2	16.4	41.4	40.8	26.5	3,221	93.9
Croghan village...............	611	594	-2.8	599	93.8	0.0	3.3	0.2	2.7	23.7	26.4	40.3	45.9	22.7	255	83.9
Croghan town (Lewis).......	3,090	3,013	-2.5	3,050	98.8	0.0	0.0	1.2	0.0	22.2	17.7	43.3	55.6	19.1	1,110	80.7
Crompond CDP	2,292	-	-	2,350	65.3	10.8	3.1	6.0	14.9	25.4	20.5	45.5	25.6	49.6	793	95.7
Croton-on-Hudson village.	8,070	8,095	0.3	8,155	74.4	4.2	3.6	3.0	14.8	26.4	17.0	41.9	21.0	60.2	2,938	94.9
Crown Heights CDP	2,840	-	-	2,850	68.1	14.3	7.7	1.0	8.9	21.7	13.8	40.5	23.4	37.4	1,035	95.5
Crown Point town (Essex).	2,019	1,880	-6.9	1,988	96.7	0.1	0.1	0.2	2.9	16.1	22.1	47.3	54.8	11.9	832	89.4
Crugers CDP	1,534	-	-	1,527	73.5	5.4	3.5	0.9	16.7	15.6	44.2	64.0	50.5	31.8	773	66.9
Crystal Beach CDP	644	-	-	735	91.7	0.1	4.1	0.0	4.1	7.6	28.3	54.8	34.3	32.2	340	94.7
Cuba village	1,572	1,474	-6.2	1,416	95.2	0.3	0.0	0.6	3.9	24.0	17.0	39.2	46.0	21.1	561	88.1
Cuba town (Allegany)	3,232	3,076	-4.8	3,118	96.4	0.1	0.0	1.7	1.8	21.6	23.4	46.1	44.9	20.7	1,295	88.0
Cumberland Head CDP....	1,627	-	-	1,463	94.5	2.7	0.0	1.5	1.2	9.5	21.1	52.8	29.6	45.8	694	88.3
Cumminsville CDP............	183	-	-	132	100.0	0.0	0.0	0.0	0.0	0.0	25.8	56.9	56.1	0.0	93	81.7
Cutchogue CDP..............	3,349	-	-	3,200	97.1	0.6	0.0	0.1	2.3	16.3	28.1	52.3	21.3	47.2	1,296	91.1
Cuyler town (Cortland)	980	916	-6.5	872	97.1	0.0	0.0	0.6	2.3	22.9	18.2	46.8	54.5	17.9	306	83.7
Cuylerville CDP	297	-	-	278	94.6	0.0	0.0	0.0	5.4	12.6	29.1	56.7	40.6	41.8	133	91.0
Dalton CDP..................	362	-	-	367	100.0	0.0	0.0	0.0	0.0	27.5	15.5	37.6	43.7	28.6	132	89.4
Danby town (Tompkins)	3,319	3,363	1.3	3,417	91.5	5.5	0.6	0.8	1.6	20.4	22.5	44.1	25.9	51.3	1,449	94.5
Dannemora village.............	3,952	3,524	-10.8	3,958	38.3	42.8	0.2	0.6	18.1	3.0	3.4	37.1	79.6	3.6	309	88.7
Dannemora town (Clinton)	4,900	4,468	-8.8	4,595	45.8	37.0	0.4	1.1	15.7	4.9	5.5	38.1	79.0	5.1	572	89.7
Dansville village...............	4,693	4,373	-6.8	4,586	89.1	2.0	0.0	3.2	5.7	24.8	15.1	39.5	48.5	17.5	1,956	84.8
Dansville town (Steuben)..	1,851	1,787	-3.5	1,931	93.8	0.7	0.2	1.2	4.0	23.8	14.4	41.6	55.5	16.2	729	85.5
Danube town (Herkimer)..	1,039	1,020	-1.8	949	98.9	0.0	0.0	1.1	0.0	20.1	18.5	40.9	48.4	16.1	349	86.0
Darien town (Genesee)	3,155	3,019	-4.3	3,051	97.2	0.0	0.0	0.1	2.7	23.8	19.4	41.4	42.0	16.7	1,067	90.4
Davenport town (Delaware)	2,974	2,705	-9.0	2,759	94.4	1.6	0.8	0.3	2.9	15.0	22.4	44.2	45.2	20.7	1,177	85.8
Davenport Center CDP.....	349	-	-	254	100.0	0.0	0.0	0.0	0.0	11.8	36.2	52.2	65.4	4.7	121	81.8
Day town (Saratoga)........	856	841	-1.8	847	96.5	2.1	0.0	1.3	0.1	10.3	29.0	55.7	56.6	21.9	396	82.8
Dayton town (Cattaraugus)	1,886	1,800	-4.6	1,881	95.1	0.7	0.2	1.1	2.9	24.7	15.7	37.8	61.2	13.9	732	73.9
Decatur town (Otsego)....	353	334	-5.4	309	86.4	1.6	0.0	9.4	2.6	19.1	21.4	48.6	52.9	16.1	114	84.2
Deerfield town (Oneida)....	4,124	4,069	-1.3	4,075	93.2	1.2	1.6	2.3	1.7	21.4	16.5	43.7	32.6	34.6	1,548	93.5
Deerpark town (Orange)...	7,909	7,751	-2.0	7,742	81.1	6.5	2.2	2.6	7.7	19.6	17.6	44.6	54.2	15.1	2,941	88.1
Deer Park CDP	27,745	-	-	27,479	56.5	12.5	10.1	2.9	18.1	21.1	16.0	42.1	39.6	31.0	8,667	93.2
Deferiet village................	296	283	-4.4	307	93.5	0.0	0.0	4.9	1.6	31.9	9.4	33.1	31.6	24.3	121	95.0
De Kalb town (St. Lawrence)	2,427	2,314	-4.7	2,674	98.2	0.1	0.1	1.0	0.6	36.9	12.0	31.0	61.9	15.5	838	70.2
DeKalb Junction CDP.......	519	-	-	657	99.5	0.5	0.0	0.0	0.0	30.4	16.6	37.3	57.2	16.4	215	67.9
Delanson village	373	384	2.9	333	94.3	0.6	0.9	0.0	4.2	26.7	6.0	36.6	28.0	29.5	101	97.0
Delaware town (Sullivan)..	2,666	2,566	-3.8	2,565	78.2	6.2	1.0	4.2	10.4	20.8	21.1	44.3	32.3	30.4	1,023	88.1
Delevan village	1,093	1,022	-6.5	1,069	98.4	0.0	0.3	1.3	0.0	26.9	13.8	40.0	55.4	12.5	420	82.4
Delhi village...................	3,087	2,949	-4.5	3,216	75.0	9.5	2.5	4.9	8.1	12.2	12.7	20.8	32.7	41.9	772	86.7
Delhi town (Delaware)	5,122	4,690	-8.4	4,793	81.8	6.7	2.0	3.5	5.9	11.9	15.2	26.2	31.5	38.0	1,488	85.7

1 May be of any race.

Table A. All Places — **Population and Housing**

STATE City, town, township, borough, or CDP (county if applicable)	Population: 2010 census total population	Population: 2019 estimated population	Population: Percent change 2010–2019	Population: ACS total population estimate 2015–2019	Race and Hispanic or Latino origin (percent): White alone, not Hispanic or Latino	Black alone, not Hispanic or Latino	Asian alone, not Hispanic or Latino	All other races or 2 or more races, not Hispanic or Latino	Hispanic or Latino[1]	Age (percent): Under 18 years old	Age 65 years and older	Median age	Educational attainment of persons age 25 and older: Percent High school diploma or less	Percent Bachelor's degree or more	Occupied housing units: Total	Percent with a computer
	1	2	3	4	5	6	7	8	9	10	11	12	13	14	15	16
NEW YORK—Con.																
Denmark town (Lewis)	2,854	2,784	-2.5	2,814	91.7	0.5	0.9	3.3	3.6	24.9	12.5	38.0	53.3	15.6	1,035	88.6
Denning town (Ulster)	553	535	-3.3	484	93.2	0.0	0.6	1.4	4.8	19.0	22.5	49.3	34.9	40.4	187	93.6
Depauville CDP	577	-	-	276	100.0	0.0	0.0	0.0	0.0	0.0	23.2	61.7	54.5	0.0	138	80.4
Depew village	15,437	15,011	-2.8	15,102	91.9	3.9	0.5	1.4	2.3	18.9	19.6	40.6	43.9	19.9	6,667	87.6
De Peyster town (St. Lawrence)	998	1,053	5.5	974	98.0	0.5	0.0	0.6	0.8	37.6	14.2	29.8	55.4	15.9	285	67.4
Deposit village	1,662	1,522	-8.4	1,625	89.9	0.5	1.9	4.0	3.7	23.1	20.4	42.4	60.6	9.9	658	79.6
Deposit town (Delaware)	1,713	1,571	-8.3	1,658	92.2	0.0	0.0	5.1	2.7	23.0	22.3	45.1	56.8	13.9	717	84.5
Dering Harbor village	11	11	0.0	-	-	-	-	-	-	-	-	-	-	-	-	-
DeRuyter village	554	524	-5.4	471	99.2	0.0	0.8	0.0	0.0	38.6	17.0	35.2	47.0	14.6	166	78.3
DeRuyter town (Madison)	1,585	1,540	-2.8	1,389	98.8	0.4	0.3	0.0	0.5	27.7	24.3	44.9	51.6	14.9	500	81.0
De Witt town (Onondaga)	25,888	25,041	-3.3	25,269	81.8	5.6	5.5	3.5	3.5	19.0	18.8	44.1	31.0	45.9	9,973	90.0
Dexter village	1,044	997	-4.5	952	93.9	1.3	0.0	2.5	2.3	27.0	11.2	31.8	49.2	14.6	371	88.4
Diana town (Lewis)	1,709	1,659	-2.9	1,405	98.8	0.0	0.0	1.2	0.0	16.8	22.0	48.0	59.5	17.8	636	93.2
Dickinson town (Broome)	5,282	5,013	-5.1	5,094	87.2	4.7	3.0	1.1	4.0	15.1	20.3	41.3	40.2	23.7	2,066	87.2
Dickinson town (Franklin)	819	796	-2.8	1,031	90.8	0.0	1.0	6.8	1.5	26.1	18.4	38.4	55.0	16.3	376	80.3
Dix town (Schuyler)	3,868	3,895	0.7	3,893	92.6	1.6	2.4	2.3	1.2	16.8	21.5	45.9	45.6	17.4	1,581	92.3
Dix Hills CDP	26,892	-	-	25,925	70.5	4.7	16.9	1.8	6.1	23.4	18.4	45.1	16.8	63.1	7,997	97.7
Dobbs Ferry village	10,924	11,027	0.9	11,070	70.7	7.9	5.9	4.3	11.2	23.8	15.0	38.6	16.6	65.4	3,670	97.8
Dolgeville village	2,201	2,069	-6.0	2,648	90.2	0.1	0.2	3.6	5.9	25.7	17.4	37.7	46.8	13.9	1,002	86.0
Dover town (Dutchess)	8,710	8,344	-4.2	8,396	75.1	3.0	1.4	1.0	19.5	19.0	16.9	44.7	53.6	16.0	3,345	90.0
Dover Plains CDP	1,323	-	-	1,096	83.5	0.5	3.7	0.0	12.2	7.5	22.0	51.5	58.9	15.9	568	84.2
Downsville CDP	617	-	-	525	95.8	0.0	0.0	4.2	0.0	14.7	22.9	47.9	60.6	5.6	228	85.1
Dresden town (Washington)	652	629	-3.5	618	95.3	0.0	0.0	4.7	0.0	13.3	32.0	56.8	46.7	25.2	278	79.5
Dresden village	304	283	-6.9	319	95.0	0.0	0.6	0.0	4.4	34.8	12.5	34.0	45.3	24.5	112	93.8
Dryden village	1,891	2,047	8.2	2,144	88.0	0.3	4.8	3.4	3.5	21.0	16.7	38.3	25.2	38.6	904	92.4
Dryden town (Tompkins)	14,438	14,265	-1.2	14,498	88.8	2.2	2.1	3.7	3.3	18.4	15.7	38.7	25.2	48.9	5,936	92.8
Duane town (Franklin)	174	174	0.0	158	98.1	0.0	0.0	0.6	1.3	10.1	33.5	56.3	41.5	31.5	86	91.9
Duane Lake CDP	323	-	-	233	100.0	0.0	0.0	0.0	0.0	26.2	18.9	45.1	14.6	39.1	81	100.0
Duanesburg CDP	391	-	-	361	78.4	0.0	0.0	0.0	21.6	13.0	23.3	35.8	8.3	48.1	153	100.0
Duanesburg town (Schenectady)	6,118	6,318	3.3	6,477	91.7	0.7	0.2	0.7	6.7	24.7	12.6	36.6	39.5	25.0	1,909	93.5
Dundee village	1,726	1,630	-5.6	1,653	95.8	0.6	0.7	1.9	1.0	30.0	17.3	35.1	51.1	14.7	673	89.0
Dunkirk city & MCD (Chautauqua)	12,554	11,756	-6.4	11,865	61.5	4.3	0.5	3.1	30.6	20.7	17.0	39.7	53.6	16.1	5,272	83.9
Dunkirk town (Chautauqua)	1,328	1,251	-5.8	1,411	72.6	0.9	0.0	0.6	25.9	15.3	34.4	57.5	54.3	24.1	550	85.6
Durham town (Greene)	2,723	2,655	-2.5	2,672	92.6	2.9	0.5	0.8	3.1	23.2	15.3	39.5	48.6	22.8	912	88.7
Durhamville CDP	584	-	-	876	100.0	0.0	0.0	0.0	0.0	42.6	8.9	23.0	39.9	22.5	271	87.1
Eagle town (Wyoming)	1,193	1,167	-2.2	1,245	97.0	0.0	1.8	1.0	0.2	22.3	15.7	40.3	56.9	11.3	452	83.2
Earlville village	872	805	-7.7	1,092	96.5	0.0	0.0	2.2	1.3	25.0	19.4	41.6	52.5	22.4	413	85.0
East Atlantic Beach CDP	2,049	-	-	1,889	88.2	0.0	0.9	0.5	10.3	11.0	21.1	48.3	21.9	55.6	754	91.5
East Aurora village	6,188	6,160	-0.5	6,184	95.0	1.4	0.7	1.7	1.2	19.6	23.4	46.8	24.5	50.3	2,565	94.5
East Avon CDP	608	-	-	636	100.0	0.0	0.0	0.0	0.0	28.0	19.0	42.2	53.3	34.0	286	95.5
East Bloomfield town (Ontario)	3,633	3,538	-2.6	3,576	97.1	0.6	0.0	0.5	1.7	23.0	21.0	42.8	33.1	31.7	1,440	88.0
Eastchester CDP	19,554	-	-	19,990	80.2	1.7	9.4	2.7	6.0	23.0	19.6	42.7	18.6	63.4	7,757	93.5
Eastchester town (Westchester)	32,327	32,906	1.8	32,983	78.4	2.6	9.2	2.6	7.1	23.0	18.1	41.8	17.5	64.4	12,762	91.7
East Farmingdale CDP	6,484	-	-	6,168	51.4	13.1	10.3	3.0	22.3	20.9	12.6	32.8	43.7	33.8	1,826	89.9
East Fishkill town (Dutchess)	29,038	29,527	1.7	29,299	81.0	2.5	4.2	4.2	8.0	22.6	16.2	44.1	32.2	40.9	9,730	94.2
East Glenville CDP	6,616	-	-	6,259	92.5	0.1	3.3	1.0	3.2	23.5	24.7	45.1	26.5	42.6	2,186	86.7
East Greenbush CDP	4,487	-	-	4,663	89.2	0.9	5.0	2.3	2.7	18.1	13.5	46.4	22.7	52.2	1,892	96.3
East Greenbush town (Rensselaer)	16,547	16,221	-2.0	16,352	89.5	2.5	3.7	1.9	2.4	20.1	18.8	44.8	27.8	44.1	6,856	92.9
East Hampton village	1,084	1,134	4.6	869	84.3	2.4	1.4	5.2	6.7	10.8	42.3	62.9	13.4	67.6	467	89.7
East Hampton town (Suffolk)	21,479	22,047	2.6	21,952	70.6	2.6	2.2	0.9	23.7	15.9	26.6	52.0	30.6	48.2	9,176	86.3
East Hampton North CDP	4,142	-	-	4,535	52.4	7.7	0.3	0.3	39.2	20.2	18.4	45.3	42.0	35.2	1,751	75.2
East Hills village	6,946	7,233	4.1	7,147	84.2	0.8	8.9	1.4	4.7	29.6	16.4	42.4	7.0	83.3	2,293	99.7
East Islip CDP	14,475	-	-	13,222	86.4	2.2	1.1	0.4	9.9	22.7	15.0	42.3	33.6	38.7	4,340	96.1
East Ithaca CDP	2,231	-	-	1,886	68.9	4.2	15.7	1.6	9.7	16.8	16.8	36.5	9.6	74.6	860	95.8
East Kingston CDP	276	-	-	469	76.3	5.8	0.0	7.9	10.0	17.7	22.2	41.3	54.4	7.3	183	100.0
East Marion CDP	926	-	-	999	92.2	1.6	0.0	2.7	3.5	12.1	36.7	60.8	34.0	37.1	457	91.5
East Massapequa CDP	19,069	-	-	17,622	75.0	11.7	2.2	1.1	9.9	18.9	21.1	45.3	30.8	42.6	6,869	91.1
East Meadow CDP	38,132	-	-	38,029	61.9	6.1	12.9	2.6	16.5	20.2	20.0	41.3	36.8	38.3	12,304	92.4
East Moriches CDP	5,249	-	-	5,445	90.4	1.9	1.9	2.6	3.2	21.5	17.4	45.4	31.4	31.3	1,860	94.5
East Nassau village	589	569	-3.4	526	96.6	0.0	0.4	1.9	1.1	23.8	9.9	39.4	34.0	28.0	204	93.6
East Northport CDP	20,217	-	-	20,190	89.5	0.6	2.5	1.0	6.4	20.7	17.2	45.7	25.2	45.7	6,957	97.2
East Norwich CDP	2,709	-	-	2,959	84.6	2.2	1.5	4.0	7.7	24.8	17.7	43.9	21.5	57.9	983	92.4
Easton town (Washington)	2,341	2,234	-4.6	2,433	99.3	0.0	0.0	0.0	0.7	22.5	18.5	44.5	41.4	32.1	941	89.7
East Otto town (Cattaraugus)	1,048	1,029	-1.8	1,054	99.2	0.2	0.0	0.3	0.3	17.0	14.9	42.2	50.0	17.0	467	76.9
East Patchogue CDP	22,469	-	-	22,172	74.1	4.1	1.9	0.5	19.5	19.9	18.5	42.8	46.3	26.4	8,135	87.7
Eastport CDP	1,831	-	-	1,917	86.5	0.5	0.0	0.0	13.0	18.8	22.3	45.3	27.6	40.7	657	83.6
East Quogue CDP	4,757	-	-	5,343	86.1	0.4	2.3	0.3	10.9	23.6	18.0	45.1	30.2	39.3	2,066	86.3
East Randolph CDP	620	-	-	621	91.3	1.8	0.6	5.3	1.0	44.1	9.5	26.8	33.2	24.4	230	87.8
East Rochester town & village (Monroe)	6,610	6,490	-1.8	6,563	85.6	4.7	0.6	5.6	3.5	18.9	15.7	37.0	30.0	35.3	2,876	88.2
East Rockaway village	9,758	9,814	0.6	9,816	79.4	4.5	4.6	0.8	10.8	21.3	15.6	42.8	29.9	47.3	3,826	96.0
East Shoreham CDP	6,666	-	-	6,801	81.4	3.4	4.0	1.8	9.4	24.2	11.1	39.5	24.5	45.7	1,981	98.0
East Syracuse village	3,084	2,920	-5.3	2,955	94.6	1.7	0.3	1.3	2.0	18.2	16.4	45.7	51.2	15.4	1,391	79.5
East Williston village	2,557	2,550	-0.3	2,572	79.0	1.0	9.2	3.6	7.3	26.4	17.6	43.2	13.4	74.9	809	98.5
Eaton town (Madison)	5,237	4,838	-7.6	4,816	88.4	6.3	2.0	1.0	2.4	14.5	14.0	26.7	44.7	21.0	1,325	89.5
Eatons Neck CDP	1,406	-	-	1,455	96.8	0.0	0.0	0.0	3.2	19.6	23.4	52.5	17.2	57.2	518	100.0
Eden CDP	3,516	-	-	3,311	94.9	0.0	1.8	0.0	3.3	20.4	16.4	49.8	37.5	27.5	1,342	82.1
Eden town (Erie)	7,691	7,611		7,631	94.9	0.0	1.1	1.0	3.0	19.1	18.2	47.7	40.3	26.8	3,098	84.8
Edinburg town (Saratoga)	1,216	1,213	-0.2	1,301	98.2	0.5	0.7	0.0	0.6	11.9	30.8	56.6	47.4	17.1	626	93.3
Edmeston CDP	657	-	-	559	95.7	0.2	2.1	0.7	1.3	27.2	15.7	37.8	34.5	27.4	216	94.0
Edmeston town (Otsego)	1,826	1,733	-5.1	1,773	94.9	1.6	0.7	0.7	2.1	21.4	20.7	42.0	45.2	19.2	639	85.1

1 May be of any race.

Table A. All Places — **Population and Housing**

STATE City, town, township, borough, or CDP (county if applicable)	Population				Race and Hispanic or Latino origin (percent)					Age (percent)			Educational attainment of persons age 25 and older		Occupied housing units	
	2010 census total population	2019 estimated population	Percent change 2010–2019	ACS total population estimate 2015–2019	White alone, not Hispanic or Latino	Black alone, not Hispanic or Latino	Asian alone, not Hispanic or Latino	All other races or 2 or more races, not Hispanic or Latino	Hispanic or Latino[1]	Under 18 years old	Age 65 years and older	Median age	Percent High school diploma or less	Percent Bachelor's degree or more	Total	Percent with a computer
	1	2	3	4	5	6	7	8	9	10	11	12	13	14	15	16
NEW YORK—Con.																
Edwards CDP	439	-	-	524	99.2	0.0	0.0	0.8	0.0	31.5	14.1	28.7	47.6	13.2	184	88.0
Edwards town (St. Lawrence)	1,154	1,096	-5.0	1,215	97.8	0.0	0.0	2.1	0.2	24.0	18.6	40.8	56.4	14.8	458	87.6
Eggertsville CDP	15,019	-	-	15,721	66.0	16.3	8.1	4.1	5.4	20.1	15.6	36.8	21.7	51.5	6,448	92.1
Elba village	675	639	-5.3	649	87.5	0.9	0.0	5.4	6.2	26.3	14.0	40.2	39.9	22.1	239	92.9
Elba town (Genesee)	2,370	2,246	-5.2	2,250	80.9	1.1	0.0	4.0	14.0	25.2	14.1	38.8	44.6	20.0	808	91.2
Elbridge village	1,053	998	-5.2	969	93.9	0.0	2.3	1.4	2.4	17.8	24.3	50.8	35.5	23.7	430	92.1
Elbridge town (Onondaga)	5,921	5,688	-3.9	5,741	93.7	0.2	0.4	3.0	2.7	20.1	20.3	47.7	46.9	23.2	2,298	91.3
Elizabethtown CDP	754	-	-	631	87.2	3.0	0.0	2.5	7.3	14.1	31.7	57.6	40.7	30.1	250	90.8
Elizabethtown town (Essex)	1,163	1,092	-6.1	1,056	90.5	1.8	1.5	1.8	4.4	13.0	30.8	56.6	39.3	30.3	438	84.0
Ellenburg town (Clinton)	1,745	1,669	-4.4	1,827	97.6	0.0	0.5	0.5	1.4	21.2	17.7	43.3	63.6	12.7	788	82.0
Ellenville village	4,139	4,014	-3.0	4,032	45.0	9.7	5.1	4.6	35.6	29.1	12.6	37.3	52.4	18.6	1,575	94.8
Ellery town (Chautauqua)	4,528	4,308	-4.9	4,351	95.9	1.7	0.0	1.8	0.6	17.4	26.6	52.0	36.2	32.1	1,881	87.2
Ellicott town (Chautauqua)	8,700	8,274	-4.9	8,384	97.1	0.6	0.3	1.1	0.9	17.5	23.1	46.4	44.3	22.4	3,648	88.7
Ellicottville village	376	382	1.6	279	93.2	0.0	0.0	6.8	0.0	14.0	41.6	55.8	35.5	52.7	142	81.7
Ellicottville town (Cattaraugus)	1,599	1,566	-2.1	1,149	96.0	0.0	0.0	3.4	0.6	15.3	27.1	53.1	38.9	36.8	552	84.6
Ellington town (Chautauqua)	1,631	1,546	-5.2	1,661	97.2	0.2	0.5	1.1	1.0	22.4	19.9	46.9	58.1	14.1	601	79.9
Ellisburg village	244	233	-4.5	223	88.3	1.3	3.1	4.0	3.1	36.8	16.1	30.9	39.5	19.4	74	86.5
Ellisburg town (Jefferson)	3,471	3,338	-3.8	3,420	94.7	0.2	0.2	2.6	2.3	28.8	19.1	38.1	47.3	22.3	1,290	87.9
Elma town (Erie)	11,317	11,775	4.0	11,732	98.4	0.1	0.4	0.8	0.3	18.4	23.2	49.4	31.5	42.2	5,076	91.0
Elma Center CDP	2,571	-	-	3,301	98.8	0.0	0.6	0.0	0.6	18.5	27.4	53.1	31.8	43.6	1,343	94.0
Elmira city & MCD (Chemung)	29,242	27,054	-7.5	27,402	73.0	14.3	0.5	6.8	5.4	24.5	13.8	34.1	55.1	14.8	9,717	86.2
Elmira town (Chemung)	6,928	6,477	-6.5	6,600	95.1	0.3	2.3	0.6	1.7	22.6	19.8	46.3	28.0	44.3	2,886	94.5
Elmira Heights village	4,097	3,805	-7.1	4,199	88.9	2.1	1.2	4.8	3.0	18.3	16.9	40.9	47.1	17.4	1,983	86.4
Elmont CDP	33,198	-	-	35,824	14.3	47.1	12.5	4.5	21.5	19.9	13.4	39.2	39.0	29.1	9,775	95.8
Elmsford village	4,682	5,216	11.4	5,085	21.9	23.8	8.9	2.9	42.5	18.4	11.8	35.6	39.9	38.6	1,614	95.4
Elwood CDP	11,177	-	-	11,498	74.1	8.9	7.6	2.7	6.6	22.6	15.6	42.1	28.8	44.9	3,566	97.0
Endicott village	13,381	12,532	-6.3	12,771	81.4	9.3	2.0	2.8	4.5	20.8	17.4	38.3	49.2	17.9	5,625	84.6
Endwell CDP	11,446	-	-	11,677	90.4	1.6	2.9	0.7	4.4	19.8	22.9	45.0	33.7	36.7	5,190	86.0
Enfield town (Tompkins)	3,522	3,409	-3.2	3,509	90.6	0.1	0.0	3.3	6.0	20.3	17.3	44.1	36.7	24.0	1,504	93.7
Ephratah town (Fulton)	1,680	1,593	-5.2	1,648	96.4	1.2	0.2	1.5	0.7	18.7	19.2	46.4	56.2	13.5	649	86.9
Erin CDP	483	-	-	395	94.7	2.3	2.0	1.0	0.0	20.5	12.2	37.8	65.2	4.8	158	88.6
Erin town (Chemung)	1,957	1,856	-5.2	1,772	97.7	0.5	0.8	1.0	0.0	19.9	18.6	44.9	52.2	16.8	751	86.7
Erwin town (Steuben)	8,073	8,136	0.8	8,259	84.0	2.6	10.2	1.9	1.2	24.0	18.6	41.3	25.5	47.5	3,497	91.5
Esopus town (Ulster)	9,044	8,711	-3.7	8,782	87.2	0.9	0.8	4.8	6.4	15.4	19.0	43.8	37.5	30.7	3,437	94.0
Esperance village	345	325	-5.8	376	93.4	1.1	1.6	1.1	2.9	16.5	16.5	47.1	51.2	13.4	156	87.2
Esperance town (Schoharie)	2,074	1,927	-7.1	2,057	96.1	0.5	0.7	0.7	2.0	17.3	22.9	47.6	51.1	15.8	878	84.4
Essex town (Essex)	671	630	-6.1	622	99.8	0.2	0.0	0.0	0.0	15.0	28.5	53.1	33.6	48.1	282	87.6
Evans town (Erie)	16,364	16,091	-1.7	16,155	94.4	1.0	0.0	1.6	3.0	19.2	20.7	47.3	43.8	24.2	6,686	87.6
Evans Mills village	610	556	-8.9	556	90.3	1.8	1.1	2.2	4.7	20.0	13.5	33.5	43.8	15.1	227	83.3
Exeter town (Otsego)	987	930	-5.8	997	96.0	1.4	0.5	0.1	2.0	15.1	18.1	48.0	49.7	21.9	421	87.2
Fabius village	352	332	-5.7	325	97.5	0.0	0.0	2.5	0.0	25.8	18.5	44.6	33.9	29.1	129	92.2
Fabius town (Onondaga)	1,973	1,944	-1.5	2,186	90.6	0.5	0.3	1.0	7.5	24.9	14.0	44.1	32.1	32.1	806	90.7
Fairfield town (Herkimer)	1,625	1,522	-6.3	1,537	96.9	0.0	0.4	2.2	0.5	25.8	15.9	39.4	48.7	21.8	586	85.2
Fair Haven village	744	717	-3.6	806	97.4	1.2	0.0	1.4	0.0	12.4	23.4	50.6	35.3	35.1	368	92.4
Fairmount CDP	10,224	-	-	10,092	90.2	1.3	2.2	1.8	4.5	20.5	18.6	42.2	32.8	35.0	4,127	89.3
Fairport village	5,356	5,305		5,349	92.2	0.1	0.5	1.9	5.3	18.2	19.5	47.1	12.7	54.4	2,472	96.3
Fairview CDP	5,515	-	-	5,486	63.5	18.1	3.4	3.5	11.5	16.3	10.7	32.1	34.4	26.2	1,708	92.8
Fairview CDP	3,099	-	-	3,535	5.6	63.2	0.7	0.6	29.9	27.5	8.3	32.4	41.7	26.0	1,170	88.5
Falconer village	2,420	2,247	-7.1	2,399	97.0	0.5	0.0	1.3	1.2	20.6	20.2	42.2	48.4	12.4	1,101	87.7
Fallsburg town (Sullivan)	12,915	13,023	0.8	12,925	62.2	10.4	2.7	3.7	21.1	23.3	14.5	39.6	48.7	22.7	4,351	86.3
Farmersville town (Cattaraugus)	1,097	1,050	-4.3	1,191	97.1	0.0	0.1	1.3	1.5	19.0	22.8	49.8	54.6	18.5	513	79.5
Farmingdale village	8,235	9,002	9.3	8,902	75.4	3.8	8.7	2.3	9.8	16.7	19.0	46.1	35.9	41.4	3,773	93.3
Farmington town (Ontario)	11,829	13,784	16.5	13,208	88.6	3.2	1.1	1.8	5.3	24.6	13.5	37.6	24.7	41.0	5,438	95.3
Farmingville CDP	15,481	-	-	15,714	74.0	3.5	4.4	3.9	14.3	20.3	13.2	40.1	39.9	28.2	4,688	95.4
Farnham village	383	371	-3.1	459	91.7	0.0	0.2	6.1	2.0	25.9	12.0	36.3	49.4	19.7	146	91.1
Fayette town (Seneca)	3,925	3,771	-3.9	3,809	96.7	0.0	0.0	0.2	3.1	21.1	24.3	50.6	48.1	18.7	1,597	87.4
Fayetteville village	4,222	4,044	-4.2	4,095	91.7	1.1	1.4	4.1	1.7	23.5	19.8	42.9	19.3	59.4	1,742	92.8
Felts Mills CDP	372	-	-	333	90.4	0.0	0.0	0.0	9.6	21.6	0.0	50.1	54.5	7.3	169	100.0
Fenner town (Madison)	1,728	1,684	-2.5	1,624	96.9	0.6	0.0	0.9	1.7	18.3	21.1	47.6	43.4	21.9	631	87.5
Fenton town (Broome)	6,675	6,227	-6.7	6,354	97.7	0.0	0.4	1.5	0.4	22.4	19.4	42.3	39.6	27.2	2,536	93.1
Fillmore CDP	603	-	-	518	97.1	0.0	0.0	0.8	2.1	27.4	16.8	44.8	42.9	25.3	190	91.6
Fine town (St. Lawrence)	1,510	1,444	-4.4	1,432	96.8	0.9	0.5	0.6	1.2	18.2	25.1	51.8	56.9	16.0	630	87.0
Fire Island CDP	292	-	-	293	67.6	0.0	1.4	0.3	30.7	16.7	22.5	51.3	42.7	31.6	96	87.5
Firthcliffe CDP	4,949	-	-	4,912	83.1	2.5	2.5	1.0	10.9	22.3	20.5	44.8	28.0	51.0	1,998	88.7
Fishers Island CDP	236	-	-	125	93.6	0.0	0.0	3.2	3.2	11.2	18.4	44.6	90.5	6.7	40	100.0
Fishers Landing CDP	89	-	-	48	100.0	0.0	0.0	0.0	0.0	0.0	62.5	81.4	50.0	10.4	23	69.6
Fishkill village	2,171	2,155	-0.7	2,014	75.2	5.9	3.1	0.9	14.9	17.9	17.5	44.4	29.0	44.5	1,007	88.3
Fishkill town (Dutchess)	23,791	24,096	1.3	24,151	63.5	12.0	6.3	2.3	15.9	16.7	18.7	43.1	36.7	34.2	8,650	92.1
Flanders CDP	4,472	-	-	5,750	28.1	10.0	0.4	1.9	59.7	33.8	10.7	34.0	58.8	15.4	1,443	96.0
Fleischmanns village	345	310	-10.1	265	71.3	0.0	0.0	0.0	28.7	22.6	32.5	42.9	47.6	37.2	115	93.0
Fleming town (Cayuga)	2,638	2,530	-4.1	2,559	97.5	0.1	0.1	0.7	1.7	14.4	22.9	53.0	40.3	30.7	1,052	92.4
Floral Park village	15,827	15,844	0.1	16,003	77.6	0.8	9.1	1.3	11.1	21.2	17.7	42.7	23.9	53.7	5,652	91.5
Florence town (Oneida)	1,025	1,058	3.2	1,030	96.9	0.6	1.4	0.0	1.2	20.6	14.9	46.3	63.0	12.0	391	81.3
Florida town (Montgomery)	2,715	2,786	2.6	2,749	92.0	0.5	1.8	0.0	5.7	17.3	20.1	48.5	49.8	17.6	1,176	81.7
Florida village	2,807	2,919	4.0	2,866	69.8	1.8	1.3	6.4	20.7	24.4	16.1	41.7	39.8	25.1	1,038	94.1
Flower Hill village	4,626	4,889	5.7	4,832	72.6	1.5	18.8	1.7	5.3	25.9	18.0	44.6	12.0	77.4	1,555	95.0
Floyd town (Oneida)	3,815	3,762	-1.4	3,769	96.7	1.5	0.0	0.9	0.8	19.6	17.4	45.4	41.4	23.9	1,512	89.7
Fonda village	788	752	-4.6	995	82.7	0.3	0.0	0.8	16.2	29.5	7.3	35.1	34.3	18.5	329	90.6
Forestburgh town (Sullivan)	819	790	-3.5	1,143	91.9	2.8	0.4	0.4	4.5	13.9	30.5	55.2	41.6	34.2	486	88.9
Forest Home CDP	572	-	-	601	40.9	3.0	37.3	10.6	8.2	16.6	5.0	30.6	6.8	84.5	289	100.0
Forestport town (Oneida)	1,535	1,530	-0.3	1,455	96.6	0.8	0.1	2.5	0.0	10.7	32.7	56.6	44.4	24.2	726	83.2
Forestville CDP	697	-	-	702	85.3	1.3	0.0	3.3	10.1	28.5	10.8	34.8	51.2	13.0	257	83.3
Fort Ann village	484	469	-3.1	341	94.4	2.3	0.0	2.3	0.9	16.4	13.2	41.8	53.1	13.6	140	93.6

1 May be of any race.

Table A. All Places — **Population and Housing**

STATE City, town, township, borough, or CDP (county if applicable)	2010 census total population	2019 estimated population	Percent change 2010–2019	ACS total population estimate 2015–2019	White alone, not Hispanic or Latino	Black alone, not Hispanic or Latino	Asian alone, not Hispanic or Latino	All other races or 2 or more races, not Hispanic or Latino	Hispanic or Latino[1]	Under 18 years old	Age 65 years and older	Median age	Percent High school diploma or less	Percent Bachelor's degree or more	Total	Percent with a computer
	1	2	3	4	5	6	7	8	9	10	11	12	13	14	15	16
NEW YORK—Con.																
Fort Ann town (Washington)	6,193	6,000	-3.1	6,052	63.7	21.8	0.4	1.8	12.3	8.9	12.8	40.6	64.3	13.0	1,372	87.7
Fort Covington town (Franklin)	1,676	1,599	-4.6	2,138	63.0	3.5	0.0	31.8	1.8	37.8	13.2	32.9	53.0	12.4	688	82.1
Fort Covington Hamlet CDP	1,308	-	-	1,535	57.7	2.5	0.1	37.2	2.5	38.0	14.5	34.2	49.6	14.9	470	86.6
Fort Drum CDP	12,955	-	-	13,020	50.6	13.9	2.9	7.4	25.2	28.8	0.1	22.1	22.5	30.0	3,299	99.7
Fort Edward village	3,371	3,268	-3.1	3,295	98.0	0.0	0.0	1.5	0.5	25.6	11.7	36.6	48.3	13.9	1,309	92.0
Fort Edward town (Washington)	6,350	6,130	-3.5	6,159	97.4	0.4	0.0	0.9	1.3	18.7	20.0	43.3	49.2	17.0	2,456	89.0
Fort Johnson village	488	464	-4.9	729	91.5	1.8	0.0	0.0	6.7	23.7	12.3	39.6	30.4	28.3	259	90.3
Fort Montgomery CDP	1,571	-	-	1,691	65.4	0.9	11.8	3.3	18.7	18.1	19.0	47.8	30.3	45.1	627	98.2
Fort Plain village	2,331	2,224	-4.6	1,765	91.4	0.5	0.9	3.2	4.0	22.7	18.3	42.2	51.9	15.9	699	86.7
Fort Salonga CDP	10,008	-	-	9,775	90.5	0.7	1.2	0.3	7.3	21.0	20.4	48.7	17.0	59.5	3,390	96.5
Fowler town (St. Lawrence)	2,202	2,119	-3.8	2,101	95.0	0.4	0.3	1.1	3.1	19.8	19.6	45.5	55.0	14.5	906	86.3
Fowlerville CDP	227	-	-	139	100.0	0.0	0.0	0.0	0.0	12.2	4.3	29.0	62.9	15.7	50	88.0
Frankfort village	2,598	2,427	-6.6	2,435	92.1	1.1	0.2	3.5	3.2	18.8	19.1	42.8	43.2	19.0	949	87.1
Frankfort town (Herkimer)	7,640	7,227	-5.4	7,344	95.3	0.8	0.1	1.9	1.8	19.8	19.5	44.8	42.1	25.2	2,924	87.3
Franklin village	374	338	-9.6	394	98.5	0.8	0.0	0.8	0.0	14.7	27.2	50.2	18.3	37.7	172	93.0
Franklin town (Delaware)	2,399	2,254	-6.0	2,481	97.0	0.2	0.5	0.6	1.7	15.2	26.5	51.1	32.9	25.7	1,024	92.2
Franklin town (Franklin)	1,145	1,124	-1.8	1,129	97.0	0.0	1.1	1.9	0.0	15.9	23.6	52.0	30.7	33.6	527	82.4
Franklin Square CDP	29,320	-	-	32,055	61.5	2.6	11.9	2.6	21.4	21.4	17.5	41.1	39.8	33.6	9,758	93.4
Franklinville village	1,743	1,630	-6.5	1,687	93.2	0.4	0.0	2.0	4.4	27.4	14.0	39.4	49.7	15.5	647	81.3
Franklinville town (Cattaraugus)	2,983	2,816	-5.6	2,860	95.2	0.2	0.0	2.0	2.6	22.7	21.5	42.8	51.0	17.9	1,165	81.4
Fredonia village	11,242	10,303	-8.4	10,464	82.6	3.9	1.4	4.0	8.1	15.1	15.2	27.4	31.6	41.7	3,627	89.5
Freedom town (Cattaraugus)	2,402	2,277	-5.2	2,232	93.1	0.0	2.2	0.8	3.9	22.7	20.2	44.0	54.5	15.5	857	80.0
Freedom Plains CDP	421	-	-	303	85.1	6.3	0.0	0.0	8.6	14.2	37.3	55.9	35.1	31.8	164	93.3
Freeport village	42,856	42,956	0.2	43,078	24.6	27.7	1.3	3.1	43.3	21.4	16.1	38.6	48.8	26.9	14,159	89.9
Freetown town (Cortland)	767	767	0.0	722	96.7	0.8	0.0	2.5	0.0	24.2	14.4	37.4	57.6	11.6	270	81.1
Freeville village	520	490	-5.8	425	88.5	0.0	0.9	3.1	7.5	14.8	24.9	51.7	19.0	52.1	194	85.1
Fremont town (Steuben)	1,007	956	-5.1	981	96.0	0.0	0.0	3.7	0.3	18.1	21.4	46.7	43.9	14.1	399	88.7
Fremont town (Sullivan)	1,375	1,332	-3.1	1,235	80.0	3.7	0.0	0.4	15.9	13.7	25.0	52.0	44.5	33.5	556	83.8
French Creek town (Chautauqua)	906	853	-5.8	926	95.2	0.0	0.0	1.1	3.7	32.1	12.2	36.3	56.6	14.6	320	87.2
Frewsburg CDP	1,906	-	-	1,713	98.0	2.0	0.0	0.0	0.0	21.9	26.4	50.7	48.3	21.8	736	85.9
Friendship CDP	1,218	-	-	1,074	97.2	2.8	0.0	0.0	0.0	26.4	19.9	38.8	47.0	12.7	452	85.8
Friendship town (Allegany)	2,004	1,869	-6.7	1,786	96.4	1.7	0.0	2.0	0.0	23.9	18.5	41.6	53.2	11.5	789	81.1
Fulton city & MCD (Oswego)	11,895	11,102	-6.7	11,300	94.3	0.4	0.4	1.1	3.7	24.6	15.1	39.1	48.2	17.6	4,758	86.3
Fulton town (Schoharie)	1,435	1,333	-7.1	1,259	97.1	1.2	0.0	1.7	0.0	17.2	23.0	47.0	56.4	16.6	543	79.6
Fultonville village	788	783	-0.6	568	96.8	0.0	0.0	1.2	1.9	27.6	12.0	33.8	46.7	20.4	249	94.4
Gaines town (Orleans)	3,373	3,148	-6.7	3,184	87.1	6.8	0.6	3.3	2.3	18.1	21.4	42.4	54.4	13.7	1,359	85.7
Gainesville village	233	218	-6.4	245	94.7	0.0	0.0	5.3	0.0	20.0	20.0	48.8	52.1	8.9	107	83.2
Gainesville town (Wyoming)	2,173	2,088	-3.9	2,140	92.3	1.3	0.7	4.6	1.0	24.9	16.4	40.6	56.2	13.8	896	79.0
Galen town (Wayne)	4,283	4,059	-5.2	4,098	91.4	1.3	0.0	1.5	5.8	28.7	13.9	39.4	58.0	10.6	1,513	85.0
Galeville CDP	4,617	-	-	4,642	89.7	4.9	0.0	5.1	0.3	20.5	21.0	42.3	45.6	18.7	2,034	76.5
Gallatin town (Columbia)	1,664	1,582	-4.9	1,575	87.4	3.1	1.5	4.0	3.9	17.0	20.4	50.2	43.4	33.1	665	88.4
Galway village	200	191	-4.5	254	95.3	0.8	0.0	0.0	3.9	29.1	22.8	35.9	44.8	30.2	90	94.4
Galway town (Saratoga)	3,550	3,543	-0.2	3,546	94.8	0.6	0.0	2.0	2.7	22.2	23.2	45.9	31.8	37.8	1,409	95.5
Gang Mills CDP	4,185	-	-	4,553	75.4	4.1	16.6	2.1	1.7	25.1	14.9	38.6	23.4	56.1	1,801	92.8
Garden City village	22,330	22,454	0.6	22,499	86.4	1.7	4.9	1.5	5.5	24.5	18.2	43.0	12.0	73.8	7,452	95.0
Garden City Park CDP	7,806	-	-	8,335	35.2	4.2	38.3	4.4	18.0	20.9	21.5	43.4	32.8	43.6	2,553	92.5
Garden City South CDP	4,024	-	-	4,250	84.9	0.0	7.0	0.6	7.6	20.8	18.1	41.1	30.3	49.1	1,312	97.9
Gardiner CDP	950	-	-	643	90.4	0.0	0.0	9.6	0.0	22.9	11.7	41.1	20.4	44.2	297	94.6
Gardiner town (Ulster)	5,723	5,598	-2.2	5,620	91.9	0.2	0.0	2.6	5.2	21.8	18.5	45.8	25.7	47.2	2,232	92.5
Gardnertown CDP	4,373	-	-	4,633	66.1	10.0	0.9	2.5	20.6	21.3	13.0	36.1	47.1	21.5	1,492	95.8
Gasport CDP	1,248	-	-	1,393	93.0	3.7	0.0	3.1	0.2	24.0	15.1	35.7	51.5	14.3	525	98.1
Gates town (Monroe)	28,498	28,251	-0.9	28,398	76.4	11.2	4.1	2.3	6.0	18.3	20.5	43.2	41.4	25.9	11,952	88.8
Gates CDP	4,910	-	-	4,872	85.4	4.4	2.3	4.7	3.2	17.6	19.6	44.2	37.1	21.6	2,026	88.9
Geddes town (Onondaga)	17,130	16,290	-4.9	16,496	85.8	4.5	0.7	5.4	3.7	22.3	20.9	41.6	35.8	31.5	6,653	88.2
Genesee town (Allegany)	1,697	1,599	-5.8	1,636	97.1	0.0	0.9	1.6	0.4	20.7	19.0	48.1	48.2	18.3	695	85.9
Genesee Falls town (Wyoming)	432	414	-4.2	354	94.6	0.0	1.1	4.2	0.0	15.8	13.0	47.3	54.9	19.1	171	88.9
Geneseo village	8,039	8,120	1.0	8,095	88.6	1.7	2.9	1.6	5.3	9.7	7.6	21.0	32.7	39.6	1,847	95.8
Geneseo town (Livingston)	10,484	10,623	1.3	10,635	89.2	1.8	3.1	1.2	4.7	11.7	12.3	21.6	32.8	42.2	2,997	92.9
Geneva city & MCD (Ontario)	13,272	12,631	-4.8	12,787	69.7	8.2	3.7	3.5	14.9	19.2	14.9	29.5	43.1	28.9	4,529	87.7
Geneva city (Seneca)	-	-	-	-	-	-	-	-	-	-	-	-	-	-	-	-
Geneva town (Ontario)	3,285	3,347	1.9	3,281	74.5	2.8	9.2	2.4	11.1	20.4	24.5	47.8	37.0	35.1	1,417	88.8
Genoa town (Cayuga)	1,931	1,933	0.1	1,839	97.0	0.0	0.4	0.3	2.3	21.3	16.9	43.7	42.0	30.5	719	86.0
Georgetown town (Madison)	970	824	-15.1	665	96.1	0.0	0.0	3.9	0.0	9.9	28.0	53.7	53.1	12.0	246	80.5
German town (Chenango)	370	353	-4.6	322	97.2	0.9	0.0	0.9	0.9	16.8	20.5	46.5	70.2	12.2	151	87.4
German Flatts town (Herkimer)	13,221	12,442	-5.9	12,601	90.3	2.2	1.8	2.1	3.7	24.9	18.8	40.0	45.8	24.5	4,921	87.5
Germantown CDP	845	-	-	796	90.8	0.0	0.9	2.5	5.8	13.7	22.7	48.7	25.9	36.2	362	89.2
Germantown town (Columbia)	1,949	1,827	-6.3	1,875	90.8	1.2	0.5	2.0	5.5	12.7	26.1	52.2	28.2	36.4	857	90.1
Gerry town (Chautauqua)	1,915	1,825	-4.7	1,592	96.8	1.4	0.0	0.0	1.8	16.0	27.3	53.5	53.7	11.8	669	86.5
Ghent CDP	564	-	-	586	64.5	10.1	0.0	0.0	25.4	27.3	5.1	39.6	49.4	37.4	199	100.0
Ghent town (Columbia)	5,398	5,071	-6.1	5,132	89.7	3.6	0.2	1.1	5.4	14.3	27.3	48.8	38.9	27.1	2,062	92.7
Gilbertsville village	401	373	-7.0	393	91.1	0.0	5.1	3.6	0.3	11.5	32.3	54.1	29.6	44.4	191	88.5
Gilboa town (Schoharie)	1,318	1,253	-4.9	1,188	97.1	0.5	0.0	0.0	2.4	12.9	27.5	54.0	51.9	18.7	551	87.3
Gilgo CDP	131	-	-	370	100.0	0.0	0.0	0.0	0.0	0.0	66.2	66.6	21.9	40.5	118	100.0
Glasco CDP	2,099	-	-	2,391	88.7	0.5	0.0	2.5	8.4	19.8	21.5	45.0	43.9	17.6	981	90.3
Glen town (Montgomery)	2,503	2,436	-2.7	2,342	88.5	2.5	0.3	4.6	4.2	29.1	11.8	37.1	51.3	18.8	740	89.7
Glen Aubrey CDP	485	-	-	319	96.2	1.9	0.0	1.9	0.0	13.5	28.5	43.8	70.8	7.1	122	76.2

1 May be of any race.

Table A. All Places — **Population and Housing**

STATE City, town, township, borough, or CDP (county if applicable)	Population 2010 census total population	2019 estimated population	Percent change 2010–2019	ACS total population estimate 2015–2019	White alone, not Hispanic or Latino	Black alone, not Hispanic or Latino	Asian alone, not Hispanic or Latino	All other races or 2 or more races, not Hispanic or Latino	Hispanic or Latino[1]	Under 18 years old	Age 65 years and older	Median age	Percent High school diploma or less	Percent Bachelor's degree or more	Occupied housing units Total	Percent with a computer
	1	2	3	4	5	6	7	8	9	10	11	12	13	14	15	16
NEW YORK—Con.																
Glen Cove city & MCD (Nassau)	26,952	27,166	0.8	27,232	54.7	8.0	5.3	6.3	25.8	20.3	19.1	40.6	44.0	38.4	9,811	89.9
Glen Head CDP	4,697	-	-	5,053	80.7	2.4	2.1	1.3	13.4	23.2	15.7	41.4	25.2	55.7	1,738	94.0
Glen Park village	490	471	-3.9	560	92.9	0.4	0.9	3.4	2.5	28.0	7.7	37.2	49.6	17.9	201	92.0
Glens Falls city & MCD (Warren)	14,700	14,262	-3.0	14,340	89.5	1.3	1.4	2.6	5.2	21.0	15.9	38.0	42.2	29.2	6,416	87.3
Glens Falls North CDP	8,443	-	-	8,817	92.9	0.5	2.9	1.6	2.2	20.0	22.3	44.9	28.8	36.9	3,923	87.8
Glenville town (Schenectady)	29,490	29,271	-0.7	29,292	91.4	1.3	1.1	2.1	4.1	22.2	20.8	42.5	30.1	39.9	10,606	92.3
Glenwood Landing CDP	3,779	-	-	3,843	83.5	3.0	5.5	2.2	5.9	18.2	16.0	45.9	20.9	56.6	1,359	93.8
Gloversville city & MCD (Fulton)	15,618	14,747	-5.6	14,878	90.2	1.6	1.1	2.3	4.7	21.6	16.6	41.6	55.7	13.1	6,225	84.5
Golden's Bridge CDP	1,630	-	-	1,792	90.9	2.1	2.8	0.0	4.2	19.6	19.6	47.8	8.8	68.4	681	100.0
Gordon Heights CDP	4,042	-	-	3,596	22.4	49.6	0.7	2.4	25.0	28.1	9.9	31.8	45.8	19.6	1,053	83.3
Gorham CDP	617	-	-	776	100.0	0.0	0.0	0.0	0.0	29.9	11.0	32.1	24.9	24.3	263	93.5
Gorham town (Ontario)	4,252	4,231	-0.5	4,248	97.1	0.1	0.7	0.8	1.3	18.9	22.4	48.2	34.3	30.3	1,747	93.4
Goshen village	5,441	5,370	-1.3	5,344	66.3	2.7	2.8	0.8	27.5	20.3	22.1	43.0	32.3	40.9	2,037	85.6
Goshen town (Orange)	13,724	14,246	3.8	13,991	71.8	5.9	2.8	1.2	18.3	19.6	20.3	43.9	35.6	37.1	4,323	90.1
Gouverneur village	3,939	3,666	-6.9	3,720	93.7	2.0	0.0	2.0	2.3	18.4	17.9	44.1	55.6	10.7	1,726	78.1
Gouverneur town (St. Lawrence)	7,090	6,939	-2.1	7,018	84.7	6.9	0.2	2.0	6.2	16.4	14.0	43.7	59.3	13.7	2,669	78.0
Gowanda village	2,711	2,547	-6.0	2,898	85.4	0.6	0.0	7.8	6.2	21.8	18.5	40.1	50.7	15.5	1,232	77.6
Grafton town (Rensselaer)	2,140	2,156	0.7	2,380	95.9	0.0	0.0	1.6	2.5	22.4	19.0	46.3	40.2	28.2	993	90.4
Granby town (Oswego)	6,822	6,438	-5.6	6,522	93.0	0.0	0.0	1.4	5.6	23.8	15.3	40.5	56.5	16.3	2,518	86.7
Grand Island town (Erie)	20,374	21,420	5.1	21,047	92.9	2.2	1.7	1.2	2.0	21.8	17.6	43.7	26.6	39.3	8,501	94.9
Grand View-on-Hudson village	288	297	3.1	290	81.0	0.0	4.1	0.7	14.1	20.0	21.7	54.0	13.3	73.3	127	98.4
Grandyle Village CDP	4,629	-	-	4,723	90.5	1.7	1.2	0.9	5.6	22.8	16.7	41.4	32.8	38.6	1,998	95.6
Granger town (Allegany)	538	511	-5.0	557	99.8	0.0	0.0	0.0	0.2	26.4	20.1	41.8	59.3	9.8	211	83.9
Granville village	2,535	2,439	-3.8	2,347	96.0	0.0	2.7	0.5	0.8	18.5	22.1	47.0	55.9	14.3	1,130	83.5
Granville town (Washington)	6,671	6,431	-3.6	6,483	96.7	0.0	1.0	1.6	0.7	20.9	23.0	48.6	61.2	14.2	2,750	83.9
Great Bend CDP	843	-	-	1,139	91.7	0.7	2.3	3.1	2.3	30.7	11.9	30.1	52.7	25.6	378	88.6
Great Neck village	10,071	10,209	1.4	10,205	77.2	1.0	10.8	0.8	10.1	29.7	18.3	35.7	28.6	53.9	3,161	92.8
Great Neck Estates village	2,761	2,879	4.3	2,852	78.2	0.0	14.8	4.2	2.8	28.9	21.9	45.5	18.0	71.8	933	98.6
Great Neck Gardens CDP	1,186	-	-	1,150	66.0	0.0	30.3	2.1	1.7	32.5	23.2	42.1	11.8	77.2	334	100.0
Great Neck Plaza village	6,715	7,027	4.6	6,957	67.7	3.2	18.3	4.5	6.2	14.5	29.5	50.0	21.4	62.2	3,678	89.3
Great River CDP	1,489	-	-	1,405	91.9	0.0	0.0	0.2	7.9	24.6	13.2	46.1	18.0	62.6	505	97.2
Great Valley town (Cattaraugus)	2,011	1,939	-3.6	1,857	97.5	0.0	0.5	2.0	0.0	18.1	24.0	53.3	48.3	18.4	860	82.2
Greece CDP	14,519	-	-	14,798	78.4	5.3	3.6	4.2	8.5	18.2	21.5	43.9	43.7	23.5	6,372	88.2
Greece town (Monroe)	95,965	95,499	-0.5	95,988	80.6	7.5	2.8	3.0	6.1	20.5	19.4	43.1	38.1	30.0	40,029	90.9
Greenburgh town (Westchester)	88,373	90,989	3.0	91,382	58.9	12.0	10.5	2.9	15.8	21.9	17.8	42.5	19.6	63.3	33,558	95.2
Greene village	1,577	1,416	-10.2	1,566	92.0	0.8	1.0	2.5	3.8	21.2	20.3	42.7	38.4	23.9	765	88.2
Greene town (Chenango)	5,604	5,016	-10.5	5,151	94.1	0.3	0.4	2.0	3.2	20.1	22.9	47.2	38.0	25.4	2,246	87.9
Greenfield town (Saratoga)	7,781	7,719	-0.8	7,763	94.3	0.4	0.8	2.6	1.9	21.3	20.5	46.4	40.6	33.7	3,200	93.4
Green Island town & village (Albany)	2,620	2,622	0.1	2,592	84.3	5.2	1.5	2.9	6.1	15.3	18.0	43.2	53.5	19.4	1,261	85.0
Greenlawn CDP	13,742	-	-	14,392	68.5	9.8	4.0	5.1	12.6	24.5	18.6	42.9	26.4	49.5	4,586	92.4
Greenport town (Columbia)	4,164	4,236	1.7	4,234	78.8	7.3	2.7	6.4	4.7	14.5	25.5	50.9	53.8	26.0	1,917	85.2
Greenport village	2,201	2,231	1.4	2,082	61.9	15.7	0.6	0.9	20.9	16.5	27.9	52.7	47.2	30.0	903	87.6
Greenport West CDP	2,124	-	-	2,283	77.0	2.4	0.6	2.7	17.3	11.2	40.4	60.4	33.8	40.6	1,094	88.2
Greenvale CDP	1,094	-	-	1,718	56.1	0.0	38.2	0.0	5.6	19.5	19.4	33.3	18.4	63.1	488	100.0
Greenville CDP	688	-	-	846	92.0	0.2	1.2	6.6	0.0	37.7	20.6	38.0	20.6	38.1	312	76.9
Greenville town (Greene)	3,724	3,562	-4.4	3,562	93.9	0.4	0.7	2.5	2.4	27.1	18.8	44.7	42.9	28.3	1,253	88.0
Greenville town (Orange)	4,639	4,699	1.3	4,689	80.3	1.7	4.5	4.4	9.1	25.1	10.8	36.8	38.9	27.2	1,471	90.8
Greenville CDP	7,116	-	-	7,814	65.7	1.1	25.8	2.7	4.8	26.9	16.8	41.7	11.2	79.5	2,443	94.2
Greenwich village	1,773	1,715	-3.3	2,149	92.6	0.7	0.5	2.9	3.3	28.5	13.5	35.8	39.7	32.1	812	92.0
Greenwich town (Washington)	4,952	4,794	-3.2	4,822	95.4	0.4	1.4	1.3	1.5	22.4	17.9	39.9	45.6	30.9	1,850	90.4
Greenwood town (Steuben)	801	763	-4.7	766	99.5	0.0	0.0	0.0	0.0	26.5	22.8	40.3	53.3	12.8	304	80.3
Greenwood Lake village	3,155	3,088	-2.1	3,091	82.8	2.3	0.0	4.4	10.5	18.6	14.5	43.6	41.9	20.3	1,238	95.1
Greig town (Lewis)	1,199	1,186	-1.1	1,255	96.3	1.1	0.0	1.5	1.0	14.1	26.7	56.0	50.7	21.2	572	87.1
Greigsville CDP	209	-	-	342	100.0	0.0	0.0	0.0	0.0	42.1	9.4	25.4	68.1	14.8	124	93.5
Groton village	2,351	2,225	-5.4	2,209	90.4	3.4	0.6	4.2	1.4	20.1	24.3	43.0	37.3	22.4	932	90.3
Groton town (Tompkins)	5,973	5,790	-3.1	5,913	89.4	1.9	1.7	2.6	4.4	20.3	18.2	44.1	42.2	24.1	2,377	91.0
Grove town (Allegany)	543	514	-5.3	536	99.6	0.0	0.0	0.0	0.4	19.4	20.7	44.2	47.2	23.3	233	85.0
Groveland town (Livingston)	3,239	3,164	-2.3	3,241	58.6	24.5	0.4	3.3	13.3	8.8	6.4	38.6	67.0	10.4	449	94.4
Groveland Station CDP	281	-	-	265	100.0	0.0	0.0	0.0	0.0	23.4	8.3	34.5	45.9	18.0	91	90.1
Guilderland town (Albany)	35,344	35,723	1.1	35,696	81.5	3.6	8.9	1.9	4.1	18.6	17.5	39.9	19.9	52.3	14,396	93.3
Guilford CDP	362	-	-	299	100.0	0.0	0.0	0.0	0.0	22.7	21.7	52.4	47.6	5.2	143	88.8
Guilford town (Chenango)	2,925	2,795	-4.4	2,821	95.9	0.0	0.0	2.3	1.8	20.2	18.6	44.6	47.6	17.6	1,264	90.1
Hadley CDP	1,009	-	-	844	97.5	0.0	0.0	1.3	1.2	20.4	22.9	49.2	52.1	16.7	359	83.8
Hadley town (Saratoga)	2,048	2,004	-2.1	1,839	95.4	0.1	0.0	3.4	1.1	17.5	23.7	50.8	51.6	17.4	745	89.4
Hagaman village	1,292	1,272	-1.5	1,455	93.0	0.0	0.0	0.2	6.8	17.1	27.4	49.6	31.1	23.7	679	88.7
Hague town (Warren)	699	674	-3.6	738	97.3	0.0	0.0	0.7	2.0	11.2	40.8	61.5	33.6	39.5	359	87.5
Hailesboro CDP	624	-	-	847	89.7	0.9	0.0	1.9	7.4	23.0	20.7	33.6	54.9	12.5	343	95.0
Halcott town (Greene)	256	249	-2.7	348	64.7	0.0	10.1	21.3	4.0	20.7	21.0	50.7	25.9	57.1	137	90.5
Halesite CDP	2,498	-	-	2,710	93.5	2.1	0.4	0.0	4.1	20.0	19.6	46.2	17.3	62.1	1,017	97.5
Halfmoon town (Saratoga)	21,514	24,635	14.5	24,224	87.6	1.6	5.2	2.4	3.2	18.7	17.0	43.3	29.1	42.2	10,810	94.8
Hall CDP	216	-	-	150	94.7	0.0	0.0	5.3	0.0	13.3	12.7	53.9	38.7	23.5	68	79.4
Hamburg village	9,422	9,712	3.1	9,636	96.1	0.6	1.4	1.4	0.5	21.1	19.3	41.0	20.8	49.3	4,204	91.7
Hamburg town (Erie)	56,949	58,730	3.1	58,266	95.3	1.1	0.6	1.1	2.0	19.8	19.7	44.3	34.1	34.7	25,079	90.2
Hamden town (Delaware)	1,316	1,207	-8.3	1,139	95.9	0.4	1.3	0.5	1.8	19.3	27.9	51.1	45.1	26.7	497	89.1
Hamilton village	4,238	4,092	-3.4	3,814	75.1	5.0	9.3	3.6	6.9	8.2	10.9	20.8	29.1	50.1	782	81.3
Hamilton town (Madison)	6,689	6,448	-3.6	6,472	82.3	3.0	5.5	2.5	6.7	15.3	12.7	22.2	30.7	44.3	1,787	88.0
Hamlin CDP	5,521	-	-	5,344	94.2	2.3	0.1	1.4	2.0	22.6	14.7	39.6	40.0	24.1	2,055	89.1

1 May be of any race.

Table A. All Places — Population and Housing

STATE City, town, township, borough, or CDP (county if applicable)	Population				Race and Hispanic or Latino origin (percent)					Age (percent)			Educational attainment of persons age 25 and older		Occupied housing units	
	2010 census total population	2019 estimated population	Percent change 2010–2019	ACS total population estimate 2015–2019	White alone, not Hispanic or Latino	Black alone, not Hispanic or Latino	Asian alone, not Hispanic or Latino	All other races or 2 or more races, not Hispanic or Latino	Hispanic or Latino[1]	Under 18 years old	Age 65 years and older	Median age	Percent High school diploma or less	Percent Bachelor's degree or more	Total	Percent with a computer
	1	2	3	4	5	6	7	8	9	10	11	12	13	14	15	16

NEW YORK—Con.

STATE City, town, township, borough, or CDP (county if applicable)	1	2	3	4	5	6	7	8	9	10	11	12	13	14	15	16
Hamlin town (Monroe)	9,051	8,963		9,003	95.3	1.7	0.1	1.5	1.4	20.8	15.7	41.5	38.3	26.8	3,430	89.9
Hammond village	280	270	-3.6	201	93.5	2.5	0.0	3.5	0.5	16.9	22.4	50.1	45.3	19.5	92	76.1
Hammond town (St. Lawrence)	1,191	1,152	-3.3	1,157	96.0	0.4	0.1	2.9	0.5	20.1	23.6	48.5	44.3	23.4	471	85.8
Hammondsport village	661	622	-5.9	495	90.7	0.0	0.0	4.6	4.6	18.4	29.5	53.3	29.8	36.4	260	82.7
Hampton town (Washington)	935	908	-2.9	691	98.6	0.0	0.0	1.0	0.4	12.3	23.4	52.9	50.9	13.8	312	86.9
Hampton Bays CDP	13,603	-	-	14,848	63.6	1.1	0.1	1.2	33.9	18.2	19.2	44.1	41.7	34.3	5,766	77.7
Hamptonburgh town (Orange)	5,546	5,585	0.7	5,516	83.1	0.7	1.0	0.9	14.2	24.9	13.9	40.9	36.0	36.5	1,562	97.1
Hampton Manor CDP	2,417	-	-	1,911	83.4	7.2	0.0	9.4	0.0	18.3	25.2	41.2	44.2	21.4	896	81.3
Hancock village	1,029	933	-9.3	1,108	86.2	2.3	0.0	5.2	6.3	18.9	22.1	44.7	58.4	12.9	532	80.6
Hancock town (Delaware)	3,232	2,988	-7.5	3,043	93.5	0.8	0.2	1.9	3.6	17.9	25.8	53.0	55.3	16.6	1,377	81.7
Hannawa Falls CDP	1,042	-	-	764	91.4	0.8	1.7	3.3	2.9	17.5	26.7	48.7	26.4	39.5	336	96.7
Hannibal village	555	525	-5.4	545	96.0	0.0	0.0	1.3	2.8	24.4	16.5	39.3	56.3	9.6	203	89.2
Hannibal town (Oswego)	4,849	4,578	-5.6	4,628	96.2	0.0	0.2	2.4	1.2	23.0	13.7	41.7	62.0	12.9	1,724	93.0
Hanover town (Chautauqua)	7,126	6,585	-7.6	6,687	92.9	1.6	0.2	3.1	2.2	20.6	20.2	45.3	47.5	21.8	2,738	84.1
Harbor Hills CDP	575	-	-	400	100.0	0.0	0.0	0.0	0.0	38.3	17.5	40.4	14.9	76.6	140	80.7
Harbor Isle CDP	1,301	-	-	1,214	80.3	0.9	0.0	0.0	18.8	21.1	25.5	48.3	20.8	48.6	413	97.8
Hardenburgh town (Ulster)	239	230	-3.8	253	94.1	0.0	3.6	2.4	0.0	19.0	20.9	43.9	34.5	41.0	113	85.0
Harford town (Cortland)	943	911	-3.4	816	96.7	0.0	0.0	2.7	0.6	22.9	17.4	40.7	44.2	20.6	301	90.7
Harmony town (Chautauqua)	2,214	2,059	-7.0	2,295	96.6	0.0	0.1	0.0	3.3	29.1	19.7	38.0	53.1	13.6	860	82.0
Harpersfield town (Delaware)	1,569	1,448	-7.7	1,363	89.4	1.3	2.5	1.4	5.4	11.2	32.3	57.2	54.8	20.3	601	85.0
Harrietstown town (Franklin)	5,702	5,455	-4.3	5,523	90.2	4.8	0.0	2.2	2.9	24.7	17.4	39.9	31.1	31.3	2,350	87.9
Harriman village	2,420	2,452	1.3	3,007	40.9	28.0	5.0	1.5	24.6	29.5	8.9	35.2	35.6	31.5	1,051	94.3
Harrisburg town (Lewis)	437	426	-2.5	511	99.8	0.0	0.0	0.2	0.0	32.3	12.1	37.5	58.4	14.5	174	77.0
Harris Hill CDP	5,508	-	-	5,847	94.0	0.6	1.9	1.2	2.2	21.9	19.5	42.4	23.0	47.2	2,398	92.7
Harrison town & village (Westchester)	27,458	28,943	5.4	28,135	72.4	4.6	7.9	2.1	12.9	21.2	14.7	36.2	26.7	54.8	8,412	95.2
Harrisville village	624	604	-3.2	518	100.0	0.0	0.0	0.0	0.0	21.0	19.9	39.8	48.3	16.9	208	95.2
Hartford town (Washington)	2,269	2,193	-3.3	2,102	93.8	0.0	2.3	0.8	3.1	21.3	19.5	45.6	48.1	22.7	814	93.6
Hartland town (Niagara)	4,109	3,973	-3.3	4,001	97.5	0.1	0.2	0.7	1.4	22.7	18.1	45.9	51.9	12.9	1,665	90.9
Hartsdale CDP	5,293	-	-	4,550	55.8	5.7	21.2	3.8	13.4	10.5	28.0	51.4	15.4	72.6	2,416	90.0
Hartsville town (Steuben)	608	576	-5.3	702	96.4	2.8	0.0	0.4	0.3	27.6	16.5	37.7	52.8	20.6	260	86.2
Hartwick CDP	629	-	-	617	98.2	0.0	0.0	1.8	0.0	19.0	12.0	41.7	25.2	36.4	257	97.7
Hartwick town (Otsego)	2,108	1,991	-5.6	2,090	94.7	0.2	1.2	3.3	0.5	21.1	16.8	41.7	33.9	32.7	865	87.7
Hastings town (Oswego)	9,477	9,192	-3.0	9,251	95.9	0.9	0.4	1.5	1.3	20.6	17.4	44.8	53.3	16.1	3,761	88.3
Hastings-on-Hudson village	7,839	7,853	0.2	7,921	81.7	2.8	5.2	3.6	6.6	25.3	18.7	44.0	14.1	74.5	2,875	95.1
Hauppauge CDP	20,882	-	-	20,005	78.7	3.7	6.6	0.9	10.1	20.1	17.1	43.6	27.5	46.3	6,892	96.0
Haverstraw village	11,910	12,045	1.1	12,065	20.1	8.1	2.3	0.7	68.7	26.1	13.0	35.2	54.7	23.0	3,733	86.1
Haverstraw town (Rockland)	36,627	37,000	1.0	37,114	32.5	12.9	4.6	2.3	47.6	25.0	15.1	38.3	43.4	27.3	12,190	91.9
Haviland CDP	3,634	-	-	3,300	84.5	3.6	1.5	0.7	9.7	16.3	22.6	47.1	37.1	30.5	1,381	97.0
Hawthorne CDP	4,586	-	-	4,658	82.3	0.9	6.4	0.2	10.2	22.2	23.2	45.8	34.2	46.0	1,669	89.5
Head of the Harbor village	1,478	1,458	-1.4	1,378	81.3	5.5	4.0	1.1	8.1	18.6	19.7	46.2	14.1	63.7	458	95.9
Hebron town (Washington)	1,853	1,793	-3.2	1,838	96.6	0.0	1.3	1.3	0.9	17.6	19.0	49.5	55.6	19.2	738	78.6
Hector town (Schuyler)	4,933	4,910	-0.5	4,917	96.8	0.0	0.2	1.9	1.1	17.7	20.0	48.2	29.0	35.7	2,121	92.4
Hemlock CDP	557	-	-	547	100.0	0.0	0.0	0.0	0.0	13.5	10.6	55.5	40.6	3.9	213	100.0
Hempstead village	54,018	55,113	2.0	55,300	5.4	43.5	1.7	2.3	47.1	26.5	10.8	33.9	58.9	18.3	15,877	90.8
Hempstead town (Nassau)	759,793	766,980	0.9	767,441	54.0	16.6	6.1	2.4	20.9	22.1	16.3	40.3	34.5	41.1	244,203	93.4
Henderson CDP	224	-	-	273	86.1	1.8	0.0	5.1	7.0	26.7	19.0	26.9	56.9	3.0	97	89.7
Henderson town (Jefferson)	1,362	1,304	-4.3	1,459	92.0	0.7	0.2	4.2	2.8	18.0	30.4	52.1	42.3	22.5	638	93.1
Henrietta town (Monroe)	42,577	43,426	2.0	43,347	72.7	10.0	9.5	3.3	4.5	18.8	15.2	34.7	34.1	36.9	15,588	91.6
Heritage Hills CDP	3,975	-	-	4,111	94.8	0.5	0.8	0.0	3.9	4.7	66.8	70.6	20.9	54.0	2,433	91.2
Herkimer village	7,737	7,262	-6.1	6,615	90.2	2.2	1.4	3.5	2.7	10.3	27.5	51.8	48.9	15.1	2,868	83.6
Herkimer town (Herkimer)	10,174	9,573	-5.9	9,716	92.9	1.6	0.9	2.6	1.9	12.3	25.3	51.2	48.9	17.1	4,119	84.7
Hermon CDP	422	-	-	338	98.8	0.0	0.0	0.3	0.9	18.0	28.7	43.7	51.4	12.9	176	81.3
Hermon town (St. Lawrence)	1,098	1,043	-5.0	963	97.9	0.0	0.0	1.6	0.5	16.3	25.6	49.5	55.6	14.3	443	87.8
Herricks CDP	4,295	-	-	4,122	41.3	0.0	44.3	11.1	3.3	18.8	23.3	46.6	24.6	60.7	1,311	96.1
Herrings CDP	90	-	-	96	92.7	0.0	2.1	1.0	4.2	3.1	7.3	57.5	63.7	14.3	43	93.0
Heuvelton village	725	722	-0.4	742	96.6	0.8	0.0	2.3	0.3	23.3	9.8	43.4	46.3	19.7	310	89.0
Hewlett CDP	6,819	-	-	6,802	69.0	7.6	10.6	0.4	12.4	19.2	22.4	47.8	33.6	46.2	2,490	91.2
Hewlett Bay Park village	406	429	5.7	350	87.7	4.6	1.7	0.3	5.7	20.6	24.9	50.0	8.1	73.4	123	98.4
Hewlett Harbor village	1,269	1,272	0.2	999	86.9	2.0	8.3	1.4	1.4	20.5	20.7	50.4	9.3	77.8	357	95.8
Hewlett Neck village	454	472	4.0	496	85.1	0.0	11.7	0.0	3.2	31.7	13.7	38.0	6.8	77.2	146	100.0
Hicksville CDP	41,547	-	-	42,709	52.6	3.4	27.7	2.4	13.8	17.9	17.5	43.1	36.4	38.8	13,549	92.7
High Falls CDP	627	-	-	525	96.8	0.4	1.3	1.0	0.6	17.9	18.1	45.8	47.4	14.7	206	96.1
Highland town (Sullivan)	2,532	2,484	-1.9	2,260	93.9	1.7	0.8	0.5	3.1	15.9	23.8	52.5	50.9	27.4	941	92.1
Highland CDP	5,647	-	-	5,707	78.3	7.3	1.3	2.3	10.8	16.5	19.5	46.9	40.7	31.2	2,246	91.5
Highland Falls village	3,887	3,829	-1.5	3,841	54.8	20.2	6.5	7.3	11.2	20.6	13.5	41.7	34.2	43.8	1,595	95.9
Highlands town (Orange)	12,487	12,183	-2.4	12,165	65.1	9.9	6.3	6.7	11.9	22.5	7.6	23.5	25.5	53.2	3,217	96.2
Hillburn village	961	983	2.3	918	36.5	16.0	9.5	11.1	26.9	25.9	15.4	39.2	48.1	25.9	287	95.5
Hillcrest CDP	7,558	-	-	7,441	11.7	47.7	8.1	2.7	29.8	22.1	16.2	38.2	39.8	31.9	1,808	91.4
Hillsdale town (Columbia)	1,923	1,802	-6.3	1,562	95.0	0.0	0.0	1.9	3.1	16.9	26.1	53.6	31.6	47.0	663	91.1
Hillside CDP	877	-	-	856	93.8	1.8	0.0	0.0	4.4	17.8	26.4	51.7	32.1	46.2	334	98.2
Hillside Lake CDP	1,084	-	-	1,200	86.5	0.0	0.0	1.3	12.3	18.4	9.9	37.6	29.3	26.0	397	94.5
Hilton village	5,881	5,777	-1.8	5,832	88.0	6.1	0.0	1.0	4.9	24.4	15.5	39.2	37.9	35.3	2,299	93.3
Hinsdale town (Cattaraugus)	2,189	2,042	-6.7	2,103	90.0	5.6	0.8	3.4	0.2	26.7	16.3	40.4	55.5	18.2	877	86.7
Hobart village	434	391	-9.9	383	97.1	1.0	1.3	0.5	0.0	18.5	16.7	42.2	49.5	24.9	157	82.8
Holbrook CDP	27,195	-	-	25,824	79.6	2.9	3.2	2.1	12.1	21.5	15.0	41.5	35.7	35.1	8,799	95.8
Holland CDP	1,206	-	-	1,329	98.0	0.0	0.0	1.3	0.7	19.8	18.1	44.8	47.2	17.9	567	84.3
Holland town (Erie)	3,401	3,343	-1.7	3,355	96.9	1.1	0.0	1.7	0.3	19.0	16.1	44.6	45.0	20.0	1,439	83.5
Holland Patent village	458	444	-3.1	308	100.0	0.0	0.0	0.0	0.0	16.6	25.6	49.6	41.8	33.2	147	91.2

1 May be of any race.

Table A. All Places — **Population and Housing**

STATE City, town, township, borough, or CDP (county if applicable)	2010 census total population	2019 estimated population	Percent change 2010–2019	ACS total population estimate 2015–2019	White alone, not Hispanic or Latino	Black alone, not Hispanic or Latino	Asian alone, not Hispanic or Latino	All other races or 2 or more races, not Hispanic or Latino	Hispanic or Latino[1]	Under 18 years old	Age 65 years and older	Median age	Percent High school diploma or less	Percent Bachelor's degree or more	Total	Percent with a computer
	1	2	3	4	5	6	7	8	9	10	11	12	13	14	15	16
NEW YORK—Con.																
Holley village	1,811	1,683	-7.1	1,749	83.3	5.9	1.0	3.7	6.1	22.5	9.9	39.8	43.7	13.6	805	88.9
Holtsville CDP	19,714	-	-	19,479	75.8	4.3	4.8	1.5	13.6	20.6	15.4	43.2	37.8	30.4	6,480	93.7
Homer village	3,285	3,101	-5.6	3,123	96.5	0.1	2.4	0.0	0.9	18.5	23.2	47.3	36.2	37.8	1,359	91.8
Homer town (Cortland)	6,402	6,181	-3.5	6,225	96.1	0.0	2.7	0.7	0.5	21.7	20.0	44.5	31.2	37.2	2,337	87.5
Honeoye CDP	579	-	-	568	63.7	6.3	0.0	0.0	29.9	30.1	16.0	32.3	32.1	10.2	206	100.0
Honeoye Falls village	2,674	2,754	3.0	2,759	95.1	0.5	0.7	3.7	0.0	23.1	19.5	41.7	18.3	49.8	1,198	91.7
Hoosick town (Rensselaer)	6,929	6,728	-2.9	6,786	94.6	0.0	0.1	0.9	4.5	24.4	18.2	43.7	46.8	21.2	2,722	82.7
Hoosick Falls village	3,493	3,347	-4.2	3,388	95.5	0.0	0.2	0.9	3.4	21.3	19.4	43.9	48.4	21.4	1,425	85.0
Hope town (Hamilton)	408	360	-11.8	850	91.1	0.0	0.0	3.9	5.1	9.8	15.8	55.1	68.4	4.6	167	79.0
Hopewell town (Ontario)	3,755	3,630	-3.3	3,686	86.2	4.2	0.0	1.2	8.4	22.1	17.6	42.2	44.9	23.5	1,233	92.3
Hopewell Junction CDP	376	-	-	510	57.6	0.0	0.0	0.0	42.4	35.9	6.7	30.6	24.1	42.2	148	90.5
Hopkinton town (St. Lawrence)	1,077	1,026	-4.7	1,098	95.9	0.3	1.0	1.8	1.0	28.1	18.9	44.1	46.4	24.3	407	90.7
Horicon town (Warren)	1,389	1,342	-3.4	1,565	94.9	0.0	0.0	4.5	0.6	13.7	31.0	55.5	41.0	30.5	716	89.0
Hornby town (Steuben)	1,697	1,648	-2.9	1,842	97.4	0.7	0.0	1.5	0.4	20.4	14.9	40.5	46.5	19.9	697	84.1
Hornell city & MCD (Steuben)	8,571	8,302	-3.1	8,281	91.0	1.1	1.9	2.9	3.1	24.4	17.1	37.5	52.8	15.6	3,329	87.4
Hornellsville town (Steuben)	4,153	3,978	-4.2	4,025	94.2	0.4	0.4	2.7	2.4	18.7	23.8	49.0	40.3	24.6	1,741	90.5
Horseheads village	6,440	6,336	-1.6	6,446	87.5	2.0	2.8	4.7	3.0	19.9	25.3	45.6	38.0	29.0	3,106	84.6
Horseheads town (Chemung)	19,477	18,866	-3.1	19,149	88.8	2.1	3.5	3.0	2.6	19.2	23.0	46.2	42.0	25.0	8,392	88.1
Horseheads North CDP	2,843	-	-	2,613	93.6	1.6	2.4	0.0	2.5	23.2	14.2	39.9	36.7	27.2	1,028	98.6
Hortonville CDP	218	-	-	193	96.9	0.0	0.0	3.1	0.0	12.4	31.6	53.1	31.4	14.8	98	94.9
Houghton CDP	1,693	-	-	1,639	82.7	5.2	6.1	1.2	4.7	17.1	10.0	20.5	20.5	72.3	249	100.0
Hounsfield town (Jefferson)	3,470	3,347	-3.5	3,432	91.3	1.0	1.9	1.8	3.9	24.0	16.5	38.2	37.0	37.9	1,502	91.9
Howard town (Steuben)	1,469	1,395	-5.0	1,668	96.8	1.0	0.5	1.4	0.4	22.4	18.3	43.1	51.7	17.0	627	89.0
Hudson city & MCD (Columbia)	6,710	6,072	-9.5	6,235	56.4	22.2	8.7	3.9	8.9	19.0	14.1	38.3	49.0	28.5	2,638	86.0
Hudson Falls village	7,292	7,056	-3.2	7,114	94.8	1.7	0.3	2.5	0.7	21.2	14.8	37.0	49.8	16.6	2,928	90.7
Hume town (Allegany)	2,071	1,974	-4.7	2,136	98.2	0.0	0.0	1.1	0.7	27.3	20.4	43.7	48.9	20.6	834	86.5
Humphrey town (Cattaraugus)	684	646	-5.6	825	97.1	0.0	0.0	2.2	0.7	30.3	11.2	38.1	51.5	17.7	304	80.3
Hunt CDP	78	-	-	136	97.8	0.0	0.0	0.0	2.2	31.6	13.2	42.8	77.4	6.5	61	68.9
Hunter village	496	475	-4.2	341	100.0	0.0	0.0	0.0	0.0	5.9	50.4	66.1	43.7	18.0	219	81.3
Hunter town (Greene)	2,722	2,629	-3.4	2,636	98.2	0.0	1.1	0.0	0.6	13.2	32.6	54.1	42.1	21.5	1,135	85.6
Huntington CDP	18,046	-	-	17,420	89.4	1.6	2.9	1.0	5.1	18.1	20.7	49.1	14.2	65.0	7,129	95.7
Huntington town (Suffolk)	203,046	200,503	-1.3	201,718	76.4	3.9	5.8	2.3	11.5	22.0	18.6	45.4	23.9	53.8	68,753	96.0
Huntington Bay village	1,445	1,437	-0.6	1,390	94.7	0.2	2.1	1.4	1.5	15.8	27.5	54.4	9.7	71.3	534	99.3
Huntington Station CDP	33,029	-	-	32,866	48.6	8.4	3.1	4.8	35.1	26.2	11.5	36.8	40.9	38.1	10,258	94.5
Hurley CDP	3,458	-	-	3,026	89.0	3.4	0.6	1.2	5.8	15.6	24.9	50.1	26.2	44.4	1,321	85.4
Hurley town (Ulster)	6,304	6,020	-4.5	6,080	92.0	1.0	0.3	2.5	4.2	16.2	25.6	52.3	29.7	44.6	2,636	88.2
Huron town (Wayne)	2,087	1,972	-5.5	2,096	79.5	8.4	0.0	0.2	11.8	18.5	20.8	46.3	43.0	30.5	819	84.5
Hyde Park CDP	1,908	-	-	1,997	86.9	4.4	0.0	2.4	6.4	20.4	14.6	44.3	31.4	37.8	830	86.3
Hyde Park town (Dutchess)	21,586	20,847	-3.4	20,954	75.7	7.8	4.0	2.5	10.1	16.6	18.8	41.4	38.1	29.9	7,624	91.1
Ilion village	8,185	7,668	-6.3	7,812	90.0	2.2	0.6	2.1	5.1	26.0	17.8	37.3	44.8	24.3	3,022	89.3
Independence town (Allegany)	1,167	1,134	-2.8	970	99.8	0.0	0.0	0.0	0.2	26.4	22.0	40.5	52.2	13.6	390	91.8
Indian Lake town (Hamilton)	1,352	1,240	-8.3	962	96.4	0.3	0.3	3.0	0.0	13.6	40.2	57.7	37.4	20.3	336	81.8
Inlet town (Hamilton)	333	304	-8.7	133	100.0	0.0	0.0	0.0	0.0	14.3	33.8	55.8	28.9	43.9	29	100.0
Interlaken village	605	599	-	583	91.1	0.7	0.7	4.8	2.7	18.9	20.1	41.4	40.8	33.8	263	79.8
Inwood CDP	9,792	-	-	9,892	30.3	17.3	4.7	0.7	47.0	25.5	11.7	33.2	58.4	19.5	3,015	89.8
Ira town (Cayuga)	2,203	2,197	-0.3	2,402	97.3	0.0	0.2	1.9	0.4	26.7	14.3	37.5	49.4	23.0	864	85.9
Irondequoit town & CDP (Monroe)	51,584	50,055	-3.0	50,302	78.4	9.5	1.3	2.1	8.8	18.8	21.5	45.2	33.9	37.2	22,020	88.2
Irvington village	6,418	6,473	0.9	6,529	84.0	0.2	7.2	2.5	6.1	28.0	17.7	41.3	9.9	73.7	2,366	96.4
Ischua town (Cattaraugus)	857	804	-6.2	719	95.7	0.6	0.0	2.1	1.7	13.1	27.0	55.4	63.4	14.0	357	75.9
Islandia village	3,336	3,309	-0.8	3,341	47.6	8.7	10.7	2.7	30.3	19.4	15.0	39.3	42.1	23.1	1,019	97.4
Island Park village	4,683	4,886	4.3	4,835	55.0	0.5	2.4	0.5	41.6	18.4	15.5	39.2	49.3	23.3	1,585	97.3
Islip CDP	18,689	-	-	17,853	75.4	5.6	1.5	1.6	15.8	19.6	13.5	41.6	35.3	37.1	5,921	94.0
Islip town (Suffolk)	335,298	329,610	-1.7	331,499	54.3	8.9	2.8	2.0	32.0	22.9	13.2	38.4	43.4	29.7	98,339	93.5
Islip Terrace CDP	5,389	-	-	5,579	78.9	0.7	3.2	1.0	16.1	24.4	12.0	38.7	39.8	29.8	1,616	94.8
Italy town (Yates)	1,147	1,155	0.7	982	95.1	0.0	0.0	2.2	2.6	17.1	17.5	47.7	47.8	27.9	373	91.2
Ithaca city & MCD (Tompkins)	30,013	30,837	2.7	30,569	64.4	5.3	17.2	6.6	6.5	7.9	6.5	21.9	19.6	66.9	10,723	95.6
Ithaca town (Tompkins)	19,925	19,663	-1.3	19,847	72.3	4.4	13.0	4.6	5.6	13.4	15.3	28.8	15.7	70.9	6,917	93.7
Jackson town (Washington)	1,800	1,743	-3.2	1,827	92.6	3.8	0.2	0.4	3.1	19.0	24.7	51.5	37.6	30.3	791	83.8
Jamesport CDP	1,710	-	-	971	93.4	0.0	3.2	0.0	3.4	5.9	33.5	59.1	35.8	39.0	400	80.8
Jamestown city & MCD (Chautauqua)	31,161	29,058	-6.7	29,504	81.9	4.1	0.5	3.6	9.9	24.0	16.6	37.7	49.7	16.9	12,659	84.9
Jamestown West CDP	2,408	-	-	2,542	97.4	0.6	0.2	0.9	0.7	17.0	29.0	51.7	32.4	36.5	1,043	90.7
Jasper town (Steuben)	1,425	1,369	-3.9	1,595	99.2	0.0	0.5	0.0	0.3	35.9	12.0	26.2	64.0	10.4	464	65.3
Java town (Wyoming)	2,052	1,961	-4.4	2,079	100.0	0.0	0.0	0.0	0.0	21.2	17.7	44.3	52.3	16.0	866	90.4
Jay town (Essex)	2,506	2,395	-4.4	2,659	96.9	0.5	0.0	1.5	1.2	20.6	16.8	46.2	32.1	37.3	1,107	90.3
Jefferson town (Schoharie)	1,399	1,434	2.5	1,331	98.0	0.0	0.0	0.5	1.4	19.9	20.3	49.3	46.5	23.9	545	83.1
Jefferson Heights CDP	1,094	-	-	1,084	93.5	4.3	0.8	0.0	1.4	10.5	40.8	61.8	49.9	22.5	457	77.2
Jefferson Valley-Yorktown CDP	14,142	-	-	14,205	78.9	4.4	4.3	3.3	9.2	21.9	20.8	47.1	26.0	52.2	5,238	92.8
Jeffersonville village	358	336	-6.1	369	78.0	0.0	2.4	6.5	13.0	12.7	17.1	42.3	43.0	21.5	143	84.6
Jericho CDP	13,567	-	-	13,889	60.3	1.3	31.4	3.6	3.4	21.4	16.2	45.2	14.5	70.2	4,707	98.2
Jerusalem town (Yates)	4,472	4,521	1.1	4,518	93.8	0.8	1.6	0.8	3.1	18.5	19.1	36.1	33.4	34.6	1,451	86.8
Jewett town (Greene)	952	942	-1.1	965	97.2	0.0	0.1	1.9	0.8	9.6	39.1	57.0	39.8	33.9	426	91.1
Johnsburg town (Warren)	2,403	2,301	-4.2	2,333	94.7	0.4	0.7	3.9	0.2	16.8	25.4	55.0	44.7	24.4	1,004	87.5
Johnson City village	15,174	14,161	-6.7	14,448	73.8	7.8	9.4	3.8	5.1	21.4	17.2	34.4	42.7	23.9	6,190	87.1
Johnstown city & MCD (Fulton)	8,657	8,230	-4.9	8,277	89.4	4.6	0.5	1.7	3.8	22.1	18.9	39.2	39.2	26.3	3,438	91.2

1 May be of any race.

Table A. All Places — **Population and Housing**

STATE City, town, township, borough, or CDP (county if applicable)	Population: 2010 census total population	Population: 2019 estimated population	Population: Percent change 2010–2019	Population: ACS total population estimate 2015–2019	Race and Hispanic or Latino origin (percent): White alone, not Hispanic or Latino	Black alone, not Hispanic or Latino	Asian alone, not Hispanic or Latino	All other races or 2 or more races, not Hispanic or Latino	Hispanic or Latino[1]	Age (percent): Under 18 years old	Age 65 years and older	Median age	Educational attainment of persons age 25 and older: Percent High school diploma or less	Percent Bachelor's degree or more	Occupied housing units: Total	Percent with a computer
	1	2	3	4	5	6	7	8	9	10	11	12	13	14	15	16
NEW YORK—Con.																
Johnstown town (Fulton)	7,218	7,278	0.8	7,331	92.9	2.7	0.1	0.5	3.8	18.5	22.3	46.9	47.5	18.6	2,975	86.1
Jordan village	1,372	1,302	-5.1	1,451	97.2	0.0	0.0	2.6	0.1	21.4	16.9	40.8	39.2	24.7	581	85.4
Junius town (Seneca)	1,467	1,425	-2.9	1,553	96.8	0.0	0.2	0.5	2.5	31.1	15.8	34.1	59.6	15.2	530	90.0
Kaser village	4,717	5,368	13.8	5,262	97.8	0.4	0.0	1.9	0.0	57.2	3.1	15.2	75.7	3.8	951	33.6
Katonah CDP	1,679	-	-	1,761	89.5	0.6	4.7	4.0	1.1	26.9	16.8	44.3	8.9	81.8	619	96.0
Keene town (Essex)	1,105	1,060	-4.1	1,195	95.9	0.0	0.1	3.2	0.8	10.9	32.1	53.6	19.7	60.0	592	87.8
Keeseville CDP	1,815	-	-	2,932	94.8	0.8	0.0	1.9	2.5	21.4	15.5	43.1	50.7	15.6	1,280	87.5
Kendall town (Orleans)	2,728	2,603	-4.6	2,612	96.5	0.0	0.0	1.3	2.2	20.4	19.0	46.5	37.7	22.8	1,107	90.2
Kenmore village	15,502	15,020	-3.1	15,132	87.4	5.9	0.9	2.7	3.1	18.4	17.4	42.6	27.4	40.1	7,089	88.0
Kennedy CDP	465	-	-	382	99.0	1.0	0.0	0.0	0.0	15.2	22.8	54.5	58.3	8.3	184	81.5
Kensington village	1,153	1,189	3.1	1,368	76.0	0.3	17.8	0.2	5.7	25.6	24.9	44.9	12.6	78.5	473	96.2
Kent town (Putnam)	13,513	13,162	-2.6	13,246	75.2	3.6	1.6	1.8	17.8	19.0	18.8	46.3	38.9	36.8	4,850	92.8
Kerhonkson CDP	1,684	-	-	2,057	68.4	4.0	0.0	19.3	8.3	27.2	14.0	32.6	33.2	31.4	670	80.4
Keuka Park CDP	1,137	-	-	1,049	88.3	3.5	4.9	1.6	1.7	3.3	7.7	20.1	9.6	80.3	138	100.0
Kiantone town (Chautauqua)	1,350	1,282	-5.0	1,323	96.5	0.3	0.0	0.0	3.2	22.0	23.4	47.3	36.5	29.3	547	88.7
Kinderhook village	1,211	1,124	-7.2	1,304	93.6	0.0	0.0	0.2	6.3	18.3	29.5	54.1	20.7	56.2	609	91.6
Kinderhook town (Columbia)	8,494	8,149	-4.1	8,271	91.7	0.7	0.4	0.7	6.6	20.9	22.6	47.7	34.2	39.0	3,246	88.8
Kingsbury town (Washington)	12,694	12,334	-2.8	12,420	91.9	1.9	0.2	2.7	3.2	20.4	14.2	37.8	49.8	18.7	5,115	94.1
Kings Park CDP	17,282	-	-	16,424	87.3	1.1	4.2	1.0	6.4	20.5	20.7	45.6	29.4	41.5	6,221	92.3
Kings Point village	5,076	5,292	4.3	5,223	89.0	0.5	2.7	2.2	5.6	26.2	17.4	31.2	28.4	51.5	1,260	97.4
Kingston city & MCD (Ulster)	23,855	22,793	-4.5	23,070	63.2	14.6	3.1	4.4	14.8	21.9	15.3	37.2	47.4	26.8	9,088	89.2
Kingston town (Ulster)	895	894	-0.1	1,026	91.9	0.0	0.5	1.4	6.2	15.2	21.2	47.1	42.4	23.7	458	93.4
Kirkland town (Oneida)	10,299	10,048	-2.4	10,087	87.5	2.1	2.5	3.1	4.8	16.8	19.3	35.8	29.6	46.0	3,556	90.7
Kirkwood town (Broome)	5,844	5,479	-6.2	5,602	87.2	1.5	2.8	0.2	8.2	24.7	18.8	45.0	43.9	19.6	2,233	93.9
Kiryas Joel village	20,365	26,813	31.7	24,571	98.3	0.0	0.0	0.2	1.5	61.4	2.2	13.8	76.9	5.8	4,169	32.3
Knox town (Albany)	2,695	2,667		2,839	99.4	0.3	0.1	0.3	0.0	22.6	15.9	42.4	32.6	38.0	1,013	96.5
Kortright town (Delaware)	1,672	1,529	-8.6	1,448	91.4	3.4	1.8	1.9	1.6	16.5	29.0	52.5	43.2	21.7	593	82.3
Kysorville CDP	110	-	-	58	100.0	0.0	0.0	0.0	0.0	10.3	34.5	61.3	41.9	14.0	26	100.0
Lackawanna city & MCD (Erie)	18,144	17,720	-2.3	17,831	75.0	10.6	0.5	4.8	9.1	24.0	16.5	37.7	53.1	16.3	7,577	79.5
Lacona village	582	547	-6.0	728	98.8	0.3	0.0	1.0	0.0	28.0	12.1	36.6	45.2	19.3	261	90.0
La Fargeville CDP	608	-	-	854	80.3	18.5	0.0	0.0	1.2	38.9	4.9	24.6	57.1	22.5	250	91.2
LaFayette town (Onondaga)	4,950	4,804	-2.9	4,847	89.7	0.8	4.1	4.5	0.8	20.8	21.9	45.4	27.0	36.2	2,035	90.1
La Grange town (Dutchess)	15,717	15,627	-0.6	15,577	82.2	3.3	4.5	1.3	8.7	21.9	16.3	44.8	24.2	49.4	5,428	96.1
Lake Carmel CDP	8,282	-	-	8,067	71.2	5.1	2.4	2.4	18.9	19.1	18.9	44.4	41.0	34.9	3,042	90.6
Lake Erie Beach CDP	3,872	-	-	3,562	96.4	1.8	0.0	0.6	1.1	16.9	23.2	49.9	46.7	23.1	1,604	88.2
Lake George village	904	874	-3.3	949	85.6	2.2	0.0	5.6	6.6	14.6	19.0	52.4	35.7	27.9	468	89.1
Lake George town (Warren)	3,519	3,402	-3.3	3,426	94.2	0.9	0.7	1.5	2.6	19.3	24.0	51.6	31.3	34.5	1,453	91.7
Lake Grove village	11,184	11,056	-1.1	11,100	80.6	1.5	6.1	2.8	9.0	21.1	16.5	40.9	32.0	38.1	3,796	90.3
Lake Katrine CDP	2,397	-	-	2,472	76.8	5.9	1.9	6.1	9.3	14.2	29.1	52.4	55.1	20.6	918	94.9
Lakeland CDP	2,786	-	-	2,571	93.2	3.5	0.2	0.7	2.5	16.4	22.2	50.0	48.5	23.4	1,073	91.7
Lake Luzerne CDP	-	-	-	1,156	98.0	1.0	0.0	0.6	0.4	18.7	24.8	48.6	42.1	25.5	522	100.0
Lake Luzerne town (Warren)	3,347	3,240	-3.2	3,266	98.7	0.3	0.0	0.2	0.8	12.6	22.8	50.3	47.9	25.6	1,492	94.0
Lake Mohegan CDP	6,010	-	-	5,808	67.1	1.8	6.0	0.4	24.7	21.0	12.0	43.9	30.0	44.5	1,934	96.4
Lake Placid village	2,526	2,357	-6.7	2,346	96.1	0.0	0.7	0.5	2.8	25.1	15.9	34.7	32.2	36.0	982	93.3
Lake Pleasant town (Hamilton)	783	718	-8.3	780	97.4	2.1	0.0	0.0	0.5	6.3	47.6	63.6	71.4	6.9	141	87.9
Lake Ronkonkoma CDP	20,155	-	-	20,667	74.6	4.4	5.8	1.9	13.4	22.1	15.3	40.7	41.8	26.1	6,726	89.7
Lake Success village	2,988	3,144	5.2	3,119	45.6	6.3	41.8	2.1	4.1	20.5	30.5	50.4	28.7	59.4	786	98.0
Lakeview CDP	5,615	-	-	6,131	2.6	73.9	6.0	2.5	14.9	24.5	12.2	35.4	33.7	35.7	1,510	98.0
Lakeville CDP	756	-	-	800	95.1	4.9	0.0	0.0	0.0	14.5	11.5	32.9	39.9	37.2	321	83.5
Lakewood village	2,989	2,797	-6.4	2,847	91.9	0.3	0.4	2.3	5.2	20.8	26.2	45.6	32.2	37.5	1,321	86.1
Lancaster village	10,296	10,109	-1.8	10,144	94.9	0.7	0.6	0.9	2.9	20.8	16.9	41.1	40.3	26.1	4,713	87.7
Lancaster town (Erie)	41,619	43,325	4.1	43,085	94.6	1.9	0.8	0.5	2.2	20.3	17.8	44.2	34.8	33.3	18,186	88.7
Lansing village	3,549	3,646	2.7	3,554	53.6	4.4	31.9	4.7	5.4	14.0	14.7	35.1	24.5	63.4	1,645	99.7
Lansing town (Tompkins)	11,031	11,634	5.5	11,385	77.2	1.6	13.2	3.5	4.5	19.0	17.5	40.5	20.4	59.1	4,981	96.6
Lapeer town (Cortland)	763	727	-4.7	977	95.1	0.6	0.7	0.8	2.8	44.0	10.0	24.3	47.2	11.3	265	72.5
Larchmont village	5,862	6,087	3.8	6,096	79.5	0.6	7.6	2.4	9.9	32.5	11.2	38.6	3.7	85.8	2,133	96.2
Lattingtown village	1,741	1,764	1.3	1,940	93.9	0.0	1.4	1.6	3.1	21.6	24.6	51.6	15.1	69.5	657	92.5
Laurel CDP	1,394	-	-	970	78.1	1.3	0.0	0.4	20.1	28.6	18.5	37.9	37.2	44.4	389	94.9
Laurel Hollow village	1,943	2,033	4.6	2,034	86.8	1.6	4.6	0.4	6.5	32.4	15.0	39.6	14.4	75.4	584	99.3
Laurens village	259	246	-5.0	209	91.9	4.3	0.0	1.0	2.9	29.2	21.5	41.8	43.2	17.6	89	82.0
Laurens town (Otsego)	2,427	2,294	-5.5	2,530	95.5	0.7	0.0	0.1	3.8	18.7	25.2	47.0	45.2	30.2	1,031	88.7
Lawrence village	6,437	6,556	1.8	6,544	95.2	0.3	1.9	0.0	2.6	31.7	22.0	36.8	8.4	71.4	2,050	95.6
Lawrence town (St. Lawrence)	1,826	1,784	-2.3	1,659	96.1	0.2	0.2	1.6	1.9	25.0	13.9	40.0	56.9	16.2	682	84.9
Lebanon town (Madison)	1,336	1,299	-2.8	1,590	94.8	0.3	0.1	4.8	0.0	26.5	14.0	39.2	49.5	23.0	534	79.0
Ledyard town (Cayuga)	1,884	1,805	-4.2	1,672	85.9	1.3	0.8	2.8	9.3	9.2	21.8	44.7	32.6	44.6	588	87.9
Lee town (Oneida)	6,499	6,369	-2.0	6,409	97.2	1.3	0.5	0.7	0.3	21.3	21.1	46.8	46.1	21.9	2,563	89.7
Leeds CDP	377	-	-	320	100.0	0.0	0.0	0.0	0.0	28.8	10.9	31.1	14.8	50.2	84	100.0
Leicester village	466	440	-5.6	518	91.7	0.0	1.2	6.2	1.0	19.9	16.0	38.4	41.9	21.9	211	90.5
Leicester town (Livingston)	2,203	2,092	-5.0	2,316	95.4	0.3	0.7	2.5	1.0	22.5	17.1	38.0	50.6	22.9	945	85.5
Lenox town (Madison)	9,211	8,823	-4.2	8,877	95.3	0.8	0.0	3.6	0.2	21.1	16.6	40.8	53.0	17.8	3,329	82.9
Leon town (Cattaraugus)	1,358	1,296	-4.6	1,231	98.0	0.0	0.0	2.0	0.0	35.3	13.7	24.5	65.6	7.8	408	43.9
Le Ray town (Jefferson)	21,779	20,957	-3.8	21,427	57.1	12.7	4.4	5.8	20.0	26.8	2.6	23.6	31.2	27.2	6,393	96.8
Le Roy village	4,390	4,260	-3.0	4,224	89.1	3.8	1.1	1.2	4.8	22.3	16.0	36.0	40.8	25.7	1,811	84.4
Le Roy town (Genesee)	7,640	7,377	-3.4	7,376	93.5	2.5	0.6	0.7	2.7	22.4	17.6	38.6	39.5	26.0	3,024	87.4
Levittown CDP	51,881	-	-	51,634	73.8	1.0	7.5	2.2	15.5	19.5	16.0	42.0	36.6	34.1	16,343	94.9
Lewis town (Essex)	1,382	1,290	-6.7	1,114	94.8	3.1	0.0	1.6	0.5	10.7	23.2	52.7	50.9	14.6	460	81.3
Lewis town (Lewis)	853	789	-7.5	815	92.6	0.0	6.4	1.0	0.0	20.7	13.0	42.4	54.5	11.0	319	85.0
Lewisboro town (Westchester)	12,408	12,522	0.9	12,599	86.4	1.7	3.5	1.6	6.8	22.5	16.1	46.2	11.5	69.6	4,703	97.9
Lewiston village	2,706	2,570	-5.0	2,587	89.5	0.1	8.4	1.6	0.4	16.2	27.8	49.6	29.0	43.7	1,302	79.3

1 May be of any race.

Table A. All Places — **Population and Housing**

STATE City, town, township, borough, or CDP (county if applicable)	2010 census total population	2019 estimated population	Percent change 2010–2019	ACS total population estimate 2015–2019	White alone, not Hispanic or Latino	Black alone, not Hispanic or Latino	Asian alone, not Hispanic or Latino	All other races or 2 or more races, not Hispanic or Latino	Hispanic or Latino[1]	Under 18 years old	Age 65 years and older	Median age	Percent High school diploma or less	Percent Bachelor's degree or more	Total	Percent with a computer
	1	2	3	4	5	6	7	8	9	10	11	12	13	14	15	16
NEW YORK—Con.																
Lewiston town (Niagara) ...	16,254	15,729	-3.2	15,830	91.3	1.0	2.1	2.5	3.1	15.7	23.2	44.9	31.8	36.6	6,256	90.4
Lexington town (Greene) ..	801	773	-3.5	713	96.6	0.0	0.0	0.0	3.4	13.7	38.0	59.8	44.9	21.9	324	73.5
Leyden town (Lewis).........	1,794	1,769	-1.4	1,934	98.9	0.2	0.1	0.0	0.9	26.5	14.9	38.5	58.0	12.8	722	86.7
Liberty village	4,360	4,199	-3.7	4,125	51.5	15.5	1.7	0.5	30.7	23.2	17.9	37.9	59.9	13.4	1,639	72.9
Liberty town (Sullivan)	9,845	9,475	-3.8	9,345	64.2	10.0	1.7	3.7	20.4	22.0	17.5	39.0	56.4	16.4	3,464	82.2
Lido Beach CDP............	2,897	-		3,024	93.2	0.2	1.9	0.8	4.0	20.5	28.1	52.2	14.0	70.3	1,181	94.6
Lima village...............	2,141	2,016	-5.8	2,278	89.4	0.4	2.2	1.0	7.0	21.7	14.0	36.4	30.7	34.3	855	93.1
Lima town (Livingston)......	4,264	4,037	-5.3	4,111	93.7	0.2	1.7	0.5	3.9	18.4	16.1	43.0	28.2	34.0	1,612	93.1
Lime Lake CDP............	867	-		815	98.8	0.0	0.0	0.7	0.5	21.2	34.8	55.5	54.0	18.8	336	73.5
Limestone CDP	389	-		357	97.8	0.8	0.0	1.1	0.3	27.5	17.6	33.0	51.2	15.9	155	93.5
Lincklaen town (Chenango)	396	377	-4.8	351	98.0	0.0	0.0	1.7	0.3	19.9	25.4	43.9	63.5	13.2	145	87.6
Lincoln town (Madison).....	2,013	1,920	-4.6	1,904	94.7	1.0	0.6	2.6	1.1	17.3	19.6	47.8	50.0	22.4	728	88.3
Lincolndale CDP...........	1,521	-		1,335	89.5	0.0	0.6	0.0	9.9	21.4	12.4	48.5	26.2	56.1	506	98.0
Lincoln Park CDP..........	2,366	-		2,291	71.8	8.6	4.2	4.1	11.3	18.1	28.4	45.8	43.0	25.2	1,183	87.2
Lindenhurst village..........	27,269	26,801	-1.7	26,979	74.4	3.7	1.9	1.9	18.0	19.3	15.7	42.2	44.7	25.1	8,783	92.6
Lindley town (Steuben).....	1,969	1,894	-3.8	1,714	98.4	0.2	0.1	1.2	0.0	22.8	16.8	42.3	48.9	16.6	663	83.4
Linwood CDP..............	74	-		66	100.0	0.0	0.0	0.0	0.0	0.0	28.8	49.3	100.0	0.0	22	100.0
Lisbon town (St. Lawrence)	4,102	4,054	-1.2	4,065	97.1	0.4	0.0	1.4	1.2	29.5	14.4	40.4	38.8	16.9	1,521	89.1
Lisle village	320	296	-7.5	228	94.7	0.0	0.0	4.4	0.9	18.9	21.9	47.5	54.9	5.8	105	76.2
Lisle town (Broome).........	2,754	2,605	-5.4	2,659	99.2	0.2	0.0	0.6	0.1	25.6	16.9	39.6	56.7	12.8	991	85.5
Litchfield town (Herkimer).	1,513	1,461	-3.4	1,506	98.7	0.0	0.0	0.9	0.3	25.8	18.6	39.5	39.4	21.4	547	87.0
Little Falls city & MCD (Herkimer).................	4,950	4,637	-6.3	4,708	93.9	1.0	0.3	0.4	4.5	23.8	18.8	40.9	48.5	25.9	1,818	87.5
Little Falls town (Herkimer)	1,579	1,477	-6.5	1,855	95.8	0.0	0.0	2.9	1.3	25.5	12.7	40.2	46.1	21.8	633	89.3
Little Valley village.........	1,142	1,079	-5.5	1,089	83.7	5.7	0.0	4.9	5.7	16.2	16.3	39.4	64.7	9.4	434	80.6
Little Valley town (Cattaraugus)...............	1,739	1,647	-5.3	1,804	90.2	3.4	0.0	2.9	3.4	18.0	17.3	41.9	60.1	9.0	743	77.9
Liverpool village.............	2,328	2,204	-5.3	2,205	93.7	0.9	1.6	1.9	2.0	15.9	23.1	48.7	29.9	42.0	1,113	91.9
Livingston town (Columbia)	3,646	3,448	-5.4	3,491	90.1	2.3	1.2	3.7	2.6	15.8	25.8	48.8	44.0	24.6	1,444	84.1
Livingston Manor CDP......	1,221	-		1,091	62.3	0.0	0.5	25.8	11.4	20.4	14.1	50.3	70.4	7.3	391	93.4
Livonia village.............	1,401	1,460	4.2	1,353	94.7	0.1	1.1	1.3	2.7	26.0	15.7	39.9	26.0	37.0	524	90.6
Livonia town (Livingston)..	7,791	7,578	-2.7	7,584	93.0	0.6	1.2	3.5	1.6	20.2	18.3	45.1	29.6	30.2	2,993	95.6
Livonia Center CDP.........	421	-		238	96.6	3.4	0.0	0.0	0.0	20.6	29.0	60.5	45.0	27.0	111	100.0
Lloyd town (Ulster).........	10,845	10,518	-3.0	10,514	80.3	5.3	1.1	2.2	11.2	18.9	18.9	46.4	37.4	33.2	4,060	89.0
Lloyd Harbor village.........	3,683	3,658	-0.7	3,677	90.7	0.6	3.7	1.7	3.3	27.3	18.6	46.8	11.2	75.1	1,196	98.3
Loch Sheldrake CDP	-	-		1,273	60.4	14.6	0.9	1.8	22.2	21.8	8.9	23.0	52.5	38.6	321	82.9
Locke town (Cayuga).......	1,959	1,887	-3.7	1,873	94.3	0.2	0.0	0.1	5.4	22.7	18.6	44.9	56.8	18.4	779	84.7
Lockport city & MCD (Niagara).................	21,186	20,305	-4.2	20,490	82.4	7.9	1.3	4.4	4.0	22.1	15.2	38.2	41.7	21.6	8,854	86.0
Lockport town (Niagara) ...	20,496	19,908	-2.9	20,027	87.7	4.4	1.0	2.4	4.5	19.8	18.2	42.8	39.1	28.3	8,071	91.4
Locust Valley CDP.........	3,406	-		3,481	80.9	3.6	1.8	4.3	9.4	24.6	16.0	38.8	24.6	48.1	1,227	88.0
Lodi village...............	291	286	-1.7	326	97.9	0.0	0.0	0.9	1.2	20.9	13.8	35.5	54.5	13.5	136	85.3
Lodi town (Seneca)..........	1,550	1,505	-2.9	1,595	98.4	0.6	0.3	0.6	0.3	18.8	22.8	46.8	42.6	20.3	727	84.9
Long Beach city & MCD (Nassau)	33,333	33,454	0.4	33,507	73.2	7.2	3.5	2.3	13.9	15.4	18.4	44.9	28.0	48.7	14,026	94.3
Long Lake CDP	547	-		352	92.6	4.0	0.0	0.0	3.4	9.1	34.7	58.5	33.3	32.0	134	82.8
Long Lake town (Hamilton)	711	648	-8.9	449	92.2	3.1	0.0	1.1	3.6	9.8	34.3	57.7	36.0	29.8	172	80.8
Lorenz Park CDP...........	2,053	-		2,140	79.1	5.7	2.8	6.1	6.3	13.8	21.6	50.2	53.4	19.9	927	84.5
Lorraine CDP..............	174	-		59	100.0	0.0	0.0	0.0	0.0	15.3	10.2	50.4	100.0	0.0	23	100.0
Lorraine town (Jefferson)..	1,035	985	-4.8	940	97.8	0.2	0.0	1.6	0.4	19.4	11.9	43.8	63.8	10.8	352	95.2
Louisville town (St. Lawrence)................	3,155	3,021	-4.2	3,058	98.0	0.0	0.3	0.4	1.3	20.8	20.2	47.1	40.5	35.7	1,262	89.5
Lowville village.............	3,455	3,312	-4.1	3,233	94.7	1.6	0.2	2.5	0.9	20.3	16.9	38.7	40.3	28.0	1,326	82.2
Lowville town (Lewis)........	4,990	4,814	-3.5	4,865	95.6	1.7	0.1	1.7	0.9	21.2	20.8	41.8	47.6	25.5	1,773	84.0
Lumberland town (Sullivan).................	2,466	2,382	-3.4	2,314	85.5	1.3	1.6	2.5	9.2	24.2	16.1	41.5	36.1	34.7	851	91.1
Lyme town (Jefferson)	2,192	2,069	-5.6	2,273	92.6	1.2	0.4	2.6	3.2	21.6	23.7	45.9	40.1	24.8	910	87.8
Lynbrook village............	19,486	19,448	-0.2	19,524	68.0	3.1	2.8	2.2	23.8	19.9	19.3	43.5	30.9	42.3	7,191	88.8
Lyncourt CDP..............	4,250	-		3,974	78.8	3.9	6.0	5.6	5.8	23.8	14.2	36.7	43.6	16.3	1,706	86.1
Lyndon town (Cattaraugus)	707	679	-4.0	739	95.4	0.0	0.1	1.9	2.6	28.3	14.7	41.3	55.8	14.5	274	82.8
Lyndonville village..........	839	781	-6.9	864	91.7	1.6	0.0	4.1	2.7	27.8	12.4	37.8	52.7	14.8	376	89.1
Lyon Mountain CDP.........	423	-		245	86.9	1.2	4.5	6.5	0.8	11.8	7.8	45.4	72.7	8.2	104	78.8
Lyons CDP................	3,619	-		3,590	80.5	10.0	0.8	5.2	3.5	22.1	18.3	41.3	51.2	12.7	1,439	86.9
Lyons town (Wayne)	5,685	5,407	-4.9	5,452	84.7	8.3	0.5	3.4	3.0	17.8	18.6	43.0	52.6	15.8	2,116	90.4
Lyonsdale town (Lewis)	1,227	1,200	-2.2	1,105	99.1	0.9	0.0	0.0	0.0	24.4	20.1	45.2	74.6	8.6	441	86.2
Lyons Falls village..........	566	549	-3.0	576	97.9	0.7	0.0	1.4	0.0	27.8	19.4	44.2	56.5	17.8	238	71.8
Lysander town (Onondaga)	21,759	22,896	5.2	22,790	93.1	1.7	0.7	1.7	2.8	22.0	17.7	45.0	25.9	43.0	9,256	93.0
McDonough town (Chenango)	886	847	-4.4	832	94.6	1.7	0.0	0.8	2.9	20.9	24.9	49.7	64.0	15.5	363	81.0
Macedon CDP.............	1,523	-		1,708	91.5	2.4	1.6	1.2	3.3	16.1	31.0	51.6	37.7	31.0	773	81.2
Macedon town (Wayne)....	9,141	8,887	-2.8	8,957	93.4	0.5	1.6	0.8	3.7	22.3	16.0	42.3	37.9	27.4	3,590	90.9
McGraw village	1,040	975	-6.3	1,023	90.7	0.3	0.0	1.1	7.9	21.8	15.2	35.4	55.2	10.0	395	83.8
Machias CDP..............	471	-		498	88.6	0.0	0.0	0.0	11.4	30.3	12.7	33.1	41.2	16.2	178	88.2
Machias town (Cattaraugus)...............	2,371	2,270	-4.3	2,389	96.8	0.0	0.0	0.7	2.6	23.9	21.4	45.8	52.8	15.0	943	79.6
Macomb town (St. Lawrence)................	906	876	-3.3	960	98.2	0.6	0.2	0.0	0.9	24.7	19.1	42.6	57.2	14.3	373	86.3
Madison village.............	302	285	-5.6	500	92.8	0.0	0.0	0.0	7.2	30.2	17.6	31.9	59.0	18.4	168	70.2
Madison town (Madison) ..	3,011	2,915	-3.2	2,934	95.8	2.3	0.6	0.0	1.2	19.1	23.6	49.5	45.6	31.2	1,351	82.0
Madrid CDP...............	757	-		757	96.8	0.4	0.4	0.8	1.6	28.7	14.0	35.5	46.2	23.0	246	96.7
Madrid town (St. Lawrence)................	1,735	1,639	-5.5	1,731	96.4	0.3	0.5	1.0	1.7	25.9	14.3	38.2	49.3	20.1	652	90.6
Mahopac CDP.............	8,369	-		8,203	82.8	0.0	2.5	2.1	12.6	20.2	18.9	45.8	33.1	38.2	3,099	96.4
Maine town (Broome)	5,393	5,058	-6.2	5,152	95.5	1.0	0.0	1.2	2.3	20.6	19.0	43.8	48.8	26.9	1,985	88.1
Malden-on-Hudson CDP ..	405	-		222	37.8	0.0	0.0	9.5	52.7	10.8	27.9	33.8	71.2	21.7	91	91.2
Malone village..............	5,917	5,600	-5.4	5,659	96.5	0.2	0.0	0.1	3.2	21.7	16.6	37.2	53.9	22.1	2,426	85.0

1 May be of any race.

Table A. All Places — **Population and Housing**

STATE City, town, township, borough, or CDP (county if applicable)	Population: 2010 census total population	Population: 2019 estimated population	Population: Percent change 2010–2019	Population: ACS total population estimate 2015–2019	Race and Hispanic or Latino origin (percent): White alone, not Hispanic or Latino	Race and Hispanic or Latino origin (percent): Black alone, not Hispanic or Latino	Race and Hispanic or Latino origin (percent): Asian alone, not Hispanic or Latino	Race and Hispanic or Latino origin (percent): All other races or 2 or more races, not Hispanic or Latino	Race and Hispanic or Latino origin (percent): Hispanic or Latino[1]	Age (percent): Under 18 years old	Age (percent): Age 65 years and older	Age (percent): Median age	Educational attainment of persons age 25 and older: Percent High school diploma or less	Educational attainment of persons age 25 and older: Percent Bachelor's degree or more	Occupied housing units: Total	Occupied housing units: Percent with a computer
	1	2	3	4	5	6	7	8	9	10	11	12	13	14	15	16
NEW YORK—Con.																
Malone town (Franklin)	14,547	14,078	-3.2	14,276	76.5	15.4	0.5	0.4	7.2	17.1	12.8	35.5	62.0	14.5	4,202	84.5
Malta town (Saratoga)	14,768	16,252	10.0	15,907	86.7	1.9	4.1	1.4	5.9	18.4	15.9	41.7	23.9	44.6	6,898	93.7
Malverne village	8,502	8,485	-0.2	8,517	77.8	5.3	4.6	4.4	7.8	18.4	22.1	48.0	24.5	53.1	3,091	93.9
Malverne Park Oaks CDP	505	-	-	276	67.4	0.0	0.0	0.0	32.6	42.8	12.0	38.1	7.6	49.4	84	100.0
Mamakating town (Sullivan)	12,082	11,430	-5.4	11,453	83.8	2.0	0.9	2.1	11.2	21.8	15.0	40.6	43.9	24.4	4,124	91.8
Mamaroneck village	18,907	19,131	1.2	19,217	64.8	4.8	3.9	1.6	24.9	22.8	18.2	41.6	31.1	53.2	6,991	92.6
Mamaroneck town (Westchester)	29,138	29,495	1.2	29,670	74.6	1.6	4.7	1.9	17.1	26.2	16.6	41.5	19.7	67.1	10,731	95.2
Manchester village	1,690	1,611	-4.7	1,798	95.4	0.2	0.0	1.9	2.5	22.4	16.7	36.3	47.6	17.4	754	88.3
Manchester town (Ontario)	9,386	9,108	-3.0	9,233	94.0	0.5	0.0	1.7	3.8	18.9	20.1	46.9	46.1	15.6	3,764	86.2
Manhasset CDP	8,080	-	-	7,985	61.5	9.0	15.3	3.3	10.9	23.6	19.7	47.3	21.1	58.7	2,655	93.8
Manhasset Hills CDP	3,592	-	-	3,615	37.8	2.4	51.4	3.0	5.4	20.6	20.5	44.8	18.3	65.1	1,105	97.7
Manheim town (Herkimer)	3,329	3,166	-4.9	3,196	93.0	0.1	0.2	2.4	4.3	23.1	20.3	43.1	49.3	15.2	1,278	84.1
Manlius village	4,656	4,434	-4.8	4,486	87.7	2.2	5.2	2.9	2.0	20.3	21.5	45.4	22.4	51.9	2,096	86.6
Manlius town (Onondaga)	32,369	31,653	-2.2	31,884	88.4	1.9	3.8	2.9	3.0	22.6	20.3	44.9	22.3	53.0	13,119	92.4
Mannsville village	350	335	-4.3	351	97.4	0.9	0.0	1.7	0.0	29.6	11.4	38.4	48.9	17.0	117	94.9
Manorhaven village	6,454	6,627	2.7	6,628	52.1	0.9	15.6	1.9	29.6	27.6	11.0	36.1	28.8	48.9	2,391	95.6
Manorville CDP	14,314	-	-	13,257	82.1	4.0	1.3	1.9	10.6	24.2	16.0	44.2	35.4	34.9	4,825	94.7
Mansfield town (Cattaraugus)	819	826	0.9	814	95.6	0.0	0.0	1.6	2.8	25.6	17.1	38.8	54.9	17.8	309	79.3
Marathon village	916	862	-5.9	926	97.5	0.8	0.0	1.3	0.4	20.5	20.6	39.5	53.4	13.9	351	90.6
Marathon town (Cortland)	1,958	1,853	-5.4	1,923	94.5	1.5	0.5	1.6	2.0	21.1	19.4	40.7	45.8	17.5	734	91.8
Marbletown town (Ulster)	5,606	5,481	-2.2	5,497	81.8	5.9	4.5	4.9	2.9	17.9	24.8	48.8	30.7	45.7	2,222	96.6
Marcellus village	1,809	1,717	-5.1	1,969	95.6	0.9	2.3	0.3	1.0	21.7	18.7	42.9	26.1	38.4	869	89.8
Marcellus town (Onondaga)	6,227	6,034	-3.1	6,081	95.6	0.5	1.2	0.9	1.8	21.5	20.2	47.3	29.1	38.8	2,458	94.0
Marcy town (Oneida)	8,988	9,460	5.3	9,465	83.6	8.3	0.3	1.1	6.7	14.8	12.7	39.6	42.5	27.3	2,546	94.7
Margaretville village	596	546	-8.4	553	89.9	1.4	0.0	6.0	2.7	16.5	49.5	64.6	46.0	20.8	242	74.4
Mariaville Lake CDP	722	-	-	358	89.9	3.1	2.8	4.2	0.0	24.3	29.3	41.5	26.9	48.1	130	84.6
Marilla town (Erie)	5,331	5,394	1.2	5,378	95.2	0.2	0.7	0.8	3.1	18.5	21.1	45.9	37.5	33.1	2,115	88.6
Marion CDP	1,511	-	-	1,167	89.8	5.9	0.0	0.0	4.3	14.1	19.5	50.0	44.8	25.7	572	77.4
Marion town (Wayne)	4,756	4,563	-4.1	4,595	89.4	2.9	0.0	4.1	3.5	20.9	17.8	43.8	49.4	20.5	1,806	88.4
Marlboro CDP	3,669	-	-	3,545	84.9	2.2	1.4	2.8	8.7	18.2	21.7	45.7	38.5	29.9	1,466	88.3
Marlborough town (Ulster)	8,819	8,603	-2.4	8,660	87.6	3.0	1.3	1.6	6.5	18.3	18.5	45.3	34.2	30.5	3,464	92.3
Marshall town (Oneida)	2,129	2,127	-0.1	2,047	96.1	0.2	0.5	0.3	2.8	18.5	19.4	43.9	39.7	33.3	897	86.4
Martinsburg town (Lewis)	1,430	1,391	-2.7	1,420	91.1	0.7	0.0	0.2	8.0	26.9	14.0	33.5	53.9	24.5	541	82.4
Maryland town (Otsego)	1,905	1,806	-5.2	2,064	94.5	0.0	0.0	2.5	3.0	19.4	20.2	47.9	46.1	21.5	828	85.0
Masonville town (Delaware)	1,313	1,231	-6.2	1,086	98.7	0.0	0.0	1.3	0.0	17.3	24.0	46.3	56.2	14.3	465	83.7
Massapequa CDP	21,685	-	-	21,784	92.6	0.4	0.8	0.7	5.7	19.9	17.8	43.9	24.2	48.4	7,259	96.3
Massapequa Park village	17,110	17,143	0.2	17,193	88.8	0.2	2.3	1.4	7.4	22.8	18.0	43.9	29.9	44.8	5,750	92.0
Massena village	10,938	10,200	-6.7	10,091	91.8	0.1	1.7	5.4	0.9	22.5	19.3	40.5	45.3	26.1	4,610	86.9
Massena town (St. Lawrence)	12,883	12,043	-6.5	12,228	90.8	0.1	1.4	6.7	0.9	23.1	19.9	41.1	49.7	23.1	5,540	85.7
Mastic CDP	15,481	-	-	15,476	64.3	7.7	0.7	2.7	24.6	27.5	9.3	32.8	56.4	15.6	4,317	93.1
Mastic Beach CDP	12,930	-	-	12,610	72.9	4.4	1.5	3.0	18.3	20.9	12.5	39.4	59.1	14.8	4,254	91.4
Matinecock village	821	833	1.5	824	92.4	0.6	4.2	0.4	2.4	27.5	17.5	48.1	6.7	82.1	269	98.9
Mattituck CDP	4,219	-	-	4,676	95.3	0.0	0.0	0.0	4.7	7.2	29.4	55.9	34.0	39.7	1,991	96.3
Mattydale CDP	6,446	-	-	5,820	85.9	1.8	1.4	3.7	7.3	23.8	14.9	36.3	55.3	13.4	2,353	89.6
Maybrook village	2,961	3,682	24.3	3,511	66.7	14.1	0.9	0.7	17.7	18.6	12.4	37.7	38.4	23.0	1,351	87.6
Mayfield village	843	791	-6.2	814	97.9	0.0	0.0	0.0	2.1	20.0	10.3	38.4	36.5	25.7	335	89.3
Mayfield town (Fulton)	6,495	6,215	-4.3	6,228	97.2	0.9	0.1	0.7	1.1	18.8	19.1	46.6	49.7	14.9	2,731	85.0
Mayville village	1,706	1,592	-6.7	1,441	89.5	5.1	0.0	0.9	4.5	20.6	19.6	39.4	42.7	24.0	549	90.2
Mechanicstown CDP	6,858	-	-	6,869	45.3	17.0	1.7	2.2	33.7	19.8	24.9	45.0	50.2	16.0	3,047	89.0
Mechanicville city & MCD (Saratoga)	5,197	5,037	-3.1	5,107	91.7	2.8	1.3	2.5	1.6	21.0	17.1	34.8	41.8	19.9	2,381	88.4
Medford CDP	24,142	-	-	24,406	66.9	8.9	1.8	1.0	21.3	19.7	17.1	42.0	40.8	29.3	8,076	94.9
Medina village	6,066	5,656	-6.8	5,847	82.8	2.8	1.6	2.6	10.2	22.0	18.8	41.5	43.3	17.8	2,714	88.9
Melrose Park CDP	2,294	-	-	2,425	98.6	0.0	0.1	0.0	1.4	24.2	17.2	45.1	23.0	42.1	882	88.7
Melville CDP	18,985	-	-	17,716	82.0	3.2	7.8	2.2	4.8	19.5	27.0	49.8	19.4	58.6	6,758	97.5
Menands village	3,994	3,864	-3.3	3,923	52.9	18.5	14.8	4.6	9.2	25.1	12.1	35.3	12.1	65.5	1,808	91.3
Mendon town (Monroe)	9,118	9,173	0.6	9,203	95.5	1.3	0.8	1.2	1.1	23.3	17.5	47.3	12.5	60.4	3,539	96.1
Mentz town (Cayuga)	2,377	2,270	-4.5	2,217	92.5	0.5	0.0	1.6	5.5	24.1	19.1	42.1	58.3	8.2	899	84.9
Meredith town (Delaware)	1,530	1,423	-7.0	1,845	93.2	0.0	2.3	0.1	4.4	13.9	20.8	49.0	38.9	28.2	747	93.6
Meridian village	309	288	-6.8	312	99.4	0.0	0.0	0.6	0.0	31.7	11.5	32.6	30.9	25.1	105	84.8
Merrick CDP	22,097	-	-	20,130	86.2	2.3	3.4	1.2	6.9	22.9	17.6	45.4	18.1	61.7	7,053	95.5
Merritt Park CDP	1,256	-	-	1,727	56.7	2.7	34.2	1.3	5.2	29.0	14.2	42.5	17.7	62.5	638	100.0
Mexico village	1,617	1,522	-5.9	1,476	94.3	0.5	0.0	4.0	1.2	24.9	15.2	36.6	44.6	24.1	568	89.1
Mexico town (Oswego)	5,188	5,062	-2.4	5,090	96.1	0.6	0.7	2.2	0.4	23.4	15.3	38.5	49.2	24.0	1,896	92.7
Middleburgh town (Schoharie)	3,732	3,520	-5.7	3,541	92.5	1.6	1.3	1.8	2.8	14.2	24.6	50.3	45.5	22.1	1,599	82.3
Middleburgh village	1,488	1,417	-4.8	1,603	89.4	1.3	2.9	1.2	5.2	16.1	18.8	47.7	42.0	22.7	752	85.5
Middlebury town (Wyoming)	1,441	1,367	-5.1	1,372	99.4	0.0	0.0	0.0	0.6	19.8	18.7	41.6	42.2	23.0	550	88.0
Middlefield town (Otsego)	2,113	2,000	-5.3	1,934	92.6	1.9	3.2	0.9	1.3	13.8	26.6	52.6	37.7	36.6	842	88.2
Middle Island CDP	10,483	-	-	10,228	72.5	11.7	2.1	1.0	12.7	19.6	23.0	45.3	40.1	29.5	4,123	90.5
Middleport village	1,840	1,743	-5.3	1,741	94.3	1.0	0.1	3.6	0.9	25.3	14.9	36.6	42.7	14.9	725	87.9
Middlesex town (Yates)	1,495	1,469	-1.7	1,389	93.4	1.5	0.6	2.2	2.3	18.9	17.7	47.0	38.9	27.7	515	88.9
Middletown town (Delaware)	3,750	3,422	-8.7	3,484	83.2	0.4	0.9	2.0	13.5	14.2	33.6	53.8	48.6	25.2	1,661	79.5
Middletown city & MCD (Orange)	28,121	28,189	0.2	27,963	32.0	19.1	3.2	4.3	41.5	24.9	13.9	35.6	50.1	19.7	10,447	91.5
Middleville village	509	487	-4.3	554	99.3	0.0	0.0	0.7	0.0	29.1	19.0	36.0	50.8	17.1	225	84.4
Milan town (Dutchess)	2,367	2,344		2,402	84.4	2.7	2.0	1.7	9.2	17.5	21.6	47.7	24.5	39.8	1,008	93.1
Milford village	418	394	-5.7	348	86.2	6.3	2.0	2.9	2.6	18.1	21.3	48.6	40.1	28.2	164	89.6
Milford town (Otsego)	3,045	2,867	-5.8	2,895	96.5	1.4	0.2	0.8	1.0	20.7	25.6	45.8	46.0	24.8	1,199	88.3
Millbrook village	1,460	1,406	-3.7	1,443	83.2	1.4	5.9	2.4	7.1	17.5	25.9	51.7	29.1	38.2	724	87.2
Miller Place CDP	12,339	-	-	12,016	88.7	0.3	1.0	0.9	9.1	25.7	16.7	41.0	21.7	50.9	3,847	98.1
Millerton village	962	925	-3.8	924	75.1	2.2	6.1	3.4	13.3	16.0	18.6	43.8	43.4	23.4	430	80.2
Mill Neck village	945	967	2.3	1,073	75.2	0.0	9.0	2.6	13.1	24.1	24.4	49.6	9.8	78.7	371	97.3

1 May be of any race.

Table A. All Places — **Population and Housing**

STATE City, town, township, borough, or CDP (county if applicable)	Population: 2010 census total population	Population: 2019 estimated population	Population: Percent change 2010–2019	Population: ACS total population estimate 2015–2019	Race and Hispanic or Latino origin (percent): White alone, not Hispanic or Latino	Race: Black alone, not Hispanic or Latino	Race: Asian alone, not Hispanic or Latino	Race: All other races or 2 or more races, not Hispanic or Latino	Race: Hispanic or Latino[1]	Age (percent): Under 18 years old	Age: Age 65 years and older	Age: Median age	Educational attainment of persons age 25 and older: Percent High school diploma or less	Educational attainment: Percent Bachelor's degree or more	Occupied housing units: Total	Occupied housing units: Percent with a computer
	1	2	3	4	5	6	7	8	9	10	11	12	13	14	15	16
NEW YORK—Con.																
Millport village	312	287	-8.0	469	93.6	0.0	0.4	6.0	0.0	23.7	19.2	38.5	59.1	7.9	155	86.5
Milo town (Yates)	7,046	6,786	-3.7	6,828	95.6	1.2	0.8	0.9	1.6	20.8	19.6	43.8	48.8	24.6	2,635	77.2
Milton town (Saratoga)	18,558	19,367	4.4	19,274	93.0	0.7	1.7	2.0	2.6	21.0	15.0	41.9	36.3	33.6	7,942	92.9
Milton CDP	3,087	-	-	3,194	97.4	0.0	0.0	1.2	1.4	18.8	18.2	47.8	23.6	49.8	1,336	93.9
Milton CDP	1,403	-	-	1,294	87.7	1.9	0.0	0.1	10.4	18.4	16.5	43.4	25.2	38.0	534	89.5
Mina town (Chautauqua)	1,105	1,040	-5.9	884	93.9	0.0	0.0	5.2	0.9	19.1	20.0	47.3	52.4	18.5	344	83.1
Minden town (Montgomery)	4,323	4,160	-3.8	4,165	91.7	0.4	0.4	4.6	3.0	30.7	13.1	34.7	54.5	12.3	1,392	83.7
Mineola village	18,865	19,207	1.8	19,186	64.0	2.5	12.5	1.7	19.2	17.0	18.0	41.8	31.7	42.0	7,592	95.4
Minerva town (Essex)	812	768	-5.4	933	98.3	0.0	0.0	1.4	0.3	18.2	25.0	50.2	48.7	21.4	394	93.4
Minetto CDP	1,069	-	-	1,059	93.4	0.0	1.3	2.5	2.8	17.6	22.9	46.7	32.0	44.7	477	90.4
Minetto town (Oswego)	1,657	1,568	-5.4	1,650	94.8	0.0	0.8	1.8	2.5	21.9	21.6	44.2	35.3	41.6	703	92.7
Mineville CDP	1,269	-	-	1,456	90.0	6.4	0.3	0.5	2.8	17.7	20.7	37.7	74.8	8.2	572	71.3
Minisink town (Orange)	4,481	4,493	0.3	4,492	78.3	0.8	0.6	1.9	18.5	26.6	13.9	40.5	34.2	34.3	1,378	97.2
Minoa village	3,452	3,415	-1.1	3,454	80.6	3.6	0.6	1.8	13.5	22.6	20.8	40.8	34.8	37.4	1,378	85.6
Mohawk village	2,702	2,526	-6.5	2,379	91.7	1.7	2.9	2.1	1.6	26.0	21.1	39.8	45.2	20.5	999	83.8
Mohawk town (Montgomery)	3,853	3,753	-2.6	3,762	88.4	0.1	0.4	1.6	9.5	18.8	17.6	45.5	40.1	20.6	1,477	86.6
Moira town (Franklin)	2,938	2,763	-6.0	2,804	98.3	0.5	0.0	1.2	0.0	20.0	20.4	46.5	57.6	19.1	1,215	82.1
Monroe village	8,355	8,586	2.8	8,586	49.9	7.6	3.7	5.1	33.7	30.3	8.7	32.7	33.2	41.6	2,552	92.6
Monroe town (Orange)	19,486	19,824	1.7	19,799	58.2	6.7	5.7	3.6	25.8	27.1	10.2	36.1	32.6	39.6	6,164	94.0
Monsey CDP	18,412	-	-	23,055	96.6	2.1	0.1	0.1	1.2	56.4	5.1	15.5	61.0	12.0	4,022	57.9
Montague town (Lewis)	78	76	-2.6	75	94.7	0.0	5.3	0.0	0.0	13.3	13.3	57.1	62.5	21.9	40	97.5
Montauk CDP	3,326	-	-	3,685	86.9	0.2	0.3	2.2	10.5	11.9	32.8	56.8	30.2	41.7	1,458	90.3
Montebello village	4,525	4,593	1.5	4,610	84.3	3.6	5.2	3.4	3.5	24.1	17.4	48.3	18.1	68.8	1,645	94.0
Montezuma town (Cayuga)	1,277	1,227	-3.9	1,560	97.3	0.2	1.1	0.4	1.0	23.3	17.5	41.7	63.9	9.4	588	83.7
Montgomery village	3,792	4,528	19.4	4,527	72.7	13.7	0.8	3.8	8.9	21.8	18.5	41.1	43.9	29.6	1,622	90.9
Montgomery town (Orange)	22,636	24,065	6.3	23,827	73.2	9.1	0.9	1.5	15.4	23.4	14.0	38.0	40.8	27.5	8,224	91.3
Monticello village	6,835	6,385	-6.6	6,433	26.2	26.9	2.5	5.9	38.5	24.2	16.5	36.0	59.0	18.8	2,405	76.8
Montour town (Schuyler)	2,310	2,190	-5.2	2,511	98.2	0.0	0.0	0.6	1.2	22.7	18.6	44.5	48.3	21.3	991	81.2
Montour Falls village	1,707	1,604	-6.0	1,638	96.2	3.0	0.0	0.2	0.5	20.2	25.3	48.8	48.4	17.5	636	76.6
Montrose CDP	2,731	-	-	3,270	78.0	2.9	1.8	1.2	16.1	18.9	14.6	44.1	30.3	38.9	1,220	95.8
Mooers CDP	442	-	-	308	97.4	0.0	0.0	0.0	2.6	11.4	15.9	47.3	35.2	17.6	160	79.4
Mooers town (Clinton)	3,597	3,556	-1.1	3,563	97.8	0.0	0.0	0.5	1.7	20.0	20.1	46.8	62.3	15.8	1,535	77.9
Moravia village	1,279	1,209	-5.5	1,306	96.0	0.0	1.1	2.0	0.9	25.1	21.2	45.1	38.7	19.5	546	85.2
Moravia town (Cayuga)	3,628	3,454	-4.8	3,477	78.7	14.8	0.7	2.3	3.6	17.3	15.1	42.0	56.6	11.0	1,032	87.2
Moreau town (Saratoga)	14,737	15,459	4.9	15,391	97.2	0.0	0.0	1.6	1.2	20.6	16.2	42.7	45.0	23.3	6,489	89.3
Morehouse town (Hamilton)	86	76	-11.6	13	100.0	0.0	0.0	0.0	0.0	0.0	69.2	69.8	69.2	0.0	9	100.0
Moriah town (Essex)	4,798	4,471	-6.8	4,588	90.1	2.2	0.5	4.9	2.3	16.2	21.7	49.6	61.7	13.5	2,014	78.5
Moriches CDP	2,838	-	-	3,073	80.7	2.3	6.9	5.2	5.0	14.9	31.3	51.7	33.5	37.4	1,507	99.0
Morris village	588	559	-4.9	575	96.7	0.0	0.0	0.0	3.3	22.6	23.7	33.4	35.0	30.6	230	84.8
Morris town (Otsego)	1,863	1,759	-5.6	1,739	95.1	0.0	0.5	1.9	2.5	18.3	18.1	42.1	43.1	24.1	674	86.6
Morrisonville CDP	1,545	-	-	1,258	91.7	0.6	3.2	4.0	0.6	15.2	19.6	48.0	39.9	29.0	523	93.1
Morristown village	393	377	-4.1	306	91.5	3.6	0.7	0.7	3.6	11.1	28.4	54.4	51.6	22.9	133	90.2
Morristown town (St. Lawrence)	1,979	1,904	-3.8	1,886	94.1	0.6	0.7	1.7	2.9	17.1	24.8	52.5	52.8	17.7	832	88.8
Morrisville village	2,166	1,849	-14.6	1,909	79.6	11.1	3.1	1.2	5.1	11.2	13.0	20.2	43.4	21.7	289	88.6
Mountain Lodge Park CDP	1,588	-	-	1,765	80.3	3.5	3.7	0.9	11.6	22.4	5.2	32.5	38.5	31.1	663	97.6
Mount Hope town (Orange)	7,025	6,664	-5.1	6,731	66.0	10.5	1.7	2.7	19.1	18.2	12.0	42.0	44.3	20.6	1,714	94.7
Mount Ivy CDP	6,878	-	-	7,075	38.8	18.7	3.5	2.8	36.1	27.5	14.9	39.7	36.8	29.1	2,703	95.0
Mount Kisco town & village (Westchester)	10,779	10,795	0.1	10,866	48.5	3.8	4.8	1.2	41.7	23.8	15.8	41.0	41.5	43.3	3,926	89.6
Mount Morris village	2,979	2,785	-6.5	2,931	77.9	7.5	0.0	0.3	14.2	19.5	19.0	43.6	38.4	26.1	1,434	91.8
Mount Morris town (Livingston)	4,458	4,185	-6.1	4,271	84.6	5.3	0.0	0.2	10.0	16.4	26.4	49.9	39.7	22.5	1,925	84.6
Mount Pleasant town (Westchester)	43,718	44,933	2.8	44,970	68.1	4.4	4.4	2.6	20.4	22.7	16.0	39.4	29.0	53.0	14,537	92.6
Mount Sinai CDP	12,118	-	-	11,101	84.9	0.9	2.5	0.3	11.4	22.6	22.7	45.7	25.4	45.8	3,975	92.9
Mount Vernon city & MCD (Westchester)	67,316	67,345	0.0	67,896	16.1	62.7	2.0	3.0	16.2	20.1	15.8	40.1	43.7	29.2	25,763	90.7
Munnsville village	490	463	-5.5	453	93.8	0.0	0.0	6.2	0.0	27.2	7.1	31.5	42.3	25.9	158	93.7
Munsey Park village	2,711	2,710	0.0	2,722	79.9	0.0	10.4	1.4	8.3	34.6	15.1	42.0	4.8	88.9	805	98.6
Munsons Corners CDP	2,728	-	-	2,938	93.2	1.8	0.0	0.4	4.6	15.4	14.4	30.4	40.1	36.6	1,083	86.9
Murray town (Orleans)	4,994	4,664	-6.6	4,723	84.3	2.2	1.0	1.8	10.8	22.9	16.3	39.6	47.5	15.9	1,979	88.1
Muttontown village	3,503	3,668	4.7	3,669	65.8	1.7	25.2	2.3	5.0	22.0	21.4	50.3	14.1	70.8	1,209	98.2
Myers Corner CDP	6,790	-	-	6,777	75.2	0.9	10.1	2.3	11.5	20.7	20.1	44.5	29.1	46.1	2,397	98.1
Nanticoke town (Broome)	1,679	1,604	-4.5	1,694	98.4	0.9	0.0	0.6	0.0	20.8	22.4	43.5	53.9	12.4	640	92.0
Nanuet CDP	17,882	-	-	17,517	56.2	15.5	12.7	3.1	12.5	19.7	20.0	45.3	31.1	46.0	6,376	92.0
Napanoch CDP	1,174	-	-	939	93.7	0.0	0.9	2.6	2.9	13.3	29.6	52.7	47.4	22.5	415	90.1
Napeague CDP	200	-	-	206	68.0	0.0	0.0	7.8	24.3	21.8	3.4	40.4	12.3	56.9	79	79.7
Naples village	1,044	994	-4.8	875	91.2	0.8	1.7	1.7	4.6	17.1	21.5	47.8	45.2	20.5	418	92.3
Naples town (Ontario)	2,501	2,443	-2.3	2,325	95.8	0.4	1.1	0.9	1.7	17.6	23.2	51.8	41.1	27.2	991	93.3
Napoli town (Cattaraugus)	1,246	1,325	6.3	1,008	95.9	0.1	0.0	4.0	0.0	20.6	15.8	45.9	53.1	15.1	402	73.6
Narrowsburg CDP	431	-	-	269	85.1	0.0	13.0	1.9	0.0	10.4	55.0	67.5	30.7	35.7	144	78.5
Nassau village	1,136	1,098	-3.3	1,062	95.9	0.3	0.0	2.0	1.9	18.7	17.1	40.7	34.9	30.4	459	91.9
Nassau town (Rensselaer)	4,784	4,758	-0.5	4,785	98.0	0.1	0.2	0.6	1.1	21.4	18.8	45.2	40.5	27.4	1,954	91.8
Natural Bridge CDP	365	-	-	289	100.0	0.0	0.0	0.0	0.0	10.4	9.3	55.5	66.0	0.0	123	78.0
Nedrow CDP	2,244	-	-	2,310	63.8	18.4	1.5	14.1	2.3	23.8	12.9	36.8	46.0	16.0	878	89.4
Nelliston village	596	570	-4.4	567	88.4	0.0	7.1	0.5	4.1	20.1	22.2	43.3	59.9	11.5	221	77.8
Nelson town (Madison)	1,985	1,947	-1.9	1,841	93.6	3.2	0.3	0.3	2.6	12.2	24.0	50.5	38.1	27.8	773	84.2
Nelsonville village	630	632	0.3	658	79.6	0.3	2.0	1.2	16.9	28.0	12.6	39.8	24.2	61.9	224	92.4
Nesconset CDP	13,387	-	-	13,293	85.5	1.0	3.9	1.3	8.2	24.1	21.1	45.4	23.6	52.0	4,506	92.7
Neversink town (Sullivan)	3,550	3,430	-3.4	3,436	90.0	2.2	0.0	0.8	7.0	23.1	14.9	43.8	37.1	31.1	1,291	82.9
New Albion town (Cattaraugus)	1,969	1,865	-5.3	2,097	94.4	0.5	0.2	1.3	3.6	22.5	18.5	44.9	52.7	15.9	879	75.9
Newark village	9,333	8,836	-5.3	8,914	80.6	6.1	1.8	3.5	8.0	22.1	19.0	42.8	45.9	18.0	3,783	85.8
Newark Valley village	999	923	-7.6	987	91.5	0.3	1.4	4.6	2.2	29.9	14.8	37.7	36.9	23.1	372	88.4

1 May be of any race.

Table A. All Places — **Population and Housing**

STATE City, town, township, borough, or CDP (county if applicable)	Population				Race and Hispanic or Latino origin (percent)					Age (percent)			Educational attainment of persons age 25 and older		Occupied housing units	
	2010 census total population	2019 estimated population	Percent change 2010–2019	ACS total population estimate 2015–2019	White alone, not Hispanic or Latino	Black alone, not Hispanic or Latino	Asian alone, not Hispanic or Latino	All other races or 2 or more races, not Hispanic or Latino	Hispanic or Latino[1]	Under 18 years old	Age 65 years and older	Median age	Percent High school diploma or less	Percent Bachelor's degree or more	Total	Percent with a computer
	1	2	3	4	5	6	7	8	9	10	11	12	13	14	15	16
NEW YORK—Con.																
Newark Valley town (Tioga)	3,948	3,701	-6.3	3,752	95.0	0.8	0.4	3.3	0.6	22.6	18.0	42.8	45.9	26.7	1,470	86.7
New Baltimore town (Greene)	3,366	3,254	-3.3	3,269	93.2	2.0	0.0	0.7	4.1	16.1	22.9	48.6	50.6	25.1	1,148	88.9
New Berlin village	1,030	989	-4.0	965	93.8	0.0	1.9	1.2	3.1	19.9	23.5	45.2	59.9	23.9	390	86.7
New Berlin town (Chenango)	2,684	2,510	-6.5	2,537	96.4	0.0	0.7	1.4	1.5	20.1	24.1	47.9	54.7	15.8	1,073	86.1
New Bremen town (Lewis)	2,707	2,636	-2.6	2,650	96.6	0.2	1.8	0.0	1.4	27.2	16.8	37.5	57.7	17.7	986	89.5
Newburgh city & MCD (Orange)	28,903	28,177	-2.5	28,255	21.4	23.2	1.4	3.7	50.3	29.6	10.3	30.7	60.3	16.7	9,967	77.9
Newburgh town (Orange)	29,728	31,494	5.9	30,905	62.2	13.8	2.5	2.6	18.8	19.5	16.4	42.4	36.1	32.0	11,111	93.4
New Cassel CDP	14,059	-	-	14,867	6.8	38.5	0.7	3.0	50.9	26.7	10.0	32.0	60.7	20.9	3,369	93.8
New Castle town (Westchester)	17,571	17,801	1.3	17,905	84.3	2.6	8.3	2.2	2.5	26.9	13.8	44.1	7.9	82.4	5,880	98.6
New City CDP	33,559	-	-	35,101	66.1	8.1	11.0	2.4	12.4	21.8	19.2	45.1	20.2	57.5	11,517	95.6
Newcomb town (Essex)	436	404	-7.3	375	94.9	0.5	0.5	2.9	1.1	9.1	46.7	62.4	45.9	29.4	207	84.1
Newfane CDP	3,822	-	-	3,376	95.5	1.0	0.0	3.2	0.3	19.1	24.5	48.6	51.2	21.8	1,447	87.7
Newfane town (Niagara)	9,674	9,149	-5.4	9,297	96.5	0.4	0.0	2.5	0.5	19.1	18.6	44.9	49.2	20.3	3,764	86.6
Newfield town (Tompkins)	5,181	5,067	-2.2	5,189	92.3	1.7	0.4	1.7	4.0	16.3	16.6	45.8	44.7	23.4	2,202	90.0
Newfield Hamlet CDP	759	-	-	451	100.0	0.0	0.0	0.0	0.0	10.9	20.8	49.7	28.1	43.5	208	69.7
New Hartford village	1,850	1,830	-1.1	1,774	91.9	0.3	1.2	1.5	5.1	18.8	22.0	45.9	17.3	53.1	798	78.2
New Hartford town (Oneida)	22,167	21,818	-1.6	21,836	90.7	1.4	4.1	1.7	2.0	18.3	25.4	47.2	26.2	45.0	9,046	90.0
New Haven town (Oswego)	2,862	2,836	-0.9	2,844	97.7	0.6	1.1	0.4	0.3	24.4	14.5	41.0	53.6	13.1	1,081	93.1
New Hempstead village	5,140	5,410	5.3	5,385	63.7	17.4	5.1	0.4	13.4	31.4	11.0	31.8	28.7	43.1	1,317	97.3
New Hudson town (Allegany)	783	763	-2.6	971	92.6	0.0	0.9	3.4	3.1	28.7	12.0	35.1	51.9	13.9	333	79.9
New Hyde Park village	9,769	9,807	0.4	9,841	41.9	0.9	30.7	4.0	22.5	21.2	15.1	40.1	29.3	47.4	2,838	97.4
New Lebanon town (Columbia)	2,301	2,152	-6.5	2,321	98.1	0.0	0.6	0.1	1.2	13.9	22.0	51.6	29.6	37.0	1,006	95.6
New Lisbon town (Otsego)	1,117	1,048	-6.2	1,218	97.1	0.0	0.7	0.7	1.4	14.7	15.9	45.4	43.6	22.8	505	86.7
New Paltz village	6,837	7,101	3.9	7,165	73.3	4.1	6.6	1.7	14.2	6.6	11.4	21.6	17.2	66.1	1,963	95.7
New Paltz town (Ulster)	14,002	14,036	0.2	14,162	78.5	4.9	3.9	2.0	10.6	15.4	15.2	25.2	17.6	60.1	4,535	95.7
Newport village	639	600	-6.1	516	98.8	1.2	0.0	0.0	0.0	17.6	24.4	44.6	32.0	19.9	243	79.0
Newport town (Herkimer)	2,307	2,225	-3.6	2,132	97.8	0.5	0.0	0.6	1.1	22.0	18.0	43.9	50.6	15.7	822	84.4
New Rochelle city & MCD (Westchester)	77,115	78,557	1.9	79,067	43.6	18.7	5.1	2.4	30.2	20.5	17.6	39.7	36.3	44.5	28,581	90.2
New Scotland town (Albany)	8,644	8,641	0.0	8,704	94.9	0.4	1.8	1.2	1.7	18.4	20.8	47.3	27.0	45.5	3,335	94.0
New Square village	6,969	8,763	25.7	8,373	98.6	0.1	0.0	0.3	1.0	59.8	2.6	14.7	74.3	3.7	1,497	17.5
Newstead town (Erie)	8,641	8,689	0.6	8,675	95.7	1.0	0.2	2.0	1.1	20.9	19.1	45.4	38.2	29.4	3,723	87.0
New Suffolk CDP	349	-	-	250	95.2	4.8	0.0	0.0	0.0	10.8	37.2	56.8	18.2	53.7	127	100.0
New Windsor CDP	8,922	-	-	9,019	57.4	12.9	3.3	1.5	25.0	18.1	17.0	41.7	44.3	23.7	3,508	91.3
New Windsor town (Orange)	25,254	27,703	9.7	27,296	56.2	13.9	3.9	2.4	23.6	22.5	14.8	38.4	36.5	32.3	9,893	91.6
New York city	8,175,031	8,336,817	2.0	8,419,316	32.1	21.8	14.0	3.0	29.1	20.8	14.5	36.7	41.9	38.1	3,167,034	89.1
New York Mills village	3,326	3,212	-3.4	3,362	93.0	0.0	2.4	3.5	1.2	17.7	22.6	45.3	42.8	32.5	1,667	83.0
Niagara town (Niagara)	8,543	8,063	-5.6	8,151	89.1	3.9	0.8	4.3	1.9	16.8	20.6	46.8	53.7	14.9	3,508	86.1
Niagara Falls city & MCD (Niagara)	50,031	47,720	-4.6	48,252	65.2	21.9	1.7	5.9	5.3	23.0	15.8	38.1	49.0	18.7	21,572	80.7
Nichols village	512	470	-8.2	560	99.6	0.0	0.0	0.4	0.0	18.4	21.8	43.3	47.7	21.0	215	94.0
Nichols town (Tioga)	2,523	2,420	-4.1	2,659	97.6	0.0	0.6	1.6	0.2	21.0	20.9	43.6	51.8	19.2	1,036	85.8
Niles town (Cayuga)	1,196	1,155	-3.4	1,235	97.0	0.6	0.8	0.8	0.8	21.7	25.0	47.7	36.5	24.9	502	87.6
Niskayuna CDP	-	-	-	4,895	83.3	1.8	5.9	3.2	5.7	27.1	16.0	40.1	14.1	62.1	1,753	94.5
Niskayuna town (Schenectady)	21,774	22,365	2.7	22,267	82.3	2.2	9.9	2.5	3.1	25.6	19.6	44.1	16.3	62.8	7,761	94.4
Nissequogue village	1,746	1,732	-0.8	1,678	83.0	5.8	3.8	0.7	6.8	18.5	20.8	48.6	12.6	67.1	541	98.2
Niverville CDP	1,662	-	-	1,228	95.6	0.9	0.0	3.0	0.5	23.3	17.1	48.2	20.3	47.0	456	87.1
Norfolk CDP	1,327	-	-	990	94.5	4.7	0.0	0.4	0.3	24.9	19.0	36.5	56.7	20.6	520	83.3
Norfolk town (St. Lawrence)	4,658	4,475	-3.9	4,512	98.0	1.0	0.0	0.6	0.4	24.3	15.7	41.4	55.0	15.9	2,014	83.1
North Amityville CDP	17,862	-	-	18,382	7.0	52.2	1.0	2.6	37.3	26.0	12.2	33.9	59.8	19.0	4,926	91.4
Northampton town (Fulton)	2,659	2,564	-3.6	2,570	98.9	0.2	0.0	0.7	0.2	19.3	26.5	49.4	43.0	25.8	1,134	86.6
Northampton CDP	570	-	-	885	20.2	63.7	0.5	1.9	13.7	21.1	15.6	33.7	36.3	48.8	278	100.0
North Babylon CDP	17,509	-	-	17,134	68.0	6.4	4.0	3.1	18.5	20.1	15.1	42.9	36.0	31.5	5,648	95.0
North Ballston Spa CDP	1,338	-	-	1,165	93.2	4.3	0.0	2.2	0.3	9.2	19.1	54.2	49.8	20.2	619	84.8
North Bay Shore CDP	18,944	-	-	21,679	13.9	12.1	1.5	6.1	66.4	28.5	8.6	31.0	60.9	13.6	4,405	94.7
North Bellmore CDP	19,941	-	-	20,718	78.6	2.1	5.6	1.7	12.0	21.1	17.3	42.6	29.8	46.9	6,512	95.4
North Bellport CDP	11,545	-	-	11,428	38.9	21.2	2.0	1.4	36.4	24.8	9.2	33.5	53.1	17.0	3,453	89.5
North Boston CDP	2,521	-	-	2,694	98.8	0.0	0.0	1.0	0.2	14.6	21.6	54.1	29.2	23.4	1,244	86.7
North Castle town (Westchester)	11,898	12,231	2.8	12,235	78.4	1.4	5.4	2.2	12.5	26.8	13.6	44.1	12.4	74.9	4,092	97.6
North Collins village	1,227	1,195	-2.6	1,370	89.2	2.0	1.6	5.3	2.0	27.2	12.8	32.5	47.0	18.3	501	86.6
North Collins town (Erie)	3,529	3,483	-1.3	3,500	94.7	1.0	0.7	2.1	1.5	23.3	14.2	39.3	49.0	22.1	1,322	89.0
North Creek CDP	616	-	-	698	92.0	0.0	2.4	5.6	0.0	12.5	32.1	56.8	47.6	19.5	266	86.5
North Dansville town (Livingston)	5,546	5,192	-6.4	5,282	90.6	1.7	0.0	2.7	4.9	22.7	16.8	42.2	46.3	17.7	2,330	85.4
North East town (Dutchess)	3,018	2,946	-2.4	2,943	81.5	3.4	2.2	1.3	11.6	21.1	21.2	44.2	42.1	34.3	1,209	86.8
Northeast Ithaca CDP	2,641	-	-	2,811	58.8	3.2	28.6	5.8	3.6	25.0	11.7	35.4	13.9	77.4	1,092	97.7
North Elba town (Essex)	8,956	8,066	-9.9	8,215	79.2	10.7	0.3	1.2	8.6	18.8	16.7	36.5	39.6	31.4	2,629	91.0
North Gates CDP	9,512	-	-	9,581	70.5	12.6	7.1	2.3	7.4	17.2	19.9	42.1	45.9	24.7	4,268	88.7
North Great River CDP	4,001	-	-	3,883	80.4	3.6	3.4	1.7	10.9	16.9	22.7	49.0	39.1	30.3	1,313	94.9
North Greenbush town (Rensselaer)	12,085	12,246	1.3	12,176	90.6	0.9	1.5	3.5	3.4	19.3	22.5	46.3	31.9	36.6	4,986	91.3
North Harmony town (Chautauqua)	2,259	2,145	-5.0	2,252	95.6	0.0	1.7	0.4	2.3	18.1	23.4	50.0	36.3	28.5	940	93.1
North Haven village	843	892	5.8	884	97.5	0.0	0.0	1.6	0.9	19.6	24.7	53.1	17.7	65.3	366	86.6
North Hempstead town (Nassau)	226,226	230,933	2.1	230,531	58.4	5.6	18.9	2.5	14.5	22.4	19.5	42.6	25.9	55.7	77,721	94.5

1 May be of any race.

Table A. All Places — **Population and Housing**

STATE City, town, township, borough, or CDP (county if applicable)	Population				Race and Hispanic or Latino origin (percent)					Age (percent)			Educational attainment of persons age 25 and older		Occupied housing units	
	2010 census total population	2019 estimated population	Percent change 2010–2019	ACS total population estimate 2015–2019	White alone, not Hispanic or Latino	Black alone, not Hispanic or Latino	Asian alone, not Hispanic or Latino	All other races or 2 or more races, not Hispanic or Latino	Hispanic or Latino[1]	Under 18 years old	Age 65 years and older	Median age	Percent High school diploma or less	Percent Bachelor's degree or more	Total	Percent with a computer
	1	2	3	4	5	6	7	8	9	10	11	12	13	14	15	16
NEW YORK—Con.																
North Hills village............	5,183	5,969	15.2	5,796	59.9	2.2	33.6	0.0	4.2	13.9	40.6	58.9	16.4	70.8	2,601	89.8
North Hornell village........	782	737	-5.8	775	95.6	0.3	1.3	1.8	1.0	12.6	38.8	57.6	35.1	38.3	313	93.0
North Hudson town (Essex)..................	240	233	-2.9	210	97.1	0.0	0.0	1.0	1.9	8.6	24.3	54.8	44.0	12.5	116	87.1
North Lindenhurst CDP....	11,652	-	-	10,624	65.2	10.1	2.4	1.9	20.4	20.7	14.2	40.7	45.6	21.8	3,607	90.4
North Lynbrook CDP........	793	-	-	464	63.6	0.0	19.8	0.0	16.6	12.3	27.4	48.7	35.2	41.0	146	94.5
North Massapequa CDP ..	17,886	-	-	18,505	92.1	0.7	1.7	1.0	4.5	20.7	17.7	43.9	31.6	39.7	6,113	93.7
North Merrick CDP...........	12,272	-	-	12,170	80.1	5.3	4.8	1.7	8.1	24.1	14.1	41.0	21.7	54.6	3,892	96.3
North New Hyde Park CDP.........................	14,899	-	-	15,080	49.6	0.1	36.9	2.3	11.2	19.1	19.8	45.0	30.0	52.6	4,735	92.5
North Norwich town (Chenango)...............	1,779	1,698	-4.6	1,643	96.2	1.2	0.0	1.2	1.4	18.7	21.1	48.4	47.7	21.1	698	89.8
North Patchogue CDP......	7,246	-	-	7,657	69.4	0.3	2.8	0.9	26.6	23.4	11.7	36.9	41.9	23.1	2,372	94.6
Northport village..............	7,404	7,273	-1.8	7,328	92.0	2.2	0.8	0.3	4.8	19.5	23.4	50.1	18.1	59.6	2,914	97.9
North Rose CDP................	636	-	-	466	84.5	1.1	1.1	2.4	10.9	12.0	32.8	54.3	52.0	18.0	257	87.2
North Salem town (Westchester).............	5,127	5,124	-0.1	5,167	78.4	4.7	5.1	4.0	7.8	21.4	20.7	48.4	20.1	60.2	1,824	97.1
North Sea CDP.................	4,458	-	-	4,597	85.9	0.0	1.6	0.0	12.4	17.3	26.8	49.0	23.5	47.6	1,855	83.2
North Syracuse village......	6,812	6,628	-2.7	6,767	87.2	3.4	0.3	6.8	2.3	18.6	18.3	43.3	44.0	23.5	3,120	84.9
North Tonawanda city & MCD (Niagara)..............	31,574	30,245	-4.2	30,487	94.5	1.0	0.5	2.2	1.7	18.0	19.4	45.6	41.4	24.7	13,577	87.2
Northumberland town (Saratoga)..................	5,103	5,076	-0.5	5,114	92.4	1.1	0.5	2.3	3.7	23.5	13.6	39.0	37.2	31.7	1,836	87.5
North Valley Stream CDP .	16,628	-	-	18,661	15.2	50.0	12.4	5.1	17.3	17.9	16.9	43.0	35.1	38.0	5,634	94.1
Northville village..............	1,099	1,053	-4.2	1,051	99.5	0.4	0.0	0.0	0.1	25.1	26.5	41.5	46.8	18.1	451	80.9
Northville CDP.................	1,340	-	-	1,370	90.7	2.6	0.0	0.0	6.7	20.7	40.1	58.3	28.2	41.3	496	100.0
North Wantagh CDP.........	11,960	-	-	11,720	84.4	0.3	2.6	1.7	11.0	19.1	20.1	45.3	29.4	42.7	4,093	90.6
Northwest Harbor CDP.....	3,317	-	-	3,557	81.6	2.4	1.1	0.8	14.2	8.5	30.8	55.5	21.0	62.8	1,770	95.3
Northwest Ithaca CDP.....	1,413	-	-	1,439	73.6	10.3	4.5	2.8	8.8	16.5	24.7	49.0	31.3	49.1	588	90.3
Norway town (Herkimer)...	758	748	-1.3	892	98.8	1.1	0.0	0.0	0.1	15.6	12.4	41.1	50.9	16.2	330	87.6
Norwich city & MCD (Chenango)...............	7,190	6,540	-9.0	6,718	91.2	2.2	0.5	2.8	3.3	21.2	19.2	37.4	51.0	21.3	2,975	83.5
Norwich town (Chenango)	4,011	3,668	-8.6	3,743	93.8	1.0	2.7	0.6	1.8	19.1	18.2	42.7	52.7	17.8	1,580	92.2
Norwood village..............	1,660	1,560	-6.0	1,651	96.2	0.2	0.8	2.5	0.3	20.2	24.5	46.6	42.2	23.8	727	84.6
Noyack CDP....................	3,568	-	-	4,372	72.4	6.7	3.3	1.7	16.0	22.6	21.3	47.2	29.2	52.2	1,589	83.2
Nunda village..................	1,358	1,283	-5.5	1,211	95.2	4.5	0.0	0.0	0.3	20.9	20.7	46.0	50.9	15.0	541	77.3
Nunda town (Livingston)...	3,054	2,889	-5.4	2,927	98.0	1.8	0.0	0.0	0.1	20.3	16.5	46.1	50.8	17.9	1,245	83.2
Nyack village..................	6,772	7,156	5.7	7,173	48.1	27.0	4.3	2.9	17.8	16.1	26.4	49.3	30.2	50.5	3,328	86.3
Oak Beach-Captree CDP .	286	-	-	36	100.0	0.0	0.0	0.0	0.0	0.0	30.6	62.2	30.6	69.4	17	100.0
Oakdale CDP...................	7,974	-	-	6,984	91.6	2.0	0.6	0.6	5.3	16.0	24.6	49.8	25.8	44.7	2,829	93.0
Oakfield village...............	1,813	1,693	-6.6	1,718	90.9	1.5	0.7	3.5	3.4	25.7	14.5	37.1	49.8	15.6	637	84.3
Oakfield town (Genesee)..	3,245	3,045	-6.2	3,080	94.6	1.2	0.4	1.9	1.9	21.2	17.6	42.5	54.3	15.3	1,212	86.6
Ocean Beach village........	81	83	2.5	32	100.0	0.0	0.0	0.0	0.0	0.0	34.4	56.0	9.4	34.4	21	66.7
Oceanside CDP................	32,109	-	-	30,604	81.0	1.1	2.8	1.1	13.9	22.1	17.7	43.4	28.8	47.6	10,466	94.2
Odessa village................	590	552	-6.4	461	94.4	0.9	0.0	2.0	2.8	13.0	23.2	51.3	44.5	24.2	202	94.1
Ogden town (Monroe).......	19,857	20,531	3.4	20,341	89.8	1.9	0.8	1.6	5.9	21.1	15.2	40.7	30.2	37.0	7,666	94.2
Ogdensburg city & MCD (St. Lawrence).............	11,131	10,436	-6.2	10,635	83.5	7.3	1.1	3.1	5.0	18.8	16.3	41.6	54.4	16.1	4,062	85.9
Ohio town (Herkimer)	1,000	997	-0.3	1,100	97.6	0.5	0.4	1.1	0.4	18.0	18.5	50.3	46.2	17.8	451	89.6
Oil Springs Reservation (Allegany)..................	1	1	0.0	2	50.0	0.0	0.0	50.0	0.0	0.0	0.0	0.0	0.0	0.0	1	100.0
Oil Springs Reservation (Cattaraugus)................	-	-	-	-	-	-	-	-	-	-	-	-	-	-	-	-
Olcott CDP......................	1,241	-	-	1,282	95.5	0.2	0.0	3.5	0.8	22.7	14.0	43.5	41.4	9.8	523	92.2
Old Bethpage CDP	5,523	-	-	5,283	85.3	0.4	8.9	1.2	4.2	24.7	18.3	44.3	22.3	61.7	1,824	89.6
Old Brookville village	2,106	2,187	3.8	1,708	74.6	0.9	18.1	1.8	4.6	23.8	19.0	48.4	12.7	69.5	577	99.5
Old Field village	918	909	-	795	87.5	1.5	7.7	1.5	1.8	20.6	20.4	49.7	5.9	80.1	287	96.9
Old Forge CDP	756	-	-	479	87.1	7.7	0.0	0.0	5.2	10.4	43.0	61.5	52.7	21.6	250	74.8
Old Westbury village........	4,703	4,614	-1.9	4,670	61.7	8.2	17.3	5.3	7.5	17.8	14.5	26.3	12.7	75.6	1,085	98.6
Olean city & MCD (Cattaraugus)................	14,428	13,437	-6.9	13,670	89.2	3.5	2.0	3.9	1.4	21.4	17.8	41.0	45.7	25.0	6,191	85.2
Olean town (Cattaraugus)	1,984	1,876	-5.4	2,036	96.1	0.3	1.6	2.0	0.0	18.4	20.5	47.4	44.4	21.8	891	87.1
Olive town (Ulster)	4,419	4,270	-3.4	4,296	85.9	0.6	3.5	5.0	5.0	12.8	27.5	52.0	36.1	40.9	1,836	89.4
Oneida city & MCD (Madison)...................	11,317	10,894	-3.7	10,948	92.2	1.6	0.4	3.3	2.5	22.4	17.3	41.8	43.2	24.2	4,504	90.1
Oneida Castle village.......	635	622	-2.0	646	96.4	0.3	1.1	2.2	0.0	27.7	22.3	45.3	38.6	20.5	266	86.1
Oneonta city & MCD (Otsego)...................	13,945	13,907	-0.3	13,893	81.7	3.8	2.9	3.3	8.4	10.8	13.4	22.4	29.1	41.8	4,398	87.8
Oneonta town (Otsego)	5,218	4,959	-5.0	5,000	90.5	4.1	0.8	0.9	3.8	18.3	25.5	45.3	28.5	37.8	1,973	91.4
Onondaga town (Onondaga)..............	23,126	22,400	-3.1	22,663	85.5	5.1	2.6	3.9	2.9	21.7	16.9	41.1	25.7	43.3	8,249	92.0
Onondaga Nation Reservation (Onondag..	461	479	3.9	156	0.0	0.0	19.9	71.2	9.0	0.0	19.2	53.6	18.6	10.3	127	100.0
Ontario CDP....................	2,160	-	-	1,942	97.3	1.0	1.7	0.0	0.0	16.6	16.3	45.8	27.9	26.2	1,016	91.2
Ontario town (Wayne).......	10,143	10,166	0.2	10,092	94.6	1.7	1.4	1.2	1.1	20.8	17.0	46.0	32.7	28.9	4,419	92.7
Oppenheim town (Fulton)..	1,923	1,871	-2.7	1,846	95.1	1.4	0.1	1.5	1.9	24.3	18.3	40.9	61.8	8.6	739	80.5
Orange town (Schuyler)....	1,609	1,401	-12.9	1,291	94.7	1.4	0.3	2.4	1.2	20.6	19.5	43.1	45.7	23.1	539	89.2
Orangeburg CDP..............	4,568	-	-	4,491	69.0	3.7	14.2	2.0	11.2	14.5	24.7	41.2	25.1	51.5	1,441	85.9
Orange Lake CDP	6,982	-	-	6,434	48.9	22.0	3.3	4.9	20.9	17.7	20.8	45.1	27.9	34.6	2,377	94.6
Orangetown town (Rockland).................	49,208	49,833	1.3	49,909	72.4	6.5	8.0	2.4	10.8	18.8	19.8	43.8	26.1	52.4	17,711	92.7
Orangeville town (Wyoming).................	1,336	1,300	-2.7	1,459	93.4	0.7	0.5	4.4	1.1	20.0	15.1	42.5	40.8	23.1	601	87.9
Orchard Park village........	3,222	3,131	-2.8	3,148	94.4	0.0	1.3	0.0	4.3	20.4	20.6	44.8	17.2	65.8	1,368	96.9
Orchard Park town (Erie)..	29,046	29,594	1.9	29,509	94.2	0.9	1.8	0.5	2.6	21.5	22.1	46.8	25.9	48.3	11,837	90.8
Orient CDP......................	743	-	-	835	92.7	0.6	0.5	3.5	2.8	9.0	48.4	64.4	22.2	48.6	392	91.8
Oriskany village...............	1,401	1,329	-5.1	1,229	96.3	2.4	0.0	0.4	0.4	17.6	28.9	47.4	46.6	22.6	597	85.3
Oriskany Falls village........	720	690	-4.2	874	96.6	1.5	0.0	1.9	0.0	28.5	15.7	37.2	51.2	19.6	347	75.8
Orleans town (Jefferson) ..	2,795	2,689	-3.8	2,754	91.0	6.1	0.0	1.3	1.6	32.3	14.2	34.1	50.4	18.1	893	89.8
Orwell town (Oswego)	1,167	1,171	0.3	1,415	94.1	1.1	0.0	1.1	3.8	31.5	14.6	37.7	54.1	19.4	462	93.1
Osceola town (Lewis)	229	221	-3.5	212	99.1	0.0	0.0	0.9	0.0	14.6	19.3	51.0	56.0	10.8	100	79.0
Ossian town (Livingston) ..	789	735	-6.8	701	99.3	0.3	0.0	0.1	0.3	20.8	25.8	53.3	41.2	20.6	289	93.1

1 May be of any race.

Table A. All Places — **Population and Housing**

STATE City, town, township, borough, or CDP (county if applicable)	Population				Race and Hispanic or Latino origin (percent)					Age (percent)			Educational attainment of persons age 25 and older		Occupied housing units	
	2010 census total population	2019 estimated population	Percent change 2010–2019	ACS total population estimate 2015–2019	White alone, not Hispanic or Latino	Black alone, not Hispanic or Latino	Asian alone, not Hispanic or Latino	All other races or 2 or more races, not Hispanic or Latino	Hispanic or Latino[1]	Under 18 years old	Age 65 years and older	Median age	Percent High school diploma or less	Percent Bachelor's degree or more	Total	Percent with a computer
	1	2	3	4	5	6	7	8	9	10	11	12	13	14	15	16
NEW YORK—Con.																
Ossining village	25,050	24,812		25,086	35.7	12.8	5.1	2.1	44.3	21.3	14.2	39.5	44.1	34.8	8,807	90.5
Ossining town (Westchester)	37,651	37,702	0.1	37,642	48.9	10.2	5.3	2.5	33.0	20.5	16.9	42.2	35.0	46.2	13,447	91.6
Oswegatchie town (St. Lawrence)	4,393	4,263	-3.0	4,312	99.0	0.3	0.0	0.6	0.0	24.5	22.8	48.1	51.1	21.3	1,651	85.9
Oswego city & MCD (Oswego)	18,151	17,236	-5.0	17,470	90.1	1.3	1.1	3.2	4.3	19.1	14.6	35.0	41.5	28.1	7,494	88.2
Oswego town (Oswego)	7,987	7,531	-5.7	7,715	82.7	6.1	2.5	1.6	7.1	11.3	9.6	20.8	41.3	29.5	1,559	96.5
Otego village	997	928	-6.9	921	93.4	0.8	1.8	3.8	0.2	14.5	22.8	42.7	28.2	34.1	438	91.8
Otego town (Otsego)	3,104	2,884	-7.1	2,914	97.2	0.3	0.6	1.8	0.1	12.9	22.0	47.3	44.2	27.9	1,218	93.6
Otisco town (Onondaga)	2,540	2,529	-0.4	2,533	98.0	0.0	0.0	1.0	0.9	17.8	18.5	46.5	35.0	35.7	993	87.5
Otisville village	1,080	1,056	-2.2	1,238	79.3	0.8	7.2	1.5	11.2	25.5	12.2	38.9	37.9	27.5	388	96.1
Otsego town (Otsego)	3,907	3,700	-5.3	3,739	86.0	2.9	3.3	3.6	4.1	14.4	26.7	51.6	20.2	56.1	1,666	94.5
Otselic town (Chenango)	1,054	1,001	-5.0	824	94.8	0.0	0.0	1.7	3.5	16.5	17.8	46.3	55.2	13.7	357	85.4
Otto town (Cattaraugus)	809	750	-7.3	795	98.4	0.5	0.0	1.0	0.1	21.3	17.7	47.4	49.8	16.6	320	75.0
Ovid village	611	598	-2.1	535	95.5	0.0	0.0	0.6	3.9	25.8	12.5	34.6	43.1	21.6	208	88.9
Ovid town (Seneca)	2,309	2,272	-1.6	2,362	94.8	1.0	0.0	2.1	2.2	22.2	18.2	38.2	49.2	22.9	1,024	78.6
Owasco town (Cayuga)	3,784	3,620	-4.3	3,656	98.8	0.0	0.1	0.0	1.1	19.3	22.4	50.5	28.1	38.8	1,526	86.8
Owego village	3,898	3,851	-1.2	3,829	91.7	1.0	1.5	1.8	4.0	21.6	17.7	38.8	44.2	25.1	1,774	85.3
Owego town (Tioga)	19,808	18,645	-5.9	18,827	93.8	0.8	1.0	1.9	2.5	19.7	21.1	46.7	35.6	35.2	7,961	89.1
Oxbow CDP	108	-	-	116	100.0	0.0	0.0	0.0	0.0	37.9	16.4	37.0	62.5	12.5	38	92.1
Oxford village	1,447	1,379	-4.7	1,477	91.2	3.2	0.0	0.5	5.1	22.8	17.5	41.1	42.2	26.1	692	88.0
Oxford town (Chenango)	3,896	3,671	-5.8	3,733	94.6	1.7	0.0	0.5	3.1	17.3	22.0	49.3	50.0	18.9	1,735	83.2
Oyster Bay CDP	6,707	-	-	5,836	78.1	3.4	2.6	1.4	14.5	19.7	23.8	46.2	33.0	42.9	2,618	87.9
Oyster Bay town (Nassau)	293,576	298,391	1.6	297,822	75.5	2.2	12.5	1.8	8.1	20.7	18.6	44.3	26.6	51.1	101,216	93.7
Oyster Bay Cove village	2,226	2,254	1.3	2,080	81.5	1.0	9.9	1.0	6.7	17.6	21.8	51.2	11.1	73.2	714	95.9
Painted Post village	1,810	1,924	6.3	1,612	91.3	1.9	3.7	2.7	0.4	22.0	20.7	41.5	25.9	45.4	805	86.3
Palatine town (Montgomery)	3,232	3,232	0.0	3,228	91.2	0.5	1.2	1.1	5.9	26.9	19.5	35.8	56.1	16.7	1,140	80.1
Palatine Bridge village	730	748	2.5	633	92.1	2.5	0.0	2.5	2.8	11.8	40.1	57.6	48.3	23.1	273	78.0
Palenville CDP	1,037	-	-	1,175	78.9	0.9	0.0	18.4	1.9	32.2	6.5	35.5	33.1	44.3	449	89.5
Palermo town (Oswego)	3,659	3,521	-3.8	3,560	92.5	4.0	1.3	1.5	0.6	21.0	14.7	39.8	56.2	11.5	1,291	91.4
Palm Tree town (Orange)	20,436	26,886	31.6	24,666	98.3	0.0	0.0	0.2	1.5	61.4	2.2	13.8	76.9	5.7	4,180	32.5
Palmyra village	3,534	3,321	-6.0	3,354	90.2	1.2	0.0	0.0	8.6	20.3	16.1	42.2	37.5	26.2	1,500	85.3
Palmyra town (Wayne)	7,966	7,512	-5.7	7,589	92.4	0.8	0.5	0.2	6.1	19.2	18.8	46.3	44.1	24.1	3,318	86.7
Pamelia town (Jefferson)	3,166	2,889	-8.7	2,968	82.6	6.5	2.0	6.4	2.6	24.6	16.6	37.7	43.4	20.3	1,143	93.4
Pamelia Center CDP	264	-	-	271	92.6	0.0	7.4	0.0	0.0	17.0	21.8	41.3	45.4	22.2	122	100.0
Panama village	479	444	-7.3	426	97.9	0.0	0.5	0.0	1.6	22.3	23.5	43.5	52.1	11.3	190	77.9
Parc CDP	254	-	-	236	69.5	15.7	0.0	3.8	11.0	2.5	0.0	19.4	45.8	0.0	24	54.2
Paris town (Oneida)	4,423	4,222	-4.5	4,261	95.6	0.4	1.5	1.1	1.3	18.7	18.2	45.8	32.5	29.4	1,778	94.3
Parish village	444	427	-3.8	488	91.6	0.0	0.2	1.6	6.6	21.3	12.7	33.3	44.2	20.8	175	91.4
Parish town (Oswego)	2,550	2,437	-4.4	2,321	95.3	0.6	0.7	2.0	1.4	18.0	16.8	43.7	48.0	16.9	945	89.9
Parishville CDP	647	-	-	781	95.6	0.0	0.0	0.9	3.5	30.3	7.3	34.7	27.1	35.4	298	85.6
Parishville town (St. Lawrence)	2,153	2,038	-5.3	2,293	95.9	0.5	0.9	1.5	1.2	23.6	13.4	41.7	36.3	28.3	945	88.1
Parma town (Monroe)	15,633	15,726	0.6	15,699	93.0	2.7	0.2	0.6	3.4	23.2	16.7	43.7	35.1	34.2	5,965	92.3
Patchogue village	11,805	12,321	4.4	12,384	59.9	3.7	4.2	1.7	30.5	19.1	11.6	37.5	39.2	31.8	5,506	93.2
Patterson town (Putnam)	11,999	11,809	-1.6	11,866	74.1	6.7	1.9	1.5	15.9	18.5	13.8	42.2	41.0	34.9	3,730	95.4
Paul Smiths CDP	671	-	-	622	82.0	10.0	4.8	0.6	2.6	0.0	0.0	19.6	0.0	0.0	0	0.0
Pavilion CDP	646	-	-	563	100.0	0.0	0.0	0.0	0.0	19.0	21.1	40.5	30.6	27.3	196	93.4
Pavilion town (Genesee)	2,471	2,351	-4.9	2,495	95.9	1.4	0.0	0.2	2.4	19.3	19.3	47.1	41.1	26.6	975	90.1
Pawling village	2,299	2,262	-1.6	2,029	73.3	1.0	4.0	0.2	21.4	17.5	20.3	45.5	42.2	33.5	884	88.7
Pawling town (Dutchess)	8,450	8,226	-2.7	8,256	81.6	3.3	1.3	0.9	12.9	19.9	18.2	45.1	36.7	37.0	3,170	92.7
Peach Lake CDP	1,629	-	-	1,604	90.1	1.0	3.0	1.1	4.8	24.2	16.5	47.6	21.5	50.3	562	96.8
Pearl River CDP	15,876	-	-	16,476	80.3	3.1	6.1	1.8	8.6	21.8	18.1	41.1	26.0	46.6	5,634	92.1
Peconic CDP	683	-	-	812	83.4	0.0	0.0	0.0	16.6	8.1	39.0	57.7	39.1	40.9	377	87.0
Peekskill city & MCD (Westchester)	23,589	24,295	3.0	24,075	29.2	22.2	2.1	3.0	43.5	24.8	15.0	38.7	45.3	29.8	9,402	85.4
Pelham village	6,861	6,947	1.3	6,941	59.2	10.7	9.5	5.2	15.3	28.0	13.6	39.9	25.9	55.8	2,285	94.4
Pelham town (Westchester)	12,379	12,481	0.8	12,510	66.5	8.9	7.7	4.1	12.7	29.6	13.5	39.1	20.1	66.2	4,006	93.9
Pelham Manor village	5,518	5,534	0.3	5,569	75.6	6.7	5.5	2.6	9.5	31.6	13.3	37.2	12.1	80.5	1,721	93.3
Pembroke town (Genesee)	4,285	4,135	-3.5	4,182	93.7	1.1	0.4	4.1	0.6	17.6	21.8	49.0	45.7	25.5	1,747	87.4
Pendleton town (Niagara)	6,396	6,829	6.8	6,700	95.9	1.1	0.5	2.0	0.5	19.9	16.5	44.5	27.0	37.4	2,335	96.4
Penfield town (Monroe)	36,293	37,301	2.8	37,252	89.2	2.5	3.4	1.4	3.6	22.0	21.5	46.5	20.0	53.4	15,179	92.7
Penn Yan village	5,173	4,925	-4.8	4,949	92.2	2.0	0.8	1.2	3.7	18.8	22.0	44.4	51.1	20.5	1,954	76.3
Perinton town (Monroe)	46,481	46,735	0.5	46,671	90.0	1.5	3.4	1.2	3.9	21.6	22.0	46.8	16.3	59.2	19,126	94.1
Perry village	3,661	3,488	-4.7	3,418	89.3	3.3	1.1	5.0	1.2	22.5	16.6	38.7	48.3	14.6	1,370	86.8
Perry town (Wyoming)	4,622	4,388	-5.1	4,389	88.3	3.1	0.9	4.9	2.9	22.0	18.4	39.6	47.0	14.6	1,793	87.0
Perrysburg CDP	401	-	-	427	97.2	1.4	0.0	1.4	0.0	20.6	29.7	51.0	65.8	9.5	129	81.4
Perrysburg town (Cattaraugus)	1,624	1,547	-4.7	1,616	97.8	0.4	0.0	1.8	0.0	18.7	23.5	47.1	53.4	14.6	612	89.2
Persia town (Cattaraugus)	2,418	2,247	-7.1	2,497	86.2	0.4	0.0	7.2	6.1	20.0	22.7	42.0	50.5	12.3	1,038	82.9
Perth town (Fulton)	3,641	3,475	-4.6	3,480	91.4	2.5	0.7	1.2	4.2	24.1	14.4	39.8	43.7	22.4	1,374	88.0
Peru CDP	1,591	-	-	1,597	97.7	0.0	2.3	0.0	0.0	16.1	29.0	50.2	25.4	41.7	679	84.2
Peru town (Clinton)	7,000	6,917	-1.2	6,927	94.3	0.4	1.2	1.4	2.7	22.6	16.8	39.8	46.1	26.3	2,563	90.8
Petersburgh town (Rensselaer)	1,517	1,473	-2.9	1,439	94.3	1.1	0.0	2.1	2.5	16.5	19.7	47.4	53.5	20.1	618	88.3
Pharsalia town (Chenango)	596	569	-4.5	589	92.0	0.0	0.0	7.1	0.8	19.4	17.1	49.4	61.4	13.6	263	75.7
Phelps village	1,993	1,898	-4.8	1,886	97.8	0.2	0.5	0.4	1.2	21.6	20.3	40.7	42.8	18.5	847	85.1
Phelps town (Ontario)	7,084	6,777	-4.3	6,858	93.2	1.4	1.0	0.4	4.0	21.6	17.2	46.2	41.4	24.9	2,722	89.7
Philadelphia village	1,236	1,125	-9.0	1,087	84.3	5.3	0.7	3.1	6.5	23.6	12.4	31.3	46.8	16.7	486	86.6
Philadelphia town (Jefferson)	1,948	1,794	-7.9	1,718	88.5	3.9	0.9	2.3	4.3	23.9	11.9	32.7	48.4	17.3	726	88.0
Philipstown town (Putnam)	9,675	9,675	0.0	9,715	86.7	1.3	1.8	1.6	8.7	20.3	20.3	47.7	25.1	51.9	3,543	95.7
Philmont village	1,371	1,258	-8.2	1,123	89.4	2.1	1.7	3.4	3.4	19.3	15.8	39.6	31.7	32.3	523	90.4
Phoenicia CDP	309	-	-	218	100.0	0.0	0.0	0.0	0.0	0.0	39.4	60.4	35.4	41.3	152	80.9
Phoenix village	2,382	2,241	-5.9	2,471	94.9	0.0	1.1	3.0	1.0	23.6	11.4	34.7	44.0	15.5	1,074	88.3
Piercefield town (St. Lawrence)	306	285	-6.9	187	97.9	0.5	0.5	1.1	0.0	13.9	46.0	62.3	36.0	37.9	94	91.5

1 May be of any race.

Table A. All Places — **Population and Housing**

STATE City, town, township, borough, or CDP (county if applicable)	Population				Race and Hispanic or Latino origin (percent)					Age (percent)			Educational attainment of persons age 25 and older		Occupied housing units	
	2010 census total population	2019 estimated population	Percent change 2010–2019	ACS total population estimate 2015–2019	White alone, not Hispanic or Latino	Black alone, not Hispanic or Latino	Asian alone, not Hispanic or Latino	All other races or 2 or more races, not Hispanic or Latino	Hispanic or Latino[1]	Under 18 years old	Age 65 years and older	Median age	Percent High school diploma or less	Percent Bachelor's degree or more	Total	Percent with a computer
	1	2	3	4	5	6	7	8	9	10	11	12	13	14	15	16
NEW YORK—Con.																
Piermont village	2,505	2,531	1.0	2,540	77.1	4.3	5.7	2.4	10.4	13.0	24.5	49.6	21.0	68.2	1,194	98.7
Pierrepont town (St. Lawrence)	2,589	2,484	-4.1	2,170	95.1	1.0	0.6	2.0	1.4	18.0	24.4	47.0	39.4	31.6	915	93.6
Pierrepont Manor CDP	228	-	-	213	92.5	0.0	0.0	7.5	0.0	43.7	0.0	24.2	93.7	6.3	52	100.0
Piffard CDP	220	-	-	286	100.0	0.0	0.0	0.0	0.0	19.2	26.2	42.2	40.2	17.8	144	100.0
Pike CDP	371	-	-	257	86.0	12.5	0.0	0.0	1.6	23.3	22.2	48.3	46.6	11.8	123	89.4
Pike town (Wyoming)	1,101	1,059	-3.8	946	95.6	3.4	0.0	0.0	1.1	22.0	19.6	48.7	53.6	16.4	387	82.2
Pinckney town (Lewis)	325	316	-2.8	301	85.7	0.0	0.0	13.6	0.7	21.3	17.3	40.7	63.2	9.6	148	89.2
Pine Bush CDP	1,780	-	-	1,732	64.8	8.2	0.0	1.0	26.0	21.0	24.5	44.6	48.8	15.3	698	86.2
Pine Hill CDP	275	-	-	215	96.7	0.0	0.0	0.0	3.3	8.8	43.7	64.3	49.5	27.5	119	96.6
Pine Plains CDP	1,353	-	-	1,260	92.8	0.0	0.0	1.1	6.1	17.9	19.2	42.3	45.2	20.5	523	87.8
Pine Plains town (Dutchess)	2,473	2,406	-2.7	2,353	94.4	0.6	0.2	0.6	4.2	14.2	19.6	47.3	49.2	22.7	1,002	90.1
Pine Valley CDP	813	-	-	674	80.6	0.0	0.0	6.2	13.2	11.3	22.8	49.9	57.9	14.2	273	94.5
Pitcairn town (St. Lawrence)	846	799	-5.6	856	97.1	0.1	0.4	1.4	1.1	25.7	16.5	41.2	52.6	10.2	329	86.0
Pitcher town (Chenango)	803	771	-4.0	721	95.6	0.0	0.0	0.6	3.9	24.7	22.7	46.1	61.7	11.9	316	80.1
Pittsfield town (Otsego)	1,368	1,290	-5.7	1,284	93.6	1.0	0.4	2.9	2.1	21.3	15.0	46.3	40.7	23.5	493	86.8
Pittsford village	1,379	1,332	-3.4	1,716	87.6	0.8	2.6	5.0	4.0	25.6	15.1	43.6	7.3	76.2	736	98.2
Pittsford town (Monroe)	29,380	29,377	0.0	29,410	83.7	1.6	8.7	2.8	3.2	22.8	19.4	42.5	9.3	76.4	10,355	95.3
Pittstown town (Rensselaer)	5,714	5,563	-2.6	5,612	92.1	0.5	0.5	0.2	6.7	22.0	16.7	40.2	50.2	20.3	2,093	89.6
Plainedge CDP	8,817	-	-	8,975	77.1	0.5	10.3	1.5	10.7	21.7	14.4	39.9	36.4	39.2	2,950	93.2
Plainfield town (Otsego)	917	868	-5.3	865	95.0	0.2	1.4	1.4	2.0	21.2	24.6	45.7	53.5	19.8	355	85.6
Plainview CDP	26,217	-	-	26,453	77.4	0.5	16.1	1.7	4.4	22.9	20.0	44.1	19.5	64.6	9,080	92.9
Plandome village	1,375	1,466	6.6	1,228	89.8	0.0	4.6	0.0	5.6	32.2	17.8	45.8	6.2	84.5	383	96.6
Plandome Heights village	1,007	1,018	1.1	967	79.3	0.0	14.4	1.8	4.6	25.4	15.2	45.6	5.4	84.5	328	98.5
Plandome Manor village	877	902	2.9	740	79.2	0.0	13.0	0.9	6.9	25.4	22.6	46.6	10.8	79.4	256	97.7
Plattekill CDP	1,260	-	-	1,029	31.7	15.7	0.0	11.8	40.8	22.4	7.9	39.0	53.3	19.6	326	86.8
Plattekill town (Ulster)	10,500	10,200	-2.9	10,254	71.1	8.7	1.1	2.7	16.4	16.6	17.0	45.9	50.7	23.6	4,025	87.8
Plattsburgh city & MCD (Clinton)	20,007	19,515	-2.5	19,465	87.6	3.8	2.8	2.7	3.1	15.1	16.1	29.2	38.2	33.6	7,836	89.5
Plattsburgh town (Clinton)	11,847	11,949	0.9	11,883	91.5	2.6	2.1	1.7	2.0	18.0	18.1	45.2	46.0	28.0	4,786	87.3
Plattsburgh West CDP	1,364	-	-	1,296	92.9	0.7	0.0	6.1	0.3	21.8	14.8	44.5	65.7	9.8	566	88.2
Pleasant Valley CDP	1,145	-	-	1,148	84.3	8.7	0.0	4.9	2.1	14.9	15.0	47.6	45.5	34.0	536	91.2
Pleasant Valley town (Dutchess)	9,676	9,685	0.1	9,703	83.9	3.3	1.1	4.6	7.1	19.3	15.2	45.0	38.7	30.4	3,853	92.7
Pleasantville village	7,076	7,260	2.6	7,221	70.8	4.3	3.0	3.2	18.7	26.1	14.7	39.1	18.4	63.3	2,417	89.0
Plessis CDP	164	-	-	196	94.9	5.1	0.0	0.0	0.0	38.8	10.2	27.6	64.1	20.4	42	100.0
Plymouth town (Chenango)	1,796	1,711	-4.7	1,825	96.0	0.9	0.0	2.0	1.1	21.3	19.6	47.1	51.2	15.0	742	87.6
Poestenkill CDP	1,061	-	-	959	99.3	0.0	0.0	0.7	0.0	15.5	26.6	52.8	39.8	13.5	430	80.9
Poestenkill town (Rensselaer)	4,514	4,499	-0.3	4,498	95.7	1.2	0.3	1.4	1.5	23.3	17.1	45.2	32.1	30.8	1,720	90.8
Point Lookout CDP	1,219	-	-	1,026	96.7	0.0	0.0	0.0	3.3	13.1	33.1	55.8	20.9	55.9	446	92.8
Poland town (Chautauqua)	2,356	2,223	-5.6	2,118	98.3	0.3	0.0	0.7	0.8	28.4	15.1	34.5	52.4	12.9	817	84.0
Poland village	508	478	-5.9	370	97.6	1.4	0.0	0.5	0.5	29.7	16.8	32.5	41.6	23.9	133	88.0
Pomfret town (Chautauqua)	14,973	13,846	-7.5	14,056	84.1	4.0	1.2	3.2	7.5	16.4	17.4	33.0	32.9	39.0	5,051	89.4
Pomona village	3,103	3,262	5.1	2,668	68.3	12.1	7.6	2.0	10.0	22.6	22.9	46.8	20.4	58.8	900	95.6
Pompey town (Onondaga)	7,074	7,276	2.9	7,284	87.4	0.0	7.7	2.6	2.4	21.8	18.2	47.5	24.2	51.8	2,536	90.2
Poospatuck Reservation (Suffolk)	324	353	9.0	654	7.0	21.1	0.0	68.8	3.1	18.2	11.0	33.8	66.9	9.2	240	89.6
Poquott village	953	928	-2.6	969	78.8	1.2	8.7	4.2	7.0	19.5	20.6	47.3	13.7	72.3	339	98.8
Portage town (Livingston)	889	836	-6.0	837	98.8	0.1	0.0	0.6	0.5	22.0	21.3	44.7	62.0	10.9	355	81.7
Port Byron village	1,255	1,189	-5.3	1,035	87.1	0.0	0.0	3.4	9.5	23.5	17.1	40.1	55.3	11.1	418	88.8
Port Chester village	28,973	29,163	0.7	29,342	30.6	3.0	1.7	0.7	63.9	22.8	13.0	37.0	52.6	27.5	9,072	91.0
Port Dickinson village	1,643	1,525	-7.2	1,931	92.9	2.1	0.6	3.0	1.4	22.5	13.3	34.6	31.5	31.8	815	94.5
Porter town (Niagara)	6,777	6,530	-3.6	6,572	96.3	0.9	0.3	1.4	1.1	20.5	21.0	47.3	35.7	31.3	2,686	89.3
Port Ewen CDP	3,546	-	-	3,315	83.4	0.9	1.6	9.2	4.9	12.5	25.8	47.9	41.1	25.6	1,466	92.3
Port Gibson CDP	453	-	-	417	83.7	0.0	0.0	16.3	0.0	18.2	21.6	54.2	42.8	15.0	173	100.0
Port Henry CDP	1,194	-	-	1,179	92.4	0.6	0.0	6.7	0.3	12.3	23.8	54.1	48.4	18.2	579	77.9
Port Jefferson village	7,744	8,145	5.2	7,939	81.4	1.9	8.1	2.1	6.5	20.4	21.1	45.1	17.9	58.2	2,993	92.9
Port Jefferson Station CDP	7,838	-	-	7,397	75.2	2.0	4.7	1.9	16.1	18.2	18.1	39.8	30.9	36.7	2,664	92.0
Port Jervis city & MCD (Orange)	8,840	8,558	-3.2	8,595	74.4	5.6	3.0	3.6	13.3	21.5	17.3	44.0	50.4	21.7	3,713	85.7
Portland town (Chautauqua)	4,825	4,619	-4.3	4,649	86.3	5.0	0.5	1.5	6.6	16.8	17.6	37.4	53.8	17.0	1,697	84.7
Port Leyden village	668	648	-3.0	617	98.9	1.0	0.2	0.0	0.0	31.0	13.9	34.6	54.6	9.2	224	92.0
Portville village	1,014	948	-6.5	983	94.8	0.0	0.0	2.5	2.6	27.5	15.8	39.1	41.6	31.2	427	83.1
Portville town (Cattaraugus)	3,734	3,518	-5.8	3,569	97.8	0.0	0.0	1.0	1.2	21.8	20.7	45.5	48.1	22.3	1,580	85.8
Port Washington CDP	15,846	-	-	15,808	75.1	2.1	10.5	1.2	11.1	24.2	22.1	42.3	15.8	68.0	5,694	95.8
Port Washington North village	3,177	3,199	0.7	3,200	73.4	0.6	8.4	0.8	16.8	23.5	25.3	44.8	26.8	55.5	1,218	93.8
Potsdam village	9,451	8,991	-4.9	9,154	80.6	5.8	3.8	3.4	6.5	9.1	6.2	20.8	28.4	49.4	2,187	88.3
Potsdam town (St. Lawrence)	16,046	15,381	-4.1	15,567	86.4	3.6	2.6	3.4	3.9	13.4	11.7	24.7	37.2	38.9	4,988	89.2
Potter town (Yates)	1,870	1,834	-1.9	1,895	95.6	0.4	0.0	2.1	1.9	29.5	15.8	35.3	55.7	12.0	627	76.7
Pottersville CDP	424	-	-	241	96.7	1.7	1.7	0.0	0.0	1.7	34.9	49.5	46.5	18.1	133	92.5
Poughkeepsie city & MCD (Dutchess)	30,812	30,515	-	30,381	40.8	35.4	1.0	6.5	16.4	19.7	16.0	37.8	44.8	23.2	12,891	86.3
Poughkeepsie town (Dutchess)	45,254	44,062	-2.6	44,177	68.1	10.5	5.0	3.5	12.9	17.9	15.7	37.7	31.9	38.4	15,364	93.6
Pound Ridge town (Westchester)	5,088	5,129	0.8	5,177	87.8	2.0	2.3	2.4	5.4	20.8	22.8	49.5	10.9	73.3	1,884	97.3
Prattsburgh CDP	656	-	-	923	95.1	0.4	1.4	2.0	1.1	29.8	9.6	34.8	58.8	20.9	324	95.7
Prattsburgh town (Steuben)	2,083	1,953	-6.2	2,112	92.7	0.2	3.2	3.2	0.7	25.9	17.7	40.7	55.1	18.8	807	86.9
Prattsville CDP	355	-	-	175	93.7	0.0	0.0	6.3	0.0	3.4	64.6	68.4	56.3	14.6	87	58.6
Prattsville town (Greene)	711	694	-2.4	704	95.5	0.0	0.0	4.5	0.0	12.1	29.8	51.0	57.2	17.4	248	82.7

1   May be of any race.

Table A. All Places — **Population and Housing**

STATE City, town, township, borough, or CDP (county if applicable)	Population				Race and Hispanic or Latino origin (percent)					Age (percent)			Educational attainment of persons age 25 and older		Occupied housing units	
	2010 census total population	2019 estimated population	Percent change 2010–2019	ACS total population estimate 2015–2019	White alone, not Hispanic or Latino	Black alone, not Hispanic or Latino	Asian alone, not Hispanic or Latino	All other races or 2 or more races, not Hispanic or Latino	Hispanic or Latino[1]	Under 18 years old	Age 65 years and older	Median age	Percent High school diploma or less	Percent Bachelor's degree or more	Total	Percent with a computer
	1	2	3	4	5	6	7	8	9	10	11	12	13	14	15	16
Preble town (Cortland)......	1,393	1,300	-6.7	1,511	97.6	0.0	0.2	2.3	0.0	14.0	24.0	51.8	38.6	31.5	647	84.4
Preston town (Chenango).	1,037	984	-5.1	998	98.8	0.0	0.6	0.3	0.3	18.9	17.4	44.8	54.8	13.2	417	91.1
Preston-Potter Hollow CDP..................	366	-	-	296	98.3	0.0	0.0	1.7	0.0	9.5	37.5	58.3	61.2	24.6	132	75.8
Princetown town (Schenectady).............	2,114	2,099	-0.7	1,896	99.6	0.2	0.0	0.2	0.0	18.0	24.6	48.1	42.7	27.3	648	89.2
Prospect CDP.................	291	-	-	426	77.5	16.2	0.5	5.9	0.0	40.6	15.3	33.5	26.6	27.5	119	93.3
Providence town (Saratoga)..................	1,995	2,056	3.1	2,165	91.2	1.5	2.8	1.5	3.0	18.9	15.7	44.6	49.2	19.6	818	88.5
Pulaski village...............	2,357	2,225	-5.6	2,067	97.2	0.0	0.1	1.4	1.2	22.9	19.5	40.4	44.2	20.3	894	82.9
Pulteney town (Steuben)..	1,285	1,261	-1.9	1,242	99.3	0.0	0.0	0.5	0.2	19.5	23.3	49.8	45.9	34.4	568	89.8
Pultneyville CDP..............	698	-	-	623	100.0	0.0	0.0	0.0	0.0	7.9	28.6	52.0	36.1	33.7	271	95.6
Putnam town (Washington)...............	609	576	-5.4	627	97.4	0.0	1.0	1.4	0.2	23.6	30.9	51.3	34.2	21.9	273	80.6
Putnam Lake CDP..........	3,844	-	-	3,455	65.2	4.0	2.0	1.2	27.7	20.3	13.0	44.5	42.1	30.5	1,226	94.2
Putnam Valley town (Putnam)..................	11,801	11,516	-2.4	11,597	78.0	5.8	1.6	2.6	12.0	18.3	15.5	44.8	33.2	43.6	4,158	97.1
Queensbury town (Warren)..................	27,881	27,359	-1.9	27,456	94.1	1.3	1.3	1.1	2.2	18.5	21.8	46.7	33.5	35.3	11,613	91.7
Quiogue CDP..................	-	-	-	767	63.0	0.0	2.7	8.5	25.8	24.4	10.6	45.7	30.5	33.3	318	79.2
Quogue village...............	973	1,014	4.2	558	87.6	3.4	3.8	1.4	3.8	14.3	44.8	59.5	12.8	70.4	246	77.2
Ramapo town (Rockland).	126,261	137,406	8.8	135,560	67.9	13.6	3.0	1.5	13.8	38.0	11.0	27.0	42.9	32.1	35,629	80.5
Randolph CDP.................	1,286	-	-	1,196	95.3	0.0	0.0	1.6	3.1	24.7	16.3	44.8	48.2	18.1	516	74.6
Randolph town (Cattaraugus).............	2,587	2,472	-4.4	2,494	95.6	0.4	0.2	2.1	1.7	27.5	17.3	42.8	48.5	19.1	1,028	78.9
Ransomville CDP...........	1,419	-	-	1,553	96.8	1.3	0.0	1.9	0.0	25.5	14.3	40.5	39.5	18.5	548	95.3
Rapids CDP....................	1,636	-	-	1,014	99.0	0.0	0.0	0.0	1.0	20.1	8.2	42.0	30.8	39.1	386	83.4
Rathbone town (Steuben).	1,126	1,092	-3.0	1,147	97.0	0.0	0.0	1.1	1.8	24.3	18.7	39.3	64.2	8.5	399	74.7
Ravena village...............	3,259	3,173	-2.6	3,210	94.4	4.2	0.0	0.9	0.6	20.9	16.0	41.1	49.7	25.4	1,331	86.5
Reading town (Schuyler) ..	1,702	1,651	-3.0	1,645	86.0	1.0	1.2	1.5	10.4	21.9	20.4	44.4	45.5	19.9	643	89.4
Red Creek village...........	532	490	-7.9	745	90.6	3.6	0.0	1.9	3.9	37.3	7.0	28.5	55.1	14.1	244	86.1
Redfield town (Oswego) ...	545	561	2.9	427	100.0	0.0	0.0	0.0	0.0	17.1	20.8	42.5	64.0	5.8	161	82.0
Redford CDP..................	477	-	-	369	93.0	0.0	0.0	0.0	7.0	37.9	31.2	33.3	66.4	6.6	153	76.5
Red Hook village	1,950	1,951	0.1	1,899	88.2	1.9	3.8	1.5	4.6	18.0	19.1	43.5	27.8	50.6	843	89.4
Red Hook town (Dutchess)................	11,338	11,124	-1.9	11,154	85.2	2.9	4.0	2.2	5.7	18.5	15.8	35.9	24.6	50.7	3,810	93.4
Red House town (Cattaraugus).............	33	35	6.1	36	100.0	0.0	0.0	0.0	0.0	13.9	16.7	47.5	33.3	40.0	20	90.0
Red Oaks Mill CDP..........	3,613	-	-	3,174	77.1	6.1	3.5	1.4	11.9	16.1	21.1	49.6	25.0	41.0	1,314	94.3
Redwood CDP.................	605	-	-	614	98.7	0.0	0.0	0.0	1.3	16.8	9.8	39.2	63.0	7.5	192	88.0
Remsen village...............	510	494	-3.1	443	94.4	0.0	0.0	0.0	5.6	18.3	25.5	48.3	55.1	10.9	177	91.0
Remsen town (Oneida).....	1,922	1,877	-2.3	1,702	97.4	0.4	0.0	0.0	2.2	15.7	21.7	50.5	46.3	20.1	737	87.1
Remsenburg-Speonk CDP	2,642	-	-	1,881	84.5	4.6	0.0	0.0	10.9	16.4	22.0	47.1	30.5	45.1	839	81.3
Rensselaer city & MCD (Rensselaer).............	9,373	9,171	-2.2	9,259	76.2	5.3	6.7	5.6	6.2	16.7	15.1	35.7	45.1	31.0	4,380	90.8
Rensselaer Falls village....	327	307	-6.1	440	98.2	1.8	0.0	0.0	0.0	38.0	9.1	31.8	36.1	25.1	150	88.7
Rensselaerville town (Albany)...................	1,844	1,811	-1.8	1,679	96.2	0.8	0.0	0.4	2.5	16.1	25.6	50.3	49.4	28.0	718	87.0
Retsof CDP....................	340	-	-	118	83.1	0.0	0.0	16.9	0.0	23.7	22.9	41.2	54.4	27.8	48	100.0
Rhinebeck village	2,653	2,563	-3.4	2,570	84.9	1.4	8.5	0.1	5.1	14.7	35.4	56.7	33.4	46.3	1,269	94.3
Rhinebeck town (Dutchess)................	7,563	7,813	3.3	7,772	87.5	2.0	3.5	1.3	5.7	17.2	31.4	53.9	30.3	48.0	3,217	95.9
Rhinecliff CDP.................	425	-	-	429	82.1	0.0	10.3	0.0	7.7	43.4	8.6	39.9	12.8	75.3	126	100.0
Richburg village.............	450	419	-6.9	396	99.7	0.0	0.0	0.0	0.3	33.6	14.9	35.5	55.0	4.6	142	85.2
Richfield town (Otsego).....	2,393	2,265	-5.3	1,998	95.7	0.3	0.9	0.3	2.9	18.3	20.1	43.8	55.6	20.9	885	83.3
Richfield Springs village ...	1,262	1,187	-5.9	1,016	92.0	0.5	1.8	0.5	5.2	19.3	14.3	37.7	51.3	19.5	433	87.3
Richford town (Tioga).......	1,172	1,119	-4.5	1,081	97.5	0.0	0.0	2.0	0.5	19.0	19.9	46.7	64.0	10.5	435	78.2
Richland town (Oswego)...	5,730	5,558	-3.0	5,595	98.2	0.3	0.1	0.9	0.4	25.6	17.4	38.4	49.5	17.3	2,141	85.6
Richmond town (Ontario).	3,378	3,213	-4.9	3,247	88.4	1.1	0.0	2.8	7.7	14.9	20.3	50.6	36.8	27.0	1,289	98.1
Richmondville village........	917	849	-7.4	841	96.3	0.1	0.0	2.0	1.5	25.8	16.1	36.3	47.0	19.6	316	84.8
Richmondville town (Schoharie)..............	2,612	2,442	-6.5	2,456	95.8	1.5	0.4	1.5	0.7	23.2	15.9	42.0	48.0	20.9	957	90.6
Richville village.............	323	302	-6.5	267	97.4	0.4	0.0	1.5	0.7	31.1	13.9	32.4	61.2	10.0	105	87.6
Ridge CDP.....................	13,336	-	-	12,854	79.8	6.8	3.6	1.8	8.1	16.5	29.8	51.3	45.3	26.3	5,542	84.9
Ridgeway town (Orleans) .	6,773	6,329	-6.6	6,398	91.3	2.3	1.3	2.5	2.6	24.5	14.9	39.1	42.8	19.8	2,742	89.4
Rifton CDP.....................	456	-	-	224	93.3	0.0	0.0	0.0	6.7	8.0	37.1	56.2	0.0	34.0	123	100.0
Riga town (Monroe).........	5,592	5,656	1.1	5,622	96.2	1.2	0.3	1.0	1.2	21.9	18.4	47.2	34.4	36.4	2,155	93.9
Ripley CDP....................	872	-	-	734	91.8	0.8	0.0	4.1	3.3	18.1	18.1	43.4	52.5	14.7	341	90.9
Ripley town (Chautauqua) .	2,416	2,279	-5.7	2,353	94.7	0.8	0.2	1.3	3.0	19.3	17.8	43.9	57.2	15.8	991	82.3
Riverhead CDP................	13,299	-	-	14,196	50.5	18.1	2.9	1.4	27.1	19.7	20.7	42.2	58.5	18.8	5,211	82.7
Riverhead town (Suffolk) ..	33,499	33,469	-0.1	33,549	72.3	9.5	2.0	0.9	15.3	18.6	23.6	46.8	43.5	29.2	12,976	88.4
Riverside village.............	496	472	-4.8	438	97.5	1.6	0.0	0.9	0.0	16.2	34.5	51.8	52.8	8.8	217	82.0
Riverside CDP.................	2,911	-	-	2,362	46.0	35.3	1.2	2.3	15.2	1.8	14.1	33.4	69.1	6.8	363	67.8
Rochester city & MCD (Monroe)..................	210,674	205,695	-2.4	206,848	36.7	37.6	3.0	3.5	19.2	22.7	10.9	32.0	45.9	25.1	86,307	84.9
Rochester town (Ulster)....	7,305	7,171	-1.8	7,177	83.4	2.1	1.0	7.3	6.2	18.9	21.5	47.1	41.4	33.1	2,960	93.1
Rock Hill CDP.................	1,742	-	-	1,516	76.0	9.4	1.5	2.8	10.4	18.4	27.3	43.1	18.3	51.0	592	92.9
Rockland town (Sullivan) ..	3,741	3,676	-1.7	3,647	77.2	0.3	0.2	16.2	6.1	22.9	20.3	48.0	50.2	26.4	1,507	83.3
Rockville Centre village	24,039	24,550	2.1	24,492	79.4	6.0	2.6	1.2	10.9	23.3	19.3	43.4	20.2	62.0	9,605	90.6
Rocky Point CDP.............	14,014	-	-	13,521	84.8	1.4	0.7	4.1	9.1	24.8	11.6	37.8	31.9	36.7	4,674	93.3
Rodman CDP..................	153	-	-	155	97.4	0.0	2.6	0.0	0.0	28.4	32.9	43.1	45.0	23.4	54	83.3
Rodman town (Jefferson) .	1,176	1,131	-3.8	1,102	96.1	0.0	1.3	1.2	1.5	25.1	13.7	39.4	46.5	19.9	399	89.7
Rome city & MCD (Oneida)..................	33,715	32,148	-4.6	32,253	83.3	6.2	1.4	2.3	6.8	21.6	17.8	39.1	47.8	21.2	12,803	85.9
Romulus CDP.................	409	-	-	381	92.9	1.0	0.0	5.2	0.8	29.4	21.0	31.6	55.9	5.1	137	89.1
Romulus town (Seneca) ...	4,315	4,169	-3.4	4,237	59.5	28.9	0.0	2.9	8.8	11.2	9.0	35.6	72.6	9.1	765	84.4
Ronkonkoma CDP...........	19,082	-	-	18,309	72.5	3.3	6.9	3.8	13.6	20.1	14.1	38.9	36.1	32.1	6,004	96.6
Roosevelt CDP................	16,258	-	-	16,899	1.4	57.0	0.5	1.1	40.0	23.7	11.5	34.0	58.2	18.3	4,414	91.8
Root town (Montgomery)..	1,726	1,668	-3.4	1,776	96.1	0.3	0.7	0.8	2.0	27.0	16.7	38.3	57.1	14.3	647	78.2
Roscoe CDP..................	541	-	-	520	97.7	0.0	0.0	0.0	2.3	22.3	26.2	48.5	45.8	37.1	226	70.4
Rose town (Wayne)	2,369	2,264	-4.4	2,016	91.8	0.9	0.7	1.2	5.4	24.6	24.2	44.7	55.4	17.0	805	85.5

1 May be of any race.

Table A. All Places — **Population and Housing**

STATE City, town, township, borough, or CDP (county if applicable)	Population				Race and Hispanic or Latino origin (percent)					Age (percent)			Educational attainment of persons age 25 and older		Occupied housing units	
	2010 census total population	2019 estimated population	Percent change 2010–2019	ACS total population estimate 2015–2019	White alone, not Hispanic or Latino	Black alone, not Hispanic or Latino	Asian alone, not Hispanic or Latino	All other races or 2 or more races, not Hispanic or Latino	Hispanic or Latino[1]	Under 18 years old	Age 65 years and older	Median age	Percent High school diploma or less	Percent Bachelor's degree or more	Total	Percent with a computer
	1	2	3	4	5	6	7	8	9	10	11	12	13	14	15	16
NEW YORK—Con.																
Roseboom town (Otsego).	715	668	-6.6	736	97.6	0.4	0.1	1.4	0.5	21.1	17.9	44.4	62.7	14.7	287	79.4
Rosendale town (Ulster)...	6,078	5,786	-4.8	5,858	87.6	2.0	1.2	3.3	5.8	17.4	20.2	44.2	29.8	37.4	2,273	93.9
Rosendale Hamlet CDP ...	1,349	-	-	1,103	88.6	3.6	2.2	2.4	3.2	14.8	27.6	46.9	35.7	25.3	508	88.4
Roslyn village	2,788	2,902	4.1	2,855	75.1	1.3	10.9	4.8	7.9	16.3	29.2	53.8	14.0	73.3	1,347	93.7
Roslyn Estates village	1,230	1,233	0.2	1,257	90.9	0.8	7.2	0.0	1.1	27.4	15.9	43.4	8.9	81.3	407	94.1
Roslyn Harbor village	1,045	1,108	6.0	898	82.4	0.8	13.3	1.2	2.3	22.6	25.8	47.9	8.2	78.0	306	97.1
Roslyn Heights CDP........	6,577	-	-	6,553	56.4	3.9	23.4	1.6	14.6	26.0	15.1	39.9	19.7	61.4	2,111	94.3
Rossie town (St. Lawrence)	877	836	-4.7	952	98.1	0.0	0.5	0.3	1.1	33.5	11.2	31.4	68.4	11.0	312	86.5
Rotterdam CDP	20,652	-	-	20,018	83.3	5.6	1.1	5.4	4.5	20.2	18.4	43.0	43.4	23.0	7,306	90.4
Rotterdam town (Schenectady)............	29,098	29,973	3.0	29,593	85.1	4.4	1.5	3.8	5.3	20.7	17.9	42.4	41.0	25.2	10,554	91.2
Round Lake village	623	770	23.6	866	96.0	0.6	0.7	2.1	0.7	15.4	15.5	45.8	24.2	53.4	388	94.1
Rouses Point village	2,209	2,126	-3.8	2,319	95.9	0.3	1.1	2.1	0.6	18.8	20.9	44.8	43.2	18.3	1,104	85.4
Roxbury town (Delaware) ..	2,500	2,304	-7.8	2,170	97.2	1.8	0.0	0.5	0.6	14.6	27.6	51.9	46.6	24.7	975	82.5
Royalton town (Niagara) ...	7,688	7,506	-2.4	7,532	93.1	1.9	0.0	1.3	3.6	22.0	16.6	41.6	46.3	21.4	2,854	92.6
Rush town (Monroe)	3,511	3,435	-2.2	3,460	95.2	2.1	1.0	0.0	1.7	21.0	21.1	49.9	26.1	47.9	1,347	96.7
Rushford CDP	363	-	-	488	87.3	0.0	0.0	9.8	2.9	33.2	14.1	38.3	51.4	7.3	159	90.6
Rushford town (Allegany) .	1,150	1,107	-3.7	1,231	94.6	0.0	0.0	4.2	1.1	21.1	23.3	44.8	45.6	20.1	531	86.6
Rushville village	681	666	-2.2	655	96.8	1.1	0.0	0.3	1.8	22.4	16.8	39.7	44.9	20.4	237	86.5
Russell town (St. Lawrence)	1,866	1,789	-4.1	1,641	99.1	0.0	0.0	0.7	0.2	22.6	19.4	42.9	48.1	22.1	658	89.4
Russell Gardens village....	944	946	0.2	993	63.2	0.0	30.7	2.5	3.5	19.8	19.5	47.5	12.7	75.5	353	95.5
Russia town (Herkimer)	2,587	2,497	-3.5	2,528	95.6	0.4	0.1	0.3	3.6	24.7	16.5	41.7	40.4	31.2	955	88.7
Rutland town (Jefferson)...	3,059	2,901	-5.2	2,974	93.5	0.3	0.8	1.7	3.7	26.3	16.6	41.0	45.7	16.8	1,188	88.0
Rye city & MCD (Westchester)...............	15,711	15,695	-0.1	15,820	82.9	1.0	5.5	3.9	6.7	29.2	15.5	43.0	11.4	74.8	5,491	95.7
Rye town (Westchester) ...	45,924	46,425	1.1	46,595	46.0	3.4	3.4	1.2	46.0	23.0	14.9	39.9	41.5	40.8	15,201	91.8
Rye Brook village	9,307	9,521	2.3	9,487	74.6	1.5	6.3	1.9	15.7	22.1	20.9	46.5	19.5	66.5	3,418	93.1
Sackets Harbor village......	1,452	1,397	-3.8	1,674	86.6	0.7	0.9	3.8	8.0	24.6	14.5	29.9	22.4	51.4	824	95.4
Saddle Rock village	884	988	11.8	722	82.3	2.5	10.1	2.6	2.5	21.5	31.6	52.4	18.5	61.2	233	96.6
Saddle Rock Estates CDP ..	466	-	-	532	92.7	0.0	7.3	0.0	0.0	41.2	10.0	32.9	6.3	85.3	144	100.0
Sagaponack village	313	323	3.2	264	96.6	0.0	0.0	0.0	3.4	18.2	37.1	57.6	17.4	69.1	108	77.8
Sag Harbor village.........	2,169	2,283	5.3	1,905	80.6	4.6	2.4	1.7	10.7	14.5	31.2	52.1	26.0	56.5	872	80.5
St. Armand town (Essex) ..	1,550	1,471	-5.1	1,571	99.2	0.0	0.0	0.4	0.3	19.5	17.6	49.8	28.1	38.3	722	87.4
St. Bonaventure CDP.......	2,044	-	-	1,909	84.2	6.4	3.7	0.8	4.9	4.3	9.0	20.1	53.3	24.6	262	76.3
St. James CDP............	13,338	-	-	13,671	86.2	0.4	4.9	1.3	7.2	21.9	19.4	45.3	24.7	48.6	4,727	93.5
St. Johnsville village	1,749	1,676	-4.2	1,947	94.2	0.6	1.3	1.1	2.8	26.8	18.1	35.2	48.9	12.1	702	84.6
St. Johnsville town (Montgomery)	2,635	2,519	-4.4	2,539	94.6	0.4	1.0	0.9	3.1	22.9	21.3	39.3	51.0	10.2	958	83.7
St. Regis Falls CDP	464	-	-	399	100.0	0.0	0.0	0.0	0.0	13.8	9.0	53.6	47.0	18.0	166	80.7
St. Regis Mohawk Reservation (Frankl......	3,228	3,353	3.9	3,325	11.4	0.1	3.0	85.5	0.0	14.1	20.6	44.5	24.9	23.6	1,360	71.7
Salamanca city & MCD (Cattaraugus)	5,810	5,402	-7.0	5,497	66.3	2.6	0.7	23.7	6.7	29.5	14.1	34.4	58.4	12.5	2,187	80.0
Salamanca town (Cattaraugus)	473	446	-5.7	426	91.8	0.0	0.0	7.7	0.5	20.7	28.2	51.3	58.0	18.8	187	87.2
Salem CDP................	946	-	-	791	96.0	0.3	0.0	2.4	1.4	22.3	20.5	37.5	44.3	21.9	329	83.6
Salem town (Washington).	2,717	2,633	-3.1	2,650	96.2	1.1	0.0	1.3	1.4	18.8	22.8	47.3	39.8	29.3	1,106	89.1
Salina town (Onondaga)...	33,649	32,232	-4.2	32,630	87.1	3.3	2.0	3.3	4.3	20.5	19.9	41.3	39.7	27.5	14,486	88.9
Salisbury town (Herkimer)	1,960	1,861	-5.1	2,146	96.4	0.0	0.0	1.3	2.3	26.0	16.5	39.8	59.3	11.5	797	78.9
Salisbury CDP..............	12,093	-	-	12,133	63.4	15.2	4.2	16.1		21.4	18.9	42.6	30.6	45.8	3,786	95.0
Salisbury Mills CDP	536	-	-	301	95.3	0.0	0.0	4.7	0.0	33.9	11.0	30.2	37.7	7.5	70	100.0
Saltaire village	41	41	0.0	8	100.0	0.0	0.0	0.0	0.0	25.0	25.0	45.5	0.0	100.0	4	100.0
Salt Point CDP	190	-	-	206	100.0	0.0	0.0	0.0	0.0	7.3	9.2	26.3	64.6	17.7	51	100.0
Sanborn CDP	1,645	-	-	987	97.5	1.6	0.0	0.5	0.4	18.3	28.0	45.9	48.5	18.1	499	80.2
Sand Lake town (Rensselaer)	8,519	8,425	-1.1	8,446	96.6	0.5	0.4	0.6	2.0	20.5	20.6	45.8	31.4	37.2	3,428	96.5
Sand Ridge CDP	849	-	-	686	97.8	0.0	0.0	1.5	0.7	15.5	19.0	50.3	61.7	3.4	248	86.7
Sands Point village	2,778	2,905	4.6	2,862	82.7	0.7	9.9	1.2	5.5	26.1	20.4	48.2	8.0	83.1	959	97.3
Sandy Creek village..........	767	721	-6.0	771	96.5	0.6	0.0	2.9	0.0	23.9	14.8	37.7	44.4	16.5	326	86.5
Sandy Creek town (Oswego)................	3,924	3,741	-4.7	3,777	98.1	0.2	0.0	1.7	0.0	18.7	21.5	49.4	48.2	13.8	1,612	93.2
Sanford town (Broome).....	2,413	2,290	-5.1	2,236	94.3	1.3	2.1	1.4	1.0	18.6	30.1	52.1	58.5	15.4	957	76.4
Sangerfield town (Oneida)	2,565	2,477	-3.4	2,374	98.9	0.5	0.0	0.5	0.1	18.7	23.5	48.3	47.9	26.0	1,020	88.4
Santa Clara town (Franklin)	351	335	-4.6	413	88.4	4.1	0.0	3.4	4.1	11.4	39.2	57.6	23.7	55.0	183	95.1
Saranac town (Clinton)	4,010	3,928	-2.0	3,935	92.1	5.1	0.8	0.3	1.7	20.5	16.7	44.0	48.2	21.9	1,659	87.0
Saranac Lake village	5,412	5,200	-3.9	5,700	89.7	4.9	0.0	2.0	3.4	22.5	17.3	39.9	29.2	32.8	2,540	84.2
Saratoga town (Saratoga)	5,666	5,695	0.5	5,709	92.9	1.1	0.4	1.8	3.8	22.7	15.5	41.2	37.3	31.3	2,288	93.1
Saratoga Springs city & MCD (Saratog...	26,568	28,212	6.2	27,943	89.1	2.5	3.5	1.5	3.4	14.5	19.9	40.3	20.4	58.4	12,370	93.7
Sardinia town (Erie).........	2,778	2,794	0.6	2,780	97.1	0.1	0.0	0.2	2.6	21.7	19.7	47.6	47.5	20.0	1,132	82.2
Saugerties village	3,993	3,808	-4.6	3,847	87.0	1.0	0.5	3.0	8.5	20.0	23.4	44.4	36.3	30.5	1,803	85.4
Saugerties town (Ulster)..	19,484	19,008	-2.4	19,066	89.6	1.3	0.4	2.6	6.1	19.1	21.3	45.8	39.6	28.1	8,133	91.1
Saugerties South CDP	2,218	-	-	1,989	84.7	3.6	0.0	3.8	7.9	24.2	21.0	40.7	34.0	32.5	839	93.6
Savannah CDP	558	-	-	600	75.2	0.3	0.0	12.8	11.7	27.5	17.8	36.9	60.8	10.8	194	86.1
Savannah town (Wayne)...	1,733	1,657	-4.4	1,888	84.1	0.3	0.5	7.6	7.5	27.9	17.1	38.4	62.7	9.0	616	83.4
Savona village	825	780	-5.5	748	89.4	0.5	5.7	1.1	3.2	24.2	15.6	39.1	51.4	9.5	309	87.7
Sayville CDP...............	16,853	-	-	15,910	91.1	0.8	2.3	1.7	4.1	21.1	19.7	44.9	29.1	46.1	5,425	92.5
Scarsdale town & village (Westchester)...............	17,124	17,871	4.4	17,837	74.4	1.3	15.0	3.4	6.0	30.1	15.8	43.1	6.0	89.2	5,577	98.7
Schaghticoke village........	592	576	-2.7	642	96.3	3.0	0.6	0.2	0.0	20.4	16.7	39.0	47.3	13.0	263	90.9
Schaghticoke town (Rensselaer)	7,660	7,495	-2.2	7,566	95.2	1.9	1.2	1.4	0.3	18.3	18.5	43.8	41.4	23.4	2,841	91.5
Schenectady city & MCD (Schenectady).............	66,157	65,273	-1.3	65,334	52.5	19.0	5.9	11.8	10.8	20.2	13.8	36.2	49.5	21.8	22,824	88.7
Schenevus CDP.............	551	-	-	652	100.0	0.0	0.0	0.0	0.0	19.6	19.6	40.2	36.9	21.6	256	84.0
Schodack town (Rensselaer)	12,801	13,108	2.4	13,126	93.0	1.3	0.9	2.5	2.4	20.2	18.6	45.2	27.5	35.8	5,146	94.4
Schoharie village	916	816	-10.9	879	89.2	4.7	2.3	0.5	3.4	22.3	22.8	47.0	51.7	18.7	350	86.0

1 May be of any race.

Table A. All Places — Population and Housing

STATE City, town, township, borough, or CDP (county if applicable)	Population				Race and Hispanic or Latino origin (percent)					Age (percent)			Educational attainment of persons age 25 and older		Occupied housing units	
	2010 census total population	2019 estimated population	Percent change 2010–2019	ACS total population estimate 2015–2019	White alone, not Hispanic or Latino	Black alone, not Hispanic or Latino	Asian alone, not Hispanic or Latino	All other races or 2 or more races, not Hispanic or Latino	Hispanic or Latino[1]	Under 18 years old	Age 65 years and older	Median age	Percent High school diploma or less	Percent Bachelor's degree or more	Total	Percent with a computer
	1	2	3	4	5	6	7	8	9	10	11	12	13	14	15	16
NEW YORK—Con.																
Schoharie town (Schoharie)	3,195	2,986	-6.5	3,006	93.7	1.4	0.7	2.1	2.1	24.7	16.5	40.1	41.2	25.1	1,123	90.2
Schroeppel town (Oswego)	8,482	8,105	-4.4	8,184	95.7	0.5	0.7	1.5	1.6	23.0	15.9	41.5	42.9	20.5	3,169	92.5
Schroon town (Essex)	1,653	1,561	-5.6	1,608	99.3	0.1	0.0	0.4	0.1	15.7	34.3	58.5	38.7	35.7	773	85.9
Schroon Lake CDP	833	-	-	769	99.6	0.3	0.0	0.1	0.0	20.7	24.3	51.7	35.6	32.9	356	86.8
Schuyler town (Herkimer)	3,424	3,311	-3.3	3,345	99.0	0.0	0.1	0.9	0.0	16.7	22.9	47.6	46.8	21.2	1,409	88.6
Schuyler Falls town (Clinton)	5,183	5,088	-1.8	5,101	97.4	0.0	1.2	1.2	0.2	14.4	18.3	45.5	56.4	17.5	2,226	91.6
Schuylerville village	1,367	1,317	-3.7	1,494	97.3	0.0	0.1	0.5	2.1	26.8	11.3	35.3	40.4	26.4	626	90.9
Scio CDP	609	-	-	589	94.7	0.5	0.0	4.1	0.7	23.3	11.4	42.9	32.9	19.9	243	94.7
Scio town (Allegany)	1,828	1,704	-6.8	1,591	95.6	0.2	1.3	2.4	0.6	15.5	20.8	48.7	44.2	16.7	678	89.5
Scipio town (Cayuga)	1,713	1,624	-5.2	1,526	96.8	0.2	0.0	0.5	2.5	21.5	18.4	40.3	43.4	22.3	621	91.5
Scotchtown CDP	9,212	-	-	9,997	36.4	28.0	7.0	2.4	26.3	22.5	10.7	35.2	33.8	21.1	3,518	97.4
Scotia village	7,744	7,642	-1.3	7,667	89.5	2.3	0.5	2.3	5.5	22.8	16.3	38.4	33.0	36.2	3,154	93.8
Scott town (Cortland)	1,181	1,125	-4.7	1,094	99.0	0.0	0.4	0.0	0.6	23.8	17.0	46.0	51.3	19.9	424	85.8
Scottsburg CDP	117	-	-	112	100.0	0.0	0.0	0.0	0.0	8.9	16.1	53.5	71.1	17.5	42	100.0
Scotts Corners CDP	711	-	-	593	84.0	5.2	7.9	1.9	1.0	13.5	20.2	50.3	19.5	68.1	233	86.3
Scottsville village	2,001	1,916	-4.2	1,921	82.1	7.1	1.5	1.3	8.1	20.5	16.2	41.7	27.9	36.2	796	95.7
Scriba town (Oswego)	6,833	6,505	-4.8	6,569	93.2	0.0	0.8	1.0	5.0	18.7	18.1	46.3	48.6	21.1	2,965	89.7
Sea Cliff village	5,014	5,020	0.1	5,038	86.1	1.2	1.5	1.6	9.5	20.9	20.4	48.3	14.5	65.4	1,899	90.7
Seaford CDP	15,294	-	-	15,040	91.0	0.0	2.1	0.8	6.1	21.7	18.7	42.8	26.5	45.3	5,110	95.8
Searingtown CDP	4,915	-	-	4,593	47.7	1.9	40.6	8.0	1.8	20.3	22.3	48.0	16.4	63.0	1,425	97.2
Selden CDP	19,851	-	-	20,093	70.3	4.2	7.1	2.5	16.0	21.1	13.7	38.5	40.9	26.7	6,243	89.3
Sempronius town (Cayuga)	889	937	5.4	865	98.6	0.1	0.0	0.7	0.6	23.8	20.9	44.5	59.1	14.9	357	79.0
Seneca town (Ontario)	2,720	2,670	-1.8	2,694	94.4	0.7	1.1	0.3	3.5	19.8	18.0	46.6	37.7	25.9	1,105	91.6
Seneca Falls CDP	6,681	-	-	6,055	89.8	3.2	2.5	1.6	2.9	19.2	18.3	41.0	45.2	27.2	2,715	93.2
Seneca Falls town (Seneca)	9,043	8,622	-4.7	8,724	89.8	2.7	2.4	1.5	3.6	19.3	18.1	41.0	45.5	28.3	3,869	91.1
Seneca Knolls CDP	2,011	-	-	2,068	89.0	0.0	0.0	4.3	6.8	18.2	22.5	50.9	48.7	12.5	948	81.5
Sennett town (Cayuga)	3,593	3,385	-5.8	3,422	91.1	3.2	1.4	2.3	2.0	16.3	21.1	48.3	35.3	34.2	1,254	95.6
Setauket-East Setauket CDP	15,477	-	-	13,235	82.1	1.1	8.1	1.9	6.8	22.1	17.4	46.1	15.7	63.1	4,777	96.6
Seward town (Schoharie)	1,737	1,667	-4.0	1,667	93.6	0.0	1.3	1.1	3.9	21.4	17.1	47.3	49.1	20.5	670	82.2
Shandaken town (Ulster)	3,087	2,937	-4.9	2,846	89.1	0.3	0.7	1.1	8.8	8.2	32.3	59.2	39.5	30.3	1,485	91.1
Sharon town (Schoharie)	1,852	1,764	-4.8	2,044	91.3	0.1	4.1	1.4	3.1	18.8	20.9	44.1	44.1	22.6	825	87.8
Sharon Springs village	563	525	-6.7	563	83.3	0.0	12.1	3.0	1.6	19.0	25.0	46.6	44.2	27.0	218	79.8
Shawangunk town (Ulster)	14,340	13,837	-3.5	13,943	74.6	7.9	1.9	2.5	13.2	16.0	10.8	39.5	43.7	23.1	3,825	94.0
Shelby town (Orleans)	5,332	5,017	-5.9	5,081	81.5	5.1	0.4	1.9	11.1	20.2	19.8	44.8	45.8	18.1	2,184	84.8
Sheldon town (Wyoming)	2,408	2,290	-4.9	2,382	92.9	0.8	0.0	2.4	3.9	19.5	21.0	45.7	50.9	21.8	986	86.1
Shelter Island CDP	1,333	-	-	2,062	81.6	0.0	3.3	7.7	7.5	35.5	24.8	31.9	29.6	47.7	819	89.3
Shelter Island town (Suffolk)	2,400	2,417	0.7	2,793	85.5	0.0	3.3	5.7	5.5	26.2	27.6	43.0	19.4	56.0	1,236	85.8
Shelter Island Heights CDP	1,048	-	-	731	96.7	0.0	3.3	0.0	0.0	0.0	35.7	62.4	2.3	70.0	417	79.1
Shenorock CDP	1,898	-	-	2,325	76.1	1.4	1.2	2.7	18.6	26.1	8.5	40.2	25.5	40.4	811	100.0
Sherburne village	1,371	1,307	-4.7	1,251	90.5	0.6	1.2	4.7	3.0	14.9	22.1	51.5	42.7	28.8	635	78.0
Sherburne town (Chenango)	4,053	3,823	-5.7	3,864	94.6	0.2	0.4	3.7	1.1	25.2	15.0	38.8	45.9	18.8	1,612	86.0
Sheridan town (Chautauqua)	2,682	2,524	-5.9	2,553	90.8	0.5	1.0	1.3	6.3	19.2	21.2	51.3	48.1	18.3	1,094	82.7
Sherman village	730	677	-7.3	685	97.8	0.0	0.4	1.8	0.0	23.8	22.2	41.3	53.7	15.2	290	84.1
Sherman town (Chautauqua)	1,653	1,590	-3.8	1,532	98.6	0.0	0.2	0.8	0.4	28.0	17.8	34.6	58.9	12.7	558	72.9
Sherrill city	3,069	2,974	-3.1	3,000	93.2	1.4	0.4	0.7	4.3	19.0	26.5	48.5	31.1	29.4	1,237	88.2
Shinnecock Hills CDP	2,188	-	-	2,202	64.8	0.2	19.3	0.8	14.9	13.2	20.1	48.4	24.7	60.1	839	87.6
Shinnecock Reservation (Suffolk)	661	708	7.1	15	0.0	0.0	66.7	33.3	0.0	0.0	33.3	60.5	0.0	66.7	10	100.0
Shirley CDP	27,854	-	-	28,583	67.1	6.9	3.8	1.2	21.0	22.7	11.4	35.5	52.6	19.5	8,303	94.1
Shokan CDP	1,183	-	-	1,336	93.7	0.0	1.6	4.7	0.0	18.7	13.0	40.4	35.7	40.4	441	97.3
Shoreham village	538	531	-1.3	447	95.7	0.0	1.8	0.7	1.8	19.7	28.9	53.9	14.1	62.2	168	97.6
Shortsville village	1,436	1,405	-2.2	1,403	97.9	0.6	0.0	1.2	0.4	18.5	21.1	48.1	39.5	20.7	546	90.1
Shrub Oak CDP	2,011	-	-	2,861	57.5	4.2	5.4	0.0	33.0	22.6	21.0	36.8	29.8	47.7	1,069	81.9
Sidney village	3,898	3,585	-8.0	3,854	90.2	0.7	0.3	4.0	4.8	26.7	18.2	42.5	54.5	16.4	1,566	77.1
Sidney town (Delaware)	5,777	5,328	-7.8	5,431	91.8	0.6	0.2	3.4	4.0	23.9	20.8	44.6	56.9	16.2	2,229	79.4
Silver Creek village	2,656	2,457	-7.5	2,426	94.2	1.2	0.0	2.9	1.6	25.0	16.9	38.7	40.3	25.0	987	89.9
Silver Springs village	776	732	-5.7	827	88.5	3.3	0.5	6.8	1.0	23.2	17.5	41.0	67.9	5.1	373	72.9
Sinclairville village	588	547	-7.0	691	94.2	2.9	0.0	2.0	0.9	27.2	19.0	37.7	58.2	19.9	287	82.6
Skaneateles village	2,457	2,465	0.3	2,368	97.2	0.2	0.6	1.9	0.0	23.9	27.3	51.5	8.1	69.8	1,053	93.6
Skaneateles town (Onondaga)	7,209	7,174	-0.5	7,201	97.3	0.1	0.2	1.4	1.0	19.6	26.4	52.0	18.0	56.2	3,078	90.1
Sleepy Hollow village	9,872	10,046	1.8	10,122	44.2	2.4	1.5	4.2	47.7	22.8	16.3	36.8	42.1	38.8	3,758	90.8
Sloan village	3,657	3,541	-3.2	3,562	89.4	5.1	2.7	1.0	1.8	17.6	15.4	45.4	47.8	17.6	1,563	80.2
Sloatsburg village	3,039	3,095	1.8	3,116	79.2	4.6	2.2	1.7	12.5	24.0	16.8	44.0	27.3	44.4	1,102	91.3
Smallwood CDP	580	-	-	616	97.2	0.0	2.8	0.0	0.0	18.5	9.4	47.2	40.2	41.6	239	95.4
Smithfield town (Madison)	1,303	1,260	-3.3	1,461	91.2	2.6	0.1	4.4	1.6	24.2	14.9	40.2	60.9	16.8	447	87.2
Smithtown CDP	26,470	-	-	26,260	90.2	0.8	3.1	0.8	5.0	20.8	18.6	45.9	26.5	48.7	8,887	93.6
Smithtown town (Suffolk)	117,764	116,022	-1.5	116,669	87.5	1.1	4.0	1.1	6.3	21.4	18.9	45.6	25.4	49.0	40,186	94.0
Smithville town (Chenango)	1,333	1,267	-5.0	1,452	94.2	0.8	0.7	1.3	3.0	24.9	17.4	39.7	49.4	18.6	567	84.8
Smithville Flats CDP	351	-	-	377	100.0	0.0	0.0	0.0	0.0	21.2	19.4	44.8	59.3	17.8	159	84.3
Smyrna village	227	216	-4.8	199	92.5	7.5	0.0	0.0	0.0	22.6	22.6	46.9	61.1	11.8	90	81.1
Smyrna town (Chenango)	1,297	1,241	-4.3	1,342	95.9	1.9	0.0	1.0	1.3	22.4	22.9	47.0	62.3	9.7	572	75.7
Sodus village	1,819	1,708	-6.1	1,654	72.7	15.3	0.0	6.4	5.6	22.4	17.2	41.4	51.4	10.7	710	84.9
Sodus town (Wayne)	8,381	8,027	-4.2	8,094	86.9	5.3	0.5	2.3	5.0	19.9	22.5	46.4	51.8	13.7	3,235	88.4
Sodus Point village	900	858	-4.7	822	92.0	2.9	0.0	4.4	0.7	11.1	41.8	61.3	35.8	25.9	446	90.8
Solon town (Cortland)	1,079	1,075	-0.4	1,092	97.5	0.0	0.0	1.6	0.8	25.8	15.7	41.2	57.6	15.7	395	81.8
Solvay village	6,589	6,234	-5.4	6,323	77.5	5.1	1.2	10.1	6.1	25.1	14.5	35.4	39.9	27.5	2,657	85.4
Somers town (Westchester)	20,516	21,574	5.2	21,487	87.6	0.9	2.3	1.3	7.8	20.7	25.9	49.8	21.4	56.3	8,172	94.9
Somerset town (Niagara)	2,657	2,548	-4.1	2,646	95.6	0.1	1.4	1.1	1.9	22.3	17.4	45.3	48.6	17.8	1,015	82.8

1 May be of any race.

Table A. All Places — Population and Housing

STATE City, town, township, borough, or CDP (county if applicable)	Population				Race and Hispanic or Latino origin (percent)					Age (percent)			Educational attainment of persons age 25 and older		Occupied housing units	
	2010 census total population	2019 estimated population	Percent change 2010–2019	ACS total population estimate 2015–2019	White alone, not Hispanic or Latino	Black alone, not Hispanic or Latino	Asian alone, not Hispanic or Latino	All other races or 2 or more races, not Hispanic or Latino	Hispanic or Latino[1]	Under 18 years old	Age 65 years and older	Median age	Percent High school diploma or less	Percent Bachelor's degree or more	Total	Percent with a computer
	1	2	3	4	5	6	7	8	9	10	11	12	13	14	15	16
NEW YORK—Con.																
Sound Beach CDP	7,612	-	-	7,821	89.6	0.1	1.5	3.1	5.7	17.9	15.2	44.5	29.5	42.2	2,723	91.1
Southampton village	3,106	3,307	6.5	3,285	78.3	7.2	1.2	1.0	12.3	12.7	35.5	56.1	25.7	58.8	1,364	80.2
Southampton town (Suffolk)	56,769	58,398	2.9	58,094	68.5	5.7	2.0	1.4	22.5	19.2	21.7	46.0	34.6	42.2	21,602	82.7
South Blooming Grove village	3,223	3,155	-2.1	3,148	66.0	11.0	3.0	1.6	18.3	27.3	16.9	37.2	42.5	25.1	1,085	92.2
South Bristol town (Ontario)	1,588	1,569	-1.2	1,727	97.1	0.2	0.5	1.4	0.8	12.3	26.0	55.2	23.4	44.1	811	94.9
South Corning village	1,152	1,084	-5.9	1,232	86.2	10.7	1.1	1.1	1.0	19.2	23.0	44.8	39.7	28.6	560	87.9
South Dayton village	620	580	-6.5	568	93.0	2.5	0.0	2.8	1.8	27.1	13.7	37.0	56.3	19.1	260	73.1
Southeast town (Putnam)	18,437	18,052	-2.1	18,153	69.5	1.6	3.6	1.5	23.7	20.9	15.1	42.3	33.1	40.3	6,471	94.7
South Fallsburg CDP	2,870	-	-	2,168	57.1	13.1	0.0	1.6	28.2	30.7	20.5	35.5	60.8	16.1	763	69.3
South Farmingdale CDP	14,486	-	-	15,229	79.2	1.5	5.7	1.6	12.0	20.2	16.6	42.7	32.1	38.0	5,042	94.8
South Floral Park village	1,777	1,790	0.7	1,999	5.9	51.9	21.0	1.7	19.6	20.1	12.8	38.1	38.0	28.3	550	96.5
South Glens Falls village	3,512	3,634	3.5	3,617	94.5	0.0	0.0	2.1	3.4	20.8	17.1	39.5	51.0	17.6	1,686	81.5
South Hempstead CDP	3,243	-	-	3,184	53.5	18.9	0.5	7.4	19.7	26.1	11.7	34.1	22.9	57.4	1,027	99.3
South Hill CDP	6,673	-	-	6,551	81.7	5.4	4.5	3.9	4.5	7.6	8.0	20.1	22.9	64.9	1,182	83.8
South Huntington CDP	9,422	-	-	10,322	77.1	1.2	6.2	1.1	14.4	19.9	18.4	45.3	29.9	47.8	3,420	92.9
South Lima village	240	-	-	207	100.0	0.0	0.0	0.0	0.0	4.3	5.8	53.1	30.4	31.5	86	100.0
South Lockport CDP	8,324	-	-	7,066	83.6	5.6	2.2	3.7	4.8	19.0	21.2	45.3	45.4	21.3	3,223	87.7
South Nyack village	3,518	3,316	-5.7	3,387	64.1	13.8	5.8	5.2	11.2	11.1	18.6	39.2	21.0	62.3	1,213	91.6
Southold CDP	5,748	-	-	5,904	86.4	0.2	2.6	0.0	10.7	17.8	32.4	54.0	28.3	42.5	2,508	91.7
Southold town (Suffolk)	21,960	22,170	1.0	22,136	86.7	2.1	0.8	0.7	9.7	14.0	31.9	55.4	32.0	41.1	9,574	91.9
Southport CDP	7,238	-	-	6,972	93.7	4.4	0.2	1.7	0.0	20.3	20.2	43.1	50.1	16.0	3,173	87.8
Southport town (Chemung)	10,909	9,761	-10.5	10,125	92.2	4.7	0.1	1.8	1.2	18.2	20.5	45.0	49.1	18.6	4,323	89.1
South Valley town (Cattaraugus)	263	256	-2.7	246	91.9	0.0	0.0	0.0	8.1	11.4	30.5	57.3	51.4	18.5	149	81.9
South Valley Stream CDP	5,962	-	-	6,775	31.5	31.5	17.6	4.3	15.1	24.0	14.9	35.6	30.5	47.1	1,992	93.7
Spackenkill CDP	4,123	-	-	4,053	81.2	2.3	6.5	0.8	9.2	25.5	19.9	45.1	20.4	51.5	1,333	96.7
Spafford town (Onondaga)	1,686	1,643	-2.6	1,723	95.1	0.0	0.4	0.6	3.9	17.6	23.3	52.0	26.8	47.2	724	92.0
Sparkill CDP	1,565	-	-	1,586	56.6	0.0	15.3	2.7	25.4	24.8	13.4	42.7	24.6	60.6	525	93.5
Sparta town (Livingston)	1,632	1,557	-4.6	1,591	96.8	2.5	0.0	0.8	0.0	19.4	21.7	48.9	51.9	20.1	642	90.3
Speculator village	320	299	-6.6	345	95.9	4.1	0.0	0.0	0.0	6.4	49.3	64.2	58.4	12.2	84	84.5
Spencer village	763	707	-7.3	694	98.4	1.4	0.0	0.0	0.1	21.3	21.9	46.8	47.7	14.8	307	80.5
Spencer town (Tioga)	3,101	2,922	-5.8	2,944	91.9	1.5	0.5	3.1	3.1	19.7	17.1	39.9	40.0	30.7	1,256	90.8
Spencerport village	3,603	3,657	1.5	3,671	95.2	0.5	1.1	2.9	0.2	24.9	13.5	39.9	35.4	39.0	1,399	98.2
Springfield town (Otsego)	1,352	1,269	-6.1	1,343	97.5	0.0	0.1	1.0	1.4	21.2	23.8	48.0	35.6	28.4	543	80.5
Springport town (Cayuga)	2,367	2,283	-3.5	2,087	91.9	0.9	0.5	2.7	4.1	21.5	21.2	46.2	42.1	24.9	868	83.3
Springs CDP	6,592	-	-	7,036	63.6	0.0	5.5	0.0	30.9	20.9	23.4	48.6	32.6	48.1	2,743	87.1
Spring Valley village	31,298	32,261	3.1	32,295	32.3	32.5	2.4	1.4	31.3	33.1	7.9	29.1	58.1	16.2	9,623	81.5
Springville village	4,294	4,288	-0.1	4,298	94.6	0.7	0.5	1.8	2.4	22.6	19.9	43.2	50.3	22.9	1,816	88.2
Springwater town (Livingston)	2,343	2,245	-4.2	2,233	96.2	1.1	0.0	1.5	1.2	23.8	19.3	43.7	45.0	23.9	890	91.5
Springwater Hamlet CDP	549	-	-	429	95.1	0.9	0.0	0.9	3.0	19.3	21.0	44.5	54.1	11.2	171	83.6
Staatsburg CDP	377	-	-	317	100.0	0.0	0.0	0.0	0.0	3.8	19.9	59.9	34.9	32.5	137	100.0
Stafford town (Genesee)	2,459	2,328	-5.3	2,212	91.8	1.5	0.7	5.3	0.7	13.7	22.1	48.2	40.1	25.6	1,008	86.7
Stamford village	1,116	1,027	-8.0	1,370	94.3	0.4	1.7	0.0	3.6	16.9	25.3	46.1	54.2	18.7	572	85.5
Stamford town (Delaware)	2,263	2,094	-7.5	2,288	96.1	0.6	0.8	0.7	1.8	15.2	21.9	48.1	49.7	22.4	960	86.1
Stanford town (Dutchess)	3,817	3,740	-2.0	3,743	83.9	1.7	3.7	1.0	9.6	17.2	21.6	50.1	22.8	42.9	1,515	94.5
Stannards CDP	798	-	-	573	100.0	0.0	0.0	0.0	0.0	14.8	27.7	52.6	41.3	26.3	260	95.0
Stark town (Herkimer)	757	711	-6.1	620	98.4	0.0	0.0	0.6	1.0	21.6	21.5	50.9	55.2	20.6	251	73.3
Starkey town (Yates)	3,567	3,510	-1.6	3,494	94.7	1.2	0.4	2.8	0.9	24.7	21.4	39.1	39.8	27.6	1,351	84.5
Star Lake CDP	809	-	-	601	94.8	0.3	0.5	2.8	1.5	16.5	27.6	55.4	47.4	17.3	301	88.0
Stephentown town (Rensselaer)	2,918	2,868	-1.7	2,884	99.8	0.0	0.0	0.2	0.0	16.0	20.1	46.9	37.8	24.4	1,270	87.2
Sterling town (Cayuga)	3,040	3,029	-0.4	3,032	98.9	0.3	0.0	0.8	0.0	19.3	22.0	47.8	43.0	22.9	1,161	95.8
Steuben town (Oneida)	1,103	1,128	2.3	1,166	98.6	0.0	0.3	1.0	0.0	18.9	19.0	46.1	46.4	20.0	465	88.0
Stewart Manor village	1,963	1,956	-0.4	2,199	77.5	0.4	5.8	2.7	13.6	23.1	22.5	47.2	21.0	58.1	801	93.0
Stillwater village	1,737	1,710	-1.6	1,943	94.1	0.8	0.2	2.2	2.7	22.3	13.7	37.5	42.6	18.8	741	89.3
Stillwater town (Saratoga)	8,308	8,972	8.0	8,764	95.3	0.2	1.3	1.0	2.2	20.4	17.4	44.9	44.1	26.3	3,408	94.0
Stockbridge town (Madison)	2,094	2,015	-3.8	2,169	93.5	0.7	0.0	1.5	4.3	20.2	19.2	42.4	52.3	13.0	777	90.9
Stockholm town (St. Lawrence)	3,665	3,601	-1.7	3,618	97.0	0.0	0.5	1.3	1.2	21.6	16.1	42.3	47.3	29.3	1,550	87.1
Stockport town (Columbia)	2,815	2,607	-7.4	2,669	90.0	1.1	0.0	1.8	7.1	19.6	16.4	42.8	53.7	18.2	1,019	86.1
Stockton town (Chautauqua)	2,242	2,072	-7.6	2,199	96.0	0.9	0.8	0.9	1.4	20.8	17.7	43.2	45.5	17.6	880	90.9
Stone Ridge CDP	1,173	-	-	1,328	64.3	10.5	16.9	7.4	0.8	20.0	19.5	49.0	26.9	48.3	522	96.4
Stony Brook CDP	13,740	-	-	12,428	81.6	1.9	9.4	1.1	6.0	21.3	23.1	47.1	14.8	65.6	4,458	94.9
Stony Brook University CDP	9,216	-	-	8,943	29.9	9.1	46.3	5.8	8.9	1.6	3.9	20.3	30.7	47.4	16	100.0
Stony Creek town (Warren)	767	738	-3.8	667	95.8	2.4	0.0	0.0	1.8	15.7	26.4	54.9	57.7	10.1	282	77.0
Stony Point CDP	12,147	-	-	12,586	68.7	9.7	2.9	1.0	17.7	20.0	19.1	43.5	34.5	34.7	4,323	94.3
Stony Point town (Rockland)	15,059	15,313	1.7	15,351	69.2	8.1	3.1	0.8	18.8	19.4	17.6	44.1	35.2	35.6	5,216	94.7
Stottville CDP	1,375	-	-	1,338	79.7	1.6	0.0	7.6	11.1	26.5	18.9	39.1	62.5	21.7	502	85.3
Stratford town (Fulton)	610	576	-5.6	400	88.5	2.3	1.3	0.0	8.0	10.8	25.8	58.2	56.9	19.3	221	61.1
Strykersville CDP	647	-	-	661	98.5	1.5	0.0	0.0	0.0	20.0	21.8	47.2	44.8	21.3	292	84.6
Stuyvesant town (Columbia)	2,010	1,869	-7.0	2,260	87.8	0.6	0.0	3.8	7.8	24.0	15.8	40.3	33.9	33.2	879	94.3
Suffern village	10,723	11,007	2.6	10,943	64.7	6.2	6.2	3.0	19.9	20.0	19.2	44.0	31.2	43.0	4,397	90.3
Sullivan town (Madison)	15,347	15,139	-1.4	15,167	96.0	0.2	0.1	1.8	1.9	20.3	17.2	45.0	40.1	25.1	5,688	93.9
Summerhill town (Cayuga)	1,209	1,157	-4.3	1,022	98.7	0.0	0.0	0.8	0.5	15.2	17.1	50.7	49.0	22.0	408	90.7
Summit town (Schoharie)	1,145	1,078	-5.9	1,179	95.8	0.5	2.5	0.0	1.3	24.8	19.6	41.0	41.5	30.2	465	85.4
Sunset Bay CDP	660	-	-	592	91.0	1.9	0.0	4.2	2.9	18.9	19.9	51.8	49.1	18.3	209	89.0
SUNY Oswego CDP	3,676	-	-	3,694	65.8	12.5	4.8	3.0	13.9	1.8	0.0	19.6	0.0	41.9	7	100.0
Sweden town (Monroe)	14,181	14,079	-0.7	14,081	86.2	3.7	2.0	2.8	5.2	16.2	13.9	25.8	29.7	39.2	4,686	93.6
Sylvan Beach village	897	879	-2.0	922	93.9	2.6	0.0	3.5	0.0	9.7	36.9	53.9	50.0	19.9	430	94.7
Syosset CDP	18,829	-	-	19,453	62.6	0.5	30.8	2.0	4.2	26.2	16.4	42.4	15.9	66.2	6,170	96.8

1 May be of any race.

Table A. All Places — **Population and Housing**

STATE City, town, township, borough, or CDP (county if applicable)	2010 census total population	2019 estimated population	Percent change 2010–2019	ACS total population estimate 2015–2019	White alone, not Hispanic or Latino	Black alone, not Hispanic or Latino	Asian alone, not Hispanic or Latino	All other races or 2 or more races, not Hispanic or Latino	Hispanic or Latino[1]	Under 18 years old	Age 65 years and older	Median age	Percent High school diploma or less	Percent Bachelor's degree or more	Total	Percent with a computer
	1	2	3	4	5	6	7	8	9	10	11	12	13	14	15	16

NEW YORK—Con.

STATE City, town, township, borough, or CDP (county if applicable)	2010 census total population	2019 estimated population	Percent change 2010–2019	ACS total population estimate 2015–2019	White alone, not Hispanic or Latino	Black alone, not Hispanic or Latino	Asian alone, not Hispanic or Latino	All other races or 2 or more races, not Hispanic or Latino	Hispanic or Latino[1]	Under 18 years old	Age 65 years and older	Median age	Percent High school diploma or less	Percent Bachelor's degree or more	Total	Percent with a computer
Syracuse city & MCD (Onondaga)	145,150	142,327	-1.9	142,874	50.0	28.5	6.5	5.6	9.4	21.5	12.6	31.2	44.4	28.4	55,275	81.5
Taconic Shores CDP	-	-	-	686	88.6	0.0	0.7	6.3	4.4	17.3	17.5	52.9	45.2	32.3	302	97.0
Taghkanic town (Columbia)	1,316	1,263	-4.0	1,100	90.6	1.3	1.3	2.0	4.8	8.9	33.4	56.3	37.4	36.1	493	80.5
Tannersville village	537	516	-3.9	858	98.0	0.0	2.0	0.0	0.0	21.1	13.5	44.8	54.4	26.3	298	94.6
Tappan CDP	6,613	-	-	7,227	72.2	3.0	13.2	1.1	10.5	21.9	19.4	45.5	26.9	51.5	2,379	94.4
Tarrytown village	11,238	11,370	1.2	11,436	60.2	5.1	8.1	0.8	25.9	18.1	16.0	44.7	24.3	58.9	4,460	97.3
Taylor town (Cortland)	523	491	-6.1	514	88.9	1.4	0.4	2.5	6.8	26.7	15.8	42.6	50.7	23.2	198	88.4
Terryville CDP	11,849	-	-	12,764	64.2	3.2	3.0	0.6	29.0	25.4	17.1	42.0	40.1	32.5	3,796	94.0
Thendara CDP	-	-	-	30	100.0	0.0	0.0	0.0	0.0	0.0	100.0	86.2	80.0	0.0	24	100.0
Theresa village	861	781	-9.3	758	89.4	0.0	1.8	5.4	3.3	21.8	12.1	38.5	43.8	15.2	311	95.2
Theresa town (Jefferson)	2,912	2,760	-5.2	2,818	94.4	0.4	0.6	2.3	2.3	24.9	11.6	37.7	49.6	16.0	1,124	88.2
Thiells CDP	5,032	-	-	4,870	56.5	12.4	10.6	0.7	19.8	22.0	16.9	42.8	29.8	42.7	1,557	98.0
Thomaston village	2,610	2,613	0.1	2,629	60.1	1.2	36.0	0.7	2.0	24.9	17.1	45.5	18.6	68.1	948	97.0
Thompson town (Sullivan)	15,311	14,993	-2.1	14,935	48.9	16.4	2.9	3.8	28.0	22.3	19.0	39.6	51.0	24.0	5,375	82.3
Thornwood CDP	3,759	-	-	4,186	75.4	3.9	4.6	0.8	15.3	20.4	15.6	40.7	28.3	52.3	1,345	92.9
Thousand Island Park CDP	31	-	-	30	100.0	0.0	0.0	0.0	0.0	0.0	76.7	81.3	43.3	13.3	22	72.7
Three Mile Bay CDP	227	-	-	225	100.0	0.0	0.0	0.0	0.0	33.3	26.2	34.1	46.7	16.0	96	84.4
Throop town (Cayuga)	1,989	1,929	-3.0	1,921	96.5	1.4	0.1	1.6	0.4	21.7	19.1	46.8	43.4	24.5	781	90.5
Thurman town (Warren)	1,218	1,180	-3.1	1,097	97.8	0.5	0.0	0.3	1.4	17.8	28.6	51.4	54.1	14.2	465	85.4
Thurston town (Steuben)	1,350	1,279	-5.3	1,261	96.2	0.0	2.4	1.0	0.5	23.6	14.6	44.8	59.6	13.7	484	81.6
Ticonderoga CDP	3,382	-	-	3,236	97.1	0.4	0.6	1.7	0.2	19.9	22.5	42.0	49.5	12.5	1,356	89.2
Ticonderoga town (Essex)	5,047	4,756	-5.8	4,845	97.9	0.3	0.5	1.1	0.2	17.8	25.0	47.3	46.9	15.6	2,152	89.9
Tillson CDP	1,586	-	-	1,657	88.4	2.8	1.4	1.4	6.0	20.4	14.5	40.9	23.3	42.9	622	94.4
Tioga town (Tioga)	4,863	4,704	-3.3	4,729	95.2	0.0	1.9	0.5	2.5	17.8	23.3	49.9	51.7	19.5	2,112	85.1
Titusville CDP	811	-	-	533	73.4	0.0	0.0	0.0	26.6	10.1	28.5	59.8	25.5	44.9	262	97.7
Tivoli village	1,116	1,081	-3.1	1,012	93.1	0.8	3.6	0.4	2.2	11.6	15.9	33.5	17.2	59.5	453	90.5
Tompkins town (Delaware)	1,246	1,140	-8.5	1,177	95.6	2.9	0.4	0.4	0.7	17.2	22.5	50.3	60.1	12.5	478	85.1
Tonawanda city & MCD (Erie)	15,166	14,745	-2.8	14,830	94.4	0.2	0.4	2.8	2.3	17.6	19.4	46.1	44.9	22.6	6,986	85.1
Tonawanda CDP	58,144	-	-	57,027	87.4	4.5	1.6	2.3	4.3	19.1	20.9	43.4	31.9	37.2	25,820	89.1
Tonawanda town (Erie)	73,516	71,675	-2.5	72,159	87.4	4.8	1.5	2.4	4.1	19.0	20.1	43.2	31.0	37.8	32,909	88.9
Tonawanda Reservation (Erie)	34	36	5.9	14	0.0	0.0	28.6	0.0	71.4	28.6	0.0	20.3	100.0	0.0	4	100.0
Tonawanda Reservation (Genesee)	483	498	3.1	458	12.2	0.0	3.1	82.5	2.2	9.4	27.1	54.3	40.0	9.6	243	83.1
Tonawanda Reservation (Niagara)	-	-	-	-	-	-	-	-	-	-	-	-	-	-	-	-
Torrey town (Yates)	1,279	1,225	-4.2	1,380	94.1	0.0	0.1	2.8	3.0	27.2	20.5	41.0	49.0	22.5	479	83.9
Town Line CDP	2,367	-	-	1,726	94.2	0.0	3.7	0.9	1.2	16.6	25.8	51.0	39.3	20.3	731	92.9
Trenton town (Oneida)	4,625	4,485	-3.0	4,530	95.6	1.9	0.0	1.9	0.7	27.6	16.9	44.2	38.2	28.8	1,717	89.4
Triangle town (Broome)	2,937	2,774	-5.5	2,817	93.5	0.7	0.0	1.3	4.4	20.8	19.6	43.4	51.3	20.6	1,132	82.6
Tribes Hill CDP	1,003	-	-	582	76.5	0.0	2.7	3.3	17.5	13.7	21.8	56.9	30.0	22.0	310	89.7
Troupsburg town (Steuben)	1,291	1,262	-2.2	1,101	97.4	0.0	0.0	2.3	0.4	26.7	16.2	37.4	56.4	12.5	389	82.3
Troy city & MCD (Rensselaer)	50,162	49,154	-2.0	49,458	63.5	16.1	4.8	6.1	9.6	19.6	11.4	30.8	42.2	26.8	19,899	88.5
Trumansburg village	1,786	1,717	-3.9	1,661	89.9	2.8	0.5	3.6	3.2	18.7	25.6	50.9	24.7	52.4	798	96.6
Truxton town (Cortland)	1,127	1,065	-5.5	920	97.5	0.0	0.3	0.0	2.2	16.3	19.9	46.9	42.6	27.6	396	86.1
Tuckahoe CDP	1,373	-	-	759	72.6	4.0	4.0	11.9	7.6	20.7	34.1	55.5	25.6	48.0	343	89.8
Tuckahoe village	6,498	6,549	0.8	6,584	69.1	7.0	10.6	2.9	10.4	19.6	16.4	39.5	21.7	54.9	2,793	85.3
Tully village	869	853	-1.8	951	95.9	2.6	1.1	0.4	0.0	15.1	16.7	45.5	37.2	32.3	428	79.2
Tully town (Onondaga)	2,735	2,666	-2.5	2,692	97.0	1.2	0.9	0.7	0.3	21.2	19.1	47.7	28.3	43.4	1,095	88.0
Tupper Lake village	3,660	3,443	-5.9	3,797	91.1	1.8	0.0	1.7	5.4	20.0	16.8	43.5	46.6	14.4	1,751	84.1
Tupper Lake town (Franklin)	5,975	5,701	-4.6	5,789	92.1	1.7	0.3	1.6	4.4	19.6	19.3	44.8	44.6	19.7	2,491	87.4
Turin village	232	227	-2.2	315	84.1	0.3	0.0	0.0	15.6	35.6	14.0	26.1	60.1	15.2	93	97.8
Turin town (Lewis)	764	743	-2.7	880	92.7	0.3	0.0	0.0	6.9	27.8	20.2	37.9	51.1	19.6	319	93.7
Tuscarora CDP	74	-	-	75	100.0	0.0	0.0	0.0	0.0	0.0	0.0	53.5	58.7	0.0	30	100.0
Tuscarora town (Steuben)	1,463	1,444	-1.3	1,321	99.2	0.0	0.0	0.8	0.0	21.2	17.6	43.0	61.6	17.5	509	86.2
Tuscarora Nation Reservation (Niagara)	1,152	1,191	3.4	1,102	17.7	0.0	4.2	77.1	1.0	22.5	23.3	43.5	60.8	8.2	410	62.0
Tusten town (Sullivan)	1,521	1,480	-2.7	1,367	86.8	3.7	3.5	2.6	3.4	16.5	28.1	52.7	34.8	29.5	625	87.0
Tuxedo town (Orange)	3,590	3,570	-0.6	3,534	77.5	4.9	0.9	3.0	13.7	20.5	19.2	45.1	18.7	55.4	1,398	92.1
Tuxedo Park village	620	600	-3.2	545	90.3	1.1	3.7	2.2	2.8	20.9	25.1	52.2	8.8	73.7	222	95.9
Tyre town (Seneca)	984	1,054	7.1	926	97.8	1.6	0.0	0.5	0.0	25.3	17.6	45.8	52.7	22.3	385	78.2
Tyrone town (Schuyler)	1,625	1,578	-2.9	1,665	97.2	1.3	0.1	0.7	0.6	22.9	24.1	45.7	54.5	12.3	601	86.0
Ulster town (Ulster)	12,356	12,598	2.0	12,474	78.7	5.3	2.0	3.8	10.2	17.3	23.1	48.1	44.1	26.7	5,178	92.1
Ulysses town (Tompkins)	4,903	4,856	-1.0	4,953	90.1	1.3	0.2	2.9	5.6	19.0	25.9	51.9	22.4	50.0	2,210	90.0
Unadilla village	1,114	1,050	-5.7	934	94.8	0.7	0.0	2.8	1.7	22.6	22.6	45.0	45.9	20.0	427	86.2
Unadilla town (Otsego)	4,382	4,104	-6.3	4,154	96.8	0.2	0.0	0.7	2.3	18.0	23.3	47.2	54.2	15.2	1,780	85.1
Union town (Broome)	56,396	52,724	-6.5	53,779	84.0	5.7	4.2	2.3	3.8	19.7	20.7	41.4	38.4	29.7	23,705	87.1
Uniondale CDP	24,759	-	-	32,007	20.2	35.4	2.7	2.5	39.2	19.8	15.5	33.2	49.9	27.2	8,196	92.2
Union Springs village	1,200	1,147	-4.4	1,042	88.8	1.2	0.6	3.2	6.2	23.8	19.0	42.3	43.9	24.2	426	84.0
Union Vale town (Dutchess)	4,697	4,606	-1.9	4,616	88.1	3.3	1.9	0.9	5.8	19.3	19.3	47.0	31.4	43.1	1,720	87.0
Unionville village	610	594	-2.6	524	70.4	1.9	0.0	6.1	21.6	20.4	25.6	45.6	42.1	26.1	199	93.5
University at Buffalo CDP	6,066	-	-	6,174	50.7	11.1	22.7	3.0	12.5	3.4	0.0	19.6	4.3	75.4	142	100.0
University Gardens CDP	4,226	-	-	4,182	47.3	1.0	42.3	1.0	8.3	19.9	18.4	45.4	22.9	59.7	1,612	96.3
Upper Brookville village	1,699	1,744	2.6	1,677	78.8	0.2	14.6	1.2	5.1	19.2	21.2	48.9	16.5	66.5	541	98.5
Upper Nyack village	2,065	2,175	5.3	2,262	78.7	6.2	1.9	3.6	9.5	25.2	20.7	46.3	16.0	66.4	781	93.7
Urbana town (Steuben)	2,343	2,233	-4.7	2,144	94.7	1.6	0.0	1.1	2.6	16.4	33.3	56.1	38.6	26.9	943	84.1
Utica city & MCD (Oneida)	62,241	59,750	-4.0	60,320	56.2	14.4	11.5	5.2	12.7	24.7	15.2	34.0	51.2	18.9	22,920	84.2
Vails Gate CDP	3,369	-	-	3,031	43.1	22.8	5.4	2.6	26.1	20.9	23.2	39.2	43.0	18.7	1,461	80.6
Valatie village	1,819	1,841	1.2	1,626	85.1	1.9	0.4	1.3	11.3	22.0	26.6	46.4	48.7	27.5	567	86.1
Valhalla CDP	3,162	-	-	3,536	68.4	7.4	3.3	2.4	18.5	18.0	15.6	41.2	31.1	47.1	1,146	94.9
Valley Cottage CDP	9,107	-	-	9,023	65.3	8.4	8.9	2.6	14.8	17.1	25.0	48.2	22.9	49.3	3,393	92.0
Valley Falls village	468	455	-2.8	443	95.3	0.0	1.1	1.8	1.8	17.4	19.6	42.1	35.7	29.8	175	90.9
Valley Stream village	37,377	37,431	0.1	37,577	28.4	25.8	14.2	6.1	25.5	21.7	14.6	41.2	33.1	39.4	11,804	94.7

1 May be of any race.

Table A. All Places — **Population and Housing**

STATE City, town, township, borough, or CDP (county if applicable)	Population				Race and Hispanic or Latino origin (percent)					Age (percent)			Educational attainment of persons age 25 and older		Occupied housing units	
	2010 census total population	2019 estimated population	Percent change 2010–2019	ACS total population estimate 2015–2019	White alone, not Hispanic or Latino	Black alone, not Hispanic or Latino	Asian alone, not Hispanic or Latino	All other races or 2 or more races, not Hispanic or Latino	Hispanic or Latino[1]	Under 18 years old	Age 65 years and older	Median age	Percent High school diploma or less	Percent Bachelor's degree or more	Total	Percent with a computer
	1	2	3	4	5	6	7	8	9	10	11	12	13	14	15	16

NEW YORK—Con.

Van Buren town (Onondaga)	13,189	13,376	1.4	13,328	93.4	0.5	0.8	2.3	3.1	20.8	18.8	42.0	35.3	27.1	5,796	90.1
Van Etten village	534	494	-7.5	636	96.9	0.0	1.1	0.0	2.0	28.9	11.9	36.1	44.4	15.4	209	86.1
Van Etten town (Chemung)	1,558	1,472	-5.5	1,522	95.5	0.7	0.5	0.3	3.1	23.7	17.0	42.1	49.0	18.9	566	87.6
Varick town (Seneca)	1,866	1,793	-3.9	1,710	93.9	0.4	0.0	1.7	4.1	27.3	23.7	38.9	46.0	25.9	643	84.1
Venice town (Cayuga)	1,374	1,373	-0.1	1,264	86.6	0.0	0.0	1.8	11.6	21.8	17.4	41.5	47.2	24.4	476	88.7
Vernon village	1,165	1,144	-1.8	1,318	93.4	0.6	0.9	1.2	3.9	21.3	17.1	43.2	39.1	17.8	545	86.6
Vernon town (Oneida)	8,475	8,295	-2.1	8,359	92.5	2.7	0.4	1.2	3.2	19.6	20.3	46.7	41.4	22.8	3,385	89.7
Verona CDP	852	-		1,024	96.0	0.0	0.0	0.0	4.0	23.5	21.5	36.9	40.6	24.6	423	89.6
Verona town (Oneida)	6,296	6,177	-1.9	6,212	95.6	2.0	0.4	1.1	0.9	21.5	17.9	42.9	51.5	18.8	2,371	94.2
Verplanck CDP	1,729	-		1,242	82.3	2.3	0.7	6.5	8.2	18.3	14.3	38.6	44.9	31.1	454	92.1
Vestal town (Broome)	28,062	28,578	1.8	28,352	78.4	4.2	11.6	1.5	4.2	15.2	16.8	28.3	27.1	45.9	8,911	91.2
Veteran town (Chemung)	3,306	3,143	-4.9	3,196	90.1	3.6	0.1	4.0	2.2	14.6	27.5	52.0	35.9	27.6	1,321	88.6
Victor village	2,776	2,680	-3.5	2,716	94.8	0.4	1.8	2.2	0.8	23.7	15.5	41.5	21.9	50.2	1,087	91.4
Victor town (Ontario)	14,272	15,033	5.3	14,877	93.5	1.0	2.0	3.0	0.5	23.9	19.0	43.6	18.2	59.2	5,979	90.3
Victory town (Cayuga)	1,658	1,565	-5.6	1,843	98.3	0.2	1.3	0.0	0.2	27.3	12.2	38.9	59.3	11.6	665	85.3
Victory village	604	580	-4.0	642	90.0	1.9	0.0	2.0	6.1	25.1	11.4	34.0	56.2	13.9	217	91.2
Vienna town (Oneida)	5,439	5,331	-2.0	5,381	98.7	0.4	0.0	0.9	0.0	21.5	17.6	42.6	48.9	15.4	2,020	92.3
Village Green CDP	3,891	-		3,729	96.6	0.0	0.6	1.7	1.0	16.6	13.0	36.4	30.8	28.9	1,803	93.4
Village of the Branch village	1,808	1,793	-0.8	1,549	89.7	1.7	4.3	0.3	3.9	19.5	22.2	47.5	24.0	56.0	575	85.7
Villenova town (Chautauqua)	1,110	1,067	-3.9	852	94.5	0.0	0.0	2.8	2.7	15.5	24.9	52.9	64.2	9.9	376	76.3
Viola CDP	6,868	-		6,898	89.7	4.7	1.3	0.8	3.5	35.2	15.5	26.8	33.3	45.7	1,823	76.6
Virgil CDP	-	-		444	91.7	0.0	0.0	8.3	0.0	44.6	7.4	27.2	47.2	31.0	116	92.2
Virgil town (Cortland)	2,399	2,373	-1.1	2,412	94.4	2.0	0.2	2.2	1.2	23.1	17.1	43.7	40.7	29.0	902	86.9
Volney town (Oswego)	5,932	5,669	-4.4	5,726	96.9	0.2	0.0	1.6	1.3	21.9	16.8	45.7	45.9	18.2	2,106	96.9
Voorheesville village	2,789	2,771	-0.6	2,801	96.3	1.1	0.9	1.0	0.7	22.4	18.3	42.6	19.5	51.8	1,063	95.9
Waddington village	972	943	-3.0	856	97.4	0.0	0.0	0.0	2.6	15.0	27.1	51.3	42.8	30.2	421	88.8
Waddington town (St. Lawrence)	2,266	2,210	-2.5	1,958	98.6	0.0	0.0	0.3	1.1	20.0	22.9	46.4	41.6	28.1	910	89.5
Wading River CDP	7,719	-		7,733	91.9	1.7	0.5	0.4	5.5	22.4	15.5	40.7	22.1	49.5	2,580	92.8
Wadsworth CDP	190	-		264	100.0	0.0	0.0	0.0	0.0	40.5	18.9	31.7	66.9	28.4	104	71.2
Wainscott CDP	650	-		349	81.4	6.6	2.0	0.9	9.2	14.9	28.7	55.9	9.4	65.8	142	68.3
Walden village	6,892	6,689	-2.9	6,724	69.4	14.6	0.4	1.1	14.6	28.9	8.0	34.2	45.2	24.7	2,219	88.7
Wales town (Erie)	3,007	3,014	0.2	3,020	94.7	0.0	3.7	1.5	0.0	20.6	16.4	46.2	33.7	31.0	1,225	91.8
Walker Valley CDP	853	-		1,275	100.0	0.0	0.0	0.0	0.0	34.2	8.2	31.3	46.9	26.3	379	100.0
Wallkill town (Orange)	27,416	28,987	5.7	28,588	50.2	18.2	3.6	3.4	24.5	21.6	16.1	40.8	40.0	22.3	10,761	93.4
Wallkill CDP	2,288	-		2,017	83.0	7.6	4.3	0.5	4.5	16.2	16.0	41.7	51.4	18.7	808	97.2
Walton village	3,088	2,798	-9.4	3,258	96.6	1.0	0.0	0.0	2.4	30.4	19.6	41.6	63.2	17.4	1,429	83.6
Walton town (Delaware)	5,575	5,076	-9.0	5,179	97.5	0.7	0.0	0.0	1.9	22.6	20.2	45.7	58.2	20.6	2,359	88.1
Walton Park CDP	2,669	-		2,668	71.6	2.8	3.3	10.4	11.8	23.6	14.4	38.8	30.9	35.0	813	92.6
Walworth town (Wayne)	9,429	9,156	-2.9	9,228	95.0	0.6	1.4	1.1	2.0	23.2	15.1	41.4	27.9	38.6	3,497	96.6
Wampsville village	635	611	-3.8	700	92.4	5.9	0.0	0.7	1.0	17.0	16.0	39.4	55.2	14.1	202	85.6
Wanakah CDP	3,199	-		3,210	93.8	0.0	2.5	2.8	0.9	18.9	22.6	48.6	34.1	28.5	1,374	87.2
Wantagh CDP	18,871	-		17,915	90.5	0.4	1.3	1.6	6.2	23.5	16.3	41.5	24.9	50.5	5,849	95.0
Wappinger town (Dutchess)	27,117	26,716	-1.5	26,660	69.4	6.3	5.3	3.0	16.0	18.2	16.6	41.0	36.2	31.6	10,205	94.5
Wappingers Falls village	5,583	5,544	-0.7	5,648	58.8	6.0	5.1	0.6	29.5	16.2	15.0	38.5	51.4	18.0	2,125	92.3
Ward town (Allegany)	380	359	-5.5	418	97.1	0.0	0.5	1.0	1.4	23.4	20.6	48.2	48.3	19.5	162	88.3
Warren town (Herkimer)	1,149	1,087	-5.4	1,186	94.9	1.3	0.3	0.7	2.7	23.0	13.8	40.0	46.4	23.1	382	82.2
Warrensburg CDP	3,103	-		3,079	98.8	0.2	0.0	0.0	1.0	20.9	18.8	42.9	49.2	15.3	1,335	80.8
Warrensburg town (Warren)	4,092	3,950	-3.5	3,985	97.9	0.1	0.1	1.0	0.9	20.0	20.5	46.2	48.1	18.9	1,723	79.1
Warsaw village	3,470	3,248	-6.4	3,205	89.5	2.7	0.4	5.7	1.7	16.8	21.1	46.2	44.6	18.3	1,471	83.4
Warsaw town (Wyoming)	5,074	4,789	-5.6	4,863	93.0	1.8	0.2	3.8	1.3	18.1	19.2	43.9	48.6	18.3	2,176	86.8
Warwick village	6,717	6,775	0.9	6,785	86.3	1.1	0.7	2.5	9.3	18.0	27.5	49.0	38.1	35.3	2,996	86.4
Warwick town (Orange)	32,062	31,327	-2.3	31,217	84.1	2.4	1.5	2.9	9.2	21.1	18.7	46.0	31.8	38.2	11,622	92.6
Washington town (Dutchess)	4,728	4,604	-2.6	4,622	82.2	4.4	2.6	2.4	8.5	19.7	21.8	50.8	32.9	39.9	2,013	89.4
Washington Heights CDP	1,689	-		1,830	33.7	13.8	8.3	10.1	34.2	21.9	13.2	36.3	32.6	24.9	605	100.0
Washington Mills CDP	1,183	-		1,428	80.1	0.0	8.8	1.3	9.8	15.5	19.6	36.5	29.0	37.7	652	92.5
Washingtonville village	5,898	5,770	-2.2	5,746	66.1	8.6	1.9	0.9	22.5	22.5	13.9	41.4	34.8	30.5	2,149	91.5
Watchtower CDP	2,381	-		2,117	43.3	15.5	7.1	3.9	30.1	0.5	3.9	36.6	46.7	16.8	0	0.0
Waterford village	1,995	2,277	14.1	2,091	83.7	2.1	4.2	1.0	9.1	17.3	13.9	40.7	44.2	23.3	969	85.9
Waterford town (Saratoga)	8,420	8,463	0.5	8,484	91.1	0.5	2.3	2.1	4.0	20.3	14.2	38.6	38.4	28.1	3,621	90.5
Waterloo village	5,166	4,872	-5.7	4,924	93.7	0.4	0.8	2.8	2.3	19.3	18.8	44.8	48.3	18.8	1,977	89.2
Waterloo town (Seneca)	7,639	7,313	-4.3	7,388	92.4	1.5	0.7	3.1	2.3	20.5	17.5	45.7	47.8	17.2	3,101	88.2
Water Mill CDP	1,559	-		1,631	77.7	0.2	3.3	4.5	14.3	11.8	22.9	53.6	19.2	63.3	676	89.9
Watertown city & MCD (Jefferson)	26,822	24,838	-7.4	25,622	78.6	7.9	1.5	4.3	7.8	23.5	12.9	32.1	47.1	20.8	10,867	87.8
Watertown town (Jefferson)	4,672	4,473	-4.3	4,597	75.0	8.1	5.5	3.3	8.1	17.9	13.4	36.8	40.7	29.6	1,648	92.3
Waterville village	1,582	1,517	-4.1	1,599	98.4	0.8	0.0	0.8	0.1	19.0	24.5	47.8	46.7	27.4	673	88.4
Watervliet city & MCD (Albany)	10,251	9,900	-3.4	10,050	72.1	9.5	3.9	6.8	7.7	15.8	15.2	39.6	45.3	21.6	4,921	84.5
Watkins Glen village	1,856	1,872	0.9	2,000	89.4	0.8	3.8	0.5	5.6	22.2	19.8	39.5	43.6	23.4	827	89.4
Watson town (Lewis)	1,880	1,790	-4.8	1,769	96.6	0.0	0.3	0.1	3.1	20.6	18.4	44.7	48.5	18.2	728	85.2
Waverly town (Franklin)	1,022	982	-3.9	914	99.3	0.0	0.0	0.7	0.0	14.8	13.1	50.7	53.4	13.6	407	68.8
Waverly village	4,427	4,115	-7.0	4,177	95.0	1.8	0.9	0.8	1.5	23.7	18.6	39.2	59.1	14.4	1,759	83.8
Wawarsing town (Ulster)	13,172	12,580	-4.5	12,799	61.3	9.0	2.3	4.8	22.6	18.9	16.3	42.2	52.1	18.6	4,450	89.0
Wawayanda town (Orange)	7,265	7,313	0.7	7,268	74.2	8.6	2.2	2.1	12.9	24.3	13.1	40.3	31.8	37.3	2,487	95.7
Wayland village	1,869	1,764	-5.6	1,694	96.0	0.8	0.0	1.5	1.8	24.6	15.1	42.8	54.4	16.7	695	89.2
Wayland town (Steuben)	4,102	3,904	-4.8	3,946	97.7	0.3	0.0	0.9	1.0	19.7	22.0	48.1	53.3	16.0	1,741	85.0
Wayne town (Steuben)	1,021	990	-3.0	1,025	98.7	0.0	0.0	0.8	0.5	14.8	28.5	55.6	36.2	34.1	456	88.8
Webb town (Herkimer)	1,804	1,782	-1.2	1,079	94.3	3.4	0.0	0.0	2.3	5.4	46.6	64.1	42.1	33.7	555	88.6
Webster village	5,349	5,667	5.9	5,606	82.0	5.1	6.5	0.6	5.7	18.6	16.0	39.5	28.3	37.0	2,578	93.9
Webster town (Monroe)	42,659	45,163	5.9	44,522	90.3	2.0	3.4	1.4	2.9	20.8	20.4	45.0	25.2	45.6	18,553	94.1
Websters Crossing CDP	69	-		44	100.0	0.0	0.0	0.0	0.0	0.0	20.5	54.3	79.3	0.0	21	100.0
Weedsport village	1,815	1,706	-6.0	1,768	93.8	0.6	1.8	1.2	2.5	21.5	19.6	45.4	40.7	20.7	761	84.6

1 May be of any race.

Items 1–16   **NY(Van Buren town (Onondaga))—NY(Weedsport village) 309**

Table A. All Places — **Population and Housing**

STATE City, town, township, borough, or CDP (county if applicable)	Population				Race and Hispanic or Latino origin (percent)					Age (percent)			Educational attainment of persons age 25 and older		Occupied housing units	
	2010 census total population	2019 estimated population	Percent change 2010–2019	ACS total population estimate 2015–2019	White alone, not Hispanic or Latino	Black alone, not Hispanic or Latino	Asian alone, not Hispanic or Latino	All other races or 2 or more races, not Hispanic or Latino	Hispanic or Latino[1]	Under 18 years old	Age 65 years and older	Median age	Percent High school diploma or less	Percent Bachelor's degree or more	Total	Percent with a computer
	1	2	3	4	5	6	7	8	9	10	11	12	13	14	15	16
NEW YORK—Con.																
Wells CDP	-	-	-	630	99.5	0.5	0.0	0.0	0.0	24.4	18.1	48.9	32.8	11.3	111	82.9
Wells town (Hamilton)	672	622	-7.4	821	99.6	0.4	0.0	0.0	0.0	22.3	17.2	47.9	43.5	12.5	160	77.5
Wellsburg village	574	536	-6.6	458	95.6	0.4	0.0	3.9	0.0	26.2	14.0	37.5	56.6	13.9	158	88.6
Wellsville village	4,680	4,375	-6.5	4,437	97.2	0.7	0.3	1.1	0.7	18.5	19.5	44.9	42.4	21.9	2,226	82.4
Wellsville town (Allegany)	7,395	6,919	-6.4	7,016	97.7	0.9	0.2	0.7	0.5	16.6	23.4	48.4	41.2	23.0	3,402	83.7
Wesley Hills village	5,623	5,919	5.3	5,885	94.8	0.3	2.4	0.6	1.9	40.7	14.4	26.7	12.6	68.9	1,466	98.9
West Almond town (Allegany)	331	325	-1.8	330	96.4	0.0	0.0	1.8	1.8	23.9	22.1	41.3	33.5	23.3	143	87.4
West Babylon CDP	43,213	-	-	42,665	65.1	11.7	3.4	1.7	18.1	20.2	16.0	40.7	44.5	27.7	13,448	94.8
West Bay Shore CDP	4,648	-	-	4,801	81.4	0.6	3.2	1.8	13.1	20.3	22.0	42.3	27.2	47.2	1,653	95.6
West Bloomfield town (Ontario)	2,514	2,482	-1.3	2,611	97.2	0.0	0.3	0.0	2.5	17.8	26.3	50.7	42.1	28.3	1,124	92.3
Westbury village	15,039	15,351	2.1	15,342	39.8	21.3	9.4	1.9	27.6	18.2	17.5	41.1	34.7	40.2	5,019	91.1
West Carthage village	2,012	1,934	-3.9	1,383	74.5	12.0	0.0	3.0	10.5	21.7	18.1	34.5	42.8	22.4	713	82.5
West Chazy CDP	529	-	-	398	98.0	0.0	0.0	2.0	0.0	13.1	34.7	51.9	45.0	28.3	192	89.6
West Elmira CDP	4,967	-	-	4,655	94.8	0.4	3.1	0.1	1.7	22.3	23.0	47.6	22.6	52.0	2,083	94.2
West End CDP	1,940	-	-	2,046	94.0	1.8	0.0	1.1	3.1	16.9	21.4	46.1	37.0	39.5	891	94.2
Westerlo town (Albany)	3,364	3,276	-2.6	3,325	97.8	0.0	0.3	0.0	1.9	12.9	21.2	50.1	45.9	21.9	1,362	84.8
Western town (Oneida)	1,953	1,923	-1.5	1,977	99.6	0.0	0.4	0.0	0.0	22.4	16.7	43.8	43.4	22.7	794	94.1
Westfield village	3,224	2,967	-8.0	2,611	91.1	0.0	4.3	0.0	4.6	20.1	24.3	49.6	38.1	36.0	1,166	86.7
Westfield town (Chautauqua)	4,896	4,566	-6.7	4,638	93.9	0.0	2.4	0.0	3.7	18.0	23.0	50.4	43.9	32.6	2,045	87.9
Westford town (Otsego)	866	820	-5.3	737	95.7	1.2	0.3	2.2	0.7	16.7	20.5	48.3	46.3	27.6	293	88.4
West Glens Falls CDP	7,071	-	-	6,860	92.3	3.9	0.5	2.0	1.3	19.5	15.7	41.8	44.2	25.0	2,813	94.0
Westhampton CDP	3,079	-	-	2,623	85.8	5.5	1.5	0.2	7.0	18.8	30.8	54.8	29.2	43.2	973	93.0
Westhampton Beach village	1,713	1,797	4.9	1,791	79.5	2.7	1.5	1.6	14.7	15.4	29.4	51.7	24.5	55.1	798	88.8
West Hampton Dunes village	55	58	5.5	68	92.6	2.9	0.0	4.4	0.0	16.2	41.2	61.5	0.0	82.5	29	100.0
West Haverstraw village	10,138	10,189	0.5	10,250	25.3	12.4	4.1	5.1	53.0	24.5	13.0	36.1	45.6	18.0	3,154	96.4
West Hempstead CDP	18,862	-	-	19,864	58.8	10.6	6.3	2.3	22.0	23.5	14.1	39.4	34.4	40.2	5,773	95.8
West Hills CDP	5,592	-	-	5,055	83.9	0.4	5.7	3.6	6.4	19.3	20.1	48.6	17.8	62.5	1,813	96.5
West Hurley CDP	1,939	-	-	1,920	98.3	0.0	1.0	0.4	0.3	12.1	29.5	55.1	29.4	43.9	892	87.7
West Islip CDP	28,335	-	-	26,844	90.8	0.5	1.6	0.6	6.5	20.9	15.8	43.1	31.8	38.8	8,398	97.3
Westmere CDP	7,284	-	-	6,933	75.3	2.8	16.1	1.7	4.1	17.6	15.5	39.0	19.3	52.0	3,077	94.5
West Monroe town (Oswego)	4,252	4,088	-3.9	4,128	97.1	0.0	0.4	1.6	0.9	23.2	16.0	42.4	53.6	13.1	1,703	94.6
Westmoreland CDP	427	-	-	658	88.4	0.0	0.0	11.6	0.0	28.6	15.3	41.1	17.7	22.8	250	100.0
Westmoreland town (Oneida)	6,149	6,066	-1.3	6,068	93.7	0.5	0.5	2.1	3.2	22.6	17.8	43.2	37.2	24.4	2,313	85.1
West Nyack CDP	3,439	-	-	3,942	76.7	0.5	6.5	1.0	15.2	18.1	19.1	48.9	19.5	50.8	1,456	94.8
Weston Mills CDP	1,472	-	-	1,189	98.1	0.1	0.0	1.7	0.1	12.3	28.9	56.8	55.4	14.1	621	79.5
West Point CDP	6,763	-	-	6,379	69.9	6.6	5.0	7.6	10.9	24.9	0.6	21.0	6.5	76.8	871	100.0
Westport CDP	518	-	-	368	98.9	1.1	0.0	0.0	0.0	7.6	36.1	56.0	29.1	46.0	221	71.9
Westport town (Essex)	1,312	1,244	-5.2	1,107	97.8	0.7	0.2	1.3	0.0	9.5	36.0	57.9	33.2	37.5	595	79.8
West Sand Lake CDP	2,660	-	-	2,697	97.3	1.4	0.0	0.0	1.3	22.5	17.8	42.3	35.6	39.7	1,016	98.4
West Sayville CDP	5,011	-	-	5,010	90.9	0.6	1.6	2.3	4.6	22.6	15.3	43.2	34.0	39.0	1,670	93.2
West Seneca town & CDP (Erie)	44,744	45,224	1.1	45,344	96.1	1.0	0.4	0.8	1.6	18.3	21.1	45.5	36.7	29.6	19,845	87.3
West Sparta town (Livingston)	1,253	1,235	-1.4	1,229	89.7	0.2	7.6	1.5	1.1	15.5	18.1	48.6	59.3	15.3	494	86.4
West Turin town (Lewis)	1,524	1,483	-2.7	1,511	95.4	2.8	0.0	0.7	1.1	24.4	18.4	48.1	56.9	15.1	603	84.4
West Union town (Steuben)	312	300	-3.8	326	93.9	0.0	0.0	6.1	0.0	18.1	23.9	49.0	59.9	8.4	140	78.6
Westvale CDP	4,963	-	-	5,000	88.7	6.1	0.3	3.6	1.3	25.6	22.4	41.2	18.9	44.7	1,904	91.5
West Valley CDP	518	-	-	561	83.8	2.7	0.0	10.0	3.6	23.7	21.2	38.0	33.3	21.5	203	92.1
Westville town (Franklin)	1,816	1,813	-0.2	1,785	95.4	0.0	0.6	3.2	0.8	16.2	19.3	48.6	59.6	11.3	808	79.8
West Winfield village	826	855	3.5	742	97.2	0.5	0.5	1.2	0.5	14.3	24.5	49.7	48.0	25.1	342	89.8
Wethersfield town (Wyoming)	885	850	-4.0	716	96.9	0.0	0.7	0.0	2.4	22.1	13.1	45.5	51.0	20.7	307	83.1
Wheatfield town (Niagara)	18,117	18,053	-0.4	18,140	94.5	1.2	1.3	1.2	1.8	19.2	23.2	48.2	30.8	33.9	7,147	89.2
Wheatland town (Monroe)	4,786	4,680	-2.2	4,711	90.0	3.8	0.6	1.6	4.0	20.8	17.4	36.5	32.9	39.0	1,933	97.5
Wheatley Heights CDP	5,130	-	-	4,942	18.9	55.8	4.8	6.8	13.7	26.7	12.1	38.5	31.6	37.3	1,307	97.3
Wheeler town (Steuben)	1,260	1,245	-1.2	1,111	93.6	0.9	0.2	1.4	3.9	21.0	18.5	44.9	49.4	20.2	429	83.0
White Creek town (Washington)	3,381	3,281	-3.0	3,292	96.2	0.0	0.8	1.3	1.7	16.0	25.5	55.3	50.0	23.6	1,491	81.3
Whitehall village	2,620	2,542	-3.0	2,293	96.6	0.3	0.0	1.7	1.4	22.9	15.2	41.7	60.3	8.2	951	81.8
Whitehall town (Washington)	4,048	3,931	-2.9	3,953	97.8	0.2	0.0	1.0	1.0	24.8	15.0	40.3	60.7	11.5	1,475	79.5
White Plains city & MCD (Westchester)	56,866	58,109	2.2	58,137	46.4	11.1	7.8	2.3	32.4	18.8	17.4	40.0	30.4	49.5	22,669	93.7
Whitesboro village	3,775	3,612	-4.3	3,643	87.9	0.0	0.0	0.4	11.6	18.1	16.3	36.9	38.1	31.0	1,686	94.2
Whitestown town (Oneida)	18,664	18,072	-3.2	18,243	91.9	1.0	2.0	0.8	4.3	19.4	20.1	42.9	35.6	32.9	7,865	88.3
Whitney Point village	961	890	-7.4	828	87.8	1.9	0.1	0.0	10.1	19.8	28.5	43.4	55.4	22.6	365	74.2
Willet town (Cortland)	1,048	1,001	-4.5	1,040	92.5	1.6	0.0	3.0	2.9	28.0	13.7	35.2	63.2	13.5	368	84.2
Williamson CDP	2,495	-	-	2,653	88.1	3.7	0.1	2.7	5.5	25.3	17.6	40.7	57.7	14.1	1,140	81.1
Williamson town (Wayne)	6,985	6,724	-3.7	6,757	86.0	2.2	0.0	3.8	8.0	21.9	17.6	42.6	44.7	25.8	2,712	87.9
Williamstown town (Oswego)	1,274	1,246	-2.2	1,384	97.9	0.0	0.0	0.9	1.2	25.1	13.6	35.9	66.8	8.2	508	80.5
Williamsville village	5,314	5,220	-1.8	5,233	89.2	3.1	3.0	3.0	1.8	17.2	23.8	44.8	17.7	61.3	2,415	95.5
Willing town (Allegany)	1,224	1,151	-6.0	1,391	100.0	0.0	0.0	0.0	0.0	24.2	19.1	43.5	44.3	16.6	537	85.1
Williston Park village	7,254	7,253	0.0	7,277	72.4	1.8	13.1	2.0	10.7	22.4	17.2	42.0	26.7	49.1	2,533	92.4
Willsboro CDP	753	-	-	763	88.2	0.7	0.0	3.4	7.7	23.1	20.1	46.9	52.4	26.4	334	93.7
Willsboro town (Essex)	2,025	1,972	-2.6	1,990	91.7	0.3	0.5	3.0	4.6	15.3	25.9	54.3	47.6	20.9	892	91.0
Wilmington CDP	937	-	-	775	92.0	0.0	0.0	5.4	2.6	10.6	20.8	52.2	39.0	26.9	366	95.4
Wilmington town (Essex)	1,253	1,252	-0.1	1,072	93.0	0.2	0.3	4.6	2.0	10.7	19.7	51.1	39.3	30.6	516	96.1
Wilna town (Jefferson)	6,429	5,846	-9.1	6,031	90.8	1.8	0.0	3.6	3.7	22.1	15.1	31.8	51.1	14.9	2,302	94.2
Wilson village	1,264	1,221	-3.4	1,120	96.3	0.0	0.5	1.6	1.6	20.1	20.9	44.9	29.6	28.7	496	85.9
Wilson town (Niagara)	5,979	5,787	-3.2	5,820	94.6	1.5	0.7	2.4	0.9	19.9	19.6	46.9	44.5	22.3	2,418	87.1
Wilton town (Saratoga)	16,154	16,918	4.7	16,877	93.4	1.3	2.5	0.9	1.8	22.0	16.3	43.9	29.5	46.0	6,766	96.7
Windham CDP	367	-	-	323	99.1	0.0	0.0	0.0	0.9	2.5	48.0	61.9	52.9	8.3	143	78.3
Windham town (Greene)	1,697	1,674	-1.4	1,586	97.2	0.0	0.0	1.5	1.3	12.1	29.6	52.7	52.9	20.0	609	85.6

1 May be of any race.

Table A. All Places — Population and Housing

STATE City, town, township, borough, or CDP (county if applicable)	2010 census total population	2019 estimated population	Percent change 2010–2019	ACS total population estimate 2015–2019	White alone, not Hispanic or Latino	Black alone, not Hispanic or Latino	Asian alone, not Hispanic or Latino	All other races or 2 or more races, not Hispanic or Latino	Hispanic or Latino[1]	Under 18 years old	Age 65 years and older	Median age	Percent High school diploma or less	Percent Bachelor's degree or more	Occupied housing units Total	Occupied housing units Percent with a computer
	1	2	3	4	5	6	7	8	9	10	11	12	13	14	15	16
NEW YORK—Con.																
Windsor village	918	860	-6.3	999	96.9	0.7	0.0	1.5	0.9	20.9	15.0	39.3	38.2	27.6	408	92.9
Windsor town (Broome)	6,265	5,886	-6.0	5,992	96.4	0.5	0.3	0.5	2.3	23.9	16.8	43.4	46.9	22.7	2,391	93.2
Winfield town (Herkimer)	2,081	2,065	-0.8	2,033	98.4	0.2	0.4	0.4	0.5	22.3	17.9	42.5	50.8	16.9	774	91.1
Winthrop CDP	510	-	-	154	90.9	0.0	0.0	9.1	0.0	0.0	18.8	52.7	22.7	33.8	97	100.0
Wirt town (Allegany)	1,105	1,036	-6.2	932	99.9	0.0	0.0	0.0	0.1	17.6	21.0	51.4	54.8	6.5	425	79.3
Witherbee CDP	347	-	-	256	68.4	0.0	6.6	25.0	0.0	32.4	11.7	34.6	43.9	0.0	132	100.0
Wolcott village	1,714	1,614	-5.8	1,673	94.9	2.0	0.0	1.7	1.4	21.6	18.4	38.6	62.3	12.8	754	81.6
Wolcott town (Wayne)	4,483	4,089	-8.8	4,144	94.3	3.1	0.3	1.1	1.2	23.0	19.2	42.0	61.3	13.8	1,807	87.2
Woodbury CDP	8,907	-	-	8,852	79.0	2.3	15.1	0.4	3.3	18.4	31.1	52.7	22.7	65.7	3,068	93.4
Woodbury village	10,691	11,089	3.7	10,810	64.9	7.3	6.1	1.3	20.4	25.5	12.7	40.0	23.7	43.1	3,328	95.6
Woodbury town (Orange)	11,327	11,730	3.6	11,570	61.7	10.1	6.9	1.4	19.8	25.8	12.6	39.1	23.8	42.5	3,547	95.8
Woodhull town (Steuben)	1,719	1,636	-4.8	1,800	97.9	0.0	0.0	2.1	0.0	26.1	13.8	36.8	56.0	12.7	624	83.0
Woodmere CDP	17,121	-	-	17,470	87.2	5.4	1.5	0.4	5.5	32.7	15.2	34.5	17.1	66.2	5,096	94.3
Woodridge village	830	777	-6.4	917	75.2	8.9	0.0	3.1	12.8	35.9	10.1	27.0	41.4	23.4	320	89.1
Woodsburgh village	776	780	0.5	808	90.2	0.7	1.9	0.0	7.2	27.0	25.7	50.0	8.2	83.5	291	96.9
Woodstock CDP	2,088	-	-	2,266	86.7	4.0	2.3	4.2	2.8	18.8	31.1	53.0	27.6	47.4	1,125	84.8
Woodstock town (Ulster)	5,893	5,767	-2.1	5,804	89.0	2.1	3.2	3.1	2.6	16.4	32.5	56.3	21.8	55.4	2,723	92.5
Woodsville CDP	80	-	-	98	100.0	0.0	0.0	0.0	0.0	27.6	6.1	33.5	57.4	11.5	34	100.0
Worcester CDP	1,113	-	-	889	83.0	1.0	0.0	7.4	8.5	19.5	30.5	47.3	39.7	27.3	362	87.6
Worcester town (Otsego)	2,220	2,087	-6.0	1,778	86.5	3.2	0.0	4.6	5.7	15.5	29.8	52.2	44.6	25.5	783	86.1
Worth town (Jefferson)	231	222	-3.9	238	100.0	0.0	0.0	0.0	0.0	18.5	20.2	49.5	58.4	8.6	94	85.1
Wright town (Schoharie)	1,536	1,467	-4.5	1,735	92.2	1.2	0.0	0.2	6.3	20.2	15.8	46.4	44.4	20.0	678	88.1
Wurtsboro village	1,240	1,149	-7.3	1,140	83.4	6.3	0.8	1.1	8.3	14.6	21.1	45.2	41.5	23.9	483	93.6
Wyandanch CDP	11,647	-	-	11,368	2.8	58.0	0.9	4.4	33.8	29.0	10.9	31.9	58.8	15.9	2,771	93.3
Wynantskill CDP	3,276	-	-	3,154	91.8	0.0	0.8	1.6	5.9	23.5	15.4	44.0	32.0	25.2	1,323	90.2
Wyoming village	437	417	-4.6	353	99.7	0.0	0.0	0.0	0.3	21.2	14.2	37.7	43.9	19.7	139	92.8
Yaphank CDP	5,945	-	-	6,338	73.4	7.0	1.3	1.2	17.2	16.1	12.1	39.3	42.3	28.1	2,118	92.4
Yates town (Orleans)	2,560	2,413	-5.7	2,558	94.4	0.5	0.0	2.7	2.3	22.4	15.1	44.5	56.4	14.5	1,120	84.1
Yonkers city & MCD (Westchester)	196,026	200,370	2.2	199,968	36.7	16.1	6.3	2.5	38.3	21.6	16.5	39.0	42.7	33.5	74,897	87.8
York town (Livingston)	3,392	3,223	-5.0	3,273	93.9	0.3	0.1	2.3	3.5	22.5	16.3	41.4	51.9	21.5	1,311	94.7
York Hamlet CDP	544	-	-	433	93.5	2.1	0.0	4.4	0.0	16.4	12.0	39.9	39.9	30.5	196	100.0
Yorkshire CDP	1,180	-	-	1,106	98.8	0.0	0.0	0.0	1.2	18.4	19.4	46.3	63.3	7.1	512	82.4
Yorkshire town (Cattaraugus)	3,921	3,690	-5.9	3,741	98.8	0.0	0.1	0.4	0.7	23.0	16.2	43.6	54.6	11.4	1,483	84.8
Yorktown town (Westchester)	36,095	36,269	0.5	36,538	74.1	4.1	5.6	2.0	14.2	21.8	18.5	45.6	27.2	51.4	12,985	92.9
Yorktown Heights CDP	1,781	-	-	1,393	89.7	0.7	4.2	1.1	4.3	8.9	27.6	55.3	40.8	44.2	622	90.8
Yorkville village	2,685	2,568	-4.4	2,595	90.8	0.5	0.6	1.1	7.0	27.4	15.4	33.1	40.8	17.7	1,074	90.1
Youngstown village	1,969	1,880	-4.5	2,019	96.0	0.6	0.9	1.3	1.1	21.8	21.2	44.8	32.7	32.0	796	88.4
Zena CDP	1,031	-	-	942	82.1	2.9	6.7	2.2	6.2	15.1	26.6	57.4	18.9	56.5	377	100.0
NORTH CAROLINA	9,535,751	10,488,084	10.0	10,264,876	63.1	21.1	2.8	3.6	9.4	22.4	15.9	38.7	37.9	31.3	3,965,482	89.1
Aberdeen town	6,369	7,988	25.4	7,595	71.1	17.6	0.0	5.3	6.0	25.4	14.8	34.4	29.6	35.2	2,891	89.4
Advance CDP	1,138	-	-	1,158	94.8	5.2	0.0	0.0	0.0	27.6	21.2	46.0	44.7	23.7	469	82.9
Ahoskie town	5,062	4,763	-5.9	4,848	23.4	64.5	2.4	4.8	5.0	20.9	19.8	39.6	53.9	18.3	1,895	77.6
Alamance village	956	1,042	9.0	1,127	92.3	6.7	0.0	0.5	0.4	19.1	20.6	47.0	26.2	39.2	454	91.4
Albemarle city	15,890	16,246	2.2	15,980	65.5	24.0	1.4	2.5	6.6	22.9	21.4	40.2	48.2	18.2	6,220	83.7
Alliance town	782	758	-3.1	809	68.5	19.0	0.0	3.2	9.3	18.4	34.4	54.8	54.9	10.6	340	75.0
Altamahaw CDP	347	-	-	319	100.0	0.0	0.0	0.0	0.0	9.7	13.8	55.0	68.0	0.0	148	94.6
Andrews town	1,777	1,846	3.9	1,837	80.2	5.9	1.4	5.7	6.8	28.8	22.7	35.2	60.8	13.5	714	80.1
Angier town	4,428	5,415	22.3	5,893	49.0	15.6	0.4	2.4	32.6	30.5	11.7	31.5	40.6	23.2	2,056	92.2
Ansonville town	626	589	-5.9	730	9.2	88.4	0.0	0.0	2.5	14.4	13.0	51.5	72.0	7.8	265	85.7
Apex town	37,727	59,300	57.2	51,370	74.2	6.3	8.8	3.3	7.3	29.9	7.9	37.1	13.5	64.3	18,197	96.9
Aquadale CDP	397	-	-	637	100.0	0.0	0.0	0.0	0.0	15.7	15.5	43.1	46.1	21.5	265	88.7
Arapahoe town	557	535	-3.9	410	85.1	8.3	0.0	2.7	3.9	11.2	32.0	48.2	54.2	5.8	203	83.3
Archdale city	11,435	11,513	0.7	11,510	77.4	7.8	7.9	3.0	3.8	22.6	17.4	42.7	44.5	19.0	4,596	90.1
Archer Lodge town	4,262	5,159	21.0	4,902	75.4	3.2	0.0	2.6	18.8	29.2	10.2	33.3	38.3	19.9	1,648	100.0
Asheboro city	25,408	25,940	2.1	25,852	58.7	10.9	0.6	4.3	25.4	23.8	16.8	37.3	49.7	18.2	10,841	87.3
Asheville city	83,420	92,870	11.3	91,560	77.9	11.2	1.7	2.4	6.8	17.8	18.1	39.0	25.2	48.9	40,791	88.8
Ashley Heights CDP	380	-	-	453	33.8	30.0	0.0	27.6	8.6	23.0	13.2	32.2	64.4	7.8	136	83.1
Askewville town	250	220	-12.0	202	88.6	0.0	0.0	2.5	8.9	13.4	38.6	55.6	63.6	6.5	93	71.0
Atkinson town	299	356	19.1	392	76.5	9.7	0.0	8.2	5.6	26.3	18.6	37.4	53.1	13.6	137	89.8
Atlantic CDP	543	-	-	522	98.9	0.0	0.0	0.0	1.1	7.9	27.8	54.3	58.4	9.2	243	90.5
Atlantic Beach town	1,497	1,512	1.0	1,747	96.6	0.6	0.0	0.9	1.9	10.3	35.1	56.6	24.0	38.2	934	86.9
Aulander town	896	783	-12.6	834	31.5	56.2	0.0	2.2	10.1	24.7	17.1	37.8	63.2	4.4	315	73.0
Aurora town	520	510	-1.9	743	35.8	59.9	0.0	4.0	0.3	14.9	21.1	46.1	69.1	3.8	313	69.3
Autryville town	200	199	-0.5	211	93.8	6.2	0.0	0.0	0.0	14.2	17.1	46.8	69.1	6.2	88	86.4
Avery Creek CDP	1,950	-	-	2,675	88.7	3.7	3.7	0.0	3.9	21.0	13.4	43.9	15.0	52.7	946	98.6
Avon CDP	776	-	-	421	100.0	0.0	0.0	0.0	0.0	5.9	35.9	58.7	32.1	41.3	328	92.4
Ayden town	5,000	5,141	2.8	5,132	50.5	41.3	2.0	1.4	4.8	25.4	20.6	38.6	41.3	16.4	2,160	84.5
Badin town	1,974	1,973	-0.1	2,009	58.6	34.3	0.0	3.9	3.2	11.6	16.7	46.9	61.4	5.7	506	88.3
Bailey town	569	562	-1.2	529	63.5	12.1	0.0	5.9	18.5	26.1	24.2	41.3	49.4	18.2	229	83.8
Bakersville town	467	445	-4.7	466	92.5	0.0	0.0	1.1	6.4	21.5	29.6	49.0	48.3	15.7	199	79.4
Bald Head Island village	158	182	15.2	230	94.3	0.0	0.0	0.0	5.7	0.0	70.9	69.0	3.0	86.1	143	98.6
Balfour CDP	1,187	-	-	1,216	79.9	2.5	3.2	3.3	11.1	8.7	19.3	44.8	48.6	34.0	659	90.9
Banner Elk town	1,057	1,149	8.7	1,332	82.7	4.1	1.5	3.7	8.0	4.4	13.5	21.2	17.3	44.2	277	97.5
Barker Heights CDP	1,254	-	-	1,354	61.5	16.8	0.0	0.0	21.7	25.1	9.3	36.3	40.9	6.1	650	80.5
Barker Ten Mile CDP	952	-	-	909	60.0	3.5	0.4	36.1	0.0	13.9	31.4	49.0	31.1	48.9	365	91.8
Bath town	249	241	-3.2	266	97.7	1.1	0.0	1.1	0.0	10.2	41.7	61.4	24.7	40.6	138	88.4
Bayboro town	1,260	1,240	-1.6	1,210	46.1	46.0	0.7	2.3	4.9	8.0	11.0	41.7	47.8	4.0	272	84.2
Bayshore CDP	3,393	-	-	4,496	91.6	6.1	0.4	1.5	0.4	28.8	15.6	33.7	23.2	45.8	1,513	94.7
Bayview CDP	346	-	-	598	87.0	6.9	0.0	0.0	6.2	10.9	27.6	48.0	53.1	28.7	190	100.0
Bear Grass town	73	66	-9.6	89	93.3	0.0	0.0	0.0	6.7	23.6	21.3	39.4	34.3	14.9	35	91.4
Beaufort town	4,184	4,452	6.4	4,343	79.8	12.3	0.4	5.4	2.1	11.4	28.3	49.8	30.4	27.7	2,156	88.2
Beech Mountain town	319	324	1.6	614	94.6	0.7	1.5	1.8	1.5	9.3	47.2	64.1	20.0	49.2	304	97.4
Belhaven town	1,692	1,579	-6.7	1,657	37.5	55.3	0.0	1.0	6.1	19.1	26.7	48.1	55.7	12.5	756	72.4
Bell Arthur CDP	466	-	-	369	89.2	9.2	0.0	1.6	0.0	34.1	6.0	32.2	41.4	32.0	146	100.0
Belmont city	10,227	12,558	22.8	12,054	72.9	13.6	3.5	7.3	2.6	24.9	12.4	34.9	29.5	43.4	4,394	88.3
Belville town	1,930	2,103	9.0	2,504	69.9	19.6	1.4	4.1	4.9	20.2	14.2	39.4	25.5	31.3	954	96.8
Belvoir CDP	307	-	-	565	90.6	9.4	0.0	0.0	0.0	43.5	8.3	28.3	43.4	17.5	152	100.0

1 May be of any race.

Table A. All Places — **Population and Housing**

STATE City, town, township, borough, or CDP (county if applicable)	Population: 2010 census total population	Population: 2019 estimated population	Population: Percent change 2010–2019	Population: ACS total population estimate 2015–2019	Race and Hispanic or Latino origin (percent): White alone, not Hispanic or Latino	Black alone, not Hispanic or Latino	Asian alone, not Hispanic or Latino	All other races or 2 or more races, not Hispanic or Latino	Hispanic or Latino[1]	Age (percent): Under 18 years old	Age 65 years and older	Median age	Educational attainment of persons age 25 and older: Percent High school diploma or less	Percent Bachelor's degree or more	Occupied housing units: Total	Percent with a computer
	1	2	3	4	5	6	7	8	9	10	11	12	13	14	15	16
NORTH CAROLINA—Con.																
Belwood town	949	954	0.5	999	94.3	0.6	0.0	1.0	4.1	20.5	19.9	41.3	57.0	12.5	349	84.2
Bennett CDP	282	-	-	476	100.0	0.0	0.0	0.0	0.0	37.6	8.8	24.1	37.7	13.2	134	70.9
Benson town	3,314	3,922	18.3	3,731	42.8	38.0	0.4	0.6	18.2	25.9	18.7	39.1	44.6	17.8	1,309	84.6
Bent Creek CDP	1,287	-	-	1,666	87.9	0.1	1.1	1.3	9.6	24.3	17.4	42.7	32.4	35.0	601	95.8
Bermuda Run town	2,592	2,709	4.5	2,666	96.5	1.9	0.6	0.4	0.6	21.8	36.9	55.6	22.3	50.7	1,128	92.5
Bessemer City city	5,328	5,577	4.7	5,471	76.2	14.3	0.0	1.2	8.3	22.3	13.7	37.5	62.7	7.1	1,994	86.4
Bethania town	328	364	11.0	374	81.6	16.8	0.0	0.0	1.6	12.3	17.9	48.4	39.8	20.7	146	96.6
Bethel town	1,577	1,611	2.2	1,789	38.2	56.1	0.0	1.0	4.8	21.0	24.4	49.4	51.2	23.8	754	72.3
Bethlehem CDP	4,214	-	-	4,227	97.5	0.0	1.3	0.4	0.9	18.2	24.5	48.1	36.3	32.0	1,900	90.7
Beulaville town	1,293	1,293	0.0	1,533	72.4	21.5	0.0	2.0	4.0	20.0	28.0	46.6	47.9	18.0	748	71.7
Biltmore Forest town	1,343	1,416	5.4	1,473	94.9	0.0	1.4	3.0	0.7	21.3	33.9	55.3	4.1	81.7	605	97.5
Biscoe town	1,742	1,716	-1.5	2,334	25.1	18.0	0.3	2.2	54.3	40.1	10.5	24.4	69.9	10.3	600	86.5
Black Creek town	767	770	0.4	890	62.7	29.9	0.0	0.0	7.4	29.9	14.3	36.4	63.5	8.8	292	87.3
Black Mountain town	7,846	8,162	4.0	8,144	88.6	6.9	1.1	2.3	1.1	13.6	29.6	54.0	30.7	49.5	3,913	88.0
Bladenboro town	1,748	1,613	-7.7	1,659	64.6	28.0	0.0	3.9	3.6	29.2	15.4	37.6	53.3	9.0	655	87.8
Blowing Rock town	1,247	1,324	6.2	1,163	95.3	2.3	1.3	1.1	0.0	6.2	43.3	63.0	13.5	65.3	619	94.7
Blue Clay Farms CDP	33	-	-	6	0.0	100.0	0.0	0.0	0.0	0.0	0.0	0.0	33.3	0.0	4	100.0
Boardman town	157	152	-3.2	275	50.2	22.2	0.0	12.4	15.3	21.1	20.0	35.2	67.7	8.6	80	80.0
Bogue town	686	703	2.5	643	88.8	0.9	0.6	3.4	6.2	19.3	22.6	52.2	41.5	17.5	279	97.1
Boiling Spring Lakes city	5,370	6,287	17.1	6,021	78.0	4.7	0.1	5.6	11.6	24.8	13.9	40.0	38.9	16.2	2,274	97.1
Boiling Springs town	4,648	4,535	-2.4	4,565	86.2	7.8	0.9	1.2	3.9	21.1	13.4	23.0	28.7	42.4	1,144	86.8
Bolivia town	143	154	7.7	195	99.0	0.0	0.0	1.0	0.0	13.3	29.2	43.7	42.9	9.8	71	95.8
Bolton town	687	641	-6.7	648	24.7	63.1	2.0	3.7	6.5	23.1	19.4	43.1	58.9	3.0	254	78.3
Bonnetsville CDP	443	-	-	506	35.4	14.8	3.0	0.0	46.8	23.3	14.8	33.7	79.4	3.8	201	89.6
Boone town	17,118	19,667	14.9	19,119	89.7	2.4	1.2	1.7	5.0	5.9	6.8	21.2	24.0	46.2	5,905	94.2
Boonville town	1,176	1,143	-2.8	1,077	84.3	12.3	0.0	1.1	2.2	20.1	24.0	46.4	32.7	25.8	522	86.4
Bostic town	385	379	-1.6	302	88.7	7.0	1.7	2.0	0.7	9.9	25.5	52.7	51.0	8.3	163	71.2
Bowmore CDP	103	-	-	70	54.3	7.1	0.0	25.7	12.9	25.7	24.3	34.7	28.8	0.0	52	71.2
Brevard city	7,680	7,926	3.2	7,824	84.7	10.7	0.0	2.9	1.7	14.1	30.9	51.8	31.0	35.2	3,530	89.0
Brices Creek CDP	3,073	-	-	4,342	75.1	11.2	3.8	5.6	4.3	32.7	14.7	35.7	24.3	44.7	1,381	99.3
Bridgeton town	470	441	-6.2	346	68.2	16.5	0.0	0.0	15.3	19.7	18.8	40.5	37.2	37.9	170	94.7
Broad Creek CDP	2,334	-	-	2,548	84.2	2.7	0.0	7.6	5.5	17.9	18.6	45.8	39.9	20.1	999	91.0
Broadway town	1,206	1,286	6.6	1,376	70.3	10.7	4.0	4.9	10.1	15.6	23.3	46.0	39.0	22.3	544	83.8
Brogden CDP	2,633	-	-	2,279	28.0	55.5	0.0	0.5	15.9	17.3	25.8	54.1	62.9	9.4	956	78.1
Brookford town	380	380	0.0	481	83.8	1.5	0.0	5.0	9.8	19.1	17.7	44.5	62.2	4.9	184	81.0
Brunswick town	1,005	933	-7.2	983	22.9	69.4	1.5	4.3	1.9	10.9	8.3	33.9	65.7	6.5	172	80.2
Bryson City town	1,422	1,452	2.1	1,723	78.1	0.0	0.0	10.8	11.1	22.1	20.4	40.7	45.6	24.0	654	76.9
Buies Creek CDP	2,942	-	-	2,585	74.7	11.3	7.0	1.2	5.9	3.4	2.4	20.6	5.0	70.3	531	98.5
Bunn town	343	385	12.2	298	64.1	25.2	0.0	6.4	4.4	22.5	23.5	43.7	48.1	14.2	135	71.9
Bunnlevel CDP	552	-	-	611	41.6	53.2	0.0	0.5	4.7	11.1	15.1	44.9	64.2	8.7	297	79.5
Burgaw town	3,854	4,149	7.7	4,080	47.2	40.7	0.3	3.3	8.5	15.3	19.3	43.7	49.7	19.0	1,249	76.5
Burlington city	51,079	54,606	6.9	53,063	47.8	27.6	3.2	2.1	19.3	22.6	17.2	38.9	43.6	25.4	22,009	88.1
Burnsville town	1,695	1,647	-2.8	1,903	84.7	5.3	0.2	3.7	6.1	19.7	25.0	42.9	40.9	26.5	822	79.8
Butner town	7,589	7,859	3.6	7,727	50.1	30.9	1.4	4.4	13.2	21.4	19.1	42.6	52.4	15.5	2,865	87.8
Butters CDP	294	-	-	199	100.0	0.0	0.0	0.0	0.0	0.0	36.2	55.9	45.2	0.0	125	90.4
Buxton CDP	1,273	-	-	1,503	77.7	0.0	0.0	6.2	16.1	28.1	12.0	34.0	27.6	25.4	572	100.0
Cajah's Mountain town	2,776	2,737	-1.4	2,735	94.7	0.9	0.0	1.0	3.4	18.9	23.0	48.9	50.3	15.2	1,184	81.9
Calabash town	1,786	2,270	27.1	1,710	81.7	3.0	0.5	12.7	2.1	16.9	33.0	55.3	44.0	18.4	812	85.3
Calypso town	530	526	-0.8	605	41.0	18.8	0.0	6.1	34.0	29.8	22.6	39.9	46.2	4.9	251	78.5
Camden CDP	599	-	-	809	77.1	22.9	0.0	0.0	0.0	13.7	8.2	39.9	36.0	21.1	274	91.2
Cameron town	284	341	20.1	394	55.1	27.7	0.0	0.0	17.3	27.2	12.4	36.8	36.4	25.4	140	80.7
Candor town	841	817	-2.9	1,068	31.1	9.8	0.0	1.5	57.6	26.2	9.1	29.9	56.0	16.6	335	88.7
Canton town	4,209	4,347	3.3	4,277	93.3	0.4	0.0	1.2	5.1	21.7	17.0	40.2	38.2	13.7	1,775	82.4
Cape Carteret town	1,986	2,061	3.8	2,403	90.8	0.9	0.0	0.9	7.4	27.5	23.8	44.9	23.7	39.3	934	95.6
Caroleen CDP	652	-	-	668	90.0	10.0	0.0	0.0	0.0	6.9	25.6	52.9	61.6	26.4	335	62.1
Carolina Beach town	5,706	6,399	12.1	6,265	95.3	0.1	0.3	2.4	1.9	14.8	19.1	47.4	23.6	43.8	2,876	97.5
Carolina Shores town	3,356	4,659	38.8	4,163	96.9	1.4	0.0	1.5	0.2	9.1	46.1	64.0	36.5	27.0	1,882	95.4
Carrboro town	19,568	21,190	8.3	21,230	68.2	10.8	9.4	4.4	7.1	20.9	9.5	32.7	13.1	70.6	9,358	93.9
Carthage town	2,293	2,553	11.3	2,480	86.2	7.2	0.0	3.9	2.7	21.7	21.8	43.3	40.5	24.3	967	76.6
Cary town	135,840	170,282	25.4	166,268	62.8	8.4	18.7	3.0	7.2	25.3	12.2	39.9	13.6	67.8	62,789	97.9
Casar town	298	293	-1.7	269	97.0	0.0	0.0	0.0	3.0	25.7	23.0	36.9	64.6	12.9	95	61.1
Cashiers CDP	157	-	-	137	100.0	0.0	0.0	0.0	0.0	0.0	61.3	70.6	54.2	35.1	70	100.0
Castalia town	265	270	1.9	360	36.4	62.8	0.0	0.0	0.8	16.1	23.6	47.4	64.2	14.2	142	57.7
Castle Hayne CDP	1,202	-	-	1,027	82.7	5.4	1.9	1.6	8.5	16.0	31.4	55.1	47.3	16.8	559	72.8
Caswell Beach town	392	431	9.9	461	91.8	0.0	5.9	1.1	1.3	5.0	49.7	64.9	15.5	58.1	226	97.3
Catawba town	614	624	1.6	462	77.7	19.0	0.0	1.7	1.5	13.0	22.3	49.5	44.8	10.9	197	88.3
Cedar Point town	1,252	1,304	4.2	1,874	83.6	1.9	2.0	8.1	4.4	25.9	17.4	44.7	25.3	46.7	739	95.9
Cedar Rock village	303	300		254	100.0	0.0	0.0	0.0	0.0	18.1	33.5	55.4	11.4	46.5	109	95.4
Centerville CDP	89	-	-	359	96.1	3.9	0.0	0.0	0.0	29.8	9.5	30.6	39.7	11.2	103	86.4
Cerro Gordo town	212	195	-8.0	204	77.5	9.8	0.0	0.0	12.7	22.1	17.2	43.6	37.0	27.5	82	78.0
Chadbourn town	1,838	1,711	-6.9	2,005	27.7	68.8	0.0	3.1	0.3	22.9	14.5	37.1	61.1	9.8	797	79.0
Chapel Hill town	57,221	64,051	11.9	60,998	66.9	10.7	12.9	3.3	6.3	16.1	11.2	25.8	11.3	76.9	20,369	97.5
Charlotte city	735,607	885,708	20.4	857,425	41.5	34.6	6.5	3.1	14.3	23.7	10.2	34.2	28.0	44.3	330,391	94.0
Cherokee CDP	2,138	-	-	2,046	12.2	1.5	2.3	83.1	0.9	19.1	19.5	45.5	52.1	15.6	867	74.5
Cherryville city	5,740	6,072	5.8	5,956	88.9	6.6	0.2	1.8	2.6	23.6	21.8	43.2	46.5	16.9	2,434	80.5
Chimney Rock Village village	119	116	-2.5	177	79.7	0.0	0.0	11.9	8.5	21.5	33.3	49.0	36.5	38.0	81	95.1
China Grove town	4,162	4,220	1.4	4,189	84.1	2.0	1.9	3.6	8.4	21.2	16.1	39.7	53.1	15.0	1,696	84.4
Chocowinity town	780	788	1.0	1,089	41.1	43.1	0.0	1.0	14.8	28.8	13.3	30.9	41.1	11.4	498	80.5
Claremont city	1,357	1,408	3.8	1,643	87.2	3.4	2.8	2.4	4.1	23.5	19.8	44.3	42.6	24.3	685	86.4
Clarkton town	841	738	-12.2	819	51.2	47.3	0.0	0.4	1.2	27.5	19.2	35.9	40.0	11.9	313	82.1
Clayton town	16,219	24,887	53.4	21,681	57.3	24.6	0.7	3.0	14.3	27.5	10.4	34.4	30.2	31.2	7,488	95.3
Clemmons village	18,624	20,867	12.0	20,313	78.5	5.9	5.4	2.0	8.2	25.1	19.1	41.0	22.8	48.6	7,733	93.1
Cleveland town	856	872	1.9	1,191	61.1	31.7	0.0	0.3	6.9	31.0	9.2	32.3	43.6	17.7	392	92.3
Cliffside CDP	611	-	-	665	96.8	3.2	0.0	0.0	0.0	11.0	7.8	30.5	66.8	14.9	223	94.2
Clinton city	8,714	8,454	-3.0	8,504	41.9	39.5	1.1	5.0	12.5	24.1	20.8	40.2	49.2	22.6	3,213	76.0
Clyde town	1,229	1,304	6.1	1,160	90.9	0.3	0.0	0.0	8.9	19.1	22.2	38.6	31.0	23.0	509	89.2
Coats town	2,104	2,500	18.8	2,418	66.7	11.6	0.0	5.5	16.1	31.1	12.0	31.0	53.0	12.5	929	86.3
Cofield village	393	369	-6.1	390	13.6	70.3	0.5	4.1	11.5	15.6	20.3	51.4	52.6	22.6	151	82.1
Coinjock CDP	335	-	-	511	78.5	9.6	2.7	0.0	9.2	12.7	13.9	39.2	33.2	22.2	191	100.0
Colerain town	204	178	-12.7	302	74.2	19.2	0.7	0.7	5.3	23.2	16.2	35.8	48.1	22.3	123	88.6
Columbia town	854	759	-11.1	789	27.1	46.9	0.0	1.1	24.8	30.7	21.0	39.8	63.2	9.6	338	68.9

1 May be of any race.

Table A. All Places — **Population and Housing**

STATE City, town, township, borough, or CDP (county if applicable)	Population				Race and Hispanic or Latino origin (percent)					Age (percent)			Educational attainment of persons age 25 and older		Occupied housing units	
	2010 census total population	2019 estimated population	Percent change 2010–2019	ACS total population estimate 2015–2019	White alone, not Hispanic or Latino	Black alone, not Hispanic or Latino	Asian alone, not Hispanic or Latino	All other races or 2 or more races, not Hispanic or Latino	Hispanic or Latino[1]	Under 18 years old	Age 65 years and older	Median age	Percent High school diploma or less	Percent Bachelor's degree or more	Total	Percent with a computer
	1	2	3	4	5	6	7	8	9	10	11	12	13	14	15	16
NORTH CAROLINA—Con.																
Columbus town	999	998	-0.1	1,167	72.2	1.5	0.7	9.8	15.9	22.5	25.7	47.8	40.4	15.3	491	87.6
Como town	91	83	-8.8	104	80.8	12.5	0.0	6.7	0.0	9.6	15.4	44.0	42.2	6.0	43	69.8
Concord city	79,389	96,341	21.4	91,980	58.7	20.5	4.8	3.2	12.7	26.1	12.0	36.8	33.3	37.5	32,528	93.2
Conetoe town	291	266	-8.6	249	28.5	56.6	0.0	7.6	7.2	18.5	29.7	44.5	70.6	6.1	106	63.2
Connelly Springs town	1,650	1,644	-0.4	1,784	87.7	2.7	4.8	1.8	2.9	16.6	25.7	49.0	63.2	14.8	727	77.0
Conover city	8,301	8,540	2.9	8,452	66.8	7.7	15.1	2.4	8.0	26.1	17.8	40.2	40.5	19.1	3,346	88.6
Conway town	834	729	-12.6	745	36.5	59.5	0.4	1.6	2.0	32.8	12.1	29.6	61.0	17.1	306	81.7
Cooleemee town	974	983	0.9	1,040	76.1	5.2	2.5	14.8	1.4	27.2	14.3	33.3	45.4	13.5	379	85.5
Cordova CDP	1,775	-	-	1,473	80.8	14.3	0.0	5.0	0.0	5.3	22.1	49.1	54.7	22.9	750	87.2
Cornelius town	24,907	30,257	21.5	29,256	79.0	8.5	2.3	1.7	8.4	23.0	15.0	41.3	16.6	53.5	12,307	97.1
Cove City town	399	388	-2.8	449	58.6	38.3	0.0	0.4	2.7	25.8	21.8	39.8	51.1	12.2	192	68.8
Cove Creek CDP	1,171	-	-	999	96.7	0.0	0.0	0.0	3.3	21.2	20.7	44.8	33.0	41.2	447	79.2
Cramerton town	4,177	4,458	6.7	4,359	85.5	5.3	3.0	3.5	2.8	23.4	12.1	40.4	32.0	37.0	1,637	93.3
Creedmoor city	4,105	4,612	12.4	4,501	61.4	26.8	0.7	3.9	7.2	27.2	13.6	36.9	32.9	38.5	1,669	99.0
Creswell town	270	234	-13.3	189	54.5	33.3	0.0	0.0	12.2	30.2	19.0	38.6	59.7	11.8	79	82.3
Cricket CDP	1,855	-	-	1,949	76.3	0.3	0.0	0.8	22.6	22.2	15.4	43.2	58.1	11.8	805	76.3
Crossnore town	191	239	25.1	131	84.7	9.2	0.0	6.1	0.0	70.2	10.7	17.0	17.9	41.0	18	100.0
Cullowhee CDP	6,228	-	-	6,377	80.5	10.6	1.0	1.6	6.4	4.3	1.4	20.5	23.6	55.1	1,269	95.0
Dallas town	4,468	4,797	7.4	4,696	66.5	17.6	0.8	2.5	12.6	26.4	10.4	39.3	59.0	10.8	1,833	84.8
Dana CDP	3,329	-	-	3,919	64.0	4.2	1.1	0.9	29.7	29.5	16.6	35.5	54.1	11.5	1,524	76.2
Danbury town	189	183	-3.2	164	83.5	7.9	4.3	4.3	0.0	6.7	18.3	46.1	33.1	40.2	46	84.8
Davidson town	10,904	13,054	19.7	12,735	85.6	5.4	1.3	2.1	5.6	24.7	14.1	37.2	9.4	73.4	4,336	97.0
Davis CDP	422	-	-	285	100.0	0.0	0.0	0.0	0.0	26.7	28.1	40.9	39.7	14.8	124	91.1
Deercroft CDP	411	-	-	482	89.2	0.0	2.5	8.3	0.0	16.4	24.9	45.7	29.3	26.6	175	100.0
Delco CDP	348	-	-	250	37.2	0.0	0.0	14.4	48.4	15.6	26.4	53.1	57.4	10.3	95	61.1
Delway CDP	203	-	-	39	66.7	33.3	0.0	0.0	0.0	0.0	100.0	75.6	66.7	0.0	24	100.0
Denton town	1,638	1,680	2.6	1,660	94.8	0.0	1.6	2.3	1.4	26.7	18.0	39.4	56.4	15.2	671	77.3
Denver CDP	2,309	-	-	3,261	83.5	4.9	5.7	2.8	3.2	23.2	16.7	41.8	34.1	23.8	1,347	97.1
Dillsboro town	232	248	6.9	213	86.4	0.9	0.0	12.2	0.5	13.1	29.6	44.1	18.7	57.9	112	93.8
Dobbins Heights town	865	839	-3.0	874	10.4	86.8	0.0	0.1	2.6	18.6	19.5	41.8	57.3	7.4	404	66.8
Dobson town	1,588	1,539	-3.1	1,646	76.7	8.1	0.7	1.5	13.1	17.4	23.6	39.4	43.7	20.3	657	75.2
Dortches town	959	963	0.4	921	74.4	20.7	0.0	4.3	0.5	22.3	24.1	47.8	41.3	27.5	354	89.3
Dover town	401	386	-3.7	240	47.1	47.9	0.0	2.5	2.5	12.5	26.7	54.1	55.5	15.2	123	70.7
Drexel town	1,884	1,854	-1.6	1,862	84.6	3.7	5.2	1.2	5.3	15.3	20.1	45.0	47.8	17.6	788	83.6
Dublin town	338	315	-6.8	412	59.5	30.3	0.2	0.0	10.0	27.2	23.5	34.5	39.9	6.7	137	92.7
Duck town	377	396	5.0	583	97.8	0.0	0.3	0.7	1.2	9.1	45.8	62.8	13.0	58.8	288	97.2
Dundarrach CDP	41	-	-	75	100.0	0.0	0.0	0.0	0.0	0.0	22.7	48.7	88.0	0.0	28	100.0
Dunn city	9,274	9,718	4.8	9,664	49.7	40.8	0.3	2.5	6.7	22.8	22.1	41.4	52.6	16.8	4,031	84.1
Durham city	229,892	278,993	21.4	269,702	39.5	38.0	5.3	3.4	13.8	21.7	11.6	33.9	28.4	49.6	109,555	92.7
Earl town	260	260	0.0	269	93.7	1.9	0.0	2.6	1.9	15.6	18.2	52.1	58.2	5.6	108	84.3
East Arcadia town	496	467	-5.8	460	0.0	93.9	0.0	6.1	0.0	24.3	11.7	30.7	54.2	7.0	181	87.3
East Bend town	623	601	-3.5	706	94.2	0.0	0.0	0.0	5.8	23.2	12.6	35.5	40.9	17.0	242	87.2
East Flat Rock CDP	4,995	-	-	5,647	63.7	5.3	1.4	0.3	29.2	24.1	12.9	35.7	56.8	13.3	2,057	83.2
East Laurinburg town	304	279	-8.2	336	60.1	19.9	0.0	15.5	4.5	24.4	13.4	33.6	75.9	2.5	128	69.5
Eastover town	3,626	3,762	3.8	3,710	74.7	12.0	0.0	8.2	5.1	26.9	22.9	43.0	45.3	23.6	1,346	88.6
East Rockingham CDP	3,736	-	-	3,086	61.8	22.7	0.0	2.4	13.0	27.8	15.2	41.0	62.3	5.3	1,237	72.7
East Spencer town	1,543	1,551	0.5	1,336	13.0	69.0	0.0	3.7	14.3	20.4	18.1	38.1	59.5	7.7	527	71.3
Eden city	15,698	14,886	-5.2	15,055	61.8	24.4	2.0	2.9	8.8	21.1	20.0	43.1	54.3	17.3	6,581	80.6
Edenton town	5,001	4,614	-7.7	4,676	36.4	60.4	0.0	1.3	2.0	22.5	25.0	41.6	47.0	22.5	2,084	81.1
Edneyville CDP	2,367	-	-	2,549	75.4	2.9	1.2	0.0	20.4	28.2	12.2	34.7	47.2	24.6	868	89.9
Efland CDP	734	-	-	668	42.5	55.1	2.4	0.0	0.0	7.5	19.5	48.7	42.9	21.4	279	87.1
Elizabeth City city	18,643	17,751	-4.8	17,629	37.6	50.1	1.3	2.9	8.0	24.4	15.1	33.6	42.9	24.6	6,526	85.8
Elizabethtown town	3,644	3,378	-7.3	3,464	52.7	42.4	0.0	1.0	3.9	19.1	23.4	44.1	48.2	24.9	1,482	77.9
Elkin town	4,025	4,011	-0.3	4,097	78.7	4.2	1.5	2.2	13.3	24.5	21.2	39.4	46.5	20.7	1,618	78.9
Elk Park town	451	444	-1.6	744	97.3	0.7	0.8	0.0	1.2	24.1	7.8	31.8	50.8	7.0	328	90.9
Ellenboro town	847	832	-1.8	684	87.7	11.3	0.4	0.6	0.0	23.1	15.4	39.0	56.3	11.4	274	78.1
Ellerbe town	1,021	978	-4.2	961	57.2	30.9	0.0	2.2	9.7	27.7	10.8	34.6	49.3	15.7	398	88.7
Elm City town	1,302	1,292	-0.8	1,445	26.8	55.5	1.2	3.0	13.5	24.4	21.8	44.3	62.0	11.7	547	79.5
Elon town	9,383	12,232	30.4	11,516	81.9	7.2	3.1	1.8	6.1	10.4	19.7	22.0	20.3	54.1	3,465	90.3
Elrod CDP	417	-	-	825	2.3	1.9	0.0	95.8	0.0	53.3	10.4	16.1	64.5	14.7	220	86.4
Elroy CDP	3,869	-	-	3,949	57.5	25.9	2.2	2.5	12.0	24.1	15.1	37.2	47.8	10.3	1,541	90.9
Emerald Isle town	3,658	3,695	1.0	3,703	94.3	0.1	0.0	4.0	1.5	13.3	30.1	55.2	20.9	48.5	1,769	97.6
Enfield town	2,537	2,274	-10.4	2,524	8.2	89.9	0.0	1.9	0.0	24.2	16.2	34.8	72.1	7.0	1,069	67.5
Engelhard CDP	445	-	-	413	75.5	0.0	0.0	4.4	20.1	39.0	11.9	18.7	100.0	0.0	120	100.0
Enochville CDP	2,925	-	-	3,232	90.1	0.4	0.0	0.8	8.7	22.4	19.6	43.3	54.0	8.7	1,235	87.6
Erwin town	4,535	5,156	13.7	5,035	66.7	20.1	0.1	3.3	9.9	20.7	20.3	43.8	56.3	11.0	1,890	87.1
Etowah CDP	6,944	-	-	7,653	88.4	2.7	1.3	4.4	3.2	15.8	32.9	54.0	38.5	26.1	3,411	92.4
Eureka town	195	196	0.5	187	70.6	20.3	0.0	0.5	8.6	19.8	26.2	46.9	40.4	17.0	81	79.0
Everetts town	155	142	-8.4	99	64.6	19.2	0.0	0.0	16.2	26.3	23.2	50.1	80.9	1.5	40	75.0
Evergreen CDP	420	-	-	164	78.0	22.0	0.0	0.0	0.0	15.9	45.1	63.1	41.7	0.0	74	77.0
Fair Bluff town	949	881	-7.2	545	37.1	58.5	0.0	3.3	1.1	8.4	36.1	56.3	55.9	17.6	297	70.0
Fairfield CDP	258	-	-	265	40.0	60.0	0.0	0.0	0.0	9.8	52.5	71.1	69.5	7.1	102	69.6
Fairfield Harbour CDP	2,952	-	-	2,770	91.9	4.5	0.7	1.3	1.6	9.2	54.8	67.1	25.4	39.6	1,342	95.5
Fairmont town	2,705	2,597	-4.0	2,641	23.7	63.3	0.0	11.7	1.2	21.9	22.2	47.8	56.2	16.0	1,046	74.0
Fairplains CDP	2,120	-	-	2,065	66.7	15.6	1.6	1.7	14.3	14.2	21.1	47.1	60.7	16.2	974	72.4
Fairview CDP	2,678	-	-	2,878	84.6	0.0	0.0	1.3	14.0	23.8	21.1	37.7	29.1	31.7	1,030	90.1
Fairview town	3,343	3,900	16.7	3,768	96.2	0.0	0.4	0.6	2.8	22.5	19.2	48.2	39.7	24.8	1,451	88.2
Faison town	958	956	-0.2	1,321	43.2	8.9	0.0	1.9	46.0	35.8	15.0	30.9	43.1	22.2	401	90.5
Faith town	792	806	1.8	817	96.9	2.6	0.0	0.0	0.5	25.1	15.5	40.1	38.5	31.1	309	86.7
Falcon town	267	270	1.1	197	75.6	2.0	0.0	11.2	11.2	37.1	14.7	31.3	39.0	26.3	65	92.3
Falkland town	96	98	2.1	80	10.0	65.0	0.0	0.0	25.0	32.5	13.8	42.2	60.0	4.0	31	58.1
Fallston town	607	605	-0.3	509	89.8	7.9	0.4	2.0	0.0	14.9	34.2	51.7	41.9	14.4	215	69.8
Farmville town	4,652	4,764	2.4	4,712	50.1	46.2	0.0	1.9	1.7	27.5	16.3	35.7	37.2	26.3	1,813	87.3
Fayetteville city	200,565	211,657	5.5	210,432	37.5	41.0	2.7	6.3	12.4	23.5	11.6	30.0	32.7	27.2	80,956	90.7
Fearrington Village CDP	2,339	-	-	2,867	96.3	1.0	0.2	2.2	0.3	9.5	71.3	72.1	7.6	77.8	1,663	95.5
Five Points CDP	689	-	-	963	72.3	19.0	0.8	7.0	0.9	22.2	16.8	33.0	22.3	30.3	323	84.5
Flat Rock village	3,116	3,383	8.6	3,328	99.1	0.0	0.1	0.3	0.6	10.8	49.0	63.7	9.3	62.7	1,590	97.9
Flat Rock CDP	1,556	-	-	1,072	90.3	9.2	0.0	0.5	0.0	13.0	16.4	44.8	54.6	10.4	516	73.8
Fletcher town	7,212	8,369	16.0	8,117	87.3	4.1	3.8	0.0	4.8	21.6	15.7	41.3	27.8	37.6	3,468	90.5
Fontana Dam town	7	7	0.0	27	81.5	0.0	0.0	18.5	0.0	25.9	0.0	38.9	65.0	0.0	15	100.0
Forest City town	7,472	7,162	-4.1	7,155	63.4	27.6	0.4	1.6	7.0	27.3	17.3	36.9	41.5	18.1	3,128	77.2
Forest Hills village	353	374	5.9	304	96.7	0.7	0.0	1.3	1.3	13.5	24.3	39.5	4.1	73.1	144	88.9

1 May be of any race.

Table A. All Places — **Population and Housing**

STATE City, town, township, borough, or CDP (county if applicable)	Population: 2010 census total population	Population: 2019 estimated population	Population: Percent change 2010–2019	Population: ACS total population estimate 2015–2019	Race and Hispanic or Latino origin (percent): White alone, not Hispanic or Latino	Black alone, not Hispanic or Latino	Asian alone, not Hispanic or Latino	All other races or 2 or more races, not Hispanic or Latino	Hispanic or Latino[1]	Age (percent): Under 18 years old	Age 65 years and older	Median age	Educational attainment of persons age 25 and older: Percent High school diploma or less	Percent Bachelor's degree or more	Occupied housing units: Total	Percent with a computer
	1	2	3	4	5	6	7	8	9	10	11	12	13	14	15	16
NORTH CAROLINA—Con.																
Forest Oaks CDP	3,890	-	-	4,108	84.9	10.2	0.6	4.0	0.3	20.6	24.0	48.4	21.7	45.2	1,473	96.5
Foscoe CDP	1,370	-	-	1,579	98.2	0.0	0.0	1.6	0.2	12.3	26.2	45.4	28.7	40.1	832	85.7
Fountain town	427	435	1.9	351	51.3	39.3	0.0	1.4	8.0	23.4	21.4	45.5	66.1	14.6	158	61.4
Four Oaks town	1,943	2,254	16.0	2,144	53.6	30.1	2.4	2.9	11.0	25.1	10.7	36.3	53.8	21.4	780	84.1
Foxfire village	916	1,042	13.8	1,434	72.3	13.0	1.8	9.5	3.3	19.3	29.4	48.2	21.0	42.7	646	93.5
Franklin town	3,880	4,105	5.8	3,980	73.5	1.7	0.4	2.0	22.4	22.7	22.9	45.1	43.5	25.1	1,817	80.4
Franklinton town	2,010	2,241	11.5	2,260	46.2	42.0	0.0	2.7	9.2	26.3	17.0	37.6	57.0	12.9	883	78.7
Franklinville town	1,172	1,187	1.3	1,798	39.1	8.7	0.0	1.9	50.3	42.4	4.4	25.0	74.6	4.0	516	90.3
Fremont town	1,279	1,262	-1.3	948	60.8	34.4	0.0	0.1	4.7	15.1	24.2	53.7	58.5	15.9	426	75.4
Frisco CDP	200	-	-	104	85.6	0.0	0.0	14.4	0.0	0.0	40.4	60.9	21.3	52.8	76	81.6
Fruitland CDP	2,031	-	-	2,373	70.4	3.9	2.4	0.0	23.3	20.9	28.4	44.4	40.2	26.1	1,026	76.4
Fuquay-Varina town	18,021	30,324	68.3	27,426	70.4	15.1	2.0	2.9	9.6	29.1	13.1	35.8	28.2	43.7	9,494	93.6
Gamewell town	4,043	3,996	-1.2	3,987	88.8	3.6	0.0	3.0	4.6	16.2	17.5	39.1	54.6	8.2	1,545	82.0
Garland town	624	617	-1.1	905	36.8	25.7	0.0	1.9	35.6	35.1	17.2	27.3	63.4	6.3	290	82.1
Garner town	25,769	31,407	21.9	29,462	58.2	27.5	2.5	2.6	9.1	22.2	14.6	37.6	28.2	39.3	11,642	95.3
Garysburg town	1,053	918	-12.8	880	1.0	97.0	0.0	1.9	0.0	22.7	19.0	44.4	57.6	11.2	414	70.3
Gaston town	1,151	1,020	-11.4	1,358	44.0	47.9	0.2	2.3	5.6	23.1	22.5	43.8	68.7	7.0	567	67.0
Gastonia city	71,720	77,273	7.7	75,887	56.2	28.3	1.9	3.3	10.2	24.3	15.6	38.4	43.2	24.2	28,973	88.6
Gatesville town	321	299	-6.9	275	91.3	8.4	0.4	0.0	0.0	25.8	20.0	46.5	37.4	18.7	120	88.3
Germanton CDP	827	-	-	955	100.0	0.0	0.0	0.0	0.0	11.8	29.7	55.4	67.1	16.9	448	69.4
Gerton CDP	254	-	-	303	100.0	0.0	0.0	0.0	0.0	3.3	46.9	58.1	51.3	35.5	172	73.8
Gibson town	540	500	-7.4	471	37.8	44.8	0.0	16.6	0.8	24.6	20.2	40.1	50.9	11.1	201	78.1
Gibsonville town	6,501	7,339	12.9	7,127	64.0	28.2	1.0	2.9	3.9	25.9	13.7	38.3	36.5	31.8	2,481	93.6
Glen Alpine town	1,501	1,483	-1.2	1,658	80.5	1.8	9.2	4.9	3.6	19.1	16.5	41.6	56.8	12.8	635	88.0
Glen Raven CDP	2,750	-	-	3,495	68.8	12.3	1.3	0.4	17.2	27.5	12.5	33.7	37.1	23.0	1,210	88.3
Glenville CDP	110	-	-	43	100.0	0.0	0.0	0.0	0.0	0.0	39.5	53.9	32.6	48.8	31	100.0
Gloucester CDP	537	-	-	525	100.0	0.0	0.0	0.0	0.0	23.8	15.4	41.4	51.3	20.0	186	97.3
Godwin town	139	143	2.9	93	50.5	44.1	0.0	1.1	4.3	12.9	29.0	52.8	48.7	20.5	45	71.1
Goldsboro city	35,425	34,186	-3.5	34,647	34.4	52.3	2.7	5.0	5.7	21.2	16.4	36.0	44.6	20.3	14,404	81.9
Goldston town	260	301	15.8	245	88.6	5.3	0.4	4.1	1.6	27.8	21.6	35.8	41.8	12.7	107	73.8
Gorman CDP	1,011	-	-	1,145	54.0	8.0	0.0	0.0	38.0	23.5	19.0	47.1	73.5	13.6	311	83.3
Graham city	14,315	15,646	9.3	14,925	50.6	27.4	0.3	4.1	17.6	25.9	17.3	38.1	46.9	19.7	6,412	87.6
Grandfather village	25	24	-4.0	68	100.0	0.0	0.0	0.0	0.0	5.9	58.8	66.3	1.7	91.5	29	100.0
Granite Falls town	4,704	4,659		4,628	85.7	2.5	1.1	2.5	8.2	23.1	21.0	42.3	40.9	27.2	1,799	90.6
Granite Quarry town	2,960	3,012	1.8	2,989	88.0	7.5	0.0	1.2	3.3	30.7	10.6	30.4	36.6	23.5	1,013	95.4
Grantsboro town	681	652	-4.3	609	79.6	7.4	0.0	4.6	8.4	20.0	14.6	41.7	49.9	11.5	247	96.8
Greenevers town	638	647	1.4	666	1.5	94.9	0.0	0.6	3.0	10.2	20.4	48.7	53.4	10.0	293	65.5
Green Level town	2,108	2,326	10.3	2,129	18.2	52.8	0.0	1.4	27.5	23.3	17.5	37.4	59.0	7.7	781	80.4
Greensboro city	268,936	296,710	10.3	291,303	42.6	41.0	5.0	3.6	7.9	21.8	13.7	35.1	31.7	38.2	116,309	86.8
Greenville city	84,711	93,400	10.3	91,921	50.4	38.8	2.5	3.7	4.7	18.2	10.2	27.3	30.1	37.7	36,926	90.2
Grifton town	2,611	2,682	2.7	2,732	41.2	42.2	0.0	1.1	15.6	21.6	12.9	41.2	49.1	13.8	1,103	81.7
Grimesland town	426	442	3.8	454	60.4	28.4	0.0	6.2	5.1	15.9	19.6	52.9	57.4	15.7	193	73.1
Grover town	708	704	-0.6	638	84.3	11.1	3.0	0.0	1.6	23.5	27.4	47.2	51.1	10.3	272	79.8
Gulf CDP	144	-	-	157	100.0	0.0	0.0	0.0	0.0	29.3	0.0	34.6	0.0	100.0	55	100.0
Half Moon CDP	8,352	-	-	8,243	60.7	23.2	2.0	7.8	6.3	26.3	10.4	31.4	42.6	20.1	2,769	96.0
Halifax town	227	204	-10.1	170	70.0	29.4	0.0	0.6	0.0	28.8	13.5	27.8	31.6	30.5	82	78.0
Hallsboro CDP	465	-	-	450	22.2	77.8	0.0	0.0	0.0	2.2	57.6	70.6	72.0	5.0	204	52.0
Hamilton town	404	370	-8.4	275	28.7	61.1	0.0	10.2	0.0	13.8	32.7	52.3	58.5	9.8	129	70.5
Hamlet city	6,565	6,328	-3.6	6,331	46.1	46.0	1.2	3.1	3.6	25.6	15.3	39.5	50.3	14.9	2,462	81.4
Hampstead CDP	4,083	-	-	5,901	89.4	3.7	0.4	4.1	2.4	25.2	22.2	42.8	24.1	41.5	1,946	93.9
Harkers Island CDP	1,207	-	-	1,260	95.3	1.6	0.0	0.0	3.1	15.1	33.6	52.9	42.0	24.6	550	82.9
Harmony town	531	595	12.1	541	94.5	2.6	0.0	0.0	3.0	26.4	17.7	39.5	58.3	11.8	199	85.9
Harrells town	202	197	-2.5	227	50.2	33.5	0.0	10.6	5.7	18.5	26.0	34.5	49.7	20.4	83	81.9
Harrellsville town	107	98	-8.4	149	75.2	22.8	0.0	0.0	2.0	29.5	8.7	36.9	50.5	23.2	47	87.2
Harrisburg town	13,439	16,576	23.3	15,806	61.5	18.7	10.6	5.3	3.9	28.7	9.4	36.7	20.3	48.3	4,865	98.5
Hassell town	84	76	-9.5	16	18.8	81.3	0.0	0.0	0.0	0.0	18.8	56.3	62.5	0.0	11	100.0
Hatteras CDP	504	-	-	460	98.7	0.0	0.0	0.2	1.1	13.9	42.8	53.9	25.6	43.8	207	100.0
Havelock city	20,792	19,854	-4.5	20,086	59.4	20.8	2.0	4.4	13.5	24.1	5.3	23.7	33.8	16.3	6,187	97.5
Haw River town	2,297	2,535	10.4	2,458	66.7	5.0	0.1	0.7	27.4	25.2	17.5	35.4	49.4	10.8	945	88.4
Hayesville town	455	483	6.2	387	89.7	1.0	0.5	1.3	7.5	27.1	19.4	41.1	53.2	20.8	161	96.3
Hays CDP	1,851	-	-	1,277	94.3	1.3	0.0	0.0	4.5	17.7	31.9	44.5	65.1	7.9	609	75.5
Hemby Bridge town	1,554	1,809	16.4	1,978	74.3	2.4	1.1	1.7	20.5	28.3	14.2	37.4	51.1	17.9	618	94.5
Henderson city	15,413	14,911	-3.3	14,948	23.4	66.7	1.4	1.7	6.8	25.5	16.5	35.9	57.1	16.8	5,715	78.2
Hendersonville city	13,121	14,157	7.9	13,908	81.1	6.6	2.0	3.1	7.2	16.8	32.3	52.1	29.8	35.6	7,274	84.6
Henrietta CDP	461	-	-	604	21.5	39.9	0.0	0.0	38.6	22.5	13.9	30.5	91.6	0.0	132	73.5
Hertford town	2,142	2,113	-1.4	2,321	62.0	30.7	0.0	1.4	5.9	23.7	23.5	37.7	49.5	13.0	1,045	69.7
Hickory city	40,035	41,171	2.8	40,634	67.0	12.4	5.0	2.8	12.8	22.3	16.9	38.1	37.4	33.3	16,690	87.7
Hiddenite CDP	536	-	-	266	68.4	0.0	0.0	0.0	31.6	4.5	0.0	43.3	81.0	0.0	132	75.8
Highlands town	930	982	5.6	1,164	87.6	1.6	1.5	2.1	7.1	11.9	37.7	59.4	23.2	46.5	639	91.9
High Point city	104,526	112,791	7.9	111,714	43.2	35.3	7.6	3.8	10.1	24.1	14.7	36.2	39.3	31.3	41,360	89.7
High Shoals city	705	748	6.1	671	94.2	2.8	0.9	1.8	0.3	24.7	21.6	42.6	66.6	5.4	298	73.8
Hightsville CDP	739	-	-	977	71.2	18.8	0.0	7.3	2.7	6.3	13.9	41.2	49.1	17.4	280	100.0
Hildebran town	2,026	2,010	-0.8	1,834	93.8	3.0	0.4	2.1	0.8	20.6	24.1	46.8	58.7	14.4	822	72.0
Hillsborough town	6,599	7,161	8.5	7,115	60.4	20.7	3.6	4.5	11.0	21.0	15.5	39.7	27.2	52.2	2,739	88.8
Hobgood town	349	317	-9.2	291	48.8	30.9	0.0	0.0	20.3	22.3	17.5	37.8	52.0	15.8	109	76.1
Hobucken CDP	129	-	-	38	100.0	0.0	0.0	0.0	0.0	63.2	0.0	11.2	50.0	0.0	7	100.0
Hoffman town	578	572		701	29.1	59.6	0.0	9.3	2.0	30.4	12.6	32.9	49.5	6.0	229	78.2
Holden Beach town	575	664	15.5	1,137	97.0	0.4	0.0	1.0	1.7	17.8	34.4	57.6	11.5	60.9	472	98.3
Hollister CDP	674	-	-	689	3.8	21.0	1.7	71.0	2.5	23.4	20.5	40.6	53.2	7.2	275	73.1
Holly Ridge town	1,279	2,827	121.0	2,421	80.0	4.1	0.5	5.8	9.7	22.5	10.9	30.9	25.2	43.5	981	97.2
Holly Springs town	24,739	37,812	52.8	34,874	73.3	11.7	2.8	5.3	7.0	33.3	7.5	35.5	15.8	58.1	11,202	96.3
Hookerton town	408	388	-4.9	499	48.3	47.9	0.0	1.0	2.8	25.7	20.8	40.6	60.6	6.8	185	79.5
Hoopers Creek CDP	1,056	-	-	1,088	97.6	0.0	0.0	0.0	2.4	14.8	22.5	53.0	39.2	18.6	487	93.0
Hope Mills town	15,088	15,849	5.0	15,769	49.4	31.6	2.2	8.1	8.7	28.3	9.5	33.2	33.6	22.2	5,759	92.9
Horse Shoe CDP	2,351	-	-	2,368	95.7	2.4	0.0	0.9	1.0	17.9	32.4	52.0	28.5	33.0	973	89.8
Hot Springs town	558	577	3.4	532	94.5	0.0	0.0	0.0	5.5	20.1	21.8	43.8	46.4	27.7	223	82.1
Hudson town	3,770	3,709	-1.6	3,701	84.6	0.1	0.0	2.3	13.0	25.9	15.3	39.3	44.9	18.8	1,527	90.8
Huntersville town	46,909	58,098	23.9	55,980	75.3	12.4	2.8	2.8	6.7	27.9	10.2	37.4	16.6	55.8	20,074	96.8
Icard CDP	2,664	-	-	2,380	78.7	0.4	18.2	0.1	2.6	20.0	14.2	38.9	59.6	7.6	929	88.3
Indian Beach town	115	119	3.5	185	97.3	2.7	0.0	0.0	0.0	5.9	49.2	64.8	27.2	46.2	96	100.0
Indian Trail town	33,619	40,252	19.7	38,822	74.2	8.9	1.9	3.7	11.3	30.3	9.4	34.7	30.6	36.6	12,743	96.9
Ingold CDP	471	-	-	676	20.0	8.6	0.0	0.0	71.4	57.7	4.7	12.3	49.0	5.6	172	100.0

1 May be of any race.

Table A. All Places — **Population and Housing**

STATE City, town, township, borough, or CDP (county if applicable)	Population: 2010 census total population	Population: 2019 estimated population	Population: Percent change 2010–2019	Population: ACS total population estimate 2015–2019	Race and Hispanic or Latino origin (percent): White alone, not Hispanic or Latino	Black alone, not Hispanic or Latino	Asian alone, not Hispanic or Latino	All other races or 2 or more races, not Hispanic or Latino	Hispanic or Latino[1]	Age (percent): Under 18 years old	Age 65 years and older	Median age	Educational attainment of persons age 25 and older: Percent High school diploma or less	Percent Bachelor's degree or more	Occupied housing units: Total	Percent with a computer
	1	2	3	4	5	6	7	8	9	10	11	12	13	14	15	16
NORTH CAROLINA—Con.																
Iron Station CDP	755	-	-	580	94.3	0.0	0.0	5.7	0.0	26.7	17.1	39.7	58.3	3.2	268	53.0
Ivanhoe CDP	264	-	-	326	9.2	85.9	0.0	0.0	4.9	42.9	23.6	31.4	83.9	0.0	94	85.1
JAARS CDP	597	-	-	443	100.0	0.0	0.0	0.0	0.0	28.0	12.2	42.6	13.8	57.4	194	96.4
Jackson town	511	454	-11.2	510	50.6	45.3	0.0	0.8	3.3	11.6	32.4	54.7	37.3	16.9	245	82.4
Jackson Heights CDP	1,141	-	-	694	67.0	12.7	0.0	0.0	20.3	8.8	34.0	54.8	82.0	0.0	318	61.0
Jacksonville city	70,327	72,436	3.0	73,025	57.1	15.7	3.0	6.8	17.3	20.8	6.2	23.1	34.8	24.1	20,979	95.0
James City CDP	5,899	-	-	5,354	80.0	8.7	1.3	2.4	7.6	23.1	18.7	44.6	37.9	23.0	2,144	88.9
Jamestown town	3,437	4,487	30.5	4,148	73.6	15.7	2.6	0.6	7.5	19.7	21.9	45.8	24.3	48.6	1,812	95.2
Jamesville town	491	447	-9.0	495	35.4	45.3	0.0	13.9	5.5	31.5	12.7	31.9	34.5	16.7	200	83.0
Jefferson town	1,600	1,533	-4.2	1,441	85.6	5.4	0.0	2.8	6.1	16.2	31.3	49.3	54.5	15.3	615	79.2
Jonesville town	2,285	2,215	-3.1	2,551	72.9	16.5	0.9	2.7	7.0	26.4	19.3	33.9	52.5	6.9	1,068	70.8
Kannapolis city	42,621	50,841	19.3	48,630	60.1	21.6	1.6	2.6	14.2	27.9	13.4	34.8	43.2	21.8	17,248	90.4
Keener CDP	567	-	-	144	55.6	44.4	0.0	0.0	0.0	0.0	55.6	71.0	71.5	5.6	125	67.2
Kelford town	251	222	-11.6	338	21.0	74.9	0.3	2.4	1.5	27.8	17.8	28.7	71.6	3.4	113	71.7
Kelly CDP	544	-	-	409	72.9	0.0	0.0	0.0	27.1	38.4	20.0	28.6	71.8	0.0	163	89.6
Kenansville town	852	841	-1.3	943	48.6	33.0	5.4	11.6	1.5	17.0	25.6	49.8	39.2	16.9	411	71.3
Kenly town	1,345	1,584	17.8	1,892	35.7	36.1	0.0	8.0	20.2	29.0	17.1	39.6	58.8	11.5	744	71.2
Kernersville town	23,101	24,660	6.7	24,576	68.2	13.7	1.8	4.1	12.3	20.0	17.4	42.0	35.7	31.7	10,564	91.2
Kill Devil Hills town	6,687	7,333	9.7	7,155	85.2	0.4	1.6	1.2	11.6	17.3	13.6	41.7	30.0	31.6	3,170	97.4
King city	6,872	6,861	-0.2	6,961	92.3	3.5	0.1	0.4	3.7	19.2	24.4	48.6	43.9	24.5	2,956	87.4
Kings Grant CDP	8,113	-	-	8,647	79.2	13.2	1.3	0.4	5.9	18.2	15.0	40.2	36.8	29.2	3,450	93.8
Kings Mountain city	10,647	10,982	3.1	11,028	72.2	22.5	1.7	0.7	2.8	26.9	18.1	39.1	57.9	14.5	4,151	79.4
Kingstown town	681	677	-0.6	492	7.1	85.6	0.0	1.2	6.1	10.0	25.6	56.6	72.5	6.5	194	66.5
Kinston city	21,749	20,041	-7.9	20,398	28.0	65.9	1.1	3.3	1.8	22.1	22.9	45.3	52.5	17.6	8,901	79.3
Kittrell town	166	162	-2.4	178	88.8	7.9	0.0	3.4	0.0	27.5	11.2	40.5	39.7	14.3	58	86.2
Kitty Hawk town	3,266	3,571	9.3	3,490	97.0	0.9	0.0	1.1	1.0	19.6	21.5	49.2	26.3	43.0	1,532	94.3
Knightdale town	11,403	17,843	56.5	16,001	39.4	44.0	1.8	2.3	12.5	24.7	8.9	36.0	26.6	38.6	6,110	95.1
Kure Beach town	2,009	2,098	4.4	2,124	96.8	0.0	0.0	0.8	2.4	10.1	31.6	57.8	22.3	52.1	951	95.5
La Grange town	2,821	2,619	-7.2	2,670	39.6	58.7	0.0	0.0	1.7	12.7	19.7	48.8	53.3	13.6	1,133	73.5
Lake Junaluska CDP	2,734	-	-	3,307	100.0	0.0	0.0	0.0	0.0	13.8	32.4	55.3	32.6	29.0	1,477	86.1
Lake Lure town	1,169	1,154	-1.3	1,498	94.7	0.6	1.4	3.2	0.1	11.4	38.5	60.9	20.6	48.1	745	93.2
Lake Norman of Catawba CDP	7,411	-	-	8,196	96.7	1.2	0.0	0.3	1.8	18.4	20.3	49.1	25.4	37.6	3,385	93.5
Lake Park village	3,423	3,909	14.2	3,798	83.6	5.0	2.0	4.1	5.3	19.4	20.0	44.0	22.3	43.6	1,453	100.0
Lake Royale CDP	2,506	-	-	3,485	70.2	27.9	1.3	0.7	0.0	26.5	17.3	39.2	28.6	30.4	1,361	92.1
Lake Santeetlah town	45	42	-6.7	52	100.0	0.0	0.0	0.0	0.0	0.0	86.5	70.0	13.5	50.0	27	100.0
Lake Waccamaw town	1,471	1,400	-4.8	1,733	77.6	13.0	0.0	6.8	2.6	25.2	32.7	52.2	40.3	28.5	654	83.9
Landis town	3,087	3,138	1.7	3,099	65.1	26.3	4.7	0.5	3.4	31.5	15.4	35.7	38.1	14.9	959	96.7
Lansing town	155	153	-1.3	202	99.0	0.0	0.0	0.5	0.5	28.2	10.9	36.5	64.4	4.4	78	79.5
Lasker town	123	106	-13.8	173	65.3	0.0	0.0	0.0	34.7	34.1	28.3	45.6	54.5	11.9	62	82.3
Lattimore town	478	448	-6.3	489	94.5	2.9	1.4	0.0	1.2	14.1	18.0	31.5	42.3	23.7	129	72.1
Laurel Hill CDP	1,254	-	-	1,194	67.3	25.4	0.0	3.4	3.9	19.7	15.2	43.9	49.6	18.0	497	90.1
Laurel Park town	2,155	2,330	8.1	2,680	84.3	3.0	0.3	0.0	12.4	11.5	43.3	61.9	18.2	51.1	1,153	94.1
Laurinburg city	15,948	15,002	-5.9	15,119	37.9	48.9	1.6	8.8	2.9	25.1	18.2	38.0	49.0	20.4	5,712	76.1
Lawndale town	600	592	-1.3	769	89.2	10.1	0.0	0.5	0.1	19.6	13.9	41.8	64.4	9.0	291	75.6
Leggett town	60	55	-8.3	44	56.8	43.2	0.0	0.0	0.0	6.8	50.0	64.0	79.5	2.6	21	47.6
Leland town	13,614	23,544	72.9	20,294	80.7	8.8	1.8	4.1	4.5	19.5	25.8	46.2	28.5	37.8	8,366	97.8
Lenoir city	18,226	17,913	-1.7	17,879	74.0	12.4	0.4	3.2	10.1	22.4	19.3	41.9	50.1	18.2	7,340	81.0
Lewiston Woodville town	549	482	-12.2	574	22.5	65.5	0.0	8.2	3.8	29.3	9.9	38.7	52.3	17.2	239	93.7
Lewisville town	12,709	14,228	12.0	13,861	88.5	6.9	0.4	1.8	2.4	21.9	19.7	45.8	28.0	40.3	5,345	95.5
Lexington city	18,944	18,933	-0.1	18,861	45.6	30.3	3.8	5.2	15.1	24.9	16.4	36.0	58.6	13.2	7,448	82.0
Liberty town	2,656	2,658	0.1	2,662	53.3	21.1	0.4	3.6	21.6	24.2	20.8	42.2	56.1	12.7	1,108	83.2
Light Oak CDP	691	-	-	1,140	5.7	94.3	0.0	0.0	0.0	12.9	24.9	45.9	88.2	2.9	388	49.2
Lilesville town	524	483	-7.8	537	37.6	62.4	0.0	0.0	0.0	20.7	10.2	33.5	53.3	16.0	210	96.2
Lillington town	3,192	3,657	14.6	3,571	42.2	32.4	0.5	6.6	18.3	13.4	14.9	39.4	55.7	12.1	924	86.1
Lincolnton city	10,325	11,200	8.5	10,832	64.0	11.7	0.1	6.1	18.0	22.7	18.9	37.7	45.1	19.0	4,668	87.3
Linden town	130	133	2.3	115	74.8	17.4	0.0	5.2	2.6	22.6	21.7	37.1	71.2	9.6	51	78.4
Littleton town	651	588	-9.7	634	42.7	38.3	0.0	0.6	18.3	23.0	31.1	54.2	54.2	20.2	319	64.3
Locust city	2,926	3,238	10.7	3,297	94.4	3.0	0.0	1.7	0.9	20.8	19.2	45.7	48.3	21.8	1,397	93.1
Long View town	4,880	4,930	1.0	4,959	70.7	12.0	3.1	1.3	13.0	18.4	18.4	41.2	53.2	12.1	2,182	79.1
Louisburg town	3,414	3,619	6.0	3,531	41.8	54.4	0.0	1.6	2.2	13.6	23.3	39.4	37.2	23.2	1,250	75.1
Love Valley town	99	112	13.1	96	95.8	0.0	0.0	4.2	0.0	2.1	22.9	60.1	59.6	5.3	56	83.9
Lowell city	3,523	3,716	5.5	3,640	65.5	15.7	2.9	3.9	12.0	17.1	20.0	41.4	60.6	11.8	1,305	91.7
Lowesville CDP	2,945	-	-	3,208	89.5	1.4	2.2	0.6	6.2	21.3	15.6	46.2	30.6	28.6	1,227	96.1
Lowgap CDP	324	-	-	425	100.0	0.0	0.0	0.0	0.0	14.8	19.5	42.3	68.8	0.0	132	91.7
Lucama town	1,136	1,152	1.4	1,186	47.0	22.1	0.0	3.8	27.1	25.5	15.4	39.1	74.5	8.0	404	77.2
Lumber Bridge town	92	88	-4.3	75	86.7	2.7	1.3	1.3	8.0	24.0	20.0	37.3	65.5	7.3	36	86.1
Lumberton city	21,523	20,484	-4.8	20,928	38.7	35.3	1.2	15.1	9.6	26.3	16.0	34.9	51.5	20.1	7,142	81.3
McAdenville town	631	673	6.7	865	99.2	0.0	0.0	0.8	0.0	21.4	10.8	41.9	31.3	49.1	330	99.4
Macclesfield town	471	426	-9.6	494	58.1	20.2	2.0	2.6	17.0	20.9	28.5	43.9	68.5	7.8	213	47.4
McDonald town	113	108	-4.4	100	44.0	15.0	0.0	41.0	0.0	12.0	32.0	54.7	42.4	21.2	41	73.2
McFarlan town	117	108	-7.7	115	100.0	0.0	0.0	0.0	0.0	14.8	34.8	50.8	35.2	18.7	46	82.6
McLeansville CDP	1,021	-	-	1,044	96.6	3.3	0.0	0.0	0.2	15.7	29.6	50.1	53.2	17.0	467	82.9
Macon town	119	110	-7.6	116	91.4	5.2	0.0	0.0	3.4	8.6	28.4	52.0	37.0	29.3	46	89.1
Madison town	2,240	2,116	-5.5	2,347	61.8	24.5	0.2	6.3	7.2	17.2	20.6	44.6	50.5	16.0	995	90.1
Maggie Valley town	1,150	1,237	7.6	1,763	90.6	1.2	0.0	1.6	6.5	16.3	34.3	55.3	30.8	31.4	833	95.2
Magnolia town	943	952	1.0	1,092	23.5	23.4	0.0	1.7	51.3	34.9	10.3	29.8	69.8	3.4	326	84.7
Maiden town	3,327	3,443	3.5	3,410	74.7	11.3	0.6	3.5	9.8	28.4	13.7	37.0	42.1	18.7	1,107	93.1
Mamers CDP	826	-	-	763	99.7	0.3	0.0	0.0	0.0	11.8	14.2	54.8	39.4	28.6	281	95.0
Manns Harbor CDP	821	-	-	782	91.4	0.0	0.0	0.0	8.6	23.4	15.0	44.9	57.4	10.2	311	100.0
Manteo town	1,325	1,456	9.9	1,950	79.4	11.8	1.6	1.4	5.8	22.1	24.4	48.6	34.6	37.4	865	91.4
Marble CDP	321	-	-	390	92.8	0.0	0.0	7.2	0.0	37.4	13.6	25.4	34.4	4.7	169	81.1
Marietta town	175	168	-4.0	139	43.9	41.7	0.0	14.4	0.0	25.2	27.3	49.8	44.9	26.5	55	70.9
Marion city	8,159	7,891	-3.3	7,834	61.1	11.7	0.9	4.3	22.0	22.4	16.6	36.3	56.7	14.0	2,844	84.9
Mar-Mac CDP	3,615	-	-	3,368	48.6	33.1	1.2	1.1	15.9	24.4	21.0	40.9	49.4	14.9	1,506	83.5
Marshall town	871	908	4.2	782	87.3	0.8	0.3	8.4	3.2	19.6	17.5	41.8	42.1	31.7	346	88.4
Marshallberg CDP	403	-	-	402	100.0	0.0	0.0	0.0	0.0	4.7	30.6	60.3	39.2	24.8	187	94.1
Mars Hill town	1,857	1,939	4.4	2,537	82.8	8.7	0.8	1.0	6.7	11.5	11.2	24.6	30.2	41.7	742	89.5
Marshville town	2,459	2,787	13.3	2,714	28.3	49.4	0.4	2.0	19.8	22.6	17.1	37.4	72.1	3.7	889	92.4
Marvin village	5,662	6,792	20.0	6,553	66.2	8.8	12.8	3.1	9.2	32.8	8.9	40.6	12.0	73.3	1,867	99.7
Matthews town	27,189	33,138	21.9	32,044	74.9	9.7	3.9	3.6	7.9	21.4	17.1	40.9	21.1	53.2	12,011	95.0
Maury CDP	1,685	-	-	1,375	42.5	42.2	0.0	7.7	7.6	9.4	6.3	42.3	62.6	3.2	187	78.1

1 May be of any race.

Table A. All Places — **Population and Housing**

STATE City, town, township, borough, or CDP (county if applicable)	Population: 2010 census total population	Population: 2019 estimated population	Population: Percent change 2010–2019	Population: ACS total population estimate 2015–2019	Race and Hispanic or Latino origin (percent): White alone, not Hispanic or Latino	Black alone, not Hispanic or Latino	Asian alone, not Hispanic or Latino	All other races or 2 or more races, not Hispanic or Latino	Hispanic or Latino[1]	Age (percent): Under 18 years old	Age 65 years and older	Median age	Educational attainment of persons age 25 and older: Percent High school diploma or less	Percent Bachelor's degree or more	Occupied housing units: Total	Percent with a computer
	1	2	3	4	5	6	7	8	9	10	11	12	13	14	15	16
NORTH CAROLINA—Con.																
Maxton town	2,447	2,346	-4.1	2,549	17.3	66.3	0.1	15.7	0.7	24.1	18.0	40.0	54.0	8.5	1,006	69.5
Mayodan town	2,477	2,382	-3.8	2,508	78.2	15.9	1.4	0.4	4.0	18.2	26.7	50.1	56.0	11.9	1,170	72.1
Maysville town	1,029	935	-9.1	1,070	47.1	36.3	0.0	11.1	5.5	25.8	14.0	33.3	46.3	14.1	401	75.6
Mebane city	11,481	16,262	41.6	14,952	63.0	24.5	2.3	3.2	6.9	29.0	10.6	34.7	26.6	39.9	5,763	94.8
Mesic town	220	210	-4.5	143	43.4	56.6	0.0	0.0	0.0	14.0	35.0	57.8	44.6	11.6	68	89.7
Micro town	447	537	20.1	672	69.0	14.3	1.2	2.4	13.1	32.1	22.9	42.4	60.0	3.4	257	73.9
Middleburg town	143	137	-4.2	201	28.4	65.7	0.0	6.0	0.0	13.4	36.3	43.9	41.2	24.8	86	48.8
Middlesex town	818	825	0.9	1,145	65.8	23.1	0.0	0.0	11.2	28.0	9.6	32.8	47.7	15.6	434	88.0
Midland town	3,093	3,805	23.0	3,622	76.4	8.9	0.0	4.8	9.9	23.9	12.5	36.0	37.9	28.4	1,182	94.3
Midway town	4,734	4,912	3.8	4,840	85.1	9.6	0.0	0.0	5.3	21.4	19.1	40.7	35.8	24.1	1,948	91.4
Millers Creek CDP	2,112	-	-	1,408	96.1	0.0	0.0	1.8	2.1	10.2	37.5	61.2	58.7	5.0	747	76.0
Millingport CDP	599	-	-	466	99.1	0.9	0.0	0.0	0.0	15.5	20.2	47.2	38.6	21.5	179	84.9
Mills River town	6,724	7,406	10.1	7,251	89.0	3.6	1.4	4.0	2.0	21.1	22.1	45.7	28.4	39.4	3,072	92.1
Milton town	159	147	-7.5	202	52.5	47.0	0.0	0.0	0.5	23.3	19.3	34.1	45.1	20.8	89	71.9
Mineral Springs town	2,656	3,111	17.1	3,008	81.6	14.9	2.1	0.0	1.5	18.3	14.1	44.4	35.4	33.8	1,155	91.3
Minnesott Beach town	437	423	-3.2	476	90.1	1.3	0.2	0.6	7.8	7.6	45.0	64.5	19.0	29.9	247	81.8
Mint Hill town	22,728	27,617	21.5	26,697	71.1	17.6	2.9	2.4	6.1	21.4	19.1	43.8	28.1	38.6	9,627	94.3
Misenheimer village	730	756	3.6	774	63.7	21.7	0.0	1.3	13.3	2.1	9.3	20.4	24.7	40.3	111	79.3
Mocksville town	5,058	5,252	3.8	5,213	64.4	12.0	1.4	3.2	19.0	21.8	17.6	38.4	50.3	21.4	2,062	85.5
Momeyer town	226	228	0.9	250	86.8	4.8	0.0	3.2	5.2	22.0	23.6	46.6	62.0	13.6	112	78.6
Moncure CDP	711	-	-	709	58.0	14.8	0.0	2.4	24.8	15.1	11.3	47.0	59.9	11.0	253	92.5
Monroe city	32,912	35,540	8.0	35,105	42.4	25.2	0.6	2.2	29.6	26.5	12.8	35.2	52.1	16.9	11,482	91.6
Montreat town	720	870	20.8	446	85.2	4.7	3.4	4.5	2.2	4.0	18.2	20.8	1.5	87.1	69	100.0
Mooresboro town	311	312	0.3	372	86.3	9.9	0.0	1.1	2.7	16.7	20.2	47.7	50.4	14.0	159	79.9
Mooresville town	34,367	39,132	13.9	37,835	72.9	10.0	5.8	2.3	8.9	26.2	12.1	35.2	26.8	40.3	14,233	95.0
Moravian Falls CDP	1,901	-	-	1,802	77.0	0.0	0.0	2.2	20.8	13.3	33.9	55.0	44.2	20.3	874	87.0
Morehead City town	8,652	9,619	11.2	9,413	77.9	9.8	2.3	2.7	7.3	16.4	24.1	46.8	33.3	35.2	4,428	87.1
Morganton city	16,882	16,577	-1.8	16,481	66.1	8.1	1.4	3.7	20.7	24.2	19.9	40.7	46.5	23.4	6,181	82.9
Morrisville town	18,583	28,846	55.2	26,280	37.9	11.9	41.3	4.4	4.5	27.5	6.4	33.8	14.3	69.4	9,699	97.1
Morven town	499	466	-6.6	548	17.0	71.7	0.0	1.5	9.9	32.3	13.9	42.5	76.5	11.3	213	69.5
Mountain Home CDP	3,622	-	-	4,173	89.7	0.6	0.0	1.7	8.0	21.9	19.6	44.9	37.6	29.2	1,709	86.9
Mountain View CDP	3,552	-	-	3,701	78.9	15.9	0.0	1.9	3.2	19.4	16.1	38.9	40.9	22.6	1,478	97.3
Mount Airy city	10,407	10,208	-1.9	10,193	79.2	8.4	0.7	2.0	9.8	19.7	26.8	47.9	42.7	25.5	4,571	78.8
Mount Gilead town	1,181	1,142	-3.3	1,228	43.6	55.5	0.0	0.8	0.1	17.7	23.9	43.8	59.0	14.0	476	70.8
Mount Holly city	13,657	16,257	19.0	15,610	75.3	15.7	4.3	1.3	3.5	21.3	12.2	36.7	36.8	30.8	6,134	91.0
Mount Olive town	4,616	4,578	-0.8	4,674	36.5	45.8	0.4	9.8	7.5	16.0	20.3	36.6	58.3	16.1	1,803	83.1
Mount Pleasant town	1,873	2,222	18.6	1,757	94.1	3.2	0.6	0.0	2.0	23.1	16.7	41.9	41.9	21.2	649	90.6
Moyock CDP	3,759	-	-	4,210	87.8	5.9	0.5	1.9	3.9	26.2	10.2	39.8	28.3	29.2	1,563	98.7
Mulberry CDP	2,332	-	-	2,239	98.9	0.0	0.0	0.0	1.1	21.3	23.4	50.1	44.9	17.0	969	86.8
Murfreesboro town	2,825	2,961	4.8	3,044	45.1	50.1	0.4	2.0	2.4	15.8	16.6	29.5	31.8	25.1	1,081	78.7
Murphy town	1,623	1,657	2.1	1,671	82.2	7.2	2.2	4.7	3.7	14.1	21.1	46.1	39.3	25.3	774	83.6
Murraysville CDP	14,215	-	-	16,542	75.3	13.0	1.5	2.2	8.0	20.8	10.8	35.4	32.3	34.1	6,646	94.9
Myrtle Grove CDP	8,875	-	-	10,753	90.2	3.8	0.3	2.8	3.0	21.5	21.6	43.4	22.8	45.0	4,172	94.0
Nags Head town	2,759	2,975	7.8	2,923	92.6	1.6	0.0	3.7	2.0	16.9	25.2	49.6	21.6	38.1	1,302	93.9
Nashville town	5,597	5,554	-0.8	5,516	48.1	47.1	0.0	4.7	0.0	19.5	19.4	43.6	29.1	27.0	2,284	84.1
Navassa town	1,480	2,306	55.8	1,758	18.2	73.5	0.0	2.7	5.6	15.9	15.1	46.0	57.3	13.9	704	82.5
Neuse Forest CDP	2,005	-	-	1,536	92.4	0.0	1.3	6.3	0.0	19.1	29.6	48.1	35.3	29.1	673	97.6
New Bern city	29,344	29,994	2.2	29,895	54.3	30.2	5.9	1.6	8.0	20.8	21.8	40.4	37.2	28.1	13,757	89.1
Newland town	703	686	-2.4	755	82.5	0.1	0.0	0.0	17.4	16.8	19.5	39.4	54.9	17.4	388	77.3
New London town	621	724	16.6	702	91.9	3.4	2.8	0.6	1.3	22.8	14.1	44.4	39.8	19.9	245	97.1
Newport town	4,130	4,591	11.2	4,606	79.2	8.6	2.3	3.0	6.9	19.0	16.5	42.5	39.8	23.0	1,772	95.6
Newton city	12,949	13,177	1.8	13,059	60.8	17.9	1.6	4.9	14.8	21.0	17.3	41.2	46.9	20.2	5,076	84.3
Newton Grove town	569	565	-0.7	557	73.4	6.6	0.5	6.8	12.6	14.9	19.0	41.4	45.2	21.8	249	85.9
Norlina town	1,125	1,047	-6.9	1,115	57.0	39.8	0.0	0.0	3.2	17.0	27.8	45.8	50.4	14.0	537	69.5
Norman town	138	132	-4.3	163	61.3	14.7	0.0	3.1	20.9	19.6	20.9	44.5	59.5	18.0	65	80.0
Northchase CDP	3,747	-	-	3,614	79.2	13.1	3.0	3.5	1.1	15.0	22.8	45.6	34.6	26.9	1,590	91.6
Northlakes CDP	1,534	-	-	1,509	84.6	1.7	1.6	5.6	6.5	24.0	23.3	52.1	22.2	45.2	617	100.0
North Topsail Beach town	741	743	0.3	846	93.9	0.0	0.0	2.7	3.4	7.1	34.2	57.2	14.4	49.3	482	96.3
Northwest city	726	785	8.1	856	22.9	66.2	0.0	9.5	1.4	13.7	19.9	48.7	55.2	17.0	326	77.6
North Wilkesboro town	4,278	4,200	-1.8	4,194	64.5	14.1	0.4	2.6	18.4	19.6	21.1	39.9	50.5	17.5	1,862	72.0
Norwood town	2,378	2,449	3.0	2,243	72.8	21.6	4.0	1.0	0.5	23.5	19.2	43.2	56.1	12.3	830	86.7
Oakboro town	1,860	1,912	2.8	2,004	76.3	15.6	1.0	0.5	6.6	24.8	14.3	38.2	46.8	20.3	766	85.6
Oak City town	314	287	-8.6	257	34.6	64.2	0.0	0.0	1.2	16.7	29.6	52.8	51.4	9.3	118	66.1
Oak Island town	6,806	8,386	23.2	7,851	98.5	0.0	0.0	0.9	0.6	9.0	34.3	59.8	27.4	38.4	3,662	94.1
Oak Ridge town	6,297	7,049	11.9	6,901	71.2	11.9	8.1	5.2	3.7	29.3	13.7	43.7	22.4	50.3	2,275	95.7
Ocean Isle Beach town	545	665	22.0	734	94.7	0.0	0.8	1.1	3.4	7.6	49.3	64.9	16.6	50.9	374	95.7
Ocracoke CDP	948	-	-	706	70.7	0.1	0.0	0.0	29.2	22.9	23.2	47.0	45.9	26.9	317	80.8
Ogden CDP	6,766	-	-	8,408	94.0	1.9	1.7	0.6	1.8	23.8	14.5	40.8	20.9	51.2	3,067	97.4
Old Fort town	905	924	2.1	1,004	91.1	7.0	0.0	1.9	0.0	19.2	18.9	42.9	53.1	6.6	463	71.5
Old Hundred CDP	287	-	-	481	55.3	5.4	0.0	39.3	0.0	32.0	8.9	27.7	59.6	0.0	139	90.6
Oriental town	901	861	-4.4	994	91.3	6.9	0.0	1.7	0.0	11.1	43.1	62.5	26.3	41.2	522	91.6
Orrum town	91	87	-4.4	61	65.6	16.4	0.0	0.0	18.0	13.1	32.8	56.5	63.3	6.1	30	83.3
Ossipee town	547	591	8.0	466	74.0	20.4	0.0	2.8	2.8	15.9	15.2	42.5	58.3	11.1	178	88.8
Oxford city	8,445	8,886	5.2	8,721	31.8	62.2	0.6	2.1	3.2	22.3	20.2	42.4	49.8	19.1	3,454	83.6
Pantego town	181	176	-2.8	201	81.6	17.4	0.0	1.0	0.0	27.4	13.9	35.1	26.0	28.1	92	93.5
Parkton town	458	439	-4.1	443	71.8	13.8	0.5	8.4	5.6	29.1	11.3	35.9	39.5	19.9	162	86.4
Parmele town	278	253	-9.0	211	18.0	82.0	0.0	0.0	0.0	13.7	31.3	57.8	52.7	20.7	97	62.9
Patterson Springs town	622	621	-0.2	934	70.0	20.9	0.0	3.0	6.1	21.3	9.4	32.2	58.1	6.3	318	75.2
Peachland town	436	402	-7.8	470	60.6	17.0	0.0	5.1	17.2	31.7	9.8	32.1	54.5	15.3	164	78.0
Peletier town	699	720	3.0	754	89.5	1.1	0.0	1.2	8.2	18.0	19.5	51.2	47.9	13.5	343	93.0
Pembroke town	3,050	2,951	-3.2	3,002	16.6	20.8	1.0	59.3	2.4	24.3	10.7	22.8	40.8	29.3	879	86.1
Pikeville town	674	674	0.0	606	77.4	15.3	0.3	3.3	3.6	20.5	15.0	35.3	35.8	22.6	263	94.3
Pilot Mountain town	1,474	1,413	-4.1	1,649	87.9	7.6	0.8	2.3	1.3	22.4	19.9	45.4	43.4	25.7	715	79.9
Pinebluff town	1,300	1,619	24.5	1,664	75.9	17.2	0.0	2.2	4.7	22.5	12.1	39.9	28.1	20.4	663	93.4
Pinehurst village	14,738	16,620	12.8	16,050	90.6	2.1	2.2	1.3	3.8	16.0	40.9	59.4	15.2	58.6	7,301	96.1
Pine Knoll Shores town	1,337	1,327	-0.7	1,343	97.1	0.4	0.0	1.2	1.3	10.6	46.6	63.9	11.9	53.4	663	94.7
Pine Level town	1,686	2,019	19.8	2,044	68.0	9.8	0.0	3.2	19.0	25.6	13.3	34.7	46.9	19.8	772	92.6
Pinetops town	1,374	1,235	-10.1	1,259	41.8	54.6	0.0	0.0	3.6	22.9	21.4	42.9	62.7	11.8	567	72.0
Pinetown CDP	155	-	-	103	100.0	0.0	0.0	0.0	0.0	8.7	81.6	72.5	24.5	10.6	66	62.1
Pineville town	7,488	9,028	20.6	8,749	45.2	31.5	5.9	3.1	14.3	23.4	19.0	36.3	25.5	44.7	3,732	89.1
Piney Green CDP	13,293	-	-	13,741	59.0	21.3	2.3	4.9	12.6	27.3	9.2	26.0	41.4	20.0	4,742	95.3
Pink Hill town	547	507	-7.3	557	57.3	22.3	0.0	6.6	13.8	20.5	19.9	45.2	60.0	9.9	247	85.4

1 May be of any race.

Table A. All Places — **Population and Housing**

STATE City, town, township, borough, or CDP (county if applicable)	Population				Race and Hispanic or Latino origin (percent)					Age (percent)			Educational attainment of persons age 25 and older		Occupied housing units	
	2010 census total population	2019 estimated population	Percent change 2010–2019	ACS total population estimate 2015–2019	White alone, not Hispanic or Latino	Black alone, not Hispanic or Latino	Asian alone, not Hispanic or Latino	All other races or 2 or more races, not Hispanic or Latino	Hispanic or Latino[1]	Under 18 years old	Age 65 years and older	Median age	Percent High school diploma or less	Percent Bachelor's degree or more	Total	Percent with a computer
	1	2	3	4	5	6	7	8	9	10	11	12	13	14	15	16
NORTH CAROLINA—Con.																
Pinnacle CDP	894	-	-	909	63.3	0.9	0.0	0.0	35.9	38.6	8.7	34.6	58.5	26.3	252	75.4
Pittsboro town	3,748	4,368	16.5	4,195	70.4	19.1	1.5	2.4	6.6	20.8	22.4	42.8	23.2	49.5	1,841	79.3
Plain View CDP	1,961	-	-	1,853	80.2	18.5	0.9	0.0	0.4	15.2	21.5	41.0	48.9	16.4	818	71.8
Pleasant Garden town	4,493	4,932	9.8	4,837	83.6	10.0	0.6	3.6	2.2	15.5	30.6	51.2	43.8	27.6	1,817	82.3
Pleasant Hill CDP	878	-	-	769	87.1	12.9	0.0	0.0	0.0	9.2	8.3	47.0	51.4	21.9	381	96.3
Plymouth town	3,873	3,361	-13.2	3,478	30.8	68.0	0.0	1.1	0.1	25.0	19.6	46.9	61.5	5.9	1,522	74.3
Polkton town	3,354	2,561	-23.6	2,921	34.7	54.3	1.5	5.5	4.0	8.2	12.1	39.3	62.4	4.0	550	73.1
Polkville city	545	544	-0.2	479	98.3	1.5	0.0	0.2	0.0	15.2	27.3	50.8	62.3	9.7	202	77.7
Pollocksville town	311	281	-9.6	216	58.8	21.3	0.0	6.9	13.0	20.8	25.5	47.0	40.1	26.1	117	80.3
Porters Neck CDP	6,204	-	-	7,538	89.8	4.0	1.1	0.8	4.3	16.6	31.2	50.3	17.0	61.1	3,087	93.2
Potters Hill CDP	481	-	-	664	97.1	0.0	0.0	2.9	0.0	36.9	11.9	30.5	43.7	6.9	216	100.0
Powellsville town	280	244	-12.9	175	56.0	40.6	0.0	3.4	0.0	5.7	50.9	65.8	60.6	13.8	89	76.4
Princeton town	1,189	1,398	17.6	1,067	65.4	23.0	0.0	8.8	2.8	23.7	20.1	43.3	46.5	15.1	497	75.5
Princeville town	2,066	1,926	-6.8	2,119	3.1	93.8	0.0	0.0	3.1	25.3	17.0	42.0	75.2	6.8	789	66.9
Proctorville town	117	114	-2.6	167	78.4	12.6	0.0	6.0	3.0	11.4	17.4	49.3	66.2	10.0	92	88.0
Prospect CDP	981	-	-	797	0.0	0.0	0.0	100.0	0.0	24.3	23.6	40.6	41.8	29.9	295	65.8
Pumpkin Center CDP	2,222	-	-	1,693	61.9	17.7	0.7	12.2	7.5	14.6	16.9	35.3	41.0	15.5	574	90.9
Raeford city	4,620	4,956	7.3	4,926	31.6	41.5	0.0	12.3	14.7	23.8	17.4	39.2	43.0	17.6	1,909	81.4
Raemon CDP	282	-	-	197	18.3	15.2	0.0	66.5	0.0	27.9	26.9	56.4	67.7	15.4	104	78.8
Raleigh city	404,068	474,069	17.3	464,485	53.1	28.2	4.6	2.9	11.2	20.9	10.6	33.6	23.8	50.9	183,335	95.9
Ramseur town	1,702	1,690	-0.7	1,817	58.4	13.8	1.9	9.0	17.0	29.3	21.7	38.5	55.0	10.5	638	80.4
Randleman city	4,117	4,115	0.0	4,101	80.9	4.8	0.9	5.3	8.1	30.5	11.9	36.6	51.7	11.3	1,662	84.6
Ranlo town	3,445	3,668	6.5	3,604	58.6	20.4	2.3	2.7	16.0	27.1	15.1	35.4	51.0	18.5	1,346	86.2
Raynham town	72	71	-1.4	38	76.3	0.0	0.0	23.7	0.0	2.6	31.6	57.0	57.1	5.7	21	52.4
Red Cross town	738	761	3.1	689	95.8	0.3	0.0	0.3	3.6	18.3	26.3	49.1	57.6	8.8	323	84.8
Red Oak town	3,420	3,468	1.4	3,445	88.3	11.3	0.0	0.0	0.4	17.3	29.1	53.8	39.1	32.5	1,433	88.8
Red Springs town	3,482	3,302	-5.2	3,378	24.3	51.9	0.0	15.2	8.6	21.9	20.7	40.4	50.3	20.7	1,342	74.5
Reidsville city	14,463	13,987	-3.3	13,915	55.0	37.8	0.1	4.3	2.7	19.6	21.0	44.8	55.8	15.2	6,166	69.9
Rennert town	383	372	-2.9	386	4.1	33.9	0.0	56.7	5.2	22.5	15.0	38.9	66.2	11.2	130	69.2
Rex CDP	55	-	-	-	-	-	-	-	-	-	-	-	-	-	-	-
Rhodhiss town	1,040	1,024	-1.5	935	86.1	0.0	2.9	2.6	8.4	21.1	11.7	37.3	77.8	4.9	366	79.5
Richfield town	608	622	2.3	545	86.1	6.2	5.7	1.5	0.6	27.0	18.0	40.6	43.1	17.8	196	89.3
Richlands town	1,494	1,703	14.0	2,364	67.8	15.5	0.6	7.0	9.1	39.6	9.2	27.8	44.8	16.7	772	93.4
Rich Square town	962	844	-12.3	780	32.7	66.2	1.2	0.0	0.0	11.9	41.8	59.3	59.7	12.6	359	76.6
Riegelwood CDP	579	-	-	840	61.3	20.1	0.0	4.3	14.3	24.0	12.4	29.1	65.1	2.9	319	97.2
River Bend town	3,111	3,026	-2.7	3,051	73.2	8.5	7.5	5.7	5.2	10.1	33.8	55.9	25.7	30.6	1,376	95.3
River Road CDP	4,394	-	-	3,826	65.0	19.8	0.0	0.0	15.2	19.6	22.3	46.5	40.5	27.6	1,800	90.9
Roanoke Rapids city	15,720	14,320	-8.9	14,741	54.1	35.5	1.9	2.7	5.9	27.0	16.6	37.0	50.0	20.9	6,051	83.9
Robbins town	1,111	1,221	9.9	1,647	40.1	11.8	2.1	0.8	45.2	30.7	12.2	33.6	75.1	6.0	526	72.1
Robbinsville town	678	637	-6.0	693	74.0	0.9	0.0	3.5	21.6	24.4	18.2	43.3	52.8	4.5	317	56.5
Robersonville town	1,488	1,343	-9.7	1,606	26.8	63.9	0.5	1.9	6.8	22.3	24.7	44.4	62.6	12.8	666	82.9
Rockfish CDP	3,298	-	-	3,523	50.9	27.4	4.9	7.0	9.9	21.2	9.3	34.1	32.9	19.6	1,348	96.2
Rockingham city	9,539	8,659	-9.2	8,865	55.4	37.1	1.0	2.3	4.2	22.8	19.1	36.4	44.9	19.5	3,602	80.6
Rockwell town	2,123	2,159	1.7	2,119	89.9	2.4	0.0	6.8	0.8	23.0	13.8	42.3	46.1	21.8	769	89.7
Rocky Mount city	57,695	53,922	-6.5	54,548	28.8	63.5	1.2	3.4	3.1	23.1	17.3	39.4	48.8	20.3	22,260	83.5
Rocky Point CDP	1,602	-	-	1,687	48.4	7.2	0.0	0.5	43.9	31.6	11.7	39.9	61.6	12.6	639	87.5
Rodanthe CDP	261	-	-	141	72.3	0.0	0.0	9.2	18.4	0.0	2.8	52.9	21.3	47.5	81	100.0
Rolesville town	3,778	8,501	125.0	7,488	62.7	23.5	2.0	5.6	6.3	38.2	10.3	35.5	19.3	52.3	2,204	98.0
Ronda town	417	411	-1.4	649	74.7	0.0	0.0	0.2	25.1	40.4	12.0	25.5	66.2	8.1	188	87.2
Roper town	622	539	-13.3	751	8.7	78.3	0.0	0.0	13.0	39.9	12.9	32.8	59.0	12.7	291	60.5
Roseboro town	1,191	1,167	-2.0	1,278	62.0	23.3	0.0	0.3	14.4	14.2	21.8	46.1	49.6	16.7	549	75.4
Rose Hill town	1,620	1,618	-0.1	2,315	38.0	36.4	0.4	2.8	22.5	31.4	14.7	33.4	58.0	12.0	823	79.6
Rosman town	577	615	6.6	486	84.2	3.1	0.0	0.4	12.3	24.7	23.0	42.0	75.5	6.5	240	75.4
Rougemont CDP	978	-	-	729	66.9	33.1	0.0	0.0	0.0	22.9	27.7	50.6	40.5	21.0	306	81.0
Rowland town	1,037	992	-4.3	1,075	20.4	69.1	0.0	10.5	0.0	18.5	21.2	49.1	58.7	14.9	441	67.6
Roxboro city	8,366	8,309	-0.7	8,298	37.4	44.5	0.2	3.2	14.8	24.8	18.7	38.8	58.6	12.8	3,348	79.1
Roxobel town	240	212	-11.7	439	18.2	68.1	0.5	0.2	13.0	26.9	14.6	40.1	59.5	6.5	152	61.8
Royal Pines CDP	4,272	-	-	4,759	77.9	7.9	7.9	2.2	4.2	21.9	19.4	48.0	25.1	46.5	1,749	92.6
Ruffin CDP	368	-	-	330	64.5	27.9	0.0	7.6	0.0	17.6	10.9	37.5	87.6	0.0	116	78.4
Rural Hall town	2,931	3,264	11.4	3,188	66.6	17.8	0.8	0.4	14.5	21.2	18.8	40.0	47.8	18.2	1,360	83.5
Ruth town	418	413	-1.2	586	73.9	8.7	0.0	6.3	11.1	24.2	25.1	46.2	57.9	11.1	190	83.7
Rutherford College town	1,321	1,304	-1.3	1,286	79.9	0.0	16.3	1.7	2.2	13.7	32.7	50.1	54.0	20.5	534	71.3
Rutherfordton town	4,185	4,087	-2.3	4,073	89.1	4.3	0.0	4.2	2.4	16.6	29.3	49.9	34.2	33.6	1,882	85.7
St. Helena village	396	424	7.1	399	78.7	11.3	0.0	2.3	7.8	17.3	16.5	47.1	31.6	24.6	169	92.9
St. James town	3,172	6,248	97.0	5,521	98.5	0.0	0.0	0.3	1.2	2.4	65.3	67.8	10.9	69.0	2,713	99.4
St. Pauls town	2,398	2,296	-4.3	2,107	42.1	22.1	0.0	6.3	29.6	25.1	23.0	45.7	64.9	8.9	884	69.7
St. Stephens CDP	8,759	-	-	9,408	71.8	7.2	3.7	0.3	17.0	23.8	16.8	39.1	50.4	18.4	3,609	86.3
Salem CDP	2,218	-	-	1,757	91.5	0.0	0.0	5.2	3.4	9.7	30.4	49.8	30.3	22.0	890	77.8
Salemburg town	422	414	-1.9	458	76.4	10.9	0.0	6.8	5.9	17.7	25.8	43.8	45.8	26.9	216	75.5
Salisbury city	33,525	33,988	1.4	33,727	49.3	35.0	0.8	2.9	12.0	21.6	18.3	37.7	43.6	22.3	12,524	85.8
Saluda city	715	697	-2.5	891	92.8	3.4	0.8	2.0	1.0	15.5	36.5	55.1	30.8	37.9	369	93.0
Salvo CDP	229	-	-	91	100.0	0.0	0.0	0.0	0.0	13.2	25.3	59.4	0.0	88.6	43	100.0
Sandy Creek town	259	304	17.4	230	91.7	0.0	0.0	4.8	3.5	11.3	25.2	52.8	42.3	9.7	107	95.3
Sandyfield town	444	418	-5.9	429	28.9	58.5	0.0	2.6	10.0	22.8	11.0	34.4	43.2	15.2	157	91.1
Sanford city	28,217	30,085	6.6	29,456	43.4	27.4	1.7	1.3	26.2	27.9	11.3	34.1	45.6	22.3	10,418	86.4
Saratoga town	408	404		413	41.9	43.3	0.0	1.9	12.8	16.5	17.2	52.9	64.3	10.2	161	82.0
Sawmills town	5,223	5,189	-0.7	5,165	87.8	1.3	1.5	2.6	6.7	18.9	17.8	46.6	57.5	11.4	1,959	87.0
Saxapahaw CDP	1,648	-	-	1,599	78.2	2.3	0.0	1.4	18.1	20.5	13.6	42.1	46.3	22.5	667	93.7
Scotch Meadows CDP	580	-	-	481	76.7	0.0	0.0	23.3	0.0	21.6	27.7	52.2	15.1	43.0	205	100.0
Scotland Neck town	2,046	1,840	-10.1	1,421	32.6	67.0	0.0	0.0	0.4	13.9	22.1	47.5	61.5	13.1	611	76.9
Seaboard town	624	543	-13.0	723	11.5	86.9	0.0	0.3	1.4	33.7	14.8	39.6	58.3	13.4	295	85.4
Sea Breeze CDP	1,969	-	-	1,785	96.7	0.0	0.0	1.4	1.9	13.1	23.2	43.0	15.7	59.7	918	100.0
Seagrove town	229	229	0.0	285	95.4	0.0	0.0	0.0	4.6	23.9	26.3	44.5	44.8	14.2	112	84.8
Sedalia town	628	684	8.9	501	13.0	81.8	0.0	1.8	3.4	11.4	39.3	56.0	46.4	15.7	213	72.3
Selma town	6,122	7,101	16.0	6,746	21.4	44.9	0.3	0.9	32.5	34.8	14.0	30.5	50.6	12.1	2,311	82.7
Seven Devils town	203	216	6.4	327	97.6	0.0	0.6	0.3	1.5	6.7	44.0	61.6	13.7	57.4	176	96.6
Seven Lakes CDP	4,888	-	-	4,903	95.0	5.0	0.0	0.0	0.0	18.4	32.0	54.7	17.0	56.6	2,134	93.8
Seven Springs town	110	111	0.9	53	86.8	13.2	0.0	0.0	0.0	22.6	17.0	50.5	74.4	5.1	22	90.9
Severn town	276	239	-13.4	212	54.2	38.7	0.0	0.0	7.1	17.5	24.5	50.8	52.4	4.3	105	79.0
Shallotte town	3,495	4,351	24.5	4,090	70.7	14.0	1.2	5.5	8.6	17.5	24.5	53.4	32.7	23.6	1,682	89.5
Shannon CDP	263	-	-	380	2.6	14.7	0.0	32.4	50.3	53.9	10.3	14.8	84.0	5.7	77	90.9
Sharpsburg town	2,024	2,013	-0.5	2,133	20.1	74.8	0.0	2.1	3.0	29.6	14.3	33.9	55.6	13.7	916	81.2

1 May be of any race.

Table A. All Places — **Population and Housing**

STATE City, town, township, borough, or CDP (county if applicable)	Population: 2010 census total population	Population: 2019 estimated population	Population: Percent change 2010–2019	Population: ACS total population estimate 2015–2019	Race and Hispanic or Latino origin (percent): White alone, not Hispanic or Latino	Race: Black alone, not Hispanic or Latino	Race: Asian alone, not Hispanic or Latino	Race: All other races or 2 or more races, not Hispanic or Latino	Race: Hispanic or Latino[1]	Age (percent): Under 18 years old	Age: Age 65 years and older	Age: Median age	Educational attainment of persons age 25 and older: Percent High school diploma or less	Educational attainment: Percent Bachelor's degree or more	Occupied housing units: Total	Occupied housing units: Percent with a computer
	1	2	3	4	5	6	7	8	9	10	11	12	13	14	15	16
NORTH CAROLINA—Con.																
Shelby city	20,363	20,026	-1.7	20,007	57.3	37.3	0.4	1.5	3.4	21.9	20.1	44.7	47.0	24.2	8,013	78.7
Siler City town	7,821	8,225	5.2	8,078	26.5	20.1	1.3	5.7	46.5	30.2	16.2	35.0	61.0	10.1	2,735	81.6
Silver City CDP	882	-	-	949	1.3	86.7	0.0	12.0	0.0	26.8	21.7	37.3	52.0	15.1	374	72.7
Silver Lake CDP	5,598	-	-	6,476	70.5	9.1	1.4	6.0	13.0	23.2	15.6	38.9	34.7	25.4	2,534	94.9
Simpson village	420	482	14.8	400	49.8	43.0	0.0	3.5	3.8	14.8	19.3	48.8	38.8	18.9	164	85.4
Sims town	282	286	1.4	599	68.1	11.9	0.0	0.0	20.0	39.9	8.5	28.3	42.1	18.9	212	98.1
Skippers Corner CDP	2,785	-	-	2,716	75.5	15.3	0.0	4.7	4.6	10.2	15.4	37.7	38.5	19.5	895	96.8
Smithfield town	11,043	12,985	17.6	12,400	51.7	24.9	0.4	1.9	21.1	21.6	21.8	44.9	47.6	20.7	4,951	83.5
Sneads Ferry CDP	2,646	-	-	2,785	96.2	0.0	3.3	0.5	0.0	23.3	16.7	36.0	38.8	21.4	1,087	96.1
Snow Hill town	1,590	1,512	-4.9	1,699	42.3	41.1	0.0	3.6	13.1	22.5	21.1	42.9	51.1	14.7	760	76.2
Southern Pines town	12,411	14,657	18.1	14,022	70.6	20.9	2.4	1.8	4.2	18.8	27.2	42.8	21.0	51.5	6,321	88.3
Southern Shores town	2,714	2,958	9.0	2,899	94.7	1.0	0.6	3.7	0.0	19.0	34.5	58.2	14.8	60.7	1,225	98.7
South Henderson CDP	1,213	-	-	1,136	19.7	54.8	0.0	0.7	24.8	28.1	17.7	37.7	72.1	4.5	403	55.8
South Mills CDP	454	-	-	456	100.0	0.0	0.0	0.0	0.0	28.5	8.6	53.8	42.6	0.0	181	93.4
Southmont CDP	1,470	-	-	1,150	94.1	5.9	0.0	0.0	0.0	17.0	21.1	57.1	44.6	24.4	543	90.2
Southport city	2,916	3,966	36.0	3,739	89.8	5.7	0.0	1.3	3.2	17.3	34.9	55.8	36.2	28.9	1,434	95.1
South Rosemary CDP	2,836	-	-	2,747	39.7	60.3	0.0	0.0	0.0	20.1	21.4	46.7	74.8	5.7	1,231	81.3
South Weldon CDP	705	-	-	840	9.5	90.5	0.0	0.0	0.0	44.2	3.6	27.6	69.8	2.0	334	66.2
Sparta town	1,741	1,723	-	1,630	85.9	2.1	0.2	0.5	11.3	19.3	27.7	49.2	64.6	11.3	732	73.0
Speed town	80	75	-6.3	79	20.3	79.7	0.0	0.0	0.0	5.1	53.2	66.5	72.9	2.9	43	69.8
Spencer town	3,268	3,257	-0.3	3,230	50.7	39.6	1.0	1.6	7.1	24.5	15.5	35.3	47.3	18.9	1,153	90.2
Spindale town	4,309	4,202	-2.5	4,190	64.3	29.9	1.9	2.5	1.5	19.2	14.8	40.2	47.7	15.3	1,564	74.3
Spivey's Corner CDP	506	-	-	462	92.0	0.0	0.0	0.0	8.0	22.9	17.7	43.2	49.1	20.1	133	81.2
Spring Hope town	1,321	1,310	-0.8	1,687	35.2	52.0	0.0	9.3	3.4	23.8	19.1	40.0	52.1	15.8	661	74.1
Spring Lake town	12,012	12,005	-0.1	12,119	38.4	35.0	2.7	7.7	16.1	25.9	5.4	25.5	31.9	27.6	4,369	94.9
Spruce Pine town	2,246	2,143	-4.6	2,273	86.3	0.4	0.4	1.6	11.3	22.3	18.9	37.5	44.9	15.0	936	87.2
Staley town	395	398	0.8	329	72.3	10.6	0.0	10.9	6.1	22.8	16.4	40.2	52.8	6.9	125	85.6
Stallings town	13,762	16,145	17.3	15,554	74.2	9.4	3.5	2.3	10.6	27.3	14.2	39.8	24.4	45.2	5,443	96.8
Stanfield town	1,489	1,548	4.0	1,264	97.2	1.3	0.0	0.7	0.9	20.6	15.0	43.3	36.3	24.0	503	92.6
Stanley town	3,533	3,762	6.5	3,679	81.1	12.8	0.0	2.0	4.1	26.4	17.7	37.2	48.3	20.4	1,395	88.5
Stantonsburg town	786	779	-0.9	633	34.4	55.8	0.0	7.6	2.2	14.8	18.6	50.3	61.4	14.9	278	82.0
Star town	876	849	-3.1	756	59.8	8.3	1.6	0.1	30.2	19.0	22.5	48.5	52.7	20.6	262	71.0
Statesville city	24,521	27,528	12.3	26,685	49.1	35.4	2.0	2.3	11.1	24.5	15.9	38.8	44.4	22.9	10,628	86.2
Stedman town	1,025	1,076	5.0	1,364	76.0	9.9	2.2	6.5	5.4	25.0	11.3	35.9	36.4	29.4	501	92.0
Stem town	452	567	25.4	1,177	68.8	9.8	0.0	3.4	18.0	27.5	7.2	29.8	31.1	20.6	389	96.9
Stokes CDP	376	-	-	777	70.5	24.2	0.0	0.0	5.3	17.8	2.6	43.3	42.4	20.2	250	76.8
Stokesdale town	5,033	5,489	9.1	5,396	75.8	13.5	1.3	2.5	6.9	28.7	8.5	38.2	30.1	34.5	1,837	94.3
Stoneville town	1,301	1,257	-3.4	1,425	73.0	12.5	0.4	2.8	11.3	26.9	17.3	39.6	45.5	13.3	474	81.4
Stonewall town	281	270	-3.9	313	62.0	26.5	3.5	1.0	7.0	18.2	23.0	49.3	36.2	3.4	151	96.7
Stony Point CDP	1,317	-	-	1,527	69.4	1.5	0.0	0.0	29.1	24.7	12.8	35.9	71.3	5.3	574	83.3
Stovall town	404	420	4.0	351	45.9	48.7	0.0	0.0	5.4	16.2	23.6	40.8	59.8	9.0	133	66.9
Sugar Mountain village	201	197	-2.0	443	95.5	0.0	4.1	0.5	0.0	14.2	46.3	62.5	15.3	55.5	219	96.8
Summerfield town	10,238	11,376	11.1	11,151	91.9	2.1	1.6	1.2	3.2	25.5	14.1	43.3	21.3	56.1	3,902	93.9
Sunbury CDP	289	-	-	300	54.7	45.3	0.0	0.0	0.0	8.0	40.7	63.1	39.1	26.4	164	100.0
Sunset Beach town	3,568	4,037	13.1	3,901	94.1	0.3	1.4	2.1	2.1	6.1	50.6	65.2	22.9	48.2	2,014	92.5
Surf City town	1,927	2,469	28.1	3,449	86.4	3.0	0.8	4.6	5.2	23.8	15.9	37.3	21.5	44.3	1,272	97.2
Swannanoa CDP	4,576	-	-	4,127	81.2	4.2	0.6	3.1	10.9	14.0	13.7	37.6	55.3	22.0	1,614	72.7
Swan Quarter CDP	324	-	-	398	62.1	2.8	0.0	2.5	32.7	14.1	20.9	39.6	80.5	0.0	164	100.0
Swansboro town	2,667	3,344	25.4	3,217	80.3	2.1	9.4	1.9	6.3	23.8	17.9	40.7	35.4	35.1	1,360	95.5
Swepsonville town	1,164	1,384	18.9	1,939	75.2	12.0	2.0	3.0	7.8	20.2	15.9	40.2	33.3	30.9	796	93.0
Sylva town	2,559	2,738	7.0	2,687	72.5	4.2	2.2	14.7	6.4	23.8	15.9	38.0	34.3	37.4	1,151	85.8
Tabor City town	4,023	4,163	3.5	4,061	45.5	39.3	0.5	5.9	8.8	16.5	14.7	37.4	66.0	7.1	968	74.2
Tarboro town	11,525	10,715	-7.0	10,915	37.1	54.7	0.2	1.5	6.5	21.2	23.0	42.2	48.5	20.2	4,635	77.3
Tar Heel town	121	115	-5.0	135	99.3	0.0	0.0	0.7	0.0	15.6	28.1	41.8	40.8	17.5	67	92.5
Taylorsville town	2,089	2,159	3.4	2,361	70.3	15.7	1.1	6.2	6.8	20.2	25.8	48.3	57.1	15.4	927	76.7
Taylortown town	776	858	10.6	1,037	49.6	42.1	1.8	2.3	4.1	20.2	17.6	46.1	53.3	13.0	440	80.9
Teachey town	424	423	-0.2	484	28.3	42.1	0.0	0.0	29.5	23.6	32.2	48.0	49.9	16.7	185	88.6
Thomasville city	26,804	26,649	-0.6	26,784	62.1	17.6	0.8	2.5	16.9	24.6	16.8	39.3	54.8	15.2	11,190	84.5
Toast CDP	1,450	-	-	1,564	88.7	5.1	0.0	0.0	6.3	23.8	22.2	46.1	44.4	15.2	641	68.5
Tobaccoville village	2,434	2,718	11.7	2,634	92.0	6.0	0.0	1.1	0.9	17.5	16.9	48.1	43.3	17.7	1,074	90.0
Topsail Beach town	368	427	16.0	409	100.0	0.0	0.0	0.0	0.0	9.5	33.0	58.8	20.0	63.2	202	96.0
Trenton town	307	280	-8.8	359	48.5	26.7	0.0	0.8	24.0	29.2	13.4	32.4	62.4	12.9	119	74.8
Trent Woods town	4,155	4,021	-3.2	4,050	93.1	0.5	0.0	2.7	3.7	20.7	27.3	49.3	17.1	53.9	1,644	95.1
Trinity city	6,600	6,606	0.1	6,579	91.7	1.4	2.4	1.0	3.5	22.9	20.6	43.9	43.2	20.8	2,576	88.0
Troutman town	2,455	2,769	12.8	2,685	74.5	20.0	1.2	2.6	1.7	24.3	13.8	35.7	33.2	32.5	995	93.4
Troy town	3,494	3,222	-7.8	3,294	49.3	35.8	0.9	9.4	4.6	16.5	13.9	40.6	55.8	14.0	1,099	70.1
Tryon town	1,638	1,615	-1.4	1,482	89.1	8.3	0.0	2.2	0.3	8.8	47.0	62.4	13.6	51.8	823	81.5
Turkey town	292	293	0.3	246	57.3	26.8	0.8	2.4	12.6	23.6	15.9	47.0	77.1	7.1	82	89.0
Tyro CDP	3,879	-	-	3,954	89.7	2.1	0.0	1.4	6.8	23.4	16.3	35.1	46.3	16.0	1,518	88.5
Unionville town	6,146	7,195	17.1	6,959	95.6	1.3	0.0	0.5	2.6	22.9	14.8	42.7	54.1	20.8	2,614	90.2
Valdese town	4,468	4,420	-1.1	4,410	93.9	0.4	1.5	1.8	2.4	19.3	22.5	45.8	55.0	21.6	1,545	86.2
Valle Crucis CDP	412	-	-	226	100.0	0.0	0.0	0.0	0.0	35.0	11.1	35.9	24.6	49.3	72	100.0
Valley Hill CDP	2,070	-	-	1,927	91.6	0.0	0.0	4.0	4.4	7.7	34.9	59.3	33.9	29.8	905	96.2
Vanceboro town	999	965	-3.4	1,065	41.1	46.4	0.0	6.2	6.3	33.3	17.3	37.9	54.0	13.1	464	85.6
Vandemere town	254	244	-3.9	234	49.1	49.1	0.0	1.7	0.0	13.2	33.3	55.2	60.0	10.5	102	83.3
Vander CDP	1,146	-	-	1,006	55.4	27.3	6.5	3.0	7.9	27.2	25.0	38.9	37.7	23.1	443	75.8
Vann Crossroads CDP	336	-	-	391	78.3	0.0	0.0	0.0	21.7	35.5	27.9	24.8	30.7	53.1	102	100.0
Varnamtown town	550	596	8.4	465	97.0	0.0	0.0	3.0	0.0	11.8	39.1	59.2	41.9	21.4	211	76.3
Vass town	705	789	11.9	841	61.7	16.4	0.0	11.8	10.1	35.3	10.5	35.4	35.1	22.0	325	86.8
Waco town	319	314	-1.6	344	93.3	6.7	0.0	0.0	0.0	11.6	25.0	50.0	70.5	11.6	131	64.1
Wade town	557	583	4.7	684	71.9	14.5	0.4	11.8	1.3	26.8	15.1	37.5	39.3	16.2	252	83.7
Wadesboro town	5,812	5,275	-9.2	5,305	25.0	72.0	2.6	0.4	0.0	20.4	18.5	36.0	60.2	12.6	2,022	77.1
Wagram town	840	777	-7.5	773	33.2	47.2	0.6	16.2	2.7	17.3	23.9	42.9	58.2	10.3	296	77.0
Wake Forest town	30,135	45,629	51.4	42,111	74.4	14.7	1.4	3.8	5.6	30.5	11.4	36.7	18.8	54.6	14,732	95.3
Wakulla CDP	105	-	-	199	0.0	0.0	0.0	100.0	0.0	51.8	0.0	15.8	25.0	17.7	54	100.0
Walkertown town	4,721	5,242	11.0	5,099	72.6	20.1	0.3	0.9	6.2	25.7	17.6	40.0	48.2	24.1	2,052	88.1
Wallace town	3,884	3,863	-0.5	3,891	59.2	20.4	0.0	4.5	15.9	29.4	21.1	44.7	51.9	13.1	1,492	75.5
Wallburg town	2,992	3,107	3.8	3,053	93.3	0.0	0.3	0.7	5.8	22.1	14.4	44.0	37.8	22.1	1,211	93.3
Walnut Cove town	1,621	1,533	-5.4	1,892	75.1	15.8	0.0	5.0	4.1	21.4	22.1	44.2	51.4	15.9	802	73.2
Walnut Creek village	848	861	1.5	994	90.6	5.1	1.5	0.8	1.9	20.4	25.5	53.1	7.6	74.6	396	96.2
Walstonburg town	219	208	-5.0	222	84.2	10.4	0.0	5.4	0.0	29.3	15.8	34.9	45.9	17.8	83	85.5
Wanchese CDP	1,642	-	-	1,732	89.9	0.0	0.0	0.0	10.1	21.5	19.7	43.0	48.1	19.4	683	95.0

1 May be of any race.

Table A. All Places — **Population and Housing**

STATE City, town, township, borough, or CDP (county if applicable)	Population				Race and Hispanic or Latino origin (percent)					Age (percent)			Educational attainment of persons age 25 and older		Occupied housing units	
	2010 census total population	2019 estimated population	Percent change 2010–2019	ACS total population estimate 2015–2019	White alone, not Hispanic or Latino	Black alone, not Hispanic or Latino	Asian alone, not Hispanic or Latino	All other races or 2 or more races, not Hispanic or Latino	Hispanic or Latino[1]	Under 18 years old	Age 65 years and older	Median age	Percent High school diploma or less	Percent Bachelor's degree or more	Total	Percent with a computer
	1	2	3	4	5	6	7	8	9	10	11	12	13	14	15	16
NORTH CAROLINA—Con.																
Warrenton town	898	833	-7.2	1,188	48.1	43.1	0.3	5.0	3.6	10.2	36.6	56.8	46.4	26.2	555	73.7
Warsaw town	3,104	3,089	-0.5	3,119	19.6	44.1	0.1	7.7	28.5	26.0	15.2	33.3	66.0	10.0	1,139	75.2
Washington city	9,845	9,497	-3.5	9,590	46.6	40.5	0.0	2.2	10.8	22.7	23.0	43.4	45.4	22.1	4,038	76.9
Washington Park town	451	428	-5.1	609	92.6	0.3	0.3	1.6	5.1	18.2	23.0	50.7	15.8	54.2	270	91.1
Watha town	188	240	27.7	185	82.2	1.6	0.0	2.7	13.5	13.0	23.2	48.5	62.2	1.4	85	70.6
Waves CDP	134	-	-	56	100.0	0.0	0.0	0.0	0.0	0.0	0.0	56.5	19.6	23.2	24	54.2
Waxhaw town	9,915	17,147	72.9	15,237	76.8	9.8	3.7	2.9	6.8	32.5	8.8	37.3	18.4	57.0	4,773	98.3
Waynesville town	9,866	10,141	2.8	9,965	88.5	2.4	0.7	2.6	5.8	18.9	29.1	48.8	42.7	27.8	4,680	83.1
Weaverville town	3,693	4,027	9.0	3,940	97.6	0.6	0.7	0.7	0.5	13.8	31.6	53.5	18.7	56.3	1,785	94.0
Webster town	361	387	7.2	362	87.6	4.7	0.0	7.5	0.3	26.8	23.5	39.3	27.0	52.0	152	94.7
Weddington town	9,532	11,182	17.3	10,794	86.4	3.6	5.3	2.9	1.9	28.5	13.7	42.6	14.1	61.7	3,424	98.8
Welcome CDP	4,162	-	-	3,804	93.8	0.0	1.6	0.1	4.5	21.6	20.0	43.2	43.5	21.8	1,612	85.8
Weldon town	1,648	1,470	-10.8	1,715	21.9	76.4	0.0	1.0	0.7	20.8	18.0	39.1	51.5	19.0	656	79.1
Wendell town	5,838	8,577	46.9	7,308	57.0	27.9	0.5	0.4	14.2	26.9	9.9	34.3	33.1	33.1	2,686	92.8
Wentworth town	2,782	2,720	-2.2	2,730	67.3	22.7	0.2	7.3	2.5	18.5	18.2	42.1	51.2	16.3	953	84.5
Wesley Chapel village	7,829	9,295	18.7	8,974	85.2	5.0	3.5	2.4	3.8	29.8	11.0	41.0	23.6	48.1	2,620	94.5
West Canton CDP	1,247	-	-	1,256	95.6	0.8	1.4	2.1	0.0	23.9	16.8	42.9	54.4	13.2	522	77.0
West Jefferson town	1,332	1,315	-1.3	1,539	86.7	3.1	4.0	1.8	4.4	18.6	24.4	46.3	54.9	16.3	663	79.6
West Marion CDP	1,348	-	-	1,392	92.2	1.1	0.0	4.2	2.6	17.9	24.2	47.2	54.2	9.1	686	83.7
Westport CDP	4,026	-	-	4,117	95.3	1.7	0.2	2.0	0.8	21.9	19.1	47.8	19.1	55.0	1,586	97.8
Whispering Pines village	2,954	3,399	15.1	3,288	91.3	2.5	1.4	2.4	2.3	31.8	19.7	39.0	21.5	51.7	1,149	98.0
Whitakers town	744	702	-5.6	649	19.6	77.3	0.0	0.9	2.2	22.2	27.0	47.8	59.9	6.6	304	69.1
White Lake town	816	769	-5.8	1,000	91.5	3.7	0.0	0.9	3.9	17.9	29.1	55.0	41.9	32.3	452	89.6
White Oak CDP	338	-	-	351	48.7	49.0	0.0	0.0	2.3	23.6	33.9	61.3	35.8	11.9	200	87.0
White Plains CDP	1,074	-	-	1,094	99.6	0.4	0.0	0.0	0.0	16.0	15.6	49.4	51.8	16.2	493	80.1
Whiteville city	5,371	5,299	-1.3	5,386	47.8	40.7	0.7	6.6	4.1	27.5	19.6	40.7	42.1	23.3	2,153	81.4
Whitsett town	590	639	8.3	732	82.4	16.5	1.0	0.1	0.0	12.3	26.1	48.8	39.4	23.4	264	84.8
Wilkesboro town	3,578	3,453	-3.5	3,495	80.4	7.4	1.6	5.7	4.9	19.6	24.9	39.5	46.8	25.3	1,386	81.3
Williamston town	5,746	5,202	-9.5	5,312	36.7	56.3	2.0	1.6	3.4	20.3	24.0	47.1	51.2	21.7	2,274	84.8
Wilmington city	106,456	123,744	16.2	120,194	71.7	18.0	1.3	2.7	6.3	17.8	16.5	36.0	28.2	41.5	52,207	91.3
Wilson city	49,168	49,459	0.6	49,272	37.3	48.2	1.2	3.1	10.2	23.2	16.7	38.6	47.6	22.8	19,667	82.8
Wilson's Mills town	2,268	2,756	21.5	2,613	49.3	21.4	0.8	2.6	25.9	28.1	7.7	31.2	51.0	14.5	840	95.4
Windsor town	3,623	3,373	-6.9	3,457	32.7	58.4	3.6	2.2	3.2	14.8	21.3	35.6	59.5	14.9	1,018	79.4
Winfall town	606	610	0.7	754	56.8	37.9	0.0	4.5	0.8	20.6	23.2	40.4	44.7	19.8	322	79.8
Wingate town	3,466	4,594	32.5	4,258	52.6	24.1	2.2	5.0	16.2	19.8	9.9	22.6	45.0	26.5	1,002	96.9
Winston-Salem city	229,627	247,945	8.0	244,115	45.7	34.2	2.5	2.6	15.0	23.8	14.1	35.5	36.7	34.5	94,957	89.5
Winterville town	9,218	9,931	7.7	9,645	54.8	36.9	1.7	3.5	3.1	25.7	12.0	39.4	23.9	45.2	3,710	90.2
Winton town	771	722	-6.4	832	30.5	63.1	0.0	3.1	3.2	28.0	13.7	38.0	55.9	15.8	291	81.1
Woodfin town	6,274	6,717	7.1	6,612	78.7	2.3	2.0	3.1	13.9	18.0	17.8	39.3	34.2	34.1	2,495	87.3
Woodland town	807	703	-12.9	785	40.4	40.6	0.0	12.4	6.6	28.8	24.7	42.0	59.3	13.9	325	79.1
Woodlawn CDP	900	-	-	646	72.9	19.5	5.3	2.3	0.0	6.2	20.0	54.3	37.1	31.7	313	100.0
Wrightsboro CDP	4,896	-	-	4,525	64.4	31.7	0.0	1.2	2.7	16.3	15.3	42.4	56.4	17.0	1,777	94.5
Wrightsville Beach town	2,488	2,556	2.7	2,565	95.2	0.2	0.0	3.0	1.6	13.3	19.6	43.7	9.4	75.3	1,166	97.9
Yadkinville town	2,973	2,876	-3.3	2,888	67.9	4.7	0.0	2.0	25.4	21.3	28.0	43.6	53.7	15.0	1,161	79.7
Yanceyville town	2,074	1,963	-5.4	2,371	37.0	56.1	0.0	2.6	4.3	18.6	22.7	40.4	66.1	10.5	891	71.0
Youngsville town	1,151	1,375	19.5	2,003	55.9	27.7	0.7	3.2	12.5	27.4	11.1	29.6	33.4	28.3	809	94.1
Zebulon town	4,459	5,917	32.7	5,404	47.4	39.8	1.2	5.2	6.4	31.9	18.5	36.1	41.2	18.5	1,884	86.9
NORTH DAKOTA	672,576	762,062	13.3	756,717	84.4	2.9	1.4	7.5	3.7	23.2	14.9	35.1	33.8	30.0	318,322	89.8
Abercrombie city	262	249	-5.0	266	97.0	0.0	0.0	3.0	0.0	17.7	21.1	50.0	50.3	8.4	110	91.8
Adams city	127	119	-6.3	149	89.3	0.0	0.0	0.0	10.7	12.8	17.4	34.8	50.0	15.6	78	85.9
Alamo city	58	78	34.5	49	100.0	0.0	0.0	0.0	0.0	42.9	6.1	39.3	18.5	22.2	14	92.9
Alexander city	223	375	68.2	258	100.0	0.0	0.0	0.0	0.0	29.5	5.4	40.2	35.7	11.9	70	95.7
Alice city	40	40	0.0	32	100.0	0.0	0.0	0.0	0.0	31.3	12.5	37.5	63.6	13.6	13	92.3
Almont city	118	119	0.8	74	94.6	0.0	0.0	5.4	0.0	9.5	17.6	47.3	61.1	0.0	43	90.7
Alsen city	35	32	-8.6	19	100.0	0.0	0.0	0.0	0.0	0.0	0.0	31.9	22.2	55.6	14	100.0
Ambrose city	25	24	-4.0	12	100.0	0.0	0.0	0.0	0.0	0.0	58.3	65.3	16.7	33.3	10	70.0
Amenia city	97	96		90	96.7	1.1	0.0	1.1	1.1	24.4	18.9	40.8	35.9	29.7	38	97.4
Amidon city	20	23	15.0	32	71.9	0.0	0.0	28.1	0.0	6.3	62.5	65.8	33.3	56.7	17	88.2
Anamoose city	227	244	7.5	256	99.2	0.0	0.0	0.8	0.0	21.9	22.7	46.8	52.4	15.2	127	81.1
Aneta city	222	210	-5.4	222	92.8	0.0	0.0	5.0	2.3	9.5	22.1	44.7	50.7	13.0	125	86.4
Antler city	27	26	-3.7	30	76.7	0.0	0.0	20.0	3.3	23.3	30.0	45.7	84.2	0.0	12	66.7
Ardoch city	73	78	6.8	35	40.0	0.0	0.0	0.0	60.0	0.0	2.9	52.7	75.0	25.0	17	70.6
Argusville city	475	468	-1.5	566	96.1	2.7	0.0	1.2	0.0	41.5	4.6	32.6	14.5	51.6	167	95.2
Arnegard city	115	175	52.2	58	70.7	0.0	0.0	19.0	10.3	8.6	29.3	61.5	30.2	1.9	28	78.6
Arthur city	337	332	-1.5	327	96.0	0.3	0.0	0.6	3.1	23.5	30.0	47.8	28.6	27.4	143	83.9
Ashley city	749	661	-11.7	574	95.1	0.0	2.3	2.1	0.5	9.4	51.0	66.0	43.7	19.9	329	76.6
Auburn CDP	48	-	-	9	100.0	0.0	0.0	0.0	0.0	0.0	55.6	0.0	100.0	0.0	4	100.0
Ayr city	17	18	5.9	3	100.0	0.0	0.0	0.0	0.0	0.0	66.7	0.0	100.0	0.0	2	0.0
Balfour city	26	27	3.8	18	100.0	0.0	0.0	0.0	0.0	0.0	11.1	57.3	88.9	5.6	13	76.9
Balta city	65	59	-9.2	100	98.0	0.0	0.0	0.0	2.0	27.0	17.0	38.5	78.5	12.3	41	68.3
Bantry city	14	14	0.0	10	100.0	0.0	0.0	0.0	0.0	0.0	30.0	51.5	42.9	28.6	6	100.0
Barney city	54	52	-3.7	53	88.7	0.0	0.0	1.9	9.4	13.2	18.9	55.5	34.1	31.8	28	92.9
Barton CDP	20	-	-	-	-	-	-	-	-	-	-	-	-	-	-	-
Bathgate city	60	58	-3.3	69	92.8	4.3	0.0	2.9	0.0	11.6	23.2	58.0	21.1	52.6	24	79.2
Beach city	1,021	1,043	2.2	1,024	85.4	0.0	0.0	11.2	3.3	18.7	23.8	48.4	33.7	28.0	545	78.7
Belcourt CDP	2,078	-	-	2,270	1.5	0.0	0.0	97.5	1.0	33.7	10.5	28.2	33.8	21.3	720	72.9
Belfield city	799	1,012	26.7	955	94.8	5.1	0.0	0.1	0.0	29.3	17.9	33.5	59.0	8.8	388	85.1
Benedict city	66	76	15.2	52	82.7	0.0	0.0	9.6	7.7	5.8	42.3	56.7	44.9	20.4	33	60.6
Bergen city	7	8	14.3	8	75.0	0.0	0.0	0.0	25.0	0.0	37.5	58.0	100.0	0.0	2	100.0
Berlin city	34	35	2.9	49	100.0	0.0	0.0	0.0	0.0	24.5	12.2	40.5	46.7	6.7	15	86.7
Berthold city	459	481	4.8	532	94.2	0.0	0.4	1.1	4.3	26.7	13.5	44.3	39.7	17.7	216	93.1
Beulah city	3,123	3,139	0.5	3,235	95.2	0.0	0.1	2.5	2.2	23.6	15.9	39.1	35.5	23.8	1,358	90.0
Binford city	183	169	-7.7	181	100.0	0.0	0.0	0.0	0.0	17.1	25.4	46.3	54.7	19.7	91	75.8
Bisbee city	126	126	0.0	139	71.9	0.0	0.0	25.9	2.2	28.1	23.7	43.3	58.0	5.0	63	63.5
Bismarck city	61,324	73,529	19.9	72,777	88.1	2.6	0.9	5.9	2.5	21.8	17.0	37.2	29.4	35.7	32,044	89.7
Blanchard CDP	26	-	-	5	100.0	0.0	0.0	0.0	0.0	0.0	40.0	0.0	60.0	40.0	2	100.0
Bottineau city	2,210	2,154	-2.5	2,094	85.6	1.7	0.0	11.1	1.6	19.9	24.4	42.9	40.3	26.4	886	81.0
Bowbells city	336	336	0.0	320	97.5	0.0	0.6	1.9	0.0	19.7	15.0	45.3	31.9	28.6	139	87.1
Bowdon city	128	120	-6.3	139	99.3	0.0	0.0	0.7	0.0	15.1	41.0	56.4	47.4	18.1	80	60.0
Bowman city	1,651	1,599	-3.1	1,560	88.1	0.1	0.0	2.1	9.7	23.7	21.9	37.3	45.8	26.2	660	90.5

1 May be of any race.

Table A. All Places — **Population and Housing**

STATE City, town, township, borough, or CDP (county if applicable)	2010 census total population	2019 estimated population	Percent change 2010–2019	ACS total population estimate 2015–2019	White alone, not Hispanic or Latino	Black alone, not Hispanic or Latino	Asian alone, not Hispanic or Latino	All other races or 2 or more races, not Hispanic or Latino	Hispanic or Latino[1]	Under 18 years old	Age 65 years and older	Median age	Percent High school diploma or less	Percent Bachelor's degree or more	Total	Percent with a computer
	1	2	3	4	5	6	7	8	9	10	11	12	13	14	15	16
NORTH DAKOTA—Con.																
Braddock city	21	27	28.6	19	100.0	0.0	0.0	0.0	0.0	5.3	21.1	22.9	22.2	33.3	15	100.0
Briarwood city	73	71	-2.7	43	95.3	0.0	4.7	0.0	0.0	14.0	16.3	50.5	18.8	40.6	18	100.0
Brinsmade city	35	34	-2.9	39	100.0	0.0	0.0	0.0	0.0	25.6	10.3	46.8	55.6	7.4	15	93.3
Brocket city	57	54	-5.3	9	100.0	0.0	0.0	0.0	0.0	0.0	22.2	60.4	0.0	11.1	6	83.3
Brooktree Park CDP	80	-	-	156	100.0	0.0	0.0	0.0	0.0	47.4	0.0	34.4	0.0	78.0	40	100.0
Buchanan city	90	110	22.2	61	96.7	0.0	0.0	3.3	0.0	34.4	0.0	31.4	59.5	8.1	19	100.0
Bucyrus city	27	26	-3.7	19	100.0	0.0	0.0	0.0	0.0	0.0	57.9	69.3	73.7	10.5	11	45.5
Buffalo city	187	184	-1.6	193	92.2	0.0	0.0	4.7	3.1	28.0	20.2	41.1	31.4	21.9	87	88.5
Burlington city	1,062	1,201	13.1	1,420	92.3	0.0	0.4	5.4	2.0	34.9	8.0	30.1	42.3	29.0	505	97.6
Butte city	68	76	11.8	95	100.0	0.0	0.0	0.0	0.0	23.2	26.3	44.4	74.2	4.8	38	86.8
Buxton city	323	320	-0.9	416	90.6	0.0	0.0	8.9	0.5	26.4	12.5	41.8	34.8	20.8	176	92.0
Caledonia CDP	39	-	-	23	100.0	0.0	0.0	0.0	0.0	0.0	73.9	68.4	43.5	0.0	15	66.7
Calio city	22	20	-9.1	3	100.0	0.0	0.0	0.0	0.0	0.0	100.0	0.0	100.0	0.0	3	100.0
Calvin city	20	18	-10.0	12	100.0	0.0	0.0	0.0	0.0	33.3	16.7	57.5	50.0	12.5	4	100.0
Cando city	1,101	1,057	-4.0	1,083	82.1	1.6	0.4	8.7	7.3	16.9	17.5	46.4	42.2	17.6	557	76.5
Cannon Ball CDP	875	-	-	935	4.1	0.0	0.0	91.1	4.8	42.6	5.9	22.9	55.4	19.5	185	61.1
Canton City (Hensel) city	38	33	-13.2	25	52.0	0.0	0.0	48.0	0.0	40.0	12.0	31.8	40.0	26.7	8	62.5
Carpio city	157	142	-9.6	133	88.7	0.0	0.0	9.8	1.5	24.8	16.5	42.4	43.2	17.9	53	83.0
Carrington city	2,062	1,980	-4.0	2,133	93.4	0.0	0.0	5.6	0.9	18.6	23.6	45.3	37.2	26.7	946	82.0
Carson city	293	269	-8.2	238	95.0	0.0	0.0	3.8	1.3	16.4	32.8	48.5	41.1	18.4	142	72.5
Casselton city	2,333	2,475	6.1	2,677	96.9	0.7	0.0	0.9	1.5	30.7	13.8	34.5	23.3	34.3	1,019	93.6
Cathay city	43	39	-9.3	17	100.0	0.0	0.0	0.0	0.0	17.6	11.8	58.5	64.3	7.1	11	100.0
Cavalier city	1,350	1,238	-8.3	1,130	91.8	0.0	0.5	4.0	3.7	20.5	27.6	47.7	40.7	27.4	557	71.8
Cayuga city	27	26	-3.7	46	93.5	0.0	0.0	6.5	0.0	26.1	10.9	51.0	50.0	0.0	19	94.7
Center city	573	578	0.9	592	90.0	0.0	0.0	2.7	7.3	32.8	25.0	38.9	36.7	20.9	236	96.6
Christine city	150	170	13.3	212	99.1	0.0	0.0	0.9	0.0	28.8	12.7	37.0	30.6	29.9	89	93.3
Churchs Ferry city	12	12	0.0	4	100.0	0.0	0.0	0.0	0.0	0.0	0.0	0.0	100.0	0.0	2	100.0
Cleveland city	81	76	-6.2	83	100.0	0.0	0.0	0.0	0.0	25.3	21.7	44.5	30.9	9.1	32	87.5
Clifford city	44	43	-2.3	43	100.0	0.0	0.0	0.0	0.0	0.0	7.0	49.5	44.2	7.0	24	95.8
Cogswell city	100	93	-7.0	55	94.5	0.0	0.0	5.5	0.0	5.5	32.7	56.8	66.7	6.3	33	81.8
Coleharbor city	79	82	3.8	72	97.2	0.0	0.0	0.0	2.8	5.6	26.4	59.2	55.4	1.5	38	94.7
Colfax city	121	152	25.6	178	100.0	0.0	0.0	0.0	0.0	28.1	20.8	36.8	18.8	41.4	69	97.1
Columbus city	133	138	3.8	121	95.0	0.0	0.0	0.0	5.0	33.1	21.5	31.1	21.0	34.6	48	87.5
Conway city	23	21	-8.7	22	100.0	0.0	0.0	0.0	0.0	18.2	31.8	52.0	77.8	0.0	14	71.4
Cooperstown city	985	903	-8.3	1,103	95.1	0.0	0.0	4.9	0.0	27.6	29.0	39.2	43.2	21.7	434	82.9
Courtenay city	45	46	2.2	64	100.0	0.0	0.0	0.0	0.0	32.8	26.6	36.6	61.0	19.5	26	96.2
Crary city	148	146	-1.4	113	73.5	0.0	0.0	11.5	15.0	19.5	12.4	40.2	49.4	16.9	42	83.3
Crosby city	1,071	1,285	20.0	1,138	84.5	6.1	1.8	0.7	6.9	19.2	30.7	50.5	51.4	17.4	531	85.7
Crystal city	138	128	-7.2	102	82.4	0.0	0.0	6.9	10.8	12.7	27.5	54.3	56.8	9.1	65	81.5
Dahlen CDP	18	-	-	9	100.0	0.0	0.0	0.0	0.0	0.0	0.0	53.9	44.4	55.6	4	100.0
Davenport city	258	272	5.4	293	76.1	0.0	0.0	2.4	21.5	27.3	3.8	39.6	45.1	18.1	113	99.1
Dawson city	61	65	6.6	43	100.0	0.0	0.0	0.0	0.0	20.9	14.0	49.6	85.3	0.0	18	83.3
Dazey city	102	93	-8.8	45	100.0	0.0	0.0	0.0	0.0	15.6	4.4	41.9	75.0	11.1	29	79.3
Deering city	100	114	14.0	139	97.1	0.0	0.7	2.2	0.0	30.9	4.3	34.8	38.2	31.5	52	100.0
De Lamere CDP	30	-	-	28	100.0	0.0	0.0	0.0	0.0	28.6	42.9	44.5	25.0	20.0	13	53.8
Denhoff CDP	20	-	-	21	71.4	0.0	0.0	28.6	0.0	19.0	42.9	35.8	29.4	23.5	11	90.9
Des Lacs city	204	201	-1.5	227	96.9	0.0	0.4	0.0	2.6	28.2	17.2	40.3	43.3	20.0	86	94.2
Devils Lake city	7,154	7,320	2.3	7,344	77.6	0.2	1.2	17.9	3.2	20.8	22.2	43.2	43.6	25.3	3,301	81.0
Dickey city	42	39	-7.1	26	100.0	0.0	0.0	0.0	0.0	15.4	34.6	49.5	71.4	14.3	14	78.6
Dickinson city	17,879	23,133	29.4	22,882	85.4	2.4	1.5	4.6	6.1	24.9	11.3	32.6	39.2	22.8	9,439	88.5
Dodge city	87	99	13.8	105	81.0	0.0	0.0	3.8	15.2	18.1	26.7	50.5	71.4	4.3	47	72.3
Donnybrook city	58	53	-8.6	76	94.7	0.0	0.0	5.3	0.0	27.6	25.0	44.5	49.1	17.0	32	71.9
Douglas city	64	63	-1.6	68	70.6	0.0	0.0	26.5	2.9	19.1	22.1	55.3	35.4	20.8	29	100.0
Drake city	275	268	-2.5	401	97.0	0.0	0.0	1.5	1.5	39.4	11.7	30.6	41.3	18.3	155	85.2
Drayton city	824	747	-9.3	751	99.5	0.0	0.0	0.5	0.0	21.7	19.2	44.9	38.1	25.4	328	86.0
Driscoll CDP	82	-	-	66	87.9	0.0	0.0	12.1	0.0	28.8	21.2	34.5	47.6	7.1	27	85.2
Dunn Center city	146	191	30.8	271	74.5	4.4	1.5	3.3	16.2	36.2	12.9	28.8	58.3	5.1	95	89.5
Dunseith city	773	764	-1.2	692	25.4	0.0	0.0	74.6	0.0	30.5	13.4	33.4	49.8	19.2	233	84.1
Dwight city	81	78	-3.7	74	86.5	0.0	0.0	0.0	13.5	27.0	5.4	35.5	40.4	12.8	29	86.2
East Dunseith CDP	500	-	-	538	0.7	0.0	0.0	99.3	0.0	37.9	1.9	26.6	51.0	3.0	134	64.9
East Fairview CDP	76	-	-	37	100.0	0.0	0.0	0.0	0.0	21.6	16.2	31.6	66.7	12.5	11	100.0
Edgeley city	572	556	-2.8	553	92.6	3.6	0.0	0.0	3.8	17.0	26.0	51.3	42.5	18.7	274	74.8
Edinburg city	196	181	-7.7	192	89.1	1.0	4.7	1.0	4.2	12.5	26.6	54.7	38.1	26.5	99	87.9
Edmore city	185	176	-4.9	175	86.9	0.0	2.9	9.1	1.1	11.4	45.1	59.4	48.3	11.9	68	79.4
Egeland city	27	27	0.0	41	75.6	0.0	0.0	9.8	14.6	7.3	26.8	53.3	39.5	5.3	28	57.1
Elgin city	642	603	-6.1	677	93.2	0.0	3.2	2.4	1.2	18.6	32.6	51.1	44.5	16.1	312	77.9
Ellendale city	1,389	1,246	-10.3	1,211	92.2	1.7	0.7	4.2	1.2	17.1	26.0	41.1	38.4	34.5	518	83.6
Elliott city	25	25	0.0	21	100.0	0.0	0.0	0.0	0.0	14.3	33.3	57.5	25.0	43.8	11	100.0
Embden CDP	59	-	-	30	100.0	0.0	0.0	0.0	0.0	20.0	20.0	51.5	50.0	25.0	12	100.0
Emerado city	432	449	3.9	442	84.2	2.5	1.6	6.6	5.2	18.1	11.5	29.7	54.5	14.6	217	86.6
Enderlin city	887	838	-5.5	919	92.1	0.0	4.0	0.3	3.6	14.7	24.3	47.8	46.2	16.6	462	82.5
Englevale CDP	40	-	-	69	100.0	0.0	0.0	0.0	0.0	37.7	0.0	31.1	31.4	0.0	10	100.0
Epping city	96	134	39.6	66	89.4	0.0	0.0	10.6	0.0	21.2	7.6	48.6	52.9	17.6	31	83.9
Erie CDP	50	-	-	31	100.0	0.0	0.0	0.0	0.0	0.0	32.3	56.9	35.5	0.0	16	100.0
Esmond city	100	97	-3.0	91	100.0	0.0	0.0	0.0	0.0	13.2	41.8	55.7	52.8	9.7	62	72.6
Fairdale city	38	34	-10.5	40	65.0	0.0	0.0	35.0	0.0	22.5	30.0	54.7	33.3	26.7	16	100.0
Fairmount city	367	359	-2.2	321	90.7	0.0	0.0	2.8	6.5	24.9	21.5	45.5	49.1	16.4	140	84.3
Fargo city	105,625	124,662	18.0	121,889	82.7	7.0	3.4	4.0	3.0	20.0	11.9	31.0	26.6	40.0	54,571	92.0
Fessenden city	479	433	-9.6	489	100.0	0.0	0.0	0.0	0.0	26.4	17.4	38.3	42.4	27.7	255	88.6
Fingal city	97	86	-11.3	110	93.6	0.0	0.0	6.4	0.0	18.2	11.8	34.7	31.9	6.9	58	87.9
Finley city	445	416	-6.5	362	98.1	0.0	0.0	0.0	1.9	12.2	26.2	52.7	40.1	24.0	191	90.6
Flasher city	232	205	-11.6	251	93.6	0.0	0.0	2.4	4.0	25.1	20.7	36.6	37.6	27.6	115	84.3
Flaxton city	66	64	-3.0	134	98.5	0.0	1.5	0.0	0.0	45.5	10.4	28.3	42.5	11.0	43	90.7
Forbes city	49	44	-10.2	41	100.0	0.0	0.0	0.0	0.0	29.3	22.0	36.8	20.7	0.0	17	100.0
Fordville city	212	198	-6.6	210	98.1	0.0	0.0	1.9	0.0	23.3	13.8	30.0	30.4	17.8	105	92.4
Forest River city	125	121	-3.2	127	60.6	0.0	0.0	5.5	33.9	7.1	25.2	51.0	55.7	14.8	66	80.3
Forman city	497	504	1.4	458	98.3	0.0	0.0	0.7	1.1	21.0	32.3	42.5	44.2	18.8	214	86.9
Fort Ransom city	79	75	-5.1	116	87.9	0.0	5.2	0.0	6.9	21.6	28.4	40.5	51.7	20.2	54	68.5
Fort Totten CDP	1,243	-	-	1,247	0.2	0.2	0.0	99.3	0.3	50.2	4.7	17.9	54.9	7.2	258	63.6
Fortuna city	22	21	-4.5	29	100.0	0.0	0.0	0.0	0.0	13.8	6.9	42.8	12.5	31.3	9	100.0
Fort Yates city	179	202	12.8	188	2.1	0.0	0.0	97.9	0.0	38.8	5.3	31.1	58.5	10.4	49	69.4
Four Bears Village CDP	517	-	-	309	4.9	0.0	0.0	95.1	0.0	46.0	4.5	23.5	45.6	18.1	89	89.9

1 May be of any race.

Table A. All Places — **Population and Housing**

STATE City, town, township, borough, or CDP (county if applicable)	Population				Race and Hispanic or Latino origin (percent)					Age (percent)			Educational attainment of persons age 25 and older		Occupied housing units	
	2010 census total population	2019 estimated population	Percent change 2010–2019	ACS total population estimate 2015–2019	White alone, not Hispanic or Latino	Black alone, not Hispanic or Latino	Asian alone, not Hispanic or Latino	All other races or 2 or more races, not Hispanic or Latino	Hispanic or Latino[1]	Under 18 years old	Age 65 years and older	Median age	Percent High school diploma or less	Percent Bachelor's degree or more	Total	Percent with a computer
	1	2	3	4	5	6	7	8	9	10	11	12	13	14	15	16
NORTH DAKOTA—Con.																
Foxholm CDP	75	-	-	30	100.0	0.0	0.0	0.0	0.0	33.3	20.0	29.7	55.0	30.0	17	64.7
Fredonia city	46	42	-8.7	36	100.0	0.0	0.0	0.0	0.0	2.8	16.7	56.4	58.6	10.3	24	91.7
Frontier city	223	213	-4.5	168	98.8	1.2	0.0	0.0	0.0	13.1	14.3	53.3	34.8	31.8	70	98.6
Fullerton city	54	53	-1.9	57	100.0	0.0	0.0	0.0	0.0	5.3	38.6	61.5	50.9	7.5	37	78.4
Gackle city	312	273	-12.5	285	96.8	0.0	0.0	2.5	0.7	14.0	34.0	55.2	44.9	19.9	123	86.2
Galesburg city	108	102	-5.6	136	100.0	0.0	0.0	0.0	0.0	23.5	13.2	43.3	41.0	13.0	67	97.0
Gardena city	29	28	-3.4	28	82.1	0.0	0.0	0.0	17.9	32.1	14.3	33.5	88.9	0.0	14	85.7
Gardner city	74	74	0.0	97	100.0	0.0	0.0	0.0	0.0	19.6	22.7	47.9	52.2	18.8	40	92.5
Garrison city	1,454	1,462	0.6	1,623	89.4	2.4	0.5	6.8	0.9	21.3	27.4	45.8	51.4	17.2	753	81.5
Gascoyne city	16	15	-6.3	11	100.0	0.0	0.0	0.0	0.0	0.0	54.5	71.3	11.1	0.0	8	87.5
Gilby city	237	232	-2.1	245	93.9	0.0	0.0	1.6	4.5	33.9	8.2	42.6	39.7	17.3	95	86.3
Gladstone city	235	348	48.1	334	66.2	0.0	0.0	11.1	22.8	43.1	7.8	26.1	68.0	10.7	108	95.4
Glenburn city	431	430	-0.2	502	95.8	0.0	0.4	3.8	0.0	34.7	5.0	29.1	39.7	19.9	159	98.7
Glenfield city	91	94	3.3	100	86.0	0.0	0.0	0.0	14.0	40.0	18.0	28.6	21.1	19.3	42	88.1
Glen Ullin city	807	717	-11.2	806	94.4	0.0	0.0	4.1	1.5	16.6	33.4	50.7	48.3	19.8	390	75.9
Golden Valley city	182	163	-10.4	240	97.1	0.0	0.4	0.4	2.1	16.3	31.7	54.8	47.2	8.2	127	70.1
Golva city	61	68	11.5	64	100.0	0.0	0.0	0.0	0.0	18.8	0.0	51.0	23.5	25.5	30	86.7
Goodrich city	98	91	-7.1	117	100.0	0.0	0.0	0.0	0.0	8.5	21.4	47.6	38.1	26.2	62	82.3
Grace City city	63	58	-7.9	85	100.0	0.0	0.0	0.0	0.0	34.1	14.1	27.2	55.3	6.4	31	74.2
Grafton city	4,287	4,157	-3.0	4,182	75.5	1.0	0.9	4.9	17.7	23.4	19.8	40.5	54.2	14.2	1,806	79.5
Grand Forks city	52,920	55,839	5.5	56,500	82.7	4.0	3.3	5.7	4.3	19.5	12.0	29.0	26.8	37.1	25,328	91.0
Grand Forks AFB CDP	2,367	-	-	2,683	67.7	10.1	2.0	8.4	11.8	29.8	0.0	22.9	14.6	30.2	718	100.0
Grandin city	173	169	-2.3	182	96.7	0.0	0.0	3.3	0.0	26.4	11.5	39.3	48.9	13.7	73	98.6
Grano city	7	6	-14.3	2	100.0	0.0	0.0	0.0	0.0	0.0	0.0	0.0	50.0	50.0	1	100.0
Granville city	241	253	5.0	275	91.3	0.0	0.0	8.7	0.0	18.2	17.8	42.3	50.0	17.4	151	86.8
Great Bend city	57	56	-1.8	76	100.0	0.0	0.0	0.0	0.0	14.5	22.4	51.6	36.9	20.0	40	80.0
Green Acres CDP	575	-	-	433	2.3	0.0	0.0	97.7	0.0	59.6	2.3	16.0	46.3	0.0	104	71.2
Grenora city	242	332	37.2	224	94.2	0.0	0.9	2.7	2.2	41.1	13.4	31.5	44.1	18.9	76	81.6
Gwinner city	753	937	24.4	1,081	83.6	8.5	0.0	1.4	6.5	26.1	13.0	32.5	45.1	20.2	493	95.5
Hague city	71	63	-11.3	85	100.0	0.0	0.0	0.0	0.0	30.6	30.6	42.8	66.1	10.2	41	53.7
Halliday city	188	204	8.5	303	94.7	0.0	0.0	0.0	5.3	33.0	17.2	29.3	47.4	22.2	132	82.6
Hamberg city	21	19	-9.5	26	84.6	0.0	0.0	0.0	15.4	0.0	34.6	60.3	59.1	22.7	20	60.0
Hamilton city	61	56	-8.2	48	100.0	0.0	0.0	0.0	0.0	33.3	22.9	38.6	62.5	0.0	20	90.0
Hampden city	48	45	-6.3	26	100.0	0.0	0.0	0.0	0.0	0.0	53.8	66.5	30.8	3.8	18	61.1
Hankinson city	919	885	-3.7	997	92.0	0.7	0.0	2.4	4.9	28.9	23.6	37.9	43.7	20.5	392	77.6
Hannaford city	131	118	-9.9	119	92.4	0.0	0.0	7.6	0.0	4.2	39.5	60.9	63.1	12.6	73	74.0
Hannah city	15	15	0.0	12	100.0	0.0	0.0	0.0	0.0	41.7	0.0	32.3	0.0	0.0	7	100.0
Hansboro city	12	13	8.3	22	100.0	0.0	0.0	0.0	0.0	36.4	0.0	36.2	16.7	50.0	10	100.0
Harmon CDP	145	-	-	239	100.0	0.0	0.0	0.0	0.0	28.5	18.4	34.0	25.5	24.8	83	100.0
Harvey city	1,800	1,646	-8.6	1,761	92.2	0.0	0.5	2.2	5.2	24.0	28.8	47.8	43.0	21.6	835	84.6
Harwood city	719	829	15.3	742	99.6	0.1	0.0	0.3	0.0	29.4	9.3	36.9	23.3	38.8	256	100.0
Hatton city	759	743	-2.1	783	88.4	0.0	0.6	5.9	5.1	23.0	21.1	42.1	35.6	21.5	345	91.6
Havana city	71	71	0.0	61	90.2	0.0	3.3	1.6	4.9	23.0	32.8	47.3	50.0	32.6	25	92.0
Haynes city	23	23	0.0	25	80.0	0.0	16.0	4.0	0.0	0.0	36.0	55.5	73.9	13.0	20	60.0
Hazelton city	235	211	-10.2	261	93.9	0.0	0.0	6.1	0.0	26.4	23.8	38.9	54.3	16.8	108	71.3
Hazen city	2,436	2,311	-5.1	2,543	86.8	2.9	0.6	6.1	3.5	24.1	17.7	39.8	36.3	20.5	1,082	89.3
Hebron city	747	675	-9.6	867	94.0	0.0	0.7	1.4	3.9	21.5	24.8	43.0	47.6	20.9	383	88.3
Heil CDP	15	-	-	15	100.0	0.0	0.0	0.0	0.0	0.0	100.0	69.5	26.7	53.3	8	100.0
Heimdal CDP	27	-	-	6	100.0	0.0	0.0	0.0	0.0	0.0	0.0	0.0	0.0	0.0	3	100.0
Hettinger city	1,228	1,155	-5.9	1,065	87.5	0.8	5.1	3.0	3.6	17.7	31.5	51.4	45.4	17.6	545	80.9
Hillsboro city	1,612	1,624	0.7	1,601	87.7	0.0	1.2	3.1	8.0	21.9	18.4	43.4	37.0	23.3	714	87.7
Hoople city	245	227	-7.3	326	72.4	0.0	0.0	1.2	26.4	29.1	13.2	35.2	38.3	27.4	143	83.9
Hope city	258	252	-2.3	286	100.0	0.0	0.0	0.0	0.0	8.4	26.2	55.2	37.4	22.0	144	79.9
Horace city	2,438	2,944	20.8	2,741	91.2	1.6	0.3	1.3	5.6	29.4	7.7	37.0	23.1	47.5	986	96.3
Hunter city	255	252	-1.2	212	98.1	0.0	0.0	0.9	0.9	17.9	12.3	47.0	36.9	20.6	102	90.2
Hurdsfield city	84	76	-9.5	36	100.0	0.0	0.0	0.0	0.0	11.1	38.9	59.7	66.7	22.2	21	100.0
Inkster city	50	47	-6.0	26	96.2	0.0	0.0	3.8	0.0	7.7	19.2	53.5	47.8	30.4	14	71.4
Jamestown city	15,421	15,084	-2.2	15,289	90.2	2.0	0.5	4.0	3.3	19.4	18.4	37.8	44.0	23.0	6,530	88.5
Jessie CDP	25	-	-	47	100.0	0.0	0.0	0.0	0.0	44.7	0.0	24.4	100.0	0.0	19	100.0
Jud city	72	70	-2.8	69	78.3	0.0	0.0	0.0	21.7	4.3	39.1	57.8	60.4	11.3	41	70.7
Karlsruhe city	82	86	4.9	54	100.0	0.0	0.0	0.0	0.0	5.6	18.5	58.2	59.6	2.1	28	78.6
Kathryn city	56	48	-14.3	46	93.5	0.0	0.0	6.5	0.0	10.9	23.9	46.7	46.3	14.6	25	96.0
Kenmare city	1,092	1,021	-6.5	939	95.4	0.0	0.0	2.9	1.7	20.0	27.6	45.1	56.5	15.8	434	82.5
Kensal city	163	156	-4.3	217	75.6	0.0	4.1	20.3	0.0	25.3	11.5	33.1	65.4	5.1	89	79.8
Kief city	13	14	7.7	17	100.0	0.0	0.0	0.0	0.0	0.0	0.0	59.7	71.4	0.0	10	80.0
Killdeer city	751	1,144	52.3	814	85.0	3.6	2.8	4.3	4.3	22.9	18.6	38.4	41.1	20.8	362	92.5
Kindred city	707	781	10.5	864	95.0	0.3	0.0	3.6	1.0	31.8	6.5	28.7	19.6	45.1	308	92.5
Knox city	25	25	0.0	33	100.0	0.0	0.0	0.0	0.0	12.1	33.3	52.1	69.0	0.0	16	81.3
Kramer city	29	28	-3.4	50	66.0	0.0	0.0	34.0	0.0	32.0	20.0	43.5	33.3	6.1	20	70.0
Kulm city	345	335	-2.9	402	94.8	1.2	0.0	2.2	1.7	19.9	27.1	47.9	35.9	28.1	209	78.0
Lakota city	672	625	-7.0	670	90.4	0.0	0.0	0.0	9.6	21.3	24.3	35.6	32.5	28.5	338	83.4
LaMoure city	887	883	-0.5	732	94.4	0.0	0.0	5.1	0.5	18.4	27.6	43.0	44.7	20.2	334	87.7
Landa city	38	36	-5.3	39	100.0	0.0	0.0	0.0	0.0	15.4	53.8	66.2	75.8	0.0	22	72.7
Langdon city	1,875	1,752	-6.6	1,924	91.9	0.1	0.0	4.6	3.4	23.3	25.2	43.6	39.7	18.0	899	88.7
Lankin city	98	90	-8.2	90	100.0	0.0	0.0	0.0	0.0	16.7	30.0	58.3	49.2	15.4	52	69.2
Lansford city	245	240	-2.0	287	94.8	0.0	0.0	1.0	4.2	27.9	8.7	28.8	47.1	15.3	126	90.5
Larimore city	1,348	1,288	-4.5	1,381	86.0	0.4	0.0	7.9	5.6	28.8	15.4	35.0	34.8	23.0	538	93.5
Larson CDP	12	-	-	13	100.0	0.0	0.0	0.0	0.0	0.0	0.0	0.0	61.5	0.0	8	100.0
Lawton city	30	31	3.3	15	100.0	0.0	0.0	0.0	0.0	0.0	66.7	67.5	53.3	13.3	11	72.7
Leal city	20	18	-10.0	16	100.0	0.0	0.0	0.0	0.0	0.0	18.8	60.7	50.0	18.8	10	70.0
Leeds city	455	460	1.1	558	98.0	0.0	0.0	1.4	0.5	24.0	18.3	41.7	38.7	16.8	250	82.0
Lehr city	80	70	-12.5	70	95.7	0.0	0.0	4.3	0.0	4.3	40.0	61.6	65.7	7.5	42	71.4
Leith city	16	15	-6.3	53	83.0	3.8	11.3	1.9	0.0	35.8	17.0	42.6	35.3	14.7	18	88.9
Leonard city	225	230	2.2	286	98.6	0.0	0.0	1.4	0.0	23.4	14.3	43.3	33.3	24.5	131	90.8
Lidgerwood city	652	616	-5.5	587	97.4	0.0	0.0	1.9	0.7	16.9	35.3	55.9	49.8	8.2	308	61.7
Lignite city	153	223	45.8	203	96.6	0.0	3.4	0.0	0.0	23.6	10.8	33.3	26.0	34.4	98	96.9
Lincoln city	2,429	3,817	57.1	3,703	90.2	0.0	0.0	4.8	5.0	34.8	5.0	30.1	28.8	28.2	1,182	97.4
Linton city	1,099	978	-11.0	972	92.1	0.0	3.7	0.3	3.9	14.4	35.5	55.4	43.7	24.5	514	72.2
Lisbon city	2,154	2,051	-4.8	2,009	92.9	2.1	0.0	4.0	0.9	18.8	25.1	48.5	41.7	21.3	941	83.5
Litchville city	172	150	-12.8	201	92.0	2.5	0.0	2.5	3.0	28.9	13.9	39.5	40.3	14.9	89	88.8
Logan CDP	194	-	-	392	76.8	0.0	0.0	23.2	0.0	42.6	2.0	33.5	66.2	20.4	113	100.0
Loma city	16	15	-6.3	16	100.0	0.0	0.0	0.0	0.0	0.0	50.0	64.0	31.3	18.8	10	100.0

1 May be of any race.

STATE City, town, township, borough, or CDP (county if applicable)	Population				Race and Hispanic or Latino origin (percent)					Age (percent)			Educational attainment of persons age 25 and older		Occupied housing units	
	2010 census total population	2019 estimated population	Percent change 2010–2019	ACS total population estimate 2015–2019	White alone, not Hispanic or Latino	Black alone, not Hispanic or Latino	Asian alone, not Hispanic or Latino	All other races or 2 or more races, not Hispanic or Latino	Hispanic or Latino[1]	Under 18 years old	Age 65 years and older	Median age	Percent High school diploma or less	Percent Bachelor's degree or more	Total	Percent with a computer
	1	2	3	4	5	6	7	8	9	10	11	12	13	14	15	16
NORTH DAKOTA—Con.																
Loraine city	9	8	-11.1	11	63.6	0.0	0.0	36.4	0.0	9.1	18.2	54.5	0.0	0.0	7	100.0
Ludden city	23	25	8.7	35	97.1	0.0	0.0	0.0	2.9	20.0	31.4	53.5	68.0	8.0	16	100.0
Luverne city	31	29	-6.5	30	100.0	0.0	0.0	0.0	0.0	36.7	20.0	43.5	68.4	21.1	12	83.3
McClusky city	380	364	-4.2	409	100.0	0.0	0.0	0.0	0.0	15.4	31.5	50.5	65.3	11.9	247	73.3
McHenry city	56	53	-5.4	33	93.9	0.0	0.0	0.0	6.1	12.1	30.3	58.3	46.4	14.3	20	100.0
McLeod CDP	27	-	-	-	-	-	-	-	-	-	-	-	-	-	-	-
McVille city	349	322	-7.7	375	98.9	0.0	0.0	1.1	0.0	18.9	30.4	51.3	30.8	15.9	215	85.1
Maddock city	382	378	-	384	87.5	0.3	0.0	7.8	4.4	22.9	26.3	49.8	43.7	23.0	187	89.8
Makoti city	156	144	-7.7	114	87.7	0.0	0.0	9.6	2.6	17.5	28.1	54.4	31.4	16.3	64	93.8
Mandan city	18,870	22,752	20.6	22,301	87.3	1.4	0.9	6.4	4.0	21.7	14.7	36.6	34.5	28.9	9,856	93.0
Mandaree CDP	596	-	-	544	3.1	0.0	0.0	88.8	8.1	55.0	2.9	14.2	48.6	10.7	92	76.1
Manning CDP	74	-	-	70	100.0	0.0	0.0	0.0	0.0	24.3	0.0	31.4	26.4	22.6	28	100.0
Mantador city	64	65	1.6	60	100.0	0.0	0.0	0.0	0.0	21.7	6.7	27.5	26.3	5.3	31	96.8
Manvel city	360	369	2.5	330	91.8	0.0	1.5	4.5	2.1	31.2	9.7	33.0	31.9	20.8	120	93.3
Mapleton city	762	1,238	62.5	1,113	87.2	6.7	0.0	2.4	3.7	31.8	6.1	33.7	26.3	26.8	376	91.5
Marion city	133	130	-2.3	141	100.0	0.0	0.0	0.0	0.0	16.3	22.7	43.4	39.4	24.0	67	89.6
Marmarth city	136	137	0.7	91	85.7	14.3	0.0	0.0	0.0	17.6	24.2	40.5	57.6	25.8	51	78.4
Martin city	75	70	-6.7	51	100.0	0.0	0.0	0.0	0.0	9.8	29.4	48.5	47.4	15.8	31	77.4
Max city	336	349	3.9	316	89.2	0.0	0.0	10.8	0.0	23.4	20.9	35.3	45.8	17.7	151	84.8
Maxbass city	82	79	-3.7	107	96.3	0.0	0.0	3.7	0.0	34.6	17.8	24.9	52.8	9.4	49	89.8
Mayville city	1,853	1,802	-2.8	1,808	86.2	4.3	0.3	2.9	6.3	18.6	21.1	34.5	36.5	31.8	722	88.1
Medina city	308	291	-5.5	291	97.9	0.0	1.0	1.0	0.0	27.5	20.3	44.8	56.7	16.9	129	78.3
Medora city	112	129	15.2	134	100.0	0.0	0.0	0.0	0.0	6.7	29.1	53.0	35.2	38.4	56	92.9
Menoken CDP	70	-	-	81	100.0	0.0	0.0	0.0	0.0	21.0	17.3	47.5	58.3	8.3	36	91.7
Mercer city	93	100	7.5	68	85.3	11.8	0.0	2.9	0.0	8.8	32.4	56.0	40.0	15.0	37	73.0
Michigan City city	297	268	-9.8	185	99.5	0.0	0.0	0.5	0.0	14.6	22.2	58.5	35.3	14.1	102	81.4
Milnor city	653	634	-2.9	754	93.8	0.0	1.2	2.7	2.4	19.4	21.2	44.4	40.4	16.1	375	86.7
Milton city	61	58	-4.7	67	95.5	0.0	0.0	4.5	0.0	13.4	32.8	56.1	64.9	3.5	30	96.7
Minnewaukan city	226	225	-0.4	197	81.7	0.0	0.0	17.3	1.0	20.8	18.3	46.3	18.8	49.7	85	87.1
Minot city	41,093	47,382	15.3	48,261	80.9	4.2	2.3	6.3	6.3	21.5	13.0	31.8	36.3	30.7	20,979	92.2
Minot AFB CDP	5,521	-	-	5,312	69.2	8.6	0.7	6.9	14.6	32.2	0.0	22.6	15.8	38.2	1,494	98.3
Minto city	604	592	-2.0	727	72.9	0.0	0.0	0.6	26.5	28.3	15.3	29.8	57.1	15.0	301	87.4
Mohall city	783	723	-7.7	704	92.0	0.6	0.4	0.3	6.7	17.6	26.4	43.5	42.6	24.2	285	93.3
Monango city	38	38	0.0	25	100.0	0.0	0.0	0.0	0.0	28.0	0.0	31.5	0.0	0.0	8	100.0
Montpelier city	87	84	-3.4	103	100.0	0.0	0.0	0.0	0.0	29.1	8.7	36.1	40.3	22.4	47	97.9
Mooreton city	197	189	-4.1	183	98.4	0.0	0.0	1.6	0.0	21.9	16.9	39.8	37.1	13.6	91	85.7
Mott city	710	724	2.0	692	98.6	0.0	0.0	1.2	0.3	20.4	31.8	56.3	45.5	17.3	332	81.9
Mountain city	92	82	-10.9	80	81.3	0.0	0.0	18.8	0.0	2.5	33.8	59.4	56.1	13.6	32	78.1
Munich city	210	195	-7.1	256	98.4	0.0	0.0	1.6	0.0	21.9	23.0	39.6	44.3	13.1	132	82.6
Mylo city	20	21	5.0	9	100.0	0.0	0.0	0.0	0.0	0.0	0.0	56.5	55.6	44.4	4	75.0
Napoleon city	792	752	-5.1	850	97.5	0.0	0.2	2.0	0.2	22.1	26.4	47.5	45.0	18.7	392	85.2
Nash CDP	32	-	-	37	100.0	0.0	0.0	0.0	0.0	0.0	0.0	53.0	100.0	0.0	18	100.0
Neche city	371	343	-7.5	338	95.9	1.5	1.5	0.6	0.6	24.3	17.2	37.4	55.7	16.1	137	79.6
Nekoma city	50	49	-2.0	34	100.0	0.0	0.0	0.0	0.0	26.5	26.5	59.4	32.0	32.0	12	100.0
Newburg city	111	108	-2.7	71	90.1	0.0	0.0	1.4	8.5	29.6	19.7	24.9	25.7	14.3	42	83.3
New England city	602	600	-0.3	824	84.2	1.2	0.0	10.7	3.9	22.2	15.4	32.5	50.0	8.0	287	87.8
New Leipzig city	221	206	-6.8	205	92.7	0.0	0.0	0.5	6.8	12.2	38.0	60.8	43.5	19.0	98	81.6
New Rockford city	1,384	1,339	-3.3	1,393	89.4	0.0	0.0	8.5	2.1	20.5	26.6	40.9	45.7	25.0	671	77.9
New Salem city	957	989	3.3	1,137	93.9	0.0	0.4	2.2	3.5	18.4	29.8	45.4	49.1	20.5	511	81.6
New Town city	1,925	2,592	34.6	2,525	14.1	0.8	0.2	73.0	12.0	30.6	7.0	29.3	39.3	19.4	689	84.9
Niagara city	53	51	-3.8	44	75.0	0.0	0.0	0.0	25.0	15.9	43.2	62.3	56.8	18.9	22	68.2
Nome city	62	56	-9.7	37	100.0	0.0	0.0	0.0	0.0	27.0	18.9	55.4	38.5	3.8	15	73.3
Noonan city	121	124	2.5	156	89.1	2.6	0.0	2.6	5.8	18.6	24.4	48.3	63.5	7.0	95	68.4
North River city	56	54	-3.6	58	100.0	0.0	0.0	0.0	0.0	24.1	27.6	53.8	18.2	43.2	22	100.0
Northwood city	938	895	-4.6	713	99.6	0.0	0.0	0.0	0.4	21.9	41.0	55.7	34.4	31.9	320	78.1
Oakes city	1,852	1,701	-8.2	2,129	91.9	1.7	0.0	0.8	5.6	27.1	14.9	36.5	35.1	26.5	909	94.6
Oberon city	105	103	-1.9	116	19.0	0.0	0.0	81.0	0.0	55.2	3.4	16.6	47.4	21.1	24	79.2
Oriska city	118	112	-5.1	109	98.2	0.0	0.0	0.0	1.8	25.7	21.1	42.5	41.6	9.1	47	85.1
Orrin CDP	22	-	-	-	-	-	-	-	-	-	-	-	-	-	-	-
Osnabrock city	134	118	-11.9	163	98.2	0.0	0.0	0.0	1.8	12.3	44.2	57.8	64.3	6.3	68	70.6
Overly city	18	17	-5.6	16	93.8	0.0	0.0	6.3	0.0	0.0	93.8	73.5	37.5	0.0	9	88.9
Oxbow city	314	306	-2.5	282	98.2	0.0	0.0	0.0	1.8	22.0	13.5	45.9	5.7	67.5	106	100.0
Page city	240	230	-4.2	198	98.5	0.0	0.0	0.5	1.0	25.3	16.2	36.4	40.2	15.2	93	81.7
Palermo city	74	98	32.4	142	97.9	0.7	0.0	1.4	0.0	16.2	14.1	38.2	64.0	12.0	49	73.5
Park River city	1,406	1,338	-4.8	1,499	97.7	0.0	0.0	0.5	1.8	23.8	25.8	44.5	48.8	17.8	668	73.1
Parshall city	900	1,288	43.1	1,119	36.1	0.8	0.5	58.8	3.8	34.3	8.9	29.7	33.5	24.2	311	87.8
Pekin city	70	65	-7.1	82	98.8	0.0	0.0	1.2	0.0	28.0	14.6	40.7	51.9	33.3	33	90.9
Pembina city	595	544	-8.6	485	96.1	0.0	1.2	0.6	2.1	19.2	28.2	49.0	38.0	18.5	229	84.7
Perth city	9	9	0.0	10	100.0	0.0	0.0	0.0	0.0	0.0	10.0	60.0	37.5	37.5	4	100.0
Petersburg city	193	173	-10.4	171	90.1	0.0	0.6	2.3	7.0	26.9	19.3	35.9	28.4	25.7	84	72.6
Pettibone city	70	68	-2.9	93	89.2	0.0	0.0	0.0	10.8	15.1	31.2	45.5	64.1	5.1	51	56.9
Pick City city	126	136	7.9	136	75.0	0.0	8.8	16.2	0.0	15.4	27.9	40.8	45.7	6.7	69	68.1
Pillsbury city	12	12	0.0	15	100.0	0.0	0.0	0.0	0.0	0.0	93.3	72.1	73.3	6.7	8	75.0
Pingree city	60	61	1.7	61	100.0	0.0	0.0	0.0	0.0	31.1	13.1	30.2	42.9	25.7	17	88.2
Pisek city	109	105	-3.7	101	79.2	0.0	0.0	3.0	17.8	45.5	22.8	32.4	61.8	1.8	36	83.3
Plaza city	171	207	21.1	186	84.9	0.0	0.5	0.0	14.5	24.7	7.5	44.5	37.2	24.1	80	82.5
Porcupine CDP	146	-	-	247	0.0	0.0	0.0	65.2	34.8	57.9	0.0	16.1	37.1	29.9	50	78.0
Portal city	126	142	12.7	148	86.5	2.7	0.0	4.1	6.8	14.2	20.3	53.0	32.2	28.1	75	88.0
Portland city	606	595	-1.8	633	91.8	0.9	0.0	7.3	0.0	23.9	19.1	41.5	30.8	38.0	292	83.6
Powers Lake city	282	285	1.1	293	97.3	0.0	0.0	2.7	0.0	31.4	17.1	36.8	41.1	12.6	114	71.1
Prairie Rose city	51	49	-3.9	47	100.0	0.0	0.0	0.0	0.0	14.9	19.1	50.8	31.6	36.8	22	100.0
Raleigh CDP	12	-	-	10	100.0	0.0	0.0	0.0	0.0	0.0	80.0	69.5	60.0	0.0	6	100.0
Ray city	592	901	52.2	495	97.6	0.0	0.0	1.8	0.6	25.7	24.2	41.8	46.1	18.7	245	77.1
Reeder city	159	148	-6.9	107	99.1	0.0	0.0	0.0	0.9	3.7	32.7	44.9	43.5	9.8	67	64.2
Regan city	43	43	0.0	34	97.1	0.0	0.0	2.9	0.0	14.7	32.4	48.5	65.4	15.4	18	66.7
Regent city	160	157	-1.9	131	93.9	0.0	0.0	6.1	0.0	12.2	39.7	60.1	35.8	19.3	76	81.6
Reile's Acres city	513	700	36.5	497	98.4	0.0	0.0	1.6	0.0	33.6	6.2	40.2	16.1	52.4	155	100.0
Reynolds city	306	299	-2.3	327	94.2	0.0	0.0	4.3	1.5	26.0	10.4	37.8	32.4	16.2	128	89.8
Rhame city	169	165	-2.4	184	97.3	0.0	0.0	0.0	2.7	22.3	8.2	47.2	57.1	8.6	87	89.7
Richardton city	525	561	6.9	851	89.1	0.0	1.2	2.4	7.4	29.3	19.2	37.6	56.2	17.4	328	85.1
Riverdale city	205	223	8.8	210	100.0	0.0	0.0	0.0	0.0	10.0	33.8	57.7	25.9	27.6	109	91.7
Robinson city	46	46	0.0	28	100.0	0.0	0.0	0.0	0.0	10.7	60.7	70.2	44.0	36.0	19	42.1

1 May be of any race.

Table A. All Places — **Population and Housing**

STATE City, town, township, borough, or CDP (county if applicable)	Population 2010 census total population	Population 2019 estimated population	Population Percent change 2010–2019	Population ACS total population estimate 2015–2019	Race White alone, not Hispanic or Latino	Race Black alone, not Hispanic or Latino	Race Asian alone, not Hispanic or Latino	Race All other races or 2 or more races, not Hispanic or Latino	Race Hispanic or Latino[1]	Age Under 18 years old	Age 65 years and older	Age Median age	Educational Percent High school diploma or less	Educational Percent Bachelor's degree or more	Occupied housing units Total	Occupied housing units Percent with a computer
	1	2	3	4	5	6	7	8	9	10	11	12	13	14	15	16
NORTH DAKOTA—Con.																
Rocklake city	101	98	-3.0	90	87.8	0.0	0.0	12.2	0.0	2.2	33.3	55.5	36.6	38.0	66	90.9
Rogers city	46	41	-10.9	48	95.8	0.0	0.0	0.0	4.2	25.0	0.0	45.0	36.1	5.6	22	86.4
Rolette city	595	593	-0.3	773	39.8	0.9	0.0	58.3	0.9	30.7	17.7	34.3	32.9	26.4	274	88.7
Rolla city	1,271	1,252	-1.5	1,299	48.0	0.5	0.4	51.1	0.0	33.4	16.2	33.1	35.3	30.2	522	81.2
Ross city	97	113	16.5	114	69.3	0.0	0.0	0.0	30.7	34.2	0.9	30.3	44.8	0.0	41	58.5
Rugby city	2,870	2,590	-9.8	2,724	90.9	0.9	0.4	7.4	0.3	18.2	28.7	48.5	43.7	21.7	1,328	82.4
Ruso city	4	4	0.0	-	-	-	-	-	-	-	-	-	-	-	-	-
Ruthville CDP	191	-	-	194	75.8	2.1	3.1	19.1	0.0	21.1	9.8	39.0	66.4	7.9	90	86.7
Rutland city	163	156	-4.3	130	100.0	0.0	0.0	0.0	0.0	18.5	27.7	53.5	48.9	13.6	67	83.6
Ryder city	85	78	-8.2	145	100.0	0.0	0.0	0.0	0.0	29.7	23.4	37.9	56.4	4.3	56	82.1
St. John city	331	350	5.7	244	19.7	0.0	0.0	75.4	4.9	31.1	13.5	41.5	43.9	18.7	108	63.9
St. Thomas city	331	311	-6.0	284	75.4	0.0	0.0	8.5	16.2	16.9	20.8	54.3	55.0	13.5	148	83.8
Sanborn city	192	170	-11.5	177	96.0	0.0	0.0	4.0	0.0	15.8	19.8	41.4	66.9	5.6	83	79.5
Sarles city	28	27	-3.6	12	100.0	0.0	0.0	0.0	0.0	33.3	16.7	37.5	25.0	75.0	6	33.3
Sawyer city	360	326	-9.4	301	94.7	0.0	0.0	2.3	3.0	18.6	14.0	42.2	42.7	23.6	130	81.5
Scranton city	273	255	-6.6	365	100.0	0.0	0.0	0.0	0.0	34.8	17.5	35.6	35.8	21.2	149	96.0
Selfridge city	160	166	3.8	219	31.1	1.4	0.0	67.6	0.0	37.0	7.8	32.9	63.7	8.1	59	67.8
Selz CDP	46	-	-	48	100.0	0.0	0.0	0.0	0.0	22.9	0.0	37.2	29.7	32.4	26	100.0
Sentinel Butte city	56	63	12.5	110	100.0	0.0	0.0	0.0	0.0	35.5	23.6	44.4	47.7	26.2	43	88.4
Sharon city	96	90	-6.3	61	100.0	0.0	0.0	0.0	0.0	8.2	47.5	60.7	22.4	40.8	36	75.0
Sheldon city	118	125	5.9	103	100.0	0.0	0.0	0.0	0.0	10.7	16.5	56.3	48.3	10.3	57	75.4
Shell Valley CDP	1,197	-	-	1,174	1.4	0.0	0.0	96.9	1.7	37.6	4.0	25.8	42.4	9.3	374	71.1
Sherwood city	242	226	-6.6	196	95.4	0.0	0.0	3.1	1.5	23.0	13.3	43.3	35.9	26.0	92	90.2
Sheyenne city	204	191	-6.4	212	61.3	0.0	0.0	38.7	0.0	15.1	27.8	52.0	30.5	17.7	102	72.5
Sibley city	30	28	-6.7	44	100.0	0.0	0.0	0.0	0.0	18.2	15.9	31.5	78.6	0.0	27	92.6
Solen city	83	86	3.6	89	34.8	0.0	0.0	59.6	5.6	22.5	16.9	43.6	59.7	12.9	36	72.2
Souris city	53	52	-1.9	69	95.7	0.0	0.0	2.9	1.4	13.0	46.4	55.5	58.3	3.3	47	91.5
South Heart city	301	429	42.5	339	85.0	0.0	1.5	8.0	5.6	16.5	17.1	43.9	55.2	13.4	133	93.2
Spiritwood CDP	18	-	-	-	-	-	-	-	-	-	-	-	-	-	-	-
Spiritwood Lake city	90	98	8.9	107	100.0	0.0	0.0	0.0	0.0	8.4	46.7	62.8	44.6	29.3	51	84.3
Springbrook city	27	40	48.1	15	93.3	0.0	0.0	6.7	0.0	13.3	20.0	47.3	7.7	23.1	8	100.0
Stanley city	1,454	2,677	84.1	2,655	80.8	4.4	1.3	0.5	13.1	28.7	14.0	34.0	44.7	21.9	964	88.4
Stanton city	366	339	-7.4	402	97.3	0.0	1.5	0.2	1.0	26.1	30.6	43.3	48.8	5.3	178	86.5
Starkweather city	117	115	-1.7	67	100.0	0.0	0.0	0.0	0.0	11.9	28.4	48.5	32.2	22.0	34	97.1
Steele city	709	711	0.3	740	95.9	0.0	0.8	1.1	2.2	18.1	19.3	50.2	45.5	21.7	384	90.6
Strasburg city	402	362	-10.0	357	99.2	0.0	0.0	0.8	0.0	12.6	40.6	59.5	56.1	13.6	175	69.1
Streeter city	170	162	-4.7	136	86.8	0.7	5.9	6.6	0.0	11.8	34.6	59.3	47.7	16.2	67	67.2
Surrey city	959	1,393	45.3	1,053	88.9	0.3	0.0	5.8	5.0	25.6	16.0	36.3	39.3	23.2	477	88.3
Sutton CDP	17	-	-	21	100.0	0.0	0.0	0.0	0.0	61.9	14.3	9.2	0.0	25.0	5	100.0
Sykeston city	117	105	-10.3	95	100.0	0.0	0.0	0.0	0.0	17.9	27.4	58.2	32.1	25.6	49	91.8
Tappen city	197	202	2.5	280	90.0	0.0	0.0	2.5	7.5	23.6	12.5	36.7	57.8	19.3	114	70.2
Taylor city	147	170	15.6	230	83.9	2.2	4.3	9.6	0.0	30.0	19.6	32.0	37.9	36.6	93	89.2
Thompson city	984	1,021	3.8	1,133	95.3	0.0	0.0	3.8	0.9	30.4	7.3	34.6	22.2	34.6	417	97.8
Tioga city	1,262	1,339	6.1	1,062	97.6	0.7	0.0	0.8	0.9	18.7	18.9	47.3	51.5	9.3	561	84.3
Tolley city	52	50	-3.8	21	100.0	0.0	0.0	0.0	0.0	0.0	57.1	65.3	33.3	33.3	19	94.7
Tolna city	166	152	-8.4	139	100.0	0.0	0.0	0.0	0.0	7.2	60.4	69.8	36.8	28.8	86	76.7
Tower City city	254	265	4.3	324	98.5	0.0	0.0	0.9	0.6	24.1	17.6	41.1	31.1	28.4	145	91.0
Towner city	533	526	-1.3	592	86.7	2.4	0.0	1.4	9.6	22.0	18.6	43.7	52.4	11.2	305	83.3
Turtle Lake city	581	554	-4.6	562	94.8	0.0	0.0	4.4	0.7	20.5	32.6	50.0	35.7	26.3	271	84.1
Tuttle city	80	81	1.3	77	100.0	0.0	0.0	0.0	0.0	11.7	31.2	59.6	57.4	7.4	48	70.8
Underwood city	776	735	-5.3	803	94.8	0.0	0.0	2.0	3.2	24.3	16.1	37.7	49.4	12.8	342	88.0
Upham city	130	138	6.2	177	95.5	0.6	1.1	2.8	0.0	18.6	14.1	43.9	38.1	15.7	87	89.7
Valley City city	6,647	6,323	-4.9	6,460	88.9	3.5	1.7	3.0	3.0	16.7	21.4	43.1	41.0	31.2	3,193	86.0
Velva city	1,085	1,190	9.7	1,379	94.1	0.2	0.2	3.6	1.9	32.0	13.3	34.2	41.3	22.1	523	90.2
Venturia city	13	12	-7.7	21	100.0	0.0	0.0	0.0	0.0	0.0	47.6	62.9	76.2	0.0	18	50.0
Verona city	89	86	-3.4	70	100.0	0.0	0.0	0.0	0.0	11.4	27.1	55.0	79.3	6.9	36	75.0
Voltaire city	42	45	7.1	34	100.0	0.0	0.0	0.0	0.0	11.8	8.8	61.5	60.0	13.3	17	94.1
Wahpeton city	7,764	7,734	-0.4	7,802	85.7	1.3	0.8	7.5	4.7	18.7	14.9	30.0	37.8	19.6	3,275	92.6
Walcott city	238	250	5.0	293	93.9	0.0	0.0	4.1	2.0	29.4	10.9	32.0	39.6	28.4	114	94.7
Wales city	31	30	-3.2	37	59.5	0.0	0.0	40.5	0.0	54.1	18.9	16.8	37.5	6.3	7	85.7
Walhalla city	990	907	-8.4	1,058	78.6	0.7	1.6	17.9	1.2	22.8	19.5	46.5	44.1	20.7	486	81.7
Warwick city	65	66	1.5	82	39.0	0.0	0.0	61.0	0.0	46.3	8.5	22.8	80.0	17.5	33	72.7
Washburn city	1,245	1,264	1.5	1,391	91.9	0.9	0.0	2.5	4.7	21.4	14.6	39.8	31.9	28.1	649	95.5
Watford City city	1,797	7,835	336.0	6,912	77.9	0.6	0.0	7.1	14.4	27.9	10.2	29.2	37.0	27.0	2,639	98.3
West Fargo city	25,845	37,058	43.4	35,397	89.3	3.2	2.5	3.0	2.1	27.7	8.7	32.8	20.5	44.2	13,840	94.6
Westhope city	429	403	-6.1	287	95.8	0.0	0.0	1.4	2.8	13.9	34.1	56.2	43.8	23.8	150	87.3
Wheatland CDP	68	-	-	36	100.0	0.0	0.0	0.0	0.0	0.0	58.3	75.3	41.7	0.0	19	100.0
White Earth city	80	91	13.8	145	97.9	0.0	0.0	0.7	1.4	54.5	3.4	16.1	46.6	15.5	20	100.0
White Shield CDP	336	-	-	212	8.5	0.0	0.0	88.7	2.8	20.8	25.0	46.3	47.1	17.4	96	82.3
Wildrose city	110	149	35.5	64	87.5	0.0	0.0	6.3	6.3	7.8	14.1	49.6	73.1	7.7	38	89.5
Williston city	15,943	29,033	82.1	27,250	76.5	5.5	1.1	7.4	9.4	27.3	7.9	30.4	35.5	25.2	11,230	92.9
Willow City city	158	150	-5.1	145	95.2	0.0	0.0	4.8	0.0	14.5	33.8	55.6	53.0	11.1	93	80.6
Wilton city	711	716	0.7	808	91.7	0.0	0.0	6.9	1.4	20.5	17.1	42.9	39.4	23.9	345	81.4
Wimbledon city	216	191	-11.6	198	93.9	0.0	0.0	6.1	0.0	13.6	21.2	50.4	35.5	22.5	107	96.3
Wing city	152	186	22.4	146	96.6	0.0	0.7	2.7	0.0	37.7	14.4	30.6	37.1	24.7	54	92.6
Wishek city	998	891	-10.7	949	89.8	1.5	0.0	1.5	7.3	16.4	30.3	52.3	51.4	18.7	480	80.2
Wolford city	36	32	-11.1	24	100.0	0.0	0.0	0.0	0.0	29.2	29.2	57.3	70.6	0.0	10	90.0
Woodworth city	50	47	-6.0	45	100.0	0.0	0.0	0.0	0.0	13.3	46.7	63.3	54.3	2.9	28	92.9
Wyndmere city	429	406	-5.4	455	92.3	0.0	0.4	0.7	6.6	26.4	20.2	38.6	37.5	17.6	196	84.2
York city	23	23	0.0	25	100.0	0.0	0.0	0.0	0.0	8.0	16.0	49.1	0.0	38.5	11	100.0
Ypsilanti CDP	104	-	-	28	100.0	0.0	0.0	0.0	0.0	0.0	32.1	0.0	100.0	0.0	28	67.9
Zap city	228	217	-4.8	171	92.4	0.0	0.0	2.9	4.7	22.8	14.0	40.3	59.3	4.9	79	91.1
Zeeland city	86	75	-12.8	87	97.7	0.0	0.0	2.3	0.0	24.1	32.2	34.8	56.6	1.9	52	82.7
OHIO	11,536,751	11,689,100	1.3	11,655,397	78.9	12.2	2.2	2.9	3.8	22.4	16.7	39.4	42.7	28.3	4,676,358	89.1
Aberdeen village	1,640	1,604	-2.2	1,552	93.9	1.2	0.0	4.0	1.0	14.4	25.5	52.6	62.2	9.9	810	87.8
Ada village	5,959	5,544	-7.0	5,941	85.6	2.2	3.9	3.2	5.0	14.3	7.8	22.4	49.3	29.6	1,694	91.1
Adamsville village	123	124	0.8	138	100.0	0.0	0.0	0.0	0.0	30.4	13.8	30.0	63.2	4.6	53	94.3
Addyston village	945	936	-1.0	884	75.5	5.4	0.0	12.7	6.4	23.9	11.1	36.8	72.4	10.6	350	94.6
Adelphi village	380	375	-1.3	329	99.1	0.0	0.0	0.9	0.0	29.8	22.5	43.4	83.7	1.4	135	68.9
Adena village	759	704	-7.2	651	95.2	0.0	0.0	4.0	0.8	25.5	17.7	40.8	62.7	7.7	278	85.3

1 May be of any race.

Table A. All Places — **Population and Housing**

STATE City, town, township, borough, or CDP (county if applicable)	Population				Race and Hispanic or Latino origin (percent)					Age (percent)			Educational attainment of persons age 25 and older		Occupied housing units	
	2010 census total population	2019 estimated population	Percent change 2010–2019	ACS total population estimate 2015–2019	White alone, not Hispanic or Latino	Black alone, not Hispanic or Latino	Asian alone, not Hispanic or Latino	All other races or 2 or more races, not Hispanic or Latino	Hispanic or Latino[1]	Under 18 years old	Age 65 years and older	Median age	Percent High school diploma or less	Percent Bachelor's degree or more	Total	Percent with a computer
	1	2	3	4	5	6	7	8	9	10	11	12	13	14	15	16
OHIO—Con.																
Akron city	199,209	197,597	-0.8	198,051	57.9	30.1	4.6	4.6	2.8	21.2	14.8	36.9	47.2	21.3	84,940	85.5
Albany village	844	891	5.6	824	96.6	1.0	0.0	0.0	2.4	19.4	24.0	42.4	49.6	22.6	360	85.6
Alexandria village	514	542	5.4	655	98.9	0.0	0.0	0.6	0.5	20.3	14.0	34.7	33.3	31.6	243	90.9
Alger village	869	839	-3.5	906	97.5	0.0	0.0	0.4	2.1	23.1	14.3	39.6	71.3	6.5	383	79.4
Alliance city	22,331	21,446	-4.0	21,842	84.6	9.0	0.6	4.2	1.7	21.4	17.6	35.3	58.4	18.7	8,859	84.6
Alvordton CDP	217	-	-	164	94.5	0.0	0.0	0.0	5.5	18.3	15.9	34.5	74.0	0.0	58	53.4
Amanda village	734	738	0.5	866	94.9	0.3	0.0	2.3	2.4	25.6	9.8	32.8	52.2	10.4	299	92.0
Amberley village	3,507	3,543	1.0	3,540	78.0	9.7	6.0	0.3	6.1	26.1	19.5	44.2	15.1	68.2	1,267	97.9
Amelia village	4,805	5,039	4.9	4,757	94.3	1.1	2.1	1.1	1.5	23.2	11.6	34.5	49.8	16.5	1,833	90.1
Amesville village	156	153	-1.9	158	100.0	0.0	0.0	0.0	0.0	13.9	25.3	56.1	27.2	27.2	66	97.0
Amherst city	11,990	12,219	1.9	12,108	88.0	0.9	2.1	2.7	6.2	20.5	23.0	47.5	36.1	26.9	4,778	89.0
Amsterdam village	511	472	-7.6	616	98.4	0.0	0.0	0.0	1.6	23.2	10.1	32.9	75.1	5.2	197	72.6
Andersonville CDP	779	-	-	763	94.8	0.0	0.0	0.3	5.0	23.3	19.0	42.4	36.0	35.2	290	94.5
Andover village	1,143	1,095	-4.2	798	95.6	0.0	0.3	3.5	0.6	18.9	34.1	53.7	67.1	9.8	339	77.3
Anna village	1,572	1,520	-3.3	1,511	97.9	0.0	0.3	0.9	0.9	31.1	10.5	30.3	42.4	24.5	521	92.9
Ansonia village	1,176	1,121	-4.7	1,368	93.9	0.1	0.0	0.0	5.9	26.6	15.9	37.5	66.5	9.7	533	84.2
Antioch village	86	79	-8.1	79	74.7	0.0	0.0	3.8	21.5	27.8	19.0	34.6	54.5	1.8	34	67.6
Antwerp village	1,736	1,683	-3.1	1,490	88.0	0.0	0.5	2.8	8.7	21.1	23.7	43.3	57.1	11.4	738	76.6
Apple Creek village	1,171	1,180	0.8	1,034	95.4	0.0	0.9	2.9	0.9	23.1	13.4	40.2	44.8	13.8	429	93.7
Apple Valley CDP	5,058	-	-	5,337	95.8	1.2	0.5	1.1	1.3	18.8	24.3	49.9	34.2	26.6	2,178	98.8
Aquilla village	340	338	-0.6	306	93.1	0.0	0.7	0.0	6.2	21.9	15.7	42.1	49.1	17.0	125	87.2
Arcadia village	599	588	-1.8	582	96.6	0.3	0.0	0.5	2.6	22.2	11.5	36.5	48.7	17.4	237	86.9
Arcanum village	2,114	2,008	-5.0	2,195	94.2	1.7	0.0	1.7	2.4	25.5	14.6	35.9	43.7	18.0	891	90.0
Archbold village	4,328	4,319	-0.2	4,468	80.6	1.1	0.0	2.4	16.0	26.8	22.7	39.2	44.4	20.1	1,761	87.8
Arlington village	1,465	1,442	-1.6	1,509	96.8	1.1	0.0	0.8	1.4	27.5	15.7	38.6	41.5	26.5	550	91.1
Arlington Heights village	752	741	-1.5	870	73.7	20.6	0.2	3.7	1.8	26.8	11.3	32.2	53.9	12.5	374	90.9
Ashland city	20,379	20,275	-0.5	20,390	93.8	1.5	1.0	2.6	1.1	20.8	19.5	35.9	48.3	27.3	8,059	85.2
Ashley village	1,330	1,608	20.9	1,758	96.4	0.0	0.0	3.2	0.4	25.6	9.2	40.2	64.7	10.5	548	91.1
Ashtabula city	19,125	18,017	-5.8	18,171	79.6	7.4	0.2	3.9	8.8	24.0	16.5	38.3	62.0	11.3	7,520	80.9
Ashville village	4,033	4,385	8.7	4,214	91.0	0.5	0.0	3.9	4.6	28.5	10.5	29.8	47.4	25.6	1,514	90.0
Athalia village	371	354	-4.6	333	93.1	0.0	1.5	5.1	0.3	30.6	15.0	37.5	54.7	17.9	112	74.1
Athens city	23,836	24,536	2.9	24,984	81.9	5.5	6.0	3.8	2.8	7.1	4.9	21.4	16.6	66.7	6,494	96.8
Attica village	897	861	-4.0	870	98.6	0.0	0.0	1.4	0.0	22.9	17.2	41.3	59.5	12.4	357	90.2
Atwater CDP	758	-	-	1,093	100.0	0.0	0.0	0.0	0.0	38.2	3.0	24.0	57.9	9.9	270	91.5
Aurora city	15,548	16,338	5.1	16,026	91.5	2.6	3.2	1.3	1.5	22.3	21.8	46.3	26.3	51.6	6,061	89.8
Austinburg CDP	516	-	-	662	81.7	0.8	0.0	16.9	0.6	23.9	32.9	36.6	61.7	22.9	233	71.2
Austintown CDP	29,677	-	-	28,488	84.5	8.0	0.9	1.3	5.3	18.4	21.7	43.1	47.9	20.3	13,016	86.0
Avon city	21,191	23,399	10.4	22,999	88.8	4.7	2.4	1.2	2.9	30.3	15.3	40.3	20.3	53.7	8,108	96.9
Avon Lake city	22,581	24,504	8.5	24,030	93.0	0.6	1.3	1.4	3.7	24.6	20.3	45.0	21.5	50.5	9,539	95.4
Bailey Lakes village	373	365	-2.1	345	98.0	0.6	0.0	0.9	0.6	13.9	18.0	45.8	45.7	18.6	158	92.4
Bainbridge CDP	3,267	-	-	3,326	96.1	0.0	2.2	0.0	1.7	29.1	16.8	40.5	7.3	74.6	1,217	96.7
Bainbridge village	862	850	-1.4	754	95.1	1.6	0.0	3.3	0.0	20.7	24.3	42.8	63.9	9.3	307	76.5
Bairdstown village	130	134	3.1	113	82.3	0.0	3.5	14.2	0.0	24.8	16.8	52.5	76.5	9.4	45	91.1
Ballville CDP	2,976	-	-	2,744	93.0	0.2	0.0	0.2	6.6	18.6	28.6	53.3	39.8	26.2	1,181	86.5
Baltic village	785	776	-1.1	766	98.3	0.0	0.5	1.2	0.0	29.1	18.7	33.1	72.2	9.9	233	86.7
Baltimore village	2,988	3,004	0.5	2,992	94.2	1.2	0.7	2.5	1.3	27.7	15.3	35.7	55.7	14.9	1,185	85.6
Bannock CDP	211	-	-	133	100.0	0.0	0.0	0.0	0.0	6.8	25.6	61.8	39.5	12.1	78	100.0
Barberton city	26,548	25,953	-2.2	26,098	86.4	8.0	0.7	2.9	2.1	21.6	19.1	41.0	61.5	14.9	11,033	80.4
Barnesville village	4,196	3,998	-4.7	3,546	97.2	0.3	1.4	1.1	0.0	23.0	22.7	43.9	52.3	19.7	1,429	79.1
Barnhill village	396	391	-1.3	359	98.1	0.0	0.0	1.9	0.0	12.8	12.3	43.1	83.3	2.3	149	79.2
Bascom CDP	390	-	-	330	94.5	0.0	0.0	5.5	0.0	21.2	20.9	40.9	52.1	17.4	154	61.7
Batavia village	1,929	1,983	2.8	1,987	83.8	6.1	0.0	6.0	4.0	16.8	13.5	35.1	61.8	12.3	588	88.3
Batesville village	101	99	-2.0	66	98.5	1.5	0.0	0.0	0.0	10.6	25.8	52.7	75.9	7.4	30	63.3
Bay View village	632	602	-4.7	798	90.1	0.8	1.6	0.9	6.6	18.5	23.4	49.4	54.6	13.4	289	89.3
Bay Village city	15,651	15,194	-2.9	15,325	93.2	1.3	0.7	2.4	2.4	26.2	17.5	43.4	13.2	67.0	6,021	96.4
Beach City village	1,024	981	-4.2	915	94.8	0.0	1.9	2.1	1.3	20.5	20.1	42.9	66.6	6.1	353	85.3
Beachwood city	11,926	11,590	-2.8	11,663	70.3	11.9	12.7	1.5	3.7	20.2	32.4	50.2	19.4	63.5	4,746	90.8
Beallsville village	409	380	-7.1	408	100.0	0.0	0.0	0.0	0.0	22.5	17.4	38.5	68.6	5.9	163	79.8
Beaver village	449	432	-3.8	556	95.1	0.0	0.0	4.9	0.0	21.2	11.5	41.0	67.6	7.2	232	81.0
Beavercreek city	45,198	47,741	5.6	46,942	84.3	2.6	6.4	4.2	2.6	20.7	18.6	42.1	19.4	51.9	19,275	94.7
Beaverdam village	385	371	-3.6	394	93.9	0.0	0.0	2.0	4.1	25.6	13.7	34.2	56.2	10.8	151	94.7
Beckett Ridge CDP	9,187	-	-	9,155	72.1	9.4	8.5	3.5	6.5	22.1	15.5	42.9	18.5	61.0	3,755	97.9
Bedford city	13,077	12,457	-4.7	12,631	37.8	55.1	0.7	2.3	4.2	21.5	17.7	40.7	45.7	20.8	5,840	84.5
Bedford Heights city	10,757	10,460	-2.8	10,565	18.0	77.7	0.5	1.3	2.5	14.6	20.0	46.9	43.6	13.4	5,589	86.9
Beechwood Trails CDP	3,020	-	-	3,106	96.2	1.2	1.6	1.0	0.0	23.0	21.5	48.7	33.4	35.3	1,116	97.3
Bellaire village	4,275	4,013	-6.1	4,097	90.2	4.3	0.0	4.2	1.3	20.4	17.2	42.9	61.7	7.5	1,779	72.3
Bellbrook city	6,962	7,344	5.5	7,212	94.5	0.7	1.1	1.3	2.4	22.6	18.9	44.2	20.5	47.5	3,092	95.9
Belle Center village	813	818	0.6	839	97.0	0.4	0.0	1.3	1.3	21.0	13.6	39.5	65.6	10.1	334	88.0
Bellefontaine city	13,364	13,249	-0.9	13,574	89.8	4.3	0.6	3.4	1.9	28.4	12.9	32.3	57.2	17.3	5,510	90.5
Belle Valley village	224	218	-2.7	226	100.0	0.0	0.0	0.0	0.0	17.7	21.2	58.3	73.0	1.7	111	85.6
Bellevue city	8,221	7,891	-4.0	7,937	94.7	0.4	0.6	0.8	3.5	24.8	17.0	39.3	50.4	15.5	3,274	89.0
Bellville village	1,922	1,931	0.5	2,219	99.7	0.0	0.3	0.0	0.0	24.7	23.7	38.5	42.2	27.8	1,015	87.6
Belmont village	451	434	-3.8	346	91.6	0.0	0.9	7.5	0.0	16.2	13.9	45.9	46.4	9.8	119	82.4
Belmore village	152	144	-5.3	86	55.8	0.0	0.0	0.0	44.2	17.4	19.8	50.1	70.1	3.0	33	72.7
Beloit village	978	924	-5.5	1,041	96.9	0.3	0.0	1.7	1.1	23.1	16.8	40.8	54.2	12.8	456	82.7
Belpre city	6,441	6,386	-0.9	6,421	90.7	2.0	0.5	5.0	1.8	17.5	23.9	45.2	46.9	14.9	2,941	85.4
Bentleyville village	864	846	-2.1	902	97.3	0.2	1.3	1.1	0.0	28.5	12.3	47.2	5.9	84.3	313	98.4
Benton Ridge village	297	292	-1.7	356	95.5	0.0	0.8	0.0	3.7	20.5	9.3	39.3	61.2	11.4	149	94.6
Bentonville CDP	287	-	-	237	100.0	0.0	0.0	0.0	0.0	9.3	56.1	66.9	81.5	4.9	142	40.1
Berea city	19,080	18,609	-2.5	18,788	84.6	6.3	2.6	3.2	3.3	17.5	16.9	37.4	33.1	34.4	7,171	91.8
Bergholz village	664	615	-7.4	619	99.0	0.2	0.0	0.8	0.0	27.8	16.2	40.0	73.2	9.5	249	71.9
Berkey village	240	236	-1.7	261	88.1	0.0	2.3	0.8	8.8	21.1	24.1	52.5	41.1	23.2	112	97.3
Berlin CDP	898	-	-	721	96.4	0.0	0.0	3.6	0.0	31.6	9.6	36.0	81.1	16.6	240	74.6
Berlin Heights village	714	713	-0.1	636	94.8	0.0	0.0	2.5	2.7	22.8	16.4	44.8	41.0	21.8	260	87.7
Bethel village	2,706	2,811	3.9	2,783	98.6	0.6	0.0	0.6	0.3	25.2	18.0	41.2	66.4	9.9	1,121	78.0
Bethesda village	1,257	1,212	-3.6	1,149	97.7	0.0	1.0	1.2	0.0	29.1	17.2	36.4	55.7	16.3	444	81.8
Bettsville village	656	622	-5.2	687	90.7	0.4	0.0	3.3	5.5	22.9	10.8	39.6	47.0	13.6	291	91.1
Beulah Beach CDP	53	-	-	11	100.0	0.0	0.0	0.0	0.0	0.0	100.0	0.0	100.0	0.0	11	0.0
Beverly village	1,312	1,332	1.5	1,496	88.1	0.0	2.1	4.3	5.4	29.7	19.2	38.8	53.8	14.9	575	78.6
Bexley city	13,054	13,770	5.5	13,786	84.5	6.8	2.9	3.1	2.7	25.6	12.8	34.6	9.7	76.4	4,752	93.8
Blacklick Estates CDP	8,682	-	-	9,727	58.7	33.3	0.8	3.7	3.6	30.2	9.9	34.8	61.4	11.5	3,364	90.2
Bladensburg CDP	191	-	-	134	100.0	0.0	0.0	0.0	0.0	13.4	20.1	48.4	64.0	30.2	46	39.1

[1] May be of any race.

Table A. All Places — **Population and Housing**

STATE City, town, township, borough, or CDP (county if applicable)	Population: 2010 census total population	Population: 2019 estimated population	Population: Percent change 2010–2019	Population: ACS total population estimate 2015–2019	Race and Hispanic or Latino origin (percent): White alone, not Hispanic or Latino	Black alone, not Hispanic or Latino	Asian alone, not Hispanic or Latino	All other races or 2 or more races, not Hispanic or Latino	Hispanic or Latino[1]	Age (percent): Under 18 years old	Age 65 years and older	Median age	Educational attainment of persons age 25 and older: Percent High school diploma or less	Percent Bachelor's degree or more	Occupied housing units: Total	Percent with a computer
	1	2	3	4	5	6	7	8	9	10	11	12	13	14	15	16
OHIO—Con.																
Blakeslee village	95	91	-4.2	88	78.4	0.0	0.0	4.5	17.0	17.0	25.0	35.3	51.6	17.7	41	68.3
Blanchester village	4,261	4,262	0.0	4,263	97.7	0.5	0.3	1.4	0.0	26.3	15.9	37.2	61.7	11.0	1,614	87.3
Bloomdale village	678	683	0.7	788	95.3	0.0	0.1	0.6	3.9	28.7	12.2	42.6	58.3	19.3	285	87.0
Bloomingburg village	938	915	-2.5	867	89.6	2.1	0.0	0.9	7.4	26.4	12.2	36.5	74.4	7.8	342	87.4
Bloomingdale village	202	188	-6.9	170	100.0	0.0	0.0	0.0	0.0	27.6	13.5	30.5	42.2	17.2	66	89.4
Bloomville village	956	911	-4.7	1,064	93.7	0.0	0.0	0.0	6.3	22.0	13.7	35.8	66.9	7.1	379	88.1
Blue Ash city	12,087	12,372	2.4	12,252	72.9	9.1	11.1	2.9	3.9	24.2	17.2	40.1	15.6	56.6	4,944	93.8
Blue Jay CDP	959	-	-	1,190	95.6	4.4	0.0	0.0	0.0	21.0	26.1	44.5	38.5	27.7	426	100.0
Bluffton village	4,200	4,082	-2.8	4,122	93.9	1.3	2.8	1.0	0.9	21.4	22.8	40.6	30.9	43.1	1,568	92.1
Boardman CDP	35,376	-	-	34,431	86.8	6.6	0.9	2.5	3.3	19.7	19.6	43.0	36.9	32.4	15,138	90.9
Bolindale CDP	2,089	-	-	2,398	94.5	3.4	0.0	2.1	0.0	24.6	20.5	38.5	71.4	8.1	1,018	85.4
Bolivar village	994	970	-2.4	1,122	98.9	0.0	0.0	1.1	0.0	19.1	23.7	40.5	43.1	17.8	439	90.9
Boston Heights village	1,317	1,314	-0.2	1,071	89.8	1.6	5.7	1.8	1.1	20.0	22.4	50.9	23.4	59.5	417	97.6
Botkins village	1,168	1,158	-0.9	1,124	93.6	0.0	0.8	4.3	1.3	24.3	18.6	42.5	51.0	16.4	492	88.8
Bourneville CDP	199	-	-	223	15.2	0.0	47.5	37.2	0.0	37.2	0.0	49.3	100.0	0.0	124	100.0
Bowerston village	398	378	-5.0	456	99.6	0.4	0.0	0.0	0.0	23.0	20.6	42.3	75.9	10.1	167	70.1
Bowersville village	333	330	-0.9	350	94.9	1.1	0.0	4.0	0.0	25.7	18.0	44.5	56.1	5.2	137	78.8
Bowling Green city	30,056	31,504	4.8	31,526	83.2	6.2	1.7	2.9	6.0	12.1	10.2	22.7	28.7	43.7	11,374	93.9
Bradford village	1,865	1,866	0.1	2,170	98.5	0.0	0.0	1.2	0.3	24.2	15.6	37.4	65.8	7.7	783	88.4
Bradner village	985	1,018	3.4	1,072	89.7	0.2	0.0	2.6	7.5	29.1	10.4	34.3	63.8	4.4	379	93.9
Brady Lake CDP	464	-	-	436	98.9	0.0	0.0	1.1	0.0	14.4	18.8	44.9	52.9	25.2	195	93.8
Bratenahl village	1,204	1,159	-3.7	1,379	83.0	13.5	0.8	1.6	1.1	8.0	41.7	62.1	10.4	66.2	770	94.5
Brecksville city	13,651	13,604	-0.3	13,537	90.0	4.2	4.0	1.5	0.3	21.1	22.4	49.3	18.8	59.0	5,539	94.2
Brecon CDP	244	-	-	486	29.6	0.0	0.0	0.0	70.4	35.8	23.7	27.5	59.6	35.4	172	70.3
Bremen village	1,426	1,452	1.8	1,382	95.5	0.0	0.0	4.3	0.2	26.8	16.6	35.0	49.6	14.5	471	93.2
Brewster village	2,168	2,153	-0.7	2,161	96.8	0.8	0.1	1.2	1.1	23.6	21.9	48.1	67.1	7.6	835	85.4
Brice village	116	120	3.4	80	88.8	2.5	0.0	5.0	3.8	18.8	12.5	47.8	57.6	10.2	30	86.7
Bridgeport village	1,839	1,728	-6.0	1,678	85.5	11.4	0.4	2.7	0.0	19.8	21.3	45.2	53.3	9.3	661	83.4
Bridgetown CDP	14,407	-	-	14,352	95.6	0.5	0.8	2.5	0.6	24.2	19.4	39.2	41.9	28.6	5,818	88.4
Brilliant CDP	1,482	-	-	1,479	96.4	0.0	0.0	3.6	0.0	23.9	21.2	42.8	61.8	6.0	642	81.2
Brimfield CDP	3,343	-	-	3,513	92.1	2.3	0.0	5.2	0.4	20.5	12.4	33.9	53.7	18.1	1,297	94.2
Broadview Heights city	19,397	19,102	-1.5	19,195	88.0	3.4	4.8	2.1	1.6	21.8	16.5	43.4	26.0	46.2	7,622	94.9
Brookfield Center CDP	1,207	-	-	1,403	96.2	3.8	0.0	0.0	0.0	20.5	21.1	41.3	49.7	21.5	575	92.2
Brooklyn city	11,169	10,646	-4.7	10,773	65.4	13.2	4.4	4.3	12.7	17.1	19.0	40.0	48.8	20.1	4,763	86.6
Brooklyn Heights village	1,539	1,497	-2.7	1,615	92.4	1.9	2.4	0.7	2.7	24.3	19.6	44.5	41.7	31.1	627	90.7
Brook Park city	19,212	18,382	-4.3	18,617	84.6	4.7	2.9	3.2	4.6	20.0	20.7	43.9	55.4	13.2	7,585	87.3
Brookside village	614	575	-6.4	795	82.1	5.8	0.0	2.4	9.7	20.9	15.6	39.1	40.1	20.6	319	90.3
Brookville city	5,872	5,874	0.0	5,919	95.8	0.6	1.1	1.2	1.4	19.7	29.0	47.2	40.9	23.7	2,818	86.4
Broughton village	120	113	-5.8	119	97.5	2.5	0.0	0.0	0.0	25.2	16.0	30.5	75.9	5.1	51	88.2
Brownsville CDP	220	-	-	116	100.0	0.0	0.0	0.0	0.0	36.2	15.5	49.6	100.0	0.0	47	100.0
Brunswick city	34,288	34,880	1.7	34,781	91.1	2.4	1.4	1.9	3.1	22.5	15.8	40.3	39.0	26.9	13,519	94.2
Bryan city	8,442	8,230	-2.5	8,251	93.8	0.8	0.1	1.8	3.6	22.9	18.9	40.4	45.4	15.0	3,777	84.3
Buchtel village	557	567	1.8	524	98.1	0.0	0.0	0.0	1.9	11.3	25.8	52.4	64.0	11.6	231	80.1
Buckeye Lake village	2,743	2,871	4.7	2,805	85.6	0.0	3.5	7.8	3.2	21.2	24.0	40.5	51.0	15.8	1,222	89.3
Buckland village	235	222	-5.5	321	99.1	0.0	0.0	0.6	0.3	34.0	15.0	30.1	54.5	3.5	126	84.9
Bucyrus city	12,386	11,764	-5.0	11,853	95.7	0.1	0.9	1.9	1.4	20.9	20.9	42.6	61.1	11.8	5,297	86.3
Buffalo CDP	401	-	-	341	97.4	0.0	0.0	2.6	0.0	28.4	26.1	40.3	65.6	3.7	120	85.8
Buford CDP	352	-	-	190	100.0	0.0	0.0	0.0	0.0	26.8	17.4	43.2	50.8	23.8	88	87.5
Burbank village	205	198	-3.4	267	98.1	1.9	0.0	0.0	0.0	19.5	34.5	51.6	66.5	4.1	82	85.4
Burgoon village	175	164	-6.3	223	89.7	0.0	0.0	0.0	10.3	30.0	13.9	30.6	42.2	9.6	68	85.3
Burkettsville village	244	273	11.9	266	95.9	0.0	0.0	0.0	4.1	25.9	13.9	33.3	62.8	16.7	104	98.1
Burlington CDP	2,676	-	-	2,521	86.5	6.1	0.0	4.4	3.0	21.7	21.9	43.6	55.5	8.7	1,022	91.2
Burton village	1,452	1,451	-0.1	1,375	96.4	1.5	0.0	0.0	2.1	17.6	29.8	49.9	43.1	23.9	600	89.8
Butler village	925	894	-3.4	781	94.6	0.0	0.0	1.9	3.5	26.8	19.1	36.4	61.9	9.3	310	82.9
Butlerville village	165	162	-1.8	224	100.0	0.0	0.0	0.0	0.0	22.8	11.2	34.0	77.3	2.7	73	93.2
Byesville village	2,444	2,352	-3.8	2,183	97.1	0.0	1.3	1.2	0.4	24.3	17.0	38.5	62.4	7.8	960	80.5
Cadiz village	3,351	3,161	-5.7	3,165	83.1	12.6	0.0	3.9	0.3	23.3	22.4	42.4	53.7	14.0	1,220	79.1
Cairo village	552	523	-5.3	512	95.9	0.0	0.8	1.0	2.3	29.1	21.5	37.7	54.7	10.5	200	84.5
Calcutta CDP	3,742	-	-	3,755	96.0	1.1	0.0	0.9	2.0	18.4	24.9	46.5	48.8	14.6	1,558	86.4
Caldwell village	1,750	1,712	-2.2	2,334	96.6	0.3	0.0	1.8	1.2	25.3	28.6	57.0	56.5	13.6	1,083	72.5
Caledonia village	582	557	-4.3	749	98.9	0.0	0.3	0.0	0.8	23.4	12.6	36.5	49.0	10.4	264	93.6
Cambridge city	10,636	10,289	-3.3	10,360	91.9	3.4	0.7	2.3	1.7	23.3	16.2	34.9	54.7	14.0	4,360	83.6
Camden village	2,044	1,973	-3.5	1,858	97.2	0.0	0.5	2.3	0.0	20.3	15.4	42.8	75.2	6.3	762	78.3
Campbell city	8,237	7,785	-5.5	7,889	51.6	20.6	0.0	4.7	23.1	24.6	18.7	40.6	57.1	9.2	3,299	82.7
Camp Dennison CDP	375	-	-	335	82.7	17.3	0.0	0.0	0.0	19.7	29.3	51.7	30.9	43.5	148	81.8
Canal Fulton city	5,432	5,408	-0.4	5,409	98.1	0.2	0.0	0.2	1.5	19.9	20.9	41.8	34.6	28.7	2,287	92.8
Canal Lewisville CDP	320	-	-	393	90.1	9.9	0.0	0.0	0.0	19.8	23.9	48.9	51.1	15.5	162	75.3
Canal Winchester city	7,117	8,818	23.9	8,611	87.4	4.7	1.3	3.8	2.8	23.8	20.7	41.8	33.8	39.4	3,192	93.5
Candlewood Lake CDP	1,147	-	-	630	100.0	0.0	0.0	0.0	0.0	31.7	14.0	34.5	39.9	6.1	219	100.0
Canfield city	7,539	7,176	-4.8	7,277	92.9	0.3	2.0	2.8	2.0	18.6	23.3	48.2	21.8	46.5	2,989	94.9
Canton city	73,403	70,447	-4.0	71,243	64.1	24.6	0.5	6.1	4.6	24.3	14.6	35.5	53.0	13.9	30,843	84.0
Carbon Hill CDP	233	-	-	291	100.0	0.0	0.0	0.0	0.0	33.0	11.0	40.8	42.4	5.1	125	74.4
Cardington village	2,041	2,071	1.5	1,923	95.6	0.3	0.0	1.7	2.5	28.8	10.0	34.0	60.4	10.2	766	88.5
Carey village	3,676	3,554	-3.3	3,507	90.3	0.0	4.2	2.2	3.3	26.7	14.5	38.3	57.5	12.2	1,455	88.3
Carlisle village	4,940	5,446	10.2	5,406	97.5	0.6	0.2	0.7	1.1	19.8	22.8	42.5	51.3	16.5	2,093	92.1
Carroll village	531	566	6.6	505	97.6	0.0	0.0	2.4	0.0	15.0	14.7	42.8	62.8	14.6	217	93.1
Carrollton village	3,242	3,026	-6.7	3,139	99.0	0.5	0.0	0.0	0.5	21.9	23.8	44.7	55.8	17.4	1,238	89.5
Casstown village	267	278	4.1	223	97.8	0.0	0.0	0.0	2.2	30.5	12.6	29.3	48.2	13.1	88	86.4
Castalia village	850	815	-4.1	953	89.6	1.0	2.0	1.3	6.1	22.2	16.7	37.3	52.9	18.6	339	92.0
Castine village	142	135	-4.9	270	99.6	0.0	0.0	0.0	0.4	42.2	2.2	23.3	51.2	1.7	89	84.3
Catawba village	285	273	-4.2	242	100.0	0.0	0.0	0.0	0.0	24.4	21.1	37.5	62.9	6.0	94	89.4
Cecil village	188	178	-5.3	126	95.2	0.0	0.0	0.0	4.8	11.1	19.8	53.0	84.8	1.8	70	92.9
Cedarville village	3,967	4,320	8.9	4,075	84.0	7.7	2.1	2.3	4.0	9.5	5.1	20.5	23.1	44.3	652	95.1
Celeryville CDP	210	-	-	107	72.9	0.0	0.0	0.0	27.1	20.6	21.5	59.8	61.2	8.2	63	54.0
Celina city	10,410	10,425	0.1	10,386	90.1	2.4	0.9	3.8	2.9	24.0	16.3	39.2	52.1	18.4	4,503	90.4
Centerburg village	1,773	2,226	25.5	1,716	94.6	1.6	0.0	2.8	1.0	21.4	23.2	46.2	57.6	15.1	712	85.5
Centerville (Thurman) village	103	98	-4.9	67	94.0	0.0	0.0	6.0	0.0	26.9	28.4	44.5	48.8	23.3	26	96.2
Centerville city	24,003	23,703	-1.2	23,796	84.8	6.0	4.8	2.3	2.1	19.8	28.1	49.6	19.7	53.7	10,788	94.1
Chagrin Falls village	4,104	3,941	-4.0	4,032	96.6	0.3	1.6	0.6	0.9	25.6	22.1	48.1	13.2	66.2	1,789	92.1
Champion Heights CDP	6,498	-	-	6,233	97.1	1.1	0.2	0.4	1.2	20.1	22.8	46.8	50.2	18.7	2,604	90.1
Chardon city	5,148	5,159	0.2	5,167	95.2	1.5	0.0	0.9	2.3	18.6	20.5	43.3	37.5	28.6	2,297	93.7

1 May be of any race.

Table A. All Places — **Population and Housing**

STATE City, town, township, borough, or CDP (county if applicable)	Population: 2010 census total population	Population: 2019 estimated population	Population: Percent change 2010–2019	Population: ACS total population estimate 2015–2019	Race and Hispanic or Latino origin (percent): White alone, not Hispanic or Latino	Black alone, not Hispanic or Latino	Asian alone, not Hispanic or Latino	All other races or 2 or more races, not Hispanic or Latino	Hispanic or Latino[1]	Age (percent): Under 18 years old	Age 65 years and older	Median age	Educational attainment of persons age 25 and older: Percent High school diploma or less	Percent Bachelor's degree or more	Occupied housing units: Total	Percent with a computer
	1	2	3	4	5	6	7	8	9	10	11	12	13	14	15	16
OHIO—Con.																
Chatfield village	187	178	-4.8	294	97.3	0.0	0.0	0.3	2.4	33.0	12.9	32.3	55.5	5.2	101	95.0
Chauncey village	1,037	1,035	-0.2	1,056	99.9	0.1	0.0	0.0	0.0	16.9	16.6	42.2	64.0	7.7	448	84.8
Cherry Fork CDP	155	-	-	326	100.0	0.0	0.0	0.0	0.0	22.7	3.4	43.0	23.4	70.3	104	93.3
Cherry Grove CDP	4,378	-	-	4,747	82.3	9.6	2.5	1.6	3.9	30.9	10.8	39.2	22.8	50.4	1,643	95.6
Chesapeake village	745	702	-5.8	875	93.3	0.5	0.0	3.4	2.9	16.1	21.7	42.7	52.9	11.7	361	86.7
Cheshire village	132	128	-3.0	177	100.0	0.0	0.0	0.0	0.0	25.4	14.7	42.5	68.1	5.3	77	70.1
Chesterhill village	289	275	-4.8	399	41.9	38.3	0.0	19.8	0.0	38.6	16.5	32.7	60.3	8.5	144	79.9
Chesterland CDP	2,521	-	-	2,215	94.1	0.5	5.3	0.1	0.0	23.2	19.1	45.1	34.7	33.8	830	86.4
Chesterville village	228	232	1.8	219	83.1	0.9	5.9	2.3	7.8	31.1	20.5	35.6	61.9	8.2	67	89.6
Cheviot city	8,347	8,209	-1.7	8,254	79.4	11.3	0.5	5.6	3.3	21.8	12.0	36.3	43.2	22.2	3,685	93.2
Chickasaw village	287	292	1.7	336	100.0	0.0	0.0	0.0	0.0	31.0	17.0	33.4	60.9	18.8	137	86.9
Chillicothe city	21,931	21,722		21,719	86.7	6.3	0.3	5.7	1.1	21.8	20.0	41.2	49.8	19.7	9,173	87.8
Chilo village	63	67	6.3	96	100.0	0.0	0.0	0.0	0.0	16.7	14.6	37.5	71.7	6.7	25	84.0
Chippewa Lake village	710	745	4.9	795	92.6	1.1	2.0	0.0	4.3	15.7	26.4	49.8	51.3	19.1	343	87.5
Chippewa Park CDP	891	-	-	702	92.6	0.0	0.0	2.0	5.4	4.4	46.9	61.7	62.0	12.7	407	77.4
Choctaw Lake CDP	1,546	-	-	1,999	95.8	0.0	0.0	4.2	0.0	19.7	19.7	49.3	28.6	35.4	752	100.0
Christiansburg village	533	505	-5.3	425	98.6	0.0	0.0	0.0	1.4	19.5	25.6	47.0	60.6	9.3	180	83.9
Churchill CDP	2,149	-	-	2,309	91.2	8.8	0.0	0.0	0.0	30.4	16.1	38.7	57.2	11.2	948	85.8
Cincinnati city	297,025	303,940	2.3	301,394	48.2	42.0	2.2	3.8	3.8	22.0	12.2	32.2	36.3	37.1	137,333	87.1
Cinnamon Lake CDP	1,243	-	-	1,430	96.0	0.0	4.0	0.0	0.0	33.6	18.8	38.3	43.1	15.1	527	97.2
Circleville city	13,506	14,050	4.0	13,928	94.5	3.2	0.1	1.9	0.3	19.9	19.6	40.1	59.1	16.4	5,607	80.7
Clarington village	385	363	-5.7	439	100.0	0.0	0.0	0.0	0.0	20.5	20.3	41.8	66.4	7.1	162	88.9
Clarksburg village	452	444	-1.8	426	93.4	2.1	0.0	4.2	0.2	32.6	13.8	31.9	64.7	9.2	156	76.3
Clarksville village	546	549	0.5	608	96.2	0.0	0.0	3.1	0.7	35.4	4.8	33.9	61.9	7.2	217	91.2
Clarktown CDP	958	-	-	596	98.5	1.5	0.0	0.0	0.0	3.2	26.0	58.4	53.7	9.0	308	86.7
Clay Center village	274	302	10.2	294	94.6	0.3	0.0	0.0	5.1	27.9	16.0	39.3	64.8	4.1	110	84.5
Clayton city	13,248	13,222	-0.2	13,205	69.9	20.8	1.2	6.1	2.0	22.3	20.7	45.6	30.2	35.9	5,171	94.3
Cleveland city	396,665	381,009	-3.9	385,282	33.8	48.2	2.5	3.6	11.9	22.1	14.0	36.3	51.9	17.5	170,549	82.4
Cleveland Heights city	46,268	43,992	-4.9	44,571	47.9	40.7	5.3	3.3	2.8	21.2	16.3	35.2	20.0	54.9	19,074	91.8
Cleves village	3,243	3,375	4.1	3,359	94.3	0.0	0.4	3.7	1.5	33.3	8.7	34.7	46.9	26.7	1,100	91.5
Clifton village	150	147	-2.0	116	84.5	0.9	0.0	2.6	12.1	16.4	11.2	39.5	21.7	27.2	52	88.5
Clinton village	1,217	1,209	-0.7	1,265	97.1	0.8	0.0	1.7	0.4	15.3	11.4	46.1	47.9	14.6	498	96.4
Cloverdale village	169	160	-5.3	175	98.3	1.1	0.0	0.0	0.6	22.3	15.4	40.8	70.7	8.1	65	72.3
Clyde city	6,403	6,166	-3.7	6,207	88.6	0.2	0.0	3.1	8.0	27.9	17.1	38.7	56.6	9.4	2,517	88.5
Coal Grove village	2,165	2,074	-4.2	1,913	92.5	0.8	0.0	4.7	2.0	17.1	18.1	45.3	57.7	15.0	805	86.0
Coalton village	479	473	-1.3	395	100.0	0.0	0.0	0.0	0.0	14.9	12.9	44.9	67.7	7.7	192	79.2
Coldstream CDP	1,173	-	-	1,255	90.6	0.0	7.6	1.0	0.7	29.2	21.7	41.5	9.2	78.2	449	96.2
Coldwater village	4,421	4,562	3.2	4,366	95.9	0.5	0.0	0.2	3.4	28.7	17.5	34.6	51.4	22.6	1,702	90.9
College Corner village	404	417	3.2	339	96.2	0.0	0.0	3.8	0.0	28.6	14.5	34.5	56.8	9.9	139	82.0
Collins CDP	631	-	-	480	100.0	0.0	0.0	0.0	0.0	20.8	3.1	37.3	62.4	17.1	206	100.0
Columbiana city	6,400	6,250	-2.3	6,247	97.4	0.2	0.3	1.3	0.8	18.6	31.6	49.0	40.9	29.5	2,884	85.3
Columbus city	789,018	898,553	13.9	878,553	55.1	28.6	5.8	4.3	6.2	22.5	10.2	32.2	35.7	36.6	357,128	92.2
Columbus Grove village	2,155	2,079	-3.5	2,179	90.7	1.7	0.0	2.2	5.5	28.5	16.7	34.2	42.9	20.1	903	90.9
Commercial Point village	1,604	1,679	4.7	2,002	93.9	0.3	1.6	2.4	1.7	33.6	7.1	33.0	47.8	27.6	623	92.3
Concorde Hills CDP	663	-	-	733	85.3	9.8	0.0	4.9	0.0	22.5	36.3	49.4	5.2	79.2	281	69.0
Conesville village	351	343	-2.3	341	99.7	0.0	0.0	0.0	0.3	23.5	19.6	40.4	69.6	6.7	148	78.4
Congress village	180	177	-1.7	202	86.6	0.0	0.0	0.0	13.4	45.0	5.4	18.7	79.0	2.5	48	75.0
Conneaut city	12,832	12,530	-2.4	12,613	86.4	7.8	0.0	2.9	2.9	17.8	18.7	42.4	58.8	12.8	4,604	83.1
Connorville CDP	-	-	-	241	100.0	0.0	0.0	0.0	0.0	21.6	14.1	34.7	53.4	15.5	101	82.2
Continental village	1,126	1,101	-2.2	1,131	96.6	2.2	0.0	0.5	0.7	20.5	20.5	43.1	54.7	14.5	519	84.6
Convoy village	1,087	1,059	-2.6	1,177	94.3	0.0	0.0	1.8	3.9	26.6	12.8	35.8	57.2	8.7	441	94.3
Coolville village	494	494	0.0	647	98.3	0.0	1.1	0.0	0.6	22.6	13.8	38.6	72.3	8.7	195	93.3
Corning village	582	568	-2.4	385	100.0	0.0	0.0	0.0	0.0	32.7	6.2	32.2	70.0	3.4	149	76.5
Cortland city	7,148	6,768	-5.3	6,836	93.3	3.8	0.0	2.8	0.2	20.0	24.9	45.3	38.2	35.3	3,069	90.9
Corwin village	416	473	13.7	527	97.2	0.0	0.0	0.0	2.8	18.8	21.8	44.7	34.7	32.9	213	92.5
Coshocton city	11,174	11,051	-1.1	11,063	93.8	2.0	0.4	2.3	1.6	20.5	20.9	40.6	57.3	15.9	4,663	83.7
Covedale CDP	6,447	-	-	6,277	88.3	5.7	1.1	2.8	2.1	24.8	19.0	41.1	35.9	41.8	2,447	91.2
Covington village	2,601	2,708	4.1	2,671	91.4	1.3	0.2	5.5	1.6	26.5	16.8	36.5	57.5	11.0	965	85.8
Craig Beach village	1,173	1,110	-5.4	1,488	99.1	0.0	0.0	0.4	0.5	24.0	13.6	41.2	58.6	14.1	596	94.5
Crestline village	4,662	4,425	-5.1	4,448	89.4	5.0	1.3	3.0	1.3	26.5	15.4	37.5	59.7	10.5	1,851	86.6
Creston village	2,143	2,170	1.3	2,009	97.9	0.0	0.0	1.8	0.3	23.9	17.6	42.4	62.8	12.4	749	88.4
Cridersville village	1,854	1,792	-3.3	1,966	87.2	5.5	0.0	3.2	4.1	22.9	22.1	43.9	54.2	16.0	874	90.6
Crooksville village	2,534	2,482	-2.1	2,556	97.5	0.0	0.0	2.0	0.5	28.1	14.4	36.7	72.8	2.7	920	84.0
Crown City village	420	402	-4.3	446	98.7	0.0	1.1	0.2	0.0	32.7	11.4	29.6	49.8	9.5	143	83.2
Crystal Lakes CDP	1,483	-	-	1,402	86.2	0.0	0.0	4.9	9.0	25.9	14.1	40.7	76.2	5.5	528	85.2
Crystal Rock CDP	176	-	-	99	100.0	0.0	0.0	0.0	0.0	35.4	34.3	40.8	73.4	26.6	47	74.5
Cumberland village	364	349	-4.1	339	98.2	0.3	0.0	1.2	0.3	23.6	10.9	37.6	61.1	10.0	124	85.5
Curtice CDP	1,526	-	-	1,240	94.5	0.0	0.0	0.0	5.5	26.8	14.1	42.7	36.5	32.0	469	91.3
Custar village	179	184	2.8	249	88.0	0.0	0.0	2.0	10.0	35.3	4.8	33.6	66.9	3.3	84	97.6
Cuyahoga Falls city	49,534	49,106	-0.9	49,192	87.7	4.8	3.0	2.8	1.8	20.1	17.4	39.6	34.4	33.3	22,053	88.6
Cuyahoga Heights village	638	607	-4.9	677	93.2	1.0	5.0	0.7	0.0	25.0	15.1	41.9	50.0	24.3	271	89.7
Cygnet village	597	618	3.5	568	93.7	0.0	0.0	0.2	6.2	25.5	15.5	36.7	62.7	11.6	203	90.1
Cynthiana CDP	68	-	-	-	-	-	-	-	-	-	-	-	-	-	-	-
Dalton village	1,870	1,888	1.0	1,637	96.2	0.4	0.0	1.3	2.1	22.5	25.0	41.7	48.1	24.4	674	80.7
Damascus CDP	443	-	-	278	100.0	0.0	0.0	0.0	0.0	16.9	11.9	41.4	62.5	30.0	115	100.0
Danville village	1,046	1,015	-3.0	1,112	95.9	0.0	0.3	0.7	3.1	24.0	15.2	35.0	49.9	21.9	467	80.1
Darbydale CDP	793	-	-	862	97.6	0.0	0.0	0.0	2.4	20.6	10.3	47.7	82.4	6.5	259	100.0
Darbyville village	223	229	2.7	175	100.0	0.0	0.0	0.0	0.0	16.0	21.1	46.3	77.7	0.8	73	69.9
Darrtown CDP	516	-	-	492	94.3	1.8	2.0	1.8	0.0	19.7	11.0	35.1	46.7	15.9	193	89.1
Day Heights CDP	2,620	-	-	2,978	94.0	0.6	0.6	0.5	4.3	29.6	20.8	35.6	31.7	26.2	1,090	97.1
Dayton city	141,989	140,407	-1.1	140,569	53.0	37.6	1.1	3.9	4.4	21.9	12.7	33.0	45.7	18.4	57,505	84.3
Deer Park city	5,668	5,566	-1.8	5,599	85.9	5.4	3.5	3.3	1.8	19.0	15.0	38.6	36.6	31.8	2,509	88.1
Deersville village	79	75	-5.1	38	100.0	0.0	0.0	0.0	0.0	13.2	15.8	50.8	65.5	20.7	20	80.0
Defiance city	17,077	16,634	-2.6	16,990	79.2	2.9	0.3	2.5	15.1	23.0	18.6	37.4	51.6	18.0	7,032	85.2
De Graff village	1,286	1,276	-0.8	1,265	93.6	1.2	0.2	4.0	0.9	26.5	19.6	40.0	61.1	12.4	495	86.5
Delaware city	34,791	41,283	18.7	40,568	85.0	5.2	3.3	3.1	3.4	24.8	12.0	35.5	33.9	35.6	14,511	94.3
Delhi Hills CDP	5,259	-	-	5,266	96.5	0.7	0.0	2.5	0.3	22.5	13.7	42.0	42.9	24.2	1,883	94.4
Dellroy village	356	330	-7.3	334	97.9	1.5	0.0	0.6	0.0	21.3	16.8	38.1	67.5	5.4	148	91.2
Delphos city	7,130	6,937	-2.7	7,020	93.2	0.9	0.1	1.2	4.6	21.6	18.2	38.7	54.5	17.3	2,906	85.5
Delshire CDP	3,180	-	-	3,483	85.9	4.9	4.2	1.5	3.4	28.7	10.3	34.4	46.1	23.5	1,161	95.5
Delta village	3,093	3,100	0.2	3,021	89.0	0.8	0.0	2.1	8.0	27.2	15.6	36.9	47.6	18.4	1,235	95.1
Dennison village	2,655	2,594	-2.3	2,662	94.8	0.7	0.0	3.1	1.4	27.8	13.6	34.5	60.8	7.9	1,092	88.1

1 May be of any race.

STATE City, town, township, borough, or CDP (county if applicable)	Population: 2010 census total population	Population: 2019 estimated population	Population: Percent change 2010–2019	Population: ACS total population estimate 2015–2019	Race and Hispanic or Latino origin (percent): White alone, not Hispanic or Latino	Race and Hispanic or Latino origin (percent): Black alone, not Hispanic or Latino	Race and Hispanic or Latino origin (percent): Asian alone, not Hispanic or Latino	Race and Hispanic or Latino origin (percent): All other races or 2 or more races, not Hispanic or Latino	Race and Hispanic or Latino origin (percent): Hispanic or Latino[1]	Age (percent): Under 18 years old	Age (percent): Age 65 years and older	Age (percent): Median age	Educational attainment of persons age 25 and older: Percent High school diploma or less	Educational attainment of persons age 25 and older: Percent Bachelor's degree or more	Occupied housing units: Total	Occupied housing units: Percent with a computer
	1	2	3	4	5	6	7	8	9	10	11	12	13	14	15	16
OHIO—Con.																
Dent CDP	10,497	-	-	11,332	93.1	3.4	0.8	0.3	2.3	24.7	16.7	39.3	26.9	42.2	4,556	95.7
Derby CDP	408	-	-	404	96.0	0.0	0.0	4.0	0.0	19.6	19.8	39.7	65.5	6.5	168	100.0
Deshler village	1,799	1,721	-4.3	1,526	86.6	1.0	0.1	1.4	10.8	27.1	17.4	36.1	64.5	9.2	645	90.7
Devola CDP	2,652	-	-	2,702	95.1	0.9	3.6	0.3	0.0	15.5	25.9	50.2	34.1	29.9	1,152	80.5
Dexter City village	126	122	-3.2	63	100.0	0.0	0.0	0.0	0.0	19.0	15.9	56.1	89.6	0.0	32	34.4
Dillonvale CDP	3,474	-	-	3,443	92.1	2.2	2.4	0.7	2.7	19.3	18.4	44.6	39.5	35.0	1,508	91.4
Dillonvale village	666	619	-7.1	715	97.6	0.7	0.4	0.8	0.4	17.2	16.1	43.2	61.7	4.9	306	86.9
Dola CDP	140	-	-	149	100.0	0.0	0.0	0.0	0.0	20.8	18.8	43.3	44.1	14.4	60	65.0
Donnelsville village	270	261	-3.3	357	98.0	0.0	0.3	1.4	0.3	29.7	9.8	35.8	45.9	20.5	130	90.0
Dover city	12,877	12,723	-1.2	12,774	89.0	1.1	1.3	2.4	6.2	23.4	24.2	42.0	46.5	26.2	5,083	83.3
Doylestown village	3,042	3,067	0.8	3,077	93.2	4.2	0.0	1.3	1.3	21.9	23.6	43.2	44.0	32.0	1,267	91.0
Dresden village	1,544	1,691	9.5	1,810	95.5	1.0	0.0	3.5	0.0	25.5	17.2	37.6	59.5	11.4	737	81.4
Drexel CDP	2,076	-	-	2,064	32.7	52.3	0.0	6.6	8.4	32.5	13.2	30.6	72.4	3.7	747	79.0
Dry Ridge CDP	2,782	-	-	2,992	90.8	3.5	0.9	3.0	1.7	18.5	21.9	48.9	29.2	40.4	1,252	96.5
Dry Run CDP	7,281	-	-	7,555	87.1	0.9	4.3	3.4	4.2	31.4	12.0	40.3	10.9	70.0	2,476	97.5
Dublin city	41,398	49,037	18.5	46,499	71.6	2.0	19.6	2.8	3.9	28.2	12.2	40.1	10.5	74.6	16,830	97.4
Duncan Falls CDP	880	-	-	1,169	100.0	0.0	0.0	0.0	0.0	20.4	16.2	31.8	63.4	5.9	413	83.8
Dundee CDP	297	-	-	209	100.0	0.0	0.0	0.0	0.0	28.2	0.0	32.5	87.0	0.0	81	88.9
Dunkirk village	871	840	-3.6	714	91.5	0.1	1.5	5.3	1.5	22.1	13.7	42.1	59.1	6.5	316	80.4
Dunlap CDP	1,719	-	-	1,355	98.7	1.3	0.0	0.0	0.0	7.1	27.3	56.8	24.0	47.7	627	98.7
Dupont village	320	303	-5.3	333	98.8	0.0	0.0	0.0	1.2	21.0	18.9	43.1	74.2	7.1	134	82.8
East Canton village	1,591	1,576	-0.9	1,464	95.7	2.2	0.0	1.8	0.3	24.0	17.3	38.8	61.0	11.3	627	86.3
East Cleveland city	17,859	16,964	-5.0	17,200	6.3	90.1	0.6	2.2	0.7	21.0	22.5	43.0	53.9	12.4	8,235	73.2
East Fultonham CDP	335	-	-	386	89.6	0.0	6.2	4.1	0.0	22.0	15.5	34.5	66.5	21.1	126	100.0
Eastlake city	18,606	18,042	-3.0	18,156	89.7	6.7	0.4	2.3	0.8	19.3	17.9	42.6	48.1	17.5	7,857	88.4
East Liberty CDP	366	-	-	320	59.7	0.0	11.9	28.4	0.0	14.7	10.3	38.9	54.6	9.2	156	79.5
East Liverpool city	11,200	10,603	-5.3	10,692	86.5	3.7	0.5	6.2	3.0	24.9	14.7	36.1	61.1	9.4	4,210	80.7
East Palestine village	4,718	4,424	-6.2	4,493	95.2	0.6	0.0	1.9	2.4	24.3	21.1	42.0	53.1	16.3	1,888	90.9
East Rochester CDP	231	-	-	142	100.0	0.0	0.0	0.0	0.0	0.0	27.5	60.2	66.7	0.0	95	85.3
East Sparta village	815	799	-2.0	937	98.7	0.1	0.0	1.2	0.0	23.8	18.1	41.9	54.0	12.2	351	91.7
East Springfield CDP	-	-	-	264	100.0	0.0	0.0	0.0	0.0	33.7	0.0	42.3	40.6	17.1	107	100.0
Eaton city	8,410	8,145	-3.2	8,183	93.8	1.3	0.9	2.7	1.3	22.8	21.2	41.6	52.4	15.6	3,399	85.0
Eaton Estates CDP	1,222	-	-	1,366	91.5	0.0	0.0	5.7	2.8	20.9	9.7	42.4	62.5	13.8	481	92.1
Edgerton village	2,007	1,999	-0.4	2,105	92.2	0.8	0.0	2.9	4.1	22.5	20.7	39.4	53.0	16.5	847	83.0
Edgewood CDP	4,432	-	-	4,253	86.2	6.0	0.0	1.2	6.5	25.4	15.6	39.8	55.8	13.9	1,754	81.9
Edison village	437	443	1.4	491	92.9	0.0	0.0	2.9	4.3	25.9	14.1	36.9	64.0	5.4	173	91.9
Edon village	838	810	-3.3	777	94.9	0.0	0.0	1.3	3.9	21.1	22.7	40.3	53.8	16.3	336	89.3
Eldorado village	511	490	-4.1	472	97.7	0.6	0.0	1.7	0.0	20.8	18.6	43.2	54.8	15.2	213	80.8
Elgin village	57	56	-1.8	96	99.0	0.0	0.0	0.0	1.0	25.0	4.2	55.5	65.2	1.4	38	97.4
Elida village	1,882	1,803	-4.2	2,233	82.2	13.5	0.2	2.3	1.8	32.5	12.9	35.8	43.3	23.6	786	90.5
Elizabethtown CDP	350	-	-	299	100.0	0.0	0.0	0.0	0.0	26.4	1.3	33.4	58.5	2.5	146	93.8
Elmore village	1,442	1,396	-3.2	1,419	95.0	0.0	0.0	1.8	3.2	21.4	19.3	44.0	45.3	22.9	638	80.1
Elmwood Place village	2,205	2,207	0.1	2,052	68.9	18.7	0.0	3.3	9.1	26.3	14.7	37.4	64.9	5.1	868	77.4
Elyria city	54,526	53,757	-1.4	53,821	71.8	15.2	1.0	4.9	7.1	22.8	15.4	39.2	46.2	15.5	22,783	88.3
Empire village	299	280	-6.4	231	100.0	0.0	0.0	0.0	0.0	13.9	19.5	50.7	68.2	0.0	101	68.3
Englewood city	13,424	13,435	0.1	13,463	77.3	15.4	2.3	3.4	1.5	22.6	23.0	44.2	35.3	30.0	5,629	89.7
Enon village	2,447	2,386	-2.5	2,504	91.7	2.4	0.7	3.0	2.2	17.1	27.2	51.0	32.9	31.8	1,100	93.5
Etna CDP	1,215	-	-	984	92.2	0.0	3.4	4.5	0.0	26.0	7.5	32.3	32.5	17.0	301	100.0
Euclid city	48,901	46,550	-4.8	47,159	33.6	61.6	0.6	2.9	1.3	21.3	17.1	41.2	42.7	19.5	22,359	82.2
Evendale village	2,739	2,727	-0.4	2,730	83.5	4.1	7.6	3.0	1.8	20.2	23.5	50.0	18.7	64.4	1,035	97.3
Fairborn city	33,028	33,876	2.6	33,462	79.3	8.7	2.6	5.6	3.8	20.4	14.4	32.9	35.0	30.0	14,519	91.2
Fairfax village	1,699	1,701	0.1	1,748	92.5	4.7	0.2	0.8	1.8	25.8	12.3	37.4	39.6	30.8	734	89.4
Fairfield city	42,500	42,558	0.1	42,634	70.4	15.6	3.3	2.7	8.1	22.5	16.4	37.7	44.3	28.7	16,946	91.4
Fairfield Beach CDP	1,292	-	-	1,041	90.3	2.7	0.0	7.0	0.0	13.8	25.3	55.1	52.4	8.5	514	87.4
Fairlawn city	7,505	7,514	0.1	7,514	78.7	8.9	6.5	5.0	0.9	20.3	24.7	43.2	23.6	46.1	3,258	89.5
Fairport Harbor village	3,112	3,067	-1.4	3,077	95.2	1.0	0.6	2.4	0.8	15.4	20.4	48.9	40.7	23.8	1,608	88.7
Fairview village	83	81	-2.4	83	96.4	3.6	0.0	0.0	0.0	28.9	19.3	42.3	45.3	20.8	36	41.7
Fairview Park city	16,827	16,161	-4.0	16,303	89.8	2.3	2.1	1.7	4.1	19.7	19.3	40.5	26.2	43.9	7,140	92.3
Farmersville village	1,009	1,002	-0.7	1,043	98.2	0.2	0.0	0.7	1.0	23.0	14.2	37.7	44.5	17.2	378	94.4
Fayette village	1,281	1,241	-3.1	1,299	84.9	0.0	1.2	1.5	12.4	25.0	13.5	35.8	51.1	15.6	556	91.2
Fayetteville village	328	316	-3.7	311	92.3	0.0	0.0	7.7	0.0	30.5	14.8	38.6	62.4	10.9	116	94.0
Felicity village	814	858	5.4	597	97.0	0.0	0.0	3.0	0.0	23.3	16.2	38.7	68.6	5.4	278	65.8
Findlay city	41,186	41,225	0.1	41,335	84.4	2.4	2.8	2.5	7.8	20.5	16.8	37.4	43.5	27.4	18,207	91.4
Finneytown CDP	12,741	-	-	12,856	55.3	36.7	1.7	5.2	1.0	24.6	17.2	41.4	32.1	36.6	5,117	92.4
Five Points CDP	1,824	-	-	1,849	93.5	0.0	0.0	1.2	5.3	28.1	15.6	45.2	17.6	65.4	639	96.6
Flat Rock CDP	233	-	-	177	95.5	0.0	0.0	4.5	0.0	16.4	21.5	50.2	50.0	33.9	44	100.0
Fletcher village	467	483	3.4	358	96.6	0.0	0.0	0.6	2.8	24.9	14.5	39.0	66.7	5.7	127	91.3
Florida village	232	214	-7.8	190	92.1	0.0	0.0	3.2	4.7	16.3	18.9	44.3	56.5	12.2	94	90.4
Flushing village	881	832	-5.6	753	92.0	2.5	0.0	3.9	1.6	24.2	17.1	36.4	57.8	10.3	309	84.8
Forest village	1,455	1,431	-1.6	1,485	95.1	0.1	0.0	1.3	3.6	29.4	12.3	39.1	58.7	9.8	569	89.8
Forest Park city	18,705	18,583	-0.7	18,657	20.1	55.9	5.7	10.2	8.2	26.4	13.9	32.7	42.3	27.4	6,833	93.7
Forestville CDP	10,532	-	-	10,415	91.1	3.9	2.2	2.3	0.5	22.9	22.9	46.5	21.7	53.5	4,363	92.8
Fort Jennings village	489	488	-0.2	414	97.8	0.5	1.0	0.7	0.0	17.6	20.3	42.8	39.5	27.6	187	85.6
Fort Loramie village	1,492	1,523	2.1	1,524	99.3	0.0	0.0	0.0	0.7	26.1	14.5	39.5	45.9	27.9	590	94.2
Fort Recovery village	1,457	1,458	0.1	1,526	91.3	0.5	0.0	0.6	7.6	32.2	13.6	35.1	52.5	21.4	614	80.5
Fort Seneca CDP	254	-	-	184	100.0	0.0	0.0	0.0	0.0	16.8	27.7	50.7	71.9	5.2	70	85.7
Fort Shawnee CDP	3,726	-	-	6,009	88.1	4.7	1.4	2.3	3.6	19.6	21.6	45.8	38.3	26.1	2,523	90.7
Fostoria city	13,453	13,225	-1.7	13,316	78.0	4.7	0.9	2.3	14.1	26.3	17.5	36.8	60.0	10.0	5,541	85.7
Four Bridges CDP	2,919	-	-	3,246	84.4	2.7	3.8	4.9	4.2	26.7	18.0	43.8	12.5	67.0	1,150	96.2
Frankfort village	1,064	1,048	-1.5	1,409	86.5	9.2	0.0	4.3	0.0	31.7	13.8	35.3	58.1	14.8	522	83.7
Franklin city	11,762	11,612	-1.3	11,705	92.4	0.6	1.5	2.3	3.2	19.6	15.1	39.2	60.6	13.5	4,952	89.3
Franklin Furnace CDP	1,660	-	-	1,559	87.9	6.0	0.0	4.5	1.6	13.0	19.0	43.7	51.1	14.5	513	80.9
Frazeysburg village	1,306	1,316	0.8	1,328	94.7	0.5	0.0	4.6	0.2	22.4	21.3	43.2	66.1	5.5	552	83.7
Fredericksburg village	415	412	-0.7	350	99.4	0.0	0.0	0.0	0.6	25.1	18.6	34.4	57.8	26.3	143	91.6
Fredericktown village	2,493	2,525	1.3	2,501	98.4	0.7	0.0	0.9	0.0	30.6	12.9	36.1	40.4	21.9	1,028	88.2
Freeport village	369	350	-5.1	405	100.0	0.0	0.0	0.0	0.0	19.0	18.5	45.7	74.3	7.2	183	71.6
Fremont city	16,641	15,917	-4.4	16,073	71.5	7.9	0.7	3.6	16.3	25.1	15.8	37.8	55.4	13.2	6,702	86.3
Fresno CDP	140	-	-	251	100.0	0.0	0.0	0.0	0.0	31.5	12.4	30.5	61.5	0.0	75	100.0
Friendship CDP	351	-	-	367	100.0	0.0	0.0	0.0	0.0	35.4	4.4	31.2	52.5	3.2	137	100.0
Fruit Hill CDP	3,755	-	-	4,156	96.7	0.5	0.0	0.4	2.4	34.4	10.4	34.7	20.8	43.9	1,416	96.0
Fulton village	256	255	-0.4	288	92.7	0.0	0.0	0.0	7.3	22.6	15.3	33.1	59.4	13.7	103	90.3
Fultonham village	162	161	-0.6	202	95.5	3.5	0.0	1.0	0.0	42.1	5.0	25.2	65.0	8.7	58	89.7

1 May be of any race.

Table A. All Places — **Population and Housing**

STATE City, town, township, borough, or CDP (county if applicable)	Population: 2010 census total population	Population: 2019 estimated population	Population: Percent change 2010–2019	Population: ACS total population estimate 2015–2019	Race and Hispanic or Latino origin (percent): White alone, not Hispanic or Latino	Black alone, not Hispanic or Latino	Asian alone, not Hispanic or Latino	All other races or 2 or more races, not Hispanic or Latino	Hispanic or Latino[1]	Age (percent): Under 18 years old	Age 65 years and older	Median age	Educational attainment of persons age 25 and older: Percent High school diploma or less	Percent Bachelor's degree or more	Occupied housing units: Total	Percent with a computer
	1	2	3	4	5	6	7	8	9	10	11	12	13	14	15	16
OHIO—Con.																
Gahanna city	33,230	35,483	6.8	35,268	79.5	11.8	3.2	2.5	3.0	24.5	15.3	39.9	24.7	48.5	13,506	96.5
Galena village	667	742	11.2	612	88.9	3.8	3.3	3.3	0.8	23.0	14.5	39.5	26.6	43.2	185	98.4
Galion city	10,611	9,982	-5.9	10,074	96.0	1.1	0.0	1.0	1.9	24.7	19.8	40.2	54.6	14.6	4,273	82.4
Gallipolis village	3,648	3,556	-2.5	3,710	81.3	5.1	2.9	6.1	4.6	24.3	21.3	36.8	45.6	21.1	1,605	85.4
Gambier village	2,391	2,486	4.0	2,442	85.5	3.8	0.9	4.7	5.2	4.7	6.4	20.5	4.0	75.8	351	91.2
Gann (Brinkhaven) village	125	121	-3.2	120	100.0	0.0	0.0	0.0	0.0	12.5	15.0	34.5	56.5	9.4	49	85.7
Garfield Heights city	28,849	27,448	-4.9	27,814	45.7	47.6	0.7	2.8	3.2	23.3	16.5	39.3	50.8	15.2	11,569	85.5
Garrettsville village	2,338	2,315		2,406	97.3	0.0	1.3	1.0	0.3	23.8	20.2	41.5	45.1	22.5	1,059	90.8
Gates Mills village	2,279	2,217	-2.7	2,189	87.3	0.9	5.3	1.8	4.7	19.6	29.9	54.2	14.5	72.8	874	95.0
Geneva city	6,207	5,937	-4.3	5,978	87.5	2.8	0.3	1.7	7.8	20.7	18.6	44.4	59.2	14.0	2,378	87.1
Geneva-on-the-Lake village	1,254	1,199	-4.4	1,169	85.8	0.0	3.8	6.5	3.9	15.1	22.1	48.9	56.8	14.1	561	84.0
Genoa village	2,334	2,277	-2.4	2,291	84.6	0.7	0.3	3.8	10.7	20.5	19.9	40.6	43.9	16.3	971	89.7
Georgetown village	4,498	4,243	-5.7	4,773	95.9	2.1	1.4	0.6	0.0	27.8	23.2	38.2	54.9	18.8	1,967	79.6
Germantown city	5,533	5,519	-0.3	5,502	99.3	0.0	0.0	0.0	0.7	27.8	15.9	41.2	39.7	22.9	2,173	95.8
Gettysburg village	516	752	45.7	576	99.0	0.0	0.0	1.0	0.0	27.3	12.0	37.4	65.9	9.9	225	87.1
Gibsonburg village	2,581	2,496	-3.3	2,592	79.2	0.8	0.0	1.2	18.8	26.9	13.8	36.2	52.3	11.0	964	89.6
Gilboa village	190	180	-5.3	199	66.8	3.0	0.0	18.1	12.1	37.7	13.1	27.2	52.2	15.0	67	91.0
Girard city	9,932	9,227	-7.1	9,368	90.7	5.2	0.0	1.9	2.3	22.0	17.1	38.3	56.4	20.3	4,239	87.6
Glandorf village	996	1,025	2.9	975	99.1	0.0	0.0	0.9	0.0	24.1	17.4	42.2	35.9	30.1	388	89.2
Glencoe CDP	310	-	-	154	100.0	0.0	0.0	0.0	0.0	0.0	6.5	33.8	75.4	8.7	49	61.2
Glendale village	2,153	2,181	1.3	2,145	78.7	13.9	1.7	4.0	1.7	19.5	26.7	50.0	14.8	62.7	946	92.8
Glenford village	173	169	-2.3	209	100.0	0.0	0.0	0.0	0.0	36.8	10.0	31.7	54.5	8.3	66	97.0
Glenmont village	273	297	8.8	282	94.3	0.0	0.0	2.1	3.5	22.3	16.7	39.8	70.9	8.0	117	65.8
Glenmoor CDP	1,987	-	-	1,853	95.3	4.7	0.0	0.0	0.0	27.3	18.5	36.6	65.0	4.0	727	85.6
Glenwillow village	911	919	0.9	1,088	41.3	36.0	17.4	4.1	1.2	28.3	18.8	44.0	35.5	43.7	340	88.2
Gloria Glens Park village	425	445	4.7	463	98.7	0.0	0.0	0.6	0.6	21.2	16.2	39.1	48.8	16.2	196	92.3
Glouster village	1,794	1,780	-0.8	1,896	92.1	0.9	0.0	6.7	0.3	27.3	12.4	39.2	62.9	7.1	691	78.9
Gnadenhutten village	1,288	1,258	-2.3	1,507	98.7	1.0	0.1	0.1	0.0	27.7	13.3	39.6	49.0	24.1	529	90.9
Golf Manor village	3,618	3,575	-1.2	3,573	29.3	58.4	4.5	5.6	2.3	20.5	14.5	37.9	41.8	26.5	1,547	89.1
Good Hope CDP	234	-	-	173	100.0	0.0	0.0	0.0	0.0	28.3	4.0	24.4	69.5	0.0	80	100.0
Gordon village	224	208	-7.1	163	94.5	0.0	0.0	5.5	0.0	17.8	10.4	45.1	55.9	10.2	66	90.9
Goshen CDP	-	-	-	793	98.0	0.0	0.0	2.0	0.0	29.9	14.6	47.2	51.6	18.1	253	94.5
Grafton village	6,636	5,707	-14.0	5,996	63.3	27.7	0.2	4.3	4.5	6.7	9.5	42.7	49.7	9.8	824	88.1
Grand Rapids village	970	1,004	3.5	993	92.8	0.5	0.0	1.8	4.8	21.1	16.7	36.8	41.7	30.5	411	94.4
Grand River village	406	402		432	94.4	1.4	0.2	2.3	1.6	18.3	27.5	45.9	51.2	17.1	183	90.2
Grandview CDP	1,466	-	-	1,056	97.0	0.0	0.0	3.0	0.0	15.3	18.0	48.9	41.8	28.0	413	90.8
Grandview Heights city	6,511	8,333	28.0	7,895	94.1	1.0	1.3	1.2	2.5	19.4	12.4	35.6	7.4	73.6	3,534	97.7
Granville village	5,675	5,916	4.2	5,815	86.8	0.7	4.4	3.5	4.6	17.8	10.6	21.4	6.2	76.1	1,333	98.0
Granville South CDP	1,410	-	-	1,506	89.1	0.3	4.4	6.1	0.0	28.2	16.7	41.8	14.9	62.8	532	86.7
Gratiot village	218	220	0.9	226	96.5	0.0	0.0	3.5	0.0	23.9	17.3	46.0	61.8	8.3	90	88.9
Gratis village	874	843	-3.5	986	98.7	0.0	0.0	0.0	1.3	24.9	12.4	32.4	48.1	9.2	374	93.0
Graysville village	78	72	-7.7	60	86.7	0.0	0.0	13.3	0.0	6.7	30.0	51.5	44.2	14.0	25	100.0
Green city	25,741	25,752	0.0	25,760	93.9	1.4	2.2	2.0	0.5	24.1	17.7	41.9	31.7	37.0	9,924	92.7
Green Camp village	374	355	-5.1	336	97.9	0.0	0.0	2.1	0.0	18.8	19.6	43.3	61.3	7.5	133	88.7
Greenfield village	4,643	4,556	-1.9	4,582	96.4	2.6	0.2	0.5	0.4	19.9	19.3	38.8	63.5	11.8	1,954	81.5
Greenhills village	3,605	3,567	-1.1	3,573	75.3	15.1	1.5	6.3	1.9	26.5	14.2	39.2	27.6	32.9	1,429	93.1
Green Meadows CDP	2,327	-	-	2,213	99.8	0.0	0.0	0.2	0.0	21.4	22.9	44.6	36.1	20.2	986	93.4
Green Springs village	1,367	1,306	-4.5	1,457	90.3	0.3	0.0	2.7	6.7	23.5	17.6	41.1	66.5	5.1	499	80.6
Greentown CDP	3,804	-	-	3,815	97.2	0.0	0.0	1.8	1.0	26.6	10.6	40.7	32.8	34.8	1,231	98.7
Greenville city	13,228	12,615	-4.6	12,766	95.4	0.8	1.5	1.1	1.1	21.1	24.3	45.0	57.8	16.4	5,805	82.2
Greenwich village	1,476	1,422	-3.7	1,481	95.9	0.7	0.0	0.5	2.9	30.2	15.4	36.9	59.9	11.7	557	88.7
Groesbeck CDP	6,788	-	-	7,038	73.5	20.9	0.2	4.9	0.5	21.6	16.3	39.7	39.1	22.0	2,904	91.3
Grove City city	35,632	41,820	17.4	40,797	90.4	3.5	1.6	2.5	2.1	25.3	15.1	38.5	35.9	34.1	15,874	93.2
Groveport city	5,372	5,621	4.6	5,617	65.0	23.5	5.7	1.4	4.4	24.8	14.1	40.7	42.9	26.0	2,066	95.9
Grover Hill village	402	376	-6.5	364	97.3	0.0	1.6	0.0	1.1	28.3	12.9	37.5	69.8	5.4	159	81.1
Hamden village	879	864	-1.7	742	98.0	0.0	0.0	2.0	0.0	30.1	13.2	36.9	71.1	5.1	268	78.7
Hamersville village	544	502	-7.7	728	99.6	0.0	0.0	0.4	0.0	30.1	10.4	36.8	61.4	6.0	260	96.2
Hamilton city	62,291	62,082	-0.3	62,182	80.2	9.3	0.9	3.7	5.8	23.6	15.4	36.6	55.1	16.2	24,731	88.1
Hamler village	576	555	-3.6	627	88.0	0.0	0.0	1.8	10.2	24.9	12.4	30.9	57.3	24.2	261	92.0
Hanging Rock village	219	209	-4.6	196	100.0	0.0	0.0	0.0	0.0	11.2	19.4	49.0	70.2	6.8	94	60.6
Hannibal CDP	411	-	-	325	100.0	0.0	0.0	0.0	0.0	16.6	23.4	51.5	64.0	23.3	136	85.3
Hanover village	919	1,204	31.0	1,111	97.5	0.4	0.0	1.6	0.5	25.0	13.7	36.8	45.9	21.9	401	89.3
Hanoverton village	414	388	-6.3	352	95.7	0.0	0.0	0.3	4.0	24.1	15.9	46.8	60.9	13.7	141	94.3
Harbor Hills CDP	1,509	-	-	1,510	99.5	0.0	0.5	0.0	0.0	17.0	25.8	56.2	44.1	35.1	667	95.2
Harbor View village	106	106	0.0	59	83.1	0.0	0.0	16.9	0.0	20.3	18.6	56.2	53.5	7.0	24	91.7
Harpster village	204	192	-5.9	169	85.2	8.3	0.0	0.0	6.5	15.4	34.3	50.9	63.6	9.8	81	75.3
Harrisburg village	321	341	6.2	519	99.6	0.0	0.0	0.0	0.4	25.8	17.5	40.2	53.8	16.4	191	90.1
Harrison city	9,941	11,896	19.7	12,006	97.1	0.5	0.0	1.4	1.0	28.4	13.5	35.9	43.9	22.0	4,808	88.2
Harrisville village	235	223	-5.1	206	98.5	0.0	0.0	0.0	1.5	8.3	24.8	49.0	74.7	9.4	99	72.7
Harrod village	419	403	-3.8	379	96.8	0.0	0.0	1.3	1.8	26.9	16.4	36.3	53.6	13.6	137	86.9
Hartford (Croton) village	397	410	3.3	323	94.7	0.0	0.0	5.3	0.0	23.8	14.6	40.0	53.6	17.6	112	95.5
Hartville village	2,965	3,079	3.8	3,039	96.7	0.0	0.4	2.2	0.7	15.4	25.0	45.9	43.8	30.9	1,326	94.9
Harveysburg village	547	567	3.7	592	91.6	2.0	0.5	4.6	1.4	26.5	6.6	33.4	49.0	22.5	236	95.8
Haskins village	1,188	1,237	4.1	1,225	94.4	1.6	0.0	0.3	3.7	29.0	8.7	32.4	25.8	34.1	415	92.8
Haviland village	210	201	-4.3	263	80.6	0.0	0.0	0.8	18.6	24.7	17.1	32.5	71.8	11.8	102	79.4
Haydenville CDP	381	-	-	419	100.0	0.0	0.0	0.0	0.0	18.1	22.7	37.5	56.8	0.0	144	85.4
Hayesville village	451	458	1.6	465	97.6	0.0	0.0	1.3	1.1	21.3	18.1	42.6	52.8	19.7	198	92.9
Heath city	10,288	10,942	6.4	10,745	87.7	3.9	1.6	4.3	2.5	21.8	20.7	42.4	48.4	20.6	4,114	88.9
Hebron village	2,336	2,477	6.0	2,389	94.9	0.6	0.6	1.4	2.5	26.4	14.2	39.1	55.3	17.4	968	88.2
Helena village	222	209	-5.9	279	93.2	0.0	0.0	1.1	5.7	19.7	20.8	45.7	52.6	12.0	101	91.1
Hemlock village	155	152	-1.9	134	94.8	0.0	0.0	0.0	5.2	20.9	18.7	47.0	47.7	14.8	56	85.7
Hessville CDP	214	-	-	166	82.5	0.0	0.0	7.8	9.6	39.2	0.0	32.4	61.4	9.9	72	88.9
Hicksville village	3,549	3,434	-3.2	3,410	88.7	0.5	0.0	1.9	8.9	26.4	15.3	35.7	55.1	15.6	1,353	87.4
Hide-A-Way Hills CDP	794	-	-	900	89.1	0.0	0.0	10.9	0.0	18.9	27.0	55.7	23.2	51.7	316	84.8
Higginsport village	251	242	-3.6	308	92.5	0.0	0.0	7.5	0.0	33.4	15.6	31.4	68.2	4.5	113	77.9
Highland village	254	250	-1.6	362	92.8	0.0	0.6	6.6	0.0	28.7	13.8	32.1	67.4	6.0	144	86.1
Highland Heights city	8,345	8,373	0.3	8,390	86.2	0.8	9.8	1.5	1.8	20.4	23.8	51.7	23.6	55.5	3,215	92.4
Highland Hills village	1,130	960	-15.0	873	9.6	83.2	0.0	4.1	3.1	10.7	22.1	38.1	50.1	11.4	282	72.7
Highland Holiday CDP	550	-	-	510	95.1	0.0	0.0	4.9	0.0	31.8	13.9	41.2	82.6	0.0	195	93.3
Highpoint CDP	1,503	-	-	1,205	91.5	2.3	0.0	0.0	6.2	20.9	18.5	38.9	55.0	25.1	533	77.5
Hilliard city	28,234	36,534	29.4	36,411	83.6	4.8	5.6	2.6	3.5	26.0	11.7	36.8	20.4	54.7	13,817	96.4

1 May be of any race.

Table A. All Places — **Population and Housing**

STATE City, town, township, borough, or CDP (county if applicable)	Population: 2010 census total population	Population: 2019 estimated population	Population: Percent change 2010–2019	Population: ACS total population estimate 2015–2019	Race and Hispanic or Latino origin (percent): White alone, not Hispanic or Latino	Race: Black alone, not Hispanic or Latino	Race: Asian alone, not Hispanic or Latino	Race: All other races or 2 or more races, not Hispanic or Latino	Race: Hispanic or Latino[1]	Age (percent): Under 18 years old	Age: Age 65 years and older	Age: Median age	Educational attainment of persons age 25 and older: Percent High school diploma or less	Educational attainment: Percent Bachelor's degree or more	Occupied housing units: Total	Occupied housing units: Percent with a computer
	1	2	3	4	5	6	7	8	9	10	11	12	13	14	15	16
OHIO—Con.																
Hills and Dales village	231	221	-4.3	310	91.3	0.0	4.8	2.6	1.3	15.8	31.3	53.8	12.0	73.0	133	98.5
Hillsboro city	6,601	6,554	-0.7	6,534	91.8	2.9	0.4	3.4	1.5	22.5	23.3	40.9	60.9	16.7	2,846	75.4
Hilltop CDP	532	-	-	912	91.6	7.1	0.0	0.0	1.3	27.2	17.3	42.1	55.3	8.8	330	75.8
Hiram village	1,406	1,159	-17.6	1,294	78.7	11.8	3.5	3.6	2.5	11.4	11.4	20.2	16.8	60.1	224	98.2
Hockingport CDP	212	-	-	120	100.0	0.0	0.0	0.0	0.0	6.7	39.2	58.5	79.5	0.0	89	66.3
Holgate village	1,109	1,059	-4.5	997	85.2	0.0	0.0	0.3	14.5	20.9	14.5	44.2	49.6	14.1	406	85.0
Holiday City village	48	47	-2.1	17	82.4	0.0	0.0	17.6	0.0	11.8	23.5	55.5	46.7	26.7	9	100.0
Holiday Lakes CDP	749	-	-	620	85.8	0.0	2.4	7.9	3.9	12.4	22.9	52.0	39.2	22.5	252	84.1
Holiday Valley CDP	1,510	-	-	1,364	88.7	1.7	0.0	2.1	7.6	17.1	24.9	49.1	37.4	24.5	556	96.9
Holland village	1,704	1,655	-2.9	1,660	77.3	7.8	0.5	3.3	11.0	17.4	29.8	53.3	44.6	24.1	694	88.2
Hollansburg village	231	216	-6.5	214	98.1	0.0	1.4	0.5	0.0	22.4	20.1	51.7	60.0	14.2	99	76.8
Holloway village	336	317	-5.7	302	100.0	0.0	0.0	0.0	0.0	17.9	21.5	51.3	72.6	0.0	119	78.2
Holmesville village	372	402	8.1	314	97.1	0.0	0.0	0.0	2.9	21.7	22.9	42.9	78.5	8.6	130	76.9
Homeworth CDP	481	-	-	532	100.0	0.0	0.0	0.0	0.0	10.5	16.2	52.6	74.4	10.3	214	94.9
Hooven CDP	534	-	-	354	97.5	0.0	0.0	0.0	2.5	12.1	26.8	52.4	79.9	9.2	158	86.1
Hopedale village	950	903	-4.9	960	94.8	1.0	0.4	3.0	0.7	13.4	25.2	51.6	58.0	9.4	342	86.8
Howard CDP	242	-	-	183	100.0	0.0	0.0	0.0	0.0	25.7	26.2	45.7	61.0	0.0	71	100.0
Howland Center CDP	6,351	-	-	6,269	92.2	2.0	1.6	3.3	0.8	20.8	24.0	45.2	41.3	28.7	2,483	93.0
Hoytville village	303	317	4.6	336	57.1	7.1	3.6	4.8	27.4	23.2	7.4	32.0	49.1	17.1	97	93.8
Hubbard city	7,895	7,419	-6.0	7,525	92.1	3.4	0.3	1.4	2.9	20.6	21.5	44.5	45.1	24.2	3,272	86.2
Huber Heights city	38,110	38,154	0.1	40,006	73.6	16.1	2.1	5.8	2.4	26.0	15.4	36.8	36.8	24.0	15,235	93.4
Huber Ridge CDP	4,604	-	-	4,468	82.3	11.6	0.0	4.0	2.1	24.9	9.7	32.7	37.4	31.6	1,495	94.8
Hudson city	22,266	22,237	-0.1	22,263	90.4	1.3	3.7	1.6	3.0	25.8	16.8	46.1	11.8	71.5	8,019	95.0
Hunter CDP	2,100	-	-	2,251	98.3	0.0	0.0	0.0	1.7	14.9	28.2	48.3	52.9	12.2	942	89.4
Hunting Valley village	707	715	1.1	763	93.1	0.5	2.8	0.9	2.8	21.9	32.5	53.6	7.9	82.1	294	94.2
Huntsville village	442	446	0.9	523	87.2	0.0	5.7	1.1	5.9	16.1	12.8	41.5	63.0	8.5	242	95.5
Huron city	7,148	6,869	-3.9	6,921	96.9	0.0	0.0	1.7	1.4	20.9	27.6	50.4	31.0	34.2	2,980	88.8
Iberia CDP	452	-	-	529	98.1	0.0	0.0	1.9	0.0	20.2	17.8	32.6	71.3	0.0	190	88.4
Independence city	7,150	7,175	0.3	7,169	94.1	0.0	1.9	1.4	2.6	21.7	20.7	48.2	27.7	48.7	2,736	92.1
Irondale village	384	358	-6.8	359	98.1	0.0	0.0	1.9	0.0	29.8	10.0	33.2	73.1	9.1	130	76.2
Ironton city	11,120	10,532	-5.3	10,599	92.9	3.9	0.1	1.7	1.4	21.0	21.2	44.5	57.3	15.5	4,381	82.2
Ithaca village	136	129	-5.1	62	100.0	0.0	0.0	0.0	0.0	11.3	14.5	46.5	66.7	9.5	33	75.8
Jackson city	6,396	6,230	-2.6	6,239	90.9	2.4	0.0	3.4	3.3	19.7	13.7	37.8	50.8	14.8	2,655	86.9
Jacksonburg village	65	65	0.0	52	92.3	0.0	0.0	0.0	7.7	26.9	17.3	37.5	59.4	6.3	17	64.7
Jackson Center village	1,462	1,465	0.2	1,484	97.8	1.8	0.0	0.3	0.1	24.2	19.7	40.0	55.5	18.4	617	89.1
Jacksonville village	484	480	-0.8	379	100.0	0.0	0.0	0.0	0.0	16.9	28.8	50.8	69.7	3.9	181	81.2
Jamestown village	2,033	2,136	5.1	2,114	98.0	1.4	0.0	0.2	0.4	22.8	21.2	44.6	50.9	19.0	860	80.8
Jefferson village	3,116	2,990	-4.0	3,553	95.0	0.6	0.6	1.2	2.6	24.8	15.3	37.6	47.3	13.2	1,384	85.3
Jeffersonville village	1,207	1,172	-2.9	1,241	93.2	3.1	0.0	1.7	2.0	23.7	10.3	33.8	62.6	8.6	524	92.7
Jenera village	221	215	-2.7	171	91.8	0.6	0.0	1.8	5.8	21.1	14.6	45.2	52.0	8.7	81	97.5
Jeromesville village	562	549	-2.3	614	98.7	0.0	0.0	1.0	0.3	30.6	13.2	34.0	48.2	16.3	241	88.4
Jerry City village	427	436	2.1	668	86.1	0.0	0.0	4.2	9.7	32.6	11.7	28.8	65.0	8.4	205	95.6
Jerusalem village	161	150	-6.8	115	100.0	0.0	0.0	0.0	0.0	13.0	37.4	52.8	73.2	3.1	59	71.2
Jewett village	692	651	-5.9	819	97.4	0.0	0.0	2.2	0.4	30.8	14.8	29.9	65.5	6.5	288	82.3
Johnstown village	4,644	5,098	9.8	5,237	94.8	0.6	0.0	0.8	3.9	24.3	17.3	35.4	46.9	23.2	1,940	81.5
Junction City village	819	805	-1.7	929	90.3	0.8	1.0	8.0	0.0	28.6	11.9	36.2	69.0	6.9	328	90.5
Kalida village	1,553	1,587	2.2	1,395	97.6	0.0	0.0	0.7	1.7	23.7	19.0	35.5	35.7	36.0	586	89.6
Kanauga CDP	175	-	-	141	100.0	0.0	0.0	0.0	0.0	40.4	7.1	38.7	48.8	0.0	66	37.9
Kansas CDP	179	-	-	52	100.0	0.0	0.0	0.0	0.0	0.0	0.0	50.5	62.5	0.0	29	79.3
Kelleys Island village	312	311	-0.3	236	92.8	0.0	0.0	1.3	5.9	2.5	50.0	65.0	29.9	39.8	120	93.3
Kent city	28,906	29,646	2.6	29,811	78.1	8.2	5.0	5.5	3.2	14.6	10.5	23.8	28.4	43.3	10,887	92.3
Kenton city	8,324	8,180	-1.7	8,284	96.1	0.5	0.0	2.4	1.1	27.2	18.3	39.2	62.1	11.6	3,441	82.4
Kenwood CDP	6,981	-	-	7,344	74.6	8.1	8.4	5.8	3.1	22.9	21.9	42.4	17.9	59.3	3,003	90.4
Kettering city	56,129	54,855	-2.3	55,390	88.1	4.1	2.5	2.9	2.4	21.7	18.4	39.3	28.1	35.4	24,960	91.4
Kettlersville village	179	170	-5.0	158	98.1	0.0	0.0	0.0	1.9	20.3	16.5	46.0	65.5	8.8	63	87.3
Kidron CDP	944	-	-	993	97.0	1.6	0.6	0.0	0.8	29.8	16.6	32.0	74.4	11.7	320	85.9
Kilbourne CDP	139	-	-	19	100.0	0.0	0.0	0.0	0.0	47.4	0.0	0.0	100.0	0.0	10	100.0
Killbuck village	852	919	7.9	879	96.9	0.0	1.3	0.5	1.4	23.1	21.0	38.8	76.7	4.6	377	81.4
Kimbolton CDP	144	-	-	65	100.0	0.0	0.0	0.0	0.0	0.0	44.6	58.9	75.4	0.0	52	100.0
Kings Mills CDP	1,319	-	-	1,511	100.0	0.0	0.0	0.0	0.0	24.2	14.7	42.3	42.4	31.9	635	92.0
Kingston village	1,033	1,017	-1.5	1,132	98.0	0.0	0.0	2.0	0.0	21.7	23.6	43.2	60.7	11.1	514	79.4
Kinsman Center CDP	616	-	-	583	89.7	0.0	0.0	10.3	0.0	15.1	26.1	52.3	53.0	14.9	221	95.0
Kipton village	243	233	-4.1	240	97.5	0.0	0.0	2.5	0.0	17.1	24.2	48.2	46.4	16.7	89	95.5
Kirby village	118	110	-6.8	96	95.8	0.0	2.1	0.0	2.1	28.1	8.3	32.5	74.1	8.6	41	85.4
Kirkersville village	525	552	5.1	414	95.7	1.9	0.5	1.9	0.0	11.6	24.4	55.1	56.7	9.0	171	92.4
Kirtland city	6,861	6,812	-0.7	6,822	94.9	0.9	0.6	2.0	1.5	20.3	22.0	48.4	28.5	41.0	2,483	95.7
Kirtland Hills village	646	644	-0.3	688	90.6	0.7	0.4	4.5	3.8	23.3	17.7	50.9	19.3	60.8	267	98.5
Kunkle CDP	246	-	-	326	100.0	0.0	0.0	0.0	0.0	14.4	0.0	26.2	83.9	0.0	127	78.7
La Croft CDP	1,144	-	-	1,360	94.7	3.4	0.0	1.4	0.5	16.8	11.1	40.7	60.8	10.3	503	91.8
Lafayette village	439	417	-5.0	427	98.8	0.0	0.0	0.0	1.2	30.9	13.6	32.5	51.0	6.5	158	86.1
Lafayette CDP	202	-	-	215	89.3	0.0	3.7	7.0	0.0	11.2	21.4	51.4	75.6	6.7	86	95.3
Lafferty CDP	304	-	-	120	100.0	0.0	0.0	0.0	0.0	10.8	27.5	51.8	38.2	0.0	80	100.0
LaGrange village	2,103	2,479	17.9	2,484	95.1	0.6	0.0	1.7	2.6	25.8	13.9	39.1	40.3	21.6	831	95.8
Lake Buckhorn CDP	601	-	-	622	90.7	0.0	0.0	9.3	0.0	21.7	22.5	30.9	67.3	22.1	202	71.8
Lake Darby CDP	4,592	-	-	4,220	90.4	1.5	1.7	3.6	2.7	34.1	5.5	31.2	28.1	34.2	1,315	95.1
Lake Lakengren CDP	3,383	-	-	3,405	91.4	0.0	0.0	7.2	1.4	23.6	13.7	38.9	42.9	25.3	1,310	93.7
Lakeline village	226	217	-4.0	253	92.5	5.1	0.0	2.4	0.0	11.9	10.3	49.1	38.3	26.2	115	89.6
Lake Lorelei CDP	1,170	-	-	1,396	88.1	0.7	0.0	4.4	6.8	24.9	19.0	36.5	50.8	11.3	512	96.7
Lake Milton CDP	-	-	-	635	100.0	0.0	0.0	0.0	0.0	8.0	32.9	54.3	62.0	21.1	360	93.9
Lake Mohawk CDP	1,652	-	-	1,872	100.0	0.0	0.0	0.0	0.0	28.4	16.0	44.9	26.9	30.4	756	98.1
Lakemore village	3,064	3,072	0.3	3,074	88.5	5.1	3.5	2.1	0.8	18.5	23.7	46.6	55.9	10.8	1,427	87.5
Lake Seneca CDP	465	-	-	540	93.7	0.0	0.0	0.0	6.3	16.7	24.3	56.5	38.9	42.4	257	96.5
Lakeside CDP	694	-	-	741	100.0	0.0	0.0	0.0	0.0	0.0	67.6	69.3	23.1	49.5	487	75.4
Lake Tomahawk CDP	485	-	-	734	98.2	0.0	0.0	1.8	0.0	25.7	29.3	42.5	29.1	21.7	272	100.0
Lakeview village	1,075	1,106	2.9	1,126	96.1	0.2	0.4	1.7	1.6	22.5	13.7	41.2	65.2	7.5	516	90.3
Lake Waynoka CDP	1,173	-	-	1,022	92.8	4.4	0.0	2.8	0.0	13.2	32.4	59.2	40.8	36.2	519	95.4
Lakewood city	52,131	49,678	-4.7	50,259	83.8	5.5	2.0	3.4	5.4	17.4	12.4	34.7	25.2	46.5	24,713	92.1
Lancaster city	38,764	40,505	4.5	40,159	92.0	2.0	0.5	3.6	2.0	22.0	18.4	39.5	51.3	17.9	16,369	85.7
Landen CDP	6,782	-	-	7,500	93.7	1.8	1.5	1.8	1.3	26.6	10.9	41.1	19.4	57.0	2,845	98.8
Lansing CDP	634	-	-	594	100.0	0.0	0.0	0.0	0.0	24.2	18.4	39.7	57.3	18.0	282	81.9
La Rue village	747	714	-4.4	675	91.1	0.0	0.0	4.3	4.6	23.6	15.0	37.6	72.3	7.5	260	86.5
Latty village	193	183	-5.2	147	87.8	10.9	0.0	0.7	0.7	19.0	10.2	38.6	50.0	8.3	66	95.5

1 May be of any race.

Table A. All Places — **Population and Housing**

STATE City, town, township, borough, or CDP (county if applicable)	Population: 2010 census total population	Population: 2019 estimated population	Population: Percent change 2010–2019	Population: ACS total population estimate 2015–2019	Race and Hispanic or Latino origin (percent): White alone, not Hispanic or Latino	Black alone, not Hispanic or Latino	Asian alone, not Hispanic or Latino	All other races or 2 or more races, not Hispanic or Latino	Hispanic or Latino[1]	Age (percent): Under 18 years old	Age 65 years and older	Median age	Educational attainment of persons age 25 and older: Percent High school diploma or less	Percent Bachelor's degree or more	Occupied housing units: Total	Percent with a computer
	1	2	3	4	5	6	7	8	9	10	11	12	13	14	15	16
OHIO—Con.																
Laura village	472	494	4.7	552	94.7	1.1	0.0	0.0	4.2	25.9	15.0	34.8	65.1	6.3	183	85.8
Laurelville village	525	503	-4.2	520	96.9	0.0	0.0	3.1	0.0	16.2	21.2	49.7	73.5	9.4	268	69.0
Leavittsburg CDP	1,973	-	-	1,602	94.8	0.0	2.0	0.7	2.5	21.3	15.9	40.3	60.3	10.9	640	98.1
Lebanon city	20,037	20,659	3.1	20,642	89.2	2.6	1.5	2.4	4.3	26.0	13.8	37.4	40.7	28.2	7,875	95.3
Leesburg village	1,317	1,323	0.5	1,455	98.6	0.0	0.3	1.1	0.0	18.4	12.7	39.5	59.8	10.2	647	79.0
Leesville village	158	146	-7.6	284	98.6	0.0	0.0	0.0	1.4	18.0	19.7	37.7	76.1	8.5	106	80.2
Leetonia village	1,967	1,832	-6.9	2,218	97.6	0.0	0.0	1.6	0.8	20.8	17.8	42.4	58.6	13.8	862	89.3
Leipsic village	2,099	2,022	-3.7	2,387	48.6	0.0	0.0	3.3	48.2	33.6	18.5	33.9	67.5	7.3	836	80.3
Lewisburg village	1,820	1,746	-4.1	1,791	98.9	0.2	0.7	0.2	0.0	25.9	13.8	38.5	50.8	12.0	715	89.8
Lewistown CDP	222	-	-	267	100.0	0.0	0.0	0.0	0.0	33.7	12.7	45.8	89.8	0.0	99	100.0
Lewisville village	176	164	-6.8	213	97.7	1.4	0.0	0.9	0.0	19.2	22.1	42.3	66.2	6.0	71	80.3
Lexington village	4,809	4,682	-2.6	4,842	92.9	4.8	0.2	0.4	1.7	20.5	22.2	44.5	36.5	28.8	2,084	84.1
Liberty Center village	1,184	1,121	-5.3	1,327	94.6	0.0	0.3	1.9	3.2	23.6	10.8	37.5	49.1	11.9	551	91.8
Lima city	38,627	36,659	-5.1	37,117	62.4	25.4	0.7	6.9	4.6	24.9	12.8	33.4	55.8	11.6	14,562	84.4
Limaville village	152	144	-5.3	238	98.7	0.0	0.0	0.4	0.8	26.9	10.1	33.0	50.3	17.9	80	95.0
Lincoln Heights village	3,286	3,349	1.9	3,354	7.9	86.7	0.3	3.7	1.4	34.1	13.5	30.4	59.6	12.7	1,375	83.3
Lincoln Village CDP	9,032	-	-	10,549	70.3	9.2	2.4	4.0	14.2	23.0	13.8	38.5	65.1	11.0	4,151	86.7
Lindsey village	446	422	-5.4	514	83.3	3.3	1.2	6.6	5.6	26.7	17.9	37.0	46.8	22.8	200	91.0
Linndale village	179	169	-5.6	160	37.5	11.3	0.0	2.5	48.8	33.8	16.9	39.4	57.5	15.1	58	89.7
Lisbon village	2,825	2,640	-6.5	2,695	93.2	1.9	0.0	4.0	0.9	26.9	19.7	38.3	56.5	14.3	1,086	88.1
Lithopolis village	1,111	1,796	61.7	1,954	93.7	0.5	0.9	3.4	1.6	28.8	12.0	32.6	34.6	25.1	701	92.9
Little Hocking CDP	263	-	-	647	100.0	0.0	0.0	0.0	0.0	22.4	23.6	46.1	54.0	19.9	210	74.8
Lockbourne village	238	249	4.6	195	98.5	0.0	0.0	0.0	1.5	19.5	16.9	46.1	69.3	8.0	78	82.1
Lockington village	141	136	-3.5	185	100.0	0.0	0.0	0.0	0.0	11.9	22.7	45.2	75.4	3.7	76	89.5
Lockland village	3,448	3,441	-0.2	3,450	46.4	36.7	1.2	4.1	11.6	25.9	11.9	33.2	75.9	4.0	1,428	78.7
Lodi village	2,753	2,899	5.3	2,857	94.1	0.3	0.0	2.5	3.2	20.0	23.9	47.2	62.6	11.4	1,326	86.3
Logan city	7,113	7,020	-1.3	6,836	96.6	0.9	0.0	1.6	0.9	25.4	19.2	36.4	50.1	16.4	2,884	84.8
Logan Elm Village CDP	1,118	-	-	1,188	81.5	1.3	17.3	0.0	0.0	23.7	22.9	42.6	70.5	9.4	398	93.0
London city	9,899	10,328	4.3	10,193	90.9	3.3	1.1	4.6	0.1	23.4	16.6	37.0	56.2	14.2	4,197	86.8
Lorain city	64,099	63,855	-0.4	63,801	51.6	15.3	0.9	3.7	28.5	24.8	15.8	37.0	52.3	12.7	25,577	84.8
Lordstown village	3,424	3,258	-4.8	3,291	93.1	1.9	1.8	2.5	0.7	19.5	25.1	48.4	58.0	16.2	1,375	89.2
Lore City village	325	308	-5.2	313	94.6	2.9	0.0	2.6	0.0	24.9	17.3	37.1	63.7	11.3	124	80.6
Loudonville village	2,641	2,617	-0.9	2,668	92.1	0.6	0.5	4.0	2.8	20.4	21.9	45.7	59.2	11.3	1,071	82.7
Louisville city	9,273	9,360	0.9	9,340	95.7	0.0	0.7	2.5	1.0	24.5	19.2	39.6	43.0	22.2	3,847	92.3
Loveland city	12,111	13,145	8.5	13,485	89.7	3.3	2.2	1.8	3.0	25.1	15.2	39.1	27.5	48.0	5,205	93.6
Loveland Park CDP	1,523	-	-	1,974	84.3	1.7	4.3	2.6	7.2	24.8	13.7	46.6	51.0	32.0	719	100.0
Lowell village	547	531	-2.9	575	97.2	0.0	1.9	0.9	0.0	26.8	15.0	35.4	53.8	14.6	246	76.8
Lowellville village	1,159	1,092	-5.8	1,185	94.4	1.9	0.0	0.8	2.9	20.0	17.8	45.1	58.4	15.6	505	81.2
Lower Salem village	86	82	-4.7	123	99.2	0.0	0.0	0.0	0.8	40.7	14.6	30.5	38.4	9.6	38	71.1
Lucas village	614	592	-3.6	456	94.3	1.5	0.0	2.9	1.3	19.1	17.8	40.7	50.4	12.5	213	80.3
Lucasville CDP	2,757	-	-	1,503	98.8	0.0	0.0	0.0	1.2	22.0	13.5	41.9	44.6	29.8	601	86.2
Luckey village	1,012	1,044	3.2	946	94.0	0.0	0.0	1.7	4.3	23.4	15.1	45.1	48.6	24.7	388	92.5
Ludlow Falls village	208	216	3.8	279	100.0	0.0	0.0	0.0	0.0	26.5	10.0	40.0	61.9	7.2	89	94.4
Lynchburg village	1,492	1,483	-0.6	1,415	98.4	0.8	0.0	0.8	0.0	30.2	15.3	34.7	51.3	10.1	577	83.9
Lyndhurst city	14,001	13,366	-4.5	13,533	81.7	13.3	2.0	1.7	1.2	15.8	26.9	48.4	22.0	50.4	6,392	91.9
Lyons village	566	548	-3.2	472	90.0	0.6	0.0	8.9	0.4	23.9	20.1	40.0	50.0	10.5	214	88.3
McArthur village	1,705	1,643	-3.6	1,453	97.0	0.0	0.1	2.5	0.5	26.5	12.8	34.3	54.8	17.9	607	86.7
McClure village	727	680	-6.5	674	92.9	0.3	0.9	1.5	4.5	18.0	15.7	38.8	64.4	5.8	324	91.0
McComb village	1,649	1,638	-0.7	1,881	86.3	0.0	1.1	1.4	11.2	26.7	16.9	38.7	53.0	13.8	714	92.7
McConnelsville village	1,780	1,749	-1.7	2,048	86.6	6.9	0.0	5.8	0.7	20.2	22.8	40.8	53.0	13.7	955	84.0
McCutchenville CDP	400	-	-	233	88.4	0.0	0.0	11.6	0.0	30.5	21.0	38.5	71.7	7.9	95	90.5
McDermott CDP	434	-	-	394	99.0	1.0	0.0	0.0	0.0	34.0	20.3	31.6	90.6	5.4	122	100.0
McDonald village	3,259	3,040	-6.7	3,087	94.2	2.6	0.0	3.2	0.0	20.4	20.3	45.3	48.4	19.6	1,349	85.5
Macedonia city	11,128	12,000	7.8	11,873	83.0	9.7	4.7	1.5	1.2	19.9	19.1	45.4	29.4	44.4	4,610	92.7
McGuffey village	503	487	-3.2	485	96.5	0.0	0.0	2.5	1.0	23.9	13.2	36.1	62.5	5.8	191	78.5
Mack CDP	11,585	-	-	11,492	95.0	0.5	0.6	0.9	3.0	25.2	16.1	44.4	31.9	42.7	4,053	95.6
McKinley Heights CDP	1,060	-	-	541	100.0	0.0	0.0	0.0	0.0	4.6	16.3	52.1	49.0	18.7	372	67.2
Macksburg village	188	182	-3.2	211	100.0	0.0	0.0	0.0	0.0	8.5	31.8	50.3	82.8	1.8	94	91.5
Madeira city	8,736	9,245	5.8	9,147	90.4	1.4	3.1	2.3	2.8	27.4	16.6	40.3	16.4	69.2	3,304	95.5
Madison village	3,184	3,166	-0.6	3,172	95.1	1.9	0.7	1.1	1.2	25.8	18.1	41.3	40.5	22.2	1,231	89.0
Magnetic Springs village	268	298	11.2	334	97.9	1.2	0.0	0.9	0.0	27.5	15.0	41.0	70.9	11.0	141	84.4
Magnolia village	985	962	-2.3	1,016	99.9	0.0	0.0	0.1	0.0	19.9	17.2	40.8	50.1	23.0	398	91.7
Maineville village	971	1,107	14.0	1,156	93.5	0.2	2.8	1.5	2.1	31.2	12.1	37.4	39.7	25.2	429	92.5
Malinta village	265	252	-4.9	287	84.7	0.0	0.0	1.4	13.9	20.9	11.8	43.3	62.9	7.9	121	88.4
Malta village	672	640	-4.8	715	73.3	24.6	0.8	1.3	0.0	24.5	15.0	37.1	59.2	14.6	316	84.2
Malvern village	1,208	1,130	-6.5	1,302	94.4	1.1	0.0	1.3	3.2	19.9	16.0	40.5	56.0	23.4	558	90.3
Manchester village	2,016	1,955	-3.0	1,998	97.7	0.0	0.0	1.1	1.2	20.4	18.2	39.8	71.7	8.3	821	67.0
Mansfield city	47,837	46,599	-2.6	46,576	69.4	21.3	0.9	5.5	2.9	20.2	17.0	38.3	54.8	15.4	18,065	83.5
Mantua village	1,033	1,020	-1.3	1,150	96.7	1.4	0.0	0.4	1.5	18.3	17.0	43.1	56.0	18.2	495	77.8
Maple Heights city	23,135	22,078	-4.6	22,383	21.3	73.9	0.6	2.1	2.1	22.4	13.3	37.6	48.8	14.7	9,359	87.8
Maple Ridge CDP	761	-	-	743	100.0	0.0	0.0	0.0	0.0	22.7	16.0	41.1	69.1	5.4	285	96.8
Maplewood Park CDP	280	-	-	286	30.4	64.7	0.0	0.0	4.9	25.9	9.4	34.7	35.3	8.6	109	100.0
Marble Cliff village	569	732	28.6	520	93.1	0.6	1.5	1.9	2.9	17.5	18.7	51.2	9.4	70.8	261	96.9
Marblehead village	886	864	-2.5	825	93.5	0.1	0.8	1.0	4.6	13.6	36.7	56.8	36.1	33.3	406	91.9
Marengo village	342	341	-0.3	294	96.9	0.0	0.0	2.0	1.0	21.4	11.9	37.3	65.7	10.4	122	95.9
Mariemont village	3,471	3,518	1.4	3,513	93.5	1.7	1.2	3.2	0.4	24.4	14.7	36.7	7.1	72.4	1,528	96.1
Marietta city	14,069	13,356	-5.1	13,588	92.3	2.2	1.0	3.0	1.5	18.2	20.3	37.4	44.3	27.2	5,876	83.4
Marion city	36,828	35,883	-2.6	36,188	82.8	9.0	0.1	4.4	3.6	21.0	14.4	37.1	59.4	9.9	13,062	85.3
Marlboro CDP	-	-	-	344	100.0	0.0	0.0	0.0	0.0	26.7	15.4	29.6	54.2	3.5	127	77.2
Marne CDP	783	-	-	540	97.4	0.0	0.0	2.6	0.0	23.7	10.6	48.6	35.8	37.8	195	92.8
Marseilles village	112	107	-4.5	85	100.0	0.0	0.0	0.0	0.0	18.8	10.6	44.6	75.4	3.3	43	83.7
Marshallville village	767	776	1.2	811	97.4	0.9	0.4	0.0	1.4	27.3	14.8	37.5	68.0	10.1	316	90.2
Martinsburg village	237	233	-1.7	224	95.5	1.8	0.0	2.7	0.0	30.4	16.5	32.0	73.6	2.8	81	85.2
Martins Ferry city	6,913	6,517	-5.7	6,646	86.5	9.0	0.0	3.2	1.2	20.8	19.9	43.1	58.0	13.2	2,672	83.3
Martinsville village	464	452	-2.6	502	98.2	0.0	0.0	0.4	1.4	34.3	10.4	33.8	60.4	6.0	162	87.7
Marysville city	22,101	24,667	11.6	23,808	88.0	4.3	2.9	2.5	2.4	23.7	11.7	35.1	39.0	31.6	8,334	92.8
Mason city	30,848	33,870	9.8	33,224	79.9	2.4	12.2	2.4	3.1	25.3	14.0	42.4	22.5	59.2	12,483	95.8
Massillon city	32,318	32,584	0.8	32,415	85.6	7.8	0.5	4.6	1.5	21.9	19.5	40.8	53.2	16.5	13,630	87.9
Masury CDP	2,064	-	-	1,921	97.8	0.7	0.0	1.0	0.4	18.4	24.1	48.3	64.9	19.1	826	87.8
Matamoras village	896	865	-3.5	672	97.5	0.0	0.0	2.5	0.0	24.0	23.8	41.8	63.9	9.5	318	77.7
Maumee city	14,282	13,669	-4.3	13,797	91.2	2.3	1.2	1.7	3.6	20.4	16.8	42.0	29.1	35.6	5,954	93.3
Mayfield village	3,451	3,337	-3.3	3,372	92.9	0.7	4.2	0.4	1.8	17.5	26.1	49.6	23.4	51.9	1,505	91.8

1 May be of any race.

Table A. All Places — **Population and Housing**

STATE City, town, township, borough, or CDP (county if applicable)	Population: 2010 census total population	Population: 2019 estimated population	Population: Percent change 2010–2019	Population: ACS total population estimate 2015–2019	Race and Hispanic or Latino origin (percent): White alone, not Hispanic or Latino	Black alone, not Hispanic or Latino	Asian alone, not Hispanic or Latino	All other races or 2 or more races, not Hispanic or Latino	Hispanic or Latino[1]	Age (percent): Under 18 years old	Age 65 years and older	Median age	Educational attainment of persons age 25 and older: Percent High school diploma or less	Percent Bachelor's degree or more	Occupied housing units: Total	Percent with a computer
	1	2	3	4	5	6	7	8	9	10	11	12	13	14	15	16
OHIO—Con.																
Mayfield Heights city	19,155	18,487	-3.5	18,669	75.9	13.5	4.5	1.6	4.5	19.2	23.9	40.5	33.4	40.0	9,155	88.1
Mechanicsburg village	1,642	1,591	-3.1	1,695	97.3	0.2	0.0	2.3	0.2	28.4	9.3	33.8	54.2	13.0	627	89.6
Medina city	26,663	25,956	-2.7	26,095	90.9	3.2	0.9	1.8	3.2	25.5	14.8	38.0	32.6	37.1	10,306	93.0
Melmore CDP	153	-	-	78	87.2	0.0	0.0	12.8	0.0	0.0	21.8	47.1	83.8	16.2	40	60.0
Melrose village	275	260	-5.5	235	91.5	3.8	0.0	4.7	0.0	28.5	12.8	37.7	75.3	10.3	98	88.8
Mendon village	662	641	-3.2	666	91.9	0.0	0.0	4.8	3.3	26.0	18.9	35.9	68.8	7.6	264	90.2
Mentor city	47,161	47,262	0.2	47,096	94.5	0.8	1.4	1.4	1.9	18.7	22.7	47.7	36.7	31.2	19,660	93.3
Mentor-on-the-Lake city	7,439	7,390	-0.7	7,391	91.2	1.6	1.3	2.2	3.8	18.6	17.5	43.2	44.4	22.3	3,373	87.3
Metamora village	629	608	-3.3	665	88.4	0.0	0.0	2.1	9.5	22.6	10.7	37.5	52.1	19.6	294	89.5
Meyers Lake village	568	565	-0.5	652	94.9	2.0	0.0	0.0	3.1	7.8	34.5	60.4	32.7	39.5	333	92.2
Miami Heights CDP	4,731	-	-	4,697	98.2	0.4	0.0	0.2	1.2	23.9	19.8	46.7	35.1	37.0	1,842	97.1
Miamisburg city	20,167	20,143	-0.1	19,993	92.1	2.4	0.6	2.8	2.1	23.8	18.0	41.1	38.1	25.6	8,196	90.1
Miamitown CDP	1,259	-	-	1,514	99.2	0.0	0.0	0.0	0.8	25.5	4.0	23.5	49.5	17.3	606	97.7
Miamiville CDP	242	-	-	264	100.0	0.0	0.0	0.0	0.0	18.2	0.0	36.2	49.4	20.9	92	100.0
Middleburg Heights city	15,950	15,432	-3.2	15,573	82.8	3.3	8.4	0.6	4.9	17.9	24.0	46.6	32.7	36.8	6,950	88.3
Middlefield village	2,690	2,700	0.4	2,704	96.1	2.7	0.3	0.9	0.1	18.6	24.1	45.4	52.9	19.3	1,243	87.9
Middle Point village	576	562	-2.4	514	96.1	2.5	0.0	0.0	1.4	21.0	16.9	40.4	60.9	6.3	226	86.7
Middleport village	2,527	2,408	-4.7	2,160	93.8	2.7	0.0	3.5	0.0	21.8	24.4	41.7	58.0	12.9	953	77.0
Middletown city	48,696	48,807	0.2	48,621	79.5	11.1	0.7	4.6	4.1	23.6	15.9	37.4	55.6	15.8	19,752	85.5
Midland village	315	308	-2.2	307	99.7	0.3	0.0	0.0	0.0	41.4	8.1	31.1	73.9	1.9	100	96.0
Midvale village	754	744	-1.3	770	94.4	1.0	0.0	4.5	0.0	24.3	15.8	41.5	70.2	9.3	294	89.8
Midway village	322	328	1.9	382	93.7	0.0	0.0	0.3	6.0	27.0	15.2	38.4	67.7	8.2	119	87.4
Mifflin village	138	134	-2.9	132	97.7	0.0	0.0	0.0	2.3	12.1	8.3	40.9	59.4	7.9	60	80.0
Milan village	1,367	1,334	-2.4	1,279	93.9	1.4	0.8	1.5	2.4	18.9	22.4	45.0	41.7	24.0	474	92.6
Milford city	6,706	6,855	2.2	6,878	91.9	1.5	0.6	2.6	3.4	19.8	20.4	43.4	37.9	37.4	3,300	86.9
Milford Center village	792	902	13.9	1,047	89.7	0.0	0.6	4.5	5.3	34.6	6.6	29.9	58.2	14.6	333	94.9
Millbury village	1,200	1,247	3.9	1,472	82.5	1.4	0.1	1.9	14.1	27.7	21.5	42.4	53.9	14.5	455	92.5
Milledgeville village	112	109	-2.7	108	85.2	0.0	7.4	6.5	0.9	17.6	20.4	45.7	72.2	5.6	57	93.0
Miller City village	143	142	-0.7	122	98.4	0.0	1.6	0.0	0.0	19.7	35.2	55.8	71.1	7.2	60	95.0
Millersburg village	3,037	3,200	5.4	3,172	95.0	0.7	0.0	1.2	3.1	18.4	17.3	42.6	65.4	13.5	1,341	90.2
Millersport village	1,055	1,074	1.8	1,282	99.1	0.9	0.0	0.0	0.0	27.7	19.6	36.5	51.6	21.7	459	81.3
Millfield CDP	341	-	-	328	90.2	0.0	0.0	9.8	0.0	10.1	23.5	60.2	70.8	10.0	161	72.7
Millville village	708	733	3.5	628	96.8	0.0	0.2	1.4	1.6	18.3	24.0	44.4	53.2	12.2	255	91.4
Milton Center village	144	146	1.4	157	59.9	0.0	0.0	0.0	40.1	22.3	7.6	35.2	66.4	14.2	51	80.4
Miltonsburg village	43	40	-7.0	107	72.9	0.0	0.0	27.1	0.0	39.3	10.3	28.1	81.4	0.0	28	78.6
Mineral City village	727	708	-2.6	705	96.6	0.0	0.0	0.0	3.4	26.8	6.2	34.0	62.3	16.0	246	84.1
Mineral Ridge CDP	3,892	-	-	3,448	95.5	3.4	0.0	0.4	0.7	12.4	29.1	50.2	49.2	27.3	1,519	88.7
Minerva village	3,723	3,620	-2.8	3,504	95.8	1.0	0.0	2.5	0.8	21.0	21.8	40.9	56.3	16.1	1,517	84.7
Minerva Park village	1,272	1,321	3.9	1,163	77.3	5.7	1.9	5.8	9.3	22.1	18.1	43.3	24.9	48.7	453	95.6
Minford CDP	693	-	-	644	100.0	0.0	0.0	0.0	0.0	23.0	23.3	48.1	56.7	11.1	281	73.7
Mingo Junction village	3,454	3,205	-7.2	3,212	93.3	0.7	0.0	2.6	3.4	14.0	21.5	46.7	42.7	21.0	1,422	86.4
Minster village	2,806	2,817	0.4	2,695	97.4	0.5	1.4	0.2	0.5	24.1	19.5	41.0	40.5	36.7	1,072	92.9
Mitiwanga CDP	-	-	-	310	79.7	0.0	0.0	15.8	4.5	0.0	35.8	59.5	46.0	37.2	169	100.0
Mogadore village	3,865	3,821	-1.1	3,536	98.0	0.1	0.0	0.0	2.0	23.9	20.1	40.8	54.5	23.9	1,301	90.2
Monfort Heights CDP	11,948	-	-	12,962	84.1	11.6	0.6	2.6	1.1	22.6	17.8	40.6	31.9	38.2	5,030	92.1
Monroe city	12,455	14,015	12.5	14,211	88.2	4.2	1.7	0.7	5.2	28.1	15.1	35.6	33.3	31.9	5,212	93.8
Monroeville village	1,400	1,350	-3.6	1,318	95.4	0.8	0.0	1.4	2.4	26.2	15.2	36.8	61.6	9.6	528	94.7
Montezuma village	161	157	-2.5	111	100.0	0.0	0.0	0.0	0.0	16.2	19.8	54.6	51.7	10.1	61	91.8
Montgomery city	10,373	10,872	4.8	10,782	85.9	2.5	6.1	2.7	2.8	24.9	21.4	44.9	12.9	71.5	4,050	96.5
Montpelier village	4,070	3,924	-3.6	3,952	91.2	0.4	2.9	0.7	4.8	22.0	16.0	38.7	59.2	12.1	1,642	87.8
Montrose-Ghent CDP	5,177	-	-	4,986	87.9	4.1	2.4	0.9	4.7	25.4	22.6	46.6	15.1	63.4	1,930	95.8
Moraine city	6,401	6,470	1.1	6,486	84.2	10.8	2.1	1.0	2.0	26.3	13.1	35.4	50.2	11.2	2,484	85.4
Moreland Hills village	3,320	3,303	-0.5	3,306	92.5	1.4	4.5	1.1	0.5	18.9	24.0	51.3	5.8	78.0	1,377	97.9
Morgandale CDP	1,224	-	-	811	90.8	3.8	0.0	0.0	5.4	12.6	26.5	55.1	83.0	6.9	389	79.9
Morral village	399	382	-4.3	383	98.7	0.5	0.0	0.8	0.0	20.6	16.7	43.9	56.8	8.6	156	86.5
Morristown village	301	288	-4.3	233	98.3	1.7	0.0	0.0	0.0	25.8	18.0	44.5	55.6	16.0	94	85.1
Morrow village	1,178	1,325	12.5	2,005	91.4	4.1	0.3	1.5	2.6	25.7	17.8	35.5	45.6	22.5	716	94.3
Moscow village	185	191	3.2	87	93.1	0.0	0.0	6.9	0.0	4.6	16.1	58.5	65.9	4.9	49	77.6
Mount Blanchard village	489	486	-0.6	426	94.4	0.0	0.0	4.2	1.4	26.3	11.7	36.4	53.4	18.2	159	89.3
Mount Carmel CDP	4,741	-	-	4,932	93.8	0.0	0.0	3.1	3.0	25.2	11.3	31.5	47.8	18.8	1,937	93.3
Mount Cory village	204	196	-3.9	185	95.1	0.0	0.0	0.0	4.9	24.3	18.4	39.3	57.4	7.0	81	88.9
Mount Eaton village	243	234	-3.7	168	100.0	0.0	0.0	0.0	0.0	26.2	13.1	35.8	75.7	8.7	67	86.6
Mount Gilead village	3,657	3,678	0.6	3,334	91.2	1.5	0.0	0.4	6.9	24.6	22.1	42.1	45.8	17.1	1,327	83.3
Mount Healthy city	6,806	6,736		6,767	51.9	41.6	3.8	1.6	1.1	17.6	20.3	43.7	51.1	13.8	3,141	77.4
Mount Healthy Heights CDP	3,264	-	-	2,724	45.3	43.1	2.3	7.5	1.8	34.7	14.5	33.0	45.3	16.8	997	96.4
Mount Orab village	3,685	3,444	-6.5	4,180	93.6	2.3	0.4	2.3	1.4	27.0	14.5	36.5	55.2	18.0	1,652	91.0
Mount Pleasant village	478	443	-7.3	442	98.4	1.4	0.0	0.2	0.0	20.4	18.6	48.5	56.8	17.0	173	91.3
Mount Repose CDP	4,672	-	-	4,249	97.4	0.9	0.2	0.1	1.4	24.4	14.8	39.2	37.8	34.2	1,626	93.8
Mount Sterling village	1,733	1,793	3.5	2,030	93.1	2.4	0.0	1.3	3.3	28.3	12.4	35.0	59.4	12.3	821	86.5
Mount Vernon city	16,965	16,769	-1.2	16,667	94.3	0.7	0.7	2.1	2.2	21.4	19.4	38.8	52.7	22.5	6,794	84.1
Mount Victory village	627	606	-3.3	616	94.0	0.0	0.0	3.4	2.6	19.0	11.0	40.1	58.5	8.9	283	79.9
Mowrystown village	362	352	-2.8	361	85.6	0.0	0.0	1.4	13.0	20.5	7.8	35.3	68.5	5.8	127	89.8
Mulberry CDP	3,323	-	-	4,143	92.2	5.9	0.2	0.5	1.2	17.7	28.2	48.5	33.4	39.4	1,789	88.5
Munroe Falls city	5,056	5,063	0.1	5,057	92.0	0.0	5.7	2.3	0.0	16.0	23.8	48.0	37.5	35.6	2,060	91.3
Murray City village	453	435	-4.0	361	97.2	0.6	1.7	0.6	0.0	13.9	27.4	44.6	71.9	1.4	157	75.2
Mutual village	107	102	-4.7	112	99.1	0.0	0.0	0.9	0.0	32.1	12.5	37.4	47.2	19.4	40	87.5
Napoleon city	8,773	8,207	-6.5	8,503	85.5	1.4	0.1	1.8	11.3	23.9	19.7	39.7	54.4	14.1	3,701	88.8
Nashville village	172	187	8.7	139	100.0	0.0	0.0	0.0	0.0	36.7	12.2	32.9	58.3	10.7	48	79.2
Navarre village	1,888	1,812	-4.0	1,648	94.7	1.9	1.0	0.4	2.0	16.8	24.9	50.1	57.9	12.5	739	84.3
Neapolis CDP	423	-	-	475	86.7	0.0	0.0	0.0	13.3	17.3	22.3	50.6	52.2	4.9	194	94.8
Neffs CDP	993	-	-	848	100.0	0.0	0.0	0.0	0.0	18.4	25.1	53.3	54.2	9.1	324	72.8
Negley CDP	281	-	-	188	100.0	0.0	0.0	0.0	0.0	21.8	22.9	48.6	85.7	0.0	82	91.5
Nellie village	134	131	-2.2	125	88.0	0.0	0.0	0.0	12.0	30.4	24.0	35.5	55.4	12.0	49	93.9
Nelsonville city	5,394	5,130	-4.9	4,769	87.5	3.5	0.7	6.2	2.1	15.1	10.4	31.5	48.6	11.6	1,693	89.3
Nettle Lake CDP	-	-	-	239	98.3	0.0	0.0	0.0	1.7	18.0	16.3	52.4	44.3	16.8	135	70.4
Nevada village	760	729	-4.1	733	98.8	0.0	0.0	0.7	0.5	27.8	16.5	39.5	67.1	4.0	294	79.3
Neville village	102	106	3.9	61	100.0	0.0	0.0	0.0	0.0	3.3	26.2	49.5	46.2	34.6	23	91.3
New Albany city	7,891	10,933	38.6	10,925	78.1	8.2	8.0	3.0	2.7	36.0	8.2	38.3	9.2	78.5	3,242	99.0
New Alexandria village	272	252	-7.4	309	100.0	0.0	0.0	0.0	0.0	12.9	25.2	46.9	62.6	5.0	122	85.2
Newark city	47,558	50,315	5.8	49,470	90.6	2.9	0.4	4.4	1.7	22.8	15.7	37.4	47.3	20.5	19,518	88.6
New Athens village	328	308	-6.1	325	100.0	0.0	0.0	0.0	0.0	23.1	17.8	40.5	68.9	5.9	143	87.4

1 May be of any race.

Table A. All Places — **Population and Housing**

STATE City, town, township, borough, or CDP (county if applicable)	Population				Race and Hispanic or Latino origin (percent)					Age (percent)			Educational attainment of persons age 25 and older		Occupied housing units	
	2010 census total population	2019 estimated population	Percent change 2010–2019	ACS total population estimate 2015–2019	White alone, not Hispanic or Latino	Black alone, not Hispanic or Latino	Asian alone, not Hispanic or Latino	All other races or 2 or more races, not Hispanic or Latino	Hispanic or Latino[1]	Under 18 years old	Age 65 years and older	Median age	Percent High school diploma or less	Percent Bachelor's degree or more	Total	Percent with a computer
	1	2	3	4	5	6	7	8	9	10	11	12	13	14	15	16
OHIO—Con.																
New Baltimore CDP	661	-	-	899	95.7	0.0	0.0	4.3	0.0	19.0	5.2	42.4	44.9	23.9	336	88.7
New Bavaria village	99	93	-6.1	98	94.9	0.0	0.0	0.0	5.1	15.3	13.3	43.5	52.1	18.3	46	89.1
New Bloomington village	520	511	-1.7	413	77.2	0.0	0.0	1.5	21.3	29.1	13.6	36.2	81.3	5.1	161	87.6
New Boston village	2,279	2,099	-7.9	2,266	93.7	0.6	0.0	4.9	0.8	20.6	24.0	44.8	65.3	11.9	1,091	71.9
New Bremen village	3,000	2,963	-1.2	3,221	95.4	0.5	2.2	1.3	0.6	27.3	13.2	41.0	32.3	40.0	1,302	93.5
Newburgh Heights village	2,167	2,049	-5.4	1,718	69.4	22.1	0.3	4.3	3.8	15.2	21.4	43.9	55.7	13.0	855	81.9
New Burlington CDP	5,069	-	-	5,088	50.9	39.9	0.0	0.2	9.1	18.2	21.6	47.3	39.1	21.8	2,173	90.0
New California CDP	1,411	-	-	1,400	93.1	0.0	4.4	0.0	2.5	34.4	7.0	36.1	15.8	62.7	396	100.0
New Carlisle city	5,782	5,568	-3.7	5,584	87.9	0.2	0.0	2.2	9.7	28.1	15.8	33.5	45.3	21.1	2,160	88.3
Newcomerstown village	3,822	3,737	-2.2	3,949	97.0	1.1	0.0	1.3	0.6	26.3	21.6	39.2	73.5	12.3	1,771	75.3
New Concord village	2,491	2,219	-10.9	2,576	88.9	2.6	1.9	3.0	3.7	13.0	9.4	21.1	33.3	45.2	527	92.0
New Franklin city	14,204	14,133	-0.5	14,150	96.5	0.6	0.0	2.1	0.8	19.0	21.9	47.7	42.3	24.6	5,566	91.4
New Hampshire CDP	174	-	-	280	100.0	0.0	0.0	0.0	0.0	29.3	11.4	31.9	92.9	0.0	76	94.7
New Haven CDP	583	-	-	406	89.9	0.0	0.0	0.0	10.1	23.4	12.3	27.4	46.5	13.8	184	89.1
New Haven CDP	399	-	-	314	100.0	0.0	0.0	0.0	0.0	25.8	11.5	46.3	72.1	3.2	119	93.3
New Holland village	801	851	6.2	783	95.4	2.0	0.0	1.7	0.9	16.7	25.0	49.3	68.4	9.3	324	84.3
New Knoxville village	879	866	-1.5	1,084	96.1	0.5	0.0	3.1	0.3	32.0	13.6	35.5	39.2	28.6	414	93.5
New Lebanon village	3,993	3,984	-0.2	4,015	89.5	1.8	1.8	6.4	0.5	27.2	14.6	33.5	50.6	7.2	1,511	95.4
New Lexington village	4,730	4,671	-1.2	4,923	98.6	0.3	0.0	1.1	0.0	23.7	14.0	37.7	63.9	7.1	1,954	85.2
New London village	2,461	2,358	-4.2	2,517	91.7	1.5	0.9	0.6	5.3	28.4	15.4	33.0	58.7	9.2	913	86.2
New Madison village	893	1,201	34.5	994	94.9	0.0	0.9	2.4	1.8	29.7	16.6	35.6	63.3	9.9	379	84.7
New Marshfield CDP	326	-	-	330	100.0	0.0	0.0	0.0	0.0	25.2	14.5	37.2	66.8	18.2	145	100.0
New Miami village	2,257	2,381	5.5	2,410	91.2	2.8	0.1	2.5	3.3	24.0	13.6	38.2	78.7	4.0	839	83.6
New Middletown village	1,634	1,550	-5.1	1,462	98.8	0.0	0.0	1.0	0.3	21.0	27.0	48.9	51.4	19.0	663	84.3
New Paris village	1,629	1,572	-3.5	1,479	98.5	0.3	0.0	1.2	0.0	26.4	14.9	33.7	57.3	10.4	622	88.6
New Philadelphia city	17,295	17,410	0.7	17,446	87.9	0.8	0.9	2.7	7.7	22.9	20.0	38.4	55.7	18.2	7,361	87.1
New Pittsburg CDP	388	-	-	422	92.7	3.8	0.0	0.0	3.6	31.0	11.4	33.0	53.3	32.9	110	100.0
Newport CDP	198	-	-	114	94.7	0.0	0.0	5.3	0.0	7.9	25.4	50.6	64.2	7.4	51	76.5
Newport CDP	1,003	-	-	949	86.6	5.2	0.0	4.4	3.8	20.7	13.3	47.7	66.6	14.0	414	70.5
New Richmond village	2,591	2,698	4.1	2,679	92.8	2.4	0.2	1.4	3.2	25.8	12.1	37.2	52.4	19.9	987	81.9
New Riegel village	249	236	-5.2	282	93.6	0.4	0.0	1.1	5.0	19.1	20.9	42.5	56.4	15.2	124	83.9
New Straitsville village	722	710	-1.7	632	94.8	0.0	1.1	4.1	0.0	28.6	9.3	35.0	55.5	7.6	258	81.0
Newton Falls village	4,755	4,471	-6.0	4,529	97.4	0.0	1.6	0.8	0.2	16.4	24.1	47.9	66.1	9.9	2,188	85.5
Newtonsville village	361	376	4.2	393	98.0	1.0	0.0	0.0	1.0	19.1	17.8	44.8	72.5	3.3	139	87.8
Newtown village	2,652	2,669	0.6	2,662	86.5	5.7	0.7	0.8	6.3	25.5	16.0	38.5	26.7	48.2	1,076	94.8
New Vienna village	1,224	1,228	0.3	1,190	93.8	0.8	0.0	1.4	3.9	25.8	8.7	35.9	56.3	7.4	517	89.9
New Washington village	968	920	-5.0	1,000	87.6	1.4	0.0	5.7	5.3	26.9	15.4	35.1	40.6	18.1	388	91.5
New Waterford village	1,239	1,180	-4.8	945	96.4	0.0	0.8	1.2	1.6	13.9	23.6	53.1	54.2	14.5	481	79.8
New Weston village	136	129	-5.1	95	100.0	0.0	0.0	0.0	0.0	25.3	17.9	40.8	80.0	2.9	44	86.4
Ney village	354	341	-3.7	256	89.5	0.0	1.6	2.3	6.6	28.9	11.3	39.0	62.0	7.0	101	92.1
Niles city	19,210	18,176	-5.4	18,468	89.9	5.9	0.7	1.5	2.0	18.6	21.3	44.6	57.1	16.0	8,335	83.8
North Baltimore village	3,429	3,545	3.4	3,467	87.8	0.6	0.2	1.0	10.3	23.1	14.2	38.6	59.7	14.0	1,253	87.1
North Bend village	861	873	1.4	809	99.4	0.0	0.2	0.0	0.4	10.6	45.4	63.4	31.9	40.0	399	89.5
Northbrook CDP	10,668	-	-	10,684	54.8	32.8	2.0	9.1	1.2	26.3	14.4	35.4	47.6	17.4	4,266	88.9
North Canton city	17,505	17,176	-1.9	17,277	91.1	2.7	2.1	2.4	1.7	18.8	22.8	41.0	33.9	36.7	7,129	89.1
North College Hill city	9,418	9,283	-1.4	9,335	36.2	55.3	0.3	8.2	0.1	22.7	12.6	39.7	46.7	20.6	3,834	88.6
North Fairfield village	560	534	-4.6	523	96.4	1.7	0.0	0.6	1.3	27.3	10.1	33.3	65.6	7.8	184	85.9
Northfield village	3,675	3,663	-0.3	3,665	76.8	9.6	7.4	5.1	1.0	20.0	15.7	37.8	45.3	18.4	1,419	86.5
Northgate CDP	7,377	-	-	6,583	72.5	20.4	2.4	2.3	2.5	20.8	19.5	42.4	55.7	17.2	2,728	87.2
North Hampton village	487	468	-3.9	490	97.1	0.0	0.0	0.2	2.7	21.6	18.4	44.3	46.7	14.5	196	92.9
North Kingsville village	2,917	2,792	-4.3	2,803	91.4	1.8	4.2	0.4	2.3	18.1	18.2	49.1	48.4	20.1	1,145	85.9
North Lawrence CDP	268	-	-	164	100.0	0.0	0.0	0.0	0.0	20.1	6.7	51.6	94.7	0.0	79	100.0
North Lewisburg village	1,498	1,465	-2.2	1,626	94.2	1.4	0.0	3.6	0.9	28.3	10.9	34.9	60.0	10.3	628	90.4
North Madison CDP	8,547	-	-	8,630	95.2	0.7	0.6	0.6	2.9	23.6	18.8	38.9	48.3	11.4	3,380	90.4
North Olmsted city	32,709	31,341	-4.2	31,710	88.6	2.0	2.8	2.3	4.3	19.9	20.6	44.4	37.0	30.9	13,093	91.1
North Perry village	893	884		758	98.3	0.3	0.3	0.7	0.5	22.6	19.9	45.9	43.5	28.1	291	90.4
North Randall village	1,027	988	-3.8	1,106	20.1	77.8	0.0	1.4	0.8	11.6	30.6	59.3	52.8	11.3	547	81.7
Northridge CDP	7,572	-	-	7,278	96.6	0.9	0.3	0.8	1.4	19.3	25.5	46.6	38.9	24.3	3,352	93.3
North Ridgeville city	29,466	34,392	16.7	33,427	89.3	2.1	1.2	1.9	5.5	23.4	19.1	41.0	35.5	32.1	12,906	94.9
North Robinson village	210	198	-5.7	306	98.4	0.7	0.0	1.0	0.0	19.9	41.5	54.6	75.7	3.0	159	57.2
North Royalton city	30,452	30,068	-1.3	30,252	90.8	2.1	4.0	1.6	1.5	19.5	19.3	43.6	30.2	40.1	12,907	91.1
North Star village	232	221	-4.7	218	100.0	0.0	0.0	0.0	0.0	28.0	17.4	30.6	51.1	28.6	82	84.1
Northwood city	5,221	5,434	4.1	5,384	89.0	0.0	0.3	2.1	8.6	22.5	15.7	37.2	46.1	17.8	2,140	93.0
North Zanesville CDP	2,816	-	-	2,423	90.4	1.2	4.7	3.7	0.0	10.5	23.3	53.5	34.2	29.3	1,102	91.8
Norton city	12,107	11,966	-1.2	12,018	94.7	3.1	0.3	0.8	1.1	21.6	17.9	43.9	43.2	26.5	4,540	87.6
Norwalk city	17,102	16,867	-1.4	16,857	86.8	1.9	0.0	1.4	9.9	23.5	19.3	38.7	57.3	16.2	6,924	89.5
Norwich village	102	101		112	100.0	0.0	0.0	0.0	0.0	18.8	14.3	43.0	61.9	26.2	41	97.6
Norwood city	19,210	19,776	2.9	19,883	80.2	11.7	1.0	2.3	4.7	18.0	10.4	31.8	42.2	31.5	8,645	88.7
Oak Harbor village	2,750	2,707	-1.6	2,710	88.2	0.0	1.2	2.1	8.5	23.8	20.5	40.1	43.6	17.6	1,246	85.7
Oak Hill village	1,560	1,522	-2.4	1,676	90.0	0.7	0.0	9.2	0.0	22.7	17.4	37.6	59.2	10.2	724	80.2
Oakwood village	3,661	3,624		3,668	34.0	60.3	0.8	4.9	0.1	14.1	25.8	51.7	39.0	31.1	1,642	89.6
Oakwood city	9,204	8,936	-2.9	8,982	93.1	0.0	2.7	2.7	1.5	27.8	15.1	42.1	8.1	69.1	3,555	96.9
Oakwood village	613	587	-4.2	619	93.7	0.0	0.0	2.4	3.9	26.7	17.4	38.1	64.6	4.0	236	87.7
Oberlin city	8,290	8,199	-1.1	8,296	70.0	13.2	6.0	5.4	5.4	12.6	17.7	22.9	24.2	53.3	2,566	93.5
Obetz village	4,537	5,196	14.5	5,024	80.9	10.5	0.7	4.4	3.6	26.9	10.4	36.8	55.5	13.8	1,831	97.2
Oceola CDP	190	-	-	91	100.0	0.0	0.0	0.0	0.0	45.1	9.9	23.4	73.7	0.0	29	69.0
Octa village	59	58	-1.7	51	92.2	0.0	0.0	0.0	7.8	5.9	37.3	58.2	87.5	2.1	31	77.4
Ohio City village	705	677	-4.0	760	88.7	0.0	0.0	0.9	10.4	22.2	16.3	39.3	73.5	5.9	338	84.6
Olde West Chester CDP	240	-	-	276	57.2	0.0	0.0	0.0	42.8	35.9	12.0	27.3	43.0	28.9	83	91.6
Old Fort CDP	186	-	-	242	91.7	0.0	0.0	0.0	8.3	31.0	30.6	37.9	76.4	20.7	81	65.4
Old Washington village	277	268	-3.2	485	75.3	0.6	0.0	23.5	0.6	29.9	8.5	35.1	41.1	9.5	154	89.6
Olmsted Falls city	9,032	8,828	-2.3	8,883	94.5	0.9	0.9	1.9	1.8	21.6	20.4	45.9	28.5	39.4	3,888	93.7
Ontario city	6,243	6,084	-2.5	6,076	91.4	4.4	2.8	1.0	0.4	18.4	21.8	47.1	40.9	24.8	2,639	90.1
Orange village	3,323	3,290		3,276	76.7	15.4	1.9	1.8	4.2	23.7	22.6	47.3	10.8	69.5	1,283	97.3
Orangeville village	189	174	-7.9	180	98.9	1.1	0.0	0.0	0.0	26.1	15.6	39.4	39.7	21.5	69	97.1
Oregon city	20,304	20,055	-1.2	20,017	87.1	2.2	1.3	2.4	7.1	19.7	20.9	45.2	45.7	20.7	8,392	89.2
Orient CDP	270	-	-	235	66.0	11.1	3.0	20.0	0.0	24.7	18.7	39.7	51.5	2.3	82	70.7
Orrville city	8,357	8,419	0.7	8,339	80.8	1.7	3.4	4.2	9.9	23.6	18.3	37.1	48.5	26.9	3,339	88.6
Orwell village	1,659	1,594	-3.9	1,563	94.8	1.0	0.0	3.1	1.2	21.6	16.6	35.6	66.8	9.5	638	83.9
Osgood village	302	282	-6.6	284	100.0	0.0	0.0	0.0	0.0	27.8	23.6	38.5	52.7	21.7	114	78.9
Ostrander village	640	749	17.0	998	95.4	0.0	0.0	1.2	3.4	33.2	9.4	37.3	41.5	33.7	307	91.9
Ottawa village	4,462	4,357	-2.4	4,359	87.6	0.9	0.3	3.6	7.6	24.6	18.9	38.7	50.9	24.9	1,900	91.1

1 May be of any race.

Table A. All Places — **Population and Housing**

STATE City, town, township, borough, or CDP (county if applicable)	Population: 2010 census total population	Population: 2019 estimated population	Population: Percent change 2010–2019	Population: ACS total population estimate 2015–2019	Race and Hispanic or Latino origin (percent): White alone, not Hispanic or Latino	Black alone, not Hispanic or Latino	Asian alone, not Hispanic or Latino	All other races or 2 or more races, not Hispanic or Latino	Hispanic or Latino[1]	Age (percent): Under 18 years old	Age 65 years and older	Median age	Educational attainment of persons age 25 and older: Percent High school diploma or less	Percent Bachelor's degree or more	Occupied housing units: Total	Percent with a computer
	1	2	3	4	5	6	7	8	9	10	11	12	13	14	15	16
OHIO—Con.																
Ottawa Hills village	4,470	4,488	0.4	4,450	80.7	2.0	9.8	4.8	2.7	28.9	16.6	41.8	8.9	78.7	1,563	98.9
Ottoville village	983	964	-1.9	856	96.7	0.0	3.3	0.0	0.0	21.5	14.3	39.4	38.7	25.8	383	90.3
Otway village	87	82	-5.7	32	100.0	0.0	0.0	0.0	0.0	9.4	37.5	62.5	72.4	6.9	26	61.5
Owensville village	794	828	4.3	883	95.8	3.1	0.1	0.7	0.3	16.9	25.0	53.3	75.6	8.5	432	75.0
Oxford city	21,387	23,110	8.1	22,700	80.1	4.8	9.1	2.3	3.7	7.6	6.6	21.2	21.2	60.1	6,322	95.6
Painesville city	19,531	19,886	1.8	19,845	53.4	15.0	0.8	4.2	26.6	27.9	10.0	31.0	54.2	16.5	7,351	86.9
Palestine village	198	184	-7.1	242	83.9	10.3	1.2	1.2	3.3	30.2	7.9	32.4	44.0	7.3	98	86.7
Pancoastburg CDP	87	-	-	65	100.0	0.0	0.0	0.0	0.0	13.8	0.0	38.5	83.9	0.0	29	100.0
Pandora village	1,145	1,107	-3.3	1,139	94.6	0.3	0.4	0.0	4.7	23.5	20.3	42.7	40.3	26.0	458	93.4
Park Layne CDP	4,343	-	-	4,264	92.1	0.8	0.0	2.6	4.6	26.2	12.9	35.9	52.6	8.2	1,653	91.2
Parkman CDP	-	-	-	154	100.0	0.0	0.0	0.0	0.0	0.0	0.0	56.3	21.4	50.0	112	57.1
Parma city	81,589	78,103	-4.3	79,091	86.5	3.3	2.0	2.5	5.7	18.7	19.0	42.0	45.8	21.7	33,424	89.5
Parma Heights city	20,722	19,790	-4.5	20,045	80.3	6.6	2.7	3.4	7.0	18.4	20.9	42.7	40.8	25.7	9,231	84.4
Parral village	218	212	-2.8	209	98.1	0.0	0.0	0.0	1.9	15.8	32.5	50.1	62.8	6.4	106	85.8
Pataskala city	14,926	15,883	6.4	15,585	81.4	10.8	1.9	3.6	2.3	27.1	12.1	35.3	39.2	25.3	5,383	92.2
Patterson village	138	133	-3.6	188	100.0	0.0	0.0	0.0	0.0	36.2	19.7	31.8	72.7	4.5	69	94.2
Paulding village	3,606	3,423	-5.1	3,536	85.9	1.0	0.1	1.2	11.7	23.0	17.8	41.5	58.8	13.9	1,496	83.2
Payne village	1,194	1,139	-4.6	1,297	94.4	2.0	0.7	2.1	0.8	20.3	16.3	41.3	64.5	10.3	562	86.3
Peebles village	1,795	1,717	-4.3	1,992	98.3	0.3	0.0	1.0	0.4	31.9	13.4	33.5	69.7	6.0	759	86.6
Pemberville village	1,373	1,420	3.4	1,501	89.4	1.5	0.0	0.6	8.5	24.0	16.3	37.8	33.7	27.1	567	90.5
Peninsula village	558	554	-0.7	643	98.1	0.5	0.0	0.0	1.4	21.5	17.6	43.1	16.2	62.6	247	96.0
Pepper Pike city	5,979	6,330	5.9	6,269	83.1	3.4	8.2	3.7	1.5	25.1	25.6	48.8	8.9	77.9	2,228	98.7
Perry village	1,635	1,626	-0.6	1,680	91.9	0.6	1.2	5.5	0.8	22.7	17.2	41.6	46.4	21.1	590	95.6
Perry Heights CDP	8,441	-	-	8,575	92.2	4.1	0.0	1.9	1.8	21.9	18.9	44.0	52.3	15.3	3,475	86.1
Perrysburg city	20,767	21,626	4.1	21,482	87.3	1.6	4.8	2.4	3.8	27.4	14.5	37.4	18.8	53.2	8,533	93.3
Perrysville village	728	717	-1.5	683	99.0	0.0	0.0	0.0	1.0	19.8	9.4	42.1	66.5	7.3	304	79.6
Pettisville CDP	498	-	-	538	75.7	3.9	3.2	0.0	17.3	26.4	25.7	42.6	44.4	24.7	210	92.4
Pheasant Run CDP	1,397	-	-	1,135	89.3	0.0	0.0	1.9	8.7	25.6	12.4	31.6	35.1	13.9	466	92.5
Phillipsburg village	556	550	-1.1	456	94.5	0.0	0.0	0.0	5.5	20.6	11.2	34.0	52.4	17.0	207	85.5
Philo village	732	728	-0.5	993	96.5	0.0	0.0	3.5	0.0	35.6	9.4	31.8	66.4	9.2	292	88.7
Pickerington city	18,278	22,158	21.2	20,631	71.8	17.9	2.8	4.5	3.0	31.3	9.2	35.0	25.9	44.6	6,986	96.6
Pigeon Creek CDP	882	-	-	827	97.9	2.1	0.0	0.0	0.0	26.4	22.1	45.5	24.0	42.2	302	96.4
Piketon village	2,180	2,140	-1.8	2,269	92.1	7.1	0.0	0.8	0.0	34.3	12.0	29.8	54.0	12.2	782	87.7
Pioneer village	1,379	1,399	1.5	1,623	94.1	0.6	0.6	0.8	4.0	25.9	13.0	32.3	51.0	17.5	686	92.7
Piqua city	20,505	21,332	4.0	21,028	90.5	2.4	1.0	5.3	0.8	23.8	16.2	38.4	53.9	13.9	8,387	85.4
Pitsburg village	386	365	-5.4	330	97.6	0.0	0.0	2.4	0.0	23.6	17.6	43.0	55.2	9.0	136	94.1
Plain City village	4,228	4,586	8.5	4,273	91.6	0.2	3.7	4.5	0.0	25.8	15.4	36.8	37.4	35.6	1,681	94.3
Plainfield village	144	158	9.7	114	98.2	0.0	0.0	0.0	1.8	14.0	24.6	54.7	59.6	18.1	53	83.0
Plainville CDP	87	-	-	175	100.0	0.0	0.0	0.0	0.0	0.0	0.0	52.4	37.1	16.0	79	100.0
Pleasant City village	443	423	-4.5	404	86.6	5.0	0.0	7.9	0.5	30.9	7.9	27.5	55.8	12.6	142	89.4
Pleasant Grove CDP	1,742	-	-	1,537	92.0	8.0	0.0	0.0	0.0	12.5	20.2	42.3	54.4	14.1	716	93.6
Pleasant Hill village	1,203	1,254	4.2	1,291	96.3	0.0	0.0	0.9	2.9	28.6	15.1	37.7	53.4	19.2	456	93.6
Pleasant Hills CDP	606	-	-	828	34.4	64.6	0.0	1.0	0.0	22.1	24.3	38.5	24.7	39.2	369	100.0
Pleasant Plain village	149	168	12.8	187	98.4	0.0	1.6	0.0	0.0	19.8	5.9	38.5	75.7	14.0	81	90.1
Pleasant Run CDP	4,953	-	-	4,887	77.8	10.4	6.4	2.7	2.8	21.2	19.3	41.9	52.6	17.9	1,802	90.1
Pleasant Run Farm CDP	4,654	-	-	4,246	50.6	46.3	0.2	1.8	1.2	25.9	12.7	38.3	29.0	35.8	1,673	96.2
Pleasantville village	956	959	0.3	1,098	86.6	2.7	0.0	7.4	3.3	27.0	11.4	37.1	63.3	4.9	380	83.7
Plumwood CDP	319	-	-	307	100.0	0.0	0.0	0.0	0.0	23.8	13.7	40.4	71.4	5.6	132	80.3
Plymouth village	1,869	1,801	-3.6	1,597	93.5	0.2	0.0	2.7	3.6	26.6	14.7	36.0	63.5	10.2	614	87.5
Poland village	2,523	2,378	-5.7	2,481	95.3	0.7	0.4	0.4	3.1	17.4	21.2	48.2	30.2	43.8	1,110	91.4
Polk village	336	330	-1.8	470	97.7	0.0	0.2	0.9	1.3	25.1	11.7	36.6	64.4	10.1	153	95.4
Pomeroy village	1,847	1,757	-4.9	1,990	92.0	2.9	0.0	4.8	0.4	22.5	11.6	39.2	56.0	7.6	728	81.6
Portage village	438	480	9.6	465	74.2	9.0	0.0	0.0	16.8	18.1	19.1	43.5	43.8	26.1	185	90.3
Portage Lakes CDP	6,968	-	-	7,087	95.0	2.2	1.1	0.7	1.0	13.0	18.6	43.5	40.1	27.7	3,387	86.4
Port Clinton city	6,349	6,176	-2.7	6,197	87.6	4.6	0.1	3.1	4.6	23.4	19.9	44.1	50.3	16.4	2,846	85.3
Port Jefferson village	369	361	-2.2	419	96.9	0.0	1.2	1.2	0.7	21.0	12.6	43.6	72.0	4.9	184	63.6
Portsmouth city	20,207	20,158	-0.2	20,311	87.7	5.9	1.1	3.3	1.9	22.1	16.5	36.1	55.5	16.0	8,582	78.9
Port Washington village	569	565	-0.7	479	97.1	0.0	0.0	1.3	1.7	24.0	19.6	47.3	77.4	6.4	184	93.5
Port William village	254	248	-2.4	338	92.9	0.0	0.0	4.1	3.0	32.5	3.0	29.6	65.3	7.7	103	88.3
Potsdam village	288	297	3.1	305	100.0	0.0	0.0	0.0	0.0	23.3	9.8	36.8	66.0	11.2	111	96.4
Pottery Addition CDP	293	-	-	147	100.0	0.0	0.0	0.0	0.0	25.2	5.4	46.2	66.7	0.0	71	88.7
Powell city	11,497	13,375	16.3	13,141	82.5	1.1	12.3	3.7	0.4	31.9	11.8	38.6	9.1	73.5	4,390	99.3
Powhatan Point village	1,592	1,520	-4.5	1,642	95.1	1.2	0.0	0.9	2.8	17.5	21.6	49.6	60.4	14.6	748	80.1
Proctorville village	574	542	-5.6	536	98.3	1.7	0.0	0.0	0.0	16.4	15.5	42.1	63.4	7.7	243	72.4
Prospect village	1,109	1,058	-4.6	1,084	94.1	0.4	0.0	3.2	2.3	29.7	18.5	37.4	47.9	22.8	400	91.5
Pulaski CDP	132	-	-	107	87.9	0.0	0.0	0.0	12.1	13.1	34.6	54.3	52.7	14.0	54	57.4
Put-in-Bay village	144	141	-2.1	71	100.0	0.0	0.0	0.0	0.0	8.5	28.2	41.2	13.8	58.5	38	100.0
Quaker City village	502	486	-3.2	461	97.0	0.0	0.0	1.3	1.7	22.1	26.2	38.8	62.3	4.8	232	73.3
Quincy village	706	704	-0.3	568	96.1	0.0	0.0	3.0	0.9	26.2	12.0	36.5	60.8	7.1	235	78.3
Racine village	696	664	-4.6	609	100.0	0.0	0.0	0.0	0.0	23.6	17.2	42.5	57.9	13.9	243	84.8
Radnor CDP	201	-	-	190	100.0	0.0	0.0	0.0	0.0	0.0	43.2	53.7	62.1	18.4	110	71.8
Rarden village	159	147	-7.5	186	100.0	0.0	0.0	0.0	0.0	13.4	19.9	47.3	72.5	3.3	74	74.3
Ravenna city	11,724	11,361	-3.1	11,485	86.1	6.8	1.2	4.1	1.8	17.7	16.1	40.2	51.3	18.5	5,052	85.7
Rawson village	572	557	-2.6	568	85.7	4.9	0.0	7.2	2.1	35.7	8.8	30.6	53.2	6.7	193	93.3
Rayland village	417	393	-5.8	407	98.0	0.0	0.0	2.0	0.0	18.7	22.1	43.7	53.8	7.4	183	82.0
Raymond CDP	257	-	-	185	100.0	0.0	0.0	0.0	0.0	21.6	4.9	43.1	32.3	36.1	72	100.0
Reading city	10,413	10,296	-1.1	10,353	81.8	8.4	1.4	4.2	4.2	20.7	13.3	38.7	49.0	21.8	4,429	89.5
Reminderville village	3,404	4,517	32.7	4,237	65.8	11.7	14.7	2.4	5.3	24.1	12.4	40.7	23.6	45.3	1,669	97.0
Remington CDP	328	-	-	362	84.5	0.0	15.5	0.0	0.0	15.2	8.0	49.2	5.9	70.8	181	100.0
Rendville village	36	36	0.0	10	20.0	0.0	0.0	80.0	0.0	0.0	20.0	49.8	10.0	0.0	9	88.9
Reno CDP	1,293	-	-	1,175	95.9	0.3	0.0	3.7	0.0	12.9	28.5	49.1	52.8	11.1	619	78.2
Republic village	549	520	-5.3	634	91.8	1.4	0.0	0.6	6.2	32.5	13.2	35.9	62.3	4.8	222	83.3
Reynoldsburg city	35,921	38,327	6.7	38,129	61.0	25.2	3.8	5.0	5.1	24.8	12.8	37.0	34.7	31.4	14,470	94.7
Richfield village	3,656	3,644	-0.3	3,650	95.7	0.5	0.8	2.5	0.5	17.8	24.1	50.4	26.6	39.5	1,421	91.8
Richmond village	481	446	-7.3	418	95.9	0.0	0.0	3.6	0.5	14.8	27.8	52.2	48.7	15.7	199	79.4
Richmond Dale CDP	377	-	-	582	83.5	0.0	0.0	16.5	0.0	43.3	6.7	26.2	84.4	0.0	204	93.6
Richmond Heights city	10,557	10,342	-2.0	10,406	38.8	52.3	2.7	3.7	2.5	16.4	23.3	47.0	34.2	35.6	4,768	87.8
Richville CDP	3,324	-	-	3,054	95.3	2.6	0.2	1.9	0.0	15.0	22.1	45.5	56.9	13.2	1,266	88.4
Richwood village	2,229	2,480	11.3	2,329	93.0	0.3	0.0	2.1	4.6	19.9	14.3	35.7	62.6	9.2	929	86.3
Ridgeville Corners CDP	435	-	-	365	89.0	0.0	0.0	0.0	11.0	21.9	15.9	32.4	36.1	22.9	148	89.2
Ridgeway village	338	329	-2.7	368	94.3	4.3	0.0	0.0	1.4	25.8	14.1	41.8	70.2	9.9	138	83.3
Rio Grande village	834	781	-6.4	896	83.5	11.4	2.3	0.9	1.9	16.6	4.8	21.4	47.1	13.1	184	95.7

1 May be of any race.

Table A. All Places — **Population and Housing**

STATE City, town, township, borough, or CDP (county if applicable)	Population: 2010 census total population	Population: 2019 estimated population	Population: Percent change 2010–2019	Population: ACS total population estimate 2015–2019	Race and Hispanic or Latino origin (percent): White alone, not Hispanic or Latino	Black alone, not Hispanic or Latino	Asian alone, not Hispanic or Latino	All other races or 2 or more races, not Hispanic or Latino	Hispanic or Latino[1]	Age (percent): Under 18 years old	Age 65 years and older	Median age	Educational attainment of persons age 25 and older: Percent High school diploma or less	Percent Bachelor's degree or more	Occupied housing units: Total	Percent with a computer
	1	2	3	4	5	6	7	8	9	10	11	12	13	14	15	16
OHIO—Con.																
Ripley village	1,749	1,697	-3.0	1,737	96.4	1.9	0.2	1.4	0.0	22.1	18.3	37.4	55.9	13.2	767	77.1
Risingsun village	610	629	3.1	569	89.3	0.2	1.1	5.1	4.4	22.8	13.7	36.9	62.8	9.3	215	86.0
Rittman city	6,465	6,506	0.6	6,503	95.2	2.6	0.0	1.7	0.5	20.9	17.3	42.2	53.7	18.0	2,711	85.9
Riverlea village	547	565	3.3	532	93.4	1.1	1.7	2.3	1.5	27.3	18.2	45.6	7.1	79.3	202	98.5
Riverside city	25,175	25,133	-0.2	25,093	77.4	10.1	2.8	4.8	5.0	24.2	16.3	35.6	43.3	22.4	10,666	90.9
Roaming Shores village	1,508	1,452	-3.7	1,545	98.4	0.7	0.0	0.1	0.8	26.9	16.2	43.5	38.4	33.2	582	93.6
Robertsville CDP	331	-	-	260	100.0	0.0	0.0	0.0	0.0	25.0	33.5	26.6	81.0	6.9	100	61.0
Rochester village	182	175	-3.8	168	97.6	0.0	0.0	0.0	2.4	28.6	21.4	41.0	59.6	19.3	68	85.3
Rockbridge CDP	182	-	-	64	100.0	0.0	0.0	0.0	0.0	26.6	43.8	40.6	59.6	0.0	28	67.9
Rock Creek village	533	507	-4.9	474	99.4	0.2	0.0	0.4	0.0	15.2	16.7	45.3	68.4	6.6	183	83.6
Rockford village	1,120	1,104	-1.4	917	95.2	1.1	0.0	0.9	2.8	15.4	28.7	49.2	55.7	20.1	426	83.6
Rocky Fork Point CDP	639	-	-	680	100.0	0.0	0.0	0.0	0.0	27.8	30.0	43.8	64.8	8.6	296	66.9
Rocky Ridge village	414	407	-1.7	385	94.0	0.0	0.0	0.0	6.0	22.9	6.8	32.5	65.5	10.7	161	92.5
Rocky River city	20,212	19,986	-1.1	20,198	92.7	1.2	1.2	2.5	2.3	21.5	24.0	46.2	18.2	59.3	9,057	89.6
Rogers village	239	224	-6.3	249	100.0	0.0	0.0	0.0	0.0	15.3	24.5	43.8	79.0	6.1	98	87.8
Rome (Stout) village	98	95	-3.1	64	100.0	0.0	0.0	0.0	0.0	21.9	29.7	47.5	83.7	4.1	30	36.7
Rose Farm CDP	-	-	-	111	100.0	0.0	0.0	0.0	0.0	22.5	9.0	40.4	37.2	17.4	46	58.7
Rosemount CDP	2,112	-	-	2,053	82.8	0.0	0.0	0.0	17.2	19.6	20.3	49.1	46.7	10.2	760	80.1
Roseville village	1,859	1,839	-1.1	2,095	87.0	0.5	0.5	10.9	1.1	27.0	11.2	35.5	64.9	8.6	744	89.1
Rosewood CDP	257	-	-	194	100.0	0.0	0.0	0.0	0.0	11.3	17.0	50.7	84.7	0.0	84	79.8
Ross CDP	3,417	-	-	3,432	98.5	0.0	0.0	0.8	0.7	27.6	13.2	36.5	44.6	31.2	1,149	95.6
Rossburg village	194	185	-4.6	248	83.9	16.1	0.0	0.0	0.0	26.2	10.5	40.0	67.9	3.1	96	88.5
Rossford city	6,337	6,562	3.6	6,539	94.9	1.0	0.4	1.3	2.4	21.8	15.1	36.4	34.1	27.7	2,699	94.1
Rossmoyne CDP	2,230	-	-	1,815	88.8	8.9	0.0	1.5	0.9	10.5	21.8	42.6	33.8	34.6	916	87.4
Roswell village	219	215	-1.8	224	96.0	0.0	0.0	2.2	1.8	17.9	9.8	50.8	75.9	10.8	95	88.4
Rudolph CDP	458	-	-	546	97.1	0.0	0.0	0.0	2.9	37.5	9.9	31.6	66.4	7.2	173	86.1
Rushsylvania village	516	530	2.7	534	98.1	0.0	0.0	0.7	1.1	22.7	12.4	40.5	70.9	7.3	210	88.1
Rushville village	307	309	0.7	360	93.6	0.8	0.0	5.6	0.0	35.3	13.1	33.7	44.6	25.4	110	87.3
Russells Point village	1,391	1,390	-0.1	1,196	93.4	0.0	4.7	1.9	0.0	21.1	15.7	44.1	65.7	9.6	606	86.6
Russellville village	554	512	-7.6	698	95.8	0.1	0.0	0.9	3.2	34.0	14.8	29.0	63.7	11.8	260	91.2
Russia village	643	664	3.3	861	97.0	1.0	0.0	0.8	1.2	34.0	11.1	31.0	41.4	22.7	302	93.4
Rutland village	396	378	-4.5	526	97.5	0.0	0.0	0.0	2.5	28.9	14.3	41.0	65.1	12.0	191	78.0
Sabina village	2,615	2,579	-1.4	2,699	90.5	0.0	0.3	6.6	2.7	22.0	17.0	41.3	63.6	8.4	1,120	89.0
St. Bernard village	4,377	4,336	-0.9	4,361	80.4	14.7	0.0	3.3	1.6	17.7	15.3	41.3	43.0	24.7	1,902	95.1
St. Clairsville city	5,189	5,141	-0.9	5,072	92.5	3.9	0.6	2.7	0.3	17.3	30.8	52.0	36.7	31.9	2,127	88.7
St. Henry village	2,439	2,555	4.8	2,508	96.8	0.6	0.0	0.0	2.6	28.7	15.9	32.5	45.0	25.6	899	90.4
St. Johns CDP	185	-	-	202	93.1	4.5	0.0	2.5	0.0	21.8	0.0	34.3	20.3	4.5	62	100.0
St. Louisville village	371	386	4.0	443	90.5	0.0	0.0	5.0	4.5	29.8	10.4	36.9	56.5	8.5	144	91.7
St. Martin CDP	129	-	-	209	100.0	0.0	0.0	0.0	0.0	9.6	18.2	48.5	56.1	27.0	102	74.5
St. Marys city	8,330	8,160	-2.0	8,202	94.8	0.0	0.6	3.9	0.7	26.1	15.6	34.8	57.6	14.9	3,347	85.2
St. Paris village	2,074	2,010	-3.1	2,173	96.2	0.0	0.3	1.0	2.5	27.0	14.4	31.6	49.9	17.1	863	90.5
Salem city	12,298	11,612	-5.6	11,774	92.9	1.8	0.0	1.6	3.7	22.2	17.7	40.0	54.7	17.3	4,751	87.6
Salem Heights CDP	3,839	-	-	3,314	92.7	1.7	3.9	0.9	0.8	17.8	18.7	45.8	26.0	51.0	1,403	91.9
Salesville CDP	129	-	-	89	100.0	0.0	0.0	0.0	0.0	7.9	24.7	46.8	83.6	0.0	45	77.8
Salineville village	1,307	1,218	-6.8	1,250	94.5	3.5	0.0	1.1	0.9	21.7	17.7	39.9	75.8	5.0	515	73.6
Sandusky city	25,919	24,564	-5.2	24,829	64.3	22.7	0.2	5.4	7.4	23.8	17.2	38.0	52.0	15.1	10,941	86.4
Sandyville CDP	368	-	-	218	100.0	0.0	0.0	0.0	0.0	37.2	0.0	35.5	86.9	0.0	79	100.0
Sarahsville village	174	169	-2.9	115	100.0	0.0	0.0	0.0	0.0	20.0	40.0	56.3	66.3	8.1	46	95.7
Sardinia village	1,175	1,136	-3.3	1,432	98.1	0.1	0.0	1.7	0.0	35.7	11.3	30.7	57.0	6.6	499	90.2
Sardis CDP	559	-	-	677	93.4	0.0	6.6	0.0	0.0	21.3	31.5	46.9	62.1	29.8	292	96.6
Savannah village	414	415	0.2	374	81.0	0.0	0.0	5.6	13.4	28.3	10.7	38.5	63.4	10.8	121	89.3
Sawyerwood CDP	1,540	-	-	1,613	95.5	0.0	0.0	0.7	3.7	7.9	24.9	52.1	71.2	10.0	722	88.9
Scio village	763	716	-6.2	730	99.0	0.0	0.0	1.0	0.0	24.1	21.9	39.8	61.8	10.4	335	77.6
Sciotodale CDP	1,081	-	-	861	94.8	0.0	2.3	2.9	0.0	16.6	27.5	53.7	54.4	11.4	382	86.4
Scott village	286	273	-4.5	298	95.0	0.0	0.0	1.3	3.7	24.8	5.4	40.1	54.6	9.7	118	89.0
Seaman village	930	895	-3.8	1,141	99.1	0.0	0.0	0.4	0.5	33.9	12.7	31.2	57.0	10.8	435	84.1
Sebring village	4,411	4,186	-5.1	4,231	98.5	0.4	0.0	1.1	0.0	17.3	28.2	47.5	62.2	14.6	1,769	83.2
Senecaville village	463	449	-3.0	314	96.5	0.6	0.0	2.2	0.6	15.9	22.3	52.3	62.4	4.1	160	81.9
Seven Hills city	11,799	11,590	-1.8	11,638	93.0	2.6	2.4	1.0	1.0	14.7	27.4	52.0	35.3	35.0	4,946	90.0
Seven Mile village	749	784	4.7	877	93.6	0.0	1.0	5.2	0.1	24.9	16.2	44.8	67.1	19.2	290	83.1
Seville village	2,308	2,425	5.1	2,673	94.7	0.2	0.0	0.2	4.9	25.6	16.6	40.2	47.0	25.8	1,048	92.3
Shadyside village	3,740	3,547	-5.2	3,727	96.9	0.3	0.9	2.0	0.0	15.3	23.4	46.0	49.2	19.9	1,585	85.3
Shaker Heights city	28,466	27,027	-5.1	27,387	54.6	35.0	4.2	4.0	2.2	25.5	18.4	40.0	13.3	66.6	11,200	94.3
Sharonville city	13,443	13,684	1.8	14,133	76.5	9.7	4.2	3.3	6.3	20.4	19.0	39.9	35.7	39.4	6,389	91.4
Shawnee CDP	724	-	-	739	98.9	0.0	0.0	1.1	0.0	16.2	10.4	51.5	61.0	21.6	300	86.0
Shawnee village	655	642	-2.0	391	97.4	0.0	0.0	1.5	1.0	34.0	15.9	37.4	65.1	11.2	133	86.5
Shawnee Hills village	677	820	21.1	895	94.6	0.0	3.0	2.3	0.0	32.1	7.4	37.0	9.2	64.0	297	98.7
Shawnee Hills CDP	2,171	-	-	2,316	98.0	0.0	0.4	0.6	1.0	20.9	19.6	44.6	44.1	25.6	902	93.2
Sheffield village	3,983	4,402	10.5	4,190	84.0	4.0	3.8	1.3	6.9	19.6	20.5	50.0	31.5	31.8	1,676	91.6
Sheffield Lake city	9,137	8,916	-2.4	8,968	84.4	1.1	0.0	1.6	12.9	20.9	18.5	41.3	45.4	18.8	3,485	91.9
Shelby city	9,328	9,031	-3.2	8,866	96.5	0.2	0.0	0.2	3.1	20.6	21.3	45.7	56.4	15.0	4,073	81.8
Sherrodsville village	304	280	-7.9	195	97.4	0.0	0.0	0.0	2.6	12.3	24.6	52.8	72.0	6.2	83	81.9
Sherwood village	827	811	-1.9	821	92.3	0.5	0.1	0.0	7.1	30.2	18.3	36.1	52.2	15.8	314	90.1
Sherwood CDP	3,719	-	-	3,328	91.7	0.0	1.7	1.7	4.9	22.9	18.1	44.7	17.1	61.3	1,307	97.1
Shiloh village	640	619	-3.3	602	99.2	0.0	0.0	0.2	0.7	25.6	11.8	39.7	66.9	2.2	207	89.4
Shreve village	1,522	1,520	-0.1	1,633	98.2	0.0	0.0	0.8	1.0	29.8	10.6	32.7	57.8	9.3	655	89.5
Sidney city	21,219	20,449	-3.6	20,590	86.8	5.4	2.0	2.9	2.9	24.4	14.9	37.1	51.2	19.4	8,233	88.0
Silver Lake village	2,522	2,494	-1.1	2,532	96.1	1.2	0.5	2.3	0.0	18.8	24.0	50.5	20.0	60.1	977	94.8
Silverton village	4,775	4,727		4,760	39.5	46.9	1.4	9.4	2.9	19.9	18.8	40.3	39.5	26.2	2,281	77.9
Sinking Spring village	134	133	-0.7	167	98.8	0.0	0.0	1.2	0.0	18.0	10.2	24.9	46.3	7.3	59	88.1
Sixteen Mile Stand CDP	2,928	-	-	2,746	67.9	5.9	22.9	2.1	1.2	23.6	18.6	41.7	9.8	77.0	1,186	94.1
Skyline Acres CDP	1,717	-	-	2,266	8.6	85.5	0.3	5.6	0.0	38.4	8.6	27.2	46.0	7.0	714	88.4
Smithfield village	852	790	-7.3	795	88.3	1.6	0.0	10.1	0.0	26.5	17.1	29.3	49.6	12.3	302	74.5
Smithville village	1,250	1,259	0.7	1,439	91.8	1.4	1.4	1.9	3.5	23.3	18.0	41.6	47.0	26.3	588	92.9
Solon city	23,360	22,779	-2.5	22,947	70.9	12.5	11.2	3.8	1.6	26.0	16.8	44.5	17.1	61.4	8,481	94.0
Somerset village	1,482	1,455	-1.8	1,728	94.4	0.8	1.9	2.3	0.6	25.1	15.6	38.3	50.6	12.8	656	89.2
Somerville CDP	281	-	-	346	100.0	0.0	0.0	0.0	0.0	23.4	11.8	41.1	76.4	8.3	119	85.7
South Amherst village	1,715	1,675	-2.3	1,820	93.9	0.0	0.7	0.7	4.7	15.1	19.0	49.6	51.1	13.0	715	90.1
South Bloomfield village	1,790	1,979	10.6	2,075	94.5	1.5	0.0	1.2	2.9	26.1	10.6	36.3	55.9	12.8	722	96.0
South Canal CDP	1,100	-	-	940	99.0	0.0	0.0	0.0	1.0	12.7	20.9	53.9	63.2	18.5	422	90.3
South Charleston village	1,681	1,619	-3.7	1,865	93.1	1.4	0.5	1.1	3.9	25.3	14.5	35.1	50.1	12.0	775	87.1
South Euclid city	22,288	21,297	-4.4	21,572	44.2	44.9	2.0	6.2	2.8	20.0	16.0	38.7	28.9	39.6	9,071	87.9

1 May be of any race.

Table A. All Places — **Population and Housing**

STATE City, town, township, borough, or CDP (county if applicable)	Population: 2010 census total population	Population: 2019 estimated population	Population: Percent change 2010–2019	Population: ACS total population estimate 2015–2019	Race and Hispanic or Latino origin (percent): White alone, not Hispanic or Latino	Race and Hispanic or Latino origin (percent): Black alone, not Hispanic or Latino	Race and Hispanic or Latino origin (percent): Asian alone, not Hispanic or Latino	Race and Hispanic or Latino origin (percent): All other races or 2 or more races, not Hispanic or Latino	Race and Hispanic or Latino origin (percent): Hispanic or Latino[1]	Age (percent): Under 18 years old	Age (percent): Age 65 years and older	Age (percent): Median age	Educational attainment of persons age 25 and older: Percent High school diploma or less	Educational attainment of persons age 25 and older: Percent Bachelor's degree or more	Occupied housing units: Total	Occupied housing units: Percent with a computer
	1	2	3	4	5	6	7	8	9	10	11	12	13	14	15	16
OHIO—Con.																
South Lebanon village	4,109	4,668	13.6	4,337	83.4	5.6	1.5	3.6	6.0	21.1	19.0	40.2	37.5	47.0	1,766	88.1
South Point village	3,958	3,839	-3.0	3,481	88.3	3.9	1.2	3.1	3.4	19.4	19.2	41.6	48.4	19.1	1,494	91.2
South Russell village	3,822	3,744	-2.0	3,776	99.4	0.0	0.0	0.0	0.6	26.8	17.6	45.2	8.5	70.9	1,400	97.9
South Salem village	204	201	-1.5	287	99.0	0.0	0.0	1.0	0.0	33.8	8.0	34.4	57.1	12.5	108	96.3
South Solon village	355	364	2.5	345	85.2	0.3	0.0	0.9	13.6	22.3	17.1	34.1	68.0	7.4	124	90.3
South Vienna village	416	400	-3.8	527	98.1	0.0	0.0	0.0	1.9	19.0	14.8	36.4	46.6	17.3	203	95.6
South Webster village	870	805	-7.5	717	97.6	0.0	0.0	2.4	0.0	21.3	29.7	50.8	57.0	17.5	345	72.8
South Zanesville village	1,986	2,095	5.5	2,194	91.0	0.8	0.0	6.0	2.2	21.8	19.9	41.4	66.6	6.1	1,001	85.6
Sparta village	161	160	-0.6	175	74.3	0.0	1.7	21.7	2.3	20.6	5.7	37.3	62.4	4.0	64	87.5
Spencer village	753	789	4.8	585	98.6	0.3	0.0	1.0	0.0	17.6	18.1	43.6	69.5	9.6	251	75.3
Spencerville village	2,225	2,161	-2.9	2,261	95.7	1.2	0.0	2.3	0.8	34.3	16.6	30.7	59.9	11.0	791	86.3
Springboro city	17,366	18,931	9.0	18,196	91.8	1.8	1.8	1.6	3.1	30.6	12.7	36.9	21.5	53.8	6,266	96.6
Springdale city	11,224	11,166	-0.5	11,217	43.0	37.0	2.4	1.0	16.6	26.3	19.8	41.2	41.7	31.7	4,554	89.1
Springfield city	60,563	58,877	-2.8	59,132	71.6	17.0	0.9	6.2	4.3	24.2	17.0	35.8	55.6	14.9	23,846	85.6
Spring Valley village	476	499	4.8	543	100.0	0.0	0.0	0.0	0.0	18.6	12.7	44.5	57.8	10.8	239	91.2
Stafford village	81	75	-7.4	98	100.0	0.0	0.0	0.0	0.0	33.7	21.4	43.5	60.0	6.2	34	79.4
Sterling CDP	457	-	-	367	90.5	1.6	0.0	7.9	0.0	22.6	9.8	36.3	35.3	10.1	165	97.6
Steubenville city	18,659	17,753	-4.9	17,988	76.7	14.7	1.3	4.5	2.8	18.0	20.3	40.0	49.3	21.3	7,228	80.7
Stewart CDP	247	-	-	411	97.3	0.0	0.0	2.7	0.0	37.5	5.4	26.1	71.6	0.0	130	91.5
Stockdale CDP	135	-	-	-	-	-	-	-	-	-	-	-	-	-	-	-
Stockport village	508	483	-4.9	575	94.3	0.5	1.7	2.3	1.2	24.2	15.5	36.5	62.6	7.5	223	76.7
Stone Creek village	177	171	-3.4	156	100.0	0.0	0.0	0.0	0.0	28.2	12.2	34.0	49.0	12.7	66	98.5
Stony Prairie CDP	1,284	-	-	1,449	55.7	6.5	0.0	0.0	37.8	18.0	13.7	40.9	71.9	4.3	513	92.4
Stony Ridge CDP	411	-	-	521	83.3	0.0	0.0	0.0	16.7	33.2	13.1	34.2	65.3	15.6	252	96.0
Stoutsville village	565	565	0.0	640	94.1	0.0	0.0	5.0	0.9	23.6	9.1	32.3	46.8	14.8	220	89.5
Stow city	34,837	34,785	-0.1	34,776	90.7	3.6	2.1	2.1	1.5	20.6	17.8	39.7	26.1	48.1	14,299	92.0
Strasburg village	2,608	2,688	3.1	2,678	99.6	0.0	0.0	0.4	0.0	16.6	26.7	46.0	53.8	19.6	1,168	84.3
Stratton village	294	275	-6.5	385	93.0	1.3	0.0	3.6	2.1	23.1	19.0	42.6	69.3	1.5	171	85.4
Streetsboro city	16,023	16,478	2.8	16,406	84.4	8.0	1.4	2.6	3.5	21.1	14.1	39.0	42.0	28.7	6,498	94.8
Strongsville city	44,750	44,660	-0.2	44,719	87.7	2.4	4.7	2.1	3.1	20.8	20.9	45.7	26.6	46.4	17,880	92.2
Struthers city	10,715	10,111	-5.6	10,242	90.5	3.0	0.3	1.5	4.7	22.8	16.6	38.8	55.2	16.3	4,235	84.5
Stryker village	1,343	1,300	-3.2	1,314	81.8	0.4	0.5	2.1	15.2	28.8	11.9	31.6	51.2	8.3	473	92.2
Sugar Bush Knolls village	185	183	-1.1	199	96.0	0.0	4.0	0.0	0.0	15.1	34.7	52.5	15.9	64.3	77	94.8
Sugarcreek village	2,218	2,234	0.7	2,245	98.8	0.0	0.3	0.8	0.2	24.3	18.4	38.4	58.6	19.1	902	89.9
Sugar Grove village	426	426	0.0	370	95.4	0.0	0.0	4.6	0.0	28.6	8.1	37.4	52.7	15.9	132	96.2
Sulphur Springs CDP	194	-	-	111	54.1	36.0	0.0	0.0	9.9	0.0	24.3	54.8	35.7	16.3	41	100.0
Summerfield village	254	248	-2.4	238	100.0	0.0	0.0	0.0	0.0	22.7	34.9	52.4	64.0	5.1	98	69.4
Summerside CDP	5,083	-	-	4,666	97.0	1.1	0.0	0.6	1.3	25.4	21.1	40.0	53.2	17.6	1,881	88.7
Summitville village	132	123	-6.8	97	97.9	0.0	0.0	0.0	2.1	23.7	22.7	43.3	74.2	6.1	37	81.1
Sunbury village	4,405	6,367	44.5	5,573	88.7	1.5	2.1	4.9	2.8	27.3	13.1	35.2	35.5	35.7	1,878	92.7
Swanton village	3,844	3,858	0.4	3,797	91.9	0.4	0.0	0.0	7.8	27.5	18.5	36.7	44.1	19.7	1,357	90.9
Sycamore village	856	814	-4.9	841	99.4	0.0	0.0	0.6	0.0	22.0	20.2	43.3	52.3	19.8	390	89.0
Sylvania city	19,095	19,311	1.1	19,143	88.5	2.1	3.2	2.3	3.9	21.3	20.9	43.1	24.1	46.5	7,802	91.2
Syracuse village	829	816	-1.6	882	96.5	0.0	0.0	3.5	0.0	26.3	16.0	36.2	44.2	21.1	340	88.5
Tallmadge city	17,545	17,519	-0.1	17,589	91.8	5.0	0.2	2.8	0.2	20.3	22.5	46.5	33.1	35.4	7,113	91.0
Tarlton village	282	290	2.8	241	90.9	0.0	0.0	2.9	6.2	13.7	13.3	41.6	62.1	18.1	94	72.3
Taylor Creek CDP	3,062	-	-	3,307	91.8	4.7	0.3	3.2	0.0	21.0	18.2	44.1	34.3	36.8	1,413	98.3
Tedrow CDP	173	-	-	189	48.1	0.0	0.0	0.0	51.9	23.3	14.3	39.3	69.5	7.8	85	63.5
Terrace Park village	2,253	2,295	1.9	2,294	96.3	0.1	0.3	0.6	2.7	33.7	10.1	39.5	5.7	83.0	766	97.8
The Plains CDP	3,080	-	-	2,946	92.0	0.8	0.4	6.8	0.0	14.6	24.8	50.0	52.4	24.0	1,362	82.3
The Village of Indian Hill city	5,712	5,786	1.3	5,762	83.9	0.5	11.8	1.7	2.1	28.2	18.2	48.8	4.0	87.0	2,032	97.9
Thornport CDP	1,004	-	-	997	100.0	0.0	0.0	0.0	0.0	12.7	38.2	60.8	44.6	37.9	465	92.0
Thornville village	995	1,008	1.3	1,042	96.2	0.9	0.0	1.7	1.2	29.9	15.8	38.5	47.1	14.5	430	87.0
Thurston village	604	604	0.0	609	96.2	0.0	0.0	3.1	0.7	32.7	11.2	36.0	62.4	8.7	224	87.1
Tiffin city	17,962	17,582	-2.1	17,577	89.6	3.7	1.7	1.4	3.6	18.8	18.0	37.2	51.3	19.5	6,981	84.3
Tiltonsville village	1,372	1,274	-7.1	1,406	95.4	0.5	0.0	2.7	1.4	21.6	16.0	43.4	57.4	14.0	628	81.1
Timberlake village	675	648	-4.0	736	94.2	0.4	0.4	3.4	1.6	15.6	22.1	51.3	35.0	24.0	306	91.2
Tipp City city	9,672	10,115	4.6	9,969	93.8	0.7	1.2	3.1	1.2	22.6	19.3	41.0	30.5	35.6	4,106	90.4
Tippecanoe CDP	121	-	-	98	100.0	0.0	0.0	0.0	0.0	0.0	19.4	54.5	100.0	0.0	49	83.7
Tiro village	280	262	-6.4	215	90.2	0.0	0.0	0.0	9.8	30.2	13.0	35.1	69.7	6.8	71	88.7
Toledo city	287,357	272,779	-5.1	276,614	58.7	27.0	1.3	4.3	8.6	23.5	14.1	35.1	46.7	18.3	118,365	87.7
Tontogany village	370	382	3.2	476	83.8	0.4	0.6	2.7	12.4	27.7	14.5	36.4	44.6	18.5	169	95.3
Toronto city	5,300	4,923	-7.1	5,280	96.1	2.3	0.0	1.2	0.4	24.5	17.6	39.5	56.5	14.5	2,275	80.6
Tremont City village	377	357	-5.3	345	95.1	1.2	0.3	0.3	3.2	24.1	18.3	42.1	54.1	15.7	141	89.4
Trenton city	11,881	13,141	10.6	12,901	94.7	1.9	0.0	1.1	2.4	30.0	12.0	33.6	47.0	14.5	4,394	94.9
Trimble village	401	404	0.7	511	92.8	0.0	0.0	6.8	0.4	29.2	10.4	35.4	59.2	6.5	172	79.1
Trinway CDP	365	-	-	184	100.0	0.0	0.0	0.0	0.0	0.0	19.0	56.8	57.6	34.2	140	68.6
Trotwood city	24,431	24,403	-0.1	24,375	26.4	67.5	0.4	4.3	1.4	21.9	20.6	42.7	48.2	15.6	10,454	87.9
Troy city	25,179	26,281	4.4	25,961	87.8	4.0	3.2	2.7	2.3	24.1	16.6	37.9	42.4	25.3	10,475	90.2
Tuppers Plains CDP	465	-	-	401	100.0	0.0	0.0	0.0	0.0	26.7	8.7	39.7	31.0	2.8	153	93.5
Turpin Hills CDP	5,099	-	-	5,870	92.8	1.2	0.5	1.4	4.1	30.9	13.5	39.2	12.4	69.0	2,078	97.3
Tuscarawas village	1,056	1,053	-0.3	1,413	97.1	0.8	0.0	2.1	0.0	23.9	13.0	38.7	66.5	9.8	580	89.7
Twinsburg city	18,510	18,856	1.9	18,707	73.1	14.0	5.6	4.0	3.4	24.1	18.9	45.0	28.7	45.5	7,822	90.7
Twinsburg Heights CDP	925	-	-	679	0.0	73.0	0.0	2.8	24.2	26.8	10.5	28.6	34.5	21.3	282	95.4
Uhrichsville city	5,413	5,314	-1.8	5,348	93.3	1.2	0.1	2.3	3.1	22.1	14.7	35.6	67.5	9.2	2,046	85.5
Union city	6,448	6,891	6.9	6,628	94.3	2.6	0.6	1.0	1.6	24.8	14.9	40.6	40.6	23.5	2,527	95.1
Union City village	1,666	1,588	-4.7	1,701	76.4	2.7	1.8	1.6	17.6	30.5	16.2	34.8	72.3	2.9	646	78.5
Uniontown CDP	3,309	-	-	3,241	96.5	0.0	1.0	1.5	1.0	25.3	17.0	44.4	38.2	31.7	1,262	88.4
Unionville Center village	237	229	-3.4	243	84.4	2.5	0.0	1.2	11.9	26.7	8.6	38.3	52.1	16.8	88	92.0
Uniopolis CDP	222	-	-	299	100.0	0.0	0.0	0.0	0.0	17.1	17.7	48.6	64.7	2.6	129	99.2
University Heights city	13,539	12,797	-5.5	13,025	69.2	23.4	1.8	2.6	3.0	22.2	11.3	29.1	17.1	58.1	4,417	93.9
Upper Arlington city	33,666	35,366	5.0	35,299	88.3	0.3	6.8	2.0	2.6	26.6	17.1	40.6	8.7	77.1	13,790	97.3
Upper Sandusky city	6,602	6,440	-2.5	6,696	94.0	0.0	0.1	0.9	4.9	23.1	20.4	38.2	50.5	21.9	2,874	88.7
Urbana city	11,872	11,404	-3.9	11,496	87.2	4.5	0.3	5.0	3.0	20.9	19.8	39.1	59.0	15.2	4,934	89.9
Urbancrest village	952	993	4.3	981	25.6	57.9	3.1	7.4	6.0	39.7	7.7	25.5	56.4	7.7	334	73.7
Utica village	2,145	2,260	5.4	1,760	96.7	0.4	0.0	2.9	0.0	19.1	23.0	44.4	55.5	12.5	712	90.7
Valley City CDP	-	-	-	520	100.0	0.0	0.0	0.0	0.0	14.2	30.2	51.2	30.5	35.2	203	100.0
Valley Hi village	214	218	1.9	181	93.4	0.0	0.0	3.9	2.8	17.1	8.8	38.3	61.6	4.8	86	93.0
Valley View village	2,034	1,997	-1.8	2,024	96.3	0.7	0.6	1.9	0.4	20.5	20.7	48.6	34.7	36.8	751	92.3
Valleyview village	616	638	3.6	525	89.3	1.3	0.0	5.5	3.8	16.6	17.7	41.5	55.4	16.0	220	83.6
Van Buren village	324	500	54.3	428	98.4	0.0	0.0	0.0	1.6	31.3	10.5	35.8	39.1	13.4	147	98.0

1 May be of any race.

Table A. All Places — **Population and Housing**

STATE City, town, township, borough, or CDP (county if applicable)	Population: 2010 census total population	Population: 2019 estimated population	Population: Percent change 2010–2019	Population: ACS total population estimate 2015–2019	Race and Hispanic or Latino origin (percent): White alone, not Hispanic or Latino	Black alone, not Hispanic or Latino	Asian alone, not Hispanic or Latino	All other races or 2 or more races, not Hispanic or Latino	Hispanic or Latino[1]	Age (percent): Under 18 years old	Age 65 years and older	Median age	Educational attainment of persons age 25 and older: Percent High school diploma or less	Percent Bachelor's degree or more	Occupied housing units: Total	Percent with a computer
	1	2	3	4	5	6	7	8	9	10	11	12	13	14	15	16
OHIO—Con.																
Vandalia city	15,256	14,997	-1.7	15,045	90.8	4.8	1.1	2.7	0.7	19.7	18.2	41.0	37.6	24.8	6,725	90.2
Vanlue village	362	355	-1.9	328	94.2	1.2	0.0	0.9	3.7	23.8	11.6	39.7	49.1	22.1	126	92.9
Van Wert city	10,857	10,676	-1.7	11,045	91.5	2.6	0.7	0.9	4.3	25.5	19.6	39.6	53.7	17.0	4,549	87.7
Vaughnsville CDP	262	-	-	197	100.0	0.0	0.0	0.0	0.0	26.4	33.0	50.9	27.6	0.0	100	66.0
Venedocia village	124	119	-4.0	127	100.0	0.0	0.0	0.0	0.0	32.3	18.1	35.5	77.6	5.9	47	80.9
Vermilion city	10,587	10,394	-1.8	10,479	97.0	0.1	0.0	0.7	2.1	19.5	26.0	49.8	44.6	27.7	4,403	91.4
Verona village	496	478	-3.6	423	100.0	0.0	0.0	0.0	0.0	23.9	13.2	37.4	60.1	6.1	166	87.3
Versailles village	2,687	2,560	-4.7	2,700	98.7	0.4	0.0	0.9	0.0	26.8	21.0	41.0	51.7	21.8	1,073	87.8
Vickery CDP	121	-	-	142	100.0	0.0	0.0	0.0	0.0	16.9	12.7	30.8	53.4	40.7	36	100.0
Vienna Center CDP	650	-	-	546	100.0	0.0	0.0	0.0	0.0	18.7	15.8	47.9	49.5	13.0	237	97.0
Vincent CDP	339	-	-	337	100.0	0.0	0.0	0.0	0.0	26.4	5.3	36.1	77.3	7.6	131	67.9
Vinton village	217	210	-3.2	267	97.8	1.9	0.0	0.4	0.0	12.4	21.0	50.2	63.9	10.6	100	87.0
Wadsworth city	21,562	24,046	11.5	23,426	95.3	1.4	0.6	1.9	0.8	22.9	17.7	38.9	33.1	38.5	9,495	92.8
Waite Hill village	471	455	-3.4	458	97.2	0.0	0.0	2.2	0.7	22.9	33.8	51.9	21.0	60.2	188	95.2
Wakeman village	1,047	1,032	-1.4	1,060	93.7	0.0	1.4	0.5	4.4	19.9	18.4	47.3	48.6	15.8	501	85.0
Walbridge village	3,014	3,153	4.6	3,123	95.3	0.0	0.0	1.4	3.2	14.2	24.9	51.0	49.8	15.8	1,570	85.2
Waldo village	339	324	-4.4	275	95.3	0.0	0.0	3.3	1.5	17.8	25.8	47.8	51.9	14.6	136	85.3
Walnut Creek CDP	878	-	-	1,107	100.0	0.0	0.0	0.0	0.0	24.7	32.4	50.0	61.9	16.6	295	72.5
Walton Hills village	2,281	2,269	-0.5	2,246	79.9	15.9	0.7	1.1	2.4	9.0	32.9	58.6	47.0	27.0	942	88.7
Wapakoneta city	9,869	9,698	-1.7	9,683	92.4	0.6	0.0	1.9	5.2	23.6	18.5	39.0	54.1	11.3	4,242	91.1
Warren city	41,584	38,752	-6.8	39,307	66.2	26.3	0.4	3.9	3.3	22.5	17.4	39.1	59.2	14.0	16,933	81.5
Warrensville Heights city	13,542	13,108	-3.2	13,203	3.9	91.6	0.4	1.9	2.1	26.4	17.5	35.0	41.6	15.1	6,054	86.3
Warsaw village	696	693	-0.4	604	100.0	0.0	0.0	0.0	0.0	24.2	16.4	42.0	55.9	8.9	249	88.0
Washington Court House city	14,234	14,091		14,114	90.9	2.5	1.2	3.1	2.2	25.0	19.0	40.0	60.7	17.3	6,057	85.2
Washingtonville village	801	750	-6.4	917	90.8	1.0	4.0	2.5	1.6	22.2	17.7	40.8	64.7	12.9	385	88.3
Waterford CDP	450	-	-	464	100.0	0.0	0.0	0.0	0.0	25.4	34.7	40.6	66.7	21.3	188	85.1
Waterville city	5,512	5,539	0.5	5,487	92.4	0.1	0.9	2.7	3.8	24.7	19.0	42.2	28.0	46.0	2,169	91.1
Wauseon city	7,389	7,410	0.3	7,413	81.6	0.2	1.1	1.5	15.6	26.3	14.9	37.3	54.0	18.2	2,793	91.0
Waverly village	4,406	4,236	-3.9	4,291	95.9	1.6	0.0	2.4	0.1	17.3	26.0	46.1	52.9	15.2	2,028	79.1
Wayne village	887	921	3.8	1,021	90.0	1.3	0.4	6.9	1.5	25.4	12.0	35.0	57.6	6.8	383	95.6
Wayne Lakes village	717	682	-4.9	715	92.7	0.4	0.0	6.9	0.0	22.0	19.4	43.8	47.1	18.1	300	87.7
Waynesburg village	918	908	-1.1	970	92.3	0.4	0.5	5.2	1.6	22.7	14.5	35.1	60.8	12.1	378	80.7
Waynesfield village	842	817	-3.0	654	94.6	0.5	1.1	2.0	1.8	19.4	13.8	34.5	62.6	11.7	278	90.6
Waynesville village	2,813	3,181	13.1	3,081	96.9	0.4	0.0	1.0	1.7	25.3	20.0	41.7	39.5	33.8	1,163	89.8
Wellington village	4,807	4,912	2.2	5,135	91.8	0.1	0.1	4.3	3.7	19.9	24.1	40.9	46.9	19.1	2,212	82.2
Wellston city	5,662	5,507	-2.7	5,520	99.3	0.2	0.0	0.2	0.3	27.4	20.3	37.3	65.1	12.6	2,206	86.9
Wellsville village	3,541	3,306	-6.6	3,352	93.1	5.0	0.0	1.3	0.7	26.7	16.1	41.7	68.7	5.5	1,477	79.7
West Alexandria village	1,379	1,325	-3.9	1,567	94.3	0.0	1.0	0.0	4.7	24.2	17.0	35.4	52.6	21.0	639	86.2
West Carrollton city	13,148	12,864	-2.2	12,913	77.0	12.4	1.0	4.7	5.0	21.8	17.5	36.6	46.9	16.7	5,822	92.5
West Elkton village	197	188	-4.6	188	100.0	0.0	0.0	0.0	0.0	30.9	10.1	37.7	69.8	0.0	80	85.0
Westerville city	36,264	41,103	13.3	39,877	84.4	7.2	2.2	3.7	2.5	22.2	19.4	41.9	22.7	52.4	14,566	94.2
West Farmington village	517	484	-6.4	461	98.7	0.0	0.0	0.2	1.1	39.5	7.2	26.0	71.3	9.0	140	77.9
Westfield Center village	1,119	1,179	5.4	1,212	97.2	0.0	0.0	0.8	2.0	18.7	24.7	49.3	31.9	43.9	499	93.0
West Hill CDP	2,273	-	-	2,033	92.9	2.1	0.0	3.5	1.5	17.6	18.3	49.0	72.0	10.5	989	78.1
West Jefferson village	4,230	4,431	4.8	4,364	96.0	0.0	0.0	1.8	2.2	19.5	18.9	43.4	61.3	14.0	1,686	88.8
West Lafayette village	2,326	2,307	-0.8	2,307	97.8	0.0	0.3	1.2	0.7	26.3	18.9	40.0	67.4	9.8	957	83.8
Westlake city	32,729	32,032	-2.1	32,275	86.5	2.9	4.9	3.1	2.6	19.9	24.0	46.9	21.1	52.6	13,809	93.1
West Leipsic village	202	190	-5.9	211	63.5	0.0	0.0	0.0	36.5	25.6	12.3	39.6	53.7	7.4	82	87.8
West Liberty village	1,802	1,799	-0.2	1,663	94.8	0.7	0.4	2.2	2.0	21.8	24.1	44.5	47.6	15.5	733	82.7
West Manchester village	468	446	-4.7	450	94.4	0.0	0.7	4.4	0.4	32.9	8.9	33.5	55.2	11.1	151	93.4
West Mansfield village	681	678	-0.4	697	93.5	0.0	1.3	5.2	0.0	23.7	17.6	37.6	69.0	8.4	287	85.0
West Millgrove village	174	176	1.1	162	100.0	0.0	0.0	0.0	0.0	25.9	14.2	36.5	34.5	8.4	52	92.3
West Milton village	4,627	4,828	4.3	4,752	97.3	0.0	0.3	1.8	0.6	19.1	20.9	44.4	58.8	13.9	2,044	90.1
Westminster CDP	-	-	-	492	96.3	0.0	0.0	0.0	3.7	31.5	4.9	31.8	50.3	2.2	165	94.5
Weston village	1,590	1,647	3.6	1,447	84.2	1.0	1.0	3.2	10.5	24.2	12.4	36.8	49.4	15.3	554	93.3
West Portsmouth CDP	3,149	-	-	3,213	99.2	0.0	0.2	0.6	0.0	22.9	17.5	39.0	60.5	8.9	1,257	88.0
West Rushville village	143	143	0.0	239	96.2	0.0	0.0	3.8	0.0	38.9	3.8	27.9	53.2	11.9	64	96.9
West Salem village	1,494	1,511	1.1	1,622	95.4	0.0	0.0	2.7	1.8	25.0	11.5	33.5	67.4	5.3	625	86.6
West Union village	3,249	3,161	-2.7	2,616	99.4	0.2	0.0	0.3	0.1	20.4	24.0	44.6	61.8	12.0	1,164	71.6
West Unity village	1,712	1,672	-2.3	1,835	89.8	0.4	0.4	1.4	8.1	27.6	11.0	32.8	56.0	14.0	718	90.7
Wetherington CDP	1,302	-	-	1,399	80.6	3.3	10.2	2.8	3.1	13.3	24.5	51.0	15.3	69.6	609	91.3
Wharton village	359	338	-5.8	354	100.0	0.0	0.0	0.0	0.0	21.2	9.6	32.6	56.7	12.9	141	89.4
Wheelersburg CDP	6,437	-	-	6,082	95.8	0.0	0.6	3.1	0.4	22.2	21.5	42.4	50.8	24.6	2,421	83.7
Whitehall city	18,135	18,926	4.4	18,915	37.3	39.2	1.0	5.8	16.7	28.5	10.0	31.6	54.5	14.5	7,243	88.4
Whitehouse village	4,133	4,845	17.2	4,735	98.0	0.3	0.0	0.1	1.6	28.0	17.0	40.1	28.1	41.2	1,813	94.4
White Oak CDP	19,167	-	-	19,271	78.6	8.9	6.9	3.4	2.1	21.8	17.3	41.6	43.0	27.3	8,078	93.5
Whites Landing CDP	375	-	-	291	100.0	0.0	0.0	0.0	0.0	4.8	13.4	58.1	65.1	22.2	149	70.5
Wickliffe city	12,756	12,744	-0.1	12,743	88.2	5.4	1.0	3.4	2.0	17.9	20.9	45.0	42.3	24.3	5,658	88.8
Wightmans Grove CDP	72	-	-	43	100.0	0.0	0.0	0.0	0.0	0.0	55.8	68.2	88.4	0.0	25	48.0
Wilberforce CDP	2,271	-	-	2,311	32.3	57.7	0.1	2.7	7.1	9.8	2.5	19.8	24.8	26.7	173	100.0
Wilkesville village	149	144	-3.4	167	100.0	0.0	0.0	0.0	0.0	22.8	19.2	38.4	52.3	15.6	64	98.4
Willard city	6,241	6,016	-3.6	6,041	77.4	2.2	1.0	3.2	16.3	24.7	16.7	34.7	63.8	11.9	2,377	86.9
Williamsburg village	2,477	2,569	3.7	2,550	98.1	0.8	0.0	0.9	0.2	24.1	15.9	37.1	55.5	8.7	1,000	85.4
Williamsdale CDP	581	-	-	893	100.0	0.0	0.0	0.0	0.0	34.7	10.4	26.3	83.8	4.2	229	88.6
Williamsport village	1,036	1,074	3.7	959	98.9	0.0	0.0	0.8	0.3	28.7	12.8	35.0	65.8	7.9	329	86.0
Williston CDP	487	-	-	423	90.8	2.4	0.0	0.0	6.9	6.9	29.6	58.5	64.0	8.1	145	100.0
Willoughby city	22,242	22,977	3.3	22,869	91.6	4.3	1.5	1.8	0.7	18.4	20.7	43.7	33.7	31.6	10,903	88.8
Willoughby Hills city	9,486	9,553	0.7	9,527	68.4	20.8	6.5	1.2	3.1	14.5	20.7	44.2	32.5	39.7	4,644	93.8
Willowick city	14,178	14,105	-0.5	14,133	91.8	4.0	0.6	1.7	2.0	21.0	17.8	40.2	39.9	22.0	6,126	88.6
Willshire village	397	381	-4.0	369	97.3	0.0	0.0	2.4	0.3	23.8	19.0	45.1	75.4	4.8	153	84.3
Wilmington city	12,517	12,366	-1.2	12,392	86.7	5.8	0.6	5.3	1.6	22.3	17.8	34.9	49.6	22.3	5,100	85.6
Wilmot village	314	304	-3.2	313	96.2	2.9	0.0	1.0	0.0	18.8	8.6	40.3	72.2	3.1	130	80.8
Wilson village	125	116	-7.2	108	97.2	0.9	0.0	1.9	0.0	25.0	19.4	38.0	57.9	6.6	46	89.1
Winchester village	1,044	1,006	-3.6	1,034	99.2	0.3	0.0	0.3	0.2	23.8	18.2	42.4	62.0	13.1	421	88.4
Windham village	2,221	2,202	-0.9	2,036	92.8	3.5	0.0	2.8	0.9	27.0	12.8	35.3	62.3	10.1	739	88.2
Winesburg CDP	352	-	-	238	100.0	0.0	0.0	0.0	0.0	0.0	39.1	54.7	53.0	13.0	74	78.4
Wintersville village	3,924	3,669	-6.5	4,328	90.1	7.0	0.0	0.0	2.9	23.5	22.6	46.0	52.6	17.8	1,743	83.9
Withamsville CDP	7,021	-	-	7,789	90.8	1.9	2.8	4.3	0.1	23.9	14.7	37.5	43.3	25.6	3,092	91.6
Wolfhurst CDP	1,239	-	-	1,036	89.7	9.1	0.0	0.0	1.3	12.5	30.5	58.0	75.9	3.9	543	61.0
Woodlawn village	3,334	3,402	2.0	3,365	27.8	55.0	2.4	11.0	3.8	16.8	18.5	37.9	35.7	30.8	1,543	87.1
Woodmere village	884	853	-3.5	698	31.5	45.1	7.9	5.6	9.9	20.6	13.2	39.6	25.4	48.4	336	91.4

1 May be of any race.

Table A. All Places — Population and Housing

STATE City, town, township, borough, or CDP (county if applicable)	Population				Race and Hispanic or Latino origin (percent)					Age (percent)			Educational attainment of persons age 25 and older		Occupied housing units	
	2010 census total population	2019 estimated population	Percent change 2010–2019	ACS total population estimate 2015–2019	White alone, not Hispanic or Latino	Black alone, not Hispanic or Latino	Asian alone, not Hispanic or Latino	All other races or 2 or more races, not Hispanic or Latino	Hispanic or Latino[1]	Under 18 years old	Age 65 years and older	Median age	Percent High school diploma or less	Percent Bachelor's degree or more	Total	Percent with a computer
	1	2	3	4	5	6	7	8	9	10	11	12	13	14	15	16
OHIO—Con.																
Woodsfield village............	2,381	2,217	-6.9	2,352	90.3	2.1	0.0	1.2	6.4	22.9	24.5	45.5	57.7	12.5	998	76.6
Woodstock village............	301	291	-3.3	261	97.3	0.0	0.0	2.7	0.0	33.7	11.5	31.1	59.7	10.1	82	93.9
Woodville village..............	2,135	2,016	-5.6	2,228	92.0	0.0	0.0	0.0	8.0	25.4	16.1	41.2	42.7	23.6	915	83.9
Wooster city....................	26,177	26,394	0.8	26,673	88.9	3.4	3.0	3.1	1.5	19.0	18.6	37.9	42.8	28.9	10,977	87.4
Worthington city...............	13,569	14,692	8.3	14,621	90.5	2.7	2.7	2.6	1.5	25.6	21.8	41.8	13.2	68.8	5,695	95.4
Wren village....................	194	187	-3.6	125	88.0	0.0	0.0	0.0	12.0	17.6	25.6	53.6	47.5	10.1	56	80.4
Wright-Patterson AFB CDP..............................	1,821	-	-	2,387	61.3	20.1	4.4	5.2	9.0	27.2	4.2	22.6	20.8	43.4	542	95.2
Wyoming city...................	8,420	8,562	1.7	8,548	79.8	15.9	1.2	2.1	0.9	29.2	14.2	42.1	10.1	71.8	3,106	96.7
Xenia city.......................	25,643	26,947	5.1	26,534	81.9	11.6	0.2	4.6	1.8	23.2	17.9	38.8	49.5	18.5	10,909	87.3
Yankee Lake village.........	79	75	-5.1	87	90.8	2.3	0.0	6.9	0.0	16.1	37.9	56.3	53.6	17.4	43	83.7
Yellow Springs village.......	3,509	3,744	6.7	3,872	79.7	11.7	1.3	3.6	3.7	18.1	27.1	49.7	16.5	63.1	1,878	91.7
Yorkshire village..............	96	139	44.8	101	100.0	0.0	0.0	0.0	0.0	25.7	5.9	35.3	93.2	0.0	45	97.8
Yorkville village...............	1,075	1,005	-6.5	987	94.7	0.7	0.0	3.0	1.5	18.6	23.3	42.5	60.7	11.4	455	84.2
Youngstown city...............	66,946	65,469	-2.2	64,783	42.9	40.7	0.6	4.9	10.9	21.8	17.3	39.3	56.4	13.6	27,883	80.3
Zaleski village.................	278	271	-2.5	305	93.1	0.0	0.0	6.9	0.0	23.3	19.7	46.8	75.8	3.7	124	89.5
Zanesfield village.............	197	196	-0.5	261	98.1	0.0	0.0	1.9	0.0	31.8	11.1	37.3	34.0	19.9	103	96.1
Zanesville city.................	25,316	25,158	-0.6	25,200	83.0	7.3	0.5	6.9	2.3	24.5	17.6	36.2	58.1	12.1	10,636	81.1
Zoar village.....................	169	178	5.3	147	100.0	0.0	0.0	0.0	0.0	5.4	54.4	67.3	41.5	39.0	73	75.3
OKLAHOMA...................	3,751,582	3,956,971	5.5	3,932,870	65.6	7.1	2.1	14.5	10.6	24.3	15.3	36.6	43.3	25.5	1,480,061	88.6
Achille town....................	491	540	10.0	368	70.4	1.1	0.0	27.7	0.8	21.5	21.5	43.5	56.3	12.9	151	72.8
Ada city.........................	16,804	17,235	2.6	17,260	61.3	4.0	1.7	26.7	6.3	21.8	14.3	31.7	41.2	30.5	6,611	86.9
Adair town......................	827	811	-1.9	816	66.7	1.7	0.0	26.6	5.0	34.8	10.9	32.6	44.8	15.3	268	88.8
Addington town................	114	107	-6.1	126	81.0	3.2	0.8	4.0	11.1	23.0	23.8	43.5	50.0	11.6	50	86.0
Afton town......................	1,045	1,020	-2.4	1,138	71.4	0.0	0.6	25.4	2.5	32.8	14.1	34.1	61.8	7.2	411	88.3
Agra town.......................	339	344	1.5	302	82.5	0.7	0.0	12.6	4.3	17.9	21.5	42.2	70.7	7.3	115	80.0
Akins CDP......................	493	-	-	586	63.5	7.2	0.0	29.4	0.0	27.3	14.2	39.1	67.7	10.6	217	87.1
Albany CDP.....................	143	-	-	64	81.3	0.0	0.0	15.6	3.1	20.3	37.5	47.8	64.7	29.4	36	55.6
Albion town.....................	106	100	-5.7	99	63.6	0.0	0.0	25.3	11.1	18.2	20.2	43.5	63.5	5.4	35	65.7
Alderson town..................	304	289	-4.9	193	60.1	3.6	0.0	28.0	8.3	19.7	15.5	49.3	59.9	1.4	88	79.5
Alex town........................	548	548	0.0	548	86.3	1.3	0.0	6.8	5.7	23.7	16.6	35.1	64.5	11.5	226	83.2
Aline town.......................	207	212	2.4	124	96.8	0.0	0.0	3.2	0.0	16.1	21.0	47.0	78.8	8.7	53	90.6
Allen town.......................	932	926	-0.6	902	64.6	0.0	0.0	30.0	5.3	23.3	21.0	43.8	59.2	15.5	325	74.5
Altus city........................	19,756	18,338	-7.2	18,744	58.3	8.4	1.5	4.9	26.9	25.1	13.0	32.8	42.0	24.9	7,264	87.9
Alva city.........................	5,032	4,953	-1.6	5,109	83.3	3.2	2.0	4.0	7.4	19.1	15.9	31.3	37.3	34.3	1,903	82.7
Amber town.....................	419	480	14.6	437	81.9	0.0	0.0	10.3	7.8	30.2	15.1	32.6	55.1	9.8	164	84.1
Ames town......................	237	241	1.7	262	96.6	0.0	0.0	0.0	3.4	31.7	21.0	36.4	60.6	11.9	108	90.7
Amorita town...................	37	38	2.7	39	79.5	0.0	0.0	20.5	0.0	30.8	17.9	40.5	34.8	21.7	12	83.3
Anadarko city..................	6,761	6,504	-3.8	6,626	31.8	6.0	1.1	49.9	11.2	30.2	14.6	35.5	53.3	16.1	2,371	78.7
Antlers city.....................	2,444	2,321	-5.0	2,556	73.9	2.2	0.1	21.9	1.9	24.3	18.7	34.9	59.0	15.3	1,031	78.9
Apache town....................	1,448	1,393	-3.8	1,436	71.0	0.0	0.0	28.3	0.7	22.3	18.4	41.4	48.5	14.2	565	88.0
Arapaho town...................	796	803	0.9	744	63.4	1.5	0.0	23.4	11.7	33.2	9.3	32.5	58.3	11.0	199	91.0
Arcadia town...................	242	270	11.6	203	26.1	57.1	0.0	16.7	0.0	11.8	22.2	51.0	50.3	15.6	99	85.9
Ardmore city...................	24,469	24,698	0.9	24,821	63.0	9.6	2.0	14.7	10.7	25.6	16.6	37.2	46.0	21.8	9,593	85.5
Arkoma town...................	1,989	1,899	-4.5	1,821	75.7	1.2	0.2	20.2	2.7	25.2	18.7	40.9	69.1	10.0	751	77.1
Armstrong town................	105	116	10.5	103	68.9	0.0	0.0	31.1	0.0	22.3	22.3	44.8	59.2	13.2	39	84.6
Arnett town.....................	524	481	-8.2	563	95.0	0.0	0.4	1.8	2.8	19.0	31.3	49.5	52.6	24.1	253	84.2
Arpelar CDP....................	272	-	-	329	77.2	0.0	0.0	21.3	1.5	15.8	22.2	45.3	52.8	14.1	148	91.2
Asher town......................	391	412	5.4	423	71.6	0.0	0.0	23.2	5.2	28.4	16.8	34.6	57.6	10.0	136	83.1
Ashland town...................	66	63	-4.5	35	77.1	0.0	0.0	22.9	0.0	22.9	17.1	45.5	48.1	25.9	17	70.6
Atoka city.......................	2,969	3,015	1.5	2,973	63.8	4.4	3.3	23.9	4.5	28.6	16.6	40.8	57.7	12.3	1,204	84.6
Atwood town....................	74	69	-6.8	70	61.4	2.9	0.0	25.7	10.0	22.9	21.4	44.3	75.5	3.8	26	69.2
Avant town......................	320	307	-4.1	269	77.3	0.0	0.0	19.7	3.0	19.7	18.6	40.6	73.1	5.2	106	89.6
Badger Lee CDP..............	76	-	-	61	55.7	23.0	0.0	21.3	0.0	23.0	45.9	62.6	87.2	12.8	26	50.0
Ballou CDP......................	176	-	-	335	61.8	0.0	0.6	12.2	25.4	21.2	11.3	43.0	48.3	30.9	110	100.0
Barnsdall city..................	1,243	1,150	-7.5	1,033	73.4	0.5	0.0	24.5	1.6	22.8	23.9	43.6	53.9	18.9	439	78.6
Bartlesville city................	35,734	36,144	1.1	36,412	72.4	3.6	3.1	13.9	7.0	23.6	18.9	38.4	40.0	32.0	14,589	87.7
Bearden town..................	133	131	-1.5	112	69.6	1.8	0.0	25.9	2.7	30.4	17.0	32.4	40.3	30.6	38	86.8
Beaver town....................	1,517	1,399	-7.8	1,461	57.9	1.4	0.0	2.9	37.8	28.1	18.2	36.0	62.2	11.4	526	83.3
Bee CDP........................	140	-	-	137	79.6	0.0	4.4	16.1	0.0	33.6	24.8	35.0	71.4	6.6	61	65.6
Beggs city......................	1,269	1,237	-2.5	1,562	50.0	12.1	1.6	26.1	10.2	29.0	18.3	35.8	55.4	11.9	528	77.7
Belfonte CDP..................	394	-	-	416	26.2	0.0	0.0	48.3	25.5	31.7	16.1	41.3	75.4	4.0	126	79.4
Bell CDP........................	535	-	-	379	31.7	0.0	0.0	59.9	8.4	24.5	21.9	42.4	79.2	2.0	139	58.3
Bennington town...............	334	366	9.6	280	56.4	0.7	0.0	35.4	7.5	25.4	13.9	38.6	66.8	17.1	109	73.4
Bernice town...................	565	580	2.7	407	76.9	0.0	0.0	22.4	0.7	14.5	33.2	53.9	52.1	11.2	199	82.9
Bessie town....................	181	174	-3.9	163	78.5	0.0	0.0	14.7	6.7	27.0	18.4	38.5	62.6	16.8	70	85.7
Bethany city....................	19,024	19,221	1.0	19,366	64.2	8.5	1.0	10.3	16.0	25.7	18.2	35.0	40.1	25.3	7,497	87.8
Bethel Acres town............	2,896	3,193	10.3	3,147	76.6	0.8	0.8	17.1	4.6	25.7	16.3	40.1	44.4	18.3	1,028	91.9
Big Cabin town................	265	250	-5.7	192	67.7	1.6	1.0	27.6	2.1	14.6	21.9	47.0	48.9	8.6	91	76.9
Billings town...................	509	496	-2.6	595	79.8	0.0	0.0	20.2	0.0	23.2	10.3	33.1	77.9	3.5	164	85.4
Binger town....................	672	632	-6.0	619	72.2	8.4	0.0	13.1	6.3	22.1	25.4	44.3	60.0	13.9	228	82.0
Bison CDP......................	65	-	-	32	84.4	0.0	0.0	0.0	15.6	0.0	12.5	56.5	40.6	0.0	25	92.0
Bixby city.......................	20,912	27,944	33.6	26,541	76.9	2.7	2.7	11.7	6.1	29.2	14.1	35.9	24.4	44.4	9,438	96.2
Blackburn town................	108	107	-0.9	82	79.3	0.0	0.0	8.5	12.2	31.7	14.6	41.7	72.5	15.7	31	87.1
Blackgum CDP................	51	-	-	76	60.5	0.0	0.0	39.5	0.0	17.1	11.8	20.9	51.4	0.0	28	100.0
Blackwell city..................	7,092	6,562	-7.5	6,696	80.4	0.4	0.0	12.2	7.1	24.7	22.7	39.5	49.8	13.9	2,733	77.2
Blair town.......................	818	742	-9.3	765	66.5	0.0	0.0	7.8	25.6	29.7	22.0	36.7	50.5	13.4	300	93.0
Blanchard city..................	7,378	8,907	20.7	8,386	81.2	1.3	0.0	12.2	5.2	27.0	14.0	37.6	33.1	31.3	2,946	94.3
Blanco CDP....................	-	-	-	107	59.8	0.0	0.0	37.4	2.8	24.3	19.6	42.2	52.2	15.9	45	80.0
Blue CDP........................	195	-	-	226	50.4	0.0	0.0	33.6	15.9	40.7	8.4	34.3	45.5	9.0	74	89.2
Bluejacket town................	339	321	-5.3	304	59.9	2.6	2.3	31.9	3.3	19.1	10.9	47.7	66.2	5.6	102	65.7
Boise City city.................	1,268	1,085	-14.4	1,138	68.8	0.4	0.5	0.4	30.0	25.7	22.6	39.9	58.8	20.6	523	81.1
Bokchito town..................	628	687	9.4	641	77.7	0.0	0.5	20.7	1.1	24.0	17.9	39.3	65.5	6.8	245	78.8
Bokoshe town..................	509	497	-2.4	455	64.6	0.7	0.7	33.0	1.1	24.2	18.2	41.6	68.0	7.4	166	72.9
Boley town......................	1,184	1,174	-0.8	1,246	45.0	37.9	0.0	14.8	2.3	3.6	12.9	43.0	79.3	3.6	84	63.1
Boswell town...................	709	682	-3.8	679	62.0	11.0	0.0	21.4	5.6	33.3	17.2	31.2	66.4	6.9	282	66.0
Bowlegs town..................	403	388	-3.7	405	62.2	0.5	0.0	26.2	11.1	23.7	17.8	45.3	62.5	6.3	145	73.8
Box CDP.........................	224	-	-	139	59.0	0.0	0.0	41.0	0.0	9.4	29.5	55.7	47.6	5.6	59	35.6
Boynton town..................	248	241	-2.8	195	33.3	46.2	0.0	20.5	0.0	34.9	15.4	32.6	50.8	5.8	83	80.7
Bradley town...................	128	133	3.9	118	92.4	0.8	0.0	5.9	0.8	23.7	16.9	45.5	72.2	3.8	44	68.2

1 May be of any race.

Table A. All Places — **Population and Housing**

STATE City, town, township, borough, or CDP (county if applicable)	Population: 2010 census total population	Population: 2019 estimated population	Population: Percent change 2010–2019	Population: ACS total population estimate 2015–2019	Race and Hispanic or Latino origin (percent): White alone, not Hispanic or Latino	Black alone, not Hispanic or Latino	Asian alone, not Hispanic or Latino	All other races or 2 or more races, not Hispanic or Latino	Hispanic or Latino[1]	Age (percent): Under 18 years old	Age 65 years and older	Median age	Educational attainment of persons age 25 and older: Percent High school diploma or less	Percent Bachelor's degree or more	Occupied housing units: Total	Percent with a computer
	1	2	3	4	5	6	7	8	9	10	11	12	13	14	15	16
OKLAHOMA—Con.																
Braggs town	259	253	-2.3	240	62.1	0.0	0.0	33.8	4.2	31.3	12.9	35.0	52.3	9.9	85	74.1
Braman town	217	202	-6.9	180	83.3	1.1	0.0	9.4	6.1	22.8	27.8	44.5	59.1	5.5	83	65.1
Bray town	1,194	1,176	-1.5	1,057	84.8	0.5	1.1	11.8	1.8	19.1	16.7	41.7	60.1	15.8	366	89.9
Breckenridge town	245	245	0.0	217	95.4	0.0	0.0	4.6	0.0	29.0	27.6	39.7	49.0	25.2	74	74.3
Brent CDP	716	-	-	896	69.8	3.2	0.0	27.0	0.0	22.3	26.0	47.2	51.2	15.1	356	87.9
Bridge Creek town	325	336	3.4	333	88.3	0.9	0.0	4.8	6.0	25.5	12.3	39.1	50.0	14.5	114	97.4
Bridgeport city	111	109	-1.8	89	68.5	0.0	1.1	16.9	13.5	20.2	24.7	51.5	79.4	5.9	34	79.4
Briggs CDP	303	-	-	341	81.5	0.0	0.0	12.3	6.2	32.8	19.6	40.8	56.8	24.9	131	59.5
Bristow city	4,222	4,200	-0.5	4,257	70.8	4.4	0.0	20.2	4.5	26.1	17.6	35.7	57.6	10.4	1,658	78.2
Broken Arrow city	98,837	110,198	11.5	108,496	71.4	4.1	3.9	12.0	8.5	25.8	14.6	37.3	28.9	33.2	39,770	96.2
Broken Bow city	4,118	4,085	-0.8	4,104	51.0	7.4	0.5	28.1	12.9	30.6	14.2	30.9	70.7	8.5	1,448	70.9
Bromide town	167	166	-0.6	98	74.5	0.0	0.0	14.3	11.2	11.2	35.7	57.3	66.7	17.3	50	62.0
Brooksville town	59	60	1.7	49	28.6	69.4	0.0	2.0	0.0	20.4	28.6	45.7	59.5	2.7	22	63.6
Brush Creek CDP	35	-	-	15	33.3	0.0	0.0	66.7	0.0	0.0	0.0	0.0	100.0	0.0	15	33.3
Brushy CDP	900	-	-	1,217	56.0	0.0	4.0	39.9	0.0	29.0	13.8	36.1	68.7	11.4	345	78.0
Buffalo town	1,293	1,287	-0.5	1,338	73.8	0.1	0.0	1.6	24.4	29.8	19.7	40.6	56.7	19.1	468	90.4
Bull Hollow CDP	67	-	-	30	63.3	0.0	0.0	36.7	0.0	0.0	36.7	61.6	66.7	0.0	20	100.0
Burbank town	141	139	-1.4	106	61.3	0.0	0.0	38.7	0.0	19.8	11.3	39.0	67.5	20.8	45	73.3
Burlington town	154	159	3.2	146	89.7	0.0	0.0	9.6	0.7	42.5	15.1	27.0	41.8	38.0	39	84.6
Burneyville CDP	-	-	-	747	74.8	0.0	0.0	21.6	3.6	30.5	24.6	40.3	43.0	27.0	254	88.6
Burns Flat town	2,057	1,901	-7.6	2,260	72.5	4.9	0.0	10.4	12.3	31.7	9.7	31.9	56.0	14.5	690	95.4
Bushyhead CDP	1,314	-	-	1,280	67.9	1.6	0.9	27.9	1.7	19.2	14.3	37.1	60.7	7.0	487	81.5
Butler town	287	295	2.8	216	76.9	0.0	0.0	0.9	22.2	17.6	21.3	47.4	58.0	12.1	108	81.5
Butler CDP	117	-	-	164	58.5	0.0	0.0	41.5	0.0	15.2	24.4	50.6	45.3	28.8	71	100.0
Byars town	255	273	7.1	177	81.4	0.6	0.0	18.1	0.0	18.6	18.1	45.8	71.1	9.4	86	82.6
Byng town	1,180	1,198	1.5	1,303	61.9	3.1	0.0	31.0	4.1	26.5	16.5	39.1	40.7	28.5	456	87.7
Byron town	34	35	2.9	30	100.0	0.0	0.0	0.0	0.0	16.7	16.7	33.3	36.0	48.0	14	85.7
Cache city	2,783	2,811	1.0	2,842	61.8	4.5	0.8	23.0	9.9	24.6	13.3	34.1	45.9	19.0	952	92.6
Caddo town	1,009	1,104	9.4	1,203	74.0	0.4	0.0	23.9	1.7	20.9	19.5	39.8	48.5	25.1	450	83.6
Calera town	2,162	2,370	9.6	2,741	67.2	2.0	0.6	24.1	6.2	27.4	12.3	30.1	45.0	15.6	981	93.9
Calumet town	507	604	19.1	420	83.3	0.0	0.0	10.2	6.4	20.2	19.8	34.9	53.4	13.3	153	90.2
Calvin town	298	275	-7.7	319	69.6	0.0	0.0	15.4	15.0	36.1	19.7	31.7	47.0	23.2	104	69.2
Camargo town	178	181	1.7	169	100.0	0.0	0.0	0.0	0.0	31.4	20.7	44.1	25.9	40.7	59	93.2
Cameron town	302	293	-3.0	326	89.9	0.0	0.0	10.1	0.0	28.5	8.3	32.0	79.4	3.3	112	66.1
Canadian town	216	203	-6.0	149	79.2	0.0	0.0	20.8	0.0	22.1	25.5	46.9	57.1	9.9	61	83.6
Caney town	205	198	-3.4	202	76.7	0.0	0.0	22.8	0.5	32.2	22.8	34.0	59.2	13.8	89	83.1
Canton town	625	589	-5.8	432	71.3	0.0	0.0	25.2	3.5	23.6	20.8	41.3	55.6	23.1	221	84.2
Canute town	541	519	-4.1	531	85.7	0.8	0.0	3.0	10.5	26.2	15.4	38.3	53.6	13.4	194	87.6
Carlisle CDP	606	-	-	512	47.1	0.0	0.0	49.4	3.5	22.3	24.8	47.1	65.8	6.8	175	80.0
Carlton Landing town	-	-	-	10	80.0	0.0	0.0	20.0	0.0	20.0	0.0	32.5	25.0	75.0	4	100.0
Carmen town	355	358	0.8	426	84.3	0.0	0.0	2.8	12.9	22.8	23.2	40.2	54.2	18.5	167	73.7
Carnegie town	1,722	1,645	-4.5	1,829	50.2	1.6	0.0	29.9	18.3	27.6	17.0	35.9	58.1	10.8	705	82.0
Carney town	647	623	-3.7	643	90.5	0.8	0.0	4.4	4.4	23.0	18.2	34.5	54.4	8.7	215	76.7
Carrier town	85	84	-1.2	44	100.0	0.0	0.0	0.0	0.0	11.4	18.2	46.6	64.1	28.2	19	100.0
Carter town	265	251	-5.3	228	78.9	0.0	0.0	9.6	11.4	16.2	15.4	42.4	51.8	4.9	88	87.5
Cartwright CDP	609	-	-	626	82.9	2.1	1.3	12.1	1.6	15.7	31.6	51.5	59.0	16.1	235	85.5
Cashion town	797	871	9.3	810	89.1	0.6	0.0	6.7	3.6	24.8	12.3	35.3	43.9	20.9	301	89.4
Castle town	106	103	-2.8	121	58.7	1.7	0.0	39.7	0.0	24.0	23.1	43.8	68.4	1.3	48	66.7
Catoosa city	7,162	6,953	-2.9	7,705	65.3	2.2	0.5	21.2	10.7	21.1	13.7	36.7	53.2	14.5	3,063	93.2
Cayuga CDP	140	-	-	132	65.9	0.0	0.0	21.2	12.9	11.4	19.7	59.2	32.4	29.4	57	100.0
Cedar Crest CDP	312	-	-	157	47.8	0.0	0.0	52.2	0.0	22.3	15.3	47.6	79.0	0.0	76	65.8
Cedar Valley city	288	330	14.6	490	76.1	0.0	0.0	16.3	7.6	14.9	35.9	56.8	17.8	41.9	196	97.4
Cement town	501	475	-5.2	418	79.9	0.5	0.0	13.9	5.7	26.1	20.8	38.2	78.9	0.7	142	87.3
Centrahoma city	97	93	-4.1	69	72.5	0.0	0.0	27.5	0.0	33.3	21.7	37.5	77.3	0.0	29	55.2
Central High town	1,198	1,164	-2.8	1,244	84.0	2.1	1.0	6.8	6.2	21.3	20.5	42.1	40.5	31.7	459	91.1
Chandler city	3,091	3,085	-0.2	3,107	72.0	6.3	0.0	18.6	3.2	28.2	15.5	37.5	51.7	17.8	1,129	87.8
Chattanooga town	469	453	-3.4	460	71.1	0.0	0.4	22.6	5.9	31.5	13.9	34.7	53.3	18.2	159	86.2
Checotah city	3,335	3,095	-7.2	3,142	51.5	7.0	0.2	36.2	5.1	21.8	18.3	40.3	65.4	10.9	1,286	78.6
Chelsea town	1,978	1,907	-3.6	2,053	64.8	0.2	0.1	33.8	1.1	26.6	14.8	34.0	57.3	13.0	810	81.9
Cherokee city	1,494	1,489	-0.3	1,554	91.6	0.4	0.0	2.7	5.3	21.0	20.9	41.7	54.3	18.8	614	84.9
Cherry Tree CDP	883	-	-	1,058	13.1	0.2	0.0	77.5	9.2	31.1	7.8	31.7	68.8	7.1	283	61.1
Chester CDP	117	-	-	133	92.5	0.0	0.0	7.5	0.0	29.3	17.3	39.4	40.5	42.9	48	81.3
Chewey CDP	135	-	-	178	5.6	0.0	72.5	21.9	0.0	41.0	11.8	42.2	90.5	0.0	57	66.7
Cheyenne town	799	774	-3.1	767	74.6	0.1	0.0	4.8	20.5	33.8	9.5	31.8	44.0	14.5	287	93.4
Chickasha city	16,030	16,431	2.5	16,337	74.9	7.3	0.6	9.3	7.9	23.2	16.8	38.2	53.9	19.5	6,355	85.4
Choctaw city	11,132	12,674	13.9	12,474	82.5	3.3	0.6	9.2	4.4	25.0	16.8	41.1	38.8	29.1	4,669	92.5
Chouteau town	2,113	2,093	-0.9	2,066	69.5	0.0	0.3	25.0	5.1	25.8	18.3	37.0	45.6	17.7	797	83.4
Christie CDP	218	-	-	139	48.9	0.0	0.0	51.1	0.0	25.9	48.9	26.0	66.0	17.5	62	53.2
Cimarron City town	150	175	16.7	209	98.1	0.0	0.0	0.0	1.9	14.4	22.0	48.1	40.9	33.3	64	100.0
Claremore city	18,599	18,743	0.8	18,753	66.0	1.7	0.6	25.6	6.1	22.6	18.5	36.4	42.2	21.1	7,671	88.7
Clarita CDP	-	-	-	69	85.5	0.0	0.0	14.5	0.0	15.9	20.3	27.6	79.5	6.8	32	37.5
Clayton town	823	786	-4.5	634	65.5	0.0	0.0	27.8	6.8	22.7	23.5	40.7	57.0	7.2	297	73.1
Clearview town	48	48	0.0	27	7.4	77.8	0.0	14.8	0.0	11.1	44.4	58.5	62.5	12.5	17	70.6
Cleora CDP	1,463	-	-	1,396	79.3	0.0	0.0	20.3	0.4	14.1	35.8	57.6	34.4	29.4	596	91.8
Cleo Springs town	338	334	-1.2	336	87.8	0.0	0.0	6.8	5.4	33.0	19.6	35.8	50.7	19.4	126	93.7
Cleveland city	3,247	3,125	-3.8	3,137	75.1	1.7	1.2	18.5	3.5	23.3	17.9	40.4	51.1	17.3	1,208	86.6
Clinton city	9,030	9,087	0.6	9,217	51.4	4.7	2.0	11.1	30.8	31.6	16.6	35.8	52.3	17.5	3,311	86.2
Cloud Creek CDP	121	-	-	39	100.0	0.0	0.0	0.0	0.0	0.0	51.3	73.1	25.6	23.1	19	47.4
Coalgate city	1,968	1,792	-8.9	1,951	64.4	0.2	0.2	28.0	7.2	24.2	22.7	42.2	60.1	14.5	810	76.0
Colbert town	1,145	1,252	9.3	1,354	68.8	12.6	0.0	13.0	5.7	20.2	21.0	39.8	58.1	13.1	530	83.4
Colcord town	819	849	3.7	862	52.8	1.2	0.0	42.6	3.5	25.1	11.5	36.1	69.1	8.3	288	81.6
Cole town	555	599	7.9	739	91.9	0.0	0.0	6.5	1.6	27.7	15.0	35.3	46.9	23.2	257	89.5
Coleman CDP	-	-	-	277	69.7	4.3	0.0	24.9	1.1	16.2	20.9	44.4	57.9	8.3	121	75.2
Collinsville city	5,592	7,236	29.4	6,882	77.1	1.8	1.1	18.5	1.5	27.8	13.5	34.4	39.7	27.5	2,494	89.7
Colony town	136	129	-5.1	107	83.2	0.0	0.0	15.0	1.9	29.0	24.3	33.5	40.9	24.2	43	95.3
Comanche city	1,667	1,559	-6.5	1,702	86.2	0.2	0.5	8.6	4.5	26.0	21.7	41.1	60.2	8.6	662	83.1
Commerce city	2,585	2,510	-2.9	2,538	60.0	0.7	0.0	17.8	21.5	27.6	17.5	37.2	68.1	9.4	900	74.0
Connerville CDP	-	-	-	150	81.3	0.0	0.0	18.7	0.0	24.7	18.7	43.1	100.0	0.0	69	71.0
Cooperton town	16	15	-6.3	8	100.0	0.0	0.0	0.0	0.0	0.0	12.5	41.8	87.5	12.5	8	37.5
Copan town	733	737	0.5	862	67.2	0.5	0.6	30.7	1.0	25.5	19.0	37.5	59.8	10.4	346	83.2
Copeland CDP	1,629	-	-	2,003	73.8	0.0	0.1	21.7	4.3	24.6	23.3	46.2	47.4	16.9	804	83.1
Corn town	503	472	-6.2	637	86.3	0.0	0.0	7.5	6.1	21.5	36.3	52.5	41.3	32.4	203	80.3

1 May be of any race.

Table A. All Places — **Population and Housing**

STATE City, town, township, borough, or CDP (county if applicable)	Population: 2010 census total population	Population: 2019 estimated population	Population: Percent change 2010–2019	Population: ACS total population estimate 2015–2019	Race and Hispanic or Latino origin (percent): White alone, not Hispanic or Latino	Black alone, not Hispanic or Latino	Asian alone, not Hispanic or Latino	All other races or 2 or more races, not Hispanic or Latino	Hispanic or Latino[1]	Age (percent): Under 18 years old	Age 65 years and older	Median age	Educational attainment of persons age 25 and older: Percent High school diploma or less	Percent Bachelor's degree or more	Occupied housing units: Total	Percent with a computer
	1	2	3	4	5	6	7	8	9	10	11	12	13	14	15	16
OKLAHOMA—Con.																
Cornish town	163	155	-4.9	149	67.8	1.3	0.0	30.2	0.7	24.2	19.5	39.2	65.6	12.5	48	70.8
Council Hill town	154	151	-1.9	116	61.2	0.0	0.0	35.3	3.4	29.3	16.4	34.2	81.7	1.4	45	84.4
Covington town	531	534	0.6	532	93.4	0.0	0.0	2.8	3.8	32.0	18.2	34.4	53.4	11.3	199	87.4
Coweta city	9,338	10,032	7.4	9,739	73.8	3.6	1.0	17.0	4.7	28.7	13.0	33.7	43.5	23.2	3,496	91.0
Cowlington town	155	152	-1.9	90	57.8	6.7	0.0	35.6	0.0	25.6	11.1	30.5	57.7	7.7	36	75.0
Coyle town	325	372	14.5	427	78.9	12.9	0.0	6.8	1.4	22.2	8.2	29.7	66.1	17.2	144	79.2
Crescent city	1,415	1,561	10.3	1,372	87.0	2.6	0.0	6.6	3.8	20.2	28.4	45.2	51.1	13.1	529	81.9
Cromwell town	286	274	-4.2	295	76.6	0.0	0.0	20.3	3.1	26.8	12.2	26.4	68.2	3.9	110	61.8
Crowder town	435	404	-7.1	421	82.2	0.0	1.7	13.3	2.9	17.1	24.2	46.3	61.9	15.6	172	89.0
Cushing city	7,826	7,615	-2.7	7,746	77.7	4.6	1.1	11.3	5.3	21.6	16.2	36.1	61.1	11.9	2,877	82.3
Custer City town	375	379	1.1	506	72.5	0.0	0.0	12.5	15.0	26.1	13.8	41.4	51.8	10.0	192	93.8
Cyril town	1,059	1,011	-4.5	981	72.0	0.0	0.0	17.9	10.1	32.0	9.5	33.4	50.0	12.9	349	73.6
Dacoma town	107	108	0.9	83	85.5	0.0	0.0	12.0	2.4	19.3	34.9	51.9	62.7	9.0	45	71.1
Dale CDP	181	-	-	180	72.8	0.0	0.0	27.2	0.0	22.2	13.9	29.2	43.0	31.2	82	100.0
Davenport town	814	807	-0.9	867	81.4	1.0	0.0	10.5	7.0	29.0	16.1	35.1	66.4	11.3	300	82.3
Davidson town	315	288	-8.6	362	47.5	8.0	0.0	10.8	33.7	24.6	17.7	39.7	70.8	3.8	123	74.0
Davis city	2,671	2,896	8.4	2,836	64.2	4.4	1.1	23.2	7.1	29.6	12.8	33.3	57.3	12.7	974	87.1
Deer Creek town	132	125	-5.3	174	79.9	12.6	0.0	4.0	3.4	44.8	5.7	21.2	57.0	2.5	56	87.5
Deer Lick CDP	46	-	-	29	48.3	0.0	0.0	51.7	0.0	0.0	48.3	0.0	0.0	51.7	14	100.0
Delaware town	417	399	-4.3	416	58.4	0.7	0.0	37.5	3.4	23.8	15.6	40.0	66.1	4.3	142	78.9
Del City city	21,327	21,712	1.8	21,822	59.9	20.9	1.7	7.1	10.3	25.2	15.7	36.3	49.5	13.9	8,683	88.1
Dennis CDP	195	-	-	144	63.2	0.0	4.2	32.6	0.0	27.8	30.6	52.6	11.5	65.4	53	84.9
Depew town	478	479	0.2	382	75.1	3.4	0.0	20.2	1.3	23.8	24.3	41.7	65.5	11.2	148	81.1
Devol town	151	141	-6.6	107	80.4	4.7	0.0	0.9	14.0	25.2	17.8	36.2	56.3	28.2	40	82.5
Dewar town	899	853	-5.1	872	62.4	1.9	0.0	31.8	3.9	28.1	19.5	36.3	60.5	7.2	305	80.7
Dewey city	3,408	3,384	-0.7	3,422	76.0	0.8	0.0	14.6	8.6	24.1	19.8	43.8	58.8	14.2	1,336	85.6
Dibble town	799	861	7.8	1,038	79.6	0.2	1.6	10.8	7.8	25.5	12.1	34.7	47.0	25.2	339	91.7
Dickson town	1,211	1,248	3.1	1,451	81.2	0.6	0.0	15.8	2.5	29.3	11.5	36.8	50.3	24.6	491	91.4
Dill City town	562	533	-5.2	414	84.1	0.0	0.0	11.4	4.6	27.8	13.0	46.0	64.6	7.9	162	83.3
Disney town	311	303	-2.6	206	76.7	0.0	0.0	21.4	1.9	11.2	28.6	56.3	56.9	10.3	108	81.5
Dodge CDP	115	-	-	91	30.8	0.0	0.0	69.2	0.0	0.0	57.1	68.3	12.0	57.8	39	100.0
Dotyville CDP	101	-	-	107	46.7	0.0	0.0	43.9	9.3	0.0	37.4	63.5	29.2	33.3	56	100.0
Dougherty town	215	222	3.3	210	83.8	0.0	0.0	16.2	0.0	27.6	14.3	37.0	62.9	11.9	85	78.8
Douglas town	32	34	6.3	19	36.8	0.0	0.0	10.5	52.6	36.8	15.8	27.8	63.6	9.1	8	50.0
Dover town	464	475	2.4	365	36.7	0.0	0.0	8.5	54.8	22.5	11.5	40.9	59.4	16.6	169	78.1
Dripping Springs CDP	50	-	-	40	25.0	0.0	0.0	75.0	0.0	22.5	20.0	44.7	86.4	0.0	13	100.0
Drowning Creek CDP	155	-	-	244	84.4	0.0	0.0	15.6	0.0	9.8	34.4	59.2	82.8	4.4	117	69.2
Drummond town	455	455	0.0	371	80.9	0.0	0.0	6.7	12.4	27.8	12.1	38.2	48.3	21.4	139	94.2
Drumright city	2,907	2,835	-2.5	2,870	83.3	2.0	0.8	9.7	4.2	22.7	18.4	43.0	62.6	10.2	1,208	82.8
Dry Creek CDP	227	-	-	172	43.0	0.0	0.0	57.0	0.0	22.7	16.9	49.0	45.2	10.3	80	75.0
Duchess Landing CDP	114	-	-	69	60.9	0.0	0.0	39.1	0.0	0.0	27.5	47.3	66.7	0.0	46	58.7
Duncan city	23,418	22,344	-4.6	22,618	75.9	2.8	0.7	9.1	11.4	24.6	17.9	38.1	52.2	18.8	8,814	86.3
Durant city	15,858	18,673	17.8	17,856	67.2	2.3	0.8	21.2	8.5	22.1	15.4	33.2	45.7	25.1	6,804	88.2
Dustin town	389	370	-4.9	498	56.4	0.0	0.0	40.0	3.6	21.9	13.3	39.8	75.4	5.3	119	52.9
Dwight Mission CDP	55	-	-	63	100.0	0.0	0.0	0.0	0.0	33.3	30.2	33.9	45.2	54.8	21	100.0
Eagletown CDP	528	-	-	539	71.4	5.9	0.0	21.5	1.1	21.7	20.4	40.4	65.9	5.3	209	65.6
Eakly town	338	325	-3.8	412	44.2	0.0	0.0	3.9	51.9	34.5	11.9	26.7	69.1	11.1	119	81.5
Earlsboro town	628	621	-1.1	476	72.1	9.7	0.0	14.9	3.4	18.5	26.9	50.2	62.7	13.1	187	69.0
East Duke town	424	387	-8.7	353	90.7	1.4	0.0	2.3	5.7	28.0	27.2	38.6	48.3	28.2	142	90.1
Edmond city	81,130	94,054	15.9	92,009	75.4	5.3	3.3	9.3	6.6	25.5	14.7	35.7	19.4	53.4	34,050	95.4
Eldon CDP	368	-	-	169	57.4	0.0	0.0	42.6	0.0	15.4	34.3	48.1	54.1	20.5	65	75.4
Eldorado town	446	406	-9.0	370	71.1	1.9	0.0	7.8	19.2	23.0	20.8	47.5	56.2	8.8	169	75.1
Elgin city	2,156	3,183	47.6	3,089	71.2	9.3	1.9	7.7	9.9	28.7	10.7	32.1	31.1	31.1	1,057	93.9
Elk City city	11,708	11,577	-1.1	11,824	75.7	2.9	0.6	5.6	15.2	26.9	13.4	34.1	49.6	17.7	4,275	88.7
Elmer town	96	89	-7.3	101	67.3	0.0	0.0	16.8	15.8	7.9	36.6	54.1	67.0	4.5	56	75.0
Elm Grove CDP	198	-	-	231	34.2	0.0	0.0	65.8	0.0	46.3	12.1	18.7	92.9	7.1	61	83.6
Elmore City town	711	712	0.1	928	88.6	0.6	0.0	5.7	5.1	28.4	15.6	39.0	65.1	8.2	339	85.5
El Reno city	16,748	19,965	19.2	19,095	63.0	6.6	0.4	15.2	14.8	23.4	12.2	35.5	58.3	11.8	5,859	86.1
Empire City town	923	893	-3.3	963	88.5	0.6	0.0	5.9	5.0	22.4	18.6	41.8	49.2	13.0	335	84.8
Enid city	49,385	49,688	0.6	50,394	70.4	2.8	1.0	11.2	14.6	25.1	15.3	35.0	49.0	22.4	19,166	87.9
Erick city	1,060	999	-5.8	839	57.8	0.7	0.0	7.4	34.1	20.9	30.5	46.8	48.1	19.3	360	94.2
Etowah town	92	99	7.6	125	90.4	0.0	0.0	9.6	0.0	18.4	16.0	42.6	60.4	9.4	49	85.7
Eufaula city	2,811	2,846	1.2	2,875	68.6	2.9	0.5	26.3	1.6	19.5	30.0	50.1	53.7	15.2	1,196	80.4
Evening Shade CDP	359	-	-	327	78.9	0.0	0.0	14.7	6.4	11.0	35.8	55.7	38.8	30.9	161	84.5
Fairfax town	1,380	1,265	-8.3	1,330	65.9	1.7	0.4	30.9	1.1	22.1	25.8	42.6	60.1	13.4	524	73.9
Fairfield CDP	584	-	-	613	28.7	0.0	0.0	59.2	12.1	26.6	20.9	39.2	71.7	12.6	223	75.3
Fairland town	1,058	1,031	-2.6	1,132	64.6	0.4	0.0	32.2	2.8	25.5	20.4	35.2	56.3	12.7	445	86.5
Fairmont town	134	131	-2.2	191	95.8	0.0	0.0	4.2	0.0	20.9	25.7	43.8	65.3	10.4	78	94.9
Fair Oaks town	89	101	13.5	103	70.9	4.9	0.0	14.6	9.7	19.4	19.4	46.3	56.6	10.8	38	84.2
Fairview city	2,577	2,594	0.7	2,618	84.6	1.2	0.7	5.8	7.7	28.6	22.0	38.2	44.0	18.2	1,016	91.3
Fallis town	27	27	0.0	47	93.6	0.0	0.0	6.4	0.0	0.0	4.3	59.6	93.6	0.0	27	92.6
Fanshawe town	419	405	-3.3	414	59.7	0.0	1.4	37.0	1.9	30.9	17.4	35.4	58.7	17.7	145	73.1
Fargo town	366	344	-6.0	354	87.3	0.0	0.6	1.1	11.0	29.9	14.1	30.1	55.0	12.4	119	87.4
Faxon town	136	130	-4.4	64	85.9	0.0	0.0	3.1	10.9	23.4	7.8	35.8	56.8	9.1	21	100.0
Felt CDP	93	-	-	107	79.4	0.0	0.0	1.9	18.7	34.6	16.8	29.1	56.3	29.7	37	100.0
Fitzhugh town	230	230	0.0	180	83.9	0.0	0.0	15.0	1.1	29.4	28.3	44.0	48.3	22.5	73	76.7
Fletcher town	1,177	1,143	-2.9	984	82.1	0.3	2.0	11.5	4.1	30.1	13.0	35.1	47.6	20.3	370	84.3
Flint Creek CDP	732	-	-	801	74.9	1.2	0.6	23.2	0.0	25.0	22.2	45.6	53.8	18.9	350	95.4
Flute Springs CDP	130	-	-	119	5.9	0.0	0.0	94.1	0.0	17.6	11.8	43.2	69.4	7.1	37	91.9
Foraker town	19	18	-5.3	17	64.7	0.0	0.0	17.6	17.6	0.0	17.6	56.2	70.6	11.8	10	70.0
Forest Park town	998	1,069	7.1	1,008	26.1	64.8	6.3	2.2	0.6	19.7	30.1	54.5	32.5	38.6	418	91.1
Forgan town	547	529	-3.3	550	83.3	0.0	0.0	1.3	15.5	29.8	13.3	35.7	60.6	14.2	178	84.8
Fort Cobb town	644	609	-5.4	586	75.4	1.4	0.0	17.6	5.6	26.8	16.0	36.7	56.3	16.7	234	89.3
Fort Coffee town	426	422	-0.9	377	19.9	59.9	0.0	18.8	1.3	20.4	25.7	45.6	53.5	10.7	166	74.1
Fort Gibson town	4,153	3,958	-4.7	4,021	63.1	0.6	0.0	34.2	2.1	23.9	15.4	38.4	42.1	36.3	1,734	88.5
Fort Supply town	330	320	-3.0	350	79.1	0.0	0.0	7.7	13.1	20.6	17.7	34.6	49.2	22.0	130	85.4
Fort Towson town	506	489	-3.4	528	80.9	0.6	0.0	17.0	1.5	15.3	30.1	55.0	57.6	11.6	232	69.0
Foss town	151	145	-4.0	147	80.3	0.0	0.7	6.1	12.9	16.3	15.6	44.2	56.2	9.9	70	80.0
Foster town	161	161	0.0	154	96.1	0.0	0.0	3.9	0.0	25.3	15.6	44.2	70.5	12.5	59	83.1
Foyil town	344	378	9.9	350	61.4	0.0	2.9	34.6	1.1	26.6	13.1	35.8	68.0	6.4	116	85.3
Francis town	315	320	1.6	330	60.3	0.9	0.0	37.9	0.9	32.4	12.4	29.0	53.7	9.4	117	82.9
Frederick city	3,940	3,545	-10.0	3,633	55.2	9.1	0.4	4.6	30.7	26.8	17.3	38.0	55.7	15.5	1,325	84.7

1 May be of any race.

Table A. All Places — **Population and Housing**

STATE City, town, township, borough, or CDP (county if applicable)	Population: 2010 census total population	Population: 2019 estimated population	Population: Percent change 2010–2019	Population: ACS total population estimate 2015–2019	Race and Hispanic or Latino origin (percent): White alone, not Hispanic or Latino	Black alone, not Hispanic or Latino	Asian alone, not Hispanic or Latino	All other races or 2 or more races, not Hispanic or Latino	Hispanic or Latino[1]	Age (percent): Under 18 years old	Age 65 years and older	Median age	Educational attainment of persons age 25 and older: Percent High school diploma or less	Percent Bachelor's degree or more	Occupied housing units: Total	Percent with a computer
	1	2	3	4	5	6	7	8	9	10	11	12	13	14	15	16
OKLAHOMA—Con.																
Freedom town	287	291	1.4	353	96.3	0.0	0.6	2.0	1.1	31.7	8.2	35.8	42.4	17.1	118	93.2
Friendship town	24	22	-8.3	37	70.3	0.0	29.7	0.0	0.0	13.5	5.4	61.3	62.5	0.0	17	100.0
Gage town	442	408	-7.7	551	78.2	0.0	0.0	11.4	10.3	29.6	17.4	39.1	69.7	8.9	194	79.9
Gans town	316	301	-4.7	291	59.8	0.0	0.0	37.8	2.4	27.1	13.7	38.5	60.7	10.9	98	85.7
Garber city	822	807	-1.8	668	81.7	0.7	0.0	14.4	3.1	31.0	14.4	32.6	56.2	14.5	258	80.6
Garvin town	253	255	0.8	275	69.1	2.2	0.0	22.9	5.8	33.8	10.5	33.3	59.3	22.2	101	71.3
Gate town	93	87	-6.5	85	90.6	0.0	0.0	9.4	0.0	24.7	21.2	45.6	42.6	29.5	40	90.0
Geary city	1,280	1,265	-1.2	1,218	59.1	2.8	0.0	29.5	8.6	31.3	12.3	32.8	51.8	10.1	505	74.7
Gene Autry town	168	165	-1.8	153	59.5	3.3	0.0	17.6	19.6	27.5	7.8	38.2	63.8	6.4	50	74.0
Geronimo town	1,268	1,215	-4.2	1,150	63.5	3.6	0.3	18.3	14.3	23.5	15.8	36.4	49.4	15.0	469	88.5
Gerty town	118	112	-5.1	36	91.7	0.0	0.0	8.3	0.0	16.7	44.4	58.5	75.9	3.4	18	66.7
Gideon CDP	49	-	-	10	0.0	0.0	0.0	100.0	0.0	0.0	60.0	71.3	30.0	40.0	7	100.0
Glencoe town	609	607	-0.3	589	80.6	0.3	0.0	17.5	1.5	22.9	26.8	47.7	49.9	15.4	272	79.0
Glenpool city	10,867	13,936	28.2	13,666	71.5	1.7	1.7	20.6	4.5	29.8	7.7	31.6	35.4	25.4	4,781	96.2
Goldsby town	1,808	2,454	35.7	2,100	75.4	0.1	0.5	13.7	10.3	24.0	17.3	42.7	34.9	35.6	793	94.5
Goltry town	249	253	1.6	255	93.3	0.0	0.0	2.4	4.3	27.1	18.0	36.2	56.5	20.0	107	86.9
Goodwell town	1,293	1,270	-1.8	1,127	67.3	4.9	4.1	8.7	15.0	16.1	6.6	22.3	30.5	42.8	376	99.2
Gore town	977	951	-2.7	958	65.2	0.1	0.0	31.5	3.1	22.4	29.2	48.6	48.5	23.5	369	79.7
Gotebo town	226	209	-7.5	188	80.9	0.0	0.0	6.9	12.2	16.0	20.2	48.8	67.3	3.9	90	82.2
Gould town	141	129	-8.5	126	28.6	0.8	0.0	11.9	58.7	27.0	20.6	29.7	37.9	6.9	50	94.0
Gowen CDP	-	-	-	371	64.7	0.0	5.1	30.2	0.0	45.3	11.9	20.4	35.5	51.6	105	100.0
Gracemont town	318	306	-3.8	237	71.3	0.0	0.0	16.0	12.7	19.4	21.1	35.8	64.4	5.7	109	76.1
Grainola town	31	31	0.0	57	47.4	0.0	0.0	21.1	31.6	36.8	12.3	33.8	55.6	30.6	15	66.7
Grandfield city	1,038	933	-10.1	783	41.4	13.8	0.0	11.0	33.8	24.9	19.4	44.2	62.1	11.9	325	72.6
Grand Lake Towne town	74	70	-5.4	77	85.7	0.0	0.0	10.4	3.9	11.7	49.4	63.8	27.3	28.8	37	100.0
Grandview CDP	394	-	-	358	34.4	0.0	0.0	65.6	0.0	43.3	0.0	20.8	54.7	11.6	134	90.3
Granite town	2,065	1,957	-5.2	1,913	67.5	9.5	0.0	14.5	8.5	10.4	14.3	39.4	63.1	11.3	504	79.0
Grant CDP	289	-	-	351	31.9	29.1	0.0	36.5	2.6	22.8	8.8	41.0	56.2	6.4	137	73.7
Grayson town	159	156	-1.9	153	6.5	71.2	0.0	20.3	2.0	15.0	42.5	58.6	47.9	9.2	64	50.0
Greasy CDP	372	-	-	323	32.8	0.0	0.0	64.7	2.5	7.4	22.6	46.1	70.9	7.2	132	50.8
Greenfield town	93	89	-4.3	168	81.0	0.0	0.0	17.9	1.2	21.4	19.0	35.7	66.0	6.0	88	84.1
Gregory CDP	171	-	-	176	85.2	0.0	9.7	5.1	0.0	26.1	8.5	37.4	34.2	41.7	60	100.0
Grove city	6,605	7,149	8.2	6,957	77.9	0.1	0.9	16.6	4.4	14.8	33.6	55.2	36.6	27.1	3,094	90.3
Guthrie city	10,206	11,661	14.3	11,376	72.9	14.6	0.1	6.8	5.6	22.1	16.9	36.5	48.2	20.4	3,751	85.9
Guymon city	11,449	10,996	-4.0	11,488	29.3	3.6	5.6	3.3	58.1	31.3	7.6	30.7	59.4	18.9	3,453	85.9
Haileyville city	806	751	-6.8	722	65.7	0.0	0.0	30.7	3.6	25.9	19.4	37.7	57.0	6.6	292	82.9
Hallett town	125	124	-0.8	112	78.6	0.0	0.0	17.0	4.5	17.9	30.4	50.5	72.1	4.7	48	81.3
Hammon town	566	557	-1.6	596	46.1	1.3	0.0	50.5	2.0	27.3	23.5	44.8	68.5	3.6	172	84.9
Hanna town	138	133	-3.6	116	44.8	0.0	0.0	55.2	0.0	37.1	8.6	27.5	81.0	7.9	40	55.0
Hardesty town	212	210	-0.9	261	41.4	0.0	0.4	11.5	46.7	31.0	7.7	35.3	57.5	14.4	91	82.4
Harrah city	5,055	6,499	28.6	6,189	80.8	0.5	0.8	10.4	7.5	25.3	19.5	41.4	47.2	20.3	2,466	89.5
Hartshorne city	2,143	1,963	-8.4	2,099	61.4	3.2	0.0	31.4	4.0	24.2	17.8	37.8	48.9	16.5	914	76.8
Haskell town	2,004	1,930	-3.7	2,073	72.6	8.7	0.2	17.3	1.2	31.4	17.4	33.8	50.2	16.2	723	84.2
Hastings town	143	132	-7.7	72	97.2	0.0	0.0	2.8	0.0	11.1	37.5	59.5	43.8	4.7	42	71.4
Haworth town	297	296	-0.3	324	78.1	2.5	0.0	9.0	10.5	27.5	14.5	34.6	70.9	9.2	122	65.6
Headrick town	94	88	-6.4	88	89.8	0.0	0.0	10.2	0.0	27.3	27.3	40.5	53.4	12.1	37	73.0
Healdton city	2,788	2,683	-3.8	2,720	85.8	1.3	0.0	6.9	6.0	23.1	20.1	39.6	66.1	11.7	1,085	77.4
Heavener city	3,414	3,301	-3.3	3,324	51.7	0.9	2.6	13.1	31.7	28.7	12.0	33.9	67.0	7.5	1,071	69.8
Helena town	1,407	1,415	0.6	1,423	58.5	12.2	0.0	22.2	7.1	7.1	15.5	45.8	62.7	6.1	147	92.5
Hendrix town	79	85	7.6	74	52.7	25.7	0.0	10.8	10.8	13.5	37.8	55.0	82.8	5.2	39	51.3
Hennessey town	2,131	2,223	4.3	2,925	61.6	0.1	1.1	7.5	29.7	26.6	11.9	36.6	63.5	18.3	983	82.6
Henryetta city	5,928	5,566	-6.1	5,633	69.3	1.5	0.0	26.9	2.3	25.1	21.4	38.0	58.4	13.2	2,275	81.7
Hickory town	71	73	2.8	136	52.2	0.0	0.0	40.4	7.4	33.8	9.6	21.9	66.7	16.7	38	94.7
Hillsdale town	121	122	0.8	85	100.0	0.0	0.0	0.0	0.0	14.1	11.8	47.4	58.8	22.1	35	100.0
Hinton town	3,199	3,219	0.6	3,232	48.1	1.1	0.1	9.3	41.5	20.9	10.8	36.0	67.1	13.9	748	86.2
Hitchcock town	121	114	-5.8	74	77.0	0.0	0.0	16.2	6.8	31.1	18.9	54.2	74.5	3.9	36	100.0
Hitchita town	88	83	-5.7	59	54.2	0.0	0.0	45.8	0.0	22.0	16.9	52.1	78.3	4.3	24	70.8
Hobart city	3,756	3,427	-8.8	3,502	69.5	4.5	1.5	8.4	16.1	26.1	16.4	38.6	57.7	11.0	1,291	75.8
Hoffman town	127	126	-0.8	109	66.1	11.0	0.0	22.9	0.0	16.5	23.9	50.5	64.6	11.4	48	75.0
Holdenville city	5,771	5,501	-4.7	5,559	56.2	11.4	0.3	25.9	6.2	19.6	13.5	34.1	65.2	8.5	1,488	67.2
Hollis city	2,062	1,873	-9.2	1,883	52.8	6.4	1.1	3.9	35.8	23.0	17.5	40.4	52.4	15.8	787	85.4
Hollister town	50	46	-8.0	52	92.3	0.0	0.0	0.0	7.7	11.5	9.6	52.8	82.6	0.0	21	95.2
Hominy city	3,563	3,388	-4.9	3,431	50.9	11.2	0.0	30.9	7.0	15.5	14.4	39.9	57.3	9.6	1,052	76.0
Hooker city	1,919	1,844	-3.9	1,730	60.5	0.2	0.0	5.5	33.8	32.8	16.3	35.2	51.1	20.4	650	87.8
Hoot Owl town	4	4	0.0	-	-	-	-	-	-	-	-	-	-	-	-	-
Horntown town	97	92	-5.2	141	80.9	0.0	0.0	7.8	11.3	30.5	22.0	29.4	48.8	8.5	44	81.8
Howe town	807	789	-2.2	1,089	80.8	3.7	0.1	12.0	3.4	20.0	15.2	43.5	68.1	8.4	295	67.5
Hugo city	5,314	5,092	-4.2	5,142	51.6	20.2	0.0	20.8	7.4	28.6	18.7	35.7	58.2	11.4	2,031	78.7
Hulbert town	590	582	-1.4	627	34.9	0.0	0.3	57.6	7.2	22.6	16.7	37.6	65.9	12.7	223	77.1
Hunter town	165	167	1.2	186	83.3	0.0	0.0	16.7	0.0	21.5	16.1	38.5	65.7	8.0	78	67.9
Hydro town	969	937	-3.3	1,020	89.6	0.1	0.2	6.6	3.5	25.6	17.6	36.0	46.7	24.6	398	87.2
Idabel city	6,985	6,843	-2.0	6,924	44.3	21.1	1.1	23.2	10.3	26.9	14.2	32.0	57.2	14.4	2,645	68.8
Indiahoma town	344	330	-4.1	303	71.9	0.0	0.0	23.4	4.6	24.8	16.2	35.6	47.9	21.1	122	75.4
Indianola CDP	48	-	-	26	100.0	0.0	0.0	0.0	0.0	0.0	50.0	0.0	50.0	0.0	13	100.0
Indianola town	162	151	-6.8	144	75.0	0.0	0.7	24.3	0.0	30.6	18.1	36.0	58.9	10.0	60	90.0
Inola town	1,787	1,803	0.9	1,828	74.1	0.7	0.0	21.9	3.3	27.1	15.5	33.5	52.0	15.1	698	90.4
Iron Post CDP	92	-	-	191	92.1	0.0	0.0	7.9	0.0	48.7	4.7	35.1	44.9	0.0	52	75.0
Isabella CDP	136	-	-	112	100.0	0.0	0.0	0.0	0.0	5.4	35.7	38.4	33.7	45.3	63	88.9
IXL town	51	50	-2.0	55	20.0	60.0	0.0	20.0	0.0	20.0	10.9	48.1	45.9	18.9	22	72.7
Jay city	2,509	2,542	1.3	2,525	44.4	1.1	0.1	45.1	9.4	24.2	15.4	35.9	63.5	10.4	858	73.5
Jefferson town	8	8	0.0	15	46.7	0.0	0.0	53.3	0.0	40.0	40.0	31.3	33.3	33.3	6	83.3
Jenks city	16,938	23,767	40.3	22,488	74.3	3.0	6.3	10.3	6.0	32.1	10.1	33.7	23.1	45.0	7,455	97.3
Jennings town	360	354	-1.7	306	68.3	0.0	0.0	31.4	0.3	28.1	15.7	34.0	73.3	6.8	121	81.0
Jet town	213	217	1.9	272	91.2	0.0	0.0	2.9	5.9	23.5	21.3	44.1	37.6	31.2	125	95.2
Johnson town	247	256	3.6	228	66.2	0.0	0.0	25.9	7.9	22.4	23.2	39.0	44.9	26.9	86	83.7
Jones town	2,696	3,169	17.5	3,077	77.5	4.9	0.0	9.9	7.6	27.3	15.3	37.3	47.5	19.7	1,034	91.1
Justice CDP	1,324	-	-	1,481	76.4	0.1	2.6	17.9	3.0	22.3	21.7	44.0	36.2	26.9	523	87.0
Kansas town	788	800	1.5	835	38.7	0.0	0.0	58.3	3.0	26.7	16.0	36.6	69.7	10.4	264	76.5
Katie town	349	354	1.4	301	85.0	2.7	0.0	10.6	1.7	18.3	20.9	47.9	66.5	12.2	127	81.9
Kaw City city	376	367	-2.4	321	80.1	0.0	0.9	18.1	0.9	17.4	35.8	54.9	49.4	6.6	140	85.0
Kellyville town	1,144	1,146	0.2	1,142	72.5	0.4	0.4	21.1	5.6	35.6	13.7	33.3	62.8	7.5	406	82.8
Kemp town	133	144	8.3	162	77.2	1.9	0.0	19.1	1.9	11.1	45.7	62.3	48.2	3.6	99	32.3

1 May be of any race.

Table A. All Places — **Population and Housing**

STATE City, town, township, borough, or CDP (county if applicable)	Population: 2010 census total population	Population: 2019 estimated population	Population: Percent change 2010–2019	Population: ACS total population estimate 2015–2019	Race and Hispanic or Latino origin (percent): White alone, not Hispanic or Latino	Race and Hispanic or Latino origin (percent): Black alone, not Hispanic or Latino	Race and Hispanic or Latino origin (percent): Asian alone, not Hispanic or Latino	Race and Hispanic or Latino origin (percent): All other races or 2 or more races, not Hispanic or Latino	Race and Hispanic or Latino origin (percent): Hispanic or Latino[1]	Age (percent): Under 18 years old	Age (percent): Age 65 years and older	Age (percent): Median age	Educational attainment of persons age 25 and older: Percent High school diploma or less	Educational attainment of persons age 25 and older: Percent Bachelor's degree or more	Occupied housing units: Total	Occupied housing units: Percent with a computer
	1	2	3	4	5	6	7	8	9	10	11	12	13	14	15	16
OKLAHOMA—Con.																
Kendrick town	139	142	2.2	98	84.7	0.0	0.0	15.3	0.0	16.3	25.5	45.5	54.7	9.4	34	76.5
Kenefic town	196	217	10.7	156	75.6	4.5	0.0	16.7	3.2	41.7	11.5	29.5	59.8	8.5	45	82.2
Kenton CDP	17	-	-	5	100.0	0.0	0.0	0.0	0.0	0.0	100.0	0.0	100.0	0.0	2	100.0
Kenwood CDP	1,224	-	-	1,113	30.6	0.2	0.3	66.8	2.2	23.9	11.5	39.6	65.6	6.5	361	76.7
Keota town	564	549	-2.7	447	73.4	0.0	0.0	24.2	2.5	29.3	16.3	30.7	68.0	8.2	174	77.0
Ketchum town	442	421	-4.8	411	76.4	0.0	0.0	22.4	1.2	22.4	19.5	43.4	50.7	10.1	182	80.2
Keyes town	324	277	-14.5	250	81.2	0.0	0.0	0.8	18.0	22.8	25.6	42.8	61.7	13.7	119	82.4
Keys CDP	565	-	-	434	77.9	0.0	0.0	22.1	0.0	23.3	24.4	40.2	31.9	38.0	141	73.0
Kiefer town	1,700	2,020	18.8	2,251	73.0	0.8	0.2	20.7	5.3	33.0	7.5	33.0	48.6	15.7	769	93.0
Kildare town	100	94	-6.0	85	76.5	0.0	0.0	17.6	5.9	22.4	18.8	50.3	63.9	8.2	29	79.3
Kingfisher city	4,633	4,908	5.9	4,875	77.4	2.6	0.6	4.5	14.9	29.6	16.7	32.4	54.8	17.3	1,731	89.4
Kingston town	1,601	1,675	4.6	1,781	70.4	1.0	0.0	21.1	7.5	27.6	15.9	38.0	58.6	8.2	631	84.8
Kinta town	324	316	-2.5	290	73.1	0.7	0.0	24.8	1.4	31.7	21.4	35.6	56.4	12.2	124	71.0
Kiowa town	730	676	-7.4	668	69.9	1.3	0.0	24.4	4.3	26.9	18.4	35.4	59.2	12.1	264	85.6
Knowles town	11	10	-9.1	14	28.6	71.4	0.0	0.0	0.0	0.0	28.6	29.9	28.6	0.0	4	100.0
Konawa city	1,298	1,197	-7.8	1,178	62.3	1.8	0.0	33.2	2.7	24.9	17.7	39.5	54.2	12.7	478	77.0
Krebs city	2,054	1,945	-5.3	2,041	63.2	1.7	0.0	28.4	6.7	23.0	17.1	36.6	49.7	11.9	864	85.1
Kremlin town	255	255	0.0	300	92.0	0.3	0.0	7.7	0.0	31.7	16.7	37.4	49.2	18.2	121	90.9
Lahoma town	611	617	1.0	526	97.9	0.0	0.0	0.6	1.5	26.2	15.8	41.1	54.8	16.6	202	90.6
Lake Aluma town	88	91	3.4	61	100.0	0.0	0.0	0.0	0.0	11.5	62.3	69.1	3.7	79.6	32	100.0
Lamar town	158	150	-5.1	160	64.4	0.0	0.0	26.9	8.8	15.6	21.9	46.4	67.5	14.3	62	64.5
Lambert town	6	6	0.0	10	100.0	0.0	0.0	0.0	0.0	0.0	40.0	54.5	80.0	10.0	5	60.0
Lamont town	416	392	-5.8	348	64.1	0.0	0.0	8.6	27.3	24.7	16.4	31.4	47.8	31.6	118	85.6
Lane CDP	414	-	-	243	78.6	0.0	0.0	14.0	7.4	24.7	10.7	37.4	46.4	17.5	103	90.3
Langley town	827	822	-0.6	636	64.2	1.3	0.5	20.3	13.8	18.2	20.1	46.1	52.8	9.5	281	83.3
Langston town	1,748	1,860	6.4	1,254	11.4	83.3	1.0	1.7	2.6	6.4	3.9	21.0	26.0	37.0	94	84.0
Latta CDP	-	-	-	1,220	51.2	3.0	0.0	42.4	3.4	30.9	7.8	29.9	22.1	31.6	413	88.9
Laverne town	1,340	1,328	-0.9	1,616	72.5	0.0	0.0	2.8	24.8	27.8	13.4	35.4	48.8	17.2	461	81.3
Lawrence Creek town	149	145	-2.7	128	65.6	0.0	0.0	27.3	7.0	29.7	14.1	39.6	45.8	12.0	46	91.3
Lawton city	96,867	93,025	-4.0	94,017	50.8	18.8	2.8	13.3	14.3	23.7	11.0	31.3	43.2	21.2	32,984	90.1
Leach CDP	237	-	-	277	36.8	0.0	1.8	56.3	5.1	32.9	13.0	31.8	43.3	28.9	97	78.4
Lebanon CDP	303	-	-	292	83.2	0.0	0.0	16.8	0.0	12.3	38.4	55.2	65.5	5.0	118	100.0
Leedey town	435	443	1.8	567	66.3	0.0	0.5	16.2	16.9	41.4	8.5	27.6	44.7	21.0	171	97.1
Le Flore town	181	175	-3.3	143	60.8	0.0	0.0	34.3	4.9	30.8	21.7	36.8	64.2	14.7	56	60.7
Lehigh city	355	332	-6.5	284	70.4	0.7	0.0	27.8	1.1	25.0	10.9	41.3	70.6	11.8	104	78.8
Lenapah town	293	280	-4.4	297	41.8	2.4	1.3	54.5	0.0	30.6	7.7	28.2	59.8	8.4	99	86.9
Leon town	91	100	9.9	126	61.9	0.0	0.0	35.7	2.4	6.3	38.1	54.3	85.1	7.4	45	64.4
Lequire CDP	-	-	-	187	76.5	0.0	0.0	15.5	8.0	23.0	20.9	51.4	67.6	11.8	77	66.2
Lexington city	2,152	2,185	1.5	2,202	76.0	3.5	0.0	9.1	11.4	24.3	17.8	36.8	63.0	12.9	790	83.9
Liberty CDP	-	-	-	310	62.6	0.0	0.0	18.7	18.7	37.4	4.8	35.0	27.4	16.0	92	72.8
Liberty town	206	206	0.0	188	78.7	0.5	0.0	18.6	2.1	19.1	19.7	40.6	48.8	24.0	73	89.0
Lima town	53	52	-1.9	55	18.2	69.1	0.0	12.7	0.0	29.1	18.2	33.8	45.7	20.0	21	57.1
Limestone CDP	629	-	-	805	84.5	0.0	6.6	1.1	7.8	29.2	17.5	40.0	37.6	31.0	253	92.1
Lindsay city	2,840	2,777	-2.2	2,807	79.8	0.2	0.0	13.6	6.3	22.4	20.0	41.4	68.2	12.6	1,150	87.9
Loco town	122	118	-3.3	97	80.4	0.0	0.0	19.6	0.0	7.2	25.8	55.8	78.6	10.7	43	65.1
Locust Grove town	1,420	1,395	-1.8	1,600	47.5	1.9	0.0	45.4	5.3	31.1	15.1	36.5	61.0	5.8	608	69.9
Lone Grove city	4,829	5,121	6.0	5,063	71.8	3.5	1.1	21.0	2.6	26.1	14.2	36.2	43.4	20.3	1,886	89.2
Lone Wolf town	438	399	-8.9	419	81.6	0.7	0.0	5.0	12.6	27.4	19.1	37.7	45.6	18.6	167	89.8
Long CDP	370	-	-	254	55.9	0.0	0.0	44.1	0.0	14.6	26.4	53.8	47.3	28.8	141	92.2
Longdale town	262	265	1.1	290	60.7	0.0	0.0	36.9	2.4	32.1	14.1	32.3	71.0	6.8	118	83.9
Longtown CDP	2,739	-	-	2,746	79.3	0.3	0.2	18.2	2.0	18.3	32.6	56.9	52.6	14.1	1,282	86.9
Lookeba town	166	162	-2.4	141	52.5	0.0	0.0	15.6	31.9	27.0	16.3	38.9	75.3	3.5	45	82.2
Lost City CDP	770	-	-	912	34.6	0.0	0.0	59.5	5.8	26.5	18.2	37.9	48.2	18.7	309	69.9
Lotsee town	2	2	0.0	6	16.7	0.0	0.0	83.3	0.0	16.7	50.0	54.0	0.0	100.0	1	100.0
Loveland town	13	12	-7.7	2	100.0	0.0	0.0	0.0	0.0	0.0	100.0	0.0	0.0	0.0	2	100.0
Loyal town	79	83	5.1	108	91.7	0.0	0.0	8.3	0.0	17.6	38.9	46.7	27.0	18.0	40	92.5
Lucien CDP	88	-	-	117	81.2	0.0	0.0	0.0	18.8	15.4	17.1	49.7	56.3	18.8	58	89.7
Luther town	1,224	1,759	43.7	1,277	68.9	3.8	0.2	24.9	2.1	25.0	14.4	40.7	43.1	27.3	450	93.8
Lyons Switch CDP	288	-	-	269	41.3	0.0	0.0	51.7	7.1	21.6	30.5	53.8	55.0	15.6	97	77.3
McAlester city	18,395	17,814	-3.2	18,045	67.7	4.9	0.6	18.9	7.8	23.1	16.7	35.8	50.6	16.9	6,936	83.7
McCord CDP	1,440	-	-	1,588	82.7	0.0	0.0	11.7	5.6	23.9	19.6	43.6	58.4	10.2	610	87.7
McCurtain town	516	502	-2.7	409	60.4	0.5	0.0	33.7	5.4	29.8	15.4	32.8	66.0	9.8	162	82.7
McLoud city	4,501	4,743	5.4	4,683	71.5	7.9	0.9	16.0	3.8	20.7	10.9	37.1	52.9	13.7	1,164	94.8
Macomb town	32	33	3.1	26	53.8	0.0	0.0	42.3	3.8	7.7	26.9	57.0	75.0	0.0	14	78.6
Madill city	3,758	4,031	7.3	3,937	47.1	4.7	0.7	8.5	38.9	29.4	14.5	34.3	64.8	12.6	1,319	86.1
Manchester town	103	99	-3.9	93	97.8	0.0	0.0	2.2	0.0	24.7	12.9	42.9	57.6	27.1	33	84.8
Mangum city	3,010	2,698	-10.4	2,778	75.0	5.4	0.0	4.1	15.5	27.2	19.6	38.1	47.6	12.5	1,085	80.7
Manitou town	181	164	-9.4	166	59.0	16.3	0.0	24.7	0.0	44.6	20.5	31.3	66.3	6.5	51	92.2
Mannford town	3,073	3,194	3.9	3,225	81.7	0.7	0.0	15.7	1.9	29.5	16.8	32.5	45.4	20.8	1,153	89.2
Mannsville town	863	862	-0.1	980	70.9	0.0	0.0	20.7	8.4	29.3	13.5	33.9	58.0	9.0	328	84.1
Maramec town	91	90	-1.1	129	78.3	0.0	1.6	20.2	0.0	32.6	18.6	37.7	64.3	3.6	48	62.5
Marble City town	263	249	-5.3	211	32.7	0.0	0.0	60.7	6.6	22.3	19.9	43.4	69.8	10.1	78	70.5
Marietta CDP	106	-	-	208	42.8	0.0	0.0	28.8	28.4	42.3	6.3	24.3	59.4	15.8	42	92.9
Marietta city	2,625	2,768	5.4	2,740	48.8	7.4	1.6	6.3	35.8	31.6	15.8	31.5	65.8	9.3	865	86.5
Marland town	225	223	-0.9	228	24.6	0.0	0.0	58.8	16.7	37.7	11.8	28.0	61.3	1.7	72	73.6
Marlow city	4,664	4,420	-5.2	4,489	84.0	0.6	0.3	12.3	2.9	24.3	23.3	41.1	61.7	12.2	1,714	85.2
Marshall town	272	307	12.9	240	96.7	0.0	0.0	2.9	0.4	18.8	6.3	41.3	43.3	11.5	79	94.9
Martha town	164	149	-9.1	138	68.8	0.0	0.0	18.1	13.0	21.7	10.1	33.3	67.7	7.5	54	88.9
Maud city	1,060	1,061	0.1	1,044	74.4	1.5	0.0	19.0	5.1	32.1	11.7	33.9	51.5	15.1	344	85.8
May town	39	41	5.1	70	100.0	0.0	0.0	0.0	0.0	14.3	7.1	30.8	81.4	1.7	12	83.3
Maysville town	1,210	1,203	-0.6	1,273	86.2	1.1	0.0	10.6	2.1	25.2	15.3	34.5	67.3	9.0	457	87.7
Mazie CDP	91	-	-	124	79.8	0.0	0.0	20.2	0.0	0.0	51.6	65.1	61.9	8.5	65	100.0
Mead town	122	134	9.8	99	71.7	0.0	0.0	26.3	2.0	14.1	25.3	44.3	30.7	20.0	43	93.0
Medford city	998	939	-5.9	1,009	92.4	0.7	0.3	5.0	1.7	18.7	21.6	43.9	51.1	19.1	429	86.2
Medicine Park town	385	452	17.4	299	94.3	1.0	1.0	2.7	1.0	7.4	33.1	60.4	31.9	35.2	145	95.2
Meeker town	1,146	1,141	-0.4	1,349	63.4	0.0	3.1	29.4	4.1	25.2	21.4	38.7	52.4	13.6	434	75.1
Meno town	235	237	0.9	217	65.0	0.0	0.0	0.0	35.0	29.0	12.9	37.2	60.3	17.5	88	83.0
Meridian town	38	43	13.2	19	15.8	78.9	0.0	0.0	5.3	10.5	52.6	66.2	0.0	29.4	15	46.7
Meridian CDP	1,493	-	-	1,513	85.9	0.0	0.0	10.8	3.2	18.8	14.1	41.8	66.9	6.5	551	93.1
Miami city	13,606	13,088	-3.8	13,289	63.4	2.0	0.7	28.1	5.8	25.3	15.4	33.3	48.0	14.9	5,041	80.9
Midwest City city	54,370	57,407	5.6	57,288	60.0	23.8	1.1	9.2	5.9	24.4	15.3	36.0	41.9	21.4	22,946	88.1
Milburn town	317	319	0.6	315	77.1	0.0	0.0	21.6	1.3	19.4	13.3	41.1	50.2	5.1	117	73.5

1 May be of any race.

Table A. All Places — **Population and Housing**

STATE City, town, township, borough, or CDP (county if applicable)	Population				Race and Hispanic or Latino origin (percent)					Age (percent)			Educational attainment of persons age 25 and older		Occupied housing units	
	2010 census total population	2019 estimated population	Percent change 2010–2019	ACS total population estimate 2015–2019	White alone, not Hispanic or Latino	Black alone, not Hispanic or Latino	Asian alone, not Hispanic or Latino	All other races or 2 or more races, not Hispanic or Latino	Hispanic or Latino[1]	Under 18 years old	Age 65 years and older	Median age	Percent High school diploma or less	Percent Bachelor's degree or more	Total	Percent with a computer
	1	2	3	4	5	6	7	8	9	10	11	12	13	14	15	16
OKLAHOMA—Con.																
Mill Creek town	319	319	0.0	311	61.7	0.0	0.0	31.8	6.4	26.7	10.0	33.7	62.8	17.3	106	74.5
Millerton town	322	315	-2.2	287	61.0	3.5	0.0	29.3	6.3	21.3	18.5	44.2	67.2	13.8	114	67.5
Minco city	1,631	1,648	1.0	1,617	83.7	1.7	0.4	8.8	5.4	20.3	17.1	39.0	55.4	19.3	644	89.3
Moffett town	128	118	-7.8	112	51.8	34.8	0.0	13.4	0.0	23.2	7.1	36.3	81.8	1.3	44	65.9
Monroe CDP	-	-	-	207	75.8	0.0	1.4	22.7	0.0	23.2	17.9	40.8	66.7	3.3	76	69.7
Moore city	55,082	62,055	12.7	60,943	71.1	5.8	2.4	10.8	9.9	24.4	11.3	34.3	36.9	26.6	23,290	94.6
Mooreland town	1,212	1,169	-3.5	1,344	87.7	0.0	0.4	4.2	7.7	32.1	16.1	30.0	40.6	25.3	449	95.1
Morris city	1,479	1,420	-4.0	1,436	60.2	1.1	0.0	34.0	4.7	31.1	11.8	34.6	43.8	14.3	518	86.3
Morrison town	733	707	-3.5	747	72.7	0.9	0.0	24.2	2.1	33.1	8.3	32.8	38.6	39.3	325	90.8
Mounds town	1,160	1,262	8.8	1,099	70.6	0.4	0.5	26.4	2.2	24.3	14.9	36.2	52.8	14.9	404	81.4
Mountain Park town	409	381	-6.8	568	75.7	0.7	0.0	7.6	16.0	32.6	9.2	27.5	57.3	9.8	199	92.0
Mountain View town	795	735	-7.5	718	72.8	0.0	0.0	23.1	4.0	21.9	18.7	45.6	57.2	16.2	335	78.2
Mulberry CDP	138	-	-	130	9.2	0.0	0.0	90.8	0.0	30.0	10.8	29.1	69.0	8.5	45	84.4
Muldrow town	3,460	3,251	-6.0	3,270	63.5	2.0	0.0	31.3	3.2	23.2	10.4	37.3	56.0	10.1	1,187	85.8
Mulhall town	225	259	15.1	260	85.8	0.0	0.0	8.1	6.2	27.7	13.1	37.3	62.6	12.6	74	87.8
Murphy CDP	219	-	-	79	88.6	0.0	0.0	11.4	0.0	0.0	12.7	56.2	64.6	35.4	43	81.4
Muskogee city	39,181	37,113	-5.3	37,624	50.5	15.1	0.8	25.3	8.3	25.1	15.5	36.2	49.1	20.9	15,101	83.5
Mustang city	17,395	22,959	32.0	21,459	81.1	1.6	1.2	9.4	6.7	25.0	15.3	37.7	37.7	24.7	7,146	93.6
Mutual town	61	61	0.0	130	90.0	0.0	0.0	2.3	7.7	32.3	6.2	29.7	42.9	27.1	40	95.0
Narcissa CDP	99	-	-	126	50.0	0.0	2.4	47.6	0.0	15.9	42.1	57.5	51.5	22.8	49	79.6
Nardin CDP	52	-	-	11	100.0	0.0	0.0	0.0	0.0	0.0	100.0	0.0	0.0	0.0	11	0.0
Nash town	203	194	-4.4	208	97.1	0.0	0.0	2.9	0.0	18.3	41.8	62.6	40.4	25.3	89	67.4
Nescatunga CDP	70	-	-	80	86.3	0.0	0.0	0.0	13.8	0.0	31.3	58.4	72.5	8.7	42	78.6
New Alluwe town	90	85	-5.6	65	47.7	0.0	1.5	50.8	0.0	30.8	12.3	35.5	61.9	7.1	27	70.4
Newcastle city	7,682	10,655	38.7	9,967	84.4	1.4	0.0	10.2	4.0	24.9	15.1	39.1	34.7	30.1	3,873	94.3
New Cordell city	2,921	2,734	-6.4	2,813	84.0	0.8	0.0	2.6	12.7	24.0	18.7	39.0	52.8	21.6	1,166	85.3
New Eucha CDP	405	-	-	497	39.0	0.0	0.0	53.5	7.4	7.6	20.5	49.8	55.1	10.1	151	100.0
Newkirk city	2,319	2,170	-6.4	2,324	76.8	0.6	0.9	16.6	5.1	26.8	18.9	37.3	54.2	10.5	893	77.9
Nichols Hills city	3,688	3,938	6.8	3,891	92.5	0.0	1.2	4.1	2.1	22.2	22.5	48.3	6.5	82.7	1,604	97.9
Nicoma Park city	2,405	2,467	2.6	2,441	81.4	2.4	0.0	11.7	4.5	25.4	17.7	38.4	50.0	13.8	897	91.9
Nicut CDP	360	-	-	277	39.0	0.0	0.0	61.0	0.0	22.0	23.5	42.1	69.7	8.0	112	55.4
Ninnekah town	1,002	1,047	4.5	1,014	80.0	0.2	0.0	11.4	8.4	23.1	20.8	38.4	55.4	18.5	374	90.1
Noble city	6,481	7,053	8.8	6,837	84.2	0.0	0.0	15.5	0.3	28.3	18.0	37.4	44.9	21.4	2,447	93.0
Norge town	145	154	6.2	138	81.2	0.0	0.0	16.7	2.2	23.2	18.1	46.0	70.5	4.8	51	82.4
Norman city	110,911	124,880	12.6	122,837	71.3	4.4	4.8	11.0	8.5	19.1	12.3	30.9	26.1	42.9	47,913	94.4
North Enid town	856	921	7.6	889	89.3	0.0	0.0	5.4	5.3	22.4	22.5	43.0	43.3	20.1	321	92.8
North Miami town	374	368	-1.6	326	59.5	0.6	0.0	32.2	7.7	19.0	20.6	39.8	67.8	8.1	133	72.9
Notchietown CDP	373	-	-	170	68.8	0.0	0.0	31.2	0.0	15.3	25.3	51.7	74.6	17.5	75	73.3
Nowata city	3,731	3,552	-4.8	3,639	61.8	4.8	0.0	28.7	4.6	21.8	20.1	40.9	60.0	7.0	1,534	79.0
Oakhurst CDP	2,185	-	-	2,272	72.2	0.2	0.0	24.0	3.6	18.3	15.4	44.4	63.4	6.7	944	81.8
Oakland town	1,057	1,140	7.9	1,109	41.3	0.6	0.3	19.2	38.6	28.2	13.3	34.2	64.7	10.8	389	89.7
Oaks town	285	283	-0.7	283	15.9	5.7	4.9	72.4	1.1	36.4	13.8	32.1	64.8	7.5	76	68.4
Oakwood town	65	66	1.5	55	63.6	0.0	0.0	18.2	18.2	0.0	32.7	58.8	54.0	14.0	28	96.4
Ochelata town	424	424	0.0	497	71.4	1.6	0.0	26.0	1.0	26.4	14.1	35.7	57.7	12.6	172	86.0
Oilton city	1,013	1,014	0.1	881	90.6	0.1	0.0	7.7	1.6	27.8	16.3	34.8	67.7	5.7	355	76.3
Okarche town	1,215	1,331	9.5	1,445	90.0	0.8	0.4	6.4	2.4	22.9	14.7	39.5	44.8	26.8	466	85.6
Okay town	617	702	13.8	521	52.6	5.6	0.0	37.0	4.8	19.0	14.8	42.9	58.0	8.8	197	86.8
Okeene town	1,204	1,138	-5.5	1,156	82.6	0.0	0.0	10.1	7.3	29.8	20.2	35.1	52.4	19.8	543	89.7
Okemah city	3,223	3,132	-2.8	3,178	56.3	4.4	0.0	35.5	3.8	23.8	17.3	37.1	59.6	10.8	1,178	76.4
Oklahoma City city	580,462	655,057	12.9	643,692	53.5	14.1	4.5	8.2	19.7	25.9	12.4	34.1	39.1	30.7	242,748	90.5
Okmulgee city	12,497	11,711	-6.3	11,846	46.8	17.7	1.1	29.9	4.5	22.9	15.9	32.5	49.9	11.7	4,453	81.6
Oktaha town	390	388	-0.5	348	60.3	4.6	0.6	32.5	2.0	25.6	12.6	39.0	61.9	9.7	127	86.6
Old Eucha CDP	52	-	-	41	2.4	0.0	0.0	97.6	0.0	9.8	0.0	50.3	66.7	0.0	14	85.7
Old Green CDP	315	-	-	396	40.2	0.0	0.0	59.8	0.0	13.1	9.3	39.5	84.6	11.5	113	88.5
Olustee town	607	555	-8.6	773	52.4	0.0	0.0	5.4	42.2	34.2	18.4	38.5	61.5	2.6	232	92.2
Oologah town	1,135	1,175	3.5	1,174	69.6	0.9	0.9	26.3	2.4	27.9	12.7	30.2	50.9	16.2	435	86.9
Optima town	356	372	4.5	413	24.0	0.0	0.0	0.0	76.0	27.6	5.3	32.9	79.0	2.9	118	74.6
Orlando town	148	167	12.8	95	82.1	0.0	0.0	12.6	5.3	25.3	17.9	30.6	66.7	6.7	38	50.0
Osage town	156	155	-0.6	140	76.4	0.0	0.0	21.4	2.1	14.3	25.0	56.3	78.8	7.1	66	71.2
Owasso city	29,884	36,957	23.7	36,173	74.3	3.2	2.3	14.2	6.1	28.0	11.3	32.9	31.8	34.4	13,342	94.4
Paden town	461	456	-1.1	468	60.0	3.2	0.0	32.1	4.7	26.9	17.9	37.7	55.3	16.4	176	80.7
Panama town	1,412	1,362	-3.5	1,334	70.2	3.9	1.3	22.9	1.7	29.2	14.7	33.9	68.1	8.7	496	72.6
Panola CDP	-	-	-	34	79.4	0.0	0.0	20.6	0.0	0.0	44.1	46.5	54.5	13.6	18	38.9
Paoli town	610	613	0.5	691	74.2	0.9	4.9	8.7	11.3	26.0	12.0	33.7	65.7	14.7	260	85.0
Paradise Hill town	85	80	-5.9	71	57.7	0.0	0.0	28.2	14.1	33.8	19.7	39.8	27.9	27.9	19	89.5
Park Hill CDP	3,909	-	-	4,001	40.3	0.3	0.0	46.1	13.2	23.0	16.0	30.3	48.3	20.0	1,207	71.8
Pauls Valley city	6,104	6,110	0.1	6,139	65.8	4.6	0.0	11.8	17.7	25.8	19.4	38.9	58.5	15.2	2,293	85.4
Pawhuska city	3,689	3,415	-7.4	3,481	53.7	2.3	0.2	38.1	5.6	22.1	15.3	39.5	49.5	14.8	1,386	82.3
Pawnee city	2,196	2,106	-4.1	2,068	58.8	3.8	0.7	33.5	3.2	25.8	18.2	40.0	57.0	15.0	751	76.3
Peavine CDP	423	-	-	377	45.1	0.0	0.0	54.9	0.0	19.6	18.3	47.0	62.6	12.6	147	86.4
Peggs CDP	813	-	-	1,014	55.3	1.0	0.2	43.2	0.3	22.1	16.7	37.9	52.8	16.4	333	76.0
Pensacola town	125	127	1.6	120	52.5	0.0	5.0	41.7	0.8	20.0	10.8	41.5	62.8	6.4	38	89.5
Peoria town	132	135	2.3	108	79.6	0.0	0.0	20.4	0.0	17.6	23.1	49.5	72.6	2.4	51	60.8
Perkins city	2,830	2,817	-0.5	2,855	87.3	6.1	0.3	3.1	3.3	29.9	17.8	30.5	41.0	21.9	1,147	89.5
Perry city	5,126	4,837	-5.6	4,942	86.9	0.4	0.0	8.9	3.7	26.4	16.2	39.1	55.3	22.7	1,951	80.4
Pettit CDP	954	-	-	927	70.2	0.0	0.0	29.8	0.0	21.3	16.2	42.4	22.1	41.5	337	89.0
Phillips town	135	127	-5.9	127	68.5	0.0	0.0	30.7	0.8	21.3	13.4	29.6	70.0	1.4	49	71.4
Piedmont city	5,720	8,551	49.5	7,747	83.1	0.7	3.4	8.3	4.6	30.0	11.7	35.8	24.9	42.6	2,511	93.4
Piney CDP	115	-	-	48	64.6	0.0	0.0	35.4	0.0	20.8	64.6	67.5	81.6	18.4	31	77.4
Pinhook Corner CDP	171	-	-	127	55.9	0.0	0.0	44.1	0.0	20.5	29.9	44.2	36.8	31.0	49	49.0
Pink town	2,058	2,181	6.0	2,020	79.5	1.3	0.3	14.4	4.5	26.1	15.1	39.8	50.5	17.9	657	87.8
Pin Oak Acres CDP	421	-	-	538	79.4	0.0	0.0	13.0	7.6	28.6	13.9	46.4	63.5	15.7	191	92.1
Pittsburg town	207	197	-4.8	215	49.3	0.0	0.0	45.1	5.6	19.5	15.8	39.4	70.1	9.0	94	75.5
Platter CDP	-	-	-	250	76.8	0.0	0.0	12.0	11.2	25.6	24.0	39.3	71.3	0.0	98	81.6
Pocasset town	203	208	2.5	158	94.9	0.0	0.0	5.1	0.0	24.7	14.6	36.5	68.1	8.0	67	85.1
Pocola town	4,048	4,121	1.8	4,071	78.8	2.6	0.7	15.2	2.7	25.2	18.0	38.3	55.0	13.1	1,469	84.3
Ponca City city	25,387	23,660	-6.8	24,134	71.6	3.4	0.5	14.7	9.9	25.1	18.0	36.7	44.7	20.4	9,617	87.8
Pond Creek city	859	834	-2.9	1,153	89.3	0.8	0.2	5.6	4.1	35.4	11.0	32.0	50.7	28.0	408	88.0
Porter town	600	682	13.7	566	75.6	4.1	0.5	15.9	3.9	24.0	19.1	37.8	65.5	7.0	216	82.9
Porum town	727	701	-3.6	755	57.5	0.0	0.0	37.9	4.6	35.6	12.7	30.6	63.3	8.1	276	76.4
Poteau city	8,512	8,863	4.1	8,843	70.3	1.1	0.2	15.1	13.3	24.1	14.6	33.4	54.4	16.9	3,199	84.2

1 May be of any race.

Table A. All Places — **Population and Housing**

STATE City, town, township, borough, or CDP (county if applicable)	Population: 2010 census total population	Population: 2019 estimated population	Population: Percent change 2010–2019	Population: ACS total population estimate 2015–2019	Race and Hispanic or Latino origin (percent): White alone, not Hispanic or Latino	Black alone, not Hispanic or Latino	Asian alone, not Hispanic or Latino	All other races or 2 or more races, not Hispanic or Latino	Hispanic or Latino[1]	Age (percent): Under 18 years old	Age 65 years and older	Median age	Educational attainment of persons age 25 and older: Percent High school diploma or less	Percent Bachelor's degree or more	Occupied housing units: Total	Percent with a computer
	1	2	3	4	5	6	7	8	9	10	11	12	13	14	15	16
OKLAHOMA—Con.																
Prague city	2,384	2,367	-0.7	1,774	82.8	3.6	0.5	11.2	1.9	16.5	25.9	49.1	54.4	15.0	780	79.7
Proctor CDP	231	-	-	454	42.1	0.0	0.0	57.9	0.0	22.7	2.6	39.4	51.9	8.0	105	88.6
Prue town	466	470	0.9	406	85.2	0.0	0.0	14.3	0.5	24.6	16.5	36.4	69.0	8.5	160	85.6
Pryor Creek city	9,537	9,379	-1.7	9,394	66.8	0.7	0.7	28.0	3.8	24.0	18.4	35.3	54.4	14.3	3,823	87.5
Pump Back CDP	175	-	-	166	42.2	0.0	0.0	57.8	0.0	13.3	18.7	38.7	43.1	4.9	69	88.4
Purcell city	6,170	6,420	4.1	6,401	69.2	2.4	0.0	10.5	17.9	24.9	16.7	38.5	53.8	18.3	2,406	87.2
Putnam town	29	29	0.0	54	81.5	0.0	0.0	18.5	0.0	9.3	7.4	51.5	46.9	26.5	14	78.6
Quapaw town	899	876	-2.6	755	59.2	0.0	0.3	34.4	6.1	24.0	20.5	39.8	56.9	6.6	285	75.1
Quinton town	1,051	985	-6.3	911	68.9	1.6	0.0	25.5	4.0	31.0	12.2	30.3	62.1	2.0	355	82.8
Ralston town	330	319	-3.3	315	74.0	0.0	0.0	22.9	3.2	27.3	16.5	38.4	64.3	9.0	112	69.6
Ramona town	539	545	1.1	620	72.3	2.9	0.0	23.7	1.1	25.5	13.5	40.1	59.7	6.6	227	81.9
Randlett town	438	413	-5.7	370	92.7	0.0	0.0	1.6	5.7	21.6	16.2	38.7	69.8	8.6	131	89.3
Ratliff City town	120	117	-2.5	90	80.0	8.9	0.0	6.7	4.4	16.7	27.8	39.0	76.9	0.0	38	76.3
Rattan town	308	296	-3.9	323	56.7	1.2	0.0	39.9	2.2	27.6	15.5	38.5	52.5	15.1	125	78.4
Ravia town	528	525	-0.6	511	61.4	0.0	0.0	35.2	3.3	23.7	17.0	39.7	66.7	6.3	194	72.7
Redbird town	137	154	12.4	81	14.8	49.4	0.0	34.6	1.2	28.4	21.0	39.9	72.7	3.6	25	84.0
Redbird Smith CDP	465	-	-	522	65.3	12.3	0.0	14.9	7.5	13.6	20.5	43.9	63.3	10.3	198	72.2
Red Oak town	549	478	-12.9	576	60.1	0.0	0.0	38.4	1.6	24.3	22.2	40.4	59.3	15.3	240	72.5
Red Rock town	283	289	2.1	311	42.8	0.0	1.3	54.3	1.6	23.5	5.5	35.2	55.0	6.3	107	85.0
Remy CDP	562	-	-	644	72.0	0.0	3.6	19.1	5.3	19.3	22.0	50.1	54.7	21.8	254	88.6
Renfrow town	12	12	0.0	7	100.0	0.0	0.0	0.0	0.0	0.0	42.9	64.5	85.7	0.0	4	100.0
Rentiesville town	128	124	-3.1	122	24.6	47.5	0.0	27.9	0.0	9.8	21.3	53.3	58.3	13.9	80	70.0
Reydon town	210	206	-1.9	139	82.7	0.0	0.0	6.5	10.8	30.2	10.8	32.7	46.3	18.8	62	74.2
Ringling town	1,037	954	-8.0	926	81.5	0.0	0.0	11.7	6.8	30.7	19.0	32.0	65.8	7.0	357	77.3
Ringwood town	497	509	2.4	611	42.6	0.0	0.0	1.8	55.6	30.1	11.8	36.9	66.0	10.8	213	85.9
Ripley town	418	409	-2.2	287	91.6	0.0	0.0	7.7	0.7	28.9	13.2	38.3	63.9	7.2	114	77.2
River Bottom CDP	154	-	-	280	61.1	0.0	0.0	33.2	5.7	21.4	28.2	51.3	56.2	8.6	119	84.9
Rock Island town	655	643	-1.8	842	86.5	0.8	0.8	11.2	0.7	27.1	12.2	38.2	65.8	10.8	297	83.5
Rocky town	162	152	-6.2	140	92.9	0.0	0.0	4.3	2.9	7.1	30.0	49.5	63.7	5.3	58	86.2
Rocky Ford CDP	61	-	-	42	40.5	0.0	0.0	59.5	0.0	28.6	7.1	29.5	48.0	16.0	15	66.7
Rocky Mountain CDP	420	-	-	514	33.3	0.0	0.0	66.7	0.0	25.9	16.0	39.4	60.1	17.2	187	61.5
Roff town	725	713	-1.7	698	66.6	0.0	0.0	27.4	6.0	34.5	15.9	31.7	67.9	10.8	245	81.2
Roland town	3,184	3,911	22.8	3,738	67.1	3.4	0.4	24.2	4.9	25.7	15.2	31.7	60.1	9.3	1,292	91.1
Roosevelt town	248	230	-7.3	289	78.9	2.4	0.0	3.5	15.2	26.0	14.5	39.8	59.5	13.5	128	81.3
Rose CDP	285	-	-	356	31.7	0.0	0.0	61.8	6.5	22.2	27.8	40.6	86.4	0.0	141	90.1
Rosedale town	68	71	4.4	51	68.6	0.0	0.0	17.6	13.7	5.9	25.5	50.3	87.2	5.1	19	73.7
Rosston town	31	32	3.2	65	47.7	0.0	0.0	3.1	49.2	27.7	7.7	35.6	42.6	38.3	20	75.0
Rush Springs town	1,234	1,256	1.8	1,248	81.3	0.3	0.0	15.6	2.8	22.9	22.7	42.3	67.6	13.5	484	87.6
Ryan town	816	750	-8.1	771	67.2	1.6	0.0	7.4	23.9	30.6	20.1	36.8	66.1	10.4	295	79.3
St. Louis town	158	161	1.9	101	84.2	0.0	0.0	13.9	2.0	16.8	15.8	51.9	71.1	9.6	42	85.7
Salem CDP	112	-	-	129	29.5	0.0	0.0	70.5	0.0	41.1	25.6	27.5	73.7	14.5	37	81.1
Salina town	1,399	1,394	-0.4	1,225	47.0	1.1	0.3	49.6	2.0	20.3	20.7	42.6	57.2	8.4	486	82.9
Sallisaw city	8,941	8,497	-5.0	8,571	59.1	0.7	0.5	32.6	7.0	25.8	16.2	36.8	56.9	16.5	3,350	86.7
Sams Corner CDP	137	-	-	183	59.0	0.0	0.0	41.0	0.0	21.9	19.7	29.7	41.2	7.6	74	85.1
Sand Hill CDP	395	-	-	330	62.7	0.0	0.0	28.2	9.1	23.6	24.2	45.8	54.0	15.9	128	82.8
Sand Springs city	18,808	19,905	5.8	19,794	78.1	2.0	0.8	14.3	4.8	24.3	17.2	37.5	42.3	20.2	7,663	89.6
Sapulpa city	20,195	21,278	5.4	21,041	73.1	3.2	1.0	17.0	5.7	24.1	18.2	38.0	50.5	18.8	7,956	86.1
Sasakwa town	145	137	-5.5	105	32.4	1.9	0.0	65.7	0.0	20.0	16.2	26.8	55.4	8.9	36	72.2
Savanna town	681	645	-5.3	601	63.1	0.0	0.2	33.3	3.5	21.8	16.6	37.9	52.6	13.8	241	86.7
Sawyer town	321	313	-2.5	316	65.5	3.2	0.0	31.0	0.3	20.6	16.8	43.7	58.8	10.7	127	81.9
Sayre city	4,374	4,486	2.6	4,549	66.3	12.9	0.2	8.2	12.5	15.7	9.5	37.6	59.5	12.1	1,067	81.5
Schulter town	510	496	-2.7	381	76.9	0.8	0.0	20.7	1.6	19.2	25.7	47.4	57.3	8.0	175	73.1
Scraper CDP	191	-	-	195	75.4	0.0	0.0	24.6	0.0	0.0	48.2	57.9	36.4	34.9	126	100.0
Seiling city	851	855	0.5	875	66.4	0.0	0.3	15.9	17.4	32.6	16.1	35.7	49.3	25.5	273	91.2
Seminole city	7,483	7,041	-5.9	7,219	63.0	4.4	1.1	25.0	6.6	27.4	14.3	33.0	50.5	14.1	2,622	82.5
Sentinel town	899	845	-6.0	825	73.0	0.2	0.0	6.4	20.4	25.1	15.5	34.4	47.1	20.2	316	84.8
Sequoyah CDP	698	-	-	957	74.1	1.3	0.0	17.9	6.8	25.5	11.7	40.2	53.1	20.3	280	93.6
Shady Grove CDP	556	-	-	533	43.9	0.0	0.0	50.5	5.6	25.1	14.8	35.6	51.1	18.2	171	87.7
Shady Grove CDP	194	-	-	183	46.4	0.0	0.0	53.6	0.0	12.0	0.0	44.9	42.6	15.7	52	100.0
Shady Point town	1,028	999	-2.8	1,144	80.4	1.0	0.2	14.9	3.5	30.6	15.0	36.0	63.4	6.6	400	80.3
Sharon town	135	134	-0.7	117	86.3	0.0	0.0	7.7	6.0	30.8	11.1	33.0	62.8	23.1	35	88.6
Shattuck town	1,356	1,257	-7.3	1,317	83.1	0.0	0.0	5.8	11.0	24.2	16.3	39.0	43.7	20.3	506	82.4
Shawnee city	29,825	31,436	5.4	31,235	68.9	4.6	0.7	19.0	6.7	22.7	16.2	35.6	46.9	20.6	12,025	85.0
Shidler city	441	430	-2.5	310	72.6	1.6	0.0	22.6	3.2	27.1	15.8	39.1	56.8	15.5	127	87.4
Short CDP	293	-	-	298	91.6	0.0	0.0	8.4	0.0	10.7	23.8	53.8	79.9	1.3	120	83.3
Silo town	335	365	9.0	412	72.8	0.0	0.0	25.5	1.7	27.9	16.7	35.5	50.6	19.4	134	85.1
Simms CDP	325	-	-	278	61.9	0.0	4.0	34.2	0.0	19.1	13.3	49.1	57.5	8.7	101	69.3
Skedee town	51	50	-2.0	27	44.4	55.6	0.0	0.0	0.0	44.4	0.0	25.5	78.6	0.0	9	100.0
Skiatook city	7,308	8,052	10.2	7,962	71.3	1.7	0.7	24.9	1.4	28.0	12.2	35.3	50.7	18.2	2,954	89.3
Slaughterville town	4,147	4,296	3.6	4,239	81.7	0.3	0.5	14.1	3.4	27.9	13.2	39.0	57.0	13.4	1,463	88.1
Slick town	180	182	1.1	158	88.0	5.7	0.0	6.3	0.0	24.1	12.7	37.7	67.0	3.5	57	71.9
Smith Village town	71	78	9.9	96	96.9	0.0	0.0	3.1	0.0	6.3	13.5	54.3	51.7	6.9	60	100.0
Snake Creek CDP	257	-	-	225	32.0	0.0	0.0	57.8	10.2	31.6	15.6	34.2	43.5	12.3	82	72.0
Snyder city	1,394	1,277	-8.4	1,554	73.1	7.8	0.3	7.4	11.5	25.9	22.7	38.6	51.0	20.0	619	83.5
Soper town	262	253	-3.4	250	63.2	2.8	1.6	22.8	9.6	23.2	25.6	41.7	62.5	9.5	106	67.9
Sour John CDP	60	-	-	74	51.4	0.0	0.0	48.6	0.0	16.2	17.6	57.1	75.9	3.7	28	71.4
South Coffeyville town	781	734	-6.0	816	67.9	2.7	0.0	27.5	2.0	26.7	15.7	36.1	51.9	11.8	322	87.0
Sparks town	169	171	1.2	158	81.6	1.3	0.0	17.1	0.0	27.2	19.0	43.5	71.0	2.8	57	77.2
Spaulding town	178	173	-2.8	119	73.1	0.0	0.0	26.1	0.8	15.1	40.3	55.1	58.9	11.1	46	37.0
Spavinaw town	437	429	-1.8	376	56.9	0.3	0.3	39.6	2.9	17.8	25.8	50.6	59.0	7.8	179	78.2
Spencer city	3,916	3,968	1.3	3,995	31.7	52.4	0.6	11.2	4.2	21.6	20.5	43.1	53.4	15.9	1,644	86.1
Sperry town	1,204	1,338	11.1	1,275	70.1	0.0	0.5	25.9	3.5	27.7	12.2	35.5	58.9	11.9	499	85.8
Spiro town	2,160	2,158	-0.1	2,560	76.2	1.9	1.5	14.4	6.0	27.6	17.5	35.2	63.9	10.7	918	79.4
Sportsmen Acres town	317	308	-2.8	378	63.5	0.3	0.5	31.0	4.8	32.8	8.2	27.5	64.2	8.8	133	94.7
Springer town	700	691	-1.3	743	63.4	1.3	0.0	29.2	6.1	33.4	12.5	32.0	58.7	13.5	269	86.2
Steely Hollow CDP	206	-	-	153	34.0	0.0	0.0	66.0	0.0	30.1	30.7	39.1	15.8	13.9	70	77.1
Sterling town	788	773	-1.9	637	68.8	0.0	1.1	24.3	5.8	24.0	14.9	39.8	63.1	10.9	241	88.0
Stidham town	20	19	-5.0	28	67.9	0.0	0.0	32.1	0.0	21.4	21.4	39.7	85.0	15.0	9	44.4
Stigler city	2,653	2,677	0.9	2,680	68.9	1.5	0.6	20.9	8.0	25.9	19.7	36.7	54.5	14.9	1,055	84.5
Stillwater city	45,721	50,299	10.0	49,952	73.6	4.6	6.7	10.5	4.7	15.9	9.2	23.5	24.1	48.7	18,585	93.6
Stilwell city	3,960	4,060	2.5	4,045	26.4	0.2	0.1	61.6	11.7	30.9	13.3	30.6	68.5	13.2	1,414	67.6
Stonewall town	518	521	0.6	506	62.6	4.2	0.0	28.9	4.3	23.1	21.9	40.3	59.4	11.7	186	75.3

1 May be of any race.

Table A. All Places — **Population and Housing**

STATE City, town, township, borough, or CDP (county if applicable)	Population				Race and Hispanic or Latino origin (percent)					Age (percent)			Educational attainment of persons age 25 and older		Occupied housing units	
	2010 census total population	2019 estimated population	Percent change 2010–2019	ACS total population estimate 2015–2019	White alone, not Hispanic or Latino	Black alone, not Hispanic or Latino	Asian alone, not Hispanic or Latino	All other races or 2 or more races, not Hispanic or Latino	Hispanic or Latino[1]	Under 18 years old	Age 65 years and older	Median age	Percent High school diploma or less	Percent Bachelor's degree or more	Total	Percent with a computer
	1	2	3	4	5	6	7	8	9	10	11	12	13	14	15	16
OKLAHOMA—Con.																
Stoney Point CDP	238	-	-	263	69.6	0.0	0.0	30.4	0.0	25.5	24.3	49.6	57.3	17.2	100	77.0
Strang town	89	89	0.0	79	50.6	0.0	0.0	49.4	0.0	25.3	7.6	33.3	61.1	0.0	32	78.1
Stratford town	1,525	1,525	0.0	1,433	72.1	0.7	0.0	24.7	2.5	28.2	14.7	31.0	61.6	15.0	584	84.2
Stringtown town	416	403	-3.1	372	70.2	2.7	0.0	26.1	1.1	30.1	23.4	39.0	64.1	12.7	162	75.9
Strong City town	47	46	-2.1	23	100.0	0.0	0.0	0.0	0.0	17.4	30.4	57.5	78.9	10.5	9	77.8
Stroud city	2,688	2,700	0.4	2,714	81.8	1.0	0.8	11.5	4.9	23.9	21.0	37.9	55.7	14.1	1,033	81.1
Stuart town	180	166	-7.8	167	91.0	0.0	0.0	7.8	1.2	24.0	15.6	40.6	64.2	2.8	60	56.7
Sugden town	43	42	-2.3	41	80.5	0.0	0.0	19.5	0.0	12.2	19.5	53.8	76.5	0.0	20	70.0
Sulphur city	4,927	5,043	2.4	5,023	72.6	1.2	1.1	16.6	8.5	25.5	19.9	36.8	53.9	17.3	1,828	88.0
Summit town	139	137	-1.4	107	15.0	82.2	0.0	2.8	0.0	24.3	23.4	52.5	77.6	1.5	31	48.4
Sweetwater town	87	83	-4.6	98	93.9	0.0	0.0	0.0	6.1	35.7	12.2	28.5	34.7	12.2	43	95.3
Swink CDP	66	-	-	50	86.0	0.0	0.0	14.0	0.0	26.0	20.0	34.9	70.3	10.8	24	66.7
Sycamore CDP	177	-	-	111	0.0	0.0	64.0	36.0	0.0	40.5	0.0	26.1	100.0	0.0	30	100.0
Taft town	250	238	-4.8	145	7.6	72.4	0.0	20.0	0.0	13.8	20.7	48.2	60.2	11.5	75	61.3
Tagg Flats CDP	13	-	-	-	-	-	-	-	-	-	-	-	-	-	-	-
Tahlequah city	15,752	16,819	6.8	16,667	48.0	2.3	1.8	39.6	8.4	20.6	14.1	29.1	37.0	33.6	5,801	87.3
Talala town	270	278	3.0	284	69.4	1.1	0.0	28.2	1.4	30.6	10.9	33.4	54.3	7.0	105	92.4
Talihina town	1,134	1,084	-4.4	992	54.7	3.0	1.7	37.5	3.0	24.3	18.8	36.9	55.2	13.2	408	69.1
Taloga town	303	312	3.0	328	89.9	2.4	0.0	5.8	1.8	18.0	24.4	44.5	52.6	33.2	156	84.6
Tamaha town	239	231	-3.3	194	54.1	0.0	16.5	19.1	10.3	9.8	22.7	52.6	55.8	20.6	95	88.4
Tatums town	151	149	-1.3	131	7.6	88.5	0.0	3.8	0.0	22.1	18.3	38.8	71.8	4.7	49	55.1
Tecumseh city	6,478	6,636	2.4	6,643	68.2	3.3	0.5	22.9	5.1	26.3	18.1	36.9	50.8	11.8	2,495	87.0
Temple town	1,002	907	-9.5	873	71.1	12.0	0.0	5.3	11.6	16.2	26.0	54.9	76.5	5.5	364	75.8
Tenkiller CDP	633	-	-	686	32.8	1.3	2.3	55.0	8.6	24.9	11.5	30.0	59.2	18.4	198	76.3
Teresita CDP	159	-	-	172	45.9	0.0	0.0	48.8	5.2	20.9	22.7	48.3	49.3	16.9	65	75.4
Terlton town	108	107	-0.9	103	75.7	0.0	0.0	20.4	3.9	28.2	24.3	46.5	64.8	7.0	40	90.0
Terral town	382	385	0.8	403	66.3	0.0	0.0	4.5	29.3	18.4	23.1	49.9	70.2	4.6	176	75.6
Texanna CDP	2,261	-	-	2,286	72.7	1.0	0.0	20.9	5.5	17.7	33.3	56.5	54.1	12.5	1,048	78.3
Texhoma town	926	901	-2.7	809	45.7	0.0	0.0	0.0	54.3	26.2	18.7	30.7	63.3	22.9	303	68.3
Texola town	36	35	-2.8	40	100.0	0.0	0.0	0.0	0.0	0.0	25.0	53.2	100.0	0.0	13	84.6
Thackerville town	463	514	11.0	440	80.2	3.2	0.0	11.8	4.8	23.9	22.7	36.5	61.6	6.0	150	84.0
The Village city	8,952	9,564	6.8	9,452	76.7	6.9	1.4	7.2	7.7	15.8	18.2	36.8	27.8	42.9	4,624	89.9
Thomas city	1,181	1,198	1.4	1,213	81.1	0.0	0.0	11.1	7.7	25.1	16.2	40.2	49.8	16.2	478	90.2
Tiawah CDP	189	-	-	189	94.2	0.0	0.0	0.0	5.8	33.9	3.2	39.9	29.6	28.7	63	90.5
Tipton town	847	759	-10.4	731	70.7	2.6	0.0	2.3	24.4	24.1	26.5	50.8	61.8	18.8	303	81.5
Tishomingo city	3,039	3,082	1.4	3,071	70.1	4.1	0.0	15.9	9.8	21.6	19.8	37.8	40.0	25.3	1,222	74.9
Titanic CDP	356	-	-	349	30.4	0.0	0.0	64.2	5.4	33.8	10.9	34.7	52.9	21.4	116	56.9
Tonkawa city	3,216	2,980	-7.3	3,052	76.0	0.7	1.3	12.5	9.7	25.3	16.0	33.5	41.6	20.9	1,229	89.7
Tribbey town	391	414	5.9	366	89.9	0.0	0.0	8.2	1.9	15.0	24.3	51.0	69.8	2.8	144	83.3
Tryon town	491	501	2.0	686	80.2	0.0	0.0	10.8	9.0	23.3	12.2	30.7	58.1	9.5	197	89.8
Tullahassee town	99	110	11.1	146	22.6	27.4	0.0	50.0	0.0	36.3	16.4	31.7	34.4	29.0	45	75.6
Tulsa city	392,004	401,190	2.3	402,324	54.0	15.0	3.3	11.1	16.5	24.5	14.0	35.1	38.0	31.5	164,000	90.0
Tupelo city	329	303	-7.9	306	58.5	0.0	0.0	33.3	8.2	26.8	14.7	38.0	64.2	12.8	115	68.7
Turley CDP	2,756	-	-	2,559	57.2	15.8	0.0	18.4	8.5	16.3	16.0	44.8	66.3	6.6	988	83.1
Turpin CDP	467	-	-	412	70.4	0.0	0.0	9.0	20.6	32.0	14.3	32.6	55.2	9.3	127	83.5
Tushka town	458	394	-14.0	525	67.0	7.4	0.0	20.0	5.5	20.2	12.6	26.6	47.3	9.2	265	73.6
Tuskahoma CDP	151	-	-	93	62.4	0.0	0.0	37.6	0.0	25.8	28.0	45.5	52.2	17.4	42	78.6
Tuttle city	6,169	7,593	23.1	7,294	84.3	0.0	0.6	11.6	3.5	25.0	16.5	41.2	40.9	28.3	2,512	93.4
Twin Oaks CDP	198	-	-	157	44.6	0.0	19.7	35.7	0.0	15.3	5.7	50.7	56.4	26.5	56	100.0
Tyrone town	762	741	-2.8	723	62.9	0.0	0.0	9.8	27.2	23.0	7.2	34.8	47.5	22.7	245	84.9
Union City town	1,641	2,157	31.4	1,651	78.3	5.4	0.7	8.2	7.4	22.2	15.3	40.4	49.4	18.1	486	92.2
Valley Brook town	774	771	-0.4	868	66.2	2.1	0.2	9.6	21.9	25.7	13.7	34.2	76.7	4.8	293	87.0
Valley Park town	65	72	10.8	118	100.0	0.0	0.0	0.0	0.0	47.5	0.0	21.2	28.3	45.7	20	90.0
Valliant town	754	738	-2.1	765	58.3	17.3	2.7	17.3	4.4	22.6	18.7	42.3	67.4	10.7	336	74.7
Velma town	620	595	-4.0	585	83.9	0.0	0.0	12.3	3.8	31.5	14.5	35.3	61.6	12.4	211	80.1
Vera town	246	247	0.4	167	76.6	0.0	0.0	16.2	7.2	19.2	22.8	45.8	65.8	10.8	63	76.2
Verden town	530	537	1.3	671	70.5	0.0	0.0	25.8	3.7	27.9	13.3	35.2	60.9	12.9	227	83.3
Verdigris town	3,940	4,590	16.5	4,460	64.4	1.0	0.5	25.7	8.4	28.3	12.6	34.2	35.5	24.0	1,623	94.7
Vian town	1,466	1,367	-6.8	1,282	38.5	6.6	0.5	45.6	8.9	26.1	16.1	37.6	63.9	12.6	471	74.9
Vici town	699	704	0.7	749	85.7	0.0	0.0	9.7	4.5	15.5	20.6	39.5	66.1	12.5	256	89.1
Vinita city	5,745	5,311	-7.6	5,423	60.1	3.8	0.7	30.9	4.6	23.3	21.1	41.6	56.5	12.5	2,157	81.9
Wagoner city	8,315	9,185	10.5	8,920	66.7	8.2	0.4	22.0	2.7	25.2	17.6	38.3	50.7	18.3	3,474	89.6
Wainwright town	165	160	-3.0	139	80.6	0.0	0.0	17.3	2.2	33.8	10.8	32.1	61.3	16.3	48	77.1
Wakita town	340	326	-4.1	296	78.4	1.0	0.3	5.1	15.2	26.4	29.4	43.5	57.6	14.8	114	76.3
Walters city	2,593	2,358	-9.1	2,621	68.9	0.9	0.0	19.6	10.6	24.7	15.5	37.6	55.1	14.8	976	85.7
Wanette town	350	359	2.6	297	84.5	0.0	0.0	15.5	0.0	26.9	16.2	40.3	65.2	9.0	112	84.8
Wann town	125	120	-4.0	114	63.2	4.4	0.0	23.7	8.8	29.8	19.3	37.0	55.1	15.4	44	68.2
Wapanucka town	438	443	1.1	426	72.1	0.0	0.0	21.8	6.1	26.5	14.1	34.1	62.8	6.7	135	71.9
Wardville CDP	-	-	-	25	88.0	0.0	0.0	12.0	0.0	0.0	84.0	69.4	52.0	24.0	19	100.0
Warner town	1,639	1,590	-3.0	1,509	62.3	5.5	0.3	30.7	1.1	20.5	19.8	31.4	50.2	18.0	490	80.8
Warr Acres city	9,895	10,118	2.3	10,180	53.6	11.5	5.3	6.7	22.9	30.3	13.4	31.0	47.3	24.1	3,656	93.8
Warwick town	148	150	1.4	191	94.8	2.1	0.0	2.1	1.0	7.9	11.5	56.5	63.4	2.9	87	88.5
Washington town	564	601	6.6	713	76.7	0.0	4.6	16.1	2.5	28.1	9.3	30.6	33.3	31.1	236	94.9
Watonga city	5,111	2,841	-44.4	2,881	47.4	11.9	0.0	12.4	28.4	7.3	12.3	42.0	67.7	7.9	834	81.8
Watts town	324	313	-3.4	322	56.8	0.9	0.0	28.3	14.0	34.8	8.4	32.3	82.9	4.4	101	69.3
Wauhillau CDP	345	-	-	474	38.6	0.0	0.0	59.5	1.9	33.5	11.0	31.5	65.0	7.0	124	61.3
Waukomis town	1,286	1,296	0.8	1,378	95.9	0.0	0.0	3.4	0.7	21.3	18.0	40.4	61.8	13.6	545	82.4
Waurika city	2,071	1,885	-9.0	2,127	81.3	2.6	0.0	9.6	6.4	26.5	20.4	38.5	58.9	14.4	746	85.7
Wayne town	688	730	6.1	601	71.5	0.0	0.0	13.3	15.1	27.1	13.3	34.8	61.5	10.5	238	78.2
Waynoka city	927	914	-1.4	854	77.0	0.0	0.0	3.4	19.6	30.0	15.3	33.3	57.2	19.0	336	88.1
Weatherford city	10,833	12,017	10.9	11,949	73.7	3.5	0.9	7.4	14.6	20.2	8.5	24.1	29.5	34.6	4,274	95.6
Webb City town	62	61	-1.6	57	96.5	0.0	0.0	3.5	0.0	8.8	17.5	51.2	55.6	0.0	25	80.0
Webbers Falls town	618	593	-4.0	545	53.6	0.0	0.0	42.0	4.4	33.2	16.5	31.1	52.3	14.4	208	69.7
Welch town	619	584	-5.7	631	65.1	0.8	0.0	23.3	10.8	29.0	12.4	34.8	53.9	16.2	217	82.5
Weleetka town	998	954	-4.4	958	55.3	5.8	0.0	33.1	5.7	25.7	15.7	35.2	65.8	8.2	301	71.8
Welling CDP	771	-	-	660	58.6	0.6	0.0	40.3	0.5	21.1	12.9	44.2	55.2	20.7	226	75.2
Wellston town	788	774	-1.8	793	89.5	1.4	0.0	6.2	2.9	21.8	17.3	39.9	58.8	11.5	324	89.2
West Peavine CDP	218	-	-	279	53.0	0.0	0.0	40.1	6.8	22.6	28.7	49.1	76.2	2.9	100	58.0
Westport town	295	296	0.3	479	84.1	1.0	0.0	10.2	4.6	18.6	21.3	47.3	44.2	23.4	192	91.7
West Siloam Springs town	835	859	2.9	978	57.7	0.9	0.5	29.1	11.8	18.2	22.2	40.5	58.7	14.7	302	83.8
Westville town	1,627	1,551	-4.7	1,661	51.7	0.0	0.6	40.6	7.2	29.7	12.3	33.3	67.5	7.8	578	74.7

1 May be of any race.

Table A. All Places — **Population and Housing**

STATE City, town, township, borough, or CDP (county if applicable)	2010 census total population	2019 estimated population	Percent change 2010–2019	ACS total population estimate 2015–2019	White alone, not Hispanic or Latino	Black alone, not Hispanic or Latino	Asian alone, not Hispanic or Latino	All other races or 2 or more races, not Hispanic or Latino	Hispanic or Latino[1]	Under 18 years old	Age 65 years and older	Median age	Percent High school diploma or less	Percent Bachelor's degree or more	Occupied housing units Total	Percent with a computer
	1	2	3	4	5	6	7	8	9	10	11	12	13	14	15	16
OKLAHOMA—Con.																
Wetumka city	1,282	1,202	-6.2	1,277	45.9	5.8	0.0	44.8	3.5	24.8	20.6	42.3	57.8	13.5	417	52.8
Wewoka city	3,430	3,224	-6.0	3,323	51.1	14.2	0.0	30.1	4.6	23.3	20.4	41.7	52.2	10.9	1,272	73.3
Whitefield town	391	387	-	494	76.5	0.0	0.6	19.8	3.0	32.0	15.2	31.0	60.6	12.5	184	88.0
White Oak CDP	263	-	-	259	49.8	0.0	0.0	45.9	4.2	16.2	18.5	43.3	51.8	17.9	111	83.8
Whitesboro CDP	250	-	-	216	49.1	0.0	0.0	50.9	0.0	29.2	17.1	34.0	67.2	9.2	88	71.6
White Water CDP	80	-	-	132	21.2	0.0	0.0	78.8	0.0	48.5	4.5	22.1	55.1	0.0	49	42.9
Wickliffe CDP	75	-	-	16	43.8	0.0	0.0	56.3	0.0	37.5	0.0	31.0	30.0	0.0	8	87.5
Wilburton city	2,836	2,542	-10.4	2,619	65.6	1.7	0.8	24.2	7.7	22.5	17.6	35.2	55.0	11.0	1,027	78.3
Willow town	149	134	-10.1	150	82.7	0.0	0.0	0.0	17.3	24.7	21.3	43.4	41.4	14.4	68	89.7
Wilson city	1,726	1,695	-1.8	1,426	87.9	1.5	0.4	7.6	2.5	24.8	17.4	36.2	60.8	14.2	516	80.2
Winchester town	516	508	-1.6	640	78.9	1.3	0.0	18.9	0.9	27.5	9.4	38.4	46.0	18.6	223	93.7
Wister town	1,102	1,062	-3.6	1,077	73.5	0.3	0.0	23.8	2.4	23.1	26.4	44.4	63.9	8.9	449	67.7
Woodall CDP	823	-	-	707	33.4	1.4	0.0	61.7	3.5	17.0	18.7	48.2	44.7	15.8	238	80.7
Woodlawn Park town	149	152	2.0	178	91.6	0.0	0.0	1.7	6.7	10.1	35.4	59.4	21.4	51.3	86	98.8
Woodward city	12,000	12,121	1.0	12,448	79.6	0.7	0.3	5.2	14.2	26.8	15.4	35.0	52.6	20.0	4,841	87.3
Wright City town	762	735	-3.5	727	46.2	4.7	0.7	42.6	5.8	29.6	13.2	34.2	68.8	14.3	295	55.9
Wyandotte town	331	324	-2.1	363	53.2	0.0	0.0	35.0	11.8	28.9	13.5	28.6	52.6	9.5	129	79.8
Wynnewood city	2,219	2,203	-0.7	1,979	70.4	8.7	0.0	11.9	9.0	22.1	19.6	42.3	58.7	13.5	784	83.7
Wynona town	437	434	-0.7	311	76.8	0.0	0.0	22.2	1.0	19.9	21.5	40.3	59.2	3.8	137	76.6
Yale city	1,252	1,225	-2.2	1,113	88.0	0.0	0.0	10.6	1.4	26.1	19.7	33.4	63.2	13.6	462	77.7
Yeager town	75	72	-4.0	104	39.4	0.0	0.0	47.1	13.5	26.9	10.6	41.0	60.5	13.2	20	70.0
Yukon city	22,706	28,084	23.7	26,943	78.6	1.0	1.7	9.1	9.5	23.7	15.8	37.7	37.0	28.3	8,739	93.5
Zeb CDP	497	-	-	492	37.2	0.0	0.0	52.0	10.8	23.2	20.1	40.1	46.8	21.3	183	79.2
Zena CDP	122	-	-	139	95.0	0.0	0.0	5.0	0.0	30.9	0.0	31.0	55.2	0.0	53	100.0
Zion CDP	41	-	-	45	8.9	0.0	0.0	91.1	0.0	13.3	28.9	41.4	57.1	25.0	14	71.4
OREGON	3,831,079	4,217,737	10.1	4,129,803	75.7	1.8	4.3	5.2	13.0	21.0	17.2	39.3	32.0	33.7	1,611,982	93.0
Adair Village city	850	874	2.8	1,119	80.5	6.0	2.9	6.0	4.6	30.8	7.5	34.4	16.1	43.4	360	96.1
Adams city	350	357	2.0	494	77.9	0.0	2.4	18.4	1.2	25.1	17.8	38.4	41.1	15.0	164	87.8
Adrian city	177	173	-2.3	198	86.4	0.0	0.0	0.0	13.6	30.8	25.8	37.2	43.9	17.5	75	53.3
Albany city	50,142	55,338	10.4	53,521	81.0	0.5	1.5	4.3	12.6	22.7	15.9	37.0	32.5	27.4	20,752	93.7
Aloha CDP	49,425	-	-	54,287	59.2	4.1	10.2	5.0	21.6	24.7	10.5	35.6	33.1	31.1	18,177	97.6
Alpine CDP	171	-	-	183	78.7	0.0	0.0	0.0	21.3	28.4	23.5	40.8	25.2	46.6	76	100.0
Alsea CDP	164	-	-	234	98.7	0.0	0.0	1.3	0.0	44.9	11.5	20.3	49.6	2.6	76	81.6
Altamont CDP	19,257	-	-	19,341	74.0	0.2	1.3	8.5	15.9	25.1	18.0	40.4	43.9	17.2	7,690	89.2
Amity city	1,614	1,724	6.8	1,650	82.3	0.0	0.8	5.0	11.9	28.1	10.7	37.7	48.4	13.4	558	92.1
Annex CDP	235	-	-	274	74.1	0.0	1.5	0.4	24.1	19.7	20.8	42.5	66.1	7.0	102	76.5
Antelope city	46	50	8.7	82	97.6	0.0	0.0	2.4	0.0	19.5	36.6	53.5	71.2	6.1	38	84.2
Arlington city	588	600	2.0	591	87.1	0.0	1.2	2.9	8.8	20.1	14.4	39.7	46.7	15.5	252	90.5
Ashland city	20,076	21,281	6.0	21,056	85.8	1.4	1.9	3.8	7.1	14.8	23.6	44.8	14.3	58.8	9,879	95.5
Astoria city	9,477	10,015	5.7	9,836	81.5	0.4	0.8	6.4	11.0	18.9	20.2	44.7	28.8	31.9	4,492	89.6
Athena city	1,135	1,144	0.8	1,246	92.0	0.9	0.0	5.1	2.1	21.7	22.6	42.5	37.4	22.7	473	92.2
Aumsville city	3,592	4,180	16.4	4,099	84.4	0.0	0.3	4.6	10.7	34.1	6.6	30.2	43.0	6.7	1,333	99.1
Aurora city	916	1,039	13.4	1,045	91.2	0.2	1.1	0.4	7.2	23.1	14.0	42.1	19.5	42.7	360	98.3
Baker City city	9,828	9,809	-0.2	9,752	89.3	1.2	0.8	3.7	4.9	20.3	22.8	43.4	40.3	23.9	4,127	88.2
Bandon city	3,040	3,148	3.6	3,100	94.1	0.5	0.5	1.1	3.9	13.9	37.9	59.2	34.2	19.2	1,647	82.1
Banks city	1,801	2,036	13.0	1,812	83.5	0.3	1.4	4.0	10.8	30.6	4.1	30.1	25.1	28.2	523	98.5
Barlow city	135	147	8.9	143	82.5	0.0	0.0	4.2	13.3	19.6	10.5	37.6	42.4	19.2	47	97.9
Barview CDP	1,844	-	-	1,879	87.3	0.4	4.2	2.9	5.3	17.7	28.6	52.6	55.2	13.8	776	78.4
Bay City city	1,284	1,404	9.3	1,675	83.2	0.0	1.1	6.8	9.0	20.4	18.0	46.2	36.2	17.5	677	88.9
Bayside Gardens CDP	880	-	-	907	99.0	0.0	0.0	1.0	0.0	25.0	27.0	55.2	29.3	24.9	411	89.5
Beatty CDP	-	-	-	-	-	-	-	-	-	-	-	-	-	-	-	-
Beaver CDP	122	-	-	103	100.0	0.0	0.0	0.0	0.0	0.0	41.7	64.8	31.1	62.1	82	87.8
Beavercreek CDP	4,485	-	-	4,075	94.9	0.5	1.2	1.4	2.0	17.1	25.3	50.3	29.4	32.5	1,645	91.1
Beaverton city	89,725	99,037	10.4	97,861	63.8	2.3	12.8	4.5	16.6	19.6	13.2	36.6	25.0	46.5	39,925	96.1
Bellfountain CDP	75	-	-	16	100.0	0.0	0.0	0.0	0.0	0.0	100.0	0.0	100.0	0.0	16	43.8
Bend city	76,660	100,421	31.0	93,917	85.5	0.5	1.7	3.0	9.2	22.1	16.7	38.9	21.7	44.0	38,312	95.6
Bethany CDP	20,646	-	-	26,501	47.5	1.7	39.0	6.6	5.3	30.3	11.3	38.2	11.6	69.6	9,112	98.3
Biggs Junction CDP	22	-	-	-	-	-	-	-	-	-	-	-	-	-	-	-
Black Butte Ranch CDP	366	-	-	206	100.0	0.0	0.0	0.0	0.0	0.0	76.2	74.5	0.0	53.4	169	100.0
Blodgett CDP	58	-	-	23	100.0	0.0	0.0	0.0	0.0	0.0	0.0	0.0	100.0	0.0	12	100.0
Boardman city	3,239	3,749	15.7	3,439	31.8	0.0	1.0	1.7	65.5	30.9	6.2	27.9	64.8	7.2	1,157	96.5
Bonanza town	415	426	2.7	464	74.8	0.0	0.0	2.2	23.1	17.9	26.3	51.0	52.5	19.4	199	83.9
Brogan CDP	90	-	-	51	100.0	0.0	0.0	0.0	0.0	0.0	15.7	54.2	82.4	0.0	25	100.0
Brookings city	6,354	6,480	2.0	6,431	86.3	1.1	0.7	4.1	7.8	18.5	29.2	48.8	32.2	25.4	2,745	90.7
Brooks CDP	398	-	-	492	52.0	0.0	1.2	0.0	46.7	39.0	8.1	23.2	75.3	6.8	151	100.0
Brownsville city	1,668	1,823	9.3	1,871	87.2	0.0	0.0	5.6	7.3	25.9	17.6	39.9	35.7	23.1	707	92.5
Bull Mountain CDP	9,133	-	-	10,005	75.4	1.7	10.0	4.0	8.9	25.0	12.8	40.6	15.5	54.3	3,313	99.7
Bunker Hill CDP	1,444	-	-	2,501	60.3	0.0	0.0	24.6	15.0	31.5	4.3	32.7	48.6	7.4	714	93.0
Burns city	2,799	2,794	-0.2	2,740	96.5	0.6	0.0	2.3	0.6	17.2	24.6	47.1	51.6	15.1	1,388	88.8
Butte Falls town	423	457	8.0	366	83.6	0.0	1.1	4.6	10.7	20.5	19.7	41.8	43.6	13.9	146	76.7
Butteville CDP	265	-	-	337	98.2	0.0	0.0	1.8	0.0	19.0	15.1	46.3	16.2	62.9	128	92.2
Camp Sherman CDP	233	-	-	215	97.7	0.0	0.0	1.4	0.9	11.6	43.3	61.5	9.5	59.5	98	100.0
Canby city	16,686	17,932	7.5	17,695	75.7	0.6	2.0	3.6	18.0	25.8	16.0	38.4	37.4	26.4	6,383	93.4
Cannon Beach city	1,687	1,768	4.8	1,491	78.9	0.3	2.1	7.1	11.7	15.2	21.5	44.2	30.9	30.7	647	93.7
Canyon City town	703	666	-5.3	702	92.3	1.0	0.6	1.6	4.6	23.4	23.5	44.9	46.1	28.0	315	83.5
Canyonville city	1,893	1,965	3.8	1,826	85.9	0.0	1.2	7.1	5.8	21.1	31.1	40.8	48.2	14.5	804	87.1
Cape Meares CDP	99	-	-	80	100.0	0.0	0.0	0.0	0.0	11.3	55.0	67.7	0.0	52.1	38	100.0
Carlton city	2,006	2,182	8.8	2,180	85.9	0.0	3.0	3.8	7.2	22.8	16.9	39.5	34.4	17.0	767	96.1
Cascade Locks city	1,141	1,161	1.8	1,285	80.6	0.7	4.0	2.6	12.1	28.6	20.4	36.8	40.2	15.3	503	88.5
Cascadia CDP	147	-	-	117	88.0	0.0	5.1	6.8	0.0	15.4	5.1	52.7	68.7	0.0	44	59.1
Cave Junction city	1,859	1,977	6.3	2,479	90.9	1.0	2.3	0.7	5.0	28.7	22.0	41.2	39.7	11.9	1,026	90.3
Cayuse CDP	68	-	-	45	75.6	0.0	0.0	24.4	0.0	13.3	35.6	52.2	34.4	18.8	18	100.0
Cedar Hills CDP	8,300	-	-	8,912	68.9	0.7	6.7	4.6	19.1	23.6	13.7	38.5	23.6	48.5	3,554	97.2
Cedar Mill CDP	14,546	-	-	17,659	68.3	2.4	16.1	6.6	6.5	28.0	12.4	40.4	12.5	64.7	6,019	97.3
Central Point city	17,269	18,848	9.1	18,376	80.0	0.1	1.1	4.1	14.7	25.4	17.2	39.0	41.5	19.4	7,052	92.9
Chenoweth CDP	1,855	-	-	1,956	77.7	0.0	0.5	1.6	20.2	28.8	13.0	34.0	50.8	15.9	715	87.7
Chiloquin city	734	755	2.9	954	39.9	0.0	0.3	47.7	12.1	19.2	16.0	36.1	54.7	9.8	362	89.5
Clatskanie city	1,753	1,830	4.4	1,646	84.1	0.0	0.3	6.9	8.7	25.0	23.6	40.2	49.3	11.2	715	78.6
Cloverdale CDP	250	-	-	177	76.8	0.0	0.0	1.7	21.5	0.0	46.9	44.5	67.2	14.1	114	90.4
Coburg city	1,028	1,170	13.8	1,011	85.0	0.5	0.4	5.6	8.5	18.8	20.5	42.4	35.1	20.9	399	100.0

1 May be of any race.

Table A. All Places — **Population and Housing**

STATE City, town, township, borough, or CDP (county if applicable)	Population: 2010 census total population	Population: 2019 estimated population	Population: Percent change 2010–2019	Population: ACS total population estimate 2015–2019	Race and Hispanic or Latino origin (percent): White alone, not Hispanic or Latino	Race and Hispanic or Latino origin (percent): Black alone, not Hispanic or Latino	Race and Hispanic or Latino origin (percent): Asian alone, not Hispanic or Latino	Race and Hispanic or Latino origin (percent): All other races or 2 or more races, not Hispanic or Latino	Race and Hispanic or Latino origin (percent): Hispanic or Latino[1]	Age (percent): Under 18 years old	Age (percent): Age 65 years and older	Age (percent): Median age	Educational attainment of persons age 25 and older: Percent High school diploma or less	Educational attainment of persons age 25 and older: Percent Bachelor's degree or more	Occupied housing units: Total	Occupied housing units: Percent with a computer
	1	2	3	4	5	6	7	8	9	10	11	12	13	14	15	16
OREGON—Con.																
Columbia City city	1,950	2,022	3.7	1,882	81.2	1.3	2.3	4.0	11.2	15.6	27.4	50.4	45.3	14.6	786	94.7
Condon city	682	697	2.2	659	96.1	0.0	1.2	0.9	1.8	10.3	42.9	61.0	36.4	13.7	352	78.7
Coos Bay city	15,996	16,361	2.3	16,229	81.9	0.7	1.0	6.8	9.5	20.5	21.4	41.3	41.3	19.3	6,853	87.3
Coquille city	3,890	3,938	1.2	3,894	91.0	0.2	0.0	3.6	5.2	16.5	28.1	48.2	42.2	10.9	1,782	90.0
Cornelius city	11,895	12,822	7.8	12,638	40.9	0.8	2.7	3.1	52.5	29.0	9.1	32.0	52.7	15.8	3,610	97.6
Corvallis city	54,494	58,856	8.0	58,028	76.4	1.3	9.8	4.7	7.8	13.6	12.7	27.4	14.4	59.1	23,083	96.0
Cottage Grove city	9,678	10,465	8.1	10,182	82.0	1.2	0.5	6.6	9.6	22.6	16.2	39.4	40.7	18.2	4,058	93.7
Cove city	623	653	4.8	653	92.5	0.2	0.0	3.4	4.0	22.4	27.9	45.1	39.8	17.6	320	83.8
Crabtree CDP	391	-	-	712	97.9	0.0	0.0	2.1	0.0	56.7	5.1	16.4	51.9	13.0	201	100.0
Crane CDP	129	-	-	107	34.6	0.0	0.0	0.0	65.4	45.8	7.5	28.9	25.9	65.5	28	78.6
Crawfordsville CDP	332	-	-	409	92.9	0.0	0.0	0.5	6.6	12.7	27.4	54.3	48.1	14.8	144	100.0
Creswell city	5,037	5,540	10.0	5,356	83.7	0.0	0.1	7.7	8.5	26.0	17.6	38.2	34.3	17.1	2,052	93.8
Crooked River Ranch CDP	-	-	-	4,026	93.2	0.1	0.3	2.3	4.0	12.3	35.3	59.5	33.1	18.8	1,737	96.3
Culver city	1,357	1,680	23.8	1,914	48.1	0.6	0.7	4.4	46.2	36.7	7.1	25.1	49.2	13.7	533	87.6
Dallas city	14,582	16,979	16.4	16,168	89.6	0.2	1.4	3.4	5.3	21.1	21.2	40.5	37.8	24.0	6,116	92.5
Damascus CDP	10,539	-	-	11,161	81.3	0.7	5.2	2.9	9.9	20.4	15.9	43.2	33.1	28.9	3,671	95.9
Days Creek CDP	272	-	-	264	90.9	0.0	0.0	9.1	0.0	11.4	41.7	61.3	53.4	12.8	136	56.6
Dayton city	2,534	2,744	8.3	2,668	60.9	0.0	0.4	3.8	34.9	30.1	13.7	33.6	51.3	17.9	754	91.5
Dayville town	149	146	-2.0	113	99.1	0.0	0.0	0.9	0.0	14.2	23.0	56.9	40.2	33.0	64	84.4
Deer Island CDP	294	-	-	147	72.1	0.0	0.0	15.0	12.9	0.0	32.0	59.2	61.7	7.8	73	68.5
Depoe Bay city	1,398	1,499	7.2	1,805	92.5	0.0	0.8	2.3	4.4	9.6	36.6	57.1	27.2	31.5	810	98.0
Deschutes River Woods CDP	5,077	-	-	6,044	89.2	0.3	0.9	2.6	7.0	21.6	12.3	40.5	41.8	17.6	2,142	90.6
Detroit city	202	225	11.4	83	97.6	0.0	0.0	2.4	0.0	3.6	32.5	58.7	41.0	38.5	46	89.1
Dillard CDP	478	-	-	568	100.0	0.0	0.0	0.0	0.0	22.2	30.6	50.4	77.8	8.8	165	100.0
Donald city	979	1,060	8.3	1,128	62.9	3.0	2.9	2.0	29.3	20.3	16.5	42.6	45.9	14.1	380	96.3
Drain city	1,159	1,194	3.0	847	88.7	0.0	0.0	5.3	6.0	14.0	22.0	48.7	55.2	9.1	377	89.1
Dufur city	604	639	5.8	572	95.6	0.0	0.0	3.7	0.7	21.0	18.7	37.8	37.7	20.3	242	84.3
Dundee city	3,147	3,274	4.0	3,234	84.0	0.1	1.5	5.9	8.5	27.6	10.8	35.8	32.7	29.0	1,130	98.1
Dunes City city	1,299	1,406	8.2	1,237	87.8	0.0	1.1	5.9	5.2	11.3	44.6	61.6	24.5	34.8	580	91.7
Durham city	1,351	1,928	42.7	1,941	62.4	1.9	4.3	10.7	20.8	25.8	10.9	38.2	19.1	51.5	732	93.4
Eagle Crest CDP	1,696	-	-	2,839	96.4	1.8	0.0	0.7	1.0	6.2	46.2	63.9	18.6	45.8	1,344	100.0
Eagle Point city	8,471	9,554	12.8	9,154	88.5	1.3	0.0	1.6	8.7	23.7	22.3	40.0	43.8	17.3	3,636	96.5
Echo city	697	710	1.9	735	86.7	1.0	2.0	4.8	5.6	25.0	10.9	39.1	53.0	16.8	286	89.9
Elgin city	1,715	1,797	4.8	1,448	94.2	1.0	0.0	1.7	3.2	19.0	31.0	51.1	59.3	7.2	680	82.6
Elkton city	193	199	3.1	174	90.2	0.0	0.0	9.8	0.0	0.6	74.7	71.8	52.7	0.0	97	92.8
Enterprise city	1,942	1,996	2.8	2,033	92.4	0.2	0.3	2.4	4.7	23.7	22.1	42.3	44.1	22.8	878	88.5
Eola CDP	45	-	-	-	-	-	-	-	-	-	-	-	-	-	-	-
Estacada city	2,706	3,770	39.3	3,426	93.8	0.1	0.6	3.1	2.4	29.3	16.3	33.3	43.0	18.8	1,286	84.8
Eugene city	156,431	172,622	10.4	168,302	77.9	1.4	4.4	6.3	10.0	17.1	16.0	34.7	23.0	41.8	70,332	94.6
Fair Oaks CDP	278	-	-	342	97.1	0.0	0.0	0.0	2.9	10.8	21.3	37.9	25.4	7.7	136	93.4
Fairview city	8,917	9,567	7.3	9,363	66.3	5.7	2.2	7.7	18.0	18.5	13.1	39.8	42.2	20.7	3,800	94.3
Falls City city	952	1,056	10.9	1,300	78.4	0.4	6.1	6.8	8.4	21.5	14.8	41.1	53.4	10.7	438	94.7
Florence city	8,484	9,151	7.9	8,921	90.0	0.0	1.8	4.0	4.2	11.7	44.3	61.1	39.9	21.2	4,462	85.9
Foots Creek CDP	799	-	-	621	94.7	0.0	0.0	5.3	0.0	30.1	10.6	42.6	33.0	16.9	251	91.6
Forest Grove city	21,298	25,553	20.0	24,457	68.2	0.5	2.5	5.7	23.1	23.8	14.4	33.2	38.7	28.4	8,486	93.5
Fort Hill CDP	129	-	-	89	82.0	0.0	0.0	18.0	0.0	0.0	100.0	82.2	62.9	0.0	52	100.0
Fossil city	473	438	-7.4	393	77.4	0.0	0.0	8.7	14.0	18.3	46.3	64.2	46.6	10.4	200	83.5
Four Corners CDP	15,947	-	-	16,399	47.1	0.9	3.9	3.7	44.5	22.9	15.1	33.6	55.8	9.8	5,565	89.9
Garden Home-Whitford CDP	6,674	-	-	7,006	88.4	1.0	3.1	4.2	3.3	19.5	18.2	42.2	11.0	61.8	2,795	95.7
Gardiner CDP	248	-	-	586	85.8	0.0	0.0	0.9	13.3	41.5	1.2	26.1	47.8	1.7	211	88.2
Garibaldi city	775	822	6.1	797	96.5	0.0	1.0	0.9	1.6	9.3	33.6	56.8	48.4	14.6	335	86.6
Gaston city	637	722	13.3	510	93.1	0.0	0.0	2.9	3.9	25.9	10.0	37.1	56.7	7.8	192	89.1
Gates city	471	513	8.9	517	83.0	1.2	0.4	10.4	5.0	13.2	31.7	54.6	41.7	11.5	234	87.2
Gearhart city	1,400	1,634	16.7	1,645	94.5	0.0	1.5	1.6	2.4	19.5	28.3	48.4	30.5	33.5	640	92.8
Gervais city	2,473	2,762	11.7	2,713	14.3	0.1	0.3	0.9	84.4	34.0	4.3	28.2	69.7	7.0	625	92.5
Gladstone city	11,486	12,324	7.3	12,170	79.2	1.1	1.5	5.1	13.1	24.2	16.8	38.5	32.9	24.9	4,661	91.8
Glasgow CDP	763	-	-	738	97.8	0.0	0.0	1.2	0.9	11.9	41.2	61.8	32.7	12.7	335	95.2
Glendale city	874	897	2.6	702	87.9	0.0	0.0	3.6	8.5	24.8	13.7	37.1	46.5	7.5	285	88.1
Glide CDP	1,795	-	-	1,366	94.8	0.0	0.0	4.0	1.2	15.7	24.0	50.3	37.5	14.0	557	93.7
Gold Beach city	2,251	2,304	2.4	2,418	85.1	0.0	0.2	6.5	8.2	12.4	28.2	54.2	34.4	20.1	1,165	92.9
Gold Hill city	1,216	1,296	6.6	1,437	90.2	0.0	1.0	2.4	6.5	24.6	18.6	38.5	44.4	16.6	552	93.7
Gopher Flats CDP	379	-	-	395	70.9	0.0	0.0	28.1	1.0	15.9	29.4	55.5	45.4	12.5	155	71.0
Government Camp CDP	193	-	-	176	90.9	9.1	0.0	0.0	0.0	14.8	35.2	61.6	20.0	52.7	89	100.0
Grand Ronde CDP	1,661	-	-	1,604	58.5	0.2	1.2	36.6	3.5	25.4	18.3	46.1	52.7	15.1	645	88.5
Granite city	38	36	-5.3	19	100.0	0.0	0.0	0.0	0.0	0.0	57.9	68.1	31.6	42.1	17	58.8
Grants Pass city	35,927	38,170	6.2	37,545	84.7	0.7	1.1	4.2	9.3	22.7	19.8	39.9	41.6	15.8	15,781	88.1
Grass Valley city	164	165	0.6	179	87.2	1.7	0.0	7.8	3.4	20.7	20.1	31.3	52.8	9.4	64	92.2
Green CDP	7,515	-	-	7,985	88.2	0.9	0.2	4.6	6.1	19.3	16.4	41.1	46.1	12.7	2,842	92.3
Gresham city	105,639	109,381	3.5	110,494	63.1	4.6	4.5	6.5	21.3	24.6	13.6	36.7	40.5	22.3	40,053	92.1
Haines city	416	422	1.4	265	95.5	0.0	0.4	4.2	0.0	13.6	27.2	59.3	54.1	10.0	138	87.7
Halfway city	290	292	0.7	314	90.1	1.0	0.0	7.3	1.6	20.4	28.0	50.7	47.2	18.4	164	93.9
Halsey city	898	1,001	11.5	1,009	92.8	0.0	0.5	4.2	2.6	22.8	10.6	40.0	47.1	13.1	370	93.5
Happy Valley city	15,251	22,553	47.9	20,971	69.5	0.8	19.4	6.0	4.3	25.6	11.3	39.2	17.9	54.7	6,951	99.2
Harbor CDP	2,391	-	-	1,958	89.7	0.2	0.0	7.3	2.9	1.7	70.9	71.7	46.0	17.0	1,222	76.3
Harper CDP	109	-	-	135	96.3	0.0	0.0	0.7	3.0	43.7	11.1	30.1	29.0	20.3	50	76.0
Harrisburg city	3,560	3,897	9.5	3,799	81.2	0.8	0.0	5.5	12.6	32.4	10.3	30.9	54.1	13.3	1,240	87.2
Hayesville CDP	19,936	-	-	21,979	43.9	3.7	3.0	5.5	43.8	27.2	14.3	32.9	52.8	14.9	7,545	90.2
Hebo CDP	232	-	-	182	100.0	0.0	0.0	0.0	0.0	12.6	20.3	51.9	20.8	5.6	72	100.0
Helix city	184	184	0.0	121	87.6	0.0	0.0	0.0	12.4	33.1	13.2	32.5	28.8	21.9	50	100.0
Heppner city	1,291	1,266	-1.9	1,110	89.1	0.9	0.4	1.8	7.8	21.0	28.8	46.1	42.3	14.3	501	87.6
Hermiston city	16,729	17,782	6.3	17,423	51.1	0.4	0.4	1.6	46.6	30.3	12.2	31.0	50.2	17.6	6,207	89.2
Hillsboro city	92,265	109,128	18.3	106,543	55.5	2.2	12.3	6.3	23.8	24.2	10.6	34.0	27.9	42.0	38,601	96.8
Hines city	1,570	1,545	-1.6	1,392	90.9	0.0	0.0	5.6	3.5	21.2	23.4	48.5	38.8	20.7	586	87.2
Holley CDP	378	-	-	402	90.8	0.0	0.0	6.5	2.7	25.9	25.4	43.1	70.8	10.7	131	88.5
Hood River city	7,235	7,801	7.8	7,715	74.8	1.4	1.3	1.6	20.9	22.6	14.5	38.6	33.4	41.2	3,486	88.9
Hubbard city	3,176	3,570	12.4	3,475	53.5	0.2	0.7	3.5	42.1	32.9	7.3	33.7	50.5	18.6	1,140	93.6
Huntington city	440	436	-0.9	407	93.6	0.0	1.2	4.2	1.0	14.5	31.2	50.7	54.2	10.1	198	72.2
Idanha city	149	161	8.1	162	90.7	0.0	0.0	1.9	7.4	6.8	37.0	61.2	78.0	4.3	74	78.4
Idaville CDP	337	-	-	312	74.0	0.0	0.0	13.1	12.8	14.7	18.9	48.5	46.6	21.1	131	91.6

1 May be of any race.

Table A. All Places — **Population and Housing**

STATE City, town, township, borough, or CDP (county if applicable)	Population				Race and Hispanic or Latino origin (percent)					Age (percent)			Educational attainment of persons age 25 and older		Occupied housing units	
	2010 census total population	2019 estimated population	Percent change 2010–2019	ACS total population estimate 2015–2019	White alone, not Hispanic or Latino	Black alone, not Hispanic or Latino	Asian alone, not Hispanic or Latino	All other races or 2 or more races, not Hispanic or Latino	Hispanic or Latino[1]	Under 18 years old	Age 65 years and older	Median age	Percent High school diploma or less	Percent Bachelor's degree or more	Total	Percent with a computer
	1	2	3	4	5	6	7	8	9	10	11	12	13	14	15	16
OREGON—Con.																
Imbler city	306	320	4.6	337	97.9	1.2	0.0	0.3	0.6	20.8	15.1	40.1	36.4	25.2	128	82.8
Independence city	8,599	10,272	19.5	9,842	58.5	0.0	0.4	1.5	39.6	30.8	8.6	27.6	40.7	19.9	3,203	98.8
Ione city	329	328	-0.3	372	68.3	0.0	0.0	7.8	23.9	22.0	16.4	48.3	44.9	9.8	152	90.8
Irrigon city	1,809	1,773	-2.0	2,053	43.7	0.8	1.6	8.7	45.3	29.4	14.1	38.1	61.7	6.1	709	90.6
Island City city	988	1,033	4.6	1,022	89.6	0.2	1.6	5.7	2.9	19.2	30.4	51.0	45.9	25.5	432	87.7
Jacksonville city	2,783	2,899	4.2	2,884	94.6	0.0	0.7	1.7	3.1	11.9	43.2	56.2	19.8	51.5	1,503	88.1
Jeffers Gardens CDP	-	-	-	348	91.4	0.0	3.4	0.0	5.2	19.8	37.4	42.7	26.2	28.1	142	79.6
Jefferson city	3,101	3,364	8.5	3,301	75.9	0.0	0.2	2.2	21.7	23.5	13.5	37.4	45.9	16.5	1,094	95.2
Jennings Lodge CDP	7,315	-	-	7,988	78.6	3.1	2.2	4.1	12.0	20.8	17.5	36.5	32.3	26.1	3,366	91.2
John Day city	1,746	1,672	-4.2	2,244	88.3	0.0	1.8	5.5	4.3	25.8	18.7	38.6	44.4	25.2	1,052	91.4
Johnson City city	570	629	10.4	514	92.0	1.9	0.0	1.8	4.3	5.8	33.5	58.3	39.9	15.7	299	89.0
Jordan Valley city	181	177	-2.2	147	98.0	0.0	0.0	0.0	2.0	25.2	28.6	50.9	25.2	16.8	64	73.4
Joseph city	1,094	1,124	2.7	989	97.9	0.2	0.8	1.1	0.0	11.3	31.6	57.3	34.3	22.0	520	80.6
Junction City city	5,349	6,229	16.5	6,053	84.7	0.1	0.6	1.0	13.6	27.0	11.5	34.2	40.3	21.2	2,182	90.1
Juntura CDP	57	-	-	26	100.0	0.0	0.0	0.0	0.0	7.7	46.2	64.7	50.0	4.2	20	70.0
Keizer city	36,434	39,713	9.0	38,980	73.6	0.3	1.8	5.9	18.4	24.1	15.8	37.4	35.4	27.0	14,232	95.1
Kerby CDP	595	-	-	578	67.8	0.0	0.0	13.1	19.0	14.5	43.1	43.7	69.5	0.0	270	60.0
King City city	3,564	4,408	23.7	4,309	79.9	3.3	4.1	2.6	10.2	15.9	44.3	60.7	24.8	40.5	2,155	92.0
Kings Valley CDP	65	-	-	132	100.0	0.0	0.0	0.0	0.0	27.3	0.0	28.7	0.0	40.5	30	100.0
Kirkpatrick CDP	179	-	-	135	32.6	0.0	0.0	67.4	0.0	25.9	15.6	35.5	49.4	13.8	46	63.0
Klamath Falls city	20,993	21,753	3.6	21,335	76.4	1.6	0.7	5.8	15.5	20.8	16.3	36.0	43.7	21.8	9,112	90.1
Labish Village CDP	412	-	-	518	21.6	0.0	0.0	0.0	78.4	18.1	0.0	42.0	82.9	1.9	164	100.0
Lacomb CDP	546	-	-	481	90.4	0.0	0.0	9.6	0.0	26.4	21.2	44.2	52.0	1.4	152	84.9
Lafayette city	3,742	4,265	14.0	4,149	59.1	0.0	0.6	6.3	34.0	23.8	8.0	37.3	49.4	13.7	1,346	98.6
La Grande city	13,097	13,614	3.9	13,310	84.8	1.0	0.9	6.6	6.6	22.5	15.3	33.2	37.1	25.9	5,367	89.1
Lake Oswego city	36,758	39,822	8.3	39,127	82.8	1.0	6.0	5.0	5.2	21.6	20.6	46.9	9.0	71.4	16,491	96.0
Lakeside city	1,699	1,798	5.8	1,765	96.4	0.3	0.0	2.9	0.4	10.2	44.6	62.5	45.1	9.1	928	87.6
Lakeview town	2,319	2,310	-0.4	2,638	79.4	0.2	1.7	8.1	10.7	23.6	20.0	41.3	41.3	20.6	1,180	84.2
Langlois CDP	177	-	-	135	100.0	0.0	0.0	0.0	0.0	0.0	21.5	59.6	16.3	48.9	88	100.0
La Pine city	1,653	1,929	16.7	2,343	85.5	0.0	0.0	6.1	8.4	17.5	25.8	46.0	48.9	14.2	944	90.5
Lebanon city	15,555	17,417	12.0	16,870	86.1	0.2	1.2	3.7	8.8	24.7	17.5	37.2	40.3	16.1	6,650	84.9
Lexington town	238	236	-0.8	146	89.0	0.0	0.0	11.0	0.0	16.4	25.3	57.1	41.5	6.8	79	77.2
Lincoln Beach CDP	2,045	-	-	2,072	91.8	0.1	2.0	3.1	2.9	7.4	51.8	65.4	21.8	33.9	1,151	82.7
Lincoln City city	8,282	9,170	10.7	8,826	81.0	0.5	2.8	6.4	9.3	18.2	27.6	50.4	37.9	25.5	3,979	87.3
Lonerock city	21	22	4.8	8	100.0	0.0	0.0	0.0	0.0	0.0	62.5	77.5	100.0	0.0	6	66.7
Long Creek city	197	190	-3.6	148	93.2	0.0	0.0	2.0	4.7	23.6	39.9	57.8	64.2	17.9	67	58.2
Lookingglass CDP	855	-	-	985	82.2	0.0	0.0	17.8	0.0	24.4	25.3	51.2	24.5	13.0	357	95.8
Lostine city	214	223	4.2	307	96.4	0.0	0.0	0.7	2.9	27.0	27.4	44.5	44.6	8.0	107	91.6
Lowell city	1,042	1,173	12.6	1,196	90.6	0.0	1.8	3.0	4.5	22.2	22.5	46.7	36.9	18.2	471	95.5
Lyons city	1,161	1,290	11.1	1,059	80.5	0.3	1.0	14.3	4.0	21.5	21.2	47.3	46.2	14.3	427	88.3
McMinnville city	32,182	34,743	8.0	34,010	71.6	1.2	1.2	3.8	22.3	22.8	18.6	37.3	37.1	26.0	12,792	91.0
Madras city	6,325	7,051	11.5	6,777	48.3	1.0	1.2	9.7	39.8	25.7	15.5	35.0	50.5	17.5	2,456	83.7
Malin city	806	832	3.2	899	31.0	0.0	0.3	1.3	67.3	28.9	12.5	34.7	70.7	8.1	285	85.3
Manzanita city	598	661	10.5	393	96.2	0.0	2.0	1.8	0.0	3.8	49.9	64.8	14.0	53.4	237	99.2
Marion CDP	313	-	-	534	94.6	0.0	0.0	5.4	0.0	21.9	42.3	38.5	45.1	8.9	191	100.0
Maupin city	418	441	5.5	508	97.0	0.0	0.0	3.0	0.0	18.1	26.0	51.4	29.3	18.8	203	88.2
Maywood Park city	752	849	12.9	995	80.4	0.4	3.4	3.1	12.7	22.4	11.3	39.7	23.9	44.0	358	96.6
Medford city	74,992	83,072	10.8	81,145	76.2	0.8	1.5	5.6	15.9	23.6	17.6	37.4	38.4	25.2	32,176	92.0
Mehama CDP	292	-	-	224	89.3	0.0	0.0	10.7	0.0	35.3	7.1	33.1	65.2	6.7	88	90.9
Melrose CDP	735	-	-	649	86.7	0.0	2.6	9.1	1.5	11.1	15.3	53.8	39.2	22.0	292	76.7
Merlin CDP	1,615	-	-	1,922	96.2	0.0	0.0	2.9	0.9	15.9	20.1	54.0	38.4	13.1	768	95.7
Merrill city	844	855	1.3	784	49.1	0.0	0.0	1.5	49.4	22.2	14.9	41.7	62.3	10.5	332	87.0
Metolius city	710	801	12.8	955	60.1	0.2	0.9	4.4	34.3	32.6	11.6	30.5	67.2	7.0	302	91.7
Metzger CDP	3,765	-	-	3,886	79.7	0.7	2.9	5.6	11.1	26.4	15.0	37.2	30.7	36.7	1,665	94.8
Mill City city	1,860	1,968	5.8	1,839	73.6	0.3	0.4	15.3	10.4	26.3	17.1	39.9	53.8	10.0	666	80.5
Millersburg city	1,329	2,557	92.4	1,998	84.1	0.4	3.9	2.7	8.9	26.7	13.4	39.1	26.4	29.8	736	94.7
Milton-Freewater city	7,052	7,074	0.3	7,037	45.0	0.0	0.5	1.7	52.7	32.6	13.8	33.5	50.3	16.4	2,417	89.6
Milwaukie city	20,522	20,990	2.3	21,009	83.1	0.7	3.3	3.7	9.2	17.6	16.4	39.8	27.0	36.2	9,205	92.0
Mission CDP	1,037	-	-	850	17.5	0.4	3.3	71.6	7.2	27.5	12.4	31.9	44.5	17.7	314	86.0
Mitchell city	133	121	-9.0	142	75.4	0.0	0.0	7.0	17.6	24.6	20.4	52.1	64.8	5.7	59	71.2
Molalla city	8,511	9,265	8.9	9,155	79.7	0.3	0.7	2.4	16.9	29.5	11.7	35.2	38.3	11.6	3,295	92.8
Monmouth city	9,535	10,586	11.0	10,282	69.4	3.2	4.3	6.3	16.7	19.4	8.9	23.6	29.7	36.5	3,315	91.3
Monroe city	617	654	6.0	640	68.4	0.0	2.3	7.7	21.6	24.5	14.5	37.0	44.1	12.6	248	92.3
Monument city	128	125	-2.3	86	90.7	0.0	2.3	2.3	4.7	10.5	43.0	54.5	50.0	5.9	59	83.1
Moro city	324	328	1.2	353	85.8	0.0	0.6	10.8	2.8	31.7	24.6	38.8	36.5	27.5	155	90.3
Mosier city	433	464	7.2	455	62.4	0.0	2.0	1.1	34.5	18.5	14.5	39.8	32.5	25.1	207	93.7
Mount Angel city	3,379	3,619	7.1	3,542	70.2	0.1	0.8	0.6	28.2	21.7	21.9	39.4	44.7	21.9	1,303	85.2
Mount Hood CDP	286	-	-	414	9.9	0.0	0.0	0.0	90.1	43.7	2.4	20.0	79.3	6.4	79	100.0
Mount Hood Village CDP	4,864	-	-	4,445	92.9	0.0	1.6	2.1	3.5	14.2	27.4	54.2	30.6	27.6	1,942	95.1
Mount Vernon city	527	512	-2.8	565	98.9	0.0	0.0	1.1	0.0	19.5	18.6	39.9	61.3	11.6	239	91.6
Mulino CDP	2,103	-	-	2,334	86.7	0.0	1.6	3.1	8.6	22.3	16.3	37.4	30.1	29.4	792	97.6
Myrtle Creek city	3,400	3,483	2.4	3,428	90.5	0.5	0.2	6.4	2.4	23.6	20.2	39.5	55.0	8.5	1,188	92.9
Myrtle Point city	2,516	2,559	1.7	2,517	84.8	0.0	0.6	13.8	0.7	17.3	27.6	47.9	52.4	13.8	1,097	88.2
Neahkahnie CDP	-	-	-	170	100.0	0.0	0.0	0.0	0.0	0.0	57.6	67.2	5.3	90.0	94	90.4
Nehalem city	273	297	8.8	355	94.4	0.0	0.0	5.6	0.0	23.1	12.1	29.1	44.4	16.1	117	80.3
Nesika Beach CDP	463	-	-	315	92.7	7.3	0.0	0.0	0.0	0.0	61.9	69.4	40.3	23.2	169	100.0
Neskowin CDP	134	-	-	164	100.0	0.0	0.0	0.0	0.0	0.0	75.0	67.9	5.5	73.2	102	100.0
Netarts CDP	748	-	-	778	88.7	0.0	0.8	6.6	4.0	23.5	41.9	61.4	35.3	36.0	365	92.3
Newberg city	22,140	23,886	7.9	23,396	77.6	0.4	2.1	5.6	14.3	23.5	13.4	33.4	31.9	31.5	8,142	96.3
New Hope CDP	1,515	-	-	1,593	95.1	0.0	0.0	0.7	4.2	15.1	28.8	51.3	46.8	16.2	682	93.8
New Pine Creek CDP	120	-	-	82	70.7	0.0	0.0	29.3	0.0	0.0	18.3	59.1	48.8	18.3	57	100.0
Newport city	10,030	10,853	8.2	10,559	70.9	1.4	1.7	5.6	20.3	18.2	25.8	46.3	34.8	27.2	4,637	94.0
North Bend city	9,689	9,768	0.8	9,652	81.6	0.4	3.1	7.7	7.2	22.4	21.6	43.2	34.4	23.1	3,889	90.4
North Plains city	1,956	2,203	12.6	2,942	78.7	0.0	5.4	5.6	10.3	18.6	10.8	34.1	27.7	39.8	1,074	94.9
North Powder city	433	460	6.2	558	74.7	0.0	0.0	3.4	21.9	30.6	18.1	37.3	49.6	11.4	203	82.3
Nyssa city	3,264	3,185	-2.4	3,163	29.8	0.0	0.6	1.0	68.6	37.6	12.3	26.9	55.0	8.4	1,079	83.3
Oak Grove CDP	16,629	-	-	17,872	81.7	0.6	1.2	4.0	12.6	16.6	21.7	42.8	33.7	31.7	7,503	91.9
Oak Hills CDP	11,333	-	-	12,308	69.5	1.7	15.6	5.2	8.0	29.8	11.8	36.4	14.7	57.5	4,196	95.9
Oakland city	927	954	2.9	885	89.0	0.0	0.2	8.4	2.4	23.3	20.5	41.9	29.7	16.6	374	88.2
Oakridge city	3,200	3,370	5.3	3,303	89.7	0.0	0.0	9.4	0.9	15.7	21.4	36.7	57.0	14.0	1,404	84.8
Oatfield CDP	13,415	-	-	14,060	86.3	1.3	3.4	3.0	5.9	17.3	23.6	48.3	30.3	33.7	5,285	91.2
O'Brien CDP	504	-	-	636	88.4	0.0	0.0	11.6	0.0	0.0	48.6	64.3	52.6	13.1	352	100.0

1 May be of any race.

Table A. All Places — **Population and Housing**

STATE City, town, township, borough, or CDP (county if applicable)	Population: 2010 census total population	Population: 2019 estimated population	Population: Percent change 2010–2019	Population: ACS total population estimate 2015–2019	Race and Hispanic or Latino origin (percent): White alone, not Hispanic or Latino	Black alone, not Hispanic or Latino	Asian alone, not Hispanic or Latino	All other races or 2 or more races, not Hispanic or Latino	Hispanic or Latino[1]	Age (percent): Under 18 years old	Age 65 years and older	Median age	Educational attainment of persons age 25 and older: Percent High school diploma or less	Percent Bachelor's degree or more	Occupied housing units: Total	Percent with a computer
	1	2	3	4	5	6	7	8	9	10	11	12	13	14	15	16
OREGON—Con.																
Oceanside CDP	361	-	-	546	96.3	0.0	0.0	0.0	3.7	7.3	51.5	65.3	19.2	44.7	309	100.0
Odell CDP	2,255	-	-	2,380	23.5	0.0	0.4	3.4	72.6	32.2	9.0	28.3	74.9	13.5	671	93.9
Ontario city	11,371	10,994	-3.3	10,966	50.8	0.2	1.0	2.4	45.5	28.4	18.1	34.4	49.2	17.5	4,268	81.9
Oregon City city	32,623	37,339	14.5	36,492	86.8	1.0	1.2	5.7	5.3	22.7	15.2	37.9	33.2	26.3	13,345	94.5
Pacific City CDP	1,035	-	-	1,076	78.4	0.0	0.0	0.6	21.0	33.0	21.8	40.4	28.1	22.0	389	76.9
Paisley city	243	242	-0.4	385	91.4	0.0	0.3	7.3	1.0	26.8	32.2	45.1	49.4	23.3	167	89.2
Parkdale CDP	311	-	-	324	74.7	0.0	0.0	0.0	25.3	12.3	15.4	40.5	55.5	0.0	84	77.4
Pendleton city	16,622	16,789	1.0	16,733	77.0	2.0	1.7	7.5	11.8	22.2	14.8	36.4	41.7	18.0	5,824	89.0
Peoria CDP	94	-	-	237	100.0	0.0	0.0	0.0	0.0	24.1	14.3	36.5	15.5	40.6	95	100.0
Philomath city	4,602	5,666	23.1	4,929	82.3	2.3	2.9	5.0	7.5	25.9	11.8	33.9	25.4	40.2	1,874	95.0
Phoenix city	4,413	4,653	5.4	4,582	88.6	0.8	1.5	3.7	5.4	13.9	33.0	50.2	30.3	20.5	2,250	87.3
Pilot Rock city	1,499	1,509	0.7	1,322	84.6	0.0	0.0	8.1	7.3	23.8	21.3	42.5	51.9	15.2	526	84.6
Pine Grove CDP	148	-	-	99	100.0	0.0	0.0	0.0	0.0	10.1	37.4	61.9	49.4	20.2	61	80.3
Pine Hollow CDP	494	-	-	488	89.3	1.6	0.0	9.0	0.0	10.7	50.8	65.2	41.6	7.7	222	93.2
Pistol River CDP	84	-	-	126	100.0	0.0	0.0	0.0	0.0	0.0	35.7	62.1	66.7	0.0	65	100.0
Plush CDP	57	-	-	95	92.6	0.0	0.0	7.4	0.0	11.6	10.5	30.7	27.4	16.7	47	78.7
Portland city	583,793	654,741	12.2	645,291	70.6	5.6	8.1	6.0	9.7	17.8	12.8	37.1	22.7	50.4	268,718	94.3
Port Orford city	1,133	1,153	1.8	954	93.2	0.0	0.0	5.3	1.5	2.7	42.2	61.2	27.7	28.4	572	81.1
Powers city	685	680	-0.7	1,030	79.0	0.0	0.0	15.0	6.0	19.9	26.1	47.1	39.3	7.0	400	75.8
Prairie City city	909	876	-3.6	735	92.5	0.0	0.0	6.8	0.7	14.6	35.0	54.4	40.4	27.4	325	84.3
Prescott city	60	63	5.0	88	95.5	0.0	0.0	3.4	1.1	5.7	35.2	58.0	40.8	26.3	42	81.0
Prineville city	9,263	10,734	15.9	10,035	81.8	0.1	0.5	4.8	12.8	22.1	21.0	41.7	48.4	16.3	4,309	86.3
Pronghorn CDP	34	-	-	44	88.6	0.0	11.4	0.0	0.0	0.0	59.1	67.8	0.0	100.0	21	100.0
Prospect CDP	455	-	-	476	91.2	0.0	0.6	8.2	0.0	14.3	30.0	56.5	44.8	8.9	231	81.8
Rainier city	1,919	2,010	4.7	2,113	77.1	0.8	1.4	14.6	6.1	22.9	18.0	38.0	44.3	14.1	776	85.2
Raleigh Hills CDP	5,896	-	-	6,146	82.4	1.0	8.9	2.7	4.9	15.8	24.2	44.4	9.5	60.3	2,795	86.8
Redmond city	26,206	32,421	23.7	30,167	81.7	1.2	0.5	4.4	12.3	22.2	15.8	37.0	40.1	18.5	11,369	95.5
Redwood CDP	2,627	-	-	2,970	88.8	1.0	0.0	8.7	1.5	22.2	30.2	55.6	35.2	17.3	1,244	92.4
Reedsport city	4,128	4,112	-0.4	4,082	85.9	1.3	0.0	6.2	6.5	18.8	27.7	50.6	50.7	9.7	1,786	88.6
Richland city	164	177	7.9	303	89.8	1.3	1.7	3.6	3.6	31.4	31.4	48.2	34.6	20.7	113	85.8
Rickreall CDP	77	-	-	-	-	-	-	-	-	-	-	-	-	-	-	-
Riddle city	1,185	1,221	3.0	1,252	84.6	0.6	0.0	5.9	8.9	25.2	12.5	35.5	58.7	10.5	482	91.7
Rivergrove city	289	372	28.7	536	78.9	3.2	11.6	5.6	0.7	26.5	18.5	46.8	10.1	67.4	191	97.9
Riverside CDP	199	-	-	165	64.2	0.0	1.2	18.2	16.4	19.4	20.6	42.5	47.5	9.3	60	95.0
Rockaway Beach city	1,309	1,416	8.2	1,166	97.0	0.1	0.7	1.3	0.9	14.2	27.5	54.5	32.8	25.6	529	88.7
Rockcreek CDP	9,316	-	-	9,893	75.9	0.6	6.8	4.2	12.4	22.0	14.0	37.8	19.4	49.5	3,628	99.4
Rogue River city	2,127	2,331	9.6	2,410	90.0	0.0	0.0	4.8	5.2	21.8	27.6	46.7	44.9	10.6	1,048	79.8
Roseburg city	22,854	23,479	2.7	23,083	86.8	0.7	1.3	4.5	6.7	20.9	22.3	41.6	37.2	25.3	10,389	89.5
Roseburg North CDP	5,912	-	-	5,059	90.3	0.0	3.2	2.8	3.7	20.5	22.5	49.0	39.1	16.3	2,211	94.5
Rose Lodge CDP	1,894	-	-	1,169	82.0	0.0	0.0	11.5	6.4	10.9	31.7	56.1	39.8	17.7	616	85.4
Rowena CDP	187	-	-	258	100.0	0.0	0.0	0.0	0.0	33.3	3.5	47.3	71.9	14.4	77	59.7
Ruch CDP	840	-	-	986	95.1	0.0	0.0	1.2	3.7	17.2	26.6	42.3	16.8	48.7	366	100.0
Rufus city	249	253	1.6	173	87.3	0.0	0.0	5.8	6.9	10.4	44.5	59.9	66.5	7.1	95	92.6
St. Helens city	13,056	13,739	5.2	13,559	84.9	0.5	1.1	6.3	7.2	25.4	10.7	36.2	43.2	15.8	5,180	90.7
St. Paul city	420	455	8.3	480	81.5	0.0	1.0	3.1	14.4	32.3	16.0	34.4	35.8	35.5	151	87.4
Salem city	154,931	174,365	12.5	169,259	66.9	1.2	2.4	6.2	23.3	24.1	14.1	35.9	36.2	28.4	60,519	93.4
Sandy city	9,602	11,387	18.6	11,070	83.0	0.6	2.3	3.9	10.2	27.4	11.5	36.2	34.7	19.1	4,066	96.9
Scappoose city	6,701	7,564	12.9	7,270	86.9	0.2	2.0	3.7	7.3	25.5	16.8	37.7	34.1	26.6	2,807	91.9
Scio city	838	1,002	19.6	927	93.2	1.6	0.0	3.8	1.4	26.8	13.8	37.4	44.6	17.0	371	87.6
Scotts Mills city	357	393	10.1	393	88.5	0.0	0.0	2.3	9.2	24.9	12.0	40.5	49.8	12.4	130	93.8
Seaside city	6,490	6,892	6.2	6,737	87.1	1.8	1.1	2.5	7.4	16.2	22.1	42.5	33.1	22.8	2,898	87.0
Selma CDP	695	-	-	591	93.1	0.0	0.0	2.7	4.2	11.8	34.9	62.3	32.8	5.7	266	100.0
Seneca city	199	229	15.1	262	97.7	0.0	0.0	2.3	0.0	14.9	35.9	54.8	53.5	3.5	128	89.8
Seventh Mountain CDP	187	-	-	371	96.5	0.0	0.0	3.5	0.0	13.5	31.3	59.3	2.9	82.5	151	100.0
Shady Cove city	2,904	3,129	7.7	3,080	87.9	1.5	0.0	1.6	9.0	13.6	28.9	57.4	52.0	10.5	1,432	78.0
Shaniko city	36	37	2.8	9	33.3	0.0	0.0	0.0	66.7	55.6	33.3	17.5	75.0	0.0	4	25.0
Shedd CDP	204	-	-	394	34.5	0.0	0.0	0.0	65.5	40.6	9.1	24.8	74.6	17.6	84	100.0
Sheridan city	6,153	6,215	1.0	6,122	69.6	5.2	3.4	6.4	15.4	17.4	12.6	38.9	49.1	10.1	1,525	90.7
Sherwood city	18,288	19,879	8.7	19,625	86.3	0.4	3.3	4.1	5.9	31.8	9.2	36.3	16.5	50.0	6,688	96.9
Siletz city	1,210	1,305	7.9	1,144	68.9	0.3	0.7	25.3	4.9	27.8	13.6	36.8	47.7	8.7	431	86.8
Silver Lake CDP	149	-	-	104	81.7	0.0	0.0	0.0	18.3	20.2	0.0	56.0	28.9	15.7	44	100.0
Silverton city	9,243	10,618	14.9	10,242	86.0	0.5	0.0	3.4	10.1	26.6	17.6	39.3	34.4	29.2	3,831	95.4
Sisters city	2,038	2,781	36.5	2,643	81.6	0.0	0.2	4.0	14.2	21.9	18.0	41.2	24.8	34.3	1,038	96.3
Sodaville city	308	345	12.0	386	84.5	0.5	1.0	12.2	1.8	17.6	15.5	46.0	38.1	23.1	142	91.5
South Lebanon CDP	1,005	-	-	970	94.8	0.0	0.0	2.6	2.6	15.9	17.0	47.8	37.7	18.3	397	86.9
Spray town	159	148	-6.9	234	99.6	0.0	0.0	0.4	0.0	15.0	35.0	59.2	59.1	3.3	102	92.2
Springfield city	59,413	63,230	6.4	62,077	79.8	0.9	1.6	6.2	11.4	21.9	14.1	36.1	42.1	17.8	24,578	91.7
Stafford CDP	1,577	-	-	1,733	98.6	1.4	0.0	0.0	0.0	26.8	24.5	48.7	12.5	76.3	737	97.3
Stanfield city	2,043	2,112	3.4	2,722	56.8	0.0	0.0	5.3	37.8	23.8	14.1	33.8	58.5	11.6	924	91.0
Stayton city	7,693	8,295	7.8	8,130	71.4	1.8	0.8	7.9	18.0	28.2	14.6	36.2	47.9	10.9	2,958	96.7
Sublimity city	2,685	2,772	3.2	2,810	88.1	0.0	2.1	1.7	8.1	23.7	27.7	46.5	35.8	28.6	1,094	88.3
Summerville town	136	144	5.9	170	95.3	0.0	0.0	1.2	3.5	18.8	21.8	45.8	48.1	23.3	66	100.0
Summit CDP	82	-	-	204	93.1	0.0	0.0	6.9	0.0	13.7	9.3	37.8	65.3	11.8	58	100.0
Sumpter city	204	206	1.0	181	96.7	0.0	0.0	1.7	1.7	0.0	58.6	68.5	56.4	11.6	109	83.5
Sunriver CDP	1,393	-	-	1,294	95.1	0.0	0.0	0.0	4.9	16.1	40.0	61.8	19.2	52.2	570	100.0
Sutherlin city	7,847	8,184	4.3	8,033	91.1	0.4	0.8	2.3	5.5	19.2	25.3	50.6	44.5	16.4	3,491	89.5
Sweet Home city	8,931	9,977	11.7	9,619	87.4	1.5	1.0	4.0	6.1	24.7	19.2	39.0	56.1	5.9	3,721	88.1
Takilma CDP	378	-	-	466	92.9	0.0	0.0	7.1	0.0	15.9	15.5	50.4	18.9	29.6	165	90.3
Talent city	6,059	6,608	9.1	6,503	74.7	0.0	5.6	3.0	16.7	21.0	20.3	35.4	26.8	39.2	3,106	87.8
Tangent city	1,164	1,347	15.7	1,414	93.6	0.0	0.0	4.0	2.5	26.0	15.3	37.1	36.8	19.5	496	95.6
Terrebonne CDP	1,257	-	-	1,658	94.2	0.0	0.0	5.8	0.0	21.0	22.6	39.6	50.9	25.1	658	95.9
Tetherow CDP	45	-	-	757	100.0	0.0	0.0	0.0	0.0	32.5	16.6	41.4	0.0	82.4	262	100.0
The Dalles city	14,950	15,761	5.4	15,448	74.5	0.4	1.0	4.5	19.6	23.2	20.7	39.6	42.6	19.6	6,300	87.8
Three Rivers CDP	3,014	-	-	3,212	90.3	0.0	1.1	5.8	2.9	17.4	23.5	44.5	28.5	28.3	1,365	92.9
Tigard city	48,205	55,514	15.2	53,312	72.8	1.0	8.1	5.4	12.6	21.3	14.6	37.6	24.0	44.2	21,233	95.2
Tillamook city	5,039	5,355	6.3	5,231	74.9	0.1	0.3	5.3	19.4	24.8	18.4	36.7	50.6	13.3	2,279	85.4
Toledo city	3,468	3,644	5.1	3,579	91.4	0.0	0.0	5.3	3.3	25.3	18.2	39.0	44.9	17.7	1,395	96.2
Trail CDP	702	-	-	552	97.3	0.0	0.0	0.0	2.7	12.7	32.1	59.0	33.9	17.1	271	100.0
Tri-City CDP	3,931	-	-	4,150	86.4	0.0	1.3	9.6	2.7	22.1	25.1	45.4	53.8	7.6	1,613	89.3
Troutdale city	15,956	16,183	1.4	16,466	70.3	2.8	5.3	6.3	15.3	24.1	10.5	34.9	35.4	22.9	5,449	95.0
Tualatin city	26,114	27,837	6.6	27,527	72.3	2.1	3.5	5.5	16.6	24.2	12.2	38.0	19.4	45.3	10,787	94.9
Tumalo CDP	488	-	-	535	96.4	0.0	0.0	0.0	3.6	22.8	15.0	46.1	10.9	74.3	223	100.0

1 May be of any race.

Table A. All Places — **Population and Housing**

STATE City, town, township, borough, or CDP (county if applicable)	Population				Race and Hispanic or Latino origin (percent)					Age (percent)			Educational attainment of persons age 25 and older		Occupied housing units	
	2010 census total population	2019 estimated population	Percent change 2010–2019	ACS total population estimate 2015–2019	White alone, not Hispanic or Latino	Black alone, not Hispanic or Latino	Asian alone, not Hispanic or Latino	All other races or 2 or more races, not Hispanic or Latino	Hispanic or Latino[1]	Under 18 years old	Age 65 years and older	Median age	Percent High school diploma or less	Percent Bachelor's degree or more	Total	Percent with a computer
	1	2	3	4	5	6	7	8	9	10	11	12	13	14	15	16
OREGON—Con.																
Turner city	1,851	2,121	14.6	2,494	82.4	0.0	2.6	1.6	13.4	26.1	17.2	35.7	31.4	19.8	965	95.6
Tutuilla CDP	487	-	-	382	68.3	0.8	0.0	28.0	2.9	19.4	27.2	52.0	39.2	20.1	154	88.3
Tygh Valley CDP	206	-	-	180	100.0	0.0	0.0	0.0	0.0	14.4	36.7	58.7	57.8	11.7	78	100.0
Ukiah city	186	208	11.8	267	83.9	0.0	4.9	8.2	3.0	14.6	21.0	35.3	54.0	12.2	85	70.6
Umapine CDP	315	-	-	361	88.6	0.0	6.9	4.4	0.0	24.9	19.4	52.6	24.7	24.0	139	84.2
Umatilla city	6,913	7,321	5.9	7,162	50.0	3.6	0.2	4.5	41.7	25.7	7.4	33.9	58.5	9.4	1,748	92.3
Union city	2,121	2,221	4.7	2,180	94.2	0.6	0.4	3.5	1.4	17.0	23.5	46.6	41.1	16.4	889	86.1
Unity city	71	70	-1.4	48	91.7	0.0	0.0	8.3	0.0	0.0	52.1	67.2	68.9	2.2	31	61.3
Vale city	1,874	1,818	-3.0	2,079	71.7	0.0	1.9	1.0	25.4	31.9	14.1	29.5	48.3	14.7	670	89.3
Veneta city	4,558	5,056	10.9	4,953	79.5	0.7	3.0	1.4	15.4	27.0	14.5	40.8	36.9	16.4	1,958	92.4
Vernonia city	2,165	2,281	5.4	1,856	95.4	0.0	0.0	1.4	3.2	22.3	17.0	42.5	50.9	12.9	737	91.2
Waldport city	2,063	2,230	8.1	2,055	88.1	0.0	0.3	4.0	7.6	15.1	30.7	57.1	35.2	17.8	997	91.6
Wallowa city	808	837	3.6	797	83.4	0.0	0.0	12.3	4.3	23.1	22.6	36.7	36.1	16.3	350	89.4
Wallowa Lake CDP	62	-	-	24	100.0	0.0	0.0	0.0	0.0	0.0	70.8	66.0	58.3	0.0	11	100.0
Wamic CDP	85	-	-	74	100.0	0.0	0.0	0.0	0.0	0.0	17.6	60.3	63.5	0.0	61	100.0
Warm Springs CDP	2,945	-	-	3,213	3.2	0.6	0.1	87.7	8.4	37.2	7.2	27.8	55.4	9.3	744	80.8
Warren CDP	1,787	-	-	1,943	96.5	0.0	0.0	0.9	2.6	19.7	18.1	45.3	39.2	25.7	659	91.4
Warrenton city	5,020	5,739	14.3	5,549	79.7	0.7	1.5	5.8	12.3	24.4	18.0	36.8	33.3	19.4	1,936	94.2
Wasco city	410	412	0.5	440	87.3	0.0	0.0	5.0	7.7	18.0	32.3	57.2	52.7	17.0	196	89.3
Waterloo town	229	256	11.8	267	92.1	0.0	0.0	3.7	4.1	21.7	25.8	41.8	50.3	5.9	86	91.9
Westfir city	251	267	6.4	296	94.3	0.0	0.0	1.0	4.7	17.6	29.7	56.1	46.2	8.9	129	86.0
West Haven-Sylvan CDP	8,001	-	-	8,888	81.1	2.2	6.1	3.4	7.1	15.4	16.0	38.1	6.8	73.3	4,194	95.1
West Linn city	25,118	26,736	6.4	26,656	81.6	1.6	6.4	4.3	6.1	25.7	15.8	42.7	13.5	61.5	9,734	96.7
Weston city	667	651	-2.4	823	83.5	0.0	0.9	3.4	12.3	35.6	13.7	27.7	62.2	3.1	261	93.1
Westport CDP	321	-	-	364	96.2	3.8	0.0	0.0	0.0	3.0	43.4	54.3	54.5	19.4	166	94.0
West Scio CDP	120	-	-	105	100.0	0.0	0.0	0.0	0.0	26.7	0.0	23.3	0.0	0.0	59	100.0
West Slope CDP	6,554	-	-	6,913	82.0	1.6	2.7	5.6	8.1	17.6	16.5	44.9	17.9	54.8	2,960	95.8
Wheeler city	414	440	6.3	357	87.7	0.0	0.0	12.3	0.0	15.1	37.8	61.1	30.7	32.0	170	84.1
White City CDP	7,975	-	-	9,890	58.1	0.9	0.9	8.6	31.6	29.1	11.7	33.2	57.1	7.0	3,007	92.4
Willamina city	2,037	2,250	10.5	2,450	90.3	0.0	0.1	5.0	4.6	25.2	15.5	35.8	43.0	7.6	900	93.4
Williams CDP	1,072	-	-	1,390	91.6	0.0	0.0	7.7	0.7	26.3	29.0	44.6	25.2	24.6	526	83.3
Wilsonville city	19,509	24,918	27.7	24,073	75.8	1.8	4.2	6.5	11.7	20.7	13.9	36.6	21.2	45.8	9,750	96.7
Wimer CDP	678	-	-	452	100.0	0.0	0.0	0.0	0.0	3.5	48.5	64.6	32.8	14.9	238	93.3
Winchester Bay CDP	382	-	-	337	99.4	0.0	0.0	0.3	0.3	9.8	39.8	62.3	22.3	10.1	155	83.2
Winston city	5,365	5,511	2.7	5,416	83.3	0.2	0.3	3.6	12.6	25.7	20.9	39.3	48.3	11.2	2,161	90.2
Woodburn city	24,118	26,273	8.9	25,738	39.5	0.6	0.7	2.3	56.8	30.8	15.9	33.9	57.1	15.9	8,018	88.3
Wood Village city	3,878	4,093	5.5	4,057	35.3	1.1	3.6	7.3	52.7	33.5	7.7	31.3	60.1	11.8	1,101	98.7
Yachats city	691	784	13.5	553	88.8	0.0	0.0	2.7	8.5	3.6	52.3	65.9	27.1	40.9	305	85.2
Yamhill city	1,024	1,169	14.2	1,346	83.1	0.4	2.3	5.9	8.4	27.5	10.5	36.8	34.4	18.0	445	98.7
Yoncalla city	1,047	1,096	4.7	1,261	88.7	0.0	0.0	11.3	0.0	21.4	26.0	47.3	49.6	9.6	539	78.1
PENNSYLVANIA	12,702,868	12,801,989	0.8	12,791,530	76.4	10.7	3.4	2.2	7.3	20.8	17.8	40.8	44.2	31.4	5,053,106	88.0
Aaronsburg CDP	613	-	-	487	95.3	0.0	0.8	3.7	0.2	11.7	24.4	50.3	59.9	22.9	224	74.1
Aaronsburg CDP	259	-	-	111	98.2	0.0	0.0	1.8	0.0	0.0	27.0	29.9	62.2	13.5	56	73.2
Abbott township (Potter)	242	228	-5.8	197	100.0	0.0	0.0	0.0	0.0	16.8	36.0	55.4	58.1	12.5	92	84.8
Abbottstown borough & MCD (Adams)	1,011	1,026	1.5	874	88.7	0.0	0.6	0.9	9.8	22.9	13.0	36.4	63.0	11.6	324	88.0
Abington township (Montgomery)	55,356	55,319	-0.1	55,459	77.0	11.7	4.1	2.9	4.4	22.0	18.5	42.4	27.1	48.9	20,930	93.1
Ackermanville CDP	610	-	-	632	71.5	0.0	24.1	0.0	4.4	29.1	16.6	40.2	55.8	23.2	206	95.6
Adams township (Butler)	11,657	13,980	19.9	13,643	95.0	0.3	2.5	0.8	1.4	24.7	14.6	42.9	18.4	65.1	4,984	96.7
Adams township (Cambria)	5,990	5,522	-7.8	5,640	99.4	0.2	0.0	0.2	0.2	22.2	21.0	40.5	50.6	23.6	2,226	88.1
Adams township (Snyder)	911	912	0.1	866	98.5	0.7	0.0	0.8	0.0	26.8	12.6	37.5	67.1	13.5	303	78.2
Adamsburg borough & MCD (Westmoreland)	172	162	-5.8	170	86.5	0.0	0.0	7.6	5.9	14.7	21.2	50.2	50.4	15.6	99	72.7
Adamstown borough	1,776	1,880	5.9	2,492	86.8	1.7	4.8	2.8	3.8	29.5	13.7	32.5	49.2	27.6	849	88.1
Adamstown borough (Berks)	20	22	10.0	92	100.0	0.0	0.0	0.0	0.0	43.5	0.0	25.5	26.9	23.1	26	100.0
Adamstown borough (Lancaster)	1,756	1,858	5.8	2,400	86.3	1.8	5.0	3.0	4.0	28.9	14.2	32.9	49.9	27.7	823	87.7
Adamsville CDP	67	-	-	57	100.0	0.0	0.0	0.0	0.0	7.0	35.1	57.7	66.7	7.8	28	64.3
Addison borough & MCD (Somerset)	207	206	-0.5	225	97.8	0.0	0.0	0.0	2.2	24.0	23.6	40.5	57.0	14.8	84	77.4
Addison township (Somerset)	974	924	-5.1	832	99.2	0.0	0.0	0.0	0.8	22.6	24.2	45.6	52.3	17.3	356	85.7
Akron borough & MCD (Lancaster)	3,884	4,015	3.4	3,997	89.1	0.6	1.0	0.0	9.3	23.1	16.0	36.5	48.5	25.4	1,623	88.7
Alba borough & MCD (Bradford)	157	145	-7.6	138	100.0	0.0	0.0	0.0	0.0	18.1	23.9	51.5	64.2	14.2	60	78.3
Albany township (Berks)	1,733	1,763	1.7	1,624	97.4	0.4	0.2	0.0	2.0	19.9	21.4	44.7	42.7	36.1	629	91.9
Albany township (Bradford)	909	905	-0.4	913	98.8	0.0	0.2	1.0	0.0	14.5	22.0	52.5	67.0	15.4	401	92.3
Albion borough & MCD (Erie)	1,511	1,449	-4.1	1,539	94.3	1.6	0.8	0.7	2.6	24.6	18.6	43.9	57.6	16.5	681	84.6
Albrightsville CDP	202	-	-	169	76.9	3.6	0.0	1.8	17.8	31.4	30.8	46.2	61.3	0.0	58	100.0
Alburtis borough & MCD (Lehigh)	2,355	2,636	11.9	2,577	80.1	4.4	0.7	2.9	11.8	23.4	8.0	35.3	36.1	38.2	965	96.6
Aldan borough & MCD (Delaware)	4,156	4,160	0.1	4,153	61.7	30.3	2.3	2.7	2.9	17.9	18.0	45.6	42.5	28.2	1,720	92.5
Aleppo township (Allegheny)	1,914	1,860	-2.8	1,878	95.8	0.9	0.0	0.8	2.4	12.2	55.8	69.7	29.1	45.7	958	79.1
Aleppo township (Greene)	505	479	-5.1	418	99.8	0.0	0.0	0.2	0.0	19.9	23.7	45.1	68.3	18.3	182	70.9
Alexandria borough & MCD (Huntingdon)	349	331	-5.2	341	93.3	0.0	0.0	0.0	6.7	28.4	11.4	40.1	51.8	29.8	133	91.7
Alfarata CDP	149	-	-	177	100.0	0.0	0.0	0.0	0.0	0.0	13.6	52.3	65.2	3.2	89	53.9
Aliquippa city & MCD (Beaver)	9,437	8,844	-6.3	9,004	57.0	34.0	0.9	4.9	3.2	20.9	20.6	43.3	50.3	12.3	4,399	74.5
Allegany township (Potter)	422	399	-5.5	404	98.8	0.0	0.2	0.5	0.5	21.8	23.0	53.5	60.5	12.3	166	78.9
Allegheny township (Blair)	6,728	6,513	-3.2	6,553	98.7	0.0	0.4	0.4	0.5	20.0	23.5	46.7	53.4	18.6	2,882	80.4

1 May be of any race.

Table A. All Places — **Population and Housing**

STATE City, town, township, borough, or CDP (county if applicable)	2010 census total population	2019 estimated population	Percent change 2010–2019	ACS total population estimate 2015–2019	White alone, not Hispanic or Latino	Black alone, not Hispanic or Latino	Asian alone, not Hispanic or Latino	All other races or 2 or more races, not Hispanic or Latino	Hispanic or Latino[1]	Under 18 years old	Age 65 years and older	Median age	Percent High school diploma or less	Percent Bachelor's degree or more	Total	Percent with a computer
	1	2	3	4	5	6	7	8	9	10	11	12	13	14	15	16
PENNSYLVANIA—Con.																
Allegheny township (Butler)	641	622	-3.0	656	85.4	8.7	0.0	2.9	3.0	25.2	18.6	41.9	64.1	10.8	240	92.9
Allegheny township (Cambria)	2,847	2,252	-20.9	3,018	77.8	12.3	0.0	2.4	7.6	13.9	10.5	42.1	51.3	20.0	681	87.5
Allegheny township (Somerset)	702	662	-5.7	598	99.8	0.0	0.0	0.2	0.0	12.2	28.8	57.3	68.6	16.8	268	80.2
Allegheny township (Venango)	277	259	-6.5	238	97.5	0.0	0.0	1.3	1.3	22.3	20.6	47.0	58.4	15.7	97	83.5
Allegheny township (Westmoreland)	8,185	8,012	-2.1	8,091	95.9	0.8	0.1	1.3	1.9	22.3	20.2	47.2	38.5	35.6	3,220	90.3
Alleghenyville CDP	1,134	-	-	1,013	88.6	1.6	0.0	8.2	1.6	19.9	13.7	49.5	36.9	41.2	376	94.1
Allen township (Northampton)	4,295	5,044	17.4	4,928	84.5	5.3	1.8	2.9	5.4	19.6	21.5	46.2	33.6	36.5	2,039	94.0
Allenport (Northampton)	648	-	-	550	93.8	4.2	0.0	2.0	0.0	14.7	24.9	50.2	69.6	11.6	263	77.6
Allenport borough & MCD (Washington)	514	495	-3.7	552	100.0	0.0	0.0	0.0	0.0	10.9	30.1	50.8	59.4	22.2	267	89.5
Allensville CDP	503	-	-	464	98.9	1.1	0.0	0.0	0.0	29.7	13.8	28.3	82.4	6.5	137	61.3
Allentown city & MCD (Lehigh)	118,095	121,442	2.8	120,915	32.4	10.2	2.8	2.1	52.5	26.4	11.9	31.6	59.0	15.3	42,245	87.0
Allenwood CDP	321	-	-	271	98.2	0.0	0.0	0.0	1.8	11.8	27.3	51.1	50.2	16.1	126	88.1
Allison township (Clinton)	200	197	-1.5	347	98.6	1.4	0.0	0.0	0.0	18.2	28.0	43.6	49.4	31.0	125	96.0
Allison CDP	625	-	-	533	92.3	4.7	0.0	3.0	0.0	21.0	19.9	44.8	62.6	23.2	208	77.4
Allison Park CDP	21,552	-	-	23,092	89.1	3.6	4.5	1.4	1.4	21.2	20.7	44.3	24.5	52.6	9,249	93.1
Allport CDP	264	-	-	397	100.0	0.0	0.0	0.0	0.0	0.0	3.3	48.4	66.0	13.8	118	100.0
Almedia CDP	1,078	-	-	992	96.4	0.0	0.0	2.1	1.5	16.6	35.3	56.5	53.7	20.9	463	79.3
Alsace township (Berks)	3,729	3,955	6.1	3,908	89.4	1.2	0.3	0.0	9.2	19.9	27.8	52.3	54.9	16.9	1,676	92.9
Alsace Manor CDP	478	-	-	490	100.0	0.0	0.0	0.0	0.0	21.8	36.7	52.1	63.7	18.7	175	72.0
Altamont CDP	602	-	-	583	99.0	0.0	1.0	0.0	0.0	7.7	42.9	60.3	51.7	25.0	299	72.9
Altoona city & MCD (Blair)	45,963	43,364	-5.7	43,987	91.0	3.4	0.2	2.9	2.4	22.2	16.5	38.3	56.9	17.6	18,847	84.9
Ambler borough & MCD (Montgomery)	6,398	6,491	1.5	6,489	69.7	11.4	3.7	2.8	12.3	21.9	14.3	35.8	33.1	44.3	2,669	91.9
Ambridge borough & MCD (Beaver)	7,048	6,601	-6.3	6,707	74.7	16.7	0.7	4.3	3.7	21.4	14.5	36.0	46.7	20.8	3,020	85.6
Amity township (Berks)	12,584	13,172	4.7	13,007	86.1	3.7	2.0	1.3	6.8	22.8	17.0	43.0	37.4	34.6	4,546	90.1
Amity township (Erie)	1,073	1,048	-2.3	950	95.9	0.0	0.6	1.8	1.7	16.9	25.3	53.4	51.8	22.2	385	82.9
Amity Gardens CDP	3,402	-	-	3,503	89.7	2.3	0.0	0.6	7.5	18.0	22.4	46.4	41.8	36.2	1,221	94.6
Amwell township (Washington)	3,746	3,640	-2.8	3,674	94.4	1.1	0.0	3.3	1.1	21.0	19.9	44.1	49.1	18.8	1,478	88.2
Ancient Oaks CDP	6,661	-	-	7,387	81.8	3.8	6.7	3.2	4.5	25.5	17.1	42.2	20.1	56.0	2,766	94.8
Annin township (McKean)	694	669	-3.6	719	96.2	0.3	0.0	3.5	0.0	17.0	18.2	43.9	64.4	10.9	310	85.2
Annville township & CDP (Lebanon)	4,782	5,056	5.7	4,973	88.3	2.1	1.7	0.7	7.1	14.2	13.7	25.1	50.6	26.7	1,496	89.0
Anthony township (Lycoming)	875	874	-0.1	839	99.2	0.0	0.0	0.0	0.8	15.7	17.4	50.9	53.2	20.5	335	89.6
Anthony township (Montour)	1,501	1,503	0.1	1,409	98.5	0.3	0.0	1.2	0.0	26.8	15.3	36.0	63.6	12.9	471	75.2
Antis township (Blair)	6,465	6,199	-4.1	6,262	96.1	1.1	0.0	2.8	0.0	19.2	22.3	48.3	49.1	21.7	2,783	84.3
Antrim township (Franklin)	14,911	15,768	5.7	15,576	91.7	0.7	1.0	2.1	4.5	23.7	16.7	41.0	56.5	19.8	5,316	93.5
Apolacon township (Susquehanna)	500	483	-3.4	422	99.3	0.0	0.0	0.0	0.7	17.1	24.2	50.2	54.3	18.8	184	79.3
Apollo borough & MCD (Armstrong)	1,647	1,523	-7.5	1,457	82.8	7.9	0.8	5.1	3.4	18.5	17.0	41.3	63.3	13.8	642	76.3
Applewold borough & MCD (Armstrong)	310	286	-7.7	315	99.0	0.0	0.3	0.3	0.3	16.8	26.3	40.3	49.4	21.8	156	81.4
Ararat township (Susquehanna)	561	522	-7.0	619	99.5	0.0	0.5	0.0	0.0	24.1	21.3	40.0	48.9	18.6	230	93.9
Arcadia University CDP	595	-	-	626	73.8	10.4	4.6	2.7	8.5	0.5	0.0	19.4	0.0	100.0	0	0.0
Archbald borough & MCD (Lackawanna)	6,987	7,030	0.6	6,988	93.6	1.9	0.9	0.8	2.8	24.6	18.1	41.0	40.9	29.2	2,883	84.9
Ardmore CDP	12,455	-	-	12,808	78.2	9.4	3.3	4.1	5.0	20.7	17.4	40.4	15.1	68.5	5,738	93.0
Arendtsville borough & MCD (Adams)	946	959	1.4	749	72.5	1.1	0.0	0.1	26.3	30.0	13.1	33.8	47.7	22.3	256	90.6
Aristes CDP	311	-	-	322	100.0	0.0	0.0	0.0	0.0	10.2	29.2	54.4	65.7	13.6	148	80.4
Arlington Heights CDP	6,333	-	-	6,129	68.0	7.3	7.9	2.4	14.4	23.7	20.4	40.2	50.4	26.9	2,065	87.7
Armagh borough & MCD (Indiana)	122	115	-5.7	100	90.0	0.0	0.0	8.0	2.0	15.0	27.0	56.3	65.0	15.0	46	80.4
Armagh township (Mifflin)	3,862	3,800	-1.6	3,804	95.2	0.0	0.7	2.4	1.7	25.2	19.0	40.2	69.2	9.7	1,503	75.2
Armenia township (Bradford)	180	173	-3.9	158	100.0	0.0	0.0	0.0	0.0	19.6	50.0	65.0	59.1	11.0	70	88.6
Armstrong township (Indiana)	3,000	2,833	-5.6	2,861	98.6	0.2	0.0	1.3	0.0	16.2	17.7	43.8	52.5	16.1	1,224	82.4
Armstrong township (Lycoming)	700	720	2.9	635	98.4	0.8	0.0	0.8	0.0	21.4	18.3	46.8	50.6	23.5	264	88.6
Arnold city & MCD (Westmoreland)	5,153	4,831	-6.2	4,902	62.0	25.5	0.0	8.8	3.8	23.7	15.6	38.3	58.9	9.7	2,227	85.6
Arnold City CDP	498	-	-	315	78.1	10.8	0.0	11.1	0.0	3.8	34.6	57.0	59.8	10.8	164	65.9
Arnot CDP	332	-	-	479	100.0	0.0	0.0	0.0	0.0	21.7	27.1	41.9	70.0	8.7	174	82.2
Arona borough & MCD (Westmoreland)	370	346	-6.5	311	90.4	0.0	0.0	7.4	2.3	15.1	16.1	49.3	61.7	13.2	141	75.9
Ashland township (Clarion)	1,114	1,056	-5.2	964	98.9	0.0	0.0	0.6	0.5	28.4	16.7	38.1	56.8	26.8	359	81.1
Ashland borough	2,817	2,679	-4.9	2,705	94.5	3.4	0.0	2.1	0.0	23.0	17.0	38.5	59.5	8.1	1,251	85.5
Ashland borough (Columbia)	-	-	-	-	-	-	-	-	-	-	-	-	-	-	-	-
Ashland borough (Schuylkill)	2,817	2,679	-4.9	2,705	94.5	3.4	0.0	2.1	0.0	23.0	17.0	38.5	59.5	8.1	1,251	85.5
Ashley borough & MCD (Luzerne)	2,797	2,723	-2.6	2,731	91.1	3.7	0.0	1.6	3.6	21.3	14.1	40.5	56.7	16.1	1,208	80.6
Ashville borough & MCD (Cambria)	230	210	-8.7	165	100.0	0.0	0.0	0.0	0.0	6.1	21.8	48.6	47.3	15.5	82	79.3
Aspers CDP	350	-	-	233	100.0	0.0	0.0	0.0	0.0	9.9	12.0	28.5	20.3	40.6	100	100.0

1 May be of any race.

Table A. All Places — **Population and Housing**

STATE City, town, township, borough, or CDP (county if applicable)	Population 2010 census total population	2019 estimated population	Percent change 2010–2019	ACS total population estimate 2015–2019	Race and Hispanic or Latino origin (percent) White alone, not Hispanic or Latino	Black alone, not Hispanic or Latino	Asian alone, not Hispanic or Latino	All other races or 2 or more races, not Hispanic or Latino	Hispanic or Latino[1]	Age (percent) Under 18 years old	Age 65 years and older	Median age	Educational attainment of persons age 25 and older Percent High school diploma or less	Percent Bachelor's degree or more	Occupied housing units Total	Percent with a computer
	1	2	3	4	5	6	7	8	9	10	11	12	13	14	15	16
PENNSYLVANIA—Con.																
Aspinwall borough & MCD (Allegheny)	2,798	2,693	-3.8	2,724	85.5	1.4	9.7	0.9	2.6	24.4	15.7	37.3	14.3	72.3	1,202	95.8
Aston township (Delaware)	16,613	16,745	0.8	16,706	90.1	4.3	2.8	1.6	1.1	19.6	16.2	41.6	40.7	32.3	6,065	90.9
Asylum township (Bradford)	1,055	1,038	-1.6	1,122	98.8	0.0	0.0	0.0	1.2	24.5	19.7	44.9	66.2	15.7	446	82.3
Atglen borough & MCD (Chester)	1,408	1,409	0.1	1,328	83.1	6.6	0.2	4.2	5.9	29.7	9.5	30.7	53.1	25.6	496	85.7
Athens borough & MCD (Bradford)	3,365	3,189	-5.2	3,225	95.0	0.0	3.3	1.7	0.0	24.7	24.6	40.4	51.2	27.2	1,401	82.1
Athens township (Bradford)	5,253	5,073	-3.4	5,101	93.1	0.0	1.0	3.2	2.8	24.3	21.8	47.2	47.5	28.2	2,204	85.3
Athens township (Crawford)	734	728	-0.8	678	98.1	0.0	0.7	0.1	1.0	15.6	25.5	52.4	62.4	15.2	305	80.0
Atkinson Mills CDP	174	-	-	106	94.3	0.0	5.7	0.0	0.0	22.6	22.6	50.4	76.8	4.9	40	100.0
Atlantic CDP	77	-	-	67	100.0	0.0	0.0	0.0	0.0	43.3	9.0	36.4	88.6	0.0	20	60.0
Atlas CDP	809	-	-	814	98.8	1.0	0.0	0.0	0.2	4.2	22.0	50.4	84.8	1.0	399	68.7
Atlasburg CDP	401	-	-	625	94.9	0.0	0.0	5.1	0.0	28.8	6.9	34.0	66.2	18.0	205	93.7
Atwood borough & MCD (Armstrong)	107	103	-3.7	110	100.0	0.0	0.0	0.0	0.0	15.5	9.1	52.9	81.8	7.8	48	75.0
Auburn borough & MCD (Schuylkill)	737	698	-5.3	564	100.0	0.0	0.0	0.0	0.0	16.3	24.1	48.4	77.5	12.3	244	84.0
Auburn township (Susquehanna)	1,939	1,846	-4.8	1,725	96.8	0.0	0.0	2.0	1.2	20.8	22.6	46.1	63.0	12.8	719	93.7
Audubon CDP	8,433	-	-	9,163	70.0	3.8	20.6	1.2	4.4	24.8	22.2	38.2	18.2	62.8	3,582	93.6
Austin borough & MCD (Potter)	559	531	-5.0	559	98.7	0.0	0.4	0.4	0.5	21.6	19.0	39.9	70.2	5.2	202	80.7
Avalon borough & MCD (Allegheny)	4,715	4,537	-3.8	4,584	82.5	9.9	0.0	5.7	1.9	12.3	21.1	40.9	35.7	33.5	2,492	80.1
Avella CDP	804	-	-	888	97.6	0.0	0.0	1.9	0.5	27.0	11.3	33.8	57.7	16.9	333	91.0
Avis borough & MCD (Clinton)	1,488	1,490	0.1	1,457	97.4	0.3	0.8	1.4	0.1	24.2	22.5	39.9	57.3	17.1	594	86.4
Avoca borough & MCD (Luzerne)	2,660	2,629	-1.2	2,623	98.9	0.0	0.0	0.3	0.8	15.7	23.1	45.1	44.7	20.0	1,155	86.8
Avon CDP	1,667	-	-	1,398	87.3	2.2	0.0	2.1	8.3	18.8	22.5	47.5	63.5	12.3	614	84.7
Avondale borough & MCD (Chester)	1,265	1,400	10.7	1,406	24.0	9.2	3.2	2.0	61.6	32.9	6.4	30.4	63.2	18.4	369	75.6
Avonia CDP	1,205	-	-	1,093	97.0	0.6	1.8	0.0	0.5	21.2	19.4	50.1	25.0	48.3	435	93.6
Avonmore borough & MCD (Westmoreland)	1,014	952	-6.1	988	94.7	0.0	0.0	5.3	0.0	18.9	23.5	45.3	56.9	13.7	456	79.4
Ayr township (Fulton)	2,091	2,004	-4.2	2,167	94.8	0.8	0.0	4.4	0.0	17.2	21.4	47.2	69.9	9.6	901	74.1
Baden borough & MCD (Beaver)	4,127	3,880	-6.0	3,948	95.0	1.3	0.3	2.7	0.7	14.3	27.5	47.8	49.0	20.5	1,765	83.9
Baidland CDP	1,563	-	-	1,560	99.0	0.0	0.0	1.0	0.0	17.6	22.6	40.1	43.4	37.8	649	95.7
Baileyville CDP	201	-	-	61	100.0	0.0	0.0	0.0	0.0	0.0	24.6	33.3	63.9	0.0	37	59.5
Bainbridge CDP	1,355	-	-	1,520	96.4	1.6	0.0	0.0	2.0	26.8	10.9	34.6	61.0	17.2	557	91.2
Bairdford CDP	698	-	-	690	96.8	0.0	0.0	3.2	0.0	12.0	12.0	47.0	51.2	29.3	306	100.0
Bakerstown CDP	1,761	-	-	2,549	96.5	0.0	3.1	0.0	0.4	19.8	31.9	53.7	16.3	64.0	954	86.1
Bald Eagle township (Clinton)	2,063	2,085	1.1	2,077	94.8	0.7	2.2	0.1	2.1	22.3	20.7	44.3	59.9	20.8	714	85.0
Baldwin borough & MCD (Allegheny)	19,967	19,554	-2.1	19,752	81.8	8.1	6.3	1.8	2.0	20.9	19.8	41.2	44.0	26.4	8,038	87.5
Baldwin township (Allegheny)	2,013	1,939	-3.7	2,050	93.6	0.0	3.2	3.3	0.0	18.6	20.1	45.2	31.6	31.4	869	94.1
Bally borough & MCD (Berks)	1,068	1,245	16.6	1,390	94.4	0.5	0.4	0.1	4.5	25.5	19.9	37.7	52.1	19.0	506	90.3
Bangor borough & MCD (Northampton)	5,264	5,228	-0.7	5,208	96.0	0.0	0.0	0.6	3.4	23.1	17.5	36.3	61.0	14.6	2,023	85.8
Banks township (Carbon)	1,263	1,221	-3.3	1,493	91.8	0.4	0.2	1.1	6.5	20.5	22.3	49.0	65.5	7.6	624	81.6
Banks township (Indiana)	1,013	946	-6.6	1,022	100.0	0.0	0.0	0.0	0.0	25.8	18.7	38.8	76.0	8.7	348	69.8
Barkeyville borough & MCD (Venango)	219	200	-8.7	314	93.9	1.0	0.0	4.1	1.0	28.0	11.8	35.0	72.1	10.8	100	98.0
Barnett township (Forest)	358	319	-10.9	301	99.3	0.0	0.0	0.0	0.7	7.6	52.8	66.7	61.9	14.7	191	73.3
Barnett township (Jefferson)	254	244	-3.9	170	98.2	0.0	0.0	1.8	0.0	15.3	25.9	59.7	51.4	13.9	81	88.9
Barr township (Cambria)	2,050	1,909	-6.9	2,071	96.9	0.1	0.8	1.9	0.3	24.2	20.9	44.3	57.1	19.5	797	77.8
Barree township (Huntingdon)	477	465	-2.5	472	99.8	0.0	0.0	0.0	0.2	12.1	23.3	49.0	51.1	21.6	194	82.0
Barrett township (Monroe)	4,219	4,142	-1.8	4,096	67.7	14.5	3.9	0.9	13.0	20.6	21.8	46.3	39.8	38.5	1,608	85.4
Barrville CDP	160	-	-	374	100.0	0.0	0.0	0.0	0.0	35.3	4.3	25.1	100.0	0.0	97	8.2
Barry township (Schuylkill)	932	881	-5.5	805	99.4	0.0	0.0	0.6	0.0	14.2	27.0	53.3	61.2	19.0	394	81.5
Bart township (Lancaster)	3,083	3,369	9.3	3,327	96.2	0.8	1.4	0.6	0.9	34.7	14.7	27.7	78.5	8.0	947	53.3
Bastress township (Lycoming)	551	547	-0.7	494	99.0	0.0	0.0	1.0	0.0	20.2	22.9	48.0	49.2	21.8	195	82.1
Bath borough & MCD (Northampton)	2,693	2,668	-0.9	2,658	83.0	4.0	0.6	2.6	9.9	24.8	15.0	38.5	54.7	17.1	1,013	85.7
Baumstown CDP	422	-	-	475	41.1	55.2	0.0	0.0	3.8	30.9	12.2	41.1	58.2	2.8	178	92.7
Beale township (Juniata)	830	834	0.5	784	90.8	3.2	2.2	3.4	0.4	18.0	16.7	49.5	70.1	14.1	322	91.0
Beallsville borough & MCD (Washington)	482	465	-3.5	510	98.6	0.4	0.0	0.0	1.0	22.7	23.5	44.5	45.4	18.7	191	84.8
Bear Creek township (Luzerne)	2,775	2,747		2,752	93.9	1.0	2.3	0.6	2.2	18.1	20.9	47.8	35.3	34.9	1,147	88.8
Bear Creek Village borough & MCD (Lu...	252	249	-1.2	241	97.9	0.0	1.2	0.0	0.8	23.2	26.1	53.9	6.8	64.2	99	92.9
Bear Lake borough & MCD (Warren)	164	155	-5.5	193	100.0	0.0	0.0	0.0	0.0	19.2	21.8	49.5	66.0	4.8	80	83.8
Bear Rocks CDP	1,048	-	-	794	100.0	0.0	0.0	0.0	0.0	10.6	27.2	53.8	38.8	27.9	366	94.8
Beaver borough & MCD (Beaver)	4,525	4,266	-5.7	4,334	93.7	2.1	1.6	1.0	1.6	18.9	25.7	48.0	26.1	44.2	2,042	88.2
Beaver township (Clarion)	1,757	1,675	-4.7	1,780	99.4	0.0	0.0	0.6	0.0	20.1	23.0	46.6	62.5	16.2	753	80.6
Beaver township (Columbia)	919	901	-2.0	814	98.6	0.0	0.0	1.4	0.0	17.0	17.1	46.8	59.7	19.5	337	87.8

1 May be of any race.

Table A. All Places — **Population and Housing**

STATE City, town, township, borough, or CDP (county if applicable)	2010 census total population	2019 estimated population	Percent change 2010–2019	ACS total population estimate 2015–2019	White alone, not Hispanic or Latino	Black alone, not Hispanic or Latino	Asian alone, not Hispanic or Latino	All other races or 2 or more races, not Hispanic or Latino	Hispanic or Latino[1]	Under 18 years old	Age 65 years and older	Median age	Percent High school diploma or less	Percent Bachelor's degree or more	Total	Percent with a computer
	1	2	3	4	5	6	7	8	9	10	11	12	13	14	15	16
PENNSYLVANIA—Con.																
Beaver township (Crawford)	900	855	-5.0	780	97.1	0.6	0.0	0.4	1.9	24.2	12.9	40.9	72.8	8.6	275	77.8
Beaver township (Jefferson)	498	479	-3.8	390	99.5	0.0	0.5	0.0	0.0	20.0	18.7	47.7	69.1	11.5	157	79.6
Beaver township (Snyder)	537	534	-0.6	494	99.2	0.0	0.0	0.0	0.8	20.4	31.0	49.0	76.2	8.6	174	79.3
Beaverdale CDP	1,035	-		778	96.3	0.9	2.4	0.0	0.4	21.1	24.0	45.2	67.9	12.3	338	69.5
Beaver Falls city & MCD (Beaver)	8,995	8,332	-7.4	8,464	71.1	17.5	1.2	8.4	1.8	20.2	15.6	31.5	54.3	17.5	3,359	83.9
Beaver Meadows borough & MCD (Carbon)	864	834	-3.5	884	86.5	0.3	0.0	0.2	12.9	17.8	21.5	47.5	62.9	12.1	383	76.2
Beaver Springs CDP	674	-		580	96.7	0.5	0.0	2.8	0.0	26.0	23.8	44.6	74.3	6.3	251	79.3
Beavertown borough & MCD (Snyder)	955	963	0.8	1,077	97.1	0.0	0.0	0.0	2.9	27.6	21.1	38.0	65.9	10.5	417	87.5
Beccaria township (Clearfield)	1,785	1,707	-4.4	1,739	95.2	0.5	0.0	2.5	1.8	20.2	21.9	45.8	64.8	13.2	667	85.0
Bechtelsville borough & MCD (Berks)	943	949	0.6	1,003	98.3	0.0	0.0	1.0	0.7	25.3	14.4	37.3	49.1	20.6	379	85.5
Bedford borough & MCD (Bedford)	2,842	2,677	-5.8	2,718	93.3	2.2	3.9	0.4	0.3	18.1	31.0	49.4	53.6	26.7	1,253	74.3
Bedford township (Bedford)	5,391	5,123	-5.0	5,171	96.9	1.8	0.0	0.1	1.3	14.9	25.4	53.2	62.6	18.2	2,187	77.7
Bedminster township (Bucks)	6,574	7,229	10.0	7,128	94.6	0.0	3.5	1.0	1.0	26.2	15.2	43.0	24.0	55.9	2,605	95.7
Beech Creek borough & MCD (Clinton)	704	692	-1.7	789	98.0	2.0	0.0	0.0	0.0	16.9	19.4	44.0	65.8	10.0	283	77.0
Beech Creek township (Clinton)	1,010	1,000		814	99.8	0.0	0.0	0.2	0.0	16.1	18.4	43.4	62.0	11.5	323	80.5
Beech Mountain Lakes CDP	2,022	-	-	1,789	90.8	0.0	0.0	2.2	7.0	16.9	18.5	48.0	28.1	41.0	746	100.0
Belfast township (Fulton)	1,450	1,425	-1.7	1,338	98.6	0.0	0.0	0.4	1.0	16.4	21.4	46.4	65.8	12.6	526	80.8
Belfast CDP	1,257	-	-	1,318	98.0	0.9	0.0	0.0	1.1	18.1	12.9	43.8	42.6	33.9	535	86.2
Bell township (Clearfield)	759	723	-4.7	753	100.0	0.0	0.0	0.0	0.0	21.1	20.2	44.6	72.5	9.0	295	80.7
Bell township (Jefferson)	2,048	1,973	-3.7	2,020	98.3	0.0	0.0	1.2	0.5	19.5	20.6	44.3	58.4	18.2	822	83.7
Bell township (Westmoreland)	2,345	2,272	-3.1	2,256	96.9	0.2	0.3	1.3	1.3	18.5	25.7	51.8	54.1	16.9	946	87.2
Bell Acres borough & MCD (Allegheny)	1,383	1,367	-1.2	1,463	93.8	1.6	1.8	2.5	0.3	24.1	18.1	47.1	28.2	52.9	527	94.1
Bellefonte borough & MCD (Centre)	6,188	6,241	0.9	6,282	91.7	4.4	0.5	0.7	2.6	16.2	20.4	42.9	40.9	38.4	2,706	90.5
Belle Vernon borough & MCD (Fayette)	1,088	1,031	-5.2	916	87.7	4.0	1.1	6.1	1.1	10.9	39.6	57.8	64.4	12.7	562	64.4
Belleville CDP	1,827	-	-	1,760	98.1	0.6	0.1	1.1	0.1	16.4	35.5	54.2	57.5	26.9	773	75.3
Bellevue borough & MCD (Allegheny)	8,352	8,036	-3.8	8,146	83.3	11.2	0.1	3.0	2.3	11.1	14.8	36.4	31.4	37.9	4,584	87.0
Bellwood borough & MCD (Blair)	1,848	1,751	-5.2	1,618	95.8	0.2	0.9	0.9	2.2	21.5	17.1	38.8	59.0	19.5	715	84.5
Belmont CDP	2,784	-	-	2,582	92.6	1.9	0.0	0.4	5.1	15.8	30.0	53.2	52.6	24.9	1,230	88.1
Ben Avon borough & MCD (Allegheny)	1,780	1,731	-2.8	1,904	93.9	1.7	0.5	3.5	0.4	24.5	12.5	38.2	16.0	61.9	782	94.9
Ben Avon Heights borough & MCD (Alle....	373	363	-2.7	392	95.4	0.0	0.8	2.6	1.3	29.6	14.3	41.8	4.6	82.0	141	100.0
Bendersville borough & MCD (Adams)	640	653	2.0	668	69.2	6.3	0.0	1.9	22.6	19.6	19.3	43.1	71.4	14.6	226	85.0
Benezette township (Elk)	207	193	-6.8	180	100.0	0.0	0.0	0.0	0.0	11.1	40.6	57.9	61.7	11.4	91	79.1
Benner township (Centre)	6,188	9,305	50.4	9,273	69.3	20.0	0.1	2.3	8.3	9.0	12.9	40.9	59.6	17.2	2,115	88.5
Bensalem township (Bucks)	60,420	60,507	0.1	60,428	65.5	8.2	12.5	3.5	10.3	18.5	15.9	40.6	44.3	28.7	24,020	91.5
Benson borough & MCD (Somerset)	201	186	-7.5	180	100.0	0.0	0.0	0.0	0.0	16.1	10.0	43.8	67.2	5.1	74	90.5
Bentleyville borough & MCD (Washington)	2,578	2,480	-3.8	2,441	94.0	1.3	0.0	3.9	0.8	21.8	17.8	45.0	53.4	19.9	1,089	85.1
Benton borough & MCD (Columbia)	830	810	-2.4	755	91.7	0.0	1.6	1.7	5.0	26.0	12.5	34.0	61.3	15.2	297	82.2
Benton township (Columbia)	1,235	1,267	2.6	1,407	96.4	0.5	0.0	0.2	2.8	16.9	25.6	53.4	57.5	17.9	564	83.0
Benton township (Lackawanna)	1,908	1,857	-2.7	1,779	99.5	0.0	0.1	0.1	0.3	16.0	29.5	55.0	46.7	32.1	754	84.5
Berlin borough & MCD (Somerset)	2,089	1,941	-7.1	2,004	97.4	0.6	0.0	0.8	1.2	19.2	31.2	49.6	69.4	12.1	770	76.8
Berlin township (Wayne)	2,591	2,470	-4.7	2,452	97.6	0.0	0.0	1.3	1.1	21.2	20.0	45.4	57.2	15.8	782	90.8
Bern township (Berks)	6,767	6,963	2.9	6,921	77.3	3.2	3.0	1.8	14.7	14.6	21.8	45.1	53.1	25.1	1,937	88.7
Bernville borough & MCD (Berks)	944	945	0.1	851	83.3	7.1	0.0	1.4	8.2	25.4	15.5	37.4	48.3	23.1	337	89.3
Berrysburg borough & MCD (Dauphin)	368	371	0.8	339	92.3	0.0	0.0	0.0	7.7	20.9	18.3	45.7	62.9	11.0	135	82.2
Berwick township (Adams)	2,379	2,412	1.4	2,258	90.2	3.3	1.9	0.8	3.7	16.5	24.5	49.6	59.1	19.9	966	87.0
Berwick borough & MCD (Columbia)	10,481	9,903	-5.5	10,073	90.7	1.4	0.0	1.1	6.8	17.8	18.6	44.0	57.3	17.1	4,476	80.6
Berwyn CDP	3,631	-	-	3,531	85.2	1.9	8.4	4.3	0.3	27.0	20.4	42.7	14.9	69.2	1,481	92.4
Bessemer borough & MCD (Lawrence)	1,109	1,051	-5.2	1,088	96.5	0.0	0.4	3.1	0.0	20.6	21.5	44.2	51.4	17.4	455	85.5
Bethany borough & MCD (Wayne)	239	224	-6.3	237	93.2	0.0	3.4	2.5	0.8	12.7	29.1	53.9	30.9	33.0	110	85.5
Bethel township (Armstrong)	1,191	1,140	-4.3	1,072	99.4	0.0	0.0	0.6	0.0	20.0	21.1	52.1	59.1	17.4	462	83.1
Bethel CDP	499	-	-	586	93.3	0.0	2.4	0.0	4.3	37.2	14.0	26.4	76.4	10.2	184	100.0
Bethel township (Berks)	4,102	4,169	1.6	4,140	96.4	0.0	0.7	0.7	2.1	28.7	14.0	36.3	65.5	14.1	1,429	87.6
Bethel township (Delaware)	8,798	9,242	5.0	9,181	84.0	1.5	11.1	1.3	2.1	23.4	17.6	44.4	27.2	53.3	3,038	94.2
Bethel township (Fulton)	1,508	1,497	-0.7	1,505	98.3	0.0	0.3	1.4	0.0	19.5	24.7	46.3	59.3	14.5	623	81.5
Bethel township (Lebanon)	5,016	5,297	5.6	5,228	91.1	0.2	0.2	1.5	7.0	28.3	15.6	37.5	65.0	13.3	1,919	84.3

1 May be of any race.

Table A. All Places — **Population and Housing**

STATE City, town, township, borough, or CDP (county if applicable)	2010 census total population	2019 estimated population	Percent change 2010–2019	ACS total population estimate 2015–2019	White alone, not Hispanic or Latino	Black alone, not Hispanic or Latino	Asian alone, not Hispanic or Latino	All other races or 2 or more races, not Hispanic or Latino	Hispanic or Latino[1]	Under 18 years old	Age 65 years and older	Median age	Percent High school diploma or less	Percent Bachelor's degree or more	Occupied housing units Total	Percent with a computer
	1	2	3	4	5	6	7	8	9	10	11	12	13	14	15	16
PENNSYLVANIA—Con.																
Bethel Park municipality & MCD (Allegheny)	32,294	32,345	0.2	32,177	91.6	2.2	2.2	2.7	1.4	19.2	23.3	46.6	27.2	46.5	13,663	91.8
Bethlehem city	74,972	75,815	1.1	75,461	57.2	7.3	3.0	2.3	30.2	18.4	16.6	35.5	45.2	29.2	29,088	88.1
Bethlehem city (Lehigh)	19,343	19,923	3.0	19,786	66.9	5.3	1.2	2.0	24.4	17.7	21.1	40.5	43.7	27.5	8,500	89.4
Bethlehem city (Northampton)	55,629	55,892	0.5	55,675	53.7	8.0	3.6	2.5	32.2	18.6	15.0	33.0	45.8	29.9	20,588	87.6
Bethlehem township (Northampton)	23,795	24,341	2.3	23,921	76.6	5.7	5.1	3.2	9.3	18.1	20.9	46.4	34.4	37.9	8,840	92.3
Beurys Lake CDP	124	-	-	74	100.0	0.0	0.0	0.0	0.0	2.7	43.2	62.8	76.4	16.7	47	76.6
Big Bass Lake CDP	1,270	-	-	1,099	92.2	3.7	0.3	0.7	3.1	19.5	24.9	50.0	45.6	23.5	474	87.1
Big Beaver borough & MCD (Beaver)	1,965	1,857	-5.5	1,784	97.8	0.3	0.0	1.9	0.0	17.6	26.8	51.4	49.4	24.4	763	84.8
Bigler CDP	398	-	-	343	88.0	0.0	0.0	0.0	12.0	15.5	15.5	36.0	62.4	37.6	175	100.0
Bigler township (Clearfield)	1,287	1,230	-4.4	1,192	98.2	1.6	0.3	0.0	0.0	19.7	18.6	43.2	70.6	9.9	486	87.2
Biglerville borough & MCD (Adams)	1,200	1,219	1.6	1,222	71.4	4.7	0.7	0.7	22.4	23.5	12.6	34.2	56.6	19.8	439	83.6
Big Run borough & MCD (Jefferson)	624	599	-4.0	424	96.7	0.0	0.0	3.3	0.0	18.9	23.6	44.6	55.2	13.3	188	83.5
Bingham township (Potter)	678	663	-2.2	526	99.2	0.0	0.0	0.0	0.8	22.4	19.4	45.3	61.9	11.8	193	69.9
Birchwood Lakes CDP	1,386	-	-	1,139	81.2	0.4	1.1	0.0	17.4	22.2	17.4	49.3	53.1	19.7	441	92.3
Bird-in-Hand CDP	402	-	-	566	100.0	0.0	0.0	0.0	0.0	30.6	12.7	37.1	69.6	9.6	172	93.0
Birdsboro borough & MCD (Berks)	5,125	5,143	0.4	5,131	92.7	1.0	1.3	1.8	3.2	20.4	13.4	41.3	43.9	27.9	2,058	92.8
Birmingham township (Chester)	4,192	4,199	0.2	4,204	87.9	2.8	4.7	1.7	2.9	24.9	16.3	44.0	10.0	77.4	1,433	96.9
Birmingham borough & MCD (Huntingdon)	90	88	-2.2	151	100.0	0.0	0.0	0.0	0.0	15.2	23.8	40.5	22.6	66.1	70	84.3
Black township (Somerset)	926	863	-6.8	979	96.5	0.0	0.0	2.1	1.3	21.1	14.8	44.1	67.5	13.2	353	85.0
Black Creek township (Luzerne)	2,020	2,076	2.8	1,749	96.8	0.0	1.5	0.0	1.7	12.3	27.1	54.4	55.3	19.4	799	82.6
Blacklick township (Cambria)	2,012	1,875	-6.8	1,876	99.7	0.1	0.0	0.2	0.0	19.2	20.2	46.8	66.5	11.0	822	81.4
Black Lick CDP	1,462	-	-	1,876	88.8	0.2	0.0	3.6	7.4	18.0	23.0	48.2	65.5	7.3	705	80.1
Black Lick township (Indiana)	1,236	1,155	-6.6	1,224	98.8	0.0	0.0	1.0	0.2	14.5	24.5	52.4	55.1	19.1	527	88.8
Blain borough & MCD (Perry)	261	263	0.8	283	97.5	0.0	0.0	1.4	1.1	32.5	16.3	33.8	50.3	10.1	93	84.9
Blaine township (Washington)	687	670	-2.5	735	93.3	0.7	0.0	6.0	0.0	26.0	12.1	40.8	60.2	20.4	263	92.4
Blair township (Blair)	4,522	4,480	-0.9	4,495	94.4	0.0	5.5	0.1	0.0	17.4	30.0	50.1	45.2	36.1	1,872	89.7
Blairsville borough & MCD (Indiana)	3,405	3,216	-5.6	3,257	93.2	2.9	1.0	2.8	0.0	20.0	19.7	41.3	50.8	19.1	1,472	83.4
Blakely borough & MCD (Lackawanna)	6,557	6,210	-5.3	6,258	99.6	0.0	0.0	0.0	0.4	13.6	30.3	53.4	45.0	27.9	2,952	78.0
Blanchard CDP	740	-	-	541	98.7	0.0	0.0	1.3	0.0	15.9	15.9	46.7	56.5	21.1	221	90.0
Blandburg CDP	402	-	-	334	100.0	0.0	0.0	0.0	0.0	27.2	16.5	41.9	64.8	10.5	136	82.4
Blandon CDP	7,152	-	-	8,111	84.8	4.5	2.2	0.4	8.1	19.5	12.9	41.6	32.7	34.4	3,035	90.0
Blawnox borough & MCD (Allegheny)	1,441	1,388	-3.7	1,606	66.4	10.5	14.3	7.0	1.9	19.6	22.5	42.8	41.5	34.2	862	83.8
Bloom township (Clearfield)	414	404	-2.4	328	96.3	0.0	0.0	0.0	3.7	16.2	27.1	51.5	63.1	15.2	147	74.8
Bloomfield township (Bedford)	1,015	985	-3.0	1,076	95.8	0.7	0.0	0.7	2.7	28.8	12.3	40.6	55.7	21.4	347	83.0
Bloomfield township (Crawford)	1,920	1,826	-4.9	1,790	99.2	0.4	0.0	0.1	0.2	22.0	21.0	46.2	64.9	13.8	742	82.6
Bloomfield borough & MCD (Perry)	1,246	1,256	0.8	1,443	90.3	0.4	0.0	5.3	4.0	23.4	21.7	40.4	58.7	22.7	484	84.7
Blooming Grove township (Pike)	4,809	4,666	-3.0	4,645	77.7	6.5	1.9	3.9	10.0	19.8	25.3	50.0	35.2	30.5	1,923	94.6
Blooming Valley borough & MCD (Crawf	337	316	-6.2	276	97.8	0.7	0.0	1.4	0.0	13.8	30.1	51.8	56.3	19.5	126	79.4
Bloomsburg town & MCD (Columbia)	14,863	13,811	-7.1	14,085	88.0	5.1	2.0	1.1	3.8	12.5	11.2	22.7	45.8	25.8	4,755	88.3
Bloss township (Tioga)	351	338	-3.7	502	100.0	0.0	0.0	0.0	0.0	21.9	25.9	40.7	67.9	10.3	184	83.2
Blossburg borough & MCD (Tioga)	1,538	1,482	-3.6	2,114	94.5	0.0	1.8	0.2	3.5	29.9	13.8	35.7	44.7	27.4	765	87.6
Blue Ball CDP	1,031	-	-	827	100.0	0.0	0.0	0.0	0.0	18.1	24.2	38.1	62.8	19.9	286	79.0
Blue Bell CDP	6,067	-	-	6,250	82.9	2.0	10.5	1.3	3.2	21.2	21.7	47.3	10.2	73.8	2,407	95.0
Blue Ridge Summit CDP	891	-	-	672	97.3	2.7	0.0	0.0	0.0	22.2	20.8	36.5	50.9	23.1	297	74.4
Blythe township (Schuylkill)	935	890	-4.8	809	96.5	0.0	0.0	0.0	3.5	14.2	19.8	46.6	62.2	10.3	350	80.0
Boalsburg CDP	3,722	-	-	4,642	90.1	1.0	1.8	4.5	2.6	19.2	19.8	43.7	17.2	69.3	1,817	99.2
Bobtown CDP	757	-	-	481	99.2	0.0	0.0	0.0	0.8	25.2	12.7	38.4	56.9	21.1	203	85.7
Boggs township (Armstrong)	939	909	-3.2	812	99.8	0.0	0.0	0.2	0.0	13.5	16.0	48.7	70.4	5.6	332	79.8
Boggs township (Centre)	2,936	2,902	-1.2	2,918	99.7	0.0	0.0	0.0	0.3	17.1	15.7	46.8	62.3	11.1	1,107	90.4
Boggs township (Clearfield)	1,759	1,715	-2.5	1,911	98.2	0.6	0.2	0.9	0.0	18.8	20.5	49.1	66.9	9.6	774	81.9
Boiling Springs CDP	3,225	-	-	3,545	93.1	0.0	0.4	4.0	2.4	22.5	23.7	48.3	27.7	45.9	1,399	96.4
Bolivar borough & MCD (Westmoreland)	465	436	-6.2	419	99.0	0.0	0.2	0.7	0.0	17.7	34.6	53.8	61.3	10.6	178	66.3
Bonneauville borough & MCD (Adams)	1,807	1,838	1.7	1,972	94.1	3.4	1.3	0.5	0.7	27.0	12.0	36.2	47.7	19.1	720	89.2
Boothwyn CDP	4,933	-	-	6,236	81.6	11.7	2.5	0.0	4.3	21.1	16.6	37.6	52.5	27.5	2,148	85.9
Boston CDP	545	-	-	304	100.0	0.0	0.0	0.0	0.0	6.3	14.8	58.5	69.5	18.6	158	83.0
Boswell borough & MCD (Somerset)	1,277	1,186	-7.1	1,385	96.8	0.3	0.4	1.5	0.9	17.5	23.0	47.9	71.1	10.8	604	78.5
Bowers CDP	326	-	-	238	100.0	0.0	0.0	0.0	0.0	24.8	20.2	43.3	62.1	26.7	89	100.0
Bowmanstown borough & MCD (Carbon)	909	884	-2.8	910	91.6	0.9	0.1	0.8	6.6	15.4	16.5	41.9	56.1	17.6	416	82.9

1 May be of any race.

Table A. All Places — **Population and Housing**

STATE City, town, township, borough, or CDP (county if applicable)	2010 census total population	2019 estimated population	Percent change 2010–2019	ACS total population estimate 2015–2019	White alone, not Hispanic or Latino	Black alone, not Hispanic or Latino	Asian alone, not Hispanic or Latino	All other races or 2 or more races, not Hispanic or Latino	Hispanic or Latino[1]	Under 18 years old	Age 65 years and older	Median age	Percent High school diploma or less	Percent Bachelor's degree or more	Total	Percent with a computer
	1	2	3	4	5	6	7	8	9	10	11	12	13	14	15	16
PENNSYLVANIA—Con.																
Bowmansville CDP	2,077	-	-	1,958	100.0	0.0	0.0	0.0	0.0	22.5	13.7	42.9	60.3	19.9	815	80.7
Boyertown borough & MCD (Berks)	4,065	4,071	0.1	4,064	86.4	6.3	1.0	0.3	5.9	22.0	22.0	44.1	58.3	19.4	1,857	79.5
Brackenridge borough & MCD (Allegheny)	3,256	3,135	-3.7	3,175	94.6	3.7	0.5	0.2	1.0	20.1	19.8	41.3	54.4	16.6	1,443	84.1
Braddock borough & MCD (Allegheny)	2,173	2,105	-3.1	1,869	21.7	66.5	0.0	9.2	2.6	21.1	23.2	49.3	61.8	12.9	789	71.6
Braddock Hills borough & MCD (Allegheny)	1,854	1,783	-3.8	1,653	61.4	32.4	0.6	3.6	2.0	13.8	23.7	50.5	39.5	24.2	942	81.1
Bradenville CDP	545	-	-	364	100.0	0.0	0.0	0.0	0.0	13.2	23.9	44.6	78.9	5.4	189	60.8
Bradford township (Clearfield)	3,031	2,969	-2.0	2,987	95.9	0.0	0.0	1.3	2.8	17.7	18.2	44.7	71.9	14.9	1,345	79.2
Bradford city & MCD (McKean)	8,802	8,210	-6.7	8,355	93.3	0.6	0.3	2.6	3.3	24.2	16.7	37.1	55.2	18.7	3,684	81.9
Bradford township (McKean)	4,808	4,583	-4.7	4,676	94.1	1.3	2.0	0.4	2.1	14.5	19.5	43.1	45.7	28.5	1,783	85.8
Bradford Woods borough & MCD (Allegheny)	1,171	1,141	-2.6	1,225	93.9	0.3	3.6	0.3	1.9	22.0	21.9	47.4	11.5	65.7	486	98.8
Brady township (Butler)	1,310	1,237	-5.6	1,171	97.6	0.0	0.5	1.3	0.6	20.2	11.4	42.2	55.5	20.1	508	90.9
Brady township (Clarion)	55	54	-1.8	31	100.0	0.0	0.0	0.0	0.0	19.4	25.8	40.8	62.5	8.3	14	71.4
Brady township (Clearfield)	1,998	1,925	-3.7	2,288	96.9	0.0	0.0	0.0	3.1	30.2	15.1	38.6	67.6	13.6	789	71.1
Brady township (Huntingdon)	1,179	1,122	-4.8	1,011	99.6	0.4	0.0	0.0	0.0	26.9	17.6	37.1	62.4	14.2	366	75.7
Brady township (Lycoming)	521	519	-0.4	541	92.2	0.6	0.4	5.9	0.9	27.4	12.9	44.3	63.0	16.5	196	95.4
Bradys Bend township (Armstrong)	770	714	-7.3	720	99.0	0.0	0.0	1.0	0.0	19.7	26.3	48.3	62.4	20.1	302	79.1
Braintrim township (Wyoming)	502	475	-5.4	518	90.9	0.8	0.0	5.2	3.1	26.6	14.1	36.9	58.1	17.4	183	90.2
Branch township (Schuylkill)	1,837	1,740	-5.3	2,001	96.6	0.3	0.0	2.9	0.2	21.0	21.7	47.7	54.9	19.0	812	91.1
Branchdale CDP	388	-	-	332	100.0	0.0	0.0	0.0	0.0	15.4	17.2	43.7	73.4	5.7	144	77.8
Brandonville CDP	197	-	-	249	98.8	0.0	0.0	0.0	1.2	30.9	19.7	41.6	81.9	1.8	101	81.2
Bratton township (Mifflin)	1,319	1,279	-3.0	1,590	99.2	0.0	0.0	0.0	0.8	21.4	19.1	44.3	76.3	8.1	611	83.3
Brave CDP	201	-	-	189	100.0	0.0	0.0	0.0	0.0	13.2	19.0	44.5	69.5	3.0	83	96.4
Brecknock township (Berks)	4,640	4,695	1.2	4,689	94.9	1.0	0.5	2.1	1.5	19.5	19.1	47.5	46.8	30.5	1,815	86.8
Brecknock township (Lancaster)	7,199	7,677	6.6	7,531	96.9	0.0	0.4	0.3	2.4	24.2	13.8	37.6	66.4	11.4	2,623	84.9
Breinigsville CDP	4,138	-	-	6,784	63.9	5.5	12.5	3.5	14.6	30.1	8.8	37.4	21.0	47.5	2,333	98.9
Brentwood borough & MCD (Allegheny)	9,634	9,268	-3.8	9,386	85.9	3.1	4.3	1.7	5.1	22.4	14.8	36.2	39.8	27.2	3,949	92.9
Bressler CDP	1,437	-	-	1,548	81.5	18.5	0.0	0.0	0.0	22.9	14.8	44.1	38.9	10.9	632	94.8
Briar Creek borough & MCD (Columbia)	662	671	1.4	845	89.3	3.1	0.7	0.9	5.9	19.3	24.1	37.9	56.8	9.4	336	74.4
Briar Creek township (Columbia)	3,016	2,935	-2.7	2,966	99.0	0.0	0.2	0.3	0.6	16.7	26.4	51.4	56.4	20.5	1,292	85.8
Brickerville CDP	1,309	-	-	1,310	96.2	0.0	1.0	2.1	0.8	21.2	14.7	42.9	54.8	26.1	467	97.6
Bridgeport borough & MCD (Montgomery)	4,555	4,570	0.3	4,579	77.4	5.1	0.0	2.6	14.9	20.2	6.2	34.4	34.2	31.2	2,124	94.5
Bridgeton township (Bucks)	1,284	1,281	-0.2	1,127	98.0	0.2	0.3	0.5	1.0	12.9	25.6	54.5	40.0	37.4	533	87.1
Bridgeville borough & MCD (Allegheny)	5,087	4,903	-3.6	4,968	92.0	4.0	0.4	3.2	0.5	18.6	20.5	41.1	36.4	29.7	2,476	84.3
Bridgewater borough & MCD (Beaver)	709	825	16.4	884	93.2	0.7	1.4	1.6	3.2	25.3	20.4	38.9	40.2	28.3	395	87.3
Bridgewater township (Susquehanna)	2,832	2,715	-4.1	2,745	95.5	1.4	0.5	1.6	1.0	19.2	25.9	47.5	46.5	27.7	1,134	88.4
Brighton township (Beaver)	8,233	8,267	0.4	8,287	93.7	1.4	1.3	1.0	2.7	21.2	23.2	47.3	31.3	39.5	3,243	89.6
Brisbin borough & MCD (Clearfield)	413	388	-6.1	358	86.3	3.9	0.8	0.0	8.9	15.4	26.0	52.1	58.9	18.9	139	82.7
Bristol borough & MCD (Bucks)	9,726	9,576	-1.5	9,605	69.1	10.0	1.6	5.7	13.6	22.0	16.3	39.2	50.4	22.7	3,897	86.8
Bristol township (Bucks)	54,556	53,473	-2.0	53,649	74.6	9.1	3.0	1.8	11.6	21.7	14.9	39.6	53.0	18.9	20,075	90.5
Brittany Farms-The Highlands CDP	3,695	-	-	3,557	87.1	2.0	6.4	0.6	3.9	18.8	22.1	48.2	31.2	44.6	1,463	93.6
Broad Top township (Bedford)	1,690	1,636	-3.2	1,490	99.4	0.0	0.0	0.6	0.0	21.6	25.4	48.5	75.9	5.8	623	75.8
Broad Top City borough & MCD (Huntingdon)	452	447	-1.1	462	99.1	0.0	0.0	0.9	0.0	17.3	21.9	45.5	64.4	9.0	180	81.1
Brockway borough & MCD (Jefferson)	2,112	2,033	-3.7	1,987	98.3	0.0	0.7	1.0	0.0	20.7	24.9	44.3	55.5	17.4	887	79.7
Brodheadsville CDP	1,800	-	-	1,460	84.6	2.9	0.0	0.7	11.8	13.4	19.5	47.9	55.0	13.6	566	91.9
Brokenstraw township (Warren)	1,884	1,777	-5.7	1,913	97.2	0.0	0.0	1.6	1.2	18.7	26.7	47.4	58.1	19.6	752	76.7
Brookfield township (Tioga)	421	404	-4.0	369	98.4	0.0	1.1	0.5	0.0	13.8	25.7	54.3	75.0	12.0	144	70.1
Brookhaven borough & MCD (Delaware)	8,012	8,049	0.5	8,038	89.3	6.2	1.3	2.2	1.0	20.1	19.0	42.8	40.6	29.1	3,418	85.8
Brooklyn township (Susquehanna)	961	901	-6.2	911	99.7	0.0	0.0	0.3	0.0	13.0	22.9	49.7	59.3	18.6	389	85.3
Brookville borough & MCD (Jefferson)	3,930	3,791	-3.5	3,823	93.8	0.4	0.0	3.4	2.4	21.3	20.7	40.5	49.5	27.9	1,687	84.4
Broomall CDP	10,789	-	-	11,222	85.9	1.5	7.8	3.3	1.5	20.7	21.0	44.5	35.2	40.8	4,068	88.9
Brothersvalley township (Somerset)	2,413	2,284	-5.3	2,364	97.0	0.0	2.4	0.5	0.0	18.5	17.2	44.1	62.0	17.5	955	85.3
Brown township (Lycoming)	96	93	-3.1	92	100.0	0.0	0.0	0.0	0.0	4.3	50.0	65.0	46.6	42.0	48	93.8
Brown township (Mifflin)	4,053	4,079	0.6	4,080	99.0	0.0	0.0	0.6	0.4	23.3	21.4	44.6	57.0	22.5	1,633	79.5

1 May be of any race.

Table A. All Places — **Population and Housing**

STATE City, town, township, borough, or CDP (county if applicable)	2010 census total population	2019 estimated population	Percent change 2010–2019	ACS total population estimate 2015–2019	White alone, not Hispanic or Latino	Black alone, not Hispanic or Latino	Asian alone, not Hispanic or Latino	All other races or 2 or more races, not Hispanic or Latino	Hispanic or Latino[1]	Under 18 years old	Age 65 years and older	Median age	Percent High school diploma or less	Percent Bachelor's degree or more	Occupied housing units Total	Percent with a computer
	1	2	3	4	5	6	7	8	9	10	11	12	13	14	15	16
PENNSYLVANIA—Con.																
Brownstown borough & MCD (Cambria)	746	677	-9.2	736	96.7	0.0	0.0	3.3	0.0	17.5	29.1	49.8	54.3	18.1	313	81.8
Brownstown CDP	2,816	-	-	2,576	94.3	1.9	1.6	0.0	2.3	15.1	21.2	48.3	42.2	29.3	1,041	84.1
Brownsville borough & MCD (Fayette)	2,347	2,224	-5.2	2,217	83.3	8.8	0.0	5.6	2.3	20.9	15.9	41.0	61.2	16.6	1,005	83.0
Brownsville township (Fayette)	684	645	-5.7	587	87.7	7.2	0.0	5.1	0.0	17.7	22.0	44.7	68.9	11.4	257	83.7
Browntown CDP	1,418	-	-	1,288	96.9	0.0	0.0	3.1	0.0	9.2	24.8	52.9	44.8	18.4	663	82.8
Bruin borough & MCD (Butler)	528	491	-7.0	483	99.0	0.0	0.4	0.0	0.6	21.5	12.4	41.5	70.9	6.9	201	79.6
Brush Creek township (Fulton)	823	810	-1.6	730	94.9	1.8	0.0	0.4	2.9	13.6	20.1	49.2	64.9	10.8	304	79.9
Brush Valley township (Indiana)	1,862	1,734	-6.9	1,976	98.4	0.0	1.0	0.2	0.5	24.6	18.5	42.4	60.9	16.1	695	76.3
Bryn Athyn borough & MCD (Montgomery)	1,367	1,404	2.7	1,368	93.3	0.6	1.0	2.3	2.9	18.7	18.6	36.8	12.7	57.9	417	97.6
Bryn Mawr CDP	3,779	-	-	3,708	66.9	12.2	12.8	4.1	4.0	10.4	14.6	23.5	17.3	67.6	1,254	90.2
Buck township (Luzerne)	437	435	-0.5	334	97.3	0.0	0.0	0.6	2.1	18.3	17.1	43.8	51.8	21.9	140	90.0
Buckhorn CDP	318	-	-	349	98.6	0.0	0.0	1.4	0.0	28.1	12.3	38.3	37.6	35.9	122	91.8
Buckingham township (Bucks)	20,074	20,240	0.8	20,248	89.2	0.7	5.3	2.2	2.7	23.2	19.6	47.7	20.2	60.5	7,306	96.7
Buckingham township (Wayne)	524	511	-2.5	417	95.4	0.0	0.2	0.0	4.3	8.9	39.1	61.7	52.2	24.2	210	78.6
Buck Run CDP	176	-	-	253	98.0	0.0	0.0	0.0	2.0	24.1	12.6	37.5	67.0	11.5	87	78.2
Buffalo township (Butler)	7,314	7,399	1.2	7,308	97.5	0.7	0.9	0.8	0.1	21.8	19.6	46.5	39.4	34.5	2,939	89.5
Buffalo township (Perry)	1,210	1,228	1.5	1,236	98.5	0.9	0.0	0.0	0.6	20.0	16.8	47.4	54.3	22.0	519	93.1
Buffalo township (Union)	3,516	3,696	5.1	3,642	96.3	1.3	0.7	0.1	1.6	25.8	21.6	41.3	62.5	17.2	1,356	83.0
Buffalo township (Washington)	2,067	2,015	-2.5	2,236	98.6	0.0	0.2	0.0	1.2	20.6	19.9	45.3	46.2	28.6	872	92.1
Buffington CDP	292	-	-	96	30.2	0.0	0.0	69.8	0.0	43.8	19.8	26.2	54.7	0.0	33	100.0
Buffington township (Indiana)	1,324	1,270	-4.1	1,220	98.2	0.2	0.2	1.5	0.0	25.5	16.6	40.7	56.4	21.6	485	80.6
Bulger CDP	407	-	-	339	100.0	0.0	0.0	0.0	0.0	16.5	17.1	33.7	50.9	21.5	168	100.0
Bullskin township (Fayette)	6,972	6,585	-5.6	6,697	99.8	0.0	0.2	0.0	0.0	19.7	19.5	45.2	57.7	17.4	2,645	88.0
Burgettstown borough & MCD (Washington)	1,379	1,309	-5.1	1,350	96.1	0.0	0.0	0.0	3.9	21.1	19.0	44.8	53.8	20.4	577	82.0
Burlington borough & MCD (Bradford)	156	146	-6.4	210	88.6	1.0	0.0	0.5	10.0	30.0	23.8	33.2	59.8	17.4	79	96.2
Burlington township (Bradford)	789	770	-2.4	741	99.1	0.9	0.0	0.0	0.0	21.6	23.5	48.1	55.6	16.1	291	90.0
Burnham borough & MCD (Mifflin)	2,058	1,993	-3.2	1,906	98.6	1.2	0.0	0.3	0.0	21.8	17.6	42.8	64.4	9.1	837	86.0
Burnside township (Centre)	437	442	1.1	459	99.6	0.0	0.0	0.0	0.4	22.0	17.6	42.3	64.2	11.4	176	89.2
Burnside borough & MCD (Clearfield)	234	223	-4.7	176	100.0	0.0	0.0	0.0	0.0	11.4	22.2	52.3	77.6	1.4	83	71.1
Burnside township (Clearfield)	1,074	1,043	-2.9	1,078	99.1	0.0	0.0	0.2	0.7	20.3	20.8	47.4	71.0	10.7	418	75.4
Burrell township (Armstrong)	685	657	-4.1	647	99.2	0.0	0.0	0.0	0.8	17.6	26.4	47.8	66.1	13.3	265	83.4
Burrell township (Indiana)	4,400	4,116	-6.5	4,165	94.0	0.1	0.0	2.1	3.7	15.0	21.7	50.6	59.0	12.6	1,655	85.4
Bushkill township (Northampton)	8,156	8,605	5.5	8,466	97.0	0.0	0.5	0.4	2.2	21.1	18.3	46.7	39.9	33.1	3,082	91.7
Butler township (Adams)	2,574	2,617	1.7	2,610	83.0	0.0	0.0	1.6	15.4	18.7	23.6	51.6	57.4	19.0	1,002	84.4
Butler city & MCD (Butler)	13,754	12,885	-6.3	13,092	88.1	3.4	0.4	4.9	3.3	21.9	13.8	38.4	49.1	20.0	5,932	82.5
Butler township (Butler)	17,248	16,469	-4.5	16,610	95.6	1.2	0.5	1.5	1.2	16.9	25.2	49.0	39.1	29.6	7,527	87.6
Butler township (Luzerne)	9,232	9,943	7.7	9,749	90.9	2.4	1.0	0.6	5.1	19.2	21.7	44.6	34.9	33.9	3,812	91.6
Butler township (Schuylkill)	5,229	4,857	-7.1	4,868	74.2	15.1	0.1	2.1	8.5	11.3	18.5	44.7	53.4	14.6	1,569	80.8
Byrnedale CDP	427	-	-	500	96.6	0.0	3.4	0.0	0.0	20.2	25.0	39.0	59.3	13.9	212	80.7
Cadogan township (Armstrong)	353	328	-7.1	315	99.0	0.0	0.0	1.0	0.0	13.0	15.2	47.7	66.4	8.0	157	86.0
Caernarvon township (Berks)	4,037	4,176	3.4	4,125	96.2	0.5	1.4	1.9	0.0	29.1	13.4	40.8	38.6	39.1	1,494	97.2
Caernarvon township (Lancaster)	4,748	4,845	2.0	4,835	98.2	0.4	0.0	0.0	1.4	29.3	18.3	35.3	65.3	17.7	1,470	69.9
Cairnbrook CDP	520	-	-	559	89.3	0.0	0.0	10.7	0.0	30.1	17.9	35.5	68.4	12.2	231	77.5
California borough & MCD (Washington)	6,786	6,276	-7.5	6,347	86.2	6.1	0.7	3.9	3.2	12.4	13.3	24.1	52.6	26.7	2,103	84.6
Callensburg borough & MCD (Clarion)	208	192	-7.7	116	100.0	0.0	0.0	0.0	0.0	25.0	18.1	38.0	74.4	7.3	53	81.1
Callery borough & MCD (Butler)	394	379	-3.8	392	98.5	0.8	0.0	0.8	0.0	14.0	11.7	46.4	40.2	31.1	169	100.0
Callimont borough & MCD (Somerset)	41	38	-7.3	63	100.0	0.0	0.0	0.0	0.0	25.4	20.6	34.4	28.9	13.3	22	95.5
Caln CDP	1,519	-	-	1,074	53.4	29.2	4.7	3.2	9.6	19.0	12.3	35.6	40.3	24.3	524	90.8
Caln township (Chester)	13,810	14,275	3.4	14,222	71.7	11.9	7.7	2.9	5.8	18.7	15.8	39.4	29.5	42.6	5,580	91.2
Calumet CDP	1,241	-	-	1,593	100.0	0.0	0.0	0.0	0.0	20.8	15.5	43.1	45.6	23.6	570	88.6
Cambria township (Cambria)	6,093	5,693	-6.6	5,807	94.2	2.6	0.0	1.5	1.6	19.1	21.9	44.8	52.2	24.3	2,128	80.0
Cambridge township (Crawford)	1,563	1,486	-4.9	1,577	99.3	0.0	0.0	0.3	0.4	19.0	19.8	47.4	46.9	25.5	655	87.3
Cambridge Springs borough & MCD (Crawford)	2,595	2,667	2.8	2,639	83.2	8.3	0.8	3.2	4.5	14.5	12.0	37.1	54.9	17.2	801	89.1
Campbelltown CDP	3,616	-	-	4,725	94.8	0.0	4.0	0.0	1.2	25.4	17.4	42.5	37.8	36.2	1,761	90.7
Camp Hill borough & MCD (Cumberland)	7,891	7,905	0.2	7,911	84.0	2.7	4.7	2.3	6.3	24.5	17.8	39.5	25.2	50.5	3,155	93.1
Canaan township (Wayne)	3,947	3,960	0.3	3,919	51.4	30.9	0.6	3.6	13.5	3.5	7.4	40.2	71.1	7.7	298	89.3
Canadohta Lake CDP	516	-	-	521	100.0	0.0	0.0	0.0	0.0	15.5	27.6	51.9	56.7	19.7	275	83.6
Canal township (Venango)	1,017	927	-8.8	792	98.5	0.3	0.0	0.3	1.0	13.0	27.7	54.0	64.2	18.4	348	86.8
Canoe township (Indiana)	1,520	1,420	-6.6	1,415	93.9	0.0	0.0	6.1	0.0	20.8	21.4	41.6	68.5	13.0	537	72.1

1 May be of any race.

Table A. All Places — **Population and Housing**

STATE City, town, township, borough, or CDP (county if applicable)	2010 census total population	2019 estimated population	Percent change 2010–2019	ACS total population estimate 2015–2019	White alone, not Hispanic or Latino	Black alone, not Hispanic or Latino	Asian alone, not Hispanic or Latino	All other races or 2 or more races, not Hispanic or Latino	Hispanic or Latino[1]	Under 18 years old	Age 65 years and older	Median age	Percent High school diploma or less	Percent Bachelor's degree or more	Total	Percent with a computer
	1	2	3	4	5	6	7	8	9	10	11	12	13	14	15	16
PENNSYLVANIA—Con.																
Canonsburg borough & MCD (Washington)	9,007	8,760	-2.7	8,844	86.2	9.0	0.6	1.4	2.8	21.5	17.3	38.9	45.9	23.5	3,908	86.5
Canton borough & MCD (Bradford)	1,964	1,861	-5.2	1,790	98.2	0.5	0.8	0.2	0.3	23.2	19.4	38.7	62.1	18.6	789	82.9
Canton township (Bradford)	2,148	2,092	-2.6	1,929	96.5	0.3	0.0	0.1	3.1	20.5	23.0	45.9	68.2	10.4	711	77.4
Canton township (Washington)	8,381	8,068	-3.7	8,134	96.3	2.2	0.0	1.2	0.3	16.1	21.2	45.9	53.7	23.4	3,368	85.8
Carbon township (Huntingdon)	377	368	-2.4	309	100.0	0.0	0.0	0.0	0.0	13.3	31.1	54.4	64.7	11.0	154	79.9
Carbondale city & MCD (Lackawanna)	8,891	8,383	-5.7	8,471	87.3	0.4	2.3	4.0	6.0	21.6	22.1	41.8	54.7	17.7	3,776	82.8
Carbondale township (Lackawanna)	1,110	1,091	-1.7	1,080	98.1	0.0	0.0	0.0	1.9	19.8	18.5	45.2	44.5	23.4	438	84.7
Carlisle borough & MCD (Cumberland)	18,691	19,198	2.7	19,153	79.1	7.3	2.2	4.5	6.9	20.8	16.1	33.4	40.6	38.8	7,563	87.6
Carmichaels borough & MCD (Greene)	479	442	-7.7	508	99.2	0.0	0.0	0.6	0.2	16.3	13.8	45.5	49.4	18.6	232	83.2
Carnegie borough & MCD (Allegheny)	7,984	7,806	-2.2	7,883	83.4	10.3	1.8	2.7	1.9	16.6	16.9	37.7	35.2	33.6	3,946	88.0
Carnot-Moon CDP	11,372	-	-	11,997	81.7	5.1	7.3	3.9	1.9	17.8	12.2	33.4	25.2	53.0	4,789	94.4
Carroll township (Perry)	5,264	5,317	1.0	5,289	97.1	1.7	0.0	1.2	0.0	19.2	16.7	45.3	66.5	8.3	2,297	87.5
Carroll township (Washington)	5,638	5,441	-3.5	5,496	95.8	1.8	0.3	1.2	0.9	15.5	26.0	51.6	43.9	32.9	2,394	85.9
Carroll township (York)	5,948	6,519	9.6	6,379	90.7	1.4	7.0	0.6	0.3	22.3	18.3	43.8	34.5	39.7	2,297	92.2
Carrolltown borough & MCD (Cambria)	850	784	-7.8	791	99.9	0.0	0.0	0.1	0.0	18.6	16.1	42.1	48.2	22.2	320	82.5
Carroll Valley borough & MCD (Adams)	3,873	3,942	1.8	3,919	95.6	0.0	0.0	2.2	2.2	21.2	16.0	43.8	32.7	27.1	1,535	95.6
Cascade township (Lycoming)	412	399	-3.2	498	96.6	0.0	1.0	0.4	2.0	24.1	15.3	43.8	52.2	19.2	178	89.9
Cashtown CDP	459	-	-	235	97.0	0.0	0.0	0.0	3.0	21.3	8.9	44.4	74.6	0.0	94	100.0
Cass township (Huntingdon)	1,117	1,078	-3.5	983	98.5	0.0	0.0	0.7	0.8	16.5	21.6	48.5	62.4	14.9	392	84.7
Cass township (Schuylkill)	1,961	1,867	-4.8	1,820	97.1	1.0	0.0	0.5	1.4	20.3	17.9	44.2	61.6	15.9	779	85.8
Cassandra borough & MCD (Cambria)	147	134	-8.8	211	99.1	0.0	0.0	0.9	0.0	36.0	9.5	30.7	55.8	9.2	71	81.7
Casselman borough & MCD (Somerset)	94	93	-1.1	85	100.0	0.0	0.0	0.0	0.0	18.8	20.0	43.4	86.4	0.0	34	97.1
Cassville borough & MCD (Huntingdon)	143	138	-3.5	141	97.9	0.0	0.0	2.1	0.0	20.6	26.2	48.1	67.6	9.5	64	84.4
Castanea township (Clinton)	1,181	1,161	-1.7	1,160	98.4	0.5	0.0	0.5	0.6	21.1	17.4	43.8	54.8	20.6	493	88.0
Castanea CDP	1,125	-	-	1,117	98.3	0.5	0.0	0.5	0.6	20.4	17.5	43.5	55.4	20.0	476	87.6
Castle Shannon borough & MCD (Allegheny)	8,318	8,216	-1.2	8,213	87.4	3.2	4.5	3.2	1.7	17.0	18.5	42.0	42.2	35.2	3,880	91.8
Catasauqua borough & MCD (Lehigh)	6,438	6,599	2.5	6,568	80.5	3.9	0.6	0.8	14.2	22.2	14.4	36.5	41.7	25.8	2,705	90.1
Catawissa borough & MCD (Columbia)	1,553	1,466	-5.6	1,556	92.4	0.4	0.0	4.9	2.2	25.2	16.5	35.5	62.6	16.9	664	78.3
Catawissa township (Columbia)	932	961	3.1	916	97.9	0.0	0.0	0.4	1.6	16.5	26.7	51.3	46.3	27.2	370	92.2
Catharine township (Blair)	723	695	-3.9	621	96.1	0.0	0.0	1.0	2.9	22.4	14.8	40.2	60.4	17.3	268	83.2
Cecil township (Washington)	11,288	13,054	15.6	12,479	96.7	0.5	0.7	1.3	0.8	21.7	17.4	41.3	33.4	40.5	5,069	93.8
Cecil-Bishop CDP	2,476	-	-	2,201	99.7	0.0	0.0	0.3	0.0	21.1	16.5	42.1	32.1	41.9	873	96.0
Cedar Crest CDP	195	-	-	268	100.0	0.0	0.0	0.0	0.0	24.3	8.6	37.4	81.3	5.7	128	80.5
Cementon CDP	1,538	-	-	1,663	66.8	4.1	2.6	6.1	20.4	23.1	11.2	40.4	42.0	26.9	696	82.2
Center township (Beaver)	11,785	11,459	-2.8	11,502	94.7	2.4	0.5	1.2	1.2	20.3	19.6	45.2	36.2	31.7	4,574	88.4
Center township (Butler)	7,893	7,594	-3.8	7,674	97.2	0.2	0.7	1.5	0.5	17.3	24.7	51.1	39.8	35.9	3,438	89.3
Center township (Greene)	1,272	1,163	-8.6	1,120	98.9	0.0	0.0	0.5	0.5	22.0	20.9	43.4	63.4	16.8	431	87.2
Center township (Indiana)	4,769	4,451	-6.7	4,510	98.9	0.0	0.0	0.9	0.2	16.7	22.9	47.8	53.3	15.8	1,975	85.8
Center township (Snyder)	2,452	2,440	-0.5	2,126	98.3	0.3	0.0	0.8	0.6	20.1	15.1	39.9	59.9	13.0	813	82.3
Centerport borough & MCD (Berks)	345	363	5.2	236	97.9	0.4	0.0	1.7	0.0	21.6	16.9	39.8	44.3	29.3	107	90.7
Centerville borough & MCD (Crawford)	218	204	-6.4	176	100.0	0.0	0.0	0.0	0.0	12.5	34.1	58.0	57.9	16.6	94	84.0
Centerville borough & MCD (Washington)	3,273	3,139	-4.1	3,163	93.0	1.6	0.0	4.6	0.8	19.7	19.3	43.3	43.5	25.4	1,273	91.8
Central City borough & MCD (Somerset)	1,121	1,029	-8.2	1,011	99.5	0.0	0.0	0.0	0.5	13.9	21.5	48.3	67.4	10.8	459	79.3
Centralia borough & MCD (Columbia)	10	11	10.0	9	44.4	0.0	0.0	55.6	0.0	0.0	11.1	64.3	33.3	0.0	6	83.3
Centre township (Berks)	4,071	4,258	4.6	4,170	95.8	0.0	0.0	0.3	4.0	19.1	18.1	46.2	51.5	21.9	1,673	86.6
Centre township (Perry)	2,484	2,512	1.1	2,488	91.8	3.5	0.0	1.0	3.7	18.4	18.6	42.3	64.4	15.8	963	83.6
Centre Hall borough & MCD (Centre)	1,250	1,228	-1.8	1,373	99.4	0.0	0.0	0.0	0.6	25.8	21.7	38.6	36.6	30.8	537	89.4
Ceres township (McKean)	909	853	-6.2	806	99.4	0.0	0.0	0.0	0.6	14.5	24.4	48.8	64.5	10.6	357	83.2
Cetronia CDP	-	-	-	2,648	83.4	0.3	3.4	0.9	12.0	22.3	18.5	40.1	36.7	35.7	999	88.8
Chadds Ford township (Delaware)	3,640	3,725	2.3	3,720	75.1	2.3	13.6	3.7	5.3	20.9	18.6	45.8	20.2	60.4	1,437	98.1
Chalfant borough & MCD (Allegheny)	800	770	-3.8	683	83.7	6.4	0.0	7.9	1.9	14.9	16.3	48.8	38.6	31.1	367	83.4
Chalfont borough & MCD (Bucks)	4,022	4,269	6.1	4,143	88.9	1.0	7.5	0.4	2.2	21.9	14.3	42.6	27.9	51.0	1,705	91.8
Chalkhill CDP	141	-	-	102	100.0	0.0	0.0	0.0	0.0	0.0	39.2	60.8	53.3	17.8	67	62.7
Chambersburg borough & MCD (Franklin)	20,201	21,143	4.7	20,832	65.1	10.8	1.2	3.1	19.8	22.7	19.1	37.6	54.4	23.5	8,604	81.8
Chanceford township (York)	6,102	6,170	1.1	6,154	92.3	4.3	0.5	2.9	0.0	22.7	15.0	42.9	61.5	11.7	2,352	82.9
Chapman township (Clinton)	848	844	-0.5	951	98.3	0.0	1.3	0.0	0.4	21.1	24.0	46.2	56.5	12.5	373	85.8

1 May be of any race.

Table A. All Places — **Population and Housing**

STATE City, town, township, borough, or CDP (county if applicable)	Population 2010 census total population	2019 estimated population	Percent change 2010–2019	ACS total population estimate 2015–2019	Race and Hispanic or Latino origin (percent) White alone, not Hispanic or Latino	Black alone, not Hispanic or Latino	Asian alone, not Hispanic or Latino	All other races or 2 or more races, not Hispanic or Latino	Hispanic or Latino[1]	Age (percent) Under 18 years old	Age 65 years and older	Median age	Educational attainment of persons age 25 and older Percent High school diploma or less	Percent Bachelor's degree or more	Occupied housing units Total	Percent with a computer
	1	2	3	4	5	6	7	8	9	10	11	12	13	14	15	16
PENNSYLVANIA—Con.																
Chapman borough & MCD (Northampton)	190	206	8.4	177	99.4	0.0	0.0	0.0	0.6	16.9	26.0	51.1	58.4	24.8	84	88.1
Chapman township (Snyder)	1,551	1,566	1.0	1,497	97.3	0.4	0.3	0.9	1.2	33.4	16.2	31.1	72.3	14.6	429	64.1
Charleroi borough & MCD (Washington)	4,098	3,901	-4.8	3,953	84.3	5.2	1.0	7.8	1.7	27.1	16.5	37.5	53.3	13.9	1,685	77.9
Charleston township (Tioga)	3,361	3,433	2.1	3,454	97.7	1.2	0.0	0.8	0.3	16.2	25.7	49.3	53.5	21.2	1,275	84.2
Charlestown township (Chester)	5,673	6,274	10.6	5,941	78.0	6.4	10.0	2.6	3.0	22.9	13.4	41.8	11.8	75.8	2,010	97.8
Chartiers township (Washington)	7,821	8,104	3.6	7,964	92.7	2.5	0.1	4.4	0.3	18.6	25.4	48.4	49.8	24.1	3,204	88.7
Chase CDP	978	-	-	968	90.4	0.0	7.6	0.0	2.0	14.5	21.6	47.0	28.5	46.1	374	94.4
Chatham township (Tioga)	597	584	-2.2	440	94.5	0.0	0.0	0.0	5.5	14.1	26.4	53.0	55.7	15.4	198	80.3
Cheltenham township (Montgomery)	36,758	37,121	1.0	37,171	49.5	34.1	6.8	4.4	5.2	20.0	17.9	39.9	21.3	54.9	14,785	93.7
Cherry township (Butler)	1,095	1,070	-2.3	1,014	95.1	1.1	0.6	2.7	0.6	18.9	20.8	47.8	58.5	13.9	395	90.4
Cherry township (Sullivan)	1,711	1,609	-6.0	1,570	99.4	0.0	0.0	0.3	0.3	13.0	26.9	50.0	63.1	13.0	745	81.6
Cherry Grove township (Warren)	216	205	-5.1	162	100.0	0.0	0.0	0.0	0.0	15.4	26.5	55.8	69.2	9.0	68	80.9
Cherryhill township (Indiana)	2,767	2,608	-5.7	2,639	96.6	0.4	0.3	0.9	1.8	19.3	20.7	47.7	50.5	29.6	1,052	88.8
Cherry Ridge township (Wayne)	1,892	1,853	-2.1	1,753	97.9	0.0	0.0	1.1	0.9	22.8	22.6	42.8	47.3	24.0	655	89.9
Cherry Tree borough & MCD (Indiana)	362	338	-6.6	343	96.5	0.0	0.0	3.5	0.0	20.1	22.2	47.1	67.1	9.7	129	80.6
Cherrytree township (Venango)	1,548	1,404	-9.3	1,496	97.3	0.3	0.0	2.5	0.0	23.3	19.7	46.4	56.8	14.1	548	86.3
Cherry Valley borough & MCD (Butler)	66	62	-6.1	68	97.1	0.0	0.0	0.0	2.9	17.6	25.0	49.5	55.4	19.6	34	79.4
Cherryville CDP	1,580	-	-	1,729	99.7	0.0	0.3	0.0	0.0	19.8	14.8	47.6	38.0	34.8	649	93.7
Chest township (Cambria)	349	340	-2.6	303	98.0	0.0	0.0	0.7	1.3	15.2	25.7	55.8	52.7	18.8	138	85.5
Chest township (Clearfield)	515	493	-4.3	481	100.0	0.0	0.0	0.0	0.0	26.2	20.0	39.8	76.3	5.7	182	68.7
Chester city & MCD (Delaware)	33,901	34,000	0.3	33,982	17.1	67.6	0.6	3.1	11.6	23.9	12.5	31.3	63.7	12.3	11,602	82.1
Chester township (Delaware)	3,930	4,073	3.6	4,068	11.4	83.7	0.1	2.7	2.1	30.9	12.6	34.3	60.2	13.8	1,543	90.7
Chesterbrook CDP	4,589	-	-	4,800	63.0	3.0	28.5	4.7	0.9	19.8	20.4	44.6	9.5	79.2	2,114	98.9
Chester Heights borough & MCD (Delaware)	2,544	2,742	7.8	2,661	88.2	4.5	3.6	1.5	2.3	22.6	19.7	39.8	28.9	46.3	1,065	93.7
Chester Hill borough & MCD (Clearfield)	883	831	-5.9	779	87.0	0.8	1.7	6.8	3.7	23.6	18.9	40.6	59.8	15.9	336	85.7
Chestnuthill township (Monroe)	17,185	17,000	-1.1	16,803	84.0	5.4	1.0	0.7	8.9	20.0	14.4	43.9	46.4	25.9	5,655	93.6
Chest Springs borough & MCD (Cambria)	149	140	-6.0	168	100.0	0.0	0.0	0.0	0.0	36.3	14.3	37.7	56.3	11.5	56	89.3
Cheswick borough & MCD (Allegheny)	1,739	1,675	-3.7	1,697	99.4	0.1	0.3	0.0	0.2	14.2	27.3	51.6	32.6	39.8	820	84.5
Chevy Chase Heights CDP	1,502	-	-	1,425	79.7	12.8	0.8	1.6	5.1	17.5	16.9	45.2	46.2	33.4	654	74.9
Chewton CDP	488	-	-	357	96.6	1.7	0.0	0.0	1.7	6.2	17.4	53.3	62.4	10.0	184	73.9
Cheyney University CDP	988	-	-	315	54.6	37.5	0.0	1.9	6.0	0.0	0.0	20.0	0.0	4.2	0	0.0
Chicora borough & MCD (Butler)	1,027	957	-6.8	982	95.7	0.9	0.0	3.4	0.0	25.1	25.7	43.8	61.5	14.0	423	80.1
Chinchilla CDP	2,098	-	-	2,161	95.4	1.7	0.0	1.3	1.5	25.1	26.3	40.4	34.5	42.0	848	86.2
Chippewa township (Beaver)	7,623	7,560	-0.8	7,644	95.1	1.1	0.3	2.6	0.9	18.7	22.7	46.3	34.2	38.4	3,152	89.2
Choconut township (Susquehanna)	713	661	-7.3	600	96.0	0.5	0.3	2.2	1.0	9.5	35.0	57.8	56.0	17.9	315	85.1
Christiana borough & MCD (Lancaster)	1,168	1,171	0.3	1,003	86.2	6.3	0.6	4.9	2.0	21.0	23.6	43.5	53.7	21.6	350	86.3
Church Hill CDP	1,627	-	-	1,649	98.9	0.0	0.0	0.0	1.1	14.7	28.7	49.9	46.2	25.4	768	91.5
Churchill borough & MCD (Allegheny)	3,033	2,921	-3.7	2,957	72.2	20.6	2.9	3.6	0.7	18.6	29.5	51.9	18.2	64.5	1,277	92.0
Churchtown CDP	470	-	-	428	100.0	0.0	0.0	0.0	0.0	28.3	30.8	31.9	68.2	11.4	156	48.1
Churchville CDP	4,128	-	-	4,412	88.1	6.6	2.7	1.3	1.3	22.2	18.4	45.2	25.5	52.8	1,418	96.0
Clairton city & MCD (Allegheny)	6,798	6,541	-3.8	6,619	59.3	37.3	0.2	1.6	1.5	18.5	20.0	41.0	50.7	14.6	3,066	81.5
Clara township (Potter)	197	186	-5.6	181	98.9	0.0	0.0	0.0	1.1	14.9	21.0	53.2	56.0	16.4	71	67.6
Clarence CDP	626	-	-	646	100.0	0.0	0.0	0.0	0.0	22.9	23.8	45.6	72.6	7.2	263	71.5
Clarendon borough & MCD (Warren)	450	424	-5.8	370	98.6	1.1	0.0	0.3	0.0	24.1	14.6	39.1	66.0	8.5	158	84.2
Clarion borough & MCD (Clarion)	5,271	5,707	8.3	5,580	90.2	5.6	1.1	0.9	2.2	15.7	14.1	25.0	40.4	38.4	2,320	89.3
Clarion township (Clarion)	4,140	3,872	-6.5	3,926	93.0	1.1	0.0	2.6	3.3	11.6	14.8	35.2	43.8	35.2	1,748	89.9
Clark borough & MCD (Mercer)	640	592	-7.5	563	98.6	0.2	0.0	1.2	0.0	17.1	20.6	47.1	42.8	20.8	231	92.2
Clarks Green borough & MCD (Lackawanna)	1,477	1,394	-5.6	1,564	79.5	1.2	16.1	0.4	2.7	22.8	21.9	46.7	22.1	55.4	643	94.7
Clarks Summit borough & MCD (Lackawanna)	5,159	4,865	-5.7	4,914	94.6	0.0	0.0	0.6	4.8	24.6	23.7	46.1	23.2	51.6	2,168	88.1
Clarksville borough & MCD (Greene)	230	218	-5.2	141	92.2	5.7	0.0	2.1	0.0	0.7	32.6	57.8	77.0	11.1	51	82.4
Clay township (Butler)	2,702	2,567	-5.0	2,594	96.1	0.1	0.0	2.6	1.2	21.7	16.1	45.5	57.7	15.0	1,027	85.9
Clay township (Huntingdon)	926	895	-3.3	755	97.9	0.1	0.0	0.0	2.0	20.0	21.7	47.4	66.0	6.5	323	83.3
Clay CDP	1,559	-	-	1,998	95.5	0.0	3.8	0.7	0.0	26.2	16.4	32.3	52.1	26.9	693	90.3
Clay township (Lancaster)	6,298	6,924	9.9	6,839	97.1	0.2	0.7	0.5	1.5	25.9	17.3	37.5	57.7	22.2	2,429	77.2
Claysburg CDP	1,625	-	-	1,337	96.3	0.5	0.0	2.3	0.8	14.6	18.8	46.2	65.8	10.6	555	85.9
Claysville borough & MCD (Washington)	828	818	-1.2	885	94.7	1.4	0.7	2.5	0.8	20.5	18.5	45.2	55.0	15.9	332	84.3

1 May be of any race.

Table A. All Places — **Population and Housing**

STATE City, town, township, borough, or CDP (county if applicable)	Population 2010 census total population	2019 estimated population	Percent change 2010–2019	ACS total population estimate 2015–2019	Race and Hispanic or Latino origin (percent) White alone, not Hispanic or Latino	Black alone, not Hispanic or Latino	Asian alone, not Hispanic or Latino	All other races or 2 or more races, not Hispanic or Latino	Hispanic or Latino[1]	Age (percent) Under 18 years old	Age 65 years and older	Median age	Educational attainment of persons age 25 and older Percent High school diploma or less	Percent Bachelor's degree or more	Occupied housing units Total	Percent with a computer
	1	2	3	4	5	6	7	8	9	10	11	12	13	14	15	16
PENNSYLVANIA—Con.																
Clearfield township (Butler)	2,648	2,552	-3.6	2,574	99.1	0.1	0.5	0.2	0.2	19.7	17.5	43.9	64.5	10.6	1,072	86.0
Clearfield township (Cambria)	1,608	1,497	-6.9	1,552	97.4	0.2	0.0	0.1	2.3	20.9	22.4	49.6	65.6	18.8	612	83.7
Clearfield borough & MCD (Clearfield)	6,209	5,839	-6.0	5,921	98.3	0.1	0.6	0.7	0.3	20.9	20.2	43.3	55.4	19.0	2,871	76.6
Cleona borough & MCD (Lebanon)	2,079	2,219	6.7	2,007	87.7	2.3	0.0	4.3	5.6	21.9	16.2	43.0	51.0	24.2	880	93.6
Cleveland township (Columbia)	1,110	1,079	-2.8	1,209	94.9	0.2	0.0	4.2	0.7	22.8	22.4	45.1	56.8	15.5	485	78.6
Clifford township (Susquehanna)	2,416	2,255	-6.7	2,503	95.6	0.0	0.9	2.4	1.2	17.2	22.0	46.6	57.3	20.9	1,043	93.4
Clifton township (Lackawanna)	1,489	1,427	-4.2	1,124	91.5	3.4	0.7	0.7	3.6	14.1	27.6	52.4	48.3	21.9	508	87.6
Clifton Heights borough & MCD (Delaware)	6,648	6,697	0.7	6,696	71.9	23.3	2.5	1.5	0.8	20.0	13.1	36.3	57.2	16.5	2,658	84.3
Clinton CDP	434	-	-	498	100.0	0.0	0.0	0.0	0.0	2.8	18.3	47.6	52.3	25.5	251	88.0
Clinton township (Butler)	2,863	2,767	-3.4	2,802	96.2	0.0	0.5	1.2	2.1	20.5	15.7	44.5	45.7	29.7	1,095	91.4
Clinton township (Lycoming)	3,712	3,676		3,676	82.6	13.5	0.2	1.1	2.6	13.1	11.9	37.4	56.3	10.7	748	84.8
Clinton township (Venango)	852	785	-7.9	952	98.2	0.1	0.0	1.1	0.6	27.1	23.5	41.5	66.4	9.5	371	73.0
Clinton township (Wayne)	2,069	2,048		2,214	93.1	0.8	0.6	1.3	4.2	18.5	20.9	46.9	54.0	20.6	878	80.0
Clinton township (Wyoming)	1,323	1,242	-6.1	1,342	95.1	1.3	0.8	1.5	1.3	24.1	17.1	42.1	47.4	25.9	496	89.5
Clintonville borough & MCD (Venango)	508	466	-8.3	441	90.2	0.0	2.7	7.0	0.0	20.4	14.3	39.9	74.1	13.4	199	81.4
Clover township (Jefferson)	450	434	-3.6	353	100.0	0.0	0.0	0.0	0.0	17.6	19.8	51.4	53.3	19.1	155	86.5
Clymer borough & MCD (Indiana)	1,358	1,266	-6.8	1,237	98.1	0.8	0.2	0.3	0.6	20.5	20.9	44.4	57.7	19.5	568	78.9
Clymer township (Tioga)	582	561	-3.6	537	97.4	0.0	0.0	2.6	0.0	14.2	34.6	53.1	66.6	9.8	223	76.7
Coal township (Northumberland)	10,376	10,208	-1.6	10,297	78.9	13.0	0.4	1.0	6.6	14.6	18.5	41.0	73.2	9.3	3,424	73.9
Coal Center borough & MCD (Washington)	139	131	-5.8	134	83.6	12.7	0.0	3.7	0.0	21.6	7.5	30.7	48.8	21.3	55	96.4
Coaldale borough & MCD (Bedford)	158	151	-4.4	123	100.0	0.0	0.0	0.0	0.0	20.3	12.2	46.8	86.0	4.7	50	68.0
Coaldale borough & MCD (Schuylkill)	2,280	2,140	-6.1	2,245	89.3	4.8	0.0	2.4	3.4	21.2	18.6	41.3	53.1	12.0	1,006	84.0
Coalmont borough & MCD (Huntingdon)	106	101	-4.7	71	98.6	0.0	0.0	1.4	0.0	16.9	32.4	43.9	73.6	5.7	28	60.7
Coalport borough & MCD (Clearfield)	523	491	-6.1	443	100.0	0.0	0.0	0.0	0.0	14.7	19.0	45.5	76.1	3.8	222	74.8
Coatesville city & MCD (Chester)	13,071	13,069	0.0	13,136	25.5	41.3	0.5	4.5	28.2	30.9	9.5	29.8	55.4	17.2	4,485	80.0
Coburn CDP	236	-	-	164	98.8	0.0	0.0	1.2	0.0	38.4	15.9	31.7	79.6	11.8	48	79.2
Cochranton borough & MCD (Crawford)	1,136	1,076	-5.3	1,151	93.4	1.3	0.9	3.9	0.5	29.6	19.9	41.0	57.2	15.1	456	94.3
Cochranville CDP	668	-	-	635	76.4	0.0	0.0	0.0	23.6	19.4	18.4	44.1	59.5	19.8	255	87.5
Codorus township (York)	3,808	3,903	2.5	3,886	91.1	1.6	0.2	1.6	5.5	21.8	18.5	43.8	56.4	22.9	1,444	85.0
Cogan House township (Lycoming)	953	927	-2.7	1,040	96.1	0.9	0.2	0.9	2.0	22.9	18.5	41.3	56.5	15.5	400	80.0
Cokeburg borough & MCD (Washington)	632	605	-4.3	537	98.5	0.0	0.0	1.5	0.0	12.1	23.6	47.5	61.7	13.3	284	78.2
Cold Spring township (Lebanon)	56	59	5.4	14	100.0	0.0	0.0	0.0	0.0	0.0	0.0	0.0	50.0	0.0	7	100.0
Colebrook township (Clinton)	198	197	-0.5	138	92.8	2.2	0.0	0.7	4.3	8.0	24.6	55.3	69.2	6.7	49	87.8
Colebrookdale township (Berks)	5,132	5,153	0.4	5,139	97.7	0.0	1.2	1.1	0.0	17.8	22.8	47.5	44.7	29.4	2,156	88.0
Colerain township (Bedford)	1,196	1,154	-3.5	1,154	97.5	0.3	0.0	0.9	1.4	19.7	27.9	51.9	68.1	10.8	451	76.7
Colerain township (Lancaster)	3,634	3,912	7.6	3,853	99.5	0.1	0.0	0.3	0.0	34.7	13.8	31.4	63.6	19.8	1,122	66.9
College township (Centre)	9,545	10,055	5.3	10,102	85.5	2.8	5.4	3.4	3.0	16.8	17.1	39.3	17.5	62.3	3,744	92.9
Collegeville borough & MCD (Montgomery)	5,098	5,174	1.5	5,152	80.8	8.9	5.6	2.4	2.3	16.1	8.9	22.2	19.3	59.4	1,326	95.9
Colley township (Sullivan)	693	673	-2.9	580	58.8	23.6	0.0	2.8	14.8	17.2	11.9	37.8	58.4	17.7	170	82.4
Collier township (Allegheny)	7,098	8,217	15.8	8,106	92.3	2.2	3.0	1.5	0.9	19.1	23.9	49.6	27.8	51.0	3,869	91.9
Collingdale borough & MCD (Delaware)	8,785	8,794	0.1	8,791	38.3	52.5	1.4	3.9	3.9	25.5	9.5	34.1	49.7	17.9	3,140	89.3
Collinsburg CDP	1,125	-	-	969	97.0	0.0	0.0	3.0	0.0	12.0	18.5	48.4	63.0	19.1	472	74.2
Colonial Park CDP	13,229	-	-	13,583	61.6	15.4	8.8	4.8	9.3	20.7	17.8	36.6	41.9	29.1	6,022	85.7
Colony Park CDP	1,076	-	-	1,289	67.9	0.0	17.9	0.0	14.2	23.7	22.4	42.0	26.9	56.2	474	94.5
Columbia township (Bradford)	1,204	1,155	-4.1	1,067	98.4	1.2	0.0	0.4	0.0	25.6	18.3	40.0	60.7	16.5	407	84.3
Columbia borough & MCD (Lancaster)	10,391	10,355	-0.3	10,382	71.7	10.9	0.6	3.1	13.6	23.7	17.5	37.6	60.8	15.4	4,383	81.6
Columbus CDP	824	-	-	857	96.5	1.2	0.0	2.3	0.0	23.9	24.4	45.5	61.6	16.1	339	87.0
Columbus township (Warren)	2,034	1,911	-6.0	1,916	94.9	0.9	0.0	2.5	1.7	19.7	19.3	47.9	59.2	12.2	767	87.5
Colver CDP	959	-	-	806	96.7	0.0	0.0	0.0	3.3	13.2	15.3	44.7	41.5	13.1	426	66.4
Colwyn borough & MCD (Delaware)	2,550	2,551	0.0	2,546	10.3	83.0	0.0	0.7	6.0	31.8	8.7	30.0	47.4	17.4	765	92.0
Commodore CDP	331	-	-	416	100.0	0.0	0.0	0.0	0.0	26.0	11.3	35.0	83.9	2.8	168	76.8
Conashaugh Lakes CDP	1,294	-	-	1,315	97.9	0.0	0.0	0.0	2.1	25.5	25.5	48.3	60.0	24.5	458	100.0
Concord township (Butler)	1,500	1,444	-3.7	1,338	96.7	0.0	0.0	3.3	0.0	16.4	22.6	49.4	60.2	22.0	611	85.3
Concord township (Delaware)	17,219	17,933	4.1	17,745	75.9	6.7	11.5	3.2	2.8	16.8	24.4	45.1	34.4	50.7	6,338	86.0
Concord township (Erie)	1,344	1,278	-4.9	1,066	99.4	0.1	0.5	0.0	0.0	16.6	26.6	49.6	55.4	16.8	461	85.2

1 May be of any race.

Table A. All Places — **Population and Housing**

STATE City, town, township, borough, or CDP (county if applicable)	Population				Race and Hispanic or Latino origin (percent)					Age (percent)			Educational attainment of persons age 25 and older		Occupied housing units	
	2010 census total population	2019 estimated population	Percent change 2010–2019	ACS total population estimate 2015–2019	White alone, not Hispanic or Latino	Black alone, not Hispanic or Latino	Asian alone, not Hispanic or Latino	All other races or 2 or more races, not Hispanic or Latino	Hispanic or Latino[1]	Under 18 years old	Age 65 years and older	Median age	Percent High school diploma or less	Percent Bachelor's degree or more	Total	Percent with a computer
	1	2	3	4	5	6	7	8	9	10	11	12	13	14	15	16
PENNSYLVANIA—Con.																
Conemaugh township (Cambria)	2,011	1,825	-9.2	2,097	96.6	0.4	0.0	2.0	1.0	18.9	23.9	47.3	56.1	15.8	858	81.7
Conemaugh township (Indiana)	2,299	2,139	-7.0	2,247	99.8	0.0	0.0	0.1	0.1	17.1	20.2	46.1	50.7	18.4	890	84.2
Conemaugh township (Somerset)	7,275	6,848	-5.9	6,913	93.6	0.0	1.1	4.3	0.9	16.1	27.1	51.3	54.8	22.8	3,046	77.0
Conestoga CDP	1,258	-	-	1,159	96.1	0.0	0.0	1.6	2.3	17.3	14.8	45.1	53.9	21.1	482	88.0
Conestoga township (Lancaster)	3,776	3,881	2.8	3,874	94.6	0.1	0.0	1.8	3.6	20.1	16.2	45.6	49.7	23.6	1,647	88.8
Conewago township (Adams)	7,111	7,230	1.7	7,193	92.8	0.7	0.0	2.4	4.1	19.1	20.4	45.7	52.4	20.6	2,819	89.6
Conewago township (Dauphin)	3,017	3,104	2.9	3,078	90.1	2.8	4.6	1.2	1.3	22.7	16.1	43.3	39.3	39.7	1,123	88.9
Conewago township (York)	7,507	8,497	13.2	8,241	77.3	12.4	1.9	1.3	7.1	25.9	13.5	37.3	51.4	21.2	3,152	87.7
Conewango township (Warren)	3,594	3,339	-7.1	3,388	96.8	0.2	0.0	2.1	0.9	19.5	22.0	48.2	49.7	18.7	1,460	83.4
Confluence borough & MCD (Somerset)	780	727	-6.8	557	96.4	2.0	0.0	0.7	0.9	8.8	28.9	52.5	53.4	21.4	285	75.1
Conneaut township (Crawford)	1,476	1,381	-6.4	1,381	99.2	0.0	0.0	0.2	0.6	19.0	22.4	51.6	63.5	11.9	603	83.4
Conneaut township (Erie)	4,298	4,412	2.7	4,381	68.2	25.8	0.0	1.4	4.6	11.0	9.6	39.7	76.2	5.4	712	83.4
Conneaut Lake borough & MCD (Crawford)	656	619	-5.6	719	96.8	0.4	0.0	1.5	1.3	21.1	12.2	41.4	53.8	22.7	310	95.8
Conneaut Lakeshore CDP	2,395	-	-	2,384	98.9	0.0	0.0	0.6	0.5	14.1	28.9	50.8	36.0	36.7	1,140	90.4
Conneautville borough & MCD (Crawford)	767	729	-5.0	713	95.9	1.7	0.0	1.5	0.8	24.5	17.8	32.8	68.3	13.5	296	80.7
Connellsville city & MCD (Fayette)	7,694	7,290	-5.3	7,411	89.4	3.3	0.5	5.0	1.8	22.7	17.9	43.4	55.3	21.9	3,576	80.3
Connellsville township (Fayette)	2,333	2,178	-6.6	2,239	95.9	0.4	0.2	1.9	1.5	17.9	25.9	48.8	57.2	19.0	1,000	81.2
Connoquenessing borough & MCD (Butler)	509	679	33.4	554	93.3	0.0	3.1	0.0	3.6	20.4	23.6	48.1	32.8	33.0	233	91.8
Connoquenessing township (Butler)	4,180	3,882	-7.1	3,948	96.8	0.0	0.0	3.2	0.0	16.7	23.0	48.7	37.2	31.0	1,660	89.4
Conoy township (Lancaster)	3,200	3,447	7.7	3,438	93.5	0.7	0.0	0.3	5.6	24.4	14.7	40.1	57.4	23.6	1,299	92.1
Conshohocken borough & MCD (Montgomery)	7,846	8,047	2.6	8,029	91.1	2.0	2.2	2.3	2.4	10.0	10.5	32.2	24.7	60.4	3,963	93.5
Conway borough & MCD (Beaver)	2,176	2,067	-5.0	2,114	97.0	0.0	0.0	1.7	1.2	18.4	22.5	46.9	44.5	26.5	1,021	82.2
Conyngham township (Columbia)	753	764	1.5	734	98.2	0.0	0.5	0.8	0.4	12.7	27.9	54.2	70.6	9.2	342	77.2
Conyngham borough & MCD (Luzerne)	1,914	1,867	-2.5	2,072	89.1	1.3	5.7	0.7	3.2	17.2	24.0	49.4	33.0	39.3	873	90.5
Conyngham township (Luzerne)	1,461	1,447		1,668	96.0	1.0	0.2	2.6	0.2	18.5	17.8	44.2	60.9	9.4	649	84.7
Cook township (Westmoreland)	2,251	2,172	-3.5	1,838	95.9	1.6	1.5	0.3	0.6	9.4	32.6	57.8	49.6	23.4	866	76.6
Cooke township (Cumberland)	179	183	2.2	216	94.4	1.9	0.0	3.2	0.5	16.2	13.0	46.9	35.3	28.7	92	95.7
Coolbaugh township (Monroe)	20,550	20,599	0.2	20,357	39.5	26.1	1.8	2.4	30.2	22.0	13.4	39.0	50.6	21.6	6,668	92.8
Coolspring township (Mercer)	2,244	2,133	-4.9	1,985	99.8	0.2	0.0	0.0	0.0	14.3	29.2	53.1	54.7	22.1	795	83.6
Cooper township (Clearfield)	2,704	2,606	-3.6	2,635	96.7	0.0	0.0	0.5	2.8	21.1	24.0	47.3	68.1	8.6	1,077	77.1
Cooper township (Montour)	932	950	1.9	891	95.4	0.3	0.0	0.4	3.8	13.7	23.0	52.9	55.4	24.9	398	85.4
Coopersburg borough & MCD (Lehigh)	2,390	2,567	7.4	2,488	88.2	4.3	0.4	2.1	4.9	15.0	24.8	47.2	53.3	21.2	1,014	87.6
Cooperstown borough & MCD (Venango)	462	420	-9.1	405	99.0	0.0	0.0	0.2	0.7	18.3	22.2	50.3	61.2	9.1	175	87.4
Coplay borough & MCD (Lehigh)	3,140	3,214	2.4	3,201	75.9	6.8	0.4	1.5	15.4	19.2	19.9	44.6	55.8	16.1	1,363	88.0
Coral CDP	325	-	-	187	100.0	0.0	0.0	0.0	0.0	0.0	67.9	68.0	74.3	0.0	101	47.5
Coraopolis borough & MCD (Allegheny)	5,642	5,424	-3.9	5,488	73.5	18.5	0.3	4.7	3.0	19.3	19.1	40.8	39.9	26.5	2,805	85.2
Cornplanter township (Venango)	2,431	2,237	-8.0	2,646	98.4	0.0	0.0	0.9	0.8	21.5	25.1	48.7	49.9	22.0	1,045	85.6
Cornwall borough & MCD (Lebanon)	4,115	4,376	6.3	4,315	93.6	1.6	1.1	0.1	3.5	15.9	35.4	55.2	46.8	33.6	1,795	90.1
Cornwells Heights CDP	1,391	-	-	1,182	85.5	3.6	5.3	3.9	1.6	18.8	19.9	45.1	40.8	37.7	438	90.4
Corry city & MCD (Erie)	6,609	6,208	-6.1	6,332	91.1	4.6	0.2	1.1	3.0	21.0	20.3	42.4	57.0	16.5	2,808	81.8
Corsica borough & MCD (Jefferson)	357	344	-3.6	355	99.2	0.3	0.0	0.6	0.0	20.6	13.2	39.6	53.4	13.7	149	83.9
Corydon township (McKean)	275	264	-4.0	262	100.0	0.0	0.0	0.0	0.0	12.6	32.4	59.8	56.1	15.8	136	84.6
Coudersport borough & MCD (Potter)	2,546	2,404	-5.6	2,766	95.7	1.1	0.4	1.2	1.5	21.8	21.5	42.7	54.8	17.8	1,107	84.5
Courtdale borough & MCD (Luzerne)	724	716	-1.1	598	96.7	0.0	1.0	1.5	0.8	15.4	29.3	52.0	55.2	20.7	264	79.2
Covington township (Clearfield)	526	498	-5.3	488	98.2	1.0	0.0	0.8	0.0	17.2	26.4	50.2	60.8	15.8	208	85.1
Covington township (Lackawanna)	2,272	2,271	0.0	1,886	92.6	1.0	1.0	0.8	4.6	19.6	24.9	46.4	49.1	24.4	784	91.7
Covington township (Tioga)	1,034	1,016	-1.7	831	100.0	0.0	0.0	0.0	0.0	14.8	25.4	54.3	53.9	20.8	348	87.4
Cowanshannock township (Armstrong)	2,901	2,742	-5.5	2,791	99.2	0.0	0.5	0.0	0.3	23.2	16.8	43.6	58.6	13.2	1,094	80.3
Crabtree CDP	277	-	-	152	100.0	0.0	0.0	0.0	0.0	42.1	5.3	37.8	44.3	0.0	49	83.7

1 May be of any race.

Table A. All Places — **Population and Housing**

STATE City, town, township, borough, or CDP (county if applicable)	2010 census total population	2019 estimated population	Percent change 2010–2019	ACS total population estimate 2015–2019	White alone, not Hispanic or Latino	Black alone, not Hispanic or Latino	Asian alone, not Hispanic or Latino	All other races or 2 or more races, not Hispanic or Latino	Hispanic or Latino[1]	Under 18 years old	Age 65 years and older	Median age	Percent High school diploma or less	Percent Bachelor's degree or more	Total	Percent with a computer
	1	2	3	4	5	6	7	8	9	10	11	12	13	14	15	16
PENNSYLVANIA—Con.																
Crafton borough & MCD (Allegheny)	5,994	5,770	-3.7	5,838	90.3	6.4	0.3	1.7	1.3	17.1	15.6	37.3	35.4	35.6	2,745	89.2
Cranberry township (Butler)	28,045	31,632	12.8	30,875	89.9	1.3	3.7	1.7	3.4	24.5	12.3	40.0	18.2	59.1	12,121	96.5
Cranberry township (Venango)	6,679	6,243	-6.5	6,359	97.6	0.1	1.1	0.4	0.8	18.5	23.0	49.4	61.6	19.5	2,819	89.0
Cranesville borough & MCD (Erie)	638	595	-6.7	602	97.8	0.0	0.3	1.3	0.5	26.1	12.1	40.1	60.1	18.4	208	88.9
Crawford township (Clinton)	937	934	-0.3	828	96.9	3.1	0.0	0.0	0.0	19.3	20.2	41.8	65.3	11.2	340	77.9
Creekside borough & MCD (Indiana)	309	289	-6.5	338	93.5	5.3	0.0	1.2	0.0	25.1	21.9	38.8	58.1	17.1	140	72.9
Crenshaw CDP	468	-	-	378	100.0	0.0	0.0	0.0	0.0	12.7	30.7	48.6	67.0	17.9	155	81.3
Crescent township (Allegheny)	2,643	2,549	-3.6	2,589	91.2	1.0	0.9	3.6	3.3	22.9	19.4	43.4	35.5	29.4	1,045	88.8
Cresson borough & MCD (Cambria)	1,707	1,553	-9.0	1,719	94.9	0.2	2.1	2.7	0.0	20.1	20.4	41.8	46.5	22.9	767	83.6
Cresson township (Cambria)	4,343	2,612	-39.9	2,682	93.4	2.4	0.2	2.3	1.6	14.7	18.2	39.7	49.9	23.3	955	81.5
Cressona borough & MCD (Schuylkill)	1,636	1,591	-2.8	1,572	91.0	2.2	0.8	1.7	4.4	22.5	17.7	41.1	54.5	13.7	648	84.1
Cromwell township (Huntingdon)	1,621	1,569	-3.2	1,573	99.0	0.8	0.0	0.3	0.0	16.8	27.4	52.2	73.6	10.5	627	81.8
Cross Creek township (Washington)	1,543	1,485	-3.8	1,646	97.5	0.0	0.0	1.3	1.2	18.7	18.3	48.6	51.3	21.4	664	85.1
Cross Creek CDP	137	-	-	166	98.2	0.0	0.0	1.8	0.0	12.7	7.2	50.5	54.5	13.8	58	94.8
Cross Roads borough & MCD (York)	511	505	-1.2	446	95.7	1.3	0.2	2.2	0.4	14.3	16.6	47.9	59.9	14.9	172	90.1
Crown CDP	183	-	-	274	100.0	0.0	0.0	0.0	0.0	25.5	19.7	49.1	68.0	15.2	127	59.8
Croydon CDP	9,950	-	-	10,034	78.4	4.8	3.2	1.7	11.9	23.4	12.3	38.4	61.1	16.5	3,844	88.4
Croyle township (Cambria)	2,338	2,215	-5.3	2,220	99.1	0.0	0.2	0.3	0.4	22.4	20.7	43.9	59.5	14.5	888	83.1
Crucible CDP	725	-	-	369	100.0	0.0	0.0	0.0	0.0	3.5	24.1	63.2	86.5	4.8	201	91.5
Cumberland township (Adams)	6,179	6,258	1.3	6,221	90.1	0.9	2.0	3.5	3.5	17.5	34.5	55.0	36.5	37.3	2,609	89.3
Cumberland township (Greene)	6,630	6,157	-7.1	6,295	98.0	0.1	0.5	0.8	0.6	22.8	19.5	42.3	58.6	15.2	2,819	82.5
Cumberland Valley township (Bedford)	1,595	1,539	-3.5	1,408	97.7	0.0	0.0	0.5	1.8	18.8	22.7	48.4	56.9	14.0	593	87.2
Cumbola CDP	443	-	-	353	94.3	0.0	0.0	0.0	5.7	14.7	17.0	46.1	56.6	12.1	164	81.1
Cummings township (Lycoming)	269	258	-4.1	282	98.9	0.0	0.0	1.1	0.0	3.2	41.5	63.0	59.1	12.3	160	72.5
Cumru township (Berks)	15,302	15,493	1.2	15,414	82.1	4.2	2.3	1.6	9.8	18.1	24.3	46.4	39.0	34.6	6,607	89.0
Curtin township (Centre)	609	589	-3.3	615	98.9	0.0	0.0	1.1	0.0	13.3	26.7	53.9	60.8	14.7	267	73.8
Curtisville CDP	1,064	-	-	1,183	100.0	0.0	0.0	0.0	0.0	12.3	11.6	45.6	44.3	33.0	631	100.0
Curwensville borough & MCD (Clearfield)	2,541	2,385	-6.1	2,314	97.6	0.1	0.0	2.3	0.0	21.0	24.5	44.3	56.0	16.7	1,036	87.9
Cussewago township (Crawford)	1,559	1,517	-2.7	1,518	96.8	0.2	0.0	1.4	1.6	21.5	18.2	46.2	51.6	26.7	627	89.0
Daisytown borough & MCD (Cambria)	323	294	-9.0	332	98.5	0.0	0.0	1.5	0.0	19.6	22.3	44.8	60.9	19.8	145	80.7
Dale borough & MCD (Cambria)	1,242	1,126	-9.3	1,088	81.1	8.2	0.6	5.2	5.0	21.1	18.6	46.7	65.6	9.5	548	73.0
Dallas borough & MCD (Luzerne)	2,837	2,792	-1.6	2,804	95.3	1.4	1.0	1.1	1.2	18.0	19.0	44.5	24.2	46.6	1,197	92.3
Dallas township (Luzerne)	8,957	9,269	3.5	9,208	95.7	1.0	0.8	1.3	1.2	19.0	24.0	43.9	32.1	40.0	3,314	80.7
Dallastown borough & MCD (York)	3,891	3,857	-0.9	3,852	92.6	4.3	0.0	1.0	2.1	17.6	17.8	41.3	52.0	15.3	1,784	88.3
Dalmatia CDP	488	-	-	437	100.0	0.0	0.0	0.0	0.0	21.3	30.2	49.1	63.8	14.7	195	73.8
Dalton borough & MCD (Lackawanna)	1,234	1,188	-3.7	1,284	94.0	1.9	0.0	0.0	4.1	21.8	24.1	48.7	27.0	50.4	528	91.9
Damascus township (Wayne)	3,657	3,624	-0.9	3,611	98.0	0.0	0.5	0.6	0.9	18.0	26.5	49.1	43.1	26.0	1,507	85.4
Danville borough & MCD (Montour)	4,699	4,648	-1.1	4,627	94.6	1.1	1.9	0.9	1.5	16.0	20.3	38.5	51.4	33.1	2,328	76.4
Darby borough & MCD (Delaware)	10,692	10,702	0.1	10,695	14.8	81.2	1.1	0.5	2.4	27.4	10.8	32.7	56.0	17.5	3,437	93.6
Darby township (Delaware)	9,264	9,279	0.2	9,272	53.8	40.5	0.6	1.5	3.7	24.3	16.4	37.0	47.7	21.3	3,849	88.2
Darlington borough & MCD (Beaver)	253	236	-6.7	199	99.0	0.0	0.0	0.0	1.0	21.1	20.6	34.7	46.1	24.8	85	89.4
Darlington township (Beaver)	1,970	1,873	-4.9	1,934	98.3	0.2	0.0	1.6	0.0	22.0	21.1	46.6	57.9	14.0	760	80.0
Dauberville CDP	848	-	-	648	96.8	0.0	0.0	1.7	1.5	23.9	15.4	48.2	53.0	17.7	269	93.3
Daugherty township (Beaver)	3,182	3,004	-5.6	3,058	98.7	0.5	0.0	0.8	0.0	14.7	19.3	50.6	46.9	23.1	1,239	85.7
Dauphin borough & MCD (Dauphin)	791	801	1.3	774	93.7	0.9	1.4	0.6	3.4	25.1	17.7	37.4	30.7	38.3	330	84.5
Davidson township (Sullivan)	575	535	-7.0	696	99.4	0.0	0.4	0.0	0.1	12.2	20.1	47.4	56.1	21.5	287	86.1
Davidsville CDP	1,130	-	-	805	81.1	0.0	9.7	7.3	1.9	16.5	38.1	58.6	45.8	33.6	399	100.0
Dawson borough & MCD (Fayette)	367	347	-5.4	448	95.5	0.4	0.0	4.0	0.0	26.8	13.8	36.1	66.0	10.0	162	81.5
Dayton borough & MCD (Armstrong)	553	510	-7.8	480	97.1	0.0	0.0	2.9	0.0	17.7	29.4	49.0	63.1	20.2	217	77.9
Dean township (Cambria)	387	356	-8.0	409	97.6	0.5	0.0	2.0	0.0	27.9	16.9	45.0	57.7	24.5	146	82.9
Decatur township (Clearfield)	4,537	4,690	3.4	4,678	64.3	12.3	3.2	1.3	18.9	11.1	19.4	47.3	72.1	8.7	1,244	71.9
Decatur township (Mifflin)	3,137	3,082	-1.8	3,089	98.5	0.7	0.0	0.8	0.0	22.0	18.8	44.6	69.2	9.5	1,190	80.3
Deemston borough & MCD (Washington)	718	697	-2.9	777	96.4	0.0	0.3	1.7	1.7	22.1	19.2	46.7	53.4	24.5	324	86.1
Deer Creek township (Mercer)	506	472	-6.7	511	100.0	0.0	0.0	0.0	0.0	19.4	24.1	50.7	69.4	13.1	209	85.2

1 May be of any race.

STATE City, town, township, borough, or CDP (county if applicable)	Population				Race and Hispanic or Latino origin (percent)					Age (percent)			Educational attainment of persons age 25 and older		Occupied housing units	
	2010 census total population	2019 estimated population	Percent change 2010–2019	ACS total population estimate 2015–2019	White alone, not Hispanic or Latino	Black alone, not Hispanic or Latino	Asian alone, not Hispanic or Latino	All other races or 2 or more races, not Hispanic or Latino	Hispanic or Latino[1]	Under 18 years old	Age 65 years and older	Median age	Percent High school diploma or less	Percent Bachelor's degree or more	Total	Percent with a computer
	1	2	3	4	5	6	7	8	9	10	11	12	13	14	15	16
PENNSYLVANIA—Con.																
Deerfield township (Tioga)	660	650	-1.5	625	96.5	0.8	0.2	0.6	1.9	13.8	22.7	49.5	57.0	16.4	239	85.8
Deerfield township (Warren)	339	316	-6.8	280	98.6	0.0	0.0	0.0	1.4	11.4	34.6	62.0	46.4	23.0	142	85.9
Deer Lake CDP	495	-	-	388	100.0	0.0	0.0	0.0	0.0	25.5	26.3	32.7	39.8	39.4	166	84.3
Deer Lake borough & MCD (Schuylkill)	683	659	-3.5	741	98.4	0.0	0.0	0.1	1.5	25.0	20.6	44.1	41.5	30.0	287	88.9
Defiance CDP	239	-	-	346	100.0	0.0	0.0	0.0	0.0	33.5	12.4	33.0	80.5	4.2	115	93.0
Delano CDP	342	-	-	267	98.9	0.0	0.0	0.7	0.4	10.1	27.3	56.4	71.7	6.6	128	60.2
Delano township (Schuylkill)	442	416	-5.9	325	99.1	0.0	0.0	0.6	0.3	11.1	26.2	56.1	67.4	5.5	161	63.4
Delaware township (Juniata)	1,565	1,562	-0.2	1,499	98.3	0.0	0.3	0.0	1.5	23.8	23.5	41.6	67.0	11.3	610	75.2
Delaware township (Mercer)	2,291	2,158	-5.8	2,261	97.5	0.0	0.0	0.5	2.0	17.2	25.0	52.0	59.5	22.1	987	80.3
Delaware township (Northumberland)	4,486	4,321	-3.7	4,376	98.4	0.8	0.5	0.0	0.4	22.5	22.0	46.5	57.5	18.6	1,839	81.1
Delaware township (Pike)	7,379	7,095	-3.8	7,063	83.8	0.3	0.4	2.4	13.2	19.4	15.1	46.6	49.1	19.2	2,601	92.3
Delaware Water Gap borough & MCD (Monroe)	748	752	0.5	699	94.0	2.9	1.7	0.0	1.4	18.7	16.0	46.8	29.8	39.0	291	94.5
Delmar township (Tioga)	2,861	2,797	-2.2	2,808	98.5	0.0	0.0	1.5	0.0	17.2	26.1	49.7	51.1	23.9	1,155	87.1
Delmont borough & MCD (Westmoreland)	2,664	2,525	-5.2	2,563	97.5	0.0	0.0	2.5	0.0	14.2	22.3	53.4	28.9	33.9	1,303	90.6
Delta borough & MCD (York)	728	723	-0.7	591	88.8	0.0	0.0	1.2	10.0	25.2	17.6	40.3	60.1	16.3	221	95.0
Dennison township (Luzerne)	1,120	1,130	0.9	888	93.4	0.0	0.0	1.1	5.5	18.5	20.4	48.7	41.6	23.1	375	86.4
Denver borough & MCD (Lancaster)	3,863	3,851	-0.3	3,861	87.2	1.0	3.4	2.5	5.9	27.8	17.4	38.1	55.5	21.9	1,492	94.4
Derry township (Dauphin)	24,679	25,249	2.3	25,093	79.3	2.8	7.1	1.6	9.2	20.2	17.6	45.2	24.5	50.2	9,872	93.5
Derry township (Mifflin)	7,330	7,301	-0.4	7,314	96.0	0.3	0.0	3.2	0.4	15.9	28.1	51.0	62.6	12.4	3,155	84.0
Derry township (Montour)	1,130	1,119	-1.0	1,086	97.9	1.3	0.0	0.0	0.8	23.1	23.1	46.6	72.2	15.4	371	77.1
Derry borough & MCD (Westmoreland)	2,680	2,512	-6.3	2,540	98.5	0.0	0.3	0.2	0.9	19.9	16.8	41.7	43.8	16.3	1,097	83.6
Derry township (Westmoreland)	14,504	13,826	-4.7	14,039	94.3	2.6	0.3	1.4	1.5	16.1	24.4	49.3	56.5	17.2	5,852	84.8
DeSales University CDP	953	-	-	913	84.6	1.5	6.6	2.2	5.1	0.5	1.3	19.7	0.0	84.2	0	0.0
Devon CDP	1,515	-	-	1,869	87.3	2.0	0.0	3.3	7.5	28.0	7.0	42.4	9.7	77.9	594	100.0
Dewart CDP	1,471	-	-	1,520	100.0	0.0	0.0	0.0	0.0	24.0	26.0	43.5	52.1	18.6	657	82.0
Dickinson township (Cumberland)	5,209	5,383	3.3	5,362	94.8	0.0	0.8	1.0	3.5	19.3	21.6	50.1	50.7	27.9	2,100	89.0
Dickson City borough & MCD (Lackawanna)	6,068	5,761	-5.1	5,802	92.7	1.7	0.4	2.8	2.4	20.3	18.8	41.8	50.5	24.0	2,528	87.5
Dicksonville CDP	467	-	-	632	83.4	0.0	0.0	16.6	0.0	40.8	10.8	35.1	47.1	19.8	229	71.2
Dillsburg borough & MCD (York)	2,578	2,582	0.2	2,580	91.6	1.4	0.3	1.2	5.5	28.2	16.6	37.3	43.7	32.8	1,052	88.2
Dimock township (Susquehanna)	1,502	1,407	-6.3	1,364	96.8	0.0	0.4	0.8	2.1	22.5	20.7	50.7	48.9	20.8	540	91.9
Dingman township (Pike)	11,938	11,711	-1.9	11,619	92.0	0.9	0.4	0.7	6.0	19.1	18.5	43.9	38.5	31.6	4,229	93.4
District township (Berks)	1,382	1,423	3.0	1,391	92.5	0.4	0.9	5.5	0.6	17.5	21.6	48.2	45.5	26.5	555	93.0
Donaldson CDP	328	-	-	261	100.0	0.0	0.0	0.0	0.0	27.6	13.8	37.8	77.5	2.2	113	87.6
Donegal township (Butler)	1,881	1,792	-4.7	1,755	97.8	0.6	0.0	0.3	1.4	17.3	19.2	47.9	52.2	19.1	642	90.5
Donegal township (Washington)	2,464	2,438	-1.1	2,287	96.7	0.0	0.8	2.5	0.0	18.9	17.7	45.0	58.8	14.0	941	88.5
Donegal borough & MCD (Westmoreland)	117	110	-6.0	179	86.0	0.0	0.0	4.5	9.5	21.8	16.2	30.8	74.6	4.3	64	79.7
Donegal township (Westmoreland)	2,405	2,328	-3.2	2,489	98.8	0.6	0.0	0.2	0.4	20.0	17.4	44.5	59.4	15.5	978	82.3
Donora borough & MCD (Washington)	4,781	4,562	-4.6	4,598	70.5	19.0	0.0	3.3	7.2	25.7	20.4	38.0	56.1	15.4	1,923	79.8
Dormont borough & MCD (Allegheny)	8,602	8,282	-3.7	8,373	89.9	3.0	1.5	2.4	3.2	15.1	11.9	36.4	23.2	49.8	4,076	93.1
Dorneyville CDP	4,406	-	-	4,224	90.4	2.9	1.8	2.8	2.2	18.1	24.0	47.9	22.8	53.0	1,705	91.7
Dorrance township (Luzerne)	2,187	2,225	1.7	2,055	98.4	0.0	0.2	1.0	0.4	17.3	18.7	47.7	43.3	30.0	829	90.5
Douglass township (Berks)	3,463	3,607	4.2	3,587	86.3	5.1	0.0	3.2	5.4	17.6	28.5	50.8	53.8	19.5	1,354	88.8
Douglass township (Montgomery)	10,194	10,549	3.5	10,506	94.5	1.1	1.5	1.4	1.5	23.4	15.2	41.1	39.8	35.7	3,788	93.2
Douglassville CDP	448	-	-	443	100.0	0.0	0.0	0.0	0.0	0.0	79.0	81.3	39.3	20.8	342	33.0
Dover borough & MCD (York)	2,007	1,988	-0.9	2,217	86.5	2.7	4.1	0.7	6.1	27.7	11.5	34.7	53.8	18.6	798	93.4
Dover township (York)	21,088	21,894	3.8	21,605	89.9	2.4	0.5	2.0	5.2	20.3	18.1	42.5	54.2	18.8	8,688	88.5
Downingtown borough & MCD (Chester)	7,887	7,897	0.1	7,926	68.6	12.6	8.0	2.4	8.3	21.1	13.2	36.4	35.3	36.1	3,175	91.5
Doylestown borough & MCD (Bucks)	8,380	8,272	-1.3	8,286	90.9	0.8	2.0	1.7	4.6	13.4	28.9	50.4	24.4	52.3	3,775	90.3
Doylestown township (Bucks)	17,669	17,398	-1.5	17,431	91.6	1.6	2.8	1.5	2.5	19.1	23.3	46.2	24.7	54.7	6,087	92.4
Dravosburg borough & MCD (Allegheny)	1,790	1,723	-3.7	1,730	95.1	2.9	0.0	0.0	2.0	13.4	23.0	49.5	46.5	20.1	896	81.8
Dreher township (Wayne)	1,408	1,371	-2.6	1,443	92.8	1.9	0.1	1.0	4.2	10.6	29.9	55.8	48.8	25.1	506	86.6
Drexel Hill CDP	28,043	-	-	27,939	71.8	15.6	5.4	3.3	4.0	22.6	13.6	38.2	32.2	41.9	11,002	93.2
Driftwood borough & MCD (Cameron)	67	58	-13.4	32	100.0	0.0	0.0	0.0	0.0	0.0	46.9	63.5	65.6	0.0	27	51.9
Drumore township (Lancaster)	2,560	2,689	5.0	2,656	96.0	0.2	0.0	0.7	3.0	29.8	10.7	28.8	64.4	14.0	828	75.6
Dry Tavern CDP	697	-	-	612	100.0	0.0	0.0	0.0	0.0	12.1	25.8	52.6	51.3	20.5	268	94.0
Dryville CDP	398	-	-	257	100.0	0.0	0.0	0.0	0.0	35.8	6.6	36.8	18.8	36.4	122	86.9
Dublin borough & MCD (Bucks)	2,158	2,133	-1.2	2,178	81.2	3.6	4.1	0.2	10.9	22.2	12.2	36.9	37.2	31.8	884	93.6
Dublin township (Fulton)	1,259	1,220	-3.1	1,103	99.4	0.4	0.0	0.3	0.0	15.3	25.9	50.1	67.8	13.0	507	81.3

1 May be of any race.

Table A. All Places — **Population and Housing**

STATE City, town, township, borough, or CDP (county if applicable)	Population 2010 census total population	2019 estimated population	Percent change 2010–2019	ACS total population estimate 2015–2019	White alone, not Hispanic or Latino	Black alone, not Hispanic or Latino	Asian alone, not Hispanic or Latino	All other races or 2 or more races, not Hispanic or Latino	Hispanic or Latino[1]	Under 18 years old	Age 65 years and older	Median age	Percent High school diploma or less	Percent Bachelor's degree or more	Occupied housing units Total	Percent with a computer
	1	2	3	4	5	6	7	8	9	10	11	12	13	14	15	16
PENNSYLVANIA—Con.																
Dublin township (Huntingdon)	1,304	1,281	-1.8	1,332	98.7	0.0	0.0	1.3	0.0	25.8	16.9	41.5	72.0	10.7	505	81.8
DuBois city & MCD (Clearfield)	7,793	7,364	-5.5	7,462	97.1	1.1	0.4	0.5	0.9	21.8	18.0	38.1	47.2	23.6	3,338	84.8
Duboistown borough & MCD (Lycoming)	1,203	1,171	-2.7	1,163	97.9	0.2	0.0	0.0	1.9	18.7	23.3	48.6	51.7	21.0	503	90.3
Dudley borough & MCD (Huntingdon)	187	180	-3.7	219	100.0	0.0	0.0	0.0	0.0	28.8	21.9	43.4	71.6	9.2	81	74.1
Dunbar borough & MCD (Fayette)	1,036	977	-5.7	1,075	95.7	0.0	0.0	1.5	2.8	24.0	14.7	40.0	63.2	12.2	449	84.0
Dunbar township (Fayette)	7,126	6,725	-5.6	6,833	98.0	0.5	0.0	1.2	0.3	17.4	21.9	49.7	59.5	16.8	2,934	79.3
Duncan township (Tioga)	208	221	6.3	255	100.0	0.0	0.0	0.0	0.0	20.8	9.0	29.3	72.5	12.1	98	89.8
Duncannon borough & MCD (Perry)	1,522	1,489	-2.2	1,463	89.2	1.5	0.6	2.7	6.0	19.2	19.1	42.7	61.9	14.4	691	83.9
Duncansville borough & MCD (Blair)	1,238	1,163	-6.1	1,161	95.1	0.0	0.3	2.2	2.4	17.6	22.5	44.2	62.5	18.9	545	81.7
Dunkard township (Greene)	2,379	2,247	-5.5	2,056	98.3	0.5	0.5	0.4	0.2	22.3	20.6	45.2	66.4	15.6	821	87.0
Dunlevy borough & MCD (Washington)	413	408	-1.2	412	92.2	2.2	0.0	3.6	1.9	16.0	27.4	48.4	61.4	17.1	204	68.6
Dunlo CDP	342	-	-	312	100.0	0.0	0.0	0.0	0.0	13.8	13.8	33.0	57.2	0.0	155	81.9
Dunmore borough & MCD (Lackawanna)	14,057	12,954	-7.8	13,111	89.3	1.3	4.2	0.5	4.7	17.6	19.8	42.9	37.7	38.1	5,499	85.0
Dunnstable township (Clinton)	1,016	1,005	-1.1	1,053	94.7	0.0	2.3	0.2	2.8	17.7	22.3	48.8	45.3	27.2	416	93.0
Dunnstown CDP	1,360	-	-	1,438	95.1	0.0	0.3	0.8	3.8	18.8	22.0	41.6	47.8	32.2	579	85.5
Dupont borough & MCD (Luzerne)	2,720	2,683	-1.4	2,692	89.9	0.1	0.0	2.2	7.8	16.4	21.8	45.8	51.1	17.5	1,186	88.0
Duquesne city & MCD (Allegheny)	5,562	5,557	-0.1	5,543	28.7	56.7	0.0	12.1	2.5	30.1	11.8	30.7	53.6	11.0	2,247	81.2
Durham township (Bucks)	1,142	1,133	-0.8	1,106	90.9	1.9	1.1	1.4	4.8	16.9	22.3	49.7	36.3	39.7	422	91.5
Duryea borough & MCD (Luzerne)	4,911	4,852	-1.2	4,863	93.5	2.5	0.0	2.1	1.9	19.5	21.0	42.6	43.8	26.6	2,103	87.7
Dushore borough & MCD (Sullivan)	601	556	-7.5	558	98.4	0.0	0.4	0.9	0.4	10.4	29.0	59.1	59.9	12.5	338	73.1
Dyberry township (Wayne)	1,426	1,408	-1.3	1,443	97.5	1.2	0.7	0.0	0.6	15.7	24.0	50.2	46.6	32.3	538	87.0
Eagle Lake CDP	12	-	-	-	-	-	-	-	-	-	-	-	-	-	-	-
Eagles Mere borough & MCD (Sullivan)	120	113	-5.8	143	100.0	0.0	0.0	0.0	0.0	12.6	42.0	61.9	11.2	76.0	77	97.4
Eagleview CDP	1,644	-	-	1,843	92.7	1.1	1.7	0.5	4.0	15.8	37.3	54.7	13.8	64.0	910	91.4
Eagleville CDP	324	-	-	536	100.0	0.0	0.0	0.0	0.0	20.3	12.3	36.4	64.8	9.5	190	73.2
Eagleville CDP	4,800	-	-	5,302	66.7	15.7	8.2	0.7	8.8	13.4	9.8	35.8	63.9	20.4	1,164	92.0
Earl township (Berks)	3,212	3,281	2.1	3,267	98.2	0.1	0.0	0.0	1.7	18.3	16.9	47.5	64.3	16.5	1,287	89.4
Earl township (Lancaster)	7,017	7,190	2.5	7,186	97.6	0.8	0.3	0.0	1.3	26.2	27.7	39.3	65.2	21.5	2,538	69.7
Earlston CDP	1,122	-	-	1,241	100.0	0.0	0.0	0.0	0.0	16.8	24.4	54.1	73.5	7.4	462	68.0
East Allen township (Northampton)	4,895	4,977	1.7	4,915	92.5	1.1	0.0	1.3	5.0	18.3	25.1	49.5	38.9	21.4	1,891	90.5
East Bangor borough & MCD (Northampton)	1,170	1,628	39.1	991	81.6	1.0	1.0	1.5	14.8	26.7	15.0	38.1	62.1	12.1	392	87.2
East Berlin borough & MCD (Adams)	1,521	1,545	1.6	1,733	93.9	1.6	0.4	1.5	2.5	19.8	12.3	39.6	51.0	21.4	685	90.9
East Berwick CDP	2,007	-	-	2,239	91.7	0.0	0.0	0.0	8.3	17.2	26.6	51.1	49.8	25.8	1,006	89.6
East Bethlehem township (Washington)	2,354	2,272	-3.5	2,030	93.0	4.3	0.0	0.6	2.2	22.7	20.0	40.5	57.8	18.9	924	80.7
East Bradford township (Chester)	9,919	9,896	-0.2	9,936	87.6	4.3	1.1	3.1	3.9	20.2	16.8	44.6	14.0	63.3	3,528	97.8
East Brady borough & MCD (Clarion)	942	906	-3.8	908	97.4	0.0	0.4	1.7	0.6	18.2	20.7	45.1	59.0	14.0	423	75.4
East Brandywine township (Chester)	6,753	9,049	34.0	8,601	81.1	4.9	7.6	3.4	2.9	27.2	16.6	42.3	23.8	58.2	3,011	98.1
East Brunswick township (Schuylkill)	1,793	1,733	-3.3	1,810	94.0	0.3	2.8	2.2	0.7	22.7	12.8	43.2	42.2	31.3	691	89.6
East Buffalo township (Union)	6,410	6,938	8.2	6,882	89.4	3.8	3.3	0.9	2.5	17.0	16.7	35.6	25.5	53.0	2,084	94.2
East Butler borough & MCD (Butler)	732	684	-6.6	757	98.2	0.0	0.0	1.1	0.8	21.4	9.8	41.9	61.5	10.9	313	89.8
East Caln township (Chester)	4,849	4,847	0.0	4,854	67.2	1.4	19.0	2.7	9.8	24.4	16.6	39.8	21.1	63.9	2,107	87.2
East Cameron township (Northumberland)	748	717	-4.1	625	98.2	0.0	0.3	0.0	1.4	19.7	19.8	45.6	57.5	13.3	285	72.3
East Carroll township (Cambria)	1,673	1,563	-6.6	1,404	99.4	0.4	0.0	0.2	0.0	16.8	19.9	49.7	57.6	22.4	593	87.5
East Chillisquaque township (Northumberland)	671	637	-5.1	729	98.9	0.0	1.1	0.0	0.0	21.0	13.4	43.6	64.1	16.3	275	92.4
East Cocalico township (Lancaster)	10,321	10,674	3.4	10,554	88.2	1.4	0.6	0.6	9.1	22.1	16.5	40.1	60.7	19.5	3,781	85.9
East Conemaugh borough & MCD (Cambria)	1,218	1,104	-9.4	905	90.4	6.3	0.0	0.7	2.7	17.9	23.4	48.3	63.3	13.7	462	78.1
East Coventry township (Chester)	6,637	6,752	1.7	6,759	86.9	3.8	5.2	0.7	3.4	25.2	15.4	42.4	31.3	45.1	2,449	96.4
East Deer township (Allegheny)	1,494	1,436	-3.9	1,449	96.2	1.4	0.0	1.7	0.6	23.1	13.0	40.1	40.3	27.1	669	86.1
East Donegal township (Lancaster)	7,759	8,366	7.8	8,310	93.2	0.4	1.1	2.5	2.8	26.5	13.8	34.0	46.2	29.2	2,863	89.8
East Drumore township (Lancaster)	3,789	3,860	1.9	3,873	93.0	1.0	3.6	0.2	2.2	25.7	24.6	42.4	63.4	16.1	1,328	79.9
East Earl CDP	1,144	-	-	1,261	90.0	0.0	0.0	0.0	10.0	33.4	6.1	38.9	51.6	29.4	354	95.2
East Earl township (Lancaster)	6,506	6,891	5.9	6,845	95.7	0.3	1.6	0.0	2.4	28.6	14.7	33.3	67.4	16.6	2,047	80.7
East Fairfield township (Crawford)	922	874	-5.2	871	96.9	1.0	0.9	0.0	1.1	20.6	20.1	43.1	63.0	15.6	347	85.9

1 May be of any race.

Table A. All Places — **Population and Housing**

STATE City, town, township, borough, or CDP (county if applicable)	Population — 2010 census total population	2019 estimated population	Percent change 2010–2019	ACS total population estimate 2015–2019	White alone, not Hispanic or Latino	Black alone, not Hispanic or Latino	Asian alone, not Hispanic or Latino	All other races or 2 or more races, not Hispanic or Latino	Hispanic or Latino[1]	Under 18 years old	Age 65 years and older	Median age	Percent High school diploma or less	Percent Bachelor's degree or more	Occupied housing units — Total	Percent with a computer
	1	2	3	4	5	6	7	8	9	10	11	12	13	14	15	16
PENNSYLVANIA—Con.																
East Fallowfield township (Chester)	7,445	7,558	1.5	7,560	85.1	6.4	1.2	2.2	5.2	26.2	13.5	41.2	27.2	44.2	2,810	94.7
East Fallowfield township (Crawford)	1,622	1,578	-2.7	1,362	99.2	0.0	0.1	0.6	0.1	22.7	18.4	39.2	69.0	10.7	520	68.5
East Finley township (Washington)	1,394	1,357	-2.7	1,545	95.8	2.2	0.0	0.4	1.6	22.5	14.6	39.7	64.1	10.3	524	85.1
East Franklin township (Armstrong)	4,083	3,842	-5.9	3,895	96.4	0.0	1.4	2.1	0.0	22.2	17.4	45.8	41.9	35.2	1,562	90.0
East Freedom CDP	972	-	-	789	100.0	0.0	0.0	0.0	0.0	16.7	14.6	45.7	59.0	13.4	373	95.4
East Goshen township (Chester)	17,998	18,149	0.8	18,204	92.7	2.2	2.3	0.4	2.3	17.0	29.5	50.3	19.6	59.5	8,337	93.5
East Greenville borough & MCD (Montgomery)	2,920	2,940	0.7	2,943	91.6	1.9	0.6	2.7	3.1	25.3	9.3	33.0	53.7	25.4	1,102	95.2
East Hanover township (Dauphin)	5,727	5,953	3.9	5,935	96.4	0.6	1.0	0.2	1.7	23.5	18.4	47.5	49.0	31.9	2,232	89.0
East Hanover township (Lebanon)	2,804	2,971	6.0	2,914	90.0	2.9	0.4	0.7	6.0	17.2	17.4	44.4	59.9	17.8	1,133	85.4
East Hempfield township (Lancaster)	23,533	24,701	5.0	24,461	83.2	2.9	3.0	2.7	8.2	20.2	22.9	43.8	30.4	46.9	10,077	90.5
East Hopewell township (York)	2,443	2,482	1.6	2,409	96.4	0.9	0.2	0.2	2.3	18.6	16.9	47.9	48.7	20.3	846	91.1
East Huntingdon township (Westmoreland)	8,007	7,648	-4.5	7,733	97.7	1.1	0.0	1.0	0.2	21.7	21.5	47.3	49.3	21.6	3,315	83.1
East Keating township (Clinton)	11	11	0.0	4	100.0	0.0	0.0	0.0	0.0	0.0	25.0	45.0	25.0	0.0	2	100.0
East Lackawannock township (Mercer)	1,682	1,620	-3.7	1,711	98.7	0.3	0.0	0.6	0.4	23.4	21.2	44.4	51.7	27.7	650	86.2
East Lampeter township (Lancaster)	16,453	17,039	3.6	16,996	76.5	5.9	6.2	1.6	9.8	25.2	15.3	38.3	50.6	27.7	6,362	88.1
East Lansdowne borough & MCD (Delaware)	2,668	2,671	0.1	2,674	23.3	51.1	16.4	4.8	4.4	19.0	14.5	37.9	51.5	20.1	893	88.9
Eastlawn Gardens CDP	3,307	-	-	3,360	83.9	0.0	1.9	0.0	14.2	25.3	14.3	42.9	35.5	33.3	1,159	94.1
East McKeesport borough & MCD (Allegheny)	2,124	2,042	-3.9	1,955	87.5	4.9	0.0	7.7	0.0	16.0	20.2	48.8	49.8	14.5	989	84.2
East Mahoning township (Indiana)	1,076	1,009	-6.2	1,027	95.6	0.0	0.0	3.1	1.3	24.5	12.7	41.5	64.3	19.0	408	73.8
East Manchester township (York)	7,259	7,810	7.6	7,640	90.4	1.5	1.8	2.0	4.2	25.6	11.6	38.9	42.4	30.4	2,751	93.4
East Marlborough township (Chester)	7,029	7,548	7.4	7,388	85.1	2.6	6.8	2.2	3.3	21.2	21.0	48.3	14.9	66.0	2,822	96.2
East Mead township (Crawford)	1,490	1,391	-6.6	1,288	97.4	0.1	0.1	1.6	0.8	20.6	19.2	43.5	62.0	11.5	551	83.8
East Nantmeal township (Chester)	1,794	1,855	3.4	1,662	93.6	1.3	0.9	0.8	3.4	19.7	23.7	50.4	23.4	56.9	598	95.3
East Norriton township (Montgomery)	13,604	13,974	2.7	14,015	77.2	11.2	5.0	1.6	5.0	14.7	27.2	48.7	35.3	42.5	5,920	89.7
East Norwegian township (Schuylkill)	865	822	-5.0	926	98.8	0.0	0.0	0.0	1.2	17.8	26.9	51.8	58.1	16.2	416	83.2
East Nottingham township (Chester)	8,624	9,085	5.3	8,975	84.8	3.2	1.4	1.6	9.0	29.7	10.0	37.6	39.1	30.6	2,789	90.4
Easton city & MCD (Northampton)	26,814	27,189	1.4	27,122	56.8	13.2	2.7	4.6	22.6	19.9	13.9	34.8	55.6	21.8	9,245	85.4
East Penn township (Carbon)	2,881	2,829	-1.8	2,813	97.1	0.5	0.2	0.4	1.8	15.0	29.0	52.7	55.3	19.9	1,171	88.8
East Pennsboro township (Cumberland)	20,566	21,458	4.3	21,432	84.8	3.6	4.8	2.4	4.4	20.3	18.0	41.8	41.5	33.7	9,143	89.8
East Petersburg borough & MCD (Lancaster)	4,506	4,504	0.0	4,520	82.8	4.1	1.7	1.4	9.9	20.4	17.1	44.0	38.0	30.7	1,871	92.0
East Pikeland township (Chester)	7,085	7,526	6.2	7,365	90.5	4.8	2.6	0.6	1.5	19.0	19.4	43.0	26.0	57.9	3,072	94.5
East Pittsburgh borough & MCD (Allegheny)	1,827	1,757	-3.8	1,576	25.8	70.8	0.4	3.0	0.0	28.7	12.9	28.7	48.8	13.2	800	80.4
East Prospect borough & MCD (York)	860	910	5.8	946	93.7	1.0	0.0	1.3	4.1	30.2	13.8	35.3	66.6	11.8	341	90.6
East Providence township (Bedford)	1,854	1,839	-0.8	1,849	93.5	1.1	0.0	3.5	1.8	22.4	17.5	43.1	66.9	11.5	758	78.6
East Rochester borough & MCD (Beaver)	567	531	-6.3	472	89.4	3.6	0.0	5.9	1.1	15.9	38.6	55.4	56.9	12.5	238	71.0
East Rockhill township (Bucks)	5,710	5,728	0.3	5,737	93.8	1.1	1.3	1.1	2.7	23.4	13.6	43.8	43.1	33.9	2,047	94.5
East St. Clair township (Bedford)	3,056	2,906	-4.9	2,939	98.1	1.9	0.0	0.0	0.0	21.2	17.3	43.4	64.8	13.6	1,257	89.3
East Salem CDP	186	-	-	221	100.0	0.0	0.0	0.0	0.0	37.6	8.1	33.2	48.0	2.4	71	85.9
East Side borough & MCD (Carbon)	315	301	-4.4	324	92.0	0.0	1.9	1.2	4.9	14.5	22.5	52.0	69.4	8.6	141	84.4
East Stroudsburg borough & MCD (Monroe)	9,862	10,433	5.8	10,333	59.2	16.0	3.2	4.7	16.8	16.5	17.0	35.7	48.8	21.9	3,291	84.8
East Taylor township (Cambria)	2,730	2,488	-8.9	2,528	97.3	0.1	0.4	0.9	1.2	19.4	18.2	46.0	54.2	14.9	1,071	88.0
Easttown township (Chester)	10,462	10,634	1.6	10,618	86.1	1.2	6.8	3.3	2.6	27.3	17.8	45.2	8.8	79.9	3,875	96.3
East Union township (Schuylkill)	1,607	1,593	-0.9	1,531	90.2	0.1	3.5	0.0	6.1	16.7	20.0	48.6	56.2	16.7	662	89.9
East Uniontown CDP	2,419	-	-	2,176	89.9	3.8	1.1	5.3	0.0	24.0	17.1	37.4	62.5	11.6	940	80.2
Eastvale borough & MCD (Beaver)	222	207	-6.8	215	94.0	1.9	0.0	4.2	0.0	23.7	13.5	34.9	79.4	9.6	79	83.5
East Vandergrift borough & MCD (Westmoreland)	677	635	-6.2	761	93.7	3.0	1.6	0.9	0.8	26.5	12.6	31.9	67.7	7.1	312	81.7
East Vincent township (Chester)	6,826	7,343	7.6	7,162	83.7	5.0	4.2	3.0	4.0	25.0	15.5	42.7	30.4	45.1	2,333	89.0
East Washington borough & MCD (Washington)	1,890	1,810	-4.2	1,986	83.8	7.3	3.9	2.8	2.2	11.0	17.7	38.9	27.5	48.6	813	96.9

1 May be of any race.

Table A. All Places — **Population and Housing**

STATE City, town, township, borough, or CDP (county if applicable)	2010 census total population	2019 estimated population	Percent change 2010–2019	ACS total population estimate 2015–2019	White alone, not Hispanic or Latino	Black alone, not Hispanic or Latino	Asian alone, not Hispanic or Latino	All other races or 2 or more races, not Hispanic or Latino	Hispanic or Latino[1]	Under 18 years old	Age 65 years and older	Median age	Percent High school diploma or less	Percent Bachelor's degree or more	Total occupied housing units	Percent with a computer
	1	2	3	4	5	6	7	8	9	10	11	12	13	14	15	16
PENNSYLVANIA—Con.																
East Waterford CDP	-	-	-	189	100.0	0.0	0.0	0.0	0.0	13.8	32.8	53.4	64.7	15.7	91	76.9
East Wheatfield township (Indiana)	2,363	2,208	-6.6	2,078	98.5	0.0	0.2	0.3	1.0	14.0	28.8	54.2	64.3	14.3	952	81.8
East Whiteland township (Chester)	10,637	12,832	20.6	11,841	68.6	5.2	16.7	1.7	7.8	21.5	14.0	35.6	18.7	65.8	4,223	95.5
East York CDP	8,777	-	-	8,495	74.8	4.5	6.9	3.3	10.6	18.6	20.5	43.6	42.8	34.6	3,492	92.6
Eaton township (Wyoming)	1,534	1,486	-3.1	1,514	95.5	1.6	0.3	0.3	2.4	18.8	23.2	45.6	55.5	21.0	620	86.0
Eau Claire borough & MCD (Butler)	318	296	-6.9	297	92.3	0.0	4.7	3.0	0.0	22.2	20.5	38.3	68.6	12.1	117	88.0
Ebensburg borough & MCD (Cambria)	3,350	3,054	-8.8	3,122	99.6	0.1	0.1	0.0	0.3	15.4	22.9	47.4	42.2	40.8	1,705	89.7
Economy borough & MCD (Beaver)	8,988	9,098	1.2	9,182	97.7	0.6	0.2	0.3	1.2	16.1	24.3	50.7	40.2	31.3	3,931	91.0
Eddington CDP	1,906	-	-	2,033	80.1	0.0	7.6	0.4	11.9	20.1	15.8	45.0	52.4	24.3	698	92.7
Eddystone borough & MCD (Delaware)	2,410	2,412	0.1	2,530	62.5	19.0	2.4	9.7	6.4	31.4	7.2	30.0	58.0	11.5	762	93.8
Eden township (Lancaster)	2,121	2,233	5.3	2,048	96.2	0.4	0.3	0.5	2.5	35.4	14.1	29.5	71.9	13.0	585	61.7
Edenborn CDP	294	-	-	199	79.4	20.6	0.0	0.0	0.0	21.6	34.2	56.5	69.2	10.3	80	58.8
Edenburg CDP	681	-	-	725	99.3	0.0	0.0	0.7	0.0	16.3	19.7	47.7	50.8	18.2	298	86.9
Edgewood borough & MCD (Allegheny)	3,128	3,004	-4.0	3,040	83.7	8.2	1.4	2.9	3.8	17.2	13.8	36.4	13.0	67.6	1,533	97.0
Edgewood CDP	2,384	-	-	2,564	90.2	1.8	0.2	0.5	7.3	21.1	20.1	36.4	62.6	10.2	1,102	75.8
Edgeworth borough & MCD (Allegheny)	1,679	1,647	-1.9	1,586	96.3	0.4	1.3	0.5	1.6	28.3	19.0	45.7	7.7	80.6	602	96.5
Edgmont township (Delaware)	3,978	4,131	3.8	4,059	86.9	1.8	7.2	3.0	1.0	18.6	30.7	45.7	13.2	65.6	1,692	96.1
Edie CDP	83	-	-	47	100.0	0.0	0.0	0.0	0.0	0.0	31.9	56.4	68.1	6.4	29	89.7
Edinboro borough & MCD (Erie)	6,445	5,515	-14.4	5,794	89.3	4.4	2.3	2.2	1.8	14.5	11.7	23.4	20.6	54.9	2,009	91.6
Edwardsville borough & MCD (Luzerne)	4,849	4,723	-2.6	4,742	75.0	8.9	2.1	2.3	11.8	26.4	23.6	37.7	50.1	25.7	2,044	87.6
Effort CDP	2,269	-	-	2,575	79.2	8.0	0.0	0.0	12.7	19.7	17.9	45.2	50.2	23.4	919	95.2
Egypt CDP	2,391	-	-	2,273	96.0	2.6	0.0	1.5	0.0	19.1	17.9	47.9	40.9	26.9	862	93.3
Ehrenfeld borough & MCD (Cambria)	228	210	-7.9	172	97.7	0.0	0.0	2.3	0.0	19.8	19.8	45.7	65.0	10.6	79	78.5
Eighty Four CDP	657	-	-	462	95.7	2.8	0.0	1.5	0.0	18.8	31.6	49.8	44.1	10.7	207	81.6
Elco borough & MCD (Washington)	323	306	-5.3	286	93.4	0.0	0.0	0.0	6.6	15.7	25.9	47.7	71.6	7.9	113	73.5
Elder township (Cambria)	1,057	980	-7.3	968	98.8	0.0	0.0	1.0	0.2	18.9	32.1	52.6	71.3	7.7	369	82.4
Elderton borough & MCD (Armstrong)	356	335	-5.9	373	97.9	0.0	0.0	0.0	2.1	18.8	27.6	42.3	64.3	17.5	163	77.9
Eldred township (Jefferson)	1,230	1,182	-3.9	1,140	100.0	0.0	0.0	0.0	0.0	17.0	24.7	52.6	68.0	14.0	514	79.2
Eldred township (Lycoming)	2,122	2,104	-0.8	2,025	92.0	1.4	0.3	1.3	4.9	19.0	24.1	51.4	41.4	29.1	818	87.4
Eldred borough & MCD (McKean)	818	761	-7.0	617	99.4	0.6	0.0	0.0	0.0	17.0	25.6	49.2	60.0	19.2	300	80.7
Eldred township (McKean)	1,582	1,505	-4.9	1,318	98.5	0.0	0.0	1.5	0.0	18.2	21.5	48.4	61.8	14.7	534	90.6
Eldred township (Monroe)	2,906	2,869	-1.3	2,881	96.0	2.4	0.0	0.5	1.2	14.2	21.6	48.1	53.9	18.1	986	87.7
Eldred township (Schuylkill)	758	720	-5.0	781	97.7	0.0	0.0	0.8	1.5	22.9	25.7	49.3	69.5	11.3	305	77.0
Eldred township (Warren)	650	608	-6.5	604	97.8	0.0	1.0	0.0	0.3	23.5	19.7	42.3	60.5	15.4	241	79.7
Elgin borough & MCD (Erie)	218	205	-6.0	190	96.8	1.1	0.0	0.0	2.1	19.5	30.5	47.5	63.7	14.4	78	84.6
Elim CDP	3,727	-	-	3,453	92.2	4.3	1.7	0.3	1.5	14.6	23.3	46.0	45.8	31.4	1,587	86.8
Elizabeth borough & MCD (Allegheny)	1,494	1,476	-1.2	1,439	95.6	1.7	0.8	0.8	1.1	20.5	17.2	43.5	49.6	16.2	663	86.3
Elizabeth township (Allegheny)	13,276	12,952	-2.4	13,067	96.2	0.7	0.5	1.2	1.4	17.9	23.0	47.6	39.6	27.2	5,479	87.0
Elizabeth township (Lancaster)	3,888	3,996	2.8	3,994	95.9	0.0	1.3	2.5	0.3	25.4	14.0	41.7	61.8	24.7	1,473	88.9
Elizabethtown borough & MCD (Lancaster)	11,514	11,445	-0.6	11,469	89.1	4.1	3.1	0.7	3.0	16.9	15.1	36.1	44.9	27.1	4,301	93.5
Elizabethville borough & MCD (Dauphin)	1,504	1,494	-0.7	1,611	93.5	0.7	0.0	0.9	4.8	20.7	18.1	40.4	51.3	16.3	637	88.9
Elk township (Chester)	1,678	1,708	1.8	1,761	93.4	0.0	0.3	0.7	5.6	22.4	16.1	44.9	40.7	42.2	622	88.1
Elk township (Clarion)	1,493	1,397	-6.4	1,563	98.5	0.2	0.0	1.3	0.0	20.9	21.5	44.1	66.6	17.7	601	87.9
Elk township (Tioga)	49	47	-4.1	33	100.0	0.0	0.0	0.0	0.0	9.1	24.2	55.5	50.0	16.7	18	72.2
Elk township (Warren)	524	490	-6.5	483	100.0	0.0	0.0	0.0	0.0	18.0	26.9	56.1	50.5	22.0	215	87.9
Elk Creek township (Erie)	1,795	1,745	-2.8	1,708	95.2	1.5	0.6	1.6	1.1	18.8	20.0	47.5	58.1	16.2	680	88.2
Elkland township (Sullivan)	578	544	-5.9	482	97.1	0.0	0.0	0.8	2.1	9.5	39.8	61.7	55.0	18.3	199	93.0
Elkland borough & MCD (Tioga)	1,821	1,739	-4.5	1,831	90.8	2.5	0.2	4.2	2.3	21.1	21.1	39.9	63.4	11.7	730	80.7
Elk Lick township (Somerset)	2,239	2,087	-6.8	2,279	99.1	0.0	0.0	0.3	0.6	30.2	17.7	36.3	74.8	12.8	733	73.0
Ellport borough & MCD (Lawrence)	1,177	1,103	-6.3	988	96.3	0.0	0.0	3.7	0.0	12.7	24.7	49.0	62.6	11.8	458	84.5
Ellsworth borough & MCD (Washington)	1,010	963	-4.7	797	89.7	4.1	0.0	6.1	0.0	20.8	21.5	41.0	60.8	12.7	322	85.1
Ellwood City borough (Lawrence)	7,857	7,286	-7.3	7,679	97.4	0.6	0.0	1.3	0.7	20.6	18.0	41.6	54.2	19.5	3,542	85.8
Ellwood City borough (Beaver)	621	583	-6.1	855	99.8	0.0	0.0	0.1	0.1	18.7	8.9	42.6	59.6	11.6	361	95.8
Ellwood City borough (Lawrence)	7,236	6,703	-7.4	6,824	97.1	0.7	0.0	1.5	0.8	20.8	19.1	39.7	53.5	20.6	3,181	84.6
Elmhurst township (Lackawanna)	894	847	-5.3	951	98.5	0.1	0.0	0.3	1.1	17.5	38.1	49.9	40.3	36.7	333	79.3
Elrama CDP	307	-	-	351	100.0	0.0	0.0	0.0	0.0	32.8	7.1	38.8	44.5	36.0	125	80.0
Elverson borough & MCD (Chester)	1,225	1,308	6.8	1,353	94.5	2.7	0.0	0.4	2.4	10.2	44.2	61.8	38.8	32.2	645	84.3

1 May be of any race.

Table A. All Places — **Population and Housing**

STATE City, town, township, borough, or CDP (county if applicable)	Population				Race and Hispanic or Latino origin (percent)					Age (percent)			Educational attainment of persons age 25 and older		Occupied housing units	
	2010 census total population	2019 estimated population	Percent change 2010–2019	ACS total population estimate 2015–2019	White alone, not Hispanic or Latino	Black alone, not Hispanic or Latino	Asian alone, not Hispanic or Latino	All other races or 2 or more races, not Hispanic or Latino	Hispanic or Latino[1]	Under 18 years old	Age 65 years and older	Median age	Percent High school diploma or less	Percent Bachelor's degree or more	Total	Percent with a computer
	1	2	3	4	5	6	7	8	9	10	11	12	13	14	15	16
PENNSYLVANIA—Con.																
Elysburg CDP..................	2,194	-	-	1,863	96.0	0.5	0.0	3.2	0.3	14.2	28.9	58.5	45.7	30.8	906	76.9
Emerald Lakes CDP........	2,886	-	-	3,495	38.7	31.5	4.3	0.0	25.5	21.2	18.0	53.0	55.3	14.3	1,060	92.2
Emigsville CDP...............	2,672	-	-	3,032	78.2	11.2	1.6	0.2	8.8	23.9	14.5	33.8	59.7	16.5	1,140	87.2
Emlenton borough...........	630	573	-9.0	693	91.1	0.1	0.7	6.9	1.2	21.1	17.3	43.0	46.8	24.0	304	92.1
Emlenton borough (Clarion)..................	8	7	-12.5	-	-	-	-	-	-	-	-	-	-	-	-	-
Emlenton borough (Venango)...............	622	566	-9.0	693	91.1	0.1	0.7	6.9	1.2	21.1	17.3	43.0	46.8	24.0	304	92.1
Emmaus borough & MCD (Lehigh)................	11,188	11,467	2.5	11,391	85.0	2.7	3.4	1.7	7.2	19.2	17.8	42.4	42.8	30.0	4,874	90.7
Emporium borough & MCD (Cameron)...........	2,068	1,816	-12.2	2,056	93.0	0.1	1.4	3.7	1.8	15.1	21.5	46.4	63.6	10.0	983	83.8
Emsworth borough & MCD (Allegheny)........	2,440	2,350	-3.7	2,503	87.7	4.8	1.9	5.0	0.6	20.7	14.3	37.5	29.8	37.2	1,258	92.0
Englewood CDP..............	532	-	-	527	100.0	0.0	0.0	0.0	0.0	19.5	33.8	50.5	34.7	31.0	237	74.7
Enhaut CDP....................	1,007	-	-	1,270	62.0	8.0	0.0	19.2	10.8	27.2	6.1	36.2	54.4	4.4	453	89.8
Enlow CDP......................	1,013	-	-	999	91.2	0.0	4.9	2.4	1.5	16.7	15.1	46.6	35.5	25.8	520	85.4
Enola CDP......................	6,111	-	-	6,251	88.6	7.2	1.2	1.4	1.7	21.1	15.1	37.8	53.9	19.7	2,741	88.5
Enon Valley borough & MCD (Lawrence).......	308	284	-7.8	368	93.2	0.5	6.3	0.0	0.0	26.4	14.4	38.8	40.8	16.3	131	93.1
Ephrata borough & MCD (Lancaster)...........	13,344	13,862	3.9	13,810	86.9	2.6	0.3	1.8	8.3	23.9	15.6	37.6	54.7	22.8	5,719	85.9
Ephrata township (Lancaster)...........	9,443	10,453	10.7	10,334	91.9	0.6	0.6	1.2	5.7	25.2	18.0	37.7	54.3	22.1	3,681	87.7
Erie city & MCD (Erie)......	101,738	95,508	-6.1	97,263	68.7	15.5	2.8	4.7	8.3	23.0	14.3	34.9	53.8	21.6	39,897	85.3
Ernest borough & MCD (Indiana).................	462	431	-6.7	523	96.4	3.6	0.0	0.0	0.0	28.7	11.3	33.9	44.7	20.4	201	85.1
Espy CDP.......................	1,642	-	-	1,602	93.4	1.1	3.8	1.7	0.0	19.0	16.3	35.8	41.1	34.5	686	90.5
Etna borough & MCD (Allegheny)................	3,440	3,308	-3.8	3,350	91.8	0.6	4.7	1.9	0.9	20.5	13.5	34.9	38.8	30.2	1,486	87.6
Eulalia township (Potter)...	895	855	-4.5	895	93.5	0.4	2.9	2.0	1.1	17.9	34.2	57.8	51.9	25.7	301	92.0
Evansburg CDP...............	2,129	-	-	2,151	63.4	12.1	15.0	1.0	8.5	22.9	12.2	42.8	15.0	58.9	773	100.0
Evans City borough & MCD (Butler)...............	1,832	1,710	-6.7	2,009	96.5	0.0	1.2	0.6	1.6	21.6	13.7	37.1	40.6	24.3	871	93.9
Everett borough & MCD (Bedford)................	1,833	1,719	-6.2	1,867	90.8	1.5	1.9	0.3	5.4	21.4	18.1	38.7	74.9	5.4	841	74.6
Everson borough & MCD (Fayette).................	792	749	-5.4	864	97.0	0.6	1.7	0.7	0.0	18.5	11.8	40.3	57.1	12.9	350	87.4
Exeter township (Berks)...	25,340	25,772	1.7	25,689	83.8	5.1	1.9	1.6	7.5	22.1	18.4	43.7	41.7	34.0	9,588	93.4
Exeter borough & MCD (Luzerne)................	5,626	5,541	-1.5	5,549	93.6	0.5	0.0	0.8	5.2	21.4	22.9	46.8	58.3	20.3	2,302	85.8
Exeter township (Luzerne)	2,375	2,354	-0.9	2,193	94.7	0.0	0.0	2.5	2.8	15.3	20.8	47.9	44.2	23.0	856	92.2
Exeter township (Wyoming)..................	683	635	-7.0	658	96.2	0.2	0.2	1.2	2.3	16.0	22.5	50.8	49.7	22.8	280	83.2
Export borough & MCD (Westmoreland)...........	911	856	-6.0	912	95.1	0.0	3.7	1.0	0.2	23.7	18.0	38.2	48.8	20.3	437	87.2
Exton CDP.....................	4,842	-	-	5,382	62.5	3.8	31.5	0.9	1.3	19.5	13.7	37.0	18.0	59.2	2,165	98.3
Eyers Grove CDP............	105	-	-	56	87.5	0.0	0.0	0.0	12.5	16.1	30.4	55.2	59.6	27.7	36	72.2
Factoryville borough & MCD (Wyoming)...........	1,201	1,167	-2.8	1,292	83.0	8.9	0.0	1.9	6.1	14.1	12.5	24.0	41.8	31.1	367	90.5
Fairchance borough & MCD (Fayette)..............	1,982	1,886	-4.8	2,230	89.2	4.6	0.1	5.4	0.7	25.9	16.1	37.1	61.4	15.1	897	85.4
Fairdale CDP...................	2,059	-	-	2,264	99.8	0.0	0.0	0.2	0.0	20.2	25.3	40.6	51.9	17.7	1,128	77.3
Fairfield borough & MCD (Adams).................	509	518	1.8	579	97.9	0.0	0.0	1.7	0.3	19.2	33.7	51.6	46.8	20.7	254	82.3
Fairfield township (Crawford)...............	1,019	960	-5.8	1,076	97.2	0.4	0.3	2.1	0.0	21.8	20.4	41.0	58.8	15.9	446	84.8
Fairfield township (Lycoming)...............	2,792	2,779	-0.5	2,780	92.3	0.9	0.1	2.0	4.7	21.4	19.4	44.1	37.3	30.8	1,169	89.6
Fairfield township (Westmoreland)...........	2,428	2,330	-4.0	2,099	96.5	0.0	0.4	0.2	2.9	20.1	22.5	49.7	64.5	15.0	873	79.4
Fairhope CDP..................	1,151	-	-	1,033	98.5	1.5	0.0	0.0	0.0	20.2	21.5	44.6	57.1	17.1	449	76.2
Fairhope township (Somerset)................	124	115	-7.3	107	100.0	0.0	0.0	0.0	0.0	15.0	24.3	50.1	72.2	8.3	42	66.7
Fairless Hills CDP............	8,466	-	-	8,379	82.8	3.4	6.2	2.3	5.3	20.0	15.6	40.8	49.1	22.7	3,267	89.4
Fairmount township (Luzerne)................	1,273	1,253	-1.6	1,420	95.5	0.5	0.0	3.2	0.8	17.6	16.7	45.1	53.9	17.0	563	92.4
Fairview borough & MCD (Butler)................	196	184	-6.1	192	91.1	8.9	0.0	0.0	0.0	25.0	13.0	31.5	68.0	9.4	55	89.1
Fairview township (Butler)	2,082	2,011	-3.4	1,993	100.0	0.0	0.0	0.0	0.0	21.5	20.4	43.1	53.8	16.1	775	89.3
Fairview CDP..................	2,348	-	-	3,099	93.4	0.8	0.8	1.8	3.2	26.4	22.6	41.2	36.9	34.7	1,006	83.2
Fairview township (Erie)...	10,100	10,037	-0.6	10,106	95.2	0.5	0.4	2.3	1.5	24.8	23.0	45.4	29.0	47.5	3,663	91.3
Fairview township (Luzerne)..................	4,512	4,514	0.0	4,498	90.5	0.5	2.7	2.4	3.9	22.4	15.6	44.5	31.4	39.9	1,573	91.1
Fairview township (Mercer).................	1,087	1,053	-3.1	913	99.9	0.1	0.0	0.0	0.0	30.9	15.6	33.4	63.5	13.2	314	67.8
Fairview township (York)...	16,677	17,607	5.6	17,399	89.0	3.5	1.8	2.0	3.7	20.0	17.1	44.1	38.5	37.1	6,947	95.3
Fairview-Ferndale CDP	2,139	-	-	2,036	99.2	0.1	0.0	0.0	0.7	16.9	21.6	49.6	69.3	11.7	989	72.1
Fallowfield township (Washington)...........	4,333	4,150	-4.2	4,193	95.2	2.3	0.0	0.2	2.3	16.4	21.3	48.6	45.6	23.5	1,850	87.9
Falls township (Bucks)......	34,024	33,520	-1.5	33,542	78.5	9.2	4.0	1.7	6.6	22.7	13.6	39.0	47.8	23.7	12,599	92.0
Falls township (Wyoming).	1,977	1,869	-5.5	2,049	96.7	0.5	0.1	0.8	1.8	21.8	19.0	45.7	52.8	19.5	760	91.4
Falls Creek borough........	1,041	999	-4.0	951	95.7	0.2	0.0	0.0	4.1	20.4	19.3	44.3	60.4	9.5	423	87.2
Falls Creek borough (Clearfield)...............	52	49	-5.8	88	100.0	0.0	0.0	0.0	0.0	22.7	3.4	34.5	61.1	5.6	28	100.0
Falls Creek borough (Jefferson)...............	989	950	-3.9	863	95.2	0.2	0.0	0.0	4.5	20.2	21.0	44.9	60.3	9.8	395	86.3
Fallston borough & MCD (Beaver)................	261	244	-6.5	227	100.0	0.0	0.0	0.0	0.0	13.2	18.1	43.9	42.5	15.5	106	84.9
Falmouth CDP.................	420	-	-	478	100.0	0.0	0.0	0.0	0.0	26.2	16.5	47.1	62.9	25.1	182	84.6
Fannett township (Franklin)................	2,548	2,601	2.1	2,594	99.1	0.0	0.0	0.6	0.3	24.9	16.5	38.5	72.2	13.8	965	75.9

1 May be of any race.

Table A. All Places — Population and Housing

STATE City, town, township, borough, or CDP (county if applicable)	2010 census total population	2019 estimated population	Percent change 2010–2019	ACS total population estimate 2015–2019	White alone, not Hispanic or Latino	Black alone, not Hispanic or Latino	Asian alone, not Hispanic or Latino	All other races or 2 or more races, not Hispanic or Latino	Hispanic or Latino[1]	Under 18 years old	Age 65 years and older	Median age	Percent High school diploma or less	Percent Bachelor's degree or more	Total	Percent with a computer
	1	2	3	4	5	6	7	8	9	10	11	12	13	14	15	16
PENNSYLVANIA—Con.																
Farmersville CDP	991	-	-	935	98.7	1.3	0.0	0.0	0.0	18.2	49.1	63.3	77.9	15.0	360	51.9
Farmington township (Clarion)	1,929	1,808	-6.3	1,790	97.3	0.0	1.2	1.5	0.0	14.0	25.5	51.6	57.5	19.5	814	74.9
Farmington CDP..............	767	-	-	964	98.7	1.3	0.0	0.0	0.0	29.4	9.8	26.8	42.3	21.0	92	39.1
Farmington township (Tioga)	645	661	2.5	544	96.9	0.0	0.0	3.1	0.0	18.8	18.8	46.1	59.2	14.1	227	89.9
Farmington township (Warren)	1,266	1,199	-5.3	1,467	94.5	2.0	0.0	1.9	1.6	32.1	14.9	37.4	51.5	14.5	476	85.3
Farrell city & MCD (Mercer)	4,953	4,580	-7.5	4,682	42.8	45.2	0.0	4.6	7.4	25.7	20.3	43.5	61.2	10.8	2,207	83.4
Fawn township (Allegheny)	2,372	2,296	-3.2	2,329	98.7	0.0	0.0	0.3	1.1	16.0	22.2	50.7	54.4	19.9	1,013	88.2
Fawn township (York)........	3,097	3,147	1.6	3,143	95.5	0.4	1.0	1.9	1.2	21.5	16.2	44.3	55.3	17.0	1,173	87.9
Fawn Grove borough & MCD (York)	452	451	-0.2	480	96.9	0.4	0.6	1.3	0.8	21.0	25.0	43.2	56.3	16.4	206	90.8
Fawn Lake Forest CDP.....	755	-	-	555	87.0	0.0	0.0	0.0	13.0	20.2	40.4	54.7	21.2	53.1	251	96.4
Faxon CDP......................	1,395	-	-	1,255	86.9	5.9	0.0	0.0	7.3	17.8	15.9	44.6	24.1	45.4	545	89.0
Fayette township (Juniata)	3,470	3,593	3.5	3,520	97.0	2.4	0.0	0.0	0.5	34.1	14.7	34.6	63.9	20.8	1,142	75.2
Fayette City borough & MCD (Fayette)..............	585	552	-5.6	502	92.0	0.0	0.0	3.4	4.6	23.5	12.5	46.1	66.8	13.9	213	80.3
Fayetteville CDP..............	3,128	-	-	3,047	89.8	0.5	0.0	4.7	5.1	16.7	25.0	53.6	53.2	16.6	1,405	86.8
Feasterville CDP..............	3,074	-	-	2,571	87.5	0.4	6.2	3.8	2.1	23.2	15.6	39.5	33.9	40.5	1,019	92.8
Fell township (Lackawanna)	2,183	2,077	-4.9	1,841	95.9	0.0	0.4	0.4	3.2	23.2	23.4	44.1	52.6	17.1	809	76.9
Fellsburg CDP..................	1,180	-	-	1,255	100.0	0.0	0.0	0.0	0.0	19.8	18.2	46.6	27.3	33.5	512	84.4
Felton borough & MCD (York)...........................	508	512	0.8	567	95.9	0.0	0.0	2.8	1.2	30.3	9.5	32.3	53.9	15.6	202	89.6
Ferguson township (Centre)	17,867	19,462	8.9	19,390	73.4	4.4	15.4	3.2	3.7	18.5	15.3	35.4	20.0	67.1	7,797	94.5
Ferguson township (Clearfield)	520	521	0.2	546	96.2	0.0	0.0	1.3	2.6	23.8	16.5	37.0	62.6	9.1	192	72.9
Fermanagh township (Juniata)	2,813	2,813	0.0	2,802	98.6	0.0	0.0	0.0	1.4	8.7	36.8	58.2	47.5	25.0	1,162	72.5
Ferndale borough & MCD (Cambria)	1,650	1,495	-9.4	1,565	91.3	1.2	0.0	3.3	4.2	24.2	16.1	37.4	45.1	25.3	688	90.1
Fernville CDP..................	556	-	-	450	90.9	0.0	3.1	6.0	0.0	14.7	15.1	48.2	30.0	49.2	190	100.0
Findlay township (Allegheny)	5,059	6,023	19.1	5,750	96.1	0.1	1.5	1.4	0.9	21.2	13.9	41.0	34.2	40.4	2,396	94.6
Findley township (Mercer)	2,907	2,835	-2.5	2,836	70.8	21.2	0.1	4.7	3.2	5.8	7.2	41.5	68.1	7.8	381	89.0
Finleyville borough & MCD (Washington)	413	393	-4.8	282	98.9	1.1	0.0	0.0	0.0	21.6	15.6	40.2	40.1	26.6	145	84.1
Fishing Creek township (Columbia)	1,419	1,387	-2.3	1,394	94.9	0.0	0.0	4.9	0.2	14.3	25.5	52.8	51.6	23.7	586	92.5
Fivepointville CDP...........	1,156	-	-	1,453	90.3	0.0	0.0	0.0	9.7	22.3	15.4	34.7	68.7	6.2	394	90.9
Fleetwood borough & MCD (Berks)	4,094	4,104	0.2	4,095	90.2	0.6	0.7	0.8	7.7	23.0	17.2	41.0	49.0	18.1	1,625	92.9
Flemington borough & MCD (Clinton)	1,331	1,326	-0.4	1,362	95.4	1.6	1.8	0.8	0.3	18.6	18.9	41.8	53.9	22.6	580	82.4
Flora Dale CDP...............	38	-	-	46	100.0	0.0	0.0	0.0	0.0	58.7	0.0	5.6	52.6	0.0	10	100.0
Flourtown CDP.................	4,538	-	-	4,331	90.6	2.2	1.3	2.2	3.7	26.2	18.4	43.5	16.4	63.9	1,611	95.8
Flying Hills CDP...............	2,568	-	-	2,030	88.5	0.0	0.0	0.0	11.5	7.4	32.9	53.1	25.5	44.1	1,200	97.4
Folcroft borough & MCD (Delaware)..................	6,623	6,632	0.1	6,627	50.7	34.8	1.5	2.4	10.6	23.9	13.5	36.4	56.9	16.7	2,345	90.9
Folsom CDP....................	8,323	-	-	8,913	88.1	4.6	0.2	1.2	5.8	23.3	11.9	38.0	45.2	27.3	3,224	92.8
Foot of Ten CDP	672	-	-	695	100.0	0.0	0.0	0.0	0.0	26.2	23.0	40.9	62.1	12.4	285	80.7
Force CDP	253	-	-	166	100.0	0.0	0.0	0.0	0.0	24.7	21.7	43.3	87.8	0.0	71	94.4
Ford City borough & MCD (Armstrong)	2,989	2,764	-7.5	2,807	93.9	1.8	0.4	0.5	3.3	20.5	20.9	42.5	59.1	12.4	1,308	79.9
Ford Cliff borough & MCD (Armstrong)	371	350	-5.7	424	95.3	0.9	1.9	0.0	1.9	13.9	22.9	48.8	54.2	10.8	192	81.8
Forest City borough & MCD (Susquehanna)	1,890	1,741	-7.9	1,891	90.2	5.6	0.0	0.7	3.5	17.2	25.9	49.2	58.1	12.7	825	80.5
Forest Hills borough & MCD (Allegheny).........	6,540	6,298	-3.7	6,377	80.2	11.9	0.9	5.8	1.2	14.9	22.8	47.5	21.3	59.5	3,147	91.4
Forest Lake township (Susquehanna)	1,193	1,108	-7.1	1,046	93.7	0.0	0.0	0.6	5.7	17.5	21.0	52.3	57.6	16.4	477	90.4
Forestville CDP...............	435	-	-	466	100.0	0.0	0.0	0.0	0.0	19.1	22.5	33.8	67.4	15.0	188	85.6
Forks township (Northampton)..............	14,719	15,769	7.1	15,470	74.3	11.0	3.7	2.1	8.8	23.1	17.7	44.0	30.6	43.4	5,748	93.7
Forks township (Sullivan)..	377	357	-5.3	299	97.3	0.0	0.0	1.7	1.0	12.0	32.4	58.4	49.2	13.1	139	83.5
Forkston township (Wyoming)	396	369	-6.8	359	95.8	0.0	0.0	2.2	1.9	26.5	19.8	38.8	53.9	15.4	128	85.9
Forksville borough & MCD (Sullivan)	145	135	-6.9	148	100.0	0.0	0.0	0.0	0.0	12.8	20.3	30.5	60.0	13.7	70	88.6
Fort Indiantown Gap CDP	143	-	-	91	100.0	0.0	0.0	0.0	0.0	36.3	0.0	44.7	31.0	27.6	29	100.0
Fort Loudon CDP.............	886	-	-	822	96.5	0.0	0.0	3.5	0.0	19.8	22.6	53.4	69.3	9.2	282	83.3
Fort Washington CDP.......	5,446	-	-	5,728	89.3	1.7	5.0	1.7	2.3	23.0	17.2	41.3	18.2	63.9	2,070	98.4
Forty Fort borough & MCD (Luzerne).................	4,161	4,041	-2.9	4,069	92.1	0.3	0.0	0.3	7.3	17.3	18.5	43.0	36.5	28.7	1,764	90.8
Forward township (Allegheny)	3,375	3,272	-3.1	3,303	97.3	1.5	0.0	1.2	0.0	16.0	24.8	48.6	51.3	21.9	1,473	82.5
Forward township (Butler).	2,537	2,852	12.4	2,709	99.2	0.1	0.3	0.4	0.0	20.2	19.1	45.8	42.2	32.2	1,128	92.2
Foster township (Luzerne)	3,483	3,452	-0.9	3,445	88.7	0.1	0.0	0.6	10.5	16.4	23.6	50.4	62.0	14.3	1,397	86.2
Foster township (McKean)	4,314	4,036	-6.4	4,102	96.6	0.0	1.7	0.2	1.5	21.8	18.0	43.3	56.2	18.8	1,710	85.5
Foster township (Schuylkill)	248	239	-3.6	308	98.4	0.0	0.0	0.0	1.6	24.0	15.6	38.5	65.8	11.0	115	77.4
Foster Brook CDP............	1,251	-	-	1,086	98.1	0.0	0.0	0.0	1.9	22.1	17.1	46.0	52.7	21.0	484	76.4
Foundryville CDP.............	256	-	-	89	93.3	0.0	0.0	0.0	6.7	0.0	32.6	57.8	57.3	0.0	51	100.0
Fountain Hill borough & MCD (Lehigh).............	4,615	4,699	1.8	4,683	58.8	6.7	2.4	1.8	30.3	19.7	19.7	39.6	45.4	23.6	1,971	84.0
Fountain Springs CDP......	278	-	-	377	96.0	2.1	0.8	1.1	0.0	9.8	22.5	46.4	33.5	15.3	148	90.5
Fox township (Elk)	3,624	3,450	-4.8	3,488	97.7	2.3	0.0	0.0	0.0	18.1	22.2	51.0	50.9	19.0	1,584	91.7

1 May be of any race.

Table A. All Places — **Population and Housing**

STATE City, town, township, borough, or CDP (county if applicable)	Population				Race and Hispanic or Latino origin (percent)					Age (percent)			Educational attainment of persons age 25 and older		Occupied housing units	
	2010 census total population	2019 estimated population	Percent change 2010–2019	ACS total population estimate 2015–2019	White alone, not Hispanic or Latino	Black alone, not Hispanic or Latino	Asian alone, not Hispanic or Latino	All other races or 2 or more races, not Hispanic or Latino	Hispanic or Latino[1]	Under 18 years old	Age 65 years and older	Median age	Percent High school diploma or less	Percent Bachelor's degree or more	Total	Percent with a computer
	1	2	3	4	5	6	7	8	9	10	11	12	13	14	15	16
PENNSYLVANIA—Con.																
Fox township (Sullivan).....	358	335	-6.4	314	100.0	0.0	0.0	0.0	0.0	13.1	28.7	51.0	67.1	13.4	140	66.4
Foxburg borough & MCD (Clarion)	183	174	-4.9	152	98.0	0.0	0.0	0.0	2.0	7.9	46.7	63.5	47.0	29.1	82	78.0
Fox Chapel borough & MCD (Allegheny)..........	5,196	5,076	-2.3	5,121	88.1	0.0	5.7	3.0	3.1	28.5	19.5	49.1	6.6	83.6	1,797	98.5
Fox Chase CDP..............	1,622	-	-	1,612	62.0	15.9	3.3	0.0	18.8	18.1	26.8	52.6	46.7	22.9	681	86.5
Frackville borough & MCD (Schuylkill)	3,805	3,611	-5.1	3,649	95.1	0.1	0.9	1.6	2.2	23.2	18.8	43.8	65.6	11.3	1,463	83.3
Frailey township (Schuylkill)	429	406	-5.4	357	99.7	0.0	0.0	0.0	0.3	26.3	12.0	38.9	77.7	3.2	151	90.1
Franconia township (Montgomery)	13,079	13,369	2.2	13,291	90.7	1.2	6.3	1.1	0.6	19.3	23.9	47.5	36.6	38.1	4,902	91.7
Frankfort Springs borough & MCD (Beaver)...........	130	122	-6.2	178	91.6	1.1	0.0	7.3	0.0	24.2	16.9	37.0	45.6	9.6	57	87.7
Franklin township (Adams)	4,882	4,968	1.8	4,939	93.7	0.3	2.5	0.0	3.5	19.1	21.6	50.4	61.0	18.8	2,043	88.7
Franklin township (Beaver)	4,042	3,834	-5.1	3,889	99.5	0.1	0.0	0.1	0.4	19.5	21.8	46.1	48.6	27.1	1,637	86.4
Franklin township (Bradford)......................	723	694	-4.0	678	98.2	0.0	0.0	1.0	0.7	19.9	21.5	46.9	67.8	5.2	272	87.9
Franklin township (Butler) .	2,623	2,764	5.4	2,729	98.4	0.3	0.0	0.5	0.8	16.0	22.6	50.6	43.4	23.4	1,211	88.8
Franklin borough & MCD (Cambria)	323	293	-9.3	224	96.0	3.1	0.0	0.4	0.4	15.2	24.6	49.5	62.8	14.2	122	68.9
Franklin township (Carbon)	4,261	4,178	-1.9	4,157	93.5	0.0	0.7	4.2	1.6	15.4	24.2	50.2	62.3	16.9	1,815	86.1
Franklin township (Chester)	4,339	4,537	4.6	4,514	92.0	0.4	2.2	0.7	4.8	25.6	13.9	44.3	17.7	57.6	1,621	94.3
Franklin township (Columbia)	595	581	-2.4	588	97.3	0.0	0.0	2.0	0.7	20.7	23.8	50.0	53.2	29.8	235	78.3
Franklin township (Erie)....	1,633	1,614	-1.2	1,548	95.8	1.0	0.7	1.7	0.8	21.4	15.7	46.3	46.1	27.2	608	88.0
Franklin township (Fayette)..................	2,530	2,382	-5.8	2,404	97.9	0.2	1.6	0.3	0.0	20.8	18.7	44.9	63.4	20.8	960	80.9
Franklin township (Greene).................	7,252	6,892	-5.0	6,937	80.3	12.4	0.1	1.9	5.2	12.4	17.9	43.3	60.6	15.3	2,067	80.7
Franklin township (Huntingdon)	472	469	-0.6	431	87.7	0.7	0.0	0.7	10.9	24.1	18.3	37.1	40.7	41.4	159	84.3
Franklin township (Luzerne)......................	1,753	1,756	0.2	1,723	96.3	0.2	0.0	1.3	2.2	21.2	17.6	45.2	39.5	32.6	693	88.2
Franklin township (Lycoming)	932	923		887	98.1	0.0	0.6	0.0	1.4	19.6	21.0	45.9	66.8	16.9	339	86.1
Franklin township (Snyder)	2,273	2,248	-1.1	2,084	97.4	0.0	0.6	1.1	0.9	19.8	22.2	44.4	62.5	11.6	853	81.6
Franklin township (Susquehanna)	936	866	-7.5	953	99.2	0.0	0.0	0.1	0.7	19.1	19.8	45.9	59.5	17.6	391	89.3
Franklin city & MCD (Venango)...................	6,553	6,013	-8.2	6,148	94.1	1.8	0.7	2.8	0.7	19.2	20.1	44.7	57.3	26.0	2,805	83.4
Franklin township (York) ...	4,650	4,884	5.0	4,865	91.6	2.1	0.9	3.5	1.8	22.7	14.8	41.7	46.6	24.4	1,920	90.9
Franklin Park borough & MCD (Allegheny)...........	13,490	14,885	10.3	14,589	79.9	2.6	12.5	2.5	2.5	28.1	14.6	42.5	13.3	71.7	5,360	96.3
Franklintown borough & MCD (York)	486	508	4.5	388	88.4	3.6	0.0	2.3	5.7	20.1	6.2	33.6	30.7	32.5	182	97.8
Frankstown township (Blair)	7,388	7,349	-0.5	7,340	97.4	0.0	0.8	1.6	0.2	17.6	27.4	51.7	42.3	33.5	2,843	90.8
Frazer township (Allegheny)..................	1,155	1,120	-3.0	1,123	99.6	0.0	0.0	0.0	0.4	17.0	21.6	48.5	47.0	20.6	468	87.4
Fredericksburg CDP	733	-	-	1,086	98.9	0.0	0.0	1.1	0.0	32.2	11.4	35.8	55.7	37.1	390	91.8
Fredericksburg CDP	1,357	-	-	1,726	93.1	0.0	0.0	0.3	6.5	34.0	11.9	34.2	63.7	9.9	622	87.5
Fredericktown CDP..........	403	-	-	552	88.0	11.1	0.0	0.7	0.2	36.6	21.2	31.9	60.4	16.6	223	78.0
Fredonia borough & MCD (Mercer)...................	494	455	-7.9	437	95.0	0.0	0.0	3.2	1.8	19.0	18.5	49.2	70.5	8.5	212	80.7
Freeburg borough & MCD (Snyder)..................	575	566	-1.6	589	97.8	0.3	0.0	0.3	1.5	17.3	17.7	45.4	56.3	16.9	233	88.8
Freedom township (Adams)	831	844	1.6	905	96.0	1.0	0.7	0.9	1.4	17.3	25.7	52.6	35.0	39.4	366	90.7
Freedom borough & MCD (Beaver)	1,569	1,472	-6.2	1,532	90.4	3.1	0.5	3.9	2.1	25.3	13.6	36.2	48.5	19.4	620	84.5
Freedom township (Blair)..	3,453	3,331	-3.5	3,353	94.3	0.0	0.9	4.9	0.0	17.0	22.5	48.2	53.4	20.5	1,463	93.2
Freehold township (Warren)	1,511	1,424	-5.8	1,245	99.5	0.0	0.0	0.5	0.0	28.9	15.2	40.2	61.0	8.2	449	77.5
Freeland borough & MCD (Luzerne)................	3,521	3,424	-2.8	3,440	78.1	1.9	0.7	1.6	17.7	26.0	17.6	40.9	60.3	9.4	1,388	83.1
Freemansburg borough & MCD (Northampton)	2,642	2,629	-0.5	2,622	60.5	11.8	1.6	1.9	24.2	24.1	9.8	37.1	56.4	17.4	992	96.0
Freeport borough & MCD (Armstrong)...............	1,814	1,677	-7.6	1,791	96.7	1.1	0.0	2.2	0.0	21.5	15.5	40.7	50.3	12.8	865	85.1
Freeport township (Greene).....................	297	280	-5.7	225	96.0	0.0	0.0	0.0	4.0	12.4	25.3	49.2	75.8	6.7	104	78.8
French Creek township (Mercer)	769	724	-5.9	788	98.6	0.0	0.0	0.1	1.3	23.4	15.6	41.4	61.3	11.0	316	87.3
Frenchcreek township (Venango)..................	1,547	1,432	-7.4	1,450	96.5	0.1	0.3	2.3	0.9	18.3	22.3	48.9	54.4	22.5	622	85.4
Friedens CDP	1,523	-	-	1,445	98.8	1.2	0.0	0.0	0.0	23.1	13.3	40.6	58.8	12.8	532	80.3
Friedensburg CDP	858	-	-	816	100.0	0.0	0.0	0.0	0.0	22.7	27.5	51.2	43.5	22.0	350	96.6
Friendsville borough & MCD (Susquehanna)	111	107	-3.6	108	100.0	0.0	0.0	0.0	0.0	18.5	20.4	46.4	42.0	8.6	42	81.0
Frizzleburg CDP	602	-	-	415	90.6	0.0	3.6	5.8	0.0	17.8	25.5	50.4	57.4	13.8	219	85.4
Frystown CDP	380	-	-	330	83.6	0.0	0.0	9.4	7.0	11.5	24.2	36.4	82.3	0.0	171	67.8
Fullerton CDP	14,925	-	-	15,787	55.3	10.6	5.1	1.6	27.4	21.6	14.7	35.3	44.8	27.0	6,383	89.3
Fulton township (Lancaster)..................	3,078	3,175	3.2	3,170	91.6	0.8	0.0	0.3	7.4	34.0	16.5	35.6	66.9	15.6	927	72.3
Gaines township (Tioga)...	544	536	-1.5	448	98.7	0.0	0.0	0.0	1.3	14.7	29.7	54.3	63.0	9.0	209	74.2
Galeton borough & MCD (Potter)	1,146	1,077	-6.0	942	99.4	0.0	0.0	0.6	0.0	16.9	21.1	51.0	57.9	10.9	428	85.7
Gallagher township (Clinton)	382	381	-0.3	463	98.1	0.0	1.9	0.0	0.0	17.5	14.0	44.9	47.0	16.6	175	88.6

1 May be of any race.

Table A. All Places — **Population and Housing**

	Population				Race and Hispanic or Latino origin (percent)					Age (percent)			Educational attainment of persons age 25 and older		Occupied housing units	
STATE City, town, township, borough, or CDP (county if applicable)	2010 census total population	2019 estimated population	Percent change 2010–2019	ACS total population estimate 2015–2019	White alone, not Hispanic or Latino	Black alone, not Hispanic or Latino	Asian alone, not Hispanic or Latino	All other races or 2 or more races, not Hispanic or Latino	Hispanic or Latino[1]	Under 18 years old	Age 65 years and older	Median age	Percent High school diploma or less	Percent Bachelor's degree or more	Total	Percent with a computer
	1	2	3	4	5	6	7	8	9	10	11	12	13	14	15	16
PENNSYLVANIA—Con.																
Gallitzin borough & MCD (Cambria)	1,669	1,534	-8.1	1,592	97.0	0.0	0.0	0.4	2.5	23.2	17.9	40.3	57.7	15.1	684	85.2
Gallitzin township (Cambria)	1,321	1,237	-6.4	1,158	99.4	0.6	0.0	0.0	0.0	17.4	20.1	49.2	57.2	15.9	479	90.4
Gamble township (Lycoming)	756	750	-0.8	788	97.5	1.4	0.0	1.1	0.0	20.4	20.3	47.5	43.2	27.1	318	89.6
Gap CDP	1,931	-	-	2,581	84.0	4.6	0.4	6.1	4.8	31.7	10.8	33.4	50.9	21.4	764	88.9
Garden View CDP	2,503	-	-	2,779	92.6	7.4	0.0	0.0	0.0	20.3	17.1	41.2	47.3	26.1	1,216	86.3
Gardners CDP	150	-	-	139	42.4	0.0	0.0	0.0	57.6	0.0	16.5	34.7	96.4	3.6	46	91.3
Garrett borough & MCD (Somerset)	461	432	-6.3	400	97.5	0.0	0.0	2.5	0.0	21.0	19.0	45.0	80.2	6.7	162	77.2
Gaskill township (Jefferson)	705	676	-4.1	831	99.5	0.0	0.0	0.0	0.5	31.4	14.2	39.3	71.5	12.3	286	68.5
Gastonville CDP	2,818	-	-	2,459	96.9	0.0	0.0	2.1	1.0	12.7	25.3	52.3	50.8	27.1	1,136	83.8
Geistown borough & MCD (Cambria)	2,470	2,271	-8.1	2,390	93.2	0.7	2.4	0.7	3.0	19.2	25.3	48.8	42.4	26.6	1,067	87.1
Genesee township (Potter)	805	764	-5.1	897	96.4	0.0	0.0	0.0	3.6	25.9	23.3	43.6	61.5	13.1	346	87.0
Geneva CDP	109	-	-	120	95.0	0.0	5.0	0.0	0.0	26.7	19.2	51.1	69.0	10.7	43	79.1
Georges township (Fayette)	6,604	6,220	-5.8	6,318	94.3	1.0	0.0	1.9	2.8	21.5	21.3	44.5	58.9	17.3	2,614	88.3
Georgetown borough & MCD (Beaver)	172	162	-5.8	174	100.0	0.0	0.0	0.0	0.0	20.7	20.7	40.5	44.4	12.6	76	84.2
Georgetown CDP	1,022	-	-	1,182	94.9	0.0	4.0	0.0	1.1	33.1	21.8	33.5	80.0	10.7	352	56.8
Georgetown CDP	1,640	-	-	1,909	74.0	1.1	5.9	6.8	12.3	23.4	17.1	41.2	63.4	10.6	790	77.6
German township (Fayette)	5,082	4,779	-6.0	4,861	92.1	5.9	0.0	1.5	0.4	21.7	18.4	40.8	67.6	13.5	2,036	76.4
Germany township (Adams)	2,700	2,745	1.7	2,728	95.3	0.0	0.3	3.6	0.8	20.3	18.2	46.2	52.5	17.6	1,020	86.3
Gettysburg borough & MCD (Adams)	7,594	7,724	1.7	7,689	78.1	5.0	1.7	2.5	12.7	13.4	12.7	24.1	43.7	34.5	2,392	81.3
Gibraltar CDP	680	-	-	781	98.0	2.0	0.0	0.0	0.0	28.0	16.0	34.8	28.9	36.2	274	100.0
Gibson township (Cameron)	164	141	-14.0	137	98.5	0.0	0.0	1.5	0.0	4.4	46.7	62.5	55.7	12.2	77	89.6
Gibson township (Susquehanna)	1,224	1,171	-4.3	1,014	91.7	2.2	2.1	0.1	3.9	19.7	28.7	52.5	46.1	23.3	443	82.2
Gibsonia CDP	2,733	-	-	2,296	96.0	0.0	0.3	0.4	3.4	25.7	16.9	39.9	34.3	46.3	845	91.4
Gilberton borough & MCD (Schuylkill)	766	723	-5.6	652	98.5	0.0	0.0	0.8	0.8	20.1	20.6	47.2	66.9	11.8	277	79.4
Gilbertsville CDP	4,832	-	-	5,438	93.6	2.0	1.2	1.1	2.1	25.9	15.3	37.0	40.5	33.3	2,010	91.7
Gilmore township (Greene)	272	244	-10.3	252	98.8	0.0	0.0	1.2	0.0	21.0	24.6	45.5	62.4	15.2	111	77.5
Gilpin township (Armstrong)	2,575	2,397	-6.9	2,522	97.3	1.9	0.4	0.0	0.3	20.3	19.6	49.0	49.7	17.5	1,048	88.7
Girard township (Clearfield)	534	505	-5.4	526	100.0	0.0	0.0	0.0	0.0	16.5	16.3	45.8	77.3	3.2	208	79.8
Girard borough & MCD (Erie)	3,104	2,913	-6.2	2,975	84.7	2.7	0.0	0.7	11.9	23.0	18.7	40.1	58.2	18.6	1,152	88.7
Girard township (Erie)	5,102	4,854	-4.9	4,935	95.5	0.0	0.0	2.1	2.4	23.0	22.9	45.5	48.4	28.1	2,060	93.6
Girardville borough & MCD (Schuylkill)	1,519	1,440	-5.2	1,454	92.6	0.0	0.0	2.1	5.3	21.7	13.9	40.6	66.5	11.2	591	81.4
Glade township (Warren)	2,310	2,162	-6.4	2,159	97.6	0.0	0.7	1.4	0.3	14.7	27.3	51.1	49.1	29.1	966	89.8
Glasgow borough & MCD (Beaver)	60	58	-3.3	112	98.2	0.0	0.0	0.0	1.8	48.2	8.0	22.5	59.3	7.4	35	100.0
Glassport borough & MCD (Allegheny)	4,488	4,315	-3.9	4,371	86.9	3.7	0.4	3.0	5.9	18.5	19.0	45.0	56.7	12.5	2,033	88.0
Glenburn CDP	953	-	-	971	86.7	1.6	6.6	3.2	1.9	18.7	23.0	48.1	31.0	48.6	413	84.3
Glenburn township (Lackawanna)	1,249	1,209	-3.2	1,213	89.1	1.6	5.3	2.6	1.5	18.5	24.9	48.9	35.7	44.3	519	86.5
Glen Campbell borough & MCD (Indiana)	245	227	-7.3	219	100.0	0.0	0.0	0.0	0.0	23.7	22.4	44.5	67.3	13.8	91	70.3
Glendon borough & MCD (Northampton)	363	358	-1.4	466	72.1	6.9	0.0	18.7	2.4	29.0	14.2	33.0	61.6	22.3	145	84.1
Glenfield borough & MCD (Allegheny)	202	201	-0.5	208	93.3	0.0	0.0	5.8	1.0	24.0	13.9	40.5	37.2	28.2	78	91.0
Glen Hope borough & MCD (Clearfield)	142	136	-4.2	138	100.0	0.0	0.0	0.0	0.0	9.4	18.1	56.6	72.0	5.1	61	90.2
Glen Lyon CDP	1,873	-	-	1,698	87.7	7.0	0.3	0.4	4.6	16.9	13.0	40.9	56.2	9.7	722	75.9
Glenolden borough & MCD (Delaware)	7,151	7,164	0.2	7,161	84.7	8.9	1.0	2.7	2.8	19.9	15.2	41.2	53.6	21.8	2,912	90.6
Glen Osborne borough & MCD (Allegheny)	544	538	-1.1	547	83.9	4.9	0.0	5.9	5.3	22.3	21.6	45.6	9.5	76.0	200	94.0
Glen Rock borough & MCD (York)	2,046	2,065	0.9	2,070	92.9	1.2	0.4	1.8	3.8	32.5	12.0	33.1	42.4	27.3	762	94.6
Glenshaw CDP	8,981	-	-	8,669	96.5	0.2	0.8	2.5	0.1	17.8	24.4	47.8	28.0	46.2	3,781	93.4
Glenside CDP	8,384	-	-	7,819	87.2	4.4	1.0	2.4	4.9	22.2	13.2	36.5	24.9	50.4	2,881	93.8
Gold Key Lake CDP	1,830	-	-	1,498	92.1	0.0	0.0	2.1	5.7	22.6	13.2	38.4	38.9	24.4	580	95.0
Goldsboro borough & MCD (York)	948	941	-0.7	1,075	89.8	0.7	0.9	6.0	2.6	30.4	11.4	32.6	52.7	16.8	344	91.6
Goodville CDP	482	-	-	580	92.1	0.0	7.9	0.0	0.0	42.2	4.5	26.2	51.8	14.7	165	89.7
Gordon borough & MCD (Schuylkill)	763	724	-5.1	821	99.4	0.0	0.0	0.0	0.6	32.2	18.3	38.5	59.9	18.4	304	83.6
Gordonville CDP	508	-	-	688	100.0	0.0	0.0	0.0	0.0	41.9	17.9	28.9	83.8	6.2	215	52.1
Goshen township (Clearfield)	435	420	-3.4	463	92.2	1.7	0.0	0.0	6.0	21.2	16.0	40.8	63.9	12.7	193	88.6
Gouglersville CDP	548	-	-	445	96.2	3.8	0.0	0.0	0.0	13.0	27.2	52.3	59.1	27.5	191	89.0
Gouldsboro CDP	890	-	-	849	99.1	0.0	0.0	0.0	0.9	13.9	12.1	48.2	45.4	16.6	301	98.3
Graceton CDP	257	-	-	98	100.0	0.0	0.0	0.0	0.0	0.0	29.6	61.8	76.4	15.7	61	75.4
Graham township (Clearfield)	1,383	1,348	-2.5	1,435	98.0	0.0	0.0	0.0	2.0	21.1	28.4	50.8	66.2	12.3	561	79.7
Grampian borough & MCD (Clearfield)	342	325	-5.0	406	91.6	0.0	2.0	0.7	5.7	22.9	16.7	40.1	64.6	10.7	137	78.1

1 May be of any race.

Table A. All Places — **Population and Housing**

STATE City, town, township, borough, or CDP (county if applicable)	Population 2010 census total population	2019 estimated population	Percent change 2010–2019	ACS total population estimate 2015–2019	Race and Hispanic or Latino origin (percent) White alone, not Hispanic or Latino	Black alone, not Hispanic or Latino	Asian alone, not Hispanic or Latino	All other races or 2 or more races, not Hispanic or Latino	Hispanic or Latino[1]	Age (percent) Under 18 years old	Age 65 years and older	Median age	Educational attainment of persons age 25 and older Percent High school diploma or less	Percent Bachelor's degree or more	Occupied housing units Total	Percent with a computer
	1	2	3	4	5	6	7	8	9	10	11	12	13	14	15	16
PENNSYLVANIA—Con.																
Grant township (Indiana)..	741	693	-6.5	634	97.5	0.0	0.5	1.7	0.3	15.9	21.9	49.8	55.4	21.5	292	77.4
Grantley CDP	3,628	-	-	3,864	87.6	3.7	1.9	1.2	5.6	12.8	11.4	21.4	31.0	45.4	810	94.4
Granville township (Bradford).....................	948	917	-3.3	883	98.1	0.3	0.0	0.7	0.9	19.9	21.2	46.4	58.4	16.6	361	78.7
Granville CDP	440	-	-	263	100.0	0.0	0.0	0.0	0.0	17.1	35.4	61.1	100.0	0.0	114	86.8
Granville township (Mifflin)	5,103	4,986	-2.3	5,016	93.1	0.1	0.7	0.9	5.2	18.1	22.3	49.1	66.9	13.9	2,086	84.1
Grapeville CDP	538	-	-	487	100.0	0.0	0.0	0.0	0.0	9.4	16.0	49.5	60.9	4.3	239	84.1
Grassflat CDP	511	-	-	800	100.0	0.0	0.0	0.0	0.0	28.5	6.6	31.7	70.7	6.8	236	90.3
Gratz borough & MCD (Dauphin)	761	756	-0.7	745	90.3	2.1	2.0	0.3	5.2	20.7	16.6	40.3	75.1	10.0	280	74.6
Gray township (Greene) ...	219	204	-6.8	156	100.0	0.0	0.0	0.0	0.0	21.2	16.7	45.7	78.5	4.7	56	87.5
Grazierville CDP	665	-	-	795	98.4	0.0	0.0	1.6	0.0	36.2	5.2	34.3	76.8	5.3	277	91.7
Great Bend borough & MCD (Susquehanna)	734	670	-8.7	973	93.6	1.1	3.9	0.0	1.3	23.4	17.5	43.0	61.0	11.7	396	85.4
Great Bend township (Susquehanna)	1,953	1,801	-7.8	1,628	99.1	0.0	0.2	0.3	0.4	17.3	27.6	53.8	55.8	17.0	725	88.1
Green township (Forest)..	526	465	-11.6	353	98.6	0.0	0.3	0.0	1.1	17.0	40.5	59.8	67.1	8.0	181	79.6
Green township (Indiana).	3,837	3,566	-7.1	3,619	95.4	0.0	0.2	4.4	0.0	21.5	20.0	44.4	67.4	14.0	1,466	76.2
Greencastle borough & MCD (Franklin)...............	3,985	3,986	0.0	4,013	88.7	5.1	0.9	4.7	0.6	22.0	19.7	39.0	44.7	29.2	1,630	89.1
Greene township (Beaver)	2,354	2,353	0.0	2,176	93.9	0.0	4.9	0.2	1.0	20.6	15.7	43.5	42.0	23.3	820	88.7
Greene township (Clinton)	1,686	1,768	4.9	1,897	96.9	0.0	2.0	0.0	1.1	33.8	12.8	28.1	63.0	22.4	591	69.4
Greene township (Erie).....	4,697	4,491	-4.4	4,555	95.9	0.0	0.7	1.8	1.6	21.3	19.8	46.4	52.4	25.0	1,783	90.8
Greene township (Franklin)....................	16,743	17,898	6.9	17,667	87.0	2.2	0.9	2.8	7.0	23.3	20.9	40.6	49.1	26.3	6,960	89.0
Greene township (Greene)	446	408	-8.5	475	96.8	0.0	0.0	2.9	0.2	23.2	17.5	46.1	47.8	26.4	185	92.4
Greene township (Mercer)	1,091	1,039	-4.8	1,284	99.2	0.1	0.0	0.5	0.2	31.0	18.8	39.3	51.5	18.6	462	86.8
Greene township (Pike)	3,960	3,846	-2.9	3,825	91.4	1.3	0.0	1.0	6.3	18.2	21.0	49.3	51.2	19.3	1,711	90.6
Greenfield township (Blair)	4,166	3,965	-4.8	4,009	97.5	0.2	0.0	1.2	1.1	23.2	15.0	40.5	61.4	10.1	1,592	85.8
Greenfield township (Erie)	1,935	1,882	-2.7	2,022	97.7	0.8	0.0	1.4	0.1	20.2	13.6	47.3	63.7	16.9	731	89.7
Greenfield township (Lackawanna)...............	2,108	2,018	-4.3	2,330	98.2	0.5	0.4	0.0	0.9	19.8	17.3	47.8	43.8	35.5	966	89.0
Greenfields CDP..............	1,170	-	-	1,056	50.4	2.1	2.8	0.0	44.7	20.6	18.6	42.8	62.5	29.9	432	88.4
Green Hills borough & MCD (Washington)........	29	28	-3.4	44	100.0	0.0	0.0	0.0	0.0	6.8	15.9	52.0	9.7	74.2	15	100.0
Green Lane borough & MCD (Montgomery)	508	506	-0.4	410	98.5	0.0	0.0	0.0	1.5	13.2	25.9	51.3	58.2	20.3	191	94.2
Greenock CDP	2,195	-	-	2,087	95.7	0.0	0.0	1.1	3.3	17.5	16.4	43.4	38.6	22.6	900	86.7
Greensboro borough & MCD (Greene)	258	241	-6.6	291	95.9	0.0	0.0	0.7	3.4	23.0	10.7	38.1	61.7	19.1	108	84.3
Greensburg city & MCD (Westmoreland)	14,897	14,113	-5.3	14,290	88.8	4.4	1.0	4.1	1.6	17.7	20.0	38.8	36.9	34.0	6,702	82.2
Greens Landing CDP	894	-	-	929	90.1	0.0	0.0	9.9	0.0	35.2	6.8	36.6	57.3	30.7	387	88.1
Green Tree borough & MCD (Allegheny)...........	4,433	4,832	9.0	4,885	87.3	2.0	8.3	0.9	1.5	17.7	20.2	42.8	22.8	51.9	2,130	95.0
Greenville borough & MCD (Mercer)	5,956	5,272	-11.5	5,459	95.4	0.8	1.0	1.7	1.2	20.3	12.3	28.7	50.1	16.3	1,980	89.0
Greenville township (Somerset)	668	632	-5.4	732	99.6	0.0	0.0	0.4	0.0	33.9	13.7	36.3	61.4	17.0	239	72.4
Greenwich township (Berks)	3,645	3,677	0.9	3,662	95.1	0.0	0.0	1.9	2.9	18.0	15.6	48.6	46.8	30.7	1,425	91.3
Greenwood CDP	2,458	-	-	2,780	97.8	1.1	1.1	0.0	0.0	19.4	14.7	43.7	55.1	20.8	1,192	90.5
Greenwood township (Clearfield)	372	358	-3.8	362	97.2	0.0	0.0	0.0	2.8	19.9	24.3	51.3	70.8	10.3	155	77.4
Greenwood township (Columbia)	1,952	1,869	-4.3	2,049	97.5	0.0	0.2	1.8	0.5	25.3	16.3	43.1	58.2	17.5	795	84.9
Greenwood township (Crawford)	1,457	1,413	-3.0	1,359	96.6	0.0	0.8	2.6	0.0	23.0	19.1	45.5	73.5	7.3	532	86.8
Greenwood township (Juniata)	616	636	3.2	517	99.4	0.0	0.0	0.6	0.0	19.1	23.8	51.3	70.3	11.8	207	84.5
Greenwood township (Perry)	993	1,006	1.3	1,098	97.4	0.0	0.0	0.8	1.8	17.4	19.9	46.8	54.8	24.1	417	87.8
Gregg township (Centre)..	2,395	2,412	0.7	2,346	93.7	0.9	0.0	2.6	2.7	22.9	16.1	44.3	54.7	27.6	856	80.4
Gregg township (Union)....	4,984	4,496	-9.8	4,607	44.0	32.9	1.0	5.4	16.7	3.6	6.2	41.6	62.1	6.5	341	83.6
Grier City CDP................	241	-	-	296	100.0	0.0	0.0	0.0	0.0	0.0	56.8	70.1	29.0	21.0	141	100.0
Grill CDP.......................	1,468	-	-	1,978	81.1	2.1	6.0	0.0	10.8	19.7	16.1	42.2	49.0	33.9	656	95.3
Grindstone CDP	498	-	-	599	94.3	2.2	0.0	0.0	3.5	27.9	12.5	33.9	66.2	3.1	261	75.9
Grove township (Cameron)..................	183	159	-13.1	141	98.6	0.0	0.0	1.4	0.0	7.8	30.5	57.3	55.5	17.6	75	89.3
Grove City borough & MCD (Mercer)	8,329	7,762	-6.8	7,945	93.1	1.5	1.1	2.5	1.8	15.3	14.1	25.2	42.2	39.9	2,486	88.3
Grugan township (Clinton)	51	51	0.0	27	100.0	0.0	0.0	0.0	0.0	7.4	48.1	62.5	64.0	12.0	17	52.9
Guilford CDP	2,138	-	-	2,624	89.0	4.9	1.1	1.0	4.0	16.7	18.9	44.2	23.4	51.2	1,083	97.7
Guilford township (Franklin)....................	14,560	14,866	2.1	14,808	89.1	4.2	1.6	2.2	2.8	17.3	26.9	50.3	42.2	31.5	6,086	86.9
Gulich township (Clearfield)	1,231	1,199	-2.6	1,173	96.2	1.9	0.0	1.0	0.9	21.4	20.6	44.7	65.2	15.9	459	79.7
Guys Mills CDP	124	-	-	118	93.2	6.8	0.0	0.0	0.0	20.3	14.4	24.1	66.0	5.7	26	76.9
Haines township (Centre).	1,557	1,576	1.2	1,796	94.8	0.0	0.7	1.3	3.2	32.5	13.5	34.5	63.7	16.7	564	63.3
Halfmoon township (Centre).....................	2,664	2,833	6.3	2,782	95.9	0.0	1.8	1.8	0.5	25.3	14.2	42.2	26.2	53.6	945	99.4
Halfway House CDP.........	2,881	-	-	2,881	77.8	5.7	6.1	5.6	4.8	24.1	10.9	36.5	38.2	37.1	1,012	94.7
Halifax borough & MCD (Dauphin)	895	887	-0.9	989	93.8	2.1	2.5	1.0	0.5	26.9	13.5	33.8	65.7	8.5	398	85.4
Halifax township (Dauphin)	3,434	3,494	1.7	3,500	94.3	0.0	2.6	0.8	2.3	25.0	19.9	42.3	56.3	19.0	1,385	81.4
Hallam borough & MCD (York)	2,664	2,645	-0.7	2,649	82.2	3.2	0.0	0.9	13.7	24.0	12.4	36.5	45.4	20.7	1,124	98.8
Hallstead borough & MCD (Susquehanna)	1,307	1,203	-8.0	1,233	99.9	0.0	0.0	0.1	0.0	19.1	17.1	46.5	60.2	15.3	575	84.7
Hamburg borough & MCD (Berks)	4,230	4,355	3.0	4,356	92.8	0.2	0.4	2.3	4.2	18.8	19.6	40.8	55.5	19.6	1,852	81.8

1 May be of any race.

Table A. All Places — **Population and Housing**

	Population				Race and Hispanic or Latino origin (percent)					Age (percent)			Educational attainment of persons age 25 and older		Occupied housing units	
STATE City, town, township, borough, or CDP (county if applicable)	2010 census total population	2019 estimated population	Percent change 2010–2019	ACS total population estimate 2015–2019	White alone, not Hispanic or Latino	Black alone, not Hispanic or Latino	Asian alone, not Hispanic or Latino	All other races or 2 or more races, not Hispanic or Latino	Hispanic or Latino[1]	Under 18 years old	Age 65 years and older	Median age	Percent High school diploma or less	Percent Bachelor's degree or more	Total	Percent with a computer
	1	2	3	4	5	6	7	8	9	10	11	12	13	14	15	16

PENNSYLVANIA—Con.

STATE	1	2	3	4	5	6	7	8	9	10	11	12	13	14	15	16
Hamilton township (Adams)	2,525	2,568	1.7	2,553	95.5	0.7	0.0	0.3	3.5	23.0	21.0	44.9	54.0	19.5	918	94.4
Hamilton township (Franklin)	10,777	11,125	3.2	11,097	86.7	2.9	1.7	1.8	6.8	25.2	15.6	39.7	55.5	23.7	4,143	89.3
Hamilton township (McKean)	543	502	-7.6	517	98.3	0.0	0.0	1.4	0.4	13.9	25.0	49.3	58.3	12.4	239	83.7
Hamilton township (Monroe)	9,052	8,966		8,866	82.3	7.3	1.7	3.3	5.3	15.9	21.5	49.5	47.3	26.3	3,084	90.7
Hamilton township (Tioga)	491	485	-1.2	462	96.1	0.2	0.0	1.7	1.9	22.9	9.7	34.7	58.3	17.2	176	88.6
Hamiltonban township (Adams)	2,367	2,407	1.7	1,969	90.9	1.0	0.6	2.8	4.7	17.7	21.3	48.1	50.1	21.2	750	84.0
Hamlin township (McKean)	734	682	-7.1	544	99.8	0.2	0.0	0.0	0.0	17.1	31.6	52.0	54.8	24.1	260	76.5
Hampden township (Cumberland)	27,703	30,692	10.8	29,966	80.3	1.5	12.4	2.8	3.0	24.1	18.4	41.9	25.1	53.2	12,039	94.0
Hampton CDP	632	-	-	692	71.5	0.0	0.0	3.3	25.1	39.7	5.2	39.3	71.2	3.3	207	100.0
Hampton township (Allegheny)	18,349	18,181	-0.9	18,282	92.1	2.0	3.7	1.1	1.2	23.1	21.1	45.2	23.2	54.4	7,271	95.0
Hannasville CDP	176	-	-	161	100.0	0.0	0.0	0.0	0.0	28.0	7.5	33.8	73.9	20.5	48	93.8
Hanover township (Beaver)	3,744	3,604	-3.7	3,634	97.7	0.1	0.0	2.0	0.2	21.9	15.7	40.5	43.7	23.2	1,345	91.8
Hanover township (Lehigh)	1,568	1,603	2.2	1,679	61.0	11.4	1.1	3.0	23.5	20.1	14.7	34.8	45.3	19.9	707	90.4
Hanover township (Luzerne)	11,052	10,824	-2.1	10,866	87.6	1.3	2.6	1.7	6.8	20.1	20.8	42.2	49.2	19.3	4,840	83.0
Hanover township (Northampton)	10,883	11,538	6.0	11,499	82.1	4.1	6.3	2.5	5.0	19.9	27.1	49.1	27.4	47.6	4,603	91.4
Hanover township (Washington)	2,673	2,600	-2.7	2,619	97.7	0.7	0.3	0.1	1.1	14.8	22.9	53.0	57.3	19.9	1,126	86.4
Hanover borough & MCD (York)	15,280	15,719	2.9	15,609	87.3	1.4	1.1	1.8	8.4	21.6	20.3	40.1	55.1	19.5	6,858	85.8
Harborcreek township (Erie)	17,235	17,091	-0.8	17,340	94.6	1.0	1.9	1.5	1.1	18.6	20.9	42.2	42.2	28.1	6,359	90.1
Harford township (Susquehanna)	1,427	1,336	-6.4	1,377	98.8	0.6	0.4	0.0	0.2	22.4	21.5	47.1	56.6	23.3	562	87.0
Harleigh CDP	1,104	-	-	1,444	81.4	0.0	0.0	0.0	18.6	18.0	22.4	57.7	70.4	11.7	536	90.7
Harleysville CDP	9,286	-	-	9,568	85.9	2.3	6.3	1.3	4.3	20.3	22.1	45.5	32.9	42.4	3,864	87.1
Harmar township (Allegheny)	2,923	2,997	2.5	3,032	94.9	1.2	0.3	0.3	3.4	11.9	37.4	58.0	34.8	33.4	1,506	82.3
Harmonsburg CDP	401	-	-	410	97.3	0.0	0.0	0.0	2.7	39.5	8.0	37.4	46.9	43.7	154	96.1
Harmony township (Beaver)	3,197	2,996	-6.3	3,049	94.4	0.7	2.7	0.6	1.7	18.1	21.2	47.1	47.9	24.7	1,340	85.1
Harmony borough & MCD (Butler)	891	840	-5.7	1,100	92.5	0.5	0.2	4.4	2.4	24.7	23.3	45.0	45.4	30.1	431	93.0
Harmony township (Forest)	666	586	-12.0	492	95.1	0.0	0.0	0.6	4.3	17.7	33.5	59.3	68.8	13.5	246	89.8
Harmony township (Susquehanna)	519	478	-7.9	526	97.7	0.4	0.0	0.4	1.5	21.7	16.5	44.6	57.9	16.5	214	93.0
Harris township (Centre)	4,901	6,040	23.2	5,770	92.0	0.8	1.4	3.6	2.1	18.2	21.6	47.0	17.4	69.0	2,350	95.9
Harrisburg city & MCD (Dauphin)	49,529	49,271	-0.5	49,209	24.1	46.7	4.6	2.8	21.8	26.7	10.4	31.0	52.4	22.1	20,543	87.3
Harrison township (Allegheny)	10,459	10,236	-2.1	10,341	89.3	3.0	1.7	4.7	1.2	19.7	20.4	45.6	47.8	21.1	4,492	82.0
Harrison township (Bedford)	974	915	-6.1	959	97.0	0.0	0.0	1.0	2.0	23.0	17.2	44.5	58.5	18.1	370	83.0
Harrison township (Potter)	1,037	975	-6.0	758	94.7	0.3	0.0	3.4	1.6	16.1	28.4	54.2	72.4	8.0	332	81.3
Harrison City CDP	134	-	-	38	100.0	0.0	0.0	0.0	0.0	0.0	100.0	71.5	34.2	0.0	38	65.8
Harrisville borough & MCD (Butler)	899	858	-4.6	932	96.6	0.0	0.0	3.0	0.4	23.4	25.3	44.8	54.7	25.7	338	92.3
Hartleton borough & MCD (Union)	284	278	-2.1	277	98.2	0.0	1.8	0.0	0.0	21.3	18.4	45.4	72.2	10.8	91	81.3
Hartley township (Union)	1,818	1,817	-0.1	1,918	95.5	0.0	0.6	0.0	3.9	27.2	19.9	40.9	68.5	9.8	636	77.7
Hartstown CDP	201	-	-	216	97.2	0.0	0.0	0.0	2.8	31.9	13.0	35.8	71.5	2.2	76	82.9
Harveys Lake borough & MCD (Luzerne)	2,780	2,774	-0.2	2,762	97.8	0.5	1.6	0.0	0.2	15.7	23.8	48.6	35.3	30.7	1,271	86.2
Harwick CDP	899	-	-	864	97.7	0.0	0.0	0.0	2.3	9.1	30.2	56.5	41.0	16.1	515	83.3
Hasson Heights CDP	1,351	-	-	1,533	97.8	0.0	0.0	1.4	0.8	23.1	22.5	47.4	41.1	27.4	629	87.6
Hastings borough & MCD (Cambria)	1,265	1,154	-8.8	1,135	98.7	0.0	0.0	0.8	0.5	23.3	17.9	39.4	54.9	19.3	481	83.2
Hatboro borough & MCD (Montgomery)	7,365	7,501	1.8	7,449	83.0	6.6	0.9	1.8	7.8	22.1	14.9	38.5	38.5	32.0	2,955	93.8
Hatfield borough & MCD (Montgomery)	3,297	3,327	0.9	3,333	54.6	12.5	25.8	1.2	6.0	20.7	14.7	36.3	39.6	32.7	1,279	90.5
Hatfield township (Montgomery)	17,249	17,850	3.5	17,646	70.9	4.9	14.8	3.1	6.3	19.3	18.1	41.1	35.7	40.4	6,850	93.2
Haverford township (Delaware)	48,509	49,526	2.1	49,283	87.9	3.0	3.8	2.7	2.6	23.1	17.3	40.8	21.3	58.6	17,458	93.7
Haverford College CDP	1,331	-	-	1,239	70.3	9.1	5.3	9.0	6.2	1.2	3.5	20.1	0.0	92.0	50	100.0
Hawk Run CDP	534	-	-	532	100.0	0.0	0.0	0.0	0.0	22.7	14.3	34.1	69.9	20.3	191	86.4
Hawley borough & MCD (Wayne)	1,203	1,153	-4.2	1,195	83.3	1.8	0.6	1.2	13.1	13.4	19.9	45.4	49.8	20.1	523	79.2
Hawthorn borough & MCD (Clarion)	494	458	-7.3	419	99.0	1.0	0.0	0.0	0.0	22.0	23.2	47.1	71.4	9.4	173	81.5
Haycock township (Bucks)	2,219	2,210	-0.4	2,100	98.3	0.0	0.7	0.0	1.0	14.8	23.7	52.5	37.8	34.0	880	92.6
Hayfield township (Crawford)	2,940	2,831	-3.7	2,852	94.8	0.0	0.5	2.9	1.7	19.0	19.9	47.4	53.2	24.9	1,223	92.2
Haysville borough & MCD (Allegheny)	77	74	-3.9	128	79.7	0.0	3.9	2.3	14.1	24.2	16.4	38.0	25.3	44.2	49	100.0
Hazle township (Luzerne)	9,560	9,556	0.0	9,550	81.1	1.0	0.2	0.2	17.4	15.8	28.2	52.4	61.6	14.3	4,226	79.3
Hazleton city & MCD (Luzerne)	25,425	24,794	-2.5	24,857	38.0	2.6	0.4	0.6	58.4	25.9	14.2	35.8	65.8	12.5	9,200	82.6

1 May be of any race.

Table A. All Places — **Population and Housing**

STATE City, town, township, borough, or CDP (county if applicable)	Population				Race and Hispanic or Latino origin (percent)					Age (percent)			Educational attainment of persons age 25 and older		Occupied housing units	
	2010 census total population	2019 estimated population	Percent change 2010–2019	ACS total population estimate 2015–2019	White alone, not Hispanic or Latino	Black alone, not Hispanic or Latino	Asian alone, not Hispanic or Latino	All other races or 2 or more races, not Hispanic or Latino	Hispanic or Latino[1]	Under 18 years old	Age 65 years and older	Median age	Percent High school diploma or less	Percent Bachelor's degree or more	Total	Percent with a computer
	1	2	3	4	5	6	7	8	9	10	11	12	13	14	15	16
PENNSYLVANIA—Con.																
Heath township (Jefferson)..................	124	118	-4.8	101	97.0	0.0	0.0	3.0	0.0	5.9	30.7	57.5	53.3	15.6	53	79.2
Hebron CDP......................	1,305	-	-	1,085	86.7	3.0	0.0	0.0	10.2	16.8	40.7	56.0	81.2	3.2	218	92.7
Hebron township (Potter)..	589	562	-4.6	707	95.9	0.0	1.1	1.8	1.1	20.7	26.2	50.2	58.7	18.6	266	86.1
Heckscherville CDP........	220	-	-	188	94.7	0.0	0.0	0.0	5.3	20.2	17.6	46.1	64.6	6.9	88	85.2
Hector township (Potter)...	386	368	-4.7	391	97.4	0.0	0.0	1.8	0.8	17.9	34.5	55.3	67.1	13.0	155	69.7
Hegins CDP	812	-	-	916	100.0	0.0	0.0	0.0	0.0	27.3	16.6	36.3	61.0	13.1	368	80.7
Hegins township (Schuylkill).................	3,516	3,363	-4.4	3,404	98.2	0.0	0.0	1.4	0.3	22.9	17.0	39.1	54.3	17.6	1,393	81.5
Heidelberg borough & MCD (Allegheny)...........	1,244	1,207	-3.0	1,271	92.8	0.9	3.6	1.7	0.9	15.9	17.9	41.3	41.5	25.7	638	85.3
Heidelberg township (Berks)	1,729	1,752	1.3	1,725	89.6	2.6	1.4	0.6	5.7	26.1	16.3	44.4	54.0	26.4	621	83.7
Heidelberg township (Lebanon).....................	4,034	4,341	7.6	4,239	97.5	0.2	0.0	0.0	2.3	23.1	19.3	40.1	63.9	15.7	1,544	82.8
Heidelberg township (Lehigh)	3,416	3,552	4.0	3,510	93.2	1.8	0.0	1.1	3.8	20.0	17.7	47.8	42.3	29.3	1,336	88.4
Heidelberg township (York)........................	3,062	3,045	-0.6	3,039	96.6	0.2	0.5	0.7	2.0	19.9	18.2	46.8	53.8	22.8	1,125	91.5
Heidlersburg CDP............	707	-	-	845	74.1	0.0	0.0	1.2	24.7	31.8	17.9	35.6	56.8	10.3	302	82.8
Heilwood CDP	711	-	-	593	99.8	0.2	0.0	0.0	0.0	16.5	15.5	49.4	68.3	12.7	257	75.9
Hellam township (York).....	6,030	5,987	-0.7	5,973	96.9	0.0	0.6	0.0	2.5	16.4	25.7	52.4	48.0	24.6	2,566	90.7
Hellertown borough & MCD (Northampton)	5,890	5,831		5,831	86.0	1.6	3.8	1.0	7.5	21.5	18.8	41.8	41.7	28.1	2,362	86.9
Hemlock township (Columbia)	2,249	2,260	0.5	2,034	96.8	0.0	1.0	1.6	0.6	22.2	16.6	44.1	40.1	39.4	780	95.0
Hemlock Farms CDP........	3,271	-	-	3,326	78.6	4.9	1.6	3.3	11.6	18.7	30.4	53.5	31.7	33.2	1,449	90.9
Hempfield township (Mercer)	3,759	3,558	-5.3	3,633	97.1	0.9	0.2	0.0	1.9	16.0	29.3	54.3	49.4	31.1	1,574	84.3
Hempfield township (Westmoreland)	43,249	40,463	-6.4	40,916	96.4	1.1	0.9	1.2	0.4	15.7	25.8	49.5	41.4	33.1	17,597	85.7
Henderson township (Huntingdon)	928	895	-3.6	952	98.8	0.4	0.0	0.5	0.2	20.7	26.2	49.8	64.4	15.0	381	89.5
Henderson township (Jefferson).....................	1,823	1,762	-3.3	1,798	97.6	0.1	0.7	0.0	1.7	30.0	15.0	31.3	77.0	6.8	588	55.4
Hendersonville CDP	325	-	-	195	95.4	4.6	0.0	0.0	0.0	15.4	29.2	50.9	59.4	20.6	89	91.0
Henry Clay township (Fayette)	2,060	1,941	-5.8	1,652	95.8	1.3	0.0	0.3	2.7	14.7	25.6	49.3	65.4	13.8	704	72.7
Hepburn township (Lycoming)	2,762	2,682	-2.9	2,695	96.9	0.3	0.4	0.6	1.9	17.7	22.7	48.8	45.9	24.9	1,125	84.4
Hereford CDP	930	-	-	963	91.4	0.0	3.2	0.0	5.4	15.4	21.0	46.8	62.5	10.8	424	80.4
Hereford township (Berks)	2,952	3,037	2.9	2,984	94.7	0.3	3.0	0.2	1.7	16.9	23.1	47.7	49.3	25.8	1,250	86.4
Herminie CDP	789	-	-	254	100.0	0.0	0.0	0.0	0.0	20.1	30.7	46.7	59.1	12.8	122	89.3
Hermitage city & MCD (Mercer)	16,419	15,471	-5.8	15,693	90.8	4.8	2.1	1.3	1.0	17.8	26.8	49.1	43.8	31.3	7,219	88.8
Herndon borough & MCD (Northumberland).........	319	300	-6.0	364	92.0	0.0	0.0	5.2	2.7	29.7	17.6	34.7	60.7	15.3	141	80.1
Herrick township (Bradford).....................	752	754	0.3	681	95.7	0.4	0.6	2.2	1.0	22.9	16.7	44.8	69.7	15.6	268	88.4
Herrick township (Susquehanna)	718	683	-4.9	574	99.0	0.0	0.3	0.0	0.7	14.6	30.8	50.8	48.8	26.9	229	93.0
Hershey CDP	14,257	-	-	14,654	79.9	2.7	5.5	1.2	10.7	18.8	16.3	46.2	26.6	45.8	5,533	92.0
Hickory township (Forest).	559	492	-12.0	294	97.6	0.0	0.3	2.0	0.0	26.2	30.3	56.3	74.2	8.0	142	76.1
Hickory township (Lawrence)	2,482	2,384	-3.9	2,499	94.6	0.4	0.0	4.1	0.9	24.2	17.0	43.1	51.0	20.4	1,016	84.5
Hickory CDP	740	-	-	561	100.0	0.0	0.0	0.0	0.0	24.2	26.6	45.0	26.2	33.7	230	90.0
Hickory Hills CDP	562	-	-	369	96.5	0.0	0.0	3.5	0.0	7.9	21.4	56.8	63.5	9.1	214	84.6
Highland township (Adams)	940	957	1.8	993	95.4	0.5	0.0	1.9	2.2	20.0	24.3	51.1	44.0	31.1	412	93.7
Highland township (Chester)	1,273	1,287	1.1	1,313	85.5	3.3	0.0	1.4	9.9	27.4	15.8	40.2	50.5	26.8	443	83.7
Highland township (Clarion)....................	525	502	-4.4	586	99.7	0.0	0.0	0.0	0.3	17.2	18.8	51.0	44.4	25.4	244	90.2
Highland township (Elk)....	492	461	-6.3	457	96.7	0.0	2.2	1.1	0.0	13.3	26.7	52.5	72.6	12.2	216	77.8
Highland Park CDP	1,380	-	-	1,504	86.6	1.7	0.0	9.7	2.1	23.3	29.1	41.5	57.6	14.9	617	81.5
Highspire borough & MCD (Dauphin)	2,399	2,373	-1.1	2,492	68.2	16.0	1.0	3.3	11.5	24.8	14.6	39.4	51.2	14.5	1,104	81.7
Hilldale CDP	1,246	-	-	1,512	95.6	0.0	0.0	1.6	2.8	10.8	24.7	51.9	38.9	40.9	643	91.4
Hiller CDP	1,155	-	-	953	95.3	4.7	0.0	0.0	0.0	9.7	23.1	49.6	50.4	18.5	434	92.6
Hillsgrove township (Sullivan)	287	270	-5.9	304	98.4	0.7	0.0	0.7	0.3	15.5	19.4	49.7	61.6	17.4	129	87.6
Hilltown township (Bucks).	15,040	15,822	5.2	15,424	89.9	1.5	4.1	1.0	3.4	22.8	15.9	43.6	36.9	39.0	5,485	93.2
Hokendauqua CDP	3,378	-	-	2,667	84.0	0.0	4.2	3.4	8.5	16.5	23.8	48.6	48.1	23.1	1,180	88.2
Holiday Pocono CDP	476	-	-	398	81.7	0.0	0.0	0.0	18.3	11.3	50.8	65.5	80.9	5.9	216	70.8
Hollenback township (Luzerne)..................	1,198	1,200	0.2	1,157	96.2	1.6	0.2	0.0	2.0	19.2	19.6	43.2	57.1	17.5	445	83.4
Hollidaysburg borough & MCD (Blair)...............	5,762	5,674	-1.5	5,701	96.8	1.7	1.4	0.1	0.0	16.6	29.2	53.2	38.1	38.5	2,885	80.2
Homeacre-Lyndora CDP ..	6,906	-	-	6,498	94.1	2.5	0.1	1.2	2.0	16.6	24.2	47.6	43.5	26.2	3,088	85.3
Homer township (Potter)...	434	409	-5.8	434	97.9	0.0	0.7	0.5	0.9	29.0	15.0	39.7	33.3	35.6	146	97.3
Homer City borough & MCD (Indiana).............	1,705	1,588	-6.9	1,688	98.0	0.8	0.0	1.1	0.1	19.5	19.5	44.0	48.6	23.4	770	83.4
Homestead borough & MCD (Allegheny)...........	3,192	3,149	-1.3	3,170	32.8	58.8	4.4	1.5	2.5	24.1	21.0	36.8	50.1	16.4	1,359	76.2
Hometown CDP	1,349	-	-	1,168	98.8	0.0	0.0	1.2	0.0	19.3	30.1	47.3	48.5	20.4	607	80.6
Homewood borough & MCD (Beaver)...............	112	105	-6.3	93	87.1	2.2	1.1	7.5	2.2	5.4	17.2	48.9	65.0	6.3	49	91.8
Honesdale borough & MCD (Wayne)...............	4,509	4,281	-5.1	4,292	91.0	0.6	0.3	1.6	6.5	21.3	24.0	45.4	55.2	19.1	1,946	79.9
Honey Brook borough & MCD (Chester).............	1,716	1,759	2.5	1,980	93.9	2.8	0.0	1.9	1.4	27.7	11.9	34.1	50.9	27.6	711	86.4

1 May be of any race.

Table A. All Places — **Population and Housing**

STATE City, town, township, borough, or CDP (county if applicable)	2010 census total population	2019 estimated population	Percent change 2010–2019	ACS total population estimate 2015–2019	White alone, not Hispanic or Latino	Black alone, not Hispanic or Latino	Asian alone, not Hispanic or Latino	All other races or 2 or more races, not Hispanic or Latino	Hispanic or Latino[1]	Under 18 years old	Age 65 years and older	Median age	Percent High school diploma or less	Percent Bachelor's degree or more	Occupied housing units Total	Percent with a computer
	1	2	3	4	5	6	7	8	9	10	11	12	13	14	15	16
PENNSYLVANIA—Con.																
Honey Brook township (Chester)	7,635	8,311	8.9	8,240	94.8	3.0	1.0	0.0	1.2	26.5	23.3	43.2	40.8	33.3	2,832	84.8
Hookstown borough & MCD (Beaver)	147	138	-6.1	144	97.9	0.0	0.0	0.0	2.1	24.3	21.5	46.8	41.3	14.4	73	89.0
Hooversville borough & MCD (Somerset)	645	594	-7.9	623	98.1	0.0	0.0	0.0	1.9	23.0	22.5	46.0	66.1	10.0	282	75.9
Hop Bottom borough & MCD (Susquehanna)	343	313	-8.7	321	99.1	0.0	0.0	0.9	0.0	20.9	16.8	45.9	65.4	10.5	134	90.3
Hopeland CDP	738	-	-	554	100.0	0.0	0.0	0.0	0.0	13.7	22.2	57.4	63.4	11.1	252	80.2
Hopewell township (Beaver)	12,602	12,585	-0.1	12,522	88.6	5.0	0.5	3.3	2.6	18.9	19.4	43.0	38.4	27.4	5,435	89.1
Hopewell borough & MCD (Bedford)	230	239	3.9	279	89.2	0.4	8.2	0.4	1.8	30.1	14.7	28.8	70.7	2.5	90	68.9
Hopewell township (Bedford)	2,003	1,949	-2.7	1,888	99.6	0.0	0.0	0.4	0.0	17.4	21.1	46.9	64.9	12.2	775	81.3
Hopewell township (Cumberland)	2,329	2,483	6.6	2,875	99.3	0.0	0.0	0.1	0.5	26.5	15.3	34.4	64.1	16.5	886	79.5
Hopewell township (Huntingdon)	580	584	0.7	519	98.8	0.0	0.0	1.2	0.0	12.1	22.2	54.4	67.8	14.2	253	85.0
Hopewell township (Washington)	957	934	-2.4	960	96.0	0.3	0.0	2.1	1.6	20.0	20.7	48.1	58.1	20.8	368	86.7
Hopewell township (York)	5,510	5,533	0.4	5,523	96.1	1.8	1.0	0.6	0.4	18.4	20.3	48.3	35.5	34.6	2,086	92.0
Hopwood CDP	2,090	-	-	2,043	99.3	0.0	0.3	0.4	0.0	19.2	23.5	45.7	51.6	23.3	806	85.6
Horsham CDP	14,842	-	-	14,611	80.8	4.8	6.6	1.5	6.2	22.3	15.0	38.6	32.0	44.2	5,827	94.6
Horsham township (Montgomery)	26,131	26,485	1.4	26,487	80.6	3.3	8.4	2.1	5.6	23.3	14.2	39.7	28.6	48.5	9,849	95.3
Horton township (Elk)	1,452	1,364	-6.1	1,330	100.0	0.0	0.0	0.0	0.0	17.8	22.3	48.1	61.9	9.8	639	85.0
Hostetter CDP	740	-	-	560	100.0	0.0	0.0	0.0	0.0	19.8	26.8	48.0	40.3	35.2	291	86.6
Houserville CDP	1,814	-	-	1,972	79.4	5.1	10.2	5.1	0.3	21.7	12.7	39.0	14.6	69.5	788	100.0
Houston borough & MCD (Washington)	1,296	1,238	-4.5	1,352	87.9	3.3	3.5	2.7	2.5	21.7	22.3	43.3	57.8	17.1	627	81.7
Houtzdale borough & MCD (Clearfield)	795	746	-6.2	747	98.5	0.3	1.2	0.0	0.0	20.1	22.2	46.2	67.0	10.9	315	79.7
Hovey township (Armstrong)	98	88	-10.2	75	100.0	0.0	0.0	0.0	0.0	9.3	30.7	57.1	68.3	9.5	29	86.2
Howard borough & MCD (Centre)	733	734	0.1	683	99.0	0.0	0.0	0.7	0.3	19.5	13.6	40.2	46.8	19.3	269	84.0
Howard township (Centre)	1,030	1,018	-1.2	896	98.8	0.0	0.0	0.9	0.3	16.9	17.0	44.3	49.3	21.5	341	94.7
Howe township (Forest)	404	388	-4.0	252	48.0	23.0	0.0	9.5	19.4	50.0	11.5	18.0	63.0	7.4	35	68.6
Howe township (Perry)	393	396	0.8	441	99.1	0.0	0.0	0.0	0.9	17.5	20.2	49.5	59.4	21.5	177	84.2
Hublersburg CDP	104	-	-	78	100.0	0.0	0.0	0.0	0.0	17.9	20.5	45.2	25.0	21.4	42	61.9
Hubley township (Schuylkill)	854	842	-1.4	780	99.0	0.0	0.0	0.8	0.3	24.4	18.7	46.1	66.3	14.8	298	83.6
Hudson CDP	1,443	-	-	1,446	87.4	9.4	0.0	0.0	3.2	21.1	19.4	38.1	46.4	20.8	660	88.9
Hughestown borough & MCD (Luzerne)	1,362	1,349		1,431	97.1	0.1	0.1	1.1	1.5	16.9	21.4	45.2	42.5	30.9	599	85.6
Hughesville borough & MCD (Lycoming)	2,116	2,029	-4.1	2,280	97.9	0.8	0.1	0.2	1.0	25.1	16.3	36.2	47.9	22.2	935	85.1
Hulmeville borough & MCD (Bucks)	1,002	999	-0.3	932	87.8	0.2	3.8	2.6	5.7	18.6	11.8	41.6	41.4	28.7	346	96.0
Hummelstown borough & MCD (Dauphin)	4,532	4,823	6.4	4,688	92.6	0.0	1.3	2.8	3.3	21.8	15.5	40.3	30.7	35.0	2,186	91.0
Hummels Wharf CDP	1,353	-	-	1,266	97.0	0.0	0.9	0.0	2.1	9.6	18.6	51.3	67.4	15.2	526	85.4
Hunker borough & MCD (Westmoreland)	287	272	-5.2	261	98.1	0.4	0.0	1.1	0.4	11.1	21.5	50.8	52.7	21.5	114	88.6
Hunlock township (Luzerne)	2,451	2,410	-1.7	2,454	97.1	0.0	0.3	1.0	1.6	21.4	18.6	44.2	52.0	16.4	947	83.0
Hunterstown CDP	547	-	-	614	71.3	0.0	0.0	0.0	28.7	16.6	6.2	37.5	70.3	6.4	266	85.3
Huntingdon borough & MCD (Huntingdon)	7,091	6,937	-2.2	6,977	91.3	1.9	2.6	2.8	1.3	16.9	21.3	34.8	38.4	33.6	2,672	84.2
Huntington township (Adams)	2,355	2,395	1.7	2,637	88.7	0.6	1.9	0.6	8.1	23.9	14.7	42.5	59.7	18.2	900	85.8
Huntington township (Luzerne)	2,245	2,214	-1.4	1,948	96.9	0.0	0.0	1.0	2.1	19.6	22.7	49.7	53.1	16.7	797	85.7
Huston township (Blair)	1,347	1,327	-1.5	1,423	94.9	0.8	0.0	0.8	3.4	27.8	16.0	38.5	70.5	11.5	484	81.8
Huston township (Centre)	1,373	1,399	1.9	1,333	98.2	0.2	0.3	1.1	0.2	15.8	17.3	49.2	47.0	29.4	512	87.5
Huston township (Clearfield)	1,436	1,366	-4.9	1,247	98.4	0.0	0.0	0.6	1.0	20.5	20.7	45.6	64.6	9.1	505	81.2
Hyde CDP	1,399	-	-	1,162	94.8	2.0	0.0	3.2	0.0	18.2	19.4	46.5	71.6	10.5	570	86.1
Hyde Park CDP	2,528	-	-	2,692	40.1	21.7	0.0	2.9	35.4	30.8	12.3	31.2	54.1	17.6	876	86.1
Hyde Park borough & MCD (Westmoreland)	502	472	-6.0	466	98.1	0.0	0.0	0.4	1.5	17.8	26.0	46.5	57.7	12.0	231	79.7
Hydetown borough & MCD (Crawford)	535	508	-5.0	833	94.6	1.0	0.5	2.8	1.2	32.8	15.6	36.6	69.5	10.9	319	84.3
Hyndman borough & MCD (Bedford)	906	857	-5.4	844	98.6	0.0	0.0	1.2	0.2	17.1	23.8	46.5	66.1	9.7	346	81.8
Idaville CDP	177	-	-	216	96.8	3.2	0.0	0.0	0.0	19.4	24.1	39.0	50.6	31.8	85	100.0
Imperial CDP	2,541	-	-	2,533	97.7	0.0	1.3	0.0	0.9	20.2	13.4	41.2	42.1	38.3	1,090	96.7
Independence township (Beaver)	2,457	2,336	-4.9	2,434	96.7	2.3	0.0	0.3	0.7	20.9	15.1	45.6	45.5	18.7	944	91.3
Independence township (Washington)	1,570	1,498	-4.6	1,579	98.9	0.0	0.0	0.9	0.0	19.7	20.5	46.6	57.3	18.1	622	83.9
Indiana township (Allegheny)	7,247	7,124	-1.7	7,189	90.9	1.5	4.1	2.2	1.4	22.6	17.7	45.5	27.8	50.7	2,645	94.4
Indiana borough & MCD (Indiana)	13,969	13,167	-5.7	13,346	85.1	6.3	2.9	3.3	2.3	9.9	5.6	21.6	32.1	46.0	3,779	94.9
Indian Lake borough & MCD (Somerset)	398	378	-5.0	365	99.7	0.0	0.0	0.3	0.0	4.1	33.4	58.6	29.6	45.4	190	91.6
Indian Mountain Lake CDP	4,372	-	-	4,719	60.7	15.8	2.8	1.0	19.7	24.0	14.1	38.3	49.1	20.8	1,533	92.4
Industry borough & MCD (Beaver)	1,833	1,711	-6.7	1,698	95.5	1.6	0.6	1.3	0.9	18.9	22.0	45.5	47.4	19.7	710	90.0

1 May be of any race.

Table A. All Places — **Population and Housing**

STATE City, town, township, borough, or CDP (county if applicable)	2010 census total population	2019 estimated population	Percent change 2010–2019	ACS total population estimate 2015–2019	White alone, not Hispanic or Latino	Black alone, not Hispanic or Latino	Asian alone, not Hispanic or Latino	All other races or 2 or more races, not Hispanic or Latino	Hispanic or Latino[1]	Under 18 years old	Age 65 years and older	Median age	Percent High school diploma or less	Percent Bachelor's degree or more	Occupied housing units Total	Percent with a computer
	1	2	3	4	5	6	7	8	9	10	11	12	13	14	15	16
PENNSYLVANIA—Con.																
Ingram borough & MCD (Allegheny)	3,322	3,198	-3.7	3,237	82.6	15.3	1.4	0.4	0.3	19.5	15.9	37.8	39.8	26.6	1,516	93.7
Inkerman CDP	1,819	-	-	1,945	97.5	0.0	0.0	0.0	2.5	11.1	44.4	61.6	42.7	23.9	1,019	80.1
Intercourse CDP	1,274	-	-	1,640	77.5	2.1	11.8	0.0	8.6	20.9	29.6	44.5	55.3	20.3	594	76.6
Iola CDP	144	-	-	197	82.2	0.0	2.5	15.2	0.0	18.8	13.2	44.4	56.3	4.0	81	93.8
Irvona borough & MCD (Clearfield)	645	611	-5.3	665	93.1	0.0	0.0	0.2	6.8	22.4	17.9	43.8	70.2	8.2	244	81.6
Irwin township (Venango)	1,382	1,250	-9.6	1,256	98.3	0.0	0.6	0.7	0.4	22.0	14.0	41.0	62.5	16.7	458	82.3
Irwin borough & MCD (Westmoreland)	3,987	3,744	-6.1	3,797	96.9	0.5	0.0	0.3	2.3	18.8	20.0	44.9	38.4	27.5	1,973	83.9
Ivyland borough & MCD (Bucks)	933	941	0.9	951	81.3	0.0	12.2	3.8	2.7	32.3	7.8	38.2	26.9	46.4	315	93.7
Jackson township (Butler)	3,707	4,258	14.9	3,979	94.5	0.0	0.3	2.4	2.7	22.1	19.5	44.7	26.4	48.9	1,649	96.5
Jackson township (Cambria)	4,376	4,005	-8.5	4,090	98.6	0.2	0.0	0.7	0.5	18.7	25.2	50.5	59.8	16.7	1,672	87.8
Jackson township (Columbia)	632	638	0.9	665	97.0	0.5	0.8	1.5	0.3	23.8	14.3	39.5	55.7	20.0	256	89.1
Jackson township (Dauphin)	1,954	2,017	3.2	1,791	99.5	0.0	0.0	0.4	0.1	19.5	20.1	48.6	54.1	21.6	719	89.3
Jackson township (Greene)	487	463	-4.9	569	99.5	0.0	0.0	0.5	0.0	27.8	12.5	33.2	58.0	16.5	207	87.0
Jackson township (Huntingdon)	864	867	0.3	887	98.9	0.0	0.8	0.3	0.0	23.2	23.4	45.1	44.9	25.8	332	85.8
Jackson township (Lebanon)	8,166	9,006	10.3	8,853	94.4	1.5	0.0	1.2	2.9	24.4	23.5	44.5	54.9	20.1	3,352	85.4
Jackson township (Luzerne)	4,649	4,661	0.3	4,663	59.6	27.7	3.0	1.0	8.7	8.3	13.2	42.2	52.9	23.2	877	92.8
Jackson township (Lycoming)	399	395		410	98.8	0.0	0.0	1.2	0.0	18.3	24.4	50.5	54.1	12.3	161	85.1
Jackson township (Mercer)	1,273	1,249	-1.9	1,129	97.4	0.0	2.3	0.3	0.0	17.8	22.2	52.0	56.9	23.2	477	86.8
Jackson township (Monroe)	7,021	6,933	-1.3	6,865	75.6	4.7	6.7	0.9	12.1	22.7	14.0	37.2	41.5	35.9	2,013	96.4
Jackson township (Northumberland)	875	859	-1.8	872	98.7	0.0	0.0	0.0	1.3	20.9	15.6	43.0	65.7	14.0	348	76.7
Jackson township (Perry)	547	554	1.3	579	94.1	0.0	1.7	1.2	2.9	38.0	10.7	29.1	80.5	7.9	168	67.3
Jackson township (Snyder)	1,391	1,454	4.5	1,598	98.1	0.0	0.0	0.0	1.9	29.0	12.8	35.5	61.5	14.1	511	83.0
Jackson township (Susquehanna)	856	779	-9.0	896	97.9	0.0	0.0	1.2	0.9	18.3	21.8	48.7	55.5	23.1	346	88.2
Jackson township (Tioga)	1,880	1,867	-0.7	1,827	96.9	0.3	0.0	0.9	1.9	19.5	22.4	46.7	62.1	8.1	666	82.1
Jackson township (Venango)	1,149	1,138		1,105	97.5	0.0	0.0	0.0	2.5	18.9	16.6	47.7	65.7	14.9	436	83.9
Jackson township (York)	7,481	8,346	11.6	8,081	89.6	2.3	3.3	1.7	3.1	21.1	16.5	41.6	59.7	20.5	3,142	89.8
Jackson Center borough & MCD (Mercer)	224	207	-7.6	181	99.4	0.0	0.0	0.6	0.0	23.8	20.4	41.6	70.7	11.3	68	89.7
Jacksonville CDP	-	-	-	73	100.0	0.0	0.0	0.0	0.0	21.9	5.5	44.2	84.4	8.9	37	94.6
Jacksonville CDP	637	-	-	612	98.7	0.0	0.0	0.0	1.3	23.7	11.9	37.2	60.9	15.1	270	78.5
Jacksonwald CDP	3,393	-	-	2,900	91.8	6.2	1.1	0.0	1.0	13.5	22.1	51.7	41.4	34.3	1,158	96.8
Jacobus borough & MCD (York)	1,835	1,833	-0.1	1,789	85.7	2.3	0.5	8.1	3.4	24.3	14.7	41.5	44.4	28.0	639	92.3
James City CDP	287	-	-	264	100.0	0.0	0.0	0.0	0.0	17.4	18.2	46.4	80.5	5.6	117	80.3
Jamestown borough & MCD (Mercer)	617	573	-7.1	731	99.6	0.3	0.0	0.1	0.0	24.6	22.7	42.6	47.8	23.5	321	90.7
Jamison City CDP	134	-	-	144	100.0	0.0	0.0	0.0	0.0	20.8	30.6	42.0	73.7	3.5	70	91.4
Jay township (Elk)	2,077	1,913	-7.9	1,997	97.6	0.0	2.0	0.4	0.0	19.4	23.7	50.7	60.9	16.9	891	78.8
Jeannette city & MCD (Westmoreland)	9,673	9,074	-6.2	9,216	79.1	11.5	0.5	7.4	1.5	20.4	17.7	41.6	49.9	18.0	4,487	84.1
Jeddo borough & MCD (Luzerne)	94	92	-2.1	328	100.0	0.0	0.0	0.0	0.0	8.2	32.6	53.0	50.0	25.3	149	61.1
Jefferson township (Berks)	1,977	2,048	3.6	2,135	89.1	0.1	3.6	1.3	5.9	21.9	18.3	44.8	52.3	24.1	714	92.3
Jefferson township (Butler)	5,500	5,242	-4.7	5,307	99.3	0.0	0.7	0.0	0.0	20.4	29.5	51.0	49.6	22.0	2,131	75.3
Jefferson township (Dauphin)	362	380	5.0	319	98.1	0.0	0.3	0.3	1.3	17.2	27.0	52.8	46.8	23.2	147	80.3
Jefferson township (Fayette)	2,015	1,912	-5.1	1,906	97.7	0.9	0.0	0.0	1.4	19.4	25.3	47.6	49.3	20.3	813	84.6
Jefferson borough & MCD (Greene)	272	253	-7.0	281	100.0	0.0	0.0	0.0	0.0	22.1	8.2	30.1	52.1	23.4	97	86.6
Jefferson township (Greene)	2,357	2,193	-7.0	2,102	96.4	2.7	0.2	0.5	0.1	17.8	23.6	46.4	49.5	21.2	940	89.3
Jefferson township (Lackawanna)	3,710	3,667	-1.2	3,660	96.3	0.0	0.7	1.1	2.0	29.5	19.0	43.2	43.8	25.0	1,403	84.7
Jefferson township (Mercer)	1,872	1,802	-3.7	1,988	98.1	0.0	0.1	1.8	0.0	20.8	19.0	45.7	60.7	17.1	808	89.2
Jefferson township (Somerset)	1,423	1,330	-6.5	1,390	94.7	0.1	0.0	0.1	5.0	18.1	24.6	49.8	55.8	25.7	581	79.9
Jefferson township (Washington)	1,142	1,130	-1.1	1,165	97.6	0.0	0.0	0.0	2.2	19.7	25.4	49.7	59.6	15.8	470	84.9
Jefferson borough & MCD (York)	723	732	1.2	629	97.0	1.4	0.6	0.0	1.0	17.5	26.7	48.2	56.9	13.4	263	82.1
Jefferson Hills borough & MCD (Allegheny)	10,620	11,101	4.5	11,200	94.3	1.9	3.0	0.5	0.3	21.8	19.7	44.7	27.9	43.5	4,523	93.3
Jenkins township (Luzerne)	4,482	4,560	1.7	4,519	94.1	2.2	0.0	0.0	3.7	15.8	31.0	55.8	44.8	24.7	2,145	82.1
Jenkintown borough & MCD (Montgomery)	4,422	4,420	0.0	4,433	79.4	10.4	1.6	1.4	7.2	24.0	17.9	40.8	20.5	64.1	1,793	95.3
Jenks township (Forest)	3,628	3,615	-0.4	4,497	50.2	39.9	0.1	2.4	7.3	5.3	11.4	36.4	80.6	4.8	430	78.1
Jenner township (Somerset)	4,121	3,792	-8.0	3,852	97.7	0.0	0.6	1.1	0.5	23.9	15.7	40.7	52.2	11.6	1,505	88.8
Jennerstown borough & MCD (Somerset)	694	640	-7.8	769	98.8	0.8	0.0	0.0	0.4	22.2	22.0	41.1	51.3	19.3	296	86.8

1 May be of any race.

Table A. All Places — Population and Housing

STATE City, town, township, borough, or CDP (county if applicable)	Population				Race and Hispanic or Latino origin (percent)					Age (percent)			Educational attainment of persons age 25 and older		Occupied housing units	
	2010 census total population	2019 estimated population	Percent change 2010–2019	ACS total population estimate 2015–2019	White alone, not Hispanic or Latino	Black alone, not Hispanic or Latino	Asian alone, not Hispanic or Latino	All other races or 2 or more races, not Hispanic or Latino	Hispanic or Latino[1]	Under 18 years old	Age 65 years and older	Median age	Percent High school diploma or less	Percent Bachelor's degree or more	Total	Percent with a computer
	1	2	3	4	5	6	7	8	9	10	11	12	13	14	15	16
PENNSYLVANIA—Con.																
Jermyn borough & MCD (Lackawanna).............	2,165	2,053	-5.2	2,080	95.5	2.6	0.7	0.5	0.7	17.1	19.7	45.3	45.9	23.5	975	84.3
Jerome CDP.....................	1,017	-	-	722	100.0	0.0	0.0	0.0	0.0	11.2	17.5	53.9	40.3	32.2	331	78.5
Jersey Shore borough & MCD (Lycoming)..........	4,357	4,139	-5.0	4,204	99.2	0.0	0.0	0.0	0.8	27.5	17.2	37.9	58.0	8.1	1,601	89.9
Jerseytown CDP..............	184	-	-	137	100.0	0.0	0.0	0.0	0.0	23.4	13.9	46.6	59.8	10.3	51	82.4
Jessup borough & MCD (Lackawanna).............	4,678	4,400	-5.9	4,441	97.0	0.0	1.5	0.0	1.5	20.1	18.0	43.6	37.5	32.2	1,810	74.5
Jessup township (Susquehanna)	536	503	-6.2	442	94.6	0.0	0.0	0.9	4.5	21.0	20.1	45.4	45.4	24.1	164	87.8
Jim Thorpe borough & MCD (Carbon)..............	4,784	4,657	-2.7	4,641	95.1	1.1	0.3	0.4	3.1	17.9	16.4	45.9	52.5	19.7	2,031	85.7
Joffre CDP......................	536	-	-	415	100.0	0.0	0.0	0.0	0.0	9.9	8.2	40.8	60.2	14.4	199	95.0
Johnsonburg borough & MCD (Elk)	2,485	2,291	-7.8	2,445	95.7	0.7	0.0	1.9	1.7	21.1	18.1	42.7	59.8	15.4	1,117	82.6
Johnstown city & MCD (Cambria).................	20,988	19,195	-8.5	19,569	74.7	14.1	0.1	7.8	3.4	23.4	21.2	42.1	60.0	11.8	9,438	74.3
Jones township (Elk)	1,624	1,533	-5.6	1,488	97.8	0.0	0.7	1.5	0.0	19.5	21.8	48.8	56.0	22.1	689	82.0
Jonestown CDP	64	-	-	94	96.8	0.0	0.0	0.0	3.2	0.0	43.6	64.1	80.2	8.6	41	100.0
Jonestown borough & MCD (Lebanon)	1,899	2,028	6.8	1,884	87.3	0.3	1.5	6.3	4.6	27.9	8.9	34.2	50.4	21.7	670	94.8
Jordan township (Clearfield)	457	445	-2.6	427	100.0	0.0	0.0	0.0	0.0	19.2	19.0	48.3	70.3	15.0	174	73.0
Jordan township (Lycoming)	864	841	-2.7	981	97.9	0.6	0.3	0.4	0.8	26.2	19.7	40.8	62.1	14.8	375	82.4
Jordan township (Northumberland)..........	792	751	-5.2	659	98.5	0.0	0.0	0.9	0.6	18.5	21.2	43.8	69.3	10.0	289	76.8
Julian CDP.....................	152	-	-	139	100.0	0.0	0.0	0.0	0.0	23.0	24.5	49.8	55.9	14.7	63	88.9
Juniata township (Bedford)	956	947	-0.9	1,020	95.6	0.0	0.0	1.6	2.8	21.3	22.2	47.8	62.4	11.7	447	74.3
Juniata township (Blair)	1,120	1,075	-4.0	957	99.7	0.0	0.0	0.3	0.0	16.1	19.5	50.3	68.2	10.1	401	90.0
Juniata township (Huntingdon)	547	533	-2.6	412	93.0	0.0	0.0	1.2	5.8	10.0	31.8	56.4	51.9	18.4	193	82.4
Juniata township (Perry)...	1,410	1,428	1.3	1,283	98.0	0.0	0.0	1.8	0.2	21.3	19.7	46.1	51.6	25.5	560	80.2
Juniata Terrace borough & MCD (Mifflin)	542	535	-1.3	505	95.2	0.0	0.0	1.6	3.2	24.8	18.6	34.6	62.7	6.0	205	82.4
Kane borough & MCD (McKean)..................	3,713	3,446	-7.2	3,507	96.5	0.9	0.1	1.1	1.4	22.7	21.4	42.6	58.0	22.1	1,577	87.2
Kapp Heights CDP	863	-	-	878	100.0	0.0	0.0	0.0	0.0	25.4	21.6	42.4	57.1	21.4	387	90.7
Karns City borough & MCD (Butler)................	213	204	-4.2	186	99.5	0.0	0.5	0.0	0.0	24.2	15.6	34.4	74.8	4.6	81	79.0
Karthaus township (Clearfield)	809	807	-0.2	654	86.7	8.9	0.0	0.3	4.1	9.9	16.8	37.3	70.8	8.0	206	74.3
Keating township (McKean)..................	3,017	2,858	-5.3	2,902	95.9	1.5	0.0	1.9	0.7	16.6	22.6	47.3	62.4	13.8	1,146	86.0
Keating township (Potter)..	312	293	-6.1	241	91.7	0.0	0.0	7.1	1.2	6.2	34.0	58.1	66.2	12.7	101	77.2
Kelayres CDP	533	-	-	487	83.6	0.0	2.1	0.0	14.4	23.8	15.0	36.5	67.0	6.3	199	83.4
Kelly township (Union)......	5,367	5,242	-2.3	5,301	68.2	13.9	3.8	4.6	9.6	13.0	23.8	45.1	48.7	31.5	1,693	76.3
Kempton CDP.................	169	-	-	114	89.5	0.0	0.0	0.0	10.5	17.5	14.9	36.7	38.0	47.8	54	94.4
Kenhorst borough & MCD (Berks)	2,802	2,805	0.1	2,803	65.8	7.5	0.0	0.6	26.2	23.9	17.1	40.1	51.6	17.9	1,097	86.9
Kenilworth CDP..............	1,907	-	-	1,987	91.7	2.3	1.4	2.5	2.2	26.8	16.6	41.0	41.5	41.0	744	94.9
Kenmar CDP..................	4,124	-	-	4,275	84.6	6.2	0.3	0.0	9.0	23.6	27.3	42.6	46.0	25.8	1,755	90.8
Kennedy township (Allegheny)	7,702	8,113	5.3	8,119	95.6	1.0	0.9	2.3	0.2	18.9	19.6	44.5	39.2	37.8	3,624	86.0
Kennerdell CDP..............	247	-	-	177	94.9	0.0	0.0	5.1	0.0	11.9	26.0	59.4	39.3	17.2	109	90.8
Kennett township (Chester)...................	7,585	8,305	9.5	8,226	76.7	5.6	2.9	1.4	13.3	21.0	24.1	48.0	24.2	62.9	3,260	90.7
Kennett Square borough & MCD (Chester).............	6,050	6,202	2.5	6,190	55.0	5.1	0.8	0.1	39.1	19.9	12.5	36.1	50.4	33.0	2,136	79.6
Kerrtown CDP.................	305	-	-	88	100.0	0.0	0.0	0.0	0.0	26.1	0.0	30.3	26.2	26.2	48	100.0
Kersey CDP...................	937	-	-	1,067	100.0	0.0	0.0	0.0	0.0	21.6	13.8	45.9	47.7	8.2	450	96.2
Kidder township (Carbon).	1,927	1,937	0.5	1,271	87.2	1.9	0.0	2.6	8.3	14.2	47.6	63.6	54.3	22.6	628	79.3
Kilbuck township (Allegheny)	704	725	3.0	700	96.6	0.4	0.6	2.4	0.0	15.1	23.3	51.6	29.0	44.7	301	94.7
Kimmel township (Bedford)	1,620	1,537	-5.1	1,611	98.9	0.0	0.0	0.0	1.1	21.1	21.9	47.3	74.6	7.8	697	74.9
King township (Bedford) ...	1,229	1,185	-3.6	1,270	95.7	0.0	0.0	2.4	2.0	23.9	17.5	42.1	70.8	8.2	476	74.8
King of Prussia CDP.........	19,936	-	-	21,313	64.4	6.2	24.5	2.5	2.5	18.5	18.3	38.0	21.7	60.2	9,439	94.3
Kingsley township (Forest)	358	315	-12.0	224	99.1	0.0	0.0	0.9	0.0	11.6	55.4	66.4	60.2	8.7	128	73.4
Kingston borough & MCD (Luzerne).................	13,160	12,812	-2.6	12,873	87.4	3.3	1.4	2.4	5.4	19.7	19.8	41.2	41.6	32.2	5,813	85.7
Kingston township (Luzerne)..................	6,992	6,898	-1.3	6,912	95.8	0.7	2.6	0.2	0.7	22.3	18.5	44.9	27.3	40.3	2,712	89.1
Kirkwood CDP	396	-	-	411	100.0	0.0	0.0	0.0	0.0	25.8	16.3	28.8	61.5	24.2	100	71.0
Kiskimere CDP	136	-	-	149	65.1	30.9	0.0	4.0	0.0	19.5	33.6	62.5	68.3	17.5	67	92.5
Kiskiminetas township (Armstrong)	4,824	4,476	-7.2	4,564	97.6	0.0	0.0	2.4	0.0	17.9	23.1	49.4	63.1	14.0	1,997	85.8
Kistler borough & MCD (Mifflin)	320	316	-1.3	345	91.9	3.8	0.0	2.0	2.3	24.3	17.7	36.6	56.6	15.8	142	90.1
Kittanning borough & MCD (Armstrong)..........	4,013	3,722	-7.3	3,789	97.5	1.7	0.1	0.3	0.3	18.3	21.5	49.4	62.8	14.7	1,751	71.6
Kittanning township (Armstrong)................	2,264	2,153	-4.9	2,073	98.7	0.0	0.0	0.9	0.4	11.8	27.8	54.6	64.8	19.2	867	86.0
Kline township (Schuylkill)	1,438	1,361	-5.4	1,427	88.6	0.4	0.7	0.6	9.7	17.4	22.6	47.1	60.3	11.4	616	80.7
Klingerstown CDP	127	-	-	90	91.1	0.0	0.0	0.0	8.9	10.0	31.1	51.4	61.8	14.5	41	90.2
Knox borough & MCD (Clarion)...................	1,148	1,069	-6.9	1,006	98.1	0.0	0.0	0.6	1.3	25.0	19.6	45.2	52.0	23.7	456	86.2
Knox township (Clarion) ...	1,031	985	-4.5	905	96.7	0.0	1.1	2.2	0.0	17.9	25.6	49.2	56.2	21.9	404	88.9
Knox township (Clearfield)	646	615	-4.8	552	96.4	0.0	2.0	0.4	1.3	21.2	23.6	48.8	71.5	12.2	221	70.6
Knox township (Jefferson)	1,048	1,007	-3.9	1,130	98.2	1.4	0.0	0.4	0.0	17.7	24.5	46.3	71.1	9.7	481	84.6
Knoxville borough & MCD (Tioga).................	629	599	-4.8	783	95.3	1.1	0.0	3.1	0.5	26.2	15.3	38.8	60.1	9.0	258	85.7

1 May be of any race.

Table A. All Places — **Population and Housing**

STATE City, town, township, borough, or CDP (county if applicable)	Population 2010 census total population	2019 estimated population	Percent change 2010– 2019	ACS total population estimate 2015–2019	Race and Hispanic or Latino origin (percent) White alone, not Hispanic or Latino	Black alone, not Hispanic or Latino	Asian alone, not Hispanic or Latino	All other races or 2 or more races, not Hispanic or Latino	Hispanic or Latino[1]	Age (percent) Under 18 years old	Age 65 years and older	Median age	Educational attainment of persons age 25 and older Percent High school diploma or less	Percent Bachelor's degree or more	Occupied housing units Total	Percent with a computer
	1	2	3	4	5	6	7	8	9	10	11	12	13	14	15	16
PENNSYLVANIA—Con.																
Koppel borough & MCD (Beaver)	762	721	-5.4	707	93.5	0.6	0.0	3.5	2.4	17.0	21.4	50.6	53.6	14.6	358	85.2
Kratzerville CDP	383	-	-	337	93.8	0.0	0.0	0.0	6.2	16.0	18.1	50.4	50.2	22.1	134	85.8
Kreamer CDP	822	-	-	724	100.0	0.0	0.0	0.0	0.0	21.5	26.0	52.7	42.4	31.3	312	81.7
Kulpmont borough & MCD (Northumberland)	2,924	2,754	-5.8	2,800	97.4	0.1	1.5	0.0	1.0	14.4	22.9	47.9	55.9	18.8	1,283	82.1
Kulpsville CDP	8,194	-	-	8,348	79.4	6.5	9.3	2.0	2.8	20.0	23.7	46.2	25.6	48.9	3,646	91.6
Kutztown borough & MCD (Berks)	4,982	5,080	2.0	5,040	93.4	0.7	3.0	0.9	2.1	14.6	17.1	36.0	34.3	41.5	2,150	90.3
Kutztown University CDP	2,918	-	-	3,604	72.2	15.2	1.3	3.4	7.9	1.0	0.1	19.8	11.9	42.9	0	0.0
Kylertown CDP	340	-	-	282	71.6	0.0	0.0	2.1	26.2	3.5	42.2	57.0	76.9	5.4	158	48.7
Laceyville borough & MCD (Wyoming)	379	348	-8.2	410	86.3	0.2	0.0	2.9	10.5	22.9	19.5	37.1	73.7	7.7	158	76.6
Lack township (Juniata)	785	765	-2.5	607	100.0	0.0	0.0	0.0	0.0	23.4	19.8	40.9	73.7	10.0	263	71.1
Lackawannock township (Mercer)	2,657	2,531	-4.7	2,570	98.5	0.9	0.0	0.6	0.0	21.1	19.0	46.1	56.0	20.5	1,069	81.2
Lackawaxen township (Pike)	5,010	5,106	1.9	5,020	87.5	4.4	0.0	2.0	6.2	16.0	30.9	51.7	39.5	25.3	2,123	94.2
Lafayette township (McKean)	2,350	2,083	-11.4	2,154	48.7	35.7	0.0	2.0	13.5	5.3	6.6	39.6	58.7	11.8	452	89.6
Laflin borough & MCD (Luzerne)	1,466	1,438	-1.9	1,513	97.9	0.9	0.7	0.1	0.3	16.9	24.1	48.2	32.5	46.7	629	90.0
Lake township (Luzerne)	2,053	2,025	-1.4	2,356	96.6	0.7	0.4	0.6	1.6	21.5	16.9	43.7	47.2	26.0	792	93.1
Lake township (Mercer)	778	743	-4.5	811	100.0	0.0	0.0	0.0	0.0	31.3	12.0	38.7	62.3	19.1	281	74.7
Lake township (Wayne)	5,258	5,094	-3.1	5,108	96.6	0.5	1.1	0.4	1.4	14.9	26.7	49.7	59.9	18.9	1,745	88.7
Lake Arthur Estates CDP	594	-	-	647	95.2	0.0	0.0	2.5	2.3	17.6	23.3	40.7	60.6	7.1	301	75.7
Lake City borough & MCD (Erie)	3,031	2,854	-5.8	2,899	94.1	0.3	0.0	1.8	3.7	26.0	11.7	36.6	58.2	16.7	1,099	91.0
Lake Heritage CDP	1,333	-	-	2,367	93.8	0.9	1.9	2.5	0.8	24.6	22.2	48.5	21.8	45.1	1,000	96.1
Lake Latonka CDP	1,012	-	-	844	96.9	0.0	3.1	0.0	0.0	14.5	26.8	54.3	28.3	40.5	375	96.3
Lake Meade CDP	2,563	-	-	2,569	96.9	0.0	0.0	0.9	2.2	22.1	18.1	47.6	31.0	45.7	906	96.6
Lakemont CDP	1,868	-	-	1,860	96.5	0.0	2.0	0.0	1.5	16.6	19.8	50.2	45.5	26.9	837	89.6
Lake Winola CDP	748	-	-	662	92.4	0.0	0.0	2.1	5.4	12.8	27.5	53.4	44.6	27.8	282	93.3
Lake Wynonah CDP	2,640	-	-	2,501	95.2	0.2	0.0	0.4	4.2	20.5	18.1	47.3	36.6	29.9	1,024	98.6
Lamar CDP	562	-	-	614	98.9	0.0	1.1	0.0	0.0	14.2	12.1	45.9	70.9	6.9	249	80.7
Lamar township (Clinton)	2,518	2,530	0.5	2,539	97.5	0.0	0.7	0.6	1.1	24.2	20.2	41.6	59.0	18.1	894	83.4
Lampeter CDP	1,669	-	-	1,358	95.9	1.5	0.0	2.5	0.0	18.9	9.4	34.7	50.4	27.4	555	82.9
Lancaster township (Butler)	2,534	2,774	9.5	2,610	98.9	0.0	0.0	0.6	0.5	21.5	18.3	46.1	36.5	33.9	1,000	94.5
Lancaster city & MCD (Lancaster)	59,263	59,265	0.0	59,433	40.1	13.0	4.4	4.1	38.3	23.3	9.8	32.0	53.9	22.9	22,092	88.3
Lancaster township (Lancaster)	16,179	17,156	6.0	17,122	56.9	9.2	4.5	1.5	27.9	22.4	18.3	38.3	42.1	32.8	6,779	92.0
Landingville borough & MCD (Schuylkill)	159	150	-5.7	144	97.2	0.0	0.0	2.1	0.7	17.4	7.6	47.0	67.3	13.1	60	81.7
Landisburg borough & MCD (Perry)	217	219	0.9	229	88.2	0.4	1.3	0.0	10.0	28.4	9.6	37.2	71.8	12.2	82	85.4
Landisville CDP	1,893	-	-	2,117	91.8	0.8	0.0	0.9	6.5	23.8	14.3	38.7	28.9	51.4	786	93.0
Lanesboro borough & MCD (Susquehanna)	497	454	-8.7	418	98.6	0.0	1.4	0.0	0.0	21.1	29.2	50.7	65.8	11.8	194	68.0
Langeloth CDP	717	-	-	742	98.4	0.0	0.0	0.0	1.6	28.4	22.1	35.9	60.7	21.7	292	78.4
Langhorne borough & MCD (Bucks)	1,615	1,580	-2.2	1,709	90.1	3.5	1.3	1.7	3.4	15.7	26.6	48.9	36.4	36.9	627	80.9
Langhorne Manor borough & MCD (Bucks)	1,440	1,424	-1.1	1,536	88.9	4.6	0.9	1.6	4.0	10.4	16.3	31.3	31.0	36.4	299	96.0
Lansdale borough & MCD (Montgomery)	16,282	17,083	4.9	16,675	70.6	5.2	14.8	3.1	6.3	20.4	14.7	38.0	37.9	36.5	6,545	92.2
Lansdowne borough & MCD (Delaware)	10,620	10,647	0.3	10,638	37.9	50.6	3.0	2.9	5.6	20.5	13.1	41.4	32.1	40.5	4,632	92.5
Lansford borough & MCD (Carbon)	3,941	3,803	-3.5	3,796	88.7	0.8	0.0	0.8	9.7	22.3	15.3	39.1	55.6	11.3	1,652	82.5
La Plume township (Lackawanna)	602	566	-6.0	365	99.7	0.0	0.3	0.0	0.0	17.8	25.5	49.8	47.7	19.7	163	79.8
Laporte borough & MCD (Sullivan)	314	298	-5.1	323	97.8	2.2	0.0	0.0	0.0	0.9	45.8	64.0	60.3	13.8	94	96.8
Laporte township (Sullivan)	351	336	-4.3	427	100.0	0.0	0.0	0.0	0.0	9.8	30.9	54.9	52.7	22.5	186	90.3
Larimer township (Somerset)	595	553	-7.1	550	92.9	0.0	3.3	0.0	3.8	18.5	14.5	49.4	68.2	11.4	225	78.7
Larksville borough & MCD (Luzerne)	4,466	4,385	-1.8	4,387	91.0	3.1	0.0	1.1	4.8	14.5	22.4	51.9	43.4	26.9	1,857	84.0
Lathrop township (Susquehanna)	837	787	-6.0	886	95.6	0.6	0.0	0.0	3.8	24.2	21.8	41.7	58.6	18.3	330	91.8
Latimore township (Adams)	2,661	2,706	1.7	2,689	85.8	1.3	0.0	2.5	10.4	23.1	16.9	44.4	46.9	24.8	1,006	94.8
Latrobe borough & MCD (Westmoreland)	8,333	7,830	-6.0	7,929	97.0	0.5	1.1	1.4	0.0	18.4	21.4	44.6	46.3	24.1	3,589	84.3
Lattimer CDP	554	-	-	395	100.0	0.0	0.0	0.0	0.0	19.2	15.4	52.8	44.3	23.0	205	91.7
Laureldale borough & MCD (Berks)	3,886	3,909	0.6	3,900	70.3	4.0	0.2	1.8	23.7	19.9	19.7	40.4	59.2	16.3	1,554	88.3
Laurel Mountain borough & MCD (Westmoreland)	165	154	-6.7	126	99.2	0.0	0.0	0.0	0.8	6.3	19.8	54.0	18.5	38.9	73	94.5
Laurel Run borough & MCD (Luzerne)	500	509	1.8	573	93.2	1.2	0.5	1.6	3.5	13.4	13.1	43.8	52.2	18.8	214	88.3
Laurelton CDP	221	-	-	415	97.1	0.0	2.9	0.0	0.0	35.9	11.6	37.3	66.4	8.7	120	84.2
Laurys Station CDP	1,243	-	-	973	98.6	0.0	1.4	0.0	0.0	19.0	12.8	48.1	31.8	38.2	372	86.8
Lausanne township (Carbon)	233	226	-3.0	234	97.0	0.0	0.0	3.0	0.0	22.6	21.8	46.8	71.7	8.8	88	83.0
Lavelle CDP	742	-	-	490	83.1	0.0	0.0	2.9	14.1	5.5	20.0	52.5	50.9	13.7	285	74.7
Lawnton CDP	3,813	-	-	3,991	43.9	22.9	21.5	1.4	10.3	25.4	16.6	37.8	49.2	25.2	1,595	81.4
Lawrence township (Clearfield)	7,683	7,523	-2.1	7,562	97.9	0.5	0.3	0.6	0.7	15.0	25.9	48.3	63.8	15.2	3,131	84.6

1 May be of any race.

Table A. All Places — **Population and Housing**

STATE City, town, township, borough, or CDP (county if applicable)	2010 census total population	2019 estimated population	Percent change 2010–2019	ACS total population estimate 2015–2019	White alone, not Hispanic or Latino	Black alone, not Hispanic or Latino	Asian alone, not Hispanic or Latino	All other races or 2 or more races, not Hispanic or Latino	Hispanic or Latino[1]	Under 18 years old	Age 65 years and older	Median age	Percent High school diploma or less	Percent Bachelor's degree or more	Total	Percent with a computer
	1	2	3	4	5	6	7	8	9	10	11	12	13	14	15	16
PENNSYLVANIA—Con.																
Lawrence township (Tioga)	1,719	1,644	-4.4	1,780	95.2	0.3	1.8	2.4	0.3	17.6	17.5	45.5	56.7	13.4	679	87.3
Lawrence CDP	540	-	-	343	100.0	0.0	0.0	0.0	0.0	13.7	23.6	36.5	47.0	10.3	185	80.5
Lawrence Park township & CDP (Erie)	3,982	3,744	-6.0	3,813	93.5	1.2	0.3	1.0	4.1	24.6	17.3	37.5	45.5	30.2	1,532	87.0
Lawrenceville borough & MCD (Tioga)	581	612	5.3	548	98.2	0.0	0.0	1.1	0.7	26.1	17.7	37.6	50.0	21.8	221	84.2
Lawson Heights CDP	2,194	-	-	2,564	92.0	0.0	3.9	4.1	0.0	23.1	13.4	36.5	38.2	20.1	984	93.0
Leacock township (Lancaster)	5,220	5,764	10.4	5,601	91.8	0.9	3.9	0.0	3.4	33.1	16.6	28.9	72.4	12.8	1,641	55.6
Lebanon city & MCD (Lebanon)	25,492	25,879	1.5	25,793	49.0	4.4	1.0	1.9	43.7	26.3	13.0	34.5	68.7	9.8	9,889	81.7
Lebanon township (Wayne)	688	673	-2.2	584	97.1	0.0	1.5	1.4	0.0	14.0	30.7	54.0	57.7	18.5	234	84.2
Lebanon South CDP	2,270	-	-	2,320	87.1	0.0	2.7	2.4	7.8	21.8	23.3	45.6	44.1	30.5	962	89.5
LeBoeuf township (Erie)	1,700	1,639	-3.6	1,619	97.5	0.0	0.6	1.1	0.8	21.4	17.4	41.0	53.3	22.6	577	93.1
Leechburg borough & MCD (Armstrong)	2,151	1,989	-7.5	2,095	95.0	1.1	0.3	3.1	0.5	21.4	18.6	43.0	48.8	19.7	963	84.8
Leeper CDP	158	-	-	152	100.0	0.0	0.0	0.0	0.0	12.5	32.9	51.8	75.9	8.3	62	85.5
Leesport borough & MCD (Berks)	1,885	1,891	0.3	2,024	90.7	0.5	1.0	0.5	7.3	25.3	10.8	36.3	52.0	18.5	751	93.6
Leet township (Allegheny)	1,647	1,586	-3.7	1,602	92.2	2.8	1.9	1.4	1.6	26.2	17.0	41.3	23.3	49.1	594	95.3
Leetsdale borough & MCD (Allegheny)	1,203	1,157	-3.8	1,189	78.3	4.7	4.5	7.7	4.7	21.2	22.5	43.6	38.7	35.4	576	82.6
Lehigh township (Carbon)	483	485	0.4	502	95.8	0.0	0.0	0.8	3.4	8.4	27.1	50.2	53.2	25.5	218	80.7
Lehigh township (Northampton)	10,500	10,433	-0.6	10,411	97.3	0.0	0.1	0.7	1.9	19.9	19.9	47.0	49.3	24.2	4,081	87.7
Lehigh township (Wayne)	1,884	1,786	-5.2	2,066	92.8	0.7	0.0	2.6	3.9	20.5	16.1	47.5	43.1	19.6	751	89.7
Lehighton borough & MCD (Carbon)	5,500	5,313	-3.4	5,304	90.4	4.1	2.1	0.5	3.0	21.9	21.5	43.6	63.6	17.7	2,219	71.7
Lehman township (Luzerne)	3,514	3,494	-0.6	3,500	98.1	1.0	0.0	0.0	0.9	20.2	19.8	44.3	38.5	38.3	1,377	93.4
Lehman township (Pike)	10,640	10,218	-4.0	10,183	45.2	21.5	1.9	3.3	28.1	19.3	16.3	44.8	37.9	23.8	3,868	94.2
Leidy township (Clinton)	184	183	-0.5	143	96.5	0.0	0.0	3.5	0.0	8.4	51.7	65.2	70.4	12.0	65	75.4
Leith-Hatfield CDP	2,546	-	-	2,344	96.2	0.9	1.7	1.0	0.0	12.5	30.7	55.4	36.4	42.5	1,040	92.6
Lemon township (Wyoming)	1,240	1,179	-4.9	1,126	97.4	0.0	1.2	1.3	0.0	15.1	27.9	53.6	52.0	27.6	500	88.0
Lemont CDP	2,270	-	-	2,188	88.8	2.1	0.3	2.8	5.9	19.6	20.6	44.0	21.6	59.8	930	85.3
Lemont Furnace CDP	827	-	-	1,011	88.4	5.0	0.0	4.1	2.5	32.9	13.8	33.3	86.4	3.0	369	84.6
Lemoyne borough & MCD (Cumberland)	4,549	4,634	1.9	4,638	77.2	10.4	3.6	5.2	3.6	18.8	15.2	37.7	27.6	36.8	2,208	91.6
Lenape Heights CDP	1,167	-	-	1,107	99.2	0.0	0.8	0.0	0.0	15.2	30.1	54.1	66.7	14.9	524	86.5
Lenhartsville borough & MCD (Berks)	172	171	-0.6	173	94.2	0.0	0.0	0.0	5.8	23.7	24.3	43.4	62.1	22.6	68	79.4
Lenkerville CDP	550	-	-	539	88.5	5.8	5.8	0.0	0.0	32.7	20.4	31.4	40.6	26.6	212	97.2
Lenox township (Susquehanna)	1,925	1,791	-7.0	1,512	94.8	0.4	0.5	1.1	3.2	16.7	23.9	49.8	58.9	15.3	622	86.7
Leola CDP	-	-	-	7,576	75.7	2.3	5.5	2.3	14.0	27.5	12.8	33.4	50.6	27.0	2,691	89.7
Le Raysville borough & MCD (Bradford)	290	276	-4.8	241	97.5	0.0	0.0	0.0	2.5	22.8	14.5	47.5	59.2	14.9	100	83.0
Leroy township (Bradford)	722	700	-3.0	646	99.4	0.3	0.0	0.3	0.0	27.6	19.0	42.9	60.3	15.4	247	85.0
Letterkenny township (Franklin)	2,323	2,377	2.3	2,397	96.9	0.6	0.5	1.8	0.3	20.2	17.1	46.9	65.3	14.1	905	84.0
Level Green CDP	4,020	-	-	3,881	96.8	0.0	1.9	0.6	0.7	21.2	23.9	48.0	41.9	32.7	1,564	96.5
Levittown CDP	52,983	-	-	51,818	84.6	4.7	1.7	1.5	7.5	22.4	15.1	39.7	49.5	22.0	18,148	92.2
Lewis township (Lycoming)	987	950	-3.7	767	97.3	2.2	0.0	0.5	0.0	8.1	22.8	53.4	54.5	18.8	369	85.9
Lewis township (Northumberland)	1,915	1,890	-1.3	1,941	98.3	0.0	0.3	0.5	1.0	28.3	18.4	42.9	53.9	19.9	704	84.5
Lewis township (Union)	1,488	1,466	-1.5	1,568	95.2	3.0	0.0	0.0	1.8	24.6	12.5	37.0	73.9	9.1	481	81.5
Lewisberry borough & MCD (York)	361	356	-1.4	482	93.4	1.5	0.4	2.1	2.7	28.4	10.8	34.8	53.2	18.5	183	86.3
Lewisburg borough & MCD (Union)	5,793	5,708	-1.5	5,723	87.7	1.7	2.9	2.5	5.1	12.1	18.2	22.3	37.6	49.7	1,986	78.5
Lewis Run borough & MCD (McKean)	609	567	-6.9	679	96.6	0.1	0.0	3.2	0.0	17.2	17.2	49.2	55.7	18.4	322	79.2
Lewistown borough & MCD (Mifflin)	8,343	8,125	-2.6	8,194	91.1	1.1	1.0	3.3	3.6	24.7	14.6	35.7	66.9	7.6	3,726	80.6
Liberty township (Adams)	1,246	1,268	1.8	1,392	96.3	1.0	0.0	2.4	0.3	20.8	19.1	45.8	52.5	23.9	553	88.1
Liberty borough & MCD (Allegheny)	2,552	2,454	-3.8	2,363	95.3	1.9	0.5	2.0	0.3	17.1	21.8	48.2	41.4	20.8	1,168	91.4
Liberty township (Bedford)	1,382	1,287	-6.9	1,425	98.6	0.2	0.0	0.0	1.2	16.7	26.8	48.4	57.2	17.5	627	80.2
Liberty township (Centre)	2,106	2,104	-0.1	2,045	97.6	0.3	0.0	1.6	0.5	17.6	19.9	46.6	66.4	11.6	807	82.8
Liberty township (McKean)	1,620	1,513	-6.6	1,427	97.0	0.0	1.1	1.3	0.7	20.3	19.8	47.6	61.5	14.4	614	90.1
Liberty township (Mercer)	1,414	1,403	-0.8	1,589	97.5	0.3	1.1	0.5	0.6	18.1	21.3	46.0	47.9	30.1	615	93.7
Liberty township (Montour)	1,578	1,589	0.7	1,822	96.9	0.7	0.4	0.0	2.0	26.4	14.7	41.2	50.9	22.8	637	83.4
Liberty township (Susquehanna)	1,285	1,194	-7.1	1,230	97.0	1.1	0.0	1.4	0.6	20.1	25.1	49.9	62.9	14.4	496	85.1
Liberty borough & MCD (Tioga)	244	234	-4.1	261	97.3	0.8	0.0	1.9	0.0	36.4	11.5	34.9	60.4	8.2	87	63.2
Liberty township (Tioga)	1,036	1,024	-1.2	975	98.2	1.4	0.0	0.4	0.0	20.6	26.3	49.2	54.4	17.6	372	86.0
Licking township (Clarion)	536	536	0.0	675	97.5	0.0	0.0	2.5	0.0	32.1	15.3	34.9	62.6	12.7	220	69.1
Licking Creek township (Fulton)	1,697	1,670	-1.6	1,569	97.1	0.2	0.0	0.6	2.1	23.9	18.5	43.0	64.1	13.0	592	79.9
Lightstreet CDP	1,093	-	-	978	94.8	0.0	5.2	0.0	0.0	18.8	22.2	45.5	49.2	32.9	442	93.2
Ligonier borough & MCD (Westmoreland)	1,569	1,510	-3.8	1,405	98.1	0.0	0.0	0.6	1.2	13.2	32.9	53.9	24.4	39.7	758	85.2
Ligonier township (Westmoreland)	6,610	6,372	-3.6	6,441	99.2	0.0	0.0	0.6	0.2	13.7	28.7	55.0	37.1	35.2	2,920	86.6
Lilly borough & MCD (Cambria)	966	880	-8.9	818	96.2	1.8	0.0	2.0	0.0	25.8	22.7	46.6	55.5	18.3	340	76.8

1 May be of any race.

STATE City, town, township, borough, or CDP (county if applicable)	Population 2010 census total population	2019 estimated population	Percent change 2010–2019	ACS total population estimate 2015–2019	White alone, not Hispanic or Latino	Black alone, not Hispanic or Latino	Asian alone, not Hispanic or Latino	All other races or 2 or more races, not Hispanic or Latino	Hispanic or Latino[1]	Under 18 years old	Age 65 years and older	Median age	Percent High school diploma or less	Percent Bachelor's degree or more	Occupied housing units Total	Percent with a computer
	1	2	3	4	5	6	7	8	9	10	11	12	13	14	15	16
PENNSYLVANIA—Con.																
Lima CDP	2,735	-	-	1,938	94.0	2.1	1.1	0.0	2.8	6.9	70.4	82.2	35.7	44.1	1,152	60.6
Limerick township (Montgomery)	18,074	19,303	6.8	18,990	87.3	3.2	4.7	2.7	2.2	24.8	13.5	40.3	32.9	44.7	7,161	95.3
Lime Ridge CDP	890	-	-	983	96.3	0.0	3.3	0.0	0.4	16.7	25.1	52.7	67.2	16.0	522	77.6
Limestone township (Clarion)	1,861	1,742	-6.4	1,856	99.1	0.3	0.0	0.6	0.0	21.2	19.0	44.7	52.8	21.1	742	89.1
Limestone township (Lycoming)	2,018	1,979	-1.9	2,105	99.4	0.0	0.2	0.0	0.4	24.9	17.1	40.0	53.9	17.5	731	86.5
Limestone township (Montour)	1,064	1,102	3.6	1,194	95.8	0.9	0.5	0.5	2.3	25.5	15.0	38.3	58.1	18.1	379	83.4
Limestone township (Union)	1,748	1,763	0.9	1,725	95.4	1.0	0.0	1.6	2.0	30.9	12.2	37.2	61.0	23.0	522	80.5
Limestone township (Warren)	402	370	-8.0	264	94.3	0.0	3.8	0.0	1.9	6.8	28.0	59.2	67.9	12.8	130	86.2
Lincoln borough & MCD (Allegheny)	1,064	1,022	-3.9	1,008	98.1	1.2	0.0	0.3	0.4	13.6	24.2	53.2	48.4	17.0	452	85.8
Lincoln township (Bedford)	444	422	-5.0	425	96.0	0.0	0.0	2.6	1.4	21.6	12.9	43.2	61.6	14.8	149	81.9
Lincoln township (Huntingdon)	338	327	-3.3	363	98.1	0.0	0.0	1.7	0.3	36.1	14.9	36.5	49.5	16.7	122	85.2
Lincoln township (Somerset)	1,506	1,413	-6.2	1,313	99.7	0.0	0.0	0.0	0.3	16.1	19.0	46.8	58.4	13.6	560	85.9
Lincoln Park CDP	1,615	-	-	1,760	74.8	3.6	0.2	1.0	20.4	18.5	16.1	41.5	31.6	37.2	756	88.2
Lincoln University CDP	1,726	-	-	1,834	23.9	64.1	3.8	4.3	3.9	1.3	0.0	20.0	13.2	18.4	0	0.0
Lincolnville CDP	96	-	-	195	100.0	0.0	0.0	0.0	0.0	42.6	6.2	28.9	79.5	8.9	58	81.0
Linesville borough & MCD (Crawford)	1,036	976	-5.8	987	92.9	0.0	0.5	3.4	3.1	27.0	22.3	39.1	59.9	20.1	421	77.0
Linglestown CDP	6,334	-	-	5,688	79.7	11.2	0.9	0.6	7.6	20.6	21.0	46.1	36.8	29.5	2,314	91.6
Linntown CDP	1,489	-	-	1,421	99.6	0.0	0.0	0.4	0.0	16.0	17.5	47.4	25.7	47.7	587	96.1
Linwood CDP	3,281	-	-	3,225	84.3	10.2	1.2	2.0	2.2	27.1	7.1	34.0	68.0	13.5	1,115	97.1
Lionville CDP	-	-	-	6,398	78.2	7.4	7.5	0.9	5.9	21.3	14.9	37.6	20.6	53.7	2,635	93.3
Litchfield township (Bradford)	1,320	1,299	-1.6	1,285	96.8	0.0	0.0	1.2	1.9	15.4	18.1	50.2	59.9	17.6	530	84.7
Lititz borough & MCD (Lancaster)	9,161	9,465	3.3	9,335	92.3	1.0	1.5	0.7	4.5	20.3	24.3	45.1	41.7	32.4	3,922	88.2
Little Beaver township (Lawrence)	1,407	1,330	-5.5	1,377	92.3	0.3	1.7	2.1	3.6	24.8	14.5	43.2	56.8	17.3	534	88.4
Little Britain CDP	372	-	-	412	100.0	0.0	0.0	0.0	0.0	19.7	10.4	35.4	55.0	7.9	109	66.1
Little Britain township (Lancaster)	4,101	4,258	3.8	4,227	99.6	0.4	0.0	0.0	0.0	20.3	18.8	47.4	67.7	9.2	1,423	80.7
Little Mahanoy township (Northumberland)	479	453	-5.4	429	96.5	0.9	0.7	1.6	0.2	27.7	18.2	45.6	70.5	14.9	156	76.9
Little Meadows borough & MCD (Susquehanna)	273	247	-9.5	187	100.0	0.0	0.0	0.0	0.0	10.7	29.9	57.1	58.8	10.6	97	91.8
Littlestown borough & MCD (Adams)	4,434	4,510	1.7	4,495	91.9	1.2	0.0	2.7	4.1	24.7	16.7	38.1	45.6	17.8	1,845	90.5
Liverpool borough & MCD (Perry)	949	958	0.9	904	96.3	0.0	2.1	1.2	0.3	17.3	22.5	42.6	59.1	15.5	420	85.5
Liverpool township (Perry)	1,048	1,060	1.1	946	98.4	0.0	1.2	0.1	0.3	24.4	17.3	44.6	51.6	24.3	351	89.2
Lock Haven city & MCD (Clinton)	9,765	9,083	-7.0	9,247	91.4	4.3	1.2	1.3	1.8	16.1	12.5	25.2	52.2	22.0	3,401	87.9
Locust township (Columbia)	1,406	1,378	-2.0	1,458	99.1	0.0	0.4	0.4	0.1	20.2	23.5	44.7	48.2	26.8	580	84.5
Locustdale CDP	177	-	-	187	100.0	0.0	0.0	0.0	0.0	10.2	12.8	47.0	39.0	0.0	90	84.4
Logan township (Blair)	12,668	12,232	-3.4	12,379	94.8	1.5	1.0	2.1	0.6	16.6	22.1	48.4	49.6	24.0	5,126	85.7
Logan township (Clinton)	817	810	-0.9	909	97.8	0.6	0.3	0.7	0.7	34.3	10.1	28.3	64.2	14.9	257	71.6
Logan township (Huntingdon)	679	655	-3.5	712	98.0	0.0	0.6	1.4	0.0	23.3	21.5	45.2	58.2	15.7	299	88.0
Loganton borough & MCD (Clinton)	475	478	0.6	497	92.8	0.0	0.0	1.4	5.8	24.1	18.7	41.5	62.4	8.0	188	74.5
Loganville borough & MCD (York)	1,241	1,313	5.8	1,320	90.2	0.4	1.4	5.5	2.6	27.8	14.5	35.7	40.1	34.3	485	90.5
London Britain township (Chester)	3,125	3,240	3.7	3,238	95.7	0.2	0.9	1.9	1.2	27.6	17.4	45.0	16.2	64.8	1,131	98.9
Londonderry township (Bedford)	1,858	1,762	-5.2	1,928	95.5	0.0	0.0	3.3	1.2	20.1	21.5	46.0	64.4	9.5	740	79.7
Londonderry township (Chester)	2,146	2,552	18.9	2,475	85.2	2.5	1.5	3.8	7.1	23.7	17.6	44.4	32.6	42.5	868	94.9
Londonderry township (Dauphin)	5,218	5,239	0.4	5,228	93.4	0.0	0.0	0.3	6.2	18.4	19.6	48.4	55.8	14.9	2,197	88.8
London Grove township (Chester)	7,462	8,829	18.3	8,696	76.0	3.3	1.8	1.2	17.6	29.1	12.4	37.1	30.1	49.6	2,712	95.4
Long Branch borough & MCD (Washington)	447	432	-3.4	461	93.1	1.7	1.7	2.4	1.1	17.1	22.1	51.4	58.5	16.4	196	87.2
Longfellow CDP	215	-	-	160	100.0	0.0	0.0	0.0	0.0	0.0	37.5	60.4	78.1	1.9	81	72.8
Longswamp township (Berks)	5,648	5,788	2.5	5,725	95.9	0.8	0.0	0.0	3.4	23.6	20.8	47.2	59.4	20.2	2,131	82.7
Lorain borough & MCD (Cambria)	764	692	-9.4	631	96.0	1.6	0.0	1.9	0.5	19.5	22.3	46.6	67.7	12.5	298	79.9
Lorane CDP	4,236	-	-	4,085	92.4	0.5	1.4	1.4	4.2	19.0	21.0	46.8	47.7	33.5	1,684	89.5
Loretto borough & MCD (Cambria)	1,302	1,190	-8.6	1,190	89.7	4.5	1.8	3.5	0.4	1.0	2.9	20.2	24.3	63.0	105	93.3
Lower Allen CDP	6,694	-	-	6,840	86.7	4.0	2.4	3.5	3.3	18.1	22.4	44.5	27.5	41.9	3,151	92.7
Lower Allen township (Cumberland)	17,937	20,260	13.0	19,418	76.5	9.1	4.4	3.5	6.6	13.1	17.9	40.4	42.4	32.6	7,095	90.4
Lower Alsace township (Berks)	4,615	4,734	2.6	4,642	82.4	1.7	1.0	2.2	12.6	19.6	18.8	44.0	48.9	19.9	1,844	88.9
Lower Augusta township (Northumberland)	1,064	1,017	-4.4	956	98.1	0.0	0.5	0.5	0.8	19.2	21.0	47.5	60.3	14.5	408	83.1
Lower Burrell city & MCD (Westmoreland)	11,757	11,078	-5.8	11,229	96.8	0.1	0.5	0.6	1.9	18.8	24.5	48.5	44.7	25.5	4,829	87.6
Lower Chanceford township (York)	3,028	3,120	3.0	3,098	97.6	0.2	0.8	0.8	0.6	22.0	15.5	42.8	57.0	19.7	1,182	81.0

1 May be of any race.

Table A. All Places — Population and Housing

STATE City, town, township, borough, or CDP (county if applicable)	Population				Race and Hispanic or Latino origin (percent)					Age (percent)			Educational attainment of persons age 25 and older		Occupied housing units	
	2010 census total population	2019 estimated population	Percent change 2010–2019	ACS total population estimate 2015–2019	White alone, not Hispanic or Latino	Black alone, not Hispanic or Latino	Asian alone, not Hispanic or Latino	All other races or 2 or more races, not Hispanic or Latino	Hispanic or Latino[1]	Under 18 years old	Age 65 years and older	Median age	Percent High school diploma or less	Percent Bachelor's degree or more	Total	Percent with a computer
	1	2	3	4	5	6	7	8	9	10	11	12	13	14	15	16
PENNSYLVANIA—Con.																
Lower Chichester township (Delaware)	3,468	3,473	0.1	3,468	78.4	16.5	1.2	1.9	2.0	29.8	6.6	33.4	66.1	13.0	1,183	97.3
Lower Frankfoot township (Cumberland)	1,734	1,825	5.2	1,864	90.9	0.2	0.2	6.7	2.0	22.4	15.8	45.2	61.0	15.0	758	88.3
Lower Frederick township (Montgomery)	4,852	4,928	1.6	4,881	90.6	1.9	1.1	0.6	5.7	23.9	15.0	39.7	31.8	40.9	1,870	96.7
Lower Gwynedd township (Montgomery)	11,405	11,497	0.8	11,520	81.9	6.1	9.2	1.9	0.8	21.6	27.1	49.8	16.4	67.5	4,519	91.4
Lower Heidelberg township (Berks)	5,280	6,154	16.6	5,965	87.6	0.1	4.1	2.2	6.1	24.6	15.0	41.3	30.2	47.8	2,087	97.5
Lower Macungie township (Lehigh)	30,644	32,690	6.7	32,218	80.5	4.7	5.3	2.2	7.3	24.0	20.8	44.3	25.0	48.1	12,601	95.0
Lower Mahanoy township (Northumberland)..........	1,689	1,620	-4.1	1,586	99.1	0.0	0.0	0.9	0.0	19.0	25.9	49.0	67.9	14.1	709	77.4
Lower Makefield township (Bucks)	32,557	32,802	0.8	32,662	84.9	3.0	5.7	2.6	3.8	22.2	17.7	47.0	12.6	70.6	12,007	97.9
Lower Merion township (Montgomery)	57,819	60,099	3.9	59,037	80.7	4.9	8.4	2.6	3.3	23.0	21.8	44.0	9.8	78.7	23,188	95.3
Lower Mifflin township (Cumberland)	1,783	1,790	0.4	1,806	98.8	0.2	0.0	0.4	0.5	24.5	17.2	39.3	65.7	17.2	667	84.7
Lower Milford township (Lehigh)	3,798	4,027	6.0	3,963	95.3	0.5	1.0	1.6	1.7	18.8	20.2	48.5	40.2	37.7	1,518	93.9
Lower Moreland township (Montgomery)	12,992	13,114	0.9	13,167	80.2	3.2	13.6	1.4	1.7	22.2	21.0	46.2	28.1	53.7	4,500	94.5
Lower Mount Bethel township (Northampton)	3,083	3,089	0.2	3,071	96.8	1.8	0.9	0.5	0.0	14.8	23.5	52.7	49.3	20.9	1,330	90.9
Lower Nazareth township (Northampton)..............	5,698	6,591	15.7	6,265	87.0	1.6	5.8	0.8	4.7	24.2	17.3	43.9	28.2	43.6	2,209	92.6
Lower Oxford township (Chester)......................	5,230	5,079	-2.9	5,064	60.3	24.4	1.4	3.8	10.1	18.9	8.8	21.7	54.1	22.5	1,005	83.3
Lower Paxton township (Dauphin).....................	47,359	49,936	5.4	49,065	68.8	15.1	7.4	3.2	5.4	20.6	17.8	41.2	35.8	37.3	20,737	88.1
Lower Pottsgrove township (Montgomery)	12,083	12,150	0.6	12,119	80.0	12.7	2.2	2.7	2.3	24.1	17.7	43.2	40.9	32.2	4,644	91.8
Lower Providence township (Montgomery)	25,473	26,873	5.5	26,650	72.7	6.0	14.0	1.5	5.8	21.1	16.5	40.1	32.1	47.5	9,103	95.1
Lower Salford township (Montgomery)	14,936	15,529	4.0	15,364	85.1	3.2	6.2	1.2	4.3	22.7	15.6	44.4	27.8	49.3	5,800	92.3
Lower Saucon township (Northampton)	10,771	10,838	0.6	10,792	87.5	1.4	2.0	1.8	7.4	21.0	22.7	48.0	34.0	45.7	4,055	91.8
Lower Southampton township (Bucks)..........	18,909	19,177	1.4	19,146	92.6	1.3	2.8	1.4	1.9	20.5	16.8	40.7	40.4	30.1	7,120	94.1
Lower Swatara township (Dauphin).....................	8,233	8,922	8.4	8,837	82.3	3.4	2.3	3.5	8.6	16.3	19.5	45.8	46.6	28.2	3,705	84.8
Lower Towamensing township (Carbon)........	3,262	3,203	-1.8	3,183	97.8	0.9	0.4	0.2	0.7	20.6	16.4	42.8	57.1	19.3	1,247	88.9
Lower Turkeyfoot township (Somerset)...................	603	564	-6.5	483	95.2	1.2	0.0	2.1	1.4	16.1	33.5	56.7	78.8	11.3	203	60.1
Lower Tyrone township (Fayette)..................	1,123	1,062	-5.4	1,121	98.3	0.3	0.4	1.1	0.0	19.7	21.2	45.9	57.3	20.3	428	82.0
Lower Windsor township (York)..................	7,388	7,576	2.5	7,545	94.7	0.1	0.1	1.8	3.3	18.3	19.2	47.9	60.3	17.7	3,049	89.4
Lower Yoder township (Cambria).....................	2,686	2,458	-8.5	2,450	98.8	0.0	0.0	1.1	0.1	15.2	30.4	56.0	60.8	14.4	1,282	76.6
Lowhill township (Lehigh) .	2,180	2,343	7.5	2,222	93.7	1.2	1.4	1.7	2.0	21.7	17.2	46.6	30.5	45.6	783	96.6
Loyalhanna CDP..............	3,428	-	-	3,456	94.8	1.0	0.0	3.0	1.2	16.0	23.4	46.9	51.4	23.1	1,538	83.5
Loyalhanna township (Westmoreland)	2,376	2,248	-5.4	1,972	95.0	0.0	0.8	1.9	2.3	17.9	13.4	38.8	55.2	12.6	832	82.3
Loyalsock township (Lycoming)	11,032	10,903	-1.2	10,999	90.4	3.6	0.2	0.8	4.9	18.9	27.8	49.5	42.5	32.9	4,455	87.3
Lucerne Mines CDP	937	-	-	999	96.0	0.1	0.0	3.9	0.0	15.8	26.4	45.8	58.6	5.8	373	93.0
Lumber township (Cameron)...................	197	172	-12.7	131	100.0	0.0	0.0	0.0	0.0	7.6	39.7	61.8	51.3	11.3	68	85.3
Lumber City CDP..............	255	-	-	284	100.0	0.0	0.0	0.0	0.0	5.3	31.7	60.0	69.9	3.0	145	100.0
Lurgan township (Franklin)	2,154	2,170	0.7	2,286	99.4	0.0	0.6	0.0	0.0	28.3	16.3	36.9	72.2	11.4	760	75.9
Luzerne township (Fayette)...................	5,959	5,904	-0.9	5,909	75.8	18.8	0.3	1.9	3.2	11.6	18.1	44.3	71.4	12.4	1,522	88.5
Luzerne borough & MCD (Luzerne)...................	2,848	2,812	-1.3	2,817	97.2	0.9	0.0	0.0	1.9	13.1	24.7	51.3	55.3	14.1	1,515	72.9
Lycoming township (Lycoming)	1,480	1,455	-1.7	1,409	95.5	2.1	0.0	1.7	0.6	16.5	23.1	51.3	51.8	15.0	575	86.1
Lykens borough & MCD (Dauphin)....................	1,780	1,769	-0.6	1,807	96.2	0.2	0.0	1.8	1.7	23.3	18.3	39.6	65.9	11.7	782	74.6
Lykens township (Dauphin)....................	1,620	1,689	4.3	1,696	96.9	0.2	0.0	0.1	2.8	36.6	12.3	28.6	73.3	10.4	469	69.5
Lynn township (Lehigh).....	4,220	4,421	4.8	4,373	92.7	0.0	0.0	3.7	3.6	20.3	16.4	43.5	39.2	34.5	1,665	92.1
Lynnwood-Pricedale CDP	2,031	-	-	1,889	95.6	3.5	0.0	0.0	0.9	10.3	28.2	52.6	58.3	24.5	972	80.6
Lyons borough & MCD (Berks)	476	479	0.6	459	94.8	0.9	0.0	0.2	4.1	14.8	20.9	45.8	62.0	21.2	202	95.5
McAdoo borough & MCD (Schuylkill)................	2,300	2,156	-6.3	2,440	81.8	0.0	0.1	0.9	17.1	25.1	13.7	37.6	62.6	9.0	1,052	80.9
McAlisterville CDP	971	-	-	1,000	93.1	6.9	0.0	0.0	0.0	37.7	17.4	31.4	56.8	29.7	341	70.7
McCalmont township (Jefferson)....................	1,077	1,036	-3.8	1,281	100.0	0.0	0.0	0.0	0.0	31.3	12.7	30.7	71.7	9.8	435	71.0
McCandless township (Allegheny)	28,481	28,193		28,471	86.4	2.5	6.4	2.3	2.5	19.5	20.6	44.2	21.2	56.7	11,883	91.8
McClure borough & MCD (Snyder)...................	942	921	-2.2	1,277	94.7	3.8	0.2	0.5	0.8	25.2	17.5	37.3	69.1	11.9	426	88.5
McConnellsburg borough & MCD (Fulton)	1,053	1,002	-4.8	1,129	94.2	2.3	0.0	2.5	1.1	29.1	18.0	38.8	58.0	18.9	506	79.1
McConnellstown CDP......	1,194	-	-	1,524	99.6	0.1	0.0	0.3	0.0	24.7	21.3	45.2	46.5	33.7	571	92.8
McDonald borough	2,143	2,050	-4.3	2,164	92.5	1.1	0.0	3.9	2.5	21.1	22.0	45.5	58.2	17.8	944	77.9

1 May be of any race.

Table A. All Places — Population and Housing

STATE City, town, township, borough, or CDP (county if applicable)	2010 census total population	2019 estimated population	Percent change 2010–2019	ACS total population estimate 2015–2019	White alone, not Hispanic or Latino	Black alone, not Hispanic or Latino	Asian alone, not Hispanic or Latino	All other races or 2 or more races, not Hispanic or Latino	Hispanic or Latino[1]	Under 18 years old	Age 65 years and older	Median age	Percent High school diploma or less	Percent Bachelor's degree or more	Total	Percent with a computer
	1	2	3	4	5	6	7	8	9	10	11	12	13	14	15	16
PENNSYLVANIA—Con.																
McDonald borough (Allegheny)	376	363	-3.5	531	82.5	2.1	0.0	15.4	0.0	29.4	21.7	40.0	75.3	9.6	181	68.0
McDonald borough (Washington)	1,767	1,687	-4.5	1,633	95.7	0.7	0.1	0.2	3.3	18.4	22.1	47.8	52.9	20.3	763	80.2
McElhattan CDP	598	-	-	385	96.9	0.0	0.0	1.3	1.8	6.0	35.6	57.3	76.8	5.1	184	91.3
McEwensville borough & MCD (Northumberland)	281	272	-3.2	334	100.0	0.0	0.0	0.0	0.0	20.7	6.0	34.7	67.1	13.4	138	92.8
McGovern CDP	2,742	-	-	2,790	96.5	0.8	0.0	2.4	0.4	23.2	23.7	43.1	42.2	28.8	1,157	89.6
McHenry township (Lycoming)	143	136	-4.9	140	97.9	0.0	0.0	2.1	0.0	13.6	36.4	60.0	51.3	24.4	79	81.0
McIntyre township (Lycoming)	521	494	-5.2	385	93.8	0.0	0.0	5.2	1.0	11.7	20.5	51.9	64.6	14.6	163	82.8
McKean borough & MCD (Erie)	390	369	-5.4	481	94.0	5.2	0.0	0.2	0.6	19.5	26.0	47.9	53.1	30.8	218	83.5
McKean township (Erie)	4,414	4,318	-2.2	4,370	95.8	0.0	0.0	3.8	0.5	22.3	18.3	42.5	51.6	24.6	1,669	96.2
McKeansburg CDP	163	-	-	149	97.3	0.0	0.0	2.7	0.0	17.4	26.8	42.8	44.8	16.4	69	85.5
McKeesport city & MCD (Allegheny)	19,730	19,009	-3.7	19,225	57.9	34.9	0.8	3.6	2.8	20.5	20.4	44.9	53.6	13.1	8,930	79.1
McKees Rocks borough & MCD (Allegheny)	6,083	5,855	-3.7	5,919	55.5	32.3	2.2	5.3	4.7	21.9	12.8	35.0	56.0	14.9	2,901	77.4
McKnightstown CDP	226	-	-	163	100.0	0.0	0.0	0.0	0.0	4.3	35.0	53.7	91.0	9.0	85	58.8
McMurray CDP	4,647	-	-	4,215	91.9	0.6	4.3	0.3	2.9	22.1	18.9	44.9	19.8	58.9	1,468	99.4
McNett township (Lycoming)	174	168	-3.4	110	100.0	0.0	0.0	0.0	0.0	11.8	38.2	59.5	67.0	11.0	57	71.9
McSherrystown borough & MCD (Adams)	3,038	3,090	1.7	3,071	91.3	0.0	1.2	2.7	4.8	24.8	17.0	39.1	46.0	13.8	1,345	75.8
Macungie borough & MCD (Lehigh)	3,074	3,178	3.4	3,155	84.5	1.2	1.9	2.5	9.8	18.1	16.4	40.7	39.1	35.6	1,410	92.4
McVeytown borough & MCD (Mifflin)	342	331	-3.2	340	97.9	1.2	0.9	0.0	0.0	18.8	26.2	48.1	58.2	23.9	156	78.2
Madison township (Armstrong)	820	762	-7.1	906	98.7	0.0	0.0	0.6	0.8	21.0	23.1	46.5	69.3	11.1	385	79.7
Madison township (Clarion)	1,211	1,129	-6.8	1,201	94.7	0.0	2.8	1.0	1.5	18.7	25.4	47.6	68.9	12.0	505	80.6
Madison township (Columbia)	1,602	1,563	-2.4	1,545	99.5	0.0	0.0	0.2	0.3	20.4	20.5	46.7	55.1	16.9	617	80.6
Madison township (Lackawanna)	2,755	2,645	-4.0	2,664	97.0	0.0	0.0	0.2	2.9	24.7	14.0	42.5	41.7	30.1	1,054	95.4
Madison borough & MCD (Westmoreland)	392	367	-6.4	367	94.8	0.0	0.0	0.8	4.4	13.1	21.8	50.0	53.4	9.2	185	87.0
Madisonburg CDP	168	-	-	223	96.4	0.0	0.0	1.8	1.8	27.8	26.0	49.4	54.8	25.8	89	80.9
Mahaffey borough & MCD (Clearfield)	373	352	-5.6	363	93.9	0.0	3.6	2.5	0.0	11.0	16.0	47.6	75.5	4.4	143	81.1
Mahanoy township (Schuylkill)	3,155	3,172	0.5	3,219	46.8	36.2	0.2	3.1	13.7	2.8	9.7	40.8	77.8	4.8	341	81.2
Mahanoy City borough & MCD (Schuylkill)	4,162	3,944	-5.2	3,982	81.2	5.3	1.5	1.9	10.2	28.6	15.5	32.7	66.2	6.4	1,573	81.0
Mahoning township (Armstrong)	1,423	1,314	-7.7	1,402	99.4	0.0	0.6	0.0	0.0	18.4	26.1	49.3	68.5	13.2	609	76.2
Mahoning township (Carbon)	4,308	4,239	-1.6	4,222	90.9	0.5	0.3	1.4	6.8	16.4	20.4	50.5	59.6	15.8	1,682	92.8
Mahoning township (Lawrence)	3,082	2,858	-7.3	2,896	100.0	0.0	0.0	0.0	0.0	20.5	20.6	41.1	54.7	21.9	1,137	85.4
Mahoning township (Montour)	4,172	4,142	-0.7	4,176	74.0	5.6	12.3	0.8	7.4	19.2	27.0	47.3	37.9	45.7	1,633	89.2
Maidencreek township (Berks)	9,112	9,478	4.0	9,434	86.0	3.8	2.6	0.3	7.3	19.1	13.4	42.5	33.6	33.3	3,634	89.9
Main township (Columbia)	1,236	1,274	3.1	1,326	98.5	0.0	0.4	0.8	0.3	21.3	18.0	44.0	43.1	31.6	504	89.3
Mainville CDP	132	-	-	96	100.0	0.0	0.0	0.0	0.0	0.0	47.9	63.0	76.0	12.5	53	62.3
Maitland CDP	357	-	-	388	100.0	0.0	0.0	0.0	0.0	0.0	21.9	51.9	52.9	7.2	190	86.3
Malvern borough & MCD (Chester)	3,012	3,455	14.7	3,447	85.7	2.5	5.0	3.2	3.6	18.6	19.4	42.7	17.9	66.2	1,575	94.5
Mammoth CDP	525	-	-	467	100.0	0.0	0.0	0.0	0.0	24.4	21.2	43.3	45.6	31.6	184	83.2
Manchester township (Wayne)	834	819	-1.8	757	93.4	0.0	0.4	2.8	3.4	18.5	25.6	49.2	55.7	18.6	288	91.3
Manchester borough & MCD (York)	2,760	2,740	-0.7	2,750	88.3	2.0	0.0	2.9	6.8	14.6	17.2	49.8	66.7	10.0	1,387	83.9
Manchester township (York)	18,168	18,648	2.6	18,545	86.9	3.8	1.0	2.4	5.9	24.7	16.4	40.8	40.2	34.3	6,910	90.4
Manheim borough & MCD (Lancaster)	4,860	4,849	-0.2	4,867	92.0	1.3	0.0	2.4	4.3	23.4	14.8	37.7	50.9	27.1	1,886	92.0
Manheim township (Lancaster)	38,159	40,548	6.3	40,028	78.4	3.3	5.2	2.5	10.5	21.9	22.6	44.5	32.1	46.7	15,954	92.0
Manheim township (York)	3,389	3,498	3.2	3,469	93.5	0.0	0.8	1.7	3.9	20.5	19.7	48.8	45.4	27.3	1,282	94.5
Mann township (Bedford)	498	476	-4.4	612	97.4	0.2	0.0	1.0	1.5	21.1	19.9	47.1	58.3	6.4	259	81.5
Manns Choice borough & MCD (Bedford)	300	284	-5.3	241	99.6	0.0	0.0	0.0	0.4	24.5	16.2	39.8	71.9	7.2	101	85.1
Manor township (Armstrong)	4,256	4,043	-5.0	4,115	99.2	0.0	0.2	0.5	0.0	17.2	28.4	49.7	60.1	16.2	1,773	79.2
Manor township (Lancaster)	19,649	21,021	7.0	20,832	83.6	4.3	2.2	1.9	8.1	21.8	16.6	39.7	44.2	29.7	8,317	91.3
Manor borough & MCD (Westmoreland)	3,200	3,344	4.5	3,318	96.8	0.0	2.4	0.4	0.5	28.8	10.3	39.1	32.2	35.3	1,230	93.7
Manorville borough & MCD (Armstrong)	410	385	-6.1	434	99.1	0.9	0.0	0.0	0.0	22.4	15.0	42.7	47.4	23.2	180	85.0
Mansfield borough & MCD (Tioga)	3,630	2,917	-19.6	3,031	90.9	1.5	1.5	2.2	3.8	20.7	17.0	31.2	40.8	34.1	1,335	87.9
Maple Glen CDP	6,742	-	-	6,726	86.3	0.5	9.3	1.4	2.5	25.2	12.8	41.2	20.6	58.9	2,323	99.0
Mapleton borough & MCD (Huntingdon)	439	414	-5.7	444	96.6	1.8	0.0	1.6	0.0	31.8	13.5	32.8	74.8	6.4	161	84.5
Mapletown CDP	130	-	-	114	100.0	0.0	0.0	0.0	0.0	10.5	46.5	63.6	80.8	6.1	52	92.3

1 May be of any race.

Table A. All Places — **Population and Housing**

STATE City, town, township, borough, or CDP (county if applicable)	Population				Race and Hispanic or Latino origin (percent)					Age (percent)			Educational attainment of persons age 25 and older		Occupied housing units	
	2010 census total population	2019 estimated population	Percent change 2010–2019	ACS total population estimate 2015–2019	White alone, not Hispanic or Latino	Black alone, not Hispanic or Latino	Asian alone, not Hispanic or Latino	All other races or 2 or more races, not Hispanic or Latino	Hispanic or Latino[1]	Under 18 years old	Age 65 years and older	Median age	Percent High school diploma or less	Percent Bachelor's degree or more	Total	Percent with a computer
	1	2	3	4	5	6	7	8	9	10	11	12	13	14	15	16
PENNSYLVANIA—Con.																
Marcus Hook borough & MCD (Delaware)	2,397	2,402	0.2	2,258	68.6	23.6	1.7	1.4	4.7	20.2	8.6	35.8	71.3	9.5	886	81.6
Marianna borough & MCD (Washington)	494	471	-4.7	450	92.4	0.0	0.0	7.6	0.0	20.7	12.7	31.2	59.9	2.5	182	76.4
Marianne CDP	1,167	-	-	1,082	89.7	2.7	1.8	4.9	0.9	15.6	24.3	47.5	38.3	38.6	424	94.3
Marienville CDP	3,137	-	-	4,045	44.9	44.4	0.1	2.5	8.1	3.8	8.3	35.5	81.2	4.4	241	82.2
Marietta borough & MCD (Lancaster)	2,588	2,604	0.6	2,610	92.0	2.2	0.0	1.8	4.0	21.8	14.3	38.6	53.0	22.5	1,101	87.7
Marion township (Beaver) .	912	869	-4.7	792	99.5	0.0	0.5	0.0	0.0	17.0	23.7	47.5	48.3	29.4	329	90.9
Marion township (Berks)...	1,620	1,927	19.0	1,627	96.4	0.9	0.2	0.5	1.9	20.0	29.2	50.0	51.1	19.2	634	81.2
Marion township (Butler)...	1,248	1,200	-3.8	1,184	98.3	0.5	0.0	1.2	0.0	14.8	16.4	45.8	63.3	19.8	498	90.8
Marion township (Centre) .	1,221	1,270	4.0	1,546	97.7	0.0	0.3	1.2	0.9	34.8	9.6	35.6	55.1	18.5	459	83.7
Marion CDP	953	-	-	1,170	62.6	24.7	4.4	8.3	0.0	36.3	8.7	37.6	41.2	27.5	382	97.4
Marion Center borough & MCD (Indiana)	451	418	-7.3	481	97.5	0.0	0.0	2.3	0.2	20.4	20.2	44.5	55.2	8.2	207	81.2
Marion Heights borough & MCD (Northumberland)	610	578	-5.2	697	100.0	0.0	0.0	0.0	0.0	20.5	16.6	43.3	52.6	14.7	287	80.8
Marklesburg borough & MCD (Huntingdon)	204	196	-3.9	282	90.8	0.0	3.9	3.9	1.4	19.9	30.5	43.6	52.7	11.3	110	86.4
Markleysburg borough & MCD (Fayette)	290	281	-3.1	305	81.3	0.0	0.0	12.1	6.6	26.9	33.8	43.3	70.0	5.3	86	74.4
Marlborough township (Montgomery)	3,208	3,385	5.5	3,372	96.6	0.4	0.5	0.1	2.4	25.0	16.5	41.5	42.2	24.1	1,233	92.0
Marlin CDP	661	-	-	420	100.0	0.0	0.0	0.0	0.0	18.3	31.0	55.4	69.3	19.0	204	75.5
Marple township (Delaware)	23,421	23,955	2.3	23,779	85.7	1.9	8.7	2.5	1.2	20.1	23.2	46.9	34.2	44.3	8,387	91.0
Mars borough & MCD (Butler)	1,699	1,612	-5.1	1,336	95.2	2.9	0.0	1.1	0.7	17.1	23.7	48.3	46.0	18.2	628	84.4
Marshall township (Allegheny)	6,907	9,598	39.0	9,053	85.6	1.9	10.3	1.0	1.2	28.7	12.2	41.3	14.1	70.4	3,190	98.3
Marshallton CDP	1,441	-	-	1,160	91.7	0.2	0.8	3.2	4.1	24.1	16.1	50.7	74.1	9.3	554	65.7
Martic township (Lancaster)	5,190	5,212	0.4	5,220	97.5	0.0	0.0	0.3	2.2	24.5	13.7	41.4	56.7	18.2	1,877	87.1
Martinsburg borough & MCD (Blair)	1,945	1,836	-5.6	1,689	99.8	0.0	0.0	0.2	0.0	16.0	23.7	49.8	54.7	23.7	802	78.9
Martins Creek CDP	631	-	-	437	96.6	0.0	0.0	3.4	0.0	9.8	38.0	63.4	43.1	17.3	244	84.0
Marysville borough & MCD (Perry)	2,534	2,559	1.0	2,543	91.2	1.8	0.7	1.5	4.8	22.1	19.0	35.9	53.1	20.3	1,157	89.5
Masontown borough & MCD (Fayette)	3,463	3,277	-5.4	3,327	88.9	4.7	0.0	6.3	0.0	22.0	19.7	42.1	61.1	11.5	1,434	75.7
Masthope CDP	685	-	-	601	79.4	0.0	0.0	6.2	14.5	10.3	45.6	52.0	30.3	40.8	298	100.0
Matamoras borough & MCD (Pike)	2,469	2,362	-4.3	2,336	83.9	0.0	5.1	4.0	7.0	20.4	20.0	41.8	44.0	25.9	955	88.5
Mather CDP	737	-	-	477	96.9	0.0	0.0	3.1	0.0	12.4	23.5	49.9	62.2	11.5	208	86.5
Mattawana CDP	276	-	-	500	99.2	0.0	0.0	0.0	0.8	17.8	14.4	43.2	81.9	9.5	189	78.3
Maxatawny township (Berks)	7,914	7,689	-2.8	7,330	83.9	8.4	0.8	2.6	4.3	9.0	8.2	20.6	60.1	20.6	1,235	90.4
Mayberry township (Montour)	246	248	0.8	261	96.9	0.0	0.0	0.0	3.1	19.9	25.7	52.5	52.2	28.4	109	75.2
Mayfield borough & MCD (Lackawanna)	1,809	1,695	-6.3	1,699	96.0	0.8	0.6	1.7	0.9	21.5	18.7	46.6	44.6	24.3	703	88.1
Maytown CDP	3,824	-	-	3,928	89.8	0.5	0.8	4.4	4.5	30.7	10.6	31.7	41.7	27.4	1,291	87.5
Mead township (Warren) ..	1,387	1,300	-6.3	1,394	98.5	1.1	0.0	0.4	0.0	15.4	22.5	50.0	58.6	14.1	631	88.3
Meadowlands CDP	822	-	-	1,249	73.3	4.1	0.0	22.6	0.0	23.2	14.9	38.7	50.8	9.8	437	86.3
Meadowood CDP	2,693	-	-	2,847	98.4	0.8	0.4	0.5	0.0	17.0	27.2	48.5	35.6	29.8	1,137	93.5
Meadville city & MCD (Crawford)	13,388	12,655	-5.5	12,864	86.2	5.2	0.7	5.5	2.3	18.2	17.3	37.9	51.6	24.6	5,442	83.8
Mechanicsburg borough & MCD (Cumberland).......	8,972	8,990	0.2	9,006	88.1	2.9	0.9	2.5	5.5	19.5	16.6	40.5	42.7	32.5	4,069	85.7
Mechanicsville borough & MCD (Schuylkill)	458	435	-5.0	467	98.5	1.1	0.0	0.0	0.4	20.6	18.6	44.1	63.5	13.5	191	86.4
Media borough & MCD (Delaware)	5,329	5,682	6.6	5,487	84.7	5.7	5.0	2.5	2.1	14.0	17.2	39.8	18.4	58.7	2,718	94.3
Mehoopany township (Wyoming)	897	881	-1.8	905	94.5	0.7	0.0	1.2	3.6	21.1	16.5	41.0	59.3	14.0	376	85.4
Menallen township (Adams)	3,517	3,568	1.5	3,553	85.6	0.5	1.0	0.7	12.3	22.9	13.8	38.7	53.5	24.1	1,336	89.4
Menallen township (Fayette)	4,203	3,986	-5.2	4,050	95.0	0.6	0.0	3.7	0.7	18.6	21.1	45.7	60.8	19.0	1,639	78.4
Menno township (Mifflin)...	1,885	1,915	1.6	1,914	97.1	2.4	0.0	0.5	0.0	38.6	10.8	25.3	77.7	9.0	557	55.7
Mercer township (Butler) ..	1,098	1,061	-3.4	1,424	99.9	0.0	0.0	0.0	0.1	19.7	15.7	41.4	53.9	18.7	534	92.7
Mercer borough & MCD (Mercer)	2,042	1,882	-7.8	1,784	96.1	0.0	0.4	3.4	0.0	16.8	22.5	44.1	49.1	24.9	901	77.2
Mercersburg borough & MCD (Franklin)	1,551	1,532	-1.2	1,633	86.4	6.3	1.2	0.6	5.5	17.5	21.0	46.5	56.9	20.0	745	88.6
Meridian CDP	3,881	-	-	3,970	94.1	0.0	1.3	3.2	1.4	19.3	23.2	47.4	39.7	30.6	1,661	85.2
Mertztown CDP	664	-	-	963	92.0	1.5	0.0	0.0	6.5	25.8	9.1	43.7	66.2	7.8	325	90.5
Meshoppen borough & MCD (Wyoming)...........	563	535	-5.0	505	90.1	0.8	0.0	2.4	6.7	26.3	3.6	32.6	70.1	4.9	165	89.7
Meshoppen township (Wyoming)	1,073	978	-8.9	838	97.0	0.0	0.1	2.3	0.6	20.0	19.1	45.4	71.5	13.0	339	90.0
Messiah College CDP	2,215	-	-	2,158	84.2	5.4	3.4	3.0	4.1	0.3	0.7	20.1	0.0	78.8	8	100.0
Metal township (Franklin)..	1,866	1,853	-0.7	1,528	100.0	0.0	0.0	0.0	0.0	18.9	21.2	48.3	69.1	11.4	637	80.7
Mexico CDP	472	-	-	367	100.0	0.0	0.0	0.0	0.0	18.8	12.0	42.8	67.8	6.1	147	86.4
Meyersdale borough & MCD (Somerset)	2,184	2,019	-7.6	2,043	96.9	0.5	0.0	1.8	0.8	17.9	23.3	47.8	63.0	10.9	925	70.4
Middleburg borough & MCD (Snyder)	1,303	1,270	-2.5	1,633	97.9	0.5	0.0	1.4	0.2	27.6	17.9	34.8	62.3	15.1	595	82.2
Middlebury township (Tioga)	1,292	1,281	-0.9	1,186	96.5	0.0	0.6	2.3	0.6	18.6	18.7	45.8	59.1	15.1	511	88.3
Middlecreek township (Snyder)	2,105	2,155	2.4	2,173	97.7	0.0	0.2	1.9	0.1	26.0	18.2	42.6	57.5	20.0	837	83.8

1 May be of any race.

Table A. All Places — Population and Housing

STATE City, town, township, borough, or CDP (county if applicable)	2010 census total population	2019 estimated population	Percent change 2010–2019	ACS total population estimate 2015–2019	White alone, not Hispanic or Latino	Black alone, not Hispanic or Latino	Asian alone, not Hispanic or Latino	All other races or 2 or more races, not Hispanic or Latino	Hispanic or Latino[1]	Under 18 years old	Age 65 years and older	Median age	Percent High school diploma or less	Percent Bachelor's degree or more	Total	Percent with a computer
	1	2	3	4	5	6	7	8	9	10	11	12	13	14	15	16
PENNSYLVANIA—Con.																
Middlecreek township (Somerset)	869	810	-6.8	711	100.0	0.0	0.0	0.0	0.0	12.9	27.6	53.8	61.8	18.1	345	76.2
Middle Paxton township (Dauphin)	4,976	5,125	3.0	5,080	97.3	1.1	0.0	1.2	0.4	18.1	21.8	46.4	40.3	35.6	2,058	90.9
Middleport borough & MCD (Schuylkill)	397	377	-5.0	373	98.7	0.0	0.8	0.5	0.0	16.6	24.7	48.4	72.5	8.9	173	71.7
Middlesex township (Butler)	5,394	5,793	7.4	5,637	95.2	0.1	2.4	1.8	0.5	21.3	19.0	42.4	31.1	42.3	2,267	94.0
Middlesex township (Cumberland)	7,021	7,411	5.6	7,335	88.8	3.5	1.8	2.6	3.3	19.3	17.5	43.5	48.1	30.7	2,553	90.4
Middle Smithfield township (Monroe) ..	15,936	15,942	0.0	15,725	64.1	15.4	2.3	1.9	16.4	19.5	15.9	43.5	44.6	21.7	5,399	95.1
Middle Taylor township (Cambria)	724	661	-8.7	784	94.6	0.0	0.0	3.7	1.7	19.1	26.4	51.2	52.1	23.1	341	82.7
Middletown township (Bucks)	45,396	44,966	-0.9	45,117	85.2	4.1	5.0	1.2	4.5	19.5	18.5	42.7	34.7	40.3	16,543	93.1
Middletown borough & MCD (Dauphin)	8,942	9,594	7.3	9,315	73.9	9.4	3.8	3.8	9.1	20.6	17.3	35.8	54.8	20.7	4,008	86.5
Middletown township (Delaware)	15,806	16,073	1.7	15,969	91.4	1.9	3.5	1.0	2.3	18.2	27.3	50.8	26.2	49.3	6,467	87.0
Middletown CDP	7,441	-	-	7,212	79.0	4.4	2.2	2.3	12.1	15.3	22.4	47.1	45.0	24.4	2,790	90.1
Middletown township (Susquehanna)	382	347	-9.2	286	93.0	0.0	0.7	6.3	0.0	12.2	27.3	56.0	63.5	11.7	140	85.7
Midland borough & MCD (Beaver)	2,637	2,469	-6.4	2,918	81.7	8.1	0.0	6.0	4.2	23.0	19.7	40.0	47.3	5.3	1,210	83.5
Midway CDP	2,125	-	-	2,062	95.2	0.0	0.0	0.4	4.4	14.4	21.6	46.3	60.3	18.9	857	94.0
Midway borough & MCD (Washington)	913	873	-4.4	867	93.2	2.2	0.0	4.6	0.0	20.5	18.9	42.3	67.3	10.7	338	92.0
Mifflin township (Columbia)	2,311	2,256	-2.4	2,134	93.9	1.7	0.0	0.0	4.4	17.0	18.7	46.1	54.0	21.2	915	87.0
Mifflin township (Dauphin)	784	821	4.7	814	99.4	0.0	0.0	0.2	0.4	36.9	14.9	33.8	72.8	9.3	244	77.5
Mifflin borough & MCD (Juniata)	640	620	-3.1	511	75.3	0.0	0.0	0.0	24.7	26.2	10.2	29.3	75.7	3.9	198	76.3
Mifflin township (Lycoming)	1,070	1,034	-3.4	1,119	96.1	0.0	1.1	0.5	2.3	23.7	15.3	45.3	58.7	13.4	443	85.8
Mifflinburg borough & MCD (Union)	3,513	3,475	-1.1	3,497	97.9	1.4	0.0	0.0	0.7	22.3	24.1	43.8	55.4	22.6	1,554	80.6
Mifflintown borough & MCD (Juniata)	936	911	-2.7	964	74.7	0.7	0.0	0.0	24.6	24.5	15.0	36.7	59.5	13.5	409	84.6
Mifflinville CDP	1,253	-	-	1,129	92.2	0.0	0.0	0.0	7.8	10.3	19.9	53.0	51.0	22.4	521	87.9
Miles township (Centre)	1,991	2,019	1.4	2,288	98.9	0.0	0.3	0.2	0.7	36.9	12.7	25.8	76.5	9.7	620	55.8
Milesburg borough & MCD (Centre)	1,099	1,076	-2.1	976	98.9	0.0	0.0	0.0	1.1	21.2	15.9	37.9	45.7	20.6	417	79.1
Milford township (Bucks)...	9,906	10,056	1.5	10,064	94.9	1.0	0.4	1.3	2.4	22.3	19.2	46.7	45.9	33.4	3,643	91.0
Milford township (Juniata).	2,090	2,099	0.4	2,242	88.5	0.4	0.0	1.3	9.8	22.7	24.4	46.0	68.2	13.0	869	88.8
Milford borough & MCD (Pike)	1,022	982	-3.9	1,172	86.9	3.2	0.9	1.0	8.0	13.7	28.7	54.4	40.3	29.3	571	82.1
Milford township (Pike)	1,539	1,489	-3.2	1,329	92.6	0.2	1.6	0.8	4.8	19.2	24.2	50.5	37.0	35.3	571	90.7
Milford township (Somerset)	1,559	1,476	-5.3	1,463	97.9	0.2	0.5	1.3	0.1	16.7	23.6	47.4	58.1	17.0	636	87.7
Milford Square CDP	897	-	-	1,034	95.2	0.0	0.0	1.6	3.2	28.1	5.7	38.0	41.1	49.3	323	93.2
Millbourne borough & MCD (Delaware)	1,159	1,160	0.1	1,184	12.3	14.4	67.5	0.4	5.4	24.3	9.0	31.0	50.3	25.6	346	92.2
Millcreek township (Clarion)	396	368	-7.1	453	99.6	0.0	0.0	0.4	0.0	21.2	27.2	52.4	62.1	14.3	183	76.0
Millcreek township (Erie) ..	53,561	52,456	-2.1	53,297	91.4	2.2	1.9	2.9	1.6	20.5	19.9	43.4	33.8	41.9	23,012	90.4
Mill Creek borough & MCD (Huntingdon)	328	317	-3.4	312	99.7	0.0	0.0	0.3	0.0	14.7	22.8	47.3	73.0	4.6	142	82.4
Millcreek township (Lebanon)	3,923	4,188	6.8	4,115	97.3	1.3	1.0	0.0	0.4	35.3	13.0	32.6	64.7	14.1	1,343	96.9
Mill Creek township (Lycoming)	604	605	0.2	597	98.0	0.2	0.7	1.2	0.0	18.8	20.8	49.5	50.4	25.2	227	94.3
Mill Creek township (Mercer)	722	705	-2.4	673	98.2	0.0	0.0	1.8	0.0	15.2	22.6	51.6	60.5	14.7	312	86.9
Miller township (Huntingdon)	462	450	-2.6	513	93.8	0.0	1.2	2.3	2.7	17.2	19.3	51.3	50.5	20.6	219	85.8
Miller township (Perry)	1,095	1,099	0.4	912	86.1	0.1	0.0	0.0	13.8	19.2	16.6	43.5	65.0	12.2	375	88.8
Millersburg borough & MCD (Dauphin)	2,529	2,516	-0.5	2,519	97.1	0.0	2.3	0.0	0.6	16.0	24.7	45.6	61.0	17.9	1,140	83.2
Millerstown borough & MCD (Perry)	674	681	1.0	704	96.0	0.1	0.6	0.0	3.3	24.3	23.2	46.4	37.3	34.2	264	86.0
Millersville borough & MCD (Lancaster)..........	8,129	8,359	2.8	8,322	83.0	4.7	2.9	2.5	6.9	10.9	17.7	27.9	35.1	42.1	3,092	90.9
Millerton CDP	316	-	-	298	100.0	0.0	0.0	0.0	0.0	11.7	29.2	51.6	57.0	5.9	118	83.1
Mill Hall borough & MCD (Clinton)	1,623	1,608	-0.9	1,774	94.2	0.8	0.9	1.0	3.0	22.0	15.9	38.6	50.9	24.5	689	84.5
Millheim borough & MCD (Centre)	892	880	-1.3	569	96.3	0.0	0.0	3.0	0.7	17.8	17.0	47.1	50.0	21.6	257	78.2
Millsboro CDP	666	-	-	472	100.0	0.0	0.0	0.0	0.0	29.7	14.2	34.2	47.1	22.7	191	92.1
Millstone township (Elk)....	82	75	-8.5	91	93.4	0.0	0.0	0.0	6.6	12.1	37.4	57.5	42.1	27.6	50	74.0
Millvale borough & MCD (Allegheny)	3,805	3,662	-3.8	3,706	86.6	8.9	0.6	3.2	0.0	15.2	16.9	43.0	48.2	18.0	1,903	81.8
Mill Village borough & MCD (Erie)	410	385	-6.1	371	93.8	1.1	1.1	3.5	0.5	21.0	17.8	44.4	58.8	15.2	147	85.7
Millville borough & MCD (Columbia)	949	922	-2.8	866	94.8	0.8	3.0	0.2	1.2	17.9	27.6	43.5	57.5	19.4	347	79.8
Millwood CDP	566	-	-	547	82.6	0.0	0.0	0.0	17.4	19.2	23.6	45.5	74.8	5.0	244	76.6
Milroy CDP	1,498	-	-	1,246	87.4	0.0	2.1	5.4	5.1	19.3	28.7	48.3	59.7	15.5	599	69.8
Milton borough & MCD (Northumberland)........	6,901	6,595	-4.4	6,697	88.4	1.6	0.3	4.0	5.7	23.3	20.2	39.5	64.2	16.5	2,660	83.5
Mineral township (Venango)	538	497	-7.6	470	90.2	0.0	0.2	8.3	1.3	15.3	30.9	53.9	54.9	19.2	213	88.7

1 May be of any race.

Table A. All Places — Population and Housing

STATE City, town, township, borough, or CDP (county if applicable)	Population				Race and Hispanic or Latino origin (percent)					Age (percent)			Educational attainment of persons age 25 and older		Occupied housing units	
	2010 census total population	2019 estimated population	Percent change 2010–2019	ACS total population estimate 2015–2019	White alone, not Hispanic or Latino	Black alone, not Hispanic or Latino	Asian alone, not Hispanic or Latino	All other races or 2 or more races, not Hispanic or Latino	Hispanic or Latino[1]	Under 18 years old	Age 65 years and older	Median age	Percent High school diploma or less	Percent Bachelor's degree or more	Total	Percent with a computer
	1	2	3	4	5	6	7	8	9	10	11	12	13	14	15	16
PENNSYLVANIA—Con.																
Minersville borough & MCD (Schuylkill)	4,404	4,157	-5.6	4,205	94.4	0.0	0.5	1.5	3.6	25.4	17.6	42.4	59.4	13.3	1,918	86.0
Mingoville CDP	503	-	-	580	100.0	0.0	0.0	0.0	0.0	28.6	11.2	34.2	50.2	26.8	248	100.0
Mocanaqua CDP	646	-	-	735	93.1	2.3	0.5	3.7	0.4	17.1	20.7	42.4	61.4	5.8	284	82.7
Modena borough & MCD (Chester)	537	530	-1.3	837	68.9	15.4	0.0	2.9	12.8	37.8	2.2	26.6	67.5	12.3	235	85.1
Mohnton borough & MCD (Berks)	2,993	3,018	0.8	3,015	85.5	0.0	0.3	0.7	13.5	23.4	10.4	41.3	48.3	31.0	1,196	88.5
Mohrsville CDP	383	-	-	589	88.6	0.0	0.0	0.0	11.4	29.4	8.7	32.2	65.0	18.9	222	88.3
Monaca borough & MCD (Beaver)	5,737	5,421	-5.5	5,521	89.7	3.3	0.0	5.9	1.1	19.2	19.4	44.3	45.6	20.4	2,644	83.9
Monaghan township (York)	2,628	2,669	1.6	2,658	95.0	1.0	0.0	2.0	2.1	18.8	22.6	48.3	38.6	36.8	991	92.0
Monessen city & MCD (Westmoreland)	7,717	7,237	-6.2	7,344	79.5	11.5	0.8	5.9	2.2	20.1	23.0	46.3	48.0	23.1	3,435	82.8
Monongahela township (Greene)	1,573	1,498	-4.8	1,870	94.2	0.9	0.0	3.9	1.1	26.3	17.8	38.0	66.3	16.2	680	87.5
Monongahela city & MCD (Washington)	4,297	4,102	-4.5	4,138	91.0	3.0	2.2	1.4	2.4	21.8	17.0	40.7	49.1	19.1	1,773	83.1
Monroe township (Bedford)	1,339	1,311	-2.1	1,439	98.2	0.2	0.0	0.0	1.6	25.9	15.6	40.0	67.3	11.0	528	80.3
Monroe borough & MCD (Bradford)	549	512	-6.7	590	98.1	0.0	0.5	0.0	1.4	22.5	17.6	40.6	57.9	20.3	261	75.9
Monroe township (Bradford)	1,245	1,187	-4.7	1,123	97.3	0.0	0.0	0.0	2.7	22.5	21.1	44.5	70.5	6.5	453	89.2
Monroe township (Clarion)	1,542	1,578	2.3	1,427	93.8	2.3	2.2	0.0	1.7	19.3	18.2	46.4	48.0	28.3	595	85.0
Monroe township (Cumberland)	5,814	6,220	7.0	6,119	96.9	0.1	1.2	0.0	1.8	18.6	17.6	45.8	35.5	35.5	2,328	96.4
Monroe township (Juniata)	2,234	2,221	-0.6	2,453	94.6	0.2	2.8	1.6	0.8	21.4	16.2	39.8	68.2	11.0	852	80.8
Monroe township (Snyder)	3,899	4,132	6.0	4,114	94.3	0.0	1.4	0.2	4.0	15.7	20.2	48.6	50.7	27.3	1,665	90.3
Monroe township (Wyoming)	1,665	1,566	-5.9	1,535	97.7	0.0	0.0	1.5	0.8	19.3	21.2	45.3	55.1	17.9	620	88.9
Monroeville municipality & MCD (Allegheny)	28,345	27,380	-3.4	27,687	75.5	12.1	6.2	3.8	2.4	17.0	23.2	46.2	29.8	41.3	12,215	93.1
Mont Alto borough & MCD (Franklin)	1,712	1,729	1.0	1,783	92.9	1.1	3.0	1.2	1.8	16.8	15.0	36.1	58.3	13.5	623	89.6
Montandon CDP	903	-	-	889	97.8	0.6	0.0	0.0	1.7	18.1	22.0	41.3	72.7	17.4	389	73.5
Montgomery township (Franklin)	6,124	6,230	1.7	6,221	98.2	1.1	0.0	0.7	0.0	22.3	17.4	44.5	55.2	19.6	2,376	90.7
Montgomery township (Indiana)	1,568	1,467	-6.4	1,548	99.2	0.0	0.0	0.0	0.8	18.3	29.9	51.1	73.0	10.7	579	75.3
Montgomery borough & MCD (Lycoming)	1,575	1,507	-4.3	1,483	94.0	1.3	1.4	2.0	1.3	27.7	10.9	34.5	55.7	12.8	559	90.0
Montgomery township (Montgomery)	24,816	26,164	5.4	26,044	71.9	5.3	18.7	2.1	1.9	21.4	16.7	44.7	22.2	58.0	9,853	93.8
Montgomeryville CDP	12,624	-	-	13,082	78.8	4.0	12.8	2.0	2.4	22.5	15.4	43.5	22.9	56.5	4,668	98.5
Montour township (Columbia)	1,345	1,285	-4.5	1,418	97.5	0.3	0.7	0.0	1.5	18.8	18.1	43.9	57.4	23.9	591	87.3
Montoursville borough & MCD (Lycoming)	4,615	4,399	-4.7	4,458	93.2	0.0	0.7	4.1	2.0	25.3	20.5	41.4	35.1	35.9	1,829	86.6
Montrose borough & MCD (Susquehanna)	1,624	1,477	-9.1	1,517	96.6	0.0	0.0	2.5	0.9	15.7	27.8	49.7	35.9	26.2	745	81.6
Montrose Manor CDP.......	604	-	-	438	76.0	16.4	0.0	2.3	5.3	17.1	26.7	51.4	61.3	25.6	213	77.5
Monument CDP	150	-	-	166	100.0	0.0	0.0	0.0	0.0	21.1	27.7	46.6	79.8	4.4	60	63.3
Moon township (Allegheny)	24,212	25,437	5.1	25,489	86.4	3.9	4.8	3.3	1.5	20.6	14.3	37.9	22.5	53.8	9,759	95.1
Moore township (Northampton).............	9,227	9,434	2.2	9,317	97.5	0.1	0.0	0.4	2.1	20.6	22.9	48.1	51.5	23.4	3,531	80.4
Moosic borough & MCD (Lackawanna)	5,719	5,832	2.0	5,767	90.3	4.0	3.8	0.1	1.7	18.3	19.8	44.7	43.6	23.5	2,442	90.9
Moreland township (Lycoming)	948	954	0.6	942	97.7	0.0	0.1	0.6	1.6	17.0	19.9	47.0	55.3	19.6	360	83.3
Morgan township (Greene)	2,579	2,358	-8.6	2,295	98.8	0.0	0.0	1.2	0.0	20.0	19.1	43.7	57.1	18.7	929	86.2
Morgantown CDP	826	-	-	676	96.2	0.0	2.1	1.8	0.0	17.5	29.3	49.4	58.6	21.9	324	82.1
Morris township (Clearfield)	2,932	2,852	-2.7	2,870	99.8	0.0	0.0	0.2	0.0	16.0	12.6	43.2	65.8	10.0	1,138	91.6
Morris township (Greene) .	818	769	-6.0	763	100.0	0.0	0.0	0.0	0.0	17.4	15.2	42.7	42.5	20.4	288	89.2
Morris township (Huntingdon)	410	409	-0.2	432	98.1	0.0	0.7	1.2	0.0	28.9	12.5	36.0	51.2	22.3	160	91.9
Morris township (Tioga)....	610	582	-4.6	514	99.2	0.2	0.0	0.0	0.6	16.1	23.3	53.4	58.4	14.5	213	81.2
Morris township (Washington)	1,107	1,097	-0.9	988	90.4	0.4	0.0	8.6	0.6	19.6	13.3	48.6	63.4	7.7	421	91.0
Morrisdale CDP	754	-	-	793	99.1	0.0	0.0	0.9	0.0	22.8	7.4	37.7	75.5	8.4	255	100.0
Morrisville borough & MCD (Bucks)	8,728	8,521	-2.4	8,573	72.0	13.6	2.4	3.8	8.2	18.5	14.0	40.9	34.5	35.6	3,599	89.3
Morrisville CDP	1,265	-	-	1,179	99.3	0.0	0.0	0.0	0.7	21.2	27.9	48.5	43.1	26.3	594	78.3
Morton borough & MCD (Delaware)....................	2,654	2,670	0.6	2,662	70.1	22.7	4.2	1.4	1.7	19.9	16.4	38.9	37.7	35.7	1,125	93.7
Moscow borough & MCD (Lackawanna)	2,025	2,035	0.5	1,834	97.5	0.3	0.3	0.2	1.6	16.4	17.0	47.4	34.5	41.1	754	91.4
Moshannon CDP	281	-	-	327	100.0	0.0	0.0	0.0	0.0	11.0	13.8	48.2	73.8	0.0	154	83.1
Mount Aetna CDP............	354	-	-	368	80.4	0.0	0.0	0.0	19.6	25.3	11.4	38.8	68.0	8.5	140	97.1
Mountainhome CDP	1,182	-	-	1,047	81.1	1.2	15.2	0.0	2.5	7.8	31.7	52.3	44.8	28.9	547	74.8
Mountain Top CDP..........	10,982	-	-	11,489	89.9	0.2	5.7	1.7	2.6	21.4	17.6	43.8	31.4	38.8	4,067	91.7
Mount Carbon borough & MCD (Schuylkill)	91	86	-5.5	61	90.2	0.0	0.0	0.0	9.8	8.2	14.8	47.7	52.4	9.5	32	84.4
Mount Carmel borough & MCD (Northumberland)	5,882	5,724	-2.7	5,667	97.1	0.6	0.2	0.4	1.7	15.5	22.1	47.0	60.6	10.7	2,876	72.7
Mount Carmel township (Northumberland)..........	3,140	2,976	-5.2	3,016	99.7	0.3	0.0	0.0	0.1	17.0	28.7	49.5	72.9	9.7	1,309	77.9
Mount Cobb CDP	1,799	-	-	1,875	94.8	0.0	0.9	1.2	3.1	28.7	17.8	41.0	34.2	29.5	684	88.7
Mount Eagle CDP............	103	-	-	65	100.0	0.0	0.0	0.0	0.0	1.5	30.8	56.4	66.7	14.3	37	94.6

1 May be of any race.

Table A. All Places — **Population and Housing**

STATE City, town, township, borough, or CDP (county if applicable)	Population				Race and Hispanic or Latino origin (percent)					Age (percent)			Educational attainment of persons age 25 and older		Occupied housing units	
	2010 census total population	2019 estimated population	Percent change 2010–2019	ACS total population estimate 2015–2019	White alone, not Hispanic or Latino	Black alone, not Hispanic or Latino	Asian alone, not Hispanic or Latino	All other races or 2 or more races, not Hispanic or Latino	Hispanic or Latino[1]	Under 18 years old	Age 65 years and older	Median age	Percent High school diploma or less	Percent Bachelor's degree or more	Total	Percent with a computer
	1	2	3	4	5	6	7	8	9	10	11	12	13	14	15	16
PENNSYLVANIA—Con.																
Mount Gretna borough & MCD (Lebanon)	198	209	5.6	270	100.0	0.0	0.0	0.0	0.0	5.2	57.0	70.4	18.3	60.2	129	100.0
Mount Gretna Heights CDP	323	-	-	342	94.2	0.0	0.0	0.0	5.8	8.2	36.0	57.0	21.1	68.8	147	100.0
Mount Holly Springs borough & MCD (Cumberland)	2,027	2,052	1.2	1,992	84.4	0.9	0.6	2.5	11.7	23.8	16.3	37.8	60.6	14.7	851	84.7
Mount Jewett borough & MCD (McKean)	914	849	-7.1	935	87.2	0.2	0.0	11.1	1.5	22.0	15.5	38.6	59.8	13.7	417	85.1
Mount Joy township (Adams)	3,688	3,742	1.5	3,728	91.5	2.1	0.5	3.7	2.1	18.8	26.2	50.6	40.3	33.1	1,524	93.3
Mount Joy borough & MCD (Lancaster)...........	7,386	8,278	12.1	8,163	81.4	3.9	1.0	2.7	11.0	20.4	14.8	37.4	51.1	21.8	3,476	90.2
Mount Joy township (Lancaster)	9,910	11,271	13.7	11,029	86.4	1.0	1.7	1.8	9.1	23.7	13.0	37.6	39.2	33.8	4,093	94.7
Mount Lebanon township (Allegheny)	33,109	31,927	-3.6	32,303	91.3	1.2	3.7	2.1	1.7	23.8	20.2	44.3	13.0	70.6	13,539	91.1
Mount Morris CDP...........	737	-	-	713	98.2	0.0	0.0	1.8	0.0	18.7	23.1	49.9	54.1	25.0	354	82.5
Mount Oliver borough & MCD (Allegheny)...........	3,412	3,281	-3.8	3,324	47.4	32.6	3.2	6.0	10.8	24.5	10.2	32.7	61.0	15.6	1,379	80.7
Mount Penn borough & MCD (Berks)	3,038	3,121	2.7	3,126	60.6	5.4	2.5	6.3	25.2	23.2	16.5	36.3	51.6	19.8	1,304	85.7
Mount Pleasant township (Adams)	4,682	4,702	0.4	4,689	92.4	2.6	0.6	2.2	2.2	21.0	20.1	47.2	60.3	18.6	1,949	85.3
Mount Pleasant township (Columbia)	1,609	1,569	-2.5	1,534	95.5	0.4	1.2	1.8	1.1	20.1	19.7	46.6	56.1	22.9	594	88.6
Mount Pleasant township (Washington)................	3,514	3,517	0.1	3,503	96.6	0.0	0.0	0.0	3.4	15.6	24.4	52.1	44.3	29.0	1,419	94.4
Mount Pleasant township (Wayne)....................	1,362	1,345	-1.2	1,416	89.1	0.0	0.5	3.7	6.6	21.0	27.0	49.3	46.3	30.1	572	86.9
Mount Pleasant borough & MCD (Westmoreland)	4,429	4,221	-4.7	4,277	94.9	2.3	0.6	0.5	1.7	17.6	21.4	46.3	48.6	21.8	1,994	83.0
Mount Pleasant township (Westmoreland)	10,923	10,442	-4.4	10,546	98.0	0.0	0.1	1.1	0.7	17.1	22.6	47.7	48.2	21.6	4,503	86.7
Mount Pleasant Mills CDP	464	-	-	385	93.2	0.0	3.9	1.6	1.3	17.7	32.7	42.1	69.8	11.6	177	70.1
Mount Pocono borough & MCD (Monroe)	3,179	3,119	-1.9	3,096	52.4	12.3	2.8	3.6	29.0	20.6	23.0	43.2	55.1	22.7	1,369	85.2
Mount Union borough & MCD (Huntingdon).......	2,448	2,339	-4.5	2,289	80.1	12.8	1.0	4.5	1.6	23.3	19.0	39.3	65.8	9.8	1,044	80.7
Mountville borough & MCD (Lancaster)..........	2,807	2,847	1.4	2,855	85.7	6.3	0.5	3.1	4.4	27.4	19.3	40.0	49.6	21.3	1,099	92.0
Mount Wolf borough & MCD (York)	1,397	1,385	-0.9	1,626	93.7	0.0	0.3	2.6	3.3	26.3	18.0	38.4	58.2	19.9	619	91.8
Muddy Creek township (Butler)	2,268	2,156	-4.9	2,232	97.0	0.0	0.3	0.7	1.9	20.7	21.2	47.0	55.1	17.8	935	86.4
Muhlenberg township (Berks)	19,677	20,345	3.4	20,223	64.7	7.7	1.8	1.5	24.3	22.6	18.2	39.0	51.3	20.7	7,563	90.5
Muhlenberg Park CDP......	1,420	-	-	1,656	63.1	2.3	3.7	4.8	26.1	18.1	27.2	47.8	50.2	24.4	681	83.0
Muir CDP......................	451	-	-	424	100.0	0.0	0.0	0.0	0.0	13.4	24.8	51.2	69.9	12.2	191	70.7
Muncy borough & MCD (Lycoming)	2,481	2,412	-2.8	2,360	97.3	0.2	0.8	0.3	1.4	23.4	21.4	41.6	43.6	28.0	1,029	87.1
Muncy township (Lycoming)	1,089	1,190	9.3	1,040	97.7	1.4	0.0	0.9	0.0	26.0	17.4	40.8	41.0	28.6	406	89.7
Muncy Creek township (Lycoming)	3,471	3,452	-0.5	3,500	97.5	0.1	0.0	0.5	2.0	16.9	26.5	48.9	47.6	29.6	1,452	85.1
Mundys Corner CDP	1,651	-	-	1,683	99.0	0.0	0.0	0.0	1.0	20.9	21.4	45.3	63.1	12.1	675	92.4
Munhall borough & MCD (Allegheny)	11,381	11,006	-3.3	11,121	81.8	14.0	1.2	1.9	1.1	19.2	20.9	46.5	39.4	27.5	5,259	83.9
Munster township (Cambria)	689	653	-5.2	665	99.5	0.0	0.0	0.0	0.5	23.5	16.5	44.4	49.9	17.8	256	86.3
Murrysville municipality & MCD (Westmoreland) ...	20,058	19,590	-2.3	19,782	92.5	1.3	4.2	0.7	1.3	20.2	24.4	48.9	20.3	58.5	8,180	95.0
Muse CDP......................	2,504	-	-	2,678	96.2	0.0	1.7	0.9	1.2	26.0	11.5	35.9	31.2	42.2	940	97.1
Myerstown borough & MCD (Lebanon)	3,050	3,251	6.6	3,201	98.5	0.0	0.0	0.4	1.1	21.4	23.0	40.4	68.7	9.6	1,316	82.1
Nanticoke city & MCD (Luzerne)	10,465	10,312	-1.5	10,304	86.6	2.1	0.1	2.4	8.9	18.2	20.8	42.9	54.9	17.0	4,478	78.9
Nanty-Glo borough & MCD (Cambria)	2,729	2,472	-9.4	2,432	96.9	0.7	0.5	0.9	1.1	18.2	22.0	44.6	64.1	11.0	1,104	78.0
Naomi CDP....................	69	-	-	73	100.0	0.0	0.0	0.0	0.0	0.0	54.8	84.2	54.8	0.0	56	28.6
Napier township (Bedford)	2,199	2,116	-3.8	2,077	97.0	1.3	0.0	1.0	0.7	12.6	21.7	50.6	63.1	13.0	867	82.2
Narberth borough & MCD (Montgomery)	4,282	4,336	1.3	4,345	78.8	6.2	5.2	5.1	4.7	23.5	15.7	40.6	12.5	76.8	1,878	95.6
Nazareth borough & MCD (Northampton).............	5,745	5,702	-0.7	5,699	90.3	0.0	0.2	3.8	5.7	22.3	18.6	39.4	42.8	30.9	2,529	84.5
Needmore CDP...............	170	-	-	133	89.5	0.0	0.0	0.0	10.5	14.3	22.6	51.2	75.6	3.3	57	84.2
Nelson township (Tioga)...	568	560	-1.4	492	97.0	0.0	0.0	0.4	2.6	18.9	21.5	46.4	55.9	12.9	190	78.9
Nemacolin CDP	937	-	-	684	96.3	0.0	0.0	2.2	1.5	13.7	4.8	41.6	49.9	2.6	366	88.8
Nescopeck borough & MCD (Luzerne)	1,585	1,544	-2.6	1,570	92.0	0.4	1.0	0.4	6.2	14.7	21.4	47.2	58.5	13.0	683	81.8
Nescopeck township (Luzerne)	1,155	1,151	-0.3	1,084	96.0	0.0	0.0	0.6	3.4	19.5	20.9	51.0	59.9	17.5	422	79.6
Neshannock township (Lawrence)	9,609	9,207	-4.2	9,254	95.2	1.6	0.8	0.9	1.5	16.9	27.5	49.4	37.9	41.8	4,180	86.5
Nesquehoning borough & MCD (Carbon).............	3,349	3,250	-3.0	3,239	85.6	3.1	0.0	2.7	8.6	18.3	25.1	42.0	59.1	18.4	1,346	84.6
Nether Providence township (Delaware)	13,709	13,780	0.5	13,767	80.6	5.2	8.3	3.6	2.3	23.3	18.4	44.2	16.6	62.3	5,083	97.1
Neville township (Allegheny)	1,084	1,044	-3.7	993	86.2	6.3	0.8	2.6	4.0	11.8	23.4	49.2	47.5	21.1	565	85.1
New Albany borough & MCD (Bradford).............	356	338	-5.1	270	100.0	0.0	0.0	0.0	0.0	23.3	14.1	31.7	69.1	4.9	111	89.2

1 May be of any race.

Table A. All Places — **Population and Housing**

STATE City, town, township, borough, or CDP (county if applicable)	2010 census total population	2019 estimated population	Percent change 2010–2019	ACS total population estimate 2015–2019	White alone, not Hispanic or Latino	Black alone, not Hispanic or Latino	Asian alone, not Hispanic or Latino	All other races or 2 or more races, not Hispanic or Latino	Hispanic or Latino[1]	Under 18 years old	Age 65 years and older	Median age	Percent High school diploma or less	Percent Bachelor's degree or more	Total	Percent with a computer
	1	2	3	4	5	6	7	8	9	10	11	12	13	14	15	16
PENNSYLVANIA—Con.																
New Alexandria borough & MCD (Westmoreland)	555	526	-5.2	554	98.0	0.0	0.0	2.0	0.0	6.3	37.9	60.9	46.6	22.9	260	75.4
New Baltimore borough & MCD (Somerset)	182	168	-7.7	161	100.0	0.0	0.0	0.0	0.0	14.9	24.2	45.2	58.4	10.4	75	84.0
New Beaver borough & MCD (Lawrence)	1,511	1,421	-6.0	1,386	98.8	0.4	0.0	0.7	0.0	17.2	20.6	49.4	65.3	10.9	640	85.2
New Bedford CDP	925	-	-	1,032	99.4	0.0	0.0	0.0	0.6	22.6	21.3	41.8	55.1	11.1	395	91.4
New Berlin borough & MCD (Union)	848	826	-2.6	879	100.0	0.0	0.0	0.0	0.0	25.3	16.0	38.9	47.8	24.6	311	88.1
New Berlinville CDP	1,368	-	-	1,634	100.0	0.0	0.0	0.0	0.0	15.5	26.5	46.1	42.3	27.8	687	95.5
Newberry township (York)	15,295	15,918	4.1	15,701	92.1	1.7	0.4	2.6	3.1	20.5	14.9	43.1	54.2	22.1	6,330	91.4
New Bethlehem borough & MCD (Clarion)	989	917	-7.3	888	99.0	0.3	0.0	0.2	0.5	19.0	31.1	47.3	59.1	15.8	456	73.7
New Brighton borough & MCD (Beaver)	6,022	5,679	-5.7	5,780	83.3	11.9	0.3	3.9	0.5	22.8	18.1	41.6	54.4	15.2	2,678	81.0
New Britain borough & MCD (Bucks)	2,978	2,969	-0.3	2,966	93.8	2.5	0.3	0.7	2.6	13.5	14.8	32.1	30.4	48.3	960	93.6
New Britain township (Bucks)	11,139	11,524	3.5	11,336	90.9	1.4	4.8	0.4	2.5	22.0	18.5	45.7	27.7	46.2	4,153	94.5
New Buffalo borough & MCD (Perry)	124	127	2.4	158	98.7	0.0	0.0	0.0	1.3	25.9	20.9	34.4	65.0	7.8	64	84.4
Newburg borough & MCD (Clearfield)	92	94	2.2	66	100.0	0.0	0.0	0.0	0.0	12.1	28.8	58.0	74.1	6.9	31	64.5
Newburg borough & MCD (Cumberland)	336	335	-0.3	295	99.0	0.3	0.0	0.0	0.7	20.0	14.6	40.9	57.5	13.2	120	85.0
New Castle city & MCD (Lawrence)	23,294	21,618	-7.2	21,991	80.8	10.7	0.2	5.2	3.1	21.5	19.3	41.2	58.4	15.4	9,580	82.2
New Castle township (Schuylkill)	414	388	-6.3	356	98.6	0.0	0.0	0.3	1.1	17.1	23.9	46.3	73.2	8.5	167	74.3
New Castle Northwest CDP	1,413	-	-	1,393	97.3	0.0	0.0	0.0	2.7	16.7	32.0	50.5	41.0	30.1	647	83.9
New Centerville borough & MCD (Somerset)	136	128	-5.9	132	100.0	0.0	0.0	0.0	0.0	12.9	28.8	49.0	59.6	20.2	54	83.3
New Columbia CDP	1,013	-	-	1,077	97.5	0.0	0.0	0.0	2.5	27.1	22.9	44.6	68.0	17.2	431	100.0
New Columbus borough & MCD (Luzerne)	228	227	-0.4	182	100.0	0.0	0.0	0.0	0.0	22.0	9.9	39.8	46.8	24.2	70	71.4
New Cumberland borough & MCD (Cumberland)	7,277	7,288	0.2	7,309	90.5	0.7	1.2	2.1	5.6	17.5	16.9	42.8	39.9	32.0	3,376	89.7
New Eagle borough & MCD (Washington)	2,189	2,085	-4.8	2,349	89.0	0.5	1.8	2.9	5.8	21.3	21.0	45.5	57.7	13.4	1,030	83.2
Newell borough & MCD (Fayette)	536	506	-5.6	586	98.5	0.0	0.0	0.2	1.4	27.0	13.0	39.5	62.7	15.5	220	86.8
New Florence borough & MCD (Westmoreland)	687	647	-5.8	666	97.3	0.5	0.0	0.3	2.0	24.9	15.0	43.3	59.0	10.7	285	84.9
New Freedom borough & MCD (York)	4,460	4,685	5.0	4,637	91.4	5.9	1.7	0.6	0.4	26.6	18.8	42.1	37.4	42.0	1,720	91.2
New Freeport CDP	112	-	-	58	100.0	0.0	0.0	0.0	0.0	12.1	24.1	49.8	91.7	6.3	26	84.6
New Galilee borough & MCD (Beaver)	378	352	-6.9	324	90.4	5.6	0.0	0.0	4.0	18.8	16.7	44.4	58.7	16.1	137	85.4
New Garden township (Chester)	12,012	12,206	1.6	12,153	63.1	3.3	3.8	1.7	28.1	22.3	14.1	40.6	36.0	47.4	4,034	89.3
New Hanover township (Montgomery)	10,934	13,212	20.8	12,841	93.4	1.7	1.4	0.6	2.8	25.6	13.7	40.5	35.5	40.7	4,423	95.6
New Holland borough & MCD (Lancaster)	5,385	5,464	1.5	5,457	80.7	1.4	1.2	5.8	10.9	24.6	27.0	43.3	56.3	20.5	2,148	89.5
New Hope borough & MCD (Bucks)	2,531	2,530	0.0	2,513	88.6	0.0	2.3	2.0	7.1	10.7	26.4	51.5	16.8	60.2	1,188	94.4
New Jerusalem CDP	649	-	-	424	100.0	0.0	0.0	0.0	0.0	15.1	22.4	47.2	59.6	8.3	178	83.1
New Kensington city & MCD (Westmoreland)	13,116	12,292	-6.3	12,468	83.3	9.9	2.7	2.3	1.8	17.5	21.6	46.8	50.0	20.3	5,846	80.6
New Kingstown CDP	495	-	-	709	88.3	9.3	0.0	2.4	0.0	21.9	38.2	58.4	55.8	29.4	331	71.3
New Lebanon borough & MCD (Mercer)	189	171	-9.5	198	99.0	1.0	0.0	0.0	0.0	31.8	11.6	37.0	47.6	17.7	69	84.1
Newlin township (Chester)	1,283	1,347	5.0	1,237	96.0	0.3	1.5	0.2	2.0	23.1	17.5	47.2	19.5	63.2	456	94.1
New London township (Chester)	5,627	5,986	6.4	5,946	87.9	0.4	1.3	1.3	9.2	27.1	11.0	41.4	26.6	49.7	1,873	94.6
Newmanstown CDP	2,478	-	-	2,449	95.4	2.2	1.6	0.0	0.7	31.1	12.8	34.8	54.7	21.2	934	97.1
New Market CDP	816	-	-	732	63.9	9.2	19.0	1.0	7.0	16.7	12.7	36.9	49.6	18.8	410	81.2
New Milford borough & MCD (Susquehanna)	868	843	-2.9	915	98.0	1.7	0.0	0.0	0.2	24.0	19.5	39.2	58.1	11.1	375	86.1
New Milford township (Susquehanna)	2,039	1,877	-7.9	1,778	95.6	0.0	0.0	0.0	4.4	14.6	24.0	51.4	62.4	15.1	731	94.9
New Morgan borough & MCD (Berks)	71	76	7.0	93	58.1	14.0	0.0	0.0	28.0	65.6	1.1	17.3	57.1	35.7	11	100.0
New Oxford borough & MCD (Adams)	1,783	1,813	1.7	2,014	68.4	1.8	1.7	1.9	26.2	30.4	17.8	34.5	62.6	14.7	752	81.9
New Paris borough & MCD (Bedford)	183	172	-6.0	184	91.3	0.0	0.0	2.2	6.5	21.2	13.0	47.5	79.6	10.2	82	85.4
New Philadelphia borough & MCD (Schuylkill)	1,086	1,031	-5.1	1,018	93.8	1.0	0.2	0.7	4.3	16.4	19.4	45.2	66.2	11.3	450	74.7
Newport township (Luzerne)	5,374	5,343	-0.6	5,346	79.5	13.6	0.7	1.7	4.5	15.9	14.4	40.6	57.3	12.9	1,646	82.9
Newport borough & MCD (Perry)	1,574	1,589	1.0	1,550	97.0	1.5	0.0	1.4	0.0	21.5	15.7	32.9	60.9	14.6	630	84.3
New Ringgold borough & MCD (Schuylkill)	276	262	-5.1	291	96.9	1.0	0.0	2.1	0.0	24.4	19.2	40.3	52.2	11.5	105	90.5
Newry borough & MCD (Blair)	270	286	5.9	234	97.9	0.0	0.0	0.0	2.1	28.2	11.1	36.0	60.8	20.9	103	86.4
New Salem CDP	579	-	-	624	100.0	0.0	0.0	0.0	0.0	16.8	13.9	38.6	68.1	9.1	227	85.5
New Salem borough & MCD (York)	723	791	9.4	739	93.5	5.1	0.0	0.7	0.7	19.5	20.6	44.3	39.5	29.4	295	90.2
New Schaefferstown CDP	223	-	-	135	100.0	0.0	0.0	0.0	0.0	13.3	27.4	47.5	47.9	16.2	67	88.1

1 May be of any race.

Table A. All Places — **Population and Housing**

STATE City, town, township, borough, or CDP (county if applicable)	Population 2010 census total population	2019 estimated population	Percent change 2010–2019	ACS total population estimate 2015–2019	White alone, not Hispanic or Latino	Black alone, not Hispanic or Latino	Asian alone, not Hispanic or Latino	All other races or 2 or more races, not Hispanic or Latino	Hispanic or Latino[1]	Under 18 years old	Age 65 years and older	Median age	Percent High school diploma or less	Percent Bachelor's degree or more	Occupied housing units Total	Percent with a computer
	1	2	3	4	5	6	7	8	9	10	11	12	13	14	15	16
PENNSYLVANIA—Con.																
New Sewickley township (Beaver)	7,366	7,160	-2.8	7,276	96.8	0.6	0.0	2.2	0.4	17.4	29.7	50.1	43.1	24.2	3,306	88.0
New Stanton borough & MCD (Westmoreland) ...	2,179	2,060	-5.5	2,199	90.6	2.7	1.5	3.0	2.2	20.3	18.2	41.8	44.4	30.2	945	91.4
Newton township (Lackawanna)................	2,838	2,790	-1.7	2,770	95.0	1.3	0.0	1.2	2.5	23.3	19.0	46.2	38.3	27.4	943	93.7
Newton Hamilton borough & MCD (Mifflin).............	205	197	-3.9	143	96.5	0.0	0.0	3.5	0.0	17.5	19.6	47.4	60.0	7.6	70	91.4
Newtown borough & MCD (Bucks)....................	2,252	2,240	-0.5	1,957	96.5	0.2	0.3	2.1	0.9	15.9	23.2	52.7	15.0	57.1	933	95.0
Newtown township (Bucks)....................	19,295	19,584	1.5	19,610	84.2	2.8	8.5	1.7	2.8	20.8	17.7	46.7	16.0	67.6	7,866	97.5
Newtown township (Delaware)................	12,218	13,943	14.1	13,351	90.0	1.3	4.9	1.7	2.1	20.5	24.6	47.2	22.0	60.0	5,329	94.0
Newtown CDP.................	243	-	-	236	100.0	0.0	0.0	0.0	0.0	6.4	30.9	56.2	71.5	11.2	120	71.7
Newtown Grant CDP	3,620	-	-	3,562	85.1	1.7	8.8	0.6	4.0	18.0	16.0	45.3	15.8	64.1	1,557	99.0
New Tripoli CDP..............	898	-	-	951	78.5	0.0	0.0	16.0	5.5	32.7	7.5	29.6	30.2	35.2	348	95.4
New Vernon township (Mercer)...................	510	504	-1.2	505	95.0	0.6	1.8	0.0	2.6	23.8	19.2	46.5	64.9	17.5	205	83.9
Newville borough & MCD (Cumberland).............	1,329	1,347	1.4	1,266	95.2	0.7	0.4	1.9	1.8	23.9	13.8	37.6	68.7	13.7	545	84.6
New Washington borough & MCD (Clearfield)........	59	55	-6.8	39	100.0	0.0	0.0	0.0	0.0	12.8	10.3	48.6	85.3	8.8	17	64.7
New Wilmington borough & MCD (Lawrence)	2,466	2,197	-10.9	2,186	89.8	4.6	1.8	2.0	1.9	11.4	17.5	21.5	32.4	51.5	538	93.7
Nicholson township (Fayette)...................	1,806	1,704	-5.6	1,766	97.7	0.0	0.0	1.5	0.8	18.6	22.3	50.3	68.1	14.4	701	79.0
Nicholson borough & MCD (Wyoming)............	765	708	-7.5	670	94.6	0.9	0.0	1.2	3.3	19.0	16.0	38.5	49.8	17.3	271	93.4
Nicholson township (Wyoming)................	1,390	1,299	-6.5	1,112	96.8	0.6	0.3	1.3	1.0	12.9	32.5	57.8	53.9	17.6	506	81.2
Nippenose township (Lycoming)................	709	744	4.9	559	99.1	0.0	0.0	0.5	0.4	14.0	29.5	51.7	54.8	24.4	249	85.5
Nittany CDP.....................	658	-	-	736	100.0	0.0	0.0	0.0	0.0	10.2	18.1	48.2	61.1	15.1	253	86.6
Nixon CDP......................	1,373	-	-	1,265	96.4	0.1	1.7	0.0	1.8	10.9	39.1	59.6	24.0	55.2	528	89.8
Noblestown CDP	575	-	-	531	100.0	0.0	0.0	0.0	0.0	27.9	15.8	42.4	33.0	40.6	187	100.0
Nockamixon township (Bucks)....................	3,441	3,376	-1.9	3,388	97.0	0.3	0.6	0.9	1.3	14.1	20.7	49.3	35.4	37.0	1,360	93.6
Norristown borough & MCD (Montgomery)	34,339	34,341	0.0	34,443	27.9	36.3	3.5	5.2	27.1	26.0	10.4	32.8	55.1	22.6	12,866	85.9
North Abington township (Lackawanna)................	702	691	-1.6	703	94.9	0.3	1.7	1.8	1.3	27.2	13.2	42.1	19.8	57.5	237	98.3
Northampton township (Bucks)....................	39,726	39,164	-1.4	39,263	89.9	1.5	4.2	1.5	2.9	21.6	19.5	46.2	22.7	53.9	13,966	94.6
Northampton borough & MCD (Northampton)	9,898	9,870	-0.3	9,847	84.4	2.4	1.1	3.2	9.0	22.9	18.9	39.8	53.2	18.2	3,946	84.2
Northampton township (Somerset)	343	323	-5.8	253	100.0	0.0	0.0	0.0	0.0	17.4	34.4	54.7	66.5	13.9	111	66.7
North Annville township (Lebanon).................	2,381	2,522	5.9	2,484	97.3	0.4	0.2	0.6	1.5	19.7	24.6	50.4	67.0	14.4	965	82.8
North Apollo borough & MCD (Armstrong)..........	1,297	1,201	-7.4	1,252	93.7	0.2	0.2	5.4	0.6	18.9	25.6	50.7	62.9	18.0	584	82.9
North Beaver township (Lawrence)...............	4,126	3,935	-4.6	3,977	98.3	0.0	0.9	0.5	0.3	20.5	21.2	45.4	47.7	25.5	1,704	87.8
North Belle Vernon borough & MCD (Westmoreland)	1,983	1,857	-6.4	1,796	89.4	2.4	2.7	1.9	3.6	18.2	19.4	41.4	38.4	30.4	810	85.9
North Bethlehem township (Washington)	1,637	1,577	-3.7	1,518	94.1	1.6	0.4	4.0	0.0	20.8	16.8	46.0	48.2	25.9	631	89.1
North Braddock borough & MCD (Allegheny)	4,858	4,669	-3.9	4,741	46.9	45.1	0.8	5.1	2.1	23.8	22.0	41.0	57.7	12.8	2,367	82.8
North Branch township (Wyoming)................	208	199	-4.3	224	98.7	0.0	0.0	1.3	0.0	18.8	27.7	53.1	63.0	8.0	91	86.8
North Buffalo township (Armstrong)................	3,010	2,889	-4.0	2,937	96.3	0.1	0.7	0.0	2.9	21.2	20.7	46.8	53.7	19.0	1,160	85.6
North Catasauqua borough & MCD (Northampton)..............	2,846	2,831	-0.5	2,831	87.4	1.7	0.0	1.4	9.5	22.6	17.6	40.0	53.9	19.1	1,068	87.6
North Centre township (Columbia)	2,097	2,110	0.6	2,210	95.6	0.5	0.6	1.4	2.0	19.6	21.1	48.0	55.8	24.0	854	86.5
North Charleroi borough & MCD (Washington)........	1,323	1,261	-4.7	1,351	95.9	1.2	0.0	1.6	1.3	19.8	21.5	47.1	60.5	17.5	573	75.6
North Codorus township (York)....................	8,941	9,074	1.5	9,051	90.2	3.2	1.4	1.6	3.6	22.7	15.8	42.2	47.8	24.4	3,456	92.1
North Cornwall township (Lebanon)....................	7,560	7,930	4.9	7,838	74.8	2.8	3.8	2.9	15.7	24.0	18.0	41.5	44.2	33.4	3,009	90.5
North Coventry township (Chester)...................	7,859	7,959	1.3	7,988	91.1	1.6	0.6	2.1	4.5	22.0	17.8	43.0	41.6	35.9	3,148	92.1
North East borough & MCD (Erie)..................	4,280	4,033	-5.8	4,108	90.1	1.8	0.1	2.8	5.3	23.2	13.8	34.5	53.9	18.6	1,707	88.6
North East township (Erie)	6,331	6,181	-2.4	6,264	95.5	1.7	0.4	1.1	1.3	19.8	20.2	43.7	38.0	31.5	2,394	92.1
Northeast Madison township (Perry)	786	792	0.8	659	94.5	0.0	0.0	5.5	0.0	18.8	19.3	49.6	65.7	10.8	272	77.2
Northern Cambria borough & MCD (Cambria)..................	3,839	3,505	-8.7	3,588	100.0	0.0	0.0	0.0	0.0	21.5	17.3	39.9	62.0	12.4	1,549	80.0
North Fayette township (Allegheny)................	13,948	14,816	6.2	14,687	90.9	2.0	1.9	3.3	1.9	19.7	12.9	38.0	32.0	35.0	6,345	94.1
North Franklin township (Washington).............	4,583	4,522	-1.3	4,549	94.9	1.3	1.9	1.4	0.6	17.0	26.0	47.0	44.2	28.5	1,852	82.3
North Heidelberg township (Berks)	1,235	1,260	2.0	1,351	97.9	0.0	0.8	1.3	0.0	15.8	24.5	53.3	48.2	25.4	533	89.5

1 May be of any race.

Table A. All Places — **Population and Housing**

STATE City, town, township, borough, or CDP (county if applicable)	2010 census total population	2019 estimated population	Percent change 2010–2019	ACS total population estimate 2015–2019	White alone, not Hispanic or Latino	Black alone, not Hispanic or Latino	Asian alone, not Hispanic or Latino	All other races or 2 or more races, not Hispanic or Latino	Hispanic or Latino[1]	Under 18 years old	Age 65 years and older	Median age	Percent High school diploma or less	Percent Bachelor's degree or more	Total	Percent with a computer
	1	2	3	4	5	6	7	8	9	10	11	12	13	14	15	16
PENNSYLVANIA—Con.																
North Hopewell township (York)	2,760	2,767	0.3	2,765	96.9	0.3	0.0	1.4	1.4	19.7	18.7	46.5	48.4	24.8	1,054	88.4
North Huntingdon township (Westmoreland)	30,605	30,378	-0.7	30,430	95.9	1.2	0.6	1.1	1.2	20.8	20.2	45.2	34.3	35.6	12,503	90.8
North Irwin borough & MCD (Westmoreland)	840	787	-6.3	840	96.5	3.0	0.0	0.2	0.2	17.0	17.3	42.7	48.8	21.0	392	94.4
North Lebanon township (Lebanon)	11,428	12,186	6.6	11,981	84.7	0.4	1.5	0.4	13.0	19.8	21.1	44.9	63.3	16.8	4,668	82.5
North Londonderry township (Lebanon)	8,069	8,598	6.6	8,451	90.4	0.0	2.9	1.7	5.0	18.1	29.0	49.5	37.2	39.0	3,550	92.3
North Mahoning township (Indiana)	1,428	1,331	-6.8	1,358	100.0	0.0	0.0	0.0	0.0	27.8	15.0	41.0	72.4	13.4	475	61.3
North Manheim township (Schuylkill)	3,766	3,661	-2.8	3,684	98.0	0.4	0.9	0.4	0.2	16.1	22.1	47.8	50.9	21.9	1,451	82.0
North Middleton township (Cumberland)	11,132	11,810	6.1	11,594	87.1	4.0	0.7	3.0	5.2	21.7	16.6	39.8	36.1	35.1	4,488	92.6
Northmoreland township (Wyoming)	1,545	1,467	-5.0	1,445	99.9	0.0	0.0	0.1	0.0	22.8	15.8	44.8	49.6	19.1	558	83.9
North Newton township (Cumberland)	2,430	2,517	3.6	2,497	98.0	0.0	0.3	1.6	0.1	28.8	15.6	37.1	66.2	16.7	836	77.5
North Philipsburg CDP	660	-	-	713	97.8	0.0	0.0	2.2	0.0	14.6	37.7	60.4	72.2	7.2	257	86.4
North Sewickley township (Beaver)	5,486	5,370	-2.1	5,415	97.6	1.2	0.2	0.9	0.0	21.1	23.2	46.3	41.4	28.0	2,120	91.8
North Shenango township (Crawford)	1,410	1,339	-5.0	1,284	98.0	0.0	0.0	1.6	0.4	11.4	35.9	55.8	56.9	16.3	611	83.0
North Strabane township (Washington)	13,387	14,475	8.1	14,437	92.9	2.5	1.1	2.4	1.1	21.0	19.5	43.5	24.5	47.9	5,912	93.8
North Towanda township (Bradford)	1,136	1,089	-4.1	1,103	94.9	3.6	0.0	0.0	1.5	15.3	40.4	58.3	57.4	17.3	499	69.9
Northumberland borough & MCD (Northumberland)	3,802	3,607	-5.1	3,655	88.9	2.7	0.5	1.9	6.0	23.8	21.5	39.8	46.8	27.8	1,593	83.8
North Union township (Fayette)	12,733	11,992	-5.8	12,200	94.3	3.2	0.0	1.9	0.6	20.3	22.7	46.9	64.2	14.2	5,369	79.0
North Union township (Schuylkill)	1,470	1,396	-5.0	1,442	95.6	0.8	0.0	0.5	3.1	14.6	27.9	52.2	55.2	15.2	700	80.0
North Vandergrift CDP	447	-	-	424	89.4	5.2	5.4	0.0	0.0	21.5	24.1	35.6	65.5	7.4	214	77.1
North Versailles township (Allegheny)	10,236	9,924	-3.0	10,037	76.4	15.9	0.2	2.7	4.8	17.2	22.5	46.7	46.3	22.9	4,782	83.7
North Wales borough & MCD (Montgomery)	3,231	3,265	1.1	3,253	88.4	4.6	1.6	2.4	2.9	19.0	12.4	39.9	29.3	40.7	1,299	91.1
North Warren CDP	1,934	-	-	1,807	98.1	0.4	0.0	0.7	0.9	12.8	25.3	50.4	48.6	17.5	774	87.3
Northwest Harborcreek CDP	8,949	-	-	9,077	96.4	0.6	0.9	1.4	0.6	20.6	24.7	49.7	42.1	27.8	3,760	89.4
North Whitehall township (Lehigh)	15,701	16,379	4.3	16,278	88.7	0.9	0.3	1.8	8.4	21.6	17.0	44.9	40.6	33.7	6,158	90.1
Northwood CDP	296	-	-	158	100.0	0.0	0.0	0.0	0.0	22.2	32.9	49.6	57.7	21.1	66	74.2
North Woodbury township (Blair)	2,647	2,595	-2.0	2,624	98.9	0.0	0.2	0.7	0.2	21.3	33.2	51.3	61.3	16.5	1,026	75.2
North York borough & MCD (York)	1,912	2,027	6.0	2,181	70.9	6.6	1.7	7.3	13.5	25.6	10.9	34.4	57.8	14.8	940	89.0
Norvelt CDP	948	-	-	770	100.0	0.0	0.0	0.0	0.0	9.4	36.0	57.3	39.7	21.8	384	89.1
Norwegian township (Schuylkill)	2,302	2,201	-4.4	1,878	98.2	0.0	0.0	0.6	1.2	15.2	28.0	52.8	58.1	24.7	863	86.7
Norwich township (McKean)	585	544	-7.0	600	98.2	0.0	0.0	1.3	0.5	23.2	22.0	45.5	64.1	16.4	267	86.1
Norwood borough & MCD (Delaware)	5,890	5,897	0.1	5,893	86.8	1.2	5.2	3.9	3.0	19.8	12.5	40.2	46.9	21.7	2,079	93.2
Nottingham township (Washington)	3,051	3,006	-1.5	3,024	97.3	0.0	0.0	0.7	2.0	15.7	25.3	51.8	37.4	35.3	1,193	97.7
Noxen CDP	633	-	-	552	98.7	0.0	0.0	1.3	0.0	13.4	27.2	48.5	69.5	9.4	226	71.2
Noxen township (Wyoming)	898	837	-6.8	878	99.1	0.0	0.0	0.8	0.1	20.2	21.9	39.5	67.9	12.7	335	72.2
Noyes township (Clinton)	360	358	-0.6	385	100.0	0.0	0.0	0.0	0.0	22.9	24.7	50.8	77.7	8.9	146	87.7
Nuangola borough & MCD (Luzerne)	678	677	-0.1	699	98.9	0.0	0.3	0.9	0.0	20.3	23.5	46.1	38.5	31.6	280	90.7
Numidia CDP	244	-	-	274	100.0	0.0	0.0	0.0	0.0	21.5	30.7	46.5	59.5	12.6	98	80.6
Nuremberg CDP	434	-	-	541	97.4	0.0	0.0	0.4	2.2	14.6	35.9	51.8	65.1	13.4	284	73.2
Oakdale borough & MCD (Allegheny)	1,455	1,432	-1.6	1,505	97.7	1.3	0.0	0.9	0.1	17.7	20.7	47.6	43.0	24.8	651	86.9
Oak Hills CDP	2,333	-	-	2,255	97.8	0.8	0.0	1.1	0.4	16.9	24.0	49.4	29.2	39.3	1,115	89.7
Oakland township (Butler)	2,987	2,838	-5.0	2,882	98.9	0.2	0.7	0.2	0.0	19.7	17.4	45.8	45.6	21.3	1,168	86.0
Oakland CDP	1,578	-	-	1,422	96.8	1.8	0.0	1.4	0.0	5.1	33.8	57.7	53.9	15.9	751	85.0
Oakland CDP	1,569	-	-	1,579	90.6	3.1	0.0	5.8	0.5	21.0	15.8	39.3	57.7	13.7	616	89.4
Oakland borough & MCD (Susquehanna)	618	562	-9.1	615	97.4	0.7	0.0	1.6	0.3	24.7	21.3	40.6	65.3	12.1	265	82.6
Oakland township (Susquehanna)	561	517	-7.8	569	98.9	0.0	0.5	0.0	0.5	34.4	13.4	40.0	65.8	14.5	196	89.3
Oakland township (Venango)	1,482	1,397	-5.7	1,342	95.9	0.0	1.2	2.9	0.0	20.1	24.9	50.9	56.6	18.7	552	81.9
Oakmont borough & MCD (Allegheny)	6,303	6,541	3.8	6,480	94.5	1.0	1.4	1.8	1.3	15.9	26.1	47.8	25.7	52.8	3,140	89.5
Oakwood CDP	2,270	-	-	2,233	87.6	5.9	0.0	3.3	3.2	19.3	25.7	51.3	55.2	17.6	906	86.5
Oberlin CDP	588	-	-	351	100.0	0.0	0.0	0.0	0.0	18.8	29.6	51.0	61.4	11.9	171	89.5
Ogle township (Somerset)	501	472	-5.8	522	98.7	0.0	0.0	0.0	1.3	16.3	22.0	49.0	60.0	17.1	207	81.2
O'Hara township (Allegheny)	8,894	8,799	-1.1	8,892	86.6	0.7	9.7	1.3	1.6	21.7	24.9	48.5	18.8	62.2	3,681	93.0
Ohio township (Allegheny)	4,804	6,925	44.2	6,565	90.6	3.0	2.7	2.2	1.4	24.8	17.4	40.0	16.7	64.8	2,483	99.2
Ohiopyle borough & MCD (Fayette)	59	56	-5.1	34	100.0	0.0	0.0	0.0	0.0	26.5	41.2	45.5	52.2	21.7	13	100.0

1 May be of any race.

Table A. All Places — Population and Housing

STATE City, town, township, borough, or CDP (county if applicable)	Population 2010 census total population	2019 estimated population	Percent change 2010–2019	ACS total population estimate 2015–2019	Race and Hispanic or Latino origin (percent) White alone, not Hispanic or Latino	Black alone, not Hispanic or Latino	Asian alone, not Hispanic or Latino	All other races or 2 or more races, not Hispanic or Latino	Hispanic or Latino[1]	Age (percent) Under 18 years old	Age 65 years and older	Median age	Educational attainment of persons age 25 and older Percent High school diploma or less	Percent Bachelor's degree or more	Occupied housing units Total	Percent with a computer
	1	2	3	4	5	6	7	8	9	10	11	12	13	14	15	16
PENNSYLVANIA—Con.																
Ohioville borough & MCD (Beaver)	3,471	3,284	-5.4	3,338	97.0	0.7	0.0	1.0	1.3	19.0	20.0	44.9	44.6	21.7	1,354	86.8
Oil City city & MCD (Venango)	10,549	9,618	-8.8	9,846	95.8	0.8	0.1	1.5	1.8	22.0	18.5	40.7	51.7	22.7	4,235	83.0
Oil Creek township (Crawford)	1,868	1,749	-6.4	1,819	97.0	1.8	0.0	0.4	0.8	18.7	22.3	47.1	58.8	16.0	796	86.8
Oil Creek township (Venango)	855	775	-9.4	704	98.9	0.0	0.0	0.0	1.1	14.3	30.3	56.3	59.0	12.2	315	80.0
Oklahoma CDP	782	-	-	878	90.4	0.9	0.0	0.0	8.7	23.9	13.0	39.1	46.6	37.2	346	70.8
Oklahoma borough & MCD (Westmoreland)	793	744	-6.2	828	90.5	1.7	0.0	3.0	4.8	11.2	26.4	57.3	60.5	13.3	386	87.6
Old Forge borough & MCD (Lackawanna)	8,313	7,894	-5.0	7,965	93.2	0.2	0.8	0.7	5.1	17.5	19.5	47.5	46.8	25.4	3,617	87.8
Old Lycoming township (Lycoming)	4,939	4,910	-0.6	4,957	93.9	4.6	0.0	0.6	1.0	17.4	24.7	47.4	46.9	23.9	2,166	85.5
Old Orchard CDP	2,434	-	-	2,185	94.5	1.1	2.9	0.0	1.6	15.7	25.4	49.0	31.5	40.0	963	96.0
Oley CDP	1,282	-	-	1,203	100.0	0.0	0.0	0.0	0.0	17.0	16.7	53.6	70.5	18.4	523	89.7
Oley township (Berks)	3,615	3,877	7.2	3,795	97.4	0.0	0.0	0.0	2.6	16.0	19.2	49.5	48.9	31.0	1,564	90.4
Oliver CDP	2,535	-	-	2,456	93.1	5.9	0.0	0.6	0.4	23.3	20.8	45.6	59.8	14.7	1,067	80.2
Oliver township (Jefferson)	1,087	1,048	-3.6	1,104	95.3	0.0	0.0	4.5	0.2	19.6	19.1	46.1	59.1	16.4	435	82.1
Oliver township (Mifflin)	2,173	2,165	-0.4	2,035	98.7	0.1	0.0	0.5	0.6	22.2	28.6	49.9	67.5	11.9	843	82.0
Oliver township (Perry)	1,934	1,941	0.4	1,872	90.8	0.0	0.0	0.4	2.2	21.3	19.2	42.7	63.9	16.4	773	80.9
Olyphant borough & MCD (Lackawanna)	5,153	5,023	-2.5	5,064	84.9	0.4	1.2	1.1	12.3	23.2	20.6	42.8	45.8	22.0	2,280	78.8
Oneida township (Huntingdon)	1,074	1,050	-2.2	914	96.5	0.5	1.0	2.0	0.0	14.9	26.4	52.6	52.6	23.3	425	88.7
Oneida CDP	200	-	-	117	97.4	0.0	0.0	0.0	2.6	2.6	22.2	45.5	80.7	0.0	68	76.5
Ontelaunee township (Berks)	1,663	2,077	24.9	2,605	81.6	4.5	2.0	2.0	9.9	28.3	13.3	36.8	44.1	28.4	915	88.7
Orange township (Columbia)	1,265	1,234	-2.5	1,019	99.6	0.0	0.0	0.4	0.0	18.6	20.0	51.2	43.9	32.4	444	91.0
Orangeville borough & MCD (Columbia)	500	479	-4.2	434	95.6	1.6	0.0	1.8	0.9	18.7	41.0	57.0	64.7	17.6	109	78.9
Orbisonia borough & MCD (Huntingdon)	426	403	-5.4	402	94.8	0.7	0.0	2.2	2.2	19.7	27.1	43.8	67.2	14.2	188	70.2
Orchard Hills CDP	1,952	-	-	2,294	97.2	0.0	0.0	2.8	0.0	19.7	16.1	43.4	71.8	8.6	892	87.7
Oregon township (Wayne)	774	758	-2.1	770	97.5	0.0	0.3	0.0	2.2	25.7	19.2	44.8	42.8	23.7	302	87.4
Oreland CDP	5,678	-	-	5,625	76.6	9.3	2.1	2.8	9.2	21.4	15.7	39.9	25.0	48.9	2,132	92.9
Orrstown borough & MCD (Franklin)	262	260	-0.8	250	96.8	2.4	0.0	0.0	0.0	24.4	21.2	42.0	77.8	5.1	90	73.3
Orrtanna CDP	173	-	-	111	94.6	0.0	0.0	0.0	5.4	27.9	17.1	39.3	37.5	23.8	49	77.6
Orviston CDP	95	-	-	131	100.0	0.0	0.0	0.0	0.0	7.6	27.5	56.3	55.6	22.2	58	55.2
Orwell township (Bradford)	1,161	1,127	-2.9	1,078	96.5	0.0	0.0	1.2	2.3	24.0	17.3	41.9	55.8	16.5	400	81.3
Orwigsburg borough & MCD (Schuylkill)	3,099	2,952	-4.7	2,974	97.7	0.0	1.0	0.8	0.5	18.0	27.2	46.6	53.3	25.5	1,215	85.7
Orwin CDP	314	-	-	292	95.2	0.0	0.0	1.7	3.1	17.5	16.4	41.5	53.1	11.4	109	100.0
Osceola township (Tioga)	656	630	-4.0	661	96.8	0.0	0.0	2.7	0.5	23.1	20.3	48.8	60.1	12.8	242	82.6
Osceola Mills borough & MCD (Clearfield)	1,141	1,069	-6.3	1,115	91.7	0.2	0.4	0.7	6.9	23.0	15.0	39.2	60.3	12.5	476	87.8
Oswayo borough & MCD (Potter)	139	131	-5.8	161	100.0	0.0	0.0	0.0	0.0	34.2	13.7	34.3	71.0	14.0	45	93.3
Oswayo township (Potter)	278	269	-3.2	258	99.6	0.0	0.0	0.4	0.0	17.1	18.2	45.3	65.2	12.9	79	77.2
Otter Creek township (Mercer)	589	563	-4.4	484	98.1	0.8	0.0	0.6	0.4	14.0	28.7	54.0	61.5	14.6	220	80.5
Otto township (McKean)	1,556	1,475	-5.2	1,657	99.0	0.0	0.0	1.0	0.0	22.4	17.7	41.9	58.2	13.2	668	90.0
Oval CDP	361	-	-	387	100.0	0.0	0.0	0.0	0.0	28.7	23.3	45.3	54.5	18.6	157	79.6
Overfield township (Wyoming)	1,670	1,599	-4.3	1,540	96.0	0.0	0.1	1.6	2.3	15.3	23.3	48.5	49.1	22.7	646	90.2
Overton township (Bradford)	250	236	-5.6	223	96.4	0.9	0.0	1.8	0.9	14.8	31.4	54.3	71.0	12.0	101	86.1
Oxford township (Adams)	5,522	5,600	1.4	5,573	94.9	0.1	0.0	2.9	2.1	18.1	28.2	51.6	54.1	16.2	2,268	84.7
Oxford borough & MCD (Chester)	5,083	5,581	9.8	5,515	55.7	6.0	0.0	3.2	35.0	31.3	14.8	33.8	61.1	21.9	1,963	78.1
Packer township (Carbon)	998	996	-0.2	1,012	99.6	0.0	0.4	0.0	0.0	13.9	20.9	51.9	57.9	14.6	407	86.5
Paint township (Clarion)	1,699	1,595	-6.1	1,554	89.4	2.1	3.0	4.8	0.6	14.9	21.4	45.4	42.2	34.2	640	93.8
Paint borough & MCD (Somerset)	1,002	935	-6.7	904	96.5	0.0	0.0	0.0	3.5	12.9	46.6	60.7	60.2	18.0	391	71.9
Paint township (Somerset)	3,141	3,019	-3.9	3,053	97.5	0.0	0.0	0.0	2.5	16.8	26.3	50.6	57.5	22.9	1,324	74.8
Palmdale CDP	1,308	-	-	1,252	81.5	5.0	2.6	0.5	10.4	19.2	19.4	41.1	44.8	39.0	570	82.8
Palmer township (Northampton)	20,681	21,422	3.6	21,345	78.8	4.8	4.4	1.3	10.7	18.4	23.1	46.2	34.1	38.0	8,494	93.7
Palmer Heights CDP	3,762	-	-	3,837	85.7	2.0	0.8	1.1	10.3	18.3	25.9	51.1	41.2	32.4	1,418	97.4
Palmerton borough & MCD (Carbon)	5,414	5,336	-1.4	5,313	99.4	0.0	0.0	0.0	0.6	24.2	18.6	41.0	59.9	17.6	1,981	89.3
Palmyra borough & MCD (Lebanon)	7,325	7,587	3.6	7,536	84.2	1.5	3.7	1.2	9.4	25.0	16.4	36.6	52.0	21.5	3,302	87.3
Palmyra township (Pike)	3,312	3,243	-2.1	3,215	93.8	0.7	1.9	3.1	0.4	11.3	37.5	57.7	36.6	36.0	1,427	89.5
Palmyra township (Wayne)	1,338	1,299	-2.9	1,140	89.9	0.0	0.6	2.6	6.8	18.0	22.1	47.2	45.2	23.0	461	88.9
Palo Alto borough & MCD (Schuylkill)	1,032	978	-5.2	830	97.5	0.0	0.7	0.1	1.7	19.3	22.5	45.4	68.4	6.3	378	83.3
Paoli CDP	5,575	-	-	5,651	79.3	4.5	8.7	3.0	4.5	20.3	25.9	46.7	26.6	59.2	2,429	91.1
Paradise CDP	1,129	-	-	1,147	91.4	1.9	0.0	4.2	2.5	21.4	18.2	41.5	56.4	19.7	405	90.9
Paradise township (Lancaster)	5,131	5,710	11.3	5,658	91.5	1.6	0.0	1.0	6.0	29.4	14.5	31.9	72.7	11.7	1,835	77.8
Paradise township (Monroe)	3,180	3,136	-1.4	3,111	67.6	10.9	0.0	4.4	17.1	17.9	12.1	34.9	43.6	24.6	901	93.9
Paradise township (York)	3,791	4,116	8.6	4,009	96.3	0.5	0.9	0.5	1.9	22.7	18.2	42.9	53.2	24.4	1,582	91.3
Pardeesville CDP	572	-	-	620	100.0	0.0	0.0	0.0	0.0	9.2	21.1	35.9	57.2	6.4	283	100.0
Paris CDP	732	-	-	842	97.4	2.3	0.0	0.4	0.0	14.7	21.3	52.1	57.3	17.9	341	96.8
Park Crest CDP	542	-	-	596	98.8	0.0	0.0	0.0	1.2	15.3	22.1	50.7	44.9	26.6	220	95.0
Parker city & MCD (Armstrong)	842	802	-4.8	648	100.0	0.0	0.0	0.0	0.0	17.4	31.6	50.6	64.7	12.7	288	71.9

1 May be of any race.

Table A. All Places — **Population and Housing**

STATE City, town, township, borough, or CDP (county if applicable)	2010 census total population	2019 estimated population	Percent change 2010–2019	ACS total population estimate 2015–2019	White alone, not Hispanic or Latino	Black alone, not Hispanic or Latino	Asian alone, not Hispanic or Latino	All other races or 2 or more races, not Hispanic or Latino	Hispanic or Latino[1]	Under 18 years old	Age 65 years and older	Median age	Percent High school diploma or less	Percent Bachelor's degree or more	Total	Percent with a computer
	1	2	3	4	5	6	7	8	9	10	11	12	13	14	15	16
Parker township (Butler)	632	608	-3.8	588	96.3	0.0	0.0	3.2	0.5	19.4	21.8	47.7	65.9	12.4	260	76.2
Parkesburg borough & MCD (Chester)	3,591	3,993	11.2	3,842	78.6	6.7	0.0	7.7	7.1	28.2	11.5	37.2	52.6	21.0	1,300	91.6
Park Forest Village CDP	9,660	-	-	10,299	72.9	5.3	15.0	3.2	3.6	20.0	10.9	31.7	23.6	64.5	3,850	98.9
Parks township (Armstrong)	2,749	2,564	-6.7	2,611	93.7	2.9	0.9	1.4	1.1	18.8	22.7	46.5	63.4	12.1	1,174	82.2
Parkside borough & MCD (Delaware)	2,326	2,330	0.2	2,227	69.7	21.6	1.3	2.5	5.0	28.4	10.2	32.9	38.0	26.3	782	94.8
Parkville CDP	6,706	-	-	7,234	92.1	2.0	1.3	1.4	3.1	23.3	15.1	37.4	59.4	15.2	2,779	91.1
Parryville borough & MCD (Carbon)	522	502	-3.8	520	99.4	0.0	0.0	0.0	0.6	17.9	11.7	43.7	73.2	4.0	215	84.7
Patterson township (Beaver)	3,022	2,850	-5.7	2,906	91.1	2.4	0.2	3.9	2.3	22.5	25.6	44.7	42.0	30.7	1,256	86.0
Patterson Heights borough & MCD (Beaver)	635	597	-6.0	508	98.4	0.4	0.4	0.8	0.0	18.7	24.2	48.2	22.8	50.6	229	93.0
Patton borough & MCD (Cambria)	1,760	1,598	-9.2	1,682	98.6	0.0	0.0	1.4	0.0	16.5	18.0	46.0	55.4	13.3	772	81.7
Patton borough & MCD (Centre)	15,155	15,805	4.3	15,828	81.0	4.9	9.3	1.3	3.5	15.6	10.9	29.6	17.7	68.5	6,294	98.4
Paupack township (Wayne)	3,847	3,737	-2.9	3,752	94.0	0.0	1.2	1.3	3.4	15.9	30.9	56.2	39.6	27.0	1,663	91.1
Pavia township (Bedford)	293	274	-6.5	299	97.0	0.0	0.0	3.0	0.0	20.4	22.7	45.6	52.5	24.7	115	87.8
Paxtang borough & MCD (Dauphin)	1,561	1,546		1,726	61.2	23.1	2.0	1.5	12.2	25.4	16.2	38.1	34.4	33.9	689	86.4
Paxtonia CDP	5,412	-	-	5,296	71.8	14.2	3.4	6.7	3.8	22.6	16.7	42.3	43.1	32.2	2,069	86.2
Paxtonville CDP	265	-	-	268	100.0	0.0	0.0	0.0	0.0	25.0	23.5	33.8	63.3	27.2	103	78.6
Peach Bottom township (York)	4,815	5,066	5.2	5,010	93.6	3.5	0.0	1.8	1.2	24.3	15.6	42.1	58.9	14.0	1,636	89.5
Pen Argyl borough & MCD (Northampton)	3,595	3,556	-1.1	3,543	90.1	1.7	0.1	0.5	7.5	22.5	11.8	34.6	54.1	19.8	1,369	89.7
Penbrook borough & MCD (Dauphin)	3,009	2,985	-0.8	2,984	44.6	40.4	0.0	3.8	11.1	27.4	11.1	29.7	44.5	29.9	1,260	90.7
Pen Mar CDP	929	-	-	1,025	87.6	2.7	0.0	6.1	3.5	29.0	10.5	39.1	37.9	20.8	354	88.4
Penn township (Berks)	2,007	2,135	6.4	2,067	91.7	0.2	0.7	1.2	6.2	18.0	20.1	49.9	49.3	21.6	797	89.2
Penn township (Butler)	5,065	4,879	-3.7	4,916	98.5	0.0	0.4	0.3	0.8	15.6	25.3	53.0	44.0	33.9	2,149	85.3
Penn township (Centre)	1,187	1,201	1.2	1,220	97.8	0.0	0.1	1.3	0.8	28.6	17.0	39.1	59.2	16.1	435	81.1
Penn township (Chester)	5,383	5,515	2.5	5,501	79.4	1.6	0.9	1.6	16.5	20.4	32.3	51.3	35.9	50.3	2,266	79.4
Penn township (Clearfield)	1,274	1,218	-4.4	1,237	96.0	0.9	0.0	0.2	2.9	20.0	23.2	46.7	67.7	13.6	491	81.3
Penn township (Cumberland)	2,924	2,991	2.3	2,984	96.1	0.8	0.0	0.6	2.4	21.9	17.8	43.8	69.4	12.6	1,050	81.1
Penn township (Huntingdon)	1,084	1,073		856	97.0	1.1	0.0	0.9	1.1	15.1	28.7	52.5	48.8	25.2	401	90.8
Penn township (Lancaster)	8,796	9,972	13.4	9,652	90.9	0.5	2.6	2.4	3.6	23.2	19.7	42.0	53.7	26.6	3,592	86.4
Penn township (Lycoming)	956	956	0.0	916	98.6	0.0	0.0	1.4	0.0	20.0	22.6	45.3	55.9	16.2	360	84.2
Penn township (Perry)	3,225	3,251	0.8	3,230	97.6	0.0	0.0	0.8	1.6	19.3	21.1	42.3	53.9	18.0	1,270	88.3
Penn township (Snyder)	4,324	4,395	1.6	4,380	95.5	1.0	1.6	0.7	1.2	13.8	22.2	47.7	50.2	31.7	1,791	81.9
Penn borough & MCD (Westmoreland)	475	465	-2.1	462	95.5	0.6	0.0	3.9	0.0	29.2	8.9	34.8	49.0	20.0	176	89.8
Penn township (Westmoreland)	20,034	19,350	-3.4	19,442	95.3	0.2	1.2	1.8	1.5	19.1	21.4	48.7	35.1	37.7	7,794	91.0
Penn township (York)	15,629	16,623	6.4	16,370	93.7	2.3	1.2	0.9	2.0	22.3	19.1	41.1	51.6	22.6	6,367	90.1
Penndel borough & MCD (Bucks)	2,322	2,157	-7.1	2,885	66.6	16.3	4.9	5.5	6.7	20.3	10.5	32.3	42.3	27.9	1,145	83.1
Penn Estates CDP	4,493	-	-	5,363	37.0	27.5	1.0	8.0	26.5	28.6	8.3	35.2	26.3	27.0	1,730	96.8
Penn Forest township (Carbon)	9,585	9,720	1.4	9,626	83.3	6.5	1.5	0.4	8.2	22.2	18.5	45.9	46.6	22.5	3,722	94.0
Penn Hills township (Allegheny)	42,385	40,807	-3.7	41,317	54.4	38.2	0.3	5.6	1.6	18.9	20.4	44.4	36.0	31.3	18,552	88.2
Penn Lake Park borough & MCD (Luzerne)	308	308	0.0	369	97.3	0.5	1.4	0.8	0.0	22.5	23.6	46.9	29.7	37.3	138	90.6
Pennsburg borough & MCD (Montgomery)	3,844	3,855	0.3	3,869	90.7	1.9	1.7	3.1	2.6	21.4	14.0	40.7	47.5	23.3	1,333	95.0
Pennsbury township (Chester)	3,590	3,650	1.7	3,640	86.2	0.7	11.1	1.1	0.9	22.5	31.6	49.6	9.7	80.2	1,309	96.5
Pennsbury Village borough & MCD (Allegheny)	661	653	-1.2	720	86.0	8.2	0.3	5.6	0.0	12.1	14.2	36.6	21.3	56.8	489	91.8
Penns Creek CDP	715	-	-	674	98.4	0.3	0.0	0.4	0.9	20.8	17.4	39.1	53.9	16.4	243	78.6
Pennside CDP	4,215	-	-	4,304	81.0	5.5	0.5	1.7	11.4	17.7	19.9	44.5	50.8	19.4	1,703	86.3
Penn State Erie (Behrend) CDP	1,629	-	-	1,626	73.7	4.2	15.1	5.4	1.6	0.3	0.0	19.4	0.0	0.0	0	0.0
Pennville CDP	1,947	-	-	2,028	92.9	5.4	0.0	0.0	1.7	22.9	23.1	36.4	58.4	23.1	862	81.3
Pennwyn CDP	780	-	-	538	98.3	0.0	0.0	0.0	1.7	8.4	15.8	50.3	48.1	35.6	272	87.1
Penn Wynne CDP	5,697	-	-	5,932	72.1	8.3	12.1	2.3	5.2	22.6	25.7	48.6	11.0	75.4	2,351	94.6
Penryn CDP	1,024	-	-	992	96.9	0.0	0.0	1.3	1.8	24.6	13.0	43.8	53.2	25.4	341	91.5
Pequea township (Lancaster)	4,596	5,339	16.2	4,978	94.3	0.0	1.7	0.5	3.5	20.1	18.2	45.1	55.2	21.9	1,905	93.1
Perkasie borough & MCD (Bucks)	8,498	8,738	2.8	8,550	93.2	1.2	1.2	1.0	3.4	23.0	14.7	40.3	36.8	38.0	3,284	91.3
Perkiomen township (Montgomery)	9,128	9,140	0.1	9,163	85.6	2.4	6.0	2.6	3.4	27.6	8.1	38.4	27.3	49.4	3,171	97.3
Perry township (Armstrong)	353	325	-7.9	459	96.1	1.7	1.1	0.0	1.1	31.8	18.3	43.2	55.7	12.1	156	89.7
Perry township (Berks)	2,421	2,483	2.6	2,430	96.8	0.0	0.3	0.0	2.9	17.1	21.2	47.2	64.8	17.4	983	84.2
Perry township (Clarion)	947	890	-6.0	925	99.5	0.0	0.0	0.4	0.1	19.6	17.5	44.8	63.1	13.0	352	84.7
Perry township (Fayette)	2,552	2,412	-5.5	2,234	97.3	0.0	0.8	0.6	1.3	13.7	28.4	52.8	58.4	16.9	1,025	86.8
Perry township (Greene)	1,514	1,402	-7.4	1,453	95.9	0.0	0.0	2.4	1.7	21.2	20.9	45.4	55.7	23.9	633	84.2
Perry township (Jefferson)	1,228	1,179	-4.0	1,072	98.4	0.0	0.2	1.2	0.2	19.6	18.1	44.4	61.0	17.3	458	85.6
Perry township (Lawrence)	1,948	1,847	-5.2	2,036	96.9	0.0	0.3	1.9	0.8	21.9	19.4	45.3	52.7	19.3	819	89.1
Perry township (Mercer)	1,448	1,352	-6.6	1,358	95.8	0.0	0.7	3.2	0.3	20.1	20.0	48.0	69.9	16.8	568	85.9
Perry township (Snyder)	2,192	2,215	1.0	2,225	96.7	0.2	0.7	1.7	0.7	23.0	17.6	39.4	68.1	10.9	783	76.6

1 May be of any race.

Table A. All Places — **Population and Housing**

STATE City, town, township, borough, or CDP (county if applicable)	2010 census total population	2019 estimated population	Percent change 2010–2019	ACS total population estimate 2015–2019	White alone, not Hispanic or Latino	Black alone, not Hispanic or Latino	Asian alone, not Hispanic or Latino	All other races or 2 or more races, not Hispanic or Latino	Hispanic or Latino[1]	Under 18 years old	Age 65 years and older	Median age	Percent High school diploma or less	Percent Bachelor's degree or more	Total	Percent with a computer
	1	2	3	4	5	6	7	8	9	10	11	12	13	14	15	16
PENNSYLVANIA—Con.																
Perryopolis borough & MCD (Fayette)	1,784	1,666	-6.6	1,790	92.3	0.2	2.6	3.1	1.7	18.4	25.0	47.7	49.1	22.3	833	80.1
Peters township (Franklin)	4,429	4,414	-0.3	4,427	96.0	0.0	0.0	0.7	3.3	25.4	17.5	38.5	68.7	8.8	1,533	86.3
Peters township (Washington)	21,202	22,044	4.0	21,983	93.8	0.8	2.8	1.1	1.5	25.7	17.5	44.4	18.1	61.3	7,733	97.3
Petersburg borough & MCD (Huntingdon)	482	464	-3.7	479	98.5	0.0	0.0	1.0	0.4	23.6	22.8	39.8	72.8	4.3	182	84.1
Petrolia borough & MCD (Butler)	213	198	-7.0	152	100.0	0.0	0.0	0.0	0.0	19.7	17.8	44.5	65.1	7.3	71	81.7
Philadelphia city	1,526,012	1,584,064	3.8	1,579,075	34.5	40.8	7.2	2.8	14.7	21.9	13.4	34.4	47.9	29.7	601,337	86.1
Philipsburg borough & MCD (Centre)	2,766	2,698	-2.5	2,719	97.9	0.4	0.0	0.3	1.4	15.9	22.0	43.4	52.5	23.0	1,402	76.9
Phoenixville borough & MCD (Chester)	16,439	16,968	3.2	16,895	81.4	8.0	2.2	2.3	6.0	21.0	11.7	35.1	32.5	44.6	7,398	91.2
Piatt township (Lycoming)	1,180	1,136	-3.7	900	98.2	0.0	0.0	1.0	0.8	19.2	17.6	47.5	65.0	17.9	359	89.7
Picture Rocks borough & MCD (Lycoming)	677	644	-4.9	603	95.4	0.0	0.2	2.2	2.3	23.7	18.4	40.8	47.3	23.5	234	93.2
Pike township (Berks)	1,717	1,755	2.2	1,595	96.7	0.0	0.2	2.2	0.9	18.2	20.1	50.6	42.5	29.2	634	91.5
Pike township (Bradford)	668	660	-1.2	569	97.0	0.0	0.7	1.4	0.9	21.3	23.2	49.3	66.5	14.2	235	74.9
Pike township (Clearfield)	2,312	2,268	-1.9	2,408	97.2	0.1	0.0	0.1	2.5	18.5	20.6	47.3	56.9	15.9	967	83.0
Pike township (Potter)	324	313	-3.4	345	98.0	0.0	0.0	1.2	0.9	17.7	24.9	52.3	61.7	19.9	134	76.9
Pikes Creek CDP	269	-	-	531	92.1	3.2	1.9	0.0	2.8	19.2	20.3	34.1	50.1	19.8	152	97.4
Pillow borough & MCD (Dauphin)	298	297	-0.3	320	89.1	8.8	0.0	0.0	2.2	28.1	14.1	37.8	72.3	9.4	118	84.7
Pine township (Allegheny)	11,484	13,741	19.7	13,118	91.6	0.8	4.9	1.0	1.6	29.4	9.1	38.8	8.0	77.2	4,530	98.9
Pine township (Armstrong)	409	380	-7.1	393	99.2	0.0	0.0	0.8	0.0	28.0	21.6	42.9	80.1	4.9	151	70.9
Pine township (Clearfield)	60	57	-5.0	58	100.0	0.0	0.0	0.0	0.0	13.8	34.5	57.5	46.0	28.0	32	75.0
Pine township (Columbia)	1,049	1,010	-3.7	1,063	96.5	0.0	0.3	1.8	1.4	21.6	24.6	48.7	61.4	15.1	425	86.6
Pine township (Crawford)	466	445	-4.5	407	98.5	0.0	0.5	0.0	1.0	14.5	31.0	56.1	65.9	13.3	200	73.5
Pine township (Indiana)	2,035	1,901	-6.6	1,645	98.4	0.1	0.2	1.3	0.0	15.7	22.4	49.9	66.3	14.1	707	70.6
Pine township (Lycoming)	294	290	-1.4	331	98.5	0.9	0.0	0.6	0.0	16.9	27.5	52.0	69.2	9.3	139	85.6
Pine township (Mercer)	5,143	4,908	-4.6	4,986	90.0	4.8	0.0	1.1	4.1	26.9	21.0	44.3	47.3	32.6	1,817	86.0
Pine Creek township (Clinton)	3,212	3,221	0.3	3,250	97.6	1.3	0.0	0.0	1.1	18.8	23.8	52.3	52.0	18.3	1,362	83.0
Pine Creek township (Jefferson)	1,353	1,313	-3.0	1,215	90.5	2.2	0.2	3.7	3.5	14.8	31.3	46.7	61.9	17.9	406	81.5
Pine Glen CDP	190	-	-	197	99.0	0.0	0.0	0.0	1.0	22.8	13.7	40.2	57.7	13.4	71	88.7
Pine Grove borough & MCD (Schuylkill)	2,186	2,069	-5.4	2,138	92.0	1.4	0.0	1.9	4.7	22.4	17.1	39.4	59.5	18.0	868	86.3
Pine Grove township (Schuylkill)	4,123	4,016	-2.6	4,041	98.2	0.0	0.3	0.1	1.4	19.5	23.3	47.9	57.8	11.9	1,686	83.3
Pinegrove township (Venango)	1,353	1,237	-8.6	1,122	97.6	0.0	0.0	1.4	1.0	19.4	20.6	50.0	61.0	14.0	472	87.1
Pine Grove township (Warren)	2,689	2,526	-6.1	2,564	95.7	0.0	1.0	1.6	1.7	16.1	29.0	51.0	43.2	27.7	1,117	91.0
Pine Grove Mills CDP	1,502	-	-	1,463	100.0	0.0	0.0	0.0	0.0	15.2	23.2	62.2	26.9	63.5	675	73.0
Pine Ridge CDP	2,707	-	-	2,703	26.6	40.0	0.4	7.5	25.5	21.0	15.5	43.7	30.8	30.3	913	91.6
Piney township (Clarion)	455	424	-6.8	316	97.8	0.9	0.6	0.6	0.0	5.7	31.6	54.7	69.0	18.5	124	81.5
Pitcairn borough & MCD (Allegheny)	3,284	3,158	-3.8	3,195	64.6	23.5	3.2	4.1	4.7	24.3	15.2	39.3	49.8	17.7	1,458	82.2
Pittsburgh city & MCD (Allegheny)	305,245	300,286	-1.6	302,205	64.7	22.8	5.8	3.6	3.2	15.1	14.7	32.9	32.5	44.6	138,058	88.3
Pittsfield township (Warren)	1,404	1,344	-4.3	1,313	94.9	0.0	1.4	2.9	0.8	21.2	16.2	42.5	59.0	11.0	500	88.8
Pittston city & MCD (Luzerne)	7,801	7,802	0.0	7,765	86.3	4.7	0.5	2.9	5.6	23.4	15.5	34.5	50.3	14.8	3,314	82.7
Pittston township (Luzerne)	3,341	3,357	0.5	3,364	97.3	0.9	0.0	1.5	0.3	14.7	18.2	47.0	47.6	20.1	1,431	81.9
Plainfield CDP	399	-	-	406	100.0	0.0	0.0	0.0	0.0	5.7	53.2	65.3	87.5	6.8	243	87.7
Plainfield township (Northampton)	6,174	6,232	0.9	6,194	97.9	0.2	0.0	0.1	1.9	16.6	23.9	50.7	52.3	25.6	2,531	80.0
Plain Grove township (Lawrence)	804	758	-5.7	863	95.8	0.9	0.8	0.9	1.5	20.3	11.6	44.6	49.9	23.8	353	89.5
Plains CDP	4,335	-	-	3,866	87.0	8.8	0.0	1.6	2.6	14.2	24.9	48.6	47.8	22.4	1,816	80.3
Plains township (Luzerne)	9,913	9,663	-2.5	9,704	88.3	6.1	0.1	2.5	3.0	13.9	25.5	49.3	47.7	26.3	4,277	82.8
Platea borough & MCD (Erie)	430	400	-7.0	434	97.7	0.0	0.0	1.2	1.2	11.3	27.9	56.6	76.3	5.9	196	87.8
Pleasant township (Warren)	2,442	2,296	-6.0	2,321	97.5	0.0	1.2	0.2	1.1	12.8	32.1	55.3	44.0	23.1	994	88.7
Pleasant Gap CDP	2,879	-	-	3,310	96.7	0.7	0.8	1.8	0.0	23.5	11.6	41.6	39.3	33.3	1,405	89.0
Pleasant Hill CDP	2,643	-	-	2,809	57.7	4.1	2.4	3.2	32.6	29.2	10.2	32.0	52.7	25.0	1,008	93.1
Pleasant Hills borough & MCD (Allegheny)	8,254	8,026	-2.8	8,113	93.6	1.0	3.0	0.7	1.8	18.8	24.7	47.4	28.3	41.4	3,603	89.0
Pleasant Valley township (Potter)	86	80	-7.0	35	100.0	0.0	0.0	0.0	0.0	11.4	57.1	67.8	48.4	35.5	19	100.0
Pleasant View CDP	780	-	-	691	95.5	0.0	0.0	0.7	3.8	9.1	23.9	49.4	58.8	12.4	353	79.3
Pleasantville borough & MCD (Bedford)	198	204	3.0	125	98.4	0.0	0.0	1.6	0.0	17.6	31.2	47.5	65.6	16.7	59	62.7
Pleasantville borough & MCD (Venango)	894	812	-9.2	876	91.8	1.0	1.3	2.7	3.2	23.6	18.5	44.2	51.7	19.8	365	92.1
Plum borough & MCD (Allegheny)	27,108	27,087	-0.1	27,195	92.5	3.2	0.3	2.8	1.2	20.1	21.0	45.3	31.5	36.8	11,366	91.7
Plum township (Venango)	1,059	973	-8.1	831	94.7	0.0	0.4	3.9	1.1	20.6	20.3	46.0	59.7	15.0	353	87.0
Plumcreek township (Armstrong)	2,381	2,210	-7.2	2,348	98.2	0.0	0.0	0.9	1.0	21.5	21.0	44.3	64.3	15.7	949	84.1
Plumstead township (Bucks)	12,444	14,483	16.4	13,980	87.1	0.6	4.4	1.3	6.7	24.6	12.7	42.6	23.4	55.7	4,965	94.6
Plumsteadville CDP	2,637	-	-	2,581	89.7	0.0	4.2	0.5	5.7	26.7	10.0	41.2	16.3	63.0	856	92.6
Plumville borough & MCD (Indiana)	307	287	-6.5	304	100.0	0.0	0.0	0.0	0.0	25.0	18.4	40.8	73.9	13.0	115	82.6
Plunketts Creek township (Lycoming)	684	671	-1.9	637	94.3	0.5	0.0	0.5	4.7	22.4	19.5	45.7	45.1	23.0	267	89.9

1 May be of any race.

Table A. All Places — **Population and Housing**

STATE City, town, township, borough, or CDP (county if applicable)	Population				Race and Hispanic or Latino origin (percent)					Age (percent)			Educational attainment of persons age 25 and older		Occupied housing units	
	2010 census total population	2019 estimated population	Percent change 2010–2019	ACS total population estimate 2015–2019	White alone, not Hispanic or Latino	Black alone, not Hispanic or Latino	Asian alone, not Hispanic or Latino	All other races or 2 or more races, not Hispanic or Latino	Hispanic or Latino[1]	Under 18 years old	Age 65 years and older	Median age	Percent High school diploma or less	Percent Bachelor's degree or more	Total	Percent with a computer
	1	2	3	4	5	6	7	8	9	10	11	12	13	14	15	16
PENNSYLVANIA—Con.																
Plymouth borough & MCD (Luzerne)	5,953	5,794	-2.7	5,820	84.9	4.3	0.9	3.3	6.6	24.7	16.3	34.6	57.4	13.1	2,418	81.1
Plymouth township (Luzerne)	1,826	1,789	-2.0	1,629	97.1	0.7	0.0	1.3	0.9	13.5	21.0	52.7	53.5	18.8	709	82.8
Plymouth township (Montgomery)	16,538	17,531	6.0	17,582	76.8	8.9	8.2	2.1	4.1	21.1	17.3	40.2	29.3	48.9	7,082	94.4
Plymouth Meeting CDP	6,177	-	-	6,947	78.4	6.4	9.0	2.1	4.1	21.3	19.2	42.0	22.8	57.5	2,995	95.5
Plymptonville CDP	981	-	-	1,192	99.8	0.1	0.0	0.1	0.0	13.8	18.4	42.6	67.4	12.8	455	91.0
Pocono township (Monroe)	11,077	11,089	0.1	10,909	66.6	13.3	1.1	1.1	17.8	21.7	18.3	43.7	41.9	29.6	3,835	92.8
Pocono Mountain Lake Estates CDP	842	-	-	731	42.3	2.6	9.0	0.0	46.1	16.7	17.9	50.1	54.2	14.8	289	91.3
Pocono Pines CDP	1,409	-	-	1,023	98.1	1.9	0.0	0.0	0.0	24.2	32.6	48.8	28.9	23.5	520	92.1
Pocono Ranch Lands CDP	1,062	-	-	1,205	81.1	3.9	1.5	0.0	13.5	13.9	16.1	47.9	60.2	7.0	460	97.4
Pocono Springs CDP	926	-	-	1,325	84.2	0.9	0.8	4.6	9.6	18.3	21.4	49.0	44.2	19.4	518	91.3
Pocono Woodland Lakes CDP	3,209	-	-	3,979	91.9	0.5	0.0	0.8	6.8	20.3	14.6	43.6	33.2	35.4	1,343	100.0
Pocopson township (Chester)	4,583	4,829	5.4	4,842	76.9	9.3	5.2	4.5	4.2	17.6	15.4	38.3	33.9	44.5	990	96.5
Point township (Northumberland)	3,687	3,593	-2.5	3,629	98.2	0.7	0.0	0.9	0.3	18.4	23.6	47.1	55.2	23.9	1,481	87.1
Point Marion borough & MCD (Fayette)	1,159	1,098	-5.3	1,280	89.8	1.3	0.0	5.9	3.0	17.3	15.2	37.5	60.0	20.4	513	80.3
Polk township (Jefferson)	265	255	-3.8	323	100.0	0.0	0.0	0.0	0.0	38.1	12.7	32.1	57.5	14.4	101	63.4
Polk township (Monroe)	7,861	7,779	-1.0	7,686	85.9	5.8	0.0	2.1	6.2	20.7	14.8	38.4	52.1	16.8	2,498	85.6
Polk borough & MCD (Venango)	814	768	-5.7	747	92.1	3.1	0.0	3.5	1.3	15.5	25.0	51.2	78.8	7.3	204	95.6
Pomeroy CDP	401	-	-	590	62.0	5.4	0.0	16.9	15.6	23.4	15.9	32.4	56.8	22.0	252	77.8
Portage borough & MCD (Cambria)	2,632	2,383	-9.5	2,439	99.1	0.4	0.4	0.1	0.1	20.3	22.5	43.9	57.5	18.0	1,144	81.7
Portage township (Cambria)	3,642	3,357	-7.8	3,424	97.5	0.3	0.0	1.0	1.2	18.4	26.7	50.3	49.4	22.3	1,447	81.3
Portage township (Cameron)	164	143	-12.8	149	100.0	0.0	0.0	0.0	0.0	21.5	36.9	57.6	48.7	24.8	70	82.9
Portage township (Potter)	231	220	-4.8	218	100.0	0.0	0.0	0.0	0.0	29.4	17.0	38.0	55.6	12.7	77	84.4
Port Allegany borough & MCD (McKean)	2,153	1,998	-7.2	2,262	98.2	0.4	0.1	0.5	0.9	25.8	18.2	42.6	51.4	21.9	942	93.5
Port Carbon borough & MCD (Schuylkill)	1,886	1,775	-5.9	1,760	95.5	0.0	0.4	0.0	4.1	21.1	18.8	43.2	59.6	15.0	800	83.9
Port Clinton borough & MCD (Schuylkill)	326	307	-5.8	313	90.1	0.0	2.6	6.1	1.3	25.9	12.1	43.8	66.1	6.4	134	88.1
Porter township (Clarion)	1,344	1,247	-7.2	1,129	99.6	0.3	0.0	0.0	0.1	15.8	23.8	48.3	62.6	16.3	453	81.0
Porter township (Clinton)	1,466	1,506	2.7	1,465	99.2	0.0	0.5	0.3	0.0	22.3	17.1	40.7	63.0	14.9	545	80.2
Porter township (Huntingdon)	1,966	1,915	-2.6	1,840	97.1	1.4	0.0	0.8	0.8	15.5	26.7	52.2	53.7	19.0	786	85.0
Porter township (Jefferson)	305	293	-3.9	401	100.0	0.0	0.0	0.0	0.0	30.2	19.5	38.2	69.6	8.4	151	64.2
Porter township (Lycoming)	1,592	1,525	-4.2	1,887	95.6	0.0	0.1	0.3	4.0	24.9	18.6	42.0	55.3	17.8	736	90.1
Porter township (Pike)	478	457	-4.4	400	89.3	2.5	0.0	1.8	6.5	17.5	36.3	57.1	41.4	21.6	195	93.3
Porter township (Schuylkill)	2,179	2,061	-5.4	2,017	98.4	0.0	0.0	0.9	0.7	15.5	26.1	47.7	66.6	10.1	916	85.3
Portersville borough & MCD (Butler)	233	224	-3.9	284	95.8	0.0	0.0	4.2	0.0	15.5	18.3	46.6	32.6	31.3	130	97.7
Portland borough & MCD (Northampton)	519	513	-1.2	600	62.7	0.3	0.0	8.2	28.8	26.8	8.8	34.5	53.3	14.6	225	96.4
Port Matilda borough & MCD (Centre)	599	587	-2.0	593	99.2	0.0	0.2	0.0	0.7	18.5	19.7	40.3	55.6	21.2	270	91.9
Port Royal borough & MCD (Juniata)	925	908	-1.8	857	90.4	0.4	0.0	0.0	9.2	13.8	25.7	48.3	66.5	14.0	396	76.8
Port Trevorton CDP	769	-	-	865	95.4	0.7	0.5	2.1	1.4	31.3	11.1	30.6	69.9	10.4	261	76.6
Port Vue borough & MCD (Allegheny)	3,797	3,651	-3.8	3,697	92.2	2.1	1.5	2.1	2.1	19.6	21.9	45.3	51.5	17.1	1,742	79.1
Potlicker Flats CDP	172	-	-	283	100.0	0.0	0.0	0.0	0.0	0.0	21.6	49.1	94.7	3.4	140	83.6
Potter township (Beaver)	548	566	3.3	501	98.4	0.0	0.2	1.4	0.0	11.2	16.2	51.9	38.0	21.6	219	94.1
Potter township (Centre)	3,532	3,604	2.0	3,588	97.4	1.5	0.0	0.3	0.9	16.8	23.0	49.3	34.9	38.9	1,518	88.9
Pottsgrove CDP	3,469	-	-	3,328	86.1	5.2	2.3	2.9	3.5	21.0	20.1	47.0	35.5	41.3	1,300	96.2
Pottstown borough & MCD (Montgomery)	22,353	22,600	1.1	22,670	62.7	22.9	0.6	6.7	7.0	23.8	13.5	35.6	50.2	20.3	9,096	87.1
Pottsville city & MCD (Schuylkill)	14,326	13,475	-5.9	13,648	90.8	4.3	0.1	0.9	3.9	20.2	19.0	42.2	53.1	19.3	5,917	79.8
President township (Venango)	540	495	-8.3	412	95.6	0.0	0.0	2.9	1.5	8.7	33.3	56.7	57.3	24.5	198	89.9
Preston township (Wayne)	1,017	1,000	-1.7	800	90.4	1.1	0.0	3.0	5.5	17.4	24.6	53.8	46.6	21.1	356	82.9
Price township (Monroe)	3,607	3,716	3.0	3,641	65.4	14.4	3.2	3.1	13.9	19.5	13.9	44.7	47.3	21.7	1,229	88.6
Pringle borough & MCD (Luzerne)	959	941	-1.9	958	88.8	6.9	0.3	1.8	2.2	17.3	19.7	41.3	49.3	19.7	429	86.0
Progress CDP	9,765	-	-	10,094	51.9	24.9	11.2	3.0	8.9	23.1	14.4	38.6	45.3	29.1	4,361	86.2
Prompton borough & MCD (Wayne)	248	234	-5.6	272	96.0	3.3	0.0	0.0	0.7	16.9	18.8	49.2	52.4	13.0	104	89.4
Prospect borough & MCD (Butler)	1,169	1,109	-5.1	1,089	94.9	0.1	0.5	1.7	2.8	18.5	20.5	49.6	46.8	21.4	458	90.0
Prospect Park CDP	327	-	-	440	100.0	0.0	0.0	0.0	0.0	24.8	18.2	47.5	35.9	15.5	191	81.7
Prospect Park borough & MCD (Delaware)	6,454	6,492	0.6	6,483	89.9	6.0	0.7	2.7	0.7	24.2	13.2	35.7	49.5	24.5	2,659	87.2
Providence township (Lancaster)	6,870	7,058	2.7	7,029	89.5	0.0	0.8	1.1	8.6	20.0	21.8	42.8	68.2	10.7	2,639	84.8
Pulaski township (Beaver)	1,507	1,405	-6.8	1,228	87.2	7.7	0.0	2.5	2.5	13.8	26.4	51.6	56.8	17.3	618	81.9
Pulaski township (Lawrence)	3,450	3,230	-6.4	3,285	96.5	2.1	0.5	0.7	0.2	20.0	22.0	45.6	57.2	16.3	1,316	83.9

1 May be of any race.

Table A. All Places — **Population and Housing**

STATE City, town, township, borough, or CDP (county if applicable)	2010 census total population	2019 estimated population	Percent change 2010–2019	ACS total population estimate 2015–2019	White alone, not Hispanic or Latino	Black alone, not Hispanic or Latino	Asian alone, not Hispanic or Latino	All other races or 2 or more races, not Hispanic or Latino	Hispanic or Latino[1]	Under 18 years old	Age 65 years and older	Median age	Percent High school diploma or less	Percent Bachelor's degree or more	Total	Percent with a computer
	1	2	3	4	5	6	7	8	9	10	11	12	13	14	15	16
PENNSYLVANIA—Con.																
Punxsutawney borough & MCD (Jefferson).............	5,948	5,704	-4.1	5,770	96.8	0.6	1.1	0.5	1.0	18.2	22.2	46.0	61.2	17.8	2,713	81.0
Putnam township (Tioga)..	423	419	-0.9	312	98.7	0.0	0.0	1.3	0.0	20.2	23.4	48.0	55.4	15.5	136	75.0
Pymatuning township (Mercer)	3,281	3,030	-7.7	3,101	95.5	1.5	1.5	1.5	0.0	20.9	17.4	42.1	55.2	22.2	1,313	80.9
Pymatuning Central CDP .	2,269	-	-	2,163	99.1	0.0	0.0	0.3	0.6	9.7	36.7	59.3	54.8	21.2	1,075	81.8
Pymatuning North CDP	311	-	-	224	98.2	0.0	0.0	0.0	1.8	6.3	35.3	61.0	65.8	5.8	141	83.7
Pymatuning South CDP....	479	-	-	297	88.2	0.0	1.3	9.1	1.3	9.4	36.7	57.1	42.7	26.8	148	87.2
Quakertown borough & MCD (Bucks).............	8,985	8,784	-2.2	8,827	85.0	4.9	1.9	2.8	5.4	22.3	16.7	37.6	48.9	23.8	3,435	87.2
Quarryville borough & MCD (Lancaster)..........	2,605	2,757	5.8	2,749	79.5	4.0	0.4	4.4	11.6	27.7	14.7	30.4	57.6	14.4	991	88.5
Queens Gate CDP............	1,464	-	-	1,437	50.0	21.0	16.4	0.0	12.7	14.8	19.8	25.7	45.2	36.5	745	93.2
Quemahoning township (Somerset)	2,032	1,904	-6.3	1,811	99.5	0.0	0.0	0.5	0.0	18.3	19.3	48.4	67.9	9.7	713	81.8
Quentin CDP	594	-	-	599	88.3	0.0	0.0	1.2	10.5	27.5	13.4	37.5	62.0	17.2	228	89.5
Quincy township (Franklin)	5,532	5,451	-1.5	5,470	93.3	2.4	0.1	1.0	3.1	20.2	25.4	47.0	65.0	12.0	1,996	78.4
Raccoon township (Beaver)	3,073	2,902	-5.6	2,950	97.9	0.5	0.0	0.7	0.9	17.4	22.4	50.9	46.4	22.5	1,163	84.8
Radnor township (Delaware)	31,550	31,875	1.0	31,820	76.8	4.7	8.3	3.8	6.4	20.8	13.4	28.9	10.8	76.2	9,419	95.7
Railroad borough & MCD (York)........................	284	280	-1.4	259	94.2	4.2	0.0	0.0	1.5	18.9	18.1	52.3	53.3	21.5	125	100.0
Rainsburg borough & MCD (Bedford).............	132	128	-3.0	70	91.4	0.0	0.0	8.6	0.0	28.6	15.7	39.7	40.0	15.6	30	76.7
Ralpho township (Northumberland)..........	4,315	4,196	-2.8	4,226	95.9	0.9	1.2	1.4	0.7	21.4	21.7	49.0	41.3	34.7	1,856	83.8
Ramblewood CDP	849	-	-	950	95.4	0.0	0.0	4.6	0.0	8.1	25.2	45.1	22.1	56.1	361	92.2
Ramey borough & MCD (Clearfield)	447	429	-4.0	413	97.3	0.0	0.0	1.5	1.2	21.1	18.6	46.0	56.5	16.7	161	84.5
Randolph township (Crawford)	1,782	1,699	-4.7	1,725	95.8	1.9	0.0	1.2	1.1	22.6	19.5	40.9	60.0	18.1	654	84.4
Rankin borough & MCD (Allegheny)................	2,108	2,027	-3.8	2,068	15.6	82.5	0.0	1.9	0.0	23.1	6.2	36.0	39.9	22.1	912	92.0
Ranshaw CDP	510	-	-	319	100.0	0.0	0.0	0.0	0.0	9.4	22.6	56.9	72.7	10.0	184	72.8
Ransom township (Lackawanna)...............	1,428	1,365	-4.4	1,646	97.4	0.0	0.5	1.1	1.0	19.7	19.1	46.3	52.1	21.8	622	89.4
Rapho township (Lancaster)..................	10,439	12,304	17.9	12,011	96.3	0.2	0.1	0.6	2.8	19.4	22.7	47.3	52.6	23.6	4,796	90.5
Raubsville CDP	1,088	-	-	1,442	68.8	23.6	6.4	1.1	0.0	28.6	14.7	45.2	36.9	35.3	467	88.9
Rauchtown CDP	726	-	-	587	99.7	0.3	0.0	0.0	0.0	20.4	17.4	43.1	66.8	12.2	256	77.3
Ravine CDP	662	-	-	754	99.5	0.0	0.0	0.0	0.5	17.1	17.9	46.1	51.0	17.0	296	82.8
Rayburn township (Armstrong)................	1,895	1,773	-6.4	1,562	97.3	1.2	0.0	1.5	0.0	14.1	17.9	46.1	71.3	9.1	624	83.7
Rayne township (Indiana).	2,992	2,793	-6.7	2,832	98.9	0.5	0.0	0.5	0.1	15.4	20.8	49.1	49.9	20.4	1,258	83.0
Reade township (Cambria)	1,618	1,496	-7.5	1,508	99.1	0.0	0.3	0.4	0.2	20.4	20.1	47.1	73.4	11.4	619	86.3
Reading township (Adams)	5,777	5,890	2.0	5,851	90.4	0.0	0.0	1.2	8.4	21.5	14.4	43.8	54.0	21.6	2,172	92.5
Reading city & MCD (Berks)	87,994	88,375	0.4	88,232	21.3	8.8	0.9	2.0	67.0	29.3	10.3	30.0	66.7	10.8	29,070	83.3
Reamstown CDP..............	3,361	-	-	3,142	99.4	0.0	0.0	0.0	0.6	23.2	16.1	42.3	53.9	23.2	1,309	84.3
Rebersburg CDP	494	-	-	569	99.6	0.0	0.4	0.0	0.0	29.9	16.3	34.1	70.0	8.0	173	80.9
Redbank township (Armstrong)................	1,064	992	-6.8	985	97.5	0.0	0.0	0.0	2.5	19.8	18.9	41.6	67.5	14.9	405	85.7
Redbank township (Clarion)	1,371	1,285	-6.3	1,337	96.5	1.2	0.0	1.3	1.0	18.9	15.9	43.1	74.3	11.7	515	80.4
Red Hill borough & MCD (Montgomery)	2,373	2,361	-0.5	2,484	88.1	6.7	0.0	1.9	3.3	19.7	26.3	46.3	50.8	21.8	1,070	82.5
Red Lion borough & MCD (York)........................	6,362	6,330	-0.5	6,322	91.0	0.6	0.6	1.8	6.0	28.6	13.0	33.0	57.7	15.3	2,401	85.2
Redstone township (Fayette)	5,566	5,264	-5.4	5,352	86.3	7.6	0.0	5.9	0.1	21.2	20.3	42.4	64.4	14.2	2,251	78.9
Reed township (Dauphin).	239	238	-0.4	216	86.1	0.0	0.0	13.9	0.0	17.6	25.9	49.0	59.3	21.0	87	87.4
Reedsville CDP	641	-	-	492	96.7	0.0	0.0	3.3	0.0	18.3	24.0	47.2	61.2	14.9	244	79.9
Refton CDP	298	-	-	490	100.0	0.0	0.0	0.0	0.0	31.0	3.5	42.7	70.0	18.4	152	100.0
Rehrersburg CDP	319	-	-	163	100.0	0.0	0.0	0.0	0.0	11.0	23.3	44.2	42.7	16.8	76	93.4
Reiffton CDP	4,178	-	-	4,651	81.9	0.0	5.2	0.8	12.1	22.2	20.1	44.5	37.7	40.2	1,616	90.3
Reilly township (Schuylkill)	729	688	-5.6	620	100.0	0.0	0.0	0.0	0.0	11.6	21.8	48.8	72.2	7.9	285	74.4
Reinerton CDP	424	-	-	517	100.0	0.0	0.0	0.0	0.0	14.9	32.9	42.9	66.8	11.5	226	91.6
Reinholds CDP	1,803	-	-	2,129	89.9	0.0	0.0	5.4	4.7	26.3	10.1	33.3	46.9	20.5	670	88.1
Rennerdale CDP	1,150	-	-	1,076	96.0	2.0	2.0	0.0	0.0	9.6	33.1	56.5	38.2	30.9	598	86.0
Renningers CDP..............	574	-	-	750	100.0	0.0	0.0	0.0	0.0	14.8	16.5	36.7	40.0	25.3	270	94.4
Renovo borough & MCD (Clinton)	1,228	1,205	-1.9	1,153	95.3	1.1	0.0	1.3	2.3	23.8	15.9	41.6	65.9	6.2	485	77.3
Republic CDP	1,096	-	-	1,152	83.4	3.8	0.0	12.8	0.0	15.1	26.1	43.8	68.4	13.1	490	82.4
Reserve township (Allegheny)................	3,346	3,225	-3.6	3,266	94.6	1.5	0.8	1.3	1.7	15.4	18.7	47.0	44.4	27.1	1,431	89.9
Revloc CDP.....................	570	-	-	586	100.0	0.0	0.0	0.0	0.0	22.9	30.5	54.1	88.7	3.4	238	72.3
Rew CDP	199	-	-	158	100.0	0.0	0.0	0.0	0.0	17.1	43.0	58.0	40.5	30.5	84	65.5
Reynolds Heights CDP.....	2,061	-	-	1,720	94.5	2.7	0.0	2.7	0.0	19.9	15.6	42.5	53.1	21.9	724	84.3
Reynoldsville borough & MCD (Jefferson)...........	2,757	2,647	-4.0	2,672	94.3	1.5	0.6	2.6	1.0	21.4	19.0	40.5	69.0	10.6	1,209	75.8
Rheems CDP	1,598	-	-	1,537	96.3	0.0	0.0	0.0	3.7	17.7	16.3	49.5	49.0	18.9	587	86.9
Rice township (Luzerne)...	3,334	3,546	6.4	3,530	87.2	0.0	9.7	1.9	1.2	24.8	11.6	40.3	33.3	41.2	1,272	95.5
Rices Landing borough & MCD (Greene)	457	424	-7.2	633	95.6	0.0	0.0	3.5	0.9	27.5	19.0	41.2	48.9	19.0	227	90.7
Riceville CDP	68	-	-	47	100.0	0.0	0.0	0.0	0.0	10.6	31.9	53.3	56.4	20.5	22	100.0
Richboro CDP.................	6,563	-	-	6,378	92.0	0.1	4.0	1.0	2.8	21.7	19.6	47.2	24.6	50.4	2,235	96.2
Richfield CDP	549	-	-	499	87.4	0.0	12.6	0.0	0.0	19.2	33.7	43.8	72.3	12.6	211	56.4
Richhill township (Greene)	896	816	-8.9	919	88.8	2.5	0.0	8.4	0.3	25.7	11.1	42.9	75.8	7.4	346	91.3

1 May be of any race.

Table A. All Places — **Population and Housing**

STATE City, town, township, borough, or CDP (county if applicable)	Population				Race and Hispanic or Latino origin (percent)					Age (percent)			Educational attainment of persons age 25 and older		Occupied housing units	
	2010 census total population	2019 estimated population	Percent change 2010–2019	ACS total population estimate 2015–2019	White alone, not Hispanic or Latino	Black alone, not Hispanic or Latino	Asian alone, not Hispanic or Latino	All other races or 2 or more races, not Hispanic or Latino	Hispanic or Latino[1]	Under 18 years old	Age 65 years and older	Median age	Percent High school diploma or less	Percent Bachelor's degree or more	Total	Percent with a computer
	1	2	3	4	5	6	7	8	9	10	11	12	13	14	15	16
PENNSYLVANIA—Con.																
Richland township (Allegheny)	11,120	11,373	2.3	11,448	95.4	0.4	1.3	0.6	2.4	24.6	19.6	44.5	24.5	55.5	4,221	92.4
Richland township (Bucks)	13,036	13,325	2.2	13,264	88.6	0.3	2.3	5.0	3.8	25.8	15.5	42.0	46.6	31.2	5,057	91.3
Richland township (Cambria)	12,796	11,818	-7.6	12,038	92.7	1.7	1.1	2.0	2.5	16.8	24.3	43.5	41.7	33.1	4,715	84.4
Richland township (Clarion)	494	456	-7.7	409	95.4	0.0	0.0	3.9	0.7	12.0	26.4	52.9	65.0	15.1	176	72.2
Richland borough & MCD (Lebanon)	1,511	1,612	6.7	1,623	95.8	0.0	0.2	1.5	2.5	21.6	18.7	39.1	57.2	16.3	604	88.1
Richland township (Venango)	774	720	-7.0	747	99.1	0.0	0.7	0.0	0.3	22.4	18.5	46.3	53.0	27.9	310	82.6
Richlandtown borough & MCD (Bucks)	1,327	1,297	-2.3	1,260	92.5	4.8	0.0	1.6	1.0	19.1	20.3	39.1	55.4	25.6	467	92.5
Richmond township (Berks)	3,431	3,613	5.3	3,561	92.4	1.0	0.0	3.8	2.9	20.0	18.3	42.9	63.0	16.3	1,450	83.6
Richmond township (Crawford)	1,475	1,414	-4.1	1,352	98.3	0.1	1.1	0.1	0.3	24.0	16.9	45.4	52.3	23.8	543	92.6
Richmond township (Tioga)	2,289	2,285	-0.2	2,110	98.0	0.0	0.4	0.7	0.9	22.0	19.2	42.6	45.2	26.8	855	86.8
Ridgebury township (Bradford)	1,972	1,912	-3.0	1,852	97.8	0.0	2.1	0.0	0.1	23.1	21.0	44.8	57.7	15.0	698	89.0
Ridgway borough & MCD (Elk)	4,079	3,751	-8.0	3,814	94.4	2.8	0.0	0.6	2.2	22.5	15.5	38.5	46.7	24.1	1,790	89.2
Ridgway township (Elk)	2,520	2,402	-4.7	2,483	97.7	1.3	0.0	0.9	0.0	19.3	19.3	47.6	53.7	16.3	1,111	88.7
Ridley township (Delaware)	30,868	31,204	1.1	31,120	87.7	6.0	2.0	0.8	3.5	21.3	15.0	40.0	47.0	26.1	12,056	92.0
Ridley Park borough & MCD (Delaware)	7,019	7,065	0.7	7,048	91.3	2.7	1.7	0.7	3.5	19.1	16.4	41.6	40.0	33.1	2,877	91.2
Riegelsville borough & MCD (Bucks)	868	852	-1.8	811	97.8	0.0	0.2	0.4	1.6	14.3	17.3	47.3	41.1	33.5	376	93.6
Rimersburg borough & MCD (Clarion)	946	881	-6.9	899	99.4	0.0	0.0	0.4	0.1	21.0	21.7	42.6	66.1	14.9	378	84.4
Ringgold township (Jefferson)	743	713	-4.0	941	97.8	0.0	0.0	0.9	1.4	25.7	24.7	47.4	65.9	9.1	346	71.4
Ringtown borough & MCD (Schuylkill)	795	756	-4.9	793	98.5	1.0	0.0	0.5	0.0	15.8	19.8	45.1	57.5	16.2	342	81.3
Riverside CDP	381	-	-	284	98.2	1.4	0.0	0.0	0.4	7.7	18.0	59.3	74.1	10.7	156	73.7
Riverside borough & MCD (Northumberland)	1,933	1,853	-4.1	2,221	91.4	1.1	3.7	3.2	0.5	19.7	25.8	49.1	45.2	40.0	957	90.2
Riverview Park CDP	3,380	-	-	2,620	85.6	2.5	3.9	0.0	8.0	22.6	22.1	45.9	49.1	30.9	989	87.3
Roaring Brook township (Lackawanna)	1,908	1,981	3.8	2,121	98.3	0.3	0.6	0.4	0.3	23.1	21.5	45.8	32.9	38.3	742	92.6
Roaring Creek township (Columbia)	545	528	-3.1	443	100.0	0.0	0.0	0.0	0.0	11.5	35.0	57.1	59.8	19.3	200	76.0
Roaring Spring borough & MCD (Blair)	2,583	2,436	-5.7	2,531	95.6	0.0	0.9	1.1	2.4	26.4	12.9	35.9	49.8	15.3	1,019	93.6
Robeson township (Berks)	7,200	7,432	3.2	7,379	94.3	1.2	0.4	1.5	2.6	22.0	17.0	43.2	45.4	27.1	2,656	92.4
Robesonia borough & MCD (Berks)	2,055	2,067	0.6	1,924	89.2	2.4	0.0	1.8	6.5	18.1	15.1	42.4	54.7	17.6	837	89.7
Robinson township (Allegheny)	13,355	13,850	3.7	13,703	92.0	4.0	2.5	0.7	0.8	17.4	18.2	43.2	30.5	49.9	6,012	96.1
Robinson CDP	614	-	-	444	100.0	0.0	0.0	0.0	0.0	15.8	26.6	52.7	69.9	6.5	211	83.4
Robinson township (Washington)	1,933	1,880	-2.7	1,819	90.9	1.3	1.9	3.8	2.1	16.3	22.5	44.5	55.6	14.5	843	79.0
Rochester borough & MCD (Beaver)	3,657	3,440	-5.9	3,502	74.1	16.8	0.6	5.2	3.3	22.0	11.4	40.4	53.4	10.8	1,565	88.6
Rochester township (Beaver)	2,802	2,635	-6.0	2,684	88.2	4.6	0.1	2.6	4.5	16.4	20.9	44.8	47.3	19.0	1,168	89.0
Rockdale township (Crawford)	1,506	1,437	-4.6	1,393	97.6	0.1	0.9	0.4	1.1	26.6	15.9	39.5	63.9	20.9	504	83.5
Rockefeller township (Northumberland)	2,273	2,196	-3.4	2,345	97.2	0.0	0.2	0.6	1.9	17.6	23.5	51.1	59.2	13.1	958	83.8
Rockhill borough & MCD (Huntingdon)	371	362	-2.4	401	100.0	0.0	0.0	0.0	0.0	24.7	16.2	45.3	66.5	6.0	157	84.1
Rockland township (Berks)	3,756	3,822	1.8	3,799	98.6	0.0	0.0	0.9	0.4	21.5	17.2	45.0	44.4	28.0	1,504	84.2
Rockland township (Venango)	1,452	1,328	-8.5	1,194	95.0	0.2	0.0	4.4	0.4	15.7	26.7	55.2	61.8	15.6	551	90.9
Rockledge borough & MCD (Montgomery)	2,539	2,530	-0.4	2,539	92.6	0.0	2.4	1.3	3.7	20.4	15.3	40.7	37.3	30.8	1,077	89.6
Rockwood borough & MCD (Somerset)	889	820	-7.8	707	97.7	0.0	0.0	1.0	1.3	21.6	23.8	41.5	61.3	18.5	345	80.9
Rogersville CDP	249	-	-	232	99.1	0.0	0.0	0.0	0.9	15.9	16.8	35.3	53.5	18.9	102	100.0
Rohrsburg CDP	145	-	-	133	100.0	0.0	0.0	0.0	0.0	15.0	21.1	40.9	55.7	22.7	57	84.2
Rome borough & MCD (Bradford)	441	405	-8.2	484	95.9	1.0	0.0	0.8	2.3	35.5	13.6	33.2	72.1	10.0	173	74.6
Rome township (Bradford)	1,187	1,197	0.8	993	97.2	0.0	1.2	1.6	0.0	19.1	19.7	52.7	53.6	19.6	401	90.8
Rome township (Crawford)	1,840	1,756	-4.6	1,850	97.9	0.9	0.2	0.4	0.6	39.3	9.4	28.0	76.9	7.6	537	60.3
Ronco CDP	256	-	-	155	80.0	8.4	0.0	11.6	0.0	16.8	29.7	50.6	53.5	11.6	87	64.4
Ronks CDP	362	-	-	133	75.9	0.0	0.0	24.1	0.0	24.1	12.0	27.0	50.6	0.0	67	76.1
Roscoe borough & MCD (Washington)	833	793	-4.8	722	97.0	0.1	0.0	2.5	0.4	15.8	24.0	49.6	51.0	26.6	347	86.7
Rose township (Jefferson)	1,237	1,189	-3.9	1,229	100.0	0.0	0.0	0.0	0.0	22.7	17.5	39.6	57.7	15.7	470	91.5
Roseto borough & MCD (Northampton)	1,548	1,540	-0.5	1,968	94.0	0.5	0.1	0.4	5.1	29.4	11.5	32.5	48.6	20.3	695	91.5
Rose Valley borough & MCD (Delaware)	913	948	3.8	934	90.9	0.5	4.8	1.7	2.0	21.4	24.2	51.8	10.0	80.1	349	97.4
Roseville borough & MCD (Tioga)	189	184	-2.6	117	92.3	0.0	0.0	5.1	2.6	11.1	17.1	55.0	60.0	11.6	54	79.6
Ross township (Allegheny)	31,104	30,473	-2.0	30,603	90.6	3.0	3.5	1.3	1.7	17.5	22.0	44.5	26.4	49.3	13,896	90.8
Ross township (Luzerne)	2,937	2,907	-	2,907	96.2	0.3	0.6	0.4	2.5	18.1	22.8	47.9	54.5	17.1	1,232	83.0
Ross township (Monroe)	5,962	5,925	-0.6	5,848	85.1	0.3	3.9	1.7	8.9	13.9	15.6	53.0	52.0	20.7	1,946	91.1

1 May be of any race.

Table A. All Places — **Population and Housing**

STATE City, town, township, borough, or CDP (county if applicable)	Population 2010 census total population	2019 estimated population	Percent change 2010–2019	ACS total population estimate 2015–2019	Race and Hispanic or Latino origin (percent) White alone, not Hispanic or Latino	Black alone, not Hispanic or Latino	Asian alone, not Hispanic or Latino	All other races or 2 or more races, not Hispanic or Latino	Hispanic or Latino[1]	Age (percent) Under 18 years old	Age 65 years and older	Median age	Educational attainment of persons age 25 and older Percent High school diploma or less	Percent Bachelor's degree or more	Occupied housing units Total	Percent with a computer
	1	2	3	4	5	6	7	8	9	10	11	12	13	14	15	16
PENNSYLVANIA—Con.																
Rossiter CDP.............	646	-	-	642	86.9	0.0	0.0	13.1	0.0	21.7	17.6	41.4	73.4	10.3	222	79.7
Rosslyn Farms borough & MCD (Allegheny)...........	437	420	-3.9	440	97.5	0.5	0.9	0.0	1.1	20.5	24.8	51.1	6.3	78.7	193	97.4
Rostraver township (Westmoreland)	11,346	11,007	-3.0	11,062	94.3	1.2	1.2	2.1	1.2	18.4	19.8	46.4	38.8	32.7	4,593	87.2
Rote CDP......................	507	-	-	546	99.3	0.0	0.0	0.0	0.7	22.0	26.0	53.1	71.6	14.3	222	87.4
Rothsville CDP.............	3,044	-	-	2,586	92.9	2.6	0.0	0.8	3.8	22.2	12.3	43.4	46.7	33.1	947	91.0
Roulette CDP................	779	-	-	882	93.0	0.0	0.0	2.8	4.2	26.5	12.4	33.3	59.6	10.8	301	95.7
Roulette township (Potter)	1,191	1,129	-5.2	1,198	93.7	0.0	0.0	3.2	3.1	22.9	16.6	42.2	59.1	12.0	438	95.0
Rouseville borough & MCD (Venango)	523	473	-9.6	458	97.4	0.0	0.0	1.7	0.9	27.9	16.2	35.4	67.6	3.6	178	81.5
Rouzerville CDP............	917	-	-	889	97.6	2.4	0.0	0.0	0.0	19.1	23.4	48.5	67.6	2.4	390	90.3
Rowes Run CDP	564	-	-	672	93.6	0.0	0.0	6.4	0.0	22.2	14.9	37.4	66.0	9.7	269	73.2
Royalton borough & MCD (Dauphin)	907	1,022	12.7	1,221	89.6	9.5	0.0	0.6	0.3	22.1	12.7	40.3	59.6	16.4	496	92.1
Royersford borough & MCD (Montgomery)	4,751	4,755	0.1	4,775	82.8	9.9	0.9	3.5	3.0	23.2	13.2	34.6	37.3	33.3	2,193	92.2
Rupert CDP...................	183	-	-	222	91.4	1.4	4.5	0.0	2.7	19.8	9.5	39.8	70.0	10.6	73	91.8
Rural Valley borough & MCD (Armstrong)..........	880	814	-7.5	923	96.7	0.0	0.0	0.0	3.3	15.8	28.5	50.5	54.9	16.6	429	89.0
Ruscombmanor township (Berks)	4,104	4,195	2.2	4,175	100.0	0.0	0.0	0.0	0.0	18.6	18.8	49.9	49.6	28.5	1,504	88.1
Rush township (Centre)....	4,024	4,042	0.4	4,018	98.7	0.4	0.2	0.7	0.0	14.9	21.1	47.9	62.3	13.8	1,504	87.5
Rush township (Dauphin) .	231	228	-1.3	307	98.4	0.7	0.0	0.0	1.0	28.7	13.4	44.5	59.2	8.7	112	82.1
Rush township (Northumberland)	1,121	1,096	-2.2	1,190	96.5	0.8	0.0	0.3	2.5	26.2	18.1	39.6	57.2	23.5	451	86.9
Rush township (Schuylkill)	3,416	3,258	-4.6	3,288	98.2	0.0	0.0	1.3	0.5	15.7	35.6	56.1	47.7	23.1	1,491	85.6
Rush township (Susquehanna)	1,267	1,182	-6.7	1,376	89.4	0.0	0.0	3.3	7.3	19.0	18.5	43.0	58.7	12.4	593	91.6
Russell CDP	1,408	-	-	1,510	93.6	0.0	1.1	2.7	2.6	16.8	29.7	50.3	42.1	31.7	661	92.9
Russellton CDP.............	1,440	-	-	1,391	99.3	0.7	0.0	0.0	0.0	13.3	19.7	48.8	33.6	24.9	710	91.3
Rutherford CDP	4,303	-	-	4,919	60.6	19.7	6.3	4.0	9.4	24.6	15.0	37.4	41.4	34.3	1,919	91.9
Rutland township (Tioga)..	821	809	-1.5	769	91.8	0.0	4.2	3.0	1.0	15.9	19.5	47.8	55.6	16.8	309	79.0
Rutledge borough & MCD (Delaware)...................	784	799	1.9	870	83.7	1.7	7.8	3.1	3.7	21.0	14.0	45.3	28.6	46.7	319	92.8
Ryan township (Schuylkill)	2,459	2,544	3.5	2,532	60.7	26.5	0.6	3.2	9.0	9.0	11.9	38.0	63.3	14.8	503	90.3
Rye township (Perry)	2,364	2,381	0.7	2,283	96.5	2.2	0.0	0.3	1.0	15.0	19.5	51.4	56.4	20.0	959	88.5
Sadsbury township (Chester)	3,571	4,110	15.1	3,983	78.4	12.7	0.9	3.2	4.8	24.3	13.7	37.8	43.1	33.2	1,503	88.8
Sadsbury township (Crawford)	2,928	2,810	-4.0	2,846	99.3	0.0	0.0	0.0	0.7	14.3	27.1	50.9	34.8	35.9	1,319	91.4
Sadsbury township (Lancaster)	3,376	3,476	3.0	3,473	96.8	0.2	0.0	1.8	1.2	37.2	13.7	30.5	67.6	14.3	910	66.6
Saegertown borough & MCD (Crawford)	996	946	-5.0	1,112	94.2	0.9	0.3	1.6	3.1	17.5	12.9	33.4	57.5	20.8	383	90.9
St. Clair borough & MCD (Schuylkill)	3,006	2,830	-5.9	2,865	97.7	0.7	0.4	0.0	1.3	17.8	21.3	46.3	64.2	10.2	1,291	80.9
St. Clair township (Westmoreland)	1,519	1,430	-5.9	1,351	99.6	0.0	0.0	0.3	0.1	17.7	24.0	49.4	55.7	11.3	588	85.2
St. Clairsville borough & MCD (Bedford)	80	75	-6.3	59	100.0	0.0	0.0	0.0	0.0	8.5	22.0	48.8	67.4	21.7	32	75.0
St. Lawrence borough & MCD (Berks)	1,831	1,840	0.5	2,022	85.7	3.1	1.5	1.9	7.8	25.9	15.1	39.2	48.2	25.1	807	86.6
St. Marys city & MCD (Elk)	13,071	12,260	-6.2	12,429	98.0	0.2	0.8	0.1	0.9	19.1	23.0	47.6	56.7	21.6	5,768	84.9
St. Michael CDP	408	-	-	345	98.3	0.0	0.0	0.0	1.7	12.8	29.6	57.1	56.3	22.9	176	67.0
St. Petersburg borough & MCD (Clarion)	400	368	-8.0	295	100.0	0.0	0.0	0.0	0.0	14.9	25.4	48.5	70.8	9.5	142	82.4
St. Thomas township (Franklin)	5,935	6,005	1.2	6,002	97.3	0.6	0.0	2.0	0.1	20.7	18.3	44.5	75.7	11.2	2,501	88.2
St. Vincent College CDP...	1,357	-	-	1,305	88.4	7.5	1.8	1.5	0.8	1.8	2.6	19.9	10.0	80.0	0	0.0
Salem township (Clarion) .	881	832	-5.6	849	98.0	0.0	0.0	0.8	1.2	24.0	15.4	35.4	55.6	19.8	319	75.5
Salem township (Luzerne)	4,255	4,196	-1.4	4,208	93.7	1.4	0.0	0.1	4.7	16.5	25.3	50.8	55.5	19.0	1,798	87.8
Salem township (Mercer)..	754	713	-5.4	653	97.9	0.0	0.3	0.0	1.8	19.6	28.0	50.8	57.0	16.6	277	75.8
Salem township (Wayne)..	4,279	4,095	-4.3	4,124	91.8	0.3	0.1	0.7	7.1	15.5	28.7	49.8	58.3	22.7	1,731	82.4
Salem township (Westmoreland)	6,622	6,417	-3.1	6,508	98.0	0.0	0.0	1.6	0.3	15.1	23.7	49.9	54.5	20.5	2,888	89.9
Salford township (Montgomery)	2,474	2,949	19.2	2,935	92.6	2.6	1.3	0.6	2.9	20.1	15.7	41.0	37.4	39.5	1,096	95.5
Salisbury township (Lancaster)	11,060	11,434	3.4	11,416	93.9	1.4	0.3	1.5	3.0	31.8	12.1	31.6	70.2	13.1	3,221	71.2
Salisbury township (Lehigh).....................	13,617	13,948	2.4	13,887	85.1	1.6	1.4	2.7	9.2	17.8	23.2	47.1	39.1	32.1	5,461	90.7
Salisbury borough & MCD (Somerset)	729	675	-7.4	771	98.4	0.0	0.0	0.0	1.6	21.4	19.1	41.3	61.3	15.9	328	79.0
Salix CDP....................	1,149	-	-	1,272	100.0	0.0	0.0	0.0	0.0	23.0	21.5	37.9	63.5	14.4	467	85.2
Salladasburg borough & MCD (Lycoming)	234	225	-3.8	225	99.1	0.0	0.0	0.9	0.0	28.0	16.4	35.8	53.4	16.2	92	87.0
Saltillo borough & MCD (Huntingdon)	350	331	-5.4	315	96.2	0.0	0.0	3.8	0.0	22.9	14.3	46.3	75.1	8.5	124	84.7
Saltlick township (Fayette)	3,467	3,273	-5.6	3,334	99.9	0.1	0.0	0.0	0.0	18.6	22.7	47.4	51.5	17.8	1,435	77.6
Saltsburg borough & MCD (Indiana).....................	864	803	-7.1	694	96.5	0.0	0.0	2.3	1.2	15.7	22.0	51.0	54.6	20.1	334	76.0
Salunga CDP................	2,695	-	-	3,139	78.7	5.2	0.4	3.1	12.6	21.7	17.3	40.0	41.7	40.2	1,152	83.9
Sanatoga CDP..............	8,378	-	-	8,588	77.1	16.0	2.3	2.7	1.9	25.4	16.8	40.4	43.7	27.7	3,276	89.8
Sand Hill CDP	2,496	-	-	2,627	82.1	1.1	0.0	0.0	16.9	18.9	19.5	43.5	67.0	15.5	1,082	88.7
Sandy CDP...................	1,429	-	-	1,401	82.6	8.3	3.6	5.6	0.0	19.8	28.6	50.3	61.8	9.4	526	85.2
Sandy township (Clearfield)	10,622	10,442	-1.7	10,523	94.3	1.3	0.7	0.8	2.9	20.7	22.0	46.6	50.1	26.7	3,957	87.8
Sandy Creek township (Mercer)	790	735	-7.0	881	97.6	0.0	0.0	1.7	0.7	22.8	18.0	43.2	61.8	13.4	341	91.8
Sandycreek township (Venango)	2,248	2,095	-6.8	2,500	89.4	3.6	0.1	5.1	1.8	21.6	23.8	50.4	49.8	20.6	966	93.1

1 May be of any race.

Table A. All Places — **Population and Housing**

STATE City, town, township, borough, or CDP (county if applicable)	Population				Race and Hispanic or Latino origin (percent)					Age (percent)			Educational attainment of persons age 25 and older		Occupied housing units	
	2010 census total population	2019 estimated population	Percent change 2010–2019	ACS total population estimate 2015–2019	White alone, not Hispanic or Latino	Black alone, not Hispanic or Latino	Asian alone, not Hispanic or Latino	All other races or 2 or more races, not Hispanic or Latino	Hispanic or Latino[1]	Under 18 years old	Age 65 years and older	Median age	Percent High school diploma or less	Percent Bachelor's degree or more	Total	Percent with a computer
	1	2	3	4	5	6	7	8	9	10	11	12	13	14	15	16
PENNSYLVANIA—Con.																
Sandy Lake borough & MCD (Mercer)	657	624	-5.0	628	96.0	1.6	0.6	1.8	0.0	20.5	17.8	39.6	58.1	22.4	279	93.9
Sandy Lake township (Mercer)	1,228	1,163	-5.3	1,264	95.2	0.0	1.1	1.8	1.9	17.5	23.5	48.8	54.0	16.3	547	86.8
Sandy Ridge CDP	407	-	-	337	100.0	0.0	0.0	0.0	0.0	4.5	21.7	54.0	74.6	2.6	162	72.2
Sankertown borough & MCD (Cambria)	672	614	-8.6	602	98.2	0.0	0.0	1.3	0.5	21.9	17.9	43.0	60.4	15.7	241	83.0
Saville township (Perry)	2,504	2,525	0.8	2,514	96.4	0.0	0.0	2.5	1.2	30.4	10.5	32.7	65.8	12.9	803	85.1
Saw Creek CDP	4,016	-	-	3,582	38.1	31.5	2.8	1.3	26.3	20.4	17.6	48.2	34.9	26.3	1,566	96.4
Saxonburg borough & MCD (Butler)	1,522	1,438	-5.5	1,609	99.1	0.1	0.5	0.3	0.0	14.0	39.0	56.5	42.7	24.2	805	81.7
Saxton borough & MCD (Bedford)	730	681	-6.7	666	89.2	0.0	0.0	7.7	3.2	24.9	15.8	35.8	56.3	16.7	281	75.8
Saylorsburg CDP	1,126	-	-	1,042	63.9	0.0	16.5	0.0	19.6	13.1	12.7	53.3	41.2	32.8	397	100.0
Sayre borough & MCD (Bradford)	5,672	5,366	-5.4	5,450	90.6	2.3	1.2	4.9	1.1	22.7	17.2	36.1	49.8	21.8	2,469	85.3
Scalp Level borough & MCD (Cambria)	773	700	-9.4	615	99.7	0.0	0.0	0.2	0.2	13.3	36.1	56.4	70.9	9.1	321	74.1
Schaefferstown CDP	941	-	-	1,118	100.0	0.0	0.0	0.0	0.0	20.8	20.4	38.0	62.4	21.2	398	95.5
Schellsburg borough & MCD (Bedford)	333	318	-4.5	341	96.5	0.0	0.0	0.0	3.5	13.8	17.0	45.5	79.3	5.2	136	77.9
Schlusser CDP	5,265	-	-	4,794	89.7	3.7	1.6	3.2	1.8	17.3	21.7	43.5	43.2	32.0	1,993	88.2
Schnecksville CDP	2,935	-	-	3,336	81.6	0.3	0.7	0.3	17.0	23.0	14.4	37.9	34.5	37.9	1,347	83.9
Schoeneck CDP	1,056	-	-	905	96.5	0.0	0.0	0.0	3.5	20.1	10.2	39.9	64.6	11.4	360	96.7
Schubert CDP	249	-	-	239	94.1	0.0	0.0	0.0	5.9	23.4	5.9	43.2	62.3	22.4	81	100.0
Schuylkill township (Chester)	8,525	8,616	1.1	8,611	88.1	1.1	3.2	0.7	6.9	25.5	13.6	39.9	19.4	65.6	2,919	94.6
Schuylkill township (Schuylkill)	1,123	1,057	-5.9	1,097	98.0	0.4	1.4	0.0	0.3	17.0	28.7	50.3	58.6	11.7	491	78.8
Schuylkill Haven borough & MCD (Schuylkill)	5,452	5,106	-6.3	5,178	96.2	0.4	0.7	1.0	1.7	23.3	20.7	37.5	59.1	22.0	2,194	85.5
Schwenksville borough & MCD (Montgomery)	1,377	1,379	0.1	1,422	90.6	2.7	0.8	2.0	3.9	22.7	17.4	38.8	37.0	30.3	628	89.8
Scotland CDP	1,395	-	-	970	74.9	11.4	0.0	5.9	7.7	24.3	34.8	51.1	38.7	18.1	444	84.5
Scott township (Allegheny)	17,033	16,428	-3.6	16,625	81.4	2.0	9.9	4.9	1.8	16.3	24.7	44.2	30.4	46.4	7,733	91.0
Scott township (Columbia)	5,113	5,055	-1.1	5,058	89.2	2.7	5.0	1.0	2.1	18.2	19.3	40.8	34.5	39.2	2,122	92.5
Scott township (Lackawanna)	4,908	4,747	-3.3	4,783	97.8	0.8	0.4	0.0	1.0	19.8	28.7	48.9	42.3	30.9	1,867	89.3
Scott township (Lawrence)	2,344	2,201	-6.1	2,151	96.7	0.0	1.2	1.9	0.2	20.5	20.6	46.9	51.9	24.2	852	89.4
Scott township (Wayne)	590	573	-2.9	454	98.7	0.0	0.4	0.0	0.9	10.8	33.3	51.8	66.6	15.2	209	85.2
Scottdale borough & MCD (Westmoreland)	4,358	4,094	-6.1	4,165	97.6	0.9	0.0	1.4	0.1	19.3	25.1	45.3	44.3	25.6	1,911	83.0
Scranton city & MCD (Lackawanna)	76,083	76,653	0.7	77,054	71.9	5.3	4.7	3.3	14.8	20.5	16.9	37.2	53.9	22.2	31,039	85.2
Scrubgrass township (Venango)	752	693	-7.8	679	98.7	0.0	0.0	0.7	0.6	14.0	22.1	52.0	53.2	15.2	297	85.5
Selinsgrove borough & MCD (Snyder)	5,654	5,902	4.4	5,927	84.2	3.9	1.7	3.5	6.7	13.2	15.6	26.0	45.0	32.1	1,845	85.7
Sellersville borough & MCD (Bucks)	4,245	4,283	0.9	4,270	86.3	1.6	0.7	3.8	7.6	23.0	11.2	37.4	43.5	32.5	1,664	90.9
Seltzer CDP	350	-	-	281	100.0	0.0	0.0	0.0	0.0	17.8	21.4	36.5	63.9	13.7	116	87.1
Seneca CDP	1,065	-	-	984	97.0	0.0	1.6	0.7	0.7	20.4	36.0	57.6	53.4	27.9	465	88.8
Sergeant township (McKean)	141	132	-6.4	90	98.9	0.0	0.0	1.1	0.0	15.6	36.7	59.6	63.5	17.6	45	86.7
Seven Fields borough & MCD (Butler)	2,887	2,736	-5.2	2,766	90.6	0.4	3.3	3.2	2.5	24.3	10.1	37.6	11.1	71.6	1,187	98.1
Seven Springs borough	26	24	-7.7	32	100.0	0.0	0.0	0.0	0.0	0.0	87.5	71.4	78.1	12.5	31	22.6
Seven Springs borough (Fayette)	15	14	-6.7	24	100.0	0.0	0.0	0.0	0.0	0.0	100.0	0.0	100.0	0.0	24	0.0
Seven Springs borough (Somerset)	11	10	-9.1	8	100.0	0.0	0.0	0.0	0.0	0.0	50.0	66.5	12.5	50.0	7	100.0
Seven Valleys borough & MCD (York)	517	511	-1.2	467	98.9	0.2	0.0	0.9	0.0	22.9	22.1	40.6	58.1	16.6	200	79.5
Seward borough & MCD (Westmoreland)	493	462	-6.3	356	99.2	0.8	0.0	0.0	0.0	17.7	17.1	47.4	62.4	10.9	149	85.2
Sewickley borough & MCD (Allegheny)	3,818	3,791	-0.7	3,829	84.4	8.7	2.4	2.8	1.7	21.4	20.7	44.1	14.2	65.4	1,825	89.4
Sewickley township (Westmoreland)	5,994	5,717	-4.6	5,777	98.3	0.5	0.0	1.0	0.2	18.3	23.0	47.0	51.1	18.8	2,362	83.6
Sewickley Heights borough & MCD (Allegheny)	817	807	-1.2	741	93.9	0.3	4.0	1.8	0.0	25.5	20.5	50.5	12.7	74.6	287	96.9
Sewickley Hills borough & MCD (Allegheny)	595	690	16.0	691	84.5	5.4	8.4	0.6	1.2	23.9	17.7	48.4	17.2	67.5	257	94.9
Shade township (Somerset)	2,769	2,568	-7.3	2,599	95.2	0.3	0.4	3.9	0.3	21.7	23.7	45.9	67.0	10.1	1,073	83.8
Shade Gap borough & MCD (Huntingdon)	91	89	-2.2	82	95.1	0.0	0.0	0.0	4.9	31.7	24.4	37.8	75.0	5.4	35	68.6
Shaler township (Allegheny)	28,703	27,720	-3.4	28,030	95.7	1.0	0.4	1.9	1.0	17.3	22.2	47.0	34.5	38.1	12,395	92.8
Shamokin city & MCD (Northumberland)	7,385	6,952	-5.9	7,051	88.0	1.0	0.0	2.6	8.5	23.2	20.6	42.0	60.9	13.2	3,497	74.9
Shamokin township (Northumberland)	2,408	2,374	-1.4	2,737	97.9	0.2	0.5	0.0	1.4	21.3	21.3	44.6	54.0	23.9	1,162	79.3
Shamokin Dam borough & MCD (Snyder)	1,685	1,706	1.2	1,919	96.7	0.2	0.0	0.4	2.7	22.9	26.9	43.9	51.7	23.3	845	83.6
Shanksville borough & MCD (Somerset)	230	212	-7.8	224	100.0	0.0	0.0	0.0	0.0	22.8	17.4	36.8	57.3	14.0	91	86.8
Shanor-Northvue CDP	5,051	-	-	5,068	96.3	0.0	1.0	2.1	0.6	19.6	25.6	49.2	33.0	43.7	2,226	90.5
Sharon city & MCD (Mercer)	14,017	12,933	-7.7	13,227	77.6	14.9	1.1	5.0	1.4	21.7	18.2	39.7	57.0	17.4	5,993	83.9
Sharon township (Potter)	865	824	-4.7	678	99.3	0.0	0.0	0.7	0.0	15.5	20.6	50.0	65.7	13.3	227	84.6

1 May be of any race.

Table A. All Places — **Population and Housing**

STATE City, town, township, borough, or CDP (county if applicable)	Population 2010 census total population	Population 2019 estimated population	Population Percent change 2010–2019	Population ACS total population estimate 2015–2019	Race and Hispanic or Latino origin (percent) White alone, not Hispanic or Latino	Black alone, not Hispanic or Latino	Asian alone, not Hispanic or Latino	All other races or 2 or more races, not Hispanic or Latino	Hispanic or Latino[1]	Age (percent) Under 18 years old	Age 65 years and older	Median age	Educational attainment of persons age 25 and older Percent High school diploma or less	Percent Bachelor's degree or more	Occupied housing units Total	Percent with a computer
	1	2	3	4	5	6	7	8	9	10	11	12	13	14	15	16
PENNSYLVANIA—Con.																
Sharon Hill borough & MCD (Delaware)	5,680	5,689	0.2	5,684	21.0	71.1	2.1	2.0	3.8	22.3	8.0	35.8	47.2	19.3	2,062	94.5
Sharpsburg borough & MCD (Allegheny)............	3,446	3,318	-3.7	3,358	85.2	8.4	1.7	2.4	2.3	16.4	11.8	42.5	52.6	22.7	1,645	78.9
Sharpsville borough & MCD (Mercer)	4,415	4,074	-7.7	4,168	97.0	1.2	0.9	0.3	0.6	21.1	21.5	44.5	49.8	19.1	1,971	81.2
Shartlesville CDP	455	-	-	469	89.8	0.0	0.0	1.9	8.3	16.4	21.5	44.5	70.5	15.0	202	79.7
Shavertown CDP	2,019	-	-	1,981	99.5	0.0	0.0	0.5	0.0	21.6	22.1	46.2	37.6	22.8	855	85.8
Sheakleyville borough & MCD (Mercer)	142	133	-6.3	206	100.0	0.0	0.0	0.0	0.0	27.7	8.3	36.2	63.9	11.8	84	88.1
Sheatown CDP	671	-	-	782	95.5	4.5	0.0	0.0	0.0	29.5	21.6	38.0	49.8	33.9	237	90.3
Sheffield CDP	1,132	-	-	1,087	95.4	2.7	0.0	0.0	1.9	27.0	15.8	43.4	61.4	13.6	483	84.5
Sheffield township (Warren).....................	2,120	1,980	-6.6	2,081	97.1	1.4	0.0	0.5	1.0	23.8	19.4	45.8	64.6	12.0	897	85.7
Shelocta borough & MCD (Indiana)	130	121	-6.9	104	100.0	0.0	0.0	0.0	0.0	28.8	15.4	27.7	64.1	6.3	43	90.7
Shenandoah borough & MCD (Schuylkill)	5,073	4,760	-6.2	4,820	66.8	4.3	0.1	3.4	25.4	26.9	17.6	38.9	64.5	13.0	1,996	73.8
Shenandoah Heights CDP	1,233	-	-	1,402	80.0	0.0	0.4	0.0	19.6	25.4	9.1	37.6	52.8	19.5	528	92.2
Shenango township (Lawrence)	7,477	7,118	-4.8	7,200	97.2	0.5	0.0	1.8	0.6	19.0	24.7	50.7	51.4	24.0	3,332	85.1
Shenango township (Mercer)	3,911	3,673	-6.1	3,727	96.1	0.5	0.0	2.2	1.2	17.2	25.7	51.8	57.3	19.3	1,739	81.5
Sheppton CDP	239	-	-	222	83.3	0.9	0.0	0.0	15.8	14.0	11.7	40.6	61.8	0.6	102	89.2
Sheshequin township (Bradford)	1,351	1,273	-5.8	1,450	93.8	0.4	0.9	0.8	4.1	28.9	12.7	36.4	55.5	17.7	542	86.0
Shickshinny borough & MCD (Luzerne)	831	813	-2.2	614	98.5	0.0	0.0	0.0	1.5	16.0	28.2	50.2	65.5	9.0	283	70.7
Shillington borough & MCD (Berks)	5,285	5,319	0.6	5,300	80.7	0.6	0.0	3.5	15.2	23.7	16.5	38.8	46.6	21.8	2,183	94.5
Shiloh CDP	11,218	-	-	11,007	87.8	3.0	1.8	0.7	6.7	18.0	25.5	46.9	48.7	25.5	4,754	78.9
Shinglehouse borough & MCD (Potter)	1,126	1,054	-6.4	1,073	97.7	0.0	0.0	0.0	2.3	26.0	24.1	40.9	66.1	8.9	414	84.5
Shippen township (Cameron)	2,242	1,958	-12.7	1,965	97.5	0.0	0.6	1.3	0.7	20.3	28.7	54.0	52.7	16.9	884	84.2
Shippen township (Tioga).	527	515	-2.3	488	92.6	1.8	1.4	3.3	0.8	24.2	14.1	33.1	63.5	18.9	154	89.0
Shippensburg borough	5,497	5,565	1.2	5,663	84.6	4.0	1.5	2.2	7.7	14.9	21.5	37.8	51.9	28.3	2,877	88.1
Shippensburg borough (Cumberland)...............	4,401	4,465	1.5	4,463	80.5	5.0	1.9	2.8	9.8	15.0	21.6	35.7	57.2	26.4	2,330	88.9
Shippensburg borough (Franklin)...................	1,096	1,100	0.4	1,200	100.0	0.0	0.0	0.0	0.0	14.5	21.3	40.6	32.5	35.4	547	84.6
Shippensburg township (Cumberland)...............	5,424	5,534	2.0	5,504	81.4	11.8	1.7	1.0	4.1	6.1	10.7	21.3	57.9	26.0	1,431	87.8
Shippensburg University CDP	2,625	-	-	1,937	78.1	9.6	4.8	1.4	6.1	0.0	0.0	19.5	30.6	61.1	82	100.0
Shippenville borough & MCD (Clarion)	479	442	-7.7	583	98.5	0.3	0.0	1.2	0.0	26.1	17.7	40.9	55.3	25.5	226	88.5
Shippingport borough & MCD (Beaver)	207	189	-8.7	174	93.1	0.0	1.1	5.7	0.0	19.5	18.4	40.0	59.4	10.9	73	84.9
Shiremanstown borough & MCD (Cumberland).......	1,622	1,628	0.4	1,556	88.2	2.8	3.0	3.7	2.2	19.6	17.7	42.0	36.6	28.9	695	92.2
Shirley township (Huntingdon)	2,529	2,454	-3.0	2,494	94.3	1.0	0.0	1.4	3.3	18.2	18.9	45.3	66.0	14.0	1,014	86.3
Shirleysburg borough & MCD (Huntingdon)........	148	139	-6.1	145	100.0	0.0	0.0	0.0	0.0	26.2	24.8	37.4	86.6	6.2	52	75.0
Shoemakersville borough & MCD (Berks)	1,384	1,388	0.3	1,391	92.7	0.0	0.8	0.6	5.8	23.8	18.5	40.4	59.1	12.7	583	87.5
Shohola township (Pike)...	2,472	2,366	-4.3	2,133	90.5	0.0	1.4	1.4	6.8	17.7	23.9	50.5	45.6	33.2	902	91.1
Shrewsbury township (Lycoming)	409	396	-3.2	510	93.3	3.3	0.0	3.3	0.0	22.7	18.0	46.2	62.0	11.1	213	82.2
Shrewsbury township (Sullivan)	319	305	-4.4	291	97.9	0.0	0.0	0.7	1.4	7.2	32.3	58.2	64.6	11.5	149	81.9
Shrewsbury borough & MCD (York)	3,825	3,855	0.8	3,851	90.1	0.4	0.0	2.9	6.6	16.7	24.1	49.3	44.5	25.4	1,616	84.3
Shrewsbury township (York).......................	6,429	6,726	4.6	6,691	95.3	2.3	0.2	0.8	1.3	18.7	24.3	48.8	38.8	37.6	2,522	91.0
Sidman CDP....................	431	-	-	437	97.9	2.1	0.0	0.0	0.0	26.1	27.5	52.7	40.6	40.6	155	82.6
Sierra View CDP	4,813	-	-	4,680	64.4	19.4	2.8	1.5	11.9	22.1	8.4	39.5	32.4	31.4	1,573	98.0
Siglerville CDP	106	-	-	143	100.0	0.0	0.0	0.0	0.0	4.2	22.4	47.9	83.0	0.0	64	100.0
Silkworth CDP	820	-	-	865	99.7	0.2	0.0	0.0	0.1	21.6	19.8	46.1	48.6	41.3	329	94.8
Silverdale borough & MCD (Bucks).................	869	854	-1.7	659	94.1	2.1	2.1	1.1	0.6	21.7	16.8	43.4	42.6	33.2	241	95.0
Silver Lake township (Susquehanna)	1,718	1,586	-7.7	1,608	97.3	0.4	0.0	0.7	1.5	12.3	21.6	54.6	42.0	27.6	708	92.1
Silver Spring township (Cumberland)...............	13,657	18,314	34.1	17,338	86.2	1.4	9.5	0.9	2.0	22.7	21.5	44.8	29.3	46.2	7,118	90.9
Simpson CDP..................	1,275	-	-	1,114	93.3	0.0	0.7	0.7	5.3	24.1	20.9	42.4	54.1	16.2	484	73.8
Sinking Spring borough & MCD (Berks)	3,987	4,106	3.0	4,101	73.8	4.2	5.7	1.5	14.8	24.1	11.6	36.3	39.9	32.3	1,646	92.8
Skippack CDP	3,758	-	-	3,775	92.6	1.0	3.9	0.0	2.6	25.4	10.8	41.0	21.6	54.3	1,435	96.3
Skippack township (Montgomery).............	13,721	14,203	3.5	14,513	77.2	15.4	2.6	1.1	3.6	19.4	16.3	43.8	40.8	39.9	4,011	98.2
Skyline View CDP............	4,003	-	-	3,929	92.5	0.6	1.1	3.3	2.5	18.7	28.8	50.4	37.0	39.7	1,626	95.9
Slabtown CDP.................	156	-	-	152	100.0	0.0	0.0	0.0	0.0	17.8	16.4	39.5	43.0	20.6	67	91.0
Slatedale CDP	455	-	-	751	95.3	1.3	0.0	3.3	0.0	39.9	6.7	35.3	64.5	29.5	226	82.3
Slatington borough & MCD (Lehigh)................	4,223	4,307	2.0	4,291	91.4	0.2	0.3	3.1	5.1	22.3	14.7	40.9	56.6	14.1	1,758	84.9
Slickville CDP.................	388	-	-	215	100.0	0.0	0.0	0.0	0.0	5.6	50.7	69.2	79.3	7.9	114	88.6
Sligo borough & MCD (Clarion)	717	666	-7.1	491	99.0	0.0	0.0	0.8	0.2	18.7	17.9	45.5	68.7	10.2	210	78.6
Slippery Rock borough & MCD (Butler)	3,625	3,531	-2.6	3,552	90.2	1.9	3.1	3.4	1.4	8.3	11.1	22.1	30.3	40.4	1,132	94.8

1 May be of any race.

Table A. All Places — **Population and Housing**

STATE City, town, township, borough, or CDP (county if applicable)	Population				Race and Hispanic or Latino origin (percent)					Age (percent)			Educational attainment of persons age 25 and older		Occupied housing units	
	2010 census total population	2019 estimated population	Percent change 2010–2019	ACS total population estimate 2015–2019	White alone, not Hispanic or Latino	Black alone, not Hispanic or Latino	Asian alone, not Hispanic or Latino	All other races or 2 or more races, not Hispanic or Latino	Hispanic or Latino[1]	Under 18 years old	Age 65 years and older	Median age	Percent High school diploma or less	Percent Bachelor's degree or more	Total	Percent with a computer
	1	2	3	4	5	6	7	8	9	10	11	12	13	14	15	16
PENNSYLVANIA—Con.																
Slippery Rock township (Butler)	5,614	6,302	12.3	6,356	93.3	1.7	0.3	3.2	1.4	10.4	7.4	21.5	34.7	32.8	1,665	95.7
Slippery Rock township (Lawrence)	3,275	3,082	-5.9	3,125	99.0	0.1	0.0	0.5	0.4	19.7	21.4	47.0	54.5	17.7	1,261	86.6
Slippery Rock University CDP	1,898	-	-	2,284	87.4	4.6	0.5	4.7	2.8	0.0	0.0	19.7	0.0	21.1	0	0.0
Slocum township (Luzerne)	1,121	1,095	-2.3	1,199	99.7	0.3	0.0	0.0	0.0	18.6	21.2	43.8	53.7	19.0	502	80.9
Slovan CDP	555	-		548	100.0	0.0	0.0	0.0	0.0	23.2	41.6	53.3	64.5	2.8	191	59.2
Smethport borough & MCD (McKean)	1,657	1,530	-7.7	1,601	98.3	0.0	0.0	0.4	1.3	23.2	24.3	45.3	43.7	29.3	682	83.0
Smicksburg borough & MCD (Indiana)	46	43	-6.5	51	100.0	0.0	0.0	0.0	0.0	15.7	29.4	55.9	69.8	2.3	22	86.4
Smith township (Washington)	4,495	4,356	-3.1	4,389	98.5	0.1	0.0	1.1	0.3	23.1	18.7	38.9	56.4	17.9	1,697	85.4
Smithfield township (Bradford)	1,503	1,449	-3.6	1,484	95.0	0.3	0.9	3.2	0.6	19.0	22.8	48.2	58.2	15.3	602	85.9
Smithfield borough & MCD (Fayette)	876	826	-5.7	810	99.6	0.0	0.0	0.4	0.0	27.0	21.7	38.5	64.6	14.8	336	83.3
Smithfield township (Huntingdon)	4,382	4,587	4.7	4,507	47.5	40.0	0.4	4.3	7.9	2.6	6.2	39.4	77.2	3.3	309	76.4
Smithfield township (Monroe)	7,435	7,558	1.7	7,462	60.7	14.1	2.2	2.0	21.0	18.2	16.4	42.0	38.1	29.6	2,430	94.6
Smithton borough & MCD (Westmoreland)	399	373	-6.5	486	96.5	0.0	0.0	2.7	0.8	24.3	14.4	39.5	55.3	12.1	178	90.4
Smock CDP	583	-		511	100.0	0.0	0.0	0.0	0.0	31.7	10.0	29.1	60.9	16.2	209	91.4
Smoketown CDP	357	-		355	96.3	0.0	3.7	0.0	0.0	41.7	1.7	25.4	78.3	15.0	98	100.0
Snake Spring township (Bedford)	1,645	1,750	6.4	1,765	97.9	0.2	0.0	0.4	1.5	14.6	35.6	55.3	54.8	22.4	688	85.8
Snow Shoe borough & MCD (Centre)	753	765	1.6	835	97.5	0.0	1.1	1.4	0.0	19.6	17.6	42.1	60.0	17.3	301	84.4
Snow Shoe township (Centre)	1,761	1,740	-1.2	1,724	97.9	0.0	0.0	0.0	2.1	17.2	21.5	49.0	72.7	8.1	712	80.5
S.N.P.J. borough & MCD (Lawrence)	19	19	0.0	26	100.0	0.0	0.0	0.0	0.0	11.5	30.8	59.5	43.5	21.7	14	64.3
Snyder township (Blair)	3,399	3,229	-5.0	3,275	97.8	0.8	0.2	0.9	0.3	20.3	19.2	45.2	61.2	18.5	1,302	87.2
Snyder township (Jefferson)	2,501	2,400	-4.0	2,422	97.1	1.4	0.0	1.2	0.4	22.7	19.8	44.9	61.2	16.3	944	85.0
Snydertown CDP	-	-		415	95.7	0.0	0.0	4.3	0.0	24.1	8.4	48.5	16.9	36.7	134	100.0
Snydertown borough & MCD (Northumberland)	334	318	-4.8	282	98.6	0.0	0.0	1.4	0.0	8.9	31.9	55.5	59.5	18.0	141	88.7
Solebury township (Bucks)	8,689	8,552	-1.6	8,577	92.0	0.5	4.2	1.4	1.9	19.8	26.1	53.7	13.3	68.8	3,635	96.1
Somerset borough & MCD (Somerset)	6,278	5,855	-6.7	5,942	94.4	0.8	0.2	2.6	2.0	22.1	20.6	40.8	54.3	24.0	2,668	77.5
Somerset township (Somerset)	12,132	12,174	0.3	12,228	80.1	13.9	0.0	1.9	4.1	12.7	15.9	43.2	66.1	11.8	3,408	85.9
Somerset township (Washington)	2,697	2,638	-2.2	2,656	97.2	0.5	0.0	1.3	1.0	17.3	20.9	49.7	44.9	25.9	1,086	90.1
Soudersburg CDP	540	-		806	96.0	0.0	0.0	0.0	4.0	44.2	7.1	20.6	87.8	9.2	238	43.7
Souderton borough & MCD (Montgomery)	6,628	7,082	6.8	6,962	75.0	2.1	5.3	0.9	16.7	23.7	12.6	35.8	52.2	25.3	2,699	86.8
South Abington township (Lackawanna)	9,028	8,888	-1.6	8,902	91.0	2.2	3.4	1.8	1.5	21.6	22.1	44.4	20.4	56.3	3,461	87.1
Southampton township (Bedford)	974	936	-3.9	795	98.9	0.0	0.0	0.6	0.5	12.5	26.8	51.4	58.7	17.5	358	76.3
Southampton township (Cumberland)	6,367	7,117	11.8	6,934	90.4	4.1	3.9	1.2	0.4	26.7	13.1	38.0	54.5	27.1	2,747	85.5
Southampton township (Franklin)	7,982	8,495	6.4	8,523	93.1	2.0	0.6	2.4	1.9	26.3	14.3	38.0	62.1	19.3	3,149	82.2
Southampton township (Somerset)	630	600	-4.8	601	96.5	0.0	0.0	1.8	1.7	10.5	24.1	52.0	68.9	8.8	264	71.2
South Annville township (Lebanon)	2,854	3,031	6.2	2,985	96.1	2.2	0.0	0.3	1.4	19.9	23.3	46.6	57.1	24.0	1,056	89.4
South Beaver township (Beaver)	2,777	2,651	-4.5	2,687	95.7	0.6	0.0	2.8	0.9	18.5	25.5	52.0	43.0	24.4	1,045	89.2
South Bend township (Armstrong)	1,172	1,097	-6.4	965	100.0	0.0	0.0	0.0	0.0	17.9	17.9	47.0	62.6	16.9	389	91.5
South Bethlehem borough & MCD (Armstrong)	481	447	-7.1	432	98.6	0.0	0.0	0.0	1.4	15.3	26.2	53.0	65.2	17.4	209	87.1
South Buffalo township (Armstrong)	2,642	2,519	-4.7	2,548	97.1	0.5	0.0	0.5	1.8	14.6	20.2	49.7	44.9	22.9	1,060	92.5
South Canaan township (Wayne)	1,797	1,764	-1.8	1,560	96.0	0.4	0.3	1.4	1.9	18.5	23.6	47.4	60.3	20.1	582	80.4
South Centre township (Columbia)	1,937	1,883	-2.8	2,047	95.1	0.0	2.6	0.7	1.5	18.0	26.5	50.1	64.7	18.6	1,010	76.6
South Coatesville borough & MCD (Chester)	1,307	1,456	11.4	1,435	37.7	49.6	0.6	3.3	8.8	23.6	14.8	33.0	58.1	13.9	559	89.6
South Connellsville borough & MCD (Fayette)	1,970	1,864	-5.4	1,961	98.5	0.0	0.0	0.5	1.1	20.8	16.3	39.8	62.7	10.7	774	73.1
South Coventry township (Chester)	2,610	2,641	1.2	2,632	94.8	0.5	3.1	0.0	1.6	26.2	14.6	43.2	26.7	52.9	979	93.6
South Creek township (Bradford)	1,132	1,091	-3.6	1,153	97.4	0.0	0.8	0.4	1.4	26.2	19.3	44.2	56.9	15.8	431	89.6
South Fayette township (Allegheny)	14,388	15,945	10.8	15,614	87.1	1.0	9.5	0.9	1.4	25.9	18.0	41.4	28.5	51.3	6,104	89.9
South Fork borough & MCD (Cambria)	929	842	-9.4	1,001	97.5	0.0	0.8	1.4	0.3	25.8	17.6	35.4	65.0	5.7	428	75.5
South Franklin township (Washington)	3,308	3,181	-3.8	3,217	98.1	0.0	0.0	1.6	0.3	15.3	21.7	49.2	51.1	30.0	1,324	91.6

1 May be of any race.

Table A. All Places — **Population and Housing**

STATE City, town, township, borough, or CDP (county if applicable)	Population 2010 census total population	2019 estimated population	Percent change 2010–2019	ACS total population estimate 2015–2019	White alone, not Hispanic or Latino	Black alone, not Hispanic or Latino	Asian alone, not Hispanic or Latino	All other races or 2 or more races, not Hispanic or Latino	Hispanic or Latino[1]	Under 18 years old	Age 65 years and older	Median age	Percent High school diploma or less	Percent Bachelor's degree or more	Occupied housing units Total	Percent with a computer
	1	2	3	4	5	6	7	8	9	10	11	12	13	14	15	16
PENNSYLVANIA—Con.																
South Greensburg borough & MCD (Westmoreland)	2,117	1,996	-5.7	2,162	96.1	0.0	0.1	0.6	3.1	15.3	24.1	48.4	51.4	19.7	1,054	82.8
South Hanover township (Dauphin)	6,239	6,897	10.5	6,797	86.2	2.3	0.7	2.5	8.3	23.7	16.6	38.9	32.1	45.5	2,589	94.7
South Heidelberg township (Berks)	7,390	7,486	1.3	7,461	84.2	5.6	1.5	2.9	5.7	18.8	17.4	45.8	46.7	30.3	2,623	94.3
South Heights borough & MCD (Beaver)	473	443	-6.3	344	98.5	0.6	0.0	0.9	0.0	14.0	14.8	46.7	52.3	17.0	165	86.7
South Huntingdon township (Westmoreland)	5,792	5,470	-5.6	5,527	97.3	2.4	0.0	0.3	0.0	15.3	24.6	51.4	59.2	16.7	2,463	81.5
South Lebanon township (Lebanon)	9,463	10,034	6.0	9,878	84.6	5.5	1.4	0.9	7.6	24.5	21.6	44.1	52.7	22.7	3,519	86.6
South Londonderry township (Lebanon)	6,996	8,516	21.7	8,174	96.3	0.0	2.5	0.0	1.2	22.9	18.7	44.2	43.8	32.6	2,999	92.7
South Mahoning township (Indiana)	1,844	1,721	-6.7	2,003	99.5	0.0	0.0	0.5	0.0	36.6	14.1	29.0	75.4	9.7	553	61.1
South Manheim township (Schuylkill)	2,518	2,491	-1.1	2,596	97.4	0.2	0.0	0.4	2.0	18.4	19.1	46.4	46.9	21.8	1,028	95.5
South Middleton township (Cumberland)	14,714	15,564	5.8	15,393	94.1	1.8	1.0	2.0	1.1	20.0	24.6	48.4	39.7	35.9	6,303	89.0
Southmont borough & MCD (Cambria)	2,284	2,076	-9.1	2,117	95.5	0.7	2.4	0.5	0.9	20.1	25.1	46.4	27.0	45.3	952	92.5
South New Castle borough & MCD (Lawrence)	714	664	-7.0	777	95.1	3.2	0.3	1.4	0.0	22.5	14.8	41.3	53.6	16.0	300	78.3
South Newton township (Cumberland)	1,383	1,440	4.1	1,335	98.6	0.6	0.0	0.8	0.0	23.4	14.4	37.9	69.7	12.3	454	78.4
South Park township & CDP (Allegheny)	13,429	13,628	1.5	13,395	88.5	4.7	2.1	2.5	2.2	19.2	19.5	45.8	32.5	36.8	5,595	93.5
South Philipsburg CDP	410	-	-	504	94.4	3.0	0.0	2.6	0.0	14.1	10.1	45.4	83.7	6.4	176	72.2
South Pottstown CDP	2,081	-	-	2,207	83.0	2.6	0.6	4.5	9.2	20.9	15.2	36.3	47.4	25.6	991	88.5
South Pymatuning township (Mercer)	2,697	2,513	-6.8	2,559	95.9	1.4	0.2	1.6	0.9	18.6	20.7	48.2	46.5	32.6	1,112	88.1
South Renovo borough & MCD (Clinton)	433	426	-1.6	500	91.2	0.4	0.0	0.4	8.0	18.8	25.2	50.4	67.3	12.6	182	79.1
South Shenango township (Crawford)	2,037	1,987	-2.5	2,003	96.8	0.0	0.2	0.4	2.6	12.3	28.3	57.0	56.1	21.0	928	84.5
South Strabane township (Washington)	9,331	9,430	1.1	9,440	91.6	1.9	3.8	0.9	1.9	18.8	29.3	50.7	37.4	35.5	4,331	82.0
South Temple CDP	1,424	-	-	2,018	62.1	0.2	0.0	0.4	37.2	28.2	13.0	36.1	49.4	20.5	660	91.7
South Union township (Fayette)	10,696	10,205	-4.6	10,393	95.0	2.3	1.3	0.9	0.4	17.3	23.8	47.7	44.7	31.7	4,375	86.8
South Uniontown CDP	1,360	-	-	1,326	93.4	1.5	1.2	1.2	2.7	16.0	20.4	44.0	47.5	25.6	625	87.2
South Versailles township (Allegheny)	347	333	-4.0	449	84.6	6.9	1.1	0.2	7.1	18.7	25.2	51.1	55.1	12.0	192	86.5
Southview CDP	276	-	-	380	100.0	0.0	0.0	0.0	0.0	10.8	23.7	42.8	76.1	6.6	141	85.1
South Waverly borough & MCD (Bradford)	1,027	1,004	-2.2	1,026	97.2	0.8	0.0	2.0	0.0	17.3	20.1	49.0	48.5	26.1	422	90.3
Southwest township (Warren)	527	495	-6.1	404	97.5	0.0	0.0	0.0	2.5	21.5	22.5	44.8	64.3	9.0	163	85.3
Southwest Greensburg borough & MCD (Westmoreland)	2,155	2,018	-6.4	2,242	88.9	4.2	0.0	5.9	1.0	19.1	17.5	40.4	39.5	31.1	1,017	90.0
Southwest Madison township (Perry)	994	999	0.5	1,298	97.4	0.0	0.0	0.0	2.6	28.9	13.3	38.4	70.3	12.4	419	82.3
South Whitehall township (Lehigh)	19,167	19,955	4.1	19,778	79.8	3.0	7.0	2.0	8.3	20.1	24.5	46.1	34.9	42.5	7,709	90.9
South Williamsport borough & MCD (Lycoming)	6,362	6,068	-4.6	6,150	90.9	2.5	4.1	1.6	0.8	20.0	17.7	41.3	43.3	26.1	2,696	91.3
South Woodbury township (Bedford)	2,165	2,094	-3.3	2,011	95.8	0.0	0.7	2.6	0.8	27.4	16.8	39.8	63.2	15.0	723	77.5
Sparta township (Crawford)	1,831	1,723	-5.9	2,134	98.7	0.2	0.0	0.6	0.5	38.1	12.5	26.6	70.7	11.2	599	56.1
Spartansburg borough & MCD (Crawford)	305	286	-6.2	296	99.3	0.7	0.0	0.0	0.0	20.3	18.6	36.7	51.8	17.6	115	86.1
Speers borough & MCD (Washington)	1,120	1,066	-4.8	1,067	96.9	1.1	0.0	1.4	0.6	14.6	27.3	52.2	39.8	32.4	483	88.2
Spinnerstown CDP	1,826	-	-	1,797	92.0	0.4	0.0	1.3	6.2	29.3	5.5	40.1	37.8	34.4	602	95.2
Spring township (Berks)	27,110	27,659	2.0	27,568	75.1	4.7	2.7	2.0	15.5	22.9	19.8	40.7	36.9	36.2	10,339	92.2
Spring township (Centre)	7,480	8,056	7.7	7,838	97.3	0.5	0.5	1.6	0.1	22.0	17.7	43.2	38.8	36.2	3,439	88.1
Spring township (Crawford)	1,550	1,495	-3.5	1,351	98.1	1.0	0.0	0.1	0.9	22.1	19.6	48.1	65.8	14.0	547	74.2
Spring township (Perry)	2,233	2,252	0.9	2,274	99.1	0.0	0.0	0.9	0.0	21.8	18.2	46.3	58.9	17.6	895	89.8
Spring township (Snyder)	1,625	1,614	-0.7	1,280	97.3	0.5	0.0	2.0	0.1	19.3	23.0	46.9	73.3	7.6	513	74.9
Springboro borough & MCD (Crawford)	477	446	-6.5	377	95.0	0.0	1.6	0.8	2.7	26.0	11.4	34.6	62.7	14.3	152	84.2
Spring Brook township (Lackawanna)	2,767	2,691	-2.7	2,692	94.9	3.6	0.4	1.0	0.0	20.6	18.2	43.9	43.5	27.0	1,042	90.7
Spring City borough & MCD (Chester)	3,321	3,303	-0.5	3,307	93.9	3.3	1.1	1.4	0.3	19.3	14.1	36.4	44.4	27.1	1,511	89.8
Spring Creek township (Elk)	233	217	-6.9	138	100.0	0.0	0.0	0.0	0.0	13.8	36.2	60.7	70.4	12.2	74	74.3
Spring Creek township (Warren)	852	788	-7.5	941	97.4	1.6	0.0	0.6	0.3	23.7	23.3	44.8	57.2	12.1	357	91.3
Springdale borough & MCD (Allegheny)	3,405	3,288	-3.4	3,326	96.8	0.2	0.2	1.8	1.0	18.7	19.5	44.3	43.9	24.1	1,598	85.0
Springdale township (Allegheny)	1,636	1,579	-3.5	1,574	97.8	0.0	0.4	0.0	1.8	10.5	29.7	55.2	44.0	18.7	846	85.1

1 May be of any race.

Table A. All Places — **Population and Housing**

STATE City, town, township, borough, or CDP (county if applicable)	Population				Race and Hispanic or Latino origin (percent)					Age (percent)			Educational attainment of persons age 25 and older		Occupied housing units	
	2010 census total population	2019 estimated population	Percent change 2010–2019	ACS total population estimate 2015–2019	White alone, not Hispanic or Latino	Black alone, not Hispanic or Latino	Asian alone, not Hispanic or Latino	All other races or 2 or more races, not Hispanic or Latino	Hispanic or Latino[1]	Under 18 years old	Age 65 years and older	Median age	Percent High school diploma or less	Percent Bachelor's degree or more	Total	Percent with a computer
	1	2	3	4	5	6	7	8	9	10	11	12	13	14	15	16

PENNSYLVANIA—Con.

STATE City, town, township, borough, or CDP (county if applicable)	1	2	3	4	5	6	7	8	9	10	11	12	13	14	15	16
Springettsbury township (York)	26,639	26,860	0.8	26,773	76.4	6.7	3.4	3.3	10.1	18.0	18.8	40.7	48.1	29.3	9,434	90.6
Springfield township (Bradford)	1,123	1,056	-6.0	1,138	95.2	0.2	0.0	2.3	2.4	22.1	19.6	44.6	58.8	16.6	453	89.2
Springfield township (Bucks)	5,044	5,033	-0.2	5,040	93.9	0.0	2.7	1.6	1.9	18.1	22.8	49.9	38.2	41.5	2,097	90.3
Springfield township (Delaware)	24,125	24,261	0.6	24,247	92.0	1.1	3.6	1.9	1.5	22.9	18.5	42.3	28.2	46.7	8,336	95.6
Springfield township (Erie)	3,428	3,280	-4.3	3,331	93.5	0.5	0.0	5.9	0.2	22.4	17.4	44.3	50.2	13.1	1,353	89.0
Springfield township (Fayette)	3,041	2,884	-5.2	2,929	98.6	0.1	0.0	1.4	0.0	20.2	15.7	44.9	73.5	7.6	1,168	88.7
Springfield township (Huntingdon)	652	638	-2.1	666	99.5	0.0	0.0	0.5	0.0	24.6	28.8	44.0	61.8	17.1	277	75.1
Springfield township (Mercer)	1,981	1,896	-4.3	1,735	99.2	0.0	0.0	0.7	0.1	19.9	18.4	45.5	54.6	22.9	719	86.5
Springfield township (Montgomery)	19,365	19,848	2.5	19,693	78.6	10.4	2.6	3.1	5.3	21.7	21.9	43.3	22.4	60.0	7,318	93.9
Springfield township (York)	5,157	5,783	12.1	5,659	92.2	3.2	1.3	0.0	3.3	24.2	19.0	40.0	36.7	40.2	2,146	97.1
Spring Garden township (York)	12,485	13,209	5.8	13,047	84.9	3.2	3.4	2.0	6.5	19.9	18.0	37.9	36.3	40.4	4,477	91.4
Spring Grove borough & MCD (York)	2,166	2,178	0.6	2,081	87.8	6.8	0.0	2.7	2.6	25.7	15.6	37.2	57.2	20.9	905	87.5
Spring Hill CDP	839	-	-	831	100.0	0.0	0.0	0.0	0.0	25.0	17.2	37.8	57.2	9.0	326	77.3
Springhill township (Fayette)	2,906	2,765	-4.9	2,802	98.1	0.9	0.0	0.0	1.0	21.1	15.0	44.0	65.1	9.8	1,092	89.6
Springhill township (Greene)	350	320	-8.6	262	98.9	0.0	0.0	1.1	0.0	18.3	26.0	51.2	76.1	8.1	122	63.1
Spring House CDP	3,804	-	-	4,045	77.3	2.9	18.0	0.9	0.9	21.1	30.0	52.5	17.3	72.6	1,534	89.2
Spring Mills CDP	268	-	-	359	89.1	0.0	0.0	0.0	10.9	8.6	16.2	46.0	73.4	23.6	124	81.5
Springmont CDP	724	-	-	1,172	61.3	1.3	0.0	3.3	34.0	29.9	13.5	28.3	33.5	20.2	395	94.9
Spring Mount CDP	2,259	-	-	2,247	86.0	3.3	0.4	0.4	9.9	27.6	14.7	37.4	32.6	45.8	908	96.1
Spring Ridge CDP	1,003	-	-	917	81.5	0.0	7.4	8.4	2.7	9.5	46.7	62.8	37.1	51.3	485	96.5
Springville township (Susquehanna)	1,641	1,514	-7.7	1,651	98.4	0.6	0.0	1.0	0.0	20.8	20.6	48.6	53.5	18.6	646	88.2
Spruce Creek township (Huntingdon)	238	227	-4.6	235	100.0	0.0	0.0	0.0	0.0	5.5	22.6	53.5	53.9	23.8	108	84.3
Spruce Hill township (Juniata)	837	861	2.9	898	89.8	10.2	0.0	0.0	0.0	25.8	16.0	38.1	61.9	12.2	324	90.7
Spry CDP	4,891	-	-	4,588	93.2	0.8	2.4	0.0	3.6	18.0	18.2	42.4	40.3	33.4	1,976	89.7
Standing Stone township (Bradford)	644	637	-1.1	647	96.6	0.2	1.5	1.7	0.0	17.6	16.1	48.1	59.3	18.7	269	90.7
Starbrick CDP	522	-	-	424	89.9	0.0	0.0	10.1	0.0	20.5	21.9	55.0	61.4	8.0	250	56.0
Star Junction CDP	616	-	-	274	100.0	0.0	0.0	0.0	0.0	11.7	33.9	47.0	71.7	15.6	156	66.7
Starrucca borough & MCD (Wayne)	173	165	-4.6	163	90.8	2.5	0.0	4.3	2.5	24.5	17.2	46.4	59.8	17.1	59	94.9
State College borough & MCD (Centre)	41,980	42,160	0.4	42,275	78.8	3.7	10.9	2.4	4.2	6.0	6.2	21.6	13.1	70.6	12,468	95.7
State Line CDP	2,709	-	-	2,491	95.0	1.5	0.7	2.8	0.0	27.0	17.4	38.4	55.7	18.0	867	97.9
Steelton borough & MCD (Dauphin)	5,992	5,962	-0.5	5,953	38.1	36.1	0.1	3.9	21.7	32.1	12.3	30.6	51.4	15.7	2,076	84.9
Sterling township (Wayne)	1,449	1,423	-1.8	1,554	90.4	1.2	0.6	2.4	5.3	22.6	19.0	41.4	50.0	21.1	534	95.9
Steuben township (Crawford)	798	769	-3.6	811	97.9	0.2	0.0	1.4	0.5	24.0	19.4	41.2	64.3	11.7	340	79.7
Stevens township (Bradford)	437	426	-2.5	406	96.6	0.0	2.0	1.5	0.0	17.2	29.8	50.4	57.8	17.9	165	95.2
Stevens CDP	612	-	-	429	46.6	26.1	0.0	0.0	27.3	30.1	5.4	40.2	68.6	12.0	155	95.5
Stewardson township (Potter)	73	68	-6.8	27	100.0	0.0	0.0	0.0	0.0	7.4	33.3	57.3	52.4	23.8	16	87.5
Stewart township (Fayette)	728	687	-5.6	660	97.7	0.0	0.0	0.0	2.3	14.4	21.8	51.7	66.7	12.0	308	73.1
Stewartstown borough & MCD (York)	2,024	2,266	12.0	1,857	95.8	0.5	1.3	0.9	1.5	23.6	17.3	48.2	39.9	32.6	848	81.0
Stiles CDP	1,113	-	-	1,166	75.5	0.0	4.2	0.0	20.3	19.6	17.8	43.8	36.1	25.5	430	100.0
Stillwater borough & MCD (Columbia)	209	205	-1.9	258	98.1	0.0	0.0	1.9	0.0	32.6	19.4	41.3	49.7	19.3	97	86.6
Stockdale borough & MCD (Washington)	506	499	-1.4	388	96.4	0.0	0.0	3.6	0.0	9.0	35.6	54.3	52.1	24.1	197	76.1
Stockertown borough & MCD (Northampton)	927	926	-0.1	999	93.7	0.4	0.4	3.6	1.9	22.5	14.8	45.0	42.2	18.7	358	94.7
Stoneboro borough & MCD (Mercer)	1,051	980	-6.8	871	98.9	0.0	0.5	0.7	0.0	16.9	29.9	51.4	55.8	18.0	449	82.4
Stonerstown CDP	376	-	-	382	99.2	0.8	0.0	0.0	0.0	22.5	16.5	38.5	53.2	12.3	160	85.6
Stonybrook CDP	2,384	-	-	2,151	86.6	1.5	4.8	3.1	4.0	27.0	21.1	42.8	31.6	43.4	815	91.4
Stonycreek township (Cambria)	2,851	2,585	-9.3	2,643	90.9	2.9	0.0	1.1	5.0	9.5	28.3	55.7	55.4	15.2	1,413	83.5
Stonycreek township (Somerset)	2,232	2,084	-6.6	2,202	99.2	0.3	0.0	0.5	0.0	22.4	19.3	46.5	60.5	15.7	860	81.2
Stony Creek Mills CDP	1,045	-	-	863	78.0	0.9	1.2	7.1	12.9	25.0	15.6	46.1	57.8	21.4	339	90.0
Stormstown CDP	2,366	-	-	2,429	95.3	0.0	2.1	2.1	0.6	26.6	12.8	41.7	23.9	57.0	822	100.0
Stouchsburg CDP	600	-	-	438	93.4	0.7	0.0	0.9	4.1	24.0	18.0	42.0	54.0	12.3	193	84.5
Stowe township (Allegheny)	6,362	6,121	-3.8	6,197	69.2	23.2	0.3	7.3	0.0	25.0	13.8	37.7	53.9	10.9	2,545	82.9
Stowe CDP	3,695	-	-	3,662	81.8	8.3	1.1	3.7	5.2	19.2	14.5	39.7	56.1	12.5	1,509	88.8
Stoystown borough & MCD (Somerset)	346	319	-7.8	393	97.5	0.0	0.0	2.5	0.0	14.0	37.2	48.2	47.3	24.0	206	76.2
Straban township (Adams)	4,921	4,978	1.2	4,954	86.0	1.5	0.1	1.0	11.5	18.9	23.2	45.5	57.8	19.9	1,714	86.5
Strasburg borough & MCD (Lancaster)	2,821	3,030	7.4	2,974	84.5	0.9	0.3	1.0	13.2	26.5	14.2	35.1	37.0	39.7	1,155	89.7
Strasburg township (Lancaster)	4,171	4,329	3.8	4,291	100.0	0.0	0.0	0.0	0.0	31.0	17.0	38.0	58.1	25.4	1,370	82.0
Strattanville borough & MCD (Clarion)	535	498	-6.9	572	97.7	0.3	0.0	0.7	1.2	21.0	14.7	41.3	59.0	9.6	262	84.0

1 May be of any race.

Table A. All Places — Population and Housing

STATE City, town, township, borough, or CDP (county if applicable)	2010 census total population	2019 estimated population	Percent change 2010–2019	ACS total population estimate 2015–2019	White alone, not Hispanic or Latino	Black alone, not Hispanic or Latino	Asian alone, not Hispanic or Latino	All other races or 2 or more races, not Hispanic or Latino	Hispanic or Latino[1]	Under 18 years old	Age 65 years and older	Median age	Percent High school diploma or less	Percent Bachelor's degree or more	Occupied housing units Total	Percent with a computer
	1	2	3	4	5	6	7	8	9	10	11	12	13	14	15	16
PENNSYLVANIA—Con.																
Strausstown CDP	342	-	-	416	96.4	0.0	0.0	0.0	3.6	33.2	8.9	31.5	72.8	13.2	147	90.5
Strodes Mills CDP	757	-	-	1,047	89.6	0.0	0.0	0.0	10.4	19.0	25.3	49.8	85.4	7.4	396	73.0
Strong CDP	147	-	-	-	-	-	-	-	-	-	-	-	-	-	-	-
Stroud township (Monroe)	19,162	19,361	1.0	18,976	58.3	16.6	3.4	3.1	18.7	23.5	16.4	41.0	40.2	28.2	6,408	91.6
Stroudsburg borough & MCD (Monroe)	5,559	5,558	0.0	5,499	66.8	13.0	2.5	3.7	14.0	22.3	19.1	40.6	39.8	26.5	2,231	84.6
Sturgeon CDP	1,710	-	-	1,580	100.0	0.0	0.0	0.0	0.0	20.3	25.6	43.4	44.9	30.5	617	92.9
Sugarcreek township (Armstrong)	1,541	1,448	-6.0	1,412	92.8	6.8	0.0	0.4	0.0	19.3	20.3	43.3	57.9	15.3	494	86.2
Sugarcreek borough & MCD (Venango)	5,312	4,904	-7.7	5,014	96.7	0.8	0.1	1.4	1.0	14.7	25.6	51.0	64.4	9.0	2,275	84.8
Sugar Grove township (Mercer)	971	901	-7.2	863	97.0	0.0	0.0	1.9	1.2	17.4	23.8	49.8	56.3	16.0	349	87.1
Sugar Grove borough & MCD (Warren)	614	573	-6.7	613	99.5	0.0	0.0	0.5	0.0	23.5	18.6	41.5	52.8	16.1	233	88.0
Sugar Grove township (Warren)	1,715	1,659	-3.3	1,561	98.4	0.0	0.0	1.6	0.0	24.7	17.6	37.5	59.1	15.2	635	77.0
Sugarloaf township (Columbia)	915	899	-1.7	803	97.9	0.0	0.6	0.0	1.5	15.1	31.0	55.6	63.7	16.1	387	75.2
Sugarloaf township (Luzerne)	4,212	3,951	-6.2	3,977	91.9	1.3	1.7	1.8	3.3	17.8	17.0	39.1	43.6	28.4	1,374	92.8
Sugar Notch borough & MCD (Luzerne)	989	962	-2.7	960	97.7	0.1	0.4	0.1	1.7	19.7	17.6	42.5	62.8	11.6	374	85.3
Sullivan township (Tioga)	1,464	1,450		1,642	95.7	1.0	0.0	1.3	2.0	21.4	20.0	43.8	55.2	21.7	665	90.1
Summerhill borough & MCD (Cambria)	488	444	-9.0	415	98.3	0.0	0.0	1.0	0.7	16.4	22.9	46.1	49.8	22.5	192	89.6
Summerhill township (Cambria)	2,464	2,257	-8.4	2,166	97.3	0.3	0.0	1.4	0.1	22.6	17.6	39.8	54.7	21.4	838	79.0
Summerhill township (Crawford)	1,234	1,195	-3.2	1,040	98.0	0.3	0.0	1.3	0.4	22.2	18.2	45.4	60.9	22.8	415	79.8
Summerville borough & MCD (Jefferson)	525	505	-3.8	486	97.3	0.0	0.0	1.4	1.2	20.2	16.5	42.4	70.0	12.7	210	86.7
Summit township (Butler)	4,890	4,657	-4.8	4,711	94.9	2.3	0.0	1.0	1.8	25.1	15.3	35.1	54.9	13.1	1,856	79.4
Summit township (Crawford)	2,029	1,942	-4.3	2,137	98.3	0.0	0.5	0.7	0.5	21.4	17.9	43.0	59.7	20.6	868	83.8
Summit township (Erie)	6,602	7,233	9.6	7,033	96.0	0.2	0.2	2.1	1.5	18.6	24.8	48.3	42.7	30.1	3,048	93.8
Summit township (Potter)	187	179	-4.3	155	94.8	0.0	0.0	5.2	0.0	21.9	43.9	53.5	56.4	24.8	70	87.1
Summit township (Somerset)	2,266	2,117	-6.6	2,240	99.6	0.2	0.0	0.2	0.0	20.0	23.3	45.8	74.8	11.0	822	74.8
Summit Hill borough & MCD (Carbon)	3,034	2,954	-2.6	2,943	87.8	1.2	0.0	2.9	8.1	21.0	15.5	42.4	47.7	16.0	1,219	86.1
Summit Station CDP	174	-	-	197	100.0	0.0	0.0	0.0	0.0	9.1	6.1	61.3	59.2	25.1	109	89.0
Sunbury city & MCD (Northumberland)	9,907	9,362	-5.5	9,480	88.7	3.5	0.0	1.8	6.0	21.2	16.9	35.7	71.2	10.5	4,225	72.8
Sunrise Lake CDP	1,387	-	-	972	78.8	7.1	0.0	0.0	14.1	16.2	14.8	43.8	20.3	62.5	398	76.9
Sun Valley CDP	2,399	-	-	2,330	97.9	0.3	0.0	0.4	1.4	25.1	14.8	35.6	53.7	19.0	766	96.2
Susquehanna township (Cambria)	2,022	1,848	-8.6	1,646	99.3	0.0	0.0	0.2	0.4	15.4	23.1	49.3	61.3	15.6	727	82.5
Susquehanna township (Dauphin)	24,030	25,114	4.5	24,954	58.0	25.6	5.6	3.7	7.0	21.9	19.8	41.9	39.8	36.6	10,529	88.5
Susquehanna township (Juniata)	1,251	1,252	0.1	1,365	98.2	1.0	0.0	0.4	0.4	27.9	13.9	39.4	76.9	6.7	471	79.2
Susquehanna township (Lycoming)	998	956	-4.2	952	99.7	0.0	0.0	0.0	0.3	20.0	21.6	48.5	61.2	15.5	399	88.2
Susquehanna Depot borough & MCD (Susquehanna)	1,651	1,513	-8.4	1,562	97.7	0.3	1.4	0.6	0.1	21.5	21.6	43.8	56.2	20.6	607	80.6
Susquehanna Trails CDP	2,264	-	-	1,821	94.9	2.6	0.0	1.7	0.8	21.4	21.0	41.0	54.9	12.3	721	87.9
Sutersville borough & MCD (Westmoreland)	603	570	-5.5	451	98.2	0.0	0.0	0.0	1.8	19.3	21.1	48.6	55.1	14.8	218	73.9
Swarthmore borough & MCD (Delaware)	6,190	6,346	2.5	6,318	81.8	4.5	5.3	4.9	3.5	22.2	15.6	32.8	10.0	78.5	1,942	94.6
Swartzville CDP	2,283	-	-	2,850	72.1	1.4	1.8	0.0	24.7	12.1	19.6	41.2	59.9	19.8	926	91.1
Swatara township (Dauphin)	23,366	25,081	7.3	24,792	57.2	22.9	6.9	3.9	9.0	22.2	15.9	39.1	45.0	25.9	9,292	90.2
Swatara township (Lebanon)	4,565	4,827	5.7	4,760	95.1	3.8	0.3	0.5	0.3	22.2	17.5	42.1	66.1	11.2	2,031	83.4
Sweden township (Potter)	872	818	-6.2	762	94.0	0.0	0.0	4.9	1.2	16.5	23.1	47.0	47.4	19.9	306	82.0
Sweden Valley CDP	223	-	-	226	87.2	0.0	0.0	10.6	2.2	16.8	23.0	38.5	52.6	17.5	72	91.7
Swissvale borough & MCD (Allegheny)	9,000	8,647	-3.9	8,760	60.8	32.3	1.2	2.5	3.2	16.7	15.1	40.1	31.9	41.2	4,436	88.0
Swoyersville borough & MCD (Luzerne)	5,117	5,009	-2.1	5,017	97.2	0.0	0.1	0.0	2.7	12.9	22.8	49.2	42.2	23.6	2,400	86.7
Sykesville borough & MCD (Jefferson)	1,162	1,115	-4.0	1,055	98.4	0.0	0.0	0.9	0.7	17.7	22.2	44.6	62.1	11.6	529	73.3
Sylvania borough & MCD (Bradford)	221	210	-5.0	205	99.0	0.0	0.0	1.0	0.0	18.0	23.4	47.1	60.4	14.5	89	85.4
Sylvania township (Potter)	77	72	-6.5	67	100.0	0.0	0.0	0.0	0.0	6.0	35.8	56.3	60.0	15.0	32	81.3
Table Rock CDP	62	-	-	42	100.0	0.0	0.0	0.0	0.0	14.3	33.3	52.6	55.6	27.8	25	44.0
Tamaqua borough & MCD (Schuylkill)	7,103	6,664	-6.2	6,731	91.2	0.5	0.0	2.0	6.3	22.5	19.0	41.6	58.0	15.5	3,146	78.3
Tarentum borough & MCD (Allegheny)	4,536	4,366	-3.7	4,413	83.1	10.6	0.0	4.6	1.7	19.4	18.2	48.7	53.5	13.0	2,231	86.0
Tatamy borough & MCD (Northampton)	1,182	1,174	-0.7	1,078	84.6	3.7	2.4	1.9	7.4	23.2	18.6	41.8	45.9	25.5	455	88.8
Taylor township (Blair)	2,477	2,425	-2.1	2,472	99.0	0.6	0.0	0.4	0.0	23.5	22.2	42.9	56.0	20.5	956	79.8
Taylor township (Centre)	848	859	1.3	829	98.2	0.5	0.0	1.3	0.0	18.5	19.4	48.0	54.0	21.5	355	76.6
Taylor township (Fulton)	1,127	1,086	-3.6	1,047	95.5	0.2	0.9	0.9	2.6	18.5	19.6	43.5	68.1	11.8	444	77.9
Taylor borough & MCD (Lackawanna)	6,263	5,913	-5.6	5,965	89.7	0.5	0.6	1.1	8.1	17.9	22.0	44.5	60.1	23.9	2,648	88.4
Taylor township (Lawrence)	1,046	969	-7.4	1,034	92.9	3.5	0.0	3.2	0.4	13.1	31.6	55.7	61.1	14.2	458	83.6

1 May be of any race.

Table A. All Places — **Population and Housing**

STATE City, town, township, borough, or CDP (county if applicable)	Population 2010 census total population	2019 estimated population	Percent change 2010–2019	ACS total population estimate 2015–2019	White alone, not Hispanic or Latino	Black alone, not Hispanic or Latino	Asian alone, not Hispanic or Latino	All other races or 2 or more races, not Hispanic or Latino	Hispanic or Latino[1]	Under 18 years old	Age 65 years and older	Median age	Percent High school diploma or less	Percent Bachelor's degree or more	Occupied housing units Total	Percent with a computer
	1	2	3	4	5	6	7	8	9	10	11	12	13	14	15	16
PENNSYLVANIA—Con.																
Taylorstown CDP	217	-	-	216	87.0	0.0	0.0	13.0	0.0	32.4	11.6	34.0	54.7	23.4	74	91.9
Telford borough	4,853	4,894	0.8	4,796	77.5	4.0	4.0	1.3	13.2	26.0	19.7	38.6	52.0	23.5	1,923	82.3
Telford borough (Bucks)	2,212	2,205	-0.3	2,141	88.4	2.4	6.2	0.7	2.4	20.0	31.9	47.5	55.1	24.7	990	75.2
Telford borough (Montgomery)	2,641	2,689	1.8	2,655	68.7	5.4	2.3	1.8	21.9	30.9	10.0	34.9	49.0	22.4	933	89.8
Tell township (Huntingdon)	662	631	-4.7	657	100.0	0.0	0.0	0.0	0.0	21.0	21.6	48.3	69.2	16.1	253	85.8
Temple CDP	1,877	-	-	1,689	73.1	0.0	0.0	2.6	24.3	25.5	9.2	38.1	51.8	7.1	699	95.1
Templeton CDP	325	-	-	294	99.0	0.0	0.0	1.0	0.0	28.6	23.5	38.5	81.0	4.1	114	66.7
Terre Hill borough & MCD (Lancaster)	1,299	1,435	10.5	1,161	91.4	0.9	0.0	3.2	4.6	25.0	15.6	38.0	69.7	14.8	383	88.5
Terry township (Bradford)	992	955	-3.7	954	97.5	0.0	0.5	2.0	0.0	21.1	17.8	43.3	58.2	18.1	380	88.2
Texas township (Wayne)	2,528	2,424	-4.1	2,622	90.0	2.5	1.2	3.1	3.2	15.9	21.1	48.8	56.1	16.7	870	92.6
Tharptown (Uniontown) CDP	498	-	-	380	98.2	0.0	0.0	0.0	1.8	8.7	50.8	65.1	64.3	13.6	213	85.4
The Hideout CDP	3,013	-	-	1,385	88.3	0.0	0.0	0.0	11.7	20.1	30.6	51.0	41.9	35.9	548	86.7
Thompson township (Fulton)	1,099	1,087	-1.1	1,045	100.0	0.0	0.0	0.0	0.0	22.4	16.3	43.6	68.9	13.5	407	80.3
Thompson borough & MCD (Susquehanna)	297	269	-9.4	330	92.4	0.0	0.0	1.2	6.4	23.9	16.1	36.6	52.5	21.1	106	91.5
Thompson township (Susquehanna)	411	380	-7.5	465	92.9	1.1	0.0	1.5	4.5	12.3	27.3	52.6	51.1	16.8	210	90.5
Thompsontown borough & MCD (Juniata)	684	664	-2.9	801	94.1	2.5	0.0	1.5	1.9	14.4	18.2	41.1	66.6	14.9	400	82.0
Thompsonville CDP	3,520	-	-	3,574	98.2	0.3	0.7	0.4	0.4	19.7	29.6	53.5	23.0	54.2	1,266	96.0
Thornburg borough & MCD (Allegheny)	430	413	-4.0	443	93.2	0.0	1.8	3.8	1.1	20.5	24.2	48.7	10.1	73.3	175	96.6
Thornbury township (Chester)	3,265	3,136	-4.0	3,139	86.4	4.9	5.4	1.5	1.9	21.6	13.9	40.5	13.0	69.6	1,161	98.6
Thornbury township (Delaware)	7,787	7,726	-0.8	7,700	84.0	7.3	5.4	1.8	1.5	29.5	16.1	43.7	20.4	62.8	2,275	98.5
Thorndale CDP	3,407	-	-	3,655	74.1	8.0	12.7	2.1	3.1	16.1	22.0	37.3	26.1	45.1	1,422	94.2
Thornhurst township (Lackawanna)	1,080	1,034	-4.3	1,072	93.3	0.0	0.0	0.0	6.7	20.0	16.0	45.7	41.6	19.1	423	94.6
Three Springs borough & MCD (Huntingdon)	444	433	-2.5	651	100.0	0.0	0.0	0.0	0.0	22.6	22.9	41.2	60.3	11.1	249	80.7
Throop borough & MCD (Lackawanna)	4,092	3,896	-4.8	3,937	88.9	1.0	5.2	3.3	1.7	19.5	19.3	39.5	47.3	23.5	1,755	85.2
Tidioute borough & MCD (Warren)	687	641	-6.7	753	97.1	0.4	0.0	0.4	2.1	18.2	29.0	52.8	59.8	14.1	341	77.7
Tilden township (Berks)	3,597	3,620	0.6	3,615	95.2	4.2	0.4	0.1	0.1	18.4	22.4	48.0	58.6	19.7	1,415	83.3
Timber Hills CDP	360	-	-	679	100.0	0.0	0.0	0.0	0.0	16.5	44.8	63.1	52.2	36.4	233	100.0
Timblin borough & MCD (Jefferson)	152	146	-3.9	193	100.0	0.0	0.0	0.0	0.0	30.6	17.1	38.1	71.9	17.5	57	71.9
Tinicum township (Bucks)	3,988	3,952	-0.9	3,954	95.8	0.2	0.8	1.9	1.2	8.4	32.7	57.8	30.6	42.3	1,932	92.7
Tinicum township (Delaware)	4,091	4,111	0.5	4,109	93.8	2.0	1.6	2.1	0.5	20.0	16.0	39.3	60.1	12.7	1,472	89.9
Tioga borough & MCD (Tioga)	665	647	-2.7	753	95.0	1.1	0.0	1.7	2.3	23.8	12.5	39.3	59.0	15.4	281	85.4
Tioga township (Tioga)	975	961	-1.4	904	97.9	0.4	0.6	0.7	0.4	16.6	25.1	40.0	60.3	14.7	405	84.7
Tionesta borough & MCD (Forest)	483	425	-12.0	404	99.3	0.0	0.0	0.7	0.0	12.6	46.5	63.4	59.8	19.7	231	76.6
Tionesta township (Forest)	727	642	-11.7	496	99.8	0.0	0.2	0.0	0.0	19.4	38.9	59.2	57.2	19.5	255	85.9
Tipton CDP	1,083	-	-	1,544	85.0	4.6	0.0	10.4	0.0	20.5	16.2	46.4	38.3	34.0	654	91.0
Titusville city & MCD (Crawford)	5,601	5,158	-7.9	5,264	95.9	1.8	1.0	0.1	1.1	20.6	21.7	39.7	56.5	19.5	2,316	81.6
Toboyne township (Perry)	443	446	0.7	406	98.5	0.0	1.2	0.2	0.0	19.2	27.8	54.8	65.3	14.6	171	73.7
Toby township (Clarion)	992	934	-5.8	1,020	95.4	0.6	1.0	2.7	0.3	20.4	14.3	45.8	66.1	16.8	383	79.6
Tobyhanna township (Monroe)	8,540	8,599	0.7	8,459	72.0	11.5	0.5	1.6	14.4	16.4	25.3	51.4	43.0	20.6	3,236	91.9
Todd township (Fulton)	1,543	1,521	-1.4	1,717	88.5	7.3	0.2	0.6	3.3	26.1	18.6	40.5	60.3	18.2	681	83.8
Todd township (Huntingdon)	952	928	-2.5	946	93.8	3.1	0.0	0.0	3.2	24.2	18.5	41.0	51.9	16.6	332	88.9
Toftrees CDP	2,053	-	-	2,500	83.4	2.7	7.8	1.2	4.8	4.1	22.6	30.8	7.2	70.8	1,508	100.0
Topton borough & MCD (Berks)	2,066	2,069	0.1	1,750	94.6	0.0	0.0	2.2	3.3	16.0	17.9	45.1	51.3	19.4	767	88.1
Toughkenamon CDP	1,492	-	-	1,282	56.8	1.6	0.0	0.0	41.7	18.2	22.1	44.2	62.2	24.4	440	73.9
Towamencin township (Montgomery)	17,592	18,441	4.8	18,330	77.7	6.8	11.3	1.5	2.6	20.4	21.7	44.8	27.4	48.9	7,642	91.8
Towamensing township (Carbon)	4,474	4,459	-0.3	4,419	98.0	0.0	0.3	0.6	1.2	15.8	21.3	49.8	49.9	20.3	1,679	91.5
Towamensing Trails CDP	2,292	-	-	1,602	85.9	12.4	1.7	0.0	0.0	18.9	17.7	50.3	46.4	18.0	628	100.0
Towanda borough & MCD (Bradford)	2,926	2,810	-4.0	2,842	96.0	0.9	0.0	0.6	2.5	25.7	13.4	33.7	50.6	21.2	1,232	83.2
Towanda township (Bradford)	1,159	1,109	-4.3	960	91.6	0.5	0.7	1.8	5.4	21.7	22.5	43.9	62.5	20.2	380	89.7
Tower City borough & MCD (Schuylkill)	1,346	1,277	-5.1	1,261	99.0	0.0	0.0	0.2	0.8	25.5	13.8	36.8	64.5	10.5	498	91.0
Townville borough & MCD (Crawford)	329	309	-6.1	268	98.9	0.0	0.0	1.1	0.0	22.8	18.7	42.7	55.7	17.0	114	86.8
Trafford borough	3,223	3,039	-5.7	3,083	97.3	0.0	0.8	1.5	0.5	22.3	17.4	39.1	40.8	28.5	1,393	79.8
Trafford borough (Allegheny)	111	107	-3.6	94	100.0	0.0	0.0	0.0	0.0	0.0	16.0	56.2	55.3	31.9	51	82.4
Trafford borough (Westmoreland)	3,112	2,932	-5.8	2,989	97.2	0.0	0.8	1.5	0.5	23.0	17.4	38.4	40.1	28.3	1,342	79.7
Trainer borough & MCD (Delaware)	1,828	1,836	0.4	1,911	55.9	29.6	0.0	7.5	7.1	33.2	11.5	30.5	62.8	15.9	588	89.1
Trappe borough & MCD (Montgomery)	3,495	3,725	6.6	3,610	82.5	2.6	6.1	0.9	7.8	19.8	11.6	39.1	26.5	41.4	1,376	98.8
Treasure Lake CDP	3,861	-	-	3,439	93.7	0.0	0.0	0.0	6.3	25.0	17.4	39.3	32.9	40.5	1,202	97.6
Tredyffrin township (Chester)	29,340	29,396	0.2	29,461	75.5	3.0	16.4	2.2	2.9	24.0	18.1	43.6	10.9	79.3	11,598	95.4

1 May be of any race.

Table A. All Places — **Population and Housing**

STATE City, town, township, borough, or CDP (county if applicable)	2010 census total population	2019 estimated population	Percent change 2010–2019	ACS total population estimate 2015–2019	White alone, not Hispanic or Latino	Black alone, not Hispanic or Latino	Asian alone, not Hispanic or Latino	All other races or 2 or more races, not Hispanic or Latino	Hispanic or Latino[1]	Under 18 years old	Age 65 years and older	Median age	Percent High school diploma or less	Percent Bachelor's degree or more	Total	Percent with a computer
	1	2	3	4	5	6	7	8	9	10	11	12	13	14	15	16
PENNSYLVANIA—Con.																
Tremont borough & MCD (Schuylkill)	1,747	1,666	-4.6	1,732	98.4	0.6	0.0	0.4	0.6	20.3	24.6	44.1	75.3	7.9	669	82.7
Tremont township (Schuylkill)	280	266	-5.0	303	97.0	0.3	0.0	1.3	1.3	17.8	24.4	47.5	68.4	8.2	116	75.9
Tresckow CDP	880	-	-	1,155	91.9	0.0	0.3	1.5	6.4	23.0	23.7	44.1	61.8	7.4	462	81.8
Trevorton CDP	1,834	-	-	1,601	97.2	0.0	0.0	1.9	0.9	19.1	18.6	43.6	74.4	9.1	701	86.4
Trevose CDP	3,550	-	-	4,030	96.6	2.0	0.4	0.0	1.0	19.1	12.0	35.4	48.9	14.0	1,474	93.4
Trexlertown CDP	1,988	-	-	1,964	65.2	14.9	7.9	5.9	6.1	21.9	15.0	39.1	30.8	53.8	805	90.7
Triumph township (Warren)	316	292	-7.6	268	92.2	0.0	0.0	4.5	3.4	27.2	26.1	47.2	72.7	12.8	110	84.5
Trooper CDP	5,744	-	-	5,965	78.5	1.5	10.3	1.8	7.8	19.4	15.7	43.3	36.8	42.2	2,107	94.8
Troutville borough & MCD (Clearfield)	238	225	-5.5	227	100.0	0.0	0.0	0.0	0.0	30.4	17.2	32.5	62.9	7.9	76	63.2
Troxelville CDP	221	-	-	322	100.0	0.0	0.0	0.0	0.0	33.2	12.7	29.3	61.7	12.4	116	82.8
Troy borough & MCD (Bradford)	1,314	1,233	-6.2	1,477	95.6	0.3	1.1	0.2	2.8	17.5	18.1	44.2	52.5	23.2	584	84.4
Troy township (Bradford)	1,685	1,641	-2.6	1,546	99.3	0.0	0.2	0.2	0.3	23.0	24.5	48.8	47.9	21.1	640	90.0
Troy township (Crawford)	1,232	1,161	-5.8	1,282	98.2	1.0	0.0	0.2	0.6	23.6	17.8	43.0	65.9	14.3	503	83.3
Trucksville CDP	2,152	-	-	2,436	97.4	1.8	0.7	0.0	0.0	26.8	12.7	38.3	21.8	46.4	865	89.6
Trumbauersville borough & MCD (Bucks)	960	935	-2.6	961	92.4	1.5	0.6	4.3	1.2	23.0	12.8	42.5	44.3	26.3	385	94.0
Tullytown borough & MCD (Bucks)	2,229	2,181	-2.2	2,169	94.5	2.0	0.0	0.1	3.4	17.6	17.7	40.6	55.3	16.9	867	91.3
Tulpehocken township (Berks)	3,281	3,457	5.4	3,378	88.7	2.0	0.0	2.0	7.3	25.0	12.0	32.7	67.6	10.6	1,046	87.5
Tunkhannock township (Monroe)	6,800	6,795	-0.1	6,720	54.6	25.3	5.3	1.5	13.2	19.0	17.7	43.4	45.9	17.9	2,020	98.5
Tunkhannock borough & MCD (Wyoming)	1,828	1,697	-7.2	1,763	93.6	1.5	0.5	2.1	2.3	19.5	22.6	47.3	44.9	24.6	821	79.3
Tunkhannock township (Wyoming)	4,285	4,154	-3.1	4,245	98.2	0.8	0.3	0.5	0.1	20.0	22.1	46.3	52.1	21.7	1,707	95.5
Tunnelhill borough	361	331	-8.3	328	99.1	0.0	0.3	0.6	0.0	18.9	20.4	46.4	61.0	13.1	150	82.7
Tunnelhill borough (Blair)	118	111	-5.9	122	100.0	0.0	0.0	0.0	0.0	9.8	18.0	48.6	64.4	9.9	52	78.8
Tunnelhill borough (Cambria)	243	220	-9.5	206	98.5	0.0	0.5	1.0	0.0	24.3	21.8	42.0	58.7	15.3	98	84.7
Turbett township (Juniata)	981	990	0.9	798	98.2	0.0	0.0	0.6	1.1	22.3	20.1	43.2	65.3	15.7	295	83.1
Turbot township (Northumberland)	1,816	1,757	-3.2	1,570	92.7	1.3	0.3	0.4	5.2	18.6	19.7	49.4	58.5	20.6	688	87.1
Turbotville borough & MCD (Northumberland)	697	665	-4.6	598	98.7	0.0	0.5	0.0	0.8	15.4	27.9	52.2	56.6	18.8	285	77.5
Turtle Creek borough & MCD (Allegheny)	5,341	5,138	-3.8	5,197	74.7	16.0	0.5	7.2	1.6	25.9	19.7	39.9	46.5	16.2	2,347	85.6
Tuscarora township (Bradford)	1,131	1,100	-2.7	1,032	95.3	0.0	0.0	3.5	1.3	17.7	28.5	53.5	66.6	9.1	452	83.0
Tuscarora township (Juniata)	1,237	1,255	1.5	1,249	99.0	0.8	0.0	0.0	0.2	20.8	21.1	47.6	76.3	7.8	528	80.7
Tuscarora township (Perry)	1,191	1,203	1.0	1,403	97.0	0.0	0.0	0.0	3.0	27.9	16.6	38.6	60.3	18.2	501	82.2
Tuscarora CDP	980	-	-	952	97.7	0.4	1.6	0.0	0.3	18.2	28.5	46.8	58.9	11.6	415	76.4
Twilight borough & MCD (Washington)	235	225	-4.3	229	96.1	2.6	0.0	1.3	0.0	24.5	21.8	47.7	43.0	23.4	81	90.1
Tyler Run CDP	1,901	-	-	2,021	82.4	3.8	0.0	0.0	13.8	17.7	29.2	47.6	36.0	36.5	903	85.4
Tylersburg CDP	196	-	-	99	100.0	0.0	0.0	0.0	0.0	9.1	10.1	47.9	53.8	13.8	50	80.0
Tyrone township (Adams)	2,303	2,338	1.5	2,058	81.8	0.6	0.0	0.8	16.8	22.9	16.4	43.7	64.8	11.0	800	82.8
Tyrone borough & MCD (Blair)	5,461	5,139	-5.9	5,217	97.6	0.2	0.2	1.4	0.5	19.0	19.9	39.9	59.4	14.8	2,360	83.6
Tyrone township (Blair)	1,879	1,844	-1.9	2,173	96.2	0.8	0.5	1.5	0.9	28.4	14.1	38.6	45.7	32.1	783	83.1
Tyrone township (Perry)	2,103	2,119	0.8	1,935	92.8	3.7	1.5	1.1	0.9	27.0	22.9	39.0	67.2	13.2	724	71.5
Ulster township (Bradford)	1,322	1,268	-4.1	1,087	93.3	0.2	3.0	3.5	0.0	14.6	20.9	50.9	64.3	14.7	494	84.2
Ulysses borough & MCD (Potter)	621	579	-6.8	723	95.0	2.2	0.0	1.2	1.5	29.2	15.9	35.5	59.3	12.9	268	77.2
Ulysses township (Potter)	633	603	-4.7	621	95.0	2.3	0.0	0.0	2.7	20.6	23.7	47.8	57.6	20.0	215	86.5
Union township (Adams)	3,148	3,203	1.7	3,181	96.5	0.5	0.5	1.4	1.1	17.3	20.8	49.1	49.9	20.0	1,204	84.6
Union township (Berks)	3,514	3,755	6.9	3,664	89.1	0.4	0.0	1.3	9.3	17.0	19.8	48.7	49.3	29.3	1,440	95.8
Union township (Centre)	1,374	1,417	3.1	1,333	98.9	0.5	0.0	0.7	0.0	18.8	20.4	46.0	56.7	19.0	510	85.7
Union township (Clearfield)	892	877	-1.7	841	98.2	1.0	0.0	0.1	0.7	9.9	21.4	55.0	54.8	16.5	369	90.2
Union township (Crawford)	1,010	967	-4.3	967	97.5	0.6	0.0	1.0	0.8	17.2	19.5	44.2	56.6	16.5	397	90.7
Union township (Erie)	1,653	1,593	-3.6	1,636	97.1	0.1	0.2	0.0	2.7	17.7	20.4	44.3	62.1	16.9	628	87.9
Union township (Fulton)	702	739	5.3	703	98.0	0.4	0.0	0.6	1.0	17.6	23.6	48.2	58.9	18.4	292	81.5
Union township (Huntingdon)	1,033	1,012	-2.0	868	100.0	0.0	0.0	0.0	0.0	10.9	37.2	60.0	75.6	10.0	413	81.8
Union township (Jefferson)	854	816	-4.4	798	94.6	0.0	0.3	0.0	5.1	20.3	22.3	45.8	60.3	15.7	338	82.8
Union township (Lawrence)	5,187	4,852	-6.5	4,938	91.4	3.7	0.0	3.3	1.6	19.3	24.9	48.3	56.5	18.0	2,108	86.0
Union township (Lebanon)	3,094	3,167	2.4	3,138	93.8	0.5	0.5	0.8	4.4	21.7	16.1	43.6	61.8	15.6	1,157	83.5
Union township (Luzerne)	2,037	2,009	-1.4	2,104	96.3	0.5	0.4	2.8	0.0	19.5	19.9	46.6	52.1	19.7	826	88.5
Union township (Mifflin)	3,460	3,523	1.8	3,493	99.1	0.3	0.0	0.6	0.1	27.5	27.4	42.3	69.0	17.2	1,284	60.4
Union township (Schuylkill)	1,295	1,229	-5.1	1,283	94.6	0.3	0.0	0.2	4.8	15.7	20.8	48.9	55.4	21.8	531	84.2
Union township (Snyder)	1,519	1,538	1.3	1,656	97.6	0.0	0.2	0.7	1.6	26.3	12.3	34.7	70.6	12.0	527	75.7
Union township (Tioga)	1,007	993	-1.4	1,015	99.0	0.0	0.3	0.7	0.0	30.4	12.9	33.9	60.7	11.3	363	87.9
Union township (Union)	1,602	1,615	0.8	1,447	95.4	1.0	0.7	2.8	0.0	19.5	23.8	48.0	43.6	33.5	571	88.8
Union township (Washington)	5,767	5,678	-1.5	5,715	95.9	0.0	0.0	0.9	3.2	14.4	24.0	49.7	50.0	25.0	2,467	84.3
Union City borough & MCD (Erie)	3,327	3,118	-6.3	3,189	97.6	0.0	0.0	1.3	1.1	23.6	18.0	40.8	64.8	13.8	1,362	83.2
Union Dale borough & MCD (Susquehanna)	262	239	-8.8	194	99.0	0.0	0.0	1.0	0.0	2.6	22.7	56.7	50.3	20.0	97	89.7
Union Deposit CDP	407	-	-	411	96.4	3.6	0.0	0.0	0.0	37.7	7.1	32.3	41.9	17.1	131	88.5

1 May be of any race.

Table A. All Places — Population and Housing

STATE City, town, township, borough, or CDP (county if applicable)	Population				Race and Hispanic or Latino origin (percent)					Age (percent)			Educational attainment of persons age 25 and older		Occupied housing units	
	2010 census total population	2019 estimated population	Percent change 2010–2019	ACS total population estimate 2015–2019	White alone, not Hispanic or Latino	Black alone, not Hispanic or Latino	Asian alone, not Hispanic or Latino	All other races or 2 or more races, not Hispanic or Latino	Hispanic or Latino[1]	Under 18 years old	Age 65 years and older	Median age	Percent High school diploma or less	Percent Bachelor's degree or more	Total	Percent with a computer
	1	2	3	4	5	6	7	8	9	10	11	12	13	14	15	16
PENNSYLVANIA—Con.																
Uniontown city & MCD (Fayette)	10,357	9,719	-6.2	9,837	71.6	19.1	1.0	5.9	2.4	18.0	20.7	41.8	58.1	15.3	4,375	79.2
Unionville CDP	962	-	-	701	97.9	0.9	0.0	1.3	0.0	5.8	19.3	55.8	60.1	17.9	388	83.5
Unionville borough & MCD (Centre)	296	289	-2.4	242	100.0	0.0	0.0	0.0	0.0	19.0	19.4	49.0	65.0	19.8	91	91.2
Unity township (Westmoreland)	22,602	21,815	-3.5	22,047	94.6	1.0	1.5	2.2	0.6	18.2	21.7	46.8	36.3	35.0	8,568	90.6
Upland borough & MCD (Delaware)	3,316	3,326	0.3	3,322	47.3	36.4	1.9	7.8	6.6	27.2	14.3	32.5	63.8	14.6	1,319	86.8
Upper Allen township (Cumberland)	18,058	20,384	12.9	19,845	86.4	5.0	4.7	2.0	1.9	19.6	18.9	38.3	28.8	47.5	7,635	92.4
Upper Augusta township (Northumberland)	2,592	2,476	-4.5	2,235	98.2	0.4	0.0	0.8	0.6	13.6	20.2	50.2	53.0	20.2	966	91.8
Upper Bern township (Berks)	1,788	1,834	2.6	1,522	95.0	0.0	0.5	1.0	3.5	15.8	22.5	47.6	63.0	15.9	647	83.9
Upper Burrell township (Westmoreland)	2,328	2,213	-4.9	2,386	95.1	0.0	2.1	0.0	2.8	16.6	18.3	45.0	48.4	22.7	954	85.6
Upper Chichester township (Delaware)	16,705	16,959	1.5	16,929	79.6	13.0	3.7	1.8	1.9	17.8	19.8	43.7	47.2	28.2	6,825	86.3
Upper Darby township (Delaware)	82,792	82,930	0.2	82,887	44.2	34.0	13.2	3.2	5.5	23.9	11.6	35.4	41.6	31.9	31,011	92.4
Upper Dublin township (Montgomery)	25,596	26,553	3.7	26,327	81.6	4.2	9.3	2.0	2.9	22.5	18.8	44.6	15.7	65.7	9,497	96.1
Upper Exeter CDP	707	-	-	756	94.4	0.0	0.0	5.6	0.0	22.6	14.0	45.2	44.1	21.3	271	91.5
Upper Fairfield township (Lycoming)	1,823	1,772	-2.8	1,843	98.9	0.1	0.0	0.3	0.7	23.1	19.5	44.9	39.0	26.5	726	88.4
Upper Frankford township (Cumberland)	2,005	2,093	4.4	1,828	91.6	0.9	1.6	0.7	5.2	19.4	19.5	48.8	62.2	13.2	745	86.6
Upper Frederick township (Montgomery)	3,519	3,663	4.1	3,608	96.9	0.0	2.0	0.5	0.6	23.6	19.5	43.0	41.6	35.4	1,431	88.5
Upper Gwynedd township (Montgomery)	15,496	15,817	2.1	15,831	78.2	3.3	14.4	1.2	3.0	18.2	24.6	46.8	23.5	56.8	6,356	95.5
Upper Hanover township (Montgomery)	6,488	8,038	23.9	7,673	89.5	4.7	1.2	1.8	2.7	23.2	17.9	42.9	43.0	29.1	2,840	93.5
Upper Leacock township (Lancaster)	8,718	8,943	2.6	8,911	81.4	2.0	4.1	2.0	10.6	29.6	13.9	33.1	58.8	21.6	3,039	79.1
Upper Macungie township (Lehigh)	20,065	25,201	25.6	24,138	75.6	3.4	10.1	2.8	8.1	24.2	14.6	40.9	26.8	49.6	9,288	92.6
Upper Mahanoy township (Northumberland)	796	791	-0.6	697	99.3	0.0	0.0	0.7	0.0	23.4	19.5	45.7	74.4	10.6	289	75.4
Upper Mahantongo township (Schuylkill)	655	619	-5.5	643	97.5	0.8	0.0	0.0	1.7	23.5	17.9	42.5	57.1	14.7	246	83.3
Upper Makefield township (Bucks)	8,193	8,600	5.0	8,417	85.2	3.4	5.1	4.3	2.0	21.0	26.6	52.6	14.7	65.2	3,139	98.6
Upper Merion township (Montgomery)	28,388	33,027	16.3	30,260	69.6	6.1	18.8	2.5	3.0	18.6	18.5	39.4	21.8	60.2	13,049	95.0
Upper Mifflin township (Cumberland)	1,304	1,378	5.7	1,418	99.3	0.5	0.0	0.2	0.0	21.8	13.2	42.6	69.9	12.2	513	84.2
Upper Milford township (Lehigh)	7,294	7,950	9.0	7,718	94.4	0.1	1.0	0.8	3.6	18.3	21.2	49.8	37.2	38.4	3,093	93.8
Upper Moreland township (Montgomery)	24,013	24,031	0.1	24,114	80.7	5.6	4.8	3.9	5.1	20.9	17.1	39.5	32.1	41.6	9,607	92.6
Upper Mount Bethel township (Northampton)	6,704	6,889	2.8	6,853	88.7	0.9	1.8	0.3	8.4	16.0	19.1	48.7	50.0	24.0	2,620	92.1
Upper Nazareth township (Northampton)	6,233	7,064	13.3	6,858	88.6	0.4	1.3	0.3	9.3	24.2	22.3	43.8	41.6	33.2	2,078	94.9
Upper Oxford township (Chester)	2,491	2,538	1.9	2,519	81.5	6.6	0.0	1.2	10.8	26.4	17.1	44.2	46.8	30.7	826	88.6
Upper Paxton township (Dauphin)	4,189	4,276	2.1	4,259	96.3	0.8	0.7	0.7	1.4	20.8	24.5	49.8	56.8	18.5	1,780	80.3
Upper Pottsgrove township (Montgomery)	5,355	5,756	7.5	5,643	85.2	4.3	3.9	3.6	3.1	21.9	11.1	38.1	42.4	33.2	1,908	94.8
Upper Providence township (Delaware)	10,133	10,444	3.1	10,416	81.2	4.5	8.8	4.1	1.3	22.7	17.0	43.6	16.3	63.7	4,106	96.1
Upper Providence township (Montgomery)	21,231	24,355	14.7	23,920	79.4	4.4	11.9	1.6	2.6	24.5	12.5	41.4	22.0	57.7	8,318	97.3
Upper St. Clair township & CDP (Allegheny)	19,317	19,744	2.2	19,737	88.7	0.5	7.8	1.5	1.5	26.7	17.7	43.5	14.4	68.9	7,193	95.1
Upper Salford township (Montgomery)	3,282	3,364	2.5	3,353	98.5	0.4	0.0	0.7	0.3	30.7	15.3	42.5	40.1	41.1	1,119	92.7
Upper Saucon township (Lehigh)	14,797	17,305	16.9	16,736	86.1	1.0	3.0	3.9	6.0	20.6	17.0	42.4	29.0	49.6	5,968	94.9
Upper Southampton township (Bucks)	15,152	14,956	-1.3	15,018	95.1	0.3	2.7	1.0	0.9	16.1	24.8	49.6	36.4	34.8	6,092	90.7
Upper Tulpehocken township (Berks)	1,909	1,918	0.5	1,896	92.6	0.5	0.1	0.2	6.6	23.3	17.3	43.0	63.0	14.6	688	84.3
Upper Turkeyfoot township (Somerset)	1,131	1,047	-7.4	1,003	100.0	0.0	0.0	0.0	0.0	19.6	23.8	48.8	64.0	9.6	425	73.9
Upper Tyrone township (Fayette)	2,069	1,941	-6.2	1,954	94.8	0.4	1.7	3.1	0.0	19.5	17.8	44.7	65.7	16.8	808	84.5
Upper Uwchlan township (Chester)	11,234	11,823	5.2	11,560	73.6	0.6	20.3	1.3	4.1	30.4	8.6	39.6	11.6	71.1	3,629	99.3
Upper Yoder township (Cambria)	5,465	5,034	-7.9	5,143	93.3	3.0	2.0	0.2	1.6	13.2	26.8	53.1	46.2	32.7	2,316	87.4
Ursina borough & MCD (Somerset)	225	208	-7.6	256	100.0	0.0	0.0	0.0	0.0	21.5	23.0	44.7	68.5	11.6	95	85.3
Utica borough & MCD (Venango)	189	169	-10.6	168	87.5	0.0	0.0	10.7	1.8	10.1	19.0	52.0	61.9	18.0	80	85.0
Uwchlan township (Chester)	18,099	18,840	4.1	18,934	85.7	3.1	6.2	0.9	4.1	25.0	14.4	40.6	15.1	64.8	7,091	96.0
Valencia borough & MCD (Butler)	549	1,362	148.1	524	99.6	0.0	0.0	0.4	0.0	9.4	61.1	77.0	39.4	28.7	300	60.0

1 May be of any race.

Table A. All Places — **Population and Housing**

STATE City, town, township, borough, or CDP (county if applicable)	Population				Race and Hispanic or Latino origin (percent)					Age (percent)			Educational attainment of persons age 25 and older		Occupied housing units	
	2010 census total population	2019 estimated population	Percent change 2010–2019	ACS total population estimate 2015–2019	White alone, not Hispanic or Latino	Black alone, not Hispanic or Latino	Asian alone, not Hispanic or Latino	All other races or 2 or more races, not Hispanic or Latino	Hispanic or Latino[1]	Under 18 years old	Age 65 years and older	Median age	Percent High school diploma or less	Percent Bachelor's degree or more	Total	Percent with a computer
	1	2	3	4	5	6	7	8	9	10	11	12	13	14	15	16
PENNSYLVANIA—Con.																
Valley township (Armstrong)	658	629	-4.4	683	99.0	0.0	0.0	0.0	1.0	16.5	25.9	53.1	55.7	17.3	295	83.7
Valley township (Chester)	6,796	7,772	14.4	7,718	60.9	21.1	1.9	8.1	8.0	23.4	17.2	40.0	47.6	28.1	2,896	88.0
Valley township (Montour)	2,158	2,149	-0.4	2,114	98.2	0.0	0.9	0.7	0.3	19.3	19.7	48.2	38.8	39.5	836	91.1
Valley Green CDP	3,429	-	-	3,785	83.7	1.9	1.5	8.7	4.3	25.2	11.9	36.3	40.2	26.7	1,479	93.3
Valley-Hi borough & MCD (Fulton)	15	15	0.0	2	100.0	0.0	0.0	0.0	0.0	0.0	100.0	0.0	0.0	0.0	1	100.0
Valley View CDP	1,683	-	-	1,572	98.0	0.0	0.0	2.0	0.0	21.1	23.5	39.8	57.3	16.3	675	82.2
Valley View CDP	2,817	-	-	2,602	87.7	1.4	5.0	0.8	5.0	23.5	18.2	39.3	35.0	40.3	1,156	83.9
Vanderbilt borough & MCD (Fayette)	476	450	-5.5	349	91.1	0.3	0.6	1.7	6.3	20.6	17.5	38.0	58.5	8.5	158	68.4
Vandergrift borough & MCD (Westmoreland)	5,201	4,875	-6.3	4,950	90.5	4.1	0.0	4.0	1.5	21.8	18.7	39.8	54.3	16.6	2,239	79.4
Vandling borough & MCD (Lackawanna)	752	705	-6.3	720	97.1	0.1	0.0	1.9	0.8	22.8	15.3	43.7	47.9	25.6	285	86.0
Vanport township (Beaver)	1,323	1,249	-5.6	1,309	97.4	0.6	0.0	1.5	0.5	12.5	39.3	57.3	48.0	18.6	717	74.6
Van Voorhis CDP	166	-	-	179	100.0	0.0	0.0	0.0	0.0	5.0	44.1	64.7	59.4	18.2	86	100.0
Venango township (Butler)	870	827	-4.9	917	96.8	0.5	0.0	1.9	0.8	21.4	21.5	43.4	64.2	12.1	365	80.5
Venango borough & MCD (Crawford)	239	249	4.2	267	95.9	0.0	0.0	2.2	1.9	23.2	19.9	33.9	64.9	17.8	106	82.1
Venango township (Crawford)	997	967	-3.0	1,016	97.3	1.4	0.0	0.2	1.1	25.0	16.1	39.5	45.5	36.0	384	92.4
Venango township (Erie)	2,296	2,245	-2.2	2,258	99.2	0.0	0.3	0.5	0.0	23.3	17.8	43.1	54.0	21.4	835	88.4
Vernon township (Crawford)	5,630	5,368	-4.7	5,423	94.5	0.3	2.7	1.9	0.7	17.4	28.0	49.4	56.7	25.4	2,457	86.9
Verona borough & MCD (Allegheny)	2,507	2,411	-3.8	2,767	82.3	12.8	0.0	4.1	0.9	18.3	20.1	43.8	45.0	24.2	1,253	82.2
Versailles borough & MCD (Allegheny)	1,519	1,461	-3.8	1,621	92.0	4.9	0.0	1.3	1.8	14.7	22.3	48.6	57.9	10.2	802	77.3
Vicksburg CDP	261	-	-	712	100.0	0.0	0.0	0.0	0.0	29.6	12.4	37.6	74.8	16.9	169	100.0
Victory township (Venango)	408	374	-8.3	413	94.7	0.0	0.5	4.4	0.5	24.0	19.1	45.1	53.7	17.7	159	88.7
Village Green-Green Ridge CDP	7,822	-	-	7,980	92.7	4.0	1.6	0.9	0.8	20.9	18.0	43.4	46.9	27.4	3,077	87.4
Village Shires CDP	3,949	-	-	3,931	93.0	0.8	2.9	0.2	3.0	18.3	28.3	48.5	24.7	53.7	1,661	87.4
Vinco CDP	1,305	-	-	1,098	99.0	0.8	0.0	0.0	0.2	13.0	31.5	55.1	61.1	20.6	477	87.2
Vintondale borough & MCD (Cambria)	414	375	-9.4	422	100.0	0.0	0.0	0.0	0.0	24.2	21.3	41.2	72.8	8.1	167	79.6
Virginville CDP	309	-	-	371	100.0	0.0	0.0	0.0	0.0	11.3	12.7	33.0	50.5	10.1	162	74.1
Volant borough & MCD (Lawrence)	165	151	-8.5	100	100.0	0.0	0.0	0.0	0.0	17.0	25.0	48.0	38.9	30.6	50	86.0
Vowinckel CDP	139	-	-	84	100.0	0.0	0.0	0.0	0.0	0.0	41.7	62.5	63.1	23.8	54	64.8
Wagner CDP	128	-	-	129	100.0	0.0	0.0	0.0	0.0	24.0	19.4	39.0	46.1	14.6	52	75.0
Wakefield CDP	609	-	-	571	96.5	0.0	0.0	0.0	3.5	37.7	18.2	36.0	60.4	16.2	169	78.1
Walker township (Centre)	4,443	4,756	7.0	4,700	99.5	0.0	0.2	0.0	0.3	19.1	18.0	44.4	52.7	25.8	1,757	92.7
Walker township (Huntingdon)	1,955	1,930	-1.3	2,385	99.5	0.0	0.0	0.5	0.0	24.9	22.3	45.1	49.0	29.0	884	93.4
Walker township (Juniata)	2,743	2,779	1.3	2,757	94.5	0.0	0.3	0.0	5.3	25.4	12.9	38.0	71.7	10.5	924	74.0
Walker township (Schuylkill)	1,054	1,006	-4.6	1,083	97.6	2.2	0.0	0.0	0.2	25.9	18.0	41.7	47.1	23.8	403	91.8
Wall borough & MCD (Allegheny)	580	557	-4.0	564	92.2	5.3	0.5	1.4	0.5	19.1	18.4	40.9	67.5	5.6	224	79.9
Wallace township (Chester)	3,458	3,675	6.3	3,676	90.3	3.8	3.7	1.1	1.2	28.2	14.0	44.1	25.3	53.9	1,167	99.1
Wallaceton borough & MCD (Clearfield)	313	304	-2.9	271	100.0	0.0	0.0	0.0	0.0	21.4	16.2	48.1	77.9	4.7	114	76.3
Wallenpaupack Lake Estates CDP	1,279	-	-	1,122	98.4	0.0	0.0	0.0	1.6	9.5	43.4	63.9	57.4	19.8	526	90.9
Waller CDP	48	-	-	39	87.2	0.0	12.8	0.0	0.0	23.1	28.2	47.2	46.7	30.0	18	77.8
Walnutport borough & MCD (Northampton)	2,071	2,087	0.8	2,038	94.5	0.0	0.3	0.5	4.7	18.3	17.6	43.6	62.7	14.1	790	90.5
Walnuttown CDP	484	-	-	618	79.6	2.8	0.0	17.6	0.0	19.6	15.7	49.3	55.8	27.7	231	90.0
Wampum borough & MCD (Lawrence)	708	658	-7.1	606	93.1	3.3	0.0	2.5	1.2	16.3	25.7	47.8	57.2	9.9	286	78.7
Wanamie CDP	612	-	-	626	89.9	5.0	5.1	0.0	0.0	20.8	19.2	45.1	41.8	14.3	249	87.6
Ward township (Tioga)	166	174	4.8	162	98.1	0.6	0.0	1.2	0.0	12.3	28.4	52.0	68.7	9.2	69	85.5
Warminster township (Bucks)	32,789	32,348	-1.3	32,489	83.6	3.4	3.9	1.7	7.4	17.1	25.4	46.3	39.3	32.5	13,314	88.6
Warminster Heights CDP	4,124	-	-	3,805	53.7	9.5	6.1	4.8	26.0	20.9	13.4	36.0	55.8	18.3	1,621	75.0
Warren township (Bradford)	959	913	-4.8	1,041	92.9	0.0	0.4	3.7	3.1	23.9	20.3	44.2	52.7	15.8	384	90.4
Warren township (Franklin)	367	368	0.3	353	99.2	0.0	0.3	0.6	0.0	13.0	20.1	48.6	53.2	22.3	144	86.1
Warren city & MCD (Warren)	9,710	9,049	-6.8	9,191	95.9	0.6	1.0	0.8	1.7	18.1	19.8	44.2	47.3	25.1	4,372	88.7
Warrington township (Bucks)	23,414	24,560	4.9	24,256	82.2	2.2	9.0	0.5	6.1	23.6	15.9	43.6	23.7	52.8	8,669	95.2
Warrington township (York)	4,518	4,650	2.9	4,620	98.6	0.2	0.0	0.7	0.5	16.6	22.9	51.0	58.0	22.9	2,039	89.6
Warrior Run borough & MCD (Luzerne)	589	581	-1.4	661	90.5	2.7	0.5	0.0	6.4	26.3	16.2	36.5	59.6	8.3	274	93.1
Warriors Mark township (Huntingdon)	1,796	1,803	0.4	2,058	96.5	0.8	0.0	1.2	1.5	19.7	19.9	44.2	44.5	29.0	783	87.7
Warsaw township (Jefferson)	1,431	1,368	-4.4	1,360	98.9	0.0	0.0	0.7	0.4	29.7	12.5	35.3	64.9	10.6	499	83.4
Warwick township (Bucks)	14,455	14,699	1.7	14,612	94.0	0.5	3.7	0.6	1.2	22.0	16.7	46.0	24.0	53.7	5,400	97.7
Warwick township (Chester)	2,506	2,546	1.6	2,545	93.9	0.0	0.8	5.0	0.3	19.6	20.4	48.3	36.4	43.8	1,045	96.4
Warwick township (Lancaster)	17,983	19,536	8.6	19,022	90.7	0.9	1.3	1.9	5.2	23.7	18.9	42.3	41.7	35.2	7,275	90.3
Washington township (Armstrong)	923	919	-0.4	749	99.5	0.0	0.0	0.5	0.0	15.6	23.0	47.2	63.9	10.4	323	88.2

1 May be of any race.

Table A. All Places — Population and Housing

STATE City, town, township, borough, or CDP (county if applicable)	2010 census total population	2019 estimated population	Percent change 2010–2019	ACS total population estimate 2015–2019	White alone, not Hispanic or Latino	Black alone, not Hispanic or Latino	Asian alone, not Hispanic or Latino	All other races or 2 or more races, not Hispanic or Latino	Hispanic or Latino[1]	Under 18 years old	Age 65 years and older	Median age	Percent High school diploma or less	Percent Bachelor's degree or more	Total	Percent with a computer
	1	2	3	4	5	6	7	8	9	10	11	12	13	14	15	16
PENNSYLVANIA—Con.																
Washington township (Berks)	3,775	4,317	14.4	4,132	99.4	0.6	0.0	0.0	0.0	13.2	22.0	52.0	49.0	19.5	1,773	91.7
Washington township (Butler)	1,298	1,232	-5.1	1,346	97.2	0.2	0.2	1.1	1.3	18.6	15.3	45.8	56.7	14.5	542	88.0
Washington township (Cambria)	881	848	-3.7	882	99.3	0.0	0.0	0.2	0.5	21.5	24.9	48.1	61.1	14.2	361	80.3
Washington township (Clarion)	1,895	1,788	-5.6	2,110	98.8	0.0	0.0	1.2	0.0	30.9	15.9	34.1	68.3	12.3	696	75.9
Washington township (Dauphin)	2,273	2,281	0.4	2,196	99.0	0.2	0.0	0.0	0.7	21.7	19.6	44.1	53.3	16.7	868	84.1
Washington township (Erie)	4,433	4,420	-0.3	4,482	95.7	0.8	0.0	1.3	2.2	20.0	15.4	45.7	26.8	49.4	1,863	92.4
Washington township (Fayette)	3,895	3,605	-7.4	3,686	97.2	1.4	0.0	0.9	0.5	14.3	25.7	53.8	56.3	18.9	1,610	78.4
Washington township (Franklin)	14,010	14,770	5.4	14,627	94.1	2.1	0.1	0.7	2.9	21.3	19.8	44.7	47.6	24.3	5,978	90.2
Washington township (Greene)	1,095	1,000	-8.7	951	97.5	0.0	0.0	1.6	0.9	14.5	23.3	52.7	54.8	21.4	413	86.0
Washington township (Indiana)	1,808	1,686	-6.7	1,623	98.9	0.0	0.0	1.0	0.1	18.1	22.9	49.5	67.8	13.1	653	78.6
Washington township (Jefferson)	1,926	1,845	-4.2	1,915	98.5	0.3	0.4	0.3	0.5	20.0	23.3	49.8	59.6	14.6	806	85.7
Washington township (Lawrence)	796	768	-3.5	576	97.2	0.0	0.3	2.3	0.2	17.0	24.8	54.2	53.9	20.5	250	94.0
Washington township (Lehigh)	6,600	6,798	3.0	6,748	97.8	0.1	0.0	1.5	0.6	22.2	16.3	44.4	54.2	24.7	2,642	87.7
Washington township (Lycoming)	1,619	1,653	2.1	1,908	96.4	0.8	1.0	1.7	0.0	28.1	14.8	36.9	60.1	16.6	634	80.0
Washington township (Northampton)	5,163	5,279	2.2	5,232	87.5	0.2	4.1	1.4	6.7	17.7	20.6	45.5	49.6	24.5	1,832	89.6
Washington township (Northumberland)	746	734	-1.6	685	99.1	0.0	0.0	0.9	0.0	22.2	21.0	43.4	68.3	16.6	264	84.8
Washington township (Schuylkill)	3,032	2,868	-5.4	2,902	95.5	0.7	0.9	0.8	2.1	24.9	18.1	44.0	60.8	17.7	1,090	84.5
Washington township (Snyder)	1,653	1,687	2.1	1,599	99.7	0.3	0.0	0.0	0.0	25.2	14.1	40.6	65.6	16.7	553	83.4
Washington city & MCD (Washington)	14,019	13,433	-4.2	13,532	78.4	12.5	1.2	4.7	3.1	16.1	14.8	36.5	54.8	21.0	5,682	84.0
Washington township (Westmoreland)	7,376	7,057	-4.3	7,109	96.2	0.4	0.0	0.8	2.6	18.3	25.3	52.6	43.0	26.2	2,978	88.3
Washington township (Wyoming)	1,420	1,306	-8.0	1,574	94.0	1.1	0.0	1.5	3.5	21.0	17.0	41.8	57.8	16.1	550	92.2
Washington township (York)	2,690	2,710	0.7	2,697	98.6	0.0	0.5	0.3	0.5	16.0	20.3	49.4	62.7	15.9	971	85.1
Washington Boro CDP	729	-	-	999	100.0	0.0	0.0	0.0	0.0	29.0	13.2	37.6	61.8	20.8	322	95.7
Washingtonville borough & MCD (Montour)	273	275	0.7	149	99.3	0.0	0.0	0.7	0.0	20.8	16.1	35.8	82.0	8.1	63	71.4
Waterford borough & MCD (Erie)	1,519	1,495	-1.6	1,316	92.8	0.2	0.2	0.9	5.9	19.5	24.7	45.5	58.8	19.1	588	82.8
Waterford township (Erie)	3,919	4,058	3.5	3,998	95.9	0.0	0.3	2.8	1.0	23.3	13.0	41.2	62.7	16.6	1,547	80.0
Watson township (Lycoming)	540	524	-3.0	554	99.5	0.0	0.2	0.0	0.4	19.9	25.3	51.5	34.9	34.0	240	89.2
Watson township (Warren)	274	256	-6.6	215	99.1	0.0	0.0	0.9	0.0	10.7	26.0	57.8	55.9	14.0	103	87.4
Watsontown borough & MCD (Northumberland)	2,355	2,252	-4.4	2,333	92.3	0.3	0.4	0.9	6.1	19.2	24.4	43.1	60.3	16.1	1,028	84.6
Watts township (Perry)	1,274	1,289	1.2	1,313	97.3	0.0	0.0	1.6	1.1	21.8	16.2	45.6	58.9	15.8	511	87.3
Wattsburg borough & MCD (Erie)	405	381	-5.9	501	93.0	0.0	0.8	4.8	1.4	27.9	14.0	38.3	61.1	12.8	189	83.6
Waverly CDP	604	-	-	727	100.0	0.0	0.0	0.0	0.0	27.5	13.3	42.7	6.1	80.9	238	95.4
Waverly township (Lackawanna)	1,744	1,683	-3.5	1,830	94.8	0.1	2.3	2.3	0.4	24.3	19.3	43.6	10.5	70.3	673	93.3
Waymart borough & MCD (Wayne)	1,342	1,269	-5.4	1,304	93.7	0.2	0.0	3.5	2.5	22.8	27.7	43.6	54.3	11.6	427	82.7
Wayne township (Armstrong)	1,192	1,112	-6.7	1,378	98.5	0.0	0.0	0.9	0.5	30.4	17.9	31.3	63.9	19.4	498	59.0
Wayne township (Clinton)	1,668	1,691	1.4	1,261	86.0	8.4	0.0	3.3	2.4	10.8	22.8	46.7	62.3	15.8	453	90.7
Wayne township (Crawford)	1,535	1,462	-4.8	1,404	97.5	0.4	0.0	1.6	0.4	23.7	17.2	40.8	57.2	23.1	560	88.8
Wayne township (Dauphin)	1,325	1,371	3.5	1,336	96.2	0.0	1.0	1.5	1.3	18.8	15.4	46.9	50.1	21.8	511	90.8
Wayne township (Erie)	1,657	1,564	-5.6	1,944	98.7	0.0	0.6	0.7	0.0	23.8	19.6	43.8	51.9	21.1	700	88.6
Wayne township (Greene)	1,197	1,184	-1.1	1,125	96.4	0.0	0.4	2.8	0.4	17.1	23.4	47.1	62.8	12.1	509	87.6
Wayne township (Lawrence)	2,695	2,537	-5.9	2,568	95.4	0.5	2.0	1.8	0.2	15.8	26.2	52.7	48.9	21.9	1,184	86.6
Wayne township (Mifflin)	2,547	2,511	-1.4	2,508	97.8	0.1	0.2	1.6	0.2	19.9	23.1	50.6	78.1	8.2	1,045	80.1
Wayne township (Schuylkill)	5,111	5,030	-1.6	5,048	97.3	0.0	0.0	1.3	1.4	19.4	20.2	49.4	44.2	27.0	2,114	91.9
Wayne Heights CDP	2,545	-	-	2,616	95.1	4.7	0.3	0.0	0.0	23.9	16.8	37.8	46.0	23.8	1,056	93.6
Waynesboro borough & MCD (Franklin)	10,563	10,886	3.1	10,860	88.7	5.8	0.3	1.8	3.4	24.7	17.6	36.6	56.0	15.8	4,750	85.4
Waynesburg borough & MCD (Greene)	4,202	3,965	-5.6	4,021	91.1	1.9	1.8	3.7	1.5	16.6	13.6	28.9	50.1	26.9	1,394	86.9
Weatherly borough & MCD (Carbon)	2,525	2,458	-2.7	2,639	94.5	1.3	0.0	1.4	2.8	20.0	24.5	44.7	54.7	18.9	985	85.7
Webster CDP	255	-	-	154	100.0	0.0	0.0	0.0	0.0	22.7	13.0	37.3	36.8	31.6	53	81.1
Weedville CDP	542	-	-	465	95.3	0.0	4.7	0.0	0.0	14.4	29.5	57.2	61.1	13.4	233	74.7
Weigelstown CDP	12,875	-	-	12,812	88.0	3.7	0.7	2.3	5.3	20.2	18.7	39.7	52.3	16.9	5,186	88.0
Weisenberg township (Lehigh)	4,934	5,276	6.9	5,182	92.2	0.0	0.2	1.1	6.5	19.5	15.5	45.8	38.1	31.5	1,889	91.3
Weissport borough & MCD (Carbon)	412	397	-3.6	442	79.0	5.7	0.2	2.3	12.9	27.8	13.3	37.8	73.2	2.8	174	82.8
Weissport East CDP	1,624	-	-	1,337	90.1	0.0	2.1	2.7	5.1	13.6	25.0	44.7	63.2	15.6	585	82.6

1 May be of any race.

STATE City, town, township, borough, or CDP (county if applicable)	Population				Race and Hispanic or Latino origin (percent)					Age (percent)			Educational attainment of persons age 25 and older		Occupied housing units	
	2010 census total population	2019 estimated population	Percent change 2010–2019	ACS total population estimate 2015–2019	White alone, not Hispanic or Latino	Black alone, not Hispanic or Latino	Asian alone, not Hispanic or Latino	All other races or 2 or more races, not Hispanic or Latino	Hispanic or Latino[1]	Under 18 years old	Age 65 years and older	Median age	Percent High school diploma or less	Percent Bachelor's degree or more	Total	Percent with a computer
	1	2	3	4	5	6	7	8	9	10	11	12	13	14	15	16

PENNSYLVANIA—Con.

STATE City, town, township, borough, or CDP (county if applicable)	1	2	3	4	5	6	7	8	9	10	11	12	13	14	15	16
Wellersburg borough & MCD (Somerset)	181	171	-5.5	184	92.4	0.0	0.0	1.1	6.5	21.7	20.1	40.0	56.5	16.8	69	82.6
Wells township (Bradford)	813	802	-1.4	1,175	98.7	0.8	0.0	0.5	0.0	26.1	19.7	44.5	48.8	23.6	456	93.9
Wells township (Fulton)	477	454	-4.8	451	99.1	0.0	0.0	0.0	0.0	13.7	28.8	51.8	61.1	9.5	205	79.5
Wellsboro borough & MCD (Tioga)	3,262	3,227	-1.1	3,256	95.2	2.1	0.7	1.3	0.7	17.8	29.5	49.3	43.8	30.3	1,419	82.5
Wellsville borough & MCD (York)	252	254	0.8	211	95.3	0.0	0.0	4.3	0.5	18.5	13.7	43.1	51.2	19.5	90	88.9
Wernersville borough & MCD (Berks)	2,749	2,799	1.8	2,793	85.2	3.7	2.8	2.1	6.2	16.8	29.3	47.7	46.2	28.0	1,279	79.7
Wescosville CDP	5,872	-	-	6,694	81.4	4.0	4.9	2.8	6.9	24.1	19.9	43.9	24.4	50.2	2,569	94.8
Wesleyville borough & MCD (Erie)	3,341	3,117	-6.7	3,185	88.5	0.8	2.3	3.7	4.8	23.9	13.0	36.3	51.0	19.9	1,379	88.5
West township (Huntingdon)	568	551	-3.0	543	83.2	0.0	0.0	0.0	16.8	24.7	19.0	44.6	50.9	30.4	220	83.6
West Abington township (Lackawanna)	250	245	-2.0	322	100.0	0.0	0.0	0.0	0.0	18.6	24.8	47.1	38.1	34.5	135	88.9
West Alexander CDP	604	-	-	479	100.0	0.0	0.0	0.0	0.0	21.1	16.5	41.0	45.5	18.6	206	85.4
West Beaver township (Snyder)	1,100	1,086	-1.3	1,027	98.8	0.0	0.0	1.2	0.0	31.5	20.4	37.4	78.7	7.9	343	65.3
West Bethlehem township (Washington)	1,458	1,412	-3.2	1,366	98.5	0.0	0.0	0.7	0.8	20.1	23.6	47.8	55.1	16.0	547	83.2
West Bradford township (Chester)	12,229	13,403	9.6	13,015	86.8	3.1	3.5	2.5	4.0	26.5	13.5	42.9	20.8	56.7	4,523	97.5
West Branch township (Potter)	397	380	-4.3	464	97.4	0.0	0.9	1.3	0.4	17.2	29.3	53.3	56.2	15.4	175	81.1
West Brandywine township (Chester)	7,400	7,467	0.9	7,470	90.9	3.4	0.3	1.4	3.9	16.4	22.8	51.5	36.4	41.2	2,818	88.4
West Brownsville borough & MCD (Washington)	992	958	-3.4	917	96.5	0.3	0.0	0.8	2.4	17.0	20.5	45.1	52.9	28.1	419	82.6
West Brunswick township (Schuylkill)	3,333	3,195	-4.1	3,218	90.4	0.3	3.5	2.5	3.4	16.4	25.1	55.6	32.3	33.0	1,497	93.1
West Buffalo township (Union)	3,027	3,018	-0.3	3,040	94.3	0.0	1.8	0.7	3.2	25.2	17.5	43.0	59.7	16.6	1,143	73.8
West Burlington township (Bradford)	699	670	-4.1	834	95.6	2.4	0.5	1.2	0.4	11.3	31.9	48.8	69.9	14.5	164	84.8
West Caln township (Chester)	9,010	9,110	1.1	9,103	87.7	5.4	1.9	2.9	2.1	16.7	20.5	46.7	48.7	29.8	3,544	88.0
West Cameron township (Northumberland)	541	527	-2.6	479	94.2	0.6	0.4	0.0	4.8	20.5	17.5	41.4	64.0	11.2	191	87.4
West Carroll township (Cambria)	1,295	1,196	-7.6	1,290	96.2	0.2	2.0	0.5	1.1	21.0	23.0	44.5	64.1	12.4	489	84.9
West Chester borough & MCD (Chester)	18,459	20,029	8.5	20,034	76.2	7.7	2.4	2.4	11.3	10.2	8.7	24.9	24.0	57.7	7,251	93.1
West Chillisquaque township (Northumberland)	2,759	2,668	-3.3	2,683	95.0	1.4	0.1	0.0	3.5	15.1	23.3	48.8	70.7	14.6	1,206	85.7
West Cocalico township (Lancaster)	7,292	7,501	2.9	7,448	94.5	0.0	0.0	3.7	1.8	26.9	11.9	36.1	60.1	15.3	2,416	89.6
West Conshohocken borough & MCD (Montgomery)	1,320	1,432	8.5	1,384	85.1	3.4	5.8	2.0	3.7	13.1	12.8	34.1	19.7	68.5	645	94.4
West Cornwall township (Lebanon)	1,956	2,068	5.7	1,961	92.9	0.5	0.2	1.5	4.9	16.0	32.9	53.9	50.7	29.1	838	85.2
West Decatur CDP	533	-	-	435	94.7	2.8	0.9	1.6	0.0	19.1	25.3	46.1	72.4	8.0	187	74.3
West Deer township (Allegheny)	11,775	11,986	1.8	11,937	97.7	0.5	0.3	0.7	0.7	17.7	23.5	49.8	38.1	31.4	5,257	89.9
West Donegal township (Lancaster)	8,254	9,063	9.8	8,814	96.4	1.5	0.2	0.0	1.9	18.6	35.1	53.9	48.6	28.2	3,320	84.7
West Earl township (Lancaster)	7,866	8,399	6.8	8,311	90.6	1.5	1.4	0.0	6.5	26.4	17.9	35.7	57.0	21.5	2,783	77.3
West Easton borough & MCD (Northampton)	1,256	1,250	-0.5	1,329	77.0	1.4	0.9	3.6	17.1	25.2	14.1	37.3	60.9	8.2	474	91.4
West Elizabeth borough & MCD (Allegheny)	516	493	-4.5	524	92.7	0.6	0.0	0.0	6.7	35.5	8.6	30.7	49.2	7.5	172	88.4
West Fairview CDP	1,282	-	-	1,181	92.8	2.6	2.6	0.0	1.9	18.1	11.3	39.3	56.8	11.4	533	94.7
Westfall township (Pike)	2,310	2,268	-1.8	2,513	94.7	1.1	2.4	0.1	1.7	14.0	30.3	54.5	49.8	22.8	1,043	85.4
West Fallowfield township (Chester)	2,567	2,590	0.9	2,590	93.4	0.0	0.0	0.0	6.6	25.0	14.6	37.5	58.3	25.8	869	80.2
West Fallowfield township (Crawford)	605	574	-5.1	637	98.4	0.0	0.0	0.6	0.9	21.5	20.9	45.2	61.5	15.6	243	84.0
West Falls CDP	382	-	-	373	95.7	0.3	0.0	0.0	4.0	22.5	25.2	46.9	43.0	29.1	171	84.2
Westfield borough & MCD (Tioga)	1,075	1,036	-3.6	1,333	96.7	0.0	0.0	1.0	2.3	23.1	16.1	39.6	66.3	10.5	472	82.4
Westfield township (Tioga)	1,033	987	-4.5	772	97.0	0.0	0.8	1.3	0.9	11.4	33.8	55.7	67.6	11.7	365	82.2
West Finley township (Washington)	875	863	-1.4	815	100.0	0.0	0.0	0.0	0.0	18.8	23.6	46.4	57.8	21.2	305	87.2
West Franklin township (Armstrong)	1,853	1,726	-6.9	1,714	99.4	0.1	0.4	0.0	0.2	23.9	22.1	46.6	59.8	18.4	714	86.8
West Goshen township (Chester)	21,855	22,973	5.1	23,001	83.8	3.0	7.6	2.5	3.1	20.7	15.0	39.5	24.0	58.8	8,870	93.4
West Grove borough & MCD (Chester)	2,857	2,839	-0.6	2,845	47.9	6.4	0.6	1.2	43.9	27.0	8.6	31.4	57.6	19.3	907	86.7
West Hamburg CDP	1,979	-	-	2,108	98.6	0.5	0.6	0.0	0.2	16.9	22.7	50.0	63.5	12.1	819	87.2
West Hanover township (Dauphin)	9,357	10,722	14.6	10,352	90.6	5.4	0.6	1.8	1.7	21.2	18.9	43.2	40.3	39.3	3,971	92.2
West Hazleton borough & MCD (Luzerne)	4,479	4,355	-2.8	4,376	37.2	0.9	0.0	0.1	61.7	23.5	12.4	30.3	66.2	11.0	1,555	80.5
West Hemlock township (Montour)	503	505	0.4	530	98.3	0.0	0.2	0.6	0.9	24.0	14.2	43.2	45.9	28.0	179	86.0
West Hempfield township (Lancaster)	16,158	16,744	3.6	16,546	84.9	1.8	1.3	2.3	9.7	24.7	16.0	40.5	47.3	28.5	6,089	90.1

1 May be of any race.

Table A. All Places — **Population and Housing**

STATE City, town, township, borough, or CDP (county if applicable)	2010 census total population	2019 estimated population	Percent change 2010–2019	ACS total population estimate 2015–2019	White alone, not Hispanic or Latino	Black alone, not Hispanic or Latino	Asian alone, not Hispanic or Latino	All other races or 2 or more races, not Hispanic or Latino	Hispanic or Latino[1]	Under 18 years old	Age 65 years and older	Median age	Percent High school diploma or less	Percent Bachelor's degree or more	Total	Percent with a computer
	1	2	3	4	5	6	7	8	9	10	11	12	13	14	15	16
PENNSYLVANIA—Con.																
West Hills CDP	1,263	-	-	1,085	94.8	0.1	5.1	0.0	0.0	20.1	23.6	48.2	44.7	31.3	526	89.7
West Homestead borough & MCD (Allegheny)	1,927	1,864	-3.3	1,782	79.0	13.2	0.0	6.3	1.4	19.3	22.6	46.0	37.2	32.5	846	87.5
West Keating township (Clinton)	29	29	0.0	13	84.6	0.0	0.0	0.0	15.4	0.0	76.9	71.5	61.5	7.7	10	40.0
West Kittanning borough & MCD (Armstrong)	1,175	1,090	-7.2	1,191	98.0	0.0	0.3	0.3	1.4	18.9	26.2	46.2	47.8	25.0	608	84.4
West Lampeter township (Lancaster)	15,189	15,950	5.0	15,888	93.2	0.5	1.3	0.3	4.7	19.2	30.5	49.8	40.4	37.9	6,412	88.1
Westland CDP	167	-	-	46	100.0	0.0	0.0	0.0	0.0	0.0	26.1	51.9	80.4	10.9	21	57.1
West Lawn CDP	1,715	-	-	1,567	65.2	10.1	0.4	5.0	19.2	22.6	10.9	34.0	41.8	30.3	600	90.2
West Lebanon township (Lebanon)	781	835	6.9	1,114	65.5	5.0	2.2	3.5	23.8	17.2	13.3	42.1	63.4	14.3	408	93.9
West Leechburg borough & MCD (Westmoreland)	1,295	1,221	-5.7	1,511	96.0	2.4	0.0	1.1	0.6	17.7	20.6	42.3	43.8	21.4	652	85.0
West Liberty borough & MCD (Butler)	343	330	-3.8	347	99.1	0.0	0.3	0.6	0.0	19.3	20.2	45.6	48.8	19.5	143	84.6
West Mahanoy township (Schuylkill)	2,872	2,710	-5.6	2,731	85.2	0.0	3.5	0.0	11.3	20.4	22.3	46.1	51.4	18.4	1,135	80.3
West Mahoning township (Indiana)	1,360	1,265	-7.0	1,499	99.7	0.0	0.0	0.1	0.2	51.4	6.1	17.3	83.9	6.9	316	32.0
West Manchester township (York)	18,866	18,814	-0.3	18,812	86.8	3.9	1.4	1.7	6.1	18.7	22.5	45.7	52.4	23.1	7,986	81.8
West Manheim township (York)	7,734	8,659	12.0	8,425	93.4	3.1	0.7	1.4	1.4	25.1	16.6	41.0	41.8	31.5	3,059	93.5
West Marlborough township (Chester)	807	815	1.0	852	90.8	2.5	0.2	1.1	5.4	12.2	27.7	51.6	29.9	47.6	379	92.3
West Mayfield borough & MCD (Beaver)	1,239	1,164	-6.1	1,081	94.9	1.3	0.0	0.8	3.0	21.2	18.0	38.1	55.1	12.5	454	92.3
West Mead township (Crawford)	5,248	5,018	-4.4	5,069	94.0	2.1	0.3	1.5	2.1	23.9	21.8	41.7	49.7	35.5	2,082	93.1
West Middlesex borough & MCD (Mercer)	863	803	-7.0	861	94.2	0.0	0.1	0.8	4.9	20.1	24.6	46.7	54.5	18.8	373	86.9
West Middletown borough & MCD (Washington)	139	133	-4.3	94	86.2	9.6	0.0	4.3	0.0	19.1	28.7	51.8	57.5	21.9	46	84.8
West Mifflin borough & MCD (Allegheny)	20,309	19,699	-3.0	19,834	86.5	7.3	0.1	4.9	1.2	19.3	21.7	46.1	43.7	21.5	8,799	85.9
West Milton CDP	900	-	-	1,588	51.4	3.4	0.6	3.3	41.2	17.6	9.2	21.4	69.2	23.2	566	89.8
Westmont borough & MCD (Cambria)	5,168	4,685	-9.3	4,797	97.7	0.6	0.7	0.0	1.0	22.8	24.4	48.4	24.3	51.5	1,963	87.2
West Nanticoke CDP	749	-	-	464	96.1	1.5	0.0	0.0	2.4	2.6	33.2	57.1	49.3	23.5	253	81.4
West Nantmeal township (Chester)	2,173	2,214	1.9	2,017	97.3	0.0	0.0	0.2	2.4	19.8	18.3	50.2	40.5	39.8	794	90.8
West Newton borough & MCD (Westmoreland)	2,647	2,480	-6.3	2,646	92.6	5.1	0.0	0.0	2.3	20.6	27.5	47.1	52.7	18.3	1,215	81.2
West Norriton township (Montgomery)	15,643	15,613	-0.2	15,659	69.8	13.6	6.5	2.8	7.2	14.9	20.0	44.0	33.4	43.1	7,281	90.7
West Nottingham township (Chester)	2,723	2,709	-0.5	2,723	77.0	1.5	0.3	0.6	20.6	24.0	15.5	39.3	63.7	14.0	971	89.6
Weston CDP	321	-	-	274	91.2	0.0	0.0	0.0	8.8	7.3	23.4	56.1	60.3	19.6	127	85.8
Westover borough & MCD (Clearfield)	389	376	-3.3	364	99.5	0.0	0.5	0.0	0.0	17.6	17.3	41.6	72.6	5.7	156	76.9
West Penn township (Schuylkill)	4,444	4,295	-3.4	4,314	95.8	1.1	0.0	0.2	2.9	15.2	23.7	50.5	51.8	21.1	1,910	90.2
West Pennsboro township (Cumberland)	5,560	5,627	1.2	5,614	94.8	2.8	0.0	2.2	0.2	19.0	24.9	47.2	55.3	17.8	2,392	89.2
West Perry township (Snyder)	1,075	1,068	-0.7	942	98.1	0.0	0.0	0.0	1.9	22.2	12.0	41.0	65.0	15.3	338	82.2
West Pikeland township (Chester)	4,017	4,066	1.2	4,075	96.1	0.0	3.4	0.2	0.4	24.5	12.5	46.6	8.8	74.5	1,450	98.0
West Pike Run township (Washington)	1,583	1,531	-3.3	1,603	91.5	5.3	0.0	1.6	1.6	16.9	23.0	48.8	62.9	17.2	690	82.9
West Pittsburg CDP	808	-	-	679	95.7	2.7	0.0	1.0	0.6	13.0	32.0	56.3	56.6	17.5	346	82.9
West Pittston borough & MCD (Luzerne)	4,900	4,761	-2.8	4,786	87.4	0.8	1.1	1.5	9.2	19.2	19.9	41.3	37.2	28.3	2,072	83.8
West Pottsgrove township (Montgomery)	3,850	3,838	-0.3	3,849	82.6	7.9	1.0	3.5	4.9	19.1	14.8	39.7	56.4	12.2	1,596	87.5
West Providence township (Bedford)	3,211	3,060	-4.7	3,084	100.0	0.0	0.0	0.0	0.0	14.8	27.8	54.2	63.2	18.6	1,391	76.2
West Reading borough & MCD (Berks)	4,278	4,296	0.4	4,268	57.7	7.0	3.0	6.3	26.0	23.5	18.6	36.4	49.1	29.8	1,570	93.8
West Rockhill township (Bucks)	5,256	5,221	-0.7	5,232	87.5	0.5	1.5	7.9	2.6	17.2	24.9	49.6	42.4	30.6	2,133	90.9
West Sadsbury township (Chester)	2,447	2,499	2.1	2,384	90.4	3.5	0.1	3.7	2.3	25.4	16.1	39.5	67.5	15.2	769	85.4
West St. Clair township (Bedford)	1,725	1,698	-1.6	1,649	94.4	0.0	0.5	3.5	1.6	21.2	21.6	45.4	63.2	14.4	623	82.7
West Salem township (Mercer)	3,527	3,330	-5.6	3,395	90.5	2.9	0.0	3.6	3.0	14.4	37.6	58.2	56.3	18.4	1,452	78.4
West Shenango township (Crawford)	504	477	-5.4	340	93.5	0.0	0.0	5.3	1.2	10.9	29.4	51.8	60.3	19.5	177	77.4
West Sunbury borough & MCD (Butler)	193	181	-6.2	186	97.3	0.0	0.0	0.0	2.7	16.1	12.4	40.0	45.1	12.5	83	85.5
West Taylor township (Cambria)	799	733	-8.3	705	96.7	0.7	0.0	0.3	2.3	11.3	26.8	53.8	71.4	5.5	313	75.7
Westtown township (Chester)	10,857	11,013	1.4	10,924	88.5	2.3	4.5	1.4	3.2	23.8	15.4	42.1	16.7	64.1	3,865	99.1
West View borough & MCD (Allegheny)	6,765	6,516	-3.7	6,601	94.0	1.6	0.3	2.2	2.0	19.8	15.1	38.0	40.5	32.6	2,893	84.2
West Vincent township (Chester)	4,569	5,911	29.4	5,429	85.8	0.9	7.5	1.6	4.3	25.3	9.4	42.0	12.1	69.4	1,821	97.7
West Waynesburg CDP	446	-	-	331	100.0	0.0	0.0	0.0	0.0	3.9	36.3	58.0	92.7	3.8	211	57.3

1 May be of any race.

Table A. All Places — **Population and Housing**

STATE City, town, township, borough, or CDP (county if applicable)	Population				Race and Hispanic or Latino origin (percent)					Age (percent)			Educational attainment of persons age 25 and older		Occupied housing units	
	2010 census total population	2019 estimated population	Percent change 2010–2019	ACS total population estimate 2015–2019	White alone, not Hispanic or Latino	Black alone, not Hispanic or Latino	Asian alone, not Hispanic or Latino	All other races or 2 or more races, not Hispanic or Latino	Hispanic or Latino[1]	Under 18 years old	Age 65 years and older	Median age	Percent High school diploma or less	Percent Bachelor's degree or more	Total	Percent with a computer
	1	2	3	4	5	6	7	8	9	10	11	12	13	14	15	16
PENNSYLVANIA—Con.																
West Wheatfield township (Indiana)	2,314	2,142	-7.4	1,768	94.8	0.0	0.0	0.0	5.2	19.6	28.2	51.5	57.9	13.8	732	78.3
West Whiteland township (Chester)	18,306	19,752	7.9	18,650	72.5	4.8	16.4	1.3	5.0	24.1	13.3	38.4	16.7	61.4	6,935	97.5
Westwood CDP	950	-	-	627	46.1	16.6	0.0	0.0	37.3	20.7	12.9	37.8	78.0	4.4	203	75.9
West Wyoming borough & MCD (Luzerne)	2,725	2,676	-1.8	2,686	95.0	2.9	0.0	0.3	1.7	16.8	23.4	47.2	43.7	26.4	1,129	86.4
West Wyomissing CDP	3,407	-	-	3,255	77.8	3.2	1.6	1.0	16.4	19.5	20.2	43.3	40.9	20.1	1,284	91.4
West York borough & MCD (York)	4,615	4,571		4,563	61.9	12.7	2.0	6.1	17.3	30.3	9.3	31.7	56.6	7.9	1,680	84.4
Wetmore township (McKean)	1,667	1,565	-6.1	1,671	98.2	0.0	0.5	1.3	0.0	20.3	20.0	46.4	51.0	20.4	702	88.0
Wharton township (Fayette)	3,575	3,410	-4.6	3,449	88.9	1.6	0.0	3.5	5.9	23.3	14.0	33.7	46.4	24.2	1,163	81.9
Wharton township (Potter)	99	93	-6.1	123	97.6	0.0	2.4	0.0	0.0	6.5	54.5	67.6	62.9	19.0	59	59.3
Wheatfield township (Perry)	3,335	3,333	-0.1	3,317	95.6	0.5	1.4	2.3	0.2	18.5	16.4	49.4	55.3	19.6	1,221	82.0
Wheatland borough & MCD (Mercer)	632	582	-7.9	589	89.8	8.1	0.0	1.2	0.8	14.9	26.0	51.7	69.4	7.6	326	80.4
Whitaker borough & MCD (Allegheny)	1,280	1,235	-3.5	1,148	77.1	17.5	0.0	3.4	2.0	20.5	14.7	43.7	47.9	17.7	532	82.3
White township (Beaver)	1,391	1,303	-6.3	1,439	83.9	10.5	0.0	4.0	1.5	18.9	18.3	40.4	46.6	16.9	686	85.7
White township (Cambria)	835	770	-7.8	763	99.0	0.4	0.4	0.0	0.3	18.0	24.6	47.7	54.6	21.2	328	91.8
White township (Indiana)	15,828	15,674		15,773	88.9	5.1	2.3	1.3	2.4	15.9	24.1	47.3	39.8	37.8	6,820	84.7
White Deer township (Union)	4,565	4,585	0.4	4,605	84.6	0.3	0.2	2.0	12.9	18.6	16.7	37.7	61.1	17.3	1,764	92.9
Whitehall borough & MCD (Allegheny)	13,772	13,393	-2.8	13,517	83.5	2.9	7.0	5.0	1.6	20.4	24.1	45.4	35.4	38.1	5,900	88.9
Whitehall township (Lehigh)	26,813	27,838	3.8	27,567	66.2	6.7	4.7	2.9	19.4	20.5	17.8	39.9	45.2	25.8	11,091	88.6
White Haven borough & MCD (Luzerne)	1,098	1,100	0.2	1,113	94.5	0.0	0.4	0.7	4.3	17.5	21.6	48.3	57.0	14.8	475	84.6
Whiteley township (Greene)	649	613	-5.5	752	99.1	0.0	0.0	0.5	0.4	27.4	15.4	39.1	46.4	23.7	278	92.4
Whitemarsh township (Montgomery)	17,371	18,344	5.6	17,938	88.5	2.8	4.4	1.5	2.8	22.2	18.9	41.9	20.4	64.4	6,969	93.4
White Mills CDP	659	-	-	965	86.7	3.2	0.0	8.5	1.6	21.6	12.4	44.3	57.2	14.3	338	93.5
White Oak borough & MCD (Allegheny)	7,839	7,441	-5.1	7,540	94.3	2.8	0.4	1.5	1.0	15.5	25.3	51.8	41.4	26.5	3,558	89.1
Whitfield CDP	4,733	-	-	4,560	80.2	2.1	1.5	1.3	14.9	25.0	23.7	43.6	31.4	46.4	1,703	92.6
Whitpain township (Montgomery)	18,878	19,240	1.9	19,195	77.3	4.6	13.3	1.7	3.1	21.0	21.8	46.0	16.6	65.6	7,366	96.2
Wickerham Manor-Fisher CDP	1,728	-	-	1,995	94.2	0.0	0.7	2.6	2.5	12.0	22.0	52.9	36.5	38.9	840	91.0
Wiconisco CDP	921	-	-	801	97.0	0.0	1.4	1.6	0.0	23.6	21.0	49.7	64.3	11.1	337	85.2
Wiconisco township (Dauphin)	1,214	1,205	-0.7	1,058	97.4	0.0	1.4	1.2	0.0	24.3	21.0	47.5	61.9	10.8	436	86.2
Wilburton Number One CDP	196	-	-	178	96.1	0.0	2.2	0.0	1.7	13.5	20.8	53.7	77.1	4.9	85	77.6
Wilburton Number Two CDP	96	-	-	93	93.5	0.0	0.0	6.5	0.0	18.3	43.0	54.7	63.6	9.1	38	73.7
Wilcox CDP	383	-	-	358	100.0	0.0	0.0	0.0	0.0	26.0	21.2	44.9	58.5	16.2	155	70.3
Wilkes-Barre city & MCD (Luzerne)	41,535	40,766	-1.9	40,867	60.6	12.1	2.3	4.1	21.0	22.9	15.8	34.5	56.8	16.5	15,581	82.8
Wilkes-Barre township (Luzerne)	2,958	2,883	-2.5	2,891	72.0	1.4	10.0	5.5	11.0	19.7	19.7	41.6	54.8	17.1	1,308	81.4
Wilkins township (Allegheny)	6,365	6,134	-3.6	6,204	76.7	16.2	0.4	5.9	0.8	15.0	22.9	45.2	30.4	36.6	3,029	90.7
Wilkinsburg borough & MCD (Allegheny)	15,860	15,292	-3.6	15,485	36.5	55.3	1.9	4.9	1.5	16.0	21.5	39.4	31.4	37.4	8,804	84.6
Williams township (Dauphin)	1,110	1,104	-0.5	1,003	82.5	5.0	0.0	0.6	12.0	19.0	20.7	50.4	63.2	11.9	442	83.0
Williams township (Northampton)	5,881	6,117	4.0	6,073	85.4	7.2	4.1	1.5	1.8	18.1	22.9	48.8	42.3	35.0	2,401	89.1
Williamsburg borough & MCD (Blair)	1,249	1,177	-5.8	1,131	95.3	0.0	0.5	3.2	1.0	25.7	18.7	38.1	59.5	15.8	474	77.2
Williamsport city & MCD (Lycoming)	29,374	28,186	-4.0	28,562	78.3	14.2	1.2	3.9	2.4	20.2	13.4	32.6	48.5	23.9	11,433	87.0
Williamstown borough & MCD (Dauphin)	1,393	1,386	-0.5	1,234	91.2	1.1	0.0	1.9	5.8	20.0	20.0	44.1	56.8	10.5	525	81.7
Willistown township (Chester)	10,507	11,014	4.8	10,947	90.0	2.5	4.4	1.7	1.4	20.8	23.7	49.1	19.0	62.9	4,295	95.5
Willow Grove CDP	15,726	-	-	14,992	75.4	8.8	5.3	5.3	5.2	21.0	15.4	39.2	30.5	42.7	5,969	93.3
Willow Street CDP	7,578	-	-	8,478	93.7	0.0	1.4	0.0	4.9	14.9	42.5	58.8	42.2	38.0	3,657	85.5
Wilmerding borough & MCD (Allegheny)	2,195	2,111	-3.8	1,860	57.7	30.1	0.0	10.1	2.0	28.9	15.6	35.9	51.3	9.1	871	82.2
Wilmington township (Lawrence)	2,722	2,567	-5.7	2,608	92.1	1.9	0.5	3.0	2.5	26.3	19.8	40.1	50.8	27.0	918	77.0
Wilmington township (Mercer)	1,412	1,348	-4.5	1,490	98.5	0.0	0.0	1.3	0.1	28.3	20.1	39.6	57.5	22.7	576	70.3
Wilmore borough & MCD (Cambria)	225	205	-8.9	240	99.6	0.0	0.0	0.0	0.4	22.1	16.3	40.2	53.7	21.5	92	94.6
Wilmot township (Bradford)	1,202	1,137	-5.4	1,422	98.0	0.0	0.0	0.6	1.5	22.6	20.2	42.6	62.4	18.3	552	85.9
Wilson borough & MCD (Northampton)	7,895	7,807	-1.1	7,797	63.2	6.7	2.0	9.7	18.4	20.3	11.9	36.2	49.6	20.1	2,932	88.4
Windber borough & MCD (Somerset)	4,156	3,816	-8.2	3,891	97.6	0.0	0.9	0.8	0.7	19.3	22.8	43.4	56.1	17.9	1,874	74.2
Wind Gap borough & MCD (Northampton)	2,717	2,738	0.8	2,720	93.3	0.4	3.3	1.0	2.1	18.4	20.3	43.1	56.1	16.4	1,135	82.7
Windham township (Bradford)	933	908	-2.7	878	91.1	0.6	0.6	2.2	5.6	19.7	24.8	50.9	64.2	12.3	378	86.2

1 May be of any race.

Table A. All Places — **Population and Housing**

	Population				Race and Hispanic or Latino origin (percent)					Age (percent)			Educational attainment of persons age 25 and older		Occupied housing units	
STATE City, town, township, borough, or CDP (county if applicable)	2010 census total population	2019 estimated population	Percent change 2010–2019	ACS total population estimate 2015–2019	White alone, not Hispanic or Latino	Black alone, not Hispanic or Latino	Asian alone, not Hispanic or Latino	All other races or 2 or more races, not Hispanic or Latino	Hispanic or Latino[1]	Under 18 years old	Age 65 years and older	Median age	Percent High school diploma or less	Percent Bachelor's degree or more	Total	Percent with a computer
	1	2	3	4	5	6	7	8	9	10	11	12	13	14	15	16
PENNSYLVANIA—Con.																
Windham township (Wyoming)	841	798	-5.1	825	97.9	0.4	0.0	0.8	0.8	17.8	25.9	51.5	72.2	6.6	313	82.1
Wind Ridge CDP	215	-	-	211	98.6	0.0	0.0	0.0	1.4	17.5	21.8	48.1	80.9	2.5	104	88.5
Windsor township (Berks)	2,341	2,412	3.0	2,520	98.2	0.0	0.0	0.2	1.6	18.5	23.3	46.8	57.4	16.2	1,018	85.5
Windsor borough & MCD (York)	1,322	1,485	12.3	1,357	84.2	4.1	0.0	6.5	5.2	29.5	6.9	32.1	54.7	12.2	489	91.0
Windsor township (York)	17,540	18,193	3.7	18,053	89.4	5.7	1.5	1.2	2.2	20.6	17.9	43.9	46.6	25.4	6,680	90.1
Winfield township (Butler)	3,526	3,389	-3.9	3,438	98.4	1.0	0.0	0.6	0.0	16.8	25.1	48.0	55.1	19.3	1,494	84.8
Winfield CDP	900	-	-	780	95.9	1.8	1.3	1.0	0.0	22.2	20.6	41.4	40.4	28.2	307	90.9
Winslow township (Jefferson)	2,615	2,505	-4.2	2,534	97.8	1.0	0.0	1.2	0.0	19.4	20.5	49.9	66.0	13.8	1,114	85.0
Winterstown borough & MCD (York)	632	627	-0.8	551	99.6	0.0	0.0	0.4	0.0	10.0	22.3	52.8	58.2	18.5	250	80.4
Witmer CDP	492	-	-	293	97.6	2.4	0.0	0.0	0.0	11.3	14.7	26.4	40.5	11.0	131	88.5
Wolf township (Lycoming)	2,921	3,054	4.6	3,012	97.5	0.0	0.5	2.0	0.0	23.6	18.8	45.1	51.2	23.3	1,160	91.9
Wolf Creek township (Mercer)	834	821	-1.6	654	96.0	2.3	0.0	0.9	0.8	15.7	26.3	50.6	54.9	24.9	291	84.9
Wolfdale CDP	2,888	-	-	2,626	96.3	1.2	0.0	1.7	0.8	9.7	22.8	54.4	59.0	19.8	1,182	80.4
Womelsdorf borough & MCD (Berks)	2,860	2,907	1.6	2,884	90.4	0.7	1.4	0.4	7.2	28.8	14.5	36.5	54.6	14.6	1,054	85.8
Wood township (Huntingdon)	679	669	-1.5	580	96.9	1.6	0.0	1.6	0.0	23.6	21.7	43.7	67.0	6.4	223	77.6
Woodbourne CDP	3,851	-	-	3,685	85.6	0.9	7.8	0.0	5.7	18.1	18.6	45.4	16.0	65.2	1,354	100.0
Woodbury borough & MCD (Bedford)	283	264	-6.7	287	99.3	0.0	0.0	0.0	0.7	23.7	20.6	40.3	56.7	16.5	107	84.1
Woodbury township (Bedford)	1,256	1,218	-3.0	1,189	98.7	0.0	0.0	1.3	0.0	27.9	16.3	37.8	55.2	19.7	425	80.0
Woodbury township (Blair)	1,698	1,633	-3.8	1,830	94.4	0.4	0.9	1.6	2.8	16.5	15.1	39.8	60.4	15.0	543	82.3
Woodcock borough & MCD (Crawford)	160	149	-6.9	131	97.7	0.0	1.5	0.8	0.0	16.0	29.0	55.1	75.0	15.7	60	86.7
Woodcock township (Crawford)	2,858	2,742	-4.1	2,770	98.4	0.0	0.3	0.4	0.9	20.0	23.1	47.6	53.1	22.1	1,163	90.6
Woodland Heights CDP	1,261	-	-	1,129	98.0	0.0	0.0	0.5	1.5	19.2	16.6	44.6	60.5	12.3	546	87.7
Woodlyn CDP	9,485	-	-	9,178	81.4	12.9	0.6	0.9	4.2	23.1	16.0	40.5	52.3	25.4	3,606	90.7
Woodside CDP	2,425	-	-	2,444	83.5	4.4	7.0	3.0	2.1	24.4	20.3	44.0	9.2	77.0	790	100.0
Woodward CDP	110	-	-	133	94.7	0.0	0.0	0.0	5.3	35.3	8.3	31.1	62.7	20.0	44	63.6
Woodward township (Clearfield)	3,998	4,139	3.5	4,111	62.1	26.1	0.6	3.7	7.5	7.0	11.6	41.1	73.5	5.6	673	81.9
Woodward township (Clinton)	2,369	2,362	-0.3	2,412	97.1	0.0	0.2	0.5	2.3	20.1	24.3	44.6	44.9	34.2	938	85.7
Woodward township (Lycoming)	2,191	2,125	-3.0	2,100	98.0	0.2	0.0	0.8	1.0	15.0	24.2	51.5	62.6	13.4	903	75.2
Worcester township (Montgomery)	9,718	10,430	7.3	10,406	79.1	4.4	13.0	1.5	2.0	22.9	21.4	47.7	25.1	56.8	3,774	95.2
Wormleysburg borough & MCD (Cumberland)	3,059	3,054	-0.2	3,062	64.2	3.6	9.1	5.7	17.3	17.7	11.8	31.6	32.3	43.6	1,519	94.2
Worth township (Butler)	1,426	1,450	1.7	1,439	96.6	1.4	0.2	1.2	0.6	15.1	16.5	45.9	38.1	37.6	640	93.6
Worth township (Centre)	825	821	-0.5	776	97.7	0.1	0.3	1.2	0.8	18.6	18.6	46.4	56.9	21.5	299	87.6
Worth township (Mercer)	895	855	-4.5	958	98.5	0.0	0.0	1.5	0.0	24.0	20.3	47.3	49.7	25.1	395	87.6
Worthington borough & MCD (Armstrong)	639	589	-7.8	693	100.0	0.0	0.0	0.0	0.0	14.6	18.6	43.4	51.0	10.6	260	90.8
Worthville borough & MCD (Jefferson)	67	65	-3.0	62	98.4	0.0	0.0	0.0	1.6	12.9	30.6	56.5	67.3	19.2	29	100.0
Woxall CDP	1,318	-	-	1,442	99.7	0.0	0.0	0.0	0.3	41.1	9.0	34.1	35.9	42.9	392	94.4
Wright township (Luzerne)	5,661	5,629	-0.6	5,622	92.3	0.0	5.4	0.9	1.4	17.5	23.0	45.8	32.4	36.1	2,023	90.9
Wrightstown township (Bucks)	2,992	3,097	3.5	3,099	89.9	1.7	4.4	2.3	1.7	22.3	13.0	44.5	24.5	56.1	1,139	97.5
Wrightsville borough & MCD (York)	2,315	2,296	-0.8	2,419	85.3	0.2	0.9	4.5	9.1	25.3	16.8	39.4	66.7	12.1	935	87.3
Wyalusing borough & MCD (Bradford)	590	555	-5.9	629	94.0	0.0	0.0	1.7	4.3	21.0	21.0	43.5	59.6	13.4	286	80.1
Wyalusing township (Bradford)	1,245	1,221	-1.9	1,280	97.4	0.0	0.4	2.2	0.0	23.9	19.5	44.3	48.2	22.1	505	91.1
Wyano CDP	484	-	-	574	100.0	0.0	0.0	0.0	0.0	23.0	8.9	42.6	69.7	10.1	225	78.7
Wylandville CDP	391	-	-	394	96.4	0.0	0.0	3.6	0.0	11.2	19.3	53.1	50.9	21.3	159	88.1
Wyncote CDP	3,044	-	-	2,900	78.8	11.3	6.3	2.2	1.3	16.6	30.3	52.3	26.3	54.5	1,115	86.4
Wyndmoor CDP	5,498	-	-	5,638	71.4	18.5	3.8	3.8	2.4	19.0	24.5	46.7	22.1	63.9	2,011	93.7
Wyoming borough & MCD (Luzerne)	3,072	3,011	-2.0	3,015	97.1	0.2	0.0	0.6	2.1	17.9	22.9	47.6	41.1	30.3	1,479	82.0
Wyomissing borough & MCD (Berks)	10,425	10,635	2.0	10,473	82.0	2.2	3.1	1.7	11.0	18.6	26.8	46.4	24.9	50.1	4,423	88.9
Wysox township (Bradford)	1,720	1,639	-4.7	1,754	98.2	0.0	0.2	0.3	1.4	19.1	23.2	49.4	57.7	19.5	723	84.8
Yardley borough & MCD (Bucks)	2,443	2,514	2.9	2,480	89.9	2.7	4.0	1.8	1.7	16.8	23.1	48.3	16.6	60.1	1,159	94.3
Yatesville borough & MCD (Luzerne)	616	611	-0.8	764	97.1	0.0	0.4	2.0	0.5	22.8	18.1	43.0	45.2	28.7	273	83.5
Yeadon borough & MCD (Delaware)	11,434	11,496	0.5	11,485	6.9	88.0	0.3	3.4	1.4	18.8	17.9	38.8	42.5	26.7	4,488	90.8
Yeagertown CDP	1,050	-	-	917	100.0	0.0	0.0	0.0	0.0	12.0	20.7	48.3	71.5	12.9	460	76.5
Yoe borough & MCD (York)	1,024	1,014	-	1,132	82.0	3.2	0.3	6.1	8.5	29.4	11.7	32.0	51.6	15.2	439	91.6
York city & MCD (York)	43,807	43,932	0.3	44,022	36.2	23.7	1.3	5.0	33.7	26.9	9.1	31.6	64.9	12.2	16,303	84.3
York township (York)	28,013	28,766	2.7	28,548	82.6	6.2	3.7	2.4	5.0	22.3	21.4	41.5	39.1	34.0	11,553	89.6
Yorkana borough & MCD (York)	231	229	-0.9	254	96.1	0.0	0.0	0.8	3.1	22.8	15.0	35.0	65.9	13.7	98	87.8
York Haven borough & MCD (York)	703	693	-1.4	713	80.6	1.7	0.0	1.3	16.4	28.1	10.8	35.5	69.0	5.7	270	85.6
Yorklyn CDP	1,912	-	-	1,977	76.3	5.3	3.2	1.8	13.4	25.0	15.4	34.7	56.7	21.6	688	87.9
York Springs borough & MCD (Adams)	764	776	1.6	811	40.0	0.0	0.0	0.2	59.8	31.6	9.1	33.8	68.1	10.8	241	88.8
Young township (Indiana)	1,766	1,636	-7.4	1,661	99.5	0.0	0.0	0.1	0.5	21.7	16.7	41.6	60.2	15.6	730	82.6

1 May be of any race.

Table A. All Places — **Population and Housing**

	Population				Race and Hispanic or Latino origin (percent)					Age (percent)			Educational attainment of persons age 25 and older		Occupied housing units	
STATE City, town, township, borough, or CDP (county if applicable)	2010 census total population	2019 estimated population	Percent change 2010–2019	ACS total population estimate 2015–2019	White alone, not Hispanic or Latino	Black alone, not Hispanic or Latino	Asian alone, not Hispanic or Latino	All other races or 2 or more races, not Hispanic or Latino	Hispanic or Latino[1]	Under 18 years old	Age 65 years and older	Median age	Percent High school diploma or less	Percent Bachelor's degree or more	Total	Percent with a computer
	1	2	3	4	5	6	7	8	9	10	11	12	13	14	15	16
PENNSYLVANIA—Con.																
Young township (Jefferson)	1,764	1,691	-4.1	1,628	98.6	0.5	0.0	0.7	0.2	16.1	21.9	50.0	55.2	25.4	734	84.2
Youngstown borough & MCD (Westmoreland) ...	324	305	-5.9	308	99.4	0.0	0.0	0.3	0.3	10.7	20.1	51.5	54.2	15.5	125	80.8
Youngsville borough & MCD (Warren)	1,730	1,612	-6.8	1,693	97.0	0.6	0.0	1.8	0.5	19.7	24.8	46.3	51.3	17.9	758	83.1
Youngwood borough & MCD (Westmoreland) ...	3,049	2,857	-6.3	2,900	98.3	0.9	0.0	0.3	0.5	17.5	18.1	44.0	47.2	16.0	1,396	85.5
Yukon CDP	677	-	-	584	100.0	0.0	0.0	0.0	0.0	4.5	42.3	62.3	65.6	11.7	302	62.3
Zelienople borough & MCD (Butler)	3,812	3,603	-5.5	3,651	99.3	0.0	0.0	0.4	0.3	18.1	24.5	48.9	26.7	50.2	1,841	81.9
Zerbe township (Northumberland)	1,857	1,754	-5.5	1,620	97.2	0.0	0.0	1.9	0.9	19.4	18.4	43.6	74.6	9.1	706	85.8
Zion CDP	2,030	-	-	2,258	99.0	0.0	0.4	0.0	0.6	23.0	13.5	39.6	41.6	41.9	851	96.8
RHODE ISLAND	1,052,964	1,059,361	0.6	1,057,231	72.0	5.7	3.3	3.5	15.4	19.6	16.8	39.9	39.5	34.2	410,489	89.1
Ashaway CDP	1,485	-	-	1,195	100.0	0.0	0.0	0.0	0.0	21.4	7.4	37.8	30.5	30.6	434	80.4
Barrington town (Bristol) ...	16,283	16,053	-1.4	16,131	89.4	0.3	3.7	2.9	3.6	26.8	16.5	44.9	13.2	69.1	6,029	95.4
Bradford CDP	1,406	-	-	1,303	95.3	4.7	0.0	0.0	0.0	26.8	11.2	38.3	53.6	14.6	432	93.5
Bristol town (Bristol)	22,918	21,915	-4.4	22,145	91.5	2.3	1.6	1.6	2.9	14.8	20.7	40.7	34.8	41.1	8,304	88.0
Burrillville town (Providence)	15,958	16,854	5.6	16,588	91.2	0.6	2.6	2.8	2.7	20.7	14.6	42.5	38.6	29.0	5,980	93.0
Carolina CDP	970	-	-	803	93.6	1.5	0.0	4.9	0.0	23.2	14.2	45.8	55.4	28.2	302	95.4
Central Falls city & MCD (Providence)	19,408	19,568	0.8	19,429	19.8	8.6	0.6	4.5	66.4	27.8	7.2	30.1	74.5	8.1	6,121	85.5
Charlestown CDP	-	-	-	1,312	99.3	0.0	0.0	0.0	0.7	5.9	44.6	62.3	27.2	46.6	694	95.2
Charlestown town (Washington)	7,842	7,826	-0.2	7,799	94.9	0.0	1.0	2.9	1.1	15.6	23.9	48.8	33.5	38.0	3,282	95.8
Chepachet CDP	1,675	-	-	1,530	95.9	0.1	1.8	0.7	1.4	15.7	14.8	45.6	45.9	22.3	635	91.0
Clayville CDP	300	-	-	284	84.2	0.0	0.0	15.8	0.0	28.2	14.8	41.6	10.8	85.1	105	100.0
Coventry town (Kent)	34,693	34,819	0.4	34,627	93.4	0.5	1.0	1.7	3.5	19.5	17.3	44.4	39.4	27.5	14,103	91.7
Cranston city & MCD (Providence)	80,627	81,456	1.0	81,254	69.4	5.3	6.1	3.7	15.5	20.2	17.0	40.0	38.4	33.2	30,481	89.4
Cumberland town (Providence)	33,511	35,263	5.2	34,846	89.0	0.6	2.4	1.1	6.9	19.8	17.7	44.6	34.9	38.9	13,276	88.6
Cumberland Hill CDP	7,934	-	-	8,249	88.1	0.3	4.4	1.8	5.4	20.6	16.1	43.7	32.5	39.4	3,141	90.4
East Greenwich town (Kent)	13,129	13,120	-0.1	13,081	86.6	0.6	5.2	3.9	3.7	26.0	17.3	44.7	19.5	62.6	5,079	92.1
East Providence city & MCD (Providence)	47,069	47,618	1.2	47,483	78.9	6.2	2.8	5.9	6.2	18.2	19.7	41.3	43.3	28.6	19,902	85.0
Exeter town (Washington)	6,423	6,519	1.5	6,664	92.5	0.2	1.2	4.8	1.4	16.3	17.7	44.5	29.9	48.6	2,412	92.3
Foster town (Providence)..	4,603	4,745	3.1	4,713	93.3	0.6	0.7	4.4	1.1	18.6	19.1	46.9	35.1	34.7	1,647	91.6
Foster Center CDP	355	-	-	289	100.0	0.0	0.0	0.0	0.0	22.1	34.9	48.4	49.0	25.7	122	81.1
Glocester town (Providence)	9,751	10,323	5.9	10,141	94.9	0.3	0.5	2.0	2.3	20.4	16.2	45.4	37.7	32.2	3,778	94.0
Greene CDP	888	-	-	987	96.6	0.0	2.5	0.0	0.9	18.8	14.0	40.3	38.9	35.2	374	93.9
Greenville CDP	8,658	-	-	8,695	92.1	0.8	1.1	2.0	4.0	17.2	23.3	50.2	34.9	35.8	3,350	83.7
Harmony CDP	985	-	-	1,207	100.0	0.0	0.0	0.0	0.0	21.3	19.6	43.5	46.7	28.4	445	97.3
Harrisville CDP	1,605	-	-	1,460	100.0	0.0	0.0	0.0	0.0	23.4	17.6	36.5	35.2	26.1	621	77.6
Hope Valley CDP	1,612	-	-	1,823	93.5	2.5	0.0	4.0	0.0	33.4	10.3	39.6	37.6	29.2	624	89.9
Hopkinton CDP	-	-	-	691	100.0	0.0	0.0	0.0	0.0	16.5	25.6	52.1	47.1	19.1	289	94.5
Hopkinton town (Washington)	8,177	8,060	-1.4	8,097	95.2	0.6	1.5	0.9	1.8	20.2	16.4	48.0	35.8	30.6	3,116	92.6
Jamestown town (Newport)	5,405	5,498	1.7	5,494	89.9	0.4	7.1	2.1	0.4	19.4	25.5	52.8	16.4	64.6	2,301	94.1
Johnston town (Providence)	28,813	29,471	2.3	29,307	84.5	1.8	3.2	1.6	9.0	17.5	19.7	43.8	46.7	23.8	11,597	87.3
Kingston CDP	6,974	-	-	6,513	78.9	4.3	3.3	2.4	11.2	4.3	5.5	19.6	14.8	68.4	605	92.6
Lincoln town (Providence)	21,052	21,987	4.4	21,731	88.1	1.4	3.4	2.6	4.5	22.3	19.0	43.4	34.8	41.1	8,066	91.1
Little Compton town (Newport)	3,491	3,474	-0.5	3,489	98.0	0.0	0.3	0.3	1.3	13.5	32.4	57.8	19.3	52.9	1,561	90.4
Melville CDP	1,320	-	-	1,276	58.9	10.3	8.4	5.6	16.8	30.7	2.0	29.9	17.1	54.1	468	100.0
Middletown town (Newport)	16,143	15,888	-1.6	16,018	79.8	5.9	2.9	4.6	6.8	18.3	19.9	42.5	28.4	45.6	6,924	92.1
Misquamicut CDP	390	-	-	398	100.0	0.0	0.0	0.0	0.0	4.8	48.5	63.5	19.5	57.2	233	82.8
Narragansett town (Washington)	15,893	15,349	-3.4	15,500	93.0	0.9	1.9	0.7	3.5	12.1	24.3	46.8	19.3	56.7	6,467	94.7
Narragansett Pier CDP	3,409	-	-	3,594	89.5	0.3	3.5	0.5	6.2	6.2	27.6	54.7	26.2	49.7	1,747	91.4
Newport city & MCD (Newport)	24,927	24,334	-2.4	24,663	77.2	6.3	2.0	4.8	9.8	14.1	18.4	35.4	25.7	52.8	10,211	88.7
Newport East CDP	11,769	-	-	11,925	77.8	7.2	2.7	4.9	7.3	16.5	21.7	43.9	30.7	41.9	5,331	90.7
New Shoreham town (Washington)	1,051	1,030	-2.0	916	93.8	0.4	2.1	2.9	0.8	17.9	23.3	52.5	29.7	36.1	440	96.1
North Kingstown town (Washington)	26,616	26,323	-1.1	26,235	90.4	0.9	2.0	3.4	3.3	20.3	19.1	45.4	23.4	51.4	10,419	93.0
North Providence town (Providence)	32,151	32,686	1.7	32,564	71.9	7.8	3.1	3.9	13.4	18.5	18.5	40.8	41.8	30.0	13,718	85.9
North Smithfield town (Providence)	11,966	12,582	5.1	12,413	92.7	0.5	1.0	0.9	4.9	19.3	22.9	48.2	41.3	31.3	4,807	89.7
Pascoag CDP	4,577	-	-	4,594	90.8	0.0	2.2	2.5	4.5	20.4	13.3	37.5	44.7	24.6	1,727	95.5
Pawtucket city & MCD (Providence)	71,153	72,117	1.4	71,844	48.2	15.9	2.4	8.3	25.3	20.9	13.0	37.6	51.3	21.8	28,545	87.3
Portsmouth town (Newport)	17,394	17,226	-	17,363	92.1	1.2	0.7	2.0	4.0	20.0	22.4	47.7	25.2	52.3	7,211	92.8
Providence city & MCD (Providence)	177,770	179,883	1.2	179,494	33.1	13.9	5.9	3.8	43.3	22.4	10.8	30.6	49.7	30.1	61,691	86.2
Quonochontaug CDP	333	-	-	535	96.3	0.0	0.0	3.7	0.0	6.7	37.9	55.5	26.5	42.4	202	96.0
Richmond town (Washington)	7,710	7,741	0.4	7,653	94.7	1.4	0.7	1.9	1.2	19.0	14.9	45.8	35.8	35.8	2,848	93.7
Scituate town (Providence)	10,377	10,730	3.4	10,634	96.5	0.3	0.9	0.9	1.5	18.3	18.7	49.0	30.2	36.6	4,009	90.2

1 May be of any race.

STATE City, town, township, borough, or CDP (county if applicable)	Population				Race and Hispanic or Latino origin (percent)					Age (percent)			Educational attainment of persons age 25 and older		Occupied housing units	
	2010 census total population	2019 estimated population	Percent change 2010–2019	ACS total population estimate 2015–2019	White alone, not Hispanic or Latino	Black alone, not Hispanic or Latino	Asian alone, not Hispanic or Latino	All other races or 2 or more races, not Hispanic or Latino	Hispanic or Latino[1]	Under 18 years old	Age 65 years and older	Median age	Percent High school diploma or less	Percent Bachelor's degree or more	Total	Percent with a computer
	1	2	3	4	5	6	7	8	9	10	11	12	13	14	15	16
RHODE ISLAND—Con.																
Smithfield town (Providence)	21,373	21,897	2.5	21,693	90.0	1.4	2.8	2.2	3.7	15.4	19.8	43.7	36.1	36.3	7,690	88.0
South Kingstown town (Washington)	30,602	30,348	-0.8	30,652	86.9	2.3	2.4	3.6	4.8	14.9	19.0	36.3	22.5	55.7	10,291	93.9
Tiverton CDP	7,557	-	-	7,804	91.6	1.3	0.4	2.0	4.7	18.5	23.8	48.3	40.5	30.7	3,313	87.2
Tiverton town (Newport)	15,781	15,662	-0.8	15,774	94.0	1.1	0.8	1.2	2.8	17.3	24.0	49.9	40.4	32.6	6,569	91.7
Valley Falls CDP	11,547	-	-	11,882	88.2	1.0	0.6	0.5	9.7	17.8	15.5	43.6	46.8	24.0	4,485	86.3
Wakefield-Peacedale CDP	8,487	-	-	9,504	83.2	3.0	2.5	7.4	3.9	19.6	16.6	37.4	29.9	48.4	3,638	94.7
Warren town (Bristol)	10,643	10,511	-1.2	10,488	94.3	0.4	0.4	2.3	2.5	16.3	21.1	48.2	37.9	36.2	4,884	85.9
Warwick city & MCD (Kent)	82,689	81,004	-2.0	80,993	87.7	1.9	3.0	2.3	5.1	17.7	20.0	44.7	35.2	33.8	35,011	90.6
Watch Hill CDP	154	-	-	141	99.3	0.0	0.0	0.0	0.7	7.8	22.7	49.3	41.4	49.1	69	92.8
Weekapaug CDP	425	-	-	417	100.0	0.0	0.0	0.0	0.0	18.2	29.3	50.1	23.9	49.5	195	97.4
Westerly CDP	17,936	-	-	17,553	89.7	1.6	2.6	2.4	3.7	16.0	21.0	46.3	36.6	33.8	7,802	88.2
Westerly town (Washington)	22,775	22,381	-1.7	22,544	90.8	1.6	2.2	2.2	3.2	17.3	21.3	46.6	36.2	34.8	9,827	89.6
West Greenwich town (Kent)	6,134	6,387	4.1	6,224	89.2	1.8	2.0	4.2	2.9	19.8	15.3	47.9	28.2	46.1	2,256	98.2
West Warwick town (Kent)	29,464	28,962	-1.7	28,944	84.7	2.7	3.0	2.3	7.4	18.5	16.4	39.1	42.2	23.3	12,973	88.0
Woonsocket city & MCD (Providence)	41,199	41,751	1.3	41,603	62.5	7.7	5.8	5.2	18.8	21.6	13.7	36.3	53.4	17.8	16,663	87.2
Wyoming CDP	270	-	-	340	66.2	0.0	15.6	0.0	18.2	15.0	60.0	66.4	50.8	0.0	170	100.0
SOUTH CAROLINA	4,625,366	5,148,714	11.3	5,020,806	63.7	26.6	1.6	2.5	5.7	22.0	17.2	39.4	41.6	28.1	1,921,862	88.3
Abbeville city	5,254	5,014	-4.6	5,045	40.4	56.1	0.0	2.2	1.3	22.6	23.0	44.0	54.9	12.4	2,256	72.6
Aiken city	29,594	30,869	4.3	30,671	64.8	30.5	1.5	1.7	1.6	18.2	26.0	47.7	32.6	41.3	12,923	89.3
Alcolu CDP	429	-	-	430	35.1	53.7	0.0	0.0	11.2	22.1	27.0	42.3	41.8	20.4	178	64.0
Allendale town	3,481	2,924	-16.0	3,009	8.6	89.7	0.3	0.2	1.2	24.8	21.6	38.3	68.2	8.5	1,244	65.1
Anderson city	26,436	27,676	4.7	27,289	61.7	30.2	0.4	3.1	4.7	22.6	19.1	37.3	46.1	23.9	11,412	84.4
Andrews town	2,860	2,859	0.0	2,964	29.6	65.1	0.0	0.2	5.1	28.5	13.8	31.8	56.4	12.3	1,049	82.8
Antreville CDP	140	-	-	61	93.4	3.3	0.0	1.6	1.6	1.6	93.4	81.0	57.6	0.0	33	100.0
Arcadia CDP	2,634	-	-	3,370	33.6	8.6	1.3	0.0	56.5	29.8	11.9	28.4	57.3	15.0	1,377	84.2
Arcadia Lakes town	861	874	1.5	759	96.8	1.6	0.4	1.2	0.0	13.2	32.8	59.0	11.7	67.5	370	91.9
Arial CDP	2,543	-	-	2,185	85.9	5.2	0.8	2.2	6.0	18.2	19.9	42.7	46.5	19.1	994	78.7
Atlantic Beach town	334	445	33.2	220	9.5	67.3	0.0	0.0	23.2	22.3	19.5	40.0	57.1	22.1	87	63.2
Awendaw town	1,317	1,443	9.6	1,384	41.8	56.1	1.4	0.7	0.0	22.0	19.0	47.6	51.0	23.1	514	75.3
Aynor town	569	967	69.9	821	81.6	14.0	0.0	4.4	0.0	23.8	15.3	42.3	46.7	22.3	298	90.3
Bamberg town	3,598	3,189	-11.4	3,267	38.6	59.5	0.0	1.4	0.6	23.5	28.3	44.6	49.7	23.4	1,311	77.0
Barnwell city	4,761	4,291	-9.9	4,424	41.2	55.6	0.0	1.8	1.4	25.6	15.7	37.6	59.3	12.2	1,685	75.4
Batesburg-Leesville town	5,376	5,415	0.7	5,647	47.4	41.6	0.2	1.7	9.2	23.6	17.5	37.6	60.0	14.0	2,046	86.5
Beaufort city	12,336	13,436	8.9	13,404	59.8	27.9	2.2	4.6	5.5	22.5	17.9	36.6	31.9	33.2	4,839	93.3
Belton city	4,164	4,455	7.0	4,366	74.9	14.2	0.1	5.8	4.9	21.1	19.0	43.7	56.5	14.2	1,956	78.6
Belvedere CDP	5,792	-	-	5,262	56.2	30.0	2.9	9.0	2.0	23.0	14.6	38.4	54.4	14.5	2,251	91.0
Bennettsville city	9,099	7,730	-15.0	8,062	29.6	62.5	0.6	4.4	2.9	21.9	15.7	37.9	66.5	9.8	2,850	74.9
Berea CDP	14,295	-	-	14,652	52.6	19.1	1.2	2.5	24.6	21.6	16.7	38.9	60.5	12.5	5,624	83.6
Bethune town	332	350	5.4	254	83.5	15.7	0.0	0.8	0.0	19.7	31.5	56.1	60.7	17.8	118	78.8
Bishopville city	3,471	3,017	-13.1	3,103	29.6	69.3	0.0	0.1	0.9	16.8	21.1	46.0	56.8	16.2	1,414	67.8
Blacksburg town	1,834	1,880	2.5	1,939	68.2	26.8	0.7	2.4	1.9	28.3	15.5	34.4	67.1	10.7	785	82.9
Blackville town	2,406	2,189	-9.0	1,844	22.8	75.5	0.0	0.0	1.6	27.2	20.0	37.2	68.1	9.8	758	73.0
Blenheim town	154	142	-7.8	181	36.5	46.4	0.0	17.1	0.0	26.5	14.9	41.7	62.9	4.8	61	83.6
Bluffton town	13,054	25,557	95.8	20,799	71.8	7.2	2.1	2.1	16.8	25.0	15.7	37.5	24.3	45.8	7,560	98.9
Blythewood town	2,057	4,150	101.8	3,324	56.8	36.9	3.5	0.3	2.5	24.8	9.0	40.6	22.3	51.1	1,057	97.2
Boiling Springs CDP	8,219	-	-	9,508	78.3	12.8	3.4	2.4	3.1	26.5	16.2	39.4	33.6	31.8	3,529	87.8
Bonneau town	452	486	7.5	710	92.0	7.0	0.0	0.0	1.0	38.2	14.4	31.3	56.7	16.1	240	82.5
Bonneau Beach CDP	1,929	-	-	1,786	97.3	0.0	0.0	2.7	0.0	17.1	33.2	56.4	41.4	18.7	708	97.7
Bowman town	965	888	-8.0	711	28.3	71.7	0.0	0.0	0.0	23.2	27.1	42.1	59.7	16.9	317	69.4
Boykin CDP	100	-	-	185	100.0	0.0	0.0	0.0	0.0	8.6	10.3	40.8	4.7	29.0	84	100.0
Bradley CDP	170	-	-	197	4.6	32.0	0.0	63.5	0.0	63.5	0.0	17.3	62.5	30.6	46	87.0
Branchville town	1,026	953	-7.1	1,242	51.0	47.0	0.0	2.0	0.0	22.4	15.1	34.9	46.5	15.0	450	74.0
Briarcliffe Acres town	457	593	29.8	479	98.1	0.0	0.8	0.0	1.0	11.9	41.5	60.8	11.5	64.6	201	98.0
Brookdale CDP	4,873	-	-	4,674	1.0	97.2	0.0	0.8	1.0	27.6	16.9	33.1	46.0	18.3	1,693	79.4
Brunson town	548	496	-9.5	555	64.7	33.5	0.0	1.6	0.2	20.5	15.5	40.0	56.7	16.3	207	87.0
Bucksport CDP	876	-	-	735	2.9	88.4	0.0	8.7	0.0	19.2	10.7	43.8	63.1	9.2	280	87.1
Buffalo CDP	1,266	-	-	1,397	76.2	21.6	0.0	1.5	0.6	23.6	13.3	48.5	66.1	4.1	569	85.8
Burnettown town	2,612	2,747	5.2	2,723	70.6	22.6	0.0	1.1	5.7	30.0	17.2	38.7	52.2	14.5	1,080	78.1
Burton CDP	6,976	-	-	9,097	42.3	39.7	0.9	0.8	16.3	25.7	10.7	28.7	52.4	13.1	2,888	87.2
Calhoun Falls town	1,999	1,902	-4.9	1,692	44.6	47.3	0.0	7.3	0.8	22.2	16.7	38.6	63.9	8.8	742	75.7
Camden city	6,826	7,220	5.8	7,100	57.2	35.5	0.0	1.4	6.0	21.0	22.2	46.6	36.4	38.1	2,905	83.5
Cameron town	424	398	-6.1	329	76.9	21.6	0.0	0.0	1.5	10.0	45.6	61.0	35.4	32.5	168	73.2
Campobello town	528	593	12.3	532	81.6	7.1	5.6	1.9	3.8	18.6	15.2	43.2	40.9	18.8	208	85.6
Cane Savannah CDP	1,117	-	-	978	57.6	37.8	0.0	0.0	4.6	20.3	13.4	45.4	53.4	16.1	468	88.2
Carlisle town	435	412	-5.3	383	10.7	84.3	0.0	3.1	1.8	16.2	23.0	44.7	57.8	8.2	178	65.2
Catawba CDP	1,343	-	-	1,108	55.0	30.5	4.3	4.9	5.3	14.4	13.6	47.7	45.0	26.0	540	86.7
Cayce city	13,074	14,009	7.2	13,600	69.4	20.1	5.4	2.9	2.2	16.5	13.8	32.4	30.5	34.2	6,017	92.5
Centerville CDP	6,586	-	-	7,173	77.9	14.2	0.1	3.4	4.4	21.7	17.0	42.1	39.5	19.4	2,990	91.8
Central town	5,202	5,385	3.5	5,270	61.6	18.2	5.2	6.0	9.1	9.6	10.8	25.7	38.2	29.9	2,483	87.4
Central Pacolet town	215	241	12.1	186	98.4	0.0	0.0	1.1	0.5	22.6	15.6	43.0	77.2	4.4	72	73.6
Chapin town	1,428	1,633	14.4	1,940	87.9	5.4	1.0	2.2	3.6	27.0	11.8	35.2	31.0	27.6	768	93.1
Charleston city	120,364	137,566	14.3	135,257	71.5	21.6	1.9	1.7	3.2	16.7	14.6	34.8	22.7	53.1	55,889	93.6
Cheraw town	5,889	5,562	-5.6	5,657	41.7	50.9	1.4	1.7	4.3	23.3	22.6	43.5	60.4	17.9	2,358	74.7
Cherryvale CDP	2,496	-	-	3,318	38.2	60.8	0.9	0.0	0.0	34.6	10.4	24.8	60.6	3.9	1,152	92.5
Chesnee city	856	957	11.8	686	78.0	16.3	0.0	2.3	3.4	9.5	17.5	46.7	59.4	12.3	324	75.9
Chester city	5,593	5,377	-3.9	5,408	34.5	63.3	0.2	0.8	1.2	24.1	14.9	34.3	57.9	11.3	2,244	77.9
Chesterfield town	1,474	1,415	-4.0	1,549	71.9	25.3	1.5	0.8	0.5	26.0	17.5	36.9	43.8	20.2	571	88.8
City View CDP	1,345	-	-	1,741	44.1	26.7	0.0	0.0	29.2	29.6	16.7	34.5	66.5	2.8	419	87.1
Clarks Hill CDP	381	-	-	320	20.3	71.9	0.0	7.8	0.0	31.3	18.8	34.9	67.2	9.1	122	82.0
Clearwater CDP	4,370	-	-	4,264	59.7	17.5	0.0	1.5	21.3	28.0	19.1	32.8	62.9	7.9	1,638	88.9
Clemson city	13,964	17,501	25.3	16,463	78.9	7.7	7.5	2.9	3.1	11.0	10.8	24.4	18.6	59.7	6,751	95.7
Clifton CDP	541	-	-	521	80.4	19.6	0.0	0.0	0.0	33.4	11.3	37.2	55.6	2.0	221	78.7
Clinton city	8,526	8,380	-1.7	8,443	57.8	35.8	1.1	3.7	1.6	17.3	21.6	38.2	54.4	22.7	3,141	72.6
Clio town	726	658	-9.4	766	29.9	61.9	0.0	8.2	0.0	29.8	10.7	35.8	51.6	13.7	258	78.3

1 May be of any race.

Table A. All Places — **Population and Housing**

STATE City, town, township, borough, or CDP (county if applicable)	Population				Race and Hispanic or Latino origin (percent)					Age (percent)			Educational attainment of persons age 25 and older		Occupied housing units	
	2010 census total population	2019 estimated population	Percent change 2010–2019	ACS total population estimate 2015–2019	White alone, not Hispanic or Latino	Black alone, not Hispanic or Latino	Asian alone, not Hispanic or Latino	All other races or 2 or more races, not Hispanic or Latino	Hispanic or Latino[1]	Under 18 years old	Age 65 years and older	Median age	Percent High school diploma or less	Percent Bachelor's degree or more	Total	Percent with a computer
	1	2	3	4	5	6	7	8	9	10	11	12	13	14	15	16
SOUTH CAROLINA—Con.																
Clover town	5,119	6,519	27.3	6,135	65.2	13.7	5.0	6.5	9.8	28.7	9.0	32.8	45.1	23.2	2,093	91.4
Cokesbury CDP	215	-	-	195	36.4	63.6	0.0	0.0	0.0	34.9	10.3	33.7	16.5	26.1	61	100.0
Columbia city	130,421	131,674	1.0	133,273	49.2	39.4	2.7	3.1	5.5	16.2	10.2	28.5	30.7	43.8	47,162	91.9
Converse CDP	608	-	-	570	79.3	20.7	0.0	0.0	0.0	20.4	10.7	39.6	62.8	8.1	210	92.9
Conway city	17,414	25,956	49.1	23,838	59.9	35.6	0.8	1.1	2.7	18.2	16.9	34.0	43.2	21.6	7,921	89.8
Cope town	77	70	-9.1	37	81.1	18.9	0.0	0.0	0.0	0.0	43.2	62.2	26.5	32.4	25	64.0
Cordova town	174	160	-8.0	310	83.5	11.9	0.0	4.5	0.0	43.5	4.8	23.6	17.2	18.5	75	94.7
Coronaca CDP	191	-	-	129	84.5	15.5	0.0	0.0	0.0	42.6	0.0	35.4	37.8	41.9	53	100.0
Cottageville town	765	745	-2.6	885	84.6	11.8	0.0	2.7	0.9	16.0	13.2	39.2	54.4	16.2	329	93.9
Coward town	755	771	2.1	671	73.9	13.1	0.0	3.3	9.7	25.8	19.7	39.9	67.7	8.0	288	77.1
Cowpens town	2,156	2,419	12.2	1,942	70.7	18.1	0.0	5.8	5.4	21.1	18.7	41.1	41.9	27.2	843	88.1
Cross Anchor CDP	126	-	-	25	100.0	0.0	0.0	0.0	0.0	0.0	100.0	0.0	100.0	0.0	25	100.0
Cross Hill town	495	505	2.0	545	42.6	52.8	0.0	3.3	1.3	23.7	17.6	43.3	76.7	5.2	217	61.8
Dalzell CDP	3,059	-	-	3,057	45.8	41.6	4.6	1.7	6.4	20.9	13.1	31.6	45.8	13.9	1,198	90.7
Darlington city	6,373	5,940	-6.8	6,043	42.4	55.3	0.0	1.6	0.7	22.7	26.5	44.0	49.2	21.2	2,692	69.2
Denmark city	3,516	2,934	-16.6	2,988	8.6	90.1	0.1	0.6	0.6	14.7	15.9	29.8	46.6	19.3	972	78.2
Dentsville CDP	14,062	-	-	15,153	17.0	72.7	5.2	1.5	3.7	23.2	12.2	34.2	37.6	25.6	6,403	93.2
Dillon city	6,779	6,311	-6.9	6,394	44.2	53.1	0.0	1.3	1.3	29.7	13.9	34.9	59.4	13.7	2,159	77.9
Donalds town	348	331	-4.9	339	87.3	10.6	0.0	0.9	1.2	19.8	14.2	41.9	56.5	10.8	125	83.2
Due West town	1,237	1,203	-2.7	1,321	74.6	14.7	0.7	6.4	3.6	16.2	12.2	21.7	41.7	33.8	249	92.4
Duncan town	3,181	3,626	14.0	3,473	60.4	23.0	0.0	7.1	9.5	30.0	10.2	29.6	47.6	24.6	1,323	84.1
Dunean CDP	3,671	-	-	3,613	61.6	30.3	0.0	3.4	4.8	16.4	20.3	42.7	60.0	16.4	1,596	73.4
Easley city	20,075	21,364	6.4	20,923	81.3	12.7	1.5	0.9	3.6	20.6	20.0	42.3	43.2	25.3	8,738	83.7
East Gaffney CDP	3,085	-	-	2,755	65.7	20.7	0.9	3.6	9.2	26.8	16.7	36.1	66.8	11.1	986	83.0
Eastover town	813	841	3.4	749	6.0	89.5	0.9	0.9	2.7	24.8	20.6	38.1	63.6	5.7	271	55.4
East Sumter CDP	1,343	-	-	1,187	47.0	53.0	0.0	0.0	0.0	17.4	13.7	41.1	56.6	8.2	505	88.7
Edgefield town	4,754	4,810	1.2	4,780	34.8	52.9	0.5	2.5	9.3	8.1	18.8	44.9	63.9	11.0	1,248	66.0
Edisto CDP	2,559	-	-	2,595	21.3	77.2	0.0	1.5	0.0	28.9	13.0	35.5	59.8	20.4	929	88.4
Edisto Beach town	414	406	-1.9	604	97.2	1.0	0.7	1.2	0.0	1.3	56.1	66.8	13.4	59.2	320	98.4
Ehrhardt town	545	482	-11.6	421	38.2	61.8	0.0	0.0	0.0	10.0	28.7	58.3	54.1	9.7	213	63.8
Elgin town	1,332	1,585	19.0	1,757	74.4	12.6	0.5	1.6	10.9	32.7	14.6	36.6	46.8	23.4	597	93.1
Elgin CDP	2,607	-	-	2,932	48.2	40.9	0.0	0.0	11.0	15.1	15.7	45.6	60.2	12.9	1,078	78.8
Elko town	193	179	-7.3	176	25.0	73.9	0.0	0.6	0.6	21.6	25.0	47.0	58.5	14.6	91	65.9
Elloree town	701	641	-8.6	631	51.2	45.2	0.0	3.6	0.0	16.6	20.9	49.3	55.3	17.8	264	67.0
Enoree CDP	665	-	-	619	48.5	2.4	0.0	4.8	44.3	30.4	16.2	38.9	77.0	2.6	234	100.0
Estill town	2,040	1,857	-9.0	3,282	9.5	85.7	0.0	0.4	4.4	30.4	16.8	30.7	66.6	10.7	889	74.9
Eureka Mill CDP	1,476	-	-	1,599	44.3	53.8	0.0	1.9	0.0	28.8	14.1	39.7	65.3	9.7	550	81.6
Eutawville town	312	290	-7.1	258	41.9	58.1	0.0	0.0	0.0	5.8	32.2	57.7	72.6	9.3	120	60.0
Fairfax town	2,025	1,675	-17.3	2,175	14.6	78.9	0.0	0.0	6.5	22.4	18.5	35.6	64.3	13.2	793	80.6
Fairforest CDP	1,693	-	-	1,539	39.6	38.7	5.1	2.5	14.1	32.0	10.9	31.5	40.7	8.8	478	96.7
Fair Play CDP	687	-	-	474	91.8	0.0	0.0	8.2	0.0	10.5	32.7	53.3	42.9	27.5	190	73.2
Fingerville CDP	134	-	-	26	100.0	0.0	0.0	0.0	0.0	0.0	100.0	0.0	100.0	0.0	13	100.0
Five Forks CDP	14,140	-	-	17,844	78.8	6.5	5.6	1.7	7.4	32.3	10.4	37.2	11.5	61.5	5,627	98.2
Florence city	37,905	38,531	1.7	38,487	46.4	47.2	2.3	2.0	2.1	24.4	18.9	39.7	39.3	31.3	15,624	84.7
Folly Beach city	2,518	2,660	5.6	2,660	99.1	0.9	0.0	0.0	0.0	3.5	18.4	49.5	17.5	54.4	1,401	93.4
Forest Acres city	10,422	10,298	-1.2	10,412	75.6	17.5	2.4	2.8	1.7	20.5	21.0	42.1	12.9	60.8	4,683	94.5
Forestbrook CDP	4,612	-	-	6,591	84.1	9.5	0.8	2.2	3.4	18.1	26.8	47.7	33.6	28.5	2,528	97.7
Fort Lawn town	895	886		940	59.6	34.9	0.0	4.8	0.7	22.7	17.0	37.0	55.8	14.1	358	76.8
Fort Mill town	11,529	22,284	93.3	17,692	75.8	15.2	1.3	3.7	4.1	31.4	9.7	35.4	22.9	48.4	6,130	96.6
Fountain Inn city	7,611	10,441	37.2	9,301	57.6	31.6	0.2	3.1	7.6	26.5	10.3	33.3	43.6	26.2	3,170	83.7
Furman town	237	218	-8.0	216	22.2	75.5	0.0	2.3	0.0	9.3	20.8	58.1	60.1	16.3	86	77.9
Gadsden CDP	1,632	-	-	1,668	0.7	99.1	0.0	0.2	0.0	13.3	13.1	36.0	42.2	10.7	546	93.8
Gaffney city	12,412	12,609	1.6	12,582	50.0	44.1	0.2	3.1	2.6	22.1	16.9	35.0	56.5	14.8	4,220	79.4
Gantt CDP	14,229	-	-	15,138	22.6	61.7	0.1	1.8	13.9	28.7	14.9	35.1	56.7	15.7	5,555	79.2
Garden City CDP	9,209	-	-	10,669	89.5	1.4	0.2	5.3	3.6	10.8	40.2	60.7	37.0	22.3	4,893	90.8
Gaston town	1,639	1,699	3.7	1,824	72.4	12.9	1.1	2.9	10.7	29.1	8.3	30.8	50.4	10.5	684	86.7
Gayle Mill CDP	913	-	-	842	31.5	68.5	0.0	0.0	0.0	25.4	11.4	36.3	78.1	0.0	247	74.5
Georgetown city	9,168	8,742	-4.6	8,866	46.5	46.2	0.0	5.8	1.4	24.8	19.9	39.2	42.6	19.9	3,649	77.9
Gifford town	287	263	-8.4	266	0.0	99.2	0.0	0.8	0.0	24.4	15.8	42.1	79.7	3.4	101	85.1
Gilbert town	562	643	14.4	701	91.4	0.9	0.0	0.7	7.0	28.1	4.7	36.1	44.1	20.4	227	89.9
Glendale CDP	307	-	-	293	91.8	0.0	0.0	8.2	0.0	14.0	8.5	38.1	48.9	20.1	131	96.2
Gloverville CDP	2,831	-	-	2,966	83.6	12.0	0.0	0.0	4.4	22.5	14.0	39.2	67.9	11.5	1,119	80.3
Golden Grove CDP	2,467	-	-	3,519	53.1	40.9	0.0	5.9	0.0	25.0	12.6	38.3	53.9	18.0	1,269	87.7
Goose Creek city	36,428	43,665	19.9	41,978	63.5	18.9	3.3	5.2	9.0	23.5	10.6	31.9	32.8	27.0	13,924	96.3
Govan town	65	56	-13.8	60	83.3	16.7	0.0	0.0	0.0	30.0	26.7	37.7	69.2	20.5	18	83.3
Gramling CDP	86	-	-	38	57.9	0.0	0.0	42.1	0.0	0.0	0.0	0.0	57.9	42.1	16	100.0
Graniteville CDP	2,614	-	-	3,320	62.5	21.2	0.0	2.6	13.6	27.9	10.5	33.5	58.9	13.4	1,220	84.1
Gray Court town	811	821	1.2	759	34.4	50.7	0.0	1.1	13.8	13.3	21.1	43.1	62.3	7.0	322	87.0
Great Falls town	1,976	1,877	-5.0	2,042	59.5	33.0	0.0	6.4	1.1	30.1	13.4	34.0	58.7	15.1	730	69.7
Greeleyville town	429	380	-11.4	365	27.7	68.2	0.0	1.1	3.0	18.4	25.5	50.6	63.5	9.0	170	60.6
Greenville city	59,280	70,635	19.2	67,737	67.3	23.0	2.4	2.5	4.9	19.0	13.4	34.3	26.3	50.3	29,942	89.2
Greenwood city	23,214	23,403	0.8	23,269	40.3	46.2	1.7	1.3	10.5	24.4	14.5	33.0	50.9	22.5	8,772	80.7
Greer city	25,879	33,373	29.0	30,854	58.2	16.0	6.6	2.8	16.3	25.9	13.5	35.1	36.7	32.5	11,531	90.2
Hampton town	2,808	2,505	-10.8	2,560	48.8	45.5	1.9	3.8	0.0	20.5	18.5	41.0	52.1	10.7	1,139	73.9
Hanahan city	17,978	26,917	49.7	24,353	68.4	14.4	4.8	2.5	9.9	25.0	11.8	34.3	33.1	33.7	8,891	92.3
Hardeeville city	3,028	7,278	140.4	6,064	70.5	16.3	0.4	1.0	11.8	11.8	35.6	57.1	32.1	38.4	2,789	96.1
Harleyville town	667	699	4.8	725	67.9	21.9	4.6	3.4	2.2	31.2	15.9	40.1	57.3	12.6	275	68.7
Hartsville city	7,764	7,542	-2.9	7,616	49.3	47.5	0.7	1.1	1.4	26.5	14.0	32.7	39.8	36.1	2,934	80.1
Heath Springs town	785	1,019	29.8	771	54.3	43.2	0.0	2.5	0.0	19.1	19.6	39.8	55.9	8.1	289	76.5
Hemingway town	460	395	-14.1	529	53.5	44.4	0.0	1.9	0.2	18.0	18.9	46.9	45.5	31.1	231	86.1
Hickory Grove town	444	551	24.1	509	80.0	19.3	0.0	0.0	0.8	18.9	15.3	44.2	64.8	18.3	202	82.7
Hilda town	438	408	-6.8	433	93.1	3.5	0.0	3.0	0.5	16.4	22.6	48.6	79.6	6.7	180	77.2
Hilton Head Island town	37,094	39,861	7.5	40,007	80.3	5.9	0.9	1.1	11.8	13.6	37.0	58.0	22.3	54.3	17,513	95.2
Hodges town	148	148	0.0	129	92.2	5.4	2.3	0.0	0.0	23.3	15.5	40.3	33.3	8.3	47	85.1
Holly Hill town	1,278	1,178	-7.8	1,335	37.1	59.1	0.0	3.0	0.8	24.6	20.3	40.8	61.5	16.3	507	64.7
Hollywood town	4,720	5,227	10.7	5,176	46.1	47.5	0.9	3.7	1.8	18.8	28.4	55.4	49.2	27.8	2,070	81.4
Homeland Park CDP	6,296	-	-	5,988	56.9	37.5	0.4	3.1	2.1	19.3	15.8	41.7	65.3	2.4	2,630	82.3
Honea Path town	3,558	3,826	7.5	3,695	81.8	14.5	0.0	3.3	0.5	25.2	12.7	36.9	36.1	23.9	1,465	84.1
Hopkins CDP	2,882	-	-	2,719	15.0	83.9	0.0	1.1	0.0	18.6	15.2	39.8	65.7	8.9	1,016	73.7
India Hook CDP	3,328	-	-	4,006	83.2	5.0	2.4	0.9	8.5	19.0	19.1	43.2	22.6	46.7	1,685	98.2
Inman city	2,179	2,430	11.5	2,759	73.8	16.1	3.9	0.5	5.6	24.8	21.9	38.2	53.0	11.7	1,141	75.7
Inman Mills CDP	1,050	-	-	849	86.8	13.2	0.0	0.0	0.0	10.2	47.7	56.5	67.5	8.2	285	93.7

1 May be of any race.

Table A. All Places — **Population and Housing**

STATE City, town, township, borough, or CDP (county if applicable)	Population: 2010 census total population	Population: 2019 estimated population	Population: Percent change 2010–2019	Population: ACS total population estimate 2015–2019	Race and Hispanic or Latino origin (percent): White alone, not Hispanic or Latino	Black alone, not Hispanic or Latino	Asian alone, not Hispanic or Latino	All other races or 2 or more races, not Hispanic or Latino	Hispanic or Latino[1]	Age (percent): Under 18 years old	Age 65 years and older	Median age	Educational attainment of persons age 25 and older: Percent High school diploma or less	Percent Bachelor's degree or more	Occupied housing units: Total	Percent with a computer
	1	2	3	4	5	6	7	8	9	10	11	12	13	14	15	16
SOUTHCAROLINA—Con.																
Irmo town	11,117	12,483	12.3	12,215	59.2	33.8	1.3	2.4	3.4	21.1	14.8	38.7	25.7	37.3	4,686	94.5
Irwin CDP	1,405	-	-	1,395	56.4	43.6	0.0	0.0	0.0	17.6	20.9	50.9	61.8	8.4	600	70.8
Islandton CDP	70	-	-	44	63.6	36.4	0.0	0.0	0.0	0.0	45.5	49.8	100.0	0.0	27	85.2
Isle of Palms city	4,133	4,360	5.5	4,360	92.9	0.0	2.2	3.0	1.9	18.0	29.9	55.2	11.8	70.1	1,799	98.4
Iva town	1,237	1,325	7.1	1,388	75.6	22.8	0.0	0.4	1.1	22.0	21.1	41.9	66.3	6.6	514	81.3
Jackson town	1,716	1,803	5.1	1,925	78.2	13.1	0.8	4.0	3.9	20.4	20.7	47.1	49.1	15.1	791	87.4
Jacksonboro CDP	478	-	-	399	34.8	65.2	0.0	0.0	0.0	3.8	16.5	45.0	54.8	24.8	178	91.0
James Island town	11,218	12,109	7.9	12,076	85.8	8.0	2.7	1.8	1.7	17.1	18.3	44.1	25.7	47.5	4,706	94.9
Jamestown town	75	82	9.3	87	39.1	52.9	0.0	8.0	0.0	0.0	12.6	50.1	47.5	20.0	56	96.4
Jefferson town	738	712	-3.5	950	62.9	29.3	2.0	5.8	0.0	26.2	18.8	40.1	65.1	12.5	350	73.1
Jenkinsville town	46	43	-6.5	56	0.0	100.0	0.0	0.0	0.0	19.6	25.0	45.3	60.0	0.0	28	50.0
Joanna CDP	1,539	-	-	1,267	86.0	4.7	1.3	0.8	7.3	18.5	22.2	41.6	63.9	16.4	484	84.5
Johnsonville city	1,487	1,485	-0.1	1,395	78.6	15.8	0.7	0.0	4.9	25.3	15.6	38.5	43.5	22.6	497	88.3
Johnston town	2,373	2,381	0.3	2,054	30.2	63.1	0.0	0.6	6.1	19.0	20.5	45.4	63.4	12.6	811	70.2
Jonesville town	908	838	-7.7	770	72.5	18.7	0.0	8.8	0.0	17.7	18.2	43.0	70.6	11.2	335	74.6
Judson CDP	2,050	-	-	1,546	19.3	48.1	0.0	2.0	30.7	22.3	7.5	33.8	78.6	7.4	610	74.6
Kershaw town	1,787	2,321	29.9	1,832	66.1	25.8	1.2	5.1	1.9	23.1	20.6	43.9	56.4	12.4	736	80.8
Kiawah Island town	1,626	1,769	8.8	1,676	95.8	1.3	1.5	0.4	1.1	1.8	58.4	67.6	3.7	81.8	869	99.0
Kingstree town	3,327	3,063	-7.9	3,096	18.4	76.9	1.9	2.8	0.0	27.6	22.9	39.7	49.9	20.1	1,414	72.8
Kline town	197	181	-8.1	128	36.7	58.6	0.0	0.0	4.7	27.3	24.2	51.0	69.0	17.9	48	77.1
Ladson CDP	13,790	-	-	15,539	66.2	23.1	1.0	4.2	5.5	27.7	10.5	35.2	51.5	16.1	5,046	92.5
Lake City city	6,674	6,497	-2.7	6,617	15.3	82.1	0.0	0.8	1.8	27.2	15.5	38.4	55.9	18.0	2,415	81.0
Lake Murray of Richland CDP	5,484	-	-	6,455	88.4	7.8	1.7	1.1	1.1	21.5	20.7	45.4	16.1	59.5	2,495	96.6
Lake Secession CDP	1,083	-	-	1,158	100.0	0.0	0.0	0.0	0.0	4.1	31.9	62.1	52.8	17.9	510	87.1
Lake View town	809	758	-6.3	773	72.3	27.0	0.0	0.6	0.0	22.0	27.9	51.2	62.7	9.1	331	59.2
Lakewood CDP	3,032	-	-	2,749	51.8	47.3	0.0	0.0	0.9	16.0	18.6	46.3	55.3	10.4	1,280	84.4
Lake Wylie CDP	8,841	-	-	12,885	78.4	10.4	1.2	1.2	8.7	26.4	16.1	43.0	18.1	50.8	4,869	96.6
Lamar town	987	935	-5.3	1,097	42.3	49.0	2.6	6.1	0.0	27.0	28.9	41.8	53.6	12.9	419	60.6
Lancaster city	8,674	9,119	5.1	9,143	40.1	50.6	0.2	2.2	7.0	26.3	16.6	39.1	55.5	16.4	3,469	79.6
Landrum city	2,370	2,677	13.0	2,563	79.1	11.0	0.7	0.0	9.2	22.8	23.2	45.6	38.7	25.1	1,125	82.0
Lane town	508	452	-11.0	467	9.4	89.3	0.0	1.3	0.0	17.6	22.3	47.5	66.5	10.5	167	69.5
Langley CDP	1,447	-	-	1,842	90.8	6.9	0.0	1.3	0.9	26.0	10.2	35.4	74.6	4.1	722	72.7
Latta town	1,374	1,285	-6.5	1,219	53.7	42.1	1.7	1.6	1.0	22.6	21.2	45.5	58.1	19.6	516	73.3
Laurel Bay CDP	5,891	-	-	6,124	56.0	24.6	0.3	2.7	16.4	30.6	5.7	25.1	46.1	13.7	2,018	95.2
Laurens city	9,033	8,849	-2.0	8,867	52.4	40.5	0.7	3.0	3.4	22.3	24.8	41.6	51.3	16.1	3,759	76.7
Lesslie CDP	3,112	-	-	3,013	81.0	12.7	0.0	6.3	0.0	25.6	14.4	43.2	49.2	18.1	1,127	94.5
Lexington town	18,507	22,157	19.7	21,334	76.5	11.1	4.4	2.7	5.3	26.2	12.4	36.2	26.5	43.5	7,907	93.0
Liberty city	3,257	3,154	-3.2	3,177	74.2	21.2	0.2	2.8	1.6	23.9	12.9	38.7	48.2	23.8	1,396	87.2
Lincolnville town	1,141	2,529	121.6	2,133	39.1	51.8	0.0	2.6	6.6	27.5	24.0	42.4	62.9	8.9	806	78.5
Little Mountain town	288	294	2.1	290	96.6	1.7	0.0	0.0	1.7	33.1	24.8	37.0	25.7	31.9	111	80.2
Little River CDP	8,960	-	-	9,792	91.2	4.8	2.4	0.2	1.4	11.9	34.1	59.2	38.4	24.4	4,885	92.2
Livingston town	132	122	-7.6	195	72.3	13.8	0.0	13.8	0.0	48.7	13.3	24.8	32.0	28.9	70	90.0
Lockhart town	489	457	-6.5	390	78.2	13.6	0.0	8.2	0.0	26.9	18.2	37.7	71.8	4.3	178	69.7
Lodge town	120	113	-5.8	95	55.8	5.3	0.0	0.0	38.9	25.3	18.9	45.1	62.1	13.8	30	83.3
Loris city	2,400	2,761	15.0	2,673	68.7	29.4	0.4	0.4	1.1	16.3	29.9	49.8	60.1	14.3	1,152	81.3
Lowndesville town	125	119	-4.8	93	60.2	39.8	0.0	0.0	0.0	22.6	19.4	50.4	69.6	5.8	54	81.5
Lowrys town	200	193	-3.5	186	85.5	11.8	0.0	0.5	2.2	14.5	21.5	47.8	47.9	21.1	75	85.3
Lugoff CDP	7,434	-	-	8,243	76.4	19.3	0.0	1.6	2.7	25.8	16.4	39.9	38.7	26.5	3,217	88.2
Luray town	127	123	-3.1	79	50.6	30.4	0.0	0.0	19.0	15.2	21.5	49.4	57.8	12.5	42	69.0
Lydia CDP	642	-	-	425	54.6	45.4	0.0	0.0	0.0	19.5	4.9	47.6	82.5	3.4	198	85.9
Lyman town	3,296	3,718	12.8	3,567	82.8	10.8	2.9	2.0	1.5	27.1	16.6	36.7	35.5	16.4	1,340	96.4
Lynchburg town	373	335	-10.2	375	11.5	82.9	0.0	5.6	0.0	24.3	18.1	38.3	68.9	6.4	143	54.5
McBee town	870	854	-1.8	1,199	34.4	64.5	0.0	0.6	0.6	33.2	9.8	34.2	59.6	6.6	365	85.2
McClellanville town	499	542	8.6	568	90.5	9.2	0.0	0.4	0.0	24.5	25.5	46.8	16.5	53.5	222	91.4
McColl town	2,174	1,970	-9.4	2,038	57.3	26.2	0.0	15.7	0.9	23.8	24.6	39.5	74.6	2.6	812	67.1
McConnells town	255	315	23.5	297	89.6	7.4	0.0	3.0	0.0	26.6	16.8	41.9	45.6	27.0	103	90.3
McCormick town	2,777	2,352	-15.3	2,992	28.5	67.7	0.1	3.1	0.5	14.2	16.4	43.3	65.1	9.0	912	72.7
Manning city	4,111	3,892	-5.3	3,943	32.0	64.5	0.9	1.3	1.3	22.9	22.3	41.5	57.4	17.8	1,485	83.0
Marion city	6,902	6,326	-8.3	6,466	17.0	80.2	2.7	0.0	0.0	27.7	15.2	35.4	56.4	20.4	2,345	71.9
Mauldin city	23,184	25,409	9.6	25,217	62.8	22.7	2.6	2.5	9.4	22.3	15.2	40.2	30.1	35.5	9,968	93.0
Mayesville town	727	715	-1.7	545	21.7	78.3	0.0	0.0	0.0	23.5	16.1	43.4	50.3	24.1	229	83.0
Mayo CDP	1,592	-	-	1,469	94.3	0.0	2.3	3.4	0.0	19.4	7.4	45.9	53.1	11.8	564	97.3
Meggett town	1,194	1,297	8.6	1,034	89.7	8.5	0.8	0.0	1.0	15.2	40.0	58.3	30.2	36.7	498	84.1
Modoc CDP	218	-	-	242	100.0	0.0	0.0	0.0	0.0	5.8	25.6	58.3	40.8	38.1	125	85.6
Monarch Mill CDP	1,811	-	-	1,452	72.9	24.0	0.0	1.8	1.4	15.2	19.4	46.5	71.6	2.9	699	78.5
Moncks Corner town	7,690	11,986	55.9	10,743	67.7	27.5	0.2	2.3	2.2	23.8	11.0	35.3	44.3	17.9	3,774	93.5
Monetta town	230	240	4.3	239	48.1	36.8	0.0	0.0	15.1	13.8	15.9	43.5	65.2	12.4	95	83.2
Mount Carmel CDP	216	-	-	233	0.0	91.0	0.0	9.0	0.0	1.7	30.5	60.8	78.6	9.2	115	62.6
Mount Croghan town	193	185	-4.1	118	79.7	7.6	1.7	5.1	5.9	16.1	21.2	47.0	55.9	16.1	56	91.1
Mount Pleasant town	68,360	91,684	34.1	86,982	89.3	4.1	1.8	2.1	2.7	23.8	16.0	40.9	14.2	63.9	34,079	95.9
Mountville CDP	108	-	-	104	22.1	66.3	0.0	0.0	11.5	16.3	26.0	40.1	30.5	13.6	27	100.0
Mulberry CDP	529	-	-	211	45.5	53.1	0.0	1.4	0.0	3.3	19.9	54.0	66.9	0.0	108	89.8
Mullins city	4,667	4,239	-9.2	4,356	31.5	66.9	0.0	0.1	1.4	24.4	22.0	39.5	65.9	17.8	1,535	76.0
Murphys Estates CDP	1,441	-	-	1,490	81.9	13.9	0.0	2.1	2.1	30.5	14.0	35.5	71.5	10.2	461	98.0
Murrells Inlet CDP	7,547	-	-	9,137	82.6	13.3	1.6	0.6	1.9	12.4	33.0	56.9	34.2	31.0	4,129	93.7
Myrtle Beach city	27,041	34,695	28.3	32,700	68.0	14.5	2.2	2.2	13.1	20.2	21.5	45.2	40.1	28.8	13,817	91.4
Neeses town	373	342	-8.3	304	84.9	12.8	0.0	2.3	0.0	15.5	18.8	45.5	57.2	12.2	120	74.2
Newberry city	10,350	10,199	-1.5	10,245	35.1	59.4	0.3	3.1	2.1	18.9	18.2	41.2	58.4	16.9	4,047	72.9
New Ellenton town	2,031	2,151	5.9	1,965	48.9	47.7	0.0	0.2	3.3	20.9	24.8	41.5	57.6	15.4	937	85.7
Newport CDP	4,136	-	-	4,602	78.7	14.3	1.8	2.1	3.1	21.7	18.8	40.5	33.4	30.1	1,704	92.1
Newry CDP	172	-	-	191	57.6	0.0	0.0	0.0	42.4	13.6	10.5	35.5	79.6	0.0	101	48.5
Nichols town	368	335	-9.0	281	56.9	39.5	0.0	0.7	2.8	18.9	22.4	45.1	55.6	23.8	124	78.2
Ninety Six town	2,039	2,042	0.1	1,918	80.9	16.3	0.0	2.1	0.7	25.5	18.7	40.1	47.6	18.0	706	87.0
Norris town	811	824	1.6	900	93.2	3.7	0.2	0.8	2.1	29.7	15.2	34.0	61.9	15.5	313	78.3
North town	771	708	-8.2	742	54.3	43.7	0.0	0.8	1.2	21.4	23.0	46.1	49.3	12.8	329	73.6
North Augusta city	21,309	23,845	11.9	22,908	71.2	18.3	0.7	3.1	6.7	21.8	17.0	40.6	32.0	36.8	9,754	93.1
North Charleston city	97,579	115,382	18.2	111,501	38.4	44.2	2.1	4.0	11.4	24.6	10.7	33.0	46.8	22.8	41,874	89.8
North Hartsville CDP	3,251	-	-	2,732	80.3	16.7	0.6	1.2	1.2	23.7	17.1	44.1	46.4	21.1	1,089	87.5
Northlake CDP	3,745	-	-	3,643	83.4	8.0	2.9	2.0	3.7	18.1	29.3	51.0	31.4	35.7	1,530	90.6
North Myrtle Beach city	13,816	16,819	21.7	16,200	87.1	1.5	2.9	1.7	6.8	10.7	35.1	58.3	33.8	34.4	7,558	96.1
Norway town	335	309	-7.8	329	42.9	52.6	0.0	4.6	0.0	19.8	19.5	42.5	19.0	26.1	116	89.7

1 May be of any race.

Table A. All Places — **Population and Housing**

STATE City, town, township, borough, or CDP (county if applicable)	Population				Race and Hispanic or Latino origin (percent)					Age (percent)			Educational attainment of persons age 25 and older		Occupied housing units	
	2010 census total population	2019 estimated population	Percent change 2010–2019	ACS total population estimate 2015–2019	White alone, not Hispanic or Latino	Black alone, not Hispanic or Latino	Asian alone, not Hispanic or Latino	All other races or 2 or more races, not Hispanic or Latino	Hispanic or Latino[1]	Under 18 years old	Age 65 years and older	Median age	Percent High school diploma or less	Percent Bachelor's degree or more	Total	Percent with a computer
	1	2	3	4	5	6	7	8	9	10	11	12	13	14	15	16
SOUTH CAROLINA—Con.																
Oak Grove CDP	10,291	-	-	10,835	73.9	12.3	0.2	3.0	10.6	21.5	17.0	38.0	46.0	18.7	4,446	87.0
Oakland CDP	1,232	-	-	1,088	48.2	35.8	0.0	12.7	3.3	23.0	14.6	34.8	43.7	15.3	515	74.8
Olanta town	561	557	-0.7	527	66.2	33.8	0.0	0.0	0.0	28.5	24.7	44.1	67.0	12.3	199	66.3
Olar town	257	228	-11.3	310	29.7	70.3	0.0	0.0	0.0	26.5	22.3	38.8	63.1	9.2	113	71.7
Orangeburg city	13,870	12,654	-8.8	12,861	21.7	74.1	0.3	1.8	2.1	18.5	14.5	31.9	31.6	28.5	4,455	87.0
Oswego CDP	84	-	-	292	93.2	6.8	0.0	0.0	0.0	17.5	17.1	59.7	76.8	15.4	130	84.6
Pacolet town	2,270	2,550	12.3	2,444	75.1	17.5	0.0	3.1	4.3	23.9	16.3	40.5	52.9	11.6	957	76.6
Pageland town	2,704	2,636	-2.5	2,661	44.7	37.1	0.0	4.1	14.1	26.7	15.1	35.3	62.2	13.7	1,019	83.2
Pamplico town	1,225	1,220	-0.4	1,223	45.9	50.1	0.0	3.8	0.2	27.1	15.3	29.7	57.0	19.8	376	83.8
Parker CDP	11,431	-	-	12,227	50.1	19.8	0.2	1.0	29.0	27.1	11.4	34.6	65.8	15.0	4,355	81.2
Parksville town	117	111	-5.1	138	87.0	8.7	0.0	1.4	2.9	12.3	20.3	58.0	56.5	15.7	70	74.3
Patrick town	346	340	-1.7	363	74.1	25.9	0.0	0.0	0.0	11.3	18.5	50.8	71.2	5.0	195	50.3
Pawleys Island town	103	108	4.9	89	98.9	0.0	0.0	0.0	1.1	0.0	59.6	67.1	2.2	78.7	52	96.2
Paxville town	184	179	-2.7	430	55.1	38.6	0.0	3.7	2.6	20.0	13.7	28.8	51.2	12.4	150	90.7
Peak town	62	63	1.6	49	42.9	57.1	0.0	0.0	0.0	20.4	32.7	56.9	30.8	48.7	22	77.3
Pelion town	688	711	3.3	695	83.7	3.2	0.0	2.6	10.5	26.2	15.1	47.1	54.2	15.5	249	87.6
Pelzer town	1,291	1,401	8.5	1,360	95.4	3.5	0.0	1.0	0.1	20.0	21.8	46.1	62.2	7.5	560	84.5
Pendleton town	3,025	3,285	8.6	3,217	70.6	17.8	2.4	5.9	3.3	14.3	14.5	43.5	38.1	36.5	1,504	78.9
Perry town	232	248	6.9	212	57.1	41.0	0.0	0.9	0.9	40.1	9.9	33.5	57.7	17.1	77	79.2
Pickens city	3,111	3,170	1.9	3,160	85.8	10.2	1.5	2.2	0.3	28.1	18.3	33.9	60.1	15.4	1,190	79.3
Piedmont CDP	5,103	-	-	5,795	87.7	3.6	0.0	1.8	6.8	20.4	17.2	42.9	66.6	13.5	1,787	90.4
Pine Ridge town	2,069	2,366	14.4	2,438	67.2	24.1	2.4	4.5	1.8	20.9	18.0	37.5	39.6	23.9	900	95.1
Pinewood town	541	534	-1.3	493	41.2	44.6	0.0	13.2	1.0	29.2	17.0	40.7	54.5	18.0	193	76.7
Pinopolis CDP	948	-	-	1,260	95.9	3.0	0.0	1.1	0.0	7.9	24.5	55.1	14.9	47.2	618	93.0
Plum Branch town	82	74	-9.8	87	100.0	0.0	0.0	0.0	0.0	13.8	12.6	47.4	45.9	44.3	31	74.2
Pomaria town	171	177	3.5	152	57.9	42.1	0.0	0.0	0.0	16.4	20.4	47.5	57.5	12.3	44	86.4
Port Royal town	10,641	13,235	24.4	12,770	62.0	18.6	2.2	4.7	12.5	19.8	9.0	25.0	28.8	33.7	3,868	93.5
Powdersville CDP	-	-	-	9,632	80.1	7.3	4.2	1.1	7.3	23.9	12.3	38.0	37.4	31.8	3,515	95.4
Princeton CDP	62	-	-	81	95.1	0.0	0.0	4.9	0.0	0.0	0.0	48.1	28.6	0.0	19	100.0
Privateer CDP	2,349	-	-	1,916	86.3	7.9	1.2	2.6	2.0	17.2	19.5	47.5	54.1	12.5	871	93.0
Promised Land CDP	511	-	-	542	0.0	100.0	0.0	0.0	0.0	6.5	36.3	54.4	57.8	11.1	217	67.7
Prosperity town	1,263	1,292	2.3	1,293	52.1	45.2	0.3	0.0	2.4	26.8	22.3	40.0	54.0	16.8	506	77.1
Quinby town	924	922	-0.2	1,149	29.3	69.2	0.4	1.0	0.0	18.4	23.9	44.9	37.5	29.1	402	83.6
Ravenel town	2,446	2,720	11.2	2,691	48.4	38.7	0.0	0.0	12.9	16.8	14.7	39.9	62.3	19.6	986	81.7
Red Bank CDP	9,617	-	-	10,106	78.8	10.0	0.7	5.7	4.7	24.0	11.8	39.4	46.7	16.4	4,137	92.0
Red Hill CDP	13,223	-	-	16,273	73.6	15.1	2.4	2.0	6.8	20.2	20.7	40.4	44.5	23.1	5,935	95.5
Reevesville town	194	204	5.2	204	86.3	12.3	1.0	0.0	0.5	25.0	33.3	43.9	50.7	22.9	83	67.5
Reidville town	595	678	13.9	1,002	75.0	7.2	5.2	3.4	9.2	27.1	8.1	35.7	35.8	43.9	355	96.3
Rembert CDP	306	-	-	286	16.4	75.9	7.7	0.0	0.0	4.9	38.8	60.1	57.7	23.9	102	100.0
Richburg town	275	260	-5.5	315	32.1	67.9	0.0	0.0	0.0	27.6	16.8	37.3	54.9	16.7	98	73.5
Ridgeland town	4,019	3,811	-5.2	3,911	35.6	48.7	0.8	1.1	13.8	27.0	9.6	30.8	53.8	16.0	1,148	77.9
Ridge Spring town	737	748	1.5	661	35.9	59.6	0.0	0.0	4.5	13.8	21.8	45.7	62.1	13.6	259	69.9
Ridgeville town	1,967	1,705	-13.3	2,029	32.7	53.3	0.0	10.6	3.4	11.2	8.3	40.6	73.3	8.3	297	85.2
Ridgeway town	317	291	-8.2	307	65.5	33.9	0.7	0.0	0.0	13.4	34.9	54.8	35.0	43.9	147	85.7
Riverview CDP	681	-	-	1,112	94.8	4.4	0.0	0.0	0.8	24.8	14.7	41.6	33.5	39.1	390	83.6
Rock Hill city	66,878	75,048	12.2	73,334	50.1	39.1	1.9	2.2	6.8	22.7	13.7	34.6	35.7	30.3	29,251	92.3
Rockville town	128	136	6.3	125	88.8	9.6	0.0	0.0	1.6	19.2	46.4	63.5	13.9	53.5	66	98.5
Roebuck CDP	2,200	-	-	2,851	69.4	17.4	0.8	0.7	11.6	19.9	23.9	45.6	56.0	14.8	986	85.5
Rowesville town	304	279	-8.2	259	42.5	57.5	0.0	0.0	0.0	15.8	19.3	46.5	55.0	16.6	88	75.0
Ruby town	351	339	-3.4	361	82.8	11.6	0.0	4.4	1.1	18.0	19.7	42.6	49.8	24.4	176	78.4
Russellville CDP	488	-	-	195	49.2	50.8	0.0	0.0	0.0	0.0	36.9	61.1	79.9	2.6	99	58.6
St. Andrews CDP	20,493	-	-	20,990	23.6	60.8	4.6	4.7	6.2	21.5	11.3	31.9	40.3	24.3	9,534	91.4
St. George town	2,067	2,202	6.5	2,352	47.7	46.9	0.0	2.0	3.4	22.7	16.4	31.6	49.5	17.1	744	73.0
St. Matthews town	2,025	1,912	-5.6	2,355	32.1	65.9	0.2	1.3	0.6	17.7	23.0	46.1	53.6	20.1	943	79.7
St. Stephen town	1,703	1,814	6.5	1,752	39.9	58.8	0.0	1.1	0.2	29.3	14.7	35.4	60.0	12.5	648	74.7
Salem town	143	152	6.3	132	97.7	0.0	0.0	2.3	0.0	23.5	13.6	43.3	64.8	12.5	43	83.7
Salley town	396	415	4.8	287	35.9	57.5	0.7	5.9	0.0	28.2	16.0	37.4	53.7	16.8	114	75.4
Saluda town	3,557	3,605	1.3	3,608	19.6	33.5	0.0	0.2	46.7	27.7	14.6	32.2	67.0	9.6	1,126	69.8
Sangaree CDP	8,220	-	-	7,840	64.0	26.3	0.2	5.4	4.1	20.1	12.6	39.5	40.4	16.6	2,836	95.2
Sans Souci CDP	7,869	-	-	9,220	47.5	24.9	1.9	3.5	22.1	24.6	11.7	33.4	52.4	20.0	3,624	81.4
Santee town	964	900	-6.6	1,000	24.9	74.7	0.4	0.0	0.0	14.7	36.7	57.1	56.8	15.4	394	81.0
Saxon CDP	3,424	-	-	3,827	34.0	33.4	0.1	2.5	30.0	27.6	12.2	29.3	68.8	6.0	1,281	76.7
Scotia town	215	197	-8.4	307	20.5	79.5	0.0	0.0	0.0	30.3	15.0	39.4	67.0	8.8	109	85.3
Scranton town	856	862	0.7	713	43.5	53.6	0.0	0.7	2.2	16.4	30.6	49.7	54.6	5.6	258	77.5
Seabrook Island town	1,717	1,865	8.6	1,762	98.0	0.6	1.1	0.2	0.1	2.0	62.1	67.9	6.9	76.5	951	98.1
Sellers town	220	200	-9.1	184	5.4	93.5	0.0	1.1	0.0	10.9	32.1	61.2	80.3	4.8	70	40.0
Seneca city	8,120	8,533	5.1	8,368	71.8	23.7	0.3	2.9	1.3	17.6	26.5	46.8	43.6	26.7	4,043	83.0
Seven Oaks CDP	15,144	-	-	15,484	55.6	36.2	2.9	2.4	2.9	20.2	17.8	37.4	28.7	37.7	6,703	93.0
Sharon town	505	625	23.8	495	84.4	8.5	0.0	6.7	0.4	22.0	17.6	42.7	55.8	14.7	196	82.7
Shell Point CDP	2,336	-	-	2,842	49.3	40.4	0.0	0.5	9.8	26.6	10.5	31.3	38.0	25.5	965	87.0
Shiloh CDP	214	-	-	260	48.1	41.9	0.0	0.0	10.0	23.5	30.0	58.5	92.5	3.8	110	96.4
Silverstreet town	162	167	3.1	143	74.1	24.5	0.0	0.0	1.4	23.1	35.0	56.1	51.8	13.6	52	90.4
Simpsonville city	18,436	24,221	31.4	22,234	66.2	21.2	1.4	1.6	9.8	24.1	14.4	37.8	32.2	35.2	8,464	95.2
Six Mile town	667	672	0.7	848	96.7	0.5	0.6	0.7	1.5	27.9	15.3	38.7	30.4	37.9	313	79.6
Slater-Marietta CDP	2,176	-	-	1,873	94.4	1.0	0.0	0.5	4.1	20.7	23.0	43.9	62.7	8.2	673	81.3
Smoaks town	126	118	-6.3	109	100.0	0.0	0.0	0.0	0.0	16.5	30.3	52.5	48.3	19.1	46	84.8
Smyrna town	43	53	23.3	27	85.2	0.0	0.0	0.0	14.8	22.2	22.2	33.5	68.4	0.0	15	73.3
Snelling town	274	258	-5.8	275	90.2	8.0	0.0	0.0	1.8	16.7	12.4	37.3	56.3	15.6	105	83.8
Socastee CDP	19,952	-	-	24,964	73.9	6.7	1.2	4.6	13.6	22.2	17.6	39.2	43.7	19.6	8,798	93.7
Society Hill town	563	528	-6.2	473	55.2	38.9	0.0	1.7	4.2	20.3	18.6	41.1	50.9	16.7	188	75.0
South Congaree town	2,304	2,484	7.8	2,513	71.3	11.8	1.7	6.7	8.5	22.2	15.4	40.2	55.4	13.2	934	88.7
Southern Shops CDP	3,767	-	-	3,592	55.4	15.0	0.8	2.1	26.7	27.8	5.7	30.5	70.7	6.3	949	80.2
South Sumter CDP	2,411	-	-	2,482	9.5	87.6	0.0	0.7	2.1	31.3	13.5	29.6	56.6	14.9	897	79.6
Spartanburg city	36,753	37,399	1.8	37,424	43.6	47.2	2.3	2.2	4.7	23.0	16.0	34.6	42.6	29.9	15,154	82.4
Springdale CDP	2,574	-	-	2,576	66.8	21.4	3.1	8.6	0.0	25.1	12.3	34.2	70.7	7.7	881	85.5
Springdale town	2,627	2,733	4.0	2,737	80.4	7.1	2.2	6.1	4.3	21.4	20.3	43.6	45.6	21.5	1,107	89.3
Springfield town	529	484	-8.5	476	54.2	43.5	0.0	2.3	0.0	21.8	26.1	46.4	45.6	18.8	187	72.2
Starr town	178	190	6.7	177	84.2	7.9	0.0	7.9	0.0	22.6	10.7	40.2	36.9	16.2	72	91.7
Startex CDP	859	-	-	954	78.5	16.9	0.0	0.0	4.6	13.8	22.5	49.2	62.8	3.1	471	72.8
Stateburg CDP	1,380	-	-	1,813	54.3	32.9	2.8	3.5	6.5	30.4	15.4	34.8	23.6	53.2	634	92.3
Stuckey town	245	219	-10.6	209	10.0	90.0	0.0	0.0	0.0	24.4	15.3	47.7	50.3	20.4	96	84.4
Sullivan's Island town	1,789	1,924	7.5	2,203	96.3	0.2	1.2	1.0	1.3	20.1	19.2	47.9	4.2	83.6	821	98.8

1 May be of any race.

Table A. All Places — **Population and Housing**

STATE City, town, township, borough, or CDP (county if applicable)	Population 2010 census total population	 2019 estimated population	 Percent change 2010–2019	 ACS total population estimate 2015–2019	Race and Hispanic or Latino origin (percent) White alone, not Hispanic or Latino	 Black alone, not Hispanic or Latino	 Asian alone, not Hispanic or Latino	 All other races or 2 or more races, not Hispanic or Latino	 Hispanic or Latino[1]	Age (percent) Under 18 years old	 Age 65 years and older	 Median age	Educational attainment of persons age 25 and older Percent High school diploma or less	 Percent Bachelor's degree or more	Occupied housing units Total	 Percent with a computer
	1	2	3	4	5	6	7	8	9	10	11	12	13	14	15	16
SOUTHCAROLINA—Con.																
Summerton town	988	927	-6.2	898	43.4	55.8	0.0	0.4	0.3	17.0	19.3	42.3	53.3	23.1	444	73.9
Summerville town	42,960	52,549	22.3	53,037	68.2	21.0	1.9	3.8	5.0	25.2	13.1	35.6	33.8	29.7	19,374	94.3
Summit town	409	476	16.4	507	86.6	3.6	2.4	1.8	5.7	32.3	8.1	33.8	41.9	27.2	168	91.7
Sumter city	40,520	39,642	-2.2	39,800	41.7	48.4	2.2	2.4	5.3	27.1	15.1	32.5	40.0	24.0	15,605	84.3
Surfside Beach town	3,833	4,525	18.1	4,385	94.5	0.3	0.5	1.2	3.4	10.8	28.8	54.0	33.9	35.1	2,111	94.1
Swansea town	847	961	13.5	897	31.8	62.2	0.0	4.6	1.4	19.4	16.4	38.0	57.1	8.8	370	86.8
Sycamore town	183	153	-16.4	177	80.2	14.7	0.0	4.0	1.1	8.5	18.1	56.9	48.6	8.2	104	64.4
Tatum town	75	69	-8.0	71	60.6	33.8	0.0	5.6	0.0	9.9	18.3	49.9	58.7	1.6	33	81.8
Taylors CDP	21,617	-	-	22,230	70.9	15.3	2.6	1.9	9.3	22.1	16.3	38.8	31.3	32.2	8,460	92.2
Tega Cay city	7,790	11,335	45.5	10,412	89.2	2.0	3.0	0.6	5.1	29.7	12.7	40.7	14.2	59.1	3,531	99.2
Tigerville CDP	1,312	-	-	2,052	75.8	9.3	2.6	7.7	4.7	2.6	1.1	20.3	27.8	41.7	27	100.0
Timmonsville town	2,350	2,366	0.7	2,412	12.5	86.9	0.0	0.4	0.2	17.9	11.1	40.7	66.3	6.2	939	77.0
Travelers Rest city	4,597	5,346	16.3	5,152	72.5	15.2	3.1	1.2	8.0	32.4	14.4	31.1	36.6	26.2	1,751	88.3
Trenton town	199	198	-0.5	298	46.6	44.0	0.0	0.7	8.7	16.4	16.8	41.4	46.5	29.2	115	72.2
Troy town	97	99	2.1	98	79.6	20.4	0.0	0.0	0.0	8.2	37.8	61.3	58.0	17.0	46	84.8
Turbeville town	836	787	-5.9	895	53.2	40.6	0.8	2.6	2.9	26.1	29.5	41.5	61.9	14.4	385	72.2
Ulmer town	87	73	-16.1	37	94.6	5.4	0.0	0.0	0.0	0.0	29.7	52.5	37.5	20.8	23	69.6
Union city	8,368	7,640	-8.7	7,769	47.3	47.2	0.0	3.4	2.1	22.5	19.4	41.5	54.5	16.9	3,452	75.8
Utica CDP	1,489	-	-	1,257	86.2	11.9	0.0	1.2	0.7	27.8	12.8	39.4	53.9	8.4	499	87.0
Valley Falls CDP	6,299	-	-	6,656	60.4	33.3	1.3	1.7	3.3	11.1	11.4	24.9	35.5	29.0	2,648	91.3
Vance town	166	153	-7.8	131	0.8	99.2	0.0	0.0	0.0	12.2	22.1	42.7	77.7	1.8	56	75.0
Van Wyck town	823	1,080	31.2	920	93.9	6.1	0.0	0.0	0.0	18.5	24.6	45.9	53.5	10.9	298	83.2
Varnville town	2,162	1,976	-8.6	1,854	45.2	53.1	0.0	0.6	1.1	23.2	19.8	46.1	54.5	19.9	728	84.2
Wade Hampton CDP	20,622	-	-	20,906	74.7	7.3	4.5	1.7	11.7	19.3	19.1	42.5	29.9	40.9	9,016	90.8
Wagener town	795	837	5.3	858	33.0	63.3	2.9	0.0	0.8	23.5	16.6	39.9	54.8	14.6	320	85.3
Walhalla city	4,250	4,472	5.2	4,370	65.3	12.2	0.0	2.1	20.4	21.7	20.4	41.4	60.4	12.0	1,668	91.2
Wallace CDP	892	-	-	689	78.1	20.6	0.0	1.3	0.0	27.0	32.9	50.8	78.4	2.5	315	53.3
Walterboro city	5,797	5,426	-6.4	5,477	51.1	47.1	0.0	1.2	0.5	22.9	21.3	37.9	49.7	21.8	2,569	85.4
Ward town	92	93	1.1	167	74.9	20.4	0.0	3.0	1.8	12.0	24.6	53.3	65.9	9.8	75	61.3
Ware Place CDP	228	-	-	110	100.0	0.0	0.0	0.0	0.0	9.1	22.7	52.3	83.7	0.0	38	100.0
Ware Shoals town	2,174	2,154	-0.9	2,830	64.6	21.6	0.0	3.3	10.5	27.6	16.9	34.3	63.5	12.0	977	77.0
Warrenville CDP	1,233	-	-	915	89.8	9.0	0.0	0.0	1.2	15.8	27.0	46.3	55.3	13.1	434	86.9
Waterloo town	149	150	0.7	151	31.1	66.2	1.3	1.3	0.0	19.2	18.5	44.6	43.4	16.0	66	68.2
Watts Mills CDP	1,635	-	-	1,377	57.8	12.2	0.0	0.0	30.0	22.2	7.7	33.3	71.3	0.0	482	93.4
Wedgefield CDP	1,615	-	-	1,994	65.1	32.8	0.4	1.7	0.0	23.9	9.4	41.9	57.0	8.1	681	87.7
Welcome CDP	6,668	-	-	7,719	47.8	28.6	0.8	3.8	19.0	25.3	14.6	33.2	63.6	9.9	3,073	74.2
Wellford city	2,409	2,718	12.8	2,590	40.6	38.7	4.9	8.3	7.5	25.6	16.3	36.4	55.8	10.0	944	84.2
West Columbia city	16,608	17,998	8.4	17,641	67.7	18.4	1.7	3.2	9.0	14.4	20.7	42.1	37.9	32.0	8,315	87.4
Westminster city	2,436	2,591	6.4	2,536	80.2	15.5	1.3	1.0	2.1	26.4	15.0	35.7	53.7	15.1	1,076	79.6
West Pelzer town	880	946	7.5	808	90.5	5.8	0.0	2.8	0.9	26.2	19.6	39.9	68.3	7.2	310	80.6
West Union town	311	334	7.4	335	49.6	1.8	0.0	15.8	32.8	22.7	17.0	36.1	63.3	10.1	134	79.9
Whitmire town	1,438	1,454	1.1	1,509	82.6	15.7	0.0	0.9	0.9	27.7	14.0	36.4	60.4	14.4	551	81.1
Wilkinson Heights CDP	2,493	-	-	1,620	2.2	97.8	0.0	0.0	0.0	14.9	30.1	51.8	41.7	22.7	798	70.6
Williams town	117	109	-6.8	193	49.2	50.8	0.0	0.0	0.0	36.3	22.8	42.2	48.3	22.9	59	100.0
Williamston town	3,960	4,260	7.6	4,180	82.4	14.6	0.0	3.0	0.0	17.8	22.9	43.1	49.2	14.2	1,963	83.4
Willington CDP	142	-	-	-	-	-	-	-	-	-	-	-	-	-	-	-
Williston town	3,139	2,925	-6.8	2,983	44.9	52.2	0.0	2.6	0.3	34.4	13.2	37.7	56.7	9.9	1,296	68.9
Windsor town	138	145	5.1	128	93.8	3.9	0.0	2.3	0.0	6.3	48.4	63.8	57.9	5.3	60	80.0
Winnsboro town	3,556	3,181	-10.5	3,237	25.6	67.8	0.0	0.0	6.5	21.9	27.9	43.2	60.3	13.0	1,329	81.3
Winnsboro Mills CDP	1,898	-	-	2,324	31.2	68.8	0.0	0.0	0.0	20.6	12.4	45.4	77.8	5.6	960	81.0
Woodfield CDP	9,303	-	-	9,459	16.0	57.4	4.0	5.8	16.8	24.8	12.8	34.0	47.9	19.7	3,764	91.0
Woodford town	183	171	-6.6	137	53.3	40.9	0.0	0.0	5.8	19.0	37.2	55.2	73.6	12.1	58	53.4
Woodruff city	4,086	4,418	8.1	4,246	51.2	40.5	0.0	1.8	6.5	24.7	17.6	32.8	49.4	19.7	1,577	87.4
Yemassee town	1,241	1,136	-8.5	979	35.0	63.5	0.4	0.5	0.5	26.5	20.5	43.2	51.2	18.4	390	80.5
York city	7,765	8,412	8.3	8,144	54.1	38.6	0.0	1.8	5.4	23.1	16.5	37.2	48.4	17.9	3,376	83.4
SOUTH DAKOTA	814,198	884,659	8.7	870,638	82.0	2.0	1.4	10.8	3.8	24.6	16.3	37.0	38.5	28.8	344,397	88.5
Aberdeen city	26,112	28,257	8.2	28,225	85.0	2.1	4.1	5.8	3.0	22.7	16.6	35.5	38.8	29.3	12,089	87.0
Agar town	75	80	6.7	75	94.7	0.0	0.0	0.0	5.3	28.0	25.3	36.8	44.4	16.7	39	76.9
Agency Village CDP	181	-	-	242	13.2	0.0	0.0	86.8	0.0	31.0	14.0	28.5	67.3	5.2	46	60.9
Akaska town	42	47	11.9	59	100.0	0.0	0.0	0.0	0.0	8.5	47.5	64.3	75.9	11.1	33	72.7
Albee town	16	15	-6.3	5	100.0	0.0	0.0	0.0	0.0	0.0	0.0	60.3	60.0	0.0	3	0.0
Alcester city	807	755	-6.4	906	98.0	0.3	0.6	1.0	0.1	15.9	35.3	51.1	48.9	20.7	434	76.3
Alexandria city	615	644	4.7	706	99.4	0.0	0.0	0.6	0.0	34.0	16.1	30.6	44.0	21.9	242	85.5
Allen CDP	420	-	-	463	0.0	0.0	0.0	100.0	0.0	45.8	2.2	18.7	85.7	0.0	57	52.6
Alpena town	286	285	-0.3	336	75.9	0.0	0.0	6.5	17.6	21.1	25.3	49.3	58.2	18.0	150	81.3
Altamont town	34	34	0.0	34	100.0	0.0	0.0	0.0	0.0	41.2	17.6	41.0	60.0	0.0	16	87.5
Anderson CDP	371	-	-	426	100.0	0.0	0.0	0.0	0.0	25.6	11.0	43.4	36.1	33.1	146	89.7
Andover town	91	82	-9.9	80	95.0	0.0	0.0	0.0	5.0	2.5	16.3	55.0	35.2	28.2	52	96.2
Antelope CDP	826	-	-	900	2.8	0.0	0.0	97.2	0.0	40.1	8.1	23.8	47.6	12.0	247	66.8
Arlington city	915	859	-6.1	1,045	90.6	0.0	0.0	0.7	8.7	20.8	18.9	35.9	53.5	28.7	483	92.1
Armour city	699	669	-4.3	739	91.9	0.0	0.0	8.1	0.0	28.1	26.8	45.2	39.1	14.2	317	82.0
Artas town	9	8	-11.1	29	100.0	0.0	0.0	0.0	0.0	0.0	65.5	76.3	34.5	65.5	18	66.7
Artesian town	138	137	-0.7	193	92.7	0.0	0.0	0.0	7.3	30.6	20.2	38.8	59.0	18.7	89	78.7
Ashland Heights CDP	754	-	-	767	82.8	0.0	0.0	15.5	1.7	29.9	15.1	42.2	35.1	16.0	342	95.3
Ashton city	122	124	1.6	115	99.1	0.0	0.0	0.9	0.0	29.6	14.8	39.1	66.3	12.5	41	70.7
Astoria town	139	135	-2.9	165	100.0	0.0	0.0	0.0	0.0	25.5	15.8	37.1	62.7	7.8	65	81.5
Aurora town	530	834	57.4	792	91.5	0.5	0.0	2.9	5.1	27.9	12.1	31.7	31.0	28.4	332	96.4
Aurora Center CDP	12	-	-	45	100.0	0.0	0.0	0.0	0.0	35.6	11.1	38.8	51.7	13.8	19	100.0
Avon city	590	590	0.0	772	90.5	0.0	0.4	5.4	3.6	27.8	22.2	35.8	46.4	27.6	335	84.5
Badger town	102	101		90	94.4	0.0	0.0	1.1	4.4	11.1	37.8	52.8	50.0	3.1	47	83.0
Baltic city	1,083	1,178	8.8	1,110	92.9	0.2	0.0	1.2	5.8	31.3	5.7	33.5	34.8	28.2	402	95.8
Bancroft town	19	19	0.0	47	100.0	0.0	0.0	0.0	0.0	42.6	2.1	33.2	11.1	14.8	17	94.1
Batesland town	108	114	5.6	45	8.9	0.0	0.0	91.1	0.0	48.9	8.9	27.2	13.0	47.8	13	61.5
Bath CDP	172	-	-	223	91.9	0.0	0.0	8.1	0.0	33.2	33.6	48.9	43.6	15.4	80	100.0
Bath Corner CDP	49	-	-	99	100.0	0.0	0.0	0.0	0.0	27.3	0.0	52.3	20.8	79.2	35	100.0
Belle Fourche city	5,594	5,702	1.9	5,616	89.3	0.9	0.2	3.9	5.6	23.3	19.2	39.3	49.8	18.1	2,373	83.5
Belvidere town	51	57	11.8	91	71.4	0.0	0.0	28.6	0.0	22.0	17.6	36.6	22.5	28.2	34	50.0
Beresford city	2,005	2,026	1.0	2,291	91.2	0.0	0.0	3.0	5.8	20.1	19.7	40.3	45.3	23.1	1,005	90.0
Big Stone City city	471	456	-3.2	667	97.5	0.0	0.6	1.3	0.6	10.8	33.7	47.8	58.4	10.3	378	78.6
Bijou Hills CDP	6	-	-	-	-	-	-	-	-	-	-	-	-	-	-	-

1 May be of any race.

Table A. All Places — **Population and Housing**

STATE City, town, township, borough, or CDP (county if applicable)	Population: 2010 census total population	Population: 2019 estimated population	Population: Percent change 2010–2019	Population: ACS total population estimate 2015–2019	Race and Hispanic or Latino origin (percent): White alone, not Hispanic or Latino	Black alone, not Hispanic or Latino	Asian alone, not Hispanic or Latino	All other races or 2 or more races, not Hispanic or Latino	Hispanic or Latino[1]	Age (percent): Under 18 years old	Age 65 years and older	Median age	Educational attainment of persons age 25 and older: Percent High school diploma or less	Percent Bachelor's degree or more	Occupied housing units: Total	Percent with a computer
	1	2	3	4	5	6	7	8	9	10	11	12	13	14	15	16
SOUTH DAKOTA—Con.																
Bison town	334	322	-3.6	308	95.5	0.0	0.0	4.5	0.0	20.8	22.7	45.9	35.8	20.5	146	86.3
Blackhawk CDP	2,892	-	-	3,057	91.2	0.0	0.9	1.2	6.7	19.3	23.1	44.3	35.1	29.6	1,279	84.5
Blucksberg Mountain CDP	462	-	-	489	100.0	0.0	0.0	0.0	0.0	22.7	23.3	35.9	25.4	54.0	186	100.0
Blunt city	354	354	0.0	409	69.9	0.0	0.0	20.0	10.0	34.2	15.2	35.4	63.7	11.6	161	78.9
Bonesteel city	275	273	-0.7	418	78.7	0.0	0.0	21.3	0.0	28.5	27.0	37.3	45.6	24.5	158	71.5
Bowdle city	526	468	-11.0	433	96.1	1.4	0.2	2.3	0.0	29.8	30.0	36.7	56.4	15.2	169	84.6
Box Elder city	7,855	10,119	28.8	9,683	77.6	3.3	1.3	9.9	7.8	26.3	5.6	25.4	36.3	25.9	3,243	94.6
Bradley town	72	78	8.3	85	100.0	0.0	0.0	0.0	0.0	27.1	10.6	46.8	71.0	6.5	40	90.0
Brandon city	8,899	10,074	13.2	9,934	95.0	1.6	0.8	2.1	0.5	31.5	10.0	35.2	23.4	37.5	3,614	95.8
Brandt town	108	107	-0.9	106	84.0	0.0	0.0	0.0	16.0	32.1	13.2	30.4	66.1	11.3	40	87.5
Brant Lake city	51	60	17.6	71	100.0	0.0	0.0	0.0	0.0	14.1	29.6	58.1	5.1	66.1	34	100.0
Brant Lake South CDP	-	-	-	179	100.0	0.0	0.0	0.0	0.0	9.5	24.6	52.0	41.3	23.9	85	96.5
Brentford town	77	80	3.9	58	100.0	0.0	0.0	0.0	0.0	5.2	17.2	53.0	50.0	12.0	34	88.2
Bridgewater city	492	461	-6.3	365	93.7	0.0	0.0	1.1	5.2	19.2	35.6	51.5	52.4	17.3	180	86.1
Bristol city	341	308	-9.7	348	95.4	0.0	0.0	0.3	4.3	12.6	42.2	57.7	45.1	19.7	170	81.8
Britton city	1,241	1,273	2.6	1,678	92.8	1.6	0.0	1.7	3.9	28.4	20.5	36.4	37.5	19.2	658	94.7
Broadland town	31	34	9.7	26	96.2	0.0	0.0	3.8	0.0	26.9	3.8	30.7	66.7	5.6	13	92.3
Brookings city	22,074	24,415	10.6	24,108	88.4	1.7	4.2	2.9	2.7	17.8	9.5	24.3	27.5	45.8	8,741	93.2
Bruce city	205	205	0.0	174	95.4	0.0	0.0	0.6	4.0	17.2	20.1	41.5	46.5	26.0	78	91.0
Bryant city	456	454	-0.4	614	89.3	0.2	0.0	1.6	9.0	28.2	22.3	26.2	69.3	8.7	223	88.8
Buffalo town	330	369	11.8	324	97.5	0.0	0.0	2.5	0.0	28.1	17.9	40.0	31.1	30.6	148	93.2
Buffalo Chip town	-	-	-	-	-	-	-	-	-	-	-	-	-	-	-	-
Buffalo Gap town	126	144	14.3	95	86.3	0.0	0.0	13.7	0.0	11.6	42.1	61.3	55.1	9.0	54	70.4
Bullhead CDP	348	-	-	363	0.0	0.0	0.0	100.0	0.0	47.1	2.5	19.4	72.8	4.4	60	50.0
Burke city	605	586	-3.1	637	92.9	0.0	0.0	7.1	0.0	18.5	30.8	47.2	39.1	29.2	312	72.1
Bushnell town	65	65	0.0	54	79.6	0.0	0.0	20.4	0.0	7.4	18.5	53.2	43.8	37.5	31	96.8
Butler town	17	17	0.0	14	100.0	0.0	0.0	0.0	0.0	0.0	57.1	67.5	85.7	7.1	9	44.4
Camp Crook town	63	66	4.8	44	100.0	0.0	0.0	0.0	0.0	9.1	52.3	65.3	45.0	17.5	28	82.1
Canistota city	656	636	-3.0	709	78.6	0.6	0.0	7.5	13.4	25.8	18.3	30.0	56.7	17.6	300	86.7
Canova town	105	100	-4.8	68	95.6	4.4	0.0	0.0	0.0	13.2	41.2	53.7	38.6	5.3	40	72.5
Canton city	3,089	3,560	15.2	3,447	93.1	1.2	0.8	4.4	0.4	21.8	18.1	38.9	44.6	16.6	1,118	88.2
Caputa CDP	-	-	-	-	-	-	-	-	-	-	-	-	-	-	-	-
Carthage city	144	130	-9.7	169	91.1	0.0	3.0	2.4	3.6	23.1	23.7	37.5	49.5	12.6	86	81.4
Castlewood city	627	641	2.2	619	97.6	0.0	0.0	0.8	1.6	28.6	13.4	32.3	44.3	22.3	257	91.1
Cavour town	114	123	7.9	123	88.6	0.0	0.0	11.4	0.0	24.4	11.4	30.5	45.3	2.3	56	89.3
Centerville city	884	872	-1.4	877	98.9	0.0	0.0	0.7	0.5	25.3	16.8	36.9	42.4	23.6	403	88.8
Central City city	134	131	-2.2	144	96.5	0.0	0.0	3.5	0.0	11.1	13.2	37.3	69.4	18.0	65	81.5
Chamberlain city	2,377	2,366	-0.5	2,565	70.4	0.9	0.5	22.9	5.2	26.2	17.2	38.4	34.9	29.9	1,074	85.8
Chancellor town	264	264	0.0	308	87.7	1.6	0.0	5.2	5.5	25.0	15.9	39.1	54.7	16.3	124	83.9
Chelsea town	27	26	-3.7	23	100.0	0.0	0.0	0.0	0.0	13.0	34.8	58.5	29.4	11.8	10	90.0
Chester CDP	261	-	-	358	100.0	0.0	0.0	0.0	0.0	27.7	11.7	43.9	34.7	25.0	150	94.0
Claire City town	76	75	-1.3	61	96.7	0.0	0.0	3.3	0.0	21.3	23.0	45.3	51.1	31.1	30	86.7
Claremont town	127	128	0.8	48	97.9	0.0	0.0	2.1	0.0	12.5	39.6	61.5	40.0	15.0	28	82.1
Clark city	1,140	1,061	-6.9	1,370	90.0	0.2	1.0	3.4	5.3	19.3	29.2	47.7	54.3	17.8	665	80.8
Clear Lake city	1,275	1,262		1,393	91.0	0.1	0.0	1.1	7.8	18.6	27.1	46.2	46.7	20.6	630	81.1
Colman city	594	579	-2.5	636	90.9	0.0	5.7	1.1	2.4	26.6	8.5	29.7	45.1	21.0	274	89.8
Colome city	296	280	-5.4	437	68.6	0.0	0.0	31.4	0.0	44.9	8.9	22.2	40.9	36.8	138	86.2
Colonial Pine Hills CDP	2,493	-	-	2,396	88.6	1.0	0.0	2.1	8.2	27.3	15.6	44.1	14.5	53.4	889	98.8
Colton city	687	669	-2.6	762	96.2	0.0	0.0	1.6	2.2	27.6	15.0	37.0	47.0	19.6	302	85.4
Columbia city	136	138	1.5	140	98.6	0.0	0.0	1.4	0.0	23.6	12.1	45.2	40.6	13.9	66	95.5
Conde city	140	142	1.4	134	100.0	0.0	0.0	0.0	0.0	5.2	50.7	66.0	66.1	13.4	82	82.9
Corn Creek CDP	105	-	-	106	0.0	0.0	0.0	100.0	0.0	25.5	9.4	30.6	83.9	0.0	28	53.6
Corona town	109	106	-2.8	19	100.0	0.0	0.0	0.0	0.0	0.0	21.1	63.4	89.5	10.5	16	62.5
Corsica city	592	575	-2.9	650	92.9	0.0	0.0	4.2	2.9	16.0	31.4	50.3	50.0	16.8	291	83.8
Cottonwood town	9	10	11.1	4	100.0	0.0	0.0	0.0	0.0	0.0	25.0	0.0	25.0	75.0	1	100.0
Cow Creek CDP	30	-	-	50	84.0	0.0	0.0	16.0	0.0	18.0	28.0	42.3	0.0	47.4	24	100.0
Cresbard town	104	99	-4.8	116	99.1	0.0	0.0	0.9	0.0	23.3	26.7	46.0	20.2	29.2	57	78.9
Crocker CDP	19	-	-	29	100.0	0.0	0.0	0.0	0.0	0.0	44.8	0.0	100.0	0.0	13	0.0
Crooks city	1,269	1,327	4.6	1,279	98.4	0.0	0.2	0.8	0.6	31.7	6.6	34.8	32.0	29.4	441	98.9
Custer city	2,007	1,969	-1.9	2,282	92.9	0.7	0.0	3.5	2.9	11.3	31.8	56.2	45.4	22.6	1,058	83.0
Dakota Dunes CDP	-	-	-	3,156	84.0	1.8	4.4	1.9	7.9	24.6	13.9	37.6	20.0	47.6	1,318	96.7
Dallas town	120	122	1.7	81	91.4	0.0	0.0	8.6	0.0	11.1	21.0	54.3	88.6	0.0	38	50.0
Dante town	84	86	2.4	103	89.3	0.0	0.0	10.7	0.0	40.8	10.7	28.5	26.8	33.9	38	94.7
Davis town	87	88	1.1	70	94.3	0.0	0.0	5.7	0.0	12.9	28.6	45.7	55.1	16.3	44	79.5
Deadwood city	1,294	1,293	-0.1	1,548	89.3	0.3	0.0	5.0	5.4	9.1	20.0	51.1	40.8	22.7	825	89.1
Dell Rapids city	3,633	3,628	-0.1	3,660	95.0	0.0	0.0	3.5	1.5	27.4	15.7	35.3	32.4	29.9	1,415	91.7
Delmont city	234	217	-7.3	233	92.7	0.0	0.0	7.3	0.0	21.5	12.0	26.8	42.9	11.1	108	68.5
De Smet city	1,089	1,052	-3.4	1,092	99.3	0.0	0.0	0.7	0.0	24.9	31.4	44.7	53.9	17.7	495	80.0
Dimock town	131	130	-0.8	156	94.9	0.0	1.9	3.2	0.0	31.4	28.8	47.7	63.7	11.8	51	84.3
Doland city	180	181	0.6	262	84.0	0.0	0.0	0.4	15.6	30.9	13.4	35.6	58.5	13.8	101	88.1
Dolton town	37	38	2.7	77	46.8	0.0	0.0	22.1	31.2	41.6	7.8	37.2	88.9	0.0	31	83.9
Draper town	82	67	-18.3	69	100.0	0.0	0.0	0.0	0.0	15.9	29.0	49.4	87.7	0.0	32	100.0
Dupree city	527	518	-1.7	525	25.5	0.0	3.2	70.3	1.0	28.8	9.1	32.8	54.9	15.9	153	67.3
Eagle Butte city	1,308	1,346	2.9	1,062	6.2	0.2	0.0	93.1	0.5	39.9	4.7	23.8	47.6	16.9	291	68.0
Eden town	89	100	12.4	84	98.8	0.0	0.0	1.2	0.0	4.8	47.6	62.8	59.0	14.1	49	83.7
Edgemont city	774	719	-7.1	716	85.3	0.0	0.0	13.7	1.0	23.3	24.9	49.1	55.8	8.3	338	71.9
Egan city	278	273	-1.8	354	93.2	0.0	0.0	3.4	3.4	21.2	24.0	50.0	51.9	12.6	167	83.8
Elk Point city	1,961	1,871	-4.6	2,176	96.0	1.9	0.0	1.3	0.8	30.8	18.8	36.9	36.4	32.5	854	88.9
Elkton city	736	726	-1.4	842	75.1	0.4	0.2	3.1	21.3	35.7	12.0	33.6	48.0	21.0	292	90.4
Emery city	448	451	0.7	557	99.8	0.0	0.0	0.2	0.0	23.2	12.7	33.7	43.9	16.1	168	89.9
Erwin town	45	44	-2.2	40	100.0	0.0	0.0	0.0	0.0	10.0	60.0	68.5	63.9	16.7	21	66.7
Estelline city	768	746	-2.9	807	89.7	0.0	0.0	3.3	6.9	26.9	19.8	36.2	50.0	21.6	353	91.5
Ethan town	331	322	-2.7	377	95.2	0.0	0.0	2.7	2.1	28.4	17.5	34.8	48.4	7.8	166	84.9
Eureka city	868	826	-4.8	1,018	90.1	4.7	1.6	0.8	2.8	12.5	39.6	58.0	56.1	18.7	535	73.5
Fairburn town	85	98	15.3	103	81.6	0.0	2.9	15.5	0.0	11.7	10.7	47.7	63.3	10.0	53	79.2
Fairfax town	115	115	0.0	135	99.3	0.0	0.0	0.7	0.0	13.3	41.5	63.7	70.1	12.8	76	60.5
Fairview town	59	74	25.4	47	100.0	0.0	0.0	0.0	0.0	4.3	38.3	57.3	41.0	17.9	19	94.7
Faith city	416	411	-1.2	363	94.2	0.0	0.0	4.7	1.1	36.4	17.9	40.0	47.8	20.8	139	77.0
Farmer town	10	10	0.0	17	100.0	0.0	0.0	0.0	0.0	58.8	11.8	11.5	100.0	0.0	4	100.0
Faulkton city	736	709	-3.7	831	97.5	0.1	0.0	2.4	0.0	23.6	25.3	44.5	42.1	26.5	375	85.9
Fedora CDP	37	-	-	14	100.0	0.0	0.0	0.0	0.0	0.0	64.3	70.4	35.7	35.7	14	100.0
Ferney CDP	43	-	-	41	100.0	0.0	0.0	0.0	0.0	0.0	100.0	69.6	80.5	19.5	41	19.5

1 May be of any race.

STATE City, town, township, borough, or CDP (county if applicable)	2010 census total population	2019 estimated population	Percent change 2010–2019	ACS total population estimate 2015–2019	White alone, not Hispanic or Latino	Black alone, not Hispanic or Latino	Asian alone, not Hispanic or Latino	All other races or 2 or more races, not Hispanic or Latino	Hispanic or Latino[1]	Under 18 years old	Age 65 years and older	Median age	Percent High school diploma or less	Percent Bachelor's degree or more	Total	Percent with a computer
	1	2	3	4	5	6	7	8	9	10	11	12	13	14	15	16
SOUTH DAKOTA—Con.																
Flandreau city	2,341	2,316	-1.1	2,458	52.6	1.1	4.0	34.0	8.3	29.7	22.3	35.2	41.8	18.8	991	87.1
Florence town	372	360	-3.2	396	91.4	0.0	0.0	8.6	0.0	31.6	12.9	36.3	39.7	10.7	154	83.8
Forestburg CDP	73	-	-	72	100.0	0.0	0.0	0.0	0.0	11.1	6.9	48.4	48.4	32.8	34	88.2
Fort Pierre city	2,094	2,217	5.9	2,240	87.9	0.0	0.0	9.8	2.3	23.4	20.2	39.9	33.4	35.7	1,050	81.9
Fort Thompson CDP	1,282	-	-	1,235	1.5	0.2	0.0	95.2	3.1	38.1	4.5	25.7	65.2	5.6	330	58.8
Frankfort city	149	151	1.3	117	95.7	0.0	0.0	4.3	0.0	17.1	29.9	55.3	59.1	8.0	60	65.0
Frederick town	199	196	-1.5	190	95.8	0.0	0.0	4.2	0.0	17.4	26.8	54.0	49.7	16.6	88	85.2
Freeman city	1,308	1,275	-2.5	1,459	88.0	0.0	1.2	3.4	7.4	24.7	27.8	43.5	48.7	21.7	576	74.8
Fruitdale town	64	68	6.3	120	100.0	0.0	0.0	0.0	0.0	26.7	25.0	45.8	76.4	15.3	41	95.1
Fulton town	91	96	5.5	144	100.0	0.0	0.0	0.0	0.0	17.4	20.8	36.9	43.9	25.4	56	91.1
Gann Valley CDP	14	-	-	16	100.0	0.0	0.0	0.0	0.0	0.0	25.0	33.7	12.5	0.0	14	100.0
Garden City town	53	58	9.4	85	78.8	0.0	3.5	17.6	0.0	25.9	9.4	24.7	32.5	20.0	31	87.1
Garretson city	1,166	1,147	-1.6	1,263	88.0	4.0	0.0	6.3	1.7	23.8	16.2	37.3	35.6	22.8	502	92.0
Gary city	227	229	0.9	297	94.3	0.0	0.0	0.7	5.1	27.6	23.9	48.8	68.6	10.5	138	79.7
Gayville town	407	396	-2.7	352	91.8	0.0	0.6	1.7	6.0	20.2	18.5	40.5	44.9	22.0	160	80.0
Geddes city	210	207	-1.4	254	83.5	0.0	0.0	16.5	0.0	36.6	14.6	31.9	59.0	9.0	89	73.0
Gettysburg city	1,178	1,081	-8.2	1,294	89.9	0.0	1.9	8.3	0.0	23.3	25.0	41.4	42.0	23.2	535	91.2
Glenham town	105	105	0.0	100	100.0	0.0	0.0	0.0	0.0	2.0	35.0	58.5	83.7	9.2	57	73.7
Goodwill CDP	513	-	-	608	1.3	0.0	0.0	96.4	2.3	44.2	8.1	24.1	56.4	2.8	130	67.7
Goodwin town	146	148	1.4	109	100.0	0.0	0.0	0.0	0.0	13.8	34.9	56.4	55.6	13.3	64	81.3
Green Grass CDP	35	-	-	22	0.0	0.0	0.0	100.0	0.0	36.4	0.0	19.4	100.0	0.0	6	0.0
Green Valley CDP	928	-	-	1,227	65.5	0.0	1.9	28.9	3.7	27.2	12.1	34.8	32.7	27.8	453	88.3
Gregory city	1,293	1,242	-3.9	1,507	85.2	0.0	4.9	7.4	2.5	23.8	22.4	46.4	43.3	21.6	677	83.3
Grenville town	53	51	-3.8	53	90.6	0.0	0.0	0.0	9.4	0.0	28.3	58.8	36.7	30.6	30	90.0
Groton city	1,458	1,475	1.2	1,673	92.2	0.0	0.0	1.6	6.3	29.1	18.8	38.5	41.9	21.5	638	81.0
Hamill CDP	11	-	-	-	-	-	-	-	-	-	-	-	-	-	-	-
Harrisburg city	4,113	6,710	63.1	6,087	93.7	0.3	0.0	4.6	1.3	35.4	2.6	29.1	25.7	39.7	1,945	100.0
Harrison CDP	52	-	-	53	100.0	0.0	0.0	0.0	0.0	7.5	79.2	67.5	81.6	16.3	25	88.0
Harrold town	124	124	0.0	81	95.1	0.0	0.0	4.9	0.0	13.6	40.7	59.9	61.5	9.2	47	72.3
Hartford city	2,537	3,354	32.2	3,220	94.7	0.4	0.2	2.9	1.8	33.0	7.7	31.6	31.5	36.3	1,153	95.1
Hayti town	381	383	0.5	366	90.7	0.0	0.3	2.2	6.8	31.4	13.4	31.9	57.1	15.1	157	88.5
Hazel town	91	86	-5.5	115	96.5	0.9	0.0	0.0	2.6	40.0	6.1	29.5	59.0	6.6	40	87.5
Hecla city	224	216	-3.6	249	88.8	0.0	0.0	0.0	11.2	19.7	38.2	61.8	48.0	13.1	122	78.7
Henry town	267	265	-0.7	239	99.6	0.0	0.0	0.4	0.0	23.0	17.2	46.6	61.1	6.8	102	95.1
Hermosa town	400	425	6.3	413	83.5	0.0	2.9	10.9	2.7	21.8	7.7	36.2	51.7	19.0	163	89.6
Herreid city	438	416	-5.0	468	100.0	0.0	0.0	0.0	0.0	23.5	23.7	50.0	49.0	26.5	204	72.1
Herrick town	105	103	-1.9	103	80.6	0.0	0.0	19.4	0.0	31.1	17.5	44.1	61.5	4.6	36	77.8
Hetland town	51	47	-7.8	9	100.0	0.0	0.0	0.0	0.0	0.0	0.0	45.5	100.0	0.0	7	71.4
Highmore city	795	726	-8.7	752	94.5	0.0	0.0	5.2	0.3	14.4	33.6	56.7	49.4	19.0	362	86.2
Hill City city	938	1,032	10.0	1,002	66.5	0.0	0.0	4.0	29.5	29.5	12.7	38.8	38.6	27.5	304	88.2
Hillsview town	3	3	0.0	-	-	-	-	-	-	-	-	-	-	-	-	-
Hitchcock town	91	95	4.4	99	91.9	0.0	0.0	0.0	8.1	11.1	22.2	49.8	24.1	36.1	47	91.5
Hosmer city	208	186	-10.6	274	100.0	0.0	0.0	0.0	0.0	27.4	26.6	46.2	57.3	16.9	111	71.2
Hot Springs city	3,725	3,502	-6.0	3,509	77.5	0.0	2.9	14.4	5.2	14.2	28.1	52.6	40.3	19.7	1,616	87.0
Hoven town	406	366	-9.9	356	100.0	0.0	0.0	0.0	0.0	19.9	34.6	55.5	59.9	8.2	139	78.4
Howard city	853	757	-11.3	907	92.7	0.3	0.3	3.6	3.0	22.1	24.9	44.3	52.2	13.2	386	85.5
Hudson town	296	345	16.6	380	99.5	0.0	0.0	0.5	0.0	19.2	15.0	40.0	56.2	12.7	175	82.9
Humboldt town	589	567	-3.7	686	97.7	0.0	0.0	2.3	0.0	30.9	17.3	33.4	42.1	19.4	261	91.2
Hurley city	413	399	-3.4	354	91.0	0.0	0.0	1.7	7.3	24.0	19.2	41.6	39.0	16.5	144	89.6
Huron city	12,610	13,380	6.1	13,282	70.0	1.6	12.6	3.2	12.6	27.9	17.2	34.4	51.2	18.2	5,495	81.2
Interior town	92	106	15.2	45	100.0	0.0	0.0	0.0	0.0	0.0	44.4	59.6	68.9	15.6	25	60.0
Ipswich city	957	891	-6.9	1,008	92.4	0.1	0.1	2.7	4.8	24.6	20.1	35.9	46.1	26.4	415	89.9
Irene city	420	406	-3.3	618	94.5	0.0	0.0	1.8	3.7	30.1	18.8	33.8	46.2	20.7	230	90.4
Iroquois city	266	259	-2.6	354	99.7	0.0	0.0	0.3	0.0	28.2	15.3	35.5	53.9	15.5	155	88.4
Isabel town	135	152	12.6	164	64.0	1.8	0.0	34.1	0.0	27.4	19.5	35.8	41.9	19.0	68	80.9
Java town	129	127	-1.6	145	93.1	0.0	0.0	4.1	2.8	15.9	27.6	30.7	53.2	24.5	62	83.9
Jefferson city	549	511	-6.9	633	95.1	0.8	0.0	3.0	1.1	23.5	18.0	38.1	37.9	17.0	290	89.7
Johnson Siding CDP	659	-	-	597	94.6	0.0	0.0	3.0	2.3	7.2	38.4	59.6	46.1	19.3	314	100.0
Kadoka city	656	717	9.3	779	78.4	0.0	0.9	20.7	0.0	25.7	22.5	35.2	52.8	24.6	284	70.8
Kaylor CDP	47	-	-	24	100.0	0.0	0.0	0.0	0.0	0.0	100.0	0.0	100.0	0.0	13	100.0
Kennebec town	240	247	2.9	308	94.2	0.0	0.0	5.8	0.0	18.2	27.3	47.2	59.2	18.5	133	85.0
Keystone town	334	343	2.7	427	79.4	0.0	2.3	5.4	12.9	21.1	11.9	34.9	45.1	21.7	150	91.3
Kidder CDP	57	-	-	-	-	-	-	-	-	-	-	-	-	-	-	-
Kimball city	699	673	-3.7	590	96.4	0.3	0.2	2.0	1.0	17.1	18.6	45.0	54.3	16.0	316	70.9
Kranzburg town	172	174	1.2	170	85.9	0.0	0.0	0.0	14.1	25.9	15.9	39.0	63.3	10.0	62	87.1
Kyle CDP	846	-	-	1,093	4.5	0.0	0.0	93.7	1.8	41.8	2.8	23.4	76.0	3.6	196	70.9
La Bolt town	68	68	0.0	90	100.0	0.0	0.0	0.0	0.0	11.1	18.9	34.4	38.0	11.3	46	84.8
Lake Andes city	820	821	0.1	897	42.6	0.6	0.2	54.2	2.5	34.4	16.9	29.2	56.3	17.9	259	73.0
Lake City town	51	52	2.0	69	100.0	0.0	0.0	0.0	0.0	11.6	23.2	51.8	32.8	15.5	27	81.5
Lake Madison CDP	683	-	-	895	95.2	0.0	0.0	4.8	0.0	10.2	39.2	58.7	27.1	47.6	406	98.3
Lake Norden city	469	522	11.3	502	99.0	0.0	0.0	1.0	0.0	20.3	27.5	45.7	59.5	15.1	204	89.7
Lake Poinsett CDP	493	-	-	520	91.0	2.7	0.0	6.3	0.0	25.0	24.2	48.3	27.1	43.4	218	94.5
Lake Preston city	599	555	-7.3	400	96.3	0.0	0.0	0.0	3.8	15.3	26.5	53.6	50.6	16.3	230	86.1
Lane town	59	60	1.7	21	100.0	0.0	0.0	0.0	0.0	0.0	42.9	63.9	85.7	0.0	17	76.5
Langford town	313	326	4.2	415	86.7	0.0	0.0	8.0	5.3	24.3	19.0	44.1	39.3	28.0	157	78.3
La Plant CDP	171	-	-	247	5.3	0.0	0.0	94.7	0.0	34.4	4.0	25.4	81.7	0.0	57	43.9
Lead city	3,123	2,943	-5.8	2,985	94.3	0.1	0.6	2.9	2.1	20.1	21.8	46.5	45.1	23.1	1,410	89.6
Lebanon town	47	43	-8.5	24	100.0	0.0	0.0	0.0	0.0	12.5	41.7	62.5	57.1	19.0	12	91.7
Lemmon city	1,235	1,174	-4.9	1,239	92.3	0.0	0.0	6.5	1.3	14.0	27.7	52.6	50.1	16.2	571	80.9
Lennox city	2,130	2,479	16.4	2,505	96.5	2.0	0.0	1.5	0.0	27.1	15.4	38.3	45.6	18.1	966	83.2
Leola city	457	427	-6.6	472	97.9	0.0	0.0	2.1	0.0	32.8	14.6	34.3	47.5	10.9	167	77.2
Lesterville town	127	131	3.1	111	92.8	0.0	2.7	4.5	0.0	3.6	29.7	60.4	52.7	6.6	56	75.0
Letcher town	173	176	1.7	201	93.0	0.0	1.5	5.5	0.0	27.9	9.5	35.7	40.2	21.4	91	90.1
Lily town	4	4	0.0	2	100.0	0.0	0.0	0.0	0.0	0.0	0.0	0.0	0.0	0.0	2	0.0
Little Eagle CDP	319	-	-	327	0.0	0.0	0.0	100.0	0.0	44.3	3.4	22.6	66.7	7.5	60	36.7
Long Hollow CDP	192	-	-	406	2.0	0.0	0.0	98.0	0.0	62.6	0.0	8.0	35.1	0.0	100	80.0
Long Lake town	31	31	0.0	42	100.0	0.0	0.0	0.0	0.0	19.0	0.0	52.5	55.9	8.8	19	78.9
Loomis CDP	34	-	-	-	-	-	-	-	-	-	-	-	-	-	-	-
Lower Brule CDP	613	-	-	897	5.9	0.4	0.3	92.9	0.4	42.1	7.1	22.5	49.4	12.9	215	68.4
Lowry town	6	6	0.0	5	100.0	0.0	0.0	0.0	0.0	0.0	40.0	64.8	60.0	0.0	3	66.7
McIntosh city	168	167	-0.6	193	70.5	0.0	0.0	28.5	1.0	27.5	18.7	44.3	45.1	30.1	81	70.4
McLaughlin city	652	653	0.2	472	26.9	0.6	0.0	72.5	0.0	30.5	10.6	31.3	38.7	29.1	167	64.7

1 May be of any race.

Table A. All Places — **Population and Housing**

STATE City, town, township, borough, or CDP (county if applicable)	Population				Race and Hispanic or Latino origin (percent)					Age (percent)			Educational attainment of persons age 25 and older		Occupied housing units	
	2010 census total population	2019 estimated population	Percent change 2010–2019	ACS total population estimate 2015–2019	White alone, not Hispanic or Latino	Black alone, not Hispanic or Latino	Asian alone, not Hispanic or Latino	All other races or 2 or more races, not Hispanic or Latino	Hispanic or Latino[1]	Under 18 years old	Age 65 years and older	Median age	Percent High school diploma or less	Percent Bachelor's degree or more	Total	Percent with a computer
	1	2	3	4	5	6	7	8	9	10	11	12	13	14	15	16
SOUTH DAKOTA—Con.																
Madison city	6,497	7,270	11.9	7,261	89.5	0.5	2.7	5.8	1.6	22.4	18.9	35.4	48.4	30.5	2,406	88.8
Manderson-White Horse Creek CDP	626	-	-	279	0.0	0.0	0.0	100.0	0.0	30.1	4.7	30.1	71.5	0.0	51	68.6
Mansfield CDP	93	-	-	165	78.2	4.2	0.0	17.6	0.0	27.9	3.6	24.8	48.1	21.0	50	84.0
Marion city	784	780	-0.5	812	97.4	0.0	0.2	1.0	1.4	18.1	28.7	51.5	39.2	14.3	361	78.1
Martin city	1,063	1,045	-1.7	973	50.4	0.2	1.4	44.1	3.9	29.0	20.1	36.3	42.1	21.0	357	78.4
Marty CDP	402	-	-	316	3.5	0.0	0.0	96.5	0.0	41.8	4.1	25.2	58.9	8.6	69	58.0
Marvin town	30	29	-3.3	20	95.0	0.0	0.0	5.0	0.0	0.0	45.0	56.0	90.0	5.0	11	81.8
Meadow View Addition CDP	538	-	-	540	79.1	3.0	0.0	10.7	7.2	14.1	20.0	41.9	51.8	20.5	224	89.3
Mellette city	210	214	1.9	192	92.7	0.0	0.0	7.3	0.0	22.4	15.1	39.6	36.1	12.8	90	95.6
Menno city	604	614	1.7	740	98.9	0.0	0.0	1.1	0.0	20.3	33.5	55.6	47.5	20.3	354	70.3
Midland town	129	127	-1.6	88	96.6	0.0	0.0	3.4	0.0	14.8	29.5	51.7	57.3	4.0	47	74.5
Milbank city	3,355	3,103	-7.5	3,166	87.8	0.2	0.0	3.5	8.5	20.1	20.6	40.9	39.0	26.3	1,507	87.2
Miller city	1,484	1,334	-10.1	1,421	97.2	0.0	1.3	0.6	0.9	19.1	28.6	49.6	42.0	25.5	721	81.8
Milltown CDP	10	-	-	21	100.0	0.0	0.0	0.0	0.0	0.0	38.1	48.6	38.1	61.9	11	63.6
Mission city	1,182	1,257	6.3	1,310	11.3	0.2	0.0	86.0	2.6	50.2	5.6	17.8	51.2	7.6	386	63.0
Mission Hill town	177	164	-7.3	209	93.8	0.0	0.0	5.3	1.0	23.9	14.8	38.8	63.0	8.1	73	91.8
Mitchell city	15,285	15,679	2.6	15,727	89.0	1.4	0.9	5.0	3.7	22.1	17.6	35.8	39.0	27.4	6,987	87.8
Mobridge city	3,462	3,444	-0.5	3,385	69.6	8.1	0.0	20.1	2.1	21.7	23.8	43.2	48.2	23.6	1,445	70.0
Monroe town	160	155	-3.1	184	91.8	0.5	0.0	3.8	3.8	31.5	6.0	27.6	54.5	17.8	84	98.8
Montrose city	472	443	-6.1	515	92.0	6.8	0.0	0.6	0.6	33.6	15.3	30.4	45.9	20.5	227	90.7
Morningside CDP	105	-	-	122	100.0	0.0	0.0	0.0	0.0	20.5	8.2	50.6	94.4	0.0	46	43.5
Morristown town	67	68	1.5	39	89.7	0.0	0.0	10.3	0.0	15.4	15.4	35.8	56.7	16.7	26	84.6
Mound City town	71	66	-7.0	70	90.0	0.0	0.0	5.7	4.3	1.4	45.7	64.0	70.6	7.4	44	81.8
Mount Vernon city	462	436	-5.6	487	92.2	0.0	0.0	0.8	7.0	29.4	10.5	35.7	33.2	19.8	201	90.5
Murdo city	488	438	-10.2	444	89.4	0.0	0.0	10.6	0.0	18.5	22.5	52.3	45.0	24.3	245	86.5
Naples town	44	48	9.1	40	100.0	0.0	0.0	0.0	0.0	42.5	12.5	22.5	82.4	5.9	9	100.0
New Effington town	256	249	-2.7	223	58.7	0.0	1.3	39.9	0.0	13.9	27.8	46.9	50.3	6.1	104	70.2
Newell city	609	597	-2.0	971	93.9	1.0	0.0	3.8	1.2	22.5	20.1	37.4	60.0	12.0	361	91.4
New Holland CDP	76	-	-	-	-	-	-	-	-	-	-	-	-	-	-	-
New Underwood city	657	673	2.4	720	64.9	2.4	0.8	15.3	16.7	27.8	17.6	34.9	44.6	27.4	200	93.0
New Witten town	79	77	-2.5	61	100.0	0.0	0.0	0.0	0.0	8.2	23.0	56.7	71.4	16.1	38	73.7
Nisland town	226	225	-0.4	281	83.3	0.0	0.0	11.0	5.7	29.2	27.4	46.2	54.4	1.6	102	92.2
Norris CDP	152	-	-	169	4.1	0.0	0.0	95.9	0.0	41.4	0.0	25.0	76.5	4.7	42	40.5
North Eagle Butte CDP	1,954	-	-	2,220	4.1	0.0	0.0	95.5	0.4	40.7	7.5	24.3	57.1	16.1	536	52.4
North Sioux City city	2,533	2,928	15.6	2,837	89.8	0.6	0.4	6.8	2.4	26.3	12.7	37.5	49.2	21.5	1,340	90.8
North Spearfish CDP	2,221	-	-	2,278	89.9	1.9	1.9	1.6	4.6	25.0	16.5	33.1	45.0	35.6	903	92.6
Northville town	143	145	1.4	124	90.3	0.0	0.0	9.7	0.0	39.5	10.5	31.8	23.6	43.1	42	97.6
Nunda town	43	51	18.6	57	94.7	0.0	0.0	5.3	0.0	28.1	33.3	57.4	51.2	39.0	28	85.7
Oacoma town	451	471	4.4	391	92.6	0.0	0.0	7.4	0.0	22.5	16.1	49.9	56.0	23.0	192	93.8
Oelrichs town	130	123	-5.4	116	81.9	0.0	0.0	18.1	0.0	18.1	32.8	62.5	46.7	23.9	61	78.7
Oglala CDP	1,290	-	-	1,612	9.4	0.0	0.0	90.6	0.0	36.8	3.6	24.1	45.5	5.4	320	46.3
Okaton CDP	36	-	-	44	100.0	0.0	0.0	0.0	0.0	29.5	27.3	37.8	67.7	19.4	15	100.0
Okreek CDP	269	-	-	245	3.7	0.0	0.0	93.1	3.3	46.9	16.7	27.5	15.4	30.0	67	70.1
Ola CDP	13	-	-	-	-	-	-	-	-	-	-	-	-	-	-	-
Oldham city	133	120	-9.8	187	89.3	0.0	0.0	10.7	0.0	31.6	13.9	32.0	47.7	15.3	97	80.4
Olivet town	74	71	-4.1	83	100.0	0.0	0.0	0.0	0.0	39.8	13.3	24.9	41.5	14.6	31	96.8
Onaka town	15	14	-6.7	4	100.0	0.0	0.0	0.0	0.0	0.0	25.0	0.0	0.0	100.0	4	75.0
Onida city	658	634	-3.6	565	95.4	0.0	0.0	2.3	2.3	27.6	26.0	42.7	37.6	30.2	250	80.8
Orient town	63	61	-3.2	44	100.0	0.0	0.0	0.0	0.0	25.0	29.5	58.3	84.8	0.0	23	69.6
Ortley town	65	64	-1.5	46	91.3	0.0	0.0	8.7	0.0	6.5	21.7	48.5	60.5	23.7	27	59.3
Parker city	1,022	1,023	0.1	911	91.8	3.1	0.0	0.9	4.3	27.2	21.2	38.6	45.5	24.4	397	83.6
Parkston city	1,516	1,477	-2.6	1,653	95.4	0.0	0.0	2.5	2.1	26.5	24.4	41.5	44.4	25.4	701	79.7
Parmelee CDP	562	-	-	717	0.0	0.0	0.0	100.0	0.0	40.7	0.0	20.8	67.4	0.0	129	53.5
Peever town	168	164	-2.4	167	20.4	0.0	0.0	75.4	4.2	33.5	2.4	27.1	64.4	5.6	55	74.5
Philip city	781	765	-2.0	852	84.0	0.1	0.0	14.3	1.5	23.7	24.2	46.5	53.3	17.1	395	79.0
Pickstown town	203	223	9.9	262	63.7	1.1	0.0	28.6	6.5	26.0	27.1	51.0	41.9	29.6	100	92.0
Piedmont city	882	903	2.4	977	86.2	1.6	0.0	8.8	3.4	26.7	13.3	36.2	43.3	21.3	381	98.2
Pierpont town	135	120	-11.1	180	96.1	0.0	0.0	3.9	0.0	21.1	15.6	49.2	60.3	9.2	87	87.4
Pierre city	13,646	13,867	1.6	13,961	81.0	0.2	0.0	15.6	3.2	21.7	16.6	37.4	35.2	35.1	6,140	85.7
Pine Lakes Addition CDP	314	-	-	330	100.0	0.0	0.0	0.0	0.0	19.4	20.9	52.7	20.3	46.9	127	96.9
Pine Ridge CDP	3,308	-	-	3,682	2.2	0.3	0.0	91.9	5.6	32.8	4.0	28.8	54.7	8.3	662	65.3
Plankinton city	712	730	2.5	691	77.0	0.0	0.0	1.6	21.4	24.2	21.3	38.3	51.3	17.2	323	85.4
Platte city	1,230	1,258	2.3	1,533	99.2	0.0	0.0	0.8	0.0	23.4	20.9	44.3	49.8	22.0	657	81.1
Pollock town	241	225	-6.6	184	97.3	0.0	0.0	2.7	0.0	8.7	32.6	56.9	57.9	14.6	105	74.3
Porcupine CDP	1,062	-	-	1,470	2.4	0.0	0.0	87.8	9.9	45.8	3.3	19.2	61.9	5.9	260	55.4
Prairie City CDP	23	-	-	4	100.0	0.0	0.0	0.0	0.0	25.0	0.0	35.5	0.0	33.3	1	100.0
Presho city	497	489	-1.6	426	93.9	0.0	0.0	4.5	1.6	16.4	22.1	55.2	48.0	24.3	195	86.7
Pringle town	112	113	0.9	154	98.1	0.0	0.0	1.9	0.0	22.7	13.6	36.9	45.7	11.4	58	87.9
Pukwana town	290	305	5.2	268	93.7	0.0	0.0	3.7	2.6	22.4	19.4	51.0	58.0	20.2	122	74.6
Quinn town	56	61	8.9	58	100.0	0.0	0.0	0.0	0.0	19.0	36.2	56.5	55.3	14.9	24	100.0
Ramona town	174	206	18.4	228	95.2	0.0	3.5	0.0	1.3	15.8	22.4	51.5	49.7	21.9	115	76.5
Rapid City city	68,994	77,503	12.3	75,258	76.8	1.3	1.6	15.0	5.3	23.0	18.2	38.0	32.5	32.8	30,578	91.0
Rapid Valley CDP	8,260	-	-	9,114	88.2	0.9	1.5	5.2	4.3	26.8	9.4	35.4	42.4	16.6	3,239	92.8
Ravinia town	61	64	4.9	59	47.5	0.0	0.0	45.8	6.8	23.7	16.9	44.5	62.5	5.0	24	54.2
Raymond town	50	54	8.0	42	100.0	0.0	0.0	0.0	0.0	4.8	57.1	67.4	62.5	22.5	21	81.0
Redfield city	2,370	2,273	-4.1	2,583	91.7	0.2	0.0	2.9	5.1	23.2	23.6	46.3	51.1	19.5	1,170	84.8
Ree Heights town	62	58	-6.5	61	65.6	6.6	0.0	27.9	0.0	27.9	34.4	60.5	56.8	18.2	30	70.0
Reliance town	191	212	11.0	135	92.6	0.0	0.0	7.4	0.0	22.2	26.7	57.1	51.5	23.3	58	74.1
Renner Corner CDP	305	-	-	352	98.9	0.0	0.0	1.1	0.0	10.2	28.4	55.3	36.1	25.0	184	81.5
Revillo town	115	105	-8.7	86	100.0	0.0	0.0	0.0	0.0	17.4	9.3	46.8	56.5	13.0	43	93.0
Richland CDP	89	-	-	164	100.0	0.0	0.0	0.0	0.0	20.1	0.0	22.6	64.2	11.9	64	85.9
Rockham town	33	33	0.0	23	100.0	0.0	0.0	0.0	0.0	34.8	26.1	34.8	73.3	0.0	8	75.0
Roscoe city	329	289	-12.2	375	92.3	0.0	0.0	0.3	7.5	24.8	11.2	30.6	51.1	19.7	137	88.3
Rosebud CDP	1,587	-	-	1,703	1.5	0.0	0.0	94.8	3.8	40.3	6.2	22.8	58.9	8.1	407	55.8
Rosholt town	422	429	1.7	456	90.6	2.0	0.0	7.5	0.0	23.5	21.5	41.1	37.7	20.9	172	81.4
Roslyn town	183	168	-8.2	217	96.8	0.0	0.0	3.2	0.0	16.6	31.3	58.6	49.7	22.9	98	85.7
Roswell CDP	15	-	-	-	-	-	-	-	-	-	-	-	-	-	-	-
Running Water CDP	36	-	-	9	100.0	0.0	0.0	0.0	0.0	0.0	100.0	0.0	100.0	0.0	9	0.0
St. Charles CDP	11	-	-	8	75.0	0.0	0.0	25.0	0.0	0.0	75.0	74.3	0.0	0.0	5	100.0
St. Francis town	536	566	5.6	654	2.9	0.5	0.3	96.3	0.0	42.4	5.5	23.9	53.1	11.7	174	63.2

1 May be of any race.

Table A. All Places — **Population and Housing**

	Population				Race and Hispanic or Latino origin (percent)					Age (percent)			Educational attainment of persons age 25 and older		Occupied housing units	
STATE City, town, township, borough, or CDP (county if applicable)	2010 census total population	2019 estimated population	Percent change 2010–2019	ACS total population estimate 2015–2019	White alone, not Hispanic or Latino	Black alone, not Hispanic or Latino	Asian alone, not Hispanic or Latino	All other races or 2 or more races, not Hispanic or Latino	Hispanic or Latino[1]	Under 18 years old	Age 65 years and older	Median age	Percent High school diploma or less	Percent Bachelor's degree or more	Total	Percent with a computer
	1	2	3	4	5	6	7	8	9	10	11	12	13	14	15	16
SOUTH DAKOTA—Con.																
St. Lawrence town	198	185	-6.6	202	98.5	0.0	0.0	0.0	1.5	23.3	17.8	41.3	59.5	6.1	87	82.8
St. Onge CDP	191	-	-	112	32.1	0.0	0.0	0.0	67.9	0.0	100.0	78.5	100.0	0.0	56	100.0
Salem city	1,351	1,285	-4.9	1,260	93.1	0.0	0.0	2.6	4.3	26.7	24.0	47.0	52.7	19.1	522	82.4
Scotland city	841	804	-4.4	659	98.5	0.0	0.0	1.5	0.0	15.3	34.3	53.8	40.1	35.2	359	77.4
Selby city	640	627	-2.0	543	88.8	0.0	0.0	4.1	7.2	16.2	33.7	57.8	55.4	18.5	223	76.2
Seneca town	38	37	-2.6	40	100.0	0.0	0.0	0.0	0.0	5.0	42.5	63.8	39.5	23.7	25	88.0
Sherman town	78	77	-1.3	43	97.7	2.3	0.0	0.0	0.0	4.7	27.9	55.5	44.7	2.6	21	71.4
Shindler CDP	584	-	-	762	95.8	0.0	0.0	3.9	0.3	21.9	12.5	44.8	33.7	37.6	249	98.4
Sinai town	120	124	3.3	88	93.2	0.0	0.0	0.0	6.8	25.0	19.3	29.0	23.0	32.8	47	97.9
Sioux Falls city	153,978	183,793	19.4	177,117	80.9	6.2	2.5	4.9	5.5	25.0	12.7	34.4	32.5	35.2	72,291	92.3
Sisseton city	2,440	2,398	-1.7	2,468	45.0	0.0	0.0	49.8	5.1	26.5	16.7	35.2	48.8	16.5	993	81.5
Soldier Creek CDP	227	-	-	300	3.3	0.0	0.0	96.7	0.0	50.0	6.3	18.0	62.9	15.2	69	53.6
South Shore town	225	215	-4.4	224	91.1	0.0	0.0	7.6	1.3	19.6	19.6	45.5	56.4	11.5	110	78.2
Spearfish city	10,465	11,756	12.3	11,547	91.4	0.7	1.0	4.4	2.5	17.6	20.6	36.1	28.4	41.4	5,011	92.1
Spencer city	154	147	-4.5	143	93.0	0.0	0.0	7.0	0.0	19.6	30.8	48.6	70.1	2.8	61	90.2
Spring Creek CDP	268	-	-	272	0.0	0.0	0.0	100.0	0.0	36.8	10.3	25.9	86.7	0.0	64	75.0
Springfield city	1,988	1,922	-3.3	2,056	68.8	5.0	0.2	22.0	4.0	10.2	11.5	36.6	62.1	8.8	329	82.7
Stickney town	284	272	-4.2	282	95.7	0.0	0.0	4.3	0.0	22.3	30.5	45.0	48.6	19.0	134	71.6
Stockholm town	108	107	-0.9	131	95.4	0.0	0.0	0.8	3.8	32.1	10.7	29.1	68.1	24.6	52	92.3
Storla CDP	6	-	-	31	100.0	0.0	0.0	0.0	0.0	41.9	16.1	25.3	16.7	0.0	18	100.0
Strandburg town	72	70	-2.8	75	96.0	0.0	0.0	4.0	0.0	26.7	18.7	49.3	54.7	3.8	34	100.0
Stratford town	72	74	2.8	52	78.8	0.0	0.0	0.0	21.2	21.2	9.6	34.5	46.2	25.6	24	87.5
Sturgis city	6,639	6,922	4.3	6,796	91.3	1.3	1.4	2.8	3.1	22.0	20.5	42.0	42.0	21.2	3,146	80.0
Summerset city	1,844	2,660	44.3	2,477	90.6	3.9	1.3	3.1	1.1	26.6	13.4	32.5	27.3	33.9	936	98.7
Summit town	297	289	-2.7	414	67.9	0.7	0.0	28.5	2.9	37.0	7.7	23.7	52.2	13.4	133	87.2
Tabor town	420	402	-4.3	417	87.1	0.0	0.0	6.2	6.7	23.3	20.4	42.8	44.3	21.5	190	90.5
Tea city	3,801	6,031	58.7	5,397	95.4	0.4	0.3	0.6	3.3	37.1	3.4	28.3	25.9	35.1	1,659	98.3
Timber Lake city	443	499	12.6	598	53.0	0.0	0.0	46.3	0.7	29.1	14.5	32.4	47.9	23.0	198	73.2
Tolstoy town	40	36	-10.0	46	100.0	0.0	0.0	0.0	0.0	15.2	28.3	46.5	41.0	25.6	27	81.5
Toronto town	212	209	-1.4	209	96.7	0.0	0.0	0.0	3.3	26.3	14.4	42.2	40.4	22.7	95	86.3
Trent town	232	230	-0.9	254	88.6	2.4	1.2	7.1	0.8	9.8	26.0	55.4	48.7	9.8	127	89.0
Tripp city	647	623	-3.7	694	96.0	0.0	0.0	3.2	0.9	24.8	30.5	50.0	48.9	19.9	289	68.5
Tulare town	207	211	1.9	241	100.0	0.0	0.0	0.0	0.0	26.1	25.3	35.5	40.5	24.8	96	93.8
Turton town	48	49	2.1	54	100.0	0.0	0.0	0.0	0.0	40.7	3.7	33.7	9.4	31.3	18	100.0
Twin Brooks town	69	70	1.4	42	100.0	0.0	0.0	0.0	0.0	19.0	26.2	54.0	63.6	6.1	20	75.0
Two Strike CDP	209	-	-	246	0.0	0.0	0.0	100.0	0.0	44.7	3.3	21.1	75.8	0.0	70	57.1
Tyndall city	1,067	1,022	-4.2	1,263	93.3	0.0	0.0	3.6	3.1	25.8	26.7	35.9	53.0	13.8	549	74.9
Utica town	65	67	3.1	94	70.2	0.0	0.0	7.4	22.3	33.0	9.2	31.6	69.5	6.8	36	86.1
Vale CDP	136	-	-	115	100.0	0.0	0.0	0.0	0.0	6.1	19.1	47.9	84.8	10.1	62	48.4
Valley Springs city	759	730	-3.8	701	97.1	0.0	0.4	2.1	0.3	25.1	11.6	39.6	39.1	16.0	298	89.9
Veblen city	531	537	1.1	462	35.5	0.0	0.0	18.8	45.7	35.3	13.4	30.4	61.6	16.1	155	76.8
Verdon town	5	5	0.0	4	100.0	0.0	0.0	0.0	0.0	0.0	0.0	0.0	100.0	0.0	2	100.0
Vermillion city	10,578	10,926	3.3	10,753	85.0	2.1	3.7	5.8	3.4	15.0	9.0	23.0	22.7	57.6	3,895	94.7
Viborg city	782	767	-1.9	786	96.7	0.5	0.0	2.8	0.0	16.7	28.9	50.0	41.0	23.2	371	74.9
Vienna town	42	45	7.1	118	75.4	0.0	0.0	24.6	0.0	66.1	0.0	7.2	42.9	25.7	24	100.0
Vilas town	20	19	-5.0	22	100.0	0.0	0.0	0.0	0.0	40.9	0.0	34.5	69.2	15.4	8	100.0
Virgil town	16	18	12.5	19	78.9	0.0	0.0	21.1	0.0	5.3	31.6	45.8	55.6	16.7	12	75.0
Vivian CDP	119	-	-	99	100.0	0.0	0.0	0.0	0.0	8.1	30.3	60.4	33.7	30.1	59	62.7
Volga city	1,785	2,028	13.6	1,926	97.5	0.0	0.7	1.3	0.5	29.1	14.3	30.9	33.1	30.6	826	93.3
Volin town	161	163	1.2	204	74.5	0.0	0.0	25.0	0.5	24.5	3.9	34.5	51.2	7.3	67	77.6
Wagner city	1,566	1,547	-1.2	1,482	58.1	0.0	0.4	32.8	8.7	25.0	25.5	43.3	48.7	21.6	571	69.4
Wakonda town	323	294	-9.0	248	92.3	4.0	0.4	3.2	0.0	20.2	34.3	56.0	47.8	17.9	112	91.1
Wall town	766	875	14.2	814	83.3	5.9	0.1	8.4	2.3	20.3	24.9	46.7	27.5	23.3	321	86.0
Wallace town	85	87	2.4	85	100.0	0.0	0.0	0.0	0.0	31.8	9.4	41.3	37.9	22.4	33	97.0
Wanblee CDP	725	-	-	975	2.3	1.0	0.0	96.3	0.4	45.9	3.6	19.9	67.4	9.8	123	49.6
Ward town	48	52	8.3	54	92.6	0.0	0.0	7.4	0.0	18.5	18.5	48.0	53.3	20.0	30	83.3
Warner town	457	468	2.4	476	84.5	0.0	0.0	0.0	15.5	25.8	14.5	41.4	41.5	26.6	177	94.9
Wasta town	80	82	2.5	130	100.0	0.0	0.0	0.0	0.0	23.1	15.4	42.5	56.8	11.6	51	96.1
Watertown city	21,531	22,174	3.0	22,166	91.7	1.0	0.5	4.0	2.8	23.8	17.4	37.8	43.3	22.1	9,731	88.7
Waubay city	576	560	-2.8	518	60.2	0.0	0.0	39.8	0.0	26.6	31.7	50.6	50.4	23.7	253	82.6
Waverly CDP	37	-	-	60	100.0	0.0	0.0	0.0	0.0	0.0	15.0	25.8	68.4	0.0	33	100.0
Webster city	1,893	1,726	-8.8	1,673	92.8	0.0	0.4	3.5	3.3	18.9	30.2	46.6	48.1	19.0	863	85.1
Wentworth village	171	194	13.5	189	90.5	0.0	3.2	0.0	6.3	11.6	22.8	54.1	65.1	16.9	90	76.7
Wessington city	168	177	5.4	354	85.3	0.0	0.0	0.6	14.1	36.4	17.5	31.3	59.5	16.6	139	86.3
Wessington Springs city	956	911	-4.7	865	96.5	0.0	0.0	3.2	0.2	16.8	41.5	58.5	54.1	18.8	437	80.5
Westport town	133	133	0.0	98	84.7	0.0	0.0	15.3	0.0	31.6	11.2	42.0	37.3	13.6	49	89.8
Wetonka town	8	8	0.0	15	100.0	0.0	0.0	0.0	0.0	0.0	13.3	49.8	0.0	54.5	5	100.0
White city	484	489	1.0	545	93.8	0.6	0.0	0.4	5.3	30.8	10.5	34.1	42.7	19.2	210	93.3
Whitehorse CDP	141	-	-	162	3.7	0.0	0.0	80.2	16.0	48.8	1.9	18.5	70.4	11.1	30	36.7
White Horse CDP	276	-	-	132	0.0	0.0	0.0	100.0	0.0	26.5	22.7	39.1	80.4	0.0	57	29.8
White Lake city	370	369	-0.3	418	96.4	0.2	0.0	3.3	0.0	21.3	24.6	40.5	41.2	20.4	180	83.9
White River city	581	574	-1.2	664	44.0	0.5	0.0	45.3	10.2	27.4	15.2	33.2	58.5	12.3	213	67.1
White Rock town	3	3	0.0	5	40.0	0.0	0.0	0.0	60.0	0.0	60.0	70.3	100.0	0.0	3	33.3
Whitewood city	928	979	5.5	1,104	88.0	0.0	0.0	6.5	5.4	21.6	15.5	45.0	55.4	15.1	454	94.7
Willow Lake city	261	243	-6.9	328	85.7	0.0	0.0	0.0	14.3	40.9	14.9	26.9	51.1	24.7	116	72.4
Wilmot city	496	501	1.0	560	83.8	0.4	0.0	3.2	12.7	22.5	33.6	45.0	42.2	19.8	264	78.8
Winfred CDP	52	-	-	56	100.0	0.0	0.0	0.0	0.0	30.4	0.0	48.0	87.2	0.0	33	100.0
Winner city	2,931	2,824	-3.7	2,826	84.9	0.0	1.0	14.0	0.0	17.6	26.2	49.9	47.7	23.8	1,324	85.2
Wolsey town	376	399	6.1	456	97.6	0.0	0.0	0.2	2.2	27.0	19.1	37.9	46.9	18.8	218	79.8
Wood town	62	63	1.6	56	64.3	0.0	0.0	35.7	0.0	16.1	37.5	54.4	29.8	29.8	34	64.7
Woonsocket city	655	648	-1.1	750	92.7	0.0	0.0	2.4	4.9	28.5	19.3	35.6	54.0	20.3	309	91.9
Worthing city	877	1,007	14.8	1,020	94.0	1.2	0.0	4.8	0.0	32.0	7.6	33.2	35.8	19.6	331	94.9
Wounded Knee CDP	382	-	-	470	0.0	0.0	0.0	100.0	0.0	47.2	0.0	18.9	82.8	0.0	72	34.7
Yale town	108	115	6.5	110	96.4	0.0	0.0	3.6	0.0	20.0	24.5	50.0	43.2	14.8	53	88.7
Yankton city	14,467	14,687	1.5	14,573	87.3	2.2	0.2	6.0	4.3	20.6	19.8	41.2	41.8	28.6	6,348	84.9
TENNESSEE	6,346,276	6,829,174	7.6	6,709,356	73.8	16.6	1.7	2.4	5.4	22.4	16.0	38.7	44.6	27.3	2,597,292	87.1
Adams city	627	671	7.0	602	92.4	2.8	0.0	1.7	3.2	27.1	10.5	33.1	61.2	17.1	210	81.4
Adamsville town	2,183	2,164	-0.9	2,307	95.1	1.1	0.2	2.4	1.2	27.1	22.5	34.8	59.9	16.3	836	85.0
Alamo town	2,361	2,277	-3.6	2,187	73.3	13.1	0.0	2.0	11.7	25.9	18.7	38.6	58.6	15.1	835	75.7
Alcoa city	8,397	9,980	18.9	9,561	77.7	11.0	1.7	3.2	6.3	25.8	16.8	37.3	46.7	25.4	3,835	84.8

1 May be of any race.

Table A. All Places — **Population and Housing**

	Population				Race and Hispanic or Latino origin (percent)					Age (percent)			Educational attainment of persons age 25 and older		Occupied housing units	
STATE City, town, township, borough, or CDP (county if applicable)	2010 census total population	2019 estimated population	Percent change 2010–2019	ACS total population estimate 2015–2019	White alone, not Hispanic or Latino	Black alone, not Hispanic or Latino	Asian alone, not Hispanic or Latino	All other races or 2 or more races, not Hispanic or Latino	Hispanic or Latino[1]	Under 18 years old	Age 65 years and older	Median age	Percent High school diploma or less	Percent Bachelor's degree or more	Total	Percent with a computer
	1	2	3	4	5	6	7	8	9	10	11	12	13	14	15	16
TENNESSEE—Con.																
Alexandria town	969	1,012	4.4	1,002	91.2	7.3	0.3	0.8	0.4	22.9	15.9	39.2	67.3	6.2	397	79.3
Algood city	3,512	4,463	27.1	4,228	94.6	0.4	0.0	4.2	0.8	25.0	22.3	39.7	53.4	21.9	1,883	80.7
Allardt city	621	627	1.0	621	99.4	0.0	0.6	0.0	0.0	12.1	33.3	54.4	58.8	23.1	266	77.8
Altamont town	1,052	1,067	1.4	1,078	73.8	1.0	0.5	24.7	0.0	26.7	17.6	35.7	78.4	5.8	362	73.5
Andersonville CDP	472	-	-	560	95.0	0.0	0.0	5.0	0.0	7.7	30.0	47.2	60.7	12.7	228	100.0
Apison CDP	2,469	-	-	2,723	95.2	0.0	0.0	0.7	4.1	17.6	23.6	50.1	46.5	27.0	987	83.9
Ardmore city	1,220	1,221	0.1	1,386	85.3	4.6	3.2	5.0	1.9	15.7	25.5	46.3	55.1	16.2	547	79.2
Arlington town	11,509	11,743	2.0	11,697	76.2	16.3	1.2	1.8	4.5	33.3	6.0	33.8	22.5	45.3	3,560	94.7
Ashland City town	4,502	4,767	5.9	4,680	86.2	3.5	1.1	2.1	7.1	20.6	17.2	42.4	51.3	19.9	1,986	85.2
Athens city	13,703	14,020	2.3	13,851	81.8	9.3	0.8	2.9	5.2	21.3	17.5	38.1	53.8	19.8	5,530	82.3
Atoka town	8,397	9,517	13.3	9,241	86.0	9.9	0.5	2.0	1.5	30.2	7.7	35.4	28.0	27.9	2,942	94.6
Atwood town	953	919	-3.6	1,047	80.4	10.7	0.0	4.1	4.8	31.1	13.1	32.6	57.6	11.2	418	77.8
Auburntown town	257	266	3.5	224	95.1	0.0	0.0	2.2	2.7	25.4	15.6	29.9	47.3	26.4	87	85.1
Baileyton town	427	451	5.6	462	97.4	1.5	0.0	0.4	0.6	27.3	18.4	33.8	57.2	17.0	193	79.8
Baneberry city	482	534	10.8	568	91.5	0.0	0.2	8.3	0.0	18.5	32.2	55.1	31.3	39.2	236	99.2
Banner Hill CDP	1,497	-	-	1,576	99.0	0.0	0.0	1.0	0.0	20.7	28.0	45.8	60.4	10.3	615	80.7
Bartlett city	56,941	59,440	4.4	59,102	69.1	21.3	3.5	2.1	4.1	23.2	16.8	41.8	30.4	36.4	20,359	93.7
Baxter town	1,357	1,531	12.8	1,546	88.9	0.8	0.0	1.8	8.5	27.9	16.0	34.0	60.1	10.0	584	79.3
Bean Station city	3,096	3,113	0.5	3,086	98.9	0.0	0.0	0.5	0.7	19.3	21.1	48.8	71.0	11.0	1,144	82.1
Beersheba Springs town ..	473	460	-2.7	543	86.7	0.0	0.0	13.3	0.0	19.5	21.9	45.2	70.8	2.7	198	68.2
Bell Buckle town	503	543	8.0	544	88.2	1.3	2.8	0.9	6.8	28.9	13.2	33.8	41.1	29.9	168	85.1
Belle Meade city	2,894	2,858	-1.2	2,280	96.5	0.8	0.6	2.1	0.0	23.5	23.9	50.2	2.4	84.9	853	96.2
Bells city	2,485	2,444	-1.6	2,736	55.2	21.6	0.5	1.8	20.9	28.9	12.9	33.4	62.8	9.7	917	81.7
Benton town	1,376	1,278	-7.1	1,526	89.5	2.7	0.0	5.4	2.4	20.1	15.3	37.2	61.0	10.2	645	83.4
Berry Hill city	535	508	-5.0	1,168	84.6	4.6	1.8	5.7	3.3	2.7	3.1	27.8	7.0	78.2	747	97.7
Bethel Springs town.........	746	727	-2.5	806	78.9	13.4	0.0	0.4	7.3	26.2	12.0	34.5	63.3	6.2	251	86.9
Bethpage CDP	288	-	-	355	67.0	26.5	0.0	6.5	0.0	20.0	3.7	26.9	25.8	18.7	103	95.1
Big Sandy town	539	521	-3.3	663	94.9	0.8	0.8	3.6	0.0	28.4	14.2	31.0	64.6	11.9	241	83.8
Blaine city	1,849	1,860	0.6	2,182	91.2	0.2	0.0	5.0	3.6	28.2	15.4	37.9	59.3	15.0	815	82.5
Bloomingdale CDP............	9,888	-	-	9,175	97.2	0.0	0.2	1.8	0.9	18.5	21.8	45.6	63.5	10.9	3,977	81.9
Blountville CDP................	3,074	-	-	3,102	96.2	1.0	0.0	1.1	1.6	10.4	20.2	42.6	55.3	17.9	1,036	90.5
Bluff City city...................	1,691	1,670	-1.2	2,062	97.4	0.4	0.0	1.7	0.4	24.1	13.4	40.7	48.5	19.4	842	89.4
Bolivar city	5,369	4,936	-8.1	5,031	36.1	60.6	0.3	2.9	0.0	21.7	19.4	45.4	64.7	11.5	2,224	71.6
Bon Aqua Junction CDP...	1,230	-	-	1,471	94.8	1.1	0.0	0.0	4.1	29.2	6.1	37.4	74.2	3.5	416	86.1
Bowman CDP	302	-	-	156	100.0	0.0	0.0	0.0	0.0	31.4	32.7	30.3	35.5	9.3	59	100.0
Braden town	280	263	-6.1	294	83.7	10.9	0.7	1.0	3.7	12.2	23.1	51.2	53.7	16.1	110	90.0
Bradford town	1,051	978	-6.9	1,238	83.8	6.4	0.0	3.9	6.0	28.3	14.6	36.9	64.1	9.9	417	81.3
Bransford CDP.................	170	-	-	444	86.7	0.0	0.0	0.0	13.3	9.9	22.5	50.0	86.5	0.0	116	100.0
Brentwood city	37,062	42,783	15.4	42,407	84.1	1.8	7.3	2.0	4.7	30.0	13.5	41.7	9.0	76.1	13,899	97.8
Brighton town	2,881	2,908	0.9	2,928	78.6	13.6	0.9	4.9	2.0	30.8	7.9	31.3	40.5	19.5	987	91.9
Bristol city	26,767	26,987	0.8	26,852	90.9	2.8	0.5	3.3	2.5	21.0	19.8	42.4	46.6	25.6	11,450	85.7
Brownsville city	10,332	9,435	-8.7	9,647	29.5	64.9	0.0	0.3	5.3	26.3	16.9	36.7	64.2	10.2	4,001	77.6
Bruceton town	1,477	1,395	-5.6	1,273	92.9	1.3	1.2	2.4	2.2	20.5	28.2	48.6	59.4	15.1	466	77.3
Bulls Gap town	746	721	-3.4	856	97.8	0.0	0.0	1.5	0.7	13.6	26.1	49.8	73.2	6.0	352	75.3
Burlison town	422	410	-2.8	348	96.0	0.0	0.0	3.7	0.3	17.5	18.4	45.3	52.0	20.8	146	78.8
Burns town	1,364	1,456	6.7	1,761	94.0	2.0	0.5	2.2	1.3	18.4	13.4	39.4	60.3	11.8	627	90.0
Byrdstown town	805	783	-2.7	999	97.0	0.9	0.0	0.2	1.9	22.3	21.7	41.0	72.2	8.1	409	76.8
Calhoun town	494	500	1.2	586	96.4	0.0	0.0	3.6	0.0	29.0	20.0	36.7	55.2	15.2	230	83.5
Camden city	3,584	3,632	1.3	3,582	97.3	1.3	0.0	0.8	0.6	24.3	24.5	43.2	54.6	16.4	1,516	79.0
Carthage town	2,303	2,338	1.5	2,466	90.6	5.8	0.0	3.2	0.4	23.5	16.3	36.8	66.9	12.5	947	80.4
Caryville town	2,324	2,148	-7.6	2,450	96.3	0.2	0.0	2.2	1.3	22.2	15.8	38.9	66.4	14.2	925	76.4
Castalian Springs CDP.....	556	-	-	428	97.7	0.0	0.0	2.3	0.0	23.4	15.0	46.2	62.6	22.9	165	88.5
Cedar Hill city	308	312	1.3	353	77.3	8.8	0.0	0.0	13.9	27.2	14.2	31.4	79.4	3.8	113	73.5
Celina city	1,500	1,420	-5.3	1,848	91.0	6.1	0.4	0.3	2.2	22.2	23.2	46.7	65.9	12.4	728	65.4
Centertown town..............	243	253	4.1	341	97.4	0.0	0.0	2.6	0.0	25.2	10.9	36.3	60.5	12.9	143	83.9
Centerville town	3,615	3,540	-2.1	3,540	92.7	3.0	0.0	1.7	2.6	18.9	27.0	49.8	59.3	13.5	1,415	66.4
Central CDP	2,279	-	-	2,217	95.8	0.0	0.0	4.2	0.0	18.6	18.4	45.8	57.6	20.4	1,002	79.6
Chapel Hill town	1,448	1,538	6.2	1,551	91.0	3.4	0.1	2.6	2.9	21.1	19.0	43.1	57.1	14.8	660	89.4
Charleston city	649	697	7.4	745	68.9	19.5	0.0	8.9	2.8	21.2	20.0	48.1	55.1	9.9	307	81.4
Charlotte town	1,508	1,634	8.4	1,736	76.4	14.8	0.0	6.6	2.1	20.3	8.8	35.4	74.4	5.1	537	80.4
Chattanooga city..............	170,322	182,799	7.3	179,690	57.3	31.1	2.7	2.7	6.3	19.5	16.6	37.5	40.2	30.0	75,940	85.4
Chesterfield CDP..............	469	-	-	683	96.9	0.0	0.0	0.0	3.1	38.4	3.2	28.8	61.3	4.0	205	86.8
Christiana CDP.................	-	-	-	3,580	85.2	7.7	0.0	5.5	1.6	26.9	18.9	37.7	38.6	31.7	1,245	91.0
Church Hill city................	6,736	6,664	-1.1	6,667	96.3	0.0	0.2	2.0	1.5	15.7	25.5	49.5	45.3	19.2	2,879	84.1
Clarkrange CDP	575	-	-	932	96.8	0.0	0.0	3.2	0.0	35.2	5.9	29.9	55.4	29.7	289	91.0
Clarksburg town...............	392	379	-3.3	571	90.4	7.7	0.0	1.1	0.9	30.1	11.2	36.8	65.7	11.2	185	84.9
Clarksville city.................	132,901	158,146	19.0	152,934	56.7	23.3	2.5	6.0	11.5	27.0	8.2	29.6	35.0	27.6	56,260	92.8
Cleveland city	41,265	45,504	10.3	44,595	76.3	7.4	2.3	3.0	11.0	21.1	15.9	35.3	44.2	25.0	16,669	85.9
Clifton city	2,693	2,655	-1.4	2,666	68.0	28.0	0.0	1.8	2.3	10.1	9.3	39.0	80.5	5.0	450	80.4
Clinton city	9,760	10,075	3.2	9,964	92.6	3.8	0.3	1.1	2.1	21.0	22.7	46.4	47.5	19.4	4,417	83.9
Coalfield CDP..................	2,463	-	-	2,580	99.5	0.0	0.0	0.0	0.5	25.8	21.1	40.8	55.2	11.4	960	85.8
Coalmont city	859	834	-2.9	940	86.9	0.0	0.0	12.8	0.3	23.2	15.6	39.4	61.6	10.9	308	77.3
Collegedale city	8,544	11,378	33.2	11,275	66.0	11.0	4.9	3.9	14.3	17.3	18.4	34.2	29.6	41.4	4,167	90.0
Collierville town	45,599	51,040	11.9	50,086	70.9	13.7	9.3	3.9	2.3	26.0	13.7	40.2	18.3	57.3	17,204	96.0
Collinwood city	985	944	-4.2	1,093	98.4	0.2	0.0	0.0	1.4	25.3	15.1	37.7	61.6	12.0	426	77.9
Colonial Heights CDP.......	6,934	-	-	3,177	94.6	1.1	1.7	1.4	1.2	15.7	18.9	45.5	43.4	29.3	1,318	95.3
Columbia city	34,649	40,335	16.4	38,380	68.4	18.4	0.4	3.6	9.2	25.3	14.2	36.5	48.4	18.8	15,070	90.8
Cookeville city	31,122	34,706	11.5	33,454	85.3	3.6	2.2	2.0	6.8	18.8	13.9	29.5	44.0	34.4	13,743	86.6
Coopertown town..............	4,278	4,586	7.2	4,496	93.5	3.4	0.4	2.7	0.0	20.5	20.6	43.1	45.7	23.9	1,614	86.4
Copperhill city	343	321	-6.4	417	80.6	0.0	1.2	2.2	16.1	31.7	18.0	36.1	56.8	13.7	184	80.4
Cornersville town	1,157	1,291	11.6	1,319	94.5	3.9	0.0	0.4	1.2	22.7	21.7	40.3	61.6	10.5	496	83.1
Cottage Grove town	89	86	-3.4	77	98.7	0.0	0.0	0.0	1.3	26.0	13.0	35.5	52.2	19.6	28	78.6
Cottontown CDP	367	-	-	320	96.9	0.0	0.0	3.1	0.0	6.3	30.0	59.3	63.0	9.2	138	86.2
Covington city	9,000	8,834	-1.8	8,857	46.9	48.4	0.0	2.9	1.8	23.0	16.4	35.0	60.0	14.3	3,456	79.4
Cowan city	1,735	1,658	-4.4	1,313	86.4	8.0	0.0	2.4	3.2	20.8	19.2	45.7	72.7	11.0	624	77.2
Crab Orchard city	755	751	-0.5	686	98.4	0.3	0.0	0.0	1.3	24.5	16.9	39.1	76.9	5.7	282	76.6
Cross Plains city..............	1,705	1,827	7.2	1,801	94.7	2.2	0.2	0.5	2.3	22.7	17.5	39.9	60.7	13.1	689	90.4
Crossville city	10,822	11,779	8.8	11,545	91.7	1.8	0.3	0.8	5.4	20.0	21.6	39.9	53.0	16.7	5,040	86.5
Crump city	1,476	1,454	-1.5	1,500	97.9	0.5	0.0	0.8	0.9	16.3	26.9	49.0	64.9	10.0	655	75.9
Cumberland City town	311	307	-1.3	326	81.6	8.0	0.6	9.2	0.6	17.8	27.6	47.6	65.8	10.1	148	72.3
Cumberland Gap town......	494	490	-0.8	326	94.2	0.6	4.6	0.3	0.3	6.7	5.2	25.3	24.3	56.8	115	100.0
Dandridge town................	2,972	3,202	7.7	3,157	88.3	6.3	0.3	2.6	2.5	15.2	20.7	42.0	49.6	17.5	1,107	86.1

1 May be of any race.

Table A. All Places — **Population and Housing**

STATE City, town, township, borough, or CDP (county if applicable)	Population				Race and Hispanic or Latino origin (percent)					Age (percent)			Educational attainment of persons age 25 and older		Occupied housing units	
	2010 census total population	2019 estimated population	Percent change 2010–2019	ACS total population estimate 2015–2019	White alone, not Hispanic or Latino	Black alone, not Hispanic or Latino	Asian alone, not Hispanic or Latino	All other races or 2 or more races, not Hispanic or Latino	Hispanic or Latino[1]	Under 18 years old	Age 65 years and older	Median age	Percent High school diploma or less	Percent Bachelor's degree or more	Total	Percent with a computer
	1	2	3	4	5	6	7	8	9	10	11	12	13	14	15	16
TENNESSEE—Con.																
Darden CDP	399	-	-	226	89.4	0.0	0.0	0.0	10.6	2.7	17.3	57.9	57.7	12.2	128	71.1
Dayton city	7,268	7,358	1.2	7,344	80.7	5.6	1.8	5.4	6.4	27.2	13.7	30.1	56.7	16.0	2,311	88.5
Decatur town	1,654	1,667	0.8	1,501	98.6	0.6	0.0	0.8	0.0	20.7	22.9	41.2	62.4	11.6	586	73.9
Decaturville town	869	862	-0.8	1,053	69.7	20.1	0.0	9.3	0.9	28.0	23.9	40.6	61.8	15.4	318	82.1
Decherd city	2,355	2,371	0.7	3,058	78.6	13.9	0.3	2.6	4.6	25.5	15.8	37.9	57.1	12.5	1,229	86.5
Dickson city	14,654	15,575	6.3	15,447	83.0	7.5	0.8	1.9	6.8	23.0	16.3	38.7	52.3	18.9	5,842	84.1
Dodson Branch CDP	1,074	-	-	1,044	95.7	0.0	0.0	2.6	1.7	9.9	21.8	48.7	51.3	10.4	411	81.0
Dover city	1,411	1,546	9.6	2,071	94.0	0.8	0.2	4.5	0.5	31.8	20.5	36.0	52.3	21.7	697	76.9
Dowelltown town	365	402	10.1	323	92.0	5.6	0.0	0.9	1.5	18.6	18.9	43.8	62.8	13.2	157	82.2
Doyle town	541	577	6.7	626	97.0	0.0	0.0	2.7	0.3	20.6	22.7	50.0	70.4	8.9	266	62.4
Dresden town	3,090	2,937	-5.0	2,940	87.8	8.5	0.0	0.3	3.3	26.5	14.8	38.4	65.4	9.6	1,170	81.0
Ducktown city	472	467	-1.1	478	95.2	1.3	0.0	2.3	1.3	11.1	39.1	55.7	57.5	8.6	174	81.6
Dunlap city	4,842	5,176	6.9	5,103	92.8	0.6	0.0	3.7	2.8	18.6	20.8	44.9	70.6	7.8	2,007	82.0
Dyer city	2,319	2,207	-4.8	2,791	77.5	18.2	0.0	1.1	3.2	28.6	20.2	37.6	62.1	14.7	1,053	77.1
Dyersburg city	17,136	16,314	-4.8	16,476	67.0	22.5	1.6	4.9	4.1	23.5	17.8	39.8	52.5	17.6	6,865	82.4
Eagleton Village CDP	5,052	-	-	5,903	82.3	2.6	0.8	3.4	10.8	25.9	12.9	33.9	43.6	13.1	2,302	87.9
Eagleville city	629	763	21.3	908	88.9	2.4	0.0	0.2	8.5	29.0	10.8	36.3	43.8	29.5	327	89.6
East Cleveland CDP	1,608	-	-	2,019	83.0	5.4	3.2	0.0	8.4	22.9	13.3	32.2	64.0	4.3	672	76.5
East Ridge city	20,991	21,182	0.9	21,168	68.7	14.8	1.0	2.0	13.4	20.7	16.3	40.2	44.6	21.9	9,027	84.3
Eastview town	733	707	-3.5	935	84.0	4.2	0.0	9.3	2.6	36.4	13.4	29.4	46.3	17.5	339	84.7
Elgin CDP	282	-	-	448	100.0	0.0	0.0	0.0	0.0	24.1	14.1	42.3	71.6	3.0	194	54.1
Elizabethton city	14,246	13,509	-5.2	13,577	89.8	5.2	0.8	0.6	3.5	19.7	21.2	42.1	49.3	19.8	5,448	82.2
Elkton city	540	524	-3.0	456	72.4	26.5	0.0	1.1	0.0	10.7	21.5	53.6	63.6	24.2	190	86.8
Englewood town	1,533	1,534	0.1	1,790	94.5	0.2	1.0	2.3	2.0	24.4	20.3	41.3	71.2	5.1	703	69.4
Enville town	192	192	0.0	168	97.6	0.0	0.0	2.4	0.0	28.6	17.9	44.0	56.9	19.8	61	82.0
Erin city	1,332	1,280	-3.9	1,654	81.0	17.5	0.0	1.5	0.0	19.4	26.0	45.1	67.1	13.2	514	71.6
Erwin town	6,091	5,918	-2.8	5,921	92.1	0.7	0.0	1.3	5.8	17.0	25.8	48.6	53.7	13.3	2,657	75.8
Estill Springs town	2,031	2,034	0.1	1,978	89.8	3.6	1.3	5.3	0.0	20.1	20.3	47.1	47.6	14.8	865	88.1
Ethridge town	465	486	4.5	853	93.2	0.0	0.7	6.1	0.0	34.7	8.8	28.1	67.9	10.2	231	83.1
Etowah city	3,495	3,494	0.0	3,468	90.1	1.8	0.0	2.5	5.7	25.0	22.1	45.4	61.4	9.1	1,256	79.3
Eva CDP	293	-	-	79	100.0	0.0	0.0	0.0	0.0	0.0	51.9	65.2	75.9	13.9	52	82.7
Fairfield CDP	131	-	-	142	100.0	0.0	0.0	0.0	0.0	33.1	7.0	20.6	36.2	0.0	47	78.7
Fairfield Glade CDP	6,989	-	-	8,985	95.1	0.0	0.6	3.0	1.3	6.6	64.5	69.5	29.2	34.0	4,574	94.9
Fairgarden CDP	529	-	-	493	100.0	0.0	0.0	0.0	0.0	26.2	5.5	48.7	52.7	12.1	186	100.0
Fairmount CDP	2,825	-	-	2,245	93.7	0.0	0.0	4.8	1.5	29.7	12.6	41.2	6.2	66.2	818	100.0
Fairview city	7,789	9,146	17.4	8,762	88.6	4.1	0.2	3.1	4.0	26.4	11.8	38.3	38.7	27.4	2,962	92.5
Fall Branch CDP	1,291	-	-	1,403	99.4	0.0	0.0	0.0	0.6	10.9	23.0	47.6	48.5	18.0	582	84.4
Falling Water CDP	1,232	-	-	1,280	99.9	0.0	0.0	0.0	0.1	27.3	17.2	42.0	36.0	31.5	476	80.5
Farragut town	20,672	23,778	15.0	22,631	88.7	0.5	6.3	1.5	3.1	23.5	23.3	47.9	13.7	64.9	8,657	95.0
Fayetteville city	6,785	7,047	3.9	7,034	66.0	26.5	0.0	3.3	4.3	20.1	22.9	40.9	62.5	16.4	3,092	71.4
Fincastle CDP	1,618	-	-	1,333	99.2	0.0	0.0	0.0	0.8	17.6	20.7	48.8	62.1	10.1	597	73.2
Finger city	298	288	-3.4	430	93.0	0.9	0.0	1.2	4.9	28.1	18.8	40.1	65.6	8.5	141	80.9
Flat Top Mountain CDP	422	-	-	338	96.2	0.0	0.0	3.8	0.0	13.3	21.0	45.6	33.3	11.9	163	91.4
Flintville CDP	627	-	-	641	100.0	0.0	0.0	0.0	0.0	22.3	13.6	31.5	83.2	6.2	243	85.2
Forest Hills city	4,814	4,820	0.1	4,939	93.5	2.5	1.4	1.5	1.1	23.2	20.3	48.2	5.2	81.8	1,796	97.7
Franklin city	62,569	83,097	32.8	77,939	77.5	6.6	6.8	2.2	6.9	24.6	12.9	38.4	17.6	61.5	29,947	95.6
Friendship city	683	664	-2.8	664	71.4	13.0	0.0	7.5	8.1	26.5	17.2	32.9	68.3	11.7	275	80.0
Friendsville city	889	903	1.6	847	94.7	0.9	0.0	0.4	4.0	14.9	22.0	44.5	66.9	9.8	336	84.8
Gadsden town	476	464	-2.5	574	89.2	7.5	0.5	0.3	2.4	24.2	21.6	41.8	61.1	11.7	212	73.1
Gainesboro town	956	959	0.3	926	94.2	3.6	0.0	1.1	1.2	16.3	22.6	43.2	62.4	12.2	347	68.9
Gallatin city	30,352	42,918	41.4	38,156	72.5	14.0	2.5	3.4	7.6	22.1	16.9	39.1	42.1	27.8	14,692	87.3
Gallaway city	671	647	-3.6	708	38.3	60.5	0.3	0.0	1.0	21.9	29.7	45.0	73.9	11.0	276	67.0
Garland town	308	298	-3.2	316	98.4	0.0	0.0	1.6	0.0	19.0	16.1	39.5	44.5	27.3	121	96.7
Gates town	659	612	-7.1	645	41.2	56.6	0.0	1.9	0.3	31.8	15.8	32.2	53.0	10.4	276	66.7
Gatlinburg city	3,974	3,860	-2.9	4,004	81.1	3.6	4.6	3.4	7.3	14.3	21.9	47.2	41.8	24.5	1,742	90.1
Germantown city	38,836	39,225	1.0	39,193	88.5	2.0	5.5	1.7	2.3	24.7	21.5	44.8	11.3	65.9	14,696	96.1
Gibson town	410	386	-5.9	460	77.6	9.3	0.9	0.9	11.3	31.7	7.0	29.4	51.6	14.7	143	96.5
Gilt Edge city	469	455	-3.0	436	94.3	1.4	0.0	4.1	0.2	24.5	14.0	36.4	61.3	12.4	159	86.8
Gleason town	1,449	1,376	-5.0	1,464	88.3	4.4	0.3	3.7	3.3	25.1	16.5	39.4	69.1	14.2	604	85.1
Goodlettsville city	15,914	16,798	5.6	16,870	68.4	21.1	2.4	3.9	4.2	21.1	17.8	40.4	35.7	33.9	6,779	91.3
Gordonsville town	1,213	1,245	2.6	1,581	91.3	6.8	0.8	1.0	0.0	21.4	12.5	37.1	64.0	9.8	594	84.2
Graball CDP	236	-	-	217	83.9	0.0	0.0	16.1	0.0	31.8	2.3	35.7	60.2	5.3	67	100.0
Grand Junction city	312	271	-13.1	392	48.5	43.9	0.0	7.7	0.0	24.5	17.9	37.9	50.6	18.1	146	81.5
Gray CDP	1,222	-	-	1,016	96.9	0.0	0.0	3.1	0.0	14.6	30.0	43.3	48.5	25.3	463	96.5
Graysville town	1,519	1,580	4.0	1,722	90.7	0.5	0.0	1.0	7.7	22.4	15.6	37.5	65.5	5.6	669	79.2
Greenback city	1,097	1,219	11.1	1,276	98.8	0.0	0.0	0.4	0.8	25.3	15.8	41.4	46.1	15.0	392	94.1
Greenbrier town	6,465	6,852	6.0	6,818	85.3	5.1	1.1	3.8	4.6	30.1	9.8	35.2	46.2	19.0	2,393	92.6
Greeneville town	15,046	14,891		14,942	87.8	4.1	0.3	2.5	5.2	21.2	20.6	42.3	49.3	22.7	6,075	80.6
Greenfield city	2,203	2,086	-5.3	2,336	88.1	6.6	0.2	2.7	2.4	22.7	16.5	40.2	55.5	17.6	1,017	74.4
Green Hill CDP	6,618	-	-	6,563	89.7	2.7	0.0	2.1	5.4	22.2	18.7	44.8	33.2	34.3	2,482	94.1
Grimsley CDP	1,167	-	-	1,013	95.9	0.0	1.8	2.4	0.0	22.0	17.4	36.3	81.9	6.9	357	63.6
Gruetli-Laager city	1,795	1,738	-3.2	2,429	91.7	0.0	0.0	6.3	2.0	29.8	14.9	31.3	76.9	4.1	747	73.2
Guys town	445	435	-2.2	360	63.3	32.8	0.0	3.6	0.3	18.6	20.6	47.3	51.4	14.9	178	73.0
Halls town	2,264	2,067	-8.7	2,182	60.2	32.9	0.0	0.9	6.0	28.7	16.7	33.7	70.8	11.5	887	76.9
Harriman city	6,350	6,132	-3.4	6,126	90.7	4.7	0.4	3.9	0.4	18.4	19.0	39.5	51.9	12.0	2,567	79.7
Harrison CDP	7,769	-	-	8,121	73.5	23.9	1.6	0.5	0.5	17.0	19.3	42.8	35.7	26.5	3,132	89.7
Harrogate city	4,366	4,348	-0.4	4,330	90.9	2.9	2.0	1.9	2.3	13.9	21.6	38.5	40.8	35.1	1,678	85.6
Hartsville/Trousdale County	7,864	11,284	43.5	10,231	84.2	10.2	0.2	4.3	1.1	18.9	13.9	35.1	53.9	13.8	3,189	82.0
Helenwood CDP	865	-	-	918	100.0	0.0	0.0	0.0	0.0	18.7	8.2	47.4	63.5	0.0	402	86.8
Henderson city	6,297	6,357	1.0	6,289	72.5	19.7	1.2	3.0	3.5	23.3	15.1	27.6	47.1	23.4	1,992	80.4
Hendersonville city	51,333	58,113	13.2	57,083	84.1	8.1	1.4	2.0	4.3	24.2	15.0	40.3	30.0	37.9	21,328	93.2
Henning town	982	931	-5.2	1,002	15.5	77.6	0.0	6.9	0.0	22.7	16.6	41.3	75.6	4.9	491	71.3
Henry town	440	447	1.6	577	71.9	4.2	0.2	2.3	21.5	26.9	8.1	36.4	74.0	8.9	181	88.4
Hickory Valley town	103	93	-9.7	90	66.7	18.9	4.4	10.0	0.0	4.4	31.1	58.2	64.0	18.6	49	83.7
Hillsboro CDP	450	-	-	380	96.6	0.0	0.0	0.0	3.4	16.1	32.6	55.6	58.6	16.0	203	57.1
Hohenwald city	3,735	3,813	2.1	3,673	88.0	4.0	3.2	3.8	1.0	26.1	19.5	42.2	53.5	8.9	1,555	63.7
Hollow Rock town	701	679	-3.1	779	89.7	6.8	1.3	0.0	2.2	23.2	18.1	45.7	64.8	10.3	307	79.2
Hopewell CDP	1,874	-	-	1,900	87.9	5.2	0.9	3.0	2.9	24.1	33.1	53.0	40.8	26.2	723	82.2
Hornbeak town	500	470	-6.0	426	91.3	0.0	1.9	6.8	0.0	22.8	21.4	47.3	70.8	8.8	166	80.1
Hornsby town	290	262	-9.7	311	92.0	8.0	0.0	0.0	0.0	21.5	14.8	32.7	63.1	15.0	133	66.2
Humboldt city	8,483	8,151	-3.9	8,169	49.3	45.5	0.0	0.5	4.7	21.4	23.7	43.9	56.9	15.2	3,561	79.1

1 May be of any race.

Table A. All Places — **Population and Housing**

STATE City, town, township, borough, or CDP (county if applicable)	Population				Race and Hispanic or Latino origin (percent)					Age (percent)			Educational attainment of persons age 25 and older		Occupied housing units	
	2010 census total population	2019 estimated population	Percent change 2010–2019	ACS total population estimate 2015–2019	White alone, not Hispanic or Latino	Black alone, not Hispanic or Latino	Asian alone, not Hispanic or Latino	All other races or 2 or more races, not Hispanic or Latino	Hispanic or Latino[1]	Under 18 years old	Age 65 years and older	Median age	Percent High school diploma or less	Percent Bachelor's degree or more	Total	Percent with a computer
	1	2	3	4	5	6	7	8	9	10	11	12	13	14	15	16
TENNESSEE—Con.																
Hunter CDP	1,854	-	-	2,390	99.5	0.0	0.0	0.0	0.5	22.1	15.5	46.6	49.7	12.3	976	73.7
Huntingdon town	3,979	3,835	-3.6	3,845	81.0	13.0	0.0	5.9	0.1	24.7	20.3	40.0	52.8	16.6	1,492	81.2
Huntland town	879	844	-4.0	818	93.2	4.0	0.0	1.6	1.2	20.7	23.3	40.6	57.8	13.7	353	76.5
Huntsville town	1,260	1,269	0.7	1,494	92.6	5.2	0.1	0.1	1.9	23.5	17.7	40.1	71.9	7.0	537	67.0
Iron City CDP	328	-	-	167	100.0	0.0	0.0	0.0	0.0	20.4	15.0	55.1	91.8	0.0	87	42.5
Jacksboro town	2,028	2,058	1.5	2,244	94.7	0.6	3.0	1.5	0.2	15.1	23.0	46.1	59.5	9.6	957	78.8
Jackson city	66,847	67,191	0.5	66,870	47.6	44.5	1.4	2.4	4.2	23.9	14.9	35.9	44.8	27.7	25,896	85.1
Jamestown city	1,964	2,106	7.2	1,949	93.6	1.6	0.2	1.5	3.0	20.4	20.4	41.4	76.3	5.7	875	66.6
Jasper town	3,340	3,447	3.2	3,403	90.4	3.8	0.0	2.9	2.9	25.9	21.8	37.1	45.9	16.2	1,376	87.9
Jefferson City city	8,247	8,194	-0.6	8,237	85.8	3.9	0.7	1.3	8.3	19.7	18.2	31.9	57.1	17.7	2,846	83.8
Jellico city	2,332	2,165	-7.2	2,170	94.0	1.2	0.0	3.8	1.0	21.8	24.9	48.6	66.3	12.9	974	77.3
Johnson City city	63,383	66,906	5.6	66,515	82.2	6.7	2.8	3.2	5.1	18.8	15.3	35.6	33.5	39.9	28,888	90.2
Jonesborough town	5,049	5,611	11.1	5,427	92.4	4.3	1.3	0.3	1.8	17.0	24.8	44.9	42.2	31.9	2,064	90.6
Kenton town	1,285	1,195	-7.0	1,188	77.6	20.0	0.5	1.9	0.0	17.5	22.4	46.6	68.3	9.7	540	80.6
Kimball town	1,427	1,449	1.5	1,841	84.7	0.3	2.2	6.2	6.6	26.1	17.1	34.5	54.3	14.9	683	83.9
Kingsport city	52,997	54,127	2.1	53,376	89.9	3.5	1.2	3.1	2.3	20.2	23.3	44.5	45.1	27.1	23,640	87.6
Kingston city	5,962	5,994	0.5	5,927	89.9	5.3	1.1	2.2	1.4	17.6	21.0	44.5	37.1	22.4	2,225	82.9
Kingston Springs town	2,743	2,727	-0.6	2,741	94.4	2.4	0.0	1.2	1.9	23.2	15.2	40.5	32.4	36.7	1,013	95.3
Knoxville city	178,134	187,603	5.3	186,173	72.4	16.9	1.8	3.6	5.3	18.8	13.6	32.7	38.1	32.4	80,966	88.1
Lafayette city	4,534	5,332	17.6	5,171	92.2	0.3	0.0	1.5	6.0	24.5	18.5	32.5	69.4	5.9	2,007	77.5
La Follette city	7,483	6,688	-10.6	6,857	94.1	0.4	0.0	2.4	3.1	22.3	21.5	44.9	67.3	6.2	2,797	75.9
La Grange town	142	132	-7.0	81	87.7	12.3	0.0	0.0	0.0	1.2	44.4	59.9	43.6	26.9	40	82.5
Lake City city	1,775	1,774	-0.1	2,283	98.3	0.4	0.0	1.3	0.0	20.2	18.8	42.0	72.3	5.5	819	69.8
Lakeland city	12,411	12,642	1.9	12,606	75.8	10.5	3.0	1.2	9.5	31.0	13.7	38.0	25.0	42.9	4,148	97.2
Lakesite city	1,829	1,864	1.9	2,028	91.9	2.3	0.1	2.9	2.8	19.3	22.4	47.4	31.5	36.3	765	91.9
Lake Tansi CDP	3,803	-	-	4,441	91.9	0.0	0.1	6.9	1.1	17.2	31.6	51.6	52.5	16.9	1,925	90.0
Lakewood Park CDP	990	-	-	795	93.6	0.0	0.0	3.0	3.4	12.7	9.7	54.1	70.4	0.0	429	81.8
La Vergne city	32,597	35,716	9.6	35,411	52.1	22.5	2.8	4.0	18.5	31.1	6.5	31.1	43.4	22.0	10,929	97.7
Lawrenceburg city	10,506	11,035	5.0	10,877	85.3	4.2	2.0	3.4	5.1	22.9	19.6	39.8	60.0	16.1	4,535	82.7
Lebanon city	26,187	36,479	39.3	33,159	74.2	13.5	2.6	3.0	6.7	22.9	16.6	36.4	46.3	25.5	11,925	89.1
Lenoir City city	8,608	9,324	8.3	9,162	74.4	0.9	1.1	4.3	19.2	25.9	14.7	32.7	55.3	18.0	3,479	84.7
Lewisburg city	11,100	12,368	11.4	11,910	69.2	17.0	0.2	2.1	11.5	25.9	15.5	35.3	63.7	11.5	4,394	86.1
Lexington city	7,659	7,889	3.0	7,848	76.8	16.8	0.3	2.2	3.9	24.2	18.9	39.3	54.9	18.1	3,150	83.9
Liberty town	318	330	3.8	374	96.5	0.0	0.0	1.1	2.4	17.4	15.5	37.5	63.6	14.8	149	82.6
Linden town	921	956	3.8	1,199	68.1	11.1	13.1	6.5	1.3	21.4	23.4	47.4	67.6	7.6	468	55.3
Livingston town	4,072	4,049	-0.6	4,032	91.5	3.6	0.6	0.0	4.3	22.7	19.9	40.1	65.4	12.7	1,677	69.5
Lobelville city	875	888	1.5	1,182	93.9	0.0	0.0	0.6	5.5	20.1	19.3	43.0	68.4	5.8	461	77.4
Lone Oak CDP	1,206	-	-	1,126	98.7	0.0	0.0	0.3	1.1	17.3	21.7	50.3	54.3	17.5	423	91.7
Lookout Mountain town	1,863	1,889	1.4	1,965	97.3	0.8	0.7	0.7	0.5	27.7	22.6	46.1	4.8	77.6	737	94.7
Loretto city	1,687	1,771	5.0	1,756	94.9	1.8	0.0	0.8	2.4	21.8	22.0	48.2	57.5	14.8	703	78.4
Loudon town	5,341	5,890	10.3	5,747	77.8	1.5	0.0	2.3	18.3	21.4	19.8	44.2	65.2	13.1	2,129	81.5
Louisville city	4,064	4,141	1.9	4,133	86.9	7.6	1.3	2.8	1.4	17.4	22.6	50.4	38.7	35.7	1,753	92.9
Luttrell town	1,024	1,080	5.5	830	97.8	0.0	0.0	0.1	2.0	14.5	17.2	49.0	76.9	3.3	366	79.2
Lyles CDP	734	-	-	1,153	96.8	0.0	0.0	3.2	0.0	33.4	11.8	35.9	69.5	7.4	317	76.7
Lynchburg, Moore County metropolitan	6,342	6,488	2.3	6,378	92.6	2.2	2.4	2.6	0.2	20.1	20.5	45.0	54.1	22.7	2,592	85.2
Lynnville town	280	305	8.9	310	86.8	3.5	1.0	6.5	2.3	23.5	31.6	40.8	53.8	19.1	127	67.7
McEwen city	1,731	1,731	0.0	1,687	97.0	0.0	0.0	0.9	2.1	16.4	18.5	46.6	63.8	14.7	605	78.2
McKenzie city	5,256	5,315	1.1	5,328	85.4	12.7	0.4	0.1	1.3	17.8	22.1	38.1	49.6	28.8	2,116	77.4
McLemoresville town	349	326	-6.6	381	74.0	8.1	0.0	12.6	5.2	16.0	25.5	50.8	54.8	20.4	178	82.6
McMinnville city	13,634	13,769	1.0	13,695	81.6	2.4	0.8	4.4	10.9	23.3	17.0	39.3	63.5	15.7	5,581	80.1
Madisonville city	4,737	5,002	5.6	4,920	89.2	5.1	0.0	1.0	4.8	19.5	22.0	40.9	58.0	14.8	1,969	80.0
Manchester city	10,111	11,038	9.2	10,721	84.4	4.3	0.9	6.5	3.8	23.0	15.7	35.2	52.7	20.6	4,141	86.7
Martin city	11,461	10,484	-8.5	10,635	74.3	18.9	0.3	3.4	3.1	14.1	12.6	23.9	37.6	31.3	3,958	86.9
Maryville city	27,453	29,742	8.3	28,974	89.4	2.1	1.7	3.4	3.4	24.9	18.1	38.6	34.2	34.6	10,719	90.9
Mascot CDP	2,411	-	-	2,310	89.2	4.2	0.0	0.5	6.1	22.1	12.1	36.8	47.7	10.4	920	90.1
Mason town	1,589	1,531	-3.7	1,242	20.0	71.9	1.5	0.5	6.0	21.0	9.6	34.3	68.5	10.3	339	73.7
Maury City town	674	659	-2.2	861	54.7	22.0	0.5	0.9	22.0	29.3	19.0	34.6	64.0	6.4	314	85.7
Maynardville city	2,366	2,428	2.6	2,526	93.0	1.9	0.0	2.6	2.5	25.4	14.2	37.6	63.3	9.5	896	86.5
Medina city	3,569	4,282	20.0	4,209	80.9	13.9	0.3	1.0	3.8	31.8	7.0	31.7	33.9	31.0	1,495	96.2
Medon city	184	183	-0.5	279	89.6	9.0	0.0	1.4	0.0	20.8	25.4	43.1	64.8	12.7	110	74.5
Memphis city	651,873	651,073	-0.1	651,932	25.7	63.8	1.7	1.6	7.2	25.0	12.8	34.0	44.9	26.2	251,732	80.6
Michie town	639	625	-2.2	916	99.3	0.0	0.0	0.0	0.7	24.5	16.4	37.1	55.5	9.5	320	80.0
Middleton city	717	635	-11.4	891	72.5	21.5	0.0	1.3	4.6	30.2	15.9	31.9	57.5	15.7	300	87.0
Middle Valley CDP	12,684	-	-	12,061	90.9	2.4	2.5	1.5	2.7	23.4	18.3	38.9	37.5	31.3	4,362	92.5
Midtown CDP	1,360	-	-	1,261	94.6	0.8	2.2	2.4	0.0	12.5	18.9	46.9	61.7	15.6	475	77.5
Milan city	7,851	7,612	-3.0	7,672	69.7	18.4	1.2	8.2	2.5	22.8	17.9	42.2	54.3	16.8	3,031	84.9
Milledgeville town	269	264	-1.9	297	92.9	5.4	1.0	0.7	0.0	17.2	27.3	52.1	52.5	5.5	128	84.4
Millersville city	6,395	6,769	5.8	6,350	81.8	8.1	1.1	1.7	7.4	18.2	15.5	37.9	44.6	15.8	2,525	89.1
Millington city	10,810	10,641	-1.6	10,645	61.5	22.5	1.8	4.6	9.7	22.7	16.0	40.7	44.9	18.0	4,136	87.4
Minor Hill city	527	531	0.8	536	90.9	2.8	0.4	6.0	0.0	32.6	10.8	31.2	60.7	7.5	205	94.1
Mitchellville city	190	196	3.2	175	94.9	0.0	1.1	1.7	2.3	24.0	15.4	48.7	79.7	1.6	55	70.9
Monteagle town	1,259	1,234	-2.0	1,836	87.7	2.3	0.0	4.6	5.3	24.8	24.1	40.7	51.5	18.3	614	87.1
Monterey town	2,828	2,898	2.5	2,840	58.7	0.5	0.2	2.2	38.4	32.5	13.9	31.1	76.6	4.9	877	73.5
Mooresburg CDP	941	-	-	611	94.9	5.1	0.0	0.0	0.0	12.1	19.5	46.7	62.2	3.7	304	96.4
Morrison town	694	722	4.0	551	66.8	5.4	1.1	2.2	24.5	25.8	14.3	36.9	68.9	9.8	202	83.2
Morristown city	29,008	30,193	4.1	29,782	68.6	7.1	0.9	3.8	19.6	23.4	16.4	37.8	60.1	14.9	11,639	81.4
Moscow city	598	557	-6.9	685	29.2	58.0	0.0	0.0	12.8	27.0	11.5	33.1	58.5	15.7	258	83.3
Mosheim town	2,372	2,337	-1.5	2,273	97.5	1.3	0.3	0.1	0.8	17.1	20.6	47.3	61.8	10.1	949	85.9
Mountain City town	2,507	2,437	-2.8	2,058	88.6	3.3	2.3	2.9	2.9	16.7	29.5	45.7	62.3	10.7	873	71.0
Mount Carmel town	5,381	5,294	-1.6	5,293	95.6	0.9	0.2	0.7	2.5	22.9	17.8	42.8	47.4	20.4	2,184	91.6
Mount Juliet city	24,785	37,029	49.4	34,377	82.0	7.7	3.6	2.2	4.5	28.8	12.0	36.3	25.7	44.6	11,969	97.7
Mount Pleasant city	4,568	4,897	7.2	4,847	78.1	17.2	0.0	3.1	1.6	21.5	21.2	44.4	47.7	21.0	1,935	85.7
Mowbray Mountain CDP	1,615	-	-	1,961	97.9	0.0	0.0	2.1	0.0	21.9	19.4	50.7	41.2	27.1	736	78.4
Munford city	5,894	6,109	3.6	6,034	75.0	17.0	2.1	1.0	5.0	26.3	13.4	41.1	38.2	20.9	2,283	93.3
Murfreesboro city	109,119	146,900	34.6	136,366	66.6	18.8	3.7	3.9	7.1	22.9	9.3	30.4	29.1	39.5	50,195	93.8
Nashville-Davidson metropolitan government	626,558	694,144	10.8	687,488	56.2	26.9	3.6	3.1	10.2	21.1	12.0	34.3	33.0	41.7	282,366	92.5
Nashville-Davidson metropolitan government (balance)	603,438	670,820	11.2	663,750	55.4	27.4	3.6	3.0	10.5	21.0	11.7	34.2	33.5	41.1	272,648	92.4

1 May be of any race.

Table A. All Places — **Population and Housing**

STATE City, town, township, borough, or CDP (county if applicable)	Population: 2010 census total population	Population: 2019 estimated population	Population: Percent change 2010–2019	Population: ACS total population estimate 2015–2019	Race and Hispanic or Latino origin (percent): White alone, not Hispanic or Latino	Black alone, not Hispanic or Latino	Asian alone, not Hispanic or Latino	All other races or 2 or more races, not Hispanic or Latino	Hispanic or Latino[1]	Age (percent): Under 18 years old	Age 65 years and older	Median age	Educational attainment of persons age 25 and older: Percent High school diploma or less	Percent Bachelor's degree or more	Occupied housing units: Total	Percent with a computer
	1	2	3	4	5	6	7	8	9	10	11	12	13	14	15	16
TENNESSEE—Con.																
Newbern town	3,315	3,292	-0.7	3,314	89.8	2.6	0.0	0.0	7.6	32.4	8.0	32.8	54.8	14.3	1,252	87.5
New Deal CDP	368	-	-	273	96.7	0.0	0.0	3.3	0.0	10.6	22.3	50.5	70.5	14.5	117	82.9
New Hope city	1,086	1,052	-3.1	840	96.3	0.0	0.0	3.7	0.0	17.0	21.3	48.3	58.8	5.9	361	83.9
New Johnsonville city	1,918	1,874	-2.3	2,027	87.3	6.5	0.4	5.6	0.2	23.9	15.5	40.6	63.8	12.8	729	85.6
New Market town	1,343	1,375	2.4	1,468	88.8	1.2	0.1	2.9	6.9	22.1	20.0	41.5	55.2	20.2	568	85.9
Newport city	6,925	6,884	-0.6	6,848	88.4	1.6	0.4	6.2	3.4	25.5	19.1	43.1	67.9	11.5	2,776	77.8
New Tazewell town	2,826	2,719	-3.8	2,730	97.1	1.1	0.0	1.0	0.9	16.7	24.1	47.4	56.8	13.0	1,293	70.4
New Union CDP	1,431	-	-	1,283	96.8	0.0	0.0	0.0	3.2	21.2	17.8	45.5	42.6	23.3	451	97.8
Niota city	718	733	2.1	981	91.1	2.0	1.0	2.3	3.5	22.0	16.6	43.0	68.5	7.7	390	83.6
Nolensville town	5,965	10,062	68.7	8,390	81.2	7.4	3.5	3.7	4.2	35.4	6.3	34.4	13.3	62.8	2,405	99.1
Normandy town	141	147	4.3	145	92.4	7.6	0.0	0.0	0.0	17.9	15.2	46.9	70.8	8.5	48	87.5
Norris city	1,593	1,602	0.6	1,272	96.1	0.4	1.3	1.6	0.6	12.4	39.9	57.7	34.9	37.4	585	76.2
Oakdale town	206	207	0.5	263	81.7	0.0	0.0	14.4	3.8	23.2	10.6	38.7	74.7	7.1	93	86.0
Oak Grove CDP	231	-	-	201	98.0	0.0	0.0	0.0	2.0	31.8	18.4	28.8	65.4	0.0	65	100.0
Oak Grove CDP	4,425	-	-	4,458	87.4	1.7	0.2	5.9	4.8	21.0	18.8	43.3	50.3	19.8	1,859	84.6
Oak Hill city	4,526	4,516	-0.2	4,587	93.7	0.7	2.5	1.4	1.7	26.9	20.4	42.1	8.4	78.9	1,668	96.9
Oakland town	6,635	8,345	25.8	7,893	88.8	8.1	0.3	1.1	1.7	25.0	17.6	37.4	29.9	22.9	3,100	95.6
Oak Ridge city	29,328	29,156	-0.6	29,037	79.3	6.7	3.0	5.1	5.9	22.3	19.4	41.3	31.9	38.1	12,008	90.6
Obion town	1,124	1,041	-7.4	1,339	86.8	5.6	0.2	3.0	4.4	29.1	13.7	31.5	68.0	5.3	514	78.0
Oliver Springs town	3,396	3,414	0.5	4,468	98.1	0.0	0.4	1.6	0.0	28.3	13.1	38.7	46.0	9.8	1,616	83.1
Olivet CDP	1,350	-	-	1,815	100.0	0.0	0.0	0.0	0.0	24.3	14.4	43.4	65.5	6.5	629	90.1
Oneida town	3,790	3,705	-2.2	3,700	96.6	0.0	0.0	0.9	2.5	25.4	17.9	38.2	58.5	18.5	1,661	85.9
Ooltewah CDP	687	-	-	756	82.7	6.1	0.0	0.0	11.2	6.6	32.1	51.2	34.1	45.3	337	63.2
Orlinda city	874	940	7.6	959	84.0	11.1	0.0	0.7	4.2	27.0	12.8	35.2	50.9	18.1	345	91.9
Orme town	113	110	-2.7	73	100.0	0.0	0.0	0.0	0.0	5.5	39.7	61.1	50.7	10.4	38	73.7
Palmer town	684	668	-2.3	696	98.3	0.0	0.0	1.7	0.0	16.7	22.4	45.0	79.9	4.1	233	80.7
Paris city	10,126	10,056	-0.7	10,043	73.8	19.7	0.2	3.5	2.8	22.8	22.0	41.3	62.5	12.7	4,335	80.0
Park City CDP	2,442	-	-	2,790	89.8	3.5	0.2	2.3	4.3	26.3	18.0	41.5	51.0	18.7	1,150	89.5
Parker's Crossroads city	313	313	0.0	239	77.0	10.5	0.4	2.1	10.0	15.9	24.7	47.8	59.8	10.1	107	85.0
Parrottsville town	289	293	1.4	279	86.4	2.5	0.0	8.6	2.5	19.7	11.1	35.6	69.6	6.0	117	70.1
Parsons city	2,362	2,290	-3.0	2,267	88.0	8.0	0.0	3.4	0.6	22.1	19.9	42.9	54.9	9.9	870	84.8
Pegram town	2,092	2,068	-1.1	2,597	95.7	2.2	0.7	0.0	1.4	21.8	18.2	42.5	43.9	26.2	911	97.1
Pelham CDP	403	-	-	408	98.3	0.0	0.0	1.7	0.0	20.8	25.2	44.4	42.3	33.2	149	83.9
Petersburg town	543	568	4.6	680	96.9	2.1	0.0	1.0	0.0	27.9	11.2	32.3	76.0	3.2	227	79.7
Petros CDP	583	-	-	715	100.0	0.0	0.0	0.0	0.0	29.5	10.3	39.8	83.2	2.0	265	92.8
Philadelphia city	652	729	11.8	882	75.7	7.4	0.0	2.7	14.2	22.7	13.6	36.1	59.8	11.2	278	82.7
Pigeon Forge city	5,866	6,266	6.8	6,229	76.4	0.0	0.0	7.7	15.9	18.5	21.9	44.3	56.5	14.7	2,346	84.7
Pikeville city	1,613	1,741	7.9	2,286	71.1	6.9	0.0	18.9	3.1	34.0	15.6	32.1	57.9	12.3	807	78.2
Pine Crest CDP	2,388	-	-	2,541	90.3	6.1	0.6	0.5	2.6	19.1	20.9	39.3	34.3	33.4	1,058	87.8
Piperton city	1,445	1,986	37.4	2,142	67.9	27.0	0.9	0.5	3.7	16.9	24.4	51.2	34.0	39.1	807	93.4
Pittman Center town	501	570	13.8	595	90.3	2.7	0.0	0.0	7.1	24.4	14.3	38.6	47.2	15.0	212	86.8
Plainview city	2,121	2,156	1.7	1,872	90.9	0.0	0.0	1.1	8.0	23.7	16.2	43.3	67.0	8.1	756	84.4
Pleasant Hill town	564	556	-1.4	462	99.4	0.0	0.0	0.6	0.0	10.6	59.3	72.5	46.2	35.2	203	84.7
Pleasant View city	4,146	4,795	15.7	4,480	96.5	1.1	0.0	0.3	2.0	24.6	11.9	36.2	38.7	30.9	1,587	92.6
Portland city	11,489	13,030	13.4	12,729	85.3	2.2	0.4	3.9	8.3	25.4	9.9	34.0	56.7	11.6	4,469	93.2
Powells Crossroads town	1,356	1,359	0.2	1,483	96.3	0.0	0.0	2.5	1.2	21.7	16.7	41.4	55.9	13.1	533	87.6
Pulaski city	7,862	7,597	-3.4	7,643	70.6	21.5	0.1	3.8	4.0	22.4	15.9	36.4	60.9	15.4	3,189	85.4
Puryear city	672	663	-1.3	677	90.4	4.1	0.3	2.2	3.0	14.9	31.8	52.4	64.8	9.8	283	82.7
Ramer city	304	296	-2.6	396	76.8	22.2	0.0	1.0	0.0	28.8	18.2	37.7	64.5	9.4	146	85.6
Red Bank city	11,647	11,840	1.7	11,745	84.2	6.0	1.0	4.0	4.8	16.8	17.0	37.7	38.7	29.0	5,683	87.5
Red Boiling Springs city	1,110	1,132	2.0	1,536	70.4	1.0	0.0	0.9	27.7	33.4	19.3	33.6	73.5	5.9	463	58.5
Riceville CDP	670	-	-	1,107	82.0	0.0	6.7	0.0	11.3	21.0	14.0	38.9	72.6	6.2	479	86.8
Ridgely town	1,795	1,623	-9.6	1,767	73.7	18.9	0.0	4.6	2.8	23.5	19.6	43.2	66.2	13.4	766	80.5
Ridgeside city	391	441	12.8	756	82.3	1.2	1.7	0.0	14.8	41.7	8.3	33.2	6.2	71.0	203	98.0
Ridgetop city	1,872	2,137	14.2	2,230	95.0	0.4	0.4	1.0	3.1	24.8	20.0	42.2	43.0	22.2	803	93.2
Ripley city	8,420	7,753	-7.9	7,947	41.9	51.7	0.4	5.4	0.5	28.2	13.5	34.5	62.7	10.0	3,269	83.6
Rives town	328	311	-5.2	356	58.1	11.8	0.0	2.0	28.1	35.7	9.8	31.0	80.0	6.7	113	86.7
Roan Mountain CDP	1,360	-	-	1,301	96.7	2.2	0.0	0.4	0.7	15.1	18.6	40.4	64.3	20.4	489	85.5
Robbins CDP	287	-	-	100	100.0	0.0	0.0	0.0	0.0	4.0	49.0	61.9	65.6	0.0	43	72.1
Rockford city	856	852	-0.5	759	94.6	0.0	0.0	1.1	4.3	23.5	22.9	46.3	47.6	25.6	294	93.2
Rockvale CDP	-	-	-	1,467	95.5	0.0	1.5	0.5	2.5	34.8	12.7	35.0	27.8	32.5	460	95.4
Rockwood city	5,571	5,425	-2.6	5,423	88.2	2.3	3.5	3.9	2.1	20.2	19.9	46.7	62.1	12.0	2,129	75.0
Rogersville town	4,459	4,377	-1.8	4,437	96.0	3.4	0.0	0.5	0.0	21.5	25.8	42.0	59.9	13.9	1,767	79.0
Rossville town	660	962	45.8	906	81.9	13.8	1.3	2.5	0.4	19.2	18.1	47.8	28.2	39.1	379	88.7
Rural Hill CDP	2,007	-	-	2,441	82.9	1.1	0.9	0.0	15.1	27.5	20.6	45.1	42.0	34.4	850	86.8
Rutherford town	1,150	1,067	-7.2	1,116	89.3	6.2	0.0	3.5	1.0	23.7	19.9	38.7	74.7	6.5	447	84.1
Rutledge town	1,290	1,355	5.0	1,587	94.0	3.8	0.8	1.4	0.0	19.4	26.7	43.5	69.6	8.1	611	70.4
St. Joseph city	796	829	4.1	943	96.5	0.0	0.6	2.5	0.3	22.1	17.4	34.9	69.8	6.0	349	74.5
Sale Creek CDP	2,845	-	-	2,781	98.7	0.5	0.0	0.0	0.7	23.3	19.8	44.0	58.4	11.3	1,006	91.7
Saltillo town	552	538	-2.5	574	72.6	27.4	0.0	0.0	0.0	8.4	28.0	52.8	66.2	7.9	258	84.9
Samburg town	210	201	-4.3	296	91.9	1.7	0.3	6.1	0.0	17.6	12.5	50.6	61.6	5.6	122	89.3
Sardis town	384	382	-0.5	366	97.5	0.0	0.0	0.8	1.6	21.6	24.9	45.6	67.2	6.1	143	79.0
Saulsbury town	102	91	-10.8	108	57.4	42.6	0.0	0.0	0.0	24.1	27.8	41.7	66.7	6.1	48	58.3
Savannah city	6,973	6,933	-0.6	6,947	84.2	7.4	0.6	1.4	6.4	25.8	23.7	39.8	59.3	11.1	2,658	81.7
Scotts Hill town	985	979	-0.6	951	92.0	0.5	0.0	0.8	6.6	19.8	20.3	45.9	65.3	12.0	357	81.2
Selmer town	4,332	4,291	-0.9	4,341	88.9	4.9	0.9	1.5	3.9	24.1	20.6	38.7	64.5	11.2	1,669	79.9
Sevierville city	14,777	17,117	15.8	16,743	81.0	0.4	0.5	1.7	16.4	22.4	21.7	39.4	54.9	15.4	6,026	87.8
Sewanee CDP	2,311	-	-	2,505	85.7	1.8	2.3	5.9	4.2	6.8	14.8	21.4	13.5	84.2	469	98.1
Seymour CDP	10,919	-	-	11,193	93.3	0.5	1.8	3.2	1.2	18.4	19.5	43.9	45.6	20.9	4,403	88.9
Shackle Island CDP	2,844	-	-	3,112	92.9	2.5	0.0	1.8	2.9	25.6	9.9	41.6	32.6	36.9	1,042	96.4
Sharon town	977	917	-6.1	1,067	82.9	14.6	1.1	1.3	0.0	23.0	22.6	46.8	55.4	16.3	487	72.5
Shelbyville city	20,315	22,101	8.8	21,591	57.3	15.1	0.0	4.1	23.5	28.8	11.9	33.0	65.3	11.1	7,257	85.3
Signal Mountain town	8,259	8,606	4.2	8,539	96.7	0.3	1.6	0.9	0.5	27.9	22.1	43.2	7.8	72.4	3,096	96.7
Silerton town	112	99	-11.6	132	93.9	0.0	0.0	0.0	6.1	10.6	25.0	55.4	46.6	38.8	77	88.3
Slayden town	191	205	7.3	147	87.1	6.8	0.0	6.1	0.0	19.7	23.1	42.9	60.3	12.1	59	88.1
Smithville city	4,529	4,886	7.9	4,711	79.2	1.1	0.4	5.9	13.4	27.7	12.3	34.4	65.2	14.7	1,631	80.0
Smyrna town	40,401	51,586	27.7	49,552	67.0	14.0	4.9	2.8	11.2	25.1	10.1	35.2	40.7	25.2	18,059	94.5
Sneedville town	1,385	1,349	-2.6	1,486	95.5	2.1	0.3	1.6	0.5	21.1	15.6	36.8	67.9	10.3	573	79.1
Soddy-Daisy city	12,915	13,619	5.5	13,398	95.9	0.9	0.1	0.4	2.7	21.4	19.8	44.2	49.3	19.8	5,628	87.0
Somerville town	3,116	3,264	4.7	3,238	46.5	45.8	0.2	6.9	0.6	25.2	15.5	36.7	61.1	17.6	1,187	80.4
South Carthage town	1,318	1,398	6.1	1,270	95.1	0.5	0.0	1.1	3.3	21.7	16.1	34.1	67.2	8.5	536	77.6
South Cleveland CDP	6,912	-	-	8,056	92.5	3.4	0.0	0.7	3.4	28.8	14.7	36.3	55.7	21.3	3,066	93.7

1 May be of any race.

Table A. All Places — **Population and Housing**

STATE City, town, township, borough, or CDP (county if applicable)	Population				Race and Hispanic or Latino origin (percent)					Age (percent)			Educational attainment of persons age 25 and older		Occupied housing units	
	2010 census total population	2019 estimated population	Percent change 2010–2019	ACS total population estimate 2015–2019	White alone, not Hispanic or Latino	Black alone, not Hispanic or Latino	Asian alone, not Hispanic or Latino	All other races or 2 or more races, not Hispanic or Latino	Hispanic or Latino[1]	Under 18 years old	Age 65 years and older	Median age	Percent High school diploma or less	Percent Bachelor's degree or more	Total	Percent with a computer
	1	2	3	4	5	6	7	8	9	10	11	12	13	14	15	16
TENNESSEE—Con.																
South Fulton city	2,392	2,214	-7.4	2,305	77.7	14.2	1.3	1.9	4.9	26.9	19.3	36.9	58.6	14.0	963	83.4
South Pittsburg city	3,101	3,029	-2.3	3,051	78.4	12.8	1.9	6.4	0.4	22.8	16.3	43.1	69.6	9.7	1,251	83.6
Sparta city	4,857	4,949	1.9	4,937	83.8	6.5	0.8	2.3	6.6	21.1	19.0	37.3	62.5	11.8	1,697	72.2
Spencer town	1,609	1,691	5.1	1,480	95.9	1.1	0.0	3.0	0.0	18.6	25.0	48.5	76.5	7.6	561	72.2
Spring City town	1,863	1,851	-0.6	2,199	95.2	2.4	0.0	1.3	1.1	22.7	23.4	41.1	65.6	10.3	935	78.2
Springfield city	16,450	17,277	5.0	17,092	58.8	21.0	0.9	2.1	17.2	25.4	12.9	34.5	58.7	15.2	6,356	85.6
Spring Hill city	29,106	43,769	50.4	39,711	85.4	4.5	1.9	2.3	6.0	32.0	9.6	33.8	21.0	46.8	12,727	96.8
Spurgeon CDP	3,957	-	-	4,666	96.3	2.2	1.2	0.2	0.2	20.4	16.5	42.9	41.2	22.2	2,014	90.6
Stanton town	457	420	-8.1	438	28.8	69.2	0.0	2.1	0.0	19.9	14.2	45.5	78.7	5.5	216	67.6
Stantonville town	267	261	-2.2	312	98.1	0.0	0.3	0.6	1.0	21.8	24.4	46.3	77.8	6.6	123	85.4
Summertown CDP	866	-	-	651	92.6	0.0	0.0	0.0	7.4	26.1	20.9	31.2	53.7	10.5	272	90.8
Sunbright city	542	519	-4.2	426	100.0	0.0	0.0	0.0	0.0	12.0	32.2	49.2	74.6	8.6	203	72.9
Surgoinsville town	1,804	1,760	-2.4	2,223	96.7	0.2	0.4	1.4	1.3	25.0	18.2	39.6	52.5	18.0	808	83.2
Sweetwater city	5,801	5,895	1.6	5,873	86.6	6.8	1.6	1.4	3.6	22.1	18.0	41.8	58.8	14.7	2,175	81.9
Tazewell town	2,236	2,276	1.8	2,451	91.1	2.4	1.0	1.6	3.9	18.2	20.0	43.4	64.5	12.0	1,022	71.5
Telford CDP	921	-	-	1,227	90.2	2.4	0.0	7.4	0.0	14.8	15.0	45.3	67.3	9.9	448	72.3
Tellico Plains town	854	909	6.4	952	97.3	0.0	0.0	2.4	0.3	26.4	19.7	35.9	65.5	9.1	370	65.7
Tellico Village CDP	5,791	-	-	5,671	98.9	0.6	0.0	0.0	0.5	0.6	73.4	71.9	19.1	55.6	3,131	95.5
Tennessee Ridge town	1,381	1,332	-3.5	1,322	97.5	0.5	0.0	2.0	0.0	23.1	25.7	42.0	67.6	14.4	501	67.1
Thompson's Station town	2,200	6,567	198.5	5,456	87.0	1.8	0.3	9.6	1.3	30.2	9.5	35.8	21.0	61.0	1,911	98.7
Three Way city	1,713	1,688	-1.5	1,676	71.1	25.6	1.2	0.8	1.3	16.8	19.4	49.0	38.4	30.9	676	92.5
Tiptonville town	4,477	3,971	-11.3	4,272	54.4	40.2	0.4	2.2	2.8	7.9	12.8	40.5	72.4	7.9	852	70.3
Toone town	369	334	-9.5	413	38.5	57.9	0.0	3.6	0.0	18.4	20.6	39.6	67.4	7.4	140	71.4
Townsend city	419	462	10.3	358	93.9	0.0	1.7	0.0	4.5	10.9	44.7	64.2	32.1	33.0	182	92.3
Tracy City town	1,457	1,397	-4.1	1,561	89.8	0.8	0.0	9.5	0.0	21.6	19.6	40.7	62.2	16.5	614	77.0
Trenton city	4,287	4,180	-2.5	4,217	60.4	26.4	0.0	8.7	4.4	17.1	20.5	36.4	59.9	12.3	1,688	72.6
Trezevant town	877	838	-4.4	772	66.5	18.8	0.0	2.3	12.4	23.7	13.0	42.2	54.9	16.1	352	80.7
Trimble town	631	611	-3.2	523	95.0	2.7	0.0	1.3	1.0	22.4	19.5	40.8	68.6	9.0	216	85.2
Troy town	1,398	1,321	-5.5	1,703	94.4	1.6	0.6	0.2	3.2	23.2	19.3	41.1	63.4	14.7	684	80.8
Tullahoma city	18,638	19,555	4.9	19,852	83.4	7.1	1.8	2.0	5.7	26.3	17.7	39.3	46.8	25.1	8,079	86.8
Tusculum city	2,670	2,689	0.7	2,726	83.2	8.8	2.2	1.3	4.5	14.6	20.2	27.0	43.8	28.2	641	81.7
Unicoi town	3,614	3,594	-0.6	3,556	91.2	0.0	0.4	0.4	8.0	14.2	21.5	44.1	50.7	20.6	1,421	80.5
Union City city	10,901	10,325	-5.3	10,424	67.8	22.7	0.1	3.5	5.9	23.8	20.3	41.0	60.1	15.4	4,461	86.3
Unionville CDP	1,368	-	-	2,109	94.4	1.1	0.0	3.4	1.2	20.6	19.4	47.9	62.4	16.4	705	73.0
Vanleer town	391	422	7.9	355	93.0	0.3	0.0	2.3	4.5	23.7	9.9	38.0	70.1	6.6	136	63.2
Viola town	131	138	5.3	105	93.3	0.0	0.0	6.7	0.0	17.1	31.4	53.9	63.2	14.9	44	70.5
Vonore town	1,486	1,552	4.4	1,677	89.7	0.0	0.2	4.7	5.4	22.7	23.9	44.9	46.1	17.1	715	84.8
Walden town	1,908	2,156	13.0	1,948	93.8	2.3	1.7	1.5	0.7	24.4	21.1	46.2	16.4	61.2	744	93.5
Walland CDP	259	-	-	357	99.4	0.0	0.0	0.0	0.6	3.6	20.4	51.9	30.1	27.7	143	80.4
Walnut Grove CDP	396	-	-	176	83.5	0.0	0.0	16.5	0.0	8.0	23.3	51.5	85.2	0.0	79	100.0
Walnut Grove CDP	864	-	-	925	97.6	0.0	0.0	2.4	0.0	15.2	22.2	45.3	66.9	6.7	312	92.6
Walnut Hill CDP	2,394	-	-	2,481	100.0	0.0	0.0	0.0	0.0	20.3	21.0	47.5	37.8	19.6	931	93.0
Walterhill CDP	401	-	-	261	100.0	0.0	0.0	0.0	0.0	8.8	31.8	63.2	34.5	28.6	148	84.5
Wartburg city	926	924	-0.2	1,045	96.6	1.8	0.0	1.6	0.0	24.6	22.7	42.7	70.8	12.3	377	79.6
Wartrace town	656	695	5.9	661	93.9	5.0	0.0	1.1	0.0	31.3	13.5	35.4	68.6	9.4	262	85.1
Watauga city	379	374	-1.3	411	98.8	0.0	0.0	0.5	0.7	20.0	18.0	43.1	67.3	11.4	133	69.2
Watertown city	1,472	1,523	3.5	1,684	75.5	14.0	0.0	3.3	7.2	25.6	15.0	37.2	60.8	11.7	641	83.0
Waverly city	4,079	4,146	1.6	4,117	90.6	5.2	0.0	0.4	3.8	20.1	20.9	37.7	65.8	16.5	1,730	82.5
Waynesboro city	2,446	2,419	-1.1	2,745	85.9	8.5	2.3	0.4	3.0	23.1	24.8	42.0	59.6	15.0	937	75.7
Westmoreland town	2,338	2,413	3.2	2,874	95.9	0.3	0.0	3.6	0.3	29.1	11.3	33.7	73.8	6.6	990	81.9
White Bluff town	3,207	3,653	13.9	3,517	95.3	1.6	0.0	1.9	1.3	21.7	13.2	36.5	66.6	13.2	1,306	82.1
White House city	10,225	12,638	23.6	11,843	91.6	1.7	1.9	1.1	3.7	25.4	14.3	36.5	38.9	26.8	4,345	94.8
White Pine town	2,277	2,346	3.0	2,139	78.1	0.3	0.0	1.8	19.8	24.7	14.5	35.9	66.9	6.5	852	87.1
Whiteville town	4,648	4,456	-4.1	4,501	41.5	51.2	0.0	1.6	5.8	5.9	5.0	36.6	83.1	3.4	289	81.0
Whitwell city	1,725	1,730	0.3	1,798	92.7	0.6	0.0	3.1	3.7	17.6	16.4	40.4	64.8	6.0	784	78.6
Wildwood CDP	1,098	-	-	1,110	90.9	0.0	0.0	3.6	5.5	15.4	28.5	53.0	50.2	16.1	367	100.0
Wildwood Lake CDP	3,124	-	-	3,639	87.1	0.5	1.0	7.7	3.7	27.7	14.2	39.1	52.4	17.4	1,309	86.6
Williston city	401	377	-6.0	449	52.1	46.5	0.0	0.7	0.7	23.4	16.9	35.7	64.0	8.1	167	79.6
Winchester city	8,607	8,982	4.4	8,706	82.2	9.2	0.5	3.1	5.0	21.0	20.6	42.0	46.6	24.9	3,556	84.1
Winfield town	1,020	1,006	-1.4	1,035	98.5	0.0	0.0	1.1	0.5	26.3	12.3	36.5	64.6	6.4	416	76.4
Woodbury town	2,642	2,889	9.3	2,784	94.1	3.5	0.1	1.1	1.1	22.8	20.8	40.2	61.6	15.1	1,139	80.5
Woodland Mills city	379	357	-5.8	323	87.9	9.6	0.3	2.2	0.0	23.5	24.1	41.6	60.3	14.6	140	90.0
Wrigley CDP	281	-	-	498	58.4	41.6	0.0	0.0	0.0	61.4	0.0	16.3	86.3	0.0	105	100.0
Yorkville city	271	255	-5.9	215	83.7	0.0	0.0	14.9	1.4	21.9	21.4	45.5	45.8	20.9	84	86.9
TEXAS	25,146,091	28,995,881	15.3	28,260,856	42.0	11.8	4.7	2.2	39.3	26.0	12.3	34.6	41.3	29.9	9,691,647	91.0
Abbott city	361	369	2.2	317	85.2	0.3	0.0	1.6	12.9	19.6	18.0	38.8	29.6	34.3	135	84.4
Abernathy city	2,812	2,706	-3.8	3,006	51.6	0.4	0.0	1.7	46.3	30.1	16.7	34.9	48.8	20.5	1,055	81.3
Abilene city	117,514	123,420	5.0	124,156	58.3	10.3	2.2	2.7	26.6	23.1	13.1	31.6	45.1	23.5	42,786	89.8
Abram CDP	2,067	-	-	2,328	0.4	0.0	0.0	0.0	99.6	40.7	7.1	24.4	73.2	3.0	597	79.9
Ackerly city	220	232	5.5	214	27.1	0.0	1.9	0.0	71.0	33.2	14.0	31.9	63.4	11.4	68	82.4
Addison town	12,537	16,263	29.7	15,302	44.6	14.0	10.3	6.5	24.6	14.6	8.1	32.2	15.5	56.3	8,279	99.1
Adrian city	166	170	2.4	120	76.7	0.0	0.0	2.5	20.8	15.0	44.2	64.2	39.6	43.6	47	93.6
Agua Dulce CDP	3,014	-	-	3,268	0.0	0.0	0.0	0.0	100.0	34.6	8.0	27.5	77.0	6.2	770	97.0
Agua Dulce city	812	801	-1.4	871	24.6	0.0	0.0	0.0	75.4	32.3	15.7	34.1	65.2	14.9	285	47.7
Aguilares CDP	21	-	-	-	-	-	-	-	-	-	-	-	-	-	-	-
Airport Heights CDP	161	-	-	22	0.0	0.0	0.0	0.0	100.0	18.2	0.0	36.5	100.0	0.0	3	100.0
Airport Road Addition CDP	93	-	-	279	0.0	0.0	0.0	0.0	100.0	39.8	19.4	33.9	39.3	35.7	48	100.0
Alamo city	18,373	19,910	8.4	19,613	14.5	0.2	0.0	0.0	85.3	35.1	16.8	31.1	67.4	12.0	5,726	80.7
Alamo Heights city	7,031	8,614	22.5	8,374	73.7	1.5	0.3	5.7	18.9	24.7	15.6	43.8	7.5	74.4	3,164	97.7
Alba town	502	545	8.6	598	82.8	2.3	0.0	0.8	14.0	23.7	27.4	42.5	63.8	15.6	225	90.7
Albany city	2,030	1,934	-4.7	1,786	83.0	0.2	0.3	3.1	13.4	24.5	21.7	42.5	38.3	26.3	739	80.9
Aldine CDP	15,869	-	-	15,318	8.5	1.0	2.0	0.1	88.4	33.7	6.7	28.7	82.1	3.1	3,822	64.5
Aledo city	2,701	4,985	84.6	4,181	81.2	0.3	1.1	6.5	10.9	33.5	8.4	35.2	23.0	43.8	1,219	96.5
Alfred CDP	91	-	-	15	0.0	0.0	0.0	0.0	100.0	0.0	0.0	0.0	100.0	0.0	7	100.0
Alice city	19,109	18,682	-2.2	19,007	12.2	1.2	1.0	1.3	84.3	26.3	15.1	35.3	59.0	14.4	6,472	72.1
Alice Acres CDP	490	-	-	254	29.9	0.0	0.0	0.0	70.1	36.6	0.0	33.4	32.3	21.7	83	54.2
Allen city	84,273	105,623	25.3	101,699	60.0	9.3	17.7	2.1	10.9	28.3	9.0	37.9	18.3	54.5	33,531	98.7
Alma town	333	385	15.6	318	70.1	0.0	0.0	2.2	27.7	15.7	23.0	48.7	52.5	14.4	107	79.4
Alpine city	5,999	5,982	-0.3	6,006	50.1	0.1	1.8	0.9	47.1	21.1	19.3	40.3	37.5	38.8	2,716	87.2

1 May be of any race.

Table A. All Places — **Population and Housing**

STATE City, town, township, borough, or CDP (county if applicable)	Population				Race and Hispanic or Latino origin (percent)					Age (percent)			Educational attainment of persons age 25 and older		Occupied housing units	
	2010 census total population	2019 estimated population	Percent change 2010–2019	ACS total population estimate 2015–2019	White alone, not Hispanic or Latino	Black alone, not Hispanic or Latino	Asian alone, not Hispanic or Latino	All other races or 2 or more races, not Hispanic or Latino	Hispanic or Latino[1]	Under 18 years old	Age 65 years and older	Median age	Percent High school diploma or less	Percent Bachelor's degree or more	Total	Percent with a computer
	1	2	3	4	5	6	7	8	9	10	11	12	13	14	15	16
TEXAS—Con.																
Alto town	1,225	1,240	1.2	1,200	43.3	26.8	0.0	1.3	28.6	21.6	19.0	39.8	56.5	7.8	498	78.1
Alto Bonito Heights CDP	342	-	-	232	0.0	0.0	0.0	0.0	100.0	21.1	19.8	42.1	100.0	0.0	46	100.0
Alton city	13,899	18,105	30.3	16,976	3.1	0.0	0.0	0.1	96.8	35.3	9.5	27.9	67.5	10.8	4,469	81.3
Alvarado city	3,752	4,530	20.7	4,156	64.3	6.9	0.0	2.6	26.3	31.1	10.8	34.1	62.5	13.2	1,424	85.1
Alvin city	24,161	26,723	10.6	26,299	55.0	2.6	1.7	0.9	39.8	27.0	12.2	33.7	44.6	16.6	9,346	90.4
Alvord town	1,338	1,573	17.6	1,260	85.3	0.7	0.0	2.9	11.0	32.6	8.0	28.2	50.7	15.3	428	91.6
Amada Acres CDP	92	-	-	28	0.0	0.0	0.0	0.0	100.0	67.9	0.0	0.0	0.0	0.0	9	100.0
Amargosa CDP	291	-	-	299	28.4	0.0	0.0	0.0	71.6	7.0	0.0	30.9	67.1	16.5	97	78.4
Amarillo city	190,666	199,371	4.6	198,955	54.0	6.3	4.1	2.4	33.1	27.0	13.5	34.2	42.7	23.7	76,319	90.8
Amaya CDP	93	-	-	26	0.0	0.0	0.0	0.0	100.0	42.3	0.0	49.3	0.0	53.3	7	100.0
Ames city	1,001	1,201	20.0	1,394	8.7	82.4	0.0	7.8	1.1	28.0	17.4	38.6	57.4	10.2	511	76.3
Amherst city	721	660	-8.5	848	40.0	5.1	0.5	0.0	54.5	20.8	19.2	44.6	59.3	11.8	286	85.3
Amistad CDP	53	-	-	44	63.6	0.0	0.0	0.0	36.4	13.6	68.2	74.7	78.9	7.9	32	100.0
Anacua CDP	12	-	-	-	-	-	-	-	-	-	-	-	-	-	-	-
Anahuac city	2,241	2,339	4.4	2,149	42.2	23.2	1.1	0.2	33.4	23.9	11.0	35.7	56.3	6.7	798	75.6
Anderson city	222	242	9.0	256	37.1	55.1	0.0	4.3	3.5	23.0	19.1	37.0	60.4	14.3	107	73.8
Andrews city	11,098	14,109	27.1	13,653	35.1	0.9	0.5	3.3	60.2	33.1	10.1	30.5	61.9	13.4	4,361	92.6
Angleton city	18,829	19,431	3.2	19,416	56.8	9.7	2.8	2.3	28.4	24.7	15.2	37.4	50.5	19.0	7,450	90.1
Angus city	416	429	3.1	436	75.0	2.8	0.5	6.2	15.6	29.6	16.3	37.1	57.7	7.3	154	90.3
Anna city	8,232	15,000	82.2	13,052	63.3	13.7	6.0	1.1	15.8	36.2	5.5	30.5	40.2	33.6	3,689	96.4
Annetta town	2,747	3,248	18.2	3,094	88.2	0.6	0.2	3.5	7.5	28.0	8.8	35.3	13.6	56.4	941	97.7
Annetta North town	497	568	14.3	567	87.7	2.1	0.4	5.6	4.2	28.6	18.0	45.8	18.9	53.7	197	96.4
Annetta South town	506	573	13.2	493	90.3	0.0	0.0	2.8	6.9	17.4	11.6	41.1	20.1	43.8	157	95.5
Annona town	315	288	-8.6	304	27.0	45.4	1.3	3.3	23.0	13.5	26.6	52.8	72.0	5.9	134	84.3
Anson city	2,430	2,297	-5.5	2,140	66.5	2.8	0.0	0.7	30.0	27.9	20.7	37.8	45.0	16.0	845	89.1
Anthony town	5,015	5,352	6.7	5,236	12.8	2.8	0.5	2.7	81.3	23.5	9.9	35.4	49.9	11.7	1,400	83.6
Anton city	1,126	1,095	-2.8	1,120	41.8	4.6	0.0	2.5	51.2	28.6	14.4	36.2	63.6	8.2	383	72.6
Appleby city	445	446	0.2	516	81.2	1.6	0.0	1.7	15.5	22.5	26.9	44.9	41.0	25.9	216	82.9
Aquilla city	108	113	4.6	208	99.0	0.0	0.0	0.0	1.0	31.3	19.7	43.5	67.4	4.3	55	98.2
Aransas Pass city	8,204	8,388	2.2	8,088	50.1	2.9	0.4	2.2	44.4	25.5	19.5	37.3	57.6	11.7	3,110	81.5
Archer City city	1,834	1,702	-7.2	1,838	82.6	3.9	0.0	1.8	11.7	25.8	14.9	37.9	51.3	24.3	776	89.0
Arcola city	1,614	2,663	65.0	2,441	5.4	11.9	0.0	0.0	82.7	35.9	6.0	28.4	77.4	10.1	541	94.1
Argyle city	3,247	4,381	34.9	4,112	96.7	2.1	0.2	0.1	0.8	22.4	14.6	48.5	13.5	58.9	1,532	98.2
Arlington city	365,098	398,854	9.2	395,477	38.6	22.3	6.5	3.1	29.6	25.6	10.4	33.3	38.6	30.3	135,333	94.7
Arp city	966	1,030	6.6	995	67.5	8.1	0.0	10.9	13.5	31.4	12.2	30.7	56.9	16.2	295	91.9
Arroyo Colorado Estates CDP	997	-	-	660	5.2	0.0	0.0	0.0	94.8	25.8	27.3	37.0	69.4	4.9	177	85.9
Arroyo Gardens CDP	456	-	-	115	0.0	0.0	0.0	0.0	100.0	11.3	66.1	68.4	100.0	0.0	73	23.3
Asherton city	1,046	1,039	-0.7	877	4.6	0.2	0.1	1.1	94.0	17.0	24.2	45.5	58.9	11.2	313	61.3
Aspermont town	917	835	-8.9	1,015	68.2	3.0	0.0	1.2	27.7	29.2	18.9	42.2	56.7	13.3	402	85.3
Atascocita CDP	65,844	-	-	81,557	45.2	22.1	2.8	2.2	27.7	29.0	8.4	34.1	28.4	37.7	25,395	98.3
Athens city	12,715	12,753	0.3	12,664	50.2	16.7	2.6	2.4	28.0	30.1	18.2	33.3	51.6	22.2	3,866	80.0
Atlanta city	5,670	5,472	-3.5	5,495	55.5	32.8	2.6	3.9	5.3	21.7	24.0	45.5	49.9	25.5	2,164	85.2
Aubrey city	2,600	4,895	88.3	3,731	86.9	1.5	0.5	3.2	7.9	28.3	12.0	34.7	37.9	24.3	1,324	90.5
Aurora city	1,222	1,512	23.7	1,452	79.7	0.0	1.5	4.8	14.0	32.5	11.2	38.0	49.9	20.1	418	88.0
Austin city	801,829	978,908	22.1	950,807	48.3	7.4	7.5	2.8	33.9	20.4	8.9	33.3	26.2	51.7	380,392	94.9
Austwell city	147	145	-1.4	133	69.9	8.3	0.0	0.0	21.8	2.3	45.1	61.8	46.6	13.8	73	68.5
Avery town	477	444	-6.9	650	79.4	0.0	0.0	0.0	20.6	20.8	14.9	37.7	71.6	11.5	251	70.9
Avinger town	444	421	-5.2	353	59.5	37.4	0.0	0.6	2.5	28.3	19.5	39.1	49.5	16.5	139	79.9
Azle city	10,862	13,351	22.9	12,796	90.1	0.4	0.4	1.8	7.3	24.2	16.6	40.4	41.6	22.4	4,650	93.3
Bacliff CDP	8,619	-	-	10,856	52.5	2.3	2.0	1.7	41.5	28.2	9.5	33.6	60.5	13.0	3,546	92.9
Bailey city	289	305	5.5	268	86.2	7.1	0.0	2.6	4.1	23.1	12.3	45.4	67.9	6.5	106	87.7
Bailey's Prairie village	724	773	6.8	661	70.7	7.3	0.0	1.5	20.6	23.6	18.2	49.0	20.6	28.4	243	91.8
Baird city	1,496	1,486	-0.7	1,722	85.4	0.1	0.6	1.7	12.1	20.0	22.3	43.6	46.1	19.3	684	75.7
Balch Springs city	23,789	25,007	5.1	25,190	19.2	22.7	1.0	0.1	57.0	34.1	6.8	28.3	66.9	7.2	6,665	92.6
Balcones Heights city	2,761	3,296	19.4	3,282	22.1	10.6	0.0	2.1	65.3	14.0	12.2	42.4	58.9	13.9	1,541	81.6
Ballinger city	3,766	3,642	-3.3	3,659	60.4	6.0	0.0	2.6	31.0	19.0	22.5	46.6	58.7	14.7	1,389	85.5
Balmorhea city	479	595	24.2	836	18.3	0.0	0.0	0.0	81.7	20.8	15.0	39.4	40.2	26.4	196	69.9
B and E CDP	518	-	-	432	0.0	0.0	0.0	0.0	100.0	31.0	28.0	45.2	96.0	0.0	77	40.3
Bandera city	857	900	5.0	833	75.2	0.0	0.0	1.7	23.2	13.4	32.2	56.6	45.3	13.3	307	91.5
Bangs city	1,613	1,527	-5.3	1,597	68.0	5.1	0.0	3.1	23.7	22.9	21.0	41.9	55.6	9.8	625	84.3
Banquete CDP	726	-	-	381	21.0	0.0	0.0	0.0	79.0	9.2	37.3	46.7	54.6	20.7	202	69.8
Bardwell city	649	689	6.2	528	31.4	11.9	0.0	0.4	56.3	27.3	18.8	38.3	75.6	4.2	170	77.6
Barrera CDP	108	-	-	228	0.0	0.0	0.0	0.0	100.0	74.6	0.0	8.5	82.5	0.0	58	87.9
Barrett CDP	3,199	-	-	3,807	9.4	60.2	0.0	2.9	27.4	22.8	13.4	39.5	55.7	8.9	1,364	90.5
Barry city	242	264	9.1	317	66.6	0.0	0.0	0.0	33.4	30.0	13.9	33.2	57.5	9.0	121	96.7
Barstow city	349	386	10.6	515	9.1	0.0	0.0	0.0	90.9	34.6	12.2	26.9	79.7	5.1	162	61.7
Bartlett city	2,699	1,758	-34.9	1,879	39.4	18.7	0.0	0.4	41.5	14.3	12.9	37.1	67.9	4.9	422	75.1
Barton Creek CDP	3,077	-	-	2,930	88.3	0.3	3.2	1.9	6.2	13.8	31.4	57.9	4.4	83.7	1,366	91.7
Bartonville town	1,566	1,785	14.0	1,558	86.4	0.6	1.0	1.3	10.7	22.8	18.8	48.1	18.9	55.2	551	98.4
Bastrop city	7,355	9,242	25.7	8,776	67.9	3.3	2.3	2.1	24.5	24.7	17.7	36.1	31.5	33.1	3,109	92.1
Batesville CDP	1,068	-	-	1,448	0.5	0.0	0.0	0.0	99.5	30.7	12.9	26.9	67.2	6.4	382	81.4
Bay City city	17,813	17,535	-1.6	17,694	31.3	14.2	0.8	1.9	51.8	28.7	15.0	34.0	52.3	17.4	6,276	81.9
Bayou Vista city	1,533	1,633	6.5	1,738	92.0	1.3	1.4	0.3	5.0	3.8	35.6	60.2	21.9	35.2	917	97.7
Bayside town	326	320	-1.8	333	62.5	7.8	0.0	3.0	26.7	15.6	27.0	56.7	40.2	18.8	138	82.6
Baytown city	71,605	77,192	7.8	76,635	31.8	17.2	1.8	2.1	47.0	27.5	11.6	32.9	49.9	15.0	26,474	89.3
Bayview town	372	389	4.6	439	56.5	0.0	0.0	1.4	42.1	22.1	22.8	49.3	30.8	43.5	164	91.5
Beach City city	2,277	2,792	22.6	2,664	79.0	5.9	0.2	1.1	13.8	25.2	13.5	36.9	21.4	31.4	900	92.3
Bear Creek village	382	480	25.7	360	90.6	0.0	2.5	0.8	6.1	21.1	24.7	50.2	15.8	63.0	142	98.6
Beasley city	650	677	4.2	638	30.7	4.9	0.0	0.0	64.4	28.2	17.1	34.8	73.5	10.3	230	79.1
Beaumont city	117,278	116,825	-0.4	118,151	32.0	46.5	3.1	1.2	17.1	25.0	14.1	33.9	43.9	24.5	45,839	85.7
Beckville city	847	823	-2.8	964	55.1	25.0	0.0	1.7	18.3	30.2	18.5	34.2	60.9	6.8	309	89.6
Bedford city	46,994	49,049	4.4	49,323	64.3	11.8	5.3	4.7	13.9	20.8	16.6	39.6	25.7	37.1	20,476	95.3
Bedias city	443	470	6.1	374	59.4	8.0	0.0	5.3	27.3	22.7	26.2	50.3	57.7	14.0	147	76.2
Bee Cave city	3,987	6,841	71.6	6,642	63.6	0.6	13.0	2.8	20.0	27.3	10.4	37.4	14.3	62.5	2,749	100.0
Beeville city	12,858	12,793	-0.5	12,912	27.0	1.8	1.0	1.2	69.0	28.0	13.5	28.9	50.5	7.1	4,285	83.1
Bellaire city	16,907	18,971	12.2	18,815	65.2	2.6	22.3	1.6	8.2	25.8	17.4	45.4	8.6	79.6	6,753	96.9
Bellevue city	362	347	-4.1	299	95.0	0.0	0.0	3.0	2.0	26.8	10.7	35.2	58.3	10.4	96	96.9
Bellmead city	9,933	10,744	8.2	10,556	40.0	16.7	0.4	4.2	38.6	27.0	11.8	33.7	58.6	12.2	3,733	81.3
Bells town	1,400	1,515	8.2	1,679	78.6	1.2	0.2	8.8	11.1	27.8	14.4	36.4	33.7	20.6	574	87.5
Bellville city	4,100	4,219	2.9	4,232	72.8	9.4	0.0	0.4	17.4	15.6	24.8	47.3	34.5	26.5	1,869	82.9
Belton city	18,233	22,885	25.5	21,685	55.1	8.4	0.9	3.8	31.8	26.8	11.1	28.3	42.1	27.4	7,412	89.8

1 May be of any race.

Table A. All Places — **Population and Housing**

STATE City, town, township, borough, or CDP (county if applicable)	Population				Race and Hispanic or Latino origin (percent)					Age (percent)			Educational attainment of persons age 25 and older		Occupied housing units	
	2010 census total population	2019 estimated population	Percent change 2010–2019	ACS total population estimate 2015–2019	White alone, not Hispanic or Latino	Black alone, not Hispanic or Latino	Asian alone, not Hispanic or Latino	All other races or 2 or more races, not Hispanic or Latino	Hispanic or Latino[1]	Under 18 years old	Age 65 years and older	Median age	Percent High school diploma or less	Percent Bachelor's degree or more	Total	Percent with a computer
	1	2	3	4	5	6	7	8	9	10	11	12	13	14	15	16
TEXAS—Con.																
Benavides city	1,496	1,406	-6.0	1,604	2.9	0.0	0.0	0.0	97.1	24.7	18.1	34.6	52.3	20.2	561	72.5
Benbrook city	21,198	23,502	10.9	23,215	78.6	5.8	0.8	3.1	11.5	21.8	18.3	39.3	26.1	38.1	9,663	95.7
Benjamin city	258	254	-1.6	145	80.7	0.7	0.0	8.3	10.3	15.2	34.5	47.2	54.6	19.6	56	73.2
Benjamin Perez CDP	34	-	-	110	0.0	0.0	0.0	0.0	100.0	21.8	0.0	28.2	100.0	0.0	15	100.0
Berryville town	970	1,064	9.7	1,127	88.7	5.9	0.0	2.4	2.9	20.1	18.0	40.4	55.8	12.4	421	82.7
Bertram city	1,348	1,476	9.5	2,254	57.6	1.0	0.0	5.9	35.4	26.5	11.9	30.8	65.7	11.4	595	91.6
Beverly Hills city	2,012	1,987	-1.2	2,494	19.8	12.7	0.0	0.7	66.8	34.2	8.5	27.7	60.8	5.9	755	94.0
Bevil Oaks city	1,274	1,225	-3.8	1,259	83.2	4.8	2.5	0.2	9.2	23.4	22.8	43.2	34.4	19.5	470	88.9
Bigfoot CDP	450	-	-	441	50.6	0.0	0.0	0.0	49.4	0.0	57.6	78.6	57.8	14.5	271	57.2
Big Lake city	2,936	3,367	14.7	3,257	22.9	1.0	0.2	0.5	75.4	33.5	7.8	29.5	63.5	10.0	920	90.8
Big Sandy town	1,355	1,412	4.2	1,495	72.0	26.9	0.0	0.5	0.7	25.5	17.9	37.1	52.9	15.5	543	87.5
Big Spring city	27,282	28,187	3.3	28,041	41.4	5.9	0.8	2.8	49.1	21.9	11.3	35.3	55.5	11.5	8,029	87.9
Big Thicket Lake Estates CDP	742	-	-	704	86.8	7.1	0.0	6.1	0.0	29.7	12.1	44.3	58.2	0.0	229	66.8
Big Wells city	697	702	0.7	930	1.6	0.0	1.4	0.0	97.0	21.1	14.6	32.2	71.1	3.3	251	71.7
Bishop city	3,134	3,056	-2.5	3,093	21.2	0.3	0.0	2.5	76.0	26.2	14.7	36.4	56.1	17.1	1,092	88.1
Bishop Hills town	193	178	-7.8	256	89.8	0.0	0.0	0.0	10.2	25.8	14.8	45.8	18.4	37.4	93	98.9
Bixby CDP	504	-	-	759	1.8	0.0	0.0	0.0	98.2	31.1	12.5	31.0	67.8	5.2	172	70.9
Blackwell city	311	310	-0.3	201	92.0	0.0	0.0	0.0	8.0	26.9	16.9	40.5	43.3	30.6	96	90.6
Blanco city	1,803	2,071	14.9	2,256	64.9	0.0	0.8	1.8	32.4	22.5	15.5	42.6	43.7	27.3	776	84.7
Blanket town	390	368	-5.6	372	86.3	0.0	0.0	1.1	12.6	22.0	18.5	44.1	54.5	9.9	153	81.0
Blessing CDP	927	-	-	538	47.0	0.0	0.0	0.0	53.0	29.4	10.2	40.6	59.5	10.0	247	72.9
Bloomburg town	402	393	-2.2	499	77.0	15.8	0.8	0.0	6.4	30.1	18.4	31.5	55.4	13.8	167	71.3
Blooming Grove town	823	835	1.5	823	90.5	1.6	0.0	2.3	5.6	27.5	15.3	33.6	54.3	9.7	326	90.8
Bloomington CDP	2,459	-	-	1,783	18.6	9.0	0.0	0.0	72.4	19.4	22.8	43.0	73.2	4.0	557	75.2
Blossom city	1,493	1,569	5.1	1,622	90.9	2.6	0.0	1.5	5.0	24.8	16.2	35.7	55.4	8.0	613	90.5
Blue Berry Hill CDP	866	-	-	623	8.8	0.0	0.0	0.0	91.2	41.6	10.9	40.1	81.0	0.0	161	87.0
Blue Mound city	2,393	2,445	2.2	2,981	35.0	1.2	3.0	1.2	59.6	28.0	7.9	34.0	64.5	8.8	931	95.0
Blue Ridge city	796	926	16.3	834	73.7	0.2	0.0	2.2	23.9	36.9	6.8	28.5	56.4	11.6	270	95.6
Bluetown CDP	356	-	-	653	4.6	0.0	0.0	0.0	95.4	41.5	13.9	28.8	88.6	0.0	150	57.3
Blum town	444	467	5.2	434	88.7	1.8	0.0	0.0	9.4	30.6	17.5	26.7	69.5	7.7	129	87.6
Boerne city	10,661	18,232	71.0	15,891	69.1	0.9	0.2	2.8	27.0	26.0	18.7	38.6	24.2	41.6	5,452	93.3
Bogata city	1,154	1,063	-7.9	1,211	92.4	0.9	0.5	2.5	3.7	25.3	23.1	40.1	60.8	9.1	467	68.5
Boling CDP	1,122	-	-	1,162	23.6	1.2	0.0	0.0	75.2	30.5	15.4	28.8	44.3	24.7	424	80.0
Bolivar Peninsula CDP	2,417	-	-	2,549	75.8	0.4	0.0	0.2	23.6	15.1	23.2	53.1	55.2	13.9	1,027	90.2
Bonanza Hills CDP	37	-	-	128	0.0	0.0	0.0	0.0	100.0	32.0	0.0	19.8	31.3	47.9	23	100.0
Bonham city	10,127	10,386	2.6	10,157	63.7	12.2	1.4	3.2	19.5	20.8	16.0	38.9	56.7	13.3	3,052	91.1
Bonney village	310	372	20.0	207	49.8	20.8	0.5	5.3	23.7	16.9	7.2	48.1	30.6	11.5	106	91.5
Booker town	1,516	1,494	-1.5	1,421	42.6	0.5	0.0	1.7	55.2	23.8	16.3	34.2	57.3	17.2	504	92.3
Borger city	13,350	12,415	-7.0	12,698	64.1	1.4	0.3	4.0	30.3	27.3	13.6	34.7	50.5	14.5	4,099	87.2
Botines CDP	117	-	-	31	67.7	0.0	0.0	0.0	32.3	0.0	32.3	62.5	32.3	67.7	31	67.7
Bovina city	1,865	1,777	-4.7	1,452	7.2	1.2	2.3	0.0	89.3	25.6	11.8	35.0	75.6	8.4	476	79.4
Bowie city	5,219	5,114	-2.0	5,050	91.8	0.9	0.0	0.0	7.4	22.5	20.9	42.3	52.1	16.2	2,019	89.0
Box Canyon CDP	34	-	-	76	32.9	0.0	0.0	0.0	67.1	15.8	59.2	66.2	56.3	34.4	33	100.0
Boyd town	1,211	1,518	25.4	1,301	73.5	0.2	0.0	4.4	22.0	19.5	14.6	34.8	58.3	21.3	442	88.5
Boys Ranch CDP	282	-	-	412	74.8	9.0	0.0	1.9	14.3	77.4	1.9	11.8	16.9	64.9	42	100.0
Brackettville city	1,688	1,686	-0.1	1,674	18.2	0.3	0.0	0.0	81.5	17.6	22.8	54.0	71.3	3.2	540	50.9
Brady city	5,541	5,302	-4.3	5,355	52.2	1.6	1.1	7.0	38.0	22.9	19.1	39.0	54.3	12.3	1,969	88.5
Brazoria city	3,029	3,056	0.9	3,078	58.2	13.5	0.4	1.5	26.3	25.5	16.2	35.5	52.8	10.7	1,145	86.6
Brazos Bend city	310	356	14.8	366	94.5	0.0	1.4	0.0	4.1	12.8	41.3	62.1	12.1	58.7	150	100.0
Brazos Country city	469	474	1.1	618	93.9	0.0	2.6	0.5	3.1	20.6	19.6	50.5	18.3	47.5	225	98.2
Breckenridge city	5,784	5,423	-6.2	5,457	60.0	3.0	0.3	3.4	33.3	28.0	15.9	35.4	53.9	16.9	1,881	91.7
Bremond city	929	966	4.0	911	59.9	30.2	0.0	2.7	7.1	12.7	24.6	42.5	59.7	13.4	418	73.9
Brenham city	15,809	17,863	13.0	17,123	52.0	22.1	2.7	3.0	20.2	22.1	18.5	34.8	48.7	24.0	5,774	77.0
Briar CDP	5,665	-	-	5,241	82.8	0.0	0.0	2.3	14.8	18.1	18.3	45.3	54.1	14.9	1,952	90.1
Briarcliff village	1,435	1,819	26.8	1,648	84.3	0.0	0.8	0.5	14.4	26.0	14.4	44.0	11.7	54.4	611	99.5
Briaroaks city	488	507	3.9	515	89.7	1.2	0.0	1.0	8.2	15.1	27.8	53.5	31.2	37.4	221	94.6
Bridge City city	7,837	7,862	0.3	7,961	96.4	0.6	0.3	0.2	2.5	28.2	11.6	34.4	38.7	21.1	2,608	88.7
Bridgeport city	5,992	6,653	11.0	6,465	52.1	3.4	0.4	0.5	43.6	25.8	9.8	35.6	57.8	17.2	1,920	85.6
Bristol CDP	668	-	-	572	78.5	5.8	0.0	2.8	12.9	11.7	18.9	36.2	70.6	7.8	203	92.1
Broaddus town	207	197	-4.8	332	97.9	0.0	0.0	0.0	2.1	30.4	6.0	40.3	36.2	18.6	103	99.0
Bronte town	999	999	0.0	949	69.1	0.0	0.0	1.1	29.8	23.3	21.0	43.4	59.4	8.9	448	85.3
Brookshire city	4,739	5,816	22.7	5,376	8.9	28.6	0.0	1.2	61.3	27.5	7.6	30.7	74.0	8.2	1,425	81.3
Brookside Village city	1,510	1,577	4.4	1,359	51.6	6.8	0.4	2.6	38.7	19.4	20.2	44.0	40.5	24.2	495	86.5
Browndell city	199	206	3.5	275	42.9	57.1	0.0	0.0	0.0	15.3	33.1	56.0	72.3	10.7	99	63.6
Brownfield city	9,657	9,358	-3.1	9,525	33.3	5.9	0.0	0.5	60.3	26.0	15.3	34.7	65.7	10.2	3,077	83.8
Brownsboro city	1,044	1,279	22.5	1,185	81.9	3.4	0.0	1.8	12.9	35.8	12.1	29.9	58.2	16.6	371	83.8
Brownsville city	174,729	182,781	4.6	182,271	4.9	0.4	0.6	0.3	93.8	30.4	12.0	30.6	58.5	18.9	52,162	79.7
Brownwood city	19,311	18,455	-4.4	18,679	64.7	5.5	1.1	1.7	26.9	23.6	15.9	34.8	52.2	18.5	7,041	87.6
Bruceville-Eddy city	1,624	1,697	4.5	1,539	80.7	0.0	0.1	2.1	17.1	27.7	14.0	41.5	54.4	10.1	564	87.9
Brundage CDP	27	-	-	-	-	-	-	-	-	-	-	-	-	-	-	-
Bruni CDP	379	-	-	378	4.5	0.0	0.0	0.0	95.5	21.7	11.9	40.3	60.0	11.3	129	90.7
Brushy Creek CDP	21,764	-	-	18,399	62.0	6.1	13.0	3.6	15.4	27.1	10.2	39.4	16.5	54.0	5,798	98.6
Bryan city	76,226	86,276	13.2	84,096	39.5	16.4	1.9	2.3	39.8	24.8	10.3	30.5	45.4	26.6	30,131	89.7
Bryson city	539	536	-0.6	587	79.7	0.7	0.9	2.4	16.4	32.9	7.8	29.9	70.7	11.9	254	81.1
Buchanan Dam CDP	1,519	-	-	1,375	87.9	0.0	0.4	1.1	10.5	13.6	29.8	58.2	45.3	21.2	631	87.8
Buchanan Lake Village CDP	692	-	-	945	98.9	0.0	0.0	0.0	1.1	8.5	48.9	64.3	45.9	10.3	467	95.9
Buckholts town	519	522	0.6	417	64.3	0.0	3.8	0.0	31.9	15.6	28.5	49.5	74.4	5.6	153	81.7
Buda city	7,270	16,906	132.5	15,565	59.0	4.9	1.2	2.2	32.8	31.5	7.0	32.3	24.0	49.3	5,117	98.8
Buena Vista CDP	102	-	-	67	0.0	0.0	0.0	0.0	100.0	19.4	0.0	48.1	100.0	0.0	16	43.8
Buffalo city	1,859	1,902	2.3	1,917	53.6	12.5	0.5	3.5	29.9	29.8	14.1	31.4	51.2	8.2	655	83.5
Buffalo Gap town	527	557	5.7	731	69.9	3.7	0.0	0.0	26.4	30.6	16.7	39.2	69.0	14.9	233	91.4
Buffalo Springs village	448	442	-1.3	428	72.4	0.7	0.0	0.7	26.2	11.0	24.8	54.0	31.7	19.0	204	91.7
Bullard town	2,465	3,727	51.2	3,227	82.0	3.0	0.0	3.7	11.3	35.9	9.5	34.2	28.6	28.3	933	93.8
Bulverde city	4,688	5,300	13.1	5,162	68.8	0.0	0.6	4.3	26.3	22.9	22.3	45.6	32.1	34.8	1,692	98.6
Buna CDP	2,142	-	-	1,737	85.7	6.8	0.0	4.5	3.0	11.9	26.1	47.3	68.9	5.8	720	88.6
Bunker Hill Village city	3,623	3,935	8.6	3,940	70.3	0.1	13.3	1.7	14.5	30.0	15.5	42.7	7.0	76.6	1,224	99.1
Burkburnett city	10,814	11,270	4.2	11,167	82.9	3.8	0.8	2.9	9.6	23.8	18.5	41.1	45.5	20.7	4,653	87.0
Burke city	731	727	-0.5	761	72.8	1.6	0.3	1.6	23.8	27.9	11.8	36.8	58.9	9.9	296	86.8
Burleson city	36,879	48,225	30.8	45,862	79.3	4.6	1.4	3.2	11.6	28.0	11.9	34.9	37.1	26.4	15,708	95.3
Burnet city	5,975	6,406	7.2	6,266	73.3	2.2	0.8	3.0	20.8	18.5	19.8	39.0	42.1	21.0	2,077	93.0

1 May be of any race.

Table A. All Places — **Population and Housing**

STATE City, town, township, borough, or CDP (county if applicable)	Population: 2010 census total population	Population: 2019 estimated population	Population: Percent change 2010–2019	Population: ACS total population estimate 2015–2019	Race and Hispanic or Latino origin (percent): White alone, not Hispanic or Latino	Black alone, not Hispanic or Latino	Asian alone, not Hispanic or Latino	All other races or 2 or more races, not Hispanic or Latino	Hispanic or Latino[1]	Age (percent): Under 18 years old	Age 65 years and older	Median age	Educational attainment of persons age 25 and older: Percent High school diploma or less	Percent Bachelor's degree or more	Occupied housing units: Total	Percent with a computer
	1	2	3	4	5	6	7	8	9	10	11	12	13	14	15	16
TEXAS—Con.																
Burton city	297	292	-1.7	387	78.6	16.0	1.0	1.8	2.6	23.3	19.6	44.8	46.1	22.9	161	62.1
Butterfield CDP	114	-	-	60	10.0	0.0	0.0	0.0	90.0	30.0	0.0	23.8	60.7	0.0	15	66.7
Byers city	485	452	-6.8	478	96.7	0.0	0.0	1.0	2.3	31.4	14.0	30.3	47.5	13.4	167	92.8
Bynum town	199	207	4.0	343	69.4	8.5	0.3	1.5	20.4	32.4	10.2	33.3	52.0	6.5	93	93.5
Cactus city	3,179	3,245	2.1	3,245	3.2	6.5	11.9	0.0	78.4	31.7	8.3	27.3	93.9	0.0	872	80.0
Caddo Mills city	1,370	1,698	23.9	1,557	82.9	3.5	0.0	4.9	8.7	29.3	10.8	34.3	52.8	20.2	569	90.7
Caldwell city	4,104	4,373	6.6	4,315	49.3	22.3	0.0	0.6	27.8	27.5	14.9	37.7	55.4	14.2	1,566	80.6
Callender Lake CDP	1,039	-	-	1,023	86.5	11.1	0.0	0.0	2.3	23.3	29.9	41.9	36.1	32.6	407	86.2
Callisburg city	353	383	8.5	381	94.8	0.0	0.8	0.5	3.9	25.5	12.3	33.9	44.4	14.4	119	87.4
Calvert city	1,192	1,126	-5.5	1,328	26.0	56.9	0.0	4.6	12.6	24.3	18.8	38.4	49.9	13.1	520	81.9
Camargito CDP	388	-	-	388	0.0	0.0	0.0	0.0	100.0	28.4	3.4	25.8	64.9	0.0	132	83.3
Cameron city	5,540	5,464	-1.4	5,489	49.8	21.4	0.5	1.1	27.1	28.4	21.8	39.7	65.2	11.2	2,000	73.4
Cameron Park CDP	6,963	-	-	6,241	4.7	0.0	0.0	0.0	95.3	30.5	7.2	27.9	75.5	6.3	1,540	78.4
Campbell city	563	632	12.3	729	83.7	2.7	1.9	5.8	5.9	28.7	15.9	41.3	54.1	13.6	291	88.7
Campo Verde CDP	132	-	-	176	0.0	0.0	0.0	0.0	100.0	0.0	8.5	49.9	85.7	14.3	50	66.0
Camp Swift CDP	6,383	-	-	6,244	38.9	5.9	1.2	2.3	51.6	18.4	10.4	38.4	66.6	11.9	1,473	90.2
Camp Wood city	705	731	3.7	934	62.7	0.0	0.0	0.0	37.3	15.3	21.3	44.5	66.7	7.2	247	59.9
Canadian city	2,649	2,699	1.9	3,029	52.9	0.2	0.0	1.1	45.8	33.8	11.2	35.0	54.2	18.2	934	89.8
Caney City town	215	220	2.3	144	60.4	30.6	0.0	9.0	0.0	6.3	34.0	61.4	59.3	11.5	71	63.4
Canton city	3,568	3,861	8.2	3,805	89.5	2.8	0.0	3.3	4.3	19.9	24.7	40.4	45.5	13.6	1,518	88.1
Cantu Addition CDP	188	-	-	92	0.0	0.0	0.0	0.0	100.0	37.0	0.0	36.9	72.4	0.0	30	100.0
Canutillo CDP	6,321	-	-	5,123	4.8	0.0	0.9	0.2	94.1	35.6	14.2	28.6	67.4	15.2	1,498	80.0
Canyon city	13,311	15,945	19.8	15,305	77.1	2.2	1.7	2.8	16.2	20.7	10.3	26.3	19.2	43.5	5,267	96.2
Canyon Creek CDP	916	-	-	1,231	86.0	2.0	0.0	0.0	11.9	33.8	7.1	32.2	52.8	11.5	330	88.2
Canyon Lake CDP	21,262	-	-	25,325	76.6	1.5	0.8	1.9	19.2	19.1	21.9	49.5	34.9	30.9	9,739	96.2
Cape Royale CDP	670	-	-	534	79.4	8.2	0.0	0.0	12.4	0.0	49.6	65.0	37.3	25.1	358	95.0
Carbon town	274	272	-0.7	348	77.6	0.0	0.0	0.3	22.1	24.1	16.4	38.3	52.5	16.2	123	84.6
Carlsbad CDP	719	-	-	551	74.0	6.2	0.0	1.6	18.1	28.9	18.0	26.5	58.7	9.4	144	60.4
Carl's Corner town	173	190	9.8	175	44.6	4.6	0.0	1.1	49.7	20.6	18.3	52.8	72.3	0.0	68	94.1
Carmine city	250	252	0.8	177	93.8	0.0	0.0	1.1	5.1	13.6	26.6	57.4	31.8	30.4	75	85.3
Carrizo Hill CDP	582	-	-	673	0.0	0.0	0.0	0.0	100.0	42.3	3.6	18.6	79.0	21.0	167	73.7
Carrizo Springs city	5,368	5,362	-0.1	5,554	8.9	0.0	0.2	0.0	90.9	34.1	18.6	31.7	79.3	8.3	1,705	61.2
Carrollton city	119,211	139,248	16.8	135,834	40.1	9.9	15.1	2.2	32.7	22.6	11.2	37.3	34.3	39.2	48,817	97.4
Carthage city	6,779	6,431	-5.1	6,535	64.3	25.1	0.3	0.3	10.0	25.5	15.1	34.9	43.8	21.9	2,309	83.4
Casa Blanca CDP	54	-	-	-	-	-	-	-	-	-	-	-	-	-	-	-
Casas CDP	39	-	-	40	0.0	0.0	0.0	0.0	100.0	0.0	0.0	28.5	53.8	0.0	7	100.0
Cashion Community city	349	355	1.7	243	93.4	0.0	1.2	2.5	2.9	19.8	28.0	49.2	46.2	30.6	113	85.8
Castle Hills city	4,122	4,470	8.4	4,447	53.1	0.7	2.1	0.2	43.9	21.8	23.6	46.8	17.8	52.9	1,652	90.3
Castroville city	2,780	3,119	12.2	3,009	51.8	1.1	0.7	4.5	41.8	25.1	20.3	41.8	34.7	31.3	1,108	89.2
Catarina CDP	118	-	-	228	0.0	0.0	0.0	0.0	100.0	3.9	32.9	62.3	85.2	4.4	68	22.1
Cedar Hill city	44,998	47,930	6.5	48,560	17.3	52.8	3.0	3.8	23.2	29.4	8.9	34.1	33.9	29.8	15,388	96.5
Cedar Park city	55,117	79,462	44.2	74,814	64.3	2.6	9.5	3.2	20.3	28.3	8.6	35.5	18.9	50.1	24,382	97.7
Cedar Point CDP	630	-	-	795	93.8	0.0	1.5	1.8	2.9	14.8	18.0	47.6	38.6	31.9	323	82.7
Celeste city	814	907	11.4	889	84.3	6.0	0.1	5.7	3.9	32.3	13.3	35.2	51.6	8.9	307	86.0
Celina city	6,315	16,299	158.1	11,116	76.7	9.0	0.7	1.7	11.9	32.2	11.1	34.1	19.3	44.5	3,466	99.2
Center city	5,346	5,175	-3.2	5,250	34.3	36.9	0.0	0.0	28.8	35.0	14.9	24.7	56.8	19.4	1,617	84.5
Centerville city	892	907	1.7	1,029	87.1	10.4	0.0	1.6	1.0	32.4	17.6	29.7	45.7	19.6	335	81.2
Central Gardens CDP	4,347	-	-	4,207	92.9	0.0	1.9	0.4	4.8	20.3	14.0	46.7	37.8	15.6	1,820	90.4
César Chávez CDP	1,929	-	-	1,200	3.7	0.0	0.0	0.9	95.4	35.3	3.9	33.2	64.3	6.7	343	96.8
Chandler city	2,741	3,180	16.0	3,003	79.6	14.8	0.1	1.2	4.4	23.1	23.9	43.4	42.1	22.4	1,165	88.7
Channelview CDP	38,289	-	-	43,055	16.7	14.5	0.5	1.3	67.0	32.7	8.1	31.0	62.1	9.1	12,204	93.2
Channing city	363	344	-5.2	257	76.3	0.4	0.0	2.7	20.6	25.7	28.8	37.1	41.0	16.9	115	87.0
Chaparrito CDP	114	-	-	119	0.0	0.0	0.0	0.0	100.0	0.0	20.2	60.4	20.2	0.0	45	46.7
Chapeno CDP	47	-	-	-	-	-	-	-	-	-	-	-	-	-	-	-
Charlotte city	1,718	1,898	10.5	1,546	13.7	0.0	0.0	2.3	84.0	25.5	12.4	36.8	83.9	2.1	536	70.0
Chester town	315	311	-1.3	391	90.3	0.0	0.0	1.5	8.2	20.7	13.6	37.6	45.4	9.6	126	92.9
Chico city	1,012	1,177	16.3	1,138	87.3	0.0	0.0	2.5	10.2	30.2	10.8	31.3	61.3	4.2	348	92.2
Childress city	6,105	6,048	-0.9	6,201	55.6	8.5	0.4	1.4	34.1	17.4	11.8	32.8	55.3	15.6	2,042	79.5
Chillicothe city	707	673	-4.8	777	54.6	5.4	0.0	2.8	37.2	26.9	13.5	34.7	58.9	18.5	260	83.5
Chilton CDP	911	-	-	734	26.8	1.9	0.0	0.8	70.4	20.3	10.2	33.7	84.3	4.9	288	84.7
China city	1,158	1,206	4.1	990	66.5	26.1	0.0	0.0	7.5	19.2	29.2	49.5	59.5	6.1	430	72.3
China Grove town	1,175	1,321	12.4	1,224	46.7	5.0	0.0	2.8	45.5	13.5	21.1	47.5	39.5	28.5	373	92.0
China Spring CDP	1,281	-	-	1,455	95.8	0.0	0.0	0.0	4.2	37.4	14.4	29.4	49.5	6.4	436	100.0
Chireno city	386	384	-0.5	414	61.4	28.5	0.0	6.0	4.1	17.6	22.2	46.0	58.9	12.7	145	73.8
Christine town	382	425	11.3	250	19.2	0.0	0.0	0.0	80.8	24.8	16.4	44.2	73.0	7.6	79	81.0
Christoval CDP	504	-	-	354	75.1	11.9	0.0	0.0	13.0	16.9	29.1	50.3	54.8	29.0	161	84.5
Chula Vista CDP	288	-	-	276	0.0	0.0	0.0	0.0	100.0	38.4	0.0	30.1	100.0	0.0	67	100.0
Chula Vista CDP	3,818	-	-	4,722	1.1	0.0	0.5	0.0	98.5	26.3	17.7	36.0	75.1	9.7	1,590	74.7
Chula Vista CDP	450	-	-	829	0.0	0.0	0.0	0.0	100.0	33.1	23.0	28.0	62.9	0.0	206	76.7
Cibolo city	20,177	31,281	55.0	28,920	48.5	15.6	2.2	3.8	30.0	28.8	8.0	34.4	23.9	39.6	8,561	98.1
Cienegas Terrace CDP	3,424	-	-	3,476	1.0	0.0	0.0	0.0	99.0	32.2	7.0	24.6	79.5	6.4	935	88.6
Cinco Ranch CDP	18,274	-	-	16,437	64.5	4.4	12.8	2.4	15.9	28.0	11.8	40.6	9.7	65.1	5,433	97.5
Circle D-KC Estates CDP	2,393	-	-	2,791	86.3	0.0	0.4	2.5	10.7	24.7	18.7	46.4	36.4	21.8	910	95.2
Cisco city	3,872	3,784	-2.3	3,778	79.2	3.5	0.2	1.1	16.0	26.4	23.7	37.6	31.2	18.4	1,417	78.3
Citrus City CDP	2,321	-	-	3,288	0.0	0.0	0.0	0.0	100.0	42.5	1.8	22.9	81.6	2.3	746	80.0
Clarendon city	2,077	1,781	-14.3	1,842	74.5	9.9	0.6	3.6	11.3	19.8	20.1	36.5	49.2	18.2	705	78.2
Clarksville city	3,352	3,072	-8.4	3,145	43.1	43.9	0.0	3.6	9.4	19.0	22.6	42.4	62.5	6.8	1,280	78.4
Clarksville City city	866	934	7.9	799	82.2	4.9	0.3	2.6	10.0	22.9	16.8	40.0	51.2	13.8	312	79.5
Claude city	1,199	1,210	0.9	1,367	85.7	0.4	0.0	3.7	10.2	25.5	21.5	43.8	40.0	22.8	470	91.5
Clear Lake Shores city	1,059	1,215	14.7	1,190	86.3	0.0	0.0	2.9	10.8	11.8	25.5	55.3	19.5	53.4	603	97.5
Cleburne city	29,639	31,295	5.6	30,289	62.8	4.2	0.9	1.4	30.6	25.2	15.4	35.3	55.6	16.9	11,121	90.0
Cleveland city	7,826	8,238	5.3	8,061	46.5	16.5	0.1	1.6	35.3	26.5	11.7	33.1	65.5	8.2	2,724	82.8
Clifton city	3,440	3,446	0.2	3,391	75.7	2.7	1.3	0.6	19.8	18.2	27.1	49.1	43.4	22.3	1,300	86.1
Clint town	926	1,112	20.1	664	8.4	0.0	0.9	0.0	90.7	18.2	37.2	51.4	59.9	14.8	272	68.0
Cloverleaf CDP	22,942	-	-	25,718	14.1	11.0	1.8	0.6	72.5	33.4	7.6	29.6	62.5	13.2	6,949	89.5
Clute city	11,234	11,690	4.1	11,590	30.6	11.9	0.0	1.8	55.8	26.6	10.1	34.3	57.7	16.7	4,350	87.1
Clyde city	3,697	3,823	3.4	3,817	84.9	2.3	0.7	4.1	8.0	30.5	11.3	34.9	51.8	20.3	1,286	85.5
Coahoma town	853	963	12.9	735	76.6	0.0	0.0	0.0	23.4	28.0	16.3	42.1	45.5	16.0	286	82.5
Cockrell Hill city	4,188	4,154	-0.8	4,240	6.2	0.6	0.0	0.5	92.8	29.4	11.8	32.6	73.1	8.0	1,133	74.2
Coffee City town	282	293	3.9	252	63.1	25.4	2.8	5.6	3.2	4.8	36.9	61.5	39.7	18.8	141	73.8
Coldspring city	867	932	7.5	1,029	69.6	16.4	0.0	8.1	5.9	22.8	18.6	36.7	54.5	20.6	327	87.5
Coleman city	4,709	4,274	-9.2	4,373	68.5	1.7	0.0	5.1	24.7	23.5	23.2	42.7	58.6	8.0	1,813	81.0

1 May be of any race.

Table A. All Places — **Population and Housing**

STATE City, town, township, borough, or CDP (county if applicable)	Population				Race and Hispanic or Latino origin (percent)					Age (percent)			Educational attainment of persons age 25 and older		Occupied housing units	
	2010 census total population	2019 estimated population	Percent change 2010–2019	ACS total population estimate 2015–2019	White alone, not Hispanic or Latino	Black alone, not Hispanic or Latino	Asian alone, not Hispanic or Latino	All other races or 2 or more races, not Hispanic or Latino	Hispanic or Latino[1]	Under 18 years old	Age 65 years and older	Median age	Percent High school diploma or less	Percent Bachelor's degree or more	Total	Percent with a computer
	1	2	3	4	5	6	7	8	9	10	11	12	13	14	15	16
TEXAS—Con.																
College Station city	94,225	117,911	25.1	113,686	64.5	7.3	10.0	2.4	15.8	16.2	6.8	23.0	17.0	58.6	40,357	97.3
Colleyville city	22,806	27,091	18.8	26,462	87.3	1.9	5.1	1.6	4.1	23.4	18.2	48.6	9.6	65.2	9,311	99.2
Collinsville town	1,624	1,959	20.6	1,701	86.8	0.5	0.0	2.7	10.0	25.0	15.0	34.2	54.5	12.6	618	91.4
Colmesneil city	601	591	-1.7	626	85.9	2.1	1.1	2.6	8.3	31.3	14.2	41.3	54.7	13.9	224	70.1
Colorado Acres CDP	296	-	-	53	0.0	0.0	0.0	0.0	100.0	26.4	0.0	38.3	100.0	0.0	19	47.4
Colorado City city	4,143	3,857	-6.9	3,920	44.3	3.9	0.8	2.7	48.3	27.0	17.9	32.0	59.9	15.4	1,385	81.4
Columbus city	3,650	3,646	-0.1	3,617	53.9	13.9	0.1	0.0	32.1	20.7	24.1	39.9	51.1	22.2	1,388	76.6
Comanche city	4,333	4,197	-3.1	4,178	57.9	0.9	0.3	0.0	40.9	23.7	22.8	41.0	58.7	18.0	1,701	77.6
Combes town	2,808	2,984	6.3	2,975	9.8	0.0	2.5	0.0	87.7	25.4	15.4	34.5	64.6	9.9	877	74.0
Combine city	2,038	2,442	19.8	2,222	65.6	0.9	1.2	1.9	30.3	25.4	15.9	41.0	54.8	15.8	647	94.7
Comfort CDP	2,363	-	-	3,717	38.3	0.1	0.0	5.4	56.2	25.6	14.1	35.2	63.6	11.8	815	91.2
Commerce city	8,073	9,680	19.9	9,293	53.0	23.4	6.1	6.6	11.0	17.8	9.0	24.2	42.9	28.7	2,837	85.4
Como town	698	727	4.2	752	67.0	0.0	0.0	1.7	31.3	27.1	18.6	32.5	66.1	1.5	246	90.2
Concepcion CDP	62	-	-	61	0.0	0.0	0.0	0.0	100.0	6.6	27.9	21.3	100.0	0.0	17	52.9
Conroe city	65,392	91,079	39.3	84,358	55.2	8.1	3.1	1.2	32.4	24.0	13.3	33.6	44.4	26.3	31,030	92.6
Converse city	21,534	28,171	30.8	26,930	25.9	22.5	2.7	6.1	42.9	31.3	7.4	31.4	32.0	25.5	7,723	96.4
Cool city	161	187	16.1	178	82.0	0.0	0.0	0.0	18.0	12.9	26.4	52.7	50.0	16.4	81	85.2
Coolidge town	955	953	-0.2	910	30.4	12.9	0.0	0.0	56.7	30.3	15.3	31.4	53.2	15.4	309	70.2
Cooper city	1,975	1,993	0.9	2,180	67.3	20.5	1.3	4.1	6.7	25.8	18.5	32.9	50.7	16.6	771	73.8
Coppell city	38,666	41,421	7.1	41,645	55.0	4.2	24.3	3.3	13.1	27.0	9.0	40.5	10.4	69.1	15,538	99.4
Copperas Cove city	32,247	33,235	3.1	32,715	55.1	14.5	2.9	9.3	18.2	26.7	10.5	32.0	33.2	19.4	12,325	93.2
Copper Canyon town	1,323	1,493	12.8	1,121	88.6	1.7	4.5	2.3	2.9	16.0	21.6	55.0	18.9	61.1	388	99.2
Corinth city	19,766	22,099	11.8	21,491	71.4	7.4	1.2	2.9	17.0	24.2	10.8	38.9	24.4	42.1	7,228	95.3
Corpus Christi city	305,226	326,586	7.0	325,780	29.5	3.9	2.2	1.2	63.2	24.6	13.8	35.2	45.7	22.2	116,952	89.2
Corral City town	27	49	81.5	8	25.0	0.0	0.0	0.0	75.0	50.0	0.0	19.5	0.0	0.0	2	100.0
Corrigan town	1,592	1,611	1.2	2,298	31.2	35.8	0.0	4.6	28.4	25.1	13.3	35.2	68.6	9.8	889	76.0
Corsicana city	23,837	23,906	0.3	23,746	39.4	17.4	1.3	4.6	37.4	28.7	14.3	34.3	53.0	14.1	8,053	85.1
Cottonwood city	167	202	21.0	237	100.0	0.0	0.0	0.0	0.0	24.5	14.8	36.7	34.7	23.5	61	100.0
Cottonwood Shores city	1,117	1,227	9.8	1,467	64.8	4.4	1.8	1.9	27.0	22.2	10.2	33.0	50.2	18.4	421	83.6
Cotulla city	3,605	4,137	14.8	4,168	6.2	0.5	0.0	1.4	91.8	20.8	19.4	36.3	75.8	8.4	1,616	70.5
Country Acres CDP	185	-	-	238	81.9	0.0	18.1	0.0	0.0	16.8	16.4	47.0	96.3	0.0	68	91.2
Coupland city	277	317	14.4	182	84.6	0.0	0.0	2.2	13.2	20.3	27.5	48.0	44.9	23.5	76	88.2
Cove city	461	559	21.3	412	86.9	0.0	0.0	1.5	11.7	22.3	24.3	43.1	35.1	14.5	146	87.0
Covington city	269	279	3.7	280	91.1	0.0	0.0	2.5	6.4	35.7	15.4	33.7	48.4	23.5	87	87.4
Coyanosa CDP	163	-	-	91	0.0	0.0	0.0	0.0	100.0	15.4	31.9	58.5	100.0	0.0	43	81.4
Coyote Acres CDP	508	-	-	1,089	2.9	0.0	0.0	0.0	97.1	47.8	10.2	20.4	46.9	0.0	197	82.7
Coyote Flats city	312	363	16.3	346	89.6	0.0	0.6	1.2	8.7	21.7	19.4	47.7	48.5	18.3	130	90.0
Crandall city	3,000	4,017	33.9	3,650	81.1	1.2	0.4	1.3	15.9	29.8	6.7	33.5	40.1	23.4	1,207	96.1
Crane city	3,348	3,682	10.0	4,138	27.3	1.8	2.3	0.1	68.5	30.5	13.0	32.2	54.7	12.8	1,203	91.9
Cranfills Gap city	281	282	0.4	340	64.7	2.6	0.0	5.9	26.8	23.8	22.9	40.4	62.4	7.7	150	86.7
Crawford town	757	827	9.2	760	83.9	10.4	0.4	1.4	3.8	34.5	12.8	30.3	45.3	16.4	273	89.4
Creedmoor city	201	224	11.4	201	52.2	0.0	0.0	0.0	47.8	24.9	11.4	30.3	61.5	18.8	63	77.8
Cresson city	735	1,338	82.0	986	87.1	2.1	0.0	2.0	8.7	17.7	16.1	49.5	45.3	16.8	333	98.2
Crockett city	6,953	6,385	-8.2	6,447	36.7	44.2	0.9	4.5	13.7	25.3	19.1	34.8	61.7	14.7	2,432	78.9
Crosby CDP	2,299	-	-	2,645	52.6	8.3	0.4	1.8	36.9	27.2	12.7	38.2	48.6	16.2	1,062	79.8
Crosbyton city	1,741	1,612	-7.4	1,787	35.4	6.1	0.0	1.1	57.5	26.4	15.4	38.5	62.8	13.1	630	75.7
Cross Mountain CDP	3,124	-	-	3,453	53.6	3.4	2.8	2.2	38.1	21.7	16.7	43.5	17.3	50.9	1,111	98.5
Cross Plains town	982	986	0.4	1,035	91.7	0.0	0.0	2.3	6.0	32.3	20.3	37.7	50.5	16.7	461	73.3
Cross Roads town	841	1,516	80.3	1,317	87.9	1.9	0.8	2.4	7.1	26.3	13.6	41.8	18.4	51.9	430	96.5
Cross Timber town	260	312	20.0	305	87.5	0.0	0.0	0.0	12.5	21.6	18.0	44.5	56.4	20.9	97	95.9
Crowell city	948	817	-13.8	745	74.8	0.0	0.0	4.2	21.1	20.0	33.0	53.3	54.5	14.1	345	89.0
Crowley city	12,838	16,460	28.2	15,439	54.2	20.0	2.3	2.8	20.7	29.7	8.9	33.7	38.4	21.8	4,903	96.5
Crystal City city	7,135	7,158	0.3	7,310	0.5	0.4	0.0	0.4	98.7	29.6	12.4	30.5	67.1	13.8	2,274	72.7
Cuero city	8,252	8,236	-0.2	8,297	38.5	17.2	0.0	0.4	43.9	21.4	15.2	39.7	62.9	7.9	2,409	71.7
Cuevitas CDP	40	-	-	-	-	-	-	-	-	-	-	-	-	-	-	-
Cumby city	777	798	2.7	693	90.3	1.7	0.0	0.0	7.9	22.4	19.0	41.1	59.5	11.6	279	90.0
Cumings CDP	981	-	-	2,481	45.2	45.1	0.0	0.0	9.7	27.0	1.7	33.8	20.0	37.0	612	100.0
Cuney town	140	140	0.0	75	53.3	37.3	0.0	2.7	6.7	13.3	34.7	58.2	63.1	0.0	29	62.1
Cushing city	609	620	1.8	465	89.0	2.6	1.3	6.5	0.6	21.9	17.4	42.9	57.4	10.3	208	89.4
Cut and Shoot city	1,062	1,438	35.4	1,113	85.6	0.2	0.2	1.3	12.8	20.6	12.5	39.0	81.4	4.8	402	92.0
Daingerfield city	2,554	2,380	-6.8	2,763	45.3	35.5	0.1	0.9	18.2	29.6	14.7	34.4	52.0	10.2	1,018	88.0
Daisetta city	960	1,124	17.1	938	93.6	0.3	0.0	1.1	5.0	24.1	11.7	39.0	66.6	7.3	347	85.3
Dalhart city	7,932	8,310	4.8	8,704	51.8	0.8	2.4	3.3	41.6	29.6	14.5	32.5	52.2	18.1	3,009	88.1
Dallas city	1,197,658	1,343,573	12.2	1,330,612	29.0	24.0	3.4	1.9	41.8	25.0	10.3	32.7	44.3	33.4	513,443	87.2
Dalworthington Gardens city	2,259	2,370	4.9	2,188	70.2	8.6	8.9	2.1	10.2	19.8	21.6	51.7	18.8	51.5	811	93.1
Damon CDP	552	-	-	299	85.3	0.0	0.0	0.0	14.7	35.8	12.0	37.5	68.9	7.2	112	89.3
Danbury city	1,719	1,760	2.4	1,201	76.5	1.0	0.8	0.8	20.8	24.8	13.6	38.8	34.8	20.8	448	93.1
Darrouzett town	350	342	-2.3	328	87.5	0.0	0.0	3.0	9.5	21.0	21.3	40.1	50.2	19.4	134	86.6
Dawson town	807	801	-0.7	767	74.7	5.0	0.9	7.0	12.4	19.6	18.9	46.1	47.6	17.5	327	81.7
Dayton city	7,364	8,389	13.9	7,952	70.2	11.6	1.5	1.3	15.4	28.0	14.5	33.1	55.1	12.9	3,024	88.0
Dayton Lakes city	93	103	10.8	47	100.0	0.0	0.0	0.0	0.0	12.8	8.5	43.3	100.0	0.0	12	75.0
Dean city	478	463	-3.1	415	93.7	0.0	1.9	1.7	2.7	18.8	30.1	49.4	48.1	20.6	182	78.6
Decatur city	6,057	7,094	17.1	6,738	58.4	2.4	1.3	1.9	36.0	27.8	18.9	33.6	44.7	18.8	2,511	87.4
DeCordova city	2,681	3,040	13.4	2,924	94.9	0.0	0.0	1.8	3.3	14.7	34.7	57.3	19.1	41.3	1,256	97.1
Deer Park city	32,010	33,474	4.6	33,855	57.5	1.2	1.5	1.9	37.8	25.3	12.3	35.5	40.8	19.1	11,130	95.7
De Kalb city	1,679	1,593	-5.1	1,490	64.5	24.2	1.0	2.3	7.9	21.7	24.9	50.1	59.1	14.5	622	70.3
De Leon city	2,247	2,198	-2.2	2,418	66.3	1.8	0.0	3.6	28.3	23.6	14.0	41.3	47.8	21.0	1,004	90.3
Dell City city	365	526	44.1	220	20.0	0.0	0.0	1.8	78.2	25.0	39.1	55.9	67.3	9.7	137	58.4
Del Mar Heights CDP	113	-	-	236	0.0	0.0	0.0	0.0	100.0	59.3	5.9	9.3	29.2	38.5	51	72.5
Delmita CDP	216	-	-	212	0.0	0.0	0.0	0.0	100.0	14.2	15.6	42.4	44.0	15.1	69	100.0
Del Rio city	35,938	35,760	-0.5	35,846	11.5	1.2	0.8	0.6	85.8	28.4	14.9	33.7	56.9	18.7	11,649	80.6
Del Sol CDP	239	-	-	129	63.6	0.0	0.0	0.0	36.4	49.6	24.0	43.0	72.3	27.7	34	52.9
Denison city	22,748	25,529	12.2	24,340	77.9	7.5	1.1	5.4	8.1	24.8	17.8	38.9	44.7	16.7	9,231	82.5
Denton city	116,326	141,541	21.7	136,195	58.9	9.4	4.2	3.1	24.5	19.5	11.4	29.4	28.3	38.9	46,687	94.5
Denver City town	4,479	4,911	9.6	4,880	23.0	0.8	0.0	0.3	75.9	32.0	10.8	29.2	66.8	7.5	1,516	88.1
Deport city	576	558	-3.1	668	92.8	2.2	0.0	2.2	2.7	22.6	19.8	40.3	57.8	11.6	283	81.6
DeSoto city	49,043	52,988	8.0	53,090	12.7	66.7	0.5	1.9	18.1	26.7	14.3	38.9	31.9	28.1	19,357	94.8
Detroit town	732	683	-6.7	1,037	65.1	24.8	0.0	4.5	5.6	40.2	18.0	32.1	50.8	9.7	346	78.9
Devers city	447	522	16.8	420	65.5	16.7	0.0	0.2	17.6	20.7	27.4	44.5	52.6	10.0	152	69.7
Devine city	4,351	4,829	11.0	4,733	36.4	0.0	1.6	0.0	62.0	32.6	13.6	37.5	50.0	18.0	1,436	84.5
Deweyville CDP	1,023	-	-	518	95.8	0.0	0.0	4.2	0.0	16.0	10.8	50.1	66.0	12.0	235	62.1

1 May be of any race.

Table A. All Places — **Population and Housing**

STATE City, town, township, borough, or CDP (county if applicable)	Population				Race and Hispanic or Latino origin (percent)					Age (percent)			Educational attainment of persons age 25 and older		Occupied housing units	
	2010 census total population	2019 estimated population	Percent change 2010–2019	ACS total population estimate 2015–2019	White alone, not Hispanic or Latino	Black alone, not Hispanic or Latino	Asian alone, not Hispanic or Latino	All other races or 2 or more races, not Hispanic or Latino	Hispanic or Latino[1]	Under 18 years old	Age 65 years and older	Median age	Percent High school diploma or less	Percent Bachelor's degree or more	Total	Percent with a computer
	1	2	3	4	5	6	7	8	9	10	11	12	13	14	15	16
TEXAS—Con.																
D'Hanis CDP	847	-	-	733	49.4	0.0	0.0	0.0	50.6	21.7	33.6	47.2	49.4	11.2	261	69.3
Diboll city	5,402	5,204	-3.7	5,266	32.2	24.1	0.3	1.2	42.1	25.6	16.3	40.6	61.3	10.2	1,438	91.2
Dickens city	286	259	-9.4	281	70.5	2.8	0.0	0.0	26.7	16.0	26.0	55.1	49.1	8.2	107	89.7
Dickinson city	19,049	21,129	10.9	20,754	54.8	7.2	1.7	2.0	34.3	24.0	13.4	40.2	43.5	22.1	7,881	91.5
Dilley city	3,894	4,489	15.3	4,401	13.0	7.9	0.5	1.1	77.3	21.2	7.1	26.5	70.2	5.5	761	77.4
Dimmitt city	4,393	4,099	-6.7	4,181	21.1	2.2	0.7	0.4	75.6	29.5	15.6	34.8	60.5	11.8	1,331	78.7
DISH town	201	439	118.4	426	89.2	0.2	0.0	0.5	10.1	20.4	11.5	43.9	32.8	35.3	158	96.8
Dodd City town	369	389	5.4	392	84.4	0.5	0.0	12.5	2.6	28.8	18.4	39.0	61.9	18.9	145	81.4
Dodson town	109	107	-1.8	160	18.8	0.0	0.0	2.5	78.8	26.9	6.3	35.4	76.7	19.0	38	68.4
Doffing CDP	5,091	-	-	5,176	0.7	0.0	0.0	0.0	99.3	38.7	5.4	22.5	67.3	7.6	1,207	84.7
Domino town	82	89	8.5	71	2.8	81.7	0.0	15.5	0.0	21.1	23.9	43.6	56.3	14.6	34	38.2
Donna city	15,736	16,338	3.8	16,409	6.3	0.0	0.6	0.4	92.7	30.6	15.3	32.0	63.7	9.0	5,011	82.2
Doolittle CDP	2,769	-	-	3,452	0.0	0.0	0.0	0.0	100.0	35.4	12.6	28.8	76.8	3.6	841	81.5
Dorchester city	87	94	8.0	71	100.0	0.0	0.0	0.0	0.0	12.7	5.6	38.5	64.6	16.7	29	86.2
Double Oak town	2,872	3,068	6.8	3,066	82.7	2.9	2.2	3.4	8.7	20.4	20.0	47.7	16.5	56.3	997	99.2
Douglassville town	229	218	-4.8	306	58.2	41.8	0.0	0.0	0.0	16.0	18.6	41.6	56.9	15.7	130	65.4
Driftwood CDP	144	-	-	176	100.0	0.0	0.0	0.0	0.0	31.3	19.9	40.5	43.8	43.8	67	100.0
Dripping Springs city	2,196	5,708	159.9	4,119	73.0	0.5	1.2	1.5	23.8	23.6	14.0	37.9	37.3	38.4	1,322	93.0
Driscoll city	746	746	0.0	631	6.2	0.0	0.0	0.0	93.8	31.1	14.6	26.8	77.4	10.4	174	76.4
Dublin city	3,618	3,553	-1.8	3,554	50.2	0.6	0.0	9.1	40.1	33.1	9.7	28.3	51.3	19.1	946	91.6
Dumas city	14,691	13,827	-5.9	14,222	35.6	3.1	6.7	1.8	52.9	31.9	10.7	30.6	55.1	16.3	4,538	94.0
Duncanville city	38,527	38,751	0.6	39,415	23.7	34.1	1.2	1.2	39.9	26.8	14.2	36.7	42.8	22.9	13,506	91.9
Eagle Lake city	3,635	3,777	3.9	3,739	16.1	19.4	0.0	4.5	60.1	30.1	11.2	32.2	67.8	9.9	1,036	84.6
Eagle Pass city	26,606	29,684	11.6	29,348	3.2	0.4	1.0	0.5	94.9	28.7	12.9	30.0	55.1	16.0	8,650	76.9
Early city	2,788	3,160	13.3	2,986	76.5	1.9	2.1	3.1	16.3	27.9	14.8	36.5	34.1	25.8	1,129	88.8
Earth city	1,065	971	-8.8	1,066	41.5	2.8	0.0	0.0	55.7	28.2	18.8	40.5	56.1	16.2	386	81.1
East Alto Bonito CDP	824	-	-	750	0.0	0.0	0.0	0.0	100.0	22.5	0.9	26.7	86.0	1.4	168	95.2
East Bernard city	2,292	2,342	2.2	2,355	68.5	1.4	0.0	0.0	30.1	31.7	16.0	34.7	39.8	34.7	876	92.0
Eastland city	3,978	3,850	-3.2	3,853	68.2	2.2	2.6	0.5	26.5	17.2	23.6	38.6	46.9	24.0	1,474	77.3
East Mountain city	808	861	6.6	1,125	76.0	1.1	0.0	9.2	13.7	23.6	15.2	40.3	53.9	22.4	333	88.9
Easton city	510	515	1.0	372	13.7	57.8	0.0	0.0	28.5	18.5	19.6	48.9	55.3	13.5	159	81.8
East Tawakoni city	877	985	12.3	810	79.0	0.6	1.0	5.6	13.8	22.6	19.8	41.0	50.1	15.8	304	87.2
Ector city	695	736	5.9	862	92.9	0.6	0.6	5.5	0.5	28.0	10.7	35.2	55.8	8.3	317	90.9
Edcouch city	3,164	3,313	4.7	3,327	0.5	0.0	0.0	0.0	99.5	24.5	20.0	38.0	67.2	11.6	1,108	74.2
Eden city	2,766	1,294	-53.2	1,899	32.8	0.6	0.7	0.8	65.1	9.5	16.3	43.4	77.3	7.5	357	81.8
Edgecliff Village town	2,776	3,026	9.0	3,016	43.7	13.8	2.6	4.5	35.4	26.8	18.5	39.5	42.7	26.7	976	94.2
Edgewater Estates CDP	72	-	-	81	11.1	0.0	0.0	0.0	88.9	0.0	25.9	58.6	69.1	14.8	34	100.0
Edgewood town	1,436	1,525	6.2	1,801	74.8	8.5	0.0	4.2	12.5	34.1	14.3	31.2	43.3	14.2	633	87.4
Edinburg city	82,018	101,170	23.4	95,847	7.5	1.6	2.2	0.4	88.3	30.7	8.1	28.8	46.0	27.7	28,172	89.4
Edmonson town	111	103	-7.2	98	32.7	0.0	0.0	0.0	67.3	35.7	7.1	26.5	62.0	4.0	33	78.8
Edna city	5,489	5,780	5.3	5,767	49.1	14.0	0.9	1.6	34.4	28.6	16.4	36.4	53.0	13.9	1,906	84.4
Edom city	373	392	5.1	287	92.7	0.0	0.0	0.7	6.6	20.2	26.1	51.8	39.2	19.1	99	94.9
Edroy CDP	331	-	-	550	0.0	0.0	0.7	0.0	99.3	38.2	15.3	34.1	76.6	0.0	140	67.9
Eidson Road CDP	8,960	-	-	9,714	0.3	0.0	0.0	0.4	99.3	35.3	8.2	28.7	78.1	4.3	2,381	73.5
Elbert CDP	30	-	-	8	100.0	0.0	0.0	0.0	0.0	0.0	100.0	67.7	0.0	62.5	6	50.0
El Brazil CDP	47	-	-	27	0.0	0.0	0.0	0.0	100.0	0.0	0.0	47.1	0.0	100.0	7	100.0
El Camino Angosto CDP	253	-	-	168	0.0	0.0	0.0	0.0	100.0	0.0	0.0	38.8	41.1	32.3	36	100.0
El Campo city	11,692	11,539	-1.3	11,630	35.7	7.9	0.0	0.5	56.0	29.3	15.7	35.3	51.7	16.6	4,159	83.2
El Castillo CDP	188	-	-	69	23.2	0.0	0.0	0.0	76.8	69.6	7.2	1.0	100.0	0.0	21	76.2
El Cenizo CDP	249	-	-	403	0.0	0.0	0.0	0.0	100.0	33.0	0.0	22.4	78.0	0.0	54	100.0
El Cenizo city	3,273	3,161	-3.4	3,221	1.2	0.0	0.0	0.0	98.8	39.7	7.2	25.5	86.3	3.7	766	60.3
El Chaparral CDP	464	-	-	416	1.4	0.0	0.0	0.0	98.6	22.8	8.2	33.5	55.6	38.0	115	80.9
Eldorado city	1,953	1,579	-19.2	2,257	31.3	0.7	0.0	0.5	67.5	30.0	14.1	34.4	52.0	14.9	814	76.3
Electra city	2,791	2,730	-2.2	2,726	75.2	2.5	0.3	9.5	12.6	18.5	22.5	52.4	59.2	12.5	1,298	76.1
Elgin city	8,289	10,314	24.4	10,064	26.8	27.1	0.3	0.9	44.9	29.4	11.5	33.5	57.9	12.9	2,750	86.7
Elias-Fela Solis CDP	30	-	-	7	0.0	0.0	0.0	0.0	100.0	0.0	100.0	0.0	100.0	0.0	7	0.0
El Indio CDP	190	-	-	21	0.0	0.0	0.0	0.0	100.0	0.0	100.0	0.0	100.0	0.0	21	0.0
Elkhart town	1,365	1,299	-4.8	1,297	79.1	12.9	0.0	0.0	8.0	30.1	15.9	35.9	53.2	9.7	494	81.6
El Lago city	2,695	2,663	-1.2	2,710	75.1	2.9	1.5	4.2	16.2	24.2	13.9	42.6	18.3	47.4	982	99.5
Elm Creek CDP	2,469	-	-	3,590	1.6	0.0	0.0	0.0	98.4	42.4	3.3	22.5	62.6	8.4	821	74.5
Elmendorf city	1,680	2,150	28.0	1,835	32.8	0.1	0.6	1.5	65.1	28.3	8.7	29.5	57.8	10.1	535	88.4
El Mesquite CDP	38	-	-	-	-	-	-	-	-	-	-	-	-	-	-	-
Elmo CDP	768	-	-	1,391	67.9	29.4	0.0	0.0	2.7	18.8	16.0	40.4	85.7	0.0	385	72.2
E. Lopez CDP	-	-	-	233	3.9	0.0	3.0	3.9	89.3	33.0	0.0	24.2	36.5	25.0	34	100.0
El Paso city	648,245	681,728	5.2	679,813	12.8	3.2	1.3	1.4	81.4	26.7	12.7	32.9	42.8	25.1	226,787	87.3
El Quiote CDP	208	-	-	172	0.0	0.0	0.0	0.0	100.0	26.2	11.6	28.8	47.0	0.0	65	92.3
El Rancho Vela CDP	274	-	-	652	0.0	0.0	0.0	0.0	100.0	37.6	11.3	33.0	80.1	0.0	156	77.6
El Refugio CDP	331	-	-	461	0.0	0.0	0.0	0.0	100.0	39.7	8.0	21.4	68.2	11.1	84	84.5
Elsa city	6,325	7,174	13.4	7,225	0.8	0.0	0.0	0.0	99.2	31.3	13.2	30.3	64.0	11.0	1,958	78.6
El Socio CDP	130	-	-	-	-	-	-	-	-	-	-	-	-	-	-	-
Emerald Bay CDP	1,047	-	-	1,255	91.8	0.0	2.3	3.1	2.8	11.5	54.3	65.7	6.6	60.6	568	97.5
Emhouse town	133	145	9.0	155	61.9	0.0	0.0	6.5	31.6	27.1	12.9	36.6	66.0	2.9	54	85.2
Emory city	1,226	1,353	10.4	1,628	75.5	10.6	1.9	1.4	10.6	20.8	17.2	37.8	54.8	12.1	556	85.8
Encantada-Ranchito-El Calaboz CDP	2,255	-	-	1,294	2.4	0.0	0.0	0.0	97.6	24.9	16.1	36.7	70.0	4.6	355	86.5
Enchanted Oaks town	326	341	4.6	315	95.6	0.3	0.0	1.6	2.5	8.3	42.2	61.6	30.8	39.9	153	91.5
Encinal city	559	591	5.7	799	4.8	0.0	0.0	0.0	95.2	23.0	14.9	37.3	74.9	10.1	215	80.0
Encino CDP	143	-	-	60	0.0	0.0	0.0	0.0	100.0	38.3	8.3	46.6	70.3	29.7	30	83.3
Ennis city	18,593	20,357	9.5	19,559	36.3	15.1	0.2	2.4	46.1	27.6	13.7	33.8	57.1	15.9	6,557	87.8
Escobares city	2,409	2,575	6.9	2,551	0.5	0.0	0.0	0.0	99.5	31.8	11.7	27.2	80.6	7.3	575	81.6
Estelline town	145	129	-11.0	135	40.7	23.0	0.0	3.0	33.3	34.1	8.1	38.8	51.3	11.3	57	86.0
Eugenio Saenz CDP	159	-	-	282	2.5	0.0	0.0	0.0	97.5	40.4	0.0	30.9	100.0	0.0	59	100.0
Euless city	51,263	57,197	11.6	55,763	50.3	12.3	11.6	4.5	21.3	23.0	10.2	35.3	31.5	35.9	21,796	96.9
Eureka city	280	307	9.6	323	75.5	1.9	0.3	9.9	12.4	18.9	18.3	44.3	41.5	19.5	128	95.3
Eustace city	996	1,006	1.0	1,087	82.5	7.9	0.9	1.7	6.9	24.7	19.2	36.7	55.8	11.3	428	76.4
Evadale CDP	1,483	-	-	1,783	83.0	0.0	1.0	7.6	8.5	29.1	12.2	30.4	68.1	7.3	450	82.4
Evant town	431	410	-4.9	494	74.1	0.0	1.2	2.2	22.5	32.4	12.8	36.5	51.1	19.9	185	86.5
Evergreen CDP	73	-	-	48	0.0	0.0	0.0	0.0	100.0	0.0	20.8	50.8	100.0	0.0	22	54.5
Everman city	6,028	6,201	2.9	6,255	21.4	24.7	0.8	1.3	51.8	29.5	10.3	33.7	67.6	9.6	1,937	89.1
Fabens CDP	8,257	-	-	5,736	3.9	0.2	0.6	0.0	95.3	30.8	13.7	34.3	77.1	3.4	1,783	76.3
Fabrica CDP	923	-	-	829	0.0	0.0	0.0	0.0	100.0	34.7	9.9	32.5	95.2	0.0	278	57.6
Fairchilds village	789	1,297	64.4	789	64.1	0.0	2.9	1.5	31.4	18.0	13.8	41.4	49.5	15.1	292	87.7

1 May be of any race.

Table A. All Places — **Population and Housing**

STATE City, town, township, borough, or CDP (county if applicable)	Population				Race and Hispanic or Latino origin (percent)					Age (percent)			Educational attainment of persons age 25 and older		Occupied housing units	
	2010 census total population	2019 estimated population	Percent change 2010–2019	ACS total population estimate 2015–2019	White alone, not Hispanic or Latino	Black alone, not Hispanic or Latino	Asian alone, not Hispanic or Latino	All other races or 2 or more races, not Hispanic or Latino	Hispanic or Latino[1]	Under 18 years old	Age 65 years and older	Median age	Percent High school diploma or less	Percent Bachelor's degree or more	Total	Percent with a computer
	1	2	3	4	5	6	7	8	9	10	11	12	13	14	15	16
TEXAS—Con.																
Fairfield city	2,960	2,892	-2.3	2,916	55.2	18.9	1.7	2.9	21.2	25.9	22.6	37.5	52.6	13.3	1,057	78.7
Fair Oaks Ranch city	6,709	10,042	49.7	9,944	78.4	3.6	1.0	3.8	13.2	22.2	23.0	46.3	13.4	65.8	3,662	99.7
Fairview town	7,239	9,141	26.3	8,832	78.5	9.9	5.7	2.3	3.5	23.1	27.8	48.0	8.0	67.3	3,519	99.2
Falconaire CDP	132	-	-	62	0.0	0.0	0.0	0.0	100.0	11.3	43.5	47.5	100.0	0.0	19	21.1
Falcon Heights CDP	53	-	-	14	0.0	0.0	0.0	0.0	100.0	0.0	0.0	0.0	0.0	0.0	8	100.0
Falcon Lake Estates CDP.	1,036	-	-	738	34.6	0.0	0.0	0.0	65.4	22.0	24.7	46.0	59.0	25.7	306	93.5
Falcon Mesa CDP	405	-	-	166	42.2	0.0	0.0	0.0	57.8	0.0	42.2	25.4	51.6	31.9	62	100.0
Falcon Village CDP	47	-	-	-	-	-	-	-	-	-	-	-	-	-	-	-
Falfurrias city	4,962	4,812	-3.0	4,365	5.6	0.0	0.0	0.4	94.0	31.7	13.9	26.7	49.6	16.5	1,488	74.2
Falls City city	611	689	12.8	1,172	64.9	0.0	0.0	1.4	33.7	28.8	12.5	31.0	53.4	27.8	414	92.5
Falman CDP	76	-	-	24	100.0	0.0	0.0	0.0	0.0	0.0	0.0	57.6	100.0	0.0	17	100.0
Fannett CDP	2,252	-	-	2,142	70.4	8.5	6.1	0.7	14.3	17.6	19.9	39.2	37.6	25.0	916	90.8
Farmers Branch city	29,141	48,158	65.3	39,039	34.9	5.5	7.4	3.1	49.1	21.6	11.5	35.7	39.0	36.8	14,295	95.5
Farmersville city	3,295	3,630	10.2	3,496	64.5	19.5	0.7	3.1	12.2	26.9	15.4	37.0	56.8	15.0	1,194	86.7
Farwell city	1,361	1,291	-5.1	1,264	49.8	0.3	0.0	0.0	49.9	20.4	21.0	44.8	57.0	15.4	554	82.9
Fate city	7,432	15,603	109.9	12,787	68.9	4.8	2.4	2.9	20.9	33.6	7.8	34.3	22.9	44.6	4,148	99.2
Fayetteville city	255	257	0.8	251	92.4	0.0	0.0	1.6	6.0	5.6	45.8	62.6	41.7	25.0	123	82.1
Faysville CDP	439	-	-	-	-	-	-	-	-	-	-	-	-	-	-	-
Fernando Salinas CDP	15	-	-	25	0.0	0.0	0.0	0.0	100.0	52.0	0.0	0.0	0.0	0.0	12	100.0
Ferris city	2,421	2,974	22.8	2,692	41.4	13.1	0.1	0.3	45.1	33.8	11.6	30.8	56.2	12.4	863	86.6
Fifth Street CDP	2,486	-	-	2,079	0.6	2.1	0.0	0.0	97.4	31.8	1.6	23.7	76.0	1.4	623	100.0
Flatonia town	1,387	1,431	3.2	1,408	49.0	6.5	0.0	0.3	44.2	20.0	22.4	44.3	67.7	13.5	436	59.9
Flor del Rio CDP	122	-	-	57	0.0	0.0	0.0	0.0	100.0	0.0	0.0	45.1	100.0	0.0	15	100.0
Florence city	1,137	1,274	12.0	850	61.6	0.0	0.0	0.4	38.0	26.4	10.0	32.6	56.6	11.6	287	86.1
Floresville city	6,398	8,045	25.7	7,585	36.3	1.4	0.8	0.8	60.8	25.3	17.4	40.0	60.2	12.7	2,427	93.0
Flowella CDP	118	-	-	16	0.0	0.0	0.0	0.0	100.0	0.0	56.3	0.0	100.0	0.0	16	43.8
Flower Mound town	64,675	79,135	22.4	76,555	71.1	3.8	10.9	3.0	11.1	27.8	9.1	39.7	14.8	62.0	25,109	98.7
Floydada city	3,038	2,676	-11.9	2,731	25.7	4.9	0.3	0.0	69.2	28.7	18.6	36.5	64.5	12.8	1,090	81.5
Follett city	459	441	-3.9	433	84.1	0.2	0.7	5.8	9.2	32.8	17.1	36.4	33.9	19.6	143	88.1
Forest Hill city	12,355	12,988	5.1	12,994	5.3	44.6	0.0	1.0	49.1	32.0	11.5	31.0	60.8	11.1	3,746	89.0
Forney city	13,819	27,236	97.1	21,459	64.2	14.3	2.2	1.5	17.8	31.8	7.8	31.5	33.9	28.8	6,549	96.9
Forsan city	210	229	9.0	169	88.8	0.0	0.0	5.3	5.9	29.6	11.2	36.8	32.5	36.0	68	97.1
Fort Bliss CDP	8,591	-	-	11,427	48.7	13.4	2.2	10.8	24.9	34.0	0.0	22.0	20.8	32.5	1,997	99.5
Fort Clark Springs CDP	1,228	-	-	1,256	70.6	0.0	0.0	0.0	29.4	4.1	32.9	55.1	38.8	25.7	643	74.0
Fort Davis CDP	1,201	-	-	1,099	25.7	0.0	0.0	1.1	73.2	26.9	26.3	39.2	61.9	14.7	401	97.5
Fort Hancock CDP	1,750	-	-	1,827	8.3	0.0	0.0	0.0	91.7	35.6	9.9	25.8	90.1	1.9	384	76.3
Fort Hood CDP	29,589	-	-	23,508	48.5	17.4	3.4	6.8	23.9	19.1	0.1	22.2	26.6	21.4	3,243	98.0
Fort Stockton city	8,349	8,421	0.9	8,424	19.8	2.4	0.5	2.2	75.1	26.7	16.1	34.5	64.7	9.6	2,771	80.3
Fort Worth city	744,824	909,585	22.1	874,401	39.2	18.5	4.5	2.7	35.1	27.7	9.7	32.6	42.7	29.7	297,498	92.8
Four Corners CDP	12,382	-	-	11,049	7.3	24.7	37.3	0.9	29.7	30.7	8.9	33.6	41.3	30.3	2,928	96.9
Four Points CDP	18	-	-	-	-	-	-	-	-	-	-	-	-	-	-	-
Fowlerton CDP	55	-	-	268	100.0	0.0	0.0	0.0	0.0	26.5	21.3	41.6	93.4	6.6	70	100.0
Franklin city	1,613	1,645	2.0	1,989	71.8	19.2	0.0	0.7	8.3	31.9	15.8	33.1	43.0	14.8	655	93.4
Frankston town	1,229	1,170	-4.8	991	75.1	12.0	1.8	8.0	3.1	19.7	27.3	50.5	53.5	15.5	403	67.7
Fredericksburg city	10,539	11,496	9.1	11,245	72.1	0.1	0.0	1.1	26.7	20.3	29.1	47.2	40.6	33.1	4,631	88.7
Freeport city	12,069	12,136	0.6	12,147	18.3	13.6	1.0	4.2	63.0	36.3	6.5	26.0	62.9	7.1	4,001	87.2
Freer city	2,820	2,666	-5.5	2,686	24.8	0.0	0.0	0.0	75.2	28.9	12.0	30.5	60.8	6.6	880	74.0
Fresno CDP	19,069	-	-	25,072	3.5	55.8	1.5	0.7	38.5	31.7	7.0	31.3	41.8	29.0	6,932	96.6
Friendswood city	35,909	40,290	12.2	39,688	70.5	3.7	7.3	2.6	15.9	27.5	14.2	39.4	22.1	48.6	13,214	96.4
Friona city	4,127	3,808	-7.7	3,865	16.2	1.5	0.0	0.7	81.6	29.2	12.7	32.6	64.9	14.5	1,287	79.5
Frisco city	117,174	200,490	71.1	177,020	56.5	7.7	20.9	3.4	11.5	30.5	8.4	37.1	13.1	63.5	60,123	99.1
Fritch city	2,113	1,952	-7.6	2,829	81.0	0.0	0.5	8.7	9.9	27.0	14.5	34.3	50.3	10.2	803	90.4
Fronton CDP	180	-	-	225	0.0	0.0	0.0	0.0	100.0	25.3	7.6	36.2	97.9	2.1	46	91.3
Fronton Ranchettes CDP	113	-	-	351	0.0	0.0	0.0	0.0	100.0	52.1	0.6	15.7	62.0	16.9	72	97.2
Frost city	640	641	0.2	800	56.1	6.6	0.0	3.3	34.0	28.5	17.9	32.9	54.5	13.1	258	90.7
Fruitvale city	408	428	4.9	540	80.7	3.1	0.2	8.3	7.6	29.6	10.2	33.1	69.3	6.3	173	86.7
Fulshear city	1,167	13,914	1092.3	9,906	59.1	3.2	13.3	3.1	21.4	33.8	6.2	35.6	8.0	68.5	2,876	99.0
Fulton town	1,358	1,487	9.5	1,503	53.0	1.0	13.6	3.3	29.1	17.2	45.0	61.2	47.6	21.1	639	87.0
Gail CDP	231	-	-	206	67.0	0.0	0.0	7.3	25.7	35.0	18.9	34.8	34.7	30.5	62	87.1
Gainesville city	16,010	16,886	5.5	16,441	55.7	6.0	1.8	3.6	32.9	27.6	13.9	33.4	55.7	13.2	6,045	83.3
Galena Park city	10,899	10,757	-1.3	10,983	9.3	9.3	0.0	0.3	81.1	31.7	7.9	28.3	69.0	8.2	2,860	88.3
Gallatin city	417	434	4.1	370	92.2	0.0	0.0	1.1	6.8	25.9	18.9	36.5	51.0	8.6	136	94.1
Galveston city	47,741	50,446	5.7	50,241	48.5	16.5	2.8	2.1	30.1	17.1	16.4	38.9	40.4	29.2	20,756	89.0
Ganado city	1,994	2,055	3.1	2,136	39.2	1.3	1.5	0.8	57.2	23.5	13.8	34.6	63.4	16.9	709	84.9
Garceno CDP	420	-	-	436	0.0	0.0	0.0	0.0	100.0	33.5	4.1	27.8	62.8	22.4	128	100.0
Garciasville CDP	46	-	-	-	-	-	-	-	-	-	-	-	-	-	-	-
Garden City CDP	334	-	-	537	57.9	0.0	0.0	0.0	42.1	21.0	7.8	35.0	44.7	17.3	115	93.0
Gardendale CDP	1,574	-	-	1,819	81.1	0.0	0.0	0.0	18.9	40.0	8.6	28.5	43.8	4.8	641	93.6
Garden Ridge city	3,257	4,130	26.8	3,961	65.2	7.9	4.0	7.0	15.9	22.2	22.7	50.1	10.1	72.3	1,456	100.0
Garfield CDP	1,698	-	-	2,239	21.0	0.6	0.9	4.5	73.0	39.4	9.4	25.7	65.3	18.1	571	93.2
Garland city	226,908	239,928	5.7	238,418	28.9	14.8	11.0	2.9	42.5	27.2	11.7	34.3	47.0	22.9	75,234	94.9
Garrett town	808	892	10.4	805	31.6	1.6	0.0	1.5	65.3	39.3	7.7	24.0	69.8	7.1	223	92.4
Garrison city	892	873	-2.1	1,266	58.3	27.8	1.4	2.9	9.6	36.3	15.1	31.6	53.1	11.4	368	86.1
Gary City town	308	300	-2.6	261	98.9	0.4	0.0	0.0	0.8	28.4	10.7	33.9	53.7	22.0	84	81.0
Garza-Salinas II CDP	719	-	-	762	0.0	0.0	0.0	2.0	98.0	40.4	7.6	28.3	79.9	10.0	160	76.9
Gatesville city	12,459	12,401	-0.5	12,377	56.5	11.8	0.3	9.0	22.5	14.4	9.0	38.1	53.2	8.3	2,721	88.0
Georgetown city	47,483	79,604	67.6	71,004	71.5	3.6	0.9	2.2	21.8	18.6	29.1	46.3	27.9	41.6	27,129	94.8
George West city	2,439	2,562	5.0	2,566	36.9	1.2	1.2	0.0	60.6	27.9	23.1	38.8	65.0	13.4	745	59.2
Geronimo CDP	1,032	-	-	630	42.1	0.0	0.0	0.0	57.9	21.1	5.9	38.7	72.8	8.1	231	100.0
Gholson city	1,061	1,118	5.4	1,193	77.1	2.6	0.8	2.8	16.7	17.2	21.0	45.4	54.5	15.6	484	90.5
Giddings city	4,875	5,099	4.6	5,055	35.1	14.8	2.7	1.5	45.9	28.5	14.0	32.2	50.7	15.9	1,686	74.8
Gilmer city	4,897	5,143	5.0	5,105	60.2	25.1	0.1	6.1	8.5	25.6	17.9	36.5	45.8	20.2	1,824	82.2
Girard CDP	50	-	-	11	100.0	0.0	0.0	0.0	0.0	0.0	81.8	82.9	90.9	9.1	6	100.0
Gladewater city	6,399	6,341	-0.9	5,991	63.1	17.9	0.5	2.9	15.7	21.6	16.6	41.9	52.0	14.6	2,277	90.0
Glenn Heights city	11,146	13,377	20.0	12,802	17.1	45.4	0.4	2.6	34.5	29.9	5.8	31.0	47.4	23.0	3,783	97.3
Glen Rose city	2,450	2,699	10.2	2,607	73.1	0.4	0.0	0.2	26.4	19.6	26.0	42.8	49.4	22.9	1,039	85.8
Glidden CDP	661	-	-	900	44.2	19.3	0.0	0.0	36.4	36.2	10.3	36.2	62.9	18.6	253	62.5
Godley city	1,004	1,373	36.8	961	85.8	0.0	0.0	0.6	13.5	26.5	7.9	35.9	53.7	13.7	343	83.7
Goldsmith city	257	294	14.4	139	81.3	0.0	0.0	5.0	13.7	14.4	31.7	49.7	34.2	24.8	73	87.7
Goldthwaite city	1,886	1,833	-2.8	2,014	66.3	0.5	0.4	0.0	32.8	19.7	27.2	49.2	43.0	17.4	778	84.2
Goliad city	1,908	2,004	5.0	2,300	31.8	9.3	1.4	0.0	57.4	29.4	21.5	37.9	52.9	19.3	670	74.8
Golinda city	555	589	6.1	657	64.1	15.4	0.0	0.0	20.5	27.5	19.5	35.0	37.9	16.6	191	95.8

1 May be of any race.

Table A. All Places — **Population and Housing**

STATE City, town, township, borough, or CDP (county if applicable)	Population: 2010 census total population	Population: 2019 estimated population	Population: Percent change 2010–2019	Population: ACS total population estimate 2015–2019	Race and Hispanic or Latino origin (percent): White alone, not Hispanic or Latino	Black alone, not Hispanic or Latino	Asian alone, not Hispanic or Latino	All other races or 2 or more races, not Hispanic or Latino	Hispanic or Latino[1]	Age (percent): Under 18 years old	Age 65 years and older	Median age	Educational attainment of persons age 25 and older: Percent High school diploma or less	Percent Bachelor's degree or more	Occupied housing units: Total	Percent with a computer
	1	2	3	4	5	6	7	8	9	10	11	12	13	14	15	16
TEXAS—Con.																
Gonzales city	7,237	7,533	4.1	7,517	32.0	11.0	0.7	0.7	55.7	30.4	13.4	32.5	69.3	14.5	2,687	77.4
Goodlow city	200	198		147	11.6	85.7	0.0	2.7	0.0	16.3	18.4	46.4	65.8	6.8	56	69.6
Goodrich city	271	323	19.2	327	16.5	24.2	0.0	3.4	56.0	28.1	5.8	40.4	84.1	4.6	124	81.5
Gordon city	472	486	3.0	400	86.8	0.0	0.0	7.3	6.0	17.3	19.8	50.6	37.2	20.8	192	93.2
Goree city	203	203	0.0	437	22.9	21.3	0.5	7.8	47.6	34.1	10.3	38.8	74.5	3.5	137	91.2
Gorman city	1,083	1,035	-4.4	1,302	67.1	0.0	0.0	4.9	28.0	32.3	15.7	22.8	58.9	8.4	436	77.8
Graford city	584	627	7.4	639	79.2	0.0	1.1	0.0	19.7	30.0	11.4	32.9	53.8	10.4	192	91.1
Graham city	8,908	8,622	-3.2	8,675	78.1	2.6	0.4	0.2	18.7	24.2	19.1	38.6	52.2	15.8	3,501	86.8
Granbury city	7,988	10,730	34.3	9,939	86.5	2.1	2.6	0.3	8.5	17.4	30.0	50.5	40.0	25.8	4,091	89.0
Grandfalls town	360	403	11.9	407	46.4	4.9	0.0	0.0	48.6	33.9	11.5	32.9	60.6	20.7	132	74.2
Grand Prairie city	175,468	194,543	10.9	192,565	21.3	22.2	6.6	2.3	47.5	28.3	9.2	33.4	47.2	23.6	60,988	91.7
Grand Saline city	3,131	3,173	1.3	3,115	71.9	1.6	0.0	1.1	25.4	28.5	18.9	35.1	65.1	7.4	1,007	78.0
Grandview city	1,561	1,798	15.2	1,841	74.3	2.4	0.5	0.5	22.3	30.5	13.9	33.7	53.5	13.0	613	87.4
Granger city	1,417	1,505	6.2	1,119	54.6	9.7	0.0	1.8	34.0	14.1	18.1	43.4	69.4	7.9	371	73.0
Granite Shoals city	5,010	5,087	1.5	5,121	53.5	0.0	0.0	0.9	45.5	25.8	12.5	36.9	56.2	19.0	1,546	97.1
Granjeno city	293	315	7.5	418	2.6	0.0	0.0	0.0	97.4	11.0	6.2	37.3	50.2	18.5	122	90.2
Grape Creek CDP	3,154	-	-	2,897	77.2	0.0	0.0	0.0	22.8	25.3	18.7	37.9	61.0	9.5	1,068	87.5
Grapeland city	1,500	1,443	-3.8	1,571	54.2	39.8	0.0	0.0	6.0	19.7	23.3	47.4	59.0	12.5	768	72.1
Grapevine city	46,336	55,281	19.3	53,317	64.7	3.9	6.7	3.1	21.6	22.8	10.6	38.2	22.7	47.7	20,647	97.5
Grays Prairie village	313	372	18.8	292	90.4	3.4	0.0	3.4	2.7	18.8	12.7	49.8	57.5	18.3	91	95.6
Green Valley Farms CDP	1,272	-	-	487	0.0	0.0	0.0	0.0	100.0	24.0	6.6	47.5	74.9	16.2	209	100.0
Greenville city	25,529	28,827	12.9	27,442	56.3	15.0	0.9	3.9	23.9	25.6	14.3	34.3	52.4	20.1	10,337	89.4
Gregory city	1,907	1,886	-1.1	1,977	9.2	0.3	0.4	1.3	88.9	25.2	15.7	35.0	66.8	6.0	630	82.2
Grey Forest city	487	564	15.8	375	87.2	0.0	0.0	3.2	9.6	18.7	29.1	54.2	21.5	39.4	165	87.9
Groesbeck city	4,320	4,253	-1.6	4,288	55.1	27.2	0.0	1.8	15.9	23.2	15.7	35.1	52.3	15.3	1,489	78.4
Groom town	574	550	-4.2	672	91.5	0.6	1.3	0.0	6.5	23.1	24.9	49.0	45.3	21.9	278	92.4
Groves city	16,144	15,480	-4.1	15,662	62.9	7.1	2.1	1.9	25.9	25.0	16.0	36.1	48.2	15.0	5,701	85.7
Groveton city	1,057	1,023	-3.2	1,238	60.3	14.9	0.0	0.7	24.1	24.1	14.8	43.6	56.0	16.2	496	85.7
Gruver city	1,194	1,135	-4.9	1,360	30.3	0.0	0.0	0.9	68.8	29.3	13.8	26.3	56.7	20.9	412	85.2
Guadalupe Guerra CDP	37	-	-	42	0.0	0.0	0.0	0.0	100.0	35.7	0.0	26.4	0.0	0.0	13	100.0
Guerra CDP	6	-	-	-	-	-	-	-	-	-	-	-	-	-	-	-
Gun Barrel City city	5,668	6,208	9.5	6,084	90.9	1.0	0.0	0.8	7.3	19.5	22.0	44.0	56.7	12.7	2,443	84.8
Gunter city	1,502	1,675	11.5	1,247	76.7	1.1	0.4	3.0	18.8	21.1	15.6	39.0	38.0	28.9	380	92.1
Gustine town	476	468	-1.7	504	45.6	0.0	0.0	0.0	54.4	33.1	19.6	41.0	59.9	11.1	182	93.4
Guthrie CDP	160	-	-	124	97.6	0.0	0.0	0.0	2.4	17.7	16.1	54.6	49.0	25.5	42	92.9
Gutierrez CDP	79	-	-	80	0.0	0.0	0.0	0.0	100.0	0.0	0.0	0.0	100.0	0.0	33	100.0
Hackberry town	996	1,077	8.1	1,863	42.7	6.1	15.8	2.3	33.1	30.3	6.3	33.7	27.1	52.6	574	96.7
Hale Center city	2,252	2,054	-8.8	2,088	30.4	2.2	0.2	1.8	65.5	26.4	16.0	37.8	59.0	11.9	769	85.7
Hallettsville city	2,563	2,637	2.9	2,627	56.2	17.5	2.8	0.7	22.8	23.0	22.1	40.6	57.0	12.7	1,056	74.7
Hallsburg city	435	468	7.6	476	87.0	0.6	0.0	0.8	11.6	26.1	16.0	37.1	41.1	14.1	170	87.6
Hallsville city	3,567	4,296	20.4	4,185	90.0	1.5	0.5	0.8	7.2	30.3	11.1	35.4	28.5	34.6	1,517	85.9
Haltom City city	42,370	43,874	3.5	44,223	36.0	5.9	8.8	2.1	47.2	29.2	9.9	32.4	60.6	11.8	13,910	93.5
Hamilton city	3,097	3,012	-2.7	2,980	85.2	0.4	0.0	1.3	13.1	24.6	25.8	42.3	55.6	17.7	1,088	79.4
Hamlin city	2,124	2,021	-4.8	1,590	62.2	11.5	0.1	6.1	20.1	34.3	24.9	35.4	56.2	11.3	725	81.5
Happy town	679	668	-1.6	697	70.7	1.3	0.0	4.6	23.4	23.7	12.2	30.9	36.0	25.5	254	90.6
Hardin city	834	935	12.1	829	82.0	0.0	0.0	4.1	13.9	25.6	23.3	38.1	68.8	11.4	326	82.8
Hargill CDP	877	-	-	963	1.3	0.0	0.0	0.0	98.7	46.3	14.4	22.6	84.1	5.3	265	52.5
Harker Heights city	26,727	32,421	21.3	30,861	46.8	20.0	4.8	6.0	22.4	27.9	9.9	35.0	30.3	35.0	10,319	93.3
Harlingen city	64,943	65,022	0.1	65,129	15.5	0.8	1.2	0.7	81.8	31.5	15.1	31.6	54.3	17.7	21,451	81.7
Harper CDP	1,192	-	-	1,217	78.1	0.0	0.0	0.8	21.1	31.9	23.3	32.9	50.3	17.7	436	72.2
Hart city	1,114	1,020	-8.4	1,178	9.5	6.0	0.3	0.0	84.1	31.5	11.1	31.4	73.2	10.6	381	69.8
Hartley CDP	540	-	-	496	35.7	0.0	0.0	1.8	62.5	33.3	10.1	35.0	65.4	18.6	213	89.2
Haskell city	3,320	3,153	-5.0	3,195	59.7	4.3	0.3	3.4	32.3	18.8	19.2	37.7	66.8	8.9	1,074	71.8
Haslet city	1,521	1,923	26.4	1,626	88.8	0.9	1.7	0.7	7.9	22.0	14.3	46.0	20.4	41.7	575	95.1
Havana CDP	407	-	-	325	0.0	0.0	0.0	0.0	100.0	0.0	33.8	57.6	81.2	0.0	105	72.4
Hawk Cove city	488	557	14.1	462	77.3	0.2	0.0	4.3	18.2	21.9	14.1	44.8	73.8	4.6	160	88.8
Hawkins city	1,264	1,321	4.5	1,337	70.9	25.0	0.0	1.2	2.9	27.4	13.3	33.6	50.4	21.7	511	92.0
Hawley city	629	623		507	87.2	0.2	0.0	3.6	9.1	22.5	29.0	49.0	50.1	9.4	259	81.5
Hays city	217	269	24.0	154	83.8	0.0	1.3	3.9	11.0	13.6	39.6	59.2	18.7	43.9	69	98.6
H. Cuellar Estates CDP	20	-	-	118	0.0	0.0	0.0	0.0	100.0	9.3	0.0	39.6	20.9	37.4	23	100.0
Hearne city	4,457	4,354	-2.3	4,433	24.4	34.8	0.0	0.2	40.6	28.7	9.2	32.2	61.9	8.4	1,521	85.9
Heath city	7,329	9,331	27.3	8,709	82.6	1.1	5.5	2.9	7.8	24.6	16.2	45.4	18.8	59.6	2,959	99.4
Hebbronville CDP	4,558	-	-	4,626	5.7	0.0	0.0	0.6	93.7	33.6	15.1	30.8	69.8	8.0	1,427	64.4
Hebron town	182	215	18.1	388	67.5	7.5	21.6	0.8	2.6	10.1	19.3	30.5	19.7	68.3	176	98.3
Hedley city	329	289	-12.2	292	89.0	0.0	0.3	0.3	10.3	15.4	28.4	51.3	43.4	23.2	135	73.3
Hedwig Village city	2,542	2,634	3.6	2,671	63.0	1.7	14.4	4.2	16.7	30.3	16.0	40.5	13.4	71.4	971	96.4
Heidelberg CDP	1,725	-	-	1,368	0.0	0.0	0.0	0.0	100.0	28.9	17.7	34.9	61.2	4.0	412	70.1
Helotes city	7,324	9,961	36.0	9,175	53.3	1.9	5.8	0.9	38.1	23.1	16.9	44.1	21.4	49.5	2,679	97.8
Hemphill city	1,251	1,244	-0.6	1,319	78.6	4.1	0.0	1.8	15.5	26.1	20.1	41.6	62.0	13.8	464	80.4
Hempstead city	5,768	8,355	44.9	7,691	21.8	42.5	0.0	2.0	33.7	32.1	10.3	26.0	60.5	16.1	2,648	86.4
Henderson city	13,712	13,154	-4.1	13,237	49.9	23.4	1.1	2.3	23.3	23.5	14.0	34.4	54.0	15.6	3,917	82.4
Henrietta city	3,144	3,118	-0.8	3,042	92.8	0.4	0.0	3.9	2.8	22.1	22.3	43.7	45.2	22.3	1,239	85.7
Hereford city	15,367	14,622	-4.8	14,815	20.3	0.8	0.8	1.1	77.1	32.5	11.6	30.0	63.1	11.5	4,929	85.2
Hermleigh CDP	345	-	-	376	55.1	0.0	0.0	1.1	43.9	23.1	23.7	47.3	72.7	6.0	143	93.0
Hewitt city	13,548	14,937	10.3	14,523	68.9	6.4	4.0	2.1	18.7	21.8	16.9	38.8	29.5	32.6	5,425	98.4
Hickory Creek town	3,412	4,795	40.5	4,574	80.5	3.7	7.0	1.4	7.4	17.1	16.0	48.0	23.4	39.6	1,683	100.0
Hico city	1,387	1,413	1.9	1,582	82.7	1.8	0.0	2.8	12.7	22.4	18.2	34.2	62.7	16.0	517	80.3
Hidalgo city	12,532	14,183	13.2	13,884	0.4	0.0	0.0	0.0	99.6	31.7	9.5	29.1	58.6	21.4	3,734	92.5
Hideaway city	2,936	3,174	8.1	3,127	96.2	0.0	1.9	0.0	2.0	9.7	48.7	64.4	24.0	36.8	1,522	95.7
Higgins city	397	391	-1.5	595	68.1	0.0	3.0	10.8	18.2	35.1	16.1	33.9	57.8	15.6	196	90.3
Highland Haven city	431	443	2.8	508	89.4	0.0	0.0	6.7	3.9	11.4	51.0	65.2	32.0	32.9	240	94.2
Highland Park town	8,560	9,083	6.1	9,168	89.0	0.3	5.7	2.3	2.7	25.9	21.6	45.8	2.6	86.4	3,656	98.7
Highlands CDP	7,522	-	-	7,720	55.0	3.2	0.5	3.0	38.3	25.9	14.2	38.3	48.8	11.7	2,713	91.5
Highland Village city	15,084	16,668	10.5	16,519	81.2	3.4	3.2	2.6	9.6	23.6	12.9	43.1	15.0	57.7	5,416	97.8
Hill Country Village city	998	1,114	11.6	584	75.7	0.9	1.4	1.9	20.2	17.3	28.8	54.0	12.1	66.3	203	97.5
Hillcrest village	730	712	-2.5	682	80.6	0.0	0.3	1.9	17.2	16.9	35.0	56.4	20.9	36.1	270	94.4
Hillsboro city	8,437	8,476	0.5	8,342	38.8	16.6	1.1	3.2	40.2	24.9	15.3	34.6	53.6	18.2	2,878	83.9
Hillside Acres CDP	30	-	-	-	-	-	-	-	-	-	-	-	-	-	-	-
Hilltop CDP	287	-	-	241	39.0	0.0	0.0	14.1	46.9	0.0	12.9	47.4	43.2	42.7	103	100.0
Hilltop CDP	77	-	-	139	0.0	0.0	0.0	0.0	100.0	49.6	5.0	23.0	100.0	0.0	42	83.3
Hilltop Lakes CDP	1,101	-	-	790	95.4	0.0	0.0	1.4	3.2	0.0	31.3	55.3	38.7	22.0	347	93.4
Hilshire Village city	746	808	8.3	875	74.9	0.0	7.2	2.1	15.9	26.2	22.7	46.6	10.2	74.4	316	98.7

1 May be of any race.

Table A. All Places — **Population and Housing**

STATE City, town, township, borough, or CDP (county if applicable)	Population: 2010 census total population	Population: 2019 estimated population	Population: Percent change 2010–2019	Population: ACS total population estimate 2015–2019	Race and Hispanic or Latino origin (percent): White alone, not Hispanic or Latino	Black alone, not Hispanic or Latino	Asian alone, not Hispanic or Latino	All other races or 2 or more races, not Hispanic or Latino	Hispanic or Latino[1]	Age (percent): Under 18 years old	Age 65 years and older	Median age	Educational attainment of persons age 25 and older: Percent High school diploma or less	Percent Bachelor's degree or more	Occupied housing units: Total	Percent with a computer
	1	2	3	4	5	6	7	8	9	10	11	12	13	14	15	16
TEXAS—Con.																
Hitchcock city	6,967	7,914	13.6	7,800	46.9	24.2	0.0	1.0	27.9	28.6	13.5	33.5	49.1	13.0	2,837	85.4
Holiday Beach CDP	514	-	-	698	78.1	0.0	0.0	0.0	21.9	12.0	9.2	50.0	54.2	5.4	305	91.5
Holiday Lakes town	1,132	1,250	10.4	851	29.4	4.7	0.0	0.8	65.1	26.7	14.3	32.7	78.7	5.0	281	86.5
Holland town	1,112	1,171	5.3	1,581	67.4	3.5	0.3	3.5	25.2	31.8	13.5	30.6	55.1	14.8	482	86.3
Holliday city	1,761	1,670	-5.2	1,533	91.3	0.0	0.0	4.6	4.1	23.2	17.7	40.9	50.3	21.4	612	83.0
Holly Lake Ranch CDP	2,774	-	-	2,529	94.6	0.0	0.0	0.6	4.8	12.0	48.2	64.2	34.4	34.2	1,248	93.8
Hollywood Park town	3,094	3,342	8.0	3,327	87.4	0.2	0.6	3.3	8.5	21.0	26.7	51.3	15.4	61.8	1,258	88.0
Homestead Meadows North CDP	5,124	-	-	5,126	14.3	0.1	0.4	0.9	84.3	28.1	7.0	32.5	55.0	20.1	1,424	88.5
Homestead Meadows South CDP	7,247	-	-	7,089	0.9	0.0	0.0	0.0	99.1	29.1	13.2	33.8	63.6	9.9	1,909	87.4
Hondo city	8,807	9,436	7.1	9,251	26.2	8.9	0.3	1.1	63.4	22.0	12.2	32.4	56.9	12.3	2,363	79.7
Honey Grove city	1,668	1,737	4.1	2,092	70.4	9.1	0.6	2.8	17.1	26.3	15.9	37.5	54.0	17.3	792	79.4
Hooks city	2,769	2,712	-2.1	2,738	77.6	12.3	0.5	4.9	4.6	28.7	15.5	35.5	48.9	17.5	1,047	79.7
Horizon City city	16,758	19,642	17.2	19,459	6.0	2.3	0.0	0.1	91.6	33.2	4.7	28.4	37.4	24.4	5,490	95.7
Hornsby Bend CDP	6,791	-	-	7,694	8.3	21.6	0.6	1.7	67.8	32.1	5.3	33.8	58.7	17.1	2,236	96.8
Horseshoe Bay city	3,510	4,024	14.6	4,100	83.1	0.0	0.0	5.2	11.7	9.4	51.5	65.4	24.4	46.8	1,997	94.3
Horseshoe Bend CDP	789	-	-	586	77.6	0.0	0.0	0.0	22.4	15.0	23.2	59.5	68.9	14.6	276	92.0
Houston city	2,095,517	2,320,268	10.7	2,310,432	24.4	22.1	6.7	1.8	45.0	25.1	10.5	33.0	43.9	32.9	858,374	89.2
Howardwick city	422	393	-6.9	453	92.5	0.0	0.0	0.0	7.5	25.6	24.7	45.8	45.1	14.4	180	90.6
Howe town	2,600	3,346	28.7	3,075	80.7	0.0	1.1	6.4	11.8	24.9	12.0	32.0	47.8	12.9	1,076	91.0
Hubbard city	1,423	1,406	-1.2	1,761	79.6	9.6	0.0	1.7	9.1	27.0	19.2	36.5	50.2	12.7	580	77.1
Hudson city	4,727	5,005	5.9	4,964	66.6	13.0	0.1	0.4	19.9	30.0	15.7	32.9	44.0	14.7	1,825	89.0
Hudson Bend CDP	2,981	-	-	2,208	83.3	0.4	5.7	4.2	6.5	16.0	21.7	53.3	16.5	60.4	1,059	99.2
Hudson Oaks city	1,681	2,479	47.5	2,383	91.6	0.0	0.0	1.0	7.5	19.0	12.8	46.3	17.6	40.4	869	98.3
Hughes Springs city	1,758	1,709	-2.8	1,479	80.3	15.9	0.0	1.1	2.7	22.7	23.9	37.6	54.7	11.1	623	69.2
Hull CDP	669	-	-	669	71.7	0.0	0.0	0.0	28.3	40.8	20.0	31.6	52.8	25.4	198	86.9
Humble city	15,127	15,824	4.6	15,864	22.6	35.4	1.5	1.5	39.0	21.4	11.6	34.3	56.1	11.2	6,118	88.4
Hungerford CDP	347	-	-	84	90.5	0.0	0.0	0.0	9.5	36.9	0.0	34.2	13.2	56.6	16	100.0
Hunters Creek Village city	4,367	4,869	11.5	4,825	88.3	0.0	6.5	0.8	4.3	30.6	14.7	42.4	2.9	87.2	1,540	97.5
Huntington city	2,112	2,111	0.0	2,470	85.5	7.7	0.2	4.0	2.6	27.4	16.4	38.6	56.7	5.7	827	80.7
Huntsville city	38,549	42,241	9.6	41,592	49.6	27.6	2.0	0.9	19.9	11.5	9.8	30.3	51.9	22.6	12,729	92.5
Hurst city	37,343	38,655	3.5	38,976	59.8	9.4	3.8	4.1	23.0	26.0	16.0	37.0	34.9	31.4	13,888	95.1
Hutchins city	5,331	5,866	10.0	5,718	23.5	33.3	0.2	3.7	39.2	22.6	5.1	32.0	70.9	6.6	1,122	87.1
Hutto city	16,461	27,947	69.8	25,320	48.7	14.6	1.9	2.7	32.0	30.1	6.1	33.5	38.2	26.0	7,561	98.0
Huxley city	380	382	0.5	479	100.0	0.0	0.0	0.0	0.0	20.3	23.6	42.3	55.3	14.0	194	85.6
Iago CDP	161	-	-	105	75.2	0.0	0.0	0.0	24.8	10.5	63.8	70.6	65.1	17.4	45	100.0
Idalou city	2,296	2,308	0.5	2,018	47.7	0.1	0.3	0.1	51.7	23.0	20.8	42.1	61.5	17.1	752	83.2
Iglesia Antigua CDP	413	-	-	290	1.0	0.0	0.0	0.0	99.0	22.4	13.4	42.9	72.0	5.0	106	37.7
Impact town	30	30	0.0	48	16.7	0.0	0.0	0.0	83.3	16.7	8.3	40.4	96.2	3.8	16	75.0
Imperial CDP	278	-	-	308	68.2	0.0	0.0	1.6	30.2	18.2	12.0	32.6	44.4	25.9	95	90.5
Indian Hills CDP	2,591	-	-	3,001	1.4	0.0	0.0	0.0	98.6	39.7	5.3	20.5	89.5	0.0	592	87.5
Indian Lake town	640	854	33.4	788	26.4	0.0	0.0	0.5	73.1	37.1	17.6	33.5	71.0	11.9	262	87.8
Indian Springs CDP	785	-	-	850	97.2	0.0	0.0	2.8	0.0	11.8	21.4	57.2	75.5	7.2	331	92.7
Indio CDP	50	-	-	-	-	-	-	-	-	-	-	-	-	-	-	-
Industry city	304	325	6.9	289	56.1	26.3	0.0	2.1	15.6	16.6	15.6	50.3	45.9	19.7	132	84.8
Inez CDP	2,098	-	-	2,702	86.6	0.0	0.0	0.0	13.4	26.9	16.3	37.6	30.3	29.8	831	86.5
Ingleside city	9,381	10,192	8.6	10,165	42.2	3.4	1.0	5.0	48.4	30.0	10.5	32.5	54.4	13.7	3,320	95.1
Ingleside on the Bay city	615	607	-1.3	802	81.9	0.0	0.1	5.4	12.6	14.0	21.9	51.1	38.5	30.1	312	94.6
Ingram city	1,772	1,850	4.4	2,003	62.7	1.0	1.3	3.3	31.7	22.6	11.8	36.7	64.5	7.3	688	88.5
Iola city	401	424	5.7	209	88.0	0.0	0.0	1.4	10.5	10.5	16.7	53.3	61.9	7.2	101	80.2
Iowa Colony village	1,163	3,233	178.0	1,811	35.9	21.8	4.4	7.8	30.1	21.9	8.0	37.9	41.3	25.6	539	98.1
Iowa Park city	6,378	6,339	-0.6	6,328	89.3	0.0	0.0	1.2	9.5	26.6	16.1	36.5	46.1	17.4	2,416	90.9
Iraan city	1,229	1,222	-0.6	1,150	46.0	0.0	3.3	3.6	47.1	23.2	8.8	37.4	47.6	17.7	413	92.0
Iredell city	339	342	0.9	348	80.7	0.0	0.0	0.6	18.7	29.6	22.1	38.0	61.0	13.6	122	84.4
Irving city	216,285	239,798	10.9	239,783	21.6	13.8	19.6	2.7	42.3	26.9	7.5	32.0	39.9	37.7	85,284	95.6
Italy town	1,872	1,923	2.7	1,934	57.1	11.0	0.0	2.7	29.2	28.2	11.6	32.6	49.8	8.9	695	90.2
Itasca city	1,644	1,733	5.4	1,392	54.3	14.3	0.0	1.5	29.9	25.2	19.0	42.1	56.9	7.0	507	82.4
Ivanhoe city	1,427	1,436	0.6	1,614	80.0	3.5	0.0	8.6	7.9	20.8	23.8	47.9	58.2	8.2	682	81.5
Jacinto City city	10,553	10,466	-0.8	10,667	9.3	3.5	0.0	0.2	86.9	27.1	10.7	35.0	73.3	5.3	3,211	82.8
Jacksboro city	4,506	4,384	-2.7	4,379	63.3	9.5	0.0	1.4	25.8	21.1	13.8	34.9	64.2	12.6	1,327	80.0
Jacksonville city	14,537	14,815	1.9	14,790	39.0	18.6	0.1	2.3	40.0	31.5	15.6	32.5	58.9	16.9	5,021	82.3
Jamaica Beach city	987	1,079	9.3	1,117	87.9	0.0	2.3	0.0	9.8	14.7	15.7	52.7	14.7	45.5	551	98.2
Jardin de San Julian CDP	22	-	-	-	-	-	-	-	-	-	-	-	-	-	-	-
Jarrell city	1,034	1,832	77.2	1,209	67.7	0.5	0.2	2.2	29.4	26.6	6.7	36.4	31.4	33.2	378	89.7
Jasper city	7,602	7,551	-0.7	7,583	40.9	54.2	0.2	0.3	4.4	28.1	18.0	35.3	57.3	16.4	2,735	84.6
Jayton city	530	502	-5.3	533	81.4	1.1	0.0	1.5	15.9	27.0	27.2	48.3	50.9	23.9	221	81.0
Jefferson city	2,106	1,915	-9.1	2,512	45.8	43.4	1.3	2.1	7.5	23.8	22.0	41.7	56.0	17.6	1,086	75.0
Jersey Village city	7,608	7,890	3.7	7,933	61.5	12.1	5.8	1.6	19.0	14.3	21.1	44.3	23.3	45.3	3,704	96.6
Jewett city	1,173	1,220	4.0	994	52.7	4.0	0.7	0.0	42.6	30.3	11.8	33.8	74.4	12.2	345	82.6
J.F. Villareal CDP	104	-	-	-	-	-	-	-	-	-	-	-	-	-	-	-
Joaquin city	822	805	-2.1	1,014	72.3	11.8	0.0	3.7	12.1	19.7	18.0	46.1	67.6	7.6	353	73.1
Johnson City city	1,645	2,131	29.5	1,860	70.9	0.2	0.8	3.0	25.1	20.5	19.9	43.6	58.6	17.6	686	96.1
Jolly city	171	163	-4.7	198	87.4	0.0	0.0	8.6	4.0	11.1	42.4	64.0	46.6	19.3	95	89.5
Jones Creek village	2,063	2,077	0.7	2,041	63.4	0.0	0.0	1.1	35.5	27.5	15.6	35.2	54.7	10.3	699	92.6
Jonestown city	1,814	2,105	16.0	1,967	86.0	0.3	0.9	1.8	11.0	22.5	16.7	46.1	25.9	37.5	782	96.4
Josephine city	795	2,094	163.4	1,366	69.1	9.8	0.9	5.5	14.7	23.7	10.0	35.1	55.9	15.4	532	94.0
Joshua city	6,407	8,101	26.4	7,477	85.1	0.0	0.3	2.8	11.8	28.1	14.5	34.0	46.7	18.2	2,763	94.4
Jourdanton city	3,886	4,405	13.4	4,291	38.4	0.4	0.0	3.6	57.6	35.3	11.7	26.9	71.4	9.7	1,330	92.3
Juarez CDP	1,017	-	-	1,653	0.0	0.0	0.0	0.0	100.0	35.9	11.7	28.2	94.1	3.0	363	100.0
Junction city	2,571	2,404	-6.5	2,507	63.8	1.9	0.0	2.2	32.1	27.5	19.5	36.9	56.8	17.8	955	79.3
Justin city	3,245	4,279	31.9	3,859	87.2	0.5	0.5	3.7	8.2	22.7	14.8	44.3	33.2	31.5	1,464	98.4
Karnes City city	3,054	3,383	10.8	3,404	21.6	4.0	0.2	0.9	73.3	24.7	11.7	33.3	67.9	16.1	695	74.1
Katy city	14,119	21,729	53.9	20,202	58.6	5.8	4.0	2.2	29.4	24.1	14.1	40.0	38.1	35.0	6,651	91.4
Kaufman city	6,600	7,788	18.0	7,330	52.8	8.9	0.0	1.5	36.8	30.2	11.1	33.9	59.7	10.9	2,081	81.2
K-Bar Ranch CDP	358	-	-	536	0.0	0.0	0.0	0.0	100.0	52.1	7.3	17.6	89.1	0.0	124	68.5
Keene city	6,121	6,568	7.3	6,396	51.2	5.7	3.0	10.3	29.8	22.1	14.7	31.6	40.3	27.8	2,009	84.8
Keller city	39,633	47,213	19.1	46,813	78.9	1.9	6.1	3.0	10.1	27.4	13.2	41.4	17.5	56.5	15,524	97.6
Kemah city	1,773	2,019	13.9	3,057	58.8	10.6	7.5	6.3	16.7	26.2	11.7	38.2	27.5	28.8	1,016	97.4
Kemp city	1,044	1,236	18.4	982	86.9	1.3	0.5	0.7	10.6	24.5	22.9	37.5	57.1	11.6	336	87.8
Kempner city	1,090	1,140	4.6	1,294	73.5	1.8	2.1	1.5	21.1	26.0	11.5	37.0	50.3	12.9	409	93.4
Kendleton city	380	454	19.5	339	5.0	77.9	0.0	0.9	16.2	19.2	19.5	47.1	57.6	11.0	144	77.8

1 May be of any race.

Table A. All Places — Population and Housing

STATE City, town, township, borough, or CDP (county if applicable)	2010 census total population	2019 estimated population	Percent change 2010–2019	ACS total population estimate 2015–2019	White alone, not Hispanic or Latino	Black alone, not Hispanic or Latino	Asian alone, not Hispanic or Latino	All other races or 2 or more races, not Hispanic or Latino	Hispanic or Latino[1]	Under 18 years old	Age 65 years and older	Median age	Percent High school diploma or less	Percent Bachelor's degree or more	Total	Percent with a computer
	1	2	3	4	5	6	7	8	9	10	11	12	13	14	15	16
TEXAS—Con.																
Kenedy city	3,312	3,353	1.2	3,384	9.0	2.7	4.5	0.3	83.5	30.3	10.8	30.7	56.4	12.6	1,072	87.4
Kenefick town	565	693	22.7	465	93.8	0.0	2.2	0.0	4.1	12.7	20.6	48.2	62.4	2.5	200	83.5
Kennard city	337	325	-3.6	295	82.4	13.9	0.0	3.7	0.0	34.6	17.3	35.4	64.3	8.6	124	62.1
Kennedale city	6,743	8,645	28.2	8,197	57.5	9.3	6.7	2.2	24.3	26.4	15.3	38.3	44.2	29.6	2,758	93.2
Kerens city	1,563	1,523	-2.6	1,881	61.8	24.0	0.0	6.6	7.6	26.3	17.5	37.9	39.9	14.1	647	82.2
Kermit city	5,713	6,486	13.5	6,503	27.4	2.5	0.0	1.8	68.4	31.4	10.8	32.2	62.8	7.2	2,185	81.8
Kerrville city	22,385	23,754	6.1	23,370	65.3	2.2	0.8	2.2	29.6	19.3	28.0	46.2	37.3	28.7	10,031	90.4
Kilgore city	13,451	14,852	10.4	14,827	62.7	12.8	1.4	3.0	20.1	24.5	16.3	33.1	45.8	17.4	5,231	84.5
Killeen city	127,747	151,666	18.7	145,686	28.1	34.9	3.7	6.7	26.6	30.3	6.2	28.8	33.5	20.2	53,363	92.7
Kingsbury city	124	133	7.3	81	100.0	0.0	0.0	0.0	0.0	32.1	39.5	32.8	41.8	34.5	33	100.0
Kingsland CDP	6,030	-	-	7,134	85.2	1.7	0.6	1.8	10.8	16.3	33.0	54.5	47.5	17.4	2,784	83.6
Kingsville city	26,450	25,315	-4.3	25,605	17.0	3.4	2.6	2.0	74.9	24.1	12.0	27.1	48.7	24.7	9,214	86.6
Kirby city	7,996	8,723	9.1	8,664	24.5	12.9	1.9	1.4	59.3	25.5	14.9	35.4	47.8	11.4	2,878	90.8
Kirbyville city	2,144	2,069	-3.5	2,631	63.7	15.8	0.0	4.4	16.2	24.2	18.5	37.8	67.7	5.5	975	80.3
Kirvin town	125	131	4.8	172	90.7	7.6	0.0	1.7	0.0	23.3	13.4	29.2	46.1	6.7	74	75.7
Knippa CDP	689	-	-	783	52.7	0.0	0.0	0.0	47.3	32.3	10.1	34.1	74.2	13.5	244	76.2
Knollwood city	432	489	13.2	590	84.6	4.4	1.7	1.0	8.3	8.5	17.1	40.3	35.5	33.3	326	96.9
Knox City town	1,130	1,119	-	1,229	56.3	1.2	0.0	1.3	41.2	31.5	18.2	34.8	51.7	18.8	426	71.4
Kosse town	464	466	0.4	664	56.5	3.8	0.8	3.6	35.4	22.6	17.6	35.6	72.5	5.8	209	67.0
Kountze city	2,134	2,108	-1.2	1,972	74.5	15.7	1.3	0.9	7.6	19.4	23.5	40.7	70.4	7.2	720	89.6
Kress city	715	681	-4.8	803	23.9	1.1	0.0	1.9	73.1	23.2	13.2	35.9	65.5	7.5	263	85.2
Krugerville city	1,573	1,836	16.7	1,699	83.8	8.3	0.7	2.4	4.9	16.7	18.1	48.8	32.8	31.1	672	93.8
Krum city	4,118	5,018	21.9	5,014	76.2	2.1	1.1	4.0	16.7	26.3	10.1	35.9	30.2	39.8	1,733	98.1
Kurten town	394	409	3.8	373	71.3	4.6	0.0	1.1	23.1	26.3	10.5	35.1	48.4	20.3	133	89.5
Kyle city	28,247	48,393	71.3	42,706	44.7	4.6	1.0	1.9	47.7	28.7	8.6	32.9	35.8	30.2	14,009	93.0
La Blanca CDP	2,488	-	-	2,316	0.0	0.0	0.0	0.0	100.0	31.4	9.5	28.4	69.5	7.4	543	74.8
La Carla CDP	70	-	-	278	0.0	0.0	0.0	0.0	100.0	43.9	0.0	22.2	41.0	7.4	33	100.0
La Casita CDP	128	-	-	-	0.0	0.0	0.0	0.0	100.0							
La Chuparosa CDP	49	-	-	34	0.0	0.0	0.0	0.0	100.0	70.6	0.0	9.4	0.0	0.0	10	100.0
Lackland AFB CDP	9,918	-	-	5,606	45.1	20.0	6.3	4.8	23.8	9.5	0.1	20.2	7.6	38.1	246	100.0
La Coma CDP	48	-	-	71	0.0	0.0	0.0	0.0	100.0	21.1	0.0	31.7	73.8	0.0	20	100.0
LaCoste city	1,119	1,247	11.4	1,297	31.8	0.0	0.0	4.3	63.8	17.8	24.5	47.1	57.6	14.5	463	88.3
Lacy-Lakeview city	6,457	6,721	4.1	6,633	50.1	22.5	2.1	1.4	23.9	28.4	11.9	32.1	48.1	8.8	2,648	89.5
Ladonia town	612	627	2.5	677	76.2	19.6	0.0	2.4	1.8	19.9	19.6	43.0	44.6	14.8	278	83.1
La Escondida CDP	153	-	-	262	0.0	0.0	0.0	0.0	100.0	63.4	0.0	16.1	100.0	0.0	53	100.0
La Esperanza CDP	229	-	-	86	0.0	0.0	0.0	0.0	100.0	17.4	0.0	36.1	47.2	32.1	27	100.0
La Feria city	7,201	7,230	0.4	7,267	10.2	0.3	0.9	0.0	88.6	33.0	18.2	35.1	56.2	12.5	2,265	68.5
La Feria North CDP	212	-	-	308	32.5	0.0	0.0	0.0	67.5	17.9	31.8	54.1	71.9	9.1	86	100.0
Lago CDP	204	-	-	428	0.0	0.0	0.0	0.0	100.0	43.5	26.4	27.3	81.0	9.5	89	32.6
Lago Vista CDP	-	-	-	39	0.0	0.0	0.0	0.0	100.0	33.3	0.0	44.5	100.0	0.0	12	100.0
Lago Vista city	6,067	7,556	24.5	6,935	74.5	3.2	0.8	1.7	19.9	18.9	19.9	48.0	32.5	33.2	2,736	94.1
La Grange city	4,653	4,677	0.5	4,667	55.7	8.5	2.0	0.5	33.3	30.2	16.7	36.0	53.8	18.1	1,544	75.3
La Grulla city	1,622	1,701	4.9	1,456	0.0	0.0	0.0	0.0	100.0	29.7	15.4	39.2	81.5	4.0	418	72.0
Laguna Heights CDP	3,488	-	-	2,090	1.2	0.0	0.0	0.0	98.8	36.0	8.4	27.3	93.0	0.0	599	100.0
Laguna Park CDP	1,276	-	-	1,518	97.4	0.0	0.0	0.0	2.6	20.0	27.0	54.5	45.4	16.1	598	80.4
Laguna Seca CDP	266	-	-	374	1.6	0.0	0.0	0.0	98.4	23.8	11.2	27.6	54.5	15.6	88	88.6
Laguna Vista town	3,142	3,180	1.2	3,157	48.2	0.4	0.9	0.6	50.0	14.9	32.4	57.7	37.4	31.6	1,425	89.8
La Homa CDP	11,985	-	-	12,729	2.6	0.0	0.0	0.2	97.2	30.8	8.4	27.9	75.0	8.6	3,216	86.4
La Joya city	3,986	4,293	7.7	4,253	2.4	0.0	1.4	0.0	96.3	40.1	11.0	28.1	65.2	11.7	1,240	93.1
Lake Bridgeport city	342	399	16.7	409	81.2	0.0	0.0	2.7	16.1	29.1	17.1	33.3	51.2	19.4	153	91.5
Lake Brownwood CDP	1,532	-	-	1,410	91.0	0.0	0.0	4.3	4.8	23.8	28.3	53.3	54.3	14.5	591	83.2
Lake Bryan CDP	1,728	-	-	1,611	49.6	4.7	1.9	2.7	41.0	35.3	3.0	30.5	45.1	18.1	489	97.3
Lake Cherokee CDP	3,071	-	-	2,942	90.7	6.2	0.0	0.0	3.1	16.8	35.4	55.1	35.1	29.6	1,309	86.4
Lake City town	509	531	4.3	545	58.9	0.0	0.0	0.0	41.1	8.3	23.7	55.8	54.7	10.0	255	91.0
Lake Colorado City CDP	588	-	-	493	90.3	0.0	0.0	0.0	9.7	18.3	17.8	37.8	57.3	14.6	196	85.2
Lake Dallas city	7,108	8,063	13.4	8,016	60.2	4.6	1.4	3.5	30.4	27.3	8.3	36.7	42.1	20.8	2,870	96.0
Lake Dunlap CDP	1,934	-	-	1,899	67.6	3.4	0.0	1.7	27.2	21.6	13.4	41.1	51.5	16.7	683	88.6
Lakehills CDP	5,150	-	-	5,631	71.5	0.0	0.6	5.3	22.6	22.4	20.8	48.2	33.2	28.7	2,085	93.5
Lake Jackson city	26,833	27,220	1.4	27,295	62.9	3.5	2.9	1.3	29.4	25.9	14.1	34.6	30.0	35.2	10,446	94.0
Lake Kiowa CDP	1,906	-	-	2,585	96.5	0.0	0.0	0.9	2.6	15.4	40.8	61.4	20.4	36.9	1,184	97.8
Lake Medina Shores CDP	1,235	-	-	1,268	68.1	2.1	0.0	3.8	25.9	9.1	22.0	54.0	50.2	3.9	525	88.6
Lake Meredith Estates CDP	437	-	-	483	100.0	0.0	0.0	0.0	0.0	0.0	31.9	54.1	53.8	11.4	170	90.6
Lakeport city	974	996	2.3	1,296	17.1	44.1	0.1	3.8	35.0	28.4	9.7	32.3	46.8	14.6	435	84.1
Lakeshore Gardens-Hidden Acres CDP	504	-	-	741	40.5	0.0	0.0	0.0	59.5	29.0	17.8	41.1	59.3	6.6	287	85.0
Lakeside town	312	303	-2.9	289	78.5	0.0	0.0	0.0	21.5	8.7	40.8	61.3	37.5	17.8	119	93.3
Lakeside town	1,499	1,593	6.3	1,616	86.3	1.5	0.1	0.7	11.4	19.7	24.3	52.6	33.5	24.6	641	95.5
Lakeside City town	969	957	-1.2	1,116	91.2	0.0	1.3	5.0	2.4	24.3	23.2	41.8	29.9	31.2	417	95.2
Lake Tanglewood village	802	886	10.5	791	94.1	0.1	2.0	1.0	2.8	9.4	30.7	60.7	13.3	55.0	382	99.2
Lakeview town	107	95	-11.2	65	33.8	9.2	0.0	4.6	52.3	20.0	29.2	57.1	71.2	1.9	33	72.7
Lake View CDP	199	-	-	100	100.0	0.0	0.0	0.0	0.0	0.0	100.0	0.0	0.0	0.0	48	100.0
Lakeway city	11,679	15,981	36.8	15,138	83.6	2.6	2.8	1.9	9.2	22.2	22.7	48.4	9.0	69.3	6,043	97.4
Lakewood Village city	537	964	79.5	562	92.9	0.0	0.9	1.8	4.4	15.7	20.8	50.4	29.5	33.2	198	97.0
Lake Worth city	4,675	4,896	4.7	4,929	67.2	0.9	0.0	0.3	31.6	23.5	16.2	40.5	55.8	11.5	1,666	94.5
La Loma de Falcon CDP	95	-	-	36	0.0	0.0	0.0	0.0	100.0	0.0	16.7	38.9	75.0	25.0	9	100.0
Lamar CDP	636	-	-	1,154	99.7	0.1	0.0	0.0	0.2	21.0	43.4	54.7	32.6	21.9	517	95.9
La Marque city	14,516	17,319	19.3	16,627	34.8	30.1	3.2	0.9	31.1	23.5	14.3	39.1	49.3	16.9	5,960	84.8
Lamesa city	9,425	9,147	-2.9	9,221	31.4	3.2	0.1	0.6	64.7	30.3	16.0	34.8	63.7	14.9	3,599	81.0
La Minita CDP	171	-	-	93	0.0	0.0	0.0	0.0	100.0	32.3	22.6	45.3	60.3	0.0	40	62.5
Lampasas city	6,735	7,982	18.5	7,760	67.5	4.4	2.0	2.3	23.7	25.9	17.9	36.6	48.7	14.8	2,864	85.1
Lancaster city	36,664	39,228	7.0	39,214	8.7	70.0	0.7	2.3	18.3	31.2	9.1	32.2	40.2	20.5	13,308	92.1
Lantana CDP	6,874	-	-	9,462	77.0	3.8	5.4	2.5	11.2	32.0	8.8	39.1	12.8	64.1	3,038	98.9
La Paloma CDP	2,903	-	-	4,063	0.0	0.0	0.0	1.8	98.2	36.5	6.9	24.7	85.7	2.9	846	67.8
La Paloma Addition CDP	330	-	-	338	13.9	0.0	0.0	0.0	86.1	24.6	12.1	44.5	49.5	0.0	105	85.7
La Paloma-Lost Creek CDP	408	-	-	613	25.6	0.0	0.0	0.0	74.4	44.4	7.0	26.6	66.0	11.0	118	79.7
La Paloma Ranchettes CDP	239	-	-	200	0.0	0.0	0.0	0.0	100.0	8.0	0.0	23.8	37.9	45.3	33	100.0
La Porte city	33,806	34,976	3.5	35,246	55.3	5.8	1.0	3.0	34.8	22.4	13.1	37.9	46.2	15.9	12,430	93.5
La Presa CDP	319	-	-	227	0.0	0.0	0.0	0.0	100.0	14.1	11.0	55.6	88.5	3.3	96	83.3
La Pryor CDP	1,643	-	-	1,466	26.7	0.0	0.0	0.0	73.3	30.8	14.5	37.0	68.8	6.0	424	72.9

1 May be of any race.

Table A. All Places — **Population and Housing**

STATE City, town, township, borough, or CDP (county if applicable)	2010 census total population	2019 estimated population	Percent change 2010–2019	ACS total population estimate 2015–2019	White alone, not Hispanic or Latino	Black alone, not Hispanic or Latino	Asian alone, not Hispanic or Latino	All other races or 2 or more races, not Hispanic or Latino	Hispanic or Latino[1]	Under 18 years old	Age 65 years and older	Median age	Percent High school diploma or less	Percent Bachelor's degree or more	Total	Percent with a computer
	1	2	3	4	5	6	7	8	9	10	11	12	13	14	15	16
La Puerta CDP	632	-	-	497	0.0	0.0	0.0	0.0	100.0	25.2	13.9	37.5	67.5	23.0	135	74.1
Laredo city	235,780	262,491	11.3	259,151	3.6	0.3	0.5	0.2	95.4	33.0	9.2	28.9	56.8	19.4	71,033	81.7
Laredo Ranchettes CDP	22	-	-	-	-	-	-	-	-	-	-	-	-	-	-	-
Laredo Ranchettes West CDP	-	-	-	-	-	-	-	-	-	-	-	-	-	-	-	-
La Rosita CDP	85	-	-	178	0.0	0.0	0.0	0.0	100.0	15.2	0.0	21.5	45.7	0.0	30	100.0
Lasana CDP	84	-	-	178	3.9	0.0	0.0	0.0	96.1	33.7	0.0	29.6	38.1	14.4	38	100.0
Lasara CDP	1,039	-	-	853	5.9	0.0	0.0	0.0	94.1	24.6	13.8	41.1	83.2	3.9	228	75.4
Las Haciendas CDP	7	-	-	-	-	-	-	-	-	-	-	-	-	-	-	-
Las Lomas CDP	3,147	-	-	2,666	0.0	0.0	0.0	0.0	100.0	32.4	7.6	27.4	92.8	2.4	657	87.4
Las Lomitas CDP	244	-	-	45	0.0	0.0	0.0	0.0	100.0	0.0	37.8	51.1	100.0	0.0	27	77.8
Las Palmas CDP	67	-	-	-	-	-	-	-	-	-	-	-	-	-	-	-
Las Palmas II CDP	1,605	-	-	1,783	0.9	0.0	0.0	0.0	99.1	47.1	15.4	20.0	86.6	0.0	482	33.4
Las Pilas CDP	28	-	-	-	-	-	-	-	-	-	-	-	-	-	-	-
Las Quintas Fronterizas CDP	3,290	-	-	1,212	0.0	2.2	0.0	0.0	97.8	32.2	21.9	39.6	69.2	6.6	373	61.4
Latexo city	322	314	-2.5	433	77.8	11.8	0.0	2.1	8.3	38.1	11.8	29.9	56.3	7.9	153	82.4
La Tina Ranch CDP	618	-	-	666	1.8	0.0	0.0	0.0	98.2	32.1	0.0	29.6	72.6	0.0	180	91.7
Laughlin AFB CDP	1,569	-	-	2,244	65.1	9.0	1.7	7.2	16.9	18.9	0.0	24.1	6.6	61.5	646	100.0
Laureles CDP	3,692	-	-	4,529	0.5	2.3	0.0	0.0	97.2	30.4	4.9	27.0	65.9	15.4	1,083	85.7
La Vernia city	1,031	1,428	38.5	925	74.7	0.0	0.0	0.0	25.3	27.9	17.2	37.1	38.9	32.0	349	83.1
La Victoria CDP	171	-	-	49	0.0	0.0	0.0	0.0	100.0	0.0	42.9	61.8	73.5	12.2	29	51.7
La Villa city	2,439	2,870	17.7	2,720	0.6	0.0	0.0	0.0	99.4	36.2	10.5	27.3	70.0	10.6	653	81.3
Lavon city	2,223	3,724	67.5	3,271	63.0	12.9	3.5	3.2	17.4	33.4	8.0	32.5	26.0	32.7	1,038	98.9
La Ward city	213	224	5.2	305	62.3	0.7	0.0	0.0	37.0	23.9	7.2	35.1	64.4	3.1	96	93.8
Lawn town	314	321	2.2	408	75.7	1.0	0.0	1.0	22.3	24.0	19.6	38.5	60.5	12.9	147	89.8
League City city	83,584	107,536	28.7	103,310	64.2	8.3	5.6	2.6	19.3	27.8	10.6	35.2	20.6	47.2	36,350	97.4
Leakey city	425	438	3.1	642	65.1	0.0	0.0	0.0	34.9	46.0	18.5	23.8	58.8	18.6	185	66.5
Leander city	27,288	62,608	129.4	53,716	62.7	5.1	4.6	4.4	23.2	31.6	7.9	34.4	25.0	41.1	15,985	97.3
Leary city	483	502	3.9	550	86.0	9.8	0.0	3.8	0.4	23.6	18.5	47.4	49.7	17.2	213	76.1
Lefors town	497	480	-3.4	614	78.3	0.0	7.0	2.6	12.1	31.4	16.4	32.5	58.4	2.8	218	84.9
Leming CDP	946	-	-	582	10.8	0.0	0.0	0.0	89.2	27.7	27.7	47.0	92.4	0.0	225	78.2
Leona city	175	180	2.9	182	96.7	0.0	0.0	0.0	3.3	38.5	17.6	24.5	63.2	24.1	70	91.4
Leonard city	1,983	2,054	3.6	2,481	82.2	2.5	0.0	3.5	11.8	27.5	12.6	34.5	53.7	12.6	850	88.4
Leon Valley city	10,998	12,306	11.9	12,199	27.7	6.7	5.6	0.5	59.6	23.1	17.7	39.2	35.1	25.8	4,407	90.9
Leroy city	336	346	3.0	366	92.9	1.9	0.0	0.0	5.2	23.8	16.7	40.0	48.8	21.5	133	80.5
Levelland city	13,555	13,502	-0.4	13,596	39.7	4.5	0.4	1.7	53.7	25.2	14.1	32.9	51.8	15.3	4,855	84.3
Lewisville city	95,459	109,212	14.4	106,386	41.6	13.2	10.3	3.4	31.5	24.5	8.4	32.8	35.4	34.1	39,038	96.6
Lexington town	1,179	1,222	3.6	1,389	74.9	6.3	0.0	1.3	17.4	18.6	23.1	44.8	50.9	8.3	541	86.5
Liberty city	8,409	9,314	10.8	9,131	60.8	9.4	0.6	1.4	27.7	24.6	12.3	32.3	50.5	16.6	3,288	90.5
Liberty City CDP	2,351	-	-	2,315	76.5	3.8	0.6	9.2	9.9	23.4	14.3	38.2	36.3	18.5	820	98.2
Liberty Hill city	927	2,931	216.2	2,041	66.8	1.3	1.8	0.9	29.1	29.3	14.3	34.0	53.1	20.4	755	81.9
Lincoln Park town	308	558	81.2	12	100.0	0.0	0.0	0.0	0.0	0.0	25.0	64.4	41.7	16.7	10	100.0
Lindale city	4,821	6,464	34.1	6,011	88.7	2.9	1.7	0.0	6.7	22.9	22.0	39.9	36.4	29.5	2,330	90.5
Linden city	1,983	1,915	-3.4	1,944	67.5	29.7	0.3	0.3	2.2	22.2	20.8	43.3	53.7	11.8	786	80.5
Lindsay city	1,023	1,149	12.3	1,257	91.2	0.0	0.0	4.9	3.9	27.6	14.1	43.4	21.2	40.0	457	97.4
Lindsay CDP	271	-	-	722	8.0	0.0	0.0	0.0	92.0	18.2	3.5	32.5	70.7	4.9	161	80.7
Linn CDP	801	-	-	693	8.9	0.0	0.0	0.0	91.1	18.6	14.6	45.6	48.4	20.9	234	85.0
Lipan city	428	488	14.0	406	88.4	0.0	0.0	1.0	10.6	31.5	15.5	32.8	49.6	15.7	143	81.1
Lipscomb CDP	37	-	-	24	54.2	4.2	0.0	0.0	41.7	0.0	41.7	57.5	42.9	19.0	9	77.8
Little Elm city	25,892	53,126	105.2	45,967	49.1	17.4	5.9	4.9	22.7	30.6	6.9	34.4	25.7	43.1	14,468	98.5
Littlefield city	6,377	5,843	-8.4	5,956	34.7	4.3	0.7	2.3	58.1	31.6	13.8	31.4	59.3	12.1	2,033	82.6
Little River-Academy city	1,967	2,038	3.6	2,020	65.6	3.1	0.9	1.4	28.9	29.3	12.2	33.4	45.5	16.7	653	89.1
Live Oak city	13,137	16,499	25.6	15,855	41.9	14.3	4.9	5.5	33.4	25.5	12.8	35.1	35.4	26.6	5,988	97.1
Liverpool city	490	551	12.4	486	79.2	0.0	1.4	1.6	17.7	21.8	18.9	45.5	53.5	6.4	198	82.8
Livingston town	5,275	5,242	-0.6	5,115	45.9	17.3	4.2	4.4	28.1	21.6	15.9	38.5	59.8	16.0	1,990	76.6
Llano city	3,259	3,497	7.3	3,443	68.0	0.6	0.0	7.1	24.2	23.2	22.3	38.7	60.9	10.2	1,086	86.0
Llano Grande CDP	3,008	-	-	2,353	5.9	0.0	0.0	0.9	93.2	20.4	26.2	44.9	73.6	5.1	798	74.6
Lockhart city	12,690	14,133	11.4	13,652	36.1	6.6	2.8	1.1	53.3	21.4	15.4	39.4	60.3	15.2	4,275	88.2
Lockney town	1,842	1,631	-11.5	1,612	26.6	1.8	0.2	3.8	67.6	21.3	17.5	36.2	54.2	15.1	609	87.5
Log Cabin city	714	772	8.1	546	89.3	1.3	0.0	1.6	7.1	26.7	16.3	41.0	67.3	4.3	223	68.6
Lolita CDP	555	-	-	619	38.6	0.0	0.0	0.0	61.4	36.5	0.0	36.2	51.7	23.4	178	100.0
Loma Grande CDP	107	-	-	274	0.0	0.0	0.0	0.0	100.0	62.4	0.0	12.6	100.0	0.0	62	69.4
Loma Linda CDP	122	-	-	106	100.0	0.0	0.0	0.0	0.0	50.9	0.0	12.0	46.2	0.0	28	100.0
Loma Linda East CDP	254	-	-	296	0.0	0.0	0.0	0.0	100.0	0.0	4.7	44.8	92.3	0.0	96	100.0
Loma Linda East CDP	44	-	-	-	-	-	-	-	-	-	-	-	-	-	-	-
Loma Linda West CDP	114	-	-	218	0.0	0.0	0.0	0.0	100.0	50.0	10.1	26.5	90.8	0.0	33	100.0
Loma Vista CDP	160	-	-	283	0.0	0.0	0.0	0.0	100.0	32.5	11.7	24.9	100.0	0.0	56	100.0
Lometa city	847	861	1.7	524	56.5	0.8	1.7	0.0	41.0	20.6	13.7	43.3	55.9	19.6	203	74.4
Lone Oak city	593	692	16.7	639	90.1	3.3	0.0	4.7	1.9	31.3	7.7	33.2	56.2	16.6	239	88.7
Lone Star city	1,581	1,482	-6.3	1,790	65.7	17.6	0.9	3.6	12.2	27.2	14.7	34.5	48.8	11.7	751	90.3
Longoria CDP	92	-	-	67	0.0	0.0	0.0	0.0	100.0	0.0	100.0	0.0	100.0	0.0	19	0.0
Longview city	80,423	81,631	1.5	81,653	54.0	22.1	1.6	2.3	20.0	26.0	14.7	34.7	44.5	21.4	30,053	88.4
Loop CDP	225	-	-	394	57.9	0.3	0.0	0.0	41.9	46.4	9.1	32.1	50.8	22.6	101	94.1
Lopeño CDP	174	-	-	188	0.0	0.0	0.0	0.0	100.0	66.0	0.0	8.3	84.4	0.0	31	100.0
Lopezville CDP	4,333	-	-	2,957	0.4	0.0	0.0	0.0	99.6	32.2	11.5	25.6	83.7	0.9	706	76.8
Loraine town	602	564	-6.3	533	57.0	0.4	0.0	5.8	36.8	34.3	15.4	35.5	67.1	7.9	179	74.3
Lorena city	1,687	1,755	4.0	1,995	73.9	0.0	3.5	0.4	22.3	27.1	13.4	33.9	27.1	30.3	721	96.0
Lorenzo city	1,147	1,138	-0.8	1,181	19.7	3.6	1.2	2.1	73.4	30.2	13.5	34.3	69.4	3.9	376	81.6
Los Altos CDP	140	-	-	261	0.0	0.0	0.0	0.0	100.0	55.2	0.0	12.0	100.0	0.0	51	76.5
Los Alvarez CDP	303	-	-	263	0.0	0.0	0.0	0.0	100.0	0.0	7.6	26.7	96.9	3.1	53	86.8
Los Angeles CDP	121	-	-	-	-	-	-	-	-	-	-	-	-	-	-	-
Los Arcos CDP	127	-	-	63	0.0	0.0	0.0	0.0	100.0	17.5	33.3	50.8	100.0	0.0	30	100.0
Los Arrieros CDP	91	-	-	-	-	-	-	-	-	-	-	-	-	-	-	-
Los Barreras CDP	288	-	-	176	0.0	0.0	0.0	0.0	100.0	33.5	3.4	20.9	30.0	26.7	42	100.0
Los Centenarios CDP	87	-	-	-	-	-	-	-	-	-	-	-	-	-	-	-
Los Corralitos CDP	35	-	-	-	-	-	-	-	-	-	-	-	-	-	-	-
Los Ebanos CDP	335	-	-	84	0.0	0.0	0.0	0.0	100.0	0.0	46.4	33.9	46.4	0.0	61	36.1
Los Ebanos CDP	280	-	-	480	0.0	0.0	0.0	0.0	100.0	27.3	3.8	25.5	51.5	23.2	83	100.0
Los Fresnos city	7,038	7,837	11.4	7,738	10.4	0.0	0.0	1.5	88.0	35.7	7.9	29.0	52.2	14.5	2,062	94.4
Los Fresnos CDP	67	-	-	54	0.0	0.0	0.0	0.0	100.0	24.1	0.0	24.4	100.0	0.0	20	50.0
Los Huisaches CDP	17	-	-	13	0.0	0.0	0.0	0.0	100.0	0.0	100.0	0.0	0.0	0.0	7	100.0

1 May be of any race.

Table A. All Places — **Population and Housing**

STATE City, town, township, borough, or CDP (county if applicable)	Population: 2010 census total population	Population: 2019 estimated population	Population: Percent change 2010–2019	Population: ACS total population estimate 2015–2019	Race and Hispanic or Latino origin (percent): White alone, not Hispanic or Latino	Black alone, not Hispanic or Latino	Asian alone, not Hispanic or Latino	All other races or 2 or more races, not Hispanic or Latino	Hispanic or Latino[1]	Age (percent): Under 18 years old	Age 65 years and older	Median age	Educational attainment of persons age 25 and older: Percent High school diploma or less	Percent Bachelor's degree or more	Occupied housing units: Total	Percent with a computer
	1	2	3	4	5	6	7	8	9	10	11	12	13	14	15	16
TEXAS—Con.																
Los Indios town	1,033	1,060	2.6	850	2.0	0.0	0.0	0.0	98.0	19.9	16.5	38.6	71.4	7.5	263	65.4
Los Lobos CDP	9	-	-	-	-	-	-	-	-	-	-	-	-	-	-	-
Los Minerales CDP	20	-	-	19	0.0	0.0	0.0	0.0	100.0	31.6	0.0	36.5	100.0	0.0	6	100.0
Los Nopalitos CDP	62	-	-	86	0.0	0.0	0.0	0.0	100.0	62.8	0.0	4.3	100.0	0.0	9	0.0
Lost Creek CDP	-	-	-	1,099	66.4	4.0	15.3	0.0	14.3	23.7	15.3	48.2	3.4	82.9	368	100.0
Los Veteranos I CDP	24	-	-	47	0.0	0.0	0.0	0.0	100.0	53.2	0.0	16.9	100.0	0.0	11	100.0
Los Veteranos II CDP	24	-	-	32	0.0	0.0	0.0	0.0	100.0	0.0	100.0	69.6	100.0	0.0	26	0.0
Los Ybanez city	19	19	0.0	23	21.7	0.0	0.0	0.0	78.3	0.0	0.0	50.6	43.5	0.0	13	30.8
Lott city	761	742	-2.5	796	61.2	16.5	0.0	9.2	13.2	22.1	16.1	36.9	61.7	17.6	229	80.8
Louise CDP	995	-	-	963	33.6	0.0	0.0	0.0	66.4	28.1	9.1	31.5	54.1	14.0	329	98.2
Lovelady city	647	627	-3.1	654	90.2	9.0	0.0	0.5	0.3	26.9	24.5	39.5	44.4	23.6	296	79.7
Lowry Crossing city	1,708	1,727	1.1	1,349	86.5	1.0	1.9	1.0	9.7	17.9	15.3	48.9	34.1	29.6	504	96.4
Lozano CDP	404	-	-	177	0.0	0.0	0.0	0.0	100.0	40.1	26.0	18.7	70.0	0.0	24	0.0
Lubbock city	229,943	258,862	12.6	253,851	51.5	7.4	2.5	2.4	36.1	23.2	11.8	29.6	38.3	31.5	95,479	91.8
Lucas city	5,405	8,553	58.2	7,763	81.5	3.7	3.5	3.3	8.0	30.6	9.9	40.6	13.5	54.6	2,228	100.0
Lueders city	345	333	-3.5	183	88.0	0.0	0.0	1.1	10.9	20.2	33.9	55.9	71.5	6.2	104	68.3
Lufkin city	35,121	35,021	-0.3	35,465	42.1	23.5	2.1	2.4	29.9	25.8	15.7	33.5	46.5	21.7	12,661	90.0
Luling city	5,401	5,869	8.7	5,830	40.8	8.0	0.4	0.8	50.0	23.6	18.0	40.7	61.9	11.1	2,136	84.4
Lumberton city	11,972	13,073	9.2	12,692	91.0	0.2	0.7	1.8	6.3	25.9	17.2	38.5	41.9	23.8	4,664	92.8
Lyford city	2,608	2,540	-2.6	2,547	4.8	0.0	0.0	0.0	95.2	26.6	17.3	36.6	75.5	9.0	717	66.2
Lytle city	2,501	3,066	22.6	2,672	33.2	0.0	0.0	0.3	66.5	17.1	18.6	45.2	58.3	16.0	862	84.6
Mabank town	2,993	3,995	33.5	3,379	86.9	2.9	1.9	0.4	7.9	17.8	19.7	44.4	55.8	12.7	1,223	81.9
McAllen city	131,547	143,268	8.9	141,968	10.7	0.8	2.5	1.1	84.8	28.3	13.2	33.4	43.5	30.3	45,705	89.6
McCamey city	1,887	2,060	9.2	2,137	28.5	7.7	0.0	0.0	63.8	31.4	15.3	37.8	69.3	8.0	742	75.3
McDade CDP	685	-	-	681	62.4	0.0	0.0	6.3	31.3	19.5	11.7	33.0	74.5	5.1	227	74.9
Macdona CDP	559	-	-	232	37.1	0.0	0.0	0.0	62.9	31.0	26.3	56.5	80.7	0.0	90	77.8
McGregor city	4,987	5,331	6.9	5,144	49.8	4.6	0.0	1.4	44.2	26.3	14.2	35.7	56.5	12.4	1,631	91.7
McKinney city	131,152	199,177	51.9	182,055	59.2	11.8	8.4	3.0	17.6	28.7	10.4	36.2	23.4	47.4	62,576	96.9
McKinney Acres CDP	815	-	-	1,143	24.8	0.0	0.0	0.0	75.2	24.2	7.6	38.7	94.9	0.0	326	77.9
McLean town	778	744	-4.4	939	83.6	0.2	0.0	4.9	11.3	29.4	19.7	39.8	57.9	9.3	357	88.0
McLendon-Chisholm city	1,408	3,455	145.4	2,912	88.9	0.7	1.1	1.8	7.5	30.0	14.1	41.0	26.5	43.5	949	94.5
McQueeney CDP	2,545	-	-	2,328	66.0	0.1	0.0	0.2	33.7	20.2	18.6	44.6	55.1	19.7	1,024	92.2
Madisonville city	4,396	4,685	6.6	4,653	37.7	23.4	5.5	3.3	30.1	29.8	15.4	36.4	64.3	13.1	1,662	77.6
Magnolia city	1,377	2,093	52.0	2,124	61.3	9.3	0.2	15.9	13.3	26.3	15.8	36.6	46.9	16.9	722	90.2
Malakoff city	2,318	2,301	-0.7	2,760	60.7	22.6	0.0	1.3	15.4	28.4	13.4	32.1	60.0	6.9	914	71.6
Malone town	269	283	5.2	290	59.7	12.4	0.0	8.6	19.3	37.9	5.5	26.6	48.7	18.7	76	94.7
Manchaca CDP	1,133	-	-	1,254	71.5	0.2	1.0	0.0	27.3	24.5	16.3	46.0	23.8	39.9	427	93.4
Manor city	4,840	13,866	186.5	9,974	13.7	22.7	3.5	4.5	55.6	36.8	4.0	29.2	48.2	21.2	2,766	96.3
Mansfield city	56,654	72,419	27.8	69,557	55.2	18.5	4.5	3.6	18.2	29.2	10.0	35.9	23.1	42.3	22,527	97.6
Manuel Garcia CDP	203	-	-	438	0.0	0.0	0.0	0.0	100.0	39.7	9.8	22.0	100.0	0.0	81	71.6
Manuel Garcia II CDP	77	-	-	-	-	-	-	-	-	-	-	-	-	-	-	-
Manvel city	5,219	12,671	142.8	10,179	45.7	18.0	0.9	1.0	34.4	30.7	10.4	33.6	25.7	30.9	3,230	98.6
Marathon CDP	430	-	-	386	47.9	0.0	0.0	4.1	47.9	11.4	38.1	59.2	37.7	39.9	199	75.9
Marble Falls city	6,070	7,038	15.9	6,542	54.9	6.1	1.7	0.0	37.3	23.3	21.9	42.8	37.4	27.1	2,885	86.6
Marfa city	1,982	1,625	-18.0	1,831	27.6	0.0	0.1	0.0	72.3	22.4	28.1	42.8	44.0	32.5	698	87.7
Marietta town	134	129	-3.7	109	76.1	5.5	0.9	0.0	17.4	12.8	30.3	50.5	60.5	11.6	46	67.4
Marion city	1,066	1,241	16.4	970	42.2	7.9	0.4	0.5	49.0	19.4	20.5	43.6	61.1	9.5	387	82.9
Markham CDP	1,082	-	-	1,271	39.0	5.0	0.0	4.8	51.2	26.0	15.1	32.6	54.1	15.8	443	72.0
Marlin city	5,969	5,581	-6.5	5,607	23.7	47.1	0.2	0.2	28.8	24.8	15.6	35.5	66.9	6.8	1,644	63.1
Marquez city	262	274	4.6	265	80.0	0.0	0.0	0.0	20.0	29.4	17.0	39.3	62.3	7.2	95	61.1
Marshall city	23,513	22,831	-2.9	23,080	41.5	36.9	1.6	1.8	18.2	26.7	17.1	34.9	52.7	16.7	7,877	76.3
Mart city	1,898	1,963	3.4	1,984	51.2	29.3	0.1	1.0	18.4	31.3	17.0	34.3	53.8	9.2	666	79.9
Martindale city	1,130	1,231	8.9	913	34.0	1.9	0.0	3.6	60.6	19.4	22.8	45.3	54.6	27.2	386	88.1
Martinez CDP	69	-	-	-	-	-	-	-	-	-	-	-	-	-	-	-
Mason city	2,115	2,305	9.0	2,265	62.7	0.1	4.0	2.2	31.0	32.2	15.7	33.7	44.9	25.2	865	77.7
Matador town	612	611	-0.2	799	63.8	2.4	0.0	4.9	28.9	34.2	23.8	28.7	38.6	13.9	281	88.6
Matagorda CDP	503	-	-	434	89.9	0.0	0.0	1.2	9.0	26.7	21.4	52.1	41.9	5.1	193	76.7
Mathis city	4,942	4,715	-4.6	4,826	7.2	1.3	0.1	0.8	90.6	27.6	14.2	33.2	75.8	3.9	1,596	77.5
Maud city	1,056	1,042	-1.3	1,138	95.0	0.4	0.0	3.5	1.1	30.0	11.2	35.6	53.4	15.6	379	84.7
Mauriceville CDP	3,252	-	-	3,267	91.1	0.0	0.1	1.3	7.5	28.9	13.9	37.6	54.4	10.7	1,109	86.9
Maypearl city	919	1,032	12.3	938	75.3	2.6	4.1	0.7	17.4	35.2	11.5	29.1	47.9	7.5	280	89.3
Meadow town	593	585	-1.3	761	41.3	0.0	0.0	4.6	54.1	34.6	17.6	33.3	55.9	12.4	231	85.7
Meadowlakes city	1,665	1,703	2.3	2,525	94.1	0.0	0.0	0.5	5.4	24.0	29.3	48.1	24.4	46.7	977	93.6
Meadows Place city	4,617	4,591	-0.6	4,653	51.9	7.0	22.2	3.7	15.1	16.1	20.9	43.2	27.2	39.9	1,557	93.5
Medina CDP	3,935	-	-	4,727	0.0	0.0	0.0	0.0	100.0	38.8	4.0	24.8	84.1	5.2	1,304	93.8
Megargel town	203	188	-7.4	168	79.2	0.0	0.0	20.8	0.0	10.1	31.5	57.2	71.4	21.8	89	77.5
Melissa city	4,772	12,117	153.9	9,487	80.1	4.9	2.7	1.3	10.9	32.3	8.4	33.4	25.4	33.1	2,705	99.3
Melvin town	178	168	-5.6	184	33.7	0.0	0.0	16.3	50.0	28.8	31.5	52.4	67.4	10.1	72	62.5
Memphis city	2,290	2,012	-12.1	2,215	52.7	5.0	0.4	3.5	38.4	24.2	19.3	42.2	52.0	13.4	889	75.4
Menard city	1,471	1,404	-4.6	1,687	45.2	0.0	0.0	3.2	51.6	15.8	27.2	46.6	65.0	9.9	741	78.3
Mentone CDP	19	-	-	29	58.6	0.0	0.0	0.0	41.4	0.0	44.8	61.8	51.9	0.0	11	81.8
Mercedes city	15,633	16,604	6.2	16,564	6.0	0.2	0.0	0.0	93.8	32.7	15.2	31.6	62.9	11.0	4,670	83.2
Meridian city	1,509	1,515	0.4	1,528	68.0	3.7	2.0	1.2	25.1	29.8	15.7	35.7	57.4	12.4	547	88.7
Merkel town	2,590	2,617	1.0	2,609	80.3	1.1	0.3	0.5	17.7	28.3	15.4	38.0	49.7	12.1	986	91.1
Mertens town	125	128	2.4	138	85.5	0.0	0.0	0.0	14.5	34.8	22.5	28.4	46.6	9.6	47	83.0
Mertzon city	781	743	-4.9	924	63.5	7.1	0.0	0.9	28.5	31.9	7.5	33.1	38.4	19.6	352	92.9
Mesquite city	139,701	140,937	0.9	143,456	27.4	25.6	2.7	2.5	41.7	29.1	10.7	33.3	49.3	17.8	46,816	92.6
Mesquite CDP	505	-	-	355	0.0	0.0	0.0	0.0	100.0	29.9	18.3	42.9	91.5	8.5	86	79.1
Mexia city	7,446	7,344	-1.4	7,356	37.1	26.6	0.7	4.0	31.7	25.0	15.3	35.9	58.2	10.5	2,486	78.3
Miami city	597	550	-7.9	483	75.8	0.0	0.0	2.1	22.2	28.2	21.3	42.5	46.6	22.9	185	94.1
Midland city	111,193	146,038	31.3	138,549	44.8	7.3	2.1	1.6	44.2	27.6	10.4	31.7	40.1	28.9	47,242	92.5
Midlothian city	22,918	33,532	46.3	29,743	74.8	4.9	0.8	4.3	15.2	28.5	10.7	36.5	31.0	32.6	9,812	96.6
Midway city	228	236	3.5	370	72.4	5.9	0.0	1.4	20.3	37.0	6.2	33.0	53.3	18.9	128	92.2
Midway North CDP	4,752	-	-	4,792	1.3	0.0	0.0	0.0	98.7	32.9	6.4	27.7	63.5	13.5	1,144	83.1
Midway South CDP	2,239	-	-	2,420	0.9	0.0	0.0	0.0	99.1	39.2	7.4	25.3	62.8	8.7	623	80.1
Miguel Barrera CDP	128	-	-	229	0.0	0.0	0.0	0.0	100.0	54.1	0.0	13.0	93.7	6.3	45	75.6
Mikes CDP	910	-	-	897	4.9	0.0	0.0	0.0	95.1	46.6	12.7	20.9	100.0	0.0	177	55.4
Mila Doce CDP	6,222	-	-	5,947	0.2	0.0	0.0	0.0	99.8	37.6	8.3	24.7	82.3	4.1	1,492	78.3
Milam CDP	1,480	-	-	1,841	95.0	1.0	0.4	2.1	1.6	26.2	25.2	40.2	48.1	17.7	625	86.1
Milano city	417	421	1.0	488	53.1	12.3	0.0	1.2	33.4	27.7	16.6	36.5	62.5	17.9	183	82.5
Mildred town	351	392	11.7	402	82.3	0.0	0.5	14.4	2.7	28.6	13.2	31.5	43.1	15.0	117	86.3
Miles city	858	872	1.6	961	59.7	0.0	0.0	0.3	40.0	32.6	10.3	31.8	53.0	21.4	301	91.0

1 May be of any race.

STATE City, town, township, borough, or CDP (county if applicable)	Population: 2010 census total population	Population: 2019 estimated population	Population: Percent change 2010–2019	Population: ACS total population estimate 2015–2019	Race and Hispanic or Latino origin (percent): White alone, not Hispanic or Latino	Race: Black alone, not Hispanic or Latino	Race: Asian alone, not Hispanic or Latino	Race: All other races or 2 or more races, not Hispanic or Latino	Race: Hispanic or Latino[1]	Age (percent): Under 18 years old	Age: Age 65 years and older	Age: Median age	Educational attainment of persons age 25 and older: Percent High school diploma or less	Educational attainment: Percent Bachelor's degree or more	Occupied housing units: Total	Occupied housing units: Percent with a computer
	1	2	3	4	5	6	7	8	9	10	11	12	13	14	15	16
TEXAS—Con.																
Milford town	726	747	2.9	782	66.5	21.9	0.0	4.9	6.8	27.7	15.5	39.0	60.1	6.9	241	85.9
Miller's Cove town	149	160	7.4	184	12.0	0.0	0.0	0.0	88.0	40.2	8.2	23.1	94.6	0.0	51	66.7
Millican town	240	243	1.3	252	52.4	9.1	0.0	1.6	36.9	31.3	13.5	38.5	66.1	26.1	87	93.1
Millsap town	400	461	15.3	289	83.4	0.0	0.7	1.0	14.9	18.3	21.1	49.8	55.1	13.3	115	88.7
Mineola city	4,499	4,766	5.9	4,685	65.5	13.5	0.0	2.3	18.7	24.4	20.4	39.1	54.5	12.8	1,584	87.1
Mineral Wells city	16,792	15,213	-9.4	15,096	63.4	4.6	1.3	1.3	29.4	24.4	16.0	35.0	54.9	12.1	5,059	84.5
Mingus city	244	257	5.3	213	85.0	1.4	0.0	0.5	13.1	9.9	28.6	52.3	68.6	5.8	111	64.0
Mi Ranchito Estate CDP	281	-	-	602	0.0	0.0	0.0	0.0	100.0	53.8	6.3	17.3	84.2	0.0	119	74.8
Mirando City CDP	375	-	-	403	5.2	0.0	0.0	0.0	94.8	40.9	16.1	24.9	75.6	6.5	119	63.0
Mission city	77,695	84,331	8.5	83,567	8.0	0.0	1.8	0.2	90.0	32.8	11.7	31.7	50.4	25.9	24,427	89.6
Mission Bend CDP	36,501	-	-	37,979	11.6	28.3	12.9	1.3	45.9	23.9	10.5	34.9	46.9	21.4	10,774	94.6
Missouri City city	66,534	75,457	13.4	74,557	21.8	41.6	17.8	2.2	16.6	22.5	13.5	39.6	28.6	43.7	24,649	97.0
Mobeetie city	101	95	-5.9	78	97.4	0.0	0.0	0.0	2.6	0.0	23.1	55.3	39.7	4.1	47	100.0
Mobile City city	188	210	11.7	125	35.2	0.0	0.0	0.0	64.8	34.4	4.0	29.7	38.7	2.7	47	91.5
Monahans city	6,961	7,816	12.3	7,618	35.7	5.7	1.5	0.9	56.1	28.6	12.4	32.8	54.5	13.9	2,554	90.0
Montague CDP	304	-	-	384	88.0	3.1	0.0	0.0	8.9	24.5	13.3	31.7	54.6	12.3	106	93.4
Mont Belvieu city	3,839	6,574	71.2	5,885	79.0	8.5	0.0	1.5	11.0	29.1	11.2	33.8	25.5	31.7	2,199	90.3
Monte Alto CDP	1,924	-	-	1,968	0.0	0.0	0.0	0.0	100.0	29.9	11.2	26.5	64.8	11.5	511	86.9
Montgomery city	619	1,360	119.7	1,575	78.5	5.7	0.3	1.5	14.0	27.7	20.1	41.0	28.7	25.5	595	93.1
Moody city	1,371	1,420	3.6	1,654	60.9	8.6	0.4	1.1	29.0	31.3	11.4	29.9	63.1	6.7	540	83.0
Moore CDP	475	-	-	199	12.6	0.0	0.0	0.0	87.4	0.0	11.1	37.8	3.1	21.5	49	100.0
Moore Station city	206	220	6.8	281	3.6	96.4	0.0	0.0	0.0	29.2	15.7	37.6	59.6	6.0	88	72.7
Moraida CDP	212	-	-	-	-	-	-	-	-	-	-	-	-	-	-	-
Morales-Sanchez CDP	84	-	-	-	-	-	-	-	-	-	-	-	-	-	-	-
Moran city	270	260	-3.7	178	89.3	0.0	0.0	0.6	10.1	22.5	13.5	55.5	57.4	10.7	73	46.6
Morgan city	490	519	5.9	462	34.4	1.5	0.0	5.2	58.9	25.1	13.4	31.2	80.2	6.5	153	85.6
Morgan Farm CDP	463	-	-	327	45.6	0.0	2.1	1.8	50.5	35.8	15.0	25.6	47.0	10.1	118	100.0
Morgan's Point city	339	342	0.9	276	56.5	4.7	0.0	1.8	37.0	30.4	22.5	47.3	19.1	41.6	110	94.5
Morgan's Point Resort city	4,208	4,685	11.3	4,460	80.6	0.8	0.0	2.5	16.0	23.8	21.4	45.6	26.5	33.7	1,673	95.1
Morning Glory CDP	651	-	-	475	2.9	0.0	0.0	0.0	97.1	39.2	15.2	36.4	73.2	18.1	130	100.0
Morse CDP	147	-	-	102	52.9	0.0	0.0	0.0	47.1	8.8	18.6	55.4	54.8	19.2	38	71.1
Morton city	2,006	1,813	-9.6	1,939	25.4	4.5	0.0	1.1	69.0	27.8	15.8	34.1	65.2	6.7	701	80.3
Moulton town	885	899	1.6	925	71.0	0.0	2.2	0.8	26.1	21.9	27.5	45.2	63.0	11.1	364	79.7
Mountain City city	648	810	25.0	739	66.2	0.9	1.8	0.1	31.0	23.8	13.4	43.9	17.8	50.3	253	100.0
Mount Calm city	317	339	6.9	330	65.2	20.0	0.0	0.0	14.8	34.8	17.3	41.3	48.0	13.1	113	82.3
Mount Enterprise city	447	436	-2.5	448	80.1	6.5	0.0	2.0	11.4	23.4	18.8	43.2	55.7	23.5	181	96.1
Mount Pleasant city	15,982	15,978	0.0	15,973	31.4	14.0	1.5	2.7	50.4	30.0	12.4	32.2	57.9	16.5	5,193	87.7
Mount Vernon town	2,778	2,738	-1.4	2,749	63.2	15.2	0.2	2.7	18.7	28.4	19.4	34.9	42.1	23.3	976	86.3
Muenster city	1,520	1,645	8.2	1,418	86.0	0.5	1.6	0.9	10.9	24.3	19.4	38.8	36.4	32.5	552	87.7
Muleshoe city	5,158	5,019	-2.7	5,798	32.8	0.4	0.8	1.4	64.6	30.5	13.2	31.0	58.1	17.9	1,570	90.7
Mullin town	179	176	-1.7	84	100.0	0.0	0.0	0.0	0.0	19.0	41.7	63.4	85.3	5.9	38	52.6
Munday city	1,300	1,275	-1.9	1,155	52.9	5.5	0.0	0.0	41.6	24.2	17.9	35.7	52.9	23.0	464	88.8
Muniz CDP	1,370	-	-	1,188	0.0	0.0	0.0	0.0	100.0	27.0	1.1	26.5	77.7	2.4	281	100.0
Murchison city	592	599	1.2	498	71.9	3.8	0.2	0.0	24.1	26.5	19.7	39.4	46.5	12.3	199	91.5
Murillo CDP	7,344	-	-	7,266	2.0	0.0	0.0	0.2	97.8	42.6	3.2	22.0	48.3	19.7	1,761	85.3
Murphy city	17,877	20,500	14.7	20,612	51.5	15.7	23.2	3.2	6.3	32.6	8.7	37.9	18.8	56.3	5,475	99.1
Mustang town	21	21	0.0	-	-	-	-	-	-	-	-	-	-	-	-	-
Mustang Ridge city	828	981	18.5	1,116	25.4	1.8	0.0	2.6	70.3	31.0	9.8	30.6	64.9	12.0	306	87.6
Myrtle Springs CDP	828	-	-	563	100.0	0.0	0.0	0.0	0.0	6.9	43.3	54.1	61.0	18.9	259	80.3
Nacogdoches city	32,854	32,877	0.1	33,200	51.0	26.1	2.3	1.8	18.8	19.7	11.5	24.4	41.5	29.9	11,963	90.8
Naples city	1,375	1,313	-4.5	1,336	72.2	18.3	0.0	3.7	5.8	33.2	19.2	34.1	56.0	14.0	536	76.7
Narciso Pena CDP	30	-	-	-	-	-	-	-	-	-	-	-	-	-	-	-
Nash city	2,963	3,827	29.2	3,464	46.2	29.3	0.0	2.3	22.1	32.0	9.0	28.1	45.6	14.1	1,329	81.5
Nassau Bay city	4,002	3,972	-0.7	4,048	66.2	2.2	5.4	0.0	26.2	15.0	17.7	39.8	17.4	57.0	1,689	97.9
Natalia city	1,420	1,590	12.0	1,220	5.7	1.1	0.0	2.6	90.5	18.9	13.0	34.6	60.7	11.5	369	75.9
Navarro town	205	220	7.3	176	88.1	1.7	0.0	1.1	9.1	25.6	7.4	33.8	60.3	0.0	70	100.0
Navasota city	7,095	7,998	12.7	7,565	43.1	22.3	0.0	2.5	32.1	27.0	13.0	34.0	56.9	14.7	2,391	85.9
Nazareth city	311	291	-6.4	329	85.1	0.0	0.3	3.3	11.2	36.5	20.7	37.4	39.7	27.3	116	77.6
Nederland city	17,014	17,371	2.1	17,357	76.9	5.5	3.9	1.9	11.8	25.7	17.0	36.5	35.4	26.9	6,800	89.3
Needville city	2,929	3,103	5.9	3,068	50.4	13.5	0.4	0.7	35.0	25.6	16.0	38.8	52.6	18.7	1,080	89.8
Netos CDP	31	-	-	-	-	-	-	-	-	-	-	-	-	-	-	-
Nevada city	834	1,257	50.7	938	81.7	1.4	0.4	1.2	15.4	26.8	13.4	39.8	38.3	30.1	315	94.9
Newark city	1,006	1,232	22.5	1,290	59.4	0.3	0.2	2.8	37.4	26.9	9.6	35.0	55.8	11.1	369	94.9
New Berlin city	586	624	6.5	757	83.4	0.0	0.0	0.0	16.6	22.1	26.0	47.4	32.2	38.6	271	94.1
New Boston city	4,799	4,609	-4.0	4,660	71.8	19.5	0.9	4.4	3.4	16.6	16.3	44.0	55.7	15.7	1,939	67.3
New Braunfels city	57,676	90,209	56.4	79,438	60.4	1.9	1.4	1.8	34.4	25.2	14.8	36.5	35.9	34.7	28,835	92.0
Newcastle city	585	573	-2.1	620	79.8	0.8	0.0	0.6	18.7	32.1	20.2	28.3	69.2	10.4	254	85.4
New Chapel Hill city	592	646	9.1	759	75.1	0.5	0.3	0.7	23.5	27.3	14.5	35.9	36.3	19.8	248	94.4
New Deal town	793	827	4.3	915	46.9	0.8	0.0	5.0	47.3	34.4	13.4	29.3	60.1	4.3	278	93.2
New Fairview city	1,252	1,544	23.3	1,347	72.5	0.4	0.0	11.3	15.7	30.8	10.6	34.7	61.1	10.8	400	91.5
New Falcon CDP	191	-	-	301	0.0	0.0	0.0	0.0	100.0	48.5	6.6	26.2	100.0	0.0	78	74.4
New Home city	334	363	8.7	789	48.9	0.0	0.0	0.0	51.1	30.0	9.6	35.3	44.2	18.8	231	88.3
New Hope town	616	628	1.9	592	83.1	0.3	0.8	2.0	13.7	17.7	18.8	47.8	42.0	32.4	207	93.2
New London city	999	1,014	1.5	1,181	87.9	1.0	0.0	7.9	3.2	23.0	19.5	42.7	55.7	10.6	421	87.9
New Summerfield city	1,111	1,170	5.3	779	28.5	0.0	0.0	0.0	71.5	29.8	9.9	25.4	64.9	4.5	201	90.5
Newton city	2,470	2,370	-4.0	2,199	63.3	26.1	0.3	3.0	7.3	24.3	21.1	38.0	56.2	16.5	823	85.5
New Waverly city	1,032	1,071	3.8	1,142	62.5	30.7	1.1	0.4	5.3	28.5	18.0	29.6	51.1	15.5	432	73.4
Neylandville town	89	97	9.0	104	12.5	31.7	0.0	3.8	51.9	39.4	4.8	30.7	42.4	0.0	24	75.0
Niederwald city	538	599	11.3	576	40.8	6.1	0.9	1.2	51.0	23.8	24.7	43.3	68.1	10.1	186	91.4
Nina CDP	141	-	-	48	0.0	0.0	0.0	0.0	100.0	25.0	27.1	59.2	75.0	0.0	22	100.0
Nixon city	2,385	2,542	6.6	2,510	14.5	2.1	0.0	0.2	83.1	31.4	7.3	27.9	83.9	2.8	761	82.8
Nocona city	3,034	3,002	-1.1	2,960	77.7	0.1	0.0	2.6	19.6	24.7	21.8	37.8	65.6	11.4	1,177	80.2
Nocona Hills CDP	675	-	-	674	96.9	0.0	0.0	0.0	3.1	8.3	34.9	60.9	37.9	25.0	341	84.5
Nolanville city	4,519	5,879	30.1	5,496	61.8	15.3	1.2	4.1	17.5	32.0	8.1	28.7	38.2	21.8	1,909	96.5
Nome city	577	595	3.1	494	78.7	14.0	0.0	0.0	7.3	20.6	21.1	40.2	34.1	29.1	177	96.0
Noonday city	675	722	7.0	471	71.5	9.8	0.2	0.8	17.6	11.7	25.7	53.8	46.6	19.1	229	88.2
Nordheim city	307	303	-1.3	313	63.3	4.5	0.0	1.3	31.0	16.3	24.0	46.9	57.9	12.4	124	76.6
Normangee town	685	706	3.1	586	72.9	16.2	0.0	4.3	6.7	27.5	11.8	41.9	58.7	20.9	190	88.9
Normanna CDP	113	-	-	137	46.7	0.0	0.0	0.0	53.3	21.2	16.1	39.1	71.4	18.7	43	93.0
North Alamo CDP	3,235	-	-	3,727	6.0	0.0	0.0	0.0	94.0	34.3	10.7	27.8	51.2	17.9	1,023	66.7
North Cleveland city	245	298	21.6	228	68.9	0.0	0.0	1.8	29.4	22.8	14.9	40.0	65.3	4.0	91	94.5
North Escobares CDP	118	-	-	64	0.0	0.0	0.0	0.0	100.0	0.0	60.9	68.4	100.0	0.0	26	100.0

1 May be of any race.

Table A. All Places — **Population and Housing**

STATE City, town, township, borough, or CDP (county if applicable)	Population: 2010 census total population	Population: 2019 estimated population	Population: Percent change 2010–2019	Population: ACS total population estimate 2015–2019	Race and Hispanic or Latino origin (percent): White alone, not Hispanic or Latino	Black alone, not Hispanic or Latino	Asian alone, not Hispanic or Latino	All other races or 2 or more races, not Hispanic or Latino	Hispanic or Latino[1]	Age (percent): Under 18 years old	Age 65 years and older	Median age	Educational attainment of persons age 25 and older: Percent High school diploma or less	Percent Bachelor's degree or more	Occupied housing units: Total	Percent with a computer
	1	2	3	4	5	6	7	8	9	10	11	12	13	14	15	16
TEXAS—Con.																
Northlake town	1,725	3,348	94.1	2,726	79.7	5.1	3.1	3.7	8.5	29.1	5.0	33.2	15.8	43.5	1,049	98.6
North Pearsall CDP	614	-	-	684	2.0	0.0	0.0	0.0	98.0	17.5	12.3	34.7	75.7	5.6	190	85.8
North Richland Hills city	63,341	70,670	11.6	70,202	68.0	6.7	4.4	4.3	16.6	23.3	15.4	38.7	31.3	33.5	26,500	96.1
North San Pedro CDP	895	-	-	645	0.0	0.0	0.0	0.0	100.0	22.3	14.3	45.3	80.0	0.0	212	64.2
Novice city	139	128	-7.9	110	47.3	0.0	0.0	6.4	46.4	17.3	14.5	56.0	74.7	0.0	39	69.2
Oak Grove town	543	669	23.2	579	84.5	1.9	0.5	2.2	10.9	24.5	26.3	42.1	38.1	22.6	186	96.8
Oakhurst CDP	233	-	-	267	100.0	0.0	0.0	0.0	0.0	0.0	16.5	46.6	100.0	0.0	69	100.0
Oak Island CDP	363	-	-	439	29.8	7.1	54.4	0.0	8.7	18.5	17.3	42.3	56.6	9.8	142	86.6
Oak Leaf city	1,390	1,484	6.8	1,613	61.6	20.3	1.2	1.6	15.4	19.8	21.1	44.8	35.9	32.7	544	97.2
Oak Point city	2,782	5,762	107.1	4,410	67.5	8.4	2.8	1.0	20.4	24.5	12.8	40.8	24.5	38.0	1,551	98.5
Oak Ridge town	141	242	71.6	237	64.6	0.0	0.0	0.8	34.6	21.5	12.7	29.7	64.7	2.3	72	95.8
Oak Ridge town	471	742	57.5	698	73.9	10.0	0.0	0.0	16.0	28.8	13.8	35.2	49.0	15.1	200	93.5
Oak Ridge North city	3,061	3,161	3.3	3,149	86.0	1.1	1.0	1.0	10.9	17.5	24.0	47.0	31.6	29.9	1,139	97.1
Oak Trail Shores CDP	2,755	-	-	3,101	56.9	0.0	0.0	0.0	43.1	33.9	13.2	32.7	66.9	6.4	944	93.6
Oak Valley town	366	421	15.0	528	91.1	1.3	0.0	1.1	6.4	23.5	20.1	43.3	49.6	9.2	191	83.2
Oakwood town	510	515	1.0	787	57.2	35.2	0.3	4.2	3.2	28.1	21.3	35.3	51.6	15.6	203	82.8
O'Brien city	106	102	-3.8	110	64.5	0.0	0.0	8.2	27.3	2.7	40.9	61.3	57.1	19.5	46	63.0
Odem city	2,445	2,360	-3.5	2,649	12.1	0.0	0.0	0.0	87.9	30.2	12.8	33.1	57.9	14.5	828	79.6
Odessa city	99,876	123,334	23.5	119,702	33.8	5.6	1.4	1.7	57.6	28.9	10.1	30.7	49.7	18.5	40,827	90.2
O'Donnell city	831	837	0.7	766	33.9	1.0	4.6	0.0	60.4	20.5	17.0	41.6	61.1	14.1	325	72.6
Oglesby city	494	465	-5.9	619	65.9	1.0	0.0	9.7	23.4	30.5	16.6	33.9	54.0	10.8	221	89.1
Oilton CDP	353	-	-	153	0.0	0.0	0.0	7.8	92.2	15.7	6.5	42.5	19.0	12.0	75	92.0
Old River-Winfree city	1,204	1,467	21.8	1,958	85.5	6.3	0.0	5.1	3.2	31.0	13.4	37.4	57.1	14.1	652	86.5
Olivarez CDP	3,827	-	-	5,621	0.2	0.0	0.0	0.0	99.8	52.3	5.7	16.1	70.3	12.7	1,074	96.6
Olivia Lopez de Gutierrez CDP	93	-	-	20	0.0	0.0	0.0	0.0	100.0	0.0	50.0	0.0	100.0	0.0	20	0.0
Olmito CDP	1,210	-	-	1,416	2.7	0.0	0.0	0.0	97.3	26.8	9.7	33.6	66.3	6.3	437	86.5
Olmito and Olmito CDP	271	-	-	188	0.0	0.0	0.0	0.0	100.0	62.8	0.0	14.5	100.0	0.0	43	100.0
Olmos Park city	2,238	2,466	10.2	1,832	72.5	4.1	0.0	0.7	22.7	23.7	18.2	43.0	11.1	76.4	687	98.4
Olney city	3,285	3,099	-5.7	3,117	75.0	0.5	0.3	1.7	22.4	23.7	21.0	40.6	50.3	23.9	1,290	83.8
Olton city	2,215	2,060	-7.0	2,013	21.6	0.6	0.0	1.5	76.2	26.1	17.7	37.6	64.9	10.8	687	73.4
Omaha city	1,031	980	-4.9	889	74.9	21.1	0.0	0.3	3.6	22.6	25.8	46.3	58.1	13.3	364	85.7
Onalaska city	2,651	2,967	11.9	2,779	90.6	0.9	0.2	1.8	6.5	21.8	18.7	43.1	60.8	6.8	1,226	85.4
Opdyke West town	174	194	11.5	222	46.8	5.4	0.0	0.0	47.7	27.5	10.4	26.7	61.1	2.4	98	87.8
Orange city	18,602	18,118	-2.6	18,762	54.0	32.1	4.2	1.8	7.9	23.0	16.2	38.4	46.6	16.9	7,766	85.0
Orange Grove city	1,318	1,302	-1.2	1,418	48.9	0.0	0.0	0.6	50.5	40.7	12.1	26.8	58.6	15.9	434	55.5
Orason CDP	129	-	-	229	3.5	0.0	0.0	0.0	96.5	49.3	5.2	21.1	27.6	0.0	43	100.0
Orchard city	349	407	16.6	212	56.6	0.0	0.0	2.4	41.0	9.4	45.3	53.9	66.7	7.8	104	78.8
Ore City city	1,141	1,228	7.6	1,071	72.5	6.6	0.0	5.6	15.2	28.6	13.9	35.2	53.4	9.0	380	81.8
Overton city	2,552	2,503	-1.9	2,896	79.6	9.9	0.1	0.5	10.0	29.0	10.0	30.9	50.5	12.5	938	83.8
Ovilla city	3,513	4,167	18.6	3,903	72.2	17.0	0.0	2.5	8.3	23.9	18.7	45.2	24.1	41.7	1,416	98.4
Owl Ranch CDP	225	-	-	117	0.0	0.0	0.0	0.0	100.0	23.9	18.8	44.0	100.0	0.0	57	61.4
Oyster Creek city	1,106	1,193	7.9	1,236	60.8	8.7	0.0	3.4	27.0	25.6	10.7	34.8	58.7	6.9	501	84.6
Ozona CDP	3,225	-	-	2,930	29.8	0.6	0.0	0.0	69.6	23.4	16.7	40.6	62.2	13.4	1,159	82.9
Pablo Pena CDP	63	-	-	14	0.0	0.0	0.0	0.0	100.0	0.0	0.0	0.0	0.0	0.0	9	100.0
Paducah town	1,188	1,094	-7.9	1,276	48.2	14.8	0.0	11.7	25.3	32.7	22.3	37.3	56.0	16.2	553	66.2
Paint Rock town	274	296	8.0	223	79.4	0.0	0.0	0.0	20.6	27.8	39.0	54.3	38.4	11.9	74	67.6
Paisano Park CDP	130	-	-	52	100.0	0.0	0.0	0.0	0.0	44.2	0.0	35.3	27.6	0.0	19	100.0
Palacios city	4,713	4,535	-3.8	4,590	18.6	2.8	11.0	1.6	65.9	29.8	11.3	31.4	67.2	14.3	1,670	82.8
Palestine city	18,713	17,730	-5.3	17,989	48.1	27.7	1.4	2.2	20.7	26.2	14.6	33.7	58.5	12.8	6,441	82.2
Palisades village	325	353	8.6	346	81.8	1.2	0.0	3.2	13.9	27.2	17.1	39.9	49.4	13.3	119	93.3
Palmer town	2,002	2,123	6.0	2,279	51.0	2.5	0.1	5.1	41.4	32.2	13.4	32.3	64.7	9.6	717	93.4
Palmhurst city	2,537	2,732	7.7	2,713	11.2	0.4	1.5	0.0	86.9	30.2	14.7	36.1	26.2	45.7	794	90.2
Palm Valley city	1,316	1,240	-5.8	1,557	55.1	0.0	0.0	0.3	44.6	18.1	36.2	55.2	15.9	46.5	713	93.1
Palmview city	5,472	5,774	5.5	5,733	2.0	0.0	0.0	0.0	98.0	27.7	11.6	29.2	68.0	13.9	1,746	82.1
Palmview South CDP	5,575	-	-	5,589	25.0	0.0	0.0	0.0	75.0	28.1	32.0	42.9	68.6	12.5	1,859	83.2
Palo Blanco CDP	204	-	-	82	0.0	0.0	0.0	0.0	100.0	28.0	0.0	32.7	76.6	23.4	20	100.0
Paloma Creek CDP	2,501	-	-	3,298	64.5	24.3	1.0	1.2	8.9	35.9	7.2	34.7	17.6	32.8	1,012	96.0
Paloma Creek South CDP	2,753	-	-	7,986	59.1	20.3	2.9	8.2	9.4	31.1	4.9	34.4	17.9	49.5	2,657	98.8
Palo Pinto CDP	333	-	-	147	78.9	18.4	0.0	0.0	2.7	15.0	13.6	39.7	53.7	2.8	33	100.0
Pampa city	17,998	17,068	-5.2	17,538	62.0	3.3	0.1	2.5	32.0	27.3	15.9	35.4	51.9	14.8	6,633	85.8
Panhandle town	2,454	2,312	-5.8	2,649	85.3	1.7	0.2	2.1	10.8	25.8	16.3	36.6	34.7	36.8	970	95.4
Panorama Village city	2,170	2,424	11.7	3,207	84.5	1.3	0.5	1.2	12.5	20.9	27.3	48.6	32.1	36.7	1,388	96.5
Pantego town	2,394	2,519	5.2	2,531	78.7	4.3	5.2	3.2	8.5	17.9	29.4	51.7	29.8	41.3	1,111	87.3
Paradise city	442	561	26.9	548	71.5	0.0	0.9	1.5	26.1	29.2	19.0	37.1	65.5	10.5	202	85.1
Paris city	25,263	24,847	-1.6	24,807	63.9	20.8	1.2	4.7	9.4	23.8	19.0	37.7	51.9	15.0	10,523	78.3
Parker city	3,733	5,177	38.7	4,722	54.9	4.2	15.8	1.9	23.2	27.8	13.1	38.1	29.7	48.4	1,291	99.5
Pasadena city	149,307	151,227	1.3	153,350	24.0	2.3	2.0	1.2	70.5	29.8	10.0	31.6	60.0	14.4	48,019	91.3
Pattison city	485	620	27.8	507	49.3	3.6	0.0	4.9	42.2	22.7	17.6	47.8	51.4	25.7	190	86.8
Patton Village city	1,597	2,157	35.1	1,457	54.8	0.3	0.0	0.5	44.5	28.6	9.7	33.2	74.4	2.6	432	88.4
Pawnee CDP	166	-	-	143	4.2	0.0	0.0	0.0	95.8	28.7	28.0	42.4	73.0	0.0	43	69.8
Payne Springs town	758	769	1.5	732	89.2	0.0	0.5	3.7	6.6	20.1	26.6	45.9	53.7	13.5	295	80.0
Pearland city	93,117	122,460	31.5	122,078	42.2	17.7	14.1	2.8	23.2	27.7	10.8	35.0	21.9	47.2	41,507	97.4
Pearsall city	9,150	10,609	15.9	10,436	14.8	1.7	1.3	0.0	82.2	21.6	11.7	32.8	70.0	5.2	2,464	69.0
Pecan Acres CDP	4,099	-	-	5,259	86.1	0.0	1.1	1.4	11.4	30.8	10.8	41.6	31.8	37.0	1,607	96.7
Pecan Gap city	198	197	-0.5	181	92.3	7.7	0.0	0.0	0.0	9.4	30.4	51.7	48.3	15.4	73	94.5
Pecan Grove CDP	15,963	-	-	17,380	60.2	8.8	2.6	1.7	26.7	22.8	14.0	41.3	20.7	46.7	6,080	98.5
Pecan Hill city	651	694	6.6	866	68.8	5.1	0.2	3.8	22.1	17.6	16.3	48.0	50.2	13.6	290	94.8
Pecan Plantation CDP	5,294	-	-	6,243	94.1	0.0	1.0	3.4	1.5	12.1	45.3	62.7	21.9	42.0	2,566	99.0
Pecos city	8,780	10,461	19.1	10,108	24.0	1.5	1.7	0.1	72.7	25.3	15.7	35.6	59.4	11.0	2,543	79.1
Pelican Bay city	1,543	2,005	29.9	1,586	85.4	0.4	0.4	1.9	11.9	24.0	11.7	35.0	63.3	6.4	543	89.3
Pena CDP	118	-	-	175	0.0	0.0	0.0	0.0	100.0	21.7	0.0	19.9	100.0	0.0	36	100.0
Penelope town	198	207	4.5	167	52.7	0.0	3.6	0.0	43.7	31.7	16.2	35.8	62.0	8.3	54	66.7
Penitas city	4,342	4,716	8.6	4,769	1.8	0.0	1.9	0.0	96.3	41.0	6.7	21.7	76.8	10.3	1,150	96.7
Perezville CDP	5,376	-	-	4,555	24.4	0.0	0.0	0.2	75.4	19.6	29.5	45.3	66.8	11.9	1,690	87.6
Perrin CDP	398	-	-	216	100.0	0.0	0.0	0.0	0.0	4.6	30.6	53.5	85.6	0.0	109	89.9
Perryton city	8,806	8,512	-3.3	9,205	39.2	0.1	0.2	2.3	58.2	32.5	9.6	31.2	61.8	13.8	3,073	89.5
Petersburg city	1,202	1,132	-5.8	1,057	28.2	0.7	0.5	0.6	70.1	27.0	13.6	36.4	61.4	12.3	378	78.0
Petrolia city	686	670	-2.3	540	93.9	0.0	0.0	2.2	3.9	19.8	30.0	53.2	66.1	4.5	239	77.0
Petronila city	113	120	6.2	103	30.1	0.0	0.0	0.0	69.9	14.6	9.7	47.5	40.5	33.3	46	100.0
Pettus CDP	558	-	-	479	66.0	0.0	0.0	0.0	34.0	21.7	25.5	42.3	35.2	10.3	168	71.4
Pflugerville city	48,370	65,380	35.2	61,737	45.2	14.7	7.0	4.1	28.9	25.9	9.3	36.1	30.4	39.0	21,186	98.8

1 May be of any race.

Table A. All Places — **Population and Housing**

STATE City, town, township, borough, or CDP (county if applicable)	Population				Race and Hispanic or Latino origin (percent)					Age (percent)			Educational attainment of persons age 25 and older		Occupied housing units	
	2010 census total population	2019 estimated population	Percent change 2010–2019	ACS total population estimate 2015–2019	White alone, not Hispanic or Latino	Black alone, not Hispanic or Latino	Asian alone, not Hispanic or Latino	All other races or 2 or more races, not Hispanic or Latino	Hispanic or Latino[1]	Under 18 years old	Age 65 years and older	Median age	Percent High school diploma or less	Percent Bachelor's degree or more	Total	Percent with a computer
	1	2	3	4	5	6	7	8	9	10	11	12	13	14	15	16
TEXAS—Con.																
Pharr city	70,457	79,112	12.3	78,073	5.3	0.1	0.3	0.0	94.3	34.5	12.2	29.2	61.2	14.9	22,095	81.7
Pilot Point city	4,010	4,525	12.8	4,364	67.2	4.3	0.0	3.5	25.0	24.1	17.3	41.0	45.6	21.6	1,718	85.0
Pine Forest city	487	519	6.6	611	82.8	0.0	0.0	1.0	16.2	22.1	17.8	38.7	59.0	11.8	209	92.8
Pine Harbor CDP	810	-	-	715	82.4	1.8	0.0	9.9	5.9	26.2	20.6	45.6	63.9	15.0	323	77.7
Pinehurst CDP	4,624	-	-	6,021	63.0	0.0	0.5	1.2	35.3	33.0	10.8	33.2	54.9	20.3	1,707	96.0
Pinehurst city	2,097	1,976	-5.8	2,380	71.5	14.0	0.0	3.1	11.4	17.4	19.4	40.5	47.7	13.6	971	92.4
Pine Island town	965	1,159	20.1	1,312	44.9	12.0	1.5	2.3	39.3	31.4	15.2	33.6	50.6	17.0	427	85.5
Pineland city	849	800	-5.8	619	69.5	26.5	0.0	1.3	2.7	18.7	26.5	49.7	69.7	10.1	275	78.9
Pinewood Estates CDP	1,678	-	-	1,628	88.4	3.9	1.1	1.7	4.9	33.0	18.5	38.5	17.4	52.0	516	96.1
Piney Point Village city	3,140	3,444	9.7	3,425	77.0	0.6	10.8	2.8	8.8	21.4	27.8	52.5	6.4	84.1	1,214	96.4
Pittsburg city	4,525	4,697	3.8	4,640	37.5	26.0	0.0	2.0	34.5	30.6	14.8	32.6	54.8	20.4	1,581	75.9
Placedo CDP	692	-	-	515	13.2	6.8	0.0	0.0	80.0	19.2	25.8	45.4	71.8	10.3	215	68.8
Plains town	1,481	1,655	11.7	1,242	25.0	0.0	0.3	0.0	74.7	28.1	13.0	39.4	63.8	10.2	428	85.7
Plainview city	22,194	20,143	-9.2	20,492	28.0	5.2	0.4	1.7	64.7	28.0	13.6	32.9	58.6	18.3	6,864	86.7
Plano city	259,859	287,677	10.7	287,064	52.4	8.5	21.1	3.1	15.0	22.5	12.8	38.7	19.4	57.2	105,854	97.7
Plantersville city	556	594	6.8	431	60.1	17.6	1.9	0.0	20.4	21.8	27.1	56.8	53.7	21.2	204	68.6
Pleak village	1,036	1,675	61.7	1,475	41.3	6.6	1.7	1.1	49.4	24.7	12.6	33.8	46.6	18.7	494	92.1
Pleasant Hill CDP	522	-	-	665	23.6	0.0	0.0	0.0	76.4	13.7	6.9	40.1	59.4	12.0	227	73.1
Pleasanton city	9,583	10,855	13.3	10,557	41.9	0.1	0.9	2.5	54.7	30.6	15.8	31.4	54.1	20.3	3,354	92.3
Pleasant Valley town	341	330	-3.2	311	87.5	1.9	0.0	2.6	8.0	17.0	22.8	54.1	47.3	21.2	139	87.8
Plum Grove city	595	726	22.0	541	64.5	0.0	0.0	2.4	33.1	23.7	13.5	36.1	68.8	1.7	207	89.9
Point city	820	926	12.9	909	70.1	6.5	0.3	7.5	15.6	27.6	13.1	34.8	64.2	5.8	302	79.8
Point Blank city	690	752	9.0	761	82.5	3.7	1.2	4.6	8.0	18.8	32.6	56.4	60.3	14.1	334	84.4
Point Comfort city	737	677	-8.1	696	56.8	6.3	1.4	6.2	29.3	22.6	13.4	35.6	49.5	12.3	268	89.9
Point Venture village	800	1,033	29.1	1,221	90.5	2.5	0.2	1.1	5.7	26.0	17.4	43.4	25.5	38.4	458	98.0
Ponder town	1,388	2,369	70.7	2,369	68.8	7.7	0.7	6.4	16.5	35.5	9.8	31.0	41.1	29.3	750	92.5
Port Aransas city	3,480	4,266	22.6	4,123	83.8	1.1	1.5	4.4	9.1	12.5	18.7	52.8	29.5	40.1	2,029	94.5
Port Arthur city	54,376	54,280	-0.2	55,109	18.7	38.1	7.3	1.4	34.5	27.1	12.7	34.5	61.1	11.7	20,010	79.8
Porter Heights CDP	1,653	-	-	2,066	97.3	1.3	0.0	1.4	0.0	10.6	20.8	50.3	53.6	3.2	668	100.0
Port Isabel city	6,350	6,256	-1.5	6,292	17.9	0.0	1.1	0.0	81.0	23.0	20.9	41.7	69.2	12.0	2,207	88.4
Portland city	15,653	17,268	10.3	17,025	55.0	1.1	1.9	0.8	41.2	26.8	13.3	35.9	34.7	27.1	5,979	94.7
Port Lavaca city	12,249	11,854	-3.2	12,147	26.2	3.3	8.7	0.5	61.3	24.4	16.1	36.8	57.5	13.5	4,254	87.6
Port Mansfield CDP	226	-	-	87	78.2	0.0	0.0	0.0	21.8	0.0	44.8	62.9	54.0	24.1	53	88.7
Port Neches city	13,042	12,655	-3.0	12,782	78.6	3.3	3.5	3.5	11.2	23.9	17.4	40.2	33.3	26.1	4,936	92.6
Port O'Connor CDP	1,253	-	-	884	76.0	0.0	0.0	8.1	15.8	20.0	20.4	36.4	40.6	9.1	306	99.0
Post city	5,376	5,115	-4.9	5,193	32.9	6.6	2.0	0.2	58.3	16.0	11.5	39.2	71.5	11.5	1,197	87.6
Post Oak Bend City town	458	587	28.2	446	86.5	10.1	0.0	0.4	2.9	30.0	14.8	36.0	32.2	22.3	150	97.3
Poteet city	3,264	3,507	7.4	3,437	10.4	0.0	1.3	1.5	86.8	20.5	12.7	35.1	70.7	9.3	1,068	84.3
Poth town	1,908	2,284	19.7	2,035	37.2	0.0	0.0	0.4	62.4	26.1	12.1	34.4	55.3	16.8	591	88.8
Potosi CDP	2,991	-	-	3,677	76.7	0.7	4.0	2.5	16.2	31.2	14.3	36.3	24.3	29.4	1,239	96.4
Pottsboro town	2,162	2,489	15.1	2,465	86.8	0.0	0.0	4.8	8.4	29.7	12.8	36.5	31.7	22.2	858	99.3
Powderly CDP	1,178	-	-	1,064	88.0	1.9	0.0	2.0	8.2	15.3	21.4	53.3	50.0	14.1	509	83.7
Powell town	135	146	8.1	96	58.3	18.8	0.0	4.2	18.8	13.5	35.4	59.5	70.0	18.8	38	73.7
Poynor town	305	306	0.3	265	70.9	0.0	0.0	0.0	29.1	34.7	16.2	38.5	47.7	5.2	85	76.5
Prado Verde CDP	246	-	-	259	17.8	0.0	0.0	0.0	82.2	29.0	3.9	39.5	21.0	28.4	100	90.0
Prairie View city	5,566	6,953	24.9	6,678	2.9	90.5	0.5	1.8	4.3	6.0	3.4	20.3	36.3	25.6	874	92.7
Premont city	2,653	2,543	-4.1	2,580	9.3	0.3	0.3	0.0	90.1	15.7	19.0	44.3	65.5	10.9	822	78.3
Presidio city	4,431	3,894	-12.1	4,019	1.9	0.0	2.0	0.0	96.1	26.8	24.7	42.6	74.7	14.0	1,425	55.4
Preston CDP	2,096	-	-	1,991	93.9	0.0	0.0	2.6	3.6	10.3	32.7	56.3	35.0	17.5	984	89.2
Primera town	4,164	5,130	23.2	4,872	10.3	2.8	0.0	0.0	86.9	34.7	7.7	27.8	56.3	19.6	1,429	76.3
Princeton city	6,822	13,894	103.7	10,846	58.0	11.4	2.2	1.8	26.5	31.0	8.0	32.6	38.8	25.2	3,582	96.1
Progreso city	5,501	5,944	8.1	5,905	0.0	0.0	0.0	0.0	100.0	31.3	12.3	29.0	70.1	13.3	1,468	85.9
Progreso Lakes city	289	291	0.7	302	30.1	0.7	0.0	0.0	69.2	33.4	12.6	37.2	32.6	37.6	81	97.5
Prosper town	9,527	24,579	158.0	22,517	77.5	7.1	4.9	3.4	7.1	33.8	6.9	35.8	17.0	57.0	6,634	98.7
Providence Village town	4,865	7,377	51.6	7,141	73.2	11.2	1.7	2.7	11.2	35.9	3.5	30.4	25.2	37.5	2,123	99.3
Pueblo East CDP	-	-	-	-	-	-	-	-	-	-	-	-	-	-	-	-
Pueblo Nuevo CDP	521	-	-	737	0.0	0.0	0.0	0.0	100.0	41.2	8.4	19.3	90.3	3.7	146	60.3
Putnam town	94	93	-1.1	93	100.0	0.0	0.0	0.0	0.0	4.3	37.6	63.6	47.1	7.1	49	73.5
Pyote town	114	132	15.8	121	66.9	0.0	0.0	13.2	19.8	28.9	9.1	30.6	62.7	9.3	51	92.2
Quail CDP	19	-	-	8	100.0	0.0	0.0	0.0	0.0	0.0	62.5	67.5	37.5	25.0	3	100.0
Quail Creek CDP	1,628	-	-	1,961	49.4	5.6	0.0	1.1	44.0	19.0	13.0	39.6	45.1	26.8	843	82.3
Quanah city	2,638	2,487	-5.7	2,474	75.9	6.0	0.0	4.6	13.5	22.8	22.4	45.8	53.5	10.2	1,070	81.9
Queen City city	1,477	1,436	-2.8	1,644	74.3	22.6	0.0	2.0	1.1	26.3	15.6	36.2	58.9	13.8	687	76.3
Quemado CDP	230	-	-	143	0.0	0.0	0.0	0.0	100.0	0.0	48.3	57.9	100.0	0.0	75	0.0
Quesada CDP	25	-	-	56	0.0	0.0	0.0	0.0	100.0	76.8	0.0	13.8	100.0	0.0	13	100.0
Quinlan city	1,379	1,524	10.5	1,560	88.7	1.3	1.7	2.1	6.3	21.9	20.5	46.5	55.9	14.9	620	88.4
Quintana town	84	94	11.9	17	70.6	0.0	0.0	0.0	29.4	0.0	17.6	54.8	23.5	52.9	16	100.0
Quitaque city	411	389	-5.4	442	47.1	2.7	0.0	9.7	40.5	17.4	21.0	42.8	51.8	19.9	185	79.5
Quitman city	1,809	1,849	2.2	2,115	81.0	5.6	0.0	2.2	11.2	21.8	24.1	38.6	47.7	16.1	773	82.7
Radar Base CDP	762	-	-	196	0.0	0.0	0.0	0.0	100.0	0.0	13.3	41.3	65.9	0.0	50	62.0
Rafael Pena CDP	17	-	-	-	-	-	-	-	-	-	-	-	-	-	-	-
Ralls city	1,944	1,806	-7.1	1,816	33.7	1.8	1.0	0.0	63.5	26.7	18.6	39.0	59.7	10.8	649	80.1
Ramireno CDP	35	-	-	69	0.0	0.0	0.0	0.0	100.0	68.1	0.0	17.5	59.1	0.0	9	100.0
Ramirez-Perez CDP	78	-	-	45	0.0	0.0	0.0	0.0	100.0	0.0	0.0	0.0	100.0	0.0	19	100.0
Ramos CDP	116	-	-	196	0.0	0.0	0.0	0.0	100.0	45.4	0.0	20.6	83.7	11.6	49	100.0
Ranchette Estates CDP	152	-	-	239	0.0	0.0	0.0	0.0	100.0	25.1	0.0	25.3	53.1	0.0	56	100.0
Ranchitos del Norte CDP	112	-	-	1,307	0.0	0.0	0.0	0.0	100.0	49.3	0.0	22.1	74.7	4.5	123	100.0
Ranchitos East CDP	212	-	-	506	0.0	0.0	0.0	0.0	100.0	47.0	2.8	24.2	94.6	5.4	117	56.4
Ranchitos Las Lomas CDP	266	-	-	400	0.0	0.0	0.0	0.0	100.0	22.5	16.3	36.4	80.9	7.4	91	78.0
Rancho Alegre CDP	1,704	-	-	1,223	5.2	0.0	0.0	0.0	94.8	24.6	14.7	40.0	77.3	5.4	337	68.5
Rancho Banquete CDP	424	-	-	484	16.5	0.0	0.0	0.0	83.5	19.4	25.0	40.7	85.5	0.0	143	71.3
Rancho Chico CDP	396	-	-	725	30.1	0.0	0.0	0.0	69.9	34.1	4.6	22.3	76.2	4.8	141	87.9
Ranchos Penitas West CDP	573	-	-	1,152	0.0	0.0	0.0	0.0	100.0	47.2	2.7	20.2	46.5	38.2	231	87.0
Rancho Viejo town	2,437	2,460	0.9	2,894	30.9	0.0	6.8	0.0	62.3	27.0	16.0	42.3	14.2	56.2	1,042	96.6
Rancho Viejo CDP	228	-	-	147	0.0	0.0	0.0	0.0	100.0	57.8	0.0	15.3	58.1	0.0	34	100.0
Randolph AFB CDP	1,241	-	-	1,123	68.0	3.9	5.0	4.5	18.5	45.0	1.2	20.9	6.2	72.7	261	99.6
Ranger city	2,469	2,469	0.0	2,865	80.2	4.8	0.2	0.9	13.9	22.1	20.0	34.5	61.6	5.9	869	76.2
Rankin city	778	851	9.4	923	59.9	5.3	1.8	0.3	32.6	25.7	14.5	42.4	64.8	9.4	330	83.0
Ransom Canyon town	1,096	1,124	2.6	1,056	87.9	0.0	0.3	0.7	11.2	18.9	22.3	54.7	20.9	53.2	432	97.9
Ratamosa CDP	254	-	-	90	100.0	0.0	0.0	0.0	0.0	0.0	43.3	55.7	100.0	0.0	20	100.0

1 May be of any race.

Table A. All Places — **Population and Housing**

STATE City, town, township, borough, or CDP (county if applicable)	Population				Race and Hispanic or Latino origin (percent)					Age (percent)			Educational attainment of persons age 25 and older		Occupied housing units	
	2010 census total population	2019 estimated population	Percent change 2010–2019	ACS total population estimate 2015–2019	White alone, not Hispanic or Latino	Black alone, not Hispanic or Latino	Asian alone, not Hispanic or Latino	All other races or 2 or more races, not Hispanic or Latino	Hispanic or Latino[1]	Under 18 years old	Age 65 years and older	Median age	Percent High school diploma or less	Percent Bachelor's degree or more	Total	Percent with a computer
	1	2	3	4	5	6	7	8	9	10	11	12	13	14	15	16
TEXAS—Con.																
Ravenna city	209	225	7.7	167	71.3	0.0	0.0	18.6	10.2	18.6	27.5	45.2	48.8	4.0	80	65.0
Raymondville city	11,270	10,880	-3.5	11,021	7.2	1.1	0.0	0.0	91.7	22.2	13.7	33.0	73.2	6.7	2,685	84.3
Realitos CDP	184	-	-	213	0.0	0.0	0.0	0.0	100.0	27.2	16.9	49.7	84.5	7.1	75	61.3
Redfield CDP	441	-	-	250	16.8	20.8	0.0	27.6	34.8	36.0	16.0	28.7	58.1	8.8	77	75.3
Redford CDP	90	-	-	121	0.0	0.0	0.0	0.0	100.0	62.8	0.0	12.3	100.0	0.0	19	0.0
Redland CDP	1,047	-	-	1,223	46.4	29.0	0.0	0.0	24.5	22.2	13.5	39.0	58.6	8.6	413	86.2
Red Lick city	1,011	1,010	-0.1	1,078	80.8	7.7	8.2	3.1	0.3	23.3	18.1	45.0	26.0	37.6	379	87.9
Red Oak city	10,733	13,464	25.4	12,724	42.6	32.3	0.8	4.0	20.4	30.7	10.8	34.3	33.9	23.9	4,040	96.0
Redwater city	1,061	1,101	3.8	1,145	86.5	7.9	0.2	1.0	4.4	29.0	13.8	32.1	48.6	14.7	379	76.3
Redwood CDP	4,338	-	-	4,033	10.6	1.5	0.0	0.5	87.4	24.1	8.7	33.8	75.8	7.9	1,153	94.6
Refugio town	2,893	2,734	-5.5	2,806	30.5	12.8	0.1	0.8	55.8	26.4	18.7	37.3	59.5	10.5	972	80.7
Regino Ramirez CDP	85	-	-	57	0.0	0.0	0.0	0.0	100.0	64.9	0.0	17.1	70.0	0.0	14	100.0
Reid Hope King CDP	786	-	-	874	0.0	0.0	0.0	0.0	100.0	47.5	13.4	24.7	73.5	18.0	192	64.1
Reklaw city	381	395	3.7	481	67.6	17.7	0.0	0.4	14.3	33.3	11.6	27.0	55.2	20.1	143	93.0
Relampago CDP	132	-	-	383	19.8	0.0	0.0	0.0	80.2	12.3	20.4	47.7	35.9	19.2	101	89.1
Rendon CDP	12,552	-	-	13,150	71.3	5.5	0.1	1.0	22.1	27.9	15.0	40.1	40.1	29.3	4,443	96.1
Reno city	3,184	3,346	5.1	3,309	87.5	5.3	2.1	2.4	2.7	19.9	24.2	47.6	31.9	29.2	1,421	90.7
Reno city	2,493	3,204	28.5	2,962	87.4	0.9	0.1	2.5	9.0	21.1	17.9	44.5	55.8	10.7	1,009	87.7
Retreat town	366	384	4.9	459	77.6	2.2	0.0	0.0	20.3	34.9	15.9	29.8	47.1	14.4	149	90.6
Rhome city	1,519	1,845	21.5	1,813	84.2	0.3	0.2	0.7	14.7	28.0	8.1	34.3	48.8	16.4	566	94.0
Ricardo CDP	1,048	-	-	674	14.4	0.0	0.0	0.0	85.6	18.8	15.0	38.2	44.7	26.1	213	81.7
Rice city	908	974	7.3	1,092	63.2	4.0	0.0	1.6	31.2	29.6	7.4	33.4	65.6	10.1	332	92.5
Richardson city	99,251	121,323	22.2	116,432	52.7	10.6	15.8	3.1	17.8	22.1	14.5	35.6	20.7	53.2	42,747	97.4
Richland town	264	273	3.4	226	79.2	15.0	0.0	0.9	4.9	14.2	27.4	53.1	49.4	10.2	94	75.5
Richland Hills city	7,787	7,953	2.1	8,051	61.0	2.4	2.7	8.6	25.3	19.4	18.0	42.6	46.6	22.7	3,094	90.1
Richland Springs town	318	309	-2.8	249	83.5	0.0	0.0	0.0	16.5	19.7	28.5	54.8	65.9	14.8	101	88.1
Richmond city	12,090	12,578	4.0	12,646	19.9	16.5	6.7	2.1	54.8	24.2	11.6	33.8	58.2	17.7	3,982	85.4
Richwood city	3,512	3,988	13.6	3,911	41.9	3.5	0.5	1.2	52.9	30.4	8.7	31.6	40.4	16.9	1,462	92.7
Riesel city	1,006	1,037	3.1	1,141	78.6	4.6	0.0	0.4	16.4	32.1	6.7	33.3	51.9	15.7	380	94.2
Rio Bravo city	4,802	4,634	-3.5	4,710	2.8	0.0	0.0	0.0	97.2	37.2	7.5	26.4	78.0	7.9	1,177	59.6
Rio Grande City city	13,808	14,511	5.1	14,408	1.3	0.1	0.0	0.1	98.5	30.0	12.7	32.1	65.7	13.9	3,906	77.8
Rio Hondo city	2,397	2,707	12.9	2,640	6.5	0.0	0.0	0.0	93.5	26.6	23.4	42.9	59.2	11.8	928	68.9
Rio Vista city	875	1,075	22.9	1,038	91.2	0.0	0.0	1.7	7.0	29.6	11.7	34.3	61.3	11.4	334	91.9
Rising Star town	835	821	-1.7	876	83.7	0.0	0.0	0.5	15.9	22.0	17.2	37.1	55.5	7.3	304	91.1
Rivereno CDP	61	-	-	22	0.0	0.0	0.0	0.0	100.0	0.0	0.0	0.0	100.0	0.0	22	100.0
River Oaks city	7,419	7,630	2.8	7,685	43.6	0.0	0.5	0.8	55.1	25.7	11.7	35.2	55.9	14.9	2,644	96.5
Riverside city	511	549	7.4	494	65.4	27.9	0.0	4.3	2.4	19.8	26.1	46.1	67.2	5.3	186	65.1
Riviera CDP	689	-	-	616	32.3	0.0	0.0	0.0	67.7	16.1	19.2	45.9	60.0	11.8	222	80.2
Roanoke city	5,962	9,388	57.5	8,341	66.4	4.0	6.9	2.7	20.0	24.3	8.4	35.0	33.0	37.4	2,776	94.9
Roaring Springs town	234	231	-1.3	187	91.4	0.0	0.0	8.6	0.0	3.2	57.8	66.7	73.7	11.1	101	75.2
Robert Lee city	1,044	1,048	0.4	1,240	73.2	0.0	0.0	1.9	24.9	26.5	20.0	40.9	47.6	21.3	562	84.5
Robinson city	10,503	11,926	13.5	11,646	74.5	3.6	0.6	3.8	17.5	29.4	15.3	36.3	33.4	26.6	3,945	94.3
Robstown city	11,486	11,261	-2.0	11,400	5.6	0.2	0.0	0.2	93.9	32.1	19.6	32.2	63.6	11.3	3,822	73.6
Roby city	643	619	-3.7	785	45.7	5.9	0.0	0.0	48.4	30.7	14.8	32.0	60.3	14.3	246	79.7
Rochester town	324	307	-5.2	464	45.9	15.1	0.0	1.3	37.7	22.4	16.2	41.0	68.9	5.1	179	70.9
Rockdale city	5,528	5,503	-0.5	5,531	50.4	11.1	0.6	0.5	37.3	27.4	16.1	34.6	61.2	6.3	1,954	91.3
Rockport city	10,022	10,604	5.8	10,841	64.0	2.8	2.2	1.7	29.2	16.0	28.6	50.3	38.4	31.7	3,960	94.6
Rocksprings town	1,179	1,135	-3.7	1,271	24.8	0.0	0.0	0.2	75.1	17.8	26.5	48.0	69.5	10.0	490	63.9
Rockwall city	37,559	45,888	22.2	44,101	71.1	5.9	3.1	2.7	17.2	25.5	12.9	38.3	23.1	42.6	15,654	95.9
Rocky Mound town	68	75	10.3	109	62.4	34.9	0.0	0.0	2.8	23.9	27.5	50.4	26.0	49.4	54	94.4
Rogers town	1,223	1,252	2.4	1,365	67.3	4.2	0.0	1.6	27.0	32.3	12.2	37.8	57.7	3.6	421	86.7
Rollingwood city	1,398	1,585	13.4	1,532	87.7	0.0	2.0	2.9	7.3	31.1	18.2	42.9	2.2	87.8	525	98.3
Roma city	10,861	11,490	5.8	11,397	0.2	0.0	0.0	0.0	99.8	28.8	17.8	34.2	75.8	10.6	3,125	71.0
Roman Forest city	1,573	2,006	27.5	1,727	83.3	2.1	0.8	3.7	10.2	19.9	18.1	41.6	35.7	22.6	623	96.3
Ropesville city	434	427	-1.6	352	28.1	0.0	0.0	2.6	69.3	28.1	10.2	36.8	54.2	9.3	144	78.5
Roscoe city	1,332	1,285	-3.5	1,361	38.7	0.0	0.0	0.0	61.3	20.9	14.0	41.4	48.8	24.0	500	83.4
Rosebud city	1,431	1,349	-5.7	1,585	46.9	11.0	0.0	0.3	41.8	27.0	18.3	34.5	73.2	8.0	424	73.1
Rose City city	502	484	-3.6	467	87.6	0.0	0.6	1.9	9.9	24.0	10.7	37.9	51.5	8.9	170	81.2
Rose Hill Acres city	441	436	-1.1	399	84.7	0.0	0.0	0.0	15.3	22.6	17.8	42.3	47.8	9.7	154	90.9
Rosenberg city	31,248	38,307	22.6	37,059	22.8	14.3	2.3	1.3	59.4	29.9	10.1	30.6	52.4	17.9	12,059	88.1
Rosharon CDP	1,152	-	-	1,115	41.1	5.0	0.0	1.2	52.7	28.8	6.9	34.5	61.9	3.2	366	96.4
Rosita CDP	2,704	-	-	2,792	0.8	0.0	0.0	14.8	84.4	38.3	3.2	23.3	76.4	1.5	595	79.7
Ross city	273	284	4.0	258	86.8	0.0	0.4	1.9	10.9	14.7	28.7	53.0	35.9	24.6	97	77.3
Rosser village	330	400	21.2	285	58.9	10.5	0.0	11.2	19.3	28.4	12.3	40.5	66.8	7.3	110	64.5
Rotan city	1,508	1,438	-4.6	1,404	48.6	4.0	0.9	7.1	39.5	21.6	22.9	44.8	56.4	12.9	643	72.2
Round Mountain town	154	169	9.7	236	84.7	0.0	0.0	0.0	15.3	16.1	8.9	44.8	53.1	23.8	93	98.9
Round Rock city	100,021	133,372	33.3	124,434	50.6	10.2	6.8	3.1	29.4	26.9	8.2	34.3	27.4	40.0	39,243	98.0
Round Top town	90	90	0.0	85	94.1	0.0	0.0	3.5	2.4	7.1	56.5	67.3	6.4	38.5	44	95.5
Rowlett city	56,242	67,339	19.7	63,793	53.2	16.6	7.3	3.2	19.7	24.9	11.5	39.3	28.9	35.5	21,161	98.1
Roxton city	650	639	-1.7	723	82.7	9.3	0.0	4.7	3.3	29.6	13.6	32.6	55.8	15.7	249	80.3
Royse City city	9,693	14,702	51.7	12,982	63.5	10.5	0.5	2.5	23.0	28.8	7.5	31.3	36.6	25.0	4,209	96.8
Rule town	634	599	-5.5	540	64.8	1.7	1.5	1.9	30.2	19.3	32.2	54.8	77.8	8.5	261	78.2
Runaway Bay city	1,286	1,576	22.6	1,845	90.0	0.0	0.2	1.0	8.7	17.6	23.1	47.6	32.9	26.9	682	95.9
Runge town	1,027	1,138	10.8	1,048	10.9	0.5	0.0	0.8	87.9	27.6	23.7	40.1	69.4	7.5	386	66.3
Rusk city	5,557	5,602	0.8	5,559	47.1	31.4	0.7	3.6	17.2	15.7	9.2	39.0	62.5	9.6	1,245	93.0
Sabinal city	1,695	1,673	-1.3	1,534	36.0	0.0	0.0	0.3	63.8	31.9	26.2	35.4	68.7	7.3	539	64.6
Sachse city	20,289	26,046	28.4	25,607	55.1	10.0	14.2	3.8	16.9	25.8	10.2	37.1	32.8	34.1	8,090	98.2
Sadler city	347	383	10.4	599	89.6	0.0	0.0	4.0	6.3	11.7	8.7	33.4	48.2	3.6	226	82.7
Saginaw city	20,048	24,310	21.3	23,321	61.3	4.7	2.5	2.0	29.5	27.8	12.2	36.3	42.4	25.1	8,037	96.7
St. Hedwig town	2,083	2,488	19.4	1,973	88.4	0.1	0.0	1.8	9.7	27.0	18.4	38.1	38.2	27.4	614	91.9
St. Jo city	1,043	1,030	-1.2	897	94.6	0.6	0.0	3.5	1.3	27.9	14.4	31.5	59.9	12.7	329	89.4
St. Paul town	1,011	1,051	4.0	865	71.9	1.3	1.6	5.4	19.8	27.9	12.1	43.1	28.1	40.5	280	98.6
St. Paul CDP	584	-	-	966	54.1	0.0	0.0	0.0	45.9	21.7	8.7	33.5	57.2	6.6	226	88.1
Salado village	2,160	2,370	9.7	3,002	79.0	2.2	0.6	3.1	15.0	26.6	25.1	41.6	22.1	51.1	1,070	97.0
Salineño CDP	201	-	-	174	0.0	0.0	0.0	0.0	100.0	27.6	1.1	20.9	49.4	0.0	46	65.2
Salineño North CDP	115	-	-	48	0.0	0.0	0.0	0.0	100.0	22.9	27.1	61.3	83.8	0.0	18	100.0
Sammy Martinez CDP	110	-	-	-	-	-	-	-	-	-	-	-	-	-	-	-
Samnorwood CDP	51	-	-	30	100.0	0.0	0.0	0.0	0.0	63.3	0.0	9.3	0.0	100.0	5	100.0
Sam Rayburn CDP	1,181	-	-	950	97.3	0.0	1.9	0.0	0.8	21.1	38.7	58.9	47.4	21.3	401	79.3
San Angelo city	93,221	101,004	8.3	100,031	49.9	4.6	1.3	1.6	42.6	23.4	15.1	33.3	43.3	24.7	37,159	87.9
San Antonio city	1,326,161	1,547,253	16.7	1,508,083	24.7	6.4	2.7	1.9	64.2	25.0	12.0	33.6	43.9	26.0	501,400	89.9
San Augustine city	2,112	1,888	-10.6	1,889	37.9	45.7	0.0	2.1	14.3	19.6	22.0	47.2	53.5	21.6	858	81.5

1 May be of any race.

Table A. All Places — **Population and Housing**

STATE City, town, township, borough, or CDP (county if applicable)	Population				Race and Hispanic or Latino origin (percent)					Age (percent)			Educational attainment of persons age 25 and older		Occupied housing units	
	2010 census total population	2019 estimated population	Percent change 2010–2019	ACS total population estimate 2015–2019	White alone, not Hispanic or Latino	Black alone, not Hispanic or Latino	Asian alone, not Hispanic or Latino	All other races or 2 or more races, not Hispanic or Latino	Hispanic or Latino[1]	Under 18 years old	Age 65 years and older	Median age	Percent High school diploma or less	Percent Bachelor's degree or more	Total	Percent with a computer
	1	2	3	4	5	6	7	8	9	10	11	12	13	14	15	16
TEXAS—Con.																
San Benito city	24,252	24,243	0.0	24,371	6.9	0.1	0.0	0.2	92.8	29.4	16.6	34.1	65.5	10.1	7,564	78.9
San Carlos CDP	3,130	-	-	4,020	1.5	0.0	0.0	0.0	98.5	34.6	6.9	25.6	71.9	4.5	973	70.7
San Carlos I CDP	316	-	-	302	0.0	0.0	0.0	0.0	100.0	20.2	23.5	45.6	100.0	0.0	74	83.8
San Carlos II CDP	261	-	-	306	0.0	0.0	0.0	0.0	100.0	58.8	0.0	13.8	78.8	10.6	65	58.5
Sanctuary town	285	321	12.6	301	92.0	1.0	0.0	1.3	5.6	21.9	18.6	42.8	49.8	12.6	99	92.9
Sanderson CDP	837	-	-	774	33.7	1.3	0.0	2.8	62.1	13.6	34.5	56.0	43.4	14.7	355	75.2
Sandia CDP	379	-	-	900	13.0	0.0	0.0	0.0	87.0	24.3	19.1	36.9	65.7	2.9	303	81.2
San Diego city	4,474	4,221	-5.7	4,018	4.9	0.0	0.0	0.0	95.1	32.3	13.8	33.7	67.8	6.3	1,308	74.7
Sandoval CDP	32	-	-	-	-	-	-	-	-	-	-	-	-	-	-	-
Sand Springs CDP	835	-	-	827	63.8	0.0	0.0	0.0	36.2	21.6	20.8	42.2	52.9	15.8	317	85.8
Sandy Hollow-Escondidas CDP	296	-	-	296	71.3	0.0	0.0	0.0	28.7	15.2	32.4	54.5	40.2	29.2	95	84.2
Sandy Oaks city	3,753	4,660	24.2	4,471	13.0	1.3	0.4	2.1	83.2	27.4	7.0	32.1	62.7	4.0	1,161	93.0
Sandy Point city	197	236	19.8	170	65.3	17.6	0.0	1.2	15.9	15.9	17.6	44.5	55.3	13.6	62	85.5
San Elizario city	9,244	9,089	-1.7	9,126	1.1	0.0	0.3	0.0	98.6	33.2	12.7	27.7	67.5	11.4	2,484	92.1
San Felipe town	746	825	10.6	766	53.1	31.5	0.0	1.3	14.1	21.7	24.9	46.7	44.9	15.0	316	75.6
San Fernando CDP	68	-	-	4	0.0	0.0	0.0	0.0	100.0	0.0	0.0	0.0	100.0	0.0	4	100.0
Sanford town	163	156	-4.3	121	81.0	4.1	0.0	2.5	12.4	20.7	19.0	39.5	60.9	16.1	36	97.2
Sanger city	6,931	8,732	26.0	8,235	70.4	6.4	0.6	2.6	20.0	25.5	12.6	33.7	47.5	20.0	2,793	93.9
San Isidro CDP	240	-	-	137	0.0	0.0	0.0	0.0	100.0	23.4	7.3	40.5	43.2	9.5	46	67.4
San Juan city	33,969	37,008	8.9	36,744	2.5	0.0	0.0	0.1	97.4	32.5	9.9	29.7	63.0	13.4	9,519	83.0
San Juan CDP	129	-	-	118	0.0	0.0	0.0	0.0	100.0	33.1	12.7	23.6	69.0	14.3	27	74.1
San Leanna village	495	507	2.4	676	79.3	0.0	0.0	0.1	20.6	14.2	19.4	37.7	34.8	45.7	243	94.2
San Leon CDP	4,970	-	-	5,336	54.2	0.2	6.1	1.4	38.1	19.3	14.7	40.4	54.0	12.1	1,958	97.5
San Marcos city	45,139	64,776	43.5	63,220	46.2	6.2	2.5	2.0	43.1	13.9	7.5	24.2	37.7	33.5	23,154	94.4
San Patricio city	390	375	-3.8	394	55.8	0.0	0.0	0.0	44.2	19.3	20.6	50.2	39.3	13.8	140	97.1
San Pedro CDP	530	-	-	438	3.4	0.0	0.0	0.0	96.6	35.6	6.2	26.9	60.9	4.9	116	71.6
San Perlita city	573	556	-3.0	730	4.0	0.0	0.0	0.0	96.0	27.1	14.0	34.8	67.2	10.6	178	61.8
San Saba city	3,208	3,168	-1.2	3,128	48.8	3.5	0.0	3.5	44.2	24.2	15.0	34.2	68.6	9.3	944	81.8
Sansom Park city	4,680	5,748	22.8	5,411	34.3	3.9	0.2	2.8	58.7	30.7	9.6	31.8	74.1	5.6	1,476	93.4
Santa Anna town	1,099	1,007	-8.4	994	71.2	6.0	0.0	4.9	17.8	22.7	16.8	43.8	48.7	10.5	361	84.5
Santa Anna CDP	13	-	-	13	0.0	0.0	0.0	0.0	100.0	0.0	0.0	0.0	61.5	0.0	13	38.5
Santa Clara city	696	751	7.9	1,032	56.7	2.8	0.4	0.9	39.2	20.2	14.3	43.5	37.0	31.3	355	95.5
Santa Cruz CDP	54	-	-	-	-	-	-	-	-	-	-	-	-	-	-	-
Santa Fe city	12,313	13,449	9.2	13,274	82.2	0.4	0.2	3.5	13.7	23.5	18.8	40.7	41.6	14.7	4,621	90.3
Santa Maria CDP	733	-	-	628	0.0	0.0	0.0	0.0	100.0	19.7	27.7	40.0	80.9	6.0	192	46.9
Santa Monica CDP	83	-	-	-	-	-	-	-	-	-	-	-	-	-	-	-
Santa Rosa town	2,873	2,723	-5.2	2,784	0.4	0.0	0.0	0.0	99.6	31.6	8.6	33.2	77.4	7.0	791	68.5
Santa Rosa CDP	241	-	-	231	0.0	0.0	0.0	0.0	100.0	33.8	19.9	35.3	77.7	9.9	62	93.5
Santel CDP	44	-	-	8	0.0	0.0	0.0	0.0	100.0	0.0	100.0	0.0	50.0	50.0	4	100.0
San Ygnacio CDP	667	-	-	695	2.9	0.0	0.0	0.0	97.1	21.0	31.8	60.8	72.3	7.7	257	54.9
Sarita CDP	238	-	-	513	3.9	0.0	0.0	0.0	96.1	31.4	26.7	39.6	96.3	0.0	166	55.4
Savannah CDP	3,318	-	-	5,953	73.1	7.4	1.4	5.0	13.2	32.2	11.3	32.8	22.2	47.2	2,032	100.0
Savoy city	836	872	4.3	867	83.5	1.6	0.0	6.3	8.5	17.6	27.5	47.1	57.7	11.4	300	82.7
Scenic Oaks CDP	4,957	-	-	6,469	65.7	1.1	6.5	4.4	22.4	32.2	14.6	38.1	15.9	58.0	1,948	100.0
Schertz city	31,824	42,042	32.1	41,199	50.7	10.7	3.0	4.3	31.4	25.8	13.3	38.0	30.1	36.6	14,149	96.9
Schulenburg city	2,854	2,913	2.1	2,899	56.8	13.3	0.8	0.4	28.7	24.0	20.7	43.7	62.4	16.3	1,052	66.2
Scissors CDP	3,186	-	-	3,594	0.4	0.0	0.0	2.2	97.4	38.7	7.4	23.4	84.6	5.5	812	73.6
Scotland city	501	474	-5.4	463	66.5	0.0	0.0	0.0	33.5	32.8	11.7	29.4	51.7	18.9	146	85.6
Scottsville city	358	354	-1.1	397	39.3	54.7	0.0	1.5	4.5	34.5	15.9	34.0	50.0	14.9	146	75.3
Scurry town	655	781	19.2	464	87.5	4.7	0.0	2.6	5.2	21.6	14.4	42.9	38.3	27.8	175	82.3
Seabrook city	11,945	14,149	18.5	13,927	71.6	4.3	2.0	1.3	20.7	23.0	10.6	37.7	20.9	42.1	5,479	97.3
Seadrift city	1,364	1,493	9.5	1,181	57.3	0.0	5.2	1.9	35.6	29.3	11.4	38.0	69.1	6.1	363	84.3
Seagoville city	14,902	16,861	13.1	16,514	37.3	16.5	0.3	1.7	44.1	28.4	10.9	35.8	64.5	9.8	4,209	85.8
Seagraves city	2,417	2,936	21.5	2,836	15.0	3.9	0.0	0.0	81.1	38.3	10.6	28.3	74.8	6.1	730	83.0
Sealy city	6,123	6,446	5.3	6,450	47.7	8.6	0.0	3.0	40.8	26.5	17.8	37.4	53.9	15.5	2,394	86.8
Sebastian CDP	1,917	-	-	1,515	3.8	0.0	0.0	0.0	96.2	27.4	17.5	36.3	63.9	7.3	518	66.8
Seco Mines CDP	560	-	-	545	13.8	0.0	0.0	0.0	86.2	46.6	12.7	19.0	64.0	13.6	138	62.3
Seguin city	25,600	29,992	17.2	28,894	39.0	6.7	2.0	1.1	51.2	24.5	17.0	35.1	59.7	17.0	10,173	84.3
Selma city	5,539	11,132	101.0	10,419	33.0	13.2	7.4	9.5	37.0	30.0	6.3	31.7	27.1	38.9	3,757	99.1
Seminole city	6,476	7,815	20.7	7,586	44.0	4.1	1.3	0.8	49.8	30.6	12.2	30.0	57.0	18.5	2,326	83.8
Serenada CDP	1,641	-	-	1,404	86.8	0.7	0.4	3.4	8.7	21.9	26.5	48.2	23.0	38.3	460	100.0
Seth Ward CDP	2,025	-	-	1,825	24.9	1.6	0.0	2.2	71.2	24.4	9.8	34.6	74.4	2.6	506	80.6
Seven Oaks city	112	129	15.2	72	30.6	69.4	0.0	0.0	0.0	12.5	23.6	47.6	51.9	3.8	24	79.2
Seven Points city	1,424	1,521	6.8	1,688	75.4	0.0	1.1	0.4	23.2	23.9	17.0	38.2	68.8	10.0	582	84.0
Seymour city	2,736	2,550	-6.8	2,817	85.8	3.9	0.0	0.0	10.3	23.1	23.6	44.5	55.2	17.2	1,203	82.2
Shadybrook CDP	1,967	-	-	2,065	76.9	4.6	0.0	2.1	16.4	21.6	23.0	45.0	41.4	23.4	798	85.7
Shady Hollow CDP	5,004	-	-	4,473	75.6	2.7	3.8	1.5	16.3	17.5	25.0	51.8	12.8	62.0	1,650	98.4
Shady Shores town	2,616	2,865	9.5	2,843	79.7	0.7	3.3	2.2	14.1	23.4	18.4	40.6	23.3	43.7	933	95.8
Shallowater city	2,455	2,574	4.8	2,551	77.5	0.9	0.0	1.3	20.3	32.5	14.0	35.0	36.6	25.3	898	95.4
Shamrock city	1,923	1,764	-8.3	1,983	60.0	7.2	0.0	4.3	28.5	24.1	17.9	39.3	53.1	10.8	899	88.2
Shavano Park city	3,035	3,979	31.1	3,787	70.7	1.4	5.8	1.7	20.4	21.0	24.1	48.7	9.6	70.2	1,282	99.0
Sheldon CDP	1,990	-	-	1,921	16.8	0.0	0.0	3.1	80.1	36.9	12.2	21.7	78.9	3.1	414	88.6
Shenandoah city	2,142	2,987	39.4	2,887	87.5	0.0	4.4	1.0	7.1	13.6	40.4	55.4	24.4	37.8	1,290	92.2
Shepherd city	2,318	2,413	4.1	3,202	74.8	10.2	0.0	2.4	12.6	28.6	12.1	30.3	56.9	6.5	975	81.0
Sherman city	38,852	44,002	13.3	42,432	59.9	9.1	3.2	4.3	23.4	25.8	14.3	34.8	42.4	20.8	15,142	88.7
Sherwood Shores CDP	1,190	-	-	911	90.0	0.0	0.0	2.6	7.4	5.6	25.1	56.4	33.8	16.4	480	92.5
Shiner city	2,073	2,162	4.3	2,192	89.7	5.0	0.0	0.2	5.0	25.2	23.9	45.5	41.7	27.2	823	82.4
Shoreacres city	1,490	1,593	6.9	1,806	81.6	1.6	0.9	1.5	14.4	20.4	14.1	40.9	24.7	32.3	637	97.0
Sienna Plantation CDP	13,721	-	-	19,486	46.5	27.1	6.3	3.4	16.7	34.9	5.7	34.9	15.0	63.1	5,331	99.0
Sierra Blanca CDP	553	-	-	764	23.7	0.0	2.5	12.8	61.0	28.4	25.8	41.8	62.6	16.4	211	91.9
Siesta Acres CDP	1,885	-	-	1,620	3.1	0.0	0.0	1.5	95.4	26.9	19.3	38.9	69.0	8.0	535	40.9
Siesta Shores CDP	1,382	-	-	1,115	1.3	0.0	10.0	0.0	88.7	37.2	9.0	27.0	59.3	19.9	325	62.5
Silsbee city	6,599	6,617	0.3	6,634	62.6	26.9	0.2	0.7	9.6	25.4	18.7	38.8	50.1	14.4	2,474	91.6
Silverton city	731	686	-6.2	660	50.6	0.0	0.0	2.9	46.5	18.9	25.6	43.9	56.1	10.6	265	80.8
Simonton city	827	884	6.9	643	76.8	11.0	0.0	0.0	12.1	26.7	17.3	39.5	33.9	37.5	226	82.3
Sinton city	5,668	5,354	-5.5	5,504	17.0	1.8	2.0	0.2	79.0	31.8	10.6	28.8	62.8	5.8	1,810	85.5
Skellytown town	473	449	-5.1	428	98.1	0.0	1.9	0.0	0.0	16.1	33.9	52.9	40.3	12.1	186	82.3
Skidmore CDP	925	-	-	1,360	26.0	0.2	0.0	0.0	73.8	23.2	17.3	39.4	61.4	7.6	425	85.4
Slaton city	6,104	5,890	-3.5	5,960	46.5	3.7	0.0	1.4	48.4	27.9	19.2	36.4	46.5	15.9	2,307	91.6
Smiley city	549	570	3.8	631	19.2	0.0	0.0	1.6	79.2	27.6	14.3	35.2	64.5	9.5	207	83.1
Smithville city	3,814	4,515	18.4	4,363	71.3	8.4	1.0	5.5	13.8	17.8	24.3	46.8	46.5	24.5	1,646	86.9

1 May be of any race.

Table A. All Places — Population and Housing

STATE City, town, township, borough, or CDP (county if applicable)	Population — 2010 census total population	2019 estimated population	Percent change 2010–2019	ACS total population estimate 2015–2019	Race and Hispanic or Latino origin (percent) — White alone, not Hispanic or Latino	Black alone, not Hispanic or Latino	Asian alone, not Hispanic or Latino	All other races or 2 or more races, not Hispanic or Latino	Hispanic or Latino[1]	Age (percent) — Under 18 years old	Age 65 years and older	Median age	Educational attainment of persons age 25 and older — Percent High school diploma or less	Percent Bachelor's degree or more	Occupied housing units — Total	Percent with a computer
	1	2	3	4	5	6	7	8	9	10	11	12	13	14	15	16
TEXAS—Con.																
Smyer town	474	478	0.8	677	67.1	3.1	0.0	1.6	28.2	26.9	12.0	31.7	49.0	20.7	214	89.3
Snook city	511	541	5.9	495	62.6	16.0	0.0	3.4	18.0	15.6	15.2	43.3	63.0	9.9	196	81.6
Snyder city	11,201	11,023	-1.6	11,323	47.6	3.3	0.5	1.2	47.5	27.2	14.3	34.8	57.4	17.0	4,192	86.6
Socorro city	32,048	34,370	7.2	33,778	2.4	0.1	0.1	1.1	96.3	27.8	11.8	32.3	65.7	7.7	9,364	88.1
Solis CDP	512	-	-	501	0.0	0.0	0.0	0.0	100.0	26.3	6.6	31.4	52.1	32.6	132	90.2
Somerset city	1,669	1,965	17.7	1,645	14.2	0.2	0.0	2.1	83.5	25.9	14.3	37.4	61.4	11.0	417	87.8
Somerville city	1,376	1,465	6.5	1,473	28.0	29.9	0.0	2.9	39.2	27.9	19.3	33.5	68.5	11.0	554	69.0
Sonora city	3,029	2,786	-8.0	3,405	31.7	0.0	0.0	0.2	68.1	27.9	18.4	38.1	59.0	17.6	1,224	76.4
Sonterra CDP	-	-	-	3,276	56.5	6.6	0.5	5.2	31.1	29.2	8.0	29.5	36.5	22.9	1,087	98.4
Sour Lake city	1,813	1,924	6.1	2,206	87.7	2.6	2.8	1.0	5.8	34.2	14.9	32.9	54.9	14.4	779	90.6
South Alamo CDP	3,361	-	-	2,954	0.0	0.0	0.0	0.0	100.0	44.8	8.5	22.2	91.4	2.1	644	53.3
South Fork Estates CDP ..	70	-	-	108	64.8	0.0	0.0	0.0	35.2	52.8	0.0	14.9	51.3	0.0	19	100.0
South Houston city	16,995	17,438	2.6	17,587	7.3	0.9	0.1	0.5	91.3	32.7	8.8	28.8	77.2	6.1	4,850	81.3
Southlake city	26,573	32,376	21.8	31,292	73.6	1.7	15.9	2.4	6.4	32.5	9.9	42.3	10.7	69.7	9,398	98.9
South La Paloma CDP	345	-	-	530	34.9	0.0	0.0	0.0	65.1	47.7	0.0	31.3	100.0	0.0	153	51.0
Southmayd city	994	1,137	14.4	1,045	77.0	1.1	1.4	3.2	17.3	29.2	16.7	37.8	56.6	5.3	372	91.1
South Mountain town	386	365	-5.4	383	83.6	0.0	0.3	1.3	14.9	14.4	21.4	48.2	43.1	25.4	152	94.7
South Padre Island town...	2,820	2,778	-1.5	2,818	72.6	0.0	0.0	0.0	27.4	7.7	29.6	58.1	16.4	45.0	1,645	96.8
South Point CDP	1,376	-	-	1,680	2.4	0.0	0.0	0.0	97.6	33.5	11.0	31.1	80.1	3.4	336	53.3
Southside Place city	1,715	1,883	9.8	1,652	69.9	2.1	15.1	4.0	9.0	28.3	11.3	39.7	7.3	86.6	556	96.2
South Toledo Bend CDP...	524	-	-	468	98.1	0.0	0.0	1.9	0.0	6.0	40.8	60.9	34.0	9.9	205	96.1
Spade CDP	73	-	-	78	66.7	0.0	0.0	0.0	33.3	12.8	32.1	57.2	44.1	23.5	34	100.0
Sparks CDP	4,529	-	-	4,104	0.0	1.5	0.0	0.0	98.5	33.1	7.7	29.5	66.3	2.2	1,079	79.3
Spearman city	3,368	3,256	-3.3	3,367	55.4	0.1	0.0	0.0	44.4	29.5	18.1	39.2	63.1	9.1	1,197	89.0
Splendora city	1,619	2,255	39.3	1,915	83.7	0.5	0.0	0.0	15.8	29.1	11.3	31.2	55.9	11.5	626	91.7
Spofford city	95	97	2.1	305	30.2	0.0	0.0	0.0	69.8	40.3	22.6	37.4	65.3	0.0	80	72.5
Spring CDP	54,298	-	-	60,976	40.2	22.1	2.9	2.9	31.9	26.0	10.2	34.8	38.3	23.9	20,329	96.9
Spring Branch city	191	254	33.0	23	82.6	0.0	8.7	8.7	0.0	17.4	17.4	34.8	47.4	36.8	12	83.3
Spring Gardens CDP	563	-	-	565	20.2	0.0	0.0	0.0	79.8	34.0	12.2	28.7	69.6	5.1	158	88.0
Springlake town	108	102	-5.6	87	54.0	1.1	0.0	0.0	44.8	8.0	24.1	58.3	69.3	12.0	44	84.1
Springtown city	2,657	3,190	20.1	2,940	91.2	0.0	0.1	3.0	5.7	24.0	15.1	35.2	41.5	18.6	1,044	95.3
Spring Valley Village city...	3,723	4,319	16.0	4,282	79.1	0.0	8.4	3.4	9.1	30.2	14.4	40.7	7.4	83.8	1,429	100.0
Spur city	1,318	1,199	-9.0	1,140	54.7	4.2	1.0	0.0	40.1	19.3	19.7	43.6	56.6	15.2	431	89.8
Stafford city	16,773	17,362	3.5	17,206	19.6	29.5	21.2	3.6	26.0	20.1	11.1	35.3	36.4	35.4	6,416	95.2
Stagecoach town	552	592	7.2	651	86.0	0.0	0.0	4.6	9.4	23.0	16.3	42.5	29.6	34.3	208	96.6
Stamford city	3,125	2,941	-5.9	2,919	47.2	3.0	0.0	2.8	46.9	29.1	20.7	40.4	56.5	18.9	1,305	82.1
Stanton city	2,506	3,000	19.7	2,946	41.2	1.6	0.0	0.0	57.2	31.4	9.8	31.5	56.3	20.8	857	76.5
Staples city	267	277	3.7	230	54.3	5.2	0.0	7.0	33.5	14.3	24.8	58.0	44.3	18.9	96	87.5
Star Harbor city	444	477	7.4	509	92.9	0.0	1.0	2.8	3.3	16.9	33.4	56.6	17.5	42.3	213	99.1
Stephenville city	17,023	21,247	24.8	20,603	73.4	3.4	1.1	1.1	21.0	18.7	10.8	24.6	33.9	32.8	6,644	95.0
Sterling City city	875	998	14.1	1,150	45.2	0.0	0.0	1.0	53.7	35.8	10.4	37.4	62.5	8.5	410	93.7
Stinnett city	1,874	1,770	-5.5	1,403	75.8	1.1	1.1	2.1	19.9	21.3	24.1	41.7	49.9	9.4	508	86.4
Stockdale city	1,446	1,649	14.0	1,269	50.0	0.2	0.0	8.4	41.4	29.5	20.5	38.3	54.6	20.4	431	89.8
Stonewall CDP	505	-	-	592	48.5	1.4	0.0	0.0	50.2	15.5	22.1	44.4	58.3	25.4	252	92.1
Stowell CDP	1,756	-	-	1,273	68.9	19.8	2.7	3.3	5.3	31.4	8.6	35.4	54.7	22.1	477	80.7
Stratford city	2,017	2,057	2.0	1,951	46.9	1.8	0.0	0.3	51.0	25.1	11.6	39.2	46.0	15.9	694	86.6
Strawn city	656	671	2.3	784	53.7	0.0	0.0	2.0	44.3	26.4	20.3	47.1	61.8	10.8	271	78.2
Streetman town	249	246	-1.2	285	72.3	6.3	0.0	3.5	17.9	15.1	28.8	49.2	46.2	25.3	119	80.7
Study Butte CDP	233	-	-	188	49.5	0.0	0.0	0.0	50.5	15.4	48.9	64.8	42.8	17.6	99	74.7
Sudan city	958	895	-6.6	1,005	45.2	2.7	1.1	0.3	50.7	27.4	16.7	37.3	56.7	16.6	399	78.4
Sugar Land city	107,835	118,488	9.9	118,709	42.7	6.9	36.5	2.5	11.4	22.7	15.6	42.2	18.9	60.1	39,298	97.7
Sullivan City city	4,004	4,170	4.1	4,176	1.9	0.0	0.0	0.0	98.1	32.7	14.1	31.4	79.8	5.7	1,258	76.0
Sulphur Springs city	15,453	16,234	5.1	16,014	69.3	13.0	0.7	2.3	14.7	23.4	18.2	37.6	55.6	18.9	6,142	88.8
Sundown city	1,397	1,425	2.0	1,249	47.9	0.8	0.8	2.1	48.4	27.3	12.3	35.4	52.5	15.7	438	84.7
Sunnyvale town	5,168	6,841	32.4	6,484	50.7	9.3	23.1	4.8	12.1	27.5	10.5	39.5	27.1	46.6	1,967	98.7
Sunray city	1,926	1,812	-5.9	2,064	45.6	0.0	1.4	2.7	50.3	32.2	12.7	34.3	58.3	15.6	717	85.8
Sunrise Beach Village city	713	796	11.6	966	96.0	0.0	0.0	0.6	3.4	13.5	37.3	58.9	20.6	39.8	409	94.4
Sunset CDP	497	-	-	644	71.7	0.0	0.0	0.0	28.3	28.6	16.9	44.3	59.6	14.4	155	74.2
Sunset CDP	47	-	-	16	0.0	0.0	0.0	0.0	100.0	50.0	0.0	27.5	50.0	0.0	4	100.0
Sunset Acres CDP	23	-	-	18	0.0	0.0	0.0	0.0	100.0	0.0	55.6	67.1	55.6	0.0	5	100.0
Sunset Valley city	648	672	3.7	548	68.2	0.4	13.1	0.2	15.3	27.4	22.3	41.6	11.0	62.0	203	98.5
Sun Valley city	76	83	9.2	48	18.8	0.0	0.0	16.7	64.6	33.3	16.7	33.1	42.9	0.0	15	100.0
Surfside Beach city	482	579	20.1	627	72.7	3.2	0.0	5.4	18.7	10.8	27.3	57.6	35.3	25.7	335	97.6
Sweeny city	3,729	3,717	-0.3	3,739	60.3	13.9	0.0	0.0	25.8	28.6	22.3	39.8	52.4	11.9	1,432	84.8
Sweetwater city	10,913	10,469	-4.1	10,626	47.5	7.6	0.4	1.2	43.3	27.7	15.8	35.1	58.1	10.3	3,745	85.6
Taft city	3,061	2,867	-6.3	2,945	16.1	1.0	0.0	1.1	81.8	25.8	15.8	34.7	63.0	4.7	1,032	77.2
Taft Southwest CDP	1,460	-	-	982	7.8	0.0	0.0	0.0	92.2	18.4	20.8	42.9	85.6	1.8	351	36.8
Tahoka city	2,673	2,649	-0.9	2,603	39.6	1.0	0.0	4.1	55.3	29.0	18.9	34.7	59.7	14.6	953	74.2
Talco city	516	497	-3.7	797	55.3	14.7	0.0	0.0	30.0	32.4	7.5	32.1	67.6	11.2	280	77.5
Talty town	1,874	2,760	47.3	2,440	73.0	10.4	0.2	1.8	14.6	33.4	9.6	39.0	30.9	34.5	696	99.6
Tanquecitos South Acres CDP	233	-	-	31	0.0	0.0	0.0	0.0	100.0	0.0	45.2	0.0	100.0	0.0	14	0.0
Tanquecitos South Acres II CDP	50	-	-	-	-	-	-	-	-	-	-	-	-	-	-	-
Tatum city	1,385	1,384	-0.1	1,272	61.2	18.1	0.0	3.3	17.4	26.7	16.7	35.1	50.1	14.6	531	78.5
Taylor city	15,281	17,383	13.8	17,001	43.8	9.3	1.1	3.6	42.2	21.1	14.7	39.0	57.5	14.9	5,599	86.0
Taylor Lake Village city	3,555	3,571	0.5	3,639	79.4	3.5	1.0	0.0	16.1	21.4	20.1	44.1	16.4	46.9	1,286	98.8
Taylor Landing city	228	240	5.3	285	75.1	0.0	0.0	0.0	24.9	27.7	21.4	40.9	24.9	29.9	95	92.6
Teague city	3,557	3,515	-1.2	3,519	53.4	15.3	0.0	1.7	29.7	27.9	13.5	35.2	45.2	12.3	1,137	80.4
Tehuacana town	283	279	-1.4	195	81.0	17.4	0.0	0.0	1.5	23.6	31.8	48.9	43.1	25.0	84	90.5
Temple city	66,082	78,439	18.7	74,762	53.5	14.8	2.0	3.2	26.4	26.8	15.0	34.2	36.2	28.9	27,618	90.3
Tenaha town	1,155	1,146	-0.8	1,198	29.2	35.8	0.0	0.5	34.5	25.7	13.7	35.6	66.9	7.5	465	70.5
Terlingua CDP	58	-	-	110	94.5	0.0	0.0	0.0	5.5	0.0	44.5	62.7	45.5	40.9	60	100.0
Terrell city	16,060	18,869	17.5	17,869	47.3	22.6	0.3	2.7	27.1	25.7	15.4	37.2	50.1	17.9	5,907	85.3
Terrell Hills city	4,878	5,447	11.7	5,371	76.8	0.9	1.0	0.8	20.5	35.3	14.0	37.9	6.0	77.9	1,672	97.5
Texarkana city	36,399	36,317	-0.2	36,688	49.4	37.7	1.9	3.4	7.6	26.0	15.2	36.0	42.3	23.3	14,025	79.1
Texas City city	45,084	50,094	11.1	48,569	38.0	28.2	0.8	4.0	29.0	24.4	15.4	36.3	50.9	15.0	17,414	86.3
Texhoma city	346	323	-6.6	437	79.9	0.0	0.0	1.6	18.5	7.8	20.8	50.4	60.2	9.4	159	72.3
Texline town	508	539	6.1	341	59.2	0.0	0.6	8.5	31.7	28.2	19.9	47.3	41.6	18.1	150	89.3
The Colony city	36,341	44,438	22.3	43,005	60.9	8.4	5.3	3.6	21.8	22.1	7.7	34.9	27.3	38.6	16,391	98.6
The Hills village	2,440	2,487	1.9	2,586	82.6	1.4	3.8	3.6	8.6	26.3	22.0	48.7	6.3	74.1	1,022	98.7
The Woodlands CDP	93,847	-	-	113,819	69.9	4.5	5.9	2.8	17.0	27.5	13.0	40.4	13.0	63.8	41,292	97.6

1 May be of any race.

Table A. All Places — **Population and Housing**

STATE City, town, township, borough, or CDP (county if applicable)	Population				Race and Hispanic or Latino origin (percent)					Age (percent)			Educational attainment of persons age 25 and older		Occupied housing units	
	2010 census total population	2019 estimated population	Percent change 2010–2019	ACS total population estimate 2015–2019	White alone, not Hispanic or Latino	Black alone, not Hispanic or Latino	Asian alone, not Hispanic or Latino	All other races or 2 or more races, not Hispanic or Latino	Hispanic or Latino[1]	Under 18 years old	Age 65 years and older	Median age	Percent High school diploma or less	Percent Bachelor's degree or more	Total	Percent with a computer
	1	2	3	4	5	6	7	8	9	10	11	12	13	14	15	16
TEXAS—Con.																
Thompsons town	218	350	60.6	243	35.8	40.7	0.4	3.7	19.3	15.6	25.5	51.3	60.8	14.6	94	90.4
Thompsonville CDP	46	-	-	198	43.9	0.0	0.0	0.0	56.1	21.2	0.0	56.1	0.0	65.4	62	100.0
Thorndale city	1,293	1,302	0.7	1,407	58.5	6.3	0.0	1.7	33.5	22.5	19.5	37.3	49.7	23.7	549	76.7
Thornton town	526	524	-0.4	671	88.7	6.6	0.0	1.2	3.6	22.4	17.7	34.6	57.2	4.5	232	85.8
Thorntonville town	476	541	13.7	566	56.4	0.0	0.0	0.9	42.8	23.7	24.2	43.0	58.0	7.0	198	72.7
Thrall city	838	977	16.6	793	51.1	3.9	0.0	1.3	43.8	34.7	8.1	35.6	57.8	11.3	201	85.1
Three Rivers city	1,848	1,949	5.5	1,821	31.1	0.1	7.2	0.0	61.6	24.5	15.4	31.6	69.5	7.2	585	65.8
Throckmorton town	839	761	-9.3	642	72.3	2.2	0.0	1.9	23.7	12.5	29.4	49.6	54.9	21.3	314	89.5
Thunderbird Bay CDP	663	-	-	661	100.0	0.0	0.0	0.0	0.0	17.9	39.9	59.5	43.6	5.3	324	92.0
Tierra Bonita CDP	141	-	-	61	0.0	0.0	0.0	0.0	100.0	0.0	0.0	26.3	62.2	37.8	14	100.0
Tierra Dorada CDP	28	-	-	-	-	-	-	-	-	-	-	-	-	-	-	-
Tierra Grande CDP	403	-	-	334	11.4	0.0	0.0	0.0	88.6	14.4	20.7	51.1	71.1	8.0	80	100.0
Tierra Verde CDP	277	-	-	441	0.0	0.0	0.0	0.0	100.0	24.3	2.0	30.5	72.5	7.0	124	100.0
Tiki Island village	968	1,065	10.0	1,051	92.7	0.7	0.0	0.9	5.8	6.1	34.3	59.2	18.3	51.9	537	98.1
Tilden CDP	261	-	-	290	40.0	0.0	0.0	3.1	56.9	47.9	12.8	25.0	24.8	38.6	101	93.1
Timbercreek Canyon village	418	471	12.7	548	85.8	0.0	2.2	3.5	8.6	19.9	27.4	54.0	26.0	48.3	200	95.0
Timberwood Park CDP	13,447	-	-	24,978	56.9	4.9	4.6	2.5	31.1	30.1	10.2	36.4	19.0	50.8	7,900	99.0
Timpson city	1,155	1,134	-1.8	1,335	46.5	42.0	1.0	0.9	9.5	29.4	14.4	34.8	52.8	12.4	573	71.0
Tioga town	812	1,051	29.4	889	80.4	0.0	0.0	0.7	18.9	25.0	19.5	38.5	45.1	17.1	361	88.6
Tira town	298	313	5.0	267	79.0	8.6	9.7	0.0	2.6	26.2	19.9	38.2	62.8	12.2	108	82.4
Tivoli CDP	479	-	-	527	42.1	2.1	2.8	0.0	52.9	22.8	18.4	37.8	45.8	21.9	192	84.4
Toco city	76	76	0.0	63	11.1	88.9	0.0	0.0	0.0	11.1	36.5	61.2	68.5	0.0	25	68.0
Todd Mission city	107	114	6.5	29	100.0	0.0	0.0	0.0	0.0	6.9	3.4	57.6	34.6	15.4	15	100.0
Tolar city	684	1,004	46.8	762	84.5	0.5	0.0	1.6	13.4	23.1	14.0	31.4	38.2	30.8	275	93.1
Tomball city	10,715	11,778	9.9	11,689	60.8	8.6	0.1	1.0	29.5	24.7	19.2	38.0	38.9	28.1	4,369	89.2
Tom Bean city	1,041	1,081	3.8	1,067	83.3	0.4	0.7	2.5	13.0	32.5	12.2	33.4	34.7	14.1	398	89.2
Tool city	2,227	2,302	3.4	2,214	82.7	4.5	0.0	3.6	9.2	13.7	28.5	52.0	50.6	18.4	982	92.6
Tornillo CDP	1,568	-	-	1,105	0.5	0.0	0.0	0.0	99.5	29.5	19.4	37.9	78.7	8.9	316	77.2
Toyah town	90	108	20.0	121	26.4	0.0	4.1	0.0	69.4	0.0	24.0	53.4	36.9	18.0	35	85.7
Tradewinds CDP	180	-	-	105	0.0	0.0	0.0	0.0	100.0	9.5	27.6	58.5	100.0	0.0	55	47.3
Travis Ranch CDP	2,556	-	-	4,265	59.5	15.9	2.3	1.1	21.2	35.4	4.2	30.9	29.0	31.4	1,226	100.0
Trent town	337	349	3.6	269	74.0	13.0	0.4	0.0	12.6	19.0	16.0	45.3	54.6	9.3	108	78.7
Trenton city	639	683	6.9	695	68.6	5.3	5.3	0.7	20.0	23.7	17.7	40.0	52.1	11.9	282	79.1
Trinidad city	886	870	-1.8	878	64.9	23.7	0.0	4.0	7.4	25.7	21.4	41.9	64.3	10.6	374	71.9
Trinity city	2,787	2,756	-1.1	2,756	42.7	27.9	0.2	4.4	24.8	26.5	13.4	34.9	67.4	6.1	1,096	74.5
Trophy Club town	8,026	12,451	55.1	11,949	85.2	2.1	4.7	2.2	5.8	29.1	9.4	40.0	9.7	65.6	3,988	98.0
Troup city	1,878	2,044	8.8	1,928	58.9	23.1	0.0	5.3	12.7	30.4	12.3	33.2	51.7	13.2	626	89.0
Troy city	1,650	2,016	22.2	2,820	78.0	0.3	0.0	0.5	21.2	35.5	10.0	29.9	43.1	18.6	854	95.1
Tuleta CDP	288	-	-	253	72.3	0.0	0.0	0.0	27.7	29.2	7.1	35.9	41.4	12.4	71	91.5
Tulia city	4,966	4,655	-6.3	4,690	35.4	8.6	0.3	4.9	50.8	26.7	17.1	35.1	63.5	11.6	1,473	82.0
Tulsita CDP	14	-	-	-	-	-	-	-	-	-	-	-	-	-	-	-
Turkey city	421	378	-10.2	316	63.3	4.4	0.0	1.9	30.4	16.1	24.7	37.5	54.6	13.8	147	81.0
Tuscola city	733	739	0.8	731	95.2	0.0	0.0	0.0	4.8	30.5	16.0	36.8	42.9	16.6	306	83.7
Tye city	1,229	1,333	8.5	1,206	68.3	0.7	0.5	5.0	25.5	25.7	18.2	40.4	67.5	7.1	438	91.6
Tyler city	96,852	106,985	10.5	104,789	50.2	23.8	2.5	1.8	21.6	23.0	15.7	33.7	34.2	29.4	36,778	91.3
Tynan CDP	278	-	-	283	13.8	0.0	0.0	0.0	86.2	22.3	16.3	37.9	47.6	16.1	79	67.1
Uhland city	1,019	1,294	27.0	1,211	20.9	4.5	0.4	4.1	70.1	30.2	10.0	33.2	64.4	11.2	333	88.3
Uncertain city	94	92	-2.1	71	66.2	33.8	0.0	0.0	0.0	0.0	50.7	65.1	59.2	14.1	43	81.4
Union Grove city	359	385	7.2	436	87.8	7.6	0.0	0.0	4.6	25.5	10.3	30.5	48.7	6.8	133	72.9
Union Valley city	311	398	28.0	366	85.5	0.0	0.0	0.5	13.9	24.3	17.8	46.0	31.1	25.0	122	94.3
Universal City city	18,526	20,890	12.8	20,459	44.1	12.8	2.6	4.4	36.1	23.9	15.1	35.8	33.2	29.5	7,212	95.3
University Park city	23,068	24,985	8.3	25,036	83.8	1.5	6.6	2.3	5.7	27.8	9.7	35.1	4.0	87.8	7,689	98.6
Utopia CDP	227	-	-	167	93.4	0.0	0.0	0.0	6.6	35.3	6.6	24.8	17.3	6.2	54	100.0
Uvalde city	15,752	16,001	1.6	16,154	14.0	0.5	1.4	0.7	83.5	28.9	13.6	31.9	52.6	14.9	4,942	79.3
Uvalde Estates CDP	2,171	-	-	1,665	8.0	0.0	0.0	0.0	92.0	16.0	18.4	46.3	61.6	13.4	671	54.7
Valentine town	134	133	-0.7	67	25.4	0.0	0.0	0.0	74.6	16.4	40.3	54.2	53.6	0.0	29	51.7
Valle Hermoso CDP	-	-	-	-	-	-	-	-	-	-	-	-	-	-	-	-
Valle Verde CDP	-	-	-	-	-	-	-	-	-	-	-	-	-	-	-	-
Valle Vista CDP	469	-	-	771	0.0	0.0	0.0	0.0	100.0	24.1	15.4	37.7	63.3	6.4	149	94.6
Valley Mills city	1,203	1,180	-1.9	1,302	73.9	3.6	0.0	2.8	19.7	29.5	14.6	33.9	56.3	10.4	455	82.2
Valley View city	757	845	11.6	953	86.0	0.4	1.3	1.7	10.6	28.1	11.0	31.9	41.9	20.5	332	93.1
Val Verde Park CDP	2,384	-	-	2,731	4.0	0.0	0.0	0.0	96.0	36.8	10.5	29.6	72.2	6.2	685	85.4
Van city	2,632	2,741	4.1	2,669	80.4	3.6	0.0	2.3	13.8	31.0	13.3	32.6	41.1	22.9	953	92.5
Van Alstyne city	3,059	4,378	43.1	3,906	70.0	7.6	0.0	4.7	17.8	25.7	18.7	35.6	46.9	16.1	1,277	95.0
Vanderbilt CDP	395	-	-	429	62.0	0.0	0.0	0.0	38.0	57.6	1.6	16.3	46.4	0.0	103	100.0
Van Horn town	2,066	1,870	-9.5	1,760	15.1	0.2	0.7	3.6	80.5	22.9	17.3	43.5	69.7	11.1	502	63.9
Van Vleck CDP	1,844	-	-	1,223	62.5	0.0	0.3	2.5	34.7	18.2	15.9	43.1	38.3	22.9	550	73.5
Vega city	884	924	4.5	1,024	76.7	1.6	3.0	3.1	15.6	16.9	14.3	41.6	53.0	12.7	360	93.6
Venus town	2,911	4,368	50.1	3,692	60.8	14.1	0.6	2.7	21.7	22.1	4.3	33.3	58.7	12.4	905	95.8
Vernon city	11,002	10,323	-6.2	10,509	51.3	11.4	1.1	2.6	33.6	22.4	18.8	38.2	60.4	12.7	4,281	82.7
Victoria city	62,624	66,916	6.9	67,055	37.0	6.5	1.6	1.9	53.0	25.6	15.2	34.4	47.1	20.7	23,400	87.5
Victoria Vera CDP	110	-	-	25	0.0	0.0	0.0	0.0	100.0	0.0	0.0	0.0	100.0	0.0	25	0.0
Vidor city	10,699	10,403	-2.8	10,725	90.5	0.1	0.0	1.3	8.2	25.9	16.1	35.0	58.3	10.2	3,929	90.9
Villa del Sol CDP	175	-	-	336	0.0	0.0	0.0	0.0	100.0	26.2	0.0	25.9	52.3	9.2	40	100.0
Villa Pancho CDP	788	-	-	612	2.3	0.0	0.0	0.0	97.7	25.3	12.7	26.7	69.5	9.7	129	65.9
Villarreal CDP	131	-	-	157	0.0	0.0	0.0	0.0	100.0	4.5	0.0	26.8	44.7	0.0	35	100.0
Villa Verde CDP	874	-	-	213	39.9	0.0	0.0	0.0	60.1	0.0	53.1	69.4	52.5	0.0	114	86.8
Vinton village	1,980	2,022	2.1	1,760	2.7	0.0	0.0	0.0	97.3	30.6	5.1	27.3	58.7	13.7	428	84.8
Volente village	520	599	15.2	619	79.5	0.0	4.4	2.7	13.4	16.2	15.5	50.1	15.4	50.8	265	99.2
Von Ormy city	1,098	1,287	17.2	1,101	6.8	3.5	0.0	0.3	89.5	28.3	12.4	31.0	69.3	8.9	266	77.1
Waco city	124,797	139,236	11.6	135,858	43.3	20.8	2.0	1.8	32.0	23.8	12.2	28.7	44.2	24.9	48,903	86.9
Waelder city	1,065	1,133	6.4	1,334	4.9	12.0	0.4	0.1	82.5	25.0	13.0	41.0	92.5	0.7	488	74.2
Wake Village city	5,492	5,327	-3.0	5,392	64.0	26.2	0.0	3.4	6.4	22.5	15.8	37.3	32.8	29.4	2,124	90.3
Waller city	2,325	3,488	50.0	3,124	49.4	15.9	1.6	0.2	32.8	27.7	16.1	25.9	49.4	12.9	1,089	89.0
Wallis city	1,248	1,303	4.4	1,571	47.4	9.0	0.0	1.5	42.1	27.6	18.8	37.3	57.2	11.4	607	75.8
Walnut Springs city	827	868	5.0	828	50.8	1.0	0.0	0.0	48.2	29.5	15.1	31.1	74.9	10.5	283	72.4
Warren CDP	757	-	-	1,060	96.6	0.0	0.0	2.8	0.6	30.6	18.7	45.2	65.8	14.3	288	86.5
Warren City city	305	305	0.0	341	66.3	18.2	0.0	3.2	12.3	25.5	16.7	35.8	44.5	15.3	120	86.7
Waskom city	2,158	2,190	1.5	1,617	66.7	13.0	0.0	6.7	13.6	23.5	18.4	40.9	60.7	10.8	528	77.8
Watauga city	23,497	24,481	4.2	24,582	61.7	4.0	7.4	2.7	24.1	25.1	10.7	33.8	41.8	21.4	7,808	96.6
Waxahachie city	29,538	37,988	28.6	35,376	60.4	12.1	0.5	1.7	25.2	26.0	12.6	32.9	39.8	22.9	12,276	94.2

1 May be of any race.

Table A. All Places — **Population and Housing**

STATE City, town, township, borough, or CDP (county if applicable)	Population: 2010 census total population	Population: 2019 estimated population	Population: Percent change 2010–2019	Population: ACS total population estimate 2015–2019	Race and Hispanic or Latino origin (percent): White alone, not Hispanic or Latino	Race: Black alone, not Hispanic or Latino	Race: Asian alone, not Hispanic or Latino	Race: All other races or 2 or more races, not Hispanic or Latino	Race: Hispanic or Latino[1]	Age (percent): Under 18 years old	Age: Age 65 years and older	Age: Median age	Educational attainment of persons age 25 and older: Percent High school diploma or less	Educational attainment: Percent Bachelor's degree or more	Occupied housing units: Total	Occupied housing units: Percent with a computer
	1	2	3	4	5	6	7	8	9	10	11	12	13	14	15	16
TEXAS—Con.																
Weatherford city	25,743	33,547	30.3	30,895	77.7	2.9	0.7	3.5	15.3	24.4	17.9	36.9	41.8	23.0	10,984	93.6
Webberville village	367	485	32.2	412	34.5	8.3	0.0	0.0	57.3	21.6	12.6	38.8	62.1	12.6	130	93.8
Webster city	10,624	11,451	7.8	11,222	41.1	19.0	4.2	2.6	33.1	20.6	10.5	30.5	36.6	31.1	4,994	94.4
Weimar city	2,151	2,226	3.5	2,561	51.5	26.3	0.1	0.1	21.9	22.8	21.0	43.3	55.7	20.1	903	70.5
Weinert city	172	162	-5.8	220	74.1	0.0	0.0	0.0	25.9	9.1	30.5	49.6	63.0	13.3	102	85.3
Weir city	453	530	17.0	379	46.7	0.0	0.0	2.9	50.4	28.2	10.6	31.5	59.8	15.9	122	91.8
Welch CDP	222	-	-	219	53.0	0.0	0.0	0.0	47.0	35.6	7.3	32.4	59.8	13.4	69	85.5
Wellington city	2,185	2,068	-5.4	2,129	51.4	11.6	0.0	2.8	34.2	25.5	16.3	40.6	57.7	10.1	785	83.6
Wellman city	203	203	0.0	190	51.1	8.9	0.0	9.5	30.5	27.9	8.9	39.5	61.2	7.5	65	89.2
Wells town	790	792	0.3	848	74.2	15.1	0.0	0.4	10.4	28.4	17.9	36.3	65.6	5.9	283	83.7
Wells Branch CDP	12,120	-	-	12,176	41.2	15.9	9.6	3.4	29.9	19.0	10.8	35.5	31.0	41.5	6,170	92.3
Weslaco city	36,756	41,629	13.3	40,464	9.2	0.7	0.9	0.2	89.0	33.7	13.7	29.3	48.1	21.3	12,255	88.8
West city	2,804	2,986	6.5	2,860	80.5	8.2	0.5	1.0	9.8	22.7	25.4	38.6	44.4	19.5	1,110	84.6
West Alto Bonito CDP	696	-	-	676	0.0	0.0	0.0	0.0	100.0	33.4	1.3	21.7	87.5	0.0	141	86.5
Westbrook city	253	244	-3.6	206	91.3	0.0	0.0	0.0	8.7	29.1	19.4	38.0	59.9	16.1	73	78.1
West Columbia city	3,898	3,830	-1.7	3,878	46.3	11.1	0.0	1.0	41.7	24.5	13.3	38.1	45.7	15.2	1,331	84.8
Westdale CDP	372	-	-	95	100.0	0.0	0.0	0.0	0.0	0.0	85.3	70.8	56.8	0.0	54	100.0
Western Lake CDP	1,525	-	-	486	51.0	0.0	3.3	2.5	43.2	17.7	15.0	38.6	68.5	6.7	228	90.8
Westlake town	988	1,709	73.0	983	78.7	0.4	10.7	4.1	6.1	26.9	10.8	45.6	11.4	69.1	342	98.2
West Lake Hills city	3,069	3,286	7.1	3,311	80.2	0.0	5.2	2.2	12.4	24.0	27.7	50.7	4.7	85.4	1,313	97.0
West Livingston CDP	8,071	-	-	8,347	58.2	16.5	0.1	0.8	24.5	15.2	11.9	41.2	67.3	8.7	1,979	92.6
Westminster CDP	861	-	-	956	49.4	0.0	0.7	0.0	49.9	22.3	9.3	31.3	63.2	11.1	328	96.6
West Odessa CDP	22,707	-	-	25,962	24.7	1.7	0.2	1.0	72.5	33.3	7.2	29.0	69.0	6.9	7,267	88.4
Weston city	300	540	80.0	263	84.4	4.2	1.1	2.3	8.0	19.0	12.2	40.5	59.5	17.4	94	89.4
Weston Lakes city	2,489	4,003	60.8	3,670	89.0	0.0	3.1	0.0	7.8	23.4	27.1	55.9	15.7	57.7	1,321	100.0
West Orange city	3,443	3,223	-6.4	3,342	61.8	17.7	0.0	4.3	16.1	24.9	16.3	35.3	53.8	11.3	1,302	84.1
Westover Hills town	636	683	7.4	553	95.8	0.4	2.2	1.3	0.4	17.4	42.3	60.6	1.8	86.4	238	92.9
West Sharyland CDP	2,309	-	-	2,338	0.0	0.0	3.2	0.0	96.8	21.4	13.9	38.9	84.1	3.9	672	87.8
West Tawakoni city	1,733	2,006	15.8	1,815	88.9	0.0	1.1	3.3	6.8	15.0	20.0	50.3	61.5	9.6	765	80.7
West University Place city	14,560	15,585	7.0	15,603	76.5	0.5	12.8	4.1	6.2	31.5	15.3	42.1	4.1	86.9	5,419	98.0
Westway CDP	4,188	-	-	3,636	1.7	0.0	0.0	0.2	98.1	31.0	13.7	31.7	78.4	9.4	1,077	79.0
Westwood Shores CDP	1,162	-	-	1,682	97.4	0.0	0.0	1.4	1.2	22.8	39.1	55.2	42.2	22.2	699	92.8
Westworth Village city	2,472	2,757	11.5	2,681	57.8	1.8	1.8	2.6	36.1	26.0	15.5	36.4	34.8	29.8	1,122	91.4
Wharton city	8,878	8,637	-2.7	8,711	33.3	28.1	0.7	0.7	37.1	22.6	18.5	38.9	56.9	12.5	3,371	73.9
Wheeler city	1,572	1,477	-6.0	1,481	53.7	1.1	0.0	1.1	44.1	27.3	22.1	38.5	53.0	21.2	586	81.6
White Deer town	1,004	955	-4.9	736	80.3	0.0	0.0	0.5	19.2	25.1	16.7	40.1	40.1	23.4	272	100.0
Whiteface town	449	412	-8.2	359	39.6	0.0	0.0	2.5	57.9	26.2	13.1	33.4	50.2	15.8	118	86.4
Whitehouse city	7,705	8,905	15.6	8,489	75.7	5.1	0.7	4.4	14.1	29.9	9.9	37.2	29.5	30.3	2,842	94.3
White Oak city	6,472	6,322	-2.3	6,331	80.9	1.7	0.6	2.1	14.7	25.7	14.8	37.9	45.7	22.2	2,182	97.4
Whitesboro city	3,786	4,120	8.8	3,998	92.0	2.2	0.0	0.7	5.1	27.5	14.9	32.5	46.3	14.1	1,550	79.1
White Settlement city	16,116	17,851	10.8	17,565	63.1	6.3	2.5	1.7	26.4	25.8	12.9	35.2	56.5	15.4	6,385	90.4
Whitewright town	1,604	1,721	7.3	1,622	82.3	10.3	0.4	4.7	2.3	27.1	17.9	36.4	48.2	22.2	668	80.8
Whitney town	2,085	2,162	3.7	2,326	73.7	9.0	1.6	1.4	14.2	28.2	20.8	39.4	56.6	9.4	825	90.7
Wichita Falls city	104,682	104,683	0.0	104,279	60.1	12.1	2.6	3.4	21.8	22.0	13.5	33.1	45.0	23.8	37,304	88.0
Wickett town	498	559	12.2	583	56.4	1.2	0.0	4.3	38.1	28.5	17.5	33.0	69.8	5.0	200	73.5
Wild Peach Village CDP	2,452	-	-	1,905	78.6	8.1	0.0	0.4	12.9	23.6	16.4	43.8	49.4	12.4	764	90.7
Wildwood CDP	1,235	-	-	1,379	100.0	0.0	0.0	0.0	0.0	28.6	29.7	41.2	32.9	9.8	497	100.0
Willis city	5,893	7,028	19.3	6,566	46.4	12.4	1.0	3.2	37.1	26.8	9.0	33.7	69.3	5.1	2,187	93.8
Willow Park city	3,962	5,842	47.5	5,365	83.6	0.0	1.8	1.1	13.4	25.8	17.4	39.6	23.2	43.0	1,905	97.7
Wills Point city	3,514	3,651	3.9	3,577	74.4	12.2	0.0	0.4	13.1	29.7	18.5	34.6	62.4	13.0	1,309	81.1
Wilmer city	3,714	4,772	28.5	4,383	25.2	29.6	0.3	2.7	42.2	27.5	9.5	33.5	57.6	7.3	1,324	89.3
Wilson city	489	490	0.2	343	24.5	0.0	1.7	2.6	71.1	22.7	16.9	52.2	71.0	7.1	127	70.9
Wimberley city	2,620	3,232	23.4	3,037	87.3	0.0	0.2	1.4	11.1	13.1	28.5	55.6	17.4	43.0	1,311	98.4
Windcrest city	5,377	5,876	9.3	5,851	55.3	8.2	6.2	1.8	28.6	15.0	28.4	49.7	27.9	42.8	2,133	98.5
Windom town	199	205	3.0	162	92.6	0.0	0.0	4.9	2.5	18.5	27.8	53.3	59.7	18.5	82	76.8
Windthorst town	404	379	-6.2	308	60.4	0.0	0.0	2.9	36.7	14.0	34.7	54.4	73.5	15.1	139	72.7
Winfield city	524	520	-0.8	520	12.5	4.4	0.0	0.0	83.1	35.4	10.0	28.6	72.2	3.7	141	77.3
Wink city	940	1,028	9.4	824	70.4	0.6	0.0	0.0	29.0	35.2	6.2	29.0	49.7	12.9	254	89.0
Winnie CDP	3,254	-	-	2,788	94.5	0.2	0.1	1.7	3.5	19.3	17.7	48.1	50.8	22.0	1,015	90.7
Winnsboro city	3,260	3,299	1.2	3,360	78.2	2.2	1.7	2.1	15.8	34.0	18.0	31.0	44.4	15.0	1,158	85.9
Winona town	576	608	5.6	547	64.5	8.0	0.0	6.4	21.0	31.4	15.5	38.2	42.8	9.2	204	85.8
Winters city	2,560	2,448	-4.4	2,858	45.2	1.5	0.4	1.0	51.9	30.4	16.4	30.3	69.8	11.7	1,025	73.5
Wixon Valley city	254	253	-0.4	213	70.4	8.9	0.0	3.8	16.9	22.5	23.5	47.6	48.1	25.0	87	74.7
Wolfe City city	1,395	1,480	6.1	1,334	78.9	15.9	0.0	0.7	4.6	21.3	23.1	42.1	63.5	7.0	500	85.2
Wolfforth city	3,658	5,486	50.0	4,821	69.5	0.7	0.3	2.2	27.4	32.4	6.3	31.3	29.4	31.2	1,701	97.0
Woodbranch city	1,279	1,441	12.7	1,935	64.7	0.5	0.5	2.3	31.9	24.3	13.9	35.6	45.7	17.6	582	93.5
Woodcreek city	1,421	1,716	20.8	1,439	89.6	0.0	0.0	1.3	9.0	13.6	40.0	59.4	15.5	51.6	678	95.4
Woodloch town	207	208	0.5	207	72.0	4.3	0.0	0.0	23.7	23.7	13.0	39.5	54.5	9.8	67	91.0
Woodsboro town	1,512	1,410	-6.7	1,344	39.5	4.2	0.3	1.4	54.5	22.3	22.8	41.5	58.9	6.0	493	76.1
Woodson town	264	241	-8.7	235	93.6	0.0	0.0	0.9	5.5	30.2	28.1	38.6	49.0	4.2	95	86.3
Woodville town	2,586	2,428	-6.1	2,776	71.9	23.9	0.1	2.7	1.4	24.9	24.1	42.4	55.8	18.1	1,054	82.4
Woodway city	8,434	9,024	7.0	8,865	80.6	2.7	2.3	1.3	13.2	24.3	26.4	45.6	15.9	52.8	3,191	94.2
Wortham town	1,076	996	-7.4	1,071	56.2	11.8	0.0	0.7	31.4	30.2	20.1	35.5	43.8	13.2	347	83.6
Wyldwood CDP	2,505	-	-	2,430	45.8	0.0	0.6	0.6	53.0	33.3	9.3	31.6	46.2	19.9	763	96.1
Wylie city	41,685	53,067	27.3	49,759	54.1	11.8	8.4	4.5	21.1	30.5	7.6	33.5	29.6	36.3	15,181	98.2
Yantis town	388	428	10.3	369	84.3	0.0	1.1	0.5	14.1	27.6	23.8	37.0	51.1	16.5	149	85.2
Yoakum city	5,809	5,940	2.3	5,996	36.8	12.2	0.0	1.4	49.6	27.1	17.1	34.1	67.7	8.5	2,186	75.2
Yorktown city	2,092	2,050	-2.0	1,916	45.1	4.3	0.0	0.0	50.6	24.3	22.3	39.8	55.8	13.2	800	65.5
Yznaga CDP	91	-	-	86	20.9	0.0	0.0	0.0	79.1	0.0	34.9	49.8	57.0	11.6	49	38.8
Zapata CDP	5,089	-	-	5,717	4.8	0.0	0.0	0.6	94.6	30.6	19.5	34.3	62.9	11.7	1,898	81.6
Zapata Ranch CDP	108	-	-	75	0.0	0.0	0.0	0.0	100.0	0.0	13.3	50.5	36.0	37.3	18	66.7
Zarate CDP	59	-	-	-	-	-	-	-	-	-	-	-	-	-	-	-
Zavalla city	713	710	-0.4	797	94.5	0.8	0.0	3.8	1.0	25.8	14.9	41.7	58.5	3.7	313	81.2
Zuehl CDP	376	-	-	339	79.1	0.0	0.0	8.8	12.1	9.7	13.9	56.5	40.1	31.5	151	100.0
UTAH	2,763,891	3,205,958	16.0	3,096,848	78.3	1.1	2.3	4.2	14.0	29.8	10.8	30.8	30.6	34.0	977,313	95.3
Alpine city	9,768	10,498	7.5	10,477	95.4	0.1	0.5	2.4	1.6	34.9	11.6	32.8	10.0	58.0	2,804	99.4
Alta town	386	379	-1.8	398	74.1	0.0	0.5	25.1	0.3	6.0	5.0	35.3	13.4	34.2	83	100.0
Altamont town	269	277	3.0	203	94.1	0.0	0.0	1.0	4.9	34.5	12.3	27.6	43.6	19.1	82	87.8
Alton town	119	120	0.8	218	94.5	0.0	0.0	5.5	0.0	53.7	13.8	16.4	15.3	20.4	53	92.5
Amalga town	490	558	13.9	530	78.9	0.4	0.0	1.1	19.6	36.4	10.9	34.4	45.3	24.1	166	78.3

1 May be of any race.

Table A. All Places — **Population and Housing**

STATE City, town, township, borough, or CDP (county if applicable)	Population				Race and Hispanic or Latino origin (percent)					Age (percent)			Educational attainment of persons age 25 and older		Occupied housing units	
	2010 census total population	2019 estimated population	Percent change 2010–2019	ACS total population estimate 2015–2019	White alone, not Hispanic or Latino	Black alone, not Hispanic or Latino	Asian alone, not Hispanic or Latino	All other races or 2 or more races, not Hispanic or Latino	Hispanic or Latino[1]	Under 18 years old	Age 65 years and older	Median age	Percent High school diploma or less	Percent Bachelor's degree or more	Total	Percent with a computer
	1	2	3	4	5	6	7	8	9	10	11	12	13	14	15	16
UTAH—Con.																
American Fork city..........	26,547	33,161	24.9	30,399	85.2	0.4	0.9	4.3	9.1	33.4	10.2	28.6	22.0	39.6	8,866	97.6
Aneth CDP....................	501	-	-	552	0.4	0.0	0.0	99.1	0.5	37.7	10.3	25.3	66.9	3.2	112	59.8
Annabella town..............	782	810	3.6	949	96.4	0.0	0.0	1.2	2.4	33.1	18.0	39.1	27.7	26.1	300	97.3
Antimony town	125	121	-3.2	86	100.0	0.0	0.0	0.0	0.0	12.8	36.0	60.4	39.1	20.3	44	95.5
Apple Valley town..........	701	844	20.4	674	98.8	0.0	0.0	1.2	0.0	30.4	17.7	36.7	40.2	22.3	223	98.7
Aurora city..................	1,016	1,052	3.5	763	95.2	0.5	0.0	0.0	4.3	24.8	25.4	48.9	53.0	14.6	304	94.4
Avon CDP....................	367	-	-	327	100.0	0.0	0.0	0.0	0.0	27.8	11.6	37.7	23.6	23.6	92	100.0
Ballard town................	810	1,093	34.9	1,053	82.2	1.4	0.0	3.5	12.8	33.9	13.0	35.0	53.7	10.7	294	92.5
Bear River City city..........	855	898	5.0	745	95.8	0.0	2.7	0.0	1.5	27.0	14.6	36.4	37.1	20.2	259	90.3
Beaver city.................	3,122	3,185	2.0	3,074	92.6	0.0	0.0	1.5	6.0	32.3	18.9	36.7	42.5	21.6	1,124	87.1
Benjamin CDP...............	1,145	-	-	960	92.5	0.0	0.0	0.0	7.5	37.3	18.6	36.7	19.6	36.0	282	91.8
Benson CDP..................	1,485	-	-	1,468	93.0	0.0	0.0	0.0	7.0	28.1	17.9	41.2	34.0	37.6	483	87.6
Beryl Junction CDP	197	-	-	89	28.1	0.0	0.0	71.9	0.0	0.0	82.0	76.3	91.0	0.0	81	9.9
Bicknell town................	349	336	-3.7	234	91.5	0.0	0.0	0.0	8.5	18.8	28.6	49.5	43.4	13.9	97	92.8
Big Water town..............	479	511	6.7	562	85.9	0.0	0.0	3.2	10.9	23.3	25.4	47.5	40.4	16.1	216	86.6
Blanding city	3,363	3,633	8.0	3,663	64.7	0.1	2.0	25.5	7.6	36.3	13.0	28.7	28.4	28.7	1,062	82.0
Bluebell CDP.................	293	-	-	236	100.0	0.0	0.0	0.0	0.0	30.1	19.9	39.4	44.2	20.4	77	100.0
Bluff town	236	245	3.8	90	88.9	0.0	0.0	11.1	0.0	0.0	42.2	63.5	37.8	25.6	45	100.0
Bluffdale city................	7,609	16,358	115.0	13,403	89.1	3.0	0.9	2.0	5.1	37.9	6.2	27.8	24.0	34.2	3,407	99.1
Bonanza CDP................	1	-	-	-	-	-	-	-	-	-	-	-	-	-	-	-
Boulder town................	226	241	6.6	270	88.1	0.0	0.0	0.0	11.9	14.4	24.1	54.0	42.5	30.4	105	97.1
Bountiful city................	42,574	43,981	3.3	43,901	89.7	0.4	1.5	2.4	6.0	29.3	15.8	33.3	20.8	45.3	14,379	94.6
Brian Head town	85	93	9.4	69	92.8	0.0	7.2	0.0	0.0	14.5	24.6	51.1	23.4	40.4	34	88.2
Brigham City city...........	17,908	19,601	9.5	19,150	84.8	0.3	0.9	3.0	11.0	30.4	14.7	32.2	37.6	24.0	6,643	91.8
Bryce Canyon City town ...	230	222	-3.5	228	75.9	0.0	0.0	0.0	24.1	24.1	11.0	27.3	50.8	20.5	58	79.3
Cache CDP...................	38	-	-	115	100.0	0.0	0.0	0.0	0.0	43.5	0.0	18.3	31.0	31.0	26	100.0
Cannonville town	178	173	-2.8	322	76.4	0.0	0.0	23.6	0.0	18.6	13.0	38.4	63.6	15.2	86	93.0
Carbonville CDP.............	1,567	-	-	1,346	83.7	0.0	0.0	3.0	13.2	19.5	15.7	46.1	44.3	14.5	606	95.9
Castle Dale city.............	1,638	1,491	-9.0	1,368	98.1	0.0	0.1	0.0	1.8	34.2	19.2	35.0	29.4	15.8	504	84.9
Castle Valley town..........	322	350	8.7	365	100.0	0.0	0.0	0.0	0.0	9.9	39.2	63.4	19.1	51.7	200	90.5
Cedar City city	28,867	34,764	20.4	32,067	83.8	0.8	0.8	4.8	9.8	28.1	10.5	26.2	28.6	34.9	10,959	96.1
Cedar Fort town............	366	395	7.9	231	98.3	1.7	0.0	0.0	0.0	19.9	23.8	41.8	45.8	7.8	86	98.8
Cedar Highlands town	60	68	13.3	164	94.5	0.0	5.5	0.0	0.0	0.0	18.3	53.6	0.0	92.2	53	100.0
Cedar Hills city.............	9,806	10,083	2.8	10,209	91.3	0.1	0.6	1.3	6.8	42.1	7.1	23.7	11.5	52.1	2,460	100.0
Centerfield town............	1,373	1,495	8.9	1,568	89.5	0.0	0.0	0.6	9.9	30.4	11.5	32.8	46.5	15.1	493	94.5
Centerville city	15,304	17,587	14.9	17,404	90.0	0.5	1.6	3.1	4.7	30.0	15.9	36.6	16.0	47.5	5,632	97.1
Central CDP	613	-	-	883	92.4	0.0	0.0	0.0	7.6	17.2	36.9	51.0	36.1	9.2	444	89.9
Central Valley town	549	570	3.8	612	94.6	0.0	0.8	1.8	2.8	28.6	19.6	38.0	28.8	25.9	211	94.3
Charleston town............	423	487	15.1	583	96.4	0.0	0.0	0.5	3.1	18.9	20.6	51.3	31.6	24.4	212	97.2
Circleville town.............	547	489	-10.6	617	91.9	0.0	0.0	1.6	6.5	27.6	25.4	51.3	42.2	22.6	207	83.6
Clarkston town	675	740	9.6	666	95.5	0.0	0.0	0.0	4.5	29.0	17.4	36.3	49.2	20.6	233	91.8
Clawson town	199	186	-6.5	136	100.0	0.0	0.0	0.0	0.0	22.8	27.9	55.8	42.9	14.3	62	80.6
Clear Creek CDP............	4	-	-	37	0.0	21.6	0.0	0.0	78.4	0.0	0.0	40.9	0.0	75.7	28	100.0
Clearfield city................	29,929	32,118	7.3	31,364	72.5	2.7	1.8	4.2	18.9	32.4	6.8	27.9	37.7	21.8	9,644	94.3
Cleveland town	470	440	-6.4	584	99.3	0.0	0.0	0.7	0.0	36.3	10.4	32.9	33.3	21.4	190	90.0
Clinton city..................	20,481	22,499	9.9	21,890	80.9	1.4	1.7	2.7	13.3	33.6	8.4	30.3	36.0	25.3	6,304	97.7
Coalville city................	1,367	1,596	16.8	1,797	60.5	1.4	0.0	1.5	36.5	33.8	8.0	28.1	53.2	17.1	466	93.1
Copperton metro township	822	835	1.6	894	82.0	0.0	0.0	3.2	14.8	26.8	13.8	31.8	49.5	14.6	336	92.0
Corinne city..................	683	763	11.7	620	81.6	0.5	0.8	2.6	14.5	30.6	19.2	34.8	35.8	24.4	211	91.9
Cornish town	297	337	13.5	250	81.6	0.0	0.0	2.0	16.4	29.2	6.8	27.0	47.4	33.1	78	97.4
Cottonwood Heights city...	33,586	33,843	0.8	34,036	87.7	0.3	2.8	3.8	5.3	21.1	16.2	39.1	16.8	52.5	12,937	96.1
Cove CDP....................	460	-	-	262	92.0	0.0	0.0	8.0	0.0	19.5	14.9	52.0	18.7	59.1	112	82.1
Dammeron Valley CDP.....	803	-	-	786	100.0	0.0	0.0	0.0	0.0	7.0	29.9	60.1	20.9	38.4	346	100.0
Daniel town..................	920	1,077	17.1	1,117	89.0	0.7	0.4	0.8	9.0	28.9	13.8	34.8	37.8	30.1	315	86.0
Delta city....................	3,437	3,602	4.8	3,534	74.6	0.6	1.4	1.3	22.0	33.5	16.6	33.8	48.1	19.3	1,156	95.6
Deseret CDP	353	-	-	305	100.0	0.0	0.0	0.0	0.0	27.5	3.0	31.0	50.3	24.3	80	100.0
Deweyville town	336	373	11.0	362	94.2	0.0	0.0	0.6	5.2	24.3	17.4	42.5	41.0	24.3	123	86.2
Draper city	42,272	48,587	14.9	48,000	85.4	1.1	3.5	3.2	6.8	32.0	7.3	32.9	18.8	50.1	13,698	98.9
Duchesne city	1,720	1,710	-0.6	1,830	93.6	0.0	0.4	1.4	4.6	34.2	13.2	32.5	48.4	11.1	652	91.0
Dugway CDP	795	-	-	576	64.4	4.5	3.8	8.7	18.6	23.6	3.0	33.7	13.6	34.0	247	100.0
Dutch John town	145	141	-2.8	89	100.0	0.0	0.0	0.0	0.0	25.8	0.0	55.2	77.3	10.6	12	75.0
Eagle Mountain city.........	21,936	38,391	75.0	32,412	83.8	0.3	0.7	3.7	11.5	46.8	2.1	20.0	21.9	32.9	7,465	99.9
East Carbon city	1,678	1,584	-5.6	1,497	80.5	0.0	0.0	1.0	18.5	25.9	20.8	39.7	50.1	10.3	554	82.7
Echo CDP....................	56	-	-	49	100.0	0.0	0.0	0.0	0.0	0.0	10.2	33.8	69.4	13.9	11	100.0
Eden CDP....................	600	-	-	794	95.1	0.0	0.0	0.0	4.9	18.8	17.3	47.9	7.1	46.2	256	100.0
Elberta CDP	256	-	-	412	70.4	0.0	0.0	4.4	25.2	49.8	7.8	25.0	53.1	0.0	79	100.0
Elk Ridge city................	2,447	4,335	77.2	3,737	94.9	0.0	0.5	1.5	3.1	41.0	7.3	24.8	15.4	41.9	915	99.2
Elmo town...................	435	402	-7.6	397	89.7	0.0	0.0	6.3	4.0	27.7	18.9	41.4	40.9	18.2	142	87.3
Elsinore town	850	882	3.8	732	89.3	0.0	0.0	8.6	2.0	17.3	30.2	45.3	45.4	12.8	300	82.7
Elwood town	1,072	1,103	2.9	1,138	96.4	0.0	1.7	0.0	1.9	34.4	9.3	33.9	35.2	28.9	329	92.1
Emery town..................	290	268	-7.6	390	95.9	0.5	0.0	2.1	1.5	33.3	14.6	40.5	36.1	23.2	130	90.8
Emigration Canyon metro township	1,568	1,592	1.5	1,976	85.3	2.8	3.7	0.7	7.4	19.2	11.2	45.3	7.6	65.3	740	98.4
Enoch city...................	5,871	7,180	22.3	6,738	87.5	0.0	0.4	3.6	8.4	38.7	7.2	26.4	31.5	26.4	1,723	96.9
Enterprise CDP..............	605	-	-	902	89.7	3.3	0.0	2.0	5.0	31.9	0.0	23.7	11.0	42.3	199	100.0
Enterprise city..............	1,711	1,890	10.5	1,505	98.7	0.0	0.0	0.0	1.3	35.3	13.8	30.8	39.0	27.5	477	97.9
Ephraim city.................	6,134	7,308	19.1	7,102	87.0	0.2	1.2	2.6	9.0	29.1	8.4	22.1	27.6	30.2	1,959	90.1
Erda CDP....................	4,642	-	-	2,635	95.0	0.0	0.0	2.6	2.4	34.5	9.6	33.3	28.9	39.0	651	96.8
Escalante city	820	798	-2.7	695	81.2	0.0	0.0	5.9	12.9	13.4	33.5	57.4	40.0	28.3	335	90.4
Eureka city..................	669	707	5.7	583	94.7	0.0	0.0	2.6	2.7	23.5	19.9	48.5	45.9	15.2	248	86.7
Fairfield town	114	145	27.2	98	87.8	0.0	0.0	0.0	12.2	19.4	13.3	47.2	53.3	2.7	32	100.0
Fairview city.................	1,245	1,358	9.1	1,410	96.3	0.0	0.0	0.8	2.9	25.7	22.0	43.3	45.6	18.7	516	89.7
Farmington city.............	18,234	25,339	39.0	23,847	91.0	0.7	1.6	2.3	4.5	34.7	8.8	31.2	17.3	47.5	6,750	97.3
Farr West city...............	5,955	7,385	24.0	7,023	89.8	0.3	0.2	3.4	6.4	28.1	12.9	36.7	34.1	24.3	2,130	95.4
Fayette town	242	263	8.7	329	91.2	0.0	0.0	0.0	8.8	42.9	7.9	20.3	15.4	31.4	84	94.0
Ferron city..................	1,666	1,495	-10.3	1,416	97.2	0.0	0.0	0.1	2.6	24.2	19.4	43.5	39.3	8.6	557	94.8
Fielding town	462	482	4.3	475	93.5	0.0	0.0	0.0	6.5	31.8	13.1	32.7	46.0	14.7	149	87.2
Fillmore city	2,461	2,650	7.7	2,544	76.7	0.0	3.3	1.8	18.3	27.2	16.2	36.7	45.2	22.5	912	94.8
Flaming Gorge CDP	83	-	-	120	100.0	0.0	0.0	0.0	0.0	30.0	20.0	50.7	50.0	27.4	51	92.2
Fort Duchesne CDP	714	-	-	594	0.0	0.0	0.0	89.6	10.4	34.2	6.1	22.4	78.4	6.1	144	72.2
Fountain Green city	1,069	1,166	9.1	944	94.6	0.0	0.0	2.1	3.3	19.8	19.0	41.1	42.9	23.0	330	93.9
Francis town	1,062	1,574	48.2	1,182	89.5	0.0	0.0	0.3	10.2	33.8	10.0	36.5	35.4	26.2	374	98.9

1 May be of any race.

Table A. All Places — **Population and Housing**

STATE City, town, township, borough, or CDP (county if applicable)	Population				Race and Hispanic or Latino origin (percent)					Age (percent)			Educational attainment of persons age 25 and older		Occupied housing units	
	2010 census total population	2019 estimated population	Percent change 2010–2019	ACS total population estimate 2015–2019	White alone, not Hispanic or Latino	Black alone, not Hispanic or Latino	Asian alone, not Hispanic or Latino	All other races or 2 or more races, not Hispanic or Latino	Hispanic or Latino[1]	Under 18 years old	Age 65 years and older	Median age	Percent High school diploma or less	Percent Bachelor's degree or more	Total	Percent with a computer
	1	2	3	4	5	6	7	8	9	10	11	12	13	14	15	16
UTAH—Con.																
Fremont CDP	145	-	-	99	96.0	4.0	0.0	0.0	0.0	0.0	19.2	36.4	20.2	56.6	57	91.2
Fruit Heights city	5,036	6,221	23.5	6,172	94.2	0.0	0.5	2.5	2.7	31.2	12.5	39.8	15.5	51.7	1,887	99.0
Garden CDP	181	-	-	262	49.6	0.0	0.0	0.0	50.4	8.0	29.4	52.3	27.2	29.1	75	100.0
Garden City town	563	617	9.6	442	83.7	0.0	0.0	0.0	16.3	36.0	16.1	30.7	30.6	14.3	124	100.0
Garland city	2,436	2,590	6.3	2,520	90.4	0.0	0.3	2.3	7.1	33.3	9.9	30.2	41.4	18.0	849	91.0
Genola town	1,372	1,567	14.2	1,426	94.5	0.8	0.0	1.1	3.6	36.7	10.3	29.0	30.7	25.3	369	92.4
Glendale town	381	407	6.8	268	95.5	0.0	0.0	1.5	3.0	23.9	26.5	41.7	25.9	16.2	89	88.8
Glenwood town	460	476	3.5	640	98.0	0.0	0.0	0.0	2.0	35.6	13.1	31.0	32.5	25.1	187	96.8
Goshen town	904	915	1.2	874	80.7	0.0	0.2	0.5	18.6	32.5	10.9	35.7	49.5	10.7	287	91.6
Granite CDP	1,932	-	-	801	92.3	2.0	0.0	5.5	0.2	28.2	23.5	43.5	6.4	62.6	266	100.0
Grantsville city	8,926	12,064	35.2	11,021	88.4	0.2	1.7	3.4	6.3	38.8	7.9	30.5	34.3	27.0	3,068	96.1
Green River city	1,030	935	-9.2	856	70.9	0.0	0.0	0.0	29.1	25.8	15.3	33.0	53.1	12.5	314	83.4
Gunnison city	3,285	3,585	9.1	3,434	64.6	4.3	2.4	7.0	21.8	14.4	6.0	36.5	48.1	9.3	418	90.0
Halchita CDP	266	-	-	408	0.0	0.0	0.0	100.0	0.0	51.5	7.4	16.9	70.7	0.0	80	20.0
Halls Crossing CDP	6	-	-	-	-	-	-	-	-	-	-	-	-	-	-	-
Hanksville town	219	220	0.5	270	71.9	0.7	0.0	11.5	15.9	25.2	23.3	45.3	41.5	10.9	94	88.3
Harrisville city	5,570	6,872	23.4	6,510	84.2	0.0	0.0	4.9	10.9	34.5	7.2	28.2	40.7	21.6	1,968	99.3
Hatch town	146	142	-2.7	148	94.6	0.0	0.0	0.0	5.4	31.1	30.4	35.5	53.2	25.5	49	89.8
Heber city	11,436	17,082	49.4	15,699	75.9	0.0	1.7	2.7	19.8	34.0	7.2	27.5	31.3	33.6	4,480	95.4
Helper city	2,203	2,105	-4.4	2,239	84.0	0.6	0.0	0.4	15.0	23.9	19.6	38.8	43.3	17.1	904	92.0
Henefer town	785	979	24.7	823	99.1	0.0	0.0	0.0	0.9	27.3	13.1	32.7	31.0	32.5	279	94.3
Henrieville town	230	225	-2.2	265	82.6	0.0	1.1	10.2	6.0	32.5	14.7	29.9	45.2	18.7	85	82.4
Herriman city	21,768	51,348	135.9	40,149	84.1	0.7	1.4	7.0	6.8	40.4	4.3	25.5	23.8	35.3	10,394	100.0
Hideout town	656	998	52.1	996	25.5	2.9	2.1	0.8	68.7	40.9	8.4	26.1	34.7	41.8	283	86.6
Highland city	15,570	19,175	23.2	18,726	94.4	1.1	1.3	1.7	1.5	40.8	7.9	24.0	9.3	61.0	4,395	99.5
Hildale city	2,745	2,896	5.5	2,910	99.5	0.0	0.0	0.0	0.5	59.6	0.4	15.8	61.0	7.2	406	98.8
Hinckley town	696	716	2.9	559	85.5	0.0	0.0	2.3	12.2	30.8	21.5	34.4	38.0	15.9	202	91.6
Holden town	378	393	4.0	514	95.5	0.0	1.8	2.5	0.2	30.0	21.0	30.2	13.1	49.1	189	98.9
Holladay city	30,127	30,325	0.7	30,636	88.1	1.8	2.1	2.7	5.3	25.2	18.4	39.2	14.4	55.8	11,065	96.2
Honeyville city	1,441	1,644	14.1	1,531	94.6	0.7	0.3	1.5	2.8	33.6	10.8	32.6	36.6	28.4	436	93.1
Hooper city	7,147	9,152	28.1	8,646	91.0	0.0	0.5	1.2	7.4	32.3	8.2	33.6	29.6	25.5	2,439	98.5
Howell town	245	254	3.7	216	93.5	0.0	1.4	0.5	4.6	19.4	23.6	40.5	42.9	9.0	89	76.4
Hoytsville CDP	607	-	-	392	100.0	0.0	0.0	0.0	0.0	30.9	14.0	44.1	42.0	30.5	142	77.5
Huntington city	2,141	1,934	-9.7	2,139	87.8	0.0	0.0	2.1	10.1	31.3	11.4	30.5	39.7	16.5	734	91.3
Huntsville town	617	642	4.1	628	96.2	0.0	1.0	0.0	2.9	20.1	24.4	48.0	24.1	33.5	225	92.0
Hurricane city	13,756	19,074	38.7	17,212	86.3	1.2	0.8	2.9	8.9	26.0	19.1	37.6	38.8	17.3	5,954	93.1
Hyde Park city	3,841	4,797	24.9	4,578	91.0	1.7	0.0	0.2	7.1	36.6	9.8	27.9	24.7	46.6	1,292	100.0
Hyrum city	7,616	8,619	13.2	8,224	79.6	0.4	0.4	2.9	16.7	36.5	7.2	26.2	37.1	27.7	2,316	99.4
Independence town	142	198	39.4	185	97.3	1.1	0.0	0.0	1.6	40.5	4.9	23.7	34.5	20.7	44	100.0
Interlaken town	157	235	49.7	118	100.0	0.0	0.0	0.0	0.0	3.4	26.3	64.1	35.1	22.8	94	100.0
Ivins city	6,757	9,192	36.0	8,530	88.4	0.4	0.9	1.7	8.6	21.1	30.0	47.6	30.5	33.5	3,481	98.2
Jensen CDP	412	-	-	222	100.0	0.0	0.0	0.0	0.0	43.7	18.9	33.4	36.8	0.0	81	75.3
Joseph town	344	358	4.1	338	91.7	0.0	0.9	4.7	2.7	23.4	21.9	42.0	46.3	18.2	130	95.4
Junction town	191	172	-9.9	253	100.0	0.0	0.0	0.0	0.0	20.2	25.7	52.2	83.9	0.0	69	89.9
Kamas city	1,850	2,276	23.0	2,539	69.5	1.0	0.0	3.4	26.1	40.0	6.5	24.9	42.3	23.5	678	97.5
Kanab city	4,326	4,931	14.0	4,636	91.1	0.0	0.5	5.3	3.0	20.0	22.1	43.3	25.8	36.6	1,681	90.7
Kanarraville town	358	407	13.7	338	93.5	2.1	0.0	0.9	3.6	20.4	26.9	42.8	33.6	24.8	133	99.2
Kanosh town	474	485	2.3	699	81.1	0.0	0.7	7.6	10.6	37.6	15.7	33.1	35.9	15.8	213	88.7
Kaysville city	27,570	32,390	17.5	31,494	93.2	0.3	0.9	1.2	4.3	36.4	9.8	30.4	14.8	49.4	8,712	98.0
Kearns metro township	35,769	36,330	1.6	36,581	49.9	2.4	3.3	6.6	37.8	34.1	6.4	28.3	55.8	11.0	9,471	95.5
Kenilworth CDP	180	-	-	204	100.0	0.0	0.0	0.0	0.0	9.3	30.9	55.6	34.6	14.6	121	94.2
Kingston town	173	155	-10.4	160	100.0	0.0	0.0	0.0	0.0	30.6	19.4	26.5	44.4	7.4	45	100.0
Koosharem town	329	330	0.3	263	83.7	7.6	0.0	1.9	6.8	44.5	23.2	31.1	39.8	15.0	73	93.2
Lake Shore CDP	817	-	-	704	100.0	0.0	0.0	0.0	0.0	18.6	9.4	48.2	24.4	16.7	240	93.8
Laketown town	252	276	9.5	270	99.6	0.0	0.0	0.0	0.4	29.3	23.0	42.8	7.4	41.3	86	91.9
La Sal CDP	395	-	-	291	42.6	0.0	0.0	0.0	57.4	22.3	10.3	46.1	57.1	0.0	78	82.1
La Verkin city	4,062	4,446	9.5	4,329	85.2	0.0	0.0	3.4	11.4	33.6	16.7	35.7	42.5	17.3	1,319	95.4
Layton city	67,529	78,014	15.5	76,197	78.8	1.5	2.3	4.6	12.8	31.4	8.8	30.7	29.2	34.2	24,061	96.1
Leamington town	226	239	5.8	316	90.8	0.0	0.0	9.2	0.0	39.6	22.2	35.6	18.3	36.6	97	95.9
Leeds town	808	873	8.0	766	91.3	0.0	1.0	0.3	7.4	14.8	44.3	60.5	32.0	28.8	325	92.6
Lehi city	47,769	69,724	46.0	64,006	85.9	0.3	1.9	4.0	7.9	42.3	5.9	25.2	17.2	46.3	16,611	98.4
Levan town	843	954	13.2	883	92.0	0.0	0.0	0.0	8.0	30.0	21.1	37.1	62.4	8.1	291	85.9
Lewiston city	1,764	1,798	1.9	2,084	83.3	0.0	0.1	3.2	13.3	33.4	13.9	31.8	32.6	27.7	638	94.4
Liberty CDP	1,257	-	-	929	85.7	0.8	0.0	1.3	12.3	25.8	7.8	36.6	42.8	28.2	307	100.0
Lindon city	10,045	11,100	10.5	10,912	88.3	0.1	1.8	4.1	5.7	32.7	10.6	29.6	20.3	42.5	2,890	98.3
Loa town	618	575	-7.0	524	93.9	0.0	0.0	2.9	3.2	36.8	16.6	31.0	47.0	16.3	176	92.6
Logan city	48,203	51,542	6.9	50,863	76.3	1.3	3.3	3.7	15.3	23.9	7.4	24.0	29.1	36.9	17,149	94.8
Lyman town	258	257	-0.4	307	97.4	0.0	2.6	0.0	0.0	20.5	20.8	46.3	36.9	13.4	109	85.3
Lynndyl town	106	117	10.4	96	97.9	0.0	0.0	2.1	0.0	35.4	27.1	42.5	53.3	20.0	40	65.0
Maeser CDP	3,601	-	-	4,123	95.9	0.6	0.0	1.4	2.1	35.0	11.2	30.9	37.6	21.3	1,244	94.9
Magna metro township	26,513	26,949	1.6	27,145	59.7	1.3	1.8	6.1	31.1	32.2	6.4	30.7	58.5	9.7	7,901	93.9
Manila town	327	307	-6.1	211	100.0	0.0	0.0	0.0	0.0	34.6	13.3	20.8	42.3	18.6	53	90.6
Manti city	3,437	3,738	8.8	3,610	90.4	1.1	0.7	2.9	4.9	27.2	16.1	35.0	28.3	25.7	1,126	94.8
Mantua town	689	963	39.8	700	92.3	0.0	0.0	4.3	3.4	18.9	18.6	47.5	25.5	34.3	245	91.4
Mapleton city	8,070	10,731	33.0	9,872	90.8	0.5	0.1	2.4	6.3	35.8	11.6	31.1	18.4	48.9	2,585	95.8
Marion CDP	685	-	-	603	97.0	0.0	0.0	0.0	3.0	24.5	2.3	27.2	30.7	49.6	160	100.0
Marriott-Slaterville city	1,696	1,898	11.9	2,037	87.8	0.6	0.7	4.2	6.7	24.8	14.9	36.8	41.6	16.1	691	96.4
Marysvale town	399	437	9.5	619	99.4	0.0	0.0	0.0	0.6	19.5	22.8	37.6	44.5	27.5	153	88.2
Mayfield town	507	552	8.9	392	98.7	0.0	0.0	1.3	0.0	30.1	22.4	37.9	24.1	23.0	143	90.9
Meadow town	310	328	5.8	219	97.3	0.0	0.0	1.4	1.4	24.2	26.0	44.1	46.6	11.6	91	80.2
Mendon city	1,341	1,396	4.1	1,214	96.2	0.0	0.0	1.1	2.7	33.6	15.7	33.8	21.6	40.6	362	93.9
Mexican Hat CDP	31	-	-	-	-	-	-	-	-	-	-	-	-	-	-	-
Midvale city	27,998	34,124	21.9	33,318	63.8	3.2	3.7	4.8	24.5	26.5	8.6	30.6	33.0	32.5	12,695	96.1
Midway city	3,901	5,280	35.3	5,035	97.4	0.0	0.2	1.4	1.0	27.8	19.0	44.1	24.1	46.3	1,930	96.6
Milford city	1,408	1,394		1,731	79.3	0.0	0.0	2.4	18.3	31.8	10.1	29.2	49.4	12.4	561	92.5
Millcreek city	58,750	61,450	4.6	60,731	80.3	1.9	4.5	3.2	10.1	22.3	15.5	36.9	21.1	50.6	24,000	94.1
Millville city	1,904	2,150	12.9	2,054	91.0	0.0	1.2	4.8	3.0	34.5	9.5	27.9	37.6	34.7	625	95.5
Minersville town	907	920	1.4	881	94.0	0.0	0.0	0.0	6.0	27.5	11.8	40.0	45.5	21.4	313	97.8
Moab city	5,066	5,336	5.3	5,268	73.6	0.6	1.9	7.3	16.6	20.9	17.5	38.3	43.7	28.8	2,209	88.3
Mona city	1,537	1,807	17.6	1,591	96.5	0.0	0.0	0.1	3.3	37.9	10.1	29.6	48.4	15.9	453	97.8
Monroe city	2,268	2,358	4.0	2,493	95.1	0.3	0.0	0.3	4.3	25.1	21.2	39.1	36.1	20.2	886	94.7
Montezuma Creek CDP	335	-	-	386	1.6	0.0	0.0	97.4	1.0	34.7	8.8	28.6	56.5	15.7	84	56.0

1 May be of any race.

Table A. All Places — **Population and Housing**

STATE City, town, township, borough, or CDP (county if applicable)	Population				Race and Hispanic or Latino origin (percent)					Age (percent)			Educational attainment of persons age 25 and older		Occupied housing units	
	2010 census total population	2019 estimated population	Percent change 2010–2019	ACS total population estimate 2015–2019	White alone, not Hispanic or Latino	Black alone, not Hispanic or Latino	Asian alone, not Hispanic or Latino	All other races or 2 or more races, not Hispanic or Latino	Hispanic or Latino[1]	Under 18 years old	Age 65 years and older	Median age	Percent High school diploma or less	Percent Bachelor's degree or more	Total	Percent with a computer
	1	2	3	4	5	6	7	8	9	10	11	12	13	14	15	16
UTAH—Con.																
Monticello city	1,981	1,969	-0.6	2,604	79.2	0.7	0.0	9.6	10.6	31.7	13.6	28.7	30.9	31.7	766	88.3
Morgan city	3,663	4,273	16.7	4,184	94.9	0.2	0.3	0.8	3.8	37.4	11.7	31.1	27.2	33.4	1,293	94.5
Moroni city	1,427	1,552	8.8	1,536	74.2	0.0	2.5	0.0	23.3	31.3	15.4	33.8	48.7	12.3	473	94.1
Mountain Green CDP	2,309	-	-	3,853	94.2	1.3	0.0	1.7	2.8	35.3	10.6	33.4	13.1	53.0	1,042	99.2
Mount Pleasant city	3,259	3,530	8.3	3,418	92.6	0.3	1.9	1.8	3.4	28.6	18.1	31.8	46.9	22.1	1,055	91.5
Murray city	46,685	48,917	4.8	49,105	80.2	1.7	2.2	4.7	11.2	21.6	16.4	36.6	29.8	33.6	19,084	93.1
Myton city	574	606	5.6	526	65.2	0.0	0.0	20.2	14.6	30.8	13.1	33.8	65.1	4.1	217	91.7
Naples city	1,736	2,082	19.9	2,714	87.7	0.0	0.0	1.5	10.8	37.8	9.8	30.2	41.8	16.3	789	93.5
Navajo Mountain CDP	354	-	-	273	0.0	0.0	0.0	98.9	1.1	33.7	9.5	23.9	54.8	15.6	68	54.4
Neola CDP	461	-	-	440	81.1	0.0	0.0	16.8	2.0	35.7	11.6	28.6	47.7	13.2	137	91.2
Nephi city	5,388	6,378	18.4	5,969	89.7	0.4	0.0	3.1	6.8	32.5	11.1	29.8	43.3	17.7	1,904	93.3
Newcastle CDP	247	-	-	267	100.0	0.0	0.0	0.0	0.0	0.0	28.1	60.7	29.2	0.0	108	100.0
New Harmony town	212	234	10.4	212	97.6	0.0	0.0	0.0	2.4	14.2	42.9	57.6	23.6	37.9	101	86.1
Newton town	794	817	2.9	780	97.1	0.0	0.0	2.3	0.6	34.7	10.3	33.8	30.7	31.7	226	95.6
Nibley city	5,466	7,135	30.5	6,819	86.1	0.0	0.4	2.7	10.8	42.3	4.5	24.9	26.4	38.0	1,691	98.8
North Logan city	8,303	11,237	35.3	10,711	86.1	0.3	4.8	2.0	6.8	30.8	10.4	27.0	18.2	47.2	3,345	96.6
North Ogden city	17,415	20,582	18.2	19,392	88.7	0.8	0.4	3.1	7.0	29.4	12.5	33.7	28.7	32.5	6,101	98.1
North Salt Lake city	16,199	20,948	29.3	20,402	78.0	0.4	3.0	4.9	13.7	31.9	7.0	29.9	24.8	43.8	6,620	97.3
Oak City town	604	649	7.5	548	89.4	0.0	0.0	9.1	1.5	36.5	12.4	33.4	17.0	27.7	163	98.8
Oakley city	1,505	1,740	15.6	1,565	99.0	0.0	0.1	0.0	0.8	24.3	13.4	36.2	33.6	27.4	518	96.7
Oasis CDP	75	-	-	28	100.0	0.0	0.0	0.0	0.0	0.0	0.0	59.6	64.3	0.0	20	100.0
Ogden city	82,887	87,773	5.9	86,833	61.3	1.7	1.2	3.9	31.9	26.3	10.7	31.8	46.2	20.8	30,556	90.7
Oljato-Monument Valley CDP	674	-	-	854	6.1	0.0	0.0	92.6	1.3	28.2	14.8	35.4	65.0	7.5	240	5.0
Ophir CDP	38	-	-	50	78.0	0.0	0.0	22.0	0.0	6.0	26.0	34.8	53.2	36.2	30	100.0
Orangeville city	1,476	1,326	-10.2	1,283	98.2	0.0	0.0	0.0	1.8	25.9	17.1	37.6	30.3	24.0	479	88.1
Orderville town	576	592	2.8	741	97.7	0.0	0.0	0.4	1.9	30.4	13.9	30.0	37.3	15.9	205	93.2
Orem city	88,328	97,828	10.8	96,725	76.0	0.6	2.1	4.5	16.8	28.2	10.1	26.5	23.1	40.0	29,049	97.0
Palmyra CDP	491	-	-	468	100.0	0.0	0.0	0.0	0.0	15.8	35.0	47.6	31.8	21.3	191	96.3
Panguitch city	1,726	1,682	-2.5	1,785	90.0	0.0	0.0	5.7	4.3	31.9	17.8	36.6	43.4	28.0	534	92.5
Paradise town	905	1,022	12.9	990	99.4	0.0	0.2	0.0	0.4	35.6	13.1	35.4	29.6	34.9	292	95.9
Paragonah town	498	545	9.4	478	93.3	0.0	0.0	4.0	2.7	25.1	18.8	40.6	39.6	12.5	169	94.1
Park City city	7,557	8,526	12.8	8,375	71.1	2.3	4.5	2.5	19.6	17.6	13.2	40.0	16.3	60.7	2,960	96.9
Parowan city	2,801	3,165	13.0	3,033	92.4	0.0	0.4	3.8	3.4	27.1	22.4	39.9	28.8	17.4	1,057	86.2
Payson city	18,515	20,303	9.7	19,842	84.7	0.0	0.6	2.9	11.9	34.6	9.9	27.1	34.4	22.8	5,483	94.5
Peoa CDP	253	-	-	247	96.0	0.0	0.0	0.0	4.0	3.2	23.9	55.2	6.7	56.5	179	100.0
Perry city	4,512	5,248	16.3	4,971	92.9	0.0	0.4	1.0	5.7	35.2	12.0	36.3	24.7	36.4	1,515	96.9
Peter CDP	324	-	-	564	94.5	1.4	0.0	0.0	4.1	47.5	5.7	25.1	13.4	36.4	147	90.5
Pine Valley CDP	186	-	-	168	100.0	0.0	0.0	0.0	0.0	27.4	22.0	32.9	16.4	60.7	68	100.0
Plain City city	5,483	7,669	39.9	6,867	96.8	0.0	0.0	1.5	1.7	37.1	9.1	30.5	34.6	24.6	1,972	94.8
Pleasant Grove city	33,550	38,258	14.0	38,380	85.5	0.4	1.4	3.6	9.1	32.2	8.9	26.8	20.0	39.8	11,501	98.0
Pleasant View city	7,945	10,839	36.4	10,162	81.9	0.0	3.7	1.6	12.7	33.1	12.3	35.2	27.8	34.3	2,808	98.6
Plymouth town	404	460	13.9	329	90.6	0.0	0.6	2.4	6.4	32.5	17.3	35.8	51.5	9.9	112	88.4
Portage town	245	273	11.4	244	95.1	0.8	0.0	3.7	0.4	28.3	16.4	34.0	54.2	9.7	88	88.6
Price city	8,727	8,332	-4.5	8,265	82.9	0.4	0.1	0.7	15.9	29.5	14.8	32.4	32.2	16.8	3,024	88.3
Providence city	6,957	7,780	11.8	7,407	91.2	0.0	1.1	2.8	5.0	32.7	13.2	30.2	15.2	49.0	2,269	97.3
Provo city	112,487	116,618	3.7	116,403	74.4	0.8	2.6	5.4	16.7	21.8	6.1	23.6	21.5	43.1	33,061	97.6
Randlett CDP	220	-	-	80	0.0	0.0	0.0	100.0	0.0	17.5	12.5	39.3	31.0	0.0	31	67.7
Randolph town	468	508	8.5	895	95.6	0.0	0.0	0.0	4.4	26.8	25.4	32.5	54.5	11.1	174	94.8
Redmond town	730	747	2.3	699	91.3	0.4	0.3	0.0	8.0	23.0	19.0	40.3	51.7	13.1	264	90.2
Richfield city	7,569	7,888	4.2	7,731	90.6	1.2	0.0	3.9	4.4	32.2	12.5	31.5	38.6	20.9	2,597	93.8
Richmond city	2,476	2,803	13.2	2,672	92.9	0.0	0.4	2.5	4.1	36.1	9.5	31.1	36.8	27.8	802	95.1
Riverdale city	8,477	8,838	4.3	8,752	78.6	2.0	2.7	1.3	15.4	24.6	14.8	32.1	38.6	21.4	3,320	94.3
River Heights city	1,842	2,076	12.7	2,162	92.0	0.0	0.9	2.5	4.6	29.9	13.6	34.9	17.1	53.4	710	99.3
Riverside CDP	760	-	-	810	98.1	0.0	1.9	0.0	0.0	21.1	14.3	37.4	18.9	22.6	283	100.0
Riverton city	38,832	44,440	14.4	43,250	87.4	0.4	1.8	1.5	8.9	36.5	7.3	30.9	23.4	38.0	11,704	98.8
Rockville town	245	269	9.8	223	98.2	0.0	0.0	0.0	1.8	7.2	38.6	57.9	10.8	43.8	110	90.0
Rocky Ridge town	733	858	17.1	963	98.8	0.0	0.0	0.0	1.2	57.4	2.0	15.4	57.2	8.2	147	94.6
Roosevelt city	6,182	7,233	17.0	7,041	76.4	0.6	1.1	8.9	13.0	36.9	8.7	28.3	42.6	19.4	2,397	91.9
Roy city	37,450	39,613	5.8	39,040	73.9	0.9	1.6	5.3	18.3	30.4	10.4	31.4	42.9	18.8	12,773	96.0
Rush Valley town	439	494	12.5	537	90.3	0.0	0.0	0.9	8.8	26.1	12.3	40.8	36.6	13.1	174	93.1
St. George city	72,759	89,587	23.1	84,500	80.5	0.8	0.9	4.9	12.9	24.8	22.7	37.2	28.9	29.3	29,943	92.3
Salem city	6,428	8,621	34.1	8,099	92.0	0.4	0.4	3.9	3.4	35.4	9.4	27.9	23.9	36.4	2,061	98.1
Salina city	2,506	2,612	4.2	2,580	87.6	0.2	0.0	2.0	10.2	26.9	12.2	35.8	53.2	14.1	948	93.4
Salt Lake City city	186,433	200,567	7.6	197,756	64.8	2.4	5.3	5.7	21.8	20.2	11.1	32.3	28.7	46.5	79,264	94.0
Samak CDP	287	-	-	369	98.1	0.0	0.0	1.9	0.0	16.0	25.5	43.7	34.8	33.3	170	88.2
Sandy city	90,180	96,380	6.9	96,127	84.0	0.6	3.7	3.0	8.7	25.2	13.8	36.5	23.4	41.8	31,388	95.4
Santa Clara city	6,145	8,417	37.0	7,495	92.0	0.8	0.5	3.5	3.2	33.8	14.7	36.0	21.6	40.0	2,231	98.8
Santaquin city	9,175	12,865	40.2	11,684	83.9	0.8	0.0	1.9	13.5	39.9	6.2	24.7	40.8	21.0	3,010	97.5
Saratoga Springs city	17,842	33,282	86.5	29,161	86.5	0.8	1.2	3.7	7.7	45.0	3.9	23.1	15.3	48.3	7,044	99.6
Scipio town	327	332	1.5	308	98.4	0.0	0.0	0.0	1.6	25.3	31.8	46.4	42.4	15.2	127	85.8
Scofield town	24	23	-4.2	62	100.0	0.0	0.0	0.0	0.0	16.1	21.0	30.5	54.8	22.6	18	72.2
Sigurd town	427	443	3.7	439	96.4	0.0	0.0	0.0	3.6	28.0	16.9	34.7	59.1	10.4	167	83.2
Silver Summit CDP	3,632	-	-	4,503	91.3	0.2	1.2	2.5	4.8	29.8	9.9	42.2	16.7	59.0	1,343	98.7
Smithfield city	9,632	12,025	24.8	11,373	89.7	0.0	1.0	2.4	6.9	37.0	9.8	26.9	23.1	37.5	3,165	97.7
Snowville town	167	173	3.6	139	89.2	0.0	0.0	0.0	10.8	18.0	11.5	32.3	72.2	4.1	36	75.0
Snyderville CDP	5,612	-	-	6,255	92.4	1.0	1.4	1.5	3.8	25.4	11.7	43.3	8.6	73.1	2,489	98.3
South Jordan city	50,473	76,598	51.8	71,198	84.7	1.0	3.8	3.4	7.1	32.9	10.0	32.6	18.9	42.2	20,833	98.1
South Ogden city	16,563	17,199	3.8	17,063	80.9	1.2	0.8	3.1	14.1	26.0	14.6	34.6	33.1	27.5	6,153	93.6
South Salt Lake city	23,574	25,582	8.5	25,017	54.4	6.9	10.4	9.2	19.1	21.8	7.5	32.2	42.2	25.3	9,544	91.0
South Weber city	6,117	7,836	28.1	7,381	88.3	0.4	0.9	1.7	8.7	33.9	8.6	31.9	16.2	42.0	2,075	97.7
South Willard CDP	1,571	-	-	1,726	90.4	0.0	0.8	1.3	7.5	28.0	11.8	36.9	36.2	28.7	582	97.6
Spanish Fork city	34,763	40,913	17.7	39,371	84.7	0.3	0.2	3.2	11.7	38.4	6.5	25.3	29.6	32.2	10,223	96.5
Spanish Valley CDP	491	-	-	577	97.9	0.0	0.0	0.0	2.1	37.4	10.1	30.4	51.2	8.9	170	71.8
Spring City city	991	1,080	9.0	1,178	92.2	0.0	0.6	0.6	6.6	17.9	30.1	51.3	38.1	26.7	447	96.0
Springdale town	529	629	18.9	346	95.1	0.0	0.0	0.0	4.9	7.8	37.6	59.9	17.9	42.1	176	93.8
Spring Glen CDP	1,126	-	-	995	98.6	0.0	0.0	0.0	1.4	15.5	23.7	55.1	35.1	15.8	465	79.4
Spring Lake CDP	458	-	-	526	97.7	2.3	0.0	0.0	0.0	23.0	13.7	35.7	41.5	16.7	167	95.2
Springville city	29,559	33,310	12.7	32,952	79.8	0.2	0.8	2.8	16.4	37.8	8.0	25.6	26.7	36.1	9,227	96.7
Stansbury Park CDP	5,145	-	-	9,325	89.1	0.6	1.6	1.7	7.0	35.9	8.5	32.2	18.1	41.9	2,813	98.3
Sterling town	293	320	9.2	259	95.0	1.2	1.5	0.4	1.9	29.0	10.4	37.1	20.8	24.7	91	87.9
Stockton town	632	682	7.9	680	91.3	0.0	0.0	0.0	8.7	19.1	19.3	50.8	55.2	9.9	259	95.4

1 May be of any race.

Table A. All Places — Population and Housing

STATE City, town, township, borough, or CDP (county if applicable)	2010 census total population	2019 estimated population	Percent change 2010–2019	ACS total population estimate 2015–2019	White alone, not Hispanic or Latino	Black alone, not Hispanic or Latino	Asian alone, not Hispanic or Latino	All other races or 2 or more races, not Hispanic or Latino	Hispanic or Latino[1]	Under 18 years old	Age 65 years and older	Median age	Percent High school diploma or less	Percent Bachelor's degree or more	Total	Percent with a computer
	1	2	3	4	5	6	7	8	9	10	11	12	13	14	15	16
UTAH—Con.																
Summit CDP	160	-	-	228	94.7	0.0	0.0	0.0	5.3	21.5	30.3	54.8	47.5	4.5	91	71.4
Summit Park CDP	7,775	-	-	8,118	87.2	0.1	2.5	1.3	9.0	22.8	14.3	42.0	15.5	67.5	2,938	98.4
Sunset city	5,147	5,364	4.2	5,278	74.3	1.2	1.9	3.4	19.2	29.5	11.1	32.5	48.8	17.4	1,678	94.8
Sutherland CDP	165	-	-	34	100.0	0.0	0.0	0.0	0.0	44.1	0.0	41.2	100.0	0.0	10	100.0
Syracuse city	24,377	31,458	29.0	29,331	86.7	3.4	1.4	2.9	5.7	37.8	7.0	28.8	24.0	37.5	7,799	99.8
Tabiona town	156	159	1.9	134	98.5	0.0	0.0	1.5	0.0	21.6	24.6	42.3	53.3	4.3	58	81.0
Taylorsville city	58,691	59,805	1.9	60,138	64.5	1.3	5.3	4.5	24.3	26.1	12.4	33.7	40.8	24.5	20,248	93.5
Teasdale CDP	191	-	-	218	100.0	0.0	0.0	0.0	0.0	47.2	2.3	26.3	19.1	56.5	67	100.0
Thatcher town	789	-	-	634	96.1	2.5	0.0	0.0	1.4	41.0	7.6	33.6	37.6	18.4	196	100.0
Thompson Springs CDP	39	-	-	99	100.0	0.0	0.0	0.0	0.0	30.3	0.0	19.8	59.1	0.0	18	100.0
Timber Lakes CDP	607	-	-	661	100.0	0.0	0.0	0.0	0.0	26.8	35.2	49.3	38.4	35.7	263	100.0
Tooele city	31,603	36,015	14.0	34,535	80.9	0.5	0.3	3.4	14.8	31.0	9.2	31.2	44.0	18.3	10,945	94.7
Toquerville city	1,372	1,735	26.5	1,802	94.7	0.3	0.0	2.7	2.2	35.6	17.6	35.0	26.2	28.7	482	97.7
Torrey town	245	244	-0.4	316	74.1	0.0	0.0	0.0	25.9	25.3	37.7	57.4	37.2	29.1	129	94.6
Tremonton city	7,679	9,206	19.9	8,638	81.0	2.3	1.0	1.9	13.8	36.4	10.5	27.0	45.6	18.7	2,755	91.2
Trenton town	489	552	12.9	508	85.0	0.0	0.0	0.0	15.0	36.0	10.8	29.7	33.6	27.3	150	98.0
Tropic town	530	514	-3.0	485	100.0	0.0	0.0	0.0	0.0	22.1	27.0	46.9	38.1	27.9	178	89.9
Tselakai Dezza CDP	109	-	-	96	0.0	0.0	0.0	96.9	3.1	21.9	10.4	49.3	64.0	2.7	30	43.3
Uintah town	1,319	1,353	2.6	1,439	84.9	0.0	0.0	4.1	11.0	29.3	15.4	39.6	25.7	33.8	454	94.3
Vernal city	9,136	10,438	14.3	10,574	78.8	0.7	0.2	7.3	13.1	30.2	12.5	30.8	52.6	17.8	3,485	88.1
Vernon town	248	356	43.5	329	87.2	0.0	0.0	9.4	3.3	37.4	15.5	31.8	40.2	16.8	97	95.9
Veyo CDP	483	-	-	822	72.4	0.0	0.0	4.7	22.9	21.7	9.4	29.7	31.2	25.0	236	100.0
Vineyard town	110	11,866	10687.3	7,103	77.9	2.9	1.8	3.7	13.7	39.3	1.6	22.5	12.4	51.4	2,015	99.6
Virgin town	598	658	10.0	595	90.4	0.3	0.0	2.5	6.7	26.4	19.5	42.3	48.6	15.9	218	98.2
Wales town	345	373	8.1	341	90.9	0.0	0.0	4.4	4.7	36.4	15.0	29.1	31.1	20.5	90	97.8
Wallsburg town	258	385	49.2	382	98.4	1.6	0.0	0.0	0.0	31.2	11.8	31.9	36.3	19.5	101	91.1
Wanship CDP	400	-	-	614	92.7	0.0	0.0	0.0	7.3	14.7	10.9	27.7	41.2	14.6	152	83.6
Washington city	18,766	29,174	55.5	26,583	86.4	0.2	0.9	3.1	9.4	29.8	16.6	34.2	28.8	30.1	8,781	94.7
Washington Terrace city	9,089	9,248	2.5	9,162	84.5	0.4	0.2	4.3	10.5	27.2	16.9	33.8	40.4	23.6	3,165	86.4
Wellington city	1,688	1,620	-4.0	1,428	86.3	0.3	0.0	1.2	12.3	25.1	16.7	36.0	39.7	14.1	595	89.7
Wellsville city	3,492	3,941	12.9	3,757	89.5	0.5	0.3	3.9	5.8	38.8	10.9	28.4	31.6	34.3	974	95.5
Wendover city	1,400	1,489	6.4	1,037	18.6	0.0	0.0	0.4	81.0	30.6	8.9	30.4	68.6	14.9	385	76.9
West Bountiful city	5,259	5,800	10.3	5,627	76.2	1.3	1.0	10.4	11.0	26.8	13.6	36.0	25.9	26.7	1,754	97.3
West Haven city	10,286	16,109	56.6	13,782	87.9	0.0	0.8	2.8	8.5	33.9	5.9	29.3	31.5	32.8	4,152	98.1
West Jordan city	103,601	116,480	12.4	114,138	71.2	1.4	3.3	4.9	19.3	30.5	8.0	31.8	37.4	25.0	33,678	97.2
West Mountain CDP	1,186	-	-	1,233	89.1	0.0	0.0	6.6	4.3	41.0	10.9	23.8	28.4	32.9	271	100.0
West Point city	9,412	10,957	16.4	10,615	84.2	0.2	2.9	5.0	7.7	32.5	7.6	31.1	30.8	26.7	2,878	97.0
West Valley City city	129,489	135,248	4.4	136,009	46.9	2.7	5.5	6.7	38.2	30.8	8.6	30.5	53.0	15.2	37,691	94.7
West Wood CDP	844	-	-	694	90.8	3.3	0.0	1.4	4.5	30.7	25.8	39.2	15.7	49.6	222	100.0
White City metro township	5,686	5,768	1.4	5,810	82.7	0.4	2.2	2.2	12.5	26.9	16.6	34.9	36.2	24.9	1,929	92.3
White Mesa CDP	242	-	-	173	0.0	0.0	0.0	100.0	0.0	31.8	32.9	34.9	64.4	0.0	80	36.3
Whiterocks CDP	289	-	-	275	6.5	0.0	0.0	93.5	0.0	55.6	0.0	15.2	68.8	10.1	41	65.9
Willard city	1,774	1,958	10.4	1,745	94.3	0.5	0.9	1.3	3.2	26.5	12.4	37.0	39.2	24.6	575	92.3
Wolf Creek CDP	1,336	-	-	1,391	92.4	4.3	3.3	0.0	0.0	19.4	14.7	42.1	28.9	43.0	534	100.0
Woodland CDP	343	-	-	245	92.2	0.0	0.0	0.0	7.8	6.1	31.8	62.1	25.8	42.3	123	74.8
Woodland Hills city	1,360	1,590	16.9	1,289	94.8	0.0	0.2	0.0	5.0	33.0	17.7	34.3	13.4	49.1	336	99.1
Woodruff town	195	212	8.7	267	100.0	0.0	0.0	0.0	0.0	46.4	7.5	28.7	32.1	22.9	69	100.0
Woods Cross city	9,767	11,431	17.0	11,340	83.5	1.8	1.3	5.1	8.3	30.7	6.8	30.4	32.4	30.8	3,460	99.0
VERMONT	625,737	623,989	-0.3	624,313	92.8	1.3	1.7	2.3	1.9	18.7	18.8	42.9	36.1	38.0	260,029	89.9
Addison town (Addison)	1,375	1,322	-3.9	1,353	97.5	0.0	0.0	1.3	1.2	19.3	21.9	45.8	32.5	41.7	525	94.1
Albany village	193	189	-2.1	178	85.4	0.0	0.0	0.6	14.0	32.6	11.8	31.8	40.4	24.6	60	90.0
Albany town (Orleans)	941	914	-2.9	942	94.2	0.0	0.0	2.7	3.2	17.4	18.3	45.2	49.4	28.2	415	81.9
Alburgh village	497	530	6.6	523	94.3	1.5	0.0	4.2	0.0	22.6	16.6	35.7	58.3	15.7	226	84.1
Alburgh town (Grand Isle)	1,998	2,132	6.7	1,766	96.8	0.5	0.8	1.9	0.0	14.5	15.7	46.5	52.9	19.7	759	86.2
Andover town (Windsor)	467	471	0.9	508	100.0	0.0	0.0	0.0	0.0	21.5	23.0	50.0	37.3	40.8	196	89.3
Arlington CDP	1,213	-	-	1,452	92.6	0.0	4.1	0.0	3.3	27.2	18.9	40.1	34.4	28.2	554	91.9
Arlington town (Bennington)	2,316	2,213	-4.4	2,662	94.1	0.0	3.0	0.3	2.6	23.0	21.9	46.8	29.4	33.6	1,057	95.9
Ascutney CDP	540	-	-	421	100.0	0.0	0.0	0.0	0.0	18.5	39.0	53.3	55.7	5.4	193	83.4
Athens town (Windham)	442	437	-1.1	408	97.3	0.0	1.7	0.0	1.0	20.1	22.3	48.0	58.9	21.4	179	78.2
Averill town (Essex)	24	25	4.2	10	100.0	0.0	0.0	0.0	0.0	0.0	100.0	72.5	70.0	0.0	7	57.1
Avery's gore (Essex)	-	-	-	-	-	-	-	-	-	-	-	-	-	-	-	-
Bakersfield town (Franklin)	1,312	1,328	1.2	1,086	87.3	0.6	0.0	9.4	2.7	14.5	18.1	47.8	46.6	19.3	461	87.6
Baltimore town (Windsor)	248	245	-1.2	329	98.5	0.0	0.0	0.6	0.9	29.2	17.3	47.0	55.0	15.8	122	91.0
Barnard town (Windsor)	951	927	-2.5	844	97.4	0.7	0.0	1.2	0.7	16.9	23.2	53.3	28.3	41.6	358	92.5
Barnet CDP	129	-	-	157	84.1	0.0	0.0	8.9	7.0	17.8	25.5	44.1	48.8	17.4	39	79.5
Barnet town (Caledonia)	1,703	1,632	-4.2	1,564	95.9	0.7	0.0	1.8	1.6	18.8	21.5	45.4	39.9	36.4	619	88.9
Barre city & MCD (Washington)	9,056	8,528	-5.8	8,646	94.7	1.1	0.2	2.2	1.7	21.7	14.1	39.7	44.4	23.7	3,983	82.9
Barre town (Washington)	7,916	7,720	-2.5	7,739	94.8	2.0	0.3	1.6	1.3	18.1	21.1	47.8	38.2	32.5	3,297	92.2
Barton village	728	643	-11.7	588	95.4	0.0	0.0	3.9	0.7	14.1	22.6	52.3	68.3	10.0	299	78.9
Barton town (Orleans)	2,810	2,498	-11.1	2,728	93.6	1.1	0.2	4.4	0.7	20.5	25.5	47.7	52.0	18.9	1,192	85.2
Beecher Falls CDP	177	-	-	193	95.3	0.0	0.0	4.7	0.0	8.8	40.4	59.5	84.7	5.7	96	83.3
Bellows Falls village	3,143	2,965	-5.7	3,007	90.9	2.9	0.5	2.9	2.8	21.8	18.1	43.1	56.7	21.5	1,349	80.2
Belvidere town (Lamoille)	348	365	4.9	431	86.3	0.0	0.0	7.2	6.5	20.2	11.6	44.9	45.9	35.2	182	84.1
Bennington CDP	9,074	-	-	8,629	93.4	0.2	0.7	3.8	1.9	15.4	23.1	45.5	44.4	28.5	3,584	88.2
Bennington town (Bennington)	15,770	14,964	-5.1	15,097	91.3	0.9	0.9	3.7	3.2	16.3	21.5	43.1	42.1	31.8	5,975	87.2
Benson CDP	308	-	-	253	96.8	0.0	0.0	3.2	0.0	16.6	28.1	55.1	55.3	15.3	115	70.4
Benson town (Rutland)	1,056	1,002	-5.1	837	95.7	0.0	1.1	2.0	1.2	16.8	22.8	49.4	48.1	24.6	376	82.4
Berkshire town (Franklin)	1,687	1,753	3.9	1,672	89.5	0.5	0.4	6.1	3.5	21.9	15.0	37.0	59.9	13.9	597	86.8
Berlin town (Washington)	2,881	2,781	-3.5	2,793	96.4	0.0	0.3	1.6	1.7	17.8	28.9	52.2	49.4	22.8	1,093	87.5
Bethel CDP	569	-	-	726	95.6	1.5	0.0	1.1	1.8	27.3	13.9	28.7	44.7	15.7	287	89.2
Bethel town (Windsor)	2,022	1,951	-3.5	2,111	94.1	0.5	0.0	4.0	1.3	22.6	14.9	39.5	36.3	30.3	805	89.3
Bloomfield town (Essex)	230	235	2.2	198	100.0	0.0	0.0	0.0	0.0	10.1	22.2	59.3	68.6	10.1	91	79.1
Bolton town (Chittenden)	1,182	1,180	-0.2	1,240	94.0	0.4	1.4	2.5	1.7	21.0	6.0	37.0	33.2	45.6	516	92.8
Bradford CDP	788	-	-	526	85.4	1.0	0.0	0.8	12.9	18.6	8.9	36.4	54.0	15.0	209	94.7
Bradford town (Orange)	2,799	2,701	-3.5	2,713	94.4	0.2	0.0	0.7	4.7	22.4	18.2	41.1	46.4	23.7	1,168	86.6
Braintree town (Orange)	1,244	1,195	-3.9	1,042	96.7	0.0	0.0	0.8	2.5	9.0	27.4	53.9	43.7	24.3	486	87.0
Brandon CDP	1,648	-	-	1,561	96.8	0.0	3.2	0.0	0.0	27.4	20.0	39.7	34.1	41.6	648	87.2

1 May be of any race.

Table A. All Places — **Population and Housing**

STATE City, town, township, borough, or CDP (county if applicable)	Population				Race and Hispanic or Latino origin (percent)					Age (percent)			Educational attainment of persons age 25 and older		Occupied housing units	
	2010 census total population	2019 estimated population	Percent change 2010–2019	ACS total population estimate 2015–2019	White alone, not Hispanic or Latino	Black alone, not Hispanic or Latino	Asian alone, not Hispanic or Latino	All other races or 2 or more races, not Hispanic or Latino	Hispanic or Latino[1]	Under 18 years old	Age 65 years and older	Median age	Percent High school diploma or less	Percent Bachelor's degree or more	Total	Percent with a computer
	1	2	3	4	5	6	7	8	9	10	11	12	13	14	15	16
VERMONT—Con.																
Brandon town (Rutland)	3,972	3,735	-6.0	3,775	97.5	0.0	1.3	0.4	0.7	21.2	20.2	46.2	41.5	30.0	1,676	86.9
Brattleboro town (Windham)	12,043	11,332	-5.9	11,524	91.8	1.1	1.7	3.1	2.3	20.4	20.0	44.2	32.1	42.6	5,478	92.2
Brattleboro CDP	7,414	-	-	6,507	92.8	0.7	1.5	3.1	2.0	19.4	20.7	45.8	32.4	40.6	3,293	91.0
Bridgewater town (Windsor)	934	963	3.1	997	98.1	0.0	0.0	1.4	0.5	13.4	19.7	55.2	47.1	29.2	486	90.9
Bridport town (Addison)	1,218	1,178	-3.3	1,241	94.0	3.3	0.2	1.2	1.2	16.3	23.7	51.4	41.6	29.8	523	83.7
Brighton town (Essex)	1,222	1,167	-4.5	1,185	95.4	0.0	1.2	3.1	0.3	16.8	24.1	48.9	59.4	17.5	527	70.2
Bristol CDP	2,030	-	-	1,855	93.5	2.6	0.6	0.0	3.3	20.8	25.1	48.2	33.8	43.4	830	91.4
Bristol town (Addison)	3,908	3,842	-1.7	3,896	95.4	1.4	1.1	0.0	2.1	22.5	19.0	43.8	43.2	34.0	1,613	89.7
Brookfield town (Orange)	1,288	1,341	4.1	1,288	89.3	2.7	0.0	7.2	0.8	18.8	22.4	48.3	34.1	42.2	557	93.5
Brookline town (Windham)	532	530	-0.4	554	98.4	0.0	0.0	1.6	0.0	22.6	12.6	40.3	42.9	27.8	228	89.9
Brownington town (Orleans)	988	965	-2.3	1,038	95.3	0.5	0.0	4.2	0.0	24.1	11.8	37.7	54.9	16.5	439	75.9
Brunswick town (Essex)	103	102		95	100.0	0.0	0.0	0.0	0.0	15.8	25.3	57.9	47.4	16.7	37	91.9
Buels gore (Chittenden)	30	31	3.3	33	84.8	0.0	0.0	15.2	0.0	48.5	0.0	35.3	17.6	58.8	9	100.0
Burke town (Caledonia)	1,757	1,693	-3.6	1,500	93.7	0.4	0.7	4.8	0.4	22.1	18.1	44.1	39.5	31.2	655	87.3
Burlington city & MCD (Chittenden)	42,414	42,819	1.0	42,545	82.9	5.5	5.8	2.7	3.1	11.8	11.9	26.8	25.8	53.3	16,552	92.0
Cabot CDP	233	-	-	182	97.8	0.0	0.0	2.2	0.0	30.2	26.4	47.6	45.7	40.5	95	76.8
Cabot town (Washington)	1,422	1,433	0.8	1,440	92.6	0.0	2.0	4.9	0.4	19.9	24.4	47.0	36.6	37.3	639	87.6
Calais town (Washington)	1,607	1,604	-0.2	1,776	95.5	0.0	1.2	2.1	1.1	17.2	22.6	50.1	31.4	46.3	745	90.7
Cambridge village	233	245	5.2	245	88.6	0.0	0.0	4.5	6.9	15.5	3.3	33.4	25.0	33.3	107	98.1
Cambridge town (Lamoille)	3,657	3,844	5.1	3,833	96.5	0.0	0.2	1.6	1.8	22.8	11.8	38.1	33.7	36.5	1,502	92.1
Canaan CDP	392	-	-	327	81.3	18.7	0.0	0.0	0.0	17.7	30.0	50.1	63.1	5.9	152	72.4
Canaan town (Essex)	972	921	-5.2	880	90.9	6.9	0.7	1.0	0.5	18.4	28.3	52.3	63.7	13.8	409	84.1
Castleton CDP	1,485	-	-	1,276	92.6	3.2	2.1	1.3	0.8	0.4	4.8	21.0	17.6	53.8	299	100.0
Castleton town (Rutland)	4,718	4,512	-4.4	4,554	97.1	0.9	0.6	0.9	0.5	11.5	19.2	43.7	44.8	29.6	1,837	87.8
Cavendish CDP	179	-	-	211	100.0	0.0	0.0	0.0	0.0	16.1	6.2	40.5	36.5	18.9	76	100.0
Cavendish town (Windsor)	1,367	1,410	3.1	1,329	98.6	0.3	0.0	0.0	1.1	18.7	20.5	49.6	39.9	31.7	525	92.6
Charleston town (Orleans)	1,028	996	-3.1	1,012	96.5	0.0	0.0	3.5	0.0	20.8	19.5	43.4	62.7	11.1	443	80.6
Charlotte town (Chittenden)	3,754	3,785	0.8	3,820	95.6	1.2	0.0	1.7	1.4	23.4	18.9	49.3	11.9	69.9	1,462	99.3
Chelsea CDP	-	-	-	475	85.7	0.4	0.0	11.4	2.5	25.7	21.7	36.1	47.9	22.6	189	86.8
Chelsea town (Orange)	1,243	1,291	3.9	1,315	92.6	0.8	0.0	5.2	1.4	21.2	25.2	48.0	45.5	26.2	557	87.3
Chester CDP	1,005	-	-	864	100.0	0.0	0.0	0.0	0.0	9.4	36.2	57.0	42.4	36.5	497	72.4
Chester town (Windsor)	3,150	3,024	-4.0	3,047	93.5	2.3	0.0	1.6	2.6	18.0	25.2	53.2	38.1	32.9	1,297	83.3
Chittenden town (Rutland)	1,259	1,181	-6.2	1,389	96.3	0.0	0.2	1.2	2.3	27.0	18.4	38.4	30.6	42.0	514	97.1
Clarendon town (Rutland)	2,572	2,413	-6.2	2,358	95.5	0.5	0.0	0.9	3.1	11.7	25.2	50.0	45.6	28.2	1,029	89.8
Colchester town (Chittenden)	17,072	17,127	0.3	17,303	91.3	2.2	1.9	1.8	2.8	17.4	13.0	38.0	28.7	43.1	6,849	95.2
Concord CDP	271	-	-	188	93.1	0.0	0.0	0.0	6.9	22.3	20.2	44.4	63.8	14.7	87	80.5
Concord town (Essex)	1,235	1,211	-1.9	1,284	96.3	0.0	0.6	1.4	1.6	18.8	18.9	47.2	58.5	13.4	541	85.2
Corinth town (Orange)	1,364	1,425	4.5	1,508	93.2	4.6	0.0	1.3	0.9	20.1	20.2	45.2	46.5	32.4	660	84.7
Cornwall town (Addison)	1,187	1,192	0.4	1,028	91.9	0.9	0.9	5.1	1.3	16.1	29.1	53.2	21.3	61.4	470	92.3
Coventry CDP	97	-	-	22	100.0	0.0	0.0	0.0	0.0	18.2	68.2	67.7	27.8	16.7	13	100.0
Coventry town (Orleans)	1,086	1,054	-2.9	985	96.9	0.6	0.0	2.5	0.0	15.4	18.3	49.1	49.2	18.0	440	83.9
Craftsbury town (Orleans)	1,206	1,176	-2.5	1,139	93.2	0.4	0.1	4.4	1.9	21.2	24.0	40.9	35.6	44.1	466	77.5
Danby town (Rutland)	1,306	1,312	0.5	1,333	98.2	0.0	0.0	0.0	1.8	24.0	26.0	45.4	53.6	27.3	521	87.1
Danville CDP	383	-	-	453	97.6	0.0	0.0	2.4	0.0	19.2	29.6	50.1	13.3	47.5	199	93.0
Danville town (Caledonia)	2,208	2,138	-3.2	2,206	94.2	1.5	1.4	1.9	1.1	18.6	24.2	53.0	34.2	39.0	984	88.3
Derby town (Orleans)	4,614	4,246	-8.0	4,298	95.1	0.0	1.3	1.8	1.9	20.1	25.5	46.8	49.7	22.3	1,848	84.4
Derby Center village	597	549	-8.0	565	99.5	0.0	0.0	0.0	0.5	20.0	28.8	51.1	68.3	11.3	253	79.1
Derby Line village	675	624	-7.6	777	96.1	0.0	0.0	2.2	1.7	24.1	17.5	32.3	42.3	27.9	333	88.0
Dorset CDP	249	-	-	213	100.0	0.0	0.0	0.0	0.0	7.0	52.1	65.9	6.1	79.8	140	96.4
Dorset town (Bennington)	2,031	1,943	-4.3	1,675	97.3	0.0	0.0	0.2	2.5	17.8	26.7	53.3	29.8	52.0	794	96.0
Dover town (Windham)	1,124	1,059	-5.8	1,027	94.2	0.0	2.2	2.7	0.9	17.6	30.8	51.8	23.1	44.4	531	96.6
Dummerston town (Windham)	1,861	1,744	-6.3	1,890	97.3	0.0	0.0	2.1	0.6	15.2	27.4	50.8	31.1	45.1	827	92.0
Duxbury town (Washington)	1,337	1,305	-2.4	1,160	95.7	0.0	2.1	1.8	0.4	15.9	16.0	47.5	24.5	47.3	519	91.1
East Barre CDP	826	-	-	711	93.8	0.0	0.0	0.0	6.2	16.0	35.9	50.3	52.0	26.8	313	89.1
East Burke CDP	132	-	-	81	100.0	0.0	0.0	0.0	0.0	16.0	23.5	53.9	16.2	30.9	49	93.9
East Haven town (Essex)	290	296	2.1	226	97.3	0.0	0.0	0.0	2.7	18.6	27.0	50.4	61.3	29.8	101	64.4
East Middlebury CDP	425	-	-	489	74.2	8.4	0.0	0.0	17.4	27.8	32.3	44.2	32.0	47.6	254	89.4
East Montpelier CDP	80	-	-	45	100.0	0.0	0.0	0.0	0.0	33.3	0.0	39.1	0.0	100.0	23	100.0
East Montpelier town (Washington)	2,585	2,551	-1.3	2,578	95.0	0.9	0.2	3.2	0.7	21.5	23.3	50.1	24.8	53.9	1,137	92.5
Eden town (Lamoille)	1,320	1,370	3.8	1,319	95.0	0.7	0.5	2.5	1.3	20.1	18.0	43.3	59.9	20.6	542	88.4
Elmore town (Lamoille)	855	863	0.9	772	97.9	0.5	0.0	0.0	1.6	18.0	19.3	49.1	18.9	53.5	345	91.6
Enosburg Falls village	1,323	1,283	-3.0	1,402	85.0	6.1	1.7	6.8	0.3	25.4	18.3	37.2	61.2	15.1	525	84.6
Enosburgh town (Franklin)	2,790	2,782	-0.3	2,766	89.8	3.1	0.9	4.4	1.7	23.4	17.1	39.8	56.8	20.3	1,033	86.8
Essex town (Chittenden)	19,593	21,890	11.7	21,467	85.6	2.6	5.1	4.7	2.1	21.8	15.1	40.2	21.0	52.2	8,830	93.4
Essex Junction village	9,291	10,852	16.8	10,603	82.2	2.4	8.0	5.0	2.4	20.7	13.1	36.3	23.8	46.1	4,295	94.6
Fairfax CDP	-	-	-	873	100.0	0.0	0.0	0.0	0.0	21.6	15.0	48.9	35.7	38.9	403	86.1
Fairfax town (Franklin)	4,286	4,803	12.1	4,692	99.2	0.0	0.0	0.8	0.0	28.9	12.0	36.2	30.4	36.9	1,843	90.6
Fairfield town (Franklin)	1,914	1,953	2.0	2,074	92.2	0.0	0.6	4.1	3.1	21.5	19.0	43.3	42.0	32.0	728	91.1
Fair Haven town (Rutland)	2,738	2,555	-6.7	2,585	96.6	0.0	0.0	0.5	2.9	24.3	17.9	38.8	53.4	18.8	1,028	88.4
Fair Haven CDP	2,269	-	-	2,247	96.1	0.0	0.0	0.5	3.3	24.0	19.0	41.2	52.5	19.7	914	87.0
Fairlee CDP	189	-	-	207	97.6	0.0	2.4	0.0	0.0	16.4	42.5	56.9	50.9	17.2	92	91.3
Fairlee town (Orange)	985	980	-0.5	994	96.0	0.0	2.7	1.1	0.2	18.0	28.2	51.8	35.8	32.3	471	90.2
Fayston town (Washington)	1,353	1,330	-1.7	1,084	97.1	0.7	0.6	0.6	1.0	17.4	22.0	49.1	17.6	57.9	492	99.4
Ferdinand town (Essex)	32	33	3.1	21	100.0	0.0	0.0	0.0	0.0	0.0	0.0	21.8	100.0	0.0	5	100.0
Ferrisburgh town (Addison)	2,777	2,690	-3.1	2,725	96.8	0.0	0.0	2.5	0.7	14.8	18.8	48.6	27.2	45.2	1,128	95.5
Fletcher town (Franklin)	1,280	1,341	4.8	1,308	97.9	0.0	0.5	1.7	0.0	19.0	14.5	44.6	36.0	38.0	529	92.8
Franklin town (Franklin)	1,420	1,425	0.4	1,453	93.8	0.0	0.4	4.3	1.5	23.1	12.9	44.7	51.7	18.2	546	90.5
Georgia town (Franklin)	4,515	4,780	5.9	4,738	91.4	0.0	1.3	2.7	4.5	24.4	12.3	39.6	36.3	31.5	1,512	95.6
Glastenbury town (Bennington)	8	7	-12.5	-	-	-	-	-	-	-	-	-	-	-	-	-

1 May be of any race.

STATE City, town, township, borough, or CDP (county if applicable)	Population				Race and Hispanic or Latino origin (percent)					Age (percent)			Educational attainment of persons age 25 and older		Occupied housing units	
	2010 census total population	2019 estimated population	Percent change 2010–2019	ACS total population estimate 2015–2019	White alone, not Hispanic or Latino	Black alone, not Hispanic or Latino	Asian alone, not Hispanic or Latino	All other races or 2 or more races, not Hispanic or Latino	Hispanic or Latino[1]	Under 18 years old	Age 65 years and older	Median age	Percent High school diploma or less	Percent Bachelor's degree or more	Total	Percent with a computer
	1	2	3	4	5	6	7	8	9	10	11	12	13	14	15	16
VERMONT—Con.																
Glover CDP	303	-	-	300	100.0	0.0	0.0	0.0	0.0	18.0	19.3	52.4	68.9	18.1	106	79.2
Glover town (Orleans)	1,122	1,099	-2.0	1,046	97.6	0.0	0.0	0.0	2.4	19.2	23.6	53.1	45.2	35.7	446	88.3
Goshen town (Addison)	164	163	-0.6	164	82.9	0.0	0.0	17.1	0.0	7.9	27.4	52.0	36.4	41.1	81	93.8
Grafton town (Windham)	679	675	-0.6	652	96.0	0.0	0.9	2.1	0.9	16.1	34.8	57.5	40.8	26.9	294	77.2
Granby town (Essex)	88	83	-5.7	81	100.0	0.0	0.0	0.0	0.0	0.0	48.1	63.6	83.6	6.8	38	50.0
Grand Isle town (Grand Isle)	2,067	2,136	3.3	2,177	86.7	0.7	0.1	8.9	3.7	17.9	19.0	45.5	30.4	44.5	904	92.9
Graniteville CDP	784	-	-	865	82.7	11.6	0.0	5.8	0.0	16.5	17.0	37.6	51.2	27.4	388	86.9
Granville town (Addison)	298	306	2.7	330	97.6	0.0	0.0	1.5	0.9	23.9	8.8	35.9	39.5	31.5	130	88.5
Greensboro CDP	109	-	-	105	100.0	0.0	0.0	0.0	0.0	5.7	50.5	67.1	11.1	74.7	69	69.6
Greensboro town (Orleans)	765	699	-8.6	731	98.6	0.0	0.0	0.0	1.4	21.8	32.0	52.2	34.4	48.6	314	86.0
Greensboro Bend CDP	232	-	-	263	100.0	0.0	0.0	0.0	0.0	39.9	14.1	39.0	46.0	26.7	89	87.6
Groton CDP	437	-	-	402	84.3	0.0	0.0	13.9	1.7	18.2	24.1	45.3	52.4	23.4	150	74.7
Groton town (Caledonia)	1,022	968	-5.3	984	91.3	0.0	0.0	5.7	3.0	19.6	24.4	42.2	52.7	20.2	402	87.6
Guildhall town (Essex)	261	248	-5.0	214	94.9	0.0	0.0	4.2	0.9	10.7	32.2	57.9	44.4	26.7	107	89.7
Guilford town (Windham)	2,124	2,109	-0.7	1,914	94.1	0.0	2.5	2.1	1.3	10.9	26.2	54.0	33.8	40.4	933	93.6
Halifax town (Windham)	728	681	-6.5	644	98.8	0.3	0.2	0.0	0.8	13.2	26.2	52.5	46.8	37.0	286	87.8
Hancock town (Addison)	324	333	2.8	337	89.6	0.0	0.6	8.0	1.8	21.4	29.4	50.1	51.4	27.7	150	88.7
Hardwick CDP	1,345	-	-	1,079	86.3	6.4	0.0	7.3	0.0	22.5	17.4	52.4	60.0	15.1	546	58.8
Hardwick town (Caledonia)	3,007	2,861	-4.9	2,889	93.6	2.4	0.0	4.0	0.0	18.2	21.6	49.9	58.1	22.2	1,349	78.2
Hartford town (Windsor)	9,948	9,556	-3.9	9,643	91.9	0.9	2.6	2.1	2.4	17.3	25.6	48.0	29.1	48.0	4,643	92.2
Hartland CDP	380	-	-	285	67.0	5.6	2.5	24.9	0.0	7.0	17.2	50.9	53.7	5.9	128	100.0
Hartland town (Windsor)	3,394	3,507	3.3	3,466	93.1	1.1	1.4	4.4	0.0	19.3	21.0	46.6	34.0	32.5	1,537	95.5
Highgate town (Franklin)	3,537	3,662	3.5	3,655	96.2	0.0	0.0	3.8	0.1	23.6	17.2	37.0	55.8	13.1	1,373	77.1
Hinesburg CDP	-	-	-	772	96.9	1.7	0.0	1.4	0.0	21.0	18.7	32.8	21.9	52.7	415	91.1
Hinesburg town (Chittenden)	4,388	4,525	3.1	4,541	99.3	0.3	0.0	0.2	0.2	23.6	13.9	40.5	30.5	45.1	1,870	93.7
Holland town (Orleans)	629	614	-2.4	557	97.8	0.0	0.0	2.2	0.0	18.5	15.6	45.1	53.0	18.2	273	94.5
Hubbardton town (Rutland)	706	665	-5.8	606	97.2	0.0	0.8	1.3	0.7	20.0	26.1	50.8	33.0	39.9	252	81.7
Huntington town (Chittenden)	1,935	1,972	1.9	1,966	93.9	0.4	1.3	2.4	2.0	19.0	12.0	43.1	29.7	47.8	805	93.8
Hyde Park village	462	479	3.7	423	94.1	0.0	4.0	1.9	0.0	13.9	21.5	49.6	21.8	47.2	191	94.2
Hyde Park town (Lamoille)	2,957	2,961	0.1	2,995	95.7	0.0	1.2	2.2	0.9	22.5	19.6	49.8	33.3	36.9	1,309	88.9
Ira town (Rutland)	432	433	0.2	424	97.2	0.0	0.9	1.4	0.5	18.2	21.0	52.7	51.3	18.6	162	91.4
Irasburg CDP	163	-	-	141	100.0	0.0	0.0	0.0	0.0	27.7	24.1	38.0	30.4	21.6	66	66.7
Irasburg town (Orleans)	1,163	1,139	-2.1	1,279	92.7	2.1	0.0	0.0	5.2	31.4	18.3	37.5	46.0	14.2	501	85.4
Island Pond CDP	821	-	-	826	94.1	0.0	1.7	3.9	0.4	18.8	22.6	45.8	63.3	14.7	362	65.5
Isle La Motte town (Grand Isle)	471	498	5.7	421	98.6	0.0	0.0	0.0	1.4	15.2	29.5	58.5	37.0	34.4	187	93.0
Jacksonville village	219	206	-5.9	240	87.1	2.1	8.8	0.0	2.1	21.3	11.7	44.5	58.9	27.8	92	94.6
Jamaica town (Windham)	1,035	1,028	-0.7	770	95.2	1.8	0.0	3.0	0.0	16.1	19.6	48.4	41.7	36.5	353	79.9
Jay town (Orleans)	515	567	10.1	627	92.5	2.6	0.0	0.0	4.9	30.3	9.4	37.8	30.5	34.1	261	91.2
Jeffersonville village	729	768	5.3	833	91.7	0.0	1.0	5.9	1.4	28.7	7.6	30.9	26.5	33.7	329	88.4
Jericho town (Chittenden)	5,005	4,994	-0.2	5,030	96.1	0.8	0.2	1.3	1.7	24.1	14.8	41.4	14.4	61.0	1,975	95.6
Johnson village	1,419	1,507	6.2	1,452	90.4	2.6	1.2	3.2	2.6	17.0	6.5	21.8	36.9	27.5	462	92.2
Johnson town (Lamoille)	3,446	3,633	5.4	3,606	95.8	1.4	0.5	1.3	1.1	14.5	10.9	29.0	32.8	26.7	1,349	92.4
Killington town (Rutland)	811	756	-6.8	675	87.3	0.0	10.7	1.3	0.7	19.7	20.1	48.1	27.2	54.8	314	97.1
Kirby town (Caledonia)	489	494	1.0	579	98.1	0.3	0.0	0.9	0.7	23.5	15.5	41.6	30.2	42.4	225	87.6
Landgrove town (Bennington)	160	157	-1.9	112	86.6	0.0	5.4	8.0	0.0	17.0	37.5	56.5	20.5	70.5	43	100.0
Leicester town (Addison)	1,097	1,086	-1.0	1,172	97.5	0.6	0.0	0.9	0.9	16.1	26.5	54.7	47.2	28.6	473	86.5
Lemington town (Essex)	104	96	-7.7	116	85.3	0.0	0.0	0.0	14.7	13.8	33.6	56.2	52.6	4.1	62	83.9
Lewis town (Essex)	-	-	-	-	-	-	-	-	-	-	-	-	-	-	-	-
Lincoln town (Addison)	1,271	1,241	-2.4	1,392	96.3	0.0	0.6	2.7	0.4	21.3	18.5	47.0	32.7	45.1	574	88.3
Londonderry town (Windham)	1,767	1,656	-6.3	1,656	96.4	0.8	0.0	1.9	0.8	13.8	23.7	54.8	42.4	33.5	748	91.8
Lowell CDP	228	-	-	139	92.1	0.0	0.0	0.0	7.9	18.0	10.1	32.0	38.2	30.0	73	84.9
Lowell town (Orleans)	879	797	-9.3	787	95.3	1.8	0.0	1.5	1.4	16.5	12.1	43.0	60.0	17.9	365	80.8
Ludlow village	808	769	-4.8	688	88.2	1.3	0.6	9.2	0.7	12.2	28.8	49.8	39.7	25.0	363	86.2
Ludlow town (Windsor)	1,963	1,864	-5.0	1,828	92.0	0.5	0.2	4.1	3.2	14.5	28.7	53.1	46.0	28.9	854	86.5
Lunenburg town (Essex)	1,302	1,326	1.8	1,470	96.9	0.0	0.0	1.3	1.8	23.0	24.5	44.2	61.3	12.9	597	82.7
Lyndon town (Caledonia)	5,982	5,674	-5.1	5,799	95.8	0.5	0.0	2.3	1.4	18.7	18.8	33.0	41.0	27.9	2,166	84.7
Lyndonville village	1,207	1,165	-3.5	1,411	98.9	0.0	0.0	1.1	0.0	19.1	17.4	28.1	43.8	19.2	671	84.2
Maidstone town (Essex)	208	195	-6.3	210	91.0	0.0	0.0	5.7	3.3	10.5	39.5	61.7	41.5	36.1	104	86.5
Manchester village	734	711	-3.1	744	95.7	0.0	0.0	0.9	3.4	10.2	55.1	69.4	32.3	47.8	460	69.8
Manchester town (Bennington)	4,393	4,224	-3.8	4,253	96.2	1.1	0.8	1.9	0.0	21.6	27.7	51.2	33.3	45.2	1,982	86.5
Manchester Center CDP	2,120	-	-	1,923	96.0	2.4	0.0	1.5	0.0	23.3	21.0	41.7	39.9	42.9	878	89.5
Marlboro town (Windham)	1,078	1,039	-3.6	1,251	90.7	1.7	2.6	0.8	4.2	10.2	17.1	34.5	25.3	55.7	380	92.4
Marshfield village	269	250	-7.1	284	90.8	0.0	0.0	4.2	4.9	33.5	18.3	30.5	22.7	36.6	100	84.0
Marshfield town (Washington)	1,582	1,473	-6.9	1,422	94.0	0.0	2.4	2.1	1.5	17.5	20.6	50.8	37.7	41.5	582	88.3
Mendon town (Rutland)	1,061	1,011	-4.7	1,082	94.9	0.0	1.9	2.0	1.1	17.5	21.5	47.5	24.0	53.2	466	89.1
Middlebury CDP	6,588	-	-	6,966	82.4	2.5	6.7	3.4	5.1	10.2	16.3	22.8	29.0	50.5	2,092	90.2
Middlebury town (Addison)	8,494	8,780	3.4	8,661	83.3	3.5	5.4	2.8	5.0	12.0	17.9	29.1	32.5	46.6	2,860	90.7
Middlesex town (Washington)	1,725	1,724	-0.1	1,676	93.2	0.2	0.7	4.4	1.4	18.7	22.8	48.7	28.8	51.2	689	91.0
Middletown Springs town (Rutland)	746	748	0.3	806	95.4	0.0	1.1	1.0	2.5	24.3	21.5	50.2	27.8	44.5	313	88.5
Milton CDP	1,861	-	-	2,507	98.6	1.4	0.0	0.0	0.0	29.0	10.4	33.8	50.7	15.3	976	93.2
Milton town (Chittenden)	10,351	10,829	4.6	10,882	97.0	1.1	0.1	1.5	0.2	20.5	13.4	40.0	40.4	25.4	4,337	91.2
Monkton town (Addison)	1,972	2,090	6.0	1,906	96.3	0.0	0.8	2.3	0.6	21.2	17.4	44.7	29.6	40.1	777	90.1
Montgomery town (Franklin)	1,202	1,201	-0.1	784	98.0	0.0	0.0	1.4	0.6	18.2	19.3	45.7	47.3	29.4	342	96.2
Montpelier city & MCD (Washington)	7,852	7,372	-6.1	7,477	92.2	1.6	1.5	2.4	2.3	17.6	20.8	45.0	20.2	61.6	3,668	90.2
Moretown town (Washington)	1,656	1,665	0.5	1,863	94.5	0.0	1.2	1.7	2.6	19.5	17.2	42.3	28.8	49.0	788	90.1
Morgan town (Orleans)	749	704	-6.0	500	92.6	0.0	0.0	1.4	6.0	11.8	41.2	60.4	50.3	23.7	236	79.7

1   May be of any race.

Table A. All Places — **Population and Housing**

STATE City, town, township, borough, or CDP (county if applicable)	Population				Race and Hispanic or Latino origin (percent)					Age (percent)			Educational attainment of persons age 25 and older		Occupied housing units	
	2010 census total population	2019 estimated population	Percent change 2010–2019	ACS total population estimate 2015–2019	White alone, not Hispanic or Latino	Black alone, not Hispanic or Latino	Asian alone, not Hispanic or Latino	All other races or 2 or more races, not Hispanic or Latino	Hispanic or Latino[1]	Under 18 years old	Age 65 years and older	Median age	Percent High school diploma or less	Percent Bachelor's degree or more	Total	Percent with a computer
	1	2	3	4	5	6	7	8	9	10	11	12	13	14	15	16
VERMONT—Con.																
Morristown town (Lamoille)	5,227	5,501	5.2	5,451	91.2	2.8	0.3	2.0	3.7	22.4	16.7	35.6	32.5	35.4	2,232	93.2
Morrisville village	1,972	2,073	5.1	2,216	91.0	3.5	0.8	1.1	3.6	21.5	18.1	35.2	23.3	34.5	996	89.8
Mount Holly town (Rutland)	1,237	1,244	0.6	1,202	99.4	0.0	0.0	0.0	0.6	15.6	27.7	53.0	34.3	39.2	523	93.7
Mount Tabor town (Rutland)	255	258	1.2	228	86.4	0.0	4.8	7.0	1.8	28.5	17.1	44.3	40.5	32.0	79	89.9
Newark town (Caledonia)	581	593	2.1	555	95.7	0.7	0.0	2.0	1.6	19.5	21.3	51.1	45.1	26.5	213	88.3
Newbury village	365	355	-2.7	381	97.9	1.0	0.0	0.0	1.0	21.5	29.4	53.1	41.2	35.7	174	83.3
Newbury town (Orange)	2,213	2,151	-2.8	2,241	95.7	0.2	0.0	3.3	0.8	22.6	24.0	45.5	45.3	29.6	951	84.4
Newfane village	120	111	-7.5	171	100.0	0.0	0.0	0.0	0.0	17.5	18.7	36.4	14.8	78.7	77	80.5
Newfane town (Windham)	1,726	1,586	-8.1	1,691	96.6	0.0	0.0	2.3	1.1	17.3	24.1	49.9	32.3	45.1	776	82.7
New Haven town (Addison)	1,720	1,705	-0.9	1,779	96.7	0.0	1.8	1.3	0.1	15.9	17.5	45.1	40.4	32.5	712	94.9
Newport city & MCD (Orleans)	4,591	4,257	-7.3	4,305	92.9	0.7	0.0	4.6	1.7	16.6	20.6	43.3	55.7	17.5	1,942	82.0
Newport town (Orleans)	1,594	2,957	85.5	2,621	97.9	0.5	0.3	1.0	0.3	14.3	26.4	53.4	58.3	16.9	1,201	82.2
Newport Center CDP	274	-	-	271	100.0	0.0	0.0	0.0	0.0	14.8	15.1	32.8	74.0	0.0	146	68.5
North Bennington village	1,643	1,697	3.3	1,715	79.6	3.0	4.4	9.9	3.0	13.0	19.7	23.8	31.4	44.1	483	86.5
Northfield CDP	2,101	-	-	2,125	92.9	0.3	0.8	2.0	4.1	19.6	17.2	32.9	46.1	29.9	802	83.3
Northfield town (Washington)	6,213	6,522	5.0	6,144	92.7	0.7	0.6	1.6	4.5	14.7	13.0	27.5	44.3	31.9	1,915	86.9
North Hartland CDP	302	-	-	228	100.0	0.0	0.0	0.0	0.0	22.8	22.8	44.2	47.7	40.9	97	100.0
North Hero town (Grand Isle)	803	814	1.4	946	93.9	0.5	0.5	2.1	3.0	20.3	26.6	51.1	25.5	45.3	405	94.8
North Springfield CDP	573	-	-	644	76.7	0.0	0.0	14.4	8.9	25.2	20.0	39.4	50.3	10.0	265	81.9
North Troy village	620	573	-7.6	608	94.9	0.8	0.7	3.6	0.0	26.0	15.0	34.1	64.9	10.5	267	74.9
North Westminster CDP	247	-	-	133	100.0	0.0	0.0	0.0	0.0	0.0	15.8	24.8	44.4	30.2	67	100.0
Norton town (Essex)	169	158	-6.5	127	92.9	0.0	1.6	5.5	0.0	9.4	20.5	57.3	64.6	22.1	67	85.1
Norwich CDP	878	-	-	592	95.1	0.0	0.0	1.7	3.2	19.6	25.2	50.3	2.4	92.0	264	100.0
Norwich town (Windsor)	3,416	3,409	-0.2	3,339	93.5	0.1	1.3	2.0	3.2	21.1	18.1	46.6	8.1	84.3	1,290	97.0
Old Bennington village	139	131	-5.8	191	95.3	0.0	0.0	4.7	0.0	20.9	23.0	52.3	6.2	71.9	81	97.5
Orange town (Orange)	1,073	1,113	3.7	1,029	95.9	0.0	0.0	1.3	2.8	15.5	19.4	52.3	59.7	12.6	424	83.5
Orleans village	816	725	-11.2	1,103	89.1	2.6	0.5	6.4	1.3	30.5	10.6	32.5	51.1	18.7	433	93.1
Orwell town (Addison)	1,245	1,215	-2.4	1,209	96.1	0.4	1.6	1.7	0.2	19.3	21.8	48.8	41.3	33.8	511	86.7
Panton town (Addison)	679	707	4.1	659	98.2	0.0	0.2	1.7	0.0	18.7	17.0	43.5	39.2	37.1	265	92.8
Pawlet town (Rutland)	1,479	1,371	-7.3	1,235	86.3	2.6	0.0	9.0	2.1	21.5	20.0	49.0	43.9	32.1	549	87.2
Peacham town (Caledonia)	741	716	-3.4	701	96.6	1.3	0.0	1.6	0.6	18.8	24.0	48.3	30.8	56.1	273	87.9
Perkinsville village	127	123	-3.1	89	96.6	0.0	0.0	3.4	0.0	18.0	27.0	54.1	47.8	27.5	41	73.2
Peru town (Bennington)	373	355	-4.8	282	88.7	0.0	3.9	0.0	7.4	11.0	25.5	58.7	36.3	37.1	135	90.4
Pittsfield town (Rutland)	550	553	0.5	351	90.0	0.0	0.0	0.0	10.0	13.7	21.9	46.9	35.1	41.0	189	95.8
Pittsford CDP	740	-	-	459	90.4	0.7	8.9	0.0	0.0	2.0	20.7	51.4	38.8	25.0	271	76.8
Pittsford town (Rutland)	2,990	2,787	-6.8	2,813	98.0	0.5	1.5	0.0	0.0	18.8	21.4	47.4	45.7	28.2	1,191	86.6
Plainfield CDP	401	-	-	321	91.0	1.2	3.7	4.0	0.0	14.3	5.3	31.5	40.3	40.3	162	84.6
Plainfield town (Washington)	1,249	1,262	1.0	1,430	91.2	0.3	2.4	5.5	0.6	19.4	17.1	38.5	32.3	44.8	564	83.3
Plymouth town (Windsor)	619	600	-3.1	536	100.0	0.0	0.0	0.0	0.0	10.1	30.8	59.1	34.4	44.8	259	88.4
Pomfret town (Windsor)	900	853	-5.2	932	96.1	1.5	1.2	0.4	0.8	17.0	20.6	54.6	17.6	61.0	392	95.9
Poultney village	1,601	1,549	-3.2	1,545	91.7	4.4	1.8	1.1	1.0	15.5	12.8	23.9	49.5	24.6	488	88.7
Poultney town (Rutland)	3,433	3,253	-5.2	3,313	94.1	2.1	0.8	1.8	1.1	15.6	17.0	39.2	41.2	32.5	1,296	83.8
Pownal town (Bennington)	3,523	3,400	-3.5	3,427	99.9	0.0	0.0	0.1	0.0	20.1	19.0	45.6	43.2	30.2	1,263	90.3
Proctor town (Rutland)	1,741	1,595	-8.4	1,704	99.1	0.1	0.0	0.9	0.0	20.1	17.8	44.7	35.8	29.9	712	94.1
Proctorsville CDP	454	-	-	323	98.8	1.2	0.0	0.0	0.0	9.0	30.0	57.3	47.4	29.2	156	84.0
Putney CDP	523	-	-	455	94.1	5.9	0.0	0.0	0.0	13.8	32.7	54.1	32.3	36.4	272	90.8
Putney town (Windham)	2,700	2,456	-9.0	2,700	93.0	2.4	0.5	2.3	1.7	16.1	18.6	38.5	30.4	42.2	1,012	91.4
Quechee CDP	656	-	-	298	100.0	0.0	0.0	0.0	0.0	35.9	10.1	36.2	19.4	75.4	143	93.0
Randolph CDP	1,974	-	-	2,158	97.5	0.0	0.0	1.4	1.1	14.9	25.7	46.1	45.8	32.3	928	86.3
Randolph town (Orange)	4,778	4,584	-4.1	4,669	98.0	0.0	0.0	1.1	0.9	16.4	21.6	42.5	44.3	33.2	1,783	86.8
Reading town (Windsor)	666	637	-4.4	462	99.4	0.0	0.0	0.0	0.6	17.5	24.2	50.6	40.2	33.2	215	92.1
Readsboro CDP	321	-	-	271	97.4	0.0	0.0	2.6	0.0	23.6	24.4	39.8	60.3	8.5	113	68.1
Readsboro town (Bennington)	763	722	-5.4	609	98.4	0.0	0.0	1.6	0.0	21.8	21.5	46.5	46.5	20.5	274	83.9
Richford CDP	1,361	-	-	1,639	88.9	0.0	0.4	7.1	3.6	20.5	11.5	42.3	72.2	8.4	626	70.1
Richford town (Franklin)	2,310	2,296	-0.6	2,723	92.5	0.0	0.3	5.1	2.2	23.9	12.0	38.1	63.5	12.0	1,001	77.2
Richmond CDP	723	-	-	387	90.4	0.0	0.0	0.0	9.6	14.5	8.8	33.9	20.6	55.2	226	100.0
Richmond town (Chittenden)	4,081	4,119	0.9	4,145	95.4	1.0	0.7	1.7	1.1	21.4	11.2	41.0	19.7	59.7	1,647	97.8
Ripton town (Addison)	588	569	-3.2	524	91.8	0.0	0.0	3.8	4.4	20.8	19.8	48.9	27.7	52.1	273	85.7
Rochester CDP	299	-	-	263	98.5	0.0	0.0	0.8	0.8	16.7	39.5	62.1	29.4	46.3	127	71.7
Rochester town (Windsor)	1,138	1,088	-4.4	1,065	98.7	0.0	0.0	0.8	0.5	11.2	35.2	59.1	38.1	36.5	527	81.0
Rockingham town (Windham)	5,275	4,981	-5.6	5,031	92.1	1.8	0.3	2.2	3.6	21.0	20.0	44.2	53.9	25.4	2,175	84.1
Roxbury town (Washington)	692	709	2.5	736	97.4	0.0	1.0	0.8	0.8	14.8	20.4	50.7	41.9	29.8	325	83.4
Royalton town (Windsor)	2,781	2,871	3.2	2,843	98.3	0.0	0.0	0.0	1.7	21.3	15.3	41.8	45.8	32.9	1,212	93.1
Rupert town (Bennington)	714	682	-4.5	645	91.5	0.0	0.3	0.0	8.2	15.2	25.4	50.7	33.1	42.8	277	92.1
Rutland city & MCD (Rutland)	16,469	15,074	-8.5	15,398	93.7	1.6	1.7	1.2	1.8	16.0	21.4	45.5	44.0	28.4	7,074	86.9
Rutland town (Rutland)	4,079	4,114	0.9	4,088	94.1	2.1	2.0	1.0	0.8	17.3	28.0	55.0	33.0	33.4	1,848	87.7
Ryegate town (Caledonia)	1,174	1,101	-6.2	1,061	96.0	0.6	0.0	0.7	2.7	25.5	23.3	47.4	39.7	34.4	410	91.2
St. Albans city & MCD (Franklin)	6,921	6,801	-1.7	6,804	90.9	2.2	0.0	4.7	2.2	22.2	13.3	36.2	39.1	32.3	2,801	87.3
St. Albans town (Franklin)	5,996	6,501	8.4	6,444	96.1	0.2	1.6	1.5	0.6	17.9	22.6	43.8	45.8	23.5	2,460	85.7
St. George town (Chittenden)	702	731	4.1	594	94.8	0.0	0.0	3.2	2.0	19.2	12.1	47.6	41.3	30.5	248	90.7
St. Johnsbury CDP	6,193	-	-	5,865	95.0	0.4	1.0	1.4	2.1	18.3	18.7	44.9	43.9	27.3	2,584	85.1
St. Johnsbury town (Caledonia)	7,603	7,157	-5.9	7,224	95.6	0.3	0.8	1.5	1.7	18.9	19.1	45.5	44.6	26.0	3,119	86.5
Salisbury town (Addison)	1,136	1,107	-2.6	1,154	96.1	0.0	1.1	2.2	0.6	19.1	19.5	45.2	38.9	34.8	434	91.7
Sandgate town (Bennington)	397	381	-4.0	413	85.5	0.0	3.9	9.7	1.0	21.8	24.0	49.9	37.8	34.9	163	85.3

1 May be of any race.

Table A. All Places — **Population and Housing**

STATE City, town, township, borough, or CDP (county if applicable)	2010 census total population	2019 estimated population	Percent change 2010–2019	ACS total population estimate 2015–2019	White alone, not Hispanic or Latino	Black alone, not Hispanic or Latino	Asian alone, not Hispanic or Latino	All other races or 2 or more races, not Hispanic or Latino	Hispanic or Latino[1]	Under 18 years old	Age 65 years and older	Median age	Percent High school diploma or less	Percent Bachelor's degree or more	Total	Percent with a computer
	1	2	3	4	5	6	7	8	9	10	11	12	13	14	15	16
VERMONT—Con.																
Saxtons River village	566	539	-4.8	442	95.9	0.2	0.0	2.5	1.4	26.7	7.9	37.5	21.8	57.1	171	98.8
Searsburg town (Bennington)	109	108	-0.9	110	86.4	0.0	5.5	8.2	0.0	10.0	15.5	49.5	72.4	17.2	55	87.3
Shaftsbury town (Bennington)	3,590	3,423	-4.7	3,448	98.8	0.0	0.0	0.4	0.8	24.9	21.3	44.1	29.8	48.0	1,283	94.1
Sharon town (Windsor)	1,501	1,530	1.9	1,437	94.5	1.7	0.7	1.9	1.2	19.8	19.8	45.9	38.5	37.3	599	93.8
Sheffield town (Caledonia)	703	718	2.1	616	94.0	0.0	0.0	3.1	2.9	18.0	21.1	49.0	54.9	21.3	263	85.2
Shelburne CDP	592	-	-	525	100.0	0.0	0.0	0.0	0.0	16.6	27.6	57.3	44.2	52.7	266	94.0
Shelburne town (Chittenden)	7,139	7,647	7.1	7,717	93.4	0.9	1.1	1.5	3.0	21.3	25.1	48.1	16.6	67.3	3,171	94.4
Sheldon town (Franklin)	2,168	2,222	2.5	2,383	97.1	0.0	1.6	1.3	0.0	21.9	16.7	45.5	66.5	11.6	872	87.8
Shoreham town (Addison)	1,265	1,229	-2.8	1,119	87.6	0.8	0.3	3.8	7.6	16.2	20.7	47.0	43.4	31.5	507	81.7
Shrewsbury town (Rutland)	1,055	983	-6.8	1,154	93.7	0.0	1.9	2.9	1.5	17.3	25.7	54.4	35.5	43.9	474	96.4
Somerset town (Windham)	3	3	-	-	-	-	-	-	-	-	-	-	-	-	-	-
South Barre CDP	1,219	-	-	1,105	94.8	1.0	0.0	2.9	1.4	15.2	19.4	45.6	37.0	30.0	515	84.5
South Burlington city & MCD (Chittenden)	17,904	19,509	9.0	19,162	87.6	1.2	5.0	2.5	3.7	17.2	18.5	41.7	20.3	55.7	8,764	92.4
South Hero town (Grand Isle)	1,631	1,655	1.5	1,712	94.5	1.8	0.8	1.5	1.5	19.5	19.5	51.5	24.0	52.4	701	96.1
South Royalton CDP	694	-	-	668	96.7	0.0	0.0	0.0	3.3	16.0	17.4	51.1	38.5	30.5	357	94.7
South Shaftsbury CDP	683	-	-	412	100.0	0.0	0.0	0.0	0.0	23.8	20.4	47.6	35.3	44.1	200	88.5
Springfield CDP	3,979	-	-	3,793	91.9	0.8	2.0	4.1	1.2	19.4	24.5	44.4	52.2	17.5	1,788	88.4
Springfield town (Windsor)	9,375	8,908	-5.0	8,989	93.5	0.7	1.1	3.1	1.6	16.7	22.7	47.1	49.2	18.7	4,050	88.4
Stamford town (Bennington)	824	809	-1.8	982	97.8	0.0	0.3	1.9	0.0	23.0	18.5	46.6	46.0	25.1	373	91.7
Stannard town (Caledonia)	218	218	0.0	247	88.3	0.0	2.0	3.6	6.1	21.9	15.4	45.3	44.7	30.9	104	83.7
Starksboro town (Addison)	1,777	1,744	-1.9	1,973	95.4	0.3	0.9	2.0	1.4	21.2	13.2	37.9	36.0	44.0	751	95.7
Stockbridge town (Windsor)	732	707	-3.4	671	99.9	0.0	0.0	0.1	0.0	14.2	19.1	48.6	41.0	33.5	316	89.6
Stowe CDP	495	-	-	201	89.1	0.0	0.0	10.9	0.0	0.0	75.1	69.9	10.9	59.2	157	58.6
Stowe town (Lamoille)	4,314	4,431	2.7	4,426	93.3	0.0	2.7	3.2	0.9	19.3	25.8	50.8	18.0	59.2	2,105	92.8
Strafford town (Orange)	1,100	1,066	-3.1	1,055	92.4	5.3	0.5	1.7	0.1	17.5	26.6	56.7	25.4	54.0	462	91.8
Stratton town (Windham)	216	198	-8.3	183	98.4	0.0	0.0	0.0	1.6	11.5	25.7	50.5	33.1	48.3	87	97.7
Sudbury town (Rutland)	561	540	-3.7	575	98.1	0.0	1.2	0.0	0.7	20.7	22.8	52.6	33.9	33.2	230	86.5
Sunderland town (Bennington)	955	952	-0.3	968	94.2	0.7	1.2	2.5	1.3	18.1	24.0	52.4	35.6	32.8	414	93.7
Sutton town (Caledonia)	1,029	1,005	-2.3	1,111	94.7	0.5	0.0	2.3	2.4	29.3	19.1	35.8	50.6	24.5	367	88.6
Swanton village	2,344	2,375	1.3	2,450	94.0	0.0	0.2	4.7	1.1	21.4	18.8	44.5	59.9	11.4	953	80.4
Swanton town (Franklin)	6,421	6,554	2.1	6,534	93.9	0.0	0.1	4.7	1.3	21.5	14.4	43.1	54.0	17.8	2,465	90.3
Thetford town (Orange)	2,589	2,531	-2.2	2,551	95.9	0.0	0.2	1.9	2.0	19.8	18.6	47.1	25.3	49.9	1,155	91.4
Tinmouth town (Rutland)	616	594	-3.6	584	100.0	0.0	0.0	0.0	0.0	21.9	17.3	39.6	46.0	25.8	255	94.5
Topsham town (Orange)	1,173	1,214	3.5	1,069	93.7	0.7	0.7	4.5	0.4	20.7	17.3	41.6	54.0	23.7	433	79.9
Townshend town (Windham)	1,232	1,239	0.6	1,024	93.3	0.0	0.0	5.8	1.0	14.5	31.5	54.9	29.7	43.0	463	89.8
Troy CDP	243	-	-	50	100.0	0.0	0.0	0.0	0.0	0.0	34.0	58.8	63.2	0.0	30	100.0
Troy town (Orleans)	1,668	1,541	-7.6	1,428	97.5	0.4	0.3	1.9	0.0	21.8	15.3	35.9	58.0	15.9	612	78.8
Tunbridge town (Orange)	1,284	1,334	3.9	1,225	98.3	0.0	0.0	1.4	0.3	17.1	13.5	46.0	40.1	33.2	548	87.4
Underhill town (Chittenden)	3,023	3,086	2.1	3,080	94.9	0.3	1.3	3.1	0.5	19.3	18.1	49.0	16.1	59.6	1,200	96.0
Vergennes city & MCD (Addison)	2,626	2,583	-1.6	2,596	95.8	0.2	0.0	2.0	2.0	18.4	16.0	43.7	37.2	25.7	1,127	93.1
Vernon town (Windham)	2,206	2,196	-0.5	2,339	90.1	0.0	2.4	1.8	5.7	20.8	20.2	42.9	41.6	29.2	852	91.8
Vershire town (Orange)	721	746	3.5	686	93.4	0.7	0.9	4.4	0.6	15.2	16.3	49.2	47.0	27.2	286	92.0
Victory town (Essex)	62	63	1.6	83	100.0	0.0	0.0	0.0	0.0	3.6	41.0	62.3	25.7	29.7	47	87.2
Waitsfield CDP	164	-	-	146	65.8	0.0	0.0	0.0	34.2	14.4	19.9	38.5	2.5	65.0	91	100.0
Waitsfield town (Washington)	1,719	1,693	-1.5	1,740	91.0	0.4	0.5	3.0	5.1	19.8	21.9	46.4	18.5	56.5	817	94.5
Walden town (Caledonia)	936	953	1.8	1,001	92.7	2.2	0.8	0.9	3.4	16.9	18.1	48.6	44.5	26.5	429	83.9
Wallingford CDP	830	-	-	907	97.1	0.0	1.2	0.0	1.7	22.4	18.0	46.9	49.6	30.4	353	89.5
Wallingford town (Rutland)	2,080	1,951	-6.2	2,117	97.5	0.0	0.5	0.8	1.2	18.2	19.3	47.8	43.8	33.9	864	91.2
Waltham town (Addison)	449	463	3.1	469	94.2	0.4	0.9	0.0	4.5	14.3	27.3	49.1	33.3	44.4	194	94.8
Wardsboro town (Windham)	900	834	-7.3	778	90.9	0.0	0.0	5.8	3.3	14.7	23.7	50.1	41.6	34.6	341	95.9
Warner's grant (Essex)	-	-	-	-	-	-	-	-	-	-	-	-	-	-	-	-
Warren town (Washington)	1,705	1,671	-2.0	1,649	94.4	0.7	0.8	2.1	2.0	28.2	22.0	40.7	22.2	63.6	678	96.5
Warren's gore (Essex)	4	4	0.0	-	-	-	-	-	-	-	-	-	-	-	-	-
Washington town (Orange)	1,039	1,010	-2.8	1,153	90.4	0.7	0.8	6.0	2.2	13.0	16.7	50.2	56.0	17.4	513	86.0
Waterbury CDP	1,763	-	-	1,841	93.0	0.0	3.7	2.4	0.9	20.5	18.1	34.8	28.2	46.0	829	89.9
Waterbury town (Washington)	5,066	5,155	1.8	5,141	95.5	0.0	1.3	1.7	1.5	20.1	15.9	38.6	26.3	48.8	2,138	90.2
Waterford town (Caledonia)	1,275	1,246	-2.3	1,444	92.9	0.3	0.7	3.3	2.8	22.7	17.2	45.8	40.7	32.7	543	85.6
Waterville town (Lamoille)	673	706	4.9	644	98.1	0.8	0.0	1.1	0.0	19.3	16.5	47.3	47.4	29.8	273	92.7
Weathersfield town (Windsor)	2,825	2,736	-3.2	2,752	95.9	0.8	0.0	2.4	0.9	21.7	20.5	43.9	42.1	26.7	1,095	90.0
Websterville CDP	550	-	-	434	88.9	4.8	0.0	4.6	1.6	29.7	3.5	35.4	44.3	21.0	164	94.5
Wells CDP	397	-	-	457	96.1	0.0	2.0	2.0	0.0	14.9	31.5	42.3	39.9	21.5	163	93.3
Wells town (Rutland)	1,148	1,154	0.5	987	98.2	0.0	0.9	0.9	0.0	14.2	26.6	51.1	39.3	27.0	422	95.5
Wells River village	397	383	-3.5	468	87.0	0.0	0.0	11.5	1.5	26.7	24.8	40.6	60.3	18.0	187	71.7
West Brattleboro CDP	2,740	-	-	2,677	89.2	2.0	1.3	3.1	4.4	22.6	19.2	38.6	35.8	37.0	1,279	92.2
West Burke village	343	328	-4.4	311	92.9	0.6	0.0	4.5	1.9	19.0	19.6	49.4	56.6	15.3	158	79.1
West Fairlee town (Orange)	653	680	4.1	894	96.9	0.0	0.8	2.3	0.0	21.1	16.9	43.1	58.1	21.3	392	81.9
Westfield town (Orleans)	536	497	-7.3	615	94.1	0.0	0.5	5.4	0.0	16.3	24.9	48.7	39.7	16.7	249	88.8
Westford town (Chittenden)	2,021	2,116	4.7	2,193	96.2	0.0	0.1	2.2	1.5	21.5	15.5	45.0	28.7	48.2	820	95.6
West Haven town (Rutland)	264	247	-6.4	361	98.1	0.0	0.0	0.8	1.1	25.8	16.3	41.8	49.2	24.0	143	92.3
Westminster village	289	269	-6.9	306	87.3	0.0	0.0	7.5	5.2	18.3	28.4	55.5	40.6	33.2	131	100.0

1 May be of any race.

Table A. All Places — **Population and Housing**

STATE City, town, township, borough, or CDP (county if applicable)	2010 census total population	2019 estimated population	Percent change 2010–2019	ACS total population estimate 2015–2019	White alone, not Hispanic or Latino	Black alone, not Hispanic or Latino	Asian alone, not Hispanic or Latino	All other races or 2 or more races, not Hispanic or Latino	Hispanic or Latino[1]	Under 18 years old	Age 65 years and older	Median age	Percent High school diploma or less	Percent Bachelor's degree or more	Total	Percent with a computer
	1	2	3	4	5	6	7	8	9	10	11	12	13	14	15	16
VERMONT—Con.																
Westminster town (Windham)	3,188	2,970	-6.8	3,009	91.0	4.3	0.2	1.7	2.8	20.0	23.3	52.2	35.0	37.5	1,315	89.4
Westmore town (Orleans)	350	317	-9.4	263	100.0	0.0	0.0	0.0	0.0	11.0	38.0	61.4	36.3	30.3	136	91.9
Weston town (Windsor)	566	544	-3.9	612	92.5	0.8	0.5	4.4	1.8	14.7	34.6	53.5	16.4	54.5	267	93.3
West Rutland town (Rutland)	2,326	2,150	-7.6	2,358	93.9	0.0	0.0	2.4	3.7	23.7	17.6	41.4	45.7	25.6	1,001	87.5
West Rutland CDP	2,024	-	-	2,175	95.3	0.0	0.0	0.6	4.0	24.8	18.3	40.1	46.7	24.8	918	87.4
West Windsor town (Windsor)	1,099	1,043	-5.1	1,207	98.2	0.0	0.3	0.9	0.6	24.1	18.4	42.8	16.3	64.7	485	89.5
Weybridge town (Addison)	833	821	-1.4	824	94.2	0.6	0.6	3.3	1.3	17.6	23.8	52.3	21.0	61.5	358	90.5
Wheelock town (Caledonia)	806	826	2.5	753	94.8	2.1	0.0	1.7	1.3	13.1	19.3	47.4	50.3	23.3	313	84.0
White River Junction CDP	2,286	-	-	2,209	85.5	0.8	9.5	3.1	1.2	19.0	19.2	40.9	37.8	35.5	1,096	83.1
Whiting town (Addison)	415	411	-	371	99.2	0.0	0.5	0.0	0.3	23.5	18.3	46.3	46.6	27.1	148	83.1
Whitingham town (Windham)	1,357	1,277	-5.9	1,567	93.9	0.5	1.3	3.2	1.0	20.8	18.5	46.2	41.7	33.7	651	93.5
Wilder CDP	1,690	-	-	1,692	92.8	2.4	0.7	1.1	3.0	20.9	23.6	45.8	28.6	51.1	745	95.4
Williamstown CDP	1,162	-	-	1,017	99.1	0.0	0.0	0.0	0.9	10.7	18.0	47.0	47.9	10.9	509	83.7
Williamstown town (Orange)	3,390	3,530	4.1	3,476	99.1	0.0	0.0	0.5	0.3	18.5	18.3	45.1	52.6	12.7	1,433	91.1
Williston town (Chittenden)	8,679	10,081	16.2	9,686	92.3	1.8	2.2	2.7	0.9	22.7	17.0	39.6	16.2	61.1	3,916	94.5
Wilmington CDP	463	-	-	355	87.3	0.0	0.0	0.0	12.7	20.8	16.9	40.5	51.6	22.2	194	87.1
Wilmington town (Windham)	1,876	1,796	-4.3	1,815	92.6	0.0	0.4	2.3	4.7	14.9	21.0	46.9	40.2	36.6	860	88.1
Windham town (Windham)	419	396	-5.5	396	97.5	0.0	0.5	0.8	1.3	16.2	27.5	54.7	36.7	40.1	174	95.4
Windsor town (Windsor)	3,553	3,298	-7.2	3,392	95.6	0.3	0.2	1.4	2.5	16.9	21.0	41.4	46.7	25.7	1,453	88.3
Windsor CDP	2,066	-	-	2,150	96.2	0.0	0.0	1.2	2.6	22.0	13.4	35.9	46.4	27.7	881	90.5
Winhall town (Bennington)	769	730	-5.1	743	85.2	0.9	6.5	5.9	1.5	17.8	23.6	49.3	30.2	40.5	347	94.2
Winooski city & MCD (Chittenden)	7,262	7,333	1.0	7,242	75.3	2.5	16.8	2.7	2.7	16.3	11.6	31.9	40.9	38.0	3,189	88.9
Wolcott town (Lamoille)	1,676	1,688	0.7	1,841	97.8	0.0	0.0	0.7	1.5	22.0	11.2	40.0	48.6	23.4	707	90.8
Woodbury town (Washington)	906	883	-2.5	831	96.1	0.0	0.0	1.4	2.4	22.0	19.3	46.4	39.1	34.3	335	86.9
Woodford town (Bennington)	424	400	-5.7	320	97.2	0.0	0.0	2.8	0.0	16.9	27.2	52.1	54.5	23.6	146	89.7
Woodstock village	893	858	-3.9	1,245	96.1	0.3	0.0	0.8	2.8	25.3	28.9	48.8	16.0	61.8	577	88.6
Woodstock town (Windsor)	3,043	2,920	-4.0	2,936	97.1	0.9	0.0	0.6	1.4	19.6	29.2	51.9	15.8	59.0	1,315	92.8
Worcester CDP	112	-	-	53	84.9	0.0	3.8	11.3	0.0	17.0	35.8	54.5	22.7	50.0	28	89.3
Worcester town (Washington)	1,002	1,028	2.6	1,025	95.2	1.8	0.2	2.1	0.7	22.3	17.3	44.4	35.6	40.0	424	89.4
VIRGINIA	8,001,049	8,535,519	6.7	8,454,463	61.8	18.8	6.3	3.7	9.4	22.1	15.0	38.2	34.3	38.8	3,151,045	91.1
Abingdon town	8,225	7,867	-4.4	7,960	94.0	2.2	1.1	2.0	0.8	18.2	23.4	46.0	33.2	37.5	3,726	87.2
Accomac town	509	485	-4.7	479	60.8	16.7	0.0	2.5	20.0	20.0	21.7	48.1	54.0	23.5	166	77.7
Adwolf CDP	1,530	-	-	1,573	98.3	1.5	0.0	0.0	0.2	21.2	19.2	45.0	37.4	20.7	655	88.5
Alberta town	298	270	-9.4	344	47.7	47.7	0.0	3.5	1.2	12.5	27.6	53.0	53.0	21.3	151	73.5
Alexandria city	139,998	159,428	13.9	157,613	51.9	21.1	5.8	4.4	16.7	18.2	11.3	36.8	18.6	63.1	70,598	95.7
Allisonia CDP	117	-	-	91	100.0	0.0	0.0	0.0	0.0	28.6	12.1	24.7	28.6	26.2	46	78.3
Altavista town	3,452	3,406	-1.3	3,442	62.8	35.9	0.5	0.1	0.7	20.3	21.8	42.1	49.0	22.0	1,484	82.6
Amelia Court House CDP	1,099	-	-	1,064	79.7	20.3	0.0	0.0	0.0	32.1	25.3	37.5	58.5	14.6	410	75.4
Amherst town	2,231	2,180	-2.3	2,732	69.8	20.5	0.1	0.7	8.9	15.8	29.8	51.5	53.3	27.4	1,150	71.6
Annandale CDP	41,008	-	-	43,295	32.6	8.8	21.8	4.8	32.1	22.0	13.8	37.3	34.9	44.9	13,882	94.6
Appalachia town	1,753	1,533	-12.5	1,444	88.2	1.9	0.0	9.3	0.5	26.8	17.6	39.2	47.4	11.1	607	76.1
Apple Mountain Lake CDP	1,396	-	-	1,369	90.9	0.4	1.6	3.9	3.1	27.7	8.7	38.3	36.2	20.6	506	100.0
Appomattox town	1,716	1,794	4.5	1,856	68.9	21.6	0.4	5.1	4.1	24.8	24.6	37.7	59.5	20.0	825	75.2
Aquia Harbour CDP	6,727	-	-	6,106	75.3	7.7	3.1	5.1	8.8	22.6	13.1	40.8	20.3	47.2	2,207	99.0
Arcola CDP	233	-	-	1,216	43.1	16.0	26.7	5.5	8.7	21.2	10.4	35.1	27.6	55.6	518	100.0
Arlington CDP	207,627	-	-	233,464	61.5	8.9	10.2	3.8	15.6	17.8	10.5	34.7	13.5	75.3	107,032	95.7
Arrington CDP	708	-	-	905	64.3	35.7	0.0	0.0	0.0	34.6	10.4	36.0	74.0	20.7	332	84.3
Ashburn CDP	43,511	-	-	49,848	59.1	7.9	17.0	4.2	11.8	26.5	12.8	37.6	14.4	62.8	17,835	97.7
Ashland town	7,256	7,875	8.5	7,750	64.0	18.6	1.1	3.5	12.9	16.2	16.2	33.2	46.5	30.3	2,798	85.2
Atkins CDP	1,143	-	-	750	83.6	2.7	4.3	0.7	8.8	9.9	30.4	51.6	60.1	8.8	443	77.2
Atlantic CDP	862	-	-	773	66.2	21.5	0.0	0.0	12.3	11.9	28.7	61.4	69.3	12.3	330	100.0
Augusta Springs CDP	257	-	-	210	100.0	0.0	0.0	0.0	0.0	9.0	24.8	52.1	81.3	0.0	99	37.4
Bailey's Crossroads CDP	23,643	-	-	24,180	31.1	17.2	12.8	4.1	34.8	24.4	13.2	34.7	37.0	45.1	9,140	91.8
Baskerville CDP	128	-	-	74	93.2	5.4	0.0	0.0	1.4	25.7	0.0	29.3	76.5	0.0	32	71.9
Bassett CDP	1,100	-	-	1,065	64.0	22.9	0.0	0.0	13.1	16.4	29.1	52.2	49.0	14.5	470	84.7
Basye CDP	1,253	-	-	953	93.6	0.0	0.0	0.0	6.4	9.2	29.6	49.3	41.9	31.4	421	94.3
Bayside CDP	120	-	-	272	0.0	100.0	0.0	0.0	0.0	46.0	4.8	37.2	38.1	0.0	88	100.0
Bealeton CDP	4,435	-	-	4,873	60.1	9.9	2.8	5.2	22.0	23.7	8.0	33.3	43.1	24.4	1,571	91.2
Bedford town	6,553	6,597	0.7	6,562	76.3	20.3	0.5	2.8	0.0	24.7	19.0	34.5	50.3	17.6	2,658	75.9
Belle Haven town	522	502	-3.8	542	76.4	16.6	0.0	2.0	5.0	29.3	20.1	35.4	44.8	23.1	225	80.4
Belle Haven CDP	6,518	-	-	6,640	76.8	4.6	5.4	3.2	9.9	19.3	18.4	44.9	17.3	66.3	2,943	96.5
Bellwood CDP	6,352	-	-	6,723	41.9	30.9	2.7	4.3	20.2	24.9	11.9	33.0	66.8	12.2	2,508	85.4
Belmont CDP	5,966	-	-	6,632	62.6	3.9	23.3	3.4	6.8	32.6	8.0	37.1	11.2	75.4	1,808	99.8
Belmont Estates CDP	1,263	-	-	1,226	71.9	0.4	0.0	2.0	25.8	21.3	34.4	50.5	32.7	45.0	496	91.7
Belspring CDP	256	-	-	199	100.0	0.0	0.0	0.0	0.0	25.6	20.6	42.1	65.2	0.0	59	78.0
Belview CDP	891	-	-	1,072	89.5	10.5	0.0	0.0	0.0	19.5	25.3	31.4	58.1	22.2	440	88.2
Benns Church CDP	872	-	-	551	63.0	22.0	5.1	10.0	0.0	14.0	15.8	48.7	65.7	4.7	232	94.4
Bensley CDP	5,819	-	-	6,092	31.7	22.8	2.0	3.5	40.0	23.7	10.5	32.2	65.1	8.3	2,263	82.0
Berryville town	4,182	4,371	4.5	4,324	75.3	8.8	1.5	3.5	10.9	23.6	21.7	42.7	45.1	28.8	1,517	84.1
Bethel Manor CDP	3,792	-	-	4,312	55.3	15.7	1.2	10.3	17.5	46.4	0.0	23.8	18.3	33.9	1,184	97.4
Big Island CDP	303	-	-	203	77.3	22.7	0.0	0.0	0.0	8.9	54.7	67.0	38.9	0.0	134	57.5
Big Stone Gap town	5,629	5,132	-8.8	5,257	76.0	19.6	1.2	1.4	1.8	17.6	13.5	40.0	49.1	20.4	1,692	85.7
Blacksburg town	42,525	44,233	4.0	44,303	75.2	4.6	12.6	3.3	4.3	10.0	6.2	22.0	14.8	71.4	13,403	97.8
Blackstone town	3,620	3,329	-8.0	3,391	37.6	55.1	0.4	0.4	6.5	27.9	17.7	37.2	59.4	16.1	1,167	77.9
Blairs CDP	916	-	-	592	80.9	19.1	0.0	0.0	0.0	13.5	19.9	46.8	54.4	11.9	267	86.5
Bland CDP	409	-	-	360	90.0	0.0	0.0	10.0	0.0	23.6	19.7	25.6	43.1	30.8	210	48.1
Bloxom town	381	366	-3.9	392	68.4	11.5	0.0	0.0	20.2	24.0	21.4	39.3	65.4	10.1	157	83.4

1 May be of any race.

Table A. All Places — **Population and Housing**

STATE City, town, township, borough, or CDP (county if applicable)	Population: 2010 census total population	Population: 2019 estimated population	Population: Percent change 2010–2019	Population: ACS total population estimate 2015–2019	Race and Hispanic or Latino origin (percent): White alone, not Hispanic or Latino	Race: Black alone, not Hispanic or Latino	Race: Asian alone, not Hispanic or Latino	Race: All other races or 2 or more races, not Hispanic or Latino	Race: Hispanic or Latino[1]	Age (percent): Under 18 years old	Age: Age 65 years and older	Age: Median age	Educational attainment of persons age 25 and older: Percent High school diploma or less	Educational attainment: Percent Bachelor's degree or more	Occupied housing units: Total	Occupied housing units: Percent with a computer
	1	2	3	4	5	6	7	8	9	10	11	12	13	14	15	16
VIRGINIA—Con.																
Bluefield town	5,405	4,837	-10.5	4,907	87.2	7.9	1.5	1.6	1.8	17.3	21.4	45.6	52.9	22.1	2,029	87.5
Blue Ridge CDP	3,084	-	-	3,288	96.4	1.4	0.3	1.9	0.0	15.7	19.3	43.0	40.4	25.6	1,261	89.7
Blue Ridge Shores CDP	813	-	-	772	100.0	0.0	0.0	0.0	0.0	13.0	12.2	44.1	49.4	25.5	277	100.0
Bobtown CDP	211	-	-	123	100.0	0.0	0.0	0.0	0.0	0.0	58.5	67.0	15.4	65.9	73	84.9
Bon Air CDP	16,366	-	-	18,052	74.1	10.2	4.3	3.0	8.4	23.1	18.2	40.9	23.6	49.4	6,944	95.9
Boones Mill town	236	233	-1.3	169	91.7	3.6	0.0	4.7	0.0	10.7	34.3	52.8	33.1	18.0	87	74.7
Boston CDP	504	-	-	928	3.3	92.9	0.0	0.0	3.8	44.1	6.0	30.2	78.7	0.0	231	73.6
Boswell's Corner CDP	1,375	-	-	1,548	18.5	15.3	1.7	5.1	59.4	25.0	3.4	31.3	65.8	15.3	452	96.2
Bowling Green town	1,109	1,175	6.0	1,249	72.0	20.4	0.3	5.0	2.3	20.8	24.7	46.4	53.5	17.8	507	75.1
Boyce town	600	627	4.5	827	78.7	5.9	1.0	8.0	6.4	31.0	12.3	37.1	29.0	35.4	283	90.5
Boydton town	433	411	-5.1	303	78.5	16.2	3.0	1.3	1.0	20.1	23.1	49.1	30.1	50.9	121	86.0
Boykins town	564	526	-6.7	748	55.5	23.0	0.0	11.8	9.8	18.6	12.7	46.3	44.7	24.1	251	84.5
Bracey CDP	1,554	-	-	1,065	93.5	5.0	0.0	0.9	0.6	3.4	39.7	62.1	42.5	28.4	544	92.3
Brambleton CDP	9,845	-	-	21,358	41.2	8.4	34.8	7.7	7.9	34.4	4.3	34.7	10.7	76.7	6,522	100.0
Branchville town	125	115	-8.0	114	66.7	33.3	0.0	0.0	0.0	16.7	10.5	39.5	42.9	14.3	36	91.7
Brandermill CDP	13,173	-	-	13,836	74.0	14.4	2.8	2.1	6.6	18.8	19.3	42.1	20.4	52.8	5,712	96.6
Bridgewater town	5,636	6,145	9.0	6,032	90.0	4.5	0.5	1.6	3.3	15.2	23.2	31.8	28.3	51.1	2,141	87.1
Brightwood CDP	1,001	-	-	1,195	94.7	0.0	0.0	4.4	0.9	25.7	22.1	39.8	54.5	20.4	430	95.1
Bristol city	17,738	16,762	-5.5	16,912	88.2	5.7	0.2	3.6	2.3	21.3	20.4	42.2	45.0	25.4	7,334	84.1
Broadlands CDP	12,313	-	-	13,576	56.3	9.5	22.6	3.9	7.7	33.2	5.1	35.9	8.9	74.2	4,176	99.6
Broadway town	3,696	3,978	7.6	3,891	88.7	1.1	0.3	2.0	7.8	28.5	13.4	34.2	44.3	26.4	1,575	94.3
Brodnax town	294	268	-8.8	240	68.8	28.8	0.0	0.8	1.7	13.8	26.7	53.3	56.0	19.4	106	79.2
Brookneal town	1,112	1,098	-1.3	876	49.5	47.7	0.0	2.7	0.0	17.5	21.3	47.4	72.7	9.4	376	80.3
Buchanan town	1,173	1,174	0.1	1,369	89.1	2.0	0.0	4.5	4.5	27.2	15.8	34.6	55.1	20.2	557	85.1
Buckhall CDP	16,293	-	-	17,708	67.1	8.4	7.1	5.1	12.4	24.1	12.5	40.7	26.1	48.7	5,353	94.9
Buckingham Courthouse CDP	133	-	-	59	71.2	28.8	0.0	0.0	0.0	23.7	28.8	33.8	37.8	51.1	31	100.0
Buena Vista city	6,607	6,478	-2.0	6,484	88.1	7.3	1.9	0.9	1.8	20.7	18.4	35.5	59.2	15.9	2,517	79.9
Bull Run CDP	14,983	-	-	16,651	24.8	18.2	11.3	4.4	41.3	27.0	5.7	30.7	47.1	29.8	5,651	95.6
Bull Run Mountain Estates CDP	1,251	-	-	1,314	76.6	12.8	1.1	0.0	9.4	23.8	11.0	36.4	28.4	32.6	427	98.1
Burke CDP	41,055	-	-	42,806	57.7	6.9	16.3	4.7	14.4	25.4	15.4	41.2	16.5	63.3	13,445	99.0
Burke Centre CDP	17,326	-	-	17,894	59.8	6.1	13.8	5.6	14.7	23.1	14.3	38.6	14.7	65.5	6,190	98.3
Burkeville town	433	399	-7.9	487	74.7	24.2	0.0	0.6	0.4	20.5	16.4	46.4	60.2	9.5	240	74.6
Callaghan CDP	348	-	-	283	77.0	5.3	3.2	0.0	14.5	5.7	19.4	48.0	71.5	12.4	104	75.0
Calverton CDP	239	-	-	107	86.0	0.0	0.0	0.0	14.0	5.6	19.6	31.9	34.8	39.1	68	61.8
Camptown CDP	766	-	-	938	23.1	67.3	0.0	9.6	0.0	25.6	19.9	34.4	60.8	12.3	400	75.3
Cana CDP	1,254	-	-	1,820	97.3	0.0	0.0	1.6	1.1	25.9	13.5	43.1	67.3	6.3	677	82.7
Cape Charles town	1,009	1,019	1.0	1,239	71.8	19.8	0.7	6.4	1.3	16.7	34.5	58.0	27.8	46.4	658	86.0
Capron town	164	151	-7.9	158	69.6	13.3	0.0	17.1	0.0	15.8	40.5	59.7	33.1	12.4	67	88.1
Captains Cove CDP	1,042	-	-	1,077	98.7	0.0	0.0	0.0	1.3	12.8	42.2	61.7	49.0	29.8	430	78.1
Carrollton CDP	4,574	-	-	6,442	74.7	15.8	1.7	2.0	5.8	24.5	12.2	38.3	28.5	34.5	2,348	97.1
Carrsville CDP	359	-	-	174	100.0	0.0	0.0	0.0	0.0	12.6	27.6	60.3	73.0	10.5	109	58.7
Cascades CDP	11,912	-	-	11,389	68.2	5.6	14.1	5.3	6.8	25.1	10.5	38.9	9.9	72.9	4,272	96.7
Castlewood CDP	2,045	-	-	1,785	100.0	0.0	0.0	0.0	0.0	23.5	20.4	44.8	57.8	8.6	749	68.2
Catlett CDP	296	-	-	162	67.3	0.0	32.7	0.0	0.0	6.8	0.0	27.7	79.6	5.8	88	100.0
Cats Bridge CDP	229	-	-	141	41.1	58.9	0.0	0.0	0.0	0.0	68.8	69.3	68.8	2.1	71	53.5
Cave Spring CDP	24,922	-	-	26,001	81.4	7.5	4.5	2.2	4.4	19.7	20.9	42.7	23.2	46.7	11,342	92.3
Cedar Bluff town	1,130	1,002	-11.3	1,045	99.4	0.3	0.0	0.3	0.0	11.9	15.6	44.3	45.6	14.8	485	79.2
Central Garage CDP	1,318	-	-	1,574	86.8	6.2	0.0	5.8	1.3	23.6	14.1	42.7	43.7	27.6	474	94.9
Centreville CDP	71,135	-	-	74,125	45.2	7.2	28.6	5.0	14.0	24.2	8.6	36.6	21.6	58.2	24,130	98.3
Chamberlayne CDP	5,456	-	-	5,888	35.3	52.2	6.6	5.1	0.7	13.7	26.3	49.2	32.0	41.6	2,287	86.3
Chantilly CDP	23,039	-	-	24,368	36.8	5.2	33.7	2.7	21.6	25.1	9.8	38.3	24.4	55.3	7,223	98.5
Charles City CDP	133	-	-	60	35.0	43.3	0.0	21.7	0.0	20.0	50.0	64.5	56.3	12.5	26	69.2
Charlotte Court House town	543	512	-5.7	538	51.5	32.7	4.3	10.8	0.7	24.7	28.6	42.1	56.7	15.5	177	65.0
Charlottesville city	43,425	47,266	8.8	47,096	65.7	18.7	7.1	3.0	5.5	15.6	11.3	31.6	25.4	54.9	18,617	92.4
Chase City town	2,341	2,215	-5.4	2,568	39.1	53.7	0.0	5.0	2.3	22.0	18.9	38.1	59.4	12.9	941	64.4
Chase Crossing CDP	377	-	-	331	0.0	100.0	0.0	0.0	0.0	6.6	10.9	62.1	85.4	0.0	160	81.9
Chatham town	1,269	1,427	12.5	1,401	73.2	14.6	0.9	3.1	8.2	19.8	17.6	43.5	39.9	34.4	560	90.7
Chatmoss CDP	1,698	-	-	1,544	64.6	29.0	1.0	1.4	4.1	14.3	23.8	46.3	14.1	49.4	648	93.8
Cheriton town	485	448	-7.6	461	62.0	32.8	0.0	3.5	1.7	13.2	35.8	55.5	59.3	20.3	207	72.0
Cherry Hill CDP	16,000	-	-	20,241	19.1	45.7	7.1	6.8	21.3	30.3	7.2	34.0	27.9	37.2	6,287	97.0
Chesapeake city	222,311	244,835	10.1	239,982	57.4	29.3	3.1	4.0	6.2	24.2	13.0	36.9	31.9	33.2	84,849	94.3
Chester CDP	20,987	-	-	22,032	64.7	22.2	0.9	3.5	8.7	24.0	13.5	37.6	35.7	32.1	8,155	94.7
Chester Gap CDP	839	-	-	1,145	98.1	0.0	0.0	0.0	1.9	30.7	16.8	36.3	46.7	18.8	386	90.4
Chilhowie town	1,816	1,702	-6.3	2,101	90.6	4.0	0.0	2.1	3.4	17.8	25.7	47.8	50.1	26.0	765	79.5
Chincoteague town	2,941	2,875	-2.2	2,899	89.9	0.4	2.1	4.3	3.2	13.1	31.9	56.5	42.3	27.7	1,539	85.4
Christiansburg town	20,965	22,473	7.2	22,163	87.2	5.5	2.8	1.5	3.0	22.3	15.7	38.9	31.9	36.1	9,324	92.1
Churchville CDP	194	-	-	174	100.0	0.0	0.0	0.0	0.0	33.3	28.2	48.3	38.8	44.8	60	66.7
Claremont town	372	336	-9.7	354	71.2	24.6	0.0	2.8	1.4	10.2	31.9	57.2	55.7	16.9	162	81.5
Clarksville town	1,233	1,166	-5.4	1,389	65.4	30.2	0.9	1.3	2.2	25.0	22.5	43.9	29.4	32.3	564	77.7
Claypool Hill CDP	1,776	-	-	1,341	96.2	1.4	0.0	0.0	2.4	19.1	27.2	48.3	46.8	13.3	629	84.1
Cleveland town	193	175	-9.3	151	100.0	0.0	0.0	0.0	0.0	14.6	28.5	49.5	75.9	0.9	64	56.3
Clifton town	282	293	3.9	264	96.2	1.1	0.8	0.4	1.5	22.3	22.0	54.2	7.7	75.0	95	97.9
Clifton Forge town	3,886	3,494	-10.1	3,581	79.6	16.3	0.2	1.7	2.2	21.8	22.5	49.1	56.7	12.8	1,586	78.1
Clinchco town	334	294	-12.0	283	98.6	0.4	0.0	0.0	1.1	16.6	25.4	50.3	75.8	10.3	146	51.4
Clinchport town	70	64	-8.6	41	100.0	0.0	0.0	0.0	0.0	14.6	22.0	48.8	78.6	0.0	16	75.0
Clintwood town	1,449	1,284	-11.4	1,452	98.3	1.0	0.0	0.1	0.5	18.7	27.3	53.4	57.9	11.6	553	70.7
Clover CDP	438	-	-	368	50.5	46.7	0.0	0.0	2.7	3.3	39.7	59.5	42.8	10.4	168	76.2
Cloverdale CDP	3,119	-	-	3,294	85.6	5.4	4.5	1.7	2.9	22.6	21.2	45.7	31.3	38.6	1,337	89.5
Cluster Springs CDP	811	-	-	764	74.3	25.7	0.0	0.0	0.0	11.1	25.3	61.4	68.6	4.3	369	74.5
Coeburn town	2,040	1,845	-9.6	1,567	95.1	3.3	0.0	1.6	0.0	24.6	16.3	43.0	60.2	13.4	676	80.9
Collinsville CDP	7,335	-	-	7,665	77.4	10.9	0.8	1.7	9.1	22.4	20.0	42.6	50.5	17.4	3,171	81.6
Colonial Beach town	3,540	3,619	2.2	3,574	70.4	11.4	2.0	8.1	8.2	24.1	29.7	45.3	41.1	25.6	1,680	89.6
Colonial Heights city	17,410	17,370	-0.2	17,428	72.3	14.6	4.2	3.0	5.9	22.8	20.4	40.6	39.9	25.5	7,036	89.2
Columbia CDP	83	-	-	126	51.6	42.9	0.0	0.0	5.6	23.8	30.2	47.3	51.0	11.5	35	82.9
Concord CDP	1,458	-	-	746	75.7	19.0	0.0	3.6	1.6	8.0	36.2	56.8	59.8	15.6	410	83.2
Countryside CDP	10,072	-	-	9,701	61.3	8.3	7.2	5.2	18.1	24.7	7.8	36.2	20.4	55.1	3,366	96.6
County Center CDP	3,270	-	-	4,045	54.2	25.0	7.4	1.4	12.1	32.5	8.7	33.8	22.2	45.7	1,115	98.4
Courtland town	1,281	1,215	-5.2	1,840	43.3	48.2	0.1	4.8	3.6	23.9	19.7	43.5	46.9	15.9	646	86.7
Covington city	5,951	5,538	-6.9	5,598	81.0	12.5	1.2	3.0	2.4	20.5	20.2	42.4	57.1	15.6	2,384	83.6

1 May be of any race.

Table A. All Places — **Population and Housing**

STATE City, town, township, borough, or CDP (county if applicable)	Population				Race and Hispanic or Latino origin (percent)					Age (percent)			Educational attainment of persons age 25 and older		Occupied housing units	
	2010 census total population	2019 estimated population	Percent change 2010–2019	ACS total population estimate 2015–2019	White alone, not Hispanic or Latino	Black alone, not Hispanic or Latino	Asian alone, not Hispanic or Latino	All other races or 2 or more races, not Hispanic or Latino	Hispanic or Latino[1]	Under 18 years old	Age 65 years and older	Median age	Percent High school diploma or less	Percent Bachelor's degree or more	Total	Percent with a computer
	1	2	3	4	5	6	7	8	9	10	11	12	13	14	15	16
VIRGINIA—Con.																
Craigsville town	918	931	1.4	687	95.9	0.0	0.0	2.6	1.5	17.3	23.0	49.6	69.0	6.2	327	81.0
Crewe town	2,326	2,129	-8.5	2,465	51.4	43.2	0.2	1.7	3.5	18.9	17.6	37.0	53.2	20.9	1,004	76.2
Crimora CDP	2,209	-	-	2,207	97.5	2.5	0.0	0.0	0.0	28.8	18.2	36.5	78.9	6.4	844	78.9
Crosspointe CDP	5,802	-	-	5,727	66.9	7.2	16.0	3.3	6.6	25.4	13.4	45.7	7.3	71.4	1,753	100.0
Crozet CDP	5,565	-	-	7,159	92.6	2.5	2.2	1.7	1.0	28.4	17.1	41.5	16.8	66.9	3,007	91.2
Culpeper town	16,658	18,873	13.3	18,342	54.9	20.1	1.9	4.0	19.1	27.4	12.0	34.5	42.4	26.1	6,246	90.0
Cumberland CDP	393	-	-	396	21.7	78.3	0.0	0.0	0.0	0.0	42.2	59.4	58.8	26.1	175	56.0
Dahlgren CDP	2,653	-	-	3,093	57.0	34.0	0.4	3.2	5.5	26.5	10.1	29.4	28.1	32.9	1,097	98.9
Dahlgren Center CDP	599	-	-	628	70.1	11.0	2.1	5.1	11.8	26.3	0.3	23.5	22.6	38.3	158	100.0
Dale City CDP	65,969	-	-	72,627	26.8	24.4	9.2	5.0	34.6	26.5	8.8	35.0	42.7	28.5	20,703	97.0
Daleville CDP	2,557	-	-	2,806	94.9	1.4	0.0	0.4	3.4	20.6	32.8	53.3	17.0	42.7	1,219	93.8
Damascus town	805	775	-3.7	614	97.2	0.5	0.0	2.3	0.0	20.0	18.4	39.9	44.1	20.8	297	73.1
Dante CDP	649	-	-	557	87.8	12.2	0.0	0.0	0.0	25.3	23.5	50.4	64.9	4.8	245	78.8
Danville city	43,071	40,044	-7.0	41,070	42.4	48.8	1.2	3.4	4.3	21.8	20.3	40.9	49.8	17.6	18,293	80.6
Dayton town	1,541	1,637	6.2	1,501	85.1	1.6	5.9	0.8	6.6	23.5	17.3	37.5	34.1	45.0	600	93.3
Deep Creek CDP	115	-	-	40	100.0	0.0	0.0	0.0	0.0	70.0	0.0	11.4	0.0	100.0	12	100.0
Deerfield CDP	132	-	-	106	74.5	0.0	0.0	25.5	0.0	7.5	8.5	31.3	71.4	0.0	50	82.0
Deltaville CDP	1,119	-	-	1,050	95.1	0.0	0.0	3.9	1.0	17.6	36.5	57.7	47.4	25.2	460	85.0
Dendron town	273	247	-9.5	377	29.2	59.2	0.0	8.0	3.7	20.4	12.5	45.3	55.1	21.1	134	85.8
Dillwyn town	444	442	-0.5	556	53.2	40.5	0.0	4.0	2.3	25.0	23.6	39.8	65.6	9.3	179	84.4
Dooms CDP	1,327	-	-	1,105	92.3	0.0	0.0	6.4	1.3	17.0	27.1	50.8	66.9	11.3	554	72.4
Drakes Branch town	533	501	-6.0	607	57.7	34.9	1.0	4.1	2.3	35.6	13.8	40.0	59.9	8.5	189	67.7
Dranesville CDP	11,921	-	-	11,661	70.8	3.9	12.3	2.2	10.9	23.5	12.8	43.1	10.2	72.5	3,726	98.3
Draper CDP	320	-	-	371	92.5	7.5	0.0	0.0	0.0	2.2	7.3	47.8	25.6	38.9	174	93.1
Dryden CDP	1,208	-	-	1,174	98.7	0.0	0.0	1.3	0.0	32.2	11.5	33.4	49.0	15.2	400	93.8
Dublin town	2,538	2,584	1.8	2,633	84.3	10.0	0.3	3.5	2.0	14.4	12.4	37.4	60.1	8.4	807	82.8
Duffield town	90	83	-7.8	81	100.0	0.0	0.0	0.0	0.0	16.0	30.9	45.4	30.6	9.7	37	70.3
Dulles Town Center CDP	4,601	-	-	5,475	34.7	11.8	19.5	3.1	30.9	24.4	4.1	32.9	32.4	49.5	2,038	99.5
Dumbarton CDP	7,879	-	-	8,714	35.3	28.7	3.3	7.9	24.7	22.1	12.7	35.7	44.1	31.4	3,640	89.2
Dumfries town	4,972	5,922	19.1	5,373	18.9	28.6	3.4	3.9	45.3	40.9	4.0	24.7	54.4	16.2	1,543	90.9
Dungannon town	322	298	-7.5	352	92.3	2.0	3.7	2.0	0.0	27.3	15.3	42.5	70.2	5.7	154	70.1
Dunn Loring CDP	8,803	-	-	9,158	59.7	4.6	18.7	5.1	11.8	26.7	17.1	41.8	14.4	72.3	2,880	98.5
East Highland Park CDP	14,796	-	-	15,498	11.5	82.0	1.0	2.5	3.0	20.4	15.4	40.1	45.1	21.5	6,211	85.9
East Lexington CDP	1,463	-	-	1,683	70.3	24.2	1.1	1.0	3.4	22.5	8.4	33.3	35.8	29.7	555	90.5
Eastville town	360	339	-5.8	611	49.3	18.0	1.3	1.5	30.0	32.6	13.3	38.9	38.1	28.1	287	77.4
Ebony CDP	161	-	-	238	51.3	48.7	0.0	0.0	0.0	6.7	6.3	24.9	100.0	0.0	106	100.0
Edinburg town	1,037	1,070	3.2	1,261	85.2	7.8	0.0	0.2	6.7	18.8	15.1	34.2	53.1	19.1	510	89.4
Elkton town	2,729	2,903	6.4	2,846	94.6	2.6	1.8	0.2	0.8	18.3	21.7	44.5	54.7	16.9	1,268	79.9
Elliston CDP	902	-	-	1,060	82.3	0.0	0.0	0.0	17.7	24.2	4.7	24.9	75.5	7.6	277	95.3
Emory CDP	1,251	-	-	1,155	79.1	11.2	2.0	3.9	3.8	2.7	12.5	21.0	24.7	47.1	190	98.4
Emporia city	5,925	5,346	-9.8	5,442	24.5	62.8	0.3	5.6	6.8	28.7	16.8	35.4	54.4	13.8	2,086	81.4
Enon CDP	3,466	-	-	4,425	63.0	26.6	2.4	1.9	6.1	25.4	14.1	36.7	37.3	30.0	1,640	96.9
Esmont CDP	528	-	-	828	12.1	61.2	0.6	0.0	26.1	35.0	11.4	27.4	48.1	16.3	269	84.4
Ettrick CDP	6,682	-	-	5,201	16.2	77.5	0.0	2.5	3.9	14.3	11.1	23.0	37.5	27.0	1,400	93.6
Ewing CDP	439	-	-	198	100.0	0.0	0.0	0.0	0.0	14.6	5.6	51.8	69.8	21.9	117	75.2
Exmore town	1,462	1,372	-6.2	1,501	44.1	48.0	0.0	0.5	7.5	24.1	22.5	41.8	68.5	11.0	655	75.4
Fairfax city	22,554	24,019	6.5	23,531	56.2	4.9	17.2	4.5	17.2	22.3	14.9	38.2	19.4	60.8	8,577	98.3
Fairfax Station CDP	12,030	-	-	12,046	70.9	3.0	14.2	4.3	7.6	19.6	19.9	46.1	11.1	70.8	4,058	98.7
Fair Lakes CDP	7,942	-	-	8,399	46.9	8.3	35.1	5.4	4.4	19.4	7.8	34.9	11.1	68.4	3,213	99.7
Fairlawn CDP	2,367	-	-	2,322	97.1	0.4	0.0	0.0	2.5	13.4	22.9	46.7	28.3	40.5	1,075	93.0
Fair Oaks CDP	30,223	-	-	33,481	48.0	8.7	28.5	4.9	9.9	20.2	8.3	34.7	14.1	66.8	14,222	97.7
Fairview CDP	240	-	-	153	62.7	37.3	0.0	0.0	0.0	0.0	81.0	83.7	96.7	3.3	35	0.0
Fairview Beach CDP	391	-	-	479	100.0	0.0	0.0	0.0	0.0	21.9	18.0	49.1	63.4	33.7	217	100.0
Falls Church city	12,244	14,617	19.4	14,128	71.7	4.6	9.9	3.1	10.7	24.9	12.9	38.7	8.4	77.6	5,493	98.2
Falmouth CDP	4,274	-	-	4,688	84.1	8.1	0.8	2.9	4.1	29.5	15.8	37.4	27.6	46.2	1,641	94.8
Fancy Gap CDP	237	-	-	54	51.9	0.0	0.0	48.1	0.0	0.0	25.9	62.1	25.9	0.0	28	100.0
Farmville town	8,218	7,846	-4.5	8,117	59.4	26.9	1.3	3.1	9.3	12.5	12.4	22.2	47.2	32.0	2,256	74.8
Ferrum CDP	2,043	-	-	2,310	75.4	19.1	0.0	1.5	4.0	11.5	7.6	21.1	59.6	18.8	429	72.7
Fieldale CDP	879	-	-	907	79.6	6.8	0.0	5.1	8.5	17.9	28.2	48.4	59.2	5.3	376	76.1
Fincastle town	355	341	-3.9	389	88.2	9.3	0.3	1.3	1.0	7.5	19.5	44.6	36.4	34.5	139	90.6
Fishersville CDP	7,462	-	-	8,647	86.9	9.6	0.3	1.6	1.7	23.0	19.6	40.7	35.5	38.5	3,308	88.1
Flint Hill CDP	209	-	-	336	81.3	0.0	0.0	0.0	18.8	25.9	26.2	35.4	63.9	22.9	158	80.4
Floris CDP	8,375	-	-	8,291	46.4	5.7	39.6	3.6	4.7	26.2	11.2	42.1	7.8	79.0	2,654	95.8
Floyd town	428	436	1.9	724	73.5	6.5	0.0	0.0	20.0	32.3	14.4	38.7	40.0	35.2	257	75.5
Forest CDP	9,106	-	-	10,836	80.6	6.9	5.8	3.0	3.7	20.8	18.1	42.4	21.5	48.8	4,398	96.7
Fort Belvoir CDP	7,100	-	-	7,967	58.8	14.8	5.1	8.3	13.0	46.6	0.2	20.4	13.2	44.4	1,865	99.5
Fort Chiswell CDP	939	-	-	960	100.0	0.0	0.0	0.0	0.0	25.1	16.1	40.4	36.9	32.4	311	94.9
Fort Hunt CDP	16,045	-	-	16,973	87.2	1.8	3.4	2.1	5.5	27.3	19.3	45.9	7.5	80.0	5,965	98.5
Fort Lee CDP	3,393	-	-	5,763	39.4	31.4	2.2	7.4	19.7	41.0	0.7	22.2	18.0	33.4	1,339	98.8
Franconia CDP	18,245	-	-	19,720	47.1	19.7	13.8	5.5	13.9	19.8	8.7	37.7	20.0	58.8	7,402	99.2
Franklin city	8,578	7,967	-7.1	8,147	36.9	56.7	1.3	4.1	1.1	25.2	19.3	39.4	42.8	19.1	3,522	81.6
Franklin Farm CDP	19,288	-	-	18,321	65.2	3.2	20.8	3.2	7.5	26.7	11.3	42.4	9.7	76.5	5,913	99.7
Fredericksburg city	24,178	29,036	20.1	28,622	59.4	20.7	2.7	6.6	10.7	21.0	10.8	30.4	33.6	40.9	10,762	93.5
Free Union CDP	193	-	-	261	55.9	34.5	9.6	0.0	0.0	18.0	11.1	29.3	0.0	45.3	97	100.0
Fries town	483	446	-7.7	476	97.7	1.1	0.0	0.0	1.3	24.6	34.5	39.0	41.4	11.7	195	72.8
Front Royal town	14,425	15,278	5.9	15,077	76.3	9.0	1.0	6.2	7.5	24.5	15.6	37.4	54.4	17.8	5,635	85.4
Gainesville CDP	11,481	-	-	17,287	55.1	13.2	16.8	4.7	10.2	31.2	7.7	34.7	18.2	55.7	5,221	99.6
Galax city	6,989	6,347	-9.2	6,517	79.1	5.0	0.6	0.8	14.5	21.7	22.4	45.0	54.7	14.8	2,663	79.9
Gargatha CDP	381	-	-	171	66.1	33.9	0.0	0.0	0.0	4.7	31.0	58.1	50.3	9.2	128	51.6
Gasburg CDP	481	-	-	529	100.0	0.0	0.0	0.0	0.0	18.5	13.4	36.8	42.2	46.4	257	94.2
Gate City town	2,048	1,869	-8.7	1,941	97.4	1.2	0.4	0.5	0.5	26.5	23.5	42.8	50.0	20.3	801	72.7
George Mason CDP	9,496	-	-	9,777	51.6	17.1	15.2	5.5	10.6	13.3	6.0	20.9	18.6	65.7	1,678	97.6
Glade Spring town	1,461	1,406	-3.8	1,616	87.1	0.5	0.0	3.0	9.3	24.4	23.4	45.0	44.9	22.8	630	86.8
Glasgow town	1,115	1,103	-1.1	1,385	76.3	13.9	0.0	1.1	8.7	22.2	22.0	38.8	68.2	12.1	533	83.9
Glen Allen CDP	14,774	-	-	15,488	58.1	28.8	4.0	4.3	4.8	25.5	15.1	39.4	26.5	40.2	6,089	97.2
Glen Lyn town	103	97	-5.8	89	100.0	0.0	0.0	0.0	0.0	21.3	4.5	41.8	63.9	0.0	35	91.4
Glenvar CDP	976	-	-	1,088	90.8	5.0	0.5	3.1	0.6	11.7	54.3	67.1	62.2	12.7	440	73.2
Gloucester Courthouse CDP	2,951	-	-	2,466	81.4	14.8	1.3	0.7	1.7	14.9	33.6	51.1	39.3	25.5	1,024	80.7
Gloucester Point CDP	9,402	-	-	9,854	85.2	7.3	0.4	3.8	3.3	21.4	20.4	44.6	42.9	24.1	4,081	95.9
Goochland CDP	861	-	-	898	92.8	7.2	0.0	0.0	0.0	29.6	7.9	43.3	27.1	44.8	290	96.9
Gordonsville town	1,481	1,624	9.7	1,758	56.5	34.5	0.0	2.0	6.9	21.6	16.6	42.1	58.2	13.0	734	86.5

1 May be of any race.

Table A. All Places — **Population and Housing**

STATE City, town, township, borough, or CDP (county if applicable)	Population				Race and Hispanic or Latino origin (percent)					Age (percent)			Educational attainment of persons age 25 and older		Occupied housing units	
	2010 census total population	2019 estimated population	Percent change 2010–2019	ACS total population estimate 2015–2019	White alone, not Hispanic or Latino	Black alone, not Hispanic or Latino	Asian alone, not Hispanic or Latino	All other races or 2 or more races, not Hispanic or Latino	Hispanic or Latino[1]	Under 18 years old	Age 65 years and older	Median age	Percent High school diploma or less	Percent Bachelor's degree or more	Total	Percent with a computer
	1	2	3	4	5	6	7	8	9	10	11	12	13	14	15	16
VIRGINIA—Con.																
Goshen town	370	368	-0.5	332	92.8	0.6	0.0	6.6	0.0	22.9	20.5	46.2	78.6	2.1	144	66.7
Gratton CDP	937	-	-	1,101	91.6	0.0	0.0	0.9	7.4	18.3	21.1	43.0	62.6	11.1	399	90.7
Great Falls CDP	15,427	-	-	14,872	71.8	1.1	17.8	4.8	4.5	22.8	21.6	49.4	8.1	80.7	4,928	99.8
Greenbackville CDP	192	-	-	29	100.0	0.0	0.0	0.0	0.0	0.0	0.0	0.0	0.0	0.0	15	100.0
Greenbriar CDP	8,166	-	-	8,686	47.0	4.2	30.0	6.6	12.3	27.1	13.6	38.4	19.9	56.5	3,060	99.5
Greenbush CDP	220	-	-	182	62.1	9.3	0.0	0.0	28.6	25.8	8.8	49.6	49.2	45.2	63	100.0
Greenville CDP	832	-	-	1,423	89.2	9.3	0.0	0.4	1.1	24.7	5.5	34.3	66.0	5.3	373	100.0
Gretna town	1,273	1,190	-6.5	1,302	57.8	34.6	0.2	6.5	1.0	17.6	33.9	55.0	55.1	14.4	633	74.1
Grottoes town	2,673	2,860	7.0	2,789	88.9	2.0	0.0	1.2	7.9	22.1	15.1	40.9	52.4	16.2	1,203	85.7
Groveton CDP	14,598	-	-	16,516	36.5	15.5	8.7	6.4	32.8	24.4	11.2	35.8	32.1	44.1	5,716	89.4
Grundy town	1,014	899	-11.3	902	72.3	22.8	0.0	3.5	1.3	28.2	23.6	35.1	50.8	32.1	327	85.6
Gwynn CDP	602	-	-	353	100.0	0.0	0.0	0.0	0.0	0.0	49.3	64.0	23.2	38.5	210	94.8
Halifax town	1,304	1,210	-7.2	1,299	59.9	35.0	0.0	0.5	4.6	15.4	23.6	50.7	50.6	28.4	538	75.7
Hallwood town	206	200	-2.9	226	74.3	8.4	0.0	3.1	14.2	27.0	14.2	42.0	65.8	4.0	88	77.3
Hamilton town	509	629	23.6	567	88.9	1.4	1.4	3.0	5.3	22.0	20.3	43.4	29.3	42.8	226	92.5
Hampden-Sydney CDP	1,450	-	-	1,729	82.0	9.8	2.0	4.0	2.2	1.2	4.9	20.2	13.4	80.6	133	86.5
Hampton city	137,464	134,510	-2.1	135,041	38.2	49.2	2.4	4.5	5.8	21.1	15.0	36.2	37.6	26.9	54,050	91.4
Hanover CDP	252	-	-	223	74.0	26.0	0.0	0.0	0.0	16.6	35.0	55.8	39.8	44.6	122	95.1
Harborton CDP	131	-	-	221	100.0	0.0	0.0	0.0	0.0	45.7	5.0	29.8	10.0	8.3	57	100.0
Harrisonburg city	48,900	53,016	8.4	53,273	66.1	6.5	3.8	3.8	19.7	16.3	9.0	25.4	41.7	36.3	16,723	90.2
Harriston CDP	909	-	-	1,193	93.9	1.8	0.0	3.8	0.5	13.0	14.9	35.8	67.3	6.6	575	78.4
Hayfield CDP	3,909	-	-	4,285	72.5	9.2	4.2	6.1	8.0	27.2	15.6	38.2	18.4	63.2	1,426	98.7
Haymarket town	1,477	1,676	13.5	1,552	63.3	17.7	7.8	3.0	8.2	32.4	6.3	33.7	18.5	50.4	464	99.4
Haysi town	497	465	-6.4	596	90.4	6.7	0.0	0.7	2.2	9.6	8.9	32.4	79.5	1.9	125	62.4
Heathsville CDP	142	-	-	109	69.7	8.3	0.0	22.0	0.0	0.0	23.9	45.9	58.7	36.7	56	100.0
Henry Fork CDP	1,234	-	-	1,294	48.2	28.3	0.0	2.6	20.9	23.0	25.4	33.9	59.6	8.7	505	74.9
Herndon town	23,292	24,601	5.6	24,532	33.7	6.9	18.4	4.1	36.9	24.8	9.9	35.6	34.9	49.0	7,748	97.2
Highland Springs CDP	15,711	-	-	16,459	22.4	72.6	0.0	2.6	2.4	24.9	12.6	37.6	49.2	16.1	6,155	84.5
Hillsboro town	139	169	21.6	149	100.0	0.0	0.0	0.0	0.0	18.1	10.7	49.7	8.0	64.6	47	100.0
Hillsville town	2,729	2,661	-2.5	2,658	96.0	0.2	0.0	0.0	3.9	13.0	27.2	46.8	48.1	20.7	1,217	73.3
Hiwassee CDP	264	-	-	310	100.0	0.0	0.0	0.0	0.0	13.9	35.5	59.1	41.4	13.7	138	86.2
Hollins CDP	14,673	-	-	14,329	82.4	8.6	2.1	2.6	4.4	18.3	24.7	45.4	37.4	27.2	6,004	91.3
Hollymead CDP	7,690	-	-	8,071	79.1	4.4	6.6	3.9	6.0	26.7	13.9	40.1	23.4	54.1	2,976	97.4
Honaker town	1,437	1,318	-8.3	1,232	98.5	1.5	0.0	0.0	0.0	17.9	20.5	47.3	56.9	11.2	552	66.1
Hopewell city	22,591	22,529	-0.3	22,456	46.5	42.2	1.4	2.0	7.9	25.7	15.5	36.2	55.4	14.8	9,224	84.0
Horntown CDP	574	-	-	524	66.2	33.8	0.0	0.0	0.0	30.7	42.7	46.5	68.6	31.4	166	86.1
Horse Pasture CDP	2,227	-	-	2,080	64.1	31.4	2.3	0.9	1.3	24.2	23.5	39.1	59.9	10.6	791	79.5
Hot Springs CDP	738	-	-	499	77.4	14.0	3.0	0.2	5.4	22.0	5.4	28.3	34.1	22.2	161	90.7
Huntington CDP	11,267	-	-	13,334	53.5	14.8	9.7	6.1	16.0	14.7	11.3	34.4	16.1	66.0	6,612	98.5
Hurt town	1,300	1,223	-5.9	1,451	73.6	23.2	0.1	2.2	1.0	16.3	23.1	47.3	50.1	17.0	737	84.4
Hybla Valley CDP	15,801	-	-	17,069	27.3	29.0	7.1	2.4	34.1	31.7	8.8	32.8	44.1	32.8	5,587	94.7
Idylwood CDP	17,288	-	-	18,273	49.4	5.0	22.6	4.5	18.4	21.1	10.7	35.2	20.8	64.1	6,688	96.4
Independence town	948	892	-5.9	1,040	87.1	10.4	0.0	0.0	2.5	17.3	33.8	50.6	54.5	14.3	502	72.9
Independent Hill CDP	7,419	-	-	9,204	60.2	18.6	6.6	3.8	10.8	29.0	7.0	38.0	18.1	57.5	2,712	99.2
Innsbrook CDP	7,753	-	-	8,888	50.7	9.5	31.5	3.5	4.8	23.9	9.2	36.1	15.1	61.6	3,278	97.1
Iron Gate town	392	357	-8.9	261	90.8	5.0	0.0	4.2	0.0	17.6	26.4	48.8	59.7	17.9	112	75.9
Irvington town	432	398	-7.9	340	94.4	2.4	0.6	0.9	1.8	6.2	49.7	64.8	28.4	47.3	170	88.8
Ivanhoe CDP	551	-	-	459	95.6	0.0	0.0	0.0	4.4	28.5	9.4	40.0	73.4	14.3	152	53.9
Ivor town	339	316	-6.8	467	81.6	8.6	0.0	9.9	0.0	27.4	16.1	40.5	44.6	12.4	179	83.8
Ivy CDP	905	-	-	459	91.9	0.0	0.0	8.1	0.0	35.5	21.1	42.1	18.9	66.6	160	90.0
Jarratt town	638	572	-10.3	773	42.9	52.3	0.8	0.3	3.8	25.9	16.2	31.4	43.3	26.3	380	85.8
Jolivue CDP	1,129	-	-	926	91.9	3.9	0.0	2.6	1.6	19.8	17.5	51.1	56.1	12.4	472	86.2
Jonesville town	1,012	928	-8.3	1,100	95.9	0.9	0.0	0.9	2.3	20.5	20.0	41.9	49.4	18.4	561	76.1
Keller town	178	169	-5.1	151	69.5	25.2	0.0	5.3	0.0	14.6	19.2	53.9	61.5	5.7	67	85.1
Kenbridge town	1,264	1,197	-5.3	984	44.7	52.0	0.1	2.1	1.0	19.3	24.2	46.8	51.5	27.1	442	57.2
Keokee CDP	416	-	-	398	100.0	0.0	0.0	0.0	0.0	20.6	15.1	52.5	79.1	1.9	130	76.2
Keysville town	832	781	-6.1	965	55.6	37.2	0.0	7.2	0.0	28.5	21.6	35.4	63.2	11.6	402	64.2
Kilmarnock town	1,488	1,394	-6.3	1,526	51.3	45.2	1.7	1.4	0.3	18.9	32.0	50.2	50.3	24.3	720	70.7
King and Queen Court House CDP	85	-	-	105	100.0	0.0	0.0	0.0	0.0	9.5	24.8	58.2	17.9	50.5	49	63.3
King George CDP	4,457	-	-	4,902	73.5	18.5	1.5	2.7	3.8	26.6	11.6	35.5	30.5	34.5	1,616	94.1
Kings Park CDP	4,333	-	-	5,109	48.6	5.8	22.6	6.0	17.0	26.2	14.9	36.5	20.9	61.3	1,492	99.0
Kings Park West CDP	13,390	-	-	14,227	63.3	5.3	16.8	3.0	11.5	22.4	13.5	37.4	13.0	67.6	4,305	98.9
Kingstowne CDP	15,556	-	-	17,517	50.7	18.5	16.2	3.1	11.5	21.6	11.3	38.1	20.3	57.9	6,861	96.7
King William CDP	252	-	-	364	75.0	25.0	0.0	0.0	0.0	33.8	4.9	22.5	30.9	24.0	96	92.7
La Crosse town	601	575	-4.3	535	59.6	30.3	0.0	0.0	10.1	10.8	25.4	57.9	50.0	11.3	195	66.7
Lafayette CDP	449	-	-	569	100.0	0.0	0.0	0.0	0.0	31.1	11.8	28.8	61.2	25.1	214	93.0
Lake Barcroft CDP	9,558	-	-	9,823	58.9	5.2	13.2	5.0	17.8	21.7	17.5	42.5	19.2	64.6	3,656	96.6
Lake Caroline CDP	2,260	-	-	1,523	72.3	26.0	0.0	0.0	1.7	18.8	25.3	44.3	46.1	30.5	757	87.3
Lake Holiday CDP	1,905	-	-	2,084	93.5	1.1	0.0	4.6	0.9	27.5	20.8	45.4	16.3	46.5	785	100.0
Lake Land'Or CDP	4,223	-	-	4,028	73.9	19.4	0.8	2.8	3.1	24.9	12.1	40.4	32.5	25.3	1,425	98.5
Lake Monticello CDP	9,920	-	-	10,862	81.1	10.3	1.0	4.4	3.3	22.4	22.4	43.5	16.0	45.5	4,242	95.6
Lake of the Woods CDP	7,177	-	-	8,406	83.7	5.6	3.5	3.8	3.3	21.0	29.0	48.3	25.2	39.0	3,447	92.7
Lake Ridge CDP	41,058	-	-	44,716	46.8	21.5	7.6	6.0	18.2	26.5	10.8	36.1	23.8	45.6	15,088	98.3
Lakeside CDP	11,849	-	-	12,374	64.0	15.8	3.8	5.1	11.3	19.4	14.3	38.6	37.3	35.3	5,203	92.6
Lake Wilderness CDP	2,669	-	-	2,871	77.3	8.2	1.6	3.3	9.6	30.0	6.6	32.1	33.7	28.1	827	97.6
Lancaster CDP	-	-	-	57	71.9	28.1	0.0	0.0	0.0	0.0	52.6	65.1	41.2	58.8	30	100.0
Lansdowne CDP	11,253	-	-	12,354	61.9	8.0	18.7	2.8	8.6	24.9	17.0	40.7	12.4	66.5	4,523	98.0
Laurel CDP	16,713	-	-	17,535	48.3	29.5	7.2	3.9	11.2	21.5	10.6	34.3	37.8	31.1	6,825	94.1
Laurel Hill CDP	6,855	-	-	8,020	43.1	16.8	30.4	3.6	6.1	25.0	9.3	38.9	19.1	58.7	2,665	100.0
Laurel Park CDP	675	-	-	841	8.9	80.4	0.0	4.9	5.8	15.5	43.6	55.4	50.4	13.5	334	68.9
Lawrenceville town	1,444	1,020	-29.4	1,557	23.5	63.0	1.3	7.3	4.9	23.6	10.9	22.7	54.4	17.0	472	83.1
Laymantown CDP	1,979	-	-	2,148	98.9	0.0	0.0	1.1	0.0	16.4	28.6	48.1	40.3	26.8	806	88.3
Lebanon town	3,422	3,147	-8.0	3,206	95.0	1.6	0.0	0.1	3.3	14.6	23.3	40.9	50.8	13.9	1,359	81.2
Lee Mont CDP	125	-	-	69	100.0	0.0	0.0	0.0	0.0	24.6	14.5	47.7	40.4	0.0	31	100.0
Leesburg town	42,643	53,727	26.0	52,994	61.8	8.0	7.8	4.6	17.7	26.7	8.5	35.2	24.7	54.2	17,900	96.6
Lexington city	7,037	7,446	5.8	7,241	79.1	8.7	3.5	2.6	6.1	9.0	15.6	22.3	30.4	46.7	2,158	83.7
Lincolnia CDP	22,855	-	-	23,933	30.7	21.5	17.6	3.5	26.7	20.5	11.5	36.9	34.3	45.7	8,303	98.1
Linton Hall CDP	35,725	-	-	41,386	61.1	12.0	9.9	5.5	11.5	33.5	5.9	33.6	20.2	55.8	11,508	99.2
Loch Lomond CDP	3,701	-	-	4,038	28.8	1.4	4.4	3.9	61.5	23.7	11.8	34.1	65.2	12.1	1,008	88.4
Long Branch CDP	7,593	-	-	8,381	60.7	3.7	18.1	2.6	14.9	24.1	19.2	43.9	19.3	65.8	2,801	95.9
Lorton CDP	18,610	-	-	20,871	29.0	30.2	16.8	4.0	20.0	27.3	9.9	35.5	29.3	44.6	6,576	96.8

1 May be of any race.

Table A. All Places — **Population and Housing**

STATE City, town, township, borough, or CDP (county if applicable)	Population: 2010 census total population	Population: 2019 estimated population	Population: Percent change 2010–2019	Population: ACS total population estimate 2015–2019	Race and Hispanic or Latino origin (percent): White alone, not Hispanic or Latino	Black alone, not Hispanic or Latino	Asian alone, not Hispanic or Latino	All other races or 2 or more races, not Hispanic or Latino	Hispanic or Latino[1]	Age (percent): Under 18 years old	Age 65 years and older	Median age	Educational attainment of persons age 25 and older: Percent High school diploma or less	Percent Bachelor's degree or more	Occupied housing units: Total	Percent with a computer
	1	2	3	4	5	6	7	8	9	10	11	12	13	14	15	16
VIRGINIA—Con.																
Loudoun Valley Estates CDP	3,656	-	-	8,020	26.6	5.9	57.3	6.9	3.3	34.1	3.0	34.3	7.3	79.2	2,378	99.4
Louisa town	1,555	1,733	11.4	1,744	60.5	23.3	1.1	5.7	9.3	21.8	23.1	38.2	55.4	21.6	768	70.4
Lovettsville town	1,620	2,198	35.7	2,551	76.8	4.4	1.6	1.8	15.5	38.2	6.2	32.2	21.1	49.7	736	97.3
Lovingston CDP	520	-	-	494	32.0	68.0	0.0	0.0	0.0	18.2	14.6	29.8	68.3	3.3	210	85.7
Lowes Island CDP	10,756	-	-	10,860	67.0	3.3	15.4	6.3	8.0	27.0	9.1	40.7	11.3	73.3	3,480	98.4
Low Moor CDP	258	-	-	207	84.5	15.5	0.0	0.0	0.0	2.9	32.9	60.3	87.6	0.0	128	43.8
Lunenburg CDP	165	-	-	203	100.0	0.0	0.0	0.0	0.0	0.0	46.8	63.8	24.9	3.5	85	83.5
Luray town	4,897	4,848		4,832	92.4	3.2	0.5	3.1	0.8	18.2	25.9	47.2	56.9	20.5	1,892	77.9
Lynchburg city	75,534	82,168	8.8	80,569	62.3	28.4	2.4	2.7	4.2	19.2	14.1	28.3	36.5	35.6	28,273	88.6
Lyndhurst CDP	1,490	-	-	1,820	80.8	2.7	2.9	0.9	12.7	25.4	20.3	41.1	42.1	25.7	636	88.5
McKenney town	483	489	1.2	469	69.9	26.0	2.3	1.1	0.6	20.0	20.7	47.4	61.7	13.0	182	72.5
McLean CDP	48,115	-	-	47,682	71.1	2.1	19.5	3.2	4.0	26.7	20.7	45.9	6.5	83.5	16,409	97.6
McMullin CDP	464	-	-	438	100.0	0.0	0.0	0.0	0.0	4.8	24.2	52.1	37.0	18.8	191	86.9
McNair CDP	17,513	-	-	21,485	28.5	17.1	40.4	3.8	10.1	26.4	3.5	32.4	17.2	68.2	8,025	98.7
Madison town	244	241	-1.2	247	91.9	4.5	0.0	3.6	0.0	19.4	21.5	41.8	57.1	10.0	84	71.4
Madison Heights CDP	11,285	-	-	11,665	68.2	24.2	0.4	6.3	0.8	20.7	20.0	43.9	52.0	16.3	4,678	81.5
Makemie Park CDP	155	-	-	316	0.0	100.0	0.0	0.0	0.0	39.2	6.6	20.4	96.8	0.0	109	100.0
Manassas city	37,799	41,085	8.7	41,174	40.8	13.2	5.1	4.2	36.6	26.9	9.7	34.2	43.1	29.6	12,898	92.4
Manassas Park city	14,243	17,478	22.7	16,986	33.1	12.8	11.1	3.3	39.7	25.6	8.5	34.7	43.7	27.9	4,641	96.8
Manchester CDP	10,804	-	-	10,919	44.0	31.8	1.9	6.2	16.1	21.3	14.4	35.9	36.6	33.5	4,444	92.3
Mantua CDP	7,135	-	-	7,342	67.4	2.5	21.5	4.2	4.5	27.4	19.7	44.3	10.6	77.3	2,554	93.5
Mappsburg CDP	60	-	-	65	75.4	0.0	0.0	0.0	24.6	12.3	21.5	35.6	12.3	59.6	33	78.8
Mappsville CDP	440	-	-	487	0.0	66.5	0.0	0.0	33.5	8.2	7.8	44.2	58.0	0.0	190	100.0
Marion town	5,978	5,559	-7.0	5,706	87.9	8.3	0.9	1.3	1.6	19.2	21.8	46.1	56.1	16.1	2,373	75.7
Marshall CDP	1,480	-	-	2,063	68.2	11.5	0.0	3.9	16.4	23.9	8.0	27.9	48.0	22.3	601	90.2
Martinsville city	13,814	12,554	-9.1	12,852	44.0	44.5	1.0	4.9	5.7	24.1	18.7	40.9	45.7	21.0	5,532	83.8
Marumsco CDP	35,036	-	-	37,770	22.6	22.6	6.0	4.5	44.2	25.6	8.3	33.8	50.6	25.9	11,606	95.5
Mason Neck CDP	2,005	-	-	1,986	82.3	4.7	2.8	2.1	8.1	22.9	19.4	47.6	17.6	54.9	755	96.2
Massanetta Springs CDP	4,833	-	-	5,884	88.6	5.7	3.8	0.5	1.4	21.5	27.3	44.0	15.4	56.3	2,286	98.0
Massanutten CDP	2,291	-	-	2,602	90.2	2.5	0.7	3.6	3.0	24.2	15.3	41.2	16.2	53.2	1,006	98.2
Mathews CDP	555	-	-	569	67.0	33.0	0.0	0.0	0.0	6.7	50.1	66.0	61.0	22.6	287	57.1
Matoaca CDP	2,403	-	-	2,490	55.6	42.6	0.0	0.9	1.0	24.0	16.7	41.1	52.6	19.9	1,008	84.5
Maurertown CDP	770	-	-	955	99.4	0.5	0.0	0.0	0.1	12.7	28.3	52.4	50.4	10.8	373	79.1
Max Meadows CDP	562	-	-	440	100.0	0.0	0.0	0.0	0.0	8.6	24.1	48.7	68.3	16.2	157	100.0
Meadowbrook CDP	18,312	-	-	19,811	30.6	44.1	4.3	2.7	18.3	21.2	15.2	39.2	48.5	22.0	6,959	91.7
Meadow View CDP	967	-	-	1,058	97.4	1.3	0.5	0.1	0.8	13.0	21.3	50.0	52.0	15.1	430	73.0
Mechanicsville CDP	36,348	-	-	37,496	83.0	9.2	1.9	3.8	2.0	22.3	18.8	43.1	33.0	36.4	14,679	93.4
Melfa town	401	387	-3.5	320	77.2	19.7	0.0	0.6	2.5	7.5	28.8	55.1	54.3	13.4	177	78.0
Merrifield CDP	15,212	-	-	18,291	43.3	7.2	31.2	5.3	13.0	16.1	7.3	33.2	12.4	75.9	7,894	99.2
Merrimac CDP	2,133	-	-	2,651	70.0	16.7	3.0	4.1	6.3	19.2	29.0	43.1	41.2	30.0	1,274	81.9
Metompkin CDP	551	-	-	504	0.0	100.0	0.0	0.0	0.0	34.9	27.2	42.4	90.8	3.4	212	46.2
Middlebrook CDP	213	-	-	115	100.0	0.0	0.0	0.0	0.0	59.1	0.0	8.5	100.0	0.0	23	100.0
Middleburg town	671	834	24.3	539	64.9	22.8	2.0	2.8	7.4	18.4	34.7	54.8	30.9	49.5	298	82.2
Middletown town	1,267	1,396	10.2	1,363	85.1	4.5	1.6	2.1	6.7	20.9	14.7	34.7	50.7	23.2	541	91.9
Midland CDP	218	-	-	97	33.0	0.0	0.0	0.0	67.0	16.5	22.7	52.8	79.0	21.0	47	100.0
Mineral town	467	523	12.0	509	93.7	1.2	0.0	5.1	0.0	23.0	12.8	39.0	73.6	8.3	180	92.8
Modest Town CDP	149	-	-	134	100.0	0.0	0.0	0.0	0.0	6.0	56.7	75.2	73.8	15.1	51	100.0
Montclair CDP	19,570	-	-	20,881	56.5	21.6	6.6	4.4	11.0	25.2	14.1	39.7	16.3	57.3	7,031	99.1
Monterey town	145	136	-6.2	112	100.0	0.0	0.0	0.0	0.0	5.4	74.1	72.9	38.7	42.5	75	68.0
Montrose CDP	7,993	-	-	7,541	21.5	71.4	0.6	3.1	3.4	24.7	14.3	35.7	50.4	10.6	3,288	82.1
Montross town	384	390	1.6	431	75.4	18.3	0.5	5.8	0.0	23.9	28.8	42.6	26.6	31.6	216	67.1
Montvale CDP	698	-	-	608	91.1	8.9	0.0	0.0	0.0	15.5	38.2	58.3	59.7	7.2	253	75.5
Moorefield Station CDP	77	-	-	1,976	47.5	8.4	25.2	4.4	14.5	27.3	2.5	32.6	13.6	68.9	817	96.9
Motley CDP	1,015	-	-	700	69.4	28.7	0.0	1.9	0.0	16.9	21.4	52.6	52.6	10.7	332	65.7
Mountain Road CDP	1,100	-	-	783	44.1	53.6	0.0	2.3	0.0	16.7	35.1	52.7	75.2	9.0	354	45.8
Mount Crawford town	433	458	5.8	393	95.7	0.0	1.0	0.8	2.5	16.3	11.5	38.1	46.5	27.2	169	91.7
Mount Hermon CDP	3,966	-	-	3,951	79.1	15.4	2.0	3.6	0.0	19.8	15.5	45.1	34.0	27.3	1,603	94.5
Mount Jackson town	2,042	2,118	3.7	2,129	60.0	1.3	1.6	6.7	30.3	25.5	13.2	38.5	59.8	17.7	828	80.1
Mount Sidney CDP	663	-	-	442	83.3	0.0	0.0	8.4	8.4	22.6	5.7	34.3	36.7	54.0	152	100.0
Mount Vernon CDP	12,416	-	-	13,113	59.5	12.7	6.7	5.4	15.7	24.0	16.7	42.5	18.8	61.3	4,443	96.6
Narrows town	2,039	1,952	-4.3	1,993	95.2	0.7	0.6	2.0	1.6	22.1	17.8	39.6	54.9	15.6	886	84.7
Nassawadox town	501	478	-4.6	486	47.9	45.3	0.6	5.1	1.0	11.9	41.8	58.1	61.2	19.8	165	82.4
Nathalie CDP	183	-	-	201	0.0	100.0	0.0	0.0	0.0	0.0	48.8	32.0	91.5	0.0	81	14.8
Neabsco CDP	12,068	-	-	20,364	24.7	43.4	11.8	5.0	15.1	26.2	5.2	35.1	21.1	48.6	6,752	99.4
Nellysford CDP	1,076	-	-	1,305	94.1	3.8	0.0	0.0	2.1	4.1	57.9	66.8	14.6	61.8	682	98.2
Nelsonia CDP	523	-	-	454	18.3	66.1	0.0	0.0	15.6	19.2	3.1	34.4	57.8	15.5	189	100.0
New Baltimore CDP	8,119	-	-	10,440	81.5	6.0	2.4	2.3	7.8	29.1	12.6	40.4	23.5	46.9	3,250	98.6
New Castle town	153	153	0.0	196	100.0	0.0	0.0	0.0	0.0	21.4	14.8	33.7	45.7	37.0	95	88.4
New Church CDP	205	-	-	93	64.5	16.1	19.4	0.0	0.0	0.0	15.1	57.8	56.4	23.1	44	68.2
New Hope CDP	797	-	-	648	94.3	0.0	0.0	2.0	3.7	20.7	24.5	51.6	51.4	26.2	328	68.3
Newington CDP	12,943	-	-	13,196	49.3	18.5	12.4	6.8	12.9	26.0	11.7	36.8	17.4	56.7	4,218	99.7
Newington Forest CDP	12,442	-	-	12,373	53.9	11.1	15.3	5.2	14.5	26.4	11.2	37.5	16.0	60.4	4,156	98.2
New Kent CDP	239	-	-	485	83.7	16.3	0.0	0.0	0.0	32.0	7.4	31.8	24.4	16.8	145	94.5
New Market town	2,181	2,253	3.3	2,180	80.1	3.6	0.0	2.2	14.1	12.2	26.0	46.0	54.1	26.8	956	76.9
Newport News city	180,955	179,225		179,673	42.9	40.0	3.2	5.0	9.0	23.2	12.7	33.5	37.5	26.3	69,835	91.2
New River CDP	244	-	-	704	58.8	36.4	0.0	4.8	0.0	3.4	21.7	51.9	38.2	48.5	298	100.0
Newsoms town	321	297	-7.5	345	54.2	41.4	0.0	4.3	0.0	17.1	14.2	47.4	42.5	16.8	145	77.9
Nickelsville town	390	360	-7.7	366	100.0	0.0	0.0	0.0	0.0	22.4	26.8	43.0	58.0	21.0	163	71.8
Nokesville CDP	1,354	-	-	1,330	92.8	0.9	0.0	2.9	3.4	18.7	15.1	43.6	42.1	33.0	428	94.4
Norfolk city	242,827	242,742	0.0	244,601	43.4	40.5	3.5	4.5	8.0	19.7	10.9	30.7	37.6	28.8	88,353	91.0
North Shore CDP	3,094	-	-	3,249	99.4	0.0	0.0	0.2	0.5	19.2	38.7	59.7	29.9	44.9	1,404	95.9
North Springfield CDP	7,274	-	-	7,303	45.7	3.8	23.7	2.5	24.3	21.9	15.7	37.9	33.8	45.4	2,139	94.6
Norton city	3,993	3,981	-0.3	3,970	88.6	3.1	4.6	2.5	1.2	23.7	16.4	37.5	40.0	22.8	1,628	84.3
Nottoway Court House CDP	84	-	-	100	15.0	85.0	0.0	0.0	0.0	0.0	50.0	64.0	66.0	27.0	43	46.5
Oak Grove CDP	1,777	-	-	2,801	23.3	2.7	47.4	0.0	26.6	25.0	4.1	32.2	25.6	50.9	794	100.0
Oak Hall CDP	255	-	-	100	0.0	100.0	0.0	0.0	0.0	0.0	45.0	0.0	100.0	0.0	100	100.0
Oak Level CDP	857	-	-	651	89.6	10.4	0.0	0.0	0.0	19.7	32.6	51.6	46.4	18.6	336	58.6
Oakton CDP	34,166	-	-	36,997	53.6	5.4	22.2	5.6	13.2	23.2	13.2	38.3	13.9	71.4	13,556	97.8
Occoquan town	929	1,086	16.9	1,174	54.2	12.7	17.2	6.6	9.4	14.1	10.0	38.4	20.5	51.4	530	99.1
Onancock town	1,261	1,211	-4.0	1,098	66.2	22.3	2.5	1.4	7.7	15.1	30.0	57.3	35.6	34.9	547	87.9

1 May be of any race.

Table A. All Places — **Population and Housing**

STATE City, town, township, borough, or CDP (county if applicable)	Population: 2010 census total population	Population: 2019 estimated population	Population: Percent change 2010–2019	Population: ACS total population estimate 2015–2019	Race and Hispanic or Latino origin (percent): White alone, not Hispanic or Latino	Black alone, not Hispanic or Latino	Asian alone, not Hispanic or Latino	All other races or 2 or more races, not Hispanic or Latino	Hispanic or Latino[1]	Age (percent): Under 18 years old	Age 65 years and older	Median age	Educational attainment of persons age 25 and older: Percent High school diploma or less	Percent Bachelor's degree or more	Occupied housing units: Total	Percent with a computer
	1	2	3	4	5	6	7	8	9	10	11	12	13	14	15	16
VIRGINIA—Con.																
Onley town	517	500	-3.3	728	54.3	11.5	2.6	14.1	17.4	29.3	19.9	40.0	49.8	31.7	296	90.2
Opal CDP	691	-	-	690	66.2	6.1	5.4	15.9	6.4	27.0	7.1	37.7	32.0	30.9	258	86.4
Orange town	4,714	5,096	8.1	4,975	65.3	21.2	0.0	7.2	6.4	28.7	14.2	34.9	51.9	21.1	1,658	92.8
Painter town	233	224	-3.9	245	56.3	19.2	0.0	0.0	24.5	33.9	9.8	32.5	46.1	20.4	86	84.9
Palmyra CDP	104	-	-	103	100.0	0.0	0.0	0.0	0.0	0.0	14.6	55.5	34.9	41.3	41	100.0
Pamplin City town	221	228	3.2	73	42.5	38.4	0.0	0.0	19.2	31.5	11.0	37.1	54.0	16.0	29	79.3
Pantops CDP	-	-	-	3,388	73.3	15.6	5.9	4.6	0.6	12.5	33.5	41.8	21.3	61.0	1,911	87.7
Parksley town	844	808	-4.3	791	56.8	36.9	0.5	3.0	2.8	23.5	14.0	40.5	60.6	12.4	311	67.8
Parrott CDP	435	-	-	256	86.3	0.0	0.0	13.7	0.0	28.1	11.7	31.8	69.3	30.7	139	41.0
Passapatanzy CDP	1,283	-	-	1,532	73.8	6.6	6.3	13.3	0.0	36.4	4.8	35.8	34.8	27.7	550	92.9
Pastoria CDP	649	-	-	996	19.2	40.5	0.0	0.0	40.4	43.9	13.6	19.6	78.0	2.8	324	67.3
Patrick Springs CDP	1,845	-	-	1,932	86.6	9.5	0.2	0.0	3.6	13.7	32.2	53.1	48.6	13.8	885	87.6
Pearisburg town	2,787	2,636	-5.4	2,652	88.3	8.7	0.0	0.0	3.0	25.9	18.4	40.0	39.2	23.7	978	89.6
Pembroke town	1,112	1,081	-2.8	1,026	93.4	5.1	0.0	1.3	0.3	15.9	24.3	42.5	59.0	17.0	480	77.9
Penhook CDP	801	-	-	1,053	83.9	0.0	0.5	0.9	14.7	13.2	34.4	57.3	31.8	43.0	451	91.4
Pennington Gap town	1,875	1,721	-8.2	2,179	89.1	7.6	0.0	3.0	0.3	18.9	23.9	46.3	67.8	9.5	872	66.7
Petersburg city	32,441	31,346	-3.4	31,362	15.1	76.3	0.9	2.8	4.9	21.4	16.7	38.1	52.9	19.8	13,165	81.1
Phenix town	228	213	-6.6	284	75.4	24.6	0.0	0.0	0.0	29.9	21.8	36.4	49.0	23.4	121	61.2
Pimmit Hills CDP	6,094	-	-	6,223	49.8	1.0	23.8	3.0	22.3	23.0	11.6	38.3	22.5	60.6	2,051	98.3
Piney Mountain CDP	1,130	-	-	1,356	71.6	14.4	0.0	2.2	11.8	28.4	11.8	36.9	30.7	26.8	555	98.0
Plum Creek CDP	1,524	-	-	1,521	94.1	1.2	0.0	1.6	3.0	22.0	17.5	42.0	70.2	4.9	732	86.3
Pocahontas town	402	353	-12.2	293	89.8	6.5	2.0	1.7	0.0	13.0	28.7	52.6	46.1	8.6	162	67.9
Poquoson city	12,159	12,271	0.9	12,090	91.4	1.1	2.5	2.2	2.8	22.1	19.6	42.4	31.0	42.2	4,593	91.2
Port Royal town	200	206	3.0	217	65.0	30.9	0.0	4.1	0.0	23.0	8.8	45.1	46.5	21.9	93	83.9
Portsmouth city	95,526	94,398	-1.2	95,097	37.7	52.2	1.4	4.3	4.5	23.4	14.5	35.3	41.8	21.9	36,370	88.6
Potomac Mills CDP	5,614	-	-	6,664	34.7	23.3	8.9	4.3	28.9	25.3	9.1	36.8	41.4	35.3	1,843	99.4
Pound town	1,021	918	-10.1	878	99.7	0.3	0.0	0.0	0.0	26.9	18.8	38.6	57.6	11.8	346	78.3
Powhatan CDP	-	-	-	348	87.1	9.5	0.0	3.4	0.0	8.3	31.6	55.5	33.9	15.8	200	100.0
Prices Fork CDP	1,066	-	-	917	90.4	0.0	0.0	0.0	9.6	24.9	8.9	38.0	35.0	34.7	417	79.9
Prince George CDP	2,066	-	-	1,878	56.1	27.4	0.0	0.0	16.5	18.5	21.6	42.6	54.9	12.7	673	95.2
Pulaski town	9,102	8,714	-4.3	8,799	85.0	6.6	0.5	5.0	2.9	19.5	19.0	42.3	48.1	14.5	3,702	86.4
Pungoteague CDP	347	-	-	230	44.3	50.4	0.0	5.2	0.0	0.0	21.3	55.7	56.5	4.1	77	62.3
Purcellville town	7,727	10,178	31.7	9,897	73.2	5.6	4.7	4.3	12.2	30.4	9.8	35.2	22.2	52.8	2,986	93.9
Quantico town	481	553	15.0	542	38.9	28.6	9.6	9.0	13.8	17.3	12.2	32.5	42.3	28.5	273	88.6
Quantico Base CDP	4,452	-	-	5,109	55.6	17.2	4.1	7.2	15.9	27.6	0.0	22.8	18.9	48.5	1,021	100.0
Quinby CDP	282	-	-	332	100.0	0.0	0.0	0.0	0.0	26.5	25.9	46.7	47.7	26.8	124	91.9
Radford city	16,395	18,249	11.3	17,691	83.3	9.8	1.6	2.5	2.9	10.6	8.7	23.4	32.6	38.0	5,573	88.6
Raven CDP	2,270	-	-	2,046	97.0	0.0	0.5	2.5	0.0	21.0	26.9	45.4	73.3	5.7	825	63.2
Ravensworth CDP	2,466	-	-	2,188	63.7	1.9	18.7	1.1	14.6	22.8	18.3	42.3	29.0	53.5	771	100.0
Remington town	598	658	10.0	764	69.0	18.1	1.0	6.5	5.4	29.5	12.0	32.7	41.3	32.9	276	79.7
Reston CDP	58,404	-	-	61,147	63.1	9.9	10.4	3.9	12.6	19.9	15.4	39.8	15.0	68.8	25,770	97.4
Rich Creek town	768	741	-3.5	887	96.1	2.5	1.1	0.3	0.0	21.3	26.5	43.9	54.2	16.4	332	83.7
Richlands town	5,834	5,234	-10.3	5,368	96.1	1.8	0.0	1.9	0.1	21.2	20.2	43.1	60.0	14.7	2,306	74.8
Richmond city	204,375	230,436	12.8	226,622	40.8	46.6	2.1	3.6	6.9	17.6	12.8	34.0	36.4	39.6	90,301	88.1
Ridgeway town	738	693	-6.1	922	77.2	10.4	0.0	0.3	12.0	29.4	17.4	34.9	44.5	14.0	360	82.5
Riner CDP	859	-	-	1,056	100.0	0.0	0.0	0.0	0.0	26.1	11.4	44.0	24.5	45.7	370	100.0
Rivanna CDP	1,860	-	-	1,851	84.5	3.5	5.7	5.6	0.6	16.7	38.7	57.3	12.4	72.1	832	93.8
Riverdale CDP	956	-	-	758	70.8	29.2	0.0	0.0	0.0	14.6	25.7	48.9	55.0	13.4	301	80.4
Riverview CDP	782	-	-	711	97.9	0.0	0.0	2.1	0.0	22.8	10.3	35.6	87.0	1.6	239	78.2
Roanoke city	96,910	99,143	2.3	99,229	58.5	28.1	2.9	4.2	6.3	21.9	16.1	38.5	47.9	23.4	41,740	85.8
Rockwood CDP	8,431	-	-	8,136	68.0	20.3	3.5	3.4	4.9	18.1	20.5	45.7	28.9	41.8	3,331	97.1
Rocky Mount town	4,777	4,724	-1.1	4,745	80.5	15.4	0.0	0.8	3.2	20.2	21.1	41.3	53.9	22.7	2,011	77.5
Rose Hill CDP	20,226	-	-	22,252	47.9	14.8	10.8	4.8	21.7	23.4	14.7	39.1	26.9	51.4	7,064	95.7
Rose Hill CDP	799	-	-	645	100.0	0.0	0.0	0.0	0.0	2.6	16.9	48.9	66.2	1.5	243	69.1
Round Hill town	533	656	23.1	674	89.6	1.2	0.7	1.9	6.5	17.5	15.1	38.5	23.2	49.1	252	92.9
Ruckersville CDP	1,141	-	-	1,335	96.6	0.0	0.7	2.7	0.0	25.2	18.7	48.1	40.1	31.0	578	93.6
Rural Retreat town	1,481	1,448	-2.2	1,702	98.4	0.2	0.0	0.8	0.6	20.7	25.7	44.4	48.9	18.5	721	84.7
Rushmere CDP	1,018	-	-	1,005	58.3	37.6	0.0	3.3	0.8	19.2	15.0	48.3	42.1	21.6	433	78.1
Rustburg CDP	1,431	-	-	1,419	71.4	26.6	0.0	0.2	1.8	17.3	22.7	38.9	60.9	10.7	558	83.3
St. Charles town	122	110	-9.8	77	100.0	0.0	0.0	0.0	0.0	35.1	9.1	38.7	74.0	0.0	36	66.7
St. Paul town	958	851	-11.2	1,008	93.1	0.0	0.0	0.8	6.2	17.9	25.0	48.8	40.0	23.7	454	77.5
Salem city	24,836	25,301	1.9	25,317	85.3	6.6	1.7	3.2	3.3	19.1	19.0	41.2	39.8	27.9	9,912	90.3
Saltville town	2,053	1,901	-7.4	2,411	93.3	0.0	0.0	0.0	6.7	25.3	13.9	41.5	57.1	8.5	926	75.9
Saluda CDP	769	-	-	639	69.8	22.2	0.5	1.4	6.1	10.2	10.0	38.1	56.1	4.7	113	100.0
Sandston CDP	7,571	-	-	7,188	48.8	43.0	1.0	3.1	4.2	22.4	15.9	39.2	60.2	11.6	3,048	85.8
Sandy Level CDP	484	-	-	491	36.9	60.3	0.0	0.0	2.9	7.5	28.1	46.0	73.0	0.0	221	60.2
Sanford CDP	212	-	-	97	83.5	0.0	0.0	0.0	16.5	16.5	46.4	64.5	50.6	0.0	55	100.0
Savage Town CDP	78	-	-	61	0.0	100.0	0.0	0.0	0.0	0.0	31.1	63.4	100.0	0.0	38	0.0
Savageville CDP	175	-	-	424	0.0	100.0	0.0	0.0	0.0	39.4	20.8	35.2	15.6	25.7	183	76.0
Saxis town	241	231	-4.1	238	92.9	0.0	0.0	5.0	2.1	9.7	31.5	56.0	50.3	13.7	111	74.8
Schuyler CDP	298	-	-	241	100.0	0.0	0.0	0.0	0.0	8.3	27.0	62.4	100.0	0.0	124	100.0
Scotland CDP	203	-	-	163	44.8	55.2	0.0	0.0	0.0	26.4	24.5	29.7	22.5	42.5	58	89.7
Scottsburg town	137	128	-6.6	187	93.0	7.0	0.0	0.0	0.0	32.1	6.4	28.9	35.0	10.0	78	41.0
Scottsville town	567	618	9.0	585	86.0	11.8	0.0	2.2	0.0	31.3	13.3	38.3	39.9	32.6	238	81.9
Sedley CDP	470	-	-	405	72.3	20.2	0.0	7.4	0.0	11.1	11.1	50.6	49.7	16.8	207	100.0
Selma CDP	529	-	-	630	88.1	2.5	0.0	9.4	0.0	28.6	26.3	47.8	54.4	13.8	230	77.4
Seven Corners CDP	9,255	-	-	8,731	34.3	5.2	19.7	2.6	38.2	23.2	12.8	36.1	44.7	44.4	3,438	89.2
Seven Mile Ford CDP	783	-	-	606	96.7	0.0	0.0	0.0	3.3	24.3	32.2	46.0	65.0	16.1	284	56.0
Shawneeland CDP	1,873	-	-	1,683	96.7	0.0	0.7	0.8	1.8	26.6	19.2	41.0	51.6	11.1	654	95.6
Shawsville CDP	1,310	-	-	1,548	94.3	5.7	0.0	0.0	0.0	19.5	16.8	46.3	58.8	10.1	541	95.7
Shenandoah town	2,371	2,331	-1.7	3,033	93.0	1.5	0.6	0.0	5.0	27.5	16.2	31.3	57.5	11.3	1,042	84.2
Shenandoah Farms CDP	3,033	-	-	3,642	94.2	0.5	0.9	1.8	2.7	27.6	8.9	34.4	50.9	21.7	1,295	97.3
Shenandoah Retreat CDP	518	-	-	626	96.5	0.0	0.0	1.8	1.8	12.5	7.2	45.8	57.6	10.8	284	100.0
Shenandoah Shores CDP	934	-	-	946	92.9	1.1	3.4	1.6	1.1	29.6	7.9	32.3	45.7	22.8	385	91.2
Sherando CDP	688	-	-	569	100.0	0.0	0.0	0.0	0.0	6.7	34.6	46.9	35.2	5.5	261	80.5
Shipman CDP	507	-	-	332	83.7	0.0	0.0	0.0	16.3	0.0	27.4	58.0	84.5	5.6	226	75.2
Short Pump CDP	24,729	-	-	28,328	61.9	7.1	24.0	2.6	4.4	26.9	9.6	37.4	11.3	72.2	10,885	97.8
Skyland Estates CDP	830	-	-	1,142	93.2	6.8	0.0	0.0	0.0	16.4	12.3	46.1	39.8	23.0	418	91.6
Smithfield town	8,093	8,475	4.7	8,367	61.7	28.8	0.3	3.9	5.4	23.1	18.0	40.2	37.3	30.0	3,321	90.4
Snowville CDP	149	-	-	76	69.7	0.0	0.0	0.0	30.3	13.2	28.9	58.2	88.9	11.1	37	67.6
Southampton Meadows CDP	-	-	-	302	39.4	45.0	0.0	15.6	0.0	15.6	30.1	50.3	69.4	0.0	95	74.7

1 May be of any race.

Table A. All Places — **Population and Housing**

STATE City, town, township, borough, or CDP (county if applicable)	Population				Race and Hispanic or Latino origin (percent)					Age (percent)			Educational attainment of persons age 25 and older		Occupied housing units	
	2010 census total population	2019 estimated population	Percent change 2010–2019	ACS total population estimate 2015–2019	White alone, not Hispanic or Latino	Black alone, not Hispanic or Latino	Asian alone, not Hispanic or Latino	All other races or 2 or more races, not Hispanic or Latino	Hispanic or Latino[1]	Under 18 years old	Age 65 years and older	Median age	Percent High school diploma or less	Percent Bachelor's degree or more	Total	Percent with a computer
	1	2	3	4	5	6	7	8	9	10	11	12	13	14	15	16
VIRGINIA—Con.																
South Boston town	8,143	7,588	-6.8	7,762	38.9	56.5	2.1	0.6	1.9	24.3	21.1	38.9	54.8	19.3	2,801	71.5
Southern Gateway CDP	2,805	-	-	3,517	32.0	32.9	4.0	6.0	25.0	20.9	5.0	28.6	35.4	26.0	1,298	98.9
South Hill town	4,603	4,349	-5.5	4,377	48.1	45.7	0.0	0.0	6.2	24.8	22.5	39.4	50.3	24.2	1,783	78.9
South Riding CDP	24,256	-	-	31,515	44.7	6.6	34.7	6.1	7.9	31.8	5.8	36.0	13.0	70.4	9,807	99.2
South Run CDP	6,389	-	-	6,243	74.7	3.2	14.7	1.5	5.9	21.7	19.1	47.8	8.7	82.2	2,151	98.9
Southside Chesconessex CDP	131	-	-	123	100.0	0.0	0.0	0.0	0.0	0.0	88.6	65.8	100.0	0.0	65	100.0
Sperryville CDP	342	-	-	228	100.0	0.0	0.0	0.0	0.0	7.9	12.3	44.4	44.6	32.8	111	79.3
Spotsylvania Courthouse CDP	4,239	-	-	4,607	70.7	15.8	1.1	5.4	6.9	24.4	13.4	33.8	42.1	26.1	1,505	86.1
Springfield CDP	30,484	-	-	32,222	40.6	11.1	22.1	3.2	23.0	20.9	18.6	39.5	35.1	42.3	10,250	92.6
Springville CDP	1,371	-	-	1,301	94.4	2.6	2.7	0.3	0.0	16.9	25.6	44.9	60.9	10.8	467	92.5
Stafford Courthouse CDP.	4,320	-	-	4,252	49.2	19.3	1.9	6.2	23.4	15.3	4.7	32.0	43.7	22.6	1,122	97.3
Stanardsville town	365	386	5.8	363	73.8	14.6	0.0	1.9	9.6	27.8	24.5	42.8	55.5	16.1	171	80.7
Stanley town	1,686	1,673	-0.8	1,865	95.0	0.3	0.0	0.3	4.3	20.3	16.2	41.5	71.7	7.7	705	73.5
Stanleytown CDP	1,422	-	-	1,379	97.2	2.8	0.0	0.0	0.0	19.4	19.5	42.2	38.0	19.4	579	87.7
Staunton city	23,745	24,932	5.0	24,432	81.1	11.0	1.4	3.5	3.1	19.0	21.0	42.8	40.1	33.4	10,597	86.6
Stephens City town	1,825	2,063	13.0	2,184	70.3	13.9	1.0	6.5	8.3	30.4	10.2	32.2	39.3	30.5	830	85.3
Sterling CDP	27,822	-	-	30,271	32.5	7.9	15.8	2.7	41.2	23.4	9.9	34.7	39.3	37.3	9,314	94.1
Stone Ridge CDP	7,214	-	-	14,220	41.8	12.8	30.2	7.4	7.8	34.3	6.4	34.2	14.1	66.5	4,341	96.8
Stony Creek town	200	178	-11.0	171	78.4	14.6	0.6	6.4	0.0	22.2	23.4	47.5	37.7	25.4	75	84.0
Strasburg town	6,431	6,676	3.8	6,609	86.2	3.7	0.5	5.1	4.5	25.9	15.2	35.0	40.7	21.6	2,657	85.0
Stuart town	1,345	1,271	-5.5	1,675	79.1	9.3	1.8	2.2	7.6	18.6	33.6	49.7	52.8	16.0	628	78.2
Stuarts Draft CDP	9,235	-	-	9,354	91.4	2.4	0.2	2.8	3.2	22.9	19.6	42.5	45.2	22.8	3,843	90.0
Sudley CDP	16,203	-	-	18,575	31.4	14.9	7.0	2.3	44.5	27.7	7.9	32.4	48.4	25.8	5,400	93.4
Suffolk city	84,565	92,108	8.9	90,093	49.3	41.0	1.9	3.4	4.4	24.3	14.2	38.0	37.3	29.5	33,774	91.4
Sugar Grove CDP	758	-	-	899	100.0	0.0	0.0	0.0	0.0	32.3	9.2	37.6	50.4	1.6	325	80.9
Sugarland Run CDP	11,799	-	-	12,956	41.7	7.8	11.0	5.7	33.8	25.9	8.4	33.3	36.2	39.7	3,640	98.9
Surry town	243	218	-10.3	357	64.1	20.7	0.0	14.3	0.8	24.4	15.1	42.2	42.2	30.7	128	89.8
Sussex CDP	256	-	-	356	76.1	23.0	0.0	0.3	0.6	21.1	12.9	51.2	50.2	26.8	134	100.0
Tangier town	725	701	-3.3	506	100.0	0.0	0.0	0.0	0.0	16.4	31.4	52.3	82.8	4.4	214	61.7
Tappahannock town	2,449	2,402	-1.9	2,068	48.1	47.3	0.4	2.4	1.7	23.3	19.5	39.1	47.8	25.0	904	82.1
Tasley CDP	300	-	-	434	18.2	11.5	0.0	0.0	70.3	46.1	9.4	22.3	79.2	0.0	78	75.6
Tazewell town	4,655	4,141	-11.0	4,250	84.7	10.8	0.2	3.3	1.0	23.5	24.1	45.6	39.2	25.8	1,626	88.3
Temperanceville CDP	358	-	-	258	42.6	29.1	0.0	3.1	25.2	36.0	12.0	39.1	30.6	20.4	110	100.0
Templeton CDP	431	-	-	158	72.8	27.2	0.0	0.0	0.0	6.3	59.5	68.1	13.5	42.6	76	85.5
The Plains town	219	236	7.8	204	88.2	3.4	0.0	6.9	1.5	16.7	21.6	51.3	36.1	40.0	96	92.7
Thynedale CDP	197	-	-	154	0.0	100.0	0.0	0.0	0.0	0.0	31.2	49.4	60.7	14.0	55	69.1
Timberlake CDP	12,183	-	-	13,247	79.8	8.3	2.1	3.9	6.0	20.3	18.6	38.8	33.1	28.5	5,466	89.4
Timberville town	2,521	2,691	6.7	2,635	87.2	0.5	0.3	2.1	9.9	24.0	15.4	37.0	57.3	14.6	1,063	87.7
Toms Brook town	265	272	2.6	409	82.6	9.0	0.0	1.0	7.3	40.8	5.9	31.1	51.1	12.6	120	86.7
Triangle CDP	8,188	-	-	8,972	28.1	34.7	7.2	5.7	24.4	25.6	7.6	32.6	33.7	37.3	2,991	94.8
Troutdale town	176	166	-5.7	149	93.3	3.4	2.7	0.0	0.7	6.0	37.6	57.1	76.6	9.4	93	58.1
Troutville town	428	427	-0.2	473	91.5	0.4	4.2	1.1	2.7	11.6	24.1	44.6	41.0	20.9	232	83.6
Tuckahoe CDP	44,990	-	-	48,799	74.8	9.9	4.9	2.8	7.6	23.9	17.8	38.8	22.4	55.0	18,501	92.6
Twin Lakes CDP	1,647	-	-	1,271	82.2	10.1	5.7	2.0	0.0	21.8	8.3	38.2	33.8	29.5	492	96.5
Tysons CDP	-	-	-	24,261	48.0	5.8	33.2	5.9	7.1	17.5	12.1	35.4	7.7	79.1	11,214	97.9
Union Hall CDP	1,138	-	-	1,105	98.0	0.9	0.5	0.5	0.0	7.0	43.8	62.8	24.4	42.9	536	91.8
Union Level CDP	188	-	-	103	75.7	24.3	0.0	0.0	0.0	19.4	18.4	49.0	68.0	14.7	51	100.0
University Center CDP	3,586	-	-	4,007	42.8	13.5	13.6	6.5	23.7	21.4	2.9	31.3	21.1	49.5	1,648	100.0
University of Virginia CDP	7,704	-	-	8,444	59.7	6.1	19.7	5.2	9.4	4.2	3.7	19.8	15.6	75.6	1,269	91.6
Urbanna town	478	458	-4.2	424	79.7	14.6	0.0	5.7	0.0	15.6	46.2	60.7	25.5	26.4	228	81.1
Vansant CDP	470	-	-	241	93.4	5.0	0.0	1.7	0.0	12.4	24.9	55.1	38.4	32.7	126	96.8
Verona CDP	4,239	-	-	4,228	92.1	3.7	0.0	1.5	2.7	18.4	11.3	36.2	66.0	13.6	1,431	84.4
Victoria town	1,725	1,626	-5.7	2,122	62.1	33.4	0.0	4.5	0.0	25.7	20.4	40.5	61.1	7.6	744	65.6
Vienna town	15,681	16,485	5.1	16,489	66.7	2.4	14.7	6.4	9.8	27.7	13.8	41.3	16.1	68.6	5,414	97.4
Villa Heights CDP	717	-	-	603	54.4	35.3	0.0	0.0	10.3	6.5	31.7	53.0	52.1	14.7	205	92.2
Vinton town	7,994	8,104	1.4	8,083	87.1	4.8	1.9	3.2	3.0	19.4	19.6	40.6	48.6	19.3	3,595	88.0
Virgilina town	148	137	-7.4	91	80.2	3.3	6.6	9.9	0.0	14.3	23.1	57.3	62.3	13.0	50	76.0
Virginia Beach city	437,903	449,974	2.8	450,201	61.7	18.4	6.6	5.1	8.2	22.3	13.7	36.2	27.4	36.0	170,798	95.0
Wachapreague town	232	223	-3.9	192	95.8	0.0	0.0	0.0	4.2	8.9	44.3	61.5	52.7	33.7	113	77.0
Wakefield CDP	11,275	-	-	11,554	65.5	2.3	21.2	2.4	8.5	24.9	20.9	45.4	11.7	72.3	3,726	96.9
Wakefield town	919	825	-10.2	1,175	48.4	45.3	0.4	3.7	2.1	22.3	20.4	34.3	58.0	12.9	454	72.9
Warfield CDP	115	-	-	100	0.0	100.0	0.0	0.0	0.0	0.0	73.0	65.7	85.0	7.0	92	20.7
Warm Springs CDP	123	-	-	-	-	-	-	-	-	-	-	-	-	-	-	-
Warrenton town	9,597	10,027	4.5	9,913	76.2	8.0	4.4	3.5	8.0	24.7	17.0	38.7	28.7	41.2	3,742	91.2
Warsaw town	1,498	1,486	-0.8	1,824	73.5	17.4	0.3	2.6	6.2	17.6	18.8	41.9	49.1	21.5	687	72.5
Washington town	130	127	-2.3	103	75.7	12.6	0.0	8.7	2.9	0.0	32.0	58.5	17.0	56.0	61	93.4
Wattsville CDP	1,128	-	-	998	81.7	18.3	0.0	0.0	0.0	17.4	30.6	50.9	47.9	28.3	535	69.3
Waverly town	2,155	1,953	-9.4	2,633	24.6	67.5	0.0	2.5	5.4	22.2	14.8	34.8	58.8	15.0	835	77.0
Waynesboro city	20,998	22,630	7.8	22,140	75.1	13.4	1.1	2.3	8.1	23.3	17.6	39.2	47.3	27.1	9,193	86.1
Weber City town	1,318	1,211	-8.1	1,623	94.2	1.2	2.9	1.7	0.0	14.2	25.4	47.4	55.6	14.7	599	72.6
West Falls Church CDP	-	-	-	29,623	41.7	5.0	18.7	3.3	31.4	20.5	12.0	37.8	34.6	45.9	10,294	96.2
Westlake Corner CDP	976	-	-	980	99.1	0.0	0.0	0.9	0.0	10.8	28.3	53.9	31.0	38.6	461	90.7
West Point town	3,308	3,257	-1.5	3,292	89.0	4.4	4.5	0.0	2.1	17.8	21.0	43.0	38.6	26.9	1,212	89.6
West Springfield CDP	22,460	-	-	24,223	54.4	8.6	16.5	4.8	15.7	24.0	14.4	40.0	17.9	61.8	8,384	97.6
Weyers Cave CDP	2,473	-	-	1,950	80.7	0.0	0.0	1.9	17.3	18.4	18.2	38.8	46.0	27.1	784	90.8
White Stone town	356	331	-7.0	263	81.7	18.3	0.0	0.0	0.0	13.3	35.0	56.3	58.7	8.9	143	80.4
Whitesville CDP	219	-	-	172	0.0	48.3	0.0	14.0	37.8	26.2	26.7	46.4	89.2	0.0	69	40.6
Williamsburg city	13,700	14,954	9.2	14,927	67.7	15.0	6.5	3.7	7.1	10.4	15.7	24.9	24.0	56.8	4,706	95.3
Winchester city	26,223	28,078	7.1	27,897	66.0	10.0	2.1	4.1	17.8	22.9	15.9	38.1	40.5	35.1	10,490	85.9
Windsor town	2,613	2,758	5.5	2,721	72.7	17.7	0.3	7.7	1.5	23.6	21.5	43.6	46.9	13.8	1,028	84.2
Wintergreen CDP	165	-	-	533	100.0	0.0	0.0	0.0	0.0	0.0	94.7	75.7	21.2	78.8	289	100.0
Wise town	3,235	2,906	-10.2	3,007	94.0	2.1	1.6	1.9	0.4	14.7	17.5	45.4	40.5	30.3	1,278	85.4
Wolf Trap CDP	16,131	-	-	16,436	71.1	2.2	16.5	3.8	6.4	25.9	19.5	46.3	5.9	82.7	5,321	99.3
Woodbridge CDP	4,055	-	-	4,373	47.9	26.6	9.0	2.0	14.5	19.5	14.7	42.8	20.8	54.2	1,779	98.5
Woodburn CDP	8,480	-	-	9,127	50.0	13.4	18.3	6.4	11.8	22.1	14.9	37.8	20.9	55.9	3,023	97.8
Woodlake CDP	7,319	-	-	7,064	80.0	7.6	6.6	2.0	3.9	28.4	12.7	40.4	13.3	64.7	2,456	99.6
Woodlawn CDP	2,343	-	-	2,168	91.4	1.4	0.2	6.6	0.4	25.2	17.9	39.1	64.4	13.8	842	90.6
Woodlawn CDP	-	-	-	24,351	15.0	30.0	9.6	4.9	40.5	29.7	7.0	31.7	46.1	24.9	7,212	92.6
Woodstock town	5,064	5,258	3.8	5,210	79.6	2.1	6.3	1.0	10.9	26.3	22.2	41.4	46.6	23.3	2,153	78.4
Wyndham CDP	9,785	-	-	10,578	71.1	2.4	21.6	1.6	3.3	30.6	10.3	40.7	6.4	80.2	3,504	99.5

1 May be of any race.

Table A. All Places — **Population and Housing**

STATE City, town, township, borough, or CDP (county if applicable)	Population				Race and Hispanic or Latino origin (percent)					Age (percent)			Educational attainment of persons age 25 and older		Occupied housing units	
	2010 census total population	2019 estimated population	Percent change 2010–2019	ACS total population estimate 2015–2019	White alone, not Hispanic or Latino	Black alone, not Hispanic or Latino	Asian alone, not Hispanic or Latino	All other races or 2 or more races, not Hispanic or Latino	Hispanic or Latino[1]	Under 18 years old	Age 65 years and older	Median age	Percent High school diploma or less	Percent Bachelor's degree or more	Total	Percent with a computer
	1	2	3	4	5	6	7	8	9	10	11	12	13	14	15	16
VIRGINIA—Con.																
Wytheville town	8,216	7,921	-3.6	7,957	86.9	7.9	1.6	3.0	0.5	15.9	24.4	48.9	45.5	24.2	3,684	83.8
Yogaville CDP	226	-	-	155	83.2	0.0	0.0	14.2	2.6	1.3	70.3	70.6	35.5	59.9	111	93.7
Yorkshire CDP	7,541	-	-	9,639	26.0	9.0	11.7	5.0	48.3	29.3	4.6	30.7	51.0	21.3	2,779	95.1
Yorktown CDP	195	-	-	317	94.3	0.0	0.0	5.7	0.0	3.5	28.4	57.9	23.6	60.6	195	94.4
WASHINGTON	6,724,540	7,614,893	13.2	7,404,107	68.5	3.7	8.5	6.7	12.7	22.2	15.1	37.7	30.7	36.0	2,848,396	93.8
Aberdeen city	16,872	16,756	-0.7	16,456	70.1	0.7	1.4	10.2	17.6	26.1	15.8	36.2	43.9	16.5	6,132	87.0
Aberdeen Gardens CDP	279	-	-	337	85.2	0.0	0.3	11.3	3.3	30.6	22.6	29.3	32.7	8.8	128	93.0
Acme CDP	246	-	-	108	100.0	0.0	0.0	0.0	0.0	0.0	0.0	0.0	0.0	50.0	54	100.0
Addy CDP	268	-	-	130	42.3	0.0	0.0	57.7	0.0	18.5	16.2	52.6	48.1	0.0	52	17.3
Ahtanum CDP	3,601	-	-	3,356	73.8	0.0	0.0	6.6	19.6	25.8	13.9	37.6	42.4	18.3	1,292	90.6
Airway Heights city	7,541	9,485	25.8	8,560	67.3	4.2	5.7	14.0	8.9	16.6	7.9	33.1	45.7	11.2	2,293	94.2
Albion town	590	604	2.4	646	92.6	0.0	0.5	3.6	3.4	14.6	12.4	34.9	32.5	39.3	281	98.6
Alder CDP	227	-	-	161	43.5	0.0	10.6	46.0	0.0	42.9	0.0	29.3	0.0	83.7	52	100.0
Alderton CDP	2,893	-	-	2,890	88.7	0.1	1.8	3.0	6.4	21.0	15.5	45.4	39.2	20.2	1,164	94.7
Alderwood Manor CDP	8,442	-	-	9,579	62.6	6.1	15.9	4.9	10.5	20.3	9.8	37.3	26.8	32.5	3,305	97.8
Alger CDP	403	-	-	184	64.7	0.0	0.0	19.6	15.8	13.0	39.7	62.3	24.4	8.8	105	88.6
Algona city	3,014	3,208	6.4	3,211	49.0	5.9	15.6	12.5	16.9	28.5	8.2	31.0	49.7	15.1	908	94.6
Allyn CDP	1,963	-	-	2,414	97.9	0.0	0.0	0.8	1.3	21.2	22.9	46.7	30.2	28.8	930	98.1
Almira town	284	280	-1.4	300	91.0	1.0	0.3	0.3	7.3	32.0	21.7	36.6	27.3	21.7	105	94.3
Altoona CDP	39	-	-	48	87.5	0.0	0.0	12.5	0.0	0.0	75.0	75.1	12.5	75.0	25	100.0
Amanda Park CDP	252	-	-	92	70.7	0.0	0.0	19.6	9.8	21.7	16.3	40.4	46.0	7.9	37	78.4
Amboy CDP	1,608	-	-	1,875	98.5	0.0	0.6	0.6	0.3	39.7	7.7	27.1	33.9	19.3	499	93.0
Ames Lake CDP	1,486	-	-	1,556	89.8	0.5	4.1	2.2	3.3	17.9	11.8	47.3	22.4	48.4	610	100.0
Anacortes city	15,768	17,527	11.2	16,977	88.8	0.5	2.5	3.8	4.5	19.2	27.4	48.6	24.6	41.4	7,388	92.5
Anderson Island CDP	1,037	-	-	1,181	91.6	1.7	2.5	4.1	0.0	7.3	38.6	59.4	19.1	31.3	628	94.7
Arlington city	17,959	20,523	14.3	19,483	78.2	1.4	4.0	6.7	9.6	24.7	13.7	38.4	40.4	19.0	7,348	94.1
Arlington Heights CDP	2,284	-	-	2,410	94.9	0.0	0.0	3.3	1.9	17.1	20.6	50.1	50.9	22.1	957	88.8
Artondale CDP	12,653	-	-	13,364	83.0	0.4	1.9	7.2	7.6	21.9	17.5	44.0	19.9	46.3	4,805	98.3
Ashford CDP	217	-	-	531	86.3	0.0	0.0	0.0	13.7	4.1	19.6	56.0	71.9	17.7	215	65.1
Asotin city	1,245	1,289	3.5	929	91.2	1.7	1.1	4.4	1.6	15.8	28.8	47.8	32.8	23.7	436	91.1
Auburn city	70,301	81,464	15.9	80,134	54.7	5.9	11.4	11.2	16.8	25.3	11.1	35.5	40.0	26.5	29,246	93.6
Bainbridge Island city	23,025	25,298	9.9	24,486	88.3	0.6	3.0	5.1	3.0	22.5	25.7	50.3	6.6	72.0	10,115	98.5
Bangor Base CDP	6,054	-	-	6,506	65.1	5.1	1.0	10.5	18.3	24.4	0.0	22.7	23.1	19.9	1,152	99.1
Banks Lake South CDP	174	-	-	146	100.0	0.0	0.0	0.0	0.0	22.6	17.8	41.9	41.7	22.3	60	100.0
Barberton CDP	5,661	-	-	6,981	87.9	0.7	3.2	3.9	4.3	22.5	19.9	44.8	28.0	37.9	2,669	96.6
Baring CDP	220	-	-	162	95.7	0.0	0.0	4.3	0.0	3.1	25.9	51.7	51.4	4.7	84	95.2
Barney's Junction CDP	146	-	-	138	80.4	0.0	0.0	19.6	0.0	22.5	0.0	27.8	80.4	0.0	48	100.0
Barstow CDP	59	-	-	105	91.4	0.0	0.0	4.8	3.8	19.0	41.0	24.8	42.9	20.4	48	81.3
Basin City CDP	1,092	-	-	1,209	0.0	0.0	0.0	0.0	100.0	35.8	0.0	22.9	100.0	0.0	237	100.0
Battle Ground city	17,794	21,252	19.4	20,406	89.3	0.2	0.8	2.8	6.9	27.5	11.3	32.0	36.4	21.3	6,901	96.0
Bay Center CDP	276	-	-	198	90.4	0.0	0.0	9.6	0.0	18.7	45.5	61.4	34.8	15.5	113	69.0
Bay View CDP	696	-	-	662	97.6	0.0	0.0	0.0	2.4	10.9	37.0	59.5	26.2	38.6	270	86.7
Beaux Arts Village town	299	324	8.4	407	91.6	0.0	4.7	2.7	1.0	32.7	18.2	45.9	1.2	88.6	134	95.5
Belfair CDP	3,931	-	-	4,564	72.8	2.7	2.8	4.3	17.4	20.3	16.0	37.5	50.8	3.8	1,745	82.7
Bellevue city	127,885	148,164	15.9	144,403	49.8	2.5	35.7	5.2	6.9	20.6	13.9	37.7	13.2	68.7	58,107	97.5
Bell Hill CDP	837	-	-	608	87.7	0.0	7.9	4.4	0.0	0.0	67.3	68.6	6.4	69.0	305	100.0
Bellingham city	81,205	92,314	13.7	88,764	78.2	1.6	5.9	5.0	9.2	14.9	14.9	31.5	23.6	44.3	36,864	94.2
Benton City city	3,033	3,495	15.2	3,373	63.9	0.0	0.1	3.3	32.7	25.7	14.5	35.5	45.5	14.8	1,245	86.7
Bethel CDP	3,713	-	-	3,851	75.1	3.3	6.5	8.2	7.0	25.2	19.4	39.4	35.0	20.8	1,452	94.6
Bickleton CDP	88	-	-	102	97.1	0.0	0.0	2.9	0.0	24.5	22.5	52.5	39.7	16.4	42	90.5
Big Lake CDP	1,835	-	-	1,774	87.0	0.0	0.7	4.3	8.0	14.8	23.7	50.2	27.8	27.0	742	97.6
Bingen city	712	742	4.2	644	56.2	0.0	0.8	0.2	42.9	22.2	13.4	37.9	53.7	28.6	241	92.5
Birch Bay CDP	8,413	-	-	9,323	85.0	0.3	2.3	6.9	5.5	18.0	25.3	51.9	31.8	27.2	4,149	94.9
Black Diamond city	4,133	4,781	15.7	4,476	86.8	0.6	3.4	2.3	6.8	20.0	15.4	42.0	22.6	41.7	1,759	95.3
Blaine city	4,694	5,607	19.5	5,313	77.1	0.7	9.1	7.4	5.8	21.6	21.5	45.5	32.5	40.2	2,242	92.5
Blyn CDP	101	-	-	60	95.0	0.0	0.0	5.0	0.0	0.0	95.0	74.5	13.3	71.7	31	100.0
Bonney Lake city	17,592	21,148	20.2	20,707	78.8	1.3	3.5	7.7	8.7	26.0	10.4	35.3	34.5	25.7	7,145	95.9
Bothell city	39,851	47,415	19.0	45,749	65.0	1.8	17.1	5.6	10.4	22.5	13.6	37.1	20.6	52.7	17,262	95.6
Bothell East CDP	8,018	-	-	11,665	45.6	3.4	40.0	6.7	4.3	28.5	8.2	34.0	16.5	58.7	3,969	97.6
Bothell West CDP	16,607	-	-	21,115	62.3	1.1	21.7	7.8	7.2	23.5	11.0	36.3	19.2	48.9	7,581	98.7
Boulevard Park CDP	5,287	-	-	3,717	35.4	8.4	13.3	6.8	36.1	17.1	13.8	35.6	51.2	21.3	1,683	91.6
Boyds CDP	34	-	-	45	46.7	0.0	0.0	53.3	0.0	0.0	20.0	54.9	100.0	0.0	23	100.0
Brady CDP	676	-	-	902	93.3	0.0	2.5	0.0	4.1	44.9	10.0	30.2	37.8	19.1	240	100.0
Bremerton city	37,865	41,405	9.3	40,631	67.9	6.2	5.8	9.0	11.1	17.0	13.6	33.0	30.0	24.8	16,733	91.5
Brewster city	2,368	2,357	-0.5	2,367	16.3	1.6	0.0	0.2	82.0	38.2	7.2	24.8	59.3	19.2	771	91.3
Bridgeport city	2,410	2,613	8.4	2,570	10.9	0.0	0.0	1.9	87.2	35.9	5.9	27.4	75.1	1.7	723	82.3
Brier city	6,243	6,970	11.6	6,843	80.0	1.5	7.1	6.4	4.9	18.5	16.2	47.0	22.7	42.7	2,410	97.2
Brinnon CDP	797	-	-	784	87.2	0.0	1.1	6.9	4.7	5.5	45.0	62.8	39.3	25.5	391	90.8
Browns Point CDP	-	-	-	1,104	90.0	1.0	1.4	2.2	5.4	11.4	26.7	53.6	25.2	45.4	486	98.8
Brush Prairie CDP	2,652	-	-	2,636	93.4	0.0	1.9	1.5	3.2	26.6	15.6	42.7	29.1	26.3	943	93.7
Bryant CDP	1,870	-	-	1,817	86.6	1.5	0.0	4.5	7.5	21.5	16.6	48.1	42.3	22.6	615	100.0
Bryn Mawr-Skyway CDP	15,645	-	-	18,414	25.4	27.6	31.1	7.5	8.4	22.5	13.2	38.9	38.4	29.6	6,834	91.0
Buckley city	4,344	5,058	16.4	4,788	91.6	0.6	1.1	2.4	4.2	23.2	12.9	36.7	42.5	20.3	1,911	91.7
Bucoda town	562	592	5.3	668	90.3	0.0	0.0	2.5	7.2	24.7	13.3	36.9	50.5	14.2	234	85.9
Buena CDP	990	-	-	1,084	13.9	0.0	0.0	0.4	85.7	44.5	11.7	19.4	85.6	1.9	266	57.1
Bunk Foss CDP	3,570	-	-	3,939	90.7	0.3	1.6	3.8	3.6	25.6	14.0	42.6	34.2	31.4	1,290	94.2
Burbank CDP	3,291	-	-	3,358	76.7	2.4	0.0	1.1	19.7	27.4	14.9	41.4	53.2	17.5	1,162	97.0
Burien city	48,081	51,500	7.1	51,477	47.9	8.0	12.9	7.5	23.8	22.5	13.7	37.9	43.0	27.7	19,231	92.9
Burley CDP	2,057	-	-	2,304	90.7	0.0	0.0	7.2	2.1	27.3	9.6	35.1	30.7	23.3	791	92.8
Burlington city	8,377	9,224	10.1	8,881	63.2	1.5	3.4	2.3	29.6	24.3	16.5	35.2	42.1	19.2	3,689	88.3
Camano CDP	-	-	-	17,042	90.9	0.6	2.4	2.4	3.6	15.7	30.3	54.7	25.9	35.8	7,232	94.9
Camas city	19,813	24,418	23.2	23,200	80.8	0.6	8.1	5.6	4.9	28.5	11.9	40.2	18.4	52.7	8,224	96.8
Canterwood CDP	3,079	-	-	3,218	85.7	1.0	2.2	0.0	11.1	20.7	29.5	53.0	14.9	52.2	1,326	98.5
Canyon Creek CDP	3,200	-	-	3,433	93.6	1.3	0.0	2.9	2.2	26.4	6.7	40.8	44.9	7.2	1,299	99.2
Carbonado town	608	735	20.9	713	94.4	0.0	0.0	0.0	5.6	26.6	12.3	33.3	54.6	12.6	243	90.1
Carlsborg CDP	995	-	-	745	100.0	0.0	0.0	0.0	0.0	0.0	58.1	67.8	23.6	23.0	331	91.5
Carnation city	1,786	2,282	27.8	1,835	79.0	0.7	1.6	3.9	14.9	22.8	11.6	40.9	29.3	38.7	689	99.4
Carson CDP	2,279	-	-	2,830	83.1	0.0	2.0	3.6	11.3	29.6	10.7	35.6	45.4	16.1	1,067	82.1
Cascade Valley CDP	2,246	-	-	1,673	80.0	2.0	0.0	0.8	17.3	10.9	21.3	54.8	44.0	21.9	823	85.8
Cashmere city	3,113	3,172	1.9	3,140	76.9	0.0	0.1	2.9	20.1	24.3	16.6	38.5	39.8	23.5	1,053	90.2

1 May be of any race.

Table A. All Places — **Population and Housing**

STATE City, town, township, borough, or CDP (county if applicable)	Population				Race and Hispanic or Latino origin (percent)					Age (percent)			Educational attainment of persons age 25 and older		Occupied housing units	
	2010 census total population	2019 estimated population	Percent change 2010–2019	ACS total population estimate 2015–2019	White alone, not Hispanic or Latino	Black alone, not Hispanic or Latino	Asian alone, not Hispanic or Latino	All other races or 2 or more races, not Hispanic or Latino	Hispanic or Latino[1]	Under 18 years old	Age 65 years and older	Median age	Percent High school diploma or less	Percent Bachelor's degree or more	Total	Percent with a computer
	1	2	3	4	5	6	7	8	9	10	11	12	13	14	15	16
WASHINGTON—Con.																
Castle Rock city	2,113	2,298	8.8	3,153	87.2	0.0	0.0	5.6	7.3	30.8	12.7	31.5	46.8	14.8	1,163	92.0
Cathcart CDP	2,458	-	-	2,426	90.3	2.3	0.0	7.3	0.0	12.6	19.9	55.0	27.3	31.2	929	100.0
Cathlamet town	532	572	7.5	621	71.8	1.6	0.0	1.8	24.8	18.0	25.3	39.6	37.6	14.1	262	85.1
Cavalero CDP	4,660	-	-	5,370	87.4	0.0	2.2	4.0	6.4	29.3	9.6	36.5	27.6	30.6	1,707	98.9
Centerville CDP	112	-	-	103	100.0	0.0	0.0	0.0	0.0	15.5	23.3	52.8	54.0	16.1	49	59.2
Centralia city	16,658	17,745	6.5	17,216	76.0	0.5	1.6	4.5	17.3	22.9	18.9	37.8	48.4	15.1	7,204	88.1
Central Park CDP	2,685	-	-	3,205	90.4	0.1	0.0	3.1	6.4	21.7	17.7	42.8	41.4	22.1	1,255	92.2
Chain Lake CDP	3,741	-	-	4,522	87.8	0.0	1.3	6.9	4.0	22.9	16.7	42.5	31.7	34.8	1,486	96.0
Chehalis city	7,259	7,654	5.4	7,497	78.0	1.7	1.1	5.4	13.8	21.2	15.6	33.6	37.2	19.2	2,968	84.8
Chelan city	3,894	4,237	8.8	4,146	69.9	0.0	0.0	0.0	30.1	21.9	18.3	42.2	49.6	21.0	1,628	85.6
Chelan Falls CDP	329	-	-	88	100.0	0.0	0.0	0.0	0.0	53.4	0.0	0.0	100.0	0.0	41	100.0
Cheney city	10,592	12,522	18.2	12,165	73.0	4.9	3.0	6.6	12.5	12.5	7.3	23.1	15.7	44.2	4,535	96.0
Cherry Grove CDP	546	-	-	738	84.7	0.0	0.0	0.0	15.3	51.5	6.6	14.8	34.3	16.4	175	100.0
Chewelah city	2,599	2,676	3.0	2,623	85.8	1.4	1.0	8.4	3.4	17.1	25.0	48.8	47.9	15.8	1,111	80.5
Chico CDP	2,259	-	-	2,846	72.7	3.6	12.1	6.6	5.0	24.6	16.0	42.3	22.6	34.8	1,030	98.5
Chinook CDP	466	-	-	154	100.0	0.0	0.0	0.0	0.0	0.0	32.5	58.7	18.8	6.5	103	69.9
Clallam Bay CDP	363	-	-	497	39.8	0.0	0.0	28.8	31.4	13.3	15.7	40.1	44.6	5.0	277	86.6
Clarkston city	7,238	7,375	1.9	7,381	86.6	0.0	1.4	4.9	7.1	21.1	14.5	36.1	41.3	16.2	2,950	88.0
Clarkston Heights-Vineland CDP	6,326	-	-	6,348	93.5	0.0	1.1	3.9	1.5	17.3	31.5	51.7	31.3	32.2	2,608	93.6
Clayton CDP	443	-	-	547	95.4	0.0	0.0	4.6	0.0	31.4	13.0	36.0	62.4	0.0	172	47.7
Clear Lake CDP	1,419	-	-	1,126	89.0	0.0	0.7	8.0	2.3	21.4	13.1	38.9	30.9	27.2	417	91.4
Clear Lake CDP	1,002	-	-	914	94.6	2.8	0.0	1.5	1.0	21.6	20.7	44.6	40.5	19.9	385	92.2
Clearview CDP	3,324	-	-	3,630	83.4	0.0	5.5	2.3	8.8	27.5	11.3	40.0	32.1	33.0	1,259	94.2
Cle Elum city	1,869	2,037	9.0	3,017	90.5	0.0	0.0	2.8	6.8	21.1	13.8	37.3	49.5	15.9	1,292	89.5
Cliffdell CDP	104	-	-	130	98.5	0.0	0.0	1.5	0.0	0.8	30.0	46.8	58.9	10.1	64	100.0
Clinton CDP	928	-	-	891	90.9	0.1	2.9	0.2	5.8	20.1	35.1	55.2	27.1	32.1	391	94.1
Clover Creek CDP	6,522	-	-	6,734	69.7	3.4	9.3	8.0	9.6	21.1	13.6	41.0	45.9	15.4	2,484	85.7
Clyde Hill city	2,988	3,386	13.3	3,329	66.1	0.9	25.4	5.9	1.6	28.0	18.0	45.7	6.0	76.8	1,131	98.9
Cohassett Beach CDP	722	-	-	691	79.6	0.0	0.0	2.2	18.2	16.6	16.2	54.2	46.9	9.6	251	100.0
Colfax city	2,795	2,872	2.8	2,891	94.9	0.0	1.3	2.0	1.8	15.4	23.5	48.1	36.8	30.1	1,148	87.3
College Place city	8,792	9,317	6.0	9,182	72.6	1.4	2.0	5.0	19.0	20.3	17.7	35.0	22.1	39.5	3,481	92.4
Colton town	429	458	6.8	436	90.4	0.0	0.9	5.7	3.0	25.5	14.0	35.9	24.3	38.0	180	93.9
Colville city	4,727	4,832	2.2	4,777	86.9	0.0	1.8	5.4	5.8	19.5	21.6	43.5	42.6	24.3	2,061	92.2
Conconully town	201	208	3.5	174	88.5	0.0	1.7	2.3	7.5	4.0	32.2	57.6	49.3	13.9	117	85.5
Concrete town	705	738	4.7	738	87.9	0.0	1.1	5.8	5.1	19.9	12.6	35.7	45.6	12.8	345	95.1
Connell city	4,210	5,545	31.7	5,517	38.7	5.5	5.0	3.9	46.9	23.9	11.7	35.0	54.5	5.6	1,118	91.1
Conway CDP	91	-	-	-	-	-	-	-	-	-	-	-	-	-	-	-
Copalis Beach CDP	415	-	-	578	79.1	1.2	0.0	16.1	3.6	7.6	24.6	50.6	52.5	5.6	295	84.4
Cosmopolis city	1,647	1,662	0.9	1,610	82.3	0.2	1.1	6.8	9.5	22.6	17.3	43.9	47.1	13.6	659	88.6
Cottage Lake CDP	22,494	-	-	22,677	82.7	0.9	9.0	4.2	3.2	24.7	14.3	44.9	12.7	64.2	7,830	98.3
Coulee City town	560	564	0.7	534	91.8	8.2	0.0	0.0	0.0	24.2	23.6	38.5	39.0	17.7	241	79.7
Coulee Dam town	1,098	1,080	-1.6	1,209	51.8	0.0	0.9	42.8	4.5	23.8	22.1	42.3	38.8	22.0	550	88.0
Country Homes CDP	5,841	-	-	6,117	79.9	1.8	5.0	6.2	7.0	14.0	12.8	22.5	21.8	40.0	1,868	93.2
Coupeville town	1,833	1,972	7.6	1,715	84.9	0.6	2.3	6.2	6.1	8.6	45.7	63.8	22.5	42.9	866	91.0
Covington city	17,565	21,175	20.6	20,825	68.1	4.5	12.4	7.0	8.0	21.9	10.8	38.3	33.3	28.4	7,272	96.9
Cowiche CDP	428	-	-	821	4.4	0.0	0.0	46.4	49.2	50.5	0.0	16.9	54.5	0.0	212	100.0
Creston town	233	229	-1.7	241	92.9	0.0	0.0	6.6	0.4	7.9	29.5	53.5	44.9	9.6	131	94.7
Crocker CDP	1,268	-	-	1,196	88.1	0.0	0.0	2.8	9.0	24.6	13.4	36.8	47.7	17.4	403	86.8
Curlew CDP	118	-	-	100	89.0	0.0	0.0	0.0	11.0	22.0	15.0	28.4	20.8	15.3	44	79.5
Curlew Lake CDP	462	-	-	610	96.4	0.0	0.0	2.3	1.3	13.4	35.9	52.0	41.9	28.6	228	96.9
Cusick town	204	217	6.4	88	95.5	0.0	0.0	0.0	4.5	11.4	19.3	55.4	50.7	13.7	48	93.8
Custer CDP	366	-	-	133	100.0	0.0	0.0	0.0	0.0	0.0	53.4	65.2	52.3	13.1	48	100.0
Dallesport CDP	1,202	-	-	1,515	91.9	0.0	1.7	6.4	0.0	22.5	16.6	42.6	49.7	0.9	539	92.4
Danville CDP	34	-	-	81	69.1	0.0	0.0	30.9	0.0	33.3	13.6	20.8	65.8	0.0	38	71.1
Darrington town	1,347	1,421	5.5	1,088	80.6	0.9	0.0	9.7	8.7	15.6	20.0	47.5	61.8	8.2	519	88.1
Dash Point CDP	931	-	-	1,105	79.8	0.3	7.8	8.6	3.5	19.7	25.1	47.6	16.2	47.8	400	98.8
Davenport city	1,734	1,744	0.6	1,819	90.8	0.1	1.2	3.5	4.5	20.0	25.3	44.5	38.5	30.5	767	94.5
Dayton city	2,535	2,442	-3.7	2,656	83.2	1.1	2.7	1.3	11.7	18.8	30.1	52.2	36.2	22.6	1,222	85.4
Deep River CDP	204	-	-	186	100.0	0.0	0.0	0.0	0.0	11.8	50.0	65.0	32.9	8.5	96	87.5
Deer Park city	3,661	4,364	19.2	4,119	93.6	0.3	0.0	2.4	3.6	28.9	18.5	33.8	41.4	13.7	1,544	87.6
Deming CDP	353	-	-	164	97.0	0.0	0.0	1.2	1.8	1.2	1.8	27.6	0.0	58.2	43	100.0
Desert Aire CDP	1,626	-	-	2,712	45.4	0.0	0.5	2.4	51.7	38.2	13.0	37.1	52.2	24.0	796	88.7
Des Moines city	29,654	32,348	9.1	31,734	51.3	7.4	11.6	9.8	19.9	20.9	16.8	40.5	38.1	26.7	12,114	95.7
Disautel CDP	78	-	-	25	0.0	0.0	0.0	100.0	0.0	0.0	28.0	55.2	72.0	0.0	25	28.0
Dixie CDP	197	-	-	190	100.0	0.0	0.0	0.0	0.0	25.8	19.5	49.0	40.1	8.8	82	87.8
Dollars Corner CDP	-	-	-	699	77.0	6.2	0.0	3.9	13.0	12.0	17.2	51.9	43.8	19.2	277	100.0
Donald CDP	91	-	-	-	-	-	-	-	-	-	-	-	-	-	-	-
Duluth CDP	1,544	-	-	1,314	91.2	0.0	0.7	1.6	6.5	21.3	19.3	49.8	42.4	23.1	541	82.3
DuPont city	8,199	9,516	16.1	9,435	67.1	9.3	5.8	8.9	8.9	28.9	8.1	31.7	11.9	58.0	3,831	94.3
Duvall city	6,713	8,107	20.8	7,901	82.6	1.0	4.0	2.7	9.6	29.7	4.6	37.0	12.7	56.8	2,681	100.0
East Cathlamet CDP	491	-	-	512	92.6	0.0	0.0	0.0	7.4	11.3	37.9	53.3	42.0	8.8	253	100.0
Eastmont CDP	20,101	-	-	21,733	74.4	1.4	10.1	6.5	7.6	24.1	13.3	39.0	26.0	42.7	7,385	96.8
Easton CDP	478	-	-	361	88.6	0.0	0.0	0.0	11.4	13.0	15.8	47.5	56.6	16.5	186	87.6
East Port Orchard CDP	5,919	-	-	5,407	75.3	2.2	3.4	9.0	10.2	27.4	13.2	33.6	37.3	20.2	2,067	88.8
East Renton Highlands CDP	11,140	-	-	11,842	81.0	0.3	6.6	7.0	5.1	22.5	16.8	44.4	28.3	40.7	4,468	95.2
East Wenatchee city	13,179	14,219	7.9	13,960	62.9	0.2	0.5	4.3	32.2	28.6	14.4	33.0	47.1	20.7	4,971	93.8
Eatonville town	2,756	3,026	9.8	2,981	85.0	0.0	0.6	6.3	8.1	26.5	11.0	35.3	41.0	18.9	1,104	95.1
Edgewood city	9,379	13,053	39.2	11,264	82.8	0.1	3.4	7.6	6.2	23.7	16.3	41.7	30.7	31.4	4,019	95.8
Edison CDP	133	-	-	147	100.0	0.0	0.0	0.0	0.0	0.0	82.3	71.9	8.8	82.3	80	100.0
Edmonds city	39,695	42,605	7.3	42,040	76.8	1.5	8.0	5.8	7.9	17.9	21.8	45.9	19.6	48.2	17,761	96.3
Elbe CDP	29	-	-	53	0.0	0.0	0.0	100.0	0.0	0.0	0.0	0.0	100.0	0.0	53	100.0
Electric City city	976	1,002	2.7	894	81.2	0.0	0.0	18.8	0.0	17.6	40.4	56.0	42.2	9.6	378	92.3
Elk Plain CDP	14,205	-	-	15,167	72.8	3.2	4.1	12.6	7.3	24.1	11.2	37.5	46.6	12.7	5,081	94.1
Ellensburg city	18,301	21,111	15.4	20,167	77.4	1.5	2.6	7.7	10.9	13.6	10.0	23.5	28.6	38.1	7,839	93.8
Elma city	3,301	3,351	1.5	3,277	87.1	0.8	0.1	8.3	3.7	18.4	27.5	40.8	50.8	17.1	1,411	78.8
Elmer City town	251	248	-1.2	298	51.0	0.0	0.0	42.6	6.4	20.1	29.5	47.7	33.3	31.1	151	84.8
Endicott town	299	305	2.0	304	98.4	0.0	0.0	0.7	1.0	27.0	11.5	35.0	34.3	23.4	121	90.1
Enetai CDP	2,286	-	-	1,921	74.9	2.1	10.7	7.7	4.5	18.3	12.5	38.4	28.8	30.4	763	99.1
Entiat city	1,111	1,280	15.2	1,029	70.5	0.0	2.9	3.2	23.4	18.9	19.3	42.1	41.5	15.6	411	97.8
Enumclaw city	11,090	12,190	9.9	11,879	80.8	0.2	1.0	4.7	13.3	23.1	15.5	39.2	38.8	23.6	4,918	89.1

1 May be of any race.

Table A. All Places — **Population and Housing**

STATE City, town, township, borough, or CDP (county if applicable)	Population				Race and Hispanic or Latino origin (percent)					Age (percent)			Educational attainment of persons age 25 and older		Occupied housing units	
	2010 census total population	2019 estimated population	Percent change 2010–2019	ACS total population estimate 2015–2019	White alone, not Hispanic or Latino	Black alone, not Hispanic or Latino	Asian alone, not Hispanic or Latino	All other races or 2 or more races, not Hispanic or Latino	Hispanic or Latino[1]	Under 18 years old	Age 65 years and older	Median age	Percent High school diploma or less	Percent Bachelor's degree or more	Total	Percent with a computer
	1	2	3	4	5	6	7	8	9	10	11	12	13	14	15	16
WASHINGTON—Con.																
Ephrata city	7,679	8,136	6.0	8,072	73.5	0.5	1.6	4.9	19.6	30.6	14.7	34.4	41.5	18.9	2,772	89.3
Erlands Point-Kitsap Lake CDP	2,935	-	-	3,116	79.6	0.7	3.2	6.1	10.3	24.8	14.7	40.1	28.9	27.8	1,311	97.4
Eschbach CDP	415	-	-	352	76.4	0.0	0.0	6.5	17.0	14.2	17.6	45.7	26.2	32.6	144	100.0
Esperance CDP	3,601	-	-	4,204	83.3	1.3	5.9	4.4	5.2	17.6	17.1	40.6	24.8	39.7	1,504	95.9
Everett city	102,953	111,475	8.3	109,766	63.8	4.7	9.1	7.3	15.1	20.6	12.5	36.1	38.6	23.3	43,428	92.8
Everson city	2,464	2,841	15.3	2,705	56.3	0.0	1.0	5.0	37.8	30.6	12.5	31.0	46.9	14.2	934	93.5
Fairchild AFB CDP	2,776	-	-	3,336	63.6	13.6	1.7	7.0	14.0	32.9	0.0	22.7	11.7	32.4	804	97.9
Fairfield town	614	626	2.0	596	92.6	0.0	0.0	4.4	3.0	25.0	23.2	43.7	40.5	13.9	217	87.6
Fairwood CDP	19,102	-	-	19,962	54.8	9.9	17.4	9.1	8.8	23.9	13.4	38.2	23.6	43.2	7,317	97.6
Fairwood CDP	7,905	-	-	8,669	86.0	0.1	2.0	4.1	7.7	29.0	19.8	36.8	16.3	39.1	3,387	96.0
Fall City CDP	1,993	-	-	2,426	70.3	0.0	6.4	10.9	12.4	25.8	19.0	40.5	29.7	38.1	785	99.0
Farmington town	150	152	1.3	125	92.8	0.0	0.0	0.8	6.4	12.0	18.4	48.5	30.6	14.3	59	88.1
Federal Way city	89,295	96,289	7.8	96,526	44.4	14.0	12.6	10.4	18.7	24.1	13.1	35.8	37.0	27.2	35,190	94.6
Felida CDP	7,385	-	-	8,959	84.1	0.8	7.0	3.8	4.2	27.8	15.4	42.8	13.3	60.0	3,170	99.6
Ferndale city	11,411	14,897	30.5	14,043	76.9	0.1	5.2	6.0	11.7	25.4	13.8	36.9	32.3	27.6	5,112	91.8
Fern Prairie CDP	1,884	-	-	1,958	97.4	0.0	0.0	0.7	1.9	21.5	13.8	44.6	37.2	17.9	691	93.6
Fife city	9,178	10,184	11.0	10,096	45.1	9.6	14.2	17.0	14.1	25.9	7.4	31.9	39.9	25.0	3,787	94.8
Fife Heights CDP	2,137	-	-	2,368	70.9	5.9	6.8	5.8	10.6	26.3	10.0	35.5	31.6	30.6	704	98.3
Finley CDP	6,012	-	-	6,021	74.5	0.0	1.0	1.2	23.4	28.5	13.4	37.2	50.3	10.7	1,966	90.7
Fircrest city	6,541	6,835	4.5	6,795	72.7	5.3	5.2	10.0	6.7	23.9	16.7	40.0	24.5	37.4	2,609	96.6
Five Corners CDP	18,159	-	-	18,908	77.9	1.5	3.6	7.2	9.8	26.2	11.8	36.3	41.8	19.6	6,358	95.6
Fobes Hill CDP	2,418	-	-	2,984	93.2	0.0	0.9	3.2	2.7	21.8	18.5	46.3	30.1	33.3	1,047	95.2
Fords Prairie CDP	1,959	-	-	2,662	84.6	0.0	2.5	1.9	11.0	29.0	18.2	39.5	36.2	18.0	816	96.2
Forks city	3,549	3,880	9.3	3,828	69.5	5.0	0.1	6.9	18.4	28.7	10.4	32.3	55.5	15.5	1,541	83.5
Fort Lewis CDP	11,046	-	-	13,054	50.5	14.8	4.6	9.9	20.2	33.3	0.1	22.5	27.7	16.7	3,193	98.6
Four Lakes CDP	512	-	-	490	99.8	0.0	0.0	0.0	0.2	12.9	36.9	52.4	25.9	33.4	247	69.6
Fox Island CDP	3,633	-	-	3,918	88.3	0.0	0.9	7.6	3.2	20.4	20.8	47.5	16.5	51.6	1,480	97.0
Frederickson CDP	18,719	-	-	22,994	57.7	9.2	8.6	13.0	11.5	29.0	8.8	32.6	37.7	18.6	7,063	97.6
Freeland CDP	2,045	-	-	2,154	87.2	3.3	0.4	4.4	4.6	14.9	34.8	56.4	34.8	30.5	990	88.0
Friday Harbor town	2,176	2,562	17.7	2,426	80.2	0.7	1.7	2.9	14.6	19.3	17.5	40.6	36.3	34.9	1,134	90.1
Garfield town	599	609	1.7	622	91.6	0.0	0.0	4.7	3.7	25.4	16.9	43.3	30.4	21.7	264	89.0
Garrett CDP	1,419	-	-	1,280	81.3	3.6	0.5	4.6	10.1	20.1	28.4	51.3	36.9	28.0	501	91.2
Geneva CDP	2,321	-	-	2,460	92.2	0.0	1.7	2.6	3.5	19.3	17.0	38.7	16.6	52.3	831	95.7
George city	502	516	2.8	745	11.8	0.0	0.0	0.0	88.2	35.8	5.6	26.7	84.2	1.8	166	95.8
Gig Harbor city	7,133	10,717	50.2	9,854	85.1	0.7	6.1	5.1	3.0	22.8	24.6	44.3	17.6	47.1	4,169	93.9
Glacier CDP	211	-	-	154	76.6	0.0	0.0	23.4	0.0	0.0	0.0	44.8	22.7	42.9	69	100.0
Gleed CDP	2,906	-	-	2,808	77.6	0.7	0.0	7.2	14.5	24.7	18.2	46.2	45.4	20.1	1,083	87.7
Glenwood CDP	-	-	-	254	66.5	0.0	0.0	33.5	0.0	29.9	20.5	36.0	51.0	10.6	101	89.1
Gold Bar city	2,158	2,352	9.0	1,858	89.6	0.0	0.0	3.2	7.2	18.8	13.3	45.4	40.4	12.8	824	90.7
Goldendale city	3,403	3,505	3.0	3,459	93.5	0.0	1.0	3.1	2.3	19.1	23.6	41.2	37.4	35.2	1,586	86.9
Gorst CDP	592	-	-	235	100.0	0.0	0.0	0.0	0.0	0.0	62.1	71.1	45.1	13.2	144	86.1
Graham CDP	23,491	-	-	28,976	76.0	3.7	3.9	7.6	8.9	27.8	10.3	35.0	39.4	18.2	9,309	95.6
Grand Coulee city	1,027	1,048	2.0	1,067	70.7	0.1	0.7	14.2	14.2	17.2	24.4	46.8	47.5	11.0	473	85.6
Grand Mound CDP	2,981	-	-	3,373	63.8	0.4	0.7	15.2	20.0	30.0	9.8	33.8	47.9	12.2	1,116	98.6
Grandview city	10,854	11,078	2.1	11,116	14.1	0.3	0.7	0.3	84.6	35.3	8.0	27.3	69.5	6.4	3,275	90.3
Granger city	3,258	3,830	17.6	3,756	10.0	0.8	0.0	0.9	88.4	38.0	7.6	24.3	78.0	3.6	863	82.4
Granite Falls city	3,390	4,234	24.9	3,737	90.8	0.9	0.0	7.9	0.5	27.7	10.5	33.3	35.1	20.7	1,491	89.9
Grapeview CDP	954	-	-	784	94.3	0.0	0.0	5.7	0.0	4.1	31.4	56.6	44.7	14.7	358	100.0
Grayland CDP	953	-	-	722	89.6	0.0	0.0	0.0	10.4	5.7	34.8	59.5	27.1	28.6	411	77.1
Grays River CDP	263	-	-	269	96.7	0.0	3.3	0.0	0.0	7.1	45.0	63.7	51.1	17.7	138	60.1
Green Bluff CDP	761	-	-	402	100.0	0.0	0.0	0.0	0.0	3.7	47.8	61.9	6.2	49.6	199	95.0
Greenwater CDP	67	-	-	56	100.0	0.0	0.0	0.0	0.0	0.0	76.8	68.9	0.0	23.2	26	100.0
Hamilton town	301	310	3.0	297	92.6	0.0	0.0	3.0	4.4	13.8	9.8	54.2	40.2	26.7	134	97.0
Hansville CDP	3,091	-	-	3,413	88.4	0.0	1.9	4.9	4.9	12.7	43.4	61.8	21.4	36.9	1,689	94.8
Harrah town	624	640	2.6	613	15.7	0.0	0.2	21.4	62.8	28.9	12.4	30.9	60.7	11.3	188	80.3
Harrington city	427	418	-2.1	409	88.0	2.9	0.0	3.4	5.6	20.5	22.0	43.8	42.4	27.3	198	86.9
Hartline town	151	154	2.0	179	97.2	0.0	0.0	2.8	0.0	31.3	21.2	38.1	35.9	19.7	69	89.9
Hat Island CDP	41	-	-	63	100.0	0.0	0.0	0.0	0.0	0.0	60.3	65.3	0.0	87.3	33	100.0
Hatton town	101	104	3.0	184	29.9	0.0	0.0	0.0	70.1	52.2	8.7	17.5	73.9	1.1	45	82.2
Hazel Dell CDP	19,435	-	-	21,196	73.8	2.0	3.8	6.0	14.5	22.8	14.5	37.5	34.7	25.7	8,242	93.9
Herron Island CDP	151	-	-	37	100.0	0.0	0.0	0.0	0.0	0.0	100.0	75.2	54.1	0.0	27	100.0
High Bridge CDP	2,994	-	-	3,148	83.0	2.0	4.2	6.5	4.4	23.1	15.6	46.4	19.8	45.8	1,092	99.0
Hobart CDP	6,221	-	-	7,262	89.5	1.4	1.9	2.5	4.8	22.7	13.7	42.8	28.4	39.0	2,620	95.7
Hockinson CDP	4,771	-	-	5,355	89.3	0.4	2.5	6.2	1.5	23.7	16.5	45.6	23.6	40.6	1,819	97.1
Hogans Corner CDP	85	-	-	70	100.0	0.0	0.0	0.0	0.0	0.0	31.4	61.5	68.6	0.0	22	100.0
Home CDP	1,377	-	-	1,477	93.6	0.0	0.1	1.6	4.6	17.9	22.1	54.6	36.9	19.6	582	98.3
Hoodsport CDP	376	-	-	134	100.0	0.0	0.0	0.0	0.0	0.0	88.1	73.8	33.6	0.0	89	100.0
Hoquiam city	8,733	8,655	-0.9	8,495	83.7	0.7	1.0	5.0	9.5	21.7	21.0	43.2	40.9	18.8	3,717	85.7
Humptulips CDP	255	-	-	243	86.8	0.0	0.0	6.2	7.0	18.5	27.2	59.2	60.2	14.6	98	90.8
Hunts Point town	396	435	9.8	389	83.5	0.0	10.3	3.9	2.3	21.1	30.6	53.2	9.4	72.5	155	95.5
Ilwaco city	941	991	5.3	1,034	88.5	0.3	0.0	3.9	7.4	22.3	27.2	39.4	40.8	16.5	395	88.4
Inchelium CDP	409	-	-	326	17.2	0.0	0.0	81.6	1.2	28.8	19.6	42.3	53.6	7.2	133	71.4
Index town	176	211	19.9	173	94.8	0.0	5.2	0.0	0.0	13.9	17.3	52.6	41.6	22.6	82	86.6
Indianola CDP	3,500	-	-	3,524	82.7	0.5	1.9	9.3	5.6	20.1	18.0	44.5	27.4	36.0	1,412	96.5
Ione town	444	472	6.3	375	92.8	0.0	0.0	7.2	0.0	19.5	27.7	46.2	43.1	19.2	169	82.2
Issaquah city	30,440	39,509	29.8	37,965	61.4	1.9	23.2	4.5	9.0	23.5	13.1	37.6	13.7	64.9	15,525	97.9
Jamestown CDP	361	-	-	395	84.3	0.0	0.0	9.6	6.1	9.1	26.8	58.2	20.1	40.9	218	100.0
Junction City CDP	18	-	-	-	-	-	-	-	-	-	-	-	-	-	-	-
Kahlotus city	189	193	2.1	215	80.5	0.0	0.0	0.0	19.5	23.3	12.6	34.8	43.8	7.2	70	84.3
Kalama city	2,361	2,798	18.5	2,629	90.8	0.0	0.0	3.0	6.2	19.5	21.6	42.1	38.9	18.4	1,115	93.1
Kapowsin CDP	333	-	-	129	100.0	0.0	0.0	0.0	0.0	0.0	10.9	48.8	49.2	10.0	60	100.0
Kayak Point CDP	-	-	-	1,704	85.5	0.9	3.5	6.6	3.5	15.7	14.9	52.5	28.0	24.5	660	97.1
Keller CDP	234	-	-	210	10.0	0.0	0.0	81.0	9.0	22.4	9.0	34.5	49.6	11.6	75	72.0
Kelso city	11,913	12,417	4.2	12,123	75.4	1.2	1.4	5.1	16.8	25.5	13.4	35.2	54.2	9.7	4,563	88.3
Kendall CDP	191	-	-	18	100.0	0.0	0.0	0.0	0.0	0.0	0.0	0.0	0.0	0.0	18	0.0
Kenmore city	20,476	23,097	12.8	22,724	73.4	1.2	13.0	4.9	7.6	21.5	14.1	39.2	17.2	56.8	8,858	96.5
Kennewick city	73,994	84,347	14.0	81,479	64.9	1.8	2.3	4.1	26.9	27.6	13.5	33.7	39.8	25.6	29,341	91.2
Kent city	118,620	132,319	11.5	131,118	42.7	12.0	20.5	8.9	16.0	24.2	11.1	34.2	40.6	25.7	44,030	94.9
Ketron Island CDP	17	-	-	-	-	-	-	-	-	-	-	-	-	-	-	-
Kettle Falls city	1,589	1,635	2.9	1,769	88.2	0.4	0.3	5.4	5.7	26.6	19.2	43.8	46.1	19.8	725	82.5
Key Center CDP	3,692	-	-	3,806	92.1	1.0	0.4	5.1	1.4	17.1	20.2	44.8	22.7	22.8	1,384	94.1

1 May be of any race.

Table A. All Places — **Population and Housing**

STATE City, town, township, borough, or CDP (county if applicable)	Population 2010 census total population	2019 estimated population	Percent change 2010–2019	ACS total population estimate 2015–2019	Race and Hispanic or Latino origin (percent) White alone, not Hispanic or Latino	Black alone, not Hispanic or Latino	Asian alone, not Hispanic or Latino	All other races or 2 or more races, not Hispanic or Latino	Hispanic or Latino[1]	Age (percent) Under 18 years old	Age 65 years and older	Median age	Educational attainment of persons age 25 and older Percent High school diploma or less	Percent Bachelor's degree or more	Occupied housing units Total	Percent with a computer
	1	2	3	4	5	6	7	8	9	10	11	12	13	14	15	16
WASHINGTON—Con.																
Keyport CDP	554	-	-	430	90.0	0.0	0.0	0.0	10.0	10.2	9.8	33.9	16.1	40.9	239	96.2
Kingston CDP	2,099	-	-	2,193	85.5	0.0	2.4	8.8	3.3	14.9	24.7	52.7	25.8	37.3	1,028	88.4
Kirkland city	80,585	93,010	15.4	89,438	71.2	1.3	14.4	5.4	7.7	20.5	13.1	37.4	14.7	61.3	36,480	97.3
Kittitas city	1,358	1,497	10.2	1,503	68.6	0.0	0.0	1.2	30.2	33.2	16.2	32.2	49.3	22.0	579	81.0
Klickitat CDP	362	-	-	243	95.5	0.0	4.5	0.0	0.0	8.6	19.3	54.1	40.1	9.9	121	78.5
Krupp (Marlin) town	48	52	8.3	54	85.2	0.0	0.0	0.0	14.8	11.1	0.0	37.5	35.7	23.8	28	100.0
La Center city	2,941	3,404	15.7	3,219	89.8	1.9	3.8	1.6	2.9	25.0	12.9	39.6	32.7	21.4	1,055	98.6
Lacey city	42,543	52,592	23.6	49,248	63.2	5.7	8.5	10.0	12.5	22.6	16.5	35.2	26.6	33.8	19,277	93.6
La Conner town	872	949	8.8	934	81.2	0.0	2.6	5.0	11.2	18.3	35.3	57.5	30.4	33.6	477	87.2
LaCrosse town	313	319	1.9	332	94.0	0.0	0.0	4.5	1.5	9.6	32.5	58.2	45.5	18.9	191	85.9
La Grande CDP	109	-	-	39	100.0	0.0	0.0	0.0	0.0	0.0	71.8	68.6	100.0	0.0	25	56.0
Lake Bosworth CDP	667	-	-	935	92.2	0.0	0.0	4.3	3.5	12.3	9.6	49.4	46.3	15.2	362	95.3
Lake Cassidy CDP	3,415	-	-	3,602	80.5	0.0	4.6	4.0	10.9	21.3	14.5	45.6	33.2	30.2	1,331	97.7
Lake Cavanaugh CDP	167	-	-	179	100.0	0.0	0.0	0.0	0.0	0.0	58.7	69.7	17.3	62.6	117	73.5
Lake Forest Park city	12,602	13,504	7.2	13,430	78.8	1.2	7.7	6.3	6.0	21.0	18.6	43.9	13.8	60.1	5,274	97.5
Lake Goodwin CDP	-	-	-	3,775	90.3	0.7	0.6	1.5	6.8	11.6	18.4	49.4	36.5	19.3	1,549	98.7
Lake Holm CDP	3,221	-	-	3,331	86.9	0.0	7.0	3.2	2.9	14.5	21.1	51.1	30.9	37.5	1,256	97.1
Lake Ketchum CDP	930	-	-	889	82.5	0.0	0.0	1.3	16.2	27.6	26.5	41.4	30.4	19.3	335	100.0
Lakeland North CDP	12,942	-	-	12,867	57.7	7.0	13.0	7.2	15.1	21.5	14.8	38.6	36.8	26.5	4,332	97.3
Lakeland South CDP	11,574	-	-	13,434	69.1	3.7	6.2	11.2	9.7	22.9	13.0	39.7	35.2	25.5	4,610	95.5
Lake McMurray CDP	192	-	-	154	96.1	3.9	0.0	0.0	0.0	5.8	39.6	62.6	51.1	16.5	66	100.0
Lake Marcel-Stillwater CDP	1,277	-	-	1,360	91.3	0.0	0.0	1.7	7.0	15.9	21.8	47.9	4.9	51.8	536	100.0
Lake Morton-Berrydale CDP	10,160	-	-	11,001	78.6	0.9	2.7	5.1	12.6	22.4	15.9	42.7	30.7	30.8	3,893	97.8
Lake Roesiger CDP	503	-	-	648	85.2	0.0	0.0	12.2	2.6	9.6	21.0	47.7	37.7	20.4	289	100.0
Lake Shore CDP	6,571	-	-	7,599	82.2	1.0	1.7	2.9	12.1	25.8	19.4	40.5	28.8	37.5	2,501	96.5
Lake Stevens city	28,108	33,911	20.6	32,487	76.6	2.1	3.8	5.6	11.9	28.0	9.6	34.7	31.3	30.4	11,186	96.7
Lake Stickney CDP	7,777	-	-	10,230	40.7	11.1	26.6	4.2	17.4	26.2	8.1	33.0	30.3	32.3	3,618	96.0
Lake Tapps CDP	11,859	-	-	12,838	85.3	0.6	2.8	5.0	6.4	24.4	12.4	41.2	29.0	35.1	4,509	97.9
Lakeview CDP	915	-	-	1,044	85.8	0.0	0.0	0.0	14.2	28.4	35.8	45.2	44.2	15.7	464	79.5
Lakewood city	57,532	61,037	6.1	60,111	50.5	12.2	8.6	11.9	16.9	21.2	15.4	35.7	39.6	22.6	24,725	92.2
Lamont town	70	74	5.7	57	87.7	0.0	0.0	0.0	12.3	26.3	19.3	54.4	45.2	16.7	24	58.3
Langley city	1,015	1,140	12.3	1,094	91.8	0.0	2.7	3.4	2.1	13.8	48.6	64.3	17.6	47.7	593	93.3
Larch Way CDP	3,318	-	-	3,851	41.9	3.9	37.9	4.6	11.6	17.8	12.4	39.1	21.9	49.6	1,440	98.8
Latah town	180	187	3.9	146	95.2	0.0	0.0	4.1	0.7	30.1	19.2	41.5	51.0	15.0	57	93.0
Laurier CDP	1	-	-	-	-	-	-	-	-	-	-	-	-	-	-	-
Leavenworth city	1,972	2,029	2.9	2,375	85.2	0.8	4.9	0.6	8.5	23.3	20.8	38.6	30.5	42.4	1,051	93.0
Lebam CDP	160	-	-	87	87.4	0.0	0.0	12.6	0.0	8.0	40.2	61.2	82.5	0.0	63	90.5
Lewisville CDP	1,722	-	-	1,721	88.8	0.0	1.3	0.0	9.9	24.0	24.6	48.3	31.2	28.8	549	98.4
Liberty Lake city	7,594	10,956	44.3	9,836	89.7	0.0	3.5	4.1	2.7	26.3	13.9	37.8	19.7	44.4	4,253	95.3
Lind town	562	563	0.2	571	85.3	0.0	0.0	11.4	3.3	23.8	11.6	32.7	52.8	11.5	200	84.5
Lochsloy CDP	2,533	-	-	2,973	83.0	0.3	1.1	12.7	2.9	17.6	14.1	45.6	41.0	14.9	1,008	95.4
Lofall CDP	2,289	-	-	1,973	91.4	2.2	0.0	2.7	3.6	14.7	19.0	54.3	20.6	43.7	867	95.7
Long Beach city	1,399	1,496	6.9	1,468	84.3	0.3	0.7	4.0	10.8	14.4	29.2	52.2	46.4	14.0	740	85.5
Longbranch CDP	3,784	-	-	3,974	83.2	0.5	3.0	11.6	1.7	25.5	24.8	38.0	28.7	25.2	1,484	90.0
Longview city	36,833	38,440	4.4	37,520	78.7	1.2	1.8	7.2	11.0	21.0	21.2	41.1	43.0	16.0	16,097	88.8
Longview Heights CDP	3,851	-	-	3,803	82.5	0.0	1.2	5.0	11.4	22.1	14.2	38.7	30.8	23.9	1,441	96.9
Loomis CDP	159	-	-	107	72.0	0.0	0.0	0.0	28.0	11.2	48.6	59.8	61.7	9.9	33	100.0
Loon Lake CDP	783	-	-	780	88.6	0.0	0.5	5.6	5.3	14.1	35.4	59.5	39.8	23.4	350	86.9
Lower Elochoman CDP	185	-	-	297	90.9	9.1	0.0	0.0	0.0	31.3	19.5	43.1	51.0	10.3	104	100.0
Lyle CDP	499	-	-	464	64.2	0.0	0.0	0.0	35.8	14.2	26.9	40.6	46.1	25.9	226	69.9
Lyman town	439	473	7.7	437	93.8	0.5	0.0	4.1	1.6	21.1	8.5	41.4	45.5	10.6	169	97.0
Lynden city	12,006	15,223	26.8	14,281	82.0	0.9	2.4	4.3	10.3	26.9	20.3	39.2	37.2	24.0	5,362	87.8
Lynnwood city	35,857	39,141	9.2	38,143	53.1	7.8	17.9	7.5	13.7	20.6	16.5	40.2	30.9	30.2	14,515	92.8
Mabton city	2,284	2,268	-0.7	2,087	5.0	0.0	1.0	0.3	93.8	36.7	13.0	25.7	83.3	2.2	528	77.7
McChord AFB CDP	2,507	-	-	3,381	52.2	6.2	5.5	10.2	25.9	33.8	0.4	22.7	23.2	27.4	827	100.0
McCleary city	1,652	1,764	6.8	2,061	81.8	1.2	2.5	3.6	11.0	25.2	17.1	37.3	44.4	14.7	777	82.9
Machias CDP	1,178	-	-	981	90.5	0.0	3.0	0.8	5.7	16.1	10.0	46.2	37.9	16.2	383	97.9
McKenna CDP	716	-	-	892	65.6	1.2	0.0	6.7	26.5	40.4	16.1	29.6	65.7	10.7	272	77.6
McMillin CDP	1,547	-	-	1,551	82.3	0.0	2.1	12.4	3.2	13.6	24.0	50.2	35.3	19.6	610	98.2
Malden town	203	206	1.5	293	94.5	0.0	0.0	5.5	0.0	24.9	18.1	43.4	50.8	11.6	110	92.7
Malo CDP	28	-	-	50	24.0	0.0	76.0	0.0	0.0	60.0	0.0	14.5	100.0	0.0	12	100.0
Malone CDP	475	-	-	524	89.3	0.0	0.0	0.0	10.7	38.7	12.4	42.3	43.9	26.5	164	100.0
Malott CDP	487	-	-	840	54.5	0.8	0.0	1.2	43.5	37.9	5.7	27.1	56.3	7.9	203	89.2
Maltby CDP	10,830	-	-	11,972	82.2	0.9	5.3	5.1	6.4	19.9	13.0	44.9	25.0	42.2	4,122	97.4
Manchester CDP	5,413	-	-	5,673	81.9	1.2	2.4	8.1	6.4	24.9	14.9	38.5	34.9	27.8	2,077	95.3
Mansfield town	320	343	7.2	343	94.2	0.0	0.3	1.7	3.8	12.2	28.3	47.7	37.9	22.4	182	89.0
Manson CDP	1,468	-	-	1,336	55.1	0.0	0.0	0.5	44.4	19.3	22.0	52.3	61.7	19.5	577	98.3
Maple Falls CDP	324	-	-	146	100.0	0.0	0.0	0.0	0.0	8.2	41.8	60.3	32.1	11.2	89	100.0
Maple Heights-Lake Desire CDP	3,152	-	-	3,641	77.4	3.3	16.5	2.0	0.8	23.5	18.3	46.5	21.9	49.4	1,350	97.0
Maple Valley city	22,722	27,202	19.7	26,352	78.6	0.9	6.4	8.3	5.8	32.7	8.3	35.2	18.5	44.4	8,666	98.2
Maplewood CDP	5,138	-	-	5,072	91.4	0.3	6.5	1.1	0.7	16.3	30.4	53.0	27.2	40.2	2,067	97.8
Marblemount CDP	203	-	-	68	100.0	0.0	0.0	0.0	0.0	58.8	0.0	10.5	0.0	0.0	15	100.0
Marcus town	171	172	0.6	113	87.6	0.0	0.0	7.1	5.3	3.5	41.6	61.9	50.0	11.3	60	70.0
Marietta-Alderwood CDP	3,906	-	-	4,086	71.4	0.7	0.0	9.0	18.9	21.2	15.4	41.7	30.9	22.9	1,815	88.9
Markham CDP	111	-	-	140	100.0	0.0	0.0	0.0	0.0	44.3	0.0	33.4	26.9	0.0	37	100.0
Marrowstone CDP	844	-	-	831	100.0	0.0	0.0	0.0	0.0	15.3	40.8	62.1	11.1	71.6	424	87.7
Martha Lake CDP	15,473	-	-	21,129	67.2	1.6	16.6	5.9	8.7	24.7	10.8	34.2	24.9	40.8	7,206	97.6
Maryhill CDP	58	-	-	62	24.2	0.0	0.0	0.0	75.8	25.8	24.2	44.2	100.0	0.0	35	57.1
Marysville city	60,013	70,298	17.1	68,633	73.1	1.2	6.1	7.5	12.1	24.8	12.7	35.7	39.1	20.6	24,610	95.0
Mattawa city	4,459	4,758	6.7	4,715	0.9	0.0	0.0	0.0	99.1	40.4	2.4	23.4	92.8	3.3	982	81.3
May Creek CDP	818	-	-	766	89.9	0.0	0.0	1.6	8.5	0.0	23.6	60.4	51.3	16.1	423	100.0
Mead CDP	7,275	-	-	7,114	90.6	0.1	0.2	2.0	7.0	22.2	19.7	46.1	28.1	31.6	2,793	95.3
Meadowdale CDP	2,826	-	-	3,151	76.5	3.5	8.9	5.4	5.7	17.0	14.6	41.3	29.2	33.3	1,030	97.3
Meadow Glade CDP	2,541	-	-	2,859	87.6	0.8	4.7	5.8	1.2	27.4	20.7	43.4	28.2	38.0	902	98.8
Medical Lake city	5,060	4,966	-1.9	4,938	86.9	0.3	1.7	9.0	2.1	27.5	10.9	32.4	31.3	30.8	1,769	95.3
Medina city	2,969	3,288	10.7	3,267	66.4	1.1	24.0	4.9	3.6	25.8	18.2	46.8	7.0	80.0	1,195	96.1
Mercer Island city	22,699	25,894	14.1	25,675	71.7	1.1	19.3	4.6	3.3	23.2	20.4	46.0	7.9	78.2	10,199	95.4
Mesa city	495	508	2.6	543	17.1	0.0	2.8	1.8	78.3	41.3	3.5	21.7	68.3	8.5	134	81.3
Metaline town	173	183	5.8	105	91.4	0.0	0.0	5.7	2.9	21.9	34.3	52.1	46.2	23.1	47	80.9

1 May be of any race.

Table A. All Places — **Population and Housing**

STATE City, town, township, borough, or CDP (county if applicable)	Population 2010 census total population	2019 estimated population	Percent change 2010–2019	ACS total population estimate 2015–2019	White alone, not Hispanic or Latino	Black alone, not Hispanic or Latino	Asian alone, not Hispanic or Latino	All other races or 2 or more races, not Hispanic or Latino	Hispanic or Latino[1]	Under 18 years old	Age 65 years and older	Median age	Percent High school diploma or less	Percent Bachelor's degree or more	Occupied housing units Total	Percent with a computer
	1	2	3	4	5	6	7	8	9	10	11	12	13	14	15	16
WASHINGTON—Con.																
Metaline Falls town	238	251	5.5	208	93.3	0.0	0.0	1.9	4.8	12.0	34.1	59.5	43.3	15.7	127	82.7
Methow CDP	68	-	-	122	97.5	0.0	0.0	0.0	2.5	31.1	4.9	38.1	72.6	15.5	40	100.0
Midland CDP	8,962	-	-	10,005	49.1	7.4	4.9	9.1	29.4	24.8	11.8	35.4	68.4	6.2	3,506	87.8
Mill Creek city	18,230	20,897	14.6	20,553	64.5	3.4	19.0	7.2	5.8	21.8	15.8	38.3	16.8	51.5	8,362	97.0
Mill Creek East CDP	15,709	-	-	24,291	59.8	1.3	24.7	5.7	8.5	31.1	6.1	35.1	17.9	52.1	7,610	98.7
Millwood city	1,786	1,800	0.8	1,629	92.3	0.4	0.7	3.4	3.1	20.4	16.6	44.0	38.1	22.2	758	92.7
Milton city	7,351	8,299	12.9	7,715	78.3	2.0	4.4	5.5	9.7	19.5	17.3	38.8	47.1	21.8	3,172	92.1
Mineral CDP	202	-	-	205	82.9	0.0	0.0	17.1	0.0	7.3	24.9	61.5	83.2	16.8	179	43.6
Minnehaha CDP	9,771	-	-	12,353	74.8	3.1	2.3	6.5	13.3	21.5	12.8	35.9	33.6	22.9	4,052	93.4
Mirrormont CDP	3,659	-	-	3,780	88.6	0.2	4.5	3.4	3.3	21.2	17.4	44.8	17.2	55.6	1,327	98.0
Moclips CDP	207	-	-	47	100.0	0.0	0.0	0.0	0.0	0.0	0.0	0.0	100.0	0.0	47	100.0
Monroe city	17,345	19,776	14.0	18,865	66.1	4.2	2.6	8.1	19.0	23.5	7.8	34.0	38.3	22.1	5,266	96.0
Monroe North CDP	1,666	-	-	1,738	82.5	0.0	1.0	1.9	14.7	33.6	18.6	38.4	24.5	42.2	586	95.2
Montesano city	3,986	4,052	1.7	3,957	83.8	0.2	2.9	10.0	3.1	25.7	20.6	43.4	32.5	24.3	1,461	94.5
Morton city	1,125	1,199	6.6	1,013	80.9	0.0	0.0	10.7	8.4	23.8	25.4	45.4	43.4	13.8	384	85.7
Moses Lake city	20,365	24,086	18.3	23,056	55.3	1.4	1.7	2.6	39.0	28.0	14.0	32.2	45.3	21.6	8,185	91.1
Moses Lake North CDP	4,418	-	-	4,526	53.2	5.1	0.8	3.0	38.0	25.9	10.7	28.5	52.0	10.0	1,319	88.6
Mossyrock city	760	820	7.9	684	49.7	0.0	0.0	7.6	42.7	29.8	17.4	32.4	67.5	2.4	289	81.0
Mountlake Terrace city	19,882	21,338	7.3	21,210	61.7	7.4	13.5	6.8	10.6	19.9	12.6	37.3	25.1	36.2	8,557	95.9
Mount Vernon city	31,724	36,006	13.5	35,026	56.9	1.0	3.0	4.8	34.3	25.7	17.2	35.3	41.4	21.9	12,396	92.7
Mount Vista CDP	7,850	-	-	9,544	86.3	0.7	4.5	4.8	3.8	21.5	18.2	40.8	19.5	41.3	3,817	98.1
Moxee city	3,459	4,104	18.6	4,012	40.4	2.3	1.2	5.0	51.1	36.7	4.3	28.3	55.4	19.5	1,063	97.4
Mukilteo city	20,249	21,441	5.9	21,336	67.1	1.7	19.7	5.3	6.1	21.6	16.1	44.4	21.0	52.7	8,176	96.8
Naches town	828	847	2.3	627	88.2	3.0	0.0	1.0	7.8	14.7	24.9	53.4	44.0	19.2	296	92.6
Napavine city	1,794	2,001	11.5	1,753	91.2	0.0	0.0	5.1	3.7	27.3	10.7	34.3	45.8	13.7	659	93.5
Naselle CDP	419	-	-	421	88.8	0.0	0.0	11.2	0.0	27.8	16.2	42.5	33.8	14.7	183	79.8
Navy Yard City CDP	2,477	-	-	3,064	76.0	2.4	1.3	12.3	8.0	17.7	12.8	33.5	36.1	11.5	1,162	94.1
Neah Bay CDP	865	-	-	1,049	6.9	0.0	0.0	86.3	6.9	34.0	10.9	27.6	48.4	9.9	323	83.6
Neilton CDP	315	-	-	281	95.0	0.0	0.0	0.0	5.0	18.5	33.1	47.1	65.5	1.5	109	78.9
Nespelem town	232	392	69.0	196	7.1	0.0	0.0	92.9	0.0	18.4	7.1	34.0	44.7	1.5	88	81.8
Nespelem Community CDP	253	-	-	180	7.8	0.0	0.0	92.2	0.0	18.9	11.7	40.6	50.5	4.5	72	84.7
Newcastle city	10,368	12,292	18.6	11,750	54.2	3.1	32.9	4.9	4.9	21.8	11.9	39.0	12.0	70.0	4,504	97.3
Newport city	2,157	2,199	1.9	2,071	92.2	2.3	0.0	3.4	2.2	20.0	28.9	51.6	42.8	15.4	911	90.3
Nile CDP	140	-	-	73	100.0	0.0	0.0	0.0	0.0	24.7	37.0	36.0	16.4	0.0	36	75.0
Nisqually Indian Community CDP	575	-	-	631	20.0	1.4	1.0	68.0	9.7	28.1	13.9	35.6	47.7	17.7	203	88.7
Nooksack city	1,330	1,631	22.6	1,724	74.4	0.5	0.0	2.1	23.1	36.9	8.9	27.9	47.7	19.3	487	94.0
Normandy Park city	6,336	6,604	4.2	6,670	85.0	0.6	8.1	0.6	5.8	17.2	27.0	51.9	20.4	52.1	2,969	91.2
North Bend city	5,850	7,423	26.9	6,983	81.0	1.2	2.5	2.0	13.3	23.9	13.0	39.7	21.5	48.4	2,600	97.6
North Bonneville city	958	1,007	5.1	1,126	88.7	0.0	0.9	3.4	7.0	16.6	15.9	43.7	33.1	23.8	473	84.1
North Fort Lewis CDP	2,699	-	-	6,355	47.9	18.6	6.0	8.8	18.8	25.4	0.0	23.4	20.1	21.6	1,024	100.0
North Lynnwood CDP	16,574	-	-	23,620	45.7	6.0	19.1	9.5	19.7	21.8	7.5	32.4	31.4	35.6	8,867	98.3
North Marysville CDP	108	-	-	142	90.1	0.0	0.0	0.0	9.9	0.0	7.7	48.8	82.4	17.6	61	82.0
North Omak CDP	688	-	-	437	15.3	0.0	5.5	79.2	0.0	15.1	24.9	32.4	57.7	12.6	238	68.5
Northport town	299	301	0.7	363	91.7	0.0	0.0	8.0	0.3	19.0	22.3	48.1	61.6	8.6	171	72.5
North Puyallup CDP	1,743	-	-	1,930	80.3	2.0	1.9	7.8	8.0	10.1	26.8	48.5	45.7	10.4	915	87.7
North Sultan CDP	264	-	-	237	100.0	0.0	0.0	0.0	0.0	8.4	27.4	41.7	45.4	23.7	82	90.2
Northwest Stanwood CDP	149	-	-	126	99.2	0.0	0.0	0.8	0.0	19.0	42.1	52.3	51.0	1.0	39	61.5
North Yelm CDP	2,906	-	-	3,365	85.2	0.2	1.8	9.9	2.9	16.4	18.5	39.5	48.5	11.9	1,349	90.3
Oakesdale town	422	439	4.0	458	96.9	1.1	0.0	2.0	0.0	22.9	20.5	45.1	30.4	25.4	163	85.9
Oak Harbor city	22,154	23,565	6.4	23,089	59.5	7.3	10.6	8.5	14.1	27.3	11.4	29.7	29.7	23.6	9,296	96.1
Oakville city	688	692	0.6	561	73.3	0.9	0.0	15.9	10.0	23.5	22.5	44.1	54.3	11.6	226	88.5
Ocean City CDP	200	-	-	213	100.0	0.0	0.0	0.0	0.0	23.5	0.0	56.4	8.6	48.5	115	100.0
Ocean Park CDP	1,573	-	-	1,745	81.6	0.0	3.1	2.0	13.3	9.2	40.7	59.7	42.2	23.5	771	85.1
Ocean Shores city	5,571	6,494	16.6	5,975	83.1	0.1	4.1	9.0	3.7	9.3	40.9	62.0	35.3	19.7	3,126	90.9
Odessa town	914	894	-2.2	988	82.0	3.6	1.7	7.9	4.8	19.0	27.7	53.7	41.0	16.7	453	85.0
Okanogan city	2,607	2,588	-0.7	2,587	65.4	0.7	2.0	6.2	25.7	24.6	13.6	37.2	53.5	15.2	1,044	90.7
Olympia city	46,884	52,882	12.8	51,534	75.9	2.6	7.0	5.7	8.9	18.0	17.5	38.4	23.9	43.6	22,409	92.8
Omak city	4,790	4,778	-0.3	4,774	61.1	0.0	0.0	18.9	20.1	28.4	16.5	35.2	55.6	9.0	2,000	84.9
Onalaska CDP	621	-	-	544	88.6	0.0	0.0	11.4	0.0	17.5	16.9	39.9	32.7	5.7	187	94.7
Orchards CDP	19,556	-	-	24,335	76.6	1.3	6.4	6.7	9.0	27.1	9.5	33.8	37.9	21.5	8,360	97.1
Orient CDP	115	-	-	82	78.0	0.0	0.0	22.0	0.0	17.1	43.9	59.4	60.3	7.4	51	58.8
Oroville city	1,709	1,675	-2.0	2,036	56.0	0.0	0.4	8.8	34.7	25.9	16.5	37.6	68.2	5.8	887	78.1
Orting city	6,737	8,610	27.8	8,012	80.4	1.5	0.9	8.8	8.4	26.2	11.9	35.2	47.6	18.1	2,572	96.0
Oso CDP	180	-	-	326	100.0	0.0	0.0	0.0	0.0	35.0	28.8	39.6	36.8	26.4	105	100.0
Othello city	7,339	8,386	14.3	8,100	18.3	0.2	1.3	0.4	79.8	36.1	8.7	25.8	66.9	11.3	2,395	83.3
Otis Orchards-East Farms CDP	6,220	-	-	6,466	92.5	0.0	0.6	1.7	5.2	25.3	15.4	41.4	32.3	20.4	2,305	97.4
Outlook CDP	292	-	-	48	0.0	0.0	0.0	0.0	100.0	33.3	0.0	20.4	0.0	100.0	14	100.0
Oyehut CDP	85	-	-	-	-	-	-	-	-	-	-	-	-	-	-	-
Pacific city	6,605	7,178	8.7	7,215	46.1	4.3	15.0	11.6	22.9	26.9	9.5	30.9	43.8	17.6	2,355	90.1
Pacific Beach CDP	291	-	-	278	68.3	0.0	12.6	19.1	0.0	16.9	13.3	31.8	50.0	32.5	89	100.0
Packwood CDP	342	-	-	315	89.2	0.0	0.0	10.8	0.0	11.4	52.4	66.3	50.2	10.0	168	85.7
Palouse city	994	1,075	8.1	1,028	84.1	1.3	3.5	4.4	6.7	18.0	22.1	49.9	22.7	46.4	482	98.8
Parker CDP	154	-	-	74	23.0	0.0	0.0	10.8	66.2	0.0	37.8	64.1	89.2	10.8	35	25.7
Parkland CDP	35,803	-	-	37,303	51.4	12.0	6.9	14.0	15.7	23.2	11.4	32.5	45.4	17.0	13,565	93.7
Parkwood CDP	7,126	-	-	7,113	76.2	2.3	5.4	8.7	7.4	23.1	17.5	36.7	36.8	23.6	2,891	90.9
Pasco city	62,163	75,432	21.3	72,899	38.1	1.7	2.1	2.6	55.5	33.6	8.5	29.5	50.5	18.4	21,824	91.7
Pateros city	678	714	5.3	653	45.8	0.0	0.0	6.3	47.9	33.4	8.0	28.3	62.6	15.4	227	78.4
Peaceful Valley CDP	3,324	-	-	4,123	78.9	0.0	1.7	4.0	15.4	26.3	12.8	33.8	62.0	6.8	1,525	85.1
Pe Ell town	632	675	6.8	555	88.3	0.0	0.0	6.5	5.2	24.7	17.7	38.9	41.9	12.5	220	92.7
Picnic Point CDP	8,809	-	-	9,064	72.1	3.4	14.6	6.5	3.5	18.7	14.1	43.6	26.1	36.4	3,462	95.5
Pine Grove CDP	145	-	-	158	100.0	0.0	0.0	0.0	0.0	22.8	22.2	45.2	39.3	0.0	55	80.0
Point Roberts CDP	1,314	-	-	1,116	87.5	0.0	2.5	2.3	7.7	10.1	33.1	57.7	28.5	38.4	643	93.5
Pomeroy city	1,431	1,395	-2.5	1,263	86.2	0.0	2.9	7.6	3.3	24.5	28.9	46.3	35.7	21.5	570	90.0
Port Angeles city	19,040	20,229	6.2	19,832	82.3	1.3	2.4	7.4	6.6	21.2	21.3	38.9	35.9	26.0	8,783	86.6
Port Angeles East CDP	3,036	-	-	3,231	92.1	1.4	0.0	1.8	4.7	18.0	24.5	49.4	39.0	15.3	1,385	92.9
Porter CDP	207	-	-	122	100.0	0.0	0.0	0.0	0.0	12.3	47.5	64.7	34.6	55.1	48	100.0
Port Gamble Tribal Community CDP	916	-	-	914	36.5	0.1	0.1	58.0	5.3	25.3	17.1	42.6	36.8	34.4	349	95.4

1 May be of any race.

Table A. All Places — **Population and Housing**

STATE City, town, township, borough, or CDP (county if applicable)	Population				Race and Hispanic or Latino origin (percent)					Age (percent)			Educational attainment of persons age 25 and older		Occupied housing units	
	2010 census total population	2019 estimated population	Percent change 2010–2019	ACS total population estimate 2015–2019	White alone, not Hispanic or Latino	Black alone, not Hispanic or Latino	Asian alone, not Hispanic or Latino	All other races or 2 or more races, not Hispanic or Latino	Hispanic or Latino[1]	Under 18 years old	Age 65 years and older	Median age	Percent High school diploma or less	Percent Bachelor's degree or more	Total	Percent with a computer
	1	2	3	4	5	6	7	8	9	10	11	12	13	14	15	16
WASHINGTON—Con.																
Port Hadlock-Irondale CDP	3,580	-	-	3,219	85.8	0.3	1.4	9.6	3.0	17.9	25.3	49.5	40.6	21.9	1,477	87.7
Port Ludlow CDP	2,603	-	-	2,828	92.2	0.0	0.8	1.8	5.3	6.7	55.7	67.6	13.9	46.3	1,424	94.0
Port Orchard city	12,195	14,597	19.7	14,062	67.9	3.5	6.4	10.8	11.3	22.1	14.9	35.7	33.6	27.1	5,175	93.8
Port Townsend city	9,112	9,831	7.9	9,551	89.7	0.6	2.2	3.1	4.4	15.7	31.1	53.9	19.9	58.3	4,682	89.6
Poulsbo city	9,237	11,168	20.9	10,602	78.9	1.3	3.9	5.9	10.0	21.4	21.6	42.5	23.0	41.3	4,451	94.3
Prairie Heights CDP	4,405	-	-	4,187	80.4	0.2	0.6	2.8	16.0	26.6	9.8	35.0	42.6	19.8	1,333	96.3
Prairie Ridge CDP	11,464	-	-	11,994	83.3	0.2	0.7	8.3	7.5	24.5	8.7	37.9	42.3	16.8	4,082	95.7
Prescott city	306	305	-0.3	328	74.7	0.0	0.0	3.4	22.0	27.7	14.0	34.3	46.6	6.9	133	85.7
Prosser city	5,748	6,380	11.0	6,202	48.7	0.6	2.3	2.0	46.4	29.0	17.5	37.2	47.2	26.9	2,534	87.6
Puget Island CDP	831	-	-	1,118	85.1	0.0	1.9	6.4	6.7	19.6	34.3	58.9	37.7	22.4	443	97.7
Pullman city	29,820	34,506	15.7	33,598	71.8	3.0	12.0	5.5	7.6	12.9	5.6	22.2	10.6	65.0	11,642	97.3
Purdy CDP	1,544	-	-	1,439	77.2	0.0	2.7	2.6	17.5	15.4	31.0	45.9	34.9	28.9	590	94.6
Puyallup city	37,241	42,361	13.7	40,991	77.7	2.5	5.1	7.0	7.7	20.6	16.1	39.9	35.1	27.5	16,428	91.9
Queets CDP	174	-	-	192	0.5	4.2	0.0	95.3	0.0	35.9	15.1	29.4	67.3	0.0	48	75.0
Quilcene CDP	596	-	-	697	93.4	0.0	4.7	1.9	0.0	18.8	21.1	41.1	55.8	21.0	259	90.7
Qui-nai-elt Village CDP	54	-	-	50	10.0	0.0	0.0	64.0	26.0	30.0	16.0	55.5	31.4	2.9	16	100.0
Quincy city	6,758	8,033	18.9	7,646	19.5	0.0	0.2	0.0	80.3	37.4	5.9	24.3	72.8	10.3	1,885	91.2
Raft Island CDP	459	-	-	434	100.0	0.0	0.0	0.0	0.0	12.2	38.9	57.2	10.3	67.4	195	100.0
Rainier city	1,787	2,287	28.0	2,385	77.6	5.4	2.4	7.9	6.8	27.5	13.8	37.2	47.3	16.0	811	91.4
Ravensdale CDP	1,101	-	-	1,773	87.0	0.0	2.3	10.2	0.6	24.9	10.7	41.0	38.4	27.1	672	77.5
Raymond city	2,869	2,994	4.4	2,918	71.7	0.0	7.9	5.7	14.6	13.0	25.7	49.5	49.0	16.2	1,179	83.6
Reardan town	571	610	6.8	446	83.0	0.0	0.0	2.2	14.8	23.1	23.1	50.5	34.2	21.5	216	87.5
Redmond city	54,511	71,929	32.0	65,558	50.8	1.6	36.4	4.4	6.8	22.4	10.8	34.5	11.1	71.8	26,437	97.6
Renton city	91,912	101,751	10.7	101,484	44.5	9.1	24.1	7.7	14.6	22.1	11.2	36.2	31.5	36.5	39,246	95.3
Republic city	1,066	1,066	0.0	1,182	81.5	0.8	0.3	13.9	3.6	21.2	24.7	45.2	45.1	23.8	526	81.0
Richland city	48,491	58,225	20.1	56,399	78.0	1.9	4.3	4.4	11.4	24.1	16.2	36.9	23.5	43.0	22,263	95.2
Ridgefield city	4,781	9,153	91.4	7,767	87.8	1.8	4.8	3.4	2.2	32.5	10.4	35.1	23.2	32.3	2,553	98.3
Ritzville city	1,684	1,654	-1.8	1,680	82.3	1.5	1.8	5.4	9.0	20.6	19.4	44.7	47.4	19.9	765	87.2
Riverbend CDP	2,132	-	-	2,562	96.2	0.0	0.8	0.8	2.2	20.3	8.2	41.9	25.2	31.9	964	100.0
River Road CDP	454	-	-	694	66.7	0.0	0.0	2.2	31.1	16.1	29.7	54.1	33.2	25.2	244	100.0
Riverside town	280	273	-2.5	287	76.0	0.0	0.0	20.2	3.8	28.2	13.2	38.2	48.3	13.9	130	88.5
Rochester CDP	2,388	-	-	3,126	81.3	0.0	0.0	3.7	15.0	27.6	12.8	37.3	35.7	15.2	1,075	95.9
Rockford town	473	486	2.7	405	93.6	0.0	0.0	5.7	0.7	21.0	21.0	52.3	33.2	12.6	169	93.5
Rock Island city	875	1,124	28.5	953	48.9	0.0	0.0	1.4	49.7	30.1	12.8	31.3	72.8	3.8	342	83.0
Rockport CDP	109	-	-	40	100.0	0.0	0.0	0.0	0.0	0.0	0.0	62.8	40.0	0.0	32	100.0
Rocky Point CDP	1,564	-	-	1,596	81.3	0.7	3.9	2.9	11.2	15.7	19.6	50.7	25.6	26.5	700	98.6
Ronald CDP	308	-	-	103	100.0	0.0	0.0	0.0	0.0	0.0	13.6	26.0	44.6	15.2	51	100.0
Roosevelt CDP	156	-	-	117	40.2	0.0	0.0	0.0	59.8	16.2	15.4	43.6	58.7	21.3	43	74.4
Rosalia town	549	558	1.6	608	85.5	0.0	1.0	4.3	9.2	21.7	18.9	46.1	39.9	21.7	243	85.2
Rosburg CDP	317	-	-	416	80.5	4.1	1.9	7.0	6.5	22.6	20.7	51.4	32.4	29.4	167	94.6
Rosedale CDP	4,044	-	-	4,472	79.9	1.9	2.6	10.3	5.3	18.3	17.1	42.4	26.3	34.4	1,238	94.7
Roslyn city	893	958	7.3	539	96.7	0.0	1.5	1.1	0.7	18.4	36.4	47.9	58.5	21.9	277	84.8
Roy city	780	822	5.4	779	86.0	0.0	2.2	8.0	3.9	22.1	16.9	40.6	37.7	12.0	321	87.2
Royal City city	2,140	2,237	4.5	1,687	7.2	0.0	0.0	0.0	92.8	34.6	4.0	25.1	83.7	4.6	439	85.2
Ruston town	749	845	12.8	1,156	84.3	0.6	4.2	5.4	5.5	20.7	17.2	43.1	24.5	46.4	490	97.3
Ryderwood CDP	395	-	-	503	100.0	0.0	0.0	0.0	0.0	0.0	85.3	72.6	39.6	15.3	322	66.1
St. John town	543	559	2.9	627	88.8	2.6	0.8	3.0	4.8	25.7	21.1	52.2	34.3	25.1	271	82.7
Salmon Creek CDP	19,686	-	-	20,956	82.2	2.2	3.3	4.9	7.4	22.7	17.5	43.0	24.4	36.9	8,004	96.6
Sammamish city	57,449	65,892	14.7	64,674	59.0	1.3	31.7	4.1	3.9	30.0	8.0	38.7	8.6	75.2	21,515	99.4
Santiago CDP	42	-	-	32	31.3	0.0	0.0	68.8	0.0	25.0	6.3	47.3	23.8	0.0	11	81.8
Satsop CDP	675	-	-	646	96.4	0.0	0.0	3.6	0.0	22.6	22.1	45.1	35.9	10.0	246	94.7
Seabeck CDP	1,105	-	-	885	94.2	0.0	0.0	5.8	0.0	13.4	34.2	59.0	31.0	45.4	434	83.6
SeaTac city	26,903	29,044	8.0	29,019	32.1	24.7	14.0	11.8	17.3	23.5	12.0	35.3	41.0	22.5	9,747	94.3
Seattle city	608,661	753,675	23.8	724,305	63.8	7.2	15.3	7.0	6.7	15.0	12.4	35.3	14.7	64.0	331,836	95.1
Sedro-Woolley city	11,076	12,072	9.0	11,739	74.8	1.1	1.3	4.3	18.5	26.1	13.0	33.2	44.6	18.9	3,964	91.3
Sekiu CDP	27	-	-	62	100.0	0.0	0.0	0.0	0.0	30.6	0.0	40.4	0.0	100.0	21	100.0
Selah city	7,347	8,087	10.1	7,856	75.2	0.9	0.7	3.0	20.2	28.9	11.4	33.1	38.4	27.0	2,935	92.9
Sequim city	6,573	7,640	16.2	7,248	79.8	1.7	3.7	8.3	6.5	14.4	36.6	56.5	33.2	28.1	3,508	84.2
Shadow Lake CDP	2,262	-	-	2,434	85.0	1.2	4.4	7.1	2.3	18.5	17.7	51.2	25.5	33.0	913	92.7
Shelton city	9,845	10,655	8.2	10,167	70.0	0.7	0.6	7.4	21.3	25.9	15.5	36.0	49.2	12.4	3,547	83.9
Shoreline city	53,031	57,027	7.5	56,267	64.1	6.0	15.5	6.4	8.0	19.1	18.4	41.8	21.6	48.9	22,068	95.4
Silvana CDP	90	-	-	14	100.0	0.0	0.0	0.0	0.0	0.0	100.0	0.0	0.0	0.0	14	0.0
Silverdale CDP	19,204	-	-	21,677	67.4	5.1	10.9	8.3	8.4	20.9	14.9	36.0	25.6	33.6	8,735	95.1
Silver Firs CDP	20,891	-	-	22,358	68.0	3.0	15.0	6.5	7.4	29.4	7.6	36.8	18.7	47.9	7,012	98.9
Sisco Heights CDP	2,696	-	-	2,754	88.7	0.8	1.5	5.5	3.5	22.5	11.7	42.6	35.8	23.7	904	96.8
Skamokawa Valley CDP	401	-	-	325	85.5	0.0	7.7	6.8	0.0	0.0	39.4	59.3	15.5	35.5	194	77.3
Skokomish CDP	617	-	-	609	15.8	0.5	0.2	79.1	4.4	29.7	8.2	25.0	53.1	9.8	150	84.0
Skykomish town	197	220	11.7	121	89.3	7.4	0.0	3.3	0.0	6.6	33.1	58.5	43.4	27.4	66	87.9
Snohomish city	9,145	10,154	11.0	9,976	83.5	0.4	2.9	6.5	6.7	23.7	14.4	37.1	36.8	23.9	4,012	90.1
Snoqualmie city	10,665	13,622	27.7	13,480	79.3	0.6	11.3	5.1	3.7	33.4	6.6	35.0	11.3	65.8	4,361	98.1
Snoqualmie Pass CDP	311	-	-	332	77.7	15.7	1.2	0.0	5.4	11.1	11.7	48.1	11.9	40.9	133	94.7
Soap Lake city	1,542	1,603	4.0	1,551	64.4	0.8	0.1	4.3	30.3	23.9	26.8	42.5	49.7	9.3	610	74.8
South Bend city	1,633	1,698	4.0	1,500	56.0	0.4	2.1	13.8	27.7	18.7	22.5	43.8	44.3	17.6	588	89.8
South Cle Elum town	530	559	5.5	653	100.0	0.0	0.0	0.0	0.0	20.2	17.5	36.5	39.4	15.7	270	92.2
South Creek CDP	2,507	-	-	2,636	90.2	2.0	0.0	3.5	4.3	18.2	11.1	45.3	41.1	12.6	1,102	95.1
South Hill CDP	52,431	-	-	60,172	67.3	3.6	6.8	9.9	12.4	28.2	11.3	34.6	32.3	27.9	19,800	96.2
South Prairie town	427	443	3.7	325	82.8	0.0	1.2	8.9	7.1	20.0	15.4	49.7	56.6	9.9	126	95.2
South Wenatchee CDP	1,553	-	-	1,821	26.9	0.0	0.0	0.0	73.1	25.0	11.3	36.5	74.3	11.0	554	77.1
Southworth CDP	2,185	-	-	2,224	87.1	0.1	1.8	5.6	5.4	17.8	19.5	48.4	35.0	30.5	898	92.1
Spanaway CDP	27,227	-	-	32,575	54.4	11.5	6.1	15.4	12.5	25.8	10.9	33.8	45.1	13.9	11,151	95.4
Spangle city	278	319	14.7	198	97.0	0.0	0.0	2.0	1.0	24.2	24.7	42.8	45.7	20.0	89	97.8
Spokane city	209,455	222,081	6.0	217,353	81.3	2.2	2.7	7.4	6.3	21.5	15.3	36.2	30.0	31.3	91,328	91.7
Spokane Valley city	89,745	101,060	12.6	97,562	86.0	1.1	1.5	4.9	6.4	22.1	16.6	37.9	34.5	23.4	40,762	91.2
Sprague city	446	460	3.1	484	85.7	0.0	0.0	7.4	6.8	21.7	26.7	44.5	49.4	13.6	203	91.1
Springdale town	281	300	6.8	392	84.7	0.0	0.0	7.4	7.9	25.5	16.1	37.5	50.2	3.7	143	90.9
Stansberry Lake CDP	2,101	-	-	2,634	87.8	1.5	0.0	4.5	6.2	35.1	13.4	32.6	25.2	18.8	759	96.0
Stanwood city	6,240	7,287	16.8	7,068	90.1	0.2	1.3	3.9	4.4	31.5	12.7	33.0	33.3	22.2	2,542	91.9
Starbuck town	126	128	1.6	137	87.6	2.2	0.0	10.2	0.0	0.0	46.0	64.2	41.0	5.2	91	70.3
Startup CDP	676	-	-	573	85.5	0.0	0.0	6.6	7.9	12.6	2.8	42.4	58.8	20.3	296	91.2
Steilacoom town	5,992	6,390	6.6	6,303	64.1	5.5	6.9	11.7	11.9	19.1	20.6	42.0	20.1	43.2	2,495	96.6
Steptoe CDP	180	-	-	190	96.3	0.0	0.0	0.0	3.7	6.8	26.3	55.8	41.3	8.4	98	94.9

1 May be of any race.

Table A. All Places — **Population and Housing**

STATE City, town, township, borough, or CDP (county if applicable)	Population 2010 census total population	2019 estimated population	Percent change 2010–2019	ACS total population estimate 2015–2019	Race and Hispanic or Latino origin (percent) White alone, not Hispanic or Latino	Black alone, not Hispanic or Latino	Asian alone, not Hispanic or Latino	All other races or 2 or more races, not Hispanic or Latino	Hispanic or Latino[1]	Age (percent) Under 18 years old	Age 65 years and older	Median age	Educational attainment of persons age 25 and older Percent High school diploma or less	Percent Bachelor's degree or more	Occupied housing units Total	Percent with a computer
	1	2	3	4	5	6	7	8	9	10	11	12	13	14	15	16
WASHINGTON—Con.																
Stevenson city	1,473	1,601	8.7	1,530	90.8	0.1	0.8	1.8	6.5	16.9	17.8	44.1	45.3	20.9	654	75.4
Sudden Valley CDP	6,441	-	-	8,072	82.9	0.6	2.8	4.8	8.9	23.4	22.6	42.6	19.7	46.4	3,024	98.1
Sultan city	4,650	5,388	15.9	5,166	78.9	0.2	1.9	5.4	13.6	24.6	9.2	37.4	44.9	15.9	1,907	92.9
Sumas city	1,307	1,534	17.4	1,703	72.6	1.3	1.5	10.3	14.3	29.4	10.5	31.1	41.0	14.0	611	91.2
Summit CDP	7,985	-	-	8,946	79.0	2.8	2.5	5.1	10.6	20.9	20.1	44.2	41.6	22.6	3,169	91.2
Summit View CDP	7,236	-	-	8,475	72.8	4.3	3.9	10.2	8.8	22.9	8.3	33.0	40.3	23.4	3,275	98.9
Summitview CDP	967	-	-	960	65.8	0.0	0.0	0.0	34.2	20.2	29.7	53.7	31.0	41.1	394	87.6
Sumner city	9,447	10,427	10.4	10,053	76.4	1.3	2.1	7.0	13.2	23.2	15.3	34.8	37.8	28.7	4,064	94.0
Sunday Lake CDP	640	-	-	613	93.5	0.0	0.0	0.0	6.5	13.2	25.4	54.2	27.5	33.5	254	87.8
Sunnyside city	15,934	16,796	5.4	16,559	13.4	0.1	0.4	0.7	85.3	38.7	8.3	25.4	70.8	6.5	4,561	92.7
Sunnyslope CDP	3,252	-	-	3,704	89.2	0.0	0.0	0.5	10.3	24.2	22.7	47.1	23.2	44.9	1,407	98.6
Suquamish CDP	4,140	-	-	4,395	71.9	0.2	2.3	18.3	7.3	19.9	22.8	45.6	28.5	34.0	1,930	95.9
Swede Heaven CDP	768	-	-	1,297	92.1	0.0	1.3	6.6	0.0	20.1	9.0	44.4	48.8	16.3	466	94.8
Tacoma city	198,247	217,827	9.9	212,869	58.5	10.2	8.6	10.7	12.0	21.6	13.0	35.7	36.5	29.7	83,688	91.7
Taholah CDP	840	-	-	665	5.9	0.0	0.0	82.9	11.3	26.5	16.2	30.7	55.2	9.7	212	85.4
Tampico CDP	312	-	-	84	100.0	0.0	0.0	0.0	0.0	0.0	21.4	34.9	45.2	0.0	55	67.3
Tanglewilde CDP	5,892	-	-	7,270	61.3	6.3	10.6	10.5	11.3	27.8	13.2	34.4	30.1	25.4	2,430	90.4
Tanner CDP	1,018	-	-	985	90.6	0.0	2.3	3.9	3.2	21.5	13.2	39.9	7.5	69.6	352	96.9
Tekoa city	781	799	2.3	731	93.7	0.0	0.0	2.6	3.7	21.9	23.5	48.2	45.0	23.1	276	97.1
Tenino city	1,685	1,865	10.7	1,716	83.9	0.4	0.7	7.7	7.3	23.2	14.6	35.8	40.8	12.5	695	86.3
Terrace Heights CDP	6,937	-	-	8,507	76.6	2.0	2.2	1.2	18.0	23.5	19.4	39.6	34.6	29.6	3,374	89.5
Thorp CDP	240	-	-	241	99.2	0.0	0.0	0.0	0.8	10.8	25.7	49.7	36.4	25.5	104	92.3
Three Lakes CDP	3,184	-	-	3,480	94.6	0.3	2.4	0.7	2.0	20.8	14.5	45.1	26.4	34.2	1,157	98.8
Tieton city	1,182	1,308	10.7	1,686	12.9	0.0	0.5	1.6	85.0	37.4	4.5	27.5	77.2	4.0	425	91.5
Tokeland CDP	151	-	-	200	77.0	0.0	0.0	23.0	0.0	13.5	35.0	56.1	44.0	12.5	80	97.5
Toledo city	721	771	6.9	654	81.5	0.0	2.1	8.0	8.4	20.0	11.6	39.5	41.8	21.5	281	91.8
Tonasket city	1,143	1,121	-1.9	1,214	70.2	0.0	0.0	16.6	13.2	24.5	22.0	38.5	54.0	9.5	537	84.5
Toppenish city	8,933	8,809	-1.4	8,873	9.0	0.1	0.4	3.8	86.6	33.6	8.5	27.8	70.1	7.3	2,448	86.0
Torboy CDP	49	-	-	105	60.0	0.0	0.0	40.0	0.0	28.6	0.0	35.9	53.3	0.0	29	69.0
Touchet CDP	421	-	-	449	76.8	0.0	0.0	0.7	22.5	23.8	9.1	38.4	24.2	12.1	171	98.2
Town and Country CDP	4,857	-	-	5,090	88.2	1.2	0.8	4.9	5.0	24.0	16.1	38.9	27.2	26.4	2,078	96.4
Tracyton CDP	5,233	-	-	5,556	59.5	5.7	8.7	16.7	9.3	21.5	16.2	37.7	32.5	22.8	2,203	94.5
Trout Lake CDP	557	-	-	624	83.5	0.0	1.0	10.3	5.3	20.5	27.4	52.2	20.8	46.6	205	96.6
Tukwila city	19,107	20,347	6.5	20,196	33.8	17.0	24.7	10.6	14.0	22.1	10.6	35.0	45.7	24.0	7,150	94.5
Tumwater city	20,167	24,024	19.1	22,974	82.1	2.2	3.1	5.8	6.9	20.3	14.3	37.2	21.2	39.8	9,568	92.6
Twin Lakes CDP	59	-	-	69	56.5	0.0	0.0	43.5	0.0	0.0	60.9	67.4	71.4	6.3	37	64.9
Twisp town	901	963	6.9	982	96.3	0.0	0.0	1.7	1.9	16.6	20.5	48.7	40.2	22.2	477	85.1
Union CDP	631	-	-	428	79.2	0.0	0.0	20.8	0.0	8.9	36.2	59.8	25.9	22.8	221	92.8
Union Gap city	6,127	6,200	1.2	6,163	40.7	0.0	0.5	2.3	56.5	27.8	13.1	34.0	73.4	7.2	2,081	83.5
Union Hill-Novelty Hill CDP	18,805	-	-	21,992	66.5	1.1	24.5	3.7	4.2	26.0	19.1	43.1	9.8	70.5	8,012	98.8
Uniontown town	294	344	17.0	306	100.0	0.0	0.0	0.0	0.0	30.4	8.8	34.7	21.4	39.6	111	89.2
University Place city	31,133	34,001	9.2	33,326	65.8	7.3	10.5	9.4	7.0	23.2	16.7	37.3	22.8	40.7	13,318	93.6
Upper Elochoman CDP	193	-	-	85	100.0	0.0	0.0	0.0	0.0	0.0	18.8	54.5	42.9	0.0	42	100.0
Vader city	622	670	7.7	880	75.0	0.0	0.0	4.2	20.8	26.6	20.2	30.0	50.9	4.6	265	84.5
Valley CDP	146	-	-	104	71.2	23.1	0.0	5.8	0.0	35.6	26.9	54.3	26.9	0.0	38	100.0
Vancouver city	167,159	184,463	10.4	180,556	71.5	2.1	5.4	7.1	13.9	22.2	15.9	36.9	33.9	29.2	72,508	93.3
Vantage CDP	74	-	-	22	100.0	0.0	0.0	0.0	0.0	0.0	0.0	0.0	100.0	0.0	10	100.0
Vashon CDP	10,624	-	-	10,291	91.9	0.1	1.3	1.9	4.9	16.3	28.6	54.2	18.5	52.8	4,664	95.5
Vaughn CDP	544	-	-	697	81.3	0.1	0.0	8.0	10.5	12.3	27.8	50.4	16.5	27.0	289	96.9
Venersborg CDP	3,745	-	-	4,227	91.2	0.9	1.8	3.1	3.1	27.8	16.8	39.9	27.2	33.9	1,344	98.2
Verlot CDP	285	-	-	651	53.9	0.0	0.0	0.0	46.1	27.0	19.2	40.7	40.4	28.0	163	66.3
Waitsburg city	1,215	1,231	1.3	1,243	92.1	0.0	0.4	3.1	4.4	22.7	17.9	41.6	33.4	22.6	494	92.9
Walla Walla city	32,445	32,900	1.4	32,793	68.2	1.9	2.3	4.4	23.2	20.0	16.9	35.7	33.3	26.0	12,377	91.1
Walla Walla East CDP	1,672	-	-	2,015	86.1	3.0	0.0	1.3	9.6	22.5	23.2	45.7	28.9	39.7	848	83.3
Waller CDP	7,922	-	-	7,647	79.7	1.8	5.1	6.6	6.8	19.4	20.8	46.9	38.0	25.1	3,033	94.8
Wallula CDP	179	-	-	342	20.8	0.0	0.0	0.0	79.2	52.3	10.5	17.5	75.5	4.9	79	100.0
Wapato city	5,016	5,010	-0.1	5,041	6.1	0.0	1.0	14.2	78.7	35.1	7.9	25.8	81.5	4.0	1,279	86.8
Warden city	2,692	2,812	4.5	2,756	14.8	0.0	1.6	4.5	79.1	32.7	7.8	28.2	70.6	10.1	816	86.0
Warm Beach CDP	2,437	-	-	2,603	89.0	0.0	4.5	2.7	3.8	22.3	22.4	51.0	26.3	36.0	974	94.1
Washougal city	14,161	16,107	13.7	15,769	83.7	1.8	3.5	4.1	6.8	25.7	14.2	39.4	29.3	32.1	5,815	97.0
Washtucna town	208	208	0.0	195	88.7	0.0	1.0	5.1	5.1	28.7	19.5	49.6	55.4	15.4	76	84.2
Waterville town	1,138	1,213	6.6	1,513	83.7	0.0	0.5	4.5	11.4	21.2	14.2	43.5	47.9	24.7	607	98.0
Wauna CDP	4,186	-	-	4,294	84.0	1.7	3.1	8.0	3.2	16.8	21.7	47.7	30.2	36.0	1,640	96.3
Waverly town	106	109	2.8	107	88.8	0.0	1.9	9.3	0.0	28.0	14.0	42.5	25.0	23.3	40	87.5
Wenatchee city	32,784	34,360	4.8	34,188	59.8	1.1	0.6	4.7	33.9	24.6	16.4	35.5	45.4	22.7	12,744	89.0
West Clarkston-Highland CDP	5,261	-	-	5,830	88.9	1.7	0.1	5.1	4.3	22.5	23.6	45.0	39.1	16.6	2,409	90.2
West Pasco CDP	3,739	-	-	1,731	60.9	6.6	1.2	6.2	25.1	27.6	17.5	33.3	33.6	32.9	474	95.8
Westport city	2,077	2,100	1.1	1,817	90.3	0.1	0.8	4.6	4.3	15.1	20.5	49.7	40.9	19.1	844	87.7
West Richland city	11,833	15,075	27.4	14,495	79.8	1.1	1.6	4.8	12.6	32.4	10.4	36.6	24.1	39.6	4,746	97.6
West Side Highway CDP	5,517	-	-	6,089	84.0	0.0	1.2	6.0	8.8	27.8	15.8	32.6	33.2	20.1	2,115	94.5
Whidbey Island Station CDP	1,541	-	-	2,371	58.3	18.4	1.8	2.6	18.9	1.8	0.0	22.6	29.5	17.4	105	100.0
White Center CDP	13,495	-	-	15,834	39.1	10.6	15.5	10.4	24.5	23.8	10.8	35.2	46.0	24.3	5,854	91.0
White Salmon city	2,344	2,691	14.8	2,554	76.8	0.0	0.0	2.7	20.4	21.9	23.7	44.7	33.7	47.0	1,172	88.3
White Swan CDP	793	-	-	851	3.8	0.0	0.0	82.6	13.6	37.5	4.2	23.8	60.2	4.8	174	82.8
Wilbur town	871	861	-1.1	779	89.6	0.5	2.3	7.1	0.5	20.5	28.1	47.1	39.0	25.4	348	94.0
Wilderness Rim CDP	1,523	-	-	1,633	83.6	6.1	1.4	6.2	2.6	18.6	15.6	37.4	26.3	41.0	601	100.0
Wilkeson town	482	514	6.6	516	97.7	0.2	0.0	2.1	0.0	26.6	12.6	34.0	50.9	9.8	187	96.8
Willapa CDP	210	-	-	160	96.3	3.8	0.0	0.0	0.0	15.0	34.4	57.7	37.7	13.8	83	81.9
Wilson Creek town	205	215	4.9	188	91.5	0.0	0.0	1.6	6.9	19.1	23.9	53.5	58.2	8.2	91	94.5
Winlock city	1,358	1,428	5.2	1,791	67.7	0.0	3.5	7.1	21.7	27.5	11.8	31.3	41.8	14.6	593	90.9
Winthrop town	403	472	17.1	386	72.0	0.0	0.0	3.4	24.6	20.7	17.6	46.2	41.2	37.5	198	72.7
Wishram CDP	342	-	-	529	82.0	0.0	0.2	15.9	1.9	21.4	15.7	45.6	59.0	7.1	184	71.2
Wollochet CDP	6,651	-	-	6,365	84.7	1.4	4.6	5.4	3.9	21.1	29.1	49.1	20.3	47.3	2,653	98.5
Woodinville city	10,941	13,263	21.2	12,383	77.8	1.1	10.8	4.6	5.7	23.3	14.2	37.6	16.5	56.9	5,094	93.7
Woodland city	5,540	6,495	17.2	6,071	84.6	1.2	0.3	1.7	12.2	32.4	15.6	33.6	42.0	13.5	2,038	95.3
Woods Creek CDP	5,589	-	-	5,706	87.6	0.0	0.9	7.1	4.3	25.4	13.3	40.1	34.2	23.3	1,928	95.7
Woodway city	1,307	1,391	6.4	1,105	85.4	0.0	11.2	1.8	1.5	22.9	22.6	49.3	9.9	68.6	421	98.1
Yacolt town	1,576	1,796	14.0	1,590	94.5	0.6	0.1	1.9	2.9	34.1	6.2	27.1	50.3	9.2	490	93.1
Yakima city	91,273	93,637	2.6	93,413	47.9	1.4	1.3	3.6	45.7	27.6	15.0	33.8	51.4	19.0	33,772	86.7

1 May be of any race.

Table A. All Places — **Population and Housing**

STATE City, town, township, borough, or CDP (county if applicable)	Population				Race and Hispanic or Latino origin (percent)					Age (percent)			Educational attainment of persons age 25 and older		Occupied housing units	
	2010 census total population	2019 estimated population	Percent change 2010–2019	ACS total population estimate 2015–2019	White alone, not Hispanic or Latino	Black alone, not Hispanic or Latino	Asian alone, not Hispanic or Latino	All other races or 2 or more races, not Hispanic or Latino	Hispanic or Latino[1]	Under 18 years old	Age 65 years and older	Median age	Percent High school diploma or less	Percent Bachelor's degree or more	Total	Percent with a computer
	1	2	3	4	5	6	7	8	9	10	11	12	13	14	15	16
WASHINGTON—Con.																
Yarrow Point town	1,001	1,149	14.8	1,202	75.4	0.0	18.0	5.5	1.2	24.6	19.4	50.0	5.0	84.2	417	98.3
Yelm city	6,817	9,456	38.7	8,985	76.5	0.5	1.2	10.9	11.0	34.7	6.4	28.5	27.8	21.2	2,746	94.2
Zillah city	3,020	3,140	4.0	3,116	57.8	0.0	0.0	8.6	33.6	23.2	16.2	39.4	53.4	16.5	1,144	84.1
WEST VIRGINIA	1,853,018	1,792,147	-3.3	1,817,305	92.0	3.6	0.8	2.0	1.6	20.3	19.4	42.5	53.4	20.6	732,585	84.2
Accoville CDP	574	-	-	980	98.7	0.0	0.0	1.3	0.0	25.5	5.6	34.5	61.6	4.4	328	100.0
Addison (Webster Springs) town	776	663	-14.6	806	98.3	0.0	0.0	1.7	0.0	17.4	20.8	39.8	56.8	13.8	412	73.8
Albright town	281	282	0.4	333	100.0	0.0	0.0	0.0	0.0	22.2	12.0	32.7	84.4	5.4	113	89.4
Alderson town	1,184	1,125	-5.0	1,135	87.4	4.0	0.0	7.4	1.2	21.1	23.4	42.1	49.7	15.5	510	90.4
Alum Creek CDP	1,749	-	-	1,805	97.0	0.0	0.0	3.0	0.0	19.4	14.1	41.8	37.4	25.3	796	87.1
Amherstdale CDP	350	-	-	519	100.0	0.0	0.0	0.0	0.0	16.8	7.9	30.8	84.0	7.7	207	83.1
Anawalt town	224	179	-20.1	140	92.9	7.1	0.0	0.0	0.0	18.6	29.3	46.5	79.5	8.0	63	76.2
Anmoore town	774	734	-5.2	660	90.6	6.2	0.0	2.7	0.5	30.3	12.6	33.8	66.6	4.6	275	91.6
Ansted town	1,406	1,305	-7.2	1,362	99.1	0.4	0.0	0.0	0.4	19.3	18.0	41.6	69.4	11.7	521	85.6
Apple Grove CDP	204	-	-	60	68.3	0.0	0.0	31.7	0.0	31.7	15.0	61.6	78.0	22.0	24	100.0
Arbovale CDP	-	-	-	152	100.0	0.0	0.0	0.0	0.0	12.5	45.4	63.2	63.9	19.5	97	90.7
Athens town	1,042	897	-13.9	1,149	87.8	8.4	1.2	1.0	1.6	9.5	13.1	22.1	23.1	50.1	280	88.2
Auburn town	97	88	-9.3	110	100.0	0.0	0.0	0.0	0.0	29.1	12.7	37.5	79.7	0.0	42	76.2
Aurora CDP	201	-	-	206	100.0	0.0	0.0	0.0	0.0	39.3	20.9	37.1	52.8	19.2	68	91.2
Bancroft town	587	591	0.7	464	98.9	0.0	0.0	1.1	0.0	14.2	32.5	49.9	81.7	5.4	210	77.1
Barboursville village	3,976	4,258	7.1	4,268	90.4	6.3	1.4	0.3	1.6	17.8	14.8	37.5	45.6	27.1	1,646	86.3
Barrackville town	1,293	1,279	-1.1	1,291	92.2	3.4	0.0	0.8	3.6	18.8	19.1	40.5	46.9	26.6	528	91.1
Bartley CDP	224	-	-	-	-	-	-	-	-	-	-	-	-	-	-	-
Bartow CDP	111	-	-	118	92.4	0.0	7.6	0.0	0.0	31.4	24.6	31.3	76.5	12.3	42	76.2
Bath (Berkeley Springs) town	624	596	-4.5	792	89.3	0.5	0.0	1.5	8.7	33.7	20.5	37.9	47.2	21.1	340	90.3
Bayard town	290	261	-10.0	217	90.3	9.7	0.0	0.0	0.0	6.0	22.6	45.3	76.3	5.6	92	79.3
Beards Fork CDP	199	-	-	173	22.0	78.0	0.0	0.0	0.0	17.3	26.6	53.9	48.3	5.6	73	100.0
Beaver CDP	1,308	-	-	1,314	88.8	0.0	0.0	11.2	0.0	10.1	23.2	48.8	54.3	13.6	580	70.3
Beckley city	17,609	15,940	-9.5	16,452	72.6	21.3	2.0	2.9	1.2	19.4	20.2	41.6	46.4	22.8	7,315	81.1
Beech Bottom village	522	469	-10.2	605	95.4	1.2	1.0	2.5	0.0	28.9	17.5	38.8	61.1	10.1	231	81.8
Belington town	1,921	1,902		2,108	98.0	0.0	0.0	1.3	0.7	29.7	16.2	35.8	69.2	9.6	725	82.3
Belle town	1,260	1,126	-10.6	1,163	97.6	0.0	0.0	0.7	1.7	20.1	20.7	40.8	50.1	25.6	545	89.5
Belmont city	900	862	-4.2	888	98.2	0.8	0.0	1.0	0.0	18.6	26.4	49.9	60.9	15.7	374	86.6
Belva CDP	95	-	-	53	100.0	0.0	0.0	0.0	0.0	0.0	66.0	66.5	66.0	0.0	26	100.0
Benwood city	1,430	1,278	-10.6	1,390	93.7	4.9	0.0	0.8	0.6	17.3	19.5	47.5	54.2	10.9	596	77.3
Bergoo CDP	94	-	-	54	100.0	0.0	0.0	0.0	0.0	20.4	27.8	53.1	100.0	0.0	29	79.3
Berwind CDP	278	-	-	384	100.0	0.0	0.0	0.0	0.0	28.1	17.7	49.2	76.4	6.6	136	89.0
Bethany town	1,036	802	-22.6	1,022	76.0	14.6	0.3	4.5	4.6	2.2	6.6	19.9	27.9	55.3	128	86.7
Bethlehem village	2,495	2,321	-7.0	2,461	97.4	0.1	1.1	1.2	0.2	19.2	20.2	43.4	23.6	41.9	1,058	90.6
Beverly town	701	666	-5.0	746	97.7	0.0	0.0	0.4	1.9	24.5	22.5	33.7	68.2	4.9	346	72.5
Big Chimney CDP	627	-	-	463	100.0	0.0	0.0	0.0	0.0	12.7	50.8	65.1	66.5	18.0	249	77.1
Big Creek CDP	237	-	-	84	100.0	0.0	0.0	0.0	0.0	33.3	0.0	26.8	100.0	0.0	26	57.7
Big Sandy CDP	168	-	-	139	67.6	32.4	0.0	0.0	0.0	0.0	79.9	68.6	63.3	0.0	65	100.0
Birch River CDP	107	-	-	136	100.0	0.0	0.0	0.0	0.0	37.5	4.4	26.7	100.0	0.0	32	100.0
Blacksville town	171	180	5.3	113	95.6	0.0	0.0	4.4	0.0	31.0	19.5	37.8	83.8	2.9	48	62.5
Blennerhassett CDP	3,089	-	-	3,330	97.1	0.4	0.0	0.0	2.5	21.7	20.7	40.3	40.5	22.4	1,183	94.1
Bluefield city	10,434	9,629	-7.7	9,889	67.8	25.9	0.1	4.5	1.6	19.5	20.9	43.4	48.4	24.8	4,365	80.4
Bluewell CDP	2,184	-	-	2,593	98.8	0.9	0.0	0.3	0.0	23.1	21.9	47.6	76.7	9.6	946	71.7
Boaz CDP	1,297	-	-	1,638	98.5	0.5	0.0	1.0	0.0	21.5	20.1	46.8	40.0	26.2	618	91.1
Bolivar town	1,038	1,022	-1.5	1,234	87.9	3.4	1.1	4.8	2.8	21.9	14.7	41.0	35.9	31.2	483	87.8
Bolt CDP	548	-	-	664	94.7	0.0	0.0	5.3	0.0	26.2	33.7	42.7	71.9	0.0	233	89.7
Boomer CDP	615	-	-	755	57.2	41.1	0.0	1.7	0.0	32.1	8.7	26.9	16.9	20.9	314	87.6
Bowden CDP	9	-	-	-	-	-	-	-	-	-	-	-	-	-	-	-
Bradley CDP	2,040	-	-	1,741	92.4	6.2	0.7	0.6	0.1	12.7	20.3	39.9	66.6	11.1	772	92.7
Bradshaw town	336	271	-19.3	212	93.9	0.0	0.0	3.3	2.8	25.0	33.5	49.5	76.6	5.8	84	71.4
Bramwell town	364	337	-7.4	312	88.1	8.7	0.3	1.9	1.0	16.3	32.1	53.6	50.4	22.8	127	75.6
Brandonville town	104	105	1.0	136	99.3	0.0	0.0	0.7	0.0	27.2	14.7	42.2	39.4	50.5	67	89.6
Brandywine CDP	218	-	-	142	100.0	0.0	0.0	0.0	0.0	10.6	18.3	54.7	82.1	0.0	108	50.0
Brenton CDP	249	-	-	169	100.0	0.0	0.0	0.0	0.0	0.0	33.1	55.4	57.4	0.0	87	51.7
Bridgeport city	8,116	8,842	8.9	8,556	93.5	0.9	3.3	1.2	1.1	20.5	20.9	45.4	22.0	56.1	3,450	91.2
Brookhaven CDP	5,171	-	-	6,043	95.3	1.4	0.6	1.4	1.2	23.3	12.0	37.1	40.3	40.1	2,052	92.7
Bruceton Mills town	85	84	-1.2	88	97.7	0.0	0.0	0.0	2.3	13.6	15.9	44.1	80.6	13.4	39	94.9
Bruno CDP	544	-	-	844	79.9	0.0	0.0	20.1	0.0	38.2	9.8	31.3	57.0	0.0	241	92.1
Brush Fork CDP	1,197	-	-	1,214	98.3	0.0	0.0	1.7	0.0	31.0	9.8	35.5	74.2	4.7	497	78.9
Buckhannon city	5,595	5,394	-3.6	5,486	88.6	7.7	0.5	1.1	2.1	14.5	18.0	35.2	49.0	24.7	2,083	88.7
Bud CDP	487	-	-	367	100.0	0.0	0.0	0.0	0.0	14.2	55.3	67.3	86.8	7.1	168	73.8
Buffalo town	1,236	1,260	1.9	1,176	99.2	0.0	0.0	0.8	0.0	24.9	21.4	44.1	64.4	10.4	448	83.3
Burlington CDP	182	-	-	123	96.7	3.3	0.0	0.0	0.0	35.0	31.7	36.0	70.0	18.8	38	65.8
Burnsville town	510	477	-6.5	542	98.9	0.0	0.0	0.0	1.1	27.5	21.6	35.2	61.9	14.2	204	88.7
Cairo town	281	254	-9.6	333	96.4	0.0	0.0	3.6	0.0	22.5	15.3	36.4	79.7	4.0	121	78.5
Camden-on-Gauley town	170	145	-14.7	182	98.9	1.1	0.0	0.0	0.0	18.7	11.0	36.7	72.7	15.6	86	66.3
Cameron city	943	843	-10.6	458	98.9	0.0	0.0	0.0	1.1	19.4	24.5	48.6	70.8	11.6	208	73.6
Capon Bridge town	357	366	2.5	463	94.6	0.0	0.0	3.2	2.2	35.4	8.9	31.1	62.3	11.3	159	79.2
Carolina CDP	411	-	-	451	63.6	22.8	0.0	13.5	0.0	12.0	17.1	46.9	71.8	12.4	209	95.7
Carpendale town	977	905	-7.4	748	97.6	2.4	0.0	0.0	0.0	18.7	22.3	42.8	51.1	11.6	339	82.0
Cass CDP	52	-	-	42	100.0	0.0	0.0	0.0	0.0	0.0	19.0	57.5	100.0	0.0	37	78.4
Cassville CDP	701	-	-	1,430	98.3	0.0	0.0	0.0	1.7	13.3	14.1	47.4	57.5	12.2	566	83.9
Cedar Grove town	997	907	-9.0	679	99.1	0.6	0.0	0.0	0.3	24.6	15.8	40.8	68.8	10.0	249	90.4
Century CDP	115	-	-	106	100.0	0.0	0.0	0.0	0.0	17.9	7.5	49.5	61.0	13.6	28	100.0
Ceredo city	1,400	1,273	-9.1	1,128	99.1	0.4	0.0	0.3	0.3	15.9	23.6	50.5	49.1	18.1	469	77.8
Chapmanville town	1,229	1,094	-11.0	1,154	98.0	1.2	0.0	0.8	0.0	22.0	29.4	44.4	62.8	16.0	554	72.7
Charleston city	51,340	46,536	-9.4	48,006	77.3	15.6	2.1	4.0	1.0	18.6	19.3	42.0	35.5	39.3	22,171	86.3
Charles Town city	5,229	6,029	15.3	5,943	71.1	10.5	2.1	5.4	10.9	26.7	15.1	38.3	36.4	35.2	2,234	90.0
Charlton Heights CDP	406	-	-	385	100.0	0.0	0.0	0.0	0.0	33.0	31.7	38.4	79.1	7.8	163	79.1
Chattaroy CDP	756	-	-	668	94.2	0.0	0.0	5.8	0.0	37.4	9.9	36.8	68.5	0.0	224	100.0
Chauncey CDP	283	-	-	422	100.0	0.0	0.0	0.0	0.0	20.1	5.9	26.3	32.7	12.7	160	84.4
Cheat Lake CDP	7,988	-	-	9,251	89.7	3.3	4.1	1.9	1.0	23.6	14.3	40.7	24.2	53.9	3,362	93.9
Chelyan CDP	776	-	-	994	94.7	0.0	0.0	5.3	0.0	19.4	6.7	27.3	89.5	3.5	285	86.0
Chesapeake town	1,554	1,414	-9.0	1,915	86.1	7.7	0.0	4.4	1.8	24.1	26.8	42.0	61.8	9.5	799	77.8

1 May be of any race.

Table A. All Places — **Population and Housing**

STATE City, town, township, borough, or CDP (county if applicable)	Population: 2010 census total population	Population: 2019 estimated population	Population: Percent change 2010–2019	Population: ACS total population estimate 2015–2019	Race and Hispanic or Latino origin (percent): White alone, not Hispanic or Latino	Black alone, not Hispanic or Latino	Asian alone, not Hispanic or Latino	All other races or 2 or more races, not Hispanic or Latino	Hispanic or Latino[1]	Age (percent): Under 18 years old	Age 65 years and older	Median age	Educational attainment of persons age 25 and older: Percent High school diploma or less	Percent Bachelor's degree or more	Occupied housing units: Total	Percent with a computer
	1	2	3	4	5	6	7	8	9	10	11	12	13	14	15	16
WEST VIRGINIA—Con.																
Chester city	2,581	2,369	-8.2	2,275	98.4	0.0	0.0	1.6	0.0	25.3	23.9	48.0	59.4	4.5	1,264	77.0
Clarksburg city	16,452	15,225	-7.5	15,553	90.8	3.0	0.3	3.9	2.0	23.0	16.8	38.1	50.8	20.3	6,154	85.7
Clay town	491	441	-10.2	706	100.0	0.0	0.0	0.0	0.0	39.2	10.5	28.0	80.1	5.9	239	85.4
Clearview village	524	482	-8.0	545	90.5	1.1	0.9	2.9	4.6	25.1	23.3	39.0	37.2	34.4	199	89.9
Clendenin town	1,227	1,100	-10.4	1,101	98.9	0.3	0.0	0.8	0.0	23.3	24.6	38.8	68.8	14.2	433	72.3
Coal City CDP	1,815	-	-	1,725	91.7	3.5	0.0	4.8	0.0	20.7	27.3	48.7	79.0	2.5	787	82.3
Coal Fork CDP	1,233	-	-	1,157	96.1	0.0	1.0	0.7	2.2	11.8	25.2	47.8	73.0	12.1	567	68.8
Comfort CDP	306	-	-	154	100.0	0.0	0.0	0.0	0.0	18.2	10.4	37.0	64.3	29.6	61	82.0
Corinne CDP	362	-	-	123	100.0	0.0	0.0	0.0	0.0	9.8	0.0	48.7	83.8	0.0	54	74.1
Covel CDP	142	-	-	30	100.0	0.0	0.0	0.0	0.0	0.0	50.0	0.0	100.0	0.0	15	100.0
Cowen town	533	468	-12.2	564	97.7	0.0	0.0	2.3	0.0	17.4	20.2	41.1	71.0	9.4	270	82.2
Crab Orchard CDP	2,678	-	-	2,579	97.0	0.7	0.5	1.8	0.0	24.6	14.3	38.6	48.4	18.8	1,049	80.7
Craigsville CDP	2,213	-	-	2,375	98.9	0.0	0.0	0.0	1.1	15.1	30.0	55.7	63.0	10.4	938	89.2
Cross Lanes CDP	9,995	-	-	9,274	86.1	4.6	1.8	3.4	4.0	22.9	15.3	39.6	38.7	33.5	3,862	91.1
Crum CDP	182	-	-	48	77.1	0.0	0.0	22.9	0.0	0.0	0.0	63.0	47.9	0.0	35	65.7
Crumpler CDP	204	-	-	133	100.0	0.0	0.0	0.0	0.0	25.6	18.8	46.1	72.7	9.1	66	77.3
Cucumber CDP	94	-	-	52	100.0	0.0	0.0	0.0	0.0	0.0	36.5	55.7	61.5	20.5	34	79.4
Culloden CDP	3,061	-	-	3,362	98.8	0.0	0.0	1.2	0.0	30.0	16.7	36.5	37.8	28.9	1,244	92.9
Dailey CDP	114	-	-	34	100.0	0.0	0.0	0.0	0.0	0.0	0.0	0.0	61.8	0.0	13	100.0
Daniels CDP	1,881	-	-	1,869	91.3	0.6	0.1	7.3	0.8	21.5	23.3	43.9	56.0	14.1	831	82.1
Danville town	691	602	-12.9	870	98.0	2.0	0.0	0.0	0.0	17.0	24.3	43.2	69.0	11.4	317	84.9
Davis town	660	631	-4.4	674	96.3	0.0	0.0	2.7	1.0	14.4	22.4	50.3	63.3	15.6	309	90.3
Davy town	423	337	-20.3	293	100.0	0.0	0.0	0.0	0.0	29.4	13.3	29.7	85.5	1.2	121	76.0
Deep Water CDP	280	-	-	313	85.0	15.0	0.0	0.0	0.0	26.8	31.0	44.3	81.1	7.5	81	100.0
Delbarton town	575	497	-13.6	537	94.0	1.5	0.0	4.5	0.0	18.8	19.0	46.4	63.7	8.8	217	85.3
Despard CDP	1,004	-	-	1,098	89.8	0.0	0.0	10.2	0.0	17.6	28.7	48.8	83.8	3.7	389	92.5
Dixie CDP	291	-	-	280	100.0	0.0	0.0	0.0	0.0	7.1	19.6	49.6	66.4	6.8	117	88.0
Dunbar city	7,902	7,093	-10.2	7,333	76.1	13.3	1.5	5.8	3.2	17.9	23.7	44.1	43.1	25.8	3,536	89.3
Durbin town	294	294	0.0	255	99.2	0.0	0.0	0.0	0.8	29.0	16.5	36.7	65.0	17.2	92	79.3
East Bank town	959	869	-9.4	891	95.1	3.7	0.0	0.6	0.7	17.1	22.8	44.9	64.1	10.5	308	90.9
East Dailey CDP	557	-	-	712	100.0	0.0	0.0	0.0	0.0	40.3	2.2	20.7	67.9	19.4	197	91.9
Eccles CDP	362	-	-	-	-	-	-	-	-	-	-	-	-	-	-	-
Eleanor town	1,518	1,587	4.5	1,380	96.0	0.0	0.0	0.8	3.2	21.7	20.9	45.1	43.4	15.8	592	85.0
Elizabeth town	823	838	1.8	719	96.8	0.7	0.0	0.0	2.5	29.8	16.8	40.3	57.1	12.3	338	71.9
Elk Garden town	228	212	-7.0	185	100.0	0.0	0.0	0.0	0.0	22.2	21.1	42.3	82.4	0.0	69	65.2
Elkins city	7,191	6,990	-2.8	7,072	91.3	3.3	2.0	2.2	1.2	24.5	17.1	35.0	48.9	30.2	2,744	85.5
Elkview CDP	1,222	-	-	1,673	88.4	0.0	3.5	4.1	4.0	20.6	19.7	46.6	77.1	5.5	754	72.9
Ellenboro town	362	363	0.3	217	100.0	0.0	0.0	0.0	0.0	15.2	23.0	56.1	66.1	8.8	99	73.7
Enterprise CDP	961	-	-	1,010	100.0	0.0	0.0	0.0	0.0	22.4	17.0	51.4	65.6	11.1	424	70.3
Fairlea CDP	1,747	-	-	1,567	96.7	3.3	0.0	0.0	0.0	22.0	22.7	43.7	56.7	13.1	632	89.2
Fairmont city	18,690	18,388	-1.6	18,458	88.2	6.9	0.8	3.2	0.9	19.9	18.2	33.8	43.4	29.1	7,574	87.2
Fairview town	408	404	-	374	88.0	0.0	0.0	12.0	0.0	27.8	29.9	40.8	69.6	8.7	132	75.0
Falling Spring town	211	202	-4.3	177	96.0	0.0	0.0	0.0	4.0	14.1	23.2	52.8	60.0	22.1	83	84.3
Falling Waters CDP	876	-	-	1,399	84.4	11.0	0.0	4.6	0.0	21.3	16.4	33.5	55.3	19.7	503	100.0
Falls View CDP	238	-	-	206	89.3	0.0	0.0	10.7	0.0	23.8	18.0	49.3	20.4	56.1	89	88.8
Farmington town	375	365	-2.7	445	97.3	1.6	0.7	0.0	0.4	23.6	20.9	39.3	62.4	9.1	169	84.0
Fayetteville town	2,962	2,720	-8.2	2,806	98.2	1.6	0.0	0.0	0.2	22.1	17.9	41.8	38.1	33.9	1,134	88.3
Fenwick CDP	116	-	-	158	100.0	0.0	0.0	0.0	0.0	12.0	3.2	46.3	100.0	0.0	54	100.0
Flatwoods town	277	265	-4.3	261	98.5	0.0	0.0	0.0	1.5	21.5	13.8	35.9	65.1	9.7	94	88.3
Flemington town	311	306	-1.6	333	99.4	0.0	0.0	0.0	0.6	20.4	22.8	45.7	56.0	20.9	122	74.6
Follansbee city	2,986	2,710	-9.2	2,768	95.8	0.0	0.0	2.7	1.5	18.9	23.7	44.9	44.1	19.0	1,304	91.1
Fort Ashby CDP	1,380	-	-	1,369	98.3	0.0	0.0	0.0	1.7	10.4	23.7	49.6	59.5	11.9	711	75.7
Fort Gay town	735	689	-6.3	891	94.2	0.0	0.0	2.0	3.8	28.3	13.8	35.7	82.7	3.4	355	68.5
Frank CDP	90	-	-	98	100.0	0.0	0.0	0.0	0.0	36.7	7.1	27.4	52.6	12.3	37	81.1
Franklin town	723	642	-11.2	622	92.0	6.6	0.0	1.4	0.0	18.5	27.2	47.6	62.0	18.1	272	73.2
Friendly town	132	121	-8.3	132	72.0	0.0	0.0	28.0	0.0	30.3	12.1	41.1	77.5	3.4	31	77.4
Gallipolis Ferry CDP	817	-	-	723	100.0	0.0	0.0	0.0	0.0	18.9	15.5	44.5	69.1	9.5	290	89.7
Galloway CDP	143	-	-	111	100.0	0.0	0.0	0.0	0.0	53.2	0.0	16.8	69.2	0.0	28	100.0
Gary city	970	788	-18.8	628	74.2	21.0	0.0	3.7	1.1	15.4	32.2	55.6	66.0	10.2	280	82.9
Gassaway town	908	846	-6.8	977	99.5	0.0	0.0	0.5	0.0	20.3	19.7	36.0	57.9	19.2	441	76.6
Gauley Bridge town	614	553	-9.9	858	98.3	1.7	0.0	0.0	0.0	27.2	10.3	27.8	75.8	13.1	321	85.7
Ghent CDP	457	-	-	536	100.0	0.0	0.0	0.0	0.0	10.6	4.5	52.0	45.8	29.9	213	88.7
Gilbert town	446	387	-13.2	364	100.0	0.0	0.0	0.0	0.0	14.0	27.5	54.8	51.7	20.0	193	88.1
Gilbert Creek CDP	1,090	-	-	1,193	98.4	0.0	1.6	0.0	0.0	9.0	23.8	55.0	74.1	16.7	513	74.1
Glasgow town	903	833	-7.8	768	98.2	0.8	0.0	1.0	0.0	20.8	36.6	51.6	55.3	16.2	297	82.8
Glen Dale city	1,526	1,371	-10.2	1,548	96.9	0.0	0.0	3.1	0.0	18.8	23.6	46.7	41.1	31.3	641	85.8
Glen Ferris CDP	203	-	-	117	100.0	0.0	0.0	0.0	0.0	11.1	54.7	66.2	0.0	44.2	58	77.6
Glen Fork CDP	487	-	-	396	100.0	0.0	0.0	0.0	0.0	30.1	3.3	31.0	66.7	0.0	132	89.4
Glen Jean CDP	210	-	-	197	41.6	58.4	0.0	0.0	0.0	0.0	23.4	52.9	100.0	0.0	52	100.0
Glenville town	1,543	1,434	-7.1	1,738	75.9	12.0	0.7	1.6	9.7	21.2	9.6	24.1	42.6	34.3	636	93.4
Glen White CDP	266	-	-	360	100.0	0.0	0.0	0.0	0.0	37.8	0.0	26.6	20.5	0.0	109	100.0
Grafton city	5,164	4,982	-3.5	5,061	93.6	0.8	1.0	3.5	1.1	19.1	20.7	44.4	59.3	17.1	2,133	82.2
Grantsville town	559	513	-8.2	495	90.9	0.6	0.0	4.8	3.6	26.7	26.3	36.1	65.6	13.6	191	69.1
Grant Town town	615	594	-3.4	527	87.7	8.2	0.0	0.0	4.2	21.6	22.2	36.7	68.5	8.5	223	76.2
Granville town	781	3,140	302.0	2,735	96.1	0.7	0.0	0.8	2.4	15.0	10.9	22.4	64.1	4.8	805	84.2
Great Cacapon CDP	386	-	-	465	98.5	0.0	0.0	1.5	0.0	26.9	23.0	53.7	74.1	0.0	179	96.1
Green Bank CDP	143	-	-	182	95.1	0.0	0.0	0.0	4.9	24.2	15.4	52.6	39.2	50.8	72	91.7
Green Spring CDP	218	-	-	160	100.0	0.0	0.0	0.0	0.0	8.1	36.9	42.9	60.2	11.7	91	68.1
Greenview CDP	378	-	-	444	100.0	0.0	0.0	0.0	0.0	30.0	2.3	27.1	59.8	0.0	149	88.6
Gypsy CDP	328	-	-	126	100.0	0.0	0.0	0.0	0.0	0.0	34.1	49.5	76.3	0.0	79	84.8
Hambleton town	230	214	-7.0	169	98.2	0.0	0.0	1.8	0.0	11.2	32.5	56.9	82.7	0.0	85	65.9
Hamlin town	1,140	1,048	-8.1	1,554	97.0	0.0	0.0	1.4	1.6	22.6	19.1	40.7	70.9	8.5	569	72.9
Handley town	349	312	-10.6	189	95.2	4.8	0.0	0.0	0.0	21.7	23.3	37.5	54.0	4.4	62	91.9
Harman town	142	139	-2.1	103	100.0	0.0	0.0	0.0	0.0	7.8	35.9	62.1	77.9	5.3	68	69.1
Harpers Ferry town	288	282	-2.1	233	89.3	2.6	0.0	4.3	3.9	21.5	22.3	49.7	39.2	49.4	99	89.9
Harrisville town	1,875	1,674	-10.7	2,111	99.4	0.0	0.0	0.0	0.6	19.3	28.7	50.8	62.5	13.4	958	76.6
Hartford City town	613	594	-3.1	660	93.3	0.0	0.0	6.7	0.0	26.7	13.2	41.3	71.6	6.8	283	77.4
Harts CDP	656	-	-	398	100.0	0.0	0.0	0.0	0.0	34.9	13.1	38.5	70.9	3.2	151	71.5
Hedgesville town	300	297	-	251	84.5	5.6	0.4	4.8	4.8	23.1	6.8	39.8	44.4	15.4	88	97.7
Helen CDP	219	-	-	14	100.0	0.0	0.0	0.0	0.0	0.0	100.0	0.0	100.0	0.0	14	100.0
Helvetia CDP	59	-	-	85	100.0	0.0	0.0	0.0	0.0	20.0	17.6	52.9	57.4	22.1	41	68.3
Henderson town	270	259	-4.1	345	100.0	0.0	0.0	0.0	0.0	25.8	12.8	30.7	75.7	11.9	114	80.7

1 May be of any race.

Table A. All Places — **Population and Housing**

STATE City, town, township, borough, or CDP (county if applicable)	Population: 2010 census total population	Population: 2019 estimated population	Population: Percent change 2010–2019	Population: ACS total population estimate 2015–2019	Race and Hispanic or Latino origin (percent): White alone, not Hispanic or Latino	Race: Black alone, not Hispanic or Latino	Race: Asian alone, not Hispanic or Latino	Race: All other races or 2 or more races, not Hispanic or Latino	Race: Hispanic or Latino[1]	Age (percent): Under 18 years old	Age: Age 65 years and older	Age: Median age	Educational attainment of persons age 25 and older: Percent High school diploma or less	Educational attainment: Percent Bachelor's degree or more	Occupied housing units: Total	Occupied housing units: Percent with a computer
	1	2	3	4	5	6	7	8	9	10	11	12	13	14	15	16
WEST VIRGINIA—Con.																
Hendricks town	274	257	-6.2	315	99.4	0.0	0.0	0.6	0.0	24.1	32.4	47.5	66.5	11.9	118	83.1
Henlawson CDP	442	-	-	90	100.0	0.0	0.0	0.0	0.0	0.0	27.8	56.1	100.0	0.0	47	46.8
Hepzibah CDP	566	-	-	518	78.2	12.9	0.0	0.0	8.9	18.3	34.7	37.7	64.9	10.5	231	94.8
Hico CDP	272	-	-	318	100.0	0.0	0.0	0.0	0.0	25.5	28.9	42.6	56.3	23.7	168	78.6
Hillsboro town	253	238	-5.9	148	100.0	0.0	0.0	0.0	0.0	19.6	28.4	50.0	63.2	5.3	71	59.2
Hilltop CDP	624	-	-	808	65.5	14.7	0.0	0.0	19.8	8.7	35.6	55.6	74.5	0.0	233	76.0
Hinton city	2,672	2,357	-11.8	2,785	86.4	9.0	0.0	2.7	2.0	22.4	23.1	41.0	60.2	10.8	1,299	77.2
Holden CDP	876	-	-	693	96.1	0.4	0.0	2.9	0.6	22.7	5.2	42.6	58.1	14.3	261	100.0
Hometown CDP	668	-	-	606	100.0	0.0	0.0	0.0	0.0	7.1	20.6	51.8	74.6	5.2	246	76.4
Hooverson Heights CDP	2,590	-	-	2,581	95.7	1.7	0.0	1.8	0.8	19.1	21.3	49.8	51.3	14.2	1,047	87.2
Hundred town	299	262	-12.4	278	100.0	0.0	0.0	0.0	0.0	2.9	15.8	53.2	79.4	4.9	137	62.0
Huntersville CDP	73	-	-	136	100.0	0.0	0.0	0.0	0.0	0.0	25.0	57.3	69.3	9.6	60	68.3
Huntington city	49,171	45,110	-8.3	46,667	84.3	8.3	1.6	3.9	1.9	18.4	15.4	35.3	43.0	27.3	19,268	84.9
Hurricane city	6,275	6,430	2.5	6,482	92.8	1.2	0.6	3.9	1.5	26.2	16.4	38.5	39.7	28.4	2,438	90.7
Huttonsville town	221	210	-5.0	237	97.9	0.8	0.0	1.3	0.0	36.7	11.4	35.2	59.0	7.2	73	89.0
Iaeger town	303	242	-20.1	264	100.0	0.0	0.0	0.0	0.0	22.7	23.1	45.9	82.5	1.6	109	84.4
Idamay CDP	611	-	-	616	93.0	0.0	0.0	0.0	7.0	20.6	8.4	38.9	44.0	15.8	270	100.0
Inwood CDP	2,954	-	-	3,330	90.7	3.7	0.6	2.5	2.5	26.7	16.7	38.1	54.8	16.0	1,256	91.7
Itmann CDP	293	-	-	258	100.0	0.0	0.0	0.0	0.0	5.4	18.6	50.8	89.5	0.0	115	58.3
Jacksonburg CDP	182	-	-	64	87.5	12.5	0.0	0.0	0.0	0.0	46.9	60.5	100.0	0.0	36	16.7
Jane Lew town	404	386	-4.5	428	94.9	0.0	3.0	0.7	1.4	26.2	18.7	41.3	53.2	15.8	182	83.0
Jefferson CDP	676	-	-	630	71.4	21.3	0.0	7.3	0.0	24.9	22.4	36.6	74.1	4.2	177	96.0
Junior town	520	486	-6.5	361	95.8	0.6	0.0	3.6	0.0	23.3	15.0	40.3	78.0	3.3	150	80.7
Justice CDP	412	-	-	654	100.0	0.0	0.0	0.0	0.0	27.1	16.4	45.1	63.6	10.6	261	84.7
Kenova city	3,247	2,961	-8.8	3,027	93.9	1.3	0.0	1.2	3.6	13.3	24.0	51.0	67.2	9.5	1,317	85.4
Kermit town	402	349	-13.2	315	99.0	0.0	0.0	1.0	0.0	20.3	13.0	49.3	61.1	9.4	148	84.5
Keyser city	5,423	4,915	-9.4	5,050	85.1	12.0	0.0	2.8	0.1	19.4	19.7	30.0	57.5	16.3	1,925	85.1
Keystone city	282	223	-20.9	99	34.3	65.7	0.0	0.0	0.0	24.2	19.2	45.3	67.7	9.7	48	47.9
Kimball town	194	153	-21.1	129	38.0	62.0	0.0	0.0	0.0	15.5	40.3	58.5	58.7	27.5	47	66.0
Kimberly CDP	287	-	-	127	45.7	21.3	0.0	33.1	0.0	0.0	34.6	40.8	85.9	14.1	27	100.0
Kincaid CDP	260	-	-	95	100.0	0.0	0.0	0.0	0.0	0.0	26.3	57.5	67.4	0.0	54	100.0
Kingwood city	3,055	3,057	0.1	3,056	95.2	3.0	0.0	0.4	1.4	25.1	21.7	39.3	54.0	25.0	1,196	82.9
Kistler CDP	528	-	-	230	63.5	36.5	0.0	0.0	0.0	3.9	47.0	59.8	51.1	0.0	161	79.5
Kopperston CDP	616	-	-	446	85.4	6.1	0.0	8.5	0.0	26.7	20.4	51.7	82.9	8.9	191	58.1
Lashmeet CDP	479	-	-	443	100.0	0.0	0.0	0.0	0.0	22.8	30.0	33.0	58.0	27.6	235	100.0
Lavalette CDP	1,073	-	-	1,356	86.9	1.7	0.4	11.0	0.0	44.4	7.9	35.6	44.2	44.4	361	89.8
Leon town	158	148	-6.3	219	99.1	0.0	0.0	0.0	0.9	24.2	7.8	30.0	95.1	0.8	77	74.0
Lesage CDP	1,358	-	-	778	100.0	0.0	0.0	0.0	0.0	6.9	32.0	53.9	66.2	7.1	403	83.9
Lester town	344	314	-8.7	454	86.8	9.5	0.0	3.5	0.2	31.1	17.4	33.6	64.2	13.6	159	82.4
Lewisburg city	3,836	3,807	-0.8	3,886	84.5	7.3	4.0	0.0	4.2	18.1	31.9	46.8	32.4	44.7	2,066	86.9
Littleton CDP	198	-	-	116	100.0	0.0	0.0	0.0	0.0	42.2	0.0	41.9	59.7	40.3	27	63.0
Logan city	1,782	1,470	-17.5	1,852	86.3	6.6	0.0	3.7	3.3	22.3	13.3	40.0	57.5	14.5	798	82.6
Lost Creek town	491	464	-5.5	481	94.4	1.0	0.0	0.8	3.7	24.7	18.7	42.1	61.6	16.3	174	90.2
Lubeck CDP	1,311	-	-	1,126	99.4	0.6	0.0	0.0	0.0	19.7	24.8	47.2	38.9	26.0	494	86.2
Lumberport town	873	840	-3.8	816	98.9	0.9	0.0	0.2	0.0	19.9	16.3	38.9	60.2	12.0	298	98.7
Mabscott town	1,408	1,263	-10.3	1,477	96.4	2.9	0.0	0.7	0.0	26.5	21.4	37.9	53.6	18.6	650	84.8
MacArthur CDP	1,500	-	-	1,680	77.4	1.9	0.0	7.0	13.7	27.3	12.6	35.2	56.9	8.7	701	92.3
McConnell CDP	514	-	-	616	100.0	0.0	0.0	0.0	0.0	13.0	27.1	52.8	50.6	3.4	296	82.8
McMechen city	1,897	1,697	-10.5	1,744	89.6	0.6	0.5	5.7	3.6	23.1	15.4	37.9	51.6	16.4	716	79.9
Madison city	3,076	2,673	-13.1	2,788	94.7	4.2	0.0	0.2	1.0	23.2	17.9	45.4	52.9	14.9	1,142	86.6
Mallory CDP	1,654	-	-	1,022	99.8	0.2	0.0	0.0	0.0	33.3	11.7	45.0	73.5	8.5	425	78.1
Man town	758	630	-16.9	943	97.5	2.0	0.0	0.0	0.5	20.8	17.9	42.3	58.4	14.2	361	91.1
Mannington city	2,068	2,023	-2.2	1,673	96.2	0.0	0.8	1.0	2.0	18.8	20.4	48.3	63.5	15.1	640	85.3
Marlinton town	1,050	961	-8.5	1,266	96.9	0.8	0.0	1.1	1.2	25.8	20.6	36.7	58.5	12.9	441	73.5
Marmet city	1,503	1,366	-9.1	1,625	97.1	0.5	0.0	2.3	0.1	18.6	23.3	43.8	58.5	15.8	604	82.1
Martinsburg city	17,194	17,454	1.5	17,475	76.6	13.9	1.3	3.5	4.8	25.0	14.5	36.9	49.1	20.4	7,179	88.5
Mason town	969	936	-3.4	831	100.0	0.0	0.0	0.0	0.0	16.7	30.8	49.4	60.7	7.7	411	74.7
Masontown town	547	538	-1.6	520	97.3	0.0	0.0	2.7	0.0	15.8	27.7	45.5	61.7	16.9	261	88.1
Matewan town	501	424	-15.4	477	90.8	7.3	0.0	1.9	0.0	13.4	21.0	54.2	80.2	7.3	298	66.4
Matheny CDP	531	-	-	276	100.0	0.0	0.0	0.0	0.0	21.0	43.1	52.5	55.0	4.3	116	37.1
Matoaka town	223	202	-9.4	221	99.5	0.0	0.5	0.0	0.0	24.0	14.9	31.1	78.6	1.9	77	88.3
Maybeury CDP	234	-	-	99	18.2	81.8	0.0	0.0	0.0	44.4	0.0	35.0	76.4	0.0	40	100.0
Meadow Bridge town	376	346	-8.0	422	95.7	0.0	0.0	4.3	0.0	28.9	16.6	35.3	63.9	13.5	180	67.8
Middlebourne town	811	738	-9.0	656	98.2	0.0	0.0	0.6	1.2	25.8	21.2	40.3	55.1	22.9	273	82.1
Middleway CDP	441	-	-	410	100.0	0.0	0.0	0.0	0.0	34.6	15.6	49.1	57.8	18.3	164	81.7
Mill Creek town	724	691	-4.6	689	98.4	0.0	0.0	0.0	1.6	18.7	17.1	45.9	85.3	7.5	291	68.0
Milton town	2,410	2,533	5.1	2,586	98.0	0.0	0.2	1.8	0.0	18.4	24.8	48.0	51.1	18.3	1,381	69.9
Mineralwells CDP	1,950	-	-	2,082	98.4	0.2	0.7	0.0	0.7	38.6	13.0	32.7	28.4	26.0	646	95.8
Mitchell Heights town	323	273	-15.5	573	95.8	0.0	1.9	1.4	0.9	30.7	15.4	37.3	23.5	40.5	211	91.5
Monaville CDP	309	-	-	337	100.0	0.0	0.0	0.0	0.0	23.1	9.2	38.0	62.2	0.0	118	94.9
Monongah town	1,043	1,149	10.2	1,184	85.6	8.9	0.0	3.8	1.7	21.5	18.2	40.4	49.8	13.7	476	85.7
Montcalm CDP	726	-	-	448	100.0	0.0	0.0	0.0	0.0	34.2	9.4	35.4	76.9	3.0	138	81.9
Montgomery city	1,638	1,508	-7.9	1,592	78.9	9.8	0.4	5.8	5.2	16.6	17.8	31.8	53.5	19.5	643	63.8
Montrose town	158	153	-3.2	158	100.0	0.0	0.0	0.0	0.0	8.9	38.0	61.0	81.0	12.0	79	74.7
Moorefield town	2,553	2,418	-5.3	3,280	72.8	15.1	6.9	0.0	5.2	20.7	22.8	44.1	72.6	8.5	1,409	81.6
Morgantown city	28,470	30,549	7.3	30,712	85.4	4.1	3.4	3.5	3.6	10.9	10.2	24.6	24.6	55.0	10,952	93.5
Moundsville city	8,995	8,252	-8.3	8,486	96.6	0.2	0.1	1.4	1.7	16.3	24.6	48.6	60.6	11.1	3,636	73.1
Mount Carbon CDP	428	-	-	389	100.0	0.0	0.0	0.0	0.0	14.4	23.1	49.0	62.2	24.6	133	75.2
Mount Gay-Shamrock CDP	1,779	-	-	1,413	97.9	2.1	0.0	0.0	0.0	10.3	30.9	49.6	72.7	0.9	629	71.7
Mount Hope city	1,411	1,274	-9.7	980	86.1	12.3	0.0	0.3	1.2	14.3	23.9	47.8	55.1	14.7	504	76.0
Mullens city	1,594	1,325	-16.9	1,435	97.5	1.3	0.0	1.0	0.2	20.6	22.7	43.9	50.2	19.9	591	86.8
Neibert CDP	183	-	-	113	100.0	0.0	0.0	0.0	0.0	0.0	31.9	63.4	26.5	61.1	54	100.0
Nettie CDP	568	-	-	438	100.0	0.0	0.0	0.0	0.0	13.7	8.0	48.9	92.9	0.0	217	70.5
Newburg town	320	315	-1.6	334	100.0	0.0	0.0	0.0	0.0	20.4	15.6	41.7	70.7	9.0	125	84.8
New Cumberland city	1,089	1,006	-7.6	1,079	94.3	0.0	0.3	0.0	5.5	14.5	31.7	52.3	58.2	9.1	541	70.8
Newell CDP	1,376	-	-	1,284	87.5	0.0	1.2	4.3	7.0	27.6	20.2	43.4	63.2	8.8	584	85.6
New Haven town	1,547	1,464	-5.4	1,644	99.3	0.0	0.0	0.0	0.7	18.9	22.6	43.8	60.4	13.1	708	72.5
New Martinsville city	5,366	5,118	-4.6	5,162	98.3	0.0	0.0	1.7	0.0	19.0	22.1	45.0	53.7	16.3	1,986	77.9
New Richmond CDP	238	-	-	365	91.8	0.0	8.2	0.0	0.0	12.6	35.9	45.4	88.4	0.0	166	81.9
Nitro city	6,935	6,373	-8.1	5,997	89.2	6.5	0.0	4.0	0.2	25.5	21.0	41.2	49.0	17.2	2,629	79.8
Northfork town	427	336	-21.3	318	55.7	42.5	0.0	1.9	0.0	36.2	16.0	41.3	68.9	5.8	111	60.4

1 May be of any race.

Table A. All Places — **Population and Housing**

STATE City, town, township, borough, or CDP (county if applicable)	Population: 2010 census total population	Population: 2019 estimated population	Population: Percent change 2010–2019	Population: ACS total population estimate 2015–2019	Race and Hispanic or Latino origin (percent): White alone, not Hispanic or Latino	Race and Hispanic or Latino origin (percent): Black alone, not Hispanic or Latino	Race and Hispanic or Latino origin (percent): Asian alone, not Hispanic or Latino	Race and Hispanic or Latino origin (percent): All other races or 2 or more races, not Hispanic or Latino	Race and Hispanic or Latino origin (percent): Hispanic or Latino[1]	Age (percent): Under 18 years old	Age (percent): Age 65 years and older	Age (percent): Median age	Educational attainment of persons age 25 and older: Percent High school diploma or less	Educational attainment of persons age 25 and older: Percent Bachelor's degree or more	Occupied housing units: Total	Occupied housing units: Percent with a computer
	1	2	3	4	5	6	7	8	9	10	11	12	13	14	15	16
WEST VIRGINIA—Con.																
North Hills town	825	774	-6.2	938	90.9	1.5	3.3	2.3	1.9	33.7	15.7	38.5	9.0	70.1	306	99.0
Nutter Fort town	1,602	1,512	-5.6	1,570	95.8	1.1	0.0	2.1	1.0	17.5	20.7	44.9	40.2	24.4	736	89.8
Oak Hill city	8,869	8,098	-8.7	8,336	88.4	8.8	0.0	2.1	0.8	26.2	22.1	41.8	58.2	18.5	3,473	80.2
Oakvale town	120	112	-6.7	61	100.0	0.0	0.0	0.0	0.0	26.2	13.1	33.9	95.1	0.0	25	84.0
Oceana town	1,390	1,204	-13.4	1,192	100.0	0.0	0.0	0.0	0.0	17.5	20.1	49.6	71.3	8.3	560	72.9
Omar CDP	552	-	-	478	100.0	0.0	0.0	0.0	0.0	32.6	8.4	32.0	42.4	13.2	159	100.0
Paden City city	2,633	2,336	-11.3	3,089	97.8	0.3	0.0	1.8	0.0	18.8	23.1	45.0	61.3	8.6	1,155	86.0
Page CDP	224	-	-	157	89.8	10.2	0.0	0.0	0.0	17.8	43.3	60.0	69.0	0.0	81	35.8
Pageton CDP	187	-	-	135	100.0	0.0	0.0	0.0	0.0	44.4	4.4	25.3	76.8	0.0	29	69.0
Parcoal CDP	-	-	-	94	100.0	0.0	0.0	0.0	0.0	18.1	31.9	46.6	62.3	21.7	41	100.0
Parkersburg city	31,287	29,306	-6.3	30,021	93.6	3.1	0.4	1.9	0.9	21.0	19.9	41.9	52.7	16.3	13,086	81.3
Parsons city	1,466	1,391	-5.1	1,592	94.2	0.7	0.0	4.1	1.0	18.3	18.5	42.0	65.3	15.2	696	84.8
Paw Paw town	508	492	-3.1	672	75.4	13.8	0.0	10.7	0.0	35.6	15.0	34.6	74.0	7.8	203	85.7
Pax town	167	152	-9.0	139	100.0	0.0	0.0	0.0	0.0	11.5	11.5	53.7	66.4	0.0	61	90.2
Pea Ridge CDP	6,650	-	-	6,632	93.2	1.9	4.2	0.6	0.0	18.2	22.2	41.5	27.8	40.0	3,196	94.4
Pennsboro city	1,147	1,003	-12.6	1,076	96.4	2.5	0.0	1.1	0.0	28.2	13.8	32.3	60.6	12.6	406	80.5
Pentress CDP	175	-	-	156	100.0	0.0	0.0	0.0	0.0	42.9	10.9	23.2	40.5	59.5	65	73.8
Petersburg city	2,410	2,655	10.2	2,574	94.5	1.9	0.0	1.5	2.1	13.5	27.7	50.3	54.5	22.3	1,102	77.0
Peterstown town	651	621	-4.6	693	88.9	0.0	0.0	10.5	0.6	33.8	23.4	36.8	56.5	15.5	251	85.3
Philippi city	2,963	3,257	9.9	3,366	89.4	4.0	1.2	4.8	0.6	19.7	17.1	36.7	53.4	20.6	1,330	82.6
Pickens CDP	66	-	-	14	100.0	0.0	0.0	0.0	0.0	0.0	0.0	0.0	0.0	0.0	14	100.0
Piedmont town	876	802	-8.4	778	54.6	29.2	0.0	12.6	3.6	22.1	23.3	49.3	73.2	4.0	330	78.5
Pinch CDP	3,262	-	-	2,746	100.0	0.0	0.0	0.0	0.0	19.0	25.2	48.2	36.0	36.3	1,183	87.2
Pine Grove town	544	482	-11.4	385	99.0	0.0	0.0	1.0	0.0	10.4	19.0	49.7	73.2	8.8	178	68.5
Pineville town	670	574	-14.3	676	97.2	2.8	0.0	0.0	0.0	16.4	23.8	44.5	52.7	18.0	268	83.6
Piney View CDP	989	-	-	1,077	99.4	0.0	0.0	0.0	0.6	24.1	23.0	42.2	62.7	16.8	467	75.6
Pleasant Valley city	3,154	3,141	-0.4	3,157	86.8	2.8	0.0	9.5	1.0	20.1	23.4	42.3	45.8	33.6	1,349	85.4
Poca town	972	974	0.2	1,052	100.0	0.0	0.0	0.0	0.0	19.9	24.5	44.7	53.2	19.8	428	85.3
Point Pleasant city	4,348	4,062	-6.6	4,146	97.9	0.3	0.1	0.9	0.8	24.7	20.6	36.4	54.9	13.7	1,823	70.6
Powellton CDP	619	-	-	763	100.0	0.0	0.0	0.0	0.0	22.7	19.5	43.1	71.4	16.2	329	78.4
Pratt town	602	556	-7.6	380	99.7	0.0	0.0	0.3	0.0	18.2	21.6	47.8	38.9	26.1	148	91.9
Prichard CDP	527	-	-	294	100.0	0.0	0.0	0.0	0.0	15.3	3.4	31.0	60.6	14.4	89	100.0
Prince CDP	116	-	-	93	100.0	0.0	0.0	0.0	0.0	51.6	0.0	3.9	100.0	0.0	21	57.1
Princeton city	6,120	5,675	-7.3	5,831	88.3	6.2	0.7	2.9	1.9	20.5	23.1	44.5	53.8	17.6	2,566	83.3
Prosperity CDP	1,498	-	-	1,815	86.5	0.0	0.0	0.0	13.5	16.2	26.8	54.8	42.7	18.6	805	95.2
Pullman town	150	136	-9.3	156	98.1	0.0	0.0	1.9	0.0	13.5	21.8	40.4	86.6	1.8	58	62.1
Quinwood town	284	263	-7.4	114	100.0	0.0	0.0	0.0	0.0	10.5	36.0	58.3	79.6	0.0	51	68.6
Rachel CDP	248	-	-	289	100.0	0.0	0.0	0.0	0.0	22.1	9.7	27.6	52.6	37.5	107	82.2
Racine CDP	256	-	-	361	100.0	0.0	0.0	0.0	0.0	13.3	28.5	47.8	65.2	13.7	143	94.4
Rainelle town	1,486	1,520	2.3	1,250	96.7	0.0	0.0	0.4	2.9	20.9	24.1	44.9	59.2	11.3	570	78.4
Rand CDP	1,631	-	-	1,497	61.2	29.1	4.4	4.3	1.1	17.9	16.4	44.2	47.2	26.4	683	77.5
Ranson corporation	4,394	5,239	19.2	5,123	73.0	13.1	2.4	5.5	6.0	24.8	10.2	36.1	50.7	20.8	1,834	94.6
Ravenswood city	3,846	3,643	-5.3	3,716	95.5	0.0	0.3	2.9	1.3	26.6	18.4	38.3	49.6	25.7	1,434	76.2
Raysal CDP	465	-	-	417	100.0	0.0	0.0	0.0	0.0	16.8	36.2	58.7	91.2	0.0	184	76.1
Reader CDP	397	-	-	336	100.0	0.0	0.0	0.0	0.0	2.7	50.0	63.0	47.6	29.7	178	74.7
Red Jacket CDP	581	-	-	362	97.0	3.0	0.0	0.0	0.0	18.5	7.5	45.7	77.8	11.5	171	71.3
Reedsville town	585	604	3.2	450	98.7	0.0	0.0	1.3	0.0	13.1	18.7	47.8	58.2	20.5	218	90.4
Reedy town	182	161	-11.5	111	80.2	0.0	0.0	1.8	18.0	31.5	26.1	42.8	70.3	2.7	41	68.3
Rhodell town	173	160	-7.5	111	97.3	0.9	0.0	1.8	0.0	15.3	17.1	41.7	83.8	5.4	54	74.1
Richwood city	2,058	1,855	-9.9	2,127	93.7	1.9	0.0	3.7	0.7	16.1	24.6	47.2	60.2	13.2	856	85.5
Ridgeley town	675	620	-8.1	657	99.1	0.0	0.0	0.9	0.0	19.3	19.9	42.2	52.1	14.6	288	70.8
Ripley city	3,232	3,159	-2.3	3,183	96.2	0.0	0.5	0.0	3.3	13.7	23.2	45.8	49.9	21.5	1,590	83.8
Rivesville town	932	903	-3.1	998	94.6	0.0	0.0	2.9	2.5	15.7	18.8	43.1	55.7	16.5	408	76.5
Robinette CDP	663	-	-	462	98.3	0.0	0.0	1.7	0.0	15.2	26.4	39.8	86.0	5.0	202	85.1
Roderfield CDP	188	-	-	111	100.0	0.0	0.0	0.0	0.0	31.5	13.5	40.2	43.3	23.3	40	62.5
Romney city	1,844	1,695	-8.1	2,107	90.0	1.7	0.0	3.1	5.2	24.3	25.6	46.0	53.3	18.7	885	69.5
Ronceverte city	1,764	1,670	-5.3	2,055	89.6	5.8	0.0	3.5	1.1	18.6	19.7	39.9	48.9	20.0	866	79.0
Rossmore CDP	301	-	-	315	100.0	0.0	0.0	0.0	0.0	13.0	14.6	50.7	63.6	0.0	93	100.0
Rowlesburg town	580	572	-1.4	434	99.1	0.0	0.0	0.9	0.0	15.4	31.8	54.1	66.1	9.8	198	73.7
Rupert town	947	894	-5.6	998	93.9	0.0	0.0	1.1	5.0	24.6	19.4	41.2	63.7	13.7	366	71.3
St. Albans city	11,039	9,918	-10.2	10,270	91.9	2.7	0.3	4.1	1.0	20.1	23.2	45.7	41.5	27.9	4,273	89.8
St. George CDP	-	-	-	161	100.0	0.0	0.0	0.0	0.0	30.4	5.0	34.7	85.9	4.3	54	90.7
St. Marys city	1,866	1,772	-5.0	1,990	100.0	0.0	0.0	0.0	0.0	18.1	21.4	45.6	57.0	17.5	843	83.7
Salem city	1,586	1,522	-4.0	1,714	90.3	5.7	0.0	2.6	1.3	19.0	13.1	31.8	47.7	21.4	605	90.1
Salt Rock CDP	388	-	-	166	100.0	0.0	0.0	0.0	0.0	0.0	56.0	65.3	75.9	0.0	109	59.6
Sand Fork town	158	148	-6.3	198	100.0	0.0	0.0	0.0	0.0	36.9	7.6	24.9	50.5	12.4	60	86.7
Sarah Ann CDP	345	-	-	47	100.0	0.0	0.0	0.0	0.0	0.0	0.0	0.0	46.8	0.0	25	100.0
Scarbro CDP	486	-	-	758	88.8	0.0	0.0	11.2	0.0	29.4	7.3	34.1	65.0	8.7	249	76.3
Shady Spring CDP	2,998	-	-	3,366	88.7	2.3	2.1	6.8	0.0	24.3	20.7	41.5	42.5	30.7	1,338	84.1
Shannondale CDP	3,358	-	-	3,459	89.0	0.8	0.8	2.7	6.8	18.4	13.2	43.5	41.4	20.9	1,395	93.3
Shenandoah Junction CDP	703	-	-	590	79.3	0.0	0.0	14.9	5.8	27.3	5.4	35.2	25.3	20.6	219	100.0
Shepherdstown town	2,150	1,911	-11.1	1,553	73.0	21.0	0.0	2.8	3.2	3.7	7.1	21.1	33.7	30.8	294	89.5
Shinnston city	2,204	2,104	-4.5	2,265	92.8	0.2	0.6	2.0	4.4	21.6	19.3	41.6	49.0	17.7	913	84.1
Shrewsbury CDP	652	-	-	802	97.4	0.0	0.0	2.6	0.0	16.2	4.9	41.5	49.9	36.0	243	100.0
Sissonville CDP	4,028	-	-	4,239	99.5	0.0	0.0	0.5	0.0	20.5	24.8	51.8	70.4	9.4	1,696	82.0
Sistersville city	1,349	1,282	-5.0	1,284	90.4	0.0	4.8	3.0	1.8	19.7	20.0	49.3	55.6	26.3	468	76.7
Smithers city	816	734	-10.0	1,104	81.8	11.1	0.4	0.0	6.7	27.3	31.6	49.1	51.1	27.0	434	89.2
Smithfield town	166	146	-12.0	179	100.0	0.0	0.0	0.0	0.0	18.4	32.4	50.4	79.0	7.3	69	69.6
Sophia town	1,340	1,231	-8.1	1,109	98.9	1.1	0.0	0.0	0.0	25.1	25.7	42.3	72.8	8.1	517	67.3
South Charleston city	13,495	12,047	-10.7	12,475	80.5	8.4	2.6	6.1	2.3	21.4	19.1	42.0	32.2	34.1	5,648	90.4
Spelter CDP	346	-	-	325	67.4	32.6	0.0	0.0	0.0	32.6	35.7	42.6	71.2	0.0	184	48.4
Spencer city	2,305	2,038	-11.6	2,079	96.9	0.0	0.0	2.2	0.9	17.2	22.0	47.6	69.8	12.1	978	73.3
Springfield CDP	477	-	-	232	100.0	0.0	0.0	0.0	0.0	8.6	55.2	70.7	60.4	13.7	150	54.7
Stanaford CDP	1,350	-	-	901	83.1	13.2	0.0	1.4	2.2	12.9	37.5	54.8	47.7	22.8	494	85.6
Star City town	1,761	1,948	10.6	2,160	85.5	6.3	4.2	1.5	2.5	13.6	14.9	32.8	35.6	42.2	937	91.0
Stollings CDP	316	-	-	205	100.0	0.0	0.0	0.0	0.0	0.0	77.1	73.9	56.6	8.3	174	45.4
Stonewood city	1,807	1,714	-5.1	1,978	92.4	3.0	0.0	3.0	1.6	16.2	21.7	49.8	57.6	14.1	899	86.4
Summersville city	3,572	3,274	-8.3	3,368	93.1	0.0	1.7	2.2	3.1	15.4	27.9	53.3	42.1	31.4	1,618	77.9
Sutton town	994	988	-0.6	1,099	98.0	1.5	0.0	0.5	0.0	26.8	18.2	40.5	60.3	18.0	456	83.8
Switzer CDP	595	-	-	529	90.2	9.8	0.0	0.0	0.0	14.4	13.8	29.1	39.9	17.9	214	92.5
Sylvester town	160	136	-15.0	240	100.0	0.0	0.0	0.0	0.0	28.8	21.7	38.8	62.9	22.6	94	77.7

1 May be of any race.

Table A. All Places — **Population and Housing**

STATE City, town, township, borough, or CDP (county if applicable)	2010 census total population	2019 estimated population	Percent change 2010–2019	ACS total population estimate 2015–2019	White alone, not Hispanic or Latino	Black alone, not Hispanic or Latino	Asian alone, not Hispanic or Latino	All other races or 2 or more races, not Hispanic or Latino	Hispanic or Latino[1]	Under 18 years old	Age 65 years and older	Median age	Percent High school diploma or less	Percent Bachelor's degree or more	Occupied housing units Total	Percent with a computer
	1	2	3	4	5	6	7	8	9	10	11	12	13	14	15	16
WEST VIRGINIA—Con.																
Teays Valley CDP	13,175	-	-	13,866	93.7	1.7	1.9	0.5	2.2	22.7	18.9	41.2	27.7	39.9	5,112	93.4
Terra Alta town	1,487	1,500	0.9	1,736	97.7	0.7	0.0	0.5	1.1	30.4	13.7	35.7	69.1	3.9	663	84.3
Thomas city	586	550	-6.1	548	99.5	0.0	0.5	0.0	0.0	12.4	36.7	54.8	71.9	12.9	218	76.1
Thurmond town	5	4	-20.0	6	100.0	0.0	0.0	0.0	0.0	0.0	33.3	64.5	0.0	100.0	4	50.0
Tioga CDP	98	-	-	107	100.0	0.0	0.0	0.0	0.0	20.6	18.7	45.2	100.0	0.0	27	74.1
Tornado CDP	-	-	-	1,187	94.9	0.5	1.1	3.5	0.0	16.0	16.2	41.3	50.7	18.7	446	86.5
Triadelphia town	813	762	-6.3	889	98.2	1.8	0.0	0.0	0.0	21.9	22.7	52.1	60.1	12.2	362	86.7
Tunnelton town	292	295	1.0	301	97.0	0.0	0.0	3.0	0.0	24.3	14.0	40.4	76.4	5.8	111	93.7
Twilight CDP	90	-	-	48	100.0	0.0	0.0	0.0	0.0	0.0	41.7	57.3	54.2	0.0	23	73.9
Union town	564	540	-4.3	428	83.6	7.5	0.0	4.2	4.7	10.5	42.3	60.3	47.4	21.9	253	69.6
Valley Bend CDP	485	-	-	497	100.0	0.0	0.0	0.0	0.0	21.3	8.9	37.5	70.5	7.7	204	76.0
Valley Grove village	376	348	-7.4	382	99.7	0.0	0.0	0.0	0.3	24.6	17.5	42.7	56.1	16.4	167	89.8
Valley Head CDP	267	-	-	181	100.0	0.0	0.0	0.0	0.0	0.0	45.3	64.3	77.3	22.7	119	69.7
Van CDP	211	-	-	178	94.4	0.0	0.0	5.6	0.0	15.7	16.9	34.0	43.8	0.0	90	100.0
Verdunville CDP	687	-	-	366	100.0	0.0	0.0	0.0	0.0	8.7	6.3	54.6	51.5	4.7	169	100.0
Vienna city	10,827	10,124	-6.5	10,348	93.6	0.3	1.9	3.5	0.6	19.0	24.1	44.9	31.5	33.1	4,465	89.0
Vivian CDP	82	-	-	62	100.0	0.0	0.0	0.0	0.0	37.1	0.0	33.4	100.0	0.0	20	100.0
Wallace CDP	-	-	-	339	77.3	0.0	0.0	5.0	17.7	29.5	20.9	33.9	71.6	10.8	107	100.0
War city	855	685	-19.9	760	96.2	3.8	0.0	0.0	0.0	22.8	25.5	41.9	84.0	10.5	334	65.6
Wardensville town	268	258	-3.7	320	93.4	1.3	0.0	2.5	2.8	18.1	16.6	45.3	57.2	24.6	137	87.6
Washington CDP	1,175	-	-	1,139	100.0	0.0	0.0	0.0	0.0	14.9	16.7	52.2	29.2	32.5	442	91.9
Waverly CDP	395	-	-	623	97.9	0.0	0.0	2.1	0.0	16.9	6.9	42.3	41.0	21.6	222	100.0
Wayne town	1,703	1,576	-7.5	1,207	100.0	0.0	0.0	0.0	0.0	22.0	19.0	41.1	65.2	12.0	549	74.5
Weirton city	19,744	18,266	-7.5	18,670	92.4	2.6	0.6	2.8	1.6	18.2	22.0	45.2	44.7	21.5	8,006	83.9
Welch city	2,398	1,644	-31.4	2,966	67.5	21.0	0.0	4.1	7.4	9.7	17.8	41.7	66.9	8.1	844	79.1
Wellsburg city	2,810	2,530	-10.0	2,595	100.0	0.0	0.0	0.0	0.0	14.4	28.0	50.3	51.9	24.3	1,383	78.0
West Hamlin town	774	714	-7.8	664	93.5	0.0	0.0	0.6	5.9	18.8	34.5	53.7	75.0	6.7	293	59.7
West Liberty town	1,735	1,447	-16.6	1,655	91.7	1.9	0.6	2.7	3.1	3.2	4.9	20.9	51.1	28.6	233	86.7
West Logan town	430	364	-15.3	427	92.3	0.0	0.0	7.7	0.0	27.2	11.9	32.5	49.8	15.1	163	87.7
West Milford town	630	607	-3.7	599	93.2	0.0	0.0	6.8	0.0	22.4	11.0	40.3	45.1	23.2	227	93.0
Weston city	4,095	3,857	-5.8	3,946	97.5	0.0	0.6	1.9	0.0	21.5	16.8	40.8	60.7	16.0	1,675	84.0
Westover city	3,983	4,173	4.8	4,196	86.8	4.6	2.6	3.1	2.9	14.5	12.9	40.5	39.1	35.5	2,003	88.1
West Union town	825	799	-3.2	647	98.3	0.0	0.0	0.5	1.2	23.2	25.0	40.9	61.2	15.5	258	69.8
Wheeling city	28,358	26,430	-6.8	27,062	90.2	5.7	0.7	2.2	1.1	19.8	22.6	44.2	42.8	30.7	11,588	80.8
White Hall town	659	666	1.1	689	95.2	3.2	0.0	1.0	0.6	14.5	18.6	40.3	35.2	31.4	348	88.5
White Sulphur Springs city	2,421	2,351	-2.9	3,036	75.0	12.4	0.5	8.4	3.7	28.1	19.2	37.5	52.7	16.3	1,260	80.7
Whitesville town	510	427	-16.3	377	98.1	0.0	0.0	1.9	0.0	14.9	15.4	45.7	78.9	4.2	171	73.1
Whitmer CDP	106	-	-	44	100.0	0.0	0.0	0.0	0.0	0.0	100.0	0.0	100.0	0.0	22	100.0
Wiley Ford CDP	1,026	-	-	852	100.0	0.0	0.0	0.0	0.0	28.3	12.7	37.9	56.6	9.6	358	84.4
Williamson city	3,194	2,676	-16.2	2,803	75.4	15.2	0.0	9.5	0.0	25.5	19.2	36.7	54.8	17.0	1,243	78.0
Williamstown city	2,910	2,869	-1.4	2,915	97.9	0.4	0.0	0.4	1.3	20.7	22.5	46.2	33.9	36.8	1,246	92.1
Windsor Heights village	423	379	-10.4	363	97.8	1.4	0.0	0.3	0.6	21.5	23.1	45.9	59.3	17.5	163	89.0
Winfield town	2,299	2,352	2.3	2,785	90.6	3.2	2.9	3.3	0.0	24.8	12.8	37.6	31.8	40.6	990	96.5
Wolf Summit CDP	272	-	-	135	76.3	0.0	0.0	0.0	23.7	0.0	50.4	66.1	74.1	11.9	81	85.2
Womelsdorf (Coalton) town	246	240	-2.4	297	96.6	3.4	0.0	0.0	0.0	24.9	16.8	45.4	76.2	8.5	112	83.0
Worthington town	153	148	-3.3	194	100.0	0.0	0.0	0.0	0.0	14.9	32.0	43.4	67.9	3.8	83	71.1
WISCONSIN	5,687,285	5,822,434	2.4	5,790,716	81.3	6.3	2.8	2.9	6.8	22.1	16.5	39.5	38.4	30.1	2,358,156	89.4
Abbotsford city	2,301	2,233	-3.0	2,239	61.4	0.3	0.0	0.9	37.4	26.6	17.3	36.2	65.4	11.2	870	87.2
Abbotsford city (Clark)	1,622	1,593	-1.8	1,510	69.1	0.5	0.0	1.1	29.4	26.2	16.6	37.7	59.3	15.4	628	84.7
Abbotsford city (Marathon)	679	640	-5.7	729	45.4	0.0	0.0	0.5	54.0	27.4	18.7	35.3	78.8	2.0	242	93.8
Abrams CDP	340	-	-	461	100.0	0.0	0.0	0.0	0.0	23.4	10.6	41.4	49.7	17.1	176	90.9
Abrams town (Oconto)	1,860	1,893	1.8	1,918	98.6	0.0	0.6	0.4	0.4	21.1	13.1	44.2	44.4	21.5	775	93.3
Ackley town (Langlade)	524	510	-2.7	493	99.6	0.0	0.0	0.0	0.4	12.4	20.1	49.0	61.1	10.1	234	85.0
Adams city & MCD (Adams)	1,972	1,893	-4.0	2,135	87.9	0.6	4.9	2.2	4.4	22.2	21.8	36.9	61.0	9.6	1,013	75.3
Adams town (Adams)	1,343	1,321	-1.6	1,111	94.0	0.0	0.5	0.1	5.5	12.6	26.3	57.0	60.6	12.9	554	84.5
Adams town (Green)	525	539	2.7	479	100.0	0.0	0.0	0.0	0.0	15.0	20.0	53.4	49.5	21.4	194	85.6
Adams town (Jackson)	1,354	1,390	2.7	1,310	93.2	0.2	0.0	5.7	0.9	16.3	32.1	57.1	44.5	20.3	625	88.3
Addison town (Washington)	3,486	3,447	-1.1	3,433	89.9	0.9	0.2	2.0	7.0	17.7	17.7	46.0	41.8	14.3	1,411	93.8
Adell village & MCD (Sheboygan)	521	512	-1.7	602	89.5	0.0	0.0	1.0	9.5	27.1	14.5	40.3	48.6	15.5	248	87.1
Adrian town (Monroe)	759	800	5.4	706	96.0	0.3	0.8	0.6	2.3	15.4	15.2	46.8	41.8	24.2	321	87.9
Agenda town (Ashland)	421	408	-3.1	294	98.3	0.0	0.0	1.0	0.7	15.3	21.8	56.1	74.2	7.5	138	82.6
Ahnapee town (Kewaunee)	935	919	-1.7	782	99.6	0.0	0.0	0.0	0.4	13.8	29.3	53.1	47.4	16.9	326	91.4
Ainsworth town (Langlade)	469	457	-2.6	484	98.3	0.0	0.0	1.4	0.0	13.8	28.9	55.7	55.1	9.8	250	79.6
Akan town (Richland)	403	390	-3.2	380	100.0	0.0	0.0	0.0	0.0	17.1	24.5	52.2	48.3	24.5	169	84.0
Alban town (Portage)	885	908	2.6	862	98.3	0.0	0.0	0.0	1.7	18.7	23.7	51.5	56.2	17.4	348	84.8
Albany village & MCD (Green)	1,018	993	-2.5	1,153	93.1	4.1	1.0	1.9	0.0	27.0	14.1	34.2	55.5	10.9	493	81.1
Albany town (Green)	1,106	1,139	3.0	1,097	92.5	2.0	0.0	2.1	3.4	24.2	19.8	42.7	43.6	20.0	405	87.4
Albany town (Pepin)	676	770	13.9	586	99.0	0.0	0.2	0.7	0.2	25.1	16.7	35.4	42.5	22.0	220	86.4
Albion town (Dane)	1,979	2,093	5.8	2,059	94.3	0.0	0.1	1.2	4.4	21.4	15.8	46.3	41.2	28.6	834	92.0
Albion town (Jackson)	1,210	1,239	2.4	1,177	95.1	0.8	0.7	2.4	1.0	22.1	21.8	49.0	43.7	18.1	497	76.9
Albion town (Trempealeau)	651	685	5.2	724	91.6	0.7	1.2	2.5	4.0	21.7	15.9	43.5	44.4	19.1	259	89.2
Alden town (Polk)	2,791	2,804	0.5	2,769	96.6	0.0	0.0	1.5	2.0	19.6	18.2	47.6	34.6	28.4	1,161	96.2
Algoma city & MCD (Kewaunee)	3,172	3,048	-3.9	3,059	95.8	1.3	0.9	1.5	0.5	20.1	26.1	47.6	43.1	21.8	1,321	80.1
Algoma town (Winnebago)	6,595	7,205	9.2	7,038	94.0	0.4	5.0	0.3	0.3	23.8	15.1	43.7	26.1	45.2	2,619	94.8
Allenton CDP	823	-	-	889	87.6	0.0	0.7	3.0	8.7	22.2	4.5	31.7	28.7	16.5	407	92.4
Allouez village & MCD (Brown)	13,977	13,894	-0.6	13,882	81.9	5.7	1.0	2.6	8.8	19.6	20.6	40.8	35.1	35.8	5,379	91.4
Alma city & MCD (Buffalo)	778	719	-7.6	688	89.8	2.0	0.0	4.5	3.6	15.0	24.1	51.5	41.8	21.4	362	86.5
Alma town (Buffalo)	297	291	-2.0	326	97.2	0.0	0.0	2.8	0.0	18.4	25.8	55.0	40.2	30.5	139	87.1
Alma town (Jackson)	1,048	1,089	3.9	1,135	73.0	0.6	1.1	0.7	24.6	22.6	15.7	42.1	59.1	14.1	413	84.0
Alma Center village & MCD (Jackson)	503	493	-2.0	430	91.2	0.0	1.2	0.9	6.7	29.5	16.5	35.5	56.3	16.7	175	88.0

1 May be of any race.

Table A. All Places — **Population and Housing**

STATE City, town, township, borough, or CDP (county if applicable)	Population 2010 census total population	2019 estimated population	Percent change 2010–2019	ACS total population estimate 2015–2019	Race and Hispanic or Latino origin (percent) White alone, not Hispanic or Latino	Black alone, not Hispanic or Latino	Asian alone, not Hispanic or Latino	All other races or 2 or more races, not Hispanic or Latino	Hispanic or Latino[1]	Age (percent) Under 18 years old	Age 65 years and older	Median age	Educational attainment of persons age 25 and older Percent High school diploma or less	Percent Bachelor's degree or more	Occupied housing units Total	Percent with a computer
	1	2	3	4	5	6	7	8	9	10	11	12	13	14	15	16
WISCONSIN—Con.																
Almena village & MCD (Barron)................	677	641	-5.3	767	88.0	0.9	0.7	5.9	4.6	21.5	15.5	38.0	58.9	10.6	339	84.4
Almena town (Barron)......	862	857	-0.6	868	99.7	0.0	0.0	0.1	0.2	16.7	29.0	56.1	37.0	26.7	376	88.3
Almon town (Shawano).....	584	575	-1.5	597	87.1	0.0	0.0	11.4	1.5	17.8	28.5	46.4	56.4	11.1	251	89.2
Almond village & MCD (Portage).....................	449	432	-3.8	485	77.1	0.0	0.0	0.0	22.9	32.0	10.3	32.8	48.5	15.1	184	88.6
Almond town (Portage)......	679	699	2.9	614	96.6	0.0	0.0	1.0	2.4	17.8	24.3	51.6	40.6	23.7	264	87.1
Alto town (Fond du Lac)....	1,051	1,071	1.9	995	97.2	0.0	0.6	1.7	0.5	23.6	13.1	46.1	53.2	15.3	349	88.5
Altoona city & MCD (Eau Claire)...................	6,714	7,870	17.2	7,625	90.6	0.8	3.5	1.6	3.5	24.1	16.9	35.7	26.1	29.8	3,224	89.4
Alvin town (Forest)...........	157	153	-2.5	112	100.0	0.0	0.0	0.0	0.0	0.0	48.2	64.8	62.7	5.5	72	72.2
Amberg CDP	180	-	-	183	97.8	0.0	0.0	2.2	0.0	14.8	30.1	52.6	48.2	15.6	102	83.3
Amberg town (Marinette)..	726	717	-1.2	644	94.7	0.9	0.0	2.6	1.7	9.2	36.0	59.2	63.6	8.8	363	79.1
Amery city & MCD (Polk)..	2,932	2,812	-4.1	2,819	95.0	0.4	1.3	2.7	0.6	22.2	26.1	43.0	50.2	17.4	1,153	78.9
Amherst village & MCD (Portage).....................	1,037	1,045	0.8	1,069	99.6	0.3	0.0	0.0	0.1	26.1	13.7	34.0	42.0	32.1	456	91.0
Amherst town (Portage)....	1,324	1,361	2.8	1,375	95.9	0.9	0.9	0.8	1.5	23.6	20.3	46.6	38.9	30.9	547	93.4
Amherst Junction village & MCD (Portage)............	377	383	1.6	395	95.4	0.0	0.0	0.0	4.6	26.8	11.9	38.5	46.5	24.5	152	93.4
Amnicon town (Douglas) ..	1,156	1,174	1.6	1,320	94.0	0.7	0.0	3.5	1.8	27.0	13.5	39.3	37.5	28.1	497	94.8
Anderson town (Burnett)..	396	400	1.0	399	97.0	0.0	0.0	2.8	0.3	20.1	16.5	47.6	41.4	17.4	185	88.1
Anderson town (Iron)........	58	57	-1.7	39	100.0	0.0	0.0	0.0	0.0	7.7	41.0	62.4	38.9	22.2	22	68.2
Angelica CDP	92	-	-	93	100.0	0.0	0.0	0.0	0.0	22.6	17.2	41.8	62.5	8.3	40	85.0
Angelica town (Shawano).	1,790	1,763	-1.5	1,900	97.6	0.0	0.5	1.7	0.3	27.5	16.5	41.4	52.2	17.0	731	85.5
Angelo town (Monroe)......	1,302	1,388	6.6	1,352	92.5	0.5	0.6	0.6	5.8	18.0	20.0	49.6	52.0	14.1	541	83.7
Aniwa village & MCD (Shawano)..................	262	249	-5.0	255	90.2	0.0	0.0	9.8	0.0	23.1	16.5	32.0	50.3	9.0	104	78.8
Aniwa town (Shawano).....	539	531	-1.5	598	95.2	0.3	0.0	2.3	2.2	25.6	14.9	40.3	58.6	7.7	220	86.8
Anson town (Chippewa)....	2,076	2,165	4.3	2,062	97.1	0.0	1.0	0.0	1.8	19.4	19.2	51.5	38.0	27.3	893	93.1
Antigo city & MCD (Langlade)...................	8,228	7,767	-5.6	7,780	90.1	2.2	0.1	4.2	3.4	23.1	20.2	40.1	51.6	16.8	3,593	82.7
Antigo town (Langlade).....	1,416	1,375	-2.9	1,475	93.6	1.6	0.9	2.9	1.0	18.2	26.2	52.4	55.3	14.4	607	89.5
Apple River town (Polk)	1,146	1,151	0.4	1,185	96.9	0.4	0.0	2.6	0.1	22.0	17.7	46.6	43.7	21.8	479	90.2
Appleton city...................	72,675	74,098	2.0	74,139	80.7	3.2	7.3	2.6	6.1	24.4	13.4	35.9	34.3	33.4	29,224	91.7
Appleton city (Calumet)....	11,082	10,926	-1.4	11,072	78.7	2.4	7.8	2.5	8.6	24.2	11.6	36.8	35.1	31.3	4,617	95.7
Appleton city (Outagamie).	59,967	61,493	2.5	61,558	81.5	3.2	6.9	2.7	5.6	24.3	13.5	35.8	34.0	34.2	23,893	91.5
Appleton city (Winnebago).	1,626	1,679	3.3	1,509	64.3	8.7	19.9	0.9	6.0	28.4	21.1	33.3	41.1	18.0	714	71.6
Arbor Vitae town (Vilas)....	3,323	3,428	3.2	3,362	82.0	0.0	0.0	14.2	3.9	26.3	28.4	49.4	36.2	29.2	1,613	76.9
Arcadia city & MCD (Trempealeau)...............	2,946	3,040	3.2	3,031	52.3	0.5	0.6	0.0	46.7	36.3	10.4	27.5	60.7	18.5	1,054	79.6
Arcadia town (Trempealeau)...............	1,751	1,839	5.0	1,622	92.8	0.0	0.0	0.0	7.2	21.8	16.5	47.9	52.2	19.5	682	86.4
Arena village & MCD (Iowa)......................	834	827	-0.8	820	93.3	0.7	0.2	5.0	0.7	26.2	12.0	37.6	50.4	14.6	345	83.8
Arena town (Iowa)............	1,455	1,498	3.0	1,468	96.4	1.8	0.8	0.6	0.4	19.6	16.0	46.0	41.3	28.7	625	91.5
Argonne CDP	160	-	-	112	78.6	2.7	0.0	0.0	18.8	19.6	17.9	52.9	60.0	6.7	59	91.5
Argonne town (Forest).....	512	506	-1.2	539	86.1	0.6	5.6	1.1	6.7	26.7	11.7	36.3	33.8	23.1	204	96.1
Argyle village & MCD (Lafayette)...................	847	811	-4.3	919	97.4	0.0	1.1	0.3	1.2	26.6	17.7	37.7	51.9	9.8	407	78.4
Argyle town (Lafayette).....	446	455	2.0	443	99.1	0.0	0.0	0.0	0.9	21.7	18.7	47.8	43.9	31.1	165	70.9
Arkansaw CDP	177	-	-	210	99.5	0.0	0.0	0.0	0.5	16.7	15.2	46.6	63.8	5.7	103	69.9
Arkdale CDP....................	158	-	-	156	100.0	0.0	0.0	0.0	0.0	19.9	32.7	48.6	67.5	9.2	75	69.3
Arland town (Barron)	789	758	-3.9	675	96.7	0.6	0.6	1.2	0.9	23.3	15.0	37.8	54.5	12.7	256	89.1
Arlington village & MCD (Columbia)	815	820	0.6	774	91.0	2.1	0.5	1.0	5.4	30.6	11.6	34.9	40.5	26.3	294	89.5
Arlington town (Columbia)	810	820	1.2	831	95.1	0.5	0.0	1.8	2.6	25.6	17.0	41.0	38.0	29.5	313	93.9
Armenia town (Juneau)	699	744	6.4	780	79.2	0.4	0.4	0.6	19.4	18.1	22.3	48.9	58.2	14.1	327	90.2
Armstrong Creek town (Forest)	409	395	-3.4	423	92.9	0.0	1.4	1.2	4.5	11.6	39.0	61.3	44.7	12.3	179	77.1
Arpin village & MCD (Wood)......................	333	309	-7.2	340	87.1	1.2	0.3	1.2	10.3	28.8	11.2	37.8	61.0	5.2	126	77.0
Arpin town (Wood)...........	929	901	-3.0	1,027	97.4	0.0	0.0	2.4	0.2	31.9	9.8	38.1	44.5	19.1	338	82.8
Arthur town (Chippewa)....	759	790	4.1	747	92.1	0.0	2.1	5.0	0.8	24.5	12.6	45.4	53.9	13.7	284	89.1
Ashford town (Fond du Lac)...........................	1,743	1,760	1.0	1,774	94.4	0.2	0.3	2.0	3.0	21.8	17.4	45.3	52.6	15.6	690	90.9
Ashippun CDP.................	333	-	-	1,069	99.4	0.0	0.0	0.0	0.6	19.6	13.7	40.8	48.5	18.2	395	94.7
Ashippun town (Dodge)....	2,560	2,581	0.8	2,553	96.5	0.0	0.6	2.4	0.5	19.3	16.5	44.9	42.0	23.1	960	92.2
Ashland city & MCD (Ashland)...................	8,216	7,843	-4.5	7,892	86.3	1.2	0.6	9.7	2.2	19.5	17.6	40.3	40.8	23.7	3,466	83.1
Ashland town (Bayfield).....	-	-	-	-	-	-	-	-	-	-	-	-	-	-	-	-
Ashland town (Ashland)....	594	581	-2.2	554	93.9	0.0	0.2	3.4	2.5	22.9	26.0	47.7	48.6	19.7	231	81.8
Ashwaubenon village & MCD (Brown)	16,943	17,161	1.3	17,149	86.6	1.9	4.0	3.6	3.9	20.9	17.3	40.2	34.8	33.4	7,723	91.1
Athelstane town (Marinette)...................	504	502	-0.4	528	95.6	0.0	0.0	4.4	0.0	13.1	32.4	60.3	64.7	8.1	258	77.5
Athens village & MCD (Marathon).................	1,095	1,077	-1.6	1,031	94.0	0.4	0.4	2.8	2.4	19.6	21.6	46.9	61.1	17.0	497	76.9
Atlanta town (Rusk)	592	597	0.8	514	96.7	0.0	0.0	1.8	1.6	16.9	20.8	53.0	50.4	13.0	241	89.6
Auburn town (Chippewa) ..	697	727	4.3	657	98.9	0.0	0.0	0.0	1.1	30.3	18.4	37.3	41.2	23.6	219	89.5
Auburn town (Fond du Lac)...........................	2,357	2,388	1.3	2,472	95.2	0.0	0.5	2.7	1.5	20.0	16.3	47.3	44.9	17.5	877	95.0
Auburndale village & MCD (Wood)................	703	665	-5.4	744	84.1	0.5	0.0	1.1	14.2	29.6	18.0	38.6	56.5	22.9	300	83.7
Auburndale town (Wood)...	860	829	-3.6	754	98.4	0.0	0.0	0.5	1.1	22.4	17.0	45.7	58.1	13.1	302	86.8
Augusta city & MCD (Eau Claire)...................	1,542	1,525	-1.1	1,431	90.8	0.0	0.0	8.4	0.8	28.9	20.4	38.5	53.8	11.3	556	86.2
Aurora town (Florence).....	1,036	1,007	-2.8	942	96.8	0.0	0.0	0.7	2.4	15.0	25.6	51.4	41.5	21.7	417	89.7
Aurora town (Taylor).........	422	403	-4.5	479	97.3	0.0	0.0	2.5	0.2	36.3	14.6	33.9	60.2	12.2	164	75.6
Aurora town (Waushara)...	986	993	0.7	1,116	91.8	0.1	0.0	3.4	4.7	25.5	16.6	44.4	53.4	14.0	453	89.6
Avoca village & MCD (Iowa)......................	637	623	-2.2	683	96.5	0.4	1.6	1.5	0.0	24.5	17.6	33.3	52.3	7.0	275	86.9
Avon town (Rock).............	606	612	1.0	567	97.0	0.0	0.0	0.9	2.1	11.8	19.9	53.9	50.0	14.7	248	86.3

1 May be of any race.

Table A. All Places — **Population and Housing**

STATE City, town, township, borough, or CDP (county if applicable)	Population				Race and Hispanic or Latino origin (percent)					Age (percent)			Educational attainment of persons age 25 and older		Occupied housing units	
	2010 census total population	2019 estimated population	Percent change 2010–2019	ACS total population estimate 2015–2019	White alone, not Hispanic or Latino	Black alone, not Hispanic or Latino	Asian alone, not Hispanic or Latino	All other races or 2 or more races, not Hispanic or Latino	Hispanic or Latino[1]	Under 18 years old	Age 65 years and older	Median age	Percent High school diploma or less	Percent Bachelor's degree or more	Total	Percent with a computer
	1	2	3	4	5	6	7	8	9	10	11	12	13	14	15	16
WISCONSIN—Con.																
Aztalan town (Jefferson)...	1,444	1,492	3.3	1,285	93.9	1.3	0.7	0.2	4.0	18.6	19.8	48.2	38.0	26.7	512	91.2
Babcock CDP..............	126	-	-	84	90.5	0.0	0.0	0.0	9.5	10.7	31.0	47.7	68.1	0.0	40	82.5
Bagley village & MCD (Grant)................	375	367	-2.1	353	97.5	0.0	0.0	2.5	0.0	15.6	35.7	55.8	51.8	11.7	173	75.1
Bagley town (Oconto).......	291	296	1.7	282	98.9	0.0	0.0	1.1	0.0	11.3	33.7	59.6	58.2	15.2	136	75.7
Baileys Harbor CDP	257	-	-	194	100.0	0.0	0.0	0.0	0.0	14.9	55.2	66.8	18.8	43.0	104	97.1
Baileys Harbor town (Door)...................	1,022	1,039	1.7	1,022	98.1	0.0	0.3	1.3	0.3	14.2	40.8	60.3	20.6	50.2	515	92.2
Baldwin village & MCD (St. Croix).............	3,978	4,072	2.4	4,016	93.3	0.8	0.5	0.0	5.4	23.4	12.7	36.8	35.5	24.3	1,784	86.0
Baldwin town (St. Croix) ...	935	955	2.1	867	98.8	0.0	0.7	0.5	0.0	20.2	22.1	48.2	38.9	25.7	337	92.9
Balsam Lake village & MCD (Polk).............	1,009	982	-2.7	800	95.3	2.8	0.0	1.3	0.8	13.8	21.8	46.0	54.2	18.4	354	87.3
Balsam Lake town (Polk)..	1,411	1,417	0.4	1,628	97.3	0.0	0.3	2.3	0.1	21.7	21.7	50.0	32.8	26.7	630	93.0
Bancroft CDP................	535	-	-	520	75.4	0.0	0.0	0.2	24.4	31.7	13.8	35.0	58.0	15.9	179	86.0
Bangor village & MCD (La Crosse).................	1,455	1,452	-0.2	1,200	98.8	0.2	0.0	0.2	0.8	19.7	17.3	41.1	33.7	22.4	544	86.4
Bangor town (La Crosse)..	615	642	4.4	528	98.9	0.4	0.0	0.8	0.0	21.6	22.9	49.9	53.0	19.8	204	82.8
Baraboo city & MCD (Sauk)...................	12,063	12,165	0.8	12,138	89.7	1.2	0.6	3.4	5.2	22.3	17.8	39.8	40.7	23.7	5,364	88.6
Baraboo town (Sauk).......	1,661	1,770	6.6	1,677	90.9	0.6	1.1	0.4	7.0	15.6	19.6	49.8	33.5	36.0	688	92.4
Barksdale town (Bayfield).	723	730	1.0	717	95.4	0.0	1.1	3.5	0.0	17.3	18.4	52.3	32.3	34.8	316	87.7
Barnes town (Bayfield)	769	779	1.3	764	95.8	1.8	0.7	1.0	0.7	5.6	49.5	64.9	30.7	38.3	416	94.2
Barneveld village & MCD (Iowa)....................	1,231	1,251	1.6	1,235	91.6	3.4	0.0	2.7	2.3	33.5	10.2	33.7	30.3	25.9	429	96.3
Barre town (La Crosse)	1,233	1,293	4.9	1,196	95.3	0.3	0.6	2.9	0.9	23.2	13.0	44.7	31.0	37.9	454	94.7
Barron city & MCD (Barron).................	3,453	3,322	-3.8	3,317	79.0	15.1	0.0	1.0	5.0	27.8	11.4	30.7	49.2	16.3	1,164	92.1
Barron town (Barron)........	841	830	-1.3	909	91.0	0.9	1.1	0.4	6.6	25.9	16.3	38.6	47.7	19.5	292	86.6
Barronett CDP	111	-	-	162	100.0	0.0	0.0	0.0	0.0	30.2	17.3	45.4	53.7	0.0	56	89.3
Barronett town (Washburn).............	440	441	0.2	467	99.6	0.0	0.0	0.0	0.4	25.5	14.3	37.7	39.6	22.1	179	89.9
Bartelme town (Shawano)	825	820	-0.6	828	23.2	0.6	0.0	75.5	0.7	24.6	23.9	44.0	55.5	13.6	316	82.3
Barton town (Washington)	2,611	2,673	2.4	2,644	93.3	0.4	0.9	3.1	2.3	21.7	19.6	49.7	39.5	29.0	955	90.7
Bashaw town (Washburn).	948	921	-2.8	988	98.2	0.0	0.2	0.5	1.1	21.0	17.6	47.0	42.4	22.4	428	86.7
Bass Lake town (Sawyer).	2,375	2,399	1.0	2,352	53.3	0.2	0.9	41.9	3.7	25.4	20.0	46.1	33.5	29.2	1,065	88.2
Bass Lake town (Washburn).............	505	510	1.0	527	94.9	0.0	0.0	0.0	5.1	14.6	18.0	52.5	38.5	23.2	248	92.7
Bay City village & MCD (Pierce)..................	500	494	-1.2	475	97.5	0.6	0.0	1.9	0.0	18.5	17.3	45.5	61.4	7.7	212	79.2
Bayfield city & MCD (Bayfield)...............	484	471	-2.7	520	78.7	6.7	2.3	10.6	1.7	10.6	38.1	56.6	25.2	47.5	280	87.9
Bayfield town (Bayfield)	683	691	1.2	736	78.5	4.5	0.0	15.2	1.8	8.0	34.4	60.4	23.9	39.4	367	95.1
Bayside village..............	4,403	4,334	-1.6	4,558	82.8	2.4	9.1	3.3	2.4	22.2	24.9	49.4	10.5	71.9	1,873	94.0
Bayside village (Milwaukee).............	4,314	4,246	-1.6	4,439	82.9	2.5	9.1	3.1	2.5	22.5	25.4	49.9	10.9	71.0	1,824	93.8
Bayside village (Ozaukee)	89	88	-1.1	119	79.0	0.0	10.1	10.9	0.0	10.9	8.4	30.4	0.0	100.0	49	100.0
Bayview town (Jackson)....	491	496	1.0	500	87.0	0.0	0.0	7.8	5.2	15.8	28.0	54.0	14.9	55.0	245	95.5
Bear Bluff town (Jackson).	138	143	3.6	158	89.9	0.0	0.0	10.1	0.0	20.9	13.9	36.3	53.2	14.7	71	84.5
Bear Creek village & MCD (Outagamie)...............	448	438	-2.2	379	61.2	2.1	0.0	5.8	30.9	19.5	13.2	36.1	63.3	4.8	155	83.2
Bear Creek town (Sauk) ...	595	633	6.4	541	96.1	0.4	0.0	0.0	3.5	21.1	17.6	51.2	49.0	27.8	224	82.1
Bear Creek town (Waupaca)...............	817	802	-1.8	688	98.1	0.0	1.3	0.1	0.4	17.3	23.1	50.2	59.7	14.6	303	79.2
Bear Lake town (Barron)...	659	656	-0.5	720	96.8	0.0	0.0	0.0	3.2	16.5	22.1	51.1	48.2	23.8	295	90.8
Beaver town (Clark)........	885	881	-0.5	687	96.5	0.0	0.0	3.1	0.4	34.9	13.8	30.6	66.7	10.4	233	76.8
Beaver town (Marinette) ...	1,146	1,141	-0.4	1,107	95.6	0.0	0.0	1.4	3.0	18.2	26.4	47.8	44.1	19.7	487	82.3
Beaver town (Polk)..........	835	839	0.5	829	95.3	0.0	0.0	3.3	1.4	19.5	19.2	50.9	51.5	15.2	325	91.7
Beaver Brook town (Washburn).............	711	717	0.8	713	92.7	0.3	1.5	3.6	1.8	20.2	21.2	41.1	35.2	22.7	296	93.9
Beaver Dam city & MCD (Dodge).................	16,210	16,403	1.2	16,345	86.1	3.0	0.6	2.2	8.1	22.9	17.8	38.9	49.5	19.8	7,027	87.7
Beaver Dam town (Dodge)	3,959	3,942	-0.4	3,919	89.1	0.0	2.5	3.3	5.1	19.8	17.5	46.9	46.1	23.4	1,604	90.1
Beecher town (Marinette).	724	711	-1.8	781	96.8	0.0	0.4	2.2	0.6	15.9	33.4	58.7	59.0	14.6	403	71.7
Beetown town (Grant).......	775	764	-1.4	662	98.9	0.0	0.0	0.5	0.6	31.7	19.6	36.6	49.3	18.7	234	85.9
Belgium village & MCD (Ozaukee)................	2,233	2,345	5.0	2,322	91.5	0.1	1.8	3.2	3.4	25.8	11.7	38.6	33.0	28.7	868	95.0
Belgium town (Ozaukee) ..	1,429	1,432	0.2	1,617	83.0	1.7	7.4	2.4	5.5	13.6	21.6	48.3	41.6	31.9	626	92.2
Bell town (Bayfield)........	263	265	0.8	340	96.2	0.0	0.0	1.8	2.1	9.4	43.8	62.1	20.1	50.2	192	91.7
Bell Center village & MCD (Crawford)..............	117	111	-5.1	120	95.8	0.0	4.2	0.0	0.0	11.7	25.0	49.5	60.6	21.2	52	76.9
Belle Plaine town (Shawano)...............	1,856	1,811	-2.4	1,927	96.4	0.0	1.3	1.7	0.6	17.9	24.5	52.0	47.5	23.6	803	86.9
Belleville village	2,374	2,463	3.7	2,556	90.3	0.7	0.6	3.9	4.5	26.5	10.2	38.2	28.9	32.8	1,027	93.3
Belleville village (Dane)....	1,853	1,931	4.2	1,898	88.6	0.9	0.8	3.6	6.1	23.9	12.3	42.1	30.8	29.7	799	92.0
Belleville village (Green)...	521	532	2.1	658	95.1	0.0	0.0	4.9	0.0	34.0	4.3	32.2	23.0	42.7	228	97.8
Bellevue village & MCD (Brown).................	14,765	15,944	8.0	15,701	79.7	0.5	4.7	3.8	11.3	22.8	16.6	40.9	38.7	28.6	6,720	90.2
Belmont village & MCD (Lafayette)...............	976	976	0.0	995	95.7	0.3	1.0	3.0	0.0	24.2	20.4	45.6	44.1	20.0	431	89.6
Belmont town (Lafayette)..	780	800	2.6	884	93.1	0.6	0.8	1.0	4.5	32.8	13.6	35.3	44.9	23.8	289	75.8
Belmont town (Portage)...	616	627	1.8	507	89.5	0.6	0.0	0.0	9.9	16.4	23.3	51.1	46.6	22.7	230	90.9
Beloit city & MCD (Rock)..	37,010	36,926	-0.2	36,836	60.7	12.1	1.5	5.6	20.2	25.9	13.6	34.0	52.5	16.7	14,037	85.0
Beloit town (Rock)...........	7,616	7,730	1.5	7,659	78.0	7.8	2.5	4.2	7.6	19.1	21.5	47.0	51.0	17.0	3,155	90.8
Belvidere town (Buffalo)....	393	385	-2.0	374	98.4	0.0	0.0	0.8	0.8	22.7	26.5	48.7	39.9	26.6	168	89.3
Bennett town (Douglas)	595	604	1.5	535	95.0	0.0	0.0	1.7	3.4	20.9	22.2	49.3	36.6	24.8	235	92.3
Benton village & MCD (Lafayette)...............	985	958	-2.7	896	96.1	2.6	0.0	0.9	0.4	23.2	21.9	42.7	45.8	16.0	399	84.0
Benton town (Lafayette)....	489	502	2.7	433	99.1	0.0	0.9	0.0	0.0	17.1	18.9	49.8	44.3	22.3	174	87.4
Bergen town (Marathon) ...	641	639	-0.3	790	98.2	0.0	1.0	0.8	0.0	24.3	18.6	42.8	41.0	25.0	284	91.9
Bergen town (Vernon).......	1,358	1,370	0.9	1,338	98.4	0.0	0.1	0.8	0.6	20.3	18.6	49.0	35.6	29.1	550	90.5
Berlin city.....................	5,541	5,385	-2.8	5,383	88.6	0.3	0.0	1.2	9.9	23.0	17.5	41.0	53.6	18.6	2,382	82.4

1 May be of any race.

Table A. All Places — Population and Housing

STATE City, town, township, borough, or CDP (county if applicable)	Population 2010 census total population	2019 estimated population	Percent change 2010–2019	ACS total population estimate 2015–2019	Race and Hispanic or Latino origin (percent) White alone, not Hispanic or Latino	Black alone, not Hispanic or Latino	Asian alone, not Hispanic or Latino	All other races or 2 or more races, not Hispanic or Latino	Hispanic or Latino[1]	Age (percent) Under 18 years old	Age 65 years and older	Median age	Educational attainment of persons age 25 and older Percent High school diploma or less	Percent Bachelor's degree or more	Occupied housing units Total	Percent with a computer
	1	2	3	4	5	6	7	8	9	10	11	12	13	14	15	16
WISCONSIN—Con.																
Berlin city (Green Lake)....	5,452	5,298	-2.8	5,275	88.4	0.3	0.0	1.2	10.1	23.1	17.4	41.3	53.9	18.5	2,326	82.7
Berlin city (Waushara)	89	87	-2.2	108	100.0	0.0	0.0	0.0	0.0	20.4	22.2	31.8	43.0	22.1	56	69.6
Berlin town (Green Lake)..	1,115	1,130	1.3	1,293	82.0	0.0	10.1	1.8	6.1	22.3	23.7	40.3	37.0	31.9	541	90.4
Berlin town (Marathon)	945	944	-0.1	895	97.3	0.0	0.2	0.9	1.6	23.8	21.9	46.1	46.0	19.0	356	81.2
Bern town (Marathon).......	593	597	0.7	733	99.6	0.0	0.0	0.4	0.0	40.5	15.1	31.3	64.3	10.3	215	65.6
Berry town (Dane)	1,115	1,187	6.5	1,127	99.2	0.0	0.0	0.5	0.3	17.3	23.1	51.4	34.3	37.0	473	91.8
Bevent town (Marathon) ...	1,118	1,107	-1.0	1,058	95.8	0.0	0.2	0.2	3.8	16.4	24.5	48.8	69.5	7.9	445	79.1
Big Bend town (Rusk).......	358	348	-2.8	421	91.0	1.4	0.0	7.1	0.5	11.9	37.1	58.3	39.5	29.3	203	87.7
Big Bend village & MCD (Waukesha)...............	1,277	1,465	14.7	1,348	98.1	0.0	0.4	0.9	0.6	19.9	16.5	45.8	37.6	17.6	537	94.4
Big Falls town (Rusk).......	140	127	-9.3	118	88.1	0.0	0.0	0.0	11.9	11.0	36.4	58.8	47.5	17.8	53	83.0
Big Falls village & MCD (Waupaca)...............	70	69	-1.4	56	83.9	0.0	0.0	0.0	16.1	0.0	51.8	65.2	78.6	3.6	38	36.8
Big Flats town (Adams)	1,018	1,005	-1.3	823	92.7	0.2	0.5	4.0	2.6	13.1	35.1	57.2	58.4	10.8	442	75.1
Birch town (Lincoln)	594	592	-0.3	651	67.3	17.7	0.9	3.1	11.1	33.5	15.5	31.0	45.5	15.9	210	78.6
Birch Creek town (Chippewa)............	517	538	4.1	430	98.6	0.0	0.5	0.9	0.0	18.4	32.1	56.4	52.4	18.3	188	87.8
Birch Hill CDP................	293	-	-	354	1.1	0.0	0.0	89.5	9.3	48.3	7.6	20.2	66.9	9.8	78	91.0
Birchwood village & MCD (Washburn)...............	444	428	-3.6	343	92.4	0.0	0.0	7.0	0.6	25.9	26.5	46.8	53.6	16.4	164	81.1
Birchwood town (Washburn)...............	476	480	0.8	521	97.1	0.0	0.0	2.9	0.0	10.4	37.4	60.9	32.4	28.4	255	93.7
Birnamwood village	815	782	-4.0	824	94.9	0.8	0.0	1.1	3.2	23.7	24.3	41.3	60.2	8.6	318	77.4
Birnamwood village (Marathon)...............	16	16	0.0	31	100.0	0.0	0.0	0.0	0.0	25.8	6.5	43.2	47.4	15.8	12	58.3
Birnamwood town (Shawano)...............	799	766	-4.1	793	94.7	0.9	0.0	1.1	3.3	23.6	25.0	40.5	60.6	8.4	306	78.1
Birnamwood town (Shawano)...............	766	753	-1.7	808	92.2	0.5	0.0	4.7	2.6	22.2	22.6	43.8	67.6	8.1	307	85.3
Biron village & MCD (Wood).................	834	772	-7.4	953	95.0	0.0	4.0	0.4	0.6	25.1	26.5	44.5	48.5	17.8	416	77.9
Black Brook town (Polk)....	1,326	1,339	1.0	1,303	97.1	0.0	0.2	0.0	2.7	23.9	12.6	44.1	44.8	17.3	542	87.1
Black Creek village & MCD (Outagamie)........	1,316	1,308	-0.6	1,236	96.0	0.0	0.3	1.9	1.8	23.3	16.0	37.2	58.1	17.1	507	88.4
Black Creek town (Outagamie).............	1,259	1,246		1,669	97.7	0.0	0.4	1.6	0.4	30.5	12.3	38.7	52.4	12.5	583	84.7
Black Earth village & MCD (Dane)..................	1,340	1,419	5.9	1,418	96.3	0.0	1.1	0.3	2.3	20.7	13.8	39.6	34.4	32.5	631	89.9
Black Earth town (Dane)...	484	513	6.0	483	98.1	0.0	0.4	0.0	1.4	19.0	19.0	48.6	35.7	34.8	182	95.1
Black River Falls city & MCD (Jackson)	3,612	3,465	-4.1	3,496	94.5	0.0	0.0	5.1	0.4	19.8	22.7	46.8	43.6	17.0	1,670	85.9
Blackwell town (Forest).....	332	319	-3.9	222	70.3	20.3	0.0	1.8	7.7	3.6	25.7	45.4	46.0	21.6	43	74.4
Black Wolf town (Winnebago)..............	2,425	2,474	2.0	2,512	97.3	0.0	0.0	0.0	2.7	20.4	23.2	52.1	36.4	31.0	1,057	90.0
Blaine town (Burnett)........	197	190	-3.6	168	96.4	0.0	0.0	3.6	0.0	16.7	29.2	53.3	49.6	14.3	77	90.9
Blair city & MCD (Trempealeau).............	1,396	1,346	-3.6	1,317	92.6	0.0	0.8	1.4	5.1	25.6	19.9	40.6	60.8	9.3	544	83.5
Blanchard town (Lafayette)..............	264	259	-1.9	193	97.9	0.0	0.0	1.6	0.5	19.7	24.8	51.9	42.0	30.7	81	88.9
Blanchardville village	825	791	-4.1	797	96.6	0.0	0.0	3.1	0.3	19.1	20.8	42.7	40.4	22.1	373	88.2
Blanchardville village (Iowa).................	177	170	-4.0	209	95.2	0.0	0.0	4.8	0.0	26.8	17.7	34.4	20.3	18.9	87	88.5
Blanchardville village (Lafayette)..............	648	621	-4.2	588	97.1	0.0	0.0	2.6	0.3	16.3	21.9	43.8	47.2	23.3	286	88.1
Bloom town (Richland)	511	496	-2.9	572	97.2	0.7	0.0	1.0	1.0	25.9	20.6	41.5	58.1	12.7	233	78.1
Bloomer city & MCD (Chippewa)............	3,541	3,505		3,497	98.4	0.0	0.5	0.0	1.1	20.4	22.0	43.8	43.3	24.1	1,626	83.0
Bloomer town (Chippewa).	1,052	1,100	4.6	1,141	99.4	0.0	0.0	0.1	0.5	24.3	13.8	41.1	54.5	15.9	463	83.8
Bloomfield village & MCD (Walworth)..............	4,671	4,746	1.6	4,708	83.0	0.6	0.0	3.9	12.4	29.9	9.7	34.3	49.6	15.7	1,528	89.9
Bloomfield town (Walworth)..............	1,592	1,606	0.9	1,508	74.7	1.9	0.7	1.1	21.6	26.1	16.5	38.9	52.1	16.7	558	90.9
Bloomfield town (Waushara)	1,053	1,058	0.5	1,013	96.2	0.0	0.3	2.9	0.7	18.1	21.9	48.7	53.2	18.2	436	82.8
Blooming Grove town (Dane)..................	1,578	1,677	6.3	1,727	85.8	3.5	0.3	2.0	8.5	16.5	13.9	42.3	33.3	32.2	764	92.9
Bloomington village & MCD (Grant).............	733	696	-5.0	735	96.5	0.0	0.3	2.9	0.4	26.0	23.3	40.0	49.5	10.5	313	80.8
Bloomington town (Grant).	358	365	2.0	409	91.2	0.0	0.0	0.0	8.8	24.7	10.3	44.3	46.1	18.1	155	87.1
Blue Mounds village & MCD (Dane)...............	857	986	15.1	1,094	96.8	0.8	0.0	1.3	1.1	30.2	10.5	35.6	40.1	28.6	395	91.6
Blue Mounds town (Dane)	862	915	6.1	856	96.3	0.8	0.9	0.0	2.0	19.0	23.9	51.6	28.7	46.0	337	89.6
Blue River village & MCD (Grant)................	440	421	-4.3	471	93.4	0.4	0.0	4.2	1.9	21.9	16.6	43.9	55.1	8.6	227	88.1
Bluffview CDP................	742	-	-	522	57.9	2.3	0.0	0.8	39.1	40.8	8.6	27.4	58.6	11.2	203	92.1
Boaz village & MCD (Richland)..............	156	146	-6.4	147	91.2	0.0	0.0	0.0	8.8	23.8	21.1	53.1	63.3	2.8	65	75.4
Bohners Lake CDP..........	2,444	-	-	2,691	97.5	0.4	0.0	0.0	2.1	21.9	18.4	45.3	39.9	26.8	1,052	89.4
Bonduel village & MCD (Shawano)...............	1,476	1,417	-4.0	1,407	96.2	0.2	0.0	3.4	0.2	24.9	16.3	40.9	47.0	18.0	588	86.7
Bone Lake town (Polk)......	717	726	1.3	657	95.6	0.0	0.0	2.6	1.8	16.9	22.8	51.5	41.1	24.7	273	86.4
Boscobel city & MCD (Grant)................	3,218	3,128	-2.8	3,134	88.1	8.8	0.3	0.7	2.1	17.2	18.8	44.2	50.2	15.9	1,186	82.0
Boscobel town (Grant)......	389	395	1.5	331	97.9	0.0	0.0	0.3	1.8	17.5	23.9	47.1	64.6	11.3	155	81.9
Boulder Junction CDP	183	-	-	172	100.0	0.0	0.0	0.0	0.0	27.9	26.7	43.8	25.0	12.1	73	91.8
Boulder Junction town (Vilas)..................	938	964	2.8	975	97.8	0.0	0.0	1.4	0.7	13.4	35.4	60.0	33.3	32.7	497	91.5
Bovina town (Outagamie).	1,147	1,184	3.2	1,059	93.8	0.0	0.0	2.4	3.9	21.7	13.5	46.1	49.8	18.5	402	89.3
Bowler village & MCD (Shawano)...............	304	290	-4.6	400	60.3	0.0	0.0	28.5	11.3	37.0	12.8	31.4	66.4	12.0	138	83.3
Boyceville village & MCD (Dunn).................	1,089	1,127	3.5	1,041	99.0	0.0	0.0	0.3	0.7	25.5	13.7	39.0	62.8	12.4	466	89.3

1 May be of any race.

Table A. All Places — **Population and Housing**

STATE City, town, township, borough, or CDP (county if applicable)	2010 census total population	2019 estimated population	Percent change 2010–2019	ACS total population estimate 2015–2019	White alone, not Hispanic or Latino	Black alone, not Hispanic or Latino	Asian alone, not Hispanic or Latino	All other races or 2 or more races, not Hispanic or Latino	Hispanic or Latino[1]	Under 18 years old	Age 65 years and older	Median age	Percent High school diploma or less	Percent Bachelor's degree or more	Occupied housing units Total	Percent with a computer
	1	2	3	4	5	6	7	8	9	10	11	12	13	14	15	16
WISCONSIN—Con.																
Boyd village & MCD (Chippewa)..........	552	532	-3.6	593	84.1	0.5	0.0	0.8	14.5	26.3	18.0	36.6	50.6	12.2	236	85.2
Bradford town (Rock)........	1,120	1,137	1.5	1,230	80.7	0.2	0.0	0.1	19.0	28.9	9.2	38.3	45.5	24.4	443	91.4
Bradley town (Lincoln)......	2,395	2,366	-1.2	2,296	95.3	0.6	0.0	2.5	1.6	11.9	32.9	57.5	45.7	22.5	1,181	88.6
Brandon village & MCD (Fond du Lac)........	879	853	-3.0	924	86.0	0.0	1.2	0.6	12.1	28.2	13.0	37.3	46.0	20.0	360	81.7
Brazeau town (Oconto).....	1,288	1,308	1.6	1,382	92.3	0.0	1.2	2.0	4.5	17.1	26.3	53.1	57.9	12.0	629	80.8
Breed town (Oconto)........	712	727	2.1	702	96.9	0.0	0.0	2.8	0.3	13.7	28.9	55.8	58.1	7.9	329	80.5
Brice Prairie CDP	1,887	-	-	2,280	91.4	0.6	4.2	2.4	1.5	23.5	15.2	42.6	28.7	31.7	828	96.3
Bridge Creek town (Eau Claire)	1,910	2,083	9.1	2,074	98.6	0.0	0.0	0.8	0.6	35.0	14.9	32.5	62.3	10.7	615	71.4
Bridgeport town (Crawford)	1,008	1,004	-0.4	910	98.1	0.0	1.2	0.0	0.7	15.2	25.6	50.2	35.6	27.4	379	87.1
Brigham town (Iowa)........	1,037	1,070	3.2	951	91.7	2.1	0.2	1.7	4.3	20.1	17.2	50.4	32.8	42.0	378	97.4
Brighton town (Kenosha)..	1,449	1,511	4.3	1,480	96.3	0.3	0.9	0.0	2.5	14.4	18.5	50.5	37.6	29.3	615	92.5
Brighton town (Marathon) .	612	646	5.6	555	91.2	0.0	0.0	0.4	8.5	28.8	14.1	44.3	54.9	11.1	195	87.2
Brillion city & MCD (Calumet)	3,147	3,077	-2.2	3,126	93.0	0.2	0.5	2.9	3.4	28.0	13.8	36.5	48.5	20.2	1,216	87.0
Brillion town (Calumet)	1,488	1,460	-1.9	1,572	94.4	0.2	1.5	1.5	2.5	22.1	12.7	36.2	40.6	17.8	618	91.6
Bristol town (Dane).........	3,695	3,945	6.8	3,945	92.5	0.7	3.0	1.7	2.1	33.7	12.8	37.7	18.0	55.6	1,265	95.9
Bristol village & MCD (Kenosha)............	4,864	5,142	5.7	5,038	94.0	0.8	0.5	0.0	4.8	21.4	21.2	49.7	34.3	27.9	1,996	91.6
Brockway town (Jackson) .	2,830	2,860	1.1	2,846	57.4	10.1	0.9	27.8	3.8	21.8	11.8	35.1	58.8	8.5	768	86.5
Brodhead city...........	3,293	3,247	-1.4	3,240	92.8	0.0	1.7	1.8	3.8	22.0	22.1	43.8	48.5	15.8	1,383	77.7
Brodhead city (Green)......	3,204	3,161	-1.3	3,170	92.6	0.0	1.7	1.8	3.8	22.5	20.4	42.0	47.5	16.3	1,340	76.9
Brodhead (Rock)........	89	86	-3.4	70	100.0	0.0	0.0	0.0	0.0	0.0	100.0	86.3	80.0	0.0	43	100.0
Brookfield city & MCD (Waukesha).........	37,919	39,115	3.2	38,358	82.4	1.0	11.4	2.5	2.6	23.1	22.0	45.8	18.5	60.7	14,633	94.8
Brookfield town (Waukesha).........	6,117	6,517	6.5	6,248	86.7	1.9	7.6	0.5	3.3	14.5	30.8	51.6	27.2	48.8	2,975	87.8
Brooklyn village	1,403	1,465	4.4	1,255	84.0	3.1	0.0	4.1	8.8	24.2	8.5	36.7	29.5	30.6	475	94.5
Brooklyn village (Dane)	938	990	5.5	850	89.4	0.5	0.0	5.3	4.8	24.9	6.8	34.3	24.3	35.8	326	97.5
Brooklyn village (Green)	465	475	2.2	405	72.6	8.6	0.0	1.7	17.0	22.7	12.1	42.8	39.8	20.1	149	87.9
Brooklyn town (Green)......	1,083	1,113	2.8	1,182	95.9	0.0	0.3	0.8	3.0	18.7	14.9	48.1	35.9	30.8	437	91.3
Brooklyn town (Green Lake)	1,844	1,875	1.7	1,652	97.3	0.5	0.0	0.7	1.4	15.2	30.5	59.0	31.1	32.7	782	88.7
Brooklyn town (Washburn)	254	256	0.8	277	96.0	0.0	0.0	3.6	0.4	20.6	26.7	51.2	45.6	24.2	129	86.8
Brothertown town (Calumet)	1,329	1,294	-2.6	1,232	93.0	0.0	0.3	4.4	2.3	22.0	17.4	44.7	46.9	18.2	532	89.8
Brown Deer village & MCD (Milwaukee).........	12,011	11,839	-1.4	11,965	49.3	31.4	5.4	8.5	5.4	22.5	18.2	41.9	30.8	33.9	5,237	90.2
Browning town (Taylor)	905	911	0.7	913	97.6	0.0	0.0	0.0	2.4	26.3	12.8	39.6	62.2	13.5	354	85.9
Browns Lake CDP............	2,039	-	-	1,799	99.4	0.0	0.0	0.0	0.6	14.1	29.2	51.0	37.3	39.2	785	92.6
Brownsville village & MCD (Dodge)...............	581	584	0.5	596	93.5	0.0	0.3	0.0	6.2	24.3	15.8	47.1	49.3	25.5	233	92.7
Browntown village & MCD (Green)...............	280	276	-1.4	258	98.1	0.0	0.0	1.9	0.0	21.7	17.4	41.9	62.8	13.3	112	80.4
Bruce village & MCD (Rusk)...............	779	705	-9.5	779	91.5	0.0	0.0	5.3	3.2	27.5	23.4	42.1	53.6	17.9	362	77.3
Brule CDP...............	254	-	-	258	95.7	0.0	0.0	3.9	0.4	26.7	23.3	43.0	33.5	32.4	110	88.2
Brule town (Douglas)........	656	667	1.7	652	92.3	0.0	0.0	7.5	0.2	19.6	21.5	49.0	43.8	22.1	304	83.6
Brunswick town (Eau Claire)	1,626	1,784	9.7	1,925	94.0	2.5	2.5	0.3	0.7	22.3	17.4	45.1	35.2	27.4	715	91.7
Brussels town (Door)........	1,134	1,104	-2.6	1,035	92.5	0.0	0.0	2.7	4.8	25.1	16.0	45.1	46.4	20.7	426	90.1
Buchanan town (Outagamie)...........	6,772	7,201	6.3	7,146	94.4	0.0	0.4	1.8	3.4	26.5	9.6	40.6	31.5	37.6	2,678	89.6
Buena Vista town (Portage)	1,198	1,237	3.3	1,039	96.8	0.0	0.0	0.4	2.8	21.3	18.6	50.0	44.4	23.9	455	90.1
Buena Vista town (Richland).............	1,870	1,820	-2.7	1,807	89.4	0.3	0.9	3.1	6.3	20.6	16.5	42.9	52.4	13.5	780	87.6
Buffalo town (Buffalo).......	705	691	-2.0	816	97.2	0.2	0.0	0.0	2.6	25.7	19.1	45.6	49.2	21.8	328	83.8
Buffalo town (Marquette) ..	1,221	1,243	1.8	1,229	93.2	0.3	1.1	2.8	2.6	27.4	17.5	42.8	53.0	13.7	459	79.3
Buffalo City city & MCD (Buffalo).............	1,023	954	-6.7	875	97.1	1.3	0.9	0.7	0.0	14.6	24.9	53.2	50.0	19.8	436	87.6
Burke town (Dane)...........	3,219	3,431	6.6	3,430	83.6	0.0	9.4	2.9	4.1	20.6	16.1	43.7	23.7	38.7	1,314	97.1
Burlington city..............	10,552	10,980	4.1	10,847	85.5	0.3	0.5	1.6	12.1	24.3	14.6	39.2	41.6	25.7	4,463	91.9
Burlington city (Racine)	10,547	10,975	4.1	10,840	85.5	0.3	0.5	1.6	12.1	24.3	14.6	39.2	41.6	25.7	4,456	92.1
Burlington city (Walworth).	5	5	0.0	7	100.0	0.0	0.0	0.0	0.0	0.0	100.0	0.0	100.0	0.0	7	0.0
Burlington town (Racine) ..	6,419	6,563	2.2	6,533	98.8	0.2	0.0	0.0	1.0	19.9	20.1	46.0	40.8	29.7	2,536	92.7
Burnett CDP...............	256	-	-	211	99.1	0.0	0.0	0.0	0.9	10.9	24.6	49.3	42.0	9.7	110	87.3
Burnett town (Dodge)	904	859	-5.0	775	99.7	0.0	0.0	0.0	0.3	14.2	22.8	50.5	52.0	13.2	347	87.6
Burns town (La Crosse)....	947	955	0.8	1,083	93.0	0.1	4.5	1.4	1.0	26.1	17.0	39.6	46.1	15.8	381	90.0
Burnside town (Trempealeau)..............	500	523	4.6	490	90.6	0.0	0.0	0.0	9.4	26.1	18.2	45.2	58.6	10.5	202	72.3
Butler town (Clark)...........	96	95		133	100.0	0.0	0.0	0.0	0.0	36.8	12.8	30.9	65.4	11.1	45	91.1
Butler village & MCD (Waukesha).........	1,841	1,798	-2.3	1,821	86.6	7.3	2.0	1.2	2.9	17.3	20.4	42.3	38.6	27.6	913	82.0
Butte des Morts CDP........	962	-	-	904	100.0	0.0	0.0	0.0	0.0	17.4	17.0	48.2	25.1	39.3	380	100.0
Butternut village & MCD (Ashland).............	371	355	-4.3	454	95.4	0.0	0.0	4.2	0.4	27.3	25.6	40.3	58.2	10.7	189	78.3
Byron town (Fond du Lac) .	1,638	1,638	0.0	1,768	94.3	0.0	1.6	1.2	2.9	21.9	16.4	45.4	42.1	23.6	691	94.5
Byron town (Monroe)........	1,341	1,349	0.6	1,170	84.6	0.3	0.5	12.5	2.1	22.8	19.6	44.0	55.9	13.2	475	82.1
Cable CDP...............	206	-	-	150	96.7	0.0	0.0	0.0	3.3	8.0	53.3	66.4	48.6	16.7	95	71.6
Cable town (Bayfield)........	820	828	1.0	712	98.0	0.0	0.0	1.3	0.7	16.2	30.2	56.8	40.2	25.3	377	80.1
Cadiz town (Green).........	818	838	2.4	719	97.6	0.0	0.0	2.4	0.0	23.5	16.7	42.4	45.3	17.8	286	92.3
Cadott village & MCD (Chippewa)............	1,436	1,424	-0.8	1,486	94.2	0.3	1.5	3.2	0.8	23.4	17.5	39.8	51.5	10.8	656	85.5
Cady town (St. Croix)........	821	873	6.3	872	99.1	0.6	0.0	0.0	0.3	22.7	17.9	43.1	39.5	25.5	310	89.0
Calamus town (Dodge).....	1,048	1,056	0.8	1,023	88.3	0.0	0.0	1.7	10.1	18.6	17.7	50.5	55.6	18.3	411	87.3
Caledonia town (Columbia)	1,378	1,394	1.2	1,576	95.2	0.3	0.0	0.8	3.7	20.7	16.6	44.7	33.7	26.8	605	92.2

1 May be of any race.

Table A. All Places — Population and Housing

STATE City, town, township, borough, or CDP (county if applicable)	Population				Race and Hispanic or Latino origin (percent)					Age (percent)			Educational attainment of persons age 25 and older		Occupied housing units	
	2010 census total population	2019 estimated population	Percent change 2010–2019	ACS total population estimate 2015–2019	White alone, not Hispanic or Latino	Black alone, not Hispanic or Latino	Asian alone, not Hispanic or Latino	All other races or 2 or more races, not Hispanic or Latino	Hispanic or Latino[1]	Under 18 years old	Age 65 years and older	Median age	Percent High school diploma or less	Percent Bachelor's degree or more	Total	Percent with a computer
	1	2	3	4	5	6	7	8	9	10	11	12	13	14	15	16
WISCONSIN—Con.																
Caledonia village & MCD (Racine)	24,875	25,277	1.6	25,120	82.8	4.5	1.5	2.3	8.9	21.1	18.3	46.0	36.7	30.8	10,021	93.0
Caledonia town (Trempealeau)	876	925	5.6	923	96.9	0.5	0.0	1.8	0.8	27.2	12.4	41.6	38.6	24.8	363	86.5
Caledonia town (Waupaca)	1,666	1,687	1.3	1,700	95.4	1.4	0.4	1.4	1.4	18.6	13.6	49.5	39.9	23.4	676	94.1
Calumet town (Fond du Lac)	1,470	1,485	1.0	1,523	96.7	0.0	0.0	1.6	1.8	20.9	19.6	47.8	43.8	21.6	602	92.5
Cambria village & MCD (Columbia)	770	748	-2.9	702	80.9	0.9	0.3	1.3	16.7	24.9	13.0	34.8	51.0	14.9	275	92.0
Cambridge village	1,454	1,535	5.6	1,332	91.7	0.3	0.3	1.9	5.8	17.1	19.2	45.9	26.3	36.3	596	94.3
Cambridge village (Dane)	1,345	1,422	5.7	1,286	91.4	0.3	0.3	1.9	6.0	17.7	18.9	45.5	25.5	37.0	573	94.9
Cambridge village (Jefferson)	109	113	3.7	46	100.0	0.0	0.0	0.0	0.0	0.0	28.3	53.8	47.2	16.7	23	78.3
Cameron village & MCD (Barron)	1,779	1,788	0.5	1,965	89.0	2.6	2.0	3.6	2.8	25.5	13.8	37.3	47.2	12.6	824	91.0
Cameron town (Wood)	500	482	-3.6	502	99.2	0.0	0.8	0.0	0.0	22.7	22.9	48.6	43.6	22.2	201	91.5
Campbell town (La Crosse)	4,316	4,299	-0.4	4,341	94.1	0.0	2.4	2.3	1.1	15.2	20.5	47.3	34.0	27.9	2,032	96.7
Campbellsport village & MCD (Fond du Lac)	2,020	1,827	-9.6	1,845	94.3	0.8	0.0	2.7	2.3	23.5	17.2	42.9	51.8	16.7	790	85.4
Camp Douglas village & MCD (Juneau)	598	623	4.2	610	91.6	1.5	3.1	1.6	2.1	28.9	14.6	36.0	49.4	10.2	248	92.3
Canton town (Buffalo)	305	298	-2.3	272	93.4	0.0	0.0	0.0	6.6	15.4	20.2	50.0	44.4	17.6	111	87.4
Carey town (Iron)	163	159	-2.5	138	92.8	0.0	1.4	0.0	5.8	13.0	25.4	52.4	25.4	29.8	65	87.7
Carlton town (Kewaunee)	1,014	1,014	0.0	1,005	98.2	0.0	0.0	1.0	0.8	18.1	18.3	47.0	45.4	15.6	422	92.9
Caroline CDP	270	-	-	229	87.8	0.0	0.0	12.2	0.0	19.2	27.9	50.7	64.7	10.0	88	73.9
Carson town (Portage)	1,303	1,337	2.6	1,357	97.4	0.0	1.0	0.8	0.7	20.9	20.6	47.7	43.5	22.3	541	88.0
Cary town (Wood)	424	402	-5.2	452	96.0	0.0	0.0	0.9	3.1	25.4	19.0	44.7	45.6	20.1	189	87.8
Cascade village & MCD (Sheboygan)	711	692	-2.7	629	93.0	0.0	0.0	3.5	3.5	18.1	13.5	40.8	48.4	20.4	265	88.3
Casco village & MCD (Kewaunee)	592	585	-1.2	645	91.3	1.4	1.1	4.8	1.4	26.4	11.8	39.9	53.7	19.6	237	88.2
Casco town (Kewaunee)	1,160	1,181	1.8	1,081	98.1	0.0	0.0	0.4	1.5	24.0	15.5	45.4	46.4	18.9	406	89.4
Casey town (Washburn)	351	353	0.6	368	97.8	1.1	0.5	0.5	0.0	8.4	35.1	60.3	30.5	31.1	197	91.9
Cashton village & MCD (Monroe)	1,104	1,112	0.7	938	89.1	1.5	0.0	3.2	6.2	21.3	16.4	40.5	51.8	21.0	424	74.5
Cassel town (Marathon)	915	925	1.1	911	95.5	0.0	0.9	0.4	3.2	25.5	17.2	42.2	48.6	23.0	348	87.1
Cassian town (Oneida)	986	980	-0.6	1,016	96.9	0.0	0.3	0.0	2.8	10.3	33.6	56.9	40.0	18.3	478	87.2
Cassville village & MCD (Grant)	923	881	-4.6	961	95.8	0.0	0.0	2.9	1.2	17.2	25.0	49.2	54.0	13.6	438	81.3
Cassville town (Grant)	443	431	-2.7	355	99.7	0.0	0.3	0.0	0.0	13.0	19.7	52.4	57.1	5.7	160	88.1
Castle Rock town (Grant)	248	254	2.4	261	100.0	0.0	0.0	0.0	0.0	23.8	22.2	47.5	44.8	26.8	106	84.9
Caswell town (Forest)	91	87	-4.4	77	97.4	0.0	0.0	2.6	0.0	10.4	20.8	52.3	50.7	13.0	39	89.7
Cataract CDP	186	-	-	172	100.0	0.0	0.0	0.0	0.0	20.9	12.2	47.6	48.5	16.9	70	91.4
Catawba village & MCD (Price)	110	100	-9.1	121	88.4	0.0	0.0	6.6	5.0	22.3	21.5	53.9	63.3	8.9	60	83.3
Catawba town (Price)	269	252	-6.3	244	98.4	0.0	0.0	0.4	1.2	17.2	33.6	55.0	51.8	11.4	122	87.7
Cato town (Manitowoc)	1,563	1,541	-1.4	1,700	98.5	0.1	0.0	0.8	0.6	25.0	15.1	43.0	44.3	20.4	632	92.4
Cazenovia village	324	310	-4.3	358	94.4	2.8	0.0	0.0	2.8	22.1	20.9	38.2	58.6	12.7	165	67.3
Cazenovia village (Richland)	314	300	-4.5	353	94.3	2.8	0.0	0.0	2.8	22.4	19.8	35.9	57.7	13.0	162	67.3
Cazenovia village (Sauk)	10	10	0.0	5	100.0	0.0	0.0	0.0	0.0	0.0	100.0	76.3	100.0	0.0	3	66.7
Cecil village & MCD (Shawano)	565	551	-2.5	635	97.0	0.0	0.0	1.9	1.1	10.1	22.7	51.6	52.7	12.7	312	89.7
Cedarburg city & MCD (Ozaukee)	11,453	11,603	1.3	11,527	93.6	0.7	1.7	1.8	2.1	20.9	18.7	44.4	18.9	57.8	4,847	92.8
Cedarburg town (Ozaukee)	5,725	6,061	5.9	5,963	96.7	0.1	1.1	2.1	0.1	26.1	15.7	45.2	24.5	48.9	2,096	98.5
Cedar Grove village & MCD (Sheboygan)	2,113	2,117	0.2	2,103	95.4	0.8	0.1	0.3	3.3	23.2	18.4	39.7	40.8	23.3	882	81.4
Cedar Lake town (Barron)	948	943	-0.5	874	97.7	0.0	0.3	0.6	1.4	10.4	35.8	57.4	38.9	23.3	433	90.8
Cedar Rapids town (Rusk)	41	42	2.4	26	100.0	0.0	0.0	0.0	0.0	19.2	50.0	63.5	42.9	23.8	13	84.6
Center town (Outagamie)	3,402	3,642	7.1	3,605	98.0	0.2	0.0	1.2	0.6	21.4	17.4	45.9	35.5	29.7	1,370	94.3
Center town (Rock)	1,062	1,117	5.2	1,003	95.4	1.0	0.2	3.4	0.0	19.1	16.9	51.5	44.2	23.4	401	90.3
Centerville town (Manitowoc)	638	624	-2.2	581	96.2	2.1	0.3	0.7	0.7	20.7	16.7	47.3	34.9	26.6	256	95.7
Centuria village & MCD (Polk)	947	910	-3.9	803	94.1	0.4	0.0	3.9	1.6	21.4	15.7	39.4	54.2	7.0	387	75.7
Chain O' Lakes CDP	981	-	-	861	99.0	0.0	0.0	0.0	1.0	12.3	42.4	61.3	22.7	53.3	473	92.0
Charlestown town (Calumet)	773	757	-2.1	828	91.9	0.1	0.0	0.7	7.2	24.5	15.3	41.6	43.3	18.1	324	96.6
Chase town (Oconto)	3,003	3,058	1.8	3,029	97.8	0.3	0.0	1.3	0.7	25.9	7.9	38.4	35.4	25.2	1,101	95.2
Chaseburg village & MCD (Vernon)	288	292	1.4	341	98.2	0.0	1.2	0.0	0.6	20.5	13.2	41.2	35.2	22.1	150	89.3
Chelsea CDP	113	-	-	115	94.8	0.0	0.0	5.2	0.0	35.7	13.0	35.5	53.1	0.0	45	84.4
Chelsea town (Taylor)	805	788	-2.1	688	98.0	0.0	0.0	1.0	1.0	21.8	21.5	47.8	61.7	14.6	301	85.4
Chenequa village & MCD (Waukesha)	564	602	6.7	560	95.2	1.8	0.7	0.0	2.3	18.8	35.5	54.6	14.2	64.9	228	96.9
Chester town (Dodge)	688	665	-3.3	702	97.4	0.0	0.0	0.9	1.7	15.5	18.9	48.7	49.4	17.1	290	84.5
Chetek city & MCD (Barron)	2,213	2,095	-5.3	2,169	95.7	0.7	1.2	1.5	0.9	18.8	29.0	47.4	54.3	17.5	892	79.7
Chetek town (Barron)	1,653	1,624	-1.8	1,691	98.0	0.0	0.8	0.7	0.5	12.7	32.5	56.8	42.0	22.1	792	90.5
Chicog town (Washburn)	234	236	0.9	228	99.1	0.0	0.0	0.9	0.0	3.5	39.5	62.5	51.9	14.8	133	89.5
Chief Lake CDP	583	-	-	565	23.2	0.0	0.0	67.6	9.2	34.5	18.8	38.6	42.0	26.7	253	81.8
Chili CDP	226	-	-	158	88.6	0.0	3.2	7.6	0.6	27.2	16.5	40.6	48.1	9.4	66	71.2
Chilton city & MCD (Calumet)	3,933	3,859	-1.9	3,831	94.1	0.2	0.0	0.8	4.9	19.5	23.0	44.3	45.8	19.1	1,719	80.0
Chilton town (Calumet)	1,141	1,120	-1.8	1,083	97.4	0.5	0.3	1.2	0.6	24.1	12.3	46.5	41.4	16.7	403	86.6
Chimney Rock town (Trempealeau)	240	252	5.0	238	98.3	0.0	0.0	0.4	1.3	18.5	20.2	44.7	57.1	20.9	102	77.5
Chippewa town (Ashland)	375	369	-1.6	406	95.3	0.0	0.0	0.7	3.9	13.5	24.1	53.1	55.7	13.3	186	89.8

1 May be of any race.

Table A. All Places — **Population and Housing**

STATE City, town, township, borough, or CDP (county if applicable)	2010 census total population	2019 estimated population	Percent change 2010–2019	ACS total population estimate 2015–2019	White alone, not Hispanic or Latino	Black alone, not Hispanic or Latino	Asian alone, not Hispanic or Latino	All other races or 2 or more races, not Hispanic or Latino	Hispanic or Latino[1]	Under 18 years old	Age 65 years and older	Median age	Percent High school diploma or less	Percent Bachelor's degree or more	Total	Percent with a computer
	1	2	3	4	5	6	7	8	9	10	11	12	13	14	15	16
WISCONSIN—Con.																
Chippewa Falls city & MCD (Chippewa).........	13,723	14,366	4.7	14,101	91.5	3.2	1.4	2.3	1.7	20.8	18.4	37.9	41.1	21.8	6,027	87.8
Christiana town (Dane).....	1,240	1,316	6.1	1,330	97.0	0.5	0.7	1.2	0.7	22.3	15.6	40.6	29.6	27.2	489	94.1
Christiana town (Vernon)..	931	970	4.2	965	99.0	0.3	0.0	0.2	0.5	26.4	16.8	40.8	37.1	21.7	356	82.9
Cicero town (Outagamie)..	1,101	1,099	-0.2	1,096	98.4	0.0	0.9	0.6	0.0	20.9	20.4	43.7	51.2	16.8	423	81.3
City Point town (Jackson) .	182	180	-1.1	179	98.9	0.0	0.0	1.1	0.0	12.3	27.4	56.6	62.4	7.6	90	91.1
Clam Falls town (Polk)......	598	584	-2.3	532	98.9	0.0	0.4	0.8	0.0	18.4	34.4	57.2	44.3	25.2	276	77.9
Clam Lake CDP...............	37	-	-	27	100.0	0.0	0.0	0.0	0.0	0.0	70.4	68.5	40.7	18.5	18	88.9
Clarno town (Green).........	1,178	1,208	2.5	1,473	97.1	0.8	0.6	0.0	1.4	25.5	13.4	40.0	46.5	21.6	539	88.1
Clay Banks town (Door).....	380	385	1.3	358	95.0	0.0	1.4	1.7	2.0	17.0	29.3	53.8	38.5	30.1	168	88.1
Clayton town (Crawford) ...	958	903	-5.7	956	94.0	1.0	0.0	2.9	2.0	24.1	18.8	46.9	46.6	18.9	371	81.7
Clayton village & MCD (Polk).........................	571	545	-4.6	424	98.6	0.0	0.0	0.0	1.4	26.2	10.6	37.0	46.0	20.3	194	83.0
Clayton town (Polk)...........	975	981	0.6	1,030	94.5	0.0	0.3	2.3	2.9	22.2	18.3	43.2	44.1	18.4	423	86.8
Clayton town (Winnebago) .	3,951	4,220	6.8	4,161	96.2	0.2	0.9	0.0	2.6	24.1	14.5	45.0	31.2	39.2	1,499	93.8
Clear Creek town (Eau Claire).......................	821	894	8.9	802	99.0	0.0	0.5	0.5	0.0	22.8	17.2	44.6	43.7	21.9	296	89.9
Clearfield town (Juneau)...	728	746	2.5	741	94.7	0.5	0.9	0.9	2.8	21.6	19.3	48.6	44.7	17.6	304	91.8
Clear Lake village & MCD (Polk).........................	1,067	1,103	3.4	1,078	98.7	0.0	0.4	0.6	0.3	27.8	16.5	39.2	54.1	10.9	467	86.5
Clear Lake town (Polk)	902	907	0.6	885	96.7	0.0	0.0	2.3	1.0	20.3	15.6	42.8	43.5	13.9	332	89.5
Cleveland town (Chippewa).................	864	903	4.5	714	98.7	1.3	0.0	0.0	0.0	15.1	18.1	52.7	50.3	9.6	309	87.1
Cleveland town (Jackson).	473	483	2.1	572	99.5	0.0	0.0	0.3	0.2	32.5	17.5	33.5	56.0	12.0	208	79.3
Cleveland village & MCD (Manitowoc)..............	1,492	1,454	-2.5	1,606	84.5	0.0	0.1	1.0	14.4	26.2	15.7	39.1	39.1	25.6	606	94.2
Cleveland town (Marathon).................	1,486	1,495	0.6	1,563	99.4	0.0	0.3	0.3	0.0	27.6	13.6	43.3	52.0	17.8	552	89.9
Cleveland town (Taylor)	268	260	-3.0	178	98.9	0.0	0.0	1.1	0.0	11.8	28.1	54.3	64.4	13.0	85	78.8
Clifton town (Grant)	385	392	1.8	495	99.2	0.0	0.0	0.8	0.0	41.2	10.5	21.8	57.1	15.9	121	69.4
Clifton town (Monroe)	690	712	3.2	669	99.7	0.0	0.0	0.1	0.1	36.3	13.5	32.5	58.4	13.9	197	81.2
Clifton town (Pierce)........	2,012	2,109	4.8	2,326	95.4	0.1	0.9	1.5	2.1	26.5	12.1	43.1	20.8	48.7	751	94.0
Clinton town (Barron).......	879	873	-0.7	742	95.0	1.3	0.0	2.3	1.3	18.3	28.0	52.9	57.4	10.5	293	79.9
Clinton village & MCD (Rock).........................	2,155	2,140	-0.7	2,036	86.8	1.2	0.0	7.4	4.6	23.9	17.6	37.8	47.5	18.0	779	87.5
Clinton town (Rock)...........	929	967	4.1	927	95.3	1.3	0.0	0.2	3.2	23.9	16.7	41.7	48.0	20.3	339	90.9
Clinton town (Vernon).......	1,348	1,432	6.2	1,217	99.2	0.0	0.0	0.8	0.0	39.1	10.8	24.3	72.3	13.1	295	51.9
Clintonville city & MCD (Waupaca)...................	4,569	4,391	-3.9	4,384	89.4	0.0	0.0	6.2	4.3	23.0	18.6	38.8	40.8	25.5	2,060	81.1
Clover town (Bayfield)......	223	226	1.3	209	92.8	1.0	0.0	1.4	4.8	11.0	33.5	57.8	22.4	34.7	105	95.2
Cloverland town (Douglas)	210	214	1.9	204	90.7	1.0	0.0	4.4	3.9	22.1	22.1	49.4	42.2	29.3	89	88.8
Cloverland town (Vilas).....	1,030	1,060	2.9	959	88.8	0.0	0.2	0.0	10.9	15.5	30.2	55.3	39.3	26.8	469	90.6
Clyde town (Iowa)............	306	314	2.6	245	95.1	2.4	0.0	1.6	0.8	13.5	25.7	53.4	36.4	26.7	112	89.3
Clyman village & MCD (Dodge).....................	422	401	-5.0	401	80.5	9.2	5.5	1.2	3.5	19.7	12.0	43.1	54.2	10.6	149	87.2
Clyman town (Dodge).......	774	769	-0.6	706	88.5	4.0	0.6	2.4	4.5	20.3	20.4	44.9	51.4	12.6	285	88.8
Cobb village & MCD (Iowa)........................	458	449	-2.0	473	100.0	0.0	0.0	0.0	0.0	18.4	17.8	40.1	38.4	22.6	229	93.9
Cochrane village & MCD (Buffalo).....................	450	411	-8.7	392	99.0	0.3	0.0	0.5	0.3	22.4	20.7	44.2	36.6	25.4	180	86.1
Colburn town (Adams)......	223	219	-1.8	248	94.0	0.0	0.0	5.6	0.4	11.3	35.5	60.0	65.2	6.7	111	83.8
Colburn town (Chippewa) .	856	888	3.7	819	98.0	0.0	0.6	0.6	0.7	20.0	22.0	45.6	52.0	16.2	337	83.1
Colby city......................	1,860	1,949	4.8	2,038	82.7	0.1	0.6	2.1	14.6	26.2	21.6	38.3	65.7	9.6	785	83.3
Colby city (Clark).............	1,364	1,434	5.1	1,444	85.5	0.1	0.8	0.3	13.2	25.8	22.1	38.0	61.4	12.2	536	86.0
Colby city (Marathon)	496	515	3.8	594	75.8	0.0	0.0	6.4	17.8	27.1	20.5	40.0	75.9	3.4	249	77.5
Colby town (Clark)...........	852	864	1.4	931	95.8	0.0	0.2	2.9	1.1	40.1	11.2	24.8	64.4	11.9	259	69.9
Cold Spring town (Jefferson)...................	730	753	3.2	702	89.5	0.9	0.4	0.7	8.5	19.1	24.9	49.4	44.5	23.1	291	93.1
Coleman village & MCD (Marinette)..................	722	688	-4.7	758	90.4	0.0	0.3	7.0	2.4	26.4	18.3	36.9	45.6	15.8	333	88.9
Colfax village & MCD (Dunn)......................	1,164	1,158	-0.5	1,151	82.5	0.0	9.6	6.5	1.3	30.0	21.7	37.4	46.3	17.5	426	88.0
Colfax town (Dunn)..........	1,186	1,242	4.7	1,105	97.6	0.0	0.0	1.4	1.0	25.3	17.0	40.8	38.5	26.3	411	95.9
Collins CDP....................	164	-	-	131	94.7	0.0	0.8	1.5	3.1	26.7	10.7	42.3	37.9	6.9	51	92.2
Coloma village & MCD (Waushara).................	450	448	-0.4	416	93.5	0.0	0.0	4.8	1.7	24.8	18.0	40.4	58.2	8.2	190	84.7
Coloma town (Waushara).	758	764	0.8	637	98.9	0.0	0.3	0.0	0.8	20.3	24.3	47.4	54.3	14.1	273	85.3
Columbus city & MCD (Columbia)..................	4,994	5,120	2.5	5,058	95.1	0.0	2.8	1.2	0.9	25.1	15.1	35.7	35.1	30.0	2,204	88.4
Columbus city (Dodge)	-	-	-	-	-	-	-	-	-	-	-	-	-	-	-	-
Columbus town (Columbia)	645	649	0.6	561	89.7	1.1	5.5	0.0	3.7	15.9	19.3	50.1	53.1	19.8	209	93.8
Combined Locks village & MCD (Outagamie).......	3,324	3,593	8.1	3,577	96.3	0.0	1.0	0.6	2.1	24.9	20.2	38.9	46.7	25.8	1,366	93.4
Commonwealth town (Florence)....................	399	388	-2.8	478	99.4	0.0	0.0	0.0	0.6	22.0	19.7	41.8	38.4	26.7	182	84.6
Como CDP......................	2,631	-	-	2,680	86.8	0.0	0.0	1.9	11.3	17.6	17.1	44.3	37.3	29.2	1,163	92.4
Concord town (Jefferson) .	2,049	2,123	3.6	2,295	98.4	0.0	0.0	0.9	0.7	18.8	24.8	50.2	44.6	21.1	858	92.9
Conover town (Vilas)	1,222	1,256	2.8	1,255	93.6	0.0	0.0	5.1	1.3	17.2	36.6	55.7	42.6	23.9	609	87.2
Conrath village & MCD (Rusk).......................	98	92	-6.1	63	81.0	0.0	0.0	0.0	19.0	9.5	27.0	55.3	73.5	16.3	32	87.5
Cooks Valley town (Chippewa).................	805	838	4.1	821	99.3	0.0	0.0	0.4	0.4	29.7	12.5	35.1	39.6	18.2	290	92.4
Coon town (Vernon)..........	728	762	4.7	809	99.1	0.0	0.0	0.5	0.4	20.5	22.2	49.9	39.1	33.0	312	92.6
Coon Valley village & MCD (Vernon)..............	765	787	2.9	889	99.2	0.0	0.1	0.3	0.3	25.3	19.9	37.9	43.6	23.8	365	81.9
Cooperstown town (Manitowoc)..............	1,292	1,274	-1.4	1,319	97.6	0.0	0.2	1.1	1.1	20.5	15.2	44.5	53.5	19.6	532	94.2
Cornell city & MCD (Chippewa).................	1,460	1,407	-3.6	1,781	90.0	0.4	0.8	2.1	6.6	27.8	17.3	35.1	55.7	9.0	695	80.1
Corning town (Lincoln)......	881	869	-1.4	676	98.8	0.4	0.0	0.4	0.3	19.1	22.3	47.9	55.4	11.2	306	83.3
Cornucopia CDP..............	98	-	-	106	96.2	0.0	0.0	3.8	0.0	0.0	47.2	64.3	17.4	54.7	77	92.2

1 May be of any race.

Table A. All Places — Population and Housing

WISCONSIN—Con.

STATE City, town, township, borough, or CDP (county if applicable)	2010 census total population	2019 estimated population	Percent change 2010–2019	ACS total population estimate 2015–2019	White alone, not Hispanic or Latino	Black alone, not Hispanic or Latino	Asian alone, not Hispanic or Latino	All other races or 2 or more races, not Hispanic or Latino	Hispanic or Latino[1]	Under 18 years old	Age 65 years and older	Median age	Percent High school diploma or less	Percent Bachelor's degree or more	Total	Percent with a computer
	1	2	3	4	5	6	7	8	9	10	11	12	13	14	15	16
Cottage Grove village & MCD (Dane)	6,366	7,143	12.2	7,020	88.4	0.1	6.8	0.6	4.1	29.7	9.5	35.7	19.1	50.4	2,408	95.1
Cottage Grove town (Dane)	3,722	3,964	6.5	3,958	91.0	0.8	0.6	6.1	1.5	21.3	17.1	47.4	34.0	32.8	1,465	96.8
Couderay village & MCD (Sawyer)	89	86	-3.4	84	50.0	0.0	0.0	50.0	0.0	13.1	20.2	51.3	38.9	23.6	44	84.1
Couderay town (Sawyer)	400	403	0.8	417	37.4	0.0	0.7	61.9	0.0	27.1	21.8	45.1	52.4	8.8	206	58.7
Courtland town (Columbia)	518	519	0.2	521	84.5	0.0	1.7	3.8	10.0	25.0	22.5	42.8	48.0	14.3	180	83.9
Crandon city & MCD (Forest)	1,922	1,800	-6.3	1,941	82.2	0.9	0.0	15.1	1.8	20.2	14.5	40.0	49.6	12.5	876	77.2
Crandon town (Forest)	650	644	-0.9	599	95.0	1.0	0.0	4.0	0.0	18.2	19.7	46.3	49.1	11.7	257	89.9
Cranmoor town (Wood)	168	158	-6.0	183	89.1	0.0	0.0	6.0	4.9	30.6	8.7	33.5	33.9	28.8	62	95.2
Crescent town (Oneida)	2,032	2,015	-0.8	2,128	97.4	0.0	1.6	1.0	0.0	17.6	21.6	52.5	37.6	29.2	932	90.5
Crivitz village & MCD (Marinette)	984	943	-4.2	1,007	92.2	0.0	0.0	2.5	5.4	17.8	26.9	50.4	64.9	11.6	444	78.4
Cross town (Buffalo)	379	371	-2.1	342	96.8	0.3	0.0	1.5	1.5	21.9	21.9	48.9	50.6	26.9	134	88.1
Cross Plains village & MCD (Dane)	3,654	4,286	17.3	4,187	93.6	0.2	1.0	2.3	3.0	27.8	11.8	37.9	27.6	37.3	1,653	94.0
Cross Plains town (Dane)	1,401	1,495	6.7	1,430	98.8	0.0	0.4	0.8	0.0	16.4	28.2	54.6	29.6	40.2	586	91.8
Crystal town (Washburn)	266	268	0.8	272	95.2	0.0	1.5	3.3	0.0	15.4	29.0	56.0	46.3	18.1	121	87.6
Crystal Lake town (Barron)	760	753	-0.9	738	97.2	1.5	0.0	1.4	0.0	21.4	25.3	47.0	44.5	20.0	294	90.5
Crystal Lake town (Marquette)	484	490	1.2	459	94.1	0.0	2.8	3.1	0.0	10.2	39.0	60.5	47.3	21.4	240	82.9
Cuba City city	2,087	2,029	-2.8	2,307	94.3	1.3	0.0	0.9	3.5	27.9	18.4	38.0	42.1	23.9	904	81.1
Cuba City city (Grant)	1,877	1,822	-2.9	1,936	93.2	1.5	0.0	1.1	4.2	26.5	19.8	39.7	46.5	23.3	795	79.7
Cuba City city (Lafayette)	210	207	-1.4	371	100.0	0.0	0.0	0.0	0.0	35.0	11.3	30.9	13.8	27.6	109	90.8
Cudahy city & MCD (Milwaukee)	18,320	18,104	-1.2	18,271	81.7	2.4	0.9	3.4	11.5	18.2	20.7	42.6	45.1	21.8	7,682	88.6
Cumberland city & MCD (Barron)	2,173	2,103	-3.2	2,291	83.1	0.0	0.0	3.1	13.8	23.9	26.1	41.7	47.7	23.9	1,039	83.1
Cumberland town (Barron)	872	865	-0.8	714	95.4	0.8	0.0	0.0	3.8	16.1	25.1	50.4	41.2	25.7	300	87.7
Curran town (Jackson)	341	343	0.6	272	98.5	0.0	0.0	1.5	0.0	13.2	26.1	49.9	57.8	19.9	131	84.0
Curtiss village & MCD (Clark)	216	212	-1.9	298	17.4	0.0	0.0	0.0	82.6	46.3	5.0	23.0	76.4	3.6	86	91.9
Cutler town (Juneau)	335	332	-0.9	325	90.5	0.6	2.2	6.8	0.0	18.5	16.6	49.7	54.8	9.7	146	87.0
Cylon town (St. Croix)	684	698	2.0	656	93.3	2.4	1.4	2.3	0.6	22.9	15.1	41.3	42.7	24.0	253	90.5
Dairyland town (Douglas)	184	188	2.2	166	97.0	0.0	0.0	0.0	3.0	14.5	39.8	59.6	65.2	8.7	80	76.3
Dakota town (Waushara)	1,233	1,246	1.1	1,219	85.9	0.0	0.0	0.2	13.9	20.4	27.7	50.3	57.3	12.1	537	80.8
Dale CDP	528	-	-	551	96.2	0.0	0.0	2.9	0.9	22.5	16.5	40.3	45.5	15.6	225	100.0
Dale town (Outagamie)	2,738	2,907	6.2	2,863	94.5	0.0	3.3	1.2	1.0	24.1	12.1	41.6	38.1	26.3	1,042	94.3
Dallas village & MCD (Barron)	406	345	-15.0	401	96.3	0.0	0.0	1.2	2.5	20.9	27.4	43.5	55.3	8.5	156	82.1
Dallas town (Barron)	570	563	-1.2	450	96.2	0.0	0.9	0.9	2.0	18.2	22.0	48.3	45.2	16.4	180	88.9
Dalton CDP	206	-	-	196	98.5	0.0	0.0	1.5	0.0	30.6	23.5	37.8	57.0	10.2	79	84.8
Danbury CDP	172	-	-	165	81.2	0.0	0.0	14.5	4.2	21.2	25.5	37.3	53.5	11.0	86	81.4
Dane village & MCD (Dane)	997	1,135	13.8	1,004	90.8	0.9	4.9	0.3	3.1	22.6	10.3	34.7	35.2	29.6	410	96.6
Dane town (Dane)	986	1,048	6.3	999	88.3	0.2	0.6	0.8	10.1	16.8	22.2	49.7	49.9	21.2	407	90.9
Daniels town (Burnett)	649	653	0.6	716	96.2	0.0	0.1	3.5	0.1	21.5	24.7	44.2	42.6	21.2	309	85.1
Darien village & MCD (Walworth)	1,580	1,590	0.6	1,704	84.2	0.2	0.0	0.2	15.4	26.5	10.0	34.6	50.1	15.7	576	87.7
Darien town (Walworth)	1,693	1,710	1.0	1,924	77.0	0.2	0.3	1.4	21.2	25.7	13.5	43.1	55.9	16.2	632	92.2
Darlington city & MCD (Lafayette)	2,451	2,337	-4.7	2,430	82.4	1.8	1.5	0.2	14.1	22.3	19.8	40.3	54.3	15.7	1,041	84.9
Darlington town (Lafayette)	883	865	-2.0	885	98.9	0.0	0.0	0.0	1.1	30.3	14.2	35.6	45.0	25.1	320	85.0
Day town (Marathon)	1,085	1,144	5.4	1,041	96.0	0.5	0.0	0.3	3.3	24.0	17.8	43.8	52.9	20.2	406	87.7
Dayton town (Richland)	693	673	-2.9	615	97.7	0.0	0.0	2.3	0.0	14.3	26.8	54.0	55.0	22.4	273	83.2
Dayton town (Waupaca)	2,748	2,692	-2.0	2,698	95.7	0.1	0.0	0.7	3.6	18.0	25.1	52.4	41.7	27.5	1,184	88.0
Decatur town (Green)	1,766	1,817	2.9	1,610	95.2	0.0	0.2	1.6	3.1	17.1	21.9	51.5	38.0	26.7	641	91.7
Deer Creek town (Outagamie)	637	657	3.1	650	94.9	0.3	0.0	0.3	4.5	22.0	18.5	48.4	66.9	6.4	257	68.5
Deer Creek town (Taylor)	768	763	-0.7	670	98.4	0.0	0.0	0.7	0.9	20.9	19.7	43.1	69.5	10.0	288	74.0
Deerfield village & MCD (Dane)	2,309	2,532	9.7	2,538	90.5	3.2	0.2	2.6	3.6	26.3	9.0	35.2	30.1	37.7	1,014	97.3
Deerfield town (Dane)	1,599	1,715	7.3	1,680	95.5	3.7	0.2	0.3	0.2	16.9	19.0	48.7	31.4	34.7	602	92.0
Deerfield town (Waushara)	737	743	0.8	645	86.4	0.0	0.5	7.1	6.0	18.0	31.5	55.4	38.6	19.4	286	89.2
Deer Park village & MCD (St. Croix)	218	213	-2.3	239	97.9	0.0	0.4	0.8	0.8	22.2	20.5	35.6	59.8	10.6	109	73.4
DeForest village & MCD (Dane)	8,975	10,691	19.1	10,179	87.4	0.6	3.2	3.5	5.2	26.7	10.4	36.6	26.4	38.2	3,833	93.1
Dekorra town (Columbia)	2,306	2,338	1.4	2,385	99.6	0.0	0.0	0.4	0.0	15.7	22.5	51.6	32.9	28.0	1,073	87.9
Delafield city & MCD (Waukesha)	7,090	7,536	6.3	7,457	94.4	0.0	0.7	1.8	3.1	19.1	23.2	48.7	19.5	52.2	3,324	95.2
Delafield town (Waukesha)	8,411	8,834	5.0	8,713	91.1	1.4	2.1	2.3	3.1	23.4	19.3	48.5	13.3	59.8	3,102	98.2
Delavan city & MCD (Walworth)	8,442	8,264	-2.1	8,303	69.7	1.0	3.0	0.3	26.1	25.0	15.0	36.1	51.3	16.6	3,287	89.7
Delavan town (Walworth)	5,295	5,333	0.7	5,313	87.2	1.6	0.0	0.7	10.5	16.3	26.5	50.1	47.1	22.2	2,251	88.9
Delavan Lake CDP	2,649	-	-	2,558	85.7	0.4	0.0	0.7	13.2	19.1	22.2	50.0	45.4	26.8	1,104	93.1
Dellona town (Sauk)	1,556	1,674	7.6	1,732	87.6	0.7	0.8	8.8	2.1	25.3	18.7	43.0	42.7	23.0	630	89.2
Dell Prairie town (Adams)	1,592	1,572	-1.3	1,566	90.8	4.6	0.3	1.1	3.2	18.3	23.4	50.6	41.6	19.1	708	87.1
Dellwood CDP	563	-	-	525	99.4	0.0	0.0	0.6	0.0	10.9	43.0	62.2	61.7	7.6	286	74.5
Delmar town (Chippewa)	933	969	3.9	1,184	97.7	0.0	0.3	1.9	0.0	32.2	10.9	37.1	45.9	17.4	398	88.7
Delta town (Bayfield)	273	276	1.1	212	93.9	0.0	1.4	4.7	0.0	14.2	30.2	60.6	25.3	41.2	98	95.9
Delton town (Sauk)	2,328	2,496	7.2	2,568	83.4	0.5	0.9	12.3	3.0	21.8	16.9	42.8	44.4	23.9	931	91.6
Denmark village & MCD (Brown)	2,122	2,277	7.3	2,200	91.4	0.0	0.3	4.3	4.0	29.9	13.2	34.2	48.7	27.4	847	84.7
De Pere city & MCD (Brown)	23,846	24,970	4.7	24,903	90.5	0.6	3.1	4.5	1.3	22.4	13.3	34.0	27.2	39.5	9,632	91.9

1 May be of any race.

Table A. All Places — **Population and Housing**

STATE City, town, township, borough, or CDP (county if applicable)	Population				Race and Hispanic or Latino origin (percent)					Age (percent)			Educational attainment of persons age 25 and older		Occupied housing units	
	2010 census total population	2019 estimated population	Percent change 2010–2019	ACS total population estimate 2015–2019	White alone, not Hispanic or Latino	Black alone, not Hispanic or Latino	Asian alone, not Hispanic or Latino	All other races or 2 or more races, not Hispanic or Latino	Hispanic or Latino[1]	Under 18 years old	Age 65 years and older	Median age	Percent High school diploma or less	Percent Bachelor's degree or more	Total	Percent with a computer
	1	2	3	4	5	6	7	8	9	10	11	12	13	14	15	16

WISCONSIN—Con.

STATE City, town, township, borough, or CDP (county if applicable)	1	2	3	4	5	6	7	8	9	10	11	12	13	14	15	16
De Soto village	287	279	-2.8	320	97.8	0.0	0.0	1.3	0.9	21.9	20.0	42.8	41.2	15.5	143	85.3
De Soto village (Crawford)	108	102	-5.6	107	97.2	0.0	0.0	0.0	2.8	29.0	14.0	41.1	31.1	13.5	41	85.4
De Soto village (Vernon)...	179	177	-1.1	213	98.1	0.0	0.0	1.9	0.0	18.3	23.0	50.0	45.9	16.4	102	85.3
Dewey town (Burnett)	511	514	0.6	485	87.4	0.0	1.0	7.0	4.5	19.4	20.6	48.7	48.0	12.2	203	86.7
Dewey town (Portage)	943	973	3.2	1,092	91.8	0.1	1.7	0.1	6.2	23.3	15.8	44.7	45.0	23.8	406	86.0
Dewey town (Rusk)	545	520	-4.6	534	94.8	1.1	0.0	2.2	1.9	20.6	20.8	47.7	40.0	26.5	224	81.7
Dewhurst town (Clark)	323	340	5.3	326	91.4	0.0	0.0	8.6	0.0	14.1	31.0	58.5	38.9	11.3	151	87.4
Dexter town (Wood)	359	345	-3.9	346	98.8	0.0	0.0	1.2	0.0	18.5	28.3	51.3	62.6	16.8	162	87.0
Diamond Bluff CDP	194	-	-	170	98.2	0.0	0.0	0.0	1.8	16.5	21.8	53.5	67.2	6.6	81	92.6
Diamond Bluff town (Pierce)	475	497	4.6	506	96.4	0.0	0.0	3.0	0.6	22.3	18.2	48.3	50.7	20.3	206	90.8
Diaperville CDP	70	-	-	37	0.0	0.0	0.0	100.0	0.0	13.5	10.8	58.1	53.1	0.0	13	69.2
Dickeyville village & MCD (Grant)	1,061	1,024	-3.5	1,231	97.7	1.6	0.0	0.2	0.5	25.0	16.0	37.1	44.4	15.1	495	90.1
Dodge CDP	121	-	-	117	100.0	0.0	0.0	0.0	0.0	12.0	21.4	37.2	57.5	9.2	65	66.2
Dodge town (Trempealeau)	394	413	4.8	431	98.6	0.2	0.5	0.0	0.7	21.8	18.6	43.1	46.0	19.9	191	82.2
Dodgeville city & MCD (Iowa)	4,848	4,695	-3.2	4,730	96.9	0.0	1.5	0.9	0.7	22.3	16.9	39.0	46.0	19.3	2,077	86.0
Dodgeville town (Iowa)	1,553	1,604	3.3	1,611	98.4	0.0	1.0	0.4	0.2	22.0	21.3	50.4	26.6	35.7	649	91.8
Dorchester village	876	865	-1.3	981	84.0	0.0	0.0	0.0	16.0	29.8	11.2	32.0	55.6	13.1	390	83.6
Dorchester village (Clark)	871	860	-1.3	981	84.0	0.0	0.0	0.0	16.0	29.8	11.2	32.0	55.6	13.1	390	83.6
Dorchester village (Marathon)	5	5	0.0	-	-	-	-	-	-	-	-	-	-	-	-	-
Doty town (Oconto)	260	264	1.5	309	99.4	0.0	0.0	0.6	0.0	1.0	53.7	66.0	49.0	14.0	180	83.9
Douglas town (Marquette)	725	733	1.1	735	97.0	0.0	0.0	0.4	2.6	14.8	26.7	52.0	51.4	16.8	332	88.3
Dousman village & MCD (Waukesha)	2,272	2,328	2.5	2,368	89.4	1.2	2.6	0.8	0.6	24.0	24.8	44.1	39.9	33.1	959	84.0
Dover town (Buffalo)	486	476	-2.1	545	99.1	0.0	0.0	0.0	0.9	31.2	13.8	36.5	54.5	14.6	188	79.8
Dover town (Racine)	4,069	4,280	5.2	4,203	87.8	3.1	0.5	3.2	5.4	16.9	19.8	45.6	40.8	25.8	1,351	92.7
Dovre town (Barron)	843	840	-0.4	885	95.9	0.0	2.9	0.2	0.9	26.6	13.3	38.5	56.1	16.4	299	84.9
Downing village & MCD (Dunn)	265	263	-0.8	199	93.5	0.0	0.0	3.0	3.5	19.1	16.1	43.5	68.9	7.3	85	89.4
Downsville CDP	146	-	-	120	100.0	0.0	0.0	0.0	0.0	18.3	10.0	41.3	25.3	26.4	58	79.3
Doyle town (Barron)	465	462	-0.6	429	98.6	0.7	0.0	0.7	0.0	15.6	12.6	48.3	47.6	15.2	179	93.3
Doylestown village & MCD (Columbia)	298	297	-0.3	256	100.0	0.0	0.0	0.0	0.0	19.1	15.2	42.7	69.4	9.4	119	85.7
Drammen town (Eau Claire)	784	857	9.3	674	96.6	0.7	0.7	1.9	0.0	12.8	25.2	52.3	38.9	24.4	301	89.7
Draper town (Sawyer)	204	205	0.5	209	97.1	0.0	0.0	1.0	1.9	3.3	41.6	63.2	47.3	15.6	116	76.7
Dresser village & MCD (Polk)	888	866	-2.5	1,004	89.3	1.2	0.4	3.0	6.1	26.4	11.2	34.2	46.5	17.4	420	87.4
Drummond CDP	154	-	-	144	92.4	0.0	0.0	0.0	7.6	16.0	16.7	53.5	50.5	18.9	88	78.4
Drummond town (Bayfield)	462	459	-0.6	402	96.0	0.0	1.2	0.0	2.7	9.2	32.6	57.4	41.6	30.7	203	82.8
Dunbar CDP	50	-	-	50	100.0	0.0	0.0	0.0	0.0	4.0	38.0	59.5	54.2	6.3	33	60.6
Dunbar town (Marinette)...	1,094	621	-43.2	706	92.4	1.7	3.4	1.6	1.0	12.6	20.8	46.6	52.6	16.5	240	79.6
Dunkirk town (Dane)	1,898	2,017	6.3	2,039	94.8	0.3	1.0	0.9	3.0	20.1	18.5	46.5	34.6	32.2	822	95.9
Dunn town (Dane)	4,925	5,257	6.7	5,237	90.9	0.8	1.6	3.3	3.4	17.6	24.7	52.1	33.8	38.6	2,212	93.5
Dunn town (Dunn)	1,524	1,600	5.0	1,465	95.2	0.3	0.3	1.4	2.7	22.5	18.4	40.9	48.8	23.2	593	87.9
Dupont town (Waupaca)...	742	725	-2.3	777	98.7	0.0	0.0	0.5	0.8	29.7	16.1	37.2	62.5	11.6	270	71.9
Durand city & MCD (Pepin)	1,929	1,800	-6.7	1,725	95.7	0.8	0.6	0.3	2.6	18.7	23.8	47.6	47.6	21.2	803	80.9
Durand town (Pepin)	744	717	-3.6	789	94.8	0.0	0.0	3.7	1.5	24.3	18.0	43.8	52.5	16.7	319	90.6
Dyckesville CDP	538	-	-	475	88.4	4.0	0.0	4.2	3.4	19.8	27.4	44.8	32.5	48.5	202	94.6
Eagle town (Richland)	531	515	-3.0	444	97.7	0.0	0.0	0.0	2.3	13.7	30.2	54.7	58.7	17.7	212	77.8
Eagle village & MCD (Waukesha)	2,005	2,159	7.7	2,063	89.2	0.4	0.3	5.6	4.6	28.0	9.2	34.5	36.5	20.9	715	90.5
Eagle town (Waukesha)	3,454	3,625	5.0	3,556	97.4	0.0	0.3	0.6	2.0	19.6	15.0	45.6	31.9	37.2	1,276	95.6
Eagle Lake CDP	1,192	-	-	1,038	98.2	0.0	0.0	1.8	0.0	15.5	14.8	45.2	29.7	31.2	471	89.8
Eagle Point town (Chippewa)	3,065	3,196	4.3	3,153	97.0	0.0	0.8	1.3	1.0	16.8	28.8	55.9	42.3	26.2	1,392	94.8
Eagle River city & MCD (Vilas)	1,400	1,592	13.7	1,626	87.6	1.2	0.1	6.3	4.8	20.4	19.2	33.5	44.6	23.3	804	87.8
Eastman village & MCD (Crawford)	428	403	-5.8	404	98.5	0.0	0.0	1.5	0.0	26.0	17.3	36.0	54.4	14.6	152	81.6
Eastman town (Crawford)	739	724	-2.0	713	95.9	0.0	1.0	3.1	0.0	17.1	23.4	51.8	45.8	19.5	294	76.5
Easton town (Adams)	1,130	1,116	-1.2	1,061	95.3	2.0	0.0	0.7	2.1	16.9	26.7	52.3	59.9	10.7	478	81.4
Easton town (Marathon) ...	1,111	1,145	3.1	1,022	96.3	0.0	0.7	2.5	0.5	21.6	16.2	45.8	43.1	18.3	408	83.1
East Troy village & MCD (Walworth)	4,315	4,313	0.0	4,316	95.8	0.0	1.4	0.7	2.1	22.5	13.5	41.1	40.6	28.1	1,862	88.7
East Troy town (Walworth)	3,992	4,053	1.5	4,044	94.7	0.0	0.4	1.0	3.9	19.6	21.2	47.3	40.0	26.1	1,621	92.3
Eaton town (Brown)	1,508	1,644	9.0	1,653	97.7	0.0	1.1	0.8	0.4	24.1	12.7	40.2	45.9	19.7	603	90.4
Eaton town (Clark)	717	717	0.0	687	99.4	0.0	0.0	0.6	0.0	33.2	9.2	35.3	58.4	12.1	226	78.3
Eaton town (Manitowoc)...	836	824	-1.4	757	92.2	0.0	0.3	0.0	7.5	18.2	14.8	45.5	44.7	22.6	322	90.7
Eau Claire city	66,230	68,802	3.9	68,187	88.2	1.4	5.5	2.5	2.5	18.6	14.0	31.7	29.0	34.1	27,440	91.3
Eau Claire city (Chippewa)	1,978	2,019	2.1	1,747	88.7	0.2	10.8	0.3	0.0	24.3	15.5	36.7	42.9	22.2	762	89.9
Eau Claire city (Eau Claire)	64,252	66,783	3.9	66,440	88.2	1.4	5.3	2.6	2.6	18.5	13.9	31.5	28.6	34.4	26,678	91.3
Eau Galle town (Dunn)	757	784	3.6	714	91.0	0.0	0.7	0.0	8.3	21.7	24.8	46.5	57.7	17.6	305	87.2
Eau Galle town (St. Croix)	1,139	1,248	9.6	1,122	98.0	0.3	0.1	0.6	1.1	28.1	16.9	40.3	38.2	27.5	407	91.2
Eau Pleine town (Marathon)	772	818	6.0	910	82.6	0.0	0.0	2.5	14.8	22.3	16.7	38.9	61.1	12.5	351	86.6
Eau Pleine town (Portage)	908	932	2.6	964	96.4	0.0	1.9	1.3	0.4	21.2	21.5	49.4	44.9	26.7	380	85.5
Eden village & MCD (Fond du Lac)	875	932	6.5	797	90.8	0.6	0.0	1.8	6.8	19.7	18.3	40.4	53.4	13.5	338	92.0
Eden town (Fond du Lac)	1,024	1,044	2.0	1,010	94.3	0.9	0.0	0.4	4.5	17.4	24.1	50.3	53.1	18.1	395	90.4
Eden town (Iowa)	353	365	3.4	409	68.5	1.0	0.0	0.0	30.6	25.7	19.8	48.8	47.6	19.1	151	84.8
Edgar village & MCD (Marathon)	1,476	1,442	-2.3	1,562	97.5	0.0	0.5	0.4	1.6	29.6	13.5	40.1	52.6	14.7	617	87.2
Edgerton city	5,412	5,631	4.0	5,550	90.9	0.0	1.7	0.5	6.8	22.8	13.9	35.8	45.4	29.7	2,214	89.9
Edgerton city (Dane)	65	68	4.6	55	100.0	0.0	0.0	0.0	0.0	0.0	0.0	26.8	68.1	0.0	28	100.0
Edgerton city (Rock)	5,347	5,563	4.0	5,495	90.8	0.0	1.7	0.5	6.9	23.1	14.0	35.8	45.1	30.1	2,186	89.8

1 May be of any race.

Table A. All Places — **Population and Housing**

STATE City, town, township, borough, or CDP (county if applicable)	2010 census total population	2019 estimated population	Percent change 2010–2019	ACS total population estimate 2015–2019	White alone, not Hispanic or Latino	Black alone, not Hispanic or Latino	Asian alone, not Hispanic or Latino	All other races or 2 or more races, not Hispanic or Latino	Hispanic or Latino[1]	Under 18 years old	Age 65 years and older	Median age	Percent High school diploma or less	Percent Bachelor's degree or more	Total	Percent with a computer
	1	2	3	4	5	6	7	8	9	10	11	12	13	14	15	16
WISCONSIN—Con.																
Edgewater town (Sawyer).	519	522	0.6	540	90.2	0.0	0.4	0.9	8.5	17.4	26.1	54.5	38.5	24.5	253	88.1
Edmund CDP..................	173	-	-	141	100.0	0.0	0.0	0.0	0.0	12.8	6.4	48.8	61.2	5.1	64	68.8
Edson town (Chippewa)....	1,089	1,132	3.9	1,068	98.4	0.0	0.0	0.5	1.1	31.0	13.5	37.9	57.5	9.6	397	73.6
Egg Harbor village & MCD (Door)........................	201	202	0.5	252	92.9	0.0	0.0	4.0	3.2	5.6	44.0	63.7	8.6	56.3	140	93.6
Egg Harbor town (Door) ...	1,342	1,349	0.5	1,416	94.4	0.0	0.0	0.1	5.4	11.6	41.2	60.0	37.3	37.5	682	88.7
Eileen town (Bayfield)......	686	692	0.9	723	92.9	1.0	0.6	2.8	2.8	24.1	13.6	41.4	24.0	24.6	320	91.9
Eisenstein town (Price).....	628	609	-3.0	584	96.7	0.0	0.0	2.4	0.9	16.1	27.9	53.6	48.7	18.7	289	80.6
Eland village & MCD (Shawano)	202	197	-2.5	195	96.4	0.0	0.0	1.5	2.1	23.6	16.4	44.8	59.0	10.4	91	90.1
Elba town (Dodge)...........	994	970	-2.4	1,141	98.9	0.0	0.0	0.6	0.5	20.2	21.2	47.8	44.5	23.9	444	89.6
Elcho CDP....................	339	-	-	249	98.4	0.0	0.0	0.8	0.8	22.5	20.5	47.5	37.6	25.8	128	89.1
Elcho town (Langlade)......	1,233	1,201	-2.6	1,105	98.8	0.0	0.8	0.2	0.2	12.5	31.3	57.5	50.2	20.5	568	87.9
Elderon village & MCD (Marathon)	181	214	18.2	308	36.7	0.0	0.0	5.2	58.1	32.8	10.7	30.4	81.7	3.2	112	79.5
Elderon town (Marathon)..	604	639	5.8	540	98.9	0.0	0.0	1.1	0.0	20.4	23.3	45.8	50.5	17.8	236	92.8
Eldorado town (Fond du Lac)..........................	1,469	1,463	-0.4	1,436	97.1	0.0	1.3	0.7	1.0	16.8	21.9	49.0	49.6	18.5	544	90.1
Eleva village & MCD (Trempealeau)..............	677	665	-1.8	688	94.8	1.3	0.0	0.6	3.3	28.1	13.4	35.1	40.4	20.4	301	85.0
Elk town (Price).............	978	949	-3.0	941	94.6	0.0	0.3	2.6	2.6	12.3	30.3	56.8	43.8	25.2	495	86.1
Elk Grove town (Lafayette)	551	567	2.9	524	97.1	0.2	0.0	0.4	2.3	28.1	15.8	34.3	44.2	26.9	168	86.3
Elkhart Lake village & MCD (Sheboygan)	963	1,016	5.5	1,116	97.1	0.0	0.0	0.4	2.5	18.9	29.9	51.4	29.8	39.6	497	91.1
Elkhorn city & MCD (Walworth).................	10,073	10,019	-0.5	9,925	85.6	0.4	1.1	1.6	11.3	23.6	17.3	37.3	41.1	26.3	4,044	88.6
Elk Mound village & MCD (Dunn).....................	878	882	0.5	1,067	83.5	0.3	7.6	2.6	6.0	30.6	10.2	31.9	39.9	22.3	371	93.5
Elk Mound town (Dunn)....	1,789	1,930	7.9	1,664	92.9	0.0	5.2	0.1	1.7	25.3	11.7	38.1	39.1	22.5	590	98.3
Ellenboro town (Grant)	525	534	1.7	554	94.0	0.0	0.0	0.2	5.8	22.9	10.5	38.0	45.8	20.9	217	82.9
Ellington town (Outagamie).................	2,758	3,135	13.7	3,023	95.5	0.0	0.0	0.5	3.9	19.4	17.3	44.5	44.4	21.2	1,185	90.0
Ellison Bay CDP	165	-	-	159	95.0	0.0	0.0	5.0	0.0	4.4	30.2	54.8	29.0	36.3	74	95.9
Ellsworth village & MCD (Pierce)...................	3,290	3,317	0.8	3,280	94.0	0.4	0.0	0.5	5.1	25.5	14.5	39.4	45.8	19.7	1,359	90.1
Ellsworth town (Pierce).....	1,138	1,190	4.6	1,227	93.6	0.2	0.3	3.9	2.0	22.2	16.5	42.5	39.5	29.7	459	93.2
Elm Grove village & MCD (Waukesha)...............	5,934	6,136	3.4	6,153	89.6	2.4	3.7	2.5	1.9	23.7	25.0	47.2	18.1	62.3	2,287	92.4
Elmwood village & MCD (Pierce)...................	818	797	-2.6	707	99.6	0.3	0.0	0.0	0.1	17.4	28.6	47.1	54.6	18.9	325	80.0
Elmwood Park village & MCD (Racine)..........	504	493	-2.2	495	87.5	4.6	3.2	1.2	3.4	18.2	28.9	53.7	22.3	36.8	201	90.0
El Paso town (Pierce).......	683	713	4.4	612	96.9	0.0	0.0	1.6	1.5	16.8	15.0	48.3	32.8	24.6	241	87.6
Elroy city & MCD (Juneau)	1,441	1,303	-9.6	1,422	92.1	3.5	0.0	2.7	1.8	17.4	20.0	46.2	56.0	14.1	618	81.4
Embarrass village & MCD (Waupaca).................	406	370	-8.9	566	98.4	0.0	0.0	0.2	1.4	26.9	27.2	47.4	66.4	12.7	216	79.6
Emerald CDP.................	161	-	-	101	85.1	0.0	0.0	9.9	5.0	14.9	26.7	56.9	64.5	10.5	48	85.4
Emerald town (St. Croix)...	853	854	0.1	773	98.8	0.0	0.0	0.6	0.5	22.5	16.8	46.9	46.3	16.1	278	91.0
Emery town (Price)...........	297	289	-2.7	379	80.5	0.0	0.5	17.9	1.1	29.6	17.9	47.5	40.2	19.2	207	61.4
Emmet town (Dodge)........	1,293	1,289	-0.3	1,211	97.0	0.4	0.2	0.1	2.3	16.7	18.2	48.1	48.1	20.0	468	92.3
Emmet town (Marathon) ...	926	938	1.3	927	99.4	0.0	0.0	0.3	0.3	27.9	13.1	39.9	42.5	20.7	342	87.7
Empire town (Fond du Lac)..........................	2,793	2,820	1.0	2,808	94.9	0.0	2.3	0.7	2.1	18.3	21.4	51.3	28.7	36.9	1,072	92.9
Endeavor village & MCD (Marquette)..............	468	465	-0.6	569	86.3	0.7	0.9	6.0	6.2	27.9	8.6	36.4	61.4	6.3	207	84.1
Enterprise town (Oneida) .	312	303	-2.9	282	98.2	0.0	0.0	1.8	0.0	10.6	28.4	51.9	37.6	21.8	125	92.0
Ephraim village & MCD (Door)........................	288	280	-2.8	268	99.6	0.0	0.0	0.4	0.0	8.2	55.2	68.1	9.3	57.3	144	88.9
Erin town (Washington) ...	3,747	3,836	2.4	3,809	96.4	0.4	0.7	0.2	2.3	17.8	21.0	50.4	30.8	36.8	1,552	95.4
Erin Prairie town (St. Croix).......................	688	705	2.5	670	88.4	0.0	9.9	0.3	1.5	17.5	11.8	49.5	33.4	34.6	249	88.0
Estella town (Chippewa) ...	434	451	3.9	338	99.1	0.0	0.0	0.9	0.0	15.1	28.1	51.7	56.9	15.2	150	88.0
Ettrick village & MCD (Trempealeau)..............	530	519	-2.1	570	98.8	0.0	0.0	0.7	0.5	26.5	15.4	41.0	53.4	10.2	247	91.1
Ettrick town (Trempealeau)..............	1,228	1,287	4.8	1,123	95.5	1.2	0.0	2.8	0.5	16.3	23.1	49.5	48.6	20.0	479	87.5
Eureka town (Polk)	1,649	1,659	0.6	1,678	99.2	0.2	0.0	0.6	0.0	18.7	16.7	49.0	43.7	17.6	713	89.3
Eureka CDP..................	220	-	-	601	58.7	0.0	0.0	8.8	32.4	27.3	3.5	33.7	68.8	9.2	198	93.9
Evansville city & MCD (Rock)......................	5,011	5,440	8.6	5,312	96.9	0.0	0.0	0.1	3.0	27.0	16.0	35.7	32.4	27.4	2,195	88.8
Evergreen town (Langlade)..................	495	479	-3.2	462	97.0	0.0	0.0	1.9	1.1	13.2	23.2	49.5	53.9	13.1	195	80.5
Evergreen town (Washburn).................	1,133	1,128	-0.4	1,067	97.3	1.1	0.0	1.5	0.1	20.4	24.6	48.1	38.6	27.9	456	95.2
Excelsior town (Sauk).......	1,567	1,673	6.8	1,733	95.0	0.3	0.8	3.3	0.5	20.0	18.5	46.4	43.2	23.2	693	91.3
Exeland village & MCD (Sawyer)....................	201	190	-5.5	168	90.5	1.2	0.0	4.8	8.0	19.6	13.1	36.8	57.1	12.6	79	78.5
Exeter town (Green)	2,033	2,099	3.2	2,305	95.4	0.0	0.7	2.1	1.7	26.8	9.5	39.8	33.1	34.3	811	93.7
Fairbanks town (Shawano)	616	605	-1.8	507	97.4	0.4	0.0	2.2	0.0	11.4	27.0	53.5	65.5	14.8	249	75.9
Fairchild village & MCD (Eau Claire)	553	603	9.0	584	91.6	0.0	0.0	6.5	1.9	25.5	8.2	34.3	70.8	4.4	244	82.8
Fairchild town (Eau Claire)	345	375	8.7	279	100.0	0.0	0.0	0.0	0.0	18.6	30.1	55.1	52.6	16.7	111	65.8
Fairfield town (Sauk)........	1,078	1,103	2.3	1,150	97.3	0.0	0.5	1.3	0.9	20.1	17.1	46.8	39.0	22.0	445	96.9
Fairwater village & MCD (Fond du Lac).............	371	357	-3.8	351	97.4	0.0	0.0	1.7	0.9	23.6	14.5	33.3	55.9	18.1	144	89.6
Fall Creek village & MCD (Eau Claire)	1,311	1,289	-1.7	1,517	94.8	0.3	0.0	2.1	2.8	27.7	16.7	35.3	37.4	26.1	599	82.6
Fall River village & MCD (Columbia).................	1,711	1,741	1.8	1,861	83.4	3.7	1.6	2.7	8.5	28.3	9.7	35.7	39.4	29.8	685	90.9
Farmington town (Jefferson)..................	1,412	1,456	3.1	1,525	99.0	0.3	0.2	0.0	0.5	22.3	18.4	46.6	46.4	20.6	550	90.9

1 May be of any race.

Table A. All Places — **Population and Housing**

	Population				Race and Hispanic or Latino origin (percent)					Age (percent)			Educational attainment of persons age 25 and older		Occupied housing units	
STATE City, town, township, borough, or CDP (county if applicable)	2010 census total population	2019 estimated population	Percent change 2010–2019	ACS total population estimate 2015–2019	White alone, not Hispanic or Latino	Black alone, not Hispanic or Latino	Asian alone, not Hispanic or Latino	All other races or 2 or more races, not Hispanic or Latino	Hispanic or Latino[1]	Under 18 years old	Age 65 years and older	Median age	Percent High school diploma or less	Percent Bachelor's degree or more	Total	Percent with a computer
	1	2	3	4	5	6	7	8	9	10	11	12	13	14	15	16
WISCONSIN—Con.																
Farmington town (La Crosse)...............	2,061	2,153	4.5	2,228	90.4	0.0	3.4	3.3	2.9	27.8	13.5	39.0	33.6	23.1	809	90.2
Farmington town (Polk).....	1,842	1,862	1.1	1,641	97.1	0.5	0.2	0.9	1.2	22.0	15.9	43.0	31.9	27.5	638	92.5
Farmington town (Washington).................	3,730	3,764	0.9	3,754	96.8	1.5	0.0	0.0	1.7	20.2	20.2	50.5	42.3	23.0	1,462	87.6
Farmington town (Waupaca)..................	3,950	3,861	-2.3	3,890	91.3	2.8	3.0	0.8	2.1	20.1	29.5	51.8	39.3	32.8	1,411	95.5
Fayette town (Lafayette) ...	384	392	2.1	381	99.0	0.0	0.0	0.5	0.5	30.4	14.7	39.6	50.6	20.1	134	76.9
Fence town (Florence)......	190	185	-2.6	213	97.2	0.0	0.0	2.8	0.0	7.5	24.4	58.2	55.0	12.2	97	78.4
Fennimore city & MCD (Grant)........................	2,514	2,456	-2.3	2,603	97.5	0.0	0.7	0.7	1.1	21.7	17.8	34.4	35.1	23.0	1,013	90.4
Fennimore town (Grant)....	594	601	1.2	607	94.2	0.0	0.0	0.0	5.8	27.5	15.3	42.9	45.4	16.5	206	86.9
Fenwood village & MCD (Marathon)...............	152	155	2.0	174	86.8	0.0	0.0	13.2	0.0	26.4	6.9	38.0	68.7	6.1	74	93.2
Fern town (Florence)	159	154	-3.1	160	98.1	0.0	0.0	0.0	1.9	10.6	29.4	59.7	44.1	20.6	84	82.1
Ferryville village & MCD (Crawford)..................	176	176	0.0	166	97.6	0.0	0.0	2.4	0.0	10.2	39.8	60.0	38.9	24.8	86	90.7
Fifield town (Price)...........	903	878	-2.8	807	98.8	0.0	0.4	0.7	0.1	18.5	27.5	52.6	51.0	18.7	390	85.6
Finley town (Juneau)........	97	95	-2.1	101	91.1	5.9	0.0	3.0	0.0	11.9	26.7	50.9	55.1	13.5	44	88.6
Fitchburg city & MCD (Dane).......................	25,161	30,792	22.4	29,450	64.7	9.2	5.1	3.7	17.3	22.3	12.8	33.9	22.5	51.1	12,449	96.4
Flambeau town (Price)	489	476	-2.7	432	94.9	0.0	0.5	0.2	4.4	13.2	26.2	53.5	53.1	16.4	219	80.8
Flambeau town (Rusk)	1,060	1,064	0.4	1,024	94.4	0.0	0.0	4.5	1.1	18.2	18.9	48.6	47.8	15.6	465	87.3
Florence CDP.................	592	-	-	457	99.1	0.0	0.0	0.0	0.9	6.6	38.7	59.5	56.4	14.5	236	83.9
Florence town (Florence)..	2,002	1,943	-2.9	1,845	96.1	0.7	0.0	1.6	1.6	16.4	26.8	54.2	43.3	21.3	840	89.0
Fond du Lac city & MCD (Fond du Lac)...............	42,992	43,263	0.6	42,909	83.6	2.6	1.7	4.1	8.1	21.5	17.1	38.9	44.0	24.0	17,709	86.4
Fond du Lac town (Fond du Lac)	3,048	4,153	36.3	3,973	96.0	0.0	2.1	0.0	1.8	25.7	13.6	41.2	33.4	32.1	1,535	97.4
Fontana-on-Geneva Lake village & MCD (Walworth)....................	1,684	1,741	3.4	1,515	95.3	0.8	1.3	0.5	2.1	13.9	37.4	59.2	15.9	61.9	700	93.7
Footville village & MCD (Rock)......................	808	831	2.8	866	98.5	1.2	0.0	0.3	0.0	20.7	22.1	37.0	61.6	5.9	338	89.3
Ford town (Taylor)	268	267	-0.4	307	99.3	0.0	0.0	0.0	0.7	22.1	28.0	47.6	50.9	17.5	127	70.9
Forest town (Fond du Lac)	1,074	1,080	0.6	967	98.7	0.0	0.7	0.6	0.0	17.8	20.6	48.6	42.3	22.0	402	88.8
Forest town (Richland)......	351	340	-3.1	393	91.6	0.5	0.3	1.3	6.4	23.9	23.4	49.4	49.3	22.0	137	83.2
Forest town (St. Croix).....	629	633	0.6	736	91.2	0.0	0.1	8.3	0.4	29.8	15.2	35.6	46.0	15.4	259	91.5
Forest town (Vernon)	634	630	-0.6	737	91.6	0.0	1.6	3.8	3.0	30.3	15.9	34.8	59.5	15.9	248	68.5
Forest Junction CDP.........	616	-	-	720	91.7	0.4	1.4	3.2	3.3	21.0	8.2	32.0	32.5	20.1	305	93.1
Forestville village & MCD (Door)......................	430	408	-5.1	477	92.5	0.0	0.0	1.3	6.3	21.4	14.0	38.6	48.1	14.5	222	89.6
Forestville town (Door)......	1,096	1,099	0.3	989	97.6	0.0	0.2	2.2	0.0	20.8	18.5	46.4	46.5	18.4	434	88.5
Fort Atkinson city & MCD (Jefferson).................	12,395	12,422	0.2	12,443	86.4	1.3	1.2	3.0	8.1	23.1	17.2	40.3	45.9	22.4	5,009	89.3
Fort Winnebago town (Columbia).................	825	835	1.2	788	98.0	0.0	0.0	1.8	0.3	21.1	25.1	47.8	46.0	16.8	356	94.7
Foster town (Clark)...........	95	96	1.1	106	100.0	0.0	0.0	0.0	0.0	12.3	46.2	64.2	64.5	19.4	51	82.4
Fountain town (Juneau)	556	585	5.2	570	97.4	1.8	0.0	0.9	0.0	17.0	21.2	48.7	47.0	19.0	247	84.2
Fountain City city & MCD (Buffalo)	859	861	0.2	821	94.3	2.7	0.0	2.2	0.9	14.9	22.0	46.2	38.6	22.1	395	91.6
Fountain Prairie town (Columbia)	885	893	0.9	751	98.1	0.0	0.3	0.7	0.9	23.8	19.4	42.9	36.8	22.4	307	93.8
Fox Crossing village & MCD (Winnebago)	18,227	19,012	4.3	18,841	87.1	1.9	3.6	2.9	4.5	18.2	16.2	37.9	38.2	29.8	8,615	93.7
Fox Lake city & MCD (Dodge).....................	1,519	1,449	-4.6	1,696	86.4	3.5	0.2	5.2	4.7	26.7	16.0	40.7	55.4	14.9	703	84.9
Fox Lake town (Dodge).....	2,468	2,740	11.0	2,704	65.8	22.1	1.1	5.1	5.8	8.7	13.3	42.0	51.6	11.1	543	90.8
Fox Point village & MCD (Milwaukee)..................	6,681	6,543	-2.1	6,650	87.3	2.8	4.9	2.3	2.7	21.2	20.9	45.6	9.7	76.7	2,806	94.9
Francis Creek village & MCD (Manitowoc)	673	640	-4.9	598	98.2	0.0	0.0	1.8	0.0	19.2	19.7	44.4	46.0	16.2	251	89.6
Frankfort town (Marathon)	670	708	5.7	574	100.0	0.0	0.0	0.0	0.0	22.0	18.8	45.1	56.3	15.0	231	77.9
Frankfort town (Pepin)	343	330	-3.8	346	99.1	0.0	0.6	0.0	0.3	16.8	24.6	53.0	48.9	17.4	145	82.8
Franklin town (Jackson)	448	461	2.9	467	96.8	0.9	0.0	1.9	0.4	24.8	20.8	40.1	51.9	17.5	177	68.4
Franklin town (Kewaunee)	993	984	-0.9	1,112	94.4	0.0	0.0	4.0	1.5	21.9	12.9	38.9	44.8	21.1	401	90.3
Franklin town (Manitowoc)	1,264	1,229	-2.8	1,125	96.4	0.0	0.6	1.4	1.5	21.3	17.2	47.2	49.8	13.9	462	89.4
Franklin city & MCD (Milwaukee)..................	35,462	35,811	1.0	36,064	78.6	4.8	6.2	4.1	6.3	21.2	18.3	43.4	31.0	41.0	13,867	91.3
Franklin town (Sauk)........	647	687	6.2	608	95.9	2.5	0.0	1.6	0.0	22.2	18.1	46.1	46.9	20.7	232	84.5
Franklin town (Vernon)......	1,140	1,188	4.2	952	98.1	0.0	0.1	0.8	0.9	24.7	16.3	43.1	42.4	16.9	382	85.9
Franks Field CDP	154	-	-	208	19.7	0.0	0.0	70.2	10.1	19.7	14.9	40.8	44.0	2.0	88	70.5
Franzen town (Marathon)..	578	572		463	94.0	0.0	0.6	0.9	4.5	21.8	20.1	47.3	68.9	8.2	199	79.9
Frederic village & MCD (Polk)......................	1,131	1,089	-3.7	1,099	86.4	1.1	0.4	2.5	9.6	24.3	23.1	39.3	56.1	12.4	479	82.7
Fredonia village & MCD (Ozaukee)	2,164	2,253	4.1	2,459	92.9	1.9	0.0	1.7	3.6	28.3	9.2	34.8	42.9	28.5	916	96.8
Fredonia town (Ozaukee) .	2,165	2,166	0.0	1,993	92.5	0.4	0.9	0.8	5.5	17.2	21.1	51.1	48.4	18.8	787	88.7
Freedom town (Forest)	345	330	-4.3	370	96.2	0.0	0.0	3.8	0.0	11.9	26.8	51.7	49.4	15.7	196	84.7
Freedom town (Outagamie)	5,846	6,200	6.1	6,149	96.6	0.4	0.0	1.1	1.9	27.3	11.1	38.1	40.8	26.0	2,143	96.7
Freedom town (Sauk).......	447	474	6.0	440	94.1	0.0	0.0	0.0	5.9	20.7	26.4	49.8	45.9	19.3	182	84.1
Freeman town (Crawford).	686	704	2.6	665	97.1	0.0	1.1	1.4	0.5	13.4	30.2	57.8	55.1	17.6	293	90.8
Fremont town (Clark)	1,265	1,280	1.2	1,135	95.4	0.0	1.1	1.1	2.4	30.7	10.3	39.4	54.4	13.1	414	75.8
Fremont village & MCD (Waupaca)...................	678	651	-4.0	629	95.2	0.0	0.0	1.3	3.5	16.2	17.0	50.9	32.0	22.8	320	90.6
Fremont town (Waupaca) .	598	589	-1.5	650	98.5	0.0	0.0	0.0	1.5	16.2	22.8	50.5	45.8	21.2	286	92.3
French Island CDP...........	4,207	-	-	4,341	94.1	0.0	2.4	2.3	1.1	15.2	20.5	47.3	34.0	27.9	2,032	96.7
Friendship village & MCD (Adams)...................	727	657	-9.6	595	81.3	6.1	0.0	2.2	10.4	11.6	23.2	48.0	65.1	11.4	233	84.5
Friendship town (Fond du Lac)...................	2,670	2,646	-0.9	2,627	87.2	1.1	1.9	0.9	8.9	15.5	24.4	48.5	50.9	15.8	1,164	88.1

1 May be of any race.

Table A. All Places — **Population and Housing**

STATE City, town, township, borough, or CDP (county if applicable)	Population				Race and Hispanic or Latino origin (percent)					Age (percent)			Educational attainment of persons age 25 and older		Occupied housing units	
	2010 census total population	2019 estimated population	Percent change 2010–2019	ACS total population estimate 2015–2019	White alone, not Hispanic or Latino	Black alone, not Hispanic or Latino	Asian alone, not Hispanic or Latino	All other races or 2 or more races, not Hispanic or Latino	Hispanic or Latino[1]	Under 18 years old	Age 65 years and older	Median age	Percent High school diploma or less	Percent Bachelor's degree or more	Total	Percent with a computer
	1	2	3	4	5	6	7	8	9	10	11	12	13	14	15	16
WISCONSIN—Con.																
Friesland village & MCD (Columbia)	356	345	-3.1	278	95.7	0.0	0.0	0.7	3.6	27.7	17.3	35.2	47.8	11.3	106	89.6
Frog Creek town (Washburn)	130	131	0.8	105	97.1	0.0	0.0	1.9	1.0	17.1	21.0	50.4	44.7	11.8	54	88.9
Fulton town (Rock)...........	3,269	3,437	5.1	3,366	89.7	6.5	0.4	2.4	1.0	18.5	20.4	43.6	43.6	24.4	1,385	91.3
Gale town (Trempealeau) .	1,657	1,738	4.9	1,759	99.5	0.0	0.0	0.3	0.2	23.8	16.7	44.9	39.7	22.0	677	92.8
Galesville city & MCD (Trempealeau)	1,513	1,596	5.5	1,698	95.9	0.0	2.4	0.9	0.8	20.6	19.0	37.6	47.0	24.9	777	84.2
Garden Valley town (Jackson)	420	428	1.9	329	96.0	0.0	0.0	4.0	0.0	18.8	26.7	55.9	45.0	18.2	138	88.4
Gardner town (Door)........	1,196	1,186	-0.8	1,273	93.6	0.2	0.0	0.8	5.4	17.1	23.0	50.5	44.9	24.3	581	90.4
Garfield town (Jackson)....	638	694	8.8	714	98.5	0.8	0.0	0.0	0.7	24.2	16.8	44.7	51.7	16.9	276	81.2
Garfield town (Polk)	1,687	1,650	-2.2	1,763	95.8	0.0	0.7	0.6	2.9	25.4	16.5	42.0	44.7	20.7	669	94.2
Gays Mills village & MCD (Crawford)	491	511	4.1	494	89.7	0.0	0.0	1.2	9.1	24.5	19.0	41.0	36.7	22.5	222	81.5
Genesee town (Waukesha)..................	7,310	7,310	0.0	7,315	95.5	0.5	0.3	2.1	1.6	21.6	18.1	48.2	29.9	38.7	2,632	95.7
Geneva town (Walworth) ..	5,000	5,040	0.8	5,027	85.6	0.1	0.1	2.1	12.1	18.0	22.5	50.0	34.9	36.9	2,177	93.0
Genoa village & MCD (Vernon)	264	261	-1.1	241	90.0	2.1	1.2	4.6	2.1	22.4	20.7	47.7	47.2	16.0	103	90.3
Genoa town (Vernon)	782	796	1.8	801	95.9	0.2	0.0	2.0	1.9	22.5	22.1	45.6	45.2	24.2	308	81.8
Genoa City village	3,048	2,985	-2.1	2,995	91.0	0.0	0.5	2.1	6.5	27.9	9.5	35.9	42.9	21.5	1,110	93.8
Genoa City village (Kenosha)	6	6	0.0	-	-	-	-	-	-	-	-	-	-	-	-	-
Genoa City village (Walworth)	3,042	2,979	-2.1	2,995	91.0	0.0	0.5	2.1	6.5	27.9	9.5	35.9	42.9	21.5	1,110	93.8
Georgetown town (Polk) ...	977	957	-2.0	906	86.0	0.3	0.0	11.8	1.9	14.0	30.1	54.7	41.9	24.5	436	88.1
Georgetown town (Price)..	171	157	-8.2	156	100.0	0.0	0.0	0.0	0.0	32.1	22.4	42.5	53.5	17.2	60	80.0
Germania town (Shawano)	332	326	-1.8	307	97.7	0.0	0.0	1.6	0.7	8.5	27.7	57.1	71.4	10.4	133	76.7
Germantown town (Juneau)	1,471	1,687	14.7	1,439	95.8	1.0	0.3	1.2	1.6	14.7	30.7	54.2	47.8	20.7	698	90.1
Germantown village & MCD (Washington)........	19,964	20,116	0.8	20,166	87.7	2.4	5.0	1.8	3.2	23.2	15.7	41.7	26.8	44.0	8,104	92.9
Germantown town (Washington)................	249	247	-0.8	303	90.4	0.0	2.3	3.6	3.6	19.1	16.5	43.7	27.0	34.2	113	90.3
Gibbsville CDP	512	-	-	435	95.2	1.8	0.9	0.0	2.1	19.3	13.6	46.4	57.0	23.7	171	97.1
Gibraltar town (Door).......	1,021	1,039	1.8	1,075	91.4	0.2	0.0	1.3	7.1	12.0	36.9	61.2	19.1	57.3	506	97.2
Gibson town (Manitowoc) .	1,344	1,324	-1.5	1,371	97.7	0.4	0.4	0.1	1.3	22.4	20.0	45.9	42.1	25.2	554	86.6
Gillett city & MCD (Oconto)	1,383	1,295	-6.4	1,166	90.2	0.5	0.3	6.3	2.7	20.6	20.2	43.1	56.3	11.4	538	84.0
Gillett town (Oconto)........	1,046	1,061	1.4	893	99.6	0.0	0.0	0.0	0.4	17.4	22.3	46.4	67.4	8.7	388	81.7
Gilman town (Pierce)........	959	1,004	4.7	1,074	96.6	0.1	0.2	0.6	2.5	31.4	11.2	36.9	35.4	26.9	373	89.8
Gilman village & MCD (Taylor)	410	392	-4.4	444	98.6	0.0	0.0	0.7	0.7	23.4	29.1	47.6	56.7	14.4	201	77.1
Gilmanton CDP...............	-	-	-	136	100.0	0.0	0.0	0.0	0.0	23.5	9.6	32.6	85.7	2.2	52	88.5
Gilmanton town (Buffalo)..	426	418	-1.9	415	99.5	0.0	0.5	0.0	0.0	22.7	14.0	44.4	65.8	10.3	163	87.1
Gingles town (Ashland)	778	770		712	85.1	0.0	0.0	10.0	4.9	17.6	14.5	48.2	29.9	19.8	282	91.1
Glenbeulah village & MCD (Sheboygan)	463	464	0.2	425	100.0	0.0	0.0	0.0	0.0	20.2	16.0	40.9	45.3	27.5	179	92.7
Glencoe town (Buffalo)	480	471	-1.9	453	85.0	0.0	0.0	0.0	15.0	26.7	19.4	42.8	58.3	16.9	194	83.0
Glendale city & MCD (Milwaukee)	13,150	12,768	-2.9	12,943	74.4	13.6	5.5	1.7	4.8	18.2	23.2	44.9	18.4	55.9	5,545	91.0
Glendale town (Monroe)...	662	666	0.6	715	99.9	0.0	0.0	0.1	0.0	20.6	23.4	50.4	50.2	14.6	291	81.4
Glen Flora village & MCD (Rusk)	92	86	-6.5	100	86.0	11.0	0.0	0.0	3.0	29.0	7.0	40.1	30.4	11.6	51	90.2
Glen Haven CDP	73	-	-	54	94.4	0.0	0.0	0.0	5.6	5.6	51.9	66.3	67.3	16.3	30	56.7
Glen Haven town (Grant)..	417	407	-2.4	356	91.6	0.0	2.0	0.0	6.5	22.5	19.4	46.2	57.8	12.4	144	79.9
Glenmore town (Brown)....	1,137	1,159	1.9	1,140	99.2	0.0	0.4	0.4	0.0	21.8	14.1	45.5	52.7	20.5	419	92.4
Glenwood town (St. Croix)	791	820	3.7	760	96.2	0.0	0.0	3.0	0.8	21.1	15.1	47.0	42.5	19.9	311	89.7
Glenwood City city & MCD (St. Croix)	1,236	1,201	-2.8	1,256	96.3	0.0	0.2	2.1	1.5	25.4	12.8	37.1	51.4	12.8	506	77.3
Glidden CDP	507	-	-	316	99.4	0.0	0.0	0.6	0.0	10.8	30.4	58.6	68.5	2.6	193	71.0
Goetz town (Chippewa)....	764	795	4.1	721	97.2	1.1	0.4	1.2	0.0	24.4	21.6	45.2	46.0	20.3	284	82.7
Goodman CDP	271	-	-	224	96.9	0.0	0.0	3.1	0.0	19.6	22.8	49.2	58.8	10.6	116	63.8
Goodman town (Marinette)..................	619	606	-2.1	646	93.2	0.6	1.5	4.6	0.0	15.8	29.7	55.3	58.9	8.4	336	74.1
Goodrich town (Taylor)......	510	511	0.2	497	99.4	0.0	0.0	0.0	0.6	23.1	17.7	41.8	54.7	13.7	185	85.4
Gordon town (Ashland)....	283	278	-1.8	284	97.2	0.0	0.0	1.4	1.4	17.3	25.7	57.4	43.2	16.2	133	78.2
Gordon CDP	176	-	-	136	82.4	0.0	0.0	12.5	5.1	12.5	33.1	54.5	36.5	11.3	72	75.0
Gordon town (Douglas)	634	653	3.0	670	89.6	1.6	0.6	6.7	1.5	7.9	31.6	59.1	41.9	18.7	337	86.4
Gotham CDP	191	-	-	179	76.5	0.0	0.0	4.5	19.0	15.1	22.9	53.8	64.4	5.9	96	85.4
Grafton village & MCD (Ozaukee)	11,495	11,715	1.9	11,646	91.5	0.5	2.2	2.6	3.2	20.6	18.9	42.2	21.0	42.7	5,227	92.8
Grafton town (Ozaukee) ...	4,016	4,174	3.9	4,153	94.0	0.3	1.4	2.0	2.2	19.5	19.6	48.6	14.7	50.5	1,710	89.2
Grand Chute town (Outagamie)................	20,967	23,305	11.2	22,734	85.0	1.6	5.3	1.8	6.3	19.1	19.4	40.1	30.0	35.9	10,293	92.9
Grand Marsh CDP	127	-	-	145	95.9	0.0	0.0	2.1	2.1	22.1	9.7	41.5	63.3	3.3	57	87.7
Grand Rapids town (Wood)	7,621	7,417	-2.7	7,429	96.2	0.8	1.6	0.4	1.0	20.4	21.4	48.8	33.0	27.9	3,148	91.9
Grand View CDP	163	-	-	90	85.6	0.0	0.0	14.4	0.0	6.7	56.7	73.0	66.2	9.1	50	60.0
Grandview town (Bayfield)	468	472	0.9	495	88.9	0.0	0.0	8.7	2.4	11.3	36.0	60.8	51.0	21.8	249	84.3
Grant town (Clark)...........	922	934	1.3	929	93.8	0.0	0.8	3.3	2.2	29.5	13.8	36.7	52.0	14.8	336	81.5
Grant town (Dunn)	383	402	5.0	376	98.7	0.0	0.0	0.3	1.1	24.7	13.0	42.0	39.3	28.2	154	94.2
Grant town (Monroe)	493	504	2.2	616	91.4	0.5	0.0	2.8	5.4	26.3	16.2	43.3	47.2	19.8	227	85.5
Grant town (Portage)........	1,906	1,969	3.3	1,936	96.5	0.0	0.0	3.5	0.0	22.1	14.4	46.6	44.1	21.8	790	91.8
Grant town (Rusk)	813	820	0.9	728	98.6	0.0	0.0	0.0	1.4	26.1	22.1	48.3	56.8	15.4	310	86.1
Grant town (Shawano)......	996	979	-1.7	862	95.9	0.0	0.8	3.2	0.0	21.2	21.0	47.4	59.5	13.2	325	81.8
Granton village & MCD (Clark)	349	344	-1.4	337	99.7	0.3	0.0	0.0	0.0	24.6	20.8	44.5	56.0	10.2	132	78.0
Grantsburg village & MCD (Burnett)	1,337	1,281	-4.2	1,384	92.6	0.0	0.6	5.4	1.4	25.9	22.9	36.4	40.9	18.1	637	88.1

1 May be of any race.

Table A. All Places — Population and Housing

STATE City, town, township, borough, or CDP (county if applicable)	Population				Race and Hispanic or Latino origin (percent)					Age (percent)			Educational attainment of persons age 25 and older		Occupied housing units	
	2010 census total population	2019 estimated population	Percent change 2010–2019	ACS total population estimate 2015–2019	White alone, not Hispanic or Latino	Black alone, not Hispanic or Latino	Asian alone, not Hispanic or Latino	All other races or 2 or more races, not Hispanic or Latino	Hispanic or Latino[1]	Under 18 years old	Age 65 years and older	Median age	Percent High school diploma or less	Percent Bachelor's degree or more	Total	Percent with a computer
	1	2	3	4	5	6	7	8	9	10	11	12	13	14	15	16
WISCONSIN—Con.																
Grantsburg town (Burnett)	1,136	1,146	0.9	949	91.4	0.9	0.2	4.0	3.5	21.9	16.3	47.4	43.2	18.5	414	90.8
Gratiot village & MCD (Lafayette)	236	226	-4.2	242	91.7	0.0	5.4	1.7	1.2	20.2	15.3	41.3	51.4	9.1	102	83.3
Gratiot town (Lafayette)	550	560	1.8	542	98.3	1.3	0.0	0.0	0.4	23.2	21.6	52.1	52.5	17.0	219	76.3
Green Bay city & MCD (Brown)	103,882	104,578	0.7	104,777	68.7	4.1	4.2	7.2	15.8	24.8	12.8	34.5	43.9	24.8	42,430	88.1
Green Bay town (Brown)	2,026	2,182	7.7	2,137	99.1	0.0	0.0	0.7	0.2	23.2	16.5	46.7	40.8	26.5	840	90.5
Greenbush CDP	162	-	-	158	91.8	0.0	7.0	1.3	0.0	37.3	10.8	34.2	43.0	23.7	63	82.5
Greenbush town (Sheboygan)	2,576	2,599	0.9	2,587	76.4	11.2	0.4	6.8	5.1	13.1	10.5	38.1	50.9	16.2	557	91.2
Greendale village & MCD (Milwaukee)	14,044	14,143	0.7	14,176	82.9	1.8	6.9	4.3	4.1	23.1	22.8	42.8	25.1	46.3	5,856	91.4
Greenfield town (La Crosse)	2,061	2,137	3.7	2,051	94.0	0.2	0.4	0.5	4.8	22.5	15.7	46.9	30.1	38.9	787	90.0
Greenfield city & MCD (Milwaukee)	36,758	37,221	1.3	37,099	77.3	3.8	4.8	2.9	11.1	18.5	21.1	42.9	38.6	29.7	16,806	86.5
Greenfield town (Monroe)	707	721	2.0	680	91.5	1.0	1.3	4.6	1.6	24.6	17.2	46.3	38.3	29.0	249	94.4
Greenfield town (Sauk)	932	995	6.8	1,098	92.4	1.2	0.4	3.9	2.1	21.1	22.2	49.2	36.8	29.5	424	91.3
Green Grove town (Clark)	756	753	-0.4	683	100.0	0.0	0.0	0.0	0.0	34.4	18.0	28.5	65.2	8.9	230	53.5
Green Lake city & MCD (Green Lake)	944	965	2.2	833	98.7	0.2	0.0	0.8	0.2	11.9	23.8	52.0	33.3	28.7	416	87.5
Green Lake town (Green Lake)	1,154	1,171	1.5	1,243	97.3	0.0	0.0	1.9	0.8	22.0	27.8	48.4	42.9	23.7	523	87.0
Greenleaf CDP	607	-	-	918	47.6	3.1	0.0	5.9	43.5	31.9	6.8	27.9	54.6	14.8	304	79.6
Green Valley town (Marathon)	545	578	6.1	407	99.5	0.0	0.5	0.0	0.0	11.5	30.5	55.9	54.0	17.6	191	76.4
Green Valley CDP	133	-	-	118	77.1	0.0	0.0	0.0	22.9	29.7	11.0	41.1	80.7	0.0	49	100.0
Green Valley town (Shawano)	1,083	1,064	-1.8	1,069	94.3	0.0	0.0	1.3	4.4	28.1	17.8	39.8	62.3	5.7	410	86.8
Greenville town (Outagamie)	10,309	12,361	19.9	12,038	96.5	0.5	0.4	1.9	0.7	28.6	11.0	39.6	31.4	35.9	4,507	95.0
Greenwood city & MCD (Clark)	1,019	998	-2.1	1,008	94.0	0.0	0.0	4.3	1.7	19.9	21.5	48.5	52.0	14.6	476	86.3
Greenwood town (Taylor)	637	634	-0.5	688	99.3	0.0	0.0	0.7	0.0	23.0	17.2	47.3	61.3	11.0	289	80.6
Greenwood town (Vernon)	847	848	0.1	832	96.5	1.3	0.0	0.0	2.2	36.9	8.5	28.8	64.5	15.1	227	62.6
Gresham village & MCD (Shawano)	586	564	-3.8	562	64.9	0.0	1.4	29.4	4.3	32.2	20.6	38.1	56.1	8.9	215	78.1
Grover town (Marinette)	1,769	1,732	-2.1	1,918	97.8	0.0	0.0	2.1	0.1	26.5	15.1	40.3	46.1	12.5	731	86.5
Grover town (Taylor)	256	264	3.1	251	100.0	0.0	0.0	0.0	0.0	21.1	14.3	51.8	46.0	12.3	103	88.3
Grow town (Rusk)	424	426	0.5	473	99.6	0.0	0.0	0.4	0.0	23.5	23.0	43.7	66.0	10.9	188	82.4
Guenther town (Marathon)	341	363	6.5	297	98.0	0.3	0.0	1.0	0.7	23.2	15.8	41.8	56.8	19.5	114	79.8
Gull Lake town (Washburn)	186	187	0.5	214	97.7	0.0	2.3	0.0	0.0	11.2	26.6	54.1	50.3	15.7	103	90.3
Gurney town (Iron)	159	157	-1.3	163	89.6	0.0	0.0	4.3	6.1	19.6	18.4	43.6	51.7	23.3	70	92.9
Hackett town (Price)	169	164	-3.0	156	99.4	0.0	0.0	0.6	0.0	20.5	15.4	49.4	44.2	15.7	67	86.6
Hager City CDP	338	-	-	287	98.6	0.0	1.4	0.0	0.0	19.2	11.5	45.4	42.1	16.2	125	96.0
Hale town (Trempealeau)	1,032	1,081	4.7	950	97.6	0.0	0.7	1.1	0.6	20.2	20.3	44.7	41.9	20.6	411	87.3
Hales Corners village & MCD (Milwaukee)	7,672	7,567	-1.4	7,646	86.3	0.9	2.6	1.7	8.5	20.4	19.6	43.7	31.3	37.6	3,188	90.3
Hallie town (Chippewa)	160	166	3.8	176	94.3	0.0	5.7	0.0	0.0	22.7	20.5	47.8	29.7	25.0	70	92.9
Halsey town (Marathon)	649	688	6.0	703	98.9	0.0	0.0	0.0	1.1	33.9	12.2	32.9	59.5	11.0	226	72.6
Hamburg town (Marathon)	920	941	2.3	952	94.5	0.0	0.0	0.2	5.3	21.3	14.9	42.6	57.7	18.3	342	80.7
Hamburg town (Vernon)	967	1,006	4.0	1,192	95.6	0.0	0.0	0.0	4.4	34.3	16.9	39.7	42.5	23.7	388	88.1
Hamilton town (La Crosse)	2,422	2,534	4.6	2,518	95.0	0.9	2.4	0.4	1.4	22.4	15.3	45.2	27.8	39.0	920	95.1
Hammel town (Taylor)	717	706	-1.5	729	97.9	0.0	0.0	1.4	0.7	13.3	25.9	55.5	59.1	10.4	357	85.2
Hammond village & MCD (St. Croix)	1,922	1,886	-1.9	2,033	93.9	0.4	0.2	2.7	2.8	24.4	12.3	36.9	40.6	25.6	807	91.3
Hammond town (St. Croix)	2,085	2,357	13.0	2,296	95.9	0.0	1.0	1.9	1.1	29.7	7.9	36.1	25.5	35.6	779	97.6
Hampden town (Columbia)	576	580	0.7	559	93.6	0.0	0.0	0.5	5.9	25.0	16.8	41.8	31.7	39.3	213	94.4
Hancock village & MCD (Waushara)	417	405	-2.9	413	78.5	0.5	0.0	2.4	18.6	24.0	20.8	41.2	59.1	10.1	178	79.8
Hancock town (Waushara)	528	532	0.8	592	90.9	0.0	0.0	2.5	6.6	25.2	29.1	49.8	54.0	16.3	248	83.1
Haney town (Crawford)	309	292	-5.5	334	100.0	0.0	0.0	0.0	0.0	21.6	29.3	48.6	43.0	17.0	137	66.4
Hanover CDP	181	-	-	137	100.0	0.0	0.0	0.0	0.0	27.7	19.7	30.7	63.6	23.9	50	94.0
Hansen town (Wood)	696	659	-5.3	914	94.7	0.0	0.0	5.3	0.0	36.2	14.8	36.6	49.6	21.1	309	85.1
Harding town (Lincoln)	374	370	-1.1	351	98.6	0.3	1.1	0.0	0.0	12.5	15.1	51.7	46.7	18.5	155	87.7
Harmony town (Price)	220	215	-2.3	192	97.4	0.0	0.0	0.5	2.1	16.1	30.2	54.1	56.1	15.5	94	79.8
Harmony town (Rock)	2,517	2,622	4.2	2,595	96.3	0.0	1.0	1.4	1.3	24.8	17.9	43.6	36.3	36.8	904	93.9
Harmony town (Vernon)	755	968	28.2	753	96.7	0.0	0.0	0.3	3.1	31.7	18.2	34.0	49.9	21.9	271	73.1
Harris town (Marquette)	795	807	1.5	739	94.2	1.1	2.2	1.8	0.8	11.5	26.5	53.5	53.0	18.2	332	84.0
Harrison village & MCD (Calumet)	10,841	12,358	14.0	12,009	93.9	0.8	1.0	0.6	3.7	28.3	10.9	39.7	30.1	38.3	4,137	95.9
Harrison village (Outagamie)	-	-	-	-	-	-	-	-	-	-	-	-	-	-	-	-
Harrison town (Calumet)	-	-	-	-	-	-	-	-	-	-	-	-	-	-	-	-
Harrison town (Grant)	490	499	1.8	425	99.8	0.0	0.2	0.0	0.0	21.4	18.8	46.2	39.9	25.4	170	88.2
Harrison town (Lincoln)	837	807	-3.6	798	97.4	0.0	0.9	1.8	0.0	16.0	25.4	54.2	40.3	18.5	382	85.6
Harrison town (Marathon)	374	373	-0.3	375	93.9	0.0	0.0	1.9	4.3	18.7	18.9	43.4	61.3	9.9	173	74.0
Harrison town (Waupaca)	467	456	-2.4	490	95.1	0.0	0.0	0.0	4.9	11.4	20.4	50.3	53.1	15.2	241	81.7
Hartford city	14,249	15,445	8.4	14,977	91.5	1.6	0.3	2.6	4.0	25.6	16.1	39.0	40.6	25.4	5,996	89.7
Hartford city (Dodge)	8	9	12.5	17	100.0	0.0	0.0	0.0	0.0	5.9	0.0	29.1	56.3	0.0	9	100.0
Hartford city (Washington)	14,241	15,436	8.4	14,960	91.5	1.6	0.3	2.6	4.0	25.6	16.1	39.1	40.6	25.4	5,987	89.7
Hartford town (Washington)	3,589	3,564	-0.7	3,569	95.1	0.0	0.5	3.1	1.3	19.7	15.3	47.9	48.8	25.8	1,410	91.0
Hartland town (Pierce)	827	867	4.8	852	97.2	0.0	0.8	1.6	0.4	20.0	12.8	45.7	48.8	18.7	360	86.9
Hartland town (Shawano)	907	895	-1.3	880	98.1	0.0	0.0	1.9	0.0	27.5	13.1	40.2	58.3	17.9	292	83.2
Hartland village & MCD (Waukesha)	9,115	9,320	2.2	9,268	90.7	0.3	1.9	0.8	6.4	24.4	14.2	37.7	42.2	42.2	3,520	94.5
Hatfield CDP	141	-	-	208	88.5	0.0	0.0	7.2	4.3	21.6	30.8	50.2	50.6	17.5	101	97.0
Hatley village & MCD (Marathon)	566	597	5.5	587	96.1	0.0	1.9	0.0	2.0	25.7	14.7	33.6	40.8	19.5	221	91.4

1 May be of any race.

Table A. All Places — Population and Housing

STATE City, town, township, borough, or CDP (county if applicable)	2010 census total population	2019 estimated population	Percent change 2010–2019	ACS total population estimate 2015–2019	White alone, not Hispanic or Latino	Black alone, not Hispanic or Latino	Asian alone, not Hispanic or Latino	All other races or 2 or more races, not Hispanic or Latino	Hispanic or Latino[1]	Under 18 years old	Age 65 years and older	Median age	Percent High school diploma or less	Percent Bachelor's degree or more	Total	Percent with a computer
	1	2	3	4	5	6	7	8	9	10	11	12	13	14	15	16
WISCONSIN—Con.																
Haugen village & MCD (Barron)	289	274	-5.2	299	90.6	0.0	0.0	3.3	6.0	26.1	18.4	38.1	46.7	12.9	124	75.0
Hawkins village & MCD (Rusk)	305	280	-8.2	387	95.3	0.0	0.0	3.6	1.0	22.5	22.2	48.2	65.6	3.5	198	83.3
Hawkins town (Rusk)	153	153	0.0	103	100.0	0.0	0.0	0.0	0.0	6.8	27.2	55.0	54.1	4.7	50	66.0
Hawthorne town (Douglas)	1,137	1,135	-0.2	991	97.3	0.0	1.3	1.4	0.0	17.2	21.4	54.5	41.3	17.6	408	91.4
Hay River town (Dunn)	558	589	5.6	650	96.5	0.0	1.5	0.6	1.4	23.4	18.0	41.0	48.2	21.9	256	85.2
Hayward city & MCD (Sawyer)	2,348	2,311	-1.6	2,780	75.7	0.1	0.8	20.9	2.5	23.1	17.0	32.7	45.9	21.6	1,267	80.2
Hayward town (Sawyer)	3,536	3,550	0.4	3,507	75.6	0.0	0.5	21.8	2.2	24.5	23.2	47.9	41.3	23.8	1,528	83.0
Hazel Green village (Grant)	1,258	1,220	-3.0	1,009	99.1	0.0	0.0	0.9	0.0	23.6	15.2	38.8	37.9	23.9	437	94.7
Hazel Green village (Grant)	1,243	1,205	-3.1	1,004	99.1	0.0	0.0	0.9	0.0	23.7	15.2	38.7	38.2	24.1	434	94.7
Hazel Green village (Lafayette)	15	15	0.0	5	100.0	0.0	0.0	0.0	0.0	0.0	0.0	0.0	0.0	0.0	3	100.0
Hazel Green town (Grant)	1,129	1,105	-2.1	1,277	98.3	0.3	0.0	0.8	0.6	17.2	35.3	53.6	33.0	42.8	411	86.1
Hazelhurst town (Oneida)	1,272	1,263	-0.7	1,203	96.9	0.0	0.0	1.9	1.2	16.1	29.2	53.8	33.4	34.9	501	90.4
Hebron CDP	224	-	-	182	96.7	0.0	0.0	0.0	3.3	6.0	21.4	52.9	65.0	6.3	98	79.6
Hebron town (Jefferson)	1,094	1,130	3.3	1,096	93.0	0.0	0.0	0.3	6.8	15.7	17.4	50.8	48.0	18.0	449	82.9
Helenville CDP	249	-	-	321	93.5	0.0	4.4	2.2	0.0	19.6	9.3	36.3	21.5	30.8	128	92.2
Helvetia town (Waupaca)	634	621	-2.1	613	98.0	0.0	0.0	2.0	0.0	11.4	24.8	52.0	56.0	11.2	319	80.6
Hendren town (Clark)	499	497	-0.4	394	91.4	0.0	1.5	1.0	6.1	23.4	22.8	51.3	55.9	17.3	172	80.8
Henrietta town (Richland)	493	478	-3.0	493	100.0	0.0	0.0	0.0	0.0	27.6	24.5	52.2	49.0	16.4	195	77.4
Herbster CDP	104	-	-	108	100.0	0.0	0.0	0.0	0.0	9.3	45.4	62.3	9.2	54.0	53	96.2
Herman town (Dodge)	1,110	1,116	0.5	1,224	94.7	0.0	0.0	0.0	5.3	23.9	10.6	39.5	52.8	16.9	452	95.4
Herman town (Shawano)	776	764	-1.5	794	84.5	0.0	0.0	14.4	1.1	29.2	16.2	43.8	55.0	11.7	275	88.7
Herman town (Sheboygan)	2,155	2,066	-4.1	2,247	88.5	3.3	4.9	0.4	2.9	17.8	15.5	31.1	47.1	20.7	646	88.5
Hewett town (Clark)	293	297	1.4	322	93.5	0.0	0.3	6.2	0.0	23.3	16.5	46.4	46.1	22.0	129	93.0
Hewitt town (Marathon)	606	642	5.9	701	88.6	0.0	0.6	0.0	10.8	23.5	16.1	46.1	47.5	20.8	276	84.4
Hewitt village & MCD (Wood)	817	778	-4.8	923	97.7	0.1	0.3	1.7	0.1	27.8	18.4	40.6	31.5	32.1	346	93.1
Hickory Grove town (Grant)	455	462	1.5	540	97.4	2.2	0.0	0.0	0.4	40.0	5.7	24.0	60.3	11.2	148	60.1
Highland town (Douglas)	311	317	1.9	352	92.3	0.0	1.7	5.7	0.3	17.3	27.6	55.5	37.6	29.7	160	90.0
Highland village & MCD (Iowa)	838	826	-1.4	966	93.4	2.4	0.8	3.1	0.3	29.7	12.5	34.8	43.1	18.3	374	88.5
Highland town (Iowa)	754	776	2.9	697	100.0	0.0	0.0	0.0	0.0	18.5	17.5	48.8	44.5	20.9	289	76.8
Hilbert village & MCD (Calumet)	1,132	1,081	-4.5	1,082	90.2	0.0	0.0	1.1	8.7	27.4	14.0	36.5	57.6	12.5	441	80.5
Hiles town (Forest)	311	308	-	360	96.7	0.6	0.0	2.8	0.0	8.3	50.3	65.1	38.2	30.5	191	85.3
Hiles town (Wood)	167	158	-5.4	198	89.4	0.0	0.0	6.6	4.0	18.7	14.6	40.5	53.2	12.2	67	92.5
Hill town (Price)	333	314	-5.7	334	96.1	0.0	0.0	0.0	3.9	21.6	17.7	50.3	46.7	19.8	148	85.1
Hillsboro city & MCD (Vernon)	1,409	1,393	-1.1	1,428	95.2	0.0	0.1	2.4	2.3	24.9	20.2	40.1	54.5	15.5	615	83.7
Hillsboro town (Vernon)	815	837	2.7	773	95.1	0.0	0.3	0.3	4.4	24.5	21.1	49.0	64.1	17.5	301	77.4
Hingham CDP	886	-	-	866	95.6	0.0	0.5	3.2	0.7	26.4	14.9	39.8	31.1	33.4	308	97.4
Hixon town (Clark)	808	799	-1.1	881	98.0	1.6	0.0	0.3	0.1	39.4	9.6	30.6	68.8	7.1	265	65.3
Hixton village & MCD (Jackson)	435	424	-2.5	424	88.0	0.0	1.2	5.2	5.7	14.4	20.8	46.8	50.9	10.9	208	79.8
Hixton town (Jackson)	652	665	2.0	608	95.7	0.0	0.0	0.3	3.9	21.9	17.3	43.6	57.7	12.9	246	88.6
Hoard town (Clark)	841	818	-2.7	867	98.3	0.0	0.0	1.7	0.0	33.9	21.8	36.8	80.0	4.2	204	60.8
Hobart village & MCD (Brown)	6,187	10,082	63.0	9,053	72.3	0.0	6.8	18.1	2.8	21.4	15.7	40.7	30.8	39.6	3,944	95.2
Holcombe CDP	267	-	-	228	100.0	0.0	0.0	0.0	0.0	13.6	18.9	54.0	46.1	17.4	108	90.7
Holland town (Brown)	1,511	1,587	5.0	1,384	98.6	0.0	0.0	1.4	0.0	25.7	16.7	44.1	48.9	16.1	523	88.9
Holland town (La Crosse)	3,696	3,884	5.1	3,865	94.0	0.3	4.8	0.4	0.5	30.8	7.8	37.5	26.7	34.5	1,215	97.0
Holland town (Sheboygan)	2,235	2,238	0.1	2,336	96.6	1.3	0.5	0.3	1.3	26.7	23.1	46.0	36.9	26.1	906	92.8
Hollandale village & MCD (Iowa)	284	275	-3.2	265	100.0	0.0	0.0	0.0	0.0	18.9	17.7	47.1	50.0	14.2	120	90.8
Holmen village & MCD (La Crosse)	9,083	10,034	10.5	9,854	87.9	1.0	6.5	2.1	2.6	27.3	15.8	37.0	31.7	31.5	3,676	92.2
Holton town (Marathon)	888	939	5.7	974	96.9	0.0	0.0	0.0	3.1	32.5	12.5	34.0	62.9	12.0	330	81.2
Holway town (Taylor)	973	954	-2.0	885	99.8	0.0	0.0	0.2	0.0	31.9	7.2	32.4	60.5	11.3	338	72.2
Homestead town (Florence)	338	329	-2.7	396	98.2	0.0	0.0	1.8	0.0	15.9	22.2	55.4	50.0	13.0	180	80.0
Honey Creek town (Sauk)	733	779	6.3	749	91.1	0.0	2.4	0.0	6.5	19.2	22.3	47.5	53.7	17.7	321	77.9
Horicon city & MCD (Dodge)	3,655	3,645	-0.3	3,620	92.7	2.8	0.0	2.0	2.5	26.8	12.8	37.3	54.2	14.6	1,422	89.0
Hortonia town (Outagamie)	1,093	1,078	-1.4	1,277	95.5	0.0	3.3	0.6	0.5	25.0	14.1	43.8	32.7	33.4	425	96.2
Hortonville village & MCD (Outagamie)	2,705	2,912	7.7	2,786	94.1	0.0	3.0	0.3	2.5	24.5	14.1	38.8	38.8	19.7	1,070	93.2
Houlton CDP	386	-	-	153	100.0	0.0	0.0	0.0	0.0	0.0	8.5	37.3	21.9	14.8	70	100.0
How town (Oconto)	516	521	1.0	554	95.3	0.0	2.3	1.1	1.3	19.9	20.0	46.2	59.0	11.8	231	81.8
Howard village & MCD (Brown)	17,425	20,177	15.8	19,658	90.5	1.5	2.7	2.0	3.3	22.6	16.2	40.9	36.1	29.7	8,097	91.1
Howard village (Outagamie)	-	-	-	-	-	-	-	-	-	-	-	-	-	-	-	-
Howard town (Chippewa)	796	814	2.3	807	99.1	0.6	0.0	0.0	0.2	27.5	14.3	39.6	46.7	21.1	305	90.5
Howards Grove village & MCD (Sheboygan)	3,184	3,272	2.8	3,254	98.9	0.9	0.0	0.0	0.2	24.8	15.6	43.7	28.2	32.5	1,262	97.4
Hubbard town (Dodge)	1,773	1,745	-1.6	1,678	97.1	0.5	0.0	0.0	2.4	18.1	18.4	50.1	53.5	18.6	674	87.2
Hubbard town (Rusk)	204	195	-4.4	198	99.0	0.0	0.0	0.0	1.0	20.2	23.2	45.3	51.0	17.2	87	86.2
Hudson city & MCD (St. Croix)	12,796	14,103	10.2	13,795	91.4	2.2	0.8	1.1	4.5	22.1	16.4	38.1	24.5	42.6	5,728	94.0
Hudson town (St. Croix)	8,367	8,779	4.9	8,717	94.2	0.8	1.8	1.7	1.5	26.7	11.9	42.6	20.2	47.8	2,999	98.5
Hughes town (Bayfield)	383	388	1.3	396	92.2	0.8	0.5	5.1	1.5	12.1	26.8	52.0	38.9	24.1	192	95.3
Hull town (Marathon)	752	793	5.5	680	94.7	0.0	0.0	1.3	4.0	28.8	16.5	37.5	55.0	17.0	246	71.1
Hull town (Portage)	5,332	5,511	3.4	5,466	98.6	0.2	0.0	1.0	0.2	17.0	17.3	47.1	28.4	40.3	2,275	86.8
Humbird CDP	266	-	-	318	98.4	0.0	0.0	1.3	0.3	33.0	7.9	33.8	68.6	1.1	112	93.8
Humboldt town (Brown)	1,302	1,358	4.3	1,342	97.8	0.4	0.0	0.6	1.3	22.1	17.1	45.2	55.0	12.3	518	87.6

1 May be of any race.

Table A. All Places — Population and Housing

STATE City, town, township, borough, or CDP (county if applicable)	2010 census total population	2019 estimated population	Percent change 2010–2019	ACS total population estimate 2015–2019	White alone, not Hispanic or Latino	Black alone, not Hispanic or Latino	Asian alone, not Hispanic or Latino	All other races or 2 or more races, not Hispanic or Latino	Hispanic or Latino[1]	Under 18 years old	Age 65 years and older	Median age	Percent High school diploma or less	Percent Bachelor's degree or more	Total occupied housing units	Percent with a computer
	1	2	3	4	5	6	7	8	9	10	11	12	13	14	15	16
WISCONSIN—Con.																
Hunter town (Sawyer)	678	686	1.2	719	64.4	0.0	0.7	31.0	3.9	13.6	38.7	59.9	43.8	25.2	397	78.6
Hurley city & MCD (Iron)	1,543	1,436	-6.9	1,472	96.3	0.2	1.3	2.0	0.3	13.5	29.5	52.4	43.2	16.4	797	78.7
Hustisford village & MCD (Dodge)	1,124	1,075	-4.4	1,064	90.5	0.8	1.3	5.5	2.0	24.0	13.3	39.0	42.6	14.6	442	93.7
Hustisford town (Dodge)	1,377	1,333	-3.2	1,525	96.9	0.0	0.0	1.4	1.7	21.6	18.0	45.2	54.4	14.7	568	92.3
Hustler village & MCD (Juneau)	194	188	-3.1	201	91.5	0.0	2.0	6.5	0.0	15.4	24.9	44.5	35.0	22.9	102	78.4
Hutchins town (Shawano)	602	597	-0.8	638	98.1	0.0	0.0	0.3	1.6	22.6	20.7	46.3	65.6	8.3	228	91.7
Independence city & MCD (Trempealeau)	1,339	1,303	-2.7	1,439	70.5	3.9	0.0	0.0	25.6	27.7	17.3	35.2	61.7	12.6	591	76.5
Ingram village & MCD (Rusk)	78	73	-6.4	65	96.9	0.0	0.0	0.0	3.1	13.8	29.2	54.6	65.4	9.6	32	81.3
Iola village & MCD (Waupaca)	1,298	1,206	-7.1	1,174	99.7	0.0	0.0	0.3	0.0	19.8	29.2	47.7	43.1	24.8	584	80.8
Iola town (Waupaca)	971	957	-1.4	912	96.1	0.0	0.7	1.0	2.3	17.5	24.1	51.1	44.8	22.8	410	90.5
Iron Belt CDP	173	-	-	180	93.3	0.0	0.0	6.7	0.0	23.3	17.8	40.0	47.9	11.8	80	87.5
Iron Ridge village & MCD (Dodge)	928	891	-4.0	1,016	98.8	0.0	0.0	0.8	0.4	21.4	10.2	37.6	52.6	11.6	428	92.1
Iron River CDP	761	-	-	637	97.8	0.0	0.0	2.2	0.0	15.5	33.0	53.5	42.9	15.9	344	75.3
Iron River town (Bayfield)	1,123	1,134	1.0	1,002	98.3	0.0	0.0	1.7	0.0	13.9	35.4	58.0	39.4	21.2	521	82.7
Ironton village & MCD (Sauk)	253	252	-0.4	248	98.8	1.2	0.0	0.0	0.0	33.9	10.5	32.3	61.0	3.9	90	87.8
Ironton town (Sauk)	650	690	6.2	573	97.7	0.0	0.0	0.0	2.3	26.9	17.8	39.2	48.2	18.7	187	75.4
Irving town (Jackson)	751	778	3.6	783	96.6	0.0	0.0	3.1	0.4	26.4	13.0	38.4	54.3	16.9	295	80.0
Isabelle town (Pierce)	281	295	5.0	241	96.7	0.0	0.0	0.8	2.5	15.8	14.1	46.7	46.0	27.5	106	83.0
Ithaca town (Richland)	619	605	-2.3	657	97.0	0.0	0.0	0.0	3.0	22.7	16.6	44.8	58.6	21.4	262	79.4
Ixonia CDP	1,624	-	-	1,911	92.3	1.2	0.0	3.2	3.3	31.9	9.7	34.0	33.8	36.6	686	95.2
Ixonia town (Jefferson)	4,385	4,556	3.9	4,517	95.9	0.5	0.5	1.5	1.6	24.2	14.4	37.5	33.4	30.8	1,631	91.7
Jackson town (Adams)	1,003	988	-1.5	1,102	96.4	1.4	0.0	0.6	1.6	12.8	31.5	56.2	56.1	14.4	520	91.0
Jackson town (Burnett)	773	780	0.9	925	92.9	0.0	0.0	4.5	2.6	12.6	48.4	64.1	29.3	33.9	481	94.2
Jackson village & MCD (Washington)	6,791	7,200	6.0	7,081	95.8	1.4	0.0	1.4	1.4	23.1	20.1	43.1	35.1	30.0	2,962	90.9
Jackson town (Washington)	4,129	4,547	10.1	4,495	95.5	1.1	0.4	1.0	2.1	20.2	17.0	48.0	31.2	32.7	1,673	96.9
Jacksonport town (Door)	705	716	1.6	781	94.2	0.0	0.0	0.1	5.6	17.0	32.3	55.5	32.1	36.1	353	91.5
Jacobs town (Ashland)	722	692	-4.2	521	98.5	0.0	0.0	0.4	1.2	13.2	27.3	54.9	58.7	8.5	289	74.0
Jamestown town (Grant)	2,081	2,118	1.8	2,141	99.3	0.0	0.0	0.0	0.7	20.4	17.6	42.7	40.8	23.7	871	93.3
Janesville city & MCD (Rock)	63,658	64,575	1.4	64,245	88.6	2.3	1.5	2.3	5.4	22.8	16.4	39.7	42.6	23.6	26,659	90.6
Janesville town (Rock)	3,421	3,612	5.6	3,544	98.8	0.0	0.3	0.9	0.0	19.6	19.4	47.4	34.0	35.6	1,388	97.0
Jefferson town (Green)	1,214	1,244	2.5	1,170	95.6	0.0	0.0	0.0	4.4	23.7	18.5	45.3	56.9	11.1	443	83.1
Jefferson city & MCD (Jefferson)	7,983	7,986	0.0	7,991	87.9	1.2	0.2	0.5	10.2	20.6	16.0	41.9	45.3	19.0	3,250	85.4
Jefferson town (Jefferson)	2,185	2,252	3.1	2,143	95.4	0.0	3.4	0.4	0.8	15.4	25.0	51.1	45.9	23.7	882	85.0
Jefferson town (Monroe)	823	911	10.7	901	98.8	0.1	0.0	0.3	0.8	36.4	9.9	31.3	59.7	13.8	261	72.4
Jefferson town (Vernon)	1,143	1,223	7.0	879	99.7	0.0	0.3	0.0	0.0	20.1	17.0	44.6	35.9	36.0	352	93.5
Jim Falls CDP	237	-	-	210	100.0	0.0	0.0	0.0	0.0	11.4	27.6	52.4	52.9	19.2	121	86.0
Johnson town (Marathon)	985	957	-2.8	924	98.8	0.0	0.0	0.4	0.8	29.3	12.7	34.5	64.4	10.4	324	72.5
Johnson Creek village & MCD (Jefferson)	2,729	3,046	11.6	2,992	89.8	1.1	0.5	2.4	6.2	27.7	11.3	36.1	33.0	31.9	1,107	94.4
Johnstown town (Polk)	534	537	0.6	537	76.5	0.0	0.4	22.0	1.1	18.1	22.5	46.5	43.6	18.7	230	84.3
Johnstown town (Rock)	776	798	2.8	869	96.0	0.3	0.0	0.8	2.9	18.3	18.9	49.0	50.5	21.7	330	91.2
Jordan town (Green)	641	659	2.8	599	92.8	0.0	0.7	0.0	6.5	23.5	14.5	44.3	46.0	20.0	231	84.4
Juda CDP	357	-	-	300	100.0	0.0	0.0	0.0	0.0	28.0	9.3	40.3	55.9	10.3	125	76.0
Jump River CDP	52	-	-	24	45.8	0.0	0.0	33.3	20.8	16.7	37.5	51.5	47.4	10.5	15	80.0
Jump River town (Taylor)	376	363	-3.5	327	93.6	0.0	0.0	4.9	1.5	25.4	16.2	41.8	50.7	12.3	138	85.5
Junction City village & MCD (Portage)	441	439	-0.5	454	84.8	2.2	0.9	1.1	11.0	30.8	15.0	36.6	57.1	14.3	176	86.9
Juneau city & MCD (Dodge)	2,814	2,668	-5.2	2,687	94.3	2.4	0.0	1.0	2.3	19.0	19.8	42.9	57.4	16.1	891	91.9
Kaukauna city	15,476	16,270	5.1	16,070	94.9	0.0	0.1	2.0	3.0	23.1	14.4	38.0	44.7	25.9	6,627	91.4
Kaukauna city (Calumet)	-	-	-	-	-	-	-	-	-	-	-	-	-	-	-	-
Kaukauna city (Outagamie)	15,476	16,270	5.1	16,070	94.9	0.0	0.1	2.0	3.0	23.1	14.4	38.0	44.7	25.9	6,627	91.4
Kaukauna town (Outagamie)	1,235	1,334	8.0	1,275	97.6	0.0	0.2	1.8	0.5	28.2	10.0	38.4	35.3	33.3	443	94.6
Kekoskee village & MCD (Dodge)	912	897	-1.6	929	97.0	0.0	0.1	1.4	1.5	19.5	17.7	49.5	47.2	19.8	367	87.2
Kellnersville village & MCD (Manitowoc)	332	318	-4.2	310	100.0	0.0	0.0	0.0	0.0	22.6	25.2	50.7	54.7	14.7	159	84.3
Kelly town (Bayfield)	463	467	0.9	414	95.4	0.0	0.2	2.4	1.9	22.0	15.7	46.0	46.3	15.5	165	89.7
Kendall town (Lafayette)	454	464	2.2	340	100.0	0.0	0.0	0.0	0.0	30.3	15.6	40.2	38.5	24.0	126	83.3
Kendall village & MCD (Monroe)	479	472	-1.5	533	90.1	0.8	1.1	3.8	4.3	24.8	19.9	38.3	52.9	14.0	215	84.7
Kennan village & MCD (Price)	132	120	-9.1	140	100.0	0.0	0.0	0.0	0.0	32.1	19.3	43.0	52.2	3.3	60	88.3
Kennan town (Price)	359	331	-7.8	294	95.6	0.0	0.0	1.4	3.1	21.1	13.3	48.7	50.9	10.6	121	91.7
Kenosha city & MCD (Kenosha)	99,279	99,944	0.7	99,688	66.1	11.0	2.0	3.1	17.8	24.7	12.9	35.8	42.0	24.4	38,072	89.3
Keshena CDP	1,262	-	-	1,438	1.5	0.5	0.0	85.1	12.9	41.6	7.5	22.9	60.1	8.3	368	73.9
Kewaskum village	4,038	4,264	5.6	4,187	90.1	1.6	0.0	0.0	8.3	26.9	18.0	37.7	39.9	25.9	1,699	88.2
Kewaskum village (Fond du Lac)	-	-	-	-	-	-	-	-	-	-	-	-	-	-	-	-
Kewaskum village (Washington)	4,038	4,264	5.6	4,187	90.1	1.6	0.0	0.0	8.3	26.9	18.0	37.7	39.9	25.9	1,699	88.2
Kewaskum town (Washington)	1,067	1,097	2.8	1,128	97.7	0.4	0.4	0.9	0.7	15.2	17.4	50.1	34.0	23.2	422	96.4
Kewaunee city & MCD (Kewaunee)	2,949	2,848	-3.4	2,858	97.4	0.1	0.0	1.8	0.7	19.2	26.9	50.2	46.1	19.4	1,419	84.4
Keystone town (Bayfield)	373	378	1.3	367	86.6	0.0	0.0	13.4	0.0	18.3	19.1	47.6	52.4	9.7	169	87.6
Kickapoo town (Vernon)	619	654	5.7	790	97.0	0.4	0.4	0.0	2.3	43.5	16.6	30.1	48.4	23.2	232	67.2
Kiel city	3,726	3,796	1.9	3,679	97.3	0.0	0.4	0.0	2.3	25.6	16.5	39.1	51.2	19.4	1,606	87.4

1 May be of any race.

Table A. All Places — **Population and Housing**

STATE City, town, township, borough, or CDP (county if applicable)	2010 census total population	2019 estimated population	Percent change 2010–2019	ACS total population estimate 2015–2019	White alone, not Hispanic or Latino	Black alone, not Hispanic or Latino	Asian alone, not Hispanic or Latino	All other races or 2 or more races, not Hispanic or Latino	Hispanic or Latino[1]	Under 18 years old	Age 65 years and older	Median age	Percent High school diploma or less	Percent Bachelor's degree or more	Occupied housing units Total	Percent with a computer
	1	2	3	4	5	6	7	8	9	10	11	12	13	14	15	16
WISCONSIN—Con.																
Kiel city (Calumet)	309	317	2.6	228	100.0	0.0	0.0	0.0	0.0	24.1	24.6	47.9	72.3	8.1	119	100.0
Kiel city (Manitowoc)........	3,417	3,479	1.8	3,451	97.1	0.0	0.4	0.0	2.5	25.7	15.9	37.7	49.7	20.2	1,487	86.4
Kieler CDP......................	497	-	-	577	100.0	0.0	0.0	0.0	0.0	20.5	17.9	38.7	36.7	20.2	218	98.2
Kildare town (Juneau).......	683	698	2.2	710	94.5	0.3	0.4	2.5	2.3	21.5	21.8	44.7	46.9	12.0	291	84.2
Kimball town (Iron)...........	502	492	-2.0	437	97.7	0.0	0.0	2.3	0.0	14.2	23.6	53.6	32.1	19.8	226	94.2
Kimberly village & MCD (Outagamie)...................	6,466	6,802	5.2	6,770	89.4	0.1	3.6	3.0	3.9	27.0	14.1	36.8	37.8	25.8	2,769	88.0
King town (Lincoln)	855	846	-1.1	1,066	96.7	0.0	1.6	1.4	0.3	13.1	24.1	54.7	40.2	24.2	471	86.2
King CDP........................	1,750	-	-	1,790	85.9	1.2	6.6	1.8	4.5	16.0	36.8	54.1	53.5	18.1	514	97.1
Kingston village & MCD (Green Lake)................	326	320	-1.8	369	98.1	0.0	0.0	1.4	0.5	16.0	17.9	42.8	51.8	10.0	183	83.6
Kingston town (Green Lake).........................	1,064	1,083	1.8	1,007	97.8	1.0	0.0	0.8	0.4	36.2	17.1	29.9	61.4	8.2	326	62.6
Kingston town (Juneau)....	90	89	-1.1	45	100.0	0.0	0.0	0.0	0.0	4.4	33.3	49.3	65.9	2.4	25	88.0
Kinnickinnic town (St. Croix)........................	1,721	1,811	5.2	1,836	93.0	1.0	3.3	2.6	0.1	25.9	14.1	43.2	25.1	42.8	647	97.1
Knapp village & MCD (Dunn).......................	463	464	0.2	556	93.3	0.5	0.0	3.6	2.5	26.8	20.9	39.5	64.6	7.5	234	84.6
Knapp town (Jackson)......	299	306	2.3	256	100.0	0.0	0.0	0.0	0.0	13.7	23.8	52.0	53.0	14.1	128	86.7
Knight town (Iron)............	211	206	-2.4	207	94.2	0.0	0.0	5.8	0.0	20.3	24.6	46.5	46.2	17.2	97	87.6
Knowlton CDP..................	120	-	-	122	100.0	0.0	0.0	0.0	0.0	7.4	27.0	56.9	48.7	8.8	64	100.0
Knowlton town (Marathon)	1,910	2,032	6.4	1,922	98.0	0.4	0.3	0.9	0.3	20.2	17.5	49.3	43.2	26.0	797	93.9
Knox town (Price)	341	332	-2.6	304	99.3	0.3	0.0	0.3	0.0	13.5	22.7	53.7	51.8	12.4	154	87.7
Kohler village & MCD (Sheboygan)................	2,112	2,059	-2.5	2,146	95.6	0.0	1.4	0.7	2.3	26.2	25.3	47.4	14.9	63.1	869	94.7
Komensky town (Jackson)	509	548	7.7	451	28.6	7.1	1.8	57.4	5.1	25.5	8.6	33.1	50.5	11.9	105	89.5
Koshkonong town (Jefferson)...................	3,653	3,780	3.5	3,765	95.5	0.4	0.1	1.8	2.2	23.0	15.4	42.7	35.9	28.5	1,410	89.7
Kossuth town (Manitowoc)	2,086	2,061	-1.2	1,793	98.3	0.0	0.2	0.9	0.6	15.2	18.9	50.4	48.1	16.3	798	87.6
Krakow CDP	354	-	-	346	95.4	0.0	2.6	2.0	0.0	19.1	21.7	46.2	59.9	17.6	169	87.6
Kronenwetter village & MCD (Marathon)	7,204	8,079	12.1	7,796	90.2	0.6	3.2	5.2	0.7	23.5	13.8	37.7	34.7	32.0	2,923	94.1
Lac du Flambeau CDP	1,969	-	-	1,522	12.5	0.9	5.0	81.1	0.5	19.3	13.6	37.0	48.9	16.8	792	81.1
Lac du Flambeau town (Vilas).......................	3,438	3,507	2.0	3,460	49.8	0.6	2.2	46.4	1.0	12.9	31.2	54.9	37.3	27.6	1,792	85.9
Lac La Belle village..........	284	299	5.3	294	95.9	0.0	0.7	1.7	1.7	26.9	18.7	47.7	10.3	65.6	110	99.1
Lac La Belle village (Jefferson)...................	1	1	0.0	-	-	-	-	-	-	-	-	-	-	-	-	-
Lac La Belle village (Waukesha).................	283	298	5.3	294	95.9	0.0	0.7	1.7	1.7	26.9	18.7	47.7	10.3	65.6	110	99.1
La Crosse city & MCD (La Crosse)......................	51,343	51,227	-0.2	51,666	88.6	2.4	4.0	2.7	2.2	14.8	13.8	29.3	32.4	35.5	21,186	89.9
Ladysmith city & MCD (Rusk).......................	3,413	3,126	-8.4	3,149	92.9	1.3	0.0	2.5	3.4	23.8	21.1	41.4	59.5	20.7	1,410	87.5
La Farge village & MCD (Vernon)...................	746	759	1.7	961	93.5	1.0	0.0	3.5	1.9	31.2	21.2	37.2	59.2	13.3	395	83.8
Lafayette town (Chippewa)	5,782	6,025	4.2	5,955	97.0	0.7	0.4	1.6	0.4	19.9	20.2	46.6	28.7	35.2	2,527	94.7
Lafayette town (Monroe)...	396	440	11.1	413	87.7	5.3	1.2	1.5	4.4	16.9	11.6	35.9	42.2	18.3	130	82.3
Lafayette town (Walworth)	1,984	2,005	1.1	1,879	97.1	0.0	0.5	0.0	2.4	19.9	19.4	48.3	34.4	32.8	741	93.8
La Follette town (Burnett).	541	544	0.6	441	73.9	0.0	1.4	22.4	2.3	14.7	31.1	53.8	41.2	29.4	214	91.6
La Grange town (Monroe) .	1,940	2,051	5.7	1,853	94.2	0.0	0.6	4.3	0.9	22.1	18.9	47.6	41.4	22.1	711	90.7
La Grange town (Walworth)...................	2,450	2,470	0.8	2,691	90.9	0.6	0.1	3.8	4.6	20.3	17.9	49.8	35.5	37.2	1,052	94.8
Lake town (Marinette).......	1,135	1,129	-0.5	1,012	98.0	0.0	1.3	0.2	0.5	14.2	31.8	56.3	55.7	13.0	494	84.8
Lake town (Price)..............	1,126	1,094	-2.8	1,077	99.9	0.0	0.1	0.0	0.0	13.4	30.2	57.5	45.4	18.9	554	87.9
Lake Arrowhead CDP.......	838	-	-	853	99.2	0.0	0.0	0.8	0.0	5.7	64.7	69.1	31.6	36.5	444	86.5
Lake Camelot CDP...........	826	-	-	787	90.2	0.0	0.0	5.0	4.8	10.7	31.0	59.0	42.1	21.8	371	95.7
Lake Delton village & MCD (Sauk)..............	2,927	2,987	2.0	2,989	84.5	5.4	3.4	0.0	6.7	17.0	17.7	44.2	39.0	25.3	1,520	88.4
Lake Geneva city & MCD (Walworth).................	7,658	8,105	5.8	7,894	85.1	0.0	1.4	2.9	10.6	22.4	16.4	40.7	34.6	38.2	3,531	91.7
Lake Hallie village & MCD (Chippewa).................	6,461	6,747	4.4	6,667	93.6	0.2	2.0	2.4	1.8	24.3	10.7	36.6	35.8	19.1	2,648	95.6
Lake Holcombe town (Chippewa).................	1,034	1,078	4.3	904	99.7	0.0	0.3	0.0	0.0	12.4	27.8	57.1	53.2	15.5	439	87.5
Lake Ivanhoe CDP............	435	-	-	479	64.7	6.1	2.3	3.5	23.4	34.9	4.4	33.1	43.5	21.9	162	84.6
Lake Koshkonong CDP	1,204	-	-	1,135	95.9	1.0	0.4	2.2	0.5	16.0	25.4	54.5	36.2	29.8	523	95.4
Lakeland town (Barron)	977	957	-2.0	1,019	95.6	0.0	0.3	0.8	3.3	18.2	24.4	51.5	41.9	20.0	416	92.1
Lake Lorraine CDP...........	324	-	-	268	100.0	0.0	0.0	0.0	0.0	7.1	25.4	50.7	62.3	16.6	125	88.0
Lake Mills city & MCD (Jefferson)...................	5,719	5,983	4.6	5,895	86.8	0.3	0.8	1.7	10.5	24.3	14.1	36.9	30.9	36.9	2,415	94.1
Lake Mills town (Jefferson)	2,062	2,139	3.7	2,276	90.2	0.0	0.4	0.3	9.2	22.6	20.6	47.2	30.2	41.3	871	96.7
Lake Nebagamon village & MCD (Douglas).........	1,069	1,049	-1.9	905	98.7	0.2	0.0	1.1	0.0	17.0	26.0	56.0	25.1	42.1	422	92.2
Lake Ripley CDP..............	1,779	-	-	1,882	99.3	0.0	0.0	0.7	0.0	21.7	16.2	50.4	21.8	46.4	784	93.1
Lake Sherwood CDP........	372	-	-	361	100.0	0.0	0.0	0.0	0.0	7.2	51.0	66.2	34.6	40.6	201	96.5
Lakeside town (Douglas)..	700	713	1.9	573	98.1	0.0	0.0	0.0	1.9	19.7	17.3	49.0	33.4	23.6	255	87.1
Lake Tomahawk CDP........	228	-	-	188	89.9	0.0	0.0	3.2	6.9	6.4	26.1	49.8	28.4	18.8	114	95.6
Lake Tomahawk town (Oneida)....................	1,043	1,030	-1.2	1,036	92.8	2.5	0.1	2.9	1.7	13.5	29.3	54.2	33.2	21.1	457	92.3
Laketown town (Polk).......	961	949	-1.2	873	87.4	0.0	8.4	4.2	0.0	15.8	33.8	57.3	46.5	17.6	387	91.2
Lake Wazeecha CDP........	2,651	-	-	2,150	100.0	0.0	0.0	0.0	0.0	20.3	23.3	48.0	32.0	23.4	959	90.0
Lake Wisconsin CDP........	4,189	-	-	4,505	95.9	0.0	0.7	1.7	1.8	18.1	19.8	50.1	27.4	35.0	2,011	93.6
Lake Wissota CDP............	2,738	-	-	2,843	97.3	0.0	0.7	1.2	0.8	18.4	21.4	44.4	31.2	32.3	1,250	95.5
Lakewood CDP.................	323	-	-	385	93.5	0.0	0.0	2.6	3.9	14.3	33.0	52.6	45.5	29.9	193	90.7
Lakewood town (Oconto)..	821	835	1.7	886	96.3	0.0	0.0	1.1	2.6	8.4	41.6	61.9	49.2	21.6	469	84.2
Lamartine town (Fond du Lac).........................	1,731	1,761	1.7	1,841	94.2	0.0	4.6	0.6	0.6	25.2	15.6	42.3	43.6	22.3	699	90.4
Lamont town (Lafayette) ...	306	313	2.3	305	98.4	0.0	0.0	0.0	1.6	26.9	16.1	38.9	49.8	17.6	120	71.7
Lanark town (Portage)......	1,530	1,575	2.9	1,604	97.1	0.2	0.9	0.4	1.3	21.1	15.3	43.6	35.8	26.6	629	96.2
Lancaster city & MCD (Grant)......................	3,873	3,701	-4.4	3,730	95.6	0.8	1.7	0.7	1.3	24.4	19.9	34.4	41.4	17.3	1,511	87.8

1 May be of any race.

Table A. All Places — **Population and Housing**

STATE City, town, township, borough, or CDP (county if applicable)	Population 2010 census total population	Population 2019 estimated population	Population Percent change 2010–2019	Population ACS total population estimate 2015–2019	Race and Hispanic or Latino origin (percent) White alone, not Hispanic or Latino	Black alone, not Hispanic or Latino	Asian alone, not Hispanic or Latino	All other races or 2 or more races, not Hispanic or Latino	Hispanic or Latino[1]	Age (percent) Under 18 years old	Age 65 years and older	Median age	Educational attainment of persons age 25 and older Percent High school diploma or less	Percent Bachelor's degree or more	Occupied housing units Total	Percent with a computer
	1	2	3	4	5	6	7	8	9	10	11	12	13	14	15	16
WISCONSIN—Con.																
Land O'Lakes town (Vilas)	867	890	2.7	829	98.4	0.0	0.0	1.0	0.6	9.2	33.4	60.2	32.2	36.1	444	89.4
Langlade town (Langlade)	473	456	-3.6	407	96.3	2.7	0.5	0.2	0.2	13.0	45.7	62.6	67.8	5.4	203	79.8
Lannon village & MCD (Waukesha)	1,107	1,232	11.3	1,213	87.3	1.5	2.3	0.7	8.2	20.1	15.0	43.7	41.1	16.6	504	89.1
Laona CDP	583	-	-	434	76.5	0.7	4.4	15.0	3.5	32.5	12.9	39.5	55.7	9.5	182	84.1
Laona town (Forest)	1,208	1,194	-1.2	1,070	86.8	0.3	1.8	8.9	2.2	23.4	20.7	44.9	50.3	18.3	448	85.9
La Pointe town (Ashland)	261	261	0.0	237	93.7	0.0	1.7	4.6	0.0	13.5	31.2	58.6	20.1	49.5	115	94.8
La Prairie town (Rock)	835	871	4.3	962	96.3	0.0	0.0	1.2	2.5	19.8	21.0	47.6	46.4	20.6	374	92.5
Larrabee town (Waupaca)	1,371	1,351	-1.5	1,470	99.9	0.0	0.0	0.1	0.0	26.3	14.4	41.6	55.7	12.3	569	82.8
Lauderdale Lakes CDP	1,172	-	-	1,259	93.2	0.4	0.3	1.8	4.2	21.9	23.7	49.9	23.1	46.2	535	95.1
La Valle village & MCD (Sauk)	365	361	-1.1	360	98.3	0.0	1.7	0.0	0.0	21.1	15.0	38.2	59.9	6.2	155	85.2
La Valle town (Sauk)	1,304	1,395	7.0	1,492	90.9	0.0	0.0	0.7	8.4	17.2	25.5	49.7	44.5	25.8	602	87.9
Lawrence town (Brown)	4,281	5,411	26.4	5,170	97.9	0.7	0.0	1.4	0.0	31.2	9.9	35.8	24.4	44.1	1,832	98.1
Lawrence town (Rusk)	311	292	-6.1	270	95.6	0.0	0.0	4.4	0.0	24.1	17.8	46.3	63.8	10.8	117	75.2
Lebanon CDP	204	-	-	249	100.0	0.0	0.0	0.0	0.0	18.1	36.9	49.9	66.8	3.2	97	58.8
Lebanon town (Dodge)	1,651	1,668	1.0	1,618	95.0	1.9	0.0	0.6	2.5	17.9	24.9	48.6	57.4	11.6	634	83.9
Lebanon town (Waupaca)	1,666	1,642	-1.4	1,755	93.6	1.6	0.2	0.2	4.3	23.9	10.8	43.1	50.8	17.5	670	92.2
Ledgeview town (Brown)	6,500	8,112	24.8	7,812	93.6	0.1	3.7	1.2	1.4	28.0	13.0	36.0	22.2	48.4	3,088	94.4
Leeds town (Columbia)	772	779	0.9	582	96.9	0.0	1.4	0.9	0.9	17.4	18.7	49.7	37.4	23.2	248	90.3
Legend Lake CDP	1,525	-	-	1,486	26.5	0.0	0.0	72.3	1.2	20.5	21.1	49.8	36.7	30.9	578	85.1
Lemonweir town (Juneau)	1,742	1,713	-1.7	1,500	95.7	0.0	0.6	3.0	0.7	18.8	21.7	50.2	52.5	12.9	681	83.0
Lena village & MCD (Oconto)	561	539	-3.9	607	90.9	0.0	0.0	7.6	1.5	24.7	14.7	35.9	61.3	6.3	256	85.5
Lena town (Oconto)	732	742	1.4	755	98.5	0.0	0.0	0.0	1.5	20.4	17.0	39.8	60.9	10.7	311	84.6
Lenroot town (Sawyer)	1,279	1,294	1.2	1,044	94.9	0.0	0.3	2.5	2.3	20.5	26.4	51.9	30.7	37.9	473	91.8
Leola town (Adams)	308	300	-2.6	289	98.6	0.0	0.0	1.4	0.0	14.9	19.7	53.1	57.2	12.2	136	79.4
Leon town (Monroe)	1,090	1,150	5.5	1,008	94.8	0.0	0.0	2.4	2.8	23.6	9.7	43.3	42.1	24.3	364	86.0
Leon town (Waushara)	1,439	1,452	0.9	1,619	97.9	1.5	0.0	0.2	0.3	20.6	23.4	52.2	55.6	13.8	673	87.1
Leopolis CDP	87	-	-	93	100.0	0.0	0.0	0.0	0.0	24.7	21.5	49.3	69.8	6.3	36	66.7
Leroy town (Dodge)	1,002	1,002	0.0	930	98.3	0.0	0.5	0.4	0.8	20.5	17.1	46.1	53.0	17.2	364	84.6
Lessor town (Shawano)	1,263	1,245	-1.4	1,173	97.6	0.0	0.0	2.2	0.2	22.3	13.0	45.0	56.0	16.5	435	89.4
Levis town (Clark)	492	498	1.2	441	95.7	0.0	0.0	1.1	3.2	14.3	27.7	49.8	66.2	6.1	201	85.1
Lewis CDP	164	-	-	154	96.1	0.0	1.3	2.6	0.0	17.5	38.3	52.7	55.2	21.6	91	72.5
Lewiston town (Columbia)	1,225	1,241	1.3	1,394	95.3	0.0	0.0	1.4	3.3	18.9	20.1	50.2	53.6	14.5	564	87.1
Liberty town (Grant)	553	561	1.4	493	98.4	0.0	0.8	0.4	0.4	34.1	15.0	36.2	55.6	14.0	181	72.9
Liberty town (Manitowoc)	1,281	1,262	-1.5	1,193	98.6	0.0	0.2	1.3	0.0	18.5	15.8	48.0	47.3	24.4	500	92.2
Liberty town (Outagamie)	874	923	5.6	838	99.4	0.0	0.0	0.0	0.6	16.8	15.5	45.9	45.9	15.8	317	95.3
Liberty town (Vernon)	252	290	15.1	289	99.3	0.0	0.0	0.0	0.7	30.8	14.9	45.3	47.5	23.5	110	86.4
Liberty Grove town (Door)	1,731	1,757	1.5	1,780	97.0	0.0	0.3	0.9	1.9	7.1	45.7	63.0	24.4	49.6	901	92.1
Lily Lake CDP	-	-	-	560	97.0	0.4	0.2	0.0	2.5	27.9	18.2	33.8	55.6	18.9	201	100.0
Lima town (Grant)	805	810	0.6	549	97.8	0.0	0.0	0.7	1.5	21.3	18.8	50.3	47.9	26.5	233	84.5
Lima town (Pepin)	702	697	-0.7	821	93.8	0.0	0.0	0.0	6.2	28.7	12.7	30.9	51.2	15.5	268	77.6
Lima town (Rock)	1,282	1,354	5.6	1,120	85.4	0.4	0.0	0.0	14.3	22.6	21.5	49.5	46.9	25.1	434	90.1
Lima town (Sheboygan)	2,975	2,963	-0.4	2,974	97.2	0.6	0.4	1.3	0.5	24.6	16.3	41.5	44.2	23.0	1,125	92.1
Lime Ridge village & MCD (Sauk)	162	163	0.6	179	98.3	0.0	0.0	1.7	0.0	20.1	31.8	49.1	62.4	14.2	69	76.8
Lincoln town (Adams)	296	300	1.4	330	91.8	0.6	2.1	0.6	4.8	14.8	29.7	55.2	54.6	15.4	142	92.3
Lincoln town (Bayfield)	287	289	0.7	315	98.7	0.0	0.3	0.0	1.0	27.0	31.4	52.9	34.7	20.4	129	76.7
Lincoln town (Buffalo)	162	158	-2.5	225	99.1	0.0	0.0	0.0	0.9	16.9	19.6	40.6	54.2	22.0	89	88.8
Lincoln town (Burnett)	306	309	1.0	257	88.7	0.0	0.8	8.2	2.3	13.2	35.8	56.7	54.4	15.2	135	82.2
Lincoln town (Eau Claire)	1,100	1,201	9.2	1,228	96.9	0.8	0.0	2.1	0.2	30.9	12.5	40.6	38.4	27.6	403	88.3
Lincoln town (Forest)	953	913	-4.2	953	62.2	0.1	0.0	36.2	1.5	19.9	28.6	53.9	51.1	20.5	432	90.3
Lincoln town (Kewaunee)	948	953	0.5	943	94.7	0.0	0.0	0.8	4.5	21.7	15.2	41.6	63.5	9.5	345	83.8
Lincoln town (Monroe)	843	859	1.9	895	98.0	0.1	0.8	1.1	0.0	21.3	15.4	45.2	45.4	13.3	349	88.8
Lincoln town (Polk)	2,174	2,186	0.6	2,018	96.0	1.1	0.1	0.8	1.8	16.5	29.3	52.1	33.4	25.3	900	91.3
Lincoln town (Trempealeau)	816	864	5.9	831	81.9	2.0	0.0	2.3	13.7	22.7	25.0	46.0	45.7	25.2	248	90.3
Lincoln town (Vilas)	2,427	2,501	3.0	2,460	99.7	0.0	0.0	0.0	0.3	16.6	28.2	52.1	35.8	29.7	1,231	90.1
Lincoln town (Wood)	1,571	1,531	-2.5	1,551	97.1	0.0	0.5	1.5	1.0	25.0	13.9	46.1	42.8	29.8	595	92.1
Lind town (Waupaca)	1,579	1,582	0.2	1,449	94.8	0.0	0.0	2.0	3.2	18.6	16.4	48.9	49.3	19.1	644	87.9
Linden village & MCD (Iowa)	549	528	-3.8	512	98.8	0.0	0.0	0.2	1.0	24.0	15.2	35.1	41.5	15.7	191	84.3
Linden town (Iowa)	847	845	-0.2	742	93.3	0.0	0.0	0.0	6.7	13.2	27.9	55.2	47.9	22.0	295	87.8
Lindina town (Juneau)	725	710	-2.1	774	80.9	0.0	0.0	2.7	16.4	28.6	16.5	40.4	54.1	17.2	284	85.9
Linn town (Walworth)	2,388	2,403	0.6	2,832	79.6	0.4	0.2	2.8	16.9	21.0	26.6	50.1	34.8	39.3	1,171	95.9
Linwood town (Portage)	1,123	1,154	2.8	944	98.1	0.0	0.8	1.1	0.0	13.3	19.0	50.7	48.0	21.2	422	82.7
Lisbon town (Juneau)	908	897	-1.2	889	96.5	0.2	0.6	2.2	0.4	24.1	21.0	47.1	46.7	17.6	362	85.6
Lisbon town (Waukesha)	10,158	10,627	4.6	10,540	96.5	0.0	1.2	0.7	1.6	20.9	19.4	49.0	28.5	35.9	4,127	95.3
Little Black town (Taylor)	1,140	1,113	-2.4	1,153	89.9	0.0	0.5	2.1	7.5	23.3	17.2	43.6	56.6	15.2	462	89.2
Little Chute village & MCD (Outagamie)	10,472	12,081	15.4	11,484	90.8	0.5	1.4	2.4	5.0	20.7	13.5	37.5	40.4	22.9	4,976	91.7
Little Falls town (Monroe)	1,520	1,600	5.3	1,494	95.2	0.7	0.0	0.1	4.0	24.6	18.3	47.0	48.2	16.6	576	92.5
Little Grant town (Grant)	283	288	1.8	320	99.1	0.0	0.3	0.6	0.0	33.8	11.9	41.3	42.8	17.5	110	82.7
Little Rice town (Oneida)	307	305	-0.7	379	98.4	0.0	0.0	1.6	0.0	14.2	32.2	56.9	51.1	17.7	174	82.2
Little River town (Oconto)	1,094	1,108	1.3	1,034	95.8	0.0	0.0	4.2	0.0	22.5	20.3	48.2	50.4	18.5	451	85.6
Little Round Lake CDP	1,081	-	-	1,080	8.0	0.5	0.0	87.8	3.8	42.4	4.4	25.5	54.3	4.9	448	67.2
Little Sturgeon CDP	136	-	-	205	97.6	0.0	0.0	2.4	0.0	12.2	31.7	58.5	42.7	29.2	99	81.8
Little Suamico town (Oconto)	4,796	4,892	2.0	4,842	95.4	1.5	0.0	1.1	2.0	23.2	11.3	43.2	45.0	24.3	1,862	100.0
Little Wolf town (Waupaca)	1,425	1,397	-2.0	1,294	97.6	0.0	0.3	0.8	1.3	19.5	20.5	46.8	59.9	12.5	541	81.3
Livingston village	664	634	-4.5	608	99.3	0.2	0.0	0.5	0.0	26.6	15.8	37.6	44.2	14.1	233	90.1
Livingston village (Grant)	656	626	-4.6	578	99.3	0.2	0.0	0.5	0.0	25.6	16.6	39.3	46.1	12.4	226	89.8
Livingston village (Iowa)	8	8	0.0	30	100.0	0.0	0.0	0.0	0.0	46.7	0.0	33.1	0.0	56.3	7	100.0
Lodi city & MCD (Columbia)	3,052	3,092	1.3	3,060	95.8	0.2	1.1	2.1	0.7	28.2	10.9	39.4	23.5	38.8	1,369	95.4
Lodi town (Columbia)	3,264	3,316	1.6	3,289	93.8	0.0	0.9	0.5	4.7	18.4	18.9	47.6	32.4	27.7	1,421	90.1
Loganville village & MCD (Sauk)	300	298	-0.7	261	98.9	0.8	0.0	0.0	0.4	20.3	18.8	41.8	53.2	10.2	110	83.6
Lohrville village & MCD (Waushara)	402	389	-3.2	385	90.6	0.0	0.8	0.8	7.8	16.1	24.7	52.5	68.6	4.4	168	75.6

1   May be of any race.

Table A. All Places — **Population and Housing**

STATE City, town, township, borough, or CDP (county if applicable)	2010 census total population	2019 estimated population	Percent change 2010–2019	ACS total population estimate 2015–2019	White alone, not Hispanic or Latino	Black alone, not Hispanic or Latino	Asian alone, not Hispanic or Latino	All other races or 2 or more races, not Hispanic or Latino	Hispanic or Latino[1]	Under 18 years old	Age 65 years and older	Median age	Percent High school diploma or less	Percent Bachelor's degree or more	Total	Percent with a computer
	1	2	3	4	5	6	7	8	9	10	11	12	13	14	15	16
WISCONSIN—Con.																
Lomira village & MCD (Dodge)	2,430	2,450	0.8	2,553	95.6	0.0	0.0	0.3	4.1	23.5	15.2	36.8	43.1	18.0	1,104	83.7
Lomira town (Dodge)	1,133	1,136	0.3	958	99.8	0.0	0.0	0.0	0.2	18.7	13.7	45.4	44.3	16.1	414	91.5
Lone Rock village & MCD (Richland)	887	835	-5.9	896	94.2	1.9	0.1	2.7	1.1	22.5	18.2	41.0	64.6	9.5	418	82.1
Long Lake CDP	50	-	-	49	100.0	0.0	0.0	0.0	0.0	4.1	32.7	57.3	77.5	0.0	31	100.0
Long Lake town (Florence)	157	150	-4.5	170	98.8	0.0	0.0	1.2	0.0	17.1	34.1	57.2	57.8	14.1	81	79.0
Long Lake town (Washburn)	627	630	0.5	551	89.7	0.0	0.0	10.0	0.4	8.7	30.9	56.4	31.2	35.9	257	92.6
Longwood town (Clark)	861	873	1.4	903	98.9	0.0	0.0	0.0	1.1	35.1	15.5	27.7	69.7	10.0	270	54.1
Lorain town (Polk)	282	276	-2.1	287	90.2	0.0	0.0	9.4	0.3	21.3	17.4	42.8	51.0	20.4	114	83.3
Lowell village & MCD (Dodge)	345	325	-5.8	253	85.8	0.0	0.0	10.3	4.0	13.4	17.4	52.4	60.8	13.9	121	85.1
Lowell town (Dodge)	1,185	1,166	-1.6	1,082	99.5	0.0	0.0	0.0	0.5	17.8	17.1	49.6	52.1	19.2	432	90.3
Lowville town (Columbia)	1,014	1,026	1.2	1,106	93.3	0.0	0.0	2.7	4.0	22.1	14.6	46.5	29.1	22.7	427	93.4
Loyal city & MCD (Clark)	1,257	1,233	-1.9	1,225	94.1	0.7	0.0	2.4	2.9	25.0	17.1	38.2	49.6	17.4	532	90.2
Loyal town (Clark)	830	849	2.3	717	91.4	0.0	0.0	1.1	7.5	36.5	12.1	33.7	58.0	14.5	225	81.8
Lublin village & MCD (Taylor)	118	113	-4.2	105	100.0	0.0	0.0	0.0	0.0	12.4	24.8	53.3	69.0	14.3	60	60.0
Lucas town (Dunn)	764	802	5.0	709	98.7	0.0	1.3	0.0	0.0	20.2	18.6	45.9	55.3	19.8	281	86.8
Luck village & MCD (Polk)	1,115	1,051	-5.7	1,227	91.4	0.5	0.0	3.7	4.3	17.2	27.0	47.4	56.1	15.6	589	80.3
Luck town (Polk)	930	934	0.4	985	97.7	0.0	0.9	0.8	0.6	19.0	20.4	49.7	43.6	18.4	441	86.8
Ludington town (Eau Claire)	1,061	1,079	1.7	1,161	98.1	0.0	1.0	0.6	0.3	22.0	18.7	45.3	48.0	16.1	430	86.3
Luxemburg village & MCD (Kewaunee)	2,520	2,571	2.0	2,561	88.9	2.1	0.0	1.4	7.5	29.2	15.5	36.5	40.6	26.3	996	83.1
Luxemburg town (Kewaunee)	1,464	1,476	0.8	1,503	95.3	0.0	1.1	1.5	2.1	21.1	17.6	44.3	47.2	16.7	557	86.2
Lyndon town (Juneau)	1,390	1,393	0.2	1,144	80.1	3.5	0.4	10.3	5.7	16.7	22.4	48.6	54.3	13.6	518	87.6
Lyndon town (Sheboygan)	1,543	1,567	1.6	1,579	97.0	0.3	0.3	0.8	1.6	19.6	17.5	47.7	43.5	21.8	618	89.2
Lyndon Station village & MCD (Juneau)	500	484	-3.2	474	88.4	1.9	0.0	6.1	3.6	16.7	23.8	45.7	67.9	6.6	210	77.6
Lynn town (Clark)	861	887	3.0	1,190	98.2	0.3	0.3	0.6	0.7	40.4	7.8	24.7	58.2	15.0	333	65.2
Lynne town (Oneida)	141	142	0.7	128	95.3	0.0	0.0	4.7	0.0	20.3	19.5	50.5	55.9	1.0	59	79.7
Lynxville village & MCD (Crawford)	132	127	-3.8	214	98.6	0.0	0.0	0.0	1.4	36.4	22.4	32.7	45.4	20.8	72	95.8
Lyons town (Walworth)	3,700	3,737	1.0	3,713	98.1	0.0	0.4	0.0	1.5	21.7	16.8	45.6	37.1	28.3	1,367	90.3
McFarland village & MCD (Dane)	7,931	9,031	13.9	8,650	94.7	2.3	1.1	1.1	0.7	22.3	16.3	42.3	26.7	40.0	3,409	96.6
Mackford town (Green Lake)	563	569	1.1	385	95.3	0.0	0.0	2.1	2.6	12.5	19.0	52.6	55.7	7.2	185	85.9
McKinley town (Polk)	347	350	0.9	257	94.6	0.0	0.8	0.4	4.3	13.6	27.2	56.3	42.7	19.2	117	88.0
McKinley town (Taylor)	457	434	-5.0	470	99.8	0.0	0.0	0.0	0.2	34.0	16.2	35.6	63.2	12.3	166	81.3
McMillan town (Marathon)	1,982	2,103	6.1	2,053	94.6	0.0	3.4	1.5	0.5	23.9	14.2	45.7	33.1	38.4	793	91.3
Madge town (Washburn)	506	509	0.6	582	96.7	1.0	0.0	1.4	0.9	13.9	42.8	59.3	30.7	33.6	267	88.8
Madison city & MCD (Dane)	233,173	259,680	11.4	254,977	73.6	6.9	8.9	3.6	7.0	16.3	11.6	31.0	18.8	57.9	110,294	95.6
Madison town (Dane)	6,451	6,873	6.5	6,871	53.8	10.6	7.0	5.0	23.7	25.5	7.8	31.3	41.0	30.9	3,085	92.3
Magnolia town (Rock)	766	807	5.4	685	88.5	0.0	0.0	0.7	10.8	20.7	18.7	46.5	46.5	18.5	280	90.7
Maiden Rock village & MCD (Pierce)	117	117	0.0	88	97.7	0.0	0.0	2.3	0.0	19.3	29.5	46.0	31.4	41.4	43	95.3
Maiden Rock town (Pierce)	591	616	4.2	627	93.9	0.2	0.3	0.5	5.1	23.8	19.6	47.9	47.5	19.1	251	94.0
Maine village & MCD (Marathon)	2,584	2,574	-0.4	2,581	96.5	0.3	2.3	0.5	0.4	20.4	17.6	46.4	35.1	32.5	1,077	94.3
Maine town (Outagamie)	866	887	2.4	966	90.3	0.0	0.0	1.6	8.2	18.6	16.6	48.8	65.6	6.6	360	86.1
Manawa city & MCD (Waupaca)	1,371	1,272	-7.2	1,352	97.9	0.4	0.3	1.5	0.0	29.1	15.0	36.9	57.3	13.5	561	85.4
Manchester town (Green Lake)	1,022	1,036	1.4	1,329	96.7	0.0	0.0	0.2	3.2	36.9	11.2	24.9	64.6	9.0	378	65.1
Manchester town (Jackson)	704	725	3.0	860	88.8	0.0	0.0	7.2	4.0	21.3	19.2	45.4	52.0	15.8	362	87.0
Manitowish Waters town (Vilas)	566	579	2.3	662	93.1	0.0	0.0	4.4	2.6	10.7	36.0	58.6	27.1	37.1	363	96.4
Manitowoc city & MCD (Manitowoc)	33,741	32,579	-3.4	32,702	84.5	1.9	6.0	2.3	5.4	21.0	21.1	43.7	46.7	20.9	14,740	86.4
Manitowoc town (Manitowoc)	1,086	1,074	-1.1	1,156	97.7	0.0	0.0	2.3	0.0	20.2	18.9	48.3	43.9	23.6	478	88.9
Manitowoc Rapids town (Manitowoc)	2,140	2,110	-1.4	2,053	99.2	0.2	0.0	0.3	0.3	15.1	24.9	53.6	32.4	36.3	863	90.8
Maple town (Douglas)	744	757	1.7	719	94.7	1.1	0.0	3.5	0.7	24.8	18.2	41.2	40.6	22.7	273	89.0
Maple Bluff village & MCD (Dane)	1,317	1,311	-0.5	1,405	92.3	0.9	0.3	1.2	5.3	20.2	22.9	50.1	9.0	73.3	585	95.9
Maple Creek town (Outagamie)	614	616	0.3	512	93.4	0.0	0.0	1.8	4.9	19.9	16.2	51.1	55.7	10.9	211	87.7
Maple Grove town (Barron)	981	975	-0.6	982	91.5	0.5	0.3	1.1	6.5	26.8	19.1	42.5	53.3	13.5	345	87.5
Maple Grove town (Manitowoc)	832	820	-1.4	822	97.8	0.0	0.0	1.9	0.2	24.3	17.0	44.1	59.6	10.8	294	84.7
Maple Grove town (Shawano)	976	960	-1.6	936	97.1	0.3	0.0	0.6	1.9	19.3	19.3	45.8	55.2	12.0	368	83.7
Maplehurst town (Taylor)	335	330	-1.5	351	99.1	0.0	0.0	0.0	0.9	21.4	22.8	48.5	64.5	5.6	152	77.0
Maple Plain town (Barron)	799	793	-0.8	679	84.7	1.2	0.0	13.5	0.6	18.7	26.7	50.7	43.9	28.4	295	94.2
Maple Valley town (Oconto)	664	674	1.5	703	93.3	0.0	0.4	5.0	1.3	21.5	24.0	50.3	54.3	11.9	323	76.8
Marathon town (Marathon)	1,044	1,106	5.9	1,018	97.7	0.0	1.9	0.4	0.0	16.9	22.3	50.9	47.8	21.2	396	88.9
Marathon City village & MCD (Marathon)	1,532	1,508	-1.6	1,376	95.9	0.0	1.5	0.8	1.9	21.5	20.7	47.4	47.8	21.3	593	82.3
Marcellon town (Columbia)	1,102	1,113	1.0	979	99.7	0.0	0.0	0.0	0.3	25.7	21.2	45.5	44.9	15.7	367	83.1
Marengo CDP	111	-	-	115	97.4	0.0	0.0	2.6	0.0	30.4	14.8	27.8	59.3	11.9	32	87.5

1 May be of any race.

Table A. All Places — **Population and Housing**

STATE City, town, township, borough, or CDP (county if applicable)	Population				Race and Hispanic or Latino origin (percent)					Age (percent)			Educational attainment of persons age 25 and older		Occupied housing units	
	2010 census total population	2019 estimated population	Percent change 2010–2019	ACS total population estimate 2015–2019	White alone, not Hispanic or Latino	Black alone, not Hispanic or Latino	Asian alone, not Hispanic or Latino	All other races or 2 or more races, not Hispanic or Latino	Hispanic or Latino[1]	Under 18 years old	Age 65 years and older	Median age	Percent High school diploma or less	Percent Bachelor's degree or more	Total	Percent with a computer
	1	2	3	4	5	6	7	8	9	10	11	12	13	14	15	16

WISCONSIN—Con.

STATE City, town, township, borough, or CDP (county if applicable)	1	2	3	4	5	6	7	8	9	10	11	12	13	14	15	16
Marengo town (Ashland) ..	388	376	-3.1	446	98.7	0.4	0.2	0.7	0.0	38.8	13.7	31.9	46.5	21.2	130	94.6
Maribel village & MCD (Manitowoc)	351	332	-5.4	414	95.2	0.0	0.0	3.6	1.2	25.6	14.0	36.7	59.6	18.8	179	85.5
Marietta town (Crawford) ..	470	453	-3.6	424	95.8	0.2	0.9	0.7	2.4	20.5	20.3	49.3	57.4	17.0	178	82.6
Marinette city & MCD (Marinette)	10,961	10,539	-3.9	10,608	95.2	1.2	0.4	0.7	2.5	20.4	20.8	43.4	47.5	17.9	5,043	87.2
Marion town (Grant)	571	581	1.8	602	97.2	0.0	0.2	0.0	2.7	24.9	13.0	35.0	59.2	12.8	216	72.2
Marion town (Juneau)	426	419	-1.6	471	96.4	0.6	0.0	1.1	1.9	18.5	24.4	47.9	52.8	12.3	209	86.6
Marion city	1,253	1,178	-6.0	1,075	96.7	0.0	0.0	1.9	1.5	25.0	23.3	44.5	65.7	7.8	466	80.5
Marion city (Shawano)	20	19	-5.0	10	0.0	0.0	0.0	50.0	50.0	80.0	0.0	8.7	0.0	0.0	2	100.0
Marion city (Waupaca)	1,233	1,159	-6.0	1,065	97.6	0.0	0.0	1.4	1.0	24.5	23.6	45.5	65.8	7.8	464	80.4
Marion town (Waushara) ..	2,038	2,056	0.9	1,928	95.1	0.1	0.8	3.5	0.5	13.3	33.9	57.3	45.5	20.2	883	90.5
Markesan city & MCD (Green Lake)	1,473	1,401	-4.9	1,284	81.5	2.4	0.0	3.5	12.6	25.9	22.0	42.8	53.4	15.6	499	82.2
Marquette village & MCD (Green Lake)	150	155	3.3	198	96.5	0.0	0.0	0.0	3.5	14.6	17.7	53.0	54.6	8.0	92	82.6
Marquette town (Green Lake)	531	539	1.5	485	96.5	0.0	0.0	1.6	1.9	20.6	27.2	53.4	55.7	11.5	198	82.8
Marshall village & MCD (Dane)	3,857	3,984	3.3	3,966	72.5	2.8	2.8	0.4	21.5	27.9	9.4	34.3	49.9	18.1	1,310	96.3
Marshall town (Richland) ..	567	549	-3.2	583	100.0	0.0	0.0	0.0	0.0	19.7	28.1	53.5	47.8	26.5	256	82.4
Marshall town (Rusk)	687	692	0.7	725	98.2	0.0	0.0	0.7	1.1	30.9	13.7	34.7	64.5	11.2	252	74.2
Marshfield town (Fond du Lac)	1,138	1,148	0.9	1,300	94.3	0.0	0.7	0.5	4.5	23.1	28.2	48.0	50.3	19.5	459	85.8
Marshfield city	19,096	18,471	-3.3	18,222	91.8	0.7	3.4	1.5	2.5	19.5	21.3	42.2	38.9	31.9	8,797	87.3
Marshfield city (Marathon)	888	881	-0.8	636	83.0	0.0	16.5	0.5	0.0	10.1	40.7	56.6	29.9	42.8	331	76.7
Marshfield city (Wood)	18,208	17,590	-3.4	17,586	92.1	0.8	2.9	1.6	2.6	19.9	20.6	41.8	39.3	31.4	8,466	87.7
Marshfield town (Wood)	790	786	-0.5	718	97.9	0.0	1.8	0.3	0.0	19.4	23.3	49.1	44.2	18.3	303	88.4
Martell town (Pierce)	1,185	1,237	4.4	1,106	97.7	0.3	0.0	1.7	0.3	24.0	17.3	49.0	35.4	31.1	431	87.0
Mason village & MCD (Bayfield)	93	94	1.1	92	96.7	0.0	0.0	1.1	2.2	41.3	9.8	31.4	42.6	9.3	35	74.3
Mason town (Bayfield)	315	319	1.3	338	95.3	0.0	0.0	4.7	0.0	30.5	17.5	39.3	40.7	15.0	136	91.2
Matteson town (Waupaca)	936	917	-2.0	911	97.4	0.0	0.3	1.0	1.3	17.5	17.1	47.5	55.7	12.0	390	85.9
Mattoon village & MCD (Shawano)	436	412	-5.5	467	78.8	0.0	0.0	0.4	20.8	34.3	11.6	33.3	68.5	4.4	163	82.2
Mauston city & MCD (Juneau)	4,419	4,355	-1.4	4,368	93.6	2.7	0.4	1.8	1.5	18.8	18.4	41.3	55.3	14.4	1,738	85.2
Maxville town (Buffalo)	309	302	-2.3	377	93.4	0.0	0.0	3.2	3.4	25.2	14.1	35.5	56.8	14.8	144	88.9
Mayville town (Clark)	967	959	-0.8	883	93.7	0.5	0.5	0.7	4.8	34.9	11.6	38.5	63.8	11.1	308	77.6
Mayville city & MCD (Dodge)	5,155	4,890	-5.1	4,895	95.5	0.0	0.0	2.8	1.7	23.0	20.0	41.2	50.7	14.6	2,134	86.0
Mazomanie village & MCD (Dane)	1,642	1,696	3.3	1,858	90.0	1.3	0.4	6.5	1.8	24.9	14.8	37.4	35.1	27.8	761	89.8
Mazomanie town (Dane) ..	1,093	1,165	6.6	1,091	93.4	0.4	0.6	4.2	1.4	22.8	18.1	49.9	36.5	30.4	453	92.3
Mead town (Clark)	321	331	3.1	312	94.9	0.0	0.6	1.9	2.6	22.8	25.3	46.1	52.9	10.6	128	58.6
Meadowbrook town (Sawyer)	131	131	0.0	115	84.3	0.0	0.9	3.5	11.3	23.5	20.9	47.1	51.8	18.8	47	80.9
Mecan town (Marquette)...	693	707	2.0	709	94.9	1.3	0.0	1.6	2.3	11.4	33.4	58.0	60.1	12.3	364	78.3
Medary town (La Crosse) .	1,438	1,506	4.7	1,859	94.6	0.0	2.3	0.0	3.1	25.9	14.7	42.3	25.6	42.9	689	94.8
Medford city & MCD (Taylor)	4,360	4,282	-1.8	4,292	95.2	1.1	0.0	2.4	1.3	20.2	22.5	43.4	50.3	17.8	2,066	77.9
Medford town (Taylor)	2,568	2,571	0.1	2,559	96.7	0.0	0.9	1.3	1.1	24.4	14.5	45.2	44.8	19.8	991	88.5
Medina town (Dane)	1,380	1,470	6.5	1,414	89.7	2.3	0.0	3.7	4.2	25.3	14.9	43.8	39.5	23.9	530	93.4
Meeme town (Manitowoc)	1,446	1,425	-1.5	1,553	95.8	1.0	0.4	1.8	1.0	19.7	20.3	44.5	49.6	17.0	630	88.1
Meenon town (Burnett)	1,170	1,179	0.8	1,262	87.5	1.3	1.0	9.7	0.5	20.4	23.1	50.1	51.9	14.5	567	89.6
Mellen city & MCD (Ashland)	729	695	-4.7	638	91.8	0.0	0.9	1.6	5.6	15.7	26.5	52.9	46.9	15.8	322	82.0
Melrose village & MCD (Jackson)	495	477	-3.6	512	95.5	0.0	0.0	1.0	3.5	25.4	13.3	35.6	42.8	16.8	217	90.3
Melrose town (Jackson)....	470	481	2.3	564	93.6	0.0	1.8	3.2	1.4	33.7	10.6	33.1	53.1	19.3	174	83.3
Melvina village & MCD (Monroe)	104	110	5.8	68	100.0	0.0	0.0	0.0	0.0	19.1	10.3	41.5	73.6	9.4	27	96.3
Menasha city	17,503	17,873	2.1	18,114	83.0	1.2	2.7	5.1	8.0	24.0	14.7	37.4	44.8	23.4	7,878	90.5
Menasha city (Calumet)....	2,221	2,202	-0.9	2,542	91.7	0.8	3.5	0.6	3.3	27.5	11.7	37.1	18.6	45.0	983	96.6
Menasha city (Winnebago)	15,282	15,671	2.5	15,572	81.6	1.2	2.6	5.8	8.8	23.5	15.2	37.5	49.2	19.9	6,895	89.6
Menominee town (Menominee)	4,232	4,556	7.7	4,558	10.1	0.3	0.2	83.4	6.1	32.7	13.0	32.0	50.7	17.9	1,408	77.9
Menomonee Falls village & MCD (Waukesha)	35,625	38,014	6.7	37,160	85.6	3.6	5.2	2.2	3.4	22.2	19.4	43.3	27.6	44.9	15,314	92.1
Menomonie city & MCD (Dunn)	16,275	16,551	1.7	16,408	91.1	1.4	3.2	3.1	1.2	12.8	11.5	23.8	32.4	35.5	5,725	88.5
Menomonie town (Dunn) ..	3,355	3,530	5.2	3,465	92.4	0.8	6.4	0.0	0.5	18.4	19.1	44.9	36.2	26.2	1,413	87.8
Mentor town (Clark)	585	584	-0.2	627	93.6	0.0	1.1	0.6	4.6	28.5	13.2	38.3	57.1	6.4	239	87.0
Mequon city & MCD (Ozaukee)	23,136	24,382	5.4	24,144	89.0	2.7	3.0	1.9	3.3	21.7	23.5	47.6	14.3	67.3	8,993	94.2
Mercer CDP	516	-		469	88.9	0.0	0.9	4.1	6.2	14.3	32.2	55.8	32.3	16.9	239	84.9
Mercer town (Iron)	1,407	1,381	-1.8	1,390	95.0	0.0	0.3	1.4	3.4	12.9	36.5	59.3	37.1	19.5	694	89.5
Merrill city & MCD (Lincoln)	9,645	9,048	-6.2	9,108	96.0	0.6	0.4	2.1	0.9	19.5	20.9	42.5	48.1	16.3	4,351	84.5
Merrill town (Lincoln)	2,976	2,943	-1.1	2,938	97.1	0.0	0.0	1.2	1.7	19.1	16.8	50.5	42.5	20.4	1,272	92.0
Merrillan village & MCD (Jackson)	536	526	-1.9	609	76.8	0.7	0.0	12.6	9.9	26.9	17.7	35.5	53.6	10.6	265	80.8
Merrimac village & MCD (Sauk)	417	440	5.5	603	94.0	0.7	0.2	0.7	4.5	20.9	16.4	41.8	35.4	30.9	224	95.1
Merrimac town (Sauk)	947	1,050	10.9	1,089	98.1	0.0	0.0	0.5	1.5	20.8	27.5	48.0	28.0	31.7	455	92.7
Merton village & MCD (Waukesha)	3,389	3,762	11.0	3,672	91.3	0.2	4.8	1.1	2.6	31.8	7.2	39.5	15.6	61.3	1,169	99.0
Merton town (Waukesha)..	8,310	8,611	3.6	8,556	95.9	0.4	0.5	1.5	1.8	21.7	16.6	47.6	20.4	54.0	3,176	95.2
Meteor town (Sawyer)	158	160	1.3	138	93.5	0.0	2.9	2.2	1.4	16.7	18.1	53.9	57.7	6.3	63	82.5
Metomen town (Fond du Lac)	741	734	-0.9	665	98.2	0.0	0.0	1.1	0.8	16.2	22.1	49.5	50.2	20.4	274	84.7

1 May be of any race.

Table A. All Places — **Population and Housing**

STATE City, town, township, borough, or CDP (county if applicable)	2010 census total population	2019 estimated population	Percent change 2010–2019	ACS total population estimate 2015–2019	White alone, not Hispanic or Latino	Black alone, not Hispanic or Latino	Asian alone, not Hispanic or Latino	All other races or 2 or more races, not Hispanic or Latino	Hispanic or Latino[1]	Under 18 years old	Age 65 years and older	Median age	Percent High school diploma or less	Percent Bachelor's degree or more	Total	Percent with a computer
	1	2	3	4	5	6	7	8	9	10	11	12	13	14	15	16
WISCONSIN—Con.																
Middle Inlet town (Marinette)	840	826	-1.7	866	99.2	0.0	0.0	0.8	0.0	15.6	27.4	55.1	58.2	10.9	411	83.2
Middleton city & MCD (Dane)	17,560	20,034	14.1	19,487	83.1	2.5	4.6	3.8	6.1	20.9	15.6	39.0	14.6	62.0	8,899	94.7
Middleton town (Dane)	5,841	6,246	6.9	6,237	89.0	0.3	5.3	4.2	1.2	28.7	15.4	45.0	13.4	63.9	2,155	100.0
Middle Village CDP	281	-	-	183	4.4	0.5	0.0	92.9	2.2	27.3	19.1	46.5	54.4	4.0	64	50.0
Mifflin town (Iowa)	583	598	2.6	688	100.0	0.0	0.0	0.0	0.0	30.4	17.9	38.8	46.2	23.0	249	68.3
Milford town (Jefferson)	1,099	1,136	3.4	1,213	96.0	0.0	0.2	1.3	2.5	17.4	15.3	46.5	40.6	25.6	496	88.9
Milladore village (Portage)	276	261	-5.4	276	94.9	0.7	0.0	0.0	4.3	25.0	11.2	35.0	45.8	11.6	119	84.0
Milladore village (Wood)	-	-	-	-	-	-	-	-	-	-	-	-	-	-	-	-
Milladore village (Wood)	276	261	-5.4	276	94.9	0.7	0.0	0.0	4.3	25.0	11.2	35.0	45.8	11.6	119	84.0
Milladore town (Wood)	690	661	-4.2	671	99.1	0.1	0.0	0.4	0.3	18.3	14.9	49.5	51.0	15.2	278	84.5
Millston CDP	125	-	-	97	99.0	0.0	0.0	1.0	0.0	9.3	24.7	42.3	49.4	6.3	47	78.7
Millston town (Jackson)	157	163	3.8	144	99.3	0.0	0.0	0.7	0.0	18.8	20.8	40.5	48.1	6.5	65	81.5
Milltown village & MCD (Polk)	917	877	-4.4	1,030	92.0	1.2	0.0	2.6	4.2	22.7	18.4	43.0	52.2	11.5	489	77.5
Milltown town (Polk)	1,226	1,232	0.5	1,390	94.6	0.1	0.3	1.2	3.7	20.6	22.4	46.8	41.7	24.0	536	89.6
Millville town (Grant)	166	169	1.8	126	90.5	0.0	0.0	8.7	0.8	14.3	28.6	52.5	59.6	11.1	53	86.8
Milton town (Buffalo)	532	524	-1.5	554	94.9	0.2	0.0	4.5	0.4	17.9	27.6	49.9	38.6	21.7	235	92.8
Milton city & MCD (Rock)	5,555	5,627	1.3	5,573	96.6	0.6	0.0	1.3	1.6	25.7	15.8	37.1	44.5	23.8	2,192	86.5
Milton town (Rock)	2,916	3,142	7.8	3,094	95.6	0.3	0.1	1.8	2.1	23.6	12.8	41.1	38.9	26.9	1,245	95.0
Milwaukee city & MCD (Milwaukee)	594,498	590,157	-0.7	594,548	35.1	38.3	4.2	3.4	19.0	25.9	10.5	31.5	46.2	24.6	230,086	85.1
Milwaukee city (Washington)	-	-	-	-	-	-	-	-	-	-	-	-	-	-	-	-
Milwaukee city (Waukesha)	-	-	-	-	-	-	-	-	-	-	-	-	-	-	-	-
Mineral Point city & MCD (Iowa)	2,499	2,465	-1.4	2,625	93.5	2.4	1.0	2.0	1.1	22.6	22.0	45.3	33.9	30.4	1,220	84.2
Mineral Point town (Iowa)	1,021	1,051	2.9	780	99.0	0.0	0.0	1.0	0.0	22.1	21.4	49.7	34.7	28.9	335	90.1
Minocqua CDP	451	-	-	326	90.8	0.0	9.2	0.0	0.0	9.5	41.1	50.7	60.9	23.2	161	94.4
Minocqua town (Oneida)	4,463	4,425	-0.9	4,406	92.5	0.5	1.0	3.3	2.7	15.3	27.8	55.2	29.6	39.6	1,951	93.8
Minong village & MCD (Washburn)	525	503	-4.2	486	90.1	0.0	2.3	6.8	0.8	23.9	21.8	49.2	62.1	12.5	244	73.4
Minong town (Washburn)	921	928	0.8	869	98.2	0.6	0.3	0.9	0.0	15.5	33.3	58.8	45.5	18.5	444	87.2
Mishicot village & MCD (Manitowoc)	1,440	1,388	-3.6	1,457	98.2	0.0	0.3	0.0	1.5	22.4	17.9	45.1	49.0	15.7	644	86.2
Mishicot town (Manitowoc)	1,283	1,267	-1.2	1,398	92.2	0.3	0.0	0.2	7.3	20.5	18.5	48.6	50.3	11.1	548	91.1
Mitchell town (Sheboygan)	1,300	1,317	1.3	1,171	94.9	1.9	0.0	1.0	2.2	21.7	19.6	46.0	39.4	26.6	446	94.2
Modena town (Buffalo)	361	353	-2.2	238	99.2	0.0	0.0	0.4	0.4	20.2	36.1	57.7	59.4	13.9	112	80.4
Mole Lake CDP	435	-	-	514	12.5	0.0	0.0	80.4	7.2	36.8	8.0	32.0	58.2	1.3	208	75.0
Molitor town (Taylor)	326	326	0.0	350	98.0	0.0	2.0	0.0	0.0	21.7	20.9	49.6	51.7	22.5	145	89.0
Mondovi city & MCD (Buffalo)	2,783	2,564	-7.9	2,603	95.5	1.5	0.0	1.5	1.5	20.4	24.0	45.9	54.2	15.2	1,198	83.9
Mondovi town (Buffalo)	468	461	-1.5	444	95.9	0.2	0.0	1.6	2.3	13.1	16.2	50.3	56.8	11.3	193	90.2
Monico town (Oneida)	309	299	-3.2	279	97.8	0.0	1.1	0.0	1.1	17.9	15.8	54.8	57.1	11.2	133	81.2
Monona city & MCD (Dane)	7,567	8,175	8.0	8,122	90.6	1.4	1.5	2.5	4.1	19.7	20.5	43.3	19.1	54.1	3,896	90.0
Monroe town (Adams)	398	393	-1.3	405	96.3	0.0	0.0	3.7	0.0	10.4	38.0	61.2	57.5	12.6	206	87.4
Monroe city & MCD (Green)	10,816	10,565	-2.3	10,625	93.6	0.7	0.7	1.6	3.4	20.7	21.4	42.0	46.3	19.5	4,864	86.8
Monroe town (Green)	1,243	1,247	0.3	1,295	95.9	0.4	0.0	1.4	2.3	26.0	22.1	44.8	41.8	27.9	418	88.5
Montana town (Buffalo)	285	279	-2.1	303	100.0	0.0	0.0	0.0	0.0	21.1	17.5	45.6	59.2	16.1	127	76.4
Montello city & MCD (Marquette)	1,488	1,466	-1.5	1,392	92.2	2.1	0.0	3.4	2.3	15.5	25.4	51.5	51.8	13.2	610	80.8
Montello town (Marquette)	1,037	1,051	1.4	1,315	89.5	0.3	0.0	2.1	8.1	23.6	22.3	39.5	48.1	17.9	540	91.7
Montfort village	720	688	-4.4	749	96.3	0.3	0.0	0.0	3.5	29.8	19.5	37.2	39.3	17.2	274	88.0
Montfort village (Grant)	622	593	-4.7	638	98.4	0.3	0.0	0.0	1.3	28.7	17.6	37.0	41.5	18.7	233	87.1
Montfort village (Iowa)	98	95	-3.1	111	83.8	0.0	0.0	0.0	16.2	36.0	30.6	46.1	26.8	8.5	41	92.7
Monticello village & MCD (Green)	1,218	1,202	-1.3	1,092	93.8	0.5	0.0	1.5	4.3	17.0	21.9	45.5	47.4	16.9	532	85.0
Monticello town (Lafayette)	133	137	3.0	120	100.0	0.0	0.0	0.0	0.0	31.7	19.2	39.8	39.5	22.2	45	95.6
Montpelier town (Kewaunee)	1,306	1,293		1,317	88.8	1.0	0.0	0.0	10.3	21.0	18.2	45.3	46.4	17.8	531	88.3
Montreal city & MCD (Iron)	807	753	-6.7	756	93.3	0.0	0.0	6.7	0.0	21.8	15.9	39.9	35.8	20.1	361	91.4
Montrose town (Dane)	1,075	1,142	6.2	1,105	89.5	0.5	0.5	3.3	6.2	19.6	19.9	47.4	25.6	41.4	455	96.5
Morgan town (Oconto)	978	993	1.5	1,080	98.1	0.0	1.3	0.2	0.4	18.2	22.4	50.2	52.7	15.0	436	88.3
Morris town (Shawano)	453	446	-1.5	373	94.4	0.0	0.0	5.1	0.5	18.0	23.6	49.2	50.0	19.7	166	84.9
Morrison town (Brown)	1,599	1,624	1.6	1,658	94.8	0.2	0.2	0.2	4.5	28.0	13.6	37.5	47.6	17.6	596	88.3
Morse town (Ashland)	495	480	-3.0	449	93.3	0.0	0.0	1.3	5.3	23.4	22.5	50.2	39.2	19.5	192	84.4
Moscow town (Iowa)	585	601	2.7	601	99.0	0.0	0.0	0.0	1.0	22.5	19.1	48.6	36.5	32.1	223	91.9
Mosel town (Sheboygan)	790	789	-0.1	783	93.2	0.0	1.9	3.1	1.8	20.8	17.9	50.2	38.1	29.1	312	93.3
Mosinee city & MCD (Marathon)	4,007	4,072	1.6	4,033	92.4	0.0	3.3	3.3	1.0	16.0	24.1	45.4	39.7	24.4	1,965	78.8
Mosinee town (Marathon)	2,161	2,193	1.5	2,683	95.9	0.6	0.3	0.9	2.2	26.5	8.9	37.7	39.9	32.7	931	92.1
Moundville town (Marquette)	552	562	1.8	506	86.2	1.4	0.0	5.7	6.7	23.1	18.2	42.3	45.4	18.0	203	77.8
Mountain CDP	363	-	-	238	95.4	0.0	0.0	0.8	3.8	8.4	38.2	59.0	60.7	10.0	130	70.0
Mountain town (Oconto)	822	839	2.1	755	95.4	0.0	1.6	1.6	1.5	15.8	31.4	57.0	60.5	12.7	377	78.0
Mount Calvary village & MCD (Fond du Lac)	764	753	-1.4	520	99.2	0.0	0.0	0.8	0.0	21.2	16.9	36.2	42.4	19.9	215	92.1
Mount Hope village & MCD (Grant)	225	216	-4.0	210	98.6	0.0	0.0	1.4	0.0	27.6	9.5	35.3	56.6	9.7	72	80.6
Mount Hope town (Grant)	300	303	1.0	349	96.6	0.3	0.0	1.1	2.0	40.1	10.0	33.3	54.5	9.5	96	69.8
Mount Horeb village & MCD (Dane)	7,134	7,534	5.6	7,449	89.4	1.8	0.7	3.1	5.0	32.8	12.6	36.6	20.5	49.4	2,709	91.8
Mount Ida town (Grant)	560	569	1.6	458	100.0	0.0	0.0	0.0	0.0	20.1	18.6	49.9	42.2	17.0	176	88.1
Mount Morris town (Waushara)	1,097	1,105	0.7	949	97.0	0.0	0.2	2.0	0.7	12.5	35.3	58.5	45.8	27.6	461	86.3

1 May be of any race.

Table A. All Places — **Population and Housing**

STATE City, town, township, borough, or CDP (county if applicable)	Population				Race and Hispanic or Latino origin (percent)					Age (percent)			Educational attainment of persons age 25 and older		Occupied housing units	
	2010 census total population	2019 estimated population	Percent change 2010–2019	ACS total population estimate 2015–2019	White alone, not Hispanic or Latino	Black alone, not Hispanic or Latino	Asian alone, not Hispanic or Latino	All other races or 2 or more races, not Hispanic or Latino	Hispanic or Latino[1]	Under 18 years old	Age 65 years and older	Median age	Percent High school diploma or less	Percent Bachelor's degree or more	Total	Percent with a computer
	1	2	3	4	5	6	7	8	9	10	11	12	13	14	15	16
WISCONSIN—Con.																
Mount Pleasant town (Green).........................	597	612	2.5	574	97.9	0.7	0.0	0.3	1.0	17.8	20.7	49.3	49.0	17.8	237	90.7
Mount Pleasant village & MCD (Racine)...............	26,697	27,082	1.4	26,928	77.3	7.2	3.4	2.8	9.4	20.2	23.2	45.9	34.1	32.5	11,165	88.5
Mount Sterling village & MCD (Crawford)...........	211	198	-6.2	159	93.7	0.0	0.0	0.0	6.3	26.4	22.0	41.8	39.2	27.5	82	75.6
Mukwa town (Waupaca) ...	2,874	2,834	-1.4	2,844	94.5	0.2	1.2	0.4	3.7	17.6	17.0	48.5	45.9	21.8	1,206	93.8
Mukwonago village	7,370	8,057	9.3	8,035	92.7	0.8	0.8	1.7	4.0	24.8	15.3	39.6	36.8	32.0	3,113	92.3
Mukwonago village (Walworth).....................	103	110	6.8	228	100.0	0.0	0.0	0.0	0.0	44.3	0.0	33.4	15.0	55.9	63	100.0
Mukwonago village (Waukesha).....................	7,267	7,947	9.4	7,807	92.5	0.8	0.9	1.8	4.1	24.3	15.7	39.8	37.3	31.5	3,050	92.1
Mukwonago town (Waukesha).....................	7,950	8,146	2.5	8,112	94.2	1.0	0.8	1.5	2.5	23.3	15.1	46.9	25.0	39.9	2,868	97.0
Murry town (Rusk)...........	277	260	-6.1	239	92.1	0.8	0.8	4.6	1.7	18.8	31.4	54.5	60.0	11.6	112	72.3
Muscoda village..............	1,324	1,243	-6.1	1,381	94.6	0.7	0.0	2.1	2.7	22.3	19.3	37.7	55.8	17.1	606	83.7
Muscoda village (Grant) ...	1,249	1,170	-6.3	1,347	94.4	0.7	0.0	2.2	2.7	22.5	19.4	37.9	55.4	17.5	585	83.6
Muscoda village (Iowa).....	75	73	-2.7	34	100.0	0.0	0.0	0.0	0.0	14.7	17.6	32.3	72.7	0.0	21	85.7
Muscoda town (Grant)......	769	782	1.7	714	98.5	0.0	0.3	0.3	1.0	22.3	17.6	41.5	48.8	11.4	285	89.1
Muskego city & MCD (Waukesha).....................	24,133	25,127	4.1	24,946	94.1	0.3	0.9	1.0	3.7	23.8	16.4	44.2	31.2	36.8	9,278	93.9
Namakagon town (Bayfield)....................	246	248	0.8	252	98.0	0.0	0.0	2.0	0.0	2.4	57.9	68.2	34.4	38.1	141	92.2
Naples town (Buffalo)........	686	672	-2.0	617	98.5	0.0	0.0	0.0	1.5	24.1	14.4	43.7	46.8	20.5	252	91.3
Nasewaupee town (Door).	2,061	2,026	-1.7	1,924	97.9	0.1	0.5	0.0	1.5	18.5	26.8	53.9	45.9	22.9	894	90.6
Nashotah village & MCD (Waukesha).....................	1,368	1,357	-0.8	1,219	88.3	0.6	2.7	6.2	2.2	22.4	16.0	48.1	18.9	54.9	492	94.5
Nashville town (Forest).....	1,064	1,029	-3.3	1,189	58.3	0.0	0.0	38.6	3.1	26.9	21.0	45.6	54.3	7.9	524	81.9
Navarino CDP..................	177	-	-	151	100.0	0.0	0.0	0.0	0.0	11.3	21.2	52.6	58.9	16.1	64	89.1
Navarino town (Shawano)	446	439	-1.6	355	97.7	0.0	1.1	1.1	0.0	13.2	21.7	54.6	53.7	16.1	160	86.3
Necedah village & MCD (Juneau).......................	914	918	0.4	957	94.1	0.6	0.0	1.5	3.8	19.7	16.8	47.9	57.4	11.8	392	85.2
Necedah town (Juneau) ...	2,329	2,357	1.2	2,529	96.0	0.5	0.0	0.3	3.2	27.8	25.8	46.2	55.5	10.7	987	88.3
Neenah city & MCD (Winnebago)	25,509	26,300	3.1	25,967	89.0	2.6	1.8	2.7	4.0	25.5	15.0	38.5	37.5	33.4	10,955	89.8
Neenah town (Winnebago).....................	3,233	3,527	9.1	3,441	92.2	0.0	0.0	1.0	6.8	23.7	15.5	41.0	32.6	36.1	1,328	93.6
Neillsville city & MCD (Clark).........................	2,461	2,409	-2.1	2,323	94.4	1.5	1.0	2.9	0.2	17.9	24.8	49.9	50.9	17.0	1,113	79.0
Nekimi town (Winnebago)	1,429	1,554	8.7	1,473	89.0	0.0	9.3	0.4	1.3	22.1	18.8	49.3	49.0	19.8	573	90.2
Nekoosa city & MCD (Wood).......................	2,580	2,422	-6.1	2,587	95.4	0.8	0.5	1.9	1.4	27.6	17.0	39.0	49.5	13.2	1,075	87.5
Nelson village & MCD (Buffalo).....................	374	344	-8.0	340	97.1	0.0	0.0	1.8	1.2	20.6	22.4	41.8	50.6	21.9	172	77.9
Nelson town (Buffalo)......	567	558	-1.6	697	92.0	0.4	0.0	0.9	6.7	22.0	24.4	48.1	50.7	22.7	276	88.8
Nelsonville village & MCD (Portage).....................	155	151	-2.6	125	100.0	0.0	0.0	0.0	0.0	34.4	17.6	35.8	45.2	26.0	47	89.4
Neopit CDP......................	690	-	-	776	1.3	0.8	0.9	95.0	2.1	39.9	7.5	23.8	59.4	8.1	211	65.4
Neosho village & MCD (Dodge).......................	574	551	-4.0	665	93.5	2.0	0.0	3.9	0.6	27.5	11.4	40.2	55.7	13.1	256	88.3
Nepeuskun town (Winnebago)	710	733	3.2	701	90.7	0.0	0.0	0.0	9.3	21.7	17.0	50.3	55.7	17.5	278	85.3
Neshkoro village & MCD (Marquette)...................	433	429	-0.9	368	98.4	0.0	0.0	0.0	1.6	12.8	34.2	58.1	55.7	11.5	190	80.5
Neshkoro town (Marquette)...................	562	570	1.4	511	95.9	1.6	0.0	0.6	2.0	11.9	44.4	62.9	51.6	15.8	245	82.0
Neva town (Langlade).......	902	875	-3.0	858	98.0	0.3	0.2	1.4	0.0	17.5	17.5	48.7	43.4	19.3	347	85.0
Newald CDP.....................	95	-	-	139	76.3	0.0	0.0	2.2	21.6	25.2	12.9	38.1	69.3	2.7	57	84.2
Newark town (Rock)	1,543	1,620	5.0	1,449	90.8	0.2	0.5	1.2	7.2	13.5	21.7	51.6	41.7	19.1	579	87.4
New Auburn village..........	554	576	4.0	564	97.5	0.0	0.0	0.4	2.1	28.0	14.0	32.3	57.5	11.7	221	83.7
New Auburn village (Barron).....................	28	29	3.6	31	77.4	0.0	0.0	0.0	22.6	41.9	6.5	24.4	41.7	33.3	11	100.0
New Auburn village (Chippewa)...................	526	547	4.0	533	98.7	0.0	0.0	0.4	0.9	27.2	14.4	33.2	58.1	11.0	210	82.9
New Berlin city & MCD (Waukesha).....................	39,591	39,691	0.3	39,718	91.2	0.8	5.1	0.8	2.1	18.7	21.7	46.8	26.8	43.3	16,701	93.1
Newbold town (Oneida)....	2,730	2,713	-0.6	2,682	97.6	0.0	0.0	0.3	2.1	15.2	29.0	55.0	38.5	29.1	1,153	90.0
Newburg village	1,248	1,209	-3.1	1,136	89.7	2.3	0.2	4.4	3.4	17.3	10.6	40.7	44.9	12.1	489	87.1
Newburg village (Ozaukee)...................	100	96	-4.0	54	100.0	0.0	0.0	0.0	0.0	22.2	3.7	55.3	40.5	23.8	27	66.7
Newburg village (Washington).................	1,148	1,113	-3.0	1,082	89.2	2.4	0.2	4.6	3.6	17.0	10.9	40.2	45.2	11.4	462	88.3
New Chester town (Adams).....................	2,254	1,892	-16.1	2,012	61.4	17.8	0.3	8.1	12.4	11.4	13.6	40.2	63.8	4.9	456	82.2
New Denmark town (Brown).....................	1,542	1,576	2.2	1,497	97.7	0.0	1.3	0.3	0.7	21.6	16.7	44.1	41.0	25.8	572	85.8
New Diggings town (Lafayette)...................	502	509	1.4	534	100.0	0.0	0.0	0.0	0.0	22.3	16.7	46.6	56.8	18.3	217	88.0
New Glarus village & MCD (Green)..............	2,168	2,151	-0.8	1,990	94.7	0.5	0.5	0.4	3.9	20.3	20.4	44.3	33.1	37.7	858	89.0
New Glarus town (Green).	1,339	1,385	3.4	1,334	98.5	0.0	0.0	0.6	0.9	26.1	12.4	44.2	20.5	48.5	485	95.5
New Haven town (Adams)	655	642	-2.0	648	97.5	0.0	0.0	1.1	1.4	18.2	23.6	51.9	51.7	13.1	269	87.7
New Haven town (Dunn)....	679	695	2.4	644	96.4	0.0	0.6	0.5	2.5	19.6	16.5	45.5	48.7	17.2	262	90.1
New Holstein city & MCD (Calumet)...................	3,237	3,102	-4.2	3,131	96.8	0.4	1.8	1.1	0.0	16.6	22.0	43.8	40.6	22.6	1,411	90.5
New Holstein town (Calumet)...................	1,509	1,478	-2.1	1,296	98.1	0.0	0.0	0.5	1.3	22.9	17.8	44.1	48.8	18.1	531	84.4
New Hope town (Portage)	718	735	2.4	720	99.2	0.0	0.0	0.0	0.8	21.9	22.6	48.6	36.2	39.7	302	87.1
New Lisbon city & MCD (Juneau).......................	2,552	2,546	-0.2	2,506	80.7	11.5	1.6	3.8	2.4	14.6	10.4	41.1	51.7	10.5	676	87.7
New London city	7,296	7,092	-2.8	6,879	89.1	0.8	2.3	1.2	6.6	24.6	16.6	36.1	51.3	17.6	3,126	85.8

1 May be of any race.

Table A. All Places — **Population and Housing**

STATE City, town, township, borough, or CDP (county if applicable)	Population				Race and Hispanic or Latino origin (percent)					Age (percent)			Educational attainment of persons age 25 and older		Occupied housing units	
	2010 census total population	2019 estimated population	Percent change 2010–2019	ACS total population estimate 2015–2019	White alone, not Hispanic or Latino	Black alone, not Hispanic or Latino	Asian alone, not Hispanic or Latino	All other races or 2 or more races, not Hispanic or Latino	Hispanic or Latino[1]	Under 18 years old	Age 65 years and older	Median age	Percent High school diploma or less	Percent Bachelor's degree or more	Total	Percent with a computer
	1	2	3	4	5	6	7	8	9	10	11	12	13	14	15	16
WISCONSIN—Con.																
New London city (Outagamie)................	1,611	1,627	1.0	1,385	74.7	0.0	11.2	0.1	14.0	33.4	8.7	31.6	52.6	19.1	568	93.0
New London city (Waupaca)................	5,685	5,465	-3.9	5,494	92.8	1.1	0.0	1.5	4.7	22.4	18.6	38.1	51.0	17.3	2,558	84.2
New Lyme town (Monroe)..	168	179	6.5	175	100.0	0.0	0.0	0.0	0.0	12.6	21.1	51.5	40.0	30.0	78	89.7
New Odanah CDP...........	472	-	-	484	3.9	4.5	0.0	89.0	2.5	30.8	13.2	38.5	60.3	7.8	164	76.8
Newport town (Columbia).	589	598	1.5	602	89.5	4.8	0.0	0.5	5.1	15.0	15.8	49.8	35.1	31.1	272	94.9
New Post CDP.................	305	-	-	232	37.1	0.0	0.0	58.2	4.7	18.5	24.6	56.0	43.1	21.3	137	70.1
New Richmond city & MCD (St. Croix).............	8,392	9,414	12.2	9,034	95.3	1.2	0.1	1.2	2.2	25.0	13.2	35.9	30.6	25.8	3,721	91.3
Newton town (Manitowoc)	2,266	2,228	-1.7	2,237	97.0	0.0	0.4	1.1	1.5	21.4	20.2	46.7	39.5	24.8	889	86.5
Newton town (Marquette) .	547	557	1.8	538	98.1	0.0	0.0	0.6	1.3	17.1	24.2	50.7	53.0	15.9	221	80.1
Niagara city & MCD (Marinette)....................	1,628	1,544	-5.2	1,509	95.8	0.1	0.0	3.0	1.0	23.3	19.4	40.5	49.2	11.3	693	82.3
Niagara town (Marinette)..	849	850	0.1	847	99.4	0.0	0.0	0.0	0.6	14.6	24.1	55.6	49.1	17.3	389	87.9
Nichols village & MCD (Outagamie)................	275	285	3.6	253	80.6	0.0	0.0	0.0	19.4	20.9	10.7	32.8	72.4	3.7	119	75.6
Nokomis town (Oneida)....	1,373	1,366	-0.5	1,362	97.1	0.9	0.0	1.4	0.6	15.7	28.9	55.2	45.9	18.0	595	91.6
Norrie town (Marathon).....	987	999	1.2	1,010	91.1	0.5	1.9	1.1	5.4	24.2	15.0	39.0	45.3	19.4	383	93.0
North Bay village & MCD (Racine)......................	241	234	-2.9	188	93.6	0.5	0.5	0.5	4.8	15.4	27.1	50.5	22.2	61.8	86	93.0
North Bend town (Jackson)...................	496	513	3.4	438	96.3	0.0	0.0	3.7	0.0	16.4	21.5	48.1	47.9	15.0	200	91.5
Northfield town (Jackson).	639	655	2.5	708	86.9	9.2	1.4	1.3	1.3	15.8	17.2	46.4	56.7	14.0	268	80.6
North Fond du Lac village & MCD (Fond du Lac) ...	5,015	5,081	1.3	5,076	88.9	3.5	0.0	1.8	5.8	24.0	17.7	38.7	44.5	17.6	2,030	85.3
North Freedom village & MCD (Sauk)	701	697	-0.6	629	98.1	0.3	0.0	0.6	1.0	23.5	16.1	39.1	52.2	10.2	255	82.7
North Hudson village & MCD (St. Croix)...........	3,774	3,811	1.0	3,796	94.4	0.0	0.0	2.3	3.3	24.7	13.7	37.6	18.2	50.1	1,696	97.9
North Lancaster town (Grant).....................	508	515	1.4	510	97.8	0.0	0.0	0.0	2.2	21.6	16.3	44.2	35.1	21.8	205	90.2
Northport CDP..................	491	-	-	503	94.4	1.2	0.0	0.6	3.8	8.7	19.1	53.7	58.0	15.5	236	100.0
North Prairie village & MCD (Waukesha).........	2,124	2,228	4.9	2,352	96.7	0.0	0.4	2.1	0.9	23.9	14.5	41.3	27.7	38.5	837	96.1
Norwalk village & MCD (Monroe)....................	652	632	-3.1	701	54.5	0.0	0.6	0.9	44.1	37.7	11.0	29.1	63.5	13.5	232	84.9
Norway town (Racine)	7,950	8,156	2.6	8,100	94.8	0.0	1.1	0.6	3.5	21.5	14.8	44.9	34.1	30.7	3,055	94.6
Norwood town (Langlade) .	913	889	-2.6	865	95.0	0.9	0.0	2.0	2.1	19.3	18.4	46.7	51.7	17.6	362	82.0
Oak Creek city & MCD (Milwaukee)................	34,449	36,325	5.4	36,066	77.7	3.6	7.4	3.0	8.3	21.8	14.2	39.9	35.0	34.0	14,714	92.8
Oakdale village & MCD (Monroe)....................	294	293	-0.3	277	94.9	0.0	1.8	0.4	2.9	14.1	17.7	48.1	49.3	7.7	105	89.5
Oakdale town (Monroe)....	775	813	4.9	857	98.5	0.4	0.0	0.4	0.8	28.8	14.0	41.6	46.6	17.5	287	90.9
Oakfield village & MCD (Fond du Lac)................	1,078	1,088	0.9	1,024	93.1	1.3	2.6	2.3	0.7	18.6	16.4	43.6	44.5	23.4	431	88.2
Oakfield town (Fond du Lac)........................	702	721	2.7	762	94.8	0.3	0.8	0.0	4.2	24.1	17.7	46.1	43.3	20.0	272	88.6
Oak Grove town (Barron)..	944	935	-1.0	846	93.7	0.0	0.7	1.4	4.1	25.4	19.9	45.9	36.7	19.7	342	89.2
Oak Grove town (Dodge)..	1,078	1,080	0.2	1,126	92.6	0.0	0.0	3.6	3.7	23.0	21.1	48.2	54.5	18.3	462	82.9
Oak Grove town (Pierce)...	2,144	2,253	5.1	2,210	96.5	1.0	0.4	1.1	1.1	26.7	11.4	42.3	27.2	40.0	749	92.1
Oakland town (Burnett)....	827	835	1.0	833	92.2	1.0	0.8	3.6	2.4	7.3	41.1	63.0	43.3	19.4	482	84.2
Oakland town (Douglas) ...	1,136	1,155	1.7	1,311	89.9	2.2	0.2	6.8	0.8	21.2	15.6	46.0	37.9	21.2	483	91.9
Oakland town (Jefferson)..	3,100	3,212	3.6	3,185	95.2	0.3	0.1	3.2	1.2	19.2	17.3	51.1	32.1	33.1	1,313	91.9
Oasis town (Waushara)	389	392	0.8	397	95.7	1.0	0.0	2.0	1.3	14.6	27.2	52.7	46.2	21.6	166	86.1
Oconomowoc city & MCD (Waukesha)................	15,807	16,981	7.4	16,698	93.5	2.0	0.6	1.3	2.6	24.6	16.1	39.9	25.1	45.8	6,807	93.5
Oconomowoc town (Waukesha)................	8,428	8,712	3.4	8,652	97.3	0.8	0.4	0.9	0.6	20.8	18.3	46.2	22.5	49.7	3,301	94.6
Oconomowoc Lake village & MCD (Waukesha)	562	600	6.8	583	92.1	0.0	5.0	0.0	2.9	19.4	19.2	49.1	12.0	71.2	216	100.0
Oconto city & MCD (Oconto)...................	4,517	4,545	0.6	4,482	91.2	0.8	1.0	3.3	3.8	21.6	19.1	43.7	55.2	15.4	1,933	88.8
Oconto town (Oconto)	1,331	1,349	1.4	1,378	94.4	0.0	0.4	4.6	0.5	20.9	19.1	47.6	49.5	18.0	571	85.3
Oconto Falls city & MCD (Oconto)...................	2,891	2,796	-3.3	2,812	92.4	0.5	0.5	5.2	1.5	19.5	20.1	37.7	54.5	10.8	1,227	82.6
Oconto Falls town (Oconto)...................	1,265	1,283	1.4	1,407	94.1	0.0	0.6	0.3	5.0	25.2	17.3	44.5	51.9	18.8	528	91.1
Odanah CDP	13	-	-	-	-	-	-	-	-	-	-	-	-	-	-	-
Ogdensburg village & MCD (Waupaca)	185	173	-6.5	168	99.4	0.0	0.0	0.6	0.0	13.1	21.4	53.9	63.6	8.6	85	82.4
Ogema CDP	186	-	-	162	88.9	9.9	0.0	0.0	1.2	16.7	21.6	51.8	62.1	12.1	73	82.2
Ogema town (Price).........	713	682	-4.3	811	95.2	2.2	0.0	0.9	1.7	16.9	19.0	47.2	58.4	11.7	354	83.3
Ojibwa town (Sawyer).......	249	252	1.2	211	97.6	0.0	0.0	0.0	2.4	7.6	27.0	57.5	53.3	15.2	123	77.2
Okauchee Lake CDP.........	4,422	-	-	4,551	97.5	1.1	0.4	0.8	0.2	20.2	17.8	47.1	21.1	52.2	1,809	94.3
Oliver village & MCD (Douglas)....................	397	411	3.5	370	87.8	0.0	1.4	10.5	0.3	21.6	15.9	46.7	48.5	20.1	169	88.2
Oma town (Iron)................	289	284	-1.7	294	95.2	1.4	0.0	1.0	2.4	3.1	43.2	61.9	28.1	30.3	151	92.7
Omro city & MCD (Winnebago)................	3,519	3,583	1.8	3,573	97.6	0.0	0.8	0.0	1.7	23.6	16.1	38.0	39.4	31.8	1,493	89.9
Omro town (Winnebago) ..	2,114	2,300	8.8	2,252	93.2	0.0	1.4	0.5	4.9	23.7	20.2	45.3	37.9	27.2	893	92.0
Onalaska city & MCD (La Crosse)...................	17,792	18,943	6.5	18,662	86.3	1.6	8.3	2.5	1.4	22.5	19.7	40.6	28.0	35.4	7,920	87.9
Onalaska town (La Crosse)...................	5,512	5,766	4.6	5,736	92.5	1.1	2.6	2.4	1.4	27.1	16.6	42.1	21.6	39.7	2,103	97.7
Oneida town (Outagamie)	4,677	4,732	1.2	4,729	50.4	0.8	0.0	43.9	4.9	24.5	14.3	36.7	49.1	15.2	1,525	87.5
Ontario village...............	554	555	0.2	465	82.6	1.7	0.6	0.9	14.2	26.7	25.2	43.8	56.0	9.4	209	76.1
Ontario village (Monroe)....	-	-	-	-	-	-	-	-	-	-	-	-	-	-	-	-
Ontario village (Vernon)....	554	555	0.2	465	82.6	1.7	0.6	0.9	14.2	26.7	25.2	43.8	56.0	9.4	209	76.1
Oostburg village & MCD (Sheboygan)...............	2,893	3,027	4.6	2,990	92.3	0.0	0.3	1.7	5.8	24.6	16.8	41.2	38.2	26.5	1,147	91.4
Orange town (Juneau)......	567	549	-3.2	543	90.8	2.9	0.4	0.7	5.2	21.9	22.5	39.9	57.4	11.9	182	85.2

1 May be of any race.

Table A. All Places — **Population and Housing**

STATE City, town, township, borough, or CDP (county if applicable)	Population 2010 census total population	2019 estimated population	Percent change 2010–2019	ACS total population estimate 2015–2019	White alone, not Hispanic or Latino	Black alone, not Hispanic or Latino	Asian alone, not Hispanic or Latino	All other races or 2 or more races, not Hispanic or Latino	Hispanic or Latino[1]	Under 18 years old	Age 65 years and older	Median age	Percent High school diploma or less	Percent Bachelor's degree or more	Occupied housing units Total	Percent with a computer
	1	2	3	4	5	6	7	8	9	10	11	12	13	14	15	16
WISCONSIN—Con.																
Oregon village & MCD (Dane)	9,315	10,571	13.5	10,353	88.2	7.3	0.2	1.9	2.3	27.8	11.9	38.8	21.6	51.4	3,991	95.7
Oregon town (Dane)	3,113	3,322	6.7	3,321	96.2	0.5	0.2	2.4	0.7	20.4	20.3	48.2	23.1	48.0	1,295	95.5
Orfordville village & MCD (Rock)	1,442	1,498	3.9	1,286	91.3	1.2	1.4	0.3	5.8	22.2	13.2	37.0	47.4	20.5	531	91.1
Orienta town (Bayfield)	122	123	0.8	138	90.6	2.2	0.0	4.3	2.9	13.0	36.2	55.7	56.9	22.0	75	94.7
Orion town (Richland)	579	562	-2.9	582	95.4	0.0	0.0	0.0	4.6	19.9	24.6	46.5	48.7	19.9	242	86.0
Osborn town (Outagamie)	1,175	1,257	7.0	1,221	96.3	0.0	0.0	3.7	0.0	23.2	10.8	41.1	37.8	22.8	431	90.5
Osceola town (Fond du Lac)	1,857	1,842	-0.8	1,767	96.5	0.5	0.5	1.0	1.5	21.0	18.6	49.3	45.7	19.0	727	90.8
Osceola village & MCD (Polk)	2,556	2,556	0.0	2,511	93.5	1.0	1.0	2.3	2.2	24.3	13.9	41.7	43.1	20.2	1,147	89.2
Osceola town (Polk)	2,868	2,888	0.7	2,848	97.3	0.2	0.2	0.9	1.4	26.1	12.7	41.8	35.2	31.0	1,090	96.4
Oshkosh city & MCD (Winnebago)	66,346	67,004	1.0	66,773	87.3	3.6	3.4	1.9	3.9	17.7	14.1	33.9	43.0	25.6	26,634	90.3
Oshkosh town (Winnebago)	2,424	2,471	1.9	2,218	96.7	0.7	0.3	1.3	1.0	15.0	32.0	55.8	40.7	28.8	1,005	87.3
Osseo city & MCD (Trempealeau)	1,703	1,676	-1.6	1,719	95.0	0.5	0.0	2.4	2.2	25.0	15.6	40.1	46.8	17.7	733	86.6
Otsego town (Columbia)	699	707	1.1	649	98.9	0.0	0.0	0.3	0.8	12.9	23.6	53.2	50.3	21.0	293	92.8
Ottawa town (Waukesha)	3,898	3,913	0.4	3,904	98.0	0.4	0.0	1.1	0.5	18.5	20.8	51.1	30.9	40.1	1,540	97.5
Otter Creek town (Dunn)	501	530	5.8	560	99.1	0.0	0.0	0.0	0.9	22.3	17.1	43.3	41.4	29.9	231	91.8
Otter Creek town (Eau Claire)	500	544	8.8	415	92.8	0.0	0.0	7.2	0.0	21.4	16.9	44.0	45.7	20.2	168	85.7
Oulu town (Bayfield)	527	531	0.8	542	97.4	0.6	0.0	2.0	0.0	19.0	20.5	48.8	41.1	18.8	250	93.2
Owen city & MCD (Clark)	937	928		885	87.9	0.3	0.3	3.5	7.9	24.0	20.2	46.1	41.3	18.7	403	83.1
Oxford village & MCD (Marquette)	603	602	-0.2	530	88.7	0.4	0.0	0.0	10.9	23.2	19.2	39.6	49.7	9.3	235	86.0
Oxford town (Marquette)	889	910	2.4	886	95.4	0.0	0.0	1.5	3.2	18.6	22.7	52.1	48.9	17.1	373	89.8
Pacific town (Columbia)	2,705	2,751	1.7	2,735	95.8	0.0	1.2	0.0	3.0	14.0	29.7	55.3	42.9	22.2	1,288	92.3
Packwaukee CDP	262	-	-	171	98.8	0.0	0.0	1.2	0.0	1.2	39.2	59.3	56.7	6.4	111	76.6
Packwaukee town (Marquette)	1,416	1,437	1.5	1,280	95.0	0.5	1.2	0.2	3.1	14.0	27.1	54.9	52.2	14.1	616	85.6
Paddock Lake village & MCD (Kenosha)	2,987	3,116	4.3	2,998	91.4	0.7	0.5	1.0	6.4	21.7	11.8	40.1	37.5	22.8	1,172	95.0
Palmyra village & MCD (Jefferson)	1,790	1,757	-1.8	1,761	93.0	0.5	0.0	0.9	5.7	18.1	17.5	42.2	48.7	14.4	763	88.7
Palmyra town (Jefferson)	1,177	1,217	3.4	1,116	90.4	0.0	0.0	0.2	9.4	20.7	19.3	49.1	32.4	32.0	446	95.5
Pardeeville village & MCD (Columbia)	2,112	2,063	-2.3	2,151	94.6	0.9	0.4	0.7	3.4	27.0	14.7	38.1	43.8	17.0	926	89.5
Paris town (Grant)	671	681	1.5	659	100.0	0.0	0.0	0.0	0.0	20.0	16.7	45.4	41.7	23.1	243	89.7
Paris town (Kenosha)	1,478	1,513	2.4	1,689	97.5	0.3	0.0	1.6	0.7	21.3	12.8	48.3	37.0	26.1	640	94.5
Park Falls city & MCD (Price)	2,464	2,230	-9.5	2,248	91.7	0.0	2.1	4.0	2.2	17.0	25.8	47.3	44.7	14.2	1,213	87.0
Parkland town (Douglas)	1,210	1,231	1.7	1,354	93.8	0.0	0.2	4.5	1.5	20.5	15.3	44.7	37.1	21.0	571	91.1
Park Ridge village & MCD (Portage)	491	494	0.6	573	92.7	0.0	1.2	3.3	2.8	22.7	29.1	45.3	19.4	52.8	253	92.9
Parrish town (Langlade)	91	89	-2.2	140	98.6	0.0	1.4	0.0	0.0	18.6	23.6	47.5	54.7	15.1	48	91.7
Patch Grove village & MCD (Grant)	198	192	-3.0	170	100.0	0.0	0.0	0.0	0.0	14.1	18.2	39.5	54.9	14.8	78	73.1
Patch Grove town (Grant)	339	332	-2.1	312	92.9	0.3	1.3	0.0	5.4	24.7	8.0	38.0	49.2	14.2	123	90.2
Peck town (Langlade)	348	338	-2.9	315	97.5	0.0	0.0	2.2	0.3	18.7	27.3	54.4	55.2	17.3	133	84.2
Peeksville town (Ashland)	145	142	-2.1	180	98.3	0.0	0.0	1.7	0.0	16.7	38.9	61.9	41.3	22.7	82	79.3
Pelican town (Oneida)	2,759	2,737	-0.8	2,724	99.1	0.0	0.0	0.9	0.0	22.5	20.1	45.3	34.5	19.7	1,033	90.6
Pella CDP	185	-	-	120	96.7	0.0	0.0	3.3	0.0	5.8	35.0	51.8	54.2	17.8	70	72.9
Pella town (Shawano)	865	863	-0.2	752	95.9	0.0	0.5	3.2	0.4	14.0	25.0	51.6	63.5	11.1	355	81.7
Pembine CDP	193	-	-	94	100.0	0.0	0.0	0.0	0.0	30.9	7.4	40.0	77.4	3.2	32	100.0
Pembine town (Marinette)	889	888	-0.1	857	91.1	2.6	0.0	2.0	4.3	21.5	20.3	48.8	52.0	13.4	353	89.8
Pence CDP	131	-	-	124	100.0	0.0	0.0	0.0	0.0	16.1	37.9	56.3	53.6	22.7	63	79.4
Pence town (Iron)	163	159	-2.5	149	100.0	0.0	0.0	0.0	0.0	16.1	35.6	58.5	48.3	21.2	74	82.4
Pensaukee town (Oconto)	1,382	1,403	1.5	1,141	97.2	0.3	0.1	2.0	0.4	14.8	22.3	51.5	45.3	18.3	529	88.1
Pepin village & MCD (Pepin)	835	781	-6.5	857	95.8	0.0	0.6	3.5	0.1	15.9	30.6	51.7	48.4	19.1	404	89.4
Pepin town (Pepin)	723	718	-0.7	633	99.8	0.0	0.0	0.0	0.2	21.2	25.6	50.9	41.8	26.1	273	86.4
Perry town (Dane)	731	776	6.2	838	87.2	3.3	0.0	0.0	9.4	21.1	15.6	44.1	24.6	38.4	301	94.7
Pershing town (Taylor)	181	176	-2.8	197	98.5	0.0	0.0	1.5	0.0	28.9	16.2	40.7	72.8	7.2	81	63.0
Peru town (Dunn)	242	252	4.1	277	98.9	0.0	1.1	0.0	0.0	20.2	11.9	37.9	36.5	22.5	110	85.5
Peshtigo city & MCD (Marinette)	3,499	3,345	-4.4	3,370	89.1	1.5	0.6	6.3	2.6	19.1	17.1	41.3	47.5	16.8	1,491	93.2
Peshtigo town (Marinette)	4,063	4,020	-1.1	4,002	96.0	1.6	0.0	1.3	1.0	17.7	23.5	54.1	46.6	20.3	1,704	91.9
Pewaukee city & MCD (Waukesha)	13,190	14,631	10.9	14,431	89.1	1.5	3.0	2.0	4.4	23.1	19.6	43.8	21.4	53.0	5,679	97.1
Pewaukee village & MCD (Waukesha)	8,211	8,113	-1.2	8,164	89.1	1.2	3.7	0.9	5.1	15.0	20.7	42.3	31.8	36.9	3,870	91.1
Phelps town (Vilas)	1,207	1,259	4.3	1,144	91.4	0.9	1.0	3.8	2.8	16.4	33.7	59.2	38.0	22.7	555	83.1
Phillips city & MCD (Price)	1,479	1,336	-9.7	1,605	87.3	1.9	1.1	6.1	3.7	17.9	21.9	38.7	52.3	14.4	812	76.5
Piehl town (Oneida)	86	85	-1.2	88	96.6	0.0	3.4	0.0	0.0	23.9	27.3	56.0	32.8	22.4	39	94.9
Pierce town (Kewaunee)	833	819	-1.7	839	96.8	0.0	0.7	1.3	1.2	19.2	20.5	48.0	50.5	18.7	352	89.8
Pigeon town (Trempealeau)	879	922	4.9	1,066	97.1	0.0	0.0	2.7	0.2	28.8	10.5	35.9	53.9	16.2	367	79.6
Pigeon Falls village & MCD (Trempealeau)	414	400	-3.4	388	100.0	0.0	0.0	0.0	0.0	9.5	41.0	62.2	61.1	18.8	196	76.0
Pilsen town (Bayfield)	210	206	-1.9	218	92.2	1.4	0.0	3.2	3.2	22.5	17.0	53.3	34.4	25.5	89	88.8
Pine Grove town (Portage)	937	929	-0.9	912	81.1	0.0	3.2	0.1	15.6	26.4	14.8	37.6	56.6	15.8	334	88.6
Pine Lake town (Oneida)	2,742	2,729	-0.5	2,703	95.9	0.0	0.0	2.0	2.1	18.2	22.3	49.1	44.1	29.4	1,147	89.0
Pine River town (Lincoln)	1,872	1,777	-5.1	1,834	94.7	0.0	1.1	0.9	3.3	22.5	18.6	46.7	50.2	19.5	744	89.8
Pine River town	147	-	-	148	100.0	0.0	0.0	0.0	0.0	14.2	29.1	54.5	52.2	13.0	66	81.8
Pine Valley town (Clark)	1,159	1,171	1.0	1,313	97.8	0.0	1.7	0.4	0.2	27.0	18.5	38.8	51.7	12.4	495	86.7
Pittsfield town (Brown)	2,608	2,818	8.1	2,758	98.0	0.0	0.4	1.4	0.3	25.2	18.1	45.4	37.4	30.1	1,005	92.9
Pittsville city & MCD (Wood)	874	824	-5.7	834	98.6	0.0	0.0	0.7	0.7	22.8	22.7	47.9	53.5	14.4	354	85.9

1 May be of any race.

Table A. All Places — **Population and Housing**

STATE City, town, township, borough, or CDP (county if applicable)	2010 census total population	2019 estimated population	Percent change 2010–2019	ACS total population estimate 2015–2019	White alone, not Hispanic or Latino	Black alone, not Hispanic or Latino	Asian alone, not Hispanic or Latino	All other races or 2 or more races, not Hispanic or Latino	Hispanic or Latino[1]	Under 18 years old	Age 65 years and older	Median age	Percent High school diploma or less	Percent Bachelor's degree or more	Total	Percent with a computer
	1	2	3	4	5	6	7	8	9	10	11	12	13	14	15	16
WISCONSIN—Con.																
Plain village & MCD (Sauk)	773	766	-0.9	755	96.0	0.0	1.7	1.6	0.7	20.1	24.5	43.1	46.9	19.4	347	84.1
Plainfield village & MCD (Waushara)	862	836	-3.0	849	74.4	0.0	0.0	1.1	24.5	29.0	17.6	35.3	66.0	7.9	301	86.4
Plainfield town (Waushara)	550	553	0.5	500	90.0	1.2	0.0	0.0	8.8	19.2	19.2	48.4	55.8	13.4	212	85.4
Platteville city & MCD (Grant)	11,280	12,087	7.2	12,264	91.1	3.0	2.7	1.0	2.3	12.0	11.1	22.5	29.0	43.5	4,125	89.9
Platteville town (Grant)	1,458	1,484	1.8	1,861	95.4	0.0	2.0	0.6	1.9	29.1	16.4	38.7	28.4	43.2	658	91.8
Pleasant Prairie village & MCD (Kenosha)	19,722	21,034	6.7	20,832	88.0	1.5	1.6	1.6	7.3	21.1	15.9	44.8	32.8	33.3	7,908	93.1
Pleasant Springs town (Dane)	3,170	3,374	6.4	3,364	96.0	0.5	0.0	1.6	1.9	19.2	16.7	48.1	24.3	45.5	1,300	93.6
Pleasant Valley town (Eau Claire)	3,122	3,418	9.5	3,329	93.1	0.3	3.2	0.6	2.9	23.0	15.7	44.7	26.5	43.5	1,155	95.3
Pleasant Valley town (St. Croix)	515	558	8.3	457	93.7	1.3	0.0	0.0	5.0	23.9	8.3	42.7	29.6	32.6	164	84.1
Plover town (Marathon)	686	685	-0.1	654	97.7	0.0	0.0	2.3	0.0	26.1	16.1	44.0	51.4	21.0	253	84.6
Plover village & MCD (Portage)	12,221	13,099	7.2	12,803	90.4	1.1	3.4	3.0	2.1	23.3	16.9	35.8	33.3	38.9	5,308	92.8
Plover town (Portage)	1,609	1,662	3.3	1,951	81.9	0.0	1.4	0.5	16.2	27.8	13.2	40.7	48.1	24.1	664	88.0
Plum City village & MCD (Pierce)	601	603	0.3	533	94.7	0.0	0.0	0.9	4.3	17.3	27.8	50.9	63.1	12.6	237	77.6
Plum Lake town (Vilas)	489	503	2.9	492	97.0	0.0	0.0	3.0	0.0	13.8	26.2	54.8	23.1	33.7	253	91.3
Plymouth town (Juneau)	596	597	0.2	556	96.2	0.7	1.3	1.3	0.5	20.5	29.0	53.3	53.7	18.4	252	76.6
Plymouth town (Rock)	1,236	1,306	5.7	1,409	89.6	1.6	0.0	2.6	6.2	28.7	17.6	38.7	48.2	18.0	470	94.3
Plymouth city & MCD (Sheboygan)	8,455	8,731	3.3	8,590	91.2	2.7	0.3	2.0	3.8	23.4	20.7	43.1	39.1	28.5	4,032	88.1
Plymouth town (Sheboygan)	3,185	3,195	0.3	3,175	98.2	0.3	0.2	0.5	0.7	18.3	22.0	53.8	42.0	29.9	1,180	92.0
Polar town (Langlade)	984	960	-2.4	953	96.4	0.9	0.0	1.6	1.0	17.5	19.8	51.4	45.0	15.7	398	87.2
Polk town (Washington)	3,944	4,029	2.2	3,999	91.1	0.0	1.9	0.6	6.4	21.3	17.3	44.1	31.4	28.5	1,459	98.5
Polonia CDP	526	-	-	512	98.8	0.0	0.0	0.0	1.2	17.8	10.0	44.1	54.0	13.1	203	92.1
Poplar village & MCD (Douglas)	603	603	0.0	599	94.2	2.2	1.2	2.5	0.0	24.9	16.5	41.9	41.2	27.9	235	91.5
Popple River town (Forest)	44	43	-2.3	39	100.0	0.0	0.0	0.0	0.0	7.7	46.2	63.6	69.4	0.0	22	77.3
Portage city & MCD (Columbia)	10,327	10,399	0.7	10,406	86.3	5.1	0.5	4.1	3.9	19.6	15.3	36.6	50.4	16.0	4,286	80.8
Port Edwards village & MCD (Wood)	1,818	1,763	-3.0	1,739	93.9	0.3	0.0	2.4	3.5	23.6	27.0	47.8	41.7	23.8	743	89.4
Port Edwards town (Wood)	1,429	1,349	-5.6	1,127	81.8	0.0	1.6	5.8	10.8	18.9	24.1	53.7	55.2	11.1	515	89.5
Porter town (Rock)	945	1,001	5.9	995	97.3	0.7	0.0	0.8	1.2	18.5	18.6	48.4	38.7	32.4	400	92.0
Porterfield town (Marinette)	1,974	1,960	-0.7	1,721	98.4	0.0	0.0	0.6	1.0	17.0	19.2	49.6	51.1	18.6	825	90.2
Portland town (Dodge)	1,072	1,055	-1.6	1,068	91.7	3.1	0.4	2.5	2.3	19.3	17.7	43.8	40.8	24.2	442	91.2
Portland town (Monroe)	804	834	3.7	1,039	88.5	0.0	0.0	1.1	10.5	34.6	10.2	33.8	45.0	19.6	325	85.8
Port Washington city & MCD (Ozaukee)	11,290	11,911	5.5	11,761	91.8	0.8	0.9	2.6	3.8	22.2	17.7	40.5	29.6	36.1	5,045	92.6
Port Washington town (Ozaukee)	1,606	1,592	-0.9	1,435	97.4	0.7	0.3	1.0	0.6	19.4	19.0	48.3	34.5	34.7	583	88.2
Port Wing CDP	164	-	-	194	87.6	4.6	0.0	4.1	3.6	8.8	34.5	55.5	37.2	16.2	111	85.6
Port Wing town (Bayfield)	368	371	0.8	371	93.0	2.4	0.0	2.7	1.9	8.9	42.9	60.9	34.1	24.5	212	83.5
Post Lake CDP	374	-	-	292	96.9	0.0	3.1	0.0	0.0	10.3	29.8	57.9	52.5	24.4	153	86.9
Potosi village & MCD (Grant)	688	665	-3.3	698	96.3	0.9	2.6	0.0	0.3	15.6	18.8	42.5	49.6	22.2	309	82.8
Potosi town (Grant)	872	886	1.6	732	99.6	0.0	0.4	0.0	0.0	20.2	23.0	49.1	41.9	23.6	301	87.4
Potter village & MCD (Calumet)	252	237	-6.0	327	94.8	0.0	0.6	1.5	3.1	19.3	11.3	41.5	50.2	12.9	118	79.7
Potter Lake CDP	1,107	-	-	1,032	94.2	0.0	0.6	2.3	2.9	16.5	24.1	47.9	22.9	29.4	418	97.6
Pound village & MCD (Marinette)	377	361	-4.2	416	83.9	0.7	0.5	0.0	14.9	25.7	9.1	34.0	55.9	7.7	164	87.2
Pound town (Marinette)	1,427	1,404	-1.6	1,386	97.3	0.5	0.0	1.3	0.9	21.9	19.0	43.0	54.9	9.4	603	85.1
Powers Lake CDP	1,615	-	-	1,095	97.8	0.1	1.2	0.0	0.9	16.3	10.3	42.9	33.9	31.0	388	92.3
Poygan town (Winnebago)	1,301	1,354	4.1	1,317	98.4	0.0	0.0	0.4	1.2	17.8	24.1	52.0	38.6	26.4	546	90.1
Poynette village & MCD (Columbia)	2,534	2,510	-0.9	2,496	94.4	0.0	0.7	4.3	0.6	22.9	14.7	40.3	42.8	17.2	1,132	87.4
Poy Sippi CDP	371	-	-	300	77.3	0.0	0.0	7.7	15.0	15.0	25.3	55.3	64.7	14.2	149	72.5
Poy Sippi town (Waushara)	936	936	0.0	898	91.5	0.0	0.0	2.9	5.6	17.5	23.7	50.9	61.9	14.2	410	72.9
Prairie du Chien city & MCD (Crawford)	5,890	5,572	-5.4	5,635	91.3	4.6	0.0	2.5	1.6	17.6	22.2	44.4	50.5	17.6	2,337	82.2
Prairie du Chien town (Crawford)	1,076	1,022	-5.0	1,082	97.0	0.0	2.7	0.3	0.0	24.3	21.7	47.0	49.4	16.8	430	87.9
Prairie du Sac village & MCD (Sauk)	4,057	4,431	9.2	4,347	90.9	0.0	0.0	0.5	8.6	26.7	17.3	36.7	41.0	31.1	1,893	85.3
Prairie du Sac town (Sauk)	1,076	1,148	6.7	1,201	90.9	1.3	0.0	1.2	6.6	21.2	21.0	47.7	43.0	23.2	455	81.3
Prairie Farm village & MCD (Barron)	473	439	-7.2	466	97.0	1.3	0.0	0.9	0.9	22.1	27.5	47.0	52.0	13.6	194	86.6
Prairie Farm town (Barron)	573	574	0.2	679	99.0	0.0	0.3	0.7	0.0	29.6	15.0	41.2	58.4	9.4	243	86.8
Prairie Lake town (Barron)	1,545	1,538	-0.5	1,546	99.7	0.1	0.2	0.0	0.0	21.3	24.1	46.3	47.4	22.7	616	86.7
Prentice village & MCD (Price)	651	597	-8.3	548	86.9	11.3	0.0	1.3	0.5	17.0	22.8	48.3	61.4	9.7	307	78.5
Prentice town (Price)	484	471	-2.7	395	97.7	0.3	0.0	1.8	0.3	15.9	26.3	51.3	56.2	10.0	183	88.0
Prescott city & MCD (Pierce)	4,258	4,295	0.9	4,258	92.7	0.2	4.6	0.8	1.9	23.6	17.2	38.3	39.0	20.6	1,719	90.6
Presque Isle town (Vilas)	613	615	0.3	552	93.1	1.6	0.0	0.9	4.3	8.5	48.2	64.2	28.6	47.5	297	93.9
Preston town (Adams)	1,395	1,380	-1.1	1,466	93.0	1.4	0.0	2.0	3.6	21.6	25.6	52.9	53.3	15.2	640	85.6
Preston town (Trempealeau)	930	975	4.8	896	99.4	0.0	0.0	0.4	0.1	29.7	19.5	37.5	47.3	17.2	319	78.1
Price town (Langlade)	228	221	-3.1	230	87.4	0.0	0.0	0.0	12.6	28.3	9.6	44.4	42.3	13.5	91	90.1

1 May be of any race.

Table A. All Places — **Population and Housing**

STATE City, town, township, borough, or CDP (county if applicable)	2010 census total population	2019 estimated population	Percent change 2010–2019	ACS total population estimate 2015–2019	White alone, not Hispanic or Latino	Black alone, not Hispanic or Latino	Asian alone, not Hispanic or Latino	All other races or 2 or more races, not Hispanic or Latino	Hispanic or Latino[1]	Under 18 years old	Age 65 years and older	Median age	Percent High school diploma or less	Percent Bachelor's degree or more	Total	Percent with a computer
	1	2	3	4	5	6	7	8	9	10	11	12	13	14	15	16
WISCONSIN—Con.																
Primrose town (Dane).......	728	774	6.3	758	94.6	0.0	0.0	1.5	4.0	21.8	21.0	47.0	42.7	29.5	290	94.1
Princeton city & MCD (Green Lake).................	1,211	1,169	-3.5	1,190	95.5	0.0	0.5	2.6	1.3	23.9	20.0	43.8	53.9	16.7	534	83.3
Princeton town (Green Lake)......................	1,433	1,437	0.3	1,491	94.8	2.3	0.0	1.8	1.1	15.3	30.7	53.7	48.5	21.5	687	87.9
Pulaski village..................	3,539	3,721	5.1	3,516	95.3	0.9	1.2	0.7	1.9	29.7	14.3	34.1	51.7	21.9	1,373	88.1
Pulaski village (Brown).....	3,325	3,505	5.4	3,387	95.1	1.0	1.2	0.7	1.9	29.5	14.9	34.1	52.3	21.7	1,337	87.8
Pulaski village (Oconto)....	-	-	-	-	-	-	-	-	-	-	-	-	-	-	-	-
Pulaski village (Shawano)	214	216	0.9	129	100.0	0.0	0.0	0.0	0.0	36.4	0.0	34.2	33.8	25.7	36	100.0
Pulaski town (Iowa)..........	375	384	2.4	354	95.5	1.4	0.0	2.0	1.1	17.5	24.6	53.8	36.5	16.2	147	83.0
Pulcifer CDP....................	134	-	-	83	97.6	0.0	0.0	2.4	0.0	8.4	33.7	62.7	63.9	16.7	42	85.7
Quincy town (Adams)........	1,161	1,143	-1.6	1,290	97.1	0.0	0.0	0.8	2.2	11.2	36.1	58.5	63.4	9.2	642	79.9
Racine city & MCD (Racine)........................	78,556	76,760	-2.3	77,081	50.9	22.3	0.9	3.6	22.4	27.3	12.4	34.7	48.1	16.6	30,684	86.8
Radisson village & MCD (Sawyer).......................	243	234	-3.7	255	65.9	1.2	0.0	32.9	0.0	21.2	16.1	24.9	72.4	6.3	150	80.7
Radisson town (Sawyer)....	403	405	0.5	323	88.9	0.0	0.3	10.5	0.3	19.2	28.5	57.3	47.7	9.2	154	87.0
Randall town (Kenosha) ...	3,213	3,276	2.0	3,242	95.9	0.2	0.5	0.2	3.2	19.8	13.6	45.8	41.1	23.1	1,201	93.5
Randolph town..................	1,814	1,747	-3.7	1,703	87.9	0.0	0.0	0.8	11.3	24.5	18.7	39.7	49.7	13.8	685	87.3
Randolph village (Columbia)....................	479	466	-2.7	459	79.5	0.0	0.0	0.0	20.5	25.5	14.6	32.1	49.0	16.6	203	86.7
Randolph village (Dodge) .	1,335	1,281	-4.0	1,244	91.0	0.0	0.0	1.0	8.0	24.2	20.3	41.5	49.9	12.9	482	87.6
Randolph town (Columbia)	770	775	0.6	652	95.9	0.6	0.6	0.2	2.8	29.6	18.9	43.9	60.0	10.0	257	83.3
Random Lake village & MCD (Sheboygan)	1,594	1,565	-1.8	1,646	92.3	0.0	1.6	1.3	4.7	22.5	14.1	43.0	43.9	22.8	713	90.7
Rantoul town (Calumet).....	798	786	-1.5	648	94.0	0.0	0.6	5.4	0.0	20.5	14.2	45.4	54.8	14.7	260	88.8
Raymond town (Racine) ...	3,875	3,963	2.3	3,916	95.2	0.8	0.0	0.9	3.0	17.1	19.2	48.8	40.0	24.5	1,586	89.5
Readstown village & MCD (Vernon)........................	413	416	0.7	435	99.5	0.2		0.0	0.2	0.0	24.8	23.4	46.0	65.6	14.6	179	78.2
Red Cedar town (Dunn)....	2,086	2,193	5.1	2,425	99.3	0.0	0.4	0.0	0.4	28.5	13.2	37.2	28.9	38.5	874	93.4
Redgranite village & MCD (Waushara)....................	2,148	2,128	-0.9	2,000	69.9	13.6	0.2	9.4	7.1	6.4	13.4	43.1	62.4	10.4	454	80.4
Red River town (Kewaunee)....................	1,393	1,405	0.9	1,338	95.7	1.4	0.0	1.3	1.5	17.6	14.3	43.7	44.1	26.5	538	91.1
Red Springs town (Shawano)....................	925	915	-1.1	871	44.8	0.6	0.0	53.4	1.3	19.6	21.8	48.3	49.2	19.3	353	78.8
Reedsburg city & MCD (Sauk)...........................	9,264	9,521	2.8	9,508	89.0	0.2	0.3	4.2	6.4	27.7	13.1	34.2	49.4	21.0	3,583	91.6
Reedsburg town (Sauk)....	1,231	1,306	6.1	1,267	99.5	0.0	0.0	0.0	0.5	20.1	26.5	46.7	47.5	22.4	434	90.6
Reedsville village & MCD (Manitowoc)..................	1,209	1,147	-5.1	1,129	95.5	0.0	0.0	3.1	1.4	24.2	20.3	40.7	53.4	15.3	464	82.1
Reeseville village & MCD (Dodge).......................	708	680	-4.0	706	83.9	2.5	1.0	2.7	9.9	22.2	9.2	39.6	56.2	9.7	313	92.3
Reid town (Marathon).......	1,215	1,290	6.2	1,244	98.3	0.0	0.0	0.0	1.7	21.5	19.0	47.5	60.9	11.1	541	81.7
Remington town (Wood)....	268	247	-7.8	218	93.1	0.0	0.9	0.9	5.0	19.3	23.9	48.6	61.4	5.4	93	81.7
Reseburg town (Clark)......	776	764	-1.5	863	94.8	0.0	0.0	3.9	1.3	38.2	13.1	23.8	67.7	10.4	233	58.8
Reserve CDP....................	429	-	-	330	15.5	0.0	1.2	83.3	0.0	23.3	22.7	44.9	53.6	11.3	177	55.4
Rewey village & MCD (Iowa).........................	294	282	-4.1	299	98.0	0.0	0.0	1.0	1.0	25.4	14.4	39.2	44.4	14.8	122	88.5
Rhine town (Sheboygan) ..	2,136	2,164	1.3	2,166	99.3	0.2	0.2	0.0	0.3	13.8	20.8	53.3	41.8	30.9	933	95.8
Rhinelander city & MCD (Oneida).......................	7,790	7,642	-1.9	7,570	89.6	2.2	0.3	6.5	1.5	22.6	19.4	40.4	46.2	22.0	3,275	81.1
Rib Falls town (Marathon).	988	1,048	6.1	1,025	95.3	0.0	0.0	2.6	2.0	28.4	12.8	42.8	48.3	18.4	367	91.0
Rib Lake village & MCD (Taylor)........................	902	863	-4.3	932	87.3	0.2	0.4	2.0	10.0	28.2	23.5	41.2	55.4	17.0	403	81.9
Rib Lake town (Taylor)......	860	858	-0.2	797	88.3	0.0	0.3	2.0	9.4	22.3	18.3	43.9	51.6	17.6	313	82.4
Rib Mountain CDP............	5,651	-	-	6,163	90.6	0.0	7.7	1.0	0.6	24.6	21.9	44.6	37.2	38.7	2,261	97.2
Rib Mountain town (Marathon)....................	6,829	6,891	0.9	6,871	91.6	0.0	6.9	0.9	0.6	23.5	21.1	45.5	37.9	37.3	2,567	97.5
Rice Lake city & MCD (Barron).......................	8,381	8,509	1.5	8,367	93.7	0.1	1.3	3.4	1.6	20.0	23.9	39.0	42.2	23.2	3,916	83.6
Rice Lake town (Barron)...	3,089	3,086	-0.1	3,090	98.4	0.0	0.0	1.2	0.3	17.3	19.5	48.3	36.7	31.7	1,421	96.1
Richfield town (Adams).....	158	156	-1.3	162	88.9	0.0	0.0	0.6	10.5	14.8	32.1	54.0	61.6	13.8	96	85.4
Richfield village & MCD (Washington).................	11,304	11,854	4.9	11,690	95.1	0.6	2.3	0.2	1.7	20.5	17.6	48.9	29.7	41.9	4,488	95.3
Richfield town (Wood).......	1,628	1,552	-4.7	1,676	96.1	0.0	0.0	0.5	3.3	22.4	16.6	44.9	49.1	27.1	597	93.6
Richford town (Waushara)	612	618	1.0	751	98.5	0.0	0.0	1.3	0.1	31.7	13.2	31.6	72.6	10.8	226	66.4
Richland town (Richland)..	1,303	1,245	-4.5	1,130	99.1	0.0	0.2	0.7	0.0	17.9	31.7	58.0	38.9	28.5	449	88.4
Richland town (Rusk).......	232	217	-6.5	181	97.2	0.0	0.0	1.1	1.7	5.5	39.2	61.9	52.5	14.2	94	68.1
Richland Center city & MCD (Richland............	5,260	4,951	-5.9	5,019	91.6	2.3	1.8	1.7	2.6	22.2	21.3	38.9	48.4	20.0	2,302	81.6
Richmond town (St. Croix)	3,249	3,745	15.3	3,586	92.3	0.0	1.2	5.5	0.9	30.9	8.1	33.9	20.8	37.6	1,173	93.6
Richmond town (Shawano)....................	1,864	1,834	-1.6	1,923	89.3	0.0	0.0	7.5	3.2	19.7	21.9	49.7	47.5	23.1	806	89.2
Richmond town (Walworth)....................	1,891	1,902	0.6	1,899	96.2	0.1	0.2	1.1	2.4	22.3	17.8	46.3	40.8	34.1	747	91.6
Richwood town (Richland)	533	517	-3.0	580	95.9	0.0	1.2	2.6	0.3	24.8	21.7	45.3	36.3	26.3	242	82.2
Ridgeland village & MCD (Dunn).........................	273	276	1.1	259	98.1	0.0	1.2	0.8	0.0	26.3	19.3	40.6	60.1	7.7	119	68.9
Ridgeville town (Monroe)..	487	511	4.9	468	89.1	1.3	0.2	2.4	7.1	24.4	24.4	47.3	43.9	25.4	172	88.4
Ridgeway village & MCD (Iowa).........................	652	630	-3.4	664	89.8	1.2	1.8	1.5	5.7	23.8	11.4	41.4	48.1	22.9	283	91.5
Ridgeway town (Iowa).......	567	584	3.0	650	96.5	0.0	0.0	2.6	0.9	24.3	20.0	41.7	38.8	24.9	243	86.4
Rietbrock town (Marathon)	989	972	-1.7	827	97.8	0.0	0.0	0.2	1.9	25.6	14.3	42.6	55.5	14.3	303	83.5
Ringle town (Marathon)	1,711	1,741	1.8	1,598	96.6	0.6	0.0	1.3	1.5	22.0	16.8	48.7	45.7	25.4	623	91.7
Rio village & MCD (Columbia)....................	1,051	1,039	-1.1	1,048	93.8	0.8	0.0	0.8	4.7	27.3	13.2	36.5	43.6	16.5	447	93.7
Ripon city & MCD (Fond du Lac).......................	7,741	7,841	1.3	7,781	91.6	0.5	1.1	2.5	4.3	20.0	20.5	39.1	47.8	23.8	3,284	80.1
Ripon town (Fond du Lac)	1,392	1,381	-0.8	1,347	98.1	0.0	0.0	1.2	0.7	17.2	22.0	49.8	41.5	24.8	570	90.4
River Falls city	15,004	16,027	6.8	15,638	91.7	1.0	1.6	3.1	2.6	16.3	12.6	25.9	27.3	38.9	5,521	91.4
River Falls city (Pierce).....	11,857	12,691	7.0	12,324	90.2	1.2	2.0	3.9	2.7	13.5	10.7	23.5	28.9	38.4	4,113	92.4

1 May be of any race.

Table A. All Places — **Population and Housing**

STATE City, town, township, borough, or CDP (county if applicable)	Population				Race and Hispanic or Latino origin (percent)					Age (percent)			Educational attainment of persons age 25 and older		Occupied housing units	
	2010 census total population	2019 estimated population	Percent change 2010–2019	ACS total population estimate 2015–2019	White alone, not Hispanic or Latino	Black alone, not Hispanic or Latino	Asian alone, not Hispanic or Latino	All other races or 2 or more races, not Hispanic or Latino	Hispanic or Latino[1]	Under 18 years old	Age 65 years and older	Median age	Percent High school diploma or less	Percent Bachelor's degree or more	Total	Percent with a computer
	1	2	3	4	5	6	7	8	9	10	11	12	13	14	15	16
WISCONSIN—Con.																
River Falls city (St. Croix) .	3,147	3,336	6.0	3,314	97.2	0.3	0.0	0.2	2.3	26.8	19.6	36.9	22.7	40.4	1,408	88.5
River Falls town (Pierce)...	2,273	2,373	4.4	2,204	96.0	0.1	0.4	1.2	2.3	19.9	13.8	47.0	26.9	41.1	863	95.2
River Hills village & MCD (Milwaukee)..................	1,600	1,575	-1.6	1,449	72.7	13.5	8.2	3.9	1.8	23.8	25.0	50.9	6.4	72.2	535	97.6
Riverview town (Oconto) ..	725	740	2.1	967	99.1	0.0	0.0	0.9	0.0	16.2	34.6	59.4	52.2	18.7	462	87.9
Roberts village & MCD (St. Croix)..................	1,651	1,889	14.4	1,903	91.4	1.1	2.3	3.2	2.0	31.4	8.5	30.6	36.2	22.7	702	87.6
Rochester village & MCD (Racine)	3,686	3,867	4.9	3,811	95.5	0.9	0.3	0.9	2.3	19.5	11.7	39.6	31.5	27.2	1,537	89.0
Rock town (Rock)	3,178	3,191	0.4	3,179	77.1	0.7	3.7	3.2	15.3	23.2	15.5	44.0	58.8	12.2	1,248	89.4
Rock town (Wood)	855	2,034	137.9	848	97.9	0.0	0.2	0.8	1.1	22.3	18.4	46.0	45.2	22.9	332	87.3
Rockbridge town (Richland)...................	734	698	-4.9	705	97.4	0.0	0.6	0.9	1.1	18.3	26.0	53.5	41.8	20.6	309	82.8
Rock Creek town (Dunn) ..	1,000	1,043	4.3	951	97.0	0.0	0.0	0.5	2.5	26.3	12.5	41.5	40.8	18.3	374	85.6
Rockdale village & MCD (Dane)	214	216	0.9	236	88.6	0.0	0.4	9.7	1.3	30.1	15.7	35.4	34.8	25.6	109	91.7
Rock Elm town (Pierce)	482	503	4.4	483	99.0	0.0	0.0	1.0	0.0	17.6	17.4	45.7	49.1	19.0	220	89.5
Rock Falls town (Lincoln)..	620	607	-2.1	658	96.5	0.0	0.2	2.9	0.5	12.8	30.5	54.9	42.9	18.9	308	89.3
Rockland town (Brown)....	1,707	1,900	11.3	1,892	93.4	0.7	0.4	4.1	1.4	27.7	9.8	39.5	29.2	39.1	649	95.5
Rockland village & MCD (La Crosse)..................	594	676	13.8	649	96.1	0.8	0.9	1.1	1.1	35.9	7.7	30.7	42.7	15.4	229	90.0
Rockland village (Monroe)	-	-	-	-	-	-	-	-	-	-	-	-	-	-	-	-
Rockland town (Manitowoc)................	998	982	-1.6	1,031	97.8	0.3	0.3	1.1	0.6	25.1	14.6	42.9	50.3	18.5	383	90.1
Rock Springs village & MCD (Sauk)..................	362	360	-0.6	296	98.3	1.7	0.0	0.0	0.0	24.7	14.2	36.8	59.1	8.4	124	91.1
Rolling town (Langlade)....	1,506	1,476	-2.0	1,503	95.5	0.9	0.0	3.4	0.2	23.2	20.6	43.8	54.2	22.9	579	88.8
Rome town (Adams)........	2,720	2,752	1.2	2,702	96.9	0.0	0.0	1.7	1.4	9.4	46.5	63.8	41.8	26.1	1,332	88.1
Rome CDP	689	-	-	711	94.0	0.0	0.0	0.4	5.6	26.0	14.2	45.0	47.3	17.3	267	88.4
Roosevelt town (Burnett) ..	202	203	0.5	217	93.1	0.0	0.0	2.8	4.1	26.7	20.3	37.7	41.5	19.0	78	85.9
Roosevelt town (Taylor)	469	451	-3.8	428	96.7	0.0	0.0	0.0	3.3	25.7	16.1	43.0	69.0	9.7	180	77.8
Rose town (Waushara)	640	646	0.9	583	95.9	1.2	0.0	0.9	2.1	13.7	23.0	52.4	54.5	20.9	250	93.2
Rosendale village & MCD (Fond du Lac)...............	1,059	1,031	-2.6	1,052	95.1	0.6	0.0	2.9	1.4	24.2	14.5	39.4	48.4	24.0	423	91.3
Rosendale town (Fond du Lac)...........................	694	697	0.4	667	92.7	0.6	0.0	0.3	6.4	22.9	20.2	49.2	43.0	24.3	266	86.8
Rosholt village & MCD (Portage)...................	504	486	-3.6	499	94.6	0.0	0.0	0.2	5.2	25.1	15.6	36.5	67.5	13.1	200	84.0
Ross town (Forest)	136	128	-5.9	185	82.2	0.0	0.0	1.6	16.2	22.2	17.8	39.9	63.5	4.3	77	77.9
Rothschild village & MCD (Marathon)	5,267	5,267	0.0	5,287	92.0	1.2	5.9	1.0	0.0	22.1	15.3	39.9	32.6	29.0	2,236	90.2
Round Lake town (Sawyer)...................	968	979	1.1	995	95.3	0.0	0.2	3.9	0.6	13.3	36.9	60.2	30.8	35.6	496	90.7
Roxbury town (Dane).......	1,792	1,917	7.0	2,117	95.4	0.0	1.5	1.6	1.6	22.6	16.6	44.0	36.5	32.5	802	93.8
Royalton town (Waupaca) ..	1,425	1,399	-1.8	1,383	98.1	0.0	0.0	1.2	0.7	16.7	25.2	53.4	54.4	15.9	626	83.9
Rubicon town (Dodge)......	2,201	2,217	0.7	1,848	98.0	1.4	0.0	0.0	0.6	16.9	17.9	49.0	50.4	13.5	770	88.6
Ruby town (Chippewa).....	491	511	4.1	411	92.9	6.1	0.0	0.0	1.0	17.8	16.3	47.9	61.8	9.2	161	82.6
Rudolph village & MCD (Wood)....................	439	416	-5.2	451	95.8	0.2	1.6	0.0	2.4	16.0	24.2	47.1	54.7	17.2	203	85.7
Rudolph town (Wood).......	1,026	973	-5.2	1,074	96.9	0.0	0.0	1.6	1.5	19.7	24.5	51.5	54.6	16.4	469	85.3
Rushford town (Winnebago)	1,560	1,631	4.6	1,844	86.2	0.4	0.0	2.9	10.6	22.0	17.2	41.6	55.1	13.0	724	87.2
Rush River town (St. Croix)......................	503	513	2.0	479	91.0	0.4	0.4	2.7	5.4	19.6	18.4	47.4	36.9	28.2	186	83.3
Rusk town (Burnett)..........	409	414	1.2	390	85.9	0.0	0.3	11.0	2.8	16.2	23.8	53.9	43.1	19.3	195	89.2
Rusk town (Rusk)............	525	517	-1.5	601	96.3	0.0	0.0	0.0	3.7	11.1	29.0	57.2	37.9	21.9	259	79.5
Russell town (Bayfield)	1,279	1,297	1.4	1,432	17.0	0.5	0.7	76.8	5.0	26.2	12.1	34.7	46.2	14.7	546	86.3
Russell town (Lincoln)	673	662	-1.6	685	89.9	1.8	0.0	4.1	4.2	24.4	13.4	40.4	48.3	15.0	273	91.9
Russell town (Sheboygan) .	377	377	0.0	408	94.9	0.0	0.0	0.2	4.9	28.7	11.8	43.3	48.9	11.4	146	87.0
Rutland town (Dane).........	1,948	2,076	6.6	1,899	94.6	0.0	1.1	1.4	2.9	18.2	18.4	50.6	29.2	37.5	792	92.2
St. Cloud town & MCD (Fond du Lac)...............	477	466	-2.3	510	94.7	0.0	0.0	3.5	1.8	19.2	19.8	43.0	49.0	18.1	218	82.6
St. Croix Falls city & MCD (Polk)......................	2,129	2,046	-3.9	1,943	98.0	0.3	0.4	1.1	0.3	21.6	27.8	49.4	44.3	27.4	928	82.2
St. Croix Falls town (Polk).	1,170	1,154	-1.4	1,205	94.9	1.5	0.0	0.3	3.3	19.1	19.1	44.5	45.8	17.1	472	90.0
St. Francis city & MCD (Milwaukee)...............	9,316	9,699	4.1	9,549	80.3	2.6	2.0	2.1	13.0	14.5	22.4	47.4	39.5	30.2	4,710	87.2
St. Germain town (Vilas)...	2,085	2,149	3.1	2,026	89.5	0.5	0.8	5.3	3.8	15.3	29.6	53.8	38.2	24.9	1,058	90.9
St. Joseph CDP	-	-	-	507	89.7	0.6	0.4	0.0	9.3	18.3	30.0	46.6	41.9	35.6	178	92.1
St. Joseph town (St. Croix)	3,849	4,139	7.5	4,050	96.9	0.4	0.6	2.1	0.0	22.7	14.1	44.6	15.5	47.6	1,463	97.6
St. Lawrence town (Waupaca).................	710	700	-1.4	722	94.3	0.0	0.0	0.7	5.0	23.0	19.3	47.3	61.2	11.3	297	81.8
St. Marie town (Green Lake)......................	355	358	0.8	327	93.6	0.9	0.0	2.8	2.8	11.6	27.8	57.4	53.6	14.1	148	91.9
St. Nazianz village & MCD (Manitowoc)................	783	750	-4.2	848	90.9	0.0	0.0	1.5	7.5	19.2	15.3	43.8	53.8	11.2	352	88.6
St. Peter CDP	1,489	-	-	1,434	95.8	0.0	0.0	0.0	4.2	31.0	13.1	37.0	26.5	41.4	512	97.5
Salem town (Pierce)	510	532	4.3	457	97.4	0.2	0.0	0.2	2.2	16.6	23.0	45.3	44.6	18.2	185	87.0
Salem Lakes village & MCD (Kenosha)...........	14,520	14,852	2.3	14,728	91.6	0.8	0.7	1.3	5.6	23.5	10.7	39.7	39.6	26.5	5,435	94.7
Sampson town (Chippewa)................	895	931	4.0	1,001	98.5	0.0	0.9	0.3	0.3	20.9	23.8	48.7	44.1	28.7	427	88.1
Sanborn town (Ashland)...	1,331	1,279	-3.9	1,517	11.7	1.5	0.7	77.1	9.0	33.4	13.4	36.1	54.2	10.7	487	78.4
Sand Creek town (Dunn)..	572	580	1.4	541	96.9	0.0	0.0	1.3	1.8	25.1	18.5	38.3	32.8	28.3	217	82.5
Sand Lake town (Burnett).	534	538	0.7	498	65.1	0.8	0.2	32.9	1.0	22.3	25.5	41.0	32.6	26.4	213	86.4
Sand Lake town (Sawyer).	815	823	1.0	648	80.6	0.9	0.9	15.4	2.2	13.3	33.5	56.0	38.5	28.4	328	84.8
Sandy Hook CDP	309	-	-	244	100.0	0.0	0.0	0.0	0.0	7.4	28.3	58.7	46.2	24.1	113	92.0
Saratoga town (Wood)......	5,142	4,949	-3.8	4,976	98.5	0.6	0.0	0.6	0.3	16.3	19.9	50.0	51.6	15.4	2,184	79.8
Sarona town (Washburn)..	384	386	0.5	379	97.6	0.0	0.0	0.0	2.4	11.1	28.2	56.5	51.8	18.7	188	86.2
Sauk City village & MCD (Sauk)	3,396	3,485	2.6	3,482	89.2	0.0	0.0	1.1	9.7	17.9	21.1	45.5	37.4	26.2	1,575	83.9

1 May be of any race.

Table A. All Places — **Population and Housing**

STATE City, town, township, borough, or CDP (county if applicable)	Population				Race and Hispanic or Latino origin (percent)					Age (percent)			Educational attainment of persons age 25 and older		Occupied housing units	
	2010 census total population	2019 estimated population	Percent change 2010–2019	ACS total population estimate 2015–2019	White alone, not Hispanic or Latino	Black alone, not Hispanic or Latino	Asian alone, not Hispanic or Latino	All other races or 2 or more races, not Hispanic or Latino	Hispanic or Latino[1]	Under 18 years old	Age 65 years and older	Median age	Percent High school diploma or less	Percent Bachelor's degree or more	Total	Percent with a computer
	1	2	3	4	5	6	7	8	9	10	11	12	13	14	15	16
WISCONSIN—Con.																
Saukville village & MCD (Ozaukee)	4,448	4,433	-0.3	4,442	89.7	0.8	1.8	4.8	2.8	25.3	14.8	32.3	35.7	28.9	1,842	90.2
Saukville town (Ozaukee)	1,832	1,845	0.7	1,805	91.1	0.2	3.5	2.1	3.1	14.6	18.1	49.7	33.8	29.5	686	92.6
Saxeville town (Waushara)	983	989	0.6	930	99.5	0.0	0.3	0.2	0.0	15.4	26.0	53.6	51.1	22.8	401	88.0
Saxon CDP	90	-	-	63	100.0	0.0	0.0	0.0	0.0	4.8	31.7	55.5	52.6	7.0	36	72.2
Saxon town (Iron)	324	318	-1.9	340	93.5	0.0	0.9	5.0	0.6	14.4	26.5	55.7	46.0	13.0	176	77.8
Sayner CDP	207	-	-	181	99.4	0.0	0.0	0.6	0.0	18.8	13.8	46.4	26.5	24.3	86	89.5
Scandinavia village & MCD (Waupaca)	363	352	-3.0	387	99.2	0.0	0.0	0.3	0.5	30.2	10.1	38.3	50.8	17.1	158	91.8
Scandinavia town (Waupaca)	1,073	1,056	-1.6	1,082	98.9	0.7	0.0	0.2	0.2	20.0	22.2	48.4	43.3	21.0	455	89.2
Schleswig town (Manitowoc)	1,977	1,955	-1.1	1,908	96.7	0.0	0.0	1.3	2.0	18.4	20.9	49.5	42.2	24.4	803	86.4
Schley town (Lincoln)	934	923	-1.2	950	99.3	0.0	0.0	0.0	0.7	25.6	14.3	42.2	56.8	11.2	385	82.1
Schoepke town (Oneida)	390	386	-1.0	349	95.4	0.0	0.3	4.3	0.0	8.6	36.4	60.3	48.8	16.6	185	86.5
Schofield city & MCD (Marathon)	2,172	2,166	-0.3	2,222	84.9	0.3	4.8	2.8	7.2	22.5	17.1	39.1	47.2	18.1	1,030	85.0
Scott town (Brown)	3,557	3,830	7.7	3,768	96.1	0.5	1.6	1.2	0.7	15.3	25.1	53.4	31.3	27.0	1,659	93.9
Scott town (Burnett)	494	498	0.8	637	96.9	0.6	0.0	2.2	0.3	10.2	50.7	65.2	32.8	32.6	318	88.7
Scott town (Columbia)	905	937	3.5	1,000	93.0	2.2	0.0	0.6	4.2	31.9	9.1	37.3	62.9	11.4	319	77.4
Scott town (Crawford)	462	480	3.9	491	99.0	0.0	0.0	1.0	0.0	22.4	26.5	47.2	46.7	17.8	199	88.9
Scott town (Lincoln)	1,447	1,429	-1.2	1,364	97.7	0.0	0.0	1.8	0.4	18.0	12.3	48.7	46.6	19.8	599	92.0
Scott town (Monroe)	136	138	1.5	119	100.0	0.0	0.0	0.0	0.0	19.3	26.1	47.1	50.0	17.5	56	82.1
Scott town (Sheboygan)	1,836	1,819	-0.9	1,742	97.4	0.0	0.6	1.4	0.7	16.5	17.8	49.9	54.1	15.5	741	88.5
Seif town (Clark)	172	172	0.0	211	95.7	0.0	0.0	4.3	0.0	29.4	23.7	40.1	55.9	7.7	87	70.1
Seneca town (Crawford)	866	896	3.5	795	94.5	0.0	0.9	0.4	4.3	19.7	26.4	50.6	44.4	18.4	334	87.7
Seneca town (Green Lake)	407	407	0.0	394	97.2	0.0	0.0	2.5	0.3	19.3	21.6	52.0	51.7	25.5	161	90.7
Seneca town (Shawano)	556	548	-1.4	421	96.2	0.0	0.0	3.8	0.0	12.8	26.1	54.4	61.7	11.6	180	78.3
Seneca town (Wood)	1,117	1,054	-5.6	1,169	91.8	0.0	0.0	8.2	0.0	23.6	15.7	47.7	42.4	18.1	449	92.4
Sevastopol town (Door)	2,625	2,666	1.6	2,633	99.1	0.0	0.0	0.0	0.9	15.7	32.4	57.7	32.8	38.1	1,239	94.0
Seven Mile Creek town (Juneau)	354	368	4.0	300	96.0	0.0	0.7	0.3	3.0	17.7	21.0	49.8	46.1	20.2	127	72.4
Sextonville CDP	551	-	-	437	97.3	0.0	0.0	0.0	2.7	27.7	9.6	35.2	58.0	7.7	192	87.0
Seymour CDP	1,418	-	-	1,345	100.0	0.0	0.0	0.0	0.0	18.6	15.8	45.6	27.1	32.2	567	92.9
Seymour town (Eau Claire)	3,171	3,361	6.0	3,310	96.7	1.4	0.8	0.7	0.5	23.1	15.6	43.8	27.1	35.0	1,276	92.6
Seymour town (Lafayette)	446	437	-2.0	434	91.5	0.0	0.0	0.0	8.5	25.3	8.1	31.5	51.9	19.6	151	79.5
Seymour city & MCD (Outagamie)	3,451	3,454	0.1	3,455	84.4	0.5	0.4	11.8	2.8	20.7	18.2	40.7	45.1	23.7	1,516	88.7
Seymour town (Outagamie)	1,193	1,214	1.8	1,213	94.8	0.0	0.0	2.2	3.0	20.3	14.6	44.4	55.6	13.9	458	90.4
Shanagolden town (Ashland)	125	123	-1.6	102	97.1	0.0	1.0	2.0	0.0	11.8	29.4	59.0	62.5	15.0	49	79.6
Sharon town (Portage)	1,984	2,044	3.0	1,957	98.4	0.0	0.0	0.3	1.3	19.2	19.8	45.7	52.1	21.5	788	89.0
Sharon village & MCD (Walworth)	1,600	1,557	-2.7	1,609	69.0	0.0	0.0	0.8	30.2	24.7	12.3	37.0	63.6	7.7	635	92.8
Sharon town (Walworth)	912	915	0.3	782	84.1	0.4	0.9	0.0	14.6	18.5	23.4	53.6	55.1	10.5	322	88.2
Shawano city & MCD (Shawano)	9,304	8,935	-4.0	8,974	76.6	1.2	0.8	15.7	5.7	23.4	18.6	38.1	47.3	16.5	3,961	83.2
Sheboygan city & MCD (Sheboygan)	49,385	47,965	-2.9	48,327	72.5	2.9	11.7	2.4	10.5	24.4	15.8	36.9	46.2	20.9	20,322	87.4
Sheboygan town (Sheboygan)	7,211	7,748	7.4	7,467	90.0	0.0	5.0	0.4	4.6	17.9	19.3	47.2	36.8	33.1	3,275	90.0
Sheboygan Falls city & MCD (Sheboygan)	7,789	7,926	1.8	7,893	90.4	0.0	1.9	1.1	6.7	19.9	18.7	44.0	45.1	24.7	3,642	89.0
Sheboygan Falls town (Sheboygan)	1,701	1,785	4.9	1,611	90.8	0.0	3.3	0.9	5.0	18.1	23.8	51.2	48.5	23.0	711	85.8
Shelby town (La Crosse)	4,703	4,918	4.6	4,884	94.2	0.8	1.3	3.1	0.6	18.0	21.8	51.1	20.7	47.1	2,154	95.3
Sheldon town (Monroe)	727	775	6.6	811	95.4	0.0	0.7	0.0	3.8	36.6	9.0	24.8	56.5	14.4	217	74.7
Sheldon village & MCD (Rusk)	237	214	-9.7	231	93.1	3.0	0.0	0.0	3.9	22.1	25.5	44.8	50.9	12.0	114	79.8
Shell Lake city & MCD (Washburn)	1,345	1,310	-2.6	1,320	93.8	0.5	0.3	4.6	0.8	23.9	32.6	49.7	39.9	24.1	578	80.4
Sheridan town (Dunn)	450	473	5.1	512	95.3	0.0	0.8	1.2	2.7	20.3	20.9	44.5	41.6	22.3	196	88.3
Sherman town (Clark)	878	918	4.6	1,041	94.3	0.6	0.0	2.6	2.5	34.6	7.8	31.7	62.7	10.9	323	75.9
Sherman town (Dunn)	851	892	4.8	767	96.6	0.0	0.0	2.0	1.4	20.2	25.3	51.3	39.5	31.8	322	87.0
Sherman town (Iron)	290	285	-1.7	302	100.0	0.0	0.0	0.0	0.0	5.3	48.7	64.2	42.3	29.9	165	88.5
Sherman town (Sheboygan)	1,500	1,516	1.1	1,275	97.5	0.0	0.0	1.6	0.9	14.4	21.8	51.4	50.7	21.5	537	95.5
Sherry town (Wood)	803	795	-1.0	824	97.7	0.0	0.0	1.2	1.1	25.5	13.2	42.6	61.4	12.0	313	86.9
Sherwood village & MCD (Calumet)	2,715	3,047	12.2	2,959	97.7	0.0	0.0	0.5	1.7	24.6	14.3	45.5	21.2	53.5	1,115	98.6
Sherwood town (Clark)	220	219	-0.5	242	97.9	0.0	0.8	1.2	0.0	20.2	17.8	51.0	50.3	10.8	107	94.4
Shields town (Dodge)	554	556	0.4	543	98.5	0.0	0.0	0.0	1.5	15.5	20.8	50.4	43.7	18.7	225	84.0
Shields town (Marquette)	541	550	1.7	485	93.2	0.0	1.2	5.2	0.4	18.1	28.2	50.9	58.6	13.2	229	80.3
Shiocton village & MCD (Outagamie)	919	913	-0.7	854	89.1	0.0	0.0	1.2	9.7	24.6	14.6	38.4	59.5	11.8	369	73.2
Shorewood village & MCD (Milwaukee)	13,148	13,145	0.0	13,290	85.5	2.9	5.2	3.5	2.9	22.5	15.8	36.8	10.8	72.8	6,054	91.5
Shorewood Hills village & MCD (Dane)	1,570	2,001	27.5	2,277	83.1	2.2	6.5	4.2	4.0	22.0	18.6	40.3	4.9	87.3	950	97.4
Shullsburg city & MCD (Lafayette)	1,239	1,193	-3.7	1,327	91.9	0.8	0.7	0.8	5.8	25.2	18.5	40.3	55.5	16.6	542	77.5
Shullsburg town (Lafayette)	341	348	2.1	300	98.0	0.7	0.0	0.0	1.3	22.0	14.0	47.1	48.3	26.6	121	82.6
Sigel town (Chippewa)	1,045	1,094	4.7	1,150	97.7	0.3	0.0	0.4	1.6	25.0	10.5	39.2	46.2	13.1	414	94.0
Sigel town (Wood)	1,051	1,007	-4.2	907	98.0	0.0	0.0	0.3	1.7	13.0	22.8	51.7	51.1	12.5	435	83.9
Silver Cliff town (Marinette)	491	493	0.4	567	94.0	0.0	0.0	6.0	0.0	21.3	36.3	59.2	57.2	11.4	239	82.8
Sioux Creek town (Barron)	665	651	-2.1	678	98.2	1.8	0.0	0.0	0.0	24.6	18.4	43.3	41.0	19.0	257	95.3

1   May be of any race.

Table A. All Places — **Population and Housing**

STATE City, town, township, borough, or CDP (county if applicable)	2010 census total population	2019 estimated population	Percent change 2010–2019	ACS total population estimate 2015–2019	White alone, not Hispanic or Latino	Black alone, not Hispanic or Latino	Asian alone, not Hispanic or Latino	All other races or 2 or more races, not Hispanic or Latino	Hispanic or Latino[1]	Under 18 years old	Age 65 years and older	Median age	Percent High school diploma or less	Percent Bachelor's degree or more	Total	Percent with a computer
	1	2	3	4	5	6	7	8	9	10	11	12	13	14	15	16
WISCONSIN—Con.																
Siren village & MCD (Burnett)	800	774	-3.3	737	93.6	0.0	0.5	2.8	3.0	16.7	19.8	46.4	46.7	18.4	380	83.2
Siren town (Burnett)	944	952	0.8	884	94.0	1.0	0.0	3.7	1.2	17.5	25.3	53.5	47.1	19.7	417	88.5
Sister Bay village & MCD (Door)	879	935	6.4	740	97.0	0.0	0.4	0.0	2.6	10.5	45.0	63.9	28.6	46.2	418	88.8
Skanawan town (Lincoln)	388	383	-1.3	367	100.0	0.0	0.0	0.0	0.0	16.9	22.1	51.1	43.1	19.7	172	89.5
Slinger village & MCD (Washington)	5,074	5,565	9.7	5,389	96.6	0.0	0.4	1.6	1.4	27.3	12.9	38.8	35.3	33.7	2,110	93.9
Smelser town (Grant)	794	803	1.1	712	100.0	0.0	0.0	0.0	0.0	17.6	19.8	52.0	49.3	20.8	304	88.2
Sobieski CDP	259	-	-	266	95.5	0.0	0.0	4.5	0.0	33.8	0.0	29.9	41.2	23.6	113	100.0
Soldiers Grove village & MCD (Crawford)	592	541	-8.6	623	97.0	1.3	0.0	0.3	0.6	23.8	25.2	41.0	62.3	12.6	241	71.8
Solon Springs village & MCD (Douglas)	600	592	-1.3	667	95.8	0.4	0.0	3.7	0.0	16.5	24.0	51.2	45.0	15.1	346	89.3
Solon Springs town (Douglas)	912	930	2.0	1,010	94.4	0.3	0.6	4.3	0.5	17.4	27.5	51.6	31.1	29.8	468	92.3
Somers town & MCD (Kenosha)	8,445	8,371	-0.9	8,336	83.3	7.8	1.5	1.1	6.3	17.4	15.4	37.8	35.3	31.9	3,062	95.3
Somers town (Kenosha)	1,124	1,137	1.2	968	68.8	4.8	0.3	0.2	25.9	14.3	17.4	44.6	57.7	18.8	407	66.6
Somerset village & MCD (St. Croix)	2,659	2,920	9.8	2,789	87.8	0.8	1.2	6.7	3.4	34.1	6.6	30.3	37.0	23.0	984	95.8
Somerset town (St. Croix)	4,017	4,367	8.7	4,235	89.2	0.6	3.6	2.1	4.5	25.3	14.6	43.6	31.9	33.8	1,467	95.6
Somo town (Lincoln)	114	107	-6.1	100	99.0	0.0	0.0	0.0	1.0	16.0	31.0	58.0	68.8	5.0	46	91.3
South Fork town (Rusk)	120	108	-10.0	89	96.6	0.0	0.0	0.0	3.4	1.1	40.4	62.9	58.0	5.7	52	80.8
South Lancaster town (Grant)	839	831		788	98.2	0.5	0.0	1.3	0.0	22.0	28.8	52.1	52.5	18.6	250	80.4
South Milwaukee city & MCD (Milwaukee)	21,155	20,696	-2.2	20,957	81.1	2.9	0.7	3.1	12.2	21.4	16.8	40.9	45.4	22.8	8,607	87.1
South Wayne village & MCD (Lafayette)	492	473	-3.9	392	91.8	0.8	0.0	7.4	0.0	22.2	19.6	46.6	66.7	7.6	187	84.5
Sparta city & MCD (Monroe)	9,523	9,832	3.2	9,717	86.6	2.5	2.4	2.5	6.0	24.3	16.7	40.2	45.7	21.9	4,157	83.3
Sparta town (Monroe)	3,127	3,282	5.0	3,247	96.2	1.2	0.1	0.8	1.7	28.4	20.3	37.2	38.7	24.8	1,117	87.4
Spencer village & MCD (Marathon)	1,919	1,878	-2.1	1,815	97.9	0.0	0.0	0.3	1.8	25.5	18.0	37.3	50.3	13.6	784	90.3
Spencer town (Marathon)	1,585	1,686	6.4	1,770	95.0	1.5	1.3	1.0	1.2	29.8	13.2	40.1	53.2	17.7	600	85.8
Spider Lake town (Sawyer)	342	339	-0.9	400	98.0	0.0	0.0	2.0	0.0	2.8	37.5	60.9	24.1	42.6	228	92.5
Spirit town (Price)	277	268	-3.2	277	94.2	0.0	0.0	5.8	0.0	18.1	34.3	57.1	50.9	17.4	129	88.4
Spooner city & MCD (Washburn)	2,688	2,571	-4.4	2,594	88.0	0.1	1.9	2.4	7.5	20.6	22.3	44.2	43.6	17.9	1,272	79.0
Spooner town (Washburn)	700	704	0.6	782	93.6	0.8	0.3	4.0	1.4	25.7	19.6	45.5	36.8	33.1	318	93.4
Spring Brook town (Dunn)	1,561	1,674	7.2	1,880	82.6	0.6	2.7	4.4	9.7	32.1	14.2	35.7	41.6	23.9	634	92.9
Springbrook CDP	-	-	-	51	94.1	0.0	5.9	0.0	0.0	7.8	35.3	56.6	48.9	12.8	33	81.8
Springbrook town (Washburn)	445	449	0.9	442	98.2	0.0	0.7	1.1	0.0	20.4	22.4	48.3	48.7	16.7	214	90.2
Springdale town (Dane)	1,886	2,008	6.5	2,044	95.5	0.3	1.6	1.4	1.2	22.4	18.3	47.8	24.7	46.9	785	93.5
Springfield town (Dane)	2,740	2,924	6.7	2,920	89.6	0.7	0.8	1.3	7.6	20.9	18.9	47.4	36.5	39.8	1,075	92.7
Springfield town (Jackson)	625	639	2.2	646	94.7	0.0	0.0	2.8	2.5	27.9	15.9	32.3	59.6	9.7	216	68.1
Springfield town (Marquette)	825	846	2.5	899	96.3	0.0	0.8	0.9	2.0	21.9	24.5	49.1	51.2	18.9	377	86.7
Springfield town (St. Croix)	932	991	6.3	759	96.4	0.0	0.1	3.0	0.4	17.9	19.6	52.4	50.6	16.2	320	91.3
Springfield CDP	158	-	-	89	100.0	0.0	0.0	0.0	0.0	0.0	50.6	68.1	47.9	0.0	37	100.0
Spring Green village & MCD (Sauk)	1,619	1,641	1.4	1,684	93.1	0.4	1.3	4.1	1.1	21.9	25.7	45.0	31.1	35.9	685	88.0
Spring Green town (Sauk)	1,706	1,830	7.3	1,734	97.2	0.0	0.8	0.7	1.3	17.8	20.2	49.4	37.3	27.4	779	89.7
Spring Grove town (Green)	874	896	2.5	860	88.5	0.0	0.5	2.0	9.1	21.3	14.7	43.9	53.6	16.1	303	80.2
Spring Lake town (Pierce)	573	596	4.0	663	99.5	0.0	0.2	0.0	0.3	27.0	16.0	42.8	41.7	28.6	238	92.4
Spring Prairie town (Walworth)	2,181	2,195	0.6	1,909	96.2	0.0	0.4	1.8	1.6	21.1	20.3	48.4	31.1	33.5	757	96.6
Springvale town (Columbia)	518	523	1.0	555	99.6	0.0	0.0	0.0	0.4	19.3	18.7	44.9	47.5	22.5	211	77.7
Springvale town (Fond du Lac)	706	700	-0.8	744	98.8	0.0	0.0	0.7	0.5	18.3	14.5	42.9	52.2	15.5	291	90.0
Spring Valley village	1,341	1,348	0.5	1,521	95.7	0.0	1.3	1.6	1.3	29.9	16.8	37.3	45.2	21.9	591	84.3
Spring Valley village (Pierce)	1,335	1,342	0.5	1,521	95.7	0.0	1.3	1.6	1.3	29.9	16.8	37.3	45.2	21.9	591	84.3
Spring Valley village (St. Croix)	6	6	0.0	-	-	-	-	-	-	-	-	-	-	-	-	-
Spring Valley town (Rock)	749	789	5.3	778	99.2	0.0	0.3	0.0	0.5	21.6	15.7	47.5	46.1	22.3	282	89.4
Springville town (Adams)	1,320	1,303	-1.3	1,132	92.8	1.2	0.0	2.6	3.4	13.9	25.4	52.4	53.8	11.0	553	86.8
Springwater town (Waushara)	1,276	1,291	1.2	1,283	96.8	0.5	0.4	0.0	2.3	8.9	32.7	58.7	50.0	24.5	572	93.0
Spruce town (Oconto)	833	844	1.3	771	98.1	1.7	0.0	0.3	0.0	24.5	22.3	48.1	58.7	13.6	313	79.2
Stanfold town (Barron)	719	710	-1.3	613	96.2	0.0	0.3	3.4	0.0	20.1	18.9	47.4	49.9	17.4	245	92.7
Stanley town (Barron)	2,529	2,516	-0.5	2,510	96.1	1.4	1.2	0.7	0.7	27.6	16.1	43.1	41.8	26.7	926	91.7
Stanley city	3,612	3,711	2.7	3,672	73.2	10.7	0.8	7.0	8.3	15.9	13.0	39.0	57.5	9.8	839	80.0
Stanley city (Chippewa)	3,603	3,702	2.7	3,664	73.2	10.7	0.8	7.0	8.3	16.0	12.8	39.0	57.7	9.9	835	79.9
Stanley city (Clark)	9	9	0.0	8	100.0	0.0	0.0	0.0	0.0	0.0	100.0	0.0	0.0	0.0	4	100.0
Stanton town (Dunn)	791	827	4.6	851	94.0	0.7	0.0	2.2	3.1	21.7	19.2	43.7	47.1	24.1	305	92.1
Stanton town (St. Croix)	892	902	1.1	927	94.9	0.0	0.0	0.9	3.8	20.4	15.7	48.9	41.3	18.6	383	94.0
Stark town (Vernon)	363	402	10.7	321	96.9	1.9	0.0	1.2	0.0	21.2	30.8	54.9	43.9	25.4	147	81.0
Star Prairie village & MCD (St. Croix)	561	556	-0.9	732	93.6	0.0	3.1	1.6	1.6	26.1	9.2	35.9	43.9	16.9	294	90.5
Star Prairie town (St. Croix)	3,510	3,619	3.1	3,589	97.3	0.5	0.6	1.6	0.0	24.1	16.0	43.4	29.4	24.6	1,397	97.3
Stella town (Oneida)	649	645	-0.6	526	98.1	0.0	0.8	1.1	0.0	10.5	24.9	51.3	40.6	17.0	228	89.5
Stephenson town (Marinette)	3,006	3,009	0.1	2,989	99.0	0.0	0.0	0.7	0.3	17.2	32.0	53.2	51.4	17.6	1,430	85.5
Sterling town (Polk)	790	767	-2.9	654	96.5	0.0	2.0	1.5	0.0	14.5	21.4	49.8	46.5	11.7	318	82.1

1 May be of any race.

Table A. All Places — Population and Housing

STATE City, town, township, borough, or CDP (county if applicable)	Population				Race and Hispanic or Latino origin (percent)					Age (percent)			Educational attainment of persons age 25 and older		Occupied housing units	
	2010 census total population	2019 estimated population	Percent change 2010–2019	ACS total population estimate 2015–2019	White alone, not Hispanic or Latino	Black alone, not Hispanic or Latino	Asian alone, not Hispanic or Latino	All other races or 2 or more races, not Hispanic or Latino	Hispanic or Latino[1]	Under 18 years old	Age 65 years and older	Median age	Percent High school diploma or less	Percent Bachelor's degree or more	Total	Percent with a computer
	1	2	3	4	5	6	7	8	9	10	11	12	13	14	15	16
WISCONSIN—Con.																
Sterling town (Vernon)	633	634	0.2	527	99.2	0.0	0.8	0.0	0.0	19.5	20.3	48.0	47.7	24.1	222	85.1
Stetsonville village & MCD (Taylor)	541	519	-4.1	644	96.1	0.0	0.8	1.4	1.7	29.7	13.4	36.1	59.3	9.8	262	84.0
Stettin town (Marathon)	2,506	2,474	-1.3	2,939	90.7	0.2	2.7	4.5	1.8	24.8	18.1	42.4	25.6	39.5	1,148	89.3
Steuben village & MCD (Crawford)	131	122	-6.9	103	97.1	2.9	0.0	0.0	0.0	27.2	7.8	41.8	50.0	13.3	41	82.9
Stevens Point city & MCD (Portage)	26,711	25,880	-3.1	26,229	87.6	1.4	4.9	2.6	3.6	15.3	13.0	27.1	34.0	37.5	10,582	90.7
Stiles town (Oconto)	1,489	1,516	1.8	1,605	97.3	0.4	0.0	0.6	1.8	20.3	18.8	47.5	49.5	15.6	666	90.4
Stinnett town (Washburn)	246	249	1.2	213	87.8	0.0	0.0	8.5	3.8	20.7	23.0	48.8	43.6	22.1	92	73.9
Stockbridge village & MCD (Calumet)	636	614	-3.5	653	95.7	0.0	0.8	2.5	1.1	15.2	16.5	43.7	51.0	23.1	315	89.8
Stockbridge town (Calumet)	1,458	1,415	-2.9	1,334	96.3	0.2	0.0	2.7	0.7	14.2	24.9	54.7	43.1	19.8	591	84.3
Stockholm village & MCD (Pepin)	66	64	-3.0	79	100.0	0.0	0.0	0.0	0.0	3.8	59.5	67.2	23.7	53.9	43	86.0
Stockholm town (Pepin)	197	195	-1.0	218	92.7	3.7	0.5	3.2	0.0	6.4	37.6	60.4	29.7	35.4	95	93.7
Stockton town (Portage)	2,915	3,005	3.1	2,986	92.8	0.5	0.5	3.2	3.0	21.5	16.0	47.1	46.9	26.3	1,196	92.9
Stoddard village & MCD (Vernon)	780	830	6.4	864	96.9	0.0	0.0	0.7	2.4	20.5	16.7	44.3	39.7	20.1	403	85.6
Stone Lake CDP	178	-	-	139	100.0	0.0	0.0	0.0	0.0	18.7	23.7	51.3	36.1	22.2	66	97.0
Stone Lake town (Washburn)	508	510	0.4	472	94.9	0.0	0.8	1.5	2.8	26.3	21.0	45.6	38.1	22.9	189	90.5
Stoughton city & MCD (Dane)	12,661	13,114	3.6	13,097	93.2	1.4	0.6	2.2	2.5	24.5	16.7	41.0	33.8	34.3	5,242	88.8
Stratford village & MCD (Marathon)	1,579	1,577	-0.1	1,562	96.4	0.2	0.5	0.1	2.8	26.2	15.4	37.8	48.7	18.2	666	87.1
Strickland town (Rusk)	280	280	0.0	267	97.4	0.0	0.0	1.9	0.7	15.7	25.8	53.6	49.5	12.0	123	87.8
Strongs Prairie town (Adams)	1,148	1,138	-0.9	980	98.7	0.0	0.0	0.0	1.3	9.4	33.9	57.1	54.8	12.3	523	75.9
Strum village & MCD (Trempealeau)	1,114	1,090	-2.2	1,178	93.5	0.1	0.8	1.5	4.0	26.7	15.5	37.9	43.8	17.1	467	85.7
Stubbs town (Rusk)	579	585	1.0	501	95.8	0.0	0.0	4.2	0.0	15.8	35.5	55.4	51.5	15.9	243	87.2
Sturgeon Bay city & MCD (Door)	9,150	8,934	-2.4	8,885	88.7	1.9	1.1	4.3	4.0	18.7	20.6	42.9	40.5	27.7	4,370	90.8
Sturgeon Bay town (Door)	817	830	1.6	824	98.8	0.0	0.0	0.7	0.5	14.3	35.7	57.5	37.8	29.9	410	85.1
Sturtevant village & MCD (Racine)	6,592	6,652	0.9	6,606	68.8	13.7	1.7	3.4	12.3	15.8	11.2	38.3	49.0	18.5	1,917	92.4
Suamico village & MCD (Brown)	11,348	13,052	15.0	12,701	97.9	0.4	0.1	0.5	1.0	25.0	12.3	40.6	28.6	37.2	4,751	96.5
Sugar Camp town (Oneida)	1,699	1,636	-3.7	1,701	99.0	0.0	0.0	0.5	0.5	16.6	25.9	51.3	34.0	29.1	750	90.1
Sugar Creek town (Walworth)	3,932	3,962	0.8	3,954	90.8	0.0	0.0	0.9	0.4	8.0	20.3	19.5	47.4	43.8	32.3	1,533	91.0
Sullivan village & MCD (Jefferson)	667	665	-0.3	686	91.4	0.0	0.0	4.7	3.9	20.3	12.0	40.8	42.1	23.4	289	86.9
Sullivan town (Jefferson)	2,212	2,297	3.8	2,272	95.1	0.0	0.3	0.8	3.8	21.3	18.2	46.3	43.6	23.6	983	86.9
Summit town (Douglas)	1,063	1,083	1.9	1,075	91.3	0.0	0.0	6.0	2.6	25.2	17.4	47.2	41.5	21.1	433	88.0
Summit town (Juneau)	647	657	1.5	848	100.0	0.0	0.0	0.0	0.0	23.7	14.9	42.8	42.9	15.2	337	87.8
Summit town (Langlade)	163	153	-6.1	132	96.2	0.0	0.0	0.0	3.8	32.6	22.0	40.5	43.2	23.5	53	71.7
Summit village & MCD (Waukesha)	4,642	5,041	8.6	4,917	95.7	0.7	0.0	0.4	3.2	20.0	22.1	51.1	20.5	46.1	1,942	96.5
Summit Lake CDP	144	-	-	151	100.0	0.0	0.0	0.0	0.0	19.9	35.8	56.3	52.5	4.2	55	80.0
Sumner town (Barron)	789	785	-0.5	675	98.7	0.0	0.6	0.6	0.1	21.9	18.5	45.1	40.8	19.4	269	86.2
Sumner town (Jefferson)	832	858	3.1	805	93.4	1.1	0.6	3.1	1.7	11.9	29.2	55.5	39.9	23.5	364	88.5
Sumner town (Trempealeau)	806	846	5.0	793	97.1	0.0	0.5	1.6	0.8	22.2	25.7	52.2	51.7	22.4	348	83.9
Sumpter town (Sauk)	1,186	1,264	6.6	864	70.8	1.4	0.0	0.5	27.3	32.9	10.1	34.7	48.9	15.8	337	92.6
Sun Prairie city & MCD (Dane)	29,540	34,661	17.3	33,321	75.5	8.1	6.7	4.4	5.3	26.3	13.4	36.5	23.2	44.7	13,479	94.8
Sun Prairie town (Dane)	2,310	2,459	6.5	2,342	83.1	0.9	4.6	0.8	10.5	22.0	19.5	48.1	29.1	33.5	884	96.3
Superior city & MCD (Douglas)	27,233	25,977	-4.6	26,223	89.9	1.9	1.8	4.2	2.1	20.0	16.2	37.8	36.3	23.6	11,727	88.0
Superior village & MCD (Douglas)	664	705	6.2	802	95.6	0.1	0.0	3.4	0.9	24.3	20.9	41.4	37.3	21.1	324	91.7
Superior town (Douglas)	2,182	2,220	1.7	2,078	97.5	0.0	0.3	2.2	0.0	19.2	19.3	48.5	42.8	29.4	865	91.6
Suring village & MCD (Oconto)	544	522	-4.0	500	86.8	0.0	0.0	11.2	2.0	20.2	28.4	48.6	61.9	10.5	221	79.2
Sussex village & MCD (Waukesha)	10,541	10,981	4.2	10,833	92.6	0.3	4.5	1.2	1.4	25.8	11.3	37.5	23.1	46.5	4,191	96.7
Swiss town (Burnett)	790	797	0.9	730	78.6	1.1	0.1	19.0	1.1	14.8	34.5	58.4	51.8	15.5	398	83.9
Sylvan town (Richland)	556	541	-2.7	551	98.2	0.0	0.0	1.8	0.0	29.0	17.2	44.8	49.2	20.3	215	63.3
Sylvester town (Green)	1,007	1,033	2.6	972	92.0	0.4	3.8	0.9	2.9	23.1	13.4	45.0	41.1	30.0	362	92.0
Taft town (Taylor)	434	419	-3.5	409	89.2	0.0	0.0	10.5	0.2	34.2	12.5	34.4	53.8	14.7	136	89.0
Tainter town (Dunn)	2,319	2,433	4.9	2,484	96.9	0.0	1.4	0.4	1.3	18.1	22.4	47.9	33.5	37.9	1,107	95.8
Tainter Lake CDP	2,242	-	-	2,494	96.9	0.0	1.4	0.4	1.3	19.2	21.8	46.0	33.4	39.8	1,103	96.6
Taycheedah CDP	704	-	-	644	100.0	0.0	0.0	0.0	0.0	12.0	16.5	52.4	34.2	30.6	286	100.0
Taycheedah town (Fond du Lac)	4,208	4,563	8.4	4,471	94.2	0.5	0.8	1.5	3.1	21.4	14.6	48.4	33.7	31.7	1,712	98.4
Taylor village & MCD (Jackson)	476	475	-0.2	434	92.6	0.0	0.0	0.7	6.7	21.4	10.6	36.0	65.8	5.4	211	77.7
Tennyson village & MCD (Grant)	358	342	-4.5	290	99.7	0.0	0.3	0.0	0.0	17.6	23.1	44.9	48.6	16.8	129	86.0
Texas town (Marathon)	1,607	1,579	-1.7	1,629	96.1	0.0	2.8	1.1	0.0	18.2	23.9	50.8	48.6	19.0	687	87.2
Theresa village & MCD (Dodge)	1,262	1,205	-4.5	1,120	96.3	0.8	0.8	0.6	1.4	15.5	16.6	48.0	45.8	10.0	547	90.3
Theresa town (Dodge)	1,079	1,051	-2.6	1,113	90.7	7.4	0.7	1.3	0.0	21.8	15.5	46.2	51.9	13.9	404	91.3
Thiensville village & MCD (Ozaukee)	3,214	3,125	-2.8	3,157	90.6	1.1	2.8	2.5	2.9	15.8	20.3	44.5	23.0	49.6	1,505	89.1
Thornapple town (Rusk)	774	784	1.3	745	90.2	0.8	0.0	8.6	0.4	20.8	22.4	48.1	52.4	15.6	339	80.8
Thornton CDP	65	-	-	75	86.7	0.0	0.0	13.3	0.0	20.0	13.3	53.9	48.1	7.4	31	90.3
Thorp city & MCD (Clark)	1,623	1,611	-0.7	1,598	94.0	0.0	0.6	0.4	5.0	24.0	23.1	42.5	52.6	14.5	698	80.9

1   May be of any race.

Table A. All Places — **Population and Housing**

STATE City, town, township, borough, or CDP (county if applicable)	Population 2010 census total population	2019 estimated population	Percent change 2010–2019	ACS total population estimate 2015–2019	Race and Hispanic or Latino origin (percent) White alone, not Hispanic or Latino	Black alone, not Hispanic or Latino	Asian alone, not Hispanic or Latino	All other races or 2 or more races, not Hispanic or Latino	Hispanic or Latino[1]	Age (percent) Under 18 years old	Age 65 years and older	Median age	Educational attainment of persons age 25 and older Percent High school diploma or less	Percent Bachelor's degree or more	Occupied housing units Total	Percent with a computer
	1	2	3	4	5	6	7	8	9	10	11	12	13	14	15	16
WISCONSIN—Con.																
Thorp town (Clark)............	805	847	5.2	931	99.9	0.0	0.1	0.0	0.0	39.2	9.5	27.6	60.2	9.0	276	75.0
Three Lakes CDP............	605	-	-	408	100.0	0.0	0.0	0.0	0.0	6.9	48.3	64.6	40.6	38.6	236	91.1
Three Lakes town (Oneida)......................	2,132	2,114	-0.8	2,002	98.1	0.0	0.5	0.0	1.3	8.1	39.3	60.2	37.7	34.3	963	87.4
Tichigan CDP	5,133	-	-	5,179	91.4	0.3	1.5	1.2	5.7	23.0	13.7	47.0	32.8	37.1	1,873	97.3
Tiffany town (Dunn)	617	649	5.2	690	99.4	0.0	0.0	0.6	0.0	21.6	20.1	48.4	39.3	29.6	278	91.4
Tigerton town & MCD (Shawano)....................	740	705	-4.7	563	95.2	0.4	0.5	3.9	0.0	13.7	19.7	47.7	60.4	16.9	288	79.9
Tilden town (Chippewa)....	1,473	1,507	2.3	1,647	97.1	0.4	0.0	1.8	0.7	30.9	16.4	41.2	32.9	24.7	568	93.7
Tilleda CDP	91	-	-	90	96.7	0.0	0.0	3.3	0.0	32.2	4.4	32.3	100.0	0.0	24	91.7
Tipler town (Florence).......	142	139	-2.1	110	96.4	0.0	0.0	3.6	0.0	2.7	28.2	57.2	53.9	6.9	67	80.6
Tomah city & MCD (Monroe)...................	9,172	9,397	2.5	9,383	87.5	4.3	0.9	2.8	4.5	23.3	16.8	36.0	41.5	23.9	4,036	85.1
Tomah town (Monroe).......	1,390	1,468	5.6	1,565	97.2	0.0	0.2	0.6	2.0	26.3	16.6	42.0	43.4	22.2	615	82.4
Tomahawk city & MCD (Lincoln)...................	3,407	3,140	-7.8	3,174	93.8	0.0	0.6	2.9	2.7	18.6	19.9	43.5	39.1	22.0	1,416	86.2
Tomahawk town (Lincoln) .	417	414	-0.7	426	97.7	0.0	0.2	1.6	0.5	10.8	26.8	56.7	49.0	15.6	207	81.2
Tony village & MCD (Rusk).....................	113	102	-9.7	121	100.0	0.0	0.0	0.0	0.0	23.1	28.1	45.3	64.0	14.6	58	72.4
Townsend CDP..............	146	-	-	94	96.8	0.0	0.0	3.2	0.0	5.3	42.6	56.5	44.9	9.0	48	100.0
Townsend town (Oconto)..	974	991	1.7	879	98.4	0.0	0.0	1.6	0.0	8.5	46.1	63.3	45.5	16.8	457	84.2
Trade Lake town (Burnett)	825	829	0.5	800	96.0	0.9	0.0	1.3	1.9	20.3	23.5	55.0	38.4	25.0	336	89.6
Trego CDP	227	-	-	176	91.5	0.0	0.0	8.5	0.0	17.0	32.4	56.5	46.7	12.6	96	92.7
Trego town (Washburn)	934	915	-2.0	908	94.1	0.0	0.0	5.8	0.1	19.1	24.3	53.6	40.1	23.4	410	94.4
Trempealeau village & MCD (Trempealeau)......	1,526	1,664	9.0	1,775	95.0	0.0	1.1	1.2	2.6	21.9	26.6	42.7	38.4	23.6	829	90.7
Trempealeau town (Trempealeau).............	1,800	1,895	5.3	1,796	96.7	0.0	0.3	2.9	0.1	20.2	15.1	44.7	33.9	25.5	750	88.8
Trenton town (Dodge).......	1,284	1,289	0.4	1,316	97.0	0.0	0.9	0.3	1.7	28.6	13.0	39.0	48.8	22.6	493	96.1
Trenton town (Pierce)	1,829	1,918	4.9	1,838	96.4	0.0	0.2	2.6	0.8	22.7	16.6	43.0	44.3	22.5	733	91.5
Trenton town (Washington).................	4,710	4,735	0.5	4,725	95.2	0.2	0.5	1.6	2.4	16.3	19.3	49.4	38.3	21.4	1,926	92.7
Trimbelle town (Pierce)	1,681	1,759	4.6	1,712	98.0	0.2	0.4	0.2	1.2	24.4	15.1	43.2	38.7	18.5	619	91.6
Tripp town (Bayfield)	231	234	1.3	207	84.1	0.0	0.5	1.9	13.5	18.8	24.2	47.5	40.7	23.5	90	88.9
Troy town (St. Croix)	4,706	5,417	15.1	5,265	95.3	0.6	0.4	1.8	1.9	24.7	11.6	44.9	19.6	50.9	1,873	97.5
Troy town (Sauk)	799	848	6.1	729	94.0	0.0	0.8	1.6	3.6	18.2	19.9	42.0	44.1	22.1	295	89.2
Troy town (Walworth)	2,349	2,371	0.9	2,140	93.8	3.6	0.2	0.7	1.8	19.0	20.1	50.5	38.1	30.2	892	91.8
True town (Rusk)	296	279	-5.7	200	100.0	0.0	0.0	0.0	0.0	13.5	24.5	54.4	48.8	10.1	96	86.5
Tunnel City CDP	106	-	-	108	92.6	0.0	1.9	5.6	0.0	16.7	24.1	38.0	65.1	5.8	45	86.7
Turtle town (Rock)	2,390	2,413	1.0	2,853	77.9	3.4	1.4	4.5	12.8	25.1	18.6	42.0	45.2	18.7	1,070	87.7
Turtle Lake village............	1,048	991	-5.4	947	88.9	0.0	2.2	6.2	2.6	29.5	22.8	37.3	59.0	8.7	434	78.6
Turtle Lake village (Barron)...................	955	901	-5.7	861	88.0	0.0	2.4	6.9	2.7	26.7	22.9	39.8	59.5	8.7	404	80.2
Turtle Lake village (Polk)...	93	90	-3.2	86	97.7	0.0	0.0	0.0	2.3	57.0	22.1	14.5	51.4	8.1	30	56.7
Turtle Lake CDP..............	343	-	-	261	95.4	0.8	0.0	0.0	3.8	17.2	19.5	54.2	38.3	37.9	120	90.8
Turtle Lake town (Barron) .	631	624	-1.1	654	96.2	0.2	0.3	1.7	1.7	26.3	15.9	42.8	51.6	16.7	252	82.5
Tustin CDP....................	117	-	-	141	95.7	0.0	0.0	4.3	0.0	16.3	31.2	51.4	44.9	7.6	77	85.7
Twin Lakes village & MCD (Kenosha)................	5,965	6,204	4.0	6,107	91.7	0.3	0.0	0.5	7.5	23.6	14.3	41.1	39.2	23.7	2,300	94.7
Two Creeks town (Manitowoc).................	442	434	-1.8	323	99.1	0.0	0.0	0.6	0.3	17.3	26.3	51.8	57.0	14.9	144	77.8
Two Rivers city & MCD (Manitowoc)................	11,728	11,041	-5.9	11,154	90.3	0.9	1.1	2.7	5.0	19.0	21.1	45.8	47.6	17.9	5,203	84.0
Two Rivers town (Manitowoc).................	1,782	1,759	-1.3	1,583	94.2	0.0	0.8	0.9	4.0	12.9	21.8	51.6	44.3	17.9	726	88.7
Underhill town (Oconto)....	882	896	1.6	807	86.9	0.0	0.0	8.1	5.1	21.8	23.0	49.6	59.2	14.1	337	86.9
Union town (Burnett)........	340	343	0.9	302	94.0	1.0	0.0	3.0	2.0	8.6	41.1	62.7	47.6	19.3	166	83.1
Union town (Door)	999	995	-0.4	890	98.3	0.1	0.4	0.4	0.7	15.1	22.5	52.8	43.1	23.2	381	92.9
Union town (Eau Claire) ...	2,608	2,812	7.8	2,785	93.1	1.2	2.4	0.3	2.9	19.4	11.8	39.1	37.8	23.5	1,023	92.6
Union town (Pierce)	610	636	4.3	653	99.1	0.0	0.0	0.3	0.6	31.2	13.9	36.5	45.0	22.1	209	87.1
Union town (Rock)	2,094	2,142	2.3	2,149	95.1	0.6	0.2	0.9	3.2	25.0	12.2	44.1	38.8	27.6	804	92.4
Union town (Vernon)........	700	696	-0.6	642	99.2	0.0	0.2	0.0	0.6	39.4	13.2	27.8	62.0	19.4	189	61.4
Union town (Waupaca)	807	802	-0.6	673	95.8	0.0	0.0	0.4	3.7	22.6	22.7	47.1	59.5	14.4	276	78.3
Union Center village & MCD (Juneau).............	202	192	-5.0	211	92.9	0.0	0.5	1.9	4.7	20.4	16.1	41.8	58.5	8.5	94	86.2
Union Grove village & MCD (Racine)	4,913	5,111	4.0	4,963	90.9	2.2	0.4	3.2	3.3	23.2	16.9	37.2	42.7	23.3	1,826	90.5
Unity town (Clark)............	882	890	0.9	818	95.6	0.7	0.9	2.7	0.1	32.3	10.9	27.9	60.4	11.6	271	81.9
Unity village	343	330	-3.8	348	94.3	0.6	0.0	0.9	4.3	21.8	12.9	44.1	61.7	7.2	159	88.1
Unity village (Clark)	139	136	-2.2	170	100.0	0.0	0.0	0.0	0.0	22.9	11.8	38.3	53.2	6.3	75	96.0
Unity village (Marathon)....	204	194	-4.9	178	88.8	1.1	0.0	1.7	8.4	20.8	14.0	45.5	69.4	8.1	84	81.0
Unity town (Trempealeau).	506	533	5.3	461	98.0	0.0	0.9	0.2	0.9	24.1	21.5	44.6	44.8	19.3	187	90.4
Upham town (Langlade) ...	677	639	-5.6	711	99.4	0.0	0.4	0.0	0.1	13.6	36.7	58.4	44.9	24.1	337	89.9
Utica town (Crawford)	661	656	-0.8	663	98.2	0.0	1.8	0.0	0.0	21.1	29.3	53.0	44.9	23.7	262	85.9
Utica town (Winnebago) ...	1,299	1,344	3.5	1,367	95.0	0.0	0.7	1.1	3.2	24.9	18.5	46.6	41.9	24.7	500	89.8
Valders village & MCD (Manitowoc)..............	962	920	-4.4	898	94.0	0.2	0.0	1.6	4.2	27.5	17.4	37.7	43.1	15.7	377	83.3
Vance Creek town (Barron)...................	664	630	-5.1	629	99.7	0.0	0.0	0.3	0.0	25.1	14.5	42.9	59.3	17.3	228	86.4
Vandenbroek town (Outagamie)................	1,442	1,546	7.2	1,603	99.0	0.0	0.2	0.6	0.2	26.0	12.4	42.3	39.0	25.3	575	93.7
Van Dyne CDP	279	-	-	218	95.4	0.0	4.6	0.0	0.0	12.4	32.6	54.7	45.5	13.1	112	83.9
Vermont town (Dane).......	826	880	6.5	836	97.0	0.0	1.2	1.8	0.0	17.2	17.8	52.3	18.9	52.8	352	96.6
Vernon town (Waukesha) .	7,618	7,658	0.5	7,654	94.3	0.9	1.0	1.1	2.7	19.9	20.1	48.3	29.6	33.3	2,888	96.6
Verona city & MCD (Dane)	10,694	13,233	23.7	13,004	89.3	4.3	3.4	2.1	0.8	29.6	10.1	37.3	16.3	59.5	5,122	93.8
Verona town (Dane).........	1,793	1,924	7.3	1,816	96.6	0.6	1.2	0.8	0.9	23.9	20.3	47.1	21.9	53.3	685	92.8
Vesper village & MCD (Wood)....................	584	548	-6.2	628	97.8	1.4	0.5	0.0	0.3	21.5	21.3	44.4	58.0	13.5	304	81.6
Vienna town (Dane).........	1,476	1,575	6.7	1,815	98.4	0.0	0.7	0.2	0.8	22.3	16.6	45.7	35.5	30.8	662	91.5
Vilas town (Langlade).......	233	228	-2.1	204	96.1	1.5	1.0	1.5	0.0	11.8	22.1	51.1	59.9	11.7	85	81.2
Vinland town (Winnebago)	1,765	1,795	1.7	1,811	97.1	0.0	1.2	1.6	0.1	14.7	23.1	53.4	35.1	31.5	791	92.7
Viola village	699	662	-5.3	749	99.2	0.0	0.0	0.0	0.8	28.8	18.2	38.1	63.4	9.5	304	76.3

1 May be of any race.

Table A. All Places — **Population and Housing**

STATE City, town, township, borough, or CDP (county if applicable)	Population				Race and Hispanic or Latino origin (percent)					Age (percent)			Educational attainment of persons age 25 and older		Occupied housing units	
	2010 census total population	2019 estimated population	Percent change 2010–2019	ACS total population estimate 2015–2019	White alone, not Hispanic or Latino	Black alone, not Hispanic or Latino	Asian alone, not Hispanic or Latino	All other races or 2 or more races, not Hispanic or Latino	Hispanic or Latino[1]	Under 18 years old	Age 65 years and older	Median age	Percent High school diploma or less	Percent Bachelor's degree or more	Total	Percent with a computer
	1	2	3	4	5	6	7	8	9	10	11	12	13	14	15	16
WISCONSIN—Con.																
Viola village (Richland)	477	441	-7.5	436	98.6	0.0	0.0	0.0	1.4	25.5	21.1	38.4	57.7	13.5	185	76.8
Viola village (Vernon)........	222	221	-0.5	313	100.0	0.0	0.0	0.0	0.0	33.5	14.1	37.9	71.1	4.0	119	75.6
Viroqua city & MCD (Vernon)....................	4,361	4,402	0.9	4,377	92.7	0.7	1.8	3.8	0.9	18.9	22.8	50.2	52.3	22.0	2,151	80.2
Viroqua town (Vernon)......	1,719	1,838	6.9	1,773	96.7	0.2	0.1	1.4	1.6	22.5	23.9	50.3	35.5	39.0	657	89.0
Wabeno CDP....................	575	-	-	316	86.7	0.0	0.0	9.2	4.1	17.7	29.4	53.3	64.8	3.4	189	66.7
Wabeno town (Forest)	1,170	1,155	-1.3	916	69.0	0.0	0.0	29.6	1.4	22.8	24.5	47.9	62.4	10.7	448	76.1
Wagner town (Marinette) ..	681	684	0.4	628	97.3	0.0	0.0	1.8	1.0	15.4	29.3	55.2	57.1	12.9	289	81.0
Waldo village & MCD (Sheboygan).................	508	501	-1.4	610	94.4	2.0	0.7	2.5	0.5	26.2	12.1	38.5	43.9	17.7	245	89.0
Waldwick town (Iowa)	467	480	2.8	460	94.1	0.7	0.0	4.8	0.4	21.5	19.6	45.6	47.7	21.4	187	87.2
Wales village & MCD (Waukesha)..................	2,546	2,585	1.5	2,581	95.0	0.0	0.9	1.9	2.1	26.3	16.5	39.9	20.6	47.3	940	96.0
Walworth village & MCD (Walworth)...................	2,819	2,827	0.3	2,824	73.8	0.2	0.7	1.2	24.0	26.1	14.3	40.3	42.2	26.1	1,051	90.6
Walworth town (Walworth)	1,701	1,715	0.8	1,644	92.9	0.2	0.2	1.8	4.8	24.0	19.0	46.1	45.9	24.9	647	88.7
Warner town (Clark).........	671	663	-1.2	671	99.9	0.0	0.0	0.0	0.1	32.3	18.2	33.5	65.0	9.5	209	72.2
Warren town (St. Croix)	1,589	1,758	10.6	1,580	95.8	0.0	1.1	0.5	2.6	24.8	11.5	41.6	26.8	32.2	586	97.3
Warren town (Waushara)..	671	658	-1.9	640	96.1	0.0	0.0	2.0	1.9	15.3	24.8	50.7	66.5	11.0	288	84.4
Warrens village & MCD (Monroe).....................	357	349	-2.2	529	91.1	0.0	0.9	7.6	0.4	29.1	10.6	37.8	47.5	23.0	209	87.6
Wascott town (Douglas).....	763	772	1.2	719	92.9	1.8	0.0	5.3	0.0	7.4	34.6	60.8	38.5	31.6	330	93.3
Washburn city & MCD (Bayfield)...................	2,113	2,036	-3.6	1,978	87.4	0.3	1.0	9.2	2.3	21.5	21.8	48.1	28.5	40.8	902	85.7
Washburn town (Bayfield).	530	536	1.1	601	91.3	0.0	0.2	8.5	0.0	26.0	17.0	44.4	23.8	54.3	237	97.9
Washburn town (Clark).....	290	289	-0.3	303	93.7	0.0	0.7	0.7	5.0	25.1	21.5	47.3	53.5	9.6	112	81.3
Washington town (Door) ...	708	718	1.4	850	95.9	0.0	1.3	0.0	2.8	11.4	46.8	62.8	24.4	45.8	407	88.2
Washington town (Eau Claire)	7,007	7,671	9.5	7,495	90.2	1.2	2.0	2.4	4.1	20.9	21.3	46.4	29.6	36.8	3,032	95.6
Washington town (Green).	815	838	2.8	752	96.3	0.0	0.0	1.1	2.7	20.3	19.5	46.3	43.8	20.2	307	89.9
Washington town (La Crosse)	558	582	4.3	569	97.9	0.7	1.2	0.0	0.2	24.3	16.0	45.6	49.4	22.3	217	83.9
Washington town (Rusk)...	339	343	1.2	346	98.6	0.0	0.0	1.4	0.0	15.9	37.0	57.3	43.3	18.8	170	72.9
Washington town (Sauk)...	1,000	1,019	1.9	1,090	97.8	0.8	0.1	0.3	1.0	34.0	12.5	33.6	60.5	13.1	339	72.3
Washington town (Shawano).................	1,906	1,887		1,945	94.1	0.0	0.8	0.8	4.2	16.7	27.2	53.0	52.7	18.7	842	85.6
Washington town (Vilas)...	1,451	1,493	2.9	1,612	93.3	0.0	1.4	3.8	1.5	15.1	27.7	55.3	35.6	29.9	742	84.6
Waterford village & MCD (Racine).....................	5,352	5,562	3.9	5,452	96.7	0.3	0.3	1.0	1.6	25.3	20.3	41.0	37.7	31.4	2,228	91.2
Waterford town (Racine) ...	6,356	6,511	2.4	6,476	92.7	0.2	1.2	1.3	4.5	20.6	15.4	48.4	34.1	38.6	2,391	97.1
Waterloo town (Grant)	547	570	4.2	494	97.2	0.0	0.4	1.6	0.8	21.3	17.4	46.3	54.6	14.5	217	84.8
Waterloo city & MCD (Jefferson)...................	3,340	3,333	-0.2	3,337	85.8	0.0	0.5	8.8	4.9	21.5	18.0	43.1	39.8	32.2	1,445	92.7
Waterloo town (Jefferson).	907	939	3.5	878	93.4	0.3	2.5	0.9	2.8	18.7	18.7	49.6	36.2	31.0	356	93.3
Watertown city	23,872	23,479	-1.6	23,633	86.5	1.8	0.2	2.2	9.3	21.5	17.0	39.4	47.7	19.6	9,402	87.2
Watertown city (Dodge)....	8,476	8,210	-3.1	8,253	85.9	3.6	0.4	2.6	7.6	19.8	21.0	43.3	47.7	17.4	3,339	87.0
Watertown city (Jefferson)	15,396	15,269	-0.8	15,380	86.8	0.8	0.1	2.0	10.3	22.4	14.9	37.3	47.8	20.9	6,063	87.2
Watertown town (Jefferson).................	1,981	2,048	3.4	2,138	94.1	0.0	1.1	0.2	4.5	24.7	19.6	44.7	47.1	17.8	813	93.5
Waterville town (Pepin).....	831	803	-3.4	795	98.2	0.0	0.0	1.0	0.8	22.9	14.6	44.7	54.0	13.2	338	79.9
Watterstown town (Grant).	326	334	2.5	374	98.9	0.0	0.0	1.1	0.0	31.0	11.8	38.5	44.4	19.1	135	85.9
Waubeek town (Pepin)......	423	412	-2.6	416	95.2	0.0	0.7	0.0	4.1	22.8	20.4	47.5	41.3	24.4	162	93.2
Waubeka CDP.................	657	-	-	681	94.3	1.2	0.0	0.0	4.6	23.5	20.4	40.6	38.6	19.0	279	87.1
Waukau CDP...................	255	-	-	220	96.8	3.2	0.0	0.0	0.0	13.2	38.2	56.3	52.1	6.9	99	86.9
Waukechon town (Shawano).................	1,023	1,009	-1.4	1,015	96.8	0.0	0.3	1.2	1.7	25.4	15.7	41.0	51.8	19.9	364	84.9
Waukesha city & MCD (Waukesha)..................	71,223	72,299	1.5	72,412	78.7	3.4	2.8	2.2	12.9	21.0	13.6	36.1	31.2	38.1	29,406	91.3
Waukesha town (Waukesha)..................	8,666	8,899	2.7	8,829	91.9	0.4	2.2	1.1	4.4	18.3	18.4	51.0	31.0	40.4	3,301	93.8
Waumandee CDP............	68	-	-	83	100.0	0.0	0.0	0.0	0.0	13.3	22.9	49.9	59.4	30.4	43	88.4
Waumandee town (Buffalo)	480	470	-2.1	409	97.8	0.0	0.0	1.5	0.7	19.3	20.0	49.8	42.9	22.1	176	85.8
Waunakee village & MCD (Dane)	12,100	14,052	16.1	13,730	93.7	0.9	1.5	1.6	2.3	29.0	13.3	39.5	18.4	53.3	5,006	94.0
Waupaca city & MCD (Waupaca)..................	6,105	5,969	-2.2	5,952	93.1	0.9	0.5	1.9	3.6	16.8	22.9	42.3	47.2	21.0	2,898	83.1
Waupaca town (Waupaca)	1,177	1,173	-0.3	1,228	98.5	0.0	0.0	0.6	1.0	21.8	18.9	44.3	52.5	17.8	482	89.6
Waupun city	11,345	11,199	-1.3	11,276	86.0	4.7	1.3	1.6	6.3	19.9	14.9	39.1	49.9	15.2	4,301	83.5
Waupun city (Dodge)........	7,863	7,738	-1.6	7,816	81.0	6.8	1.9	1.4	8.9	18.5	13.2	38.2	51.8	13.2	2,836	82.5
Waupun city (Fond du Lac)..........................	3,482	3,461	-0.6	3,460	97.5	0.0	0.0	2.0	0.5	23.3	18.8	42.3	45.3	19.9	1,465	85.4
Waupun town (Fond du Lac)..........................	1,364	1,355	-0.7	1,431	96.2	0.0	0.5	3.0	0.3	20.2	21.6	46.5	51.6	20.3	544	88.8
Wausau city & MCD (Marathon).................	39,201	38,561	-1.6	38,735	81.2	0.6	11.6	3.3	3.3	22.0	17.3	38.9	38.2	29.0	17,113	89.3
Wausau town (Marathon) .	2,201	2,209	0.4	2,370	97.2	0.0	1.1	0.3	1.4	21.9	18.5	44.8	44.8	21.9	923	88.0
Wausaukee village & MCD (Marinette)	573	554	-3.3	521	91.9	0.0	0.0	6.7	1.3	23.6	24.0	43.1	53.7	13.5	266	77.4
Wausaukee town (Marinette).................	1,068	1,083	1.4	997	97.9	0.0	1.3	0.6	0.2	13.7	32.1	56.9	47.1	18.7	484	86.6
Wautoma city & MCD (Waushara).................	2,208	2,142	-3.0	2,209	72.0	0.2	1.8	1.7	24.3	27.8	16.8	36.5	64.8	16.0	921	77.4
Wautoma town (Waushara).................	1,282	1,292	0.8	1,263	96.5	0.5	0.0	2.1	0.9	17.3	27.1	55.1	47.1	19.8	535	83.2
Wauwatosa city & MCD (Milwaukee).................	46,425	48,118	3.6	47,971	84.4	5.2	4.0	3.4	2.9	22.0	17.0	37.9	18.3	58.6	20,273	91.4
Wauzeka village & MCD (Crawford)..................	711	735	3.4	836	91.7	3.5	0.0	2.3	2.5	31.2	10.2	32.4	44.3	12.4	306	84.6
Wauzeka town (Crawford)	422	399	-5.5	341	95.0	0.0	0.0	5.0	0.0	21.4	23.5	45.5	52.9	20.2	145	82.8
Wayne town (Lafayette)	481	491	2.1	499	98.0	0.0	0.0	1.2	0.8	21.8	19.8	46.7	63.6	10.5	193	78.2
Wayne town (Washington)	2,182	2,258	3.5	2,175	92.1	1.3	0.3	0.9	5.5	22.8	12.2	40.8	45.2	21.4	805	94.2

1 May be of any race.

Table A. All Places — **Population and Housing**

STATE City, town, township, borough, or CDP (county if applicable)	Population				Race and Hispanic or Latino origin (percent)					Age (percent)			Educational attainment of persons age 25 and older		Occupied housing units	
	2010 census total population	2019 estimated population	Percent change 2010–2019	ACS total population estimate 2015–2019	White alone, not Hispanic or Latino	Black alone, not Hispanic or Latino	Asian alone, not Hispanic or Latino	All other races or 2 or more races, not Hispanic or Latino	Hispanic or Latino[1]	Under 18 years old	Age 65 years and older	Median age	Percent High school diploma or less	Percent Bachelor's degree or more	Total	Percent with a computer
	1	2	3	4	5	6	7	8	9	10	11	12	13	14	15	16
WISCONSIN—Con.																
Webb Lake town (Burnett)	311	314	1.0	372	97.8	0.0	0.0	0.8	1.3	9.1	41.7	63.3	41.0	24.3	195	88.7
Webster village & MCD (Burnett)	646	619	-4.2	678	86.0	0.6	0.0	8.0	5.5	22.4	18.1	40.3	49.8	18.2	339	83.2
Webster town (Vernon)	778	825	6.0	971	99.6	0.0	0.0	0.0	0.4	28.8	12.5	34.7	49.9	24.1	301	85.0
Weirgor town (Sawyer)	327	330	0.9	290	84.8	0.0	0.0	11.4	3.8	8.6	25.9	57.3	52.4	11.5	159	81.1
Wellington town (Monroe)	621	653	5.2	666	94.3	2.7	0.9	2.0	0.2	31.7	17.0	33.3	62.2	14.4	218	83.9
Wells town (Monroe)	515	541	5.0	521	99.2	0.0	0.0	0.4	0.4	24.8	25.7	46.7	37.6	25.1	213	87.3
Wescott town (Shawano)	3,184	3,144	-1.3	3,134	89.1	0.0	0.3	10.4	0.3	15.0	31.9	54.0	50.7	16.4	1,471	85.7
West Allis city & MCD (Milwaukee)	60,401	59,890	-0.8	60,025	73.5	6.4	2.7	3.8	13.6	20.4	15.3	37.9	41.4	24.6	27,245	85.3
West Baraboo village & MCD (Sauk)	1,411	1,424	0.9	1,708	82.6	4.3	1.8	1.6	9.8	29.4	10.2	30.5	47.8	22.9	672	95.4
West Bend city & MCD (Washington)	31,186	31,563	1.2	31,596	92.9	1.8	0.6	1.0	3.7	22.8	17.4	39.1	37.5	27.9	13,459	87.9
West Bend town (Washington)	4,695	4,726	0.7	4,740	98.2	0.0	0.0	1.5	0.3	17.6	27.6	50.8	33.5	42.0	1,843	94.0
Westboro CDP	190	-	-	175	100.0	0.0	0.0	0.0	0.0	19.4	30.9	45.9	46.7	24.8	77	77.9
Westboro town (Taylor)	684	672	-1.8	582	98.6	0.0	0.0	1.4	0.0	17.9	26.6	50.5	52.5	14.3	267	77.2
Westby city & MCD (Vernon)	2,216	2,255	1.8	2,472	95.1	0.4	0.6	1.8	2.1	28.6	18.7	37.6	43.1	24.6	978	83.5
Westfield village & MCD (Marquette)	1,252	1,266	1.1	1,369	92.3	1.6	0.0	2.6	3.5	30.8	15.6	36.1	49.8	13.8	529	85.6
Westfield town (Marquette)	868	883	1.7	785	93.9	0.0	1.0	2.2	2.9	19.2	22.8	50.0	48.7	16.5	346	92.5
Westfield town (Sauk)	571	604	5.8	653	100.0	0.0	0.0	0.0	0.0	27.4	13.3	38.3	48.2	18.8	208	83.7
Westford town (Dodge)	1,242	1,202	-3.2	1,076	98.7	0.0	0.0	0.9	0.4	16.0	23.9	53.1	54.2	18.4	491	88.8
Westford town (Richland)	530	513	-3.2	599	93.3	0.0	0.2	3.3	3.2	27.9	18.9	43.6	61.4	12.9	209	79.9
West Kewaunee town (Kewaunee)	1,299	1,338	3.0	1,344	90.1	0.7	0.4	1.6	7.2	21.9	19.6	43.8	56.2	10.6	490	89.2
West Marshland town (Burnett)	367	371	1.1	324	86.4	2.5	0.3	10.2	0.6	21.9	22.5	46.0	49.8	12.6	138	93.5
West Milwaukee village & MCD (Milwau	4,199	4,096	-2.5	4,146	49.4	13.2	1.0	2.4	34.0	21.7	10.6	37.3	50.6	18.4	1,914	75.1
Weston town (Clark)	699	693	-0.9	624	94.7	0.6	0.5	0.0	4.2	26.4	14.9	46.7	56.2	10.2	252	82.1
Weston town (Dunn)	594	621	4.5	615	82.3	0.0	0.2	15.8	1.8	28.3	14.1	42.0	55.0	18.3	208	80.3
Weston village & MCD (Marathon)	14,908	15,167	1.7	15,110	82.6	2.2	9.8	2.4	3.0	22.1	16.0	36.4	40.5	23.1	6,047	91.4
Weston town (Marathon)	585	634	8.4	541	95.4	0.0	0.7	0.6	3.3	22.9	12.9	44.6	28.6	29.7	215	91.2
West Point town (Columbia)	1,962	1,990	1.4	2,198	93.5	0.1	0.8	3.4	2.2	18.8	22.3	52.0	27.0	41.9	921	94.6
Westport town (Dane)	3,930	4,194	6.7	4,184	89.9	0.0	3.3	1.1	5.7	19.7	28.3	52.0	16.4	58.9	1,989	95.5
West Salem village & MCD (La Crosse)	4,809	5,015	4.3	5,005	92.2	0.3	2.9	1.8	2.8	24.2	20.0	40.8	31.2	32.2	1,998	90.2
West Sweden town (Polk)	705	707	0.3	754	95.9	0.0	0.3	1.1	2.8	16.7	18.0	50.6	42.6	22.3	311	84.9
Weyauwega city & MCD (Waupaca)	1,890	1,761	-6.8	1,736	83.8	0.6	0.0	5.1	10.4	23.2	17.7	42.2	55.8	15.1	705	87.8
Weyauwega town (Waupaca)	593	585	-1.3	697	83.8	0.4	0.0	1.4	14.3	23.1	15.9	39.9	57.3	14.5	274	85.8
Weyerhaeuser village & MCD (Rusk)	238	215	-9.7	282	90.1	4.3	0.0	4.6	1.1	19.1	19.1	42.7	53.0	10.7	136	72.8
Wheatland town (Kenosha)	3,372	3,455	2.5	3,418	94.0	0.6	0.8	2.2	2.5	20.6	17.2	42.5	51.2	22.5	1,303	92.9
Wheatland town (Vernon)	561	581	3.6	557	99.3	0.0	0.0	0.7	0.0	12.7	30.9	55.7	45.4	15.0	273	78.8
Wheaton town (Chippewa)	2,711	2,828	4.3	2,792	92.3	0.7	5.3	0.4	1.4	24.4	13.4	43.5	35.8	22.8	982	95.7
Wheeler village & MCD (Dunn)	348	349	0.3	297	87.9	0.0	0.0	7.4	4.7	25.6	15.2	35.0	63.2	6.0	121	86.0
Whitefish Bay village & MCD (Milwaukee)	14,125	13,783	-2.4	13,972	84.0	4.6	5.2	2.6	3.6	30.9	13.9	39.1	9.1	75.8	5,226	94.5
Whitehall city & MCD (Trempealeau)	1,591	1,572	-1.2	1,593	91.3	1.3	0.0	0.5	6.9	26.3	18.6	38.9	52.5	14.2	681	83.3
White Lake village & MCD (Langlade)	354	352	-0.6	297	95.3	0.0	0.0	4.4	0.3	11.4	26.3	51.0	61.5	8.2	157	79.0
Whitelaw village & MCD (Manitowoc)	760	740	-2.6	715	97.9	0.0	0.0	0.4	1.7	23.1	14.8	43.3	49.3	16.9	287	89.5
White Oak Springs town (Lafayette)	118	115	-2.5	98	94.9	0.0	0.0	5.1	0.0	12.2	33.7	55.8	59.8	11.0	42	83.3
White River town (Ashland)	923	910	-1.4	931	97.5	0.0	0.0	2.5	0.0	40.2	12.5	29.6	51.1	14.1	274	88.7
Whitestown town (Vernon)	499	524	5.0	516	98.3	0.4	0.6	0.6	0.2	32.0	14.1	37.3	57.0	14.2	181	71.3
Whitewater city	14,395	14,895	3.5	14,722	78.7	3.9	1.9	3.5	12.0	10.4	8.5	21.5	34.5	33.6	4,686	89.7
Whitewater city (Jefferson)	3,237	2,806	-13.3	2,959	74.5	3.4	2.7	2.4	17.0	9.4	4.7	19.7	38.5	35.2	376	89.9
Whitewater city (Walworth)	11,158	12,089	8.3	11,763	79.8	4.0	1.7	3.8	10.7	10.7	9.5	21.9	33.9	33.4	4,310	89.7
Whitewater town (Walworth)	1,456	1,467	0.8	1,420	90.2	0.8	0.1	0.4	8.4	15.9	21.8	50.0	33.2	39.7	573	95.3
Whiting village & MCD (Portage)	1,725	1,705	-1.2	1,714	85.5	0.2	11.4	1.1	1.8	18.2	30.1	46.9	43.0	29.6	746	81.8
Whittlesey CDP	105	-	-	139	97.8	0.0	0.0	0.0	2.2	22.3	22.3	47.6	55.6	16.2	56	87.5
Wien town (Marathon)	828	874	5.6	900	99.7	0.0	0.0	0.1	0.2	33.9	13.9	37.5	51.2	17.0	276	81.9
Wild Rose village & MCD (Waushara)	725	684	-5.7	850	91.5	0.9	0.8	1.6	5.1	21.6	27.2	51.0	52.1	15.5	356	79.8
Wilkinson town (Rusk)	40	42	5.0	38	86.8	0.0	0.0	13.2	0.0	0.0	28.9	61.6	31.6	50.0	20	70.0
Willard town (Rusk)	505	486	-3.8	521	98.3	0.0	0.0	1.7	0.0	18.2	24.2	54.6	56.6	12.6	232	84.5
Williams Bay village & MCD (Walworth)	2,564	2,639	2.9	2,604	89.7	0.5	1.2	0.1	8.4	23.5	27.4	47.7	19.0	45.2	1,129	91.8
Willow town (Richland)	586	568	-3.1	485	96.5	0.0	0.6	2.5	0.4	19.4	18.1	45.6	53.9	18.4	201	81.6
Willow Springs town (Lafayette)	747	757	1.3	829	95.5	0.2	0.0	0.0	4.2	25.6	17.7	40.6	39.6	24.8	304	86.2
Wilson town (Dunn)	531	557	4.9	436	95.0	0.0	0.0	0.0	5.0	18.6	26.8	53.1	45.4	20.9	191	82.2
Wilson town (Eau Claire)	454	497	9.5	440	98.2	0.0	0.0	0.0	1.8	23.2	15.0	42.8	57.0	7.8	155	79.4
Wilson town (Lincoln)	314	310	-1.3	302	98.3	0.0	0.3	1.3	0.0	12.3	34.4	59.2	54.3	10.7	147	83.7

1 May be of any race.

Table A. All Places — **Population and Housing**

STATE City, town, township, borough, or CDP (county if applicable)	Population				Race and Hispanic or Latino origin (percent)					Age (percent)			Educational attainment of persons age 25 and older		Occupied housing units	
	2010 census total population	2019 estimated population	Percent change 2010–2019	ACS total population estimate 2015–2019	White alone, not Hispanic or Latino	Black alone, not Hispanic or Latino	Asian alone, not Hispanic or Latino	All other races or 2 or more races, not Hispanic or Latino	Hispanic or Latino[1]	Under 18 years old	Age 65 years and older	Median age	Percent High school diploma or less	Percent Bachelor's degree or more	Total	Percent with a computer
	1	2	3	4	5	6	7	8	9	10	11	12	13	14	15	16
WISCONSIN—Con.																
Wilson town (Rusk)	106	108	1.9	93	95.7	0.0	0.0	0.0	4.3	17.2	28.0	42.2	54.9	7.0	40	77.5
Wilson village & MCD (St. Croix)	184	185	0.5	224	95.1	0.0	0.0	4.0	0.9	24.1	12.5	44.6	50.3	9.0	87	93.1
Wilson town (Sheboygan)	3,301	3,350	1.5	3,326	89.9	2.2	2.0	2.0	3.9	21.3	15.4	46.7	34.3	36.4	1,302	95.7
Wilton village & MCD (Monroe)	514	500	-2.7	511	82.4	1.2	0.0	0.8	15.7	35.6	11.9	33.3	49.5	11.2	192	83.3
Wilton town (Monroe)	1,015	1,068	5.2	1,017	95.7	0.0	0.7	1.4	2.3	36.7	8.1	31.4	65.4	7.6	273	71.4
Winchester town (Vilas)	388	399	2.8	337	95.5	0.0	0.0	1.8	2.7	5.0	49.9	65.0	24.9	42.1	194	99.0
Winchester CDP	671	-	-	635	95.6	0.0	0.9	0.6	2.8	20.2	17.5	45.2	35.1	31.0	278	93.5
Winchester town (Winnebago)	1,763	1,832	3.9	1,609	95.6	0.0	0.4	2.3	1.7	18.1	17.7	48.6	39.3	26.9	690	88.6
Wind Lake CDP	5,342	-	-	5,364	94.8	0.0	0.8	0.6	3.8	19.8	17.7	46.6	34.4	31.3	2,086	94.9
Wind Point village & MCD (Racine)	1,723	1,695	-1.6	1,776	90.4	0.3	6.4	0.7	2.2	18.7	29.0	55.1	18.4	62.3	746	94.2
Windsor village & MCD (Dane)	6,308	7,644	21.2	7,110	91.9	0.7	2.8	0.8	3.8	26.2	16.0	40.0	22.1	44.7	2,710	90.0
Winfield town (Sauk)	859	919	7.0	880	99.1	0.0	0.0	0.0	0.9	19.8	15.9	48.6	43.6	17.6	350	88.9
Wingville town (Grant)	358	363	1.4	382	91.4	0.0	0.5	1.8	6.3	32.2	12.0	34.5	48.7	22.4	131	80.9
Winneconne village & MCD (Winnebago)	2,369	2,484	4.9	2,708	93.7	0.0	0.2	2.4	3.7	25.5	19.6	46.4	41.0	29.8	1,203	87.6
Winneconne town (Winnebago)	2,364	2,524	6.8	2,488	99.7	0.0	0.0	0.3	0.0	19.1	22.7	49.9	32.6	33.1	1,016	92.1
Winter village & MCD (Sawyer)	313	300	-4.2	335	83.6	0.0	0.0	3.3	13.1	15.2	22.7	43.3	61.6	15.9	185	84.3
Winter town (Sawyer)	960	959	-0.1	869	91.9	2.8	0.6	2.6	2.1	5.2	40.3	61.4	54.3	12.0	435	73.8
Wiota CDP	-	-	-	122	94.3	0.0	0.0	5.7	0.0	20.5	35.2	54.8	67.4	8.7	50	80.0
Wiota town (Lafayette)	859	877	2.1	806	91.4	0.0	0.0	1.6	6.9	17.4	23.0	52.3	60.3	15.5	346	80.1
Wisconsin Dells city	2,716	2,992	10.2	2,841	92.0	0.4	0.1	1.3	6.2	20.5	21.6	42.3	40.8	23.9	1,320	85.3
Wisconsin Dells city (Adams)	46	50	8.7	37	100.0	0.0	0.0	0.0	0.0	59.5	0.0	13.5	0.0	100.0	8	100.0
Wisconsin Dells city (Columbia)	2,458	2,700	9.8	2,607	91.3	0.4	0.2	1.4	6.7	20.1	21.8	42.4	40.7	23.2	1,227	85.0
Wisconsin Dells city (Juneau)	-	-	-	9	100.0	0.0	0.0	0.0	0.0	0.0	0.0	0.0	100.0	0.0	9	100.0
Wisconsin Dells city (Sauk)	212	242	14.2	188	100.0	0.0	0.0	0.0	0.0	18.1	23.9	47.0	42.9	25.6	76	86.8
Wisconsin Rapids city & MCD (Wood)	18,400	17,610	-4.3	17,770	84.7	1.4	4.2	3.8	5.9	22.3	20.6	40.7	50.3	15.0	8,228	84.8
Withee village & MCD (Clark)	487	476	-2.3	369	90.0	0.0	0.8	9.2	0.0	15.7	14.6	42.7	51.5	7.5	190	81.1
Withee town (Clark)	964	978	1.5	885	98.8	0.5	0.0	0.8	0.0	39.5	14.1	30.5	63.6	9.7	263	73.0
Wittenberg village & MCD (Shawano)	1,087	988	-9.1	998	86.3	0.2	0.7	7.4	5.4	17.6	18.7	44.5	64.2	17.0	423	78.0
Wittenberg town (Shawano)	827	817	-1.2	903	89.6	2.4	0.0	4.2	3.8	23.3	16.4	44.0	48.6	16.0	337	86.1
Wolf River town (Langlade)	740	724	-2.2	732	95.8	0.0	0.0	1.9	2.3	8.6	37.3	58.0	53.3	15.6	372	87.9
Wolf River town (Winnebago)	1,189	1,210	1.8	1,236	98.3	0.0	0.6	1.1	0.0	17.0	29.5	53.3	47.1	18.7	566	85.9
Wonewoc village & MCD (Juneau)	826	788	-4.6	748	88.2	0.0	0.8	10.3	0.7	25.1	18.9	45.9	57.0	9.3	361	81.7
Wonewoc town (Juneau)	676	654	-3.3	707	93.2	0.0	0.6	0.7	5.5	23.8	17.7	48.3	56.9	12.8	283	82.3
Wood town (Wood)	790	752	-4.8	717	99.3	0.0	0.4	0.3	0.0	18.5	23.7	50.1	51.6	19.4	311	78.1
Woodboro town (Oneida)	811	804	-0.9	906	96.0	0.2	0.0	1.4	2.3	17.4	24.0	51.4	39.1	19.4	365	84.4
Woodford CDP	69	-	-	50	36.0	0.0	0.0	0.0	64.0	0.0	18.0	29.0	88.0	0.0	29	51.7
Woodland town (Sauk)	790	842	6.6	674	99.3	0.0	0.0	0.7	0.0	26.0	20.8	44.2	46.2	26.6	266	83.8
Woodman village & MCD (Grant)	132	129	-2.3	81	100.0	0.0	0.0	0.0	0.0	16.0	9.9	50.2	50.8	3.4	38	97.4
Woodman town (Grant)	185	187	1.1	118	99.2	0.0	0.0	0.0	0.8	17.8	28.0	54.4	45.2	22.6	50	88.0
Woodmohr town (Chippewa)	924	963	4.2	1,125	98.3	0.2	0.0	0.2	1.3	28.2	16.4	41.9	43.7	15.1	409	92.9
Wood River town (Burnett)	953	931	-2.3	901	96.3	0.4	0.0	2.1	1.1	14.4	26.6	53.9	43.1	21.4	428	91.1
Woodruff CDP	966	-	-	746	89.8	0.0	0.0	5.4	4.8	14.6	32.7	50.8	38.8	19.8	375	72.5
Woodruff town (Oneida)	1,986	1,976	-0.5	1,911	93.7	0.0	0.0	2.4	3.9	15.4	30.2	52.2	32.5	34.6	878	85.3
Woodville town (Calumet)	980	959	-2.1	975	90.7	0.0	1.0	3.4	4.9	25.5	17.1	39.4	49.9	17.7	357	89.4
Woodville village & MCD (St. Croix)	1,338	1,353	1.1	1,369	94.4	0.2	0.3	4.5	0.7	31.8	13.1	34.8	51.5	18.1	515	89.5
Worcester town (Price)	1,566	1,487	-5.0	1,371	97.0	0.0	0.4	0.9	1.7	17.8	26.3	53.8	40.4	21.4	650	86.6
Worden town (Clark)	666	702	5.4	624	100.0	0.0	0.0	0.0	0.0	29.2	17.0	42.6	63.6	11.7	208	74.0
Wrightstown village	2,843	3,508	23.4	3,459	92.0	1.6	1.0	2.9	2.5	31.3	11.8	34.6	32.1	33.3	1,288	92.2
Wrightstown village (Brown)	2,692	3,323	23.4	3,232	91.4	1.7	1.0	3.1	2.7	31.2	12.1	34.6	34.0	31.4	1,203	91.7
Wrightstown village (Outagamie)	151	185	22.5	227	100.0	0.0	0.0	0.0	0.0	33.5	7.0	34.5	4.4	62.0	85	100.0
Wrightstown town (Brown)	2,213	2,378	7.5	2,514	80.5	1.1	0.0	2.5	15.9	26.0	8.8	36.0	43.0	24.3	904	85.2
Wyalusing town (Grant)	346	342	-1.2	333	98.2	1.2	0.0	0.3	0.3	23.4	21.6	46.5	47.2	18.3	138	84.1
Wyeville village & MCD (Monroe)	147	143	-2.7	157	75.2	3.2	0.0	0.6	21.0	33.1	10.8	34.3	43.5	9.8	55	87.3
Wyocena village & MCD (Columbia)	775	725	-6.5	795	90.8	0.8	0.0	3.0	5.4	18.2	22.5	42.8	50.8	13.2	308	90.3
Wyocena town (Columbia)	1,659	1,683	1.4	1,469	97.3	1.3	0.2	0.6	0.6	14.4	23.9	53.1	36.9	24.1	687	91.4
Wyoming town (Iowa)	302	311	3.0	306	94.8	0.0	0.0	0.0	5.2	13.7	26.1	54.1	26.5	44.3	146	92.5
Wyoming town (Waupaca)	328	324	-1.2	356	99.4	0.0	0.0	0.0	0.6	26.7	14.9	43.5	58.5	7.0	128	86.7
York town (Clark)	886	873	-1.5	743	93.1	0.0	0.4	0.4	6.1	29.2	17.6	37.7	57.1	12.6	273	76.2
York town (Dane)	652	691	6.0	785	92.6	3.1	0.3	1.3	2.8	25.2	20.5	47.4	35.3	28.1	296	91.6
York town (Green)	910	938	3.1	1,124	97.5	0.0	0.9	1.6	0.0	27.5	15.2	40.6	33.5	34.1	372	95.2
Yorkville village & MCD (Racine)	3,073	3,130	1.9	3,114	93.8	0.1	0.6	1.4	4.1	21.8	20.3	48.5	36.8	27.4	1,188	91.7
Yuba village & MCD (Richland)	75	69	-8.0	32	100.0	0.0	0.0	0.0	0.0	6.3	50.0	65.0	62.1	0.0	22	68.2
Zoar CDP	98	-	-	128	8.6	0.0	0.0	91.4	0.0	26.6	18.0	38.1	47.9	0.0	40	100.0

1 May be of any race.

Table A. All Places — **Population and Housing**

STATE City, town, township, borough, or CDP (county if applicable)	Population				Race and Hispanic or Latino origin (percent)					Age (percent)			Educational attainment of persons age 25 and older		Occupied housing units	
	2010 census total population	2019 estimated population	Percent change 2010–2019	ACS total population estimate 2015–2019	White alone, not Hispanic or Latino	Black alone, not Hispanic or Latino	Asian alone, not Hispanic or Latino	All other races or 2 or more races, not Hispanic or Latino	Hispanic or Latino[1]	Under 18 years old	Age 65 years and older	Median age	Percent High school diploma or less	Percent Bachelor's degree or more	Total	Percent with a computer
	1	2	3	4	5	6	7	8	9	10	11	12	13	14	15	16
WYOMING	563,775	578,759	2.7	581,024	84.1	0.9	0.8	4.3	9.9	23.5	15.7	37.7	35.9	27.4	230,101	91.8
Afton town	1,920	2,041	6.3	2,058	86.8	0.0	0.2	5.7	7.3	25.9	15.5	34.7	28.0	28.5	694	96.0
Albany CDP	55	-	-	46	100.0	0.0	0.0	0.0	0.0	0.0	23.9	60.9	0.0	76.1	19	100.0
Albin town	186	206	10.8	119	42.9	0.0	0.0	0.0	57.1	39.5	4.2	34.1	63.9	8.3	40	72.5
Alcova CDP	76	-	-	-	-	-	-	-	-	-	-	-	-	-	-	-
Alpine town	853	924	8.3	639	91.2	0.5	0.5	4.1	3.8	18.8	5.5	45.3	42.6	19.1	276	90.9
Alpine Northeast CDP	196	-	-	55	100.0	0.0	0.0	0.0	0.0	0.0	0.0	0.0	0.0	0.0	55	100.0
Alpine Northwest CDP	244	-	-	172	0.0	0.0	0.0	0.0	100.0	55.2	0.0	15.7	100.0	0.0	29	100.0
Alta CDP	394	-	-	460	100.0	0.0	0.0	0.0	0.0	22.0	33.0	55.6	3.4	43.8	205	100.0
Antelope Hills CDP	97	-	-	-	-	-	-	-	-	-	-	-	-	-	-	-
Arapahoe CDP	1,656	-	-	1,829	10.4	0.4	0.0	84.3	4.8	36.5	8.3	25.2	47.8	9.3	451	78.3
Arlington CDP	25	-	-	-	-	-	-	-	-	-	-	-	-	-	-	-
Arrowhead Springs CDP	63	-	-	120	100.0	0.0	0.0	0.0	0.0	33.3	28.3	46.3	16.3	57.5	53	100.0
Arvada CDP	43	-	-	22	81.8	0.0	0.0	9.1	9.1	31.8	13.6	33.7	33.3	0.0	9	44.4
Atlantic City CDP	37	-	-	-	-	-	-	-	-	-	-	-	-	-	-	-
Auburn CDP	328	-	-	481	100.0	0.0	0.0	0.0	0.0	51.1	13.1	13.9	31.9	40.4	135	91.1
Baggs town	440	417	-5.2	485	73.0	0.0	0.0	0.0	27.0	31.8	8.9	34.8	65.6	17.5	179	82.7
Bairoil town	106	97	-8.5	178	100.0	0.0	0.0	0.0	0.0	18.5	23.6	40.7	51.7	5.6	49	95.9
Bar Nunn town	2,203	2,812	27.6	2,782	84.9	0.0	0.2	11.4	3.5	29.2	5.3	29.4	41.0	12.5	919	99.1
Basin town	1,287	1,282	-0.4	1,388	93.4	0.2	0.2	2.9	3.2	15.3	23.2	42.9	52.1	16.2	475	83.6
Bear River town	519	506	-2.5	642	86.3	0.0	0.0	1.4	12.3	35.2	8.6	36.1	45.5	13.9	216	99.1
Bedford CDP	201	-	-	289	91.0	0.0	0.0	9.0	0.0	42.9	0.0	26.2	83.6	16.4	39	100.0
Bessemer Bend CDP	199	-	-	232	100.0	0.0	0.0	0.0	0.0	7.8	18.5	43.7	65.4	11.2	102	91.2
Beulah CDP	73	-	-	-	-	-	-	-	-	-	-	-	-	-	-	-
Big Horn CDP	490	-	-	483	100.0	0.0	0.0	0.0	0.0	22.4	8.5	51.5	14.0	38.9	237	81.0
Big Piney town	560	517	-7.7	527	80.6	0.0	0.0	19.4	0.0	33.6	6.1	29.0	66.1	15.3	129	96.9
Bondurant CDP	93	-	-	59	100.0	0.0	0.0	0.0	0.0	0.0	0.0	0.0	100.0	0.0	59	100.0
Boulder CDP	170	-	-	32	100.0	0.0	0.0	0.0	0.0	0.0	100.0	0.0	100.0	0.0	32	100.0
Boulder Flats CDP	408	-	-	250	27.6	0.0	0.0	66.0	6.4	21.6	12.8	43.2	33.5	22.0	94	92.6
Brookhurst CDP	185	-	-	180	100.0	0.0	0.0	0.0	0.0	0.0	0.0	58.8	44.4	30.6	111	100.0
Buffalo city	4,583	4,575	-0.2	4,578	88.6	0.7	0.0	6.5	4.2	22.2	20.8	45.5	29.1	34.4	2,205	88.1
Burlington town	288	342	18.8	257	73.2	0.0	0.0	13.6	13.2	32.3	7.4	37.3	43.8	22.5	85	92.9
Burns town	301	312	3.7	315	95.6	0.0	0.0	1.0	3.5	28.9	21.0	42.3	34.3	21.6	131	99.2
Byron town	591	604	2.2	519	94.8	0.0	0.0	0.0	5.2	26.4	19.7	40.7	39.3	19.0	178	93.8
Carpenter CDP	94	-	-	350	88.6	11.4	0.0	0.0	0.0	16.3	4.3	50.4	66.1	7.0	129	100.0
Carter CDP	10	-	-	-	-	-	-	-	-	-	-	-	-	-	-	-
Casper city	55,316	57,931	4.7	58,446	86.5	1.3	0.6	3.0	8.6	24.2	14.4	35.9	35.4	25.1	24,219	92.1
Casper Mountain CDP	401	-	-	835	84.3	0.0	0.0	0.0	15.7	34.4	10.4	29.3	14.5	52.7	217	100.0
Centennial CDP	270	-	-	308	85.1	0.0	0.0	1.9	13.0	1.6	40.3	62.0	7.3	62.4	171	100.0
Cheyenne city	59,552	64,235	7.9	63,607	78.5	1.8	1.5	3.5	14.7	22.3	16.7	36.6	31.8	30.4	27,344	92.0
Chugcreek CDP	156	-	-	216	100.0	0.0	0.0	0.0	0.0	58.8	0.0	17.6	27.0	42.7	49	100.0
Chugwater town	212	201	-5.2	185	95.7	0.0	2.2	0.0	2.2	27.0	27.0	51.0	36.6	19.4	97	96.9
Clearmont town	146	157	7.5	154	100.0	0.0	0.0	0.0	0.0	25.3	4.5	39.3	48.0	21.6	75	93.3
Clearview Acres CDP	795	-	-	1,208	56.9	0.0	0.0	0.0	43.1	27.2	11.2	32.7	67.3	6.1	318	100.0
Cody city	9,520	9,788	2.8	9,764	91.2	0.6	0.5	2.4	5.4	21.6	21.1	43.2	23.4	37.5	4,315	90.8
Cokeville town	535	554	3.6	536	100.0	0.0	0.0	0.0	0.0	32.8	15.1	39.1	34.1	27.1	167	95.2
Cora CDP	142	-	-	49	100.0	0.0	0.0	0.0	0.0	0.0	24.5	59.5	24.5	28.6	26	100.0
Cowley town	659	761	15.5	623	95.8	0.0	0.0	2.4	1.8	31.1	14.9	35.9	29.6	20.8	230	91.3
Crowheart CDP	141	-	-	150	56.0	0.0	0.0	44.0	0.0	22.0	30.7	51.4	29.8	28.8	65	75.4
Daniel CDP	150	-	-	94	100.0	0.0	0.0	0.0	0.0	0.0	58.5	76.7	57.4	0.0	82	100.0
Dayton town	760	828	8.9	771	97.4	0.0	0.0	1.4	1.2	29.1	24.0	44.5	31.8	35.4	309	90.9
Deaver town	177	181	2.3	140	98.6	0.0	0.7	0.0	0.7	23.6	13.6	36.0	25.8	11.3	65	92.3
Diamondville town	737	757	2.7	651	83.6	0.6	0.0	7.4	8.4	21.2	23.8	48.4	56.6	5.6	307	86.3
Dixon town	97	94	-3.1	91	98.9	0.0	0.0	0.0	1.1	36.3	18.7	31.8	19.0	22.4	43	69.8
Douglas city	6,109	6,364	4.2	6,393	82.5	0.0	0.5	3.7	13.3	25.0	18.4	40.7	49.4	15.0	2,560	91.8
Dubois town	982	959	-2.3	842	92.0	3.3	0.0	2.1	2.5	18.4	28.6	56.1	42.8	24.7	446	93.5
East Thermopolis town	256	238	-7.0	238	91.2	0.0	0.0	5.5	3.4	12.2	42.0	58.8	43.6	15.4	160	66.9
Eden CDP	281	-	-	195	100.0	0.0	0.0	0.0	0.0	23.6	15.4	43.0	55.3	37.4	86	100.0
Edgerton town	199	204	2.5	153	100.0	0.0	0.0	0.0	0.0	18.3	15.7	35.9	65.8	3.6	70	81.4
Elk Mountain town	191	185	-3.1	194	84.0	0.0	0.0	0.0	16.0	26.3	16.5	32.7	24.2	26.6	78	84.6
Encampment town	450	426	-5.3	443	95.5	0.0	0.0	1.8	2.7	26.6	18.3	32.8	41.2	41.9	207	91.3
Esterbrook CDP	52	-	-	87	80.5	0.0	0.0	19.5	0.0	0.0	48.3	63.8	34.5	17.2	40	100.0
Ethete CDP	1,553	-	-	1,486	3.3	0.0	0.5	93.5	2.7	39.4	7.5	25.5	42.9	11.0	306	80.1
Etna CDP	164	-	-	-	-	-	-	-	-	-	-	-	-	-	-	-
Evanston city	12,398	11,641	-6.1	11,848	84.6	0.1	0.2	2.8	12.3	28.5	12.7	35.3	51.0	13.4	4,372	94.0
Evansville town	2,536	2,964	16.9	2,963	76.4	2.6	1.5	0.9	18.6	30.9	11.2	29.2	53.2	10.2	1,101	91.4
Fairview CDP	275	-	-	101	85.1	0.0	0.0	0.0	14.9	66.3	0.0	15.1	0.0	44.1	19	100.0
Farson CDP	313	-	-	143	100.0	0.0	0.0	0.0	0.0	35.7	34.3	38.7	0.0	30.4	69	100.0
Fontenelle CDP	13	-	-	26	100.0	0.0	0.0	0.0	0.0	0.0	0.0	0.0	76.9	0.0	26	100.0
Fort Bridger CDP	345	-	-	181	100.0	0.0	0.0	0.0	0.0	22.1	6.1	41.1	100.0	0.0	90	100.0
Fort Laramie town	230	227	-1.3	232	93.5	0.0	0.0	2.2	4.3	13.8	23.7	51.5	33.9	17.0	97	88.7
Fort Washakie CDP	1,759	-	-	1,741	5.1	0.0	0.8	90.2	3.8	36.1	11.0	27.4	49.6	10.2	453	80.4
Fox Farm-College CDP	3,647	-	-	4,549	56.2	0.5	0.1	7.2	36.0	26.4	9.3	27.0	59.7	2.6	1,565	83.9
Fox Park CDP	-	-	-	8	100.0	0.0	0.0	0.0	0.0	0.0	0.0	0.0	0.0	0.0	8	100.0
Frannie town	157	159	1.3	149	88.6	0.0	0.0	1.3	10.1	21.5	25.5	48.1	41.4	9.1	59	74.6
Freedom CDP	214	-	-	268	82.5	0.0	0.0	0.0	17.5	37.7	14.2	18.9	25.8	35.0	61	100.0
Garland CDP	115	-	-	202	77.7	0.0	0.0	0.0	22.3	0.0	59.4	67.7	49.2	10.8	95	100.0
Gillette city	31,401	32,030	2.0	32,857	84.4	0.5	0.6	3.6	11.0	29.7	8.2	31.4	42.3	19.2	11,967	95.2
Glendo town	205	201	-2.0	203	95.6	0.0	0.0	4.4	0.0	28.6	32.0	56.2	57.6	10.4	99	73.7
Glenrock town	2,641	2,575	-2.5	2,594	93.4	0.0	0.0	2.2	4.4	31.8	11.4	30.8	42.8	19.3	936	92.4
Granger town	139	128	-7.9	40	90.0	0.0	0.0	0.0	10.0	10.0	27.5	60.3	77.8	0.0	26	80.8
Green River city	12,515	11,759	-6.0	12,069	78.3	0.0	1.3	4.0	16.4	25.0	12.6	37.3	36.8	22.1	4,303	92.6
Greybull town	1,848	1,838	-0.5	1,981	72.9	0.0	0.5	0.9	25.8	24.5	19.1	38.4	47.6	15.9	741	85.3
Grover CDP	147	-	-	438	93.2	0.0	3.4	3.4	0.0	9.6	19.6	32.3	66.3	18.2	95	100.0
Guernsey town	1,147	1,124	-2.0	956	90.5	0.1	0.0	2.4	7.0	21.8	25.5	43.6	48.2	12.8	454	86.3
Hanna town	841	769	-8.6	725	87.7	3.2	0.0	6.9	2.2	36.1	15.2	35.8	41.2	26.7	252	73.8
Hartrandt CDP	693	-	-	808	87.7	0.0	0.0	0.0	12.3	14.4	17.7	49.2	74.7	2.1	305	82.6
Hartville town	62	60	-3.2	48	89.6	0.0	0.0	0.0	10.4	0.0	22.9	57.1	58.3	16.7	33	63.6
Hawk Springs CDP	45	-	-	7	100.0	0.0	0.0	0.0	0.0	0.0	100.0	0.0	0.0	100.0	7	100.0
Hillsdale CDP	47	-	-	-	-	-	-	-	-	-	-	-	-	-	-	-
Hill View Heights CDP	170	-	-	80	100.0	0.0	0.0	0.0	0.0	0.0	100.0	73.5	35.0	18.8	44	79.5

1 May be of any race.

Table A. All Places — **Population and Housing**

STATE City, town, township, borough, or CDP (county if applicable)	Population				Race and Hispanic or Latino origin (percent)					Age (percent)			Educational attainment of persons age 25 and older		Occupied housing units	
	2010 census total population	2019 estimated population	Percent change 2010–2019	ACS total population estimate 2015–2019	White alone, not Hispanic or Latino	Black alone, not Hispanic or Latino	Asian alone, not Hispanic or Latino	All other races or 2 or more races, not Hispanic or Latino	Hispanic or Latino[1]	Under 18 years old	Age 65 years and older	Median age	Percent High school diploma or less	Percent Bachelor's degree or more	Total	Percent with a computer
	1	2	3	4	5	6	7	8	9	10	11	12	13	14	15	16
WYOMING—Con.																
Hoback CDP	1,176	-	-	1,439	75.6	0.0	2.8	5.1	16.5	28.3	5.8	39.6	26.8	46.8	548	100.0
Homa Hills CDP	278	-	-	239	100.0	0.0	0.0	0.0	0.0	17.2	25.9	51.1	67.7	0.0	108	88.9
Hudson town	461	445	-3.5	446	86.3	0.0	0.0	6.5	7.2	22.2	15.0	39.0	46.2	14.9	175	88.6
Hulett town	379	427	12.7	386	96.1	0.0	0.0	0.8	3.1	15.5	15.8	41.4	45.0	10.3	160	84.4
Huntley town	30	-	-	-	-	-	-	-	-	-	-	-	-	-	-	-
Hyattville CDP	75	-	-	97	66.0	0.0	0.0	34.0	0.0	0.0	42.3	57.9	0.0	43.3	39	100.0
Jackson town	9,628	10,559	9.7	10,553	72.9	0.5	0.3	1.1	25.2	20.9	7.9	32.6	26.7	53.9	3,970	93.0
James Town CDP	536	-	-	663	84.2	0.0	0.0	0.0	15.8	17.5	20.1	47.8	27.2	30.3	268	100.0
Jeffrey City CDP	58	-	-	29	100.0	0.0	0.0	0.0	0.0	0.0	48.3	0.0	100.0	0.0	15	0.0
Johnstown CDP	242	-	-	184	45.1	0.0	0.0	54.9	0.0	18.5	26.6	44.5	36.8	16.8	74	85.1
Kaycee town	269	278	3.3	284	84.2	0.0	0.0	11.6	4.2	25.7	20.8	46.8	45.9	14.4	118	78.8
Kelly CDP	138	-	-	122	100.0	0.0	0.0	0.0	0.0	0.0	0.0	0.0	0.0	0.0	64	100.0
Kemmerer city	2,656	2,749	3.5	2,747	90.5	0.1	0.4	2.7	6.3	27.3	16.3	37.7	31.7	23.9	1,152	89.9
Kirby town	92	84	-8.7	69	89.9	0.0	0.0	5.8	4.3	11.6	27.5	56.8	60.7	14.8	32	78.1
La Barge town	551	569	3.3	315	91.4	0.0	4.1	2.5	1.9	33.3	7.9	35.6	42.2	4.2	115	83.5
La Grange town	448	442	-1.3	303	89.8	0.3	0.0	3.3	6.6	13.2	13.5	24.3	26.6	30.8	92	85.9
Lakeview North CDP	84	-	-	99	100.0	0.0	0.0	0.0	0.0	29.3	29.3	53.2	27.1	35.7	35	100.0
Lance Creek CDP	43	-	-	32	100.0	0.0	0.0	0.0	0.0	0.0	59.4	74.3	71.9	12.5	18	100.0
Lander city	7,597	7,458	-1.8	7,555	87.3	0.3	0.5	9.3	2.7	23.9	20.5	38.7	31.5	36.4	2,958	89.7
Laramie city	30,816	32,711	6.1	32,381	80.5	1.8	3.6	3.7	10.4	16.0	8.9	25.9	17.6	52.7	13,350	95.5
Lingle town	468	456	-2.6	479	87.7	0.0	0.0	4.2	8.1	14.8	30.9	53.3	26.8	27.6	203	86.7
Little America CDP	68	-	-	45	100.0	0.0	0.0	0.0	0.0	0.0	0.0	0.0	100.0	0.0	45	100.0
Lonetree CDP	49	-	-	-	-	-	-	-	-	-	-	-	-	-	-	-
Lost Springs town	4	4	0.0	1	100.0	0.0	0.0	0.0	0.0	0.0	100.0	0.0	100.0	0.0	1	100.0
Lovell town	2,360	2,366	0.3	2,237	80.3	1.3	0.8	2.5	15.1	27.1	21.1	39.3	48.8	13.2	852	90.5
Lucerne CDP	535	-	-	462	86.4	0.0	0.0	9.7	3.9	17.5	13.0	46.5	30.0	24.8	187	100.0
Lusk town	1,567	1,526	-2.6	1,558	87.8	0.3	0.0	7.6	4.4	25.4	16.0	36.0	53.0	12.8	547	82.3
Lyman town	2,111	2,070	-1.9	2,285	91.4	0.0	0.2	5.4	3.0	32.7	14.2	34.6	38.1	27.4	799	94.6
McKinnon CDP	60	-	-	51	100.0	0.0	0.0	0.0	0.0	49.0	0.0	39.0	0.0	50.0	13	100.0
Mammoth CDP	263	-	-	49	81.6	6.1	8.2	0.0	4.1	0.0	12.2	32.9	15.0	47.5	0	0.0
Manderson town	114	113	-0.9	74	100.0	0.0	0.0	0.0	0.0	10.8	35.1	57.6	45.5	15.2	41	78.0
Manville town	95	87	-8.4	97	72.2	0.0	0.0	0.0	27.8	3.1	29.9	57.4	53.3	9.8	47	78.7
Marbleton town	1,115	1,111	-0.4	1,404	68.5	0.0	0.0	13.1	18.4	27.7	15.6	30.7	53.6	16.1	387	96.4
Meadow Acres CDP	198	-	-	130	76.9	0.0	0.0	23.1	0.0	8.5	0.0	52.8	27.7	14.3	78	100.0
Medicine Bow town	284	259	-8.8	284	97.2	0.0	0.0	2.8	0.0	10.6	37.0	60.5	55.7	16.0	159	71.1
Meeteetse town	327	323	-1.2	459	72.5	24.6	0.0	1.3	1.5	29.0	31.6	41.7	24.1	18.2	194	96.9
Midwest town	404	394	-2.5	233	96.6	0.0	0.0	0.0	3.4	21.9	18.5	50.3	61.0	9.9	105	87.6
Mills town	3,468	3,979	14.7	3,919	89.2	0.0	0.6	2.1	8.1	23.7	18.8	37.2	57.2	5.9	1,753	84.7
Moorcroft town	1,009	1,084	7.4	846	98.6	0.0	0.0	0.0	1.4	36.6	14.1	28.3	41.9	11.5	301	93.7
Moose Wilson Road CDP	1,821	-	-	1,398	98.1	0.0	1.6	0.1	0.1	1.7	33.5	54.7	23.6	52.6	645	98.0
Mountain View CDP	96	-	-	35	100.0	0.0	0.0	0.0	0.0	0.0	22.9	0.0	22.9	0.0	35	0.0
Mountain View town	1,280	1,226	-4.2	1,227	84.6	0.6	0.0	8.7	6.1	27.5	19.0	36.1	50.1	15.9	492	90.2
Newcastle city	3,533	3,397	-3.8	3,445	96.6	0.2	0.8	0.8	1.6	20.5	18.7	40.1	41.7	20.6	1,308	90.7
Nordic CDP	602	-	-	337	100.0	0.0	0.0	0.0	0.0	8.6	7.1	57.3	51.3	0.0	203	100.0
North Rock Springs CDP	2,207	-	-	2,567	84.5	0.0	0.0	0.0	15.5	30.8	8.0	31.8	47.6	10.1	863	96.5
Oakley CDP	49	-	-	-	-	-	-	-	-	-	-	-	-	-	-	-
Opal town	96	109	13.5	121	96.7	0.0	0.8	2.5	0.0	9.9	16.5	55.1	63.6	0.9	49	85.7
Orin CDP	46	-	-	89	100.0	0.0	0.0	0.0	0.0	0.0	57.1	0.0	0.0	73.0	24	100.0
Osage CDP	208	-	-	152	100.0	0.0	0.0	0.0	0.0	0.0	0.0	45.5	100.0	0.0	67	68.7
Osmond CDP	397	-	-	669	84.3	0.0	0.0	9.7	6.0	50.7	9.6	15.8	34.5	40.0	157	100.0
Owl Creek CDP	5	-	-	-	-	-	-	-	-	-	-	-	-	-	-	-
Parkman CDP	151	-	-	126	100.0	0.0	0.0	0.0	0.0	6.3	6.3	59.8	33.9	6.8	59	59.3
Pavillion town	233	230	-1.3	194	77.8	0.0	0.0	7.2	14.9	29.4	13.4	38.5	37.5	14.8	74	93.2
Pine Bluffs town	1,161	1,159	-0.2	944	70.6	0.0	0.0	0.0	29.4	24.3	23.2	44.9	48.3	16.0	400	90.3
Pinedale town	2,013	1,871	-7.1	1,962	83.6	0.0	0.0	0.7	15.7	25.6	10.0	37.6	43.0	22.9	638	91.7
Pine Haven town	490	548	11.8	497	94.2	0.0	3.6	0.8	1.4	25.4	15.7	45.9	35.4	15.9	170	94.1
Point of Rocks CDP	-	-	-	56	100.0	0.0	0.0	0.0	0.0	0.0	0.0	31.1	17.9	0.0	35	100.0
Powder River CDP	44	-	-	-	-	-	-	-	-	-	-	-	-	-	-	-
Powell city	6,323	6,180	-2.3	6,295	85.7	0.2	0.7	3.7	9.7	23.1	16.6	33.1	36.3	30.4	2,479	97.9
Purple Sage CDP	535	-	-	818	39.6	0.0	0.0	0.0	60.4	39.1	6.8	26.2	90.4	3.4	222	100.0
Rafter J Ranch CDP	1,075	-	-	1,750	82.9	0.0	0.0	3.0	14.1	20.4	13.4	46.4	17.6	64.5	735	94.6
Ralston CDP	280	-	-	564	84.8	0.0	0.0	0.0	15.2	33.5	16.5	39.6	41.8	3.3	183	100.0
Ranchester town	862	1,041	20.8	1,117	96.5	0.0	0.0	0.0	3.5	35.5	12.4	34.5	44.2	23.4	384	96.1
Ranchettes CDP	5,798	-	-	6,289	85.5	0.3	0.8	2.1	11.4	24.5	19.7	45.8	25.7	40.4	2,345	96.2
Rawlins city	9,261	8,510	-8.1	8,820	67.5	1.6	1.3	3.5	26.1	26.1	10.2	33.9	51.0	17.6	3,230	90.5
Red Butte CDP	449	-	-	815	96.0	0.0	0.0	4.0	0.0	29.9	8.8	39.4	16.7	33.3	293	100.0
Reliance CDP	714	-	-	386	77.7	0.0	4.4	11.7	6.2	0.0	8.8	53.8	76.1	0.0	235	63.4
Riverside town	52	52	0.0	27	100.0	0.0	0.0	0.0	0.0	0.0	40.7	64.4	59.3	22.2	20	100.0
Riverton city	10,760	10,772	0.1	10,891	70.9	1.1	0.5	13.1	14.4	22.9	17.8	38.5	39.7	19.5	4,329	86.5
Robertson CDP	97	-	-	45	100.0	0.0	0.0	0.0	0.0	31.1	28.9	51.5	41.9	58.1	13	100.0
Rock River town	245	254	3.7	204	71.6	0.0	3.4	0.0	25.0	22.5	25.5	51.3	37.8	23.0	90	81.1
Rock Springs city	23,066	22,653	-1.8	23,319	82.6	2.1	0.5	2.7	12.1	27.6	10.4	33.8	37.4	26.7	8,352	94.4
Rolling Hills town	444	424	-4.5	471	89.0	0.0	0.0	4.7	6.4	25.1	13.4	38.7	47.8	22.6	142	89.4
Ryan Park CDP	38	-	-	26	100.0	0.0	0.0	0.0	0.0	0.0	100.0	0.0	50.0	0.0	13	100.0
Saratoga town	1,690	1,615	-4.4	1,377	90.6	0.0	0.6	1.4	7.5	12.6	25.3	52.2	45.4	20.0	664	84.3
Shell CDP	83	-	-	95	100.0	0.0	0.0	0.0	0.0	33.7	0.0	36.5	0.0	0.0	50	100.0
Sheridan city	17,477	17,940	2.6	17,844	90.5	0.2	0.4	2.7	6.1	21.7	18.9	37.9	29.9	30.3	8,009	84.4
Shoshoni town	650	644	-0.9	515	92.8	0.0	0.0	2.7	4.5	19.0	23.9	54.0	65.7	7.1	257	80.9
Sinclair town	433	395	-8.8	418	79.9	0.5	0.7	0.0	18.9	15.8	17.5	48.9	41.8	16.4	197	86.8
Slater CDP	80	-	-	94	100.0	0.0	0.0	0.0	0.0	40.4	41.5	60.4	69.6	23.2	26	50.0
Sleepy Hollow CDP	1,308	-	-	1,368	98.0	0.0	0.0	1.0	1.1	18.0	6.7	37.3	34.9	25.6	505	100.0
Smoot CDP	195	-	-	217	88.9	0.0	0.0	0.0	11.1	0.0	18.4	13.8	53.1	19.2	60	100.0
South Greeley CDP	4,217	-	-	4,134	70.4	1.2	0.6	3.1	24.7	26.6	10.7	35.8	49.1	8.6	1,532	95.6
South Park CDP	1,731	-	-	1,812	84.3	8.1	0.7	0.0	6.9	28.9	7.3	41.7	4.7	56.7	719	100.0
Star Valley Ranch town	1,527	1,659	8.6	1,961	95.9	0.0	0.2	1.9	2.0	18.6	26.0	51.3	34.6	27.4	819	97.8
Story CDP	828	-	-	660	95.6	0.0	0.0	0.0	4.4	3.9	30.2	63.1	21.1	18.9	396	87.6
Sundance town	1,182	1,292	9.3	1,705	87.4	0.0	0.0	9.4	3.2	28.4	13.1	32.2	38.3	25.5	615	95.8
Superior town	341	312	-8.5	212	78.8	0.0	0.0	0.0	21.2	18.9	13.2	40.8	48.1	7.7	95	84.2
Table Rock CDP	-	-	-	-	-	-	-	-	-	-	-	-	-	-	-	-
Taylor CDP	90	-	-	110	100.0	0.0	0.0	0.0	0.0	49.1	22.7	31.1	23.2	0.0	30	100.0
Ten Sleep town	259	250	-3.5	214	98.1	0.0	0.0	1.9	0.0	15.9	27.6	54.5	36.0	29.2	111	98.2
Teton Village CDP	330	-	-	440	97.3	0.0	0.0	0.0	2.7	16.8	41.4	62.0	13.4	86.6	164	100.0

1 May be of any race.

Table A. All Places — **Population and Housing**

STATE City, town, township, borough, or CDP (county if applicable)	Population				Race and Hispanic or Latino origin (percent)					Age (percent)			Educational attainment of persons age 25 and older		Occupied housing units	
	2010 census total population	2019 estimated population	Percent change 2010–2019	ACS total population estimate 2015–2019	White alone, not Hispanic or Latino	Black alone, not Hispanic or Latino	Asian alone, not Hispanic or Latino	All other races or 2 or more races, not Hispanic or Latino	Hispanic or Latino[1]	Under 18 years old	Age 65 years and older	Median age	Percent High school diploma or less	Percent Bachelor's degree or more	Total	Percent with a computer
	1	2	3	4	5	6	7	8	9	10	11	12	13	14	15	16
WYOMING—Con.																
Thayne town	366	394	7.7	514	94.2	0.0	0.0	0.8	5.1	26.5	18.7	36.0	57.4	10.7	177	96.6
Thermopolis town	3,016	2,764	-8.4	2,703	96.1	0.0	0.0	2.2	1.7	20.9	25.7	44.7	38.2	25.3	1,244	87.1
Torrington city	6,501	6,624	1.9	6,675	82.8	0.1	0.9	1.9	14.3	21.1	18.5	39.5	38.9	24.5	2,510	85.2
Turnerville CDP	192	-	-	106	100.0	0.0	0.0	0.0	0.0	25.5	21.7	56.0	0.0	36.7	52	100.0
Upton town	1,100	1,056	-4.0	1,075	92.1	0.8	0.0	5.8	1.3	27.3	16.3	43.5	51.0	23.0	477	87.0
Urie CDP	262	-	-	318	100.0	0.0	0.0	0.0	0.0	10.1	0.0	29.7	33.0	0.0	78	100.0
Van Tassell town	18	18	0.0	21	100.0	0.0	0.0	0.0	0.0	0.0	23.8	39.5	26.3	36.8	12	100.0
Veteran CDP	23	-	-	48	100.0	0.0	0.0	0.0	0.0	18.8	0.0	18.8	52.4	0.0	11	100.0
Vista West CDP................	951	-	-	856	92.1	0.0	0.0	6.9	1.1	24.9	15.7	49.4	35.8	28.7	352	93.5
Wamsutter town................	451	467	3.5	171	70.8	0.0	4.1	5.8	19.3	11.7	17.5	48.9	63.6	15.9	88	86.4
Warren AFB CDP	3,072	-	-	2,456	57.8	13.2	3.0	5.4	20.6	29.9	0.0	22.0	14.2	46.6	539	100.0
Washam CDP....................	51	-	-	-	-	-	-	-	-	-	-	-	-	-	-	-
Westview Circle CDP.........	52	-	-	-	-	-	-	-	-	-	-	-	-	-	-	-
Wheatland town................	3,625	3,462	-4.5	3,558	82.2	0.0	2.7	4.4	10.7	13.1	21.2	49.0	49.8	16.5	1,737	80.5
Whiting CDP	83	-	-	134	100.0	0.0	0.0	0.0	0.0	0.0	28.4	61.3	71.6	0.0	73	83.6
Wilson CDP	1,482	-	-	1,463	92.3	5.3	0.0	0.0	2.3	30.1	22.9	43.6	0.0	79.6	551	100.0
Woods Landing-Jelm CDP	97	-	-	113	100.0	0.0	0.0	0.0	0.0	7.1	22.1	53.6	58.9	17.8	40	85.0
Worland city.....................	5,487	5,024	-8.4	5,180	76.3	0.0	0.0	3.6	20.1	27.1	20.1	38.9	41.8	23.0	2,182	85.3
Wright town	1,807	1,753	-3.0	1,266	81.6	0.9	3.4	2.8	11.2	23.8	9.7	35.9	44.9	22.0	525	98.3
Yoder town.......................	151	154	2.0	169	98.8	0.0	0.0	0.0	1.2	4.1	29.6	57.4	61.7	20.3	71	64.8
Y-O Ranch CDP................	195	-	-	115	100.0	0.0	0.0	0.0	0.0	24.3	44.3	48.6	81.5	0.0	32	100.0

1 May be of any race.

TABLE B.

Incorporated Places, Census Designated Places (CDPs), and Minor Civil Divisions (MCDs) of 10,000 or More Population

(For explanation of symbols see page xvi)

Table B—Incorporated Places, Census Designated Places (CDPs), and Minor Civil Divisions (MCDs) of 10,000 or More Population

STATE City, town, township, borough, or CDP (county if applicable)	Land area 2010 (sq mi)	Population — Total persons 2010	Total persons 2019	Percent change 2010–2019	Persons per square mile 2019	Population characteristics 2015–2019 — Percent foreign born	Percent living in the same house as previous year	Income and poverty 2015–2019 — Median household income	Percent of households with income below poverty level	Median value of owner-occupied housing units	Employment, 2015–2019 — Percent in civilian labor force	Unemployment rate	Households, 2015–2019 (percent of households) — Family households	One person households
	1	2	3	4	5	6	7	8	9	10	11	12	13	14
UNITED STATES	3533043.75	305,758,105	328,239,523	7.4	92.9	13.6	85.8	62,843	12.9	217,500	63.0	5.3	65.5	27.9
ALABAMA	50646.64	4,780,125	4,903,185	2.6	96.8	3.5	86.3	50,536	16.7	142,700	57.1	5.9	65.7	29.8
Alabaster city	25.25	31,112	33,487	7.6	1326.2	6.0	88.2	80,072	7.0	173,000	67.0	4.4	74.9	21.5
Albertville city	26.78	21,209	21,711	2.4	810.7	14.2	86.9	45,867	20.5	120,100	58.0	2.0	70.3	25.8
Alexander City city	42.00	14,984	14,317	-4.5	340.9	2.8	88.5	38,328	22.1	101,700	51.5	6.5	67.8	29.9
Anniston city	45.76	22,987	21,287	-7.4	465.2	1.9	80.9	36,051	24.3	97,600	49.6	10.1	58.8	37.6
Athens city	39.86	21,878	27,366	25.1	686.6	4.3	85.5	53,165	14.9	161,400	57.3	8.0	64.7	31.8
Atmore city	21.86	10,167	9,107	-10.4	416.6	0.3	94.0	26,118	32.2	94,300	32.6	15.7	51.5	45.6
Auburn city	60.08	53,439	66,259	24.0	1102.8	10.4	70.2	47,318	28.5	266,200	58.5	4.4	52.7	33.2
Bessemer city	40.54	27,667	26,472	-4.3	653.0	3.1	82.1	32,301	27.3	86,500	54.5	14.9	60.8	34.4
Birmingham city	146.08	212,585	209,403	-1.5	1433.5	3.8	78.8	37,375	24.8	91,100	60.2	9.0	51.5	41.2
Calera city	24.17	11,608	14,717	26.8	608.9	4.7	90.7	61,594	7.2	148,000	68.4	0.8	68.0	26.4
Center Point city	6.19	16,880	16,110	-4.6	2602.6	1.7	84.4	43,515	23.4	97,800	59.7	11.1	66.6	29.1
Chelsea city	23.08	10,680	14,126	32.3	612.0	3.7	88.5	97,727	2.2	232,700	71.8	4.5	81.0	18.3
Cullman city	21.84	15,158	16,034	5.8	734.2	4.5	83.0	48,712	14.3	142,800	59.2	4.6	65.9	30.2
Daphne city	17.18	21,622	26,869	24.3	1564.0	3.8	87.7	71,882	10.7	201,400	62.3	3.4	66.1	27.4
Decatur city	54.16	55,786	54,445	-2.4	1005.3	7.1	85.5	48,429	17.4	134,500	57.8	5.7	62.4	31.6
Dothan city	89.76	65,922	68,941	4.6	768.1	3.0	86.3	47,081	18.2	150,700	57.2	7.2	62.8	33.1
Enterprise city	30.63	26,534	28,376	6.9	926.4	5.0	78.5	62,695	15.1	170,100	58.9	5.7	69.4	27.1
Eufaula city	59.52	13,134	11,709	-10.8	196.7	3.5	85.1	33,132	28.0	128,100	53.8	9.6	64.7	33.8
Fairfield city	3.47	11,106	10,568	-4.8	3045.5	0.8	79.9	40,652	18.8	99,100	54.6	11.5	57.0	41.1
Fairhope city	13.99	16,265	22,677	39.4	1620.9	6.7	88.3	75,197	7.3	299,200	54.8	4.6	72.0	25.6
Florence city	26.48	39,560	40,797	3.1	1540.7	3.1	73.3	40,526	23.7	142,400	55.1	4.9	55.6	34.8
Foley city	32.49	15,358	20,391	32.8	627.6	6.8	88.1	43,614	14.5	177,600	50.3	5.4	53.1	39.5
Forestdale CDP	6.75	10,162	NA	NA	NA	2.4	88.5	59,041	10.9	122,800	62.9	9.3	65.8	31.8
Fort Payne city	56.19	14,096	14,074	-0.2	250.5	10.7	82.6	40,273	21.4	124,900	55.5	6.6	63.5	33.1
Gadsden city	37.31	36,964	35,000	-5.3	938.1	4.7	80.9	32,642	26.3	73,600	52.4	7.5	59.1	36.5
Gardendale city	22.89	13,983	14,177	1.4	619.4	1.2	87.4	72,351	9.5	171,700	60.2	4.3	68.3	30.5
Gulf Shores city	28.18	10,843	12,757	17.7	452.7	4.4	86.5	53,476	7.1	243,100	62.0	5.5	57.6	37.7
Hartselle city	16.44	14,281	14,466	1.3	879.9	2.2	93.5	59,697	9.7	148,600	60.5	3.7	71.2	25.9
Helena city	20.38	16,963	19,925	17.5	977.7	3.5	91.3	87,781	3.8	195,100	70.1	1.2	76.2	21.8
Homewood city	8.34	25,143	25,377	0.9	3042.8	7.6	80.6	84,157	8.9	347,800	71.2	2.7	61.3	32.3
Hoover city	47.89	80,823	85,768	6.1	1790.9	9.4	82.2	89,452	5.9	291,000	68.6	3.3	72.1	24.5
Hueytown city	19.68	16,141	15,322	-5.1	778.6	0.7	85.1	51,519	10.5	116,700	58.8	6.1	70.6	27.1
Huntsville city	214.36	180,395	200,574	11.2	935.7	6.6	78.7	55,305	16.2	182,900	62.6	5.3	57.9	35.7
Irondale city	17.32	12,415	12,893	3.9	744.4	7.0	89.5	56,445	10.3	142,500	65.5	5.3	58.6	33.8
Jacksonville city	10.91	13,175	12,544	-4.8	1149.8	2.4	68.7	41,268	28.3	147,900	56.5	11.0	54.7	32.8
Jasper city	29.06	14,417	13,431	-6.8	462.2	2.7	82.5	49,201	17.6	150,300	53.3	6.3	60.3	32.8
Leeds city	22.48	11,772	12,040	2.3	535.6	3.4	90.9	60,863	7.4	160,500	65.6	3.3	70.7	26.2
Madison city	30.32	43,192	51,593	19.5	1701.6	7.8	84.9	99,188	5.5	253,000	67.3	3.8	71.9	24.6
Millbrook city	14.02	14,995	15,896	6.0	1133.8	1.9	82.9	62,839	12.5	154,300	67.3	3.0	69.7	27.8
Mobile city	139.47	194,659	188,720	-3.1	1353.1	3.4	85.2	42,321	20.0	123,600	57.2	6.2	54.6	39.8
Montgomery city	159.88	205,501	198,525	-3.4	1241.7	4.9	78.0	48,011	18.7	121,200	60.0	6.8	60.0	35.0
Moody city	24.53	11,705	13,065	11.6	532.6	1.6	85.2	63,607	9.6	162,200	66.8	4.3	71.3	25.6
Mountain Brook city	12.83	20,467	20,297	-0.8	1582.0	2.5	89.2	152,355	3.4	628,800	60.5	1.7	78.7	18.2
Muscle Shoals city	16.54	13,154	14,575	10.8	881.2	3.2	92.2	60,629	9.0	147,100	59.1	3.5	69.6	28.3
Northport city	16.89	23,828	26,115	9.6	1546.2	2.8	85.2	59,836	13.8	177,200	65.2	3.7	67.8	26.0
Opelika city	59.07	26,491	30,908	16.7	523.2	3.8	86.8	48,459	18.1	151,300	64.6	5.2	60.7	34.3
Oxford city	31.77	21,533	21,225	-1.4	668.1	7.1	87.2	57,887	9.9	145,300	63.9	4.4	71.2	24.6
Ozark city	34.09	14,894	14,284	-4.1	419.0	3.8	85.0	41,027	19.2	115,500	48.5	10.8	61.4	33.8
Pelham city	38.82	21,466	23,911	11.4	615.9	10.0	89.4	80,510	6.2	189,000	69.5	3.4	69.3	25.9
Pell City city	24.88	12,712	14,045	10.5	564.5	1.7	81.4	54,674	13.0	183,800	59.9	5.6	63.7	31.4
Phenix City city	28.00	32,862	36,487	11.0	1303.1	4.7	81.9	42,089	22.1	129,000	58.0	7.2	62.3	33.2
Pleasant Grove city	9.88	10,119	9,604	-5.1	972.1	0.1	94.0	70,526	5.2	157,400	63.0	5.1	73.6	23.5
Prattville city	33.86	34,041	35,957	5.6	1061.9	3.9	83.9	61,110	14.9	162,700	59.5	4.4	68.6	26.7
Prichard city	25.31	22,633	21,428	-5.3	846.6	0.4	92.6	29,009	31.6	66,100	46.2	12.2	63.9	34.5
Saks CDP	12.18	10,744	NA	NA	NA	3.9	84.7	39,336	18.3	98,200	52.5	11.7	68.7	27.6
Saraland city	32.06	13,801	14,649	6.1	456.9	1.6	83.6	60,633	8.7	149,000	59.3	5.2	69.9	25.6
Scottsboro city	50.66	14,786	14,436	-2.4	285.0	1.7	93.3	42,651	16.2	117,900	53.3	3.7	64.5	32.2
Selma city	13.81	20,756	17,231	-17.0	1247.7	2.0	88.2	27,030	32.4	87,300	49.1	14.6	59.3	37.2
Sylacauga city	20.25	12,803	12,034	-6.0	594.3	1.5	79.2	36,068	26.3	131,600	52.6	8.9	60.6	36.4
Talladega city	25.51	16,054	15,457	-3.7	605.9	2.0	81.3	27,719	26.2	86,600	41.8	14.5	60.0	36.5
Tillmans Corner CDP	12.97	17,398	NA	NA	NA	9.1	92.9	44,701	15.8	114,400	62.6	5.0	68.5	27.7
Troy city	28.34	18,192	18,957	4.2	668.9	5.8	78.3	31,515	30.8	154,000	55.1	5.6	47.1	42.2
Trussville city	34.35	19,874	22,635	13.9	659.0	1.5	91.1	97,226	5.8	255,100	65.2	3.3	80.6	17.0
Tuscaloosa city	61.85	90,275	101,129	12.0	1635.1	4.6	75.5	45,268	21.7	178,900	55.8	6.7	54.9	35.4
Vestavia Hills city	19.87	33,766	34,413	1.9	1731.9	6.3	86.5	109,485	4.3	376,200	66.7	2.0	73.1	23.0
ALASKA	571016.95	710,249	731,545	3.0	1.3	7.8	82.1	77,640	9.4	270,400	65.5	7.2	65.7	26.1
Anchorage municipality	1706.80	291,836	288,000	-1.3	168.7	10.9	80.2	84,928	7.6	314,800	68.5	5.7	64.4	26.3
Badger CDP	65.64	19,482	NA	NA	NA	3.1	86.1	81,111	8.2	224,900	67.0	7.6	71.7	20.5
College CDP	18.72	12,964	NA	NA	NA	9.4	82.0	80,561	9.3	244,700	69.6	4.3	59.7	30.2
Fairbanks city	31.76	31,556	30,917	-2.0	973.5	6.6	71.6	62,602	8.7	211,500	54.3	7.7	64.6	24.9
Juneau city and borough	2703.98	31,276	31,974	2.2	11.8	8.8	81.0	88,390	6.9	345,900	69.0	4.6	61.3	29.1
Knik-Fairview CDP	83.21	14,923	NA	NA	NA	3.2	86.5	87,331	9.9	243,200	62.3	7.8	74.7	18.5
Lakes CDP	12.59	8,364	NA	NA	NA	2.2	83.2	86,925	11.2	277,400	59.1	9.1	78.4	15.8
Tanaina CDP	30.35	8,197	NA	NA	NA	4.6	83.6	77,140	9.6	257,100	64.1	10.5	76.7	17.4
Wasilla city	12.40	7,806	10,838	38.8	874.0	6.0	81.7	63,587	11.6	243,400	53.4	8.0	66.3	27.7
ARIZONA	113653.15	6,392,288	7,278,717	13.9	64.0	13.3	82.6	58,945	13.6	225,500	59.4	5.9	65.3	27.3
Anthem CDP	7.91	21,700	NA	NA	NA	4.5	81.3	102,719	5.3	346,800	62.0	4.3	76.4	19.9
Apache Junction city	35.07	35,709	42,571	19.2	1213.9	6.5	79.8	45,653	14.3	105,600	45.7	8.4	56.1	36.6
Arizona City CDP	6.13	10,475	NA	NA	NA	8.5	80.6	40,355	17.3	112,500	45.9	10.1	60.7	36.9
Avondale city	45.25	76,132	87,931	15.5	1943.2	16.2	84.8	61,825	11.9	215,100	68.8	5.9	75.6	18.3
Buckeye city	393.11	50,851	79,620	56.6	202.5	10.4	85.3	71,707	8.7	222,700	55.4	5.6	82.3	13.2

Table B. Incorporated Places, Census Designated Places (CDPs), and Minor Civil Divisions (MCDs) of 10,000 or More Population — **Crime, Residential Construction and Local Government Finance**

	Serious crimes known to police, 2018[1]				New residential construction authorized by building permits, 2019			Local government finance, 2017						
	Violent crime		Property crime					General revenue				General expenditure		
									Intergovernmental				Per capita[3]		
STATE City, town, township, borough, or CDP (county if applicable)	Number	Rate[2]	Number	Rate[2]	Value ($1,000)	Number of housing units	Percent single family	Total (mil dol)	Total (mil dol)	Percent from state gov.	Taxes per capita[3]	Total (mil dol)	Total	Capital outlays	Debt outstanding (mil dol)
	15	16	17	18	19	20	21	22	23	24	25	26	27	28	29
UNITED STATES	1,206,836	369	7,196,045	2,200	280,534,198	1,386,048	62.2	X	X	X	X	X	X	X	X
ALABAMA	25,399	520	137,700	2,817	3,545,271	17,748	82.9	X	X	X	X	X	X	X	X
Alabaster city	92	275	579	1,728	15,850	47	100.0	39.5	0.8	51.1	883	27.7	833	48	113.1
Albertville city	24	112	802	3,743	5,817	34	85.3	28.7	1.5	54.1	740	25.7	1,194	149	39.8
Alexander City city	314	2,158	610	4,193	3,638	17	100.0	24.3	2.0	100.0	1,037	27.7	1,902	235	19.9
Anniston city	646	2,992	1,696	7,855	193	2	100.0	44.0	4.9	52.4	1,620	40.4	1,863	77	37.2
Athens city	13	50	768	2,934	59,146	276	100.0	24.7	2.7	48.3	849	20.5	798	68	171.4
Atmore city	NA	NA	NA	NA	646	4	100.0	11.5	2.4	100.0	882	8.8	940	64	10.9
Auburn city	240	366	1,396	2,129	322,197	1,477	35.9	122.1	1.2	41.6	1,435	88.5	1,384	296	305.1
Bessemer city	NA	NA	NA	NA	5,534	38	100.0	64.1	4.8	86.0	1,813	74.3	2,791	379	152.1
Birmingham city	4,025	1,912	13,295	6,314	28,805	196	39.8	517.2	49.6	71.5	1,954	531.4	2,512	433	1451.7
Calera city	265	1,849	429	2,993	31,447	213	100.0	18.7	0.0	0.0	962	24.3	1,744	577	57.4
Center Point city	NA	NA	NA	NA	1,787	18	100.0	3.2	0.0	0.0	188	3.5	215	0	0.0
Chelsea city	NA	NA	NA	NA	46,434	161	100.0	5.8	0.1	100.0	417	4.1	311	27	5.2
Cullman city	32	207	629	4,066	31,293	209	71.3	53.1	3.2	99.9	1,959	53.3	3,387	691	162.6
Daphne city	36	135	463	1,739	86,344	389	100.0	35.6	3.4	100.0	1,093	30.2	1,161	189	33.3
Decatur city	228	421	2,308	4,258	14,732	74	100.0	125.1	15.5	63.0	1,250	93.8	1,723	414	200.5
Dothan city	670	978	2,799	4,084	53,534	246	78.9	112.3	5.2	29.5	1,144	126.9	1,858	387	122.5
Enterprise city	127	446	809	2,842	34,294	290	37.2	37.0	0.8	98.1	1,050	25.7	913	49	87.7
Eufaula city	75	630	469	3,940	2,262	9	100.0	20.1	0.9	99.9	985	16.3	1,355	58	10.5
Fairfield city	224	2,108	855	8,047	0	0	0.0	12.6	0.0	0.0	939	9.4	878	0	57.8
Fairhope city	43	198	537	2,476	128,203	448	90.2	33.0	1.5	48.6	843	34.3	1,638	441	45.3
Florence city	206	516	1,663	4,165	10,653	97	73.2	72.6	3.6	91.0	1,273	63.6	1,588	154	99.0
Foley city	48	256	755	4,029	75,920	515	72.0	48.5	9.7	8.3	1,470	66.1	3,615	1618	159.0
Forestdale CDP	NA	NA	NA	NA	NA	NA	NA	NA	NA	NA	NA	NA	NA	NA	NA
Fort Payne city	NA	NA	NA	NA	2,679	18	100.0	25.4	2.4	0.1	1,057	25.2	1,779	23	16.3
Gadsden city	372	1,057	2,495	7,087	0	0	0.0	66.4	2.8	25.7	1,419	58.0	1,631	64	93.1
Gardendale city	94	676	347	2,495	9,308	48	100.0	18.7	0.8	98.7	1,131	17.6	1,260	138	8.2
Gulf Shores city	24	200	497	4,137	107,734	460	54.3	33.0	1.3	100.0	2,458	31.6	2,574	179	37.8
Hartselle city	61	424	353	2,454	3,696	30	100.0	16.7	0.6	100.0	788	15.3	1,066	49	37.2
Helena city	61	315	131	676	54,130	186	100.0	8.8	0.4	100.0	345	8.0	419	11	3.1
Homewood city	75	294	956	3,746	19,953	43	100.0	56.0	0.9	100.0	2,037	45.3	1,778	418	65.6
Hoover city	NA	NA	NA	NA	188,289	456	100.0	126.2	8.8	62.7	1,216	129.2	1,516	351	141.6
Hueytown city	71	462	531	3,456	1,489	7	100.0	14.9	0.3	100.0	838	13.5	874	77	3.1
Huntsville city	NA	NA	NA	NA	84,644	1,603	89.6	440.2	35.8	93.6	1,575	413.8	2,117	620	983.4
Irondale city	74	593	350	2,803	21,015	108	100.0	18.7	0.3	6.8	1,186	15.9	1,266	18	27.1
Jacksonville city	85	678	433	3,455	3,583	29	100.0	14.1	0.4	100.0	877	14.7	1,168	253	16.8
Jasper city	74	548	1,035	7,660	6,247	32	100.0	24.8	0.6	100.0	1,319	14.7	1,080	3	11.5
Leeds city	NA	NA	NA	NA	4,898	38	100.0	22.8	0.2	100.0	1,765	14.7	1,219	269	0.0
Madison city	NA	NA	NA	NA	123,722	369	100.0	53.5	1.3	100.0	843	53.2	1,081	269	276.7
Millbrook city	44	286	728	4,724	7,320	34	100.0	14.9	0.2	100.0	700	11.4	728	1	17.3
Mobile city	NA	NA	NA	NA	27,413	133	100.0	401.3	18.8	47.7	1,499	358.2	1,883	362	483.5
Montgomery city	1,216	612	8,480	4,269	40,298	263	97.7	270.3	30.4	77.7	984	225.3	1,126	69	356.0
Moody city	56	426	206	1,568	8,883	65	100.0	4.2	0.0	0.0	313	1.7	133	0	0.9
Mountain Brook city	16	79	228	1,119	25,937	34	100.0	38.0	0.8	94.9	1,669	35.6	1,744	255	0.0
Muscle Shoals city	86	608	800	5,657	16,194	137	100.0	23.8	1.0	56.8	1,147	21.8	1,550	182	58.7
Northport city	89	351	772	3,045	40,884	164	100.0	30.1	4.4	22.1	740	35.3	1,360	339	51.2
Opelika city	168	545	1,214	3,939	75,726	330	95.5	74.7	1.5	51.6	1,892	53.6	1,769	228	204.8
Oxford city	67	317	928	4,388	6,855	66	100.0	43.2	0.6	100.0	1,801	58.8	2,755	983	127.1
Ozark city	148	1,031	619	4,311	634	6	100.0	20.1	1.4	50.1	1,032	18.1	1,253	136	0.0
Pelham city	36	151	404	1,699	32,642	103	100.0	52.6	0.0	0.0	1,547	44.8	1,911	103	87.9
Pell City city	NA	NA	NA	NA	18,065	101	96.0	24.2	2.8	100.0	1,367	20.8	1,516	417	65.0
Phenix City city	235	641	1,326	3,616	8,739	58	96.6	47.6	1.5	100.0	938	50.3	1,395	233	121.9
Pleasant Grove city	16	158	127	1,257	6,348	28	100.0	6.1	1.3	100.0	344	6.8	705	139	0.0
Prattville city	83	233	1,221	3,421	69,004	242	100.0	45.9	1.3	38.6	994	37.9	1,069	190	60.5
Prichard city	263	1,217	930	4,303	263	2	100.0	11.5	0.0	0.0	187	15.0	692	0	20.0
Saks CDP	NA	NA	NA	NA	NA	NA	NA	NA	NA	NA	NA	NA	NA	NA	NA
Saraland city	51	347	490	3,332	10,705	41	100.0	20.7	0.0		1,135	17.6	1,205	0	41.5
Scottsboro city	193	1,336	671	4,646	3,834	21	100.0	30.7	1.3	90.2	1,227	29.1	2,002	210	76.0
Selma city	NA	NA	NA	NA	50	1	100.0	23.6	1.8	100.0	990	24.0	1,309	64	24.7
Sylacauga city	77	632	614	5,039	587	4	100.0	20.3	1.0	57.2	1,020	18.2	1,490	67	58.6
Talladega city	124	808	805	5,247	235	3	100.0	19.7	1.5	70.6	854	18.3	1,193	192	28.9
Tillmans Corner CDP	NA	NA	NA	NA	NA	NA	NA	NA	NA	NA	NA	NA	NA	NA	NA
Troy city	303	1,582	961	5,016	10,851	89	100.0	48.2	1.1	71.6	715	74.6	3,910	955	78.3
Trussville city	113	511	654	2,960	70,457	203	100.0	41.8	1.2	57.5	1,717	34.7	1,598	323	134.9
Tuscaloosa city	514	505	4,415	4,339	212,032	1,165	27.6	191.2	52.2	36.2	896	157.0	1,576	355	191.8
Vestavia Hills city	30	87	435	1,266	41,010	90	100.0	36.2	0.0		1,029	18.6	542	0	46.5
ALASKA	6,526	885	24,339	3,301	412,921	1,680	68.3	X	X	X	X	X	X	X	X
Anchorage municipality	3,824	1,310	14,389	4,928	298,202	1,059	79.1	1432.3	620.4	93.7	2,070	1395.3	4,741	734	1569.1
Badger CDP	NA	NA	NA	NA	NA	NA	NA	NA	NA	NA	NA	NA	NA	NA	NA
College CDP	NA	NA	NA	NA	NA	NA	NA	NA	NA	NA	NA	NA	NA	NA	NA
Fairbanks city	193	610	1,354	4,280	0	0	0.0	60.0	20.9	99.4	767	49.4	1,558	484	4.8
Juneau city and borough	264	827	1,550	4,856	NA	NA	NA	341.6	89.2	91.3	3,206	327.3	10,198	1922	149.8
Knik-Fairview CDP	NA	NA	NA	NA	NA	NA	NA	NA	NA	NA	NA	NA	NA	NA	NA
Lakes CDP	NA	NA	NA	NA	NA	NA	NA	NA	NA	NA	NA	NA	NA	NA	NA
Tanaina CDP	NA	NA	NA	NA	NA	NA	NA	NA	NA	NA	NA	NA	NA	NA	NA
Wasilla city	61	580	637	6,054	9,165	37	67.6	22.0	2.2	82.1	1,326	21.9	2,162	491	2.0
ARIZONA	34,058	475	191,974	2,677	10,850,556	46,580	73.0	X	X	X	X	X	X	X	X
Anthem CDP	NA	NA	NA	NA	NA	NA	NA	NA	NA	NA	NA	NA	NA	NA	NA
Apache Junction city	81	196	773	1,874	15,494	108	100.0	24.7	10.1	100.0	323	37.5	923	0	6.1
Arizona City CDP	NA	NA	NA	NA	NA	NA	NA	NA	NA	NA	NA	NA	NA	NA	NA
Avondale city	286	336	2,739	3,215	28,613	104	100.0	112.5	33.6	96.8	630	103.1	1,216	200	60.1
Buckeye city	125	175	1,348	1,890	710,666	2,652	100.0	80.9	19.3	96.6	659	68.0	993	33	89.2

1 Data for serious crimes have not been adjusted for underreporting. This may affect comparability between geographic areas over time.
2 Per 100,000 population estimated by the FBI.   3 Based on population estimated as of July 1 of the year shown.

Table B. Incorporated Places, Census Designated Places (CDPs), and Minor Civil Divisions (MCDs) of 10,000 or More Population — Land Area, Population, and Households, and Employment

STATE City, town, township, borough, or CDP (county if applicable)	Land area 2010 (sq mi)	Population Total persons 2010	Population Total persons 2019	Population Percent change 2010–2019	Population Persons per square mile 2019	Population characteristics 2015–2019 Percent foreign born	Population characteristics 2015–2019 Percent living in the same house as previous year	Income and poverty 2015–2019 Median household income	Income and poverty 2015–2019 Percent of households with income below poverty level	Median value of owner-occupied housing units	Employment, 2015–2019 Percent in civilian labor force	Employment, 2015–2019 Unemployment rate	Households, 2015–2019 (percent of households) Family households	Households, 2015–2019 (percent of households) One person households
	1	2	3	4	5	6	7	8	9	10	11	12	13	14
ARIZONA—Con.														
Bullhead City city	59.38	39,541	40,884	3.4	688.5	8.5	80.6	41,507	17.0	140,300	46.8	8.5	61.8	30.8
Camp Verde town	43.12	10,875	11,187	2.9	259.4	6.1	85.5	39,681	22.4	193,100	45.2	5.6	67.4	27.2
Casa Grande city	110.63	48,564	58,632	20.7	530.0	10.3	79.2	52,841	15.2	150,400	56.2	6.6	70.7	23.1
Casas Adobes CDP	26.65	66,795	NA	NA	NA	9.9	81.6	64,224	9.1	206,500	62.8	5.7	60.7	31.8
Catalina Foothills CDP	41.85	50,796	NA	NA	NA	11.9	83.9	92,929	6.4	440,100	53.4	4.4	62.7	32.2
Chandler city	65.12	236,157	261,165	10.6	4010.5	15.7	81.3	82,925	7.2	300,800	71.2	3.7	68.7	24.5
Chino Valley town	63.37	10,817	12,375	14.4	195.3	6.3	88.1	49,631	9.0	229,100	53.4	4.8	62.5	29.6
Coolidge city	72.93	11,845	13,130	10.8	180.0	6.0	82.5	49,266	16.7	113,100	56.3	12.7	77.5	16.1
Cottonwood city	16.70	11,184	12,253	9.6	733.7	4.7	78.1	42,500	12.7	189,400	54.4	3.5	48.3	42.2
Douglas city	9.98	17,509	16,193	-7.5	1622.5	23.8	76.7	35,514	29.1	100,300	32.4	11.4	69.9	27.1
Drexel Heights CDP	19.46	27,749	NA	NA	NA	14.2	88.0	57,790	14.4	137,200	61.6	6.4	78.7	16.7
El Mirage city	9.90	31,797	35,753	12.4	3611.4	12.9	88.5	58,216	12.7	160,800	69.1	5.6	77.1	17.2
Eloy city	113.49	16,665	19,625	17.8	172.9	19.1	79.0	39,835	26.7	100,100	23.1	10.4	73.2	22.4
Flagstaff city	66.02	66,006	75,038	13.7	1136.6	5.8	65.6	58,748	18.6	351,600	66.5	7.6	52.1	27.3
Florence town	62.62	25,452	27,422	7.7	437.9	14.0	73.9	49,534	12.8	153,500	14.3	10.8	64.9	29.6
Flowing Wells CDP	3.81	16,419	NA	NA	NA	17.9	82.7	38,434	22.9	65,100	59.5	8.3	59.3	33.4
Fort Mohave CDP	16.70	14,364	NA	NA	NA	6.6	78.6	50,931	13.4	163,200	46.7	8.6	71.3	21.4
Fortuna Foothills CDP	40.06	26,265	NA	NA	NA	12.6	82.4	50,749	10.4	126,300	33.9	6.7	65.7	27.2
Fountain Hills town	20.28	22,489	25,200	12.1	1242.6	8.3	84.0	85,200	4.8	402,100	52.3	3.7	64.9	31.2
Gilbert town	68.48	208,462	254,114	21.9	3710.8	9.3	81.4	96,857	5.4	328,700	70.6	4.1	77.6	16.6
Glendale city	61.59	226,172	252,381	11.6	4097.8	17.4	82.5	55,020	16.8	214,700	63.7	5.8	66.8	26.2
Gold Canyon CDP	22.36	0	NA	0.0	NA	5.1	85.5	75,518	8.5	298,100	33.0	3.3	71.7	24.2
Goodyear city	191.20	65,261	86,840	33.1	454.2	12.1	86.3	83,866	7.1	290,800	57.1	4.5	78.2	16.5
Green Valley CDP	32.06	21,391	NA	NA	NA	8.0	84.2	49,147	6.5	175,400	15.4	7.8	56.6	39.7
Kingman city	37.55	28,076	31,013	10.5	825.9	3.6	74.5	49,029	12.9	152,900	49.0	6.4	65.0	28.7
Lake Havasu City city	46.34	52,531	55,865	6.3	1205.5	7.6	81.0	53,605	10.0	248,200	47.2	5.9	63.2	28.5
Marana town	121.10	34,556	49,030	41.9	404.9	10.1	85.2	85,812	5.4	252,100	58.6	4.3	77.2	16.9
Maricopa city	42.80	43,488	52,127	19.9	1217.9	11.6	82.5	74,515	9.4	202,100	64.4	3.9	77.0	17.7
Mesa city	138.09	440,092	518,012	17.7	3751.3	11.8	80.6	58,181	12.9	226,500	64.2	4.9	66.1	26.0
New Kingman-Butler CDP	4.97	12,134	NA	NA	NA	3.2	78.4	36,823	21.3	71,200	46.6	13.5	64.6	26.9
New River CDP	56.13	14,952	NA	NA	NA	6.1	91.8	85,294	4.2	376,700	61.8	3.2	70.9	22.1
Nogales city	20.81	20,839	20,103	-3.5	966.0	41.6	87.1	29,339	32.6	119,700	50.8	9.6	71.3	26.4
Oro Valley town	34.87	41,045	46,044	12.2	1320.4	8.3	80.6	83,341	6.0	311,800	48.1	5.7	69.2	25.9
Paradise Valley town	15.38	12,755	14,637	14.8	951.7	10.0	92.2	211,393	3.6	1,516,200	55.3	2.1	81.2	15.2
Payson town	19.35	15,299	15,813	3.4	817.2	5.0	83.0	51,280	9.2	236,300	44.3	4.9	65.6	28.4
Peoria city	175.99	154,048	175,961	14.2	999.8	9.1	85.1	75,323	7.1	264,500	63.2	5.1	72.0	23.3
Phoenix city	517.67	1,446,691	1,680,992	16.2	3247.2	19.4	83.7	57,459	15.4	235,400	67.1	5.4	63.9	27.9
Prescott city	44.94	39,770	44,299	11.4	985.7	5.1	80.6	55,734	10.8	347,700	42.5	5.9	58.1	34.9
Prescott Valley town	40.89	38,877	46,515	19.6	1137.6	7.8	81.8	51,909	11.5	228,700	52.1	6.9	65.2	28.6
Queen Creek town	32.39	26,736	50,890	90.3	1571.2	6.0	83.9	105,729	5.9	348,600	66.3	3.5	81.7	15.3
Rio Rico CDP	62.26	18,962	NA	NA	NA	31.0	88.6	51,475	14.5	146,300	58.5	6.1	84.4	13.6
Saddlebrooke CDP	29.24	9,614	NA	NA	NA	6.0	91.2	80,154	6.1	361,600	17.4	4.8	72.6	25.0
Sahuarita town	31.69	26,000	31,421	20.9	991.5	9.9	84.6	80,525	6.2	214,100	52.3	3.6	77.4	19.6
San Luis city	34.09	27,909	34,778	24.6	1020.2	50.2	89.4	37,255	23.8	117,400	56.6	14.2	90.8	7.3
San Tan Valley CDP	36.67	81,321	NA	NA	NA	7.2	82.3	67,880	8.8	212,900	63.1	5.7	75.2	19.9
Scottsdale city	183.99	217,492	258,069	18.7	1402.6	12.0	82.8	88,213	7.3	475,300	62.1	3.3	55.2	35.9
Sedona city	19.03	10,034	10,339	3.0	543.3	11.9	85.8	61,470	12.7	507,400	45.8	5.9	55.9	38.2
Show Low city	65.50	10,667	11,442	7.3	174.7	6.9	75.8	46,310	18.8	170,800	51.7	6.1	70.7	24.1
Sierra Vista city	152.22	45,276	43,045	-4.9	282.8	8.8	77.8	59,585	12.3	172,600	47.8	6.0	65.9	29.0
Sierra Vista Southeast CDP	110.87	14,797	NA	NA	NA	5.1	91.9	66,011	9.7	188,900	55.6	4.3	73.7	24.4
Somerton city	7.42	14,297	16,554	15.8	2231.0	40.5	90.9	38,315	28.9	127,000	63.3	8.7	85.5	12.4
Sun City CDP	14.42	37,499	NA	NA	NA	5.7	86.1	40,586	10.5	159,900	18.8	5.8	48.9	46.4
Sun City West CDP	10.85	24,535	NA	NA	NA	5.6	88.0	52,196	8.7	221,500	12.6	7.4	56.9	39.3
Sun Lakes CDP	5.37	13,975	NA	NA	NA	6.3	85.9	56,779	6.8	272,400	21.3	5.4	62.1	35.8
Surprise city	108.06	117,473	141,664	20.6	1311.0	8.5	86.7	69,076	6.7	239,500	55.5	5.8	74.8	20.2
Tanque Verde CDP	32.32	16,901	NA	NA	NA	7.1	90.2	101,508	4.2	386,800	50.6	3.0	76.0	19.6
Tempe city	39.98	161,774	195,805	21.0	4897.6	16.0	71.9	57,994	17.8	272,900	69.1	5.1	48.0	33.1
Tucson city	238.01	526,634	548,073	4.1	2302.7	15.3	75.8	43,425	20.6	155,300	60.5	7.8	55.0	34.6
Tucson Estates CDP	12.99	12,192	NA	NA	NA	7.6	88.2	48,566	8.6	132,200	44.4	3.0	64.9	30.3
Vail CDP	22.68	10,208	NA	NA	NA	6.0	87.3	85,927	6.1	237,500	62.1	3.8	81.4	14.2
Valencia West CDP	9.91	9,355	NA	NA	NA	15.1	85.3	63,368	12.9	187,600	64.2	3.4	80.8	15.0
Verde Village CDP	6.86	11,605	NA	NA	NA	9.6	86.0	52,204	14.3	208,800	52.5	4.9	68.3	22.5
Yuma city	121.21	90,717	98,285	8.3	810.9	19.7	79.1	47,998	18.3	143,400	55.9	9.9	72.2	22.2
ARKANSAS	52037.53	2,916,031	3,017,804	3.5	58.0	4.8	84.6	47,597	16.7	127,800	57.9	5.1	66.1	28.6
Arkadelphia city	7.39	10,704	10,726	0.2	1451.4	3.4	67.8	33,133	28.1	121,200	55.3	2.5	52.4	36.4
Batesville city	11.60	10,244	10,878	6.2	937.8	6.5	79.2	45,202	16.8	124,600	57.6	5.0	61.4	32.5
Bella Vista city	45.31	26,510	28,872	8.9	637.2	2.0	84.7	67,550	5.0	168,000	52.5	3.0	70.9	24.9
Benton city	22.73	30,766	36,820	19.7	1619.9	3.3	84.2	59,029	10.2	149,400	65.9	3.9	68.1	29.1
Bentonville city	33.77	35,356	54,909	55.3	1626.0	15.5	81.3	80,392	7.5	232,600	69.7	2.3	67.0	24.4
Blytheville city	20.74	15,614	13,455	-13.8	648.7	1.8	77.2	38,765	25.5	79,400	61.9	9.5	64.2	28.8
Bryant city	20.49	16,666	20,968	25.8	1023.3	3.5	84.6	66,688	7.3	165,400	70.8	2.5	64.1	29.8
Cabot city	20.76	24,119	26,352	9.3	1269.4	3.4	84.3	60,591	10.6	154,000	61.6	3.1	71.2	24.1
Camden city	16.53	12,182	10,749	-11.8	650.3	0.7	90.2	30,199	32.7	77,000	55.0	7.7	59.8	39.1
Centerton city	13.58	9,583	16,244	69.5	1196.2	5.1	82.1	75,631	8.0	185,400	73.1	2.0	75.6	18.8
Conway city	46.03	58,874	67,638	14.9	1469.4	4.4	84.0	47,221	20.3	171,600	63.0	3.2	57.7	31.0
El Dorado city	16.20	18,895	17,651	-6.6	1089.6	2.7	87.9	42,595	21.6	88,600	55.1	6.4	62.3	34.6
Fayetteville city	54.03	73,580	87,590	19.0	1621.1	6.8	70.7	43,690	23.6	207,600	62.7	5.0	47.2	35.9
Forrest City city	20.25	15,422	13,820	-10.4	682.5	2.1	84.7	30,817	28.5	65,100	37.8	5.3	60.9	32.5
Fort Smith city	63.29	86,266	87,891	1.9	1388.7	12.4	80.0	41,724	19.8	121,800	59.5	4.8	60.7	33.2
Harrison city	11.20	12,949	13,080	1.0	1167.9	0.6	78.0	40,271	19.8	117,900	60.1	6.2	57.3	36.3
Helena-West Helena city	13.09	12,474	10,299	-17.4	786.8	0.5	77.8	22,177	36.6	73,400	50.2	11.8	60.0	36.5
Hope city	10.68	10,119	9,599	-5.1	898.8	8.3	85.1	37,832	23.1	77,900	60.3	4.6	72.5	22.8
Hot Springs city	37.44	37,941	38,797	2.3	1036.2	6.7	81.5	37,552	22.5	122,900	52.2	5.7	51.7	42.6
Hot Springs Village CDP	56.94	12,807	NA	NA	NA	2.3	84.2	58,899	6.9	207,800	28.2	4.1	69.3	27.0
Jacksonville city	28.56	28,354	28,235	-0.4	988.6	4.0	82.4	48,727	17.8	125,800	53.7	6.0	68.0	27.7

Table B. Incorporated Places, Census Designated Places (CDPs), and Minor Civil Divisions (MCDs) of 10,000 or More Population — Crime, Residential Construction and Local Government Finance

STATE City, town, township, borough, or CDP (county if applicable)	Serious crimes known to police, 2018[1] Violent crime Number	Violent crime Rate[2]	Property crime Number	Property crime Rate[2]	New residential construction authorized by building permits, 2019 Value ($1,000)	Number of housing units	Percent single family	Local government finance, 2017 General revenue Total (mil dol)	Intergovernmental Total (mil dol)	Intergovernmental Percent from state gov.	Taxes per capita[3]	General expenditure Total (mil dol)	Per capita[3] Total	Per capita Capital outlays	Debt outstanding (mil dol)
	15	16	17	18	19	20	21	22	23	24	25	26	27	28	29
ARIZONA—Con.															
Bullhead City city	149	369	1,444	3,578	56,969	248	99.2	54.2	17.2	100.0	358	53.4	1,327	205	42.5
Camp Verde town	31	276	212	1,885	4,802	21	100.0	5.6	2.0	97.4	269	5.5	487	4	2.6
Casa Grande city	346	613	1,478	2,617	132,998	567	100.0	83.0	23.6	90.5	633	79.4	1,426	154	90.7
Casas Adobes CDP	NA	NA	NA	NA	NA	NA	NA	NA	NA	NA	NA	NA	NA	NA	NA
Catalina Foothills CDP	NA	NA	NA	NA	NA	NA	NA	NA	NA	NA	NA	NA	NA	NA	NA
Chandler city	606	237	5,430	2,121	311,470	1,033	56.2	375.8	99.9	91.8	691	449.0	1,771	404	318.9
Chino Valley town	42	355	179	1,512	12,854	78	100.0	11.8	4.9	100.0	428	12.3	1,047	49	21.3
Coolidge city	37	289	433	3,379	33,771	241	80.5	16.5	7.8	77.6	488	16.1	1,269	206	7.9
Cottonwood city	NA	NA	NA	NA	25,642	247	17.8	30.0	7.9	70.3	1,239	31.4	2,619	906	50.2
Douglas city	NA	NA	NA	NA	777	9	44.4	24.3	6.8	90.8	542	21.7	1,342	64	18.2
Drexel Heights CDP	NA	NA	NA	NA	NA	NA	NA	NA	NA	NA	NA	NA	NA	NA	NA
El Mirage city	77	216	933	2,611	26,910	123	100.0	37.5	11.3	100.0	339	41.4	1,168	105	25.6
Eloy city	81	414	351	1,796	24,373	127	100.0	22.8	9.3	95.3	438	19.3	1,007	327	10.3
Flagstaff city	342	469	2,465	3,384	69,666	472	60.0	146.3	37.1	86.3	924	133.5	1,854	273	79.8
Florence town	34	131	127	489	111,946	385	100.0	28.0	12.0	90.8	294	22.7	878	57	70.6
Flowing Wells CDP	NA	NA	NA	NA	NA	NA	NA	NA	NA	NA	NA	NA	NA	NA	NA
Fort Mohave CDP	NA	NA	NA	NA	NA	NA	NA	NA	NA	NA	NA	NA	NA	NA	NA
Fortuna Foothills CDP	NA	NA	NA	NA	NA	NA	NA	NA	NA	NA	NA	NA	NA	NA	NA
Fountain Hills town	NA	NA	NA	NA	21,395	65	84.6	20.9	7.1	100.0	520	19.8	801	18	9.3
Gilbert town	234	95	3,273	1,323	401,587	1,705	67.0	317.7	88.6	94.1	679	260.6	1,074	161	407.8
Glendale city	1,167	467	10,186	4,078	113,567	583	42.2	390.7	98.4	88.8	808	401.4	1,620	269	804.4
Gold Canyon CDP	NA	NA	NA	NA	NA	NA	NA	NA	NA	NA	NA	NA	NA	NA	NA
Goodyear city	203	247	2,081	2,533	510,953	2,058	77.8	152.2	31.4	100.0	1,066	136.3	1,705	357	269.2
Green Valley CDP	NA	NA	NA	NA	NA	NA	NA	NA	NA	NA	NA	NA	NA	NA	NA
Kingman city	118	398	1,152	3,883	49,195	295	94.6	49.9	13.2	91.4	656	41.2	1,402	179	36.0
Lake Havasu City city	88	161	830	1,518	64,073	353	87.5	105.1	27.6	80.7	599	88.8	1,633	130	259.3
Marana town	33	71	1,076	2,317	259,358	808	100.0	98.7	44.7	34.4	1,062	87.0	1,936	787	104.3
Maricopa city	93	191	489	1,005	253,632	1,003	100.0	56.0	22.4	87.0	573	65.7	1,368	411	41.4
Mesa city	1,837	364	10,024	1,985	513,528	1,985	86.1	651.7	206.3	77.4	439	699.2	1,398	157	1536.5
New Kingman-Butler CDP	NA	NA	NA	NA	NA	NA	NA	NA	NA	NA	NA	NA	NA	NA	NA
New River CDP	NA	NA	NA	NA	NA	NA	NA	NA	NA	NA	NA	NA	NA	NA	NA
Nogales city	41	205	610	3,054	626	2	100.0	30.8	11.4	82.9	555	31.2	1,542	8	33.5
Oro Valley town	17	38	610	1,360	85,547	221	97.3	47.3	19.0	100.0	479	48.2	1,081	117	47.5
Paradise Valley town	3	21	196	1,350	128,741	95	87.4	25.8	4.3	100.0	1,125	27.3	1,901	150	8.7
Payson town	63	405	403	2,592	22,552	76	94.7	21.3	8.1	84.4	630	22.0	1,418	40	17.9
Peoria city	388	228	3,241	1,905	297,709	1,990	68.5	266.7	67.5	100.0	683	253.6	1,508	168	274.9
Phoenix city	12,110	733	57,732	3,492	1,893,626	9,898	42.2	3254.8	900.6	75.3	767	2422.3	1,483	157	7724.4
Prescott city	136	315	896	2,075	151,393	542	80.1	85.6	21.9	75.6	877	91.6	2,146	485	98.9
Prescott Valley town	67	148	776	1,712	157,689	720	63.1	57.3	18.3	88.6	564	49.4	1,111	172	68.4
Queen Creek town	NA	NA	NA	NA	545,472	1,485	100.0	88.5	11.2	100.0	1,029	57.7	1,335	137	154.7
Rio Rico CDP	NA	NA	NA	NA	NA	NA	NA	NA	NA	NA	NA	NA	NA	NA	NA
Saddlebrooke CDP	NA	NA	NA	NA	NA	NA	NA	NA	NA	NA	NA	NA	NA	NA	NA
Sahuarita town	38	127	348	1,164	100,674	342	100.0	26.2	12.3	98.6	312	26.3	883	123	46.0
San Luis city	8	24	472	1,427	50,573	339	100.0	27.7	10.5	99.4	270	31.3	955	74	197.1
San Tan Valley CDP	NA	NA	NA	NA	NA	NA	NA	NA	NA	NA	NA	NA	NA	NA	NA
Scottsdale city	422	166	5,683	2,229	394,520	1,259	46.9	495.2	97.2	90.8	1,115	496.6	1,975	371	1218.6
Sedona city	NA	NA	NA	NA	26,218	55	100.0	30.5	5.5	100.0	1,761	25.9	2,510	442	41.8
Show Low city	59	529	427	3,828	28,828	115	96.5	23.8	5.4	98.6	1,070	23.2	2,093	641	21.4
Sierra Vista city	104	244	1,121	2,633	13,506	75	100.0	58.2	17.4	99.8	521	59.6	1,388	187	19.9
Sierra Vista Southeast CDP	NA	NA	NA	NA	NA	NA	NA	NA	NA	NA	NA	NA	NA	NA	NA
Somerton city	19	116	218	1,331	7,156	39	100.0	15.1	7.5	100.0	163	13.2	813	132	18.8
Sun City CDP	NA	NA	NA	NA	NA	NA	NA	NA	NA	NA	NA	NA	NA	NA	NA
Sun City West CDP	NA	NA	NA	NA	NA	NA	NA	NA	NA	NA	NA	NA	NA	NA	NA
Sun Lakes CDP	NA	NA	NA	NA	NA	NA	NA	NA	NA	NA	NA	NA	NA	NA	NA
Surprise city	165	121	2,103	1,539	569,966	1,944	88.2	158.0	43.3	100.0	530	196.0	1,454	345	73.8
Tanque Verde CDP	NA	NA	NA	NA	NA	NA	NA	NA	NA	NA	NA	NA	NA	NA	NA
Tempe city	913	484	7,802	4,138	246,804	1,401	7.3	392.5	81.3	75.2	1,112	351.6	1,892	261	446.0
Tucson city	3,958	737	26,623	4,954	377,542	1,816	55.0	745.4	264.8	75.1	578	721.2	1,332	185	1005.8
Tucson Estates CDP	NA	NA	NA	NA	NA	NA	NA	NA	NA	NA	NA	NA	NA	NA	NA
Vail CDP	NA	NA	NA	NA	NA	NA	NA	NA	NA	NA	NA	NA	NA	NA	NA
Valencia West CDP	NA	NA	NA	NA	NA	NA	NA	NA	NA	NA	NA	NA	NA	NA	NA
Verde Village CDP	NA	NA	NA	NA	NA	NA	NA	NA	NA	NA	NA	NA	NA	NA	NA
Yuma city	491	511	2,041	2,123	91,010	536	98.9	223.8	34.0	93.8	1,613	133.1	1,380	141	24.2
ARKANSAS	16,384	544	87,793	2,913	2,171,607	12,723	61.8	X	X	X	X	X	X	X	X
Arkadelphia city	45	423	256	2,404	1,729	14	85.7	8.6	1.3	90.5	336	9.2	877	216	5.1
Batesville city	46	427	311	2,884	3,449	20	75.0	25.6	7.6	100.0	864	10.8	1,019	512	31.0
Bella Vista city	53	184	193	670	75,019	278	100.0	14.4	10.4	33.0	5	15.7	549	42	0.0
Benton city	182	498	NA	NA	24,938	112	92.9	32.2	3.2	89.3	574	36.4	1,013	354	98.6
Bentonville city	106	205	705	1,366	218,757	1,076	44.0	84.0	14.9	51.0	788	83.7	1,694	699	59.1
Blytheville city	137	990	837	6,046	800	4	100.0	41.7	3.9	42.0	358	40.1	2,858	50	714.2
Bryant city	32	154	889	4,287	24,914	136	97.1	24.2	2.1	65.6	836	20.7	1,027	110	38.5
Cabot city	39	147	403	1,523	17,190	103	100.0	23.7	5.0	44.8	462	22.2	841	78	12.3
Camden city	127	1,167	488	4,485	1,550	8	75.0	11.1	1.5	90.9	607	11.3	1,025	134	15.8
Centerton city	59	399	130	879	134,611	560	73.2	6.5	2.0	33.8	186	4.7	336	38	13.9
Conway city	361	541	2,229	3,341	53,777	332	64.2	113.6	9.1	67.7	574	120.1	1,822	548	438.3
El Dorado city	NA	NA	1,069	5,967	1,748	10	100.0	27.8	10.5	17.0	527	29.9	1,662	351	13.2
Fayetteville city	496	570	3,768	4,331	254,470	1,616	34.3	139.3	27.3	43.7	801	129.7	1,516	452	107.0
Forrest City city	132	933	882	6,236	0	0	0.0	13.6	4.6	31.8	403	11.4	793	42	5.8
Fort Smith city	707	801	4,265	4,831	64,707	326	50.9	173.9	40.9	49.7	749	154.1	1,754	639	745.0
Harrison city	65	496	468	3,573	2,379	12	100.0	13.2	3.0	37.3	473	12.7	968	0	6.0
Helena-West Helena city	157	1,499	471	4,496	1,084	46	4.3	13.2	4.1	40.0	506	11.6	1,079	11	8.5
Hope city	75	770	392	4,023	0	0	0.0	10.3	2.6	30.9	318	9.6	980	159	3.4
Hot Springs city	194	524	2,592	7,004	20,378	117	40.2	73.3	6.4	56.4	838	83.2	2,162	544	100.4
Hot Springs Village CDP	NA	NA	NA	NA	NA	NA	NA								
Jacksonville city	331	1,160	1,322	4,634	13,256	142	43.7	32.6	10.9	44.6	377	34.3	1,205	148	43.5

1 Data for serious crimes have not been adjusted for underreporting. This may affect comparability between geographic areas over time.
2 Per 100,000 population estimated by the FBI. 3 Based on population estimated as of July 1 of the year shown.

Table B. Incorporated Places, Census Designated Places (CDPs), and Minor Civil Divisions (MCDs) of 10,000 or More Population — **Land Area, Population, and Households, and Employment**

STATE City, town, township, borough, or CDP (county if applicable)	Land area 2010 (sq mi)	Population Total persons 2010	Total persons 2019	Percent change 2010–2019	Persons per square mile, 2019	Population characteristics 2015–2019 Percent foreign born	Percent living in the same house as previous year	Income and poverty 2015–2019 Median household income	Percent of households with income below poverty level	Median value of owner-occupied housing units	Employment, 2015–2019 Percent in civilian labor force	Unemployment rate	Households, 2015–2019 (percent of households) Family households	One person households
	1	2	3	4	5	6	7	8	9	10	11	12	13	14
ARKANSAS—Con.														
Jonesboro city	80.17	67,295	78,394	16.5	977.8	5.3	74.5	45,931	17.6	152,900	64.1	6.9	62.5	30.3
Little Rock city	119.99	193,538	197,312	2.0	1644.4	7.7	83.5	51,485	15.5	167,600	65.7	4.1	56.9	36.7
Magnolia city	13.21	11,559	11,467	-0.8	868.1	2.2	76.8	33,474	24.0	96,100	55.5	10.8	59.4	36.0
Malvern city	9.87	10,443	10,931	4.7	1107.5	2.2	77.0	33,549	25.6	93,200	45.1	8.3	61.5	33.4
Marion city	20.29	12,505	12,310	-1.6	606.7	2.2	83.8	73,459	6.8	153,900	72.4	6.8	70.4	24.6
Maumelle city	12.07	17,170	18,199	6.0	1507.8	4.0	87.4	84,341	5.3	223,800	64.7	3.3	70.2	26.2
Mountain Home city	11.90	12,458	12,569	0.9	1056.2	2.3	79.5	40,408	10.8	126,100	52.4	4.4	55.1	39.6
North Little Rock city	52.34	62,350	65,903	5.7	1259.1	3.2	81.4	43,703	21.5	135,200	60.6	6.8	57.7	35.1
Paragould city	31.84	26,319	28,986	10.1	910.4	1.1	73.0	45,841	16.7	129,100	59.0	6.2	69.2	24.7
Pine Bluff city	43.77	49,066	41,474	-15.5	947.5	1.5	85.4	34,723	25.1	75,500	52.7	11.4	56.8	37.8
Rogers city	38.69	56,109	68,669	22.4	1774.9	20.7	88.5	61,551	10.6	178,000	70.4	2.4	70.7	24.2
Russellville city	28.31	28,106	29,175	3.8	1030.6	10.4	74.8	36,562	20.5	128,300	58.5	8.6	57.5	34.1
Searcy city	18.32	22,849	23,660	3.5	1291.5	4.5	69.4	41,014	19.6	145,000	53.0	6.0	58.6	35.1
Sherwood city	20.84	29,619	31,436	6.1	1508.4	3.0	87.7	63,131	10.7	154,800	63.4	2.8	67.5	28.9
Siloam Springs city	11.38	15,108	17,101	13.2	1502.7	10.6	82.3	47,016	22.3	135,500	58.7	3.7	74.0	21.7
Springdale city	46.89	70,800	81,125	14.6	1730.1	23.4	84.9	50,343	14.8	150,900	68.0	5.4	73.7	21.2
Texarkana city	41.89	29,903	29,657	-0.8	708.0	2.3	81.6	39,622	22.0	119,700	55.7	8.1	64.4	30.6
Van Buren city	15.40	22,811	23,683	3.8	1537.9	8.0	81.2	45,714	18.6	116,200	60.9	6.0	66.9	29.0
West Memphis city	28.86	26,245	24,402	-7.0	845.5	1.2	76.1	33,103	21.3	86,800	59.4	9.9	60.0	32.2
CALIFORNIA	155854.04	37,254,519	39,512,223	6.1	253.5	26.8	87.1	75,235	12.5	505,000	63.3	6.1	68.7	23.8
Adelanto city	52.91	31,760	34,049	7.2	643.5	19.9	82.6	45,380	24.7	195,800	51.3	12.9	83.9	12.1
Agoura Hills city	7.80	20,336	20,222	-0.6	2592.6	21.9	89.6	122,998	5.4	815,000	64.2	4.6	74.3	22.6
Alameda city	10.45	73,812	77,624	5.2	7428.1	25.2	87.4	104,756	7.6	859,900	66.9	3.6	62.5	28.4
Alamo CDP	9.67	14,570	NA	NA	NA	15.5	88.9	239,545	4.2	1,670,500	54.3	1.8	83.6	13.8
Albany city	1.79	18,515	19,696	6.4	11003.4	31.7	82.9	95,400	7.9	882,500	69.1	3.5	70.8	21.9
Alhambra city	7.63	83,119	83,750	0.8	10976.4	49.2	91.6	61,384	13.7	612,700	61.8	4.3	68.6	23.4
Aliso Viejo city	6.92	47,674	50,887	6.7	7353.6	22.2	85.4	112,689	5.1	632,900	75.5	3.7	69.1	24.3
Alpine CDP	26.79	14,236	NA	NA	NA	6.7	79.7	87,930	7.2	606,200	64.8	5.1	71.5	26.9
Altadena CDP	8.47	42,777	NA	NA	NA	19.7	91.8	98,693	7.8	742,800	64.4	5.6	72.4	22.7
Alum Rock CDP	0.84	15,536	NA	NA	NA	35.3	92.5	90,405	10.1	633,800	64.5	6.2	85.9	11.1
American Canyon city	6.09	19,560	20,475	4.7	3362.1	35.1	90.5	101,792	10.2	499,300	66.5	5.2	84.2	12.5
Anaheim city	50.32	336,109	350,365	4.2	6962.7	36.5	88.7	71,763	13.4	575,600	67.3	5.2	73.9	18.5
Anderson city	7.03	9,968	10,630	6.6	1512.1	5.0	87.0	42,649	18.8	200,200	55.3	4.8	62.3	32.5
Antelope CDP	6.84	45,770	NA	NA	NA	24.6	89.3	80,998	10.2	325,300	67.1	3.4	82.3	12.9
Antioch city	29.35	102,745	111,502	8.5	3799.0	22.4	86.8	76,601	13.3	397,400	63.8	8.4	76.4	18.6
Apple Valley town	74.93	69,146	73,453	6.2	980.3	10.3	89.7	54,527	14.5	250,000	53.3	10.5	76.2	19.8
Arcadia city	10.93	56,303	57,939	2.9	5300.9	49.0	89.7	93,574	10.0	1,097,600	58.5	4.7	79.9	16.9
Arcata city	9.37	17,410	18,431	5.9	1967.0	6.0	64.0	35,506	36.5	341,000	64.2	11.7	34.6	35.8
Arden-Arcade CDP	17.77	92,186	NA	NA	NA	20.1	81.5	50,501	19.2	367,700	61.5	8.5	56.3	34.6
Arroyo Grande city	5.94	17,275	17,976	4.1	3026.3	8.3	86.8	80,833	7.1	591,800	59.3	2.1	67.7	26.9
Artesia city	1.62	16,522	16,601	0.5	10247.5	46.9	93.7	67,647	7.5	542,200	59.7	5.4	82.8	12.0
Arvin city	4.82	19,304	21,851	13.2	4533.4	38.1	92.9	38,464	29.7	166,900	61.4	9.5	91.6	7.1
Ashland CDP	1.84	21,925	NA	NA	NA	39.8	92.7	63,406	13.8	498,500	68.3	7.3	70.4	23.9
Atascadero city	26.06	28,306	30,075	6.2	1154.1	7.0	89.6	79,658	7.2	493,200	65.6	3.1	68.0	24.7
Atwater city	6.09	28,215	29,559	4.8	4853.7	22.3	81.8	55,674	19.6	229,400	63.2	11.2	77.3	18.1
Auburn city	7.18	13,312	14,195	6.6	1977.0	7.7	86.3	66,314	13.6	447,600	56.2	5.8	58.7	35.3
Avenal city	19.49	15,504	13,496	-13.0	692.5	36.7	79.8	41,114	32.1	152,500	41.7	12.5	85.6	11.8
Avocado Heights CDP	2.71	15,411	NA	NA	NA	36.2	94.8	75,142	8.9	478,800	60.4	8.1	88.8	7.9
Azusa city	9.67	46,574	49,974	7.3	5167.9	28.6	88.6	68,216	12.6	418,800	65.5	6.2	75.8	16.5
Bakersfield city	149.76	347,817	384,145	10.4	2565.1	18.9	85.6	63,139	15.3	247,000	63.6	8.4	75.0	19.6
Baldwin Park city	6.63	75,397	75,251	-0.2	11350.1	44.4	95.0	65,904	13.8	408,600	64.3	5.8	85.4	11.2
Banning city	23.27	29,592	31,221	5.5	1341.7	19.0	87.0	42,274	17.9	234,900	44.5	9.1	63.6	32.3
Barstow city	41.28	22,750	23,915	5.1	579.3	9.0	76.7	40,633	29.3	117,100	52.6	9.2	64.9	27.5
Bay Point CDP	6.45	21,349	NA	NA	NA	40.3	90.6	65,098	14.9	302,900	67.7	8.1	84.4	11.0
Beaumont city	30.32	36,867	51,063	38.5	1684.1	18.3	86.9	84,105	10.0	320,500	61.3	6.7	79.0	16.6
Bell city	2.50	35,469	35,521	0.1	14208.4	41.4	93.7	44,327	22.8	413,400	63.4	7.4	84.6	13.0
Bellflower city	6.12	76,625	76,435	-0.2	12489.4	31.6	92.0	60,011	13.5	458,600	64.4	5.8	74.6	20.9
Bell Gardens city	2.46	42,053	42,012	-0.1	17078.0	42.1	94.8	42,223	28.6	388,100	63.3	7.4	87.2	9.0
Belmont city	4.63	25,833	26,941	4.3	5818.8	30.5	86.5	156,052	4.6	1,527,500	68.6	3.2	71.5	23.6
Benicia city	12.84	27,035	28,240	4.5	2199.4	13.1	88.3	103,413	6.1	585,600	64.8	2.7	69.9	25.2
Berkeley city	10.47	112,513	121,363	7.9	11591.5	21.1	72.0	85,530	15.9	1,004,900	61.7	5.3	45.6	34.4
Beverly Hills city	5.71	33,921	33,792	-0.4	5918.0	34.1	89.0	106,936	9.6	2,000,000	60.9	6.0	57.5	37.3
Big Bear City CDP	31.95	12,304	NA	NA	NA	6.4	85.1	51,875	17.0	257,200	55.2	6.0	66.2	27.7
Bloomington CDP	6.07	23,851	NA	NA	NA	25.8	93.3	52,085	17.8	270,000	59.5	5.6	84.0	12.2
Blythe city	26.61	20,877	19,682	-5.7	739.6	16.8	77.8	45,385	24.0	150,000	35.5	8.3	63.9	31.7
Bonita CDP	5.02	12,538	NA	NA	NA	23.6	94.1	99,427	6.4	662,400	60.5	8.5	73.0	20.9
Bostonia CDP	1.93	15,379	NA	NA	NA	20.7	78.4	55,368	15.1	368,300	64.9	8.3	68.2	22.9
Brawley city	8.12	24,976	26,227	5.0	3229.9	26.0	87.3	42,326	28.2	188,900	52.3	18.0	78.0	18.9
Brea city	12.16	39,195	43,255	10.4	3557.2	21.7	85.6	94,492	6.7	660,400	68.5	5.1	72.5	22.2
Brentwood city	14.86	51,627	64,474	24.9	4338.8	14.6	87.4	108,994	6.0	580,500	63.4	6.7	80.6	15.9
Buena Park city	10.52	80,619	81,788	1.5	7774.5	37.3	89.0	78,932	10.8	579,100	66.1	5.2	81.9	14.0
Burbank city	17.32	103,357	102,511	-0.8	5918.6	31.7	88.8	75,827	12.7	730,100	66.2	6.1	59.1	32.2
Burlingame city	4.41	28,806	30,889	7.2	7004.3	29.5	83.8	128,447	4.9	1,901,900	71.2	4.7	64.4	27.5
Calabasas city	13.68	23,462	23,853	1.7	1743.6	26.3	85.1	125,814	7.2	1,076,600	65.8	4.1	75.2	19.2
Calexico city	8.62	38,573	39,825	3.2	4620.1	43.9	88.2	43,592	26.9	207,600	56.2	15.3	79.9	17.8
California City city	203.61	14,120	14,198	0.6	69.7	9.0	76.3	49,022	20.0	124,500	43.6	19.1	65.8	26.1
Camarillo city	19.68	65,156	69,888	7.3	3551.2	15.7	88.5	93,512	7.9	602,000	61.7	4.0	68.5	26.1
Cameron Park CDP	11.23	18,228	NA	NA	NA	9.5	86.1	79,814	9.1	438,700	56.5	4.6	68.4	25.3
Campbell city	6.07	40,580	41,793	3.0	6885.2	25.6	84.0	124,525	6.4	1,079,000	71.3	2.1	63.8	25.8
Camp Pendleton South CDP	3.92	10,616	NA	NA	NA	6.1	59.3	49,851	10.2	0	35.0	8.7	96.0	4.0
Canyon Lake city	3.91	10,553	11,280	6.9	2884.9	6.4	84.2	100,682	6.2	442,900	58.4	3.4	74.8	21.1
Capitola city	1.59	9,917	10,010	0.9	6295.6	12.4	82.0	71,059	12.9	721,900	61.3	1.2	54.0	37.2
Carlsbad city	37.75	105,328	115,382	9.5	3056.5	14.4	87.0	110,478	5.2	814,700	64.6	4.9	71.0	22.8
Carmichael CDP	13.45	61,762	NA	NA	NA	15.0	83.5	64,710	12.3	380,200	61.1	5.8	60.6	30.9
Carpinteria city	2.59	13,003	13,385	2.9	5168.0	24.3	89.2	76,521	8.1	705,300	65.8	5.2	63.6	27.3

Table B. Incorporated Places, Census Designated Places (CDPs), and Minor Civil Divisions (MCDs) of 10,000 or More Population — **Crime, Residential Construction and Local Government Finance**

STATE City, town, township, borough, or CDP (county if applicable)	Violent crime Number (15)	Violent crime Rate[2] (16)	Property crime Number (17)	Property crime Rate[2] (18)	Value ($1,000) (19)	Number of housing units (20)	Percent single family (21)	General revenue Total (mil dol) (22)	Intergovernmental Total (mil dol) (23)	Intergovernmental Percent from state gov. (24)	Taxes per capita[3] (25)	General expenditure Total (mil dol) (26)	Per capita[3] Total (27)	Per capita[3] Capital outlays (28)	Debt outstanding (mil dol) (29)
ARKANSAS—Con.															
Jonesboro city	425	551	3,143	4,075	77,647	663	60.5	79.1	22.7	27.0	370	75.6	995	130	272.8
Little Rock city	2,882	1,446	13,049	6,548	175,700	1,019	47.1	461.4	90.4	24.4	939	513.3	2,589	710	592.8
Magnolia city	22	193	NA	NA	3,730	21	71.4	32.0	1.3	85.9	628	30.8	2,674	55	45.6
Malvern city	NA	NA	NA	NA	1,024	5	100.0	8.5	2.0	48.0	343	7.0	642	35	19.5
Marion city	125	1,006	500	4,024	7,329	32	100.0	18.1	1.8	46.6	366	13.7	1,104	78	165.3
Maumelle city	47	256	326	1,776	17,671	66	100.0	17.7	5.2	25.0	527	22.9	1,259	495	24.5
Mountain Home city	22	179	590	4,791	2,201	16	18.8	15.6	3.2	38.5	603	13.9	1,132	23	9.8
North Little Rock city	494	744	2,287	3,443	45,684	436	24.3	104.1	20.4	26.0	793	109.4	1,661	285	146.2
Paragould city	NA	NA	NA	NA	22,628	212	50.0	33.8	6.0	39.4	251	33.4	1,169	142	14.3
Pine Bluff city	679	1,609	2,278	5,399	1,354	10	100.0	47.5	14.3	39.1	478	48.7	1,129	102	23.4
Rogers city	294	432	1,925	2,830	119,149	734	60.9	93.3	23.7	40.6	694	87.2	1,309	540	117.6
Russellville city	114	387	904	3,069	6,951	83	71.1	35.1	7.4	33.9	605	39.5	1,354	529	47.5
Searcy city	NA	NA	NA	NA	13,458	70	82.9	28.0	6.4	38.4	473	22.2	932	37	46.8
Sherwood city	180	575	978	3,126	36,497	199	100.0	25.6	9.3	26.2	284	25.1	809	94	12.2
Siloam Springs city	78	456	NA	NA	23,630	225	67.6	24.7	5.2	41.0	555	29.0	1,716	503	21.0
Springdale city	388	480	2,702	3,340	76,410	284	100.0	92.0	27.1	36.9	490	81.1	1,016	253	198.8
Texarkana city	200	660	1,256	4,145	5,863	28	100.0	32.0	6.6	59.3	510	29.0	964	24	32.4
Van Buren city	134	568	771	3,266	9,762	90	75.6	21.8	5.0	46.5	432	22.3	951	115	15.3
West Memphis city	486	1,970	1,262	5,116	2,305	12	100.0	31.4	7.6	32.3	611	32.6	1,309	191	19.0
CALIFORNIA	176,982	447	941,618	2,380	26,583,348	110,197	53.2	X	X	X	X	X	X	X	X
Adelanto city	239	694	610	1,772	16,179	63	100.0	19.0	0.3	84.0	347	19.6	577	70	27.8
Agoura Hills city	27	130	274	1,321	1,690	3	100.0	38.3	2.5	91.1	958	25.0	1,214	353	13.4
Alameda city	184	230	2,123	2,655	135,046	135,047	135048	173.1	14.1	38.1	1,217	128.2	1,622	63	142.2
Alamo CDP	NA	NA	NA	NA	NA	NA	NA	NA	NA	NA	NA	NA	NA	NA	NA
Albany city	37	182	608	2,984	1,191	12	100.0	33.5	2.3	70.9	977	32.6	1,622	279	20.3
Alhambra city	193	225	1,930	2,252	22,754	126	31.0	98.6	3.5	86.4	665	102.9	1,212	144	56.1
Aliso Viejo city	43	82	445	853	0	0	0.0	24.2	2.6	58.7	344	33.5	657	95	31.2
Alpine CDP	NA	NA	NA	NA	NA	NA	NA	NA	NA	NA	NA	NA	NA	NA	NA
Altadena CDP	NA	NA	NA	NA	NA	NA	NA	NA	NA	NA	NA	NA	NA	NA	NA
Alum Rock CDP	NA	NA	NA	NA	NA	NA	NA	NA	NA	NA	NA	NA	NA	NA	NA
American Canyon city	56	275	405	1,991	45	1	100.0	33.5	1.9	57.7	1,041	41.0	2,045	118	38.9
Anaheim city	1,192	336	8,702	2,453	49,807	669	18.4	796.8	150.7	10.4	1,052	705.4	2,013	241	1823.7
Anderson city	64	613	388	3,719	10,040	39	100.0	11.1	1.0	37.2	699	10.8	1,042	188	6.8
Antelope CDP	NA	NA	NA	NA	NA	NA	NA	NA	NA	NA	NA	NA	NA	NA	NA
Antioch city	602	533	3,330	2,948	75,551	330	70.3	81.7	6.2	56.5	466	74.9	672	95	30.1
Apple Valley town	227	308	1,459	1,982	16,318	105	96.2	65.8	11.5	85.7	381	73.3	1,005	111	16.8
Arcadia city	76	129	1,420	2,401	61,231	145	58.6	82.7	4.7	38.9	886	76.4	1,309	143	11.8
Arcata city	64	354	665	3,680	2,671	27	100.0	27.5	4.4	59.0	659	29.3	1,616	539	6.4
Arden-Arcade CDP	NA	NA	NA	NA	NA	NA	NA	NA	NA	NA	NA	NA	NA	NA	NA
Arroyo Grande city	24	132	286	1,568	13,227	32	100.0	21.9	2.6	51.3	836	31.3	1,731	171	1.6
Artesia city	82	484	335	1,975	4,769	11	100.0	11.9	0.8	85.1	517	11.4	681	129	0.0
Arvin city	207	960	382	1,772	23,157	121	100.0	16.4	7.2	79.1	251	14.6	693	54	9.1
Ashland CDP	NA	NA	NA	NA	NA	NA	NA	NA	NA	NA	NA	NA	NA	NA	NA
Atascadero city	99	322	428	1,393	11,821	71	49.3	30.9	2.4	40.5	660	32.3	1,065	306	40.7
Atwater city	179	605	910	3,078	505	3	100.0	35.4	2.6	68.1	393	46.1	1,574	573	77.1
Auburn city	72	511	192	1,362	4,666	11	100.0	22.4	2.6	43.9	805	18.1	1,292	186	15.4
Avenal city	44	364	118	977	1,904	17	100.0	8.7	1.7	36.0	270	12.0	968	209	17.3
Avocado Heights CDP	NA	NA	NA	NA	NA	NA	NA	NA	NA	NA	NA	NA	NA	NA	NA
Azusa city	193	383	1,122	2,227	25,578	185	5.4	57.5	2.5	81.1	634	51.7	1,038	37	171.8
Bakersfield city	1,895	491	16,097	4,174	403,835	1,472	96.4	444.4	118.4	11.1	462	467.9	1,238	485	661.7
Baldwin Park city	287	375	1,386	1,811	2,651	20	60.0	47.8	10.4	77.3	364	49.6	653	52	13.9
Banning city	135	429	531	1,688	2,230	11	100.0	30.6	6.8	72.7	345	29.7	954	248	63.2
Barstow city	285	1,183	1,102	4,574	150	1	100.0	29.6	2.8	91.0	738	37.0	1,545	236	9.1
Bay Point CDP	NA	NA	NA	NA	NA	NA	NA	NA	NA	NA	NA	NA	NA	NA	NA
Beaumont city	208	428	871	1,794	164,595	535	100.0	82.2	5.5	7.7	390	95.8	2,046	957	216.6
Bell city	184	513	495	1,381	8,700	63	17.5	33.2	4.4	37.1	569	36.5	1,024	248	69.0
Bellflower city	335	430	1,688	2,166	3,833	19	15.8	39.3	4.0	54.2	373	38.1	493	78	36.5
Bell Gardens city	117	273	633	1,477	1,281	7	42.9	43.7	2.1	58.8	627	38.8	912	86	20.6
Belmont city	40	146	424	1,552	487	1	100.0	66.3	2.5	54.7	1,114	50.4	1,863	64	66.6
Benicia city	34	119	382	1,339	2,240	6	100.0	51.9	2.1	75.2	1,287	63.0	2,231	715	59.7
Berkeley city	586	474	5,381	4,349	59,834	266	30.1	381.9	35.9	58.7	1,528	364.8	2,986	172	201.8
Beverly Hills city	106	307	1,757	5,084	40,695	25	68.0	340.2	3.5	32.8	6,251	308.6	9,012	1169	214.1
Big Bear City CDP	NA	NA	NA	NA	NA	NA	NA	NA	NA	NA	NA	NA	NA	NA	NA
Bloomington CDP	NA	NA	NA	NA	NA	NA	NA	NA	NA	NA	NA	NA	NA	NA	NA
Blythe city	71	364	684	3,505	320	1	100.0	15.3	3.1	83.2	327	15.5	787	136	21.3
Bonita CDP	NA	NA	NA	NA	NA	NA	NA	NA	NA	NA	NA	NA	NA	NA	NA
Bostonia CDP	NA	NA	NA	NA	NA	NA	NA	NA	NA	NA	NA	NA	NA	NA	NA
Brawley city	154	579	657	2,471	16,226	112	46.4	22.8	2.3	82.3	403	32.7	1,249	334	19.2
Brea city	83	192	1,293	2,988	95,918	709	5.6	75.4	5.8	21.8	1,053	91.7	2,153	615	75.2
Brentwood city	152	237	1,317	2,054	65,988	323	100.0	141.4	5.2	48.2	752	106.1	1,704	231	177.3
Buena Park city	257	308	2,583	3,100	0	0	0.0	88.2	4.1	85.8	764	107.4	1,300	279	96.2
Burbank city	229	218	2,625	2,499	4,974	43	100.0	249.2	21.0	38.4	1,360	318.8	3,060	0	281.5
Burlingame city	58	187	921	2,975	17,321	20	100.0	112.1	1.3	99.3	2,173	82.4	2,693	481	88.6
Calabasas city	26	107	363	1,493	14,405	7	100.0	51.0	17.6	8.8	1,050	45.6	1,898	541	40.9
Calexico city	87	214	1,064	2,621	1,752	10	100.0	34.3	5.5	30.7	369	30.2	754	106	63.6
California City city	47	335	393	2,797	1,463	8	100.0	15.4	1.8	74.6	761	19.0	1,368	372	6.4
Camarillo city	78	114	841	1,233	31,299	260	18.8	85.5	9.2	34.0	652	106.9	1,586	278	82.4
Cameron Park CDP	NA	NA	NA	NA	NA	NA	NA	NA	NA	NA	NA	NA	NA	NA	NA
Campbell city	119	284	1,379	3,295	18,165	51	100.0	56.2	3.6	34.8	969	68.9	1,619	167	10.4
Camp Pendleton South CDP	NA	NA	NA	NA	NA	NA	NA	NA	NA	NA	NA	NA	NA	NA	NA
Canyon Lake city	12	106	101	893	5,071	14	100.0	5.4	0.6	100.0	413	8.9	799	269	0.3
Capitola city	26	255	507	4,962	6,348	15	86.7	17.8	1.6	24.2	1,265	16.3	1,609	137	3.3
Carlsbad city	243	208	2,100	1,799	82,531	293	77.5	226.5	19.6	44.8	1,233	213.3	1,863	385	37.0
Carmichael CDP	NA	NA	NA	NA	NA	NA	NA	NA	NA	NA	NA	NA	NA	NA	NA
Carpinteria city	22	160	212	1,546	14,515	34	35.3	13.4	1.5	99.5	734	12.1	890	22	0.2

1   Data for serious crimes have not been adjusted for underreporting. This may affect comparability between geographic areas over time.
2   Per 100,000 population estimated by the FBI.   3   Based on population estimated as of July 1 of the year shown.

Table B. Incorporated Places, Census Designated Places (CDPs), and Minor Civil Divisions (MCDs) of 10,000 or More Population — **Land Area, Population, and Households, and Employment**

STATE City, town, township, borough, or CDP (county if applicable)		Population				Population characteristics 2015–2019		Income and poverty 2015–2019			Employment, 2015–2019		Households, 2015–2019 (percent of households)	
	Land area 2010 (sq mi)	Total persons 2010	Total persons 2019	Percent change 2010–2019	Persons per square mile, 2019	Percent foreign born	Percent living in the same house as previous year	Median household income	Percent of households with income below poverty level	Median value of owner-occupied housing units	Percent in civilian labor force	Unemployment rate	Family households	One person households
	1	2	3	4	5	6	7	8	9	10	11	12	13	14
CALIFORNIA—Con.														
Carson city	18.73	91,711	91,394	-0.3	4879.6	34.7	92.6	82,305	8.5	462,600	63.0	6.0	81.3	15.8
Casa de Oro-Mount Helix CDP	6.85	18,762	NA	NA	NA	12.1	86.8	100,097	7.5	661,500	63.9	5.1	77.5	18.1
Castaic CDP	7.26	19,015	NA	NA	NA	19.3	92.8	117,031	4.5	553,600	67.5	5.2	83.7	13.2
Castro Valley CDP	16.59	61,388	NA	NA	NA	25.7	90.4	108,488	7.0	741,500	65.9	4.2	72.6	20.7
Cathedral City city	22.49	51,230	55,007	7.4	2445.8	32.0	90.2	46,521	20.2	279,500	57.1	6.4	61.3	31.2
Ceres city	9.36	45,843	48,706	6.2	5203.6	24.4	87.0	58,667	14.4	270,500	61.7	11.9	84.0	13.0
Cerritos city	8.72	49,043	49,859	1.7	5717.8	43.6	92.1	106,190	5.5	685,300	56.9	6.0	85.9	11.5
Charter Oak CDP	0.93	9,310	NA	NA	NA	25.9	87.0	74,503	12.1	423,400	67.8	8.2	75.2	18.5
Cherryland CDP	1.20	14,728	NA	NA	NA	34.8	90.8	69,721	17.2	490,100	63.4	7.6	66.6	22.0
Chico city	33.46	86,798	103,301	19.0	3087.3	7.6	75.8	53,324	21.8	327,700	65.0	8.0	52.6	29.5
Chino city	29.64	78,069	94,371	20.9	3183.9	24.1	81.7	81,711	8.7	459,100	53.5	5.1	79.2	16.1
Chino Hills city	44.68	74,792	83,853	12.1	1876.7	29.6	86.9	106,347	6.3	622,300	65.0	4.9	83.3	12.6
Chowchilla city	11.09	18,785	18,310	-2.5	1651.0	15.7	80.5	53,563	18.1	216,400	28.5	6.8	72.5	25.1
Chula Vista city	49.64	243,923	274,492	12.5	5529.7	31.1	89.9	81,272	10.2	492,700	64.0	9.0	79.6	16.4
Citrus CDP	0.89	10,866	NA	NA	NA	31.6	94.1	78,865	7.2	425,800	64.7	5.4	81.6	12.4
Citrus Heights city	14.23	83,184	87,796	5.5	6169.8	13.4	83.9	62,276	10.2	297,700	64.3	6.2	61.7	29.3
Claremont city	13.35	34,878	36,266	4.0	2716.6	18.9	85.1	101,420	6.0	672,500	60.5	5.4	70.6	23.6
Clayton city	3.84	10,918	12,265	12.3	3194.0	10.9	89.8	157,768	1.5	771,400	63.2	3.1	78.0	18.2
Clearlake city	10.13	15,250	15,267	0.1	1507.1	9.0	80.1	31,551	30.6	110,500	49.2	18.4	56.5	33.3
Clovis city	25.41	95,980	114,584	19.4	4509.4	12.2	85.1	77,904	9.7	324,600	65.7	5.5	72.8	22.0
Coachella city	30.08	40,708	45,743	12.4	1520.7	39.1	95.4	34,224	24.5	219,400	70.7	14.3	55.9	41.5
Coalinga city	6.58	18,342	17,179	-6.3	2610.8	19.1	78.9	62,522	18.6	170,100	46.1	7.8	74.3	20.4
Colton city	15.54	52,148	54,824	5.1	3527.9	21.4	91.5	53,838	14.9	257,500	61.2	7.1	76.9	17.6
Commerce city	6.54	12,840	12,661	-1.4	1935.9	35.9	94.0	47,518	16.0	411,200	58.9	6.1	76.3	20.0
Compton city	10.03	96,404	95,605	-0.8	9531.9	29.3	93.5	52,883	20.0	355,200	60.9	9.4	82.9	14.1
Concord city	30.56	122,169	129,295	5.8	4230.9	27.5	85.9	89,564	9.1	551,300	67.2	5.0	68.2	23.9
Corcoran city	7.37	24,823	21,960	-11.5	2979.6	19.4	75.5	40,159	28.0	149,300	26.9	11.6	75.2	21.1
Corona city	39.99	152,315	169,868	11.5	4247.8	24.2	88.7	83,752	10.1	467,000	66.7	5.1	76.8	19.0
Coronado city	7.97	24,701	23,731	-3.9	2977.5	9.6	78.4	108,967	6.4	1,617,000	42.9	4.3	67.2	28.7
Costa Mesa city	15.80	110,078	113,003	2.7	7152.1	25.0	85.8	84,138	10.5	749,400	72.7	4.2	59.5	26.0
Coto de Caza CDP	7.72	14,866	NA	NA	NA	11.8	92.0	199,056	3.7	1,043,700	66.3	3.6	89.1	8.0
Covina city	7.03	47,786	47,450	-0.7	6749.6	25.4	88.8	70,780	9.0	509,200	66.9	5.8	73.3	20.4
Crestline CDP	13.86	10,770	NA	NA	NA	6.8	88.4	61,953	13.3	258,100	56.7	3.7	63.9	26.3
Cudahy city	1.18	23,809	23,569	-1.0	19973.7	42.9	94.7	46,642	24.7	420,700	65.2	8.5	88.1	7.4
Culver City city	5.11	38,895	39,185	0.7	7668.3	25.8	89.4	95,044	7.0	892,000	71.2	4.2	56.7	35.4
Cupertino city	11.31	58,559	59,276	1.2	5241.0	53.1	85.7	171,917	6.8	1,711,300	60.2	3.6	77.1	18.5
Cypress city	6.61	47,865	49,006	2.4	7413.9	29.3	91.0	93,137	6.3	632,900	63.4	4.2	80.9	14.8
Daly City city	7.64	101,116	106,280	5.1	13911.0	51.9	91.4	94,550	7.7	783,400	68.4	5.1	73.6	18.4
Dana Point city	6.49	33,290	33,577	0.9	5173.7	14.3	86.6	99,409	5.6	878,300	63.0	3.9	60.3	31.6
Danville town	18.08	41,865	44,510	6.3	2461.8	16.0	89.7	160,808	3.7	1,091,900	62.7	3.4	77.6	19.0
Davis city	9.89	65,639	69,413	5.7	7018.5	21.0	66.9	69,379	24.7	652,300	57.5	5.8	50.1	23.3
Del Aire CDP	1.01	10,001	NA	NA	NA	20.3	84.1	103,697	8.2	631,400	69.4	3.5	70.6	22.3
Delano city	14.29	53,044	53,573	1.0	3749.0	37.8	88.6	43,641	22.2	182,900	52.5	11.9	87.6	10.0
Delhi CDP	3.51	10,755	NA	NA	NA	35.9	89.8	63,081	15.8	239,700	61.2	10.6	88.7	9.5
Desert Hot Springs city	30.22	27,054	28,878	6.7	955.6	24.6	85.4	33,046	26.8	194,500	53.7	9.7	58.2	34.3
Diamond Bar city	14.87	55,568	55,720	0.3	3747.1	45.5	89.8	99,083	6.7	664,400	62.7	5.6	82.5	14.8
Diamond Springs CDP	16.64	11,037	NA	NA	NA	5.9	84.4	62,370	7.2	326,400	51.1	4.8	62.1	33.4
Dinuba city	6.51	21,460	24,461	14.0	3757.5	27.4	88.4	44,289	23.5	197,500	62.4	11.6	86.6	10.5
Discovery Bay CDP	3.78	13,352	NA	NA	NA	9.0	87.7	130,547	4.7	615,900	64.9	4.4	81.0	12.4
Dixon city	7.07	18,417	20,698	12.4	2927.6	21.9	89.4	82,570	7.4	385,400	69.7	5.7	80.4	14.8
Downey city	12.41	111,775	111,126	-0.6	8954.6	32.6	91.3	75,878	9.0	569,300	65.8	5.2	79.7	15.9
Duarte city	6.71	21,325	21,271	-0.3	3170.0	32.8	94.2	75,083	11.6	482,200	63.5	6.9	68.6	25.7
Dublin city	15.23	46,036	64,826	40.8	4256.5	39.0	82.5	150,299	3.9	882,200	70.4	3.5	78.2	16.7
East Hemet CDP	5.20	17,418	NA	NA	NA	16.6	84.3	53,964	19.7	243,100	58.0	10.7	80.2	15.4
East Los Angeles CDP	7.45	126,496	NA	NA	NA	39.8	96.3	46,082	19.4	415,600	63.6	9.1	81.1	15.0
East Palo Alto city	2.52	28,155	29,314	4.1	11632.5	39.2	89.4	67,087	13.2	821,200	72.4	4.4	75.3	16.5
East Rancho Dominguez CDP	0.82	15,135	NA	NA	NA	34.8	93.3	54,317	18.7	355,600	61.2	8.1	87.2	8.1
East San Gabriel CDP	1.56	14,874	NA	NA	NA	45.5	92.2	82,716	13.4	796,600	59.4	2.9	73.9	21.5
Eastvale city	12.67	53,712	64,157	19.4	5063.7	26.3	88.5	119,213	6.8	574,500	69.1	4.8	88.3	9.5
East Whittier CDP	1.09	0	NA	0.0	NA	15.8	91.4	76,373	8.4	584,400	63.4	5.0	70.3	24.0
El Cajon city	14.51	99,584	102,708	3.1	7078.4	29.0	81.7	55,309	18.0	445,600	62.4	8.0	71.3	21.9
El Centro city	11.51	42,588	44,079	3.5	3829.6	31.1	86.7	47,864	23.8	192,600	55.8	13.1	78.0	18.8
El Cerrito city	3.66	23,585	25,508	8.2	6969.4	31.3	86.1	108,298	7.1	804,700	64.5	4.4	67.7	23.6
El Dorado Hills CDP	48.46	42,108	NA	NA	NA	12.7	85.7	137,726	3.6	630,000	62.0	4.3	83.8	13.5
Elk Grove city	42.03	152,995	174,775	14.2	4158.3	24.1	89.1	93,780	7.8	406,300	63.7	5.5	79.9	17.1
El Monte city	9.56	113,531	115,487	1.7	12080.2	50.6	93.7	49,003	19.7	454,900	60.8	6.2	80.1	15.4
El Paso de Robles (Paso Robles) city	19.64	29,747	32,153	8.1	1637.1	18.4	87.7	62,601	9.8	456,000	65.3	3.5	69.9	23.6
El Segundo city	5.46	16,656	16,610	-0.3	3042.1	13.9	86.2	109,577	5.1	1,094,300	76.3	6.5	64.8	27.1
El Sobrante CDP	2.77	12,669	NA	NA	NA	25.7	90.0	86,626	6.4	497,400	69.6	5.6	70.8	20.9
El Sobrante CDP	7.23	12,723	NA	NA	NA	26.6	91.6	120,049	7.2	549,600	64.0	5.3	84.4	13.8
Emeryville city	1.27	10,112	12,086	19.5	9516.5	30.0	73.1	102,725	11.2	489,400	73.5	2.5	35.6	47.1
Encinitas city	19.05	59,526	62,709	5.3	3291.8	12.6	87.1	116,022	6.9	947,700	64.5	3.8	65.1	25.4
Escondido city	37.31	143,976	151,625	5.3	4063.9	27.8	86.0	64,038	13.5	450,200	65.9	4.7	71.5	21.2
Eureka city	9.38	27,196	26,710	-1.8	2847.5	7.3	78.6	42,890	17.0	281,400	60.4	7.4	49.8	39.1
Exeter city	2.46	10,332	10,485	1.5	4262.2	13.7	89.0	44,602	25.1	205,400	58.7	13.1	75.8	21.0
Fairfield city	41.19	105,467	117,133	11.1	2843.7	22.2	83.3	84,557	8.4	409,000	64.8	5.8	76.2	18.4
Fair Oaks CDP	10.86	30,912	NA	NA	NA	11.4	86.7	84,717	8.2	476,100	60.1	4.5	66.6	26.8
Fairview CDP	2.75	10,003	NA	NA	NA	22.0	94.9	114,306	3.7	641,700	67.2	2.0	70.3	23.5
Fallbrook CDP	17.54	30,534	NA	NA	NA	22.5	87.7	63,244	12.8	522,700	56.5	5.3	76.3	18.5
Farmersville city	2.24	10,588	10,703	1.1	4778.1	31.6	93.6	39,720	24.2	153,800	63.7	12.5	80.6	13.5
Fillmore city	3.36	14,987	15,870	5.9	4723.2	18.8	93.1	76,590	8.8	426,600	64.4	3.3	80.9	14.5
Florence-Graham CDP	3.51	63,387	NA	NA	NA	41.2	93.6	44,328	25.3	357,000	63.2	8.4	83.9	11.2
Florin CDP	8.70	47,513	NA	NA	NA	33.8	88.2	44,618	23.8	248,900	56.2	11.4	69.1	25.6
Folsom city	27.89	72,147	81,328	12.7	2916.0	17.0	85.0	114,405	5.4	524,100	61.6	3.1	71.6	23.6
Fontana city	43.07	196,458	214,547	9.2	4981.4	26.8	90.1	72,918	11.7	371,700	66.4	6.9	85.6	11.0
Foothill Farms CDP	4.20	33,121	NA	NA	NA	22.4	80.7	54,426	17.4	252,900	62.3	8.0	70.2	21.0

Table B. Incorporated Places, Census Designated Places (CDPs), and Minor Civil Divisions (MCDs) of 10,000 or More Population — **Crime, Residential Construction and Local Government Finance**

STATE City, town, township, borough, or CDP (county if applicable)	Serious crimes known to police, 2018[1] Violent crime Number	Violent crime Rate[2]	Property crime Number	Property crime Rate[2]	New residential construction authorized by building permits, 2019 Value ($1,000)	Number of housing units	Percent single family	Local government finance, 2017 General revenue Total (mil dol)	Intergovernmental Total (mil dol)	Intergovernmental Percent from state gov.	Taxes per capita[3]	General expenditure Total (mil dol)	Per capita[3] Total	Per capita[3] Capital outlays	Debt outstanding (mil dol)
	15	16	17	18	19	20	21	22	23	24	25	26	27	28	29
CALIFORNIA—Con.															
Carson city	435	468	1,971	2,122	26,604	209	4.3	166.8	42.6	6.6	1,058	242.2	2,627	429	204.7
Casa de Oro-Mount Helix CDP	NA	NA	NA	NA	NA	NA	NA	NA	NA	NA	NA	NA	NA	NA	NA
Castaic CDP	NA	NA	NA	NA	NA	NA	NA	NA	NA	NA	NA	NA	NA	NA	NA
Castro Valley CDP	NA	NA	NA	NA	NA	NA	NA	NA	NA	NA	NA	NA	NA	NA	NA
Cathedral City city	172	312	717	1,302	29,207	144	98.6	60.3	11.5	14.7	617	61.6	1,132	141	195.3
Ceres city	228	464	1,452	2,957	12,999	61	100.0	56.3	6.5	45.0	350	55.9	1,157	94	22.5
Cerritos city	162	316	1,794	3,497	0	0	0.0	65.1	1.7	97.2	1,032	79.6	1,570	181	11.0
Charter Oak CDP	NA	NA	NA	NA	NA	NA	NA	NA	NA	NA	NA	NA	NA	NA	NA
Cherryland CDP	NA	NA	NA	NA	NA	NA	NA	NA	NA	NA	NA	NA	NA	NA	NA
Chico city	611	648	2,403	2,549	120,146	822	35.6	111.0	16.6	33.2	736	102.8	1,105	310	128.4
Chino city	259	283	2,216	2,421	127,195	531	100.0	169.7	15.9	97.5	719	129.7	1,448	148	69.6
Chino Hills city	77	95	1,079	1,329	20,683	76	100.0	118.1	3.8	49.9	589	104.1	1,299	209	115.1
Chowchilla city	42	226	293	1,579	2,919	11	100.0	12.8	1.3	69.7	363	26.3	1,426	855	33.5
Chula Vista city	835	304	3,611	1,316	183,617	839	33.6	494.5	23.3	41.6	508	298.0	1,108	224	669.1
Citrus CDP	NA	NA	NA	NA	NA	NA	NA	NA	NA	NA	NA	NA	NA	NA	NA
Citrus Heights city	324	366	2,478	2,797	3,479	15	100.0	53.7	5.7	55.1	411	59.7	681	143	26.6
Claremont city	66	182	930	2,571	19,018	140	17.9	42.5	2.4	48.7	696	48.2	1,346	128	13.7
Clayton city	1	8	146	1,184	NA	NA	NA	8.5	1.7	29.4	459	9.1	754	262	10.2
Clearlake city	109	725	506	3,365	3,898	17	100.0	9.3	1.0	94.8	373	8.5	550	30	14.2
Clovis city	221	198	2,438	2,182	264,554	1,142	66.5	162.5	15.3	30.7	540	140.0	1,281	213	177.8
Coachella city	104	226	1,143	2,479	1,012	6	100.0	41.1	9.3	95.3	426	54.5	1,203	535	93.3
Coalinga city	73	440	244	1,471	17,220	70	100.0	22.8	6.6	74.9	288	15.2	896	82	22.2
Colton city	184	333	1,600	2,898	12,605	65	100.0	70.4	5.9	44.7	478	81.5	1,490	134	94.4
Commerce city	128	988	995	7,677	0	0	0.0	109.0	15.8	80.0	6,160	104.6	8,134	736	128.3
Compton city	1,174	1,201	2,559	2,617	6,663	42	69.0	83.0	15.1	17.1	461	122.5	1,262	118	103.5
Concord city	473	362	4,126	3,153	6,557	38	100.0	193.1	37.8	21.5	775	160.4	1,238	106	76.2
Corcoran city	75	349	380	1,769	11,347	51	96.1	12.2	2.1	45.9	226	11.6	530	83	24.9
Corona city	263	155	3,264	1,920	118,417	593	36.4	238.9	18.6	60.0	682	300.5	1,796	709	218.3
Coronado city	18	74	314	1,282	23,811	32	68.8	74.4	3.4	87.2	1,995	90.3	3,714	1114	138.6
Costa Mesa city	344	301	3,792	3,316	40,824	185	40.0	139.3	7.5	94.0	1,036	130.7	1,150	145	25.0
Coto de Caza CDP	NA	NA	NA	NA	NA	NA	NA	NA	NA	NA	NA	NA	NA	NA	NA
Covina city	188	387	1,117	2,300	1,127	4	100.0	52.1	2.1	87.3	651	47.3	981	145	64.5
Crestline CDP	NA	NA	NA	NA	NA	NA	NA	NA	NA	NA	NA	NA	NA	NA	NA
Cudahy city	90	373	187	776	434	2	100.0	11.4	1.7	45.3	326	16.0	667	9	24.0
Culver City city	188	478	1,756	4,464	2,710	31	45.2	192.9	53.9	10.5	2,279	166.5	4,268	531	15.0
Cupertino city	72	118	956	1,565	34,785	68	100.0	107.6	2.6	70.2	1,080	87.7	1,448	86	33.7
Cypress city	58	118	704	1,430	35,091	190	100.0	45.6	3.9	42.7	659	47.0	962	245	1.8
Daly City city	242	224	1,528	1,416	26,497	72	100.0	115.4	7.9	55.4	623	116.1	1,088	126	29.2
Dana Point city	69	203	504	1,482	60,230	92	89.1	40.3	1.8	97.3	1,044	55.3	1,636	132	18.8
Danville town	16	35	326	721	55,882	184	21.7	37.0	2.0	100.0	564	40.1	897	248	10.4
Davis city	117	168	1,690	2,432	11,923	38	73.7	118.3	15.5	24.7	832	102.4	1,488	159	154.1
Del Aire CDP	NA	NA	NA	NA	NA	NA	NA	NA	NA	NA	NA	NA	NA	NA	NA
Delano city	238	448	1,437	2,704	12,538	70	100.0	62.7	7.4	53.0	446	42.6	805	70	65.2
Delhi CDP	NA	NA	NA	NA	NA	NA	NA	NA	NA	NA	NA	NA	NA	NA	NA
Desert Hot Springs city	309	1,066	638	2,201	5,387	22	100.0	27.6	1.9	99.5	603	29.4	1,026	233	75.9
Diamond Bar city	58	102	936	1,647	5,954	16	100.0	30.6	3.0	64.6	381	44.7	794	349	9.6
Diamond Springs CDP	NA	NA	NA	NA	NA	NA	NA	NA	NA	NA	NA	NA	NA	NA	NA
Dinuba city	184	754	597	2,446	33,221	236	100.0	44.5	6.6	50.7	960	43.6	1,825	320	81.2
Discovery Bay CDP	NA	NA	NA	NA	NA	NA	NA	NA	NA	NA	NA	NA	NA	NA	NA
Dixon city	53	259	368	1,798	25,182	105	100.0	32.2	5.7	11.6	933	33.4	1,659	322	36.9
Downey city	367	324	2,615	2,309	9,891	36	55.6	111.2	19.1	37.6	568	107.6	957	62	28.4
Duarte city	62	284	403	1,847	31,393	186	11.8	17.6	1.7	87.7	555	24.5	1,131	66	1.7
Dublin city	108	170	1,188	1,872	100,854	241	60.2	120.9	3.3	82.5	1,632	86.1	1,416	109	10.4
East Hemet CDP	NA	NA	NA	NA	NA	NA	NA	NA	NA	NA	NA	NA	NA	NA	NA
East Los Angeles CDP	NA	NA	NA	NA	NA	NA	NA	NA	NA	NA	NA	NA	NA	NA	NA
East Palo Alto city	141	470	567	1,891	583	6	100.0	39.8	5.0	39.0	805	29.1	981	159	27.1
East Rancho Dominguez CDP	NA	NA	NA	NA	NA	NA	NA	NA	NA	NA	NA	NA	NA	NA	NA
East San Gabriel CDP	NA	NA	NA	NA	NA	NA	NA	NA	NA	NA	NA	NA	NA	NA	NA
Eastvale city	63	98	956	1,479	75,742	301	100.0	26.7	2.0	77.1	358	31.5	505	4	0.0
East Whittier CDP	NA	NA	NA	NA	NA	NA	NA	NA	NA	NA	NA	NA	NA	NA	NA
El Cajon city	515	493	2,269	2,171	35,287	151	98.7	105.2	6.5	47.2	661	110.7	1,070	173	61.5
El Centro city	126	283	1,625	3,643	8,207	86	16.3	191.6	8.4	11.5	596	215.7	4,890	918	157.7
El Cerrito city	171	663	1,314	5,094	10,123	49	69.4	52.3	11.5	15.3	836	49.4	1,938	343	36.9
El Dorado Hills CDP	NA	NA	NA	NA	NA	NA	NA	NA	NA	NA	NA	NA	NA	NA	NA
Elk Grove city	414	237	2,359	1,351	158,597	764	100.0	226.4	24.4	53.8	405	112.2	654	122	14.4
El Monte city	362	311	2,242	1,925	18,782	87	40.2	98.8	9.8	38.9	662	101.6	880	144	72.6
El Paso de Robles (Paso Robles) city	43	133	797	2,473	6,609	36	66.7	65.9	3.1	51.7	1,238	53.3	1,677	326	87.9
El Segundo city	62	367	714	4,230	4,803	11	72.7	81.6	1.0	71.3	3,811	83.6	4,991	532	9.3
El Sobrante CDP	NA	NA	NA	NA	NA	NA	NA	NA	NA	NA	NA	NA	NA	NA	NA
El Sobrante CDP	NA	NA	NA	NA	NA	NA	NA	NA	NA	NA	NA	NA	NA	NA	NA
Emeryville city	170	1,415	2,014	16,761	182	1	100.0	80.2	4.2	74.6	3,801	96.7	8,233	1841	10.4
Encinitas city	114	179	795	1,248	36,498	185	100.0	88.6	5.2	31.5	982	126.4	2,010	420	60.8
Escondido city	535	350	2,736	1,787	3,838	23	100.0	175.6	12.6	60.9	595	180.6	1,195	122	242.8
Eureka city	197	725	1,491	5,487	480	4	100.0	75.2	30.1	12.4	965	58.5	2,158	302	60.6
Exeter city	16	151	279	2,636	NA	NA	NA	8.2	1.7	52.7	373	7.3	699	46	10.5
Fairfield city	587	498	3,280	2,782	102,737	348	100.0	170.2	42.3	10.2	913	135.2	1,167	236	162.8
Fair Oaks CDP	NA	NA	NA	NA	NA	NA	NA	NA	NA	NA	NA	NA	NA	NA	NA
Fairview CDP	NA	NA	NA	NA	NA	NA	NA	NA	NA	NA	NA	NA	NA	NA	NA
Fallbrook CDP	NA	NA	NA	NA	NA	NA	NA	NA	NA	NA	NA	NA	NA	NA	NA
Farmersville city	45	416	190	1,758	NA	NA	NA	10.8	2.6	63.0	459	8.1	753	114	1.3
Fillmore city	39	245	135	848	26,126	94	100.0	24.7	0.9	88.5	392	18.1	1,151	248	76.3
Florence-Graham CDP	NA	NA	NA	NA	NA	NA	NA	NA	NA	NA	NA	NA	NA	NA	NA
Florin CDP	NA	NA	NA	NA	NA	NA	NA	NA	NA	NA	NA	NA	NA	NA	NA
Folsom city	85	108	1,245	1,578	177,947	681	66.5	133.3	13.5	49.9	913	117.5	1,510	228	219.5
Fontana city	709	331	3,218	1,504	225,133	836	76.8	297.6	16.5	39.6	799	224.3	1,063	269	390.2
Foothill Farms CDP	NA	NA	NA	NA	NA	NA	NA	NA	NA	NA	NA	NA	NA	NA	NA

1 Data for serious crimes have not been adjusted for underreporting. This may affect comparability between geographic areas over time.
2 Per 100,000 population estimated by the FBI.   3 Based on population estimated as of July 1 of the year shown.

Table B. Incorporated Places, Census Designated Places (CDPs), and Minor Civil Divisions (MCDs) of 10,000 or More Population — Land Area, Population, and Households, and Employment

STATE City, town, township, borough, or CDP (county if applicable)	Land area 2010 (sq mi)	Population Total persons 2010	Total persons 2019	Percent change 2010–2019	Persons per square mile 2019	Population characteristics 2015–2019 Percent foreign born	Percent living in the same house as previous year	Income and poverty 2015–2019 Median household income	Percent of households with income below poverty level	Median value of owner-occupied housing units	Employment, 2015–2019 Percent in civilian labor force	Unemploy-ment rate	Households, 2015–2019 (percent of households) Family households	One person households
	1	2	3	4	5	6	7	8	9	10	11	12	13	14
CALIFORNIA—Con.														
Fortuna city	5.25	12,039	12,259	1.8	2335.0	9.0	83.1	46,193	16.0	283,400	58.4	7.4	65.3	27.6
Foster City city	3.80	30,568	33,901	10.9	8921.3	45.1	78.2	158,529	4.5	1,245,800	67.2	3.1	72.8	19.8
Fountain Valley city	9.07	55,360	55,357	0.0	6103.3	30.7	89.6	93,075	7.3	734,800	59.8	4.1	77.0	17.7
Fremont city	77.47	214,074	241,110	12.6	3112.3	48.6	89.4	133,354	4.6	931,600	66.3	3.6	81.5	14.2
French Valley CDP	10.87	23,067	NA	NA	NA	15.1	80.9	111,052	5.3	430,400	62.3	8.8	86.9	8.2
Fresno city	114.73	497,172	531,576	6.9	4633.3	20.4	83.4	50,432	22.5	242,000	61.8	9.4	68.3	24.8
Fullerton city	22.43	135,233	138,632	2.5	6180.7	30.0	84.2	79,978	11.0	650,000	65.9	6.5	69.8	21.5
Galt city	6.80	23,703	26,536	12.0	3902.4	16.9	86.0	75,638	9.0	331,100	64.1	6.6	79.7	14.3
Gardena city	5.83	58,829	59,329	0.8	10176.5	36.5	91.4	58,447	13.4	474,700	62.3	4.6	66.9	26.9
Garden Acres CDP	2.58	10,648	NA	NA	NA	33.9	88.6	41,385	21.0	167,600	59.5	11.9	75.7	18.9
Garden Grove city	17.96	170,958	171,644	0.4	9557.0	44.3	91.7	69,278	13.6	554,400	63.8	4.5	78.2	15.7
Gilroy city	16.54	48,879	59,032	20.8	3569.0	24.8	86.7	101,616	7.8	663,100	70.3	5.6	79.6	14.5
Glendale city	30.47	191,692	199,303	4.0	6541.0	53.1	89.9	66,130	16.1	769,900	62.1	6.5	67.4	26.8
Glendora city	19.51	50,267	51,544	2.5	2641.9	19.4	87.8	96,132	8.8	601,800	63.7	6.0	77.8	17.4
Goleta city	7.85	30,096	30,911	2.7	3937.7	22.2	84.3	98,005	8.3	797,700	69.8	5.5	64.1	25.2
Grand Terrace city	3.51	12,040	12,584	4.5	3585.2	11.8	84.9	71,788	6.6	324,400	64.6	6.3	73.3	23.8
Granite Bay CDP	21.51	20,402	NA	NA	NA	11.8	88.6	143,401	4.9	794,000	58.4	3.9	79.8	18.0
Grass Valley city	5.25	12,876	12,817	-0.5	2441.3	5.1	81.6	37,548	19.7	331,400	54.1	7.7	42.2	46.3
Greenfield city	2.14	16,334	17,516	7.2	8185.0	40.7	92.6	59,595	11.6	305,000	63.9	3.8	88.2	9.4
Grover Beach city	2.31	13,161	13,459	2.3	5826.4	8.7	84.5	64,217	10.6	493,700	65.1	3.6	63.8	27.3
Hacienda Heights CDP	11.18	54,038	NA	NA	NA	40.4	93.4	85,953	9.3	595,700	59.6	4.8	83.3	14.1
Half Moon Bay city	6.43	11,324	12,932	14.2	2011.2	24.3	92.3	134,177	6.4	999,500	65.5	3.0	69.2	26.0
Hanford city	17.40	54,436	57,703	6.0	3316.3	17.8	83.9	62,413	13.7	221,300	60.6	7.4	75.3	18.5
Hawaiian Gardens city	0.95	14,273	14,159	-0.8	14904.2	42.8	92.9	49,483	22.9	363,500	61.0	5.7	82.0	15.0
Hawthorne city	6.08	84,290	86,068	2.1	14155.9	35.6	88.8	54,215	15.5	564,300	70.0	6.0	65.7	27.8
Hayward city	45.54	144,427	159,203	10.2	3495.9	38.7	90.3	86,744	7.7	581,200	67.2	4.4	73.9	18.3
Healdsburg city	4.46	11,255	11,845	5.2	2655.8	15.1	85.9	96,016	8.7	724,700	66.9	2.9	66.3	27.1
Hemet city	29.27	78,630	85,334	8.5	2915.4	16.2	83.9	39,726	19.8	196,700	47.5	12.9	65.0	29.7
Hercules city	6.41	24,089	26,276	9.1	4099.2	33.5	90.6	117,018	4.5	561,600	68.8	3.9	77.7	19.3
Hermosa Beach city	1.43	19,508	19,320	-1.0	13510.5	10.9	80.4	136,702	5.0	1,542,900	76.5	4.0	47.1	38.4
Hesperia city	72.70	90,100	95,750	6.3	1317.1	18.1	90.4	53,561	18.2	235,700	56.4	10.3	80.4	15.7
Highland city	18.75	53,106	55,417	4.4	2955.6	21.0	89.6	64,868	16.7	330,200	63.3	8.3	79.5	17.1
Hillsborough town	6.19	10,839	11,387	5.1	1839.6	24.2	92.9	250	1.8	2,000,000	55.7	3.0	89.1	8.2
Hollister city	7.35	34,805	40,740	17.1	5542.9	22.1	88.2	80,629	9.7	476,800	70.4	7.9	80.9	14.3
Home Gardens CDP	1.51	11,570	NA	NA	NA	34.7	93.8	67,985	13.1	352,000	62.2	5.7	80.6	16.5
Huntington Beach city	27.00	191,038	199,223	4.3	7378.6	16.1	87.0	95,046	7.6	771,100	66.9	4.3	65.1	25.9
Huntington Park city	3.01	58,125	57,509	-1.1	19106.0	46.2	92.7	42,447	23.7	412,600	65.2	8.3	84.0	11.4
Imperial city	6.24	14,733	18,120	23.0	2903.8	19.8	88.4	85,654	6.9	239,900	64.6	11.2	79.5	18.7
Imperial Beach city	4.30	26,329	27,440	4.2	6381.4	20.7	83.2	53,690	16.0	563,600	61.3	8.7	66.2	25.5
Indio city	33.23	79,166	91,765	15.9	2761.5	22.8	90.0	53,669	17.0	281,400	58.1	8.5	63.9	31.8
Inglewood city	9.07	109,649	108,151	-1.4	11924.0	28.5	89.3	54,400	16.6	483,000	67.1	8.0	66.3	28.6
Irvine city	65.62	212,107	287,401	35.5	4379.8	41.2	77.7	105,126	13.0	838,000	63.1	4.5	66.1	23.0
Isla Vista CDP	1.85	23,096	NA	NA	NA	19.2	21.8	24,545	57.6	466,700	49.6	14.4	15.7	22.8
Jurupa Valley city	42.94	94,986	109,527	15.3	2550.7	26.6	90.5	70,642	12.7	363,000	63.3	8.7	81.4	14.2
Kerman city	3.27	13,567	15,282	12.6	4673.4	30.6	93.6	46,449	20.8	224,500	63.6	8.3	81.5	16.0
King City city	3.90	12,874	14,077	9.3	3609.5	49.2	93.5	49,375	16.9	252,500	61.2	2.9	85.1	9.1
Kingsburg city	3.71	11,454	12,108	5.7	3263.6	11.8	94.4	68,738	15.8	276,800	59.2	5.7	71.9	25.5
La Cañada Flintridge city	8.63	20,256	20,009	-1.2	2318.5	24.5	93.8	175,788	3.8	1,518,000	58.7	3.1	84.9	13.4
La Crescenta-Montrose CDP ...	3.43	19,653	NA	NA	NA	32.4	93.3	102,989	7.7	823,400	63.0	4.9	74.9	21.3
Ladera Ranch CDP	4.91	22,980	NA	NA	NA	14.8	83.4	161,348	4.0	820,100	72.0	4.2	85.0	12.3
Lafayette city	15.05	23,791	26,638	12.0	1770.0	15.2	87.6	178,889	2.9	1,428,900	61.8	4.5	76.8	16.3
Laguna Beach city	8.89	22,733	22,827	0.4	2567.7	13.2	87.9	129,983	5.0	1,771,600	61.3	6.0	58.5	32.4
Laguna Hills city	6.60	30,673	31,207	1.7	4728.3	26.3	89.8	100,985	7.4	707,700	66.1	4.2	70.0	21.2
Laguna Niguel city	14.74	62,989	66,385	5.4	4503.7	21.5	87.1	108,537	7.1	827,100	65.3	4.0	71.8	23.2
Laguna Woods city	3.35	15,991	15,850	-0.9	4731.3	34.7	87.1	44,020	12.3	288,400	19.9	3.5	36.2	59.2
La Habra city	7.35	59,016	60,513	2.5	8233.1	28.8	86.3	79,325	10.4	539,200	68.2	7.5	76.1	17.8
Lake Arrowhead CDP	17.73	12,424	NA	NA	NA	15.3	86.5	61,732	15.3	373,700	52.6	7.5	70.4	23.9
Lake Elsinore city	38.27	53,313	69,283	30.0	1810.4	21.5	87.3	71,476	13.2	352,600	65.2	8.2	81.9	14.4
Lake Forest city	16.63	77,445	85,531	10.4	5143.2	24.8	87.2	109,492	6.7	647,500	71.1	4.2	73.5	20.5
Lakeland Village CDP	8.78	11,541	NA	NA	NA	20.7	86.6	52,913	14.6	293,800	57.2	8.1	74.5	18.8
Lake Los Angeles CDP	9.74	12,328	NA	NA	NA	10.6	95.6	45,881	26.3	180,200	43.5	10.0	82.2	14.8
Lakeside CDP	6.93	20,648	NA	NA	NA	6.7	87.7	74,823	9.6	428,200	61.1	7.0	71.3	21.6
Lakewood city	9.41	80,086	79,307	-1.0	8427.9	21.5	92.4	93,432	6.7	568,600	65.7	5.2	76.6	18.5
La Mesa city	9.10	57,016	59,249	3.9	6510.9	15.6	81.2	66,051	11.2	530,400	66.2	7.0	58.8	32.0
La Mirada city	7.82	48,527	48,183	-0.7	6161.5	25.3	91.0	95,685	5.9	569,500	60.6	6.1	81.2	16.0
Lamont CDP	4.59	15,120	NA	NA	NA	38.3	94.6	43,297	27.4	139,800	63.8	8.9	85.7	8.5
Lancaster city	94.28	156,649	157,601	0.6	1671.6	10.6	91.8	55,237	21.4	261,400	51.7	6.5	73.9	21.9
La Palma city	1.78	15,525	15,428	-0.6	8667.4	34.4	91.9	107,724	4.7	659,100	60.1	4.1	81.2	14.4
La Presa CDP	5.50	34,169	NA	NA	NA	23.5	87.9	66,158	11.8	421,300	62.2	8.4	78.1	16.6
La Puente city	3.48	39,832	39,614	-0.5	11383.3	40.3	93.4	64,592	14.3	419,800	64.5	6.2	87.2	10.2
La Quinta city	35.26	37,465	41,748	11.4	1184.0	15.5	88.5	77,839	10.5	398,200	55.3	7.5	69.5	25.6
La Riviera CDP	1.90	10,802	NA	NA	NA	11.3	72.8	64,518	12.5	290,800	66.8	6.3	57.4	27.2
Larkspur city	3.02	11,908	12,254	2.9	4057.6	17.3	86.1	109,426	8.7	1,309,200	66.8	2.6	56.4	36.3
Lathrop city	19.83	17,589	24,483	39.2	1234.6	35.2	85.7	85,805	9.5	358,900	63.0	6.6	87.6	8.6
La Verne city	8.43	31,096	31,974	2.8	3792.9	16.3	88.9	88,131	7.1	588,300	59.8	7.4	71.9	23.4
Lawndale city	1.97	32,769	32,389	-1.2	16441.1	37.6	91.0	62,013	12.7	518,000	68.7	4.2	74.1	20.7
Lemon Grove city	3.88	25,318	26,811	5.9	6910.1	20.3	87.5	63,548	10.8	432,000	62.0	8.1	70.4	21.4
Lemon Hill CDP	1.64	13,729	NA	NA	NA	33.0	86.5	39,430	30.2	177,000	57.6	9.9	73.5	18.5
Lemoore city	8.81	24,534	26,725	8.9	3033.5	15.0	78.8	63,605	11.9	229,100	63.5	6.2	73.5	19.9
Lennox CDP	1.09	22,753	NA	NA	NA	45.5	89.5	49,316	18.3	454,800	70.6	5.8	84.4	12.3
Lincoln city	23.51	42,926	48,275	12.5	2053.4	14.3	88.2	88,734	8.2	447,600	53.0	3.5	72.6	23.2
Linda CDP	8.59	17,773	NA	NA	NA	17.6	83.0	46,373	22.5	217,800	55.4	9.2	72.7	19.9
Lindsay city	2.73	11,756	13,463	14.5	4931.5	38.3	87.4	31,489	33.5	142,200	56.6	16.0	76.4	14.5
Live Oak CDP	3.24	17,158	NA	NA	NA	16.0	89.5	83,750	10.8	718,600	63.7	3.5	61.9	29.3
Livermore city	27.02	81,426	90,189	10.8	3337.9	15.7	88.3	127,452	3.9	744,200	70.1	3.1	74.4	20.7
Livingston city	3.68	13,020	14,896	14.4	4047.8	39.3	89.5	54,886	17.2	229,900	67.7	7.3	84.9	13.1
Lodi city	13.64	62,121	67,586	8.8	4955.0	18.0	83.1	58,763	13.9	323,400	62.8	7.1	69.5	25.1

Table B. Incorporated Places, Census Designated Places (CDPs), and Minor Civil Divisions (MCDs) of 10,000 or More Population — Crime, Residential Construction and Local Government Finance

STATE City, town, township, borough, or CDP (county if applicable)	Serious crimes known to police, 2018[1]				New residential construction authorized by building permits, 2019			Local government finance, 2017							
	Violent crime		Property crime					General revenue				General expenditure			
									Intergovernmental				Per capita[3]		
	Number	Rate[2]	Number	Rate[2]	Value ($1,000)	Number of housing units	Percent single family	Total (mil dol)	Total (mil dol)	Percent from state gov.	Taxes per capita[3]	Total (mil dol)	Total	Capital outlays	Debt outstanding (mil dol)
	15	16	17	18	19	20	21	22	23	24	25	26	27	28	29
CALIFORNIA—Con.															
Fortuna city	46	376	352	2,879	5,588	24	83.3	15.7	4.5	96.1	428	13.8	1,123	143	20.3
Foster City city	35	100	376	1,075	14,722	20	100.0	83.7	1.2	100.0	1,198	46.9	1,366	53	0.0
Fountain Valley city	52	92	1,496	2,651	22,296	130	18.5	60.2	5.5	35.7	715	69.1	1,233	219	44.7
Fremont city	502	211	4,687	1,969	260,851	1,148	14.7	311.6	20.1	58.8	1,042	283.4	1,208	128	204.3
French Valley CDP	NA	NA	NA	NA	NA	NA	NA	NA	NA	NA	NA	NA	NA	NA	NA
Fresno city	2,953	555	17,787	3,345	421,046	1,611	71.6	767.4	154.7	39.0	613	440.5	838	4	1206.3
Fullerton city	332	235	3,660	2,593	50,293	423	5.4	171.6	30.6	86.1	636	170.1	1,217	287	106.7
Galt city	96	362	462	1,740	8,261	57	100.0	34.2	1.5	70.7	509	30.6	1,170	97	41.7
Gardena city	326	540	1,306	2,161	5,384	43	100.0	106.7	46.4	11.0	800	81.6	1,363	161	21.9
Garden Acres CDP	NA	NA	NA	NA	NA	NA	NA	NA	NA	NA	NA	NA	NA	NA	NA
Garden Grove city	507	290	4,040	2,313	26,680	577	29.3	219.2	9.9	56.9	697	248.1	1,431	418	127.7
Gilroy city	209	354	1,609	2,726	80,653	191	100.0	82.8	3.1	67.7	727	90.6	1,575	375	84.8
Glendale city	202	99	3,110	1,519	27,039	200	69.0	379.8	20.7	57.5	906	322.1	1,596	90	382.6
Glendora city	122	231	1,523	2,889	8,589	41	100.0	42.2	4.8	51.6	566	35.6	684	66	34.3
Goleta city	42	134	352	1,125	37,972	154	94.8	44.5	2.4	47.4	812	41.2	1,326	419	14.9
Grand Terrace city	37	292	254	2,004	4,807	18	100.0	8.3	1.1	73.2	344	9.9	785	176	0.0
Granite Bay CDP	NA	NA	NA	NA	NA	NA	NA	NA	NA	NA	NA	NA	NA	NA	NA
Grass Valley city	70	538	517	3,976	7,335	52	46.2	24.8	1.5	50.9	1,011	17.9	1,382	65	18.8
Greenfield city	97	549	193	1,092	2,141	10	100.0	18.1	5.7	66.7	340	13.8	797	139	12.0
Grover Beach city	28	205	249	1,818	9,037	50	62.0	15.6	3.0	50.7	590	15.8	1,163	63	13.1
Hacienda Heights CDP	NA	NA	NA	NA	NA	NA	NA	NA	NA	NA	NA	NA	NA	NA	NA
Half Moon Bay city	NA	NA	NA	NA	2,693	8	75.0	22.4	0.6	71.1	1,110	19.0	1,479	274	10.9
Hanford city	274	482	1,264	2,225	61,751	235	89.4	52.2	3.7	56.8	507	58.1	1,031	125	41.6
Hawaiian Gardens city	81	560	250	1,727	1,248	5	100.0	24.4	5.1	9.2	1,262	34.1	2,379	636	30.0
Hawthorne city	617	698	1,705	1,929	20,425	31	83.9	99.1	7.4	54.1	755	106.4	1,219	103	70.2
Hayward city	669	411	4,770	2,929	331,731	1,348	51.6	250.4	23.7	56.5	1,034	226.4	1,412	262	211.4
Healdsburg city	20	168	223	1,871	10,072	26	100.0	30.9	2.1	32.7	1,304	36.3	3,077	157	46.7
Hemet city	432	502	2,863	3,327	14,949	76	100.0	55.4	4.7	66.2	440	64.6	762	134	10.1
Hercules city	30	117	350	1,359	0	0	0.0	51.3	14.5	53.3	911	30.5	1,197	269	153.0
Hermosa Beach city	30	152	477	2,417	25,131	42	100.0	41.0	1.7	57.1	1,464	41.8	2,132	110	11.3
Hesperia city	406	425	2,035	2,131	59,911	391	51.2	66.9	5.5	46.8	512	97.6	1,033	326	185.2
Highland city	208	374	1,143	2,054	16,889	62	100.0	28.0	3.8	51.8	383	47.5	861	214	11.2
Hillsborough town	9	78	90	777	11,174	8	100.0	41.2	2.1	100.0	2,047	40.0	3,491	192	67.8
Hollister city	98	252	496	1,274	152,569	422	98.8	56.8	7.1	19.6	539	38.8	1,010	13	69.0
Home Gardens CDP	NA	NA	NA	NA	NA	NA	NA	NA	NA	NA	NA	NA	NA	NA	NA
Huntington Beach city	429	211	3,993	1,963	59,405	165	93.3	276.3	14.8	68.9	888	265.2	1,320	135	142.1
Huntington Park city	429	728	1,800	3,055	120	3	100.0	62.4	8.7	52.6	633	54.1	925	74	259.7
Imperial city	9	50	77	428	34,623	178	100.0	16.6	1.9	25.9	407	17.4	1,000	257	24.9
Imperial Beach city	79	287	352	1,277	2,461	18	100.0	26.3	2.6	93.2	428	26.8	982	88	37.8
Indio city	495	542	2,242	2,454	41,514	261	100.0	96.2	10.1	49.7	666	105.8	1,183	132	181.1
Inglewood city	683	617	2,744	2,478	5,332	25	12.0	191.4	30.2	9.2	1,095	240.1	2,184	279	236.9
Irvine city	160	56	3,659	1,270	522,341	2,509	36.6	307.9	12.6	60.1	777	305.3	1,106	84	1066.9
Isla Vista CDP	NA	NA	NA	NA	NA	NA	NA	NA	NA	NA	NA	NA	NA	NA	NA
Jurupa Valley city	332	309	2,839	2,638	67,527	355	100.0	39.5	2.6	94.6	250	35.2	333	0	7.9
Kerman city	59	390	358	2,367	21,314	132	53.8	12.5	2.4	43.5	338	9.9	667	102	12.3
King City city	32	225	175	1,230	4,332	19	100.0	13.5	1.8	27.7	430	9.1	656	56	7.0
Kingsburg city	40	331	306	2,531	16,536	84	39.3	12.5	1.8	32.5	527	11.6	965	207	3.0
La Cañada Flintridge city	13	64	330	1,615	13,908	13	100.0	21.2	1.1	66.8	756	22.5	1,107	158	29.6
La Crescenta-Montrose CDP	NA	NA	NA	NA	NA	NA	NA	NA	NA	NA	NA	NA	NA	NA	NA
Ladera Ranch CDP	NA	NA	NA	NA	NA	NA	NA	NA	NA	NA	NA	NA	NA	NA	NA
Lafayette city	10	37	231	861	NA	NA	NA	25.6	3.1	23.2	585	29.4	1,113	225	4.8
Laguna Beach city	90	388	443	1,909	14,410	22	100.0	90.5	4.9	40.2	2,562	80.1	3,477	402	11.5
Laguna Hills city	55	175	402	1,277	220	3	100.0	24.2	1.8	61.8	634	30.9	978	258	8.7
Laguna Niguel city	81	121	640	958	70,776	279	1.8	46.6	2.5	69.8	581	58.8	890	195	0.3
Laguna Woods city	10	62	108	666	0	0	0.0	6.4	0.6	77.5	343	12.1	751	174	0.0
La Habra city	111	177	1,155	1,840	5,794	29	100.0	70.0	12.2	59.7	610	89.7	1,472	318	112.3
Lake Arrowhead CDP	NA	NA	NA	NA	NA	NA	NA	NA	NA	NA	NA	NA	NA	NA	NA
Lake Elsinore city	161	235	1,919	2,804	89,494	397	79.1	71.6	6.0	94.4	455	72.6	1,099	172	246.2
Lake Forest city	159	186	761	892	117,782	416	86.1	90.9	4.9	40.8	541	95.5	1,139	355	14.4
Lakeland Village CDP	NA	NA	NA	NA	NA	NA	NA	NA	NA	NA	NA	NA	NA	NA	NA
Lake Los Angeles CDP	NA	NA	NA	NA	NA	NA	NA	NA	NA	NA	NA	NA	NA	NA	NA
Lakeside CDP	NA	NA	NA	NA	NA	NA	NA	NA	NA	NA	NA	NA	NA	NA	NA
Lakewood city	270	333	1,848	2,279	7,254	31	22.6	60.0	7.4	86.5	495	57.4	712	89	2.0
La Mesa city	160	265	1,049	1,736	17,700	202	7.4	64.2	4.4	76.6	705	72.1	1,207	186	43.6
La Mirada city	89	181	829	1,686	3,502	7	100.0	54.3	6.4	17.5	742	57.1	1,169	438	70.8
Lamont CDP	NA	NA	NA	NA	NA	NA	NA	NA	NA	NA	NA	NA	NA	NA	NA
Lancaster city	1,193	742	3,805	2,366	56,845	258	80.2	116.7	9.7	57.7	539	149.5	937	185	233.7
La Palma city	20	127	334	2,121	0	0	0.0	13.3	1.9	42.9	610	16.3	1,039	121	6.5
La Presa CDP	NA	NA	NA	NA	NA	NA	NA	NA	NA	NA	NA	NA	NA	NA	NA
La Puente city	162	401	501	1,240	4,472	18	100.0	18.8	1.7	78.1	319	18.2	455	83	33.7
La Quinta city	42	100	1,154	2,758	42,668	139	100.0	79.8	6.9	22.5	1,332	64.0	1,555	228	211.7
La Riviera CDP	NA	NA	NA	NA	NA	NA	NA	NA	NA	NA	NA	NA	NA	NA	NA
Larkspur city	NA	NA	NA	NA	877	1	100.0	23.8	1.6	52.2	1,461	19.3	1,571	153	4.0
Lathrop city	NA	NA	NA	NA	137,095	425	93.6	64.8	1.7	37.1	1,085	35.4	1,594	191	60.5
La Verne city	87	266	742	2,272	3,295	6	100.0	41.5	1.9	86.0	700	41.8	1,295	58	10.6
Lawndale city	129	390	348	1,051	1,724	8	75.0	18.7	3.5	23.9	413	29.3	892	217	19.6
Lemon Grove city	155	566	468	1,710	613	6	100.0	24.9	3.4	96.0	498	34.3	1,272	196	27.7
Lemon Hill CDP	NA	NA	NA	NA	NA	NA	NA	NA	NA	NA	NA	NA	NA	NA	NA
Lemoore city	188	706	385	1,446	18,695	82	100.0	20.2	2.1	67.1	283	22.5	856	207	5.8
Lennox CDP	NA	NA	NA	NA	NA	NA	NA	NA	NA	NA	NA	NA	NA	NA	NA
Lincoln city	35	72	418	864	83,784	260	100.0	90.3	4.5	56.1	429	56.7	1,192	150	27.9
Linda CDP	NA	NA	NA	NA	NA	NA	NA	NA	NA	NA	NA	NA	NA	NA	NA
Lindsay city	34	251	214	1,580	1,592	9	100.0	11.5	1.3	58.1	386	16.9	1,279	502	16.3
Live Oak CDP	NA	NA	NA	NA	NA	NA	NA	NA	NA	NA	NA	NA	NA	NA	NA
Livermore city	186	203	1,696	1,851	26,223	102	52.0	172.3	7.9	46.6	1,043	203.7	2,260	338	124.3
Livingston city	41	287	308	2,154	14,626	67	100.0	13.4	1.9	41.7	376	11.8	841	61	8.8
Lodi city	277	417	1,701	2,561	75,729	403	29.5	102.0	17.6	62.1	640	117.6	1,789	210	152.6

1 Data for serious crimes have not been adjusted for underreporting. This may affect comparability between geographic areas over time.
2 Per 100,000 population estimated by the FBI.   3 Based on population estimated as of July 1 of the year shown.

Table B. Incorporated Places, Census Designated Places (CDPs), and Minor Civil Divisions (MCDs) of 10,000 or More Population — Land Area, Population, and Households, and Employment

STATE / City, town, township, borough, or CDP (county if applicable)	Land area 2010 (sq mi)	Population				Population characteristics 2015–2019		Income and poverty 2015–2019		Median value of owner-occupied housing units	Employment, 2015–2019		Households, 2015–2019 (percent of households)	
		Total persons 2010	Total persons 2019	Percent change 2010–2019	Persons per square mile 2019	Percent foreign born	Percent living in the same house as previous year	Median household income	Percent of households with income below poverty level		Percent in civilian labor force	Unemploy-ment rate	Family households	One person households
	1	2	3	4	5	6	7	8	9	10	11	12	13	14
CALIFORNIA—Con.														
Loma Linda city	7.66	23,306	24,482	5.0	3196.1	28.3	85.4	55,607	15.8	367,400	53.7	5.7	67.0	28.2
Lomita city	1.91	20,256	20,320	0.3	10638.7	20.1	90.4	71,606	10.9	604,300	66.1	3.2	62.5	31.2
Lompoc city	11.62	42,438	42,853	1.0	3687.9	21.4	82.8	54,855	15.6	315,900	59.3	10.0	69.1	25.0
Long Beach city	50.70	462,221	462,628	0.1	9124.8	25.2	88.7	63,017	14.6	556,100	65.9	6.0	59.6	31.0
Los Alamitos city	4.02	11,376	11,399	0.2	2835.6	15.6	88.3	88,729	8.7	761,200	62.7	4.7	70.5	24.4
Los Altos city	6.48	29,024	30,089	3.7	4643.4	31.3	89.8	235,278	3.2	2,000,000	60.2	3.3	80.9	16.4
Los Angeles city	468.96	3,793,139	3,979,576	4.9	8486.0	36.9	88.4	62,142	17.3	636,900	66.5	6.3	59.5	30.3
Los Banos city	9.99	35,971	41,036	14.1	4107.7	28.3	88.9	62,874	17.0	293,400	62.7	13.3	80.6	16.2
Los Gatos town	11.39	29,715	30,222	1.7	2653.4	21.8	86.5	155,863	4.2	1,694,000	61.0	4.5	69.1	25.5
Los Osos CDP	12.76	14,276	NA	NA	NA	10.0	87.0	77,807	9.3	551,500	57.0	4.3	72.0	21.8
Lynwood city	4.84	69,763	69,887	0.2	14439.5	36.9	93.5	52,213	17.9	399,100	60.6	8.4	87.6	9.4
McFarland city	2.67	12,707	15,506	22.0	5807.5	36.6	94.8	35,346	28.6	171,000	56.3	13.4	87.8	12.0
McKinleyville CDP	20.88	15,177	NA	NA	NA	2.8	85.2	54,614	16.5	296,700	61.0	6.8	58.3	29.9
Madera city	16.33	61,513	65,860	7.1	4033.1	29.0	88.7	45,163	24.6	224,100	62.2	9.2	79.6	16.4
Magalia CDP	14.01	11,310	NA	NA	NA	1.6	83.8	50,415	14.3	172,900	46.6	7.2	63.6	25.5
Malibu city	19.85	12,634	11,820	-6.4	595.5	11.3	88.0	150,747	7.6	2,000,000	59.5	3.5	61.5	33.7
Manhattan Beach city	3.94	35,131	35,183	0.1	8929.7	13.3	89.2	153,023	3.9	2,000,000	62.2	5.1	71.4	22.6
Manteca city	21.39	67,348	83,028	23.3	3881.6	17.0	86.6	72,867	10.0	386,400	59.9	8.2	76.1	18.0
Marina city	8.89	19,718	22,781	15.5	2562.5	23.6	85.2	64,258	11.5	513,000	65.3	5.1	62.2	30.2
Martinez city	12.63	36,032	38,297	6.3	3032.2	12.2	86.0	107,328	4.6	596,400	68.4	3.9	65.3	27.8
Marysville city	3.46	12,072	12,476	3.3	3605.8	10.7	77.3	44,839	21.4	207,200	58.8	7.1	57.2	34.1
Maywood city	1.18	27,382	26,973	-1.5	22858.5	46.7	95.0	44,241	24.1	387,000	66.4	7.8	84.3	10.7
Mead Valley CDP	19.08	18,510	NA	NA	NA	33.0	89.8	59,079	20.1	268,900	54.7	9.1	87.8	9.9
Mendota city	3.39	11,306	11,511	1.8	3395.6	54.0	96.3	31,237	35.6	158,700	66.7	19.2	83.9	10.1
Menifee city	46.47	77,382	94,756	22.5	2039.1	14.5	85.6	70,224	9.2	334,600	55.6	7.3	73.2	22.6
Menlo Park city	10.01	32,019	34,698	8.4	3466.3	26.1	82.6	160,784	7.4	2,000,000	66.5	3.6	66.3	24.7
Merced city	23.23	78,958	83,676	6.0	3602.1	22.7	84.6	45,232	26.1	237,500	57.1	12.7	69.3	23.3
Millbrae city	3.25	21,537	22,394	4.0	6890.5	39.4	89.5	128,494	5.9	1,403,100	64.5	3.5	73.3	20.7
Mill Valley city	4.76	13,905	14,259	2.5	2995.6	13.0	87.4	163,614	6.3	1,598,700	60.5	2.3	65.9	28.4
Milpitas city	13.65	66,820	84,196	26.0	6168.2	52.3	84.7	132,320	6.8	858,600	66.3	3.7	80.8	12.4
Mission Viejo city	17.70	93,103	94,381	1.4	5332.3	20.0	86.1	118,477	5.1	693,000	65.2	4.1	76.9	18.5
Modesto city	42.98	203,114	215,196	5.9	5006.9	18.0	86.1	59,287	13.1	283,800	59.8	8.9	70.0	24.0
Monrovia city	13.63	36,600	36,331	-0.7	2665.5	26.2	90.3	77,111	8.1	663,400	68.0	5.9	67.8	24.3
Montclair city	5.52	36,645	40,083	9.4	7261.4	33.7	90.1	62,024	14.0	354,500	64.6	7.5	80.3	14.5
Montebello city	8.33	62,488	61,954	-0.9	7437.5	37.8	92.1	56,150	14.2	492,300	63.2	7.0	77.8	18.4
Monterey city	8.64	27,691	28,178	1.8	3261.3	16.7	74.3	80,694	9.4	782,500	56.2	3.0	48.1	39.3
Monterey Park city	7.67	60,225	59,669	-0.9	7779.5	53.6	90.8	61,819	14.2	616,000	56.8	5.2	75.8	18.6
Moorpark city	12.58	34,523	36,375	5.4	2891.5	16.8	91.7	107,820	4.4	632,900	69.2	4.3	79.8	15.8
Moraga town	9.47	16,006	17,783	11.1	1877.8	14.8	87.3	140,378	6.3	1,140,700	55.9	4.0	74.2	19.8
Moreno Valley city	51.26	193,301	213,055	10.2	4156.4	25.0	88.9	66,134	13.1	312,000	63.6	8.4	83.9	11.7
Morgan Hill city	13.00	37,969	45,952	21.0	3534.8	18.0	88.3	124,419	4.1	855,100	67.4	4.0	78.9	16.8
Morro Bay city	5.32	10,235	10,543	3.0	1981.8	5.2	87.9	68,262	11.3	607,300	51.9	7.4	53.8	38.3
Mountain House CDP	3.19	9,675	NA	NA	NA	35.0	83.6	140,801	4.8	595,700	67.1	5.3	90.2	7.3
Mountain View city	11.99	74,008	82,739	11.8	6900.7	42.2	79.5	139,720	6.8	1,413,500	73.7	3.3	56.6	30.5
Murrieta city	33.61	103,731	116,223	12.0	3458.0	15.2	83.8	90,535	7.1	414,100	63.0	7.6	79.7	15.6
Muscoy CDP	3.02	10,644	NA	NA	NA	35.8	85.3	46,969	23.7	251,400	55.9	17.3	86.2	10.7
Napa city	17.96	77,088	78,130	1.4	4350.2	20.8	88.1	84,043	7.6	616,700	68.5	4.4	66.2	27.1
National City city	7.29	58,560	61,394	4.8	8421.7	39.2	88.3	47,119	18.5	402,000	54.2	6.6	73.1	21.9
Newark city	13.88	42,573	49,149	15.4	3541.0	36.7	90.5	116,856	5.1	742,100	68.3	4.1	81.2	13.0
Newman city	2.06	10,261	11,784	14.8	5720.4	23.1	88.8	62,877	6.9	263,000	61.1	13.5	83.9	14.9
Newport Beach city	23.82	85,211	84,534	-0.8	3548.9	14.6	85.3	127,223	7.3	1,898,900	61.9	3.1	57.8	32.8
Nipomo CDP	14.85	16,714	NA	NA	NA	17.7	90.9	82,543	9.0	537,700	60.3	5.4	82.4	13.1
Norco city	13.83	27,212	26,604	-2.2	1923.6	11.5	85.4	102,817	6.8	544,900	55.7	3.7	76.1	19.7
North Auburn CDP	7.79	13,022	NA	NA	NA	8.7	82.3	60,308	13.3	356,200	52.0	2.3	58.0	35.7
North Fair Oaks CDP	1.20	14,687	NA	NA	NA	43.5	87.9	77,899	12.5	941,600	71.6	3.1	72.7	20.9
North Highlands CDP	8.81	42,694	NA	NA	NA	25.4	86.8	45,488	21.6	217,500	59.8	5.1	71.0	22.0
North Tustin CDP	6.61	24,917	NA	NA	NA	14.4	90.4	156,176	3.5	926,100	60.6	3.3	83.6	13.2
Norwalk city	9.71	105,549	103,949	-1.5	10705.4	34.1	93.3	70,667	10.5	440,800	62.7	5.8	83.1	12.7
Novato city	27.45	51,869	55,516	7.0	2022.4	20.0	88.4	101,342	6.8	782,500	64.4	3.6	64.6	28.3
Oakdale city	6.18	20,744	23,596	13.7	3818.1	10.6	87.8	64,555	11.8	310,100	62.3	12.2	70.8	24.2
Oak Hills CDP	24.35	8,879	NA	NA	NA	19.2	92.2	87,429	10.2	347,900	56.7	2.5	87.8	8.5
Oakland city	55.89	390,765	433,031	10.8	7747.9	26.8	86.5	73,692	15.4	687,400	68.7	6.1	54.5	33.3
Oakley city	15.86	35,423	42,543	20.1	2682.4	16.3	91.7	104,893	7.6	441,900	67.8	3.9	83.2	14.5
Oak Park CDP	5.29	13,811	NA	NA	NA	20.9	86.0	132,578	4.2	760,200	67.0	5.3	68.7	27.2
Oceanside city	41.26	167,547	175,742	4.9	4259.4	19.8	83.2	72,697	8.9	492,600	64.3	6.0	67.6	25.1
Oildale CDP	6.53	32,684	NA	NA	NA	5.2	78.7	38,099	25.1	160,300	57.1	15.0	62.2	27.9
Olivehurst CDP	7.46	13,656	NA	NA	NA	16.2	85.1	48,598	16.1	173,100	57.1	7.8	72.7	20.6
Ontario city	49.96	163,936	185,010	12.9	3703.2	27.9	89.1	65,046	12.8	375,000	67.7	6.5	78.0	16.4
Orange city	25.67	136,776	138,669	1.4	5402.0	22.8	87.3	91,793	10.5	656,100	64.9	4.4	73.2	18.9
Orange Cove city	1.79	9,735	10,273	5.5	5739.1	35.5	87.2	25,677	45.9	152,300	59.6	14.7	85.0	11.8
Orangevale CDP	11.47	33,960	NA	NA	NA	7.6	84.6	81,801	7.1	372,500	63.2	5.4	68.2	24.6
Orcutt CDP	11.13	28,905	NA	NA	NA	7.5	89.9	91,343	5.8	422,600	63.9	6.6	75.2	20.2
Orinda city	12.85	17,759	19,926	12.2	1550.7	17.0	89.1	223,217	3.9	1,464,400	60.8	3.8	79.2	17.7
Oroville city	13.83	18,725	20,737	10.7	1499.4	6.0	74.9	34,428	24.1	183,600	45.7	8.7	61.0	30.2
Oxnard city	26.53	198,047	208,881	5.5	7873.4	34.6	90.6	72,843	12.5	453,900	67.8	5.7	80.7	13.6
Pacifica city	12.66	37,338	38,546	3.2	3044.7	20.6	90.5	125,500	4.1	882,800	68.9	3.2	70.2	21.1
Pacific Grove city	2.86	15,039	15,413	2.5	5389.2	11.2	81.0	88,250	7.7	857,900	57.5	3.9	57.5	36.0
Palmdale city	106.08	152,733	155,079	1.5	1461.9	24.7	90.0	62,865	15.2	280,000	59.6	8.0	79.8	16.1
Palm Desert city	26.81	48,449	53,275	10.0	1987.1	19.2	86.1	59,977	12.0	350,400	49.6	5.2	56.3	35.8
Palm Springs city	94.55	44,555	48,518	8.9	513.1	20.0	82.6	53,441	14.4	389,800	50.6	8.6	42.2	45.8
Palo Alto city	23.85	64,387	65,364	1.5	2740.6	35.3	83.5	158,271	7.3	2,000,000	62.0	3.2	66.5	26.2
Palos Verdes Estates city	4.77	13,438	13,273	-1.2	2782.6	22.1	89.7	194,543	5.9	2,000,000	51.5	2.3	82.9	14.9
Paradise town	18.32	26,219	4,476	-82.9	244.3	2.4	85.6	51,566	14.7	223,400	48.1	7.4	58.9	34.9
Paramount city	4.73	54,098	53,955	-0.3	11407.0	34.7	91.6	55,670	16.5	343,800	64.1	5.3	82.0	14.5
Parkway CDP	2.40	14,670	NA	NA	NA	26.6	87.0	44,097	23.8	233,900	60.0	13.1	72.9	20.1
Parlier city	2.41	14,596	15,618	7.0	6480.5	41.2	89.7	34,905	37.5	161,600	65.1	6.7	84.4	12.7
Pasadena city	22.96	137,114	141,029	2.9	6142.4	30.0	86.8	83,068	14.3	785,700	65.8	4.2	56.6	33.5

Table B.   Incorporated Places, Census Designated Places (CDPs), and Minor Civil Divisions (MCDs) of 10,000 or More Population — **Crime, Residential Construction and Local Government Finance**

STATE City, town, township, borough, or CDP (county if applicable)	Serious crimes known to police, 2018[1] Violent crime Number	Violent crime Rate[2]	Property crime Number	Property crime Rate[2]	New residential construction authorized by building permits, 2019 Value ($1,000)	Number of housing units	Percent single family	Local government finance, 2017 General revenue Total (mil dol)	Intergovernmental Total (mil dol)	Percent from state gov.	Taxes per capita[3]	General expenditure Total (mil dol)	Per capita[3] Total	Capital outlays	Debt outstanding (mil dol)
	15	16	17	18	19	20	21	22	23	24	25	26	27	28	29
CALIFORNIA—Con.															
Loma Linda city	40	165	608	2,500	8,559	89	21.3	26.0	1.1	63.1	516	28.5	1,180	137	5.8
Lomita city	66	318	312	1,502	6,884	23	69.6	12.8	4.8	70.9	293	12.5	607	118	7.0
Lompoc city	218	499	951	2,175	1,203	5	100.0	74.0	8.9	33.8	468	67.0	1,549	185	41.1
Long Beach city	3,284	698	11,922	2,534	228,993	1,161	8.6	1548.9	258.1	27.0	939	1647.7	3,531	933	2367.5
Los Alamitos city	8	69	156	1,342	5,466	26	0.0	14.2	1.1	91.1	916	15.1	1,310	220	3.9
Los Altos city	13	42	284	917	46,711	53	100.0	48.7	2.3	54.4	1,112	47.1	1,535	191	1.4
Los Angeles city	30,126	748	101,267	2,513	3,311,094	14,387	18.4	10825.2	1131.0	26.5	1,184	9618.2	2,419	399	27626.9
Los Banos city	144	363	1,071	2,701	47,355	95	100.0	42.4	2.4	87.9	479	34.2	878	150	2.0
Los Gatos town	10	32	459	1,486	19,683	29	86.2	41.5	1.8	97.4	1,073	51.1	1,653	437	24.6
Los Osos CDP	NA	NA	NA	NA	NA	NA	NA	NA	NA	NA	NA	NA	NA	NA	NA
Lynwood city	426	597	1,438	2,016	2,849	20	70.0	49.1	6.3	92.4	393	47.5	671	126	40.3
McFarland city	61	394	212	1,370	877	8	100.0	13.2	4.8	22.2	298	10.2	681	120	14.7
McKinleyville CDP	NA	NA	NA	NA	NA	NA	NA	NA	NA	NA	NA	NA	NA	NA	NA
Madera city	399	604	1,346	2,036	29,340	171	100.0	58.4	10.0	35.2	366	61.5	947	233	94.5
Magalia CDP	NA	NA	NA	NA	NA	NA	NA	NA	NA	NA	NA	NA	NA	NA	NA
Malibu city	37	287	380	2,943	95,363	64	100.0	65.7	0.9	36.6	2,231	59.1	4,614	2206	58.3
Manhattan Beach city	57	158	844	2,342	68,348	98	98.0	88.6	4.2	40.2	1,503	86.2	2,415	205	25.0
Manteca city	256	316	2,288	2,822	190,213	689	75.0	112.8	7.4	56.0	561	113.5	1,435	392	69.7
Marina city	49	218	317	1,408	10,709	34	100.0	40.3	3.2	65.7	723	78.8	3,582	2222	66.3
Martinez city	73	189	524	1,354	926	4	100.0	29.9	1.6	99.2	654	27.3	711	54	33.7
Marysville city	112	899	533	4,278	0	0	0.0	12.5	1.3	87.2	480	13.4	1,086	91	49.4
Maywood city	87	315	302	1,094	903	7	42.9	11.1	1.2	50.2	318	12.4	454	27	2.8
Mead Valley CDP	NA	NA	NA	NA	NA	NA	NA	NA	NA	NA	NA	NA	NA	NA	NA
Mendota city	86	749	197	1,717	0	0	0.0	7.3	1.7	84.6	249	7.1	613	129	6.1
Menifee city	155	168	1,945	2,102	322,427	1,349	75.4	49.7	4.5	76.4	350	88.6	983	190	18.3
Menlo Park city	43	124	606	1,747	92,075	245	20.0	74.1	3.2	58.0	1,650	71.0	2,076	363	78.5
Merced city	465	556	2,219	2,652	185,661	668	100.0	93.5	7.8	72.2	467	107.0	1,296	274	49.6
Millbrae city	NA	NA	NA	NA	0	0	0.0	51.1	1.7	49.1	1,112	42.6	1,879	223	64.7
Mill Valley city	9	62	196	1,359	23,761	35	71.4	48.7	1.4	70.6	2,219	40.2	2,813	243	27.6
Milpitas city	87	109	1,934	2,421	111,190	359	36.5	177.5	4.8	40.4	1,282	133.4	1,713	410	125.6
Mission Viejo city	113	117	937	972	0	0	0.0	83.9	4.0	59.8	626	101.3	1,060	131	38.0
Modesto city	1,904	882	7,727	3,580	54,711	198	98.5	285.6	70.5	69.9	505	214.1	1,005	131	516.5
Monrovia city	69	186	914	2,462	3,196	20	90.0	66.4	8.2	16.0	1,142	73.2	1,986	229	149.8
Montclair city	239	603	1,646	4,152	0	0	0.0	63.7	3.6	40.7	1,117	61.8	1,579	455	86.9
Montebello city	218	344	1,643	2,596	4,474	11	100.0	132.5	36.4	14.0	1,140	82.4	1,312	178	130.2
Monterey city	112	390	1,143	3,977	6,200	14	28.6	143.5	7.0	74.5	2,407	136.1	4,790	363	97.5
Monterey Park city	124	203	1,589	2,598	4,255	13	100.0	70.1	7.6	76.0	701	65.7	1,083	51	90.6
Moorpark city	33	89	261	703	328	4	100.0	34.9	2.8	27.0	426	38.5	1,053	85	29.0
Moraga town	12	67	94	526	NA	NA	NA	13.0	2.0	100.0	468	9.9	562	74	7.7
Moreno Valley city	775	371	6,161	2,946	82,834	329	95.7	149.0	14.7	73.5	486	212.2	1,026	177	144.4
Morgan Hill city	52	113	740	1,604	59,915	199	66.8	71.1	1.4	96.9	769	75.3	1,674	425	90.4
Morro Bay city	36	337	135	1,263	7,801	31	83.9	25.8	1.3	80.2	1,156	27.4	2,589	370	1.9
Mountain House CDP	NA	NA	NA	NA	NA	NA	NA	NA	NA	NA	NA	NA	NA	NA	NA
Mountain View city	157	190	2,103	2,549	128,688	669	11.8	300.9	4.1	65.6	1,827	272.8	3,360	740	44.0
Murrieta city	92	80	1,412	1,231	72,903	328	49.4	70.0	5.8	59.5	428	95.9	849	299	52.1
Muscoy CDP	NA	NA	NA	NA	NA	NA	NA	NA	NA	NA	NA	NA	NA	NA	NA
Napa city	269	336	1,241	1,548	137,400	714	14.0	139.8	17.2	22.1	951	138.2	1,747	158	56.9
National City city	306	495	1,167	1,890	16,252	163	8.6	92.6	18.8	28.8	888	100.6	1,646	378	60.4
Newark city	97	201	1,318	2,730	128,024	443	60.0	72.2	3.5	46.7	1,059	55.8	1,177	85	18.3
Newman city	19	165	134	1,163	13,900	56	100.0	9.5	0.6	67.9	256	9.2	813	105	0.4
Newport Beach city	124	144	2,073	2,403	120,567	175	71.4	259.8	10.8	20.0	2,029	296.0	3,452	1350	226.9
Nipomo CDP	NA	NA	NA	NA	NA	NA	NA	NA	NA	NA	NA	NA	NA	NA	NA
Norco city	63	236	675	2,527	1,834	5	100.0	32.4	1.4	72.7	559	55.6	2,070	522	149.1
North Auburn CDP	NA	NA	NA	NA	NA	NA	NA	NA	NA	NA	NA	NA	NA	NA	NA
North Fair Oaks CDP	NA	NA	NA	NA	NA	NA	NA	NA	NA	NA	NA	NA	NA	NA	NA
North Highlands CDP	NA	NA	NA	NA	NA	NA	NA	NA	NA	NA	NA	NA	NA	NA	NA
North Tustin CDP	NA	NA	NA	NA	NA	NA	NA	NA	NA	NA	NA	NA	NA	NA	NA
Norwalk city	449	423	1,948	1,835	1,527	6	100.0	101.3	33.2	24.6	535	73.6	698	64	119.3
Novato city	97	171	773	1,366	31,516	124	60.5	54.3	3.2	58.5	685	58.8	1,055	220	66.4
Oakdale city	48	204	555	2,361	7,568	63	7.9	27.4	3.5	91.2	573	21.9	951	148	36.6
Oak Hills CDP	NA	NA	NA	NA	NA	NA	NA	NA	NA	NA	NA	NA	NA	NA	NA
Oakland city	5,480	1,274	23,190	5,390	360,872	1,862	15.1	1639.3	137.8	49.4	1,915	1319.3	3,109	273	2230.3
Oakley city	42	99	508	1,191	72,636	262	100.0	34.6	1.2	100.0	432	31.7	762	250	61.8
Oak Park CDP	NA	NA	NA	NA	NA	NA	NA	NA	NA	NA	NA	NA	NA	NA	NA
Oceanside city	669	377	3,836	2,162	64,921	356	19.9	270.0	23.3	44.3	616	277.8	1,579	262	171.6
Oildale CDP	NA	NA	NA	NA	NA	NA	NA	NA	NA	NA	NA	NA	NA	NA	NA
Olivehurst CDP	NA	NA	NA	NA	NA	NA	NA	NA	NA	NA	NA	NA	NA	NA	NA
Ontario city	670	377	4,584	2,582	326,080	1,431	81.6	416.0	25.1	35.3	1,333	458.7	2,616	619	250.9
Orange city	160	113	2,478	1,756	63,074	440	17.0	147.1	9.9	56.4	754	170.6	1,217	330	107.7
Orange Cove city	25	258	94	971	0	0	0.0	7.3	2.9	57.4	235	7.4	718	22	3.1
Orangevale CDP	NA	NA	NA	NA	NA	NA	NA	NA	NA	NA	NA	NA	NA	NA	NA
Orcutt CDP	NA	NA	NA	NA	NA	NA	NA	NA	NA	NA	NA	NA	NA	NA	NA
Orinda city	9	45	110	550	NA	NA	NA	20.1	2.7	21.5	701	20.1	1,020	70	51.3
Oroville city	112	584	982	5,118	15,353	72	83.3	25.9	3.7	33.5	637	26.2	1,372	249	5.3
Oxnard city	801	378	5,055	2,387	41,996	140	45.0	374.7	21.2	48.0	636	301.2	1,442	24	442.7
Pacifica city	71	181	402	1,022	4,800	3	100.0	52.4	3.6	45.5	692	50.3	1,289	119	72.2
Pacific Grove city	23	146	312	1,976	2,994	12	100.0	31.0	4.1	97.5	1,319	28.4	1,821	203	18.3
Palmdale city	591	374	2,442	1,544	23,491	153	47.7	171.9	15.6	66.9	839	101.3	647	100	184.4
Palm Desert city	91	170	1,989	3,713	99,678	398	22.1	125.3	2.9	50.5	1,052	128.0	2,424	451	416.8
Palm Springs city	274	563	2,078	4,272	63,893	208	96.2	207.4	13.3	24.7	2,258	184.2	3,834	753	211.4
Palo Alto city	72	107	1,513	2,240	73,761	102	100.0	274.2	6.8	36.9	1,899	338.4	5,054	1472	132.9
Palos Verdes Estates city	6	44	104	767	15,341	21	100.0	19.9	0.9	73.6	863	22.9	1,699	225	0.0
Paradise town	65	243	279	1,043	78,572	312	100.0	19.4	5.8	56.6	471	19.6	736	20	15.6
Paramount city	329	598	1,427	2,594	861	3	100.0	33.7	5.9	70.5	452	35.8	656	100	5.0
Parkway CDP	NA	NA	NA	NA	NA	NA	NA	NA	NA	NA	NA	NA	NA	NA	NA
Parlier city	111	723	335	2,182	9,840	52	100.0	8.2	1.6	31.8	240	8.6	561	101	2.0
Pasadena city	547	381	2,928	2,041	56,289	252	13.9	403.5	42.8	27.6	1,535	323.3	2,281	0	946.5

1   Data for serious crimes have not been adjusted for underreporting. This may affect comparability between geographic areas over time.
2   Per 100,000 population estimated by the FBI.   3   Based on population estimated as of July 1 of the year shown.

Table B. Incorporated Places, Census Designated Places (CDPs), and Minor Civil Divisions (MCDs) of 10,000 or More Population — Land Area, Population, and Households, and Employment

STATE City, town, township, borough, or CDP (county if applicable)	Land area 2010 (sq mi)	Population Total persons 2010	Total persons 2019	Percent change 2010–2019	Persons per square mile, 2019	Population characteristics 2015–2019 Percent foreign born	Percent living in the same house as previous year	Income and poverty 2015–2019 Median household income	Percent of households with income below poverty level	Median value of owner-occupied housing units	Employment, 2015–2019 Percent in civilian labor force	Unemployment rate	Households, 2015–2019 (percent of households) Family households	One person households
	1	2	3	4	5	6	7	8	9	10	11	12	13	14
CALIFORNIA—Con.														
Patterson city	7.80	20,629	22,524	9.2	2887.7	25.5	91.8	69,233	12.1	306,900	63.9	8.9	84.6	12.0
Perris city	31.56	68,564	79,291	15.6	2512.4	30.4	89.8	63,829	16.0	281,600	64.1	7.4	86.6	9.9
Petaluma city	14.42	57,968	60,520	4.4	4196.9	15.7	87.8	91,528	7.1	633,900	65.7	4.0	67.8	25.6
Phelan CDP	60.09	14,304	NA	NA	NA	10.4	90.0	59,375	16.2	237,800	55.1	11.9	82.8	13.8
Pico Rivera city	8.30	62,958	62,027	-1.5	7473.1	29.7	94.7	67,636	11.0	440,600	62.4	5.1	79.5	17.4
Piedmont city	1.70	10,695	11,135	4.1	6550.0	10.8	92.5	224,659	2.8	2,000,000	63.7	3.9	82.2	16.3
Pinole city	5.10	18,330	19,250	5.0	3774.5	26.6	87.8	100,315	5.2	500,900	65.6	5.3	71.1	22.5
Pittsburg city	17.64	63,259	72,588	14.7	4115.0	32.1	88.0	74,459	14.0	386,200	66.2	8.3	76.0	17.2
Placentia city	6.61	50,915	51,233	0.6	7750.8	24.4	89.8	95,757	7.0	630,500	68.5	4.1	76.3	17.8
Placerville city	5.84	10,488	11,175	6.6	1913.5	6.8	77.7	59,247	16.9	355,500	53.4	4.7	59.4	31.4
Pleasant Hill city	7.07	33,076	34,839	5.3	4927.7	19.3	87.8	118,947	7.1	716,300	65.8	3.9	64.9	26.1
Pleasanton city	24.15	70,280	81,777	16.4	3386.2	32.0	87.5	156,400	4.7	986,800	66.0	3.1	78.9	17.7
Pomona city	22.98	149,061	151,691	1.8	6601.0	34.1	88.0	60,598	17.0	394,500	63.8	7.1	76.8	16.1
Porterville city	18.61	58,104	59,599	2.6	3202.5	22.4	86.0	43,823	25.1	172,500	57.7	12.4	76.0	19.1
Port Hueneme city	4.42	21,743	21,926	0.8	4960.6	22.7	82.6	64,126	12.1	412,200	59.4	5.0	66.4	25.8
Poway city	39.08	47,805	49,323	3.2	1262.1	20.0	87.2	107,902	5.6	686,400	62.4	5.6	80.8	14.4
Prunedale CDP	46.06	17,560	NA	NA	NA	22.0	91.7	89,137	6.2	566,700	63.6	5.1	80.5	14.6
Quartz Hill CDP	3.76	10,912	NA	NA	NA	8.8	91.9	74,071	14.1	335,500	55.1	5.2	73.0	20.3
Ramona CDP	38.44	20,292	NA	NA	NA	13.1	88.6	84,289	5.7	476,800	67.6	4.7	75.6	19.2
Rancho Cordova city	35.02	64,804	75,087	15.9	2144.1	23.9	84.2	65,307	11.8	299,800	67.3	7.5	67.9	24.1
Rancho Cucamonga city	40.12	165,380	177,603	7.4	4426.8	19.9	85.5	90,953	7.7	495,800	66.0	5.4	76.5	18.9
Rancho Mirage city	25.35	17,142	18,528	8.1	730.9	14.3	87.1	78,682	10.6	498,700	37.7	6.5	53.7	37.1
Rancho Palos Verdes city	13.47	41,688	41,530	-0.4	3083.1	27.5	89.5	138,557	5.5	1,156,700	55.7	4.0	75.3	21.7
Rancho San Diego CDP	8.70	21,208	NA	NA	NA	21.0	88.0	95,892	6.0	611,000	63.0	5.8	74.6	21.2
Rancho Santa Margarita city	12.90	47,855	47,896	0.1	3712.9	16.5	87.6	121,017	4.5	662,200	74.4	3.1	75.9	19.5
Red Bluff city	7.56	14,071	14,539	3.3	1923.1	6.5	81.8	31,450	29.6	174,300	53.8	11.0	55.6	34.2
Redding city	59.65	89,857	92,590	3.0	1552.2	6.8	83.1	54,278	15.7	264,900	57.5	5.2	61.7	30.0
Redlands city	35.86	68,679	71,513	4.1	1994.2	14.1	88.1	74,839	10.4	390,700	60.2	5.9	69.3	24.5
Redondo Beach city	6.20	66,931	66,749	-0.3	10766.0	19.5	86.2	113,499	4.1	926,500	72.2	3.8	60.3	30.2
Redwood City city	19.27	76,817	85,925	11.9	4459.0	34.0	85.4	117,123	7.1	1,251,000	70.8	2.9	65.0	25.2
Reedley city	5.45	24,306	25,668	5.6	4707.9	32.3	91.7	46,490	18.3	207,500	60.2	13.0	83.1	13.6
Rialto city	24.00	99,103	103,526	4.5	4313.6	27.4	88.8	61,518	15.7	313,400	64.7	10.6	82.6	14.1
Richmond city	30.06	103,255	110,567	7.1	3678.2	35.2	88.4	68,472	13.8	462,600	65.5	6.0	67.2	25.4
Ridgecrest city	20.88	27,616	28,973	4.9	1387.6	8.7	83.6	69,577	14.1	180,300	60.3	7.5	62.3	29.5
Rio Linda CDP	9.89	15,106	NA	NA	NA	15.2	89.4	70,825	14.3	274,200	58.9	4.9	79.8	12.6
Ripon city	5.33	14,415	16,386	13.7	3074.3	11.8	91.2	84,313	8.7	452,000	63.1	4.9	77.3	19.8
Riverbank city	4.05	22,675	24,881	9.7	6143.5	25.2	91.7	70,549	11.3	294,200	66.1	6.8	81.3	13.0
Riverside city	81.26	303,933	331,360	9.0	4077.8	22.6	86.6	69,045	13.3	365,300	63.0	6.6	72.3	20.4
Rocklin city	19.81	57,131	68,823	20.5	3474.2	12.0	82.8	98,566	6.3	481,900	65.9	4.4	72.1	22.1
Rodeo CDP	3.74	8,679	NA	NA	NA	27.4	85.7	74,688	14.2	459,100	62.1	8.4	77.6	16.6
Rohnert Park city	7.00	40,818	43,291	6.1	6184.4	16.5	81.7	71,585	10.6	456,500	68.3	2.4	60.4	25.7
Rosamond CDP	52.12	18,150	NA	NA	NA	12.1	86.4	61,807	13.3	208,600	59.4	10.3	71.3	21.4
Rosedale CDP	29.27	14,058	NA	NA	NA	5.5	91.0	113,766	5.7	412,500	57.9	6.1	85.2	12.4
Rosemead city	5.16	53,771	54,058	0.5	10476.4	56.6	94.2	57,999	13.8	556,600	58.6	4.6	84.8	11.3
Rosemont CDP	4.37	22,681	NA	NA	NA	15.4	84.4	69,794	12.4	293,400	65.3	4.7	66.9	22.7
Roseville city	44.08	119,277	141,500	18.6	3210.1	13.8	85.6	89,082	8.9	444,400	63.0	4.6	69.6	24.7
Rossmoor CDP	1.54	10,244	NA	NA	NA	12.2	90.0	127,891	2.5	948,700	60.0	4.8	79.9	14.4
Rowland Heights CDP	13.08	48,993	NA	NA	NA	54.1	90.1	75,587	11.1	637,900	60.9	5.9	81.9	13.5
Sacramento city	97.73	466,383	513,624	10.1	5255.5	22.2	83.2	62,335	15.2	336,900	63.6	7.0	59.4	30.9
Salida CDP	5.29	13,722	NA	NA	NA	21.0	91.9	82,745	6.2	301,700	71.7	7.1	80.9	14.5
Salinas city	23.43	150,607	155,465	3.2	6635.3	37.3	91.6	61,527	15.8	415,000	63.7	4.9	78.9	16.3
San Anselmo town	2.68	12,309	12,476	1.4	4655.2	7.4	89.0	128,212	4.7	1,066,800	72.8	4.5	66.9	27.6
San Bernardino city	62.11	210,422	215,784	2.5	3474.2	22.6	85.3	45,834	24.0	249,400	59.4	9.2	75.3	19.6
San Bruno city	5.47	41,109	42,807	4.1	7825.8	37.5	89.0	109,387	5.0	908,300	71.4	4.0	67.6	24.8
San Buenaventura (Ventura) city	21.88	107,217	109,106	1.8	4986.6	14.2	86.7	78,882	9.2	570,100	63.6	4.9	64.4	28.8
San Carlos city	5.51	28,379	30,185	6.4	5478.2	20.3	88.9	182,083	4.1	1,625,700	72.0	3.4	71.6	21.7
San Clemente city	18.35	63,500	64,558	1.7	3518.1	12.0	85.9	110,434	6.0	906,100	64.1	4.4	71.2	22.9
San Diego city	325.88	1,301,929	1,423,851	9.4	4369.2	26.1	83.1	79,673	11.4	602,600	65.2	5.8	60.5	27.5
San Diego Country Estates CDP	16.78	10,109	NA	NA	NA	4.6	88.1	120,446	2.7	508,700	64.2	3.7	87.0	7.8
San Dimas city	15.04	33,375	33,621	0.7	2235.4	20.1	87.6	86,410	8.8	576,800	60.3	3.0	70.5	24.8
San Fernando city	2.37	23,640	24,322	2.9	10262.4	37.7	91.9	58,425	13.9	431,100	62.4	4.1	81.4	16.3
San Francisco city	46.90	805,184	881,549	9.5	18796.4	34.3	85.6	112,449	10.9	1,097,800	71.1	4.2	47.9	35.6
San Gabriel city	4.15	39,644	39,899	0.6	9614.2	56.8	93.5	62,541	13.6	680,700	61.7	5.8	76.6	17.5
Sanger city	5.76	24,262	25,339	4.4	4399.1	23.9	92.8	48,929	22.6	218,900	61.4	5.9	78.8	17.6
San Jacinto city	25.71	44,213	49,215	11.3	1914.2	19.7	85.5	52,009	16.3	241,000	56.0	9.2	78.1	17.8
San Jose city	177.81	952,528	1,021,795	7.3	5746.6	39.7	87.1	109,593	8.6	864,600	68.3	4.7	73.1	19.4
San Juan Capistrano city	14.43	34,426	35,911	4.3	2488.6	21.4	88.8	91,600	7.9	720,200	59.8	3.1	71.2	24.0
San Leandro city	13.34	84,977	88,815	4.5	6657.8	36.7	90.6	78,003	8.8	590,800	66.9	5.2	66.6	26.4
San Lorenzo CDP	2.78	23,452	NA	NA	NA	32.1	94.6	97,286	5.8	586,400	64.5	4.7	79.7	14.4
San Luis Obispo city	13.33	45,121	47,459	5.2	3560.3	8.8	67.6	56,071	26.2	643,200	62.6	3.7	39.5	31.3
San Marcos city	24.36	83,631	96,664	15.6	3968.1	24.0	86.6	78,797	10.7	538,200	65.8	3.9	73.9	19.3
San Marino city	3.77	13,101	13,048	-0.4	3461.0	41.9	92.7	166,607	7.0	2,000,000	55.5	1.8	86.0	12.5
San Mateo city	12.17	97,195	104,430	7.4	8580.9	34.7	85.6	124,842	6.5	1,098,400	71.2	3.7	63.4	28.5
San Pablo city	2.63	29,512	30,990	5.0	11783.3	46.2	90.8	53,198	17.5	355,000	65.2	6.7	73.8	21.3
San Rafael city	16.57	57,698	58,440	1.3	3526.9	27.3	84.6	91,742	9.9	923,100	65.5	4.2	58.4	33.2
San Ramon city	18.69	71,412	75,995	6.4	4066.1	37.0	86.4	160,783	4.8	958,800	68.8	3.2	79.0	17.6
Santa Ana city	27.36	324,774	332,318	2.3	12146.1	43.3	90.2	66,145	14.5	491,300	67.6	5.1	81.7	12.3
Santa Barbara city	19.50	88,380	91,364	3.4	4685.3	22.2	81.1	76,606	11.8	1,051,500	68.3	3.8	53.2	32.2
Santa Clara city	18.23	116,453	130,365	11.9	7151.1	43.8	79.0	126,006	5.9	1,034,000	69.2	3.7	67.6	22.3
Santa Clarita city	70.76	208,778	212,979	2.0	3009.9	20.8	87.8	99,666	7.1	537,000	67.9	5.0	75.7	18.9
Santa Cruz city	12.74	59,944	64,608	7.8	5071.3	14.6	72.6	77,921	18.8	854,200	62.5	7.7	48.5	32.7
Santa Fe Springs city	8.87	16,218	17,630	8.7	1987.6	27.6	93.3	68,685	13.7	447,400	60.8	3.6	77.5	19.2
Santa Maria city	22.81	99,596	107,263	7.7	4702.5	34.9	87.4	63,341	13.3	344,100	66.8	4.9	79.6	15.7
Santa Monica city	8.42	89,742	90,401	0.7	10736.5	23.5	84.9	96,570	11.4	1,382,700	69.5	5.4	41.7	46.8
Santa Paula city	4.54	29,267	29,806	1.8	6565.2	29.6	93.3	60,468	13.8	383,700	64.5	7.3	76.3	19.3

Table B. Incorporated Places, Census Designated Places (CDPs), and Minor Civil Divisions (MCDs) of 10,000 or More Population — **Crime, Residential Construction and Local Government Finance**

STATE City, town, township, borough, or CDP (county if applicable)	Serious crimes known to police, 2018[1] — Violent crime — Number	Rate[2]	Property crime — Number	Rate[2]	New residential construction authorized by building permits, 2019 — Value ($1,000)	Number of housing units	Percent single family	Local government finance, 2017 — General revenue — Total (mil dol)	Intergovernmental — Total (mil dol)	Percent from state gov.	Taxes per capita[3]	General expenditure — Total (mil dol)	Per capita[3] — Total	Capital outlays	Debt outstanding (mil dol)
	15	16	17	18	19	20	21	22	23	24	25	26	27	28	29
CALIFORNIA—Con.															
Patterson city	53	237	387	1,731	5,721	49	100.0	40.5	2.2	70.0	512	34.1	1,540	83	309.9
Perris city	214	270	2,000	2,524	25,332	157	87.3	60.3	4.6	79.9	379	87.6	1,129	150	311.0
Petaluma city	197	321	889	1,451	14,597	64	73.4	103.1	16.4	31.3	694	90.5	1,491	229	136.4
Phelan CDP	NA	NA	NA	NA	NA	NA	NA	NA	NA	NA	NA	NA	NA	NA	NA
Pico Rivera city	228	359	1,159	1,822	2,990	13	100.0	59.3	12.6	42.1	588	76.7	1,214	345	69.4
Piedmont city	21	183	195	1,699	1,300	1	100.0	33.6	1.1	51.3	1,961	31.6	2,778	233	12.3
Pinole city	70	359	747	3,829	0	0	0.0	27.8	1.7	51.2	874	24.5	1,265	160	18.3
Pittsburg city	422	574	1,679	2,286	20,916	99	100.0	141.1	50.7	8.2	567	109.5	1,520	198	367.7
Placentia city	120	229	904	1,728	38,367	222	2.3	41.0	3.1	50.8	546	56.1	1,081	129	14.3
Placerville city	54	490	278	2,523	3,895	12	100.0	23.2	5.9	9.9	771	22.8	2,066	332	54.2
Pleasant Hill city	57	162	1,584	4,493	6,388	20	100.0	29.5	3.0	58.6	677	42.2	1,208	220	11.9
Pleasanton city	110	129	1,445	1,700	50,915	149	47.7	171.1	6.6	67.3	1,374	130.7	1,578	0	65.9
Pomona city	877	571	4,697	3,060	15,992	108	90.7	180.3	22.1	26.2	657	171.9	1,127	154	275.6
Porterville city	209	352	1,561	2,628	30,666	112	92.9	67.1	14.5	44.9	427	55.9	936	180	78.6
Port Hueneme city	61	272	421	1,878	0	0	0.0	30.4	5.0	16.5	395	27.8	1,250	160	9.3
Poway city	65	129	509	1,011	13,228	74	27.0	116.0	1.9	91.9	1,786	141.5	2,840	930	159.2
Prunedale CDP	NA	NA	NA	NA	NA	NA	NA	NA	NA	NA	NA	NA	NA	NA	NA
Quartz Hill CDP	NA	NA	NA	NA	NA	NA	NA	NA	NA	NA	NA	NA	NA	NA	NA
Ramona CDP	NA	NA	NA	NA	NA	NA	NA	NA	NA	NA	NA	NA	NA	NA	NA
Rancho Cordova city	272	363	1,388	1,854	156,537	561	100.0	91.1	11.0	34.5	907	107.3	1,462	309	17.8
Rancho Cucamonga city	290	162	3,854	2,152	77,613	434	31.6	210.2	17.9	47.5	883	193.8	1,095	233	298.0
Rancho Mirage city	24	130	708	3,835	51,542	194	100.0	58.3	1.0	62.6	1,966	53.4	2,928	387	113.7
Rancho Palos Verdes city	32	75	389	916	13,181	14	100.0	36.1	1.7	79.9	711	32.6	773	72	25.9
Rancho San Diego CDP	NA	NA	NA	NA	NA	NA	NA	NA	NA	NA	NA	NA	NA	NA	NA
Rancho Santa Margarita city	46	94	316	646	0	0	0.0	20.4	1.6	73.4	342	19.6	404	63	9.6
Red Bluff city	165	1,153	719	5,023	579	2	100.0	16.5	2.5	30.3	631	14.5	1,019	20	1.3
Redding city	620	673	3,433	3,729	73,290	294	77.2	156.2	21.3	32.8	616	146.5	1,600	127	231.1
Redlands city	264	367	2,491	3,462	33,874	113	100.0	115.4	6.2	73.8	771	110.8	1,553	311	61.2
Redondo Beach city	171	251	1,452	2,134	40,672	116	81.0	123.4	6.9	79.8	948	122.5	1,815	106	32.0
Redwood City city	177	201	1,254	1,422	56,922	201	20.4	210.3	12.6	40.6	1,284	221.0	2,559	262	96.0
Reedley city	105	407	289	1,120	2,405	13	100.0	38.3	18.0	4.0	318	21.3	830	90	36.1
Rialto city	543	521	3,038	2,916	11,763	42	100.0	191.8	13.8	91.1	662	126.7	1,227	1	312.1
Richmond city	1,046	943	4,353	3,922	5,218	50	100.0	293.7	44.7	30.8	1,395	295.9	2,693	389	627.7
Ridgecrest city	171	589	500	1,721	7,924	56	89.3	27.3	4.2	45.0	434	21.2	740	141	32.3
Rio Linda CDP	NA	NA	NA	NA	NA	NA	NA	NA	NA	NA	NA	NA	NA	NA	NA
Ripon city	10	63	225	1,417	18,196	72	97.2	17.3	0.9	51.6	498	15.9	1,012	206	9.8
Riverbank city	24	96	447	1,786	2,946	16	100.0	13.9	1.3	86.6	297	19.0	773	132	7.9
Riverside city	1,686	509	10,226	3,089	100,227	679	25.0	451.5	47.0	68.3	686	404.3	1,237	92	1790.3
Rocklin city	52	79	952	1,443	154,147	439	100.0	73.2	4.2	62.4	641	65.9	1,020	66	70.5
Rodeo CDP	NA	NA	NA	NA	NA	NA	NA	NA	NA	NA	NA	NA	NA	NA	NA
Rohnert Park city	222	515	745	1,727	42,616	195	100.0	80.3	3.5	67.8	674	66.5	1,557	291	61.4
Rosamond CDP	NA	NA	NA	NA	NA	NA	NA	NA	NA	NA	NA	NA	NA	NA	NA
Rosedale CDP	NA	NA	NA	NA	NA	NA	NA	NA	NA	NA	NA	NA	NA	NA	NA
Rosemead city	194	355	1,274	2,331	15,095	84	89.3	27.5	2.5	75.1	385	50.2	927	295	45.3
Rosemont CDP	NA	NA	NA	NA	NA	NA	NA	NA	NA	NA	NA	NA	NA	NA	NA
Roseville city	299	217	3,252	2,362	277,010	1,213	82.3	382.4	49.9	36.9	800	251.2	1,859	129	996.9
Rossmoor CDP	NA	NA	NA	NA	NA	NA	NA	NA	NA	NA	NA	NA	NA	NA	NA
Rowland Heights CDP	NA	NA	NA	NA	NA	NA	NA	NA	NA	NA	NA	NA	NA	NA	NA
Sacramento city	3,329	657	15,417	3,041	632,277	3,001	51.2	1022.4	59.0	46.8	913	776.0	1,550	8	2283.1
Salida CDP	NA	NA	NA	NA	NA	NA	NA	NA	NA	NA	NA	NA	NA	NA	NA
Salinas city	981	619	4,304	2,714	18,537	96	83.3	172.1	18.9	50.3	817	160.6	1,026	131	57.8
San Anselmo town	NA	NA	NA	NA	3,387	8	75.0	21.5	1.3	82.8	1,420	27.5	2,198	162	8.3
San Bernardino city	2,906	1,333	9,014	4,135	21,294	91	64.8	204.8	9.3	64.2	592	195.1	900	97	220.1
San Bruno city	123	282	984	2,256	14,596	33	9.1	79.9	1.5	85.8	757	70.9	1,641	133	29.8
San Buenaventura (Ventura) city	445	400	3,482	3,129	34,360	257	5.4	160.9	7.0	77.9	830	172.0	1,562	156	151.2
San Carlos city	NA	NA	NA	NA	14,034	36	8.3	67.6	1.3	72.8	1,244	55.9	1,841	159	3.9
San Clemente city	114	174	900	1,374	22,379	45	95.6	86.1	3.8	68.1	780	96.0	1,478	316	82.5
San Diego city	5,360	373	27,416	1,909	692,028	3,941	14.7	3177.9	331.0	12.6	1,001	2575.2	1,823	217	2779.5
San Diego Country Estates CDP	NA	NA	NA	NA	NA	NA	NA	NA	NA	NA	NA	NA	NA	NA	NA
San Dimas city	80	232	751	2,179	8,965	20	100.0	28.8	1.5	84.5	612	40.2	1,179	110	15.2
San Fernando city	102	410	312	1,255	4,303	75	94.7	29.1	2.0	51.4	846	30.8	1,255	48	2.7
San Francisco city	6,144	691	49,214	5,534	913,794	3,200	0.7	9978.8	2985.9	47.3	4,255	10297.3	11,728	921	16803.8
San Gabriel city	136	335	691	1,700	2,074	15	100.0	42.8	2.6	78.2	754	49.2	1,223	193	10.8
Sanger city	88	348	362	1,432	9,054	52	100.0	31.5	4.6	54.5	451	24.7	986	114	25.7
San Jacinto city	132	270	1,461	2,992	19,391	147	100.0	28.5	2.6	76.5	351	28.5	593	42	26.2
San Jose city	4,444	424	25,753	2,459	329,550	2,345	21.9	2270.4	98.5	51.3	1,200	1558.9	1,510	112	4767.7
San Juan Capistrano city	84	231	351	967	41,285	99	87.9	48.2	3.9	64.4	871	40.9	1,140	183	89.7
San Leandro city	473	518	3,584	3,923	3,447	38	89.5	157.1	14.0	29.2	1,100	151.4	1,674	144	100.9
San Lorenzo CDP	NA	NA	NA	NA	NA	NA	NA	NA	NA	NA	NA	NA	NA	NA	NA
San Luis Obispo city	192	401	1,809	3,778	77,690	511	33.5	103.5	6.4	29.3	1,279	105.3	2,225	372	66.7
San Marcos city	202	206	1,052	1,073	36,719	205	83.9	130.3	5.0	63.0	806	154.1	1,612	288	291.6
San Marino city	11	82	203	1,520	0	0	0.0	28.4	1.1	63.5	1,532	28.5	2,152	317	3.8
San Mateo city	285	269	2,163	2,044	108,726	339	2.7	207.2	7.8	62.0	1,197	177.3	1,698	256	223.2
San Pablo city	180	573	979	3,118	634	6	100.0	52.2	2.4	100.0	1,271	50.7	1,631	394	46.4
San Rafael city	257	434	1,695	2,861	4,304	10	100.0	103.5	6.4	43.4	1,170	102.4	1,741	51	28.2
San Ramon city	43	56	786	1,027	27,516	94	78.7	90.1	19.4	20.1	599	85.2	1,125	164	89.4
Santa Ana city	1,571	468	6,390	1,905	107,820	643	15.1	403.8	93.2	23.6	634	470.9	1,416	212	223.3
Santa Barbara city	415	448	2,333	2,519	18,483	114	11.4	270.3	18.5	35.9	1,181	236.5	2,584	222	211.0
Santa Clara city	208	162	3,741	2,907	167,301	628	40.9	494.1	28.3	15.1	1,158	407.6	3,217	304	704.2
Santa Clarita city	292	135	2,437	1,125	179,705	894	43.5	191.7	46.0	48.5	483	187.6	878	180	57.5
Santa Cruz city	390	594	2,905	4,423	10,859	42	100.0	154.6	5.8	49.8	1,187	157.4	2,429	335	124.5
Santa Fe Springs city	105	576	991	5,433	0	0	0.0	59.9	3.9	48.5	2,477	78.9	4,417	1136	12.5
Santa Maria city	497	460	1,932	1,787	50,881	489	22.5	144.0	21.0	26.1	598	140.1	1,318	239	53.7
Santa Monica city	797	860	4,732	5,106	67,473	97	76.3	690.5	116.4	22.6	3,685	501.6	5,468	194	345.2
Santa Paula city	90	296	458	1,504	56,212	146	100.0	30.7	2.5	63.2	350	32.2	1,068	160	124.9

1 Data for serious crimes have not been adjusted for underreporting. This may affect comparability between geographic areas over time.
2 Per 100,000 population estimated by the FBI.   3 Based on population estimated as of July 1 of the year shown.

Table B. Incorporated Places, Census Designated Places (CDPs), and Minor Civil Divisions (MCDs) of 10,000 or More Population — Land Area, Population, and Households, and Employment

STATE City, town, township, borough, or CDP (county if applicable)	Land area 2010 (sq mi)	Population				Population characteristics 2015–2019		Income and poverty 2015–2019			Employment, 2015–2019		Households, 2015–2019 (percent of households)	
		Total persons 2010	Total persons 2019	Percent change 2010–2019	Persons per square mile 2019	Percent foreign born	Percent living in the same house as previous year	Median household income	Percent of households with income below poverty level	Median value of owner-occupied housing units	Percent in civilian labor force	Unemployment rate	Family households	One person households
	1	2	3	4	5	6	7	8	9	10	11	12	13	14
CALIFORNIA—Con.														
Santa Rosa city	42.52	175,038	176,753	1.0	4156.9	20.1	85.2	75,630	9.0	540,600	66.4	4.7	62.2	28.2
Santee city	16.54	53,420	58,081	8.7	3511.5	10.6	84.6	87,098	6.3	445,500	63.5	5.3	72.9	20.0
Saratoga city	12.77	29,995	30,153	0.5	2361.2	40.1	92.5	191,677	4.7	2,000,000	54.7	3.7	82.6	14.8
Scotts Valley city	4.62	11,573	11,757	1.6	2544.8	12.0	85.9	108,289	4.8	815,600	64.1	3.6	69.9	21.5
Seal Beach city	11.28	24,076	23,896	-0.7	2118.4	15.6	88.4	68,852	6.8	371,600	47.2	4.1	48.4	45.7
Seaside city	9.24	33,025	33,748	2.2	3652.4	27.9	82.0	63,575	12.4	488,400	62.1	6.1	68.0	23.7
Selma city	5.77	23,380	24,825	6.2	4302.4	25.1	90.8	40,815	22.3	186,300	58.8	7.0	76.6	19.7
Shafter city	38.72	17,104	20,401	19.3	526.9	29.5	91.0	45,854	22.4	175,300	56.3	9.1	81.6	16.5
Shasta Lake city	10.92	10,164	10,413	2.4	953.6	2.2	84.2	48,902	19.5	183,000	55.1	6.4	67.8	26.5
Sierra Madre city	2.95	10,917	10,793	-1.1	3658.6	14.0	91.1	100,988	7.3	969,700	63.4	7.0	63.0	32.3
Signal Hill city	2.19	11,018	11,421	3.7	5215.1	27.3	89.4	75,508	12.7	505,900	65.9	5.2	52.9	35.0
Simi Valley city	41.53	124,242	125,613	1.1	3024.6	18.1	91.7	99,151	5.7	584,900	67.3	4.5	73.6	20.4
Solana Beach city	3.41	12,867	13,296	3.3	3899.1	13.5	86.1	108,118	4.1	1,192,600	64.3	3.2	59.3	30.3
Soledad city	4.48	25,738	25,999	1.0	5803.3	29.9	85.7	64,472	14.2	370,800	33.5	3.0	84.2	12.6
Sonoma city	2.74	10,657	11,024	3.4	4023.4	10.9	83.7	84,352	11.6	785,900	58.6	6.8	53.3	38.7
Soquel CDP	4.60	9,644	NA	NA	NA	10.1	91.2	93,305	9.2	712,300	64.4	4.1	67.5	25.7
South El Monte city	2.84	20,096	20,574	2.4	7244.4	44.3	92.6	52,204	18.4	445,500	58.9	5.8	83.3	13.3
South Gate city	7.24	94,412	93,444	-1.0	12906.6	42.4	93.1	52,321	16.9	408,200	65.5	9.6	85.3	11.6
South Lake Tahoe city	10.15	21,397	22,197	3.7	2186.9	20.6	81.5	49,390	13.1	403,600	68.4	7.3	50.8	37.5
South Pasadena city	3.41	25,605	25,329	-1.1	7427.9	24.9	88.8	104,308	7.1	1,071,000	70.3	4.0	66.4	25.7
South San Francisco city	9.23	63,622	67,789	6.5	7344.4	40.3	91.6	105,459	6.5	844,000	69.3	3.0	75.4	16.9
South San Jose Hills CDP	1.51	20,551	NA	NA	NA	42.1	95.0	70,218	13.1	369,300	60.6	7.7	90.7	7.5
South Whittier CDP	5.34	57,156	NA	NA	NA	25.4	93.6	71,458	9.0	474,800	62.3	5.4	81.7	13.3
Spring Valley CDP	7.34	28,205	NA	NA	NA	20.4	88.9	72,178	9.8	450,900	66.1	8.4	75.0	17.3
Stanford CDP	2.75	13,809	NA	NA	NA	27.3	56.5	58,906	23.7	2,000,000	48.7	4.7	30.6	38.3
Stanton city	3.10	37,827	38,139	0.8	12302.9	44.0	90.4	57,598	16.0	386,400	65.7	4.6	73.0	22.7
Stevenson Ranch CDP	6.36	17,557	NA	NA	NA	25.7	83.9	135,179	5.8	732,400	67.2	5.6	72.6	20.0
Stockton city	62.17	292,182	312,697	7.0	5029.7	25.7	87.1	54,614	18.1	273,400	59.5	8.8	71.5	22.9
Suisun City city	4.06	28,059	29,663	5.7	7306.2	22.5	89.8	83,320	7.8	357,500	66.0	5.6	75.8	19.8
Sunnyvale city	22.03	140,060	152,703	9.0	6931.6	48.6	81.4	140,631	5.4	1,223,600	71.4	4.0	67.7	21.7
Sun Village CDP	10.80	11,565	NA	NA	NA	24.1	92.1	46,502	20.1	233,500	52.9	8.7	84.7	10.6
Susanville city	7.94	17,943	15,010	-16.3	1890.4	6.6	61.2	52,488	16.4	183,700	22.9	5.0	58.4	37.7
Tamalpais-Homestead Valley CDP	4.69	10,735	NA	NA	NA	13.7	92.4	163,071	4.2	1,243,500	67.0	3.1	69.4	24.1
Tehachapi city	10.15	14,420	13,011	-9.8	1281.9	12.3	73.6	54,083	17.5	211,200	33.7	7.4	59.6	34.1
Temecula city	37.27	100,013	114,761	14.7	3079.2	15.8	83.5	96,183	6.8	444,800	65.4	5.8	80.5	14.6
Temescal Valley CDP	19.34	0	NA	0.0	NA	16.5	88.3	108,934	4.1	453,600	62.4	5.1	80.7	15.6
Temple City city	4.00	35,554	35,811	0.7	8952.8	49.9	93.0	78,516	9.3	715,300	59.9	3.3	79.6	16.6
Thousand Oaks city	55.26	126,490	126,813	0.3	2294.8	18.3	90.3	109,378	5.7	726,100	64.1	4.5	70.1	24.2
Torrance city	20.52	145,151	143,592	-1.1	6997.7	29.8	87.8	93,492	7.1	762,700	64.1	4.0	69.4	25.6
Tracy city	25.89	83,423	94,740	13.6	3659.3	26.9	86.6	92,046	7.3	446,200	68.1	5.3	82.1	14.2
Truckee town	32.33	16,163	16,735	3.5	517.6	7.9	86.8	97,092	7.0	593,400	71.8	1.8	73.8	18.4
Tulare city	20.37	59,293	65,496	10.5	3215.3	18.8	87.4	54,037	18.6	207,000	60.8	6.9	78.5	16.0
Turlock city	16.92	68,712	73,631	7.2	4351.7	22.2	87.7	59,681	16.2	310,100	61.9	7.2	70.5	23.2
Tustin city	11.12	75,317	79,348	5.4	7135.6	32.0	83.7	84,697	9.3	647,500	71.8	4.0	70.4	21.4
Twentynine Palms city	58.76	25,048	26,073	4.1	443.7	6.9	65.1	44,226	22.4	146,400	38.9	10.4	66.0	27.5
Ukiah city	4.78	16,083	15,995	-0.5	3346.2	18.2	84.2	49,889	19.3	349,600	62.4	11.4	60.1	32.9
Union City city	19.40	69,531	74,107	6.6	3819.9	45.1	91.0	114,681	4.5	765,500	65.1	3.4	83.3	11.5
Upland city	15.61	73,718	77,140	4.6	4941.7	18.1	86.5	72,782	11.9	525,700	65.4	4.8	71.0	21.7
Vacaville city	29.22	92,422	100,670	8.9	3445.2	12.2	84.5	87,823	7.7	422,400	57.9	4.6	71.6	22.3
Valinda CDP	2.01	22,822	NA	NA	NA	39.7	93.5	84,134	9.6	447,100	66.5	6.8	88.4	8.3
Vallejo city	30.83	115,914	121,692	5.0	3947.2	26.0	85.9	69,405	12.2	370,000	63.5	8.2	67.7	25.1
Valle Vista CDP	6.87	14,578	NA	NA	NA	10.9	86.0	53,327	16.4	184,600	53.4	8.4	70.1	23.5
Valley Center CDP	27.47	9,277	NA	NA	NA	11.2	89.4	101,331	9.1	614,800	62.5	3.6	85.3	13.1
Victorville city	73.62	115,899	122,385	5.6	1662.4	18.7	83.7	53,957	18.5	221,200	55.3	12.9	77.8	17.4
View Park-Windsor Hills CDP	1.84	11,075	NA	NA	NA	7.7	93.0	92,625	9.6	760,000	61.3	11.3	55.4	35.8
Vincent CDP	1.47	0	NA	0.0	NA	34.1	94.9	86,011	4.5	436,300	66.1	5.9	86.0	11.3
Vineyard CDP	17.20	24,836	NA	NA	NA	26.5	89.3	94,939	7.6	384,100	64.1	4.7	81.2	13.2
Visalia city	37.92	124,528	134,605	8.1	3549.7	14.1	88.1	62,263	13.6	236,400	61.0	4.9	73.2	22.1
Vista city	18.75	93,186	101,638	9.1	5420.7	25.3	87.3	72,125	10.2	480,900	68.2	4.4	73.2	19.2
Walnut city	8.99	29,177	29,685	1.7	3302.0	49.9	92.8	108,669	7.2	774,400	58.4	4.4	87.0	10.4
Walnut Creek city	19.76	64,157	70,166	9.4	3550.9	23.3	83.7	105,948	5.5	793,100	56.9	3.7	57.6	35.1
Walnut Park CDP	0.75	15,966	NA	NA	NA	47.8	94.8	52,226	16.4	410,300	63.9	6.6	85.4	8.9
Wasco city	9.39	25,549	28,710	12.4	3057.5	28.2	82.4	39,250	22.9	168,500	43.8	10.3	85.5	14.1
Watsonville city	6.69	51,214	53,856	5.2	8050.2	36.0	92.4	55,470	14.7	464,200	67.1	7.5	76.6	19.4
West Carson CDP	2.27	21,699	NA	NA	NA	39.4	90.9	73,472	9.1	473,900	60.1	4.5	68.4	24.7
West Covina city	16.04	106,108	105,101	-0.9	6552.4	36.0	89.4	82,938	8.2	540,500	64.3	5.6	78.9	16.0
West Hollywood city	1.89	34,351	36,475	6.2	19298.9	24.7	83.9	74,044	13.9	755,400	78.6	5.3	21.5	60.3
Westminster city	10.04	89,619	90,643	1.1	9028.2	44.5	91.3	62,625	16.4	603,700	59.9	5.3	77.7	18.6
Westmont CDP	1.85	31,853	NA	NA	NA	28.9	91.5	38,600	28.3	419,900	59.0	8.3	71.1	24.8
West Puente Valley CDP	1.87	22,636	NA	NA	NA	35.7	94.5	75,856	11.3	441,600	60.7	7.5	87.9	9.9
West Rancho Dominguez CDP	3.97	5,669	NA	NA	NA	23.2	94.0	60,155	20.4	367,400	60.9	7.4	76.4	21.0
West Sacramento city	21.47	48,744	53,519	9.8	2492.7	25.8	86.8	70,699	14.6	349,800	65.2	7.3	68.1	24.8
West Whittier-Los Nietos CDP	2.52	25,540	NA	NA	NA	27.1	95.7	76,397	8.4	435,500	58.8	4.7	82.5	13.9
Whittier city	14.65	85,313	85,098	-0.3	5808.7	16.8	90.7	77,270	9.5	574,400	63.2	4.0	71.8	22.1
Wildomar city	23.69	32,210	37,229	15.6	1571.5	17.3	83.5	74,991	10.8	356,700	60.8	7.7	80.2	14.8
Willowbrook CDP	1.55	35,983	NA	NA	NA	33.2	91.6	43,781	26.9	340,200	63.9	10.8	82.1	16.2
Windsor town	7.27	26,791	27,128	1.3	3731.5	15.0	89.7	106,899	4.5	597,500	69.9	4.1	76.7	18.3
Winter Gardens CDP	4.42	20,631	NA	NA	NA	12.3	83.3	69,063	8.2	414,000	65.1	5.8	72.3	20.7
Winton CDP	3.04	10,613	NA	NA	NA	35.8	91.2	45,858	16.4	171,900	65.2	17.2	80.1	14.9
Woodcrest CDP	11.38	14,347	NA	NA	NA	13.9	92.1	102,625	5.0	487,100	61.4	3.6	86.5	10.8
Woodland city	15.31	55,553	60,548	9.0	3954.8	23.3	87.3	69,612	10.6	365,000	63.3	5.6	73.3	21.8
Yorba Linda city	19.84	64,167	67,644	5.4	3409.5	19.8	89.6	129,995	4.3	858,300	63.0	3.6	82.7	14.7
Yuba City city	14.90	65,634	67,010	2.1	4497.3	24.8	83.6	56,816	14.9	277,400	58.0	8.7	71.6	22.5
Yucaipa city	28.29	51,347	53,921	5.0	1906.0	11.2	89.7	69,104	12.6	327,400	61.9	4.4	71.3	25.3
Yucca Valley town	39.83	20,652	21,777	5.4	546.7	7.9	81.1	44,757	18.0	172,600	53.4	11.8	62.5	30.4

STATE City, town, township, borough, or CDP (county if applicable)	Serious crimes known to police, 2018[1]				New residential construction authorized by building permits, 2019			Local government finance, 2017							
	Violent crime		Property crime		Value ($1,000)	Number of housing units	Percent single family	General revenue				General expenditure			Debt outstanding (mil dol)
	Number	Rate[2]	Number	Rate[2]				Total (mil dol)	Intergovernmental Total (mil dol)	Intergovernmental Percent from state gov.	Taxes per capita[3]	Total (mil dol)	Per capita[3] Total	Per capita[3] Capital outlays	
	15	16	17	18	19	20	21	22	23	24	25	26	27	28	29
CALIFORNIA—Con.															
Santa Rosa city	823	467	3,118	1,768	471,567	1,190	78.9	302.6	56.3	79.2	643	318.4	1,753	301	404.9
Santee city	109	185	886	1,507	14,744	135	1.5	53.5	4.7	38.6	619	74.9	1,295	192	58.1
Saratoga city	22	71	237	764	46,802	54	100.0	24.9	2.1	45.3	620	33.0	1,070	192	9.6
Scotts Valley city	17	142	191	1,592	1,344	6	100.0	17.6	0.5	86.8	929	17.6	1,482	118	8.6
Seal Beach city	39	160	601	2,468	5,872	12	100.0	34.7	2.0	52.7	947	51.7	2,136	470	17.1
Seaside city	92	268	445	1,297	0	0	0.0	32.8	2.7	81.0	760	32.0	945	207	13.2
Selma city	240	961	725	2,902	4,870	26	100.0	26.1	5.3	97.1	535	20.9	848	121	6.3
Shafter city	44	220	544	2,722	33,089	190	100.0	49.2	1.5	49.5	1,050	55.5	2,851	743	1.7
Shasta Lake city	NA	NA	NA	NA	14,802	72	58.3	13.6	1.9	67.0	343	14.1	1,387	397	7.5
Sierra Madre city	7	63	95	859	0	0	0.0	15.2	0.9	60.4	939	15.5	1,413	150	16.9
Signal Hill city	86	734	690	5,892	125	1	100.0	32.1	10.3	71.8	1,641	35.2	3,050	989	4.3
Simi Valley city	214	168	1,491	1,172	40,509	142	100.0	113.4	15.7	38.8	543	107.1	849	135	180.0
Solana Beach city	23	170	206	1,523	5,502	9	100.0	29.7	3.8	66.4	1,135	32.8	2,453	367	16.9
Soledad city	70	266	101	384	23,588	72	100.0	21.0	2.7	31.0	309	18.0	688	48	38.2
Sonoma city	44	394	164	1,468	13,983	72	100.0	18.9	0.7	99.7	1,364	23.2	2,097	518	3.1
Soquel CDP	NA	NA	NA	NA	NA	NA	NA	NA	NA	NA	NA	NA	NA	NA	NA
South El Monte city	126	597	621	2,941	7,724	38	76.3	18.4	2.1	57.1	663	25.3	1,211	273	2.5
South Gate city	634	663	2,364	2,474	36,957	293	14.0	90.0	12.9	43.5	495	75.7	798	135	84.8
South Lake Tahoe city	182	825	454	2,058	18,146	26	30.8	65.6	5.6	47.6	1,966	50.9	2,320	428	139.8
South Pasadena city	32	123	522	2,014	1,884	8	100.0	34.7	2.7	43.7	894	29.1	1,134	0	55.4
South San Francisco city	181	266	1,444	2,124	61,618	204	15.7	146.8	4.5	80.0	1,319	144.8	2,156	262	48.4
South San Jose Hills CDP	NA	NA	NA	NA	NA	NA	NA	NA	NA	NA	NA	NA	NA	NA	NA
South Whittier CDP	NA	NA	NA	NA	NA	NA	NA	NA	NA	NA	NA	NA	NA	NA	NA
Spring Valley CDP	NA	NA	NA	NA	NA	NA	NA	NA	NA	NA	NA	NA	NA	NA	NA
Stanford CDP	NA	NA	NA	NA	NA	NA	NA	NA	NA	NA	NA	NA	NA	NA	NA
Stanton city	135	350	618	1,600	26,609	114	100.0	26.8	3.0	81.9	479	37.1	967	228	80.6
Stevenson Ranch CDP	NA	NA	NA	NA	NA	NA	NA	NA	NA	NA	NA	NA	NA	NA	NA
Stockton city	4,383	1,400	11,800	3,768	118,076	464	65.1	401.2	37.4	30.9	732	320.3	1,033	16	589.0
Suisun City city	93	312	627	2,100	3,980	19	42.1	20.0	4.3	20.6	296	21.7	735	122	4.4
Sunnyvale city	255	164	2,541	1,633	116,047	677	21.7	373.0	27.0	70.5	923	290.0	1,893	92	72.2
Sun Village CDP	NA	NA	NA	NA	NA	NA	NA	NA	NA	NA	NA	NA	NA	NA	NA
Susanville city	197	1,312	274	1,825	1,476	8	50.0	9.9	3.0	96.2	338	10.8	707	23	72.3
Tamalpais-Homestead Valley CDP	NA	NA	NA	NA	NA	NA	NA	NA	NA	NA	NA	NA	NA	NA	NA
Tehachapi city	82	661	276	2,225	3,291	15	100.0	30.6	3.3	34.6	474	15.6	1,243	339	7.6
Temecula city	139	119	2,711	2,329	25,246	223	24.2	118.3	9.4	30.8	685	180.1	1,580	527	151.3
Temescal Valley CDP	NA	NA	NA	NA	NA	NA	NA	NA	NA	NA	NA	NA	NA	NA	NA
Temple City city	64	175	472	1,294	20,991	76	100.0	19.2	3.2	75.3	321	18.2	502	15	6.4
Thousand Oaks city	126	97	1,480	1,145	9,091	31	100.0	151.8	12.3	30.0	687	178.4	1,391	218	74.2
Torrance city	267	182	2,702	1,839	17,457	81	96.3	287.9	51.9	8.4	1,247	239.5	1,643	2	82.3
Tracy city	199	216	2,331	2,534	176,221	821	72.7	182.9	29.4	12.1	780	151.2	1,667	399	91.6
Truckee town	17	102	143	861	72,980	177	51.4	43.0	5.0	51.1	1,567	35.0	2,124	606	8.6
Tulare city	251	389	1,818	2,818	112,153	584	63.0	101.5	10.5	36.7	549	103.4	1,628	464	262.9
Turlock city	420	566	2,233	3,007	34,965	127	81.9	85.6	7.1	56.0	510	101.8	1,389	436	104.2
Tustin city	122	150	1,874	2,307	61,666	238	100.0	140.3	4.2	80.5	642	112.9	1,409	334	164.0
Twentynine Palms city	81	303	278	1,039	304	5	100.0	11.9	1.2	100.0	344	13.0	491	101	11.5
Ukiah city	95	592	284	1,771	387	4	100.0	31.4	1.7	88.4	921	34.0	2,131	386	73.5
Union City city	261	343	1,653	2,169	4,272	15	100.0	109.2	21.9	54.3	854	124.9	1,660	319	163.3
Upland city	290	374	2,072	2,675	70,858	483	27.7	81.3	3.1	88.4	546	78.7	1,025	64	8.4
Vacaville city	230	227	2,158	2,134	108,373	378	100.0	199.7	29.9	16.0	883	192.1	1,929	553	52.6
Valinda CDP	NA	NA	NA	NA	NA	NA	NA	NA	NA	NA	NA	NA	NA	NA	NA
Vallejo city	942	766	4,508	3,666	14,789	54	100.0	191.9	33.5	23.0	743	172.0	1,415	128	126.1
Valle Vista CDP	NA	NA	NA	NA	NA	NA	NA	NA	NA	NA	NA	NA	NA	NA	NA
Valley Center CDP	NA	NA	NA	NA	NA	NA	NA	NA	NA	NA	NA	NA	NA	NA	NA
Victorville city	809	656	2,718	2,204	129,367	439	100.0	151.4	33.7	18.0	492	212.0	1,738	191	412.3
View Park-Windsor Hills CDP	NA	NA	NA	NA	NA	NA	NA	NA	NA	NA	NA	NA	NA	NA	NA
Vincent CDP	NA	NA	NA	NA	NA	NA	NA	NA	NA	NA	NA	NA	NA	NA	NA
Vineyard CDP	NA	NA	NA	NA	NA	NA	NA	NA	NA	NA	NA	NA	NA	NA	NA
Visalia city	450	335	3,978	2,964	168,916	699	97.0	227.5	55.7	38.4	618	156.9	1,185	239	27.1
Vista city	330	321	1,497	1,457	86,794	540	44.8	138.9	8.9	71.4	711	176.0	1,747	208	222.8
Walnut city	22	73	483	1,592	6,777	14	100.0	18.7	3.0	29.6	354	23.1	769	29	28.7
Walnut Creek city	109	154	2,249	3,186	58,459	379	4.5	107.6	2.6	76.0	908	110.7	1,589	128	0.9
Walnut Park CDP	NA	NA	NA	NA	NA	NA	NA	NA	NA	NA	NA	NA	NA	NA	NA
Wasco city	NA	NA	NA	NA	9,200	80	85.0	20.1	4.1	16.6	260	17.6	657	79	1.5
Watsonville city	243	446	1,330	2,440	10,047	110	50.0	84.7	4.7	41.1	656	91.2	1,691	117	4.9
West Carson CDP	NA	NA	NA	NA	NA	NA	NA	NA	NA	NA	NA	NA	NA	NA	NA
West Covina city	292	271	2,513	2,331	14,359	57	100.0	108.8	7.5	52.1	628	120.4	1,126	314	81.7
West Hollywood city	301	803	2,100	5,603	48,601	185	8.6	141.9	3.4	63.9	2,129	157.3	4,274	682	155.2
Westminster city	286	312	2,433	2,650	23,351	192	38.5	78.1	6.6	38.4	669	130.0	1,426	529	126.7
Westmont CDP	NA	NA	NA	NA	NA	NA	NA	NA	NA	NA	NA	NA	NA	NA	NA
West Puente Valley CDP	NA	NA	NA	NA	NA	NA	NA	NA	NA	NA	NA	NA	NA	NA	NA
West Rancho Dominguez CDP	NA	NA	NA	NA	NA	NA	NA	NA	NA	NA	NA	NA	NA	NA	NA
West Sacramento city	225	415	1,412	2,604	66,198	319	50.5	123.0	7.0	62.1	1,138	152.7	2,864	838	334.7
West Whittier-Los Nietos CDP	NA	NA	NA	NA	NA	NA	NA	NA	NA	NA	NA	NA	NA	NA	NA
Whittier city	233	268	2,225	2,556	8,816	39	64.1	85.8	4.6	63.1	569	85.0	984	119	61.6
Wildomar city	48	128	724	1,924	1,587	7	100.0	15.6	4.0	83.6	252	18.3	498	38	0.0
Willowbrook CDP	NA	NA	NA	NA	NA	NA	NA	NA	NA	NA	NA	NA	NA	NA	NA
Windsor town	74	268	249	900	11,773	85	29.4	30.7	1.7	43.6	583	36.0	1,312	280	15.2
Winter Gardens CDP	NA	NA	NA	NA	NA	NA	NA	NA	NA	NA	NA	NA	NA	NA	NA
Winton CDP	NA	NA	NA	NA	NA	NA	NA	NA	NA	NA	NA	NA	NA	NA	NA
Woodcrest CDP	NA	NA	NA	NA	NA	NA	NA	NA	NA	NA	NA	NA	NA	NA	NA
Woodland city	220	363	1,602	2,640	121,899	386	100.0	119.7	3.5	62.5	891	107.5	1,794	417	381.6
Yorba Linda city	44	64	812	1,180	35,458	108	100.0	63.3	4.8	31.7	557	67.7	997	284	20.0
Yuba City city	264	394	1,846	2,754	17,019	49	100.0	68.5	7.7	28.7	476	65.2	979	162	100.6
Yucaipa city	101	187	822	1,522	17,217	107	43.0	28.8	2.4	95.0	350	39.5	738	131	38.1
Yucca Valley town	85	388	340	1,553	4,318	33	100.0	13.4	0.7	96.5	497	16.5	763	228	10.7

1 Data for serious crimes have not been adjusted for underreporting. This may affect comparability between geographic areas over time.
2 Per 100,000 population estimated by the FBI. 3 Based on population estimated as of July 1 of the year shown.

Table B. Incorporated Places, Census Designated Places (CDPs), and Minor Civil Divisions (MCDs) of 10,000 or More Population — Land Area, Population, and Households, and Employment

STATE City, town, township, borough, or CDP (county if applicable)	Land area 2010 (sq mi)	Population				Population characteristics 2015–2019		Income and poverty 2015–2019		Median value of owner-occupied housing units	Employment, 2015–2019		Households, 2015–2019 (percent of households)	
		Total persons 2010	Total persons 2019	Percent change 2010–2019	Persons per square mile 2019	Percent foreign born	Percent living in the same house as previous year	Median household income	Percent of households with income below poverty level		Percent in civilian labor force	Unemployment rate	Family households	One person households
	1	2	3	4	5	6	7	8	9	10	11	12	13	14
COLORADO	103637.50	5,029,319	5,758,736	14.5	55.6	9.7	82.0	72,331	10.2	343,300	67.6	4.3	63.7	27.4
Arvada city	38.79	106,760	121,272	13.6	3126.4	5.0	84.8	84,717	6.0	384,500	70.0	3.8	66.4	26.5
Aurora city	154.27	324,659	379,289	16.8	2458.6	20.1	81.5	65,100	9.7	290,000	71.3	4.6	65.7	26.7
Berkley CDP	3.61	11,207	NA	NA	NA	20.5	84.9	61,788	12.4	288,400	71.2	2.7	61.3	23.5
Black Forest CDP	100.64	13,116	NA	NA	NA	4.7	88.0	119,747	2.0	547,000	63.0	3.8	83.1	14.1
Boulder city	26.29	97,612	105,673	8.3	4019.5	11.0	65.3	69,520	19.3	700,000	66.2	4.6	42.0	33.8
Brighton city	21.18	33,540	41,554	23.9	1961.9	10.0	85.6	75,355	8.3	308,900	67.5	4.0	72.1	22.8
Broomfield city	33.00	55,861	70,465	26.1	2135.3	8.9	78.6	96,416	6.0	413,500	73.4	3.2	65.3	26.0
Cañon City city	12.39	16,417	16,725	1.9	1349.9	0.7	85.3	46,494	16.9	160,800	48.1	5.3	63.2	31.8
Castle Pines city	9.59	10,333	10,763	4.2	1122.3	6.8	86.5	163,819	2.1	615,400	69.7	2.4	87.3	9.5
Castle Rock town	34.29	48,251	68,484	41.9	1997.2	5.0	81.5	109,700	3.8	422,100	74.0	2.9	77.6	17.2
Centennial city	29.58	100,635	110,937	10.2	3750.4	9.1	85.9	109,324	3.3	433,800	70.0	3.1	75.1	19.9
Cherry Creek CDP	1.67	11,120	NA	NA	NA	14.9	82.7	110,988	5.5	628,200	72.4	5.0	74.6	20.2
Cimarron Hills CDP	5.94	16,161	NA	NA	NA	7.7	76.5	64,780	10.5	197,500	70.1	6.2	75.5	16.8
Clifton CDP	6.05	19,889	NA	NA	NA	3.8	82.0	43,452	24.9	143,500	65.9	8.8	65.6	23.9
Colorado Springs city	195.00	417,447	478,221	14.6	2452.4	7.5	77.3	64,712	11.1	269,800	64.7	5.7	63.3	28.6
Columbine CDP	6.63	24,280	NA	NA	NA	4.5	89.5	101,731	3.9	402,700	66.9	2.3	75.8	20.1
Commerce City city	35.73	45,864	60,336	31.6	1688.7	15.7	86.7	77,065	9.7	320,100	72.5	4.4	79.5	16.3
Dakota Ridge CDP	9.39	32,005	NA	NA	NA	5.0	87.2	100,438	3.1	373,400	74.2	4.0	76.2	18.2
Denver city	153.29	599,825	727,211	21.2	4744.0	15.0	79.9	68,592	12.1	390,600	72.2	3.8	48.4	38.2
Durango city	14.69	16,889	18,973	12.3	1291.6	1.9	79.2	66,160	9.6	463,700	69.5	4.8	51.8	36.6
Edwards CDP	26.65	10,266	NA	NA	NA	23.4	89.9	77,459	9.4	682,000	75.5	3.6	68.9	20.9
Englewood city	6.55	30,258	34,911	15.4	5330.8	7.6	77.8	59,774	12.9	344,400	72.6	5.7	46.6	41.9
Erie town	19.71	18,186	27,003	48.5	1370.0	7.0	82.9	119,555	5.2	468,600	73.9	3.8	79.5	15.2
Evans city	10.18	18,505	21,205	14.6	2083.0	14.0	76.3	59,527	12.9	223,500	73.7	3.4	70.8	19.3
Federal Heights city	1.78	11,461	12,827	11.9	7206.2	23.8	79.8	45,395	17.1	64,300	69.5	2.0	66.8	25.7
Firestone town	13.50	10,200	16,177	58.6	1198.3	4.7	84.9	100,288	3.1	354,000	74.7	2.7	81.7	13.4
Fort Carson CDP	8.59	13,813	NA	NA	NA	3.5	47.6	48,321	13.6	0	15.2	11.3	94.7	5.3
Fort Collins city	57.18	144,879	170,243	17.5	2977.3	6.8	73.4	65,866	16.6	367,900	70.0	5.4	53.9	24.7
Fort Morgan city	5.13	11,363	11,463	0.9	2234.5	24.7	74.4	50,823	10.9	169,900	67.2	4.6	66.8	25.8
Fountain city	22.49	25,905	30,735	18.6	1366.6	8.8	76.3	64,582	7.1	229,200	61.5	6.8	77.8	18.4
Frederick town	14.79	8,665	13,960	61.1	943.9	4.0	88.5	105,827	2.3	363,200	77.9	3.5	83.6	13.3
Fruita city	7.88	12,689	13,478	6.2	1710.4	1.8	83.9	58,531	11.7	223,500	63.8	9.3	70.8	24.7
Golden city	9.64	18,890	20,767	9.9	2154.3	7.3	71.3	72,349	15.2	522,200	60.3	4.6	51.7	31.6
Grand Junction city	39.53	59,034	63,597	7.7	1608.8	5.4	74.4	52,504	15.1	237,100	62.1	6.9	54.5	35.1
Greeley city	48.86	92,950	108,649	16.9	2223.7	11.5	79.2	57,586	15.2	247,700	63.3	5.2	65.8	26.1
Greenwood Village city	8.26	13,919	15,735	13.0	1905.0	15.8	81.1	129,035	7.4	927,900	62.5	4.1	67.4	25.9
Gunbarrel CDP	6.29	9,263	NA	NA	NA	8.0	78.4	86,107	9.7	531,900	67.6	5.3	51.7	33.0
Highlands Ranch CDP	24.27	96,713	NA	NA	NA	9.2	87.3	125,454	3.0	467,500	72.7	3.0	78.5	18.4
Johnstown town	13.76	9,860	15,198	54.1	1104.5	5.3	85.3	100,025	3.8	336,100	73.9	3.9	73.2	19.4
Ken Caryl CDP	9.83	32,438	NA	NA	NA	4.5	87.4	93,856	4.8	370,600	72.8	3.3	71.7	22.0
Lafayette city	9.42	24,491	30,687	25.3	3257.6	10.3	83.5	83,342	6.2	422,000	72.9	3.3	61.9	29.3
Lakewood city	43.05	142,600	157,935	10.8	3668.6	9.4	82.3	66,740	9.1	364,800	69.0	3.5	56.9	32.8
Littleton city	12.63	41,632	48,065	15.5	3805.6	7.5	80.7	76,015	8.5	410,900	69.5	3.5	58.8	32.1
Lone Tree city	9.81	10,234	13,082	27.8	1333.5	13.5	69.7	120,392	3.5	634,000	71.2	2.8	63.4	26.9
Longmont city	28.74	86,327	97,261	12.7	3384.2	11.7	82.2	74,242	9.3	362,500	69.8	5.0	65.0	28.3
Louisville city	7.98	18,408	20,816	13.1	2608.5	9.7	84.9	103,017	6.8	587,000	72.4	3.7	63.5	26.8
Loveland city	34.41	66,992	78,877	17.7	2292.3	3.3	84.7	68,592	8.1	313,900	65.9	4.3	63.6	27.8
Montrose city	18.45	19,092	19,782	3.6	1072.2	7.3	84.5	46,250	18.5	211,700	55.5	7.0	64.6	31.9
Northglenn city	7.35	35,758	38,819	8.6	5281.5	10.3	83.0	66,300	10.1	297,900	72.3	4.5	65.1	26.5
Parker town	22.20	45,357	57,706	27.2	2599.4	7.3	82.3	110,934	3.9	420,000	77.2	2.9	76.7	17.7
Pueblo city	54.96	106,542	112,361	5.5	2044.4	3.3	81.5	40,450	21.8	141,000	55.2	8.4	58.5	34.2
Pueblo West CDP	70.43	29,637	NA	NA	NA	2.6	89.7	71,553	6.7	221,700	61.7	4.3	76.1	19.7
Security-Widefield CDP	13.00	32,882	NA	NA	NA	5.3	84.5	69,352	6.8	211,300	62.0	8.7	80.5	15.7
Sherrelwood CDP	2.43	18,287	NA	NA	NA	20.0	88.4	62,169	9.7	273,500	69.0	3.4	68.6	25.3
Steamboat Springs city	9.89	12,134	13,214	8.9	1336.1	6.9	84.7	77,419	11.4	584,200	73.0	3.8	53.0	30.8
Sterling city	7.43	14,799	14,495	-2.1	1950.9	4.4	71.5	45,647	15.2	136,800	63.1	3.7	53.5	40.0
Superior town	3.95	12,481	13,087	4.9	3313.2	20.0	79.9	127,292	4.9	576,800	76.7	2.5	75.6	15.5
The Pinery CDP	10.38	10,517	NA	NA	NA	2.4	90.5	127,857	1.9	503,300	70.9	1.8	85.8	11.6
Thornton city	35.89	118,787	141,464	19.1	3941.6	13.4	84.4	79,411	7.7	322,200	73.6	3.6	72.0	20.9
Welby CDP	3.71	14,846	NA	NA	NA	23.7	84.9	56,923	12.5	213,500	72.3	2.8	69.8	23.4
Westminster city	31.59	106,135	113,166	6.6	3582.3	9.1	83.1	76,142	6.5	340,900	72.7	4.0	63.9	27.0
Wheat Ridge city	9.34	30,176	31,324	3.8	3353.7	4.4	82.9	57,659	12.7	383,900	66.9	3.7	53.2	35.5
Windsor town	25.08	18,649	30,477	63.4	1215.2	3.5	84.1	99,732	4.1	406,100	69.8	3.2	79.3	16.6
CONNECTICUT	4842.68	3,574,147	3,565,287	-0.2	736.2	14.6	87.9	78,444	10.0	275,400	66.1	6.0	65.2	28.5
Ansonia city and town (New Haven)	6.02	19,277	18,654	-3.2	3098.7	11.4	93.5	54,901	14.7	214,200	65.4	7.3	58.8	37.5
Avon town (Hartford)	23.16	18,091	18,276	1.0	789.1	18.1	89.5	131,130	3.3	383,200	63.4	3.4	73.4	23.9
Berlin town (Hartford)	26.32	19,874	20,436	2.8	776.4	10.2	92.9	101,127	5.0	283,300	64.9	3.6	72.6	23.9
Bethel town (Fairfield)	16.96	18,604	19,800	6.4	1167.5	15.8	93.0	101,968	4.1	342,400	71.8	4.2	70.1	24.4
Bethel CDP	4.09	9,549	NA	NA	NA	17.4	91.5	73,393	5.4	295,600	73.8	3.1	60.4	32.8
Bloomfield town (Hartford)	26.09	20,480	21,211	3.6	813.0	24.1	89.2	76,717	6.9	214,600	58.1	5.3	63.7	31.5
Branford town (New Haven)	21.84	28,026	27,900	-0.4	1277.5	9.4	87.1	77,640	5.9	293,100	65.1	4.1	59.5	34.1
Bridgeport city and town (Fairfield)	16.06	144,246	144,399	0.1	8991.2	30.3	83.1	46,662	22.0	174,700	66.8	12.5	63.3	29.5
Bristol city and town (Hartford)	26.41	60,499	59,947	-0.9	2269.9	8.5	87.3	67,507	9.6	197,800	67.7	5.4	60.9	32.0
Brookfield town (Fairfield)	19.74	16,442	16,973	3.2	859.8	12.3	88.2	114,615	4.8	377,900	68.1	4.4	75.7	19.9
Canton town (Hartford)	24.59	10,292	10,254	-0.4	417.0	6.7	91.4	87,567	3.2	322,500	67.5	3.4	70.5	26.8
Cheshire town (New Haven)	33.08	29,279	28,937	-1.2	874.8	9.6	89.0	120,546	1.7	334,900	63.4	3.4	74.4	21.4
Clinton town (Middlesex)	16.21	13,263	12,925	-2.5	797.3	6.7	92.1	79,554	7.8	282,000	68.3	3.5	68.5	25.9
Colchester town (New London)	49.03	16,003	15,809	-1.2	322.4	4.5	90.2	105,281	6.7	255,500	72.7	5.1	71.2	21.0
Coventry town (Tolland)	37.57	12,433	12,407	-0.2	330.2	2.9	90.7	96,143	3.6	252,700	73.1	4.4	75.9	18.0
Cromwell town (Middlesex)	12.45	14,003	13,839	-1.2	1111.6	8.6	89.9	89,243	4.8	236,300	70.3	2.5	59.3	35.1

Table B. Incorporated Places, Census Designated Places (CDPs), and Minor Civil Divisions (MCDs) of 10,000 or More Population — Crime, Residential Construction and Local Government Finance

STATE City, town, township, borough, or CDP (county if applicable)	Serious crimes known to police, 2018[1] Violent crime Number	Violent crime Rate[2]	Property crime Number	Property crime Rate[2]	New residential construction authorized by building permits, 2019 Value ($1,000)	Number of housing units	Percent single family	Local government finance, 2017 General revenue Total (mil dol)	Intergovernmental Total (mil dol)	Percent from state gov.	Taxes per capita[3]	General expenditure Total (mil dol)	Per capita[3] Total	Capital outlays	Debt outstanding (mil dol)
	15	16	17	18	19	20	21	22	23	24	25	26	27	28	29
COLORADO	22,624	397	152,163	2,672	9,638,045	38,633	64.1	X	X	X	X	X	X	X	X
Arvada city	272	226	3,544	2,938	80,483	294	100.0	5.5	0.0		46	0.0	0	0	71.8
Aurora city	2,716	729	11,122	2,983	548,351	2,328	65.4	505.2	45.7	47.5	857	493.8	1,343	228	809.7
Berkley CDP	NA	NA	NA	NA	NA	NA	NA	NA	NA	NA	NA	NA	NA	NA	NA
Black Forest CDP	NA	NA	NA	NA	NA	NA	NA	NA	NA	NA	NA	NA	NA	NA	NA
Boulder city	292	269	3,666	3,383	100,159	327	12.5	359.7	29.1	75.3	1,934	346.4	3,254	629	125.5
Brighton city	114	274	1,135	2,728	126,967	437	100.0	62.8	7.1	100.0	1,005	56.3	1,396	256	61.4
Broomfield city	82	117	1,707	2,428	120,364	343	97.1	248.1	15.6	98.1	1,962	145.7	2,134	227	261.2
Cañon City city	94	568	757	4,572	10,502	43	76.7	14.8	1.8	90.8	523	14.8	895	93	13.5
Castle Pines city	NA	NA	NA	NA	83,008	254	100.0	5.6	1.2	24.2	395	7.5	718	173	0.0
Castle Rock town	36	56	969	1,502	266,061	1,013	92.3	111.2	4.7	100.0	908	89.6	1,438	176	93.4
Centennial city	202	181	1,958	1,754	30,417	110	94.5	89.5	11.6	0.0	574	74.6	676	164	2.9
Cherry Creek CDP	NA	NA	NA	NA	NA	NA	NA	NA	NA	NA	NA	NA	NA	NA	NA
Cimarron Hills CDP	NA	NA	NA	NA	NA	NA	NA	NA	NA	NA	NA	NA	NA	NA	NA
Clifton CDP	NA	NA	NA	NA	NA	NA	NA	NA	NA	NA	NA	NA	NA	NA	NA
Colorado Springs city	2,617	556	15,752	3,344	NA	NA	NA	591.9	59.6	43.2	707	480.5	1,033	192	2481.6
Columbine CDP	NA	NA	NA	NA	NA	NA	NA	NA	NA	NA	NA	NA	NA	NA	NA
Commerce City city	385	670	1,826	3,177	184,446	629	100.0	77.5	2.5	73.9	1,138	65.0	1,162	0	312.5
Dakota Ridge CDP	NA	NA	NA	NA	NA	NA	NA	NA	NA	NA	NA	NA	NA	NA	NA
Denver city	5,262	730	26,464	3,672	1,267,641	7,330	30.8	3390.9	279.3	90.4	1,893	3002.8	4,260	770	6263.5
Durango city	81	433	661	3,532	20,587	129	54.3	62.6	7.0	100.0	2,049	59.5	3,220	106	28.3
Edwards CDP	NA	NA	NA	NA	NA	NA	NA	NA	NA	NA	NA	NA	NA	NA	NA
Englewood city	83	237	2,139	6,106	28,245	156	76.9	69.6	4.1	48.3	1,140	61.2	1,775	4	55.5
Erie town	25	99	258	1,023	169,565	572	100.0	50.7	1.8	86.0	689	30.3	1,255	423	87.8
Evans city	108	521	423	2,039	28,928	175	57.1	28.4	4.0	100.0	646	19.1	933	89	0.0
Federal Heights city	86	665	554	4,285	0	0	0.0	15.4	2.0	49.3	791	14.6	1,143	235	1.4
Firestone town	18	125	122	846	84,672	420	62.1	14.9	1.6	95.5	638	10.5	754	219	4.5
Fort Carson CDP	NA	NA	NA	NA	NA	NA	NA	NA	NA	NA	NA	NA	NA	NA	NA
Fort Collins city	392	233	3,701	2,201	159,239	948	33.3	333.0	50.6	39.7	1,065	271.2	1,638	177	143.2
Fort Morgan city	38	337	300	2,663	530	2	100.0	25.3	4.9	91.9	894	20.6	1,818	238	21.3
Fountain city	120	395	632	2,081	NA	NA	NA	20.3	1.5	8.0	575	28.6	962	104	49.4
Frederick town	4	30	NA	NA	74,576	285	100.0	12.2	1.1	70.6	569	11.1	867	191	6.4
Fruita city	30	224	217	1,621	NA	NA	NA	15.2	4.4	40.5	387	13.5	1,019	282	58.7
Golden city	44	212	537	2,586	2,700	7	100.0	61.5	15.0	90.7	1,381	57.9	2,755	1113	23.1
Grand Junction city	275	437	2,733	4,340	NA	NA	NA	118.1	16.4	40.4	940	128.1	2,066	240	92.6
Greeley city	424	395	2,739	2,552	133,840	867	19.6	159.2	15.9	53.7	936	147.4	1,380	343	158.8
Greenwood Village city	94	588	728	4,553	20,090	14	100.0	51.8	4.1	22.9	2,618	49.0	3,111	624	0.0
Gunbarrel CDP	NA	NA	NA	NA	NA	NA	NA	NA	NA	NA	NA	NA	NA	NA	NA
Highlands Ranch CDP	NA	NA	NA	NA	NA	NA	NA	NA	NA	NA	NA	NA	NA	NA	NA
Johnstown town	9	55	222	1,346	20,197	86	100.0	20.2	1.8	71.8	1,074	5.4	393	56	0.0
Ken Caryl CDP	NA	NA	NA	NA	NA	NA	NA	NA	NA	NA	NA	NA	NA	NA	NA
Lafayette city	60	208	711	2,459	32,149	178	54.5	54.0	1.6	100.0	882	40.4	1,419	155	30.3
Lakewood city	NA	NA	NA	NA	134,900	915	25.7	221.3	27.3	33.1	896	212.5	1,371	173	37.1
Littleton city	43	88	1,560	3,208	18,858	96	30.2	101.2	17.9	100.0	935	87.6	1,833	105	42.8
Lone Tree city	43	309	1,010	7,249	18,051	47	100.0	47.7	15.6	6.7	2,243	36.1	2,782	1116	18.4
Longmont city	415	434	2,586	2,707	216,548	966	44.2	173.3	25.8	25.7	969	194.3	2,054	524	191.2
Louisville city	16	74	NA	NA	7,619	32	100.0	45.4	6.7	67.8	1,224	56.8	2,682	1506	47.6
Loveland city	201	257	1,749	2,237	76,661	297	79.8	146.6	8.5	95.8	1,105	137.1	1,783	287	2.5
Montrose city	66	341	894	4,624	23,260	141	88.7	27.8	2.6	94.3	952	26.8	1,391	258	3.2
Northglenn city	145	368	1,302	3,306	1,800	10	20.0	41.8	3.8	100.0	703	35.1	900	202	0.2
Parker town	55	99	781	1,405	158,531	475	87.8	79.5	9.0	30.8	943	82.1	1,514	474	65.0
Pueblo city	1,110	993	6,231	5,576	NA	NA	NA	158.4	18.4	74.1	820	144.0	1,297	103	120.5
Pueblo West CDP	NA	NA	NA	NA	NA	NA	NA	NA	NA	NA	NA	NA	NA	NA	NA
Security-Widefield CDP	NA	NA	NA	NA	NA	NA	NA	NA	NA	NA	NA	NA	NA	NA	NA
Sherrelwood CDP	NA	NA	NA	NA	NA	NA	NA	NA	NA	NA	NA	NA	NA	NA	NA
Steamboat Springs city	17	130	264	2,015	NA	NA	NA	54.3	5.9	94.4	2,587	41.3	3,180	487	49.6
Sterling city	88	632	487	3,497	163	1	100.0	0.8	0.0		52	1.6	112	0	28.1
Superior town	NA	NA	NA	NA	21,584	74	100.0	27.1	0.7	100.0	1,427	23.2	1,780	536	68.0
The Pinery CDP	NA	NA	NA	NA	NA	NA	NA	NA	NA	NA	NA	NA	NA	NA	NA
Thornton city	378	271	4,647	3,327	242,060	880	85.5	208.1	28.6	84.5	914	178.3	1,303	288	112.8
Welby CDP	NA	NA	NA	NA	NA	NA	NA	NA	NA	NA	NA	NA	NA	NA	NA
Westminster city	318	280	3,669	3,226	58,414	350	30.9	243.5	29.5	16.8	1,168	245.1	2,170	712	397.6
Wheat Ridge city	76	242	1,031	3,278	12,790	50	84.0	34.1	1.8	63.8	919	45.1	1,440	262	0.1
Windsor town	6	23	163	617	239,111	898	89.3	29.0	1.5	69.0	558	27.0	1,016	349	11.0
CONNECTICUT	7,411	207	60,055	1,681	1,354,391	5,854	40.4	X	X	X	X	X	X	X	X
Ansonia city and town (New Haven)	25	133	442	2,357	90	1	100.0	79.0	32.2	100.0	1,939	63.6	3,385	31	31.8
Avon town (Hartford)	4	22	186	1,012	3,755	13	100.0	93.5	7.8	86.6	4,240	85.9	4,690	168	21.7
Berlin town (Hartford)	15	73	281	1,365	5,075	25	68.0	98.3	22.9	99.9	3,290	74.7	3,650	50	79.2
Bethel town (Fairfield)	4	20	144	721	26,491	80	92.5	75.7	10.7	96.2	3,239	65.4	3,325	22	24.1
Bethel CDP	NA	NA	NA	NA	NA	NA	NA	NA	NA	NA	NA	NA	NA	NA	NA
Bloomfield town (Hartford)	60	279	573	2,660	3,955	32	50.0	98.9	21.0	95.8	3,536	97.3	4,557	306	52.5
Branford town (New Haven)	17	61	476	1,693	6,854	24	100.0	116.7	8.6	97.7	3,481	102.9	3,675	454	35.3
Bridgeport city and town (Fairfield)	945	644	2,833	1,930	5,094	45	57.8	786.6	412.0	97.2	2,188	813.6	5,597	834	686.8
Bristol city and town (Hartford)	62	103	970	1,612	6,752	39	100.0	236.3	76.2	98.8	2,408	223.4	3,716	424	89.1
Brookfield town (Fairfield)	5	29	158	917	5,022	16	100.0	73.0	10.8	98.7	3,530	52.2	3,067	491	32.6
Canton town (Hartford)	1	10	70	680	2,728	11	100.0	43.3	7.2	94.8	3,247	44.7	4,351	540	16.4
Cheshire town (New Haven)	5	17	244	832	4,040	17	100.0	121.2	25.2	98.2	2,971	126.6	4,333	655	45.5
Clinton town (Middlesex)	2	16	323	2,501	5,529	23	100.0	53.7	13.9	100.0	2,970	55.6	4,303	666	83.5
Colchester town (New London)	NA	NA	NA	NA	3,723	12	100.0	63.6	20.8	99.2	2,472	60.1	3,776	338	19.2
Coventry town (Tolland)	10	80	90	724	3,963	22	90.9	62.3	24.6	99.1	2,478	56.9	4,579	454	18.0
Cromwell town (Middlesex)	7	50	251	1,799	2,841	10	100.0	53.8	7.9	97.2	3,035	49.5	3,559	155	16.4

1 Data for serious crimes have not been adjusted for underreporting. This may affect comparability between geographic areas over time.
2 Per 100,000 population estimated by the FBI. 3 Based on population estimated as of July 1 of the year shown.

Table B. Incorporated Places, Census Designated Places (CDPs), and Minor Civil Divisions (MCDs) of 10,000 or More Population — Land Area, Population, and Households, and Employment

STATE City, town, township, borough, or CDP (county if applicable)	Land area 2010 (sq mi)	Population				Population characteristics 2015–2019		Income and poverty 2015–2019		Median value of owner-occupied housing units	Employment, 2015–2019		Households, 2015–2019 (percent of households)	
		Total persons 2010	Total persons 2019	Percent change 2010–2019	Persons per square mile 2019	Percent foreign born	Percent living in the same house as previous year	Median household income	Percent of households with income below poverty level		Percent in civilian labor force	Unemploy-ment rate	Family households	One person households
	1	2	3	4	5	6	7	8	9	10	11	12	13	14
CONNECTICUT—Con.														
Danbury city and town (Fairfield)	41.95	80,893	84,694	4.7	2018.9	31.5	86.1	73,297	11.1	299,600	71.3	6.0	65.2	28.5
Darien town (Fairfield)	12.65	20,716	21,728	4.9	1717.6	11.8	92.9	232,523	3.9	1,471,700	62.3	4.9	82.8	16.4
Derby city and town (New Haven)	5.06	12,876	12,339	-4.2	2438.5	16.4	90.7	56,357	14.3	206,300	67.7	10.4	56.8	36.2
East Hampton town (Middlesex)	35.65	12,960	12,800	-1.2	359.0	6.3	89.4	95,513	6.0	267,700	69.0	7.3	71.5	20.7
East Hartford town (Hartford)	18.00	51,254	49,872	-2.7	2770.7	19.9	86.1	55,967	15.5	164,200	68.8	7.2	64.1	29.2
East Haven town (New Haven)	12.30	29,212	28,569	-2.2	2322.7	11.7	88.9	67,390	8.9	212,800	61.9	6.5	62.2	31.9
East Lyme town (New London)	34.01	19,164	18,462	-3.7	542.8	8.8	84.9	95,217	6.5	312,200	58.0	4.9	64.8	27.0
East Windsor town (Hartford)	26.25	11,162	11,668	4.5	444.5	14.3	85.1	76,824	5.9	216,000	70.0	5.2	62.1	31.9
Ellington town (Tolland)	34.06	15,593	16,467	5.6	483.5	7.7	88.1	91,510	5.2	282,300	71.2	4.4	59.0	31.9
Enfield town (Hartford)	33.32	44,653	43,659	-2.2	1310.3	6.5	86.5	79,730	6.8	190,400	63.7	6.1	64.0	29.2
Fairfield town (Fairfield)	29.90	59,403	62,045	4.4	2075.1	12.4	88.8	139,122	5.4	611,500	63.6	4.9	75.2	20.6
Farmington town (Hartford)	27.94	25,350	25,497	0.6	912.6	21.3	91.0	93,053	9.1	332,000	65.1	4.4	63.7	31.0
Glastonbury town (Hartford)	51.27	34,427	34,482	0.2	672.6	12.6	90.6	120,837	5.1	348,000	67.4	4.4	70.0	25.2
Granby town (Hartford)	40.71	11,290	11,507	1.9	282.7	4.4	90.7	121,250	3.5	310,600	69.5	4.4	80.4	17.4
Greenwich town (Fairfield)	47.72	61,198	62,840	2.7	1316.8	23.2	87.8	152,577	6.7	1,251,200	61.9	4.7	72.8	23.2
Greenwich CDP	4.11	12,942	NA	NA	NA	27.5	83.4	109,500	9.2	1,128,800	62.4	4.7	60.0	33.8
Griswold town (New London)	34.71	11,951	11,534	-3.5	332.3	2.8	86.2	64,365	5.5	180,600	68.9	5.6	69.9	25.6
Groton town (New London)	31.11	40,125	38,436	-4.2	1235.5	8.9	76.7	66,657	8.9	242,600	59.6	6.4	58.6	34.9
Guilford town (New Haven)	47.08	22,373	22,133	-1.1	470.1	7.5	92.4	111,870	2.8	399,600	65.9	3.9	73.8	23.2
Hamden town (New Haven)	32.63	60,880	60,556	-0.5	1855.8	13.3	86.5	77,274	9.0	225,300	67.1	5.4	60.6	31.6
Hartford city and town (Hartford)	17.38	124,765	122,105	-2.1	7025.6	21.5	82.1	36,278	29.1	165,300	60.6	12.0	55.9	37.1
Killingly town (Windham)	48.35	17,375	17,336	-0.2	358.6	4.7	85.5	62,550	12.6	192,000	68.1	3.9	61.0	29.5
Ledyard town (New London)	38.21	15,048	14,621	-2.8	382.6	4.5	88.7	94,099	3.1	235,200	64.6	4.3	71.2	21.9
Madison town (New Haven)	36.15	18,258	18,030	-1.2	498.8	6.0	87.9	113,798	3.9	428,600	64.5	5.4	73.9	23.5
Manchester CDP	6.46	30,577	NA	NA	NA	11.0	86.1	62,622	12.9	165,900	71.0	7.1	57.9	32.4
Manchester town (Hartford)	27.40	58,253	57,584	-1.1	2101.6	16.8	85.2	74,503	10.0	184,600	69.3	5.6	62.3	29.2
Mansfield town (Tolland)	44.64	26,610	25,487	-4.2	570.9	11.2	70.4	51,911	24.9	244,900	52.8	5.0	46.7	28.3
Meriden city and town (New Haven)	23.80	60,825	59,395	-2.4	2495.6	10.2	88.2	58,843	9.5	171,900	64.9	6.0	55.7	38.7
Middletown city and town (Middlesex)	41.02	47,648	46,258	-2.9	1127.7	11.8	82.2	65,572	12.8	231,300	66.0	5.9	53.7	37.8
Milford city (consolidated city) and town (New Haven)	22.18	52,756	54,747	3.8	2468.3	11.7	89.5	91,799	5.9	313,400	67.0	4.8	63.3	30.3
Milford city (balance)	21.91	51,261	53,195	3.8	2427.9	11.9	89.5	91,783	5.8	312,500	66.9	4.8	63.7	30.0
Monroe town (Fairfield)	26.07	19,476	19,434	-0.2	745.5	9.9	94.9	118,669	2.8	370,200	68.1	3.2	77.0	18.5
Montville town (New London)	41.96	19,569	18,508	-5.4	441.1	8.6	88.2	74,106	8.4	201,700	59.7	7.3	71.2	21.0
Naugatuck borough and town (New Haven)	16.30	31,872	31,108	-2.4	1908.5	13.0	92.2	74,944	7.1	183,400	69.5	6.4	68.9	24.8
New Britain city and town (Hartford)	13.36	73,203	72,495	-1.0	5426.3	19.3	87.9	46,499	20.1	160,800	62.3	8.0	59.6	32.8
New Canaan town (Fairfield)	22.20	19,778	20,233	2.3	911.4	13.2	89.4	190,227	2.9	1,355,800	56.1	5.0	76.4	20.8
New Fairfield town (Fairfield)	20.44	13,890	13,878	-0.1	679.0	7.5	93.7	112,457	2.8	348,800	65.4	4.3	78.1	18.2
New Haven city and town (New Haven)	18.69	129,884	130,250	0.3	6969.0	17.8	79.5	42,222	25.2	199,000	63.9	9.0	51.4	38.4
Newington town (Hartford)	13.14	30,538	30,014	-1.7	2284.2	19.4	91.3	81,646	5.2	230,500	67.7	4.5	62.6	31.1
New London city and town (New London)	5.62	27,620	26,858	-2.8	4779.0	18.3	77.7	46,298	23.0	181,900	60.9	8.5	54.2	38.7
New Milford town (Litchfield)	61.57	28,094	26,805	-4.6	435.4	10.8	90.2	89,969	4.8	301,300	72.9	4.6	68.9	23.8
Newtown town (Fairfield)	57.53	27,560	27,891	1.2	484.8	7.7	92.6	127,602	3.0	398,200	66.6	5.0	78.0	19.1
North Branford town (New Haven)	24.76	14,424	14,146	-1.9	571.3	4.7	94.2	90,461	2.3	291,000	68.1	3.5	71.6	22.9
North Haven town (New Haven)	20.84	24,088	23,683	-1.7	1136.4	7.4	91.7	96,598	4.7	298,300	67.2	5.0	71.5	22.5
Norwalk city and town (Fairfield)	22.89	85,612	88,816	3.7	3880.1	28.1	90.6	85,769	9.8	435,800	71.1	6.7	64.2	29.3
Norwich city and town (New London)	28.06	40,493	38,768	-4.3	1381.6	13.4	84.7	57,052	13.3	164,200	66.2	7.0	60.0	33.1
Old Saybrook town (Middlesex)	15.06	10,242	10,061	-1.8	668.1	9.7	93.4	83,132	3.8	382,700	63.0	3.5	64.7	26.2
Orange town (New Haven)	17.18	13,955	13,926	-0.2	810.6	12.0	93.4	121,308	3.8	389,900	65.5	3.2	77.4	18.4
Oxford town (New Haven)	32.75	12,696	13,255	4.4	404.7	7.2	94.5	110,111	2.2	354,100	68.5	5.4	78.6	15.6
Plainfield town (Windham)	42.41	15,405	15,125	-1.8	356.6	3.1	86.2	70,206	9.7	182,500	66.7	7.0	69.8	23.6
Plainville town (Hartford)	9.71	17,658	17,534	-0.7	1805.8	12.0	87.5	72,175	8.0	219,700	70.0	4.4	58.1	36.0
Plymouth town (Litchfield)	21.87	12,243	11,598	-5.3	530.3	3.7	91.7	82,063	4.3	198,500	70.0	3.0	63.7	29.3
Ridgefield town (Fairfield)	34.50	24,645	24,959	1.3	723.4	11.3	92.0	163,945	2.7	653,100	64.8	3.9	77.8	18.9
Rocky Hill town (Hartford)	13.46	19,708	20,115	2.1	1494.4	25.4	85.1	85,125	4.2	268,700	66.3	3.7	62.4	33.5
Seymour town (New Haven)	14.52	16,528	16,437	-0.6	1132.0	9.2	89.0	76,195	5.3	253,300	71.1	6.0	65.6	29.0
Shelton city and town (Fairfield)	30.63	39,558	41,129	4.0	1342.8	13.1	90.5	97,131	6.5	349,300	67.1	5.5	69.2	25.7
Simsbury town (Hartford)	33.93	23,511	25,395	8.0	748.5	9.5	90.7	123,905	3.4	332,800	66.6	3.8	71.0	24.6
Somers town (Tolland)	28.46	11,451	10,784	-5.8	378.9	4.2	90.8	108,560	2.9	323,300	53.8	3.0	76.5	18.0
Southbury town (New Haven)	39.01	19,903	19,571	-1.7	501.7	5.8	92.3	98,790	4.6	325,000	57.4	4.2	65.0	32.3
Southington town (Hartford)	35.90	43,103	43,834	1.7	1221.0	8.6	94.7	94,463	4.5	277,000	65.6	3.4	70.2	25.9
South Windsor town (Hartford)	28.06	25,703	26,162	1.8	932.4	15.6	89.6	107,374	4.9	287,100	66.4	3.8	73.3	23.8
Stafford town (Tolland)	58.04	12,080	11,893	-1.5	204.9	2.2	89.9	74,386	7.5	191,600	67.6	5.2	63.3	27.3
Stamford city and town (Fairfield)	37.62	122,633	129,638	5.7	3446.0	34.4	83.6	93,059	8.8	532,700	73.3	6.3	62.5	28.4
Stonington town (New London)	38.64	18,538	18,559	0.1	480.3	5.7	89.7	81,667	7.4	335,100	61.4	4.6	63.4	31.0
Storrs CDP	5.59	15,344	NA	NA	NA	11.3	64.5	27,035	48.2	230,900	46.9	4.9	22.8	36.3
Stratford town (Fairfield)	17.48	51,380	51,849	0.9	2966.2	14.2	92.6	79,430	7.8	258,400	68.0	6.7	68.8	27.3
Suffield town (Hartford)	42.29	15,735	15,814	0.5	373.9	7.6	88.4	114,208	0.8	310,500	59.9	3.6	77.1	18.9
Tolland town (Tolland)	39.63	15,056	14,618	-2.9	368.9	4.9	91.1	118,194	5.1	287,100	70.7	2.6	79.2	15.3
Torrington city and town (Litchfield)	39.77	36,391	34,044	-6.4	856.0	10.9	87.6	63,172	9.2	153,700	64.6	6.0	59.9	33.4
Trumbull town (Fairfield)	23.24	36,005	35,673	-0.9	1535.0	14.2	90.7	122,451	3.0	399,200	65.5	5.9	79.8	18.2

Table B. Incorporated Places, Census Designated Places (CDPs), and Minor Civil Divisions (MCDs) of 10,000 or More Population — Crime, Residential Construction and Local Government Finance

STATE City, town, township, borough, or CDP (county if applicable)	Serious crimes known to police, 2018[1] Violent crime Number	Violent crime Rate[2]	Property crime Number	Property crime Rate[2]	New residential construction authorized by building permits, 2019 Value ($1,000)	Number of housing units	Percent single family	Local government finance, 2017 General revenue Total (mil dol)	Intergovernmental Total (mil dol)	Percent from state gov.	Taxes per capita[3]	General expenditure Total (mil dol)	Per capita[3] Total	Capital outlays	Debt outstanding (mil dol)
	15	16	17	18	19	20	21	22	23	24	25	26	27	28	29
CONNECTICUT—Con.															
Danbury city and town (Fairfield)	133	155	1,163	1,355	25,843	106	84.9	313.9	77.3	98.3	2,449	284.1	3,357	249	232.3
Darien town (Fairfield)	4	18	259	1,175	54,272	41	100.0	153.4	5.6	100.0	6,256	149.4	6,882	676	62.2
Derby city and town (New Haven)	38	303	291	2,322	590	3	100.0	47.7	13.1	99.3	2,171	70.2	5,611	206	10.5
East Hampton town (Middlesex)	11	85	87	675	2,375	14	100.0	54.3	17.5	94.5	2,619	54.2	4,219	670	33.1
East Hartford town (Hartford)	117	233	1,206	2,403	750	4	100.0	223.8	84.0	90.6	2,665	253.5	5,054	230	47.4
East Haven town (New Haven)	21	73	593	2,059	2,845	33	33.3	115.9	47.6	99.9	2,295	95.2	3,311	41	16.3
East Lyme town (New London)	8	43	88	470	16,576	82	43.9	73.4	14.0	78.4	2,913	78.3	4,192	530	0.0
East Windsor town (Hartford)	17	149	362	3,169	2,880	19	100.0	52.1	10.2	96.0	2,677	43.5	3,827	407	11.0
Ellington town (Tolland)	NA	NA	NA	NA	18,713	126	29.4	60.9	16.0	95.9	2,513	55.3	3,419	80	19.7
Enfield town (Hartford)	55	123	687	1,541	5,178	48	6.3	156.0	50.4	96.9	2,100	165.8	3,729	419	11.9
Fairfield town (Fairfield)	34	54	955	1,529	39,681	232	16.4	325.3	25.2	97.2	4,441	313.8	5,072	279	199.6
Farmington town (Hartford)	14	55	555	2,168	10,237	56	85.7	117.7	13.1	94.3	3,638	111.6	4,375	118	30.4
Glastonbury town (Hartford)	20	58	456	1,318	11,548	36	100.0	172.8	17.4	93.6	4,184	161.9	4,691	368	67.0
Granby town (Hartford)	3	26	79	695	4,253	42	38.1	51.1	11.1	86.8	3,174	49.0	4,326	499	19.1
Greenwich town (Fairfield)	6	10	396	628	148,850	159	71.7	454.9	26.0	96.4	6,039	510.1	8,178	994	251.6
Greenwich CDP	NA	NA	NA	NA	NA	NA	NA	NA	NA	NA	NA	NA	NA	NA	NA
Griswold town (New London)	NA	NA	NA	NA	9,867	85	15.3	39.2	17.9	89.4	1,680	35.8	3,077	14	0.0
Groton town (New London)	37	126	383	1,304	6,426	78	23.1	135.8	37.9	96.3	2,173	122.7	3,160	95	37.5
Guilford town (New Haven)	11	49	320	1,437	7,466	29	100.0	103.3	11.0	99.8	3,939	99.0	4,461	546	106.5
Hamden town (New Haven)	205	335	1,168	1,907	3,659	73	5.5	254.7	73.6	99.1	2,891	252.4	4,138	4	306.8
Hartford city and town (Hartford)	1,313	1,067	4,435	3,602	942	7	100.0	843.8	535.8	87.8	2,173	801.4	6,521	381	619.6
Killingly town (Windham)	NA	NA	NA	NA	4,127	26	100.0	58.3	25.1	87.5	1,829	96.1	5,590	84	16.8
Ledyard town (New London)	8	54	52	351	1,371	11	81.8	59.8	19.3	89.8	2,397	61.5	4,162	265	13.0
Madison town (New Haven)	NA	NA	111	610	5,759	11	100.0	93.1	13.6	97.5	4,208	80.2	4,427	334	23.9
Manchester CDP	101	175	1,275	2,203	NA	NA	NA	NA	NA	NA	NA	NA	NA	NA	NA
Manchester town (Hartford)	NA	NA	NA	NA	3,343	30	86.7	248.7	85.1	96.9	2,451	202.6	3,505	198	111.9
Mansfield town (Tolland)	NA	NA	NA	NA	2,026	4	100.0	61.0	22.1	98.2	1,246	49.8	1,924	225	1.4
Meriden city and town (New Haven)	215	360	1,216	2,034	550	3	100.0	264.9	120.4	98.7	2,054	265.4	4,449	547	157.0
Middletown city and town (Middlesex)	36	78	584	1,261	3,084	17	100.0	211.6	45.0	95.5	2,389	230.4	4,958	313	107.0
Milford city (consolidated city) and town (New Haven)	37	68	1,119	2,044	15,473	195	14.4	NA	NA	NA	NA	NA	NA	NA	NA
Milford city (balance)	NA	NA	NA	NA	NA	NA	NA	230.1	27.6	97.1	3,452	228.5	4,327	259	102.6
Monroe town (Fairfield)	10	51	105	534	2,880	9	100.0	94.0	10.7	98.6	3,970	90.1	4,623	295	27.4
Montville town (New London)	NA	NA	NA	NA	3,820	10	100.0	75.0	19.6	98.5	2,379	66.9	3,566	145	0.0
Naugatuck borough and town (New Haven)	26	83	502	1,599	0	0	0.0	125.3	40.5	89.5	2,460	133.6	4,261	14	30.8
New Britain city and town (Hartford)	310	427	2,014	2,773	2,269	18	50.0	242.9	120.2	99.1	1,679	176.8	2,434	20	189.1
New Canaan town (Fairfield)	NA	NA	101	494	8,950	11	81.8	176.9	4.8	100.0	6,814	155.9	7,700	1319	117.6
New Fairfield town (Fairfield)	NA	NA	NA	NA	1,958	6	100.0	61.1	11.8	92.4	3,371	70.9	5,085	839	23.6
New Haven city and town (New Haven)	1,105	842	5,111	3,896	79,944	699	0.6	846.0	506.3	91.8	2,051	872.2	6,675	998	605.0
Newington town (Hartford)	21	69	780	2,567	354	2	100.0	118.9	21.8	78.1	3,105	119.6	3,965	366	5.2
New London city and town (New London)	122	452	568	2,104	5,958	36	100.0	130.0	63.2	92.6	1,839	132.6	4,918	110	44.8
New Milford town (Litchfield)	20	74	263	976	2,811	13	84.6	120.2	20.2	93.4	3,031	107.1	3,966	268	30.0
Newtown town (Fairfield)	6	21	122	436	9,329	59	49.2	131.3	12.6	93.0	3,755	130.3	4,699	542	72.6
North Branford town (New Haven)	9	64	146	1,030	2,500	10	100.0	62.2	13.9	98.0	2,944	52.8	3,727	180	0.0
North Haven town (New Haven)	13	55	524	2,211	5,416	17	100.0	116.5	23.3	100.0	3,603	125.9	5,316	1541	76.7
Norwalk city and town (Fairfield)	252	282	1,347	1,506	63,736	194	9.3	402.6	51.9	98.5	3,524	383.0	4,335	353	261.1
Norwich city and town (New London)	108	275	498	1,267	1,387	9	33.3	224.3	127.5	94.6	2,034	171.1	4,355	209	67.6
Old Saybrook town (Middlesex)	5	49	48	474	2,822	15	60.0	46.2	1.8	87.8	4,293	42.5	4,201	229	36.3
Orange town (New Haven)	7	50	465	3,321	3,834	21	100.0	71.9	4.3	100.0	4,463	51.1	3,668	206	28.8
Oxford town (New Haven)	NA	NA	NA	NA	5,450	34	100.0	49.4	8.3	100.0	2,929	45.9	3,536	152	0.0
Plainfield town (Windham)	22	146	74	492	2,355	15	100.0	68.0	37.7	95.4	1,839	48.7	3,227	57	28.8
Plainville town (Hartford)	34	192	509	2,876	2,089	11	100.0	74.3	21.0	99.1	2,661	67.6	3,844	273	39.2
Plymouth town (Litchfield)	11	95	151	1,297	600	5	100.0	47.2	12.3	99.2	2,586	46.3	3,957	385	4.2
Ridgefield town (Fairfield)	1	4	64	253	9,421	38	21.1	146.8	4.5	100.0	5,150	140.7	5,622	203	69.8
Rocky Hill town (Hartford)	6	30	265	1,314	2,197	8	100.0	85.2	17.0	100.0	3,214	82.2	4,074	523	25.1
Seymour town (New Haven)	10	60	153	922	1,201	5	100.0	62.7	15.3	100.0	2,646	54.4	3,291	53	31.1
Shelton city and town (Fairfield)	23	55	286	687	8,168	42	95.2	132.3	19.1	94.1	2,520	114.9	2,798	75	48.1
Simsbury town (Hartford)	5	20	150	596	8,473	66	81.8	97.9	10.7	99.7	3,460	89.7	3,602	63	58.4
Somers town (Tolland)	NA	NA	NA	NA	2,472	14	100.0	30.8	10.0	100.0	1,869	27.3	2,512	30	13.7
Southbury town (New Haven)	NA	NA	NA	NA	3,000	32	56.3	73.4	7.9	94.8	3,177	73.2	3,722	487	5.4
Southington town (Hartford)	32	73	734	1,670	8,736	103	100.0	168.9	36.5	97.2	2,703	160.6	3,671	274	123.1
South Windsor town (Hartford)	14	54	358	1,379	7,813	32	100.0	148.6	41.4	99.3	3,687	132.0	5,101	725	83.9
Stafford town (Tolland)	NA	NA	NA	NA	2,112	10	100.0	45.5	14.9	98.3	2,279	41.6	3,485	229	6.4
Stamford city and town (Fairfield)	218	165	2,120	1,606	319,672	1,140	3.6	621.5	69.0	99.3	4,037	542.9	4,180	36	559.7
Stonington town (New London)	13	70	164	882	9,781	51	41.2	73.8	7.5	100.0	3,203	75.2	4,067	645	51.9
Storrs CDP	NA	NA	NA	NA	NA	NA	NA	NA	NA	NA	NA	NA	NA	NA	NA
Stratford town (Fairfield)	53	101	1,080	2,058	4,930	75	9.3	249.7	61.3	99.8	3,373	203.8	3,924	223	313.2
Suffield town (Hartford)	2	13	77	491	11,080	30	100.0	68.6	21.3	79.0	2,549	67.1	4,296	622	6.7
Tolland town (Tolland)	NA	NA	NA	NA	2,817	15	46.7	61.9	15.7	97.8	2,945	67.1	4,564	750	22.9
Torrington city and town (Litchfield)	46	134	564	1,645	315	3	100.0	146.8	40.0	97.1	2,643	130.7	3,798	82	16.2
Trumbull town (Fairfield)	46	127	850	2,350	290	1	100.0	187.4	16.0	89.2	4,227	190.4	5,302	466	143.5

1 Data for serious crimes have not been adjusted for underreporting. This may affect comparability between geographic areas over time.
2 Per 100,000 population estimated by the FBI.   3 Based on population estimated as of July 1 of the year shown.

Table B. Incorporated Places, Census Designated Places (CDPs), and Minor Civil Divisions (MCDs) of 10,000 or More Population — **Land Area, Population, and Households, and Employment**

STATE City, town, township, borough, or CDP (county if applicable)	Land area 2010 (sq mi)	Population				Population characteristics 2015–2019		Income and poverty 2015–2019			Employment, 2015–2019		Households, 2015–2019 (percent of households)	
		Total persons 2010	Total persons 2019	Percent change 2010–2019	Persons per square mile, 2019	Percent foreign born	Percent living in the same house as previous year	Median household income	Percent of households with income below poverty level	Median value of owner-occupied housing units	Percent in civilian labor force	Unemploy-ment rate	Family households	One person households
	1	2	3	4	5	6	7	8	9	10	11	12	13	14
CONNECTICUT—Con.														
Vernon town (Tolland)	17.70	29,183	29,359	0.6	1658.7	10.5	84.9	64,587	9.5	203,600	68.7	8.4	54.6	32.7
Wallingford town (New Haven)	39.04	45,123	44,326	-1.8	1135.4	9.1	92.4	80,793	6.0	267,800	64.8	3.5	62.2	32.5
Wallingford Center CDP	7.26	18,209	NA	NA	NA	10.6	91.7	67,143	8.2	238,200	63.7	4.0	55.2	38.9
Waterbury city and town (New Haven)	28.52	110,309	107,568	-2.5	3771.7	16.6	87.0	42,401	21.9	130,700	61.5	9.6	60.5	33.9
Waterford town (New London)	32.70	19,519	18,746	-4.0	573.3	6.5	89.6	90,893	6.3	252,200	66.6	5.2	65.8	27.0
Watertown town (Litchfield)	29.01	22,538	21,578	-4.3	743.8	10.4	92.8	79,576	5.8	234,900	69.7	5.6	69.2	26.8
West Hartford town (Hartford)	21.84	63,296	62,965	-0.5	2883.0	16.7	87.8	104,281	7.5	334,300	68.1	3.8	62.9	29.6
West Haven city and town (New Haven)	10.75	55,564	54,620	-1.7	5080.9	18.0	86.1	62,985	12.1	193,800	67.7	9.3	60.8	30.4
Weston town (Fairfield)	19.77	10,191	10,252	0.6	518.6	12.2	94.1	222,535	3.0	868,200	69.3	3.5	84.9	11.0
Westport town (Fairfield)	19.96	26,395	28,491	7.9	1427.4	13.8	89.9	206,466	4.1	1,150,400	61.4	4.0	76.3	20.9
Wethersfield town (Hartford)	12.30	26,668	26,008	-2.5	2114.5	15.8	91.8	86,216	7.2	255,300	68.6	3.8	63.2	31.6
Willimantic CDP	4.40	17,737	NA	NA	NA	12.5	79.6	40,122	29.7	148,900	60.7	9.6	53.2	35.8
Wilton town (Fairfield)	26.79	18,036	18,343	1.7	684.7	12.9	89.5	193,292	2.3	793,200	65.4	3.8	81.9	14.4
Winchester town (Litchfield)	32.52	11,244	10,604	-5.7	326.1	4.8	82.9	68,750	15.5	168,200	66.7	7.5	58.8	30.9
Windham town (Windham)	26.85	25,209	24,561	-2.6	914.7	10.6	81.3	47,481	23.8	159,700	62.0	9.1	56.8	32.4
Windsor town (Hartford)	29.52	29,052	28,733	-1.1	973.3	16.6	91.2	92,199	5.5	225,600	69.7	4.7	67.2	26.2
Windsor Locks town (Hartford)	9.02	12,498	12,854	2.8	1425.1	9.2	91.7	70,067	8.5	188,200	68.7	5.2	62.9	32.2
Wolcott town (New Haven)	20.44	16,700	16,587	-0.7	811.5	6.2	94.6	95,257	5.3	247,500	68.9	3.3	74.6	22.6
DELAWARE	1948.51	897,937	973,764	8.4	499.7	9.6	87.4	68,287	11.2	251,100	62.0	5.5	66.1	27.5
Bear CDP	5.71	19,371	NA	NA	NA	17.4	85.5	72,192	7.9	209,700	72.7	9.3	62.5	29.2
Brookside CDP	3.94	14,353	NA	NA	NA	15.6	86.0	58,555	8.8	197,200	68.3	5.2	64.1	29.1
Dover city	23.67	35,802	38,166	6.6	1612.4	8.3	75.8	47,669	19.8	175,300	57.6	6.2	56.1	35.7
Glasgow CDP	9.93	14,303	NA	NA	NA	12.8	90.7	93,209	5.0	274,000	73.3	5.8	73.2	17.9
Hockessin CDP	10.04	13,527	NA	NA	NA	12.8	95.8	128,412	1.9	441,200	60.4	5.7	81.2	16.9
Middletown town	11.81	18,869	22,900	21.4	1939.0	9.0	88.8	90,134	5.0	301,700	65.1	7.0	74.1	23.5
Milford city	9.77	9,591	11,732	22.3	1200.8	16.1	85.9	47,824	13.3	190,900	60.6	4.4	63.5	29.5
Newark city	9.19	31,467	33,515	6.5	3646.9	13.5	71.1	58,434	20.6	277,800	52.2	4.4	48.1	32.3
Pike Creek Valley CDP	2.58	11,217	NA	NA	NA	11.3	81.5	74,871	6.4	252,400	69.9	3.5	53.6	36.1
Smyrna town	6.28	10,047	11,813	17.6	1881.1	4.4	86.5	67,277	9.2	206,400	69.6	5.4	67.9	25.8
Wilmington city	10.90	70,875	70,166	-1.0	6437.2	6.0	80.8	45,032	23.8	168,000	61.6	8.4	49.3	43.8
DISTRICT OF COLUMBIA	61.14	601,767	705,749	17.3	11543.2	13.7	80.5	86,420	14.6	601,500	69.9	6.9	43.5	44.1
Washington city	61.14	601,767	705,749	17.3	11543.2	13.7	80.5	86,420	14.6	601,500	69.9	6.9	43.5	44.1
FLORIDA	53647.88	18,804,564	21,477,737	14.2	400.3	20.7	84.5	55,660	13.3	215,300	58.5	5.6	64.6	28.6
Alafaya CDP	30.41	78,113	NA	NA	NA	19.1	81.8	75,307	10.8	269,300	69.0	4.7	73.5	17.3
Altamonte Springs city	9.08	41,569	44,143	6.2	4861.6	19.7	79.8	52,888	10.6	184,100	69.6	5.3	52.6	38.5
Apollo Beach CDP	19.81	14,055	NA	NA	NA	8.5	82.4	88,919	7.0	276,600	65.4	4.7	74.4	20.9
Apopka city	33.63	42,194	53,447	26.7	1589.3	15.2	92.0	66,057	8.8	228,400	68.2	5.5	72.1	21.6
Asbury Lake CDP	17.05	8,700	NA	NA	NA	4.8	81.4	82,431	6.9	216,600	64.0	5.8	87.8	12.2
Atlantic Beach city	3.49	12,671	13,872	9.5	3974.8	6.3	86.4	78,059	7.0	362,300	65.2	2.8	59.9	31.2
Auburndale city	13.56	13,455	16,650	23.7	1227.9	6.9	86.5	54,066	14.4	180,800	58.8	4.7	71.0	23.7
Aventura city	2.65	35,742	36,987	3.5	13957.4	51.0	86.0	63,892	12.2	355,200	56.2	5.0	52.0	43.4
Avon Park city	9.74	10,050	10,689	6.4	1097.4	12.4	76.6	30,750	28.9	70,300	53.0	19.1	68.5	28.9
Azalea Park CDP	3.05	12,556	NA	NA	NA	21.3	88.4	45,188	17.8	154,500	64.6	6.3	71.2	19.7
Bartow city	46.22	17,172	20,147	17.3	435.9	7.1	86.4	47,779	17.1	137,100	58.7	4.9	69.5	26.4
Bayonet Point CDP	5.76	23,467	NA	NA	NA	7.1	81.7	39,916	20.0	92,500	47.8	10.3	56.3	33.7
Bayshore Gardens CDP	3.52	16,323	NA	NA	NA	18.7	86.3	43,290	13.1	96,400	56.5	8.6	57.3	36.9
Bellair-Meadowbrook Terrace CDP	4.10	13,343	NA	NA	NA	12.3	64.7	47,211	12.3	123,900	64.7	6.7	66.5	27.7
Belle Glade city	7.10	18,206	20,134	10.6	2835.8	30.3	86.4	24,322	42.3	113,400	55.4	14.9	56.6	39.3
Bellview CDP	11.64	23,355	NA	NA	NA	4.8	85.1	54,103	6.1	113,700	61.6	4.7	61.8	31.0
Bloomingdale CDP	8.13	22,711	NA	NA	NA	9.3	88.1	88,081	6.0	243,600	62.6	4.1	80.5	16.2
Boca Raton city	29.18	84,409	99,805	18.2	3420.3	20.4	81.6	83,114	9.9	458,600	58.0	5.0	55.3	36.9
Bonita Springs city	38.33	43,930	59,637	35.8	1555.9	22.2	86.3	70,249	6.4	311,900	43.3	3.5	67.5	27.6
Boynton Beach city	16.15	68,293	78,679	15.2	4871.8	25.0	81.5	57,563	11.2	207,500	63.8	7.4	56.2	34.4
Bradenton city	14.37	49,273	59,439	20.6	4136.3	11.9	82.2	46,776	14.3	169,800	54.3	6.4	57.6	36.7
Brandon CDP	33.14	103,483	NA	NA	NA	16.4	79.5	61,120	10.2	187,000	65.5	5.2	63.6	27.7
Brent CDP	10.37	21,804	NA	NA	NA	5.9	85.1	39,549	19.2	82,100	59.1	8.3	55.9	32.6
Brownsville CDP	2.28	15,313	NA	NA	NA	29.3	89.1	25,440	38.4	160,700	58.2	13.3	61.3	35.8
Buenaventura Lakes CDP	5.58	26,079	NA	NA	NA	25.5	85.8	48,974	15.5	182,600	63.0	7.1	74.5	20.8
Callaway city	9.41	14,318	14,060	-1.8	1494.2	6.9	74.1	50,383	13.3	148,400	58.6	7.8	67.5	25.7
Cape Canaveral city	2.22	9,987	10,470	4.8	4716.2	6.1	81.9	54,653	9.5	244,900	49.0	4.4	50.2	43.4
Cape Coral city	105.95	154,309	194,495	26.0	1835.7	15.2	87.5	61,599	10.1	229,400	58.1	6.0	70.9	23.8
Carrollwood CDP	9.22	33,365	NA	NA	NA	18.5	88.1	68,422	7.9	246,000	66.6	5.0	64.0	29.3
Casselberry city	6.93	26,032	28,757	10.5	4149.6	15.1	83.4	50,529	17.0	159,300	61.6	5.5	56.1	32.7
Cheval CDP	5.95	10,702	NA	NA	NA	15.1	85.6	70,735	5.9	355,800	70.7	6.3	62.5	32.1
Citrus Park CDP	10.16	24,252	NA	NA	NA	21.2	87.4	68,834	10.3	240,600	69.0	2.9	65.2	26.9
Clearwater city	26.08	109,139	116,946	7.2	4484.1	16.6	83.0	48,691	14.6	206,300	58.9	7.0	55.9	35.6
Clermont city	15.93	28,823	38,654	34.1	2426.5	14.9	78.6	64,736	10.0	233,000	56.5	2.6	71.5	23.5
Cocoa city	13.34	17,167	18,603	8.4	1394.5	10.5	84.6	38,892	18.2	115,500	56.1	7.5	57.2	37.6
Cocoa Beach city	4.66	11,198	11,705	4.5	2511.8	10.1	81.7	58,636	6.7	318,000	45.8	4.8	50.1	43.4
Coconut Creek city	11.17	53,042	61,248	15.5	5483.3	28.8	83.6	62,973	9.5	192,500	66.3	4.8	61.2	31.6
Conway CDP	3.42	13,467	NA	NA	NA	11.7	88.9	75,800	6.3	252,800	67.3	4.1	73.7	20.8
Cooper City city	8.04	28,537	35,800	25.5	4452.7	24.5	90.0	106,795	5.1	378,100	68.7	3.2	82.6	14.6
Coral Gables city	12.93	46,746	49,700	6.3	3843.8	39.5	82.1	100,843	9.0	846,100	60.9	3.2	62.4	31.2
Coral Springs city	22.86	122,588	133,759	9.1	5851.2	29.8	85.5	77,360	9.0	354,100	71.1	6.7	77.3	18.4
Coral Terrace CDP	3.36	24,376	NA	NA	NA	64.4	92.2	62,547	14.6	335,100	60.5	2.0	80.9	13.8
Country Club CDP	4.17	47,105	NA	NA	NA	58.8	83.1	48,184	18.4	224,900	68.5	5.3	73.2	21.5
Country Walk CDP	2.58	15,997	NA	NA	NA	45.7	91.2	82,445	6.7	337,100	65.1	2.1	86.5	9.0
Crestview city	16.08	21,065	25,274	20.0	1571.8	3.7	71.3	54,972	12.7	164,300	57.7	9.6	67.8	26.9

Table B. Incorporated Places, Census Designated Places (CDPs), and Minor Civil Divisions (MCDs) of 10,000 or More Population — **Crime, Residential Construction and Local Government Finance**

STATE City, town, township, borough, or CDP (county if applicable)	Serious crimes known to police, 2018[1] — Violent crime — Number	Rate[2]	Property crime — Number	Rate[2]	New residential construction authorized by building permits, 2019 — Value ($1,000)	Number of housing units	Percent single family	Local government finance, 2017 — General revenue — Total (mil dol)	Intergovernmental Total (mil dol)	Percent from state gov.	Taxes per capita[3]	General expenditure — Per capita[3] Total (mil dol)	Total	Capital outlays	Debt outstanding (mil dol)
	15	16	17	18	19	20	21	22	23	24	25	26	27	28	29
CONNECTICUT—Con.															
Vernon town (Tolland)	21	72	367	1,252	9,732	117	9.4	113.1	30.8	95.8	2,400	106.3	3,636	329	40.7
Wallingford town (New Haven)..	30	67	597	1,336	3,985	22	100.0	177.5	40.8	96.7	2,672	174.6	3,919	177	34.8
Wallingford Center CDP	NA	NA	NA	NA	NA	NA	NA	NA	NA	NA	NA	NA	NA	NA	NA
Waterbury city and town (New Haven)	481	444	4,252	3,923	1,125	15	100.0	531.0	249.6	98.6	2,238	576.6	5,325	358	448.9
Waterford town (New London)..	11	58	329	1,737	12,996	100	28.0	100.6	6.4	93.9	4,424	91.3	4,821	212	86.9
Watertown town (Litchfield)	21	97	491	2,270	5,139	23	73.9	72.3	16.1	99.5	2,513	63.0	2,901	4	53.3
West Hartford town (Hartford) ..	45	71	1,742	2,761	7,191	93	12.9	317.9	54.2	96.6	3,760	286.4	4,546	760	150.5
West Haven city and town (New Haven)	105	192	1,175	2,147	9,217	57	15.8	199.3	76.8	99.3	1,813	197.6	3,602	135	30.7
Weston town (Fairfield)	NA	NA	27	261	13,677	9	100.0	80.6	2.2	97.1	7,158	73.3	7,137	173	22.6
Westport town (Fairfield)	3	11	241	852	47,789	55	92.7	222.3	9.8	90.2	6,772	189.6	6,816	122	94.1
Wethersfield town (Hartford)	23	88	384	1,470	944	2	100.0	121.9	33.5	97.2	3,248	104.5	3,998	316	64.0
Willimantic CDP	29	164	136	769	NA	NA	NA	NA	NA	NA	NA	NA	NA	NA	NA
Wilton town (Fairfield)	5	27	154	826	872	2	100.0	141.3	17.8	100.0	6,361	154.3	8,370	1918	81.9
Winchester town (Litchfield)	8	75	97	909	675	3	100.0	40.2	13.8	98.2	2,236	38.0	3,548	46	4.6
Windham town (Windham)	NA	NA	NA	NA	994	5	100.0	100.8	53.1	95.2	1,512	96.7	3,926	177	17.1
Windsor town (Hartford)	27	94	783	2,712	3,528	20	100.0	137.4	36.8	98.9	3,291	121.2	4,205	352	38.3
Windsor Locks town (Hartford) .	10	80	171	1,362	328	2	100.0	56.0	17.2	94.6	2,710	52.8	4,212	222	17.9
Wolcott town (New Haven)	8	48	240	1,440	4,025	37	75.7	59.9	19.0	98.3	2,209	58.9	3,543	200	17.0
DELAWARE	4,097	424	22,481	2,324	849,102	6,539	85.2	X	X	X	X	X	X	X	X
Bear CDP	NA	NA	NA	NA	NA	NA	NA	NA	NA	NA	NA	NA	NA	NA	NA
Brookside CDP	NA	NA	NA	NA	NA	NA	NA	NA	NA	NA	NA	NA	NA	NA	NA
Dover city	301	797	1,810	4,791	8,173	48	95.8	38.6	5.3	41.6	449	47.6	1,272	137	36.9
Glasgow CDP	NA	NA	NA	NA	NA	NA	NA	NA	NA	NA	NA	NA	NA	NA	NA
Hockessin CDP	NA	NA	NA	NA	NA	NA	NA	NA	NA	NA	NA	NA	NA	NA	NA
Middletown town	64	286	437	1,955	20,140	323	46.1	15.7	0.4	100.0	446	14.9	688	26	38.0
Milford city	85	752	565	5,000	18,994	169	100.0	13.7	0.4	93.5	499	14.3	1,297	48	14.8
Newark city	100	292	667	1,950	8,287	51	100.0	25.0	1.5	86.4	292	38.2	1,135	133	9.9
Pike Creek Valley CDP	NA	NA	NA	NA	NA	NA	NA	NA	NA	NA	NA	NA	NA	NA	NA
Smyrna town	50	424	268	2,273	16,893	164	40.2	7.6	0.4	100.0	464	12.6	1,094	450	24.0
Wilmington city	1,099	1,545	3,502	4,922	25,580	208	12.5	217.8	54.1	36.6	1,681	184.0	2,604	186	367.9
DISTRICT OF COLUMBIA	6,996	996	30,724	4,374	680,539	5,945	2.8	X	X	X	X	X	X	X	X
Washington city	6,613	941	29,993	4,270	680,539	5,945	2.8	13057.2	4055.8	5.5	10,729	13938.0	20,057	2232	14417.4
FLORIDA	81,980	385	486,017	2,282	33,210,471	154,302	64.7	X	X	X	X	X	X	X	X
Alafaya CDP	NA	NA	NA	NA	NA	NA	NA	NA	NA	NA	NA	NA	NA	NA	NA
Altamonte Springs city	136	305	1,446	3,238	0	0	0.0	56.5	5.7	97.3	588	65.9	1,490	618	0.0
Apollo Beach CDP	NA	NA	NA	NA	NA	NA	NA	NA	NA	NA	NA	NA	NA	NA	NA
Apopka city	218	411	1,508	2,840	98,028	331	100.0	57.7	10.4	93.8	399	56.8	1,087	68	24.8
Asbury Lake CDP	NA	NA	NA	NA	NA	NA	NA	NA	NA	NA	NA	NA	NA	NA	NA
Atlantic Beach city	30	218	246	1,789	14,503	38	100.0	23.8	4.4	44.9	629	21.4	1,575	203	18.4
Auburndale city	36	220	578	3,533	46,659	241	100.0	24.9	3.2	46.8	664	27.1	1,705	427	55.7
Aventura city	82	213	1,963	5,093	0	0	0.0	54.7	13.1	89.1	845	48.8	1,296	148	20.2
Avon Park city	NA	NA	NA	NA	NA	NA	NA	10.0	2.1	44.8	311	10.6	1,010	129	0.0
Azalea Park CDP	NA	NA	NA	NA	NA	NA	NA	NA	NA	NA	NA	NA	NA	NA	NA
Bartow city	114	571	756	3,789	6,609	38	100.0	28.4	5.2	56.0	347	37.0	1,901	335	29.6
Bayonet Point CDP	NA	NA	NA	NA	NA	NA	NA	NA	NA	NA	NA	NA	NA	NA	NA
Bayshore Gardens CDP	NA	NA	NA	NA	NA	NA	NA	NA	NA	NA	NA	NA	NA	NA	NA
Bellair-Meadowbrook Terrace CDP	NA	NA	NA	NA	NA	NA	NA	NA	NA	NA	NA	NA	NA	NA	NA
Belle Glade city	206	1,036	787	3,959	425	3	100.0	15.4	4.5	83.8	284	14.2	723	60	0.0
Bellview CDP	NA	NA	NA	NA	NA	NA	NA	NA	NA	NA	NA	NA	NA	NA	NA
Bloomingdale CDP	NA	NA	NA	NA	NA	NA	NA	NA	NA	NA	NA	NA	NA	NA	NA
Boca Raton city	205	205	2,361	2,357	95,631	120	94.2	253.8	34.3	33.5	1,358	238.8	2,431	185	68.8
Bonita Springs city	NA	NA	NA	NA	234,702	606	77.1	28.0	6.0	92.4	261	27.6	491	219	23.0
Boynton Beach city	477	603	2,964	3,745	83,289	769	2.9	139.5	11.3	86.3	889	134.4	1,729	194	108.1
Bradenton city	388	673	1,564	2,713	43,793	362	17.7	78.5	9.4	71.4	541	64.5	1,138	56	43.3
Brandon CDP	NA	NA	NA	NA	NA	NA	NA	NA	NA	NA	NA	NA	NA	NA	NA
Brent CDP	NA	NA	NA	NA	NA	NA	NA	NA	NA	NA	NA	NA	NA	NA	NA
Brownsville CDP	NA	NA	NA	NA	NA	NA	NA	NA	NA	NA	NA	NA	NA	NA	NA
Buenaventura Lakes CDP	NA	NA	NA	NA	NA	NA	NA	NA	NA	NA	NA	NA	NA	NA	NA
Callaway city	NA	NA	NA	NA	10,714	55	100.0	12.0	2.6	100.0	281	10.4	681	61	22.3
Cape Canaveral city	NA	NA	NA	NA	2,232	7	100.0	21.9	7.2	36.0	631	21.0	2,017	858	8.1
Cape Coral city	267	142	2,701	1,438	462,340	2,688	69.9	295.7	50.1	91.6	613	286.5	1,560	106	820.4
Carrollwood CDP	NA	NA	NA	NA	NA	NA	NA	NA	NA	NA	NA	NA	NA	NA	NA
Casselberry city	152	529	946	3,291	40,470	407	5.7	36.9	3.8	91.7	449	42.3	1,494	434	21.6
Cheval CDP	NA	NA	NA	NA	NA	NA	NA	NA	NA	NA	NA	NA	NA	NA	NA
Citrus Park CDP	NA	NA	NA	NA	NA	NA	NA	NA	NA	NA	NA	NA	NA	NA	NA
Clearwater city	510	438	3,087	2,650	38,084	125	31.2	247.2	31.1	48.2	768	229.3	1,986	143	205.6
Clermont city	58	160	723	1,995	104,474	505	85.7	47.9	4.9	67.0	596	49.8	1,416	373	22.8
Cocoa city	141	752	1,021	5,449	85,267	93	95.7	32.1	5.9	32.8	498	50.9	2,744	350	90.5
Cocoa Beach city	41	347	407	3,447	4,800	6	100.0	25.9	3.0	96.6	1,030	33.9	2,902	792	29.6
Coconut Creek city	89	143	1,027	1,650	1,633	12	100.0	76.0	7.2	90.4	558	69.4	1,136	151	6.3
Conway CDP	NA	NA	NA	NA	NA	NA	NA	NA	NA	NA	NA	NA	NA	NA	NA
Cooper City city	36	98	433	1,174	434	2	100.0	42.0	4.5	73.2	659	41.8	1,171	48	0.7
Coral Gables city	68	132	1,225	2,369	33,704	26	100.0	172.9	6.4	89.0	2,077	185.2	3,659	687	100.2
Coral Springs city	209	155	2,027	1,506	11,377	59	83.1	155.2	15.5	85.5	657	155.9	1,168	151	121.0
Coral Terrace CDP	NA	NA	NA	NA	NA	NA	NA	NA	NA	NA	NA	NA	NA	NA	NA
Country Club CDP	NA	NA	NA	NA	NA	NA	NA	NA	NA	NA	NA	NA	NA	NA	NA
Country Walk CDP	NA	NA	NA	NA	NA	NA	NA	NA	NA	NA	NA	NA	NA	NA	NA
Crestview city	86	354	702	2,890	48,632	182	100.0	24.6	4.1	76.9	519	20.2	842	100	27.7

1 Data for serious crimes have not been adjusted for underreporting. This may affect comparability between geographic areas over time.
2 Per 100,000 population estimated by the FBI.   3 Based on population estimated as of July 1 of the year shown.

Table B. Incorporated Places, Census Designated Places (CDPs), and Minor Civil Divisions (MCDs) of 10,000 or More Population — **Land Area, Population, and Households, and Employment**

STATE City, town, township, borough, or CDP (county if applicable)	Land area 2010 (sq mi)	Total persons 2010	Total persons 2019	Percent change 2010–2019	Persons per square mile 2019	Percent foreign born	Percent living in the same house as previous year	Median household income	Percent of households with income below poverty level	Median value of owner-occupied housing units	Percent in civilian labor force	Unemployment rate	Family households	One person households
	1	2	3	4	5	6	7	8	9	10	11	12	13	14
FLORIDA—Con.														
Cutler Bay town	9.89	40,289	43,718	8.5	4420.4	40.8	91.9	75,101	9.8	287,000	67.7	4.3	77.9	15.9
Cypress Gardens CDP	3.47	8,917	NA	NA	NA	4.8	87.6	62,963	6.8	168,000	58.4	3.7	71.5	22.7
Cypress Lake CDP	3.86	11,846	NA	NA	NA	7.8	84.3	50,945	8.2	159,000	48.9	4.9	48.6	46.1
Dania Beach city	7.81	29,738	32,271	8.5	4132.0	29.4	82.0	47,135	16.7	194,700	64.0	7.6	60.7	30.4
Davie town	34.92	91,950	106,306	15.6	3044.3	29.9	84.5	71,780	12.7	309,600	69.3	4.3	69.4	21.4
Daytona Beach city	65.65	61,591	69,186	12.3	1053.9	9.1	81.2	35,893	23.0	153,000	53.6	6.7	47.5	42.0
DeBary city	18.95	19,312	21,305	10.3	1124.3	6.1	87.4	65,316	8.5	211,100	55.4	2.6	68.0	23.0
Deerfield Beach city	14.95	75,008	81,066	8.1	5422.5	34.8	78.5	48,124	16.2	168,600	63.1	7.1	54.1	37.8
DeLand city	18.82	26,852	34,851	29.8	1851.8	7.6	81.8	47,925	16.2	209,200	48.8	6.0	59.2	34.2
Delray Beach city	15.91	60,611	69,451	14.6	4365.2	24.5	80.8	60,746	10.3	280,200	60.9	6.4	52.3	38.4
Deltona city	37.27	85,131	92,757	9.0	2488.8	8.2	90.5	52,616	11.9	155,000	58.2	5.2	75.2	18.3
Destin city	7.69	12,150	14,247	17.3	1852.7	10.1	81.1	79,000	7.5	332,000	66.0	3.8	59.6	29.7
Doctor Phillips CDP	3.18	10,981	NA	NA	NA	26.5	90.2	105,714	5.1	366,900	61.4	3.5	74.6	20.3
Doral city	13.82	45,712	65,741	43.8	4756.9	66.8	81.3	77,493	12.4	394,900	67.3	3.5	82.2	13.6
Dunedin city	10.41	35,355	36,537	3.3	3509.8	9.7	82.9	50,356	10.9	198,700	53.2	4.2	50.9	42.3
East Lake CDP	28.71	30,962	NA	NA	NA	12.1	86.7	81,498	7.8	346,400	54.4	6.7	68.6	26.7
East Lake-Orient Park CDP	15.97	22,753	NA	NA	NA	15.1	78.7	40,838	18.5	115,400	68.2	7.6	64.5	28.4
East Milton CDP	28.71	11,074	NA	NA	NA	3.9	73.3	54,559	13.0	116,500	32.0	3.6	65.8	22.7
Edgewater city	24.58	21,813	23,918	9.7	973.1	3.3	85.9	49,878	11.1	155,900	51.4	4.2	63.0	29.5
Egypt Lake-Leto CDP	5.91	35,282	NA	NA	NA	42.9	80.5	43,936	16.8	174,800	69.0	6.1	60.3	28.4
Elfers CDP	3.55	13,986	NA	NA	NA	9.9	87.5	41,176	14.0	81,200	56.6	4.8	59.6	35.4
Englewood CDP	9.86	14,863	NA	NA	NA	8.8	85.3	47,862	9.6	169,300	34.7	9.3	55.2	35.7
Ensley CDP	12.18	20,602	NA	NA	NA	10.0	84.1	45,245	13.9	114,000	63.1	6.5	56.7	33.3
Estero village	24.34	27,991	33,871	21.0	1391.6	10.7	86.7	82,054	6.4	339,600	39.9	4.4	69.4	24.9
Eustis city	10.48	18,460	21,303	15.4	2032.7	8.8	86.1	46,755	16.7	162,000	57.4	5.8	66.3	28.1
Fairview Shores CDP	2.97	10,239	NA	NA	NA	13.0	84.3	49,963	14.5	206,200	69.7	3.2	54.9	37.1
Fernandina Beach city	11.44	11,382	13,169	15.7	1151.1	9.9	85.9	63,942	11.7	333,900	49.5	5.7	64.3	32.1
Ferry Pass CDP	13.94	28,921	NA	NA	NA	7.0	75.5	49,517	17.7	149,800	61.1	6.3	53.0	36.6
Fish Hawk CDP	16.22	14,087	NA	NA	NA	10.3	84.8	119,208	5.3	350,300	66.6	3.7	83.6	13.6
Fleming Island CDP	15.84	27,126	NA	NA	NA	6.6	81.8	94,154	3.7	269,600	62.7	6.1	78.3	19.4
Florida City city	5.99	11,252	11,771	4.6	1965.1	26.8	83.9	35,253	39.7	153,100	63.7	14.0	79.7	16.1
Florida Ridge CDP	10.77	18,164	NA	NA	NA	14.1	88.6	48,946	9.9	141,200	56.0	8.9	66.9	28.2
Forest City CDP	4.29	13,854	NA	NA	NA	15.6	83.3	66,679	6.7	250,900	63.1	3.1	68.4	22.7
Fort Lauderdale city	34.59	165,754	182,437	10.1	5274.3	24.7	81.9	59,450	13.8	334,000	65.1	7.0	48.9	39.6
Fort Myers city	39.84	62,305	87,103	39.8	2186.3	20.1	80.2	46,409	16.5	238,700	54.9	5.4	57.4	35.1
Fort Pierce city	23.68	41,942	46,103	9.9	1946.9	18.1	86.9	35,198	26.2	113,600	56.6	7.0	58.7	34.0
Fort Walton Beach city	7.65	19,635	22,521	14.7	2943.9	8.9	78.5	54,330	12.2	185,900	60.6	5.9	56.8	37.1
Fountainebleau CDP	3.99	59,764	NA	NA	NA	71.0	86.7	51,041	14.3	190,300	66.5	4.4	74.0	19.6
Four Corners CDP	47.43	26,116	NA	NA	NA	14.7	79.8	57,207	9.6	182,800	66.9	4.2	65.7	23.7
Fruit Cove CDP	16.07	29,362	NA	NA	NA	9.3	86.7	107,557	4.0	333,400	63.8	4.9	84.3	13.8
Fruitville CDP	6.81	13,224	NA	NA	NA	11.9	83.3	75,693	6.8	258,700	65.1	3.0	61.1	26.9
Fuller Heights CDP	4.31	8,758	NA	NA	NA	9.3	90.5	66,678	7.9	170,100	66.3	8.7	69.1	18.9
Gainesville city	63.07	124,504	133,997	7.6	2124.6	11.6	69.5	37,264	27.9	161,900	57.3	5.2	38.5	44.3
Gateway CDP	5.62	8,401	NA	NA	NA	11.4	85.5	100,101	4.9	297,800	65.5	2.3	71.8	22.3
Gibsonton CDP	12.81	14,234	NA	NA	NA	14.1	82.9	52,696	19.7	188,400	65.3	7.9	71.1	21.0
Gifford CDP	6.79	9,590	NA	NA	NA	8.0	87.9	36,323	24.4	231,100	40.4	10.9	52.0	44.5
Gladeview CDP	2.56	11,535	NA	NA	NA	23.4	88.3	30,482	36.8	119,200	55.7	12.2	68.7	26.4
Glenvar Heights CDP	4.12	16,898	NA	NA	NA	47.6	84.1	63,627	11.3	385,200	67.1	3.7	55.5	33.7
Golden Gate CDP	3.91	23,961	NA	NA	NA	53.9	81.5	48,958	15.7	233,800	72.8	4.1	77.8	15.6
Golden Glades CDP	4.83	33,145	NA	NA	NA	49.2	85.4	45,964	19.7	231,300	63.2	9.4	73.1	22.9
Goldenrod CDP	2.53	12,039	NA	NA	NA	13.7	77.6	48,734	15.7	218,000	69.0	5.2	52.4	28.1
Gonzalez CDP	15.11	13,273	NA	NA	NA	3.2	92.4	77,492	5.6	172,200	61.8	2.2	70.9	24.1
Goulds CDP	2.91	10,103	NA	NA	NA	40.7	92.2	41,051	24.2	260,600	58.4	8.1	81.5	14.8
Greenacres city	5.85	37,592	41,117	9.4	7028.5	38.7	84.9	49,884	12.6	162,600	66.1	6.1	67.5	26.6
Groveland city	16.11	8,715	16,423	88.4	1019.4	17.3	86.9	62,384	9.1	199,100	56.4	5.7	72.6	15.3
Gulf Gate Estates CDP	2.70	10,911	NA	NA	NA	12.6	82.2	50,450	9.6	224,200	53.6	3.4	45.3	47.2
Gulfport city	2.77	12,035	12,342	2.6	4455.6	8.2	83.5	52,705	9.6	185,600	50.8	5.2	45.9	45.1
Haines City city	18.85	20,404	26,009	27.5	1379.8	18.0	88.9	44,279	20.8	141,400	58.4	5.6	75.4	19.7
Hallandale Beach city	4.21	37,113	39,847	7.4	9464.8	48.5	80.9	39,184	20.5	215,600	61.8	7.3	51.8	41.2
Hialeah city	21.58	224,704	233,339	3.8	10812.7	74.4	91.8	35,068	26.4	228,600	58.4	4.6	72.5	22.8
Hialeah Gardens city	3.22	21,740	23,474	8.0	7290.1	71.2	92.2	53,423	14.6	208,900	66.2	3.5	84.6	11.4
Highland City CDP	7.80	10,834	NA	NA	NA	9.0	94.5	68,563	9.1	167,300	63.9	7.2	75.2	18.1
Hobe Sound CDP	7.11	11,521	NA	NA	NA	8.7	88.9	50,030	11.7	206,300	53.1	7.9	55.9	36.8
Holiday CDP	5.32	22,403	NA	NA	NA	9.5	89.9	36,032	18.7	76,300	52.8	8.5	56.1	36.4
Holly Hill city	3.96	11,648	12,357	6.1	3120.5	5.8	86.0	35,113	23.3	105,600	49.0	7.5	51.4	42.6
Hollywood city	27.27	140,769	154,817	10.0	5677.2	37.7	85.2	54,251	12.2	254,000	66.1	6.5	61.7	32.3
Homestead city	15.08	60,748	69,523	14.4	4610.3	37.3	85.6	47,508	21.7	222,300	67.6	7.1	79.9	16.2
Homosassa Springs CDP	25.17	13,791	NA	NA	NA	2.5	86.7	40,870	16.1	83,300	43.5	9.0	63.4	28.9
Horizon West CDP	32.87	14,000	NA	NA	NA	24.0	74.7	98,247	8.1	343,600	74.8	3.4	76.6	15.5
Hudson CDP	6.36	12,158	NA	NA	NA	5.2	83.7	41,754	16.0	154,000	37.1	6.3	52.2	42.0
Hunters Creek CDP	7.04	14,321	NA	NA	NA	38.1	80.1	69,078	7.2	289,900	70.6	4.4	72.3	20.0
Immokalee CDP	22.71	24,154	NA	NA	NA	43.9	80.8	30,885	34.2	121,200	68.2	10.6	75.5	15.1
Iona CDP	6.62	15,369	NA	NA	NA	5.8	87.4	58,075	9.6	246,100	35.3	4.6	53.2	39.3
Ives Estates CDP	2.55	19,525	NA	NA	NA	47.2	81.2	56,613	8.1	195,700	68.9	7.2	67.2	27.9
Jacksonville city	747.47	821,750	911,507	10.9	1219.5	11.3	80.8	54,701	13.8	173,200	64.3	5.9	62.4	30.4
Jacksonville Beach city	7.32	21,362	23,628	10.6	3227.9	5.6	83.9	91,037	6.9	368,200	68.5	2.4	54.5	34.2
Jasmine Estates CDP	3.55	18,989	NA	NA	NA	14.5	86.4	37,268	20.4	94,100	54.9	6.1	62.2	28.4
Jensen Beach CDP	6.97	11,707	NA	NA	NA	7.2	87.6	54,778	11.6	232,600	51.4	4.7	51.2	41.8
Jupiter town	21.63	55,312	65,791	18.9	3041.7	13.0	85.7	86,027	8.1	372,800	63.6	3.8	63.1	30.7
Jupiter Farms CDP	14.92	11,994	NA	NA	NA	11.3	93.9	108,443	3.8	392,700	65.1	1.5	82.3	12.7
Kendale Lakes CDP	8.08	56,148	NA	NA	NA	62.7	91.2	59,252	14.3	259,200	63.0	4.5	79.9	15.7
Kendall CDP	16.11	75,371	NA	NA	NA	45.7	89.0	73,612	10.0	382,400	65.5	3.5	68.2	25.5
Kendall West CDP	2.75	36,154	NA	NA	NA	67.2	89.7	58,009	16.6	256,400	65.0	3.7	82.3	13.5
Key Biscayne village	1.25	12,344	12,846	4.1	10276.8	50.6	87.9	151,310	5.5	1,211,000	60.9	5.3	73.8	24.3
Key Largo CDP	12.05	10,433	NA	NA	NA	16.7	86.7	65,864	15.4	421,900	56.6	2.6	62.2	29.5
Keystone CDP	35.12	24,039	NA	NA	NA	13.4	89.6	116,626	4.1	379,000	65.0	3.7	82.0	15.3
Key West city	5.59	24,635	24,118	-2.1	4314.5	21.0	77.7	69,630	9.2	611,400	66.6	2.2	52.2	33.8

Table B. Incorporated Places, Census Designated Places (CDPs), and Minor Civil Divisions (MCDs) of 10,000 or More Population — Crime, Residential Construction and Local Government Finance

STATE City, town, township, borough, or CDP (county if applicable)	Serious crimes known to police, 2018[1] Violent crime Number	Rate[2]	Property crime Number	Rate[2]	New residential construction authorized by building permits, 2019 Value ($1,000)	Number of housing units	Percent single family	Local government finance, 2017 General revenue Total (mil dol)	Intergovernmental Total (mil dol)	Percent from state gov.	Taxes per capita[3]	General expenditure Total (mil dol)	Per capita[3] Total	Capital outlays	Debt outstanding (mil dol)
	15	16	17	18	19	20	21	22	23	24	25	26	27	28	29
FLORIDA—Con.															
Cutler Bay town	97	212	1,278	2,790	2,290	10	100.0	23.1	8.5	55.8	271	22.4	504	7	15.7
Cypress Gardens CDP	NA	NA	NA	NA	NA	NA	NA	NA	NA	NA	NA	NA	NA	NA	NA
Cypress Lake CDP	NA	NA	NA	NA	NA	NA	NA	NA	NA	NA	NA	NA	NA	NA	NA
Dania Beach city	209	646	1,210	3,737	8,268	40	100.0	58.6	3.7	84.9	919	60.0	1,867	698	29.6
Davie town	270	252	2,763	2,579	18,861	186	26.9	123.5	15.1	80.3	725	129.3	1,230	98	186.7
Daytona Beach city	764	1,107	3,358	4,865	83,677	436	34.9	147.0	15.6	54.6	739	130.4	1,916	201	138.9
DeBary city	NA	NA	NA	NA	26,653	71	100.0	14.4	1.8	92.2	401	14.1	679	123	5.5
Deerfield Beach city	329	404	2,490	3,060	33,432	215	100.0	134.4	17.0	63.1	755	139.6	1,733	74	64.4
DeLand city	182	545	1,256	3,762	138,092	474	99.6	49.6	6.4	83.5	623	43.2	1,336	89	9.3
Delray Beach city	409	585	2,522	3,604	63,815	122	87.7	183.4	31.3	25.7	1,391	141.7	2,062	155	68.6
Deltona city	NA	NA	NA	NA	114,170	441	96.8	59.1	10.4	90.8	315	55.8	615	100	166.8
Destin city	NA	NA	NA	NA	20,111	35	88.6	15.9	3.2	79.8	817	13.5	989	230	26.9
Doctor Phillips CDP	NA	NA	NA	NA	NA	NA	NA	NA	NA	NA	NA	NA	NA	NA	NA
Doral city	77	121	1,464	2,299	197,286	1,058	24.5	72.5	8.3	84.1	875	74.0	1,228	466	21.5
Dunedin city	52	142	652	1,776	20,935	64	90.6	49.5	5.0	81.6	574	61.5	1,686	97	35.2
East Lake CDP	NA	NA	NA	NA	NA	NA	NA	NA	NA	NA	NA	NA	NA	NA	NA
East Lake-Orient Park CDP	NA	NA	NA	NA	NA	NA	NA	NA	NA	NA	NA	NA	NA	NA	NA
East Milton CDP	NA	NA	NA	NA	NA	NA	NA	NA	NA	NA	NA	NA	NA	NA	NA
Edgewater city	25	110	410	1,811	5,746	30	93.3	24.6	2.8	74.8	390	22.4	955	53	19.4
Egypt Lake-Leto CDP	NA	NA	NA	NA	NA	NA	NA	NA	NA	NA	NA	NA	NA	NA	NA
Elfers CDP	NA	NA	NA	NA	NA	NA	NA	NA	NA	NA	NA	NA	NA	NA	NA
Englewood CDP	NA	NA	NA	NA	NA	NA	NA	NA	NA	NA	NA	NA	NA	NA	NA
Ensley CDP	NA	NA	NA	NA	NA	NA	NA	NA	NA	NA	NA	NA	NA	NA	NA
Estero village	NA	NA	NA	NA	32,402	270	23.0	20.6	3.5	97.7	382	21.8	662	46	0.0
Eustis city	39	184	522	2,464	7,241	24	91.7	23.8	2.2	83.1	644	23.3	1,122	141	6.0
Fairview Shores CDP	NA	NA	NA	NA	NA	NA	NA	NA	NA	NA	NA	NA	NA	NA	NA
Fernandina Beach city	19	153	280	2,256	36,846	165	100.0	34.9	1.8	85.9	1,391	34.5	2,817	302	40.1
Ferry Pass CDP	NA	NA	NA	NA	NA	NA	NA	NA	NA	NA	NA	NA	NA	NA	NA
Fish Hawk CDP	NA	NA	NA	NA	NA	NA	NA	NA	NA	NA	NA	NA	NA	NA	NA
Fleming Island CDP	NA	NA	NA	NA	NA	NA	NA	NA	NA	NA	NA	NA	NA	NA	NA
Florida City city	375	3,053	875	7,123	9,986	14	100.0	17.3	3.7	40.8	397	15.9	1,327	94	0.1
Florida Ridge CDP	NA	NA	NA	NA	NA	NA	NA	NA	NA	NA	NA	NA	NA	NA	NA
Forest City CDP	NA	NA	NA	NA	NA	NA	NA	NA	NA	NA	NA	NA	NA	NA	NA
Fort Lauderdale city	1,006	552	9,050	4,968	349,936	1,247	10.2	444.4	48.0	44.3	1,145	400.8	2,228	92	719.8
Fort Myers city	582	703	2,285	2,760	402,814	1,978	41.4	180.2	13.7	71.5	994	183.9	2,298	177	342.2
Fort Pierce city	283	614	1,184	2,568	35,989	138	100.0	74.1	8.0	55.9	571	78.2	1,718	49	151.0
Fort Walton Beach city	69	310	655	2,942	7,692	35	74.3	33.8	4.8	67.6	678	39.6	1,796	212	33.5
Fountainebleau CDP	NA	NA	NA	NA	NA	NA	NA	NA	NA	NA	NA	NA	NA	NA	NA
Four Corners CDP	NA	NA	NA	NA	NA	NA	NA	NA	NA	NA	NA	NA	NA	NA	NA
Fruit Cove CDP	NA	NA	NA	NA	NA	NA	NA	NA	NA	NA	NA	NA	NA	NA	NA
Fruitville CDP	NA	NA	NA	NA	NA	NA	NA	NA	NA	NA	NA	NA	NA	NA	NA
Fuller Heights CDP	NA	NA	NA	NA	NA	NA	NA	NA	NA	NA	NA	NA	NA	NA	NA
Gainesville city	989	741	5,229	3,920	54,218	1,214	10.6	209.3	36.9	50.5	470	226.8	1,717	263	1090.1
Gateway CDP	NA	NA	NA	NA	NA	NA	NA	NA	NA	NA	NA	NA	NA	NA	NA
Gibsonton CDP	NA	NA	NA	NA	NA	NA	NA	NA	NA	NA	NA	NA	NA	NA	NA
Gifford CDP	NA	NA	NA	NA	NA	NA	NA	NA	NA	NA	NA	NA	NA	NA	NA
Gladeview CDP	NA	NA	NA	NA	NA	NA	NA	NA	NA	NA	NA	NA	NA	NA	NA
Glenvar Heights CDP	NA	NA	NA	NA	NA	NA	NA	NA	NA	NA	NA	NA	NA	NA	NA
Golden Gate CDP	NA	NA	NA	NA	NA	NA	NA	NA	NA	NA	NA	NA	NA	NA	NA
Golden Glades CDP	NA	NA	NA	NA	NA	NA	NA	NA	NA	NA	NA	NA	NA	NA	NA
Goldenrod CDP	NA	NA	NA	NA	NA	NA	NA	NA	NA	NA	NA	NA	NA	NA	NA
Gonzalez CDP	NA	NA	NA	NA	NA	NA	NA	NA	NA	NA	NA	NA	NA	NA	NA
Goulds CDP	NA	NA	NA	NA	NA	NA	NA	NA	NA	NA	NA	NA	NA	NA	NA
Greenacres city	159	386	836	2,030	3,980	23	100.0	26.6	5.2	89.5	408	29.5	725	122	2.4
Groveland city	24	167	190	1,325	156,745	553	100.0	14.2	1.2	80.0	568	14.4	1,069	240	16.1
Gulf Gate Estates CDP	NA	NA	NA	NA	NA	NA	NA	NA	NA	NA	NA	NA	NA	NA	NA
Gulfport city	15	121	398	3,204	2,420	11	100.0	19.5	2.7	62.1	598	22.2	1,796	225	0.0
Haines City city	36	145	528	2,122	206,561	696	100.0	34.7	2.4	91.2	600	27.2	1,133	72	54.3
Hallandale Beach city	217	540	1,296	3,222	4,522	19	47.4	90.6	10.6	35.9	888	111.4	2,798	525	110.6
Hialeah city	533	221	5,355	2,215	70,908	591	14.9	254.1	63.3	73.3	428	241.2	1,021	37	155.7
Hialeah Gardens city	30	122	517	2,109	595	1	100.0	18.4	5.3	76.2	423	20.7	869	105	5.5
Highland City CDP	NA	NA	NA	NA	NA	NA	NA	NA	NA	NA	NA	NA	NA	NA	NA
Hobe Sound CDP	NA	NA	NA	NA	NA	NA	NA	NA	NA	NA	NA	NA	NA	NA	NA
Holiday CDP	NA	NA	NA	NA	NA	NA	NA	NA	NA	NA	NA	NA	NA	NA	NA
Holly Hill city	63	512	495	4,024	704	4	100.0	16.1	2.2	48.9	565	13.6	1,118	65	24.0
Hollywood city	363	233	4,343	2,793	59,275	231	95.7	316.5	29.1	64.7	955	282.9	1,844	165	329.1
Homestead city	714	1,001	2,282	3,200	54,290	225	100.0	84.6	16.7	62.7	355	112.8	1,632	354	27.4
Homosassa Springs CDP	NA	NA	NA	NA	NA	NA	NA	NA	NA	NA	NA	NA	NA	NA	NA
Horizon West CDP	NA	NA	NA	NA	NA	NA	NA	NA	NA	NA	NA	NA	NA	NA	NA
Hudson CDP	NA	NA	NA	NA	NA	NA	NA	NA	NA	NA	NA	NA	NA	NA	NA
Hunters Creek CDP	NA	NA	NA	NA	NA	NA	NA	NA	NA	NA	NA	NA	NA	NA	NA
Immokalee CDP	NA	NA	NA	NA	NA	NA	NA	NA	NA	NA	NA	NA	NA	NA	NA
Iona CDP	NA	NA	NA	NA	NA	NA	NA	NA	NA	NA	NA	NA	NA	NA	NA
Ives Estates CDP	NA	NA	NA	NA	NA	NA	NA	NA	NA	NA	NA	NA	NA	NA	NA
Jacksonville city	5,381	596	30,112	3,334	1,278,709	6,805	61.1	2264.4	558.5	39.1	1,114	1680.4	1,884	121	8768.9
Jacksonville Beach city	143	600	915	3,838	27,835	86	100.0	43.6	4.5	68.6	933	38.1	1,620	424	16.1
Jasmine Estates CDP	NA	NA	NA	NA	NA	NA	NA	NA	NA	NA	NA	NA	NA	NA	NA
Jensen Beach CDP	NA	NA	NA	NA	NA	NA	NA	NA	NA	NA	NA	NA	NA	NA	NA
Jupiter town	132	199	959	1,443	54,333	104	82.7	68.3	9.7	73.5	651	56.6	872	73	40.7
Jupiter Farms CDP	NA	NA	NA	NA	NA	NA	NA	NA	NA	NA	NA	NA	NA	NA	NA
Kendale Lakes CDP	NA	NA	NA	NA	NA	NA	NA	NA	NA	NA	NA	NA	NA	NA	NA
Kendall CDP	NA	NA	NA	NA	NA	NA	NA	NA	NA	NA	NA	NA	NA	NA	NA
Kendall West CDP	NA	NA	NA	NA	NA	NA	NA	NA	NA	NA	NA	NA	NA	NA	NA
Key Biscayne village	5	38	90	677	27,159	27	100.0	36.1	2.1	66.6	2,207	34.4	2,650	372	30.4
Key Largo CDP	NA	NA	NA	NA	NA	NA	NA	NA	NA	NA	NA	NA	NA	NA	NA
Keystone CDP	NA	NA	NA	NA	NA	NA	NA	NA	NA	NA	NA	NA	NA	NA	NA
Key West city	100	396	808	3,195	5,909	24	83.3	117.3	20.7	48.5	1,198	121.8	4,865	1125	21.3

1 Data for serious crimes have not been adjusted for underreporting. This may affect comparability between geographic areas over time.
2 Per 100,000 population estimated by the FBI. 3 Based on population estimated as of July 1 of the year shown.

Table B. Incorporated Places, Census Designated Places (CDPs), and Minor Civil Divisions (MCDs) of 10,000 or More Population — Land Area, Population, and Households, and Employment

STATE City, town, township, borough, or CDP (county if applicable)	Land area 2010 (sq mi)	Population				Population characteristics 2015–2019		Income and poverty 2015–2019		Median value of owner-occupied housing units	Employment, 2015–2019		Households, 2015–2019 (percent of households)	
		Total persons 2010	Total persons 2019	Percent change 2010–2019	Persons per square mile, 2019	Percent foreign born	Percent living in the same house as previous year	Median household income	Percent of households with income below poverty level	Median value of owner-occupied housing units	Percent in civilian labor force	Unemployment rate	Family households	One person households
	1	2	3	4	5	6	7	8	9	10	11	12	13	14
FLORIDA—Con.														
Kissimmee city	20.81	59,558	72,717	22.1	3494.3	24.5	83.9	40,826	21.1	173,200	64.6	5.4	67.7	25.2
Lady Lake town	8.28	14,033	16,020	14.2	1934.8	5.2	79.9	42,483	11.9	146,300	35.9	4.3	58.3	35.6
Lake Butler CDP	11.40	15,400	NA	NA	NA	23.2	86.4	128,695	6.7	642,300	62.8	1.9	88.9	9.2
Lake City city	11.85	11,901	12,352	3.8	1042.4	5.7	71.0	38,000	21.1	106,800	57.9	7.9	50.9	42.7
Lakeland city	66.14	97,270	112,136	15.3	1695.4	10.9	78.9	47,511	14.9	149,500	55.0	6.4	59.7	33.2
Lakeland Highlands CDP	4.86	11,056	NA	NA	NA	8.8	89.0	92,955	3.6	262,900	59.0	3.9	76.5	18.1
Lake Magdalene CDP	10.21	28,509	NA	NA	NA	15.3	86.9	63,270	11.1	231,000	62.9	4.3	61.9	31.1
Lake Mary city	9.08	13,803	17,479	26.6	1925.0	15.4	82.4	96,983	3.9	320,100	63.3	3.1	76.8	19.3
Lakeside CDP	13.45	30,943	NA	NA	NA	5.9	81.9	63,605	10.1	167,800	61.2	5.7	72.6	24.2
Lake Wales city	18.84	14,154	16,759	18.4	889.5	8.1	82.0	44,186	18.9	167,400	55.6	7.7	62.3	31.7
Lakewood Park CDP	6.65	11,323	NA	NA	NA	8.7	89.7	49,529	14.3	131,100	52.7	5.7	61.2	28.3
Lake Worth city	5.89	34,894	38,526	10.4	6540.9	38.7	83.6	42,500	21.8	194,300	65.9	6.5	54.3	32.9
Land O' Lakes CDP	19.07	31,996	NA	NA	NA	10.2	87.2	80,860	6.3	241,100	64.7	3.7	74.7	21.4
Lantana town	2.37	10,592	12,581	18.8	5308.4	31.5	87.7	49,801	14.6	225,600	63.5	7.9	55.0	38.3
Largo city	18.49	79,439	84,948	6.9	4594.3	12.9	83.2	44,323	13.1	124,700	58.1	5.7	51.9	38.2
Lauderdale Lakes city	3.68	32,784	36,194	10.4	9835.3	51.2	85.4	35,532	23.9	119,800	62.4	9.7	63.2	33.5
Lauderhill city	8.52	66,936	71,868	7.4	8435.2	37.3	84.8	41,723	19.3	154,400	65.0	8.1	65.2	30.5
Lealman CDP	4.03	19,879	NA	NA	NA	18.5	89.8	35,818	18.4	99,100	60.8	6.5	52.2	37.3
Leesburg city	36.62	20,335	23,671	16.4	646.4	10.2	77.2	37,092	19.4	153,000	50.8	8.3	58.8	34.4
Lehigh Acres CDP	92.65	86,784	NA	NA	NA	27.8	84.8	48,483	17.9	158,900	62.1	6.3	76.3	18.1
Leisure City CDP	3.40	22,655	NA	NA	NA	46.4	88.4	36,609	26.6	194,400	62.9	8.9	81.2	13.6
Lighthouse Point city	2.31	10,358	11,270	8.8	4878.8	12.1	88.1	81,445	6.2	538,700	58.9	3.1	60.5	34.8
Lockhart CDP	4.44	13,060	NA	NA	NA	18.5	82.5	53,449	8.5	158,200	72.7	5.3	62.6	28.4
Longwood city	5.48	13,651	15,561	14.0	2839.6	12.4	87.5	65,805	11.4	213,600	66.4	5.1	64.6	26.4
Lutz CDP	24.40	19,344	NA	NA	NA	9.3	88.5	85,000	4.6	310,500	64.9	2.0	73.5	21.2
Lynn Haven city	10.44	18,727	20,525	9.6	1966.0	4.0	81.4	65,650	9.7	200,100	65.4	4.0	74.8	20.8
Maitland city	5.37	15,852	17,652	11.4	3287.2	11.7	77.8	75,944	10.3	372,500	69.0	3.0	59.8	32.0
Mango CDP	4.67	11,313	NA	NA	NA	12.7	85.1	39,455	24.8	132,200	56.7	5.6	59.1	32.3
Marco Island city	12.16	16,413	17,947	9.3	1475.9	13.4	90.3	86,215	7.4	678,900	40.6	3.1	68.2	27.5
Margate city	8.76	53,120	58,796	10.7	6711.9	36.8	86.3	45,594	14.8	183,800	64.4	5.4	58.4	36.8
Meadow Woods CDP	11.17	25,558	NA	NA	NA	26.6	85.8	70,341	7.4	228,700	70.6	5.2	78.6	14.7
Medulla CDP	5.59	8,892	NA	NA	NA	9.1	84.8	51,541	10.0	180,900	65.3	4.4	70.6	19.6
Melbourne city	44.06	76,217	83,029	8.9	1884.5	11.0	82.8	48,673	14.0	169,000	56.7	4.3	53.8	38.6
Merritt Island CDP	17.52	34,743	NA	NA	NA	6.9	84.9	64,865	10.0	264,600	58.1	4.4	62.1	32.3
Miami city	36.00	399,481	467,963	17.1	12999.0	58.3	86.3	39,049	25.3	317,700	62.4	6.0	54.9	37.4
Miami Beach city	7.69	87,380	88,885	1.7	11558.5	55.8	77.4	53,971	15.6	459,000	69.2	3.8	44.8	45.2
Miami Gardens city	18.23	107,163	110,001	2.6	6034.1	32.3	90.3	44,064	20.1	190,200	58.8	7.7	73.8	22.6
Miami Lakes town	5.66	29,373	31,367	6.8	5541.9	51.1	88.3	75,762	6.2	386,900	67.8	2.8	70.9	22.9
Miami Shores village	2.49	10,360	10,365	0.0	4162.7	27.6	90.0	123,478	5.6	558,700	68.6	7.6	72.1	19.9
Miami Springs city	2.88	13,809	13,917	0.8	4832.3	52.8	93.1	61,795	11.9	410,400	65.6	2.1	70.0	25.9
Middleburg CDP	19.63	13,008	NA	NA	NA	1.8	83.4	58,327	10.5	138,800	61.0	8.3	75.2	15.2
Midway CDP	12.01	16,115	NA	NA	NA	6.3	85.7	59,367	6.1	236,000	61.6	3.2	69.1	24.8
Minneola city	11.12	9,419	12,595	33.7	1132.6	12.0	79.3	61,549	5.6	219,200	70.8	5.3	82.0	14.4
Miramar city	28.85	121,958	141,191	15.8	4894.0	37.2	92.6	70,669	9.6	299,900	69.7	5.0	77.5	15.9
Mount Dora city	8.04	12,135	14,516	19.6	1805.5	6.8	88.6	48,690	12.6	244,100	48.9	5.9	59.9	35.6
Myrtle Grove CDP	6.64	15,870	NA	NA	NA	9.8	78.0	47,941	11.5	113,200	53.7	9.3	57.9	34.5
Naples city	12.30	19,519	22,088	13.2	1795.8	13.1	85.6	107,013	8.1	988,500	36.0	3.2	59.7	35.0
Naranja CDP	1.50	8,303	NA	NA	NA	34.9	73.0	37,594	23.1	172,700	68.5	9.9	84.6	10.6
Navarre CDP	23.07	31,378	NA	NA	NA	7.8	79.4	78,282	9.9	235,800	56.7	5.9	78.9	16.9
New Port Richey city	4.55	14,919	16,737	12.2	3678.5	8.7	84.8	35,384	19.1	87,500	46.2	7.5	52.2	41.2
New Port Richey East CDP	3.75	10,036	NA	NA	NA	4.7	81.3	39,581	15.4	102,500	50.1	7.6	53.3	39.0
New Smyrna Beach city	37.71	23,441	27,843	18.8	738.3	5.6	84.4	57,043	9.3	256,100	42.5	2.2	55.7	37.7
Niceville city	13.51	12,978	15,972	23.1	1182.2	3.8	81.3	76,823	5.2	238,800	61.1	3.8	74.6	22.0
Nocatee CDP	26.38	4,524	NA	NA	NA	8.9	79.7	119,276	1.5	389,500	59.4	5.0	86.5	12.3
Northdale CDP	8.09	22,079	NA	NA	NA	16.0	85.8	78,517	5.4	254,300	70.9	3.5	65.4	27.5
North Fort Myers CDP	50.62	39,407	NA	NA	NA	8.4	84.5	46,964	9.7	97,900	38.5	4.4	55.1	38.1
North Lauderdale city	4.62	41,089	44,262	7.7	9580.5	46.1	83.7	43,759	19.6	167,100	74.9	8.1	66.5	27.7
North Miami city	8.43	60,134	62,822	4.5	7452.2	54.5	85.8	41,611	19.4	202,600	65.1	7.6	66.5	28.3
North Miami Beach city	4.85	40,870	43,041	5.3	8874.4	54.0	89.2	43,788	19.2	194,300	66.2	6.9	68.1	27.4
North Palm Beach village	3.27	12,018	13,127	9.2	4014.4	12.5	86.5	72,027	6.4	328,100	56.0	2.5	56.6	37.6
North Port city	99.32	57,320	70,724	23.4	712.1	10.0	87.1	62,097	6.5	188,700	53.2	3.6	75.2	18.7
Oakland Park city	7.53	41,299	45,202	9.5	6002.9	34.1	83.7	51,377	14.4	214,600	72.0	7.6	53.2	34.7
Oakleaf Plantation CDP	16.43	20,315	NA	NA	NA	13.8	83.6	87,485	5.3	231,600	68.8	5.7	88.0	9.6
Oak Ridge CDP	3.55	22,685	NA	NA	NA	40.8	84.4	38,364	21.2	130,500	71.8	4.2	63.5	24.4
Ocala city	47.30	56,568	60,786	7.5	1285.1	8.5	78.7	41,755	19.4	142,200	56.0	8.1	57.0	36.8
Ocoee city	15.31	35,734	48,263	35.1	3152.4	20.6	84.1	75,329	9.8	242,200	71.7	5.0	77.0	19.1
Ojus CDP	2.65	18,036	NA	NA	NA	51.2	89.4	49,756	13.9	217,000	65.6	4.4	60.9	34.8
Oldsmar city	8.94	13,730	15,061	9.7	1684.7	9.5	85.1	57,283	8.2	228,400	66.3	6.4	68.4	25.3
Olympia Heights CDP	2.66	13,488	NA	NA	NA	61.8	94.2	61,776	14.8	348,500	56.7	2.6	76.7	17.8
Opa-locka city	4.31	15,185	15,887	4.6	3686.1	32.8	89.9	21,523	44.5	154,300	52.1	12.6	63.1	33.5
Orange City city	7.81	11,324	12,335	8.9	1579.4	7.8	79.2	40,450	14.3	116,600	49.2	1.9	56.5	37.8
Orlando city	110.56	238,836	287,442	20.4	2599.9	22.0	76.8	51,757	16.2	240,000	72.0	5.4	54.4	33.6
Ormond Beach city	33.09	39,429	43,759	11.0	1322.4	7.7	86.1	54,432	8.5	208,800	52.6	3.4	59.8	33.5
Oviedo city	15.49	33,471	41,860	25.1	2702.4	12.6	86.4	95,935	6.2	289,000	68.3	3.9	81.0	13.7
Pace CDP	24.23	20,039	NA	NA	NA	3.6	83.1	70,292	8.7	186,000	61.5	3.9	78.6	18.3
Palatka city	9.75	10,624	10,451	-1.6	1071.9	2.7	85.5	26,881	30.6	75,200	48.2	10.4	48.5	47.0
Palm Bay city	97.81	104,006	115,552	11.1	1181.4	12.1	86.8	51,408	12.4	155,200	56.9	6.2	68.2	25.4
Palm Beach Gardens city	58.71	49,896	57,704	15.6	982.9	15.3	85.0	87,969	7.5	378,500	57.1	2.4	61.6	31.2
Palm City CDP	13.86	23,120	NA	NA	NA	9.6	89.4	84,711	5.9	350,900	53.5	4.0	68.7	27.4
Palm Coast city	95.09	75,199	89,800	19.4	944.4	14.1	88.4	54,360	9.3	209,300	50.4	5.0	71.7	21.7
Palmetto city	5.31	12,641	13,748	8.8	2589.1	15.4	83.1	48,301	15.9	156,700	53.0	9.3	63.1	30.4
Palmetto Bay village	8.29	23,413	24,523	4.7	2958.1	31.9	88.5	123,477	5.0	562,300	65.6	6.2	84.6	12.1
Palmetto Estates CDP	2.16	13,535	NA	NA	NA	46.7	92.0	62,910	8.9	236,000	62.5	6.5	81.8	14.9
Palm Harbor CDP	17.34	57,439	NA	NA	NA	13.0	84.5	59,557	7.0	232,900	55.7	4.5	62.5	32.6
Palm River-Clair Mel CDP	11.43	21,024	NA	NA	NA	23.8	85.7	47,856	17.6	133,300	64.4	6.1	65.0	25.5
Palm Springs village	4.21	23,165	25,216	8.9	5989.5	45.5	84.2	44,162	15.0	148,800	70.0	5.2	68.0	23.5
Palm Valley CDP	12.18	20,019	NA	NA	NA	7.2	82.8	109,000	5.7	476,800	59.3	3.3	67.4	28.9

Table B. Incorporated Places, Census Designated Places (CDPs), and Minor Civil Divisions (MCDs) of 10,000 or More Population — **Crime, Residential Construction and Local Government Finance**

STATE City, town, township, borough, or CDP (county if applicable)	Serious crimes known to police, 2018[1] Violent crime Number	Rate[2]	Property crime Number	Rate[2]	New residential construction authorized by building permits, 2019 Value ($1,000)	Number of housing units	Percent single family	Local government finance, 2017 General revenue Total (mil dol)	Intergovernmental Total (mil dol)	Percent from state gov.	Taxes per capita[3]	General expenditure Total (mil dol)	Per capita[3] Total	Capital outlays	Debt outstanding (mil dol)
	15	16	17	18	19	20	21	22	23	24	25	26	27	28	29
FLORIDA—Con.															
Kissimmee city	288	395	1,839	2,523	101,922	719	36.7	104.6	42.0	43.7	430	100.5	1,407	248	305.3
Lady Lake town	16	103	227	1,463	14,129	104	100.0	13.5	1.5	88.4	559	11.6	757	29	0.5
Lake Butler CDP	NA	NA	NA	NA	NA	NA	NA	NA	NA	NA	NA	NA	NA	NA	NA
Lake City city	148	1,215	858	7,043	295	2	100.0	27.0	7.3	42.6	732	24.2	2,010	491	42.7
Lakeland city	361	329	3,417	3,117	230,020	1,559	38.9	230.0	26.2	67.3	529	230.6	2,141	340	988.0
Lakeland Highlands CDP	NA	NA	NA	NA	NA	NA	NA	NA	NA	NA	NA	NA	NA	NA	NA
Lake Magdalene CDP	NA	NA	NA	NA	NA	NA	NA	NA	NA	NA	NA	NA	NA	NA	NA
Lake Mary city	36	213	270	1,598	12,494	52	80.8	26.2	1.7	90.6	1,003	26.1	1,588	44	3.2
Lakeside CDP	NA	NA	NA	NA	NA	NA	NA	NA	NA	NA	NA	NA	NA	NA	NA
Lake Wales city	57	349	369	2,257	45,788	431	20.0	20.5	3.1	55.0	580	20.2	1,264	166	16.7
Lakewood Park CDP	NA	NA	NA	NA	NA	NA	NA	NA	NA	NA	NA	NA	NA	NA	NA
Lake Worth city	369	957	1,153	2,989	19,360	126	60.3	57.1	6.7	79.6	422	61.9	1,627	107	65.7
Land O' Lakes CDP	NA	NA	NA	NA	NA	NA	NA	NA	NA	NA	NA	NA	NA	NA	NA
Lantana town	91	758	612	5,098	4,794	7	57.1	15.6	2.4	94.1	559	12.6	1,066	163	2.4
Largo city	322	376	2,593	3,030	20,408	74	100.0	121.7	13.3	83.9	545	168.2	1,986	657	36.2
Lauderdale Lakes city	312	853	1,209	3,306	13,854	315	0.0	35.3	7.4	63.7	438	28.6	790	28	20.5
Lauderhill city	551	758	2,313	3,182	0	0	0.0	84.8	11.1	79.7	481	78.6	1,093	28	99.6
Lealman CDP	NA	NA	NA	NA	NA	NA	NA	NA	NA	NA	NA	NA	NA	NA	NA
Leesburg city	175	760	1,214	5,272	36,212	211	99.1	48.2	4.2	62.8	721	52.0	2,299	274	117.9
Lehigh Acres CDP	NA	NA	NA	NA	NA	NA	NA	NA	NA	NA	NA	NA	NA	NA	NA
Leisure City CDP	NA	NA	NA	NA	NA	NA	NA	NA	NA	NA	NA	NA	NA	NA	NA
Lighthouse Point city	12	106	173	1,521	7,065	14	100.0	17.2	1.2	90.7	1,100	18.0	1,604	150	2.3
Lockhart CDP	NA	NA	NA	NA	NA	NA	NA	NA	NA	NA	NA	NA	NA	NA	NA
Longwood city	46	301	441	2,887	69,366	596	11.7	15.7	1.7	88.5	724	17.1	1,140	136	2.1
Lutz CDP	NA	NA	NA	NA	NA	NA	NA	NA	NA	NA	NA	NA	NA	NA	NA
Lynn Haven city	28	132	202	949	43,090	200	48.5	21.7	2.6	96.5	394	16.7	783	88	18.1
Maitland city	37	207	303	1,698	640	4	100.0	38.3	3.9	82.9	1,007	35.8	2,004	275	32.7
Mango CDP	NA	NA	NA	NA	NA	NA	NA	NA	NA	NA	NA	NA	NA	NA	NA
Marco Island city	6	33	98	541	87,265	108	100.0	41.1	5.0	75.5	1,289	42.0	2,345	763	192.3
Margate city	98	166	997	1,685	6,142	47	53.2	78.0	7.5	82.4	602	75.0	1,289	123	26.3
Meadow Woods CDP	NA	NA	NA	NA	NA	NA	NA	NA	NA	NA	NA	NA	NA	NA	NA
Medulla CDP	NA	NA	NA	NA	NA	NA	NA	NA	NA	NA	NA	NA	NA	NA	NA
Melbourne city	601	726	2,941	3,550	78,429	377	26.3	172.2	57.3	84.5	665	138.1	1,688	62	97.8
Merritt Island CDP	NA	NA	NA	NA	NA	NA	NA	NA	NA	NA	NA	NA	NA	NA	NA
Miami city	2,978	630	16,837	3,559	1,332,215	4,468	2.4	929.9	173.7	37.2	1,196	894.4	1,959	193	652.3
Miami Beach city	871	937	6,947	7,476	38,880	38	100.0	565.7	66.3	17.5	3,834	646.2	7,129	1755	982.5
Miami Gardens city	816	712	4,530	3,951	17,562	195	30.8	92.6	16.5	78.9	466	83.7	746	42	160.8
Miami Lakes town	33	105	653	2,085	45,439	208	100.0	24.6	6.1	78.3	489	23.2	756	144	8.6
Miami Shores village	34	319	523	4,900	2,023	4	100.0	22.3	5.5	29.3	1,055	20.5	1,964	186	10.2
Miami Springs city	48	331	446	3,074	840	4	100.0	19.9	3.1	68.8	770	23.6	1,662	335	8.5
Middleburg CDP	NA	NA	NA	NA	NA	NA	NA	NA	NA	NA	NA	NA	NA	NA	NA
Midway CDP	NA	NA	NA	NA	NA	NA	NA	NA	NA	NA	NA	NA	NA	NA	NA
Minneola city	19	160	114	961	112,425	490	39.4	10.2	1.1	91.8	507	6.4	554	51	12.1
Miramar city	337	236	2,128	1,487	14,031	91	53.8	169.4	19.1	71.6	602	195.4	1,394	225	213.8
Mount Dora city	67	473	548	3,865	28,983	150	96.0	27.9	3.6	68.8	740	20.4	1,472	51	16.7
Myrtle Grove CDP	NA	NA	NA	NA	NA	NA	NA	NA	NA	NA	NA	NA	NA	NA	NA
Naples city	9	40	320	1,435	196,506	126	92.9	95.2	9.6	37.6	1,708	88.9	4,053	201	19.9
Naranja CDP	NA	NA	NA	NA	NA	NA	NA	NA	NA	NA	NA	NA	NA	NA	NA
Navarre CDP	NA	NA	NA	NA	NA	NA	NA	NA	NA	NA	NA	NA	NA	NA	NA
New Port Richey city	160	972	599	3,639	5,964	58	20.7	28.8	4.6	51.0	843	27.5	1,694	170	30.1
New Port Richey East CDP	NA	NA	NA	NA	NA	NA	NA	NA	NA	NA	NA	NA	NA	NA	NA
New Smyrna Beach city	96	356	684	2,539	185,600	549	100.0	60.6	5.0	43.9	856	51.6	1,952	474	23.3
Niceville city	23	147	187	1,197	28,175	117	100.0	20.5	2.7	87.4	450	20.6	1,342	201	15.4
Nocatee CDP	NA	NA	NA	NA	NA	NA	NA	NA	NA	NA	NA	NA	NA	NA	NA
Northdale CDP	NA	NA	NA	NA	NA	NA	NA	NA	NA	NA	NA	NA	NA	NA	NA
North Fort Myers CDP	NA	NA	NA	NA	NA	NA	NA	NA	NA	NA	NA	NA	NA	NA	NA
North Lauderdale city	246	551	805	1,803	1,631	29	100.0	43.1	5.5	91.8	371	40.0	906	25	1.7
North Miami city	524	837	2,329	3,721	6,618	97	26.8	92.9	10.1	76.4	520	89.1	1,438	26	18.7
North Miami Beach city	323	726	1,683	3,783	3,048	12	83.3	72.7	6.7	80.4	679	90.2	2,107	174	99.0
North Palm Beach village	12	91	105	795	3,975	6	100.0	25.6	1.5	95.2	1,344	25.1	1,922	99	2.4
North Port city	117	173	1,186	1,752	351,960	1,352	97.4	104.1	10.3	72.6	481	96.6	1,457	288	70.2
Oakland Park city	277	608	1,606	3,525	3,156	28	42.9	68.5	8.8	49.2	614	63.3	1,410	99	56.6
Oakleaf Plantation CDP	NA	NA	NA	NA	NA	NA	NA	NA	NA	NA	NA	NA	NA	NA	NA
Oak Ridge CDP	NA	NA	NA	NA	NA	NA	NA	NA	NA	NA	NA	NA	NA	NA	NA
Ocala city	405	681	2,871	4,825	69,394	225	100.0	136.2	15.3	69.7	750	130.0	2,199	252	173.3
Ocoee city	162	337	1,430	2,971	170,315	490	100.0	58.7	12.4	98.0	399	51.7	1,109	123	38.8
Ojus CDP	NA	NA	NA	NA	NA	NA	NA	NA	NA	NA	NA	NA	NA	NA	NA
Oldsmar city	31	210	336	2,276	1,602	4	100.0	21.8	2.5	52.8	723	21.9	1,489	175	10.1
Olympia Heights CDP	NA	NA	NA	NA	NA	NA	NA	NA	NA	NA	NA	NA	NA	NA	NA
Opa-locka city	391	2,347	880	5,281	205	1	100.0	23.2	3.1	61.2	735	29.6	1,822	180	7.9
Orange City city	45	381	782	6,624	34,622	138	100.0	11.8	1.5	94.5	611	13.2	1,097	142	1.7
Orlando city	2,282	796	13,803	4,815	555,715	2,634	28.4	873.9	254.3	23.9	954	851.2	3,020	169	1241.5
Ormond Beach city	131	302	1,367	3,156	17,348	49	100.0	58.4	10.5	44.0	603	57.2	1,340	215	45.0
Oviedo city	66	157	374	892	8,634	23	100.0	48.1	10.2	41.0	542	50.1	1,228	133	74.1
Pace CDP	NA	NA	NA	NA	NA	NA	NA	NA	NA	NA	NA	NA	NA	NA	NA
Palatka city	110	1,061	630	6,078	0	0	0.0	17.7	2.5	66.5	619	16.3	1,566	117	13.4
Palm Bay city	404	358	2,109	1,868	201,813	782	100.0	92.1	15.6	88.0	419	87.5	780	104	134.5
Palm Beach Gardens city	83	148	1,409	2,516	109,990	291	75.6	89.6	7.3	87.4	1,183	93.2	1,655	215	12.7
Palm City CDP	NA	NA	NA	NA	NA	NA	NA	NA	NA	NA	NA	NA	NA	NA	NA
Palm Coast city	NA	NA	NA	NA	257,371	1,240	65.9	64.3	10.2	51.6	295	88.6	1,028	205	166.2
Palmetto city	72	522	439	3,180	37,364	60	100.0	21.3	1.7	86.9	869	19.7	1,441	173	12.9
Palmetto Bay village	42	169	711	2,857	846	5	100.0	18.6	2.7	98.0	566	17.0	696	49	16.6
Palmetto Estates CDP	NA	NA	NA	NA	NA	NA	NA	NA	NA	NA	NA	NA	NA	NA	NA
Palm Harbor CDP	NA	NA	NA	NA	NA	NA	NA	NA	NA	NA	NA	NA	NA	NA	NA
Palm River-Clair Mel CDP	NA	NA	NA	NA	NA	NA	NA	NA	NA	NA	NA	NA	NA	NA	NA
Palm Springs village	126	501	981	3,901	17,900	79	100.0	24.0	2.9	96.5	364	21.4	860	67	17.0
Palm Valley CDP	NA	NA	NA	NA	NA	NA	NA	NA	NA	NA	NA	NA	NA	NA	NA

1 Data for serious crimes have not been adjusted for underreporting. This may affect comparability between geographic areas over time.
2 Per 100,000 population estimated by the FBI. 3 Based on population estimated as of July 1 of the year shown.

Table B. Incorporated Places, Census Designated Places (CDPs), and Minor Civil Divisions (MCDs) of 10,000 or More Population — **Land Area, Population, and Households, and Employment**

STATE City, town, township, borough, or CDP (county if applicable)	Land area 2010 (sq mi)	Population				Population characteristics 2015–2019		Income and poverty 2015–2019		Median value of owner-occupied housing units	Employment, 2015–2019		Households, 2015–2019 (percent of households)	
		Total persons 2010	Total persons 2019	Percent change 2010–2019	Persons per square mile 2019	Percent foreign born	Percent living in the same house as previous year	Median household income	Percent of households with income below poverty level		Percent in civilian labor force	Unemployment rate	Family households	One person households
	1	2	3	4	5	6	7	8	9	10	11	12	13	14
FLORIDA—Con.														
Panama City city	35.02	34,660	34,667	0.0	989.9	8.4	77.3	43,953	19.2	155,800	60.0	7.6	54.5	38.1
Panama City Beach city	19.30	11,549	12,583	9.0	652.0	11.6	76.9	63,912	4.4	243,300	62.6	2.8	58.2	33.6
Parkland city	12.50	22,513	34,170	51.8	2733.6	24.4	85.5	154,844	3.6	611,800	61.1	3.6	86.9	11.2
Pasadena Hills CDP	30.03	7,570	NA	NA	NA	11.5	83.5	66,582	11.4	222,000	52.6	2.6	73.0	19.0
Pebble Creek CDP	2.83	7,622	NA	NA	NA	30.0	83.6	95,200	10.9	276,800	66.5	3.1	78.0	20.6
Pembroke Pines city	32.67	154,898	173,591	12.1	5313.5	37.2	89.3	68,745	11.9	288,700	64.1	5.4	70.5	24.1
Pensacola city	22.64	52,008	52,975	1.9	2339.9	3.4	80.9	50,493	14.8	182,800	61.3	5.6	53.8	37.3
Pine Castle CDP	2.42	10,805	NA	NA	NA	30.5	81.6	41,914	24.0	161,200	68.5	7.4	60.7	27.8
Pinecrest village	7.45	18,217	19,155	5.1	2571.1	35.6	89.5	156,875	5.3	949,400	64.3	3.9	81.8	15.4
Pine Hills CDP	12.20	60,076	NA	NA	NA	31.0	82.9	40,894	22.2	140,100	68.5	9.1	75.3	20.8
Pinellas Park city	16.06	49,553	53,637	8.2	3339.8	15.2	85.3	49,652	13.1	154,700	59.1	5.4	60.4	32.1
Pine Ridge CDP	24.85	9,598	NA	NA	NA	7.2	85.1	55,503	12.3	232,800	30.0	7.4	69.2	27.5
Pinewood CDP	1.75	16,520	NA	NA	NA	40.1	87.5	35,352	24.6	182,800	59.7	10.3	70.3	24.9
Plantation city	21.67	84,883	94,580	11.4	4364.6	31.0	83.7	74,903	7.7	330,900	67.6	4.3	68.0	24.8
Plant City city	27.55	34,732	39,744	14.4	1442.6	13.9	83.9	54,235	13.7	169,400	64.8	5.3	69.4	25.0
Poinciana CDP	71.86	53,193	NA	NA	NA	19.9	85.6	49,878	16.2	170,900	53.3	5.7	78.8	18.1
Pompano Beach city	24.02	99,839	112,118	12.3	4667.7	29.3	79.5	49,518	16.6	213,700	59.8	7.7	56.1	35.1
Port Charlotte CDP	28.48	54,392	NA	NA	NA	13.8	87.0	46,603	12.3	164,000	48.9	6.2	62.4	29.5
Port Orange city	26.81	56,628	64,842	14.5	2418.6	9.0	85.6	51,883	14.1	179,400	56.1	5.4	60.2	32.1
Port St. John CDP	3.88	12,267	NA	NA	NA	4.1	90.9	56,955	7.1	149,900	63.6	5.7	71.5	23.7
Port St. Lucie city	119.20	164,203	201,846	22.9	1693.3	18.7	86.4	60,587	9.2	207,200	58.7	4.7	73.6	20.4
Port Salerno CDP	3.57	10,091	NA	NA	NA	13.2	81.9	54,098	12.5	220,400	53.7	4.3	62.5	30.7
Princeton CDP	7.42	22,038	NA	NA	NA	46.9	86.4	65,390	15.2	260,400	69.9	6.0	84.5	11.0
Progress Village CDP	3.03	5,392	NA	NA	NA	11.6	76.0	57,140	12.2	168,700	67.1	4.1	62.8	25.0
Punta Gorda city	15.52	17,120	20,369	19.0	1312.4	7.8	84.2	61,395	9.0	325,800	30.2	6.7	62.2	32.0
Richmond Heights CDP	1.59	8,541	NA	NA	NA	28.3	93.6	49,067	12.5	211,000	59.7	7.1	80.7	16.6
Richmond West CDP	4.17	31,973	NA	NA	NA	45.8	92.8	75,842	7.7	311,000	64.0	5.2	88.7	8.1
Riverview CDP	46.21	71,050	NA	NA	NA	14.1	84.2	74,622	7.5	214,100	69.6	5.7	73.6	20.5
Riviera Beach city	8.28	32,540	35,463	9.0	4283.0	17.8	83.6	47,193	18.3	189,500	61.5	9.4	66.8	27.7
Rockledge city	12.13	24,921	28,227	13.3	2327.0	5.7	88.6	68,265	8.7	204,800	58.7	4.3	68.0	27.4
Royal Palm Beach village	11.34	34,196	40,396	18.1	3562.3	28.1	90.4	82,582	5.3	273,900	68.8	3.5	77.3	18.2
Ruskin CDP	18.05	17,208	NA	NA	NA	15.5	89.4	57,836	15.3	183,700	64.4	4.9	73.9	19.7
Safety Harbor city	4.92	16,913	18,016	6.5	3661.8	9.5	87.9	78,026	6.4	268,800	63.0	3.5	69.4	24.7
St. Augustine city	9.45	13,004	15,415	18.5	1631.2	7.1	75.5	54,468	15.3	271,000	50.0	4.1	49.9	39.1
St. Cloud city	20.28	37,787	54,579	44.4	2691.3	11.5	88.7	55,440	11.6	197,500	62.4	6.2	70.9	23.9
St. Petersburg city	61.86	245,177	265,351	8.2	4289.5	10.8	83.5	56,982	12.0	205,000	63.3	5.1	53.3	37.5
San Carlos Park CDP	4.73	16,824	NA	NA	NA	15.9	87.0	61,963	12.8	193,900	73.8	5.3	69.3	18.5
Sanford city	23.35	53,933	61,448	13.9	2631.6	13.9	80.4	47,217	19.1	156,600	64.2	7.2	63.3	29.2
Sarasota city	14.72	52,107	58,285	11.9	3959.6	18.0	81.6	53,669	13.3	268,400	54.5	4.0	48.3	42.5
Sarasota Springs CDP	3.50	14,395	NA	NA	NA	12.9	84.3	65,222	7.8	207,300	66.8	3.9	64.5	27.9
Satellite Beach city	2.92	10,080	11,130	10.4	3811.6	8.0	84.7	79,082	5.1	300,200	56.7	2.9	70.2	23.3
Sebastian city	14.00	21,935	26,118	19.1	1865.6	5.2	88.0	53,707	10.8	195,500	44.1	6.2	67.1	27.7
Sebring city	10.12	10,064	10,600	5.3	1047.4	9.9	79.0	25,737	27.0	96,600	47.4	16.5	49.3	42.9
Seminole city	5.17	17,330	18,838	8.7	3643.7	9.1	85.8	53,975	11.4	203,800	49.3	2.6	54.4	39.5
Shady Hills CDP	28.64	11,523	NA	NA	NA	3.7	90.7	51,369	17.1	139,200	48.2	5.7	69.5	22.8
South Bradenton CDP	4.49	22,178	NA	NA	NA	16.2	85.6	36,933	18.9	83,900	53.9	7.0	54.1	40.3
Southchase CDP	6.92	15,921	NA	NA	NA	34.0	87.7	60,026	10.0	239,800	62.2	4.6	83.6	10.8
South Daytona city	3.70	12,257	13,080	6.7	3535.1	6.4	84.0	40,632	15.9	146,800	54.3	6.0	55.5	33.9
South Miami city	2.27	11,676	11,911	2.0	5247.1	35.2	85.1	62,067	16.9	569,300	60.7	9.0	59.6	29.6
South Miami Heights CDP	4.90	35,696	NA	NA	NA	55.9	89.9	43,562	22.2	226,300	60.8	5.6	78.6	17.5
South Venice CDP	6.03	13,949	NA	NA	NA	7.0	85.2	57,092	8.7	191,000	54.0	5.3	63.3	29.9
Spring Hill CDP	59.86	98,621	NA	NA	NA	8.1	85.0	51,395	13.3	147,200	50.9	6.3	71.3	22.8
Stuart city	6.76	15,277	16,237	6.3	2401.9	9.5	83.6	47,921	13.4	185,700	53.9	2.8	49.0	43.3
Sun City Center CDP	15.75	19,258	NA	NA	NA	7.9	85.9	50,613	9.8	182,900	22.6	5.1	53.6	42.7
Sunny Isles Beach city	1.01	20,828	21,804	4.7	21588.1	61.6	85.4	55,350	11.8	359,600	60.4	3.4	54.5	41.3
Sunrise city	16.18	84,306	95,166	12.9	5881.7	41.6	86.8	54,744	13.1	205,100	65.4	5.8	65.0	29.9
Sunset CDP	3.50	16,389	NA	NA	NA	51.7	91.7	84,552	14.9	388,800	62.1	3.8	75.4	20.1
Sweetwater city	2.19	19,918	20,994	5.4	9586.3	74.5	89.5	39,920	24.6	178,700	61.1	3.8	73.9	19.0
Tallahassee city	100.47	181,050	194,500	7.4	1935.9	8.1	69.4	45,734	24.4	203,800	66.0	8.0	45.6	35.1
Tamarac city	11.67	60,778	66,721	9.8	5717.3	36.8	82.3	48,930	11.3	168,900	61.7	4.9	57.6	36.4
Tamiami CDP	7.05	55,271	NA	NA	NA	66.4	93.1	57,531	13.7	297,700	58.4	2.8	82.1	14.4
Tampa city	114.02	336,150	399,700	18.9	3505.5	17.2	78.6	53,833	17.5	238,900	65.0	6.3	55.0	35.8
Tarpon Springs city	9.13	23,526	25,577	8.7	2801.4	12.0	86.0	50,012	14.4	209,400	50.3	6.9	62.4	32.7
Tavares city	12.16	13,987	17,749	26.9	1459.6	8.4	77.6	45,319	10.2	144,900	43.4	9.3	58.7	36.9
Temple Terrace city	7.29	24,425	26,639	9.1	3654.2	16.1	77.3	63,018	13.3	228,900	69.2	1.7	57.9	28.4
The Acreage CDP	34.30	38,704	NA	NA	NA	20.0	90.0	90,034	7.6	315,600	67.8	4.0	80.7	13.5
The Crossings CDP	3.45	22,758	NA	NA	NA	49.0	92.4	76,376	12.6	297,400	64.4	3.0	76.0	19.8
The Hammocks CDP	7.89	51,003	NA	NA	NA	54.8	87.8	70,014	11.9	316,300	65.6	4.2	81.3	14.1
The Villages CDP	31.31	51,442	NA	NA	NA	5.2	91.1	63,841	5.6	280,300	13.1	0.9	67.9	29.0
Thonotosassa CDP	26.48	13,014	NA	NA	NA	6.2	86.3	48,099	17.2	158,000	54.0	6.5	69.5	25.8
Three Lakes CDP	3.21	15,047	NA	NA	NA	43.4	90.5	67,955	11.9	294,100	69.2	3.3	78.0	14.7
Titusville city	29.22	43,618	46,580	6.8	1594.1	4.4	83.8	46,609	13.8	143,700	54.9	7.6	57.6	35.4
Town 'n' Country CDP	22.09	78,442	NA	NA	NA	30.5	81.8	54,444	13.5	170,800	67.2	5.3	65.3	25.5
Trinity CDP	4.47	10,907	NA	NA	NA	10.4	91.2	79,509	6.0	281,600	53.8	3.9	78.0	18.6
Union Park CDP	3.06	9,765	NA	NA	NA	17.3	83.8	54,963	19.3	177,100	67.9	3.9	68.3	17.8
University CDP	6.33	41,163	NA	NA	NA	23.1	70.7	28,495	33.4	106,400	64.4	10.3	38.7	42.9
University CDP	9.06	31,084	NA	NA	NA	9.4	65.9	43,520	28.6	193,800	37.6	6.2	48.7	27.2
University Park CDP	3.99	26,995	NA	NA	NA	60.8	88.6	54,667	14.2	312,200	59.0	4.8	76.1	18.2
Upper Grand Lagoon CDP	8.09	13,963	NA	NA	NA	7.2	82.7	59,698	13.2	229,000	64.5	4.5	61.0	29.4
Valrico CDP	13.81	35,545	NA	NA	NA	11.5	87.1	75,221	6.7	231,600	63.9	4.6	75.8	20.5
Venice city	15.08	20,800	23,985	15.3	1590.5	9.4	82.3	60,086	7.6	252,200	30.2	3.9	55.1	39.5
Vero Beach city	11.45	15,201	17,503	15.1	1528.6	10.0	85.7	48,844	13.7	259,800	53.3	5.0	47.7	47.0
Vero Beach South CDP	10.25	23,092	NA	NA	NA	12.2	86.3	55,085	10.2	184,200	57.3	5.1	59.2	33.8
Viera East CDP	4.98	10,757	NA	NA	NA	10.7	86.3	73,929	5.2	267,000	51.3	4.8	64.3	31.6
Viera West CDP	8.93	6,641	NA	NA	NA	9.4	86.7	68,345	3.9	296,100	49.0	1.2	67.5	27.4
Villas CDP	4.63	11,569	NA	NA	NA	18.4	84.0	53,500	7.0	162,400	59.0	3.2	52.0	37.9
Warrington CDP	6.93	14,531	NA	NA	NA	2.5	83.8	38,574	17.4	93,200	54.1	8.9	52.5	38.4

Table B. Incorporated Places, Census Designated Places (CDPs), and Minor Civil Divisions (MCDs) of 10,000 or More Population — Crime, Residential Construction and Local Government Finance

STATE City, town, township, borough, or CDP (county if applicable)	Serious crimes known to police, 2018[1] Violent crime Number	Rate[2]	Property crime Number	Rate[2]	New residential construction authorized by building permits, 2019 Value ($1,000)	Number of housing units	Percent single family	Local government finance, 2017 General revenue Total (mil dol)	Intergovernmental Total (mil dol)	Percent from state gov.	Taxes per capita[3]	General expenditure Total (mil dol)	Per capita[3] Total	Capital outlays	Debt outstanding (mil dol)
	15	16	17	18	19	20	21	22	23	24	25	26	27	28	29
FLORIDA—Con.															
Panama City city	234	627	2,150	5,761	55,123	172	97.7	70.8	10.1	89.8	888	60.7	1,634	156	53.6
Panama City Beach city	110	850	960	7,422	69,136	223	100.0	51.1	11.2	14.0	1,509	49.9	3,891	1275	91.7
Parkland city	38	113	240	711	218,650	405	100.0	43.9	3.0	82.9	723	33.5	1,060	255	10.7
Pasadena Hills CDP	NA	NA	NA	NA	NA	NA	NA	NA	NA	NA	NA	NA	NA	NA	NA
Pebble Creek CDP	NA	NA	NA	NA	NA	NA	NA	NA	NA	NA	NA	NA	NA	NA	NA
Pembroke Pines city	314	181	3,333	1,926	60,928	460	15.9	281.9	67.5	90.0	625	368.2	2,157	318	327.5
Pensacola city	285	541	2,012	3,820	19,686	89	95.5	133.3	44.9	20.4	841	133.4	2,539	460	203.0
Pine Castle CDP	NA	NA	NA	NA	NA	NA	NA	NA	NA	NA	NA	NA	NA	NA	NA
Pinecrest village	26	131	473	2,382	47,497	40	100.0	23.9	3.0	68.8	843	23.9	1,234	188	12.8
Pine Hills CDP	NA	NA	NA	NA	NA	NA	NA	NA	NA	NA	NA	NA	NA	NA	NA
Pinellas Park city	224	420	2,423	4,539	69,471	684	5.3	76.0	10.6	77.2	658	82.7	1,563	164	19.2
Pine Ridge CDP	NA	NA	NA	NA	NA	NA	NA	NA	NA	NA	NA	NA	NA	NA	NA
Pinewood CDP	NA	NA	NA	NA	NA	NA	NA	NA	NA	NA	NA	NA	NA	NA	NA
Plantation city	239	251	2,706	2,842	154,540	862	5.6	133.9	11.4	83.9	835	117.8	1,256	100	43.9
Plant City city	186	473	1,198	3,048	4,426	42	100.0	58.3	9.5	70.5	623	56.4	1,437	304	36.9
Poinciana CDP	NA	NA	NA	NA	NA	NA	NA	NA	NA	NA	NA	NA	NA	NA	NA
Pompano Beach city	876	782	4,307	3,844	44,836	408	18.4	186.5	21.7	67.8	919	209.6	1,899	300	104.8
Port Charlotte CDP	NA	NA	NA	NA	NA	NA	NA	NA	NA	NA	NA	NA	NA	NA	NA
Port Orange city	25	39	1,397	2,176	46,283	129	100.0	68.6	7.5	90.5	406	69.2	1,097	61	101.9
Port St. John CDP	NA	NA	NA	NA	NA	NA	NA	NA	NA	NA	NA	NA	NA	NA	NA
Port St. Lucie city	218	113	1,851	958	552,753	3,039	85.3	265.6	31.7	71.6	504	253.7	1,341	219	806.9
Port Salerno CDP	NA	NA	NA	NA	NA	NA	NA	NA	NA	NA	NA	NA	NA	NA	NA
Princeton CDP	NA	NA	NA	NA	NA	NA	NA	NA	NA	NA	NA	NA	NA	NA	NA
Progress Village CDP	NA	NA	NA	NA	NA	NA	NA	NA	NA	NA	NA	NA	NA	NA	NA
Punta Gorda city	11	55	330	1,636	33,126	85	95.3	43.5	8.5	68.0	744	41.2	2,092	140	16.8
Richmond Heights CDP	NA	NA	NA	NA	NA	NA	NA	NA	NA	NA	NA	NA	NA	NA	NA
Richmond West CDP	NA	NA	NA	NA	NA	NA	NA	NA	NA	NA	NA	NA	NA	NA	NA
Riverview CDP	NA	NA	NA	NA	NA	NA	NA	NA	NA	NA	NA	NA	NA	NA	NA
Riviera Beach city	413	1,180	1,333	3,810	26,308	124	80.6	99.2	9.6	43.5	1,633	124.3	3,583	557	176.6
Rockledge city	61	219	408	1,465	18,937	67	64.2	28.3	2.9	99.8	519	26.3	962	85	3.0
Royal Palm Beach village	61	155	759	1,934	56,765	173	100.0	56.2	4.7	94.8	392	27.7	717	120	0.0
Ruskin CDP	NA	NA	NA	NA	NA	NA	NA	NA	NA	NA	NA	NA	NA	NA	NA
Safety Harbor city	24	133	227	1,262	3,954	16	100.0	25.9	3.1	56.3	600	24.2	1,355	202	10.5
St. Augustine city	93	645	571	3,958	82,143	532	41.0	44.3	3.0	78.4	1,067	53.5	3,690	462	59.5
St. Cloud city	76	142	666	1,244	413,693	1,246	100.0	82.9	7.0	65.0	351	67.7	1,310	106	96.6
St. Petersburg city	1,660	624	8,784	3,303	316,124	2,118	17.8	428.7	81.9	37.9	616	438.3	1,669	153	653.5
San Carlos Park CDP	NA	NA	NA	NA	NA	NA	NA	NA	NA	NA	NA	NA	NA	NA	NA
Sanford city	421	700	2,133	3,546	52,482	224	98.2	139.1	36.8	23.1	643	101.2	1,700	265	72.0
Sarasota city	337	584	1,877	3,252	129,248	335	29.0	158.5	23.4	57.3	1,114	151.6	2,650	420	109.2
Sarasota Springs CDP	NA	NA	NA	NA	NA	NA	NA	NA	NA	NA	NA	NA	NA	NA	NA
Satellite Beach city	3	27	41	366	7,027	23	100.0	13.3	1.5	61.2	813	15.8	1,437	296	6.5
Sebastian city	31	121	279	1,087	43,184	181	100.0	19.7	3.4	99.4	497	15.9	631	71	3.2
Sebring city	80	745	431	4,013	4,362	14	100.0	22.7	3.6	47.9	665	22.3	2,141	105	16.8
Seminole city	24	128	604	3,214	7,213	56	100.0	19.3	2.4	74.3	479	16.7	892	81	1.9
Shady Hills CDP	NA	NA	NA	NA	NA	NA	NA	NA	NA	NA	NA	NA	NA	NA	NA
South Bradenton CDP	NA	NA	NA	NA	NA	NA	NA	NA	NA	NA	NA	NA	NA	NA	NA
Southchase CDP	NA	NA	NA	NA	NA	NA	NA	NA	NA	NA	NA	NA	NA	NA	NA
South Daytona city	56	430	319	2,447	32,196	258	0.8	16.4	3.3	39.6	545	17.4	1,349	219	16.3
South Miami city	41	332	487	3,939	8,697	30	33.3	21.4	1.8	88.1	1,098	19.8	1,637	184	11.4
South Miami Heights CDP	NA	NA	NA	NA	NA	NA	NA	NA	NA	NA	NA	NA	NA	NA	NA
South Venice CDP	NA	NA	NA	NA	NA	NA	NA	NA	NA	NA	NA	NA	NA	NA	NA
Spring Hill CDP	NA	NA	NA	NA	NA	NA	NA	NA	NA	NA	NA	NA	NA	NA	NA
Stuart city	50	300	493	2,954	17,005	301	3.0	34.9	4.4	61.6	912	35.5	2,187	195	31.3
Sun City Center CDP	NA	NA	NA	NA	NA	NA	NA	NA	NA	NA	NA	NA	NA	NA	NA
Sunny Isles Beach city	34	151	302	1,339	10,590	90	1.1	45.1	2.6	92.3	1,509	52.0	2,360	1073	38.9
Sunrise city	186	194	2,350	2,453	0	0	0.0	218.9	14.3	73.2	807	196.2	2,081	261	258.1
Sunset CDP	NA	NA	NA	NA	NA	NA	NA	NA	NA	NA	NA	NA	NA	NA	NA
Sweetwater city	17	80	341	1,610	0	0	0.0	17.8	4.0	73.1	341	16.9	815	33	2.0
Tallahassee city	1,404	730	8,695	4,518	235,116	1,682	24.2	381.8	68.3	56.9	540	350.7	1,830	159	1413.0
Tamarac city	206	310	1,239	1,864	42,842	307	35.8	105.1	13.6	50.8	609	101.6	1,537	128	52.3
Tamiami CDP	NA	NA	NA	NA	NA	NA	NA	NA	NA	NA	NA	NA	NA	NA	NA
Tampa city	1,598	407	6,576	1,674	834,087	4,777	24.3	700.5	94.9	65.7	791	732.5	1,873	273	1675.3
Tarpon Springs city	51	199	530	2,070	23,488	88	100.0	41.7	5.2	57.6	673	45.2	1,792	325	33.7
Tavares city	48	277	250	1,444	9,240	40	100.0	23.8	2.0	78.4	611	23.3	1,384	125	57.8
Temple Terrace city	67	250	571	2,132	9,346	78	38.5	36.8	4.0	81.7	648	43.2	1,617	160	39.5
The Acreage CDP	NA	NA	NA	NA	NA	NA	NA	NA	NA	NA	NA	NA	NA	NA	NA
The Crossings CDP	NA	NA	NA	NA	NA	NA	NA	NA	NA	NA	NA	NA	NA	NA	NA
The Hammocks CDP	NA	NA	NA	NA	NA	NA	NA	NA	NA	NA	NA	NA	NA	NA	NA
The Villages CDP	NA	NA	NA	NA	NA	NA	NA	NA	NA	NA	NA	NA	NA	NA	NA
Thonotosassa CDP	NA	NA	NA	NA	NA	NA	NA	NA	NA	NA	NA	NA	NA	NA	NA
Three Lakes CDP	NA	NA	NA	NA	NA	NA	NA	NA	NA	NA	NA	NA	NA	NA	NA
Titusville city	289	620	1,397	2,995	16,949	103	100.0	63.8	9.9	51.9	535	51.1	1,108	39	37.7
Town 'n' Country CDP	NA	NA	NA	NA	NA	NA	NA	NA	NA	NA	NA	NA	NA	NA	NA
Trinity CDP	NA	NA	NA	NA	NA	NA	NA	NA	NA	NA	NA	NA	NA	NA	NA
Union Park CDP	NA	NA	NA	NA	NA	NA	NA	NA	NA	NA	NA	NA	NA	NA	NA
University CDP	NA	NA	NA	NA	NA	NA	NA	NA	NA	NA	NA	NA	NA	NA	NA
University CDP	NA	NA	NA	NA	NA	NA	NA	NA	NA	NA	NA	NA	NA	NA	NA
University Park CDP	NA	NA	NA	NA	NA	NA	NA	NA	NA	NA	NA	NA	NA	NA	NA
Upper Grand Lagoon CDP	NA	NA	NA	NA	NA	NA	NA	NA	NA	NA	NA	NA	NA	NA	NA
Valrico CDP	NA	NA	NA	NA	NA	NA	NA	NA	NA	NA	NA	NA	NA	NA	NA
Venice city	25	107	323	1,383	90,931	498	33.7	61.1	14.1	38.8	1,044	69.5	3,009	944	43.1
Vero Beach city	34	198	415	2,417	NA	NA	NA	38.4	5.8	73.7	717	44.2	2,620	469	49.9
Vero Beach South CDP	NA	NA	NA	NA	NA	NA	NA	NA	NA	NA	NA	NA	NA	NA	NA
Viera East CDP	NA	NA	NA	NA	NA	NA	NA	NA	NA	NA	NA	NA	NA	NA	NA
Viera West CDP	NA	NA	NA	NA	NA	NA	NA	NA	NA	NA	NA	NA	NA	NA	NA
Villas CDP	NA	NA	NA	NA	NA	NA	NA	NA	NA	NA	NA	NA	NA	NA	NA
Warrington CDP	NA	NA	NA	NA	NA	NA	NA	NA	NA	NA	NA	NA	NA	NA	NA

1 Data for serious crimes have not been adjusted for underreporting. This may affect comparability between geographic areas over time.
2 Per 100,000 population estimated by the FBI. 3 Based on population estimated as of July 1 of the year shown.

Table B. Incorporated Places, Census Designated Places (CDPs), and Minor Civil Divisions (MCDs) of 10,000 or More Population — **Land Area, Population, and Households, and Employment**

STATE City, town, township, borough, or CDP (county if applicable)	Land area 2010 (sq mi)	Total persons 2010	Total persons 2019	Percent change 2010–2019	Persons per square mile, 2019	Percent foreign born	Percent living in the same house as previous year	Median household income	Percent of households with income below poverty level	Median value of owner-occupied housing units	Percent in civilian labor force	Unemploy-ment rate	Family households	One person households
	1	2	3	4	5	6	7	8	9	10	11	12	13	14
FLORIDA—Con.														
Wekiwa Springs CDP	8.63	21,998	NA	NA	NA	11.6	86.5	87,468	5.5	295,100	64.0	5.0	74.2	21.7
Wellington village	44.97	56,697	65,398	15.3	1454.3	23.4	86.3	92,586	6.6	382,000	63.7	5.0	77.9	18.7
Wesley Chapel CDP	43.92	44,092	NA	NA	NA	15.4	85.7	84,951	6.1	231,600	68.8	4.5	77.2	17.1
Westchase CDP	9.94	21,747	NA	NA	NA	19.0	82.6	94,989	5.3	359,600	68.5	3.3	69.6	24.4
Westchester CDP	3.96	29,862	NA	NA	NA	65.4	92.8	55,716	14.4	332,600	57.5	2.5	79.0	17.0
West Lealman CDP	3.15	15,651	NA	NA	NA	12.9	86.2	39,133	15.9	107,700	52.1	3.2	49.5	43.4
West Little River CDP	4.59	34,699	NA	NA	NA	39.8	93.5	36,730	23.6	159,700	57.7	7.8	71.3	24.5
West Melbourne city	10.60	18,314	24,259	32.5	2288.6	14.6	82.1	68,277	8.1	224,400	54.5	3.8	61.0	33.0
Weston city	24.59	65,419	71,166	8.8	2894.1	46.1	84.7	107,908	6.8	481,800	64.6	4.5	86.8	10.6
West Palm Beach city	53.81	100,665	111,955	11.2	2080.6	27.8	80.9	54,334	14.0	251,700	64.4	7.7	54.0	36.6
West Park city	2.20	14,064	15,089	7.3	6858.6	29.9	86.5	46,765	20.3	174,800	66.0	6.6	74.9	19.6
West Pensacola CDP	7.17	21,339	NA	NA	NA	4.0	83.7	35,068	16.7	65,900	57.8	11.0	51.7	39.4
Westview CDP	3.03	9,650	NA	NA	NA	40.7	94.0	33,984	22.5	208,400	52.9	8.6	79.1	20.8
Westwood Lakes CDP	1.66	11,838	NA	NA	NA	62.1	95.3	51,500	15.2	319,500	62.4	2.5	79.4	16.8
Wilton Manors city	1.97	11,633	12,756	9.7	6475.1	14.2	82.6	70,465	8.2	326,600	63.5	4.4	31.0	50.7
Winter Garden city	16.25	34,754	46,051	32.5	2833.9	25.0	85.4	73,739	10.8	313,600	67.8	3.5	73.9	21.4
Winter Haven city	32.24	34,624	44,955	29.8	1394.4	6.8	83.0	46,669	15.0	154,100	49.5	5.4	62.7	32.3
Winter Park city	8.74	27,715	30,825	11.2	3526.9	10.1	83.1	77,899	9.5	447,800	58.3	3.4	58.6	34.6
Winter Springs city	14.86	33,306	37,312	12.0	2510.9	11.4	86.3	71,898	6.1	246,500	63.6	4.3	69.5	26.5
World Golf Village CDP	26.84	12,310	NA	NA	NA	9.0	86.4	91,875	3.6	273,500	65.1	6.0	77.3	11.6
Wright CDP	5.50	23,127	NA	NA	NA	11.5	80.6	51,349	14.4	168,500	60.1	3.5	52.1	37.7
Yulee CDP	23.16	11,491	NA	NA	NA	3.0	84.3	68,571	13.9	186,400	61.1	5.8	76.8	14.9
Zephyrhills city	9.48	13,859	16,456	18.7	1735.9	8.7	85.3	36,260	17.7	98,800	42.5	5.4	61.1	35.5
GEORGIA	57716.33	9,688,729	10,617,423	9.6	184.0	10.1	84.9	58,700	14.2	176,000	62.6	5.7	67.2	27.2
Acworth city	8.98	20,491	22,818	11.4	2541.0	15.8	87.5	68,860	8.9	182,900	70.4	5.4	65.6	29.1
Albany city	55.07	77,436	72,130	-6.9	1309.8	1.8	76.9	36,615	27.9	99,800	57.9	13.7	58.4	36.3
Alpharetta city	26.90	57,383	67,213	17.1	2498.6	26.2	83.8	113,802	5.5	422,800	71.0	4.4	72.5	22.6
Americus city	11.30	17,116	15,108	-11.7	1337.0	2.0	78.8	33,347	27.5	86,200	60.0	12.2	57.7	37.6
Athens-Clarke County unified government	NA	116,688	128,331	10.0	NA	10.0	70.2	38,623	27.5	170,700	60.9	5.2	49.4	33.3
Athens-Clarke County unified government (balance)	116.33	115,387	126,913	10.0	1091.0	10.1	70.1	38,311	27.7	171,000	60.8	5.3	49.2	33.4
Atlanta city	135.74	427,059	506,811	18.7	3733.7	7.6	78.9	59,948	17.4	290,400	65.6	6.4	42.2	46.8
Augusta-Richmond County consolidated government	NA	200,594	202,518	1.0	NA	3.7	82.1	42,728	20.5	108,000	56.3	9.0	60.7	33.8
Augusta-Richmond County consolidated government (balance)	302.27	195,859	197,888	1.0	654.7	3.8	81.9	42,592	20.6	108,000	56.2	9.0	60.4	34.0
Bainbridge city	18.53	12,798	12,081	-5.6	652.0	0.9	85.2	37,985	26.4	99,900	50.6	7.6	69.6	27.0
Belvedere Park CDP	4.90	15,152	NA	NA	NA	5.9	82.1	46,432	15.3	158,100	66.1	9.6	53.4	34.6
Braselton town	13.02	7,544	12,961	71.8	995.5	6.8	90.5	105,096	6.9	318,700	67.8	1.3	82.0	15.5
Brookhaven city	11.61	49,640	55,554	11.9	4785.0	21.8	83.1	92,604	9.6	484,400	78.6	2.6	50.7	38.5
Brunswick city	17.06	15,291	16,256	6.3	952.9	6.8	77.8	28,032	36.2	108,600	59.1	7.4	58.3	34.8
Buford city	17.47	12,562	15,522	23.6	888.5	17.6	85.3	59,855	11.8	239,100	62.8	3.0	72.1	21.4
Calhoun city	15.62	16,253	17,271	6.3	1105.7	16.1	83.6	35,761	24.7	150,800	59.7	3.5	65.7	27.9
Candler-McAfee CDP	6.97	23,025	NA	NA	NA	2.7	83.8	41,673	17.6	114,400	60.5	11.2	59.8	33.2
Canton city	18.15	23,518	30,528	29.8	1682.0	16.1	81.8	61,259	13.0	215,600	69.1	5.7	69.8	21.9
Carrollton city	22.32	24,380	27,259	11.8	1221.3	7.7	68.2	42,942	28.0	155,300	60.4	9.7	57.7	30.3
Cartersville city	29.00	19,785	21,760	10.0	750.3	6.0	82.0	51,351	18.1	188,900	58.1	5.1	67.5	29.0
Chamblee city	7.70	26,846	30,307	12.9	3936.0	31.6	84.6	61,797	13.5	283,300	78.0	3.3	47.6	37.9
Clarkston city	1.81	12,103	12,637	4.4	6981.8	53.1	68.7	41,070	24.4	122,900	71.5	10.2	62.8	26.4
College Park city	11.09	14,633	15,169	3.6	1366.9	4.5	80.5	35,470	21.7	183,700	69.4	6.9	49.7	46.0
Columbus city	216.48	190,570	195,769	2.7	904.3	5.3	78.1	46,408	19.6	141,300	56.2	9.2	61.6	33.8
Conyers city	11.68	15,238	16,256	6.7	1391.8	11.4	79.9	44,367	21.7	140,400	64.6	7.3	61.1	32.0
Cordele city	10.14	11,186	10,521	-5.9	1037.6	1.9	86.9	21,350	45.3	75,100	57.3	14.4	63.3	35.1
Covington city	15.73	13,127	14,206	8.2	903.1	3.6	84.0	39,845	24.8	171,600	60.2	6.1	65.4	27.5
Cusseta-Chattahoochee County unified	248.74	11,263	10,907	-3.2	43.8	4.5	55.0	47,096	18.7	71,300	29.8	11.3	73.4	21.6
Dallas city	7.38	11,502	13,981	21.6	1894.4	5.5	83.8	43,209	14.9	154,300	58.9	1.3	66.2	31.5
Dalton city	20.55	33,090	33,665	1.7	1638.2	26.8	88.7	44,696	19.0	146,300	63.5	5.2	66.1	27.8
Decatur city	4.44	19,630	25,696	30.9	5787.4	8.1	86.5	106,088	10.4	521,900	67.0	3.4	63.3	32.9
Doraville city	4.91	9,700	10,265	5.8	2090.6	46.3	82.7	51,647	15.2	177,600	75.5	4.0	62.7	29.3
Douglas city	14.44	11,627	11,695	0.6	809.9	6.7	87.3	33,276	26.2	103,900	54.6	4.2	60.2	34.9
Douglasville city	22.56	30,404	33,992	11.8	1506.7	8.7	79.4	58,560	12.6	171,600	69.4	8.8	61.8	31.9
Druid Hills CDP	2.96	14,568	NA	NA	NA	13.0	81.5	129,740	9.0	645,600	64.2	1.4	55.2	33.5
Dublin city	15.93	16,184	15,881	-1.9	996.9	2.5	85.4	32,128	29.5	102,400	46.0	6.7	60.4	35.8
Duluth city	10.22	26,663	29,609	11.0	2897.2	33.5	84.4	71,220	10.4	229,600	69.3	3.9	68.1	24.6
Dunwoody city	13.03	46,427	49,356	6.3	3787.9	23.2	83.5	96,057	5.4	432,900	69.4	3.3	61.6	34.1
East Point city	14.69	33,452	34,875	4.3	2374.1	6.5	81.5	43,453	18.0	139,800	69.0	6.5	47.3	44.5
Evans CDP	25.26	29,011	NA	NA	NA	6.9	88.8	110,036	4.5	262,100	60.4	5.0	79.6	18.6
Fairburn city	16.88	13,100	16,768	28.0	993.4	13.7	81.3	46,785	21.0	140,600	73.5	5.1	68.1	31.9
Fayetteville city	12.88	16,154	17,991	11.4	1396.8	11.9	86.3	73,526	8.0	224,100	60.9	7.2	70.7	26.6
Forest Park city	9.31	18,463	20,020	8.4	2150.4	16.5	81.6	36,792	20.7	67,100	57.3	9.4	61.0	31.8
Gainesville city	32.95	34,035	43,232	27.0	1312.0	23.4	82.3	51,520	17.3	219,300	62.4	3.1	66.1	27.6
Georgetown CDP	8.22	11,823	NA	NA	NA	8.8	78.5	63,403	7.3	178,800	63.6	11.3	75.3	19.5
Griffin city	13.94	23,226	22,813	-1.8	1636.5	3.9	88.6	36,890	22.9	102,800	62.3	5.3	59.8	32.8
Grovetown city	5.28	11,224	15,152	35.0	2869.7	9.8	85.7	68,756	8.7	158,900	58.8	4.4	74.1	15.8
Hinesville city	18.17	33,347	33,273	-0.2	1831.2	7.5	68.1	47,563	16.2	123,700	58.7	10.1	70.2	24.7
Holly Springs city	7.02	9,290	15,442	66.2	2199.7	6.4	87.9	95,941	3.1	268,900	70.9	7.0	77.3	18.5
Jefferson city	22.47	9,501	12,032	26.6	535.5	5.8	91.0	58,451	14.5	201,300	56.7	3.0	73.4	22.8
Jesup city	16.55	10,209	9,841	-3.6	594.6	3.3	85.1	39,933	20.7	99,700	51.5	7.1	63.0	33.1
Johns Creek city	30.81	76,638	84,579	10.4	2745.2	31.0	86.3	122,514	4.1	400,100	69.4	4.7	81.0	16.5
Kennesaw city	9.72	30,603	34,077	11.4	3505.9	13.6	85.1	70,930	9.6	194,800	74.9	4.3	64.4	25.9
Kingsland city	44.71	15,866	17,949	13.1	401.5	8.4	78.8	51,779	16.9	156,700	61.6	4.6	74.3	20.4
LaGrange city	42.10	29,338	30,305	3.3	719.8	6.0	83.9	34,808	26.8	127,100	59.2	6.7	61.0	34.4

STATE City, town, township, borough, or CDP (county if applicable)	Serious crimes known to police, 2018[1] Violent crime Number	Rate[2]	Property crime Number	Rate[2]	New residential construction authorized by building permits, 2019 Value ($1,000)	Number of housing units	Percent single family	Local government finance, 2017 General revenue Total (mil dol)	Intergovernmental Total (mil dol)	Percent from state gov.	Taxes per capita[3]	General expenditure Total (mil dol)	Per capita[3] Total	Capital outlays	Debt outstanding (mil dol)
	15	16	17	18	19	20	21	22	23	24	25	26	27	28	29
FLORIDA—Con.															
Wekiwa Springs CDP	NA	NA	NA	NA	NA	NA	NA	NA	NA	NA	NA	NA	NA	NA	NA
Wellington village	81	123	832	1,259	13,870	39	89.7	69.4	8.9	72.0	530	75.1	1,159	266	5.5
Wesley Chapel CDP	NA	NA	NA	NA	NA	NA	NA	NA	NA	NA	NA	NA	NA	NA	NA
Westchase CDP	NA	NA	NA	NA	NA	NA	NA	NA	NA	NA	NA	NA	NA	NA	NA
Westchester CDP	NA	NA	NA	NA	NA	NA	NA	NA	NA	NA	NA	NA	NA	NA	NA
West Lealman CDP	NA	NA	NA	NA	NA	NA	NA	NA	NA	NA	NA	NA	NA	NA	NA
West Little River CDP	NA	NA	NA	NA	NA	NA	NA	NA	NA	NA	NA	NA	NA	NA	NA
West Melbourne city	27	119	550	2,427	138,097	1,218	19.0	20.2	3.6	73.5	447	19.3	882	324	13.6
Weston city	41	57	374	521	5,690	24	100.0	85.2	6.2	100.0	498	107.2	1,512	53	68.3
West Palm Beach city	1,026	919	4,249	3,805	91,222	529	13.0	266.9	46.7	31.3	1,181	272.2	2,467	138	452.1
West Park city	109	713	490	3,203	2,000	8	100.0	13.0	1.8	82.9	416	13.4	893	46	0.0
West Pensacola CDP	NA	NA	NA	NA	NA	NA	NA	NA	NA	NA	NA	NA	NA	NA	NA
Westview CDP	NA	NA	NA	NA	NA	NA	NA	NA	NA	NA	NA	NA	NA	NA	NA
Westwood Lakes CDP	NA	NA	NA	NA	NA	NA	NA	NA	NA	NA	NA	NA	NA	NA	NA
Wilton Manors city	54	417	427	3,300	14,821	72	6.9	21.2	1.6	78.5	900	22.6	1,768	227	6.5
Winter Garden city	155	345	1,018	2,266	221,461	391	100.0	55.1	10.7	76.4	552	58.2	1,332	312	36.2
Winter Haven city	236	558	1,032	2,442	183,243	757	100.0	67.9	6.7	85.5	572	68.4	1,675	231	73.8
Winter Park city	60	192	767	2,449	52,952	100	98.0	67.6	9.4	66.3	1,031	78.9	2,555	327	145.9
Winter Springs city	57	154	274	738	20,493	155	31.0	34.6	4.4	79.0	429	28.8	787	171	22.1
World Golf Village CDP	NA	NA	NA	NA	NA	NA	NA	NA	NA	NA	NA	NA	NA	NA	NA
Wright CDP	NA	NA	NA	NA	NA	NA	NA	NA	NA	NA	NA	NA	NA	NA	NA
Yulee CDP	NA	NA	NA	NA	NA	NA	NA	NA	NA	NA	NA	NA	NA	NA	NA
Zephyrhills city	47	303	612	3,947	50,661	178	100.0	23.0	3.6	84.1	607	21.5	1,377	175	18.8
GEORGIA	34,355	327	270,738	2,574	10,681,578	53,823	79.8	X	X	X	X	X	X	X	X
Acworth city	24	104	503	2,184	5,168	24	100.0	28.7	9.6	2.4	450	26.2	1,156	288	19.9
Albany city	809	1,114	3,704	5,102	36,531	238	7.6	112.3	27.8	20.8	382	118.2	1,614	5	29.9
Alpharetta city	42	63	1,204	1,796	87,972	228	89.5	116.0	31.6	21.4	790	115.0	1,749	695	222.0
Americus city	130	856	921	6,066	488	2	100.0	19.0	4.1	3.7	427	16.6	1,076	20	11.5
Athens-Clarke County unified government	NA	NA	NA	NA	NA	NA	NA	227.6	61.2	4.7	634	216.1	1,704	241	264.0
Athens-Clarke County unified government (balance)	NA	NA	NA	NA	NA	NA	NA	NA	NA	NA	NA	NA	NA	NA	NA
Atlanta city	3,814	769	23,091	4,654	503,095	3,283	22.2	1874.4	322.1	4.6	1,300	1608.0	3,270	839	7204.2
Augusta-Richmond County consolidated government	NA	NA	NA	NA	NA	NA	NA	NA	NA	NA	NA	NA	NA	NA	NA
Augusta-Richmond County consolidated government (balance)	NA	NA	NA	NA	NA	NA	NA	393.7	123.9	3.7	627	325.8	1,654	217	604.8
Bainbridge city	91	756	456	3,790	5,379	35	77.1	14.2	3.9	13.6	387	13.7	1,121	16	14.5
Belvedere Park CDP	NA	NA	NA	NA	NA	NA	NA	NA	NA	NA	NA	NA	NA	NA	NA
Braselton town	1	9	65	563	50,805	281	100.0	15.8	4.6	6.9	439	10.7	977	149	69.5
Brookhaven city	187	345	1,456	2,689	81,992	207	96.1	85.2	19.9	3.4	431	96.4	1,797	224	21.5
Brunswick city	175	1,065	862	5,246	NA	NA	NA	19.3	8.4	9.6	498	18.4	1,139	88	0.8
Buford city	NA	NA	NA	NA	38,617	160	95.6	33.5	3.4	16.1	1,234	57.5	3,873	380	39.1
Calhoun city	NA	NA	NA	NA	16,126	133	100.0	34.7	8.9	4.6	444	23.8	1,407	113	54.8
Candler-McAfee CDP	NA	NA	NA	NA	NA	NA	NA	NA	NA	NA	NA	NA	NA	NA	NA
Canton city	34	119	668	2,329	121,995	718	63.0	34.1	7.2	4.4	421	21.6	762	132	38.1
Carrollton city	160	589	1,122	4,127	27,965	91	100.0	37.1	8.4	3.1	444	35.8	1,339	208	13.3
Cartersville city	NA	NA	NA	NA	44,321	152	100.0	57.6	9.9	13.1	1,346	37.2	1,771	218	30.8
Chamblee city	NA	NA	NA	NA	61,731	200	93.0	24.1	2.1	37.8	529	19.6	667	72	0.0
Clarkston city	63	486	415	3,203	324	2	100.0	5.5	0.2	39.2	279	5.4	421	51	1.0
College Park city	156	1,038	1,035	6,884	7,791	42	100.0	94.0	4.6	0.0	2,649	74.6	4,912	793	46.8
Columbus city	NA	NA	NA	NA	109,463	681	43.0	331.5	90.7	8.2	728	329.2	1,698	185	452.8
Conyers city	NA	NA	NA	NA	42,989	167	100.0	24.2	3.0	7.0	848	23.9	1,496	9	2.3
Cordele city	64	600	561	5,258	250	1	100.0	14.4	3.5	16.0	497	14.5	1,352	33	4.6
Covington city	51	360	666	4,697	24,227	96	100.0	31.8	5.5	7.7	603	33.9	2,421	140	13.0
Cusseta-Chattahoochee County unified	NA	NA	NA	NA	NA	NA	NA	6.7	3.3	0.0	193	4.9	480	22	1.0
Dallas city	37	274	303	2,245	26,784	156	100.0	10.8	3.4	19.5	261	10.0	755	207	25.4
Dalton city	93	275	987	2,917	NA	NA	NA	88.1	17.4	1.8	434	75.6	2,252	290	70.8
Decatur city	41	167	576	2,352	9,946	28	75.0	36.3	7.5	2.2	737	43.1	1,812	251	143.9
Doraville city	53	499	637	5,995	4,032	17	100.0	14.1	0.9	29.1	840	16.5	1,612	386	0.0
Douglas city	NA	NA	NA	NA	550	6	100.0	21.8	6.6	15.9	384	22.0	1,928	227	0.0
Douglasville city	193	566	1,841	5,403	71,243	220	100.0	34.3	7.6	11.4	557	27.3	828	27	46.5
Druid Hills CDP	NA	NA	NA	NA	NA	NA	NA	NA	NA	NA	NA	NA	NA	NA	NA
Dublin city	127	806	774	4,912	2,601	14	100.0	24.9	7.1	4.6	481	25.3	1,600	101	6.3
Duluth city	20	67	537	1,797	31,900	101	31.7	27.1	7.8	5.3	505	21.8	741	90	16.5
Dunwoody city	79	158	2,032	4,056	18,088	50	100.0	38.0	8.7	6.0	434	52.0	1,048	363	1.5
East Point city	441	1,243	4,260	12,005	9,088	93	100.0	56.9	14.2	1.4	640	41.1	1,174	0	116.1
Evans CDP	NA	NA	NA	NA	NA	NA	NA	NA	NA	NA	NA	NA	NA	NA	NA
Fairburn city	52	327	660	4,150	38,743	138	100.0	19.4	1.6	0.4	589	19.9	1,280	62	35.0
Fayetteville city	29	161	467	2,588	42,819	124	98.4	14.9	2.5	0.5	373	16.9	947	176	24.5
Forest Park city	134	669	962	4,804	530	1	100.0	34.3	10.5	7.7	690	29.9	1,514	6	26.4
Gainesville city	158	382	1,280	3,094	71,746	533	33.0	116.3	17.4	4.9	714	82.0	2,032	241	779.5
Georgetown CDP	NA	NA	NA	NA	NA	NA	NA	NA	NA	NA	NA	NA	NA	NA	NA
Griffin city	261	1,149	1,080	4,756	314	4	100.0	40.7	7.9	7.5	352	25.3	1,112	79	69.7
Grovetown city	14	96	186	1,279	62,576	570	30.0	10.1	3.3	44.9	233	8.5	606	22	2.5
Hinesville city	147	443	1,201	3,622	102,065	696	32.8	30.2	4.3	10.0	395	29.9	906	26	31.0
Holly Springs city	3	24	123	994	135,732	398	100.0	11.0	3.8	59.7	507	15.5	1,293	665	3.0
Jefferson city	12	105	151	1,325	19,994	110	100.0	16.7	3.1	13.8	566	13.7	1,226	141	35.8
Jesup city	36	371	524	5,403	1,689	11	100.0	9.9	2.4	3.9	351	9.1	930	95	10.4
Johns Creek city	34	40	532	623	70,375	174	100.0	57.3	22.1	9.5	368	79.1	939	427	3.9
Kennesaw city	57	163	428	1,226	53,415	353	11.9	33.5	7.6	3.1	499	39.4	1,151	479	32.1
Kingsland city	NA	NA	NA	NA	30,920	139	87.1	18.7	4.4	17.2	438	14.4	844	119	14.5
LaGrange city	130	425	1,408	4,600	75,121	316	24.1	49.5	11.9	3.3	202	52.2	1,714	110	37.9

1 Data for serious crimes have not been adjusted for underreporting. This may affect comparability between geographic areas over time.
2 Per 100,000 population estimated by the FBI.   3 Based on population estimated as of July 1 of the year shown.

Table B. Incorporated Places, Census Designated Places (CDPs), and Minor Civil Divisions (MCDs) of 10,000 or More Population — **Land Area, Population, and Households, and Employment**

STATE City, town, township, borough, or CDP (county if applicable)	Land area 2010 (sq mi)	Population				Population characteristics 2015–2019		Income and poverty 2015–2019		Median value of owner-occupied housing units	Employment, 2015–2019		Households, 2015–2019 (percent of households)	
		Total persons 2010	Total persons 2019	Percent change 2010–2019	Persons per square mile, 2019	Percent foreign born	Percent living in the same house as previous year	Median household income	Percent of households with income below poverty level		Percent in civilian labor force	Unemployment rate	Family households	One person households
	1	2	3	4	5	6	7	8	9	10	11	12	13	14
GEORGIA—Con.														
Lawrenceville city	13.61	27,219	30,834	13.3	2265.5	26.4	84.2	52,585	17.6	171,600	68.6	6.3	67.2	28.7
Lilburn city	6.40	11,648	12,810	10.0	2001.6	35.1	92.1	58,151	12.2	175,300	65.0	4.0	75.5	20.5
Lithia Springs CDP	13.57	15,491	NA	NA	NA	14.6	85.0	48,988	14.4	130,800	72.2	4.7	64.6	26.5
Loganville city	7.34	10,412	12,880	23.7	1754.8	19.6	88.6	61,502	13.6	202,300	63.0	5.8	75.9	19.4
Mableton CDP	20.58	37,115	NA	NA	NA	17.1	87.4	69,840	8.7	182,800	72.4	5.3	75.7	21.5
McDonough city	12.62	22,015	26,768	21.6	2121.1	8.6	79.1	63,108	10.0	164,100	67.0	7.3	67.6	26.7
Macon-Bibb County	249.40	155,783	153,159	-1.7	614.1	3.3	83.0	41,334	24.1	120,200	56.9	7.2	60.1	35.0
Marietta city	23.41	56,486	60,867	7.8	2600.0	17.4	78.5	57,452	12.4	287,600	68.5	4.5	56.2	34.8
Martinez CDP	14.50	35,795	NA	NA	NA	8.6	89.2	75,330	7.6	162,600	63.2	3.7	69.2	27.3
Milledgeville city	20.34	18,428	18,704	1.5	919.6	2.0	70.5	28,632	32.3	121,900	45.7	13.6	48.4	37.6
Milton city	38.54	32,837	39,587	20.6	1027.2	18.3	87.5	128,559	3.8	541,000	68.8	3.4	76.6	20.0
Monroe city	15.68	12,847	13,673	6.4	872.0	1.9	78.8	31,740	26.4	127,400	58.9	11.5	68.4	27.4
Moultrie city	16.66	14,258	14,211	-0.3	853.0	11.1	74.5	27,129	29.9	94,400	56.8	12.3	60.4	31.5
Mountain Park CDP	5.79	11,554	NA	NA	NA	19.3	89.0	75,885	9.8	187,800	64.4	4.7	78.8	19.2
Newnan city	19.32	32,905	41,581	26.4	2152.2	9.1	80.4	63,606	13.7	206,300	66.5	4.2	66.2	28.6
Norcross city	6.10	14,952	16,592	11.0	2720.0	36.3	92.3	58,236	12.9	177,400	70.9	4.7	72.2	22.2
North Decatur CDP	4.91	16,698	NA	NA	NA	15.3	77.3	79,449	10.6	295,800	69.0	2.7	43.1	42.6
North Druid Hills CDP	4.54	18,947	NA	NA	NA	16.6	77.3	66,660	11.7	366,800	73.7	4.9	37.1	44.0
Panthersville CDP	3.67	9,749	NA	NA	NA	4.5	81.8	37,740	17.4	107,700	63.3	11.0	55.8	39.1
Peachtree City city	24.56	34,366	36,223	5.4	1474.9	11.4	86.8	101,121	5.4	338,900	60.7	2.9	73.1	24.0
Peachtree Corners city	16.11	38,014	43,905	15.5	2725.3	18.4	89.0	71,149	7.8	344,600	70.8	3.6	63.1	31.9
Perry city	26.76	13,737	17,894	30.3	668.7	5.0	77.8	49,219	14.4	150,500	59.9	10.5	66.6	31.4
Pooler city	27.65	18,489	25,694	39.0	929.3	7.5	81.4	79,426	5.5	214,500	73.8	6.4	69.7	22.6
Powder Springs city	7.36	13,938	15,758	13.1	2141.0	11.8	88.0	69,807	6.8	167,500	68.3	6.2	76.1	19.8
Redan CDP	8.09	33,015	NA	NA	NA	10.2	84.8	49,464	16.1	115,100	69.3	8.5	62.3	32.5
Richmond Hill city	23.55	9,376	13,839	47.6	587.6	7.5	76.5	71,438	15.3	210,700	64.8	6.1	79.2	17.3
Rincon city	9.74	8,916	10,361	16.2	1063.8	5.3	87.7	64,625	12.3	164,500	67.1	3.7	66.3	29.1
Riverdale city	4.42	14,276	15,594	9.2	3528.1	13.2	82.6	50,145	16.3	101,300	68.0	8.6	61.7	31.9
Rome city	31.54	36,372	36,716	0.9	1164.1	12.8	80.6	38,443	23.8	151,200	57.1	5.3	62.6	33.3
Roswell city	40.72	88,332	94,763	7.3	2327.2	18.5	86.9	99,726	5.3	374,700	71.1	3.6	69.5	23.8
St. Marys city	22.82	17,084	18,567	8.7	813.6	2.3	79.4	59,869	12.9	182,400	53.6	8.9	71.7	20.4
St. Simons CDP	16.48	12,743	NA	NA	NA	4.1	89.2	87,248	4.6	371,600	56.5	1.6	63.6	31.9
Sandy Springs city	37.65	93,826	109,452	16.7	2907.1	20.6	82.2	78,613	6.2	471,800	73.3	3.0	53.0	38.6
Savannah city	103.91	136,918	144,464	5.5	1390.3	6.2	72.9	43,307	21.1	156,500	63.6	8.6	56.6	33.5
Scottdale CDP	3.35	10,631	NA	NA	NA	26.4	83.6	56,832	11.9	197,000	74.1	4.8	52.7	35.2
Smyrna city	15.55	51,037	56,666	11.0	3644.1	17.3	79.5	76,444	8.1	284,000	77.6	4.5	55.3	35.5
Snellville city	10.47	18,259	20,077	10.0	1917.6	14.8	89.5	74,535	6.9	169,600	64.7	3.5	79.6	18.0
South Fulton city	84.79	85,589	99,155	15.9	1169.4	4.5	88.2	65,919	9.8	162,800	68.8	8.0	63.2	31.2
Statesboro city	14.89	28,365	32,954	16.2	2213.2	4.0	54.9	29,203	38.7	113,600	56.9	12.3	44.7	31.2
Stockbridge city	13.67	26,431	29,904	13.1	2187.6	15.8	83.4	61,291	9.9	180,700	71.0	5.7	73.7	22.9
Stonecrest city	37.40	50,207	54,903	9.4	1468.0	7.0	80.2	49,865	14.5	126,400	68.9	7.9	57.9	36.8
Sugar Hill city	11.09	18,484	24,617	33.2	2219.7	21.6	87.3	87,090	9.0	232,500	69.4	4.1	80.7	15.6
Suwanee city	10.88	15,343	20,907	36.3	1921.6	21.1	84.4	90,436	7.0	308,900	70.6	3.4	74.7	20.7
Thomasville city	15.01	18,556	18,518	-0.2	1233.7	2.3	77.1	32,378	26.2	163,500	57.0	6.3	66.2	29.8
Tifton city	12.61	16,411	16,838	2.6	1335.3	8.3	86.6	38,316	28.9	119,200	57.2	2.3	64.0	29.6
Tucker city	20.12	33,380	36,395	9.0	1808.9	17.3	83.9	70,522	10.2	256,200	68.4	4.7	60.5	32.3
Union City city	19.66	19,317	22,399	16.0	1139.3	3.9	82.2	45,324	14.2	132,300	68.5	6.5	57.9	39.3
Valdosta city	35.97	54,764	56,457	3.1	1569.6	3.4	80.4	32,595	30.8	121,800	57.7	6.9	53.1	36.8
Vidalia city	17.88	10,424	10,402	-0.2	581.8	7.2	82.8	40,621	23.0	118,600	54.8	10.5	61.8	35.0
Villa Rica city	14.08	14,046	16,058	14.3	1140.5	7.6	76.5	63,241	10.5	162,800	70.1	6.2	72.9	22.5
Vinings CDP	3.13	9,734	NA	NA	NA	11.7	67.1	81,973	2.9	481,000	74.4	2.2	46.0	41.7
Warner Robins city	37.22	69,596	77,617	11.5	2085.4	7.2	82.4	51,779	15.8	117,100	65.9	6.4	66.4	27.1
Waycross city	11.88	14,600	13,480	-7.7	1134.7	1.0	82.0	27,381	31.7	70,100	49.1	5.2	55.6	40.7
Wilmington Island CDP	8.30	15,138	NA	NA	NA	5.2	86.3	82,500	3.1	263,700	65.0	3.0	66.7	31.2
Winder city	13.66	14,379	17,937	24.7	1313.1	7.0	87.3	48,429	16.8	162,700	63.9	4.8	67.0	28.1
Woodstock city	12.42	23,803	33,039	38.8	2660.1	10.7	84.5	76,191	7.5	243,500	74.4	2.9	65.7	30.3
HAWAII	6422.43	1,360,307	1,415,872	4.1	220.5	18.5	86.6	81,275	9.8	615,300	61.8	4.3	69.5	24.2
East Honolulu CDP	23.01	49,914	NA	NA	NA	14.9	90.5	133,165	4.0	959,800	62.0	2.0	78.0	18.2
Ewa Beach CDP	1.19	14,955	NA	NA	NA	34.0	93.2	100,151	6.9	551,200	69.1	3.1	84.3	12.8
Ewa Gentry CDP	2.13	22,690	NA	NA	NA	19.4	86.7	111,272	2.7	568,300	69.5	2.8	84.0	10.0
Halawa CDP	2.37	14,014	NA	NA	NA	19.1	88.1	101,010	6.2	785,200	64.7	3.2	75.8	18.2
Hawaiian Paradise Park CDP	15.21	11,404	NA	NA	NA	12.7	95.9	54,870	10.9	303,300	57.0	3.6	75.6	20.5
Hilo CDP	53.39	43,263	NA	NA	NA	7.6	91.1	63,283	17.2	329,200	57.3	5.8	64.1	29.1
Kahului CDP	14.39	26,337	NA	NA	NA	33.3	88.9	86,129	8.0	606,600	65.7	3.9	81.9	14.1
Kailua CDP	35.69	11,975	NA	NA	NA	20.2	86.4	72,267	10.0	461,900	65.7	3.0	69.1	20.0
Kailua CDP	7.77	38,635	NA	NA	NA	9.5	86.1	114,292	5.6	959,200	62.0	3.8	73.7	19.5
Kalaoa CDP	39.17	9,644	NA	NA	NA	12.5	89.7	77,830	9.7	554,900	70.2	3.0	74.0	18.4
Kaneohe CDP	6.53	34,597	NA	NA	NA	8.5	90.8	108,761	4.2	770,700	63.4	3.1	75.1	19.8
Kaneohe Station CDP	4.40	9,517	NA	NA	NA	4.8	71.7	59,939	6.6	1,069,400	23.8	7.5	95.7	3.7
Kapaa CDP	10.03	10,699	NA	NA	NA	16.3	91.3	90,925	12.1	543,900	66.0	3.7	69.2	26.2
Kapolei CDP	4.14	15,186	NA	NA	NA	13.3	87.8	103,547	5.2	570,800	70.9	4.7	82.3	13.6
Kihei CDP	9.36	20,881	NA	NA	NA	17.5	84.4	78,869	7.7	590,200	69.4	4.0	63.6	26.0
Lahaina CDP	7.78	11,704	NA	NA	NA	30.8	81.5	75,850	7.4	686,800	72.2	5.5	68.8	20.6
Maili CDP	1.72	9,488	NA	NA	NA	10.1	85.0	88,395	13.6	464,900	61.8	8.7	77.8	16.6
Makakilo CDP	3.82	18,248	NA	NA	NA	17.2	86.3	113,244	4.0	622,900	68.7	5.6	80.9	15.3
Mililani Mauka CDP	3.98	21,039	NA	NA	NA	13.1	90.2	114,886	2.5	691,200	68.1	1.7	75.6	20.2
Mililani Town CDP	4.01	27,629	NA	NA	NA	9.9	89.5	99,460	3.9	639,800	62.8	2.3	78.7	16.9
Nanakuli CDP	2.99	12,666	NA	NA	NA	6.3	93.7	75,031	18.7	370,600	62.6	11.9	81.7	14.2
Ocean Pointe CDP	2.02	8,361	NA	NA	NA	16.9	76.5	119,934	4.0	665,200	65.1	3.1	83.5	13.0
Pearl City CDP	9.11	47,698	NA	NA	NA	12.2	88.4	100,057	4.3	667,000	56.0	2.8	76.5	19.5
Royal Kunia CDP	3.01	14,525	NA	NA	NA	32.0	91.0	116,290	3.4	624,900	72.7	3.4	82.6	12.3
Schofield Barracks CDP	2.77	16,370	NA	NA	NA	6.2	66.7	60,966	6.5	0	24.0	12.7	90.2	7.1
Urban Honolulu CDP	60.54	337,721	345,064	2.2	5699.8	27.4	85.2	71,465	11.4	683,000	63.2	3.7	59.0	33.5
Wahiawa CDP	2.08	17,821	NA	NA	NA	16.1	89.7	62,092	17.9	590,900	60.6	4.5	68.8	25.9
Waianae CDP	5.36	13,177	NA	NA	NA	7.7	89.2	62,172	22.9	375,100	57.8	13.5	80.9	16.0

Table B. Incorporated Places, Census Designated Places (CDPs), and Minor Civil Divisions (MCDs) of 10,000 or More Population — **Crime, Residential Construction and Local Government Finance**

STATE City, town, township, borough, or CDP (county if applicable)	Violent crime Number	Violent crime Rate[2]	Property crime Number	Property crime Rate[2]	Value ($1,000)	Number of housing units	Percent single family	General revenue Total (mil dol)	Intergovernmental Total (mil dol)	Intergovernmental Percent from state gov.	Taxes per capita[3]	General expenditure Total (mil dol)	Per capita[3] Total	Per capita[3] Capital outlays	Debt outstanding (mil dol)
	15	16	17	18	19	20	21	22	23	24	25	26	27	28	29
GEORGIA—Con.															
Lawrenceville city	NA	NA	NA	NA	18,245	77	100.0	21.7	6.1	9.8	191	43.1	1,455	393	0.0
Lilburn city	47	366	407	3,168	36,401	112	100.0	9.6	2.1	6.9	395	8.2	651	83	4.3
Lithia Springs CDP	NA	NA	NA	NA	NA	NA	NA	NA	NA	NA	NA	NA	NA	NA	NA
Loganville city	16	130	320	2,600	25,733	140	100.0	19.3	2.9	4.5	611	17.6	1,467	214	12.3
Mableton CDP	NA	NA	NA	NA	NA	NA	NA	NA	NA	NA	NA	NA	NA	NA	NA
McDonough city	37	147	662	2,632	68,208	446	100.0	22.6	4.8	3.8	363	23.0	932	211	9.8
Macon-Bibb County	NA	NA	NA	NA	23,339	132	100.0	136.5	57.0	3.3	261	138.4	906	70	35.9
Marietta city	214	347	1,948	3,159	61,969	266	100.0	104.6	19.1	0.6	642	104.2	1,717	485	115.1
Martinez CDP	NA	NA	NA	NA	NA	NA	NA	NA	NA	NA	NA	NA	NA	NA	NA
Milledgeville city	66	355	764	4,103	166	2	100.0	21.5	4.7	10.5	418	16.7	895	0	5.3
Milton city	11	28	288	723	34,116	144	100.0	31.8	11.3	3.4	445	33.0	850	302	9.6
Monroe city	89	656	629	4,634	40,055	127	100.0	26.4	3.5	1.2	364	23.1	1,724	10	20.9
Moultrie city	73	516	707	5,001	5,111	30	86.7	25.0	2.7	6.6	507	24.0	1,712	13	21.2
Mountain Park CDP	NA	NA	NA	NA	NA	NA	NA	NA	NA	NA	NA	NA	NA	NA	NA
Newnan city	182	457	1,052	2,641	126,714	666	50.8	42.7	15.2	2.3	389	38.3	985	156	32.3
Norcross city	81	474	569	3,330	74,760	534	9.6	19.3	3.8	14.3	496	18.5	1,113	261	0.8
North Decatur CDP	NA	NA	NA	NA	NA	NA	NA	NA	NA	NA	NA	NA	NA	NA	NA
North Druid Hills CDP	NA	NA	NA	NA	NA	NA	NA	NA	NA	NA	NA	NA	NA	NA	NA
Panthersville CDP	NA	NA	NA	NA	NA	NA	NA	NA	NA	NA	NA	NA	NA	NA	NA
Peachtree City city	18	51	466	1,317	51,016	181	100.0	57.1	7.7	5.1	650	39.6	1,122	82	13.0
Peachtree Corners city	NA	NA	NA	NA	32,629	105	100.0	38.6	7.6	5.1	304	39.6	916	18	0.0
Perry city	NA	NA	NA	NA	93,357	547	86.8	22.1	2.4	21.1	555	22.3	1,343	140	14.9
Pooler city	24	97	758	3,074	68,828	231	100.0	34.7	9.9	5.4	468	46.0	1,945	987	18.0
Powder Springs city	33	217	285	1,873	13,771	63	100.0	17.1	3.4	5.2	402	14.4	962	247	13.0
Redan CDP	NA	NA	NA	NA	NA	NA	NA	NA	NA	NA	NA	NA	NA	NA	NA
Richmond Hill city	NA	NA	NA	NA	63,760	269	100.0	15.8	3.4	0.1	459	15.1	1,203	120	30.8
Rincon city	13	130	314	3,128	60,547	150	94.0	10.6	3.2	17.1	161	9.2	929	333	5.5
Riverdale city	NA	NA	NA	NA	0	0	0.0	17.3	6.0	0.0	340	17.1	1,117	156	16.0
Rome city	NA	NA	NA	NA	NA	NA	NA	73.4	20.2	3.4	635	92.4	2,541	342	43.9
Roswell city	126	132	1,500	1,568	97,443	245	100.0	102.6	28.0	4.6	469	131.2	1,385	191	23.9
St. Marys city	NA	NA	NA	NA	26,438	127	100.0	20.2	4.3	6.5	356	18.2	1,012	27	78.5
St. Simons CDP	NA	NA	NA	NA	NA	NA	NA	NA	NA	NA	NA	NA	NA	NA	NA
Sandy Springs city	128	118	2,015	1,855	59,383	201	100.0	117.1	31.0	4.3	660	208.1	1,951	1186	178.3
Savannah city	NA	NA	NA	NA	69,331	339	100.0	375.3	86.7	1.1	838	378.2	2,594	304	158.9
Scottdale CDP	NA	NA	NA	NA	NA	NA	NA	NA	NA	NA	NA	NA	NA	NA	NA
Smyrna city	117	204	1,459	2,538	48,387	204	100.0	72.5	12.1	4.2	606	50.0	889	2	86.0
Snellville city	64	321	795	3,986	22,451	94	100.0	18.6	4.0	5.2	412	17.7	899	236	2.5
South Fulton city	NA	NA	NA	NA	28,581	269	100.0	NA	NA	NA	NA	NA	NA	NA	NA
Statesboro city	110	346	845	2,656	9,196	118	84.7	35.0	6.1	6.2	341	29.7	948	53	15.0
Stockbridge city	NA	NA	NA	NA	36,852	125	100.0	16.2	6.7	7.2	167	10.9	375	24	14.5
Stonecrest city	NA	NA	NA	NA	70,352	297	100.0	NA	NA	NA	NA	NA	NA	NA	NA
Sugar Hill city	NA	NA	NA	NA	23,329	142	100.0	22.0	3.2	6.4	271	17.2	748	434	0.0
Suwanee city	29	143	523	2,586	66,579	375	37.9	18.6	4.7	6.3	617	26.3	1,348	353	16.2
Thomasville city	33	178	860	4,647	9,346	54	96.3	73.1	7.5	5.3	207	58.0	3,124	409	23.1
Tifton city	NA	NA	NA	NA	12,511	119	24.8	23.4	5.9	3.9	542	14.8	891	0	5.1
Tucker city	NA	NA	NA	NA	43,364	183	100.0	61.7	16.9	8.2	730	61.3	1,701	185	66.5
Union City city	NA	NA	NA	NA	51,354	389	100.0	28.6	5.7	10.5	652	21.8	1,025	35	19.2
Valdosta city	NA	NA	NA	NA	107,949	533	100.0	75.0	24.2	6.6	461	67.2	1,199	106	89.7
Vidalia city	65	620	493	4,701	957	8	50.0	13.1	4.8	15.0	392	13.9	1,337	247	0.0
Villa Rica city	57	367	583	3,753	73,689	278	100.0	27.6	5.2	9.0	450	18.7	1,222	80	37.2
Vinings CDP	NA	NA	NA	NA	NA	NA	NA	NA	NA	NA	NA	NA	NA	NA	NA
Warner Robins city	444	587	4,200	5,551	67,131	403	77.2	68.2	8.0	12.1	423	70.3	932	87	34.5
Waycross city	71	516	770	5,592	0	0	0.0	20.4	5.9	7.4	523	17.2	1,253	10	7.6
Wilmington Island CDP	NA	NA	NA	NA	NA	NA	NA	NA	NA	NA	NA	NA	NA	NA	NA
Winder city	NA	NA	NA	NA	19,243	120	100.0	23.9	4.0	10.7	290	24.6	1,518	212	24.1
Woodstock city	42	128	491	1,495	89,399	241	100.0	32.7	4.3	12.0	543	22.7	717	0	3.3
HAWAII	3,532	249	40,772	2,870	1,283,822	4,093	62.2	X	X	X	X	X	X	X	X
East Honolulu CDP	NA	NA	NA	NA	NA	NA	NA	NA	NA	NA	NA	NA	NA	NA	NA
Ewa Beach CDP	NA	NA	NA	NA	NA	NA	NA	NA	NA	NA	NA	NA	NA	NA	NA
Ewa Gentry CDP	NA	NA	NA	NA	NA	NA	NA	NA	NA	NA	NA	NA	NA	NA	NA
Halawa CDP	NA	NA	NA	NA	NA	NA	NA	NA	NA	NA	NA	NA	NA	NA	NA
Hawaiian Paradise Park CDP	NA	NA	NA	NA	NA	NA	NA	NA	NA	NA	NA	NA	NA	NA	NA
Hilo CDP	NA	NA	NA	NA	NA	NA	NA	NA	NA	NA	NA	NA	NA	NA	NA
Kahului CDP	NA	NA	NA	NA	NA	NA	NA	NA	NA	NA	NA	NA	NA	NA	NA
Kailua CDP	NA	NA	NA	NA	NA	NA	NA	NA	NA	NA	NA	NA	NA	NA	NA
Kailua CDP	NA	NA	NA	NA	NA	NA	NA	NA	NA	NA	NA	NA	NA	NA	NA
Kalaoa CDP	NA	NA	NA	NA	NA	NA	NA	NA	NA	NA	NA	NA	NA	NA	NA
Kaneohe CDP	NA	NA	NA	NA	NA	NA	NA	NA	NA	NA	NA	NA	NA	NA	NA
Kaneohe Station CDP	NA	NA	NA	NA	NA	NA	NA	NA	NA	NA	NA	NA	NA	NA	NA
Kapaa CDP	NA	NA	NA	NA	NA	NA	NA	NA	NA	NA	NA	NA	NA	NA	NA
Kapolei CDP	NA	NA	NA	NA	NA	NA	NA	NA	NA	NA	NA	NA	NA	NA	NA
Kihei CDP	NA	NA	NA	NA	NA	NA	NA	NA	NA	NA	NA	NA	NA	NA	NA
Lahaina CDP	NA	NA	NA	NA	NA	NA	NA	NA	NA	NA	NA	NA	NA	NA	NA
Maili CDP	NA	NA	NA	NA	NA	NA	NA	NA	NA	NA	NA	NA	NA	NA	NA
Makakilo CDP	NA	NA	NA	NA	NA	NA	NA	NA	NA	NA	NA	NA	NA	NA	NA
Mililani Mauka CDP	NA	NA	NA	NA	NA	NA	NA	NA	NA	NA	NA	NA	NA	NA	NA
Mililani Town CDP	NA	NA	NA	NA	NA	NA	NA	NA	NA	NA	NA	NA	NA	NA	NA
Nanakuli CDP	NA	NA	NA	NA	NA	NA	NA	NA	NA	NA	NA	NA	NA	NA	NA
Ocean Pointe CDP	NA	NA	NA	NA	NA	NA	NA	NA	NA	NA	NA	NA	NA	NA	NA
Pearl City CDP	NA	NA	NA	NA	NA	NA	NA	NA	NA	NA	NA	NA	NA	NA	NA
Royal Kunia CDP	NA	NA	NA	NA	NA	NA	NA	NA	NA	NA	NA	NA	NA	NA	NA
Schofield Barracks CDP	NA	NA	NA	NA	NA	NA	NA	NA	NA	NA	NA	NA	NA	NA	NA
Urban Honolulu CDP	NA	NA	NA	NA	NA	NA	NA	NA	NA	NA	NA	NA	NA	NA	NA
Wahiawa CDP	NA	NA	NA	NA	NA	NA	NA	NA	NA	NA	NA	NA	NA	NA	NA
Waianae CDP	NA	NA	NA	NA	NA	NA	NA	NA	NA	NA	NA	NA	NA	NA	NA

1 Data for serious crimes have not been adjusted for underreporting. This may affect comparability between geographic areas over time.
2 Per 100,000 population estimated by the FBI. 3 Based on population estimated as of July 1 of the year shown.

Items 15–29

Table B.   Incorporated Places, Census Designated Places (CDPs), and Minor Civil Divisions (MCDs) of 10,000 or More Population — **Land Area, Population, and Households, and Employment**

STATE City, town, township, borough, or CDP (county if applicable)	Land area 2010 (sq mi)	Total persons 2010	Total persons 2019	Percent change 2010–2019	Persons per square mile, 2019	Percent foreign born	Percent living in the same house as previous year	Median household income	Percent of households with income below poverty level	Median value of owner-occupied housing units	Percent in civilian labor force	Unemploy-ment rate	Family households	One person households
	1	2	3	4	5	6	7	8	9	10	11	12	13	14
HAWAII—Con.														
Wailuku CDP	5.27	15,313	NA	NA	NA	12.0	83.3	73,576	10.7	544,900	69.7	6.0	67.1	28.2
Waimalu CDP	1.83	13,730	NA	NA	NA	20.5	86.0	81,054	5.9	446,800	59.9	3.1	61.5	31.5
Waimea CDP	39.29	9,212	NA	NA	NA	18.4	81.9	91,074	13.8	449,200	66.0	4.3	72.9	20.0
Waipahu CDP	2.65	38,216	NA	NA	NA	42.3	89.7	78,204	11.9	626,600	61.7	4.3	82.7	13.8
Waipio CDP	1.25	11,674	NA	NA	NA	16.9	85.5	89,882	6.9	536,300	68.7	2.0	76.1	19.3
IDAHO	82645.13	1,567,657	1,787,065	14.0	21.6	6.0	82.8	55,785	12.9	212,300	62.4	4.3	67.6	26.3
Ammon city	7.59	13,971	17,115	22.5	2254.9	3.2	83.4	67,545	6.7	199,400	66.1	3.1	73.3	23.8
Blackfoot city	5.92	11,975	12,034	0.5	2032.8	3.2	83.7	48,750	15.2	136,700	64.4	5.3	65.7	30.5
Boise City city	83.67	209,384	228,959	9.3	2736.5	6.4	82.2	60,035	13.2	253,400	68.3	4.5	56.7	34.1
Burley city	6.24	10,286	10,582	2.9	1695.8	13.3	80.4	48,265	21.2	128,100	60.9	2.3	73.5	22.3
Caldwell city	22.61	46,346	58,481	26.2	2586.5	11.3	78.3	49,046	16.8	152,400	63.6	6.8	70.3	23.4
Chubbuck city	5.90	13,982	15,588	11.5	2642.0	5.8	81.5	59,459	13.5	176,300	63.8	4.6	66.3	28.1
Coeur d'Alene city	16.06	44,168	52,414	18.7	3263.6	2.9	78.7	51,073	14.4	234,900	64.0	4.1	57.8	32.6
Eagle city	30.57	19,982	29,796	49.1	974.7	4.7	88.2	92,807	7.6	426,000	55.4	2.0	76.2	21.3
Garden City city	4.08	10,976	11,969	9.0	2933.6	5.0	82.1	49,318	15.5	238,100	56.6	3.6	51.4	40.1
Hayden city	10.42	13,301	15,434	16.0	1481.2	1.9	85.3	56,930	7.3	256,100	58.3	4.2	68.9	26.4
Idaho Falls city	24.00	57,833	62,888	8.7	2620.3	5.8	78.6	53,148	13.8	164,500	63.3	3.9	66.0	28.8
Jerome city	5.58	10,873	11,994	10.3	2149.5	15.7	78.3	45,148	18.5	128,800	67.6	1.8	67.9	23.3
Kuna city	19.78	15,451	22,257	44.0	1125.2	6.8	82.9	68,017	8.4	207,700	78.1	3.4	78.7	17.3
Lewiston city	17.30	31,891	32,788	2.8	1895.3	2.2	83.5	56,479	13.1	189,400	62.5	3.3	63.2	30.3
Meridian city	33.97	76,986	114,161	48.3	3360.6	5.8	85.5	71,389	8.8	274,900	67.4	3.7	69.8	26.4
Moscow city	6.91	23,802	25,702	8.0	3719.5	8.2	69.3	41,896	23.6	229,900	64.7	5.1	44.7	33.6
Mountain Home city	6.06	14,216	14,562	2.4	2403.0	10.4	77.8	49,404	13.1	144,200	50.5	6.6	62.9	27.0
Nampa city	32.82	81,879	99,277	21.2	3024.9	7.6	80.3	48,846	14.2	167,200	64.5	5.6	65.9	27.3
Pocatello city	33.24	54,236	56,637	4.4	1703.9	4.2	79.2	46,617	18.4	148,200	61.0	5.8	60.2	29.6
Post Falls city	15.13	27,787	36,250	30.5	2395.9	2.1	83.1	54,021	13.2	218,100	66.2	2.9	69.8	24.9
Rexburg city	10.01	25,490	29,400	15.3	2937.1	5.6	55.3	31,128	36.5	211,700	67.1	7.0	80.2	12.7
Twin Falls city	19.22	44,320	50,197	13.3	2611.7	10.8	80.8	50,739	14.6	162,000	67.6	3.0	65.9	27.7
ILLINOIS	55513.72	12,831,572	12,671,821	-1.2	228.3	14.1	87.3	65,886	12.3	194,500	65.1	5.9	64.2	29.6
Addison village	9.84	37,084	36,482	-1.6	3707.5	32.0	89.7	67,337	11.5	250,100	70.2	3.7	70.4	24.1
Algonquin village	12.30	30,065	30,897	2.8	2512.0	12.2	90.8	102,856	4.5	255,700	74.5	5.0	76.0	19.0
Alsip village	6.53	19,271	18,709	-2.9	2865.1	10.0	93.4	63,312	9.7	171,400	68.7	7.8	59.9	35.6
Alton city	15.50	27,932	26,208	-6.2	1690.8	1.5	85.2	40,211	21.9	79,900	61.4	9.2	53.5	38.5
Antioch village	8.20	14,475	14,175	-2.1	1728.7	5.2	90.8	96,069	6.1	221,100	70.1	3.2	78.7	17.1
Arlington Heights village	16.61	75,185	74,760	-0.6	4500.9	19.5	89.0	96,340	5.5	358,300	66.4	3.2	65.9	29.2
Aurora city	45.01	197,975	197,757	-0.1	4393.6	25.4	85.2	71,749	10.2	184,400	72.3	5.2	73.3	20.7
Barrington village	4.61	10,320	10,217	-1.0	2216.3	10.0	87.5	117,931	6.2	483,400	63.4	3.2	71.1	27.5
Bartlett village	15.75	41,236	40,647	-1.4	2580.8	19.8	89.8	108,592	4.3	279,200	71.6	3.0	78.9	18.5
Batavia city	10.53	26,238	26,420	0.7	2509.0	5.8	87.2	93,789	5.9	304,400	71.4	4.2	71.5	23.8
Beach Park village	7.07	13,630	13,701	0.5	1937.9	16.1	92.6	71,867	9.1	150,900	68.5	6.1	77.4	18.0
Belleville city	23.22	44,301	40,897	-7.7	1761.3	2.0	84.9	48,099	13.9	93,700	64.9	5.7	53.9	39.5
Bellwood village	2.40	19,055	18,672	-2.0	7780.0	8.3	89.4	56,557	12.2	151,200	65.2	8.9	69.6	28.9
Belvidere city	12.07	25,652	25,143	-2.0	2083.1	14.7	87.8	51,166	15.2	110,300	64.8	7.1	67.3	27.3
Bensenville village	5.48	18,348	18,044	-1.7	3292.7	34.9	88.7	62,756	9.6	217,300	70.6	4.0	65.5	27.7
Berwyn city	3.90	56,653	54,391	-4.0	13946.4	27.3	90.5	62,758	12.0	211,700	67.7	4.2	69.6	23.1
Bloomingdale village	6.77	22,059	21,779	-1.3	3217.0	18.8	87.5	86,350	6.5	302,400	68.2	4.4	64.4	30.0
Bloomington city	27.13	76,724	77,330	0.8	2850.4	10.1	83.4	67,507	13.9	168,300	66.4	3.5	59.8	32.3
Blue Island city	4.07	23,701	22,899	-3.4	5626.3	22.0	92.5	48,398	16.6	122,700	64.6	10.0	65.5	29.5
Bolingbrook village	24.62	73,365	74,545	1.6	3027.8	23.1	90.7	91,290	6.9	223,600	73.5	4.2	79.3	16.4
Boulder Hill CDP	1.46	8,108	NA	NA	NA	5.9	87.4	67,124	6.4	161,400	69.4	6.9	77.0	19.0
Bourbonnais village	9.47	18,690	19,462	4.1	2055.1	5.3	83.7	73,882	9.8	173,700	63.3	3.6	63.8	30.2
Bradley village	6.93	15,895	15,314	-3.7	2209.8	5.1	92.8	60,012	8.5	135,200	67.1	5.7	66.6	27.3
Bridgeview village	4.15	16,439	16,096	-2.1	3878.6	26.6	90.7	55,687	16.6	183,400	60.4	7.1	69.7	25.4
Brookfield village	3.06	18,974	18,310	-3.5	5983.7	9.9	90.1	82,435	7.1	245,200	70.0	3.1	68.0	27.7
Buffalo Grove village	9.49	41,503	40,494	-2.4	4267.0	32.9	88.4	115,951	4.5	332,300	72.5	3.5	74.6	23.0
Burbank city	4.17	28,925	28,289	-2.2	6783.9	26.1	89.9	62,573	9.6	192,600	64.2	6.4	73.3	23.7
Burr Ridge village	7.07	10,535	10,758	2.1	1521.6	23.9	95.4	159,335	5.4	686,600	58.2	3.2	77.5	20.2
Cahokia village	9.76	15,238	13,880	-8.9	1422.1	1.7	87.1	35,663	25.0	47,900	58.8	13.4	64.3	29.2
Calumet City city	7.18	37,116	35,913	-3.2	5001.8	10.1	87.3	44,456	16.8	106,000	65.4	16.9	61.9	35.5
Campton Hills village	16.89	11,065	11,091	0.2	656.7	3.4	91.2	154,375	2.8	426,000	69.0	3.4	88.9	7.6
Canton city	7.86	14,715	13,506	-8.2	1718.3	2.0	79.9	44,299	17.6	90,200	47.8	6.4	55.1	37.6
Carbondale city	17.39	26,414	25,083	-5.0	1442.4	9.5	58.1	22,152	41.6	117,500	55.0	10.0	34.5	46.7
Carol Stream village	9.11	39,541	39,203	-0.9	4303.3	24.1	87.6	82,062	8.5	247,600	71.9	5.3	72.5	20.5
Carpentersville village	7.87	37,669	37,254	-1.1	4733.7	27.9	89.4	68,997	13.9	171,600	74.0	5.8	77.1	17.4
Cary village	6.23	18,341	18,067	-1.5	2900.0	9.0	90.8	100,339	5.0	232,500	74.5	4.1	77.7	19.5
Centralia city	8.19	13,029	12,210	-6.3	1490.8	1.4	83.4	37,675	20.8	69,400	56.9	10.1	52.1	40.0
Champaign city	22.83	81,246	88,909	9.4	3894.4	14.7	73.9	48,415	23.3	161,800	61.5	4.6	44.0	40.4
Channahon village	15.76	12,578	13,239	5.3	840.0	3.0	91.3	91,897	3.6	224,500	69.5	3.8	83.3	13.4
Charleston city	8.88	21,844	20,117	-7.9	2265.4	3.7	64.0	40,863	31.5	104,900	61.8	5.5	48.1	34.4
Chatham village	7.30	11,732	13,008	10.9	1781.9	2.8	86.6	88,822	4.8	188,900	71.5	1.8	73.7	21.0
Chicago city	227.37	2,695,652	2,693,976	-0.1	11848.4	20.6	85.0	58,247	17.3	258,000	66.9	8.1	53.1	37.2
Chicago Heights city	10.28	30,367	29,322	-3.4	2852.3	14.9	91.8	50,186	22.7	105,900	62.7	13.1	67.5	28.4
Chicago Ridge village	2.27	14,304	13,928	-2.6	6135.7	24.1	88.9	48,886	14.9	160,500	59.5	6.6	64.6	32.1
Cicero town	5.87	84,241	80,796	-4.1	13764.2	38.8	91.9	49,367	16.2	165,100	65.5	5.3	78.8	16.4
Collinsville city	14.74	25,654	24,395	-4.9	1655.0	3.8	83.2	53,490	11.8	127,300	69.0	6.7	60.8	31.8
Columbia city	10.31	9,698	10,513	8.4	1019.7	3.0	90.9	98,977	6.4	217,300	72.2	3.3	73.6	24.2
Country Club Hills city	4.98	16,783	16,482	-1.8	3309.6	5.1	93.5	61,982	11.5	131,800	60.6	16.7	65.5	30.8
Crest Hill city	9.02	20,800	20,376	-2.0	2259.0	12.2	82.0	56,616	8.3	169,200	51.8	4.5	60.4	33.8
Crestwood village	3.05	10,948	10,706	-2.2	3510.2	7.5	86.2	61,132	8.6	154,300	58.6	5.1	49.2	43.4
Crystal Lake city	18.89	40,752	39,829	-2.3	2108.5	9.9	88.9	87,578	5.9	221,300	71.1	4.4	73.5	22.2
Danville city	17.98	33,033	30,479	-7.7	1695.2	3.6	86.7	36,172	25.0	66,700	48.3	9.3	57.8	37.2
Darien city	6.20	21,951	21,628	-1.5	3488.4	17.9	93.8	96,275	6.0	330,000	64.5	3.7	67.8	26.6
Decatur city	42.32	76,131	70,746	-7.1	1671.7	2.0	81.5	42,701	20.6	83,000	57.7	9.2	54.3	39.9

STATE City, town, township, borough, or CDP (county if applicable)	Serious crimes known to police, 2018[1] Violent crime Number	Rate[2]	Property crime Number	Rate[2]	New residential construction authorized by building permits, 2019 Value ($1,000)	Number of housing units	Percent single family	Local government finance, 2017 General revenue Total (mil dol)	Intergovernmental Total (mil dol)	Percent from state gov.	Taxes per capita[3]	General expenditure Total (mil dol)	Per capita[3] Total	Capital outlays	Debt outstanding (mil dol)
	15	16	17	18	19	20	21	22	23	24	25	26	27	28	29
HAWAII—Con.															
Wailuku CDP	NA	NA	NA	NA	NA	NA	NA	NA	NA	NA	NA	NA	NA	NA	NA
Waimalu CDP	NA	NA	NA	NA	NA	NA	NA	NA	NA	NA	NA	NA	NA	NA	NA
Waimea CDP	NA	NA	NA	NA	NA	NA	NA	NA	NA	NA	NA	NA	NA	NA	NA
Waipahu CDP	NA	NA	NA	NA	NA	NA	NA	NA	NA	NA	NA	NA	NA	NA	NA
Waipio CDP	NA	NA	NA	NA	NA	NA	NA	NA	NA	NA	NA	NA	NA	NA	NA
IDAHO	3,983	227	25,636	1,461	3,401,488	17,716	73.3	X	X	X	X	X	X	X	X
Ammon city	NA	NA	NA	NA	35,137	175	100.0	10.1	1.6	100.0	179	8.1	522	84	32.7
Blackfoot city	40	336	315	2,645	4,740	23	100.0	14.9	4.3	84.0	351	14.3	1,203	126	4.4
Boise City city	635	277	4,627	2,018	323,624	1,581	44.1	349.8	37.5	63.7	640	321.0	1,410	270	109.3
Burley city	NA	NA	NA	NA	6,042	44	100.0	17.3	2.5	84.0	542	17.7	1,693	0	26.6
Caldwell city	183	327	1,202	2,149	121,353	931	79.4	48.2	7.2	57.6	322	45.9	838	154	25.4
Chubbuck city	55	367	678	4,521	10,728	116	82.8	13.2	1.9	89.7	355	10.2	682	37	17.9
Coeur d'Alene city	188	364	972	1,882	98,192	574	49.5	59.1	10.6	56.7	529	58.8	1,162	208	35.7
Eagle city	NA	NA	NA	NA	208,877	870	52.9	7.0	2.1	100.0	172	6.0	229	0	3.4
Garden City city	82	682	354	2,944	3,640	38	100.0	11.7	1.3	100.0	437	12.2	1,027	20	1.3
Hayden city	NA	NA	NA	NA	34,918	150	88.7	10.5	2.4	84.3	143	10.7	731	21	7.9
Idaho Falls city	206	334	960	1,557	49,058	314	100.0	87.3	18.6	87.5	538	79.1	1,280	271	29.3
Jerome city	31	264	179	1,525	6,455	49	100.0	13.3	1.5	100.0	397	8.7	748	0	22.3
Kuna city	NA	NA	NA	NA	131,836	665	90.1	10.9	1.1	77.6	100	8.3	427	0	0.0
Lewiston city	48	146	1,007	3,056	13,542	67	62.7	55.4	11.6	100.0	649	51.2	1,565	84	4.2
Meridian city	165	159	1,260	1,214	602,167	3,024	71.5	63.0	7.8	99.7	343	66.9	665	177	0.6
Moscow city	13	51	394	1,555	13,956	64	59.4	27.9	6.3	49.1	287	25.9	1,019	161	10.3
Mountain Home city	38	267	260	1,828	9,108	56	100.0	14.7	1.9	84.5	440	11.3	793	81	10.6
Nampa city	268	281	2,424	2,541	207,391	1,755	63.4	104.6	12.6	95.8	508	89.0	950	93	0.0
Pocatello city	209	378	1,568	2,835	12,629	117	91.5	72.2	16.3	60.3	577	60.0	1,085	85	40.0
Post Falls city	69	202	578	1,693	170,305	1,161	45.0	29.7	6.2	100.0	332	20.5	617	37	5.9
Rexburg city	5	17	135	469	32,882	242	19.4	22.7	4.8	99.7	144	23.7	830	103	6.9
Twin Falls city	225	451	1,180	2,364	84,831	585	60.7	60.0	12.5	47.2	631	45.4	922	176	109.0
ILLINOIS	51,490	404	246,264	1,933	3,726,457	20,524	42.6	X	X	X	X	X	X	X	X
Addison village	61	166	464	1,261	6,351	28	100.0	45.9	15.4	92.6	465	64.9	1,756	476	59.2
Algonquin village	27	87	265	851	6,470	49	100.0	27.7	12.9	94.2	418	36.0	1,165	353	29.9
Alsip village	24	126	427	2,242	0	0	0.0	33.9	7.4	100.0	925	32.5	1,704	0	94.3
Alton city	171	644	994	3,742	180	1	100.0	54.8	21.1	68.7	632	70.2	2,627	1106	12.1
Antioch village	20	141	165	1,162	5,303	35	100.0	15.6	5.8	98.5	461	15.8	1,111	129	26.0
Arlington Heights village	28	37	628	830	17,848	60	61.7	183.9	38.4	97.1	1,737	170.3	2,257	174	66.3
Aurora city	538	267	2,301	1,143	20,788	74	97.3	231.6	70.3	91.8	702	236.7	1,181	81	1034.8
Barrington village	1	10	124	1,205	4,440	25	32.0	25.2	6.9	94.1	690	23.7	2,305	255	52.0
Bartlett village	21	51	169	411	6,444	19	100.0	38.1	8.1	93.7	486	59.3	1,441	374	77.8
Batavia city	34	128	369	1,387	22,151	96	16.7	35.0	10.7	94.0	626	34.5	1,302	226	35.9
Beach Park village	NA	NA	NA	NA	0	0	0.0	5.1	2.4	91.4	130	5.3	380	129	2.4
Belleville city	171	414	1,261	3,055	9,240	49	100.0	59.5	21.2	100.0	595	77.8	1,865	675	74.5
Bellwood village	NA	NA	NA	NA	280	1	100.0	29.5	3.7	97.9	1,088	29.5	1,555	81	168.8
Belvidere city	60	239	270	1,075	1,037	9	100.0	21.4	7.3	100.0	358	23.8	946	104	32.4
Bensenville village	20	109	272	1,484	550	3	100.0	30.0	11.8	70.2	662	27.4	1,492	320	81.6
Berwyn city	191	345	818	1,477	899	8	100.0	72.7	16.4	86.9	825	76.1	1,373	57	264.9
Bloomingdale village	32	145	488	2,217	11,867	49	53.1	28.7	11.8	97.8	475	28.7	1,303	233	24.0
Bloomington city	339	434	1,193	1,528	9,420	76	50.0	136.1	29.6	98.3	907	131.3	1,681	115	257.7
Blue Island city	93	399	288	1,236	0	0	0.0	25.5	7.1	90.4	502	24.5	1,052	177	4.2
Bolingbrook village	112	148	592	785	10,897	66	100.0	105.9	26.6	90.5	720	104.4	1,392	106	236.7
Boulder Hill CDP	NA	NA	NA	NA	NA	NA	NA	NA	NA	NA	NA	NA	NA	NA	NA
Bourbonnais village	33	180	154	838	6,160	31	100.0	14.3	5.9	91.8	87	15.7	803	130	17.4
Bradley village	17	111	442	2,894	2,361	12	100.0	15.7	8.4	99.7	298	16.4	1,071	25	23.5
Bridgeview village	30	184	319	1,955	1,300	8	100.0	38.3	14.8	86.3	911	42.4	2,597	187	300.6
Brookfield village	NA	NA	NA	NA	850	6	0.0	23.3	4.6	90.2	722	27.5	1,475	278	52.6
Buffalo Grove village	7	17	268	651	903	2	100.0	53.0	11.7	100.0	624	54.5	1,323	138	68.8
Burbank city	60	209	242	841	935	6	100.0	22.8	7.3	100.0	475	23.7	823	87	83.9
Burr Ridge village	3	28	190	1,751	21,297	32	100.0	10.3	4.0	87.1	411	9.7	902	47	6.4
Cahokia village	75	536	604	4,313	0	0	0.0	11.3	3.8	92.3	430	11.1	784	35	1.5
Calumet City city	187	512	980	2,681	0	0	0.0	53.3	13.3	80.0	940	55.7	1,524	144	44.4
Campton Hills village	1	9	17	150	5,687	22	100.0	3.0	1.7	91.3	103	2.6	230	4	0.4
Canton city	NA	NA	NA	NA	270	2	100.0	14.5	5.1	100.0	382	10.7	774	16	13.5
Carbondale city	111	430	760	2,944	620	4	100.0	38.1	13.0	87.3	627	37.7	1,473	109	72.0
Carol Stream village	33	83	411	1,027	200	1	100.0	33.4	14.2	98.0	377	28.8	723	3	7.0
Carpentersville village	34	89	496	1,298	0	0	0.0	41.7	11.9	82.1	565	41.3	1,088	116	99.4
Cary village	20	112	110	617	3,297	19	100.0	10.9	3.8	100.0	252	9.2	512	13	6.3
Centralia city	157	1,269	499	4,033	1,000	12	100.0	14.9	5.2	95.9	260	15.1	1,221	94	4.5
Champaign city	602	682	1,998	2,262	118,365	846	8.4	109.6	36.0	85.2	696	104.6	1,191	206	136.1
Channahon village	9	70	58	452	19,900	104	92.3	19.7	3.2	100.0	872	18.7	1,465	97	35.8
Charleston city	29	139	61	292	389	1	100.0	19.4	7.4	90.6	300	19.2	944	75	8.2
Chatham village	18	141	82	642	16,678	100	32.0	7.6	2.3	99.0	187	11.9	929	60	13.2
Chicago city	27,357	1,006	86,513	3,182	913,567	7,914	5.2	8260.8	1710.7	63.4	1,314	7769.2	2,866	464	23539.6
Chicago Heights city	260	872	NA	NA	0	0	0.0	43.6	9.9	86.9	901	45.9	1,538	99	182.5
Chicago Ridge village	18	127	358	2,527	605	4	100.0	19.4	2.2	100.0	1,029	22.9	1,617	116	49.3
Cicero town	314	382	1,770	2,150	214	1	100.0	107.6	24.4	88.4	823	129.2	1,568	206	299.4
Collinsville city	NA	NA	NA	NA	2,069	14	100.0	33.3	17.0	95.0	355	32.7	1,321	156	41.3
Columbia city	NA	NA	NA	NA	13,025	93	21.5	10.8	3.7	86.7	363	8.8	854	173	5.9
Country Club Hills city	71	429	589	3,556	0	0	0.0	28.5	5.1	90.3	1,070	26.8	1,595	57	82.3
Crest Hill city	42	198	203	957	0	0	0.0	13.0	5.5	93.0	271	14.3	694	136	21.1
Crestwood village	NA	NA	NA	NA	1,060	7	42.9	18.1	9.8	99.8	380	21.4	1,973	614	48.4
Crystal Lake city	38	94	648	1,606	19,238	95	93.7	55.5	17.9	99.4	618	53.7	1,341	118	45.3
Danville city	559	1,792	1,508	4,833	1,050	6	100.0	49.7	31.1	87.9	319	48.1	1,535	60	5.3
Darien city	25	113	231	1,047	1,100	4	100.0	16.4	9.0	98.0	301	13.0	593	20	26.0
Decatur city	358	500	2,050	2,862	0	0	0.0	91.9	32.5	94.6	544	86.9	1,210	6	133.5

1   Data for serious crimes have not been adjusted for underreporting. This may affect comparability between geographic areas over time.
2   Per 100,000 population estimated by the FBI.   3   Based on population estimated as of July 1 of the year shown.

Table B. Incorporated Places, Census Designated Places (CDPs), and Minor Civil Divisions (MCDs) of 10,000 or More Population — **Land Area, Population, and Households, and Employment**

STATE City, town, township, borough, or CDP (county if applicable)	Land area 2010 (sq mi)	Population: Total persons 2010	Population: Total persons 2019	Population: Percent change 2010–2019	Population: Persons per square mile, 2019	Population characteristics 2015–2019: Percent foreign born	Population characteristics 2015–2019: Percent living in the same house as previous year	Income and poverty 2015–2019: Median household income	Income and poverty 2015–2019: Percent of households with income below poverty level	Median value of owner-occupied housing units	Employment, 2015–2019: Percent in civilian labor force	Employment, 2015–2019: Unemployment rate	Households, 2015–2019 (percent of households): Family households	Households, 2015–2019 (percent of households): One person households
	1	2	3	4	5	6	7	8	9	10	11	12	13	14
ILLINOIS—Con.														
Deerfield village	5.53	18,227	18,646	2.3	3371.8	10.0	91.9	153,431	3.6	518,500	68.3	2.7	76.4	21.1
DeKalb city	16.14	44,123	42,847	-2.9	2654.7	9.3	70.1	45,020	29.4	157,900	65.9	9.5	50.3	31.0
Des Plaines city	14.23	58,383	58,899	0.9	4139.1	32.5	90.6	69,760	9.1	256,700	66.8	4.5	65.7	29.0
Dixon city	7.75	15,766	15,115	-4.1	1950.3	3.4	80.4	47,171	17.3	90,700	50.8	3.3	52.2	39.7
Dolton village	4.57	23,074	22,348	-3.1	4890.2	2.9	85.6	46,614	20.4	102,600	63.1	17.6	70.9	26.8
Downers Grove village	14.52	48,882	49,057	0.4	3378.6	11.6	89.1	94,893	6.8	353,100	66.4	4.1	62.8	33.1
East Moline city	14.60	21,311	20,645	-3.1	1414.0	13.0	81.3	53,660	13.7	110,800	58.5	6.1	63.2	32.2
East Peoria city	20.21	23,454	22,546	-3.9	1115.6	3.1	87.6	58,984	7.9	139,800	63.3	5.0	62.2	31.4
East St. Louis city	13.91	26,935	26,047	-3.3	1872.5	0.9	91.6	24,343	38.2	54,500	52.8	18.3	50.6	46.3
Edwardsville city	19.94	24,410	25,233	3.4	1265.4	4.9	75.2	77,411	13.8	228,300	65.7	6.4	61.4	24.5
Effingham city	10.23	12,340	12,511	1.4	1223.0	4.1	77.0	47,582	15.6	126,800	62.8	2.9	57.7	35.4
Elgin city	37.50	108,219	110,849	2.4	2956.0	26.5	89.7	69,041	11.1	186,000	68.4	5.7	71.9	23.6
Elk Grove Village village	11.62	33,383	32,400	-2.9	2788.3	22.2	89.0	81,895	4.1	271,900	67.9	3.9	66.2	29.9
Elmhurst city	10.26	44,136	46,746	5.9	4556.1	9.5	90.0	118,609	4.3	432,600	67.5	4.1	73.6	22.9
Elmwood Park village	1.91	24,883	24,098	-3.2	12616.8	27.1	89.9	59,963	9.8	258,000	67.6	4.5	68.0	29.1
Evanston city	7.78	74,483	73,473	-1.4	9443.8	19.0	81.8	78,904	12.6	391,400	61.1	4.2	53.6	36.0
Evergreen Park village	3.16	19,848	19,147	-3.5	6059.2	8.5	91.4	75,657	8.5	193,300	64.8	3.6	69.8	26.9
Fairview Heights city	11.43	17,078	16,303	-4.5	1426.3	3.5	83.8	64,495	10.5	135,400	65.5	5.2	59.1	36.1
Forest Park village	2.40	14,167	13,704	-3.3	5710.0	10.6	80.8	62,664	9.7	234,100	71.4	5.4	44.6	46.6
Fox Lake village	7.83	10,667	10,451	-2.0	1334.7	6.0	86.8	60,230	8.2	161,100	61.9	6.0	54.2	36.2
Frankfort village	16.09	17,808	19,373	8.8	1204.0	5.4	92.5	139,145	2.8	384,900	68.1	3.5	84.2	15.3
Franklin Park village	4.77	18,311	17,627	-3.7	3695.4	32.2	95.6	63,971	12.3	203,800	67.4	6.0	69.2	27.2
Freeport city	11.65	25,634	23,775	-7.3	2040.8	3.2	81.4	39,975	17.1	72,100	59.3	10.5	58.3	37.9
Gages Lake CDP	2.98	10,198	NA	NA	NA	11.4	85.7	96,123	4.0	231,800	72.1	7.2	73.6	21.4
Galesburg city	17.74	32,195	30,197	-6.2	1702.2	4.8	89.4	36,547	20.1	75,900	49.6	6.3	49.8	42.7
Geneva city	9.93	21,592	21,809	1.0	2196.3	6.7	90.6	111,916	5.0	338,300	66.9	3.7	75.9	20.8
Glen Carbon village	10.26	12,917	12,850	-0.5	1252.4	4.3	88.1	89,236	9.3	226,500	64.6	4.0	67.6	24.3
Glendale Heights village	5.42	34,296	33,617	-2.0	6202.4	33.7	83.5	68,495	7.7	194,400	74.6	4.6	71.1	22.3
Glen Ellyn village	6.79	27,773	27,714	-0.2	4081.6	9.8	87.6	110,678	7.2	453,900	64.7	3.3	69.0	27.6
Glenview village	14.02	44,726	47,308	5.8	3374.3	21.2	90.3	115,198	5.1	499,900	59.6	3.6	73.0	25.2
Godfrey village	34.40	17,989	17,400	-3.3	505.8	1.7	84.7	73,238	6.3	148,300	62.3	3.1	67.7	27.0
Granite City city	19.25	29,798	28,158	-5.5	1462.8	3.1	87.5	51,469	18.2	83,500	60.4	7.7	61.4	32.1
Grayslake village	10.98	21,053	20,725	-1.6	1887.5	13.1	85.3	97,265	8.6	235,400	72.7	5.3	67.8	24.6
Gurnee village	13.51	31,238	30,378	-2.8	2248.6	15.8	86.9	96,104	6.2	259,500	72.7	4.9	67.8	26.6
Hanover Park village	6.34	38,092	37,426	-1.7	5903.2	32.1	88.4	76,615	9.5	195,300	72.5	4.8	82.1	14.1
Harvey city	6.21	25,265	24,408	-3.4	3930.4	12.4	89.3	30,306	31.5	73,700	57.3	15.1	61.9	34.5
Hazel Crest village	3.39	14,009	13,565	-3.2	4001.5	3.6	88.7	54,347	14.1	113,200	61.3	10.3	64.3	33.1
Herrin city	9.67	12,522	12,687	1.3	1312.0	3.4	84.4	44,989	17.3	87,700	56.3	6.2	59.2	33.0
Hickory Hills city	2.83	14,049	13,710	-2.4	4844.5	29.3	93.0	65,226	10.1	229,700	63.4	5.0	71.0	25.8
Highland city	6.70	9,928	9,834	-0.9	1467.8	2.6	82.7	59,922	9.4	152,100	66.1	4.9	63.1	30.7
Highland Park city	12.24	29,745	29,515	-0.8	2411.4	12.0	88.4	150,269	5.1	584,500	64.4	3.3	75.4	21.6
Hinsdale village	4.62	16,845	17,637	4.7	3817.5	11.9	87.9	203,368	3.3	884,700	62.5	2.9	82.0	16.8
Hoffman Estates village	21.06	51,891	50,932	-1.8	2418.4	30.0	89.3	91,917	5.2	283,300	70.5	3.4	77.7	18.2
Homer Glen village	22.13	24,210	24,472	1.1	1105.8	11.7	93.5	106,818	5.0	330,600	66.1	3.9	81.5	15.8
Homewood village	5.22	19,307	18,703	-3.1	3583.0	6.9	92.2	74,450	8.0	163,100	63.9	4.2	68.9	29.6
Huntley village	14.29	24,312	27,228	12.0	1905.4	10.2	89.0	75,100	8.7	251,400	53.9	2.3	65.4	32.0
Jacksonville city	10.56	19,444	18,603	-4.3	1761.6	2.4	78.7	43,976	15.1	103,900	54.5	7.3	55.1	39.3
Joliet city	64.15	147,308	147,344	0.0	2296.9	14.7	88.2	70,509	10.9	181,100	70.6	6.0	70.9	24.3
Justice village	2.84	12,925	12,608	-2.5	4439.4	26.2	89.4	51,017	15.2	180,600	66.5	6.7	68.2	30.3
Kankakee city	15.03	27,540	26,024	-5.5	1731.5	9.1	90.4	37,894	27.7	88,500	55.7	6.9	60.3	33.3
Kewanee city	6.60	12,919	12,339	-4.5	1869.5	3.7	93.9	41,664	19.0	60,000	56.8	7.6	61.3	33.6
La Grange village	2.53	15,554	15,322	-1.5	6056.1	6.0	90.5	123,965	3.8	501,700	62.7	3.9	73.7	24.9
La Grange Park village	2.23	13,580	13,178	-3.0	5909.4	7.8	89.3	105,783	5.4	361,500	66.5	4.0	69.6	27.9
Lake Forest city	17.20	19,379	19,446	0.3	1130.6	14.2	86.0	172,165	3.4	842,900	55.6	4.0	74.2	23.9
Lake in the Hills village	10.21	28,948	28,634	-1.1	2804.5	10.5	88.0	92,872	5.2	227,100	76.9	3.2	77.6	18.0
Lake Zurich village	6.83	19,693	19,877	0.9	2910.2	18.1	92.5	119,349	3.2	337,300	73.7	2.8	83.3	11.8
Lansing village	7.46	28,353	27,402	-3.4	3673.2	9.0	87.8	53,940	13.1	129,900	64.2	11.0	63.4	32.9
Lemont village	8.27	16,051	17,291	7.7	2090.8	14.2	94.1	99,724	5.6	363,000	64.2	3.6	76.8	20.6
Libertyville village	8.81	20,405	20,205	-1.0	2293.4	10.8	88.3	134,110	4.3	447,900	66.5	3.3	74.2	22.4
Lincoln city	6.25	14,549	13,524	-7.0	2163.8	1.7	82.8	48,931	12.4	88,300	58.7	8.1	57.4	36.0
Lincolnwood village	2.69	12,590	12,245	-2.7	4552.0	34.3	92.1	95,030	7.8	396,100	53.3	3.7	74.0	24.8
Lindenhurst village	4.52	14,577	14,216	-2.5	3145.1	7.8	90.2	108,044	3.8	219,700	72.1	5.9	75.6	20.5
Lisle village	6.90	22,552	23,270	3.2	3372.5	16.1	82.6	90,588	6.1	356,900	70.2	4.8	57.0	36.0
Lockport city	11.38	24,819	25,615	3.2	2250.9	7.2	89.7	90,475	6.3	242,600	71.6	3.4	75.0	21.4
Lombard village	10.21	43,466	44,303	1.9	4339.2	15.4	85.0	82,461	7.1	261,200	67.7	4.0	63.6	30.6
Loves Park city	16.42	23,994	23,371	-2.6	1423.3	5.2	89.0	59,059	11.7	111,900	68.8	7.2	62.8	30.2
Lyons village	2.19	10,733	10,372	-3.4	4736.1	19.0	89.3	60,168	10.3	169,800	65.8	6.1	61.9	35.2
McHenry city	14.46	27,039	27,061	0.1	1871.4	9.4	89.4	75,811	6.8	181,300	68.0	3.9	68.9	25.7
Machesney Park village	12.69	23,508	22,677	-3.5	1787.0	3.5	88.7	63,662	6.4	120,700	67.4	5.7	72.1	22.2
Macomb city	10.83	19,298	17,413	-9.8	1607.8	5.2	70.4	39,384	28.1	101,400	53.0	8.9	45.3	41.2
Marion city	16.52	17,227	17,520	1.7	1060.5	1.8	85.4	43,502	18.5	115,500	53.7	5.5	56.5	36.8
Markham city	5.41	12,533	12,314	-1.7	2276.2	5.7	93.3	43,011	15.3	90,000	60.1	15.6	70.1	27.9
Matteson village	9.30	19,026	19,448	2.2	2091.2	5.1	92.4	83,729	11.2	165,100	68.5	9.1	62.8	34.2
Mattoon city	10.31	18,563	17,615	-5.1	1708.5	0.9	81.7	39,852	20.2	85,400	60.2	6.6	55.9	38.0
Maywood village	2.72	24,100	23,158	-3.9	8514.0	12.1	90.7	50,176	18.1	151,300	63.6	11.5	67.7	27.9
Melrose Park village	4.24	25,414	24,703	-2.8	5826.2	33.2	88.7	50,870	16.2	192,000	67.0	4.6	69.8	25.3
Midlothian village	2.82	14,817	14,346	-3.2	5087.2	12.6	94.2	60,160	13.3	150,400	64.2	4.8	64.9	31.8
Minooka village	9.41	10,953	11,397	4.1	1211.2	4.2	89.7	92,902	6.0	212,500	74.6	4.7	74.8	19.6
Mokena village	8.80	18,646	20,159	8.1	2290.8	4.6	94.9	109,108	3.9	319,200	71.0	3.3	76.7	20.6
Moline city	16.75	43,440	41,356	-4.8	2469.0	9.0	86.4	54,431	11.4	119,500	63.9	4.7	60.3	35.5
Montgomery village	9.26	18,307	19,638	7.3	2120.7	12.1	84.6	98,050	5.1	221,500	75.9	5.5	76.4	18.3
Morris city	9.91	13,639	15,053	10.4	1519.0	5.5	87.7	63,562	9.1	200,000	62.6	3.0	63.5	31.5
Morton village	12.78	16,355	16,277	-0.5	1273.6	2.8	86.6	77,214	6.2	199,400	62.0	2.6	67.7	29.5
Morton Grove village	5.09	23,222	22,796	-1.8	4478.6	39.0	94.7	85,360	6.7	317,200	60.0	2.4	72.0	25.5
Mount Prospect village	10.72	55,037	53,719	-2.4	5011.1	29.3	89.6	79,733	7.8	330,200	68.3	4.2	73.1	23.9
Mount Vernon city	14.58	15,241	14,723	-3.4	1009.8	2.2	79.9	40,625	18.6	78,600	58.4	8.6	58.1	37.8
Mundelein village	9.54	30,986	31,051	0.2	3254.8	30.7	89.7	93,027	4.8	237,500	70.9	3.5	76.6	19.6

Table B. Incorporated Places, Census Designated Places (CDPs), and Minor Civil Divisions (MCDs) of 10,000 or More Population — Crime, Residential Construction and Local Government Finance

STATE City, town, township, borough, or CDP (county if applicable)	Violent crime Number	Violent crime Rate[2]	Property crime Number	Property crime Rate[2]	Value ($1,000)	Number of housing units	Percent single family	Total (mil dol)	Intergovernmental Total (mil dol)	Intergovernmental Percent from state gov.	Taxes per capita[3]	Total (mil dol)	Per capita[3] Total	Per capita[3] Capital outlays	Debt outstanding (mil dol)
	15	16	17	18	19	20	21	22	23	24	25	26	27	28	29
ILLINOIS—Con.															
Deerfield village	4	21	137	719	4,360	9	100.0	49.8	15.6	96.7	1,244	33.1	1,751	60	109.8
DeKalb city	228	529	1,105	2,566	500	4	0.0	55.5	17.6	93.5	699	57.4	1,341	262	33.7
Des Plaines city	39	67	725	1,247	11,524	44	100.0	122.0	50.6	96.2	1,016	109.0	1,876	332	200.2
Dixon city	32	212	222	1,467	1,248	19	57.9	15.2	5.7	100.0	303	13.8	899	115	22.3
Dolton village	NA	NA	NA	NA	0	0	0.0	25.9	5.7	99.6	650	24.1	1,057	4	25.6
Downers Grove village	49	99	563	1,135	27,386	50	100.0	71.0	28.6	94.7	612	65.1	1,313	78	75.7
East Moline city	NA	NA	NA	NA	529	3	100.0	25.6	7.3	96.5	428	28.1	1,342	149	68.2
East Peoria city	114	504	584	2,580	1,680	10	100.0	52.0	19.3	100.0	943	44.1	1,936	229	106.2
East St. Louis city	317	1,190	NA	NA	0	0	0.0	38.1	23.0	82.7	530	38.8	1,457	0	13.3
Edwardsville city	13	52	185	738	12,070	34	91.2	35.5	13.2	100.0	502	41.5	1,654	573	30.5
Effingham city	43	341	340	2,693	11,810	66	21.2	23.3	10.7	100.0	680	26.9	2,144	605	17.6
Elgin city	235	208	1,713	1,515	28,789	133	100.0	157.5	43.0	96.2	681	147.7	1,318	182	87.5
Elk Grove Village village	23	70	485	1,482	300	1	100.0	94.2	16.8	97.9	1,570	73.0	2,213	136	75.6
Elmhurst city	23	49	445	946	48,448	90	100.0	79.1	21.2	99.0	851	96.7	2,075	548	90.0
Elmwood Park village	54	221	250	1,021	1,200	5	100.0	26.9	4.2	97.8	792	29.2	1,194	56	24.0
Evanston city	140	187	1,702	2,276	7,769	26	53.8	147.8	26.7	81.6	1,063	171.5	2,298	245	393.9
Evergreen Park village	54	277	921	4,724	720	3	100.0	31.0	10.1	94.6	657	39.5	2,027	93	25.9
Fairview Heights city	67	406	695	4,208	1,056	5	100.0	23.7	11.2	92.6	674	19.7	1,183	0	1.6
Forest Park village	66	474	531	3,815	0	0	0.0	23.7	7.4	97.2	874	32.0	2,297	315	66.3
Fox Lake village	17	161	256	2,430	2,307	25	100.0	20.0	5.1	99.5	488	18.3	1,744	263	8.9
Frankfort village	9	47	187	975	28,470	85	100.0	15.5	8.5	96.9	289	18.0	948	232	27.3
Franklin Park village	47	262	242	1,347	0	0	0.0	40.7	8.2	100.0	1,277	42.0	2,336	111	152.2
Freeport city	49	205	572	2,395	416	2	100.0	32.8	13.9	83.0	371	32.2	1,338	109	50.1
Gages Lake CDP	NA	NA	NA	NA	NA	NA	NA	NA	NA	NA	NA	NA	NA	NA	NA
Galesburg city	NA	NA	NA	NA	0	0	0.0	41.3	13.6	97.6	692	40.3	1,312	154	105.2
Geneva city	6	27	154	697	6,154	18	100.0	25.0	8.5	100.0	586	26.0	1,183	67	69.0
Glen Carbon village	9	69	129	993	8,336	28	100.0	15.7	6.8	98.3	384	14.1	1,092	12	19.6
Glendale Heights village	18	53	397	1,167	0	0	0.0	39.5	13.6	91.2	569	40.7	1,190	164	34.4
Glen Ellyn village	21	75	217	773	12,763	24	100.0	44.4	8.2	88.7	683	44.6	1,590	322	23.2
Glenview village	34	71	422	878	10,187	21	100.0	117.6	27.8	98.4	1,458	102.0	2,146	192	62.2
Godfrey village	NA	NA	NA	NA	7,091	33	87.9	9.8	5.6	100.0	73	9.8	557	105	0.8
Granite City city	219	766	729	2,550	905	7	100.0	47.2	12.9	92.6	762	45.9	1,603	105	100.4
Grayslake village	27	129	168	802	225	1	100.0	16.8	4.7	99.7	228	15.3	730	175	0.0
Gurnee village	44	143	1,085	3,534	230	1	100.0	45.8	28.0	87.5	396	41.0	1,335	109	52.4
Hanover Park village	43	113	194	511	0	0	0.0	45.9	11.1	97.7	674	43.4	1,140	111	66.9
Harvey city	NA	NA	NA	NA	0	0	0.0	32.1	7.6	99.2	756	42.5	1,708	168	63.9
Hazel Crest village	52	377	424	3,070	0	0	0.0	15.0	2.9	100.0	632	15.0	1,083	29	0.9
Herrin city	35	271	376	2,908	2,197	16	75.0	12.9	5.8	97.1	303	12.1	940	91	4.8
Hickory Hills city	16	115	189	1,356	685	3	100.0	11.6	3.9	95.2	303	13.6	979	226	1.3
Highland city	9	92	79	805	9,113	110	14.5	19.5	6.3	91.1	402	19.0	1,939	338	25.0
Highland Park city	24	81	198	665	19,484	57	36.8	58.8	13.4	98.5	1,101	58.7	1,976	301	53.2
Hinsdale village	2	11	98	550	35,201	40	100.0	27.9	8.5	84.9	810	24.4	1,375	277	20.3
Hoffman Estates village	48	93	417	810	11,258	61	100.0	99.5	17.6	82.4	1,042	79.1	1,537	126	205.4
Homer Glen village	9	37	149	605	7,285	19	100.0	13.2	10.9	87.9	75	12.0	489	104	10.6
Homewood village	46	241	786	4,125	0	0	0.0	22.8	6.9	99.7	562	24.5	1,284	88	46.8
Huntley village	9	33	99	358	16,911	110	100.0	21.7	6.1	95.9	374	24.3	897	72	24.6
Jacksonville city	65	355	519	2,833	1,500	16	25.0	23.3	9.0	84.7	514	20.3	1,076	77	47.8
Joliet city	486	327	2,312	1,556	42,633	238	72.3	228.2	72.2	97.7	601	191.7	1,297	312	84.2
Justice village	7	55	29	226	350	2	100.0	10.9	4.4	55.3	293	13.7	1,071	288	25.0
Kankakee city	230	884	871	3,346	0	0	0.0	54.7	11.1	83.2	878	67.5	2,585	552	171.9
Kewanee city	35	282	489	3,939	297	1	100.0	12.6	4.3	99.9	326	13.5	1,082	36	13.5
La Grange village	15	96	153	982	5,974	19	68.4	24.9	7.2	78.6	963	29.5	1,894	284	20.5
La Grange Park village	5	37	62	462	1,400	3	100.0	9.4	2.6	100.0	393	15.3	1,138	446	27.0
Lake Forest city	NA	NA	NA	NA	19,839	28	78.6	60.5	7.5	100.0	2,054	53.6	2,734	373	48.3
Lake in the Hills village	32	111	117	405	0	0	0.0	20.1	7.4	95.4	296	20.9	726	85	16.3
Lake Zurich village	5	25	259	1,300	2,354	7	100.0	64.4	29.6	64.6	1,299	65.0	3,272	684	81.3
Lansing village	88	315	1,525	5,465	0	0	0.0	38.1	9.8	88.6	740	35.4	1,267	102	106.4
Lemont village	22	128	142	824	24,726	96	65.6	13.5	4.8	100.0	392	14.6	854	137	44.9
Libertyville village	NA	NA	NA	NA	20,061	39	100.0	43.8	10.6	95.7	809	58.1	2,843	1135	48.5
Lincoln city	52	379	253	1,844	295	3	100.0	16.5	7.2	100.0	162	16.3	1,185	476	6.6
Lincolnwood village	15	120	380	3,048	342	1	100.0	23.8	7.4	92.6	1,066	29.7	2,385	269	34.9
Lindenhurst village	13	90	58	401	0	0	0.0	7.1	3.2	89.4	137	9.0	626	82	18.4
Lisle village	16	70	106	462	3,265	15	46.7	24.2	8.3	81.4	558	22.7	966	167	41.4
Lockport city	17	67	177	694	29,149	183	23.5	23.7	9.0	92.4	364	22.1	875	113	16.7
Lombard village	52	119	856	1,955	7,643	29	100.0	99.3	29.3	90.0	447	109.0	2,485	141	210.5
Loves Park city	86	369	456	1,957	10,511	77	79.2	18.0	11.7	99.8	205	22.9	979	184	22.1
Lyons village	11	104	115	1,089	440	2	100.0	12.8	3.5	99.8	655	18.7	1,769	746	28.0
McHenry city	48	179	288	1,071	17,586	143	100.0	30.1	12.8	98.8	247	53.2	1,983	1081	38.3
Machesney Park village	57	252	416	1,839	6,626	62	100.0	18.9	13.9	76.6	201	16.6	730	294	10.1
Macomb city	56	309	228	1,258	226	1	100.0	18.2	10.2	89.8	212	22.4	1,258	288	9.7
Marion city	NA	NA	NA	NA	5,268	34	94.1	35.0	10.9	96.7	994	31.6	1,795	152	34.5
Markham city	NA	NA	NA	NA	45	1	100.0	18.7	4.5	100.0	763	23.7	1,893	56	37.8
Matteson village	NA	NA	NA	NA	4,253	30	100.0	31.8	7.8	100.0	668	34.3	1,769	59	124.7
Mattoon city	99	556	281	1,579	427	3	100.0	32.9	14.0	71.0	460	37.6	2,101	441	97.7
Maywood village	135	573	570	2,418	500	2	100.0	34.3	5.0	98.7	1,098	37.5	1,590	205	12.6
Melrose Park village	85	338	316	1,256	180	1	100.0	51.3	19.7	99.9	1,033	57.0	2,268	28	271.2
Midlothian village	26	178	330	2,259	640	4	100.0	17.2	5.0	80.1	533	12.9	880	20	53.5
Minooka village	NA	NA	NA	NA	8,519	55	100.0	10.5	3.7	100.0	326	9.6	847	244	10.0
Mokena village	11	54	295	1,439	13,540	35	100.0	17.0	10.4	100.0	178	17.2	854	115	5.9
Moline city	228	542	1,050	2,497	2,864	36	38.9	66.5	25.5	97.3	818	97.8	2,333	669	182.0
Montgomery village	17	85	287	1,442	18,977	207	30.4	18.3	6.8	93.0	377	16.0	815	175	29.4
Morris city	16	108	238	1,608	8,125	135	8.1	17.1	7.7	98.6	463	19.9	1,359	372	4.8
Morton village	18	110	103	632	6,238	43	16.3	17.4	7.3	96.6	251	16.1	980	349	1.9
Morton Grove village	10	43	285	1,233	3,266	14	100.0	36.7	7.9	96.6	991	31.9	1,383	32	20.5
Mount Prospect village	32	59	558	1,036	19,432	102	6.9	78.3	11.8	72.8	1,020	81.9	1,498	60	157.4
Mount Vernon city	228	1,529	773	5,183	2,816	30	26.7	25.5	9.2	98.3	679	27.2	1,830	358	66.4
Mundelein village	27	86	183	582	6,101	43	100.0	40.6	16.9	99.5	463	39.4	1,257	109	12.6

1 Data for serious crimes have not been adjusted for underreporting. This may affect comparability between geographic areas over time.
2 Per 100,000 population estimated by the FBI.   3 Based on population estimated as of July 1 of the year shown.

Table B. Incorporated Places, Census Designated Places (CDPs), and Minor Civil Divisions (MCDs) of 10,000 or More Population — Land Area, Population, and Households, and Employment

STATE City, town, township, borough, or CDP (county if applicable)	Land area 2010 (sq mi)	Population Total persons 2010	Total persons 2019	Percent change 2010–2019	Persons per square mile, 2019	Population characteristics 2015–2019 Percent foreign born	Percent living in the same house as previous year	Income and poverty 2015–2019 Median household income	Percent of households with income below poverty level	Median value of owner-occupied housing units	Employment, 2015–2019 Percent in civilian labor force	Unemployment rate	Households, 2015–2019 (percent of households) Family households	One person households
	1	2	3	4	5	6	7	8	9	10	11	12	13	14
ILLINOIS—Con.														
Naperville city	38.81	142,170	148,449	4.4	3825.0	20.0	87.2	125,926	4.6	416,700	69.1	4.0	75.5	20.1
New Lenox village	15.51	24,288	26,926	10.9	1736.0	3.0	92.6	110,313	4.4	294,800	72.1	4.6	79.1	17.9
Niles village	5.85	29,825	28,938	-3.0	4946.7	40.8	92.5	64,772	11.1	284,400	57.4	4.6	66.4	30.3
Normal town	18.30	52,549	54,469	3.7	2976.4	5.7	77.5	58,111	23.5	170,200	64.4	2.9	52.8	29.4
Norridge village	1.81	14,574	14,152	-2.9	7818.8	31.1	94.5	72,570	6.1	286,400	55.0	3.5	68.5	28.0
North Aurora village	7.24	16,621	18,057	8.6	2494.1	11.8	89.3	86,537	7.2	246,800	71.5	3.6	66.0	27.5
Northbrook village	13.24	33,200	32,958	-0.7	2489.3	20.8	91.1	124,863	3.9	534,800	56.9	2.3	75.0	24.2
North Chicago city	7.99	32,594	29,615	-9.1	3706.5	16.8	62.7	43,094	21.5	108,100	44.6	7.2	59.5	33.4
Northlake city	3.17	12,325	12,161	-1.3	3836.3	28.8	92.4	55,305	15.3	181,700	63.7	6.2	69.8	26.1
Oak Forest city	6.01	27,966	27,173	-2.8	4521.3	12.2	94.3	76,945	5.2	194,200	70.6	4.8	69.4	24.7
Oak Lawn village	8.57	56,690	55,022	-2.9	6420.3	18.0	92.6	64,476	10.1	204,000	60.2	6.0	64.8	32.4
Oak Park village	4.70	51,878	52,381	1.0	11144.9	8.6	88.4	94,646	9.4	387,300	70.9	4.9	59.3	34.8
O'Fallon city	15.37	28,759	29,583	2.9	1924.7	4.5	85.0	90,349	5.1	207,900	65.3	4.5	73.3	24.1
Orland Park village	22.03	56,607	57,857	2.2	2626.3	15.7	90.8	90,345	4.8	287,700	62.0	3.8	71.8	25.5
Oswego village	14.89	30,452	36,252	19.0	2434.7	11.4	91.5	102,110	1.7	254,900	73.6	3.6	81.8	14.8
Ottawa city	12.80	18,818	18,063	-4.0	1411.2	4.2	83.7	51,288	15.4	128,000	64.6	6.2	61.3	33.8
Palatine village	13.60	68,551	67,482	-1.6	4961.9	26.4	85.6	80,526	7.9	284,400	73.3	3.3	64.8	28.4
Palos Heights city	3.77	12,515	12,520	0.0	3321.0	8.3	93.9	89,286	5.7	282,100	53.7	3.8	70.7	25.3
Palos Hills city	4.25	17,480	17,060	-2.4	4014.1	25.6	90.5	61,143	11.0	203,800	61.5	5.0	62.8	32.7
Park Forest village	4.96	21,981	21,210	-3.5	4276.2	3.7	91.1	53,938	13.3	73,600	63.2	7.9	58.0	38.7
Park Ridge city	7.09	37,479	36,950	-1.4	5211.6	14.5	91.7	111,642	3.9	437,000	63.6	2.9	71.1	25.8
Pekin city	14.59	34,018	32,045	-5.8	2196.4	1.0	85.5	50,973	13.3	106,200	59.0	5.5	58.4	35.3
Peoria city	48.00	115,150	110,417	-4.1	2300.4	7.6	84.7	51,771	19.2	125,700	60.8	9.3	55.6	38.2
Peru city	9.63	10,329	9,730	-5.8	1010.4	5.1	88.8	51,321	9.3	127,400	61.6	4.5	57.4	38.3
Plainfield village	24.26	39,884	44,308	11.1	1826.4	10.1	91.6	130,614	2.6	319,500	75.1	4.0	85.8	12.0
Plano city	8.98	10,850	11,665	7.5	1299.0	13.7	84.2	73,233	11.3	165,500	74.7	7.2	71.9	24.7
Pontiac city	8.10	11,930	11,253	-5.7	1389.3	2.4	83.7	45,285	18.5	97,000	49.9	5.3	62.1	34.2
Prospect Heights city	4.25	16,258	15,887	-2.3	3738.1	40.8	88.3	73,084	7.8	284,300	68.7	3.2	71.8	23.0
Quincy city	15.71	40,709	39,949	-1.9	2542.9	1.4	85.5	46,189	13.8	116,300	63.5	5.3	59.2	34.6
Rantoul village	8.49	12,956	12,493	-3.6	1471.5	5.3	86.3	42,149	18.7	85,900	64.0	6.0	60.6	35.2
Richton Park village	4.39	13,670	13,292	-2.8	3027.8	2.4	91.8	62,858	16.0	146,000	64.1	13.2	63.4	35.0
Riverdale village	3.58	13,549	13,077	-3.5	3652.8	2.2	84.4	35,711	23.4	79,000	63.9	20.1	59.4	37.6
River Forest village	2.48	11,176	10,816	-3.2	4361.3	9.1	88.2	129,928	3.9	596,900	64.6	2.2	71.1	28.4
River Grove village	2.39	10,246	9,883	-3.5	4135.1	33.9	90.7	59,814	10.7	211,200	68.9	5.5	69.0	28.3
Rockford city	64.38	153,285	145,609	-5.0	2261.7	11.8	83.8	44,252	20.1	91,600	61.7	10.7	59.6	35.2
Rock Island city	16.87	38,985	37,176	-4.6	2203.7	10.0	80.5	48,680	18.7	104,600	63.5	7.9	58.0	34.4
Rolling Meadows city	5.62	24,091	23,532	-2.3	4187.2	25.5	91.1	74,134	5.8	241,200	71.5	3.5	65.2	28.1
Romeoville village	19.07	39,652	39,746	0.2	2084.2	23.0	91.5	79,183	5.3	186,100	69.6	4.4	71.9	22.6
Roscoe village	10.27	10,847	10,510	-3.1	1023.4	7.0	92.4	92,138	4.6	163,000	73.1	3.6	77.9	17.9
Roselle village	5.47	22,724	22,463	-1.1	4106.6	17.2	88.4	90,257	5.4	256,800	73.0	3.4	70.7	23.5
Round Lake village	5.56	18,342	18,100	-1.3	3255.4	24.2	84.8	82,521	8.5	197,800	76.7	6.0	79.1	14.8
Round Lake Beach village	5.05	28,093	27,100	-3.5	5366.3	23.5	89.0	70,474	9.3	142,900	71.7	4.9	76.3	19.5
St. Charles city	14.40	32,301	32,887	1.8	2283.8	9.1	86.1	98,393	4.9	293,300	67.1	3.4	69.3	26.4
Sauk Village village	4.00	10,553	10,246	-2.9	2561.5	4.6	89.9	38,788	25.2	70,400	72.8	16.3	72.0	24.4
Schaumburg village	19.30	74,233	72,887	-1.8	3776.5	31.6	86.8	83,096	6.5	251,100	71.0	3.8	63.1	31.7
Schiller Park village	2.77	11,793	11,403	-3.3	4116.6	46.7	89.7	54,099	13.7	203,200	66.8	5.3	71.3	23.7
Shiloh village	11.02	12,557	13,586	8.2	1232.8	8.1	84.9	86,021	7.6	220,500	64.0	3.5	66.7	30.8
Shorewood village	7.89	15,630	17,509	12.0	2219.1	6.4	92.7	105,938	4.3	262,600	66.4	2.7	77.9	19.2
Skokie village	10.06	64,845	62,700	-3.3	6232.6	40.4	90.7	73,046	10.2	318,800	60.0	4.2	73.0	23.9
South Elgin village	7.06	21,993	24,755	12.6	3506.4	12.9	90.9	99,451	5.8	235,500	74.7	4.7	78.6	16.7
South Holland village	7.24	21,999	21,296	-3.2	2941.4	5.1	91.2	63,170	11.6	150,600	64.0	12.6	73.3	24.4
Springfield city	60.94	116,996	114,230	-2.4	1874.5	4.5	81.9	54,648	16.5	133,400	61.5	7.1	55.2	38.0
Sterling city	5.78	15,426	14,463	-6.2	2502.2	5.8	82.9	43,685	12.0	88,100	62.2	4.1	58.2	35.0
Streamwood village	7.79	39,839	39,228	-1.5	5035.7	30.7	89.6	80,651	5.9	192,800	71.3	3.6	75.0	21.6
Streator city	7.22	14,001	13,113	-6.3	1816.2	3.4	88.8	39,736	17.8	70,800	59.8	6.7	55.1	40.1
Summit village	2.12	11,054	11,116	0.6	5243.4	39.4	89.9	47,377	15.9	170,800	65.2	8.7	73.5	23.1
Swansea village	6.47	13,454	13,350	-0.8	2063.4	4.5	90.4	77,517	6.8	167,000	67.3	4.9	66.1	28.4
Sycamore city	9.83	17,521	18,322	4.6	1863.9	4.5	85.0	71,698	8.1	189,400	68.5	3.0	66.2	26.1
Taylorville city	10.32	11,275	10,360	-8.1	1003.9	0.8	87.1	39,979	15.3	88,900	54.0	2.6	52.2	38.6
Tinley Park village	16.11	56,827	55,773	-1.9	3462.0	10.6	91.6	78,343	6.7	231,400	67.6	5.4	68.7	27.5
Troy city	5.52	9,949	10,375	4.3	1879.5	1.8	88.4	71,381	9.8	178,800	64.3	1.7	68.7	27.1
Urbana city	11.82	42,136	42,214	0.2	3571.4	20.2	67.2	37,102	29.4	155,000	57.2	6.4	39.1	43.9
Vernon Hills village	7.74	25,005	26,521	6.1	3426.5	32.8	88.8	104,199	7.1	348,900	69.5	3.7	72.2	23.4
Villa Park village	4.72	22,025	21,483	-2.5	4551.5	16.8	88.9	77,739	9.6	245,800	71.1	3.4	67.6	25.9
Warrenville city	5.45	13,182	13,174	-0.1	2417.2	12.4	90.4	87,871	6.8	221,700	75.6	4.0	65.0	27.8
Washington city	8.46	15,231	16,516	8.4	1952.2	2.4	87.4	76,508	4.1	180,900	63.8	2.9	69.8	27.3
Waterloo city	8.14	9,982	10,578	6.0	1299.5	1.6	90.7	67,682	5.9	192,100	63.5	3.2	68.2	27.9
Wauconda village	5.07	13,622	13,504	-0.9	2663.5	15.4	87.1	81,313	6.2	226,600	72.6	3.8	70.1	23.8
Waukegan city	24.26	89,115	86,075	-3.4	3548.0	30.5	82.3	49,803	17.0	132,200	68.7	7.7	67.7	27.0
Westchester village	3.69	16,718	16,111	-3.6	4367.8	12.6	93.1	86,623	5.9	241,100	65.9	4.4	66.7	28.6
West Chicago city	15.36	27,221	26,816	-1.5	1745.8	32.6	90.9	78,116	10.6	249,500	71.8	4.4	80.0	14.6
Western Springs village	2.79	12,948	13,359	3.2	4788.2	3.8	91.9	174,760	4.0	609,900	65.4	2.3	84.9	15.0
Westmont village	5.00	24,662	24,443	-0.9	4888.6	23.1	87.3	64,416	14.6	301,900	65.4	3.4	56.2	39.0
Wheaton city	11.30	53,045	52,745	-0.6	4667.7	12.4	85.4	103,376	5.6	358,000	65.6	3.5	69.9	25.0
Wheeling village	8.67	37,644	38,646	2.7	4457.4	43.1	86.9	68,615	9.1	198,700	72.4	3.0	64.5	29.1
Wilmette village	5.40	27,060	27,089	0.1	5016.5	17.0	91.3	164,681	3.9	707,800	61.5	4.2	77.9	20.5
Winnetka village	3.81	12,192	12,316	1.0	3232.5	8.9	91.8	250	3.5	1,091,700	56.7	2.4	81.8	16.4
Wood Dale city	4.75	13,769	13,607	-1.2	2864.6	27.1	91.3	70,552	8.2	236,900	68.4	5.8	70.1	22.3
Woodridge village	9.67	32,976	33,432	1.4	3457.3	19.9	87.6	86,094	5.8	271,800	74.7	3.7	66.6	27.0
Wood River city	7.00	10,633	10,051	-5.5	1435.9	1.4	84.1	46,860	19.2	81,600	64.7	6.2	56.7	34.6
Woodstock city	13.08	24,794	25,240	1.8	1929.7	12.0	80.9	61,478	12.6	179,700	67.2	4.2	67.6	26.5
Worth village	2.37	10,789	10,466	-3.0	4416.0	23.8	91.5	60,516	11.5	171,200	64.5	7.4	66.7	28.3
Yorkville city	20.00	16,950	20,613	21.6	1030.7	3.4	80.8	97,610	6.9	245,200	72.3	5.3	73.9	20.2
Zion city	9.79	24,394	23,487	-3.7	2399.1	13.2	87.5	51,702	17.5	124,000	64.8	9.1	69.4	27.6

Table B. Incorporated Places, Census Designated Places (CDPs), and Minor Civil Divisions (MCDs) of 10,000 or More Population — Crime, Residential Construction and Local Government Finance

STATE City, town, township, borough, or CDP (county if applicable)	Serious crimes known to police, 2018[1] Violent crime Number	Violent crime Rate[2]	Property crime Number	Property crime Rate[2]	New residential construction authorized by building permits, 2019 Value ($1,000)	Number of housing units	Percent single family	Local government finance, 2017 General revenue Total (mil dol)	Intergovernmental Total (mil dol)	Intergovernmental Percent from state gov.	Taxes per capita[3]	General expenditure Total (mil dol)	Per capita[3] Total	Per capita[3] Capital outlays	Debt outstanding (mil dol)
	15	16	17	18	19	20	21	22	23	24	25	26	27	28	29
ILLINOIS—Con.															
Naperville city	102	69	NA	NA	97,981	314	78.3	266.4	106.0	94.7	930	255.7	1,732	133	154.5
New Lenox village	35	130	299	1,111	44,638	144	82.6	36.1	9.1	98.1	442	32.8	1,240	199	53.9
Niles village	34	116	605	2,056	936	2	100.0	60.3	25.7	99.5	957	64.4	2,187	459	8.9
Normal town	119	218	985	1,807	6,673	76	51.3	81.4	18.9	99.2	791	92.6	1,700	396	92.3
Norridge village	20	139	413	2,865	550	2	100.0	15.6	7.3	100.0	508	15.1	1,047	13	2.9
North Aurora village	24	130	240	1,299	12,825	89	91.0	16.0	6.8	99.7	436	16.8	930	174	14.5
Northbrook village	6	18	512	1,532	21,048	37	100.0	65.3	17.7	99.2	1,074	74.0	2,219	195	100.5
North Chicago city	NA	NA	NA	NA	1,349	7	100.0	28.9	7.2	89.4	548	36.5	1,218	143	121.3
Northlake city	10	81	268	2,167	735	4	100.0	22.5	5.3	90.5	1,009	15.0	1,216	1	17.1
Oak Forest city	37	134	304	1,100	150	1	100.0	26.4	5.9	90.1	587	31.2	1,129	234	63.8
Oak Lawn village	81	145	758	1,354	3,040	13	100.0	77.6	20.0	96.2	705	67.1	1,199	2	71.7
Oak Park village	NA	NA	NA	NA	16,200	65	27.7	90.3	17.8	72.6	1,099	95.1	1,825	361	288.3
O'Fallon city	81	276	543	1,850	34,339	126	100.0	42.6	17.4	96.6	447	37.9	1,294	187	54.9
Orland Park village	20	34	1,015	1,719	17,789	63	61.9	88.8	30.5	98.6	506	93.4	1,594	526	109.6
Oswego village	17	48	298	840	16,150	92	100.0	24.1	14.9	98.7	131	23.6	676	121	49.9
Ottawa city	15	83	310	1,713	15,528	82	26.8	26.6	10.0	100.0	688	27.6	1,520	365	19.1
Palatine village	28	41	358	522	10,965	62	9.7	83.0	21.8	84.1	659	84.1	1,228	151	197.8
Palos Heights city	3	24	135	1,090	0	0	0.0	21.9	3.1	97.1	1,257	22.9	1,848	437	35.5
Palos Hills city	18	104	84	485	1,730	6	100.0	10.7	3.3	100.0	284	12.1	698	8	21.0
Park Forest village	61	282	344	1,590	0	0	0.0	39.5	13.2	49.2	921	42.8	1,979	92	55.5
Park Ridge city	21	56	341	910	10,061	18	100.0	53.3	8.8	99.5	1,049	46.7	1,249	84	35.8
Pekin city	136	418	NA	NA	3,079	27	25.9	46.0	12.8	96.9	420	50.5	1,552	347	11.4
Peoria city	860	764	4,509	4,005	11,716	33	100.0	185.9	55.2	92.1	752	197.8	1,756	250	191.9
Peru city	10	102	149	1,525	650	3	100.0	22.3	9.5	99.3	755	17.1	1,740	0	13.2
Plainfield village	54	121	328	737	52,525	202	100.0	42.6	10.9	93.7	412	38.4	876	131	60.4
Plano city	9	77	72	616	7,945	59	100.0	9.1	3.4	93.5	248	10.2	876	172	5.4
Pontiac city	40	339	172	1,458	592	3	100.0	13.3	5.0	100.0	326	13.0	1,136	146	5.2
Prospect Heights city	25	155	82	507	1,560	4	100.0	13.1	3.6	80.6	363	10.0	621	57	15.7
Quincy city	252	626	1,288	3,200	12,074	59	100.0	47.4	25.0	85.7	368	33.8	838	4	15.4
Rantoul village	35	275	349	2,739	54	1	100.0	18.8	4.0	90.1	647	24.2	1,884	541	36.2
Richton Park village	55	408	331	2,455	0	0	0.0	11.2	3.9	89.3	330	14.5	1,071	270	2.8
Riverdale village	99	743	377	2,830	0	0	0.0	17.4	4.6	66.3	644	20.4	1,534	102	81.7
River Forest village	14	126	233	2,094	2,391	3	100.0	20.6	4.6	96.4	941	23.0	2,088	158	56.7
River Grove village	NA	NA	NA	NA	204	7	14.3	11.8	3.2	89.8	665	13.1	1,303	342	31.7
Rockford city	2,027	1,387	5,368	3,672	11,734	88	37.5	252.5	107.4	66.7	618	240.9	1,639	286	104.8
Rock Island city	99	261	986	2,596	193	1	100.0	63.7	18.4	90.0	640	73.5	1,945	290	66.4
Rolling Meadows city	15	63	284	1,185	0	0	0.0	42.8	7.4	92.2	1,154	47.9	2,002	147	98.7
Romeoville village	58	146	431	1,088	13,281	135	18.5	61.5	14.1	85.7	685	71.2	1,797	440	169.3
Roscoe village	10	96	93	889	NA	NA	NA	5.5	3.5	98.8	158	4.7	445	4	5.7
Roselle village	9	40	206	904	15,855	104	5.8	18.6	3.7	97.3	519	20.5	899	191	34.5
Round Lake village	18	98	108	585	0	0	0.0	9.5	3.6	91.0	264	9.3	504	60	12.2
Round Lake Beach village	34	124	509	1,849	185	1	100.0	15.3	7.9	97.2	225	17.3	627	182	20.0
St. Charles city	45	137	232	708	10,446	44	100.0	57.2	16.9	99.2	875	59.3	1,822	384	105.9
Sauk Village village	NA	NA	271	2,597	0	0	0.0	12.3	2.0	100.0	829	8.5	815	22	45.6
Schaumburg village	61	82	1,516	2,044	685	2	100.0	168.9	48.1	91.1	915	196.8	2,658	351	519.0
Schiller Park village	17	146	219	1,885	360	2	100.0	24.6	5.8	98.5	1,170	23.7	2,040	0	58.2
Shiloh village	22	167	159	1,208	14,872	61	100.0	10.6	4.1	97.5	330	9.5	725	44	16.4
Shorewood village	14	80	101	578	13,973	60	100.0	21.9	6.6	100.0	536	17.3	1,004	109	17.0
Skokie village	172	269	1,606	2,515	58,687	206	2.4	115.0	29.8	98.1	1,013	100.9	1,580	187	57.5
South Elgin village	24	106	97	429	3,814	25	100.0	21.3	8.2	84.9	377	24.4	1,087	357	28.8
South Holland village	68	314	541	2,494	170	1	100.0	32.6	6.3	98.8	888	30.3	1,400	137	20.7
Springfield city	955	833	5,487	4,787	26,784	169	33.7	160.6	54.6	86.9	723	204.1	1,763	454	1436.9
Sterling city	34	232	436	2,971	377	2	100.0	242.3	9.0	95.9	574	224.7	15,277	14	32.5
Streamwood village	NA	NA	NA	NA	0	0	0.0	33.3	10.0	98.8	500	29.4	736	58	4.5
Streator city	31	238	302	2,316	0	0	0.0	17.4	6.4	100.0	398	17.9	1,351	128	44.9
Summit village	40	354	241	2,131	0	0	0.0	12.8	4.3	91.8	547	12.4	1,098	47	31.6
Swansea village	14	104	192	1,422	5,888	25	100.0	11.3	4.2	100.0	233	9.1	676	128	1.5
Sycamore city	10	55	172	951	11,042	53	73.6	40.7	13.2	97.3	1,155	38.1	2,112	1042	9.6
Taylorville city	7	66	134	1,268	600	3	100.0	10.7	5.5	99.5	272	13.1	1,235	229	14.8
Tinley Park village	23	41	694	1,225	7,308	33	100.0	68.2	21.5	98.0	681	57.6	1,018	165	67.8
Troy city	13	127	81	793	11,047	47	95.7	8.4	3.6	100.0	266	8.0	779	116	10.0
Urbana city	150	357	1,233	2,934	5,509	29	75.9	46.8	15.9	76.4	553	43.7	1,022	111	11.5
Vernon Hills village	15	57	295	1,116	22,104	31	100.0	31.5	17.5	100.0	399	28.8	1,098	35	50.8
Villa Park village	27	124	232	1,064	2,885	10	100.0	31.3	12.5	79.9	551	36.9	1,690	159	75.6
Warrenville city	13	98	108	813	34,337	165	27.3	16.3	3.9	98.8	704	15.1	1,136	68	12.5
Washington city	30	176	193	1,132	5,766	19	100.0	15.0	7.1	92.6	273	17.5	1,051	389	0.6
Waterloo city	13	125	73	701	10,278	39	100.0	9.3	3.9	100.0	217	8.9	855	136	0.0
Wauconda village	NA	NA	NA	NA	864	4	100.0	13.0	4.1	96.8	377	13.2	963	76	30.7
Waukegan city	355	406	NA	NA	1,015	7	100.0	90.9	29.2	92.3	598	118.0	1,347	267	339.5
Westchester village	19	116	172	1,047	0	0	0.0	17.5	3.9	99.6	726	22.5	1,371	91	55.6
West Chicago city	34	125	245	902	143	1	100.0	30.0	8.6	99.8	329	30.0	1,101	36	49.4
Western Springs village	2	15	154	1,136	16,343	31	100.0	16.4	2.7	96.6	736	14.6	1,083	20	11.9
Westmont village	19	77	270	1,090	4,151	15	100.0	31.6	11.8	96.8	762	30.6	1,234	123	49.4
Wheaton city	39	73	629	1,178	7,420	15	100.0	59.3	14.1	100.0	663	52.9	990	57	23.9
Wheeling village	27	70	322	832	56,000	321	0.0	57.4	14.4	85.4	891	63.5	1,650	281	66.3
Wilmette village	13	47	259	943	18,061	29	100.0	48.1	7.4	99.4	1,083	48.4	1,769	192	135.7
Winnetka village	3	24	108	863	14,960	12	100.0	29.2	3.2	95.7	1,388	34.3	2,753	194	20.3
Wood Dale city	10	73	191	1,384	1,330	3	100.0	24.0	9.5	57.5	546	21.0	1,522	349	52.0
Woodridge village	32	95	392	1,164	16,331	72	100.0	33.5	11.5	91.6	490	28.3	843	58	54.5
Wood River city	59	578	528	5,171	629	3	100.0	15.1	5.6	100.0	212	14.1	1,383	147	6.7
Woodstock city	24	95	298	1,175	7,056	53	100.0	27.6	9.7	88.2	446	24.8	984	117	34.0
Worth village	26	244	123	1,156	0	0	0.0	9.9	3.2	87.8	359	10.3	969	12	34.7
Yorkville city	18	91	200	1,013	25,215	167	87.4	22.7	5.8	89.1	551	23.3	1,200	324	47.6
Zion city	148	620	721	3,019	0	0	0.0	26.2	6.4	99.6	634	26.9	1,123	15	78.2

1 Data for serious crimes have not been adjusted for underreporting. This may affect comparability between geographic areas over time.
2 Per 100,000 population estimated by the FBI.   3 Based on population estimated as of July 1 of the year shown.

Table B. Incorporated Places, Census Designated Places (CDPs), and Minor Civil Divisions (MCDs) of 10,000 or More Population — **Land Area, Population, and Households, and Employment**

STATE City, town, township, borough, or CDP (county if applicable)	Land area 2010 (sq mi)	Total persons 2010	Total persons 2019	Percent change 2010–2019	Persons per square mile, 2019	Percent foreign born	Percent living in the same house as previous year	Median household income	Percent of households with income below poverty level	Median value of owner-occupied housing units	Percent in civilian labor force	Unemployment rate	Family households	One person households
	1	2	3	4	5	6	7	8	9	10	11	12	13	14
INDIANA	35826.44	6,484,051	6,732,219	3.8	187.9	5.2	85.3	56,303	12.8	141,700	63.8	4.8	64.7	29.0
Anderson city	41.60	56,082	54,765	-2.3	1316.5	2.7	81.3	37,038	22.7	72,900	57.3	7.8	56.6	36.7
Auburn city	7.66	12,794	13,484	5.4	1760.3	1.0	80.4	50,180	10.5	119,700	67.0	5.7	59.2	37.8
Avon town	18.72	13,529	18,706	38.3	999.3	7.4	84.7	94,213	4.3	210,600	76.0	7.3	74.6	20.5
Bedford city	12.21	13,406	13,212	-1.4	1082.1	1.9	84.7	43,700	18.8	94,800	56.9	4.5	57.9	34.8
Beech Grove city	4.48	14,227	14,937	5.0	3334.2	2.6	91.5	43,802	13.1	101,600	64.1	6.7	56.9	37.3
Bloomington city	23.24	80,293	85,755	6.8	3690.0	11.7	58.1	37,077	31.9	200,700	57.8	6.7	38.8	38.7
Brownsburg town	15.79	21,946	27,001	23.0	1710.0	5.6	85.7	78,877	4.2	195,700	72.0	3.0	73.8	22.4
Carmel city	49.06	83,887	101,068	20.5	2060.1	12.2	85.1	112,765	3.7	333,200	71.3	2.5	73.3	22.0
Cedar Lake town	8.46	11,579	13,183	13.9	1558.3	2.6	89.0	65,322	7.3	182,600	67.6	7.1	70.1	24.1
Chesterton town	9.32	13,087	14,088	7.6	1511.6	4.4	90.6	73,977	7.7	190,400	61.7	6.5	68.0	27.1
Clarksville town	9.96	21,527	21,558	0.1	2164.5	7.0	88.3	45,440	11.9	119,300	64.8	3.8	56.1	37.2
Columbus city	28.10	44,089	48,046	9.0	1709.8	15.0	80.3	63,405	11.9	166,200	64.9	4.1	60.8	31.6
Connersville city	7.68	13,510	12,796	-5.3	1666.1	0.8	83.7	34,201	25.6	71,500	54.4	6.6	59.2	33.8
Crawfordsville city	9.67	15,960	16,118	1.0	1666.8	5.0	74.6	44,077	15.6	107,500	63.0	5.5	57.1	34.8
Crown Point city	17.83	27,870	30,488	9.4	1709.9	7.0	84.6	76,927	7.0	194,600	61.0	3.8	68.4	27.2
Dyer town	6.24	16,367	15,976	-2.4	2560.3	6.9	92.4	84,202	2.3	212,400	66.1	5.0	71.3	24.4
East Chicago city	14.09	29,698	27,871	-6.3	1974.2	14.9	86.0	32,839	28.6	74,500	52.9	9.1	65.0	32.1
Elkhart city	27.51	51,908	52,358	0.9	1903.2	12.3	83.6	40,750	19.4	95,900	63.1	7.7	58.1	35.0
Evansville city	47.32	120,069	117,979	-1.7	2493.2	2.9	79.3	40,178	19.6	94,200	62.6	5.9	53.5	38.5
Fishers city	35.47	77,293	95,310	23.3	2687.1	9.2	86.6	109,454	3.1	264,200	75.1	2.6	73.9	20.8
Fort Wayne city	110.64	253,739	270,402	6.6	2444.0	8.2	83.6	49,411	14.7	115,100	66.5	5.5	60.7	32.1
Frankfort city	8.06	16,420	15,884	-3.3	1970.7	12.3	85.3	41,120	15.4	83,400	61.4	5.5	61.2	34.0
Franklin city	13.44	23,729	25,608	7.9	1905.4	1.7	82.3	59,930	9.7	129,200	65.9	4.7	67.0	26.6
Gary city	49.73	80,256	74,879	-6.7	1505.7	1.8	83.2	31,936	28.7	66,100	51.4	12.4	58.2	37.5
Goshen city	17.59	32,572	34,217	5.1	1945.3	14.0	83.8	48,626	14.7	121,100	64.2	4.7	63.8	30.9
Granger CDP	24.91	30,465	NA	NA	NA	9.4	94.6	101,904	3.5	219,900	64.5	2.5	81.0	16.7
Greencastle city	5.24	10,311	10,270	-0.4	1959.9	6.0	67.1	47,471	10.4	105,700	52.4	2.3	52.7	42.0
Greenfield city	13.56	20,641	23,006	11.5	1696.6	1.5	80.7	53,270	9.9	139,000	61.0	3.3	59.3	32.1
Greensburg city	9.26	11,489	11,891	3.5	1284.1	3.7	84.1	54,099	11.2	120,800	65.8	3.8	57.6	35.1
Greenwood city	27.91	51,116	59,458	16.3	2130.3	7.6	79.5	63,474	6.8	155,300	66.7	3.4	64.9	28.6
Griffith town	7.74	16,919	16,060	-5.1	2074.9	3.2	86.0	65,534	7.6	141,700	68.4	4.4	61.8	32.7
Hammond city	22.74	80,825	75,522	-6.6	3321.1	12.0	86.4	46,406	20.1	91,700	60.4	7.6	62.8	31.6
Highland town	6.98	23,741	22,316	-6.0	3197.1	6.7	90.9	67,281	7.1	161,100	66.6	4.9	64.4	29.6
Hobart city	26.22	29,336	27,939	-4.8	1065.6	4.2	88.9	58,829	10.7	142,700	64.7	7.2	66.0	28.8
Huntington city	9.01	17,524	17,138	-2.2	1902.1	1.8	85.1	43,955	15.1	81,800	63.7	3.8	61.6	31.5
Indianapolis city (consolidated city)	NA	829,709	886,220	6.8	NA	9.6	85.1	48,031	16.4	137,200	66.8	6.3	54.2	37.8
Indianapolis city (balance)	361.57	820,457	876,384	6.8	2423.8	9.7	85.0	47,873	16.5	137,000	66.8	6.4	54.1	37.8
Jasper city	13.26	15,127	15,724	3.9	1185.8	5.1	89.7	57,062	11.2	155,300	67.7	1.9	63.2	30.9
Jeffersonville city	34.11	45,026	48,126	6.9	1410.9	4.0	88.1	56,223	9.4	136,900	65.8	5.7	62.9	31.5
Kokomo city	36.68	58,187	58,020	-0.3	1581.8	2.2	82.2	45,797	17.3	89,100	58.2	5.8	59.3	35.5
Lafayette city	29.38	68,864	71,721	4.1	2441.2	8.3	76.8	46,374	15.3	114,800	69.6	5.2	52.7	38.3
Lake Station city	8.31	12,671	11,845	-6.5	1425.4	6.0	78.4	47,857	19.3	84,400	63.4	9.9	67.7	24.8
La Porte city	11.67	22,063	21,569	-2.2	1848.2	5.5	83.7	41,231	14.6	99,300	60.3	7.3	58.9	33.9
Lawrence city	20.20	45,915	49,462	7.7	2448.6	8.0	90.9	56,819	13.2	148,700	72.6	5.7	59.9	34.7
Lebanon city	15.52	15,739	16,065	2.1	1035.1	3.1	79.8	53,020	10.3	124,500	67.7	0.6	58.8	32.5
Logansport city	10.47	18,271	17,584	-3.8	1679.5	17.1	82.8	37,670	18.8	66,800	59.3	4.6	58.2	37.7
Madison city	8.63	11,918	11,861	-0.5	1374.4	1.6	77.3	40,231	19.5	133,000	50.0	5.6	50.9	42.9
Marion city	15.60	29,918	27,930	-6.6	1790.4	1.8	84.0	32,977	22.4	67,800	54.2	8.6	54.8	38.4
Martinsville city	4.53	11,753	11,669	-0.7	2575.9	1.1	73.0	44,898	17.7	98,500	56.8	7.4	58.1	34.3
Merrillville town	33.19	34,969	34,792	-0.5	1048.3	5.8	86.9	60,803	11.0	136,100	65.9	6.6	60.0	34.8
Michigan City city	19.68	31,401	31,015	-1.2	1576.0	2.7	78.6	40,631	20.0	89,900	55.9	8.2	55.9	37.3
Mishawaka city	17.65	48,236	50,363	4.4	2853.4	5.3	84.6	43,248	14.6	102,900	66.2	5.4	51.8	40.9
Muncie city	27.40	70,206	67,999	-3.1	2481.7	2.3	69.2	33,944	28.8	73,500	57.5	7.9	50.4	35.3
Munster town	7.55	23,580	22,476	-4.7	2977.0	8.9	90.1	84,254	4.8	228,400	63.9	3.9	70.4	26.7
New Albany city	15.41	36,374	36,843	1.3	2390.9	2.5	84.8	48,734	15.4	122,800	63.0	4.1	56.1	36.9
New Castle city	7.35	18,103	17,113	-5.5	2328.3	0.2	83.5	38,545	21.5	73,300	52.3	7.1	58.3	35.3
New Haven city	11.92	14,843	15,922	7.3	1335.7	0.9	85.2	51,306	7.4	103,400	64.7	7.6	69.0	27.4
Noblesville city	34.35	52,374	64,668	23.5	1882.6	3.8	82.1	82,218	5.8	209,100	73.7	3.2	69.9	23.0
Peru city	5.51	11,588	11,023	-4.9	2000.5	0.7	81.7	39,267	21.0	61,200	59.6	8.7	59.1	37.5
Plainfield town	25.80	27,700	35,287	27.4	1367.7	6.3	79.0	61,046	8.8	170,400	65.8	4.4	67.1	28.8
Plymouth city	7.57	10,138	9,982	-1.5	1318.6	10.1	84.5	37,610	25.7	93,600	57.5	5.9	60.8	32.1
Portage city	25.54	36,828	36,988	0.4	1448.2	4.8	87.4	58,486	15.0	152,500	61.7	5.0	64.5	29.3
Richmond city	24.01	36,779	35,342	-3.9	1472.0	3.8	80.9	39,724	18.9	88,400	57.2	6.4	59.0	33.6
St. John town	12.45	14,831	18,796	26.7	1509.7	4.3	94.3	105,852	3.9	290,200	65.2	4.3	81.7	16.1
Schererville town	15.01	29,217	28,527	-2.4	1900.5	11.1	90.8	72,035	5.6	222,400	66.1	3.9	65.6	29.6
Seymour city	12.14	18,047	19,959	10.6	1644.1	9.0	82.9	44,944	18.8	119,800	65.4	4.6	64.3	30.3
Shelbyville city	12.45	19,059	19,407	1.8	1558.8	4.9	82.8	52,901	14.1	102,100	64.8	4.3	60.4	30.5
South Bend city	41.96	101,249	102,026	0.8	2431.5	8.8	85.0	40,265	21.5	85,200	63.9	6.3	58.3	35.3
Speedway town	4.75	11,812	12,193	3.2	2566.9	17.9	83.4	42,188	17.0	122,000	66.5	4.7	51.5	43.6
Terre Haute city	34.55	60,785	60,622	-0.3	1754.6	3.2	73.8	36,406	26.7	78,700	55.4	9.0	53.1	37.0
Valparaiso city	16.32	31,743	33,897	6.8	2077.0	5.2	76.9	59,533	12.8	185,800	60.7	4.7	54.9	34.2
Vincennes city	7.41	18,422	16,862	-8.5	2275.6	1.9	73.3	38,412	19.9	77,700	60.9	5.0	56.6	35.8
Wabash city	9.64	10,665	9,941	-6.8	1031.2	0.7	80.2	44,973	15.5	82,400	62.0	5.6	59.0	34.7
Warsaw city	13.36	13,695	15,150	10.6	1134.0	9.7	68.6	55,982	12.9	135,200	68.3	5.1	61.8	28.3
Washington city	6.63	11,773	12,528	6.4	1889.6	7.6	81.4	41,824	18.5	86,300	62.5	6.3	61.4	34.9
Westfield city	30.40	30,133	43,649	44.9	1435.8	6.9	85.1	98,376	5.8	254,800	73.4	2.8	79.1	15.7
West Lafayette city	13.58	41,997	50,996	21.4	3755.2	24.3	54.5	34,650	36.0	224,000	51.9	3.8	36.8	35.9
Yorktown town	31.93	11,301	11,111	-1.7	348.0	1.9	87.8	65,395	10.3	141,900	63.8	3.9	72.6	24.2
Zionsville town	67.25	24,392	28,357	16.3	421.7	5.7	87.3	137,377	4.5	385,700	67.8	2.5	80.3	17.4
IOWA	55853.72	3,046,871	3,155,070	3.6	56.5	5.3	85.2	60,523	11.4	147,800	67.3	3.7	63.4	29.3
Altoona city	10.91	14,594	19,221	31.7	1761.8	2.9	81.3	77,581	7.1	196,600	71.9	1.5	73.3	22.2
Ames city	27.34	59,035	66,258	12.2	2423.5	12.8	61.1	48,105	27.4	205,900	63.3	5.8	40.8	31.6

Table B. Incorporated Places, Census Designated Places (CDPs), and Minor Civil Divisions (MCDs) of 10,000 or More Population — **Crime, Residential Construction and Local Government Finance**

STATE City, town, township, borough, or CDP (county if applicable)	Serious crimes known to police, 2018[1] — Violent crime — Number	Violent crime — Rate[2]	Property crime — Number	Property crime — Rate[2]	New residential construction authorized by building permits, 2019 — Value ($1,000)	Number of housing units	Percent single family	Local government finance, 2017 — General revenue — Total (mil dol)	Intergovernmental — Total (mil dol)	Intergovernmental — Percent from state gov.	Taxes per capita[3]	General expenditure — Total (mil dol)	Per capita[3] — Total	Per capita[3] — Capital outlays	Debt outstanding (mil dol)
	15	16	17	18	19	20	21	22	23	24	25	26	27	28	29
INDIANA	25,581	382	145,838	2,179	4,988,366	22,309	73.1	X	X	X	X	X	X	X	X
Anderson city	227	413	2,340	4,260	7,400	58	96.6	65.9	9.6	48.7	544	172.4	3,140	78	189.0
Auburn city	7	53	169	1,278	17,170	71	100.0	23.9	6.2	98.9	406	13.1	993	129	17.8
Avon town	NA	NA	NA	NA	63,096	237	100.0	9.5	2.0	92.2	387	10.8	624	69	12.6
Bedford city	16	121	283	2,131	3,738	23	100.0	22.3	4.0	86.3	578	14.7	1,105	133	15.6
Beech Grove city	NA	NA	NA	NA	0	0	0.0	14.0	2.2	91.1	340	15.5	1,045	72	5.3
Bloomington city	463	540	2,275	2,654	NA	NA	NA	188.3	58.2	35.3	932	263.9	3,110	107	350.1
Brownsburg town	33	124	264	995	47,376	204	81.4	30.4	3.5	93.1	511	36.6	1,414	292	35.5
Carmel city	43	46	716	761	186,779	468	76.1	102.8	23.2	88.3	477	123.4	1,267	54	753.7
Cedar Lake town	7	56	193	1,532	32,020	188	100.0	16.4	1.6	81.6	369	11.4	917	142	19.5
Chesterton town	11	81	111	819	20,993	89	55.1	17.8	1.5	87.3	510	12.1	894	57	51.9
Clarksville town	NA	NA	NA	NA	7,957	36	61.1	29.5	0.0	0.0	878	27.6	1,276	10	61.8
Columbus city	76	160	1,706	3,584	NA	NA	NA	46.4	14.7	29.1	536	46.8	992	175	14.9
Connersville city	NA	NA	NA	NA	NA	NA	NA	12.9	11.0	5.4	11	19.5	1,516	51	9.7
Crawfordsville city	71	438	342	2,110	6,528	46	93.5	12.9	2.0	59.4	512	11.6	721	0	1.5
Crown Point city	6	20	335	1,121	69,590	215	100.0	36.5	4.4	84.2	428	24.8	839	99	27.2
Dyer town	10	63	133	838	2,285	4	100.0	22.6	2.5	93.3	592	12.5	788	84	34.2
East Chicago city	NA	NA	NA	NA	0	0	0.0	83.4	31.3	97.0	1,329	73.6	2,614	393	98.2
Elkhart city	624	1,185	1,869	3,549	7,425	45	75.6	84.0	13.2	96.2	658	62.0	1,184	55	47.7
Evansville city	675	568	5,301	4,463	28,827	157	88.5	196.3	45.3	74.1	553	197.1	1,665	283	745.6
Fishers city	46	49	815	867	220,329	855	73.5	86.7	6.6	88.0	656	66.7	728	57	325.6
Fort Wayne city	1,024	383	7,007	2,618	NA	NA	NA	240.6	46.2	100.0	694	183.4	692	51	497.7
Frankfort city	NA	NA	469	2,979	685	7	71.4	21.4	5.6	96.9	508	21.2	1,344	159	13.2
Franklin city	129	510	708	2,800	19,162	93	100.0	21.8	3.0	88.6	514	35.3	1,414	144	21.7
Gary city	374	496	2,723	3,610	1,503	8	100.0	125.1	22.3	84.0	516	133.1	1,757	240	84.3
Goshen city	47	141	1,128	3,379	19,854	57	100.0	38.2	4.0	92.1	517	33.9	1,012	144	85.8
Granger CDP	NA	NA	NA	NA	NA	NA	NA	NA	NA	NA	NA	NA	NA	NA	NA
Greencastle city	NA	NA	NA	NA	9,385	104	11.5	9.0	0.9	39.9	445	7.0	681	45	1.7
Greenfield city	NA	NA	NA	NA	42,973	163	97.5	22.4	1.7	77.2	849	17.2	780	78	3.3
Greensburg city	NA	NA	NA	NA	7,125	57	100.0	15.0	3.3	73.4	483	11.7	988	191	49.2
Greenwood city	83	142	1,777	3,047	71,360	288	93.8	62.6	7.3	92.8	391	36.7	639	41	58.3
Griffith town	8	50	381	2,374	473	2	100.0	15.2	2.3	89.5	451	8.1	501	63	22.5
Hammond city	365	480	2,652	3,487	2,490	16	37.5	168.6	61.9	98.7	680	170.7	2,231	365	260.5
Highland town	NA	NA	567	2,528	1,907	8	100.0	32.4	5.8	95.9	503	20.5	907	84	24.9
Hobart city	71	253	1,112	3,957	4,445	16	100.0	43.0	4.9	93.2	598	37.1	1,318	311	26.8
Huntington city	NA	NA	NA	NA	4,219	19	100.0	15.8	1.0	68.5	491	5.9	345	14	2.4
Indianapolis city (consolidated city)	11,170	1,273	36,237	4,129	499,309	2,382	48.4	NA	NA	NA	NA	NA	NA	NA	NA
Indianapolis city (balance)	NA	NA	NA	NA	NA	NA	NA	3008.5	919.2	61.9	492	2462.1	2,851	95	3572.6
Jasper city	NA	NA	NA	NA	13,197	67	49.3	57.7	1.6	92.0	448	14.0	899	160	6.1
Jeffersonville city	65	136	1,239	2,597	52,148	403	39.0	91.7	2.1	100.0	988	58.9	1,246	332	115.6
Kokomo city	364	630	1,426	2,467	26,613	221	31.2	82.7	29.4	45.6	655	60.4	1,044	59	31.1
Lafayette city	338	464	2,623	3,598	29,334	372	12.4	122.9	19.0	86.6	649	91.6	1,271	380	148.0
Lake Station city	31	261	321	2,702	0	0	0.0	11.3	1.5	89.9	364	10.3	862	43	22.6
La Porte city	111	513	495	2,289	1,846	10	100.0	26.9	5.2	89.0	523	31.9	1,470	437	24.4
Lawrence city	210	428	1,083	2,206	18,411	81	100.0	36.2	4.4	86.5	302	30.7	631	17	26.3
Lebanon city	NA	NA	NA	NA	12,629	70	85.7	34.5	2.0	90.7	415	16.9	1,062	162	52.5
Logansport city	NA	NA	NA	NA	NA	NA	NA	20.2	3.3	97.7	419	21.7	1,229	107	0.9
Madison city	NA	NA	NA	NA	3,435	11	100.0	17.8	1.3	92.2	601	16.6	1,421	43	17.1
Marion city	128	455	1,038	3,692	6,114	31	100.0	40.6	8.6	97.2	692	30.1	1,067	72	22.7
Martinsville city	NA	NA	NA	NA	2,774	15	73.3	24.4	17.7	6.1	575	14.2	1,221	0	31.2
Merrillville town	NA	NA	NA	NA	13,788	87	65.5	15.5	0.6	100.0	427	11.5	332	58	31.2
Michigan City city	230	742	1,373	4,429	3,856	17	100.0	74.6	22.2	98.5	673	65.1	2,099	353	80.9
Mishawaka city	114	231	2,525	5,121	8,757	52	100.0	95.6	3.7	0.0	1,446	98.6	2,014	760	76.1
Muncie city	219	320	2,281	3,335	2,287	23	100.0	143.2	20.0	81.2	342	96.7	1,405	349	176.4
Munster town	21	93	375	1,660	11,420	24	100.0	26.4	3.9	68.0	577	21.5	948	119	65.4
New Albany city	NA	NA	NA	NA	8,382	44	100.0	71.7	6.7	92.1	637	56.1	1,538	228	74.7
New Castle city	NA	NA	NA	NA	262	5	100.0	23.4	4.7	21.7	705	23.6	1,366	623	12.7
New Haven city	NA	NA	NA	NA	NA	NA	NA	26.4	4.7	68.0	385	16.9	1,084	248	21.3
Noblesville city	59	93	589	930	169,450	678	86.0	88.8	18.0	88.6	706	64.9	1,050	167	233.6
Peru city	51	465	370	3,372	1,273	6	100.0	23.1	1.8	79.0	506	19.8	1,771	116	23.1
Plainfield town	93	276	794	2,358	79,689	375	65.1	54.8	5.2	94.5	886	55.2	1,677	635	168.9
Plymouth city	5	50	218	2,191	1,266	10	80.0	27.4	3.2	98.5	495	16.8	1,675	365	21.7
Portage city	68	186	740	2,019	17,386	121	100.0	46.0	1.2	100.0	730	31.1	846	78	68.2
Richmond city	NA	NA	NA	NA	1,263	6	100.0	52.0	15.0	80.1	449	55.1	1,554	99	70.1
St. John town	3	17	111	630	86,304	324	100.0	14.5	1.9	98.7	375	12.6	735	87	7.3
Schererville town	NA	NA	NA	NA	15,636	50	84.0	34.0	2.7	87.8	316	18.9	661	42	46.2
Seymour city	41	208	995	5,056	18,482	166	37.3	40.1	2.9	36.6	728	25.7	1,316	232	47.9
Shelbyville city	215	1,127	563	2,952	5,569	34	100.0	204.4	74.3	64.4	696	181.1	9,505	3120	126.9
South Bend city	1,064	1,039	4,406	4,303	NA	NA	NA	222.5	56.4	85.4	806	191.1	1,873	278	219.6
Speedway town	35	287	522	4,283	930	45	0.0	20.9	1.6	86.9	576	20.5	1,687	25	78.0
Terre Haute city	NA	NA	NA	NA	5,436	33	51.5	102.6	20.5	62.6	551	89.2	1,467	429	223.0
Valparaiso city	37	110	402	1,196	29,414	100	90.0	55.7	4.7	93.1	792	45.6	1,364	214	81.6
Vincennes city	NA	NA	NA	NA	224	2	0.0	23.6	1.7	95.2	472	12.7	735	38	8.1
Wabash city	NA	NA	NA	NA	1,385	7	71.4	9.0	1.2	100.0	397	14.0	1,387	0	17.6
Warsaw city	NA	NA	NA	NA	4,536	106	17.9	29.7	2.8	72.8	984	27.4	1,847	292	16.6
Washington city	NA	NA	NA	NA	3,496	26	61.5	15.3	2.2	94.5	221	15.1	1,217	426	43.5
Westfield city	11	27	390	950	297,131	1,038	72.4	28.2	4.8	76.6	474	48.8	1,236	369	100.3
West Lafayette city	31	66	401	855	64,750	529	3.6	74.3	4.6	92.8	365	56.2	1,184	581	150.3
Yorktown town	NA	NA	NA	NA	0	0	0.0	5.9	1.2	93.4	216	4.4	391	23	7.9
Zionsville town	NA	NA	60	221	106,305	449	48.3	31.5	14.2	99.7	455	23.7	862	49	22.1
IOWA	7,893	250	53,385	1,692	2,500,495	11,870	66.4	X	X	X	X	X	X	X	X
Altoona city	NA	NA	NA	NA	54,130	232	100.0	33.9	4.2	59.6	1,113	25.7	1,377	74	121.2
Ames city	NA	NA	NA	NA	41,194	338	18.6	279.3	24.1	60.4	595	247.2	3,729	504	221.7

1 Data for serious crimes have not been adjusted for underreporting. This may affect comparability between geographic areas over time.
2 Per 100,000 population estimated by the FBI. 3 Based on population estimated as of July 1 of the year shown.

Table B. Incorporated Places, Census Designated Places (CDPs), and Minor Civil Divisions (MCDs) of 10,000 or More Population — Land Area, Population, and Households, and Employment

STATE City, town, township, borough, or CDP (county if applicable)	Land area 2010 (sq mi)	Population Total persons 2010	Total persons 2019	Percent change 2010–2019	Persons per square mile 2019	Population characteristics 2015–2019 Percent foreign born	Percent living in the same house as previous year	Income and poverty 2015–2019 Median household income	Percent of households with income below poverty level	Median value of owner-occupied housing units	Employment, 2015–2019 Percent in civilian labor force	Unemploy-ment rate	Households, 2015–2019 (percent of households) Family households	One person households
	1	2	3	4	5	6	7	8	9	10	11	12	13	14
IOWA—Con.														
Ankeny city	30.14	45,608	67,355	47.7	2234.7	4.2	80.4	86,486	4.9	220,100	78.9	3.0	66.6	22.6
Bettendorf city	21.30	33,205	36,543	10.1	1715.6	6.4	85.8	82,153	6.7	225,300	67.7	2.9	68.0	27.7
Boone city	9.09	12,671	12,384	-2.3	1362.4	1.6	80.4	57,943	8.3	112,200	70.0	1.8	62.9	32.6
Burlington city	14.40	25,611	24,713	-3.5	1716.2	2.1	81.1	47,540	18.1	93,200	64.3	6.3	59.7	34.7
Carroll city	5.73	10,128	9,833	-2.9	1716.1	2.2	86.8	47,534	11.2	148,500	66.8	2.4	59.6	37.7
Cedar Falls city	28.93	39,250	40,536	3.3	1401.2	5.1	71.7	61,420	16.7	189,100	72.1	3.1	53.3	30.4
Cedar Rapids city	71.62	126,580	133,562	5.5	1864.9	6.1	83.8	58,511	11.4	141,800	69.3	4.0	56.9	34.2
Clinton city	35.16	26,878	25,093	-6.6	713.7	1.7	81.7	44,094	15.8	99,500	59.2	5.7	58.8	33.8
Clive city	7.67	15,421	17,242	11.8	2248.0	8.6	89.0	104,839	5.4	264,300	72.9	3.1	73.2	22.9
Coralville city	12.56	18,910	22,290	17.9	1774.7	19.4	74.0	60,321	14.2	227,700	69.7	3.1	55.2	31.4
Council Bluffs city	42.93	62,226	62,166	-0.1	1448.1	5.5	85.0	53,524	13.0	120,100	65.7	4.3	61.2	31.4
Davenport city	63.54	99,701	101,590	1.9	1598.8	4.5	87.9	51,029	15.2	131,700	62.9	4.5	56.7	35.4
Des Moines city	88.18	204,220	214,237	4.9	2429.5	12.5	80.7	53,525	15.0	133,200	70.2	5.8	56.4	34.2
Dubuque city	30.62	57,605	57,882	0.5	1890.3	3.3	81.2	54,234	14.8	143,500	65.6	4.7	58.0	34.0
Fairfield city	6.54	9,467	10,425	10.1	1594.0	12.6	78.8	40,920	20.6	114,200	60.1	8.7	55.5	41.3
Fort Dodge city	16.04	25,205	23,888	-5.2	1489.3	3.9	82.6	40,886	15.1	93,600	56.2	4.9	52.5	40.7
Fort Madison city	9.67	11,099	10,321	-7.0	1067.3	0.5	88.3	42,694	12.8	81,600	56.9	8.9	60.5	32.3
Grimes city	11.71	8,255	14,804	79.3	1264.2	3.4	81.6	81,950	5.5	225,800	80.6	6.6	69.6	24.9
Indianola city	11.32	14,780	16,015	8.4	1414.8	2.3	78.6	60,854	15.0	163,300	66.3	3.8	63.1	31.9
Iowa City city	25.60	67,961	75,130	10.5	2934.8	14.3	69.4	49,075	26.6	215,100	69.3	4.7	43.8	33.9
Johnston city	16.76	17,272	22,582	30.7	1347.4	9.7	86.8	96,948	3.5	268,300	76.4	2.4	69.8	25.2
Keokuk city	9.08	10,776	10,157	-5.7	1118.6	2.2	87.7	39,779	21.6	71,200	61.5	9.3	60.4	34.5
Marion city	17.71	35,172	40,359	14.7	2278.9	2.2	88.4	72,150	7.4	168,700	71.1	3.6	64.8	28.0
Marshalltown city	19.28	27,557	26,666	-3.2	1383.1	18.7	86.1	52,035	14.5	94,300	62.7	5.4	62.0	28.9
Mason City city	27.79	28,072	26,931	-4.1	969.1	2.4	87.2	50,397	13.5	114,900	66.2	5.1	56.1	37.9
Muscatine city	18.18	23,777	23,631	-0.6	1299.8	6.9	91.8	52,660	13.7	110,800	66.2	3.8	64.4	29.2
Newton city	11.26	15,254	15,182	-0.5	1348.3	2.8	83.3	48,481	14.5	114,200	63.0	5.6	63.2	32.2
North Liberty city	9.02	13,393	19,501	45.6	2162.0	7.5	75.7	83,949	5.8	220,800	82.5	1.1	65.1	21.2
Norwalk city	11.55	8,990	11,938	32.8	1033.6	1.0	85.4	83,403	7.1	202,900	75.9	2.4	71.2	24.8
Oskaloosa city	8.02	11,503	11,506	0.0	1434.7	3.2	81.2	47,429	19.1	96,300	64.7	4.7	59.8	33.3
Ottumwa city	15.84	25,021	24,368	-2.6	1538.4	10.2	83.0	41,722	16.6	74,100	63.0	6.0	62.1	33.0
Pella city	8.99	10,358	10,237	-1.2	1138.7	3.3	69.3	68,963	4.3	187,400	66.1	1.3	64.9	31.4
Sioux City city	58.46	82,693	82,651	-0.1	1413.8	9.8	89.4	55,433	14.3	116,600	69.4	4.8	64.4	28.5
Spencer city	10.93	11,247	10,952	-2.6	1002.0	2.0	77.5	46,545	12.8	128,800	62.0	5.0	60.3	34.9
Storm Lake city	5.27	10,641	10,322	-3.0	1958.6	32.9	83.9	50,565	14.6	121,300	71.8	8.0	64.4	31.8
Urbandale city	22.48	39,461	44,379	12.5	1974.2	8.2	86.0	90,858	5.3	237,500	73.6	3.1	70.0	23.2
Waterloo city	61.39	68,496	67,328	-1.7	1096.7	9.2	81.5	47,327	16.4	117,400	65.4	5.7	59.1	34.3
Waukee city	20.75	13,809	24,089	74.4	1160.9	8.0	83.1	94,580	4.7	238,900	79.4	2.3	68.3	25.1
Waverly city	11.26	9,874	10,198	3.3	905.7	2.6	81.6	64,949	9.1	173,700	65.1	2.8	67.5	26.7
West Des Moines city	47.09	56,707	67,899	19.7	1441.9	12.4	81.5	76,368	5.8	218,500	73.5	2.3	59.0	32.9
KANSAS	81758.48	2,853,123	2,913,314	2.1	35.6	7.1	83.8	59,597	12.0	151,900	65.9	4.1	64.7	29.1
Andover city	10.10	11,800	13,405	13.6	1327.2	6.9	85.4	89,302	8.8	201,000	67.4	2.5	76.7	20.7
Arkansas City city	9.32	12,417	11,669	-6.0	1252.0	6.2	84.3	42,576	17.6	64,100	57.9	6.0	59.9	35.5
Atchison city	8.01	11,022	10,476	-5.0	1307.9	1.0	83.6	46,465	16.0	89,900	62.4	3.8	63.3	32.8
Coffeyville city	9.46	10,306	9,275	-10.0	980.4	4.0	81.4	33,750	26.1	55,800	53.9	6.0	51.7	41.5
Derby city	10.26	22,294	24,943	11.9	2431.1	3.5	84.5	73,322	6.1	165,200	66.8	3.4	72.7	23.4
Dodge City city	14.58	27,326	27,104	-0.8	1859.0	29.1	81.8	50,338	13.0	109,100	72.0	6.0	71.9	22.3
El Dorado city	9.16	13,235	12,954	-2.1	1414.2	2.3	78.5	43,314	14.9	88,500	65.1	7.5	61.7	31.6
Emporia city	11.98	24,942	24,598	-1.4	2053.3	12.9	72.0	40,525	21.8	88,900	69.5	6.6	54.6	30.5
Garden City city	10.79	26,727	26,408	-1.2	2447.5	24.8	83.2	55,987	12.1	149,300	72.2	3.9	66.8	27.5
Gardner city	10.29	19,134	22,031	15.1	2141.0	4.0	81.0	78,180	7.5	189,100	78.0	3.4	78.5	17.9
Great Bend city	10.50	16,005	14,974	-6.4	1426.1	7.8	80.6	47,574	15.3	95,800	66.0	3.6	61.4	33.4
Hays city	8.39	20,539	20,744	1.0	2472.5	2.7	73.6	50,040	18.7	176,900	71.8	3.3	53.7	35.2
Haysville city	4.65	10,830	11,338	4.7	2438.3	0.9	88.6	54,484	8.9	102,500	64.9	3.5	68.5	29.1
Hutchinson city	24.58	42,180	40,383	-4.3	1642.9	3.7	81.6	46,927	14.7	96,300	61.0	4.7	58.5	33.8
Junction City city	11.11	23,361	21,482	-8.0	1933.6	7.3	71.4	53,932	11.7	143,100	57.3	4.4	68.1	25.9
Kansas City city	124.82	145,783	152,960	4.9	1225.4	17.9	85.5	45,665	19.0	95,600	66.2	6.8	63.1	30.9
Lansing city	12.31	11,261	11,949	6.1	970.7	5.0	81.3	89,213	2.9	173,000	52.8	3.9	77.5	21.3
Lawrence city	34.14	87,918	98,193	11.7	2876.2	8.6	69.9	53,639	19.4	195,500	71.6	4.3	48.6	32.2
Leavenworth city	24.24	35,245	35,957	2.0	1483.4	3.0	70.0	59,132	14.3	123,800	51.4	4.7	65.9	30.1
Leawood city	15.11	31,888	34,727	8.9	2298.3	5.8	90.2	157,515	1.7	463,200	63.6	2.7	78.8	18.6
Lenexa city	34.07	48,216	55,625	15.4	1632.7	8.6	81.9	87,102	5.0	260,900	72.6	2.6	66.8	26.6
Liberal city	11.44	20,531	19,174	-6.6	1676.0	31.4	82.7	48,629	16.7	106,400	72.8	5.0	69.9	24.3
McPherson city	7.43	13,161	13,061	-0.8	1757.9	2.6	82.2	58,337	11.7	143,700	71.1	2.2	63.4	29.8
Manhattan city	19.85	52,158	54,604	4.7	2750.8	9.2	67.5	50,537	21.9	209,700	65.7	5.2	44.9	35.1
Merriam city	4.32	11,017	11,081	0.6	2565.0	6.8	83.7	63,806	8.8	169,400	69.0	3.6	51.4	38.3
Newton city	14.51	19,116	18,861	-1.3	1299.9	3.8	84.6	55,405	11.5	107,500	64.7	3.1	66.6	29.9
Olathe city	61.64	125,922	140,545	11.6	2280.1	10.6	85.9	90,435	6.0	238,100	74.2	2.8	74.4	20.9
Ottawa city	9.87	12,652	12,254	-3.1	1241.5	2.1	83.6	46,808	12.8	109,000	65.1	5.3	60.3	31.9
Overland Park city	75.18	173,329	195,494	12.8	2600.3	11.6	82.0	86,487	5.0	276,100	71.5	3.0	63.6	30.2
Parsons city	10.61	10,499	9,477	-9.7	893.2	0.6	84.1	39,949	21.2	65,000	64.6	3.9	63.4	33.3
Pittsburg city	13.06	20,237	20,050	-0.9	1535.2	6.7	69.5	34,956	28.2	88,500	62.1	5.7	51.1	34.0
Prairie Village city	6.21	21,447	22,295	4.0	3590.2	2.6	85.8	91,136	5.1	290,600	69.5	2.5	59.7	34.4
Salina city	25.74	47,777	46,550	-2.6	1808.5	6.5	82.4	50,490	13.7	129,300	65.7	3.4	58.4	35.2
Shawnee city	41.97	62,203	65,807	5.8	1568.0	6.2	85.6	87,120	8.3	237,500	74.0	2.9	71.1	24.2
Topeka city	61.44	127,630	125,310	-1.8	2039.6	5.1	83.5	47,999	14.0	103,200	63.4	4.7	55.0	38.5
Wichita city	161.66	382,437	389,938	2.0	2412.1	10.2	81.9	52,620	15.4	133,400	66.7	5.6	60.2	33.4
Winfield city	11.15	12,332	11,943	-3.2	1071.1	3.3	76.4	45,923	16.2	91,500	55.7	4.8	64.3	29.7
KENTUCKY	39491.38	4,339,333	4,467,673	3.0	113.1	3.9	84.9	50,589	17.0	141,000	59.0	5.6	65.5	28.6
Ashland city	10.74	21,691	20,146	-7.1	1875.8	1.8	85.0	40,917	24.9	102,800	52.6	8.6	63.5	31.4
Bardstown city	12.17	12,527	13,253	5.8	1089.0	1.0	79.1	54,328	10.7	123,500	64.3	5.9	56.3	31.9
Berea city	16.51	13,558	16,026	18.2	970.7	4.6	77.5	44,292	20.6	139,300	59.9	4.9	64.0	31.3
Bowling Green city	39.44	59,407	70,543	18.7	1788.6	12.8	68.9	42,216	22.6	161,000	65.9	5.5	52.8	34.5

Table B. Incorporated Places, Census Designated Places (CDPs), and Minor Civil Divisions (MCDs) of 10,000 or More Population — Crime, Residential Construction and Local Government Finance

STATE City, town, township, borough, or CDP (county if applicable)	Violent crime Number	Violent crime Rate[2]	Property crime Number	Property crime Rate[2]	Value ($1,000)	Number of housing units	Percent single family	Total (mil dol)	Intergov. Total (mil dol)	Intergov. Percent from state gov.	Taxes per capita[3]	Total (mil dol)	Per capita[3] Total	Per capita[3] Capital outlays	Debt outstanding (mil dol)
	15	16	17	18	19	20	21	22	23	24	25	26	27	28	29
IOWA—Con.															
Ankeny city	NA	NA	NA	NA	276,441	1,126	83.6	81.8	8.7	94.3	723	68.9	1,104	228	148.9
Bettendorf city	NA	NA	NA	NA	54,295	205	95.1	69.7	11.7	60.9	984	68.3	1,908	569	133.4
Boone city	NA	NA	NA	NA	6,042	26	38.5	14.6	2.5	70.3	633	11.7	938	124	21.4
Burlington city	NA	NA	NA	NA	3,150	29	58.6	41.9	7.2	72.7	815	36.7	1,472	223	57.3
Carroll city	NA	NA	NA	NA	2,273	7	100.0	15.2	2.1	75.6	839	12.7	1,286	365	9.1
Cedar Falls city	NA	NA	NA	NA	25,366	99	91.9	83.0	14.2	55.4	834	73.4	1,788	694	67.3
Cedar Rapids city	NA	NA	NA	NA	52,799	370	46.8	381.2	99.4	38.3	1,037	387.8	2,925	1067	489.6
Clinton city	NA	NA	NA	NA	4,813	41	31.7	49.1	8.4	60.8	865	51.4	2,024	360	121.2
Clive city	NA	NA	NA	NA	39,676	111	100.0	31.8	3.6	75.6	1,154	30.1	1,759	371	24.6
Coralville city	NA	NA	NA	NA	15,773	116	14.7	69.9	11.8	87.0	1,801	80.5	3,824	1250	273.1
Council Bluffs city	NA	NA	NA	NA	25,496	106	79.2	131.3	37.5	66.4	1,073	114.8	1,840	507	90.8
Davenport city	NA	NA	NA	NA	38,607	318	38.4	188.2	41.4	54.1	961	167.1	1,633	381	317.3
Des Moines city	NA	NA	NA	NA	142,998	670	58.4	463.7	96.0	39.3	846	411.3	1,898	251	561.4
Dubuque city	NA	NA	NA	NA	27,650	78	92.3	147.4	46.1	38.9	918	125.0	2,144	533	271.2
Fairfield city	NA	NA	NA	NA	5,010	41	7.3	14.7	1.6	75.8	712	15.4	1,497	12	15.6
Fort Dodge city	NA	NA	NA	NA	2,518	14	100.0	58.0	12.5	53.7	891	59.8	2,459	1168	79.4
Fort Madison city	NA	NA	NA	NA	440	2	100.0	17.5	3.0	90.6	654	16.6	1,582	313	37.1
Grimes city	NA	NA	NA	NA	33,374	409	31.5	19.8	2.2	96.0	666	24.4	1,919	1082	42.5
Indianola city	NA	NA	NA	NA	10,427	58	96.6	20.3	2.3	89.0	675	13.6	856	85	30.8
Iowa City city	NA	NA	NA	NA	115,921	569	17.2	146.2	39.2	60.6	845	128.1	1,693	507	128.7
Johnston city	NA	NA	NA	NA	37,733	213	32.4	33.8	4.7	79.6	984	40.8	1,892	764	92.5
Keokuk city	NA	NA	NA	NA	0	0	0.0	17.8	2.8	76.6	795	15.1	1,465	44	42.3
Marion city	NA	NA	NA	NA	24,360	212	68.9	51.0	6.9	76.0	754	55.2	1,399	438	59.9
Marshalltown city	NA	NA	NA	NA	3,240	15	86.7	38.7	9.3	50.5	670	35.6	1,314	305	58.8
Mason City city	NA	NA	NA	NA	3,214	11	100.0	40.6	7.3	69.5	793	42.0	1,538	324	36.6
Muscatine city	NA	NA	NA	NA	6,703	53	9.4	67.1	10.4	41.0	810	52.9	2,230	469	25.9
Newton city	NA	NA	NA	NA	3,809	19	89.5	24.5	4.2	52.3	786	25.0	1,647	444	24.4
North Liberty city	NA	NA	NA	NA	22,754	93	77.4	26.5	4.9	47.7	724	26.1	1,386	473	59.8
Norwalk city	NA	NA	NA	NA	53,098	202	100.0	15.8	1.4	90.4	882	18.2	1,668	695	22.4
Oskaloosa city	NA	NA	NA	NA	4,581	27	40.7	14.7	2.3	67.5	587	13.9	1,200	429	10.9
Ottumwa city	NA	NA	NA	NA	345	3	100.0	44.8	5.8	59.1	781	40.3	1,648	284	46.3
Pella city	NA	NA	NA	NA	12,843	57	100.0	18.0	3.5	45.1	723	12.3	1,199	298	27.2
Sioux City city	NA	NA	NA	NA	46,907	341	22.9	155.2	34.8	62.7	922	157.5	1,915	438	255.9
Spencer city	NA	NA	NA	NA	9,144	99	4.0	120.9	5.2	35.3	838	118.9	10,773	1628	45.1
Storm Lake city	NA	NA	NA	NA	1,190	8	100.0	15.4	2.4	87.4	755	18.5	1,746	299	42.3
Urbandale city	NA	NA	NA	NA	39,417	130	100.0	55.8	9.1	71.1	842	55.9	1,282	536	77.7
Waterloo city	NA	NA	NA	NA	64,619	237	20.3	144.8	46.8	41.1	964	129.8	1,916	485	112.0
Waukee city	NA	NA	NA	NA	169,609	645	96.3	29.3	4.2	67.5	725	32.2	1,556	502	67.7
Waverly city	NA	NA	NA	NA	NA	NA	NA	72.7	4.5	35.1	875	16.8	1,668	444	32.5
West Des Moines city	NA	NA	NA	NA	135,639	569	39.7	121.3	24.1	64.0	1,088	127.0	1,937	640	128.9
KANSAS	NA	NA	NA	NA	1,682,921	7,961	63.9	X	X	X	X	X	X	X	X
Andover city	12,782	439	76,686	2,634	29,310	143	55.2	21.2	0.5	98.2	867	13.9	1,062	187	69.1
Arkansas City city	50	424	510	4,325	6,369	54	11.1	35.5	2.2	99.8	805	31.9	2,690	283	40.4
Atchison city	43	406	269	2,540	918	4	100.0	11.8	0.7	94.0	714	11.2	1,054	166	67.1
Coffeyville city	57	608	472	5,035	0	0	0.0	16.8	1.3	86.2	928	27.7	2,932	1201	86.1
Derby city	37	155	505	2,118	19,718	87	77.0	30.3	5.6	27.0	636	27.2	1,150	243	64.6
Dodge City city	90	324	592	2,133	7,980	55	67.3	48.6	8.1	47.4	752	49.4	1,793	438	233.4
El Dorado city	28	216	383	2,955	1,520	9	100.0	16.8	0.5	100.0	682	16.2	1,248	18	16.4
Emporia city	28	113	429	1,737	5,548	60	20.0	31.5	5.6	43.5	583	24.5	994	74	26.1
Garden City city	123	457	608	2,260	9,227	65	100.0	63.0	16.3	5.6	571	55.5	2,086	588	41.0
Gardner city	56	255	308	1,404	30,780	155	100.0	25.6	5.6	63.2	373	22.7	1,054	195	97.3
Great Bend city	112	734	577	3,783	410	2	100.0	20.8	2.2	16.6	894	20.5	1,340	310	7.3
Hays city	NA	NA	NA	NA	7,668	37	51.4	29.6	1.7	59.2	978	27.1	1,297	283	16.1
Haysville city	46	406	283	2,495	5,157	26	100.0	12.0	0.8	55.7	528	8.7	773	83	8.7
Hutchinson city	166	409	1,624	4,003	1,824	13	100.0	55.4	8.0	48.2	841	83.1	2,032	932	78.3
Junction City city	NA	NA	NA	NA	NA	NA	NA	44.4	4.6	45.2	969	42.0	1,832	378	151.9
Kansas City city	NA	NA	NA	NA	32,896	183	92.3	398.0	65.7	90.9	1,525	397.1	2,600	393	1749.6
Lansing city	30	249	136	1,129	2,511	10	80.0	10.9	0.8	95.9	508	7.2	603	0	25.1
Lawrence city	NA	NA	NA	NA	67,792	373	46.6	389.1	24.2	49.3	771	374.2	3,873	598	388.7
Leavenworth city	345	950	1,130	3,110	4,684	24	100.0	39.6	6.6	26.9	605	37.9	1,047	202	29.1
Leawood city	27	77	543	1,548	28,964	35	100.0	52.6	5.4	57.2	1,163	54.6	1,576	225	48.9
Lenexa city	107	197	838	1,542	99,103	328	76.5	110.3	17.8	47.3	1,269	134.2	2,507	1242	397.5
Liberal city	NA	NA	NA	NA	1,900	17	76.5	36.0	16.4	78.3	620	35.5	1,782	505	6.6
McPherson city	23	174	NA	NA	5,112	25	52.0	24.1	3.6	37.7	880	19.5	1,481	210	77.8
Manhattan city	NA	NA	NA	NA	20,798	115	41.7	100.8	9.0	35.2	1,197	76.7	1,391	228	373.6
Merriam city	NA	NA	NA	NA	6,345	47	4.3	27.6	9.2	20.5	1,464	21.8	1,944	511	4.4
Newton city	131	696	560	2,974	1,591	9	100.0	32.7	3.2	19.1	639	30.9	1,646	133	82.8
Olathe city	305	219	1,957	1,406	205,461	631	58.6	208.3	13.0	62.7	858	224.7	1,634	444	964.4
Ottawa city	63	512	313	2,545	5,810	35	85.7	11.9	2.1	31.1	534	22.5	1,826	495	32.2
Overland Park city	440	227	3,739	1,929	250,848	1,189	27.6	303.5	66.1	20.9	656	229.9	1,202	268	480.0
Parsons city	91	942	345	3,570	95	2	100.0	14.8	1.6	52.0	787	15.2	1,561	204	8.3
Pittsburg city	NA	NA	NA	NA	2,859	24	100.0	28.8	6.3	21.5	796	26.3	1,304	169	46.0
Prairie Village city	NA	NA	NA	NA	38,309	68	100.0	25.6	5.0	76.7	612	31.8	1,422	456	58.7
Salina city	NA	NA	NA	NA	7,550	38	84.2	68.3	4.8	55.8	857	63.7	1,361	104	135.1
Shawnee city	165	250	1,076	1,631	52,430	307	53.7	77.4	19.9	55.8	704	70.6	1,078	230	128.3
Topeka city	766	606	6,560	5,190	16,631	101	91.1	196.4	25.9	75.3	976	193.8	1,532	380	392.1
Wichita city	4,622	1,180	22,011	5,619	143,267	982	62.9	638.0	175.1	49.8	471	575.7	1,475	346	2489.8
Winfield city	22	182	524	4,341	2,007	10	40.0	16.0	1.8	70.2	623	17.3	1,433	193	67.6
KENTUCKY	9,467	212	87,695	1,963	2,135,837	11,811	63.2	X	X	X	X	X	X	X	X
Ashland city	30	146	774	3,771	346	2	100.0	38.1	5.5	17.2	1,033	22.3	1,082	88	141.8
Bardstown city	26	196	NA	NA	NA	NA	NA	23.7	0.7	74.5	504	22.9	1,749	199	10.7
Berea city	20	126	326	2,051	8,073	78	55.1	17.8	1.2	57.6	833	19.0	1,222	488	98.6
Bowling Green city	208	305	3,312	4,852	44,470	295	49.5	118.3	11.8	29.8	1,082	83.0	1,223	173	165.8

1 Data for serious crimes have not been adjusted for underreporting. This may affect comparability between geographic areas over time.
2 Per 100,000 population estimated by the FBI. 3 Based on population estimated as of July 1 of the year shown.

Table B. Incorporated Places, Census Designated Places (CDPs), and Minor Civil Divisions (MCDs) of 10,000 or More Population — Land Area, Population, and Households, and Employment

STATE City, town, township, borough, or CDP (county if applicable)	Land area 2010 (sq mi)	Total persons 2010	Total persons 2019	Percent change 2010–2019	Persons per square mile 2019	Percent foreign born	Percent living in the same house as previous year	Median household income	Percent of households with income below poverty level	Median value of owner-occupied housing units	Percent in civilian labor force	Unemployment rate	Family households	One person households
	1	2	3	4	5	6	7	8	9	10	11	12	13	14
KENTUCKY—Con.														
Burlington CDP	8.81	15,926	NA	NA	NA	4.9	80.7	73,344	7.2	168,900	71.0	4.2	76.9	20.1
Campbellsville city	7.50	10,676	11,482	7.5	1530.9	3.4	66.4	31,107	27.2	107,300	53.9	6.1	57.8	35.0
Covington city	13.20	40,506	40,341	-0.4	3056.1	3.8	79.6	43,437	21.0	111,500	65.0	7.9	49.9	39.9
Danville city	17.18	16,206	16,769	3.5	976.1	3.6	72.9	39,906	19.9	148,700	51.3	7.0	58.8	36.3
Elizabethtown city	26.75	28,055	30,289	8.0	1132.3	4.2	75.6	46,754	15.5	180,000	61.9	5.9	57.5	35.3
Erlanger city	8.37	18,138	19,246	6.1	2299.4	4.0	85.2	64,460	8.8	136,100	68.6	3.4	64.5	28.1
Florence city	10.67	29,531	33,004	11.8	3093.2	8.2	78.3	57,348	8.9	153,700	69.3	5.1	62.3	32.3
Fort Campbell North CDP	5.07	13,685	NA	NA	NA	7.2	60.3	39,917	11.7	0	17.6	14.5	94.7	4.7
Fort Knox CDP	20.29	10,124	NA	NA	NA	6.3	38.1	59,323	5.3	0	33.7	5.3	80.5	17.3
Fort Thomas city	5.67	16,165	16,263	0.6	2868.3	2.1	86.4	78,972	5.9	227,600	68.8	2.9	67.3	28.6
Frankfort city	14.77	27,269	27,755	1.8	1879.1	5.8	76.8	50,211	12.5	130,900	63.3	4.0	51.4	42.1
Georgetown city	16.66	29,138	34,992	20.1	2100.4	3.5	79.3	65,812	10.9	170,000	72.2	3.6	69.5	23.5
Glasgow city	15.86	14,050	14,485	3.1	913.3	3.5	78.5	35,138	20.6	121,600	51.0	8.4	58.7	33.6
Henderson city	16.12	28,924	28,207	-2.5	1749.8	2.1	82.3	39,887	21.2	120,700	55.2	5.0	59.2	35.4
Hopkinsville city	31.83	31,988	30,680	-4.1	963.9	2.2	79.1	41,597	21.7	116,600	54.7	7.0	58.8	36.4
Independence city	17.56	24,759	28,521	15.2	1624.2	2.9	87.8	81,657	4.1	173,300	74.7	3.0	75.7	18.5
Jeffersontown city	10.34	27,813	27,715	-0.4	2680.4	10.9	86.8	68,803	5.5	181,500	70.0	3.8	64.6	29.0
Lawrenceburg city	6.02	11,018	11,509	4.5	1911.8	0.7	78.3	50,382	16.8	131,100	69.3	8.9	63.5	28.0
Lexington-Fayette urban county	283.64	295,870	323,152	9.2	1139.3	9.7	75.6	57,291	15.5	189,800	67.8	5.1	57.6	31.6
Louisville/Jefferson County metro government	NA	741,075	766,757	3.5	NA	7.8	84.5	54,474	5.5	170,100	64.7	0.0	64.6	32.1
Louisville/Jefferson County metro government (balance)	263.43	595,710	617,638	3.7	2344.6	7.7	84.2	53,436	15.0	158,700	65.1	6.0	59.4	33.4
Lyndon city	3.60	11,002	11,423	3.8	3173.1	11.4	77.4	57,472	7.5	191,300	75.2	4.2	44.2	45.9
Madisonville city	17.76	19,841	18,621	-6.1	1048.5	1.9	80.5	44,720	21.1	125,000	58.3	7.2	63.9	30.6
Mayfield city	7.31	10,033	9,817	-2.2	1343.0	5.4	88.4	32,289	32.6	100,200	50.0	11.6	57.3	39.3
Middlesborough city	7.38	10,190	9,084	-10.9	1230.9	0.7	84.8	25,488	35.7	91,500	38.0	8.5	61.7	33.5
Mount Washington city	9.29	13,521	14,817	9.6	1594.9	2.0	89.1	69,214	8.5	170,400	69.2	3.7	72.6	25.5
Murray city	11.61	17,735	19,327	9.0	1664.7	6.6	72.1	30,576	33.8	157,500	58.0	3.7	48.5	42.1
Newport city	2.73	15,440	14,932	-3.3	5469.6	3.5	84.7	37,435	26.3	144,000	55.0	5.6	51.7	40.1
Nicholasville city	14.47	28,021	30,865	10.1	2133.0	4.3	81.2	48,242	19.6	144,800	64.1	7.4	69.4	23.1
Owensboro city	20.50	57,482	60,131	4.6	2933.2	3.6	81.0	43,369	19.6	113,400	60.0	5.4	59.0	34.8
Paducah city	20.18	25,027	24,865	-0.6	1232.2	1.9	85.5	39,266	20.4	118,400	57.1	4.6	49.1	43.9
Radcliff city	13.30	22,309	22,914	2.7	1722.9	6.5	75.1	46,105	17.4	129,100	60.8	9.0	62.5	31.0
Richmond city	20.33	31,321	36,157	15.4	1778.5	3.0	66.3	36,302	28.9	152,600	62.8	7.2	47.9	38.0
St. Matthews city	4.38	17,577	18,105	3.0	4133.6	8.1	78.7	62,152	7.0	235,000	72.9	3.1	43.1	46.6
Shelbyville city	8.75	14,195	16,585	16.8	1895.4	9.3	84.5	61,269	13.4	178,600	69.0	3.8	68.9	25.3
Shepherdsville city	14.52	11,343	12,442	9.7	856.9	2.2	80.6	52,448	15.5	144,200	65.0	3.6	64.8	29.9
Shively city	4.57	15,262	15,689	2.8	3433.0	4.4	91.9	39,048	20.6	107,000	64.7	6.3	55.5	41.0
Somerset city	11.72	11,234	11,585	3.1	988.5	3.4	82.1	29,611	33.3	118,800	48.5	9.2	58.1	34.9
Winchester city	9.14	18,359	18,548	1.0	2029.3	1.8	78.8	44,747	19.5	128,200	60.5	7.0	61.0	29.7
LOUISIANA	43204.49	4,533,487	4,648,794	2.5	107.6	4.2	87.2	49,469	18.8	163,100	59.1	6.5	64.0	30.3
Abbeville city	6.05	12,227	12,038	-1.5	1989.8	5.5	86.6	38,900	28.0	95,400	53.1	12.9	57.8	33.9
Alexandria city	28.49	47,918	46,180	-3.6	1620.9	3.1	82.7	43,497	22.2	148,900	57.1	9.0	61.0	33.0
Baker city	8.41	13,854	13,194	-4.8	1568.8	0.5	84.5	53,082	13.5	129,800	70.2	5.0	66.0	28.8
Bastrop city	8.90	11,361	10,023	-11.8	1126.2	0.8	89.5	20,117	46.2	72,200	46.7	7.3	59.3	35.4
Baton Rouge city	86.45	229,423	220,236	-4.0	2547.6	5.5	81.4	44,470	22.7	174,000	64.1	8.4	53.9	36.2
Bayou Blue CDP	23.27	12,352	NA	NA	NA	3.2	91.7	66,201	14.4	156,500	59.0	7.0	78.4	16.8
Bayou Cane CDP	7.60	19,355	NA	NA	NA	4.0	84.7	53,668	15.3	164,500	59.3	4.2	63.5	26.8
Belle Chasse CDP	24.92	12,679	NA	NA	NA	4.6	87.4	66,653	9.5	263,400	59.3	2.3	80.4	16.5
Bogalusa city	9.51	12,251	11,504	-6.1	1209.7	0.4	74.5	31,976	30.3	87,800	54.7	13.2	60.0	33.0
Bossier City city	43.48	61,768	68,159	10.3	1567.6	4.5	85.8	50,340	18.2	163,500	54.9	5.3	65.0	27.7
Broussard city	17.55	8,377	12,700	51.6	723.6	5.1	87.2	82,677	11.7	214,400	74.0	4.2	65.9	23.2
Central city	62.26	27,211	29,357	7.9	471.5	1.6	89.2	80,015	5.8	217,700	61.4	3.0	76.0	20.4
Chalmette CDP	7.17	16,751	NA	NA	NA	6.9	86.2	43,976	22.3	152,900	60.8	10.9	67.8	25.7
Claiborne CDP	9.96	11,507	NA	NA	NA	1.9	86.5	56,318	9.8	153,400	63.4	1.9	62.9	32.0
Covington city	8.07	8,850	10,564	19.4	1309.0	2.6	78.4	71,548	12.6	232,900	49.1	2.8	68.6	26.6
Crowley city	5.85	13,265	12,588	-5.1	2151.8	2.8	86.2	26,972	34.5	115,300	47.4	8.3	61.0	32.6
Denham Springs city	7.29	10,370	9,753	-5.9	1337.9	2.7	85.8	53,435	8.0	161,600	63.5	4.1	62.4	31.3
DeRidder city	9.23	10,577	10,588	0.1	1147.1	4.5	79.8	45,536	20.9	144,500	56.4	9.0	65.4	30.4
Destrehan CDP	5.97	11,535	NA	NA	NA	3.4	94.5	93,831	5.1	239,500	65.6	5.2	78.3	16.8
Estelle CDP	4.64	16,377	NA	NA	NA	10.6	96.5	68,051	13.6	157,700	66.6	7.9	82.0	14.4
Eunice city	5.14	10,398	9,814	-5.6	1909.3	3.6	78.4	34,573	26.7	114,200	56.7	11.4	67.8	28.2
Gardere CDP	3.32	10,580	NA	NA	NA	13.4	76.6	39,418	21.6	168,700	81.8	4.0	50.9	33.4
Gonzales city	9.14	9,783	10,957	12.0	1198.8	8.5	88.9	52,923	13.8	161,200	62.5	5.4	67.5	28.7
Gretna city	4.04	17,745	17,647	-0.6	4368.1	13.5	86.9	47,244	20.1	171,800	58.8	7.3	55.3	38.1
Hammond city	14.04	20,007	21,437	7.1	1526.9	2.5	74.9	36,921	28.2	159,300	58.9	7.6	57.8	32.3
Harvey CDP	6.49	20,348	NA	NA	NA	9.8	87.8	41,559	17.0	139,300	60.1	5.5	58.6	36.3
Houma city	14.43	33,664	32,696	-2.9	2265.8	2.9	85.6	42,949	23.6	157,600	58.6	6.7	63.2	28.2
Jefferson CDP	2.71	11,193	NA	NA	NA	7.5	86.5	50,972	12.2	185,600	63.7	4.9	44.3	46.2
Jennings city	10.40	10,383	9,800	-5.6	942.3	0.1	83.9	29,819	27.4	113,000	52.2	8.3	61.9	34.7
Kenner city	14.88	66,631	66,340	-0.4	4458.3	19.8	88.7	54,975	15.7	182,100	65.2	4.6	65.3	29.7
Lafayette city	55.50	121,667	126,185	3.7	2273.6	4.3	81.4	51,264	19.3	195,400	64.4	5.1	55.8	35.2
Lake Charles city	44.89	72,398	78,396	8.3	1746.4	3.4	83.0	42,942	20.0	155,700	60.3	6.2	54.8	37.7
Laplace CDP	20.90	29,872	NA	NA	NA	4.9	87.7	63,253	15.0	161,000	64.6	6.9	75.0	20.4
Luling CDP	23.29	12,119	NA	NA	NA	3.9	89.6	89,034	9.2	219,000	65.1	4.1	79.9	15.1
Mandeville city	7.12	12,058	12,475	3.5	1752.1	5.3	82.6	72,989	12.3	288,900	60.7	2.7	65.5	27.8
Marrero CDP	7.20	33,141	NA	NA	NA	6.6	89.0	44,866	20.9	138,700	59.2	7.0	66.3	30.0
Metairie CDP	23.26	138,481	NA	NA	NA	15.1	87.3	59,346	11.9	236,900	65.2	3.7	60.3	33.4
Minden city	15.04	13,087	11,840	-9.5	787.2	1.5	89.8	24,894	34.0	97,200	47.4	4.3	60.2	35.6
Monroe city	29.30	48,878	47,294	-3.2	1614.1	2.2	84.6	30,438	34.5	139,600	53.4	8.5	56.6	38.2
Morgan City city	5.98	12,404	10,742	-13.4	1796.3	5.8	81.5	40,240	20.4	132,400	54.2	10.4	52.7	42.7
Moss Bluff CDP	15.22	11,557	NA	NA	NA	2.5	90.2	54,788	10.2	189,600	65.2	4.1	73.5	18.6
Natchitoches city	22.73	18,545	17,485	-5.7	769.2	1.8	83.3	21,715	43.2	164,700	41.2	18.3	44.6	37.9
New Iberia city	11.14	30,617	28,454	-7.1	2554.2	3.3	84.1	38,221	26.6	114,600	58.3	10.7	66.5	28.1

Table B. Incorporated Places, Census Designated Places (CDPs), and Minor Civil Divisions (MCDs) of 10,000 or More Population — Crime, Residential Construction and Local Government Finance

STATE City, town, township, borough, or CDP (county if applicable)	Serious crimes known to police, 2018[1] Violent crime Number	Rate[2]	Property crime Number	Rate[2]	New residential construction authorized by building permits, 2019 Value ($1,000)	Number of housing units	Percent single family	Local government finance, 2017 General revenue Total (mil dol)	Intergovernmental Total (mil dol)	Percent from state gov.	Taxes per capita[3]	General expenditure Total (mil dol)	Per capita[3] Total	Capital outlays	Debt outstanding (mil dol)
	15	16	17	18	19	20	21	22	23	24	25	26	27	28	29
KENTUCKY—Con.															
Burlington CDP	NA	NA	NA	NA	NA	NA	NA	NA	NA	NA	NA	NA	NA	NA	NA
Campbellsville city	32	278	522	4,538	1,930	6	100.0	17.1	5.8	10.7	530	9.7	851	193	42.4
Covington city	164	406	1,097	2,712	0	0	0.0	73.7	16.1	15.1	1,134	70.5	1,739	553	106.0
Danville city	34	202	283	1,684	NA	NA	NA	21.6	3.2	19.6	829	15.2	909	107	49.1
Elizabethtown city	64	212	400	1,325	16,468	81	67.9	51.5	6.0	45.2	1,107	36.8	1,247	138	54.1
Erlanger city	22	96	186	809	17,738	51	100.0	19.1	0.8	89.7	823	14.1	746	260	1.8
Florence city	59	180	1,240	3,792	NA	NA	NA	47.0	3.4	91.6	1,034	27.4	847	236	18.3
Fort Campbell North CDP	NA	NA	NA	NA	NA	NA	NA	NA	NA	NA	NA	NA	NA	NA	NA
Fort Knox CDP	NA	NA	NA	NA	NA	NA	NA	NA	NA	NA	NA	NA	NA	NA	NA
Fort Thomas city	6	37	68	418	2,550	5	100.0	14.5	0.7	100.0	712	10.4	638	70	5.5
Frankfort city	71	257	1,052	3,803	2,556	13	100.0	77.8	3.5	49.5	1,021	63.9	2,309	412	60.1
Georgetown city	62	181	992	2,888	NA	NA	NA	36.5	3.8	40.2	684	25.5	756	35	443.9
Glasgow city	33	229	452	3,137	2,590	25	56.0	20.8	3.0	61.0	919	15.5	1,082	270	55.6
Henderson city	95	332	NA	NA	10,258	95	16.8	43.6	12.8	10.6	709	39.8	1,388	269	116.1
Hopkinsville city	85	278	997	3,258	15,601	127	17.3	40.1	6.0	8.4	932	33.1	1,078	57	165.1
Independence city	23	82	154	549	20,086	113	100.0	9.1	0.7	94.2	292	6.7	242	73	5.9
Jeffersontown city	44	160	NA	NA	5,974	24	100.0	50.0	21.0	15.8	755	40.0	1,422	119	102.5
Lawrenceburg city	4	35	142	1,248	5,631	31	87.1	7.6	0.8	41.7	318	5.6	491	106	17.1
Lexington-Fayette urban county	982	302	10,329	3,173	217,839	1,383	41.9	690.2	86.8	23.5	1,277	589.9	1,832	481	919.4
Louisville/Jefferson County metro government	NA	NA	NA	NA	NA	NA	NA	1127.6	192.7	37.9	838	1215.3	1,579	151	2142.7
Louisville/Jefferson County metro government (balance)	NA	NA	NA	NA	NA	NA	NA	NA	NA	NA	NA	NA	NA	NA	NA
Lyndon city	NA	NA	NA	NA	NA	NA	NA	2.5	0.2	96.9	199	3.9	338	26	48.2
Madisonville city	37	195	NA	NA	8,676	77	24.7	29.0	1.6	68.2	798	26.5	1,403	118	11.7
Mayfield city	35	357	454	4,624	304	2	100.0	10.1	0.6	99.3	753	7.2	727	75	10.5
Middlesborough city	13	139	424	4,530	880	11	100.0	12.9	4.1	10.9	463	8.2	875	27	0.5
Mount Washington city	12	82	131	891	NA	NA	NA	9.0	0.3	100.0	245	9.9	678	292	12.5
Murray city	23	119	NA	NA	4,496	40	35.0	130.3	3.8	82.6	484	123.6	6,448	246	110.6
Newport city	46	307	569	3,800	269	2	100.0	27.9	2.4	47.5	1,068	22.1	1,465	55	43.5
Nicholasville city	60	194	824	2,665	18,430	123	87.8	25.4	2.4	64.4	604	16.5	543	57	35.8
Owensboro city	160	268	2,638	4,420	29,224	320	86.6	112.1	20.8	17.6	707	91.5	1,537	220	450.1
Paducah city	93	373	NA	NA	9,460	45	42.2	68.5	14.3	52.9	1,459	52.6	2,106	561	180.3
Radcliff city	82	363	NA	NA	3,747	24	100.0	15.3	3.5	28.9	457	13.0	576	156	3.6
Richmond city	66	184	1,066	2,965	15,916	231	59.7	49.2	9.2	16.7	728	27.6	780	104	74.4
St. Matthews city	37	203	NA	NA	NA	NA	NA	13.3	0.6	100.0	686	9.4	517	50	26.6
Shelbyville city	20	124	273	1,692	NA	NA	NA	11.6	0.8	35.7	595	9.0	564	69	9.4
Shepherdsville city	26	210	257	2,074	NA	NA	NA	16.2	0.6	99.2	812	15.7	1,281	379	24.2
Shively city	55	346	578	3,641	NA	NA	NA	10.1	0.8	100.0	569	7.9	503	67	36.1
Somerset city	30	262	247	2,157	9,000	116	86.2	23.7	2.3	20.6	770	22.0	1,924	59	53.7
Winchester city	NA	NA	NA	NA	NA	NA	NA	35.4	4.9	24.7	807	26.9	1,463	125	68.2
LOUISIANA	25,049	538	152,661	3,276	3,136,086	15,793	88.7	X	X	X	X	X	X	X	X
Abbeville city	89	725	241	1,963	1,657	10	100.0	9.4	2.0	67.4	379	14.9	1,218	207	5.0
Alexandria city	685	1,450	3,973	8,411	18,197	69	100.0	85.5	19.2	4.6	1,064	103.6	2,204	375	201.5
Baker city	44	326	335	2,484	904	6	100.0	15.7	1.6	90.5	530	14.1	1,044	88	1.6
Bastrop city	138	1,344	1,006	9,796	0	0	0.0	19.0	2.0	45.3	922	11.2	1,084	47	0.0
Baton Rouge city	2,067	920	11,965	5,323	96,848	354	100.0	991.7	113.8	42.8	2,451	1138.2	5,072	742	1319.4
Bayou Blue CDP	NA	NA	NA	NA	NA	NA	NA	NA	NA	NA	NA	NA	NA	NA	NA
Bayou Cane CDP	NA	NA	NA	NA	NA	NA	NA	NA	NA	NA	NA	NA	NA	NA	NA
Belle Chasse CDP	NA	NA	NA	NA	NA	NA	NA	NA	NA	NA	NA	NA	NA	NA	NA
Bogalusa city	124	1,057	584	4,979	NA	NA	NA	18.4	3.3	23.4	933	19.3	1,648	53	6.4
Bossier City city	576	828	2,998	4,311	55,857	338	100.0	134.8	4.4	42.7	1,152	95.4	1,393	230	528.8
Broussard city	52	410	500	3,946	41,633	155	100.0	13.2	0.1	100.0	943	9.3	784	0	46.6
Central city	NA	NA	NA	NA	24,494	150	93.3	16.5	5.1	5.8	330	8.4	287	251	0.0
Chalmette CDP	NA	NA	NA	NA	NA	NA	NA	NA	NA	NA	NA	NA	NA	NA	NA
Claiborne CDP	NA	NA	NA	NA	NA	NA	NA	NA	NA	NA	NA	NA	NA	NA	NA
Covington city	30	282	223	2,092	7,968	31	100.0	20.0	3.6	13.3	1,253	19.8	1,894	522	6.2
Crowley city	228	1,784	916	7,168	2,015	13	100.0	19.7	3.8	30.4	950	17.4	1,358	147	7.3
Denham Springs city	44	451	669	6,854	6,208	31	100.0	26.2	7.8	97.5	1,069	24.4	2,480	65	54.8
DeRidder city	10	92	301	2,782	350	2	100.0	10.4	0.4	49.8	802	11.3	1,057	135	0.5
Destrehan CDP	NA	NA	NA	NA	NA	NA	NA	NA	NA	NA	NA	NA	NA	NA	NA
Estelle CDP	NA	NA	NA	NA	NA	NA	NA	NA	NA	NA	NA	NA	NA	NA	NA
Eunice city	44	437	487	4,835	800	9	100.0	11.8	0.5	38.6	718	11.4	1,138	158	1.6
Gardere CDP	NA	NA	NA	NA	NA	NA	NA	NA	NA	NA	NA	NA	NA	NA	NA
Gonzales city	62	568	775	7,100	23,685	126	100.0	21.6	0.9	37.8	1,725	161.1	14,917	603	141.7
Gretna city	86	479	555	3,089	2,689	16	100.0	39.2	8.1	83.9	863	36.6	2,054	293	9.7
Hammond city	299	1,455	2,124	10,336	28,193	194	40.7	38.4	3.9	0.0	1,387	49.6	2,427	0	19.3
Harvey CDP	NA	NA	NA	NA	NA	NA	NA	NA	NA	NA	NA	NA	NA	NA	NA
Houma city	158	476	1,625	4,891	NA	NA	NA	482.7	85.3	11.7	3,121	524.9	15,790	2430	113.8
Jefferson CDP	NA	NA	NA	NA	NA	NA	NA	NA	NA	NA	NA	NA	NA	NA	NA
Jennings city	19	191	187	1,880	1,712	10	60.0	13.9	1.2	59.8	788	14.1	1,413	246	5.1
Kenner city	155	229	2,040	3,020	14,087	47	100.0	102.1	51.4	4.8	467	107.2	1,601	333	91.1
Lafayette city	681	534	5,882	4,610	NA	NA	NA	378.0	37.9	19.2	1,847	399.6	3,158	621	484.1
Lake Charles city	575	739	3,777	4,852	99,532	723	61.0	140.1	24.1	52.8	1,152	122.0	1,573	270	56.8
Laplace CDP	NA	NA	NA	NA	NA	NA	NA	NA	NA	NA	NA	NA	NA	NA	NA
Luling CDP	NA	NA	NA	NA	NA	NA	NA	NA	NA	NA	NA	NA	NA	NA	NA
Mandeville city	16	129	217	1,754	15,696	40	100.0	30.3	1.8	90.0	1,751	20.6	1,655	358	1.4
Marrero CDP	NA	NA	NA	NA	NA	NA	NA	NA	NA	NA	NA	NA	NA	NA	NA
Metairie CDP	NA	NA	NA	NA	NA	NA	NA	NA	NA	NA	NA	NA	NA	NA	NA
Minden city	18	147	251	2,055	3,143	8	100.0	9.9	0.5	60.6	532	14.8	1,210	75	1.6
Monroe city	677	1,402	3,278	6,788	28,111	173	48.0	134.6	22.5	14.2	1,752	106.1	2,199	145	206.8
Morgan City city	96	868	535	4,835	351	3	33.3	17.9	2.6	20.5	780	22.5	2,023	264	9.0
Moss Bluff CDP	NA	NA	NA	NA	NA	NA	NA	NA	NA	NA	NA	NA	NA	NA	NA
Natchitoches city	159	884	1,141	6,346	2,469	12	100.0	29.4	5.3	35.8	804	30.0	1,668	136	25.0
New Iberia city	NA	NA	NA	NA	3,493	18	44.4	35.1	6.4	6.8	724	31.5	1,066	169	1.2

1 Data for serious crimes have not been adjusted for underreporting. This may affect comparability between geographic areas over time.
2 Per 100,000 population estimated by the FBI. 3 Based on population estimated as of July 1 of the year shown.

Table B. Incorporated Places, Census Designated Places (CDPs), and Minor Civil Divisions (MCDs) of 10,000 or More Population — Land Area, Population, and Households, and Employment

STATE City, town, township, borough, or CDP (county if applicable)	Land area 2010 (sq mi)	Population Total persons 2010	Total persons 2019	Percent change 2010–2019	Persons per square mile 2019	Population characteristics 2015–2019 Percent foreign born	Percent living in the same house as previous year	Income and poverty 2015–2019 Median household income	Percent of households with income below poverty level	Median value of owner-occupied housing units	Employment, 2015–2019 Percent in civilian labor force	Unemploy-ment rate	Households, 2015–2019 (percent of households) Family households	One person households
	1	2	3	4	5	6	7	8	9	10	11	12	13	14
LOUISIANA—Con.														
New Orleans city	169.43	343,828	390,144	13.5	2302.7	5.5	85.6	41,604	23.8	231,500	61.7	7.9	47.0	45.9
Opelousas city	7.93	16,758	15,911	-5.1	2006.4	0.3	84.9	22,646	43.6	98,100	44.2	8.8	56.5	40.5
Pineville city	12.59	14,511	14,122	-2.7	1121.7	0.6	83.4	45,088	18.8	157,100	60.4	4.7	60.5	32.2
Prairieville CDP	22.00	26,895	NA	NA	NA	3.7	90.8	99,953	5.8	236,500	70.1	5.2	77.1	19.3
Raceland CDP	21.57	10,193	NA	NA	NA	2.0	88.6	45,128	16.3	133,500	56.8	7.7	70.8	22.0
River Ridge CDP	2.80	13,494	NA	NA	NA	2.4	91.3	69,929	6.7	265,300	59.1	3.5	64.5	31.2
Ruston city	21.14	21,887	21,854	-0.2	1033.8	4.8	70.6	29,128	37.3	169,600	56.9	4.5	49.4	30.5
Shenandoah CDP	6.20	18,399	NA	NA	NA	6.1	89.0	92,432	6.4	261,900	67.0	3.6	76.6	21.2
Shreveport city	107.36	200,976	187,112	-6.9	1742.8	2.6	87.6	39,090	23.8	148,100	57.8	6.8	58.2	36.3
Slidell city	15.33	27,265	27,633	1.3	1802.5	4.2	84.3	54,906	16.4	161,700	61.5	7.0	65.5	26.2
Sulphur city	11.22	20,390	20,065	-1.6	1788.3	2.9	84.1	53,287	12.6	141,700	60.0	4.6	62.0	33.4
Terrytown CDP	3.67	23,319	NA	NA	NA	19.1	89.5	46,638	18.4	162,700	70.0	7.2	67.0	27.5
Thibodaux city	6.13	14,502	14,425	-0.5	2353.2	2.5	80.4	38,269	20.1	166,800	59.0	6.1	53.4	40.0
Timberlane CDP	1.50	10,243	NA	NA	NA	13.2	88.8	54,702	7.4	162,500	63.5	11.8	72.6	25.6
Waggaman CDP	5.51	10,015	NA	NA	NA	3.2	93.1	46,075	22.9	112,800	59.1	15.3	76.8	21.4
West Monroe city	8.02	13,080	12,227	-6.5	1524.6	1.8	85.8	34,454	26.0	133,100	60.3	6.1	46.9	45.1
Woodmere CDP	3.65	12,080	NA	NA	NA	5.0	95.6	54,363	15.3	133,200	64.0	4.3	70.9	25.3
Youngsville city	12.07	8,308	14,704	77.0	1218.2	5.3	79.4	89,038	11.5	222,800	70.6	4.6	88.3	9.4
Zachary city	26.08	15,146	17,949	18.5	688.2	2.2	88.3	84,795	7.5	224,500	68.2	4.4	73.7	22.0
MAINE	30844.80	1,328,358	1,344,212	1.2	43.6	3.6	86.6	57,918	12.2	190,400	62.8	4.1	62.0	29.6
Auburn city & MCD (Androscoggin)	59.34	23,057	23,414	1.5	394.6	3.3	82.5	49,719	11.9	165,200	66.7	3.2	56.1	33.9
Augusta city & MCD (Kennebec)	55.15	19,132	18,697	-2.3	339.0	3.3	81.0	43,796	19.2	144,800	57.9	5.3	45.3	44.1
Bangor city & MCD (Penobscot)	34.26	33,031	32,262	-2.3	941.7	4.8	78.9	46,625	18.4	157,000	59.4	5.3	50.8	37.8
Biddeford city & MCD (York)	30.09	21,276	21,504	1.1	714.7	5.8	80.0	53,120	10.8	245,900	67.1	4.4	58.9	28.0
Brunswick CDP	14.52	15,175	NA	NA	NA	5.1	82.4	54,083	12.7	210,500	60.8	4.4	50.3	40.9
Brunswick town (Cumberland)	46.78	20,281	20,535	1.3	439.0	4.4	83.7	59,922	10.4	243,500	62.9	3.8	55.0	37.4
Falmouth town (Cumberland)	29.40	11,176	12,312	10.2	418.8	6.3	88.9	121,285	4.9	439,800	68.9	2.5	70.6	25.4
Gorham town (Cumberland)	50.59	16,368	17,978	9.8	355.4	3.2	84.6	84,767	5.8	268,700	72.5	2.2	67.2	23.3
Kennebunk town (York)	35.10	10,793	11,625	7.7	331.2	4.0	87.6	75,517	5.1	331,400	60.1	7.5	65.6	29.3
Lewiston city & MCD (Androscoggin)	34.15	36,592	36,225	-1.0	1060.8	6.8	79.5	44,523	17.0	140,600	62.2	4.6	54.6	35.1
Orono town (Penobscot)	18.18	10,359	10,799	4.2	594.0	7.8	58.8	47,528	26.5	176,100	56.3	8.6	42.9	32.6
Portland city & MCD (Cumberland)	21.57	66,191	66,215	0.0	3069.8	11.1	78.8	60,467	15.4	289,000	71.7	2.8	43.4	38.3
Saco city & MCD (York)	38.48	18,495	19,964	7.9	518.8	3.2	83.9	70,517	6.9	258,900	72.5	2.3	65.5	23.9
Sanford city & MCD (York)	47.79	20,793	21,223	2.1	444.1	3.7	83.4	52,513	14.0	183,800	64.7	6.4	58.8	31.1
Scarborough town (Cumberland)	47.61	18,919	20,991	11.0	440.9	5.4	89.0	94,905	5.1	367,700	66.3	1.1	69.7	24.9
South Portland city & MCD (Cumberland)	12.07	25,022	25,532	2.0	2115.3	9.4	86.5	69,290	9.4	257,200	71.2	4.8	59.1	31.5
Standish town (Cumberland)	59.06	9,872	10,099	2.3	171.0	0.8	92.6	74,688	7.9	234,600	68.2	2.3	72.8	24.2
Waterville city & MCD (Kennebec)	13.53	15,719	16,558	5.3	1223.8	4.8	74.8	38,862	20.5	125,000	53.5	4.1	53.1	39.8
Wells town (York)	57.56	9,589	10,675	11.3	185.5	5.9	89.4	66,578	10.0	287,800	60.4	4.0	69.3	26.9
Westbrook city & MCD (Cumberland)	17.19	17,520	19,074	8.9	1109.6	6.9	83.9	59,460	15.2	232,900	69.3	6.0	53.7	34.3
Windham town (Cumberland)	46.58	16,997	18,540	9.1	398.0	2.3	88.6	78,284	5.9	248,400	69.1	2.7	70.0	22.1
York town (York)	54.70	12,517	13,290	6.2	243.0	2.3	88.4	93,333	5.4	410,200	65.5	3.9	64.0	31.0
MARYLAND	9711.14	5,773,794	6,045,680	4.7	622.6	15.2	86.4	84,805	8.9	314,800	67.1	5.1	66.6	27.4
Aberdeen city	6.48	14,982	16,019	6.9	2472.1	7.8	86.0	63,842	16.4	205,900	64.2	4.3	57.4	34.0
Accokeek CDP	27.43	10,573	NA	NA	NA	12.3	92.6	130,655	3.2	384,000	74.3	4.7	73.5	22.0
Adelphi CDP	2.72	15,086	NA	NA	NA	53.5	82.7	75,248	12.3	313,700	74.4	4.4	66.7	19.6
Annapolis city	7.21	38,335	39,223	2.3	5440.1	14.9	82.3	85,636	10.4	420,500	71.4	5.0	59.2	32.9
Annapolis Neck CDP	6.93	10,950	NA	NA	NA	4.3	90.6	142,625	0.9	602,900	68.0	3.3	68.5	26.6
Arbutus CDP	6.53	20,483	NA	NA	NA	9.6	85.9	76,801	8.7	234,500	70.8	5.4	61.9	30.4
Arnold CDP	10.82	23,106	NA	NA	NA	5.5	89.3	126,310	3.7	441,300	71.3	3.5	77.0	17.5
Aspen Hill CDP	9.60	48,759	NA	NA	NA	39.8	85.9	87,055	8.8	423,300	73.5	6.0	74.6	21.6
Ballenger Creek CDP	10.81	18,274	NA	NA	NA	16.7	83.8	91,143	7.1	267,300	74.5	3.7	66.9	27.4
Baltimore city	80.95	620,770	593,490	-4.4	7331.6	8.1	83.6	50,379	20.0	160,100	61.8	8.3	50.3	39.8
Bel Air town	3.04	10,100	10,119	0.2	3328.6	6.2	83.2	71,122	11.6	245,400	66.6	3.3	55.2	36.0
Bel Air North CDP	15.96	30,568	NA	NA	NA	2.7	91.6	107,689	3.5	340,700	68.9	3.6	78.2	18.8
Bel Air South CDP	15.66	47,709	NA	NA	NA	7.3	89.2	91,153	6.4	281,800	68.6	4.1	68.8	26.3
Beltsville CDP	7.21	16,772	NA	NA	NA	36.6	82.2	81,115	9.8	314,200	71.1	6.3	63.2	30.7
Bensville CDP	16.89	0	NA	0.0	NA	6.2	89.8	127,096	7.3	366,600	68.1	3.4	79.7	16.5
Bethesda CDP	13.26	60,858	NA	NA	NA	22.5	84.7	164,142	3.5	911,000	68.5	3.1	62.8	31.5
Bowie city	19.78	55,296	58,643	6.1	2964.8	14.9	90.3	113,338	3.4	338,100	71.1	4.8	70.1	25.1
Brock Hall CDP	13.62	9,552	NA	NA	NA	9.9	91.0	152,059	3.1	426,200	77.0	3.3	76.2	21.6
Brooklyn Park CDP	4.21	14,373	NA	NA	NA	9.6	91.3	61,250	9.0	210,800	61.9	6.0	67.4	27.8
California CDP	12.87	11,857	NA	NA	NA	5.7	78.8	84,690	7.7	268,700	69.0	5.2	65.5	27.2
Calverton CDP	4.59	17,724	NA	NA	NA	39.6	90.6	89,796	5.6	358,000	65.2	5.3	63.8	34.5
Cambridge city	10.65	12,416	12,260	-1.3	1151.2	4.6	82.0	43,120	20.7	163,200	62.2	9.5	57.7	37.1
Camp Springs CDP	7.68	19,096	NA	NA	NA	10.1	86.7	95,484	5.5	281,500	67.1	6.9	65.4	30.9
Carney CDP	6.97	29,941	NA	NA	NA	15.6	85.7	66,776	5.7	244,600	61.0	4.0	59.8	35.1
Catonsville CDP	13.96	41,567	NA	NA	NA	8.8	87.3	89,219	5.6	327,900	62.3	2.9	62.2	31.9
Chesapeake Ranch Estates CDP	4.32	10,519	NA	NA	NA	1.5	88.8	92,083	4.6	215,300	77.6	3.4	73.4	17.6
Chillum CDP	3.40	33,513	NA	NA	NA	51.4	83.8	63,795	10.5	292,900	73.0	5.4	67.4	24.5
Clarksburg CDP	8.21	13,766	NA	NA	NA	33.2	85.7	147,070	5.3	482,500	76.6	4.3	86.1	10.8
Clinton CDP	25.01	35,970	NA	NA	NA	7.6	93.6	112,771	5.7	299,800	68.4	6.0	77.1	21.0
Cloverly CDP	10.00	15,126	NA	NA	NA	26.5	91.6	134,964	5.5	487,800	70.6	6.7	84.3	11.7

Table B. Incorporated Places, Census Designated Places (CDPs), and Minor Civil Divisions (MCDs) of 10,000 or More Population — **Crime, Residential Construction and Local Government Finance**

STATE City, town, township, borough, or CDP (county if applicable)	Serious crimes known to police, 2018[1] Violent crime Number	Rate[2]	Property crime Number	Rate[2]	New residential construction authorized by building permits, 2019 Value ($1,000)	Number of housing units	Percent single family	Local government finance, 2017 General revenue Total (mil dol)	Intergovernmental Total (mil dol)	Percent from state gov.	Taxes per capita[3]	General expenditure Total (mil dol)	Per capita[3] Total	Capital outlays	Debt outstanding (mil dol)
	15	16	17	18	19	20	21	22	23	24	25	26	27	28	29
LOUISIANA—Con.															
New Orleans city	4,611	1,163	18,063	4,557	244,557	1,306	42.7	1508.9	379.6	17.7	1,416	1359.1	3,472	920	2414.1
Opelousas city	348	2,140	1,180	7,256	2,070	11	100.0	23.5	3.6	6.2	944	22.8	1,400	34	15.8
Pineville city	91	631	796	5,522	19,531	108	74.1	24.7	3.8	49.7	1,070	25.1	1,756	165	4.9
Prairieville CDP	NA	NA	NA	NA	NA	NA	NA	NA	NA	NA	NA	NA	NA	NA	NA
Raceland CDP	NA	NA	NA	NA	NA	NA	NA	NA	NA	NA	NA	NA	NA	NA	NA
River Ridge CDP	NA	NA	NA	NA	NA	NA	NA	NA	NA	NA	NA	NA	NA	NA	NA
Ruston city	82	368	628	2,819	29,633	235	36.2	32.9	6.9	41.0	713	32.2	1,461	260	17.6
Shenandoah CDP	NA	NA	NA	NA	NA	NA	NA	NA	NA	NA	NA	NA	NA	NA	NA
Shreveport city	1,588	832	9,884	5,180	67,030	300	100.0	393.6	43.1	35.0	1,249	378.3	1,970	218	206.4
Slidell city	87	311	815	2,914	2,104	10	100.0	38.8	0.0		1,117	13.7	491	0	0.0
Sulphur city	95	469	879	4,341	19,733	183	74.3	36.3	5.0	14.3	1,138	33.8	1,679	246	50.8
Terrytown CDP	NA	NA	NA	NA	NA	NA	NA	NA	NA	NA	NA	NA	NA	NA	NA
Thibodaux city	68	461	534	3,622	13,877	41	95.1	23.2	4.1	27.2	933	22.4	1,529	130	6.6
Timberlane CDP	NA	NA	NA	NA	NA	NA	NA	NA	NA	NA	NA	NA	NA	NA	NA
Waggaman CDP	NA	NA	NA	NA	NA	NA	NA	NA	NA	NA	NA	NA	NA	NA	NA
West Monroe city	103	818	1,008	8,004	1,360	13	46.2	33.9	2.6	46.9	1,838	32.4	2,565	257	4.1
Woodmere CDP	NA	NA	NA	NA	NA	NA	NA	NA	NA	NA	NA	NA	NA	NA	NA
Youngsville city	12	84	221	1,538	32,318	183	100.0	16.5	2.7	99.4	790	15.3	1,148	479	35.7
Zachary city	110	615	624	3,489	34,669	199	100.0	16.9	0.1	22.9	683	19.0	1,103	311	20.6
MAINE	1,501	112	18,173	1,358	1,004,740	4,760	73.0	X	X	X	X	X	X	X	X
Auburn city & MCD (Androscoggin)	50	217	765	3,322	13,247	69	20.3	84.8	33.2	95.1	2,013	79.1	3,421	306	48.8
Augusta city & MCD (Kennebec)	60	324	618	3,336	3,337	17	100.0	71.9	20.9	91.6	1,688	78.3	4,204	616	49.9
Bangor city & MCD (Penobscot)	56	176	1,300	4,095	5,592	28	57.1	147.3	41.4	94.0	1,935	143.1	4,465	506	134.0
Biddeford city & MCD (York)	64	297	673	3,128	2,505	14	100.0	73.5	16.9	95.8	2,316	69.5	3,236	24	63.7
Brunswick CDP	NA	NA	NA	NA	NA	NA	NA	NA	NA	NA	NA	NA	NA	NA	NA
Brunswick town (Cumberland)	28	135	361	1,746	18,684	60	100.0	67.8	17.0	98.8	2,290	62.4	3,051	157	23.9
Falmouth town (Cumberland)	7	57	87	707	19,643	66	54.5	54.7	10.7	99.9	3,168	56.4	4,637	697	50.1
Gorham town (Cumberland)	4	23	93	528	13,510	70	77.1	55.5	21.7	99.8	1,705	50.1	2,857	88	40.0
Kennebunk town (York)	6	52	51	445	12,103	46	95.7	15.4	1.3	100.0	992	14.3	1,248	134	10.3
Lewiston city & MCD (Androscoggin)	84	232	598	1,653	3,945	19	100.0	149.3	67.9	95.1	1,680	143.4	3,987	476	125.1
Orono town (Penobscot)	10	87	90	786	175	1	100.0	10.6	2.1	100.0	577	10.3	962	107	28.7
Portland city & MCD (Cumberland)	192	287	1,626	2,427	75,670	385	7.0	296.3	49.7	91.9	2,512	330.9	4,964	237	392.1
Saco city & MCD (York)	21	107	309	1,574	16,268	101	56.4	65.7	15.7	97.7	2,205	52.7	2,698	16	10.9
Sanford city & MCD (York)	56	266	568	2,697	3,803	19	89.5	70.6	31.3	96.5	1,692	98.1	4,658	1882	107.7
Scarborough town (Cumberland)	7	35	253	1,261	44,210	266	38.3	84.9	9.2	98.0	3,224	83.0	4,166	376	91.6
South Portland city & MCD (Cumberland)	36	141	455	1,780	22,920	222	8.1	100.0	18.4	90.3	2,701	100.6	3,950	570	56.6
Standish town (Cumberland)	NA	NA	NA	NA	7,548	37	100.0	6.5	0.8	99.5	494	7.7	766	169	5.9
Waterville city & MCD (Kennebec)	30	179	536	3,204	1,276	8	75.0	40.2	19.4	87.5	1,151	39.8	2,387	87	34.4
Wells town (York)	6	58	79	759	39,775	138	100.0	18.3	0.9	100.0	1,288	16.3	1,572	236	2.7
Westbrook city & MCD (Cumberland)	33	175	358	1,893	9,617	103	27.2	71.1	21.8	93.8	2,189	61.6	3,288	507	53.2
Windham town (Cumberland)	9	49	220	1,207	49,996	166	89.2	36.9	1.8	100.0	1,798	18.2	996	126	15.4
York town (York)	8	61	91	691	19,422	52	100.0	54.5	2.9	99.4	3,602	62.1	4,767	1012	34.4
MARYLAND	28,320	469	122,864	2,033	3,754,023	18,491	65.2	X	X	X	X	X	X	X	X
Aberdeen city	116	716	314	1,937	3,621	9	100.0	23.6	2.7	53.7	844	21.4	1,336	0	20.9
Accokeek CDP	NA	NA	NA	NA	NA	NA	NA	NA	NA	NA	NA	NA	NA	NA	NA
Adelphi CDP	NA	NA	NA	NA	NA	NA	NA	NA	NA	NA	NA	NA	NA	NA	NA
Annapolis city	215	545	910	2,306	61,854	241	15.4	97.1	10.0	44.7	1,495	89.8	2,289	20	161.8
Annapolis Neck CDP	NA	NA	NA	NA	NA	NA	NA	NA	NA	NA	NA	NA	NA	NA	NA
Arbutus CDP	NA	NA	NA	NA	NA	NA	NA	NA	NA	NA	NA	NA	NA	NA	NA
Arnold CDP	NA	NA	NA	NA	NA	NA	NA	NA	NA	NA	NA	NA	NA	NA	NA
Aspen Hill CDP	NA	NA	NA	NA	NA	NA	NA	NA	NA	NA	NA	NA	NA	NA	NA
Ballenger Creek CDP	NA	NA	NA	NA	NA	NA	NA	NA	NA	NA	NA	NA	NA	NA	NA
Baltimore city	11,100	1,833	27,217	4,495	77,309	510	25.5	3446.7	1447.1	96.3	2,438	3478.8	5,698	601	818.8
Bel Air town	23	229	231	2,304	10,222	93	49.5	14.7	0.8	97.0	950	15.0	1,493	106	3.8
Bel Air North CDP	NA	NA	NA	NA	NA	NA	NA	NA	NA	NA	NA	NA	NA	NA	NA
Bel Air South CDP	NA	NA	NA	NA	NA	NA	NA	NA	NA	NA	NA	NA	NA	NA	NA
Beltsville CDP	NA	NA	NA	NA	NA	NA	NA	NA	NA	NA	NA	NA	NA	NA	NA
Bensville CDP	NA	NA	NA	NA	NA	NA	NA	NA	NA	NA	NA	NA	NA	NA	NA
Bethesda CDP	NA	NA	NA	NA	NA	NA	NA	NA	NA	NA	NA	NA	NA	NA	NA
Bowie city	80	135	817	1,376	NA	NA	NA	52.8	3.1	86.1	726	49.8	850	0	13.2
Brock Hall CDP	NA	NA	NA	NA	NA	NA	NA	NA	NA	NA	NA	NA	NA	NA	NA
Brooklyn Park CDP	NA	NA	NA	NA	NA	NA	NA	NA	NA	NA	NA	NA	NA	NA	NA
California CDP	NA	NA	NA	NA	NA	NA	NA	NA	NA	NA	NA	NA	NA	NA	NA
Calverton CDP	NA	NA	NA	NA	NA	NA	NA	NA	NA	NA	NA	NA	NA	NA	NA
Cambridge city	128	1,035	602	4,869	2,581	15	100.0	18.2	3.3	99.9	711	17.9	1,448	15	16.2
Camp Springs CDP	NA	NA	NA	NA	NA	NA	NA	NA	NA	NA	NA	NA	NA	NA	NA
Carney CDP	NA	NA	NA	NA	NA	NA	NA	NA	NA	NA	NA	NA	NA	NA	NA
Catonsville CDP	NA	NA	NA	NA	NA	NA	NA	NA	NA	NA	NA	NA	NA	NA	NA
Chesapeake Ranch Estates CDP	NA	NA	NA	NA	NA	NA	NA	NA	NA	NA	NA	NA	NA	NA	NA
Chillum CDP	NA	NA	NA	NA	NA	NA	NA	NA	NA	NA	NA	NA	NA	NA	NA
Clarksburg CDP	NA	NA	NA	NA	NA	NA	NA	NA	NA	NA	NA	NA	NA	NA	NA
Clinton CDP	NA	NA	NA	NA	NA	NA	NA	NA	NA	NA	NA	NA	NA	NA	NA
Cloverly CDP	NA	NA	NA	NA	NA	NA	NA	NA	NA	NA	NA	NA	NA	NA	NA

1 Data for serious crimes have not been adjusted for underreporting. This may affect comparability between geographic areas over time.
2 Per 100,000 population estimated by the FBI.   3 Based on population estimated as of July 1 of the year shown.

Table B. Incorporated Places, Census Designated Places (CDPs), and Minor Civil Divisions (MCDs) of 10,000 or More Population — Land Area, Population, and Households, and Employment

STATE City, town, township, borough, or CDP (county if applicable)	Land area 2010 (sq mi)	Population — Total persons 2010	Total persons 2019	Percent change 2010-2019	Population characteristics 2015-2019 — Persons per square mile 2019	Percent foreign born	Percent living in the same house as previous year	Income and poverty 2015-2019 — Median household income	Percent of households with income below poverty level	Median value of owner-occupied housing units	Employment, 2015-2019 — Percent in civilian labor force	Unemployment rate	Households, 2015-2019 (percent of households) — Family households	One person households
	1	2	3	4	5	6	7	8	9	10	11	12	13	14
MARYLAND—Con.														
Cockeysville CDP	11.39	20,776	NA	NA	NA	20.9	80.8	65,420	10.5	333,000	72.6	3.7	50.9	40.0
Colesville CDP	5.12	14,647	NA	NA	NA	33.1	92.6	125,497	6.8	463,000	61.9	5.0	74.5	21.1
College Park city	5.61	30,397	32,163	5.8	5733.2	22.1	63.1	66,679	27.1	330,300	52.4	4.2	45.4	33.4
Columbia CDP	31.94	99,615	NA	NA	NA	20.5	84.7	108,352	6.7	378,300	70.7	4.1	66.5	26.3
Crofton CDP	6.61	27,348	NA	NA	NA	10.4	85.8	123,858	2.3	387,400	74.5	3.0	77.3	18.9
Cumberland city	10.05	20,824	19,284	-7.4	1918.8	1.8	82.0	36,145	23.8	94,100	53.9	8.3	51.8	39.8
Damascus CDP	11.56	15,257	NA	NA	NA	15.0	91.7	124,612	4.2	396,700	73.2	3.8	81.0	15.0
Dundalk CDP	13.07	63,597	NA	NA	NA	7.8	89.0	55,757	14.3	149,800	62.2	6.6	63.5	29.8
Easton town	11.46	16,210	16,671	2.8	1454.7	8.9	79.4	61,651	10.4	276,900	60.5	2.3	59.2	34.2
East Riverdale CDP	1.62	15,509	NA	NA	NA	50.5	89.5	63,712	9.8	249,700	73.7	4.7	74.7	21.2
Edgewood CDP	17.78	25,562	NA	NA	NA	7.6	84.2	68,952	12.1	182,300	66.5	5.7	71.9	24.8
Eldersburg CDP	39.84	30,531	NA	NA	NA	5.0	93.4	120,688	4.0	386,700	67.8	2.5	77.3	18.4
Elkridge CDP	8.39	15,593	NA	NA	NA	21.0	79.6	100,068	5.8	364,700	76.4	3.4	70.7	24.6
Elkton town	8.89	15,482	15,622	0.9	1757.3	7.7	83.7	56,250	17.3	194,800	61.5	6.2	66.6	26.3
Ellicott City CDP	29.97	65,834	NA	NA	NA	26.7	88.8	131,534	4.3	537,400	68.4	3.2	76.8	20.1
Essex CDP	9.26	39,262	NA	NA	NA	8.2	87.4	57,780	12.4	191,400	65.5	6.9	61.5	32.4
Fairland CDP	4.96	23,681	NA	NA	NA	36.2	85.2	84,426	10.0	349,300	73.9	6.6	69.6	24.6
Ferndale CDP	3.98	16,746	NA	NA	NA	9.3	84.4	72,168	10.8	247,800	69.5	5.0	68.6	26.0
Forestville CDP	3.93	12,353	NA	NA	NA	7.8	87.4	68,507	10.4	228,500	70.4	8.2	66.0	28.5
Fort Meade CDP	8.21	9,327	NA	NA	NA	7.7	66.5	77,412	4.3	0	35.7	10.8	84.0	10.0
Fort Washington CDP	13.79	23,717	NA	NA	NA	19.8	92.8	117,950	5.1	358,500	65.5	5.8	74.9	21.8
Frederick city	23.79	65,289	72,244	10.7	3036.7	20.4	81.7	76,118	10.4	270,400	71.1	5.1	61.4	30.0
Friendly CDP	4.88	9,250	NA	NA	NA	17.7	91.6	130,577	3.3	320,700	68.7	5.9	77.0	18.9
Gaithersburg city	10.32	59,899	67,985	13.5	6587.7	38.1	78.6	89,763	8.7	392,200	73.4	5.5	66.1	27.3
Germantown CDP	17.03	86,395	NA	NA	NA	34.5	83.6	94,559	6.8	345,400	75.4	3.4	73.7	22.5
Glassmanor CDP	2.36	17,295	NA	NA	NA	16.9	79.4	58,019	12.2	242,200	75.6	6.6	58.2	36.4
Glen Burnie CDP	17.32	67,639	NA	NA	NA	9.4	83.0	70,769	8.6	256,500	68.8	4.7	62.9	29.6
Glenmont CDP	2.80	13,529	NA	NA	NA	46.8	86.8	95,482	8.4	422,500	73.5	4.7	78.3	17.7
Glen Dale CDP	7.15	13,466	NA	NA	NA	22.5	90.4	130,017	3.6	412,500	73.4	7.6	79.1	18.0
Greenbelt city	6.24	22,128	23,224	5.0	3721.8	28.6	79.3	71,734	9.1	227,400	77.4	5.2	58.6	37.4
Hagerstown city	12.17	39,752	40,100	0.9	3295.0	7.9	79.8	40,800	24.8	155,700	62.1	7.6	58.4	34.9
Halfway CDP	4.65	10,701	NA	NA	NA	3.4	92.9	66,052	7.0	178,200	68.4	3.4	65.9	30.2
Havre de Grace city	5.85	13,003	14,018	7.8	2396.2	5.3	88.1	77,690	10.8	287,500	63.9	6.3	59.8	33.7
Hillcrest Heights CDP	2.49	16,469	NA	NA	NA	5.4	81.7	63,767	7.9	239,200	71.4	8.9	50.8	42.7
Hyattsville city	2.68	17,535	18,230	4.0	6802.2	31.6	85.8	81,736	8.5	336,300	76.8	3.4	60.0	30.0
Ilchester CDP	10.73	23,476	NA	NA	NA	18.4	89.5	126,566	3.3	390,600	76.0	2.7	75.0	19.9
Joppatowne CDP	6.73	12,616	NA	NA	NA	4.7	93.3	89,423	6.8	260,900	72.5	4.3	73.7	19.7
Kemp Mill CDP	2.50	12,564	NA	NA	NA	31.4	91.7	116,542	4.6	424,700	70.2	4.0	77.9	18.3
Kettering CDP	5.49	12,790	NA	NA	NA	13.8	94.1	93,698	5.3	301,500	62.5	5.4	60.9	36.8
Lake Shore CDP	13.43	19,477	NA	NA	NA	3.1	90.2	108,904	4.1	382,500	71.4	3.6	76.4	19.2
Landover CDP	4.00	23,078	NA	NA	NA	29.5	84.8	59,935	11.9	207,400	72.2	7.6	66.2	29.0
Langley Park CDP	0.99	18,755	NA	NA	NA	61.4	89.4	63,105	15.9	269,400	78.1	5.6	73.6	16.6
Lanham CDP	3.53	10,157	NA	NA	NA	33.2	90.5	85,577	7.8	306,800	67.6	7.8	76.9	20.3
Largo CDP	3.06	10,709	NA	NA	NA	22.9	87.0	87,482	4.2	283,900	73.3	7.1	61.1	32.0
Laurel city	4.82	24,901	25,631	2.9	5317.6	28.8	81.6	78,313	6.3	269,000	76.5	4.9	56.4	36.5
Lexington Park CDP	5.62	11,626	NA	NA	NA	9.9	75.5	74,598	10.2	203,200	69.6	2.2	59.0	33.5
Linthicum CDP	5.46	10,324	NA	NA	NA	4.1	90.5	96,875	3.2	305,600	68.0	3.0	70.4	23.4
Lochearn CDP	5.59	25,333	NA	NA	NA	17.7	91.7	64,392	9.6	206,500	62.7	6.0	63.6	30.7
Maryland City CDP	7.72	16,093	NA	NA	NA	22.9	77.3	103,112	6.2	315,500	79.4	5.5	63.9	30.9
Mays Chapel CDP	3.71	11,420	NA	NA	NA	15.7	92.0	108,297	4.1	395,300	66.3	2.5	70.1	27.8
Middle River CDP	7.78	25,191	NA	NA	NA	11.0	86.3	57,621	10.2	168,300	66.5	5.6	65.9	27.3
Milford Mill CDP	6.95	29,042	NA	NA	NA	17.4	85.9	67,747	11.1	210,100	71.4	4.2	62.4	32.4
Mitchellville CDP	4.94	10,967	NA	NA	NA	16.8	90.8	125,625	3.0	354,300	74.7	7.5	78.9	18.5
Montgomery Village CDP	3.97	32,032	NA	NA	NA	39.3	85.3	80,440	9.5	305,400	73.4	5.0	71.5	23.4
New Carrollton city	1.54	12,348	12,928	4.7	8394.8	44.2	91.7	66,991	9.2	271,100	73.4	10.9	64.7	33.3
North Bethesda CDP	8.87	43,828	NA	NA	NA	32.5	81.6	107,220	6.5	567,500	69.7	3.2	54.2	38.1
North Laurel CDP	6.48	4,474	NA	NA	NA	26.7	83.1	104,352	4.6	359,000	77.2	4.2	74.5	18.1
North Potomac CDP	6.52	24,410	NA	NA	NA	37.1	88.1	171,066	3.9	672,900	69.0	2.7	87.0	11.3
Ocean Pines CDP	6.66	11,710	NA	NA	NA	5.8	88.4	71,990	5.7	278,600	46.8	3.4	69.8	25.7
Odenton CDP	14.77	37,132	NA	NA	NA	9.8	83.0	99,601	4.2	323,500	68.0	3.2	63.5	30.1
Olney CDP	16.19	33,844	NA	NA	NA	20.3	91.2	143,396	3.7	506,400	71.8	2.7	82.3	15.4
Overlea CDP	3.00	12,275	NA	NA	NA	10.0	87.1	64,868	10.7	201,400	68.5	5.3	61.5	32.4
Owings Mills CDP	9.53	30,622	NA	NA	NA	23.5	84.2	81,569	7.1	260,700	73.4	5.7	58.4	33.1
Oxon Hill CDP	6.62	17,722	NA	NA	NA	15.0	87.0	88,327	7.2	244,800	71.8	8.0	62.5	31.5
Parkville CDP	4.29	30,734	NA	NA	NA	9.9	88.9	66,363	7.5	202,400	71.6	5.5	63.0	29.8
Parole CDP	10.27	15,922	NA	NA	NA	5.5	79.0	104,006	4.3	454,300	59.1	3.2	52.0	40.0
Pasadena CDP	14.94	24,287	NA	NA	NA	5.6	84.1	96,575	4.8	314,400	75.6	4.3	73.0	19.6
Perry Hall CDP	6.97	28,474	NA	NA	NA	10.5	89.5	88,825	6.6	265,400	69.4	3.5	69.9	26.4
Pikesville CDP	12.35	30,764	NA	NA	NA	16.6	86.9	86,655	9.0	319,900	63.2	3.5	61.1	33.9
Potomac CDP	25.13	44,965	NA	NA	NA	27.7	90.7	195,884	3.4	893,800	61.9	3.6	79.3	18.6
Randallstown CDP	10.22	32,430	NA	NA	NA	11.7	87.8	83,549	8.2	242,600	65.3	5.6	68.9	27.4
Redland CDP	7.04	17,242	NA	NA	NA	38.4	89.6	117,944	4.8	418,500	70.0	3.1	81.8	13.1
Reisterstown CDP	5.17	25,968	NA	NA	NA	20.6	90.4	70,507	11.5	240,000	70.3	5.8	71.0	24.3
Riviera Beach CDP	2.63	12,677	NA	NA	NA	3.2	92.3	96,359	5.0	268,100	69.5	4.0	70.8	23.4
Rockville city	13.59	61,242	68,079	11.2	5009.5	34.1	80.9	106,576	6.7	540,000	69.7	4.4	65.4	27.5
Rosaryville CDP	9.19	10,697	NA	NA	NA	8.3	93.7	127,721	5.2	332,800	68.5	5.7	80.9	17.0
Rosedale CDP	6.89	19,257	NA	NA	NA	11.7	90.4	73,047	8.5	205,700	66.9	5.1	72.0	22.7
Rossville CDP	5.38	15,147	NA	NA	NA	21.8	82.5	66,522	8.0	221,400	71.1	6.7	57.8	37.4
Salisbury city	13.71	30,264	32,935	8.8	2402.3	13.0	71.8	41,905	19.9	158,700	65.6	8.3	52.5	33.4
Seabrook CDP	3.08	17,287	NA	NA	NA	39.4	82.3	75,825	6.5	293,600	71.4	7.9	72.5	23.6
Severn CDP	18.32	44,231	NA	NA	NA	14.3	80.6	107,155	4.3	362,300	70.6	4.7	75.2	20.4
Severna Park CDP	16.53	37,634	NA	NA	NA	4.7	88.6	151,499	2.8	546,800	67.5	3.5	80.7	15.9
Silver Spring CDP	7.89	71,452	NA	NA	NA	36.5	80.2	83,782	9.0	516,900	78.1	5.7	56.4	33.8
South Laurel CDP	8.07	26,112	NA	NA	NA	31.1	79.9	79,227	6.4	343,500	76.4	6.0	63.5	31.6
Suitland CDP	4.25	25,825	NA	NA	NA	8.9	79.0	62,073	7.9	225,400	75.5	7.2	59.1	33.8
Summerfield CDP	3.64	10,898	NA	NA	NA	13.6	77.0	82,904	7.2	257,700	76.2	5.6	58.9	36.9
Takoma Park city	2.09	16,739	17,725	5.9	8480.9	30.1	85.1	84,591	9.8	583,800	76.0	5.6	65.4	27.0

Table B. Incorporated Places, Census Designated Places (CDPs), and Minor Civil Divisions (MCDs) of 10,000 or More Population — Crime, Residential Construction and Local Government Finance

STATE City, town, township, borough, or CDP (county if applicable)	Serious crimes known to police, 2018[1] Violent crime Number	Violent crime Rate[2]	Property crime Number	Property crime Rate[2]	New residential construction authorized by building permits, 2019 Value ($1,000)	Number of housing units	Percent single family	Local government finance, 2017 General revenue Total (mil dol)	Intergovernmental Total (mil dol)	Percent from state gov.	Taxes per capita[3]	General expenditure Total (mil dol)	Per capita[3] Total	Capital outlays	Debt outstanding (mil dol)
	15	16	17	18	19	20	21	22	23	24	25	26	27	28	29
MARYLAND—Con.															
Cockeysville CDP	NA	NA	NA	NA	NA	NA	NA	NA	NA	NA	NA	NA	NA	NA	NA
Colesville CDP	NA	NA	NA	NA	NA	NA	NA	NA	NA	NA	NA	NA	NA	NA	NA
College Park city	NA	NA	NA	NA	NA	NA	NA	20.5	1.8	80.6	456	16.0	496	2	12.3
Columbia CDP	NA	NA	NA	NA	NA	NA	NA	NA	NA	NA	NA	NA	NA	NA	NA
Crofton CDP	NA	NA	NA	NA	NA	NA	NA	NA	NA	NA	NA	NA	NA	NA	NA
Cumberland city	146	747	881	4,505	0	0	0.0	34.4	6.3	37.4	674	37.8	1,926	9	73.9
Damascus CDP	NA	NA	NA	NA	NA	NA	NA	NA	NA	NA	NA	NA	NA	NA	NA
Dundalk CDP	NA	NA	NA	NA	NA	NA	NA	NA	NA	NA	NA	NA	NA	NA	NA
Easton town	36	218	400	2,417	13,566	44	100.0	41.7	1.7	88.3	913	21.2	1,283	0	56.6
East Riverdale CDP	NA	NA	NA	NA	NA	NA	NA	NA	NA	NA	NA	NA	NA	NA	NA
Edgewood CDP	NA	NA	NA	NA	NA	NA	NA	NA	NA	NA	NA	NA	NA	NA	NA
Eldersburg CDP	NA	NA	NA	NA	NA	NA	NA	NA	NA	NA	NA	NA	NA	NA	NA
Elkridge CDP	NA	NA	NA	NA	NA	NA	NA	NA	NA	NA	NA	NA	NA	NA	NA
Elkton town	199	1,269	989	6,307	1,455	11	100.0	17.5	0.8	0.0	641	18.4	1,178	67	12.4
Ellicott City CDP	NA	NA	NA	NA	NA	NA	NA	NA	NA	NA	NA	NA	NA	NA	NA
Essex CDP	NA	NA	NA	NA	NA	NA	NA	NA	NA	NA	NA	NA	NA	NA	NA
Fairland CDP	NA	NA	NA	NA	NA	NA	NA	NA	NA	NA	NA	NA	NA	NA	NA
Ferndale CDP	NA	NA	NA	NA	NA	NA	NA	NA	NA	NA	NA	NA	NA	NA	NA
Forestville CDP	NA	NA	NA	NA	NA	NA	NA	NA	NA	NA	NA	NA	NA	NA	NA
Fort Meade CDP	NA	NA	NA	NA	NA	NA	NA	NA	NA	NA	NA	NA	NA	NA	NA
Fort Washington CDP	NA	NA	NA	NA	NA	NA	NA	NA	NA	NA	NA	NA	NA	NA	NA
Frederick city	285	394	1,490	2,061	86,087	515	54.6	122.6	18.9	65.5	945	92.6	1,305	25	210.7
Friendly CDP	NA	NA	NA	NA	NA	NA	NA	NA	NA	NA	NA	NA	NA	NA	NA
Gaithersburg city	NA	NA	NA	NA	8,588	66	3.0	66.7	4.5	54.7	683	57.3	842	19	102.7
Germantown CDP	NA	NA	NA	NA	NA	NA	NA	NA	NA	NA	NA	NA	NA	NA	NA
Glassmanor CDP	NA	NA	NA	NA	NA	NA	NA	NA	NA	NA	NA	NA	NA	NA	NA
Glen Burnie CDP	NA	NA	NA	NA	NA	NA	NA	NA	NA	NA	NA	NA	NA	NA	NA
Glenmont CDP	NA	NA	NA	NA	NA	NA	NA	NA	NA	NA	NA	NA	NA	NA	NA
Glen Dale CDP	NA	NA	NA	NA	NA	NA	NA	NA	NA	NA	NA	NA	NA	NA	NA
Greenbelt city	116	490	722	3,051	NA	NA	NA	30.2	3.1	40.3	993	28.5	1,226	56	5.3
Hagerstown city	255	631	1,052	2,605	6,164	41	100.0	64.4	4.0	44.0	843	62.5	1,554	5	109.4
Halfway CDP	NA	NA	NA	NA	NA	NA	NA	NA	NA	NA	NA	NA	NA	NA	NA
Havre de Grace city	32	234	217	1,589	19,095	86	86.0	20.7	2.9	30.3	819	23.7	1,748	424	27.7
Hillcrest Heights CDP	NA	NA	NA	NA	NA	NA	NA	NA	NA	NA	NA	NA	NA	NA	NA
Hyattsville city	79	428	927	5,025	NA	NA	NA	21.6	0.7	100.0	1,102	16.6	910	4	8.3
Ilchester CDP	NA	NA	NA	NA	NA	NA	NA	NA	NA	NA	NA	NA	NA	NA	NA
Joppatowne CDP	NA	NA	NA	NA	NA	NA	NA	NA	NA	NA	NA	NA	NA	NA	NA
Kemp Mill CDP	NA	NA	NA	NA	NA	NA	NA	NA	NA	NA	NA	NA	NA	NA	NA
Kettering CDP	NA	NA	NA	NA	NA	NA	NA	NA	NA	NA	NA	NA	NA	NA	NA
Lake Shore CDP	NA	NA	NA	NA	NA	NA	NA	NA	NA	NA	NA	NA	NA	NA	NA
Landover CDP	NA	NA	NA	NA	NA	NA	NA	NA	NA	NA	NA	NA	NA	NA	NA
Langley Park CDP	NA	NA	NA	NA	NA	NA	NA	NA	NA	NA	NA	NA	NA	NA	NA
Lanham CDP	NA	NA	NA	NA	NA	NA	NA	NA	NA	NA	NA	NA	NA	NA	NA
Largo CDP	NA	NA	NA	NA	NA	NA	NA	NA	NA	NA	NA	NA	NA	NA	NA
Laurel city	115	442	929	3,568	11,554	40	75.0	36.1	2.3	65.0	1,018	34.5	1,339	0	7.1
Lexington Park CDP	NA	NA	NA	NA	NA	NA	NA	NA	NA	NA	NA	NA	NA	NA	NA
Linthicum CDP	NA	NA	NA	NA	NA	NA	NA	NA	NA	NA	NA	NA	NA	NA	NA
Lochearn CDP	NA	NA	NA	NA	NA	NA	NA	NA	NA	NA	NA	NA	NA	NA	NA
Maryland City CDP	NA	NA	NA	NA	NA	NA	NA	NA	NA	NA	NA	NA	NA	NA	NA
Mays Chapel CDP	NA	NA	NA	NA	NA	NA	NA	NA	NA	NA	NA	NA	NA	NA	NA
Middle River CDP	NA	NA	NA	NA	NA	NA	NA	NA	NA	NA	NA	NA	NA	NA	NA
Milford Mill CDP	NA	NA	NA	NA	NA	NA	NA	NA	NA	NA	NA	NA	NA	NA	NA
Mitchellville CDP	NA	NA	NA	NA	NA	NA	NA	NA	NA	NA	NA	NA	NA	NA	NA
Montgomery Village CDP	NA	NA	NA	NA	NA	NA	NA	NA	NA	NA	NA	NA	NA	NA	NA
New Carrollton city	40	305	181	1,380	NA	NA	NA	10.0	0.6	82.6	539	9.2	709	111	1.8
North Bethesda CDP	NA	NA	NA	NA	NA	NA	NA	NA	NA	NA	NA	NA	NA	NA	NA
North Laurel CDP	NA	NA	NA	NA	NA	NA	NA	NA	NA	NA	NA	NA	NA	NA	NA
North Potomac CDP	NA	NA	NA	NA	NA	NA	NA	NA	NA	NA	NA	NA	NA	NA	NA
Ocean Pines CDP	14	114	52	425	NA	NA	NA	NA	NA	NA	NA	NA	NA	NA	NA
Odenton CDP	NA	NA	NA	NA	NA	NA	NA	NA	NA	NA	NA	NA	NA	NA	NA
Olney CDP	NA	NA	NA	NA	NA	NA	NA	NA	NA	NA	NA	NA	NA	NA	NA
Overlea CDP	NA	NA	NA	NA	NA	NA	NA	NA	NA	NA	NA	NA	NA	NA	NA
Owings Mills CDP	NA	NA	NA	NA	NA	NA	NA	NA	NA	NA	NA	NA	NA	NA	NA
Oxon Hill CDP	NA	NA	NA	NA	NA	NA	NA	NA	NA	NA	NA	NA	NA	NA	NA
Parkville CDP	NA	NA	NA	NA	NA	NA	NA	NA	NA	NA	NA	NA	NA	NA	NA
Parole CDP	NA	NA	NA	NA	NA	NA	NA	NA	NA	NA	NA	NA	NA	NA	NA
Pasadena CDP	NA	NA	NA	NA	NA	NA	NA	NA	NA	NA	NA	NA	NA	NA	NA
Perry Hall CDP	NA	NA	NA	NA	NA	NA	NA	NA	NA	NA	NA	NA	NA	NA	NA
Pikesville CDP	NA	NA	NA	NA	NA	NA	NA	NA	NA	NA	NA	NA	NA	NA	NA
Potomac CDP	NA	NA	NA	NA	NA	NA	NA	NA	NA	NA	NA	NA	NA	NA	NA
Randallstown CDP	NA	NA	NA	NA	NA	NA	NA	NA	NA	NA	NA	NA	NA	NA	NA
Redland CDP	NA	NA	NA	NA	NA	NA	NA	NA	NA	NA	NA	NA	NA	NA	NA
Reisterstown CDP	NA	NA	NA	NA	NA	NA	NA	NA	NA	NA	NA	NA	NA	NA	NA
Riviera Beach CDP	NA	NA	NA	NA	NA	NA	NA	NA	NA	NA	NA	NA	NA	NA	NA
Rockville city	NA	NA	NA	NA	155,381	745	10.1	111.6	8.8	51.2	896	104.8	1,545	28	130.8
Rosaryville CDP	NA	NA	NA	NA	NA	NA	NA	NA	NA	NA	NA	NA	NA	NA	NA
Rosedale CDP	NA	NA	NA	NA	NA	NA	NA	NA	NA	NA	NA	NA	NA	NA	NA
Rossville CDP	NA	NA	NA	NA	NA	NA	NA	NA	NA	NA	NA	NA	NA	NA	NA
Salisbury city	272	820	1,548	4,665	9,320	72	44.4	58.8	12.6	76.7	808	51.9	1,591	54	102.0
Seabrook CDP	NA	NA	NA	NA	NA	NA	NA	NA	NA	NA	NA	NA	NA	NA	NA
Severn CDP	NA	NA	NA	NA	NA	NA	NA	NA	NA	NA	NA	NA	NA	NA	NA
Severna Park CDP	NA	NA	NA	NA	NA	NA	NA	NA	NA	NA	NA	NA	NA	NA	NA
Silver Spring CDP	NA	NA	NA	NA	NA	NA	NA	NA	NA	NA	NA	NA	NA	NA	NA
South Laurel CDP	NA	NA	NA	NA	NA	NA	NA	NA	NA	NA	NA	NA	NA	NA	NA
Suitland CDP	NA	NA	NA	NA	NA	NA	NA	NA	NA	NA	NA	NA	NA	NA	NA
Summerfield CDP	NA	NA	NA	NA	NA	NA	NA	NA	NA	NA	NA	NA	NA	NA	NA
Takoma Park city	57	316	393	2,177	NA	NA	NA	23.4	2.8	45.8	956	25.0	1,411	117	2.1

1 Data for serious crimes have not been adjusted for underreporting. This may affect comparability between geographic areas over time.
2 Per 100,000 population estimated by the FBI.   3 Based on population estimated as of July 1 of the year shown.

Table B. Incorporated Places, Census Designated Places (CDPs), and Minor Civil Divisions (MCDs) of 10,000 or More Population — **Land Area, Population, and Households, and Employment**

STATE City, town, township, borough, or CDP (county if applicable)	Land area 2010 (sq mi)	Total persons 2010	Total persons 2019	Percent change 2010–2019	Persons per square mile, 2019	Percent foreign born	Percent living in the same house as previous year	Median household income	Percent of households with income below poverty level	Median value of owner-occupied housing units	Percent in civilian labor force	Unemployment rate	Family households	One person households
	1	2	3	4	5	6	7	8	9	10	11	12	13	14
MARYLAND—Con.														
Timonium CDP	5.35	9,925	NA	NA	NA	10.2	89.6	97,055	3.6	380,700	60.1	3.0	67.7	28.9
Towson CDP	14.15	55,197	NA	NA	NA	10.8	80.5	88,786	11.6	363,800	61.3	4.3	55.5	32.7
Travilah CDP	15.87	12,159	NA	NA	NA	33.9	94.6	241,369	1.5	1,081,200	65.0	3.5	91.6	8.2
Urbana CDP	6.62	9,175	NA	NA	NA	21.1	88.5	155,000	2.3	524,100	81.0	3.0	84.7	11.3
Waldorf CDP	36.26	67,752	NA	NA	NA	8.0	88.6	95,695	5.9	279,100	70.7	3.6	70.4	25.5
Walker Mill CDP	3.16	11,302	NA	NA	NA	7.6	88.8	70,349	8.0	254,900	65.9	6.1	63.1	34.3
Westminster city	6.68	18,496	18,640	0.8	2790.4	7.9	86.5	60,518	13.1	242,700	59.6	5.1	58.1	37.1
Wheaton CDP	6.90	48,284	NA	NA	NA	43.6	88.0	85,617	10.6	371,700	75.7	5.3	74.7	19.7
White Oak CDP	3.78	17,403	NA	NA	NA	42.7	85.6	73,877	12.6	401,800	73.3	9.0	69.3	25.4
Woodlawn CDP	9.54	37,879	NA	NA	NA	20.0	88.7	68,623	8.4	219,000	69.2	6.0	67.2	27.4
MASSACHUSETTS	7800.96	6,547,785	6,892,503	5.3	883.5	16.8	87.3	81,215	10.8	381,600	67.2	4.8	63.4	28.5
Abington town (Plymouth)	9.96	16,026	16,668	4.0	1673.5	8.7	85.8	99,381	6.3	357,300	72.9	4.3	71.4	23.0
Acton town (Middlesex)	19.87	21,912	23,662	8.0	1190.8	26.8	88.8	141,665	6.1	581,400	68.7	4.3	72.6	22.1
Acushnet town (Bristol)	18.43	10,304	10,625	3.1	576.5	11.0	93.5	80,221	4.8	296,000	66.2	3.6	73.7	20.0
Agawam Town city & MCD (Hampden)	23.32	28,438	28,613	0.6	1227.0	8.0	92.4	68,944	9.7	230,700	65.2	3.5	60.9	32.7
Amesbury Town city & MCD (Essex)	12.29	16,286	17,532	7.7	1426.5	4.3	88.2	82,468	6.7	336,200	70.8	3.6	63.9	29.5
Amherst town (Hampshire)	27.63	37,819	39,924	5.6	1445.0	17.7	50.0	56,905	24.6	358,700	55.4	8.9	49.6	29.3
Amherst Center CDP	4.94	19,065	NA	NA	NA	14.6	34.2	45,098	31.2	350,600	48.0	12.2	39.8	39.3
Andover town (Essex)	30.81	33,071	36,356	9.9	1180.0	17.4	89.4	151,334	4.4	620,500	67.9	3.2	74.8	22.7
Arlington town (Middlesex)	5.14	42,823	45,531	6.3	8858.2	19.6	88.0	108,389	5.7	642,200	71.5	3.3	60.9	31.9
Ashland town (Middlesex)	12.34	16,615	17,807	7.2	1443.0	21.9	90.1	124,130	5.3	401,900	74.7	2.2	70.5	20.8
Athol town (Worcester)	32.30	11,579	11,732	1.3	363.2	4.7	84.8	54,142	13.6	156,700	59.6	8.1	63.0	28.0
Attleboro city & MCD (Bristol)	26.78	43,568	45,237	3.8	1689.2	10.3	90.9	74,962	8.0	292,900	68.2	4.8	65.6	28.1
Auburn town (Worcester)	15.49	16,219	16,766	3.4	1082.4	6.4	94.8	84,740	3.7	263,700	65.6	5.0	64.3	29.5
Barnstable Town city & MCD (Barnstable)	59.93	45,188	44,477	-1.6	742.1	15.4	90.5	72,733	8.3	380,400	65.1	4.4	63.0	29.7
Bedford town (Middlesex)	13.66	13,316	14,123	6.1	1033.9	18.8	85.6	128,354	3.5	655,300	66.8	5.5	68.3	26.4
Belchertown town (Hampshire)	52.60	14,649	15,098	3.1	287.0	6.1	89.8	91,191	6.3	276,900	74.2	4.2	73.3	18.7
Bellingham town (Norfolk)	18.34	16,411	17,270	5.2	941.7	7.0	91.1	101,477	3.7	316,200	76.5	4.5	68.6	23.3
Belmont town (Middlesex)	4.65	24,650	26,116	5.9	5616.3	24.9	86.1	129,380	6.2	859,600	68.0	4.0	71.2	24.2
Beverly city & MCD (Essex)	15.09	39,504	42,174	6.8	2794.8	8.0	86.2	80,586	9.9	437,300	68.1	3.4	58.0	34.4
Billerica town (Middlesex)	25.57	40,235	43,367	7.8	1696.0	12.6	90.3	105,343	4.4	404,800	70.1	4.7	76.7	18.4
Boston city & MCD (Suffolk)	48.34	617,792	692,600	12.1	14327.7	28.3	80.2	71,115	18.7	532,700	69.7	6.6	48.1	36.2
Bourne town (Barnstable)	40.67	19,748	19,762	0.1	485.9	4.0	88.3	75,534	6.0	370,100	61.2	2.4	59.5	33.5
Braintree Town city & MCD (Norfolk)	13.76	35,726	37,190	4.1	2702.8	17.0	89.8	96,522	6.3	456,500	69.2	3.5	66.8	27.6
Bridgewater Town city & MCD (Plymouth)	27.25	26,569	27,619	4.0	1013.5	5.2	85.8	95,675	8.8	358,900	66.9	6.1	69.8	21.7
Brockton city & MCD (Plymouth)	21.33	93,767	95,708	2.1	4487.0	30.9	84.3	58,469	16.8	264,800	68.6	8.3	68.0	27.7
Brookline town (Norfolk)	6.76	58,613	59,121	0.9	8745.7	29.1	79.2	117,326	13.3	933,200	68.3	2.8	52.5	30.4
Burlington town (Middlesex)	11.75	24,492	28,627	16.9	2436.3	23.8	89.9	118,721	4.8	533,800	66.9	2.8	73.9	21.1
Cambridge city & MCD (Middlesex)	6.39	105,148	118,927	13.1	18611.4	28.9	73.3	103,154	12.5	768,300	70.5	4.0	42.9	35.8
Canton town (Middlesex)	18.75	21,581	23,805	10.3	1269.6	16.1	91.4	105,919	6.4	510,500	68.0	3.9	65.6	28.4
Carver town (Plymouth)	37.31	11,490	11,767	2.4	315.4	3.9	88.0	70,959	5.5	291,500	64.6	4.1	64.0	29.0
Charlton town (Worcester)	42.18	12,986	13,713	5.6	325.1	5.0	90.7	101,111	4.6	297,700	69.8	5.8	71.8	22.8
Chelmsford town (Middlesex)	22.38	33,792	35,391	4.7	1581.4	10.9	91.2	116,111	4.6	400,500	67.9	4.4	72.0	23.9
Chelsea city & MCD (Suffolk)	2.22	35,181	39,690	12.8	17878.4	45.4	85.4	56,802	20.0	350,800	70.9	4.7	59.1	31.6
Chicopee city & MCD (Hampden)	22.91	55,307	55,126	-0.3	2406.2	8.4	87.9	53,225	13.7	182,100	62.2	5.9	60.0	33.3
Clinton town (Worcester)	5.65	13,600	14,000	2.9	2477.9	15.5	86.7	67,634	8.9	248,200	71.4	4.2	59.1	29.8
Concord town (Middlesex)	24.51	17,680	18,918	7.0	771.8	10.8	87.2	152,318	4.1	875,400	55.9	2.8	74.2	23.8
Danvers town (Essex)	13.28	26,500	27,549	4.0	2074.5	10.5	89.4	89,250	8.8	427,400	67.6	3.7	67.2	28.5
Dartmouth town (Bristol)	60.93	34,033	34,188	0.5	561.1	11.3	88.9	84,220	9.1	362,100	59.2	4.8	70.5	24.4
Dedham town (Norfolk)	10.27	24,723	25,219	2.0	2455.6	12.6	89.0	100,757	5.0	461,200	67.5	3.7	64.7	29.9
Dennis town (Barnstable)	20.60	14,221	13,871	-2.5	673.3	6.2	89.8	65,616	9.4	381,000	53.9	5.2	59.0	35.1
Dracut town (Middlesex)	20.68	29,407	31,634	7.6	1529.7	9.3	91.8	90,273	6.6	333,200	69.5	4.1	70.0	25.4
Dudley town (Worcester)	20.83	11,375	11,773	3.5	565.2	7.1	89.2	69,071	6.8	263,900	66.4	6.2	69.0	24.3
Duxbury town (Plymouth)	23.70	15,060	15,921	5.7	671.8	3.3	93.6	128,173	5.0	651,000	60.6	4.3	78.6	19.6
East Bridgewater town (Plymouth)	17.23	13,796	14,526	5.3	843.1	5.2	93.8	90,528	5.2	352,300	69.9	4.2	76.6	17.9
Easthampton Town city & MCD (Hampshi)	13.32	16,049	15,829	-1.4	1188.4	3.4	91.2	63,507	7.7	255,000	68.6	7.0	55.8	33.3
East Longmeadow town (Hampden)	12.94	15,767	16,192	2.7	1251.3	4.7	91.2	87,748	5.5	268,400	60.0	3.6	70.0	26.1
Easton town (Bristol)	28.76	23,116	25,105	8.6	872.9	8.2	90.3	112,268	4.2	414,100	69.9	4.5	73.7	21.3
Everett city & MCD (Middlesex)	3.42	41,553	46,451	11.8	13582.2	43.1	86.3	65,528	12.9	405,800	72.0	5.2	68.0	25.6
Fairhaven town (Bristol)	12.38	15,873	16,078	1.3	1298.7	8.9	88.7	67,394	8.7	281,000	61.2	5.2	60.3	33.3
Fall River city & MCD (Bristol)	33.11	88,865	89,541	0.8	2704.3	20.0	84.9	43,503	19.5	242,200	59.3	8.4	58.3	35.1
Falmouth town (Barnstable)	44.06	31,532	30,993	-1.7	703.4	6.6	92.4	75,820	6.0	422,300	57.1	4.0	61.3	32.9
Fitchburg city & MCD (Worcester)	27.82	40,325	40,638	0.8	1460.7	10.0	85.0	57,207	14.9	196,600	66.0	8.3	61.6	28.5
Foxborough town (Norfolk)	19.86	16,872	18,399	9.1	926.4	9.5	87.9	96,062	6.3	427,500	68.0	5.0	66.4	27.2
Framingham city & MCD (Middlesex)	25.04	68,323	74,416	8.9	2971.9	28.4	86.2	82,709	9.7	409,400	72.7	5.0	65.1	28.5
Franklin Town city & MCD (Norfolk)	26.64	31,633	34,087	7.8	1279.5	6.8	89.9	122,607	5.0	432,700	72.7	4.1	72.6	23.0
Gardner city & MCD (Worcester)	22.07	20,233	20,683	2.2	937.2	6.9	88.6	49,679	14.6	185,700	60.5	3.9	61.5	31.0
Gloucester city & MCD (Essex)	26.20	28,789	30,430	5.7	1161.5	8.6	91.3	72,574	9.8	425,400	64.1	4.4	62.8	30.3
Grafton town (Worcester)	22.80	17,763	18,883	6.3	828.2	11.9	90.9	106,250	6.1	357,500	72.7	5.0	66.8	24.5

Table B. Incorporated Places, Census Designated Places (CDPs), and Minor Civil Divisions (MCDs) of 10,000 or More Population — Crime, Residential Construction and Local Government Finance

STATE City, town, township, borough, or CDP (county if applicable)	Serious crimes known to police, 2018[1] Violent crime Number	Rate[2]	Property crime Number	Rate[2]	New residential construction authorized by building permits, 2019 Value ($1,000)	Number of housing units	Percent single family	Local government finance, 2017 General revenue Total (mil dol)	Intergovernmental Total (mil dol)	Percent from state gov.	Taxes per capita[3]	General expenditure Total (mil dol)	Per capita[3] Total	Capital outlays	Debt outstanding (mil dol)
	15	16	17	18	19	20	21	22	23	24	25	26	27	28	29
MARYLAND—Con.															
Timonium CDP	NA	NA	NA	NA	NA	NA	NA	NA	NA	NA	NA	NA	NA	NA	NA
Towson CDP	NA	NA	NA	NA	NA	NA	NA	NA	NA	NA	NA	NA	NA	NA	NA
Travilah CDP	NA	NA	NA	NA	NA	NA	NA	NA	NA	NA	NA	NA	NA	NA	NA
Urbana CDP	NA	NA	NA	NA	NA	NA	NA	NA	NA	NA	NA	NA	NA	NA	NA
Waldorf CDP	NA	NA	NA	NA	NA	NA	NA	NA	NA	NA	NA	NA	NA	NA	NA
Walker Mill CDP	NA	NA	NA	NA	NA	NA	NA	NA	NA	NA	NA	NA	NA	NA	NA
Westminster city	84	452	579	3,112	NA	NA	NA	26.7	4.6	29.0	683	19.8	1,070	115	18.2
Wheaton CDP	NA	NA	NA	NA	NA	NA	NA	NA	NA	NA	NA	NA	NA	NA	NA
White Oak CDP	NA	NA	NA	NA	NA	NA	NA	NA	NA	NA	NA	NA	NA	NA	NA
Woodlawn CDP	NA	NA	NA	NA	NA	NA	NA	NA	NA	NA	NA	NA	NA	NA	NA
MASSACHUSETTS	23,337	338	87,196	1,263	3,679,201	17,365	36.2	X	X	X	X	X	X	X	X
Abington town (Plymouth)	41	249	147	894	7,405	37	35.1	80.4	38.2	96.9	2,265	121.6	7,405	4109	55.3
Acton town (Middlesex)	26	108	156	649	8,560	22	100.0	94.6	4.4	97.8	3,581	96.3	4,061	137	29.5
Acushnet town (Bristol)	19	180	69	652	5,458	17	100.0	30.8	9.4	99.8	1,714	28.2	2,680	128	14.6
Agawam Town city & MCD (Hampden)	105	363	428	1,478	NA	NA	NA	101.2	30.5	96.6	2,147	115.5	4,027	196	25.8
Amesbury Town city & MCD (Essex)	32	182	143	811	2,439	12	100.0	66.0	15.5	96.7	2,480	59.5	3,411	25	36.4
Amherst town (Hampshire)	120	298	175	435	35,368	188	12.8	85.7	21.1	95.3	1,323	83.8	2,123	131	16.3
Amherst Center CDP	NA	NA	NA	NA	NA	NA	NA	NA	NA	NA	NA	NA	NA	NA	NA
Andover town (Essex)	7	19	173	476	22,471	86	30.2	179.2	21.5	95.1	4,041	163.4	4,567	339	101.8
Arlington town (Middlesex)	34	74	191	416	7,293	23	73.9	160.0	30.4	92.8	2,644	165.8	3,653	481	80.4
Ashland town (Middlesex)	22	123	90	504	17,491	94	31.9	72.5	14.2	97.6	2,638	71.6	4,026	359	30.3
Athol town (Worcester)	57	486	143	1,220	4,645	24	100.0	26.2	8.1	88.0	1,251	24.3	2,073	76	25.1
Attleboro city & MCD (Bristol)	98	219	529	1,183	19,145	98	75.5	149.9	54.0	98.0	1,672	133.3	2,976	164	60.0
Auburn town (Worcester)	29	173	318	1,896	4,111	23	65.2	68.0	15.6	97.0	2,699	62.6	3,747	369	47.3
Barnstable Town city & MCD (Barnstable)	166	377	462	1,050	40,559	89	67.4	185.8	28.1	84.0	2,848	183.8	4,143	394	105.5
Bedford town (Middlesex)	7	49	58	405	12,686	25	100.0	91.0	15.2	95.0	4,738	91.1	6,429	452	50.7
Belchertown town (Hampshire)	25	165	78	514	15,375	41	100.0	53.7	21.5	95.4	1,857	53.6	3,562	5	18.1
Bellingham town (Norfolk)	19	111	210	1,222	13,040	52	100.0	66.0	17.4	97.0	2,367	63.4	3,703	310	47.5
Belmont town (Middlesex)	5	19	167	626	1,949	4	100.0	120.5	14.5	97.4	3,429	131.7	5,003	1131	74.4
Beverly city & MCD (Essex)	42	100	243	577	4,659	13	100.0	171.4	44.1	92.5	2,426	162.2	3,869	1021	87.5
Billerica town (Middlesex)	37	83	171	384	6,188	26	100.0	183.0	45.6	98.7	2,852	178.8	4,088	826	175.2
Boston city & MCD (Suffolk)	4,324	623	14,007	2,016	586,333	2,993	1.2	3800.8	945.0	91.1	3,439	3728.9	5,422	605	1929.8
Bourne town (Barnstable)	46	231	266	1,337	5,991	21	85.7	83.2	13.7	88.0	2,497	77.2	3,891	251	43.6
Braintree Town city & MCD (Norfolk)	52	139	487	1,304	3,537	13	84.6	140.0	35.0	95.9	2,578	133.2	3,574	177	121.4
Bridgewater Town city & MCD (Plymouth)	57	207	116	421	9,326	45	95.6	60.3	7.1	94.8	1,694	58.7	2,150	113	19.8
Brockton city & MCD (Plymouth)	868	905	2,071	2,159	5,874	35	71.4	415.3	229.7	98.4	1,518	375.7	3,927	65	199.6
Brookline town (Norfolk)	56	95	632	1,068	9,577	12	83.3	283.1	37.1	95.2	3,685	315.6	5,323	940	106.2
Burlington town (Middlesex)	40	145	378	1,372	10,560	28	100.0	142.7	15.8	93.7	4,106	134.3	4,817	269	52.7
Cambridge city & MCD (Middlesex)	339	295	2,068	1,800	120,053	635	5.4	1207.0	357.5	73.2	3,692	1102.8	9,436	808	422.1
Canton town (Norfolk)	81	342	118	498	9,354	129	0.0	106.0	14.0	98.2	3,296	95.5	4,093	419	54.5
Carver town (Plymouth)	30	256	70	596	1,758	8	100.0	44.1	15.5	93.8	2,215	57.5	4,903	1679	36.5
Charlton town (Worcester)	13	95	88	645	7,610	29	100.0	38.2	4.0	81.5	1,676	27.6	2,032	126	12.1
Chelmsford town (Middlesex)	31	88	381	1,080	31,459	195	7.2	139.7	24.5	98.4	2,921	138.5	3,957	19	95.7
Chelsea city & MCD (Suffolk)	277	676	584	1,425	7,523	48	0.0	207.0	112.4	98.5	1,722	196.4	4,875	717	38.0
Chicopee city & MCD (Hampden)	NA	NA	NA	NA	6,720	43	69.8	221.8	88.8	98.6	1,558	207.4	3,748	80	179.9
Clinton town (Worcester)	10	71	18	129	4,203	23	100.0	51.7	18.9	96.6	1,809	46.8	3,352	80	21.2
Concord town (Middlesex)	8	41	111	570	12,530	30	93.3	110.0	9.0	99.4	4,673	104.5	5,480	525	57.0
Danvers town (Essex)	54	195	420	1,516	5,075	17	88.2	112.5	16.8	98.9	2,985	113.2	4,112	324	93.7
Dartmouth town (Bristol)	66	192	458	1,334	16,858	43	100.0	106.1	19.3	99.1	1,909	105.9	3,106	183	50.8
Dedham town (Norfolk)	7	28	339	1,333	14,241	67	28.4	113.8	14.1	99.7	3,429	127.5	5,049	910	82.2
Dennis town (Barnstable)	63	454	231	1,665	18,969	54	100.0	59.2	2.8	96.5	3,339	56.7	4,068	261	17.8
Dracut town (Middlesex)	41	129	277	868	8,891	34	100.0	94.0	31.6	98.6	1,653	90.5	2,875	29	88.1
Dudley town (Worcester)	24	203	33	280	3,737	13	100.0	17.8	2.7	96.8	1,124	17.5	1,486	30	4.3
Duxbury town (Plymouth)	7	44	92	573	9,843	20	100.0	86.1	12.2	98.4	4,033	75.9	4,759	145	88.7
East Bridgewater town (Plymouth)	22	151	94	646	2,768	11	100.0	51.5	16.6	97.0	2,118	50.3	3,470	102	52.8
Easthampton Town city & MCD (Hampshi)	34	212	122	760	NA	NA	NA	43.9	15.7	91.6	1,622	43.4	2,709	91	17.0
East Longmeadow town (Hampden)	28	171	262	1,598	0	0	0.0	62.4	16.2	99.7	2,634	64.1	3,940	134	18.5
Easton town (Bristol)	45	178	173	686	6,139	32	100.0	83.1	18.0	98.1	2,321	88.1	3,528	202	47.2
Everett city & MCD (Middlesex)	173	368	685	1,457	4,389	34	8.8	202.2	89.5	97.3	2,213	189.0	4,099	291	85.9
Fairhaven town (Bristol)	55	342	293	1,823	3,245	9	100.0	59.1	18.8	82.3	1,879	47.0	2,929	256	13.3
Fall River city & MCD (Bristol)	908	1,015	1,361	1,521	6,807	62	90.3	329.3	178.6	93.9	1,176	287.9	3,224	161	262.7
Falmouth town (Barnstable)	109	351	329	1,060	53,556	140	68.6	137.5	18.8	95.7	3,408	145.9	4,686	806	166.6
Fitchburg city & MCD (Worcester)	238	583	526	1,288	3,505	17	100.0	156.4	80.9	94.7	1,374	137.9	3,384	257	72.0
Foxborough town (Norfolk)	44	249	154	872	4,932	26	61.5	85.9	18.4	99.5	2,961	92.9	5,278	523	85.7
Framingham city & MCD (Middlesex)	253	349	820	1,131	16,077	124	31.5	312.1	76.7	98.5	2,726	322.3	4,490	249	239.1
Franklin Town city & MCD (Norfolk)	5	15	85	256	NA	NA	NA	129.9	36.9	99.8	2,336	139.5	4,208	376	98.8
Gardner city & MCD (Worcester)	92	444	364	1,758	2,123	15	100.0	67.2	30.9	92.2	1,316	64.0	3,102	15	21.1
Gloucester city & MCD (Essex)	72	237	216	712	29,608	72	36.1	129.8	21.6	95.7	2,838	129.9	4,307	530	159.0
Grafton town (Worcester)	21	111	61	323	12,879	36	66.7	62.6	15.5	96.8	2,216	79.3	4,226	1111	74.9

1 Data for serious crimes have not been adjusted for underreporting. This may affect comparability between geographic areas over time.
2 Per 100,000 population estimated by the FBI.   3 Based on population estimated as of July 1 of the year shown.

Table B. Incorporated Places, Census Designated Places (CDPs), and Minor Civil Divisions (MCDs) of 10,000 or More Population — **Land Area, Population, and Households, and Employment**

STATE City, town, township, borough, or CDP (county if applicable)	Land area 2010 (sq mi)	Population Total persons 2010	Total persons 2019	Percent change 2010–2019	Persons per square mile 2019	Population characteristics 2015–2019 Percent foreign born	Percent living in the same house as previous year	Income and poverty 2015–2019 Median household income	Percent of households with income below poverty level	Median value of owner-occupied housing units	Employment, 2015–2019 Percent in civilian labor force	Unemployment rate	Households, 2015–2019 (percent of households) Family households	One person households
	1	2	3	4	5	6	7	8	9	10	11	12	13	14
MASSACHUSETTS—Con.														
Greenfield Town city & MCD (Franklin)	21.41	17,450	17,258	-1.1	806.1	4.8	84.2	50,478	11.8	194,200	63.0	5.1	48.3	39.9
Groton town (Middlesex)	32.77	10,643	11,325	6.4	345.6	5.7	89.2	129,085	4.1	473,000	65.8	3.4	74.6	20.7
Hanover town (Plymouth)	15.54	13,873	14,570	5.0	937.6	2.4	90.6	127,981	4.7	512,000	71.3	4.1	77.0	19.0
Hanson town (Plymouth)	15.02	10,203	10,914	7.0	726.6	4.6	93.6	96,693	5.5	363,700	70.6	3.2	75.5	23.0
Harwich town (Barnstable)	20.89	12,223	12,142	-0.7	581.2	6.0	91.1	76,822	7.4	399,500	56.9	6.0	63.3	29.5
Haverhill city & MCD (Essex)	33.04	60,878	64,014	5.2	1937.5	10.7	89.1	69,426	11.7	300,600	72.2	5.2	64.1	28.0
Hingham town (Plymouth)	22.20	22,155	24,679	11.4	1111.7	5.3	91.4	142,435	5.6	771,600	62.2	3.5	71.3	26.7
Holbrook town (Norfolk)	7.26	10,806	11,033	2.1	1519.7	16.3	95.0	76,055	4.6	324,800	63.2	2.5	66.1	30.0
Holden town (Worcester)	35.08	17,464	19,300	10.5	550.3	6.0	92.7	108,964	4.3	318,000	70.8	4.2	73.0	22.1
Holliston town (Middlesex)	18.65	13,546	14,912	10.1	799.6	8.8	92.5	135,340	2.9	448,600	72.2	3.9	82.2	15.5
Holyoke city & MCD (Hampden)	21.17	39,881	40,117	0.6	1895.0	5.3	89.0	40,769	27.4	195,800	55.1	6.0	61.3	31.5
Hopkinton town (Middlesex)	26.23	14,909	18,470	23.9	704.2	12.5	89.5	157,353	4.5	577,600	70.1	3.9	82.7	15.5
Hudson town (Middlesex)	11.53	19,075	19,864	4.1	1722.8	15.1	94.0	91,706	4.9	353,700	70.5	3.8	68.6	24.5
Hudson CDP	5.74	14,907	NA	NA	NA	17.4	94.2	82,431	5.9	332,300	69.7	3.2	65.4	27.7
Hull town (Plymouth)	2.87	10,293	10,475	1.8	3649.8	4.5	94.0	88,476	5.5	406,600	68.8	6.7	53.9	38.2
Ipswich town (Essex)	32.11	13,176	14,074	6.8	438.3	6.5	93.5	93,212	8.0	485,600	66.2	4.2	64.5	31.8
Kingston town (Plymouth)	18.64	12,628	13,863	9.8	743.7	2.3	93.9	96,104	7.2	378,500	67.6	4.6	72.9	21.2
Lakeville town (Plymouth)	29.60	10,610	11,561	9.0	390.6	4.1	93.5	106,633	3.9	371,300	69.7	3.2	76.1	18.5
Lawrence city & MCD (Essex)	6.93	76,343	80,028	4.8	11548.1	40.6	88.2	44,613	24.6	271,100	67.0	9.3	69.0	24.9
Leicester town (Worcester)	23.26	10,892	11,341	4.1	487.6	6.0	93.5	88,505	6.2	259,500	70.7	2.9	68.8	25.5
Leominster city & MCD (Worcester)	28.82	40,760	41,716	2.3	1447.5	14.9	89.8	61,825	11.8	241,800	68.1	5.9	63.2	29.3
Lexington town (Middlesex)	16.43	31,406	33,132	5.5	2016.6	28.8	87.1	186,201	4.6	889,700	64.8	3.6	79.8	18.7
Littleton town (Middlesex)	16.52	8,910	10,227	14.8	619.1	9.7	92.5	123,413	4.4	459,000	69.6	4.5	76.6	20.5
Longmeadow town (Hampden)	9.09	15,783	15,705	-0.5	1727.7	9.9	92.4	122,035	3.7	343,700	61.9	2.7	77.3	20.3
Lowell city & MCD (Middlesex)	13.61	106,525	110,997	4.2	8155.5	28.4	85.2	56,878	19.3	269,800	66.2	5.8	61.5	28.4
Ludlow town (Hampden)	27.20	21,099	21,233	0.6	780.6	15.0	91.7	73,458	8.4	232,300	62.4	4.5	71.5	23.6
Lunenburg town (Worcester)	26.39	10,076	11,736	16.5	444.7	5.8	93.3	103,228	6.2	308,800	69.4	3.9	73.8	20.8
Lynn city & MCD (Essex)	10.74	90,324	94,299	4.4	8780.2	36.7	87.4	56,181	19.5	323,100	68.2	5.9	65.0	28.9
Lynnfield town (Essex)	9.86	11,593	12,999	12.1	1318.4	7.8	92.5	128,641	3.3	670,700	68.8	5.2	77.6	20.5
Malden city & MCD (Middlesex)	5.04	59,536	60,477	1.6	11998.0	42.6	84.0	65,975	16.6	401,900	68.1	5.0	63.2	26.9
Mansfield town (Bristol)	20.10	23,183	24,470	5.6	1217.4	8.6	88.0	120,613	4.4	412,300	78.6	5.2	76.4	19.2
Marblehead town (Essex)	4.38	19,808	20,555	3.8	4692.9	10.5	90.7	123,333	4.8	675,400	66.3	4.9	73.5	23.3
Marlborough city & MCD (Middlesex)	20.86	38,501	39,597	2.8	1898.2	27.6	85.5	80,943	6.3	348,500	74.1	4.0	62.9	27.6
Marshfield town (Plymouth)	28.65	25,125	25,967	3.4	906.4	3.0	93.9	102,560	7.3	460,900	66.9	4.7	71.2	23.7
Mashpee town (Barnstable)	23.40	14,004	14,229	1.6	608.1	5.9	91.0	77,019	5.1	363,100	61.4	3.7	64.1	31.7
Maynard town (Middlesex)	5.21	10,112	11,336	12.1	2175.8	9.3	92.0	105,254	4.5	350,200	73.1	1.2	68.3	26.6
Medfield town (Norfolk)	14.41	12,027	12,955	7.7	899.0	8.3	92.8	160,963	4.9	667,500	67.2	2.7	84.8	13.7
Medford city & MCD (Middlesex)	8.10	56,280	57,341	1.9	7079.1	21.9	84.3	96,455	8.8	500,800	71.6	2.8	55.4	29.9
Medway town (Norfolk)	11.54	12,754	13,479	5.7	1168.0	6.8	93.5	132,823	5.0	413,600	73.0	2.7	76.7	19.2
Melrose city & MCD (Middlesex)	4.68	26,967	28,016	3.9	5986.3	12.2	90.7	106,955	5.7	570,300	71.6	2.8	62.8	29.6
Methuen Town city & MCD (Essex)	22.21	47,328	50,706	7.1	2283.0	22.3	88.5	77,484	9.4	333,200	69.9	6.0	73.0	22.5
Middleborough town (Plymouth)	69.04	23,114	25,463	10.2	368.8	3.1	92.6	83,631	7.4	308,100	66.7	3.7	68.4	26.1
Milford town (Worcester)	14.75	27,989	29,101	4.0	1972.9	20.8	90.3	83,243	8.6	314,800	72.6	5.0	68.3	26.8
Milford CDP	10.15	25,055	NA	NA	NA	21.5	89.5	80,371	9.4	303,300	72.6	5.3	67.3	27.5
Millbury town (Worcester)	15.72	13,261	13,947	5.2	887.2	8.2	91.7	85,781	6.4	290,300	70.2	6.9	68.9	24.5
Milton town (Norfolk)	13.01	27,007	27,593	2.2	2120.9	14.8	88.9	133,718	5.8	618,800	68.5	3.6	77.6	19.2
Nantucket town (Nantucket)	46.17	10,172	11,399	12.1	246.9	11.6	89.4	107,717	5.6	1,084,700	72.8	2.9	62.4	30.2
Natick town (Middlesex)	14.96	33,012	36,050	9.2	2409.8	18.8	88.7	115,545	3.8	566,400	72.7	3.0	67.7	29.0
Needham town (Norfolk)	12.30	28,973	31,388	8.3	2551.9	13.9	91.5	165,547	4.3	855,300	65.4	4.0	78.5	19.5
New Bedford city & MCD (Bristol)	20.00	95,071	95,363	0.3	4768.2	19.8	86.1	46,321	20.0	226,900	61.8	6.4	58.5	33.7
Newburyport city & MCD (Essex)	8.35	17,410	18,289	5.0	2190.3	7.5	90.4	109,839	6.0	548,400	69.3	3.5	62.3	32.0
Newton city & MCD (Middlesex)	17.83	85,089	88,414	3.9	4958.7	22.2	86.0	151,068	4.5	914,700	65.8	2.8	72.5	21.2
Norfolk town (Norfolk)	14.90	11,215	12,003	7.0	805.6	6.5	88.9	151,279	1.3	506,300	54.6	3.4	82.7	14.0
North Adams city & MCD (Berkshire)	20.35	13,693	12,730	-7.0	625.6	4.2	86.2	41,471	20.1	140,900	57.2	5.5	53.5	37.7
Northampton city & MCD (Hampshire)	34.25	28,560	28,451	-0.4	830.7	7.5	81.5	66,522	13.9	332,100	62.8	3.7	51.8	35.3
North Andover town (Essex)	26.28	28,358	31,188	10.0	1186.8	11.9	86.7	108,070	8.4	505,400	66.7	3.8	71.1	24.2
North Attleborough town (Bristol)	18.86	28,699	29,364	2.3	1556.9	11.1	89.5	92,886	9.7	351,800	72.8	3.4	66.4	27.8
Northborough town (Worcester)	18.48	14,199	15,109	6.4	817.6	12.9	90.5	128,613	4.4	447,100	72.3	3.1	79.2	16.8
Northbridge town (Worcester)	17.27	15,701	16,679	6.2	965.8	5.3	88.9	81,504	7.1	321,800	68.3	4.7	69.4	25.2
North Reading town (Middlesex)	13.16	14,891	15,865	6.5	1205.5	8.9	93.0	128,651	3.0	536,700	71.5	4.3	75.6	18.6
Norton town (Bristol)	27.83	19,025	19,948	4.9	716.8	4.8	89.9	111,042	6.3	351,600	70.8	4.3	73.0	21.5
Norwell town (Plymouth)	20.93	10,514	11,153	6.1	532.9	5.5	92.9	157,987	4.0	608,300	68.9	3.4	81.8	16.7
Norwood town (Norfolk)	10.38	28,609	29,725	3.9	2863.7	18.1	85.7	90,133	9.0	439,300	71.7	3.0	63.6	29.4
Oxford town (Worcester)	26.52	13,711	14,009	2.2	528.2	7.1	92.7	76,373	8.9	260,600	68.5	4.6	63.4	28.0
Palmer Town city & MCD (Hampden)	31.57	12,138	12,232	0.8	387.5	5.4	85.1	64,651	10.6	197,000	66.7	6.4	59.4	27.7
Peabody city & MCD (Essex)	16.23	51,266	53,070	3.5	3269.9	15.4	88.0	73,217	9.6	387,400	64.0	4.0	62.2	33.0
Pembroke town (Plymouth)	21.79	17,844	18,509	3.7	849.4	3.8	94.5	103,905	3.6	398,400	71.6	4.1	71.8	22.3
Pepperell town (Middlesex)	22.57	11,498	12,114	5.4	536.7	4.2	92.2	104,130	7.0	343,400	69.7	3.5	73.9	21.5
Pittsfield city & MCD (Berkshire)	40.47	44,743	42,142	-5.8	1041.3	6.6	89.0	51,411	13.7	174,300	63.5	5.7	54.9	37.7
Plymouth town (Plymouth)	96.43	56,468	61,528	9.0	638.1	6.5	88.9	90,279	6.9	370,100	64.6	4.3	70.9	24.1

Table B. Incorporated Places, Census Designated Places (CDPs), and Minor Civil Divisions (MCDs) of 10,000 or More Population — Crime, Residential Construction and Local Government Finance

STATE City, town, township, borough, or CDP (county if applicable)	Serious crimes known to police, 2018[1] Violent crime Number	Rate[2]	Property crime Number	Rate[2]	New residential construction authorized by building permits, 2019 Value ($1,000)	Number of housing units	Percent single family	Local government finance, 2017 General revenue Total (mil dol)	Intergovernmental Total (mil dol)	Percent from state gov.	Taxes per capita[3]	General expenditure Total (mil dol)	Per capita[3] Total	Capital outlays	Debt outstanding (mil dol)
	15	16	17	18	19	20	21	22	23	24	25	26	27	28	29
MASSACHUSETTS—Con.															
Greenfield Town city & MCD (Franklin)	101	579	325	1,863	1,080	6	66.7	86.0	26.9	81.9	1,918	73.2	4,208	675	52.3
Groton town (Middlesex)	11	96	36	314	5,860	24	83.3	37.6	2.3	95.8	2,866	36.8	3,244	188	20.3
Hanover town (Plymouth)	2	14	120	826	5,205	21	100.0	65.9	14.4	99.5	3,208	66.1	4,571	78	56.1
Hanson town (Plymouth)	30	276	58	534	2,066	13	38.5	24.6	1.9	93.1	1,955	23.9	2,218	247	8.2
Harwich town (Barnstable)	24	198	125	1,031	17,488	24	100.0	62.2	3.5	85.9	4,022	61.1	5,033	305	26.5
Haverhill city & MCD (Essex)	358	559	895	1,398	11,643	61	72.1	250.3	102.9	98.3	1,702	230.2	3,616	480	109.5
Hingham town (Plymouth)	37	157	180	763	12,542	27	85.2	113.0	15.7	93.9	3,678	114.0	4,864	148	79.2
Holbrook town (Norfolk)	23	208	110	995	2,849	7	100.0	74.4	40.5	98.4	2,682	89.9	8,137	4367	61.8
Holden town (Worcester)	NA	NA	NA	NA	10,928	36	100.0	52.0	8.5	97.5	2,091	49.6	2,605	342	48.6
Holliston town (Middlesex)	12	80	40	268	11,024	43	93.0	67.2	15.7	93.4	3,254	61.9	4,204	197	28.2
Holyoke city & MCD (Hampden)	391	966	1,640	4,052	1,846	8	50.0	185.1	109.1	95.9	1,415	176.0	4,375	34	86.8
Hopkinton town (Middlesex)	2	11	30	162	27,613	117	100.0	86.4	17.9	94.5	3,419	112.2	6,242	1728	71.1
Hudson town (Middlesex)	48	239	90	449	4,575	23	100.0	81.3	22.5	89.2	2,662	86.1	4,322	660	69.2
Hudson CDP	NA	NA	NA	NA	NA	NA	NA	NA	NA	NA	NA	NA	NA	NA	NA
Hull town (Plymouth)	NA	NA	NA	NA	2,966	8	100.0	45.9	9.6	96.4	2,846	43.2	4,125	364	28.5
Ipswich town (Essex)	14	99	74	525	3,399	13	100.0	57.9	10.4	94.9	3,007	55.2	3,943	431	36.8
Kingston town (Plymouth)	26	190	102	745	12,384	63	100.0	49.2	9.1	99.1	2,483	48.1	3,546	277	37.4
Lakeville town (Plymouth)	14	122	114	989	11,885	57	100.0	27.7	2.1	100.0	2,098	26.1	2,287	135	3.1
Lawrence city & MCD (Essex)	500	620	934	1,158	2,185	21	33.3	335.3	249.5	84.5	937	326.4	4,080	130	142.6
Leicester town (Worcester)	35	306	142	1,242	670	3	100.0	35.1	17.7	92.2	1,398	37.0	3,260	46	5.0
Leominster city & MCD (Worcester)	219	525	824	1,975	7,034	55	25.5	149.3	63.5	95.5	1,732	134.7	3,238	234	50.9
Lexington town (Middlesex)	8	24	113	332	25,098	64	100.0	250.8	25.4	99.8	5,361	300.2	8,971	1780	183.9
Littleton town (Middlesex)	9	87	56	544	15,850	44	100.0	52.1	9.1	93.8	3,739	52.1	5,165	839	33.4
Longmeadow town (Hampden)	15	94	183	1,151	1,760	3	100.0	68.1	10.4	96.3	3,324	66.3	4,208	134	49.6
Lowell city & MCD (Middlesex)	363	324	1,718	1,534	55,594	362	3.6	405.0	222.8	93.0	1,236	399.9	3,579	212	252.2
Ludlow town (Hampden)	46	213	228	1,056	8,962	35	94.3	68.3	22.2	97.5	1,895	79.2	3,716	219	16.4
Lunenburg town (Worcester)	18	157	180	1,566	4,222	63	22.2	46.8	15.5	97.7	2,387	57.8	5,115	1771	54.7
Lynn city & MCD (Essex)	563	595	1,359	1,437	9,251	68	42.6	366.0	218.6	97.5	1,401	387.6	4,127	66	63.2
Lynnfield town (Essex)	4	30	93	708	7,061	18	100.0	58.6	8.2	99.6	3,573	59.8	4,620	261	23.1
Malden city & MCD (Middlesex)	180	293	588	957	1,280	6	66.7	195.3	85.7	99.6	1,518	167.7	2,746	134	86.1
Mansfield town (Bristol)	34	141	205	852	5,725	19	57.9	105.3	30.3	99.0	2,626	114.2	4,771	512	57.2
Marblehead town (Essex)	20	97	102	494	5,789	9	100.0	90.3	11.0	99.6	3,329	95.4	4,644	439	75.8
Marlborough city & MCD (Middlesex)	167	417	456	1,139	3,381	24	100.0	161.2	40.1	99.6	2,587	157.5	3,959	89	147.3
Marshfield town (Plymouth)	33	127	83	320	11,571	38	100.0	106.6	24.1	94.5	2,690	110.0	4,252	432	99.5
Mashpee town (Barnstable)	47	331	134	943	28,240	49	83.7	62.0	8.5	94.9	3,415	62.5	4,403	144	16.7
Maynard town (Middlesex)	21	196	52	484	2,271	24	0.0	45.8	9.8	94.0	2,880	46.7	4,385	121	43.2
Medfield town (Norfolk)	NA	NA	NA	NA	8,370	38	47.4	61.5	10.0	100.0	3,558	69.0	5,359	752	49.0
Medford city & MCD (Middlesex)	73	126	548	945	70,704	1,780	0.2	176.5	37.5	94.6	2,020	176.8	3,060	81	56.5
Medway town (Norfolk)	21	157	73	545	855	4	100.0	58.6	16.0	96.9	2,700	60.7	4,547	45	40.2
Melrose city & MCD (Middlesex)	15	53	146	511	1,548	7	100.0	100.8	20.1	96.7	2,234	107.4	3,808	173	60.7
Methuen Town city & MCD (Essex)	44	87	486	959	28,004	92	100.0	175.5	67.6	99.1	1,823	155.7	3,094	200	66.5
Middleborough town (Plymouth)	111	442	215	856	17,989	104	48.1	78.0	27.3	99.4	1,747	102.6	4,121	77	59.7
Milford town (Worcester)	61	210	233	802	8,273	31	100.0	115.9	39.3	98.3	2,353	128.1	4,429	901	56.1
Milford CDP	NA	NA	NA	NA	NA	NA	NA	NA	NA	NA	NA	NA	NA	NA	NA
Millbury town (Worcester)	19	138	155	1,123	15,243	53	100.0	45.3	13.7	98.8	1,942	47.5	3,458	241	23.8
Milton town (Norfolk)	12	43	60	217	8,339	19	89.5	111.7	16.5	99.2	2,872	100.3	3,635	268	39.3
Nantucket town (Nantucket)	37	325	225	1,976	153,682	156	98.7	146.4	6.7	83.6	9,162	153.1	13,661	4625	186.2
Natick town (Middlesex)	56	153	419	1,141	9,835	32	75.0	147.0	20.5	96.3	3,205	153.8	4,253	408	83.4
Needham town (Norfolk)	16	51	144	461	76,494	110	87.3	177.8	21.0	98.0	4,400	178.4	5,749	549	91.1
New Bedford city & MCD (Bristol)	603	634	2,425	2,550	3,120	21	66.7	418.3	235.2	96.1	1,359	425.1	4,471	1168	244.0
Newburyport city & MCD (Essex)	18	99	121	667	19,441	103	26.2	81.2	12.4	97.8	3,167	83.5	4,625	726	109.0
Newton city & MCD (Middlesex)	58	65	629	703	50,337	232	9.1	456.5	57.7	89.2	3,882	459.3	5,170	747	316.4
Norfolk town (Norfolk)	1	8	21	177	4,640	10	100.0	40.1	5.5	99.6	2,740	39.9	3,381	7	21.0
North Adams city & MCD (Berkshire)	100	778	421	3,274	0	0	0.0	51.4	28.9	85.2	1,404	52.3	4,035	557	15.6
Northampton city & MCD (Hampshire)	113	395	540	1,889	7,217	30	66.7	107.4	22.5	88.9	2,131	98.5	3,447	136	55.5
North Andover town (Essex)	35	112	173	551	2,175	6	100.0	107.8	17.9	100.0	2,493	115.1	3,714	214	51.2
North Attleborough town (Bristol)	28	96	357	1,222	8,374	32	100.0	97.2	29.9	97.8	1,879	96.6	3,319	184	62.8
Northborough town (Worcester)	NA	NA	111	734	2,335	12	41.7	64.0	9.4	95.5	3,342	70.6	4,686	651	30.8
Northbridge town (Worcester)	27	161	186	1,110	8,100	28	78.6	53.0	23.9	88.7	1,437	53.3	3,204	111	7.0
North Reading town (Middlesex)	16	101	44	278	12,429	67	25.4	71.5	14.0	99.5	3,293	73.8	4,755	460	89.0
Norton town (Bristol)	14	70	23	115	1,838	7	100.0	64.0	19.4	97.9	1,988	64.6	3,251	185	29.5
Norwell town (Plymouth)	9	81	51	458	2,934	8	100.0	57.1	9.3	99.7	4,044	61.1	5,506	552	20.2
Norwood town (Norfolk)	39	133	265	906	7,205	39	28.2	119.5	16.6	98.9	2,734	132.3	4,522	6	125.3
Oxford town (Worcester)	33	236	171	1,220	3,418	12	100.0	42.9	15.9	98.6	1,673	42.4	3,033	161	11.7
Palmer Town city & MCD (Hampden)	57	463	98	796	1,205	5	100.0	40.4	16.4	95.7	1,647	42.4	3,463	122	21.5
Peabody city & MCD (Essex)	159	299	532	1,000	6,488	22	90.9	182.5	47.1	88.6	2,185	196.7	3,714	469	88.6
Pembroke town (Plymouth)	15	81	86	466	5,372	21	100.0	65.2	18.6	99.9	2,307	73.0	3,967	351	28.6
Pepperell town (Middlesex)	13	106	41	335	5,600	13	100.0	27.3	2.8	98.2	1,721	26.8	2,211	70	8.7
Pittsfield city & MCD (Berkshire)	356	842	1,196	2,828	990	5	100.0	194.8	95.9	97.7	2,054	216.1	5,054	1134	133.3
Plymouth town (Plymouth)	230	381	519	860	86,482	406	100.0	269.5	76.5	94.8	2,855	343.2	5,721	2460	241.3

1 Data for serious crimes have not been adjusted for underreporting. This may affect comparability between geographic areas over time.
2 Per 100,000 population estimated by the FBI.   3 Based on population estimated as of July 1 of the year shown.

Table B. Incorporated Places, Census Designated Places (CDPs), and Minor Civil Divisions (MCDs) of 10,000 or More Population — Land Area, Population, and Households, and Employment

STATE City, town, township, borough, or CDP (county if applicable)	Land area 2010 (sq mi)	Total persons 2010	Total persons 2019	Percent change 2010–2019	Persons per square mile 2019	Percent foreign born	Percent living in the same house as previous year	Median household income	Percent of households with income below poverty level	Median value of owner-occupied housing units	Percent in civilian labor force	Unemployment rate	Family households	One person households
	1	2	3	4	5	6	7	8	9	10	11	12	13	14
MASSACHUSETTS—Con.														
Quincy city & MCD (Norfolk).....	16.57	92,262	94,470	2.4	5701.3	33.1	85.1	77,562	11.7	428,600	70.0	5.1	52.0	37.4
Randolph Town city & MCD (Norfolk)	9.83	32,100	34,362	7.0	3495.6	35.3	90.5	82,510	9.5	331,300	69.2	6.5	70.3	24.0
Raynham town (Bristol)	20.48	13,425	14,470	7.8	706.5	5.5	94.2	100,938	6.7	351,300	69.3	4.4	72.0	21.4
Reading town (Middlesex)	9.98	23,987	25,400	5.9	2545.1	8.2	95.2	132,731	3.2	562,800	70.9	3.1	76.4	19.2
Rehoboth town (Bristol)	46.93	11,606	12,385	6.7	263.9	6.9	93.9	116,585	2.0	400,800	74.0	2.8	76.5	17.5
Revere city & MCD (Suffolk).....	5.70	51,713	53,073	2.6	9311.1	39.0	88.2	62,568	13.7	373,800	67.1	5.4	63.4	28.1
Rockland town (Plymouth)........	10.03	17,478	17,986	2.9	1793.2	6.3	90.2	78,011	9.5	310,800	69.4	3.3	63.1	28.8
Salem city & MCD (Essex)	8.29	41,312	43,226	4.6	5214.2	14.6	85.7	68,808	14.4	367,200	68.0	4.0	53.9	36.2
Sandwich town (Barnstable).....	42.88	20,676	20,169	-2.5	470.4	3.5	91.9	98,827	3.1	382,000	65.0	3.5	72.2	21.2
Saugus town (Essex)	10.78	26,634	28,361	6.5	2630.9	13.2	92.2	88,667	10.8	394,900	67.4	5.0	71.2	22.7
Scituate town (Plymouth).........	17.21	18,135	18,924	4.4	1099.6	5.4	88.1	128,864	4.7	593,500	68.0	3.0	72.9	24.8
Seekonk town (Bristol)..........	18.40	13,722	15,770	14.9	857.1	7.2	92.1	90,078	4.3	339,300	69.9	3.0	77.2	18.0
Sharon town (Norfolk)...........	23.44	17,554	18,895	7.6	806.1	23.6	93.4	141,423	2.6	559,600	70.6	4.3	82.4	13.8
Shrewsbury town (Worcester) ..	20.74	35,561	38,526	8.3	1857.6	23.7	89.1	104,766	4.4	416,000	67.3	3.8	75.4	20.5
Somerset town (Bristol)	7.90	18,153	18,129	-0.1	2294.8	5.9	92.9	84,115	4.9	279,200	62.3	3.3	72.4	22.8
Somerville city & MCD (Middlesex)	4.12	75,701	81,360	7.5	19747.6	25.0	76.5	97,328	10.6	664,700	79.2	3.3	42.4	29.8
Southborough town (Worcester)	14.01	9,767	10,208	4.5	728.6	16.6	91.9	146,554	3.4	604,400	71.3	3.6	76.8	19.5
Southbridge Town city & MCD (Worcester)	20.24	16,709	16,878	1.0	833.9	4.0	83.5	51,270	20.0	198,400	64.7	8.8	61.7	31.1
South Hadley town (Hampshire)	17.72	17,522	17,625	0.6	994.6	7.5	82.8	69,346	9.9	243,500	62.1	4.8	60.3	31.9
South Yarmouth CDP..............	6.96	11,092	NA	NA	NA	9.5	88.5	61,088	6.6	329,600	61.0	5.9	62.6	30.7
Spencer town (Worcester)........	32.85	11,708	11,935	1.9	363.3	5.7	90.3	72,821	11.4	255,900	68.9	4.9	65.9	27.0
Springfield city & MCD (Hampden)	31.87	153,132	153,606	0.3	4819.8	10.0	86.3	39,432	26.6	156,200	57.7	8.2	62.4	32.2
Stoneham town (Middlesex)	6.02	21,286	24,126	13.3	4007.6	13.5	90.0	101,549	7.0	494,600	70.9	3.1	63.4	29.5
Stoughton town (Norfolk).........	16.09	26,995	28,915	7.1	1797.1	20.8	88.5	83,519	8.8	348,300	69.7	4.3	69.3	24.9
Sudbury town (Middlesex)........	24.27	17,675	19,655	11.2	809.8	12.7	93.3	191,310	2.2	720,800	67.2	3.6	85.9	11.5
Swampscott town (Essex)	3.02	13,790	15,298	10.9	5065.6	12.9	88.6	113,407	3.8	475,500	69.1	3.3	67.8	26.1
Swansea town (Bristol)	22.68	15,858	16,834	6.2	742.2	8.3	93.2	86,637	6.4	288,700	66.3	4.7	74.9	18.5
Taunton city & MCD (Bristol)	46.71	55,826	57,464	2.9	1230.2	13.1	89.4	62,865	13.7	271,800	67.5	6.5	63.8	29.6
Tewksbury town (Middlesex).....	20.72	29,069	31,178	7.3	1504.7	7.9	91.3	102,500	5.6	387,800	69.2	3.5	68.2	26.1
Tyngsborough town (Middlesex)	16.80	11,314	12,527	10.7	745.7	11.6	94.4	114,067	4.8	387,600	72.9	4.4	73.1	21.8
Uxbridge town (Worcester).......	29.59	13,455	14,195	5.5	479.7	3.8	91.0	108,060	7.3	315,400	72.0	5.3	78.2	17.3
Wakefield town (Middlesex)......	7.39	25,101	27,045	7.7	3659.7	8.0	90.9	100,278	5.2	505,800	70.7	3.1	68.3	27.4
Walpole town (Norfolk)	20.45	24,069	25,200	4.7	1232.3	11.1	91.1	119,846	4.1	484,800	68.1	3.7	75.8	20.4
Waltham city & MCD (Middlesex)	12.74	60,638	62,495	3.1	4905.4	27.5	81.0	95,964	7.7	536,500	70.8	3.0	53.8	32.4
Wareham town (Plymouth)	35.82	21,836	22,745	4.2	635.0	3.9	91.7	65,825	11.7	277,000	65.7	5.9	64.0	30.7
Watertown Town city & MCD (Middlesex)	4.00	31,986	35,939	12.4	8984.8	21.4	84.3	101,103	7.7	559,700	75.2	3.5	54.6	32.0
Wayland town (Middlesex)........	15.04	12,940	13,835	6.9	919.9	14.8	92.6	185,375	3.8	711,500	67.4	1.4	81.0	16.7
Webster town (Worcester)	12.36	16,772	16,949	1.1	1371.3	8.4	85.2	62,281	8.6	233,500	65.0	7.0	64.5	28.8
Webster CDP......................	2.97	11,412	NA	NA	NA	8.2	82.3	49,051	10.3	202,900	65.8	7.9	59.7	32.0
Wellesley town (Norfolk)	10.02	27,898	28,670	2.8	2861.3	16.9	86.4	197,132	4.5	1,149,100	59.3	4.6	79.6	18.2
Westborough town (Worcester)	20.60	18,278	19,144	4.7	929.3	26.7	82.0	112,153	5.2	458,100	69.1	2.3	71.7	22.9
Westfield city & MCD (Hampden)	46.26	41,090	41,204	0.3	890.7	9.2	83.8	67,862	8.3	234,400	61.9	4.3	65.0	28.4
Westford town (Middlesex)	30.24	21,962	24,817	13.0	820.7	15.4	91.1	144,917	2.6	531,300	70.1	3.0	80.5	16.7
Weston town (Middlesex).........	16.82	11,260	12,124	7.7	720.8	17.6	89.0	207,702	7.7	1,312,300	53.9	4.0	81.4	17.2
Westport town (Bristol)	49.82	15,531	16,034	3.2	321.8	8.6	93.4	79,895	6.0	363,100	61.8	3.5	70.3	23.8
West Springfield Town city & MCD (Hampden)	16.73	28,391	28,517	0.4	1704.5	13.2	87.7	53,053	13.3	225,100	66.4	5.6	54.1	39.9
Westwood town (Norfolk).........	10.88	14,625	16,400	12.1	1507.4	14.2	94.0	160,132	3.5	713,800	66.4	4.8	77.1	22.4
Weymouth Town city & MCD (Norfolk)	16.77	53,762	57,746	7.4	3443.4	13.0	87.5	84,942	6.1	375,400	71.6	5.8	62.7	29.7
Whitman town (Plymouth)	6.94	14,485	15,216	5.0	2192.5	3.9	92.4	86,570	6.7	327,100	72.6	3.7	68.8	25.8
Wilbraham town (Hampden)	22.04	14,219	14,689	3.3	666.5	4.5	89.8	109,191	4.7	303,000	65.7	1.4	77.1	18.8
Wilmington town (Middlesex)....	16.97	22,341	23,445	4.9	1381.6	11.0	93.1	125,922	3.9	473,800	72.3	3.2	79.6	15.7
Winchendon town (Worcester) .	43.02	10,332	10,905	5.5	253.5	4.1	91.9	80,096	10.4	206,700	71.0	5.5	72.2	22.2
Winchester town (Middlesex)....	6.03	21,389	22,799	6.6	3780.9	18.0	91.9	169,623	3.2	943,800	66.0	2.0	77.4	20.2
Winthrop Town city & MCD (Suffolk)	1.99	17,497	18,544	6.0	9318.6	15.9	87.8	74,069	9.1	439,800	70.7	3.6	55.9	35.6
Woburn city & MCD (Middlesex)	12.65	38,882	40,228	3.5	3180.1	20.2	88.2	91,022	6.7	453,900	71.2	3.0	65.5	26.7
Worcester city & MCD (Worcester)	37.36	180,891	185,428	2.5	4963.3	20.9	85.7	48,139	19.7	227,100	60.3	5.6	52.8	37.9
Wrentham town (Norfolk).........	21.71	11,037	12,023	8.9	553.8	6.0	92.5	126,613	6.1	443,900	71.5	4.5	69.8	24.9
Yarmouth town (Barnstable)	24.16	23,797	23,203	-2.5	960.4	9.2	89.4	63,432	7.1	337,400	57.8	4.1	62.9	31.3
MICHIGAN............................	56605.93	9,884,116	9,986,857	1.0	176.4	6.9	86.2	57,144	13.6	154,900	61.5	5.9	64.0	29.6
Ada township (Kent)	36.03	13,123	14,832	13.0	411.7	5.8	90.7	123,848	3.5	352,800	67.4	1.8	84.6	13.7
Adrian city & MCD (Lenawee) ..	8.00	21,189	20,600	-2.8	2575.0	5.1	78.8	36,236	21.2	76,800	58.0	4.2	53.6	38.7
Algoma township (Kent).........	34.40	9,939	12,752	28.3	370.7	2.4	91.9	88,627	7.0	233,200	66.5	2.1	79.7	16.3
Allendale CDP.....................	22.73	17,579	NA	NA	NA	3.0	60.1	53,214	27.0	196,500	66.4	7.4	56.7	13.3
Allendale charter township (Ottawa)	31.13	20,708	26,709	29.0	858.0	2.8	61.4	55,646	26.3	203,700	67.1	6.4	56.8	12.6
Allen Park city & MCD (Wayne)	7.00	28,212	26,940	-4.5	3848.6	4.1	91.9	67,130	8.4	123,800	63.5	3.6	67.6	27.6
Alpena city & MCD (Alpena).....	8.17	10,505	9,956	-5.2	1218.6	1.0	80.3	40,012	20.1	74,600	58.1	8.0	53.9	37.0
Alpine township (Kent)...........	36.03	13,318	13,941	4.7	386.9	7.8	83.2	53,834	10.2	160,700	71.2	3.2	61.7	26.0
Ann Arbor city & MCD (Washtenaw)	27.91	113,988	119,980	5.3	4298.8	19.1	66.1	65,745	18.3	323,400	61.5	3.9	44.4	34.7

Table B. Incorporated Places, Census Designated Places (CDPs), and Minor Civil Divisions (MCDs) of 10,000 or More Population — **Crime, Residential Construction and Local Government Finance**

STATE City, town, township, borough, or CDP (county if applicable)	Violent crime Number	Violent crime Rate[2]	Property crime Number	Property crime Rate[2]	Value ($1,000)	Number of housing units	Percent single family	Total (mil dol)	Intergovernmental Total (mil dol)	Intergovernmental Percent from state gov.	Taxes per capita[3]	Total (mil dol)	Per capita[3] Total	Per capita[3] Capital outlays	Debt outstanding (mil dol)
	15	16	17	18	19	20	21	22	23	24	25	26	27	28	29
MASSACHUSETTS—Con.															
Quincy city & MCD (Norfolk).....	352	373	1,190	1,261	16,085	143	9.8	381.7	81.4	91.5	2,419	445.3	4,721	383	257.5
Randolph Town city & MCD (Norfolk)	108	313	456	1,320	3,878	17	100.0	112.6	32.5	99.7	1,865	130.5	3,799	660	71.1
Raynham town (Bristol)	27	189	235	1,641	7,402	33	100.0	44.6	2.1	99.8	2,649	42.5	2,982	276	19.3
Reading town (Middlesex)........	5	19	144	548	27,017	148	16.9	104.4	20.0	96.5	2,739	113.0	4,493	515	44.9
Rehoboth town (Bristol)	8	65	97	791	8,495	41	100.0	27.1	2.3	100.0	1,959	26.1	2,143	74	0.0
Revere city & MCD (Suffolk).....	259	477	885	1,630	6,865	43	18.6	185.6	87.1	99.2	1,652	196.3	3,631	382	135.9
Rockland town (Plymouth)........	NA	NA	NA	NA	725	3	100.0	67.7	21.1	97.2	2,152	69.8	3,882	70	47.3
Salem city & MCD (Essex)	83	190	824	1,888	27,491	163	25.8	191.3	54.4	91.2	2,133	172.8	3,992	7	79.2
Sandwich town (Barnstable).....	23	114	102	504	6,728	19	100.0	86.8	15.4	93.9	3,112	92.3	4,546	245	29.4
Saugus town (Essex)..............	66	232	370	1,300	3,406	77	6.5	91.4	14.6	95.5	2,441	94.1	3,335	10	48.5
Scituate town (Plymouth).........	15	80	63	336	18,127	56	73.2	108.0	32.6	96.5	3,460	164.5	8,791	4409	123.3
Seekonk town (Bristol)............	26	164	267	1,688	6,891	30	100.0	55.2	8.7	99.9	2,765	56.0	3,606	23	10.3
Sharon town (Norfolk).............	13	71	51	278	4,583	13	38.5	90.2	14.7	99.8	3,735	92.2	5,034	772	66.9
Shrewsbury town (Worcester) ..	4	11	114	303	49,367	352	9.7	156.7	36.3	99.4	2,097	161.6	4,329	489	70.2
Somerset town (Bristol)	39	215	155	853	0	0	0.0	57.4	10.6	100.0	2,258	59.1	3,260	65	10.9
Somerville city & MCD (Middlesex)	177	215	1,020	1,242	28,618	146	15.8	266.5	70.4	93.4	1,917	274.1	3,376	167	154.7
Southborough town (Worcester)	11	108	23	226	7,586	21	100.0	50.6	7.0	99.9	4,064	52.3	5,156	265	15.9
Southbridge Town city & MCD (Worcester)	89	526	304	1,795	2,382	14	100.0	69.7	36.9	96.9	1,266	61.6	3,646	216	45.5
South Hadley town (Hampshire)	24	135	251	1,410	1,183	4	100.0	56.9	21.8	93.6	1,641	56.7	3,182	274	33.8
South Yarmouth CDP..............	NA	NA	NA	NA	NA	NA	NA	NA	NA	NA	NA	NA	NA	NA	NA
Spencer town (Worcester)........	18	150	69	576	5,002	20	100.0	22.3	3.0	98.5	1,310	20.5	1,710	94	8.4
Springfield city & MCD (Hampden)	1,534	989	4,089	2,635	767	4	100.0	729.9	475.9	94.2	1,368	727.3	4,716	336	200.5
Stoneham town (Middlesex)	33	149	243	1,098	2,966	14	35.7	78.2	13.3	98.6	2,320	70.4	3,074	73	32.2
Stoughton town (Norfolk).........	76	265	327	1,138	6,600	36	58.3	111.7	30.9	98.3	2,324	111.7	3,907	610	45.8
Sudbury town (Middlesex)	21	110	63	331	4,715	11	100.0	98.8	9.8	99.8	4,535	97.2	5,165	103	27.5
Swampscott town (Essex)	9	59	170	1,105	19,355	74	8.1	66.6	9.9	72.3	3,435	67.7	4,519	297	31.9
Swansea town (Bristol)............	29	175	193	1,161	12,703	62	96.8	49.1	12.5	99.2	2,045	49.2	2,979	99	11.9
Taunton city & MCD (Bristol)	243	424	356	621	9,524	66	56.1	220.1	89.0	96.9	1,827	221.4	3,885	193	144.8
Tewksbury town (Middlesex).....	82	260	345	1,093	5,840	30	60.0	122.1	21.8	99.8	2,788	103.5	3,309	147	124.1
Tyngsborough town (Middlesex)	20	160	53	424	12,868	85	41.2	43.7	11.4	95.9	2,310	50.1	4,055	533	18.6
Uxbridge town (Worcester).......	NA	NA	NA	NA	27,868	100	56.0	49.2	15.8	94.1	2,102	55.1	3,939	491	41.0
Wakefield town (Middlesex)......	42	153	175	638	27,971	114	9.6	103.1	16.0	97.7	2,698	103.2	3,808	147	57.5
Walpole town (Norfolk)	42	167	262	1,040	37,493	588	7.5	101.1	15.0	99.8	2,921	108.5	4,313	334	45.5
Waltham city & MCD (Middlesex)	117	187	561	895	24,483	67	67.2	260.4	33.3	96.5	3,090	224.3	3,571	209	93.7
Wareham town (Plymouth)	160	703	384	1,688	7,673	35	100.0	76.8	22.1	95.3	1,901	80.1	3,538	242	26.4
Watertown Town city & MCD (Middlesex)	29	80	283	779	55,014	265	4.5	138.2	18.9	97.1	2,817	127.2	3,560	237	34.1
Wayland town (Middlesex)........	1	7	1	7	1,650	3	100.0	86.6	9.2	99.2	4,868	103.3	7,448	1489	81.3
Webster town (Worcester)........	108	633	206	1,208	0	0	0.0	54.6	21.8	96.4	1,519	50.2	2,949	372	59.2
Webster CDP........................	NA	NA	NA	NA	NA	NA	NA	NA	NA	NA	NA	NA	NA	NA	NA
Wellesley town (Norfolk)	12	40	124	418	35,783	34	100.0	205.7	21.6	98.5	4,887	215.8	7,501	229	138.2
Westborough town (Worcester)	17	88	181	941	7,914	23	100.0	112.3	23.2	91.2	3,854	127.9	6,697	1377	116.7
Westfield city & MCD (Hampden)	111	265	464	1,109	8,664	44	100.0	151.2	56.9	93.5	1,820	141.0	3,405	513	98.1
Westford town (Middlesex)	12	49	64	260	38,242	247	21.1	112.0	26.8	97.5	3,228	116.6	4,804	103	47.1
Weston town (Middlesex)	5	41	45	367	24,815	14	100.0	93.1	9.9	99.8	6,420	97.2	8,007	492	87.0
Westport town (Bristol)	33	207	115	721	3,912	26	100.0	41.4	10.2	99.4	1,809	43.0	2,702	174	8.1
West Springfield Town city & MCD (Hampden)	168	583	1,020	3,541	NA	NA	NA	113.9	38.9	94.4	2,349	101.8	3,564	238	71.4
Westwood town (Norfolk)..........	10	62	136	836	13,155	19	100.0	96.6	15.9	68.1	4,637	107.4	6,669	1100	51.0
Weymouth Town city & MCD (Norfolk)	160	280	514	901	37,686	260	8.1	183.3	49.4	97.6	1,941	176.6	3,115	190	77.9
Whitman town (Plymouth)	38	252	111	735	5,457	32	50.0	31.2	3.5	99.1	1,680	31.0	2,063	138	13.2
Wilbraham town (Hampden)......	22	149	170	1,152	6,917	26	100.0	44.1	2.4	100.0	2,634	46.5	3,184	406	12.7
Wilmington town (Middlesex)....	20	83	125	521	4,446	21	100.0	110.1	19.8	99.8	3,503	99.4	4,248	84	43.6
Winchendon town (Worcester) .	38	348	149	1,363	1,126	7	100.0	33.2	16.7	97.7	1,215	32.7	3,012	121	13.9
Winchester town (Middlesex)....	6	26	112	486	17,829	35	82.9	121.9	21.4	99.8	3,973	159.7	7,005	2346	149.2
Winthrop Town city & MCD (Suffolk)	28	149	112	596	19,650	85	0.0	56.6	17.9	95.1	1,768	66.6	3,568	785	56.3
Woburn city & MCD (Middlesex)	46	115	377	945	27,179	112	39.3	156.6	26.9	99.2	2,758	160.1	3,966	428	74.3
Worcester city & MCD (Worcester)	1,271	683	3,979	2,137	10,734	70	85.7	757.5	367.1	95.0	1,659	808.0	4,360	644	722.7
Wrentham town (Norfolk).........	5	42	218	1,824	11,936	41	100.0	43.5	7.6	98.1	2,867	45.1	3,807	117	9.0
Yarmouth town (Barnstable)	113	486	291	1,251	4,399	13	100.0	84.6	4.1	89.4	2,763	81.5	3,492	283	11.3
MICHIGAN.............................	44,918	449	165,280	1,654	4,580,486	20,600	71.0	X	X	X	X	X	X	X	X
Ada township (Kent)	NA	NA	NA	NA	NA	NA	NA	7.3	1.4	100.0	231	10.6	733	26	6.8
Adrian city & MCD (Lenawee) ..	115	558	474	2,298	0	0	0.0	31.3	8.7	59.1	279	24.0	1,168	86	21.0
Algoma township (Kent)..........	NA	NA	NA	NA	15,890	64	82.8	2.2	1.0	100.0	70	2.9	243	63	0.0
Allendale CDP.......................	NA	NA	NA	NA	NA	NA	NA	NA	NA	NA	NA	NA	NA	NA	NA
Allendale charter township (Ottawa)	NA	NA	NA	NA	23,422	110	87.3	9.1	1.7	100.0	111	9.1	350	26	4.7
Allen Park city & MCD (Wayne)	68	252	500	1,851	197	2	100.0	60.4	8.4	61.7	830	58.5	2,148	308	74.2
Alpena city & MCD (Alpena).....	41	413	194	1,953	1,490	7	28.6	23.2	5.5	55.4	410	18.9	1,887	0	6.8
Alpine township (Kent)............	NA	NA	NA	NA	3,434	9	100.0	4.7	1.3	100.0	84	6.0	429	4	3.0
Ann Arbor city & MCD (Washtenaw)........................	270	220	1,932	1,576	24,434	96	100.0	258.5	61.0	37.2	844	255.8	2,105	318	313.7

1 Data for serious crimes have not been adjusted for underreporting. This may affect comparability between geographic areas over time.
2 Per 100,000 population estimated by the FBI. 3 Based on population estimated as of July 1 of the year shown.

Table B. Incorporated Places, Census Designated Places (CDPs), and Minor Civil Divisions (MCDs) of 10,000 or More Population — Land Area, Population, and Households, and Employment

STATE City, town, township, borough, or CDP (county if applicable)	Land area 2010 (sq mi)	Total persons 2010	Total persons 2019	Percent change 2010–2019	Persons per square mile 2019	Percent foreign born	Percent living in the same house as previous year	Median household income	Percent of households with income below poverty level	Median value of owner-occupied housing units	Percent in civilian labor force	Unemployment rate	Family households	One person households
													Households, 2015–2019 (percent of households)	
	1	2	3	4	5	6	7	8	9	10	11	12	13	14
MICHIGAN—Con.														
Antwerp township (Van Buren).	34.68	12,182	12,308	1.0	354.9	3.1	88.5	74,761	8.3	160,500	70.1	3.0	76.7	19.0
Auburn Hills city & MCD (Oakland)	16.63	21,414	24,748	15.6	1488.2	22.6	74.8	64,186	10.5	158,600	68.6	6.0	52.9	31.9
Bangor charter township (Bay).	14.11	14,642	13,946	-4.8	988.4	0.8	86.9	46,145	15.3	119,200	53.4	4.9	66.4	30.8
Bath charter township (Clinton)	31.96	11,616	13,004	11.9	406.9	5.8	82.9	68,313	14.6	204,900	64.2	5.9	63.5	26.8
Battle Creek city & MCD (Calhoun)	42.61	52,401	51,093	-2.5	1199.1	6.4	83.1	42,298	19.1	86,500	60.5	7.6	58.1	36.6
Bay City city & MCD (Bay)	10.17	34,929	32,717	-6.3	3217.0	1.6	85.5	37,893	22.8	66,800	60.8	8.9	57.7	33.9
Bedford township (Monroe)	39.20	31,091	32,083	3.2	818.4	4.1	92.5	70,131	7.1	173,000	61.8	3.0	69.2	27.1
Beecher CDP	5.88	10,232	NA	NA	NA	1.9	80.1	28,272	35.9	29,300	54.4	23.7	59.7	31.7
Benton charter township (Berrien)	32.42	14,757	14,300	-3.1	441.1	2.3	81.9	32,202	29.9	87,000	59.1	9.6	57.8	34.1
Benton Harbor city & MCD (Berrien)	4.38	10,030	9,741	-2.9	2224.0	1.5	80.0	21,916	42.3	63,300	55.5	14.0	56.2	38.9
Berkley city & MCD (Oakland)..	2.62	14,970	15,366	2.6	5864.9	4.1	90.4	86,905	5.3	199,200	75.7	1.6	58.3	32.5
Beverly Hills village	4.02	10,251	10,352	1.0	2575.1	7.2	90.2	127,419	2.4	387,400	66.7	2.4	72.1	25.6
Big Rapids city & MCD (Mecosta)	4.45	10,433	10,363	-0.7	2328.8	3.4	63.7	26,227	38.0	93,900	59.5	8.3	40.3	42.6
Birmingham city & MCD (Oakland)	4.80	20,107	21,389	6.4	4456.0	11.2	86.4	122,804	6.1	541,500	68.1	2.4	61.8	34.5
Blackman charter township (Jackson)	31.71	23,987	23,470	-2.2	740.1	2.4	70.1	46,449	13.8	112,000	39.1	5.2	52.9	40.7
Bloomfield charter township (Oakland)	24.58	40,875	41,945	2.6	1706.5	15.7	90.1	132,929	4.4	427,700	59.9	3.6	73.9	23.0
Brandon charter township (Oakland)	35.12	15,184	16,061	5.8	457.3	1.4	92.0	89,541	6.4	227,900	67.8	6.8	75.8	19.4
Bridgeport charter township (Saginaw)	34.60	10,514	9,809	-6.7	283.5	1.8	91.4	50,144	17.0	80,700	52.1	7.0	66.1	28.1
Brighton township (Livingston) .	32.97	17,789	18,865	6.0	572.2	3.8	92.6	106,250	2.3	290,400	66.2	3.1	79.3	15.9
Brownstown charter township (Wayne)	22.16	30,623	32,081	4.8	1447.7	6.4	91.5	75,871	10.2	181,000	63.6	3.0	71.5	24.9
Burton city & MCD (Genesee)..	23.36	29,999	28,574	-4.8	1223.2	1.7	84.8	48,019	17.9	87,600	59.9	7.8	63.1	30.4
Byron township (Kent)	36.11	20,324	24,913	22.6	689.9	5.2	88.4	70,094	6.6	216,200	68.3	3.1	74.2	21.1
Cadillac city & MCD (Wexford) .	7.06	10,354	10,497	1.4	1486.8	0.3	80.6	36,734	21.7	77,300	57.6	7.3	58.2	36.5
Caledonia township (Kent)	34.93	12,340	14,890	20.7	426.3	2.9	89.5	93,202	3.8	263,400	71.1	2.4	81.5	16.0
Cannon township (Kent)	35.58	13,334	15,167	13.7	426.3	2.9	90.6	96,794	3.9	267,900	74.0	7.1	81.9	14.4
Canton charter township (Wayne)	36.11	90,176	93,704	3.9	2595.0	19.6	87.6	93,483	6.3	251,900	68.7	4.1	74.8	21.3
Cascade charter township (Kent)	33.87	17,157	19,406	13.1	573.0	7.4	88.3	108,657	2.7	336,400	63.8	3.2	75.0	21.4
Chesterfield township (Macomb)	27.55	43,387	46,680	7.6	1694.4	4.7	88.3	77,059	6.3	199,300	69.1	4.9	70.9	23.4
Clawson city & MCD (Oakland)	2.20	11,833	11,845	0.1	5384.1	6.1	88.2	67,717	7.4	177,500	69.6	2.8	50.9	41.5
Clinton charter township (Macomb)	28.02	96,798	100,471	3.8	3585.7	8.0	85.7	56,796	11.6	158,200	64.6	5.4	58.8	35.1
Coldwater city & MCD (Branch)	9.65	13,612	12,215	-10.3	1265.8	9.7	85.0	43,200	15.2	88,200	49.0	4.1	58.7	33.4
Commerce charter township (Oakland)	27.43	40,106	44,065	9.9	1606.5	10.7	91.0	96,053	5.5	261,200	68.1	3.7	74.5	20.9
Comstock charter township (Kalamazoo)	33.32	14,851	15,594	5.0	468.0	4.5	85.9	60,978	10.4	150,700	71.5	5.7	62.2	28.5
Comstock Park CDP	3.88	10,088	NA	NA	NA	8.6	81.3	46,677	11.6	152,100	71.6	3.6	57.7	31.2
Cooper charter township (Kalamazoo)	36.33	10,117	11,067	9.4	304.6	1.2	85.5	66,512	8.2	154,600	64.9	4.1	71.8	20.6
Cutlerville CDP	5.84	14,470	NA	NA	NA	7.9	81.0	53,209	11.0	146,600	71.5	3.7	66.7	24.9
Davison township (Genesee)....	33.31	19,547	19,231	-1.6	577.3	2.6	84.8	53,777	8.6	150,400	63.0	3.8	58.0	34.9
Dearborn city & MCD (Wayne) .	24.23	98,146	93,932	-4.3	3876.7	29.1	86.9	53,670	22.0	143,000	55.8	6.6	67.8	27.6
Dearborn Heights city & MCD (Wayne)	11.74	57,774	55,353	-4.2	4714.9	21.5	88.8	49,750	15.9	113,800	56.6	6.0	66.3	28.8
Delhi charter township (Ingham)	28.59	25,873	28,082	8.5	982.2	5.8	86.2	66,498	8.8	163,700	67.9	5.5	64.2	29.7
Delta charter township (Eaton).	32.40	32,393	33,408	3.1	1031.1	8.2	82.9	67,930	7.2	173,500	65.4	4.7	58.2	35.5
Detroit city & MCD (Wayne)......	138.72	713,898	670,031	-6.1	4830.1	6.2	85.2	30,894	32.8	49,200	54.4	15.7	53.3	40.7
DeWitt charter township (Clinton)	28.13	14,342	15,608	8.8	554.9	3.1	91.7	66,213	7.6	176,600	62.9	4.0	66.9	25.8
East Bay township (Grand Traverse)	39.98	10,688	11,621	8.7	290.7	1.5	87.9	74,015	6.6	195,000	68.6	4.4	69.6	22.4
East Grand Rapids city & MCD (Kent)	2.93	10,687	11,956	11.9	4080.5	5.3	89.5	144,922	2.2	374,000	70.6	2.5	83.9	15.2
East Lansing city	13.43	48,561	48,145	-0.9	3584.9	14.4	50.7	39,867	37.0	192,800	56.2	8.6	34.6	36.1
East Lansing city (Ingham)	10.02	46,614	46,176	-0.9	4608.4	14.4	49.4	38,349	37.9	186,200	55.5	8.9	33.1	37.1
Eastpointe city & MCD (Macomb)	5.16	32,403	32,081	-1.0	6217.2	2.3	85.9	49,849	14.4	77,200	63.3	8.3	64.4	30.4
Egelston township (Muskegon)	33.19	9,910	10,325	4.2	311.1	1.3	86.2	51,755	10.1	104,500	60.0	6.7	69.9	19.5
Emmett charter township (Calhoun)	32.05	11,791	11,627	-1.4	362.8	4.8	88.6	59,228	10.7	129,700	62.8	5.9	66.7	26.0
Escanaba city & MCD (Delta)...	12.75	12,615	12,160	-3.6	953.7	1.2	81.4	35,813	20.4	86,100	54.0	6.0	54.4	38.7
Farmington city & MCD (Oakland)	2.66	10,381	10,491	1.1	3944.0	19.1	85.6	76,102	8.5	210,000	68.4	2.7	59.9	33.1
Farmington Hills city & MCD (Oakland)	33.27	79,725	80,612	1.1	2423.0	21.7	85.8	83,268	7.3	257,300	65.8	3.9	62.2	32.0
Fenton city	6.65	11,740	11,403	-2.9	1714.7	1.0	86.1	63,036	10.8	144,600	64.6	4.4	56.6	38.7
Fenton city (Genesee)	6.55	11,738	11,401	-2.9	1740.6	1.0	86.1	62,950	10.8	144,300	64.7	4.4	56.5	38.8
Fenton charter township (Genesee)	23.82	15,572	15,688	0.7	658.6	2.9	89.5	91,467	4.9	240,600	61.8	3.0	75.5	19.5
Ferndale city & MCD (Oakland)	3.88	19,891	20,033	0.7	5163.1	4.0	84.2	71,807	9.9	162,000	80.7	2.5	36.8	44.3
Flint city & MCD (Genesee)......	33.43	102,266	95,538	-6.6	2857.9	2.0	82.6	28,834	35.7	29,500	53.4	19.7	56.3	36.9

560 **MI(Antwerp township (Van Buren))—MI(Flint city & MCD (Genesee))** Items 1–14

Table B. Incorporated Places, Census Designated Places (CDPs), and Minor Civil Divisions (MCDs) of 10,000 or More Population — Crime, Residential Construction and Local Government Finance

STATE City, town, township, borough, or CDP (county if applicable)	Serious crimes known to police, 2018[1] — Violent crime — Number	Violent crime — Rate[2]	Property crime — Number	Property crime — Rate[2]	New residential construction authorized by building permits, 2019 — Value ($1,000)	Number of housing units	Percent single family	Local government finance, 2017 — General revenue — Total (mil dol)	Intergovernmental — Total (mil dol)	Intergovernmental — Percent from state gov.	Taxes per capita[3]	General expenditure — Total (mil dol)	Per capita[3] — Total	Per capita[3] — Capital outlays	Debt outstanding (mil dol)
	15	16	17	18	19	20	21	22	23	24	25	26	27	28	29
MICHIGAN—Con.															
Antwerp township (Van Buren).	NA	NA	NA	NA	7,544	32	100.0	2.0	0.8	91.2	51	1.8	147	20	0.0
Auburn Hills city & MCD (Oakland)	94	399	530	2,248	24,953	151	58.9	48.8	7.2	97.7	893	39.9	1,705	83	7.0
Bangor charter township (Bay).	NA	NA	NA	NA	2,175	9	100.0	7.1	2.0	91.7	141	9.9	706	9	0.0
Bath charter township (Clinton)	14	108	106	816	8,025	64	45.3	6.9	1.3	86.0	232	7.3	572	21	7.0
Battle Creek city & MCD (Calhoun)	600	990	1,958	3,230	2,779	9	100.0	107.9	26.0	63.0	950	101.7	1,984	308	105.2
Bay City city & MCD (Bay)	231	701	732	2,221	8,337	23	100.0	55.3	16.0	51.5	440	46.0	1,388	287	81.2
Bedford township (Monroe)	NA	NA	NA	NA	26,831	108	100.0	12.1	2.7	94.9	120	11.5	368	6	12.1
Beecher CDP	NA	NA	NA	NA	NA	NA	NA	NA	NA	NA	NA	NA	NA	NA	NA
Benton charter township (Berrien)	231	1,606	857	5,959	4,376	16	100.0	18.0	1.4	91.6	414	14.4	1,000	63	42.7
Benton Harbor city & MCD (Berrien)	213	2,166	422	4,290	1,039	4	100.0	24.5	11.4	48.1	293	23.7	2,408	199	24.4
Berkley city & MCD (Oakland)..	5	33	87	566	10,163	30	100.0	18.5	3.0	99.3	604	24.4	1,583	0	1.1
Beverly Hills village	5	48	57	546	3,121	10	100.0	17.1	1.8	95.8	653	16.1	1,542	83	3.7
Big Rapids city & MCD (Mecosta)	24	232	86	829	NA	NA	NA	19.2	4.2	67.1	557	17.1	1,654	117	13.2
Birmingham city & MCD (Oakland)	10	47	137	643	33,949	62	100.0	79.7	4.8	72.7	1,635	74.3	3,500	431	19.3
Blackman charter township (Jackson)	97	263	1,321	3,582	31,957	134	11.9	9.7	3.6	66.6	109	11.0	472	12	2.5
Bloomfield charter township (Oakland)	21	50	327	775	59,583	73	100.0	73.7	4.4	94.6	1,125	39.0	925	70	131.8
Brandon charter township (Oakland)	13	81	50	313	8,700	25	100.0	8.4	1.2	96.9	365	9.2	577	39	0.6
Bridgeport charter township (Saginaw)	40	406	138	1,401	160	1	100.0	5.0	1.1	97.5	175	7.3	735	73	0.5
Brighton township (Livingston) .	NA	NA	NA	NA	NA	NA	NA	6.6	1.5	100.0	67	4.9	260	27	6.6
Brownstown charter township (Wayne)	78	244	281	881	19,603	79	100.0	30.6	2.9	96.9	510	36.0	1,132	64	32.3
Burton city & MCD (Genesee)..	127	446	685	2,407	3,292	28	100.0	24.2	6.9	84.1	269	34.3	1,198	229	30.2
Byron township (Kent)	NA	NA	NA	NA	53,491	189	100.0	9.7	1.8	100.0	98	12.6	527	82	0.0
Cadillac city & MCD (Wexford) .	68	650	226	2,162	NA	NA	NA	18.2	4.2	82.6	414	13.3	1,273	84	11.0
Caledonia township (Kent).......	NA	NA	NA	NA	14,230	94	0.0	5.4	1.4	100.0	102	5.9	405	17	2.9
Cannon township (Kent)	NA	NA	NA	NA	11,979	39	84.6	4.4	1.3	97.4	111	4.8	322	9	6.6
Canton charter township (Wayne)	134	146	986	1,071	119,222	437	61.8	100.4	8.1	92.5	459	92.0	1,001	30	55.1
Cascade charter township (Kent)	NA	NA	NA	NA	92,694	319	53.6	10.6	1.5	97.8	429	8.7	457	35	3.6
Chesterfield township (Macomb)	59	129	630	1,379	39,628	148	100.0	31.6	4.2	99.8	328	32.7	721	79	31.0
Clawson city & MCD (Oakland)	12	100	69	577	0	0	0.0	12.7	2.1	99.9	777	18.8	1,568	32	28.2
Clinton charter township (Macomb)	322	318	1,422	1,404	20,710	121	17.4	86.0	9.6	88.7	433	86.5	859	61	75.6
Coldwater city & MCD (Branch)	49	456	312	2,906	1,862	9	77.8	25.4	6.7	60.6	409	70.6	5,783	799	38.1
Commerce charter township (Oakland)	15	38	195	500	50,345	196	33.2	38.5	3.2	99.1	332	38.1	878	61	106.5
Comstock charter township (Kalamazoo)	NA	NA	NA	NA	12,980	58	100.0	6.0	1.5	100.0	122	6.3	406	47	0.6
Comstock Park CDP	NA	NA	NA	NA	NA	NA	NA	NA	NA	NA	NA	NA	NA	NA	NA
Cooper charter township (Kalamazoo)	NA	NA	NA	NA	11,531	70	31.4	1.8	0.8	100.0	44	2.0	180	42	0.7
Cutlerville CDP	NA	NA	NA	NA	NA	NA	NA	NA	NA	NA	NA	NA	NA	NA	NA
Davison township (Genesee)....	40	209	171	892	10,267	64	100.0	10.3	1.9	93.1	80	17.4	905	36	0.0
Dearborn city & MCD (Wayne) .	314	334	1,871	1,990	8,861	36	100.0	207.9	41.5	86.3	1,059	229.5	2,423	287	226.7
Dearborn Heights city & MCD (Wayne)	243	438	911	1,642	2,532	19	47.4	69.1	15.6	91.2	586	66.8	1,195	62	48.2
Delhi charter township (Ingham)	NA	NA	NA	NA	40,727	197	84.8	21.0	2.7	93.3	332	19.6	710	62	28.6
Delta charter township (Eaton).	NA	NA	NA	NA	8,308	27	100.0	24.8	3.1	85.3	338	26.5	800	123	14.2
Detroit city & MCD (Wayne)......	13,478	2,008	28,897	4,305	54,299	399	7.5	1894.3	608.6	59.6	1,108	2108.5	3,125	876	3188.4
DeWitt charter township (Clinton)	18	119	127	836	19,653	86	39.5	9.1	1.2	100.0	232	11.0	728	62	0.6
East Bay township (Grand Traverse)	NA	NA	NA	NA	NA	NA	NA	4.2	0.9	94.1	179	6.6	574	25	7.9
East Grand Rapids city & MCD (Kent)	6	51	122	1,026	NA	NA	NA	15.8	2.0	100.0	861	17.8	1,516	171	9.5
East Lansing city	107	219	807	1,651	NA	NA	NA	67.1	14.0	84.6	509	74.2	1,512	312	62.1
East Lansing city (Ingham).......	NA	NA	NA	NA	722	6	100.0	0.0	0.0	0.0	0	0.0	0	0	0.0
Eastpointe city & MCD (Macomb)	222	683	1,063	3,268	0	0	0.0	30.5	6.9	97.7	400	39.6	1,219	79	16.6
Egelston township (Muskegon)	NA	NA	NA	NA	4,147	25	100.0	3.7	1.0	100.0	124	4.1	402	27	3.6
Emmett charter township (Calhoun)	42	362	606	5,216	0	0	0.0	4.5	1.4	100.0	125	4.9	423	32	3.4
Escanaba city & MCD (Delta)...	41	337	337	2,769	NA	NA	NA	14.8	5.0	87.1	470	29.3	2,402	357	5.4
Farmington city & MCD (Oakland)	20	189	58	547	200	1	100.0	19.2	2.1	91.6	483	15.9	1,495	87	15.1
Farmington Hills city & MCD (Oakland)	69	85	681	838	11,323	47	100.0	100.0	17.0	89.4	597	115.9	1,423	182	51.9
Fenton city	17	151	207	1,844	NA	NA	NA	12.8	2.2	96.6	491	12.2	1,082	71	15.4
Fenton city (Genesee)	NA	NA	NA	NA	3,440	18	66.7	NA	NA	NA	NA	NA	NA	NA	NA
Fenton charter township (Genesee)	NA	NA	NA	NA	36,096	127	98.4	11.7	1.3	99.8	63	10.8	702	7	21.3
Ferndale city & MCD (Oakland)	39	194	341	1,697	21,389	193	24.4	53.0	12.0	37.8	756	50.8	2,522	270	29.1
Flint city & MCD (Genesee)......	1,739	1,818	2,584	2,701	9,113	33	30.3	614.5	175.2	89.6	372	577.5	5,987	164	145.4

1 Data for serious crimes have not been adjusted for underreporting. This may affect comparability between geographic areas over time.
2 Per 100,000 population estimated by the FBI. 3 Based on population estimated as of July 1 of the year shown.

Table B. Incorporated Places, Census Designated Places (CDPs), and Minor Civil Divisions (MCDs) of 10,000 or More Population — **Land Area, Population, and Households, and Employment**

STATE City, town, township, borough, or CDP (county if applicable)	Land area 2010 (sq mi)	Population Total persons 2010	Total persons 2019	Percent change 2010–2019	Persons per square mile 2019	Population characteristics 2015–2019 Percent foreign born	Percent living in the same house as previous year	Income and poverty 2015–2019 Median household income	Percent of households with income below poverty level	Median value of owner-occupied housing units	Employment, 2015–2019 Percent in civilian labor force	Unemploy-ment rate	Households, 2015–2019 (percent of households) Family households	One person households
	1	2	3	4	5	6	7	8	9	10	11	12	13	14
MICHIGAN—Con.														
Flint charter township (Genesee)	23.21	32,085	30,357	-5.4	1307.9	4.7	86.0	41,167	17.6	89,600	56.2	9.0	60.2	36.0
Flushing charter township (Genesee)	31.38	10,639	10,181	-4.3	324.4	4.2	90.0	67,344	5.4	149,900	59.9	4.6	74.1	20.5
Forest Hills CDP	49.27	25,867	NA	NA	NA	5.8	90.9	119,404	3.3	347,500	65.3	2.6	80.7	16.7
Fort Gratiot charter township (St. Clair)	15.95	11,108	10,991	-1.1	689.1	2.7	84.9	59,767	9.9	165,200	57.5	6.6	62.5	29.5
Fraser city & MCD (Macomb)	4.14	14,480	14,480	0.0	3497.6	6.9	89.7	59,089	11.0	149,100	64.0	4.1	64.5	32.0
Frenchtown township (Monroe)	41.75	20,511	19,980	-2.6	478.6	1.3	86.1	53,103	17.0	136,700	55.3	5.9	63.8	30.2
Fruitport charter township (Muskegon)	29.97	13,604	14,386	5.7	480.0	0.8	92.9	63,352	9.6	145,800	65.8	5.5	75.0	18.9
Gaines charter township (Kent)	35.70	25,145	27,345	8.7	766.0	8.2	85.9	67,942	6.3	196,900	71.7	3.6	74.6	19.3
Garden City city & MCD (Wayne)	5.86	27,636	26,408	-4.4	4506.5	5.2	92.0	56,521	8.6	111,000	63.5	3.6	61.9	32.2
Garfield charter township (Grand Traverse)	26.59	16,217	17,740	9.4	667.2	2.3	81.5	50,372	12.3	190,300	61.4	5.9	56.7	34.6
Genesee charter township (Genesee)	29.06	21,559	20,440	-5.2	703.4	1.3	86.4	45,527	16.4	81,200	55.7	10.4	65.1	27.8
Genoa township (Livingston)	33.84	19,790	20,690	4.5	611.4	3.4	90.1	80,757	5.9	271,800	63.5	4.3	70.0	26.2
Georgetown charter township (Ottawa)	33.16	46,985	52,637	12.0	1587.4	3.0	89.3	78,481	7.4	196,800	70.1	2.7	75.2	20.1
Grand Blanc charter township (Genesee)	32.70	37,528	36,593	-2.5	1119.1	4.9	87.0	66,743	8.1	162,000	64.3	3.8	64.5	29.9
Grand Haven city & MCD (Ottawa)	5.72	10,363	11,047	6.6	1931.3	2.2	86.6	58,307	6.8	161,000	60.5	5.5	61.1	34.6
Grand Haven charter township (Ottawa)	28.70	15,227	17,614	15.7	613.7	2.6	86.1	79,355	4.7	225,600	70.2	3.9	73.9	19.7
Grand Rapids city & MCD (Kent)	44.76	188,036	201,013	6.9	4490.9	10.9	77.2	50,103	17.4	143,400	68.7	6.3	54.9	33.1
Grand Rapids charter township (Kent)	15.33	16,662	18,722	12.4	1221.3	7.7	92.2	103,325	3.8	291,000	64.5	2.8	75.7	21.3
Grandville city & MCD (Kent)	7.25	15,372	15,858	3.2	2187.3	5.1	85.4	62,827	7.1	161,800	68.7	2.6	68.4	25.7
Green Oak township (Livingston)	34.20	17,471	18,976	8.6	554.9	4.0	93.9	90,706	4.7	263,300	64.9	3.5	76.2	19.5
Grosse Ile township (Wayne)	9.03	10,371	10,137	-2.3	1122.6	6.3	93.1	105,833	3.0	286,200	57.4	2.7	77.9	19.9
Grosse Pointe Park city & MCD (Wayne)	2.17	11,553	11,050	-4.4	5092.2	5.9	92.7	115,341	5.6	358,400	71.4	3.0	72.3	23.7
Grosse Pointe Woods city & MCD (Wayne)	3.24	15,947	15,332	-3.9	4732.1	7.2	93.4	104,848	5.7	244,500	63.5	2.9	75.8	20.8
Hamburg township (Livingston)	32.24	21,161	21,794	3.0	676.0	2.4	94.6	93,245	3.3	260,700	67.2	3.5	75.4	19.6
Hamtramck city & MCD (Wayne)	2.10	22,448	21,599	-3.8	10285.2	41.4	88.8	27,166	42.0	69,700	42.9	9.6	67.5	27.0
Harper Woods city & MCD (Wayne)	2.63	14,396	13,746	-4.5	5226.6	3.5	84.1	48,418	17.6	83,600	64.7	11.0	63.8	31.2
Harrison charter township (Macomb)	14.24	24,589	24,977	1.6	1754.0	3.1	84.2	64,883	9.9	193,100	65.3	3.9	57.9	35.2
Hartland township (Livingston)	35.87	14,665	15,170	3.4	422.9	2.8	93.5	90,577	4.4	265,000	67.9	3.6	74.4	20.8
Haslett CDP	15.39	19,220	NA	NA	NA	12.2	80.1	69,601	10.7	198,400	65.3	3.3	53.2	38.4
Hazel Park city & MCD (Oakland)	2.82	16,422	16,347	-0.5	5796.8	4.3	83.5	38,903	22.6	73,600	63.0	6.8	51.7	36.2
Highland charter township (Oakland)	34.06	19,208	20,172	5.0	592.2	2.2	93.4	87,011	6.1	231,200	65.4	3.7	71.2	23.4
Highland Park city & MCD (Wayne)	2.97	11,776	10,775	-8.5	3627.9	0.6	88.1	18,474	46.3	45,700	44.9	22.6	46.4	48.4
Holland city	16.68	33,101	33,216	0.3	1991.4	8.7	79.1	57,002	10.4	151,300	65.1	3.5	59.8	32.8
Holland city (Ottawa)	8.45	26,104	26,128	0.1	3092.1	9.9	76.2	59,527	9.4	154,200	65.8	3.7	59.4	32.0
Holland charter township (Ottawa)	26.98	35,569	38,690	8.8	1434.0	15.9	85.8	63,985	10.7	170,600	73.7	4.0	72.7	21.4
Holly township (Oakland)	34.39	11,360	11,687	2.9	339.8	2.2	87.3	63,872	11.5	155,600	61.9	5.3	65.8	30.4
Holt CDP	15.66	23,973	NA	NA	NA	6.0	85.6	66,316	9.0	162,500	68.4	5.5	63.8	29.9
Huron charter township (Wayne)	35.35	15,879	16,247	2.3	459.6	1.7	89.7	67,216	6.1	187,600	61.7	5.4	74.1	22.1
Independence charter township (Oakland)	35.01	34,626	37,026	6.9	1057.6	4.7	89.4	94,018	4.7	269,600	67.9	4.6	75.6	18.2
Inkster city & MCD (Wayne)	6.25	25,366	24,284	-4.3	3885.4	4.3	81.5	32,014	30.4	48,700	58.7	11.4	60.4	33.3
Ionia city & MCD (Ionia)	5.41	11,326	11,168	-1.4	2064.3	2.4	78.9	48,902	18.8	97,600	39.1	6.9	58.6	32.1
Jackson city & MCD (Jackson)	10.86	33,477	32,440	-3.1	2987.1	2.3	83.5	35,464	28.2	68,400	60.6	8.8	57.9	35.3
Jenison CDP	5.86	16,538	NA	NA	NA	3.0	91.5	69,481	6.8	171,100	65.6	3.5	72.0	26.1
Kalamazoo city & MCD (Kalamazoo)	24.67	74,263	76,200	2.6	3088.8	5.7	68.0	41,774	24.9	106,600	66.5	7.6	44.8	37.2
Kalamazoo charter township (Kalamazoo)	11.67	21,913	22,651	3.4	1941.0	6.0	82.7	54,158	14.2	107,800	68.1	6.4	56.0	31.9
Kentwood city & MCD (Kent)	20.92	48,701	51,898	6.6	2480.8	17.6	82.6	54,197	9.7	158,700	70.5	3.0	62.5	30.9
Lansing city	39.19	114,265	118,210	3.5	3016.3	10.0	76.6	41,674	20.4	83,500	66.9	8.4	49.4	39.4
Lansing city (Ingham)	33.29	109,516	113,328	3.5	3404.3	9.9	76.5	41,784	20.3	83,700	66.9	8.1	49.2	39.6
Lenox township (Macomb)	38.68	10,457	10,953	4.7	283.2	1.9	88.5	65,360	10.3	161,100	52.7	7.0	70.6	21.5
Leoni township (Jackson)	48.63	13,785	13,637	-1.1	280.4	1.9	91.4	54,876	10.8	132,800	60.4	5.8	68.8	25.1
Lincoln charter township (Berrien)	17.91	14,691	14,597	-0.6	815.0	7.0	88.5	73,567	5.8	187,400	65.0	3.3	70.8	25.8
Lincoln Park city & MCD (Wayne)	5.84	38,085	36,321	-4.6	6219.3	8.5	88.9	44,554	19.8	73,700	60.8	6.7	61.1	33.7
Livonia city & MCD (Wayne)	35.70	96,857	93,665	-3.3	2623.7	7.8	91.3	80,149	5.7	191,500	64.5	3.8	69.4	26.5
Lyon charter township (Oakland)	30.96	14,557	20,975	44.1	677.5	6.4	89.9	117,308	5.4	346,100	71.9	3.6	78.8	16.8
Macomb township (Macomb)	36.25	79,574	91,574	15.1	2526.2	10.6	93.3	101,570	4.3	271,600	69.5	3.6	79.3	17.4
Madison Heights city & MCD (Oakland)	7.09	29,694	29,886	0.6	4215.2	15.4	83.0	53,439	13.9	124,000	67.8	3.7	54.4	38.1

Table B. Incorporated Places, Census Designated Places (CDPs), and Minor Civil Divisions (MCDs) of 10,000 or More Population — Crime, Residential Construction and Local Government Finance

STATE City, town, township, borough, or CDP (county if applicable)	Serious crimes known to police, 2018[1] Violent crime Number	Rate[2]	Property crime Number	Rate[2]	New residential construction authorized by building permits, 2019 Value ($1,000)	Number of housing units	Percent single family	Local government finance, 2017 General revenue Total (mil dol)	Intergovernmental Total (mil dol)	Percent from state gov.	Taxes per capita[3]	General expenditure Total (mil dol)	Per capita[3] Total	Capital outlays	Debt outstanding (mil dol)
	15	16	17	18	19	20	21	22	23	24	25	26	27	28	29
MICHIGAN—Con.															
Flint charter township (Genesee)	266	876	1,214	3,996	627	3	100.0	17.0	3.2	82.2	295	14.3	468	11	2.1
Flushing charter township (Genesee)	5	49	45	442	NA	NA	NA	3.5	1.0	95.8	102	5.8	570	50	0.0
Forest Hills CDP	NA	NA	NA	NA	NA	NA	NA	NA	NA	NA	NA	NA	NA	NA	NA
Fort Gratiot charter township (St. Clair)	NA	NA	NA	NA	2,059	9	100.0	6.1	0.9	94.9	260	10.2	925	32	3.0
Fraser city & MCD (Macomb)	23	157	198	1,354	0	0	0.0	32.2	1.5	93.6	947	30.2	2,067	273	23.6
Frenchtown township (Monroe)	NA	NA	NA	NA	11,612	46	100.0	15.6	1.6	100.0	541	13.0	653	2	0.0
Fruitport charter township (Muskegon)	15	106	544	3,840	NA	NA	NA	4.3	1.1	99.8	152	6.8	478	45	3.4
Gaines charter township (Kent)	NA	NA	NA	NA	32,532	139	65.5	9.7	2.0	100.0	48	12.4	462	18	0.0
Garden City city & MCD (Wayne)	105	396	241	909	0	0	0.0	31.1	7.2	74.1	456	39.0	1,459	51	34.3
Garfield charter township (Grand Traverse)	NA	NA	NA	NA	27,206	253	30.4	8.0	1.3	100.0	178	10.3	591	25	0.5
Genesee charter township (Genesee)	73	357	256	1,252	214	1	100.0	9.7	1.9	98.4	103	11.4	555	3	0.5
Genoa township (Livingston)	NA	NA	NA	NA	NA	NA	NA	9.8	1.6	100.0	64	11.5	571	59	8.2
Georgetown charter township (Ottawa)	NA	NA	NA	NA	66,410	234	100.0	19.6	3.8	99.9	94	26.9	521	92	0.0
Grand Blanc charter township (Genesee)	49	134	448	1,228	39,203	164	39.0	26.7	3.5	96.0	259	21.7	594	59	9.8
Grand Haven city & MCD (Ottawa)	21	191	173	1,575	6,009	24	58.3	19.3	4.0	33.4	823	17.8	1,629	248	33.7
Grand Haven charter township (Ottawa)	NA	NA	NA	NA	33,125	207	24.6	7.4	1.2	100.0	284	9.5	564	31	7.2
Grand Rapids city & MCD (Kent)	1,313	655	3,830	1,911	37,193	336	45.5	361.4	81.9	48.0	776	371.7	1,866	207	676.1
Grand Rapids charter township (Kent)	NA	NA	NA	NA	NA	NA	NA	3.7	1.4	94.5	102	5.5	299	93	0.0
Grandville city & MCD (Kent)	28	174	516	3,214	850	3	100.0	24.8	2.9	92.2	491	18.2	1,138	41	7.5
Green Oak township (Livingston)	25	133	140	742	19,745	55	100.0	10.5	1.5	100.0	341	12.7	674	220	30.7
Grosse Ile township (Wayne)	3	30	34	336	5,006	11	100.0	16.6	2.2	53.9	948	18.0	1,773	100	36.4
Grosse Pointe Park city & MCD (Wayne)	NA	NA	175	1,581	2,200	1	100.0	22.1	1.9	99.5	924	21.7	1,943	51	6.7
Grosse Pointe Woods city & MCD (Wayne)	13	84	225	1,452	425	1	100.0	32.6	2.7	99.1	931	32.9	2,124	471	27.8
Hamburg (Livingston)	10	45	67	304	NA	NA	NA	13.1	1.8	99.1	342	17.0	783	39	11.0
Hamtramck city & MCD (Wayne)	166	766	493	2,275	0	0	0.0	38.0	9.5	62.1	500	31.2	1,427	159	10.3
Harper Woods city & MCD (Wayne)	128	936	677	4,951	138	1	100.0	15.5	2.7	92.1	634	20.2	1,457	17	5.7
Harrison charter township (Macomb)	NA	NA	NA	NA	5,151	18	100.0	26.8	2.5	89.8	306	26.3	1,050	17	19.9
Hartland (Livingston)	NA	NA	NA	NA	NA	NA	NA	10.4	1.2	100.0	183	16.0	1,070	20	28.4
Haslett CDP	NA	NA	NA	NA	NA	NA	NA	NA	NA	NA	NA	NA	NA	NA	NA
Hazel Park city & MCD (Oakland)	53	321	284	1,721	640	8	100.0	32.2	4.8	74.5	344	28.5	1,720	141	8.9
Highland charter township (Oakland)	15	75	99	492	8,799	23	100.0	8.6	1.8	91.5	228	7.2	360	18	1.1
Highland Park city & MCD (Wayne)	188	1,742	344	3,187	0	0	0.0	29.5	5.4	84.3	958	31.5	2,903	23	35.5
Holland city	142	425	728	2,179	NA	NA	NA	53.4	11.8	78.8	542	77.0	2,304	1046	243.1
Holland city (Ottawa)	NA	NA	NA	NA	2,466	9	100.0	0.0	0.0	0.0	0	0.0	0	0	0.0
Holland charter township (Ottawa)	NA	NA	NA	NA	33,886	171	98.2	27.4	3.1	100.0	214	32.5	856	60	10.1
Holly township (Oakland)	NA	NA	NA	NA	10,436	39	100.0	2.1	0.5	100.0	118	1.9	165	2	0.0
Holt CDP	NA	NA	NA	NA	NA	NA	NA	NA	NA	NA	NA	NA	NA	NA	NA
Huron charter township (Wayne)	34	213	120	753	7,800	37	100.0	12.7	2.0	69.7	295	13.8	865	47	5.9
Independence charter township (Oakland)	16	43	191	517	17,587	83	100.0	29.4	3.8	97.1	319	25.6	695	36	14.2
Inkster city & MCD (Wayne)	262	1,077	656	2,696	0	0	0.0	48.7	25.5	61.8	401	33.3	1,358	63	38.2
Ionia city & MCD (Ionia)	48	430	120	1,074	NA	NA	NA	11.9	2.8	76.6	311	14.0	1,256	254	31.7
Jackson city & MCD (Jackson)	366	1,123	1,387	4,254	10,969	132	0.8	60.4	21.9	36.7	627	61.2	1,872	366	45.6
Jenison CDP	NA	NA	NA	NA	NA	NA	NA	NA	NA	NA	NA	NA	NA	NA	NA
Kalamazoo city & MCD (Kalamazoo)	1,008	1,326	3,825	5,032	8,074	36	94.4	129.0	32.1	65.7	546	98.8	1,303	131	512.6
Kalamazoo charter township (Kalamazoo)	98	398	660	2,680	268	1	100.0	10.2	2.7	84.7	206	17.0	752	45	10.1
Kentwood city & MCD (Kent)	193	370	1,100	2,108	17,540	84	97.6	42.2	11.1	87.1	404	47.2	912	96	16.4
Lansing city	1,301	1,108	3,557	3,030	NA	NA	NA	238.2	55.9	49.7	697	218.3	1,854	80	565.6
Lansing city (Ingham)	NA	NA	NA	NA	36,455	269	9.3	NA	NA	NA	NA	NA	NA	NA	NA
Lenox township (Macomb)	NA	NA	NA	NA	15,431	62	100.0	5.1	0.8	67.0	137	7.5	697	77	22.3
Leoni township (Jackson)	NA	NA	NA	NA	0	0	0.0	7.9	1.2	99.9	96	6.4	467	6	21.6
Lincoln charter township (Berrien)	12	82	177	1,214	6,735	22	100.0	7.2	1.6	80.4	230	7.6	523	27	1.3
Lincoln Park city & MCD (Wayne)	208	570	1,023	2,805	0	0	0.0	37.7	9.7	84.6	362	36.7	1,000	85	11.9
Livonia city & MCD (Wayne)	138	147	1,313	1,401	11,417	39	100.0	121.6	18.8	92.8	619	111.0	1,178	30	47.6
Lyon charter township (Oakland)	14	67	NA	NA	32,575	183	100.0	15.4	1.3	98.3	362	14.3	719	25	33.9
Macomb township (Macomb)	NA	NA	NA	NA	147,836	452	73.9	43.6	8.6	94.1	163	34.8	389	32	66.6
Madison Heights city & MCD (Oakland)	89	296	435	1,445	2,159	20	100.0	40.1	7.7	94.0	627	44.0	1,455	211	23.2

1 Data for serious crimes have not been adjusted for underreporting. This may affect comparability between geographic areas over time.
2 Per 100,000 population estimated by the FBI.   3 Based on population estimated as of July 1 of the year shown.

Table B. Incorporated Places, Census Designated Places (CDPs), and Minor Civil Divisions (MCDs) of 10,000 or More Population — **Land Area, Population, and Households, and Employment**

STATE City, town, township, borough, or CDP (county if applicable)	Land area 2010 (sq mi)	Population Total persons 2010	Total persons 2019	Percent change 2010–2019	Persons per square mile 2019	Population characteristics 2015–2019 Percent foreign born	Percent living in the same house as previous year	Income and poverty 2015–2019 Median household income	Percent of households with income below poverty level	Median value of owner-occupied housing units	Employment, 2015–2019 Percent in civilian labor force	Unemploy-ment rate	Households, 2015–2019 (percent of households) Family households	One person households
	1	2	3	4	5	6	7	8	9	10	11	12	13	14
MICHIGAN—Con.														
Marion township (Livingston)....	34.90	10,020	11,165	11.4	319.9	2.2	94.1	92,420	3.3	261,700	68.0	3.5	81.2	16.6
Marquette city & MCD (Marquette)	11.34	21,366	20,995	-1.7	1851.4	2.3	69.7	43,977	23.5	187,300	60.4	6.8	44.8	35.9
Melvindale city & MCD (Wayne)	2.72	10,727	10,248	-4.5	3767.6	14.0	86.8	41,629	26.5	64,300	56.9	12.6	58.2	39.5
Meridian charter township (Ingham)	30.56	39,690	43,196	8.8	1413.5	17.6	78.3	72,463	13.2	227,600	64.7	4.3	55.0	33.0
Midland charter township	34.36	41,866	41,701	-0.4	1213.6	6.8	82.3	63,812	11.7	150,400	60.7	5.1	62.0	31.0
Midland city (Midland)	33.96	41,717	41,546	-0.4	1223.4	6.9	82.2	63,910	11.7	150,800	60.7	5.1	61.9	31.1
Milford charter township (Oakland)	33.04	15,739	16,905	7.4	511.7	5.3	90.8	86,997	6.9	308,500	62.4	2.4	71.1	24.4
Monitor charter township (Bay)	36.78	10,735	10,456	-2.6	284.3	1.6	93.4	60,382	7.8	146,100	54.7	3.5	67.4	28.1
Monroe city & MCD (Monroe)...	9.05	20,676	19,552	-5.4	2160.4	2.1	86.6	46,550	19.7	122,300	60.3	5.1	60.7	35.9
Monroe charter township (Monroe)	16.87	14,534	14,183	-2.4	840.7	2.6	83.7	54,789	12.5	150,800	60.5	7.9	64.2	29.2
Mount Clemens city & MCD (Macomb)	4.09	16,312	16,163	-0.9	3951.8	1.8	80.7	43,018	20.3	103,100	56.0	6.8	51.0	42.3
Mount Morris township (Genesee)	31.55	21,580	20,336	-5.8	644.6	2.3	84.0	38,919	24.6	64,700	54.3	15.6	63.9	30.7
Mount Pleasant city & MCD (Isabella)	7.72	26,032	24,797	-4.7	3212.0	5.7	58.7	37,714	31.4	137,700	59.6	8.8	42.3	35.3
Mundy township (Genesee)......	36.03	15,092	14,473	-4.1	401.7	4.1	93.2	65,847	5.4	138,000	58.5	4.1	67.9	29.0
Muskegon city & MCD (Muskegon)	14.14	38,399	36,565	-4.8	2585.9	2.4	74.5	32,433	26.1	73,000	50.3	9.5	53.3	38.9
Muskegon charter township (Muskegon)	23.47	17,820	18,000	1.0	766.9	1.4	84.4	52,615	12.3	93,400	60.1	7.0	69.0	22.2
Muskegon Heights city & MCD (Muskegon)	3.19	10,852	10,736	-1.1	3365.5	1.7	79.7	30,795	33.0	43,900	59.6	16.5	64.2	31.6
New Baltimore city & MCD (Macomb)	4.60	12,084	12,347	2.2	2684.1	2.0	91.2	77,730	8.2	225,400	63.1	4.5	70.7	26.7
Niles city	5.79	11,596	11,149	-3.9	1925.6	2.6	81.3	34,486	23.3	85,400	62.5	7.0	56.8	34.5
Niles city (Berrien)	5.15	11,596	11,149	-3.9	2164.9	2.6	81.3	34,486	23.3	85,400	62.5	7.0	56.8	34.5
Niles township (Berrien)	37.31	14,160	13,801	-2.5	369.9	2.9	88.8	49,335	11.4	115,400	62.7	3.9	63.7	28.0
Northview CDP	10.30	14,541	NA	NA	NA	4.4	83.9	60,829	9.5	167,700	69.3	3.6	62.3	30.1
Northville township (Wayne).....	16.19	28,571	29,342	2.7	1812.4	18.0	88.2	113,918	3.7	419,600	64.4	3.8	70.9	25.3
Norton Shores city & MCD (Muskegon)	23.24	23,998	24,664	2.8	1061.3	2.3	87.6	63,805	8.5	140,400	64.7	4.3	66.9	27.5
Novi city & MCD (Oakland).......	30.25	55,232	60,896	10.3	2013.1	25.9	87.1	98,020	4.7	322,100	68.1	2.8	66.9	28.5
Oakland charter township (Oakland)	36.27	16,779	19,547	16.5	538.9	16.1	89.8	146,228	2.2	416,500	66.1	4.7	85.5	13.0
Oak Park city & MCD (Oakland)	5.16	29,408	29,431	0.1	5703.7	9.9	89.2	52,584	14.1	117,700	65.6	5.6	55.2	36.9
Oceola township (Livingston) ...	36.13	11,973	14,812	23.7	410.0	2.9	88.8	95,778	3.6	254,000	66.5	2.1	78.0	16.5
Okemos CDP	16.86	21,369	NA	NA	NA	21.5	77.4	78,600	15.0	243,200	64.4	5.0	57.7	27.5
Orion charter township (Oakland)	33.16	35,406	39,816	12.5	1200.7	7.1	87.8	96,323	5.6	269,100	70.2	3.6	72.5	20.9
Oshtemo charter township (Kalamazoo)	35.69	21,704	23,190	6.8	649.8	8.7	77.1	49,591	13.1	212,100	63.5	5.3	51.5	38.4
Owosso city & MCD (Shiawassee)	5.25	15,180	14,441	-4.9	2750.7	1.0	86.7	45,203	17.0	84,300	64.0	6.3	59.1	32.0
Oxford charter township (Oakland)	33.84	20,532	22,886	11.5	676.3	5.7	89.8	83,550	6.5	249,800	67.2	4.4	75.8	20.9
Park township (Ottawa)	19.20	17,801	18,905	6.2	984.6	4.6	90.7	90,871	3.9	235,500	67.0	2.4	81.5	15.4
Pittsfield charter township (Washtenaw)	27.12	34,789	38,921	11.9	1435.1	18.8	80.9	79,965	10.8	292,500	65.4	3.0	59.9	31.3
Plainfield charter township (Kent)	35.02	30,970	34,147	10.3	975.1	3.3	88.6	71,853	7.1	190,400	69.2	3.0	70.2	24.1
Plymouth charter township (Wayne)	15.93	27,521	27,035	-1.8	1697.1	9.3	91.5	86,439	4.7	313,800	61.7	4.6	69.2	26.8
Pontiac city & MCD (Oakland)..	19.89	59,695	59,438	-0.4	2988.3	8.6	78.5	33,568	29.5	67,100	62.1	11.9	54.9	38.5
Portage city & MCD (Kalamazoo)	32.28	46,304	49,445	6.8	1531.8	5.9	84.9	62,941	8.9	164,300	69.0	5.7	62.7	30.3
Port Huron city & MCD (St. Clair)	8.10	30,199	28,749	-4.8	3549.3	3.6	77.1	38,808	24.0	86,700	60.6	9.3	55.1	35.4
Port Huron charter township (St. Clair)	12.83	10,639	10,356	-2.7	807.2	2.2	82.2	46,300	16.2	133,300	55.9	5.7	69.0	26.0
Redford charter township (Wayne)	11.24	48,289	46,674	-3.3	4152.5	4.2	89.9	57,216	12.7	87,700	66.0	6.8	62.6	31.1
Riverview city & MCD (Wayne).	4.40	12,486	12,032	-3.6	2734.5	4.1	86.9	58,246	9.7	149,400	55.7	4.1	59.1	35.3
Rochester city & MCD (Oakland)	3.83	12,714	13,296	4.6	3471.5	10.4	86.1	89,904	8.3	366,100	67.6	5.1	62.6	31.7
Rochester Hills city & MCD (Oakland)	32.80	70,987	74,516	5.0	2271.8	20.1	89.2	93,953	5.0	295,000	63.4	2.9	70.4	25.6
Romulus city & MCD (Wayne) ..	35.61	23,989	23,573	-1.7	662.0	3.2	86.4	51,504	16.8	97,300	63.2	10.6	67.2	28.0
Roseville city & MCD (Macomb)	9.84	47,324	47,018	-0.6	4778.3	3.6	85.9	47,648	15.2	86,400	64.5	7.4	59.1	34.2
Royal Oak city & MCD (Oakland)	11.79	57,232	59,277	3.6	5027.7	7.7	84.0	81,665	6.8	224,600	74.6	3.2	46.9	41.0
Saginaw city & MCD (Saginaw)	17.08	51,469	48,115	-6.5	2817.0	1.6	81.7	29,582	33.2	40,100	55.8	13.7	57.7	35.7
Saginaw charter township (Saginaw)	24.50	40,855	39,150	-4.2	1598.0	6.4	86.6	51,680	12.7	127,200	59.0	4.5	58.3	34.1
St. Clair Shores city & MCD (Macomb)	11.68	59,765	58,984	-1.3	5050.0	3.6	90.1	60,805	7.7	135,800	64.4	5.7	57.4	36.8
St. Joseph charter township (Berrien)	6.65	10,028	9,676	-3.5	1455.0	7.7	90.8	70,266	3.1	169,500	61.0	2.9	69.6	26.3
Sault Ste. Marie city & MCD (Chippewa)	14.76	14,144	13,420	-5.1	909.2	3.1	74.9	38,341	20.7	92,500	60.8	9.2	49.3	41.8

Table B. Incorporated Places, Census Designated Places (CDPs), and Minor Civil Divisions (MCDs) of 10,000 or More Population — **Crime, Residential Construction and Local Government Finance**

STATE City, town, township, borough, or CDP (county if applicable)	Serious crimes known to police, 2018[1] Violent crime Number	Rate[2]	Property crime Number	Rate[2]	New residential construction authorized by building permits, 2019 Value ($1,000)	Number of housing units	Percent single family	Local government finance, 2017 General revenue Total (mil dol)	Intergovernmental Total (mil dol)	Percent from state gov.	Taxes per capita[3]	General expenditure Total (mil dol)	Per capita[3] Total	Capital outlays	Debt outstanding (mil dol)
	15	16	17	18	19	20	21	22	23	24	25	26	27	28	29
MICHIGAN—Con.															
Marion township (Livingston)....	NA	NA	NA	NA	NA	NA	NA	2.2	0.9	100.0	43	2.9	261	1	5.4
Marquette city & MCD (Marquette)	23	112	204	994	NA	NA	NA	51.6	6.7	71.0	836	34.1	1,651	65	137.9
Melvindale city & MCD (Wayne)	68	661	243	2,361	791	4	100.0	25.8	5.7	47.6	780	23.7	2,291	17	8.7
Meridian charter township (Ingham)	98	228	1,090	2,531	11,546	35	94.3	34.8	4.1	95.6	332	34.6	805	53	10.5
Midland city	55	131	354	844	NA	NA	NA	81.6	21.3	85.8	869	70.1	1,674	104	22.6
Midland city (Midland)	NA	NA	NA	NA	6,129	44	86.4	NA	NA	NA	NA	NA	NA	NA	NA
Milford charter township (Oakland)	10	60	67	399	1,831	9	100.0	8.8	1.0	98.4	378	11.5	687	31	10.8
Monitor charter township (Bay).	NA	NA	NA	NA	3,036	9	100.0	5.8	1.6	83.7	222	6.8	644	4	6.8
Monroe city & MCD (Monroe)...	114	577	383	1,939	102	1	100.0	36.9	6.8	93.4	881	54.6	2,764	16	106.8
Monroe charter township (Monroe)	NA	NA	NA	NA	1,700	11	63.6	3.5	1.2	99.8	133	5.9	418	33	0.4
Mount Clemens city & MCD (Macomb)	NA	NA	NA	NA	0	0	0.0	32.4	5.3	80.9	458	24.5	1,501	172	14.7
Mount Morris township (Genesee)	137	675	401	1,976	135	1	100.0	11.1	2.3	92.3	204	16.8	819	9	1.6
Mount Pleasant city & MCD (Isabella)	76	294	323	1,251	3,985	36	22.2	27.3	5.8	98.3	314	26.8	1,037	51	7.5
Mundy township (Genesee)......	NA	NA	NA	NA	6,971	37	100.0	8.2	1.3	99.7	179	10.5	723	63	0.0
Muskegon city & MCD (Muskegon)	245	643	1,717	4,504	8,492	42	100.0	56.0	12.1	74.2	490	56.4	1,484	66	20.1
Muskegon charter township (Muskegon)	40	224	781	4,368	2,371	12	100.0	9.9	2.0	77.2	193	11.8	660	4	25.7
Muskegon Heights city & MCD (Muskegon)	240	2,239	630	5,877	0	0	0.0	10.3	5.5	54.2	279	16.2	1,508	39	15.3
New Baltimore city & MCD (Macomb)	8	64	57	459	5,748	21	71.4	12.8	1.9	98.0	480	11.4	923	147	25.6
Niles city	70	628	273	2,448	NA	NA	NA	12.3	3.4	73.4	305	28.0	2,505	28	6.0
Niles city (Berrien)	NA	NA	NA	NA	475	2	100.0	12.3	3.4	73.4	305	28.0	2,505	28	6.0
Niles township (Berrien)	NA	NA	NA	NA	5,195	25	80.0	5.1	1.3	98.9	140	6.6	476	2	0.7
Northview CDP	NA	NA	NA	NA	NA	NA	NA	NA	NA	NA	NA	NA	NA	NA	NA
Northville township (Wayne)	21	73	302	1,044	23,938	77	75.3	51.0	2.7	91.7	600	36.7	1,265	0	30.8
Norton Shores city & MCD (Muskegon)	37	151	695	2,828	2,873	10	100.0	29.4	4.8	98.4	485	26.0	1,063	129	2.7
Novi city & MCD (Oakland)......	43	71	532	881	34,874	190	100.0	70.4	10.4	97.0	593	71.4	1,191	312	23.4
Oakland charter township (Oakland)	4	21	30	154	26,737	128	34.4	12.6	1.5	97.7	420	14.5	757	82	3.9
Oak Park city & MCD (Oakland)	83	280	455	1,533	7,917	69	7.2	41.6	6.1	91.1	604	46.4	1,558	27	40.2
Oceola township (Livingston) ...	NA	NA	NA	NA	NA	NA	NA	4.4	1.0	100.0	79	5.8	402	16	1.8
Okemos CDP	NA	NA	NA	NA	NA	NA	NA	NA	NA	NA	NA	NA	NA	NA	NA
Orion charter township (Oakland)	20	55	200	553	1,818	16	6.3	27.0	3.3	94.6	282	36.6	939	59	5.1
Oshtemo charter township (Kalamazoo)	NA	NA	NA	NA	21,104	84	83.3	6.3	2.0	99.0	43	9.6	416	37	0.0
Owosso city & MCD (Shiawassee)	76	526	169	1,169	1,339	13	84.6	21.9	5.7	91.7	287	19.3	1,329	214	12.3
Oxford charter township (Oakland)	12	63	81	423	13,105	49	100.0	15.7	1.5	96.6	381	16.9	749	30	11.4
Park township (Ottawa)	NA	NA	NA	NA	19,139	64	84.4	6.8	1.5	100.0	239	13.1	699	170	0.0
Pittsfield charter township (Washtenaw)	76	193	582	1,480	42,835	208	53.8	33.8	3.6	86.4	355	20.5	530	11	9.3
Plainfield charter township (Kent)	NA	NA	NA	NA	34,613	140	77.9	14.9	3.0	94.2	180	26.3	778	267	19.3
Plymouth charter township (Wayne)	24	89	165	610	6,990	23	56.5	19.6	4.8	50.4	318	20.4	752	17	8.6
Pontiac city & MCD (Oakland)..	799	1,336	1,286	2,150	429	3	100.0	52.2	16.9	93.5	463	48.1	800	73	22.5
Portage city & MCD (Kalamazoo)	117	238	1,442	2,932	28,229	193	38.9	57.0	11.9	96.2	493	51.9	1,063	181	67.5
Port Huron city & MCD (St. Clair)	230	796	746	2,581	527	4	100.0	62.9	20.0	45.2	653	54.1	1,865	144	89.3
Port Huron charter township (St. Clair)	NA	NA	NA	NA	1,555	8	100.0	7.0	1.9	95.2	246	11.8	1,141	42	3.0
Redford charter township (Wayne)	302	644	1,044	2,226	643	4	100.0	50.2	8.1	82.5	523	44.4	943	17	23.2
Riverview city & MCD (Wayne).	14	116	116	962	1,049	5	100.0	26.2	3.0	94.7	550	29.4	2,424	121	14.4
Rochester city & MCD (Oakland)	8	61	48	367	3,886	10	70.0	21.9	2.9	94.4	708	23.8	1,818	24	15.9
Rochester Hills city & MCD (Oakland)	53	71	442	592	38,956	83	100.0	80.4	15.2	77.0	459	78.4	1,053	57	28.1
Romulus city & MCD (Wayne)..	190	812	532	2,275	3,076	32	100.0	46.1	8.9	75.5	714	42.3	1,801	191	38.9
Roseville city & MCD (Macomb)	187	394	1,528	3,215	380	6	100.0	55.0	12.7	90.4	470	52.2	1,099	83	12.0
Royal Oak city & MCD (Oakland)	56	94	481	810	39,713	137	100.0	107.6	13.0	81.4	869	108.0	1,819	331	221.1
Saginaw city & MCD (Saginaw)	783	1,621	886	1,834	1,191	7	71.4	83.1	31.9	44.3	435	92.3	1,896	114	62.8
Saginaw charter township (Saginaw)	79	202	796	2,031	8,702	59	49.2	30.4	3.5	98.4	291	34.2	867	15	7.7
St. Clair Shores city & MCD (Macomb)	132	221	591	991	5,128	30	100.0	79.2	13.6	80.9	569	80.7	1,353	243	24.1
St. Joseph charter township (Berrien)	7	72	88	900	2,981	8	100.0	5.9	0.8	100.0	351	5.3	539	10	0.3
Sault Ste. Marie city & MCD (Chippewa)	30	221	225	1,660	10,290	67	0.0	29.9	6.7	59.5	563	25.2	1,852	198	43.2

1 Data for serious crimes have not been adjusted for underreporting. This may affect comparability between geographic areas over time.
2 Per 100,000 population estimated by the FBI. 3 Based on population estimated as of July 1 of the year shown.

Table B. Incorporated Places, Census Designated Places (CDPs), and Minor Civil Divisions (MCDs) of 10,000 or More Population — Land Area, Population, and Households, and Employment

STATE City, town, township, borough, or CDP (county if applicable)	Land area 2010 (sq mi)	Population Total persons 2010	Population Total persons 2019	Population Percent change 2010–2019	Population Persons per square mile, 2019	Population characteristics 2015–2019 Percent foreign born	Population characteristics 2015–2019 Percent living in the same house as previous year	Income and poverty 2015–2019 Median household income	Income and poverty 2015–2019 Percent of households with income below poverty level	Median value of owner-occupied housing units	Employment, 2015–2019 Percent in civilian labor force	Employment, 2015–2019 Unemploy-ment rate	Households, 2015–2019 (percent of households) Family households	Households, 2015–2019 (percent of households) One person households
	1	2	3	4	5	6	7	8	9	10	11	12	13	14
MICHIGAN—Con.														
Scio township (Washtenaw)	32.01	16,442	17,921	9.0	559.9	15.0	82.7	123,906	3.2	385,400	66.6	2.0	74.7	18.3
Shelby charter township (Macomb).............................	34.39	73,832	80,628	9.2	2344.5	13.9	86.8	76,380	6.3	249,200	63.3	4.4	70.3	25.1
Southfield city & MCD (Oakland)............................	26.26	71,715	72,689	1.4	2768.1	7.6	84.7	55,705	11.5	155,700	61.0	6.9	52.9	41.3
Southfield township (Oakland)..	8.06	14,545	14,759	1.5	1831.1	8.4	91.3	138,309	3.0	412,500	63.7	2.7	73.8	23.8
Southgate city & MCD (Wayne)	6.88	30,047	28,959	-3.6	4209.2	7.7	85.8	57,133	9.6	112,300	63.2	5.7	57.2	36.6
South Lyon city & MCD (Oakland)............................	3.74	11,315	11,821	4.5	3160.7	5.9	88.0	73,200	8.6	192,100	69.4	3.2	62.2	32.6
Springfield charter township (Oakland)............................	35.41	13,940	14,489	3.9	409.2	3.6	86.0	93,252	6.0	272,900	65.4	5.7	77.5	18.4
Spring Lake township (Ottawa).	16.51	14,303	15,100	5.6	914.6	2.6	85.5	67,598	6.6	219,800	62.5	3.6	67.0	26.8
Sterling Heights city & MCD (Macomb).............................	36.43	129,675	132,438	2.1	3635.4	27.1	88.8	64,833	10.4	187,600	62.1	4.1	69.1	26.2
Sturgis city & MCD (St. Joseph).............................	6.74	11,139	10,861	-2.5	1611.4	9.8	86.8	41,630	20.8	84,900	63.5	6.7	66.0	27.1
Summit township (Jackson)......	29.14	22,626	22,518	-0.5	772.8	2.7	88.7	60,810	9.6	135,500	57.9	3.5	67.1	30.0
Superior charter township (Washtenaw)......................	35.22	13,060	14,287	9.4	405.7	8.4	86.4	69,688	12.4	201,800	65.2	5.5	71.3	24.0
Taylor city & MCD (Wayne).......	23.61	63,131	60,922	-3.5	2580.3	4.0	87.3	50,053	15.0	96,300	61.4	7.7	64.5	28.5
Texas charter township (Kalamazoo).......................	34.75	14,694	17,250	17.4	496.4	8.1	87.2	114,056	4.7	293,100	67.5	2.2	85.9	11.8
Thomas township (Saginaw)	30.84	11,985	11,465	-4.3	371.8	1.6	93.3	65,758	6.1	145,700	57.7	1.9	69.8	27.3
Traverse City city	8.33	14,731	15,788	6.8	1889.3	2.8	81.5	57,076	12.8	266,100	64.1	4.6	53.7	37.8
Traverse City city (Grand Traverse)	7.97	14,540	15,547	6.9	1950.7	2.8	81.4	56,948	12.8	263,800	64.2	4.7	53.6	38.1
Trenton city & MCD (Wayne)	7.24	18,853	18,157	-3.7	2507.9	4.0	93.3	67,294	7.9	150,800	58.1	3.1	61.7	34.8
Troy city & MCD (Oakland).......	33.45	80,972	84,090	3.9	2514.0	29.0	89.3	101,882	6.0	301,500	63.6	3.5	72.6	23.8
Tyrone township (Livingston)	35.46	10,019	10,562	5.4	297.9	1.7	89.2	100,444	3.8	274,300	64.2	6.4	79.3	16.8
Union charter township (Isabella)............................	28.17	12,911	13,701	6.1	486.4	3.1	56.6	31,544	38.6	140,200	66.7	5.7	42.9	29.4
Van Buren charter township (Wayne).............................	34.01	28,823	28,396	-1.5	834.9	4.8	85.5	60,191	10.0	168,600	67.9	4.6	59.2	34.5
Vienna charter township (Genesee)............................	34.99	13,255	12,626	-4.7	360.8	1.2	88.1	55,487	9.9	130,900	56.7	6.4	68.6	23.9
Walker city & MCD (Kent)........	24.58	23,545	24,869	5.6	1011.8	3.8	85.1	65,170	8.1	174,700	70.7	2.9	63.2	29.7
Warren city & MCD (Macomb)..	34.36	134,070	133,943	-0.1	3898.2	14.2	87.1	49,619	15.1	122,300	61.1	7.7	63.8	31.0
Washington township (Macomb).............................	35.58	25,154	28,651	13.9	805.3	7.7	89.0	89,447	6.3	295,900	63.4	4.3	73.5	23.1
Waterford charter township (Oakland)............................	30.62	71,688	72,631	1.3	2372.0	6.7	88.6	62,321	9.4	165,000	66.8	4.5	60.3	32.0
Waverly CDP	9.07	23,925	NA	NA	NA	9.8	79.5	63,362	8.0	164,100	66.0	5.2	54.9	38.3
Wayne city & MCD (Wayne)	6.02	17,593	16,814	-4.4	2793.0	3.0	83.8	46,875	18.7	85,100	61.8	6.6	64.8	30.8
West Bloomfield charter township (Oakland)	26.95	64,676	65,610	1.4	2434.5	21.9	91.1	104,368	5.0	310,600	62.9	4.4	74.2	22.3
Westland city & MCD (Wayne) .	20.43	84,150	81,511	-3.1	3989.8	8.9	86.6	50,710	13.0	121,100	64.5	5.4	55.0	38.6
White Lake charter township (Oakland)............................	33.40	30,019	31,356	4.5	938.8	4.0	89.2	85,384	6.2	241,200	66.6	4.0	73.8	20.0
Wixom city & MCD (Oakland)...	9.15	13,505	14,049	4.0	1535.4	15.3	88.6	53,259	9.4	249,300	76.3	2.1	55.6	40.0
Woodhaven city & MCD (Wayne).............................	6.39	12,879	12,469	-3.2	1951.3	7.4	92.0	64,501	5.5	159,800	61.1	7.4	62.9	32.4
Wyandotte city & MCD (Wayne).............................	5.29	25,883	24,859	-4.0	4699.2	2.6	88.8	54,462	13.4	109,300	63.4	6.2	57.0	36.7
Wyoming city & MCD (Kent)	24.63	72,117	75,667	4.9	3072.1	12.4	83.4	54,328	10.7	127,700	71.5	4.5	66.4	25.2
Ypsilanti city & MCD (Washtenaw)......................	4.23	19,569	20,171	3.1	4768.6	7.2	61.3	39,332	28.4	151,300	70.0	8.5	34.8	38.7
Ypsilanti charter township (Washtenaw)......................	30.03	53,362	55,216	3.5	1838.7	9.0	79.1	54,232	14.4	155,600	69.9	5.7	58.9	31.3
Zeeland charter township (Ottawa).............................	34.38	9,971	11,564	16.0	336.4	6.6	90.2	78,833	3.5	198,400	70.1	4.0	74.3	22.5
MINNESOTA..........................	79625.88	5,303,927	5,639,632	6.3	70.8	8.5	85.9	71,306	9.5	223,900	69.6	3.6	64.1	28.5
Albert Lea city & MCD (Freeborn)...........................	13.27	18,203	17,656	-3.0	1330.5	7.5	86.0	47,508	13.8	97,100	61.3	4.6	60.9	32.8
Alexandria city & MCD (Douglas)............................	17.21	12,508	13,822	10.5	803.1	2.4	80.0	52,984	11.0	177,100	64.6	1.8	51.8	41.5
Andover city & MCD (Anoka)....	33.89	30,588	33,140	8.3	977.9	3.9	90.9	109,930	3.3	289,500	74.3	2.3	82.8	13.1
Anoka city & MCD (Anoka).......	6.66	17,149	17,549	2.3	2635.0	6.3	87.2	58,576	8.4	203,100	63.9	4.4	60.4	33.5
Apple Valley city & MCD (Dakota)..............................	16.96	49,092	55,135	12.3	3250.9	11.9	86.3	89,251	5.1	258,000	73.0	3.2	71.6	23.7
Arden Hills city & MCD (Ramsey).............................	8.46	9,552	10,281	7.6	1215.2	6.4	80.5	91,250	3.4	292,900	64.0	5.3	71.6	24.0
Austin city & MCD (Mower).......	13.06	24,909	25,233	1.3	1932.1	17.0	78.9	48,127	13.6	107,800	63.5	4.5	60.3	33.7
Bemidji city & MCD (Beltrami) ..	14.55	14,248	15,434	8.3	1060.8	1.4	71.4	32,193	29.8	139,900	58.8	6.3	46.6	43.5
Big Lake city & MCD (Sherburne)..........................	7.04	10,085	11,226	11.3	1594.6	4.4	85.4	80,889	6.2	193,000	77.5	0.9	76.3	15.7
Blaine city & MCD (Anoka).......	32.91	57,179	65,607	14.7	1993.5	12.2	89.1	84,933	5.7	230,900	72.7	3.6	73.3	21.7
Bloomington city	34.70	82,893	84,943	2.5	2447.9	14.1	86.0	75,130	6.7	251,300	69.5	3.4	60.2	32.5
Brainerd city & MCD (Crow Wing)...............................	12.16	13,587	13,434	-1.1	1104.8	1.9	80.4	34,371	19.0	117,900	63.4	3.2	48.9	41.3
Brooklyn Center city	8.00	30,180	30,690	1.7	3836.3	23.8	86.7	59,550	13.4	172,800	74.4	5.4	66.5	26.3
Brooklyn Park city	26.08	75,776	80,389	6.1	3082.4	23.0	90.7	73,940	8.4	224,300	72.9	3.7	71.8	24.1
Buffalo city & MCD (Wright)......	7.50	15,471	16,442	6.3	2192.3	1.8	88.0	73,955	8.7	203,700	71.9	5.0	68.7	25.5
Burnsville city & MCD (Dakota)	24.83	60,286	61,339	1.7	2470.4	14.4	84.4	73,529	7.1	247,500	73.2	4.7	65.7	26.9
Champlin city...........................	8.15	23,097	25,268	9.4	3100.4	8.1	92.9	92,858	5.6	237,800	77.2	2.5	74.0	22.1

Table B.   Incorporated Places, Census Designated Places (CDPs), and Minor Civil Divisions (MCDs) of 10,000 or More Population — **Crime, Residential Construction and Local Government Finance**

STATE City, town, township, borough, or CDP (county if applicable)	Serious crimes known to police, 2018[1] Violent crime Number	Rate[2]	Property crime Number	Rate[2]	New residential construction authorized by building permits, 2019 Value ($1,000)	Number of housing units	Percent single family	Local government finance, 2017 General revenue Total (mil dol)	Intergovernmental Total (mil dol)	Percent from state gov.	Taxes per capita[3]	General expenditure Total (mil dol)	Per capita[3] Total	Capital outlays	Debt outstanding (mil dol)
	15	16	17	18	19	20	21	22	23	24	25	26	27	28	29
MICHIGAN—Con.															
Scio township (Washtenaw)	NA	NA	NA	NA	NA	NA	NA	12.6	1.5	89.9	275	19.7	1,123	77	16.7
Shelby charter township (Macomb)............	119	149	500	626	132,701	625	35.0	66.0	7.1	92.0	390	55.2	697	28	26.6
Southfield city & MCD (Oakland)............	204	278	1,509	2,055	6,075	17	100.0	104.3	23.0	61.3	878	113.2	1,542	265	76.0
Southfield township (Oakland)..	NA	NA	NA	NA	3,118	2	100.0	0.7	0.0	100.0	42	0.7	45	0	0.0
Southgate city & MCD (Wayne)	46	159	789	2,725	41,141	178	1.1	34.4	6.4	87.3	563	34.0	1,168	3	14.8
South Lyon city & MCD (Oakland)............	12	102	40	339	14,609	56	78.6	8.6	1.9	90.9	440	10.4	881	34	11.4
Springfield charter township (Oakland)............	11	76	54	374	6,437	30	100.0	7.0	1.4	81.5	302	8.0	556	15	2.5
Spring Lake township (Ottawa).	NA	NA	NA	NA	18,154	58	100.0	7.1	1.4	97.8	136	11.8	787	274	11.4
Sterling Heights city & MCD (Macomb)............	240	180	1,334	1,003	51,380	214	80.4	152.6	36.8	75.4	486	172.6	1,301	207	147.8
Sturgis city & MCD (St. Joseph)............	61	565	259	2,399	557	3	100.0	17.3	3.9	81.0	356	38.8	3,561	54	24.0
Summit township (Jackson)......	NA	NA	NA	NA	4,648	14	100.0	6.9	1.9	100.0	82	10.2	453	11	2.1
Superior charter township (Washtenaw)............	NA	NA	NA	NA	25,961	112	100.0	8.5	1.7	79.8	256	12.3	876	8	3.0
Taylor city & MCD (Wayne).......	366	600	1,346	2,205	5,383	21	100.0	104.3	25.8	54.6	707	100.5	1,637	20	67.1
Texas charter township (Kalamazoo)............	NA	NA	NA	NA	21,456	62	100.0	4.0	1.2	100.0	89	5.1	303	59	0.0
Thomas township (Saginaw)	8	70	68	592	4,807	14	100.0	12.2	1.4	99.6	186	9.5	824	53	0.2
Traverse City city	74	473	253	1,619	NA	NA	NA	39.5	7.4	51.4	848	37.2	2,396	157	15.0
Traverse City city (Grand Traverse)............	NA	NA	NA	NA	NA	NA	NA	NA	NA	NA	NA	NA	NA	NA	NA
Trenton city & MCD (Wayne) ...	22	121	104	572	930	2	100.0	44.5	5.4	93.3	924	33.4	1,827	74	32.7
Troy city & MCD (Oakland)	52	62	1,157	1,374	24,976	92	100.0	103.7	17.4	88.7	625	102.4	1,217	230	34.5
Tyrone township (Livingston)	NA	NA	NA	NA	NA	NA	NA	3.2	0.8	100.0	62	2.9	278	0	18.8
Union charter township (Isabella)	NA	NA	NA	NA	1,516	8	50.0	6.1	1.1	100.0	154	8.1	591	8	15.8
Van Buren charter township (Wayne)............	86	305	540	1,914	17,658	70	90.0	20.8	2.7	94.4	259	25.9	914	41	69.1
Vienna charter township (Genesee)............	NA	NA	NA	NA	4,690	10	100.0	6.1	1.4	78.2	173	6.2	487	0	2.0
Walker city & MCD (Kent).........	63	252	522	2,087	28,572	243	18.1	24.1	4.8	88.3	622	23.8	958	137	4.5
Warren city & MCD (Macomb)..	688	509	2,808	2,078	18,294	136	31.6	191.1	49.0	89.8	721	167.7	1,241	94	189.7
Washington township (Macomb)............	NA	NA	NA	NA	200	1	100.0	17.7	2.3	99.9	292	21.8	783	60	23.6
Waterford charter township (Oakland)............	146	200	750	1,027	9,820	84	60.7	67.6	8.8	88.1	335	80.1	1,094	77	39.2
Waverly CDP	NA	NA	NA	NA	NA	NA	NA	NA	NA	NA	NA	NA	NA	NA	NA
Wayne city & MCD (Wayne)	132	783	266	1,578	95	1	100.0	40.9	5.1	73.9	58	30.5	1,794	28	25.2
West Bloomfield charter township (Oakland)	38	58	386	586	45,557	239	19.7	64.6	5.8	92.3	508	60.6	917	22	60.3
Westland city & MCD (Wayne) .	316	388	1,234	1,515	7,545	58	100.0	103.2	26.6	62.0	412	105.4	1,286	27	34.5
White Lake charter township (Oakland)............	13	42	266	852	26,690	193	37.3	18.9	2.6	94.0	301	16.3	523	12	4.2
Wixom city & MCD (Oakland)...	26	187	169	1,218	18,054	76	96.1	20.8	4.5	97.5	718	18.3	1,319	0	8.8
Woodhaven city & MCD (Wayne)............	12	97	117	941	1,130	8	25.0	23.5	3.2	95.0	930	26.4	2,105	0	10.0
Wyandotte city & MCD (Wayne)............	61	245	397	1,597	2,149	9	100.0	45.2	6.3	91.7	651	97.8	3,905	135	83.9
Wyoming city & MCD (Kent)	350	458	1,477	1,931	60,640	609	12.3	74.2	23.3	56.0	370	69.7	916	46	69.6
Ypsilanti city & MCD (Washtenaw)............	186	873	612	2,874	309	4	100.0	24.4	6.3	80.1	555	19.8	938	74	34.2
Ypsilanti charter township (Washtenaw)............	NA	NA	NA	NA	21,922	121	40.5	29.4	4.9	99.7	317	34.0	614	20	16.2
Zeeland charter township (Ottawa)	NA	NA	NA	NA	11,208	39	100.0	4.2	0.8	97.5	257	4.4	401	0	2.9
MINNESOTA............	12,369	220	111,874	1,994	6,147,907	28,586	48.0	X	X	X	X	X	X	X	X
Albert Lea city & MCD (Freeborn)............	26	147	466	2,640	1,509	5	100.0	26.3	7.9	76.5	454	29.2	1,636	529	22.5
Alexandria city & MCD (Douglas)............	51	371	390	2,835	12,581	54	100.0	16.4	5.3	49.8	536	25.2	1,853	900	36.6
Andover city & MCD (Anoka)....	NA	NA	NA	NA	37,259	116	100.0	22.2	1.6	87.0	382	17.8	542	121	27.6
Anoka city & MCD (Anoka).......	27	154	393	2,236	183	1	100.0	21.8	2.2	96.1	497	27.3	1,564	486	17.3
Apple Valley city & MCD (Dakota)............	63	119	956	1,806	9,899	29	100.0	55.9	2.7	74.9	525	43.1	823	188	42.3
Arden Hills city & MCD (Ramsey)............	NA	NA	NA	NA	1,500	3	100.0	8.6	0.4	94.5	387	9.2	887	143	0.0
Austin city & MCD (Mower).......	66	265	544	2,182	18,886	96	14.6	34.6	14.2	84.4	314	40.2	1,602	440	50.1
Bemidji city & MCD (Beltrami) ..	79	509	1,094	7,045	2,247	21	100.0	26.5	5.9	94.1	419	31.5	2,052	451	62.6
Big Lake city & MCD (Sherburne)............	11	100	53	480	21,385	115	67.0	12.0	1.0	36.0	502	9.0	821	173	42.7
Blaine city & MCD (Anoka).......	64	98	1,705	2,597	108,458	441	68.0	48.3	3.4	78.6	403	50.4	784	185	45.2
Bloomington city	165	191	2,592	3,004	NA	NA	NA	152.9	20.6	44.3	912	163.4	1,909	388	72.4
Brainerd city & MCD (Crow Wing)............	61	455	453	3,380	7,250	37	94.6	25.8	10.0	58.2	593	23.2	1,732	602	32.0
Brooklyn Center city	117	376	1,065	3,421	624	3	100.0	48.4	4.0	67.7	721	47.5	1,534	276	99.2
Brooklyn Park city	302	372	2,465	3,033	26,448	99	100.0	82.7	7.8	71.6	610	73.2	911	183	70.8
Buffalo city & MCD (Wright)......	17	104	317	1,944	34,327	200	24.0	21.9	1.7	83.0	425	21.3	1,315	319	160.9
Burnsville city & MCD (Dakota)	114	185	1,613	2,619	75,492	552	3.1	66.5	5.2	55.4	580	63.9	1,040	278	66.2
Champlin city	26	103	234	925	11,915	43	100.0	23.5	2.0	96.9	423	23.9	959	230	40.7

1   Data for serious crimes have not been adjusted for underreporting. This may affect comparability between geographic areas over time.
2   Per 100,000 population estimated by the FBI.   3   Based on population estimated as of July 1 of the year shown.

Table B. Incorporated Places, Census Designated Places (CDPs), and Minor Civil Divisions (MCDs) of 10,000 or More Population — Land Area, Population, and Households, and Employment

STATE City, town, township, borough, or CDP (county if applicable)	Land area 2010 (sq mi)	Population Total persons 2010	Total persons 2019	Percent change 2010–2019	Persons per square mile 2019	Population characteristics 2015–2019 Percent foreign born	Percent living in the same house as previous year	Income and poverty 2015–2019 Median household income	Percent of households with income below poverty level	Median value of owner-occupied housing units	Employment, 2015–2019 Percent in civilian labor force	Unemployment rate	Households, 2015–2019 (percent of households) Family households	One person households
	1	2	3	4	5	6	7	8	9	10	11	12	13	14
MINNESOTA—Con.														
Chanhassen city & MCD (Carver)	20.39	22,929	26,389	15.1	1294.2	7.0	88.8	124,125	3.9	381,300	74.6	1.8	76.2	19.2
Chaska city & MCD (Carver)	17.01	23,865	26,989	13.1	1586.7	7.4	86.1	85,143	5.5	266,200	76.3	2.0	68.2	24.7
Cloquet city & MCD (Carlton)	35.21	12,130	12,009	-1.0	341.1	1.7	90.0	54,065	11.9	142,700	67.3	4.8	64.7	27.2
Columbia Heights city & MCD (Anoka)	3.39	19,480	20,427	4.9	6025.7	18.9	83.9	57,882	10.6	177,300	68.5	5.7	55.5	35.8
Coon Rapids city & MCD (Anoka)	22.61	61,485	62,998	2.5	2786.3	9.2	86.9	71,267	5.7	204,700	71.2	4.0	65.6	27.0
Cottage Grove city & MCD (Washington)	33.64	34,601	37,604	8.7	1117.8	6.7	92.5	102,039	2.4	249,800	74.5	1.8	80.0	16.2
Crystal city	5.79	22,103	22,899	3.6	3954.9	12.2	89.1	67,342	6.7	197,300	74.3	3.9	58.5	33.7
Duluth city & MCD (St. Louis)	71.65	86,266	85,618	-0.8	1194.9	3.5	76.0	52,463	17.3	163,300	66.7	4.4	50.0	36.2
Eagan city & MCD (Dakota)	31.19	64,150	66,372	3.5	2128.0	14.4	87.2	90,515	5.8	288,200	75.6	4.2	66.8	25.4
East Bethel city & MCD (Anoka)	44.58	11,591	12,038	3.9	270.0	1.9	92.7	93,375	2.9	251,100	75.5	2.9	77.6	15.1
Eden Prairie city	32.52	60,797	64,893	6.7	1995.5	17.1	84.7	111,981	4.9	368,100	72.6	3.1	71.4	23.1
Edina city	15.46	47,980	52,857	10.2	3419.0	11.8	87.7	104,244	6.2	476,300	64.8	3.1	64.0	31.3
Elk River city & MCD (Sherburne)	42.34	22,960	25,213	9.8	595.5	5.6	84.8	89,596	5.5	241,400	72.9	4.5	73.3	19.2
Fairmont city & MCD (Martin)	15.02	10,669	10,030	-6.0	667.8	2.0	84.7	47,876	17.9	123,700	62.8	5.4	57.8	36.5
Faribault city & MCD (Rice)	15.17	23,344	23,897	2.4	1575.3	14.3	86.6	50,702	14.6	153,500	57.1	5.2	61.5	33.1
Farmington city & MCD (Dakota)	14.62	21,084	23,091	9.5	1579.4	3.1	86.8	95,331	2.9	254,200	79.2	1.8	73.7	20.1
Fergus Falls city & MCD (Otter Tail)	14.43	13,450	13,794	2.6	955.9	2.4	83.0	43,528	12.1	132,300	62.2	2.8	53.9	40.0
Forest Lake city & MCD (Washington)	30.54	18,405	20,933	13.7	685.4	3.8	88.7	79,840	7.4	272,200	72.7	2.9	71.5	22.4
Fridley city & MCD (Anoka)	10.17	27,222	27,826	2.2	2736.1	18.4	84.2	63,836	8.5	198,200	70.2	4.1	62.3	30.6
Golden Valley city	10.20	20,357	21,886	7.5	2145.7	8.5	86.4	98,058	6.3	304,700	66.0	2.2	58.6	34.1
Grand Rapids city & MCD (Itasca)	22.57	10,869	11,214	3.2	496.9	0.6	86.4	48,287	16.8	151,300	59.4	2.6	57.6	37.4
Ham Lake city & MCD (Anoka)	34.42	15,296	16,783	9.7	487.6	4.3	95.4	103,655	3.9	306,700	70.8	2.7	80.2	15.9
Hastings city & MCD (Dakota)	10.29	22,220	22,886	3.0	2224.1	1.6	83.4	71,264	7.6	214,900	68.5	2.5	63.6	29.4
Hibbing city & MCD (St. Louis)	181.97	16,358	15,855	-3.1	87.1	4.0	86.5	49,009	15.5	109,800	57.4	4.9	61.6	34.7
Hopkins city	4.07	17,584	18,468	5.0	4537.6	19.9	81.0	56,390	8.1	227,500	75.2	3.1	43.4	47.4
Hugo city & MCD (Washington)	33.46	13,332	15,267	14.5	456.3	2.4	88.2	89,969	2.8	259,300	75.1	1.8	70.7	21.1
Hutchinson city & MCD (McLeod)	8.48	14,173	13,983	-1.3	1648.9	2.6	84.6	57,672	8.7	149,200	69.5	3.6	55.0	35.3
Inver Grove Heights city & MCD (Dakota)	27.86	33,986	35,672	5.0	1280.4	10.5	85.4	78,347	6.5	254,500	69.1	4.3	64.3	27.9
Lakeville city & MCD (Dakota)	36.32	56,001	67,317	20.2	1853.4	8.8	88.6	110,212	4.3	311,100	77.3	2.8	79.3	16.9
Lino Lakes city & MCD (Anoka)	28.22	20,219	22,119	9.4	783.8	3.2	89.1	115,368	2.4	293,100	71.8	1.9	82.5	14.5
Little Canada city & MCD (Ramsey)	3.90	9,777	10,501	7.4	2692.6	13.9	82.0	52,842	14.4	242,500	66.1	3.9	50.5	41.4
Mankato city & MCD (Blue Earth)	19.08	39,847	42,931	7.7	2250.1	7.4	73.3	47,924	22.2	179,400	71.7	4.2	48.0	29.9
Maple Grove city	32.57	61,548	72,622	18.0	2229.7	10.0	90.3	109,557	2.8	293,400	73.8	2.7	72.9	22.5
Maplewood city & MCD (Ramsey)	17.04	38,016	40,885	7.5	2399.4	13.0	86.1	70,484	7.6	217,300	67.3	4.3	65.1	26.8
Marshall city & MCD (Lyon)	10.22	13,691	13,487	-1.5	1319.7	13.0	79.8	48,958	18.6	154,100	69.2	3.7	60.6	32.0
Mendota Heights city & MCD (Dakota)	9.08	11,072	11,343	2.4	1249.2	3.7	89.7	121,214	5.8	392,600	63.2	2.4	69.6	27.0
Minneapolis city	54.00	382,603	429,606	12.3	7955.7	15.6	76.7	62,583	16.5	251,600	74.4	5.1	44.5	40.4
Minnetonka city	26.91	49,735	54,064	8.7	2009.1	11.5	84.9	95,630	5.3	347,900	68.7	3.0	60.2	31.9
Monticello city & MCD (Wright)	8.76	12,793	13,824	8.1	1578.1	5.3	86.7	70,394	7.2	199,900	72.6	3.7	64.9	25.5
Moorhead city & MCD (Clay)	22.27	39,437	43,652	10.7	1960.1	6.7	79.3	60,315	15.4	194,600	71.2	3.3	58.5	31.8
Mounds View city & MCD (Ramsey)	4.06	12,155	13,324	9.6	3281.8	10.5	86.6	67,402	8.0	206,700	72.0	5.0	64.3	28.7
New Brighton city & MCD (Ramsey)	6.50	21,390	22,753	6.4	3500.5	14.9	86.0	74,644	8.5	256,600	70.0	4.4	66.3	26.4
New Hope city	5.06	20,329	20,907	2.8	4131.8	14.5	84.6	60,675	10.0	225,100	66.1	3.7	62.6	31.3
New Ulm city & MCD (Brown)	10.14	13,524	13,212	-2.3	1303.0	2.7	88.3	61,597	8.3	141,300	69.8	1.7	62.3	30.7
North Branch city & MCD (Chisago)	35.60	10,125	10,767	6.3	302.4	1.3	85.1	79,826	8.8	191,400	71.4	3.8	67.9	24.8
Northfield city	8.50	20,017	20,742	3.6	2440.2	7.5	79.9	70,148	9.9	226,000	70.3	3.7	60.9	32.4
Northfield city (Rice)	7.04	18,870	19,536	3.5	2775.0	7.8	79.2	67,640	10.5	219,700	70.7	3.8	60.1	33.2
North Mankato city & MCD (Nicollet)	6.24	13,403	13,948	4.1	2235.3	3.4	85.6	67,278	9.0	193,400	74.0	4.0	63.9	30.8
North St. Paul city & MCD (Ramsey)	2.85	11,460	12,506	9.1	4388.1	7.4	90.9	64,722	9.8	206,100	68.0	4.5	61.8	33.1
Oakdale city & MCD (Washington)	10.96	27,364	27,933	2.1	2548.6	8.1	88.1	72,511	6.4	227,700	71.0	3.8	64.0	31.6
Otsego city & MCD (Wright)	29.61	13,571	18,113	33.5	611.7	3.4	93.2	105,290	3.7	261,600	79.1	1.7	80.3	11.9
Owatonna city & MCD (Steele)	14.54	25,622	25,704	0.3	1767.8	5.8	84.2	62,642	10.5	166,600	68.9	3.8	63.9	31.4
Plymouth city	32.71	70,591	79,768	13.0	2438.6	13.4	84.2	105,958	3.8	351,700	71.9	2.5	68.4	24.8
Prior Lake city & MCD (Scott)	15.90	22,997	27,241	18.5	1713.3	6.2	89.5	109,604	5.2	322,400	72.1	2.8	72.9	22.7
Ramsey city & MCD (Anoka)	28.85	23,683	27,721	17.1	960.9	6.2	89.3	95,014	3.6	251,900	76.7	2.7	78.1	16.6
Red Wing city & MCD (Goodhue)	34.86	16,457	16,320	-0.8	468.2	3.7	80.7	54,785	13.5	174,000	62.6	5.0	61.0	32.1
Richfield city	6.72	35,094	36,354	3.6	5409.8	16.7	85.0	66,908	9.0	225,200	72.9	3.4	54.6	35.2
Robbinsdale city	2.80	13,953	14,389	3.1	5138.9	6.8	88.7	70,348	8.9	201,100	73.0	3.4	53.1	38.0
Rochester city & MCD (Olmsted)	55.20	106,823	118,935	11.3	2154.6	14.1	83.6	73,106	9.8	200,100	70.7	3.5	61.3	31.0
Rogers city	25.41	11,197	13,490	20.5	530.9	7.7	92.1	127,629	3.2	331,200	74.0	2.4	81.8	13.1
Rosemount city & MCD (Dakota)	33.26	21,881	25,207	15.2	757.9	7.6	91.5	104,743	3.1	279,000	79.3	2.6	77.8	18.0
Roseville city & MCD (Ramsey)	13.02	33,661	36,457	8.3	2800.1	12.4	84.3	71,180	8.8	254,200	65.2	3.7	55.5	38.0

Table B. Incorporated Places, Census Designated Places (CDPs), and Minor Civil Divisions (MCDs) of 10,000 or More Population — Crime, Residential Construction and Local Government Finance

STATE City, town, township, borough, or CDP (county if applicable)	Serious crimes known to police, 2018[1] — Violent crime Number	Violent crime Rate[2]	Property crime Number	Property crime Rate[2]	New residential construction authorized by building permits, 2019 — Value ($1,000)	Number of housing units	Percent single family	Local government finance, 2017 — General revenue Total (mil dol)	Intergovernmental Total (mil dol)	Percent from state gov.	Taxes per capita[3]	General expenditure Total (mil dol)	Per capita[3] Total	Capital outlays	Debt outstanding (mil dol)
	15	16	17	18	19	20	21	22	23	24	25	26	27	28	29
MINNESOTA—Con.															
Chanhassen city & MCD (Carver).............	NA	NA	NA	NA	30,284	59	100.0	19.2	1.0	57.8	469	19.3	755	117	29.0
Chaska city & MCD (Carver)....	21	78	227	842	31,603	113	100.0	34.7	2.9	77.1	483	40.1	1,511	289	108.3
Cloquet city & MCD (Carlton)...	12	101	181	1,520	10,929	77	7.8	12.8	3.9	98.2	337	14.9	1,248	544	71.1
Columbia Heights city & MCD (Anoka).............	57	270	504	2,387	809	3	100.0	23.1	4.1	76.0	580	27.9	1,384	456	27.6
Coon Rapids city & MCD (Anoka).............	83	132	1,322	2,105	4,666	17	100.0	59.4	5.6	83.0	502	68.6	1,099	321	95.9
Cottage Grove city & MCD (Washington).................	25	67	546	1,472	81,003	293	100.0	31.0	4.2	64.3	441	0.0	0	0	46.2
Crystal city.......................	34	146	487	2,089	1,338	6	100.0	23.8	3.1	97.1	451	26.9	1,166	370	45.6
Duluth city & MCD (St. Louis)...	308	358	3,688	4,286	76,726	440	15.9	223.9	79.1	70.4	742	227.7	2,649	727	263.8
Eagan city & MCD (Dakota)	59	88	1,289	1,924	14,487	35	100.0	63.3	4.9	87.1	520	67.4	1,013	278	64.0
East Bethel city & MCD (Anoka).............	NA	NA	NA	NA	5,877	27	100.0	7.0	0.4	78.0	505	6.8	570	170	19.7
Eden Prairie city	39	60	873	1,345	78,027	352	4.5	64.0	2.4	59.2	632	74.1	1,154	259	83.0
Edina city	23	44	803	1,528	63,932	162	40.7	70.6	6.1	97.2	761	73.5	1,419	407	135.3
Elk River city & MCD (Sherburne).............	29	117	429	1,735	27,572	125	93.6	31.6	2.2	97.6	547	32.9	1,342	736	69.9
Fairmont city & MCD (Martin)...	12	119	244	2,427	898	3	100.0	10.9	3.8	89.9	381	13.7	1,355	111	50.4
Faribault city & MCD (Rice)......	77	323	423	1,777	7,802	61	27.9	28.0	6.9	87.6	452	24.4	1,024	171	36.7
Farmington city & MCD (Dakota).............	13	56	174	745	8,067	38	100.0	21.7	1.7	92.6	554	20.2	876	152	39.0
Fergus Falls city & MCD (Otter Tail).............	30	217	488	3,526	4,239	17	100.0	23.3	7.6	88.7	504	21.5	1,559	223	45.9
Forest Lake city & MCD (Washington).............	NA	NA	NA	NA	32,631	192	27.1	20.7	5.5	78.0	513	20.3	1,021	297	43.6
Fridley city & MCD (Anoka)......	85	304	1,014	3,629	8,272	39	100.0	34.3	7.6	97.9	493	32.6	1,175	323	13.8
Golden Valley city	22	101	410	1,890	6,457	13	100.0	35.3	2.2	97.7	1,018	39.7	1,852	725	92.1
Grand Rapids city & MCD (Itasca).............	9	80	145	1,284	1,206	8	75.0	20.8	7.3	55.5	643	20.3	1,805	578	58.1
Ham Lake city & MCD (Anoka).	NA	NA	NA	NA	16,028	65	100.0	8.6	2.8	98.2	307	8.2	498	240	1.9
Hastings city & MCD (Dakota)..	42	184	412	1,807	10,078	74	18.9	29.4	4.3	71.2	598	29.0	1,275	310	28.6
Hibbing city & MCD (St. Louis) .	44	275	182	1,138	2,075	11	100.0	46.0	18.5	85.3	382	35.4	2,209	331	12.8
Hopkins city	32	170	334	1,773	1,425	4	100.0	25.4	3.0	52.8	742	35.6	1,914	549	52.9
Hugo city & MCD (Washington)	NA	NA	NA	NA	29,274	104	100.0	10.5	1.8	56.8	428	8.2	558	141	7.2
Hutchinson city & MCD (McLeod).............	28	202	227	1,638	8,930	61	37.7	18.8	3.4	88.3	599	20.5	1,474	533	59.9
Inver Grove Heights city & MCD (Dakota).............	90	253	560	1,573	44,713	146	72.6	34.9	2.8	37.2	606	35.7	1,008	266	51.7
Lakeville city & MCD (Dakota)..	39	60	532	820	224,012	955	64.5	69.5	9.3	69.3	469	71.3	1,119	591	126.5
Lino Lakes city & MCD (Anoka)	12	56	181	839	28,706	114	100.0	19.3	0.7	82.0	481	13.1	612	108	29.2
Little Canada city & MCD (Ramsey).............	NA	NA	NA	NA	490	1	100.0	11.3	2.3	24.6	388	13.5	1,299	621	9.5
Mankato city & MCD (Blue Earth).............	140	329	1,418	3,328	27,721	134	63.4	95.3	20.1	67.0	646	102.9	2,438	789	120.9
Maple Grove city....................	44	61	1,117	1,541	97,714	461	51.2	78.0	7.7	93.7	528	68.1	962	282	197.9
Maplewood city & MCD (Ramsey).............	90	218	1,859	4,497	21,490	158	1.3	49.4	5.6	98.8	597	36.5	896	95	117.7
Marshall city & MCD (Lyon)....	25	182	250	1,823	7,703	69	20.3	23.3	9.1	95.7	657	28.2	2,049	784	91.3
Mendota Heights city & MCD (Dakota).............	16	141	207	1,819	16,457	75	13.3	13.2	1.0	97.2	690	12.4	1,093	207	14.9
Minneapolis city......................	3,395	793	16,750	3,911	897,180	4,813	2.5	1215.6	223.1	41.2	1,120	1582.3	3,759	1427	2903.4
Minnetonka city	28	52	810	1,512	192,395	953	5.2	65.4	6.1	89.3	744	63.0	1,190	272	136.2
Monticello city & MCD (Wright)	NA	NA	NA	NA	10,940	57	71.9	23.3	4.2	52.4	764	23.9	1,758	637	22.9
Moorhead city & MCD (Clay)....	61	140	1,024	2,346	34,987	206	60.7	72.2	27.1	87.4	219	74.0	1,712	743	381.7
Mounds View city & MCD (Ramsey).............	23	174	449	3,393	19,435	137	6.6	11.3	1.6	3.6	526	14.4	1,105	380	12.8
New Brighton city & MCD (Ramsey).............	25	109	564	2,455	24,442	172	10.5	27.4	2.3	77.6	407	35.3	1,561	382	61.3
New Hope city	14	66	396	1,871	1,830	7	100.0	21.3	2.2	76.9	561	31.2	1,485	580	38.8
New Ulm city & MCD (Brown)...	9	68	162	1,227	6,403	32	75.0	25.0	8.5	70.8	643	32.3	2,443	972	27.3
North Branch city & MCD (Chisago).............	12	114	246	2,340	8,355	49	100.0	8.6	1.1	91.4	455	6.1	585	24	45.7
Northfield city........................	28	136	199	969	NA	NA	NA	126.3	3.9	89.5	442	121.2	5,900	288	70.7
Northfield city (Rice)...............	NA	NA	NA	NA	6,984	39	33.3	0.0	0.0	0.0	0	0.0	0	0	0.0
North Mankato city & MCD (Nicollet).............	19	138	144	1,044	8,676	32	75.0	15.9	3.3	91.9	524	15.6	1,132	250	29.9
North St. Paul city & MCD (Ramsey).............	15	119	220	1,748	9,409	44	100.0	12.9	2.4	94.8	433	16.7	1,347	498	30.7
Oakdale city & MCD (Washington).................	37	131	663	2,353	0	0	0.0	23.9	1.1	88.1	416	24.2	863	146	23.7
Otsego city & MCD (Wright)	NA	NA	NA	NA	107,966	335	100.0	15.7	2.1	51.7	404	11.9	709	373	61.8
Owatonna city & MCD (Steele).	26	101	438	1,696	12,933	63	55.6	27.7	7.0	84.4	466	24.6	956	146	45.8
Plymouth city........................	44	55	904	1,136	129,545	391	93.9	92.1	18.8	75.5	478	103.0	1,319	406	75.0
Prior Lake city & MCD (Scott)...	40	149	574	2,132	55,908	197	100.0	23.3	1.7	52.2	493	24.1	913	296	45.9
Ramsey city & MCD (Anoka)....	27	100	349	1,292	49,499	290	48.3	18.2	1.5	91.1	427	16.0	606	124	40.5
Red Wing city & MCD (Goodhue).............	40	244	427	2,603	13,992	127	15.0	44.9	5.5	86.4	1,265	49.2	3,001	1141	54.2
Richfield city	81	223	771	2,124	24,586	120	6.7	46.3	10.3	37.8	617	54.0	1,499	496	116.0
Robbinsdale city	49	335	232	1,586	950	3	100.0	17.6	2.3	90.3	471	20.6	1,417	171	80.0
Rochester city & MCD (Olmsted).............	227	194	2,435	2,081	133,850	774	38.2	289.2	56.0	76.0	766	326.3	2,823	1037	2610.2
Rogers city............................	10	75	236	1,780	31,817	106	97.2	14.6	1.6	82.7	667	14.7	1,133	368	12.1
Rosemount city & MCD (Dakota).............	16	65	187	757	65,211	274	66.1	21.1	0.7	85.8	492	21.6	888	222	25.8
Roseville city & MCD (Ramsey)	86	234	1,829	4,984	35,300	173	4.6	32.5	3.4	68.0	566	37.4	1,036	273	31.8

1 Data for serious crimes have not been adjusted for underreporting. This may affect comparability between geographic areas over time.
2 Per 100,000 population estimated by the FBI.   3 Based on population estimated as of July 1 of the year shown.

Table B. Incorporated Places, Census Designated Places (CDPs), and Minor Civil Divisions (MCDs) of 10,000 or More Population — Land Area, Population, and Households, and Employment

STATE City, town, township, borough, or CDP (county if applicable)	Land area 2010 (sq mi)	Population — Total persons 2010	Population — Total persons 2019	Population — Percent change 2010–2019	Population — Persons per square mile, 2019	Population characteristics 2015–2019 — Percent foreign born	Population characteristics 2015–2019 — Percent living in the same house as previous year	Income and poverty 2015–2019 — Median household income	Income and poverty 2015–2019 — Percent of households with income below poverty level	Median value of owner-occupied housing units	Employment, 2015–2019 — Percent in civilian labor force	Employment, 2015–2019 — Unemployment rate	Households, 2015–2019 (percent of households) — Family households	Households, 2015–2019 (percent of households) — One person households
	1	2	3	4	5	6	7	8	9	10	11	12	13	14
MINNESOTA—Con.														
St. Cloud city...............	40.00	65,905	68,462	3.9	1711.6	11.5	71.2	49,135	19.7	155,500	69.8	7.2	53.7	32.5
St. Cloud city (Stearns).............	31.85	52,710	54,683	3.7	1716.9	12.0	72.0	50,019	19.0	158,900	71.4	7.8	55.5	31.1
St. Louis Park city.............	10.63	45,205	48,662	7.6	4577.8	10.6	78.9	80,627	6.8	271,600	76.3	2.5	46.6	40.1
St. Michael city & MCD (Wright).............	32.67	16,380	18,204	11.1	557.2	3.8	94.5	114,015	2.5	270,600	80.0	1.6	83.3	14.4
St. Paul city & MCD (Ramsey)..	51.98	285,112	308,096	8.1	5927.2	20.0	79.4	57,876	16.6	208,000	70.3	5.0	54.8	34.9
St. Peter city & MCD (Nicollet)..	6.10	11,188	11,953	6.8	1959.5	8.2	80.0	55,774	13.5	170,200	71.2	3.0	61.4	30.2
Sartell city.............	10.07	16,075	18,926	17.7	1879.4	4.5	85.4	74,169	5.2	201,500	74.8	3.2	62.8	31.2
Sartell city (Stearns).............	9.00	13,835	16,416	18.7	1824.0	5.0	85.7	80,313	3.6	215,900	78.6	3.2	66.0	27.3
Sauk Rapids city & MCD (Benton)	6.28	12,840	14,146	10.2	2252.5	3.7	85.8	52,106	13.4	170,000	71.6	3.2	61.1	28.0
Savage city & MCD (Scott)......	15.59	26,911	32,362	20.3	2075.8	11.0	89.8	119,291	4.1	307,500	78.7	2.9	81.7	13.7
Shakopee city & MCD (Scott)...	28.12	36,988	41,570	12.4	1478.3	16.8	88.7	87,719	5.4	265,500	76.1	3.5	71.7	21.9
Shoreview city & MCD (Ramsey)	10.77	25,043	27,130	8.3	2519.0	10.2	89.1	92,826	4.6	275,800	67.5	3.2	67.1	29.1
South St. Paul city & MCD (Dakota)	5.62	20,118	20,060	-0.3	3569.4	6.5	84.9	63,247	11.3	192,100	71.9	4.1	63.0	28.8
Stillwater city & MCD (Washington)	8.05	18,620	19,627	5.4	2438.1	2.6	88.9	91,350	6.5	291,400	70.2	2.0	67.8	27.6
Vadnais Heights city & MCD (Ramsey)	6.97	12,298	13,607	10.6	1952.2	9.1	90.3	77,413	4.9	242,500	68.2	3.2	65.0	30.5
Waconia city & MCD (Carver)...	4.62	10,778	12,370	14.8	2677.5	2.3	93.0	99,602	3.7	303,700	74.6	1.5	73.2	22.0
West St. Paul city & MCD (Dakota)	4.91	19,541	19,961	2.1	4065.4	10.1	85.8	56,097	12.6	199,400	68.7	6.3	55.3	36.7
White Bear township (Ramsey)	7.31	10,908	11,774	7.9	1610.7	3.3	90.1	102,330	2.3	279,000	68.6	1.7	76.4	20.0
White Bear Lake city.............	8.06	23,849	25,875	8.5	3210.3	5.8	86.2	71,709	5.8	226,000	66.3	3.2	63.0	31.5
White Bear Lake city (Ramsey)	7.98	23,455	25,468	8.6	3191.5	5.7	86.2	71,399	6.0	225,300	66.5	3.2	63.7	30.8
Willmar city & MCD (Kandiyohi)	13.96	19,578	19,869	1.5	1423.3	16.4	83.8	47,826	14.6	133,000	67.7	4.8	61.4	30.9
Winona city & MCD (Winona)...	19.04	27,610	26,594	-3.7	1396.7	3.5	73.0	48,677	18.3	148,800	68.2	4.5	45.9	39.6
Woodbury city & MCD (Washington)	34.89	61,963	72,828	17.5	2087.4	12.1	86.7	108,539	3.6	323,000	73.7	2.3	73.0	21.8
Worthington city & MCD (Nobles)	7.83	12,776	13,099	2.5	1672.9	31.0	90.9	48,854	16.0	132,500	66.8	3.8	69.0	27.6
MISSISSIPPI	46925.53	2,968,130	2,976,149	0.3	63.4	2.4	86.9	45,081	19.7	119,000	56.7	7.5	66.5	29.2
Bay St. Louis city	14.69	9,262	14,034	51.5	955.3	2.2	86.9	39,721	18.7	172,600	54.0	7.7	59.4	34.8
Biloxi city	42.99	44,250	46,212	4.4	1074.9	7.3	72.8	48,137	18.5	161,700	54.7	8.0	60.9	32.2
Brandon city	25.66	22,062	24,289	10.1	946.6	2.6	84.2	78,573	4.4	181,900	66.6	2.5	75.1	22.6
Brookhaven city	21.64	12,510	11,947	-4.5	552.1	1.4	89.6	32,331	24.4	100,300	54.1	8.9	65.0	30.2
Byram city	18.36	11,487	11,428	-0.5	622.4	1.3	87.6	66,641	7.3	141,700	70.7	2.2	69.2	25.2
Canton city	21.29	12,012	12,094	0.7	568.1	5.9	85.9	33,634	22.3	119,200	60.6	4.3	61.9	34.8
Clarksdale city	13.89	17,962	14,894	-17.1	1072.3	0.5	83.1	30,223	32.8	65,400	53.1	14.9	65.1	30.3
Cleveland city	7.58	12,341	11,073	-10.3	1460.8	3.2	84.4	35,278	26.6	128,300	50.9	5.3	61.2	32.3
Clinton city	41.87	25,226	24,440	-3.1	583.7	5.8	86.6	62,685	12.0	169,500	63.7	4.3	68.4	27.2
Columbus city	25.05	25,183	23,573	-6.4	941.0	1.6	82.3	36,336	26.6	121,900	51.5	11.5	55.9	39.4
Corinth city	30.16	14,565	14,472	-0.6	479.8	2.0	81.5	38,460	20.7	123,300	53.7	9.4	58.4	36.8
D'Iberville city	10.58	11,567	14,012	21.1	1324.4	5.4	77.0	46,115	15.0	146,500	67.1	8.2	63.0	28.3
Gautier city	30.26	18,572	18,490	-0.4	611.0	3.8	85.6	47,399	14.5	138,900	58.8	9.4	65.3	30.6
Greenville city	26.90	34,403	29,085	-15.5	1081.2	1.0	87.5	27,025	33.4	78,300	52.5	14.1	61.0	35.2
Greenwood city	12.34	16,152	13,561	-16.0	1098.9	1.2	95.1	26,965	36.2	87,900	49.9	6.1	56.7	40.3
Grenada city	30.01	13,083	12,219	-6.6	407.2	0.3	85.9	33,226	25.9	97,600	54.4	8.2	58.6	37.1
Gulfport city	55.63	67,785	71,705	5.8	1289.0	4.4	77.2	39,171	24.6	122,300	58.4	11.6	63.8	30.5
Hattiesburg city	53.43	45,758	45,863	0.2	858.4	3.6	73.8	34,735	31.2	113,200	62.9	10.5	51.6	37.3
Hernando city	25.30	14,046	16,399	16.8	648.2	2.8	86.8	79,195	5.8	197,100	66.8	2.8	73.4	24.6
Horn Lake city	16.05	26,068	27,272	4.6	1699.2	4.2	81.7	48,622	12.8	106,400	68.8	8.5	66.6	26.4
Indianola city	8.57	10,618	9,037	-14.9	1054.5	0.4	92.1	28,941	26.6	76,400	57.2	14.9	63.4	31.8
Jackson city	111.09	173,551	160,628	-7.4	1445.9	1.2	80.8	38,888	21.9	90,700	62.4	11.3	58.5	35.1
Laurel city	16.24	18,529	18,338	-1.0	1129.2	4.4	92.5	31,968	29.6	85,800	57.2	8.1	62.7	32.7
Long Beach city	10.26	14,814	16,023	8.2	1561.7	5.3	77.3	53,951	12.8	151,400	59.9	7.0	64.8	30.1
McComb city	11.78	12,764	13,013	2.0	1104.7	0.3	88.2	27,823	39.9	88,800	48.5	3.8	49.4	48.0
Madison city	25.24	24,086	25,661	6.5	1016.7	6.1	92.3	114,521	3.2	261,900	68.6	2.0	79.4	19.0
Meridian city	53.74	41,130	36,347	-11.6	676.3	1.9	82.8	32,422	26.1	83,300	54.9	7.3	58.2	37.5
Moss Point city	24.12	13,704	13,350	-2.6	553.5	1.1	91.2	42,173	22.1	90,800	55.5	8.5	64.0	32.5
Natchez city	15.82	15,750	14,615	-7.2	923.8	0.8	94.4	26,443	32.6	97,500	46.3	11.2	52.3	43.7
Ocean Springs city	11.55	17,442	17,862	2.4	1546.5	4.8	85.4	58,713	9.5	174,000	60.8	5.8	66.6	31.0
Olive Branch city	37.21	33,487	38,924	16.2	1046.1	4.1	84.9	74,680	5.9	175,600	68.7	4.3	72.8	22.5
Oxford city	26.62	22,136	28,122	27.0	1056.4	4.5	70.0	44,283	24.3	248,200	63.1	6.0	49.2	34.3
Pascagoula city	15.38	22,392	21,699	-3.1	1410.9	6.2	82.1	39,887	24.1	110,900	56.3	11.7	57.8	38.0
Pearl city	25.47	25,688	26,510	3.2	1040.8	2.1	84.6	49,944	9.0	120,700	66.0	7.2	63.7	31.1
Petal city	16.77	10,434	10,632	1.9	634.0	3.0	80.5	55,946	12.1	141,600	63.0	5.7	75.1	22.4
Picayune city	18.04	11,626	10,904	-6.2	604.4	2.3	84.2	30,006	35.0	110,100	56.1	13.8	66.2	29.3
Ridgeland city	21.38	24,300	24,104	-0.8	1127.4	7.3	81.1	60,823	8.0	186,500	73.0	4.5	56.9	35.6
Southaven city	41.33	48,979	55,780	13.9	1349.6	4.4	84.0	61,026	10.0	153,200	67.3	4.6	71.3	23.2
Starkville city	25.51	23,874	25,653	7.5	1005.6	5.9	76.0	35,048	31.5	176,900	56.3	7.3	48.5	35.1
Tupelo city	64.38	37,673	38,312	1.7	595.1	3.1	84.0	50,694	16.6	145,400	62.9	5.3	65.4	31.0
Vicksburg city	32.98	23,856	21,653	-9.2	656.5	2.7	88.9	32,072	29.6	108,500	54.2	7.4	54.2	40.9
West Point city	20.88	11,309	10,404	-8.0	498.3	1.0	89.0	30,664	30.5	89,600	49.2	11.1	59.9	36.2
Yazoo City city	9.84	11,394	10,869	-4.6	1104.6	0.7	87.7	24,688	37.4	70,900	53.6	20.5	55.9	39.0
MISSOURI	68745.46	5,988,950	6,137,428	2.5	89.3	4.2	84.8	55,461	13.3	157,200	62.6	4.6	64.0	29.5
Affton CDP	4.57	20,307	NA	NA	NA	11.9	90.6	60,969	11.2	149,300	69.1	4.1	57.7	35.2
Arnold city	11.53	20,839	21,091	1.2	1829.2	4.0	87.5	66,670	10.4	157,600	62.7	4.9	68.4	26.3
Ballwin city	8.98	30,417	30,082	-1.1	3349.9	8.2	86.7	98,750	3.1	261,900	69.2	2.8	71.2	25.0
Bellefontaine Neighbors city	4.40	10,780	10,397	-3.6	2363.0	1.4	86.0	46,163	17.1	63,400	60.8	7.8	63.2	28.0
Belton city	14.14	23,099	23,642	2.4	1672.0	3.6	82.8	62,754	9.3	135,800	70.2	3.3	71.6	22.7

STATE City, town, township, borough, or CDP (county if applicable)	Serious crimes known to police, 2018[1]				New residential construction authorized by building permits, 2019			Local government finance, 2017							
	Violent crime		Property crime					General revenue				General expenditure			
									Intergovernmental				Per capita[3]		
	Number	Rate[2]	Number	Rate[2]	Value ($1,000)	Number of housing units	Percent single family	Total (mil dol)	Total (mil dol)	Percent from state gov.	Taxes per capita[3]	Total (mil dol)	Total	Capital outlays	Debt outstanding (mil dol)
	15	16	17	18	19	20	21	22	23	24	25	26	27	28	29
MINNESOTA—Con.															
St. Cloud city	262	384	2,575	3,771	20,857	88	100.0	118.2	24.7	92.7	599	125.8	1,847	821	398.0
St. Cloud city (Stearns)	NA	NA	NA	NA	NA	NA	NA	NA	NA	NA	NA	NA	NA	NA	NA
St. Louis Park city	70	141	1,227	2,474	76,525	442	0.0	60.9	4.5	85.1	719	71.5	1,464	437	187.1
St. Michael city & MCD (Wright)	NA	NA	NA	NA	34,659	118	93.2	12.8	1.2	62.8	390	7.9	447	57	27.9
St. Paul city & MCD (Ramsey)	1,941	627	10,082	3,255	159,855	1,575	4.7	658.5	197.0	57.5	574	811.0	2,660	316	2381.0
St. Peter city & MCD (Nicollet)	14	117	152	1,265	1,392	6	100.0	33.5	0.0	0.0	159	29.3	2,456	122	13.2
Sartell city	11	61	301	1,671	14,153	54	100.0	15.7	1.5	98.7	437	18.0	1,001	330	82.7
Sartell city (Stearns)	NA	NA	NA	NA	NA	NA	NA	0.0	0.0	0.0	0	0.0	0	0	0.0
Sauk Rapids city & MCD (Benton)	6	43	283	2,043	23,154	161	16.1	13.1	3.2	94.9	348	12.1	881	298	35.4
Savage city & MCD (Scott)	36	112	433	1,352	70,979	362	47.5	35.8	5.7	99.2	573	35.7	1,142	438	62.5
Shakopee city & MCD (Scott)	75	181	810	1,955	168,174	783	17.9	34.2	3.3	97.6	532	65.1	1,598	880	93.5
Shoreview city & MCD (Ramsey)	NA	NA	NA	NA	24,224	162	7.4	27.5	1.4	99.9	504	25.7	965	116	52.8
South St. Paul city & MCD (Dakota)	46	227	505	2,493	2,015	8	100.0	27.1	4.3	87.3	672	31.6	1,562	239	24.2
Stillwater city & MCD (Washington)	18	93	151	776	23,966	78	59.0	25.7	2.0	96.2	688	30.6	1,585	209	68.1
Vadnais Heights city & MCD (Ramsey)	NA	NA	NA	NA	19,560	158	11.4	7.9	0.7	100.0	327	4.0	298	0	6.8
Waconia city & MCD (Carver)	NA	NA	NA	NA	7,433	20	100.0	18.7	1.6	71.1	658	20.5	1,675	712	54.3
West St. Paul city & MCD (Dakota)	74	374	960	4,849	1,666	5	100.0	27.9	9.3	25.0	687	37.3	1,888	903	40.0
White Bear township (Ramsey)	NA	NA	NA	NA	3,469	10	100.0	7.2	0.1	76.1	346	7.5	646	161	4.8
White Bear Lake city	37	141	704	2,688	12,576	13	100.0	20.9	3.7	79.2	229	23.0	895	190	5.3
White Bear Lake city (Ramsey)	NA	NA	NA	NA	NA	NA	NA	0.0	0.0	0.0	0	0.0	0	0	0.0
Willmar city & MCD (Kandiyohi)	55	280	499	2,541	8,142	86	16.3	150.9	6.4	94.4	398	160.9	8,189	840	105.6
Winona city & MCD (Winona)	43	160	615	2,291	4,267	44	18.2	32.3	13.1	93.8	333	32.0	1,192	390	3.1
Woodbury city & MCD (Washington)	50	71	941	1,327	177,001	695	100.0	80.3	6.2	87.4	522	71.1	1,022	329	95.4
Worthington city & MCD (Nobles)	35	263	111	834	1,772	10	40.0	17.3	5.6	87.9	354	20.2	1,544	502	9.3
MISSISSIPPI	6,999	234	71,766	2,403	1,240,886	6,952	88.7	X	X	X	X	X	X	X	X
Bay St. Louis city	NA	NA	NA	NA	62,608	472	69.9	6.3	3.4	99.5	136	4.7	358	7	15.0
Biloxi city	149	323	2,577	5,584	28,475	155	100.0	111.4	64.0	55.6	499	107.8	2,343	605	113.5
Brandon city	30	124	186	766	21,630	77	100.0	19.9	7.0	88.5	265	18.4	768	55	15.2
Brookhaven city	93	767	346	2,854	2,422	16	100.0	15.4	7.1	87.1	392	13.0	1,068	8	5.6
Byram city	18	154	283	2,421	2,197	16	100.0	7.9	3.1	95.3	282	9.1	784	230	8.8
Canton city	NA	NA	NA	NA	553	2	100.0	18.8	6.7	72.0	491	17.6	1,444	151	14.7
Clarksdale city	NA	NA	NA	NA	863	6	100.0	17.7	3.7	90.2	377	25.4	1,616	45	126.1
Cleveland city	NA	NA	NA	NA	1,348	6	100.0	20.5	9.8	44.6	459	20.5	1,768	648	7.4
Clinton city	15	60	538	2,140	8,674	38	100.0	22.8	7.3	94.7	369	21.3	839	121	34.2
Columbus city	NA	NA	NA	NA	1,000	8	75.0	36.0	14.8	81.9	527	37.4	1,551	167	58.4
Corinth city	NA	NA	NA	NA	2,632	15	100.0	206.0	10.1	100.0	264	198.0	13,574	225	152.2
D'Iberville city	15	126	827	6,933	8,323	41	100.0	22.3	8.9	93.3	305	16.8	1,233	336	31.3
Gautier city	62	335	573	3,097	4,090	18	100.0	14.2	3.8	82.1	255	17.3	937	195	21.5
Greenville city	NA	NA	NA	NA	921	5	100.0	34.6	11.5	68.2	461	31.4	1,026	158	17.0
Greenwood city	NA	NA	NA	NA	191	2	100.0	145.4	8.3	87.8	411	152.3	10,873	1021	57.6
Grenada city	NA	NA	NA	NA	400	2	100.0	16.1	5.9	100.0	412	17.7	1,423	220	0.0
Gulfport city	387	535	3,662	5,058	46,737	189	98.9	597.0	45.1	93.7	449	586.8	8,156	509	177.0
Hattiesburg city	92	198	NA	NA	15,869	83	47.0	80.5	32.7	79.9	620	86.7	1,883	400	126.5
Hernando city	NA	NA	NA	NA	37,320	214	100.0	11.3	3.0	92.5	288	11.3	714	22	9.9
Horn Lake city	28	103	650	2,386	3,356	38	100.0	21.3	6.0	100.0	290	21.9	806	102	24.6
Indianola city	NA	NA	NA	NA	786	4	100.0	9.6	4.4	91.2	354	10.2	1,074	336	7.1
Jackson city	NA	NA	7,855	4,731	37,063	330	3.0	219.6	57.8	68.0	483	201.3	1,206	166	443.6
Laurel city	103	557	870	4,706	837	4	100.0	32.3	13.3	91.3	400	33.8	1,832	483	51.5
Long Beach city	NA	NA	NA	NA	19,156	121	96.7	14.2	2.6	64.1	331	12.7	813	3	2.0
McComb city	NA	NA	NA	NA	800	2	100.0	162.6	11.4	86.5	337	157.5	12,383	741	51.3
Madison city	18	70	241	933	41,417	100	100.0	31.5	12.1	70.3	503	29.7	1,160	270	57.5
Meridian city	155	413	1,477	3,939	1,801	7	100.0	44.5	15.4	99.1	488	38.4	1,012	68	51.6
Moss Point city	NA	NA	NA	NA	0	0	0.0	18.2	3.8	55.9	476	23.4	1,742	634	18.4
Natchez city	NA	NA	NA	NA	54	1	100.0	30.4	10.9	100.0	601	28.7	1,902	259	13.1
Ocean Springs city	36	203	589	3,323	11,102	41	100.0	20.0	8.9	89.1	271	20.7	1,168	127	18.0
Olive Branch city	NA	NA	NA	NA	40,118	311	100.0	42.7	9.9	100.0	502	39.0	1,039	114	47.5
Oxford city	NA	NA	666	2,733	37,232	203	84.2	43.0	15.0	81.4	559	36.1	1,333	149	44.2
Pascagoula city	73	337	1,325	6,119	2,586	8	100.0	29.4	8.6	100.0	515	36.8	1,690	292	28.2
Pearl city	NA	NA	NA	NA	10,363	61	100.0	33.2	13.7	91.9	332	32.6	1,232	83	81.1
Petal city	NA	NA	59	554	5,852	34	88.2	9.3	2.6	100.0	459	12.4	1,174	168	21.5
Picayune city	NA	NA	NA	NA	1,956	20	60.0	18.4	7.4	94.0	415	19.3	1,742	565	4.7
Ridgeland city	NA	NA	NA	NA	6,089	10	100.0	42.9	23.3	86.6	466	35.4	1,458	201	84.4
Southaven city	68	124	1,633	2,982	56,040	400	100.0	61.0	21.2	75.6	514	54.8	1,011	207	81.9
Starkville city	43	168	NA	NA	18,619	109	61.5	27.8	14.7	87.2	211	20.9	823	54	24.8
Tupelo city	NA	NA	NA	NA	23,684	141	100.0	63.2	32.0	85.0	421	74.4	1,949	748	97.9
Vicksburg city	NA	NA	1,140	5,113	5,457	26	88.5	41.2	11.1	85.7	834	44.6	1,991	479	15.1
West Point city	33	312	273	2,577	700	6	100.0	12.4	6.0	79.7	404	9.5	896	2	16.5
Yazoo City city	NA	NA	NA	NA	0	0	0.0	12.2	2.9	97.9	400	11.5	1,038	75	0.8
MISSOURI	30,758	502	162,173	2,647	3,388,568	17,460	62.7	0.0	0.0	0.0	0	0.0	0	0	0.0
Affton CDP	NA	NA	NA	NA	NA	NA	NA								
Arnold city	22	104	767	3,626	6,278	30	100.0	29.8	2.7	100.0	869	26.3	1,245	263	70.0
Ballwin city	9	30	245	813	12,906	34	100.0	21.3	2.8	74.0	471	19.2	637	115	16.6
Bellefontaine Neighbors city	100	944	462	4,360	0	0	0.0	5.0	0.4	91.5	349	5.4	516	0	4.7
Belton city	NA	NA	NA	NA	16,024	84	59.5	36.8	2.3	100.0	857	47.9	2,048	705	78.0

1 Data for serious crimes have not been adjusted for underreporting. This may affect comparability between geographic areas over time.
2 Per 100,000 population estimated by the FBI.   3 Based on population estimated as of July 1 of the year shown.

STATE City, town, township, borough, or CDP (county if applicable)	Land area 2010 (sq mi)	Total persons 2010	Total persons 2019	Percent change 2010-2019	Persons per square mile, 2019	Percent foreign born	Percent living in the same house as previous year	Median household income	Percent of households with income below poverty level	Median value of owner-occupied housing units	Percent in civilian labor force	Unemployment rate	Family households	One person households
	1	2	3	4	5	6	7	8	9	10	11	12	13	14
MISSOURI—Con.														
Blue Springs city	22.42	52,593	55,829	6.2	2490.1	3.1	86.6	75,767	6.0	166,000	70.9	3.0	75.8	19.3
Bolivar city	8.29	10,334	11,067	7.1	1335.0	0.9	71.7	38,396	15.3	111,600	59.7	3.8	59.0	32.5
Branson city	21.17	10,543	11,630	10.3	549.4	10.7	75.8	46,319	14.9	157,500	61.3	3.6	64.1	28.6
Bridgeton city	14.56	11,516	11,520	0.0	791.2	7.9	86.0	59,940	8.7	168,700	62.1	5.7	67.9	26.0
Cape Girardeau city	29.06	37,973	40,559	6.8	1395.7	4.6	73.9	45,733	20.8	151,800	59.9	4.4	54.7	32.9
Carthage city	11.65	14,378	14,746	2.6	1265.8	16.5	85.3	41,226	21.8	88,600	60.8	6.3	70.4	26.4
Chesterfield city	31.88	47,483	47,538	0.1	1491.2	14.1	85.2	113,315	4.9	379,800	61.9	2.5	69.8	26.3
Clayton city	2.51	15,977	16,747	4.8	6672.1	12.6	71.9	107,596	9.6	633,400	52.7	2.2	55.7	35.2
Columbia city	65.57	109,044	123,195	13.0	1878.8	9.1	70.5	51,276	20.4	191,800	66.2	4.4	51.8	32.8
Concord CDP	5.50	16,421	NA	NA	NA	4.0	89.1	75,831	5.5	204,100	62.6	2.8	64.8	29.3
Crestwood city	3.59	11,885	11,834	-0.4	3296.4	4.8	91.6	84,714	5.9	208,600	67.7	1.6	69.0	26.9
Creve Coeur city	10.28	17,811	18,622	4.6	1811.5	14.3	83.3	96,319	3.6	402,300	59.8	2.3	58.8	36.7
Dardenne Prairie city	5.39	11,633	13,348	14.7	2476.4	4.4	92.1	132,192	2.4	301,500	72.1	2.5	86.5	10.8
Eureka city	10.51	10,179	10,946	7.5	1041.5	4.3	87.9	111,058	2.6	277,800	67.4	3.9	82.1	16.5
Excelsior Springs city	10.83	11,081	11,731	5.9	1083.2	0.6	85.3	49,428	12.4	135,400	58.2	4.6	64.3	32.0
Farmington city	9.13	16,293	19,113	17.3	2093.4	2.3	76.6	45,528	12.6	134,200	46.8	3.5	57.5	33.8
Ferguson city	6.17	21,190	20,525	-3.1	3326.6	2.4	84.9	40,000	21.6	83,500	65.2	7.5	67.6	28.9
Festus city	5.79	11,587	12,036	3.9	2078.8	0.7	87.0	55,236	7.3	137,100	63.5	5.8	69.3	25.8
Florissant city	12.55	52,260	50,952	-2.5	4059.9	3.5	82.0	54,978	9.2	97,600	68.3	8.6	63.2	31.1
Fort Leonard Wood CDP	23.03	15,061	NA	NA	NA	9.3	25.9	51,364	6.8	0	23.4	9.7	65.6	19.8
Fulton city	12.33	12,793	12,596	-1.5	1021.6	1.3	74.7	47,040	20.1	126,800	44.5	4.3	62.5	31.1
Gladstone city	8.08	25,439	27,489	8.1	3402.1	4.7	80.7	59,018	9.5	144,400	66.5	5.7	61.3	33.3
Grain Valley city	6.14	12,855	14,526	13.0	2365.8	1.4	90.6	73,698	4.5	174,400	75.6	2.9	71.9	21.8
Grandview city	14.73	24,455	24,856	1.6	1687.4	5.6	82.0	47,103	14.5	108,600	68.0	4.7	57.6	34.7
Hannibal city	15.99	17,784	17,346	-2.5	1084.8	1.0	81.4	42,906	16.9	105,300	59.0	6.7	58.6	33.8
Harrisonville city	9.88	10,019	10,078	0.6	1020.0	1.7	81.1	47,404	13.9	137,000	66.1	6.9	59.4	34.9
Hazelwood city	16.04	25,726	25,117	-2.4	1565.9	7.5	85.7	54,573	11.4	118,900	67.6	5.7	57.8	36.6
Independence city	77.99	116,812	116,672	-0.1	1496.0	4.9	90.7	50,592	14.2	114,100	62.6	4.9	61.1	32.5
Jackson city	10.75	13,754	14,836	7.9	1380.1	0.4	78.4	64,497	10.6	164,800	66.8	7.3	70.5	21.2
Jefferson City city	36.05	43,124	42,708	-1.0	1184.7	4.5	80.4	52,253	12.0	147,800	58.9	3.4	54.9	38.8
Jennings city	3.73	14,776	14,575	-1.4	3907.5	2.9	82.1	33,425	20.4	64,800	62.9	9.9	54.1	40.8
Joplin city	38.11	50,798	50,925	0.3	1336.3	3.6	82.5	45,449	17.7	125,900	63.7	6.0	58.0	33.2
Kansas City city	314.89	459,902	495,327	7.7	1573.0	8.2	81.5	54,194	14.8	154,600	69.0	4.8	53.7	37.0
Kearney city	13.33	8,376	10,858	29.6	814.6	0.7	84.7	85,561	3.3	188,700	73.8	0.7	77.8	20.1
Kennett city	7.00	10,934	10,094	-7.7	1442.0	2.6	76.5	38,297	23.9	91,600	54.8	6.0	57.6	33.4
Kirksville city	14.39	17,505	17,602	0.6	1223.2	5.3	67.6	33,575	30.5	118,400	48.7	7.1	44.0	39.8
Kirkwood city	9.18	27,567	27,807	0.9	3029.1	4.2	88.0	90,730	4.5	315,000	65.5	2.4	63.7	31.7
Lake St. Louis city	8.53	14,558	16,864	15.8	1977.0	4.6	88.1	92,298	5.0	274,400	63.5	3.0	72.8	22.8
Lebanon city	14.64	14,471	14,798	2.3	1010.8	1.1	84.5	39,911	21.4	99,800	62.6	6.2	66.5	29.0
Lee's Summit city	63.82	91,368	99,357	8.7	1556.8	4.2	87.7	89,969	5.1	223,700	69.9	2.8	73.1	22.4
Lemay CDP	4.10	16,645	NA	NA	NA	12.6	88.3	49,938	13.6	105,500	65.0	5.9	60.8	32.8
Liberty city	28.83	29,244	32,100	9.8	1113.4	2.0	82.0	76,577	6.6	182,000	68.3	2.5	67.6	26.3
Manchester city	5.03	18,081	18,073	0.0	3593.0	10.1	89.2	77,983	8.6	229,700	67.3	4.3	66.1	28.0
Marshall city	10.12	13,036	12,841	-1.5	1268.9	10.2	81.9	42,584	16.8	110,200	60.4	2.4	58.5	35.7
Maryland Heights city	21.88	27,471	26,956	-1.9	1232.0	19.2	81.1	66,686	6.7	158,800	71.4	4.1	57.3	34.0
Maryville city	6.37	12,034	11,599	-3.6	1820.9	3.4	66.2	34,258	29.5	130,500	57.2	3.3	46.8	34.2
Mehlville CDP	7.47	28,380	NA	NA	NA	12.3	85.9	58,125	8.2	158,000	66.6	3.4	55.0	37.6
Mexico city	12.13	11,554	11,517	-0.3	949.5	2.7	85.7	40,538	15.8	92,500	59.5	5.1	62.7	31.0
Moberly city	12.86	13,984	13,615	-2.6	1058.7	2.2	84.4	37,021	20.6	94,100	49.8	5.6	57.5	38.6
Neosho city	15.75	11,830	12,054	1.9	765.3	6.3	78.7	38,214	21.8	93,300	58.6	3.1	66.1	28.4
Nixa city	9.11	19,055	22,515	18.2	2471.5	3.5	85.9	58,402	10.1	160,600	63.6	3.7	70.5	26.0
Oakville CDP	15.88	36,143	NA	NA	NA	4.2	91.5	85,972	4.5	234,800	64.9	1.9	73.6	22.4
O'Fallon city	29.78	79,597	88,673	11.4	2977.6	4.1	90.7	90,025	3.8	226,300	72.7	2.8	75.7	20.1
Old Jamestown CDP	14.93	19,184	NA	NA	NA	4.0	88.3	88,904	6.7	176,800	64.4	5.9	78.0	19.9
Overland city	4.39	16,055	15,551	-3.1	3542.4	9.9	87.4	44,516	12.5	89,000	64.4	5.1	62.2	31.9
Ozark city	11.20	17,811	20,482	15.0	1828.8	1.9	82.2	55,774	8.8	154,000	69.4	4.0	63.5	28.7
Poplar Bluff city	13.14	17,035	16,937	-0.6	1289.0	1.5	71.2	30,370	32.5	92,400	54.3	8.9	58.1	35.6
Raymore city	17.31	19,210	22,194	15.5	1282.1	2.4	91.4	84,697	6.0	202,100	66.6	1.3	73.1	23.7
Raytown city	9.93	29,611	28,991	-2.1	2919.5	5.3	89.8	52,662	11.1	105,700	65.1	3.9	57.1	36.3
Republic city	15.53	14,920	16,938	13.5	1090.7	1.0	78.5	55,964	11.9	131,000	69.3	3.0	70.3	22.7
Rolla city	12.13	19,540	20,431	4.6	1684.3	10.0	67.5	37,600	28.1	131,100	52.2	5.6	48.3	36.3
St. Ann city	3.16	13,031	12,629	-3.1	3996.5	7.1	86.0	47,727	17.5	89,900	70.3	6.4	62.2	32.8
St. Charles city	24.82	66,218	71,028	7.3	2861.7	6.4	84.5	68,486	8.1	200,400	67.9	2.2	58.1	33.6
St. Joseph city	44.03	76,783	74,875	-2.5	1700.5	4.5	81.3	48,197	17.0	114,100	60.7	4.7	59.3	33.4
St. Louis city	61.74	319,289	300,576	-5.9	4868.4	7.2	81.7	43,896	20.7	138,700	65.9	7.0	45.3	45.3
St. Peters city	22.40	52,595	58,212	10.7	2598.8	3.7	90.0	78,786	3.8	182,200	72.2	3.9	67.5	28.3
Sedalia city	13.48	21,514	21,629	0.5	1604.5	7.1	79.7	39,804	16.1	90,500	61.0	8.8	57.7	36.5
Sikeston city	17.90	16,334	16,023	-1.9	895.1	1.5	84.5	39,803	21.2	121,400	54.3	4.3	62.0	34.0
Spanish Lake CDP	7.37	19,650	NA	NA	NA	2.0	83.5	37,153	19.1	98,800	66.3	8.2	58.6	34.6
Springfield city	82.39	159,341	167,882	5.4	2037.7	3.4	76.2	36,856	22.7	118,100	59.2	4.9	48.3	38.9
Town and Country city	11.49	10,820	11,109	2.7	966.8	14.1	91.0	192,983	5.6	734,800	52.9	2.6	78.0	20.4
Troy city	7.74	10,599	12,820	21.0	1656.3	1.3	83.4	54,915	9.9	148,000	64.9	4.3	69.3	25.1
Union city	9.09	10,288	11,990	16.5	1319.0	2.1	77.6	52,577	13.0	148,800	65.6	3.8	67.0	25.9
University City city	5.88	35,292	34,165	-3.2	5810.4	7.9	78.4	61,274	16.0	273,500	61.5	4.6	51.0	36.7
Warrensburg city	9.41	18,866	20,418	8.2	2169.8	4.2	59.5	46,315	25.0	160,400	61.7	5.4	50.4	27.5
Washington city	9.45	13,999	14,081	0.6	1490.1	2.7	90.3	60,882	8.6	165,000	64.5	3.0	65.4	29.0
Webb City city	8.64	10,999	12,134	10.3	1404.4	2.4	83.0	50,033	13.1	99,600	68.1	6.0	63.4	31.5
Webster Groves city	5.93	23,019	22,819	-0.9	3848.1	2.9	88.0	102,759	5.7	296,800	67.3	3.0	68.8	25.9
Wentzville city	19.93	29,144	41,784	43.4	2096.5	2.4	87.6	90,403	4.9	228,400	73.1	3.2	78.3	17.8
West Plains city	13.27	12,009	12,304	2.5	927.2	0.7	86.3	36,865	22.9	99,700	57.3	1.6	55.1	39.7
Wildwood city	66.64	35,305	35,432	0.4	531.7	7.3	90.7	135,202	3.2	378,000	67.7	2.4	84.6	12.6
MONTANA	145547.71	989,407	1,068,778	8.0	7.3	2.2	84.1	54,970	13.3	230,600	63.0	4.0	61.6	30.6
Billings city	44.61	104,284	109,577	5.1	2456.3	2.5	81.5	59,656	10.6	221,100	67.6	3.3	58.7	32.5
Bozeman city	20.34	37,273	49,831	33.7	2449.9	4.5	67.2	55,569	19.6	365,600	72.9	3.2	44.5	31.0

STATE City, town, township, borough, or CDP (county if applicable)	Serious crimes known to police, 2018[1]				New residential construction authorized by building permits, 2019			Local government finance, 2017							
	Violent crime		Property crime					General revenue				General expenditure			
									Intergovernmental				Per capita[3]		
	Number	Rate[2]	Number	Rate[2]	Value ($1,000)	Number of housing units	Percent single family	Total (mil dol)	Total (mil dol)	Percent from state gov.	Taxes per capita[3]	Total (mil dol)	Total	Capital outlays	Debt outstanding (mil dol)
	15	16	17	18	19	20	21	22	23	24	25	26	27	28	29
MISSOURI—Con.															
Blue Springs city	134	242	1,599	2,893	40,219	417	34.1	50.1	3.9	100.0	571	46.4	845	85	123.5
Bolivar city	30	274	443	4,040	2,400	17	47.1	10.0	1.2	65.6	593	11.2	1,027	18	12.5
Branson city	85	734	1,224	10,562	11,888	94	48.9	62.1	11.2	100.0	3,101	52.1	4,573	452	217.4
Bridgeton city	68	583	680	5,830	0	0	0.0	22.4	2.1	100.0	1,523	19.8	1,707	150	19.1
Cape Girardeau city	192	489	1,537	3,911	19,138	772	12.4	72.6	6.5	100.0	1,214	69.5	1,775	755	40.1
Carthage city	NA	NA	NA	NA	3,705	62	29.0	17.1	3.0	100.0	669	13.2	895	26	31.5
Chesterfield city	22	46	732	1,538	NA	NA	NA	35.2	3.3	100.0	671	35.3	743	210	43.8
Clayton city	25	148	265	1,565	23,259	31	41.9	35.6	1.9	69.0	1,358	28.9	1,719	205	38.2
Columbia city	446	361	3,483	2,818	129,680	504	67.1	182.1	38.8	12.9	605	156.7	1,289	337	365.2
Concord CDP	NA	NA	NA	NA	NA	NA	NA	NA	NA	NA	NA	NA	NA	NA	NA
Crestwood city	15	126	NA	NA	NA	NA	NA	10.9	0.8	82.9	772	11.1	936	125	0.1
Creve Coeur city	22	117	289	1,535	12,933	21	100.0	18.8	1.7	99.2	763	20.2	1,083	239	10.6
Dardenne Prairie city	NA	NA	NA	NA	6,425	38	100.0	3.5	0.7	63.5	159	3.2	237	36	3.8
Eureka city	11	104	130	1,223	24,269	149	100.0	13.2	1.4	100.0	724	12.7	1,201	160	16.5
Excelsior Springs city	22	189	351	3,019	3,207	14	100.0	45.4	1.5	71.1	1,005	60.2	5,218	1420	59.6
Farmington city	29	155	621	3,314	5,432	34	82.4	19.4	2.0	47.3	540	19.1	1,040	347	1.7
Ferguson city	129	624	946	4,578	0	0	0.0	19.2	7.1	0.0	389	21.9	1,057	203	8.0
Festus city	56	463	202	1,671	11,865	47	87.2	12.3	0.6	62.8	691	9.5	793	104	11.3
Florissant city	115	224	1,079	2,102	0	0	0.0	36.3	15.5	5.5	265	32.2	627	60	16.4
Fort Leonard Wood CDP	NA	NA	NA	NA	NA	NA	NA	NA	NA	NA	NA	NA	NA	NA	NA
Fulton city	29	226	500	3,889	2,422	16	100.0	19.0	1.6	100.0	520	16.5	1,287	108	9.6
Gladstone city	116	424	660	2,410	726	6	66.7	32.3	4.0	59.0	632	29.2	1,079	204	41.9
Grain Valley city	25	177	201	1,419	34,928	145	86.2	10.8	0.8	70.8	481	7.6	542	63	22.2
Grandview city	173	685	924	3,659	707	5	100.0	30.2	3.7	100.0	675	29.2	1,160	266	20.6
Hannibal city	102	581	896	5,107	3,524	22	100.0	25.9	1.1	100.0	785	29.5	1,692	492	24.4
Harrisonville city	36	356	298	2,947	2,106	10	100.0	10.3	1.0	73.7	500	12.6	1,251	106	36.5
Hazelwood city	99	392	734	2,909	0	0	0.0	34.1	1.9	49.9	1,181	36.7	1,451	99	32.2
Independence city	521	444	6,115	5,210	50,013	384	22.4	140.0	11.0	92.8	694	162.7	1,388	233	464.8
Jackson city	19	126	179	1,185	3,352	22	50.0	8.7	1.5	45.1	252	10.3	692	0	3.6
Jefferson City city	151	352	1,277	2,980	13,863	55	87.3	63.2	6.7	100.0	848	63.1	1,471	315	88.2
Jennings city	NA	NA	NA	NA	6,026	59	8.5	11.2	3.8	16.8	402	14.3	971	70	12.4
Joplin city	NA	NA	NA	NA	35,182	243	78.6	135.2	59.2	7.9	988	120.1	2,380	1063	37.6
Kansas City city	7,842	1,590	21,236	4,307	225,121	1,498	41.3	1617.5	101.0	39.7	1,513	1710.9	3,504	476	3583.8
Kearney city	6	58	149	1,447	16,991	71	100.0	5.0	0.3	100.0	465	0.4	37	0	8.5
Kennett city	50	484	654	6,334	3,483	19	100.0	6.3	0.4	100.0	469	4.0	388	12	0.0
Kirksville city	44	251	507	2,891	9,219	42	100.0	32.6	12.5	25.7	615	20.2	1,148	380	25.3
Kirkwood city	30	108	381	1,377	28,248	73	100.0	27.9	1.9	100.0	780	27.5	993	124	15.6
Lake St. Louis city	12	74	248	1,537	57,966	177	95.5	15.5	1.4	49.0	807	13.9	872	209	10.5
Lebanon city	57	390	731	4,999	3,878	25	68.0	38.0	0.9	100.0	748	15.1	1,034	317	6.2
Lee's Summit city	118	120	2,105	2,145	182,841	1,095	31.0	160.3	22.0	13.8	870	143.0	1,472	356	62.7
Lemay CDP	NA	NA	NA	NA	NA	NA	NA	NA	NA	NA	NA	NA	NA	NA	NA
Liberty city	93	292	511	1,605	11,407	40	100.0	43.7	1.0	1.0	865	57.1	1,812	572	0.2
Manchester city	16	88	267	1,474	NA	NA	NA	14.6	7.1	6.8	376	9.1	502	0	6.6
Marshall city	29	229	300	2,371	315	3	33.3	16.1	1.6	98.6	437	14.3	1,110	196	3.6
Maryland Heights city	93	345	692	2,570	509	2	100.0	39.3	11.9	21.0	815	61.4	2,275	1209	23.5
Maryville city	7	60	169	1,443	2,687	27	40.7	12.1	1.7	100.0	659	10.6	909	194	22.6
Mehlville CDP	NA	NA	NA	NA	NA	NA	NA	NA	NA	NA	NA	NA	NA	NA	NA
Mexico city	14	122	289	2,512	3,022	27	70.4	12.5	0.1	100.0	653	11.1	962	174	27.1
Moberly city	120	873	253	1,840	5,235	30	100.0	16.8	1.7	98.6	781	18.5	1,345	308	12.3
Neosho city	29	241	526	4,363	3,591	27	100.0	11.9	0.7	82.6	652	11.5	954	438	23.4
Nixa city	26	120	249	1,150	57,737	297	83.2	14.3	1.6	90.4	292	13.4	627	174	9.9
Oakville CDP	NA	NA	NA	NA	NA	NA	NA	NA	NA	NA	NA	NA	NA	NA	NA
O'Fallon city	145	163	952	1,073	99,780	571	70.6	73.2	8.9	59.3	524	70.6	807	280	207.8
Old Jamestown CDP	NA	NA	NA	NA	NA	NA	NA	NA	NA	NA	NA	NA	NA	NA	NA
Overland city	NA	NA	NA	NA	163	1	100.0	9.6	0.7	63.8	515	9.2	585	64	0.0
Ozark city	41	203	436	2,158	30,049	193	75.1	14.8	1.0	70.1	366	12.7	638	59	42.4
Poplar Bluff city	85	498	1,163	6,812	688	10	100.0	22.6	1.4	100.0	1,138	19.3	1,136	110	16.5
Raymore city	9	42	474	2,210	34,499	139	100.0	19.7	1.4	59.8	605	23.2	1,098	314	29.0
Raytown city	153	525	1,295	4,439	846	7	100.0	28.9	1.7	100.0	578	24.9	849	92	51.5
Republic city	43	261	311	1,885	40,938	228	45.2	11.4	0.9	88.0	547	14.1	865	165	19.4
Rolla city	121	594	683	3,351	7,594	84	38.1	27.7	4.2	93.3	689	27.2	1,346	377	19.8
St. Ann city	36	284	275	2,166	0	0	0.0	12.9	1.4	96.0	520	12.6	990	48	0.2
St. Charles city	147	207	1,610	2,270	116,669	522	73.6	98.3	10.3	27.9	917	105.1	1,493	396	209.1
St. Joseph city	NA	NA	3,768	4,931	22,759	143	32.9	119.4	10.2	81.3	872	115.6	1,520	374	726.2
St. Louis city	5,525	1,800	18,142	5,912	45,033	381	30.2	919.8	110.5	55.9	1,875	1030.2	3,342	243	1902.6
St. Peters city	106	183	1,248	2,158	10,577	49	100.0	89.6	7.8	28.3	806	103.0	1,801	372	126.3
Sedalia city	183	848	944	4,372	2,039	19	100.0	138.2	0.9	98.3	1,204	126.8	5,848	292	53.4
Sikeston city	97	601	644	3,993	1,034	14	85.7	21.1	1.1	100.0	724	22.1	1,367	475	73.8
Spanish Lake CDP	NA	NA	NA	NA	NA	NA	NA	NA	NA	NA	NA	NA	NA	NA	NA
Springfield city	2,218	1,316	11,830	7,019	22,170	132	72.7	348.8	57.1	68.6	1,037	306.3	1,833	334	896.0
Town and Country city	2	18	132	1,183	24,970	24	100.0	14.5	0.5	100.0	1,083	13.5	1,222	214	0.0
Troy city	26	213	244	1,996	19,511	151	65.6	11.3	0.5	91.2	556	9.1	759	152	9.1
Union city	52	444	533	4,552	9,518	66	100.0	10.6	1.0	41.5	622	9.8	849	87	7.4
University City city	108	314	1,147	3,331	800	4	100.0	36.5	2.2	100.0	765	35.6	1,034	67	3.4
Warrensburg city	78	383	692	3,400	13,552	87	31.0	20.1	1.5	87.8	638	17.7	878	180	39.0
Washington city	34	244	526	3,767	14,865	109	30.3	24.8	1.7	98.1	1,080	18.4	1,316	246	59.0
Webb City city	10	88	309	2,716	15,198	138	35.5	10.6	1.9	16.2	499	9.5	819	89	5.9
Webster Groves city	25	109	164	717	12,205	69	36.2	22.4	2.3	46.2	709	22.0	961	162	8.3
Wentzville city	106	258	427	1,040	141,667	558	64.2	49.6	5.6	38.8	778	41.3	1,056	246	62.0
West Plains city	44	358	585	4,765	3,876	34	35.3	16.6	1.8	100.0	760	15.6	1,270	155	8.4
Wildwood city	NA	NA	NA	NA	NA	NA	NA	16.1	9.2	15.4	164	14.7	415	176	1.3
MONTANA	3,974	374	26,518	2,496	855,745	4,776	63.1	X	X	X	X	X	X	X	X
Billings city	598	542	5,276	4,779	93,735	380	81.1	163.2	26.0	60.8	424	152.7	1,391	332	198.4
Bozeman city	104	216	885	1,840	142,397	834	30.5	64.9	9.1	100.0	526	62.0	1,323	234	36.7

1 Data for serious crimes have not been adjusted for underreporting. This may affect comparability between geographic areas over time.
2 Per 100,000 population estimated by the FBI. 3 Based on population estimated as of July 1 of the year shown.

Table B. Incorporated Places, Census Designated Places (CDPs), and Minor Civil Divisions (MCDs) of 10,000 or More Population — Land Area, Population, and Households, and Employment

STATE City, town, township, borough, or CDP (county if applicable)	Land area 2010 (sq mi)	Population Total persons 2010	Total persons 2019	Percent change 2010-2019	Persons per square mile 2019	Population characteristics 2015–2019 Percent foreign born	Percent living in the same house as previous year	Income and poverty 2015–2019 Median household income	Percent of households with income below poverty level	Median value of owner-occupied housing units	Employment, 2015–2019 Percent in civilian labor force	Unemployment rate	Households, 2015–2019 (percent of households) Family households	One person households
	1	2	3	4	5	6	7	8	9	10	11	12	13	14
MONTANA—Con.														
Butte-Silver Bow (consolidated city)		34,209	34,915	2.1	0.0	2.8	83.6	45,718	19.4	149,800	58.8	4.6	53.4	39.7
Butte-Silver Bow (balance)	715.76	33,505	34,207	2.1	47.8	2.8	83.3	45,794	19.5	150,600	58.8	4.6	53.2	39.8
Great Falls city	22.97	59,121	58,434	-1.2	2543.9	2.2	80.6	46,965	15.6	176,500	60.9	3.8	58.6	34.1
Helena city	16.82	28,809	33,124	15.0	1969.3	1.3	75.5	61,324	12.6	244,300	64.8	3.1	52.5	37.9
Kalispell city	12.01	20,042	24,565	22.6	2045.4	1.8	81.1	50,294	12.5	233,500	64.5	5.6	59.0	35.8
Missoula city	34.47	67,358	75,516	12.1	2190.8	3.4	74.0	47,426	18.4	279,700	73.0	4.9	48.2	36.4
NEBRASKA	76816.50	1,826,305	1,934,408	5.9	25.2	7.2	84.1	61,439	11.1	155,800	69.3	3.3	63.7	29.4
Beatrice city	9.39	12,686	12,279	-3.2	1307.7	2.0	87.1	44,991	14.3	106,600	64.7	3.8	54.7	39.6
Bellevue city	16.57	51,520	53,544	3.9	3231.4	8.7	80.4	65,308	9.9	148,900	67.4	5.2	67.2	25.3
Chalco CDP	2.82	10,994	NA	NA	NA	2.2	89.6	80,896	6.9	153,100	80.8	2.5	68.6	26.4
Columbus city	10.54	22,286	23,468	5.3	2226.6	12.7	84.6	60,110	9.3	145,500	70.6	3.2	62.0	33.2
Fremont city	10.42	26,413	26,383	-0.1	2532.0	8.2	83.0	49,474	13.3	132,700	67.1	5.6	62.2	29.8
Grand Island city	29.75	48,655	51,267	5.4	1723.3	16.0	82.1	54,965	12.1	140,800	70.7	4.2	66.1	27.3
Hastings city	14.59	25,234	24,692	-2.1	1692.4	7.4	82.8	48,644	13.6	119,800	64.1	2.5	57.6	36.7
Kearney city	14.46	30,952	33,867	9.4	2342.1	5.1	71.0	57,064	15.6	178,900	73.1	2.8	58.0	30.7
La Vista city	5.43	16,610	17,170	3.4	3162.1	4.5	84.2	68,551	5.8	154,300	75.0	2.1	61.4	28.9
Lexington city	4.50	10,230	10,115	-1.1	2247.8	37.4	83.0	52,885	11.9	92,400	72.2	5.5	68.4	22.2
Lincoln city	96.22	258,794	289,102	11.7	3004.6	8.5	77.6	57,746	13.1	169,800	71.5	3.4	57.4	31.6
Norfolk city	11.35	24,231	24,449	0.9	2154.1	6.1	79.6	49,372	17.5	145,400	69.8	3.7	58.4	33.8
North Platte city	13.24	24,738	23,639	-4.4	1785.4	3.6	79.8	54,357	14.7	118,900	65.4	4.1	60.4	35.4
Omaha city	140.98	458,989	478,192	4.2	3391.9	10.7	83.2	60,092	12.9	159,700	70.0	4.3	59.8	32.6
Papillion city	9.87	20,067	20,471	2.0	2074.1	4.4	87.0	80,619	5.8	189,900	72.1	2.5	69.5	24.9
Scottsbluff city	6.63	15,047	14,556	-3.3	2195.5	5.2	82.3	44,354	18.7	116,600	65.9	6.4	57.1	34.9
South Sioux City city	6.41	13,365	12,809	-4.2	1998.3	35.2	91.6	54,806	13.9	116,200	72.9	3.9	70.0	19.8
NEVADA	109860.37	2,700,677	3,080,156	14.1	28.0	19.4	82.1	60,365	12.6	267,900	63.3	6.2	63.5	28.5
Boulder City city	208.27	15,020	16,207	7.9	77.8	4.8	84.9	61,787	8.8	287,000	50.1	6.7	63.1	31.4
Carson City	144.66	55,269	55,916	1.2	386.5	12.7	82.9	55,718	11.6	273,800	60.3	5.1	62.2	32.3
Elko city	17.86	18,341	20,452	11.5	1145.1	9.6	76.9	79,205	12.0	232,100	71.1	5.0	66.9	27.0
Enterprise CDP	51.13	108,481	NA	NA	NA	23.8	82.8	81,461	7.7	315,300	73.6	4.4	67.0	22.7
Fernley city	122.58	19,368	21,476	10.9	175.2	5.0	86.0	62,929	8.5	221,200	59.2	5.8	69.3	23.6
Gardnerville Ranchos CDP	14.95	11,312	NA	NA	NA	4.1	83.9	59,511	5.6	310,300	61.0	3.7	68.9	21.0
Henderson city	106.08	257,001	320,189	24.6	3018.4	12.9	83.7	74,147	8.1	318,800	61.5	5.8	65.1	27.9
Las Vegas city	141.77	584,489	651,319	11.4	4594.2	21.0	81.1	56,354	15.0	258,600	62.3	6.7	62.0	30.6
Mesquite city	31.58	15,276	19,726	29.1	624.6	11.3	79.7	55,542	7.0	236,700	39.3	7.6	66.9	28.4
North Las Vegas city	98.02	216,667	251,974	16.3	2570.6	21.3	82.9	59,835	13.1	233,600	63.6	6.5	74.1	20.5
Pahrump CDP	301.73	36,441	NA	NA	NA	6.4	85.6	47,535	15.3	173,900	39.4	10.5	60.7	31.8
Paradise CDP	46.73	223,167	NA	NA	NA	26.9	79.2	48,312	16.4	239,400	67.2	6.9	54.7	33.9
Reno city	108.74	225,317	255,601	13.4	2350.6	15.9	78.0	58,790	12.4	335,000	68.0	5.4	55.1	33.0
Spanish Springs CDP	55.64	15,064	NA	NA	NA	4.8	88.8	96,797	5.5	378,100	62.0	2.9	76.9	19.3
Sparks city	35.82	91,117	105,006	15.2	2931.5	14.8	83.0	64,645	9.5	301,500	66.7	5.9	67.3	25.9
Spring Creek CDP	58.77	12,361	NA	NA	NA	3.1	82.1	99,854	6.3	232,900	67.2	4.0	74.6	21.5
Spring Valley CDP	33.25	178,395	NA	NA	NA	31.8	82.3	58,388	11.2	262,000	68.6	5.0	61.7	29.8
Summerlin South CDP	9.69	24,085	NA	NA	NA	16.2	84.6	93,899	5.5	426,400	58.7	3.7	62.9	29.7
Sunrise Manor CDP	33.38	189,372	NA	NA	NA	28.7	80.6	43,241	21.0	170,700	63.2	8.8	67.1	26.8
Sun Valley CDP	14.87	19,299	NA	NA	NA	18.9	90.2	57,368	12.4	169,000	67.3	4.8	78.5	16.3
Whitney CDP	6.71	38,585	NA	NA	NA	25.4	82.4	49,699	16.2	183,500	65.8	8.0	63.0	27.0
Winchester CDP	4.40	27,978	NA	NA	NA	37.4	78.1	39,020	17.8	162,400	68.6	9.4	51.9	37.5
NEW HAMPSHIRE	8953.40	1,316,462	1,359,711	3.3	151.9	6.1	86.1	76,768	7.9	261,700	67.5	3.6	65.7	26.3
Amherst town (Hillsborough)	33.91	11,196	11,393	1.8	336.0	5.1	92.2	138,994	1.3	354,200	68.1	4.1	82.1	14.2
Bedford town (Hillsborough)	32.78	21,222	22,628	6.6	690.3	6.6	89.4	135,021	2.6	407,300	69.4	3.5	82.0	15.7
Berlin city & MCD (Coos)	61.35	10,051	10,122	0.7	165.0	3.2	80.2	39,130	19.0	92,100	47.6	8.0	56.2	38.5
Claremont city & MCD (Sullivan)	43.15	13,351	12,932	-3.1	299.7	3.8	85.6	47,649	13.2	133,500	58.6	2.2	60.5	32.0
Concord city & MCD (Merrimack)	63.95	42,686	43,627	2.2	682.2	9.5	85.4	66,719	10.2	230,200	64.3	4.0	58.3	33.0
Conway town (Carroll)	69.48	10,102	10,252	1.5	147.6	0.8	85.7	62,198	13.4	194,000	68.4	2.1	58.4	32.1
Derry CDP	15.20	22,015	NA	NA	NA	4.5	84.6	67,073	10.1	225,600	74.8	6.5	65.1	26.5
Derry town (Rockingham)	35.48	33,219	33,485	0.8	943.8	4.6	88.3	76,536	8.4	245,200	75.4	5.6	70.7	21.5
Dover city & MCD (Strafford)	26.73	29,986	32,191	7.4	1204.3	7.2	79.5	71,631	9.8	264,700	70.9	3.3	55.1	31.3
Durham CDP	2.68	10,345	NA	NA	NA	7.4	36.9	53,523	33.8	348,500	64.4	6.9	44.0	32.0
Durham town (Strafford)	22.41	14,638	16,293	11.3	727.0	7.3	44.8	81,995	27.4	380,000	66.3	5.7	52.8	23.5
Exeter town (Rockingham)	19.60	14,301	15,313	7.1	781.3	4.5	88.5	77,120	7.3	280,400	66.4	3.5	58.6	32.5
Goffstown town (Hillsborough)	37.01	17,632	18,053	2.4	487.8	4.3	85.8	89,317	7.1	258,800	64.1	3.2	72.0	21.0
Hampton town (Rockingham)	12.91	14,987	15,495	3.4	1200.2	3.7	91.1	85,549	4.8	373,200	67.7	2.6	61.0	31.6
Hanover town (Grafton)	49.03	11,260	11,473	1.9	234.0	15.4	70.1	137,344	7.2	564,000	50.3	2.3	62.1	27.6
Hooksett town (Merrimack)	36.06	13,465	14,542	8.0	403.3	5.6	87.9	84,568	6.7	254,100	71.0	3.9	70.2	18.8
Hudson town (Hillsborough)	28.28	24,471	25,619	4.7	905.9	4.9	91.4	104,597	3.2	291,700	74.7	3.7	73.6	19.4
Keene city & MCD (Cheshire)	37.09	23,563	22,786	-3.3	614.3	4.9	74.4	56,971	12.4	190,500	61.2	4.3	51.2	38.7
Laconia city & MCD (Belknap)	19.87	15,974	16,581	3.8	834.5	2.7	86.7	57,960	11.1	193,300	63.1	3.3	60.3	31.4
Lebanon city & MCD (Grafton)	40.31	13,147	13,651	3.8	338.7	9.4	80.9	67,698	12.3	245,400	66.6	1.3	51.8	40.2
Londonderry CDP	12.22	11,037	NA	NA	NA	4.8	91.8	97,596	2.8	310,200	72.6	2.9	77.3	19.4
Londonderry town (Rockingham)	42.00	24,023	26,490	10.3	630.7	5.2	92.0	107,868	2.2	321,000	73.5	3.0	79.4	16.6
Manchester city & MCD (Hillsborough)	33.08	109,549	112,673	2.9	3406.1	14.5	77.3	60,711	13.1	227,600	70.1	4.9	56.0	31.4
Merrimack town (Hillsborough)	32.58	25,485	26,490	3.9	813.1	5.3	91.2	107,232	4.3	283,200	72.8	3.8	71.8	21.3
Milford town (Hillsborough)	25.41	15,116	16,411	8.6	645.8	6.6	87.6	79,647	5.4	251,400	71.6	4.2	65.2	26.3
Nashua city & MCD (Hillsborough)	30.83	86,475	89,355	3.3	2898.3	15.7	82.4	74,995	9.4	267,900	70.0	4.4	60.1	31.2
Pelham town (Hillsborough)	26.34	12,906	14,220	10.2	539.9	3.8	91.6	106,686	2.3	349,000	71.1	2.9	79.3	16.6

Table B. Incorporated Places, Census Designated Places (CDPs), and Minor Civil Divisions (MCDs) of 10,000 or More Population — Crime, Residential Construction and Local Government Finance

STATE City, town, township, borough, or CDP (county if applicable)	Serious crimes known to police, 2018[1] Violent crime Number	Rate[2]	Property crime Number	Rate[2]	New residential construction authorized by building permits, 2019 Value ($1,000)	Number of housing units	Percent single family	Local government finance, 2017 General revenue Total (mil dol)	Intergovernmental Total (mil dol)	Percent from state gov.	Taxes per capita[3]	General expenditure Total (mil dol)	Per capita[3] Total	Capital outlays	Debt outstanding (mil dol)
	15	16	17	18	19	20	21	22	23	24	25	26	27	28	29
MONTANA—Con.															
Butte-Silver Bow (consolidated city)	NA	NA	NA	NA	NA	NA	NA	70.0	14.8	94.8	947	89.0	2,558	739	41.6
Butte-Silver Bow (balance)	NA	NA	NA	NA	7,145	65	72.3	NA	NA	NA	NA	NA	NA	NA	NA
Great Falls city	NA	NA	NA	NA	10,015	54	77.8	64.9	11.6	77.8	377	60.1	1,021	120	57.9
Helena city	196	615	1,694	5,311	34,156	204	23.5	46.1	10.1	53.2	410	39.2	1,223	127	23.5
Kalispell city	72	304	675	2,848	42,702	248	41.1	31.7	6.5	97.0	430	25.8	1,109	151	18.8
Missoula city	333	448	3,521	4,739	86,980	445	56.9	89.1	23.0	96.4	546	90.8	1,226	110	66.5
NEBRASKA	5,494	285	40,126	2,080	1,325,156	8,025	58.2	X	X	X	X	X	X	X	X
Beatrice city	33	270	293	2,393	4,001	20	85.0	15.8	3.1	86.5	473	20.7	1,682	612	3.2
Bellevue city	113	211	983	1,831	61,827	371	45.0	53.8	6.9	95.9	582	54.1	1,013	147	52.5
Chalco CDP	NA	NA	NA	NA	NA	NA	NA	NA	NA	NA	NA	NA	NA	NA	NA
Columbus city	26	112	357	1,535	46,970	321	22.1	37.3	4.4	71.2	858	43.4	1,865	586	11.5
Fremont city	59	223	534	2,018	18,175	211	13.7	42.9	5.5	72.3	640	51.2	1,931	366	71.0
Grand Island city	241	466	1,505	2,907	19,156	105	67.6	76.4	5.7	100.0	679	86.1	1,685	581	86.2
Hastings city	51	204	830	3,325	29,323	164	30.5	34.9	9.0	57.5	516	35.3	1,408	413	33.7
Kearney city	85	248	801	2,338	30,145	112	63.4	47.4	7.3	100.0	560	56.5	1,683	597	55.8
La Vista city	16	93	270	1,572	5,081	99	3.0	43.0	3.3	77.3	1,121	27.1	1,586	216	69.6
Lexington city	10	100	141	1,411	5,738	41	17.1	14.1	2.9	82.5	463	20.1	2,009	645	12.6
Lincoln city	1,045	362	8,307	2,879	287,607	1,727	50.0	350.3	70.6	35.0	600	373.6	1,313	297	1368.8
Norfolk city	29	119	444	1,815	30,294	230	38.3	32.6	3.6	89.5	721	21.7	886	60	31.6
North Platte city	97	408	1,006	4,232	3,228	27	85.2	39.4	6.5	64.2	730	66.1	2,767	985	38.0
Omaha city	2,628	560	16,314	3,476	234,540	2,144	55.0	717.8	70.6	65.3	898	540.2	1,134	81	1386.7
Papillion city	39	199	367	1,874	82,552	408	64.2	44.0	11.6	19.2	863	37.4	1,828	372	65.2
Scottsbluff city	55	343	486	3,032	2,130	5	100.0	19.2	2.3	95.3	589	33.1	2,238	472	6.3
South Sioux City city	24	187	389	3,028	4,711	23	100.0	18.3	6.0	69.3	534	23.9	1,866	506	37.7
NEVADA	16,420	541	73,985	2,438	3,681,836	20,143	65.0	X	X	X	X	X	X	X	X
Boulder City city	13	81	147	912	11,030	33	100.0	46.8	14.6	74.2	429	33.8	2,137	188	12.7
Carson City	NA	NA	NA	NA	53,457	248	69.4	144.0	47.5	62.8	873	129.7	2,379	315	277.0
Elko city	95	458	443	2,134	9,429	48	100.0	40.5	15.0	96.6	534	36.0	1,768	307	11.9
Enterprise CDP	NA	NA	NA	NA	NA	NA	NA	NA	NA	NA	NA	NA	NA	NA	NA
Fernley city	NA	NA	NA	NA	49,403	175	100.0	11.3	2.5	18.7	220	5.5	280	6	72.0
Gardnerville Ranchos CDP	NA	NA	NA	NA	NA	NA	NA	NA	NA	NA	NA	NA	NA	NA	NA
Henderson city	583	188	6,072	1,961	660,246	2,826	81.9	393.0	141.9	79.6	492	368.1	1,230	97	230.9
Las Vegas city	NA	NA	NA	NA	613,199	2,665	70.7	851.6	399.8	74.1	354	796.5	1,254	161	797.5
Mesquite city	32	168	298	1,564	68,186	317	96.2	49.8	21.0	95.7	680	34.2	1,866	179	43.0
North Las Vegas city	2,386	966	5,202	2,107	297,917	2,178	84.2	290.7	116.1	95.7	390	259.9	1,081	128	415.5
Pahrump CDP	NA	NA	NA	NA	NA	NA	NA	NA	NA	NA	NA	NA	NA	NA	NA
Paradise CDP	NA	NA	NA	NA	NA	NA	NA	NA	NA	NA	NA	NA	NA	NA	NA
Reno city	1,636	648	6,053	2,399	615,899	3,320	35.4	392.3	90.5	88.5	594	348.5	1,413	235	621.2
Spanish Springs CDP	NA	NA	NA	NA	NA	NA	NA	NA	NA	NA	NA	NA	NA	NA	NA
Sparks city	508	496	2,440	2,384	207,279	1,338	28.1	129.3	41.6	94.3	448	117.5	1,175	158	198.9
Spring Creek CDP	NA	NA	NA	NA	NA	NA	NA	NA	NA	NA	NA	NA	NA	NA	NA
Spring Valley CDP	NA	NA	NA	NA	NA	NA	NA	NA	NA	NA	NA	NA	NA	NA	NA
Summerlin South CDP	NA	NA	NA	NA	NA	NA	NA	NA	NA	NA	NA	NA	NA	NA	NA
Sunrise Manor CDP	NA	NA	NA	NA	NA	NA	NA	NA	NA	NA	NA	NA	NA	NA	NA
Sun Valley CDP	NA	NA	NA	NA	NA	NA	NA	NA	NA	NA	NA	NA	NA	NA	NA
Whitney CDP	NA	NA	NA	NA	NA	NA	NA	NA	NA	NA	NA	NA	NA	NA	NA
Winchester CDP	NA	NA	NA	NA	NA	NA	NA	NA	NA	NA	NA	NA	NA	NA	NA
NEW HAMPSHIRE	2,349	173	16,935	1,249	1,059,428	4,743	57.9	X	X	X	X	X	X	X	X
Amherst town (Hillsborough)	6	53	127	1,131	7,213	28	92.9	10.8	0.9	100.0	737	13.7	1,214	80	9.2
Bedford town (Hillsborough)	12	53	190	839	29,935	152	12.5	28.3	2.4	89.6	938	22.5	996	2	20.2
Berlin city & MCD (Coos)	16	156	103	1,004	282	1	100.0	44.5	19.1	78.4	1,709	44.6	4,450	812	20.7
Claremont city & MCD (Sullivan)	58	449	247	1,910	544	7	100.0	20.5	2.4	20.3	1,031	35.9	2,773	109	24.9
Concord city & MCD (Merrimack)	103	239	849	1,971	13,359	83	20.5	13.7	0.0		0	21.2	489	0	46.1
Conway town (Carroll)	18	177	204	2,009	15,322	57	49.1	13.5	1.2	100.0	1,107	13.9	1,375	14	0.1
Derry CDP	NA	NA	NA	NA	NA	NA	NA	NA	NA	NA	NA	NA	NA	NA	NA
Derry town (Rockingham)	45	133	315	934	9,349	43	79.1	36.4	2.5	96.4	910	37.7	1,126	36	14.4
Dover city & MCD (Strafford)	35	111	353	1,117	25,921	184	29.3	126.3	28.7	86.1	2,637	128.6	4,070	976	165.5
Durham CDP	NA	NA	NA	NA	NA	NA	NA	NA	NA	NA	NA	NA	NA	NA	NA
Durham town (Strafford)	11	65	53	315	63,569	162	7.4	18.3	4.9	100.0	519	15.5	919	93	19.5
Exeter town (Rockingham)	15	98	114	745	3,400	18	5.6	22.9	2.5	100.0	1,002	22.9	1,514	187	0.0
Goffstown town (Hillsborough)	24	134	134	745	7,424	36	72.2	22.5	1.7	100.0	919	24.2	1,340	82	1.3
Hampton town (Rockingham)	34	217	159	1,014	17,930	71	49.3	32.4	1.4	100.0	1,606	26.1	1,685	15	19.6
Hanover town (Grafton)	8	70	96	833	6,470	29	17.2	25.2	1.1	100.0	1,382	18.9	1,652	0	14.8
Hooksett town (Merrimack)	18	126	207	1,449	19,877	77	87.0	21.8	1.2	97.6	1,263	49.2	3,450	105	4.8
Hudson town (Hillsborough)	25	99	246	975	9,747	48	60.4	28.8	2.1	93.1	868	28.1	1,106	44	11.9
Keene city & MCD (Cheshire)	46	201	560	2,449	846	7	100.0	53.3	4.4	75.9	1,323	52.5	2,288	415	27.6
Laconia city & MCD (Belknap)	40	240	554	3,326	8,523	38	94.7	71.1	19.1	91.1	2,649	68.7	4,164	291	40.0
Lebanon city & MCD (Grafton)	22	162	236	1,738	11,778	55	45.5	37.7	2.4	73.5	1,653	32.9	2,415	454	59.8
Londonderry CDP	NA	NA	NA	NA	NA	NA	NA	NA	NA	NA	NA	NA	NA	NA	NA
Londonderry town (Rockingham)	39	147	194	729	16,791	107	33.6	37.1	2.0	100.0	1,079	34.5	1,321	27	10.5
Manchester city & MCD (Hillsborough)	661	593	2,878	2,583	25,524	132	80.3	431.5	144.0	88.3	1,769	376.7	3,356	80	437.7
Merrimack town (Hillsborough)	6	23	148	576	60,027	410	15.1	32.9	3.4	89.4	769	30.9	1,193	216	9.2
Milford town (Hillsborough)	8	52	94	607	14,346	54	100.0	16.8	1.1	99.6	804	18.9	1,218	16	5.0
Nashua city & MCD (Hillsborough)	124	140	1,144	1,291	9,315	63	85.7	331.6	71.6	99.0	2,421	291.4	3,274	188	189.4
Pelham town (Hillsborough)	13	94	96	696	10,453	51	92.2	36.6	0.1	100.0	2,643	8.7	629	78	3.6

1 Data for serious crimes have not been adjusted for underreporting. This may affect comparability between geographic areas over time.
2 Per 100,000 population estimated by the FBI. 3 Based on population estimated as of July 1 of the year shown.

Table B. Incorporated Places, Census Designated Places (CDPs), and Minor Civil Divisions (MCDs) of 10,000 or More Population — Land Area, Population, and Households, and Employment

STATE City, town, township, borough, or CDP (county if applicable)	Land area 2010 (sq mi)	Population				Population characteristics 2015–2019		Income and poverty 2015–2019		Median value of owner-occupied housing units	Employment, 2015–2019		Households, 2015–2019 (percent of households)	
		Total persons 2010	Total persons 2019	Percent change 2010–2019	Persons per square mile 2019	Percent foreign born	Percent living in the same house as previous year	Median household income	Percent of households with income below poverty level		Percent in civilian labor force	Unemployment rate	Family households	One person households
	1	2	3	4	5	6	7	8	9	10	11	12	13	14
NEW HAMPSHIRE—Con.														
Portsmouth city & MCD (Rockingham)	15.66	21,233	21,927	3.3	1400.2	7.6	80.1	83,923	7.8	425,600	69.6	2.1	50.7	34.3
Raymond town (Rockingham)	28.82	10,150	10,529	3.7	365.3	2.1	87.1	76,234	7.9	229,700	74.4	4.1	68.5	21.0
Rochester city & MCD (Strafford)	45.02	29,787	31,526	5.8	700.3	3.4	86.8	62,179	11.2	172,300	63.8	4.3	64.1	27.2
Salem town (Rockingham)	24.84	28,753	29,791	3.6	1199.3	9.4	90.1	86,587	6.3	325,600	69.6	3.9	68.2	27.3
Somersworth city & MCD (Strafford)	9.80	11,765	11,968	1.7	1221.2	8.4	83.2	66,663	9.7	184,700	70.6	4.8	64.7	28.5
Windham town (Rockingham)	26.74	13,578	14,853	9.4	555.5	5.6	91.1	148,459	1.4	450,300	69.1	3.2	84.4	14.2
NEW JERSEY	7354.80	8,791,978	8,882,190	1.0	1207.7	22.4	89.8	82,545	10.0	335,600	65.5	5.5	68.9	26.0
Aberdeen township (Monmouth)	5.45	18,142	19,332	6.6	3547.2	13.9	89.1	101,363	4.0	331,300	73.5	4.2	68.7	23.9
Asbury Park city & MCD (Monmouth)	1.43	16,114	15,408	-4.4	10774.8	17.7	82.0	47,841	23.7	377,400	70.1	10.0	43.2	45.9
Atlantic City city & MCD (Atlantic)	10.76	39,552	37,743	-4.6	3507.7	31.6	81.3	29,232	32.9	156,700	59.3	12.6	51.4	41.4
Avenel CDP	3.48	17,011	NA	NA	NA	29.1	86.2	70,035	10.8	262,800	49.0	5.4	72.3	25.5
Barnegat township (Ocean)	34.00	20,930	23,655	13.0	695.7	7.3	91.0	73,498	6.8	252,800	53.9	7.7	74.9	22.3
Bayonne city & MCD (Hudson)	5.82	63,015	64,897	3.0	11150.7	30.9	90.1	63,947	13.3	333,700	64.3	6.0	64.2	31.5
Beachwood borough & MCD (Ocean)	2.76	11,042	11,312	2.4	4098.6	5.1	92.5	79,777	7.7	231,500	70.5	5.7	77.8	17.2
Belleville township (Essex)	3.30	35,854	36,497	1.8	11059.7	30.1	90.6	70,311	9.6	295,700	68.5	6.4	70.0	24.8
Bellmawr borough & MCD (Camden)	2.98	11,614	11,359	-2.2	3811.7	18.0	87.5	59,646	13.4	167,700	63.6	7.1	63.2	30.2
Bergenfield borough & MCD (Bergen)	2.90	26,839	27,327	1.8	9423.1	37.0	93.8	96,335	9.2	358,200	69.4	3.8	74.4	21.3
Berkeley township (Ocean)	42.72	41,377	42,036	1.6	984.0	8.5	91.7	54,942	8.6	194,900	46.3	5.3	58.0	38.1
Berkeley Heights township (Union)	6.22	13,134	13,363	1.7	2148.4	19.6	94.0	183,056	1.5	617,500	67.8	4.7	83.3	14.7
Bernards township (Somerset)	24.20	26,690	27,038	1.3	1117.3	23.0	90.6	151,871	4.4	673,000	61.5	4.3	73.1	24.2
Bloomfield township (Essex)	5.34	47,366	49,973	5.5	9358.2	25.0	91.1	78,034	8.2	329,900	71.2	6.7	62.2	32.1
Bordentown township (Burlington)	8.66	11,380	11,914	4.7	1375.8	14.4	91.7	93,288	5.3	298,600	64.6	2.7	71.4	25.5
Bound Brook borough & MCD (Somerset)	1.66	10,421	10,180	-2.3	6132.5	32.5	87.8	70,540	7.7	273,700	72.1	2.7	67.8	26.1
Bradley Gardens CDP	4.49	14,206	NA	NA	NA	34.7	91.5	139,716	3.1	460,500	69.0	3.8	78.5	19.3
Branchburg township (Somerset)	20.07	14,456	14,499	0.3	722.4	11.5	94.1	138,603	3.0	479,100	71.8	4.8	73.3	21.3
Brick township (Ocean)	25.61	75,049	76,100	1.4	2971.5	7.0	91.1	78,288	6.7	291,700	64.7	5.4	66.2	28.5
Bridgeton city & MCD (Cumberland)	6.23	25,404	24,160	-4.9	3878.0	21.4	83.1	37,804	30.8	109,200	50.4	6.9	67.9	27.0
Bridgewater township (Somerset)	31.89	44,420	43,968	-1.0	1378.7	27.4	90.3	133,342	3.9	488,600	67.4	3.7	76.8	20.9
Browns Mills CDP	5.37	11,223	NA	NA	NA	8.8	87.0	63,833	9.0	157,600	65.2	10.6	70.6	23.9
Burlington township (Burlington)	13.45	22,569	22,594	0.1	1679.9	15.0	91.1	89,545	5.4	256,100	73.7	7.4	70.5	24.8
Camden city & MCD (Camden)	8.92	76,866	73,562	-4.3	8246.9	14.0	85.2	27,015	36.5	84,000	55.8	12.9	65.6	29.7
Carteret borough & MCD (Middlesex)	4.39	22,851	23,408	2.4	5332.1	31.9	87.0	73,347	15.0	272,200	64.8	5.7	74.0	22.3
Cedar Grove township (Essex)	4.24	12,420	12,489	0.6	2945.5	13.7	93.0	123,768	4.6	473,100	61.5	2.6	71.1	25.8
Chatham township (Morris)	9.08	10,412	10,117	-2.8	1114.2	15.1	92.8	189,297	2.3	901,000	63.4	2.1	70.6	25.9
Cherry Hill township (Camden)	24.07	70,871	71,245	0.6	2959.9	17.3	89.6	105,022	6.0	277,300	67.2	4.0	71.1	25.5
Cherry Hill Mall CDP	3.65	14,171	NA	NA	NA	21.9	92.1	84,694	6.0	241,900	71.9	5.8	65.8	28.9
Cinnaminson township (Burlington)	7.42	15,562	16,342	5.0	2202.4	5.4	93.7	110,227	3.3	272,400	67.6	4.0	76.6	19.9
City of Orange township (Essex)	2.21	30,347	30,551	0.7	13824.0	38.4	90.0	42,966	21.2	236,400	63.4	8.3	57.6	38.2
Clark township (Union)	4.27	14,742	15,911	7.9	3726.2	15.7	93.9	109,678	5.2	446,800	69.1	3.3	69.8	26.7
Cliffside Park borough & MCD (Bergen)	0.96	23,565	26,133	10.9	27221.9	46.5	87.3	72,633	11.7	447,900	63.5	3.2	66.4	29.4
Clifton city & MCD (Passaic)	11.27	84,117	85,052	1.1	7546.8	36.9	91.3	76,646	9.4	345,400	65.3	4.0	71.2	25.0
Clinton township (Hunterdon)	29.87	13,510	12,565	-7.0	420.7	8.0	89.6	142,162	4.7	438,800	56.5	4.9	72.1	25.7
Collingswood borough & MCD (Camden)	1.83	13,939	13,884	-0.4	7586.9	4.9	87.8	73,594	7.9	260,900	72.2	6.1	57.2	34.7
Colonia CDP	3.93	17,795	NA	NA	NA	24.8	94.3	112,590	3.8	363,900	69.0	4.5	81.2	17.9
Colts Neck township (Monmouth)	30.72	10,138	9,822	-3.1	319.7	9.4	90.9	176,280	4.1	801,500	63.0	2.4	86.2	12.4
Cranford township (Union)	4.84	22,635	24,054	6.3	4969.8	10.8	91.3	129,781	3.8	486,600	68.1	4.7	72.3	24.2
Delran township (Burlington)	6.63	16,925	16,492	-2.6	2487.5	11.4	93.0	89,346	5.9	248,100	68.9	5.3	71.6	23.9
Denville township (Morris)	11.99	16,679	16,446	-1.4	1371.6	10.2	94.1	125,655	5.3	419,500	69.4	4.5	70.0	25.9
Deptford township (Gloucester)	17.33	30,619	30,349	-0.9	1751.2	6.9	90.3	72,261	7.3	194,500	68.1	6.4	65.5	28.8
Dover town & MCD (Morris)	2.68	18,158	17,725	-2.4	6613.8	45.9	91.4	71,903	11.5	268,000	74.1	4.9	74.4	21.1
Dumont borough & MCD (Bergen)	1.95	17,392	17,516	0.7	8982.6	27.9	92.7	100,219	6.3	376,100	70.0	5.6	73.8	22.1
East Brunswick township (Middlesex)	21.78	47,465	47,611	0.3	2186.0	32.3	93.4	115,445	7.5	398,400	67.9	6.2	77.8	18.9
East Greenwich township (Gloucester)	14.44	9,508	10,719	12.7	742.3	6.3	92.3	129,353	3.7	320,100	67.4	4.3	85.0	12.8
East Hanover township (Morris)	7.88	11,155	10,921	-2.1	1385.9	22.2	94.9	136,016	2.3	608,700	66.6	4.1	81.6	15.1
East Orange city & MCD (Essex)	3.93	64,169	64,367	0.3	16378.4	27.4	84.4	48,072	18.5	219,300	66.3	12.6	58.2	36.5
East Windsor township (Mercer)	15.57	27,179	27,288	0.4	1752.6	33.9	90.5	88,795	7.9	301,700	68.1	3.9	71.0	26.4
Eatontown borough & MCD (Monmouth)	5.84	12,685	12,157	-4.2	2081.7	21.1	89.0	66,223	13.7	336,200	67.2	5.1	55.6	39.8

Table B. Incorporated Places, Census Designated Places (CDPs), and Minor Civil Divisions (MCDs) of 10,000 or More Population — Crime, Residential Construction and Local Government Finance

STATE — City, town, township, borough, or CDP (county if applicable)	Serious crimes known to police, 2018[1] Violent crime — Number (15)	Violent crime — Rate[2] (16)	Property crime — Number (17)	Property crime — Rate[2] (18)	New residential construction authorized by building permits, 2019 — Value ($1,000) (19)	Number of housing units (20)	Percent single family (21)	Local government finance, 2017 — General revenue — Total (mil dol) (22)	Intergovernmental — Total (mil dol) (23)	Intergovernmental — Percent from state gov. (24)	Taxes per capita[3] (25)	General expenditure — Total (mil dol) (26)	Per capita[3] — Total (27)	Per capita[3] — Capital outlays (28)	Debt outstanding (mil dol) (29)
NEW HAMPSHIRE—Con.															
Portsmouth city & MCD (Rockingham)	36	163	341	1,547	15,580	111	8.1	155.3	26.2	70.5	3,895	145.0	6,644	1511	139.3
Raymond town (Rockingham)	10	95	54	515	11,921	45	100.0	8.6	0.5	100.0	761	7.0	675	0	1.4
Rochester city & MCD (Strafford)	117	378	902	2,915	14,916	158	24.1	114.2	36.3	94.0	1,695	75.4	2,429	232	39.3
Salem town (Rockingham)	30	102	475	1,621	57,914	374	24.9	46.4	0.8	90.6	1,197	41.7	1,437	163	6.6
Somersworth city & MCD (Strafford)	30	252	319	2,676	20,103	172	14.0	59.5	26.5	89.8	2,435	49.2	4,102	515	26.6
Windham town (Rockingham)	5	34	52	351	22,186	48	100.0	12.7	1.2	100.0	742	13.4	917	69	0.2
NEW JERSEY	18,537	208	125,156	1,405	4,453,654	36,505	31.6	X	X	X	X	X	X	X	X
Aberdeen township (Monmouth)	11	60	163	887	1,020	16	12.5	25.0	2.6	88.8	896	26.3	1,446	262	20.1
Asbury Park city & MCD (Monmouth)	174	1,107	653	4,155	1,918	8	75.0	64.6	28.1	55.4	1,172	58.2	3,714	631	42.4
Atlantic City city & MCD (Atlantic)	276	721	1,181	3,086	17,673	146	4.1	263.3	125.2	79.9	3,131	213.7	5,653	178	188.2
Avenel CDP	NA	NA	NA	NA	NA	NA	NA	NA	NA	NA	NA	NA	NA	NA	NA
Barnegat township (Ocean)	13	57	120	527	28,445	201	80.1	27.3	1.4	82.1	1,029	27.7	1,219	57	7.4
Bayonne city & MCD (Hudson)	114	171	773	1,157	51,281	1,143	0.7	234.7	90.2	87.3	1,352	278.2	4,257	70	238.9
Beachwood borough & MCD (Ocean)	6	54	130	1,166	1,876	11	100.0	25.1	0.0	0.0	1,717	23.4	2,089	128	13.3
Belleville township (Essex)	62	172	589	1,633	39,934	239	0.4	50.6	0.0		1,386	33.0	918	0	12.9
Bellmawr borough & MCD (Camden)	8	71	158	1,397	200	1	100.0	12.0	1.2	93.7	855	9.6	842	0	8.5
Bergenfield borough & MCD (Bergen)	1	4	76	275	6,690	51	47.1	35.9	2.6	90.5	1,177	33.7	1,226	133	8.9
Berkeley township (Ocean)	25	61	378	915	15,326	98	100.0	57.6	5.7	83.1	844	50.8	1,218	0	56.3
Berkeley Heights township (Union)	4	29	60	440	4,667	16	100.0	18.3	1.6	96.7	1,158	17.1	1,273	78	15.4
Bernards township (Somerset)	2	8	87	325	7,194	37	35.1	33.9	3.6	86.8	1,096	18.4	677	0	2.8
Bloomfield township (Essex)	50	99	647	1,274	40,109	495	19.0	78.6	9.7	89.6	1,310	60.3	1,202	5	65.8
Bordentown township (Burlington)	14	114	99	803	6,182	46	6.5	11.6	1.0	77.3	678	10.4	860	5	6.8
Bound Brook borough & MCD (Somerset)	13	126	114	1,100	21,148	278	4.3	12.9	1.2	99.0	920	14.3	1,388	250	9.6
Bradley Gardens CDP	NA	NA	NA	NA	NA	NA	NA	NA	NA	NA	NA	NA	NA	NA	NA
Branchburg township (Somerset)	4	27	80	549	4,088	21	100.0	19.8	2.8	100.0	886	22.1	1,530	294	6.4
Brick township (Ocean)	65	87	904	1,210	31,747	104	100.0	117.0	12.7	73.9	1,067	61.6	818	2	50.6
Bridgeton city & MCD (Cumberland)	203	832	720	2,953	0	0	0.0	35.6	8.1	61.2	591	33.9	1,386	33	14.3
Bridgewater township (Somerset)	16	36	331	735	18,655	81	35.8	41.4	6.9	100.0	545	37.9	849	0	77.4
Browns Mills CDP	NA	NA	NA	NA	NA	NA	NA	NA	NA	NA	NA	NA	NA	NA	NA
Burlington township (Burlington)	35	153	274	1,199	5,766	77	100.0	29.8	4.7	96.3	562	24.7	1,094	39	14.0
Camden city & MCD (Camden)	1,198	1,638	2,219	3,034	12,282	141	57.4	262.1	21.3	3.7	656	180.7	2,451	0	3.2
Carteret borough & MCD (Middlesex)	45	188	295	1,233	1,269	11	45.5	50.9	13.6	0.0	1,154	40.7	1,722	0	54.1
Cedar Grove township (Essex)	4	32	86	684	28,175	219	100.0	17.1	1.3	95.5	911	17.3	1,383	67	0.0
Chatham township (Morris)	NA	NA	33	321	12,997	23	100.0	18.0	1.1	85.4	1,346	17.5	1,694	182	9.0
Cherry Hill township (Camden)	92	130	2,026	2,871	40,666	384	2.6	69.7	11.4	99.8	715	50.6	713	58	82.3
Cherry Hill Mall CDP	NA	NA	NA	NA	NA	NA	NA	NA	NA	NA	NA	NA	NA	NA	NA
Cinnaminson township (Burlington)	14	84	286	1,720	12,867	134	20.9	16.8	2.0	88.5	607	17.1	1,041	120	11.9
City of Orange township (Essex)	NA	NA	NA	NA	15,647	188	4.3	172.3	113.2	93.3	1,636	187.0	6,151	257	27.5
Clark township (Union)	4	25	227	1,412	3,564	25	88.0	26.3	1.9	97.4	1,248	25.2	1,590	11	7.0
Cliffside Park borough & MCD (Bergen)	15	60	150	600	12,771	75	32.0	42.7	7.6	25.1	1,242	39.0	1,582	122	42.0
Clifton city & MCD (Passaic)	97	113	1,354	1,579	2,953	14	85.7	122.3	14.3	80.2	1,052	112.4	1,318	185	84.9
Clinton township (Hunterdon)	1	8	50	390	7,290	68	2.9	10.5	1.3	73.3	602	12.3	960	83	12.6
Collingswood borough & MCD (Camden)	30	217	279	2,016	0	0	0.0	19.3	2.0	80.1	816	15.8	1,133	121	32.3
Colonia CDP	NA	NA	NA	NA	NA	NA	NA	NA	NA	NA	NA	NA	NA	NA	NA
Colts Neck township (Monmouth)	8	81	51	513	5,221	6	100.0	11.3	1.9	100.0	857	9.5	959	37	6.8
Cranford township (Union)	7	29	145	595	7,017	110	14.5	35.2	2.9	99.5	1,059	31.4	1,305	95	22.1
Delran township (Burlington)	8	48	176	1,062	2,792	24	100.0	21.7	1.3	99.1	912	15.6	945	61	6.7
Denville township (Morris)	2	12	90	538	4,605	16	100.0	18.0	0.5	0.0	832	17.3	1,033	103	29.9
Deptford township (Gloucester)	47	156	1,153	3,826	2,769	23	100.0	45.8	3.4	95.1	896	30.9	1,016	19	20.4
Dover town & MCD (Morris)	26	145	187	1,040	20,591	217	0.5	26.4	6.5	54.5	845	46.8	2,596	1478	16.8
Dumont borough & MCD (Bergen)	5	28	49	275	17,149	116	0.0	22.7	1.4	94.7	1,141	21.2	1,197	22	8.0
East Brunswick township (Middlesex)	32	66	632	1,307	16,646	111	25.2	73.5	8.5	98.8	983	53.5	1,117	22	83.2
East Greenwich township (Gloucester)	4	38	68	647	6,447	60	73.3	8.7	1.8	94.8	457	11.4	1,084	148	10.9
East Hanover township (Morris)	2	18	106	956	5,071	18	100.0	21.1	0.0	100.0	1,475	25.7	2,318	341	47.1
East Orange city & MCD (Essex)	333	515	904	1,399	41,539	484	1.9	388.8	267.5	93.5	1,575	403.7	6,278	121	78.6
East Windsor township (Mercer)	18	66	171	624	2,178	29	3.4	27.5	4.8	76.3	530	24.4	897	17	29.3
Eatontown borough & MCD (Monmouth)	30	243	277	2,240	1,004	10	100.0	26.2	1.8	99.7	1,561	24.5	1,992	240	14.2

1 Data for serious crimes have not been adjusted for underreporting. This may affect comparability between geographic areas over time.
2 Per 100,000 population estimated by the FBI.   3 Based on population estimated as of July 1 of the year shown.

Table B. Incorporated Places, Census Designated Places (CDPs), and Minor Civil Divisions (MCDs) of 10,000 or More Population — Land Area, Population, and Households, and Employment

STATE City, town, township, borough, or CDP (county if applicable)	Land area 2010 (sq mi)	Population				Population characteristics 2015–2019		Income and poverty 2015–2019		Median value of owner-occupied housing units	Employment, 2015–2019		Households, 2015–2019 (percent of households)	
		Total persons 2010	Total persons 2019	Percent change 2010–2019	Persons per square mile, 2019	Percent foreign born	Percent living in the same house as previous year	Median household income	Percent of households with income below poverty level		Percent in civilian labor force	Unemploy-ment rate	Family households	One person households
	1	2	3	4	5	6	7	8	9	10	11	12	13	14
NEW JERSEY—Con.														
Echelon CDP	2.80	10,743	NA	NA	NA	28.4	78.2	73,671	13.8	223,600	66.7	5.7	55.9	35.8
Edgewater borough & MCD (Bergen)	0.97	11,516	13,364	16.0	13777.3	45.9	80.7	127,221	9.1	600,600	71.0	3.5	59.1	33.5
Edison township (Middlesex)	30.06	100,323	99,758	-0.6	3318.6	46.9	87.6	103,076	5.8	390,700	65.6	5.1	77.4	18.9
Egg Harbor township (Atlantic)	67.05	43,420	42,249	-2.7	630.1	16.5	92.0	82,117	7.4	212,100	69.5	6.7	76.2	20.0
Elizabeth city & MCD (Union)	12.32	124,973	129,216	3.4	10488.3	46.6	88.1	48,407	17.4	282,700	68.1	5.8	71.9	23.6
Elmwood Park borough & MCD (Bergen)	2.64	19,488	19,966	2.5	7562.9	31.8	94.8	77,334	9.7	362,700	66.7	3.9	75.3	19.7
Englewood city & MCD (Bergen)	4.93	27,116	28,402	4.7	5761.1	36.4	92.1	85,899	11.9	388,300	68.9	6.1	65.1	30.2
Evesham township (Burlington)	29.16	45,534	45,188	-0.8	1549.7	9.3	91.5	100,720	3.9	290,300	70.3	3.5	67.5	27.9
Ewing township (Mercer)	15.21	35,729	36,303	1.6	2386.8	14.0	82.2	78,876	8.5	215,500	61.9	7.4	59.2	33.0
Fair Lawn borough & MCD (Bergen)	5.14	32,385	32,896	1.6	6400.0	30.6	93.1	123,159	5.5	424,000	69.4	3.7	78.6	18.9
Fairview borough & MCD (Bergen)	0.84	13,835	14,189	2.6	16891.7	54.5	95.0	57,698	14.7	364,900	69.0	5.9	64.4	26.3
Florence township (Burlington)	9.77	12,122	12,486	3.0	1278.0	10.2	91.5	84,897	6.2	226,600	70.3	4.4	66.6	27.5
Florham Park borough & MCD (Morris)	7.31	11,736	11,496	-2.0	1572.6	12.6	87.8	128,071	5.7	645,800	62.6	3.8	66.1	27.0
Fords CDP	2.67	15,187	NA	NA	NA	29.2	90.9	94,948	5.3	314,200	67.4	3.9	75.5	19.3
Fort Lee borough & MCD (Bergen)	2.52	35,433	38,605	9.0	15319.4	51.1	90.6	83,767	10.4	324,600	61.3	3.2	57.4	38.3
Franklin township (Gloucester)	55.83	16,778	16,300	-2.8	292.0	2.4	93.3	83,654	7.9	196,700	67.2	6.8	72.8	21.0
Franklin township (Somerset)	46.17	62,337	65,642	5.3	1421.7	28.9	91.0	93,347	6.8	337,100	66.1	5.6	67.4	28.3
Franklin Lakes borough & MCD (Bergen)	9.41	10,579	11,119	5.1	1181.6	16.9	92.7	172,766	1.4	945,900	61.4	5.2	84.9	13.1
Franklin Park CDP	2.61	13,295	NA	NA	NA	34.0	92.9	92,904	5.5	283,100	73.2	5.2	64.5	30.8
Freehold borough & MCD (Monmouth)	1.93	12,045	11,682	-3.0	6052.8	31.1	90.1	61,314	14.3	291,800	72.7	3.4	65.2	28.4
Freehold township (Monmouth)	38.65	36,206	34,624	-4.4	895.8	12.4	90.6	110,432	4.1	432,100	63.5	3.5	73.4	22.3
Galloway township (Atlantic)	88.67	37,241	35,618	-4.4	401.7	13.3	87.6	74,196	6.8	210,500	64.8	6.9	69.3	25.4
Garfield city & MCD (Bergen)	2.11	30,494	31,802	4.3	15072.0	43.0	92.6	62,939	15.6	338,400	65.1	3.3	69.7	23.7
Glassboro borough & MCD (Gloucester)	9.32	18,578	20,288	9.2	2176.8	7.1	71.2	74,222	19.0	202,800	61.4	6.8	63.2	24.2
Glen Rock borough & MCD (Bergen)	2.70	11,581	11,707	1.1	4335.9	15.2	92.1	187,000	3.2	646,600	67.4	3.9	85.6	13.3
Gloucester township (Camden)	22.95	64,660	63,903	-1.2	2784.4	7.0	90.3	80,053	7.1	197,700	69.8	6.0	69.2	26.0
Gloucester City city & MCD (Camden)	2.31	11,453	11,219	-2.0	4856.7	7.0	89.3	59,394	10.7	125,800	66.4	6.8	69.8	27.9
Greentree CDP	4.65	11,367	NA	NA	NA	20.0	87.3	137,346	3.1	325,600	66.9	5.0	78.6	19.9
Guttenberg town & MCD (Hudson)	0.19	11,157	11,121	-0.3	58531.6	54.5	90.4	62,450	16.2	323,100	71.2	6.3	61.7	32.4
Hackensack city & MCD (Bergen)	4.19	43,024	44,188	2.7	10546.1	38.9	84.6	70,090	13.3	296,300	69.3	4.1	52.3	39.1
Haddon township (Camden)	2.69	14,688	14,541	-1.0	5405.6	4.2	93.0	92,578	6.1	262,700	68.2	5.5	62.2	33.1
Haddonfield borough & MCD (Camden)	2.80	11,610	11,317	-2.5	4041.8	3.6	89.3	150,958	1.8	511,700	67.8	2.3	75.7	21.7
Hamilton township (Atlantic)	110.90	26,498	25,746	-2.8	232.2	14.2	81.7	74,329	8.8	211,900	69.7	10.3	68.9	25.5
Hamilton township (Mercer)	39.44	88,442	87,065	-1.6	2207.5	16.6	89.8	78,177	8.1	248,000	67.3	5.1	67.5	27.3
Hamilton Square CDP	4.28	12,784	NA	NA	NA	8.3	93.5	113,578	1.6	302,900	69.2	4.2	79.1	19.3
Hammonton town & MCD (Atlantic)	40.75	14,771	13,934	-5.7	341.9	11.5	91.6	73,048	8.5	235,500	65.7	6.9	67.1	26.8
Hanover township (Morris)	10.52	13,718	14,252	3.9	1354.8	18.3	92.6	126,658	3.2	506,300	67.3	3.7	67.8	28.2
Harrison township (Gloucester)	18.93	12,384	13,116	5.9	692.9	4.4	91.4	145,366	3.6	359,400	74.0	2.7	81.9	16.9
Harrison town & MCD (Hudson)	1.21	13,537	20,061	48.2	16579.3	53.8	82.1	69,604	14.0	333,700	70.6	5.6	66.0	23.5
Hasbrouck Heights borough & MCD (Bergen)	1.52	11,887	11,992	0.9	7889.5	29.2	94.6	94,801	7.9	429,100	68.8	3.9	75.6	19.6
Hawthorne borough & MCD (Passaic)	3.32	18,786	18,753	-0.2	5648.5	15.6	90.1	97,692	6.2	381,000	72.9	3.6	66.9	28.4
Hazlet township (Monmouth)	5.57	20,321	19,664	-3.2	3530.3	8.5	94.8	100,247	5.2	335,800	66.2	4.7	74.6	22.1
Highland Park borough & MCD (Middlesex)	1.82	13,982	13,711	-1.9	7533.5	27.5	85.4	81,402	10.8	373,700	70.3	5.6	59.8	31.4
Hillsborough township (Somerset)	54.61	38,316	39,950	4.3	731.6	20.6	93.0	129,284	3.0	438,400	73.4	4.1	76.5	20.2
Hillsdale borough & MCD (Bergen)	2.90	10,184	10,307	1.2	3554.1	14.1	91.3	146,080	5.7	566,200	68.3	2.6	80.2	16.5
Hillside township (Union)	2.77	21,463	21,967	2.3	7930.3	29.2	91.7	75,239	8.9	259,300	71.4	9.1	73.2	21.9
Hoboken city & MCD (Hudson)	1.25	50,020	52,677	5.3	42141.6	17.1	79.6	147,620	8.3	720,700	80.0	3.0	42.0	34.5
Holiday City-Berkeley CDP	5.97	12,831	NA	NA	NA	10.8	89.2	40,065	8.2	161,600	26.0	10.6	46.0	49.5
Holmdel township (Monmouth)	17.85	16,785	16,731	-0.3	937.3	22.2	89.2	149,432	5.2	661,800	57.6	3.6	80.4	18.2
Hopatcong borough & MCD (Sussex)	10.89	15,136	14,186	-6.3	1302.7	11.9	92.3	89,400	3.1	237,000	74.4	4.6	70.4	21.7
Hopewell township (Mercer)	58.07	18,304	17,725	-3.2	305.2	12.7	92.0	136,231	3.3	460,100	62.4	3.8	78.8	18.2
Howell township (Monmouth)	60.27	51,088	51,952	1.7	862.0	13.0	93.6	105,082	5.2	341,200	69.4	5.3	78.5	17.1
Irvington township (Essex)	2.91	53,838	54,312	0.9	18663.9	35.7	90.7	45,176	18.8	182,400	70.7	11.1	58.7	37.8
Iselin CDP	3.19	18,695	NA	NA	NA	47.3	91.5	98,250	7.1	306,700	63.5	5.5	77.3	20.7
Jackson township (Ocean)	99.17	54,890	57,731	5.2	582.1	7.7	88.7	95,069	5.2	361,600	65.8	3.0	76.2	20.9
Jefferson township (Morris)	38.90	21,289	20,716	-2.7	532.5	10.6	95.6	106,892	5.6	342,500	70.0	4.3	71.4	23.1
Jersey City city & MCD (Hudson)	14.74	247,608	262,075	5.8	17779.9	41.8	84.4	70,752	16.9	373,700	68.4	5.7	60.8	28.7
Keansburg borough & MCD (Monmouth)	1.07	10,097	9,632	-4.6	9001.9	10.9	87.4	52,321	28.5	193,600	64.7	9.9	64.9	32.1
Kearny town & MCD (Hudson)	8.84	40,714	41,058	0.8	4644.6	46.0	89.9	70,702	9.3	333,100	63.9	4.6	75.9	20.1
Kinnelon borough & MCD (Morris)	18.03	10,125	9,896	-2.3	548.9	11.4	94.0	158,000	2.8	570,800	69.4	5.4	86.1	10.4
Lacey township (Ocean)	83.25	27,642	29,295	6.0	351.9	4.0	92.5	84,567	7.6	276,300	63.6	4.5	69.1	23.9

STATE City, town, township, borough, or CDP (county if applicable)	Serious crimes known to police, 2018[1] Violent crime Number	Rate[2]	Property crime Number	Rate[2]	New residential construction authorized by building permits, 2019 Value ($1,000)	Number of housing units	Percent single family	Local government finance, 2017 General revenue Total (mil dol)	Intergovernmental Total (mil dol)	Percent from state gov.	Taxes per capita[3]	General expenditure Total (mil dol)	Per capita[3] Total	Capital outlays	Debt outstanding (mil dol)
	15	16	17	18	19	20	21	22	23	24	25	26	27	28	29
NEW JERSEY—Con.															
Echelon CDP	NA	NA	NA	NA	NA	NA	NA	NA	NA	NA	NA	NA	NA	NA	NA
Edgewater borough & MCD (Bergen)	13	106	137	1,112	9,919	34	82.4	53.1	1.0	81.9	4,290	15.2	1,247	41	77.0
Edison township (Middlesex)	120	118	1,147	1,132	43,246	230	23.9	292.8	44.0	99.3	2,176	363.7	3,615	128	51.7
Egg Harbor township (Atlantic)	62	143	902	2,084	11,849	114	55.3	42.0	10.5	79.7	610	27.2	638	8	0.0
Elizabeth city & MCD (Union)	897	695	4,002	3,100	43,243	550	2.5	307.8	58.5	62.1	1,476	276.9	2,160	245	183.8
Elmwood Park borough & MCD (Bergen)	33	163	342	1,687	4,249	32	68.8	62.2	1.1	100.0	2,817	23.2	1,151	191	15.0
Englewood city & MCD (Bergen)	85	293	281	969	6,578	42	16.7	90.4	27.5	70.3	1,907	146.8	5,129	455	71.7
Evesham township (Burlington)	34	75	506	1,116	25,710	326	4.3	46.9	6.0	61.7	567	25.1	556	7	57.4
Ewing township (Mercer)	69	191	685	1,895	3,500	52	26.9	59.1	13.0	79.2	1,070	47.2	1,313	36	5.8
Fair Lawn borough & MCD (Bergen)	19	57	304	910	25,537	194	31.4	49.7	4.2	97.2	1,308	43.0	1,300	129	34.7
Fairview borough & MCD (Bergen)	35	243	144	998	8,729	259	0.8	18.2	0.5	100.0	1,157	16.7	1,168	0	10.9
Florence township (Burlington)	13	102	89	698	7,065	46	13.0	12.2	1.9	70.6	636	10.1	801	93	16.5
Florham Park borough & MCD (Morris)	3	26	65	560	25,176	265	34.3	23.7	1.4	90.0	1,491	19.9	1,710	152	15.1
Fords CDP	NA	NA	NA	NA	NA	NA	NA	NA	NA	NA	NA	NA	NA	NA	NA
Fort Lee borough & MCD (Bergen)	22	58	271	718	31,677	186	9.7	83.6	9.3	24.7	1,844	81.1	2,174	186	57.6
Franklin township (Gloucester)	9	56	236	1,455	2,547	20	100.0	43.1	1.6	100.0	2,521	43.1	2,624	0	8.7
Franklin township (Somerset)	48	72	670	1,006	20,062	402	10.0	72.6	5.1	100.0	741	47.6	725	132	23.2
Franklin Lakes borough & MCD (Bergen)	1	9	59	527	24,961	76	100.0	17.2	1.9	100.0	1,249	15.7	1,416	188	14.9
Franklin Park CDP	NA	NA	NA	NA	NA	NA	NA	NA	NA	NA	NA	NA	NA	NA	NA
Freehold borough & MCD (Monmouth)	16	135	129	1,087	0	0	0.0	18.0	1.4	87.5	1,032	17.0	1,442	155	5.8
Freehold township (Monmouth)	41	118	451	1,292	5,983	38	100.0	46.7	8.7	92.0	741	38.8	1,114	0	46.4
Galloway township (Atlantic)	73	200	399	1,094	3,372	121	20.7	32.7	3.4	93.2	581	19.4	540	5	20.9
Garfield city & MCD (Bergen)	79	245	585	1,817	2,106	33	3.0	79.0	1.8	1.1	1,739	31.3	984	73	43.8
Glassboro borough & MCD (Gloucester)	38	191	327	1,640	5,621	127	1.6	35.5	7.3	58.1	742	35.0	1,758	286	51.4
Glen Rock borough & MCD (Bergen)	NA	NA	49	411	1,675	5	100.0	18.2	1.0	100.0	1,272	17.6	1,486	0	17.6
Gloucester township (Camden)	78	123	945	1,495	4,545	38	100.0	62.8	8.6	80.0	720	51.2	804	15	60.0
Gloucester City city & MCD (Camden)	34	305	269	2,409	0	0	0.0	20.2	4.7	98.1	1,092	17.7	1,578	277	23.2
Greentree CDP	NA	NA	NA	NA	NA	NA	NA	NA	NA	NA	NA	NA	NA	NA	NA
Guttenberg town & MCD (Hudson)	28	241	99	853	8,816	40	42.5	22.7	4.1	20.3	1,428	22.5	1,980	72	3.0
Hackensack city & MCD (Bergen)	116	258	649	1,445	126,029	784	0.0	103.5	7.1	73.1	1,940	110.2	2,476	369	57.0
Haddon township (Camden)	19	131	247	1,703	1,482	9	100.0	14.7	2.3	59.1	649	16.6	1,142	225	11.1
Haddonfield borough & MCD (Camden)	6	53	100	889	5,008	14	100.0	15.8	1.2	93.1	1,184	28.2	2,482	1420	25.7
Hamilton township (Atlantic)	57	216	857	3,249	23,246	224	25.0	28.9	4.1	81.0	783	27.6	1,064	153	7.1
Hamilton township (Mercer)	116	132	1,700	1,934	8,821	96	63.5	115.7	21.0	99.3	830	91.3	1,044	8	123.8
Hamilton Square CDP	NA	NA	NA	NA	NA	NA	NA	NA	NA	NA	NA	NA	NA	NA	NA
Hammonton town & MCD (Atlantic)	9	63	149	1,041	3,163	54	22.2	9.7	0.0		690	4.6	323	0	22.9
Hanover township (Morris)	4	27	161	1,104	8,182	33	69.7	32.1	3.2	91.7	1,241	31.0	2,142	343	13.2
Harrison township (Gloucester)	2	16	67	519	4,245	17	100.0	8.9	0.7	100.0	478	11.1	854	170	38.4
Harrison town & MCD (Hudson)	41	227	373	2,066	74,841	1,289	2.5	81.0	49.6	96.3	1,282	80.7	4,708	102	34.8
Hasbrouck Heights borough & MCD (Bergen)	1	8	51	419	1,263	5	100.0	21.2	1.2	89.6	1,617	18.6	1,534	42	4.1
Hawthorne borough & MCD (Passaic)	2	11	177	938	4,366	59	6.8	20.8	1.7	97.0	928	18.9	1,006	119	17.7
Hazlet township (Monmouth)	23	115	208	1,042	497	14	7.1	24.6	2.4	100.0	795	23.7	1,193	15	5.8
Highland Park borough & MCD (Middlesex)	8	57	166	1,187	16,377	368	4.1	13.7	1.3	100.0	887	0.3	23	0	2.3
Hillsborough township (Somerset)	15	38	240	603	20,390	124	60.5	33.1	4.0	96.1	566	35.5	900	89	5.2
Hillsdale borough & MCD (Bergen)	3	29	41	391	2,384	10	50.0	14.0	1.3	94.5	1,050	13.9	1,338	71	4.9
Hillside township (Union)	41	186	540	2,446	119	1	100.0	44.3	4.0	100.0	1,724	40.6	1,848	0	2.4
Hoboken city & MCD (Hudson)	119	216	862	1,565	91,467	175	1.7	136.9	25.0	55.1	1,288	178.6	3,328	1145	132.1
Holiday City-Berkeley CDP	NA	NA	NA	NA	NA	NA	NA	NA	NA	NA	NA	NA	NA	NA	NA
Holmdel township (Monmouth)	4	24	129	776	6,209	27	85.2	25.2	3.0	72.5	1,087	27.8	1,682	386	11.0
Hopatcong borough & MCD (Sussex)	6	42	42	296	916	6	100.0	21.2	1.5	99.7	1,065	17.1	1,198	135	43.3
Hopewell township (Mercer)	8	44	76	422	1,123	6	100.0	21.3	2.6	79.3	890	16.7	929	13	74.6
Howell township (Monmouth)	36	68	351	666	12,732	72	95.8	53.7	11.4	100.0	599	40.6	779	36	78.6
Irvington township (Essex)	354	653	1,277	2,355	195	2	100.0	256.9	164.8	95.4	1,472	246.6	4,571	12	89.2
Iselin CDP	NA	NA	NA	NA	NA	NA	NA	NA	NA	NA	NA	NA	NA	NA	NA
Jackson township (Ocean)	27	48	360	635	6,931	40	100.0	43.3	4.0	92.5	658	37.5	658	56	29.1
Jefferson township (Morris)	5	24	84	399	929	6	100.0	22.9	0.4	76.1	1,000	17.9	850	0	31.3
Jersey City city & MCD (Hudson)	1,233	456	4,781	1,770	367,509	4,675	42.8	796.7	175.1	49.5	1,055	622.6	2,365	136	661.4
Keansburg borough & MCD (Monmouth)	33	338	160	1,638	1,097	11	100.0	25.5	7.6	44.1	1,330	30.2	3,104	1085	21.9
Kearny town & MCD (Hudson)	38	90	677	1,599	0	0	0.0	78.4	24.3	100.0	1,116	73.0	1,754	100	69.8
Kinnelon borough & MCD (Morris)	1	10	25	248	1,228	4	100.0	13.7	0.8	100.0	1,215	12.1	1,199	102	5.7
Lacey township (Ocean)	18	63	257	897	18,987	109	100.0	27.8	11.6	99.0	528	15.5	542	52	12.1

1 Data for serious crimes have not been adjusted for underreporting. This may affect comparability between geographic areas over time. 2 Per 100,000 population estimated by the FBI. 3 Based on population estimated as of July 1 of the year shown.

Table B. Incorporated Places, Census Designated Places (CDPs), and Minor Civil Divisions (MCDs) of 10,000 or More Population — **Land Area, Population, and Households, and Employment**

STATE City, town, township, borough, or CDP (county if applicable)	Land area 2010 (sq mi)	Population				Population characteristics 2015–2019		Income and poverty 2015–2019		Median value of owner-occupied housing units	Employment, 2015–2019		Households, 2015–2019 (percent of households)	
		Total persons 2010	Total persons 2019	Percent change 2010–2019	Persons per square mile 2019	Percent foreign born	Percent living in the same house as previous year	Median household income	Percent of households with income below poverty level		Percent in civilian labor force	Unemployment rate	Family households	One person households
	1	2	3	4	5	6	7	8	9	10	11	12	13	14
NEW JERSEY—Con.														
Lakewood township (Ocean)	24.68	92,799	106,300	14.5	4307.1	11.3	91.5	52,148	19.0	335,600	55.0	5.3	73.5	23.3
Lakewood CDP.......................	7.08	53,805	NA	NA	NA	10.4	92.6	50,897	26.7	474,400	57.3	4.3	87.3	10.9
Lawrence township (Mercer)	21.73	33,483	32,435	-3.1	1492.6	23.3	84.8	103,690	6.9	326,400	66.7	4.8	66.3	28.4
Lincoln Park borough & MCD (Morris).............................	6.40	10,539	10,111	-4.1	1579.8	15.1	90.2	97,003	2.3	330,900	66.3	4.0	71.1	23.8
Linden city & MCD (Union).......	10.69	40,533	42,361	4.5	3962.7	33.9	89.3	73,386	9.2	281,800	67.8	7.2	71.1	24.5
Lindenwold borough & MCD (Camden)...........................	3.90	17,620	17,263	-2.0	4426.4	13.9	84.7	45,789	14.6	124,200	69.7	7.0	53.8	39.8
Little Egg Harbor township (Ocean).............................	47.35	20,053	21,712	8.3	458.5	6.0	89.1	66,974	7.1	229,400	55.7	5.5	64.7	28.1
Little Falls township (Passaic)...	2.80	14,423	14,474	0.4	5169.3	15.4	89.2	101,651	5.6	369,100	69.5	4.3	67.2	27.1
Little Ferry borough & MCD (Bergen).............................	1.48	10,638	10,739	0.9	7256.1	43.8	88.1	66,098	12.1	329,300	70.0	6.0	68.6	27.9
Livingston township (Essex)	13.79	29,382	30,303	3.1	2197.5	25.9	92.4	166,629	3.6	627,000	63.5	2.9	81.7	16.5
Lodi borough & MCD (Bergen) .	2.27	24,091	24,347	1.1	10725.6	40.7	88.6	66,595	11.7	373,000	66.1	5.3	65.3	26.9
Long Branch city & MCD (Monmouth)........................	5.12	30,717	30,241	-1.5	5906.4	30.9	88.3	59,892	16.8	362,400	69.4	7.6	59.7	31.7
Lower township (Cape May)	27.38	22,874	21,339	-6.7	779.4	5.7	88.5	64,238	9.2	241,800	60.3	6.6	66.6	26.7
Lumberton township (Burlington)	12.88	12,544	12,192	-2.8	946.6	9.5	84.6	88,017	6.1	323,600	66.1	6.1	72.2	25.9
Lyndhurst township (Bergen)....	4.58	20,554	22,918	11.5	5003.9	27.4	91.6	79,985	10.6	375,600	65.5	4.6	65.8	30.0
Madison borough & MCD (Morris).............................	4.31	15,813	17,654	11.6	4096.1	15.9	90.7	146,157	5.4	724,700	67.1	3.9	68.6	25.4
Mahwah township (Bergen)	25.39	25,883	26,200	1.2	1031.9	19.0	86.7	107,081	5.4	498,400	64.8	6.2	66.8	30.5
Manalapan township (Monmouth)........................	30.65	38,975	39,325	0.9	1283.0	14.5	95.6	122,304	4.1	466,900	65.0	3.9	76.3	20.5
Manchester township (Ocean)..	81.42	43,057	43,723	1.5	537.0	7.4	89.5	43,878	8.8	139,600	38.4	7.0	48.4	47.4
Mantua township (Gloucester)..	16.01	15,286	14,840	-2.9	926.9	3.9	92.1	91,321	5.4	215,200	68.3	4.9	71.0	20.5
Manville borough & MCD (Somerset)........................	2.36	10,344	10,121	-2.2	4288.6	15.0	92.2	69,625	11.6	262,000	68.6	4.1	65.5	28.9
Maple Shade township (Burlington)	3.83	19,147	18,476	-3.5	4824.0	12.3	85.3	61,335	8.7	187,500	68.7	5.1	53.1	40.0
Maplewood township (Essex) ...	3.87	23,841	25,380	6.5	6558.1	19.1	92.3	139,081	5.4	527,900	73.7	6.0	75.7	20.3
Marlboro township (Monmouth)	30.34	40,061	39,640	-1.1	1306.5	22.1	93.5	152,489	2.4	550,100	65.2	4.3	84.7	12.9
Marlton CDP...........................	3.25	10,133	NA	NA	NA	9.2	88.3	79,216	4.2	249,200	69.9	3.2	64.6	30.8
Martinsville CDP......................	12.15	11,980	NA	NA	NA	18.8	90.0	156,327	1.9	559,800	68.1	4.1	79.4	17.9
Medford township (Burlington)..	38.80	23,004	23,394	1.7	602.9	5.5	90.9	124,471	2.8	363,700	65.4	4.4	78.6	17.8
Mercerville CDP......................	3.69	13,230	NA	NA	NA	9.0	93.3	98,107	4.3	259,300	69.0	4.6	67.4	24.3
Metuchen borough & MCD (Middlesex)	2.85	13,581	14,543	7.1	5102.8	20.6	88.1	128,619	4.1	437,400	72.0	3.0	72.8	22.9
Middle township (Cape May)	70.24	18,933	18,175	-4.0	258.8	3.4	92.4	64,976	10.7	246,500	61.3	9.5	67.2	25.4
Middlesex borough & MCD (Middlesex)	3.49	13,635	13,679	0.3	3919.5	21.8	89.8	75,460	5.5	307,000	70.2	4.2	75.2	21.6
Middletown township (Monmouth)........................	40.95	66,507	65,305	-1.8	1594.7	7.4	92.3	118,351	3.8	425,300	66.7	5.0	75.1	21.6
Millburn township (Essex).........	9.33	20,141	20,080	-0.3	2152.2	26.1	93.3	225,227	4.3	1,130,100	66.5	4.8	84.2	14.2
Millstone township (Monmouth)	36.61	10,666	10,397	-2.5	284.0	9.8	92.7	163,981	5.6	584,400	71.3	4.1	86.1	11.1
Millville city & MCD (Cumberland)......................	42.00	28,417	27,391	-3.6	652.2	4.2	88.5	58,138	16.5	159,000	61.9	8.9	66.7	27.8
Monroe township (Gloucester) .	46.42	36,119	36,865	2.1	794.2	5.9	91.5	85,399	6.0	210,200	67.7	5.3	69.1	26.5
Monroe township (Middlesex)...	41.94	39,176	45,030	14.9	1073.7	22.5	93.3	90,451	5.4	375,900	49.7	4.4	68.4	29.5
Montclair township (Essex).......	6.24	37,671	38,564	2.4	6180.1	13.5	89.4	126,844	7.3	624,700	70.4	4.2	64.9	27.9
Montgomery township (Somerset)........................	32.30	22,255	23,124	3.9	715.9	31.9	91.6	195,807	4.4	609,200	69.1	5.3	84.9	13.4
Montville township (Morris).......	18.63	21,505	21,058	-2.1	1130.3	20.9	93.4	145,292	3.5	598,400	69.2	4.1	81.3	16.0
Moorestown township (Burlington)	14.73	20,741	20,516	-1.1	1392.8	9.0	89.7	148,060	4.2	516,100	66.2	2.6	78.2	19.1
Moorestown-Lenola CDP	7.03	14,217	NA	NA	NA	6.8	88.9	121,853	4.9	414,000	69.5	2.3	72.1	24.2
Morris township (Morris)..........	15.68	22,413	22,156	-1.1	1413.0	13.1	85.5	151,776	5.0	593,500	65.2	4.1	71.9	24.2
Morristown town & MCD (Morris).............................	2.91	18,352	19,261	5.0	6618.9	26.3	86.1	96,545	8.9	472,000	74.7	2.5	46.5	36.7
Mount Laurel township (Burlington)	21.72	41,860	41,250	-1.5	1899.2	12.4	89.3	94,832	4.2	272,800	66.3	4.2	64.3	29.2
Mount Olive township (Morris)..	29.62	28,181	28,926	2.6	976.6	17.1	89.9	88,073	7.3	367,900	70.5	4.5	69.7	24.4
Neptune township (Monmouth)	8.13	27,991	27,384	-2.2	3368.3	12.9	88.8	76,463	11.0	309,700	66.6	5.7	60.9	32.8
Newark city & MCD (Essex)	24.14	277,135	282,011	1.8	11682.3	31.8	88.3	35,199	28.7	245,200	61.2	11.3	59.6	35.4
New Brunswick city & MCD (Middlesex)	5.23	54,500	55,676	2.2	10645.5	31.5	84.3	43,783	32.3	251,100	52.7	5.8	59.5	25.2
New Milford borough & MCD (Bergen).............................	2.28	16,347	16,429	0.5	7205.7	28.2	90.4	94,344	5.6	426,800	70.8	4.6	72.2	24.1
New Providence borough & MCD (Union)	3.69	12,207	13,595	11.4	3684.3	17.4	91.0	143,672	3.7	607,100	67.7	5.1	75.4	20.3
North Arlington borough & MCD (Bergen)	2.48	15,392	15,683	1.9	6323.8	33.5	94.1	84,527	7.2	363,400	67.0	3.5	68.5	26.2
North Bergen township (Hudson)	5.14	60,790	60,666	-0.2	11802.7	49.7	89.9	63,908	14.2	350,600	68.7	6.5	70.2	24.8
North Brunswick township (Middlesex)	12.03	41,423	41,431	0.0	3444.0	34.6	90.2	96,546	7.9	341,000	67.1	4.8	72.6	22.5
North Plainfield borough & MCD (Somerset)..................	2.81	21,774	21,289	-2.2	7576.2	30.3	90.1	69,566	11.0	272,900	75.1	6.4	68.2	27.8
Nutley township (Essex)	3.37	28,376	28,434	0.2	8437.4	19.6	90.4	99,276	5.4	387,600	70.2	3.1	65.7	30.1
Oakland borough & MCD (Bergen).............................	8.50	12,753	12,926	1.4	1520.7	13.7	93.5	126,319	2.5	468,700	69.9	3.7	86.3	10.8
Ocean township (Monmouth) ...	10.87	27,293	26,542	-2.8	2441.8	16.4	91.1	94,284	6.9	431,600	64.9	4.3	69.0	28.1
Ocean Acres CDP	5.83	16,142	NA	NA	NA	2.2	92.6	88,750	6.3	264,600	68.2	3.6	79.2	17.8
Ocean City city & MCD (Cape May)	6.72	11,702	10,971	-6.2	1632.6	5.1	84.1	81,076	7.2	574,100	52.6	3.6	60.5	35.9

Table B. Incorporated Places, Census Designated Places (CDPs), and Minor Civil Divisions (MCDs) of 10,000 or More Population — **Crime, Residential Construction and Local Government Finance**

STATE City, town, township, borough, or CDP (county if applicable)	Serious crimes known to police, 2018[1] Violent crime Number	Rate[2]	Property crime Number	Rate[2]	New residential construction authorized by building permits, 2019 Value ($1,000)	Number of housing units	Percent single family	Local government finance, 2017 General revenue Total (mil dol)	Intergovernmental Total (mil dol)	Percent from state gov.	Taxes per capita[3]	General expenditure Total (mil dol)	Per capita[3] Total	Capital outlays	Debt outstanding (mil dol)
	15	16	17	18	19	20	21	22	23	24	25	26	27	28	29
NEW JERSEY—Con.															
Lakewood township (Ocean)	129	125	779	757	77,133	554	71.3	88.4	23.2	37.3	618	51.9	508	1	45.1
Lakewood CDP..........	NA	NA	NA	NA	NA	NA	NA	NA	NA	NA	NA	NA	NA	NA	NA
Lawrence township (Mercer)	30	92	596	1,826	9,478	40	100.0	48.9	4.7	95.2	931	42.1	1,291	0	17.6
Lincoln Park borough & MCD (Morris)	NA	NA	60	582	5	2	0.0	18.5	1.4	99.8	1,358	14.7	1,417	76	24.1
Linden city & MCD (Union)	122	285	1,126	2,631	25,582	355	8.7	107.0	25.5	81.8	1,689	101.9	2,404	286	52.9
Lindenwold borough & MCD (Camden)	111	645	455	2,645	4,805	82	13.4	16.2	2.6	91.9	690	15.6	901	30	2.2
Little Egg Harbor township (Ocean)	4	19	241	1,143	5,806	34	100.0	21.3	0.5	100.0	750	14.4	682	99	28.6
Little Falls township (Passaic)...	16	112	113	790	769	3	100.0	16.2	1.4	85.9	961	16.2	1,118	94	12.9
Little Ferry borough & MCD (Bergen)	7	64	94	863	972	5	100.0	15.7	1.5	69.1	1,272	14.6	1,354	128	9.2
Livingston township (Essex)	23	77	277	929	18,637	80	81.3	49.1	4.7	98.1	1,225	35.9	1,209	27	91.5
Lodi borough & MCD (Bergen) .	28	113	254	1,028	831	4	50.0	33.1	8.2	29.1	796	31.2	1,274	75	22.7
Long Branch city & MCD (Monmouth)	124	403	639	2,078	65,512	460	15.4	77.8	18.7	27.0	1,438	80.5	2,633	366	82.5
Lower township (Cape May)	35	162	163	754	8,415	104	49.0	26.4	2.9	76.5	1,045	18.8	865	12	17.3
Lumberton township (Burlington)	10	82	212	1,730	1,228	15	100.0	8.9	2.0	74.0	512	7.0	576	107	10.3
Lyndhurst township (Bergen)....	12	54	168	751	3,768	32	31.3	43.1	2.1	78.1	1,623	29.1	1,321	141	57.4
Madison borough & MCD (Morris)	3	19	76	480	5,768	24	50.0	25.5	4.5	24.5	1,145	29.1	1,834	244	24.7
Mahwah township (Bergen)	3	11	98	370	5,012	18	100.0	24.2	0.0		917	0.9	34	0	20.7
Manalapan township (Monmouth)	13	32	218	543	1,937	36	16.7	34.2	3.8	96.8	747	36.3	912	161	16.6
Manchester township (Ocean)..	15	35	238	554	14,419	174	100.0	37.8	5.4	92.5	552	29.5	680	13	36.6
Mantua township (Gloucester)..	7	47	190	1,286	7,378	60	81.7	14.7	1.9	84.3	724	13.0	870	71	11.3
Manville borough & MCD (Somerset)	18	175	214	2,076	749	2	100.0	16.4	1.7	94.4	1,188	15.1	1,479	42	4.5
Maple Shade township (Burlington)	38	202	305	1,625	125	1	100.0	18.1	2.7	90.2	660	17.6	945	183	29.9
Maplewood township (Essex) ...	22	89	394	1,599	7,843	111	10.8	31.7	0.4	100.0	1,192	22.8	934	12	0.0
Marlboro township (Monmouth)	25	62	271	672	4,493	16	100.0	37.5	3.1	100.0	766	30.4	759	68	75.9
Marlton CDP.....................	NA	NA	NA	NA	NA	NA	NA	NA	NA	NA	NA	NA	NA	NA	NA
Martinsville CDP..................	NA	NA	NA	NA	NA	NA	NA	NA	NA	NA	NA	NA	NA	NA	NA
Medford township (Burlington)..	47	200	176	747	6,831	45	100.0	61.0	41.7	97.0	660	15.8	680	37	44.7
Mercerville CDP..................	NA	NA	NA	NA	NA	NA	NA	NA	NA	NA	NA	NA	NA	NA	NA
Metuchen borough & MCD (Middlesex)	5	35	128	898	4,396	15	100.0	17.9	1.6	94.2	967	16.6	1,177	45	12.8
Middle township (Cape May)	51	278	394	2,146	14,531	32	84.4	55.8	3.7	99.5	2,616	18.2	989	41	11.0
Middlesex borough & MCD (Middlesex)	11	80	100	730	2,008	14	57.1	14.7	0.5	100.0	983	14.9	1,093	0	12.6
Middletown township (Monmouth)	14	21	388	593	26,677	101	100.0	72.0	9.5	99.7	873	54.5	836	29	29.8
Millburn township (Essex).........	8	40	369	1,822	13,103	19	100.0	56.7	2.7	99.5	2,383	41.4	2,053	0	14.0
Millstone township (Monmouth) ...	NA	NA	NA	NA	2,704	14	57.1	5.3	1.1	99.4	356	5.3	503	44	8.1
Millville city & MCD (Cumberland)	127	456	1,217	4,372	1,060	15	100.0	35.4	5.3	100.0	799	36.0	1,302	0	31.1
Monroe township (Gloucester) .	47	129	462	1,266	13,219	71	100.0	47.8	4.5	99.7	770	37.3	1,016	12	29.9
Monroe township (Middlesex)...	5	11	158	347	57,039	306	78.4	34.9	4.5	100.0	636	27.3	614	10	12.5
Montclair township (Essex).......	37	95	502	1,291	101,510	290	3.1	151.1	18.7	93.8	3,025	187.3	4,846	102	66.2
Montgomery township (Somerset)	7	30	97	413	14,157	130	33.8	32.7	1.9	95.0	822	26.3	1,133	0	28.2
Montville township (Morris).......	4	19	173	809	6,091	33	100.0	36.3	2.4	97.9	1,134	28.8	1,345	131	34.2
Moorestown township (Burlington)	13	63	251	1,224	10,960	45	88.9	28.1	2.0	100.0	930	22.7	1,116	135	43.6
Moorestown-Lenola CDP	NA	NA	NA	NA	NA	NA	NA	NA	NA	NA	NA	NA	NA	NA	NA
Morris township (Morris)...........	6	27	120	541	25,279	140	100.0	80.0	3.7	100.0	1,266	31.3	1,406	0	37.0
Morristown town & MCD (Morris)	30	159	202	1,071	8,875	62	12.9	58.7	6.3	47.9	1,405	55.1	2,930	596	67.7
Mount Laurel township (Burlington)	52	125	664	1,595	68,052	1,488	7.7	36.7	3.8	89.4	705	25.5	617	7	23.5
Mount Olive township (Morris)..	6	21	77	266	12,048	73	100.0	39.5	0.4	57.0	739	26.4	913	0	26.5
Neptune township (Monmouth)	106	381	851	3,058	6,533	56	71.4	51.6	14.1	39.3	1,105	320.2	11,577	9575	31.2
Newark city & MCD (Essex)	2,069	733	5,674	2,010	75,696	564	0.0	845.4	353.0	39.2	1,234	891.1	3,168	187	433.8
New Brunswick city & MCD (Middlesex)	309	546	1,210	2,139	46,848	258	1.2	300.6	192.9	92.9	664	347.2	6,186	237	575.5
New Milford borough & MCD (Bergen)	5	30	52	311	6,498	44	20.5	16.7	0.4	50.0	969	19.6	1,184	133	15.1
New Providence borough & MCD (Union)	NA	NA	65	489	3,465	15	40.0	19.5	1.7	93.1	1,287	16.6	1,266	103	4.5
North Arlington borough & MCD (Bergen)	5	32	148	933	1,276	12	33.3	21.5	2.7	91.7	1,088	22.0	1,398	118	12.0
North Bergen township (Hudson)	98	155	435	689	17,140	134	1.5	119.5	20.3	53.4	1,136	100.3	1,620	64	105.9
North Brunswick township (Middlesex)	53	126	683	1,618	6,597	38	100.0	49.6	4.9	8.7	808	36.9	881	117	72.7
North Plainfield borough & MCD (Somerset)	39	179	338	1,548	0	0	0.0	24.7	0.1	100.0	968	23.8	1,106	0	29.2
Nutley township (Essex)..........	27	94	197	689	5,054	37	24.3	54.3	9.0	97.5	1,544	41.7	1,464	11	16.5
Oakland borough & MCD (Bergen)	7	53	48	366	1,329	6	16.7	16.7	0.0	68.2	1,210	12.6	970	0	20.5
Ocean township (Monmouth) ...	20	74	586	2,175	14,314	51	100.0	40.0	4.0	96.5	1,261	27.8	1,036	50	42.3
Ocean Acres CDP.................	NA	NA	NA	NA	NA	NA	NA	NA	NA	NA	NA	NA	NA	NA	NA
Ocean City city & MCD (Cape May)	5	45	283	2,541	69,319	206	52.4	71.9	4.7	71.6	5,052	89.1	7,990	2549	142.7

1 Data for serious crimes have not been adjusted for underreporting. This may affect comparability between geographic areas over time.
2 Per 100,000 population estimated by the FBI. 3 Based on population estimated as of July 1 of the year shown.

Table B. Incorporated Places, Census Designated Places (CDPs), and Minor Civil Divisions (MCDs) of 10,000 or More Population — Land Area, Population, and Households, and Employment

STATE City, town, township, borough, or CDP (county if applicable)	Land area 2010 (sq mi)	Population				Population characteristics 2015–2019		Income and poverty 2015–2019		Median value of owner-occupied housing units	Employment, 2015–2019		Households, 2015–2019 (percent of households)	
		Total persons 2010	Total persons 2019	Percent change 2010–2019	Persons per square mile, 2019	Percent foreign born	Percent living in the same house as previous year	Median household income	Percent of households with income below poverty level		Percent in civilian labor force	Unemployment rate	Family households	One person households
	1	2	3	4	5	6	7	8	9	10	11	12	13	14
NEW JERSEY—Con.														
Old Bridge CDP	7.11	23,753	NA	NA	NA	18.3	96.1	105,562	6.2	365,600	69.5	5.8	77.9	19.2
Old Bridge township (Middlesex)	38.18	65,406	65,590	0.3	1717.9	22.1	93.2	91,919	5.9	351,000	69.9	4.9	71.2	24.5
Palisades Park borough & MCD (Bergen)	1.24	19,589	20,715	5.7	16705.6	63.7	89.4	68,245	12.8	558,400	64.9	3.9	74.6	18.3
Paramus borough & MCD (Bergen)	10.45	26,342	26,264	-0.3	2513.3	30.3	91.2	128,306	3.5	600,200	59.8	4.5	80.9	17.6
Parsippany-Troy Hills township (Morris)	23.63	53,185	51,561	-3.1	2182.0	38.4	90.0	102,408	4.7	438,200	68.2	5.8	70.5	25.2
Passaic city & MCD (Passaic)	3.13	69,811	69,703	-0.2	22269.3	38.8	92.3	40,865	30.2	332,700	62.0	5.3	74.2	22.5
Paterson city & MCD (Passaic)	8.41	146,181	145,233	-0.6	17269.1	40.6	92.5	41,360	27.8	244,200	60.3	4.8	72.6	23.2
Pemberton township (Burlington)	61.56	27,913	26,979	-3.3	438.3	7.9	85.7	64,444	8.5	169,100	61.3	9.4	70.0	24.0
Pennsauken township (Camden)	10.48	36,015	35,761	-0.7	3412.3	15.6	89.6	67,300	13.5	158,200	65.9	7.8	71.7	23.9
Pennsville CDP	10.08	11,888	NA	NA	NA	3.2	89.2	67,043	9.5	153,700	64.2	4.0	63.9	32.9
Pennsville township (Salem)	21.27	13,422	12,418	-7.5	583.8	3.4	89.1	68,181	9.5	155,000	64.0	3.9	63.2	33.6
Pequannock township (Morris)	6.79	15,538	14,965	-3.7	2204.0	9.2	93.6	105,316	7.0	425,100	62.2	7.0	66.7	30.7
Perth Amboy city & MCD (Middlesex)	4.66	50,827	51,390	1.1	11027.9	41.5	92.2	52,563	20.2	261,800	62.5	3.9	77.0	18.7
Phillipsburg town & MCD (Warren)	3.19	14,950	14,212	-4.9	4455.2	10.2	87.5	54,459	16.2	136,800	67.3	5.2	60.7	32.8
Pine Hill borough & MCD (Camden)	3.91	10,230	10,417	1.8	2664.2	3.3	88.5	56,058	15.2	136,900	68.0	9.6	58.7	33.7
Piscataway township (Middlesex)	18.79	55,984	56,837	1.5	3024.9	32.6	87.2	99,925	6.9	334,300	57.2	5.5	76.9	19.0
Plainfield city & MCD (Union)	5.96	49,595	50,317	1.5	8442.4	37.4	89.5	56,339	19.5	257,200	67.8	7.9	68.6	26.5
Plainsboro township (Middlesex)	11.74	22,995	22,884	-0.5	1949.2	53.3	76.3	113,131	3.8	488,400	68.6	4.5	68.3	26.7
Pleasantville city & MCD (Atlantic)	5.72	20,272	20,149	-0.6	3522.6	29.2	80.0	40,991	23.5	131,800	64.0	8.8	64.8	27.6
Point Pleasant borough & MCD (Ocean)	3.49	18,373	18,772	2.2	5378.8	6.3	87.5	98,401	2.9	386,200	71.8	4.9	67.8	25.7
Pompton Lakes borough & MCD (Passaic)	2.89	11,097	10,986	-1.0	3801.4	20.9	92.8	102,371	6.7	302,700	74.0	4.4	71.3	26.3
Princeton & MCD (Mercer)	17.95	28,584	31,187	9.1	1737.4	28.5	75.4	137,672	8.0	866,200	59.7	3.3	68.1	24.9
Princeton Meadows CDP	2.07	13,834	NA	NA	NA	55.8	70.3	104,245	4.4	392,800	72.2	4.8	66.4	27.7
Rahway city & MCD (Union)	3.90	27,324	29,895	9.4	7665.4	24.4	87.8	78,946	6.8	272,700	69.6	4.4	63.3	32.5
Ramsey borough & MCD (Bergen)	5.50	14,521	14,884	2.5	2706.2	15.4	94.3	147,875	2.3	598,900	65.8	3.0	75.1	21.8
Randolph township (Morris)	20.91	25,701	25,378	-1.3	1213.7	21.2	92.5	142,459	5.0	539,900	68.5	2.9	78.1	19.7
Raritan township (Hunterdon)	37.48	22,196	22,382	0.8	597.2	12.2	92.9	135,115	3.1	438,000	68.9	4.1	77.1	20.5
Readington township (Hunterdon)	47.56	16,120	15,843	-1.7	333.1	11.2	93.6	131,755	3.6	479,500	64.9	3.9	74.2	20.5
Red Bank borough & MCD (Monmouth)	1.75	12,227	11,966	-2.1	6837.7	24.8	87.7	74,181	10.9	404,400	74.7	5.0	47.6	42.8
Ridgefield borough & MCD (Bergen)	2.54	11,041	11,171	1.2	4398.0	46.8	94.2	71,699	7.9	442,500	65.7	5.7	75.0	21.0
Ridgefield Park village & MCD (Bergen)	1.71	12,722	12,901	1.4	7544.4	36.8	89.4	86,923	7.1	349,100	72.4	3.7	71.6	24.7
Ridgewood village & MCD (Bergen)	5.74	24,951	25,056	0.4	4365.2	21.0	90.0	184,355	4.1	763,300	64.7	3.4	80.1	17.7
Ringwood borough & MCD (Passaic)	25.59	12,261	12,198	-0.5	476.7	11.1	91.9	125,476	1.5	366,400	70.2	4.1	81.2	16.5
River Edge borough & MCD (Bergen)	1.83	11,340	11,435	0.8	6248.6	27.8	93.1	124,598	4.8	520,800	68.4	2.6	81.2	16.4
Robbinsville township (Mercer)	20.44	13,648	14,543	6.6	711.5	22.3	91.4	155,107	1.3	412,800	74.6	3.4	76.2	22.2
Robertsville CDP	5.90	11,297	NA	NA	NA	17.9	93.7	151,397	2.8	496,900	67.6	4.6	84.8	10.6
Rockaway township (Morris)	41.73	24,136	25,876	7.2	620.1	15.2	93.9	111,026	4.1	359,000	66.7	4.1	70.3	26.8
Roselle borough & MCD (Union)	2.64	21,067	21,811	3.5	8261.7	29.5	91.6	64,718	9.5	225,100	69.1	8.7	70.8	25.8
Roselle Park borough & MCD (Union)	1.23	13,290	13,588	2.2	11047.2	29.8	92.7	75,000	5.3	284,000	71.2	5.3	72.1	24.1
Roxbury township (Morris)	20.85	23,308	22,551	-3.2	1081.6	12.5	92.8	113,957	4.2	354,900	65.9	4.1	77.1	19.8
Rutherford borough & MCD (Bergen)	2.78	18,061	18,303	1.3	6583.8	26.8	89.7	101,473	6.4	473,500	66.5	4.2	71.7	24.1
Saddle Brook township (Bergen)	2.69	13,658	13,562	-0.7	5041.6	23.2	90.9	106,776	5.1	379,000	66.3	2.4	68.0	26.6
Sayreville borough & MCD (Middlesex)	15.83	42,770	44,173	3.3	2790.5	28.5	89.7	81,883	7.0	302,800	69.2	4.9	70.1	25.7
Scotch Plains township (Union)	9.02	23,646	24,274	2.7	2691.1	15.8	94.8	131,732	4.9	497,900	68.9	4.9	75.3	21.2
Secaucus town & MCD (Hudson)	5.83	16,264	21,893	34.6	3755.2	34.7	90.7	114,821	8.1	460,800	64.6	3.8	69.6	25.2
Short Hills CDP	5.25	13,165	NA	NA	NA	24.2	93.8	250	3.9	1,386,600	65.3	5.8	91.2	8.3
Somerset CDP	6.33	22,083	NA	NA	NA	26.5	89.8	96,197	6.8	315,900	70.0	5.9	64.8	30.3
Somers Point city & MCD (Atlantic)	4.01	10,795	10,174	-5.8	2537.2	10.2	88.5	61,366	13.2	221,500	67.6	5.3	63.3	30.3
Somerville borough & MCD (Somerset)	2.34	12,093	12,063	-0.2	5155.1	24.9	87.0	77,104	8.3	322,000	69.2	5.2	58.2	33.6
Southampton township (Burlington)	43.96	10,440	10,095	-3.3	229.6	3.1	88.3	62,757	7.6	201,600	53.1	4.8	60.5	36.5
South Brunswick township (Middlesex)	40.61	43,419	45,685	5.2	1125.0	42.6	90.5	120,546	4.1	430,100	68.3	3.9	81.2	17.3
South Orange Village township (Essex)	2.85	16,175	16,691	3.2	5856.5	14.6	84.9	139,037	9.6	604,300	64.5	5.8	69.0	23.4
South Plainfield borough & MCD (Middlesex)	8.30	23,392	24,052	2.8	2897.8	22.8	91.5	101,565	3.4	340,200	71.0	6.9	81.1	16.2

Table B. Incorporated Places, Census Designated Places (CDPs), and Minor Civil Divisions (MCDs) of 10,000 or More Population — **Crime, Residential Construction and Local Government Finance**

STATE City, town, township, borough, or CDP (county if applicable)	Serious crimes known to police, 2018[1] Violent crime Number	Rate[2]	Property crime Number	Rate[2]	New residential construction authorized by building permits, 2019 Value ($1,000)	Number of housing units	Percent single family	Local government finance, 2017 General revenue Total (mil dol)	Intergovernmental Total (mil dol)	Percent from state gov.	Taxes per capita[3]	General expenditure Total (mil dol)	Per capita[3] Total	Capital outlays	Debt outstanding (mil dol)
	15	16	17	18	19	20	21	22	23	24	25	26	27	28	29
NEW JERSEY—Con.															
Old Bridge CDP	NA	NA	NA	NA	NA	NA	NA	NA	NA	NA	NA	NA	NA	NA	NA
Old Bridge township (Middlesex)	28	42	490	739	15,583	577	4.5	70.0	7.6	87.5	610	57.2	869	13	47.2
Palisades Park borough & MCD (Bergen)	17	81	130	622	22,980	144	18.1	22.6	1.0	96.3	938	20.9	1,015	80	6.3
Paramus borough & MCD (Bergen)	24	90	1,067	3,990	19,417	34	100.0	60.0	5.1	89.5	1,812	65.0	2,443	292	37.7
Parsippany-Troy Hills township (Morris)	29	55	362	690	6,016	27	100.0	86.1	8.1	100.0	1,001	64.1	1,218	37	100.2
Passaic city & MCD (Passaic)	406	576	1,298	1,843	3,272	62	51.6	124.4	37.1	40.7	963	124.7	1,778	57	5.6
Paterson city & MCD (Passaic)	1,076	733	3,564	2,426	15,986	483	4.3	340.1	108.9	54.7	1,202	333.3	2,283	141	82.4
Pemberton township (Burlington)	90	331	547	2,010	603	6	100.0	42.1	3.7	100.0	1,190	32.1	1,184	6	26.2
Pennsauken township (Camden)	101	285	909	2,566	15,381	380	3.7	43.8	7.6	78.2	745	47.9	1,345	115	24.2
Pennsville CDP	NA	NA	NA	NA	NA	NA	NA	NA	NA	NA	NA	NA	NA	NA	NA
Pennsville township (Salem)	6	49	236	1,907	14	1	100.0	17.7	4.9	99.7	620	10.1	810	22	5.7
Pequannock township (Morris)	3	20	93	613	2,725	8	100.0	21.2	2.3	74.6	881	20.8	1,364	75	5.9
Perth Amboy city & MCD (Middlesex)	165	315	721	1,377	17,745	122	100.0	111.5	24.1	44.3	1,171	98.4	1,899	110	175.2
Phillipsburg town & MCD (Warren)	44	306	295	2,049	370	4	100.0	26.8	5.7	56.2	912	20.6	1,440	171	14.3
Pine Hill borough & MCD (Camden)	25	240	162	1,553	219	3	100.0	10.2	0.9	94.7	641	8.5	814	46	6.4
Piscataway township (Middlesex)	54	94	425	741	9,673	146	10.3	74.2	9.5	100.0	888	52.3	918	5	49.3
Plainfield city & MCD (Union)	195	384	820	1,614	5,867	72	4.2	124.7	23.1	1.0	1,902	129.5	2,571	32	36.3
Plainsboro township (Middlesex)	10	43	118	508	1,492	5	100.0	24.0	3.5	98.7	794	19.1	829	20	41.6
Pleasantville city & MCD (Atlantic)	92	442	306	1,471	80	1	100.0	37.5	9.3	23.0	1,030	26.5	1,299	0	32.5
Point Pleasant borough & MCD (Ocean)	14	76	115	623	15,101	42	100.0	23.0	2.0	78.7	910	22.3	1,200	164	29.3
Pompton Lakes borough & MCD (Passaic)	15	136	89	805	5,447	96	1.0	13.4	0.8	69.9	916	8.0	721	59	10.7
Princeton & MCD (Mercer)	11	35	224	703	0	0	0.0	60.0	3.8	90.3	1,211	59.8	1,908	436	95.1
Princeton Meadows CDP	NA	NA	NA	NA	NA	NA	NA	NA	NA	NA	NA	NA	NA	NA	NA
Rahway city & MCD (Union)	34	113	245	814	17,833	267	4.9	57.5	5.0	88.8	1,450	50.9	1,719	88	79.0
Ramsey borough & MCD (Bergen)	2	13	106	701	3,406	12	100.0	25.5	1.8	100.0	1,310	25.0	1,669	183	11.3
Randolph township (Morris)	2	8	128	501	2,638	15	100.0	33.6	2.3	78.1	1,013	31.8	1,244	91	6.4
Raritan township (Hunterdon)	5	23	95	430	15,399	228	34.2	18.2	2.1	94.7	700	17.3	787	23	22.1
Readington township (Hunterdon)	2	13	82	514	17,363	172	24.4	17.1	1.5	100.0	909	17.3	1,084	71	52.6
Red Bank borough & MCD (Monmouth)	21	173	162	1,336	9,167	57	31.6	25.2	2.1	100.0	1,709	13.0	1,081	0	26.7
Ridgefield borough & MCD (Bergen)	3	27	68	600	2,688	14	50.0	14.1	5.9	100.0	662	12.4	1,102	0	9.9
Ridgefield Park village & MCD (Bergen)	13	100	99	760	3,528	51	9.8	21.7	1.5	94.8	1,270	18.1	1,403	24	8.7
Ridgewood village & MCD (Bergen)	5	20	155	610	12,416	170	7.6	44.6	2.3	92.3	1,502	49.3	1,950	263	57.7
Ringwood borough & MCD (Passaic)	6	49	48	390	2,139	11	100.0	11.9	0.2	0.0	945	7.6	623	0	10.5
River Edge borough & MCD (Bergen)	NA	NA	64	551	12,802	77	16.9	15.7	1.2	93.8	1,241	16.9	1,466	175	7.2
Robbinsville township (Mercer)	2	14	59	401	12,579	166	17.5	22.0	2.0	87.8	1,100	23.7	1,636	0	47.5
Robertsville CDP	NA	NA	NA	NA	NA	NA	NA	NA	NA	NA	NA	NA	NA	NA	NA
Rockaway township (Morris)	6	24	294	1,161	13,984	232	14.7	44.7	2.0	93.3	1,431	34.7	1,377	71	23.0
Roselle borough & MCD (Union)	45	207	281	1,290	3,256	37	5.4	38.1	3.3	94.7	1,481	30.0	1,387	0	35.4
Roselle Park borough & MCD (Union)	5	37	104	759	0	0	0.0	18.1	1.4	89.9	1,065	16.3	1,197	115	17.8
Roxbury township (Morris)	1	4	127	552	2,046	15	20.0	35.0	2.5	98.8	1,145	33.2	1,440	169	7.9
Rutherford borough & MCD (Bergen)	19	102	164	881	2,204	6	100.0	29.6	2.0	98.8	1,406	26.0	1,409	108	13.4
Saddle Brook township (Bergen)	1	7	192	1,368	1,715	10	60.0	16.1	0.0		1,159	9.5	681	0	26.2
Sayreville borough & MCD (Middlesex)	44	98	301	668	4,184	69	15.9	56.1	12.1	80.9	814	57.0	1,280	187	51.1
Scotch Plains township (Union)	10	41	171	700	4,211	17	100.0	27.3	2.4	98.9	825	25.6	1,054	72	4.3
Secaucus town & MCD (Hudson)	30	147	526	2,568	2,551	22	4.5	59.4	10.9	32.6	2,114	77.6	3,939	9	45.6
Short Hills CDP	NA	NA	NA	NA	NA	NA	NA	NA	NA	NA	NA	NA	NA	NA	NA
Somerset CDP	NA	NA	NA	NA	NA	NA	NA	NA	NA	NA	NA	NA	NA	NA	NA
Somers Point city & MCD (Atlantic)	14	134	246	2,357	10,111	11	100.0	38.5	1.5	99.0	3,262	2.4	236	0	15.4
Somerville borough & MCD (Somerset)	16	130	131	1,063	23,618	454	0.7	21.4	1.5	99.3	1,325	19.8	1,619	225	13.1
Southampton township (Burlington)	NA	NA	NA	NA	0	0	0.0	28.0	0.8	34.3	2,669	3.0	294	0	5.5
South Brunswick township (Middlesex)	23	50	276	596	46,510	193	37.8	71.9	5.7	95.5	927	52.8	1,156	12	68.6
South Orange Village township (Essex)	22	130	293	1,736	2,471	23	4.3	36.9	2.6	91.4	1,464	32.7	1,949	98	13.6
South Plainfield borough & MCD (Middlesex)	23	95	397	1,638	2,449	26	61.5	36.8	3.7	93.9	983	35.2	1,470	83	0.0

1 Data for serious crimes have not been adjusted for underreporting. This may affect comparability between geographic areas over time. 2 Per 100,000 population estimated by the FBI. 3 Based on population estimated as of July 1 of the year shown.

Table B. Incorporated Places, Census Designated Places (CDPs), and Minor Civil Divisions (MCDs) of 10,000 or More Population — **Land Area, Population, and Households, and Employment**

STATE City, town, township, borough, or CDP (county if applicable)	Land area 2010 (sq mi)	Total persons 2010	Total persons 2019	Percent change 2010–2019	Persons per square mile 2019	Percent foreign born	Percent living in the same house as previous year	Median household income	Percent of households with income below poverty level	Median value of owner-occupied housing units	Percent in civilian labor force	Unemployment rate	Family households	One person households
	1	2	3	4	5	6	7	8	9	10	11	12	13	14
NEW JERSEY—Con.														
South River borough & MCD (Middlesex)	2.79	16,050	15,779	-1.7	5655.6	30.0	94.6	78,162	7.9	299,600	71.2	9.8	71.4	25.4
Sparta township (Sussex)	36.79	19,581	18,575	-5.1	504.9	7.4	91.7	138,061	2.2	381,600	69.6	4.4	77.0	19.0
Springdale CDP	5.35	14,518	NA	NA	NA	17.3	91.9	151,431	3.9	364,900	63.3	2.5	76.9	22.8
Springfield township (Union)	5.16	15,799	17,464	10.5	3384.5	27.5	88.1	111,899	7.2	436,900	70.7	3.8	67.7	28.5
Stafford township (Ocean)	46.11	26,541	27,845	4.9	603.9	4.9	90.7	81,548	7.9	277,500	62.8	4.7	68.2	27.2
Summit city & MCD (Union)	5.99	21,460	21,897	2.0	3655.6	23.6	89.6	157,835	3.9	890,100	68.5	5.5	74.8	22.5
Teaneck township (Bergen)	6.04	39,760	40,284	1.3	6669.5	23.1	89.9	111,821	6.3	408,500	63.4	3.4	75.9	20.3
Tenafly borough & MCD (Bergen)	4.59	14,513	14,453	-0.4	3148.8	35.0	90.7	172,926	3.5	829,600	64.8	4.5	85.6	12.9
Tinton Falls borough & MCD (Monmouth)	15.48	18,032	17,451	-3.2	1127.3	12.7	89.8	87,157	5.4	354,300	61.2	3.4	54.4	40.0
Toms River CDP	39.00	88,791	NA	NA	NA	8.9	89.0	79,889	8.3	289,400	64.2	4.9	68.2	26.7
Toms River township (Ocean)	40.55	91,261	94,108	3.1	2320.8	8.9	88.8	79,607	8.4	294,700	63.7	4.9	67.6	27.2
Totowa borough & MCD (Passaic)	4.00	10,807	10,792	-0.1	2698.0	22.0	93.7	105,637	3.2	371,200	68.7	3.1	76.8	18.2
Trenton city & MCD (Mercer)	7.58	84,959	83,203	-2.1	10976.6	24.1	81.6	35,402	29.0	95,800	58.7	11.4	59.4	34.4
Union township (Union)	9.05	56,717	58,488	3.1	6462.8	30.9	92.1	88,496	6.2	329,000	66.8	5.2	73.9	23.0
Union City city & MCD (Hudson)	1.29	66,467	67,982	2.3	52699.2	58.0	93.6	48,992	20.1	340,800	69.1	4.5	67.4	24.5
Upper township (Cape May)	62.03	12,379	11,917	-3.7	192.1	1.7	93.1	91,167	6.4	306,600	68.4	5.0	72.4	24.2
Upper Montclair CDP	2.49	11,565	NA	NA	NA	11.9	89.1	211,221	1.6	766,100	69.1	3.7	82.2	15.5
Ventnor City city & MCD (Atlantic)	1.96	10,650	9,895	-7.1	5048.5	20.0	86.8	59,219	9.8	273,500	61.0	10.7	61.6	31.2
Vernon township (Sussex)	67.60	23,605	21,989	-6.8	325.3	6.6	92.0	95,883	3.7	236,400	71.3	5.5	74.8	20.3
Verona township (Essex)	2.79	13,343	13,390	0.4	4799.3	12.9	93.0	128,060	3.1	457,400	71.4	3.7	69.5	26.3
Vineland city & MCD (Cumberland)	68.39	60,734	59,439	-2.1	869.1	11.3	87.7	54,476	14.5	167,300	60.3	7.2	68.5	26.2
Voorhees township (Camden)	11.47	29,310	29,175	-0.5	2543.6	22.5	87.7	98,906	9.0	324,300	62.1	5.0	68.8	26.5
Wall township (Monmouth)	30.66	26,156	25,554	-2.3	833.5	4.8	93.7	107,685	6.1	501,100	64.5	5.0	68.7	26.8
Wallington borough & MCD (Bergen)	0.99	11,335	11,495	1.4	11611.1	43.0	93.8	68,845	9.6	375,800	66.4	4.5	64.8	29.0
Wanaque borough & MCD (Passaic)	8.07	11,072	11,762	6.2	1457.5	12.7	92.8	95,023	4.6	318,000	65.0	5.2	67.3	26.5
Wantage township (Sussex)	66.76	11,364	10,902	-4.1	163.3	5.8	97.7	96,964	5.2	285,200	67.0	3.7	78.2	17.6
Warren township (Somerset)	19.57	15,320	15,625	2.0	798.4	25.6	94.9	170,264	2.6	790,300	63.0	2.9	85.7	11.8
Washington township (Gloucester)	21.35	49,035	47,753	-2.6	2236.7	6.1	92.8	97,247	3.8	245,500	67.8	5.4	76.4	20.5
Washington township (Morris)	44.58	18,542	18,152	-2.1	407.2	9.1	95.6	149,129	4.7	462,300	64.0	3.0	86.7	11.1
Waterford township (Camden)	36.00	10,662	10,684	0.2	296.8	5.7	92.6	105,119	5.1	205,100	69.2	3.1	76.2	17.3
Wayne township (Passaic)	23.72	54,713	53,369	-2.5	2250.0	20.0	91.8	123,204	3.7	468,500	63.5	4.5	74.0	21.1
Weehawken township (Hudson)	0.78	12,553	14,638	16.6	18766.7	36.6	89.0	101,449	10.7	650,400	75.5	3.4	51.2	33.9
West Caldwell township (Essex)	5.10	10,694	10,837	1.3	2124.9	12.2	95.8	127,989	2.9	504,200	66.6	4.3	71.8	24.1
West Deptford township (Gloucester)	15.36	21,656	20,980	-3.1	1365.9	5.3	88.6	76,950	5.4	214,500	65.4	4.1	62.0	32.5
Westfield town & MCD (Union)	6.72	30,300	29,512	-2.6	4391.7	11.7	91.1	170,798	4.5	743,400	65.8	2.7	75.9	22.0
West Freehold CDP	5.91	13,613	NA	NA	NA	13.4	93.5	116,413	3.1	415,000	64.2	2.9	72.4	24.6
West Milford township (Passaic)	75.93	26,242	26,331	0.3	346.8	9.7	94.1	100,461	4.6	286,000	68.4	4.1	72.5	22.5
West New York town & MCD (Hudson)	0.99	49,710	52,723	6.1	53255.6	61.0	88.8	56,436	18.4	326,900	70.3	5.7	64.9	25.4
West Orange township (Essex)	12.00	46,164	47,563	3.0	3963.6	30.1	91.7	105,537	5.7	385,200	67.7	4.1	72.2	23.0
West Windsor township (Mercer)	25.55	27,153	27,895	2.7	1091.8	40.0	87.8	169,312	2.5	620,600	68.6	5.1	82.5	15.9
Westwood borough & MCD (Bergen)	2.26	10,928	11,078	1.4	4901.8	21.3	90.6	110,473	7.4	463,500	72.2	1.8	67.7	27.7
Williamstown CDP	7.42	15,567	NA	NA	NA	4.4	93.1	83,232	5.4	205,900	64.3	3.9	67.6	28.8
Willingboro township (Burlington)	7.73	31,615	32,005	1.2	4140.4	14.2	88.5	75,428	6.9	166,000	65.0	10.8	75.5	19.2
Winslow township (Camden)	57.42	39,784	38,629	-2.9	672.7	6.9	89.2	78,445	8.7	192,400	67.7	7.1	70.8	24.9
Woodbridge CDP	3.89	19,265	NA	NA	NA	35.3	88.8	85,857	6.4	278,100	67.6	5.8	70.1	26.0
Woodbridge township (Middlesex)	23.26	99,385	100,145	0.8	4305.5	32.6	90.7	88,900	6.5	310,000	63.5	4.8	74.9	21.8
Woodbury city & MCD (Gloucester)	2.02	10,138	9,794	-3.4	4848.5	8.1	91.3	55,226	18.3	166,400	63.6	6.4	59.1	36.0
Woodland Park borough & MCD (Passaic)	2.94	11,819	12,581	6.4	4279.3	27.3	90.5	77,250	8.4	365,900	62.8	3.7	67.5	27.6
Woolwich township (Gloucester)	21.07	10,214	12,960	26.9	615.1	8.1	92.1	141,875	2.6	344,600	72.1	3.3	82.1	13.8
Wyckoff township (Bergen)	6.59	16,731	16,947	1.3	2571.6	11.2	92.4	153,736	2.7	742,900	61.2	3.6	78.7	19.9
NEW MEXICO	121312.24	2,059,199	2,096,829	1.8	17.3	9.4	86.7	49,754	18.0	171,400	57.3	6.7	63.2	30.8
Alamogordo city	21.39	30,409	31,980	5.2	1495.1	6.3	78.7	42,204	18.4	113,500	54.5	6.4	55.3	37.6
Albuquerque city	187.22	546,153	560,513	2.6	2993.9	9.9	84.0	52,911	16.0	198,200	63.6	5.6	57.8	34.7
Artesia city	10.99	11,513	12,356	7.3	1124.3	5.6	83.4	51,839	20.6	177,800	60.8	6.8	68.6	28.4
Carlsbad city	31.21	26,251	29,810	13.6	955.1	5.5	86.0	69,193	13.0	141,300	63.4	3.8	69.5	25.3
Chaparral CDP	59.06	14,631	NA	NA	NA	32.2	88.2	24,665	43.0	78,000	50.2	11.2	72.6	23.5
Clovis city	23.61	37,794	38,319	1.4	1623.0	10.3	78.1	43,111	21.3	125,600	57.7	7.2	62.0	32.8
Deming city	16.70	14,821	13,880	-6.3	831.1	18.7	85.0	27,079	33.0	95,200	51.1	12.1	58.3	38.7
Espa ola city	7.80	10,267	10,044	-2.2	1287.7	7.8	91.4	34,368	28.5	160,100	51.0	3.1	53.3	39.8
Farmington city	34.46	45,954	44,372	-3.4	1287.6	3.7	83.3	54,480	16.1	186,800	60.3	6.5	68.1	26.4
Gallup city	19.99	21,758	21,493	-1.2	1075.2	4.8	88.3	48,065	24.2	132,000	58.1	7.4	66.8	28.0
Hobbs city	26.40	34,167	39,141	14.6	1482.6	16.8	89.3	59,020	17.5	140,600	60.1	6.8	71.3	24.7
Las Cruces city	76.93	97,706	103,432	5.9	1344.5	12.2	82.9	43,022	23.2	155,200	58.5	7.3	61.2	29.6

Table B. Incorporated Places, Census Designated Places (CDPs), and Minor Civil Divisions (MCDs) of 10,000 or More Population — **Crime, Residential Construction and Local Government Finance**

STATE City, town, township, borough, or CDP (county if applicable)	Serious crimes known to police, 2018[1] Violent crime Number	Rate[2]	Property crime Number	Rate[2]	New residential construction authorized by building permits, 2019 Value ($1,000)	Number of housing units	Percent single family	Local government finance, 2017 General revenue Total (mil dol)	Intergovernmental Total (mil dol)	Percent from state gov.	Taxes per capita[3]	General expenditure Total (mil dol)	Per capita[3] Total	Capital outlays	Debt outstanding (mil dol)
	15	16	17	18	19	20	21	22	23	24	25	26	27	28	29
NEW JERSEY—Con.															
South River borough & MCD (Middlesex)	19	118	122	755	1,539	20	25.0	13.3	1.3	94.3	644	18.6	1,163	250	7.8
Sparta township (Sussex)	5	27	54	289	13,604	113	57.5	25.5	5.2	0.0	1,086	15.3	818	0	8.8
Springdale CDP	NA	NA	NA	NA	NA	NA	NA	NA	NA	NA	NA	NA	NA	NA	NA
Springfield township (Union)	4	23	144	811	708	3	100.0	32.0	2.4	95.8	1,561	31.0	1,779	130	5.3
Stafford township (Ocean)	15	55	183	674	31,419	204	56.9	54.1	5.1	99.4	1,369	35.9	1,316	4	117.3
Summit city & MCD (Union)	7	32	143	646	9,255	34	35.3	149.5	5.1	88.4	6,142	100.4	4,570	65	1.6
Teaneck township (Bergen)	45	110	419	1,024	7,702	81	3.7	66.3	3.7	100.0	1,461	54.4	1,339	10	32.8
Tenafly borough & MCD (Bergen)	4	27	37	251	17,054	53	66.0	27.8	1.2	100.0	1,772	25.1	1,710	199	18.4
Tinton Falls borough & MCD (Monmouth)	5	28	182	1,025	14,769	64	100.0	28.7	1.7	99.5	1,179	25.6	1,448	106	21.0
Toms River CDP	NA	NA	NA	NA	NA	NA	NA	NA	NA	NA	NA	NA	NA	NA	NA
Toms River township (Ocean)	55	60	1,317	1,429	56,162	294	89.8	136.6	13.6	91.9	1,052	106.5	1,155	126	11.1
Totowa borough & MCD (Passaic)	12	113	219	2,053	16,000	240	0.0	17.7	1.7	95.3	1,339	16.8	1,551	136	0.0
Trenton city & MCD (Mercer)	973	1,162	2,467	2,946	5,542	67	0.0	467.1	382.8	92.0	651	512.0	6,131	103	321.1
Union township (Union)	45	77	954	1,621	11,882	646	1.2	90.6	1.1	99.8	1,355	77.6	1,327	23	24.7
Union City city & MCD (Hudson)	233	333	1,078	1,541	5,598	59	3.4	356.8	265.5	97.4	1,029	386.4	5,642	312	108.9
Upper township (Cape May)	NA	NA	NA	NA	6,133	23	91.3	60.7	6.8	96.8	2,799	42.8	3,610	233	4.2
Upper Montclair CDP	NA	NA	NA	NA	NA	NA	NA	NA	NA	NA	NA	NA	NA	NA	NA
Ventnor City city & MCD (Atlantic)	17	167	259	2,544	11,232	36	77.8	25.2	3.6	93.0	2,090	39.0	3,868	66	41.5
Vernon township (Sussex)	1	5	100	453	62	2	100.0	22.7	3.0	90.4	870	21.4	964	95	16.6
Verona township (Essex)	NA	NA	89	662	1,583	6	16.7	21.0	1.1	0.0	1,251	21.2	1,578	0	22.4
Vineland city & MCD (Cumberland)	258	428	2,021	3,350	9,239	100	100.0	96.1	18.4	22.9	604	86.8	1,450	428	59.6
Voorhees township (Camden)	42	145	375	1,290	413	3	100.0	30.0	3.4	80.5	804	29.3	1,002	183	34.2
Wall township (Monmouth)	6	23	262	1,009	17,060	105	19.0	42.9	4.3	85.4	1,218	33.0	1,279	41	35.5
Wallington borough & MCD (Bergen)	5	43	120	1,028	745	5	20.0	12.7	0.7	100.0	848	12.4	1,072	81	8.3
Wanaque borough & MCD (Passaic)	11	92	71	594	95	1	100.0	17.8	1.1	96.8	920	15.9	1,357	91	11.8
Wantage township (Sussex)	NA	NA	NA	NA	1,880	9	100.0	34.0	1.2	84.2	2,940	33.2	3,048	171	12.8
Warren township (Somerset)	3	19	52	326	6,196	22	100.0	22.6	0.0		1,094	18.1	1,152	341	21.7
Washington township (Gloucester)	66	140	554	1,178	12,214	98	51.0	37.9	4.1	100.0	673	29.7	622	9	14.5
Washington township (Morris)	7	38	50	271	292	2	100.0	19.7	2.1	73.0	810	18.0	972	73	10.4
Waterford township (Camden)	7	66	64	601	590	3	100.0	11.4	1.6	91.0	787	8.7	818	5	13.7
Wayne township (Passaic)	64	118	986	1,815	4,022	22	40.9	76.4	5.0	100.0	1,281	47.2	874	184	66.2
Weehawken township (Hudson)	23	148	223	1,433	575	2	100.0	45.0	3.7	100.0	2,029	34.6	2,321	12	89.8
West Caldwell township (Essex)	2	18	68	623	0	0	0.0	20.2	1.9	74.4	1,448	21.8	2,009	329	1.2
West Deptford township (Gloucester)	19	91	290	1,388	894	8	100.0	37.9	6.5	74.0	1,098	24.0	1,136	22	112.8
Westfield town & MCD (Union)	4	13	217	723	19,408	55	100.0	47.1	4.1	79.0	1,244	41.1	1,374	117	25.7
West Freehold CDP	NA	NA	NA	NA	NA	NA	NA	NA	NA	NA	NA	NA	NA	NA	NA
West Milford township (Passaic)	10	38	158	595	1,686	7	100.0	36.3	3.8	98.8	1,101	36.8	1,392	142	19.3
West New York town & MCD (Hudson)	138	255	567	1,048	15,126	154	0.0	212.3	137.3	94.9	787	241.7	4,584	336	46.5
West Orange township (Essex)	91	189	615	1,279	7,820	48	20.8	74.6	7.0	97.1	1,269	75.8	1,589	110	19.5
West Windsor township (Mercer)	11	39	298	1,054	8,258	72	38.9	42.7	2.3	0.0	939	40.0	1,429	0	48.7
Westwood borough & MCD (Bergen)	11	98	57	508	2,044	4	100.0	48.6	1.3	87.8	4,192	15.1	1,357	81	16.5
Williamstown CDP	NA	NA	NA	NA	NA	NA	NA	NA	NA	NA	NA	NA	NA	NA	NA
Willingboro township (Burlington)	112	349	476	1,482	114	1	100.0	40.7	4.3	89.9	1,071	35.5	1,113	31	32.2
Winslow township (Camden)	64	167	512	1,334	5,783	29	100.0	33.7	6.8	96.4	499	29.0	750	1	27.8
Woodbridge CDP	NA	NA	NA	NA	NA	NA	NA	NA	NA	NA	NA	NA	NA	NA	NA
Woodbridge township (Middlesex)	113	112	1,554	1,540	26,183	413	6.1	180.7	41.2	81.8	990	160.2	1,601	204	222.3
Woodbury city & MCD (Gloucester)	53	544	423	4,340	274	3	100.0	14.9	1.7	100.0	1,184	15.3	1,555	87	6.4
Woodland Park borough & MCD (Passaic)	10	78	149	1,164	0	0	0.0	19.2	1.1	0.0	1,401	13.8	1,093	0	21.7
Woolwich township (Gloucester)	NA	NA	50	396	9,446	67	88.1	9.1	1.3	48.9	615	8.1	649	97	14.7
Wyckoff township (Bergen)	6	35	84	490	38,365	198	4.0	21.6	1.1	100.0	967	20.4	1,196	37	0.0
NEW MEXICO	17,949	857	71,657	3,420	1,121,875	5,020	85.4	X	X	X	X	X	X	X	X
Alamogordo city	96	306	1,022	3,262	NA	NA	NA	48.3	14.7	76.8	605	39.5	1,260	311	63.6
Albuquerque city	7,646	1,365	34,619	6,179	214,597	1,094	82.8	979.8	270.0	87.5	690	814.4	1,455	218	1567.1
Artesia city	NA	NA	NA	NA	15,616	52	100.0	34.1	4.7	22.9	1,950	39.7	3,266	1374	29.6
Carlsbad city	148	508	844	2,895	55,673	213	90.1	79.2	5.3	93.6	1,908	71.8	2,489	862	52.0
Chaparral CDP	NA	NA	NA	NA	NA	NA	NA	NA	NA	NA	NA	NA	NA	NA	NA
Clovis city	NA	NA	NA	NA	17,868	100	54.0	56.3	10.0	60.5	780	55.9	1,435	463	22.0
Deming city	141	1,000	734	5,208	894	5	100.0	22.6	8.4	9.5	450	16.3	1,149	140	3.3
Espa ola city	NA	NA	NA	NA	NA	NA	NA	17.5	0.9	100.0	1,159	14.7	1,460	108	21.9
Farmington city	593	1,307	1,769	3,900	10,026	58	74.1	87.9	33.5	11.4	659	93.5	2,060	126	1684.2
Gallup city	338	1,538	1,515	6,893	375	2	100.0	54.8	11.8	57.4	1,415	52.3	2,396	296	38.9
Hobbs city	251	655	1,579	4,121	35,938	164	100.0	127.2	50.8	98.1	1,428	98.4	2,601	451	39.9
Las Cruces city	413	404	3,627	3,549	152,897	686	85.1	180.7	17.6	55.4	1,210	101.7	998	174	202.4

1 Data for serious crimes have not been adjusted for underreporting. This may affect comparability between geographic areas over time.
2 Per 100,000 population estimated by the FBI.   3 Based on population estimated as of July 1 of the year shown.

Table B. Incorporated Places, Census Designated Places (CDPs), and Minor Civil Divisions (MCDs) of 10,000 or More Population — **Land Area, Population, and Households, and Employment**

STATE City, town, township, borough, or CDP (county if applicable)	Land area 2010 (sq mi)	Population				Population characteristics 2015–2019		Income and poverty 2015–2019		Median value of owner-occupied housing units	Employment, 2015–2019		Households, 2015–2019 (percent of households)	
		Total persons 2010	Total persons 2019	Percent change 2010–2019	Persons per square mile, 2019	Percent foreign born	Percent living in the same house as previous year	Median household income	Percent of households with income below poverty level		Percent in civilian labor force	Unemploy-ment rate	Family households	One person households
	1	2	3	4	5	6	7	8	9	10	11	12	13	14
NEW MEXICO—Con.														
Las Vegas city	7.82	14,043	12,919	-8.0	1652.0	3.1	84.5	26,561	37.7	117,600	45.1	9.4	52.2	42.9
Los Alamos CDP	11.13	12,019	NA	NA	NA	12.3	86.7	116,116	6.7	308,100	70.1	2.7	58.5	35.6
Los Lunas village	18.73	15,030	16,061	6.9	857.5	5.2	86.6	56,250	11.8	161,000	58.5	6.5	68.9	26.3
Lovington city	11.36	11,058	11,489	3.9	1011.4	22.9	84.4	51,620	16.0	116,800	54.8	8.7	74.6	21.6
North Valley CDP	6.95	11,333	NA	NA	NA	10.0	86.2	53,744	15.2	221,500	56.7	3.7	60.7	32.3
Portales city	7.94	12,306	11,610	-5.7	1462.2	8.6	67.3	37,921	28.6	116,200	59.1	11.5	58.3	31.4
Rio Rancho city	103.42	87,387	99,178	13.5	959.0	5.3	87.6	66,856	8.8	190,800	63.0	6.7	72.2	21.8
Roswell city	29.72	48,417	47,551	-1.8	1600.0	12.7	82.9	43,372	18.6	105,100	57.0	5.1	65.6	30.8
Santa Fe city	52.23	80,871	84,683	4.7	1621.3	14.6	88.5	57,972	12.2	280,800	61.4	4.3	54.9	38.2
Silver City town	10.12	10,301	9,386	-8.9	927.5	3.3	81.9	31,620	30.3	134,400	57.2	6.7	51.4	39.5
South Valley CDP	29.02	40,976	NA	NA	NA	15.6	92.4	39,714	21.6	147,400	55.9	7.8	63.4	31.5
Sunland Park city	13.02	14,260	17,978	26.1	1380.8	35.5	92.4	27,266	37.6	111,100	56.8	7.6	76.2	22.3
NEW YORK	47123.77	19,378,144	19,453,561	0.4	412.8	22.6	89.5	68,486	13.9	313,700	63.0	5.5	63.1	29.9
Albany city & MCD (Albany)	21.40	97,845	96,460	-1.4	4507.5	14.2	77.6	45,825	20.4	179,100	65.0	7.0	41.2	44.3
Alden town (Erie)	34.31	10,875	9,918	-8.8	289.1	3.2	85.8	74,858	7.2	171,300	53.2	3.0	71.3	25.8
Amherst town (Erie)	53.20	122,376	126,082	3.0	2370.0	13.3	85.5	76,704	10.1	202,400	60.3	3.0	61.0	32.1
Amsterdam city & MCD (Montgomery)	5.87	18,606	17,766	-4.5	3026.6	6.0	81.8	37,457	22.5	86,100	57.8	9.0	60.2	31.9
Arcadia town (Wayne)	52.03	14,252	13,536	-5.0	260.2	2.9	87.5	50,290	12.9	97,500	58.0	5.0	58.8	33.6
Auburn city & MCD (Cayuga)	8.34	27,690	26,173	-5.5	3138.2	3.1	79.0	44,049	17.5	102,000	55.9	6.3	50.1	39.7
Aurora town (Erie)	36.39	13,783	13,753	-0.2	377.9	2.4	91.3	80,963	6.1	226,500	64.3	3.2	67.5	26.5
Babylon village	2.43	12,157	11,992	-1.4	4935.0	7.6	91.1	131,134	3.9	475,400	69.8	3.0	72.7	20.6
Babylon town (Suffolk)	52.18	213,580	210,141	-1.6	4027.2	19.1	92.6	94,011	7.3	361,300	67.8	5.0	72.6	22.3
Baldwin CDP	2.96	24,033	NA	NA	NA	24.6	96.0	112,352	4.9	390,800	69.0	4.7	79.0	15.7
Ballston town (Saratoga)	29.58	9,757	11,464	17.5	387.6	4.3	91.3	95,000	7.2	290,800	62.3	3.7	72.5	23.0
Batavia city & MCD (Genesee)	5.20	15,390	14,379	-6.6	2765.2	2.1	84.8	47,712	19.3	96,900	61.2	4.3	52.7	39.2
Bath town (Steuben)	95.32	12,378	11,929	-3.6	125.1	1.8	81.4	39,621	14.7	91,100	49.5	6.1	55.6	35.8
Bay Shore CDP	5.40	26,337	NA	NA	NA	23.9	91.6	80,341	11.6	335,300	66.2	5.1	72.2	23.2
Beacon city & MCD (Dutchess)	4.74	13,806	13,968	1.2	2946.8	10.2	89.3	71,193	11.1	278,700	64.9	5.0	59.6	31.8
Bedford town (Westchester)	37.18	17,436	17,651	1.2	474.7	16.4	90.6	129,140	6.0	737,500	58.7	2.6	80.9	17.4
Beekman town (Dutchess)	30.20	14,743	14,387	-2.4	476.4	8.8	90.6	98,483	4.9	299,400	56.2	3.8	76.1	20.9
Bellmore CDP	2.36	16,218	NA	NA	NA	11.8	95.7	136,684	2.9	502,100	71.4	3.2	79.6	18.0
Bethlehem town (Albany)	49.03	33,634	34,895	3.7	711.7	6.6	88.4	97,867	5.6	276,900	66.3	2.6	63.6	30.5
Bethpage CDP	3.58	16,429	NA	NA	NA	15.8	93.1	123,427	4.7	471,600	66.6	3.9	77.8	19.2
Binghamton city & MCD (Broome)	10.48	47,404	44,399	-6.3	4236.5	10.3	75.2	34,487	29.1	91,000	57.2	10.4	46.1	41.4
Blooming Grove town (Orange)	34.73	18,026	17,623	-2.2	507.4	8.7	95.0	97,479	5.5	286,500	65.4	3.3	73.0	23.9
Bohemia CDP	8.61	10,180	NA	NA	NA	7.9	91.1	92,113	6.8	390,300	73.0	2.9	66.6	26.7
Brentwood CDP	10.97	60,664	NA	NA	NA	42.8	94.3	82,165	10.7	312,100	68.6	3.9	84.0	13.1
Brighton town (Monroe)	15.41	36,592	35,928	-1.8	2331.5	18.2	78.3	75,807	8.8	184,600	62.8	3.7	53.7	36.1
Brookhaven town (Suffolk)	259.39	486,336	480,763	-1.1	1853.4	12.2	92.9	96,760	6.9	347,200	64.4	4.4	71.6	23.4
Brunswick town (Rensselaer)	44.35	11,952	13,046	9.2	294.2	4.5	88.5	87,896	5.3	226,100	68.4	2.6	65.0	24.5
Buffalo city & MCD (Erie)	40.38	261,346	255,284	-2.3	6322.0	10.4	82.2	37,354	27.5	89,800	59.8	7.1	50.6	39.9
Camillus town (Onondaga)	34.35	24,145	24,105	-0.2	701.7	6.0	92.3	73,110	7.0	147,800	66.3	3.7	65.8	28.5
Canandaigua city & MCD (Ontario)	4.58	10,591	10,156	-4.1	2217.5	2.8	83.0	49,130	9.4	164,400	61.9	3.1	49.9	40.9
Canandaigua town (Ontario)	56.80	9,962	11,302	13.5	199.0	4.5	85.1	84,965	6.1	250,900	59.1	2.9	63.1	28.8
Canton town (St. Lawrence)	104.73	10,993	11,041	0.4	105.4	5.7	81.5	62,540	17.0	120,200	48.1	8.7	60.7	30.8
Carmel town (Putnam)	35.92	34,229	34,106	-0.4	949.5	11.6	95.2	104,016	3.3	379,300	64.8	5.3	74.2	22.7
Catskill town (Greene)	60.44	11,785	11,334	-3.8	187.5	5.6	91.3	40,850	17.5	173,100	51.5	5.6	51.8	44.3
Centereach CDP	8.73	31,578	NA	NA	NA	11.4	93.3	107,184	5.3	346,300	66.6	5.4	78.8	18.5
Central Islip CDP	7.11	34,450	NA	NA	NA	34.9	92.5	74,458	10.3	275,800	67.7	3.5	70.0	26.0
Cheektowaga CDP	25.38	75,178	NA	NA	NA	5.8	91.8	54,002	10.3	114,100	65.2	3.5	56.7	35.3
Cheektowaga town (Erie)	29.45	88,170	85,884	-2.6	2916.3	5.5	92.0	54,191	10.2	113,900	65.0	3.6	57.1	35.1
Chenango town (Broome)	33.83	11,212	10,505	-6.3	310.5	3.3	90.8	71,623	12.4	145,300	60.3	3.0	71.3	21.6
Chester town (Orange)	25.05	12,003	12,185	1.5	486.4	7.7	91.5	107,396	3.5	301,800	66.4	4.1	73.0	21.3
Chili town (Monroe)	39.50	28,629	28,527	-0.4	722.2	7.7	90.1	74,415	6.0	147,100	68.8	5.8	69.8	23.4
Cicero town (Onondaga)	48.28	31,566	30,721	-2.7	636.3	3.3	92.8	80,625	6.5	155,800	67.4	3.7	69.2	24.5
Clarence town (Erie)	53.51	30,654	32,906	7.3	615.0	5.9	91.1	101,831	3.2	294,000	66.3	3.1	71.2	24.3
Clarkstown town (Rockland)	38.46	84,536	86,237	2.0	2242.3	22.1	93.2	121,167	4.6	456,800	64.8	4.3	74.9	21.0
Clay town (Onondaga)	47.96	58,320	59,250	1.6	1235.4	5.1	90.0	72,214	8.3	148,700	68.4	3.9	63.9	28.0
Clifton Park town (Saratoga)	48.20	36,733	36,366	-1.0	754.5	9.8	90.2	108,116	4.0	289,900	65.3	2.1	73.0	21.5
Cohoes city & MCD (Albany)	3.77	16,177	16,687	3.2	4426.3	5.4	84.9	55,054	13.7	156,000	65.6	6.8	49.2	42.5
Colonie town (Albany)	55.95	81,588	82,798	1.5	1479.9	12.8	87.8	80,921	5.6	240,800	65.4	3.1	64.0	29.7
Commack CDP	11.96	36,124	NA	NA	NA	9.5	93.5	138,098	3.4	495,000	66.3	2.5	82.9	14.6
Copiague CDP	3.09	22,993	NA	NA	NA	27.8	93.4	82,258	9.0	328,600	65.7	6.6	74.4	20.5
Coram CDP	13.83	39,113	NA	NA	NA	14.3	91.4	84,022	6.4	323,600	68.8	3.4	61.2	32.7
Corning city & MCD (Steuben)	3.08	11,184	10,538	-5.8	3421.4	4.5	86.0	50,321	16.9	112,800	66.2	6.1	50.7	42.9
Cornwall town (Orange)	26.66	12,596	12,465	-1.0	467.6	4.3	93.3	105,563	3.1	328,200	69.1	4.3	71.4	23.3
Cortland city & MCD (Cortland)	3.89	19,184	18,670	-2.7	4799.5	1.9	73.6	44,317	25.4	109,400	57.9	5.1	49.6	34.2
Cortlandt town (Westchester)	39.26	41,585	42,294	1.7	1077.3	14.0	91.1	115,572	4.8	429,400	67.6	4.5	74.1	22.9
Deer Park CDP	6.17	27,745	NA	NA	NA	20.3	93.7	94,645	7.6	369,500	67.2	4.8	73.9	20.5
Depew village	5.08	15,437	15,011	-2.8	2954.9	2.7	92.6	58,458	6.2	120,200	65.9	4.6	60.6	32.4
De Witt town (Onondaga)	33.77	25,888	25,041	-3.3	741.5	11.4	85.2	71,490	8.8	168,300	60.2	4.1	61.4	32.4
Dix Hills CDP	15.94	26,892	NA	NA	NA	19.8	94.2	166,334	2.6	730,500	61.8	4.0	90.4	7.7
Dobbs Ferry village	2.43	10,924	11,027	0.9	4537.9	16.2	81.8	143,462	3.7	671,700	69.3	5.1	74.7	20.3
Dryden town (Tompkins)	93.64	14,438	14,265	-1.2	152.3	4.5	82.6	69,118	13.1	188,300	66.5	4.5	61.3	26.6
Dunkirk city & MCD (Chautauqua)	4.51	12,554	11,756	-6.4	2606.7	4.5	85.6	35,146	23.7	67,300	57.8	7.4	57.4	36.9
Eastchester CDP	3.29	19,554	NA	NA	NA	18.4	89.3	130,926	5.0	595,200	67.8	3.9	68.4	28.9
Eastchester town (Westchester)	4.85	32,327	32,906	1.8	6784.7	19.2	90.5	127,212	6.7	628,000	65.7	4.0	67.2	29.4
East Fishkill town (Dutchess)	56.53	29,038	29,527	1.7	522.3	10.6	92.6	113,087	3.0	358,700	65.3	3.3	83.6	11.8
East Greenbush town (Rensselaer)	24.02	16,547	16,221	-2.0	675.3	6.8	89.1	91,127	4.7	218,100	65.8	2.3	62.5	32.0

STATE City, town, township, borough, or CDP (county if applicable)	Serious crimes known to police, 2018[1]				New residential construction authorized by building permits, 2019			Local government finance, 2017							
	Violent crime		Property crime					General revenue				General expenditure			
									Intergovernmental				Per capita[3]		
	Number	Rate[2]	Number	Rate[2]	Value ($1,000)	Number of housing units	Percent single family	Total (mil dol)	Total (mil dol)	Percent from state gov.	Taxes per capita[3]	Total (mil dol)	Total	Capital outlays	Debt outstanding (mil dol)
	15	16	17	18	19	20	21	22	23	24	25	26	27	28	29
NEW MEXICO—Con.															
Las Vegas city	111	848	457	3,493	140	1	100.0	26.4	6.2	80.7	916	24.8	1,885	419	36.8
Los Alamos CDP	24	127	110	583	NA	NA	NA	NA	NA	NA	NA	NA	NA	NA	NA
Los Lunas village	189	1,214	681	4,374	12,170	75	100.0	27.7	2.4	81.2	951	24.3	1,563	223	72.0
Lovington city	15	134	271	2,425	NA	NA	NA	13.9	1.2	97.1	630	15.5	1,380	152	8.9
North Valley CDP	NA	NA	NA	NA	NA	NA	NA	NA	NA	NA	NA	NA	NA	NA	NA
Portales city	66	561	306	2,600	3,363	22	100.0	13.3	4.0	97.8	396	13.7	1,155	278	26.2
Rio Rancho city	197	202	1,595	1,638	119,292	560	97.5	113.0	15.7	46.9	634	89.6	931	133	228.9
Roswell city	396	831	2,008	4,212	7,016	45	91.1	66.7	42.3	94.4	163	64.8	1,351	264	8.8
Santa Fe city	333	396	3,388	4,025	108,721	589	58.4	185.8	70.3	80.8	577	231.5	2,758	332	259.0
Silver City town	NA	NA	NA	NA	1,621	10	100.0	15.8	0.5	97.7	1,174	11.7	1,221	8	14.2
South Valley CDP	NA	NA	NA	NA	NA	NA	NA	NA	NA	NA	NA	NA	NA	NA	NA
Sunland Park city	NA	NA	NA	NA	27,215	122	100.0	6.5	0.1	42.7	341	6.6	384	0	0.0
NEW YORK	68,495	351	281,507	1,441	7,746,335	45,219	20.8	X	X	X	X	X	X	X	X
Albany city & MCD (Albany)	823	837	3,147	3,201	1,317	11	63.6	189.8	62.4	36.0	659	188.6	1,930	240	288.2
Alden town (Erie)	NA	NA	NA	NA	2,231	10	40.0	4.1	1.3	13.6	268	3.6	357	25	1.2
Amherst town (Erie)	145	120	1,766	1,455	59,289	238	40.3	146.4	54.6	3.6	637	155.7	1,241	121	122.9
Amsterdam city & MCD (Montgomery)	25	141	201	1,133	350	1	100.0	23.8	10.0	47.5	358	26.4	1,481	170	19.4
Arcadia town (Wayne)	NA	NA	NA	NA	431	3	100.0	3.8	0.8	37.3	206	3.8	277	51	4.3
Auburn city & MCD (Cayuga)	137	516	718	2,702	175	1	100.0	49.3	19.6	50.5	487	45.3	1,702	184	67.1
Aurora town (Erie)	1	7	79	568	15,582	53	100.0	11.1	2.4	29.2	392	8.7	631	51	18.3
Babylon village	NA	NA	NA	NA	650	2	100.0	10.9	1.3	25.6	616	10.0	835	79	6.5
Babylon town (Suffolk)	NA	NA	NA	NA	17,228	66	74.2	177.6	22.3	19.2	512	171.5	813	97	197.5
Baldwin CDP	NA	NA	NA	NA	NA	NA	NA	NA	NA	NA	NA	NA	NA	NA	NA
Ballston town (Saratoga)	NA	NA	NA	NA	28,424	152	50.7	5.2	3.1	7.1	173	5.2	471	58	2.1
Batavia city & MCD (Genesee)	63	433	370	2,540	0	0	0.0	22.0	4.8	61.7	823	21.3	1,459	254	8.2
Bath town (Steuben)	NA	NA	NA	NA	1,225	14	100.0	4.2	1.4	36.2	197	3.6	302	47	0.0
Bay Shore CDP	NA	NA	NA	NA	NA	NA	NA	NA	NA	NA	NA	NA	NA	NA	NA
Beacon city & MCD (Dutchess)	26	183	190	1,334	7,242	25	100.0	24.3	8.8	25.9	883	31.0	2,303	814	49.2
Bedford town (Westchester)	4	22	41	227	1,150	2	100.0	35.1	4.3	10.0	1,517	32.2	1,805	148	33.1
Beekman town (Dutchess)	NA	NA	NA	NA	10,000	20	100.0	4.6	0.9	18.6	206	4.1	288	0	3.0
Bellmore CDP	NA	NA	NA	NA	NA	NA	NA	NA	NA	NA	NA	NA	NA	NA	NA
Bethlehem town (Albany)	27	76	498	1,395	20,123	83	90.4	35.7	13.8	11.9	431	32.7	930	107	27.6
Bethpage CDP	NA	NA	NA	NA	NA	NA	NA	NA	NA	NA	NA	NA	NA	NA	NA
Binghamton city & MCD (Broome)	326	726	1,893	4,218	11,617	62	0.0	111.1	50.1	34.4	850	125.6	2,788	1159	172.1
Blooming Grove town (Orange)	8	67	81	681	884	5	100.0	13.6	2.0	11.6	588	11.9	676	24	7.0
Bohemia CDP	NA	NA	NA	NA	NA	NA	NA	NA	NA	NA	NA	NA	NA	NA	NA
Brentwood CDP	NA	NA	NA	NA	NA	NA	NA	NA	NA	NA	NA	NA	NA	NA	NA
Brighton town (Monroe)	32	88	613	1,681	5,805	8	100.0	27.8	5.2	22.0	470	30.1	832	105	6.2
Brookhaven town (Suffolk)	NA	NA	NA	NA	1,593	6	100.0	311.7	30.9	31.6	396	338.1	699	138	682.3
Brunswick town (Rensselaer)	NA	NA	NA	NA	5,612	32	50.0	7.2	1.9	33.6	371	5.9	456	27	1.5
Buffalo city & MCD (Erie)	2,692	1,043	9,852	3,815	63,103	291	10.0	1439.0	1218.1	89.2	415	1482.7	5,785	348	1263.9
Camillus town (Onondaga)	14	57	275	1,124	27,700	109	58.7	19.3	0.9	83.1	583	19.9	821	80	3.4
Canandaigua city & MCD (Ontario)	24	234	194	1,892	2,177	8	100.0	16.3	3.7	44.1	953	16.5	1,600	209	16.6
Canandaigua town (Ontario)	NA	NA	NA	NA	16,185	43	100.0	8.8	5.0	8.7	296	8.0	716	64	2.1
Canton town (St. Lawrence)	NA	NA	NA	NA	1,514	13	100.0	2.8	1.2	30.3	117	2.7	245	49	0.0
Carmel town (Putnam)	17	49	132	384	13,323	100	20.0	40.4	2.0	64.5	973	36.2	1,058	77	26.0
Catskill town (Greene)	NA	NA	NA	NA	2,286	13	100.0	5.5	0.1	85.2	307	9.5	834	366	4.7
Centereach CDP	NA	NA	NA	NA	NA	NA	NA	NA	NA	NA	NA	NA	NA	NA	NA
Central Islip CDP	NA	NA	NA	NA	NA	NA	NA	NA	NA	NA	NA	NA	NA	NA	NA
Cheektowaga CDP	NA	NA	NA	NA	NA	NA	NA	NA	NA	NA	NA	NA	NA	NA	NA
Cheektowaga town (Erie)	189	243	2,156	2,777	624	2	100.0	89.0	14.5	16.9	807	97.4	1,127	197	45.3
Chenango town (Broome)	NA	NA	NA	NA	906	6	100.0	6.3	2.9	13.2	227	5.6	524	70	9.5
Chester town (Orange)	NA	NA	NA	NA	5,357	20	100.0	10.5	1.5	10.0	639	10.0	824	13	3.2
Chili town (Monroe)	NA	NA	NA	NA	14,253	109	22.0	15.6	4.4	10.1	338	14.4	503	37	0.6
Cicero town (Onondaga)	11	38	218	752	11,617	44	100.0	15.9	1.0	64.2	455	16.0	520	63	4.9
Clarence town (Erie)	NA	NA	NA	NA	69,315	120	93.3	21.3	6.8	6.7	418	22.5	696	116	27.0
Clarkstown town (Rockland)	71	87	1,209	1,475	5,215	17	100.0	140.2	9.7	28.1	1,395	136.5	1,577	128	109.9
Clay town (Onondaga)	NA	NA	NA	NA	11,507	44	100.0	25.3	1.2	62.6	386	24.9	419	17	4.0
Clifton Park town (Saratoga)	NA	NA	NA	NA	16,718	59	100.0	24.2	15.2	14.7	141	24.1	656	134	10.8
Cohoes city & MCD (Albany)	46	271	195	1,149	1,400	13	23.1	21.8	9.6	42.2	489	21.7	1,292	130	15.7
Colonie town (Albany)	80	100	1,856	2,325	27,489	99	84.8	85.6	28.4	5.0	371	93.6	1,128	72	107.9
Commack CDP	NA	NA	NA	NA	NA	NA	NA	NA	NA	NA	NA	NA	NA	NA	NA
Copiague CDP	NA	NA	NA	NA	NA	NA	NA	NA	NA	NA	NA	NA	NA	NA	NA
Coram CDP	NA	NA	NA	NA	NA	NA	NA	NA	NA	NA	NA	NA	NA	NA	NA
Corning city & MCD (Steuben)	52	489	244	2,293	14,696	133	1.5	18.8	2.9	98.2	1,043	18.7	1,750	273	9.0
Cornwall town (Orange)	NA	NA	NA	NA	1,075	4	100.0	11.1	2.8	33.0	601	10.5	843	37	3.7
Cortland city & MCD (Cortland)	28	150	316	1,696	0	0	0.0	25.2	10.3	41.7	506	31.8	1,701	513	24.0
Cortlandt town (Westchester)	NA	NA	NA	NA	12,427	83	100.0	40.2	7.5	17.8	562	40.6	956	139	10.2
Deer Park CDP	NA	NA	NA	NA	NA	NA	NA	NA	NA	NA	NA	NA	NA	NA	NA
Depew village	12	79	250	1,649	480	3	33.3	14.1	2.5	27.0	646	13.3	884	65	8.2
De Witt town (Onondaga)	34	135	584	2,311	0	0	0.0	20.3	0.7	92.5	716	20.4	810	61	7.8
Dix Hills CDP	NA	NA	NA	NA	NA	NA	NA	NA	NA	NA	NA	NA	NA	NA	NA
Dobbs Ferry village	3	27	93	832	9,165	27	7.4	18.3	2.6	19.7	1,247	17.4	1,572	169	14.3
Dryden town (Tompkins)	NA	NA	NA	NA	3,596	23	73.9	6.8	2.7	15.4	242	6.9	473	55	0.6
Dunkirk city & MCD (Chautauqua)	24	204	170	1,446	2,321	16	100.0	19.0	3.3	80.0	641	20.5	1,738	184	23.3
Eastchester CDP	NA	NA	NA	NA	NA	NA	NA	NA	NA	NA	NA	NA	NA	NA	NA
Eastchester town (Westchester)	NA	NA	NA	NA	7,213	8	75.0	38.9	6.7	8.4	695	38.0	1,147	57	12.4
East Fishkill town (Dutchess)	9	30	136	459	19,235	72	90.3	20.3	2.1	15.6	525	22.3	760	114	28.6
East Greenbush town (Rensselaer)	12	74	404	2,474	0	0	0.0	16.3	3.1	9.0	613	14.7	898	34	17.4

1   Data for serious crimes have not been adjusted for underreporting. This may affect comparability between geographic areas over time.
2   Per 100,000 population estimated by the FBI.   3   Based on population estimated as of July 1 of the year shown.

Table B. Incorporated Places, Census Designated Places (CDPs), and Minor Civil Divisions (MCDs) of 10,000 or More Population — **Land Area, Population, and Households, and Employment**

STATE City, town, township, borough, or CDP (county if applicable)	Land area 2010 (sq mi)	Population Total persons 2010	Population Total persons 2019	Population Percent change 2010–2019	Population Persons per square mile 2019	Population characteristics 2015–2019 Percent foreign born	Population characteristics 2015–2019 Percent living in the same house as previous year	Income and poverty 2015–2019 Median household income	Income and poverty 2015–2019 Percent of households with income below poverty level	Income and poverty 2015–2019 Median value of owner-occupied housing units	Employment, 2015–2019 Percent in civilian labor force	Employment, 2015–2019 Unemployment rate	Households, 2015–2019 (percent of households) Family households	Households, 2015–2019 (percent of households) One person households
	1	2	3	4	5	6	7	8	9	10	11	12	13	14
NEW YORK—Con.														
East Hampton town (Suffolk)....	74.32	21,479	22,047	2.6	296.6	21.9	94.3	96,687	9.1	869,600	60.5	2.3	62.9	29.7
East Islip CDP	3.98	14,475	NA	NA	NA	5.6	95.8	125,000	4.4	416,000	63.8	3.7	74.4	21.1
East Massapequa CDP	3.42	19,069	NA	NA	NA	11.0	93.5	106,790	5.2	442,200	63.6	2.7	68.3	28.6
East Meadow CDP	6.30	38,132	NA	NA	NA	19.3	91.9	106,409	5.1	454,500	60.2	4.1	79.4	19.2
East Northport CDP	5.17	20,217	NA	NA	NA	7.8	96.4	115,651	4.0	472,800	64.6	4.6	77.3	20.7
East Patchogue CDP	8.32	22,469	NA	NA	NA	11.2	96.7	81,890	11.5	335,300	65.9	5.4	64.9	29.2
Eggertsville CDP	2.86	15,019	NA	NA	NA	15.2	87.3	72,652	12.3	155,900	66.9	3.7	64.3	27.7
Elma town (Erie)	34.52	11,317	11,775	4.0	341.1	2.4	90.1	75,718	5.2	251,100	62.8	3.0	65.6	28.6
Elmira city & MCD (Chemung) .	7.25	29,242	27,054	-7.5	3731.6	2.6	86.5	36,909	26.8	74,500	53.2	9.0	57.8	34.6
Elmont CDP	3.41	33,198	NA	NA	NA	44.7	94.9	104,671	5.4	402,400	68.5	5.4	82.8	14.3
Elwood CDP	4.78	11,177	NA	NA	NA	12.7	96.4	116,144	3.8	537,200	65.8	3.9	85.4	12.5
Endicott village	3.19	13,381	12,532	-6.3	3928.5	5.7	81.8	41,339	17.0	88,300	60.6	8.6	52.1	40.9
Endwell CDP	3.74	11,446	NA	NA	NA	5.3	93.0	58,662	11.1	134,300	60.3	3.6	59.9	34.9
Evans town (Erie)	41.53	16,364	16,091	-1.7	387.5	3.2	91.4	61,833	11.3	126,300	61.2	4.6	64.7	28.7
Fairmount CDP	3.33	10,224	NA	NA	NA	5.1	94.1	69,875	6.0	130,400	69.3	3.6	65.8	27.8
Fallsburg town (Sullivan)	77.62	12,915	13,023	0.8	167.8	11.8	87.7	40,631	17.8	140,200	53.1	7.5	58.1	35.3
Farmington town (Ontario)	39.43	11,829	13,784	16.5	349.6	3.1	86.3	70,679	6.1	159,700	72.4	2.1	62.7	29.7
Farmingville CDP	4.12	15,481	NA	NA	NA	13.6	97.7	110,246	3.1	349,400	67.3	5.6	85.2	11.3
Fishkill town (Dutchess)	27.34	23,791	24,096	1.3	881.3	12.4	82.9	88,606	7.7	296,100	54.2	4.8	62.6	32.0
Floral Park village	1.41	15,827	15,844	0.1	11236.9	14.9	93.7	117,857	2.9	593,900	65.7	3.1	74.4	19.9
Fort Drum CDP	14.34	12,955	NA	NA	NA	8.1	55.9	50,711	8.8	0	21.6	12.3	86.0	12.8
Fort Salonga CDP	9.80	10,008	NA	NA	NA	7.4	94.2	158,041	3.4	671,400	59.2	1.4	77.0	19.3
Franklin Square CDP	2.88	29,320	NA	NA	NA	24.0	95.0	107,415	4.2	476,100	64.1	4.1	81.8	15.2
Fredonia village	5.19	11,242	10,303	-8.4	1985.2	4.8	72.7	49,071	22.8	130,700	53.2	9.1	56.6	31.3
Freeport village	4.58	42,856	42,956	0.2	9379.0	31.5	93.9	81,958	11.1	339,100	64.5	4.0	70.1	25.4
Fulton city & MCD (Oswego)	3.82	11,895	11,102	-6.7	2906.3	2.5	82.2	45,639	22.5	80,700	58.4	6.5	60.0	31.5
Garden City village	5.33	22,330	22,454	0.6	4212.8	10.7	93.9	174,886	2.6	860,000	62.3	3.8	80.4	17.5
Gates town (Monroe)	15.20	28,498	28,251	-0.9	1858.6	10.7	89.8	58,838	6.8	121,200	67.2	3.9	63.4	29.2
Geddes town (Onondaga)	9.16	17,130	16,290	-4.9	1778.4	6.3	91.0	59,369	10.5	134,800	61.9	4.2	64.0	30.5
Geneseo town (Livingston)	43.94	10,484	10,623	1.3	241.8	6.8	70.7	46,112	30.4	172,800	43.5	2.4	54.7	26.7
Geneva city & MCD (Ontario)	4.21	13,272	12,631	-4.8	3000.2	6.6	75.0	44,050	17.0	96,200	59.1	6.3	53.9	39.8
German Flatts town (Herkimer)	33.70	13,221	12,442	-5.9	369.2	2.7	90.9	53,185	19.3	87,100	60.3	6.2	61.0	31.3
Glen Cove city & MCD (Nassau)	6.66	26,952	27,166	0.8	4079.0	29.2	92.4	80,702	15.2	508,300	62.4	2.2	67.9	25.7
Glens Falls city & MCD (Warren)	3.85	14,700	14,262	-3.0	3704.4	4.6	82.0	50,071	15.8	156,200	66.0	6.6	51.5	38.5
Glenville town (Schenectady) ...	49.25	29,490	29,271	-0.7	594.3	3.7	90.8	79,037	6.4	189,400	63.8	3.4	64.1	31.4
Gloversville city & MCD (Fulton)	5.05	15,618	14,747	-5.6	2920.2	2.3	85.8	38,896	22.2	76,100	55.5	7.5	59.3	32.0
Goshen town (Orange)	43.64	13,724	14,246	3.8	326.4	11.2	91.6	103,796	6.4	336,400	58.8	3.6	71.2	23.2
Grand Island town (Erie)	28.27	20,374	21,420	5.1	757.7	6.1	89.1	80,733	6.1	207,100	69.4	4.6	66.5	28.4
Great Neck village	1.33	10,071	10,209	1.4	7675.9	33.0	93.6	100,766	8.3	843,700	62.5	4.7	79.6	18.4
Greece CDP	4.37	14,519	NA	NA	NA	12.9	88.8	61,365	7.1	122,700	65.6	4.0	56.7	35.0
Greece town (Monroe)	47.46	95,965	95,499	-0.5	2012.2	7.5	88.5	63,113	8.6	135,500	65.6	4.1	63.3	30.6
Greenburgh town (Westchester)	30.28	88,373	90,989	3.0	3004.9	22.4	88.8	129,165	5.0	580,400	69.2	4.6	69.7	25.7
Greenlawn CDP	3.72	13,742	NA	NA	NA	16.1	93.9	112,333	5.8	489,900	63.5	3.5	76.1	20.7
Guilderland town (Albany)	57.90	35,344	35,723	1.1	617.0	11.3	88.9	86,180	5.1	250,900	65.7	2.9	61.8	31.7
Halfmoon town (Saratoga)	32.58	21,514	24,635	14.5	756.1	9.6	84.2	87,169	6.1	270,600	69.8	3.0	60.3	31.8
Hamburg town (Erie)	41.32	56,949	58,730	3.1	1421.3	3.0	91.4	70,408	8.3	166,100	65.6	2.6	64.2	30.8
Hampton Bays CDP	12.84	13,603	NA	NA	NA	27.5	92.2	81,250	8.2	489,100	64.2	2.4	67.8	27.9
Harrison village and town (Westchester)	16.76	27,458	28,943	5.4	1726.9	23.0	88.7	123,030	6.2	850,500	59.5	6.1	73.1	20.0
Hauppauge CDP	10.73	20,882	NA	NA	NA	11.1	90.4	116,124	3.4	486,200	65.2	3.1	73.1	20.1
Haverstraw village	1.98	11,910	12,045	1.1	6083.3	37.3	85.7	63,191	15.5	255,200	69.8	8.8	71.1	22.7
Haverstraw town (Rockland)	22.15	36,627	37,000	1.0	1670.4	30.3	86.6	73,306	12.3	297,800	67.5	7.8	71.8	21.8
Hempstead village	3.68	54,018	55,113	2.0	14976.4	40.6	92.4	62,569	19.8	321,200	67.5	4.5	72.8	23.0
Hempstead town (Nassau)	118.52	759,793	766,980	0.9	6471.3	22.7	93.5	111,072	6.2	455,700	66.0	4.2	77.7	19.1
Henrietta town (Monroe)	35.35	42,577	43,426	2.0	1228.5	15.2	77.6	63,819	13.1	145,500	61.5	4.5	61.0	29.0
Herkimer town (Herkimer)	31.66	10,174	9,573	-5.9	302.4	4.1	84.4	50,809	15.3	93,000	56.6	4.7	54.4	38.2
Hicksville CDP	6.79	41,547	NA	NA	NA	32.8	91.8	113,063	4.5	454,800	65.3	3.7	81.4	14.8
Highlands town (Orange)	30.40	12,487	12,183	-2.4	400.8	10.9	79.2	98,022	4.5	239,300	47.4	2.3	66.3	28.4
Holbrook CDP	7.17	27,195	NA	NA	NA	7.3	94.7	105,619	5.7	377,100	70.3	3.9	72.7	22.0
Holtsville CDP	7.11	19,714	NA	NA	NA	10.7	94.3	106,556	5.4	362,600	69.7	4.3	75.7	21.2
Horseheads town (Chemung)	35.61	19,477	18,866	-3.1	529.8	5.9	85.4	57,181	9.1	124,800	59.7	3.9	59.2	33.9
Huntington CDP	7.59	18,046	NA	NA	NA	8.6	94.4	123,797	6.9	615,000	63.4	3.9	61.0	32.0
Huntington town (Suffolk)	94.15	203,046	200,503	-1.3	2129.6	14.0	94.3	124,490	5.2	560,400	64.2	3.7	76.2	19.8
Huntington Station CDP	5.48	33,029	NA	NA	NA	25.5	93.0	93,400	9.2	376,500	69.3	3.8	74.6	20.6
Hyde Park town (Dutchess)	36.66	21,586	20,847	-3.4	568.7	7.5	88.6	76,093	9.1	220,600	60.1	6.7	68.1	25.9
Irondequoit town (Monroe)	14.99	51,584	50,055	-3.0	3339.2	6.5	88.5	62,225	9.0	123,800	65.3	4.3	60.8	33.7
Islip CDP	4.83	18,689	NA	NA	NA	12.4	92.2	110,387	5.7	378,600	69.5	3.6	73.0	23.0
Islip town (Suffolk)	103.79	335,298	329,610	-1.7	3175.7	21.1	93.4	98,387	7.3	365,900	67.8	4.1	75.7	20.1
Ithaca city & MCD (Tompkins) ..	5.39	30,013	30,837	2.7	5721.2	17.8	58.5	34,424	36.6	239,100	52.4	4.8	27.7	42.0
Ithaca town (Tompkins)	28.95	19,925	19,663	-1.3	679.2	20.4	73.7	67,350	11.7	272,500	55.5	3.9	50.5	36.2
Jamestown city & MCD (Chautauqua)	8.93	31,161	29,058	-6.7	3254.0	1.9	85.8	33,420	26.7	63,200	56.8	7.5	53.9	38.6
Jefferson Valley-Yorktown CDP	6.95	14,142	NA	NA	NA	12.7	95.5	129,797	4.0	422,000	63.8	3.0	73.9	23.6
Jericho CDP	3.96	13,567	NA	NA	NA	26.1	91.2	173,709	5.1	797,400	66.9	5.7	81.9	15.8
Johnson City village	4.55	15,174	14,161	-6.7	3112.3	10.3	80.8	42,299	18.8	89,300	61.2	6.0	52.5	36.7
Kenmore village	1.44	15,502	15,200	-3.1	10430.6	4.1	92.1	68,110	8.2	133,600	66.9	1.6	54.0	38.5
Kent town (Putnam)	40.51	13,513	13,162	-2.6	324.9	13.9	94.9	100,385	3.6	289,900	65.8	4.6	69.8	25.8
Kingsbury town (Washington)...	39.69	12,694	12,334	-2.8	310.8	2.5	79.9	53,134	12.0	138,400	69.8	8.3	61.8	26.2
Kings Park CDP	6.23	17,282	NA	NA	NA	7.2	93.5	100,110	5.0	443,700	62.2	5.5	66.3	30.8
Kingston city & MCD (Ulster)....	7.48	23,855	22,793	-4.5	3047.2	11.3	82.4	51,299	16.1	177,500	66.9	6.8	55.5	35.8
Kirkland town (Oneida)	33.76	10,299	10,048	-2.4	297.6	4.6	87.1	72,714	10.1	204,700	58.6	3.5	56.0	36.3
Kiryas Joel village	1.36	20,365	26,813	31.7	19715.4	5.3	95.1	31,277	42.9	517,400	47.2	4.5	97.3	2.6
Lackawanna city & MCD (Erie).	6.55	18,144	17,720	-2.3	2705.3	9.8	87.0	38,289	21.5	94,700	58.8	5.9	54.7	38.0

Table B. Incorporated Places, Census Designated Places (CDPs), and Minor Civil Divisions (MCDs) of 10,000 or More Population — **Crime, Residential Construction and Local Government Finance**

STATE City, town, township, borough, or CDP (county if applicable)	Violent crime Number	Violent crime Rate²	Property crime Number	Property crime Rate²	Value ($1,000)	Number of housing units	Percent single family	General revenue Total (mil dol)	Intergovernmental Total (mil dol)	Intergovernmental Percent from state gov.	Taxes per capita³	General expenditure Total (mil dol)	Per capita³ Total	Per capita³ Capital outlays	Debt outstanding (mil dol)
	15	16	17	18	19	20	21	22	23	24	25	26	27	28	29
NEW YORK—Con.															
East Hampton town (Suffolk)....	11	55	176	880	60,285	83	100.0	109.8	36.2	6.5	2,712	72.6	3,309	360	100.9
East Islip CDP	NA	NA	NA	NA	NA	NA	NA	NA	NA	NA	NA	NA	NA	NA	NA
East Massapequa CDP	NA	NA	NA	NA	NA	NA	NA	NA	NA	NA	NA	NA	NA	NA	NA
East Meadow CDP	NA	NA	NA	NA	NA	NA	NA	NA	NA	NA	NA	NA	NA	NA	NA
East Northport CDP	NA	NA	NA	NA	NA	NA	NA	NA	NA	NA	NA	NA	NA	NA	NA
East Patchogue CDP	NA	NA	NA	NA	NA	NA	NA	NA	NA	NA	NA	NA	NA	NA	NA
Eggertsville CDP	NA	NA	NA	NA	NA	NA	NA	NA	NA	NA	NA	NA	NA	NA	NA
Elma town (Erie)	NA	NA	NA	NA	5,310	17	100.0	6.0	2.9	9.7	168	6.4	546	36	0.0
Elmira city & MCD (Chemung) .	70	254	702	2,548	30,141	194	0.0	33.7	15.0	40.8	492	39.2	1,437	184	26.8
Elmont CDP..........................	NA	NA	NA	NA	NA	NA	NA	NA	NA	NA	NA	NA	NA	NA	NA
Elwood CDP	NA	NA	NA	NA	NA	NA	NA	NA	NA	NA	NA	NA	NA	NA	NA
Endicott village	70	549	397	3,113	0	0	0.0	19.2	6.2	25.8	656	21.0	1,644	326	10.2
Endwell CDP.........................	NA	NA	NA	NA	NA	NA	NA	NA	NA	NA	NA	NA	NA	NA	NA
Evans town (Erie)	22	136	177	1,091	0	0	0.0	14.6	2.5	22.0	662	16.4	1,015	127	17.0
Fairmount CDP.......................	NA	NA	NA	NA	NA	NA	NA	NA	NA	NA	NA	NA	NA	NA	NA
Fallsburg town (Sullivan).........	15	123	109	893	13,473	74	100.0	17.8	0.9	67.4	842	17.0	1,319	37	11.0
Farmington town (Ontario).......	NA	NA	NA	NA	20,867	81	85.2	12.2	3.6	7.7	184	10.5	795	177	10.1
Farmingville CDP....................	NA	NA	NA	NA	NA	NA	NA	NA	NA	NA	NA	NA	NA	NA	NA
Fishkill town (Dutchess)..........	10	46	161	748	6,916	57	17.5	15.4	1.3	17.3	363	13.0	540	91	19.2
Floral Park village	8	50	46	285	948	3	100.0	27.7	0.8	100.0	1,555	28.3	1,780	183	12.1
Fort Drum CDP......................	NA	NA	NA	NA	NA	NA	NA	NA	NA	NA	NA	NA	NA	NA	NA
Fort Salonga CDP..................	NA	NA	NA	NA	NA	NA	NA	NA	NA	NA	NA	NA	NA	NA	NA
Franklin Square CDP...............	NA	NA	NA	NA	NA	NA	NA	NA	NA	NA	NA	NA	NA	NA	NA
Fredonia village	7	67	159	1,518	NA	NA	NA	7.7	2.2	4.7	305	8.0	766	100	6.6
Freeport village	70	161	422	968	3,901	11	100.0	66.8	1.8	82.2	1,059	76.9	1,782	73	109.3
Fulton city & MCD (Oswego)	8	71	396	3,522	0	0	0.0	23.3	5.5	60.6	1,208	24.7	2,178	309	11.3
Garden City village	10	44	358	1,574	450	1	100.0	60.7	1.4	90.5	2,323	60.6	2,687	328	29.5
Gates town (Monroe)..............	56	195	823	2,866	6,235	50	82.0	16.5	3.4	18.5	410	17.0	601	20	0.0
Geddes town (Onondaga)........	7	69	215	2,113	794	3	100.0	9.8	0.6	90.5	542	9.7	589	72	1.7
Geneseo town (Livingston).......	NA	NA	NA	NA	558	6	16.7	2.7	0.5	45.1	151	2.3	212	55	0.1
Geneva city & MCD (Ontario)..	31	241	221	1,721	3,142	18	83.3	24.4	5.0	81.6	852	27.3	2,129	573	106.3
German Flatts town (Herkimer)	NA	NA	NA	NA	0	0	0.0	3.0	1.4	71.7	111	2.8	221	3	0.8
Glen Cove city & MCD (Nassau)	4	15	111	403	1,297	7	14.3	59.7	19.7	43.5	1,226	54.0	1,982	213	57.5
Glens Falls city & MCD (Warren)	24	167	150	1,041	150	1	100.0	27.4	6.3	66.9	941	27.3	1,896	210	44.5
Glenville town (Schenectady) ...	19	88	293	1,352	5,686	51	37.3	15.0	4.0	20.8	334	14.7	503	53	15.2
Gloversville city & MCD (Fulton)	83	559	363	2,443	0	0	0.0	19.0	4.3	86.8	761	18.1	1,212	90	5.7
Goshen town (Orange)	NA	NA	NA	NA	2,435	24	100.0	8.6	1.7	17.9	405	8.0	572	34	2.4
Grand Island town (Erie)..........	NA	NA	NA	NA	27,586	193	25.4	18.3	4.1	5.5	507	18.7	879	181	20.5
Great Neck village	NA	NA	NA	NA	3,570	8	100.0	9.7	0.5	100.0	831	8.4	827	44	8.4
Greece CDP	NA	NA	NA	NA	NA	NA	NA	NA	NA	NA	NA	NA	NA	NA	NA
Greece town (Monroe).............	189	196	2,040	2,111	17,680	101	89.1	57.0	11.1	14.9	438	67.3	701	209	30.2
Greenburgh town (Westchester)......................	NA	NA	NA	NA	11,173	19	100.0	104.7	8.8	21.7	877	104.2	1,136	120	82.3
Greenlawn CDP......................	NA	NA	NA	NA	NA	NA	NA	NA	NA	NA	NA	NA	NA	NA	NA
Guilderland town (Albany)	27	79	687	2,005	11,795	98	30.6	30.6	12.9	6.1	292	28.2	790	58	20.5
Halfmoon town (Saratoga)........	NA	NA	NA	NA	40,646	154	100.0	20.6	8.1	14.4	219	12.8	524	93	30.8
Hamburg town (Erie)	41	88	888	1,910	27,124	178	66.3	42.4	8.7	10.3	498	41.3	709	40	10.8
Hampton Bays CDP	NA	NA	NA	NA	NA	NA	NA	NA	NA	NA	NA	NA	NA	NA	NA
Harrison village and town (Westchester)......................	NA	NA	101	351	23,233	61	100.0	59.0	7.4	1.9	1,592	64.4	2,306	8	0.0
Hauppauge CDP	NA	NA	NA	NA	NA	NA	NA	NA	NA	NA	NA	NA	NA	NA	NA
Haverstraw village	NA	NA	NA	NA	808	10	20.0	12.2	2.5	83.0	615	12.6	1,046	394	21.9
Haverstraw town (Rockland).....	NA	NA	NA	NA	0	0	0.0	41.1	2.2	9.4	844	36.1	970	44	34.3
Hempstead village	322	574	589	1,051	1,590	10	60.0	80.6	2.0	65.7	1,218	75.8	1,369	58	49.2
Hempstead town (Nassau)	NA	NA	NA	NA	127,791	825	41.3	498.9	93.4	13.4	462	612.2	797	57	456.3
Henrietta town (Monroe)...........	NA	NA	NA	NA	28,178	112	100.0	17.3	5.2	12.2	166	25.5	587	218	0.6
Herkimer town (Herkimer)	NA	NA	NA	NA	500	3	100.0	2.0	0.5	21.7	124	2.0	205	6	0.9
Hicksville CDP	NA	NA	NA	NA	NA	NA	NA	NA	NA	NA	NA	NA	NA	NA	NA
Highlands town (Orange).........	NA	NA	NA	NA	335	3	100.0	5.4	1.0	19.7	255	4.6	377	11	1.2
Holbrook CDP.......................	NA	NA	NA	NA	NA	NA	NA	NA	NA	NA	NA	NA	NA	NA	NA
Holtsville CDP.......................	NA	NA	NA	NA	NA	NA	NA	NA	NA	NA	NA	NA	NA	NA	NA
Horseheads town (Chemung)...	NA	NA	NA	NA	1,891	9	77.8	3.6	2.3	12.0	56	4.2	218	10	0.1
Huntington CDP.....................	NA	NA	NA	NA	NA	NA	NA	NA	NA	NA	NA	NA	NA	NA	NA
Huntington town (Suffolk)	NA	NA	NA	NA	12,165	46	100.0	191.1	7.9	81.6	701	180.3	894	83	112.6
Huntington Station CDP	NA	NA	NA	NA	NA	NA	NA	NA	NA	NA	NA	NA	NA	NA	NA
Hyde Park town (Dutchess)......	9	43	91	432	0	0	0.0	9.8	1.7	30.4	346	8.8	422	32	10.3
Irondequoit town (Monroe)	91	181	922	1,836	764	7	71.4	33.6	7.6	23.1	471	33.6	672	74	25.0
Islip CDP..............................	NA	NA	NA	NA	NA	NA	NA	NA	NA	NA	NA	NA	NA	NA	NA
Islip town (Suffolk)	NA	NA	NA	NA	16,944	67	91.0	202.2	27.2	42.1	407	202.3	611	78	165.4
Ithaca city & MCD (Tompkins) ..	72	231	815	2,617	57,856	424	3.5	66.0	10.2	63.2	1,246	67.2	2,191	286	127.5
Ithaca town (Tompkins)...........	NA	NA	NA	NA	12,675	99	6.1	16.0	3.6	10.1	408	14.7	744	80	16.5
Jamestown city & MCD (Chautauqua)....................	227	773	817	2,780	132	1	100.0	76.2	35.4	57.8	562	82.7	2,803	72	32.4
Jefferson Valley-Yorktown CDP	NA	NA	NA	NA	NA	NA	NA	NA	NA	NA	NA	NA	NA	NA	NA
Jericho CDP	NA	NA	NA	NA	NA	NA	NA	NA	NA	NA	NA	NA	NA	NA	NA
Johnson City village................	63	437	596	4,134	NA	NA	NA	29.7	13.3	31.2	746	44.1	3,051	1473	68.1
Kenmore village	14	92	185	1,219	0	0	0.0	15.9	3.2	22.0	668	16.7	1,105	200	18.0
Kent town (Putnam)	1	8	51	383	0	0	0.0	18.1	1.2	52.0	1,165	17.7	1,335	118	1.7
Kingsbury town (Washington)....	NA	NA	NA	NA	NA	NA	NA	3.3	0.4	66.5	161	2.7	217	45	0.8
Kings Park CDP.....................	NA	NA	NA	NA	NA	NA	NA	NA	NA	NA	NA	NA	NA	NA	NA
Kingston city & MCD (Ulster)....	70	303	477	2,067	695	3	100.0	48.8	21.0	31.4	837	52.4	2,275	285	36.1
Kirkland town (Oneida)............	NA	NA	NA	NA	1,826	19	21.1	6.3	2.6	10.6	270	6.0	599	42	3.9
Kiryas Joel village	NA	NA	NA	NA	NA	NA	NA	11.3	5.5	22.8	144	10.1	415	35	44.0
Lackawanna city & MCD (Erie).	70	391	315	1,759	525	2	100.0	28.8	16.4	49.9	586	29.1	1,633	46	7.1

1 Data for serious crimes have not been adjusted for underreporting. This may affect comparability between geographic areas over time.
2 Per 100,000 population estimated by the FBI. 3 Based on population estimated as of July 1 of the year shown.

STATE City, town, township, borough, or CDP (county if applicable)	Land area 2010 (sq mi)	Population Total persons 2010	Total persons 2019	Percent change 2010–2019	Persons per square mile, 2019	Population characteristics 2015–2019 Percent foreign born	Percent living in the same house as previous year	Income and poverty 2015–2019 Median household income	Percent of households with income below poverty level	Median value of owner-occupied housing units	Employment, 2015–2019 Percent in civilian labor force	Unemployment rate	Households, 2015–2019 (percent of households) Family households	One person households
	1	2	3	4	5	6	7	8	9	10	11	12	13	14
NEW YORK—Con.														
La Grange town (Dutchess)......	39.88	15,717	15,627	-0.6	391.9	8.6	93.1	117,229	2.4	302,700	67.0	3.9	77.9	19.2
Lake Grove village..................	2.96	11,184	11,056	-1.1	3735.1	10.4	94.2	114,676	4.5	417,800	65.8	3.6	77.7	19.9
Lake Ronkonkoma CDP	4.94	20,155	NA	NA	NA	12.1	93.4	95,080	10.5	366,400	64.5	4.9	72.6	23.3
Lancaster village...................	2.70	10,296	10,109	-1.8	3744.1	2.2	87.8	54,875	7.6	123,700	70.3	3.3	51.9	38.6
Lancaster town (Erie)............	37.71	41,619	43,325	4.1	1148.9	3.5	91.9	72,591	5.2	181,100	68.5	3.5	64.2	29.0
Lansing town (Tompkins).........	60.49	11,031	11,634	5.5	192.3	18.9	74.1	72,587	10.2	237,900	67.5	1.6	59.9	28.3
Le Ray town (Jefferson).........	73.61	21,779	20,957	-3.8	284.7	8.0	60.7	53,227	7.4	182,500	34.1	6.6	78.1	17.2
Levittown CDP......................	6.81	51,881	NA	NA	NA	14.4	94.3	124,995	3.7	406,200	68.4	3.5	82.1	15.6
Lewisboro town (Westchester) .	27.75	12,408	12,522	0.9	451.2	12.6	92.9	158,299	4.2	620,500	68.1	4.5	79.6	18.9
Lewiston town (Niagara)..........	37.12	16,254	15,729	-3.2	423.7	7.4	89.5	69,967	4.6	179,700	57.3	3.0	63.8	32.2
Lindenhurst village................	3.75	27,269	26,801	-1.7	7146.9	14.8	91.2	97,253	5.7	367,000	69.2	4.3	75.1	21.4
Lloyd town (Ulster)..................	31.27	10,845	10,518	-3.0	336.4	7.5	91.3	77,384	9.0	248,000	63.3	4.4	60.8	29.3
Lockport city & MCD (Niagara).	8.40	21,186	20,305	-4.2	2417.3	3.2	87.3	45,018	16.6	93,000	63.0	6.0	54.4	37.0
Lockport town (Niagara)	44.84	20,496	19,908	-2.9	444.0	2.4	89.8	65,797	11.0	141,400	59.3	5.7	65.0	28.7
Long Beach city & MCD (Nassau)	2.22	33,333	33,454	0.4	15069.4	13.4	87.9	97,022	6.4	508,800	67.1	4.4	55.6	36.3
Lynbrook village...................	2.01	19,486	19,448	-0.2	9675.6	15.7	91.3	102,686	4.5	454,100	67.6	4.3	69.7	27.8
Lysander town (Onondaga)......	61.71	21,759	22,896	5.2	371.0	2.6	92.6	87,078	7.4	184,200	66.0	3.2	72.1	22.7
Malone town (Franklin)	101.52	14,547	14,078	-3.2	138.7	5.0	71.4	47,500	24.3	102,900	36.4	5.2	64.9	31.3
Malta town (Saratoga)...........	27.92	14,768	16,252	10.0	582.1	5.9	85.5	91,558	4.0	264,100	70.2	5.0	63.8	27.7
Mamakating town (Sullivan)......	96.11	12,082	11,430	-5.4	118.9	6.3	92.7	76,467	10.3	201,900	66.0	7.6	72.9	22.0
Mamaroneck village................	3.17	18,907	19,131	1.2	6035.0	28.5	88.3	102,138	5.7	623,400	66.3	4.0	69.5	25.8
Mamaroneck town (Westchester)......	6.65	29,138	29,495	1.2	4435.3	22.4	90.6	137,135	4.6	863,500	67.4	3.8	72.8	23.7
Manlius town (Onondaga)	49.22	32,369	31,653	-2.2	643.1	8.1	87.0	81,222	6.2	196,800	65.2	3.2	64.9	30.5
Manorville CDP.....................	25.40	14,314	NA	NA	NA	6.7	92.4	98,109	7.1	416,300	58.3	2.3	66.8	29.1
Massapequa CDP	3.56	21,685	NA	NA	NA	4.7	94.5	132,133	3.3	536,400	65.5	2.4	81.6	13.9
Massapequa Park village	2.19	17,110	17,143	0.2	7827.9	5.5	95.9	129,525	3.7	471,200	64.3	2.9	82.5	15.8
Massena village....................	4.52	10,938	10,200	-6.7	2256.6	4.8	86.0	44,626	17.2	76,400	57.2	9.2	56.6	36.5
Massena town (St. Lawrence) ..	44.35	12,883	12,043	-6.5	271.5	5.3	88.1	44,220	18.9	78,700	56.2	8.0	57.3	35.7
Mastic CDP.........................	3.90	15,481	NA	NA	NA	12.5	96.8	98,811	7.6	248,400	66.0	4.9	81.6	13.1
Mastic Beach CDP	4.72	12,930	NA	NA	NA	9.4	96.3	72,137	12.0	225,100	59.5	5.2	70.2	20.2
Medford CDP.......................	10.80	24,142	NA	NA	NA	12.3	94.7	95,603	9.0	324,800	65.6	4.9	71.6	24.6
Melville CDP........................	12.09	18,985	NA	NA	NA	11.1	93.0	127,359	4.1	670,400	60.9	3.3	72.3	23.2
Merrick CDP........................	3.98	22,097	NA	NA	NA	11.6	94.8	158,306	4.1	573,200	66.5	3.3	82.0	14.8
Middle Island CDP.................	8.22	10,483	NA	NA	NA	10.0	91.7	78,301	9.4	274,000	60.0	4.8	59.2	36.2
Middletown city & MCD (Orange)......	5.31	28,121	28,189	0.2	5308.7	13.6	87.1	55,245	16.1	182,000	65.0	4.3	60.1	34.9
Miller Place CDP	6.55	12,339	NA	NA	NA	6.3	95.4	130,341	5.4	443,200	59.5	4.7	82.5	12.6
Milton town (Saratoga)	35.69	18,558	19,367	4.4	542.6	3.1	91.8	72,382	10.1	206,900	67.5	4.0	65.5	28.7
Mineola village.....................	1.88	18,865	19,207	1.8	10216.5	28.7	94.8	100,891	4.6	512,800	71.3	2.9	63.4	30.6
Monroe town (Orange)	18.55	19,486	19,824	1.7	1068.7	15.8	92.4	108,246	4.6	328,000	65.6	3.2	81.7	15.1
Monsey CDP........................	2.27	18,412	NA	NA	NA	7.4	93.5	45,399	34.9	676,400	52.0	7.4	94.4	4.2
Montgomery town (Orange)......	50.26	22,636	24,065	6.3	478.8	5.9	89.3	83,034	7.9	245,800	65.6	3.6	72.3	22.7
Moreau town (Saratoga)..........	41.94	14,737	15,459	4.9	368.6	1.2	84.1	66,095	6.6	186,900	70.0	2.8	65.9	28.9
Mount Kisco village and town (Westchester)......	3.04	10,779	10,795	0.1	3551.0	34.6	89.3	86,654	4.3	429,900	70.1	4.0	61.2	34.8
Mount Pleasant town (Westchester)...............	27.44	43,718	44,933	2.8	1637.5	20.6	88.7	120,676	6.8	667,000	63.6	5.4	76.4	18.5
Mount Sinai CDP	6.00	12,118	NA	NA	NA	8.5	93.8	135,975	3.8	454,100	62.4	5.4	78.6	18.6
Mount Vernon city & MCD (Westchester)...............	4.38	67,316	67,345	0.0	15375.6	31.5	90.2	59,907	15.6	362,200	65.1	6.6	58.6	35.8
Nanuet CDP.........................	5.43	17,882	NA	NA	NA	26.1	88.8	104,315	5.4	382,200	62.6	3.3	67.3	27.0
Nesconset CDP.....................	3.82	13,387	NA	NA	NA	9.6	97.8	125,245	4.3	458,500	62.7	5.8	81.3	17.2
Newburgh city & MCD (Orange)...............	3.81	28,903	28,177	-2.5	7395.5	21.7	89.2	41,769	23.9	159,000	64.2	6.6	59.2	34.5
Newburgh town (Orange)	43.36	29,728	31,494	5.9	726.3	11.6	92.9	91,596	5.2	262,500	65.5	4.7	72.7	22.7
New Cassel CDP...................	1.48	14,059	NA	NA	NA	47.0	94.6	87,604	11.6	362,900	68.7	4.6	80.6	16.9
New Castle town (Westchester)	23.17	17,571	17,801	1.3	768.3	13.5	95.4	247,090	2.2	897,900	65.8	5.4	88.2	9.7
New City CDP.......................	15.57	33,559	NA	NA	NA	21.1	94.5	138,638	4.0	489,600	66.5	4.7	81.4	15.2
New Hartford town (Oneida).....	25.38	22,167	21,818	-1.6	859.7	6.5	91.5	67,056	5.6	165,000	59.2	2.5	62.0	33.1
New Paltz town (Ulster)	33.88	14,002	14,036	0.2	414.3	9.0	79.1	76,335	15.7	314,900	57.9	7.1	55.2	29.6
New Rochelle city & MCD (Westchester)...............	10.35	77,115	78,557	1.9	7590.0	31.0	88.9	81,311	11.6	575,300	65.3	6.1	65.5	30.2
New Windsor town (Orange)	34.08	25,254	27,703	9.7	812.9	14.5	92.4	82,144	7.0	261,600	65.9	3.3	65.8	27.7
New York city.....................	300.38	8,175,031	8,336,817	2.0	27754.2	36.8	90.0	63,998	17.7	606,000	63.6	6.3	59.6	32.3
Niagara Falls city & MCD (Niagara).........	14.09	50,031	47,720	-4.6	3386.4	5.3	88.9	36,346	25.6	77,400	58.1	6.9	53.8	38.7
Niskayuna town (Schenectady)	14.15	21,774	22,365	2.7	1580.6	14.2	90.5	110,855	3.5	275,800	60.9	5.3	71.1	27.2
North Amityville CDP..............	2.35	17,862	NA	NA	NA	27.3	93.1	75,529	11.4	313,100	70.7	4.9	67.3	28.4
North Babylon CDP................	3.37	17,509	NA	NA	NA	14.5	93.5	95,306	6.8	356,400	66.8	4.5	71.4	22.6
North Bay Shore CDP	3.21	18,944	NA	NA	NA	40.2	93.4	89,275	9.4	298,400	74.7	8.6	86.5	9.9
North Bellmore CDP...............	2.62	19,941	NA	NA	NA	9.8	93.6	136,879	5.6	482,000	66.5	4.1	79.9	15.7
North Bellport CDP.................	4.90	11,545	NA	NA	NA	21.7	93.7	75,531	13.1	284,800	64.4	3.7	76.0	17.7
North Castle town (Westchester)...............	23.86	11,898	12,231	2.8	512.6	15.1	91.9	186,591	1.9	919,300	68.8	3.9	85.3	12.5
North Greenbush town (Rensselaer)...............	18.54	12,085	12,246	1.3	660.5	5.7	89.0	78,462	2.8	215,400	67.1	4.8	63.3	30.8
North Hempstead town (Nassau)...............	53.52	226,226	230,933	2.1	4314.9	29.3	92.9	125,364	5.3	710,400	63.0	3.6	76.2	20.8
North Lindenhurst CDP	1.93	11,652	NA	NA	NA	26.3	93.2	85,491	8.1	339,400	68.8	3.5	71.2	22.5
North Massapequa CDP	2.99	17,886	NA	NA	NA	6.1	96.1	119,485	4.1	457,900	63.7	3.6	81.1	16.8
North Merrick CDP.................	1.72	12,272	NA	NA	NA	9.6	92.4	135,469	2.7	505,100	71.4	2.4	84.5	13.2
North New Hyde Park CDP	1.98	14,899	NA	NA	NA	33.5	94.7	128,142	2.6	621,000	61.8	3.3	84.8	14.5
North Tonawanda city & MCD (Niagara).........	10.10	31,574	30,245	-4.2	2994.6	3.5	91.2	58,211	9.8	122,700	63.8	4.8	58.2	35.6
North Valley Stream CDP	1.87	16,628	NA	NA	NA	39.1	92.7	116,224	3.7	412,600	66.7	4.7	78.9	16.7

Table B. Incorporated Places, Census Designated Places (CDPs), and Minor Civil Divisions (MCDs) of 10,000 or More Population — Crime, Residential Construction and Local Government Finance

STATE City, town, township, borough, or CDP (county if applicable)	Serious crimes known to police, 2018[1] Violent crime Number	Violent crime Rate[2]	Property crime Number	Property crime Rate[2]	New residential construction authorized by building permits, 2019 Value ($1,000)	Number of housing units	Percent single family	Local government finance, 2017 General revenue Total (mil dol)	Intergovernmental Total (mil dol)	Percent from state gov.	Taxes per capita[3]	General expenditure Total (mil dol)	Per capita[3] Total	Capital outlays	Debt outstanding (mil dol)
	15	16	17	18	19	20	21	22	23	24	25	26	27	28	29
NEW YORK—Con.															
La Grange town (Dutchess)......	NA	NA	NA	NA	6,716	36	44.4	10.2	1.1	26.6	414	9.6	615	39	17.9
Lake Grove village..................	NA	NA	NA	NA	6,037	9	100.0	4.6	0.4	93.8	269	4.7	421	44	0.0
Lake Ronkonkoma CDP	NA	NA	NA	NA	NA	NA	NA	NA	NA	NA	NA	NA	NA	NA	NA
Lancaster village....................	21	56	405	1,072	NA	NA	NA	8.1	1.8	47.3	494	7.1	700	115	49.0
Lancaster town (Erie)	NA	NA	NA	NA	22,477	78	92.3	32.7	6.6	6.5	513	32.2	745	85	71.3
Lansing town (Tompkins)........	NA	NA	NA	NA	18,021	181	0.6	5.5	1.8	15.3	203	5.0	445	33	3.2
Le Ray town (Jefferson)...........	NA	NA	NA	NA	NA	NA	NA	4.7	2.2	24.0	72	4.0	187	32	13.2
Levittown CDP.......................	NA	NA	NA	NA	NA	NA	NA	NA	NA	NA	NA	NA	NA	NA	NA
Lewisboro town (Westchester) .	NA	NA	NA	NA	5,908	6	100.0	12.5	2.2	16.2	681	12.4	979	64	12.5
Lewiston town (Niagara)..........	13	82	155	974	4,000	10	100.0	14.4	6.8	26.6	199	13.6	856	78	12.3
Lindenhurst village.................	NA	NA	NA	NA	192	1	100.0	14.4	2.2	83.2	328	13.3	493	78	9.0
Lloyd town (Ulster).................	9	86	75	714	12,867	94	21.3	8.6	0.6	48.9	637	7.9	749	97	10.3
Lockport city & MCD (Niagara).	NA	NA	NA	NA	0	0	0.0	30.8	9.3	44.8	743	35.2	1,716	124	18.1
Lockport town (Niagara)	NA	NA	NA	NA	10,157	38	100.0	14.4	6.0	5.7	324	13.3	665	99	17.2
Long Beach city & MCD (Nassau)...........................	29	86	80	237	3,400	17	100.0	82.5	11.3	63.3	1,280	89.9	2,679	253	142.6
Lynbrook village.....................	12	61	105	532	375	1	100.0	39.3	0.6	65.6	1,700	36.9	1,889	119	22.3
Lysander town (Onondaga)	NA	NA	NA	NA	252	1	100.0	4.8	0.5	51.8	175	4.6	203	1	3.6
Malone town (Franklin)	NA	NA	NA	NA	1,100	13	100.0	4.1	1.0	55.1	198	3.8	268	73	0.4
Malta town (Saratoga)............	NA	NA	NA	NA	16,424	57	100.0	11.4	5.0	3.6	183	10.4	644	65	2.8
Mamakating town (Sullivan)......	NA	NA	NA	NA	3,711	23	100.0	6.7	0.9	74.4	421	6.5	572	104	1.1
Mamaroneck village................	13	67	127	651	8,720	16	43.8	39.6	6.9	4.1	1,410	38.0	1,978	148	42.0
Mamaroneck town (Westchester).....................	NA	NA	NA	NA	7,096	9	100.0	42.3	9.2	7.8	912	45.4	1,529	202	32.9
Manlius town (Onondaga)	18	74	260	1,065	6,452	27	100.0	18.6	0.8	52.7	503	18.0	566	28	0.4
Manorville CDP	NA	NA	NA	NA	NA	NA	NA	NA	NA	NA	NA	NA	NA	NA	NA
Massapequa CDP	NA	NA	NA	NA	NA	NA	NA	NA	NA	NA	NA	NA	NA	NA	NA
Massapequa Park village	NA	NA	NA	NA	794	3	100.0	7.1	0.8	94.0	310	6.6	381	68	6.3
Massena village......................	NA	NA	NA	NA	NA	NA	NA	12.5	2.7	22.8	571	13.5	1,307	260	5.9
Massena town (St. Lawrence) ..	NA	NA	NA	NA	0	0	0.0	60.8	7.5	86.1	214	60.0	4,911	59	1.9
Mastic CDP...........................	NA	NA	NA	NA	NA	NA	NA	NA	NA	NA	NA	NA	NA	NA	NA
Mastic Beach CDP	NA	NA	NA	NA	0	0	0.0	NA	NA	NA	NA	NA	NA	NA	NA
Medford CDP.........................	NA	NA	NA	NA	NA	NA	NA	NA	NA	NA	NA	NA	NA	NA	NA
Melville CDP	NA	NA	NA	NA	NA	NA	NA	NA	NA	NA	NA	NA	NA	NA	NA
Merrick CDP..........................	NA	NA	NA	NA	NA	NA	NA	NA	NA	NA	NA	NA	NA	NA	NA
Middle Island CDP..................	NA	NA	NA	NA	NA	NA	NA	NA	NA	NA	NA	NA	NA	NA	NA
Middletown city & MCD (Orange)............................	110	395	510	1,829	15,451	64	100.0	44.1	14.2	24.4	731	47.8	1,711	208	56.3
Miller Place CDP	NA	NA	NA	NA	NA	NA	NA	NA	NA	NA	NA	NA	NA	NA	NA
Milton town (Saratoga)...........	NA	NA	NA	NA	5,130	14	100.0	5.6	3.3	8.6	95	6.0	310	42	0.0
Mineola village.......................	NA	NA	NA	NA	36,938	196	1.0	22.0	0.8	63.9	837	18.9	984	29	8.9
Monroe town (Orange)	NA	NA	NA	NA	4,468	8	100.0	12.5	2.4	32.1	268	11.4	574	19	0.7
Monsey CDP..........................	NA	NA	NA	NA	NA	NA	NA	NA	NA	NA	NA	NA	NA	NA	NA
Montgomery town (Orange)......	NA	NA	NA	NA	4,765	21	100.0	11.0	1.9	17.6	322	9.9	415	16	5.1
Moreau town (Saratoga).........	NA	NA	NA	NA	13,960	119	47.9	7.1	2.9	8.6	171	6.5	419	17	7.6
Mount Kisco village and town (Westchester).....................	NA	NA	NA	NA	NA	NA	NA	25.9	3.9	14.0	1,644	23.8	2,181	176	16.1
Mount Pleasant town (Westchester).....................	NA	NA	NA	NA	5,626	13	100.0	44.6	7.3	8.8	727	41.2	915	34	62.7
Mount Sinai CDP....................	NA	NA	NA	NA	NA	NA	NA	NA	NA	NA	NA	NA	NA	NA	NA
Mount Vernon city & MCD (Westchester).....................	351	510	975	1,415	0	0	0.0	115.4	14.9	64.6	1,251	114.0	1,677	63	29.5
Nanuet CDP...........................	NA	NA	NA	NA	NA	NA	NA	NA	NA	NA	NA	NA	NA	NA	NA
Nesconset CDP.......................	NA	NA	NA	NA	NA	NA	NA	NA	NA	NA	NA	NA	NA	NA	NA
Newburgh city & MCD (Orange)............................	329	1,163	657	2,323	1,255	10	100.0	55.5	19.3	46.5	820	59.6	2,114	54	91.0
Newburgh town (Orange)	34	109	978	3,135	14,900	158	17.7	33.4	5.4	12.5	660	29.3	951	85	23.0
New Cassel CDP.....................	NA	NA	NA	NA	NA	NA	NA	NA	NA	NA	NA	NA	NA	NA	NA
New Castle town (Westchester)	1	6	53	291	400	1	100.0	30.5	3.4	15.9	1,310	28.7	1,598	78	14.0
New City CDP........................	NA	NA	NA	NA	NA	NA	NA	NA	NA	NA	NA	NA	NA	NA	NA
New Hartford town (Oneida).....	5	25	691	3,415	7,325	46	23.9	14.9	6.7	8.8	316	13.0	596	14	8.9
New Paltz town (Ulster)	20	142	145	1,030	1,300	3	100.0	10.9	0.6	59.1	604	13.0	914	144	1.3
New Rochelle city & MCD (Westchester).....................	98	122	666	829	308,202	1,284	0.2	148.7	22.9	40.5	1,210	143.1	1,809	129	125.9
New Windsor town (Orange)	40	142	329	1,169	10,815	41	100.0	27.2	4.9	16.4	571	27.0	980	84	9.2
New York city	46,113	541	128,051	1,502	NA	NA	NA	106595.1	37653.5	81.2	6,555	102551.2	12,154	1303	140617.8
Niagara Falls city & MCD (Niagara)...........................	418	867	1,962	4,068	0	0	0.0	113.7	62.5	73.5	870	125.2	2,594	346	55.1
Niskayuna town (Schenectady)	23	102	390	1,734	3,227	12	100.0	20.0	3.9	8.1	435	18.5	829	45	13.9
North Amityville CDP..............	NA	NA	NA	NA	NA	NA	NA	NA	NA	NA	NA	NA	NA	NA	NA
North Babylon CDP	NA	NA	NA	NA	NA	NA	NA	NA	NA	NA	NA	NA	NA	NA	NA
North Bay Shore CDP	NA	NA	NA	NA	NA	NA	NA	NA	NA	NA	NA	NA	NA	NA	NA
North Bellmore CDP	NA	NA	NA	NA	NA	NA	NA	NA	NA	NA	NA	NA	NA	NA	NA
North Bellport CDP.................	NA	NA	NA	NA	NA	NA	NA	NA	NA	NA	NA	NA	NA	NA	NA
North Castle town (Westchester).....................	6	48	55	442	8,094	10	100.0	32.4	2.9	34.1	2,103	31.3	2,562	323	22.3
North Greenbush town (Rensselaer).......................	9	74	156	1,277	11,697	46	69.6	8.7	1.8	19.2	335	7.3	597	24	17.0
North Hempstead town (Nassau)...........................	NA	NA	NA	NA	19,065	37	100.0	244.8	21.3	15.9	699	230.7	999	82	338.1
North Lindenhurst CDP	NA	NA	NA	NA	NA	NA	NA	NA	NA	NA	NA	NA	NA	NA	NA
North Massapequa CDP	NA	NA	NA	NA	NA	NA	NA	NA	NA	NA	NA	NA	NA	NA	NA
North Merrick CDP	NA	NA	NA	NA	NA	NA	NA	NA	NA	NA	NA	NA	NA	NA	NA
North New Hyde Park CDP	NA	NA	NA	NA	NA	NA	NA	NA	NA	NA	NA	NA	NA	NA	NA
North Tonawanda city & MCD (Niagara)...........................	46	152	400	1,319	1,478	8	100.0	43.1	17.0	33.9	615	44.6	1,465	139	13.6
North Valley Stream CDP	NA	NA	NA	NA	NA	NA	NA	NA	NA	NA	NA	NA	NA	NA	NA

1 Data for serious crimes have not been adjusted for underreporting. This may affect comparability between geographic areas over time.
2 Per 100,000 population estimated by the FBI. 3 Based on population estimated as of July 1 of the year shown.

STATE City, town, township, borough, or CDP (county if applicable)	Land area 2010 (sq mi)	Population Total persons 2010	Total persons 2019	Percent change 2010–2019	Persons per square mile 2019	Population characteristics 2015–2019 Percent foreign born	Percent living in the same house as previous year	Income and poverty 2015–2019 Median household income	Percent of households with income below poverty level	Median value of owner-occupied housing units	Employment, 2015–2019 Percent in civilian labor force	Unemploy-ment rate	Households, 2015–2019 (percent of households) Family households	One person households
	1	2	3	4	5	6	7	8	9	10	11	12	13	14
NEW YORK—Con.														
North Wantagh CDP	1.90	11,960	NA	NA	NA	7.3	95.9	134,260	2.0	444,800	64.6	2.9	77.2	19.6
Oceanside CDP	4.93	32,109	NA	NA	NA	13.0	94.8	118,196	5.3	472,100	66.6	5.1	77.3	20.5
Ogden town (Monroe)	36.48	19,857	20,531	3.4	562.8	4.6	89.1	77,500	6.3	163,400	69.3	4.7	71.3	23.2
Ogdensburg city & MCD (St. Lawrence)	4.96	11,131	10,436	-6.2	2104.0	3.9	78.8	41,965	22.8	67,900	44.2	6.8	60.8	32.8
Olean city & MCD (Cattaraugus)	5.90	14,428	13,437	-6.9	2277.5	2.3	84.7	41,742	21.2	80,200	62.6	5.4	52.1	40.6
Oneida city & MCD (Madison)	22.05	11,317	10,894	-3.7	494.1	2.4	85.4	50,746	13.9	114,600	61.5	5.0	56.5	35.6
Oneonta city & MCD (Otsego)	4.36	13,945	13,907	-0.3	3189.7	5.8	71.2	45,971	22.0	153,200	52.9	7.2	47.5	37.6
Onondaga town (Onondaga)	57.74	23,126	22,400	-3.1	387.9	7.2	87.1	84,248	5.9	180,000	64.4	3.8	69.9	24.0
Ontario town (Wayne)	32.41	10,143	10,166	0.2	313.7	2.8	90.3	71,513	4.4	166,600	70.7	2.5	66.1	28.8
Orangetown town (Rockland)	24.05	49,208	49,833	1.3	2072.1	17.1	90.6	108,074	4.6	481,600	65.0	4.5	67.2	27.4
Orchard Park town (Erie)	38.43	29,046	29,594	1.9	770.1	4.1	89.5	90,245	4.7	245,500	65.3	2.8	69.8	25.8
Ossining village	3.16	25,050	24,812	-1.0	7851.9	35.6	88.1	70,177	11.3	360,300	65.9	4.0	66.1	29.5
Ossining town (Westchester)	11.57	37,651	37,702	0.1	3258.6	28.7	89.6	94,046	8.7	433,700	64.4	4.5	69.7	25.9
Oswego city & MCD (Oswego)	7.61	18,151	17,236	-5.0	2264.9	3.2	77.5	43,258	22.7	87,500	59.6	10.0	50.2	35.4
Owego town (Tioga)	104.14	19,808	18,645	-5.9	179.0	2.6	88.8	72,156	8.7	133,400	60.8	3.6	65.6	29.3
Oyster Bay town (Nassau)	103.72	293,576	298,391	1.6	2876.9	16.5	93.5	129,232	4.6	530,100	64.4	3.2	78.3	18.9
Palm Tree town (Orange)	1.46	20,436	26,886	31.6	18415.1	5.3	95.1	31,203	43.0	514,600	47.2	4.5	97.3	2.6
Parma town (Monroe)	42.02	15,633	15,726	0.6	374.3	3.6	89.8	72,348	7.2	153,800	67.1	3.8	72.7	22.4
Patchogue village	2.26	11,805	12,321	4.4	5451.8	15.9	92.0	71,235	10.6	319,300	73.0	4.8	52.3	42.1
Patterson town (Putnam)	32.21	11,999	11,809	-1.6	366.6	11.9	91.9	103,714	3.8	332,100	61.6	3.7	76.9	18.1
Pearl River CDP	6.80	15,876	NA	NA	NA	14.5	91.8	114,619	3.6	456,200	65.0	4.3	75.8	21.8
Peekskill city & MCD (Westchester)	4.37	23,589	24,295	3.0	5559.5	27.6	88.8	57,206	12.5	294,100	68.5	5.6	58.8	34.3
Pelham town (Westchester)	2.17	12,379	12,481	0.8	5751.6	17.4	89.6	157,143	3.5	786,300	66.9	4.3	81.1	16.6
Penfield town (Monroe)	37.22	36,293	37,301	2.8	1002.2	7.0	91.9	84,916	4.6	208,400	64.7	2.8	68.2	26.6
Perinton town (Monroe)	34.18	46,481	46,735	0.5	1367.3	7.9	91.1	90,481	6.4	207,900	63.5	2.9	70.9	25.0
Pittsford town (Monroe)	23.17	29,380	29,377	0.0	1267.9	11.1	84.3	123,625	2.5	277,900	61.3	3.0	75.6	20.1
Plainview CDP	5.72	26,217	NA	NA	NA	17.7	93.9	146,853	4.8	594,000	64.6	3.0	80.3	18.0
Plattekill town (Ulster)	35.11	10,500	10,200	-2.9	290.5	7.8	90.0	63,646	8.1	209,100	62.1	3.6	65.8	29.8
Plattsburgh city & MCD (Clinton)	5.04	20,007	19,515	-2.5	3872.0	5.3	69.2	49,065	19.6	148,700	57.4	4.8	45.1	38.4
Plattsburgh town (Clinton)	45.92	11,847	11,949	0.9	260.2	4.9	89.0	60,768	13.4	139,700	56.9	4.1	64.9	25.8
Pomfret town (Chautauqua)	43.86	14,973	13,846	-7.5	315.7	4.4	77.3	50,523	19.6	129,700	52.2	7.8	61.3	29.8
Port Chester village	2.33	28,973	29,163	0.7	12516.3	44.4	85.9	74,920	10.6	446,900	70.6	8.2	73.6	20.7
Port Washington CDP	4.18	15,846	NA	NA	NA	16.9	91.9	141,667	5.4	815,300	60.4	2.2	75.5	21.9
Potsdam town (St. Lawrence)	101.38	16,046	15,381	-4.1	151.7	5.2	79.3	53,977	19.2	106,000	51.1	8.5	53.4	34.2
Poughkeepsie city & MCD (Dutchess)	5.14	30,812	30,515	-1.0	5936.8	17.5	84.5	43,794	19.2	196,800	63.4	9.4	52.2	38.7
Poughkeepsie town (Dutchess)	28.52	45,254	44,062	-2.6	1545.0	14.7	86.9	86,233	7.7	248,200	64.3	5.1	66.9	26.9
Putnam Valley town (Putnam)	41.18	11,801	11,516	-2.4	279.7	13.4	94.0	106,315	6.3	350,200	70.0	4.6	74.7	17.8
Queensbury town (Warren)	62.80	27,881	27,359	-1.9	435.7	3.4	88.0	73,723	7.7	228,500	63.4	2.6	63.8	29.6
Ramapo town (Rockland)	61.14	126,261	137,406	8.8	2247.4	20.2	92.1	69,655	19.0	448,800	61.9	6.1	78.8	18.8
Red Hook town (Dutchess)	36.15	11,338	11,124	-1.9	307.7	8.6	84.0	85,881	10.2	292,100	59.9	3.0	64.4	26.8
Ridge CDP	13.20	13,336	NA	NA	NA	9.0	91.4	71,738	7.0	298,600	52.4	4.2	59.9	35.6
Riverhead CDP	15.09	13,299	NA	NA	NA	28.9	89.9	52,126	13.1	334,100	60.8	6.2	59.5	35.3
Riverhead town (Suffolk)	67.41	33,499	33,469	-0.1	496.5	16.8	93.8	73,161	10.9	369,900	59.4	5.2	64.1	30.3
Rochester city & MCD (Monroe)	35.77	210,674	205,695	-2.4	5750.5	9.1	77.7	35,590	28.6	83,100	62.3	10.2	48.2	41.3
Rockville Centre village	3.25	24,039	24,550	2.1	7553.8	9.4	93.4	113,769	4.8	651,700	66.2	3.6	67.3	30.8
Rocky Point CDP	11.32	14,014	NA	NA	NA	6.6	95.7	98,913	3.7	301,400	68.2	4.2	70.7	24.0
Rome city & MCD (Oneida)	74.85	33,715	32,148	-4.6	429.5	3.4	86.7	48,120	18.5	98,400	53.4	4.0	57.7	35.1
Ronkonkoma CDP	7.82	19,082	NA	NA	NA	12.3	92.6	106,434	5.1	345,900	68.9	3.4	75.7	18.5
Roosevelt CDP	1.77	16,258	NA	NA	NA	33.0	94.1	90,423	10.5	309,100	68.6	6.0	83.1	14.6
Rotterdam CDP	6.89	20,652	NA	NA	NA	4.6	90.2	65,820	8.5	161,400	63.4	4.9	61.8	33.8
Rotterdam town (Schenectady)	35.68	29,098	29,973	3.0	840.1	5.3	89.8	71,835	8.1	169,800	65.2	4.5	63.6	31.2
Rye city & MCD (Westchester)	5.85	15,711	15,695	-0.1	2682.9	18.5	90.1	192,688	4.4	1,392,100	62.2	4.1	73.1	25.0
Rye town (Westchester)	6.92	45,924	46,425	1.1	6708.8	35.5	87.3	91,415	7.8	567,100	68.3	7.7	75.0	20.8
St. James CDP	4.56	13,338	NA	NA	NA	6.9	93.4	115,580	3.3	459,600	63.7	4.7	71.0	25.6
Salina town (Onondaga)	13.75	33,649	32,232	-4.2	2344.1	5.8	90.1	58,207	9.0	113,700	65.1	3.8	57.6	34.6
Salisbury CDP	1.75	12,093	NA	NA	NA	25.0	95.4	130,688	3.5	471,800	65.7	3.4	82.8	15.2
Saratoga Springs city & MCD (Saratoga)	28.07	26,568	28,212	6.2	1005.1	7.2	79.8	82,816	6.2	365,900	62.2	4.1	54.1	35.9
Saugerties town (Ulster)	64.57	19,484	19,008	-2.4	294.4	5.3	88.9	57,928	9.8	222,500	64.7	6.0	58.7	35.0
Sayville CDP	5.31	16,853	NA	NA	NA	4.7	93.8	116,005	6.3	451,400	63.7	3.2	76.0	19.9
Scarsdale village	6.66	17,124	17,871	4.4	2683.3	23.1	90.3	250	1.5	1,448,300	61.8	2.5	89.1	9.2
Scarsdale village and town (Westchester)	6.66	17,124	17,871	4.4	2683.3	23.1	90.3	250	1.5	1,448,300	61.8	2.5	89.1	9.2
Schenectady city & MCD (Schenectady)	10.79	66,157	65,273	-1.3	6049.4	17.2	85.6	45,438	17.1	108,700	60.3	9.2	51.5	42.0
Schodack town (Rensselaer)	61.93	12,801	13,108	2.4	211.7	2.6	89.6	81,234	4.1	226,800	67.0	4.9	68.4	26.7
Seaford CDP	2.61	15,294	NA	NA	NA	7.8	93.7	133,278	2.9	481,900	68.1	4.3	79.7	17.4
Selden CDP	4.32	19,851	NA	NA	NA	15.1	91.3	95,801	6.3	330,100	68.5	3.7	78.2	18.0
Setauket-East Setauket CDP	8.50	15,477	NA	NA	NA	11.8	93.4	154,130	1.5	485,300	64.8	2.7	76.3	19.7
Shawangunk town (Ulster)	56.06	14,340	13,837	-3.5	246.8	6.6	89.6	79,778	10.9	236,400	49.4	1.2	77.6	19.0
Shirley CDP	11.47	27,854	NA	NA	NA	13.3	93.0	87,242	9.5	265,600	63.9	5.4	78.2	14.4
Sleepy Hollow village	2.20	9,872	10,046	1.8	4566.4	36.9	93.0	68,125	11.6	693,500	67.4	7.1	68.5	26.2
Smithtown CDP	11.62	26,470	NA	NA	NA	6.4	95.5	137,347	3.4	535,300	61.9	2.5	75.9	20.6
Smithtown town (Suffolk)	53.75	117,764	116,022	-1.5	2158.5	7.8	94.8	126,510	3.5	486,300	64.0	3.5	76.1	20.8
Somers town (Westchester)	29.64	20,516	21,574	5.2	727.9	10.5	92.6	125,797	3.7	501,000	60.7	3.1	71.1	25.1
Southampton town (Suffolk)	139.39	56,769	58,398	2.9	419.0	19.1	90.1	95,281	7.3	671,600	60.0	2.9	66.2	28.6
Southeast town (Putnam)	31.73	18,437	18,052	-2.1	568.9	18.0	91.6	103,253	4.7	351,200	68.1	3.5	71.4	23.6
South Farmingdale CDP	2.22	14,486	NA	NA	NA	9.1	95.4	124,073	5.1	426,000	67.3	2.0	80.5	18.2
South Huntington CDP	3.42	9,422	NA	NA	NA	12.8	93.7	115,978	4.4	434,800	67.5	4.6	76.1	16.3
Southold town (Suffolk)	53.77	21,960	22,170	1.0	412.3	11.5	95.3	81,094	7.2	591,800	55.0	4.2	65.2	30.1
Southport town (Chemung)	46.41	10,909	9,761	-10.5	210.3	0.8	91.7	54,572	12.3	92,500	52.8	3.5	61.6	32.7

STATE City, town, township, borough, or CDP (county if applicable)	Serious crimes known to police, 2018[1] Violent crime Number	Rate[2]	Property crime Number	Rate[2]	New residential construction authorized by building permits, 2019 Value ($1,000)	Number of housing units	Percent single family	Local government finance, 2017 General revenue Total (mil dol)	Intergovernmental Total (mil dol)	Percent from state gov.	Taxes per capita[3]	General expenditure Per capita[3] Total (mil dol)	Total	Capital outlays	Debt outstanding (mil dol)
	15	16	17	18	19	20	21	22	23	24	25	26	27	28	29
NEW YORK—Con.															
North Wantagh CDP	NA	NA	NA	NA	NA	NA	NA	NA	NA	NA	NA	NA	NA	NA	NA
Oceanside CDP	NA	NA	NA	NA	NA	NA	NA	NA	NA	NA	NA	NA	NA	NA	NA
Ogden town (Monroe)	8	39	195	961	0	0	0.0	11.4	2.5	9.4	363	10.4	514	54	0.0
Ogdensburg city & MCD (St. Lawrence)	32	301	395	3,716	519	3	100.0	17.4	5.0	78.8	815	17.4	1,639	168	7.7
Olean city & MCD (Cattaraugus)	44	323	403	2,960	0	0	0.0	25.4	8.3	70.9	855	36.4	2,662	1298	44.3
Oneida city & MCD (Madison)	53	485	377	3,446	632	3	100.0	16.6	4.9	48.5	814	17.3	1,590	234	13.2
Oneonta city & MCD (Otsego)	33	235	191	1,357	0	0	0.0	21.9	11.7	34.7	394	21.8	1,563	311	10.5
Onondaga town (Onondaga)	NA	NA	NA	NA	0	0	0.0	10.5	0.8	45.9	410	14.1	623	235	1.9
Ontario town (Wayne)	NA	NA	NA	NA	6,739	42	64.3	7.7	1.2	15.2	311	5.8	573	11	2.3
Orangetown town (Rockland)	NA	NA	NA	NA	4,210	11	100.0	68.0	5.2	28.8	1,115	74.4	1,490	105	68.9
Orchard Park town (Erie)	28	94	331	1,112	18,495	111	36.0	22.8	5.9	11.7	522	27.4	930	223	19.9
Ossining village	15	59	188	739	650	3	33.3	40.0	10.9	5.5	923	45.3	1,803	176	33.7
Ossining town (Westchester)	NA	NA	NA	NA	4,249	37	21.6	14.8	1.3	21.3	327	13.1	350	16	7.3
Oswego city & MCD (Oswego)	36	207	455	2,620	7,190	57	7.0	45.3	8.0	45.8	1,445	40.1	2,296	130	43.8
Owego town (Tioga)	NA	NA	NA	NA	1,485	9	100.0	10.3	4.0	33.1	184	8.6	455	29	7.2
Oyster Bay town (Nassau)	NA	NA	NA	NA	79,878	165	62.4	330.1	23.1	19.2	877	333.8	1,120	55	840.7
Palm Tree town (Orange)	NA	NA	NA	NA	67,887	526	0.2	0.0	0.0	0.0	0	0.0	0	0	0.0
Parma town (Monroe)	NA	NA	NA	NA	8,775	43	100.0	5.4	1.5	16.5	185	5.0	318	18	0.0
Patchogue village	NA	NA	NA	NA	2,072	6	100.0	18.9	3.8	70.2	767	16.4	1,326	296	9.5
Patterson town (Putnam)	NA	NA	NA	NA	1,150	4	100.0	11.3	0.6	96.4	836	10.6	891	90	5.8
Pearl River CDP	NA	NA	NA	NA	NA	NA	NA	NA	NA	NA	NA	NA	NA	NA	NA
Peekskill city & MCD (Westchester)	50	205	224	919	1,312	5	100.0	46.7	15.4	27.2	779	51.8	2,159	281	78.0
Pelham town (Westchester)	NA	NA	NA	NA	NA	NA	NA	4.5	0.8	22.7	201	4.5	363	1	0.0
Penfield town (Monroe)	NA	NA	NA	NA	14,139	54	100.0	19.2	4.9	9.5	280	17.2	463	46	13.3
Perinton town (Monroe)	NA	NA	NA	NA	21,416	102	44.1	27.5	5.2	12.3	289	25.1	535	37	19.3
Pittsford town (Monroe)	NA	NA	NA	NA	12,775	27	100.0	17.3	3.9	9.0	402	19.5	664	150	15.7
Plainview CDP	NA	NA	NA	NA	NA	NA	NA	NA	NA	NA	NA	NA	NA	NA	NA
Plattekill town (Ulster)	NA	NA	31	303	3,622	15	86.7	3.5	0.2	23.0	288	3.3	321	12	0.2
Plattsburgh city & MCD (Clinton)	35	178	312	1,588	8,839	63	9.5	27.4	8.6	44.0	572	34.6	1,785	198	30.2
Plattsburgh town (Clinton)	NA	NA	NA	NA	4,398	14	100.0	10.7	4.2	7.3	368	9.0	761	71	6.0
Pomfret town (Chautauqua)	NA	NA	NA	NA	180	1	100.0	2.9	1.2	30.5	97	2.9	204	3	3.3
Port Chester village	22	74	185	621	0	0	0.0	40.0	5.6	17.6	863	43.2	1,468	181	43.2
Port Washington CDP	6	31	188	961	NA	NA	NA	NA	NA	NA	NA	NA	NA	NA	NA
Potsdam town (St. Lawrence)	NA	NA	NA	NA	972	29	100.0	3.7	1.6	31.6	119	3.8	246	35	0.2
Poughkeepsie city & MCD (Dutchess)	216	706	494	1,615	16,400	118	1.7	60.4	23.5	28.2	778	61.4	2,018	141	71.0
Poughkeepsie town (Dutchess)	NA	NA	NA	NA	812	2	100.0	40.5	2.8	14.4	675	39.6	898	131	38.9
Putnam Valley town (Putnam)	NA	NA	NA	NA	1,528	3	100.0	12.6	0.5	64.2	961	12.0	1,033	118	1.2
Queensbury town (Warren)	NA	NA	NA	NA	15,200	61	100.0	23.9	9.6	5.3	320	22.2	807	61	10.9
Ramapo town (Rockland)	NA	NA	NA	NA	27,656	219	6.8	110.5	5.5	10.7	639	112.1	827	37	78.7
Red Hook town (Dutchess)	NA	NA	NA	NA	4,500	16	75.0	5.3	0.9	40.6	354	4.6	413	105	3.5
Ridge CDP	NA	NA	NA	NA	NA	NA	NA	NA	NA	NA	NA	NA	NA	NA	NA
Riverhead CDP	NA	NA	NA	NA	NA	NA	NA	NA	NA	NA	NA	NA	NA	NA	NA
Riverhead town (Suffolk)	50	148	603	1,783	6,644	30	100.0	70.7	4.4	27.8	1,668	70.1	2,090	46	152.1
Rochester city & MCD (Monroe)	1,615	778	7,036	3,388	51,153	346	2.6	1347.3	1042.1	79.9	586	1473.5	7,139	748	804.2
Rockville Centre village	20	80	180	721	1,423	3	100.0	44.2	4.3	28.1	1,285	54.7	2,220	379	60.7
Rocky Point CDP	NA	NA	NA	NA	NA	NA	NA	NA	NA	NA	NA	NA	NA	NA	NA
Rome city & MCD (Oneida)	49	152	540	1,672	25,161	111	7.2	50.6	14.9	86.9	813	51.3	1,592	101	73.5
Ronkonkoma CDP	NA	NA	NA	NA	NA	NA	NA	NA	NA	NA	NA	NA	NA	NA	NA
Roosevelt CDP	NA	NA	NA	NA	NA	NA	NA	NA	NA	NA	NA	NA	NA	NA	NA
Rotterdam CDP	NA	NA	NA	NA	NA	NA	NA	NA	NA	NA	NA	NA	NA	NA	NA
Rotterdam town (Schenectady)	37	124	909	3,042	11,601	97	25.8	23.0	6.3	10.4	462	23.9	808	166	12.5
Rye city & MCD (Westchester)	6	37	56	349	29,248	26	76.9	41.3	4.2	40.7	1,719	44.1	2,784	140	13.0
Rye town (Westchester)	NA	NA	NA	NA	NA	NA	NA	3.8	0.4	75.9	50	2.8	61	3	2.0
St. James CDP	NA	NA	NA	NA	6,000	108	0.0	14.9	0.7	89.4	417	14.3	439	41	19.5
Salina town (Onondaga)	NA	NA	NA	NA	NA	NA	NA	NA	NA	NA	NA	NA	NA	NA	NA
Salisbury CDP	NA	NA	NA	NA	NA	NA	NA	NA	NA	NA	NA	NA	NA	NA	NA
Saratoga Springs city & MCD (Saratog)	63	223	468	1,657	39,911	138	44.2	54.0	3.9	50.3	1,239	58.8	2,101	224	52.5
Saugerties town (Ulster)	NA	NA	NA	NA	0	0	0.0	15.7	2.9	29.8	586	15.4	808	36	9.0
Sayville CDP	NA	NA	NA	NA	NA	NA	NA	NA	NA	NA	NA	NA	NA	NA	NA
Scarsdale village	2	11	123	675	NA	NA	NA	60.2	4.9	15.9	2,467	56.7	3,172	221	20.7
Scarsdale village and town (Westchester)	NA	NA	NA	NA	17,830	14	100.0	0.0	0.0	0.0	0	0.0	0	0	0.0
Schenectady city & MCD (Schenectady)	620	946	2,106	3,213	1,379	8	100.0	102.2	38.5	55.0	546	109.7	1,680	257	113.6
Schodack town (Rensselaer)	11	94	48	409	3,169	10	100.0	9.7	2.2	27.5	494	8.8	671	90	11.2
Seaford CDP	NA	NA	NA	NA	NA	NA	NA	NA	NA	NA	NA	NA	NA	NA	NA
Selden CDP	NA	NA	NA	NA	NA	NA	NA	NA	NA	NA	NA	NA	NA	NA	NA
Setauket-East Setauket CDP	NA	NA	NA	NA	225	1	100.0	5.9	1.3	25.3	297	5.5	396	45	4.5
Shawangunk town (Ulster)	NA	NA	NA	NA	NA	NA	NA	NA	NA	NA	NA	NA	NA	NA	NA
Shirley CDP	NA	NA	NA	NA	NA	NA	NA	NA	NA	NA	NA	NA	NA	NA	NA
Sleepy Hollow village	NA	NA	1	10	9,293	40	57.5	20.2	4.0	29.4	1,302	18.8	1,861	182	34.2
Smithtown CDP	NA	NA	NA	NA	NA	NA	NA	NA	NA	NA	NA	NA	NA	NA	NA
Smithtown town (Suffolk)	NA	NA	NA	NA	6,753	37	100.0	96.0	6.2	55.2	559	98.7	847	105	21.4
Somers town (Westchester)	NA	NA	NA	NA	6,567	28	100.0	15.5	3.7	17.8	448	13.5	622	81	9.1
Southampton town (Suffolk)	52	102	523	1,021	116,670	155	100.0	166.3	13.0	55.1	2,324	172.3	2,965	1281	120.8
Southeast town (Putnam)	NA	NA	NA	NA	700	2	100.0	12.3	0.8	93.7	492	11.1	614	25	10.3
South Farmingdale CDP	NA	NA	NA	NA	NA	NA	NA	NA	NA	NA	NA	NA	NA	NA	NA
South Huntington CDP	NA	NA	NA	NA	NA	NA	NA	NA	NA	NA	NA	NA	NA	NA	NA
Southold town (Suffolk)	17	85	216	1,075	2,436	19	0.0	60.3	12.0	18.7	1,751	55.9	2,529	402	37.7
Southport town (Chemung)	NA	NA	NA	NA	244	1	100.0	3.6	2.3	16.3	97	4.1	410	53	0.0

1   Data for serious crimes have not been adjusted for underreporting. This may affect comparability between geographic areas over time.
2   Per 100,000 population estimated by the FBI.   3   Based on population estimated as of July 1 of the year shown.

Table B. Incorporated Places, Census Designated Places (CDPs), and Minor Civil Divisions (MCDs) of 10,000 or More Population — **Land Area, Population, and Households, and Employment**

STATE City, town, township, borough, or CDP (county if applicable)	Land area 2010 (sq mi)	Population				Population characteristics 2015–2019		Income and poverty 2015–2019			Employment, 2015–2019		Households, 2015–2019 (percent of households)	
		Total persons 2010	Total persons 2019	Percent change 2010–2019	Persons per square mile, 2019	Percent foreign born	Percent living in the same house as previous year	Median household income	Percent of households with income below poverty level	Median value of owner-occupied housing units	Percent in civilian labor force	Unemployment rate	Family households	One person households
	1	2	3	4	5	6	7	8	9	10	11	12	13	14
NEW YORK—Con.														
Spring Valley village	2.01	31,298	32,261	3.1	16050.2	40.3	88.1	45,428	24.9	295,500	69.1	7.4	70.2	25.1
Stony Brook CDP	5.81	13,740	NA	NA	NA	13.6	94.7	120,476	4.9	461,800	65.1	2.6	73.4	21.4
Stony Point CDP	5.44	12,147	NA	NA	NA	10.8	88.9	107,012	5.0	369,200	66.3	6.5	75.3	21.4
Stony Point town (Rockland)	27.63	15,059	15,313	1.7	554.2	11.0	89.3	112,893	5.1	381,400	67.2	6.3	75.9	20.2
Suffern village	2.10	10,723	11,007	2.6	5241.4	21.1	91.0	81,845	9.5	310,900	66.0	5.4	62.3	34.5
Sullivan town (Madison)	73.13	15,347	15,139	-1.4	207.0	1.7	92.9	74,987	8.2	155,200	66.4	3.1	71.9	21.5
Sweden town (Monroe)	33.68	14,181	14,079	-0.7	418.0	4.6	73.4	50,630	18.8	137,800	58.9	7.4	55.5	28.9
Syosset CDP	4.98	18,829	NA	NA	NA	25.6	93.4	163,589	3.3	663,400	64.4	2.8	85.4	13.1
Syracuse city & MCD (Onondaga)	25.03	145,150	142,327	-1.9	5686.3	13.1	76.7	38,276	27.0	94,400	55.9	9.3	49.0	38.8
Tarrytown village	2.93	11,238	11,370	1.2	3880.5	25.2	89.4	124,046	3.6	609,400	68.0	4.5	64.5	27.6
Terryville CDP	3.23	11,849	NA	NA	NA	17.3	97.4	110,504	8.2	369,900	64.4	2.1	80.9	17.5
Thompson town (Sullivan)	84.09	15,311	14,993	-2.1	178.3	12.7	92.8	45,367	20.0	166,700	58.1	11.1	58.3	34.3
Tonawanda city & MCD (Erie)	3.80	15,166	14,745	-2.8	3880.3	3.6	91.2	53,115	13.7	108,800	62.5	3.7	56.6	38.5
Tonawanda CDP	17.30	58,144	NA	NA	NA	5.3	90.0	59,845	9.4	139,300	63.5	3.0	57.2	36.8
Tonawanda town (Erie)	18.74	73,516	71,675	-2.5	3824.7	5.1	90.4	61,571	9.1	138,000	64.2	2.7	56.5	37.1
Troy city & MCD (Rensselaer)	10.36	50,162	49,154	-2.0	4744.6	8.0	73.6	45,728	21.2	149,800	61.3	6.8	49.0	38.4
Ulster town (Ulster)	26.81	12,356	12,598	2.0	469.9	7.6	91.7	58,982	12.9	190,000	58.5	6.9	59.2	34.8
Union town (Broome)	35.47	56,396	52,724	-6.5	1486.4	6.3	86.4	50,719	13.5	112,300	60.7	5.1	56.2	37.0
Uniondale CDP	5.71	24,759	NA	NA	NA	36.6	87.7	85,471	10.0	361,000	59.7	4.7	71.5	23.5
Utica city & MCD (Oneida)	16.76	62,241	59,750	-4.0	3565.0	20.0	82.0	37,760	26.7	95,900	57.0	8.2	57.2	36.5
Valley Stream village	3.48	37,377	37,431	0.1	10756.0	35.3	93.1	110,189	4.9	427,100	68.5	5.8	82.5	14.9
Van Buren town (Onondaga)	35.47	13,189	13,376	1.4	377.1	3.9	87.9	58,962	10.4	122,000	63.1	5.1	59.2	33.5
Vestal town (Broome)	51.73	28,062	28,578	1.8	552.4	12.4	82.7	67,910	13.0	148,700	47.7	4.5	64.6	26.4
Victor town (Ontario)	35.92	14,272	15,033	5.3	418.5	5.1	90.7	98,793	2.1	288,500	66.8	2.1	69.4	26.5
Wallkill town (Orange)	61.88	27,416	28,987	5.7	468.4	12.8	91.8	69,952	11.1	250,400	61.3	5.2	66.3	28.8
Wantagh CDP	3.83	18,871	NA	NA	NA	5.2	95.3	155,426	3.0	518,200	66.6	3.6	83.9	13.5
Wappinger town (Dutchess)	27.06	27,117	26,716	-1.5	987.3	12.4	90.8	82,428	7.9	285,500	67.1	4.2	71.3	23.8
Warwick town (Orange)	101.29	32,062	31,327	-2.3	309.3	5.9	90.1	98,730	5.3	325,000	63.8	3.7	70.9	24.5
Watertown city & MCD (Jefferson)	9.03	26,822	24,838	-7.4	2750.6	4.6	78.8	40,253	23.5	133,400	56.4	7.5	52.3	39.4
Watervliet city & MCD (Albany)	1.35	10,251	9,900	-3.4	7333.3	10.8	81.4	43,803	16.7	145,200	67.9	4.7	44.2	44.5
Wawarsing town (Ulster)	130.51	13,172	12,580	-4.5	96.4	10.5	86.8	48,743	16.8	138,100	50.5	8.3	58.5	35.5
Webster town (Monroe)	33.53	42,659	45,163	5.9	1346.9	8.5	90.4	81,329	5.0	189,400	67.1	2.1	67.6	27.3
West Babylon CDP	7.78	43,213	NA	NA	NA	15.0	91.6	100,470	4.3	358,200	68.2	4.8	72.2	22.4
Westbury village	2.34	15,039	15,351	2.1	6560.3	35.7	93.0	101,250	7.4	458,500	66.6	4.3	72.5	21.1
West Haverstraw village	1.52	10,138	10,189	0.5	6703.3	29.1	89.0	64,782	14.9	265,900	67.5	8.3	73.8	20.3
West Hempstead CDP	2.66	18,862	NA	NA	NA	22.3	95.8	120,747	5.6	461,300	66.1	4.7	82.0	13.7
West Islip CDP	6.30	28,335	NA	NA	NA	6.0	95.1	125,779	4.2	426,700	66.5	4.2	82.6	14.1
West Seneca town (Erie)	21.39	44,744	45,224	1.1	2114.3	2.5	91.4	67,617	6.9	151,700	65.0	3.1	60.5	33.5
Wheatfield town (Niagara)	27.91	18,117	18,053	-0.4	646.8	4.7	91.7	82,083	7.2	216,000	62.4	2.5	71.6	24.2
White Plains city & MCD (Westchester)	9.79	56,866	58,109	2.2	5935.5	30.7	86.3	90,427	11.1	568,400	66.9	5.1	60.6	32.0
Whitestown town (Oneida)	27.32	18,664	18,072	-3.2	661.5	2.9	91.1	57,389	9.4	133,900	60.4	4.3	58.5	36.2
Wilton town (Saratoga)	35.84	16,154	16,918	4.7	472.0	3.6	88.5	94,429	4.8	292,400	67.0	3.4	74.8	21.5
Woodbury village	35.58	10,691	11,089	3.7	311.7	17.4	96.0	130,541	6.1	319,500	70.3	5.9	78.8	19.6
Woodbury town (Orange)	36.10	11,327	11,730	3.6	324.9	19.5	94.8	128,364	6.2	317,200	70.8	5.7	78.8	19.4
Woodmere CDP	2.58	17,121	NA	NA	NA	12.4	95.2	142,904	2.6	706,200	62.5	3.0	83.6	14.5
Wyandanch CDP	4.46	11,647	NA	NA	NA	22.1	93.8	59,076	22.5	252,700	66.4	6.2	79.6	16.4
Yonkers city & MCD (Westchester)	18.01	196,026	200,370	2.2	11125.5	31.4	90.6	63,849	15.2	403,900	63.4	6.6	63.4	32.4
Yorktown town (Westchester)	36.65	36,095	36,269	0.5	989.6	17.4	93.4	127,763	5.1	432,800	65.7	4.4	75.8	21.4
NORTH CAROLINA	48620.28	9,535,751	10,488,084	10.0	215.7	8.0	84.8	54,602	13.9	172,500	61.3	5.6	65.4	28.5
Albemarle city	17.43	15,890	16,246	2.2	932.1	5.0	82.8	44,269	18.3	119,000	58.7	7.8	66.0	30.3
Apex town	20.80	37,727	59,300	57.2	2851.0	11.9	83.9	111,435	4.8	327,800	74.9	3.0	77.1	18.2
Archdale city	8.77	11,435	11,513	0.7	1312.8	6.0	85.0	53,030	8.5	138,000	63.6	5.0	64.8	27.5
Asheboro city	18.85	25,408	25,940	2.1	1376.1	13.7	81.5	38,211	20.2	120,900	60.1	6.1	56.5	39.2
Asheville city	45.57	83,420	92,870	11.3	2038.0	7.4	82.3	49,930	12.4	270,400	64.9	2.8	47.2	41.1
Belmont city	12.11	10,227	12,558	22.8	1037.0	4.9	84.7	71,650	12.1	210,600	65.9	4.5	66.5	26.7
Boone town	6.31	17,118	19,667	14.9	3116.8	1.9	50.3	22,434	50.8	268,100	50.5	14.4	27.8	31.9
Burlington city	29.80	51,079	54,606	6.9	1832.4	12.3	84.0	43,225	17.4	134,100	65.2	6.6	59.0	34.2
Carrboro town	6.48	19,568	21,190	8.3	3270.1	15.3	71.6	58,702	17.9	368,800	74.5	4.5	49.6	37.1
Cary town	58.73	135,840	170,282	25.4	2899.4	22.1	82.6	104,669	4.9	356,400	70.8	3.2	73.5	22.0
Chapel Hill town	21.53	57,221	64,051	11.9	2975.0	15.8	66.2	73,614	16.9	399,700	60.5	3.4	51.8	33.0
Charlotte city	307.24	735,607	885,708	20.4	2882.8	16.7	81.5	62,817	11.3	220,300	71.6	5.0	58.8	32.9
Clayton town	15.14	16,219	24,887	53.4	1643.8	11.5	78.1	62,676	10.2	192,900	69.6	3.4	70.7	24.3
Clemmons village	11.88	18,624	20,867	12.0	1756.5	9.1	88.0	70,659	6.5	226,600	62.1	4.0	69.8	27.2
Concord city	63.50	79,389	96,341	21.4	1517.2	10.8	83.6	67,984	9.7	206,600	69.7	5.3	71.3	24.7
Cornelius town	12.88	24,907	30,257	21.5	2349.1	9.4	85.5	90,542	9.4	322,400	67.0	3.9	63.8	29.1
Davidson town	5.97	10,904	13,054	19.7	2186.6	5.3	74.9	124,853	3.9	448,300	62.7	2.8	69.4	23.7
Durham city	112.22	229,892	278,993	21.4	2486.1	15.0	79.0	58,905	13.7	224,100	69.4	4.6	56.3	33.9
Eden city	14.20	15,698	14,886	-5.2	1048.3	6.1	85.9	34,917	21.5	87,500	54.5	7.5	60.4	36.9
Elizabeth City city	11.69	18,643	17,751	-4.8	1518.5	4.4	80.6	38,917	22.4	137,800	54.1	8.1	58.8	35.7
Elon town	3.97	9,383	12,232	30.4	3081.1	5.8	76.3	65,313	20.0	253,500	39.7	3.3	54.5	27.1
Fayetteville city	147.85	200,565	211,657	5.5	1431.6	7.1	75.4	45,024	17.5	131,000	52.2	9.1	59.3	35.6
Fuquay-Varina town	15.19	18,021	30,324	68.3	1996.3	9.4	86.6	79,000	7.9	255,900	67.6	4.4	75.3	21.0
Garner town	15.90	25,769	31,407	21.9	1975.3	7.3	77.9	65,064	9.1	190,000	69.0	4.5	65.6	25.3
Gastonia city	51.65	71,720	77,273	7.7	1496.1	7.3	83.5	49,460	15.8	155,200	63.9	7.2	63.2	29.2
Goldsboro city	28.55	35,425	34,186	-3.5	1197.4	5.9	74.5	34,083	25.3	127,300	49.4	12.5	57.8	37.3
Graham city	9.77	14,315	15,646	9.3	1601.4	8.6	85.2	36,310	22.9	133,800	59.6	4.9	61.8	33.2
Greensboro city	129.07	268,936	296,710	10.3	2298.8	11.1	82.4	48,964	16.5	156,300	64.3	6.1	57.6	34.3
Greenville city	35.63	84,711	93,400	10.3	2621.4	4.7	66.9	40,875	26.8	161,200	63.2	8.9	47.3	35.6
Harrisburg town	11.28	13,439	16,576	23.3	1469.5	11.7	88.5	108,942	5.7	288,900	69.8	5.4	85.6	10.7
Havelock city	17.08	20,792	19,854	-4.5	1162.4	3.7	67.9	52,439	10.0	138,500	46.3	5.5	73.6	18.8
Henderson city	8.51	15,413	14,911	-3.3	1752.2	6.4	80.4	31,408	25.9	100,100	55.2	9.5	62.1	34.1

Table B. Incorporated Places, Census Designated Places (CDPs), and Minor Civil Divisions (MCDs) of 10,000 or More Population — Crime, Residential Construction and Local Government Finance

STATE City, town, township, borough, or CDP (county if applicable)	Serious crimes known to police, 2018[1] Violent crime Number	Violent crime Rate[2]	Property crime Number	Property crime Rate[2]	New residential construction authorized by building permits, 2019 Value ($1,000)	Number of housing units	Percent single family	Local government finance, 2017 General revenue Total (mil dol)	Intergovernmental Total (mil dol)	Intergovernmental Percent from state gov.	Taxes per capita[3]	General expenditure Total (mil dol)	Per capita[3] Total	Per capita[3] Capital outlays	Debt outstanding (mil dol)
	15	16	17	18	19	20	21	22	23	24	25	26	27	28	29
NEW YORK—Con.															
Spring Valley village..................	120	365	403	1,225	4,356	24	16.7	37.0	11.4	8.0	757	43.8	1,356	12	11.1
Stony Brook CDP	NA	NA	NA	NA	NA	NA	NA	NA	NA	NA	NA	NA	NA	NA	NA
Stony Point CDP	NA	NA	NA	NA	NA	NA	NA	NA	NA	NA	NA	NA	NA	NA	NA
Stony Point town (Rockland).....	5	32	51	326	1,936	5	100.0	22.4	0.8	20.7	1,142	21.6	1,405	42	20.1
Suffern village.........................	NA	NA	NA	NA	0	0	0.0	16.4	0.9	99.5	1,043	15.6	1,434	58	10.9
Sullivan town (Madison)............	NA	NA	NA	NA	385	2	100.0	6.7	1.8	18.3	300	6.0	399	72	11.0
Sweden town (Monroe)	NA	NA	NA	NA	10,055	61	16.4	5.0	1.4	10.8	208	4.3	308	12	1.3
Syosset CDP	NA	NA	NA	NA	NA	NA	NA	NA	NA	NA	NA	NA	NA	NA	NA
Syracuse city & MCD (Onondaga)......................	1,006	703	4,420	3,088	867	10	100.0	712.0	591.5	83.3	464	765.2	5,378	223	441.8
Tarrytown village.....................	7	60	41	353	0	0	0.0	23.8	3.1	14.2	1,506	27.4	2,394	357	54.7
Terryville CDP.........................	NA	NA	NA	NA	NA	NA	NA	NA	NA	NA	NA	NA	NA	NA	NA
Thompson town (Sullivan).........	NA	NA	NA	NA	9,056	60	100.0	16.7	3.3	93.6	573	11.9	799	159	5.9
Tonawanda city & MCD (Erie) ..	27	182	245	1,648	3,320	41	2.4	24.0	9.0	42.0	798	25.7	1,733	285	18.5
Tonawanda CDP.......................	NA	NA	NA	NA	NA	NA	NA	NA	NA	NA	NA	NA	NA	NA	NA
Tonawanda town (Erie).............	89	155	763	1,333	35	1	100.0	84.3	14.3	16.4	626	94.0	1,304	145	76.3
Troy city & MCD (Rensselaer) ..	283	572	1,411	2,851	3,069	30	6.7	73.4	33.1	44.6	502	74.3	1,503	122	70.2
Ulster town (Ulster).................	13	103	232	1,841	18,507	77	5.2	15.4	0.9	73.5	972	13.8	1,109	137	5.5
Union town (Broome)................	NA	NA	NA	NA	275	1	100.0	22.4	10.0	8.4	207	22.8	424	77	7.3
Uniondale CDP.........................	NA	NA	NA	NA	NA	NA	NA	NA	NA	NA	NA	NA	NA	NA	NA
Utica city & MCD (Oneida)	381	631	1,914	3,168	0	0	0.0	90.4	35.8	72.5	719	83.2	1,378	157	68.6
Valley Stream village	NA	NA	NA	NA	523	3	100.0	39.5	2.3	48.3	849	41.3	1,098	140	30.3
Van Buren town (Onondaga)	NA	NA	NA	NA	1,280	5	100.0	5.1	0.9	62.8	272	4.7	352	78	2.9
Vestal town (Broome)	18	64	521	1,846	12,268	215	3.7	24.8	6.9	8.4	421	23.6	837	149	19.1
Victor town (Ontario)...............	NA	NA	NA	NA	12,585	42	100.0	10.7	5.7	4.6	241	10.7	715	79	5.4
Wallkill town (Orange)..............	47	161	541	1,858	47,799	280	8.6	28.2	6.7	26.2	402	27.3	957	154	24.2
Wantagh CDP	NA	NA	NA	NA	NA	NA	NA	NA	NA	NA	NA	NA	NA	NA	NA
Wappinger town (Dutchess)	NA	NA	NA	NA	15,429	58	100.0	16.6	2.6	19.6	390	13.5	509	88	24.5
Warwick town (Orange)	NA	NA	NA	NA	12,740	43	100.0	22.3	8.1	38.8	403	22.5	721	110	7.5
Watertown city & MCD (Jefferson).........................	175	686	904	3,542	0	0	0.0	48.9	31.7	22.6	393	62.4	2,430	315	35.9
Watervliet city & MCD (Albany)	36	356	225	2,224	0	0	0.0	14.0	6.8	29.1	471	15.1	1,505	229	8.8
Wawarsing town (Ulster)..........	NA	NA	NA	NA	410	2	100.0	11.1	3.1	59.9	556	9.9	770	129	7.6
Webster town (Monroe)	35	78	361	802	33,411	152	73.7	28.4	5.7	8.2	382	26.8	603	75	14.5
West Babylon CDP	NA	NA	NA	NA	NA	NA	NA	NA	NA	NA	NA	NA	NA	NA	NA
Westbury village	NA	NA	NA	NA	2,274	17	100.0	8.6	0.8	57.6	454	9.5	617	166	7.7
West Haverstraw village	NA	NA	NA	NA	0	0	0.0	6.9	0.6	45.6	580	6.5	630	28	2.2
West Hempstead CDP	NA	NA	NA	NA	NA	NA	NA	NA	NA	NA	NA	NA	NA	NA	NA
West Islip CDP	NA	NA	NA	NA	NA	NA	NA	NA	NA	NA	NA	NA	NA	NA	NA
West Seneca town (Erie).........	NA	NA	NA	NA	10,222	57	47.4	47.5	8.4	21.3	742	58.3	1,286	284	59.9
Wheatfield town (Niagara)	NA	NA	NA	NA	9,103	25	100.0	10.6	5.1	8.4	238	11.2	619	100	8.3
White Plains city & MCD (Westchester)...................	NA	NA	NA	NA	43,106	316	0.9	175.5	7.3	96.7	2,010	184.9	3,167	198	160.2
Whitestown town (Oneida)	NA	NA	NA	NA	1,389	7	100.0	7.2	2.9	11.1	209	6.3	342	22	3.0
Wilton town (Saratoga)	NA	NA	NA	NA	15,871	68	52.9	8.7	6.0	5.0	100	8.1	481	87	0.2
Woodbury village	NA	NA	NA	NA	NA	NA	NA	9.2	1.1	13.8	732	8.1	742	96	0.1
Woodbury town (Orange)	7	63	416	3,743	12,217	33	100.0	12.4	0.9	8.7	917	10.5	908	28	3.9
Woodmere CDP	NA	NA	NA	NA	NA	NA	NA	NA	NA	NA	NA	NA	NA	NA	NA
Wyandanch CDP	NA	NA	NA	NA	NA	NA	NA	NA	NA	NA	NA	NA	NA	NA	NA
Yonkers city & MCD (Westchester)...................	706	348	1,771	873	53,220	557	1.8	1011.1	527.2	98.9	2,010	1167.9	5,843	306	732.1
Yorktown town (Westchester) ...	14	38	185	499	2,040	6	100.0	49.1	9.4	16.9	831	45.4	1,241	82	24.7
NORTH CAROLINA................	39,210	378	258,979	2,494	13,849,671	71,307	72.4	X	X	X	X	X	X	X	X
Albemarle city.........................	NA	NA	853	5,334	NA	NA	NA	24.7	5.6	54.2	593	29.4	1,841	567	18.7
Apex town	NA	NA	663	1,261	372,294	1,918	97.4	62.9	8.4	68.1	722	57.1	1,130	217	81.0
Archdale city...........................	NA	NA	235	2,038	NA	NA	NA	10.4	1.8	97.5	412	8.7	754	77	4.5
Asheboro city..........................	NA	NA	1,168	4,506	4,647	52	84.6	37.2	6.2	96.4	799	31.9	1,236	31	5.8
Asheville city..........................	NA	NA	4,798	5,149	92,165	428	80.1	142.3	24.4	51.5	960	132.6	1,445	226	118.4
Belmont city............................	NA	NA	550	4,460	NA	NA	NA	14.7	1.2	100.0	712	11.5	950	97	10.0
Boone town.............................	NA	NA	289	1,480	44,712	299	3.3	19.7	2.3	97.3	591	18.3	949	53	32.5
Burlington city.........................	NA	NA	1,877	3,516	74,961	670	40.6	55.8	9.0	67.6	766	50.9	957	113	38.2
Carrboro town.........................	NA	NA	407	1,864	15,626	46	100.0	21.3	3.1	98.8	801	17.7	825	44	5.2
Cary town	NA	NA	1,666	977	251,592	1,523	52.9	248.7	23.3	71.8	786	178.3	1,075	232	407.8
Chapel Hill town.......................	NA	NA	NA	NA	28,400	65	96.9	0.0	0.0		0	2.2	37	0	59.5
Charlotte city...........................	NA	NA	34,881	3,746	NA	NA	NA	2085.7	502.2	46.8	999	1536.3	1,786	485	4073.0
Clayton town...........................	NA	NA	417	1,874	80,476	590	100.0	34.9	8.2	100.0	521	26.5	1,237	179	26.9
Clemmons village	NA	NA	NA	NA	NA	NA	NA	6.4	2.4	99.9	159	7.7	378	135	0.0
Concord city............................	NA	NA	1,679	1,786	NA	NA	NA	133.7	30.0	59.0	734	110.5	1,199	159	106.6
Cornelius town.........................	NA	NA	NA	NA	NA	NA	NA	25.5	6.3	84.8	603	23.2	790	212	11.2
Davidson town.........................	NA	NA	127	980	NA	NA	NA	12.5	1.9	74.6	717	11.8	929	90	3.4
Durham city............................	NA	NA	9,755	3,563	651,164	3,829	50.8	376.8	58.6	61.8	783	308.6	1,144	164	332.3
Eden city...............................	NA	NA	530	3,545	1,398	7	100.0	17.7	3.4	73.1	601	19.5	1,299	76	16.0
Elizabeth City city	NA	NA	939	5,327	9,451	66	100.0	20.5	6.0	56.6	653	18.6	1,062	62	4.8
Elon town...............................	NA	NA	NA	NA	NA	NA	NA	9.1	0.4	92.8	440	6.6	562	0	0.1
Fayetteville city......................	NA	NA	NA	NA	72,675	522	46.0	200.8	64.8	42.7	518	192.2	919	110	312.5
Fuquay-Varina town.................	NA	NA	NA	NA	165,717	764	100.0	34.4	5.0	50.1	676	30.6	1,101	153	58.2
Garner town............................	NA	NA	NA	NA	52,295	366	100.0	30.0	3.2	95.0	836	33.9	1,178	283	36.5
Gastonia city..........................	NA	NA	3,839	4,965	92,210	352	77.3	88.1	15.5	79.5	597	91.4	1,198	155	78.9
Goldsboro city........................	NA	NA	NA	NA	9,860	41	80.5	39.1	7.8	95.3	747	37.5	1,095	95	57.6
Graham city............................	NA	NA	NA	NA	17,352	97	100.0	16.0	2.3	19.8	595	14.2	960	109	5.5
Greensboro city.......................	NA	NA	9,831	3,352	150,248	933	58.7	385.0	52.6	74.1	709	415.0	1,423	219	496.9
Greenville city........................	NA	NA	2,707	2,903	106,687	701	42.2	151.2	24.4	86.8	535	138.2	1,502	236	303.6
Harrisburg town	NA	NA	NA	NA	NA	NA	NA	0.0	0.0		0	0.5	30	0	12.9
Havelock city..........................	NA	NA	530	2,667	7,243	90	20.0	16.4	2.3	89.6	379	14.3	706	50	9.7
Henderson city........................	NA	NA	804	5,440	NA	NA	NA	27.7	10.7	22.3	604	13.4	902	0	22.2

1 Data for serious crimes have not been adjusted for underreporting. This may affect comparability between geographic areas over time.
2 Per 100,000 population estimated by the FBI. 3 Based on population estimated as of July 1 of the year shown.

Table B. Incorporated Places, Census Designated Places (CDPs), and Minor Civil Divisions (MCDs) of 10,000 or More Population — **Land Area, Population, and Households, and Employment**

STATE City, town, township, borough, or CDP (county if applicable)	Land area 2010 (sq mi)	Total persons 2010	Total persons 2019	Percent change 2010–2019	Persons per square mile 2019	Percent foreign born	Percent living in the same house as previous year	Median household income	Percent of households with income below poverty level	Median value of owner-occupied housing units	Percent in civilian labor force	Unemployment rate	Family households	One person households
	1	2	3	4	5	6	7	8	9	10	11	12	13	14
NORTH CAROLINA—Con.														
Hendersonville city	7.28	13,121	14,157	7.9	1944.6	6.5	82.4	38,696	17.3	188,100	49.5	1.8	45.9	50.4
Hickory city	29.64	40,035	41,171	2.8	1389.0	9.0	82.7	47,652	17.7	168,600	62.1	8.5	58.9	34.9
High Point city	55.98	104,526	112,791	7.9	2014.8	13.4	82.0	47,234	15.7	151,900	62.1	6.9	66.2	28.3
Holly Springs town	17.04	24,739	37,812	52.8	2219.0	7.2	84.8	112,029	3.2	320,900	72.4	3.7	83.1	13.4
Hope Mills town	7.41	15,088	15,849	5.0	2138.9	4.8	85.7	48,948	16.8	134,900	60.6	6.9	66.6	29.4
Huntersville town	40.73	46,909	58,098	23.9	1426.4	8.0	85.4	102,016	4.3	301,500	71.5	3.4	74.5	20.2
Indian Trail town	21.97	33,619	40,252	19.7	1832.1	10.2	84.7	83,905	6.8	216,100	72.2	3.7	80.1	16.5
Jacksonville city	48.65	70,327	72,436	3.0	1488.9	4.8	60.4	44,956	13.1	154,900	34.9	11.2	69.4	25.0
Kannapolis city	32.61	42,621	50,841	19.3	1559.1	7.8	86.4	53,365	12.6	144,400	67.5	6.2	70.1	24.7
Kernersville town	17.78	23,101	24,660	6.7	1387.0	9.6	84.0	51,645	13.0	181,300	65.8	5.3	57.3	38.0
Kings Mountain city	13.42	10,647	10,982	3.1	818.3	2.0	81.0	39,195	24.6	123,600	57.6	12.2	61.1	36.4
Kinston city	18.39	21,749	20,041	-7.9	1089.8	2.7	82.0	33,066	25.8	101,800	51.7	15.4	56.7	39.3
Knightdale town	7.46	11,403	17,843	56.5	2391.8	12.2	85.8	69,684	3.4	196,600	76.0	4.7	67.3	26.1
Laurinburg city	12.53	15,948	15,002	-5.9	1197.3	3.0	81.8	30,862	30.0	103,200	49.7	14.6	62.0	32.5
Leland town	19.80	13,614	23,544	72.9	1189.1	5.3	83.5	68,924	9.5	243,200	56.6	4.9	71.3	24.5
Lenoir city	20.66	18,226	17,913	-1.7	867.0	4.2	83.2	36,755	19.9	111,300	53.8	7.5	61.8	34.2
Lewisville town	14.38	12,709	14,228	12.0	989.4	2.4	90.5	78,464	6.9	195,400	63.7	4.1	73.4	20.6
Lexington city	17.98	18,944	18,933	-0.1	1053.0	10.1	77.8	29,938	28.0	104,200	52.8	11.0	61.9	28.6
Lincolnton city	8.65	10,325	11,200	8.5	1294.8	11.1	79.5	37,027	23.1	153,800	59.0	8.0	56.8	39.1
Lumberton city	17.73	21,523	20,484	-4.8	1155.3	7.1	88.0	36,935	29.0	109,800	47.8	7.8	63.5	32.2
Matthews town	17.12	27,189	33,138	21.9	1935.6	11.9	85.8	84,594	5.1	265,300	66.8	3.3	70.7	25.1
Mebane city	9.75	11,481	16,262	41.6	1667.9	6.6	85.0	64,726	10.7	189,600	67.2	5.7	65.0	31.7
Mint Hill town	24.16	22,728	27,617	21.5	1143.1	7.9	89.6	75,084	5.8	268,300	61.4	3.5	76.7	21.3
Monroe city	30.32	32,912	35,540	8.0	1172.2	16.0	85.3	51,754	15.1	164,000	66.0	8.6	75.4	19.8
Mooresville town	24.61	34,367	39,132	13.9	1590.1	11.2	77.8	69,188	10.6	232,700	68.2	3.7	69.3	25.1
Morganton city	19.24	16,882	16,577	-1.8	861.6	11.0	81.7	42,137	17.3	160,100	51.5	5.2	63.2	33.4
Morrisville town	8.72	18,583	28,846	55.2	3308.0	36.8	67.7	101,738	6.7	331,800	75.3	3.5	69.9	24.2
Mount Airy city	11.69	10,407	10,208	-1.9	873.2	4.3	86.4	38,515	22.9	153,700	48.7	6.3	55.3	41.1
Mount Holly city	10.86	13,657	16,257	19.0	1497.0	5.8	84.5	60,574	8.3	172,300	70.9	4.6	62.7	29.8
Murraysville CDP	8.61	14,215	NA	NA	NA	7.3	83.6	62,331	9.2	192,300	76.9	3.0	65.8	24.8
Myrtle Grove CDP	6.71	8,875	NA	NA	NA	1.7	83.3	78,000	11.2	280,500	57.8	5.8	77.2	19.4
New Bern city	28.28	29,344	29,994	2.2	1060.6	7.7	82.3	43,204	16.5	155,900	57.9	8.1	58.7	35.4
Newton city	13.78	12,949	13,177	1.8	956.2	6.5	82.3	46,063	11.1	110,200	55.8	4.9	65.6	24.7
Pinehurst village	16.69	14,738	16,620	12.8	995.8	5.7	84.3	82,081	3.6	293,100	40.4	3.0	68.4	28.8
Piney Green CDP	13.62	13,293	NA	NA	NA	5.2	74.3	45,787	16.6	150,600	56.0	6.2	72.3	19.9
Raleigh city	145.89	404,068	474,069	17.3	3249.5	13.4	79.0	67,266	10.4	248,300	70.3	4.1	56.1	33.1
Reidsville city	14.69	14,463	13,987	-3.3	952.1	2.4	84.6	32,339	23.3	103,500	52.4	9.5	57.8	38.4
Roanoke Rapids city	9.91	15,720	14,320	-8.9	1445.0	3.6	86.8	37,575	25.0	112,400	56.4	6.5	62.2	34.1
Rocky Mount city	44.19	57,695	53,922	-6.5	1220.2	3.4	82.9	40,633	20.9	113,100	60.8	7.3	64.4	31.4
Salisbury city	22.29	33,525	33,988	1.4	1524.8	5.8	78.3	41,901	20.1	129,100	57.1	9.6	58.5	35.0
Sanford city	29.06	28,217	30,085	6.6	1035.3	12.5	85.0	46,915	17.0	142,200	64.9	6.3	64.5	30.1
Shelby city	22.31	20,363	20,026	-1.7	897.6	2.7	80.7	38,559	25.1	119,300	54.1	9.2	61.0	35.8
Smithfield town	11.92	11,043	12,985	17.6	1089.3	11.2	87.6	36,335	22.8	142,200	51.6	5.6	59.0	37.5
Southern Pines town	17.05	12,411	14,657	18.1	859.6	5.3	76.8	58,843	14.4	289,400	51.7	6.7	55.5	39.7
Spring Lake town	23.53	12,012	12,005	-0.1	510.2	5.2	58.3	39,559	17.3	94,300	41.6	11.8	60.7	31.9
Stallings town	8.34	13,762	16,145	17.3	1935.9	10.9	86.1	85,193	5.4	250,300	68.6	2.1	78.7	16.9
Statesville city	24.74	24,521	27,528	12.3	1112.7	7.9	81.8	39,987	16.8	151,800	64.1	6.7	61.5	33.2
Summerfield town	26.39	10,238	11,376	11.1	431.1	3.0	91.0	103,769	8.2	361,100	65.0	3.1	82.7	15.5
Tarboro town	11.56	11,525	10,715	-7.0	926.9	3.8	92.0	29,738	26.6	112,100	56.3	9.2	61.4	34.8
Thomasville city	16.77	26,804	26,649	-0.6	1589.1	9.9	84.8	40,648	17.5	116,800	58.1	6.3	60.7	34.4
Wake Forest town	17.63	30,135	45,629	51.4	2588.1	6.6	79.6	92,210	5.0	297,300	69.7	3.9	75.4	19.8
Waxhaw town	11.96	9,915	17,147	72.9	1433.7	8.0	86.9	111,642	3.3	329,400	70.9	3.2	84.9	13.8
Weddington town	17.53	9,532	11,182	17.3	637.9	8.7	85.6	136,891	2.5	457,900	60.7	1.9	89.5	10.1
Wilmington city	51.40	106,456	123,744	16.2	2407.5	5.4	78.4	47,580	20.5	246,400	61.4	5.7	49.1	38.2
Wilson city	31.11	49,168	49,459	0.6	1589.8	7.0	86.3	42,036	22.8	142,700	59.8	8.6	58.6	34.7
Winston-Salem city	132.61	229,627	247,945	8.0	1869.7	9.9	84.2	45,750	18.6	147,900	60.5	6.0	58.5	35.7
NORTH DAKOTA	68994.77	672,576	762,062	13.3	11.0	4.1	82.2	64,894	11.2	193,900	69.2	2.8	59.5	31.7
Bismarck city	34.30	61,324	73,529	19.9	2143.7	2.8	83.1	64,444	10.0	245,300	68.5	2.3	57.4	34.8
Dickinson city	14.14	17,879	23,133	29.4	1636.0	3.2	77.9	68,718	11.0	238,000	70.3	2.7	55.0	35.2
Fargo city	49.74	105,625	124,662	18.0	2506.3	9.0	72.6	55,551	13.5	212,100	75.3	3.2	49.7	36.5
Grand Forks city	27.49	52,920	55,839	5.5	2031.2	6.4	74.1	50,076	19.5	210,300	71.3	4.2	48.6	36.9
Jamestown city	13.28	15,421	15,084	-2.2	1135.8	2.1	75.6	51,789	13.9	144,800	63.5	3.2	51.3	41.1
Mandan city	13.50	18,870	22,752	20.6	1685.3	1.9	85.1	69,014	8.3	215,300	77.0	2.3	61.3	26.0
Minot city	27.25	41,093	47,382	15.3	1738.8	5.6	78.3	66,194	11.5	208,700	69.2	2.7	54.1	36.3
West Fargo city	16.04	25,845	37,058	43.4	2310.3	5.2	81.2	85,120	6.1	241,000	79.3	1.5	69.3	21.8
Williston city	23.17	15,943	29,033	82.1	1253.0	7.4	77.9	84,710	6.8	238,700	75.5	2.6	57.9	32.8
OHIO	40858.76	11,536,751	11,689,100	1.3	286.1	4.6	85.3	56,602	13.7	145,700	63.2	5.3	63.2	30.5
Akron city	61.93	199,209	197,597	-0.8	3190.7	6.6	84.5	38,739	22.1	82,400	62.4	8.1	53.1	38.8
Alliance city	9.01	22,331	21,446	-4.0	2380.2	1.5	74.7	35,718	24.4	81,400	55.5	7.1	55.7	37.9
Amherst city	7.06	11,990	12,219	1.9	1730.7	3.7	91.1	71,775	7.8	164,600	59.2	5.9	72.9	22.8
Ashland city	11.29	20,379	20,275	-0.5	1795.8	2.1	77.7	47,869	13.0	109,300	61.0	3.0	56.1	35.1
Ashtabula city	7.77	19,125	18,017	-5.8	2318.8	1.9	85.0	29,566	31.7	72,200	51.1	8.1	57.0	38.2
Athens city	9.83	23,836	24,536	2.9	2496.0	9.3	41.0	32,360	40.8	191,700	52.1	8.2	35.0	36.2
Aurora city	22.91	15,548	16,338	5.1	713.1	5.4	91.6	97,848	3.4	272,300	62.5	4.1	70.4	26.9
Austintown CDP	11.62	29,677	NA	NA	NA	1.6	87.6	45,242	13.9	97,300	62.9	6.3	58.0	37.4
Avon city	20.81	21,191	23,399	10.4	1124.4	2.9	86.9	109,916	4.7	296,900	69.2	3.5	77.4	18.7
Avon Lake city	11.13	22,581	24,504	8.5	2201.6	4.4	90.7	83,018	7.0	256,400	63.2	2.3	69.8	25.6
Barberton city	9.02	26,548	25,953	-2.2	2877.3	2.2	90.5	42,813	17.9	86,800	58.0	7.6	58.7	34.5
Bay Village city	4.57	15,651	15,194	-2.9	3324.7	3.4	92.0	103,582	4.8	247,900	67.7	1.3	71.3	24.2
Beachwood city	5.26	11,926	11,590	-2.8	2203.4	20.2	79.2	89,190	5.9	302,500	55.0	3.3	61.1	36.3
Beavercreek city	26.59	45,198	47,741	5.6	1795.4	7.8	87.0	91,217	6.4	194,400	61.4	2.8	70.4	24.1
Bedford city	5.35	13,077	12,457	-4.7	2328.4	3.4	83.7	46,020	10.2	91,400	63.6	6.1	50.4	45.9
Bedford Heights city	4.54	10,757	10,460	-2.8	2304.0	3.7	85.4	46,485	20.5	102,600	63.3	5.9	46.2	47.1

Table B. Incorporated Places, Census Designated Places (CDPs), and Minor Civil Divisions (MCDs) of 10,000 or More Population — Crime, Residential Construction and Local Government Finance

STATE City, town, township, borough, or CDP (county if applicable)	Serious crimes known to police, 2018[1]				New residential construction authorized by building permits, 2019			Local government finance, 2017							
	Violent crime		Property crime					General revenue				General expenditure			
									Intergovernmental				Per capita[3]		
	Number	Rate[2]	Number	Rate[2]	Value ($1,000)	Number of housing units	Percent single family	Total (mil dol)	Total (mil dol)	Percent from state gov.	Taxes per capita[3]	Total (mil dol)	Total	Capital outlays	Debt outstanding (mil dol)
	15	16	17	18	19	20	21	22	23	24	25	26	27	28	29
NORTH CAROLINA—Con.															
Hendersonville city	NA	NA	NA	NA	NA	NA	NA	22.4	3.0	91.7	856	21.0	1,507	171	27.5
Hickory city	NA	NA	1,884	4,629	NA	NA	NA	67.5	10.8	73.8	925	58.4	1,431	198	31.2
High Point city	NA	NA	3,682	3,272	59,701	407	94.1	175.5	32.5	64.3	762	156.2	1,398	79	225.3
Holly Springs town	NA	NA	267	722	152,777	755	100.0	42.1	13.9	100.0	565	30.3	861	88	81.4
Hope Mills town	NA	NA	681	4,199	1,373	8	0.0	13.5	1.7	100.0	604	12.4	783	86	4.7
Huntersville town	NA	NA	884	1,533	NA	NA	NA	42.7	6.2	80.5	521	39.7	704	148	41.1
Indian Trail town	NA	NA	NA	NA	NA	NA	NA	14.3	2.2	37.6	254	17.4	448	171	15.5
Jacksonville city	NA	NA	1,763	2,458	2,986	24	50.0	70.8	9.7	74.7	490	59.6	819	99	92.1
Kannapolis city	NA	NA	968	1,946	NA	NA	NA	48.9	7.0	65.5	713	49.2	1,009	130	96.6
Kernersville town	NA	NA	970	3,948	41,098	199	100.0	29.8	1.8	100.0	945	30.5	1,254	200	15.8
Kings Mountain city	NA	NA	400	3,701	8,106	40	90.0	14.8	2.5	84.1	690	18.9	1,748	358	30.9
Kinston city	NA	NA	1,305	6,416	1,245	8	75.0	33.8	4.8	98.0	684	35.1	1,727	202	15.3
Knightdale town	NA	NA	NA	NA	30,259	139	100.0	13.7	1.9	92.8	615	10.9	692	60	9.8
Laurinburg city	NA	NA	NA	NA	NA	NA	NA	10.6	3.4	23.3	298	9.7	641	88	5.8
Leland town	NA	NA	320	1,523	188,894	993	49.3	14.8	1.6	92.0	492	13.4	679	82	9.4
Lenoir city	NA	NA	845	4,720	NA	NA	NA	23.3	5.9	33.7	678	20.3	1,132	54	11.6
Lewisville town	NA	NA	NA	NA	NA	NA	NA	4.3	1.1	97.4	222	3.5	252	13	1.0
Lexington city	NA	NA	489	2,607	19,039	113	18.6	26.5	3.7	97.6	813	33.6	1,796	172	16.6
Lincolnton city	NA	NA	NA	NA	NA	NA	NA	14.0	1.3	97.9	729	12.6	1,173	172	10.7
Lumberton city	NA	NA	NA	NA	1,751	8	100.0	34.3	4.8	88.8	818	25.5	1,218	69	7.2
Matthews town	NA	NA	949	2,887	NA	NA	NA	25.5	4.0	71.3	532	20.1	625	106	6.4
Mebane city	NA	NA	NA	NA	40,076	246	73.2	19.9	3.2	90.8	831	16.9	1,120	118	14.6
Mint Hill town	NA	NA	471	1,721	NA	NA	NA	13.8	2.0	100.0	318	13.7	512	20	1.1
Monroe city	NA	NA	NA	NA	12,342	76	100.0	51.7	10.3	61.3	759	61.5	1,747	755	74.5
Mooresville town	NA	NA	1,018	2,655	NA	NA	NA	83.0	8.9	75.3	1,201	76.8	2,030	462	192.3
Morganton city	NA	NA	NA	NA	6,083	86	12.8	29.8	3.2	86.6	821	26.3	1,589	180	24.8
Morrisville town	NA	NA	NA	NA	82,647	686	18.2	31.9	3.8	97.0	966	30.5	1,155	272	19.3
Mount Airy city	NA	NA	NA	NA	NA	NA	NA	15.1	2.1	73.3	887	15.3	1,500	132	10.0
Mount Holly city	NA	NA	302	1,895	NA	NA	NA	15.3	1.6	98.1	599	13.8	886	101	17.3
Murraysville CDP	NA	NA	NA	NA	NA	NA	NA	NA	NA	NA	NA	NA	NA	NA	NA
Myrtle Grove CDP	NA	NA	NA	NA	NA	NA	NA	NA	NA	NA	NA	NA	NA	NA	NA
New Bern city	NA	NA	940	3,176	38,035	202	100.0	0.0	0.0		0	2.5	85	0	56.7
Newton city	NA	NA	453	3,453	NA	NA	NA	17.1	2.7	87.8	747	15.2	1,160	122	20.9
Pinehurst village	NA	NA	111	685	43,824	153	100.0	17.8	2.8	97.4	831	15.5	966	93	0.8
Piney Green CDP	NA	NA	NA	NA	NA	NA	NA	NA	NA	NA	NA	NA	NA	NA	NA
Raleigh city	NA	NA	NA	NA	222,539	1,207	31.5	724.2	109.0	54.2	765	552.4	1,186	194	1680.4
Reidsville city	NA	NA	693	5,031	3,274	18	77.8	0.1	0.0		7	1.3	97	0	25.3
Roanoke Rapids city	NA	NA	NA	NA	753	5	100.0	0.0	0.0		0	0.7	48	0	16.7
Rocky Mount city	NA	NA	1,577	2,916	1,150	10	100.0	82.8	17.9	58.2	658	78.4	1,436	146	57.0
Salisbury city	NA	NA	1,579	4,658	NA	NA	NA	59.4	6.1	91.3	749	61.1	1,812	87	55.6
Sanford city	NA	NA	782	2,652	17,491	102	100.0	41.0	5.6	73.0	730	39.6	1,347	51	59.4
Shelby city	NA	NA	NA	NA	1,436	9	100.0	27.7	4.2	86.9	656	27.4	1,370	43	33.2
Smithfield town	NA	NA	454	3,630	NA	NA	NA	18.1	1.8	100.0	740	14.9	1,204	172	12.3
Southern Pines town	NA	NA	312	2,186	40,084	176	100.0	20.4	2.4	99.8	896	18.6	1,327	110	5.2
Spring Lake town	NA	NA	NA	NA	965	5	100.0	8.0	3.1	100.0	293	7.8	648	5	5.5
Stallings town	NA	NA	NA	NA	NA	NA	NA	7.2	1.4	98.9	324	6.2	398	4	0.0
Statesville city	NA	NA	NA	NA	NA	NA	NA	44.3	10.5	99.8	539	36.0	1,350	173	33.1
Summerfield town	NA	NA	NA	NA	NA	NA	NA	1.1	0.5	100.0	46	1.3	114	30	0.0
Tarboro town	NA	NA	NA	NA	761	9	100.0	0.0	0.0		0	0.0	2	0	0.5
Thomasville city	NA	NA	1,009	3,795	7,310	46	100.0	23.8	4.9	94.7	631	25.4	955	135	32.4
Wake Forest town	NA	NA	653	1,473	136,333	681	100.0	46.4	7.5	47.6	842	45.0	1,067	291	22.5
Waxhaw town	NA	NA	NA	NA	44,446	289	100.0	11.0	1.2	99.7	539	11.2	739	85	0.0
Weddington town	NA	NA	NA	NA	NA	NA	NA	7.6	1.4	100.0	467	7.1	656	41	1.1
Wilmington city	NA	NA	3,639	3,009	NA	NA	NA	150.3	20.4	74.4	793	150.5	1,245	156	185.7
Wilson city	NA	NA	1,719	3,482	11,979	101	96.0	81.9	10.8	91.9	619	70.3	1,430	133	74.2
Winston-Salem city	NA	NA	NA	NA	178,528	1,185	100.0	324.1	51.4	57.9	701	412.9	1,689	523	778.9
NORTH DAKOTA	2,133	281	15,507	2,040	537,457	2,495	70.8	X	X	X	X	X	X	X	X
Bismarck city	223	299	2,034	2,725	67,697	344	63.4	128.8	25.4	55.2	608	161.7	2,211	740	222.9
Dickinson city	56	245	500	2,186	20,214	62	100.0	54.9	25.3	100.0	660	41.3	1,856	667	85.7
Fargo city	522	418	3,931	3,147	96,380	483	64.4	278.9	77.2	92.7	750	373.1	3,048	1949	795.4
Grand Forks city	148	257	1,410	2,445	33,307	143	62.9	116.8	24.1	58.9	743	63.8	1,124	139	352.1
Jamestown city	40	260	341	2,218	1,424	6	100.0	20.2	2.6	95.6	645	20.0	1,298	361	40.2
Mandan city	82	361	690	3,034	26,921	179	34.1	23.1	6.3	100.0	448	26.5	1,186	124	90.8
Minot city	134	274	1,011	2,071	14,201	64	100.0	138.2	63.8	29.5	839	119.5	2,487	990	108.4
West Fargo city	67	179	527	1,410	104,165	545	57.2	52.2	2.9	100.0	635	65.3	1,832	1119	250.1
Williston city	142	518	776	2,833	14,031	55	100.0	109.7	23.7	59.5	2,648	53.5	2,061	246	249.5
OHIO	32,723	280	254,496	2,177	5,421,691	23,047	69.8	X	X	X	X	X	X	X	X
Akron city	1,704	862	7,159	3,621	NA	NA	NA	445.0	37.7	36.9	1,082	416.1	2,100	70	674.3
Alliance city	43	198	515	2,371	1,140	7	100.0	33.6	5.0	88.5	1,009	25.0	1,149	264	50.2
Amherst city	11	91	187	1,546	9,251	69	100.0	12.6	1.0	91.4	605	10.3	851	199	13.3
Ashland city	20	98	369	1,805	983	3	100.0	26.3	2.7	100.0	594	22.4	1,095	78	0.0
Ashtabula city	NA	NA	NA	NA	NA	NA	NA	21.7	5.7	92.0	490	21.1	1,165	286	5.6
Athens city	31	122	453	1,787	2,580	10	100.0	10.1	2.7	100.0	114	16.8	667	105	25.7
Aurora city	10	62	148	922	24,015	76	100.0	26.2	1.1	97.8	1,310	23.7	1,484	194	15.8
Austintown CDP	42	120	667	1,904	NA	NA	NA	NA	NA	NA	NA	NA	NA	NA	NA
Avon city	NA	NA	NA	NA	70,141	147	83.0	39.2	5.3	100.0	971	42.7	1,855	766	108.1
Avon Lake city	NA	NA	NA	NA	36,574	144	69.4	36.2	5.0	100.0	808	34.5	1,430	310	17.1
Barberton city	94	361	833	3,197	945	7	100.0	35.9	6.0	87.2	582	35.0	1,342	119	4.5
Bay Village city	NA	NA	NA	NA	6,472	12	100.0	23.8	1.0	30.2	980	20.6	1,343	117	11.4
Beachwood city	11	94	289	2,474	4,680	10	100.0	40.6	0.8	100.0	3,132	38.6	3,311	357	16.8
Beavercreek city	40	85	1,145	2,426	NA	NA	NA	36.7	10.2	100.0	456	33.5	714	211	6.3
Bedford city	27	215	182	1,446	352	2	100.0	34.9	2.4	37.5	1,077	36.4	2,888	685	20.3
Bedford Heights city	20	189	223	2,109	0	0	0.0	20.1	1.4	100.0	1,328	18.1	1,716	83	0.6

1 Data for serious crimes have not been adjusted for underreporting. This may affect comparability between geographic areas over time.
2 Per 100,000 population estimated by the FBI.   3 Based on population estimated as of July 1 of the year shown.

STATE City, town, township, borough, or CDP (county if applicable)	Land area 2010 (sq mi)	Population Total persons 2010	Total persons 2019	Percent change 2010–2019	Persons per square mile, 2019	Population characteristics 2015–2019 Percent foreign born	Percent living in the same house as previous year	Income and poverty 2015–2019 Median household income	Percent of households with income below poverty level	Median value of owner-occupied housing units	Employment, 2015–2019 Percent in civilian labor force	Unemploy- ment rate	Households, 2015–2019 (percent of households) Family households	One person households
	1	2	3	4	5	6	7	8	9	10	11	12	13	14
OHIO—Con.														
Bellefontaine city	10.05	13,364	13,249	-0.9	1318.3	1.4	79.0	49,237	17.2	99,300	66.8	6.2	62.7	28.4
Berea city	5.66	19,080	18,609	-2.5	3287.8	3.3	81.5	59,511	12.7	138,200	64.2	4.1	55.9	36.0
Bexley city	2.42	13,054	13,770	5.5	5690.1	7.1	80.9	109,036	8.5	379,200	70.8	4.6	70.5	23.4
Blue Ash city	7.58	12,087	12,372	2.4	1632.2	12.0	82.5	91,563	5.8	284,700	68.6	3.0	67.8	28.4
Boardman CDP	15.13	35,376	NA	NA	NA	3.3	88.3	55,813	10.0	118,900	65.6	6.0	58.0	35.4
Bowling Green city	12.67	30,056	31,504	4.8	2486.5	3.7	53.6	37,346	30.5	168,000	71.2	6.2	39.0	37.1
Brecksville city	19.52	13,651	13,604	-0.3	696.9	7.5	90.7	108,606	4.7	283,000	64.6	5.4	70.4	27.6
Bridgetown CDP	4.31	14,407	NA	NA	NA	2.4	90.7	65,886	7.5	125,800	65.0	3.9	62.4	32.0
Broadview Heights city	13.05	19,397	19,102	-1.5	1463.8	8.5	90.0	89,224	2.1	228,500	72.0	1.8	69.4	26.8
Brooklyn city	4.25	11,169	10,646	-4.7	2504.9	10.4	80.4	48,552	13.1	110,600	65.6	6.7	54.5	36.3
Brook Park city	7.53	19,212	18,382	-4.3	2441.2	7.6	88.5	53,390	10.3	118,400	64.0	6.8	65.8	29.1
Brunswick city	12.92	34,288	34,880	1.7	2699.7	4.0	90.8	69,884	7.6	169,200	68.6	2.4	67.5	27.2
Bucyrus city	7.38	12,386	11,764	-5.0	1594.0	1.3	82.9	41,314	17.0	79,800	58.0	4.5	52.7	40.2
Cambridge city	6.35	10,636	10,289	-3.3	1620.3	1.1	80.6	33,011	28.6	88,700	57.5	8.2	55.4	33.9
Canton city	26.14	73,403	70,447	-4.0	2695.0	2.9	81.6	32,287	26.4	71,100	61.5	11.1	54.3	39.3
Celina city	4.98	10,410	10,425	0.1	2093.4	2.3	85.8	47,776	9.0	118,300	66.8	3.8	61.2	33.5
Centerville city	10.97	24,003	23,703	-1.2	2160.7	7.8	83.2	73,904	6.9	186,900	58.8	2.2	61.8	33.4
Chillicothe city	10.42	21,931	21,722	-1.0	2084.6	0.8	81.6	44,323	18.1	116,800	56.5	5.9	59.6	34.0
Cincinnati city	77.84	297,025	303,940	2.3	3904.7	6.0	74.9	40,640	24.1	138,000	66.0	8.0	45.3	44.4
Circleville city	7.19	13,506	14,050	4.0	1954.1	0.5	78.6	42,103	20.6	124,800	51.4	6.2	60.9	35.2
Clayton city	18.52	13,248	13,222	-0.2	713.9	5.0	87.0	74,437	6.3	135,000	64.4	4.7	75.7	19.5
Cleveland city	77.69	396,665	381,009	-3.9	4904.2	5.9	81.0	30,907	30.9	69,600	59.1	13.2	48.2	44.4
Cleveland Heights city	8.10	46,268	43,992	-4.9	5431.1	9.1	83.8	57,768	17.3	128,700	64.5	6.9	54.0	36.3
Columbus city	219.20	789,018	898,553	13.9	4099.2	12.7	77.9	53,745	16.3	151,600	70.6	5.5	53.3	35.6
Conneaut city	26.44	12,832	12,530	-2.4	473.9	0.6	82.2	45,034	17.1	89,500	49.5	7.9	65.2	29.3
Coshocton city	8.00	11,174	11,051	-1.1	1381.4	1.1	81.1	42,767	15.7	82,200	56.8	5.5	61.1	33.6
Cuyahoga Falls city	25.80	49,534	49,106	-0.9	1903.3	5.0	89.8	57,101	10.3	127,600	67.8	3.7	56.0	37.1
Dayton city	55.40	141,989	140,407	-1.1	2534.4	5.0	72.8	32,540	29.2	66,800	56.8	10.7	50.6	41.7
Defiance city	12.53	17,077	16,634	-2.6	1327.5	3.2	81.6	49,628	13.8	112,900	62.8	5.4	62.8	29.0
Delaware city	19.30	34,791	41,283	18.7	2139.0	4.2	84.0	69,087	10.2	186,900	69.1	3.9	64.4	29.1
Dent CDP	5.93	10,497	NA	NA	NA	3.3	88.9	80,786	7.1	198,200	70.7	5.3	67.8	23.6
Dover city	5.69	12,877	12,723	-1.2	2236.0	4.4	85.5	56,898	8.4	133,500	60.9	4.0	59.9	32.9
Dublin city	24.67	41,398	49,037	18.5	1987.7	19.1	86.5	137,867	3.4	377,500	70.4	2.5	77.7	19.2
East Cleveland city	3.09	17,859	16,964	-5.0	5490.0	2.5	79.9	20,743	39.6	58,100	50.3	18.8	46.2	49.0
Eastlake city	6.40	18,606	18,042	-3.0	2819.1	3.3	89.7	54,698	9.9	133,000	66.5	6.0	62.0	31.1
East Liverpool city	4.70	11,200	10,603	-5.3	2256.0	2.2	88.4	32,119	26.7	55,600	58.0	10.4	63.4	30.9
Elyria city	20.57	54,526	53,757	-1.4	2613.4	2.8	82.8	44,324	21.9	99,100	62.2	6.9	58.6	34.8
Englewood city	6.55	13,424	13,435	0.1	2051.1	3.2	88.1	60,684	8.6	129,300	59.3	6.5	61.5	33.4
Euclid city	10.65	48,901	46,550	-4.8	4370.9	3.4	87.3	38,242	22.5	82,600	61.4	9.1	49.5	45.8
Fairborn city	14.57	33,028	33,876	2.6	2325.1	4.8	75.7	47,440	19.8	118,100	63.7	7.3	53.2	35.7
Fairfield city	20.83	42,500	42,558	0.1	2043.1	11.0	86.9	60,340	8.9	159,300	67.6	3.0	63.7	29.8
Fairview Park city	4.69	16,827	16,161	-4.0	3445.8	7.3	90.2	61,020	9.0	161,100	68.5	3.9	59.9	34.9
Findlay city	19.63	41,186	41,225	0.1	2100.1	5.5	78.5	51,002	13.8	136,700	66.0	4.3	55.3	34.6
Finneytown CDP	4.03	12,741	NA	NA	NA	5.6	89.3	65,313	10.0	127,800	67.2	3.6	70.4	24.9
Forest Park city	6.45	18,705	18,583	-0.7	2881.1	15.3	86.5	55,694	12.1	112,400	68.1	4.5	64.5	30.9
Forestville CDP	3.70	10,532	NA	NA	NA	2.2	86.1	76,950	5.8	223,200	62.2	5.1	67.5	30.7
Fostoria city	7.54	13,453	13,225	-1.7	1754.0	2.3	82.2	39,688	21.1	66,600	58.7	6.8	56.3	33.7
Franklin city	9.18	11,762	11,612	-1.3	1264.9	3.7	86.4	51,337	15.1	112,100	64.2	4.3	64.9	28.6
Fremont city	8.53	16,641	15,917	-4.4	1866.0	1.8	86.2	41,305	18.6	85,900	59.7	5.5	56.4	36.7
Gahanna city	12.43	33,230	35,483	6.8	2854.6	4.5	85.9	88,475	5.2	216,100	70.6	2.4	71.1	24.0
Galion city	7.39	10,611	9,982	-5.9	1350.7	1.8	87.3	35,738	20.9	71,400	54.2	10.6	59.0	35.3
Garfield Heights city	7.23	28,849	27,448	-4.9	3796.4	2.9	86.8	43,971	16.1	72,700	65.0	9.0	58.1	36.0
Green city	32.03	25,741	25,752	0.0	804.0	3.8	89.0	75,566	8.9	201,200	64.6	3.7	70.5	26.0
Greenville city	6.64	13,228	12,615	-4.6	1899.8	1.5	84.6	41,647	16.4	98,800	56.3	7.1	55.3	38.0
Grove City city	17.17	35,632	41,820	17.4	2435.6	2.8	88.8	74,284	7.9	188,300	70.0	3.0	71.1	24.9
Hamilton city	21.45	62,291	62,082	-0.3	2894.3	3.7	83.2	47,064	16.6	107,200	60.5	6.6	59.6	34.1
Harrison city	5.29	9,941	11,896	19.7	2248.8	0.5	86.1	61,731	7.5	143,800	68.6	2.4	63.7	31.7
Heath city	10.73	10,288	10,942	6.4	1019.8	2.4	82.3	55,956	13.2	150,700	63.3	3.1	62.4	31.1
Hilliard city	14.27	28,234	36,534	29.4	2560.2	7.0	87.5	96,959	5.4	254,700	72.5	3.4	71.7	25.0
Huber Heights city	22.20	38,110	38,154	0.1	1718.6	5.5	86.6	62,461	9.9	112,100	65.4	5.5	70.7	23.8
Hudson city	25.63	22,266	22,237	-0.1	867.6	5.8	91.8	134,963	2.8	345,500	66.3	3.7	82.8	15.2
Ironton city	4.16	11,120	10,532	-5.3	2531.7	0.5	84.4	35,666	26.5	95,900	45.9	2.9	54.0	40.8
Kent city	9.18	28,906	29,646	2.6	3229.4	7.8	70.0	32,993	30.5	146,700	64.0	7.9	47.5	38.8
Kettering city	18.69	56,129	54,855	-2.3	2935.0	5.3	84.0	58,970	10.9	133,800	65.5	4.1	57.0	36.4
Lakewood city	5.54	52,131	49,678	-4.7	8967.1	8.6	81.5	53,290	13.6	158,100	74.3	4.6	43.2	44.8
Lancaster city	18.85	38,764	40,505	4.5	2148.8	1.3	80.0	43,720	16.4	125,900	57.5	5.8	59.1	32.5
Lebanon city	12.82	20,037	20,659	3.1	1611.5	4.4	87.8	65,477	9.1	183,500	67.3	2.5	67.3	24.9
Lima city	13.54	38,627	36,659	-5.1	2707.5	1.7	78.8	35,799	23.4	66,600	61.1	7.9	55.9	36.7
Lincoln Village CDP	1.83	9,032	NA	NA	NA	9.7	84.9	49,541	12.3	103,200	65.9	7.4	57.4	29.7
London city	8.39	9,899	10,328	4.3	1231.0	0.8	77.3	56,801	8.8	135,200	61.6	4.5	60.1	28.7
Lorain city	23.67	64,099	63,855	-0.4	2697.7	2.6	84.7	38,291	25.3	87,300	57.8	8.7	60.9	34.6
Loveland city	5.06	12,111	13,145	8.5	2597.8	5.3	85.3	71,405	13.4	201,000	67.9	3.2	67.7	26.6
Lyndhurst city	4.43	14,001	13,366	-4.5	3017.2	8.4	88.8	73,164	3.7	143,600	63.2	4.4	59.3	37.6
Macedonia city	9.73	11,128	12,000	7.8	1233.3	4.1	92.0	97,440	1.4	223,400	70.1	2.2	76.1	20.7
Mack CDP	9.23	11,585	NA	NA	NA	1.9	92.3	103,258	2.6	231,900	68.7	2.1	81.9	17.4
Mansfield city	30.85	47,837	46,599	-2.6	1510.5	2.2	76.9	37,683	21.5	79,600	48.5	8.5	54.5	38.5
Maple Heights city	5.17	23,135	22,078	-4.6	4270.4	2.3	86.9	42,805	16.6	68,200	65.4	9.2	57.8	37.9
Marietta city	8.43	14,069	13,356	-5.1	1584.3	1.6	81.5	38,729	25.7	108,300	55.1	3.4	55.2	39.6
Marion city	11.79	36,828	35,883	-2.6	3043.5	1.8	80.4	38,221	18.8	74,600	49.1	9.2	57.5	36.5
Marysville city	16.35	22,101	24,667	11.6	1508.7	3.8	74.6	75,116	7.7	190,600	60.0	1.3	67.2	26.0
Mason city	19.25	30,848	33,870	9.8	1759.5	12.3	87.7	100,594	2.8	267,300	66.9	2.1	74.4	22.5
Massillon city	18.97	32,318	32,584	0.8	1717.7	1.3	86.5	45,809	16.8	102,100	60.5	5.5	60.3	32.8
Maumee city	10.06	14,282	13,669	-4.3	1358.7	2.8	88.2	71,419	5.5	144,600	69.6	3.6	64.1	31.1
Mayfield Heights city	4.17	19,155	18,487	-3.5	4433.3	17.7	83.3	53,450	10.6	145,400	64.2	4.6	48.9	46.0
Medina city	11.57	26,663	25,956	-2.7	2243.4	2.6	87.1	66,155	9.4	175,200	69.1	2.4	66.6	29.9
Mentor city	27.80	47,161	47,262	0.2	1700.1	4.5	92.2	72,615	5.3	172,400	64.1	3.4	65.8	28.3
Miamisburg city	12.20	20,167	20,143	-0.1	1651.1	2.2	86.9	63,042	9.7	144,600	63.1	4.8	69.2	26.5

Table B. Incorporated Places, Census Designated Places (CDPs), and Minor Civil Divisions (MCDs) of 10,000 or More Population — Crime, Residential Construction and Local Government Finance

STATE City, town, township, borough, or CDP (county if applicable)	Serious crimes known to police, 2018[1] Violent crime Number	Violent crime Rate[2]	Property crime Number	Property crime Rate[2]	New residential construction authorized by building permits, 2019 Value ($1,000)	Number of housing units	Percent single family	Local government finance, 2017 General revenue Total (mil dol)	Intergovernmental Total (mil dol)	Percent from state gov.	Taxes per capita[3]	General expenditure Total (mil dol)	Per capita[3] Total	Capital outlays	Debt outstanding (mil dol)
	15	16	17	18	19	20	21	22	23	24	25	26	27	28	29
OHIO—Con.															
Bellefontaine city	12	91	282	2,147	NA	NA	NA	17.6	2.6	100.0	650	15.7	1,199	185	3.1
Berea city	10	53	116	616	3,047	17	100.0	27.7	4.1	96.1	892	35.1	1,866	844	16.8
Bexley city	13	94	398	2,865	517	1	100.0	24.4	3.8	100.0	1,095	22.6	1,632	408	17.5
Blue Ash city	14	115	247	2,020	8,844	34	100.0	58.5	4.1	100.0	3,821	53.2	4,335	1675	53.4
Boardman CDP	NA	NA	NA	NA	NA	NA	NA	NA	NA	NA	NA	NA	NA	NA	NA
Bowling Green city	24	75	386	1,206	NA	NA	NA	40.4	3.3	100.0	872	36.6	1,150	122	13.3
Brecksville city	10	73	44	322	13,289	26	100.0	32.4	2.7	63.2	1,668	26.8	1,965	397	10.5
Bridgetown CDP	NA	NA	NA	NA	NA	NA	NA	NA	NA	NA	NA	NA	NA	NA	NA
Broadview Heights city	2	10	18	94	11,023	40	70.0	24.7	2.1	100.0	933	22.4	1,166	162	17.1
Brooklyn city	NA	NA	566	5,261	0	0	0.0	26.6	1.4	100.0	2,197	25.2	2,333	362	3.0
Brook Park city	NA	NA	NA	NA	0	0	0.0	31.7	3.1	100.0	1,352	31.1	1,671	380	0.0
Brunswick city	22	63	173	495	15,821	78	48.7	34.1	4.3	63.7	640	25.4	730	68	7.4
Bucyrus city	30	256	354	3,015	1,746	6	100.0	12.2	2.1	91.4	464	17.2	1,456	495	0.0
Cambridge city	NA	NA	396	3,819	265	1	100.0	7.5	0.1	100.0	718	0.2	21	0	5.2
Canton city	845	1,197	3,790	5,368	2,401	14	100.0	122.5	20.0	100.0	934	164.0	2,305	712	2.4
Celina city	NA	NA	NA	NA	1,959	11	100.0	20.7	9.1	88.4	637	8.8	856	107	20.9
Centerville city	8	34	292	1,229	1,418	8	100.0	22.6	1.0	32.3	655	28.4	1,196	328	55.7
Chillicothe city	104	485	1,622	7,565	1,956	9	100.0	28.4	4.2	66.6	761	24.0	1,109	78	10.2
Cincinnati city	2,535	840	13,710	4,541	170,956	1,127	12.0	1158.1	403.9	11.7	1,810	928.7	3,079	635	858.4
Circleville city	43	307	530	3,788	NA	NA	NA	93.3	2.0	68.1	561	80.7	5,797	528	34.3
Clayton city	5	38	135	1,022	NA	NA	NA	9.3	1.2	5.2	468	11.0	834	162	10.4
Cleveland city	5,576	1,450	16,970	4,412	12,414	97	80.4	985.2	205.9	83.4	1,225	1056.0	2,741	374	2408.9
Cleveland Heights city	93	209	711	1,601	1,178	15	0.0	55.1	5.9	54.6	869	54.6	1,225	153	23.5
Columbus city	4,416	495	31,512	3,531	468,926	2,770	18.5	1640.6	186.4	27.9	1,074	1749.5	1,984	416	4294.7
Conneaut city	19	151	256	2,029	NA	NA	NA	10.4	1.4	100.0	413	11.8	932	231	17.9
Coshocton city	NA	NA	NA	NA	900	3	33.3	5.1	0.7	100.0	218	1.6	144	101	15.8
Cuyahoga Falls city	57	116	1,040	2,114	NA	NA	NA	71.2	1.1	55.9	908	63.9	1,299	209	0.6
Dayton city	1,291	922	6,323	4,513	230	1	100.0	314.5	46.9	63.0	1,026	276.9	1,973	164	53.5
Defiance city	25	150	313	1,883	2,725	16	100.0	25.3	3.2	35.2	675	25.6	1,534	370	42.2
Delaware city	64	160	601	1,505	137,683	741	50.9	65.8	7.8	30.9	706	60.3	1,532	319	110.0
Dent CDP	NA	NA	NA	NA	NA	NA	NA	NA	NA	NA	NA	NA	NA	NA	NA
Dover city	11	86	97	761	1,700	10	60.0	17.8	3.3	100.0	733	18.3	1,435	498	15.8
Dublin city	29	60	413	850	39,994	117	100.0	129.7	3.7	100.0	2,094	239.4	5,013	3117	158.6
East Cleveland city	112	654	311	1,816	0	0	0.0	20.8	5.3	62.9	559	27.6	1,607	7	0.0
Eastlake city	7	39	399	2,203	1,315	9	100.0	17.9	2.8	40.3	607	16.0	881	36	11.8
East Liverpool city	NA	NA	NA	NA	0	0	0.0	7.2	0.3	100.0	428	5.5	513	17	5.9
Elyria city	NA	NA	NA	NA	13,528	76	89.5	66.2	5.4	80.9	723	62.4	1,161	107	48.4
Englewood city	14	104	400	2,969	5,060	31	3.2	14.6	1.2	61.2	675	15.0	1,113	252	0.0
Euclid city	291	619	1,224	2,602	0	0	0.0	101.9	43.2	97.9	649	132.4	2,806	829	31.1
Fairborn city	106	315	673	2,003	35,695	167	59.3	42.7	4.9	64.7	666	33.5	995	150	12.2
Fairfield city	84	197	909	2,135	1,801	8	100.0	64.5	6.0	100.0	913	53.8	1,262	158	16.3
Fairview Park city	16	99	140	862	890	3	100.0	23.0	1.9	69.9	859	18.8	1,152	86	19.5
Findlay city	90	218	1,043	2,522	10,146	56	53.6	53.8	5.3	100.0	718	49.0	1,181	260	10.9
Finneytown CDP	NA	NA	NA	NA	NA	NA	NA	NA	NA	NA	NA	NA	NA	NA	NA
Forest Park city	NA	NA	NA	NA	140	1	100.0	25.4	0.7	1.8	961	22.1	1,184	104	0.0
Forestville CDP	NA	NA	NA	NA	400	4	100.0	10.5	0.9	73.8	415	10.0	751	82	11.2
Fostoria city	NA	NA	NA	NA	335	2	100.0	9.2	0.6	100.0	216	0.5	45	0	10.6
Franklin city	NA	NA	870	5,395	330	3	100.0	24.3	3.3	83.2	645	35.2	2,183	1073	96.4
Fremont city	31	87	588	1,652	9,600	26	15.4	42.6	3.4	91.9	640	38.8	1,097	194	23.1
Gahanna city	17	171	220	2,210	180	1	100.0	11.7	1.3	74.6	558	14.4	1,428	517	20.3
Galion city	NA	NA	NA	NA	0	0	0.0	33.7	6.0	100.0	721	32.0	1,149	196	19.5
Garfield Heights city	NA	NA	NA	NA	NA	NA	NA	32.3	5.5	36.5	974	36.9	1,430	167	75.5
Green city	48	378	226	1,779	NA	NA	NA	14.0	2.5	28.2	704	13.4	1,050	229	0.9
Greenville city	43	103	1,156	2,763	47,507	210	29.5	46.1	10.6	99.9	719	56.7	1,378	606	54.5
Grove City city	315	508	2,686	4,328	9,832	64	100.0	88.8	9.6	78.7	634	97.5	1,570	288	227.6
Hamilton city	2	17	156	1,355	18,715	130	100.0	12.3	0.5	64.2	673	11.8	1,038	26	26.2
Harrison city	25	232	546	5,068	NA	NA	NA	13.2	1.7	100.0	747	11.6	1,083	127	4.4
Heath city	35	94	242	651	34,611	98	100.0	46.0	3.2	56.0	833	25.3	701	70	63.9
Hilliard city	57	150	916	2,413	NA	NA	NA	36.0	5.7	40.7	567	37.5	985	246	83.3
Huber Heights city	1	5	126	567	NA	NA	NA	59.4	1.6	99.9	1,354	41.6	1,870	296	36.8
Hudson city	25	234	340	3,188	379	7	42.9	11.5	2.7	100.0	317	13.8	1,294	132	6.4
Ironton city	36	120	421	1,400	1,319	4	100.0	37.7	7.3	43.1	663	34.6	1,155	350	30.0
Kent city	54	98	838	1,523	4,650	15	100.0	86.6	7.2	89.2	1,097	83.0	1,506	205	14.7
Kettering city	58	116	674	1,346	3,410	8	100.0	68.6	8.5	70.6	796	64.4	1,282	229	79.7
Lakewood city	116	286	1,687	4,166	16,645	112	54.5	76.4	9.7	92.0	712	63.8	1,585	233	0.0
Lancaster city	41	198	365	1,764	3,711	19	100.0	31.3	3.4	100.0	701	28.7	1,393	358	0.0
Lebanon city	240	650	1,664	4,504	10,129	103	5.8	71.1	29.4	68.5	523	77.0	2,075	739	115.5
Lima city	NA	NA	NA	NA	NA	NA	NA	NA	NA	NA	NA	NA	NA	NA	NA
Lincoln Village CDP	20	197	239	2,349	4,406	16	100.0	4.7	0.0		66	0.1	13	0	3.1
London city	NA	NA	NA	NA	10,454	87	100.0	47.1	13.1	24.5	436	51.4	806	115	125.1
Lorain city	5	39	102	792	2,433	9	100.0	17.6	2.0	100.0	671	16.3	1,266	50	6.9
Loveland city	14	104	154	1,139	0	0	0.0	23.0	2.5	100.0	1,048	21.4	1,583	0	0.0
Lyndhurst city	3	25	271	2,248	9,456	32	100.0	18.3	1.0	49.2	922	14.7	1,235	42	5.6
Macedonia city	NA	NA	NA	NA	NA	NA	NA	NA	NA	NA	NA	NA	NA	NA	NA
Mack CDP	237	516	2,087	4,543	1,345	5	100.0	64.2	9.8	50.6	826	59.9	1,299	61	6.9
Mansfield city	NA	NA	NA	NA	0	0	0.0	17.6	2.0	38.3	518	16.2	724	30	14.9
Maple Heights city	25	184	265	1,946	NA	NA	NA	21.0	2.9	9.8	830	26.0	1,906	232	18.0
Marietta city	101	282	940	2,620	650	4	100.0	39.4	5.3	100.0	537	36.0	997	92	24.0
Marion city	NA	NA	NA	NA	NA	NA	NA	35.1	1.3	74.8	818	35.7	1,496	121	188.0
Marysville city	6	18	264	786	43,810	118	100.0	79.8	5.1	100.0	1,361	79.7	2,398	742	70.0
Mason city	75	232	747	2,308	11,258	130	35.4	44.8	4.8	100.0	655	41.3	1,275	53	0.0
Massillon city	18	131	340	2,478	2,272	9	55.6	30.4	5.5	100.0	1,374	31.2	2,263	475	22.1
Maumee city	5	27	113	606	3,535	11	100.0	27.6	0.9	90.6	1,343	24.7	1,322	14	0.0
Mayfield Heights city	27	103	272	1,041	2,344	17	76.5	63.3	2.9	43.0	2,036	43.4	1,659	281	12.6
Medina city	41	87	709	1,505	14,175	51	100.0	74.0	6.7	98.6	1,156	74.5	1,580	0	18.1
Mentor city	49	246	443	2,220	340	1	100.0	64.0	32.2	100.0	1,079	43.7	2,193	929	13.9
Miamisburg city															

1 Data for serious crimes have not been adjusted for underreporting. This may affect comparability between geographic areas over time.
2 Per 100,000 population estimated by the FBI.   3 Based on population estimated as of July 1 of the year shown.

Table B. Incorporated Places, Census Designated Places (CDPs), and Minor Civil Divisions (MCDs) of 10,000 or More Population — **Land Area, Population, and Households, and Employment**

STATE City, town, township, borough, or CDP (county if applicable)	Land area 2010 (sq mi)	Population: Total persons 2010	Population: Total persons 2019	Population: Percent change 2010–2019	Population: Persons per square mile, 2019	Population characteristics 2015–2019: Percent foreign born	Population characteristics 2015–2019: Percent living in the same house as previous year	Income and poverty 2015–2019: Median household income	Income and poverty 2015–2019: Percent of households with income below poverty level	Median value of owner-occupied housing units	Employment, 2015–2019: Percent in civilian labor force	Employment, 2015–2019: Unemployment rate	Households, 2015–2019 (percent of households): Family households	Households, 2015–2019 (percent of households): One person households
	1	2	3	4	5	6	7	8	9	10	11	12	13	14
OHIO—Con.														
Middleburg Heights city	8.08	15,950	15,432	-3.2	1909.9	16.2	87.3	63,619	5.8	162,000	58.7	3.1	57.8	37.4
Middletown city	26.14	48,696	48,807	0.2	1867.1	2.5	80.1	40,347	21.7	97,700	58.7	8.4	60.5	32.7
Monfort Heights CDP	5.95	11,948	NA	NA	NA	3.5	91.1	71,038	5.8	151,800	66.8	4.2	70.8	24.8
Monroe city	15.87	12,455	14,015	12.5	883.1	3.6	82.2	86,935	3.1	180,800	71.6	3.5	73.3	23.2
Montgomery city	5.31	10,373	10,872	4.8	2047.5	7.6	89.7	131,111	3.3	374,000	63.4	1.7	76.2	21.8
Mount Vernon city	9.57	16,965	16,769	-1.2	1752.2	2.0	82.8	42,668	20.3	118,000	55.3	5.9	61.6	32.9
New Albany city	15.21	7,891	10,933	38.6	718.8	8.1	88.7	203,409	1.4	497,800	71.3	4.6	87.7	8.3
Newark city	20.88	47,558	50,315	5.8	2409.7	2.2	82.8	45,039	18.2	123,100	61.2	6.6	60.1	32.0
New Franklin city	24.99	14,204	14,133	-0.5	565.5	1.5	94.0	72,866	4.1	149,200	64.0	3.7	71.7	22.7
New Philadelphia city	8.21	17,295	17,410	0.7	2120.6	4.5	81.7	44,603	18.8	126,100	60.3	5.0	59.5	34.3
Niles city	8.61	19,210	18,176	-5.4	2111.0	1.8	89.6	44,020	16.1	85,200	59.4	5.7	55.2	37.1
Northbrook CDP	1.93	10,668	NA	NA	NA	3.9	86.8	48,842	10.3	80,800	69.5	3.9	64.6	30.5
North Canton city	6.41	17,505	17,176	-1.9	2679.6	2.9	84.4	62,128	7.5	155,300	63.0	3.2	57.7	34.6
North Olmsted city	11.67	32,709	31,341	-4.2	2685.6	11.9	87.3	64,236	9.3	156,400	63.7	3.8	63.6	31.5
North Ridgeville city	23.42	29,466	34,392	16.7	1468.5	4.6	88.4	77,221	4.7	182,300	65.9	3.2	70.6	24.8
North Royalton city	21.31	30,452	30,068	-1.3	1411.0	10.8	86.4	70,665	5.3	208,600	67.1	3.2	61.0	32.5
Norton city	20.19	12,107	11,966	-1.2	592.7	2.4	91.1	68,457	5.8	140,500	65.6	5.0	73.3	19.7
Norwalk city	8.86	17,102	16,867	-1.4	1903.7	2.3	87.5	45,752	17.2	126,300	62.3	4.9	61.5	31.6
Norwood city	3.14	19,210	19,776	2.9	6298.1	4.5	79.3	45,581	17.9	135,200	69.9	4.2	45.2	39.1
Oregon city	28.52	20,304	20,055	-1.2	703.2	2.8	88.5	60,078	9.9	144,000	63.0	6.0	64.5	30.9
Oxford city	7.51	21,387	23,110	8.1	3077.2	10.9	47.1	31,546	42.2	217,100	44.3	4.1	34.7	36.1
Painesville city	6.83	19,531	19,886	1.8	2911.6	13.7	79.3	49,448	16.6	103,300	66.4	7.2	62.0	30.0
Parma city	20.02	81,589	78,103	-4.3	3901.2	10.0	86.0	57,120	9.0	115,500	65.8	5.6	62.3	31.5
Parma Heights city	4.19	20,722	19,790	-4.5	4723.2	9.6	85.8	52,068	10.3	116,500	64.7	4.5	52.6	39.8
Pataskala city	28.97	14,926	15,883	6.4	548.3	5.0	87.3	77,514	5.2	184,400	68.6	4.3	74.0	18.6
Perrysburg city	11.89	20,767	21,626	4.1	1818.8	6.9	82.3	90,633	5.7	224,000	69.7	3.3	66.6	28.0
Pickerington city	9.85	18,278	22,158	21.2	2249.5	5.6	85.2	97,192	4.3	218,400	74.2	2.4	78.1	20.4
Piqua city	11.65	20,505	21,332	4.0	1831.1	1.2	78.0	43,061	13.2	87,100	63.2	6.6	58.6	33.1
Portsmouth city	10.73	20,207	20,158	-0.2	1878.7	2.0	75.4	28,840	33.8	78,400	48.5	11.2	54.1	39.5
Powell city	5.64	11,497	13,375	16.3	2371.5	11.7	90.0	157,149	1.0	372,700	72.0	2.4	84.3	14.9
Ravenna city	5.63	11,724	11,361	-3.1	2017.9	2.6	87.3	42,382	21.0	98,600	64.6	10.0	51.2	38.9
Reading city	2.89	10,413	10,296	-1.1	3562.6	6.7	87.6	56,137	12.0	129,400	71.2	4.9	57.2	36.2
Reynoldsburg city	11.11	35,921	38,327	6.7	3449.8	9.5	82.2	67,120	8.4	160,800	70.2	4.6	66.4	27.1
Richmond Heights city	4.44	10,557	10,342	-2.0	2329.3	11.3	89.0	51,505	12.4	141,100	62.2	7.0	56.7	39.7
Riverside city	9.73	25,175	25,133	-0.2	2583.0	6.7	86.6	48,626	14.4	90,300	61.8	3.8	62.2	30.3
Rocky River city	4.73	20,212	19,986	-1.1	4225.4	7.4	88.5	74,950	5.8	245,800	63.3	3.5	56.1	38.5
Salem city	6.42	12,298	11,612	-5.6	1808.7	3.6	79.5	40,134	21.3	96,900	61.9	9.1	60.1	33.9
Sandusky city	9.66	25,919	24,564	-5.2	2542.9	2.0	84.8	38,380	20.0	86,600	62.4	7.5	54.3	38.6
Seven Hills city	4.91	11,799	11,590	-1.8	2360.5	10.7	95.3	82,255	5.9	174,400	60.7	4.9	68.5	25.7
Shaker Heights city	6.31	28,466	27,027	-5.1	4283.2	7.8	84.8	87,235	9.3	229,500	66.9	6.2	65.2	31.0
Sharonville city	9.81	13,443	13,684	1.8	1394.9	11.0	85.1	61,378	8.2	157,600	67.0	1.2	54.1	38.8
Sidney city	11.97	21,219	20,449	-3.6	1708.4	3.1	81.5	53,505	11.4	111,100	68.6	6.1	63.1	30.9
Solon city	20.37	23,360	22,779	-2.5	1118.3	14.8	89.8	107,286	5.0	286,200	67.8	2.9	77.2	20.6
South Euclid city	4.65	22,288	21,297	-4.4	4580.0	5.9	90.3	61,078	14.8	100,200	65.8	5.8	59.9	32.3
Springboro city	9.33	17,366	18,931	9.0	2029.0	3.8	88.5	107,225	4.1	227,600	71.1	3.0	80.6	16.2
Springdale city	4.98	11,224	11,166	-0.5	2242.2	15.4	83.0	56,789	11.4	128,700	63.7	5.5	60.6	34.7
Springfield city	25.74	60,563	58,877	-2.8	2287.4	2.6	74.5	39,332	21.5	80,700	59.1	10.0	58.2	34.3
Steubenville city	10.54	18,659	17,753	-4.9	1684.3	3.0	81.6	38,600	27.0	90,300	51.6	8.5	50.0	40.8
Stow city	17.09	34,837	34,785	-0.1	2035.4	4.2	86.4	73,201	6.8	181,400	67.0	2.9	65.0	29.1
Streetsboro city	23.49	16,023	16,478	2.8	701.5	6.3	84.7	65,742	7.2	148,800	68.8	2.8	64.9	26.9
Strongsville city	24.62	44,750	44,660	-0.2	1814.0	10.3	87.0	88,176	4.2	206,300	66.5	4.5	69.5	25.5
Struthers city	3.64	10,715	10,111	-5.6	2777.7	0.6	89.3	39,315	16.1	70,800	62.2	7.5	64.7	30.2
Sylvania city	6.63	19,095	19,311	1.1	2912.7	5.2	86.8	76,923	8.5	178,800	63.6	5.0	65.7	28.8
Tallmadge city	14.04	17,545	17,519	-0.1	1247.8	2.9	89.1	75,622	7.0	172,900	60.9	4.1	68.6	27.6
Tiffin city	6.87	17,962	17,582	-2.1	2559.2	3.2	78.1	41,996	15.0	97,100	60.1	5.1	55.2	35.5
Toledo city	80.49	287,357	272,779	-5.1	3389.0	3.4	80.8	37,752	24.6	80,800	61.7	9.1	54.5	37.6
Trenton city	4.56	11,881	13,141	10.6	2881.8	0.9	81.2	77,739	8.4	136,900	70.1	5.6	77.3	18.9
Trotwood city	30.49	24,431	24,403	-0.1	800.4	1.5	82.6	36,778	21.9	72,400	58.2	9.8	58.9	35.2
Troy city	12.07	25,179	26,281	4.4	2177.4	3.5	85.2	54,161	13.7	139,200	65.4	7.0	57.8	33.9
Twinsburg city	13.76	18,510	18,856	1.9	1370.3	6.9	89.6	76,674	6.5	218,200	68.3	2.2	64.1	31.7
University Heights city	1.82	13,539	12,797	-5.5	7031.3	6.5	82.1	77,256	10.3	164,300	69.3	3.5	61.4	29.6
Upper Arlington city	9.79	33,666	35,366	5.0	3612.5	8.3	88.3	123,548	2.5	397,300	68.4	2.6	70.7	24.6
Urbana city	7.91	11,872	11,404	-3.9	1441.7	1.2	80.1	45,515	16.2	109,400	56.9	6.5	54.3	38.1
Vandalia city	12.35	15,256	14,997	-1.7	1214.3	3.4	83.9	58,277	7.0	143,200	68.6	2.7	58.1	35.2
Van Wert city	7.61	10,857	10,676	-1.7	1402.9	0.6	85.5	44,318	18.6	87,600	58.7	4.8	65.8	31.3
Vermilion city	10.64	10,587	10,394	-1.8	976.9	1.8	89.6	63,715	7.7	140,800	54.6	3.8	65.2	29.9
Wadsworth city	11.29	21,562	24,046	11.5	2129.8	1.1	85.8	71,478	6.9	171,200	66.6	3.5	65.2	29.0
Warren city	15.97	41,584	38,752	-6.8	2426.5	1.4	86.4	28,898	32.8	62,100	47.4	8.2	53.7	39.6
Warrensville Heights city	4.13	13,542	13,108	-3.2	3173.8	1.6	81.1	38,433	19.1	81,000	63.4	10.4	58.9	38.4
Washington Court House city	8.79	14,234	14,091	-1.0	1603.1	2.1	84.2	42,238	18.0	106,300	57.8	6.6	64.6	30.5
West Carrollton city	6.43	13,148	12,864	-2.2	2000.6	6.1	77.0	44,413	12.7	99,000	65.3	8.4	53.1	36.3
Westerville city	12.60	36,264	41,103	13.3	3262.1	6.7	87.6	93,717	6.8	237,300	67.2	3.0	73.4	23.0
Westlake city	15.93	32,729	32,032	-2.1	2010.8	9.6	88.3	86,008	5.3	258,600	63.3	3.4	60.4	33.6
Whitehall city	5.28	18,135	18,926	4.4	3584.5	15.6	77.7	42,526	20.5	88,900	69.6	7.5	61.0	32.8
White Oak CDP	6.22	19,167	NA	NA	NA	8.5	88.1	65,711	7.5	148,800	66.2	2.4	61.6	32.5
Wickliffe city	4.61	12,756	12,744	-0.1	2764.4	4.2	88.4	61,105	6.4	121,500	67.7	4.8	59.2	33.9
Willoughby city	10.25	22,242	22,977	3.3	2241.7	5.3	89.8	60,332	8.4	152,700	66.2	2.7	52.2	40.7
Willowick city	2.54	14,178	14,105	-0.5	5553.1	3.3	91.7	62,016	7.6	119,100	71.0	5.1	58.6	34.2
Wilmington city	10.89	12,517	12,366	-1.2	1135.5	2.4	81.7	35,833	18.9	108,500	60.7	7.8	56.3	39.8
Wooster city	17.05	26,177	26,394	0.8	1548.0	4.0	74.3	47,944	14.2	143,100	60.9	5.4	55.8	39.5
Worthington city	5.47	13,569	14,692	8.3	2685.9	4.9	89.2	104,362	3.4	285,300	65.4	2.4	71.6	23.6
Xenia city	13.02	25,643	26,947	5.1	2069.7	1.3	84.6	45,812	18.9	100,500	58.4	7.9	59.8	32.4
Youngstown city	33.93	66,946	65,469	-2.2	1929.5	2.0	81.6	28,822	32.2	44,800	53.1	14.3	51.9	42.1
Zanesville city	11.77	25,316	25,158	-0.6	2137.5	0.9	76.5	30,345	25.5	79,600	53.3	10.2	54.7	38.9

Table B. Incorporated Places, Census Designated Places (CDPs), and Minor Civil Divisions (MCDs) of 10,000 or More Population — **Crime, Residential Construction and Local Government Finance**

STATE City, town, township, borough, or CDP (county if applicable)	Serious crimes known to police, 2018[1] Violent crime Number	Rate[2]	Property crime Number	Rate[2]	New residential construction authorized by building permits, 2019 Value ($1,000)	Number of housing units	Percent single family	Local government finance, 2017 General revenue Total (mil dol)	Intergovernmental Total (mil dol)	Percent from state gov.	Taxes per capita[3]	General expenditure Total (mil dol)	Per capita[3] Total	Capital outlays	Debt outstanding (mil dol)
	15	16	17	18	19	20	21	22	23	24	25	26	27	28	29
OHIO—Con.															
Middleburg Heights city	NA	NA	NA	NA	575	3	100.0	31.2	1.2	100.0	1,595	27.7	1,778	246	37.0
Middletown city	NA	NA	NA	NA	11,845	66	100.0	63.3	13.1	43.5	587	57.9	1,184	289	204.9
Monfort Heights CDP	NA	NA	NA	NA	NA	NA	NA	NA	NA	NA	NA	NA	NA	NA	NA
Monroe city	15	92	407	2,495	10,830	65	100.0	23.1	5.2	100.0	869	20.5	1,499	96	2.0
Montgomery city	7	65	97	898	10,345	26	100.0	30.6	1.7	4.2	1,766	8.0	743	0	2.2
Mount Vernon city	20	120	510	3,071	1,180	8	50.0	23.1	4.2	37.3	707	17.6	1,057	236	22.8
New Albany city	2	18	82	733	20,539	47	100.0	51.0	7.0	100.0	2,966	42.3	3,927	1081	34.0
Newark city	152	306	2,166	4,359	NA	NA	NA	62.7	16.0	97.4	583	65.9	1,332	303	20.2
New Franklin city	4	28	120	848	NA	NA	NA	7.3	0.1	0.0	451	7.5	530	0	0.0
New Philadelphia city	7	40	212	1,215	2,381	16	50.0	28.5	7.0	93.7	681	31.0	1,774	110	0.2
Niles city	43	234	505	2,749	1,334	7	100.0	9.7	0.8	76.2	445	20.8	1,133	770	6.0
Northbrook CDP	NA	NA	NA	NA	NA	NA	NA	NA	NA	NA	NA	NA	NA	NA	NA
North Canton city	19	110	267	1,547	6,155	15	100.0	20.5	0.9	100.0	731	14.9	862	49	24.4
North Olmsted city	13	41	397	1,254	480	2	100.0	47.6	14.1	9.0	780	44.4	1,401	123	76.8
North Ridgeville city	9	27	97	285	96,000	312	100.0	35.6	3.1	100.0	546	42.0	1,258	318	18.1
North Royalton city	15	50	122	402	7,266	28	100.0	32.3	2.0	97.8	694	31.3	1,033	138	23.6
Norton city	11	92	215	1,791	NA	NA	NA	10.5	1.6	47.2	701	10.3	860	12	11.8
Norwalk city	14	83	311	1,851	713	6	66.7	12.3	0.9	65.4	84	9.6	568	17	9.3
Norwood city	55	275	738	3,694	0	0	0.0	28.5	1.3	50.0	975	16.8	843	0	85.1
Oregon city	31	156	630	3,162	7,311	33	87.9	54.3	21.4	21.3	1,231	49.7	2,487	969	32.4
Oxford city	23	100	463	2,010	3,362	20	50.0	23.4	2.0	52.0	511	22.2	971	68	2.0
Painesville city	NA	NA	NA	NA	2,875	22	100.0	23.6	3.1	76.8	535	27.9	1,405	378	4.5
Parma city	124	157	846	1,071	360	2	100.0	85.9	12.9	100.0	751	85.5	1,081	20	24.3
Parma Heights city	NA	NA	NA	NA	0	0	0.0	18.8	1.5	74.3	627	18.6	926	107	4.6
Pataskala city	NA	NA	NA	NA	NA	NA	NA	11.6	2.6	60.7	401	10.9	701	269	20.2
Perrysburg city	9	42	240	1,112	NA	NA	NA	38.6	1.8	98.3	1,128	30.8	1,436	284	37.8
Pickerington city	28	135	264	1,274	48,767	196	100.0	17.7	2.0	65.1	460	13.4	659	81	46.1
Piqua city	45	214	806	3,828	NA	NA	NA	31.4	6.0	95.6	733	25.9	1,234	196	0.0
Portsmouth city	118	576	1,021	4,987	0	0	0.0	13.1	3.8	93.3	174	0.0	0	0	4.5
Powell city	6	45	109	810	17,117	47	91.5	16.2	2.3	0.0	666	14.0	1,062	298	28.4
Ravenna city	NA	NA	NA	NA	175	1	100.0	20.1	3.5	100.0	942	18.4	1,606	262	0.0
Reading city	NA	NA	NA	NA	125	1	100.0	14.6	0.6	60.5	952	13.9	1,345	0	2.0
Reynoldsburg city	88	231	942	2,471	215	1	100.0	35.7	4.4	26.9	423	24.5	647	28	17.8
Richmond Heights city	37	355	179	1,719	1,738	11	100.0	12.9	1.2	100.0	933	10.5	1,013	43	4.6
Riverside city	25	100	287	1,144	NA	NA	NA	7.2	1.9	95.8	171	9.8	392	19	8.8
Rocky River city	3	15	65	321	12,285	31	22.6	43.7	9.2	100.0	1,145	41.3	2,044	342	10.4
Salem city	22	188	414	3,535	676	4	100.0	10.8	0.6	72.8	611	10.3	874	0	9.6
Sandusky city	71	287	920	3,725	1,716	6	100.0	40.6	6.0	72.8	897	28.7	1,156	26	14.4
Seven Hills city	3	26	52	446	2,416	21	100.0	13.5	0.7	48.1	854	12.7	1,093	37	16.7
Shaker Heights city	NA	NA	NA	NA	0	0	0.0	66.1	8.6	30.5	1,542	70.8	2,584	315	15.2
Sharonville city	NA	NA	NA	NA	565	3	100.0	37.3	3.7	91.6	2,155	28.0	2,043	230	30.4
Sidney city	54	263	688	3,350	1,702	5	100.0	38.1	5.8	73.0	1,033	32.1	1,560	435	46.4
Solon city	10	44	210	915	3,882	8	100.0	60.0	2.1	100.0	1,974	63.0	2,741	792	0.0
South Euclid city	31	144	518	2,405	250	1	100.0	27.9	3.6	71.6	840	23.7	1,100	371	19.3
Springboro city	4	21	101	538	16,892	91	54.9	27.7	1.3	100.0	845	26.8	1,441	566	28.6
Springdale city	NA	NA	NA	NA	5,928	30	100.0	20.0	1.0	11.5	1,516	20.2	1,797	328	11.1
Springfield city	336	569	3,141	5,322	3,123	16	62.5	66.0	14.9	78.9	602	86.8	1,467	267	43.3
Steubenville city	55	307	958	5,348	0	0	0.0	32.9	7.0	91.6	824	32.8	1,821	379	40.1
Stow city	26	75	510	1,467	6,343	47	31.9	42.8	7.7	98.7	749	38.4	1,104	197	6.8
Streetsboro city	10	61	215	1,310	20,586	131	100.0	19.0	2.3	91.8	891	7.2	441	0	0.8
Strongsville city	12	27	642	1,432	16,930	44	100.0	75.1	5.7	42.2	1,029	68.3	1,527	260	49.2
Struthers city	11	108	141	1,383	NA	NA	NA	11.0	3.4	100.0	474	13.2	1,292	534	0.0
Sylvania city	49	166	658	2,225	NA	NA	NA	23.4	2.4	100.0	743	22.8	1,191	17	23.6
Tallmadge city	20	114	290	1,652	NA	NA	NA	22.9	1.3	100.0	876	21.9	1,248	160	9.3
Tiffin city	2	11	458	2,618	10,163	57	1.8	21.9	3.5	100.0	607	14.8	845	86	9.5
Toledo city	2,333	848	10,222	3,717	2,203	21	76.2	499.8	101.1	92.9	777	480.1	1,735	249	422.8
Trenton city	NA	NA	NA	NA	4,824	35	94.3	6.8	0.4	100.0	219	7.1	551	16	6.8
Trotwood city	165	677	893	3,663	NA	NA	NA	24.1	2.6	82.4	538	23.6	966	157	12.9
Troy city	33	127	535	2,061	NA	NA	NA	43.5	1.6	63.6	910	36.2	1,399	177	9.8
Twinsburg city	12	63	109	574	3,629	65	15.4	47.4	2.8	100.0	1,698	32.9	1,763	166	7.1
University Heights city	21	162	217	1,672	0	0	0.0	18.5	3.3	79.0	1,003	19.6	1,507	362	23.2
Upper Arlington city	10	28	391	1,099	22,106	23	100.0	56.5	8.9	100.0	1,015	47.4	1,338	391	68.7
Urbana city	22	194	363	3,202	NA	NA	NA	14.5	1.7	40.6	657	13.8	1,212	122	32.1
Vandalia city	31	206	286	1,904	1,331	5	100.0	31.6	2.6	100.0	1,205	31.0	2,061	224	7.0
Van Wert city	30	282	319	3,001	1,652	8	100.0	15.0	1.9	100.0	856	14.1	1,318	222	0.0
Vermilion city	4	38	132	1,265	4,283	22	36.4	13.9	1.8	87.2	544	19.7	1,886	502	18.0
Wadsworth city	26	110	371	1,563	11,837	51	100.0	34.9	4.7	98.9	596	37.5	1,600	343	27.8
Warren city	245	624	1,500	3,819	0	0	0.0	56.2	7.5	59.2	479	52.2	1,324	124	30.6
Warrensville Heights city	NA	NA	NA	NA	240	1	100.0	23.4	1.5	13.3	1,594	20.0	1,510	24	0.0
Washington Court House city	23	162	489	3,441	9,174	74	28.4	14.2	1.3	74.2	600	10.5	746	62	16.7
West Carrollton city	36	279	261	2,024	92	1	100.0	13.1	0.9	100.0	605	13.1	1,013	157	9.1
Westerville city	46	114	717	1,783	34,901	159	32.1	99.2	11.1	54.2	1,694	135.1	3,392	1197	65.2
Westlake city	NA	NA	NA	NA	18,095	39	100.0	77.7	8.4	88.4	1,367	75.2	2,329	967	90.4
Whitehall city	119	626	1,074	5,646	211	2	100.0	33.2	2.6	62.4	1,357	33.2	1,751	323	9.3
White Oak CDP	NA	NA	NA	NA	NA	NA	NA	NA	NA	NA	NA	NA	NA	NA	NA
Wickliffe city	9	71	155	1,217	1,780	9	100.0	15.5	0.6	100.0	947	12.1	950	124	1.4
Willoughby city	30	131	385	1,678	14,606	75	100.0	37.9	3.3	88.9	976	36.8	1,608	250	33.8
Willowick city	NA	NA	NA	NA	NA	NA	NA	14.7	3.6	100.0	526	14.5	1,028	25	2.2
Wilmington city	17	137	703	5,676	1,858	11	100.0	16.2	1.3	61.8	618	13.9	1,121	6	13.9
Wooster city	87	326	797	2,986	4,562	23	47.8	170.2	5.0	93.2	850	181.4	6,808	293	17.2
Worthington city	NA	NA	NA	NA	3,636	37	13.5	34.0	1.1	52.7	1,952	31.2	2,122	218	6.0
Xenia city	71	266	789	2,956	NA	NA	NA	32.8	5.1	97.5	609	22.7	855	412	1.2
Youngstown city	428	666	2,285	3,555	NA	NA	NA	128.6	18.3	33.3	1,155	102.3	1,584	38	8.6
Zanesville city	120	473	946	3,729	1,631	3	100.0	35.8	6.3	100.0	780	35.7	1,415	104	4.0

1 Data for serious crimes have not been adjusted for underreporting. This may affect comparability between geographic areas over time.
2 Per 100,000 population estimated by the FBI. 3 Based on population estimated as of July 1 of the year shown.

Table B. Incorporated Places, Census Designated Places (CDPs), and Minor Civil Divisions (MCDs) of 10,000 or More Population — Land Area, Population, and Households, and Employment

STATE City, town, township, borough, or CDP (county if applicable)	Land area 2010 (sq mi)	Population Total persons 2010	Total persons 2019	Percent change 2010–2019	Persons per square mile 2019	Population characteristics 2015–2019 Percent foreign born	Percent living in the same house as previous year	Income and poverty 2015–2019 Median household income	Percent of households with income below poverty level	Median value of owner-occupied housing units	Employment, 2015–2019 Percent in civilian labor force	Unemployment rate	Households, 2015–2019 (percent of households) Family households	One person households
	1	2	3	4	5	6	7	8	9	10	11	12	13	14
OKLAHOMA	68595.95	3,751,582	3,956,971	5.5	57.7	6.0	83.2	52,919	15.0	136,800	60.6	5.1	65.9	28.3
Ada city	19.75	16,804	17,235	2.6	872.7	3.3	77.6	40,175	21.1	106,900	58.8	4.2	53.7	37.2
Altus city	18.37	19,756	18,338	-7.2	998.3	6.4	74.0	47,691	16.0	107,200	57.2	5.6	65.4	29.1
Ardmore city	49.93	24,469	24,698	0.9	494.7	4.9	79.3	47,860	17.4	107,400	59.4	6.4	59.7	35.2
Bartlesville city	22.84	35,734	36,144	1.1	1582.5	5.5	81.7	54,778	13.6	123,200	58.3	5.7	65.7	29.6
Bethany city	5.23	19,024	19,221	1.0	3675.1	6.8	81.1	50,867	11.9	119,900	64.1	5.0	61.7	33.4
Bixby city	24.87	20,912	27,944	33.6	1123.6	4.2	85.1	83,119	6.6	223,900	67.6	2.9	75.4	20.6
Broken Arrow city	61.78	98,837	110,198	11.5	1783.7	6.9	85.2	73,119	7.2	166,900	69.2	4.2	73.9	21.5
Chickasha city	22.03	16,030	16,431	2.5	745.8	3.6	82.5	42,175	19.3	85,900	55.1	3.2	61.5	32.8
Choctaw city	27.29	11,132	12,674	13.9	464.4	1.4	92.3	77,917	6.3	178,600	60.6	2.8	76.4	21.4
Claremore city	14.78	18,599	18,743	0.8	1268.1	2.5	77.6	46,295	15.3	124,200	60.5	5.2	62.0	32.1
Del City city	7.52	21,327	21,712	1.8	2887.2	3.5	80.3	46,485	14.5	84,200	62.6	5.6	62.0	32.9
Duncan city	42.91	23,418	22,344	-4.6	520.7	3.6	83.4	44,404	17.0	108,900	58.8	6.1	62.5	32.4
Durant city	26.70	15,858	18,673	17.8	699.4	4.0	75.5	38,603	23.4	123,300	58.2	6.1	56.7	35.7
Edmond city	84.70	81,130	94,054	15.9	1110.4	6.4	81.7	81,473	9.1	240,600	66.4	3.6	71.9	21.9
Elk City city	16.28	11,708	11,577	-1.1	711.1	4.7	80.1	47,850	18.4	155,600	59.8	3.9	65.7	27.8
El Reno city	79.24	16,748	19,965	19.2	252.0	4.7	83.6	48,060	14.9	109,700	60.4	7.4	65.0	30.5
Enid city	73.96	49,385	49,688	0.6	671.8	9.7	83.2	51,952	13.6	108,300	62.2	4.9	64.1	30.2
Glenpool city	11.00	10,867	13,936	28.2	1266.9	3.9	81.0	67,703	8.5	139,000	74.6	3.4	76.1	19.0
Guthrie city	18.77	10,206	11,661	14.3	621.3	0.5	82.0	41,739	14.3	125,400	52.8	3.8	61.6	33.6
Guymon city	7.78	11,449	10,996	-4.0	1413.4	37.4	79.3	53,164	16.9	124,900	75.5	2.5	69.2	24.3
Jenks city	17.15	16,938	23,767	40.3	1385.8	8.1	83.2	94,132	5.7	214,300	71.5	4.3	79.6	16.9
Lawton city	81.43	96,867	93,025	-4.0	1142.4	6.3	67.8	47,779	17.8	112,800	53.1	8.2	62.2	31.7
McAlester city	16.20	18,395	17,814	-3.2	1099.6	3.7	75.6	43,879	18.6	101,600	51.9	6.9	60.7	33.5
Miami city	10.84	13,606	13,088	-3.8	1207.4	2.9	79.9	36,908	21.9	80,200	56.2	5.4	61.6	32.8
Midwest City city	24.42	54,370	57,407	5.6	2350.8	2.9	81.6	49,914	13.8	113,400	62.2	5.5	60.6	33.3
Moore city	21.88	55,082	62,055	12.7	2836.2	4.7	84.0	65,915	9.3	139,300	70.9	4.4	69.5	23.3
Muskogee city	43.16	39,181	37,113	-5.3	859.9	4.0	79.2	38,194	24.9	92,300	54.9	7.3	64.9	31.4
Mustang city	11.98	17,395	22,959	32.0	1916.4	2.4	87.2	74,071	7.4	160,200	67.6	2.7	75.0	21.8
Norman city	178.83	110,911	124,880	12.6	698.3	7.5	74.5	58,119	16.7	183,200	64.4	4.5	58.8	29.1
Oklahoma City city	606.45	580,462	655,057	12.9	1080.2	11.8	80.8	55,557	14.8	158,500	66.1	4.3	61.7	31.1
Okmulgee city	17.09	12,497	11,711	-6.3	685.3	1.0	77.4	31,884	23.5	70,400	50.6	11.1	61.6	32.2
Owasso city	17.67	29,884	36,957	23.7	2091.5	4.4	79.6	72,443	6.4	172,700	70.5	3.3	69.8	24.4
Ponca City city	18.39	25,387	23,660	-6.8	1286.6	2.8	77.8	44,043	15.7	96,600	59.5	6.6	60.6	32.7
Sand Springs city	19.38	18,808	19,905	5.8	1027.1	2.0	86.9	58,153	9.1	127,800	62.1	3.2	71.5	24.8
Sapulpa city	23.54	20,195	21,278	5.4	903.9	3.2	86.5	51,655	16.3	118,700	58.4	2.7	67.7	28.2
Shawnee city	43.59	29,825	31,436	5.4	721.2	2.6	78.8	40,473	20.0	109,600	56.7	6.7	61.3	33.5
Stillwater city	29.54	45,721	50,299	10.0	1702.7	10.5	63.3	34,309	34.8	184,900	57.6	4.6	42.7	36.3
Tahlequah city	12.48	15,752	16,819	6.8	1347.7	5.9	75.9	37,177	24.6	124,600	54.9	7.8	52.0	40.9
Tulsa city	197.48	392,004	401,190	2.3	2031.5	11.2	79.5	47,650	17.5	139,900	65.5	6.3	57.3	35.1
Warr Acres city	2.80	9,895	10,118	2.3	3613.6	14.5	81.1	48,616	14.5	117,700	63.1	3.0	67.2	26.8
Weatherford city	6.76	10,833	12,017	10.9	1777.7	6.6	71.6	47,770	26.4	169,600	67.0	3.2	55.0	32.5
Woodward city	13.08	12,000	12,121	1.0	926.7	8.2	78.9	53,903	12.5	117,800	64.5	4.5	66.1	30.1
Yukon city	26.53	22,706	28,084	23.7	1058.6	4.1	88.3	66,419	7.4	143,100	69.8	4.4	74.8	22.9
OREGON	95988.00	3,831,079	4,217,737	10.1	43.9	9.9	82.9	62,818	12.6	312,200	62.3	5.5	63.1	27.5
Albany city	17.54	50,142	55,338	10.4	3155.0	5.6	81.1	60,624	11.8	226,200	63.2	6.4	63.5	27.5
Aloha CDP	7.35	49,425	NA	NA	NA	18.2	85.0	78,148	9.8	325,600	69.6	5.7	72.2	18.4
Altamont CDP	8.11	19,257	NA	NA	NA	6.3	84.3	46,930	20.4	157,500	52.4	7.9	65.1	27.0
Ashland city	6.64	20,076	21,281	6.0	3205.0	5.9	76.0	56,315	17.0	441,900	57.6	5.0	47.5	37.3
Beaverton city	19.58	89,725	99,037	10.4	5058.1	21.1	80.7	71,806	10.4	376,500	71.0	4.7	58.5	30.9
Bend city	33.10	76,660	100,421	31.0	3033.9	5.1	80.2	65,662	11.0	384,800	67.0	4.8	63.7	26.7
Bethany CDP	5.44	20,646	NA	NA	NA	36.5	85.7	135,800	4.6	557,300	68.2	5.9	80.2	15.9
Bull Mountain CDP	1.95	9,133	NA	NA	NA	13.5	87.4	120,523	1.7	478,100	71.9	2.5	84.8	12.7
Canby city	4.48	16,686	17,932	7.5	4002.7	10.3	85.2	73,038	7.8	329,700	65.2	3.9	73.3	22.1
Cedar Mill CDP	3.33	14,546	NA	NA	NA	19.0	86.5	145,057	3.9	598,500	68.9	4.1	77.9	18.9
Central Point city	3.93	17,269	18,848	9.1	4795.9	4.4	82.9	57,432	10.8	260,600	65.5	5.6	70.6	23.9
Coos Bay city	10.63	15,996	16,361	2.3	1539.1	4.1	81.9	48,919	15.7	181,200	58.5	9.0	57.3	35.2
Cornelius city	2.27	11,895	12,822	7.8	5648.5	29.3	85.2	67,207	5.5	263,000	70.1	3.3	74.7	17.2
Corvallis city	14.27	54,494	58,856	8.0	4124.5	12.5	65.9	52,942	23.5	330,500	59.6	6.0	49.0	30.3
Cottage Grove city	3.87	9,678	10,465	8.1	2704.1	4.1	81.2	47,752	19.2	192,600	57.4	8.7	59.8	30.2
Dallas city	4.91	14,582	16,979	16.4	3458.0	2.9	82.1	56,429	13.1	222,700	56.0	6.8	66.2	26.9
Damascus CDP	17.68	10,539	NA	NA	NA	11.0	84.8	93,963	4.5	434,200	61.7	5.8	83.0	13.9
Eugene city	44.14	156,431	172,622	10.4	3910.8	7.6	72.4	50,962	19.5	288,600	62.3	7.0	51.3	33.6
Forest Grove city	5.85	21,298	25,553	20.0	4368.0	9.6	81.8	64,172	11.5	319,200	65.9	5.0	64.1	27.8
Four Corners CDP	2.47	15,947	NA	NA	NA	20.9	87.2	52,995	13.4	174,900	65.0	5.2	68.2	25.1
Gladstone city	2.40	11,486	12,324	7.3	5135.0	4.7	80.1	64,045	9.5	302,200	65.9	6.1	63.8	29.1
Grants Pass city	11.52	35,927	38,170	6.2	3313.4	4.2	80.9	44,185	18.1	231,800	56.2	6.4	61.5	31.0
Gresham city	23.35	105,639	109,381	3.5	4684.4	16.4	85.5	54,084	14.2	287,900	65.4	6.2	65.3	26.6
Happy Valley city	11.37	15,251	22,553	47.9	1983.6	16.0	87.4	125,676	3.4	508,400	69.3	2.4	80.0	15.0
Hayesville CDP	3.03	19,936	NA	NA	NA	21.2	84.5	52,438	17.0	201,700	61.0	8.2	71.3	22.1
Hermiston city	8.18	16,729	17,782	6.3	2173.8	17.2	81.4	54,123	16.8	164,300	67.5	7.9	68.8	23.6
Hillsboro city	25.69	92,265	109,128	18.3	4247.9	20.6	80.2	82,275	8.0	342,500	70.5	4.7	67.7	23.3
Keizer city	7.15	36,434	39,713	9.0	5554.3	8.3	85.3	64,638	10.3	260,200	62.7	5.1	66.6	24.5
Klamath Falls city	20.04	20,993	21,753	3.6	1085.5	4.6	73.5	41,444	22.4	159,500	58.6	9.3	54.1	34.0
La Grande city	4.57	13,097	13,614	3.9	2979.0	3.7	73.6	42,375	19.8	170,500	62.0	7.9	59.9	26.9
Lake Oswego city	10.78	36,758	39,822	8.3	3694.1	11.2	85.8	108,927	4.4	637,200	63.1	3.9	67.4	27.9
Lebanon city	6.97	15,555	17,417	12.0	2498.9	3.8	78.1	45,642	17.3	177,900	59.5	7.7	64.4	30.0
McMinnville city	10.58	32,182	34,743	8.0	3283.8	10.9	82.6	54,254	13.4	247,400	58.7	3.7	62.5	29.8
Medford city	25.78	74,992	83,072	10.8	3222.3	7.3	79.7	50,116	16.5	265,400	61.3	5.8	61.6	29.5
Milwaukie city	4.90	20,522	20,990	2.3	4283.7	5.2	83.6	61,902	10.7	323,500	68.4	4.1	55.5	32.8
Monmouth city	2.17	9,535	10,586	11.0	4878.3	14.0	70.6	39,704	31.0	225,100	60.5	5.1	55.6	24.2
Newberg city	5.91	22,140	23,886	7.9	4041.6	9.3	81.9	64,202	15.4	320,400	65.5	4.0	67.9	24.5
Newport city	9.98	10,030	10,853	8.2	1087.5	10.0	79.6	49,039	15.1	258,000	53.2	5.7	55.1	37.0
Oak Grove CDP	3.90	16,629	NA	NA	NA	8.6	85.6	66,655	8.2	324,000	64.4	5.6	56.4	34.2

Table B. Incorporated Places, Census Designated Places (CDPs), and Minor Civil Divisions (MCDs) of 10,000 or More Population — **Crime, Residential Construction and Local Government Finance**

STATE City, town, township, borough, or CDP (county if applicable)	Serious crimes known to police, 2018[1] — Violent crime Number	Violent crime Rate[2]	Property crime Number	Property crime Rate[2]	New residential construction authorized by building permits, 2019 — Value ($1,000)	Number of housing units	Percent single family	Local government finance, 2017 — General revenue Total (mil dol)	Intergovernmental Total (mil dol)	Intergovernmental Percent from state gov.	Taxes per capita[3]	General expenditure Total (mil dol)	Per capita[3] Total	Per capita[3] Capital outlays	Debt outstanding (mil dol)
	15	16	17	18	19	20	21	22	23	24	25	26	27	28	29
OKLAHOMA	18,380	466	113,364	2,875	2,482,605	12,152	85.5	X	X	X	X	X	X	X	X
Ada city	84	485	640	3,691	1,780	18	44.4	25.1	2.6	49.3	1,015	33.6	1,944	690	39.8
Altus city	43	230	385	2,058	2,959	19	89.5	24.3	1.6	83.2	571	19.7	1,049	46	4.2
Ardmore city	159	641	1,083	4,364	4,517	30	100.0	46.0	6.3	28.8	1,186	38.4	1,549	192	40.4
Bartlesville city	103	282	1,213	3,326	2,535	16	100.0	44.2	2.0	69.8	698	45.2	1,242	286	86.5
Bethany city	49	252	577	2,967	3,726	17	100.0	15.1	0.2	25.3	329	15.0	776	0	23.6
Bixby city	34	123	419	1,515	48,032	186	100.0	23.4	0.7	92.5	599	17.2	645	120	20.7
Broken Arrow city	156	142	2,283	2,082	135,040	575	100.0	116.7	12.0	92.4	629	110.7	1,021	211	226.6
Chickasha city	63	386	436	2,673	2,476	10	100.0	21.3	0.4	32.9	817	20.8	1,277	256	8.2
Choctaw city	21	165	210	1,650	12,722	48	100.0	5.8	0.2	59.8	312	7.8	625	124	16.5
Claremore city	47	251	558	2,976	24,928	214	27.1	21.4	1.4	6.7	694	25.6	1,368	207	55.0
Del City city	172	787	1,062	4,858	697	5	100.0	19.0	0.6	85.6	570	20.7	950	188	10.7
Duncan city	39	175	692	3,096	1,307	8	100.0	28.4	7.6	99.4	497	26.9	1,197	63	39.8
Durant city	53	294	911	5,049	13,665	140	74.3	34.0	4.9	29.8	1,075	25.2	1,415	148	34.7
Edmond city	127	136	1,424	1,522	196,323	573	83.2	124.9	8.7	89.1	789	106.8	1,165	169	129.0
Elk City city	7	61	231	2,001	2,385	9	100.0	26.3	0.9	21.8	1,325	19.7	1,706	241	29.9
El Reno city	43	223	341	1,769	13,979	124	75.8	15.9	0.4	100.0	791	2.0	105	0	46.9
Enid city	173	345	1,428	2,844	6,412	26	100.0	71.4	2.5	51.3	784	65.2	1,300	182	65.6
Glenpool city	66	462	215	1,506	5,127	31	100.0	8.7	2.6	1.1	0	8.3	602	36	41.0
Guthrie city	39	339	339	2,943	2,137	11	100.0	14.4	1.7	54.5	664	15.4	1,346	284	21.4
Guymon city	11	95	121	1,048	195	1	100.0	17.7	1.5	36.2	761	18.3	1,587	128	27.0
Jenks city	26	111	307	1,308	46,276	183	100.0	24.1	0.4	51.9	548	23.0	1,023	250	46.5
Lawton city	840	902	3,338	3,584	8,674	37	100.0	109.7	12.3	64.3	617	127.3	1,354	402	124.2
McAlester city	115	639	1,031	5,728	1,667	8	100.0	119.1	3.6	46.9	916	113.2	6,264	227	56.7
Miami city	55	418	439	3,335	695	11	100.0	14.9	0.8	94.6	554	18.5	1,397	202	24.6
Midwest City city	180	312	1,795	3,110	21,989	152	93.4	57.8	4.7	14.7	253	63.2	1,106	114	76.5
Moore city	108	173	1,314	2,104	71,374	426	36.2	75.6	12.8	4.1	708	87.8	1,441	190	95.1
Muskogee city	377	1,001	1,536	4,079	1,993	11	100.0	53.5	6.5	37.9	809	55.7	1,475	370	66.9
Mustang city	30	138	231	1,059	42,419	225	88.0	19.1	0.3	51.9	564	18.2	856	155	29.4
Norman city	336	270	3,466	2,782	119,143	449	93.3	560.6	9.8	33.7	836	544.1	4,410	588	407.2
Oklahoma City city	5,663	867	26,298	4,028	705,270	3,371	96.2	1268.2	197.6	44.4	999	1026.0	1,596	398	1836.8
Okmulgee city	62	520	548	4,598	1,160	8	100.0	13.1	0.9	84.7	590	11.9	1,001	93	48.7
Owasso city	65	175	856	2,300	25,902	150	57.3	48.9	2.3	40.1	919	42.9	1,180	384	42.3
Ponca City city	169	702	951	3,952	512	2	100.0	33.4	0.8	62.2	695	45.5	1,887	52	23.7
Sand Springs city	19	95	683	3,406	10,896	56	82.1	31.4	2.8	45.5	749	27.2	1,369	427	54.9
Sapulpa city	42	201	529	2,525	19,519	149	35.6	27.7	2.7	59.5	755	25.8	1,217	112	87.6
Shawnee city	424	1,349	1,616	5,143	11,424	66	97.0	37.0	4.2	76.2	716	39.0	1,246	219	23.3
Stillwater city	168	333	959	1,901	22,479	128	54.7	55.4	2.2	63.3	656	43.3	866	132	94.3
Tahlequah city	23	136	685	4,059	10,907	107	62.6	114.1	3.2	7.4	425	115.0	6,872	160	72.3
Tulsa city	4,294	1,065	21,893	5,431	246,350	1,209	52.0	821.1	74.2	10.1	967	720.9	1,793	554	1412.1
Warr Acres city	43	415	386	3,722	660	4	100.0	10.1	0.7	85.9	675	9.9	979	108	0.5
Weatherford city	25	209	251	2,095	8,560	34	100.0	14.7	0.9	52.8	796	14.6	1,228	195	13.9
Woodward city	35	284	329	2,670	262	3	100.0	20.4	1.4	55.7	1,016	21.2	1,722	351	43.0
Yukon city	48	175	524	1,909	15,453	76	68.4	35.7	2.2	87.0	914	26.8	997	33	31.9
OREGON	11,966	286	121,278	2,894	4,447,105	22,037	52.6	X	X	X	X	X	X	X	X
Albany city	NA	NA	NA	NA	71,070	430	51.2	76.2	9.9	51.9	715	84.7	1,582	447	90.4
Aloha CDP	NA	NA	NA	NA	NA	NA	NA	NA	NA	NA	NA	NA	NA	NA	NA
Altamont CDP	NA	NA	NA	NA	NA	NA	NA	NA	NA	NA	NA	NA	NA	NA	NA
Ashland city	38	179	701	3,296	14,279	102	43.1	42.9	2.6	90.3	1,116	41.0	1,944	52	31.2
Beaverton city	189	192	2,039	2,068	78,653	392	44.9	108.9	19.8	56.1	572	90.6	926	69	8.4
Bend city	162	166	2,079	2,134	150,442	756	84.9	126.6	13.2	59.6	732	125.8	1,330	367	152.2
Bethany CDP	NA	NA	NA	NA	NA	NA	NA	NA	NA	NA	NA	NA	NA	NA	NA
Bull Mountain CDP	NA	NA	NA	NA	NA	NA	NA	NA	NA	NA	NA	NA	NA	NA	NA
Canby city	45	251	260	1,451	NA	NA	NA	26.2	3.7	62.7	610	27.1	1,522	296	29.2
Cedar Mill CDP	NA	NA	NA	NA	NA	NA	NA	NA	NA	NA	NA	NA	NA	NA	NA
Central Point city	35	190	462	2,511	20,379	151	17.9	14.4	2.3	100.0	423	12.3	670	59	9.6
Coos Bay city	46	282	775	4,742	3,817	17	88.2	20.9	3.8	44.5	642	30.7	1,890	857	25.6
Cornelius city	32	254	297	2,361	32,180	129	93.8	10.7	2.6	89.1	331	9.0	713	79	3.6
Corvallis city	94	161	1,835	3,137	76,926	416	22.1	83.7	13.3	50.5	681	78.3	1,337	137	41.0
Cottage Grove city	27	264	415	4,052	6,051	44	100.0	10.5	1.1	100.0	572	9.6	944	54	19.6
Dallas city	45	272	492	2,971	25,513	119	98.3	15.7	1.7	84.5	460	13.0	795	71	11.3
Damascus CDP	NA	NA	NA	NA	NA	NA	NA	6.0	1.4	55.4		4.4			0.0
Eugene city	661	387	5,503	3,222	113,463	640	48.8	313.9	42.6	46.5	848	284.7	1,681	228	307.6
Forest Grove city	42	171	435	1,771	26,334	96	87.5	26.1	1.9	100.0	435	29.1	1,203	18	123.8
Four Corners CDP	NA	NA	NA	NA	NA	NA	NA	NA	NA	NA	NA	NA	NA	NA	NA
Gladstone city	NA	NA	NA	NA	NA	NA	NA	10.6	1.7	55.0	522	10.4	847	114	2.0
Grants Pass city	135	357	1,342	3,549	22,595	114	70.2	41.1	5.0	73.1	674	46.1	1,223	315	7.9
Gresham city	472	422	3,823	3,420	125,991	817	25.1	132.1	36.2	30.6	534	129.8	1,167	140	80.5
Happy Valley city	NA	NA	NA	NA	105,250	425	60.9	16.3	4.7	34.1	463	11.1	517	39	0.0
Hayesville CDP	NA	NA	NA	NA	NA	NA	NA	NA	NA	NA	NA	NA	NA	NA	NA
Hermiston city	42	240	584	3,334	21,259	110	56.4	14.5	3.0	73.7	412	15.2	872	32	45.8
Hillsboro city	287	263	2,077	1,903	253,510	1,304	36.5	189.9	12.9	87.3	940	165.3	1,538	110	92.7
Keizer city	85	214	888	2,235	11,039	42	85.7	20.8	3.6	89.6	216	19.4	494	28	15.5
Klamath Falls city	91	409	744	3,345	NA	NA	NA	26.3	5.8	41.1	492	24.9	1,170	270	55.2
La Grande city	12	91	264	2,002	4,146	15	73.3	14.8	1.6	23.0	402	15.1	1,135	50	5.4
Lake Oswego city	20	51	530	1,340	39,314	80	81.3	98.4	19.2	18.5	1,210	88.0	2,239	446	183.1
Lebanon city	NA	NA	NA	NA	10,814	78	48.7	23.6	1.7	92.2	765	21.4	1,268	242	37.6
McMinnville city	84	242	1,064	3,069	52,740	290	54.1	41.8	5.1	66.4	556	49.2	1,441	365	33.9
Medford city	403	487	4,463	5,390	78,388	335	90.4	131.9	15.9	49.9	892	134.0	1,651	339	535.1
Milwaukie city	36	173	309	1,480	11,881	37	100.0	30.6	4.5	63.4	603	32.1	1,522	124	18.4
Monmouth city	13	124	144	1,377	3,666	18	44.4	10.4	2.1	99.8	290	9.2	888	165	21.7
Newberg city	42	155	394	1,453	23,633	100	80.0	31.2	4.0	76.9	651	28.5	1,216	185	42.1
Newport city	30	281	346	3,239	15,400	126	12.7	28.3	2.2	78.2	1,727	22.4	2,108	307	24.2
Oak Grove CDP	NA	NA	NA	NA	NA	NA	NA	NA	NA	NA	NA	NA	NA	NA	NA

1 Data for serious crimes have not been adjusted for underreporting. This may affect comparability between geographic areas over time.
2 Per 100,000 population estimated by the FBI. 3 Based on population estimated as of July 1 of the year shown.

Table B. Incorporated Places, Census Designated Places (CDPs), and Minor Civil Divisions (MCDs) of 10,000 or More Population — Land Area, Population, and Households, and Employment

STATE City, town, township, borough, or CDP (county if applicable)	Land area 2010 (sq mi)	Population Total persons 2010	Total persons 2019	Percent change 2010–2019	Persons per square mile 2019	Population characteristics 2015–2019 Percent foreign born	Percent living in the same house as previous year	Income and poverty 2015–2019 Median household income	Percent of households with income below poverty level	Median value of owner-occupied housing units	Employment, 2015–2019 Percent in civilian labor force	Unemploy-ment rate	Households, 2015–2019 (percent of households) Family households	One person households
	1	2	3	4	5	6	7	8	9	10	11	12	13	14
OREGON—Con.														
Oak Hills CDP........................	1.56	11,333	NA	NA	NA	21.1	87.8	96,323	8.4	452,400	66.6	1.9	77.0	18.2
Oatfield CDP........................	3.41	13,415	NA	NA	NA	8.2	86.1	85,995	6.5	366,400	57.9	5.7	74.0	22.1
Ontario city........................	5.17	11,371	10,994	-3.3	2126.5	11.0	79.7	36,922	26.0	117,800	57.8	8.8	59.7	35.1
Oregon City city................	9.88	32,623	37,339	14.5	3779.3	3.9	81.5	76,149	7.8	359,200	68.3	5.3	70.0	21.3
Pendleton city....................	11.72	16,622	16,789	1.0	1432.5	4.5	80.2	51,315	18.5	172,100	55.8	8.6	61.9	28.3
Portland city......................	133.42	583,793	654,741	12.2	4907.4	13.5	80.8	71,005	13.4	412,000	70.3	4.8	51.2	34.0
Prineville city....................	12.83	9,263	10,734	15.9	836.6	4.3	81.6	35,871	17.5	188,500	54.6	9.7	58.5	33.9
Redmond city......................	16.82	26,206	32,421	23.7	1927.5	4.7	77.5	65,088	12.7	258,300	68.0	6.0	66.0	25.4
Roseburg city....................	10.74	22,854	23,479	2.7	2186.1	4.1	78.6	44,970	12.4	195,400	55.3	6.3	52.4	37.7
St. Helens city....................	4.80	13,056	13,739	5.2	2862.3	3.3	82.2	51,199	15.9	228,500	61.9	6.2	64.0	25.0
Salem city........................	48.69	154,931	174,365	12.5	3581.1	11.5	81.6	55,920	13.6	242,800	61.6	5.8	63.2	29.0
Sandy city........................	3.47	9,602	11,387	18.6	3281.6	6.8	86.3	73,443	8.0	281,300	68.7	4.1	70.0	22.6
Sherwood city....................	4.45	18,288	19,879	8.7	4467.2	7.4	84.2	103,512	3.7	405,900	71.7	1.8	75.4	21.7
Silverton city....................	3.50	9,243	10,618	14.9	3033.7	3.4	85.4	64,296	8.2	296,400	59.9	7.5	69.2	26.5
Springfield city..................	15.84	59,413	63,230	6.4	3991.8	6.1	81.0	47,695	17.4	204,700	65.9	7.8	60.7	29.1
The Dalles city..................	6.66	14,950	15,761	5.4	2366.5	8.2	84.3	50,678	11.3	204,400	58.6	4.5	60.1	31.2
Tigard city........................	12.75	48,205	55,514	15.2	4354.0	14.5	85.4	79,809	9.1	408,400	70.5	3.7	64.0	25.9
Troutdale city....................	5.94	15,956	16,183	1.4	2724.4	11.1	86.5	76,598	8.5	309,600	74.0	4.3	74.6	16.6
Tualatin city......................	8.17	26,114	27,837	6.6	3407.2	9.9	86.0	85,772	7.6	419,400	71.7	3.6	65.6	27.9
West Linn city....................	7.41	25,118	26,736	6.4	3608.1	10.7	88.9	111,042	6.4	493,900	65.6	4.9	75.9	21.2
Wilsonville city................	7.28	19,509	24,918	27.7	3422.8	9.3	78.1	72,312	11.4	425,900	64.1	3.9	59.0	30.1
Woodburn city....................	5.84	24,118	26,273	8.9	4498.8	26.2	93.7	50,093	13.7	205,300	62.4	3.6	72.6	23.6
PENNSYLVANIA...............	44741.69	12,702,868	12,801,989	0.8	286.1	6.9	87.6	61,744	12.1	180,200	62.7	5.3	64.0	29.7
Abington township (Montgomery)	15.52	55,356	55,319	-0.1	3564.4	8.2	92.3	94,863	5.6	286,200	67.4	4.4	72.4	23.4
Adams township (Butler)	22.40	11,657	13,980	19.9	624.1	3.6	92.4	128,484	2.4	396,500	67.4	2.8	81.2	15.5
Allentown city & MCD (Lehigh).	17.55	118,095	121,442	2.8	6919.8	19.2	79.8	41,167	22.4	131,300	63.1	10.0	64.0	27.7
Allison Park CDP................	13.84	21,552	NA	NA	NA	6.6	89.3	83,594	5.3	235,600	64.9	4.0	67.0	28.9
Altoona city & MCD (Blair)........	9.79	45,963	43,364	-5.7	4429.4	0.9	86.1	41,403	22.5	88,500	57.2	4.9	60.9	32.5
Amity township (Berks)...........	18.08	12,584	13,172	4.7	728.5	2.3	91.5	102,547	5.7	252,900	67.2	1.3	76.1	20.6
Antrim township (Franklin)........	70.24	14,911	15,768	5.7	224.5	2.7	92.7	77,939	3.9	204,900	67.5	3.9	80.5	14.6
Ardmore CDP....................	1.97	12,455	NA	NA	NA	9.8	85.4	96,780	9.7	355,400	70.1	3.2	57.4	33.6
Aston township (Delaware).......	5.84	16,613	16,745	0.8	2867.3	4.8	91.1	91,188	4.9	246,800	66.7	5.0	70.1	26.5
Baldwin borough & MCD (Allegheny)	5.77	19,967	19,554	-2.1	3388.9	9.5	86.8	65,420	6.7	135,800	65.3	4.6	66.2	29.1
Bensalem township (Bucks)	19.86	60,420	60,507	0.1	3046.7	20.1	86.5	64,126	10.1	266,200	67.1	5.5	64.0	29.0
Berwick borough & MCD (Columbia)	3.08	10,481	9,903	-5.5	3215.3	2.0	91.7	40,227	22.8	106,400	61.5	6.3	58.1	33.3
Bethel Park municipality & MCD (Allegheny)................	11.67	32,294	32,345	0.2	2771.6	5.0	92.4	79,894	5.6	188,600	64.6	4.6	68.8	28.0
Bethlehem city (Lehigh)..........	19.12	74,972	75,815	1.1	3965.2	9.6	81.9	55,809	13.6	173,500	60.4	5.2	57.3	33.3
Bethlehem city (Lehigh)..........	4.30	19,343	19,923	3.0	4633.3	7.7	87.4	53,984	10.1	170,100	62.8	3.9	54.9	37.6
Bethlehem city (Northampton)..	14.82	55,629	55,892	0.5	3771.4	10.2	80.0	56,424	15.1	176,100	59.6	5.7	58.3	31.6
Bethlehem township (Northampton)................	14.42	23,795	24,341	2.3	1688.0	10.0	89.1	90,491	3.9	256,100	64.8	3.9	75.8	20.3
Bloomsburg town & MCD (Columbia)	4.35	14,863	13,811	-7.1	3174.9	2.5	73.4	32,217	29.0	136,000	45.5	6.7	41.9	44.3
Bristol township (Bucks)	15.88	54,556	53,473	-2.0	3367.3	8.7	90.1	65,384	10.7	207,500	69.0	5.8	67.3	26.4
Broomall CDP....................	2.89	10,789	NA	NA	NA	11.5	91.1	91,594	6.1	340,500	64.3	3.5	74.6	22.0
Buckingham township (Bucks)..	32.88	20,074	20,240	0.8	615.6	8.3	95.2	138,789	2.4	486,600	62.4	3.4	80.8	17.0
Butler city & MCD (Butler)........	2.72	13,754	12,885	-6.3	4737.1	1.6	81.9	31,361	27.8	100,200	57.3	8.1	51.0	40.0
Butler township (Butler)...........	21.62	17,248	16,469	-4.5	761.7	1.3	88.5	64,995	4.5	165,700	63.1	2.2	64.1	30.6
Caln township (Chester).........	8.86	13,810	14,275	3.4	1611.2	9.0	82.7	92,792	7.8	229,300	69.0	4.5	62.2	27.6
Carlisle borough & MCD (Cumberland)................	5.53	18,691	19,198	2.7	3471.6	6.9	73.8	48,612	13.0	187,800	61.9	5.4	53.8	39.2
Carnot-Moon CDP................	5.98	11,372	NA	NA	NA	11.7	78.3	72,744	6.4	198,100	69.0	4.8	53.8	35.4
Cecil township (Washington)	26.30	11,288	13,054	15.6	496.3	1.5	89.8	81,984	6.1	240,000	71.5	3.2	68.9	24.5
Center township (Beaver)	15.05	11,785	11,459	-2.8	761.4	2.6	87.3	80,982	6.4	175,200	61.1	5.8	71.8	23.4
Chambersburg borough & MCD (Franklin)	6.93	20,201	21,143	4.7	3050.9	12.2	86.6	49,023	12.3	154,700	61.3	4.7	56.2	37.4
Cheltenham township (Montgomery)	9.03	36,758	37,121	1.0	4110.9	12.2	87.6	85,217	9.2	278,400	66.3	4.7	62.5	31.4
Chester city & MCD (Delaware)	4.83	33,901	34,000	0.3	7039.3	4.5	82.4	32,403	28.8	72,400	53.7	12.1	57.5	34.7
Chestnuthill township (Monroe)	37.39	17,185	17,000	-1.1	454.7	5.0	90.7	72,705	5.6	171,500	65.0	7.4	75.0	19.8
Coal township (Northumberland)................	26.36	10,376	10,208	-1.6	387.3	1.3	83.3	37,352	18.4	69,900	37.4	11.4	61.1	34.5
Coatesville city & MCD (Chester)................	1.81	13,071	13,069	0.0	7220.4	13.2	84.8	45,265	22.4	123,500	67.9	8.8	64.1	28.8
College township (Centre)........	18.55	9,545	10,055	5.3	542.0	8.7	80.7	84,500	5.8	270,600	58.3	4.8	67.6	26.5
Colonial Park CDP................	4.76	13,229	NA	NA	NA	14.0	81.5	52,306	13.2	157,100	67.7	5.0	53.8	36.3
Columbia borough & MCD (Lancaster)................	2.41	10,391	10,355	-0.3	4296.7	3.5	82.1	41,475	17.8	107,900	60.1	6.6	58.4	36.6
Concord township (Delaware) ..	13.62	17,219	17,933	4.1	1316.7	13.0	77.7	110,592	2.9	446,800	48.0	3.9	67.5	30.9
Coolbaugh township (Monroe) .	86.10	20,550	20,599	0.2	239.2	15.8	92.8	58,033	13.8	128,900	62.6	9.3	72.3	21.7
Cranberry township (Butler)......	22.82	28,045	31,632	12.8	1386.2	7.0	86.6	106,024	3.3	303,900	71.5	3.1	71.4	23.0
Croydon CDP....................	2.48	9,950	NA	NA	NA	7.5	88.0	56,599	12.4	196,400	66.3	7.4	62.8	30.3
Cumru township (Berks)..........	20.91	15,302	15,493	1.2	740.9	5.9	88.5	75,007	5.9	187,500	64.4	4.3	60.2	31.8
Darby borough & MCD (Delaware)	0.84	10,692	10,702	0.1	12740.5	20.3	88.6	49,292	24.7	78,700	64.1	8.9	65.6	25.5
Derry township (Dauphin)........	27.13	24,679	25,249	2.3	930.7	12.1	80.1	80,575	6.7	251,000	68.8	2.5	63.5	29.2
Derry township (Westmoreland)	95.57	14,504	13,826	-4.7	144.7	0.9	91.9	56,403	8.3	136,100	57.4	4.8	67.1	26.2
Dingman township (Pike)..........	58.19	11,938	11,711	-1.9	201.3	7.2	92.8	93,171	4.5	226,300	66.1	7.2	74.7	18.6
Douglass township (Montgomery)	15.28	10,194	10,549	3.5	690.4	3.6	93.6	97,904	5.5	286,500	72.9	1.0	80.7	15.0

Table B. Incorporated Places, Census Designated Places (CDPs), and Minor Civil Divisions (MCDs) of 10,000 or More Population — Crime, Residential Construction and Local Government Finance

STATE City, town, township, borough, or CDP (county if applicable)	Serious crimes known to police, 2018[1] Violent crime Number	Violent crime Rate[2]	Property crime Number	Property crime Rate[2]	New residential construction authorized by building permits, 2019 Value ($1,000)	Number of housing units	Percent single family	Local government finance, 2017 General revenue Total (mil dol)	Intergovernmental Total (mil dol)	Percent from state gov.	Taxes per capita[3]	General expenditure Total (mil dol)	Per capita[3] Total	Per capita Capital outlays	Debt outstanding (mil dol)
	15	16	17	18	19	20	21	22	23	24	25	26	27	28	29
OREGON—Con.															
Oak Hills CDP	NA	NA	NA	NA	NA	NA	NA	NA	NA	NA	NA	NA	NA	NA	NA
Oatfield CDP	NA	NA	NA	NA	NA	NA	NA	NA	NA	NA	NA	NA	NA	NA	NA
Ontario city	56	511	577	5,266	210	1	100.0	17.5	1.5	83.1	575	22.7	2,071	36	7.1
Oregon City city	134	363	868	2,351	64,955	320	36.9	57.0	7.9	100.0	631	39.1	1,074	75	23.9
Pendleton city	44	264	451	2,704	4,412	18	88.9	24.9	4.9	74.1	609	26.4	1,578	382	40.8
Portland city	3,418	520	35,884	5,460	779,225	5,094	13.8	1734.3	204.2	41.5	1,371	1449.1	2,236	419	3150.5
Prineville city	43	422	371	3,643	70,793	289	65.7	20.1	5.9	41.1	517	19.9	1,980	881	22.1
Redmond city	73	239	1,106	3,615	134,422	768	47.0	59.0	12.1	51.4	644	67.1	2,236	894	80.6
Roseburg city	58	259	1,338	5,982	NA	NA	NA	28.0	2.7	80.1	932	30.5	1,317	279	7.1
St. Helens city	21	152	204	1,478	17,969	129	17.1	10.0	1.1	100.0	311	12.3	902	158	16.7
Salem city	719	418	7,170	4,168	189,804	1,034	41.8	313.6	73.5	61.1	751	285.2	1,682	224	416.0
Sandy city	NA	NA	NA	NA	16,138	59	96.6	13.2	2.2	68.7	600	14.0	1,252	401	11.7
Sherwood city	NA	NA	NA	NA	8,943	26	100.0	22.4	3.1	56.3	669	16.5	839	133	39.4
Silverton city	12	115	214	2,043	10,137	33	93.9	11.5	0.9	98.0	495	11.1	1,075	186	16.5
Springfield city	182	290	2,120	3,377	14,274	61	93.4	149.8	9.5	99.0	715	101.0	1,619	129	122.3
The Dalles city	33	210	466	2,961	NA	NA	NA	19.3	4.0	65.9	402	16.6	1,068	205	25.1
Tigard city	114	212	1,558	2,892	102,567	567	45.0	63.9	10.3	61.9	585	52.0	974	107	119.4
Troutdale city	NA	NA	NA	NA	14,784	165	3.0	15.1	2.0	79.1	302	12.3	745	61	6.1
Tualatin city	60	217	729	2,635	370	1	100.0	33.3	4.9	48.9	497	32.3	1,168	71	10.0
West Linn city	24	89	234	869	12,947	28	100.0	27.1	5.2	59.9	481	28.2	1,054	281	16.5
Wilsonville city	NA	NA	NA	NA	30,532	111	100.0	57.6	5.5	60.2	1,171	27.8	1,151	278	70.7
Woodburn city	111	426	962	3,696	3,950	17	88.2	29.0	2.8	95.8	590	19.6	760	21	36.9
PENNSYLVANIA	39,192	306	190,816	1,490	4,677,483	23,539	63.2	X	X	X	X	X	X	X	X
Abington township (Montgomery)	44	79	949	1,706	2,869	11	100.0	60.9	6.3	61.0	635	62.9	1,134	100	15.6
Adams township (Butler)	3	21	46	326	16,176	39	100.0	7.2	0.7	98.9	407	9.9	719	174	0.0
Allentown city & MCD (Lehigh)	412	338	2,821	2,317	0	0	0.0	149.9	31.8	50.9	584	182.3	1,506	101	97.4
Allison Park CDP	NA	NA	NA	NA	NA	NA	NA	NA	NA	NA	NA	NA	NA	NA	NA
Altoona city & MCD (Blair)	165	376	686	1,565	567	4	100.0	34.7	6.4	52.1	539	34.4	783	69	25.3
Amity township (Berks)	4	31	84	642	2,157	11	100.0	7.0	0.7	100.0	315	7.8	603	103	3.0
Antrim township (Franklin)	NA	NA	NA	NA	9,091	41	100.0	7.6	0.9	85.9	164	5.8	375	72	3.4
Ardmore CDP	NA	NA	NA	NA	NA	NA	NA	NA	NA	NA	NA	NA	NA	NA	NA
Aston township (Delaware)	6	36	164	982	191	2	100.0	12.2	1.7	95.5	540	11.2	671	19	3.9
Baldwin borough & MCD (Allegheny)	17	87	104	531	0	0	0.0	15.8	1.1	89.6	437	18.4	932	212	23.8
Bensalem township (Bucks)	70	116	1,292	2,132	21,022	80	100.0	44.8	16.8	94.7	340	45.5	753	19	47.3
Berwick borough & MCD (Columbia)	37	369	181	1,805	0	0	0.0	4.0	0.6	90.7	316	4.0	393	13	0.3
Bethel Park municipality & MCD (Allegheny)	11	34	282	870	1,199	3	100.0	32.3	3.2	57.4	555	36.7	1,136	170	20.2
Bethlehem city	207	273	1,281	1,690	4,722	34	11.8	96.8	23.1	92.4	566	97.3	1,288	0	195.1
Bethlehem city (Lehigh)	NA	NA	NA	NA	NA	NA	NA	0.0	0.0	0.0	0	0.0	0	0	0.0
Bethlehem city (Northampton)	NA	NA	NA	NA	NA	NA	NA	0.0	0.0	0.0	0	0.0	0	0	0.0
Bethlehem township (Northampton)	18	75	323	1,347	12,075	105	100.0	23.8	2.1	96.3	568	22.4	937	71	11.9
Bloomsburg town & MCD (Columbia)	35	247	194	1,372	671	4	50.0	8.2	2.5	62.6	272	11.9	854	206	1.2
Bristol township (Bucks)	95	177	973	1,813	1,253	14	100.0	40.1	4.5	62.7	425	38.9	726	77	36.0
Broomall CDP	NA	NA	NA	NA	NA	NA	NA	NA	NA	NA	NA	NA	NA	NA	NA
Buckingham township (Bucks)	1	5	70	345	12,530	38	92.1	19.2	1.2	95.2	500	12.1	596	86	12.2
Butler city & MCD (Butler)	40	307	347	2,666	0	0	0.0	8.9	1.6	60.3	454	12.6	964	303	8.2
Butler township (Butler)	25	151	431	2,606	3,356	17	100.0	8.1	1.2	100.0	383	8.9	533	64	2.7
Caln township (Chester)	39	272	272	1,900	750	1	100.0	11.4	2.4	35.7	407	13.5	949	251	6.2
Carlisle borough & MCD (Cumberland)	18	93	145	750	8,094	58	17.2	19.4	2.4	58.1	416	22.9	1,200	276	25.0
Carnot-Moon CDP	NA	NA	NA	NA	NA	NA	NA	NA	NA	NA	NA	NA	NA	NA	NA
Cecil township (Washington)	2	16	54	428	24,432	93	86.0	9.3	1.2	100.0	593	12.4	996	194	0.1
Center township (Beaver)	38	332	324	2,832	4,918	42	38.1	6.5	0.6	100.0	457	7.7	672	112	11.4
Chambersburg borough & MCD (Franklin)	60	286	577	2,753	2,740	14	50.0	40.3	3.3	70.7	430	47.0	2,250	672	27.1
Cheltenham township (Montgomery)	70	187	995	2,653	0	0	0.0	40.3	3.0	85.3	599	39.3	1,056	74	58.1
Chester city & MCD (Delaware)	474	1,391	1,151	3,377	1,200	8	50.0	56.7	9.9	87.5	653	55.4	1,633	14	6.7
Chestnuthill township (Monroe)	NA	NA	NA	NA	1,262	5	100.0	4.7	1.2	87.2	196	5.1	303	45	4.5
Coal township (Northumberland)	57	552	163	1,578	181	2	100.0	4.7	1.5	55.2	287	4.0	390	0	0.1
Coatesville city & MCD (Chester)	NA	NA	NA	NA	105	2	100.0	10.7	1.0	92.7	581	12.3	941	114	4.0
College township (Centre)	NA	NA	NA	NA	5,505	13	100.0	6.9	1.0	96.1	544	8.5	844	66	5.3
Colonial Park CDP	NA	NA	NA	NA	NA	NA	NA	NA	NA	NA	NA	NA	NA	NA	NA
Columbia borough & MCD (Lancaster)	19	182	176	1,687	0	0	0.0	5.9	0.7	86.4	401	7.4	710	0	9.8
Concord township (Delaware)	NA	NA	NA	NA	2,114	8	100.0	12.3	0.9	98.8	273	10.8	608	123	13.9
Coolbaugh township (Monroe)	NA	NA	NA	NA	4,868	19	100.0	8.4	1.0	100.0	337	7.2	354	39	3.3
Cranberry township (Butler)	8	26	302	969	79,522	220	100.0	39.8	2.4	91.0	601	44.0	1,434	294	79.5
Croydon CDP	NA	NA	NA	NA	NA	NA	NA	NA	NA	NA	NA	NA	NA	NA	NA
Cumru township (Berks)	13	85	170	1,105	3,060	21	23.8	16.9	1.2	95.6	580	13.8	898	58	2.7
Darby borough & MCD (Delaware)	149	1,392	346	3,233	0	0	0.0	9.3	0.9	89.2	510	10.1	943	12	1.8
Derry township (Dauphin)	40	159	379	1,508	7,377	32	53.1	30.1	12.0	97.3	591	39.9	1,590	448	32.2
Derry township (Westmoreland)	NA	NA	NA	NA	266	1	100.0	3.7	1.2	99.2	159	3.4	243	6	0.0
Dingman township (Pike)	NA	NA	NA	NA	5,776	19	100.0	2.2	0.4	100.0	143	1.9	165	6	0.2
Douglass township (Montgomery)	8	75	50	470	2,226	17	100.0	5.0	0.8	94.9	318	4.9	465	14	0.0

1 Data for serious crimes have not been adjusted for underreporting. This may affect comparability between geographic areas over time.
2 Per 100,000 population estimated by the FBI.   3 Based on population estimated as of July 1 of the year shown.

Table B. Incorporated Places, Census Designated Places (CDPs), and Minor Civil Divisions (MCDs) of 10,000 or More Population — Land Area, Population, and Households, and Employment

STATE City, town, township, borough, or CDP (county if applicable)	Land area 2010 (sq mi)	Population — Total persons 2010	Total persons 2019	Percent change 2010-2019	Persons per square mile 2019	Population characteristics 2015–2019 — Percent foreign born	Percent living in the same house as previous year	Income and poverty 2015–2019 — Median household income	Percent of households with income below poverty level	Median value of owner-occupied housing units	Employment, 2015–2019 — Percent in civilian labor force	Unemploy-ment rate	Households, 2015–2019 (percent of households) — Family households	One person households
	1	2	3	4	5	6	7	8	9	10	11	12	13	14
PENNSYLVANIA—Con.														
Dover township (York)..............	41.55	21,088	21,894	3.8	526.9	1.8	87.9	61,865	6.2	154,100	67.4	2.7	69.3	25.6
Doylestown township (Bucks)...	15.44	17,669	17,398	-1.5	1126.8	5.5	87.9	115,237	4.4	467,100	56.9	2.9	69.9	25.6
Drexel Hill CDP........................	3.20	28,043	NA	NA	NA	8.5	87.0	71,326	8.2	182,200	71.3	4.1	64.3	31.4
Dunmore borough & MCD (Lackawanna)	8.92	14,057	12,954	-7.8	1452.2	5.3	85.4	59,806	10.6	160,900	63.4	4.5	55.0	35.9
East Cocalico township (Lancaster)..........................	20.43	10,321	10,674	3.4	522.5	7.1	96.6	76,607	7.0	197,700	68.1	3.6	72.5	20.7
East Goshen township (Chester)...........................	10.05	17,998	18,149	0.8	1805.9	7.3	87.4	86,358	4.0	427,200	58.4	3.6	62.1	34.2
East Hempfield township (Lancaster)..........................	21.07	23,533	24,701	5.0	1172.3	5.3	87.3	77,961	6.3	254,200	63.8	2.7	68.8	24.8
East Lampeter township (Lancaster)..........................	19.66	16,453	17,039	3.6	866.7	10.7	83.4	62,288	12.0	234,900	67.8	5.8	66.5	25.6
East Norriton township (Montgomery).....................	6.06	13,604	13,974	2.7	2305.9	8.8	88.8	80,686	4.7	264,800	62.2	4.6	62.6	28.8
Easton city & MCD (Northampton)....................	4.26	26,814	27,189	1.4	6382.4	11.5	76.9	51,698	14.8	124,800	58.1	4.9	63.2	29.4
East Pennsboro township (Cumberland)......................	10.54	20,566	21,458	4.3	2035.9	7.3	90.2	64,879	8.1	185,900	67.4	2.9	63.1	31.9
East Stroudsburg borough & MCD (Monroe)	2.84	9,862	10,433	5.8	3673.6	8.7	71.9	51,016	16.5	146,800	59.0	10.9	59.5	34.1
Easttown township (Chester)....	8.23	10,462	10,634	1.6	1292.1	9.9	92.7	153,343	3.5	681,700	64.4	4.4	76.3	19.4
East Whiteland township (Chester)..........................	10.93	10,637	12,832	20.6	1174.0	19.5	86.3	114,486	2.7	415,200	74.2	2.1	69.2	23.0
Elizabeth township (Allegheny)	22.84	13,276	12,952	-2.4	567.1	1.4	95.0	65,810	6.2	128,100	62.1	3.8	69.8	25.9
Elizabethtown borough & MCD (Lancaster)........................	2.65	11,514	11,445	-0.6	4318.9	4.4	84.9	62,219	9.0	180,000	63.7	3.7	68.0	26.9
Emmaus borough & MCD (Lehigh)............................	2.90	11,188	11,467	2.5	3954.1	4.5	88.5	59,026	7.5	184,900	68.3	3.5	63.9	29.3
Ephrata borough & MCD (Lancaster)........................	3.42	13,344	13,862	3.9	4053.2	5.5	88.1	51,954	10.8	155,400	68.7	4.3	65.5	29.6
Ephrata township (Lancaster)...	16.24	9,443	10,453	10.7	643.7	3.6	85.1	64,848	7.5	216,200	65.7	2.9	73.4	21.0
Erie city & MCD (Erie)	19.14	101,738	95,508	-6.1	4990.0	7.3	80.3	37,894	23.8	89,100	59.0	7.9	54.5	35.9
Exeter township (Berks)	24.22	25,340	25,772	1.7	1064.1	4.5	90.5	82,889	5.0	191,600	67.3	4.2	75.1	20.5
Fairview township (Erie)	28.88	10,100	10,037	-0.6	347.5	1.6	89.8	94,892	5.2	216,400	58.1	1.4	77.4	21.3
Fairview township (York)..........	35.58	16,677	17,607	5.6	494.9	3.3	88.9	80,683	4.5	222,700	66.5	3.2	73.3	21.0
Falls township (Bucks).............	21.33	34,024	33,520	-1.5	1571.5	10.4	92.4	75,316	9.4	241,100	72.2	5.2	70.8	23.6
Ferguson township (Centre).....	47.70	17,867	19,462	8.9	408.0	17.9	80.1	74,560	16.1	290,300	62.9	2.8	57.8	27.1
Forks township (Northampton) .	12.10	14,719	15,769	7.1	1303.2	7.5	93.5	97,370	3.5	269,700	66.0	4.2	76.3	20.7
Franconia township (Montgomery)	13.88	13,079	13,369	2.2	963.2	6.3	94.2	93,710	4.7	329,600	65.2	3.6	77.1	19.5
Franklin Park borough & MCD (Allegheny).....................	13.52	13,490	14,885	10.3	1101.0	11.0	91.2	134,688	3.8	350,200	69.2	3.9	79.6	19.3
Fullerton CDP...........................	3.67	14,925	NA	NA	NA	21.0	82.2	59,368	9.0	177,900	71.0	4.9	65.4	27.1
Greene township (Franklin)	57.30	16,743	17,898	6.9	312.4	4.6	88.2	70,678	7.0	188,400	61.6	7.2	72.5	24.1
Greensburg city & MCD (Westmoreland)	4.06	14,897	14,113	-5.3	3476.1	2.3	87.3	42,058	21.2	134,000	58.4	4.2	47.3	44.3
Guilford township (Franklin).....	51.02	14,560	14,866	2.1	291.4	3.9	88.4	74,117	7.2	205,100	57.2	4.0	70.5	25.6
Hamilton township (Franklin)	35.54	10,777	11,125	3.2	313.0	4.0	88.9	68,731	8.0	199,200	72.1	5.2	77.9	19.3
Hampden township (Cumberland)......................	17.26	27,703	30,692	10.8	1778.2	12.5	88.7	94,617	4.5	271,600	68.7	2.9	67.6	27.3
Hampton township (Allegheny).	16.20	18,349	18,181	-0.9	1122.3	4.8	90.7	91,651	4.6	248,300	65.6	3.5	70.9	25.9
Hanover township (Luzerne).....	18.87	11,052	10,824	-2.1	573.6	2.2	90.6	49,360	18.1	92,000	63.3	6.4	60.1	35.9
Hanover township (Northampton).....................	6.55	10,883	11,538	6.0	1761.5	11.9	89.8	92,629	4.3	299,400	57.9	1.4	68.8	29.0
Hanover borough & MCD (York)...............................	3.70	15,280	15,719	2.9	4248.4	3.7	82.6	51,909	11.8	155,300	65.5	4.4	57.4	36.4
Harborcreek township (Erie).....	34.09	17,235	17,091	-0.8	501.3	3.8	84.8	62,855	8.2	165,900	55.1	4.5	68.9	26.6
Harrisburg city & MCD (Dauphin).......................	8.12	49,529	49,271	-0.5	6067.9	10.1	74.1	39,685	22.2	80,800	67.1	8.6	51.7	39.9
Harrison township (Allegheny)..	7.36	10,459	10,236	-2.1	1390.8	2.2	84.9	54,250	14.4	105,300	61.2	5.4	64.4	31.7
Hatfield township (Montgomery)	9.94	17,249	17,850	3.5	1795.8	17.2	91.3	84,781	5.7	302,100	67.3	3.0	68.3	25.2
Haverford township (Delaware)	9.95	48,509	49,526	2.1	4977.5	7.5	92.0	111,287	4.0	337,600	68.8	4.7	74.0	22.4
Hazleton city & MCD (Luzerne)	6.01	25,425	24,794	-2.5	4125.5	32.6	82.0	40,467	21.5	97,900	65.0	8.2	66.3	29.1
Hempfield township (Westmoreland)	76.73	43,249	40,463	-6.4	527.3	1.8	92.3	65,132	8.7	172,800	57.7	3.8	64.1	30.3
Hermitage city & MCD (Mercer)	29.46	16,419	15,471	-5.8	525.2	2.0	89.1	56,026	7.1	149,000	60.2	4.4	60.7	33.2
Hershey CDP............................	14.31	14,257	NA	NA	NA	13.9	75.6	69,688	8.6	272,100	69.0	2.5	59.2	32.0
Hilltown township (Bucks)........	26.97	15,040	15,822	5.2	586.7	6.4	89.9	98,538	3.2	340,000	71.1	3.5	78.5	19.8
Hopewell township (Beaver)	16.75	12,602	12,585	-0.1	751.3	1.8	88.8	67,109	8.3	138,400	64.6	4.1	63.0	30.8
Horsham CDP...........................	5.47	14,842	NA	NA	NA	11.0	91.0	82,098	3.0	288,100	74.6	3.2	65.7	30.6
Horsham township (Montgomery)	17.32	26,131	26,485	1.4	1529.2	10.9	88.2	97,663	2.8	349,300	73.6	3.4	69.5	25.3
Indiana borough & MCD (Indiana)..........................	1.76	13,969	13,167	-5.7	7481.3	4.9	44.7	30,647	38.1	113,900	52.7	10.0	37.3	30.7
Jefferson Hills borough & MCD (Allegheny).....................	16.55	10,620	11,101	4.5	670.8	2.9	95.3	93,140	3.5	228,600	66.2	2.3	72.2	23.9
Johnstown city & MCD (Cambria).........................	5.89	20,988	19,195	-8.5	3258.9	1.1	83.9	24,561	34.6	38,100	48.9	13.9	50.6	44.0
King of Prussia CDP................	8.49	19,936	NA	NA	NA	24.4	85.6	90,136	4.3	320,800	69.5	3.7	58.1	34.5
Kingston borough & MCD (Luzerne)........................	2.13	13,160	12,812	-2.6	6015.0	3.8	85.1	51,554	14.4	130,800	63.4	5.4	49.4	42.4
Lancaster city & MCD (Lancaster)........................	7.23	59,263	59,265	0.0	8197.1	11.3	79.0	45,514	21.4	114,600	67.3	7.2	58.8	30.7
Lancaster township (Lancaster)	5.86	16,179	17,156	6.0	2927.6	8.9	87.1	58,716	10.4	178,200	65.1	3.2	63.0	29.0

Table B. Incorporated Places, Census Designated Places (CDPs), and Minor Civil Divisions (MCDs) of 10,000 or More Population — Crime, Residential Construction and Local Government Finance

STATE City, town, township, borough, or CDP (county if applicable)	Serious crimes known to police, 2018[1] Violent crime Number	Rate[2]	Property crime Number	Rate[2]	New residential construction authorized by building permits, 2019 Value ($1,000)	Number of housing units	Percent single family	Local government finance, 2017 General revenue Total (mil dol)	Intergovernmental Total (mil dol)	Percent from state gov.	Taxes per capita[3]	General expenditure Total (mil dol)	Per capita[3] Total	Capital outlays	Debt outstanding (mil dol)
	15	16	17	18	19	20	21	22	23	24	25	26	27	28	29
PENNSYLVANIA—Con.															
Dover township (York)...............	NA	NA	NA	NA	22,748	215	33.0	12.2	2.4	61.6	236	11.0	509	40	3.1
Doylestown township (Bucks)...	15	86	141	809	1,747	8	100.0	12.3	2.0	74.2	500	11.6	666	99	0.4
Drexel Hill CDP.......................	NA	NA	NA	NA	NA	NA	NA	NA	NA	NA	NA	NA	NA	NA	NA
Dunmore borough & MCD (Lackawanna).......................	23	178	169	1,307	160	4	0.0	10.2	2.9	100.0	500	12.0	918	128	20.9
East Cocalico township (Lancaster)............................	8	76	63	596	10,300	68	88.2	5.4	1.3	64.2	343	5.4	509	23	2.3
East Goshen township (Chester).............................	NA	NA	NA	NA	175	1	100.0	16.0	1.4	99.9	473	15.4	846	94	3.2
East Hempfield township (Lancaster)............................	32	130	244	988	20,863	69	100.0	14.7	2.1	81.8	370	14.9	609	87	1.3
East Lampeter township (Lancaster)............................	9	53	457	2,667	4,227	20	90.0	15.9	3.1	33.7	419	12.8	753	50	6.4
East Norriton township (Montgomery).......................	43	305	267	1,896	0	0	0.0	14.2	1.6	74.1	615	12.1	863	16	1.4
Easton city & MCD (Northampton).......................	69	254	388	1,429	452	4	100.0	54.0	9.3	57.4	705	52.9	1,951	80	47.7
East Pennsboro township (Cumberland).......................	11	51	113	520	1,870	7	100.0	18.1	2.1	97.8	326	15.5	724	33	26.3
East Stroudsburg borough & MCD (Monroe)	NA	NA	NA	NA	0	0	0.0	7.2	0.6	76.9	351	8.3	805	104	4.7
Easttown township (Chester)....	17	159	56	525	4,147	11	100.0	12.6	0.9	94.5	616	11.9	1,117	19	4.8
East Whiteland township (Chester).............................	3	25	107	885	17,196	141	100.0	17.5	0.9	89.5	909	18.5	1,560	222	26.8
Elizabeth township (Allegheny)	NA	NA	NA	NA	1,057	4	100.0	9.9	0.7	96.0	340	10.0	761	31	29.7
Elizabethtown borough & MCD (Lancaster)............................	21	181	88	759	12,161	93	5.4	10.0	0.9	89.4	379	9.3	810	135	4.4
Emmaus borough & MCD (Lehigh).............................	7	61	164	1,427	877	7	100.0	11.4	0.8	83.9	566	10.7	936	46	5.5
Ephrata borough & MCD (Lancaster)............................	23	165	175	1,254	474	5	60.0	17.2	1.0	95.8	272	20.6	1,491	122	12.4
Ephrata township (Lancaster)...	10	96	155	1,481	6,565	33	100.0	3.4	0.5	89.8	247	3.4	326	26	0.0
Erie city & MCD (Erie)	299	309	1,880	1,943	845	3	100.0	120.0	23.3	35.3	554	108.3	1,114	65	178.4
Exeter township (Berks)	24	93	247	952	1,152	9	100.0	20.0	1.7	99.8	388	17.7	690	26	44.1
Fairview township (Erie)	NA	NA	NA	NA	7,781	28	85.7	3.8	0.6	96.5	299	4.5	443	35	0.0
Fairview township (York)..........	39	222	137	780	8,526	28	100.0	7.6	1.1	99.5	323	9.5	547	40	0.0
Falls township (Bucks)..............	42	124	448	1,323	3,126	31	51.6	24.3	1.9	95.6	132	23.3	695	49	0.0
Ferguson township (Centre)	8	41	88	450	39,547	162	69.1	13.5	1.6	93.9	564	13.1	674	132	0.6
Forks township (Northampton) .	8	52	98	630	20,133	122	100.0	15.2	1.0	92.2	496	14.9	963	144	7.7
Franconia township (Montgomery).......................	3	23	47	352	8,145	52	100.0	8.1	0.9	89.4	429	5.9	443	5	7.6
Franklin Park borough & MCD (Allegheny).......................	3	20	43	292	16,632	38	100.0	9.4	0.8	100.0	484	10.5	722	139	4.9
Fullerton CDP.........................	NA	NA	NA	NA	NA	NA	NA	NA	NA	NA	NA	NA	NA	NA	NA
Greene township (Franklin)	NA	NA	NA	NA	8,564	53	100.0	5.6	1.0	100.0	148	5.4	307	66	0.0
Greensburg city & MCD (Westmoreland)	58	408	292	2,054	78	1	100.0	15.7	3.9	98.7	565	13.9	970	100	6.8
Guilford township (Franklin)......	NA	NA	NA	NA	7,912	29	100.0	3.4	0.9	100.0	142	2.8	188	5	0.0
Hamilton township (Franklin)	NA	NA	NA	NA	5,237	24	100.0	2.0	0.5	95.3	130	2.3	206	20	18.0
Hampden township (Cumberland).......................	10	33	156	513	68,589	446	23.3	30.8	1.9	95.3	349	33.9	1,129	68	55.5
Hampton township (Allegheny).	14	76	67	366	9,342	28	100.0	15.6	1.2	99.0	542	14.7	802	54	15.3
Hanover township (Luzerne).....	49	313	437	2,792	938	5	100.0	8.5	1.2	100.0	618	9.6	888	173	2.1
Hanover township (Northampton).......................	41	378	205	1,891	0	0	0.0	11.4	0.7	100.0	572	11.3	980	164	1.8
Hanover borough & MCD (York)............................	NA	NA	NA	NA	8,259	62	6.5	22.5	1.9	73.8	527	21.8	1,397	35	51.1
Harborcreek township (Erie).....	NA	NA	NA	NA	2,779	12	100.0	5.0	0.9	95.4	206	6.3	363	71	0.2
Harrisburg city & MCD (Dauphin)............................	531	1,080	1,252	2,548	5,676	42	0.0	89.4	19.2	54.3	909	139.6	2,838	1046	98.9
Harrison township (Allegheny)..	NA	NA	NA	NA	794	3	100.0	6.1	0.6	98.6	385	5.8	557	55	2.0
Hatfield township (Montgomery).......................	22	105	194	922	7,398	28	100.0	13.1	1.1	86.2	509	11.4	646	33	5.0
Haverford township (Delaware)	24	49	563	1,139	1,183	5	100.0	48.8	4.2	81.8	602	55.1	1,118	150	51.8
Hazleton city & MCD (Luzerne)	117	475	229	930	1,319	46	2.2	22.2	7.4	92.0	522	13.3	535	11	8.4
Hempfield township (Westmoreland)	NA	NA	NA	NA	22,479	189	12.2	13.6	2.2	100.0	251	14.3	349	27	8.4
Hermitage city & MCD (Mercer)	19	122	497	3,200	18,089	68	100.0	20.7	1.7	74.6	671	17.4	1,110	97	12.5
Hershey CDP	NA	NA	NA	NA	NA	NA	NA	NA	NA	NA	NA	NA	NA	NA	NA
Hilltown township (Bucks).........	10	65	156	1,009	27,824	105	100.0	8.4	1.0	93.0	372	7.6	493	52	1.0
Hopewell township (Beaver).....	22	173	98	771	6,665	33	100.0	9.5	0.8	100.0	370	7.3	575	13	8.7
Horsham CDP	NA	NA	NA	NA	NA	NA	NA	NA	NA	NA	NA	NA	NA	NA	NA
Horsham township (Montgomery).......................	7	26	190	714	5,105	25	100.0	18.3	1.7	99.4	548	16.6	625	35	5.7
Indiana borough & MCD (Indiana)............................	117	897	140	1,074	0	0	0.0	12.4	2.0	85.2	258	14.5	1,106	149	9.8
Jefferson Hills borough & MCD (Allegheny).......................	20	177	60	531	11,142	49	100.0	12.5	0.9	79.7	664	13.1	1,167	86	5.8
Johnstown city & MCD (Cambria)............................	240	1,150	620	2,970	0	0	0.0	33.2	13.8	84.5	550	48.2	2,452	1620	12.5
King of Prussia CDP................	NA	NA	NA	NA	NA	NA	NA	NA	NA	NA	NA	NA	NA	NA	NA
Kingston borough & MCD (Luzerne)............................	23	179	201	1,566	0	0	0.0	9.4	1.2	96.0	514	10.8	838	131	11.1
Lancaster city & MCD (Lancaster)............................	419	701	1,580	2,644	200	1	100.0	94.4	10.8	67.2	638	133.5	2,244	382	258.7
Lancaster township (Lancaster)	36	208	319	1,847	2,740	19	100.0	5.4	0.6	100.0	200	5.5	323	10	0.0

1 Data for serious crimes have not been adjusted for underreporting. This may affect comparability between geographic areas over time.
2 Per 100,000 population estimated by the FBI.   3 Based on population estimated as of July 1 of the year shown.

Table B. Incorporated Places, Census Designated Places (CDPs), and Minor Civil Divisions (MCDs) of 10,000 or More Population — **Land Area, Population, and Households, and Employment**

STATE City, town, township, borough, or CDP (county if applicable)	Land area 2010 (sq mi)	Population — Total persons 2010	Total persons 2019	Percent change 2010–2019	Persons per square mile 2019	Population characteristics 2015–2019 — Percent foreign born	Percent living in the same house as previous year	Income and poverty 2015–2019 — Median household income	Percent of households with income below poverty level	Median value of owner-occupied housing units	Employment, 2015–2019 — Percent in civilian labor force	Unemployment rate	Households, 2015–2019 (percent of households) — Family households	One person households
	1	2	3	4	5	6	7	8	9	10	11	12	13	14
PENNSYLVANIA—Con.														
Lansdale borough & MCD (Montgomery)	2.99	16,282	17,083	4.9	5713.4	19.3	89.9	66,794	7.9	232,800	71.8	4.6	62.9	29.0
Lansdowne borough & MCD (Delaware)	1.18	10,620	10,647	0.3	9022.9	11.3	89.4	55,536	9.7	161,100	69.7	5.3	55.6	40.1
Lebanon city & MCD (Lebanon)	4.17	25,492	25,879	1.5	6206.0	8.0	76.6	39,427	22.6	96,100	63.9	8.0	59.9	31.4
Lehigh township (Northampton)	29.34	10,500	10,433	-0.6	355.6	1.1	96.8	65,166	8.6	198,200	64.3	5.6	71.4	23.5
Lehman township (Pike)	48.94	10,640	10,218	-4.0	208.8	15.6	93.9	59,776	13.8	136,900	56.8	8.9	73.4	23.1
Levittown CDP	10.16	52,983	NA	NA	NA	5.4	91.6	81,107	6.8	226,500	69.8	5.7	74.6	20.8
Limerick township (Montgomery)	22.50	18,074	19,303	6.8	857.9	6.4	90.7	96,914	3.9	299,600	73.6	5.8	73.4	22.2
Logan township (Blair)	46.51	12,668	12,232	-3.4	263.0	1.2	89.6	59,714	12.9	153,000	57.1	3.8	64.8	27.5
Lower Allen township (Cumberland)	10.06	17,937	20,260	13.0	2013.9	6.5	75.1	73,435	5.9	183,500	51.4	3.3	56.5	34.1
Lower Burrell city & MCD (Westmoreland)	11.26	11,757	11,078	-5.8	983.8	1.0	90.0	64,696	6.3	143,800	58.7	3.9	68.1	28.0
Lower Gwynedd township (Montgomery)	9.31	11,405	11,497	0.8	1234.9	10.1	88.9	102,725	5.9	508,600	55.8	3.2	68.3	30.5
Lower Macungie township (Lehigh)	22.37	30,644	32,690	6.7	1461.3	10.2	93.2	90,011	3.7	278,300	64.6	3.6	72.1	24.5
Lower Makefield township (Bucks)	17.87	32,557	32,802	0.8	1835.6	9.0	91.5	150,572	2.5	465,500	67.9	4.0	81.7	15.2
Lower Merion township (Montgomery)	23.61	57,819	60,099	3.9	2545.5	13.3	85.8	136,288	5.4	611,400	64.3	3.6	67.7	28.0
Lower Moreland township (Montgomery)	7.28	12,992	13,114	0.9	1801.4	21.0	95.5	105,890	6.4	412,800	62.4	3.3	80.4	18.5
Lower Paxton township (Dauphin)	28.16	47,359	49,936	5.4	1773.3	10.9	86.5	70,814	6.5	196,600	67.9	4.2	63.1	30.7
Lower Pottsgrove township (Montgomery)	7.93	12,083	12,150	0.6	1532.2	4.5	91.1	79,868	7.2	207,700	67.6	3.5	72.1	23.4
Lower Providence township (Montgomery)	15.25	25,473	26,873	5.5	1762.2	15.1	86.4	97,670	4.1	338,500	58.8	4.5	71.4	23.8
Lower Salford township (Montgomery)	14.47	14,936	15,529	4.0	1073.2	7.4	91.9	111,219	3.3	368,900	71.4	2.9	77.6	20.0
Lower Saucon township (Northampton)	24.27	10,771	10,838	0.6	446.6	4.6	93.9	91,526	5.1	310,400	58.9	4.8	72.9	22.3
Lower Southampton township (Bucks)	6.68	18,909	19,177	1.4	2870.8	13.8	92.2	88,714	4.6	293,700	69.7	3.9	72.0	22.6
Loyalsock township (Lycoming)	21.15	11,032	10,903	-1.2	515.5	3.3	84.5	56,074	13.4	200,800	51.3	2.3	66.2	30.9
McCandless township (Allegheny)	16.50	28,481	28,193	-1.0	1708.7	8.2	88.0	86,221	5.8	247,000	64.1	3.2	64.2	31.2
McKeesport city & MCD (Allegheny)	5.04	19,730	19,009	-3.7	3771.6	1.6	88.9	29,094	30.3	48,000	55.5	12.1	48.9	44.7
Manchester township (York)	15.84	18,168	18,648	2.6	1177.3	5.8	90.1	85,833	7.3	196,700	69.2	4.3	72.1	21.8
Manheim township (Lancaster)	23.87	38,159	40,548	6.3	1698.7	8.3	87.1	78,294	6.7	237,700	64.4	2.6	69.4	25.8
Manor township (Lancaster)	38.33	19,649	21,021	7.0	548.4	4.4	89.3	66,747	9.3	196,700	68.5	2.6	64.5	25.2
Marple township (Delaware)	10.20	23,421	23,955	2.3	2348.5	11.2	92.4	103,135	4.4	365,100	62.8	3.4	75.8	21.5
Meadville city & MCD (Crawford)	4.37	13,388	12,655	-5.5	2895.9	2.6	76.9	36,793	21.8	110,100	57.3	8.3	52.8	39.2
Middle Smithfield township (Monroe)	53.16	15,936	15,942	0.0	299.9	13.8	86.6	66,972	9.3	152,500	62.7	5.4	72.1	23.6
Middletown township (Bucks)	18.89	45,396	44,966	-0.9	2380.4	8.3	88.3	91,171	4.9	320,300	66.8	4.4	71.7	23.4
Middletown township (Delaware)	13.47	15,806	16,073	1.7	1193.2	5.0	91.4	97,266	5.4	367,700	57.8	4.1	63.5	33.1
Milford township (Bucks)	27.89	9,906	10,056	1.5	360.6	1.7	92.4	98,516	5.9	297,500	66.2	3.0	80.9	17.0
Millcreek township (Erie)	32.07	53,561	52,456	-2.1	1635.7	5.0	87.8	64,003	9.4	170,800	63.7	4.0	61.3	31.7
Monroeville municipality & MCD (Allegheny)	19.72	28,345	27,380	-3.4	1388.4	7.6	90.6	68,743	7.8	150,400	62.6	4.5	61.5	32.6
Montgomery township (Montgomery)	10.63	24,816	26,164	5.4	2461.3	16.2	91.7	110,043	3.7	358,400	71.0	4.1	71.6	23.0
Montgomeryville CDP	4.76	12,624	NA	NA	NA	11.7	94.4	114,970	2.7	350,200	74.1	4.7	77.4	16.4
Moon township (Allegheny)	23.85	24,212	25,437	5.1	1066.5	8.3	84.8	91,349	4.6	227,600	69.3	3.8	66.6	25.7
Mountain Top CDP	15.04	10,982	NA	NA	NA	7.0	92.4	85,560	6.1	211,800	67.6	2.2	80.0	16.8
Mount Joy township (Lancaster)	27.84	9,910	11,271	13.7	404.8	3.7	84.6	71,932	3.5	223,400	75.4	3.8	76.2	18.6
Mount Lebanon township (Allegheny)	6.08	33,109	31,927	-3.6	5251.2	7.9	89.4	100,011	6.3	268,500	63.9	2.6	64.8	31.9
Mount Pleasant township (Westmoreland)	55.94	10,923	10,442	-4.4	186.7	1.3	92.0	53,646	9.2	147,400	59.2	6.0	72.3	24.3
Muhlenberg township (Berks)	11.80	19,677	20,345	3.4	1724.2	9.5	85.5	67,389	8.8	158,400	65.9	5.1	69.8	23.1
Munhall borough & MCD (Allegheny)	2.30	11,381	11,006	-3.3	4785.2	2.5	91.0	47,649	13.6	91,100	63.3	5.4	50.0	43.6
Murrysville municipality & MCD (Westmoreland)	36.84	20,058	19,590	-2.3	531.8	4.2	91.9	102,081	3.3	257,400	63.0	2.1	74.1	22.0
Nanticoke city & MCD (Luzerne)	3.46	10,465	10,312	-1.5	2980.3	2.5	90.2	42,735	19.2	80,300	59.7	7.1	56.8	36.0
Nether Providence township (Delaware)	4.71	13,709	13,780	0.5	2925.7	10.8	91.9	122,326	3.5	350,200	67.1	4.5	77.6	21.1
Newberry township (York)	30.41	15,295	15,918	4.1	523.4	2.9	91.4	69,964	7.4	159,600	69.7	4.4	67.6	24.7
New Britain township (Bucks)	14.68	11,139	11,524	3.5	785.0	7.7	89.5	103,836	5.3	358,300	68.6	3.1	77.6	18.2
New Castle city & MCD (Lawrence)	8.31	23,294	21,618	-7.2	2601.4	1.8	82.2	34,133	25.8	61,900	56.6	10.9	58.3	35.9
New Garden township (Chester)	16.11	12,012	12,206	1.6	757.7	22.0	88.7	116,875	4.6	398,100	70.4	4.0	82.3	14.6
New Hanover township (Montgomery)	21.63	10,934	13,212	20.8	610.8	1.9	96.0	102,522	3.4	316,300	73.3	3.2	79.8	18.0
New Kensington city & MCD (Westmoreland)	3.95	13,116	12,292	-6.3	3111.9	3.2	89.1	42,264	20.4	104,100	60.9	4.3	52.8	40.4

Table B. Incorporated Places, Census Designated Places (CDPs), and Minor Civil Divisions (MCDs) of 10,000 or More Population — Crime, Residential Construction and Local Government Finance

STATE City, town, township, borough, or CDP (county if applicable)	Serious crimes known to police, 2018[1]				New residential construction authorized by building permits, 2019			Local government finance, 2017							
	Violent crime		Property crime					General revenue				General expenditure			
									Intergovernmental				Per capita[3]		
	Number	Rate[2]	Number	Rate[2]	Value ($1,000)	Number of housing units	Percent single family	Total (mil dol)	Total (mil dol)	Percent from state gov.	Taxes per capita[3]	Total (mil dol)	Total	Capital outlays	Debt outstanding (mil dol)
	15	16	17	18	19	20	21	22	23	24	25	26	27	28	29
PENNSYLVANIA—Con.															
Lansdale borough & MCD (Montgomery)	15	90	176	1,058	14,433	122	25.4	15.6	1.2	98.9	426	23.5	1,420	161	32.1
Lansdowne borough & MCD (Delaware)	26	244	237	2,225	0	0	0.0	9.4	1.2	97.4	461	10.2	964	137	3.1
Lebanon city & MCD (Lebanon)	83	322	469	1,817	1,128	7	100.0	17.0	2.7	67.3	410	14.1	548	15	0.2
Lehigh township (Northampton)	18	172	87	830	4,060	17	100.0	4.6	1.0	75.4	334	4.1	395	53	0.3
Lehman township (Pike)	NA	NA	NA	NA	278	2	100.0	2.8	0.5	84.3	210	2.6	251	20	0.4
Levittown CDP	NA	NA	NA	NA	NA	NA	NA	NA	NA	NA	NA	NA	NA	NA	NA
Limerick township (Montgomery)	8	42	309	1,614	16,088	85	17.6	17.4	1.6	95.3	524	17.5	923	77	11.9
Logan township (Blair)	16	129	137	1,108	5,243	16	100.0	10.6	1.1	72.3	388	9.3	754	81	21.8
Lower Allen township (Cumberland)	14	72	231	1,182	16,783	62	74.2	14.0	1.4	98.1	463	11.2	578	44	11.3
Lower Burrell city & MCD (Westmoreland)	9	81	84	753	1,492	6	100.0	8.8	0.7	97.2	417	8.0	716	40	0.2
Lower Gwynedd township (Montgomery)	3	26	145	1,256	6,855	20	100.0	13.5	1.0	77.8	666	11.8	1,026	80	1.6
Lower Macungie township (Lehigh)	NA	NA	NA	NA	6,572	27	100.0	18.4	1.6	100.0	295	16.1	499	84	1.5
Lower Makefield township (Bucks)	10	31	219	668	10,970	50	100.0	27.0	1.9	94.0	347	37.6	1,150	217	46.9
Lower Merion township (Montgomery)	32	54	973	1,642	61,845	291	8.9	89.6	10.9	81.4	929	90.2	1,529	177	105.8
Lower Moreland township (Montgomery)	4	30	122	924	0	0	0.0	15.5	1.0	86.5	634	11.6	882	59	10.0
Lower Paxton township (Dauphin)	87	177	665	1,349	62,391	382	40.3	26.5	3.0	100.0	360	36.4	741	154	132.2
Lower Pottsgrove township (Montgomery)	39	322	136	1,121	11,312	47	100.0	6.5	0.8	93.0	382	6.1	504	39	0.0
Lower Providence township (Montgomery)	33	122	154	569	9,417	57	33.3	13.3	1.5	86.3	368	11.7	437	37	5.6
Lower Salford township (Montgomery)	7	45	60	389	5,341	19	100.0	11.8	1.2	98.2	541	10.8	704	13	12.8
Lower Saucon township (Northampton)	10	92	76	702	1,050	4	100.0	10.6	1.1	95.0	724	7.2	670	84	3.5
Lower Southampton township (Bucks)	68	354	278	1,446	1,840	23	100.0	22.2	2.1	63.7	597	19.9	1,037	85	7.4
Loyalsock township (Lycoming)	NA	NA	NA	NA	3,284	16	37.5	4.2	0.8	94.2	251	4.9	449	111	2.4
McCandless township (Allegheny)	5	18	140	492	4,436	10	100.0	15.7	1.7	93.3	451	19.3	680	138	0.0
McKeesport city & MCD (Allegheny)	320	1,530	506	2,419	0	0	0.0	19.6	2.0	77.2	352	18.6	971	16	22.3
Manchester township (York)	NA	NA	NA	NA	5,236	20	100.0	14.9	1.6	73.1	412	12.1	651	6	4.8
Manheim township (Lancaster)	50	124	556	1,376	29,158	130	58.5	30.7	5.7	46.6	462	31.8	794	74	12.1
Manor township (Lancaster)	24	114	129	612	7,019	63	34.9	8.0	1.2	100.0	245	7.2	347	18	0.0
Marple township (Delaware)	4	17	355	1,487	853	7	100.0	21.8	1.6	97.7	537	29.1	1,222	230	13.9
Meadville city & MCD (Crawford)	21	163	157	1,216	805	1	100.0	14.0	3.8	24.0	404	13.3	1,033	76	38.0
Middle Smithfield township (Monroe)	NA	NA	NA	NA	4,254	16	100.0	7.6	0.7	100.0	259	7.3	464	51	9.6
Middletown township (Bucks)	33	73	610	1,350	4,169	16	100.0	34.1	3.3	70.0	515	30.3	671	51	27.0
Middletown township (Delaware)	NA	NA	NA	NA	4,288	11	100.0	8.5	0.7	97.2	300	5.7	357	53	9.1
Milford township (Bucks)	NA	NA	NA	NA	1,016	3	100.0	4.5	0.6	90.5	337	6.2	613	191	4.5
Millcreek township (Erie)	137	256	564	1,056	6,747	34	52.9	61.6	3.8	88.4	458	39.8	746	59	10.7
Monroeville municipality & MCD (Allegheny)	63	228	481	1,741	11,270	99	7.1	31.3	2.7	91.5	986	27.1	981	37	19.3
Montgomery township (Montgomery)	7	27	338	1,285	3,555	33	100.0	18.4	1.7	95.3	579	17.2	660	52	8.7
Montgomeryville CDP	NA	NA	NA	NA	NA	NA	NA	NA	NA	NA	NA	NA	NA	NA	NA
Moon township (Allegheny)	20	78	233	905	5,169	22	100.0	15.6	1.3	99.2	517	15.7	615	51	8.5
Mountain Top CDP	NA	NA	NA	NA	NA	NA	NA	NA	NA	NA	NA	NA	NA	NA	NA
Mount Joy township (Lancaster)	NA	NA	NA	NA	5,122	24	83.3	5.2	0.6	97.8	293	9.7	879	249	1.6
Mount Lebanon township (Allegheny)	23	71	241	748	1,047	4	100.0	47.6	2.5	84.9	850	48.9	1,517	177	25.3
Mount Pleasant township (Westmoreland)	NA	NA	NA	NA	1,782	7	100.0	2.8	0.7	95.5	179	2.5	233	12	1.2
Muhlenberg township (Berks)	22	108	503	2,478	3,916	24	100.0	16.1	1.5	90.1	542	17.7	874	124	16.8
Munhall borough & MCD (Allegheny)	NA	NA	NA	NA	0	0	0.0	8.5	0.8	86.2	559	7.5	672	14	1.0
Murrysville municipality & MCD (Westmoreland)	4	20	92	466	4,059	9	100.0	12.0	1.5	94.7	485	10.8	549	35	2.9
Nanticoke city & MCD (Luzerne)	15	146	154	1,502	120	1	100.0	8.9	1.4	23.7	508	6.7	648	0	3.9
Nether Providence township (Delaware)	12	87	135	980	859	3	100.0	10.1	1.3	95.3	381	10.6	773	99	4.0
Newberry township (York)	22	140	200	1,270	7,222	44	100.0	9.1	0.9	92.4	253	6.5	413	10	7.8
New Britain township (Bucks)	3	27	56	498	6,408	18	100.0	7.3	1.0	74.6	474	6.8	606	54	1.7
New Castle city & MCD (Lawrence)	123	561	596	2,720	60	1	100.0	18.2	2.0	71.3	553	15.6	712	44	26.1
New Garden township (Chester)	NA	NA	NA	NA	5,609	32	50.0	15.8	6.6	25.2	420	16.5	1,363	618	0.8
New Hanover township (Montgomery)	2	15	69	523	24,397	97	100.0	7.7	0.7	100.0	329	7.6	590	68	5.7
New Kensington city & MCD (Westmoreland)	70	566	382	3,086	0	0	0.0	7.3	0.9	91.8	373	7.5	600	31	1.3

1 Data for serious crimes have not been adjusted for underreporting. This may affect comparability between geographic areas over time.
2 Per 100,000 population estimated by the FBI. 3 Based on population estimated as of July 1 of the year shown.

Table B.   Incorporated Places, Census Designated Places (CDPs), and Minor Civil Divisions (MCDs) of 10,000 or More Population — **Land Area, Population, and Households, and Employment**

STATE City, town, township, borough, or CDP (county if applicable)	Land area 2010 (sq mi)	Population Total persons 2010	Total persons 2019	Percent change 2010-2019	Persons per square mile 2019	Population characteristics 2015-2019 Percent foreign born	Percent living in the same house as previous year	Income and poverty 2015-2019 Median household income	Percent of households with income below poverty level	Median value of owner-occupied housing units	Employment, 2015-2019 Percent in civilian labor force	Unemploy-ment rate	Households, 2015-2019 (percent of households) Family households	One person households
	1	2	3	4	5	6	7	8	9	10	11	12	13	14
PENNSYLVANIA—Con.														
Newtown township (Bucks).......	11.90	19,295	19,584	1.5	1645.7	12.3	91.5	123,958	2.9	428,200	69.5	3.4	70.9	25.8
Newtown township (Delaware) .	10.02	12,218	13,943	14.1	1391.5	8.7	88.7	110,344	4.8	419,600	59.0	3.3	67.9	28.3
Norristown borough & MCD (Montgomery)	3.52	34,339	34,341	0.0	9756.0	19.6	84.0	48,414	17.5	152,900	70.8	7.7	62.9	30.7
Northampton township (Bucks)	25.68	39,726	39,164	-1.4	1525.1	11.1	93.0	120,343	3.8	413,200	66.4	3.5	78.4	18.6
North Fayette township (Allegheny)	25.18	13,948	14,816	6.2	588.4	6.1	84.9	78,707	9.1	191,500	73.5	3.9	59.7	32.8
North Huntingdon township (Westmoreland)	27.26	30,605	30,378	-0.7	1114.4	1.3	94.0	75,006	5.1	170,300	64.5	3.4	72.1	24.6
North Lebanon township (Lebanon)..........................	16.75	11,428	12,186	6.6	727.5	5.5	92.0	63,459	7.2	165,500	66.4	3.8	67.5	24.4
North Middleton township (Cumberland	23.19	11,132	11,810	6.1	509.3	4.9	79.6	76,398	3.7	169,000	64.3	3.3	71.0	23.0
North Strabane township (Washington)..................	27.26	13,387	14,475	8.1	531.0	3.0	89.0	91,468	4.4	246,500	69.4	3.5	65.9	29.0
North Union township (Fayette)	39.02	12,733	11,992	-5.8	307.3	0.4	92.0	41,968	16.7	91,700	51.1	7.0	56.1	38.0
North Versailles township (Allegheny)	8.03	10,236	9,924	-3.0	1235.9	2.1	89.4	44,133	9.1	82,900	60.2	6.1	57.3	39.4
North Whitehall township (Lehigh)..........................	28.10	15,701	16,379	4.3	582.9	4.1	91.3	82,019	4.0	268,000	65.5	4.2	75.1	22.2
Oil City city & MCD (Venango) .	4.49	10,549	9,618	-8.8	2142.1	0.5	86.1	39,750	17.4	51,700	58.9	8.8	55.1	38.4
Palmer township (Northampton)...................	10.26	20,681	21,422	3.6	2087.9	12.1	88.7	86,133	3.5	234,000	65.6	3.0	70.8	23.2
Park Forest Village CDP...........	2.49	9,660	NA	NA	NA	17.0	71.8	72,083	13.8	289,800	65.3	6.8	59.5	27.1
Patton township (Centre).........	24.53	15,155	15,805	4.3	644.3	11.5	72.5	67,842	15.9	290,200	64.8	6.7	51.2	29.9
Penn township (Westmoreland)	30.76	20,034	19,350	-3.4	629.1	2.1	93.5	82,162	7.6	197,100	64.5	3.0	75.4	21.4
Penn township (York)	12.98	15,629	16,623	6.4	1280.7	3.1	90.5	72,802	4.7	175,200	65.4	3.3	72.3	23.3
Penn Hills township (Allegheny)	19.12	42,385	40,807	-3.7	2134.3	1.8	88.8	55,491	9.4	95,000	65.4	5.6	60.8	34.1
Peters township (Washington)..	19.55	21,202	22,044	4.0	1127.6	3.8	92.2	127,837	2.4	355,200	62.6	3.2	84.6	13.3
Philadelphia city...................	134.28	1,526,012	1,584,064	3.8	11796.7	14.1	85.6	45,927	22.9	163,000	60.9	9.2	54.2	37.5
Phoenixville borough & MCD (Chester)	3.51	16,439	16,968	3.2	4834.2	7.0	82.2	73,004	11.4	237,200	75.5	4.3	51.4	37.8
Pine township (Allegheny)	16.97	11,484	13,741	19.7	809.7	7.6	86.3	153,302	3.1	427,600	69.9	3.1	80.8	12.9
Pittsburgh city & MCD (Allegheny)........................	55.38	305,245	300,286	-1.6	5422.3	9.0	77.5	48,711	19.7	125,000	63.7	5.6	42.2	43.6
Plum borough & MCD (Allegheny)........................	28.58	27,108	27,087	-0.1	947.8	1.4	91.9	78,709	4.3	153,700	66.1	3.0	71.5	24.9
Plumstead township (Bucks)	27.16	12,444	14,483	16.4	533.2	9.4	94.2	115,428	4.4	421,100	71.6	1.7	76.7	18.5
Plymouth township (Montgomery)	8.40	16,538	17,531	6.0	2087.0	9.3	85.1	83,857	6.4	341,700	68.8	3.8	67.6	26.9
Pocono township (Monroe).......	34.24	11,077	11,089	0.1	323.9	10.2	91.1	65,710	12.8	173,700	61.8	4.3	68.8	26.0
Pottstown borough & MCD (Montgomery)	4.85	22,353	22,600	1.1	4659.8	3.8	82.9	50,331	17.4	124,400	69.0	6.5	61.5	30.7
Pottsville city & MCD (Schuylkill).......................	4.17	14,326	13,475	-5.9	3231.4	1.5	85.2	42,083	19.8	71,400	58.1	8.9	57.0	37.6
Progress CDP........................	2.80	9,765	NA	NA	NA	13.8	81.4	59,632	9.4	155,100	68.3	3.7	57.6	36.0
Radnor township (Delaware)	13.77	31,550	31,875	1.0	2314.8	12.5	81.1	127,161	8.6	663,900	56.9	5.6	69.2	26.3
Rapho township (Lancaster).....	47.43	10,439	12,304	17.9	259.4	1.0	91.4	72,418	3.8	221,000	66.3	3.0	74.4	21.1
Reading city & MCD (Berks).....	9.84	87,994	88,375	0.4	8981.2	19.1	78.1	32,176	32.0	73,200	61.5	12.9	63.3	30.0
Richland township (Allegheny) .	14.63	11,120	11,373	2.3	777.4	3.6	93.9	105,844	6.1	262,800	64.3	1.8	73.9	22.2
Richland township (Bucks).......	20.65	13,036	13,325	2.2	645.3	6.3	95.6	77,250	6.1	250,800	66.0	6.0	71.0	23.2
Richland township (Cambria) ...	20.59	12,796	11,818	-7.6	574.0	2.0	85.4	61,594	6.7	155,600	49.5	2.1	58.8	36.9
Ridley township (Delaware)......	5.12	30,868	31,204	1.1	6094.5	4.5	90.7	75,215	7.7	193,300	69.8	4.2	62.3	32.0
Robinson township (Allegheny)	15.23	13,355	13,850	3.7	909.4	5.7	86.0	84,762	3.7	201,400	66.4	2.0	63.9	28.2
Ross township (Allegheny)	14.48	31,104	30,473	-2.0	2104.5	5.3	88.2	77,170	5.3	174,600	67.0	3.2	58.2	35.1
Rostraver township (Westmoreland)	32.28	11,346	11,007	-3.0	341.0	1.1	92.7	74,386	7.3	177,300	62.6	4.0	66.4	28.8
St. Marys city & MCD (Elk).......	99.32	13,071	12,260	-6.2	123.4	1.3	91.1	53,516	9.1	122,600	64.8	3.7	60.0	34.1
Salisbury township (Lancaster)	41.76	11,060	11,434	3.4	273.8	1.0	93.8	81,277	5.7	289,900	66.2	1.5	86.7	12.4
Salisbury township (Lehigh)	11.17	13,617	13,948	2.4	1248.7	5.9	92.6	76,746	8.0	209,700	59.4	3.1	69.9	25.5
Sandy township (Clearfield)......	51.96	10,622	10,442	-1.7	201.0	1.1	90.6	58,681	9.8	142,800	58.1	5.8	73.7	22.8
Scott township (Allegheny)	3.91	17,033	16,428	-3.6	4201.5	13.0	87.1	70,346	5.5	161,700	62.7	2.6	56.9	37.7
Scranton city & MCD (Lackawanna)....................	25.31	76,083	76,653	0.7	3028.6	10.1	82.5	40,608	21.6	103,000	56.8	5.2	56.5	36.3
Shaler township (Allegheny).....	11.08	28,703	27,720	-3.4	2501.8	2.6	93.9	75,064	5.0	174,100	67.6	3.5	65.0	30.2
Sharon city & MCD (Mercer)	3.77	14,017	12,933	-7.7	3430.5	3.0	85.2	32,470	27.3	65,400	57.7	9.2	56.9	38.8
Shiloh CDP............................	4.22	11,218	NA	NA	NA	3.0	87.2	62,993	6.8	178,300	60.3	2.7	59.6	33.6
Silver Spring township (Cumberland)	32.31	13,657	18,314	34.1	566.8	8.3	87.3	84,710	4.3	252,600	64.2	2.1	70.1	25.3
Skippack township (Montgomery)	13.86	13,721	14,203	3.5	1024.7	4.4	92.3	123,403	2.8	386,000	50.5	3.7	81.3	15.2
Somerset township (Somerset)	64.20	12,132	12,174	0.3	189.6	0.8	84.0	53,438	7.8	121,100	34.6	4.6	67.2	27.2
South Fayette township (Allegheny)	20.38	14,388	15,945	10.8	782.4	7.4	87.9	86,858	6.3	248,100	66.0	2.3	64.9	30.4
South Middleton township (Cumberland)	48.74	14,714	15,564	5.8	319.3	2.0	92.8	76,357	4.2	220,500	62.4	2.3	68.5	27.7
South Park township (Allegheny)	9.27	13,429	13,628	1.5	1470.1	4.1	89.7	74,022	7.8	167,000	69.3	4.4	69.4	26.6
South Union township (Fayette)	16.76	10,696	10,205	-4.6	608.9	2.4	93.1	62,515	13.6	166,200	52.4	5.9	66.2	29.4
South Whitehall township (Lehigh)..........................	17.08	19,167	19,955	4.1	1168.3	10.0	88.1	82,258	3.6	238,000	59.1	3.6	70.3	23.4
Spring township (Berks)	18.40	27,110	27,659	2.0	1503.2	7.4	87.6	78,363	5.0	194,100	67.0	4.1	72.6	23.2
Springettsbury township (York).	16.37	26,639	26,860	0.8	1640.8	9.9	80.9	64,595	8.9	174,200	56.5	4.2	67.6	24.9
Springfield township (Delaware).........................	6.32	24,125	24,261	0.6	3838.8	4.8	94.2	116,313	1.6	315,000	68.8	4.1	80.8	16.3
Springfield township (Montgomery)	6.73	19,365	19,848	2.5	2949.2	6.3	88.4	104,417	5.6	341,600	68.3	4.2	68.7	26.7

Table B. Incorporated Places, Census Designated Places (CDPs), and Minor Civil Divisions (MCDs) of 10,000 or More Population — Crime, Residential Construction and Local Government Finance

STATE City, town, township, borough, or CDP (county if applicable)	Serious crimes known to police, 2018[1] Violent crime Number	Rate[2]	Property crime Number	Rate[2]	New residential construction authorized by building permits, 2019 Value ($1,000)	Number of housing units	Percent single family	Local government finance, 2017 General revenue Total (mil dol)	Intergovernmental Total (mil dol)	Percent from state gov.	Taxes per capita[3]	General expenditure Total (mil dol)	Per capita[3] Total	Capital outlays	Debt outstanding (mil dol)
	15	16	17	18	19	20	21	22	23	24	25	26	27	28	29
PENNSYLVANIA—Con.															
Newtown township (Bucks).......	5	22	128	559	2,612	7	100.0	14.7	2.7	58.2	480	19.6	996	323	9.4
Newtown township (Delaware) .	5	37	100	737	19,455	115	77.4	10.4	1.2	97.4	520	11.5	864	169	13.3
Norristown borough & MCD (Montgomery)	139	403	511	1,480	3,000	16	100.0	32.6	4.1	58.3	671	27.8	807	41	14.4
Northampton township (Bucks)	12	31	144	367	3,479	8	100.0	27.9	2.9	99.4	448	32.1	818	142	23.6
North Fayette township (Allegheny)..................	6	40	214	1,433	20,098	97	100.0	14.3	0.9	97.7	554	17.9	1,213	149	21.3
North Huntingdon township (Westmoreland)	15	49	291	957	21,521	78	94.9	14.9	1.9	95.0	385	15.3	502	63	0.0
North Lebanon township (Lebanon).....................	29	241	176	1,462	NA	NA	NA	4.8	1.0	90.1	283	4.2	354	0	0.2
North Middleton township (Cumberland).....................	6	51	67	574	9,571	92	47.8	3.7	0.6	96.1	235	3.5	301	14	0.7
North Strabane township (Washington)...................	27	184	86	585	0	0	0.0	11.8	3.9	99.4	479	10.8	742	47	6.4
North Union township (Fayette)	NA	NA	NA	NA	NA	NA	NA	3.4	1.0	100.0	165	2.6	210	24	0.0
North Versailles township (Allegheny)..................	35	289	85	701	0	0	0.0	6.9	0.6	97.4	501	6.7	673	34	0.4
North Whitehall township (Lehigh)......................	NA	NA	NA	NA	5,382	11	100.0	5.5	0.9	100.0	251	4.7	290	17	2.1
Oil City city & MCD (Venango) .	18	184	126	1,290	0	0	0.0	10.9	1.3	97.8	368	11.8	1,194	135	12.4
Palmer township (Northampton).................	13	60	264	1,227	14,650	30	100.0	21.8	1.5	100.0	522	34.4	1,610	452	17.7
Park Forest Village CDP..........	NA	NA	NA	NA	NA	NA	NA	NA	NA	NA	NA	NA	NA	NA	NA
Patton township (Centre).........	5	31	125	774	8,516	31	100.0	9.6	1.0	100.0	514	10.3	651	127	5.9
Penn township (Westmoreland)	30	156	1	5	28,413	125	88.0	9.9	1.4	91.4	405	9.8	507	20	1.0
Penn township (York)............	22	133	143	866	16,806	100	100.0	15.3	1.9	70.8	451	16.5	1,010	136	15.4
Penn Hills township (Allegheny)	169	411	674	1,638	0	0	0.0	40.2	3.5	59.8	540	40.1	973	132	88.6
Peters township (Washington)..	12	54	135	610	35,311	55	100.0	17.8	2.0	100.0	580	23.9	1,089	419	18.2
Philadelphia city.................	14,420	909	49,145	3,097	747,902	4,566	19.6	7149.5	2318.6	66.7	2,346	6861.4	4,341	276	4997.9
Phoenixville borough & MCD (Chester)........................	32	188	192	1,129	841	12	33.3	17.2	2.1	54.1	480	15.4	910	114	16.8
Pine township (Allegheny)	NA	NA	NA	NA	55,377	109	100.0	12.5	0.8	100.0	732	13.1	1,001	259	4.1
Pittsburgh city & MCD (Allegheny).....................	1,751	579	9,125	3,016	77,141	660	11.8	628.6	115.8	64.2	1,385	757.1	2,511	54	473.2
Plum borough & MCD (Allegheny).....................	65	238	150	550	8,672	41	100.0	15.5	1.7	85.0	398	17.1	629	70	17.0
Plumstead township (Bucks)	11	77	66	463	6,035	23	100.0	8.8	1.0	75.9	508	8.0	571	46	20.5
Plymouth township (Montgomery).................	26	146	448	2,523	2,069	10	100.0	29.7	1.9	100.0	1,143	29.5	1,680	163	0.0
Pocono township (Monroe).......	29	267	241	2,220	4,200	16	100.0	11.5	0.8	100.0	573	15.6	1,430	342	23.9
Pottstown borough & MCD (Montgomery).................	196	860	753	3,304	525	2	100.0	31.6	5.7	73.4	523	25.9	1,143	80	2.6
Pottsville city & MCD (Schuylkill)....................	44	325	227	1,678	0	0	0.0	10.6	1.4	59.9	495	11.0	808	124	4.4
Progress CDP......................	NA	NA	NA	NA	NA	NA	NA	NA	NA	NA	NA	NA	NA	NA	NA
Radnor township (Delaware)....	31	97	223	698	13,700	34	100.0	42.6	2.5	97.5	966	45.0	1,419	125	60.7
Rapho township (Lancaster).....	NA	NA	NA	NA	9,282	34	100.0	5.6	0.9	94.4	329	5.0	419	39	0.0
Reading city & MCD (Berks).....	621	702	1,984	2,243	120	2	0.0	129.9	14.0	94.7	668	125.2	1,421	26	257.4
Richland township (Allegheny) .	NA	NA	NA	NA	1,548	5	100.0	8.2	0.7	100.0	463	7.5	654	25	9.3
Richland township (Bucks)	18	134	180	1,345	3,408	19	100.0	6.5	0.8	99.0	377	5.5	412	24	3.3
Richland township (Cambria) ...	7	59	420	3,518	1,329	7	100.0	7.5	1.6	98.4	416	6.2	512	15	0.3
Ridley township (Delaware)......	27	87	323	1,036	210	3	100.0	27.1	1.7	97.6	503	31.3	1,007	147	10.8
Robinson township (Allegheny)	20	146	272	1,989	19,560	65	100.0	11.9	1.0	96.5	685	12.9	950	31	10.2
Ross township (Allegheny)	20	66	582	1,906	9,647	50	100.0	28.3	1.8	99.8	518	35.4	1,160	191	9.1
Rostraver township (Westmoreland)................	8	73	260	2,359	5,987	20	100.0	7.1	0.9	82.2	420	7.3	666	64	4.2
St. Marys city & MCD (Elk).......	13	106	138	1,124	2,403	10	100.0	10.9	1.0	93.6	492	10.7	863	132	10.9
Salisbury township (Lancaster)	NA	NA	NA	NA	4,389	18	100.0	3.6	0.7	94.1	168	4.3	379	133	1.5
Salisbury township (Lehigh)	8	57	154	1,102	3,309	5	100.0	11.2	1.3	89.9	459	11.3	813	93	6.3
Sandy township (Clearfield)......	31	296	134	1,279	2,410	8	100.0	7.0	1.1	60.9	346	7.3	690	80	0.5
Scott township (Allegheny)	18	109	157	948	0	0	0.0	14.3	0.9	87.2	536	20.3	1,222	264	16.0
Scranton city & MCD (Lackawanna).................	811	1,042	1,505	1,934	749	3	100.0	115.7	9.2	76.7	952	107.4	1,391	6	152.8
Shaler township (Allegheny).....	20	71	211	753	582	2	100.0	19.1	1.2	100.0	350	19.8	707	52	0.4
Sharon city & MCD (Mercer)	65	494	414	3,147	0	0	0.0	9.6	1.6	57.2	520	8.9	675	34	1.6
Shiloh CDP.........................	NA	NA	NA	NA	NA	NA	NA	NA	NA	NA	NA	NA	NA	NA	NA
Silver Spring township (Cumberland).....................	3	17	67	371	37,872	173	82.1	12.1	1.1	100.0	476	11.7	676	64	12.3
Skippack township (Montgomery).....................	NA	NA	NA	NA	3,251	22	100.0	8.5	0.7	100.0	328	4.6	309	70	2.0
Somerset township (Somerset)	NA	NA	NA	NA	830	3	100.0	2.6	0.9	100.0	104	2.3	190	0	0.0
South Fayette township (Allegheny)..................	2	13	59	374	13,795	49	100.0	12.5	1.0	84.9	659	11.2	718	74	6.6
South Middleton township (Cumberland).....................	NA	NA	NA	NA	9,247	47	100.0	6.0	0.9	93.5	231	5.9	384	99	2.3
South Park township (Allegheny)..................	3	23	23	173	2,205	13	100.0	9.6	0.9	96.9	385	9.2	689	58	3.7
South Union township (Fayette)	NA	NA	NA	NA	1,105	5	100.0	5.7	0.9	94.4	253	6.2	593	56	0.0
South Whitehall township (Lehigh)........................	13	65	483	2,425	6,384	24	100.0	19.9	2.1	93.9	722	21.7	1,098	105	0.0
Spring township (Berks)	NA	NA	NA	NA	14,656	216	2.8	22.2	1.9	83.5	446	23.4	848	77	19.8
Springettsbury township (York).	43	160	845	3,149	1,200	6	100.0	24.3	2.0	76.5	398	23.8	889	19	25.1
Springfield township (Delaware).....................	13	54	507	2,090	110	1	100.0	25.4	1.7	97.9	543	23.7	980	54	3.4
Springfield township (Montgomery).....................	24	122	193	977	3,743	11	63.6	16.7	1.7	85.8	542	37.4	1,904	606	10.2

1 Data for serious crimes have not been adjusted for underreporting. This may affect comparability between geographic areas over time.
2 Per 100,000 population estimated by the FBI.   3 Based on population estimated as of July 1 of the year shown.

Table B. Incorporated Places, Census Designated Places (CDPs), and Minor Civil Divisions (MCDs) of 10,000 or More Population — **Land Area, Population, and Households, and Employment**

STATE City, town, township, borough, or CDP (county if applicable)	Land area 2010 (sq mi)	Population Total persons 2010	Total persons 2019	Percent change 2010–2019	Persons per square mile 2019	Population characteristics 2015–2019 Percent foreign born	Percent living in the same house as previous year	Income and poverty 2015–2019 Median household income	Percent of households with income below poverty level	Median value of owner-occupied housing units	Employment, 2015–2019 Percent in civilian labor force	Unemployment rate	Households, 2015–2019 (percent of households) Family households	One person households
	1	2	3	4	5	6	7	8	9	10	11	12	13	14
PENNSYLVANIA—Con.														
Spring Garden township (York).	6.73	12,485	13,209	5.8	1962.7	3.9	88.9	76,762	6.1	170,700	61.1	5.2	69.3	26.0
State College borough & MCD (Centre)	4.56	41,980	42,160	0.4	9245.6	15.5	48.3	34,005	37.0	312,400	46.2	5.7	28.6	41.2
Stroud township (Monroe)	31.06	19,162	19,361	1.0	623.3	14.4	91.5	68,371	9.6	192,600	65.6	6.0	73.4	20.8
Susquehanna township (Dauphin)	13.35	24,030	25,114	4.5	1881.2	9.0	83.8	68,674	8.0	166,600	64.3	4.8	57.4	36.5
Swatara township (Dauphin)	13.05	23,366	25,081	7.3	1921.9	10.4	82.4	61,758	8.1	155,000	62.9	5.5	63.6	31.7
Towamencin township (Montgomery)	9.68	17,592	18,441	4.8	1905.1	11.8	89.6	85,811	5.2	318,900	64.4	3.1	66.3	31.0
Tredyffrin township (Chester)	19.77	29,340	29,396	0.2	1486.9	18.2	87.2	136,429	4.3	558,600	66.1	3.7	67.9	26.5
Uniontown city & MCD (Fayette)	2.04	10,357	9,719	-6.2	4764.2	3.2	85.0	35,150	26.2	85,100	54.0	12.4	48.5	40.4
Unity township (Westmoreland)	67.44	22,602	21,815	-3.5	323.5	1.3	89.4	67,722	7.7	195,800	60.2	3.7	72.6	23.5
Upper Allen township (Cumberland)	13.20	18,058	20,384	12.9	1544.2	7.4	87.3	80,597	4.5	219,300	65.1	4.6	65.2	31.0
Upper Chichester township (Delaware)	6.69	16,705	16,959	1.5	2535.0	4.7	91.2	76,620	7.7	217,000	63.4	3.8	64.5	30.3
Upper Darby township (Delaware)	7.83	82,792	82,930	0.2	10591.3	21.3	88.9	55,908	14.3	148,100	69.5	4.9	65.5	29.4
Upper Dublin township (Montgomery)	13.23	25,596	26,553	3.7	2007.0	11.0	92.1	128,463	2.9	415,800	69.0	3.9	79.2	18.4
Upper Gwynedd township (Montgomery)	8.12	15,496	15,817	2.1	1947.9	15.7	90.4	95,784	3.2	355,800	64.1	5.2	69.3	25.7
Upper Macungie township (Lehigh)	26.09	20,065	25,201	25.6	965.9	13.0	87.3	100,170	3.2	315,000	69.4	3.8	73.5	22.1
Upper Merion township (Montgomery)	16.97	28,388	33,027	16.3	1946.2	20.1	86.8	95,921	4.2	339,900	70.0	3.8	61.4	31.3
Upper Moreland township (Montgomery)	7.97	24,013	24,031	0.1	3015.2	8.1	89.2	77,832	6.6	273,900	69.8	4.6	61.7	31.7
Upper Providence township (Delaware)	5.60	10,133	10,444	3.1	1865.0	11.9	90.8	121,406	1.6	460,400	71.0	3.2	70.2	25.7
Upper Providence township (Montgomery)	17.81	21,231	24,355	14.7	1367.5	11.0	91.8	131,453	3.9	376,500	73.3	3.0	80.9	16.6
Upper St. Clair township (Allegheny)	9.83	19,317	19,744	2.2	2008.5	9.3	89.9	128,482	2.4	295,600	64.8	3.1	80.3	17.3
Upper Saucon township (Lehigh)	24.47	14,797	17,305	16.9	707.2	6.6	89.0	104,477	2.6	313,100	67.1	3.1	81.0	15.4
Upper Southampton township (Bucks)	6.62	15,152	14,956	-1.3	2259.2	11.6	92.4	85,963	4.8	334,400	64.3	3.7	69.1	27.5
Upper Uwchlan township (Chester)	10.89	11,234	11,823	5.2	1085.7	17.1	90.3	173,385	2.1	442,300	72.4	3.5	86.6	11.4
Uwchlan township (Chester)	10.40	18,099	18,840	4.1	1811.5	8.0	85.4	112,375	3.6	396,600	72.3	2.5	74.4	21.3
Warminster township (Bucks)	10.16	32,789	32,348	-1.3	3183.9	11.5	90.9	77,118	6.1	304,600	63.3	3.8	64.6	31.1
Warrington township (Bucks)	13.69	23,414	24,560	4.9	1794.0	10.3	92.4	106,386	3.6	401,800	70.5	2.4	76.0	21.0
Warwick township (Bucks)	10.97	14,455	14,699	1.7	1339.9	12.0	95.6	125,423	1.8	418,700	70.7	3.2	78.2	17.6
Warwick township (Lancaster)	19.77	17,983	19,536	8.6	988.2	3.2	88.3	75,514	5.5	245,400	67.2	3.7	74.1	19.6
Washington township (Franklin)	39.09	14,010	14,770	5.4	377.8	1.6	91.7	65,285	8.7	193,200	64.7	4.7	71.1	22.3
Washington city & MCD (Washington)	2.95	14,019	13,433	-4.2	4553.6	2.4	72.3	42,533	20.3	100,700	63.4	7.3	51.3	41.9
Waynesboro borough & MCD (Franklin)	3.41	10,563	10,886	3.1	3192.4	1.0	83.3	43,557	17.3	142,600	61.3	5.6	58.1	36.1
Weigelstown CDP	5.81	12,875	NA	NA	NA	2.3	88.4	54,298	7.3	148,300	66.0	2.8	66.3	28.2
West Bradford township (Chester)	18.50	12,229	13,403	9.6	724.5	5.2	92.4	125,572	3.3	356,000	75.5	4.0	85.2	10.4
West Chester borough & MCD (Chester)	1.85	18,459	20,029	8.5	10826.5	6.6	67.2	61,837	19.1	378,400	70.6	5.3	36.0	35.0
West Deer township (Allegheny)	28.87	11,775	11,986	1.8	415.2	1.7	92.6	67,577	5.6	166,300	64.0	3.9	67.4	31.6
West Goshen township (Chester)	11.86	21,855	22,973	5.1	1937.0	9.6	86.4	101,452	10.1	384,700	70.0	4.2	67.1	24.7
West Hanover township (Dauphin)	23.21	9,357	10,722	14.6	462.0	4.6	88.3	89,219	5.2	223,100	66.4	2.4	74.6	19.1
West Hempfield township (Lancaster)	18.46	16,158	16,744	3.6	907.0	4.6	95.2	79,037	7.6	211,500	68.3	3.6	78.3	19.6
West Lampeter township (Lancaster)	16.40	15,189	15,950	5.0	972.6	3.8	91.0	83,698	3.7	252,700	55.9	1.2	71.3	26.0
West Manchester township (York)	19.94	18,866	18,814	-0.3	943.5	2.4	88.3	62,241	7.7	164,700	62.3	2.8	61.5	32.5
West Mifflin borough & MCD (Allegheny)	14.21	20,309	19,699	-3.0	1386.3	1.2	91.7	52,679	13.3	99,000	61.2	6.7	62.9	32.7
West Norriton township (Montgomery)	5.89	15,643	15,613	-0.2	2650.8	14.9	83.7	75,342	8.1	219,200	69.4	4.5	57.5	35.8
Westtown township (Chester)	8.66	10,857	11,013	1.4	1271.7	7.8	88.4	119,177	6.5	446,700	68.6	1.7	78.1	18.2
West Whiteland township (Chester)	12.84	18,306	19,752	7.9	1538.3	16.2	87.2	114,837	4.4	344,600	73.3	3.6	71.8	21.9
White township (Indiana)	42.35	15,828	15,674	-1.0	370.1	2.7	87.8	56,688	13.9	173,600	52.9	4.2	55.4	37.7
Whitehall borough & MCD (Allegheny)	3.33	13,772	13,393	-2.8	4021.9	9.8	90.6	66,484	10.1	162,600	58.3	2.8	60.3	35.6
Whitehall township (Lehigh)	12.58	26,813	27,838	3.8	2212.9	16.3	86.4	63,707	6.7	187,700	68.8	4.7	67.9	26.3
Whitemarsh township (Montgomery)	14.65	17,371	18,344	5.6	1252.2	7.3	86.6	121,446	3.5	407,000	68.4	2.2	69.2	25.1
Whitpain township (Montgomery)	12.85	18,878	19,240	1.9	1497.3	13.6	88.9	128,828	3.4	458,500	64.7	4.8	75.0	20.2
Wilkes-Barre city & MCD (Luzerne)	6.98	41,535	40,766	-1.9	5840.4	10.2	78.2	37,902	23.6	75,100	57.6	9.1	57.3	37.1
Wilkinsburg borough & MCD (Allegheny)	2.25	15,860	15,292	-3.6	6796.4	3.5	80.2	36,743	21.2	87,800	64.2	6.9	36.2	56.2

Table B. Incorporated Places, Census Designated Places (CDPs), and Minor Civil Divisions (MCDs) of 10,000 or More Population — Crime, Residential Construction and Local Government Finance

STATE City, town, township, borough, or CDP (county if applicable)	Serious crimes known to police, 2018[1] Violent crime Number	Violent crime Rate[2]	Property crime Number	Property crime Rate[2]	New residential construction authorized by building permits, 2019 Value ($1,000)	Number of housing units	Percent single family	Local government finance, 2017 General revenue Total (mil dol)	Intergovernmental Total (mil dol)	Percent from state gov.	Taxes per capita[3]	General expenditure Total (mil dol)	Per capita[3] Total	Capital outlays	Debt outstanding (mil dol)
	15	16	17	18	19	20	21	22	23	24	25	26	27	28	29
PENNSYLVANIA—Con.															
Spring Garden township (York).	51	389	339	2,584	10,824	61	39.3	11.4	0.8	100.0	477	11.3	870	0	0.0
State College borough & MCD (Centre)	20	34	448	762	273	1	100.0	44.0	4.9	58.0	386	41.4	975	129	36.3
Stroud township (Monroe)	NA	NA	NA	NA	7,219	23	100.0	10.3	0.9	99.7	414	9.5	503	58	6.4
Susquehanna township (Dauphin)	46	183	296	1,175	4,690	27	100.0	16.7	2.0	80.7	522	17.2	686	27	7.1
Swatara township (Dauphin)	94	354	866	3,264	6,008	25	100.0	16.1	2.5	76.3	527	15.3	619	45	10.6
Towamencin township (Montgomery)	12	65	45	244	2,149	5	100.0	16.2	1.4	92.0	420	13.1	716	58	10.8
Tredyffrin township (Chester)	12	41	238	805	0	0	0.0	40.7	2.5	87.5	532	43.6	1,477	668	8.7
Uniontown city & MCD (Fayette)	136	1,395	455	4,666	491	8	0.0	8.8	1.2	75.0	464	8.6	883	36	5.1
Unity township (Westmoreland)	NA	NA	NA	NA	5,497	21	100.0	6.8	1.2	100.0	250	5.6	253	3	2.1
Upper Allen township (Cumberland)	7	35	68	338	21,633	145	75.2	16.7	1.3	83.7	456	17.2	870	127	21.6
Upper Chichester township (Delaware)	43	253	303	1,782	376	2	100.0	14.5	1.2	86.3	640	12.2	723	56	4.2
Upper Darby township (Delaware)	439	529	873	1,053	0	0	0.0	83.3	7.3	67.4	704	74.6	901	8	15.7
Upper Dublin township (Montgomery)	NA	NA	NA	NA	4,907	25	100.0	28.7	2.1	99.7	928	40.3	1,533	279	33.1
Upper Gwynedd township (Montgomery)	9	56	52	326	2,648	30	100.0	17.6	1.8	95.3	609	18.7	1,178	148	6.9
Upper Macungie township (Lehigh)	7	28	164	656	44,939	215	56.3	27.6	4.1	39.4	431	21.2	875	87	0.0
Upper Merion township (Montgomery)	23	75	1,105	3,603	9,102	55	29.1	43.6	5.0	95.0	915	45.4	1,499	206	29.0
Upper Moreland township (Montgomery)	22	91	419	1,733	490	3	100.0	21.6	1.8	94.3	709	20.5	851	78	3.0
Upper Providence township (Delaware)	4	38	18	172	122	1	100.0	5.9	0.6	95.1	481	5.8	559	31	2.0
Upper Providence township (Montgomery)	11	45	250	1,023	18,666	75	93.3	18.4	1.3	100.0	478	18.6	777	101	0.0
Upper St. Clair township (Allegheny)	8	41	119	602	13,827	31	100.0	34.3	2.5	74.9	978	36.1	1,829	228	53.6
Upper Saucon township (Lehigh)	2	12	79	461	13,963	43	100.0	14.6	1.4	74.8	557	12.8	761	121	10.0
Upper Southampton township (Bucks)	6	40	87	579	0	0	0.0	12.6	1.3	71.0	558	11.8	788	53	4.1
Upper Uwchlan township (Chester)	NA	NA	56	487	12,165	76	100.0	20.5	0.9	84.4	454	16.7	1,459	692	6.2
Uwchlan township (Chester)	16	84	111	583	0	0	0.0	15.0	1.6	71.4	401	15.6	825	0	1.5
Warminster township (Bucks)	25	77	282	871	1,302	10	100.0	24.2	2.3	95.0	459	22.0	679	54	4.1
Warrington township (Bucks)	18	73	158	643	14,544	55	100.0	22.0	2.6	50.0	473	25.5	1,045	185	40.8
Warwick township (Bucks)	12	82	54	369	8,335	30	100.0	9.7	0.9	100.0	529	8.1	553	55	5.8
Warwick township (Lancaster)	NA	NA	NA	NA	15,219	63	93.7	5.9	1.0	87.4	202	5.8	303	37	0.0
Washington township (Franklin)	12	82	214	1,459	14,651	81	100.0	5.6	1.5	55.8	207	5.6	385	59	1.0
Washington city & MCD (Washington)	101	748	418	3,095	468	3	100.0	16.9	3.1	55.6	842	11.9	876	78	11.9
Waynesboro borough & MCD (Franklin)	13	119	189	1,731	3,974	16	87.5	6.3	0.6	87.5	283	6.2	573	4	4.9
Weigelstown CDP	NA	NA	NA	NA	NA	NA	NA	NA	NA	NA	NA	NA	NA	NA	NA
West Bradford township (Chester)	NA	NA	NA	NA	31,557	131	100.0	7.9	0.6	100.0	272	6.5	499	81	9.9
West Chester borough & MCD (Chester)	37	182	309	1,522	6,826	46	100.0	28.5	3.0	55.1	549	32.5	1,624	224	41.9
West Deer township (Allegheny)	1	8	48	401	9,998	57	78.9	5.3	0.7	91.7	326	5.3	442	23	0.0
West Goshen township (Chester)	34	147	223	963	8,831	41	56.1	23.8	1.7	87.9	605	20.9	912	32	5.8
West Hanover township (Dauphin)	NA	NA	NA	NA	10,987	58	94.8	4.8	0.7	82.7	308	4.4	423	67	9.5
West Hempfield township (Lancaster)	18	108	143	862	9,068	86	25.6	7.3	1.0	88.3	275	6.4	390	4	0.0
West Lampeter township (Lancaster)	9	56	93	578	14,151	52	92.3	6.8	0.8	96.5	269	6.3	396	54	2.1
West Manchester township (York)	27	143	551	2,926	1,042	5	100.0	16.4	1.4	96.7	374	15.5	826	20	0.0
West Mifflin borough & MCD (Allegheny)	29	147	93	470	904	12	100.0	15.7	1.5	91.4	652	15.1	764	42	19.7
West Norriton township (Montgomery)	32	204	259	1,649	19,500	39	100.0	15.7	1.3	83.1	581	16.2	1,035	361	6.7
Westtown township (Chester)	NA	NA	NA	NA	5,966	13	100.0	11.3	0.8	82.3	562	10.1	928	124	22.1
West Whiteland township (Chester)	12	65	431	2,343	24,892	140	35.7	16.8	1.4	100.0	552	15.5	842	63	11.7
White township (Indiana)	NA	NA	NA	NA	6,585	17	100.0	6.3	0.8	100.0	179	7.4	467	60	0.0
Whitehall borough & MCD (Allegheny)	9	66	41	299	1,407	7	28.6	13.8	0.9	82.7	598	13.7	1,013	18	2.1
Whitehall township (Lehigh)	21	76	898	3,244	3,214	22	100.0	22.3	1.9	86.0	589	21.4	776	71	1.4
Whitemarsh township (Montgomery)	9	50	134	746	20,958	105	100.0	21.5	1.4	95.6	958	23.5	1,314	207	16.7
Whitpain township (Montgomery)	6	31	165	854	8,925	24	75.0	23.1	1.3	96.8	881	22.3	1,162	92	7.4
Wilkes-Barre city & MCD (Luzerne)	210	516	965	2,370	75	1	100.0	54.7	14.0	55.1	699	50.9	1,244	133	67.4
Wilkinsburg borough & MCD (Allegheny)	NA	NA	NA	NA	0	0	0.0	13.4	1.1	78.4	512	13.0	840	1	9.7

1 Data for serious crimes have not been adjusted for underreporting. This may affect comparability between geographic areas over time.
2 Per 100,000 population estimated by the FBI.   3 Based on population estimated as of July 1 of the year shown.

Table B. Incorporated Places, Census Designated Places (CDPs), and Minor Civil Divisions (MCDs) of 10,000 or More Population — **Land Area, Population, and Households, and Employment**

STATE City, town, township, borough, or CDP (county if applicable)	Land area 2010 (sq mi)	Total persons 2010	Total persons 2019	Percent change 2010–2019	Persons per square mile 2019	Percent foreign born	Percent living in the same house as previous year	Median household income	Percent of households with income below poverty level	Median value of owner-occupied housing units	Percent in civilian labor force	Unemployment rate	Family households	One person households
	1	2	3	4	5	6	7	8	9	10	11	12	13	14
PENNSYLVANIA—Con.														
Williamsport city & MCD (Lycoming)	8.73	29,374	28,186	-4.0	3228.6	2.8	79.2	39,990	24.5	110,700	59.1	6.1	54.4	37.5
Willistown township (Chester)	18.11	10,507	11,014	4.8	608.2	7.7	89.7	114,614	4.5	432,500	62.1	3.7	71.2	23.9
Willow Grove CDP	3.66	15,726	NA	NA	NA	8.0	91.7	79,162	8.1	262,800	69.5	5.1	62.9	31.0
Windsor township (York)	27.28	17,540	18,193	3.7	666.9	3.6	93.1	82,736	3.9	197,300	67.6	2.4	78.0	15.3
Worcester township (Montgomery)	16.22	9,718	10,430	7.3	643.0	13.0	92.4	128,417	4.5	458,000	61.9	5.0	76.9	21.7
Wyomissing borough & MCD (Berks)	4.51	10,425	10,635	2.0	2358.1	8.7	84.7	81,178	5.7	245,600	60.2	4.3	64.5	30.0
Yeadon borough & MCD (Delaware)	1.60	11,434	11,496	0.5	7185.0	18.0	87.0	54,487	12.8	140,500	69.1	7.8	62.6	30.9
York city & MCD (York)	5.29	43,807	43,932	0.3	8304.7	9.6	77.8	33,906	28.2	75,900	62.5	11.4	59.1	31.0
York township (York)	25.25	28,013	28,766	2.7	1139.2	6.5	87.9	69,451	7.1	191,900	61.6	2.0	65.5	27.5
RHODE ISLAND	1033.90	1,052,964	1,059,361	0.6	1024.6	13.6	87.4	67,167	13.1	261,900	64.4	5.4	62.1	31.0
Barrington town (Bristol)	8.19	16,283	16,053	-1.4	1960.1	7.5	91.2	125,431	4.3	433,200	69.2	2.6	77.0	20.4
Bristol town (Bristol)	9.79	22,918	21,915	-4.4	2238.5	10.9	84.9	72,610	9.3	337,700	59.2	3.6	62.0	30.6
Burrillville town (Providence)	54.92	15,958	16,854	5.6	306.9	2.7	84.7	84,680	9.8	253,200	70.1	5.2	71.4	22.0
Central Falls city & MCD (Providence)	1.20	19,408	19,568	0.8	16306.7	37.3	82.6	32,982	31.0	159,100	61.6	6.8	70.3	25.0
Coventry town (Kent)	59.06	34,693	34,819	0.4	589.6	3.3	93.7	73,392	9.1	241,300	67.0	4.4	68.0	25.9
Cranston city & MCD (Providence)	28.34	80,627	81,456	1.0	2874.2	14.0	89.1	72,017	9.9	243,500	63.9	4.3	63.1	31.1
Cumberland town (Providence)	26.49	33,511	35,263	5.2	1331.2	12.0	94.8	91,726	8.5	288,200	67.3	2.5	70.4	25.6
East Greenwich town (Kent)	16.37	13,129	13,120	-0.1	801.5	7.8	94.4	114,147	8.2	437,500	67.7	4.2	69.0	27.9
East Providence city & MCD (Providence)	13.29	47,069	47,618	1.2	3583.0	15.1	87.4	59,142	12.7	221,700	64.7	4.0	58.3	35.6
Glocester town (Providence)	54.23	9,751	10,323	5.9	190.4	2.8	91.7	89,391	6.5	292,000	69.8	5.0	70.6	22.8
Johnston town (Providence)	23.48	28,813	29,471	2.3	1255.2	8.9	90.7	65,125	8.1	231,400	65.1	6.0	58.5	34.9
Lincoln town (Providence)	18.07	21,052	21,987	4.4	1216.8	9.8	90.6	81,045	9.0	319,800	65.0	4.3	67.8	27.0
Middletown town (Newport)	12.69	16,143	15,888	-1.6	1252.0	10.7	83.9	73,609	9.6	379,100	63.3	3.8	63.0	29.3
Narragansett town (Washington)	13.87	15,893	15,349	-3.4	1106.6	5.4	82.9	86,920	13.8	444,300	54.2	4.6	59.1	28.2
Newport city & MCD (Newport)	7.66	24,927	24,334	-2.4	3176.8	8.7	73.1	67,102	14.6	448,800	58.2	5.2	49.0	39.4
Newport East CDP	5.75	11,769	NA	NA	NA	11.0	85.7	69,368	11.4	361,100	64.8	4.1	58.4	33.0
North Kingstown town (Washington)	43.17	26,616	26,323	-1.1	609.8	4.4	93.1	91,796	9.2	350,400	66.4	4.4	69.8	25.8
North Providence town (Providence)	5.64	32,151	32,686	1.7	5795.4	13.9	89.7	57,135	13.8	217,900	63.4	6.9	54.8	40.7
North Smithfield town (Providence)	23.90	11,966	12,582	5.1	526.4	5.2	89.4	78,617	5.9	295,900	64.1	5.3	67.2	26.6
Pawtucket city & MCD (Providence)	8.67	71,153	72,117	1.4	8318.0	25.8	88.4	50,476	17.4	194,600	69.0	7.1	59.9	33.6
Portsmouth town (Newport)	23.03	17,394	17,226	-1.0	748.0	4.3	87.5	100,453	8.2	386,600	63.1	2.0	69.0	26.6
Providence city & MCD (Providence)	18.41	177,770	179,883	1.2	9770.9	28.7	80.7	45,610	25.7	200,300	61.2	7.8	56.7	33.3
Scituate town (Providence)	48.13	10,377	10,730	3.4	222.9	2.8	94.2	96,179	2.3	323,000	69.6	3.3	68.3	22.9
Smithfield town (Providence)	26.24	21,373	21,897	2.5	834.5	4.4	91.1	85,337	5.9	288,700	59.0	3.2	59.8	34.3
South Kingstown town (Washington)	56.37	30,602	30,348	-0.8	538.4	5.2	85.9	89,917	8.6	371,400	60.5	7.4	68.3	24.9
Tiverton town (Newport)	29.06	15,781	15,662	-0.8	539.0	5.0	92.4	75,295	6.3	277,500	63.1	6.1	69.9	25.0
Valley Falls CDP	3.53	11,547	NA	NA	NA	18.2	94.7	83,090	12.5	239,000	69.5	3.2	66.2	27.4
Warren town (Bristol)	6.16	10,643	10,511	-1.2	1706.3	8.5	88.9	59,926	13.5	297,300	66.1	4.0	56.0	38.9
Warwick city & MCD (Kent)	35.00	82,689	81,004	-2.0	2314.4	6.6	90.1	73,757	7.3	225,300	66.7	3.7	61.3	32.4
Westerly CDP	15.83	17,936	NA	NA	NA	6.5	89.7	66,909	10.8	294,600	67.9	7.7	59.0	34.7
Westerly town (Washington)	29.47	22,775	22,381	-1.7	759.5	6.3	90.4	70,784	10.3	302,600	66.9	7.5	61.4	32.0
West Warwick town (Kent)	7.83	29,464	28,962	-1.7	3698.9	6.8	85.7	55,927	14.0	205,800	68.6	4.5	53.2	36.2
Woonsocket city & MCD (Providence)	7.75	41,199	41,751	1.3	5387.2	12.3	84.7	42,595	20.7	173,300	63.3	7.9	55.9	36.1
SOUTH CAROLINA	30063.72	4,625,366	5,148,714	11.3	171.3	5.0	85.7	53,199	14.9	162,300	59.7	5.8	65.6	28.9
Aiken city	21.08	29,594	30,869	4.3	1464.4	3.2	81.4	56,199	12.2	188,600	52.6	5.1	65.6	31.0
Anderson city	14.51	26,436	27,676	4.7	1907.4	3.9	79.5	33,351	22.2	136,800	58.7	6.4	53.6	42.1
Beaufort city	24.43	12,336	13,436	8.9	550.0	5.4	81.4	54,873	17.9	214,700	52.6	4.1	68.5	28.3
Berea CDP	7.70	14,295	NA	NA	NA	16.4	78.0	37,125	18.2	114,900	60.5	7.4	63.0	31.5
Bluffton town	51.97	13,054	25,557	95.8	491.8	11.2	83.2	82,481	4.0	290,800	66.3	1.4	71.5	22.4
Cayce city	16.80	13,074	14,009	7.2	833.9	5.7	78.3	52,582	15.1	129,900	66.3	4.5	46.4	37.9
Charleston city	110.55	120,364	137,566	14.3	1244.4	4.8	81.8	68,438	12.6	330,600	66.9	3.4	52.6	35.5
Clemson city	7.55	13,964	17,501	25.3	2318.0	9.8	58.8	43,568	36.2	236,500	57.1	3.6	38.1	25.2
Columbia city	136.00	130,421	131,674	1.0	968.2	5.0	64.2	47,286	20.9	181,100	56.4	6.7	48.1	40.6
Conway city	22.97	17,414	25,956	49.1	1130.0	2.5	78.8	42,508	21.1	155,000	55.8	9.4	61.6	31.2
Dentsville CDP	6.70	14,062	NA	NA	NA	6.6	81.7	38,675	17.5	123,600	69.3	10.1	56.2	37.4
Easley city	12.46	20,075	21,364	6.4	1714.6	3.5	83.3	52,414	11.8	159,800	61.4	4.4	63.8	28.8
Five Forks CDP	7.57	14,140	NA	NA	NA	9.9	85.3	114,049	4.0	300,700	69.3	3.7	89.4	9.8
Florence city	22.62	37,905	38,531	1.7	1703.4	4.4	86.3	49,525	19.4	158,600	61.0	5.2	61.9	34.1
Forest Acres city	4.60	10,422	10,298	-1.2	2238.7	5.6	86.7	69,212	7.3	193,700	63.9	4.5	58.0	39.2
Fort Mill town	19.49	11,529	22,284	93.3	1143.4	4.5	79.9	91,061	6.1	289,200	70.1	2.7	79.2	15.8
Gaffney city	8.35	12,412	12,609	1.6	1510.1	0.8	80.5	31,047	25.1	111,100	50.9	7.8	50.1	46.3
Gantt CDP	9.79	14,229	NA	NA	NA	7.5	88.8	38,341	24.5	103,700	59.1	9.0	62.8	33.0
Garden City CDP	5.31	9,209	NA	NA	NA	3.0	86.0	44,862	10.1	145,800	43.3	3.9	56.5	37.6
Goose Creek city	41.22	36,428	43,665	19.9	1059.3	6.8	78.0	68,893	9.8	188,300	61.1	4.9	74.3	21.0
Greenville city	29.64	59,280	70,635	19.2	2383.1	6.6	74.2	56,609	13.9	292,400	69.0	4.3	49.3	41.8
Greenwood city	16.32	23,214	23,403	0.8	1434.0	6.8	85.5	33,699	26.2	97,400	61.8	9.5	55.6	35.9
Greer city	22.87	25,879	33,373	29.0	1459.2	18.0	83.8	61,744	11.5	173,100	70.3	3.7	65.1	29.4
Hanahan city	10.53	17,978	26,917	49.7	2556.2	9.7	83.6	70,043	10.0	228,800	69.1	3.7	67.8	25.2

Table B. Incorporated Places, Census Designated Places (CDPs), and Minor Civil Divisions (MCDs) of 10,000 or More Population — Crime, Residential Construction and Local Government Finance

STATE City, town, township, borough, or CDP (county if applicable)	Serious crimes known to police, 2018[1] Violent crime Number	Rate[2]	Property crime Number	Rate[2]	New residential construction authorized by building permits, 2019 Value ($1,000)	Number of housing units	Percent single family	Local government finance, 2017 General revenue Total (mil dol)	Intergovernmental Total (mil dol)	Percent from state gov.	Taxes per capita[3]	General expenditure Total (mil dol)	Per capita[3] Total	Capital outlays	Debt outstanding (mil dol)
	15	16	17	18	19	20	21	22	23	24	25	26	27	28	29
PENNSYLVANIA—Con.															
Williamsport city & MCD (Lycoming)	71	251	646	2,280	120	1	100.0	37.4	15.5	69.5	698	26.6	933	107	22.5
Willistown township (Chester)	3	27	29	264	12,398	11	100.0	12.5	0.7	99.7	790	16.2	1,482	62	14.9
Willow Grove CDP	NA	NA	NA	NA	NA	NA	NA	NA	NA	NA	NA	NA	NA	NA	NA
Windsor township (York)	NA	NA	NA	NA	2,831	14	100.0	10.4	1.6	67.1	215	9.3	518	107	0.2
Worcester township (Montgomery)	NA	NA	NA	NA	6,728	21	100.0	6.0	0.5	92.6	317	5.9	567	99	2.5
Wyomissing borough & MCD (Berks)	13	124	259	2,478	800	1	100.0	14.5	1.0	95.8	859	13.8	1,327	49	0.2
Yeadon borough & MCD (Delaware)	86	747	384	3,336	0	0	0.0	9.4	0.5	97.6	490	8.8	767	43	3.1
York city & MCD (York)	450	1,019	1,137	2,574	10,374	68	17.6	76.8	7.8	61.0	685	66.9	1,519	48	94.3
York township (York)	NA	NA	NA	NA	9,544	67	29.9	20.8	1.7	100.0	338	22.1	777	105	0.0
RHODE ISLAND	2,317	219	17,561	1,661	280,414	1,400	72.9	X	X	X	X	X	X	X	X
Barrington town (Bristol)	8	50	113	701	7,599	19	68.4	86.7	18.0	100.0	3,648	80.4	4,992	438	87.7
Bristol town (Bristol)	10	45	89	402	10,188	22	100.0	57.0	4.2	100.0	2,006	56.2	2,534	251	58.4
Burrillville town (Providence)	19	113	97	578	2,985	24	100.0	59.9	23.0	98.6	1,898	56.5	3,395	246	15.0
Central Falls city & MCD (Providence)	83	430	293	1,519	480	8	100.0	20.9	4.4	100.0	790	16.8	871	0	11.1
Coventry town (Kent)	35	101	452	1,298	8,642	54	81.5	117.5	40.2	94.4	2,041	119.4	3,454	173	52.8
Cranston city & MCD (Providence)	118	146	1,140	1,406	7,614	56	71.4	332.8	96.2	87.6	2,346	306.0	3,777	209	93.9
Cumberland town (Providence)	23	66	304	868	12,353	63	65.1	102.0	28.3	99.6	1,920	96.8	2,786	147	46.2
East Greenwich town (Kent)	10	77	115	881	2,846	11	100.0	77.6	7.4	100.0	4,452	70.5	5,395	201	69.1
East Providence city & MCD (Providence)	50	105	515	1,084	0	0	0.0	121.8	53.9	96.7	966	174.6	3,686	132	86.1
Glocester town (Providence)	5	49	30	295	6,473	39	74.4	29.1	4.0	98.6	2,420	28.8	2,851	126	2.2
Johnston town (Providence)	40	136	344	1,173	5,653	31	100.0	120.0	24.5	99.6	2,725	119.4	4,082	241	14.1
Lincoln town (Providence)	17	78	386	1,763	12,270	38	100.0	88.4	26.7	98.2	2,538	83.8	3,869	151	30.5
Middletown town (Newport)	13	81	209	1,304	8,323	42	90.5	79.6	18.6	93.7	3,128	76.8	4,783	264	39.2
Narragansett town (Washington)	8	52	123	796	8,616	29	100.0	74.0	11.6	96.1	3,319	67.8	4,371	495	27.6
Newport city & MCD (Newport)	85	342	600	2,413	4,532	8	100.0	140.5	26.4	92.9	3,199	146.8	5,955	1028	171.6
Newport East CDP	NA	NA	NA	NA	NA	NA	NA	NA	NA	NA	NA	NA	NA	NA	NA
North Kingstown town (Washington)	10	38	231	885	6,893	44	81.8	114.2	27.7	76.7	2,938	116.0	4,427	399	48.7
North Providence town (Providence)	38	117	316	973	1,136	9	100.0	111.4	36.0	88.2	2,197	108.4	3,341	224	10.8
North Smithfield town (Providence)	13	104	261	2,093	2,329	28	100.0	48.1	9.9	100.0	2,749	47.8	3,863	353	35.2
Pawtucket city & MCD (Providence)	321	447	1,882	2,618	1,521	13	100.0	236.7	122.6	95.0	1,456	239.4	3,343	193	188.3
Portsmouth town (Newport)	7	40	77	441	10,807	30	100.0	66.4	11.1	86.8	2,922	73.3	4,204	511	25.2
Providence city & MCD (Providence)	819	455	5,679	3,152	12,705	197	7.1	898.0	401.5	93.5	2,075	790.6	4,411	148	711.1
Scituate town (Providence)	8	75	38	358	5,346	23	100.0	35.6	5.4	99.6	2,668	35.6	3,357	99	7.4
Smithfield town (Providence)	21	97	189	869	9,940	27	100.0	77.1	11.8	100.0	2,750	78.8	3,646	211	30.7
South Kingstown town (Washington)	16	52	203	659	23,720	129	75.2	98.2	15.2	96.3	2,376	103.6	3,362	159	9.8
Tiverton town (Newport)	16	101	167	1,055	8,894	35	94.3	54.6	9.8	98.5	2,586	48.7	3,084	70	43.6
Valley Falls CDP	NA	NA	NA	NA	NA	NA	NA	NA	NA	NA	NA	NA	NA	NA	NA
Warren town (Bristol)	18	173	114	1,097	1,251	6	100.0	27.0	1.1	91.9	2,335	23.6	2,263	272	1.1
Warwick city & MCD (Kent)	73	91	1,372	1,707	9,832	96	40.6	337.8	55.9	96.2	2,974	334.7	4,141	181	145.6
Westerly CDP	NA	NA	NA	NA	NA	NA	NA	NA	NA	NA	NA	NA	NA	NA	NA
Westerly town (Washington)	17	75	288	1,278	16,435	44	77.3	95.9	17.6	99.9	3,149	87.7	3,880	74	75.3
West Warwick town (Kent)	65	228	306	1,075	832	10	20.0	107.6	31.9	99.0	2,179	114.9	3,980	192	51.0
Woonsocket city & MCD (Providence)	246	590	898	2,153	2,848	19	100.0	176.1	86.4	95.2	1,567	162.0	3,903	229	152.8
SOUTH CAROLINA	24,825	488	153,421	3,018	8,006,648	36,034	86.2	X	X	X	X	X	X	X	X
Aiken city	120	389	NA	NA	27,355	135	63.0	49.4	1.9	50.1	936	44.4	1,445	145	0.0
Anderson city	NA	NA	NA	NA	11,781	120	100.0	44.7	2.7	20.5	808	39.5	1,448	92	179.0
Beaufort city	81	582	581	4,174	25,758	74	67.6	23.3	3.0	14.7	1,126	22.5	1,672	321	18.3
Berea CDP	NA	NA	NA	NA	NA	NA	NA	NA	NA	NA	NA	NA	NA	NA	NA
Bluffton town	50	222	252	1,116	408,535	1,190	100.0	25.1	2.4	67.4	919	23.4	1,139	305	15.1
Cayce city	112	787	661	4,643	1,575	12	100.0	22.5	0.4	55.3	679	20.7	1,470	251	105.0
Charleston city	415	303	2,848	2,077	149,548	1,188	69.7	262.8	12.4	45.3	1,302	176.9	1,304	117	26.3
Clemson city	NA	NA	NA	NA	27,650	172	31.4	24.2	5.4	36.4	718	20.5	1,235	397	9.2
Columbia city	986	738	6,753	5,057	87,671	474	97.9	262.9	66.2	40.5	738	309.0	2,306	614	595.0
Conway city	141	569	960	3,874	37,598	248	99.2	25.3	3.5	40.6	495	29.4	1,235	317	2.1
Dentsville CDP	NA	NA	NA	NA	NA	NA	NA	NA	NA	NA	NA	NA	NA	NA	NA
Easley city	105	495	1,254	5,914	36,153	169	85.8	28.2	5.8	100.0	569	29.0	1,375	119	46.0
Five Forks CDP	NA	NA	NA	NA	NA	NA	NA	NA	NA	NA	NA	NA	NA	NA	NA
Florence city	362	957	2,462	6,510	49,076	382	61.3	54.7	3.4	49.5	742	66.3	1,719	684	191.7
Forest Acres city	50	482	654	6,304	9,002	38	100.0	8.0	0.6	68.2	666	7.8	751	83	0.0
Fort Mill town	31	167	328	1,762	327,818	1,010	80.7	14.4	1.0	54.6	489	11.1	634	35	0.0
Gaffney city	104	812	908	7,085	312	4	100.0	14.1	2.7	47.9	805	13.5	1,076	84	0.5
Gantt CDP	NA	NA	NA	NA	NA	NA	NA	NA	NA	NA	NA	NA	NA	NA	NA
Garden City CDP	NA	NA	NA	NA	NA	NA	NA	NA	NA	NA	NA	NA	NA	NA	NA
Goose Creek city	105	241	955	2,193	62,583	363	100.0	24.8	1.2	3.3	448	23.5	563	71	26.7
Greenville city	368	529	2,810	4,037	156,145	933	29.3	181.3	8.3	100.0	1,357	120.2	1,755	201	108.8
Greenwood city	392	1,685	1,594	6,852	NA	NA	NA	18.6	4.8	47.6	487	19.6	840	101	31.3
Greer city	134	422	1,144	3,606	162,152	851	87.5	37.6	3.1	26.0	735	31.1	1,002	76	78.1
Hanahan city	60	230	346	1,328	39,999	464	20.5	11.0	2.3	100.0	252	11.0	447	44	1.6

1 Data for serious crimes have not been adjusted for underreporting. This may affect comparability between geographic areas over time.
2 Per 100,000 population estimated by the FBI.   3 Based on population estimated as of July 1 of the year shown.

Table B. Incorporated Places, Census Designated Places (CDPs), and Minor Civil Divisions (MCDs) of 10,000 or More Population — Land Area, Population, and Households, and Employment

STATE City, town, township, borough, or CDP (county if applicable)	Land area 2010 (sq mi)	Population Total persons 2010	Total persons 2019	Percent change 2010–2019	Persons per square mile, 2019	Population characteristics 2015–2019 Percent foreign born	Percent living in the same house as previous year	Income and poverty 2015–2019 Median household income	Percent of households with income below poverty level	Median value of owner-occupied housing units	Employment, 2015–2019 Percent in civilian labor force	Unemployment rate	Households, 2015–2019 (percent of households) Family households	One person households
	1	2	3	4	5	6	7	8	9	10	11	12	13	14
SOUTH CAROLINA—Con.														
Hilton Head Island town	41.36	37,094	39,861	7.5	963.8	10.6	86.6	84,575	8.4	483,600	50.5	3.8	66.8	27.8
Irmo town	6.85	11,117	12,483	12.3	1822.3	2.2	92.2	66,313	8.1	125,000	71.0	8.1	71.0	26.4
James Island town	4.74	11,218	12,109	7.9	2554.6	2.3	91.2	81,674	4.9	300,600	68.0	1.2	64.3	28.9
Ladson CDP	7.03	13,790	NA	NA	NA	3.2	86.7	63,808	9.1	163,600	63.3	5.8	74.7	20.1
Lake Wylie CDP	7.86	8,841	NA	NA	NA	4.8	80.1	99,335	4.4	322,200	66.6	1.7	80.0	16.8
Lexington town	11.84	18,507	22,157	19.7	1871.4	7.3	77.2	72,996	9.1	190,500	63.2	3.7	66.6	27.6
Mauldin city	10.91	23,184	25,409	9.6	2329.0	9.7	84.8	67,860	5.9	163,800	70.4	4.8	63.6	32.6
Moncks Corner town	8.61	7,690	11,986	55.9	1392.1	2.4	78.3	65,540	11.3	203,200	62.6	2.4	74.1	22.6
Mount Pleasant town	49.34	68,360	91,684	34.1	1858.2	5.2	84.1	103,232	5.7	461,000	68.1	2.1	66.8	26.1
Myrtle Beach city	23.56	27,041	34,695	28.3	1472.6	12.2	84.4	43,200	18.4	216,100	58.9	7.0	55.6	38.2
Newberry city	8.94	10,350	10,199	-1.5	1140.8	3.2	82.2	31,831	21.6	95,300	53.9	9.3	55.2	37.3
North Augusta city	20.51	21,309	23,845	11.9	1162.6	4.8	86.2	59,931	11.2	161,100	62.6	6.0	66.2	28.6
North Charleston city	77.50	97,579	115,382	18.2	1488.8	9.6	81.8	45,510	18.9	174,800	63.9	5.0	54.0	38.3
North Myrtle Beach city	21.41	13,816	16,819	21.7	785.6	9.0	86.6	60,982	7.8	266,200	51.5	7.9	60.6	31.7
Oak Grove CDP	6.43	10,291	NA	NA	NA	5.4	91.2	49,390	13.2	130,300	65.9	10.1	59.4	34.2
Orangeburg city	9.01	13,870	12,654	-8.8	1404.4	2.0	86.8	31,455	27.3	105,600	53.7	11.0	51.2	44.7
Parker CDP	6.84	11,431	NA	NA	NA	16.9	83.6	34,181	26.8	81,400	59.2	4.8	54.9	34.0
Port Royal town	16.96	10,641	13,235	24.4	780.4	5.0	68.6	49,797	9.0	233,300	40.3	7.2	59.2	37.0
Red Bank CDP	11.81	9,617	NA	NA	NA	3.5	91.3	53,693	15.5	127,800	69.1	6.2	73.4	25.8
Red Hill CDP	11.06	13,223	NA	NA	NA	5.6	81.9	46,799	17.2	167,900	58.2	8.1	67.1	24.0
Rock Hill city	38.59	66,878	75,048	12.2	1944.8	5.7	80.7	50,444	15.2	155,800	66.9	5.7	59.5	32.8
St. Andrews CDP	6.19	20,493	NA	NA	NA	8.1	71.0	37,042	20.0	100,500	71.0	9.7	45.8	44.3
Seven Oaks CDP	7.63	15,144	NA	NA	NA	5.5	79.7	56,048	7.9	150,100	69.2	5.4	62.3	32.4
Simpsonville city	9.23	18,436	24,221	31.4	2624.2	7.8	83.0	71,990	4.1	173,400	71.9	3.6	72.1	23.9
Socastee CDP	13.35	19,952	NA	NA	NA	8.6	86.0	50,147	15.0	165,400	61.4	4.8	67.1	22.3
Spartanburg city	19.77	36,753	37,399	1.8	1891.7	4.3	80.6	40,053	21.0	125,600	60.4	7.3	57.0	37.3
Summerville town	19.69	42,960	52,549	22.3	2668.8	4.6	83.3	59,180	11.3	207,800	66.1	5.4	67.8	26.8
Sumter city	32.63	40,520	39,642	-2.2	1214.9	4.2	80.2	40,662	18.4	138,900	54.3	10.0	63.6	32.6
Taylors CDP	10.57	21,617	NA	NA	NA	7.8	88.1	61,667	9.5	165,200	65.1	5.2	69.1	24.7
Tega Cay city	4.52	7,790	11,335	45.5	2507.7	6.4	86.5	130,918	0.8	331,100	68.8	5.0	85.3	14.0
Wade Hampton CDP	8.91	20,622	NA	NA	NA	13.4	85.4	54,331	12.1	185,900	63.5	4.6	59.5	34.1
West Columbia city	8.90	16,608	17,998	8.4	2022.2	7.9	81.6	46,623	13.8	142,800	62.7	4.6	45.3	41.0
SOUTH DAKOTA	75809.69	814,198	884,659	8.7	11.7	3.7	84.2	58,275	11.5	167,100	67.7	3.4	63.4	30.0
Aberdeen city	16.04	26,112	28,257	8.2	1761.7	4.7	81.5	52,651	11.5	161,800	68.6	3.1	56.6	36.6
Brookings city	13.46	22,074	24,415	10.6	1813.9	7.8	71.8	53,863	14.5	181,000	71.1	4.1	46.1	36.2
Huron city	9.51	12,610	13,380	6.1	1406.9	18.5	84.2	46,106	14.1	91,900	64.9	1.6	56.8	38.4
Mitchell city	11.47	15,285	15,679	2.6	1367.0	1.9	76.9	46,661	13.8	147,200	68.5	2.3	55.8	37.8
Pierre city	13.03	13,646	13,867	1.6	1064.2	1.3	77.7	62,192	12.8	175,600	68.0	3.3	55.5	39.2
Rapid City city	54.71	68,994	77,503	12.3	1416.6	2.5	81.1	52,351	13.1	184,700	63.4	5.7	57.8	36.1
Sioux Falls city	78.23	153,978	183,793	19.4	2349.4	8.5	79.4	59,912	10.2	189,800	73.8	3.0	60.1	32.1
Spearfish city	16.45	10,465	11,756	12.3	714.7	2.4	74.0	46,193	14.4	212,700	63.5	1.5	50.4	39.3
Vermillion city	4.57	10,578	10,926	3.3	2390.8	5.2	56.5	40,874	28.5	159,600	71.6	6.0	46.0	31.4
Watertown city	18.12	21,531	22,174	3.0	1223.7	2.0	83.8	50,971	14.6	170,500	70.3	2.4	58.2	32.8
Yankton city	8.58	14,467	14,687	1.5	1711.8	1.7	81.5	50,582	13.7	148,700	62.0	2.6	57.0	35.7
TENNESSEE	41237.96	6,346,276	6,829,174	7.6	165.6	5.1	85.5	53,320	14.7	167,200	61.0	5.3	65.8	28.3
Arlington town	23.02	11,509	11,743	2.0	510.1	3.6	88.4	102,114	3.1	238,500	72.2	1.8	85.6	13.3
Athens city	15.51	13,703	14,020	2.3	903.9	5.0	79.8	31,913	29.6	148,800	49.6	6.6	54.1	40.3
Bartlett city	32.28	56,941	59,440	4.4	1841.4	6.1	88.6	84,688	6.0	185,100	63.8	4.0	78.4	18.7
Brentwood city	41.10	37,062	42,783	15.4	1040.9	9.1	89.8	168,688	3.3	655,400	65.6	2.6	85.9	12.5
Bristol city	32.66	26,767	26,987	0.8	826.3	1.8	86.3	42,010	18.8	133,600	57.0	7.9	59.5	35.2
Brownsville city	9.86	10,332	9,435	-8.7	956.9	4.1	88.3	33,789	25.2	88,100	58.2	5.6	60.7	36.5
Chattanooga city	142.96	170,322	182,799	7.3	1278.7	6.4	83.6	45,527	16.0	167,500	61.9	6.1	52.0	40.5
Clarksville city	98.80	132,901	158,146	19.0	1600.7	5.3	77.2	53,604	14.6	154,300	58.0	6.9	68.2	24.7
Cleveland city	27.09	41,265	45,504	10.3	1679.7	9.4	78.2	44,633	18.5	171,500	60.6	4.8	60.0	31.9
Collegedale city	12.05	8,544	11,378	33.2	944.2	10.3	76.0	59,015	17.0	229,000	62.0	3.3	59.6	31.4
Collierville town	36.20	45,599	51,040	11.9	1409.9	10.4	88.1	113,996	4.6	319,300	67.0	2.1	81.8	16.2
Columbia city	32.98	34,649	40,335	16.4	1223.0	4.1	85.0	49,284	13.7	151,000	62.0	4.1	65.4	29.0
Cookeville city	35.39	31,122	34,706	11.5	980.7	6.1	73.9	38,256	24.1	166,700	57.6	8.1	53.4	33.8
Crossville city	20.40	10,822	11,779	8.8	577.4	3.8	73.0	34,113	21.4	147,000	50.3	8.3	55.1	37.1
Dickson city	20.07	14,654	15,575	6.3	776.0	3.3	84.3	49,805	15.7	156,500	59.3	2.5	63.2	28.1
Dyersburg city	17.32	17,136	16,314	-4.8	941.9	2.6	80.8	38,614	25.4	105,800	56.8	8.7	65.5	29.3
East Ridge city	8.28	20,991	21,182	0.9	2558.2	9.6	87.3	47,203	12.0	130,400	63.6	4.3	56.3	36.5
Elizabethton city	9.55	14,246	13,509	-5.2	1414.6	2.4	82.2	36,863	23.4	124,000	49.6	5.8	60.6	32.7
Farragut town	15.97	20,672	23,778	15.0	1488.9	7.4	88.7	108,511	4.0	370,400	57.5	1.9	77.9	20.1
Franklin city	41.58	62,569	83,097	32.8	1998.5	11.7	80.3	98,231	6.2	412,400	70.8	3.2	72.5	21.7
Gallatin city	31.83	30,352	42,918	41.4	1348.4	6.8	84.5	59,745	11.8	222,800	61.3	2.6	67.7	27.3
Germantown city	19.99	38,836	39,225	1.0	1962.2	7.8	86.4	118,163	3.3	331,700	63.5	2.9	79.5	18.8
Goodlettsville city	14.32	15,914	16,798	5.6	1173.0	7.1	84.1	60,268	9.4	218,800	65.9	5.1	64.1	31.3
Greeneville town	17.00	15,046	14,891	-1.0	875.9	2.1	83.4	37,121	20.5	129,000	47.2	5.0	58.4	38.8
Hartsville/Trousdale County	114.34	7,864	11,284	43.5	98.7	1.0	87.4	56,321	8.7	155,700	57.5	6.3	65.3	30.7
Hendersonville city	31.39	51,333	58,113	13.2	1851.3	5.4	85.3	72,539	6.1	266,100	69.8	3.5	69.3	27.1
Jackson city	58.30	66,847	67,191	0.5	1152.5	3.7	87.4	43,621	21.3	133,200	58.3	5.9	62.4	32.3
Johnson City city	43.09	63,383	66,906	5.6	1552.7	6.1	76.6	41,682	21.5	167,500	61.0	5.5	53.7	36.9
Kingsport city	52.54	52,997	54,127	2.1	1030.2	2.4	84.1	42,856	17.8	145,800	53.0	6.4	60.4	35.5
Knoxville city	98.71	178,134	187,603	5.3	1900.5	5.8	76.7	40,341	21.9	136,300	64.2	5.4	49.5	39.2
Lakeland city	23.48	12,411	12,642	1.9	538.4	5.7	89.7	103,074	5.2	257,400	69.0	3.5	80.1	16.2
La Vergne city	24.58	32,597	35,716	9.6	1453.1	13.6	89.4	64,531	9.0	160,900	74.7	4.3	79.4	16.7
Lawrenceburg city	12.67	10,506	11,035	5.0	871.0	3.2	84.9	34,086	25.0	101,500	48.2	7.8	54.9	36.5
Lebanon city	39.65	26,187	36,479	39.3	920.0	6.8	82.8	54,228	13.4	223,600	62.3	4.4	70.0	24.1
Lewisburg city	13.51	11,100	12,368	11.4	915.5	6.0	88.6	42,298	15.8	96,800	57.6	8.9	62.8	31.3
McMinnville city	11.06	13,634	13,769	1.0	1244.9	7.7	82.5	35,909	26.5	98,400	52.6	6.9	56.1	39.3
Manchester city	14.26	10,111	11,038	9.2	774.1	3.3	81.4	50,009	16.5	129,700	58.1	1.8	62.4	32.0
Martin city	12.41	11,461	10,484	-8.5	844.8	3.2	71.3	32,364	30.4	128,600	52.4	5.6	51.8	31.9

Table B. Incorporated Places, Census Designated Places (CDPs), and Minor Civil Divisions (MCDs) of 10,000 or More Population — **Crime, Residential Construction and Local Government Finance**

STATE City, town, township, borough, or CDP (county if applicable)	Serious crimes known to police, 2018[1]: Violent crime: Number	Violent crime: Rate[2]	Property crime: Number	Property crime: Rate[2]	New residential construction authorized by building permits, 2019: Value ($1,000)	Number of housing units	Percent single family	Local government finance, 2017: General revenue: Total (mil dol)	Intergovernmental: Total (mil dol)	Intergovernmental: Percent from state gov.	Taxes per capita[3]	General expenditure: Total (mil dol)	Per capita[3]: Total	Per capita[3]: Capital outlays	Debt outstanding (mil dol)
	15	16	17	18	19	20	21	22	23	24	25	26	27	28	29
SOUTH CAROLINA—Con.															
Hilton Head Island town	NA	NA	NA	NA	58,862	105	100.0	73.0	1.8	57.9	1,476	63.2	1,572	349	90.1
Irmo town	64	516	447	3,601	NA	NA	NA	5.2	0.3	100.0	337	5.0	409	0	0.0
James Island town	NA	NA	NA	NA	NA	NA	NA	1.8	1.5	100.0	22	0.4	31	0	0.0
Ladson CDP	NA	NA	NA	NA	NA	NA	NA	NA	NA	NA	NA	NA	NA	NA	NA
Lake Wylie CDP	NA	NA	NA	NA	NA	NA	NA	NA	NA	NA	NA	NA	NA	NA	NA
Lexington town	79	364	662	3,054	53,667	220	100.0	29.5	1.5	65.2	651	25.7	1,208	344	85.8
Mauldin city	42	165	439	1,727	16,881	102	100.0	19.8	1.7	1.5	607	17.0	674	65	4.2
Moncks Corner town	68	592	409	3,562	55,782	175	94.3	8.4	0.4	100.0	578	10.9	1,020	407	7.5
Mount Pleasant town	138	154	1,221	1,361	216,214	547	100.0	146.0	7.3	57.7	1,014	145.8	1,670	714	226.4
Myrtle Beach city	473	1,404	3,553	10,547	155,479	525	97.0	211.7	18.1	76.5	3,409	133.5	4,089	352	208.4
Newberry city	91	884	457	4,440	237	2	100.0	16.0	2.6	18.7	502	20.1	1,946	499	57.0
North Augusta city	43	186	893	3,856	51,162	166	100.0	32.0	3.6	19.7	602	29.8	1,298	173	36.2
North Charleston city	1,039	921	6,567	5,820	137,694	1,439	38.2	148.4	9.4	31.1	1,101	134.6	1,214	193	199.6
North Myrtle Beach city	105	629	NA	NA	76,756	294	98.6	72.7	9.4	73.9	1,872	63.9	3,930	956	19.2
Oak Grove CDP	NA	NA	NA	NA	NA	NA	NA	NA	NA	NA	NA	NA	NA	NA	NA
Orangeburg city	170	1,326	750	5,850	306	3	100.0	35.2	1.1	62.4	653	26.7	2,074	0	1.0
Parker CDP	NA	NA	NA	NA	NA	NA	NA	NA	NA	NA	NA	NA	NA	NA	NA
Port Royal town	16	121	198	1,497	79,363	633	18.5	7.3	0.3	82.0	379	7.1	554	21	0.8
Red Bank CDP	NA	NA	NA	NA	NA	NA	NA	NA	NA	NA	NA	NA	NA	NA	NA
Red Hill CDP	NA	NA	NA	NA	NA	NA	NA	NA	NA	NA	NA	NA	NA	NA	NA
Rock Hill city	361	488	2,794	3,773	100,888	433	59.6	105.3	11.1	22.6	616	102.3	1,394	317	287.3
St. Andrews CDP	NA	NA	NA	NA	NA	NA	NA	NA	NA	NA	NA	NA	NA	NA	NA
Seven Oaks CDP	NA	NA	NA	NA	NA	NA	NA	NA	NA	NA	NA	NA	NA	NA	NA
Simpsonville city	41	181	694	3,065	50,154	421	70.5	43.8	18.1	5.3	488	43.2	1,964	812	29.7
Socastee CDP	NA	NA	NA	NA	NA	NA	NA	NA	NA	NA	NA	NA	NA	NA	NA
Spartanburg city	NA	NA	NA	NA	6,857	29	100.0	68.0	23.8	10.1	963	42.6	1,138	63	192.7
Summerville town	140	272	1,740	3,374	46,430	213	100.0	39.8	3.9	77.4	537	35.3	684	81	7.1
Sumter city	366	917	1,873	4,695	NA	NA	NA	61.5	6.9	23.6	715	48.0	1,209	168	34.8
Taylors CDP	NA	NA	NA	NA	NA	NA	NA	NA	NA	NA	NA	NA	NA	NA	NA
Tega Cay city	7	65	219	2,035	35,030	110	100.0	14.3	0.2	100.0	719	12.3	1,193	145	19.6
Wade Hampton CDP	NA	NA	NA	NA	NA	NA	NA	NA	NA	NA	NA	NA	NA	NA	NA
West Columbia city	181	1,042	1,292	7,439	12,200	95	35.8	16.6	0.6	85.3	602	14.3	816	88	80.4
SOUTH DAKOTA	3,570	405	15,251	1,729	836,315	4,415	70.8	X	X	X	X	X	X	X	X
Aberdeen city	124	432	602	2,097	3,433	51	100.0	45.9	8.4	13.9	992	32.6	1,144	0	62.0
Brookings city	46	190	324	1,339	19,219	173	39.9	125.6	1.2	77.5	799	141.4	5,826	1510	57.1
Huron city	56	425	221	1,675	767	5	60.0	17.7	0.9	93.7	872	15.5	1,154	112	0.0
Mitchell city	81	518	573	3,661	5,221	32	62.5	39.7	3.2	80.7	1,821	18.7	1,186	247	27.9
Pierre city	70	498	380	2,705	1,200	6	100.0	12.4	1.2	44.8	39	18.2	1,299	0	28.8
Rapid City city	492	654	2,194	2,914	65,956	368	55.4	146.3	13.5	53.6	1,137	96.2	1,278	104	148.0
Sioux Falls city	788	437	5,288	2,932	279,303	1,656	61.2	292.5	18.1	50.7	1,152	270.6	1,523	550	380.9
Spearfish city	25	213	375	3,188	19,972	66	81.8	21.0	1.1	60.5	1,061	18.3	1,571	360	25.2
Vermillion city	26	241	216	1,999	7,083	17	100.0	14.3	1.2	66.4	594	11.7	1,084	107	28.8
Watertown city	67	300	382	1,711	8,991	67	58.2	26.5	1.2	100.0	532	30.7	1,379	467	44.7
Yankton city	75	516	379	2,610	8,468	66	42.4	26.0	4.1	39.8	934	23.7	1,632	561	28.7
TENNESSEE	42,226	624	191,279	2,825	7,876,497	41,361	71.6	X	X	X	X	X	X	X	X
Arlington town	NA	NA	NA	NA	NA	NA	NA	10.3	3.3	45.8	341	6.2	531	112	17.0
Athens city	119	873	1,043	7,654	2,047	20	100.0	39.7	23.1	58.2	656	34.2	2,472	156	26.8
Bartlett city	190	320	1,119	1,884	6,891	30	100.0	65.4	23.9	40.6	403	66.0	1,116	224	46.1
Brentwood city	35	80	403	926	58,750	109	100.0	58.7	25.6	37.8	468	51.3	1,204	285	44.9
Bristol city	151	562	857	3,190	12,725	149	16.8	114.3	57.2	43.5	1,379	75.3	2,804	156	2.2
Brownsville city	106	1,117	385	4,057	0	0	0.0	11.9	5.3	34.0	435	12.3	1,274	1	0.0
Chattanooga city	1,891	1,048	10,930	6,059	161,842	1,130	38.4	533.7	132.3	32.3	940	391.0	2,178	187	706.5
Clarksville city	1,041	666	4,514	2,889	156,985	1,588	89.9	158.6	54.0	69.4	275	123.3	806	100	795.3
Cleveland city	412	917	2,512	5,588	37,022	300	56.7	138.1	89.8	50.5	633	136.6	3,069	837	121.3
Collegedale city	5	41	181	1,485	7,555	28	100.0	13.2	3.9	30.9	475	10.9	946	204	1.8
Collierville town	83	163	868	1,703	80,813	199	100.0	68.5	5.8	100.0	925	45.6	908	64	123.5
Columbia city	246	634	1,246	3,211	54,953	490	65.1	61.0	16.8	9.1	426	52.2	1,361	87	57.4
Cookeville city	143	423	1,418	4,197	40,477	303	70.3	306.3	19.4	36.1	429	316.2	9,463	494	91.8
Crossville city	95	824	538	4,664	87,424	405	100.0	21.9	2.2	100.0	1,114	17.8	1,550	284	36.3
Dickson city	133	851	757	4,841	9,522	46	100.0	16.1	7.7	5.2	466	13.9	893	95	20.2
Dyersburg city	204	1,245	943	5,756	3,009	24	91.7	82.8	48.3	66.1	1,015	66.2	4,030	532	10.2
East Ridge city	100	473	749	3,544	5,898	45	100.0	16.2	4.0	97.6	460	15.7	739	85	7.4
Elizabethton city	62	454	680	4,979	30	2	0.0	47.2	27.0	69.7	812	47.8	3,507	173	59.0
Farragut town	NA	NA	NA	NA	33,826	78	100.0	9.0	1.0	100.0	322	2.6	113	113	0.0
Franklin city	119	147	982	1,215	289,324	1,099	46.0	128.0	55.8	41.4	387	91.3	1,167	86	195.9
Gallatin city	121	315	538	1,399	125,850	579	77.2	59.2	31.7	58.4	443	39.7	1,061	103	68.0
Germantown city	30	77	605	1,544	NA	NA	NA	68.7	17.3	45.7	834	59.4	1,518	122	32.0
Goodlettsville city	78	459	534	3,141	31,513	97	100.0	18.6	4.9	48.6	675	20.4	1,923	412	13.5
Greeneville town	65	437	636	4,278	3,088	17	100.0	68.9	39.9	49.1	1,105	52.2	3,490	188	48.8
Hartsville/Trousdale County	NA	NA	NA	NA	NA	NA	NA	19.9	12.8	89.7	429	23.5	2,167	391	0.0
Hendersonville city	113	193	914	1,564	126,357	432	100.0	44.9	15.1	48.4	389	43.8	760	115	4.8
Jackson city	670	1,002	2,866	4,287	34,172	156	100.0	75.7	16.4	12.6	562	82.5	1,236	168	124.2
Johnson City city	274	410	2,622	3,925	37,161	231	58.4	251.9	136.2	41.3	892	200.8	3,035	199	382.6
Kingsport city	404	756	2,801	5,239	14,277	66	87.9	197.0	110.3	42.0	988	179.2	3,350	605	241.2
Knoxville city	1,508	799	8,827	4,679	201,120	1,224	35.1	402.4	43.6	51.1	1,198	290.1	1,552	498	542.4
Lakeland city	NA	NA	NA	NA	NA	NA	NA	6.2	2.6	88.8	69	6.6	526	131	10.6
La Vergne city	157	434	820	2,267	13,820	78	100.0	36.6	17.7	73.2	288	22.7	637	68	35.7
Lawrenceburg city	67	620	556	5,145	1,980	10	80.0	17.0	3.2	42.8	787	16.1	1,485	122	42.0
Lebanon city	185	558	940	2,833	133,761	834	89.4	34.6	17.8	33.3	402	41.6	1,279	288	69.5
Lewisburg city	80	669	216	1,805	NA	NA	NA	11.8	3.3	43.8	465	9.8	824	32	38.8
McMinnville city	86	629	489	3,578	2,904	14	100.0	16.3	2.9	74.3	628	14.3	1,044	49	10.9
Manchester city	62	578	401	3,741	9,643	75	68.0	34.9	21.9	48.6	658	29.2	2,752	34	68.3
Martin city	27	259	245	2,352	1,939	20	100.0	2.4	1.3	94.6	84	2.9	274	0	0.0

1 Data for serious crimes have not been adjusted for underreporting. This may affect comparability between geographic areas over time.
2 Per 100,000 population estimated by the FBI. 3 Based on population estimated as of July 1 of the year shown.

STATE City, town, township, borough, or CDP (county if applicable)	Land area 2010 (sq mi)	Population Total persons 2010	Total persons 2019	Percent change 2010–2019	Persons per square mile, 2019	Population characteristics 2015–2019 Percent foreign born	Percent living in the same house as previous year	Income and poverty 2015–2019 Median household income	Percent of households with income below poverty level	Median value of owner-occupied housing units	Employment, 2015–2019 Percent in civilian labor force	Unemployment rate	Households, 2015–2019 (percent of households) Family households	One person households
	1	2	3	4	5	6	7	8	9	10	11	12	13	14
TENNESSEE—Con.														
Maryville city	17.25	27,453	29,742	8.3	1724.2	3.9	88.0	61,384	11.8	204,500	56.8	4.2	66.5	29.3
Memphis city	317.36	651,873	651,073	-0.1	2051.5	6.2	84.0	41,228	22.4	101,800	63.3	8.7	56.6	37.1
Middle Valley CDP	9.76	12,684	NA	NA	NA	3.2	88.5	68,925	5.8	171,500	66.0	4.4	78.2	19.1
Millington city	22.41	10,810	10,641	-1.6	474.8	3.9	87.2	52,500	14.8	129,000	57.2	10.3	65.7	30.7
Morristown city	27.34	29,008	30,193	4.1	1104.4	9.2	86.3	32,193	26.0	115,900	53.2	7.7	60.0	33.4
Mount Juliet city	24.88	24,785	37,029	49.4	1488.3	8.7	85.5	91,303	6.5	274,800	70.8	3.3	78.6	18.5
Murfreesboro city	61.71	109,119	146,900	34.6	2380.5	6.8	76.5	62,003	13.0	238,000	71.5	5.1	62.2	24.4
Nashville-Davidson metropolitan government		626,558	694,144	10.8	0.0	13.0	80.9	60,388	13.0	241,700	71.4	4.1	55.4	33.7
Nashville-Davidson metropolitan government (balance)	475.54	603,438	670,820	11.2	1410.6	13.3	80.8	59,828	13.2	239,000	71.6	4.1	55.1	33.9
Oak Ridge city	85.25	29,328	29,156	-0.6	342.0	7.5	82.0	55,230	14.2	155,800	59.1	5.4	63.6	32.0
Paris city	12.91	10,126	10,056	-0.7	778.9	0.4	81.7	30,902	22.7	94,700	48.4	5.0	59.0	36.3
Portland city	13.34	11,489	13,030	13.4	976.8	4.7	79.6	55,722	13.0	144,500	67.8	3.7	72.7	22.7
Red Bank city	6.56	11,647	11,840	1.7	1804.9	3.5	81.9	42,618	15.0	148,900	62.6	2.2	46.9	44.4
Sevierville city	23.97	14,777	17,117	15.8	714.1	9.5	82.3	43,233	15.5	188,300	57.8	3.0	65.5	25.5
Seymour CDP	12.63	10,919	NA	NA	NA	1.9	86.6	57,773	7.2	171,700	64.7	7.2	72.2	22.6
Shelbyville city	18.44	20,315	22,101	8.8	1198.5	11.1	85.4	41,716	19.8	124,500	65.7	5.3	69.2	22.1
Smyrna town	30.31	40,401	51,586	27.7	1701.9	10.7	84.8	62,635	9.4	189,800	73.3	4.9	68.0	24.7
Soddy-Daisy city	23.15	12,915	13,619	5.5	588.3	1.3	92.6	48,097	13.8	145,800	58.0	3.3	60.0	35.9
Springfield city	12.92	16,450	17,277	5.0	1337.2	10.5	83.3	46,897	18.5	154,800	60.7	6.1	68.6	26.6
Spring Hill city	26.79	29,106	43,769	50.4	1633.8	6.9	80.8	90,778	3.8	286,800	72.0	2.6	83.1	12.8
Tullahoma city	23.44	18,638	19,555	4.9	834.3	3.6	82.8	48,770	14.9	146,500	59.3	4.4	64.1	31.9
Union City city	12.07	10,901	10,325	-5.3	855.4	3.1	82.5	28,580	28.7	96,700	53.0	7.2	58.7	36.9
White House city	11.21	10,225	12,638	23.6	1127.4	4.4	88.7	78,041	6.7	215,600	67.4	2.6	80.8	18.3
TEXAS	261263.08	25,146,091	28,995,881	15.3	111.0	17.0	84.4	61,874	13.7	172,500	64.2	5.1	69.3	25.2
Abilene city	106.67	117,514	123,420	5.0	1157.0	6.8	76.0	50,659	16.0	120,400	57.2	3.6	63.9	27.5
Addison town	4.35	12,537	16,263	29.7	3738.6	22.4	69.9	74,986	8.0	335,300	83.1	4.0	39.6	48.5
Alamo city	7.51	18,373	19,910	8.4	2651.1	25.1	90.2	39,858	26.8	72,000	50.5	5.4	81.9	16.4
Aldine CDP	7.85	15,869	NA	NA	NA	41.8	90.3	38,925	25.3	87,800	58.3	3.0	82.2	11.7
Alice city	11.99	19,109	18,682	-2.2	1558.1	7.5	87.9	36,059	26.5	77,600	56.9	5.1	68.2	26.7
Allen city	26.40	84,273	105,623	25.3	4000.9	19.6	86.9	105,925	4.4	303,300	72.0	4.6	80.2	16.2
Alton city	7.31	13,899	18,105	30.3	2476.7	32.1	90.4	32,495	34.4	73,900	64.6	13.0	86.3	9.9
Alvin city	24.21	24,161	26,723	10.6	1103.8	10.2	84.9	56,504	15.1	151,100	64.1	5.2	70.5	22.6
Amarillo city	101.74	190,666	199,371	4.6	1959.6	11.8	81.4	52,725	14.4	132,500	66.6	3.6	65.0	30.4
Andrews city	6.95	11,098	14,109	27.1	2030.1	16.9	84.8	76,342	9.9	147,400	63.8	4.2	77.4	19.2
Angleton city	11.62	18,829	19,431	3.2	1672.2	7.6	87.0	55,933	11.7	122,000	61.2	2.8	65.5	30.1
Anna city	16.05	8,232	15,000	82.2	934.6	13.6	77.2	95,136	7.5	210,100	72.5	0.4	87.0	9.7
Arlington city	95.78	365,098	398,854	9.2	4164.3	20.8	84.5	60,571	12.7	170,700	69.0	4.6	69.4	24.9
Atascocita CDP	23.84	65,844	NA	NA	NA	9.8	87.0	100,292	5.9	198,500	68.1	4.0	80.3	16.3
Athens city	17.83	12,715	12,753	0.3	715.3	11.1	83.9	38,149	24.7	87,200	52.7	5.9	69.3	28.7
Austin city	319.94	801,829	978,908	22.1	3059.7	18.8	79.0	71,576	11.6	337,400	73.8	3.7	52.0	34.5
Azle city	8.79	10,862	13,351	22.9	1518.9	3.1	87.9	72,614	9.3	151,100	60.4	6.0	71.4	22.7
Bacliff CDP	2.74	8,619	NA	NA	NA	17.2	83.1	46,063	16.9	128,100	65.9	6.6	70.3	24.3
Balch Springs city	9.02	23,789	25,007	5.1	2772.4	28.3	85.1	51,446	15.7	106,000	70.4	5.3	80.3	15.7
Bay City city	9.26	17,813	17,535	-1.6	1893.6	13.1	89.9	50,182	21.2	99,200	60.0	6.1	65.7	31.8
Baytown city	36.89	71,605	77,192	7.8	2092.5	18.2	81.9	57,270	15.3	119,900	64.2	8.2	68.8	26.2
Beaumont city	82.34	117,278	116,825	-0.4	1418.8	10.5	85.8	50,632	17.2	113,600	60.4	4.2	62.1	33.1
Bedford city	10.02	46,994	49,004	4.4	4895.1	10.8	76.1	70,362	5.3	217,300	69.1	3.6	62.1	31.8
Beeville city	6.17	12,858	12,793	-0.5	2073.4	3.0	81.1	33,995	29.5	77,400	58.5	8.5	70.6	27.0
Bellaire city	3.60	16,907	18,971	12.2	5269.7	21.6	94.1	206,734	2.5	842,700	65.3	2.0	82.6	15.6
Bellmead city	6.86	9,933	10,744	8.2	1566.2	16.3	82.6	41,696	19.3	74,600	59.1	4.1	67.9	21.2
Belton city	20.22	18,233	22,885	25.5	1131.8	9.7	75.5	55,539	16.4	158,400	62.8	5.1	58.2	36.5
Benbrook city	10.76	21,198	23,502	10.9	2184.2	4.2	83.4	72,699	8.5	182,600	68.0	4.0	63.0	32.0
Big Spring city	19.11	27,282	28,187	3.3	1475.0	14.5	81.5	52,275	18.9	90,500	50.6	8.1	63.2	31.9
Boerne city	11.30	10,661	18,232	71.0	1613.5	6.4	78.3	70,745	8.0	286,300	61.2	1.7	71.0	26.8
Bonham city	9.83	10,127	10,386	2.6	1056.6	8.9	65.8	43,793	17.3	84,700	37.7	4.1	59.9	37.3
Borger city	8.79	13,350	12,415	-7.0	1412.4	5.9	86.5	46,183	18.0	76,900	59.8	8.1	66.9	29.1
Brenham city	12.90	15,809	17,863	13.0	1384.7	9.0	83.1	45,197	15.2	163,800	53.7	6.2	61.9	33.8
Brownsville city	132.32	174,729	182,781	4.6	1381.4	28.6	90.0	38,588	29.2	90,000	56.3	6.0	81.5	16.9
Brownwood city	14.97	19,311	18,455	-4.4	1232.8	5.6	89.2	41,404	15.9	95,400	58.4	4.9	63.2	29.7
Brushy Creek CDP	6.51	21,764	NA	NA	NA	15.5	84.8	110,179	2.7	294,000	72.4	3.9	77.4	17.8
Bryan city	45.87	76,226	86,276	13.2	1880.9	14.8	75.0	45,771	21.6	147,600	62.7	4.1	61.2	30.1
Buda city	6.23	7,270	16,906	132.5	2713.6	10.2	82.3	89,688	4.5	257,800	76.0	2.0	79.7	13.7
Burkburnett city	11.54	10,814	11,270	4.2	976.6	1.7	83.9	48,236	14.9	102,400	58.4	6.0	65.9	29.2
Burleson city	28.26	36,879	48,225	30.8	1706.5	2.5	84.0	79,784	4.8	184,600	70.6	3.6	77.6	19.0
Canyon city	7.06	13,311	15,945	19.8	2258.5	3.9	72.6	60,171	17.3	162,700	70.6	3.2	61.6	30.3
Canyon Lake CDP	142.71	21,262	NA	NA	NA	5.3	88.6	74,401	10.1	247,500	55.2	2.5	73.4	23.5
Carrollton city	36.67	119,211	139,248	16.8	3797.3	27.7	86.1	78,306	6.9	238,300	72.9	3.5	68.7	25.3
Cedar Hill city	35.79	44,998	47,930	6.5	1339.2	11.0	87.6	72,463	9.7	168,800	70.7	5.7	73.4	22.4
Cedar Park city	25.40	55,117	79,462	44.2	3128.4	13.9	81.2	104,019	4.3	301,600	72.9	3.0	74.1	19.6
Celina city	27.93	6,315	16,299	158.1	583.6	5.9	84.6	124,375	1.2	318,300	72.6	1.0	84.3	13.2
Channelview CDP	14.48	38,289	NA	NA	NA	27.0	88.3	63,581	14.2	124,900	64.6	7.7	80.8	14.2
Cibolo city	20.65	20,177	31,281	55.0	1514.8	6.8	83.6	104,601	4.1	230,800	63.4	4.1	87.6	10.0
Cinco Ranch CDP	4.31	18,274	NA	NA	NA	30.2	87.7	141,752	5.8	373,600	61.6	5.8	83.6	14.7
Cleburne city	35.54	29,639	31,295	5.6	880.6	5.5	88.6	50,848	11.6	112,700	59.4	4.2	68.0	28.0
Cloverleaf CDP	3.08	22,942	NA	NA	NA	31.5	91.1	50,494	23.5	116,200	60.8	6.7	81.1	14.3
Clute city	5.32	11,234	11,690	4.1	2197.4	16.0	84.2	56,768	15.2	112,800	66.9	5.9	64.9	29.9
College Station city	51.15	94,225	117,911	25.1	2305.2	13.4	63.4	45,820	28.0	241,600	59.2	4.0	48.0	29.7
Colleyville city	13.11	22,806	27,091	18.8	2066.4	7.4	89.5	163,509	3.7	516,500	63.6	3.6	85.1	13.2
Conroe city	71.95	65,392	91,079	39.3	1265.9	17.7	81.3	60,343	10.8	187,300	67.0	4.2	64.3	27.8
Converse city	8.46	21,534	28,171	30.8	3329.9	9.3	84.1	72,911	10.1	165,400	63.5	4.7	77.9	18.2
Coppell city	14.50	38,666	41,421	7.1	2856.6	25.5	87.2	122,340	2.8	388,800	73.6	2.2	78.2	20.1
Copperas Cove city	18.04	32,247	33,235	3.1	1842.3	8.2	75.6	52,284	12.6	112,000	57.1	8.3	69.1	25.4

Table B. Incorporated Places, Census Designated Places (CDPs), and Minor Civil Divisions (MCDs) of 10,000 or More Population — **Crime, Residential Construction and Local Government Finance**

STATE City, town, township, borough, or CDP (county if applicable)	Serious crimes known to police, 2018[1] Violent crime Number	Violent crime Rate[2]	Property crime Number	Property crime Rate[2]	New residential construction authorized by building permits, 2019 Value ($1,000)	Number of housing units	Percent single family	Local government finance, 2017 General revenue Total (mil dol)	Intergovernmental Total (mil dol)	Intergovernmental Percent from state gov.	Taxes per capita[3]	General expenditure Total (mil dol)	Per capita[3] Total	Per capita[3] Capital outlays	Debt outstanding (mil dol)
	15	16	17	18	19	20	21	22	23	24	25	26	27	28	29
TENNESSEE—Con.															
Maryville city	47	162	480	1,657	36,328	181	100.0	115.4	59.0	48.8	1,471	85.3	2,936	212	104.2
Memphis city	12,674	1,943	41,779	6,406	NA	NA	NA	1242.1	318.8	34.2	696	1048.8	1,611	143	2006.0
Middle Valley CDP	NA	NA	NA	NA	NA	NA	NA	NA	NA	NA	NA	NA	NA	NA	NA
Millington city	101	917	586	5,320	NA	NA	NA	17.7	10.1	28.8	374	17.0	1,603	406	14.4
Morristown city	242	810	1,388	4,645	13,625	93	95.7	63.3	19.7	28.0	506	61.7	2,074	335	231.6
Mount Juliet city	72	198	630	1,731	210,186	698	86.2	41.9	12.4	99.2	480	34.8	1,005	426	13.7
Murfreesboro city	613	436	4,417	3,139	381,813	2,154	61.1	224.3	109.0	62.9	738	260.0	1,909	614	368.8
Nashville-Davidson metropolitan government	7,641	1,113	27,537	4,011	NA	NA	NA	2657.7	644.9	94.4	2,329	2894.0	4,212	698	14599.2
Nashville-Davidson metropolitan government (balance)	NA	NA	NA	NA	1,430,865	9,765	39.2	NA	NA	NA	NA	NA	NA	NA	NA
Oak Ridge city	164	564	734	2,525	8,168	64	100.0	149.5	89.2	33.4	1,493	113.2	3,900	218	125.2
Paris city	45	446	283	2,805	1,536	18	88.9	12.6	4.0	41.6	351	20.7	2,059	821	15.6
Portland city	36	279	227	1,762	25,118	91	100.0	14.6	2.6	97.2	500	18.2	1,423	577	25.8
Red Bank city	52	442	296	2,515	10,455	40	100.0	7.7	3.1	30.0	266	6.7	573	22	0.4
Sevierville city	92	541	833	4,900	49,399	841	37.3	61.6	9.4	80.4	1,936	46.9	2,790	359	222.1
Seymour CDP	NA	NA	NA	NA	NA	NA	NA	NA	NA	NA	NA	NA	NA	NA	NA
Shelbyville city	153	705	657	3,027	33,906	149	93.3	27.4	5.9	48.3	559	33.7	1,561	783	11.3
Smyrna town	NA	NA	NA	NA	116,943	776	60.4	66.5	22.7	25.1	314	53.3	1,067	190	61.2
Soddy-Daisy city	20	145	316	2,289	8,819	43	100.0	9.3	4.7	53.9	324	7.4	547	123	0.0
Springfield city	145	858	530	3,137	11,893	101	100.0	25.7	2.4	98.9	707	28.8	1,690	672	65.0
Spring Hill city	43	104	446	1,079	203,126	857	100.0	31.8	5.2	92.1	358	30.0	759	227	32.0
Tullahoma city	106	549	618	3,199	13,865	71	100.0	82.7	51.3	51.1	819	66.3	3,455	263	49.3
Union City city	NA	NA	NA	NA	338	2	100.0	38.4	22.8	52.9	928	31.2	2,982	144	12.6
White House city	36	305	201	1,701	28,970	122	100.0	13.2	4.4	32.5	317	13.3	1,145	257	15.3
TEXAS	117,927	411	679,430	2,367	37,413,284	209,895	61.5	X	X	X	X	X	X	X	X
Abilene city	591	483	3,528	2,881	70,660	349	95.4	150.3	11.5	24.2	815	185.5	1,518	545	256.2
Addison town	72	455	872	5,505	21,611	197	0.0	62.9	1.4	100.0	3,078	41.4	2,772	108	101.9
Alamo city	130	655	953	4,803	23,779	304	88.2	12.1	0.2	40.7	354	19.7	1,008	20	16.3
Aldine CDP	NA	NA	NA	NA	NA	NA	NA	NA	NA	NA	NA	NA	NA	NA	NA
Alice city	91	481	939	4,962	1,844	9	100.0	17.8	0.6	82.6	533	20.9	1,098	22	29.6
Allen city	111	108	1,277	1,238	238,951	1,230	40.2	150.6	1.4	39.5	1,024	97.5	963	145	149.6
Alton city	57	320	217	1,219	21,791	214	67.3	8.9	1.3	49.8	153	8.2	478	155	9.6
Alvin city	57	213	467	1,743	39,768	217	100.0	29.2	0.3	13.3	725	22.9	870	109	30.3
Amarillo city	1,622	807	8,433	4,194	111,563	472	94.5	285.4	34.4	43.6	757	289.4	1,449	217	366.7
Andrews city	55	397	200	1,445	15,803	168	16.7	12.7	2.4	0.6	504	15.3	1,146	439	12.7
Angleton city	32	163	241	1,227	19,920	68	100.0	16.6	0.0	0.0	576	13.4	686	33	15.0
Anna city	16	118	174	1,281	114,044	637	100.0	10.6	0.5	29.8	552	9.7	764	15	34.7
Arlington city	1,784	445	11,780	2,938	681,128	1,662	50.5	514.4	28.7	23.4	714	463.3	1,166	129	1049.6
Atascocita CDP	NA	NA	NA	NA	NA	NA	NA	NA	NA	NA	NA	NA	NA	NA	NA
Athens city	55	433	286	2,251	2,757	17	58.8	12.9	0.0		773	13.0	1,034	155	10.4
Austin city	3,720	382	33,655	3,458	2,157,939	14,709	31.1	1949.7	96.4	22.6	937	2010.4	2,113	417	5394.5
Azle city	25	196	254	1,994	35,118	152	100.0	16.5	0.5	14.6	672	13.9	1,115	45	20.3
Bacliff CDP	NA	NA	NA	NA	NA	NA	NA	NA	NA	NA	NA	NA	NA	NA	NA
Balch Springs city	179	700	883	3,454	4,028	45	100.0	17.4	1.3	43.0	567	22.7	899	328	9.8
Bay City city	73	417	686	3,916	3,031	17	100.0	17.5	1.2	3.4	534	18.4	1,040	61	30.9
Baytown city	302	390	2,911	3,754	53,886	312	99.4	135.9	8.8	74.7	782	130.7	1,704	322	204.4
Beaumont city	1,265	1,060	4,516	3,783	47,536	232	100.0	206.3	46.5	77.5	845	192.2	1,616	248	372.6
Bedford city	90	181	1,057	2,121	113	1	100.0	47.4	0.7	100.0	655	50.8	1,024	118	49.7
Beeville city	40	309	390	3,011	1,751	17	64.7	15.8	2.7	93.0	494	11.2	874	31	10.7
Bellaire city	26	136	265	1,389	60,140	93	100.0	28.0	0.2	14.1	1,143	30.2	1,604	375	77.4
Bellmead city	137	1,294	656	6,196	140	3	100.0	8.0	0.1	100.0	551	5.4	515	0	10.8
Belton city	57	256	511	2,297	27,318	147	72.8	20.5	2.1	43.8	536	21.9	1,015	252	16.0
Benbrook city	29	121	411	1,718	16,209	59	100.0	17.7	0.6	0.0	701	23.4	995	0	0.9
Big Spring city	152	543	795	2,839	7,956	41	90.2	24.9	1.2	60.4	479	18.3	662	31	27.4
Boerne city	27	159	341	2,005	85,710	365	100.0	38.5	2.3	35.5	1,098	29.6	1,841	530	63.9
Bonham city	17	167	174	1,705	2,310	21	100.0	3.6	0.2	72.4	277	3.2	315	32	0.9
Borger city	40	316	499	3,937	0	0	0.0	16.7	0.8	40.2	730	17.5	1,376	80	15.4
Brenham city	65	380	367	2,144	6,792	55	100.0	26.8	1.2	37.7	980	36.4	2,165	77	51.3
Brownsville city	694	376	4,834	2,621	98,817	937	72.5	191.7	21.5	18.3	443	175.0	960	98	311.4
Brownwood city	79	421	550	2,930	1,937	12	100.0	29.0	3.9	69.7	768	26.5	1,426	94	31.9
Brushy Creek CDP	NA	NA	NA	NA	NA	NA	NA	NA	NA	NA	NA	NA	NA	NA	NA
Bryan city	332	390	2,073	2,435	119,225	709	86.2	88.2	2.4	6.5	633	144.1	1,711	173	440.9
Buda city	20	111	277	1,537	37,721	184	100.0	14.5	0.9	73.8	578	14.4	898	236	56.3
Burkburnett city	33	294	267	2,380	1,871	20	0.0	8.0	0.0	9.3	392	8.4	754	88	34.7
Burleson city	133	279	776	1,630	88,968	533	38.6	62.5	0.5	78.3	911	60.4	1,312	376	158.2
Canyon city	14	90	120	769	21,581	93	95.7	10.1	0.5	2.1	335	8.7	575	5	12.7
Canyon Lake CDP	NA	NA	NA	NA	NA	NA	NA	NA	NA	NA	NA	NA	NA	NA	NA
Carrollton city	191	138	2,364	1,710	95,360	349	100.0	156.7	2.9	82.0	862	151.3	1,112	262	192.5
Cedar Hill city	85	173	1,379	2,800	37,207	225	34.2	61.9	0.8	9.7	876	56.6	1,160	104	138.5
Cedar Park city	97	123	966	1,221	68,026	332	100.0	97.2	6.9	100.0	770	79.8	1,057	259	52.2
Celina city	15	142	88	833	452,188	1,238	100.0	0.0	0.0		0	0.1	8	0	1.4
Channelview CDP	NA	NA	NA	NA	NA	NA	NA	NA	NA	NA	NA	NA	NA	NA	NA
Cibolo city	37	120	271	881	130,424	827	42.0	21.7	0.3	9.1	448	15.4	531	44	52.2
Cinco Ranch CDP	NA	NA	NA	NA	NA	NA	NA	NA	NA	NA	NA	NA	NA	NA	NA
Cleburne city	77	254	543	1,791	41,210	254	93.7	51.7	2.6	36.2	979	53.4	1,768	611	172.8
Cloverleaf CDP	NA	NA	NA	NA	NA	NA	NA	NA	NA	NA	NA	NA	NA	NA	NA
Clute city	39	334	290	2,480	18,913	61	100.0	14.6	0.7	28.8	590	15.1	1,297	274	14.2
College Station city	237	203	2,422	2,078	108,491	617	64.5	111.1	3.0	36.1	608	104.6	914	184	278.9
Colleyville city	8	29	149	547	60,630	109	100.0	39.6	0.6	100.0	1,153	33.2	1,245	99	13.6
Conroe city	219	250	2,183	2,494	394,885	2,232	52.9	108.1	10.9	10.2	926	118.9	1,402	494	265.3
Converse city	172	711	482	1,993	45,049	221	100.0	17.6	0.6	2.2	368	14.2	526	35	19.6
Coppell city	30	71	532	1,254	13,375	36	100.0	91.7	3.4	2.3	1,805	106.3	2,531	963	106.6
Copperas Cove city	143	437	629	1,920	21,031	165	97.6	28.8	0.2	18.8	581	19.3	593	0	70.3

1 Data for serious crimes have not been adjusted for underreporting. This may affect comparability between geographic areas over time.
2 Per 100,000 population estimated by the FBI. 3 Based on population estimated as of July 1 of the year shown.

Table B. Incorporated Places, Census Designated Places (CDPs), and Minor Civil Divisions (MCDs) of 10,000 or More Population — **Land Area, Population, and Households, and Employment**

STATE City, town, township, borough, or CDP (county if applicable)	Land area 2010 (sq mi)	Population Total persons 2010	Total persons 2019	Percent change 2010–2019	Persons per square mile 2019	Population characteristics 2015–2019 Percent foreign born	Percent living in the same house as previous year	Income and poverty 2015–2019 Median household income	Percent of households with income below poverty level	Median value of owner-occupied housing units	Employment, 2015–2019 Percent in civilian labor force	Unemploy-ment rate	Households, 2015–2019 (percent of households) Family households	One person households
	1	2	3	4	5	6	7	8	9	10	11	12	13	14
TEXAS—Con.														
Corinth city	7.79	19,766	22,099	11.8	2836.8	6.4	87.2	103,099	6.8	257,600	74.6	3.1	81.4	14.6
Corpus Christi city	159.70	305,226	326,586	7.0	2045.0	9.3	82.4	56,333	16.3	141,100	62.4	5.5	67.1	26.3
Corsicana city	22.99	23,837	23,906	0.3	1039.8	20.1	83.9	42,352	18.8	88,800	62.8	5.1	68.0	26.2
Crowley city	7.31	12,838	16,460	28.2	2251.7	6.9	88.8	76,720	5.8	157,900	71.9	5.6	79.2	15.4
Dallas city	339.74	1,197,658	1,343,573	12.2	3954.7	24.8	83.1	52,580	16.4	188,100	68.5	4.7	56.6	35.3
Deer Park city	10.47	32,010	33,474	4.6	3197.1	10.9	86.8	80,592	6.7	173,400	68.6	7.6	78.7	18.8
Del Rio city	20.42	35,938	35,760	-0.5	1751.2	23.1	83.7	44,959	22.7	100,600	56.5	5.1	72.3	24.3
Denison city	28.58	22,748	25,529	12.2	893.2	3.2	82.7	43,586	15.5	98,300	58.1	7.4	63.4	32.2
Denton city	96.24	116,326	141,541	21.7	1470.7	12.7	74.2	60,018	15.7	218,800	67.1	5.2	58.4	28.1
DeSoto city	21.63	49,043	52,988	8.0	2449.7	8.2	88.0	71,578	8.6	169,800	68.4	5.2	69.3	27.8
Dickinson city	10.12	19,049	21,129	10.9	2087.8	15.2	86.1	66,875	15.0	159,300	65.0	5.6	70.5	25.9
Donna city	8.29	15,736	16,338	3.8	1970.8	18.6	88.1	29,724	38.5	59,500	51.6	5.3	74.8	22.2
Dumas city	5.53	14,691	13,827	-5.9	2500.4	20.9	87.2	57,117	11.2	132,100	71.8	6.2	72.1	25.2
Duncanville city	11.20	38,527	38,751	0.6	3459.9	13.0	92.2	56,412	12.6	149,600	62.7	8.0	73.9	23.8
Eagle Pass city	9.42	26,606	29,684	11.6	3151.2	31.5	87.9	42,901	28.1	128,200	57.2	8.9	82.2	15.0
Edinburg city	44.74	82,018	101,170	23.4	2261.3	19.9	87.0	48,673	24.0	121,900	63.9	7.1	75.0	18.8
El Campo city	9.76	11,692	11,539	-1.3	1182.3	11.9	87.6	49,182	18.4	146,000	62.6	4.3	71.2	25.6
Elgin city	6.42	8,289	10,314	24.4	1606.5	13.1	80.1	58,816	12.2	155,900	68.7	10.0	73.3	22.3
El Paso city	257.42	648,245	681,728	5.2	2648.3	23.1	84.3	47,568	19.0	127,400	60.1	6.1	70.9	25.6
Ennis city	32.44	18,593	20,357	9.5	627.5	16.6	89.2	57,619	13.0	111,200	66.2	3.2	72.7	23.7
Euless city	16.13	51,263	57,197	11.6	3546.0	21.7	78.3	65,921	7.7	200,500	74.3	3.4	62.5	29.7
Farmers Branch city	11.88	29,141	48,158	65.3	4053.7	27.7	84.5	74,464	6.5	196,300	73.4	3.4	66.8	26.9
Fate city	11.85	7,432	15,603	109.9	1316.7	10.2	85.3	110,373	1.1	256,800	73.6	3.8	83.6	13.6
Flower Mound town	41.93	64,675	79,135	22.4	1887.3	13.3	84.8	137,285	3.0	361,900	72.5	3.8	84.9	13.0
Forest Hill city	4.17	12,355	12,988	5.1	3114.6	22.6	90.2	41,496	21.7	94,400	57.3	8.1	76.9	20.8
Forney city	14.80	13,819	27,236	97.1	1840.3	4.6	80.5	102,716	6.6	204,600	75.8	5.4	79.9	15.4
Fort Bliss CDP	6.22	8,591	NA	NA	NA	5.1	51.6	54,707	13.1	0	17.9	8.0	93.0	6.7
Fort Hood CDP	15.68	29,589	NA	NA	NA	7.2	55.3	44,718	14.4	92,000	19.0	12.6	93.2	6.0
Fort Worth city	345.58	744,824	909,585	22.1	2632.1	16.8	83.1	62,187	13.6	169,700	67.3	5.4	67.9	26.1
Four Corners CDP	2.51	12,382	NA	NA	NA	52.3	93.0	64,859	13.7	176,500	60.6	3.1	94.9	4.4
Fredericksburg city	9.06	10,539	11,496	9.1	1268.9	11.2	83.1	50,497	8.9	275,500	62.5	4.5	58.9	37.4
Freeport city	15.40	12,069	12,136	0.6	788.1	12.4	76.5	38,462	25.7	81,100	62.9	9.8	67.8	29.0
Fresno CDP	8.53	19,069	NA	NA	NA	20.8	87.7	79,115	10.7	173,600	70.8	3.4	81.5	13.7
Friendswood city	20.63	35,909	40,290	12.2	1953.0	8.9	86.2	111,478	4.2	284,100	66.7	5.6	80.6	16.2
Frisco city	68.13	117,174	200,490	71.1	2942.8	22.8	83.4	127,055	3.9	395,900	71.8	3.6	77.2	19.7
Gainesville city	19.30	16,010	16,886	5.5	874.9	13.2	75.6	44,753	19.2	107,900	66.6	6.5	67.6	25.5
Galena Park city	4.79	10,899	10,757	-1.3	2245.7	31.9	86.4	48,533	26.0	80,700	65.2	6.4	83.7	10.0
Galveston city	41.13	47,741	50,446	5.7	1226.5	13.6	76.1	49,319	19.3	182,800	57.8	7.2	53.5	37.7
Garland city	57.06	226,908	239,928	5.7	4204.8	29.6	87.9	61,211	11.3	160,800	69.2	5.2	74.4	20.4
Gatesville city	8.67	12,459	12,401	-0.5	1430.3	5.4	82.4	42,122	16.8	79,800	29.6	9.9	57.9	36.5
Georgetown city	54.85	47,483	79,604	67.6	1451.3	7.3	84.7	73,822	6.3	266,900	51.7	5.9	67.3	28.9
Glenn Heights city	7.21	11,146	13,377	20.0	1855.3	13.8	90.9	68,739	12.3	162,600	69.6	8.3	79.5	16.6
Grand Prairie city	72.26	175,468	194,543	10.9	2692.3	22.8	90.0	67,388	9.8	162,400	70.3	4.6	75.8	20.0
Grapevine city	31.97	46,336	55,281	19.3	1729.2	15.9	78.7	91,143	5.2	320,400	76.6	3.8	64.8	26.9
Greenville city	32.29	25,529	28,827	12.9	892.8	9.7	78.4	44,622	16.4	104,400	62.1	5.5	60.8	34.1
Groves city	5.17	16,144	15,480	-4.1	2994.2	9.4	80.4	55,652	10.5	112,900	60.8	7.9	65.3	25.1
Haltom city	12.37	42,370	43,874	3.5	3546.8	26.0	81.4	52,709	13.7	111,300	68.5	5.3	72.7	21.8
Harker Heights city	15.66	26,727	32,421	21.3	2070.3	11.4	77.0	74,839	12.9	201,400	54.6	7.6	76.8	18.6
Harlingen city	40.08	64,943	65,022	0.1	1622.3	14.7	89.6	39,752	26.0	87,500	57.7	6.2	70.8	24.5
Henderson city	11.95	13,712	13,154	-4.1	1100.8	10.8	73.0	48,672	16.6	121,600	45.9	6.4	68.2	27.9
Hereford city	6.14	15,367	14,622	-4.8	2381.4	17.1	90.0	49,338	17.0	90,500	66.6	4.6	72.3	24.3
Hewitt city	7.02	13,548	14,937	10.3	2127.8	5.0	80.7	72,077	4.8	167,500	65.1	2.9	75.6	20.0
Hidalgo city	8.35	12,532	14,183	13.2	1698.6	39.5	95.9	33,576	34.3	101,100	61.0	9.4	85.4	13.8
Highland Village city	5.53	15,084	16,668	10.5	3014.1	6.0	89.0	147,222	2.0	360,600	70.1	4.3	83.4	15.0
Horizon City city	8.71	16,758	19,642	17.2	2255.1	22.1	87.3	60,431	11.7	121,500	68.0	5.9	84.1	12.2
Houston city	640.19	2,095,517	2,320,268	10.7	3624.3	29.3	81.5	52,338	17.7	171,800	67.2	5.9	60.8	32.3
Humble city	9.76	15,127	15,824	4.6	1621.3	16.7	87.2	41,845	16.1	122,900	70.5	7.4	55.0	42.7
Huntsville city	35.85	38,549	42,241	9.6	1178.3	11.2	73.7	34,890	30.9	165,000	43.8	2.7	47.4	33.8
Hurst city	9.97	37,343	38,655	3.5	3877.1	13.1	86.0	63,722	8.9	190,800	66.7	3.9	70.8	24.0
Hutto city	8.38	16,461	27,947	69.8	3335.0	8.5	84.9	78,942	6.3	194,000	77.4	6.2	76.7	17.4
Ingleside city	16.82	9,381	10,192	8.6	605.9	10.3	76.7	64,877	9.4	145,100	62.4	5.3	74.8	21.4
Irving city	67.06	216,285	239,798	10.9	3575.9	38.4	79.0	64,868	10.4	177,500	74.0	4.4	66.0	27.3
Jacinto City city	1.85	10,553	10,466	-0.8	5657.3	36.6	89.9	41,875	22.1	79,500	60.3	9.4	73.0	22.6
Jacksonville city	14.19	14,537	14,815	1.9	1044.0	18.3	86.3	43,574	24.0	89,000	60.7	7.0	68.9	27.9
Katy city	14.54	14,119	21,729	53.9	1494.4	18.9	91.0	83,091	3.4	197,300	66.0	5.9	81.3	15.4
Keller city	18.46	39,633	47,213	19.1	2557.6	9.2	85.9	141,364	3.3	386,200	67.8	3.1	85.1	13.1
Kerrville city	21.92	22,385	23,754	6.1	1083.7	4.7	80.4	48,446	11.2	179,200	51.3	4.6	60.9	34.9
Kilgore city	18.56	13,451	14,852	10.4	800.2	8.3	83.3	56,715	14.7	122,200	63.1	7.2	66.1	26.9
Killeen city	54.55	127,747	151,666	18.7	2780.3	9.7	71.3	49,630	14.7	126,200	60.1	10.4	68.3	27.5
Kingsville city	13.87	26,450	25,315	-4.3	1825.2	7.3	78.6	42,452	27.4	89,600	58.3	8.0	61.6	29.1
Kyle city	30.46	28,247	48,393	71.3	1588.7	6.7	85.0	79,348	4.6	196,700	72.7	3.5	69.8	22.7
La Homa CDP	6.74	11,985	NA	NA	NA	37.0	93.0	31,563	34.1	66,900	58.9	14.3	87.8	11.5
Lake Jackson city	19.74	26,833	27,220	1.4	1378.9	10.1	79.5	82,465	8.2	185,500	68.7	4.3	70.1	24.8
Lakeway city	12.21	11,679	15,981	36.8	1308.8	7.1	84.0	132,899	3.8	472,700	59.2	3.0	79.4	18.7
La Marque city	13.93	14,516	17,319	19.3	1243.3	7.4	82.9	53,964	14.2	117,000	61.3	10.8	68.8	26.3
Lancaster city	33.24	36,664	39,228	7.0	1180.1	6.3	86.1	57,259	14.2	136,700	71.6	6.2	73.8	23.1
La Porte city	18.63	33,806	34,976	3.5	1877.4	9.3	87.1	75,262	10.3	148,100	66.3	6.6	74.8	20.7
Laredo city	105.74	235,780	262,491	11.3	2482.4	25.9	89.2	47,593	24.8	129,900	60.2	4.8	80.2	17.2
League City city	51.26	83,584	107,536	28.7	2097.9	10.3	85.9	109,073	5.7	245,100	70.5	4.6	74.6	20.3
Leander city	37.48	27,288	62,608	129.4	1670.4	10.7	82.1	101,872	4.1	263,400	72.3	3.1	80.8	16.3
Leon Valley city	3.47	10,998	12,306	11.9	3546.4	13.0	85.2	55,777	12.5	165,900	60.3	5.3	65.3	31.1
Levelland city	10.21	13,555	13,502	-0.4	1322.4	11.2	81.4	46,473	17.0	98,300	62.9	8.0	67.1	29.9
Lewisville city	36.70	95,459	109,212	14.4	2975.8	22.3	77.2	64,493	8.0	209,000	76.2	3.6	62.3	30.0
Little Elm city	17.82	25,892	53,126	105.2	2981.3	18.7	84.4	98,803	4.5	255,200	77.3	5.5	79.6	16.9
Live Oak city	4.76	13,137	16,499	25.6	3466.2	9.8	83.8	61,294	9.1	151,200	65.4	6.0	57.7	36.8
Lockhart city	15.61	12,690	14,133	11.4	905.4	7.5	85.2	55,644	17.1	141,000	52.8	2.2	68.2	26.1
Longview city	55.76	80,423	81,631	1.5	1464.0	10.2	79.0	49,086	16.8	139,600	60.4	5.0	62.7	30.8

STATE City, town, township, borough, or CDP (county if applicable)	Serious crimes known to police, 2018[1] Violent crime Number	Rate[2]	Property crime Number	Rate[2]	New residential construction authorized by building permits, 2019 Value ($1,000)	Number of housing units	Percent single family	Local government finance, 2017 General revenue Total (mil dol)	Intergovernmental Total (mil dol)	Percent from state gov.	Taxes per capita[3]	General expenditure Total (mil dol)	Per capita[3] Total	Capital outlays	Debt outstanding (mil dol)
	15	16	17	18	19	20	21	22	23	24	25	26	27	28	29
TEXAS—Con.															
Corinth city	12	56	190	890	14,532	35	100.0	25.3	0.1	100.0	692	29.7	1,394	298	30.1
Corpus Christi city	2,488	757	11,975	3,644	309,595	1,074	100.0	448.0	30.4	41.2	722	436.0	1,339	248	1675.1
Corsicana city	135	571	764	3,229	8,054	48	66.7	34.8	1.6	63.8	815	41.2	1,737	261	51.4
Crowley city	18	114	378	2,396	102,903	478	100.0	15.8	0.9	0.9	637	13.8	897	25	30.7
Dallas city	10,422	765	44,266	3,249	1,068,187	8,093	25.9	3128.3	142.0	62.3	990	3235.6	2,410	631	10912.7
Deer Park city	30	88	492	1,441	2,175	12	66.7	47.0	0.2	32.7	682	43.5	1,281	75	41.5
Del Rio city	22	61	742	2,061	17,550	90	91.1	43.6	4.9	53.7	532	41.6	1,158	177	38.3
Denison city	92	374	467	1,897	32,862	194	100.0	27.7	0.3	13.9	612	28.3	1,161	140	53.0
Denton city	439	315	3,228	2,318	421,725	1,881	52.8	211.0	10.9	57.7	858	216.0	1,593	330	569.3
DeSoto city	183	338	1,235	2,279	63,990	251	52.2	58.2	2.6	100.0	690	52.6	982	124	106.1
Dickinson city	44	214	410	1,990	25,549	101	100.0	17.7	2.3	47.9	550	17.7	850	65	15.2
Donna city	NA	NA	NA	NA	3,579	43	100.0	0.0	0.0		0	7.0	424	0	48.5
Dumas city	22	149	259	1,751	1,897	11	100.0	11.5	0.1	77.6	435	10.9	757	19	22.5
Duncanville city	215	543	1,253	3,163	883	4	100.0	42.1	0.6	35.1	618	37.4	945	15	6.5
Eagle Pass city	55	188	600	2,046	21,021	92	95.7	33.1	3.4	100.0	417	256.8	8,761	209	63.4
Edinburg city	304	329	3,248	3,516	141,078	975	38.9	82.3	6.1	80.7	512	83.1	871	162	93.0
El Campo city	43	366	241	2,049	2,869	14	100.0	14.4	1.0	10.2	678	14.9	1,271	119	9.8
Elgin city	12	121	94	948	9,455	83	88.0	7.6	1.0	9.9	464	6.6	663	0	26.5
El Paso city	2,554	371	10,365	1,506	501,344	2,286	81.9	868.3	87.0	35.9	673	744.6	1,093	214	2275.1
Ennis city	44	227	343	1,771	16,427	75	94.7	23.7	0.9	96.5	926	19.3	996	36	45.2
Euless city	91	163	1,187	2,130	84,111	385	26.2	82.2	0.7	46.8	1,025	92.3	1,671	322	62.5
Farmers Branch city	65	169	929	2,413	309,420	1,582	15.6	61.0	0.6	24.4	1,302	61.6	1,639	287	103.3
Fate city	9	69	63	485	195,794	544	100.0	8.2	0.1	100.0	417	12.1	978	395	17.6
Flower Mound town	45	57	663	844	162,837	557	77.7	93.1	2.7	21.1	956	78.7	1,026	110	145.9
Forest Hill city	54	414	403	3,091	10,088	45	91.1	11.0	0.0		534	9.6	737	23	5.5
Forney city	18	84	267	1,244	73,318	308	100.0	23.3	0.2	100.0	865	36.9	1,825	882	76.3
Fort Bliss CDP	NA	NA	NA	NA	NA	NA	NA	NA	NA	NA	NA	NA	NA	NA	NA
Fort Hood CDP	NA	NA	NA	NA	NA	NA	NA	NA	NA	NA	NA	NA	NA	NA	NA
Fort Worth city	4,482	502	25,433	2,846	1,621,821	11,339	44.7	1311.3	102.9	69.5	875	1299.6	1,486	214	1482.3
Four Corners CDP	NA	NA	NA	NA	NA	NA	NA	NA	NA	NA	NA	NA	NA	NA	NA
Fredericksburg city	13	113	120	1,044	13,488	68	94.1	21.8	0.4	18.5	1,151	23.9	2,127	314	15.3
Freeport city	50	410	160	1,313	3,616	20	100.0	15.5	0.2	11.4	503	17.4	1,424	69	6.0
Fresno CDP	NA	NA	NA	NA	NA	NA	NA	NA	NA	NA	NA	NA	NA	NA	NA
Friendswood city	34	84	332	821	40,836	76	100.0	33.0	0.7	77.3	609	36.5	915	238	67.7
Frisco city	163	87	2,562	1,364	625,471	3,041	68.4	413.0	46.0	1.7	903	374.1	2,105	1072	809.1
Gainesville city	95	577	363	2,203	8,816	39	100.0	27.8	0.4	31.3	874	23.8	1,452	0	49.9
Galena Park city	29	264	156	1,418	70	1	100.0	11.1	0.4	78.3	753	10.0	907	130	6.1
Galveston city	265	521	1,539	3,024	39,489	159	100.0	203.8	59.1	87.4	1,540	166.1	3,284	1001	209.7
Garland city	659	275	6,454	2,694	99,952	678	35.8	237.9	17.5	6.5	515	219.5	921	62	963.3
Gatesville city	24	194	209	1,689	3,602	25	52.0	7.9	0.4	4.1	340	7.1	572	78	17.0
Georgetown city	78	104	731	979	366,748	2,085	72.4	89.0	4.0	99.9	738	100.4	1,421	460	127.0
Glenn Heights city	35	262	209	1,563	92,723	367	100.0	9.1	0.2	37.0	401	10.6	813	121	5.6
Grand Prairie city	496	252	3,886	1,977	162,212	1,186	17.5	281.1	34.0	13.0	784	243.5	1,255	143	268.0
Grapevine city	87	158	1,288	2,336	70,127	476	9.2	149.9	3.1	76.6	2,132	146.8	2,720	716	164.5
Greenville city	83	300	579	2,089	23,757	242	100.0	49.2	1.8	4.5	787	18.6	679	446	98.3
Groves city	71	452	307	1,953	6,798	36	83.3	11.3	0.3	100.0	431	12.9	818	0	9.7
Haltom City city	140	313	1,154	2,581	15,002	64	100.0	44.7	0.2	28.2	687	40.2	904	130	50.7
Harker Heights city	63	199	749	2,362	44,911	182	78.0	28.2	0.6	98.9	618	29.4	951	247	45.8
Harlingen city	272	415	2,792	4,261	29,873	325	57.5	87.8	7.4	39.0	704	83.6	1,283	136	99.8
Henderson city	86	650	516	3,897	0	0	0.0	15.0	0.3	100.0	750	14.2	1,078	205	7.9
Hereford city	97	655	348	2,349	390	2	100.0	57.9	0.1	100.0	363	54.8	3,700	65	922.9
Hewitt city	18	124	204	1,402	12,332	70	57.1	10.8	0.0	100.0	397	7.3	507	0	43.8
Hidalgo city	44	311	147	1,040	7,782	85	100.0	3.6	0.2	72.4	203	3.2	232	23	0.9
Highland Village city	8	48	132	786	8,549	47	100.0	21.9	0.2	35.6	1,007	19.8	1,185	39	30.1
Horizon City city	12	60	111	556	48,996	234	100.0	8.0	1.6	76.0	308	8.4	432	150	15.8
Houston city	24,062	1,026	94,033	4,010	2,539,169	15,463	33.1	4568.5	320.9	35.7	1,080	4066.6	1,755	271	14092.4
Humble city	145	899	1,562	9,689	190	2	100.0	33.7	5.8	3.4	1,171	27.5	1,714	138	8.2
Huntsville city	134	322	666	1,599	37,221	279	15.8	37.8	2.9	97.3	413	36.6	876	185	29.8
Hurst city	95	242	1,422	3,619	4,847	22	100.0	57.7	1.1	44.0	1,025	57.1	1,458	184	67.0
Hutto city	11	41	87	323	182,276	533	100.0	14.6	0.1	100.0	364	16.2	638	104	46.6
Ingleside city	14	134	206	1,971	25,866	225	14.7	8.1	2.2	100.0	542	5.8	567	0	24.6
Irving city	510	209	5,759	2,361	390,995	1,987	30.9	325.6	15.8	80.6	1,002	349.4	1,452	254	668.0
Jacinto City city	17	159	232	2,173	945	7	100.0	3.6	0.2	72.4	264	3.2	301	30	0.9
Jacksonville city	77	515	375	2,507	633	5	100.0	16.0	0.8	100.0	664	14.6	988	37	10.3
Katy city	49	258	560	2,953	210,882	858	62.8	33.3	5.4	100.0	1,243	22.3	1,232	98	18.5
Keller city	25	52	321	663	56,767	98	100.0	64.1	5.9	62.8	886	53.8	1,142	160	84.0
Kerrville city	68	289	400	1,700	17,791	89	95.5	33.3	0.8	8.6	1,007	28.5	1,220	0	34.7
Kilgore city	42	280	409	2,731	2,540	24	100.0	23.7	1.4	79.1	1,058	24.3	1,647	346	3.9
Killeen city	577	390	3,336	2,254	153,892	858	81.6	131.7	6.4	21.1	474	157.8	1,087	152	284.6
Kingsville city	81	319	754	2,971	4,665	37	100.0	19.9	0.1	100.0	504	13.0	511	53	27.0
Kyle city	80	173	538	1,166	206,693	892	70.5	21.0	1.6	24.4	297	24.9	576	143	63.8
La Homa CDP	NA	NA	NA	NA	NA	NA	NA	NA	NA	NA	NA	NA	NA	NA	NA
Lake Jackson city	50	181	553	2,006	13,024	49	100.0	33.2	0.0	100.0	661	31.9	1,166	117	53.1
Lakeway city	22	140	154	980	48,105	251	91.6	12.6	0.2	32.7	656	13.2	865	49	4.2
La Marque city	73	427	904	5,284	43,605	194	100.0	17.8	2.8	52.7	536	20.3	1,214	180	11.9
Lancaster city	171	430	983	2,472	42,672	222	100.0	44.1	0.3	15.0	728	41.6	1,056	33	135.2
La Porte city	65	183	457	1,284	42,964	511	31.5	65.7	1.0	9.5	1,042	48.7	1,378	137	35.5
Laredo city	890	337	6,367	2,410	294,265	1,602	81.3	426.9	40.9	42.8	584	370.2	1,427	193	524.2
League City city	109	101	1,814	1,675	189,990	742	100.0	103.7	3.4	75.8	635	88.1	844	154	210.4
Leander city	48	90	501	934	464,088	2,239	79.0	44.5	5.6	1.6	589	46.0	923	350	127.2
Leon Valley city	34	293	489	4,216	712	3	100.0	12.7	2.0	2.1	637	7.8	637	57	9.6
Levelland city	124	909	426	3,122	1,842	9	100.0	14.2	1.2	42.9	645	14.3	1,054	109	12.0
Lewisville city	275	256	2,396	2,228	144,311	929	31.9	126.6	1.5	54.3	852	130.2	1,223	341	164.0
Little Elm city	88	174	275	544	198,543	962	99.8	44.1	0.8	59.4	667	30.7	667	13	92.5
Live Oak city	42	259	505	3,112	17,881	82	100.0	18.3	0.3	36.0	927	20.4	1,290	384	15.0
Lockhart city	12	86	171	1,226	11,011	57	89.5	13.6	0.6	71.5	517	16.1	1,171	43	15.0
Longview city	326	399	2,506	3,069	30,868	166	91.6	128.3	11.1	30.8	993	111.7	1,379	135	69.9

1 Data for serious crimes have not been adjusted for underreporting. This may affect comparability between geographic areas over time.
2 Per 100,000 population estimated by the FBI. 3 Based on population estimated as of July 1 of the year shown.

Table B. Incorporated Places, Census Designated Places (CDPs), and Minor Civil Divisions (MCDs) of 10,000 or More Population — **Land Area, Population, and Households, and Employment**

STATE City, town, township, borough, or CDP (county if applicable)	Land area 2010 (sq mi)	Population Total persons 2010	Total persons 2019	Percent change 2010–2019	Persons per square mile 2019	Population characteristics 2015–2019 Percent foreign born	Percent living in the same house as previous year	Income and poverty 2015–2019 Median household income	Percent of households with income below poverty level	Median value of owner-occupied housing units	Employment, 2015–2019 Percent in civilian labor force	Unemployment rate	Households, 2015–2019 (percent of households) Family households	One person households
	1	2	3	4	5	6	7	8	9	10	11	12	13	14
TEXAS—Con.														
Lubbock city	134.72	229,943	258,862	12.6	1921.5	6.3	72.3	50,453	19.3	140,800	65.0	3.7	59.4	29.3
Lufkin city	34.21	35,121	35,021	-0.3	1023.7	11.2	80.5	48,588	19.5	116,800	59.7	6.6	67.8	28.0
Lumberton city	13.41	11,972	13,073	9.2	974.9	2.1	87.5	71,563	9.8	170,500	62.4	2.1	76.1	21.0
McAllen city	65.70	131,547	143,268	8.9	2180.6	26.5	87.4	46,804	21.9	126,000	62.4	6.3	75.0	20.9
McKinney city	66.94	131,152	199,177	51.9	2975.5	16.4	83.4	93,354	6.9	309,200	69.9	3.2	76.2	20.4
Mansfield city	36.67	56,654	72,419	27.8	1974.9	10.9	84.0	99,510	4.1	257,100	70.7	3.9	79.4	17.5
Manvel city	25.52	5,219	12,671	142.8	496.5	8.4	92.9	86,585	4.2	252,800	63.8	2.9	72.8	26.3
Marshall city	29.59	23,513	22,831	-2.9	771.6	8.6	86.2	41,250	22.9	99,400	55.9	5.5	66.3	27.8
Mercedes city	11.80	15,633	16,604	6.2	1407.1	15.3	87.0	34,677	30.1	71,000	55.0	7.4	79.9	18.6
Mesquite city	47.25	139,701	140,937	0.9	2982.8	19.7	82.7	57,824	12.2	143,000	68.0	4.8	72.5	23.4
Midland city	74.38	111,193	146,038	31.3	1963.4	14.1	80.1	79,329	8.8	219,500	71.2	3.3	68.4	26.1
Midlothian city	63.41	22,918	33,532	46.3	528.8	3.8	86.2	95,306	6.5	228,000	70.8	2.8	84.2	13.3
Mineral Wells city	20.40	16,792	15,213	-9.4	745.7	9.7	76.0	42,052	18.8	93,700	58.2	9.9	64.3	27.5
Mission city	35.54	77,695	84,331	8.5	2372.8	29.1	88.5	48,815	21.5	112,400	58.6	7.8	81.6	16.4
Mission Bend CDP	4.64	36,501	NA	NA	NA	41.1	94.6	63,486	10.4	146,800	66.4	5.1	81.7	14.7
Missouri City city	29.04	66,534	75,457	13.4	2598.4	23.4	89.9	87,915	4.3	197,200	68.7	6.7	78.7	18.2
Mount Pleasant city	15.57	15,982	15,978	0.0	1026.2	24.2	88.9	48,567	15.7	100,600	65.2	4.2	74.5	22.8
Murphy city	5.68	17,877	20,500	14.7	3609.2	25.5	91.5	126,196	4.0	351,400	68.3	4.9	90.6	8.4
Nacogdoches city	27.59	32,854	32,877	0.1	1191.6	7.2	64.5	36,553	27.5	149,900	59.3	11.3	52.0	34.0
Nederland city	5.92	17,014	17,371	2.1	2934.3	6.6	86.2	79,903	7.2	132,700	65.6	2.3	65.3	28.9
New Braunfels city	45.19	57,676	90,209	56.4	1996.2	7.2	83.6	71,044	7.9	219,200	66.0	3.4	70.8	24.3
North Richland Hills city	18.13	63,341	70,670	11.6	3898.0	9.5	82.5	71,076	6.9	203,800	68.6	4.8	69.6	26.0
Odessa city	45.22	99,876	123,334	23.5	2727.4	12.6	80.3	63,847	11.5	151,500	69.4	6.0	66.5	28.4
Orange city	22.08	18,602	18,114	-2.6	820.6	6.0	76.5	48,169	19.6	100,900	63.6	8.0	62.4	31.2
Palestine city	19.42	18,713	17,730	-5.3	913.0	8.7	87.2	37,868	17.7	99,400	59.3	4.3	68.3	29.3
Pampa city	9.02	17,998	17,068	-5.2	1892.2	11.2	85.0	46,432	15.7	76,600	60.4	5.6	64.7	29.0
Paris city	35.19	25,263	24,847	-1.6	706.1	4.2	77.0	32,544	24.6	81,100	55.7	4.2	58.0	36.3
Pasadena city	43.59	149,307	151,227	1.3	3469.3	26.6	81.0	55,039	15.4	124,200	65.3	9.4	74.1	21.2
Pearland city	48.16	93,117	122,460	31.5	2542.8	16.9	89.8	104,504	3.8	244,800	71.3	3.2	74.3	21.3
Pearsall city	5.93	9,150	10,609	15.9	1789.0	23.2	79.7	45,865	22.6	71,400	45.1	1.9	74.3	25.0
Pecan Grove CDP	8.32	15,963	NA	NA	NA	7.0	89.2	111,594	6.5	251,000	68.9	3.3	82.8	14.7
Pecos city	7.31	8,780	10,461	19.1	1431.1	7.6	91.9	60,582	16.0	68,200	57.9	7.2	68.9	27.3
Pflugerville city	24.92	48,370	65,380	35.2	2623.6	14.3	85.4	93,627	4.3	238,700	72.8	4.1	73.6	21.3
Pharr city	23.63	70,457	79,112	12.3	3347.9	31.9	94.1	39,884	28.9	80,900	56.0	5.0	82.6	15.2
Plainview city	13.89	22,194	20,143	-9.2	1450.2	11.5	85.1	48,430	18.2	84,400	63.7	5.6	71.5	26.7
Plano city	71.68	259,859	287,677	10.7	4013.4	27.0	88.0	95,602	6.9	320,100	69.8	3.7	71.0	23.7
Pleasanton city	8.92	9,583	10,855	13.3	1216.9	3.8	85.5	65,016	16.0	158,900	58.2	4.3	76.2	20.7
Port Arthur city	76.92	54,376	54,280	-0.2	705.7	23.2	88.7	36,557	26.8	65,800	53.2	7.3	64.0	31.4
Portland city	11.14	15,653	17,268	10.3	1550.1	5.5	79.6	76,123	9.4	167,400	64.8	2.3	75.1	20.3
Port Lavaca city	10.15	12,249	11,854	-3.2	1167.9	19.0	85.9	57,748	9.8	106,600	63.6	5.2	66.4	26.5
Port Neches city	8.63	13,042	12,655	-3.0	1466.4	6.1	80.8	71,740	8.2	165,900	60.0	4.4	72.9	22.6
Princeton city	10.10	6,822	13,894	103.7	1375.6	11.7	86.4	67,204	10.3	185,200	71.4	4.1	76.9	20.6
Prosper town	25.19	9,527	24,579	158.0	975.7	8.9	83.7	146,733	2.6	459,500	68.4	2.1	89.7	8.0
Raymondville city	4.12	11,270	10,880	-3.5	2640.8	13.9	91.6	29,750	31.2	47,000	49.9	17.6	80.3	16.3
Red Oak city	15.55	10,733	13,464	25.4	865.9	5.3	81.8	71,957	8.0	207,600	72.7	4.4	80.5	18.0
Rendon CDP	24.70	12,552	NA	NA	NA	5.3	91.9	79,375	8.7	231,400	58.1	3.2	83.1	15.1
Richardson city	28.57	99,251	121,323	22.2	4246.5	23.7	81.4	85,678	9.3	274,200	67.2	3.8	67.0	25.5
Richmond city	4.12	12,090	12,578	4.0	3052.9	21.4	82.0	43,071	17.5	157,600	57.2	4.2	68.6	27.4
Rio Grande City city	11.35	13,808	14,511	5.1	1278.5	23.1	87.1	33,084	33.8	72,100	57.9	14.9	69.9	29.7
Robinson city	31.23	10,503	11,926	13.5	381.9	3.2	90.2	80,184	6.4	165,300	66.6	3.9	84.0	14.7
Robstown city	15.50	11,486	11,261	-2.0	726.5	5.1	86.0	35,504	35.0	64,000	51.8	15.4	69.5	27.2
Rockport city	16.55	10,022	10,604	5.8	640.7	11.3	81.5	58,871	15.4	175,800	58.7	5.7	68.4	26.2
Rockwall city	29.34	37,559	45,888	22.2	1564.0	9.4	85.0	95,653	5.1	261,400	67.9	3.8	77.0	20.2
Roma city	5.87	10,861	11,490	5.8	1957.4	38.4	91.5	23,763	36.5	73,700	49.1	7.9	82.5	15.6
Rosenberg city	36.87	31,248	38,307	22.6	1039.0	18.2	84.4	52,138	12.9	154,300	67.1	4.7	70.3	25.9
Round Rock city	36.21	100,021	133,372	33.3	3683.3	14.5	80.8	82,676	6.2	244,300	74.7	5.2	73.3	20.7
Rowlett city	20.89	56,242	67,339	19.7	3223.5	14.9	86.4	101,085	5.9	228,800	72.2	5.1	82.9	13.5
Royse City city	18.30	9,693	14,702	51.7	803.4	7.8	82.9	82,860	6.2	188,700	72.3	4.7	81.4	13.5
Sachse city	9.77	20,289	26,046	28.4	2665.9	21.1	85.3	102,175	3.5	241,800	70.9	4.4	83.2	14.8
Saginaw city	7.65	20,048	24,310	21.3	3177.8	9.2	89.9	83,402	5.4	168,900	66.1	3.9	78.8	16.5
San Angelo city	59.64	93,221	101,004	8.3	1693.6	6.5	82.0	51,928	13.8	138,000	61.4	3.9	62.3	31.3
San Antonio city	485.11	1,326,161	1,547,253	16.7	3189.5	14.3	83.3	52,455	16.8	146,400	63.7	5.5	63.8	29.9
San Benito city	15.79	24,252	24,243	0.0	1535.3	14.2	93.6	27,460	32.2	57,000	47.6	6.8	74.8	22.7
San Juan city	11.62	33,969	37,008	8.9	3184.9	26.1	95.2	40,773	28.9	90,300	58.3	6.1	87.1	11.5
San Marcos city	34.14	45,139	64,776	43.5	1897.4	9.1	67.2	40,370	30.2	171,500	67.2	7.5	43.4	31.6
Santa Fe city	17.40	12,313	13,449	9.2	772.9	0.7	84.1	72,486	10.0	184,700	60.6	6.6	76.9	20.6
Schertz city	32.00	31,824	42,042	32.1	1313.8	7.1	82.8	87,059	5.9	211,700	64.6	4.0	77.9	18.3
Seabrook city	5.33	11,945	14,149	18.5	2654.6	10.1	76.0	89,817	7.5	250,200	71.7	3.4	63.5	28.9
Seagoville city	18.82	14,902	16,861	13.1	895.9	16.8	90.1	52,378	13.9	114,200	50.4	5.4	75.7	20.3
Seguin city	37.98	25,600	29,992	17.2	789.7	7.1	85.9	49,039	18.0	134,100	57.9	4.2	66.3	27.7
Selma city	5.04	5,539	11,132	101.0	2208.7	9.4	73.7	73,175	7.1	188,300	72.4	4.1	67.2	27.2
Sherman city	45.55	38,852	44,002	13.3	966.0	11.7	78.9	47,397	15.9	126,200	63.6	3.7	63.4	32.0
Sienna Plantation CDP	12.94	13,721	NA	NA	NA	10.2	86.0	149,018	5.6	359,600	74.2	4.9	88.8	9.7
Snyder city	8.99	11,201	11,023	-1.6	1226.1	6.9	89.6	54,191	12.0	79,300	61.3	5.1	66.3	29.0
Socorro city	21.95	32,048	34,370	7.2	1565.8	33.3	90.8	38,111	25.5	93,200	57.4	5.9	84.9	13.1
South Houston city	3.05	16,995	17,438	2.6	5717.4	34.4	85.8	45,852	20.7	94,500	64.3	6.8	78.2	19.4
Southlake city	21.83	26,573	32,376	21.8	1483.1	13.8	89.2	240,248	2.6	676,900	62.2	2.2	89.2	8.3
Spring CDP	22.49	54,298	NA	NA	NA	12.9	90.2	71,376	9.4	155,600	69.0	5.0	74.3	20.8
Stafford city	7.00	16,773	17,362	3.5	2480.3	31.7	84.2	62,264	12.4	180,400	70.3	5.6	68.3	24.5
Stephenville city	11.89	17,023	21,247	24.8	1787.0	8.1	72.2	47,161	23.5	141,500	62.8	5.1	51.0	36.3
Sugar Land city	40.49	107,835	118,488	9.9	2926.4	34.9	89.5	121,274	4.7	323,300	64.2	4.7	80.8	16.8
Sulphur Springs city	20.24	15,453	16,234	5.1	802.1	5.3	79.7	45,945	18.8	102,500	61.6	5.2	66.3	27.2
Sweetwater city	11.07	10,913	10,469	-4.1	945.7	5.4	81.6	41,549	17.7	68,100	60.2	5.8	65.0	31.7
Taylor city	18.38	15,281	17,383	13.8	945.8	12.5	87.2	52,672	12.6	158,400	60.4	5.6	65.4	29.4
Temple city	70.48	66,082	78,439	18.7	1112.9	7.1	77.7	54,873	14.2	143,400	61.3	5.5	64.8	29.2
Terrell city	22.74	16,060	18,869	17.5	829.8	7.9	78.0	47,636	17.6	118,600	62.8	7.3	72.8	22.5
Texarkana city	29.05	36,399	36,317	-0.2	1250.2	4.9	87.9	45,080	23.5	130,600	55.8	8.5	63.6	31.6

Table B. Incorporated Places, Census Designated Places (CDPs), and Minor Civil Divisions (MCDs) of 10,000 or More Population — **Crime, Residential Construction and Local Government Finance**

STATE City, town, township, borough, or CDP (county if applicable)	Violent crime Number	Violent crime Rate[2]	Property crime Number	Property crime Rate[2]	Value ($1,000)	Number of housing units	Percent single family	General revenue Total (mil dol)	Intergovernmental Total (mil dol)	Intergovernmental Percent from state gov.	Taxes per capita[3]	General expenditure Total (mil dol)	Per capita[3] Total	Per capita[3] Capital outlays	Debt outstanding (mil dol)
	15	16	17	18	19	20	21	22	23	24	25	26	27	28	29
TEXAS—Con.															
Lubbock city	2,565	997	11,743	4,563	363,710	2,086	67.3	322.9	37.2	12.6	662	366.4	1,440	487	1242.5
Lufkin city	134	373	1,403	3,904	11,474	56	100.0	47.9	1.5	73.5	780	49.7	1,397	110	158.4
Lumberton city	18	139	153	1,182	19,025	123	57.7	3.6	0.2	80.3	182	2.6	201	0	0.0
McAllen city	122	85	3,856	2,671	100,749	865	62.0	218.2	11.1	13.2	806	205.1	1,442	299	253.6
McKinney city	288	152	1,980	1,045	683,996	3,195	46.7	269.3	8.6	10.8	889	220.2	1,209	260	383.2
Mansfield city	73	103	766	1,081	163,167	466	100.0	106.2	1.0	99.1	1,050	122.4	1,778	523	199.3
Manvel city	13	117	72	649	193,569	465	100.0	5.1	0.1	68.6	480	4.4	437	68	2.9
Marshall city	136	588	687	2,968	5,122	25	100.0	29.1	1.2	91.1	805	29.9	1,297	230	26.5
Mercedes city	81	480	646	3,830	5,389	60	96.7	12.3	0.2	8.2	538	16.0	967	19	22.9
Mesquite city	573	396	5,238	3,624	15,149	64	100.0	171.2	13.7	7.2	685	166.9	1,157	118	145.4
Midland city	403	288	2,764	1,973	209,964	1,290	100.0	201.0	10.0	29.8	970	154.6	1,135	141	78.3
Midlothian city	22	84	336	1,275	111,404	476	99.6	43.1	8.5	2.8	893	47.2	1,600	427	90.3
Mineral Wells city	52	353	396	2,689	2,049	10	100.0	10.8	0.0		433	13.2	882	91	0.3
Mission city	94	110	1,594	1,867	47,975	385	97.9	79.0	8.1	45.4	480	69.6	833	73	361.0
Mission Bend CDP	NA	NA	NA	NA	NA	NA	NA	NA	NA	NA	NA	NA	NA	NA	NA
Missouri City city	102	135	815	1,078	135,350	570	100.0	66.8	5.4	33.9	621	70.2	941	185	160.9
Mount Pleasant city	63	387	555	3,407	5,560	34	100.0	18.7	0.6	10.4	664	17.9	1,122	95	36.2
Murphy city	10	47	113	536	37,023	75	100.0	19.9	0.0	100.0	698	20.1	972	170	39.2
Nacogdoches city	102	303	979	2,905	3,816	25	84.0	35.1	1.2	69.7	547	35.2	1,059	126	46.6
Nederland city	47	268	309	1,759	6,111	31	100.0	19.1	0.9	1.1	657	14.3	818	165	14.3
New Braunfels city	241	291	1,197	1,447	388,172	1,737	89.2	103.4	0.7	54.9	786	102.6	1,300	268	112.8
North Richland Hills city	104	146	1,387	1,940	126,193	959	24.2	91.2	19.9	64.5	582	85.6	1,213	338	136.7
Odessa city	1,049	878	2,996	2,506	297,179	1,782	41.7	141.4	3.3	59.9	792	122.2	1,049	93	52.9
Orange city	NA	NA	NA	NA	8,182	40	100.0	26.6	1.0	40.5	569	27.3	1,435	188	14.7
Palestine city	NA	NA	NA	NA	9,907	155	12.3	20.6	1.1	100.0	776	27.2	1,501	39	18.5
Pampa city	103	592	653	3,750	900	1	100.0	19.0	0.9	38.1	524	17.0	978	42	21.4
Paris city	218	881	725	2,931	10,781	82	28.0	36.3	2.1	100.0	888	42.0	1,694	145	15.5
Pasadena city	679	441	3,467	2,250	27,417	189	100.0	174.4	19.0	46.1	640	159.7	1,038	275	215.9
Pearland city	118	95	1,841	1,483	145,278	651	100.0	153.6	1.9	64.2	901	130.9	1,098	188	231.7
Pearsall city	14	133	209	1,986	508	5	100.0	3.6	0.2	72.4	270	3.2	308	31	0.9
Pecan Grove CDP	NA	NA	NA	NA	NA	NA	NA	NA	NA	NA	NA	NA	NA	NA	NA
Pecos city	124	1,229	164	1,625	13,728	67	100.0	3.6	0.2	72.4	287	3.2	328	33	0.9
Pflugerville city	NA	NA	NA	NA	218,553	867	100.0	59.3	2.9	4.1	533	65.9	1,041	451	222.8
Pharr city	238	295	1,585	1,961	72,256	360	65.3	50.0	4.0	48.7	236	0.0	0	0	109.7
Plainview city	59	287	503	2,445	0	0	0.0	24.3	0.8	68.2	568	22.7	1,105	131	10.4
Plano city	402	139	4,955	1,709	178,577	1,345	14.6	457.1	8.4	67.3	1,050	369.7	1,285	111	135.4
Pleasanton city	30	282	406	3,821	4,319	24	100.0	8.3	0.0	100.0	613	14.6	1,394	50	0.9
Port Arthur city	390	701	1,445	2,597	43,273	326	39.6	117.2	13.6	86.7	857	105.1	1,896	171	57.3
Portland city	25	143	376	2,143	15,216	69	100.0	20.0	0.1	35.0	811	18.3	1,060	155	30.3
Port Lavaca city	NA	NA	NA	NA	4,413	32	87.5	12.8	0.1	100.0	642	11.4	938	84	8.8
Port Neches city	56	435	178	1,382	10,504	52	100.0	8.5	0.1	89.9	436	10.2	797	28	1.4
Princeton city	19	177	183	1,703	154,347	650	100.0	7.5	0.4	0.5	398	7.9	781	245	14.5
Prosper town	63	279	188	833	273,862	847	100.0	44.2	0.1	56.3	1,052	23.1	1,139	2	83.0
Raymondville city	106	967	318	2,902	1,024	5	100.0	6.1	1.2	0.0	290	4.4	403	1	8.2
Red Oak city	22	168	336	2,566	73,644	217	100.0	3.6	0.2	72.4	221	3.2	252	25	2.1
Rendon CDP	NA	NA	NA	NA	NA	NA	NA	NA	NA	NA	NA	NA	NA	NA	NA
Richardson city	135	113	2,522	2,111	69,465	315	21.9	203.1	5.0	77.6	1,195	195.5	1,682	188	238.9
Richmond city	46	379	255	2,102	0	0	0.0	17.6	0.7	70.7	707	21.9	1,732	308	28.7
Rio Grande City city	59	404	194	1,327	NA	NA	NA	9.9	0.8	66.1	469	11.5	798	135	25.4
Robinson city	25	212	156	1,325	14,124	60	100.0	7.0	0.0		396	6.6	567	0	14.1
Robstown city	NA	NA	NA	NA	5,699	24	100.0	9.8	0.0		427	7.4	652	0	15.9
Rockport city	22	205	443	4,127	43,426	203	100.0	15.6	1.0	73.0	840	11.6	1,045	32	47.6
Rockwall city	42	93	750	1,660	109,042	546	47.3	55.5	0.3	100.0	1,080	39.6	897	0	125.1
Roma city	25	217	82	713	NA	NA	NA	3.6	0.2	72.4	247	3.2	282	28	0.9
Rosenberg city	157	407	615	1,596	118,728	500	100.0	45.0	5.4	29.3	736	32.7	878	159	17.0
Round Rock city	154	121	2,494	1,958	215,422	1,010	64.8	171.4	1.2	49.6	1,098	150.9	1,220	285	247.2
Rowlett city	114	179	912	1,428	92,609	628	38.7	64.3	2.4	7.1	637	63.0	1,000	196	98.5
Royse City city	20	153	129	984	60,838	243	100.0	9.6	0.3	1.3	466	10.1	774	112	21.5
Sachse city	15	56	208	775	22,808	45	100.0	38.7	0.4	9.3	1,355	35.5	1,368	709	40.4
Saginaw city	NA	NA	NA	NA	81,678	265	100.0	23.6	2.9	100.0	655	24.7	1,060	256	24.2
San Angelo city	373	369	3,383	3,347	61,492	283	100.0	114.5	5.2	11.1	712	120.3	1,207	234	207.7
San Antonio city	9,647	627	61,478	3,994	1,505,994	9,196	42.3	2328.5	464.5	36.9	626	2273.7	1,505	273	11712.5
San Benito city	65	265	1,018	4,145	3,902	48	91.7	17.3	0.9	39.9	374	16.3	666	0	38.0
San Juan city	155	415	858	2,294	13,055	152	92.1	20.5	1.1	30.8	316	21.7	592	93	19.6
San Marcos city	263	398	1,415	2,139	105,400	577	100.0	103.9	19.8	100.0	789	87.5	1,377	240	70.8
Santa Fe city	17	125	171	1,257	13,298	56	100.0	7.3	1.8	99.2	389	6.2	464	60	0.0
Schertz city	95	230	670	1,619	74,372	310	100.0	54.8	3.2	8.9	780	45.9	1,144	255	70.3
Seabrook city	25	179	144	1,032	9,953	30	100.0	16.3	0.3	100.0	790	15.5	1,130	141	28.0
Seagoville city	12	71	384	2,261	25,950	215	100.0	13.1	1.0	1.8	452	10.9	657	77	1.8
Seguin city	88	298	745	2,527	31,489	172	77.9	142.7	16.4	93.8	581	172.4	5,928	1084	228.6
Selma city	24	204	240	2,044	87,195	750	2.7	14.7	0.1	100.0	1,008	12.9	1,212	20	19.1
Sherman city	147	346	1,068	2,516	91,019	560	40.2	48.9	1.3	61.2	681	53.2	1,257	114	175.0
Sienna Plantation CDP	NA	NA	NA	NA	NA	NA	NA	NA	NA	NA	NA	NA	NA	NA	NA
Snyder city	34	300	198	1,747	800	3	100.0	11.3	0.7	2.6	483	11.3	1,008	102	14.1
Socorro city	45	131	251	731	84,572	488	64.8	10.3	0.2	30.2	263	8.3	247	0	23.4
South Houston city	73	414	422	2,395	4,900	84	14.3	3.6	0.2	72.4	160	3.2	183	18	0.9
Southlake city	11	34	450	1,379	86,427	84	100.0	89.5	0.7	65.5	2,303	84.3	2,655	496	171.2
Spring CDP	NA	NA	NA	NA	NA	NA	NA	NA	NA	NA	NA	NA	NA	NA	NA
Stafford city	NA	NA	NA	NA	1,509	7	100.0	35.3	11.7	27.0	1,136	32.9	1,882	701	22.2
Stephenville city	30	140	404	1,888	22,382	336	8.9	18.8	0.3	79.7	603	18.1	881	142	19.4
Sugar Land city	82	91	1,537	1,709	36,855	124	100.0	167.8	6.0	38.5	857	226.1	1,900	931	469.7
Sulphur Springs city	37	230	157	975	6,215	42	61.9	20.8	0.8	100.0	688	21.4	1,338	286	29.5
Sweetwater city	50	475	307	2,916	420	2	100.0	19.3	0.3	100.0	700	17.7	1,674	98	18.0
Taylor city	50	290	387	2,247	41,147	150	97.3	19.3	0.2	31.2	763	19.8	1,167	131	48.2
Temple city	236	312	1,940	2,563	125,381	1,006	99.4	108.4	4.6	95.0	784	101.4	1,363	242	49.6
Terrell city	73	403	581	3,209	7,495	45	100.0	33.8	8.2	61.6	1,006	28.4	1,586	196	0.0
Texarkana city	171	457	1,914	5,110	8,436	37	100.0	49.3	1.5	25.8	987	43.3	1,175	139	55.6

1 Data for serious crimes have not been adjusted for underreporting. This may affect comparability between geographic areas over time.
2 Per 100,000 population estimated by the FBI. 3 Based on population estimated as of July 1 of the year shown.

Table B. Incorporated Places, Census Designated Places (CDPs), and Minor Civil Divisions (MCDs) of 10,000 or More Population — **Land Area, Population, and Households, and Employment**

STATE City, town, township, borough, or CDP (county if applicable)	Land area 2010 (sq mi)	Population — Total persons 2010	Total persons 2019	Percent change 2010–2019	Persons per square mile 2019	Population characteristics 2015–2019 — Percent foreign born	Percent living in the same house as previous year	Income and poverty 2015–2019 — Median household income	Percent of households with income below poverty level	Median value of owner-occupied housing units	Employment, 2015–2019 — Percent in civilian labor force	Unemploy-ment rate	Households, 2015–2019 (percent of households) — Family households	One person households
	1	2	3	4	5	6	7	8	9	10	11	12	13	14
TEXAS—Con.														
Texas City city	64.31	45,084	50,094	11.1	778.9	7.7	79.7	48,839	17.1	124,200	59.9	7.5	68.9	24.7
The Colony city	14.01	36,341	44,438	22.3	3171.9	13.0	83.2	87,187	4.7	231,700	79.4	2.5	64.3	27.6
The Woodlands CDP	43.21	93,847	NA	NA	NA	19.8	82.2	122,634	5.3	374,200	63.5	3.5	75.3	22.1
Timberwood Park CDP	20.40	13,447	NA	NA	NA	9.6	86.7	108,358	3.4	339,400	67.7	4.3	78.2	19.2
Tomball city	13.00	10,715	11,778	9.9	906.0	10.8	78.3	59,164	12.1	211,700	61.7	8.3	61.2	34.1
Trophy Club town	3.95	8,026	12,451	55.1	3152.2	6.1	87.2	147,477	4.4	400,500	74.0	4.3	86.1	10.4
Tyler city	57.46	96,852	106,985	10.5	1861.9	10.3	84.3	52,932	16.2	160,000	62.0	5.5	62.9	30.8
Universal City city	5.57	18,526	20,890	12.8	3750.4	10.6	81.9	63,192	8.5	168,300	63.3	4.5	68.5	27.1
University Park city	3.69	23,068	24,985	8.3	6771.0	6.9	83.3	224,485	4.3	1,295,500	59.4	3.5	80.4	14.9
Uvalde city	7.66	15,752	16,001	1.6	2088.9	13.6	85.3	41,713	17.7	77,700	61.9	4.6	71.1	23.2
Vernon city	7.90	11,002	10,323	-6.2	1306.7	5.1	78.9	42,533	17.6	64,600	62.0	6.4	60.0	35.3
Victoria city	37.19	62,624	66,916	6.9	1799.3	8.1	81.3	54,192	15.9	136,400	63.9	5.8	67.2	26.7
Vidor city	12.02	10,699	10,403	-2.8	865.5	2.4	86.2	43,637	17.3	85,800	55.0	3.5	67.0	28.5
Waco city	88.86	124,797	139,236	11.6	1566.9	10.6	77.2	40,190	24.4	125,300	59.6	4.8	59.0	31.3
Watauga city	4.16	23,497	24,481	4.2	5884.9	11.6	86.0	71,897	8.0	136,300	70.4	4.3	77.4	16.0
Waxahachie city	48.84	29,538	37,988	28.6	777.8	6.0	82.7	65,589	11.0	176,300	66.5	3.4	71.6	24.0
Weatherford city	27.12	25,743	33,547	30.3	1237.0	6.6	81.3	63,708	13.0	169,400	59.5	4.5	65.0	30.4
Webster city	6.39	10,624	11,451	7.8	1792.0	19.5	64.2	55,497	12.6	186,400	77.5	6.6	46.4	44.1
Wells Branch CDP	2.43	12,120	NA	NA	NA	21.3	78.6	54,421	12.4	246,600	74.7	2.6	42.4	49.6
Weslaco city	17.59	36,756	41,629	13.3	2366.6	16.6	85.2	45,060	23.2	83,900	58.3	3.8	77.1	21.0
West Odessa CDP	62.72	22,707	NA	NA	NA	18.6	93.0	61,460	14.0	101,700	66.3	7.5	77.6	18.7
West University Place city	2.00	14,560	15,585	7.0	7792.5	17.0	89.8	250	2.3	1,113,500	62.8	2.6	85.0	14.3
White Settlement city	5.04	16,116	17,851	10.8	3541.9	8.8	83.1	48,996	10.6	99,200	64.6	5.5	61.0	32.4
Wichita Falls city	72.01	104,682	104,683	0.0	1453.7	7.9	78.0	47,476	18.4	102,400	54.8	5.1	61.3	32.3
Wylie city	22.06	41,685	53,067	27.3	2405.6	17.7	87.4	92,395	5.0	227,700	75.5	4.5	81.7	14.1
UTAH	82376.89	2,763,891	3,205,958	16.0	38.9	8.5	83.1	71,621	9.7	279,100	68.3	3.6	74.6	19.4
Alpine city	7.95	9,768	10,498	7.5	1320.5	2.5	87.9	129,239	2.2	569,300	64.4	3.4	92.5	6.7
American Fork city	10.76	26,547	33,161	24.9	3081.9	5.8	87.3	77,857	4.4	286,800	65.2	4.1	85.4	13.1
Bluffdale city	11.14	7,609	16,358	115.0	1468.4	1.5	85.9	116,454	5.3	485,400	74.6	2.6	95.5	3.5
Bountiful city	13.20	42,574	43,981	3.3	3331.9	4.9	85.3	77,823	6.5	316,300	64.2	1.9	76.9	20.2
Brigham City city	24.52	17,908	19,601	9.5	799.4	4.0	82.7	53,504	11.8	181,500	62.2	6.4	74.8	23.0
Cedar City city	35.86	28,867	34,764	20.4	969.4	4.3	78.9	48,346	20.4	215,900	64.2	4.7	68.7	22.0
Cedar Hills city	2.72	9,806	10,083	2.8	3707.0	3.1	85.0	104,808	5.0	371,300	63.0	3.0	91.1	7.6
Centerville city	5.97	15,304	17,587	14.9	2945.9	3.2	89.5	93,344	4.2	321,700	65.7	1.8	79.0	18.5
Clearfield city	7.71	29,929	32,118	7.3	4165.8	6.8	79.1	60,260	9.9	194,300	69.2	3.2	74.7	20.0
Clinton city	5.93	20,481	22,499	9.9	3794.1	4.4	88.1	82,161	2.8	243,400	70.7	2.3	85.6	12.0
Cottonwood Heights city	9.22	33,586	33,843	0.8	3670.6	7.1	85.7	93,564	5.4	382,900	70.9	3.0	66.6	26.7
Draper city	29.96	42,272	48,587	14.9	1621.7	6.6	82.4	117,266	5.0	469,000	68.1	3.1	83.8	10.8
Eagle Mountain city	50.42	21,936	38,391	75.0	761.4	5.6	80.3	83,290	5.7	280,700	73.5	3.0	94.9	3.0
Farmington city	9.95	18,234	25,339	39.0	2546.6	2.5	86.5	106,488	3.6	386,500	65.5	2.5	80.5	16.0
Grantsville city	37.47	8,926	12,064	35.2	322.0	2.1	84.8	72,378	7.8	254,700	66.3	5.4	85.0	12.3
Heber city	8.87	11,436	17,082	49.4	1925.8	10.4	80.3	74,665	8.0	348,100	75.0	2.4	76.5	16.2
Herriman city	21.63	21,768	51,348	135.9	2373.9	4.5	83.4	101,460	2.9	375,100	75.1	3.5	83.8	12.4
Highland city	8.64	15,570	19,175	23.2	2219.3	2.4	91.2	139,453	3.5	559,600	64.3	3.3	95.3	4.3
Holladay city	8.49	30,127	30,325	0.7	3571.8	5.8	85.9	88,728	5.8	442,900	64.6	1.9	74.1	22.2
Hurricane city	52.76	13,756	19,074	38.7	361.5	4.4	87.3	55,190	11.4	238,800	56.3	5.4	71.0	25.4
Kaysville city	10.50	27,570	32,390	17.5	3084.8	2.2	90.1	99,597	4.6	339,500	65.4	2.9	88.7	10.4
Kearns metro township	4.63	35,769	36,330	1.6	7846.7	19.7	89.6	64,337	8.3	202,000	73.1	4.6	85.8	10.5
Layton city	22.49	67,529	78,014	15.5	3468.8	5.4	83.8	77,426	6.9	260,400	70.0	3.3	79.5	17.0
Lehi city	28.04	47,769	69,724	46.0	2486.6	5.8	83.8	95,510	5.8	353,100	69.5	2.7	87.6	9.8
Lindon city	8.36	10,045	11,100	10.5	1327.8	5.8	84.6	90,978	5.4	401,200	64.7	4.4	88.7	9.4
Logan city	17.66	48,203	51,542	6.9	2918.6	9.8	69.3	41,833	24.1	198,500	71.1	2.8	64.1	20.5
Magna metro township	15.11	26,513	26,949	1.6	1783.5	14.7	83.8	63,075	10.3	205,000	75.0	5.2	77.6	17.1
Midvale city	5.91	27,998	34,124	21.9	5773.9	15.1	79.5	60,216	12.8	261,400	74.1	4.2	59.8	29.7
Millcreek city	12.76	58,750	61,450	4.6	4815.8	11.4	82.4	72,134	8.6	366,100	69.0	3.3	61.4	30.0
Murray city	12.32	46,685	48,917	4.8	3970.5	8.3	83.9	64,470	7.4	287,100	70.7	3.3	62.2	29.8
North Logan city	7.13	8,303	11,227	35.3	1576.0	6.5	78.9	71,351	13.9	274,900	66.7	2.7	73.7	17.5
North Ogden city	7.45	17,415	20,582	18.2	2762.7	1.2	86.3	81,198	6.7	263,800	69.0	2.0	81.5	14.7
North Salt Lake city	8.47	16,199	20,948	29.3	2473.2	9.2	81.6	85,185	4.7	303,200	76.5	2.5	79.2	13.8
Ogden city	27.53	82,887	87,773	5.9	3188.3	12.3	80.2	50,061	17.1	170,100	65.3	4.8	63.5	29.2
Orem city	18.48	88,328	97,828	10.8	5293.7	12.0	77.4	64,590	11.5	272,000	69.5	3.9	78.1	14.4
Payson city	12.63	18,515	20,303	9.7	1607.5	6.0	86.6	67,272	10.6	231,000	68.4	5.3	81.8	14.4
Pleasant Grove city	9.18	33,550	38,258	14.0	4167.5	6.0	82.5	72,327	9.3	296,900	70.6	4.1	75.6	17.4
Pleasant View city	6.98	7,945	10,839	36.4	1552.9	5.3	89.5	98,765	5.6	323,400	65.3	3.7	89.6	8.9
Provo city	41.67	112,487	116,618	3.7	2798.6	11.0	62.1	48,888	24.7	271,300	71.0	4.6	69.4	13.3
Riverton city	12.59	38,832	44,440	14.4	3529.8	4.2	90.5	101,619	2.4	349,600	72.8	2.1	89.1	9.3
Roy city	8.14	37,450	39,613	5.8	4866.5	5.6	86.0	70,032	9.0	191,800	70.1	4.4	75.5	20.4
St. George city	76.89	72,759	89,587	23.1	1165.1	6.7	83.0	58,259	10.8	286,000	55.3	3.7	71.0	23.2
Salt Lake City city	110.70	186,433	200,567	7.6	1811.8	17.1	78.4	60,676	14.7	314,500	71.7	3.6	50.4	36.2
Sandy city	24.10	90,180	96,380	6.9	3999.2	9.0	86.1	94,018	5.5	356,500	68.3	2.8	78.2	16.9
Santaquin city	10.29	9,175	12,865	40.2	1250.2	4.3	86.9	72,171	5.8	251,600	73.1	3.5	86.3	10.3
Saratoga Springs city	22.86	17,842	33,282	86.5	1455.9	4.7	80.3	102,531	2.4	340,700	70.5	3.4	89.3	7.5
Smithfield city	5.21	9,632	12,025	24.8	2308.1	3.6	84.8	71,118	7.9	237,100	67.2	2.9	86.8	11.2
South Jordan city	22.22	50,473	76,598	51.8	3447.3	6.3	84.6	104,597	2.8	405,400	70.9	1.6	82.1	14.9
South Ogden city	3.89	16,563	17,199	3.8	4421.3	6.9	83.0	68,585	6.8	213,800	67.7	1.6	72.6	23.3
South Salt Lake city	6.94	23,574	25,582	8.5	3686.2	24.6	78.4	47,813	17.5	226,000	70.4	5.5	59.2	31.7
Spanish Fork city	16.20	34,763	40,913	17.7	2525.5	5.7	83.6	78,490	6.8	273,600	69.2	2.1	85.9	11.9
Springville city	14.34	29,559	33,310	12.7	2322.9	7.7	82.2	69,139	8.2	260,200	66.8	2.3	82.0	13.9
Syracuse city	10.16	24,377	31,458	29.0	3096.3	2.1	87.7	99,625	4.0	316,200	72.2	2.3	89.9	8.4
Taylorsville city	10.85	58,691	59,805	1.9	5512.0	16.0	85.5	66,311	8.8	239,400	72.0	4.2	72.7	22.1
Tooele city	24.09	31,603	36,015	14.0	1495.0	4.1	83.3	63,851	8.4	195,300	68.0	6.0	76.6	20.2
Vernal city	4.62	9,136	10,438	14.3	2259.3	6.1	76.4	48,325	16.8	166,400	65.1	11.5	59.8	34.1
Washington city	34.72	18,766	29,174	55.5	840.3	4.8	85.0	66,479	9.9	291,900	61.3	0.6	78.2	16.2
West Haven city	10.46	10,286	16,109	56.6	1540.1	1.4	81.0	77,733	7.0	301,900	77.8	2.4	82.3	12.8
West Jordan city	32.33	103,601	116,480	12.4	3602.8	11.2	85.6	80,955	5.6	284,200	74.6	4.0	80.4	14.5

STATE City, town, township, borough, or CDP (county if applicable)	Serious crimes known to police, 2018[1] Violent crime Number	Violent crime Rate[2]	Property crime Number	Property crime Rate[2]	New residential construction authorized by building permits, 2019 Value ($1,000)	Number of housing units	Percent single family	Local government finance, 2017 General revenue Total (mil dol)	Intergovernmental Total (mil dol)	Percent from state gov.	Taxes per capita[3]	General expenditure Total (mil dol)	Per capita[3] Total	Capital outlays	Debt outstanding (mil dol)
	15	16	17	18	19	20	21	22	23	24	25	26	27	28	29
TEXAS—Con.															
Texas City city	236	481	1,489	3,036	106,458	814	60.9	61.0	1.7	83.3	899	70.1	1,448	199	69.9
The Colony city	100	229	477	1,092	80,991	291	100.0	51.5	5.0	92.3	877	37.9	883	49	121.3
The Woodlands CDP	NA	NA	NA	NA	NA	NA	NA	NA	NA	NA	NA	NA	NA	NA	NA
Timberwood Park CDP	NA	NA	NA	NA	NA	NA	NA	NA	NA	NA	NA	NA	NA	NA	NA
Tomball city	NA	NA	NA	NA	21,151	98	100.0	23.4	0.3	14.2	1,434	19.0	1,633	72	14.2
Trophy Club town	2	15	69	527	17,893	34	100.0	14.2	0.6	5.4	829	21.5	1,734	675	35.5
Tyler city	412	388	3,133	2,951	111,255	416	94.2	139.8	18.1	7.0	760	126.2	1,205	228	55.5
Universal City city	63	303	546	2,622	17,334	73	100.0	18.3	0.1	100.0	563	17.0	828	163	40.9
University Park city	5	20	302	1,184	58,116	94	51.1	57.4	0.2	100.0	994	59.4	2,353	222	640.9
Uvalde city	36	220	621	3,792	2,979	28	100.0	9.2	1.6	100.0	450	14.3	879	256	27.3
Vernon city	46	448	269	2,622	325	2	100.0	9.6	0.2	3.7	451	11.5	1,117	9	6.6
Victoria city	280	413	1,885	2,782	41,538	201	70.1	86.5	3.5	30.2	833	88.3	1,318	298	163.7
Vidor city	NA	NA	NA	NA	0	0	0.0	8.5	0.7	94.6	563	8.2	754	127	6.5
Waco city	878	636	4,851	3,513	152,534	938	66.5	320.4	51.1	25.6	896	194.5	1,420	146	269.6
Watauga city	48	194	319	1,289	631	4	100.0	21.5	0.2	100.0	554	23.3	943	160	26.1
Waxahachie city	73	202	527	1,455	135,461	683	84.3	51.1	0.2	100.0	1,037	41.8	1,185	71	159.0
Weatherford city	58	185	508	1,618	45,462	269	70.3	37.5	1.7	48.3	780	43.1	1,403	192	107.3
Webster city	47	420	774	6,914	6,496	26	100.0	30.8	1.3	77.0	2,276	24.0	2,154	132	27.1
Wells Branch CDP	NA	NA	NA	NA	NA	NA	NA	NA	NA	NA	NA	NA	NA	NA	NA
Weslaco city	162	397	1,595	3,904	128,282	854	25.2	35.3	1.8	91.3	538	32.5	808	80	80.5
West Odessa CDP	NA	NA	NA	NA	NA	NA	NA	NA	NA	NA	NA	NA	NA	NA	NA
West University Place city	2	13	111	704	51,316	62	100.0	29.4	0.4	2.0	1,370	28.0	1,788	299	72.9
White Settlement city	33	183	338	1,869	7,783	54	100.0	16.9	0.2	48.4	623	17.4	974	100	37.4
Wichita Falls city	387	370	3,234	3,088	35,079	128	71.9	114.8	16.7	37.5	630	124.1	1,189	131	186.9
Wylie city	52	102	398	780	104,068	428	99.1	57.6	4.6	64.4	788	50.0	1,010	109	89.5
UTAH	7,368	233	75,156	2,378	6,453,593	28,779	63.2	X	X	X	X	X	X	X	X
Alpine city	NA	NA	NA	NA	24,826	37	100.0	9.2	0.5	99.1	331	6.5	618	56	3.6
American Fork city	22	55	702	1,739	107,068	349	69.6	49.1	7.5	17.8	596	42.8	1,451	229	0.0
Bluffdale city	13	89	177	1,208	110,776	501	100.0	21.9	4.1	14.4	690	12.6	935	475	0.0
Bountiful city	43	97	642	1,449	19,615	66	37.9	32.9	3.0	58.4	354	43.0	978	204	0.0
Brigham City city	28	145	362	1,870	10,080	37	100.0	11.7	1.2	60.5	385	14.3	748	163	3.2
Cedar City city	70	217	751	2,329	50,855	231	82.7	28.5	2.3	69.2	519	23.3	737	97	1.6
Cedar Hills city	NA	NA	NA	NA	4,239	7	100.0	8.8	0.4	100.0	297	6.3	607	53	0.0
Centerville city	23	128	380	2,110	3,812	13	100.0	8.4	0.1	31.3	370	8.6	487	37	6.0
Clearfield city	59	187	462	1,464	5,177	52	0.0	34.8	1.3	73.8	474	29.9	956	103	2.4
Clinton city	13	59	301	1,357	28,540	109	100.0	15.1	0.9	97.6	286	13.7	627	97	1.0
Cottonwood Heights city	43	126	787	2,311	21,739	55	100.0	23.2	1.4	97.1	484	27.4	806	336	4.1
Draper city	84	173	976	2,012	93,951	261	73.9	117.0	8.7	40.0	1,274	67.5	1,415	555	13.5
Eagle Mountain city	NA	NA	NA	NA	304,268	1,105	100.0	19.1	1.1	100.0	193	20.9	651	150	24.1
Farmington city	15	60	306	1,224	24,500	80	100.0	24.6	0.9	90.8	657	19.4	808	129	0.0
Grantsville city	29	256	192	1,695	26,716	129	100.0	7.5	0.8	55.9	331	5.6	509	46	6.4
Heber city	26	157	228	1,380	48,774	167	56.9	12.8	0.7	91.8	485	10.4	663	115	0.0
Herriman city	NA	NA	NA	NA	288,101	1,532	67.6	38.6	7.8	48.1	393	45.8	1,169	887	21.8
Highland city	NA	NA	NA	NA	36,113	76	100.0	10.7	0.9	85.1	303	10.2	540	11	13.3
Holladay city	NA	NA	NA	NA	23,782	57	42.1	2.1	0.0	0.0	56	2.9	94	1	0.0
Hurricane city	22	125	283	1,601	56,190	359	99.4	13.5	0.8	84.7	354	11.8	689	107	0.0
Kaysville city	24	74	246	759	49,560	111	100.0	23.3	1.2	100.0	352	19.3	610	53	0.0
Kearns metro township	NA	NA	NA	NA	NA	NA	NA	0.0	0.0	0.0	0	0.0	0	0	0.0
Layton city	134	172	1,561	2,000	91,526	456	97.8	49.3	6.8	23.0	258	52.7	689	143	0.0
Lehi city	59	91	694	1,066	339,098	1,303	100.0	74.4	3.2	28.2	423	77.5	1,217	413	120.3
Lindon city	NA	NA	NA	NA	28,490	136	94.9	14.2	0.5	59.0	803	13.5	1,236	233	0.0
Logan city	70	136	852	1,654	68,900	464	32.5	70.4	9.9	62.4	511	52.8	1,034	118	0.0
Magna metro township	NA	NA	NA	NA	NA	NA	NA	0.0	0.0	0.0	0	0.0	0	0	0.0
Midvale city	NA	NA	NA	NA	67,877	425	2.1	29.7	2.2	56.1	421	26.8	798	289	18.5
Millcreek city	NA	NA	NA	NA	22,732	77	71.4	3.7	1.3	0.0	39	3.9	64	0	0.0
Murray city	216	435	3,027	6,094	46,186	161	100.0	57.2	4.6	45.2	745	91.5	1,855	279	10.3
North Logan city	NA	NA	NA	NA	21,651	105	29.5	8.3	0.5	92.0	438	8.0	750	30	0.0
North Ogden city	6	30	232	1,173	45,097	212	48.6	16.6	0.7	100.0	430	12.7	650	104	1.3
North Salt Lake city	27	127	405	1,911	21,786	123	70.7	16.7	1.2	93.0	507	15.3	747	133	1.0
Ogden city	417	476	3,218	3,673	23,234	164	65.2	101.2	9.9	71.6	568	100.6	1,155	201	117.4
Orem city	69	70	1,827	1,841	163,172	753	14.9	86.3	6.0	88.2	469	71.5	732	151	3.7
Payson city	10	50	318	1,584	54,604	304	63.5	20.3	1.1	74.4	302	19.0	956	32	5.1
Pleasant Grove city	29	73	424	1,070	50,973	145	71.0	29.6	1.3	99.8	293	23.3	600	25	15.7
Pleasant View city	11	103	108	1,013	8,075	20	100.0	7.2	0.5	90.4	327	5.6	545	63	1.1
Provo city	207	175	2,090	1,771	61,263	314	55.4	81.0	6.1	51.3	321	91.3	776	23	4.6
Riverton city	NA	NA	NA	NA	59,666	226	63.7	21.2	1.6	82.1	209	16.7	385	54	427.2
Roy city	53	137	514	1,324	14,836	116	51.7	25.8	1.6	91.2	332	20.9	532	68	1.8
St. George city	196	227	1,388	1,610	232,942	1,527	71.3	108.1	6.0	58.0	604	86.4	1,022	251	109.0
Salt Lake City city	1,480	730	12,516	6,177	532,128	3,486	3.6	639.8	16.5	11.4	1,316	776.5	3,865	1588	1677.2
Sandy city	159	164	2,613	2,692	22,300	111	27.9	90.3	5.1	81.7	524	107.7	1,117	581	0.0
Santaquin city	4	29	114	839	57,880	226	63.3	9.1	0.5	100.0	281	7.5	641	88	0.5
Saratoga Springs city	32	101	226	711	163,134	727	100.0	26.7	1.3	84.8	365	17.5	593	115	15.1
Smithfield city	NA	NA	NA	NA	0	0	0.0	10.1	1.3	58.3	289	7.7	675	47	0.4
South Jordan city	77	104	1,453	1,955	224,821	1,031	74.2	61.4	3.1	89.1	642	37.1	523	418	23.7
South Ogden city	25	146	329	1,916	5,401	51	5.9	15.3	1.9	100.0	512	14.6	853	153	0.4
South Salt Lake city	242	962	1,796	7,138	27,261	92	71.7	34.2	4.3	13.2	963	33.3	1,334	118	13.5
Spanish Fork city	12	30	352	878	73,561	282	99.3	34.7	1.5	76.0	279	26.5	672	164	0.0
Springville city	23	68	627	1,854	56,529	206	85.4	33.2	1.8	93.0	573	40.8	1,229	322	35.8
Syracuse city	23	76	235	776	66,486	310	100.0	24.6	2.6	64.9	310	15.5	528	64	10.4
Taylorsville city	NA	NA	NA	NA	43,419	270	24.4	23.4	0.6	100.0	309	20.9	348	20	0.5
Tooele city	104	297	1,143	3,260	50,720	391	41.7	24.8	1.6	84.9	437	18.8	543	21	11.4
Vernal city	32	305	261	2,490	2,311	11	100.0	9.8	2.3	75.9	587	12.7	1,232	95	11.5
Washington city	35	126	477	1,722	210,148	1,178	53.7	27.2	1.2	94.5	453	28.8	1,090	65	18.3
West Haven city	NA	NA	NA	NA	94,076	658	37.2	11.1	3.3	94.0	363	11.7	865	116	0.0
West Jordan city	298	258	3,036	2,631	135,507	702	47.7	83.0	4.8	87.4	411	74.3	652	138	55.3

1 Data for serious crimes have not been adjusted for underreporting. This may affect comparability between geographic areas over time.
2 Per 100,000 population estimated by the FBI. 3 Based on population estimated as of July 1 of the year shown.

Table B. Incorporated Places, Census Designated Places (CDPs), and Minor Civil Divisions (MCDs) of 10,000 or More Population — Land Area, Population, and Households, and Employment

STATE City, town, township, borough, or CDP (county if applicable)	Land area 2010 (sq mi)	Population — Total persons 2010	Total persons 2019	Percent change 2010–2019	Persons per square mile, 2019	Population characteristics 2015–2019 — Percent foreign born	Percent living in the same house as previous year	Income and poverty 2015–2019 — Median household income	Percent of households with income below poverty level	Median value of owner-occupied housing units	Employment, 2015–2019 — Percent in civilian labor force	Unemployment rate	Households, 2015–2019 (percent of households) — Family households	One person households
	1	2	3	4	5	6	7	8	9	10	11	12	13	14
UTAH—Con.														
West Point city	7.11	9,412	10,957	16.4	1541.1	3.4	85.1	92,655	2.4	254,500	71.7	1.6	91.1	6.9
West Valley City city	35.47	129,489	135,248	4.4	3813.0	22.3	83.4	66,342	10.4	219,500	72.5	4.2	78.0	15.0
Woods Cross city	3.83	9,767	11,431	17.0	2984.6	3.3	86.0	77,433	5.3	268,700	76.7	3.5	72.3	19.5
VERMONT	9217.88	625,737	623,989	-0.3	67.7	4.7	86.7	61,973	11.2	227,700	65.4	3.6	60.1	30.6
Bennington town (Bennington)	42.25	15,770	14,964	-5.1	354.2	2.7	87.0	50,892	15.2	164,600	57.2	3.4	56.0	35.0
Brattleboro town (Windham)	31.84	12,043	11,332	-5.9	355.9	4.0	82.3	38,176	20.2	214,000	62.7	5.2	51.4	41.8
Burlington city & MCD (Chittenden)	10.31	42,414	42,819	1.0	4153.2	11.8	64.9	51,394	24.4	284,500	65.6	4.3	36.1	37.1
Colchester town (Chittenden)	36.33	17,072	17,127	0.3	471.4	7.1	80.7	71,090	10.7	265,000	71.1	4.1	57.3	29.3
Essex town (Chittenden)	38.82	19,593	21,890	11.7	563.9	10.6	87.1	84,588	8.5	301,000	73.7	2.7	65.5	24.9
Essex Junction village	4.57	9,291	10,852	16.8	2374.6	14.3	84.0	80,019	9.7	298,200	76.7	2.9	62.4	26.1
Milton town (Chittenden)	51.38	10,351	10,829	4.6	210.8	2.3	86.1	84,992	5.0	248,800	75.9	5.3	76.5	18.5
Rutland city & MCD (Rutland)	7.54	16,469	15,074	-8.5	1999.2	2.8	89.9	48,212	14.7	153,300	62.0	3.7	51.5	41.3
South Burlington city & MCD (Chittenden)	16.49	17,904	19,509	9.0	1183.1	11.1	83.7	73,065	6.2	307,500	69.2	3.7	56.4	31.7
VIRGINIA	39482.15	8,001,049	8,535,519	6.7	216.2	12.4	84.7	74,222	10.3	273,100	64.1	4.6	66.4	27.1
Alexandria city	14.93	139,998	159,428	13.9	10678.4	27.2	79.0	100,939	7.5	572,900	76.1	3.0	48.9	41.3
Annandale CDP	7.85	41,008	NA	NA	NA	46.6	86.9	96,533	10.3	489,100	72.1	3.9	68.1	22.9
Arlington CDP	26.00	207,627	NA	NA	NA	23.2	79.6	120,071	6.5	705,400	77.1	2.7	46.0	39.2
Ashburn CDP	17.18	43,511	NA	NA	NA	23.1	85.8	132,331	3.4	493,400	73.5	3.0	71.1	23.1
Bailey's Crossroads CDP	2.05	23,643	NA	NA	NA	51.7	85.6	66,995	14.8	357,900	67.4	5.4	56.5	34.7
Blacksburg town	19.72	42,525	44,233	4.0	2243.1	12.6	62.7	43,173	37.3	298,400	49.5	5.1	37.5	27.2
Bon Air CDP	8.36	16,366	NA	NA	NA	10.0	86.8	81,896	4.0	241,000	66.1	3.2	64.6	31.7
Brambleton CDP	5.75	9,845	NA	NA	NA	29.0	84.1	181,905	0.7	600,700	80.9	2.2	90.1	7.2
Brandermill CDP	6.16	13,173	NA	NA	NA	7.8	88.1	101,426	3.5	257,000	69.3	3.5	70.3	26.7
Bristol city	12.90	17,738	16,762	-5.5	1299.4	1.1	86.0	37,500	20.0	111,700	54.2	6.1	57.7	37.8
Broadlands CDP	3.23	12,313	NA	NA	NA	19.6	88.1	184,475	2.1	618,400	78.3	1.5	84.0	11.3
Buckhall CDP	20.20	16,293	NA	NA	NA	13.8	90.2	143,602	1.9	449,400	68.5	3.0	84.7	12.5
Bull Run CDP	2.60	14,983	NA	NA	NA	41.0	78.9	68,502	11.9	247,500	79.7	4.5	64.8	26.1
Burke CDP	8.61	41,055	NA	NA	NA	24.9	88.3	145,234	2.8	541,900	65.7	5.0	84.8	12.3
Burke Centre CDP	3.13	17,326	NA	NA	NA	22.8	85.8	132,034	5.7	462,400	67.6	3.1	73.2	19.4
Cascades CDP	3.69	11,912	NA	NA	NA	22.1	89.9	151,111	4.3	486,000	74.8	4.1	69.4	24.0
Cave Spring CDP	11.94	24,922	NA	NA	NA	8.3	84.0	64,793	7.6	215,500	63.7	3.3	62.8	31.9
Centreville CDP	11.94	71,135	NA	NA	NA	34.9	85.8	118,158	5.2	437,500	76.3	3.9	75.3	19.0
Chantilly CDP	12.00	23,039	NA	NA	NA	41.2	91.5	124,930	3.1	501,200	73.8	3.8	82.0	13.9
Charlottesville city	10.25	43,425	47,266	8.8	4611.3	12.2	71.3	59,471	20.7	299,600	64.1	4.2	45.5	34.6
Cherry Hill CDP	7.81	16,000	NA	NA	NA	24.4	85.1	99,831	9.7	332,500	71.0	4.4	74.3	19.5
Chesapeake city	338.51	222,311	244,835	10.1	723.3	5.9	85.5	78,640	7.7	273,700	61.9	4.7	74.5	21.4
Chester CDP	13.21	20,987	NA	NA	NA	7.7	88.1	70,519	6.0	221,900	67.1	4.6	71.6	24.4
Christiansburg town	14.10	20,965	22,473	7.2	1593.8	4.6	83.8	60,856	9.6	190,000	64.0	3.4	62.1	33.1
Colonial Heights city	7.52	17,410	17,370	-0.2	2309.8	7.3	82.5	54,550	12.4	171,700	61.1	8.1	63.2	32.7
Countryside CDP	2.57	10,072	NA	NA	NA	22.0	87.6	126,786	1.3	428,300	75.7	3.5	73.7	19.6
Culpeper town	7.27	16,658	18,873	13.3	2596.0	16.0	84.2	68,208	12.5	263,600	71.7	5.1	68.4	22.9
Dale City CDP	14.24	65,969	NA	NA	NA	30.8	91.2	95,297	7.2	314,200	72.3	5.1	79.7	16.5
Danville city	42.80	43,071	40,044	-7.0	935.6	3.5	86.3	37,203	23.5	90,500	54.4	8.5	56.9	37.1
Dranesville CDP	3.84	11,921	NA	NA	NA	18.0	94.2	179,031	1.4	576,100	71.6	2.0	84.5	11.7
East Highland Park CDP	8.78	14,796	NA	NA	NA	3.9	89.0	52,286	11.8	150,700	69.8	3.8	55.2	38.3
Fairfax city	6.24	22,554	24,019	6.5	3849.2	28.9	83.8	116,979	9.4	560,400	70.2	4.1	69.0	20.5
Fairfax Station CDP	9.08	12,030	NA	NA	NA	18.2	91.8	177,600	1.1	662,400	65.1	4.9	81.4	14.3
Fair Oaks CDP	4.99	30,223	NA	NA	NA	36.8	75.4	106,875	5.7	453,500	74.5	2.6	56.1	33.5
Falls Church city	2.05	12,244	14,617	19.4	7130.2	19.2	80.5	127,610	3.3	789,300	74.4	3.9	65.6	28.8
Forest CDP	13.60	9,106	NA	NA	NA	9.0	80.4	76,367	8.2	234,500	64.4	2.6	70.1	26.4
Fort Hunt CDP	5.85	16,045	NA	NA	NA	7.7	89.7	188,142	1.6	702,200	63.3	2.1	79.9	18.0
Franconia CDP	3.48	18,245	NA	NA	NA	29.9	87.2	125,031	1.4	421,100	77.3	4.5	63.8	29.1
Franklin Farm CDP	4.75	19,288	NA	NA	NA	22.1	92.4	183,247	2.7	633,600	72.6	2.7	87.9	10.1
Fredericksburg city	10.45	24,178	29,036	20.1	2778.6	10.2	71.8	65,641	15.2	367,200	71.3	4.8	52.3	37.1
Front Royal town	10.27	14,425	15,278	5.9	1487.6	5.3	86.4	51,871	13.3	214,500	65.4	7.2	61.6	30.5
Gainesville CDP	10.11	11,481	NA	NA	NA	19.7	87.4	141,609	4.1	491,500	75.6	3.7	85.0	12.6
Glen Allen CDP	8.80	14,774	NA	NA	NA	9.8	85.0	75,429	5.5	241,500	71.0	3.2	68.1	28.5
Great Falls CDP	25.36	15,427	NA	NA	NA	22.1	92.0	238,125	3.7	1,142,000	59.7	3.8	90.6	8.7
Groveton CDP	4.35	14,598	NA	NA	NA	34.6	85.7	95,259	4.8	443,600	71.4	3.0	65.4	30.2
Hampton city	51.46	137,464	134,510	-2.1	2613.9	4.7	81.2	56,287	13.5	186,700	60.2	6.1	59.7	32.6
Harrisonburg city	17.34	48,900	53,016	8.4	3057.4	17.1	69.9	46,679	22.1	203,600	59.7	4.9	53.9	29.8
Herndon town	4.29	23,292	24,601	5.6	5734.5	43.8	84.8	111,371	3.4	442,700	77.6	4.1	72.3	21.6
Highland Springs CDP	7.97	15,711	NA	NA	NA	2.5	88.1	48,886	12.4	145,800	71.2	6.8	62.0	33.8
Hollins CDP	8.61	14,673	NA	NA	NA	6.8	88.6	65,000	8.4	173,200	58.5	3.2	62.9	31.7
Hopewell city	10.35	22,591	22,529	-0.3	2176.7	3.7	81.9	39,030	24.6	122,900	58.8	6.9	62.5	30.2
Huntington CDP	1.13	11,267	NA	NA	NA	25.7	73.4	95,930	5.5	403,300	76.7	2.6	44.0	44.6
Hybla Valley CDP	2.05	15,801	NA	NA	NA	38.9	84.0	59,063	17.4	357,100	71.0	6.9	71.9	23.6
Idylwood CDP	2.80	17,288	NA	NA	NA	42.1	82.5	113,481	6.1	571,900	75.2	1.7	64.4	24.7
Kings Park West CDP	2.96	13,390	NA	NA	NA	22.6	84.4	141,789	4.9	574,400	68.6	5.0	81.8	12.2
Kingstowne CDP	2.87	15,556	NA	NA	NA	26.5	84.4	131,185	3.1	486,300	71.9	4.1	64.7	28.0
Lake Monticello CDP	8.85	9,920	NA	NA	NA	4.5	91.7	80,759	2.2	228,900	57.7	2.6	75.1	21.9
Lake Ridge CDP	9.34	41,058	NA	NA	NA	22.0	88.2	102,244	4.5	341,400	69.9	3.8	71.6	24.4
Lakeside CDP	4.32	11,849	NA	NA	NA	11.0	88.8	56,131	10.3	186,100	73.8	3.9	54.8	34.8
Lansdowne CDP	3.98	11,253	NA	NA	NA	23.9	87.1	131,165	3.5	527,100	64.4	1.6	68.3	27.9
Laurel CDP	5.39	16,713	NA	NA	NA	16.0	75.5	59,126	7.2	195,900	74.0	4.5	56.0	33.3
Leesburg town	12.40	42,643	53,727	26.0	4332.8	21.3	87.3	114,444	5.0	434,300	76.9	3.4	74.4	18.4
Lincolnia CDP	4.74	22,855	NA	NA	NA	42.8	84.1	94,854	7.7	474,700	73.2	3.8	65.0	25.7
Linton Hall CDP	12.73	35,725	NA	NA	NA	16.4	90.5	144,420	1.7	446,100	78.3	4.1	88.0	9.1
Lorton CDP	5.34	18,610	NA	NA	NA	35.0	81.9	106,847	6.8	461,200	73.6	3.8	75.7	19.1
Lowes Island CDP	3.02	10,756	NA	NA	NA	18.3	89.6	176,830	2.6	596,500	76.6	4.5	83.0	11.7
Lynchburg city	48.97	75,534	82,168	8.8	1677.9	5.2	78.8	46,409	18.1	160,100	58.3	5.8	57.3	32.0

Table B. Incorporated Places, Census Designated Places (CDPs), and Minor Civil Divisions (MCDs) of 10,000 or More Population — Crime, Residential Construction and Local Government Finance

STATE City, town, township, borough, or CDP (county if applicable)	Serious crimes known to police, 2018[1] Violent crime Number	Violent crime Rate[2]	Property crime Number	Property crime Rate[2]	New residential construction authorized by building permits, 2019 Value ($1,000)	Number of housing units	Percent single family	Local government finance, 2017 General revenue Total (mil dol)	Intergovernmental Total (mil dol)	Percent from state gov.	Taxes per capita[3]	General expenditure Total (mil dol)	Per capita[3] Total	Per capita Capital outlays	Debt outstanding (mil dol)
	15	16	17	18	19	20	21	22	23	24	25	26	27	28	29
UTAH—Con.															
West Point city	NA	NA	NA	NA	23,998	130	53.8	6.3	1.2	100.0	225	5.0	474	115	1.0
West Valley City city	945	689	4,915	3,584	91,468	375	46.4	125.9	13.4	40.4	574	125.1	918	18	76.2
Woods Cross city	11	95	176	1,517	23,895	94	52.1	13.8	0.6	84.3	437	8.0	707	161	0.0
VERMONT	1,077	172	8,036	1,283	351,910	1,801	54.8	X	X	X	X	X	X	X	X
Bennington town (Bennington)	31	208	415	2,785	879	8	100.0	15.1	1.3	100.0	697	16.5	1,097	394	12.3
Brattleboro town (Windham)	40	351	457	4,005	3,800	18	0.0	22.9	2.2	96.4	1,271	27.3	2,370	761	42.2
Burlington city & MCD (Chittenden)	115	272	837	1,983	28,402	157	4.5	136.5	22.6	44.8	1,065	120.2	2,835	661	185.1
Colchester town (Chittenden)	16	92	196	1,132	12,665	36	100.0	20.5	1.7	100.0	767	17.2	993	122	5.9
Essex town (Chittenden)	13	60	297	1,362	8,092	33	75.8	17.1	1.1	94.9	585	16.3	754	118	6.1
Essex Junction village	NA	NA	NA	NA	NA	NA	NA	8.6	2.9	76.8	247	7.4	689	192	17.9
Milton town (Chittenden)	16	145	104	943	7,588	58	19.0	10.3	1.8	87.7	637	9.4	852	107	8.9
Rutland city & MCD (Rutland)	60	392	383	2,503	246	1	100.0	25.7	2.5	95.3	1,071	26.5	1,719	178	17.3
South Burlington city & MCD (Chittenden)	32	166	572	2,961	15,367	94	41.5	29.9	0.8	56.8	938	26.3	1,369	87	31.8
VIRGINIA	17,032	200	141,885	1,666	5,793,753	32,418	65.0	X	X	X	X	X	X	X	X
Alexandria city	260	160	2,482	1,527	16,653	65	100.0	931.2	216.1	74.5	3,842	953.5	5,989	792	802.7
Annandale CDP	NA	NA	NA	NA	NA	NA	NA	NA	NA	NA	NA	NA	NA	NA	NA
Arlington CDP	NA	NA	NA	NA	NA	NA	NA	NA	NA	NA	NA	NA	NA	NA	NA
Ashburn CDP	NA	NA	NA	NA	NA	NA	NA	NA	NA	NA	NA	NA	NA	NA	NA
Bailey's Crossroads CDP	NA	NA	NA	NA	NA	NA	NA	NA	NA	NA	NA	NA	NA	NA	NA
Blacksburg town	41	91	322	718	27,663	174	25.9	46.5	15.2	48.5	449	37.4	841	161	0.0
Bon Air CDP	NA	NA	NA	NA	NA	NA	NA	NA	NA	NA	NA	NA	NA	NA	NA
Brambleton CDP	NA	NA	NA	NA	NA	NA	NA	NA	NA	NA	NA	NA	NA	NA	NA
Brandermill CDP	NA	NA	NA	NA	NA	NA	NA	NA	NA	NA	NA	NA	NA	NA	NA
Bristol city	42	253	513	3,088	670	5	100.0	79.7	40.4	88.5	1,898	81.1	4,803	434	99.5
Broadlands CDP	NA	NA	NA	NA	NA	NA	NA	NA	NA	NA	NA	NA	NA	NA	NA
Buckhall CDP	NA	NA	NA	NA	NA	NA	NA	NA	NA	NA	NA	NA	NA	NA	NA
Bull Run CDP	NA	NA	NA	NA	NA	NA	NA	NA	NA	NA	NA	NA	NA	NA	NA
Burke CDP	NA	NA	NA	NA	NA	NA	NA	NA	NA	NA	NA	NA	NA	NA	NA
Burke Centre CDP	NA	NA	NA	NA	NA	NA	NA	NA	NA	NA	NA	NA	NA	NA	NA
Cascades CDP	NA	NA	NA	NA	NA	NA	NA	NA	NA	NA	NA	NA	NA	NA	NA
Cave Spring CDP	NA	NA	NA	NA	NA	NA	NA	NA	NA	NA	NA	NA	NA	NA	NA
Centreville CDP	NA	NA	NA	NA	NA	NA	NA	NA	NA	NA	NA	NA	NA	NA	NA
Chantilly CDP	NA	NA	NA	NA	NA	NA	NA	NA	NA	NA	NA	NA	NA	NA	NA
Charlottesville city	174	358	1,161	2,390	23,017	88	68.2	284.7	117.4	65.7	2,442	279.0	5,879	627	140.6
Cherry Hill CDP	NA	NA	NA	NA	NA	NA	NA	NA	NA	NA	NA	NA	NA	NA	NA
Chesapeake city	979	404	5,191	2,142	284,887	991	100.0	1034.6	456.8	82.5	1,939	974.9	4,060	455	548.2
Chester CDP	NA	NA	NA	NA	NA	NA	NA	NA	NA	NA	NA	NA	NA	NA	NA
Christiansburg town	43	192	532	2,370	14,922	119	96.6	39.6	8.2	70.6	568	30.2	1,361	245	26.1
Colonial Heights city	50	280	676	3,786	434	3	100.0	72.0	24.1	97.4	2,496	91.2	5,236	227	42.9
Countryside CDP	NA	NA	NA	NA	NA	NA	NA	NA	NA	NA	NA	NA	NA	NA	NA
Culpeper town	31	166	296	1,585	NA	NA	NA	19.2	2.4	100.0	526	18.5	1,006	64	37.6
Dale City CDP	NA	NA	NA	NA	NA	NA	NA	NA	NA	NA	NA	NA	NA	NA	NA
Danville city	216	530	1,632	4,002	925	7	100.0	227.3	124.1	77.6	1,369	228.3	5,562	202	136.3
Dranesville CDP	NA	NA	NA	NA	NA	NA	NA	NA	NA	NA	NA	NA	NA	NA	NA
East Highland Park CDP	NA	NA	NA	NA	NA	NA	NA	NA	NA	NA	NA	NA	NA	NA	NA
Fairfax city	24	99	405	1,670	3,835	12	100.0	147.6	18.0	92.2	4,840	175.1	7,470	223	216.7
Fairfax Station CDP	NA	NA	NA	NA	NA	NA	NA	NA	NA	NA	NA	NA	NA	NA	NA
Fair Oaks CDP	NA	NA	NA	NA	NA	NA	NA	NA	NA	NA	NA	NA	NA	NA	NA
Falls Church city	12	81	176	1,183	133,974	346	6.9	105.1	13.4	83.1	5,046	96.3	6,763	204	0.0
Forest CDP	NA	NA	NA	NA	NA	NA	NA	NA	NA	NA	NA	NA	NA	NA	NA
Fort Hunt CDP	NA	NA	NA	NA	NA	NA	NA	NA	NA	NA	NA	NA	NA	NA	NA
Franconia CDP	NA	NA	NA	NA	NA	NA	NA	NA	NA	NA	NA	NA	NA	NA	NA
Franklin Farm CDP	NA	NA	NA	NA	NA	NA	NA	NA	NA	NA	NA	NA	NA	NA	NA
Fredericksburg city	108	374	999	3,455	37,826	274	22.6	219.2	87.6	50.6	2,842	170.1	5,970	511	84.7
Front Royal town	33	215	279	1,817	NA	NA	NA	19.2	6.2	100.0	268	40.2	2,678	1719	44.9
Gainesville CDP	NA	NA	NA	NA	NA	NA	NA	NA	NA	NA	NA	NA	NA	NA	NA
Glen Allen CDP	NA	NA	NA	NA	NA	NA	NA	NA	NA	NA	NA	NA	NA	NA	NA
Great Falls CDP	NA	NA	NA	NA	NA	NA	NA	NA	NA	NA	NA	NA	NA	NA	NA
Groveton CDP	NA	NA	NA	NA	NA	NA	NA	NA	NA	NA	NA	NA	NA	NA	NA
Hampton city	316	236	NA	NA	11,417	183	100.0	602.6	274.9	77.6	1,814	585.8	4,348	378	309.3
Harrisonburg city	110	201	834	1,520	11,706	73	100.0	203.2	81.0	85.6	1,479	220.5	4,111	1090	6.2
Herndon town	32	130	259	1,049	1,580	5	100.0	46.4	7.9	72.8	1,041	45.2	1,844	257	1.4
Highland Springs CDP	NA	NA	NA	NA	NA	NA	NA	NA	NA	NA	NA	NA	NA	NA	NA
Hollins CDP	NA	NA	NA	NA	NA	NA	NA	NA	NA	NA	NA	NA	NA	NA	NA
Hopewell city	99	439	553	2,451	5,048	56	58.9	123.7	53.7	87.0	1,743	123.7	5,497	885	0.0
Huntington CDP	NA	NA	NA	NA	NA	NA	NA	NA	NA	NA	NA	NA	NA	NA	NA
Hybla Valley CDP	NA	NA	NA	NA	NA	NA	NA	NA	NA	NA	NA	NA	NA	NA	NA
Idylwood CDP	NA	NA	NA	NA	NA	NA	NA	NA	NA	NA	NA	NA	NA	NA	NA
Kings Park West CDP	NA	NA	NA	NA	NA	NA	NA	NA	NA	NA	NA	NA	NA	NA	NA
Kingstowne CDP	NA	NA	NA	NA	NA	NA	NA	NA	NA	NA	NA	NA	NA	NA	NA
Lake Monticello CDP	NA	NA	NA	NA	NA	NA	NA	NA	NA	NA	NA	NA	NA	NA	NA
Lake Ridge CDP	NA	NA	NA	NA	NA	NA	NA	NA	NA	NA	NA	NA	NA	NA	NA
Lakeside CDP	NA	NA	NA	NA	NA	NA	NA	NA	NA	NA	NA	NA	NA	NA	NA
Lansdowne CDP	NA	NA	NA	NA	NA	NA	NA	NA	NA	NA	NA	NA	NA	NA	NA
Laurel CDP	NA	NA	NA	NA	NA	NA	NA	NA	NA	NA	NA	NA	NA	NA	NA
Leesburg town	100	179	626	1,117	45,507	257	58.0	74.1	22.4	90.3	599	69.9	1,292	277	124.3
Lincolnia CDP	NA	NA	NA	NA	NA	NA	NA	NA	NA	NA	NA	NA	NA	NA	NA
Linton Hall CDP	NA	NA	NA	NA	NA	NA	NA	NA	NA	NA	NA	NA	NA	NA	NA
Lorton CDP	NA	NA	NA	NA	NA	NA	NA	NA	NA	NA	NA	NA	NA	NA	NA
Lowes Island CDP	NA	NA	NA	NA	NA	NA	NA	NA	NA	NA	NA	NA	NA	NA	NA
Lynchburg city	275	337	1,627	1,994	33,774	330	12.1	379.8	190.6	73.1	1,699	330.5	4,104	978	332.2

1 Data for serious crimes have not been adjusted for underreporting. This may affect comparability between geographic areas over time.
2 Per 100,000 population estimated by the FBI. 3 Based on population estimated as of July 1 of the year shown.

Table B. Incorporated Places, Census Designated Places (CDPs), and Minor Civil Divisions (MCDs) of 10,000 or More Population — Land Area, Population, and Households, and Employment

STATE City, town, township, borough, or CDP (county if applicable)	Land area 2010 (sq mi)	Population Total persons 2010	Total persons 2019	Percent change 2010–2019	Persons per square mile, 2019	Population characteristics 2015–2019 Percent foreign born	Percent living in the same house as previous year	Income and poverty 2015–2019 Median household income	Percent of households with income below poverty level	Median value of owner-occupied housing units	Employment, 2015–2019 Percent in civilian labor force	Unemploy-ment rate	Households, 2015–2019 (percent of households) Family households	One person households
	1	2	3	4	5	6	7	8	9	10	11	12	13	14
VIRGINIA—Con.														
McLean CDP	24.78	48,115	NA	NA	NA	23.9	89.5	207,184	3.4	1,031,200	61.6	2.9	79.0	18.8
McNair CDP	2.04	17,513	NA	NA	NA	44.2	70.1	104,761	5.0	432,400	82.6	4.6	61.6	26.8
Madison Heights CDP	19.17	11,285	NA	NA	NA	1.1	89.4	46,183	13.4	138,400	60.5	5.6	65.6	29.3
Manassas city	9.85	37,799	41,085	8.7	4171.1	26.2	85.5	81,493	8.4	324,600	73.2	5.0	73.4	22.0
Manassas Park city	2.53	14,243	17,478	22.7	6908.3	36.1	83.1	88,046	4.4	308,000	74.8	4.5	70.6	21.8
Manchester CDP	5.93	10,804	NA	NA	NA	11.9	84.5	63,112	7.8	188,500	72.3	4.1	61.4	28.5
Martinsville city	10.96	13,814	12,554	-9.1	1145.4	3.8	82.0	34,371	23.9	87,700	54.9	6.0	59.2	35.8
Marumsco CDP	7.42	35,036	NA	NA	NA	40.9	83.3	66,713	9.0	270,600	73.2	7.4	69.4	24.2
Meadowbrook CDP	8.15	18,312	NA	NA	NA	16.3	90.1	64,106	8.3	191,500	68.0	8.6	70.0	21.9
Mechanicsville CDP	28.35	36,348	NA	NA	NA	3.4	89.4	79,692	6.1	241,400	68.1	2.0	69.9	25.7
Merrifield CDP	2.70	15,212	NA	NA	NA	43.1	73.3	114,219	8.7	494,700	78.7	2.0	51.6	34.6
Montclair CDP	6.01	19,570	NA	NA	NA	14.1	87.4	127,194	3.6	414,200	66.5	4.2	76.5	20.7
Mount Vernon CDP	5.23	12,416	NA	NA	NA	22.8	88.6	146,250	6.2	627,900	66.8	2.9	78.5	17.0
Neabsco CDP	4.61	12,068	NA	NA	NA	26.7	82.2	120,264	3.9	381,000	75.0	3.5	73.3	22.0
New Baltimore CDP	12.02	8,119	NA	NA	NA	4.6	91.8	135,261	2.1	474,400	66.1	3.3	88.6	8.5
Newington CDP	4.59	12,943	NA	NA	NA	26.9	87.4	135,843	3.2	455,800	72.1	2.5	83.0	14.8
Newington Forest CDP	3.31	12,442	NA	NA	NA	23.9	87.9	137,975	3.0	453,900	69.9	2.2	80.0	17.3
Newport News city	68.99	180,955	179,225	-1.0	2597.8	7.5	82.6	53,215	14.5	194,000	61.2	6.2	60.4	32.9
Norfolk city	53.28	242,827	242,742	0.0	4556.0	7.2	73.2	51,590	17.4	206,700	56.5	7.6	57.1	34.0
Oakton CDP	9.76	34,166	NA	NA	NA	33.4	83.2	132,256	6.4	631,700	70.7	3.5	68.1	24.7
Petersburg city	22.72	32,441	31,346	-3.4	1379.7	3.9	76.7	38,679	23.2	108,100	58.7	11.7	50.5	42.5
Poquoson city	15.38	12,159	12,271	0.9	797.9	4.3	87.5	97,118	6.0	323,100	59.6	2.0	75.8	20.7
Portsmouth city	33.30	95,526	94,398	-1.2	2834.8	2.9	83.4	52,175	14.7	170,900	59.9	7.8	58.3	34.5
Radford city	9.68	16,395	18,249	11.3	1885.2	2.6	73.9	36,297	29.4	170,800	54.2	4.5	42.3	41.4
Reston CDP	15.33	58,404	NA	NA	NA	24.6	82.1	120,396	6.2	499,200	74.0	3.9	59.5	32.3
Richmond city	59.92	204,375	230,436	12.8	3845.7	7.0	76.2	47,250	20.1	230,500	65.6	6.5	44.3	43.4
Roanoke city	42.52	96,910	99,143	2.3	2331.7	6.7	80.5	44,230	20.0	135,100	64.0	6.3	53.9	38.2
Rose Hill CDP	5.62	20,226	NA	NA	NA	27.6	88.2	124,058	5.6	482,600	70.9	3.8	74.2	19.0
Salem city	14.52	24,836	25,301	1.9	1742.5	3.4	84.9	57,165	9.7	181,900	61.1	4.4	62.1	33.1
Short Pump CDP	8.96	24,729	NA	NA	NA	24.2	80.7	107,321	4.9	413,900	74.0	2.3	67.2	27.8
South Riding CDP	6.86	24,256	NA	NA	NA	32.0	90.9	158,996	3.0	528,400	76.9	3.8	87.0	10.6
Springfield CDP	7.85	30,484	NA	NA	NA	41.6	91.6	101,814	6.4	468,100	64.3	5.4	70.1	27.0
Staunton city	19.92	23,745	24,932	5.0	1251.6	3.7	81.1	52,611	11.4	169,000	62.1	3.7	57.0	36.9
Sterling CDP	5.45	27,822	NA	NA	NA	41.5	89.4	97,647	5.9	359,000	78.8	5.1	70.5	22.9
Stone Ridge CDP	2.50	7,214	NA	NA	NA	29.4	86.3	153,628	1.8	473,800	79.7	1.9	82.2	14.8
Sudley CDP	2.76	16,203	NA	NA	NA	38.5	79.1	73,669	6.7	296,700	78.3	4.3	74.2	19.4
Suffolk city	399.15	84,565	92,108	8.9	230.8	3.5	85.0	74,884	10.4	254,400	64.1	6.2	73.2	22.5
Sugarland Run CDP	2.01	11,799	NA	NA	NA	31.9	85.5	114,432	5.3	413,000	75.6	5.9	83.2	12.2
Timberlake CDP	11.26	12,183	NA	NA	NA	5.0	90.5	52,245	7.2	184,700	65.2	3.7	62.4	30.3
Tuckahoe CDP	20.44	44,990	NA	NA	NA	13.0	84.0	79,503	8.9	313,300	66.9	5.0	64.9	28.7
Tysons CDP	4.27	0	NA	0.0	NA	44.6	70.0	107,388	7.4	563,000	74.1	4.7	51.6	38.5
Vienna town	4.40	15,681	16,485	5.1	3746.6	22.9	85.3	161,196	3.5	743,500	69.5	2.4	81.2	16.5
Virginia Beach city	244.72	437,903	449,974	2.8	1838.7	9.4	82.3	76,610	6.8	280,800	64.4	4.6	68.4	24.5
Wakefield CDP	3.77	11,275	NA	NA	NA	21.5	88.3	155,729	1.5	632,600	64.0	4.2	87.4	11.2
Waynesboro city	14.97	20,998	22,630	7.8	1511.7	3.8	83.2	45,011	14.7	174,100	62.5	4.7	55.1	38.1
West Falls Church CDP	4.99	0	NA	0.0	NA	39.3	86.1	103,867	7.3	514,900	76.4	4.6	67.6	23.0
West Springfield CDP	4.81	22,460	NA	NA	NA	24.6	89.6	129,936	3.4	472,000	67.5	2.4	74.8	21.5
Williamsburg city	8.94	13,700	14,954	9.2	1672.7	6.9	62.6	57,463	14.9	306,000	49.9	5.8	46.7	40.4
Winchester city	9.19	26,223	28,078	7.1	3055.3	13.2	82.0	58,818	12.4	244,900	65.2	3.2	57.4	34.3
Wolf Trap CDP	9.80	16,131	NA	NA	NA	21.1	88.7	227,022	1.3	912,900	63.9	3.8	88.2	10.6
Woodlawn CDP	2.29	0	NA	0.0	NA	37.4	86.5	75,622	15.0	301,100	74.8	6.5	75.1	19.5
Wyndham CDP	3.64	9,785	NA	NA	NA	21.0	89.1	182,803	2.1	493,200	68.1	1.9	88.0	10.6
WASHINGTON	66455.12	6,724,540	7,614,893	13.2	114.6	14.3	82.3	73,775	10.3	339,000	63.6	5.0	64.7	26.7
Aberdeen city	10.87	16,872	16,756	-0.7	1541.5	7.6	81.7	44,444	22.8	124,300	53.8	7.6	60.8	30.8
Anacortes city	11.70	15,768	17,527	11.2	1498.0	6.4	82.8	71,844	8.8	406,400	51.9	4.0	64.3	28.8
Arlington city	9.72	17,959	20,523	14.3	2111.4	8.7	83.4	82,626	5.1	323,200	67.3	4.0	70.0	25.1
Artondale CDP	13.38	12,653	NA	NA	NA	6.3	86.5	110,651	6.2	470,300	59.6	1.8	78.7	15.6
Auburn city	29.57	70,301	81,464	15.9	2755.0	21.1	82.4	72,822	9.3	327,200	67.9	4.9	66.0	25.6
Bainbridge Island city	27.61	23,025	25,298	9.9	916.3	7.2	86.1	117,990	4.8	705,400	58.5	3.1	70.1	23.8
Battle Ground city	8.51	17,794	21,252	19.4	2497.3	9.4	87.0	75,208	7.9	282,900	66.3	4.5	75.4	19.9
Bellevue city	33.46	127,885	148,164	15.9	4428.1	38.9	79.4	120,456	6.5	809,200	66.9	3.4	66.1	26.0
Bellingham city	27.69	81,205	92,314	13.7	3333.8	9.7	71.4	53,396	21.2	374,700	64.2	6.2	45.8	33.9
Bonney Lake city	8.22	17,592	21,148	20.2	2572.7	5.6	85.6	97,055	4.2	331,200	71.0	2.3	75.6	17.5
Bothell city	13.64	39,851	47,415	19.0	3476.2	21.4	82.6	99,965	5.7	530,300	69.3	4.3	67.7	23.5
Bothell East CDP	2.10	8,018	NA	NA	NA	35.7	83.5	122,004	4.7	640,700	68.2	2.8	81.5	13.7
Bothell West CDP	4.15	16,607	NA	NA	NA	23.2	87.4	111,705	4.1	464,700	72.6	2.6	78.3	15.5
Bremerton city	28.48	37,865	41,405	9.3	1453.8	8.1	75.8	52,716	15.7	238,600	50.4	6.5	50.9	37.6
Bryn Mawr-Skyway CDP	2.84	15,645	NA	NA	NA	33.6	81.4	70,968	10.7	393,800	66.7	2.6	64.9	27.6
Burien city	10.04	48,081	51,500	7.1	5129.5	25.5	84.7	67,402	11.1	380,300	69.0	5.6	63.2	27.9
Camano CDP	39.76	0	NA	0.0	NA	6.3	89.7	80,965	6.3	398,200	53.1	5.9	75.7	18.3
Camas city	14.07	19,813	24,418	23.2	1735.5	9.7	87.5	111,584	4.3	441,400	67.5	3.3	78.7	16.9
Centralia city	7.58	16,658	17,745	6.5	2341.0	8.3	83.2	42,449	17.7	157,300	55.0	8.0	53.0	37.7
Cheney city	4.34	10,592	12,522	18.2	2885.3	6.3	58.1	40,573	35.0	203,500	63.6	9.7	42.1	27.5
Cottage Lake CDP	22.75	22,494	NA	NA	NA	13.5	91.2	161,233	2.1	798,200	63.6	3.3	87.1	9.8
Covington city	5.93	17,565	21,175	20.6	3570.8	14.3	85.7	105,154	5.7	357,300	71.7	2.1	73.2	18.8
Des Moines city	6.41	29,654	32,348	9.1	5046.5	21.1	82.0	70,222	7.6	359,100	65.5	6.0	65.8	27.3
Eastmont CDP	5.11	20,101	NA	NA	NA	15.3	90.9	111,482	5.2	433,800	67.4	3.8	80.6	14.8
East Renton Highlands CDP	11.17	11,140	NA	NA	NA	9.0	91.3	105,755	3.2	506,600	68.4	5.0	76.2	18.6
East Wenatchee city	3.79	13,179	14,219	7.9	3751.7	14.2	83.5	54,223	13.5	274,800	64.0	4.0	71.8	22.0
Edgewood city	8.39	9,379	13,053	39.2	1555.8	4.2	79.4	100,110	2.4	409,100	67.3	3.4	76.5	16.0
Edmonds city	8.92	39,695	42,605	7.3	4776.3	14.0	85.4	89,229	3.8	536,900	64.6	3.5	62.3	28.8
Elk Plain CDP	7.69	14,205	NA	NA	NA	6.0	88.5	70,041	13.1	228,700	63.6	6.4	75.2	17.0
Ellensburg city	7.58	18,301	21,111	15.4	2785.1	7.1	58.6	39,645	33.1	264,200	61.5	7.4	36.8	37.9
Enumclaw city	5.17	11,090	12,190	9.9	2357.8	8.8	86.8	61,010	11.1	299,000	66.8	5.3	61.1	31.9
Everett city	33.20	102,953	111,475	8.3	3357.7	18.6	79.9	60,759	12.2	322,700	65.1	5.2	56.9	32.6

Table B. Incorporated Places, Census Designated Places (CDPs), and Minor Civil Divisions (MCDs) of 10,000 or More Population — **Crime, Residential Construction and Local Government Finance**

STATE City, town, township, borough, or CDP (county if applicable)	Serious crimes known to police, 2018[1] Violent crime Number	Violent crime Rate[2]	Property crime Number	Property crime Rate[2]	New residential construction authorized by building permits, 2019 Value ($1,000)	Number of housing units	Percent single family	Local government finance, 2017 General revenue Total (mil dol)	Intergovernmental Total (mil dol)	Percent from state gov.	Taxes per capita[3]	General expenditure Total (mil dol)	Per capita[3] Total	Capital outlays	Debt outstanding (mil dol)
	15	16	17	18	19	20	21	22	23	24	25	26	27	28	29
VIRGINIA—Con.															
McLean CDP	NA	NA	NA	NA	NA	NA	NA	NA	NA	NA	NA	NA	NA	NA	NA
McNair CDP	NA	NA	NA	NA	NA	NA	NA	NA	NA	NA	NA	NA	NA	NA	NA
Madison Heights CDP	NA	NA	NA	NA	NA	NA	NA	NA	NA	NA	NA	NA	NA	NA	NA
Manassas city	105	251	636	1,518	26,086	111	98.2	219.2	85.2	84.8	2,423	209.5	5,092	470	110.0
Manassas Park city	25	148	111	658	0	0	0.0	73.8	35.8	91.4	1,973	74.0	4,314	361	121.6
Manchester CDP	NA	NA	NA	NA	NA	NA	NA	NA	NA	NA	NA	NA	NA	NA	NA
Martinsville city	54	415	471	3,616	0	0	0.0	73.6	39.9	77.6	1,433	72.0	5,613	778	16.2
Marumsco CDP	NA	NA	NA	NA	NA	NA	NA	NA	NA	NA	NA	NA	NA	NA	NA
Meadowbrook CDP	NA	NA	NA	NA	NA	NA	NA	NA	NA	NA	NA	NA	NA	NA	NA
Mechanicsville CDP	NA	NA	NA	NA	NA	NA	NA	NA	NA	NA	NA	NA	NA	NA	NA
Merrifield CDP	NA	NA	NA	NA	NA	NA	NA	NA	NA	NA	NA	NA	NA	NA	NA
Montclair CDP	NA	NA	NA	NA	NA	NA	NA	NA	NA	NA	NA	NA	NA	NA	NA
Mount Vernon CDP	NA	NA	NA	NA	NA	NA	NA	NA	NA	NA	NA	NA	NA	NA	NA
Neabsco CDP	NA	NA	NA	NA	NA	NA	NA	NA	NA	NA	NA	NA	NA	NA	NA
New Baltimore CDP	NA	NA	NA	NA	NA	NA	NA	NA	NA	NA	NA	NA	NA	NA	NA
Newington CDP	NA	NA	NA	NA	NA	NA	NA	NA	NA	NA	NA	NA	NA	NA	NA
Newington Forest CDP	NA	NA	NA	NA	NA	NA	NA	NA	NA	NA	NA	NA	NA	NA	NA
Newport News city	942	527	5,148	2,880	28,248	218	56.0	904.3	403.4	73.8	2,051	911.6	5,080	625	993.6
Norfolk city	1,134	464	8,463	3,464	125,388	819	40.7	1219.1	544.7	73.0	1,814	1240.6	5,073	704	1518.8
Oakton CDP	NA	NA	NA	NA	NA	NA	NA	NA	NA	NA	NA	NA	NA	NA	NA
Petersburg city	224	710	916	2,902	1,350	10	100.0	147.0	79.1	86.4	1,772	145.4	4,669	116	21.8
Poquoson city	19	158	101	841	5,147	26	100.0	45.4	18.4	90.4	1,820	43.1	3,580	66	35.5
Portsmouth city	749	795	4,977	5,282	9,879	93	100.0	418.6	204.0	83.7	1,755	491.0	5,177	314	589.7
Radford city	52	292	237	1,332	3,102	24	91.7	46.4	24.1	91.7	757	55.0	3,146	189	20.7
Reston CDP	NA	NA	NA	NA	NA	NA	NA	NA	NA	NA	NA	NA	NA	NA	NA
Richmond city	1,190	518	8,807	3,830	128,721	1,240	28.5	1288.8	545.0	79.3	2,312	1217.7	5,359	668	1610.3
Roanoke city	427	427	4,434	4,432	38,925	278	14.4	488.0	259.4	83.9	1,868	450.1	4,547	298	120.4
Rose Hill CDP	NA	NA	NA	NA	NA	NA	NA	NA	NA	NA	NA	NA	NA	NA	NA
Salem city	24	93	503	1,939	7,589	32	100.0	118.2	39.8	89.6	2,380	124.0	4,888	743	9.6
Short Pump CDP	NA	NA	NA	NA	NA	NA	NA	NA	NA	NA	NA	NA	NA	NA	NA
South Riding CDP	NA	NA	NA	NA	NA	NA	NA	NA	NA	NA	NA	NA	NA	NA	NA
Springfield CDP	NA	NA	NA	NA	NA	NA	NA	NA	NA	NA	NA	NA	NA	NA	NA
Staunton city	46	187	608	2,473	6,372	42	90.5	98.1	45.6	88.9	1,518	89.9	3,697	152	56.2
Sterling CDP	NA	NA	NA	NA	NA	NA	NA	NA	NA	NA	NA	NA	NA	NA	NA
Stone Ridge CDP	NA	NA	NA	NA	NA	NA	NA	NA	NA	NA	NA	NA	NA	NA	NA
Sudley CDP	NA	NA	NA	NA	NA	NA	NA	NA	NA	NA	NA	NA	NA	NA	NA
Suffolk city	251	276	2,340	2,577	104,021	695	71.9	393.1	171.0	88.9	1,874	396.4	4,399	928	628.7
Sugarland Run CDP	NA	NA	NA	NA	NA	NA	NA	NA	NA	NA	NA	NA	NA	NA	NA
Timberlake CDP	NA	NA	NA	NA	NA	NA	NA	NA	NA	NA	NA	NA	NA	NA	NA
Tuckahoe CDP	NA	NA	NA	NA	NA	NA	NA	NA	NA	NA	NA	NA	NA	NA	NA
Tysons CDP	NA	NA	NA	NA	NA	NA	NA	NA	NA	NA	NA	NA	NA	NA	NA
Vienna town	8	48	149	894	NA	NA	NA	34.7	5.9	58.6	1,174	37.3	3,253	463	14.4
Virginia Beach city	528	117	7,772	1,723	153,826	1,350	49.4	1932.4	740.4	80.9	2,107	1859.0	4,132	485	1484.0
Wakefield CDP	NA	NA	NA	NA	NA	NA	NA	NA	NA	NA	NA	NA	NA	NA	NA
Waynesboro city	50	223	477	2,123	22,832	222	45.0	95.6	43.7	80.8	1,703	84.3	3,791	277	64.0
West Falls Church CDP	NA	NA	NA	NA	NA	NA	NA	NA	NA	NA	NA	NA	NA	NA	NA
West Springfield CDP	NA	NA	NA	NA	NA	NA	NA	NA	NA	NA	NA	NA	NA	NA	NA
Williamsburg city	20	132	193	1,271	5,427	29	100.0	52.7	7.0	86.9	2,327	45.2	3,013	251	13.3
Winchester city	93	331	692	2,460	2,539	37	100.0	221.6	109.2	45.2	2,683	157.8	5,600	561	182.7
Wolf Trap CDP	NA	NA	NA	NA	NA	NA	NA	NA	NA	NA	NA	NA	NA	NA	NA
Woodlawn CDP	NA	NA	NA	NA	NA	NA	NA	NA	NA	NA	NA	NA	NA	NA	NA
Wyndham CDP	NA	NA	NA	NA	NA	NA	NA	NA	NA	NA	NA	NA	NA	NA	NA
WASHINGTON	23,472	312	222,011	2,946	10,223,055	48,424	48.1	X	X	X	X	X	X	X	X
Aberdeen city	85	518	834	5,084	525	2	100.0	26.2	3.4	93.0	804	24.6	1,497	204	14.8
Anacortes city	30	175	380	2,218	24,771	66	100.0	45.5	3.6	31.5	1,038	36.2	2,129	243	75.5
Arlington city	60	309	662	3,413	26,481	247	4.0	32.9	1.8	89.9	836	26.8	1,395	217	47.5
Artondale CDP	NA	NA	NA	NA	NA	NA	NA	NA	NA	NA	NA	NA	NA	NA	NA
Auburn city	360	437	3,334	4,047	8,386	23	100.0	145.3	13.7	74.7	751	122.3	1,504	244	69.3
Bainbridge Island city	25	101	242	978	41,595	94	100.0	32.3	2.8	100.0	863	26.1	1,062	176	33.2
Battle Ground city	32	152	404	1,924	52,511	217	95.4	23.0	1.2	97.1	616	18.4	893	53	25.0
Bellevue city	194	132	4,294	2,923	180,028	404	48.3	414.6	47.4	27.0	1,526	402.8	2,773	690	284.6
Bellingham city	204	226	3,346	3,709	150,488	1,072	17.5	169.4	13.8	60.9	1,101	139.2	1,564	165	106.3
Bonney Lake city	33	156	451	2,128	84,150	523	18.5	30.4	1.8	89.9	634	30.2	1,446	300	45.3
Bothell city	65	140	1,017	2,192	48,360	167	100.0	89.7	10.8	90.1	968	77.7	1,701	385	130.1
Bothell East CDP	NA	NA	NA	NA	NA	NA	NA	NA	NA	NA	NA	NA	NA	NA	NA
Bothell West CDP	NA	NA	NA	NA	NA	NA	NA	NA	NA	NA	NA	NA	NA	NA	NA
Bremerton city	NA	NA	NA	NA	62,118	367	50.4	71.9	4.6	83.1	898	60.0	1,476	129	71.1
Bryn Mawr-Skyway CDP	NA	NA	NA	NA	NA	NA	NA	NA	NA	NA	NA	NA	NA	NA	NA
Burien city	NA	NA	1,900	3,641	12,952	53	64.2	41.5	4.0	68.6	525	30.5	586	58	33.2
Camano CDP	NA	NA	NA	NA	NA	NA	NA	NA	NA	NA	NA	NA	NA	NA	NA
Camas city	19	80	219	918	145,364	643	58.9	49.7	5.0	97.1	889	43.1	1,849	395	71.2
Centralia city	88	509	794	4,590	7,716	42	81.0	23.9	1.8	81.1	530	18.0	1,042	63	54.2
Cheney city	43	338	203	1,597	27,140	219	24.2	15.6	2.2	99.8	532	13.1	1,057	139	14.0
Cottage Lake CDP	NA	NA	NA	NA	NA	NA	NA	NA	NA	NA	NA	NA	NA	NA	NA
Covington city	NA	NA	584	2,724	50,005	189	52.9	20.0	1.9	90.8	608	17.7	843	149	10.4
Des Moines city	111	353	1,092	3,471	24,662	69	79.7	42.2	9.1	94.7	618	35.8	1,140	332	17.9
Eastmont CDP	NA	NA	NA	NA	NA	NA	NA	NA	NA	NA	NA	NA	NA	NA	NA
East Renton Highlands CDP	NA	NA	NA	NA	NA	NA	NA	NA	NA	NA	NA	NA	NA	NA	NA
East Wenatchee city	14	99	377	2,674	1,502	10	10.0	11.0	2.2	99.2	518	10.7	763	249	2.6
Edgewood city	15	130	231	2,007	42,082	149	63.1	8.8	1.1	100.0	430	7.3	653	112	19.2
Edmonds city	65	153	842	1,978	15,167	51	49.0	67.4	8.8	78.0	859	60.4	1,432	180	73.3
Elk Plain CDP	NA	NA	NA	NA	NA	NA	NA	NA	NA	NA	NA	NA	NA	NA	NA
Ellensburg city	42	204	601	2,915	7,715	51	70.6	24.2	2.4	98.6	692	24.3	1,200	119	35.3
Enumclaw city	9	76	229	1,927	44,729	179	100.0	23.4	5.2	97.6	706	15.2	1,281	96	23.8
Everett city	373	336	4,683	4,216	101,448	723	15.5	228.6	15.2	75.1	1,268	198.5	1,802	219	349.2

1 Data for serious crimes have not been adjusted for underreporting. This may affect comparability between geographic areas over time.
2 Per 100,000 population estimated by the FBI. 3 Based on population estimated as of July 1 of the year shown.

Table B. Incorporated Places, Census Designated Places (CDPs), and Minor Civil Divisions (MCDs) of 10,000 or More Population — Land Area, Population, and Households, and Employment

STATE City, town, township, borough, or CDP (county if applicable)	Land area 2010 (sq mi)	Total persons 2010	Total persons 2019	Percent change 2010–2019	Persons per square mile, 2019	Percent foreign born	Percent living in the same house as previous year	Median household income	Percent of households with income below poverty level	Median value of owner-occupied housing units	Percent in civilian labor force	Unemploy-ment rate	Family households	One person households
	1	2	3	4	5	6	7	8	9	10	11	12	13	14
WASHINGTON—Con.														
Fairwood CDP	4.73	19,102	NA	NA	NA	18.7	84.2	97,398	5.6	424,800	68.6	5.9	74.0	20.7
Federal Way city	22.30	89,295	96,289	7.8	4317.9	24.7	81.3	67,347	11.6	328,800	67.0	5.6	67.6	25.6
Ferndale city	6.99	11,411	14,897	30.5	2131.2	12.1	84.6	73,074	14.2	300,600	64.2	5.4	69.2	22.1
Fife city	5.72	9,178	10,184	11.0	1780.4	18.9	76.7	66,144	9.6	288,500	72.9	4.5	60.0	31.5
Five Corners CDP	5.82	18,159	NA	NA	NA	9.6	83.1	71,802	6.7	277,300	68.1	6.4	74.6	18.7
Fort Lewis CDP	10.23	11,046	NA	NA	NA	5.3	55.8	42,157	13.7	0	25.4	6.4	93.3	4.6
Frederickson CDP	11.56	18,719	NA	NA	NA	10.7	80.6	89,012	4.5	272,400	65.2	5.7	77.4	16.6
Graham CDP	34.99	23,491	NA	NA	NA	4.9	86.7	86,943	6.8	288,000	64.9	5.8	78.9	15.4
Grandview city	6.43	10,854	11,078	2.1	1722.9	31.6	89.4	49,002	16.4	145,400	70.5	8.8	79.8	18.4
Hazel Dell CDP	4.84	19,435	NA	NA	NA	11.2	82.3	61,520	10.8	279,700	66.5	3.4	63.8	25.6
Issaquah city	12.13	30,440	39,509	29.8	3257.1	26.2	80.0	109,676	6.7	642,300	71.5	4.0	66.3	26.1
Kelso city	8.14	11,913	12,417	4.2	1525.4	6.6	78.2	39,044	21.2	148,100	53.6	8.6	61.7	32.5
Kenmore city	6.15	20,476	23,097	12.8	3755.6	18.4	86.2	109,810	7.2	572,900	70.0	3.6	68.5	23.2
Kennewick city	27.45	73,994	84,347	14.0	3072.8	12.7	83.8	59,533	13.5	215,500	61.4	6.0	66.0	27.1
Kent city	33.75	118,620	132,319	11.5	3920.6	31.8	80.8	72,062	11.2	346,400	68.2	5.5	70.0	22.1
Kirkland city	17.81	80,585	93,010	15.4	5222.3	23.3	81.1	117,190	6.1	662,300	70.7	3.3	63.8	27.2
Lacey city	17.10	42,543	52,592	23.6	3075.6	11.1	76.6	67,687	8.3	262,500	58.3	5.9	64.8	27.3
Lake Forest Park city	3.52	12,602	13,504	7.2	3836.4	14.3	88.1	126,750	2.4	623,500	70.3	4.0	73.0	22.5
Lakeland North CDP	3.25	12,942	NA	NA	NA	20.4	91.0	93,413	6.0	319,800	65.9	4.8	76.5	15.7
Lakeland South CDP	4.96	11,574	NA	NA	NA	16.7	87.4	79,183	5.5	324,400	66.5	5.3	77.0	16.3
Lake Morton-Berrydale CDP	12.33	10,160	NA	NA	NA	9.4	92.1	102,458	5.3	414,300	66.6	3.6	81.4	11.9
Lake Stevens city	8.91	28,108	33,911	20.6	3805.9	7.2	84.6	93,381	5.9	356,900	70.7	3.8	75.1	17.5
Lake Stickney CDP	1.53	7,777	NA	NA	NA	34.8	75.9	81,765	11.0	432,700	71.0	6.7	64.8	23.7
Lake Tapps CDP	12.26	11,859	NA	NA	NA	4.0	90.2	116,942	2.6	431,000	71.5	3.6	80.8	14.0
Lakewood city	17.06	57,532	61,037	6.1	3577.8	15.7	79.8	51,972	15.6	269,200	57.9	6.7	60.4	32.6
Longview city	14.84	36,833	38,440	4.4	2590.3	5.0	76.9	44,957	18.1	190,400	53.7	6.5	56.0	36.6
Lynden city	5.42	12,006	15,223	26.8	2808.7	10.6	86.1	66,085	7.9	348,100	64.9	3.7	69.4	26.2
Lynnwood city	7.88	35,857	39,141	9.2	4967.1	29.3	84.8	63,743	15.0	395,300	63.3	3.6	62.5	27.8
Maltby CDP	19.31	10,830	NA	NA	NA	9.1	90.0	124,857	5.8	586,800	69.8	4.9	77.4	14.7
Maple Valley city	6.00	22,722	27,202	19.7	4533.7	8.1	84.7	114,159	3.3	414,400	73.8	5.3	81.9	13.9
Martha Lake CDP	4.55	15,473	NA	NA	NA	20.8	85.1	102,316	4.6	459,300	71.8	3.6	73.9	16.3
Marysville city	20.75	60,013	70,298	17.1	3387.9	9.8	83.8	80,453	7.3	325,300	66.3	4.5	70.6	22.8
Mercer Island city	6.38	22,699	25,894	14.1	4058.6	21.0	82.4	147,566	6.2	1,218,200	63.0	4.0	70.4	23.1
Midland CDP	3.04	8,962	NA	NA	NA	20.0	87.8	50,845	12.2	211,200	65.0	4.6	64.6	26.2
Mill Creek city	4.64	18,230	20,897	14.6	4503.7	18.7	82.1	103,750	3.6	536,800	68.5	3.2	67.8	25.0
Mill Creek East CDP	4.45	15,709	NA	NA	NA	25.2	82.8	133,794	3.7	523,300	74.7	3.4	86.2	11.8
Minnehaha CDP	2.21	9,771	NA	NA	NA	11.6	86.3	84,568	6.5	282,000	69.0	7.1	79.9	13.0
Monroe city	6.09	17,345	19,776	14.0	3247.3	11.1	82.1	85,896	7.2	357,000	58.4	4.2	73.3	18.5
Moses Lake city	17.89	20,365	24,086	18.3	1346.3	11.7	82.3	51,272	11.6	164,700	62.7	6.0	63.8	29.5
Mountlake Terrace city	4.06	19,882	21,338	7.3	5255.7	23.6	80.6	72,955	7.5	392,600	69.4	3.6	63.1	26.9
Mount Vernon city	12.30	31,724	36,006	13.5	2927.3	18.0	81.3	62,056	13.4	269,100	63.0	5.7	67.8	25.8
Mukilteo city	6.26	20,249	21,441	5.9	3425.1	21.9	84.4	108,536	2.4	582,700	64.6	5.1	71.2	21.9
Newcastle city	4.45	10,368	12,292	18.6	2762.2	31.0	84.5	129,828	3.8	759,500	72.2	3.8	72.9	21.4
North Lynnwood CDP	3.13	16,574	NA	NA	NA	28.9	72.6	73,565	9.3	363,700	71.9	4.0	61.5	25.3
Oak Harbor city	9.64	22,154	23,565	6.4	2444.5	12.7	77.7	55,647	10.9	277,500	52.3	5.6	64.2	27.8
Olympia city	18.24	46,884	52,882	12.8	2899.2	9.5	74.5	59,878	15.0	297,200	61.1	5.3	53.2	35.3
Orchards CDP	5.35	19,556	NA	NA	NA	12.4	81.9	73,417	8.5	282,700	72.7	5.6	72.9	19.0
Parkland CDP	8.64	35,803	NA	NA	NA	14.9	80.6	55,346	14.7	223,400	63.3	8.4	64.7	27.2
Pasco city	33.92	62,163	75,432	21.3	2223.8	23.1	81.9	62,775	13.7	199,400	68.4	6.2	74.9	20.0
Port Angeles city	10.71	19,040	20,229	6.2	1888.8	5.2	81.3	47,256	16.0	217,100	55.2	7.4	54.9	36.3
Port Orchard city	9.64	12,195	14,597	19.7	1514.2	7.9	77.8	69,962	12.9	324,200	55.0	6.0	67.6	22.7
Poulsbo city	4.74	9,237	11,168	20.9	2356.1	7.5	82.6	73,388	8.2	360,200	56.8	5.2	62.0	33.7
Prairie Ridge CDP	4.09	11,464	NA	NA	NA	3.4	85.8	85,536	6.2	273,000	69.5	4.3	75.6	18.5
Pullman city	10.67	29,820	34,506	15.7	3233.9	15.7	53.2	31,487	34.2	272,400	59.0	10.5	39.1	34.9
Puyallup city	14.14	37,241	42,361	13.7	2995.8	7.5	81.1	73,248	7.6	329,000	62.9	4.4	62.0	29.2
Redmond city	16.57	54,511	71,929	32.0	4340.9	40.5	77.2	132,188	5.4	703,000	71.7	3.5	65.6	25.5
Renton city	23.43	91,912	101,751	10.7	4342.8	28.7	80.5	77,739	9.4	400,500	71.2	3.7	62.1	26.2
Richland city	39.22	48,491	58,225	20.1	1484.6	8.2	80.2	77,686	7.6	263,500	64.3	4.0	65.4	28.0
Salmon Creek CDP	6.35	19,686	NA	NA	NA	7.7	88.1	79,593	9.1	332,100	60.3	5.5	70.5	22.9
Sammamish city	20.43	57,449	65,892	14.7	3225.3	30.1	88.8	174,003	2.7	830,000	68.7	2.8	87.2	10.4
SeaTac city	10.06	26,903	29,044	8.0	2887.1	38.7	81.5	63,009	10.9	321,300	70.3	6.0	64.5	26.9
Seattle city	83.86	608,661	753,675	23.8	8987.3	18.8	76.8	92,263	10.2	663,100	73.5	4.1	45.2	38.5
Sedro-Woolley city	4.31	11,076	12,072	9.0	2800.9	5.9	79.6	60,863	10.2	244,000	62.8	5.5	67.7	23.5
Shelton city	5.81	9,845	10,655	8.2	1833.9	12.7	82.7	40,809	21.1	162,700	55.1	7.6	58.0	31.6
Shoreline city	11.64	53,031	57,027	7.5	4899.2	21.5	83.7	86,827	7.7	519,900	67.3	3.8	63.9	27.1
Silverdale CDP	12.63	19,204	NA	NA	NA	9.5	76.1	77,299	5.9	332,700	57.0	4.3	64.9	26.8
Silver Firs CDP	6.85	20,891	NA	NA	NA	17.4	90.8	131,337	1.6	487,100	72.4	1.9	86.3	10.3
Snoqualmie city	7.18	10,665	13,622	27.7	1897.2	12.6	83.9	145,580	1.8	610,700	79.9	3.1	89.3	8.3
South Hill CDP	18.36	52,431	NA	NA	NA	9.5	83.7	86,568	5.6	303,100	66.0	6.0	79.5	15.4
Spanaway CDP	8.75	27,227	NA	NA	NA	9.9	86.5	71,659	10.8	240,800	62.0	7.6	73.5	19.0
Spokane city	68.76	209,455	222,081	6.0	3229.8	6.0	78.1	50,306	16.4	187,600	61.5	5.9	56.6	34.1
Spokane Valley city	37.72	89,745	101,060	12.6	2679.2	5.6	82.0	51,961	12.4	204,700	63.2	5.4	61.4	30.9
Sumner city	7.53	9,447	10,427	10.4	1384.7	6.4	85.2	63,043	8.1	333,000	65.2	5.8	60.7	30.5
Sunnyside city	7.54	15,934	16,796	5.4	2227.6	28.0	89.7	42,780	19.1	129,400	63.8	8.1	80.7	16.9
Tacoma city	49.76	198,247	217,827	9.9	4377.6	13.0	81.1	62,358	13.7	277,900	64.4	5.2	57.6	33.4
Tukwila city	9.19	19,107	20,347	6.5	2214.0	40.4	83.8	58,097	14.4	315,000	73.6	7.6	58.7	29.6
Tumwater city	17.43	20,167	24,024	19.1	1378.3	4.6	79.8	69,685	9.5	286,700	65.8	7.1	62.1	26.8
Union Hill-Novelty Hill CDP	24.23	18,805	NA	NA	NA	26.5	88.7	150,239	2.8	809,000	60.1	3.0	80.2	16.8
University Place city	8.34	31,133	34,001	9.2	4076.9	12.7	83.2	71,697	8.2	367,200	61.8	4.0	63.7	29.2
Vancouver city	48.74	167,159	184,463	10.4	3784.6	13.9	78.4	61,714	10.7	286,500	64.5	5.0	59.6	30.4
Vashon CDP	36.93	10,624	NA	NA	NA	5.6	87.6	78,966	6.7	524,200	56.4	1.6	59.6	34.4
Walla Walla city	13.72	32,445	32,900	1.4	2398.0	10.4	74.0	50,550	16.8	203,500	53.9	4.7	58.0	33.8
Washougal city	5.79	14,161	16,107	13.7	2781.9	5.5	84.6	91,100	7.2	325,500	65.0	3.7	74.6	17.6
Wenatchee city	10.11	32,784	34,360	4.8	3398.6	14.9	82.7	53,167	12.6	253,600	60.9	3.2	60.1	33.9
West Richland city	22.11	11,833	15,075	27.4	681.8	4.7	89.7	99,817	6.1	270,500	63.9	4.4	76.9	17.3
White Center CDP	2.26	13,495	NA	NA	NA	30.7	81.5	58,704	16.0	383,900	71.6	6.1	64.9	24.3
Woodinville city	5.62	10,941	13,263	21.2	2360.0	16.4	81.1	106,145	5.7	623,600	68.6	3.5	59.2	31.3
Yakima city	27.80	91,273	93,637	2.6	3368.2	17.9	81.5	44,950	17.6	173,000	60.7	6.3	64.8	28.9

Table B. Incorporated Places, Census Designated Places (CDPs), and Minor Civil Divisions (MCDs) of 10,000 or More Population — **Crime, Residential Construction and Local Government Finance**

STATE City, town, township, borough, or CDP (county if applicable)	Serious crimes known to police, 2018[1] Violent crime Number	Rate[2]	Property crime Number	Rate[2]	New residential construction authorized by building permits, 2019 Value ($1,000)	Number of housing units	Percent single family	Local government finance, 2017 General revenue Total (mil dol)	Intergovernmental Total (mil dol)	Percent from state gov.	Taxes per capita[3]	General expenditure Total (mil dol)	Per capita[3] Total	Capital outlays	Debt outstanding (mil dol)
	15	16	17	18	19	20	21	22	23	24	25	26	27	28	29
WASHINGTON—Con.															
Fairwood CDP	NA	NA	NA	NA	NA	NA	NA	NA	NA	NA	NA	NA	NA	NA	NA
Federal Way city	458	469	4,480	4,583	55,414	266	24.8	90.4	22.8	74.2	497	92.2	948	295	51.6
Ferndale city	16	111	308	2,133	31,482	134	82.1	17.5	1.9	95.5	665	17.1	1,219	375	26.7
Fife city	NA	NA	NA	NA	11,305	57	40.4	33.1	3.6	36.2	1,629	30.5	3,007	525	26.8
Five Corners CDP	NA	NA	NA	NA	NA	NA	NA	NA	NA	NA	NA	NA	NA	NA	NA
Fort Lewis CDP	NA	NA	NA	NA	NA	NA	NA	NA	NA	NA	NA	NA	NA	NA	NA
Frederickson CDP	NA	NA	NA	NA	NA	NA	NA	NA	NA	NA	NA	NA	NA	NA	NA
Graham CDP	NA	NA	NA	NA	NA	NA	NA	NA	NA	NA	NA	NA	NA	NA	NA
Grandview city	7	63	205	1,836	2,615	12	83.3	12.1	1.2	82.5	482	11.4	1,029	144	11.1
Hazel Dell CDP	NA	NA	NA	NA	NA	NA	NA	NA	NA	NA	NA	NA	NA	NA	NA
Issaquah city	30	78	1,357	3,515	50,208	199	32.2	78.4	8.7	80.9	1,146	68.3	1,812	354	39.3
Kelso city	52	428	486	3,995	1,683	14	64.3	24.1	5.1	57.0	728	21.9	1,810	360	15.4
Kenmore city	NA	NA	259	1,116	13,442	42	100.0	23.2	6.3	95.2	511	25.0	1,087	489	12.2
Kennewick city	158	191	2,126	2,571	104,597	356	96.9	88.9	8.2	87.6	661	86.9	1,065	208	82.0
Kent city	452	348	5,953	4,584	119,024	389	79.7	197.9	23.2	69.2	772	169.4	1,286	257	263.8
Kirkland city	101	113	2,004	2,232	239,765	1,383	21.0	166.4	8.7	65.8	1,120	151.3	1,700	270	46.5
Lacey city	96	189	1,374	2,702	119,023	685	35.5	78.1	6.5	61.3	685	56.2	1,132	96	37.8
Lake Forest Park city	14	104	262	1,940	3,036	8	100.0	17.8	3.5	59.0	587	14.0	1,040	92	5.8
Lakeland North CDP	NA	NA	NA	NA	NA	NA	NA	NA	NA	NA	NA	NA	NA	NA	NA
Lakeland South CDP	NA	NA	NA	NA	NA	NA	NA	NA	NA	NA	NA	NA	NA	NA	NA
Lake Morton-Berrydale CDP	NA	NA	NA	NA	NA	NA	NA	NA	NA	NA	NA	NA	NA	NA	NA
Lake Stevens city	63	188	356	1,063	100,146	315	99.4	19.8	2.2	99.9	435	18.3	558	151	18.2
Lake Stickney CDP	NA	NA	NA	NA	NA	NA	NA	NA	NA	NA	NA	NA	NA	NA	NA
Lake Tapps CDP	NA	NA	NA	NA	NA	NA	NA	NA	NA	NA	NA	NA	NA	NA	NA
Lakewood city	393	648	2,818	4,643	10,566	41	75.6	61.1	15.6	70.9	591	56.9	943	281	12.5
Longview city	110	292	1,350	3,579	6,149	49	30.6	69.2	9.6	49.4	780	61.8	1,644	158	60.1
Lynden city	18	123	205	1,403	33,405	136	72.8	20.2	2.3	97.1	697	16.6	1,160	203	62.6
Lynnwood city	101	262	1,646	4,262	11,983	30	100.0	84.4	6.9	71.5	1,283	77.0	2,012	209	85.7
Maltby CDP	NA	NA	NA	NA	NA	NA	NA	NA	NA	NA	NA	NA	NA	NA	NA
Maple Valley city	NA	NA	354	1,351	61,758	182	100.0	19.5	2.7	96.9	500	18.2	703	136	7.6
Martha Lake CDP	NA	NA	NA	NA	NA	NA	NA	NA	NA	NA	NA	NA	NA	NA	NA
Marysville city	170	242	1,549	2,206	109,453	502	92.4	82.6	4.4	83.4	653	75.7	1,099	177	75.1
Mercer Island city	10	39	452	1,763	68,970	84	100.0	49.2	1.4	78.5	1,176	46.6	1,814	151	33.5
Midland CDP	NA	NA	NA	NA	NA	NA	NA	NA	NA	NA	NA	NA	NA	NA	NA
Mill Creek city	19	90	333	1,568	0	0	0.0	18.5	1.0	97.9	627	16.4	784	101	3.7
Mill Creek East CDP	NA	NA	NA	NA	NA	NA	NA	NA	NA	NA	NA	NA	NA	NA	NA
Minnehaha CDP	NA	NA	NA	NA	NA	NA	NA	NA	NA	NA	NA	NA	NA	NA	NA
Monroe city	69	363	458	2,410	68,350	337	35.3	34.9	4.6	99.2	713	31.5	1,673	476	37.8
Moses Lake city	80	337	1,049	4,414	30,184	138	95.7	36.9	1.4	84.3	780	32.9	1,411	7	30.0
Mountlake Terrace city	39	181	538	2,497	9,136	30	100.0	25.1	1.9	91.5	609	23.8	1,115	82	27.5
Mount Vernon city	99	279	1,308	3,679	23,519	86	97.7	47.9	2.8	92.6	677	48.5	1,379	150	38.6
Mukilteo city	37	171	433	2,001	2,143	5	100.0	22.7	1.5	85.4	763	21.4	997	64	14.2
Newcastle city	NA	NA	243	2,046	57,343	280	14.6	11.5	1.0	44.6	767	9.7	826	131	9.5
North Lynnwood CDP	NA	NA	NA	NA	NA	NA	NA	NA	NA	NA	NA	NA	NA	NA	NA
Oak Harbor city	24	103	162	694	4,336	21	42.9	37.1	9.2	99.7	537	50.1	2,161	1065	57.2
Olympia city	246	470	2,020	3,861	44,418	401	7.2	126.6	11.5	35.9	1,320	125.2	2,424	259	98.6
Orchards CDP	NA	NA	NA	NA	NA	NA	NA	NA	NA	NA	NA	NA	NA	NA	NA
Parkland CDP	NA	NA	NA	NA	NA	NA	NA	NA	NA	NA	NA	NA	NA	NA	NA
Pasco city	166	223	1,328	1,781	126,771	504	94.6	83.7	5.0	79.2	519	73.8	1,013	126	67.7
Port Angeles city	106	530	823	4,117	7,931	57	78.9	46.5	4.7	46.4	752	54.2	2,727	621	71.4
Port Orchard city	67	470	633	4,436	31,228	98	100.0	24.0	6.1	36.6	721	20.2	1,442	205	12.8
Poulsbo city	19	175	227	2,085	15,222	47	100.0	21.9	1.3	87.2	904	19.3	1,811	323	16.9
Prairie Ridge CDP	NA	NA	NA	NA	NA	NA	NA	NA	NA	NA	NA	NA	NA	NA	NA
Pullman city	41	121	371	1,095	72,489	388	26.0	53.8	19.2	15.8	590	32.2	958	156	9.4
Puyallup city	108	260	2,337	5,622	27,438	123	57.7	72.8	5.7	96.6	1,015	61.8	1,508	337	67.5
Redmond city	89	135	1,854	2,817	83,989	455	25.9	185.4	25.0	35.3	1,518	163.0	2,512	562	136.5
Renton city	331	322	4,915	4,784	57,887	168	61.9	253.4	57.8	30.8	1,092	198.6	1,948	240	144.1
Richland city	127	221	1,281	2,230	160,214	760	48.7	97.0	11.9	53.5	906	100.1	1,766	163	196.5
Salmon Creek CDP	NA	NA	NA	NA	NA	NA	NA	NA	NA	NA	NA	NA	NA	NA	NA
Sammamish city	NA	NA	371	566	88,320	175	100.0	88.7	3.5	66.2	755	46.9	722	128	2.8
SeaTac city	NA	NA	1,402	4,759	5,358	14	71.4	61.9	13.1	53.4	1,425	55.1	1,882	504	4.5
Seattle city	5,052	680	38,246	5,149	1,693,658	10,784	4.7	2791.7	256.3	67.1	1,966	2586.2	3,549	749	5049.0
Sedro-Woolley city	10	84	309	2,585	8,991	37	94.6	16.5	2.7	99.8	564	14.6	1,236	310	12.7
Shelton city	52	510	657	6,449	13,381	61	96.7	22.4	3.5	99.9	790	20.6	2,032	426	54.5
Shoreline city	NA	NA	1,100	1,942	102,898	575	18.8	54.2	9.7	62.3	635	48.6	860	140	44.9
Silverdale CDP	NA	NA	NA	NA	NA	NA	NA	NA	NA	NA	NA	NA	NA	NA	NA
Silver Firs CDP	NA	NA	NA	NA	NA	NA	NA	NA	NA	NA	NA	NA	NA	NA	NA
Snoqualmie city	3	22	169	1,212	4,113	9	100.0	29.0	2.8	96.0	1,079	26.1	1,923	301	18.9
South Hill CDP	NA	NA	NA	NA	NA	NA	NA	NA	NA	NA	NA	NA	NA	NA	NA
Spanaway CDP	NA	NA	NA	NA	NA	NA	NA	NA	NA	NA	NA	NA	NA	NA	NA
Spokane city	1,742	798	15,439	7,075	90,370	421	66.3	411.8	42.1	62.2	790	404.4	1,860	278	408.0
Spokane Valley city	346	349	4,165	4,206	143,085	963	15.0	59.5	12.0	93.4	439	61.2	627	191	20.0
Sumner city	26	255	532	5,220	11,870	64	28.1	36.8	8.1	89.7	1,301	31.7	3,143	1432	27.7
Sunnyside city	37	225	422	2,563	10,431	68	97.1	19.3	2.3	88.2	620	18.1	1,093	112	22.6
Tacoma city	1,869	867	11,362	5,268	159,490	1,076	15.1	584.1	62.6	36.7	1,050	560.1	2,625	341	1703.7
Tukwila city	148	730	3,401	16,764	8,237	20	100.0	85.1	10.3	68.9	2,571	83.5	4,119	619	101.0
Tumwater city	84	359	703	3,004	18,852	143	52.4	47.8	1.8	99.1	1,191	40.5	1,762	238	19.1
Union Hill-Novelty Hill CDP	NA	NA	NA	NA	NA	NA	NA	NA	NA	NA	NA	NA	NA	NA	NA
University Place city	72	213	719	2,131	19,758	67	100.0	28.5	6.8	100.0	479	29.9	895	256	42.0
Vancouver city	819	461	5,852	3,295	162,327	1,372	21.9	284.4	29.9	49.8	794	239.2	1,326	217	180.5
Vashon CDP	NA	NA	NA	NA	NA	NA	NA	NA	NA	NA	NA	NA	NA	NA	NA
Walla Walla city	128	389	1,194	3,629	16,906	63	90.5	66.9	6.5	66.8	800	68.6	2,087	401	69.8
Washougal city	25	157	251	1,574	14,728	60	90.0	22.4	2.8	87.5	722	24.2	1,534	471	41.4
Wenatchee city	100	293	851	2,491	12,924	58	69.0	48.3	5.8	72.5	750	36.3	1,060	127	38.2
West Richland city	11	73	125	833	44,259	172	78.5	13.9	1.1	95.9	484	18.7	1,285	593	19.0
White Center CDP	NA	NA	NA	NA	NA	NA	NA	NA	NA	NA	NA	NA	NA	NA	NA
Woodinville city	NA	NA	308	2,534	112,780	816	7.5	17.2	1.4	99.9	1,075	14.2	1,177	345	4.1
Yakima city	421	448	3,343	3,558	67,297	580	26.4	142.6	25.8	29.2	738	114.5	1,225	122	90.6

1 Data for serious crimes have not been adjusted for underreporting. This may affect comparability between geographic areas over time.
2 Per 100,000 population estimated by the FBI.   3 Based on population estimated as of July 1 of the year shown.

Table B. Incorporated Places, Census Designated Places (CDPs), and Minor Civil Divisions (MCDs) of 10,000 or More Population — Land Area, Population, and Households, and Employment

STATE City, town, township, borough, or CDP (county if applicable)	Land area 2010 (sq mi)	Total persons 2010	Total persons 2019	Percent change 2010–2019	Persons per square mile, 2019	Percent foreign born	Percent living in the same house as previous year	Median household income	Percent of households with income below poverty level	Median value of owner-occupied housing units	Percent in civilian labor force	Unemploy-ment rate	Family households	One person households
	1	2	3	4	5	6	7	8	9	10	11	12	13	14
WEST VIRGINIA	24041.13	1,853,018	1,792,147	-3.3	74.5	1.7	88.3	46,711	17.3	119,600	53.2	6.5	64.7	29.7
Beckley city	9.50	17,609	15,940	-9.5	1677.9	2.8	84.0	39,455	20.3	110,000	56.3	6.4	59.4	34.1
Bluefield city	9.03	10,434	9,629	-7.7	1066.3	1.6	83.4	36,793	20.5	84,100	47.2	11.0	64.5	32.6
Charleston city	31.50	51,340	46,536	-9.4	1477.3	3.9	84.7	43,344	19.6	145,800	57.4	5.2	52.0	40.8
Clarksburg city	9.73	16,452	15,225	-7.5	1564.7	0.4	77.5	43,518	20.9	86,200	58.4	6.6	55.8	35.1
Fairmont city	8.59	18,690	18,388	-1.6	2140.6	1.4	78.6	43,319	19.2	110,900	56.3	6.2	57.8	34.1
Huntington city	16.22	49,171	45,110	-8.3	2781.1	2.2	79.5	31,162	31.7	98,200	50.6	6.8	47.5	41.8
Martinsburg city	6.63	17,194	17,454	1.5	2632.6	3.3	78.5	42,835	24.8	157,200	61.0	11.2	52.7	39.2
Morgantown city	9.98	28,470	30,549	7.3	3061.0	7.6	60.0	42,966	28.2	210,300	55.6	9.7	40.7	38.4
Parkersburg city	11.77	31,287	29,306	-6.3	2489.9	1.0	85.7	35,778	24.2	91,100	51.4	7.3	57.8	36.4
St. Albans city	3.62	11,039	9,918	-10.2	2739.8	0.5	89.1	50,755	15.7	113,300	55.0	6.9	64.1	29.8
South Charleston city	7.89	13,495	12,047	-10.7	1526.9	2.5	84.2	53,713	12.2	130,700	63.9	4.8	57.6	37.5
Teays Valley CDP	7.18	13,175	NA	NA	NA	2.4	85.5	89,045	4.7	227,200	64.9	4.3	74.4	21.5
Vienna city	3.96	10,827	10,124	-6.5	2556.6	2.4	91.4	55,562	14.3	134,900	55.9	3.7	63.0	30.9
Weirton city	18.06	19,744	18,266	-7.5	1011.4	1.9	83.8	49,496	12.4	94,800	60.4	6.6	58.4	33.9
Wheeling city	13.78	28,358	26,430	-6.8	1918.0	1.8	89.1	44,119	17.5	110,100	56.3	6.6	50.7	43.3
WISCONSIN	54167.44	5,687,285	5,822,434	2.4	107.5	5.0	86.0	61,747	11.0	180,600	66.4	3.6	62.9	29.5
Allouez village & MCD (Brown)	4.56	13,977	13,894	-0.6	3046.9	4.3	89.8	70,915	4.9	159,200	58.4	2.6	63.0	30.8
Appleton city	24.73	72,675	74,098	2.0	2996.3	6.5	87.2	58,112	9.6	147,800	69.3	3.6	63.1	30.8
Appleton city (Calumet)	3.31	11,082	10,926	-1.4	3300.9	7.4	89.8	60,836	9.4	155,700	72.1	4.8	70.0	24.8
Appleton city (Outagamie)	21.02	59,967	61,493	2.5	2925.5	6.2	87.3	58,489	9.6	145,900	69.0	3.4	62.5	31.3
Ashwaubenon village & MCD (Brown)	12.38	16,943	17,161	1.3	1386.2	4.1	85.3	59,413	9.4	170,600	67.7	3.5	61.4	32.2
Baraboo city & MCD (Sauk)	7.35	12,063	12,165	0.8	1655.1	1.4	81.3	52,109	12.1	152,600	66.9	6.4	56.0	36.4
Beaver Dam city & MCD (Dodge)	7.29	16,210	16,403	1.2	2250.1	3.0	84.5	50,742	8.8	133,200	67.6	5.0	55.5	34.0
Bellevue village & MCD (Brown)	14.33	14,765	15,944	8.0	1112.6	6.7	82.4	55,704	9.5	188,400	70.2	3.6	65.7	29.2
Beloit city & MCD (Rock)	17.33	37,010	36,926	-0.2	2130.8	9.6	82.0	43,651	19.5	89,900	62.0	8.8	59.9	33.1
Brookfield city & MCD (Waukesha)	27.29	37,919	39,115	3.2	1433.3	11.9	88.7	108,198	3.6	318,800	62.0	2.9	75.5	21.0
Brown Deer village & MCD (Milwaukee)	4.40	12,011	11,839	-1.4	2690.7	9.4	85.9	63,884	11.1	167,100	63.4	2.7	59.1	37.0
Burlington city	7.74	10,552	10,980	4.1	1418.6	5.2	83.0	68,564	10.2	185,300	70.1	2.3	65.3	28.2
Burlington city (Racine)	7.47	10,547	10,975	4.1	1469.2	5.2	83.0	68,640	10.2	185,300	70.2	2.3	65.4	28.1
Caledonia village & MCD (Racine)	45.23	24,875	25,277	1.6	558.9	3.3	90.3	80,659	4.8	208,600	64.6	3.8	72.7	23.3
Cedarburg city & MCD (Ozaukee)	4.84	11,453	11,603	1.3	2397.3	4.1	86.7	88,487	8.9	303,500	68.2	1.6	65.1	31.1
Chippewa Falls city & MCD (Chippewa)	11.32	13,723	14,366	4.7	1269.1	1.9	77.2	46,909	12.4	135,100	61.9	6.0	57.1	36.4
Cudahy city & MCD (Milwaukee)	4.77	18,320	18,104	-1.2	3795.4	6.3	89.3	56,795	10.4	152,900	63.1	2.7	58.7	33.9
DeForest village & MCD (Dane)	8.18	8,975	10,691	19.1	1307.0	3.2	90.5	88,151	7.6	234,800	74.5	1.0	71.7	20.5
De Pere city & MCD (Brown)	11.96	23,846	24,970	4.7	2087.8	3.6	80.1	72,286	7.3	177,500	70.5	2.6	64.5	28.4
Eau Claire city	32.70	66,230	68,802	3.9	2104.0	4.5	75.8	55,477	14.9	155,000	70.3	4.0	51.7	34.9
Eau Claire city (Eau Claire)	28.71	64,252	66,783	3.9	2326.1	4.5	75.3	55,469	15.2	155,300	70.2	4.0	51.3	35.0
Elkhorn city & MCD (Walworth)	8.04	10,073	10,019	-0.5	1246.1	6.7	84.9	54,475	12.0	176,700	65.7	2.5	63.4	30.0
Fitchburg city & MCD (Dane)	34.92	25,161	30,792	22.4	881.8	12.3	83.9	72,324	8.7	315,900	71.3	3.2	58.9	29.0
Fond du Lac city & MCD (Fond du Lac)	19.22	42,992	43,263	0.6	2250.9	4.9	83.0	52,724	11.9	126,200	64.3	4.6	57.8	34.5
Fort Atkinson city & MCD (Jefferson)	5.66	12,395	12,422	0.2	2194.7	4.9	86.0	55,404	13.3	157,000	68.3	2.1	64.4	27.4
Fox Crossing village & MCD (Winnebago)	12.26	18,227	19,012	4.3	1550.7	5.2	83.2	58,090	6.0	158,600	67.7	2.3	55.5	35.0
Franklin city & MCD (Milwaukee)	34.58	35,462	35,811	1.0	1035.6	8.3	84.6	82,569	4.7	251,400	59.4	3.4	66.8	29.6
Germantown village & MCD (Washington)	34.37	19,964	20,116	0.8	585.3	6.0	91.7	87,562	4.3	264,100	71.8	2.5	71.0	23.9
Glendale city & MCD (Milwaukee)	5.77	13,150	12,768	-2.9	2212.8	13.8	84.7	77,584	10.1	220,900	62.6	1.7	58.9	35.1
Grafton village & MCD (Ozaukee)	5.09	11,495	11,715	1.9	2301.6	4.2	86.0	75,963	6.9	234,800	72.0	3.3	64.9	28.9
Grand Chute town (Outagamie)	22.90	20,967	23,305	11.2	1017.7	4.9	86.3	60,419	7.2	180,500	68.4	2.9	54.0	37.7
Green Bay city & MCD (Brown)	45.48	103,882	104,578	0.7	2299.4	9.9	82.9	49,251	15.1	135,900	69.2	3.6	57.2	34.1
Greendale village & MCD (Milwaukee)	5.57	14,044	14,143	0.7	2539.1	11.2	87.0	71,786	4.7	216,800	63.6	2.6	63.3	30.8
Greenfield city & MCD (Milwaukee)	11.53	36,758	37,221	1.3	3228.2	8.5	86.6	60,788	8.9	177,800	64.6	3.5	52.5	39.8
Greenville town (Outagamie)	35.72	10,309	12,361	19.9	346.1	0.7	91.2	101,502	3.8	241,200	74.4	2.0	76.0	18.9
Harrison village & MCD (Calumet)	31.89	10,841	12,358	14.0	387.5	0.9	94.5	107,225	4.4	223,300	74.6	0.9	85.7	12.6
Hartford city	8.41	14,249	15,445	8.4	1836.5	2.1	88.3	56,784	9.2	188,000	68.8	3.8	65.7	28.4
Hartford city (Washington)	7.85	14,241	15,436	8.4	1966.4	2.1	88.4	56,756	9.2	188,000	68.7	3.8	65.7	28.4
Howard village	18.45	17,425	20,177	15.8	1093.6	3.5	87.2	70,385	6.4	212,500	69.3	2.6	66.3	26.8
Howard village (Brown)	18.44	17,425	20,177	15.8	1094.2	3.5	87.2	70,385	6.4	212,500	69.3	2.6	66.3	26.8
Hudson city & MCD (St. Croix)	6.69	12,796	14,103	10.2	2108.1	6.3	83.8	75,000	8.9	243,400	69.6	2.2	63.5	27.3
Janesville city & MCD (Rock)	34.05	63,658	64,575	1.4	1896.5	3.2	85.3	56,293	11.2	142,500	66.2	4.6	61.1	31.2
Kaukauna city & MCD (Outagamie)	7.73	15,476	16,270	5.1	2104.8	0.8	88.6	62,822	8.3	142,500	71.6	1.6	64.6	26.4
Kenosha city & MCD (Kenosha)	27.99	99,279	99,944	0.7	3570.7	7.6	83.1	55,417	14.7	152,500	67.5	6.9	61.3	30.8

Table B. Incorporated Places, Census Designated Places (CDPs), and Minor Civil Divisions (MCDs) of 10,000 or More Population — Crime, Residential Construction and Local Government Finance

STATE City, town, township, borough, or CDP (county if applicable)	Serious crimes known to police, 2018[1] Violent crime Number	Violent crime Rate[2]	Property crime Number	Property crime Rate[2]	New residential construction authorized by building permits, 2019 Value ($1,000)	Number of housing units	Percent single family	Local government finance, 2017 General revenue Total (mil dol)	Intergovernmental Total (mil dol)	Percent from state gov.	Taxes per capita[3]	General expenditure Total (mil dol)	Per capita[3] Total	Capital outlays	Debt outstanding (mil dol)
	15	16	17	18	19	20	21	22	23	24	25	26	27	28	29
WEST VIRGINIA......	5,236	290	26,827	1,486	500,116	3,010	84.8	X	X	X	X	X	X	X	X
Beckley city......	147	906	836	5,150	0	0	0.0	33.4	1.6	6.5	1,240	26.1	1,593	79	30.2
Bluefield city......	92	940	103	1,052	617	4	100.0	24.5	0.8	73.2	580	22.2	2,243	0	2.0
Charleston city......	331	697	2,853	6,010	4,980	34	100.0	151.7	9.0	41.9	1,758	168.9	3,516	1075	97.1
Clarksburg city......	NA	NA	NA	NA	0	0	0.0	22.6	0.3	18.7	834	15.3	982	38	22.8
Fairmont city......	63	342	261	1,416	5,168	42	88.1	23.7	0.3	100.0	574	20.7	1,125	25	46.7
Huntington city......	NA	NA	NA	NA	6,385	52	9.6	70.6	6.4	38.9	657	73.0	1,562	18	35.7
Martinsburg city......	55	316	540	3,099	5,377	46	95.7	29.8	2.3	59.0	1,002	25.8	1,478	296	42.4
Morgantown city......	82	266	500	1,621	3,608	18	55.6	65.2	1.6	40.9	902	63.4	2,048	578	187.8
Parkersburg city......	NA	NA	NA	NA	2,157	24	33.3	40.8	1.6	12.9	521	39.5	1,314	114	61.4
St. Albans city......	NA	NA	NA	NA	610	3	100.0	11.3	0.2	78.0	727	11.9	1,163	15	13.8
South Charleston city......	47	380	577	4,669	0	0	0.0	36.3	0.5	12.1	1,455	37.2	2,982	0	4.2
Teays Valley CDP......	NA	NA	NA	NA	NA	NA	NA	NA	NA	NA	NA	NA	NA	NA	NA
Vienna city......	23	223	351	3,406	1,825	4	100.0	8.7	0.2	33.7	565	9.6	925	91	3.8
Weirton city......	9	49	166	895	1,596	5	100.0	24.8	1.7	100.0	673	17.8	955	41	33.0
Wheeling city......	229	853	321	1,195	100	1	100.0	79.8	3.6	58.0	1,025	75.4	2,809	135	96.8
WISCONSIN......	17,176	295	90,686	1,560	3,968,450	17,480	64.6	X	X	X	X	X	X	X	X
Allouez village & MCD (Brown)	NA	NA	NA	NA	1,668	9	55.6	12.4	2.3	97.9	475	14.3	1,031	48	23.8
Appleton city......	165	220	1,151	1,536	NA	NA	NA	109.9	32.9	58.2	619	111.6	1,498	325	167.6
Appleton city (Calumet)......	NA	NA	NA	NA	NA	NA	NA	NA	NA	NA	NA	NA	NA	NA	NA
Appleton city (Outagamie)......	NA	NA	NA	NA	22,547	89	60.7	NA	NA	NA	NA	NA	NA	NA	NA
Ashwaubenon village & MCD (Brown)	13	75	528	3,049	4,887	13	46.2	26.5	3.0	73.7	809	44.1	2,562	1111	42.8
Baraboo city & MCD (Sauk)	24	197	358	2,940	2,221	11	81.8	18.5	5.4	82.9	745	18.2	1,495	332	22.9
Beaver Dam city & MCD (Dodge)	25	153	239	1,458	6,705	57	5.3	23.3	4.5	87.4	725	25.7	1,573	381	32.2
Bellevue village & MCD (Brown)	NA	NA	NA	NA	12,971	85	54.1	11.0	1.6	73.1	266	10.7	682	68	23.0
Beloit city & MCD (Rock)......	171	465	979	2,664	7,097	101	19.8	63.9	24.7	88.6	636	60.9	1,654	228	75.6
Brookfield city & MCD (Waukesha)	28	74	815	2,141	18,819	38	71.1	62.9	7.1	60.6	1,105	67.7	1,780	121	72.3
Brown Deer village & MCD (Milwaukee)	51	426	548	4,581	15,911	175	9.1	17.2	2.3	79.5	846	18.6	1,556	161	24.0
Burlington city......	15	136	108	978	NA	NA	NA	16.9	2.7	64.7	949	14.2	1,297	103	35.1
Burlington city (Racine)......	NA	NA	NA	NA	4,134	16	75.0	NA	NA	NA	NA	NA	NA	NA	NA
Caledonia village & MCD (Racine)	21	84	151	603	NA	NA	NA	29.5	4.3	77.4	556	41.3	1,644	557	77.1
Cedarburg city & MCD (Ozaukee)	3	26	54	471	22,339	103	37.9	14.4	1.7	74.1	757	23.7	2,058	918	18.0
Chippewa Falls city & MCD (Chippewa)	26	185	175	1,243	10,470	80	25.0	23.8	6.7	82.5	658	26.3	1,872	745	36.6
Cudahy city & MCD (Milwaukee)	24	131	221	1,208	297	1	100.0	28.1	5.8	94.4	771	28.2	1,539	212	57.0
DeForest village & MCD (Dane)	9	85	98	928	28,276	95	72.6	14.9	2.0	75.6	794	25.5	2,457	1338	38.3
De Pere city & MCD (Brown)....	38	151	205	814	14,111	96	33.3	33.0	4.4	91.4	599	38.2	1,525	488	33.5
Eau Claire city......	199	289	1,688	2,449	NA	NA	NA	93.8	23.9	66.4	648	94.5	1,378	226	158.5
Eau Claire city (Eau Claire)......	NA	NA	NA	NA	39,594	218	47.7	NA	NA	NA	NA	NA	NA	NA	NA
Elkhorn city & MCD (Walworth)	13	131	113	1,138	4,618	29	72.4	14.4	2.6	52.3	656	11.8	1,191	101	29.8
Fitchburg city & MCD (Dane)....	86	285	581	1,927	14,930	57	93.0	39.1	5.0	84.8	918	37.8	1,281	387	47.4
Fond du Lac city & MCD (Fond du Lac)...	101	236	1,012	2,366	18,025	149	24.8	61.0	15.6	68.2	640	58.0	1,358	165	153.9
Fort Atkinson city & MCD (Jefferson)	25	200	169	1,353	1,836	11	45.5	14.8	2.8	83.0	624	15.4	1,236	191	13.6
Fox Crossing village & MCD (Winnebago)	20	104	189	978	NA	NA	NA	30.7	4.2	77.3	791	25.3	1,342	179	51.0
Franklin city & MCD (Milwaukee)	13	36	527	1,454	27,761	68	100.0	38.4	4.5	76.7	702	37.9	1,049	122	32.6
Germantown village & MCD (Washington)	8	40	422	2,109	5,840	14	100.0	26.7	2.9	87.6	697	32.3	1,602	518	26.3
Glendale city & MCD (Milwaukee)	53	417	965	7,592	0	0	0.0	33.7	3.4	98.9	1,893	33.0	2,551	452	123.3
Grafton village & MCD (Ozaukee)	7	60	136	1,166	9,207	34	94.1	18.2	2.6	69.7	970	16.8	1,437	225	38.9
Grand Chute town (Outagamie)	52	227	683	2,987	21,712	79	87.3	26.1	2.3	68.8	603	23.7	1,049	194	21.8
Green Bay city & MCD (Brown)	483	459	1,798	1,708	18,036	63	100.0	147.7	42.2	72.8	565	144.1	1,373	160	262.5
Greendale village & MCD (Milwaukee)	12	85	251	1,770	0	0	0.0	17.1	1.7	90.0	841	20.3	1,434	329	28.7
Greenfield city & MCD (Milwaukee)	64	174	898	2,437	1,628	6	100.0	41.5	5.6	81.8	666	60.4	1,641	626	77.0
Greenville town (Outagamie)....	NA	NA	NA	NA	16,403	59	93.2	4.1	0.6	100.0	211	4.0	330	56	2.9
Harrison village & MCD (Calumet)	NA	NA	NA	NA	NA	NA	NA	3.7	0.6	82.8	199	4.1	334	125	2.1
Hartford city......	17	112	204	1,344	NA	NA	NA	19.1	3.2	62.5	596	21.7	1,443	332	44.4
Hartford city (Washington)......	NA	NA	NA	NA	22,852	132	37.9	NA	NA	NA	NA	NA	NA	NA	NA
Howard village......	NA	NA	NA	NA	NA	NA	NA	15.2	2.2	92.8	355	21.4	1,090	424	12.1
Howard village (Brown)......	NA	NA	NA	NA	23,214	132	54.5	15.2	2.2	92.8	355	21.4	1,090	424	12.1
Hudson city & MCD (St. Croix).	19	137	383	2,766	16,610	54	79.6	15.9	2.6	43.6	601	19.1	1,388	398	15.8
Janesville city & MCD (Rock) ...	167	259	1,800	2,792	50,332	312	29.5	90.4	18.7	60.4	637	109.5	1,702	522	112.9
Kaukauna city & MCD (Outagamie)	25	155	135	835	9,314	44	90.9	24.4	4.1	94.5	604	25.6	1,593	261	109.0
Kenosha city & MCD (Kenosha)......	338	338	1,495	1,496	20,625	226	10.6	146.4	31.1	73.3	821	129.9	1,302	158	111.1

1 Data for serious crimes have not been adjusted for underreporting. This may affect comparability between geographic areas over time.
2 Per 100,000 population estimated by the FBI.   3 Based on population estimated as of July 1 of the year shown.

Table B. Incorporated Places, Census Designated Places (CDPs), and Minor Civil Divisions (MCDs) of 10,000 or More Population — Land Area, Population, and Households, and Employment

STATE City, town, township, borough, or CDP (county if applicable)	Land area 2010 (sq mi)	Population Total persons 2010	Total persons 2019	Percent change 2010–2019	Persons per square mile 2019	Population characteristics 2015–2019 Percent foreign born	Percent living in the same house as previous year	Income and poverty 2015–2019 Median household income	Percent of households with income below poverty level	Median value of owner-occupied housing units	Employment, 2015–2019 Percent in civilian labor force	Unemployment rate	Households, 2015–2019 (percent of households) Family households	One person households
	1	2	3	4	5	6	7	8	9	10	11	12	13	14
WISCONSIN—Con.														
La Crosse city & MCD (La Crosse)	21.71	51,343	51,227	-0.2	2359.6	2.8	72.5	45,233	19.2	142,500	66.0	4.3	43.8	37.2
Lisbon town (Waukesha)	27.19	10,158	10,627	4.6	390.8	1.9	95.7	100,665	2.9	298,900	67.1	0.8	78.2	19.8
Little Chute village & MCD (Outagamie)	6.40	10,472	12,081	15.4	1887.7	2.3	84.7	61,111	6.1	150,900	72.2	3.2	61.0	32.3
Madison city & MCD (Dane)	79.34	233,173	259,680	11.4	3273.0	12.1	73.8	65,332	14.9	246,300	72.2	3.1	46.1	35.3
Manitowoc city & MCD (Manitowoc)	17.78	33,741	32,579	-3.4	1832.3	4.0	90.3	47,861	12.6	107,100	60.4	3.1	54.8	37.8
Marinette city & MCD (Marinette)	7.01	10,961	10,539	-3.9	1503.4	1.0	86.0	42,788	17.5	86,400	59.5	3.4	53.0	39.5
Marshfield city	13.64	19,096	18,471	-3.3	1354.2	3.8	83.6	52,615	11.6	141,300	66.0	2.7	53.7	39.3
Marshfield city (Wood)	11.77	18,208	17,590	-3.4	1494.5	3.5	83.9	52,212	11.6	140,900	66.9	2.6	54.4	38.4
Menasha city	6.06	17,503	17,873	2.1	2949.3	5.0	85.5	54,274	11.2	131,100	69.8	4.4	56.7	35.1
Menasha city (Winnebago)	4.51	15,282	15,671	2.5	3474.7	5.4	84.3	51,043	12.2	118,400	68.7	5.0	53.5	37.4
Menomonee Falls village & MCD (Waukesha)	32.91	35,625	38,014	6.7	1155.1	5.6	89.6	82,396	3.5	247,300	68.8	2.9	65.8	30.0
Menomonie city & MCD (Dunn)	13.68	16,275	16,551	1.7	1209.9	3.2	63.7	44,121	21.3	145,200	64.4	3.3	42.0	39.9
Mequon city & MCD (Ozaukee)	46.28	23,136	24,382	5.4	526.8	9.0	89.1	116,486	4.6	407,000	59.4	2.0	78.4	18.6
Middleton city & MCD (Dane)	8.93	17,560	20,034	14.1	2243.4	9.2	83.9	76,011	5.4	336,900	71.9	2.5	58.5	33.0
Milwaukee city & MCD (Milwaukee)	96.18	594,498	590,157	-0.7	6136.0	10.0	82.4	41,838	23.2	122,100	64.6	6.8	54.3	36.3
Monroe city & MCD (Green)	5.61	10,816	10,565	-2.3	1883.2	2.4	88.2	50,537	9.0	126,100	68.6	1.6	54.9	39.7
Mount Pleasant village & MCD (Racine)	33.88	26,697	27,082	1.4	799.4	6.2	90.3	69,485	6.9	190,800	59.6	3.1	68.1	27.1
Muskego city & MCD (Waukesha)	31.60	24,133	25,127	4.1	795.2	2.0	92.5	95,242	3.6	291,700	70.0	4.2	76.5	18.6
Neenah city & MCD (Winnebago)	9.29	25,509	26,300	3.1	2831.0	3.3	85.6	59,820	10.7	141,100	68.7	3.3	60.7	31.8
New Berlin city & MCD (Waukesha)	36.46	39,591	39,691	0.3	1088.6	6.2	91.5	83,488	4.1	259,800	64.9	2.5	68.9	27.4
Oak Creek city & MCD (Milwaukee)	28.45	34,449	36,325	5.4	1276.8	10.0	86.6	74,840	6.7	231,200	69.5	3.1	64.7	27.8
Oconomowoc city & MCD (Waukesha)	11.65	15,807	16,981	7.4	1457.6	2.3	86.7	88,662	5.5	259,200	71.9	2.1	63.8	29.1
Onalaska city & MCD (La Crosse)	10.25	17,792	18,943	6.5	1848.1	5.8	88.6	61,429	6.3	196,600	64.8	3.0	59.7	30.6
Oregon village & MCD (Dane)	4.49	9,315	10,571	13.5	2354.3	1.5	89.8	83,885	5.8	256,500	76.1	1.3	66.8	28.7
Oshkosh city & MCD (Winnebago)	26.99	66,346	67,004	1.0	2482.5	3.4	76.6	50,892	15.0	125,000	62.0	3.4	51.4	34.8
Pewaukee city & MCD (Waukesha)	19.49	13,190	14,631	10.9	750.7	4.2	86.1	104,645	2.4	315,300	68.4	1.7	71.2	22.1
Platteville city & MCD (Grant)	6.32	11,280	12,087	7.2	1912.5	3.4	63.4	46,690	23.1	152,400	60.5	4.1	40.0	32.5
Pleasant Prairie village & MCD (Kenosha)	33.38	19,722	21,034	6.7	630.1	6.4	87.7	86,687	6.4	231,200	66.4	4.9	70.7	23.4
Plover village & MCD (Portage)	10.60	12,221	13,099	7.2	1235.8	5.9	81.0	60,482	10.0	175,300	66.9	2.2	63.4	26.9
Portage city & MCD (Columbia)	8.91	10,327	10,399	0.7	1167.1	3.0	79.7	45,448	13.4	125,200	60.7	5.8	54.9	38.8
Port Washington city & MCD (Ozaukee)	5.83	11,290	11,911	5.5	2043.1	2.6	84.2	68,167	5.7	197,900	69.2	3.8	62.1	31.2
Racine city & MCD (Racine)	15.47	78,556	76,760	-2.3	4961.9	6.1	83.5	44,056	19.7	108,700	63.3	6.4	61.2	31.9
Richfield village & MCD (Washington)	35.91	11,304	11,854	4.9	330.1	2.4	94.9	105,441	2.0	323,700	70.5	1.9	83.1	14.9
River Falls city	7.15	15,004	16,027	6.8	2241.5	2.1	60.2	59,440	12.1	197,000	68.1	2.1	51.3	33.2
River Falls city (Pierce)	3.97	11,857	12,691	7.0	3196.7	2.5	53.9	55,920	14.1	199,400	68.3	2.1	47.0	33.0
Salem Lakes village & MCD (Kenosha)	30.48	14,520	14,852	2.3	487.3	3.4	90.0	74,201	7.9	202,100	71.0	5.3	72.4	22.4
Sheboygan city & MCD (Sheboygan)	15.63	49,385	47,965	-2.9	3068.8	9.0	86.9	51,104	9.8	114,500	66.5	5.0	58.0	34.8
Shorewood village & MCD (Milwaukee)	1.59	13,148	13,145	0.0	8267.3	13.8	81.3	74,745	12.1	338,400	68.8	3.0	53.1	38.5
South Milwaukee city & MCD (Milwaukee)	4.83	21,155	20,696	-2.2	4284.9	6.9	86.3	52,678	14.2	162,000	63.3	4.5	61.3	31.4
Stevens Point city & MCD (Portage)	17.17	26,711	25,880	-3.1	1507.3	5.0	69.1	45,471	21.4	140,100	68.2	4.1	44.6	35.9
Stoughton city & MCD (Dane)	5.81	12,661	13,114	3.6	2257.1	3.4	86.6	67,329	10.2	218,100	70.8	1.5	63.4	28.3
Suamico village & MCD (Brown)	36.34	11,348	13,052	15.0	359.2	1.1	88.7	101,479	1.4	249,400	76.0	2.4	80.3	12.2
Sun Prairie city & MCD (Dane)	12.49	29,540	34,661	17.3	2775.1	8.0	89.5	77,139	5.6	239,200	73.9	1.4	62.4	31.6
Superior city & MCD (Douglas)	36.65	27,233	25,977	-4.6	708.8	3.1	82.3	46,957	14.9	120,800	66.0	3.3	55.6	35.6
Sussex village & MCD (Waukesha)	7.78	10,541	10,981	4.2	1411.4	4.8	87.1	91,387	6.5	286,300	75.1	3.0	68.9	23.0
Two Rivers city & MCD (Manitowoc)	6.04	11,728	11,041	-5.9	1828.0	3.5	90.1	47,228	11.4	94,300	64.2	3.6	57.2	37.6
Verona city & MCD (Dane)	7.43	10,694	13,233	23.7	1781.0	4.2	82.9	96,990	3.3	310,700	76.7	2.3	65.4	27.7
Watertown city	12.07	23,872	23,479	-1.6	1945.2	3.6	87.4	51,534	9.7	153,100	68.9	4.0	65.5	29.1
Watertown city (Jefferson)	7.98	15,396	15,269	-0.8	1913.4	4.0	86.5	51,544	10.4	146,500	70.5	3.9	65.0	28.7
Waukesha city & MCD (Waukesha)	25.52	71,223	72,299	1.5	2833.0	6.9	84.9	65,260	11.2	212,700	71.7	3.0	60.2	31.9
Waunakee village & MCD (Dane)	7.13	12,100	14,052	16.1	1970.8	3.4	88.1	112,845	4.2	346,300	70.4	2.5	71.8	22.5
Waupun city & MCD (Dodge)	4.64	11,345	11,199	-1.3	2413.6	2.8	87.5	56,587	11.3	120,600	58.5	2.7	62.9	31.2
Wausau city & MCD (Marathon)	19.22	39,201	38,561	-1.6	2006.3	6.7	85.6	46,824	13.3	121,900	65.2	4.0	56.1	35.3
Wauwatosa city & MCD (Milwaukee)	13.23	46,425	48,118	3.6	3637.0	4.9	86.8	82,392	7.6	242,800	68.7	2.2	58.7	32.8
West Allis city & MCD (Milwaukee)	11.38	60,401	59,890	-0.8	5262.7	6.4	85.7	52,325	13.0	146,100	68.6	3.7	50.5	41.4

Table B. Incorporated Places, Census Designated Places (CDPs), and Minor Civil Divisions (MCDs) of 10,000 or More Population — **Crime, Residential Construction and Local Government Finance**

STATE City, town, township, borough, or CDP (county if applicable)	Serious crimes known to police, 2018[1] — Violent crime Number	Violent crime Rate[2]	Property crime Number	Property crime Rate[2]	New residential construction authorized by building permits, 2019 Value ($1,000)	Number of housing units	Percent single family	Local government finance, 2017 — General revenue Total (mil dol)	Intergovernmental Total (mil dol)	Percent from state gov.	Taxes per capita[3]	General expenditure Total (mil dol)	Per capita[3] Total	Per capita[3] Capital outlays	Debt outstanding (mil dol)
	15	16	17	18	19	20	21	22	23	24	25	26	27	28	29
WISCONSIN—Con.															
La Crosse city & MCD (La Crosse)	145	279	1,924	3,707	17,001	119	29.4	101.1	25.7	78.4	920	94.8	1,833	332	63.5
Lisbon town (Waukesha)	NA	NA	NA	NA	10,465	26	100.0	6.6	1.0	71.4	376	11.1	1,053	626	13.5
Little Chute village & MCD (Outagamie)	NA	NA	NA	NA	9,371	33	75.8	16.7	4.8	52.0	509	15.4	1,355	258	23.4
Madison city & MCD (Dane)	1,043	404	6,722	2,601	325,679	1,658	25.7	481.5	105.0	66.8	962	423.1	1,654	173	906.4
Manitowoc city & MCD (Manitowoc)	71	218	661	2,030	1,632	9	55.6	52.5	15.2	62.8	577	43.2	1,324	171	84.7
Marinette city & MCD (Marinette)	9	85	182	1,723	0	0	0.0	19.4	8.2	84.8	634	18.4	1,735	320	23.6
Marshfield city	12	66	382	2,086	NA	NA	NA	38.1	8.6	90.5	790	41.5	2,256	459	85.9
Marshfield city (Wood)	NA	NA	NA	NA	10,993	94	14.9	0.0	0.0	0.0	0	0.0	0	0	0.0
Menasha city	45	253	367	2,063	NA	NA	NA	25.5	7.8	81.4	668	26.5	1,489	91	58.0
Menasha city (Winnebago)	NA	NA	NA	NA	3,611	14	100.0	0.0	0.0	0.0	0	0.0	0	0	0.0
Menomonee Falls village & MCD (Waukesha)	21	56	408	1,082	44,687	135	86.7	51.2	4.7	93.6	828	57.9	1,547	173	94.8
Menomonie city & MCD (Dunn)	28	170	306	1,860	3,987	25	68.0	20.3	5.8	85.8	490	19.2	1,171	95	23.3
Mequon city & MCD (Ozaukee)	5	21	241	991	26,895	151	36.4	30.2	2.8	85.0	934	45.1	1,880	421	47.3
Middleton city & MCD (Dane) ...	52	260	276	1,382	21,513	97	23.7	45.4	4.2	68.2	1,507	36.3	1,845	315	49.0
Milwaukee city & MCD (Milwaukee)	8,416	1,413	17,699	2,972	24,330	193	7.8	940.5	378.3	76.2	482	1116.7	1,881	235	1507.0
Monroe city & MCD (Green)	11	104	127	1,201	1,040	4	100.0	17.8	3.3	86.0	743	16.9	1,596	211	36.2
Mount Pleasant village & MCD (Racine)	23	87	569	2,141	17,328	65	90.8	38.4	5.5	57.7	745	39.5	1,465	219	39.3
Muskego city & MCD (Waukesha)	9	36	143	569	23,449	81	53.1	25.8	3.1	90.3	550	33.9	1,356	173	37.6
Neenah city & MCD (Winnebago)	NA	NA	NA	NA	14,860	108	27.8	37.5	6.7	71.5	806	38.2	1,473	193	65.0
New Berlin city & MCD (Waukesha)	15	38	432	1,086	24,180	62	64.5	48.5	4.6	85.5	654	58.6	1,474	204	50.0
Oak Creek city & MCD (Milwaukee)	46	126	739	2,017	15,198	47	100.0	47.8	10.2	93.6	704	59.4	1,637	456	115.1
Oconomowoc city & MCD (Waukesha)	7	42	133	789	24,205	89	100.0	22.2	4.3	46.0	727	23.3	1,392	310	14.2
Onalaska city & MCD (La Crosse)	6	32	415	2,203	14,386	132	3.8	20.1	3.2	78.5	654	20.6	1,105	216	47.3
Oregon village & MCD (Dane) ..	4	38	97	920	24,795	76	100.0	10.3	1.4	63.6	606	10.9	1,050	201	12.7
Oshkosh city & MCD (Winnebago)	115	172	1,107	1,659	8,136	38	84.2	98.4	24.3	79.3	637	105.2	1,578	227	305.9
Pewaukee city & MCD (Waukesha)	NA	NA	NA	NA	16,392	37	100.0	22.2	3.4	44.0	715	25.9	1,789	212	19.2
Platteville city & MCD (Grant) ...	31	245	208	1,645	2,200	14	28.6	15.8	5.6	82.8	504	17.9	1,463	538	40.8
Pleasant Prairie village & MCD (Kenosha)	36	172	390	1,865	35,040	217	35.5	50.2	4.1	92.1	1,109	55.1	2,656	804	86.6
Plover village & MCD (Portage)	14	109	175	1,362	17,133	97	42.3	13.8	2.6	91.2	543	11.6	906	68	22.8
Portage city & MCD (Columbia)	25	238	156	1,486	1,071	5	100.0	12.6	3.9	93.9	523	13.5	1,286	210	22.8
Port Washington city & MCD (Ozaukee)	19	161	73	617	16,219	110	58.2	15.8	4.7	94.3	487	19.0	1,610	332	35.1
Racine city & MCD (Racine)	435	562	1,662	2,148	826	4	100.0	141.7	50.4	80.1	725	145.3	1,882	202	179.5
Richfield village & MCD (Washington)	NA	NA	NA	NA	16,496	37	94.6	6.3	0.7	100.0	255	7.2	614	374	1.0
River Falls city	16	103	259	1,663	NA	NA	NA	18.8	5.2	62.8	453	20.8	1,333	123	20.5
River Falls city (Pierce)	NA	NA	NA	NA	28,230	212	35.8	0.0	0.0	0.0	0	0.0	0	0	0.0
Salem Lakes village & MCD (Kenosha)	NA	NA	NA	NA	NA	NA	NA	0.0	0.0	0.0	0	0.0	0	0	0.0
Sheboygan city & MCD (Sheboygan)	183	380	826	1,714	5,906	30	30.0	61.7	19.8	84.6	570	62.9	1,302	129	56.0
Shorewood village & MCD (Milwaukee)	18	135	374	2,798	0	0	0.0	20.0	2.4	76.8	1,033	24.9	1,872	472	56.1
South Milwaukee city & MCD (Milwaukee)	35	167	366	1,745	291	2	0.0	24.4	6.0	82.8	594	25.8	1,231	182	39.6
Stevens Point city & MCD (Portage)	40	153	392	1,494	19,745	155	7.1	43.4	9.9	69.1	652	40.8	1,555	329	59.6
Stoughton city & MCD (Dane) ..	22	167	238	1,810	8,696	59	23.7	18.3	2.6	77.4	677	24.1	1,835	691	37.3
Suamico village & MCD (Brown)	NA	NA	NA	NA	16,251	40	100.0	9.8	0.9	97.9	459	8.2	644	76	19.5
Sun Prairie city & MCD (Dane) .	27	81	676	2,025	60,831	220	50.9	41.0	5.3	86.9	733	36.3	1,103	154	69.9
Superior city & MCD (Douglas)	76	292	1,114	4,276	1,981	10	60.0	56.6	22.0	89.6	582	47.8	1,821	230	44.6
Sussex village & MCD (Waukesha)	NA	NA	NA	NA	13,475	50	100.0	14.0	1.8	71.8	629	29.0	2,677	1532	46.1
Two Rivers city & MCD (Manitowoc)	36	325	136	1,228	253	1	100.0	19.7	7.8	94.8	524	18.8	1,681	313	25.3
Verona city & MCD (Dane)	19	141	207	1,535	29,202	137	34.3	31.3	3.0	66.5	1,784	47.6	3,623	912	52.3
Watertown city	46	195	220	931	NA	NA	NA	31.8	5.9	90.4	632	28.2	1,191	148	57.8
Watertown city (Jefferson)	NA	NA	NA	NA	14,868	53	54.7	0.0	0.0	0.0	0	0.0	0	0	0.0
Waukesha city & MCD (Waukesha)	92	127	750	1,032	12,472	60	66.7	113.0	24.2	80.1	879	104.3	1,438	307	301.2
Waunakee village & MCD (Dane)	20	143	92	657	26,849	62	100.0	17.0	1.7	82.6	773	21.6	1,568	603	39.2
Waupun city	12	107	92	817	NA	NA	NA	11.1	4.0	98.3	307	10.5	928	86	23.0
Wausau city & MCD (Marathon)	119	308	626	1,618	19,648	144	24.3	56.4	13.8	85.6	776	65.2	1,684	572	75.1
Wauwatosa city & MCD (Milwaukee)	55	113	1,249	2,572	3,293	24	8.3	76.9	10.3	65.6	952	92.5	1,927	439	126.1
West Allis city & MCD (Milwaukee)	195	326	1,673	2,794	200	1	100.0	89.6	23.4	64.6	732	84.3	1,408	88	72.2

1 Data for serious crimes have not been adjusted for underreporting. This may affect comparability between geographic areas over time.
2 Per 100,000 population estimated by the FBI. 3 Based on population estimated as of July 1 of the year shown.

Table B. Incorporated Places, Census Designated Places (CDPs), and Minor Civil Divisions (MCDs) of 10,000 or More Population — **Land Area, Population, and Households, and Employment**

STATE City, town, township, borough, or CDP (county if applicable)	Land area 2010 (sq mi)	Population				Population characteristics 2015–2019		Income and poverty 2015–2019		Median value of owner-occupied housing units	Employment, 2015–2019		Households, 2015–2019 (percent of households)	
		Total persons 2010	Total persons 2019	Percent change 2010–2019	Persons per square mile, 2019	Percent foreign born	Percent living in the same house as previous year	Median household income	Percent of households with income below poverty level		Percent in civilian labor force	Unemployment rate	Family households	One person households
	1	2	3	4	5	6	7	8	9	10	11	12	13	14
WISCONSIN—Con.														
West Bend city & MCD (Washington)........................	15.14	31,186	31,563	1.2	2084.7	2.1	86.5	60,910	8.0	174,500	68.5	2.4	60.8	33.7
Weston village & MCD (Marathon)	21.62	14,908	15,167	1.7	701.5	4.8	85.8	66,716	7.3	160,200	70.9	1.9	66.2	24.7
Whitefish Bay village & MCD (Milwaukee).........................	2.12	14,125	13,783	-2.4	6501.4	7.9	87.8	124,397	4.1	387,000	70.4	2.2	74.1	21.8
Whitewater city	8.84	14,395	14,895	3.5	1685.0	4.5	55.1	36,176	39.1	168,700	63.5	6.0	38.8	35.1
Whitewater city (Walworth).......	5.99	11,158	12,089	8.3	2018.2	3.9	54.6	35,513	41.4	171,700	65.0	5.6	36.3	36.3
Wisconsin Rapids city & MCD (Wood)	13.85	18,400	17,610	-4.3	1271.5	3.0	82.1	42,531	13.7	91,100	57.6	5.5	51.2	42.4
WYOMING.............................	97088.70	563,775	578,759	2.7	6.0	3.4	83.2	64,049	10.9	220,500	65.8	4.5	64.6	28.2
Casper city............................	26.53	55,316	57,931	4.7	2183.6	2.5	84.8	61,979	11.0	207,400	69.3	3.8	60.6	31.8
Cheyenne city........................	32.14	59,552	64,235	7.9	1998.6	2.9	81.7	64,598	10.4	214,300	64.7	5.4	60.6	33.1
Evanston city	10.29	12,398	11,641	-6.1	1131.3	4.1	82.8	58,566	10.6	169,400	66.8	7.5	67.6	25.5
Gillette city.............................	22.99	31,401	32,030	2.0	1393.2	3.8	82.1	79,789	12.7	216,400	72.1	3.3	69.2	24.8
Green River city......................	13.70	12,515	11,759	-6.0	858.3	3.8	83.2	75,087	10.9	213,800	67.0	5.0	75.6	19.3
Jackson town..........................	2.96	9,628	10,559	9.7	3567.2	16.5	76.7	73,411	6.4	652,100	83.1	1.4	46.8	32.6
Laramie city............................	18.33	30,816	32,711	6.1	1784.6	8.1	63.4	46,117	24.8	216,300	69.5	4.8	43.5	33.1
Riverton city...........................	10.33	10,760	10,772	0.1	1042.8	2.3	78.3	52,463	12.8	156,800	64.4	5.1	58.6	32.9
Rock Springs city....................	19.38	23,066	22,653	-1.8	1168.9	3.9	81.1	76,722	10.8	211,800	72.0	4.9	66.5	28.5
Sheridan city..........................	12.68	17,477	17,940	2.6	1414.8	2.3	81.3	54,278	8.5	228,200	62.9	3.4	54.5	36.0

Table B. Incorporated Places, Census Designated Places (CDPs), and Minor Civil Divisions (MCDs) of 10,000 or More Population — **Crime, Residential Construction and Local Government Finance**

STATE City, town, township, borough, or CDP (county if applicable)	Serious crimes known to police, 2018[1] Violent crime Number	Rate[2]	Property crime Number	Rate[2]	New residential construction authorized by building permits, 2019 Value ($1,000)	Number of housing units	Percent single family	Local government finance, 2017 General revenue Total (mil dol)	Intergovernmental Total (mil dol)	Percent from state gov.	Taxes per capita[3]	General expenditure Total (mil dol)	Per capita[3] Total	Capital outlays	Debt outstanding (mil dol)
	15	16	17	18	19	20	21	22	23	24	25	26	27	28	29
WISCONSIN—Con.															
West Bend city & MCD (Washington)	56	177	528	1,668	6,868	34	47.1	37.9	6.8	77.3	747	32.4	1,029	110	63.7
Weston village & MCD (Marathon)	NA	NA	NA	NA	5,819	52	40.4	23.0	8.5	29.7	703	12.4	818	0	38.2
Whitefish Bay village & MCD (Milwaukee)	10	72	191	1,371	3,528	8	100.0	18.1	1.9	79.3	865	21.5	1,545	265	57.7
Whitewater city	24	165	104	714	NA	NA	NA	16.9	5.9	85.6	358	15.9	1,086	149	34.3
Whitewater city (Walworth)	NA	NA	NA	NA	2,099	13	69.2	0.0	0.0	0.0	0	0.0	0	0	0.0
Wisconsin Rapids city & MCD (Wood)	27	152	599	3,379	9,034	98	8.2	29.6	7.9	84.2	702	28.6	1,608	181	37.7
WYOMING	1,226	212	10,313	1,785	541,013	1,708	89.1	0.0	0.0	0.0	0	0.0	0	0	0.0
Casper city	117	201	1,630	2,801	18,529	74	83.8	109.5	52.4	65.1	202	121.0	2,092	543	15.8
Cheyenne city	207	323	2,559	3,987	40,028	211	78.2	116.7	64.2	51.9	244	110.4	1,739	488	83.0
Evanston city	11	93	212	1,797	2,943	12	100.0	14.9	9.1	75.2	138	14.4	1,215	138	0.0
Gillette city	56	183	667	2,176	6,473	24	83.3	101.0	65.0	73.3	127	67.6	2,098	414	158.6
Green River city	14	116	102	848	2,348	6	100.0	23.9	15.9	44.7	182	21.2	1,758	341	0.2
Jackson town	NA	NA	NA	NA	18,815	56	41.1	41.2	28.0	39.5	195	29.0	2,734	751	1.3
Laramie city	32	98	395	1,215	12,935	69	76.8	52.4	30.6	62.6	163	51.4	1,583	544	23.5
Riverton city	26	235	332	2,998	809	4	100.0	20.4	13.7	59.5	141	18.0	1,645	348	3.2
Rock Springs city	43	184	314	1,342	15,905	57	100.0	47.1	24.5	59.2	159	52.6	2,257	389	9.8
Sheridan city	17	95	313	1,747	14,099	75	57.3	46.3	25.8	66.8	237	36.5	2,045	908	15.2

1 Data for serious crimes have not been adjusted for underreporting. This may affect comparability between geographic areas over time.
2 Per 100,000 population estimated by the FBI.   3 Based on population estimated as of July 1 of the year shown.

TABLE C.

Incorporated Places, Census Designated Places (CDPs), and Minor Civil Divisions (MCDs) of 10,000 or More Population— Economic Census

(For explanation of symbols see page xvi)

Table C. Incorporated Places, Census Designated Places (CDPs), and Minor Civil Divisions (MCDs) of 10,000 or More Population — Economic Census

STATE City, town, township, borough, or CDP (county if applicable)	Retail Trade Number of establish-ments	Number of employees	Wholesale trade[1] Number of establish-ments	Number of employees	Transportation and warehousing Number of establish-ments	Number of employees	Information Number of establish-ments	Number of employees	Finance and insurance Number of establish-ments	Number of employees	Real estate and rental and leasing Number of establish-ments	Number of employees	Professional, scientific, and technical services Number of establish-ments	Number of employees
	1	2	3	4	5	6	7	8	9	10	11	12	13	14
UNITED STATES............	1,064,087	15,938,821	352,065	5,156,359	237,095	4,954,931	153,928	3,565,063	475,780	6,499,871	410,820	2,194,885	913,624	9,015,366
ALABAMA......................	17,958	230,069	4,410	63,468	3,098	61,687	1,735	34,078	7,349	72,311	4,362	22,778	9,496	100,857
Alabaster city...............	96	2,013	42	981	D	D	13	187	D	D	20	79	62	455
Albertville city.............	125	1,386	25	566	20	281	9	155	59	378	25	435	42	206
Alexander City city.........	98	1,052	7	45	6	351	D	D	39	218	15	41	30	145
Anniston city...............	151	2,050	40	626	20	474	15	319	84	515	35	182	113	541
Athens city.................	148	1,980	19	306	D	D	20	615	78	357	39	100	72	514
Auburn city.................	211	3,609	37	477	19	338	20	615	86	690	86	344	158	820
Bessemer city..............	172	2,610	59	1,163	33	2,074	18	248	53	276	25	134	53	577
Birmingham city............	906	11,179	472	8,998	198	6,683	181	3,747	511	11,335	303	3,308	909	11,420
Calera city.................	48	767	13	413	18	274	D	D	D	D	9	34	10	60
Center Point city...........	43	521	D	D	4	5	NA	NA	16	73	D	D	6	27
Chelsea city................	39	659	8	45	4	16	D	D	13	48	NA	NA	28	127
Cullman city...............	204	2,978	31	548	26	1,258	D	D	91	709	41	156	79	327
Daphne city................	102	2,548	41	303	11	109	D	D	61	267	50	115	90	443
Decatur city................	D	D	78	1,316	43	840	20	283	137	1,205	69	297	133	1,716
Dothan city................	461	7,378	D	D	61	1,784	43	732	186	1,188	D	D	197	1,044
Enterprise city.............	164	2,150	9	197	D	D	D	D	64	332	31	144	52	728
Eufaula city................	74	799	D	D	D	D	D	D	D	D	12	29	26	79
Fairfield city...............	43	404	D	D	D	D	NA	NA	7	73	NA	NA	6	21
Fairhope city...............	118	1,504	17	96	9	54	7	57	66	409	45	142	87	297
Florence city...............	283	4,404	46	945	13	116	D	D	139	815	D	D	126	645
Foley city..................	235	3,278	17	87	6	62	20	117	62	325	32	130	34	189
Fort Payne city.............	112	1,429	19	351	16	445	D	D	48	217	12	40	46	218
Gadsden city...............	214	3,079	30	283	23	270	20	246	102	741	40	141	91	454
Gardendale city............	69	1,184	7	35	8	59	11	151	43	220	12	34	39	314
Gulf Shores city............	94	1,314	9	29	13	97	11	100	34	179	64	854	42	259
Hartselle city..............	70	895	8	65	D	D	7	16	28	196	12	27	24	482
Helena city................	19	322	7	53	D	D	5	18	13	56	D	D	D	D
Homewood city............	208	3,108	67	910	20	665	40	812	121	4,740	71	473	176	1,551
Hoover city................	398	7,989	80	706	24	147	61	3,774	278	5,840	119	559	326	2,571
Hueytown city.............	56	1,004	15	114	NA	NA	4	15	22	110	7	33	11	65
Huntsville city.............	952	15,387	210	3,744	113	2,347	124	4,640	379	3,287	321	1,509	1,146	33,606
Irondale city...............	34	666	56	1,053	16	332	D	D	22	191	17	121	29	290
Jacksonville city...........	41	642	3	18	D	D	5	31	19	95	7	22	13	27
Jasper city.................	143	1,799	18	174	D	D	D	D	61	346	30	154	58	362
Leeds city.................	91	1,594	14	156	5	40	NA	NA	20	88	D	D	20	56
Madison city...............	137	2,050	48	776	29	1,255	20	120	69	482	57	247	130	1,793
Millbrook city..............	46	706	D	D	D	D	D	D	24	142	15	38	20	106
Mobile city................	987	15,065	355	4,062	198	4,323	115	3,334	501	5,631	319	1,869	707	8,917
Montgomery city...........	869	12,352	250	4,664	137	3,774	D	D	385	4,329	248	1,556	580	5,887
Moody city................	32	350	16	674	5	15	D	D	17	73	9	23	18	271
Mountain Brook city........	101	847	16	103	3	23	9	49	88	646	61	359	124	478
Muscle Shoals city.........	104	1,740	32	330	14	230	D	D	61	465	16	67	17	87
Northport city.............	141	2,115	23	386	14	45	D	D	62	318	28	271	60	423
Opelika city................	199	3,063	36	500	30	1,789	D	D	84	429	44	216	80	421
Oxford city................	151	2,865	22	401	28	422	8	106	52	271	15	51	20	97
Ozark city.................	76	909	8	92	D	D	D	D	31	140	12	31	23	73
Pelham city................	183	2,498	133	1,680	21	427	D	D	D	D	58	349	101	1,044
Pell City city..............	80	1,291	D	D	8	69	D	D	39	307	14	36	44	150
Phenix City city...........	115	1,691	9	59	19	99	D	D	D	D	D	D	45	174
Prattville city..............	156	2,930	D	D	D	D	D	D	D	D	46	124	46	257
Prichard city...............	51	443	9	385	19	473	NA	NA	5	18	11	115	NA	NA
Saks CDP..................	15	152	NA	NA	NA	NA	NA	NA	4	13	7	11	NA	NA
Saraland city..............	73	1,102	12	210	13	384	6	31	49	210	9	45	26	187
Scottsboro city............	112	1,465	D	D	7	33	D	D	41	233	23	61	46	165
Selma city.................	101	1,109	12	91	D	D	D	D	45	283	19	69	41	163
Sylacauga city.............	83	1,104	10	143	10	302	9	42	39	256	15	53	17	53
Talladega city..............	86	948	11	94	D	D	6	76	30	180	13	45	17	77
Tillmans Corner CDP	31	326	5	23	8	79	NA	NA	D	D	D	D	12	42
Troy city..................	103	1,424	17	318	D	D	D	D	49	314	29	57	27	422
Trussville city.............	127	1,810	31	208	18	143	D	D	52	237	29	80	65	292
Tuscaloosa city............	470	7,117	84	873	56	1,316	41	612	176	1,449	143	1,386	D	D
Vestavia Hills city..........	145	2,084	34	178	7	115	20	934	137	1,617	88	466	D	D
ALASKA......................	2,480	34,498	643	7,529	1,177	18,923	416	6,553	784	7,279	965	4,622	1,959	17,869
Anchorage municipality	849	15,445	338	5,162	324	10,413	179	4,381	412	4,918	437	2,519	1,188	14,219
Badger CDP................	15	87	4	6	22	107	NA	NA	NA	NA	9	9	15	34
College CDP...............	31	259	NA	NA	12	109	D	D	8	45	20	58	28	121
Fairbanks city..............	195	3,783	44	492	41	970	27	446	84	632	92	537	116	984
Juneau city and borough ..	148	1,790	33	278	69	855	27	250	49	330	64	195	91	471
Knik-Fairview CDP.........	4	7	D	D	7	47	NA	NA	NA	NA	6	11	8	30
Lakes CDP.................	15	87	NA	NA	D	D	NA	NA	8	30	7	61	9	38
Tanaina CDP	NA	NA	NA	NA	D	D	NA	NA	NA	NA	NA	NA	5	6
Wasilla city................	125	2,681	13	69	18	95	D	D	37	307	34	126	44	209
ARIZONA.....................	17,918	324,912	5,508	79,541	3,415	92,227	2,521	55,357	9,602	161,152	9,937	48,305	18,100	146,970
Anthem CDP...............	25	666	8	70	6	49	8	97	35	134	D	D	63	167
Apache Junction city.......	102	1,835	13	116	D	D	D	D	25	121	38	130	20	54
Arizona City CDP...........	7	36	NA	NA	NA	NA	NA	NA	NA	NA	6	8	NA	NA
Avondale city..............	120	4,077	12	208	36	245	13	392	50	198	50	149	68	357
Buckeye city...............	65	1,422	17	150	35	1,734	6	30	28	131	41	100	63	165
Bullhead City city..........	109	2,192	11	75	13	167	D	D	44	199	62	268	39	198
Camp Verde town	39	461	6	42	12	120	NA	NA	9	36	14	21	16	50
Casa Grande city...........	182	3,417	25	451	28	1,210	16	266	67	487	53	246	52	249
Casas Adobes CDP........	147	2,300	22	81	16	75	17	188	132	858	D	D	196	1,257
Catalina Foothills CDP	125	1,617	20	54	12	77	15	600	127	809	187	714	245	1,687
Chandler city...............	760	15,938	273	4,128	107	2,521	103	5,028	434	11,458	459	1,494	801	13,130

1 Merchant wholesalers, except manufacturers' sales branches and offices.

Table C. Incorporated Places, Census Designated Places (CDPs), and Minor Civil Divisions (MCDs) of 10,000 or More Population — **Economic Census**

	Economic activity by sector, 2017											
	Administration and support and waste management and mediation services		Educational services		Health care and social assistance		Arts, entertainment, and recreation		Accommodation and food services		Other services (except public administration)	
STATE City, town, township, borough, or CDP (county if applicable)	Number of establish-ments	Number of employees	Number of establish-ments	Number of employees	Number of establish-ments	Number of employees	Number of establish-ments	Number of employees	Number of establish-ments	Number of employees	Number of establish-ments	Number of employees
	15	16	17	18	19	20	21	22	23	24	25	26
UNITED STATES............	417,259	11,889,169	77,334	722,823	892,245	20,506,502	142,938	2,390,279	726,081	14,002,624	560,845	3,696,831
ALABAMA....................	4,436	143,954	604	5,287	10,636	258,399	1,168	17,939	9,085	183,590	6,149	38,476
Alabaster city...................	41	571	4	7	82	2,649	11	261	54	1,373	D	D
Albertville city.................	16	1,243	3	D	59	968	4	22	36	654	17	78
Alexander City city...........	17	1,800	NA	NA	61	1,678	NA	NA	44	638	33	186
Anniston city..................	30	840	D	D	167	4,547	8	42	66	1,299	74	333
Athens city....................	23	275	3	16	98	1,980	D	D	77	1,784	48	271
Auburn city....................	77	1,118	17	180	132	1,631	15	256	226	4,598	95	501
Bessemer city.................	23	551	NA	NA	87	2,594	8	103	91	1,807	50	547
Birmingham city..............	341	19,061	39	342	730	40,064	83	1,873	608	13,704	407	4,323
Calera city.....................	8	21	3	D	26	198	5	57	25	556	12	39
Center Point city..............	D	D	NA	NA	19	517	NA	NA	17	384	D	D
Chelsea city...................	11	34	NA	NA	29	215	3	21	24	367	D	D
Cullman city...................	19	618	D	D	141	3,594	8	82	106	2,006	D	D
Daphne city....................	40	266	10	78	92	1,580	D	D	77	1,650	58	325
Decatur city...................	78	3,334	11	85	285	4,439	21	264	149	3,322	D	D
Dothan city....................	99	4,078	D	D	312	9,741	D	D	239	5,102	174	888
Enterprise city................	17	320	D	D	87	1,547	D	D	91	1,560	D	D
Eufaula city....................	5	136	NA	NA	33	556	3	7	49	611	16	74
Fairfield city...................	5	130	NA	NA	D	D	D	D	19	207	7	34
Fairhope city..................	31	221	5	16	120	2,435	D	D	83	1,881	52	296
Florence city..................	D	D	D	D	208	4,768	16	250	136	3,898	D	D
Foley city......................	25	306	4	32	100	1,857	7	324	87	1,753	38	241
Fort Payne city...............	24	751	NA	NA	69	1,323	D	D	51	1,062	29	98
Gadsden city..................	34	1,188	NA	NA	211	5,388	8	168	115	2,641	D	D
Gardendale city..............	15	138	NA	NA	47	940	4	29	D	D	D	D
Gulf Shores city..............	31	324	5	17	D	D	18	242	91	2,245	38	131
Hartselle city..................	10	90	NA	NA	39	394	NA	NA	39	611	30	116
Helena city....................	21	124	4	13	24	166	D	D	20	284	D	D
Homewood city...............	72	3,831	14	133	208	6,546	13	160	139	2,629	84	1,625
Hoover city....................	122	3,323	28	211	258	3,618	33	683	220	5,140	115	640
Hueytown city.................	12	216	NA	NA	18	213	NA	NA	33	477	31	171
Huntsville city.................	279	11,295	57	1,492	773	21,639	88	1,943	580	13,530	336	3,146
Irondale city...................	34	450	NA	NA	16	176	D	D	19	220	19	105
Jacksonville city..............	4	18	NA	NA	26	728	NA	NA	D	D	D	D
Jasper city....................	14	121	NA	NA	121	2,760	4	D	57	1,103	D	D
Leeds city.....................	11	79	NA	NA	16	176	6	20	36	711	D	D
Madison city..................	50	2,443	15	234	147	2,469	14	242	120	2,157	57	511
Millbrook city.................	6	10	NA	NA	26	352	NA	NA	D	D	D	D
Mobile city....................	302	17,830	42	249	627	18,940	73	1,465	510	11,756	381	3,075
Montgomery city..............	258	9,743	D	D	649	18,128	53	1,283	492	11,361	412	2,611
Moody city....................	12	218	NA	NA	D	D	NA	NA	16	315	21	111
Mountain Brook city.........	25	133	7	59	82	907	15	723	70	1,567	56	275
Muscle Shoals city...........	14	2,243	NA	NA	51	1,109	7	24	54	1,204	D	D
Northport city.................	33	1,155	8	78	99	3,141	D	D	75	1,468	D	D
Opelika city...................	D	D	D	D	102	5,116	D	D	112	2,796	D	D
Oxford city....................	25	568	NA	NA	51	726	5	39	93	2,186	D	D
Ozark city.....................	8	34	D	D	37	982	D	D	D	D	23	102
Pelham city...................	72	3,259	7	58	67	716	12	234	74	1,482	84	597
Pell City city..................	19	1,057	D	D	44	1,239	D	D	43	922	24	109
Phenix City city..............	D	D	NA	NA	62	1,407	6	36	78	1,429	50	248
Prattville city.................	D	D	D	D	86	1,447	D	D	D	D	D	D
Prichard city..................	12	86	NA	NA	27	439	NA	NA	13	192	D	D
Saks CDP......................	D	D	NA	NA	D	D	NA	NA	4	22	9	48
Saraland city..................	17	898	NA	NA	D	D	NA	NA	43	831	27	186
Scottsboro city...............	16	204	NA	NA	82	1,291	D	D	54	1,033	D	D
Selma city.....................	9	551	NA	NA	84	1,528	6	41	40	639	D	D
Sylacauga city................	D	D	NA	NA	D	D	NA	NA	D	D	19	116
Talladega city.................	13	1,824	NA	NA	39	1,038	D	D	33	571	16	47
Tillmans Corner CDP	13	71	3	41	6	77	D	D	9	179	10	84
Troy city.......................	D	D	3	16	D	D	D	D	D	D	29	126
Trussville city.................	D	D	6	63	62	841	10	239	63	1,645	52	281
Tuscaloosa city...............	102	3,140	13	111	303	9,957	35	388	332	8,245	144	1,117
Vestavia Hills city............	51	2,443	15	102	156	2,826	21	758	83	1,836	66	381
ALASKA......................	1,176	18,886	212	1,669	2,679	52,125	575	5,433	2,214	28,853	1,357	7,271
Anchorage municipality	574	14,499	98	882	1,291	27,333	158	2,795	798	15,618	571	3,928
Badger CDP...................	11	101	D	D	10	82	3	12	6	57	D	D
College CDP..................	19	152	D	D	47	339	6	17	27	384	D	D
Fairbanks city.................	61	671	17	198	216	5,826	47	508	155	2,470	110	568
Juneau city and borough ..	61	462	14	119	133	2,288	38	593	124	1,390	76	393
Knik-Fairview CDP...........	8	18	NA	NA	13	59	D	D	6	38	3	14
Lakes CDP....................	18	276	NA	NA	31	221	7	68	6	26	9	17
Tanaina CDP..................	12	46	NA	NA	13	348	NA	NA	3	5	3	14
Wasilla city....................	28	279	5	92	132	1,921	D	D	83	1,173	56	251
ARIZONA.....................	8,663	263,739	1,463	15,105	18,816	379,015	2,041	47,060	13,079	299,628	9,271	68,350
Anthem CDP..................	28	81	D	D	49	389	8	243	31	518	20	321
Apache Junction city........	30	247	NA	NA	76	990	9	140	48	869	43	217
Arizona City CDP............	5	37	NA	NA	8	102	NA	NA	D	D	4	13
Avondale city.................	42	209	14	318	124	1,519	10	D	113	2,255	72	453
Buckeye city..................	37	134	D	D	38	385	9	154	49	1,101	21	84
Bullhead City city............	31	284	NA	NA	120	1,774	7	49	89	1,286	50	270
Camp Verde town	15	76	3	D	23	356	3	74	30	858	19	66
Casa Grande city............	42	858	5	25	188	3,444	10	113	102	2,531	71	436
Casas Adobes CDP..........	108	724	19	99	368	7,282	30	379	106	2,574	92	432
Catalina Foothills CDP	52	335	28	357	174	2,601	23	671	73	3,933	72	576
Chandler city..................	329	30,159	106	1,518	839	14,927	89	1,974	556	14,304	356	2,389

Table C. Incorporated Places, Census Designated Places (CDPs), and Minor Civil Divisions (MCDs) of 10,000 or More Population — **Economic Census**

STATE City, town, township, borough, or CDP (county if applicable)	Retail Trade Number of establishments	Retail Trade Number of employees	Wholesale trade[1] Number of establishments	Wholesale trade[1] Number of employees	Transportation and warehousing Number of establishments	Transportation and warehousing Number of employees	Information Number of establishments	Information Number of employees	Finance and insurance Number of establishments	Finance and insurance Number of employees	Real estate and rental and leasing Number of establishments	Real estate and rental and leasing Number of employees	Professional, scientific, and technical services Number of establishments	Professional, scientific, and technical services Number of employees
	1	2	3	4	5	6	7	8	9	10	11	12	13	14
ARIZONA—Con.														
Chino Valley town	36	388	3	D	10	67	NA	NA	13	43	19	32	18	90
Coolidge city	29	552	6	202	NA	NA	D	D	8	34	7	18	6	20
Cottonwood city	88	1,341	9	26	5	87	11	152	34	142	31	112	47	172
Douglas city	56	811	D	D	11	133	6	12	D	D	11	25	D	D
Drexel Heights CDP	29	416	NA	NA	3	2	NA	NA	D	D	D	D	6	20
El Mirage city	31	548	4	40	11	103	NA	NA	7	19	16	55	10	47
Eloy city	23	257	4	D	D	D	NA	NA	NA	NA	D	D	D	D
Flagstaff city	328	5,763	74	682	51	530	31	780	127	778	160	657	273	1,419
Florence town	12	172	NA	NA	NA	NA	NA	NA	8	40	7	35	15	29
Flowing Wells CDP	39	334	15	204	13	378	D	D	D	D	13	56	25	208
Fort Mohave CDP	45	465	6	30	D	D	NA	NA	10	46	11	22	13	89
Fortuna Foothills CDP	37	268	5	8	3	9	NA	NA	14	50	9	31	8	28
Fountain Hills town	74	908	18	59	7	10	11	109	47	184	57	84	D	D
Gilbert town	526	11,863	160	1,175	73	579	80	1,121	353	2,214	491	1,220	739	4,785
Glendale city	673	14,394	122	1,462	86	934	66	501	289	2,087	239	1,017	339	2,031
Gold Canyon CDP	10	148	9	25	NA	NA	NA	NA	18	58	9	49	18	56
Goodyear city	149	4,398	30	559	32	1,729	12	219	79	374	98	1,004	134	504
Green Valley CDP	40	561	4	5	NA	NA	4	27	D	D	24	296	34	238
Kingman city	137	2,654	17	318	29	517	15	150	51	268	34	94	51	269
Lake Havasu City city	236	3,146	45	546	22	165	25	283	71	419	113	318	96	308
Marana town	179	3,671	29	244	21	225	14	259	D	D	45	154	78	221
Maricopa city	34	926	6	15	11	24	10	72	29	105	19	34	48	207
Mesa city	1,283	23,696	334	4,852	158	3,455	134	1,967	675	5,055	669	2,481	1,168	6,599
New Kingman-Butler CDP	10	48	4	19	NA	NA	NA	NA	NA	NA	NA	NA	4	13
New River CDP	15	62	14	27	8	20	5	16	4	D	9	10	42	105
Nogales city	136	1,905	92	625	121	1,305	D	D	29	171	31	92	34	135
Oro Valley town	87	2,182	24	93	12	33	7	121	80	314	77	131	144	397
Paradise Valley town	11	38	11	23	NA	NA	5	8	30	51	69	185	92	229
Payson town	74	1,040	7	69	D	D	9	66	30	113	38	80	44	155
Peoria city	400	10,761	63	413	57	405	28	560	225	1,338	212	688	306	871
Phoenix city	3,753	73,994	1,823	36,641	937	48,292	737	17,558	2,661	72,545	2,336	16,218	5,288	53,825
Prescott city	271	4,206	54	685	27	228	32	249	136	541	159	349	229	845
Prescott Valley town	106	1,920	27	462	29	266	14	232	44	193	43	111	62	350
Queen Creek town	81	1,257	14	18	10	66	11	69	32	111	55	101	98	225
Rio Rico CDP	11	108	D	D	41	393	NA	NA	4	22	4	7	11	31
Saddlebrooke CDP	D	D	NA	NA	NA	NA	NA	NA	5	11	NA	NA	10	7
Sahuarita town	31	918	9	40	D	D	8	51	D	D	18	23	11	31
San Luis city	33	653	D	D	16	106	NA	NA	7	18	D	D	10	36
San Tan Valley CDP	30	935	D	D	16	36	5	11	D	D	30	30	54	130
Scottsdale city	1,358	21,051	481	4,119	137	1,799	275	5,787	1,257	17,524	1,223	6,842	2,332	17,664
Sedona city	180	1,176	10	65	14	376	17	127	36	137	50	270	82	212
Show Low city	92	1,675	15	135	14	121	12	327	23	103	32	85	31	110
Sierra Vista city	148	2,714	9	67	13	150	16	197	54	304	56	283	97	1,507
Sierra Vista Southeast CDP	20	172	3	5	D	D	NA	NA	NA	NA	D	D	10	38
Somerton city	33	344	NA	NA	5	16	NA	NA	5	32	4	14	D	D
Sun City CDP	74	987	5	10	4	14	D	D	64	339	31	284	54	272
Sun City West CDP	31	635	4	6	NA	NA	D	D	39	177	15	48	22	80
Sun Lakes CDP	16	261	6	11	NA	NA	NA	NA	19	71	17	32	25	58
Surprise city	200	5,435	20	504	32	283	24	287	108	495	89	221	D	D
Tanque Verde CDP	13	50	5	9	NA	NA	4	4	D	D	24	42	68	135
Tempe city	771	16,650	379	6,993	140	4,539	181	6,917	434	26,082	469	2,844	D	D
Tucson city	1,812	32,262	410	4,469	189	5,881	231	5,757	723	7,754	739	3,980	1,574	12,594
Tucson Estates CDP	6	43	NA	NA	6	66	NA	NA	D	D	3	D	NA	NA
Vail CDP	7	46	NA	NA	D	D	NA	NA	NA	NA	5	11	10	27
Valencia West CDP	5	27	NA	NA	4	17	NA	NA	NA	NA	NA	NA	D	D
Verde Village CDP	4	22	D	D	D	D	NA	NA	3	2	5	9	8	7
Yuma city	313	6,228	74	1,287	79	869	D	D	119	1,084	145	612	170	786
ARKANSAS	10,925	142,857	2,812	36,528	2,456	51,508	1,152	20,864	4,448	38,275	3,115	12,776	5,914	38,088
Arkadelphia city	65	1,112	D	D	NA	NA	D	D	D	D	D	D	29	200
Batesville city	96	1,352	15	153	10	198	10	97	41	405	15	74	44	150
Bella Vista city	26	386	12	49	D	D	8	20	D	D	22	94	38	97
Benton city	145	2,224	26	187	18	165	D	D	60	269	35	117	69	385
Bentonville city	141	3,347	97	1,137	44	3,007	58	1,146	D	D	88	358	264	4,158
Blytheville city	77	1,093	26	268	25	332	D	D	21	139	18	97	17	63
Bryant city	92	1,448	D	D	12	28	D	D	D	D	31	105	47	285
Cabot city	85	1,239	13	82	10	115	D	D	50	290	28	95	49	270
Camden city	77	821	14	80	8	66	D	D	30	175	D	D	D	D
Centerton city	16	266	NA	NA	D	D	NA	NA	D	D	9	14	14	49
Conway city	296	5,085	52	595	32	539	D	D	137	936	115	486	184	717
El Dorado city	133	1,740	28	189	16	229	D	D	D	D	D	D	54	212
Fayetteville city	428	7,523	64	761	42	428	53	982	170	1,356	180	667	413	2,501
Forrest City city	70	789	11	344	D	D	11	91	23	179	19	124	D	D
Fort Smith city	515	7,673	165	2,568	84	1,558	47	943	188	1,460	143	1,137	D	D
Harrison city	128	1,794	18	163	19	968	D	D	54	846	35	98	39	195
Helena-West Helena city	48	352	11	185	9	71	D	D	D	D	10	35	20	63
Hot Springs city	354	4,926	42	317	21	147	28	468	138	893	72	375	148	798
Hot Springs Village CDP	23	328	D	D	6	29	6	29	D	D	18	29	22	54
Jacksonville city	93	1,375	14	136	7	25	D	D	33	491	43	194	41	335
Jonesboro city	408	6,221	91	1,129	73	1,239	D	D	144	1,145	117	483	183	1,321
Little Rock city	1,065	15,813	376	7,115	147	4,599	210	8,603	760	12,079	432	2,196	1,245	9,394
Magnolia city	74	543	19	105	10	101	D	D	33	236	D	D	D	D
Malvern city	59	693	D	D	8	145	D	D	D	D	D	D	20	55
Marion city	24	278	11	85	D	D	NA	NA	15	64	D	D	D	D
Maumelle city	23	733	15	440	11	299	9	147	D	D	24	73	49	117
Mountain Home city	129	1,746	D	D	6	29	D	D	59	514	24	194	52	362
North Little Rock city	396	6,015	162	3,705	72	3,009	33	425	128	748	109	495	D	D
Paragould city	126	1,785	20	176	D	D	9	93	44	392	31	70	48	336

1   Merchant wholesalers, except manufacturers' sales branches and offices.

STATE City, town, township, borough, or CDP (county if applicable)	Administration and support and waste management and mediation services		Educational services		Health care and social assistance		Arts, entertainment, and recreation		Accommodation and food services		Other services (except public administration)	
	Number of establishments	Number of employees	Number of establishments	Number of employees	Number of establishments	Number of employees	Number of establishments	Number of employees	Number of establishments	Number of employees	Number of establishments	Number of employees
	15	16	17	18	19	20	21	22	23	24	25	26
ARKANSAS—Con.												
Chino Valley town	9	58	NA	NA	22	155	NA	NA	27	346	14	32
Coolidge city	9	90	NA	NA	20	491	NA	NA	15	235	10	51
Cottonwood city	14	116	NA	NA	94	2,200	3	46	61	772	34	177
Douglas city	D	D	NA	NA	21	369	NA	NA	30	323	D	D
Drexel Heights CDP	9	16	NA	NA	10	88	NA	NA	13	224	D	D
El Mirage city	24	295	NA	NA	10	88	NA	NA	12	183	D	D
Eloy city	D	D	NA	NA	8	221	NA	NA	14	214	10	152
Flagstaff city	113	1,183	23	122	346	6,592	56	874	329	7,249	166	932
Florence town	9	1,972	NA	NA	24	601	D	D	18	311	D	D
Flowing Wells CDP	36	1,903	NA	NA	14	201	6	54	6	119	22	129
Fort Mohave CDP	10	51	NA	NA	26	449	NA	NA	24	259	14	40
Fortuna Foothills CDP	9	12	NA	NA	15	188	D	D	28	339	D	D
Fountain Hills town	45	199	D	D	60	700	D	D	55	732	46	225
Gilbert town	368	4,828	62	759	827	11,909	69	1,767	420	9,804	332	1,816
Glendale city	245	5,037	31	228	713	14,020	52	2,386	420	9,413	285	1,476
Gold Canyon CDP	6	27	NA	NA	16	115	6	258	D	D	D	D
Goodyear city	77	988	19	210	176	5,066	16	553	138	4,035	66	384
Green Valley CDP	20	85	NA	NA	67	1,976	D	D	22	431	34	143
Kingman city	37	592	D	D	126	3,496	7	42	105	1,927	51	331
Lake Havasu City city	98	578	NA	NA	191	2,571	15	210	139	2,824	147	598
Marana town	59	560	12	21	69	1,220	19	370	116	2,646	D	D
Maricopa city	20	49	NA	NA	45	475	5	D	41	726	D	D
Mesa city	600	22,146	96	1,102	1,432	31,274	113	2,023	841	17,855	631	4,133
New Kingman-Butler CDP	3	18	NA	NA	D	D	NA	NA	4	22	D	D
New River CDP	30	95	NA	NA	10	42	5	37	5	96	21	36
Nogales city	D	D	D	D	60	1,682	D	D	55	771	31	124
Oro Valley town	56	428	12	58	149	2,038	20	415	74	1,916	58	526
Paradise Valley town	17	57	10	20	111	725	13	290	13	2,062	16	140
Payson town	17	58	NA	NA	84	1,114	D	D	53	783	31	114
Peoria city	197	2,599	49	408	501	7,793	39	702	293	7,172	232	1,393
Phoenix city	2,430	105,547	347	3,355	4,267	107,483	416	10,741	2,958	69,330	2,204	20,997
Prescott city	93	552	18	99	365	7,049	26	472	176	2,921	130	620
Prescott Valley town	67	830	D	D	139	2,746	9	203	76	1,329	82	350
Queen Creek town	D	D	6	32	89	587	D	D	48	1,114	41	180
Rio Rico CDP	D	D	NA	NA	D	D	NA	NA	10	88	7	16
Saddlebrooke CDP	NA	NA	NA	NA	NA	NA	NA	NA	NA	NA	D	D
Sahuarita town	19	66	NA	NA	23	111	NA	NA	28	527	20	139
San Luis city	8	1,143	NA	NA	27	388	NA	NA	15	178	D	D
San Tan Valley CDP	46	165	3	22	51	467	6	51	37	650	D	D
Scottsdale city	666	17,295	181	2,387	1,726	25,334	220	5,835	886	26,231	743	6,676
Sedona city	31	307	12	31	D	D	21	194	105	2,561	52	290
Show Low city	21	174	NA	NA	102	1,810	4	96	49	761	26	163
Sierra Vista city	41	687	D	D	167	2,918	D	D	97	1,783	67	338
Sierra Vista Southeast CDP	12	43	4	28	13	65	D	D	11	79	D	D
Somerton city	6	32	NA	NA	13	338	D	D	D	D	6	23
Sun City CDP	14	72	5	18	130	4,082	18	455	31	480	40	290
Sun City West CDP	10	81	NA	NA	112	3,279	NA	NA	12	171	D	D
Sun Lakes CDP	7	8	NA	NA	D	D	D	D	8	114	7	311
Surprise city	103	663	8	69	256	3,111	14	452	178	4,625	101	964
Tanque Verde CDP	17	47	5	25	D	D	6	154	D	D	10	36
Tempe city	457	19,770	64	907	633	11,539	82	1,551	633	14,895	378	3,909
Tucson city	652	20,336	149	1,104	1,822	44,082	165	2,921	1,271	27,909	935	6,299
Tucson Estates CDP	6	19	NA	NA	4	24	NA	NA	8	118	7	55
Vail CDP	6	7	NA	NA	4	39	D	D	5	169	D	D
Valencia West CDP	NA	NA	NA	NA	NA	NA	NA	NA	NA	NA	3	16
Verde Village CDP	15	40	NA	NA	6	27	NA	NA	NA	NA	7	7
Yuma city	103	2,821	8	67	328	7,066	D	D	244	5,753	152	819
ARKANSAS	2,794	65,017	422	2,361	7,878	182,126	787	9,919	5,977	106,280	3,910	21,132
Arkadelphia city	8	104	3	27	44	997	D	D	D	D	20	73
Batesville city	19	1,275	NA	NA	83	3,313	D	D	44	978	38	215
Bella Vista city	19	109	4	10	29	435	6	73	22	282	22	206
Benton city	25	529	6	62	114	2,776	D	D	73	1,281	D	D
Bentonville city	110	2,053	18	116	156	2,936	20	579	159	3,352	D	D
Blytheville city	13	207	NA	NA	62	1,045	D	D	48	776	25	118
Bryant city	14	157	4	9	72	962	5	19	64	1,418	D	D
Cabot city	17	203	D	D	68	830	D	D	57	1,085	31	153
Camden city	8	121	NA	NA	49	1,566	D	D	31	486	D	D
Centerton city	8	28	NA	NA	9	62	NA	NA	9	142	4	9
Conway city	66	1,604	D	D	253	5,012	16	224	180	3,851	106	566
El Dorado city	D	D	4	36	109	2,156	D	D	67	1,023	D	D
Fayetteville city	105	1,968	23	173	375	9,954	48	700	367	7,796	164	874
Forrest City city	D	D	NA	NA	D	D	NA	NA	D	D	D	D
Fort Smith city	131	6,071	17	D	374	10,671	28	288	273	5,742	D	D
Harrison city	16	498	NA	NA	107	2,457	D	D	56	883	36	173
Helena-West Helena city	3	5	NA	NA	43	629	D	D	D	D	D	D
Hot Springs city	53	1,851	13	D	256	7,527	37	1,445	218	4,441	115	520
Hot Springs Village CDP	8	233	NA	NA	22	619	6	78	D	D	D	D
Jacksonville city	14	70	5	30	61	1,765	4	35	58	835	31	125
Jonesboro city	84	4,882	D	D	325	9,650	20	354	D	D	113	724
Little Rock city	453	10,252	79	535	1,049	37,064	92	1,681	660	13,362	501	3,692
Magnolia city	D	D	3	D	57	1,119	3	D	D	D	24	83
Malvern city	D	D	D	D	42	1,072	D	D	30	546	17	78
Marion city	7	109	NA	NA	29	D	3	D	D	D	D	D
Maumelle city	15	57	NA	NA	47	488	D	D	36	816	D	D
Mountain Home city	14	107	NA	NA	141	3,905	D	D	69	1,149	47	267
North Little Rock city	92	4,454	20	207	245	5,693	D	D	237	4,761	147	908
Paragould city	21	4,001	D	D	94	1,840	D	D	D	D	32	146

Table C. Incorporated Places, Census Designated Places (CDPs), and Minor Civil Divisions (MCDs) of 10,000 or More Population — **Economic Census**

STATE City, town, township, borough, or CDP (county if applicable)	Retail Trade Number of establishments	Number of employees	Wholesale trade[1] Number of establishments	Number of employees	Transportation and warehousing Number of establishments	Number of employees	Information Number of establishments	Number of employees	Finance and insurance Number of establishments	Number of employees	Real estate and rental and leasing Number of establishments	Number of employees	Professional, scientific, and technical services Number of establishments	Number of employees
	1	2	3	4	5	6	7	8	9	10	11	12	13	14
ARKANSAS—Con.														
Pine Bluff city...............	233	2,714	39	319	16	179	D	D	D	D	49	173	D	D
Rogers city.................	341	6,215	50	702	41	728	31	639	D	D	98	410	238	2,763
Russellville city............	215	2,860	43	507	22	693	D	D	86	803	67	175	121	701
Searcy city.................	186	2,591	29	277	31	1,537	18	167	70	498	44	129	63	342
Sherwood city...............	99	1,817	30	275	10	25	D	D	39	1,126	43	126	39	163
Siloam Springs city.........	84	1,341	14	82	D	D	10	235	D	D	22	72	39	171
Springdale city.............	268	4,261	133	1,486	82	3,038	25	340	108	853	71	290	149	988
Texarkana city..............	120	1,253	D	D	D	D	D	D	D	D	38	147	D	D
Van Buren city..............	75	1,081	41	556	27	2,994	9	74	D	D	25	136	48	172
West Memphis city	99	1,597	31	868	50	1,763	D	D	21	138	31	173	31	154
CALIFORNIA................	108,233	1,723,278	52,861	735,916	24,817	545,870	25,103	678,261	50,972	650,176	57,434	314,273	127,023	1,241,452
Adelanto city...............	18	222	5	102	D	D	D	D	8	50	9	15	4	79
Agoura Hills city............	100	1,060	60	592	10	58	68	558	104	1,281	71	555	254	2,353
Alameda city...............	180	2,415	60	1,746	31	261	40	599	D	D	90	349	248	2,483
Alamo CDP.................	29	446	D	D	NA	NA	D	D	40	499	D	D	83	277
Albany city.................	52	680	14	77	NA	NA	D	D	D	D	D	D	69	235
Alhambra city..............	251	4,511	255	977	97	376	29	297	117	1,011	140	469	281	1,058
Aliso Viejo city.............	72	1,546	74	687	D	D	46	800	119	2,887	86	1,883	307	4,789
Alpine CDP.................	32	251	3	3	D	D	D	D	D	D	D	D	36	109
Altadena CDP...............	53	520	17	34	15	58	34	66	21	93	35	60	130	587
Alum Rock CDP.............	D	D	NA	NA	NA	NA	NA	NA	NA	NA	NA	NA	5	14
American Canyon city......	26	739	13	259	28	411	D	D	D	D	15	76	15	40
Anaheim city...............	841	12,856	792	10,365	167	4,628	123	2,034	342	5,295	446	3,853	D	D
Anderson city..............	53	780	D	D	D	D	D	D	17	92	9	27	10	53
Antelope CDP...............	35	1,411	D	D	50	132	7	108	21	52	20	61	18	48
Antioch city................	222	4,012	27	491	33	422	D	D	62	336	65	395	90	529
Apple Valley town...........	118	2,452	18	108	29	1,423	9	143	42	360	44	137	77	301
Arcadia city................	298	5,034	309	1,348	62	631	34	197	193	1,093	275	890	314	1,023
Arcata city.................	104	1,035	16	195	12	125	5	19	23	143	19	60	55	720
Arden-Arcade CDP..........	366	6,011	29	114	18	38	48	1,592	172	1,574	205	1,142	352	1,914
Arroyo Grande city..........	78	1,192	8	21	5	55	7	85	54	301	D	D	62	213
Artesia city................	87	781	33	123	7	36	NA	NA	36	162	25	69	35	103
Arvin city..................	69	903	D	D	D	D	NA	NA	4	19	D	D	5	21
Ashland CDP...............	42	423	NA	NA	12	50	NA	NA	9	19	26	39	7	32
Atascadero city............	117	1,224	23	128	8	59	13	93	53	231	D	D	75	285
Atwater city...............	70	1,253	6	76	3	5	3	33	33	144	12	37	11	64
Auburn city................	88	787	22	259	11	229	20	269	52	243	41	151	D	D
Avenal city................	13	81	NA	NA	NA	NA	NA	NA	NA	NA	5	16	NA	NA
Avocado Heights CDP	66	318	137	769	20	154	NA	NA	3	D	12	33	9	44
Azusa city.................	101	1,378	90	1,064	D	D	D	D	21	96	30	65	42	422
Bakersfield city	989	20,027	283	3,708	258	9,901	108	2,638	435	4,974	377	2,017	790	5,270
Baldwin Park city...........	133	2,330	147	829	72	1,008	D	D	30	159	23	75	40	196
Banning city...............	61	757	10	247	10	67	5	27	18	90	25	89	14	122
Barstow city...............	127	2,257	8	51	10	175	6	25	18	90	32	204	21	644
Bay Point CDP.............	21	169	NA	NA	D	D	3	3	NA	NA	9	102	10	62
Beaumont city..............	78	1,574	8	30	16	69	D	D	19	101	28	93	33	77
Bell city...................	59	566	82	1,874	23	202	NA	NA	24	167	D	D	26	244
Bellflower city..............	183	1,962	35	240	36	538	12	219	47	182	71	286	63	218
Bell Gardens city...........	74	1,153	41	617	19	57	D	D	18	69	D	D	9	128
Belmont city...............	50	782	17	61	D	D	10	1,370	D	D	39	D	102	429
Benicia city................	64	1,129	61	1,149	37	930	D	D	37	161	44	180	111	964
Berkeley city...............	483	6,425	108	1,225	18	151	154	1,696	D	D	216	904	663	4,639
Beverly Hills city...........	485	6,976	133	929	23	124	341	16,139	286	3,415	604	3,494	1,053	6,182
Big Bear City CDP..........	24	100	D	D	NA	NA	4	24	NA	NA	11	49	11	22
Bloomington CDP...........	36	223	11	70	37	1,136	NA	NA	D	D	6	28	7	12
Blythe city.................	45	591	5	61	11	70	8	27	12	41	12	35	10	71
Bonita CDP................	13	37	14	44	NA	NA	NA	NA	D	D	D	D	40	101
Bostonia CDP..............	34	212	18	91	5	34	NA	NA	5	27	17	67	7	33
Brawley city...............	51	784	19	203	12	94	D	D	22	119	31	109	D	D
Brea city..................	315	5,969	327	5,016	52	1,365	45	880	159	7,871	131	633	312	2,532
Brentwood city.............	155	2,722	13	62	17	42	D	D	68	373	58	154	100	399
Buena Park city	228	4,460	190	4,392	82	1,985	29	338	90	2,073	78	309	141	758
Burbank city...............	418	7,965	199	3,680	94	1,602	572	31,925	204	2,085	297	3,111	665	8,516
Burlingame city............	165	2,368	137	1,350	107	4,637	D	D	161	1,558	165	830	307	2,963
Calabasas city.............	95	1,605	57	639	11	305	99	832	151	4,442	138	404	379	1,784
Calexico city...............	159	2,461	53	309	56	389	11	64	32	128	34	118	41	115
California City city..........	18	145	NA	NA	NA	NA	D	D	NA	NA	7	43	D	D
Camarillo city..............	330	5,612	137	2,467	36	775	51	1,340	114	653	115	598	339	2,751
Cameron Park CDP.........	50	618	NA	NA	D	D	6	30	D	D	30	82	70	311
Campbell city..............	D	D	77	754	14	332	D	D	153	911	99	376	327	3,576
Canyon Lake city	11	55	D	D	4	19	4	14	14	32	27	86	34	134
Capitola city...............	138	2,427	10	209	4	36	4	79	D	D	D	D	50	164
Carlsbad city...............	487	8,305	281	5,854	65	1,108	127	2,555	386	3,124	394	1,345	1,089	8,040
Carmichael CDP............	122	1,611	24	118	18	81	4	8	58	191	80	329	107	644
Carpinteria city............	44	253	29	405	4	34	D	D	20	187	17	44	41	242
Carson city................	221	4,827	346	6,630	373	9,237	32	1,031	53	385	80	1,227	115	855
Casa de Oro-Mount Helix CDP	50	535	7	22	4	5	6	7	21	58	34	68	56	130
Castaic CDP................	23	297	6	7	10	55	D	D	D	D	D	D	33	57
Castro Valley CDP..........	89	1,229	17	108	21	102	D	D	D	D	88	193	104	424
Cathedral City city	134	2,455	21	89	12	54	D	D	28	125	38	160	43	95
Ceres city.................	102	1,795	23	482	42	1,416	6	90	31	128	33	133	30	433
Cerritos city................	251	7,796	237	5,003	94	3,268	34	1,974	100	2,293	101	410	206	1,389
Charter Oak CDP	19	240	4	42	NA	NA	NA	NA	6	20	9	25	6	11
Cherryland CDP	23	192	3	8	D	D	NA	NA	D	D	11	47	3	16
Chico city..................	393	7,340	81	1,187	33	609	44	893	216	2,425	165	705	303	1,949
Chino city.................	298	4,951	526	7,891	186	4,510	23	195	89	603	82	417	164	940
Chino Hills city.............	165	2,535	126	428	37	124	15	164	85	1,828	97	223	194	644

1 Merchant wholesalers, except manufacturers' sales branches and offices.

	Economic activity by sector, 2017											
	Administration and support and waste management and mediation services		Educational services		Health care and social assistance		Arts, entertainment, and recreation		Accommodation and food services		Other services (except public administration)	
STATE City, town, township, borough, or CDP (county if applicable)	Number of establishments	Number of employees	Number of establishments	Number of employees	Number of establishments	Number of employees	Number of establishments	Number of employees	Number of establishments	Number of employees	Number of establishments	Number of employees
	15	16	17	18	19	20	21	22	23	24	25	26
ARKANSAS—Con.												
Pine Bluff city	36	1,394	D	D	167	3,541	D	D	99	1,584	57	340
Rogers city	92	1,891	15	76	229	4,669	17	362	194	5,028	87	574
Russellville city	37	1,375	D	D	160	3,425	12	D	127	2,624	74	416
Searcy city	21	502	6	15	134	4,420	12	140	88	1,851	57	382
Sherwood city	43	1,064	5	27	62	1,095	D	D	42	833	54	247
Siloam Springs city	14	654	3	39	53	824	D	D	60	952	30	193
Springdale city	100	3,590	16	74	165	4,952	D	D	144	2,633	119	939
Texarkana city	33	717	D	D	D	D	D	D	67	1,347	33	163
Van Buren city	D	D	NA	NA	63	1,223	D	D	55	974	D	D
West Memphis city	17	320	D	D	90	1,380	D	D	65	1,181	34	225
CALIFORNIA	45,082	1,563,794	10,917	115,799	113,390	2,043,117	26,390	349,752	89,596	1,739,010	62,302	437,372
Adelanto city	D	D	NA	NA	16	199	NA	NA	17	228	D	D
Agoura Hills city	65	582	24	154	138	1,182	72	254	82	1,271	57	372
Alameda city	D	D	36	397	228	4,027	42	1,149	237	3,611	155	1,493
Alamo CDP	D	D	D	D	52	280	7	D	D	D	24	97
Albany city	D	D	7	30	67	609	10	102	67	675	46	232
Alhambra city	95	1,410	32	245	302	3,588	24	250	256	4,275	125	503
Aliso Viejo city	71	3,170	23	277	140	2,692	25	491	90	1,689	63	472
Alpine CDP	25	119	3	12	25	456	4	12	29	356	D	D
Altadena CDP	37	297	9	45	121	1,669	59	110	D	D	30	218
Alum Rock CDP	D	D	NA	NA	D	D	NA	NA	4	5	7	22
American Canyon city	20	388	NA	NA	45	D	6	195	26	382	D	D
Anaheim city	446	31,962	79	613	970	20,597	94	34,259	799	27,327	430	3,672
Anderson city	4	148	NA	NA	21	371	D	D	28	603	30	137
Antelope CDP	26	93	NA	NA	28	228	5	50	33	623	28	126
Antioch city	95	928	12	79	261	5,922	28	375	139	2,028	98	554
Apple Valley town	43	412	6	14	208	3,512	8	117	95	1,565	48	310
Arcadia city	84	2,415	53	300	441	5,310	71	2,277	224	4,170	119	555
Arcata city	21	129	9	27	68	1,523	10	129	92	1,986	45	244
Arden-Arcade CDP	133	4,540	26	229	408	11,565	32	578	238	4,634	197	1,293
Arroyo Grande city	28	187	D	D	93	1,138	3	D	56	956	36	173
Artesia city	24	164	7	77	86	1,366	NA	NA	110	1,292	D	D
Arvin city	NA	NA	NA	NA	10	162	NA	NA	26	239	D	D
Ashland CDP	6	25	NA	NA	19	728	NA	NA	22	209	D	D
Atascadero city	40	391	8	28	119	3,123	12	180	78	1,087	47	193
Atwater city	12	57	NA	NA	29	621	D	D	39	536	21	117
Auburn city	22	219	5	35	88	1,066	5	27	58	908	60	281
Avenal city	NA	NA	NA	NA	D	D	NA	NA	5	41	NA	NA
Avocado Heights CDP	17	1,010	D	D	15	219	3	31	24	290	D	D
Azusa city	34	1,317	D	D	60	698	6	84	95	1,319	78	402
Bakersfield city	365	13,204	53	469	1,210	23,324	79	1,580	799	15,215	454	3,674
Baldwin Park city	48	730	6	D	86	5,226	NA	NA	103	1,504	50	137
Banning city	17	153	NA	NA	59	1,619	NA	NA	57	730	33	203
Barstow city	17	140	NA	NA	58	763	NA	NA	93	1,625	31	329
Bay Point CDP	16	137	NA	NA	D	D	NA	NA	11	140	6	19
Beaumont city	21	145	NA	NA	50	686	5	62	58	966	D	D
Bell city	21	4,737	NA	NA	38	531	NA	NA	63	863	33	154
Bellflower city	63	3,345	4	10	176	2,584	17	181	136	1,855	125	539
Bell Gardens city	11	45	NA	NA	39	1,012	NA	NA	66	2,578	D	D
Belmont city	32	454	18	128	71	650	5	57	68	824	57	317
Benicia city	56	913	8	64	64	320	16	137	68	1,055	79	749
Berkeley city	D	D	95	1,333	491	8,402	115	1,619	538	8,416	326	2,358
Beverly Hills city	214	3,435	37	657	1,209	6,751	1,036	5,821	238	9,436	404	2,441
Big Bear City CDP	8	10	NA	NA	13	71	NA	NA	12	88	10	24
Bloomington CDP	7	33	NA	NA	D	D	NA	NA	14	129	30	220
Blythe city	8	19	NA	NA	22	304	NA	NA	39	547	15	43
Bonita CDP	18	71	6	40	D	D	D	D	29	378	11	119
Bostonia CDP	21	111	NA	NA	9	133	D	D	13	130	46	249
Brawley city	10	77	NA	NA	54	1,540	D	D	46	570	27	136
Brea city	111	5,681	30	846	187	2,463	D	D	180	4,673	103	768
Brentwood city	69	665	16	112	150	1,392	11	270	128	2,151	96	528
Buena Park city	71	1,788	22	308	220	2,215	D	D	231	4,492	96	615
Burbank city	225	150,610	54	400	629	9,383	447	1,793	353	8,431	281	2,509
Burlingame city	106	11,720	30	439	211	4,729	24	433	161	5,155	141	866
Calabasas city	91	1,940	18	135	143	882	198	298	64	1,423	59	425
Calexico city	14	319	NA	NA	25	360	NA	NA	62	896	D	D
California City city	5	41	NA	NA	12	103	NA	NA	9	89	4	7
Camarillo city	111	7,105	21	202	274	4,745	33	474	177	3,362	134	1,027
Cameron Park CDP	15	75	6	34	51	704	D	D	50	613	D	D
Campbell city	98	5,663	43	639	221	3,215	20	195	153	3,485	183	1,409
Canyon Lake city	19	77	NA	NA	13	82	NA	NA	11	245	13	177
Capitola city	17	403	7	96	55	802	8	117	74	1,489	31	214
Carlsbad city	246	5,413	78	1,600	450	7,009	86	3,603	314	9,150	230	1,896
Carmichael CDP	67	1,066	10	92	240	6,216	20	302	84	1,281	93	778
Carpinteria city	34	139	8	139	27	161	10	25	51	909	29	77
Carson city	102	5,272	D	D	197	2,260	19	561	186	3,440	127	1,854
Casa de Oro-Mount Helix CDP	32	373	D	D	45	388	D	D	D	D	D	D
Castaic CDP	15	63	NA	NA	10	44	9	12	32	420	16	34
Castro Valley CDP	D	D	17	179	201	7,108	24	159	109	1,440	72	288
Cathedral City city	81	485	NA	NA	70	765	12	261	109	1,777	101	725
Ceres city	17	206	D	D	56	677	6	67	75	1,067	48	472
Cerritos city	55	1,535	28	274	245	3,003	12	169	208	4,794	71	1,113
Charter Oak CDP	6	55	NA	NA	22	D	NA	NA	D	D	D	D
Cherryland CDP	D	D	NA	NA	23	453	NA	NA	3	D	D	D
Chico city	116	2,538	27	159	443	9,129	26	540	292	5,709	178	2,840
Chino city	109	2,578	27	211	231	2,926	28	815	190	3,425	163	1,715
Chino Hills city	63	466	26	174	166	1,722	23	389	178	3,343	72	433

STATE City, town, township, borough, or CDP (county if applicable)	Retail Trade		Wholesale trade[1]		Transportation and warehousing		Information		Finance and insurance		Real estate and rental and leasing		Professional, scientific, and technical services	
	Number of establish-ments	Number of employees	Number of establish-ments	Number of employees	Number of establish-ments	Number of employees	Number of establish-ments	Number of employees	Number of establish-ments	Number of employees	Number of establish-ments	Number of employees	Number of establish-ments	Number of employees
	1	2	3	4	5	6	7	8	9	10	11	12	13	14
CALIFORNIA—Con.														
Chowchilla city	32	297	7	135	6	22	NA	NA	12	70	11	20	5	14
Chula Vista city	624	12,160	289	2,134	104	1,679	69	794	235	1,660	310	931	455	2,438
Citrus Heights city	246	4,525	15	67	29	81	16	880	102	596	83	320	104	649
Claremont city	86	1,268	25	351	11	71	12	75	57	348	D	D	152	575
Clayton city	12	188	NA	NA	5	10	D	D	11	35	7	18	24	81
Clearlake city	39	716	NA	NA	D	D	3	39	9	55	16	36	6	27
Clovis city	306	6,679	45	216	46	312	28	458	120	529	98	344	186	1,595
Coachella city	60	1,000	18	272	12	132	NA	NA	16	94	21	65	7	39
Coalinga city	29	311	4	69	8	231	D	D	4	20	11	32	9	49
Colton city	112	2,051	41	758	32	671	6	67	31	110	40	240	45	1,800
Commerce city	222	6,379	423	11,480	122	4,701	20	263	25	224	53	723	60	734
Compton city	160	2,414	122	2,107	154	3,945	20	284	29	200	21	198	18	325
Concord city	420	8,211	151	1,391	60	1,468	59	1,263	218	6,760	182	1,414	298	4,687
Corcoran city	25	204	9	97	7	79	NA	NA	3	15	D	D	D	D
Corona city	441	8,810	305	7,018	150	1,564	51	817	196	2,365	203	765	384	3,434
Coronado city	69	494	12	16	9	196	10	41	42	154	90	270	119	518
Costa Mesa city	766	15,676	262	3,735	57	604	83	2,295	276	5,088	347	3,889	812	8,989
Coto de Caza CDP	14	157	14	28	NA	NA	9	25	20	27	20	29	80	134
Covina city	173	3,350	70	535	26	101	12	115	110	835	99	589	183	934
Cudahy city	23	262	12	161	7	156	NA	NA	D	D	D	D	4	46
Culver City city	301	5,726	109	1,363	25	517	238	13,814	94	483	128	1,475	459	5,140
Cupertino city	D	D	61	791	10	28	D	D	113	1,118	122	696	413	2,420
Cypress city	90	1,569	112	3,556	28	455	31	930	76	2,917	83	236	146	1,553
Daly City city	190	4,048	28	148	43	204	D	D	D	D	57	367	81	437
Dana Point city	97	1,027	58	159	9	66	14	51	62	166	90	191	204	606
Danville town	121	1,633	34	152	4	27	D	D	107	623	128	439	212	827
Davis city	122	2,136	20	213	D	D	30	457	D	D	130	586	238	1,627
Delano city	92	1,683	12	133	26	340	D	D	30	154	17	46	D	D
Delhi CDP	22	155	NA	NA	9	137	NA	NA	3	4	NA	NA	NA	NA
Desert Hot Springs city	44	588	4	9	4	23	5	29	11	67	18	43	11	282
Diamond Bar city	144	1,000	289	1,205	78	324	23	359	136	2,201	145	D	273	1,194
Diamond Springs CDP	56	931	25	138	11	87	D	D	D	D	D	D	30	255
Dinuba city	56	998	7	122	D	D	8	63	20	94	15	29	13	41
Discovery Bay CDP	10	156	6	D	D	D	NA	NA	7	27	21	74	18	43
Dixon city	40	1,318	13	343	18	501	4	43	17	179	D	D	20	69
Downey city	294	5,829	86	921	99	1,752	24	326	150	1,157	165	990	162	665
Duarte city	59	1,423	49	419	8	42	4	23	13	62	18	94	D	D
Dublin city	189	4,330	63	477	12	107	38	1,530	D	D	60	251	276	1,972
East Hemet CDP	8	94	NA	NA	D	D	NA	NA	NA	NA	5	9	9	14
East Los Angeles CDP	186	1,232	74	696	38	223	11	98	50	522	37	260	75	373
East Palo Alto city	22	858	8	38	5	15	NA	NA	D	D	18	76	24	469
East Rancho Dominguez CDP	13	195	NA	NA	NA	NA	NA	NA	NA	NA	NA	NA	NA	NA
East San Gabriel CDP	18	111	18	30	D	D	D	D	D	D	15	20	27	18
Eastvale city	78	1,362	77	675	75	3,742	10	125	23	74	D	D	D	D
East Whittier CDP	D	D	NA	NA	D	D	NA	NA	NA	NA	4	2	3	3
El Cajon city	456	7,318	124	1,324	61	937	27	327	107	573	144	920	208	1,187
El Centro city	194	4,454	57	424	32	319	19	347	59	502	50	229	91	494
El Cerrito city	62	1,551	12	51	5	40	D	D	26	135	24	37	70	187
El Dorado Hills CDP	68	1,122	48	298	12	77	25	308	D	D	88	350	247	1,306
Elk Grove city	279	7,241	D	D	D	D	28	563	171	746	136	413	241	1,053
El Monte city	308	3,677	312	2,338	133	909	28	320	80	2,899	75	361	129	588
El Paso de Robles (Paso Robles) city	143	2,245	42	352	13	149	22	453	67	360	63	284	82	368
El Segundo city	107	2,657	92	3,866	65	1,463	149	7,580	193	3,224	129	1,511	497	17,080
El Sobrante CDP (Contra Costa County)	29	162	NA	NA	D	D	NA	NA	D	D	5	8	25	76
El Sobrante CDP (Riverside County)	D	D	5	4	6	29	NA	NA	D	D	12	26	20	25
Emeryville city	99	1,914	48	1,490	10	152	52	4,517	D	D	47	340	214	6,080
Encinitas city	284	4,402	87	432	13	36	57	463	159	585	243	647	621	2,235
Escondido city	511	10,528	132	998	48	417	59	575	189	1,153	205	825	339	1,776
Eureka city	222	3,418	47	448	21	236	18	253	73	615	49	257	91	789
Exeter city	26	245	6	139	NA	NA	NA	NA	11	79	8	18	10	39
Fairfield city	313	5,691	77	1,377	66	995	41	846	122	1,860	109	499	163	909
Fair Oaks CDP	70	711	15	29	7	13	8	51	80	257	58	212	99	449
Fairview CDP	3	10	NA	NA	NA	NA	NA	NA	NA	NA	D	D	8	13
Fallbrook CDP	65	722	29	132	13	61	13	46	29	128	35	88	80	259
Farmersville city	17	148	NA	NA	NA	NA	NA	NA	4	15	6	19	NA	NA
Fillmore city	38	345	5	D	9	50	D	D	D	D	6	14	13	35
Florence-Graham CDP	90	1,176	63	502	22	113	D	D	13	80	6	10	5	13
Florin CDP	112	2,654	17	166	34	372	7	76	30	143	34	216	15	163
Folsom city	288	6,285	32	240	19	84	49	1,235	192	1,988	123	782	411	10,954
Fontana city	337	7,334	184	3,468	303	8,516	26	281	97	613	112	570	131	474
Foothill Farms CDP	32	447	D	D	10	28	D	D	15	64	D	D	9	178
Fortuna city	61	612	D	D	6	13	NA	NA	25	99	16	45	20	101
Foster City city	31	788	35	586	6	20	28	2,919	D	D	64	651	139	1,523
Fountain Valley city	213	3,139	102	1,474	26	138	30	328	114	735	126	407	233	2,226
Fremont city	447	8,938	454	9,727	119	1,547	103	1,611	D	D	284	1,174	1,251	13,598
French Valley CDP	11	111	7	8	10	76	NA	NA	14	36	21	25	31	117
Fresno city	1,537	25,256	510	8,150	350	5,900	184	3,582	751	8,201	558	3,657	1,150	8,428
Fullerton city	428	5,476	291	2,839	92	2,435	38	584	161	909	247	917	448	2,968
Galt city	39	629	8	328	15	47	D	D	22	80	7	11	21	60
Gardena city	172	2,534	172	1,688	85	1,649	13	172	52	477	55	284	79	283
Garden Grove city	444	5,988	227	2,364	64	664	51	1,077	142	733	167	818	275	1,724
Gilroy city	302	5,409	47	593	31	388	D	D	51	211	46	171	73	470
Glendale city	726	12,197	241	1,913	141	863	268	3,392	402	5,194	401	2,913	1,086	6,902
Glendora city	132	2,743	48	405	20	118	20	283	74	626	87	295	141	934
Goleta city	123	2,414	58	1,147	15	421	34	3,098	43	413	47	288	D	D
Grand Terrace city	24	231	12	123	D	D	5	18	13	55	7	70	16	103

1 Merchant wholesalers, except manufacturers' sales branches and offices.

Table C. Incorporated Places, Census Designated Places (CDPs), and Minor Civil Divisions (MCDs) of 10,000 or More Population — **Economic Census**

STATE City, town, township, borough, or CDP (county if applicable)	Administration and support and waste management and mediation services — Number of establishments	Administration and support and waste management and mediation services — Number of employees	Educational services — Number of establishments	Educational services — Number of employees	Health care and social assistance — Number of establishments	Health care and social assistance — Number of employees	Arts, entertainment, and recreation — Number of establishments	Arts, entertainment, and recreation — Number of employees	Accommodation and food services — Number of establishments	Accommodation and food services — Number of employees	Other services (except public administration) — Number of establishments	Other services (except public administration) — Number of employees
	15	16	17	18	19	20	21	22	23	24	25	26
CALIFORNIA—Con.												
Chowchilla city..................	9	40	NA	NA	D	D	NA	NA	26	348	D	D
Chula Vista city................	226	2,826	39	314	613	10,464	60	1,968	431	7,956	275	1,852
Citrus Heights city............	79	1,647	16	224	166	2,475	15	590	D	D	90	562
Claremont city..................	31	151	18	93	182	2,377	18	469	121	1,918	50	214
Clayton city.....................	D	D	NA	NA	12	97	D	D	11	165	12	29
Clearlake city..................	6	41	NA	NA	33	728	NA	NA	28	288	17	38
Clovis city......................	98	2,682	22	171	272	5,829	29	580	247	4,677	145	1,047
Coachella city..................	31	141	NA	NA	22	204	D	D	54	751	16	59
Coalinga city...................	D	D	NA	NA	17	90	NA	NA	22	340	D	D
Colton city......................	41	796	NA	NA	120	5,057	NA	NA	93	1,304	57	500
Commerce city.................	63	5,207	3	125	40	676	D	D	69	3,926	43	1,003
Compton city...................	40	2,637	D	D	91	1,038	D	D	D	D	D	D
Concord city....................	220	9,606	37	517	432	8,766	49	1,046	299	5,364	251	1,589
Corcoran city...................	NA	NA	NA	NA	13	170	NA	NA	18	159	4	11
Corona city.....................	229	8,324	49	314	424	5,741	43	487	346	6,667	240	1,634
Coronado city..................	18	82	15	76	70	1,006	17	180	83	3,622	48	354
Costa Mesa city...............	252	10,366	53	518	454	5,715	73	1,894	471	10,378	386	2,850
Coto de Caza CDP..........	14	25	D	D	D	D	D	D	7	73	12	42
Covina city......................	84	3,725	13	100	242	4,622	13	128	143	2,147	141	681
Cudahy city.....................	5	227	NA	NA	17	257	NA	NA	D	D	11	38
Culver City city...............	141	8,830	40	447	236	4,667	184	572	247	4,719	167	1,521
Cupertino city..................	59	722	61	546	233	2,482	28	538	192	3,440	79	470
Cypress city....................	46	1,738	17	D	132	1,424	D	D	129	2,082	86	733
Daly City city..................	58	810	12	96	263	4,620	14	553	198	3,416	98	442
Dana Point city................	48	404	7	175	129	1,248	D	D	112	3,795	76	378
Danville town...................	63	590	24	216	168	1,796	33	497	114	2,217	77	374
Davis city.......................	58	496	24	162	172	2,626	25	289	188	3,392	97	532
Delano city.....................	D	D	NA	NA	74	1,507	D	D	64	922	20	69
Delhi CDP......................	7	23	NA	NA	7	225	NA	NA	6	27	4	20
Desert Hot Springs city.....	23	105	NA	NA	37	497	D	D	47	470	13	52
Diamond Bar city.............	85	1,627	41	248	208	1,587	11	185	141	1,950	81	369
Diamond Springs CDP	20	229	NA	NA	46	655	6	59	27	321	37	121
Dinuba city.....................	D	D	NA	NA	25	384	D	D	D	D	D	D
Discovery Bay CDP..........	9	47	NA	NA	D	D	D	D	14	150	D	D
Dixon city.......................	20	137	D	D	27	237	D	D	37	692	D	D
Downey city....................	85	1,339	16	123	355	12,312	20	262	292	5,840	162	895
Duarte city......................	16	243	NA	NA	66	5,363	3	18	51	801	31	161
Dublin city......................	D	D	32	346	184	1,850	D	D	183	3,288	107	671
East Hemet CDP.............	10	41	NA	NA	15	253	NA	NA	10	160	3	6
East Los Angeles CDP.....	45	549	7	78	168	3,077	D	D	133	1,604	D	D
East Palo Alto city...........	25	155	5	56	35	483	D	D	23	565	17	98
East Rancho Dominguez CDP	NA	NA	NA	NA	11	85	NA	NA	D	D	3	7
East San Gabriel CDP......	16	37	4	17	19	139	4	41	8	176	D	D
Eastvale city...................	37	534	8	31	59	262	D	D	53	1,096	D	D
East Whittier CDP............	9	29	NA	NA	3	16	NA	NA	NA	NA	NA	NA
El Cajon city...................	117	2,155	29	284	287	6,238	15	333	229	3,532	213	1,678
El Centro city..................	33	521	D	D	153	2,915	11	104	123	2,311	72	324
El Cerrito city.................	22	227	D	D	83	597	9	38	58	694	36	248
El Dorado Hills CDP	85	5,387	14	161	126	1,118	24	389	62	1,268	58	395
Elk Grove city.................	128	1,464	44	369	384	4,044	27	546	276	5,122	180	1,265
El Monte city..................	106	1,574	18	106	216	3,203	9	D	204	2,109	129	497
El Paso de Robles (Paso Robles) city.................	46	402	7	50	88	1,154	14	325	133	2,514	62	300
El Segundo city...............	115	6,917	25	259	96	1,201	D	D	151	4,028	77	617
El Sobrante CDP (Contra Costa County)...............	13	70	D	D	24	137	3	6	26	171	20	167
El Sobrante CDP (Riverside County)	13	37	NA	NA	20	54	NA	NA	9	136	6	27
Emeryville city	D	D	9	485	69	3,755	D	D	83	2,269	42	401
Encinitas city..................	141	1,233	43	304	438	5,156	70	853	230	4,455	183	1,141
Escondido city.................	219	3,446	21	384	426	8,246	34	708	276	4,875	279	1,541
Eureka city.....................	42	740	6	47	153	3,477	17	150	147	2,034	90	552
Exeter city......................	D	D	NA	NA	21	200	D	D	D	D	13	97
Fairfield city....................	103	3,643	22	542	283	7,141	22	580	210	3,507	150	1,131
Fair Oaks CDP................	39	338	14	135	112	986	11	224	50	857	60	287
Fairview CDP..................	D	D	NA	NA	13	188	NA	NA	NA	NA	D	D
Fallbrook CDP................	40	495	6	42	89	1,007	14	65	51	782	59	285
Farmersville city.............	5	161	NA	NA	7	69	NA	NA	15	361	4	6
Fillmore city...................	5	17	NA	NA	20	378	NA	NA	D	D	12	73
Florence-Graham CDP.....	16	308	NA	NA	19	287	NA	NA	42	526	34	208
Florin CDP.....................	18	109	3	10	84	1,159	D	D	91	1,428	D	D
Folsom city....................	116	1,146	D	D	292	4,017	36	605	231	4,867	129	974
Fontana city...................	117	3,934	22	114	207	8,480	18	370	270	4,779	212	1,257
Foothill Farms CDP	10	50	NA	NA	21	131	NA	NA	20	276	D	D
Fortuna city....................	6	97	NA	NA	38	655	4	33	34	483	24	80
Foster City city...............	50	971	21	146	101	1,249	5	232	72	1,394	31	148
Fountain Valley city..........	84	950	28	458	430	7,277	D	D	193	3,109	102	739
Fremont city...................	218	9,226	117	1,104	732	12,827	52	966	464	7,787	350	2,386
French Valley CDP...........	11	50	NA	NA	20	133	D	D	7	49	14	100
Fresno city.....................	540	21,182	83	1,052	1,734	35,901	123	3,647	1,018	20,209	661	6,346
Fullerton city..................	152	1,920	55	368	449	8,509	40	762	365	7,803	238	2,771
Galt city........................	8	109	NA	NA	30	249	5	39	D	D	D	D
Gardena city...................	63	1,691	5	42	144	2,797	13	1,260	235	3,065	117	625
Garden Grove city............	149	3,423	33	203	509	6,152	D	D	484	8,175	271	1,572
Gilroy city......................	54	802	6	38	D	D	D	D	155	2,711	111	890
Glendale city..................	264	19,314	47	1,296	1,167	16,964	236	1,382	489	8,105	410	1,865
Glendora city..................	62	828	12	114	223	3,712	D	D	118	1,711	92	554
Goleta city.....................	62	583	11	84	132	1,728	14	372	107	2,812	D	D
Grand Terrace city	10	161	NA	NA	D	D	NA	NA	11	162	D	D

Table C. Incorporated Places, Census Designated Places (CDPs), and Minor Civil Divisions (MCDs) of 10,000 or More Population — **Economic Census**

STATE City, town, township, borough, or CDP (county if applicable)	Retail Trade Number of establishments	Retail Trade Number of employees	Wholesale trade[1] Number of establishments	Wholesale trade[1] Number of employees	Transportation and warehousing Number of establishments	Transportation and warehousing Number of employees	Information Number of establishments	Information Number of employees	Finance and insurance Number of establishments	Finance and insurance Number of employees	Real estate and rental and leasing Number of establishments	Real estate and rental and leasing Number of employees	Professional, scientific, and technical services Number of establishments	Professional, scientific, and technical services Number of employees
	1	2	3	4	5	6	7	8	9	10	11	12	13	14
CALIFORNIA—Con.														
Granite Bay CDP	35	397	11	22	6	18	8	62	54	1,099	49	144	114	383
Grass Valley city	148	2,264	10	197	13	123	15	209	67	883	38	135	70	337
Greenfield city	25	219	6	115	13	57	NA	NA	4	32	10	22	3	16
Grover Beach city	48	465	8	108	6	74	3	7	15	53	21	71	31	88
Hacienda Heights CDP	95	697	111	317	72	129	9	24	51	245	72	144	93	386
Half Moon Bay city	56	594	9	27	NA	NA	D	D	D	D	23	89	57	381
Hanford city	160	2,778	27	386	21	348	13	197	57	411	63	250	61	368
Hawaiian Gardens city	30	298	9	28	D	D	NA	NA	9	41	10	55	5	46
Hawthorne city	154	3,841	72	1,354	83	1,547	28	184	41	420	79	342	73	606
Hayward city	412	6,899	442	6,836	248	3,732	44	588	D	D	188	1,450	319	5,858
Healdsburg city	101	1,095	25	348	6	21	6	24	38	462	35	132	75	255
Hemet city	212	4,534	18	82	16	70	17	299	68	386	84	416	58	379
Hercules city	18	383	D	D	8	25	NA	NA	12	204	9	16	28	215
Hermosa Beach city	78	839	27	169	8	18	39	177	56	299	86	291	195	685
Hesperia city	179	2,602	42	194	68	713	9	100	49	286	52	227	57	238
Highland city	57	764	11	81	15	77	5	17	17	80	14	31	34	155
Hillsborough town	D	D	D	D	NA	NA	D	D	D	D	42	134	42	78
Hollister city	79	1,267	20	167	24	279	5	80	D	D	37	96	48	179
Home Gardens CDP	10	46	10	120	NA	NA	NA	NA	NA	NA	4	25	4	10
Huntington Beach city	624	10,253	372	4,541	76	837	70	826	336	2,051	403	1,436	837	4,436
Huntington Park city	184	2,301	60	775	21	92	D	D	46	327	28	146	33	194
Imperial city	16	356	16	273	17	254	NA	NA	7	27	15	64	D	D
Imperial Beach city	35	251	6	12	3	2	NA	NA	12	70	19	64	35	115
Indio city	169	3,206	44	514	30	189	D	D	40	210	65	353	79	403
Inglewood city	239	4,197	77	615	180	2,572	24	352	52	368	76	736	86	604
Irvine city	700	11,702	1,095	19,409	128	3,247	415	17,376	1,141	26,240	945	12,200	3,259	47,066
Isla Vista CDP	10	137	NA	NA	NA	NA	NA	NA	NA	NA	18	101	NA	NA
Jurupa Valley city	142	1,995	102	2,654	202	6,048	9	62	35	158	45	455	48	253
Kerman city	31	540	9	153	12	35	D	D	5	42	12	24	10	37
King City city	36	374	7	63	D	D	D	D	11	53	6	14	7	25
Kingsburg city	27	346	5	23	10	66	NA	NA	19	132	14	24	14	97
La Cañada Flintridge city	59	961	24	34	D	D	26	83	40	224	D	D	108	220
La Crescenta-Montrose CDP	40	453	27	134	12	19	14	67	33	145	46	119	91	215
Ladera Ranch CDP	34	350	19	28	7	8	10	91	35	156	59	82	132	333
Lafayette city	81	1,267	22	111	10	113	22	165	86	673	54	144	216	1,010
Laguna Beach city	176	1,150	46	135	8	42	29	131	76	288	121	256	238	1,054
Laguna Hills city	171	1,819	105	568	20	310	24	144	150	655	96	594	367	1,995
Laguna Niguel city	157	2,890	77	486	14	150	30	587	126	614	159	481	354	922
Laguna Woods city	22	536	D	D	NA	NA	NA	NA	D	D	7	D	31	73
La Habra city	183	3,876	60	332	28	191	11	168	68	293	70	255	94	461
Lake Elsinore city	193	3,314	35	207	26	99	14	183	37	220	40	232	67	397
Lake Forest city	214	3,951	216	3,427	39	358	47	715	127	2,543	129	970	465	3,203
Lakeland Village CDP	14	41	D	D	4	20	NA	NA	NA	NA	3	16	7	8
Lake Los Angeles CDP	7	46	NA	NA	D	D	NA	NA	NA	NA	NA	NA	NA	NA
Lakeside CDP	30	170	17	222	19	101	D	D	D	D	33	278	19	51
Lakewood city	215	5,494	26	118	30	127	21	282	69	394	54	300	97	531
La Mesa city	224	4,099	21	220	20	100	22	178	153	925	151	824	252	1,091
La Mirada city	91	1,547	130	3,395	66	1,212	15	174	54	330	56	585	74	292
Lamont CDP	27	259	NA	NA	6	12	NA	NA	D	D	NA	NA	NA	NA
Lancaster city	310	5,519	63	642	59	1,718	28	405	107	604	125	533	145	1,179
La Palma city	30	316	30	436	14	185	5	57	26	216	13	38	45	1,004
La Presa CDP	61	682	4	29	5	20	4	8	10	39	21	43	11	38
La Puente city	102	1,258	22	101	29	56	5	13	31	228	23	72	19	436
La Quinta city	90	2,405	24	44	10	63	12	141	56	228	99	270	98	337
La Riviera CDP	17	81	D	D	NA	NA	NA	NA	7	27	8	18	12	73
Larkspur city	50	719	13	57	4	11	15	165	86	495	D	D	118	563
Lathrop city	26	482	15	724	58	2,454	NA	NA	10	39	16	55	7	99
La Verne city	80	1,224	58	545	11	143	13	124	36	193	43	154	73	402
Lawndale city	83	751	16	113	14	93	5	92	32	185	23	285	38	110
Lemon Grove city	78	1,629	12	59	10	75	D	D	21	107	27	75	24	156
Lemon Hill CDP	26	262	D	D	NA	NA	NA	NA	5	16	NA	NA	NA	NA
Lemoore city	52	559	5	27	D	D	D	D	D	D	24	57	20	66
Lennox CDP	24	206	9	46	48	342	NA	NA	7	18	4	10	D	D
Lincoln city	68	1,220	18	140	22	261	8	35	48	201	42	101	58	478
Linda CDP	27	244	3	D	8	102	NA	NA	D	D	7	18	6	22
Lindsay city	26	261	4	93	5	14	NA	NA	4	28	12	19	3	8
Live Oak CDP	59	665	16	243	D	D	NA	NA	7	97	22	73	52	278
Livermore city	366	6,829	164	2,753	54	877	34	1,222	D	D	110	716	250	12,580
Livingston city	25	303	NA	NA	D	D	NA	NA	D	D	4	11	NA	NA
Lodi city	214	3,991	40	280	30	604	13	196	107	1,643	65	441	99	418
Loma Linda city	34	634	8	36	8	28	4	54	15	55	19	97	36	219
Lomita city	64	509	21	74	15	35	D	D	16	79	39	101	41	153
Lompoc city	108	1,553	9	53	D	D	D	D	37	287	38	217	41	272
Long Beach city	921	13,603	309	4,118	372	20,288	153	2,365	435	9,067	571	3,040	1,123	8,457
Los Alamitos city	66	524	72	540	13	133	14	67	70	415	59	261	136	856
Los Altos city	D	D	15	87	D	D	D	D	103	617	110	446	277	4,124
Los Angeles city	11,728	151,931	8,196	79,204	2,195	65,382	6,185	88,119	5,265	87,943	7,059	44,587	16,741	155,056
Los Banos city	80	1,473	8	110	18	54	10	76	27	134	25	58	22	114
Los Gatos town	D	D	21	D	D	D	D	D	103	879	140	571	270	1,786
Los Osos CDP	27	313	5	D	4	22	D	D	12	43	16	51	38	118
Lynwood city	102	1,250	39	487	32	192	11	83	40	185	13	129	26	92
McFarland city	18	185	NA	NA	8	27	NA	NA	NA	NA	NA	NA	NA	NA
McKinleyville CDP	36	581	9	79	6	51	NA	NA	15	101	23	35	26	173
Madera city	156	2,282	27	363	27	93	D	D	51	296	47	177	38	152
Magalia CDP	9	118	NA	NA	NA	NA	NA	NA	NA	NA	NA	NA	7	22
Malibu city	97	860	17	71	NA	NA	55	190	41	187	106	298	120	831
Manhattan Beach city	175	2,822	40	364	6	101	74	442	117	1,334	171	546	407	3,584
Manteca city	193	3,614	29	462	59	677	16	503	D	D	63	269	61	274
Marina city	46	954	7	151	7	28	5	43	12	51	20	63	D	D

1 Merchant wholesalers, except manufacturers' sales branches and offices.

Table C. Incorporated Places, Census Designated Places (CDPs), and Minor Civil Divisions (MCDs) of 10,000 or More Population — **Economic Census**

	Economic activity by sector, 2017											
	Administration and support and waste management and mediation services		Educational services		Health care and social assistance		Arts, entertainment, and recreation		Accommodation and food services		Other services (except public administration)	
STATE City, town, township, borough, or CDP (county if applicable)	Number of establishments	Number of employees	Number of establishments	Number of employees	Number of establishments	Number of employees	Number of establishments	Number of employees	Number of establishments	Number of employees	Number of establishments	Number of employees
	15	16	17	18	19	20	21	22	23	24	25	26
CALIFORNIA—Con.												
Granite Bay CDP	37	442	11	123	69	569	12	202	34	575	27	185
Grass Valley city	36	165	8	64	149	3,833	19	148	87	1,257	71	357
Greenfield city	NA	NA	NA	NA	8	94	6	46	14	155	9	16
Grover Beach city	23	136	5	48	20	157	4	46	39	516	18	73
Hacienda Heights CDP	50	535	23	343	135	817	D	D	97	1,294	46	140
Half Moon Bay city	18	131	3	D	28	232	9	125	55	1,458	36	252
Hanford city	30	317	8	60	165	4,184	D	D	D	D	69	311
Hawaiian Gardens city	5	80	NA	NA	26	403	D	D	29	329	D	D
Hawthorne city	58	757	8	102	172	2,666	D	D	129	1,955	119	683
Hayward city	D	D	37	289	331	7,052	25	D	326	4,417	259	2,031
Healdsburg city	21	234	5	12	56	707	8	146	74	1,225	43	161
Hemet city	47	384	5	31	222	4,585	D	D	149	2,374	95	461
Hercules city	12	108	NA	NA	45	274	NA	NA	33	358	D	D
Hermosa Beach city	41	840	18	90	105	988	D	D	113	2,200	61	295
Hesperia city	50	404	9	25	104	1,050	12	77	121	2,192	101	601
Highland city	32	459	D	D	58	1,684	D	D	60	1,038	35	155
Hillsborough town	4	4	NA	NA	18	67	7	101	7	63	D	D
Hollister city	32	707	9	39	77	1,168	11	141	63	946	D	D
Home Gardens CDP	7	33	NA	NA	NA	NA	NA	NA	D	D	8	16
Huntington Beach city	276	5,323	74	611	751	6,662	113	1,459	546	12,331	411	2,525
Huntington Park city	41	3,107	D	D	124	1,823	3	69	128	1,772	D	D
Imperial city	10	44	NA	NA	26	230	4	70	D	D	9	61
Imperial Beach city	12	118	6	93	25	436	4	9	45	431	32	138
Indio city	102	1,008	NA	NA	131	2,200	14	532	140	3,549	85	664
Inglewood city	69	933	D	D	264	5,128	27	1,699	186	2,872	142	1,308
Irvine city	636	35,670	225	3,098	1,294	15,404	154	2,714	736	16,000	410	3,869
Isla Vista CDP	NA	NA	NA	NA	D	D	NA	NA	47	688	D	D
Jurupa Valley city	74	1,873	D	D	78	1,253	D	D	91	1,379	D	D
Kerman city	7	271	NA	NA	16	346	NA	NA	24	287	11	34
King City city	7	96	NA	NA	D	D	4	22	30	356	12	25
Kingsburg city	12	44	NA	NA	30	312	NA	NA	39	421	13	50
La Cañada Flintridge city	20	163	9	61	128	802	69	603	55	873	44	245
La Crescenta-Montrose CDP	22	110	17	94	57	244	16	D	27	244	D	D
Ladera Ranch CDP	28	102	16	53	56	345	D	D	29	596	23	115
Lafayette city	D	D	25	271	139	1,546	27	336	67	1,643	76	467
Laguna Beach city	51	244	11	87	132	877	D	D	123	4,432	82	451
Laguna Hills city	88	2,286	17	128	374	5,753	D	D	90	1,956	86	458
Laguna Niguel city	96	627	22	102	241	1,891	D	D	122	1,796	109	482
Laguna Woods city	6	24	3	7	39	999	NA	NA	16	350	11	95
La Habra city	51	1,448	17	98	130	1,265	D	D	145	2,128	112	559
Lake Elsinore city	36	159	8	40	80	519	16	509	108	1,654	72	330
Lake Forest city	140	3,016	47	433	252	2,526	43	452	230	3,814	140	881
Lakeland Village CDP	4	21	NA	NA	NA	NA	NA	NA	7	35	D	D
Lake Los Angeles CDP	NA	NA	NA	NA	4	41	NA	NA	NA	NA	NA	NA
Lakeside CDP	21	143	NA	NA	25	332	4	28	21	300	28	110
Lakewood city	39	690	12	48	203	2,719	14	283	D	D	82	607
La Mesa city	89	806	19	208	351	8,597	21	546	176	3,565	130	814
La Mirada city	28	318	5	45	108	1,430	14	224	107	1,407	48	166
Lamont CDP	D	D	NA	NA	11	141	NA	NA	17	225	D	D
Lancaster city	90	3,304	19	150	423	10,408	19	274	239	3,950	170	840
La Palma city	13	240	9	47	73	1,151	D	D	36	382	11	155
La Presa CDP	18	298	NA	NA	36	474	NA	NA	34	425	32	187
La Puente city	22	2,898	NA	NA	63	472	4	15	90	1,106	44	188
La Quinta city	66	566	12	84	104	841	23	1,049	D	D	50	299
La Riviera CDP	9	296	3	17	18	398	NA	NA	20	245	9	24
Larkspur city	22	535	7	275	121	1,267	10	166	45	874	34	374
Lathrop city	20	445	NA	NA	21	99	NA	NA	34	469	D	D
La Verne city	47	416	9	71	79	927	D	D	74	1,443	D	D
Lawndale city	36	707	8	121	79	459	7	14	52	700	D	D
Lemon Grove city	30	591	NA	NA	50	969	3	18	55	907	55	174
Lemon Hill CDP	NA	NA	NA	NA	D	D	NA	NA	9	60	14	129
Lemoore city	8	70	D	D	26	178	3	D	D	D	D	D
Lennox CDP	7	42	NA	NA	15	177	NA	NA	9	81	6	50
Lincoln city	31	89	8	58	87	949	11	190	63	942	D	D
Linda CDP	D	D	NA	NA	D	D	NA	NA	D	D	D	D
Lindsay city	5	481	NA	NA	17	187	NA	NA	D	D	D	D
Live Oak CDP	30	217	10	56	130	4,104	6	41	18	203	53	341
Livermore city	D	D	33	335	214	2,551	38	1,079	219	3,592	148	828
Livingston city	NA	NA	NA	NA	10	165	NA	NA	D	D	5	17
Lodi city	63	726	10	95	195	3,498	14	352	144	2,288	123	606
Loma Linda city	D	D	NA	NA	157	12,707	D	D	38	480	16	53
Lomita city	26	365	9	24	70	552	5	22	61	702	61	192
Lompoc city	26	281	7	15	84	1,582	5	46	90	1,224	51	351
Long Beach city	372	9,354	108	808	1,263	29,063	145	2,242	993	20,426	699	5,912
Los Alamitos city	34	394	10	154	224	3,009	D	D	58	1,245	36	326
Los Altos city	39	427	36	339	172	1,962	20	D	88	1,323	78	726
Los Angeles city	4,868	134,145	1,167	11,871	12,429	226,723	10,363	49,334	9,300	179,751	7,114	53,813
Los Banos city	23	100	NA	NA	54	774	D	D	73	1,044	29	175
Los Gatos town	48	284	32	269	339	3,386	24	762	127	2,550	112	715
Los Osos CDP	22	112	NA	NA	33	170	D	D	25	205	15	47
Lynwood city	18	528	NA	NA	135	3,667	NA	NA	87	1,400	D	D
McFarland city	D	D	NA	NA	9	77	NA	NA	6	24	NA	NA
McKinleyville CDP	12	68	NA	NA	38	292	D	D	23	398	D	D
Madera city	37	702	D	D	135	2,349	8	78	98	1,339	55	239
Magalia CDP	D	D	NA	NA	D	D	NA	NA	6	70	NA	NA
Malibu city	41	235	10	204	73	1,156	96	234	71	2,056	49	161
Manhattan Beach city	61	464	30	366	237	1,416	96	428	151	4,437	90	705
Manteca city	63	1,756	4	36	167	4,019	D	D	144	2,779	90	440
Marina city	31	282	6	221	36	600	5	D	64	927	D	D

Table C. Incorporated Places, Census Designated Places (CDPs), and Minor Civil Divisions (MCDs) of 10,000 or More Population — **Economic Census**

STATE City, town, township, borough, or CDP (county if applicable)	Retail Trade Number of establishments	Retail Trade Number of employees	Wholesale trade[1] Number of establishments	Wholesale trade[1] Number of employees	Transportation and warehousing Number of establishments	Transportation and warehousing Number of employees	Information Number of establishments	Information Number of employees	Finance and insurance Number of establishments	Finance and insurance Number of employees	Real estate and rental and leasing Number of establishments	Real estate and rental and leasing Number of employees	Professional, scientific, and technical services Number of establishments	Professional, scientific, and technical services Number of employees
	1	2	3	4	5	6	7	8	9	10	11	12	13	14
CALIFORNIA—Con.														
Martinez city	69	1,060	23	212	17	195	D	D	34	177	46	204	91	402
Marysville city	50	888	9	409	6	141	8	104	28	122	16	41	34	215
Maywood city	45	508	16	652	16	138	NA	NA	14	42	5	11	4	10
Mead Valley CDP	9	83	4	18	27	373	NA	NA	NA	NA	NA	NA	4	6
Mendota city	20	160	D	D	17	38	NA	NA	NA	NA	4	8	NA	NA
Menifee city	109	2,109	15	58	23	378	13	286	36	178	55	204	65	175
Menlo Park city	113	1,798	32	745	14	498	D	D	199	4,428	80	320	346	6,125
Merced city	225	4,134	37	643	19	400	19	329	94	772	69	359	90	462
Millbrae city	68	1,073	30	109	15	87	D	D	D	D	39	110	70	415
Mill Valley city	72	1,000	10	D	D	D	27	98	69	276	41	120	151	415
Milpitas city	295	5,471	160	8,560	34	555	55	1,119	83	416	93	762	343	7,472
Mission Viejo city	336	6,221	102	530	29	275	40	186	250	1,212	170	750	496	2,675
Modesto city	691	11,082	100	2,035	80	1,397	58	762	278	1,973	213	952	377	3,116
Monrovia city	105	2,918	86	855	22	256	27	296	49	341	70	298	173	1,927
Montclair city	217	4,086	90	695	22	84	9	97	29	193	32	226	36	224
Montebello city	209	3,885	109	1,709	81	1,115	D	D	49	275	63	412	71	325
Monterey city	200	2,232	35	335	23	378	32	422	85	672	95	411	240	4,470
Monterey Park city	194	1,787	185	1,227	125	504	30	300	100	3,428	112	279	190	1,597
Moorpark city	60	900	55	1,072	9	82	16	64	35	433	40	185	114	388
Moraga town	33	435	9	31	NA	NA	D	D	24	75	9	20	68	209
Moreno Valley city	326	9,094	D	D	111	7,110	33	306	77	561	88	336	87	538
Morgan Hill city	D	D	56	2,108	14	31	D	D	66	437	74	255	130	858
Morro Bay city	66	538	5	16	10	57	7	38	18	82	24	61	33	64
Mountain House CDP	3	4	NA	NA	NA	NA	NA	NA	NA	NA	6	6	19	23
Mountain View city	210	4,054	92	1,867	18	181	276	42,388	74	1,345	145	812	537	13,889
Murrieta city	228	4,930	106	968	35	266	39	279	146	764	167	603	282	1,317
Muscoy CDP	8	21	NA	NA	5	18	NA	NA	NA	NA	4	4	NA	NA
Napa city	295	4,518	75	505	46	612	34	310	150	991	120	569	D	D
National City city	295	6,265	93	1,571	38	1,612	15	152	55	703	55	306	54	585
Newark city	161	4,149	55	1,167	38	1,191	19	670	D	D	51	247	157	2,442
Newman city	18	181	4	23	D	D	NA	NA	5	17	6	9	9	80
Newport Beach city	472	7,370	224	1,915	55	779	104	1,768	738	11,359	841	4,996	1,348	9,092
Nipomo CDP	25	345	17	92	5	33	3	8	14	49	15	45	25	73
Norco city	108	1,527	28	534	25	68	5	24	34	158	37	89	79	1,338
North Auburn CDP	89	2,003	10	118	3	19	7	21	28	142	29	92	D	D
North Fair Oaks CDP	37	230	12	106	D	D	D	D	D	D	6	34	32	185
North Highlands CDP	148	2,347	49	812	40	407	9	230	40	224	56	290	61	345
North Tustin CDP	12	50	17	61	9	27	9	28	14	38	D	D	D	D
Norwalk city	172	3,479	96	1,431	52	1,286	15	303	59	549	55	204	68	1,383
Novato city	162	2,656	67	627	24	156	51	1,350	128	832	81	391	247	2,294
Oakdale city	78	970	16	155	10	57	3	24	37	226	26	157	36	579
Oak Hills CDP	7	35	NA	NA	D	D	NA	NA	3	4	4	4	8	14
Oakland city	995	11,810	341	4,811	276	15,198	252	6,799	382	6,892	544	3,196	1,628	14,453
Oakley city	37	403	7	D	D	D	NA	NA	11	54	21	61	23	121
Oak Park CDP	12	59	6	23	D	D	D	D	D	D	D	D	59	104
Oceanside city	398	6,639	144	1,563	43	737	53	673	136	766	187	678	350	1,814
Oildale CDP	53	597	4	43	8	116	NA	NA	8	40	20	156	20	80
Olivehurst CDP	17	110	D	D	6	43	NA	NA	NA	NA	4	6	NA	NA
Ontario city	590	14,963	775	13,440	368	17,898	64	2,450	218	2,766	218	1,786	D	D
Orange city	538	8,816	334	4,361	75	1,313	76	1,014	335	5,826	300	2,196	744	9,814
Orange Cove city	18	92	NA	NA	NA	NA	NA	NA	NA	NA	NA	NA	NA	NA
Orangevale CDP	43	773	D	D	5	19	3	24	52	152	38	122	72	264
Orcutt CDP	36	340	9	37	11	34	NA	NA	18	59	26	75	39	132
Orinda city	28	265	9	81	NA	NA	10	96	62	706	59	147	124	349
Oroville city	100	1,425	10	100	5	82	6	52	46	175	19	54	29	139
Oxnard city	437	8,471	211	3,685	120	1,248	55	720	179	1,211	168	627	257	2,222
Pacifica city	58	681	10	29	D	D	D	D	25	93	30	52	83	236
Pacific Grove city	54	491	NA	NA	NA	NA	4	22	19	86	D	D	28	124
Palmdale city	308	7,566	30	147	48	406	41	643	99	590	112	373	157	3,894
Palm Desert city	453	6,849	77	569	31	355	34	554	137	871	165	1,056	296	1,079
Palm Springs city	208	3,280	32	182	30	1,299	32	559	80	399	151	676	190	639
Palo Alto city	323	5,426	87	4,217	27	1,340	266	20,082	267	3,824	209	1,820	904	17,354
Palos Verdes Estates city	14	49	19	57	NA	NA	7	5	34	134	D	D	84	309
Paradise town	67	872	7	49	7	29	11	49	32	139	30	215	36	158
Paramount city	123	1,632	219	2,167	39	1,032	D	D	21	149	28	190	37	370
Parkway CDP	36	645	D	D	D	D	NA	NA	11	46	8	36	10	30
Parlier city	21	171	NA	NA	4	6	NA	NA	NA	NA	5	7	NA	NA
Pasadena city	559	9,940	167	1,143	45	631	218	3,072	503	10,934	434	2,153	1,352	17,626
Patterson city	45	1,756	10	467	15	401	5	32	17	63	9	76	10	35
Perris city	103	3,071	29	348	58	2,688	D	D	24	131	29	130	39	121
Petaluma city	273	3,900	103	2,461	39	1,407	50	559	123	1,344	72	360	D	D
Phelan CDP	18	236	NA	NA	D	D	3	16	NA	NA	D	D	11	37
Pico Rivera city	117	2,477	86	2,223	66	1,201	8	103	44	175	43	215	33	197
Piedmont city	8	99	NA	NA	NA	NA	D	D	D	D	21	42	47	90
Pinole city	63	1,653	D	D	D	D	4	24	26	110	D	D	36	133
Pittsburg city	106	2,234	33	771	28	180	12	211	33	168	34	219	49	283
Placentia city	99	1,337	106	1,078	20	143	9	18	69	227	70	388	121	465
Placerville city	99	1,286	NA	NA	NA	NA	5	84	D	D	17	54	41	139
Pleasant Hill city	135	3,149	25	139	17	123	D	D	78	613	55	340	160	840
Pleasanton city	314	6,397	129	3,227	43	528	94	10,441	248	4,458	218	1,075	634	8,558
Pomona city	330	4,329	316	3,279	114	1,639	27	452	87	657	102	652	132	1,085
Porterville city	151	2,652	24	207	22	1,472	15	209	54	523	25	90	44	184
Port Hueneme city	34	429	6	20	D	D	3	8	D	D	20	57	38	229
Poway city	140	3,001	95	1,987	40	1,268	23	545	D	D	92	343	265	1,479
Prunedale CDP	23	279	8	133	5	66	D	D	7	35	10	36	20	51
Quartz Hill CDP	24	134	NA	NA	D	D	NA	NA	7	9	10	18	12	35
Ramona CDP	72	822	12	26	17	79	7	39	25	88	40	98	53	141
Rancho Cordova city	282	3,851	165	2,261	50	650	62	3,230	169	12,456	90	447	243	5,602
Rancho Cucamonga city	476	8,566	377	4,598	186	2,652	45	649	244	3,431	256	1,003	491	3,294
Rancho Mirage city	72	1,132	D	D	D	D	10	195	37	132	D	D	78	372

1 Merchant wholesalers, except manufacturers' sales branches and offices.

STATE City, town, township, borough, or CDP (county if applicable)	Administration and support and waste management and mediation services		Educational services		Health care and social assistance		Arts, entertainment, and recreation		Accommodation and food services		Other services (except public administration)	
	Number of establishments	Number of employees	Number of establishments	Number of employees	Number of establishments	Number of employees	Number of establishments	Number of employees	Number of establishments	Number of employees	Number of establishments	Number of employees
	15	16	17	18	19	20	21	22	23	24	25	26
CALIFORNIA—Con.												
Martinez city	54	556	D	D	97	5,436	7	35	90	999	62	248
Marysville city	9	61	NA	NA	50	2,403	5	29	40	570	D	D
Maywood city	8	1,287	NA	NA	26	336	NA	NA	41	462	D	D
Mead Valley CDP	9	25	NA	NA	10	228	NA	NA	NA	NA	NA	NA
Mendota city	NA	NA	NA	NA	D	D	NA	NA	13	89	3	7
Menifee city	43	262	3	15	119	2,141	12	174	95	2,379	54	314
Menlo Park city	74	1,797	42	925	163	2,418	20	243	97	1,690	93	584
Merced city	54	741	8	74	288	5,102	20	221	138	2,513	77	433
Millbrae city	25	167	12	90	66	587	7	D	123	2,102	51	385
Mill Valley city	29	210	17	202	96	672	30	576	50	949	53	425
Milpitas city	72	2,118	40	397	285	3,405	26	584	314	5,598	133	1,011
Mission Viejo city	141	1,588	46	420	508	7,651	39	661	214	3,880	215	1,253
Modesto city	178	6,225	38	372	683	16,649	47	858	430	8,484	309	1,761
Monrovia city	50	904	12	81	104	1,651	23	182	119	2,024	85	575
Montclair city	39	753	5	41	126	2,517	D	D	93	1,627	D	D
Montebello city	43	945	7	7	194	3,248	7	182	142	2,355	106	571
Monterey city	73	3,961	16	293	307	6,055	39	994	234	6,544	99	897
Monterey Park city	104	2,188	32	222	282	4,342	12	132	242	3,327	87	378
Moorpark city	43	464	6	39	67	692	15	45	54	817	33	148
Moraga town	18	94	D	D	D	D	7	91	22	285	26	234
Moreno Valley city	106	6,402	13	819	248	6,376	22	310	257	4,746	132	572
Morgan Hill city	57	473	21	129	D	D	15	368	128	1,904	93	388
Morro Bay city	22	349	NA	NA	32	437	D	D	94	1,071	24	137
Mountain House CDP	4	43	NA	NA	15	57	NA	NA	NA	NA	NA	NA
Mountain View city	109	2,985	60	895	324	7,574	24	838	366	6,514	152	901
Murrieta city	133	2,059	26	207	340	5,494	37	548	195	3,737	186	1,259
Muscoy CDP	5	70	NA	NA	6	89	NA	NA	5	3	3	3
Napa city	143	2,440	32	327	306	5,637	30	451	229	5,716	173	1,100
National City city	47	662	D	D	177	3,842	12	139	177	2,997	124	687
Newark city	D	D	25	177	104	773	4	52	176	2,471	92	587
Newman city	NA	NA	NA	NA	D	D	NA	NA	14	130	4	14
Newport Beach city	240	13,977	71	534	1,036	13,306	131	1,708	411	13,281	322	2,215
Nipomo CDP	22	619	NA	NA	21	235	D	D	26	452	9	44
Norco city	50	824	9	58	47	557	9	117	D	D	72	412
North Auburn CDP	25	421	6	156	99	2,059	6	131	63	1,080	D	D
North Fair Oaks CDP	30	333	NA	NA	D	D	5	96	26	185	36	105
North Highlands CDP	63	1,429	5	45	67	2,416	8	148	86	1,679	84	352
North Tustin CDP	23	150	9	29	52	309	D	D	8	85	9	38
Norwalk city	54	4,445	5	39	160	4,090	11	209	148	2,106	89	419
Novato city	134	2,250	21	598	194	2,670	27	438	127	2,081	113	881
Oakdale city	11	79	D	D	D	D	D	D	55	885	D	D
Oak Hills CDP	11	36	NA	NA	4	14	NA	NA	6	51	5	10
Oakland city	410	10,057	185	3,274	1,279	30,875	164	3,257	1,108	17,173	945	7,498
Oakley city	D	D	4	24	39	248	3	D	D	D	D	D
Oak Park CDP	D	D	4	11	18	90	28	80	13	129	13	33
Oceanside city	182	16,244	36	252	363	5,870	47	1,100	359	7,350	231	1,596
Oildale CDP	12	177	NA	NA	17	509	NA	NA	41	572	12	25
Olivehurst CDP	NA	NA	NA	NA	11	141	NA	NA	5	51	D	D
Ontario city	257	37,813	19	548	268	6,152	30	872	364	7,906	231	2,627
Orange city	290	32,330	53	519	687	20,941	53	731	450	8,572	353	2,549
Orange Cove city	D	D	NA	NA	4	74	NA	NA	3	8	4	7
Orangevale CDP	40	247	4	23	59	743	4	68	35	430	55	330
Orcutt CDP	30	100	6	23	48	227	6	25	34	505	22	48
Orinda city	22	197	D	D	77	532	16	163	31	363	22	109
Oroville city	13	123	NA	NA	81	2,678	5	136	59	909	53	242
Oxnard city	194	5,686	23	89	455	7,068	36	398	312	6,273	227	1,132
Pacifica city	21	105	13	112	45	563	D	D	72	1,008	52	157
Pacific Grove city	27	154	NA	NA	54	822	8	163	76	1,245	36	178
Palmdale city	66	417	13	77	261	2,704	17	520	235	4,743	121	664
Palm Desert city	141	3,069	17	96	286	3,891	48	2,602	195	6,563	189	1,388
Palm Springs city	81	2,001	8	60	283	5,879	49	1,363	276	6,406	114	868
Palo Alto city	120	1,566	76	717	412	27,393	57	1,219	321	7,457	185	1,962
Palos Verdes Estates city	19	109	7	49	51	156	22	311	15	213	8	34
Paradise town	23	104	4	14	114	2,715	13	124	D	D	46	185
Paramount city	44	2,663	5	44	70	1,603	4	42	69	830	66	480
Parkway CDP	13	77	NA	NA	30	410	NA	NA	19	301	D	D
Parlier city	NA	NA	NA	NA	8	147	NA	NA	12	73	3	3
Pasadena city	258	9,696	98	1,244	1,104	19,293	249	2,311	557	11,645	448	2,941
Patterson city	12	183	NA	NA	25	196	4	15	D	D	15	52
Perris city	31	666	NA	NA	57	829	D	D	77	1,310	39	166
Petaluma city	132	1,637	27	169	193	3,342	41	631	180	2,830	139	899
Phelan CDP	8	34	NA	NA	14	69	3	6	14	206	5	10
Pico Rivera city	36	1,423	6	50	83	1,570	5	98	115	2,022	67	518
Piedmont city	D	D	D	D	26	82	NA	NA	NA	NA	8	22
Pinole city	22	64	3	7	95	1,232	6	23	77	1,260	D	D
Pittsburg city	44	398	4	12	85	1,059	5	80	94	1,514	80	681
Placentia city	76	2,719	13	72	137	1,375	D	D	106	1,479	D	D
Placerville city	20	142	D	D	87	2,395	D	D	67	855	44	241
Pleasant Hill city	56	552	25	184	157	2,631	18	446	114	2,104	75	513
Pleasanton city	D	D	73	599	338	7,384	44	1,109	252	4,537	169	1,401
Pomona city	83	1,604	16	424	322	9,677	18	394	237	4,464	163	968
Porterville city	19	640	5	26	154	3,293	D	D	92	1,422	43	281
Port Hueneme city	17	117	D	D	24	229	NA	NA	D	D	21	77
Poway city	74	1,032	27	331	191	2,727	31	452	112	1,542	108	540
Prunedale CDP	23	71	NA	NA	D	D	3	9	15	171	D	D
Quartz Hill CDP	17	370	3	D	6	27	NA	NA	12	178	D	D
Ramona CDP	26	227	3	4	46	401	D	D	37	614	53	198
Rancho Cordova city	155	4,773	20	244	133	5,321	24	491	165	3,165	118	761
Rancho Cucamonga city	216	7,540	51	529	535	6,858	51	658	402	8,913	282	1,496
Rancho Mirage city	26	206	4	5	226	6,349	19	939	73	4,676	32	358

Table C. Incorporated Places, Census Designated Places (CDPs), and Minor Civil Divisions (MCDs) of 10,000 or More Population — **Economic Census**

STATE City, town, township, borough, or CDP (county if applicable)	Retail Trade — Number of establishments	Retail Trade — Number of employees	Wholesale trade[1] — Number of establishments	Wholesale trade[1] — Number of employees	Transportation and warehousing — Number of establishments	Transportation and warehousing — Number of employees	Information — Number of establishments	Information — Number of employees	Finance and insurance — Number of establishments	Finance and insurance — Number of employees	Real estate and rental and leasing — Number of establishments	Real estate and rental and leasing — Number of employees	Professional, scientific, and technical services — Number of establishments	Professional, scientific, and technical services — Number of employees
	1	2	3	4	5	6	7	8	9	10	11	12	13	14
CALIFORNIA—Con.														
Rancho Palos Verdes city	50	482	35	95	12	61	13	137	46	230	76	172	157	642
Rancho San Diego CDP	47	885	14	40	7	15	3	46	27	105	D	D	42	134
Rancho Santa Margarita city	73	1,967	65	488	8	32	22	1,067	75	642	75	249	221	1,731
Red Bluff city	76	1,103	9	71	D	D	D	D	35	162	22	62	27	152
Redding city	442	7,306	110	1,223	57	701	49	881	198	1,683	165	672	288	1,748
Redlands city	213	4,753	53	622	51	1,597	24	2,807	128	973	98	477	245	1,199
Redondo Beach city	261	4,055	73	425	36	621	69	397	106	597	168	888	476	7,910
Redwood City city	222	4,818	69	2,137	17	173	135	18,023	156	2,000	163	858	477	10,934
Reedley city	54	562	14	124	8	178	8	47	27	135	D	D	23	70
Rialto city	150	3,299	54	1,109	120	5,938	D	D	38	231	49	211	39	266
Richmond city	228	4,845	100	1,730	86	2,669	34	467	50	243	78	395	172	2,147
Ridgecrest city	78	1,333	5	29	10	55	13	105	22	235	26	104	56	848
Rio Linda CDP	20	180	8	102	D	D	NA	NA	NA	NA	11	28	7	20
Ripon city	29	405	8	98	10	170	NA	NA	12	60	11	26	25	97
Riverbank city	50	1,036	D	D	16	120	D	D	12	67	12	19	9	51
Riverside city	867	15,315	324	5,890	201	5,217	107	2,011	363	3,676	370	1,809	674	5,250
Rocklin city	171	2,627	70	1,816	26	459	28	1,633	111	2,058	127	352	211	1,853
Rodeo CDP	8	110	D	D	NA	NA	NA	NA	D	D	NA	NA	D	D
Rohnert Park city	110	2,176	34	698	9	105	14	693	47	440	55	232	75	459
Rosamond CDP	27	260	4	D	D	D	NA	NA	NA	NA	16	38	10	44
Rosedale CDP	21	274	10	72	16	508	NA	NA	7	49	10	32	38	158
Rosemead city	177	1,807	129	593	60	386	22	135	57	422	55	156	100	358
Rosemont CDP	20	268	7	50	11	47	NA	NA	24	1,451	11	34	28	118
Roseville city	613	14,350	98	1,165	66	1,246	68	963	487	7,265	337	2,177	560	5,821
Rossmoor CDP	4	42	6	12	3	5	3	9	NA	NA	19	35	33	44
Rowland Heights CDP	178	1,423	168	655	101	182	16	77	83	477	101	285	137	361
Sacramento city	1,198	19,969	454	8,275	296	5,119	220	4,151	592	7,445	634	3,406	1,847	17,260
Salida CDP	36	772	26	617	9	66	D	D	16	100	13	86	25	261
Salinas city	443	7,831	134	2,729	147	1,419	50	732	138	1,265	116	542	D	D
San Anselmo town	48	356	16	267	D	D	7	15	22	99	D	D	79	219
San Bernardino city	515	13,661	135	3,386	108	11,340	54	489	163	2,271	118	523	220	1,925
San Bruno city	138	1,990	31	366	34	225	D	D	37	252	44	164	77	707
San Buenaventura (Ventura) city	497	7,449	162	1,753	67	908	58	628	193	1,029	217	996	497	3,948
San Carlos city	137	3,217	94	943	24	668	28	866	53	430	61	341	243	2,208
San Clemente city	239	3,320	163	1,672	D	D	43	340	143	591	154	887	448	1,530
San Diego city	4,240	66,413	1,866	22,288	941	15,446	903	28,147	2,729	42,625	3,293	18,066	8,428	115,825
San Diego Country Estates CDP	5	21	NA	NA	6	12	NA	NA	D	D	4	6	21	36
San Dimas city	128	1,816	100	571	14	107	15	103	67	513	61	518	148	2,068
San Fernando city	75	900	39	721	16	162	13	176	49	237	23	328	34	149
San Francisco city	3,396	49,883	963	14,014	386	10,482	1,775	83,500	2,328	64,847	2,132	19,351	7,193	117,838
San Gabriel city	218	1,627	126	513	63	238	18	72	91	607	92	194	160	905
Sanger city	50	715	11	97	D	D	3	28	16	79	D	D	13	40
San Jacinto city	68	1,092	15	71	20	56	5	49	9	42	D	D	23	113
San Jose city	2,204	43,442	1,055	35,492	339	7,658	521	23,324	1,060	12,709	1,139	6,062	3,276	45,002
San Juan Capistrano city	126	1,975	62	323	12	1,277	21	88	83	460	104	323	234	1,209
San Leandro city	301	7,348	234	3,337	119	3,171	39	1,112	D	D	137	834	131	686
San Lorenzo CDP	18	160	9	375	D	D	NA	NA	D	D	6	38	19	81
San Luis Obispo city	342	5,770	74	933	28	1,015	53	2,328	132	1,013	142	876	358	2,507
San Marcos city	268	4,415	134	1,139	48	889	34	600	106	541	148	494	263	1,510
San Marino city	44	152	43	122	D	D	10	22	48	259	89	229	113	325
San Mateo city	349	6,371	83	2,791	D	D	142	4,961	292	5,077	199	1,107	577	6,189
San Pablo city	78	1,024	10	61	8	33	D	D	19	120	17	51	13	110
San Rafael city	318	5,235	112	936	37	1,005	87	2,631	186	2,444	170	948	518	2,619
San Ramon city	109	1,975	97	1,608	27	547	89	5,634	228	5,139	128	878	566	5,263
Santa Ana city	841	12,828	540	6,092	130	2,444	125	1,963	427	9,445	315	2,503	1,067	10,446
Santa Barbara city	544	6,220	112	2,017	55	664	115	2,483	288	2,063	353	1,362	670	4,249
Santa Clara city	335	4,802	344	9,949	80	1,072	227	13,110	120	1,555	204	2,162	1,000	21,327
Santa Clarita city	555	10,464	219	3,121	D	D	164	949	252	1,763	285	1,204	630	3,375
Santa Cruz city	268	4,052	62	851	18	344	49	651	D	D	83	267	308	1,607
Santa Fe Springs city	147	2,362	671	14,529	152	3,763	21	206	45	318	91	948	126	1,107
Santa Maria city	357	6,048	105	1,347	91	1,241	33	516	112	891	88	403	154	983
Santa Monica city	672	10,704	156	2,220	35	924	680	15,976	304	3,009	523	3,086	1,259	10,777
Santa Paula city	51	693	15	283	16	124	D	D	D	D	23	135	D	D
Santa Rosa city	679	11,842	156	1,909	63	736	76	1,237	311	3,272	246	1,106	617	3,918
Santee city	146	3,306	41	368	21	76	14	252	34	207	56	189	93	411
Saratoga city	D	D	14	33	D	D	D	D	49	178	D	D	178	554
Scotts Valley city	54	760	18	1,036	4	6	18	223	D	D	21	292	84	650
Seal Beach city	80	1,598	24	803	7	31	15	76	81	548	D	D	137	613
Seaside city	91	1,585	12	35	4	10	D	D	14	54	14	99	D	D
Selma city	68	1,424	14	240	14	62	7	34	17	85	15	45	18	65
Shafter city	33	323	19	506	25	1,715	NA	NA	9	38	7	29	8	17
Shasta Lake city	17	173	D	D	NA	NA	NA	NA	NA	NA	NA	NA	NA	NA
Sierra Madre city	17	105	14	49	D	D	D	D	15	73	22	36	48	109
Signal Hill city	89	2,928	84	716	29	378	11	66	27	128	35	188	90	947
Simi Valley city	410	6,234	149	1,332	46	407	71	962	176	2,324	142	508	377	2,085
Solana Beach city	94	939	33	480	6	56	25	256	74	367	104	454	233	1,370
Soledad city	29	255	7	53	8	39	NA	NA	9	33	13	46	NA	NA
Sonoma city	97	1,029	18	196	6	105	11	122	64	473	38	122	81	318
Soquel CDP	46	874	12	60	D	D	3	9	20	45	18	52	60	183
South El Monte city	151	1,297	504	3,553	44	172	7	75	17	50	D	D	43	251
South Gate city	161	3,177	54	795	67	1,305	11	161	46	225	54	160	35	664
South Lake Tahoe city	134	1,643	9	22	D	D	14	93	D	D	62	531	55	187
South Pasadena city	56	831	35	203	D	D	28	148	48	431	D	D	D	D
South San Francisco city	213	3,774	289	4,212	270	9,250	D	D	58	408	97	917	239	9,444
South San Jose Hills CDP	27	159	35	321	9	26	NA	NA	NA	NA	9	53	NA	NA
South Whittier CDP	48	335	14	56	21	92	D	D	D	D	12	34	15	32
Spring Valley CDP	28	136	19	178	14	44	3	5	D	D	24	106	34	102

1 Merchant wholesalers, except manufacturers' sales branches and offices.

Table C. Incorporated Places, Census Designated Places (CDPs), and Minor Civil Divisions (MCDs) of 10,000 or More Population — **Economic Census**

STATE City, town, township, borough, or CDP (county if applicable)	Administration and support and waste management and mediation services — Number of establishments	Number of employees	Educational services — Number of establishments	Number of employees	Health care and social assistance — Number of establishments	Number of employees	Arts, entertainment, and recreation — Number of establishments	Number of employees	Accommodation and food services — Number of establishments	Number of employees	Other services (except public administration) — Number of establishments	Number of employees
	15	16	17	18	19	20	21	22	23	24	25	26
CALIFORNIA—Con.												
Rancho Palos Verdes city .	28	94	10	30	132	914	20	328	40	1,532	40	100
Rancho San Diego CDP...	19	83	4	18	38	435	7	37	46	727	D	D
Rancho Santa Margarita city...	59	1,366	34	369	97	900	26	365	78	1,861	71	346
Red Bluff city	17	250	NA	NA	82	1,601	6	60	61	764	32	85
Redding city.................	125	4,110	22	170	565	10,007	35	494	260	4,767	206	1,272
Redlands city	85	2,859	32	200	379	7,221	27	602	185	3,318	143	970
Redondo Beach city	89	696	55	385	260	1,792	D	D	231	4,891	158	762
Redwood City city...........	154	2,440	43	1,106	346	6,563	38	931	244	3,724	163	1,846
Reedley city	7	117	3	12	54	1,631	3	39	D	D	D	D
Rialto city	40	778	4	16	96	936	8	123	113	1,999	81	388
Richmond city	98	2,059	10	207	150	4,940	35	1,417	138	1,408	133	719
Ridgecrest city	19	247	D	D	67	1,315	D	D	68	1,012	34	149
Rio Linda CDP...............	26	124	NA	NA	D	D	NA	NA	14	133	D	D
Ripon city....................	9	52	NA	NA	D	D	6	55	26	387	D	D
Riverbank city	13	113	NA	NA	25	236	NA	NA	45	834	18	73
Riverside city	306	12,934	62	398	969	21,881	69	1,186	628	12,935	456	2,928
Rocklin city	73	1,322	27	193	192	1,663	18	409	132	1,950	90	483
Rodeo CDP..................	3	12	NA	NA	D	D	NA	NA	9	47	4	13
Rohnert Park city............	55	890	D	D	93	1,001	13	255	102	4,092	71	418
Rosamond CDP..............	D	D	NA	NA	8	36	5	139	19	254	8	38
Rosedale CDP...............	22	346	NA	NA	20	58	5	70	7	136	19	151
Rosemead city	43	800	23	165	147	2,155	D	D	177	2,780	100	300
Rosemont CDP...............	26	1,598	D	D	D	D	NA	NA	D	D	13	63
Roseville city	208	5,814	41	228	583	15,615	58	1,894	405	8,923	250	2,574
Rossmoor CDP...............	7	72	NA	NA	D	D	D	D	5	78	6	14
Rowland Heights CDP.....	45	306	29	158	127	699	11	116	207	2,642	80	239
Sacramento city.............	574	20,947	135	1,916	1,351	46,565	148	3,862	1,210	24,804	1,017	8,213
Salida CDP..................	21	619	7	63	25	1,705	NA	NA	27	442	13	62
Salinas city	136	2,083	20	127	345	7,217	26	451	300	4,775	214	1,236
San Anselmo town..........	22	185	13	172	43	297	12	311	38	554	34	146
San Bernardino city	143	15,038	17	961	452	12,967	22	467	362	6,183	226	1,537
San Bruno city	58	890	7	94	107	1,131	D	D	117	1,655	95	670
San Buenaventura (Ventura) city	177	2,640	40	272	583	11,196	72	718	353	6,364	262	1,266
San Carlos city	65	1,106	25	375	113	1,787	21	145	105	1,698	97	963
San Clemente city	109	1,254	26	202	249	2,870	48	444	174	2,918	129	745
San Diego city	1,996	92,527	566	5,802	4,712	97,758	629	18,611	4,076	98,278	2,801	23,453
San Diego Country Estates CDP...............	11	60	NA	NA	5	16	3	18	4	29	D	D
San Dimas city..............	56	547	7	19	141	2,450	18	244	89	1,800	60	924
San Fernando city	18	1,175	3	28	67	814	NA	NA	60	931	59	319
San Francisco city	1,431	56,436	496	7,183	3,330	69,425	616	15,360	4,559	89,123	2,470	25,451
San Gabriel city	73	322	21	95	231	3,617	10	127	184	2,381	141	477
Sanger city..................	D	D	NA	NA	39	367	3	14	38	766	18	228
San Jacinto city	20	34	NA	NA	36	283	NA	NA	48	629	38	131
San Jose city	1,146	46,838	335	3,475	2,617	38,211	251	8,417	2,215	39,154	1,569	10,237
San Juan Capistrano city..	64	1,104	18	130	151	1,867	D	D	76	1,463	73	336
San Leandro city............	D	100	16	152	279	8,061	20	D	233	3,441	201	1,346
San Lorenzo CDP...........	D	D	NA	NA	31	112	NA	NA	30	432	D	D
San Luis Obispo city........	85	1,667	24	225	389	6,129	25	311	237	5,150	139	837
San Marcos city	147	3,758	34	263	201	3,183	23	237	211	3,820	178	1,179
San Marino city	20	99	15	80	74	312	D	D	39	422	26	92
San Mateo city..............	181	8,099	57	601	553	7,558	40	818	371	5,655	245	1,601
San Pablo city...............	15	166	5	23	57	1,357	NA	NA	71	878	D	D
San Rafael city	153	1,877	50	364	365	6,843	80	602	228	3,418	258	1,899
San Ramon city	180	4,610	46	628	360	4,323	33	502	158	2,702	148	980
Santa Ana city	450	23,257	58	951	876	14,624	58	1,140	602	9,481	469	3,298
Santa Barbara city	261	3,673	71	790	590	9,902	117	1,434	487	9,711	306	2,304
Santa Clara city	209	13,209	71	1,561	304	9,674	46	2,126	455	7,951	292	2,126
Santa Clarita city	255	5,322	70	603	619	8,461	177	1,201	384	7,810	333	2,013
Santa Cruz city	78	737	56	644	263	3,569	41	2,033	279	5,496	138	1,169
Santa Fe Springs city	93	3,260	12	476	74	1,983	D	D	100	1,576	123	1,321
Santa Maria city.............	105	2,607	10	61	335	6,512	23	340	197	3,198	165	1,181
Santa Monica city	207	3,618	116	1,224	949	10,936	772	3,131	503	13,766	482	3,854
Santa Paula city.............	D	D	NA	NA	43	390	D	D	43	723	45	261
Santa Rosa city	233	5,140	51	586	766	14,989	81	1,419	422	6,895	348	2,603
Santee city..................	58	579	15	96	120	956	D	D	133	2,420	109	602
Saratoga city................	17	131	19	131	116	1,411	16	258	57	628	44	108
Scotts Valley city	23	178	14	71	47	1,704	D	D	49	532	37	469
Seal Beach city..............	25	391	8	12	93	828	D	D	97	2,199	42	470
Seaside city.................	42	206	4	15	21	290	NA	NA	80	1,451	54	251
Selma city...................	10	41	NA	NA	46	1,067	5	65	54	816	D	D
Shafter city..................	D	D	D	D	14	280	3	8	D	D	12	52
Shasta Lake city	5	8	D	D	13	220	NA	NA	10	74	D	D
Sierra Madre city	14	126	D	D	44	751	12	45	19	249	21	88
Signal Hill city	52	3,230	5	133	55	581	11	99	42	1,112	66	659
Simi Valley city..............	203	2,611	D	D	375	4,312	73	634	247	4,200	190	1,043
Solana Beach city...........	41	177	20	189	119	1,235	19	274	53	1,300	55	485
Soledad city	9	28	NA	NA	14	159	NA	NA	22	302	5	14
Sonoma city................	24	6,134	7	103	81	1,360	D	D	72	1,856	35	163
Soquel CDP.................	27	218	D	D	62	560	8	68	28	358	23	191
South El Monte city..........	39	707	NA	NA	34	1,119	4	6	63	916	74	325
South Gate city	38	525	7	29	83	895	9	204	127	2,090	74	269
South Lake Tahoe city	32	286	6	37	91	1,190	D	D	194	3,880	66	433
South Pasadena city........	38	1,734	18	61	128	731	68	296	66	1,057	41	168
South San Francisco city..	135	4,661	12	112	203	3,351	22	295	262	5,006	129	1,495
South San Jose Hills CDP	9	25	NA	NA	12	99	NA	NA	D	D	D	D
South Whittier CDP..........	16	84	3	D	49	287	NA	NA	29	341	D	D
Spring Valley CDP	25	326	3	11	31	526	3	2	22	354	30	134

Table C. Incorporated Places, Census Designated Places (CDPs), and Minor Civil Divisions (MCDs) of 10,000 or More Population — **Economic Census**

STATE City, town, township, borough, or CDP (county if applicable)	Retail Trade Number of establishments	Number of employees	Wholesale trade[1] Number of establishments	Number of employees	Transportation and warehousing Number of establishments	Number of employees	Information Number of establishments	Number of employees	Finance and insurance Number of establishments	Number of employees	Real estate and rental and leasing Number of establishments	Number of employees	Professional, scientific, and technical services Number of establishments	Number of employees
	1	2	3	4	5	6	7	8	9	10	11	12	13	14
CALIFORNIA—Con.														
Stanford CDP	D	D	3	15	NA	NA	3	42	6	34	NA	NA	14	142
Stanton city	96	1,347	31	298	19	111	NA	NA	20	81	25	93	44	274
Stevenson Ranch CDP	39	924	D	D	7	22	12	70	32	234	42	122	71	174
Stockton city	702	11,974	228	5,449	248	4,966	55	1,204	267	3,717	215	1,352	359	2,836
Suisun City city	32	604	D	D	8	55	NA	NA	D	D	9	30	19	74
Sunnyvale city	256	4,782	163	8,817	29	1,088	205	25,725	122	2,181	198	1,109	835	26,102
Sun Village CDP	7	44	D	D	D	D	NA	NA	NA	NA	NA	NA	NA	NA
Susanville city	52	751	NA	NA	NA	NA	D	D	D	D	15	33	17	64
Tamalpais-Homestead Valley CDP	15	88	6	8	NA	NA	D	D	D	D	15	52	71	120
Tehachapi city	38	819	NA	NA	NA	NA	6	33	18	79	D	D	D	D
Temecula city	460	9,426	163	2,442	59	540	53	597	225	1,420	224	710	430	2,149
Temescal Valley CDP	15	138	17	270	15	80	NA	NA	D	D	6	51	21	43
Temple City city	103	1,188	74	247	41	88	9	49	54	226	68	153	77	258
Thousand Oaks city	531	9,044	191	3,365	45	649	126	1,858	510	4,318	311	1,224	D	D
Torrance city	709	13,168	620	5,573	196	2,241	124	1,628	390	4,038	401	1,907	D	D
Tracy city	230	4,578	71	2,418	115	10,398	21	224	84	405	93	216	140	580
Truckee town	96	940	12	68	17	76	12	83	21	121	59	120	105	337
Tulare city	187	3,241	54	726	42	470	10	190	62	352	52	219	41	285
Turlock city	239	4,311	64	891	43	702	14	232	103	685	64	230	101	749
Tustin city	297	6,742	185	2,558	33	564	63	2,273	235	2,786	196	1,123	626	3,688
Twentynine Palms city	32	286	4	18	6	138	D	D	8	61	15	166	12	90
Ukiah city	129	1,800	13	149	14	185	17	136	44	436	46	228	64	298
Union City city	112	2,177	143	4,672	71	699	24	290	D	D	48	175	117	523
Upland city	253	4,112	119	754	36	446	31	546	120	577	120	1,096	230	1,530
Vacaville city	328	6,309	40	333	30	448	21	280	92	907	107	485	133	1,077
Valinda CDP	15	52	NA	NA	D	D	NA	NA	3	10	7	16	7	16
Vallejo city	237	4,529	30	592	42	639	25	260	66	876	77	272	105	526
Valle Vista CDP	20	228	NA	NA	NA	NA	NA	NA	NA	NA	9	27	10	19
Valley Center CDP	28	171	11	34	D	D	D	D	D	D	16	27	40	154
Victorville city	314	6,756	44	281	51	1,160	36	738	97	751	101	451	90	699
View Park-Windsor Hills CDP	16	104	NA	NA	4	7	10	27	NA	NA	9	22	18	31
Vincent CDP	12	53	D	D	4	11	NA	NA	NA	NA	NA	NA	NA	NA
Vineyard CDP	14	459	NA	NA	D	D	NA	NA	10	35	9	21	21	32
Visalia city	423	7,865	138	1,934	81	2,529	38	638	183	2,112	154	923	256	1,457
Vista city	258	4,526	193	3,641	30	308	37	320	81	406	155	724	267	1,561
Walnut city	125	1,172	240	884	46	153	22	127	45	223	75	164	153	444
Walnut Creek city	301	6,960	69	700	D	D	76	2,067	415	6,402	238	1,482	724	6,893
Walnut Park CDP	22	198	NA	NA	8	89	NA	NA	16	58	NA	NA	9	34
Wasco city	36	450	4	20	D	D	NA	NA	7	21	15	46	5	21
Watsonville city	150	2,378	63	1,053	35	353	14	155	58	321	57	255	78	470
West Carson CDP	62	810	24	149	25	107	9	69	D	D	22	85	D	D
West Covina city	284	5,745	91	234	62	310	28	327	120	770	107	453	155	710
West Hollywood city	306	3,710	100	620	8	34	243	2,051	70	377	185	1,104	446	3,140
Westminster city	397	5,144	113	535	36	177	28	346	98	891	124	406	162	755
Westmont CDP	30	134	NA	NA	4	5	NA	NA	3	12	4	37	7	28
West Puente Valley CDP	5	17	6	31	12	122	NA	NA	NA	NA	NA	NA	D	D
West Rancho Dominguez CDP	70	783	131	1,771	103	2,153	NA	NA	6	37	21	261	15	160
West Sacramento city	157	2,413	144	4,360	101	3,491	D	D	D	D	94	765	93	1,262
West Whittier-Los Nietos CDP	26	294	8	34	D	D	NA	NA	5	29	11	36	5	5
Whittier city	215	3,587	63	399	42	215	22	226	107	541	D	D	176	1,057
Wildomar city	34	424	7	51	16	60	6	34	12	45	20	154	40	94
Willowbrook CDP	18	184	4	55	D	D	NA	NA	NA	NA	NA	NA	NA	NA
Windsor town	61	1,179	23	525	16	267	6	19	28	121	25	494	55	244
Winter Gardens CDP	26	251	5	10	D	D	3	3	9	28	16	54	22	58
Winton CDP	14	107	NA	NA	NA	NA	NA	NA	NA	NA	3	4	D	D
Woodcrest CDP	10	40	5	37	10	70	NA	NA	NA	NA	5	10	16	36
Woodland city	152	2,362	71	1,253	40	1,562	11	118	D	D	53	241	85	446
Yorba Linda city	133	1,732	131	1,361	23	66	19	121	116	516	135	387	278	906
Yuba City city	243	4,174	38	378	74	306	D	D	97	631	66	306	97	456
Yucaipa city	99	1,081	20	106	14	119	9	31	28	109	53	164	68	198
Yucca Valley town	78	1,441	3	7	5	42	6	93	22	116	24	102	21	46
COLORADO	19,056	279,982	5,953	80,365	3,764	70,347	3,610	91,856	10,393	111,376	12,087	47,642	26,404	192,964
Arvada city	258	3,970	93	1,033	40	294	38	251	175	933	158	347	413	1,662
Aurora city	973	17,442	229	6,441	252	4,852	129	1,990	362	2,535	403	1,857	733	7,726
Berkley CDP	42	278	10	82	14	95	D	D	D	D	17	41	13	36
Black Forest CDP	11	35	D	D	8	9	9	22	D	D	D	D	74	156
Boulder city	593	9,518	210	3,228	26	581	225	3,749	328	2,422	393	1,608	1,524	16,400
Brighton city	106	2,210	25	712	34	127	D	D	53	286	50	143	64	415
Broomfield city	286	5,338	70	845	25	279	66	4,606	129	2,548	150	425	404	4,147
Cañon City city	84	1,380	6	14	8	159	9	63	37	168	26	139	33	106
Castle Pines city	29	364	8	17	NA	NA	6	10	32	58	40	89	83	208
Castle Rock town	206	3,790	D	D	11	29	34	289	108	374	122	324	258	828
Centennial city	293	5,719	185	3,450	D	D	145	5,991	444	8,432	356	1,100	744	4,758
Cherry Creek CDP	5	9	NA	NA	NA	NA	7	10	13	23	25	21	68	102
Cimarron Hills CDP	46	448	32	376	15	214	D	D	19	30	24	65	13	41
Clifton CDP	22	260	7	93	11	69	NA	NA	7	34	8	25	9	21
Colorado Springs city	1,698	26,651	347	3,869	180	3,188	256	8,939	1,044	11,136	1,092	3,867	2,097	20,579
Columbine CDP	46	610	D	D	4	13	16	158	32	136	D	D	103	326
Commerce City city	131	1,949	142	3,380	161	7,302	12	70	D	D	60	672	D	D
Dakota Ridge CDP	34	485	17	83	5	11	5	7	43	168	D	D	97	244
Denver city	2,471	32,753	1,191	20,941	523	26,441	751	19,634	1,789	27,906	2,033	11,307	5,133	50,003
Durango city	230	2,901	31	399	21	391	36	230	89	1,139	102	311	241	1,013
Englewood city	206	3,574	105	1,508	26	568	20	333	70	446	96	430	D	D
Erie town	29	453	10	82	D	D	8	27	31	81	D	D	119	215

1 Merchant wholesalers, except manufacturers' sales branches and offices.

Table C. Incorporated Places, Census Designated Places (CDPs), and Minor Civil Divisions (MCDs) of 10,000 or More Population — **Economic Census**

STATE City, town, township, borough, or CDP (county if applicable)	Administration and support and waste management and mediation services — Number of establishments (15)	Number of employees (16)	Educational services — Number of establishments (17)	Number of employees (18)	Health care and social assistance — Number of establishments (19)	Number of employees (20)	Arts, entertainment, and recreation — Number of establishments (21)	Number of employees (22)	Accommodation and food services — Number of establishments (23)	Number of employees (24)	Other services (except public administration) — Number of establishments (25)	Number of employees (26)
CALIFORNIA—Con.												
Stanford CDP	D	D	5	49	D	D	5	10	52	511	D	D
Stanton city	27	1,944	NA	NA	41	801	D	D	84	1,072	D	D
Stevenson Ranch CDP	16	1,157	3	D	48	266	20	47	D	D	D	D
Stockton city	211	7,485	29	225	761	19,134	50	989	492	7,809	364	2,813
Suisun City city	17	250	NA	NA	23	144	D	D	39	609	D	D
Sunnyvale city	118	4,703	58	477	475	5,651	48	958	431	6,502	197	1,086
Sun Village CDP	7	15	NA	NA	4	10	NA	NA	NA	NA	D	D
Susanville city	8	32	NA	NA	42	692	D	D	33	593	19	60
Tamalpais-Homestead Valley CDP	23	78	7	46	17	108	12	22	17	225	15	50
Tehachapi city	10	71	D	D	25	540	NA	NA	53	743	22	268
Temecula city	172	6,003	51	286	422	4,413	51	741	332	7,648	255	1,450
Temescal Valley CDP	14	90	D	D	15	118	6	D	7	112	D	D
Temple City city	39	114	26	165	111	1,140	4	6	74	1,338	63	191
Thousand Oaks city	263	2,902	64	508	723	8,242	123	1,455	335	7,485	259	1,238
Torrance city	275	8,926	107	1,324	1,112	17,983	88	1,430	480	10,197	307	2,220
Tracy city	71	1,387	22	137	197	2,677	21	418	185	3,065	124	598
Truckee town	55	424	12	43	63	930	26	576	67	2,544	47	278
Tulare city	39	428	4	12	115	1,602	D	D	89	1,527	53	302
Turlock city	67	822	7	94	213	4,512	17	325	173	3,395	116	1,104
Tustin city	148	2,082	38	399	472	4,110	40	541	293	5,630	166	1,415
Twentynine Palms city	8	37	NA	NA	15	236	4	46	48	773	18	95
Ukiah city	19	121	7	49	113	2,098	8	30	79	1,064	56	284
Union City city	D	D	26	205	165	2,453	D	D	128	2,158	94	880
Upland city	125	3,238	23	119	387	6,621	32	484	185	3,288	189	1,091
Vacaville city	76	1,890	17	246	215	5,747	24	436	198	3,994	143	883
Valinda CDP	12	21	NA	NA	13	81	NA	NA	9	125	D	D
Vallejo city	89	916	12	143	291	8,968	28	1,760	190	2,998	132	711
Valle Vista CDP	3	3	NA	NA	NA	NA	NA	NA	6	108	4	16
Valley Center CDP	24	79	NA	NA	22	98	4	12	D	D	10	31
Victorville city	58	1,392	16	109	257	6,432	15	343	190	3,915	122	585
View Park-Windsor Hills CDP	9	32	4	7	26	132	12	8	11	175	17	36
Vincent CDP	7	35	NA	NA	6	64	3	D	D	D	5	23
Vineyard CDP	16	151	NA	NA	30	194	6	13	16	244	D	D
Visalia city	D	D	22	153	467	10,168	29	589	271	4,990	182	1,184
Vista city	117	1,457	11	98	257	4,034	28	360	200	2,926	141	834
Walnut city	43	430	20	147	98	632	17	41	62	747	63	328
Walnut Creek city	150	5,469	39	444	533	13,584	60	655	235	4,912	222	3,127
Walnut Park CDP	7	68	NA	NA	29	170	NA	NA	13	193	7	10
Wasco city	D	D	NA	NA	18	427	NA	NA	D	D	11	37
Watsonville city	57	1,196	11	133	190	2,927	10	D	105	1,508	83	391
West Carson CDP	19	611	NA	NA	52	6,384	NA	NA	47	797	24	133
West Covina city	86	3,360	22	656	345	7,319	18	437	231	3,955	109	518
West Hollywood city	109	1,078	25	121	302	14,861	D	D	258	10,190	241	1,936
Westminster city	63	1,020	21	98	301	2,899	D	D	277	3,077	147	852
Westmont CDP	5	32	NA	NA	19	171	NA	NA	14	158	8	30
West Puente Valley CDP	5	38	NA	NA	10	83	NA	NA	NA	NA	NA	NA
West Rancho Dominguez CDP	24	645	NA	NA	22	447	4	16	21	363	24	168
West Sacramento city	54	1,519	10	74	92	1,445	11	737	D	D	115	985
West Whittier-Los Nietos CDP	6	338	D	D	20	403	NA	NA	28	389	21	93
Whittier city	83	1,392	13	338	319	10,435	13	486	215	3,604	131	820
Wildomar city	31	335	D	D	66	1,695	13	161	47	581	39	243
Willowbrook CDP	NA	NA	NA	NA	18	1,145	NA	NA	17	378	7	18
Windsor town	39	403	6	32	45	603	D	D	48	994	48	174
Winter Gardens CDP	26	292	NA	NA	20	156	3	6	18	230	D	D
Winton CDP	NA	NA	NA	NA	NA	NA	NA	NA	3	16	4	4
Woodcrest CDP	25	107	NA	NA	21	121	NA	NA	NA	NA	4	16
Woodland city	56	1,142	6	28	130	2,586	20	288	D	D	96	490
Yorba Linda city	92	715	34	233	211	1,644	D	D	113	1,908	96	582
Yuba City city	76	1,175	D	D	216	3,527	17	283	129	2,191	109	557
Yucaipa city	41	182	4	15	98	1,310	18	145	75	1,374	58	301
Yucca Valley town	12	31	3	13	64	590	5	36	51	756	33	150
COLORADO	9,308	261,328	2,239	17,276	16,659	320,813	3,028	58,229	14,121	290,915	11,667	74,317
Arvada city	176	1,906	34	176	281	4,503	44	672	208	4,129	202	1,187
Aurora city	397	12,240	74	552	791	26,587	69	D	680	13,457	526	3,512
Berkley CDP	16	317	NA	NA	NA	NA	NA	NA	12	57	19	111
Black Forest CDP	33	140	4	5	20	45	NA	NA	9	90	D	D
Boulder city	213	3,022	140	1,092	671	8,626	148	1,525	433	10,606	387	2,873
Brighton city	36	706	10	29	88	1,851	4	D	85	1,534	59	290
Broomfield city	110	2,538	46	399	197	2,472	35	398	178	3,689	145	732
Cañon City city	15	267	D	D	79	1,838	D	D	57	984	28	144
Castle Pines city	12	47	7	22	26	259	D	D	21	283	22	137
Castle Rock town	79	558	32	156	180	2,166	D	D	116	2,307	133	636
Centennial city	258	11,069	75	1,785	450	6,621	48	897	245	6,353	259	1,657
Cherry Creek CDP	7	160	NA	NA	19	127	NA	NA	3	3	NA	NA
Cimarron Hills CDP	46	526	3	D	D	D	4	35	22	355	D	D
Clifton CDP	D	D	NA	NA	6	22	D	D	20	466	12	35
Colorado Springs city	698	18,856	188	1,345	1,850	35,415	219	3,178	1,111	26,615	995	8,956
Columbine CDP	32	132	6	35	D	D	7	9	32	519	D	D
Commerce City city	83	1,999	10	122	44	630	D	D	78	1,207	106	722
Dakota Ridge CDP	40	96	12	49	42	357	5	83	20	259	D	D
Denver city	1,449	88,370	372	3,207	2,302	56,165	473	11,883	2,354	55,545	1,874	15,112
Durango city	67	311	17	99	181	3,058	34	200	170	3,745	98	461
Englewood city	111	2,026	D	D	232	8,097	D	D	117	1,934	137	862
Erie town	27	159	7	25	45	259	6	53	25	408	26	152

Table C. Incorporated Places, Census Designated Places (CDPs), and Minor Civil Divisions (MCDs) of 10,000 or More Population — **Economic Census**

STATE City, town, township, borough, or CDP (county if applicable)	Retail Trade — Number of establishments	Retail Trade — Number of employees	Wholesale trade[1] — Number of establishments	Wholesale trade[1] — Number of employees	Transportation and warehousing — Number of establishments	Transportation and warehousing — Number of employees	Information — Number of establishments	Information — Number of employees	Finance and insurance — Number of establishments	Finance and insurance — Number of employees	Real estate and rental and leasing — Number of establishments	Real estate and rental and leasing — Number of employees	Professional, scientific, and technical services — Number of establishments	Professional, scientific, and technical services — Number of employees
	1	2	3	4	5	6	7	8	9	10	11	12	13	14
COLORADO—Con.														
Evans city	33	444	15	247	D	D	NA	NA	D	D	6	38	11	59
Federal Heights city	47	658	D	D	5	16	NA	NA	D	D	24	112	13	67
Firestone town	25	945	D	D	7	3	NA	NA	14	55	12	28	26	97
Fort Carson CDP	7	52	NA	NA	NA	NA	NA	NA	7	26	NA	NA	34	381
Fort Collins city	606	10,749	129	2,126	47	432	126	1,782	368	2,231	420	1,369	943	5,898
Fort Morgan city	55	766	10	68	15	126	13	217	27	154	12	30	21	79
Fountain city	58	1,731	NA	NA	15	731	8	20	22	102	12	41	23	93
Frederick town	18	489	21	331	D	D	NA	NA	D	D	15	70	30	163
Fruita city	30	316	D	D	D	D	NA	NA	11	43	14	72	27	94
Golden city	102	1,562	50	845	8	173	15	169	51	1,102	62	346	216	1,597
Grand Junction city	433	6,851	147	1,390	81	1,442	D	D	210	1,344	222	727	359	3,120
Greeley city	311	5,520	88	833	68	1,145	34	950	159	2,598	142	754	213	1,068
Greenwood Village city	113	2,190	55	554	16	75	125	7,991	467	12,341	205	1,006	556	6,938
Gunbarrel CDP	5	13	5	7	NA	NA	NA	NA	4	16	17	23	61	69
Highlands Ranch CDP	191	4,288	80	545	17	60	55	1,320	194	3,237	233	403	577	2,303
Johnstown town	23	522	11	164	11	115	D	D	12	102	11	17	39	123
Ken Caryl CDP	73	948	15	127	12	53	23	356	87	537	84	139	186	1,151
Lafayette city	79	1,114	38	384	7	53	19	86	38	139	D	D	202	2,330
Lakewood city	677	11,479	140	920	61	1,003	95	1,016	359	2,969	295	1,151	871	7,165
Littleton city	228	4,331	63	1,245	14	254	D	D	135	680	116	376	379	2,009
Lone Tree city	212	5,694	16	97	D	D	D	D	57	948	53	205	111	516
Longmont city	292	5,383	75	654	34	515	41	981	151	766	136	393	402	5,245
Louisville city	79	1,381	44	1,093	D	D	30	1,639	66	494	67	493	247	1,732
Loveland city	336	6,144	77	1,489	43	1,566	29	1,215	154	950	146	433	301	2,032
Montrose city	120	1,854	29	201	25	405	D	D	52	304	43	131	76	476
Northglenn city	120	2,346	18	123	18	32	D	D	54	435	35	71	64	307
Parker town	193	3,741	35	199	27	132	26	172	114	417	121	223	247	802
Pueblo city	383	6,341	59	647	46	945	37	925	181	1,019	110	567	D	D
Pueblo West CDP	59	901	19	246	12	189	6	80	22	77	25	49	31	75
Security-Widefield CDP	28	198	D	D	10	22	NA	NA	18	53	20	28	24	61
Sherrelwood CDP	23	305	NA	NA	D	D	D	D	NA	NA	9	38	14	292
Steamboat Springs city	167	1,603	36	310	19	178	D	D	43	250	124	526	169	595
Sterling city	86	1,043	11	37	17	179	D	D	D	D	14	43	22	87
Superior town	34	832	6	7	NA	NA	12	280	16	28	16	46	85	122
The Pinery CDP	8	17	4	6	5	16	NA	NA	13	27	16	13	61	152
Thornton city	220	5,547	34	182	51	207	37	951	100	501	121	434	182	1,160
Welby CDP	33	204	19	363	18	79	NA	NA	D	D	26	120	7	31
Westminster city	325	6,752	66	905	40	265	52	1,840	234	3,277	198	645	D	D
Wheat Ridge city	177	2,271	69	711	13	228	20	122	57	331	69	188	201	1,360
Windsor town	65	669	22	271	13	67	12	89	D	D	59	302	102	418
CONNECTICUT	12,391	186,297	3,504	62,298	1,660	44,938	1,796	42,615	5,924	115,871	3,459	20,224	9,184	108,479
Ansonia city	45	692	8	63	D	D	NA	NA	D	D	D	D	20	70
Avon town	78	1,098	10	40	4	65	D	D	69	583	D	D	80	522
Berlin town	75	1,090	42	983	14	400	D	D	28	253	13	65	46	313
Bethel town	56	809	27	254	9	482	4	84	31	189	15	82	50	1,097
Bloomfield town	64	1,004	56	914	29	1,442	D	D	D	D	31	235	58	387
Branford town	153	2,102	60	982	14	145	21	248	59	450	36	974	94	609
Bridgeport city	284	3,179	D	D	41	504	32	491	79	2,357	92	518	197	1,285
Bristol city	161	2,904	39	434	16	293	D	D	51	333	33	101	71	322
Brookfield town	87	1,610	D	D	10	304	8	59	28	87	14	25	57	364
Canton town	80	1,222	D	D	NA	NA	D	D	18	63	6	17	35	168
Cheshire town	63	1,037	51	2,131	9	611	13	118	52	819	31	134	95	900
Clinton town	116	1,798	10	57	4	34	8	44	15	53	D	D	D	D
Colchester town	49	949	D	D	4	34	5	34	19	75	12	42	22	230
Coventry town	18	202	NA	NA	4	41	NA	NA	4	15	4	8	14	33
Cromwell town	41	1,018	16	D	5	105	10	198	26	100	16	102	28	294
Danbury city	444	8,143	90	1,302	49	646	48	1,506	131	2,114	90	1,951	222	2,269
Darien town	101	1,577	16	217	11	334	14	144	90	597	28	116	87	539
Derby city	55	1,085	4	82	NA	NA	D	D	D	D	7	15	10	41
East Hampton town	23	304	NA	NA	4	42	D	D	12	39	7	8	16	60
East Hartford town	138	2,504	70	2,057	25	1,071	D	D	77	984	60	335	93	2,025
East Haven town	73	1,340	29	262	19	256	10	77	17	176	18	48	36	187
East Lyme town	61	791	6	87	6	72	4	45	20	113	26	64	45	130
East Windsor town	62	1,000	30	843	8	54	D	D	19	66	12	143	21	115
Ellington town	28	545	D	D	NA	NA	NA	NA	7	24	10	118	19	75
Enfield town	171	3,833	37	2,093	24	1,006	D	D	D	D	18	72	58	361
Fairfield town	235	3,772	50	618	24	420	24	208	167	1,040	77	351	298	1,741
Farmington town	188	3,532	32	651	8	177	34	656	157	4,761	46	273	147	2,101
Glastonbury town	116	1,874	30	402	7	361	21	478	172	2,039	D	D	164	2,290
Granby town	31	494	D	D	NA	NA	NA	NA	14	47	4	7	15	118
Greenwich town	348	4,059	77	795	31	370	48	2,043	391	7,466	158	1,330	314	1,740
Griswold (balance)	18	110	NA	NA	3	121	NA	NA	NA	NA	NA	NA	D	D
Groton town (balance)	106	1,597	14	185	12	278	13	136	29	324	30	86	D	D
Guilford town	100	1,291	37	384	8	783	19	216	78	778	20	47	101	797
Hamden town	173	2,674	47	802	20	579	D	D	85	540	47	255	118	832
Hartford city	371	3,334	94	1,962	65	2,809	83	2,092	250	29,318	169	1,270	410	8,800
Killingly town	48	744	8	719	9	838	4	24	16	99	D	D	16	105
Ledyard town	66	729	NA	NA	NA	NA	NA	NA	7	32	11	74	17	157
Madison town	60	661	15	79	D	D	D	D	43	221	23	93	64	390
Manchester town	326	6,411	42	818	21	570	22	504	75	376	55	268	102	1,153
Mansfield town	54	865	D	D	D	D	5	45	22	114	20	73	27	225
Meriden city	227	3,049	39	337	23	594	D	D	51	620	45	491	64	841
Middletown city	124	1,633	45	1,190	13	276	26	361	44	854	45	301	101	1,022
Milford city	312	6,036	95	1,239	24	506	28	438	84	849	58	264	181	1,189
Monroe town	62	907	26	511	5	99	D	D	32	128	16	27	58	225
Montville town	61	867	7	64	D	D	5	21	10	45	10	33	14	49
Naugatuck borough	60	1,139	18	469	8	269	4	38	20	306	D	D	35	210
New Britain city	162	1,797	41	378	15	542	D	D	37	799	38	174	74	601

1 Merchant wholesalers, except manufacturers' sales branches and offices.

Table C. Incorporated Places, Census Designated Places (CDPs), and Minor Civil Divisions (MCDs) of 10,000 or More Population — **Economic Census**

	Economic activity by sector, 2017											
	Administration and support and waste management and mediation services		Educational services		Health care and social assistance		Arts, entertainment, and recreation		Accommodation and food services		Other services (except public administration)	
STATE City, town, township, borough, or CDP (county if applicable)	Number of establish-ments	Number of employees	Number of establish-ments	Number of employees	Number of establish-ments	Number of employees	Number of establish-ments	Number of employees	Number of establish-ments	Number of employees	Number of establish-ments	Number of employees
	15	16	17	18	19	20	21	22	23	24	25	26
COLORADO—Con.												
Evans city	14	84	NA	NA	18	457	NA	NA	24	412	11	83
Federal Heights city	11	129	NA	NA	18	D	NA	NA	29	400	D	D
Firestone town	D	D	NA	NA	17	109	3	72	29	526	17	58
Fort Carson CDP	8	471	NA	NA	D	D	NA	NA	6	107	6	44
Fort Collins city	259	3,508	83	664	713	11,970	105	1,269	483	10,162	358	2,052
Fort Morgan city	15	749	NA	NA	41	832	3	45	42	760	25	90
Fountain city	16	65	NA	NA	D	D	D	D	54	1,187	24	148
Frederick town	19	401	3	25	10	120	NA	NA	9	188	D	D
Fruita city	13	42	NA	NA	19	585	D	D	30	454	12	26
Golden city	42	611	20	100	71	1,108	17	143	87	1,697	71	456
Grand Junction city	D	D	28	213	367	10,487	39	524	247	5,101	251	1,478
Greeley city	110	2,010	25	179	334	6,318	32	275	220	4,284	170	1,085
Greenwood Village city	140	19,370	33	393	278	4,694	29	D	172	4,204	124	1,140
Gunbarrel CDP	10	20	D	D	15	81	D	D	D	D	7	17
Highlands Ranch CDP	137	699	52	384	210	2,643	50	972	128	3,057	163	1,022
Johnstown town	12	50	NA	NA	29	449	D	D	D	D	D	D
Ken Caryl CDP	42	297	20	145	104	1,116	D	D	66	1,282	79	454
Lafayette city	41	298	23	90	152	4,464	10	518	74	D	64	305
Lakewood city	280	7,457	65	525	665	13,975	67	815	413	8,801	352	2,080
Littleton city	89	1,530	30	354	275	4,712	39	666	152	2,885	146	965
Lone Tree city	27	733	15	86	169	2,886	9	138	95	2,706	52	412
Longmont city	154	2,189	34	208	312	4,766	45	248	239	4,154	202	1,224
Louisville city	42	363	20	114	142	2,550	14	62	71	1,412	55	375
Loveland city	125	1,826	25	197	275	5,868	41	246	224	4,916	154	1,173
Montrose city	37	359	NA	NA	140	2,802	D	D	85	1,223	63	288
Northglenn city	37	244	10	57	79	868	11	D	57	1,668	66	411
Parker town	63	1,039	37	412	216	3,788	22	755	137	2,732	158	992
Pueblo city	89	3,347	D	D	369	12,940	34	674	273	4,962	179	1,056
Pueblo West CDP	29	253	NA	NA	28	298	5	62	34	515	D	D
Security-Widefield CDP	26	81	NA	NA	D	D	D	D	10	114	21	72
Sherrelwood CDP	13	63	4	43	8	51	NA	NA	17	259	D	D
Steamboat Springs city	73	623	11	58	124	1,405	37	345	141	5,067	91	479
Sterling city	9	40	NA	NA	62	1,092	D	D	36	636	41	162
Superior town	15	42	7	20	26	194	9	84	25	425	D	D
The Pinery CDP	11	95	NA	NA	D	D	7	D	NA	NA	8	10
Thornton city	99	1,143	19	112	209	3,899	31	D	189	4,025	138	1,196
Welby CDP	24	625	NA	NA	D	D	3	38	8	134	25	164
Westminster city	156	3,442	55	291	304	6,846	47	880	258	6,014	191	1,227
Wheat Ridge city	75	1,591	15	148	206	5,239	19	119	91	1,515	123	585
Windsor town	44	234	16	62	85	983	15	118	50	693	53	287
CONNECTICUT	5,417	89,113	1,166	10,179	11,065	295,083	1,744	30,320	8,762	146,456	7,507	46,490
Ansonia city	9	30	NA	NA	29	417	NA	NA	23	171	27	94
Avon town	29	171	13	81	124	2,512	D	D	D	D	50	457
Berlin town	40	401	6	20	62	1,858	11	89	55	571	68	305
Bethel town	42	584	6	26	43	799	9	D	61	574	41	214
Bloomfield town	46	403	D	D	123	2,306	D	D	41	770	45	421
Branford town	42	630	13	149	119	2,130	21	360	94	1,517	113	733
Bridgeport city	106	2,677	18	143	350	15,223	35	838	239	2,581	211	1,092
Bristol city	49	954	5	12	172	4,618	16	403	104	1,421	98	458
Brookfield town	37	494	12	67	56	820	13	274	42	582	D	D
Canton town	17	135	9	16	26	639	10	30	35	507	D	D
Cheshire town	44	1,263	11	45	102	2,323	12	138	D	D	59	429
Clinton town	23	131	4	12	33	490	D	D	25	266	D	D
Colchester town	18	16	4	30	52	718	NA	NA	36	523	30	127
Coventry town	12	24	NA	NA	D	D	3	D	12	131	6	29
Cromwell town	22	97	D	D	64	1,956	7	129	52	1,071	44	352
Danbury city	146	2,590	28	227	286	9,809	29	467	232	3,958	198	1,205
Darien town	46	312	15	123	69	639	25	835	71	1,124	78	578
Derby city	16	84	NA	NA	46	2,051	4	105	38	711	25	89
East Hampton town	10	32	NA	NA	18	287	5	33	17	267	D	D
East Hartford town	79	5,857	8	210	101	2,952	11	133	80	1,241	96	832
East Haven town	27	161	D	D	54	1,029	D	D	D	D	47	157
East Lyme town	19	119	9	39	53	760	13	131	D	D	42	143
East Windsor town	32	1,795	NA	NA	24	509	3	27	43	727	D	D
Ellington town	14	130	7	40	28	249	5	45	D	D	D	D
Enfield town	42	448	12	119	133	1,969	D	D	88	2,057	80	551
Fairfield town	116	1,787	41	351	263	3,813	52	803	202	3,230	162	1,845
Farmington town	84	1,363	13	63	132	5,830	19	374	86	1,907	68	1,103
Glastonbury town	61	958	17	72	171	3,041	29	349	82	1,884	95	498
Granby town	19	66	NA	NA	26	397	3	330	23	198	D	D
Greenwich town	139	819	48	222	245	4,680	78	1,858	170	3,250	219	1,304
Griswold town (balance)	6	25	NA	NA	5	112	NA	NA	11	80	6	33
Groton town (balance)	26	67	8	69	91	1,430	18	229	96	2,074	54	305
Guilford town	35	177	16	155	104	2,074	16	126	D	D	73	374
Hamden town	82	1,003	25	142	227	4,551	31	406	126	2,155	114	610
Hartford city	140	5,591	35	224	471	24,473	35	1,477	340	5,544	293	2,187
Killingly town	21	168	3	13	50	1,071	NA	NA	22	427	D	D
Ledyard town	21	86	NA	NA	27	309	4	8	33	6,907	19	140
Madison town	33	133	5	D	66	797	13	98	D	D	39	222
Manchester town	53	469	19	144	214	6,074	21	322	174	3,391	129	659
Mansfield town	10	44	D	D	D	D	D	D	63	1,340	28	281
Meriden city	59	2,212	14	85	148	5,315	7	483	119	1,316	101	477
Middletown city	58	835	13	106	183	9,759	20	334	126	1,535	106	513
Milford city	75	970	13	83	189	3,429	33	522	194	3,121	157	1,010
Monroe town	51	1,103	11	118	46	1,107	8	77	55	711	51	199
Montville town	15	84	NA	NA	29	458	7	188	55	8,305	23	127
Naugatuck borough	16	76	4	20	51	1,326	3	120	49	546	43	163
New Britain city	52	782	5	54	169	8,866	15	397	103	1,280	97	434

Table C. Incorporated Places, Census Designated Places (CDPs), and Minor Civil Divisions (MCDs) of 10,000 or More Population — Economic Census

	Economic activity by sector, 2017													
	Retail Trade		Wholesale trade¹		Transportation and warehousing		Information		Finance and insurance		Real estate and rental and leasing		Professional, scientific, and technical services	
STATE City, town, township, borough, or CDP (county if applicable)	Number of establishments	Number of employees	Number of establishments	Number of employees	Number of establishments	Number of employees	Number of establishments	Number of employees	Number of establishments	Number of employees	Number of establishments	Number of employees	Number of establishments	Number of employees
	1	2	3	4	5	6	7	8	9	10	11	12	13	14
CONNECTICUT—Con.														
New Canaan town	82	705	19	73	15	424	9	107	71	500	D	D	93	369
New Fairfield town	17	222	13	216	NA	NA	D	D	8	139	6	5	D	D
New Haven city	344	3,671	69	2,269	43	1,178	D	D	126	2,235	132	809	356	3,485
Newington town	134	2,950	40	904	13	51	D	D	39	240	35	120	51	776
New London city	105	1,538	16	726	12	564	14	455	33	215	26	139	86	642
New Milford town	107	1,492	33	178	11	134	11	57	25	176	22	60	70	419
Newtown town (balance)	66	873	20	205	9	142	18	523	29	127	14	57	72	522
North Branford town	35	365	D	D	7	132	D	D	9	30	6	10	16	91
North Haven town	113	2,080	57	1,202	24	731	D	D	47	363	38	278	77	687
Norwalk city	345	6,332	131	2,254	46	922	91	3,133	168	4,700	110	393	325	5,218
Norwich city	128	1,912	18	419	17	1,032	13	163	43	511	35	126	56	878
Old Saybrook town	111	2,079	18	183	9	55	9	295	29	93	19	42	44	224
Orange town	126	2,388	22	1,178	16	416	D	D	27	267	22	163	46	458
Oxford town	27	321	20	242	21	339	D	D	11	73	NA	NA	22	141
Plainfield town	56	625	7	142	9	613	D	D	D	D	11	18	12	39
Plainville town	83	1,363	28	427	11	162	D	D	20	166	D	D	30	311
Plymouth town	27	219	6	119	6	129	NA	NA	4	17	4	11	10	36
Ridgefield town	99	1,071	D	D	D	D	18	102	51	372	D	D	D	D
Rocky Hill town	61	1,315	40	1,232	16	766	18	478	66	1,399	29	137	116	2,679
Seymour town	42	441	D	D	8	157	D	D	11	67	7	13	35	146
Shelton city	91	1,817	60	1,926	19	623	35	947	89	2,121	47	331	154	2,421
Simsbury town	65	1,111	D	D	NA	NA	D	D	50	950	D	D	75	456
Somers town	28	177	9	74	5	43	NA	NA	8	26	D	D	19	93
Southbury town	65	923	16	92	5	125	D	D	35	192	17	66	49	253
Southington town	147	2,764	38	966	20	462	D	D	53	278	43	123	86	437
South Windsor town	127	1,495	69	1,314	28	1,241	D	D	47	434	18	245	67	658
Stafford town	34	386	D	D	10	86	NA	NA	12	88	4	8	11	63
Stamford city	460	6,250	236	5,349	105	1,427	198	6,076	618	16,736	246	1,605	743	16,984
Stonington town	121	1,431	15	97	D	D	12	88	34	160	24	41	69	672
Stratford town	128	1,998	83	1,326	43	1,523	18	736	61	409	35	112	109	700
Suffield town	24	182	17	361	16	189	4	16	15	65	10	44	21	148
Tolland town	32	293	9	241	NA	NA	D	D	8	31	11	30	21	115
Torrington city	151	2,666	24	190	8	145	10	68	39	311	22	87	56	377
Trumbull town	144	2,658	D	D	9	518	17	271	43	316	D	D	112	943
Vernon town	108	1,721	10	69	NA	NA	6	46	37	146	D	D	47	265
Wallingford town	145	2,916	92	1,688	39	1,612	34	1,743	70	2,520	56	556	118	1,806
Waterbury city	432	5,994	68	770	34	550	30	725	74	641	87	344	121	742
Waterford town	163	3,243	21	337	8	424	12	233	34	365	21	100	38	512
Watertown town	71	1,423	12	71	D	D	7	88	25	135	13	70	28	146
West Hartford town	245	3,808	45	346	14	322	D	D	175	1,265	71	323	206	2,418
West Haven city	111	1,295	55	1,291	23	723	D	D	24	119	39	110	60	315
Weston town	7	109	D	D	NA	NA	D	D	D	D	D	D	D	D
Westport town	225	4,016	44	351	20	250	31	314	189	2,862	61	142	275	1,369
Wethersfield town	84	1,164	20	130	10	27	D	D	53	359	20	52	75	809
Wilton town	70	1,010	36	1,382	11	146	15	156	75	890	D	D	113	5,196
Winchester town	27	137	D	D	4	80	4	85	9	46	5	21	17	80
Windham town	69	1,476	10	241	7	79	12	227	13	230	12	35	29	138
Windsor town	56	1,338	50	882	47	1,952	11	705	79	4,908	35	165	80	2,584
Windsor Locks town	39	300	D	D	44	2,108	3	23	13	165	22	302	22	101
Wolcott town	34	260	15	100	6	101	NA	NA	14	54	10	21	15	56
DELAWARE	3,648	58,201	962	9,315	708	10,604	580	7,169	1,925	44,120	1,286	6,096	2,991	29,716
Bear CDP	39	566	7	94	10	39	NA	NA	11	130	10	49	17	200
Brookside CDP	29	389	15	176	10	118	4	18	6	25	14	89	21	726
Dover city	258	4,087	46	232	24	335	69	434	108	863	80	334	189	1,347
Glasgow CDP	47	1,046	6	41	8	67	D	D	24	143	12	110	45	519
Hockessin CDP	43	646	8	15	D	D	NA	NA	29	107	15	166	65	210
Middletown town	88	4,764	D	D	9	97	14	126	38	150	20	45	51	193
Milford city	89	1,327	16	214	10	92	11	78	27	127	25	224	26	185
Newark city	147	2,924	42	346	19	170	12	349	76	2,029	52	219	140	1,560
Pike Creek Valley CDP	20	544	NA	NA	NA	NA	NA	NA	12	63	13	61	19	94
Smyrna town	47	803	NA	NA	D	D	D	D	17	52	D	D	11	262
Wilmington city	287	3,360	129	1,078	74	1,185	115	1,324	409	13,713	202	833	686	9,685
DISTRICT OF COLUMBIA	1,743	23,133	321	3,851	159	4,137	778	23,787	997	18,843	1,350	11,000	5,812	108,016
Washington city	1,743	23,133	321	3,851	159	4,137	778	23,787	997	18,843	1,350	11,000	5,812	108,016
FLORIDA	74,496	1,086,052	27,230	283,295	15,619	265,209	9,386	175,393	32,200	372,525	37,660	176,886	79,224	513,798
Alafaya CDP	196	4,267	26	54	30	98	25	214	62	746	94	262	181	540
Altamonte Springs city	317	6,186	67	568	20	42	52	667	127	1,169	116	982	275	2,978
Apollo Beach CDP	38	607	18	39	10	24	5	18	44	109	48	95	63	171
Apopka city	155	2,489	55	985	36	248	D	D	61	282	52	139	115	400
Asbury Lake CDP	8	116	NA	NA	3	7	NA	NA	D	D	6	5	5	12
Atlantic Beach city	52	261	11	76	D	D	D	D	20	152	D	D	82	214
Auburndale city	79	1,218	15	55	20	574	D	D	22	147	22	179	28	157
Aventura city	399	8,877	137	586	22	81	36	387	159	1,105	285	907	440	1,156
Avon Park city	58	890	7	81	D	D	D	D	13	71	12	40	9	38
Azalea Park CDP	50	454	11	39	D	D	NA	NA	9	40	15	67	19	65
Bartow city	55	1,081	17	244	17	414	D	D	28	249	13	28	68	462
Bayonet Point CDP	53	884	D	D	4	10	4	10	16	92	14	29	25	114
Bayshore Gardens CDP	49	985	NA	NA	D	D	NA	NA	26	159	11	52	21	50
Bellair-Meadowbrook Terrace CDP	159	2,271	21	287	D	D	7	138	25	126	22	89	35	1,825
Belle Glade city	74	595	21	317	8	77	NA	NA	14	88	12	32	17	47
Bellview CDP	31	514	6	32	NA	NA	D	D	D	D	8	17	13	37
Bloomingdale CDP	50	517	12	24	4	11	6	10	49	123	29	72	53	155
Boca Raton city	742	10,317	436	5,801	118	1,184	192	5,212	697	8,660	578	4,591	1,769	13,203

1 Merchant wholesalers, except manufacturers' sales branches and offices.

Table C. Incorporated Places, Census Designated Places (CDPs), and Minor Civil Divisions (MCDs) of 10,000 or More Population — **Economic Census**

STATE City, town, township, borough, or CDP (county if applicable)	Administration and support and waste management and mediation services		Educational services		Health care and social assistance		Arts, entertainment, and recreation		Accommodation and food services		Other services (except public administration)	
	Number of establishments	Number of employees	Number of establishments	Number of employees	Number of establishments	Number of employees	Number of establishments	Number of employees	Number of establishments	Number of employees	Number of establishments	Number of employees
	15	16	17	18	19	20	21	22	23	24	25	26
CONNECTICUT—Con.												
New Canaan town	35	245	17	118	54	1,024	20	515	D	D	48	249
New Fairfield town	14	39	D	D	D	D	10	46	17	161	18	51
New Haven city	94	3,050	33	535	422	21,715	44	639	366	4,686	256	1,708
Newington town	61	579	9	100	99	2,857	13	246	84	1,508	75	490
New London city	23	335	10	45	132	4,300	17	146	99	1,383	69	439
New Milford town	46	437	12	D	79	1,061	20	181	66	806	78	324
Newtown town (balance) ..	54	738	16	81	74	838	14	107	56	769	53	361
North Branford town	29	265	3	29	14	384	4	65	30	255	29	121
North Haven town	58	893	7	75	87	1,377	D	D	80	1,817	70	424
Norwalk city	256	4,227	44	224	298	6,606	73	1,559	297	3,778	231	1,432
Norwich city	18	143	9	73	192	5,301	11	113	82	1,487	76	518
Old Saybrook town	D	D	6	15	64	1,190	D	D	60	974	53	277
Orange town	39	814	8	41	D	D	18	242	65	1,313	D	D
Oxford town	26	151	3	46	19	201	D	D	22	510	D	D
Plainfield town	8	82	NA	NA	27	797	D	D	40	499	36	126
Plainville town	23	457	D	D	59	1,599	4	310	64	1,000	42	307
Plymouth town	11	39	NA	NA	15	222	NA	NA	D	D	D	D
Ridgefield town	42	461	26	128	94	1,585	28	310	D	D	64	471
Rocky Hill town	58	1,436	13	188	82	2,050	11	113	63	1,103	85	532
Seymour town	19	158	6	55	28	396	4	37	30	333	D	D
Shelton city	85	4,395	12	56	133	3,368	19	246	117	1,752	73	514
Simsbury town	43	319	7	65	66	1,079	19	268	62	1,004	46	220
Somers town	D	D	D	D	13	74	5	52	10	93	14	73
Southbury town	29	203	10	84	83	1,867	D	D	39	644	37	349
Southington town	57	598	10	118	146	2,318	21	835	135	2,517	91	475
South Windsor town	50	1,423	D	D	81	995	16	254	49	854	67	617
Stafford town	13	25	NA	NA	16	856	D	D	14	154	D	D
Stamford city	508	10,335	73	1,151	475	10,082	79	1,789	410	6,333	340	1,882
Stonington town	29	122	8	58	56	947	26	933	95	1,795	50	216
Stratford town	72	601	20	172	145	3,257	18	286	106	1,338	104	672
Suffield town	21	86	4	30	24	483	D	D	17	152	D	D
Tolland town	21	56	3	28	38	761	3	65	12	143	15	125
Torrington city	42	591	7	56	156	4,105	17	229	92	1,010	83	414
Trumbull town	60	1,066	10	101	165	3,917	12	328	69	1,084	48	300
Vernon town	24	254	5	15	98	2,376	8	489	71	1,252	59	396
Wallingford town	73	1,586	14	135	147	5,088	21	410	130	2,028	134	797
Waterbury city	64	2,554	21	336	346	11,499	15	347	237	3,084	159	1,251
Waterford town	35	415	5	36	64	1,704	11	109	51	879	D	D
Watertown town	25	159	6	149	48	713	D	D	44	510	D	D
West Hartford town	70	815	27	189	252	5,482	34	563	D	D	168	973
West Haven city	42	348	8	171	82	3,470	NA	NA	114	1,463	88	427
Weston town	11	27	7	31	D	D	16	156	NA	NA	D	D
Westport town	65	361	31	293	157	2,836	51	900	D	D	120	1,129
Wethersfield town	34	199	8	64	87	3,695	11	128	65	1,009	54	308
Wilton town	53	1,553	D	D	69	1,108	17	443	45	497	50	493
Winchester town	16	66	NA	NA	29	315	6	44	13	142	13	56
Windham town	13	187	3	13	84	2,879	D	D	63	982	33	152
Windsor town	55	2,555	4	86	94	2,266	D	D	61	1,127	47	570
Windsor Locks town.........	23	568	4	2	17	256	4	63	53	1,143	39	470
Wolcott town	15	165	NA	NA	39	587	3	13	D	D	D	D
DELAWARE....................	1,521	27,667	237	1,752	2,648	68,348	440	8,466	2,141	39,950	1,608	10,252
Bear CDP	16	596	8	75	25	225	NA	NA	30	536	13	112
Brookside CDP	24	575	NA	NA	12	553	5	36	20	304	17	86
Dover city........................	72	1,189	D	D	240	7,734	D	D	135	4,329	91	627
Glasgow CDP	19	93	7	20	57	1,056	D	D	39	727	17	139
Hockessin CDP................	20	271	10	58	45	913	8	424	34	589	28	166
Middletown town	20	210	7	16	73	1,078	13	99	70	1,419	46	324
Milford city	13	442	NA	NA	NA	NA	D	D	D	D	38	177
Newark city	46	1,411	15	136	162	10,649	21	271	140	3,456	65	503
Pike Creek Valley CDP	10	49	5	26	18	283	D	D	15	234	D	D
Smyrna town	11	417	NA	NA	NA	NA	D	D	33	436	D	D
Wilmington city	177	3,996	33	259	373	9,984	55	741	222	3,407	226	1,638
DISTRICT OF COLUMBIA	1,139	35,895	423	6,980	2,203	74,134	380	9,817	2,733	72,890	3,502	73,756
Washington city	1,139	35,895	423	6,980	2,203	74,134	380	9,817	2,733	72,890	3,502	73,756
FLORIDA........................	36,718	1,729,126	5,240	40,403	61,554	1,127,155	8,883	208,733	42,071	955,006	38,932	222,512
Alafaya CDP	88	487	24	162	166	1,227	28	287	119	3,152	60	358
Altamonte Springs city......	128	9,478	21	94	243	5,741	23	229	156	3,722	125	592
Apollo Beach CDP...........	D	D	8	33	33	206	10	122	20	264	25	62
Apopka city.....................	90	603	11	56	112	1,499	15	60	76	1,484	69	335
Asbury Lake CDP.............	5	7	NA	NA	3	32	NA	NA	4	92	5	18
Atlantic Beach city	D	D	NA	NA	D	D	10	162	41	1,101	D	D
Auburndale city	24	250	NA	NA	25	410	D	D	41	694	D	D
Aventura city	D	D	18	69	295	3,544	32	262	111	3,330	112	1,287
Avon Park city	D	D	NA	NA	43	864	NA	NA	24	424	22	95
Azalea Park CDP.............	19	560	NA	NA	13	95	5	50	14	181	28	114
Bartow city......................	31	421	NA	NA	72	1,659	NA	NA	40	767	28	86
Bayonet Point CDP	D	D	NA	NA	48	635	D	D	23	290	D	D
Bayshore Gardens CDP ...	27	175	4	16	31	232	NA	NA	28	349	D	D
Bellair-Meadowbrook Terrace CDP	24	2,098	4	12	86	2,727	6	74	77	1,922	D	D
Belle Glade city...............	D	D	NA	NA	D	D	NA	NA	19	278	D	D
Bellview CDP...................	12	45	NA	NA	D	D	NA	NA	23	573	D	D
Bloomingdale CDP...........	31	98	11	28	D	D	9	275	23	416	D	D
Boca Raton city	505	14,213	77	525	849	11,616	120	2,287	439	12,240	492	2,666

Table C. Incorporated Places, Census Designated Places (CDPs), and Minor Civil Divisions (MCDs) of 10,000 or More Population — **Economic Census**

STATE City, town, township, borough, or CDP (county if applicable)	Retail Trade		Wholesale trade[1]		Transportation and warehousing		Information		Finance and insurance		Real estate and rental and leasing		Professional, scientific, and technical services	
	Number of establishments	Number of employees	Number of establishments	Number of employees	Number of establishments	Number of employees	Number of establishments	Number of employees	Number of establishments	Number of employees	Number of establishments	Number of employees	Number of establishments	Number of employees
	1	2	3	4	5	6	7	8	9	10	11	12	13	14
FLORIDA—Con.														
Bonita Springs city	195	2,501	48	357	23	87	32	337	134	728	147	539	219	1,097
Boynton Beach city	332	5,615	113	928	41	560	33	364	134	639	114	455	328	1,364
Bradenton city	244	3,834	31	317	16	40	22	527	121	989	97	269	228	1,315
Brandon CDP	497	11,028	112	1,047	57	604	43	399	257	4,445	142	508	333	2,538
Brent CDP	144	2,392	69	831	25	263	10	112	34	607	27	139	38	1,494
Brownsville CDP	58	388	56	755	22	860	NA	NA	4	D	14	125	12	93
Buenaventura Lakes CDP	39	410	NA	NA	21	23	NA	NA	11	72	24	44	11	38
Callaway city	36	659	NA	NA	NA	NA	3	11	12	61	9	15	11	185
Cape Canaveral city	37	183	9	102	11	345	7	40	7	29	32	135	61	725
Cape Coral city	455	6,550	118	494	90	286	48	428	206	953	413	667	456	1,409
Carrollwood CDP	116	1,347	34	332	13	100	16	309	96	770	D	D	221	1,274
Casselberry city	149	2,571	29	296	14	52	17	141	49	213	51	218	85	350
Cheval CDP	11	314	D	D	D	D	4	33	20	63	14	117	54	117
Citrus Park CDP	120	2,086	15	37	16	75	8	155	30	138	D	D	71	375
Clearwater city	682	10,337	160	1,850	57	1,234	79	891	330	4,012	330	1,187	726	5,378
Clermont city	160	3,289	22	85	29	54	24	236	75	406	99	247	107	342
Cocoa city	151	2,039	22	138	14	211	D	D	35	159	29	76	73	361
Cocoa Beach city	58	739	6	D	D	D	9	22	21	103	35	154	72	435
Coconut Creek city	169	3,510	53	304	32	65	26	217	77	540	67	294	198	1,234
Conway CDP	22	212	8	21	4	5	NA	NA	14	40	9	11	33	67
Cooper City city	96	1,753	49	159	17	21	16	66	66	278	D	D	208	671
Coral Gables city	326	4,954	199	1,657	46	696	98	1,204	440	6,923	450	1,736	1,708	10,129
Coral Springs city	470	8,318	238	2,010	64	252	67	453	309	2,390	267	1,222	D	D
Coral Terrace CDP	69	543	25	195	11	19	D	D	29	95	21	72	65	181
Country Club CDP	72	1,470	89	344	33	454	7	62	24	233	36	108	71	315
Country Walk CDP	39	398	65	274	20	75	5	16	4	D	15	D	43	417
Crestview city	109	1,672	5	12	7	98	D	D	33	147	30	68	49	248
Cutler Bay town	157	2,524	27	113	11	60	6	57	39	178	34	59	85	196
Cypress Gardens CDP	12	53	NA	NA	NA	NA	NA	NA	13	68	15	48	13	14
Cypress Lake CDP	31	678	9	21	NA	NA	D	D	31	132	32	67	45	350
Dania Beach city	155	1,846	129	1,005	38	784	D	D	29	305	72	578	145	600
Davie town	443	7,614	268	1,753	89	536	50	444	176	814	223	1,049	597	2,084
Daytona Beach city	519	7,165	74	679	49	2,195	53	604	123	1,358	166	825	309	2,256
DeBary city	39	392	16	97	10	16	NA	NA	14	41	D	D	54	216
Deerfield Beach city	315	3,668	213	3,650	70	2,231	69	1,795	132	1,743	139	944	403	2,764
DeLand city	164	2,872	48	401	19	529	24	1,408	76	429	62	240	127	664
Delray Beach city	401	5,475	129	1,019	46	300	42	393	181	1,198	216	539	488	2,350
Deltona city	114	1,930	13	27	33	133	13	68	33	173	25	31	57	178
Destin city	163	2,633	20	61	33	148	14	157	57	356	115	619	109	508
Doctor Phillips CDP	51	1,416	23	68	D	D	14	55	47	284	74	211	89	360
Doral city	546	7,535	1,480	14,646	639	10,522	126	4,734	232	4,136	360	2,441	691	4,103
Dunedin city	134	1,462	26	256	6	124	11	53	85	833	D	D	177	544
East Lake CDP	41	778	18	22	14	37	12	109	57	494	58	90	152	311
East Lake-Orient Park CDP	100	794	155	3,168	50	1,719	20	316	109	8,863	49	631	122	3,500
East Milton CDP	D	D	6	313	8	75	NA	NA	4	7	5	21	4	18
Edgewater city	65	584	8	24	11	19	6	34	19	139	19	53	28	89
Egypt Lake-Leto CDP	98	1,230	28	412	36	67	24	214	64	1,052	45	194	94	1,212
Elfers CDP	54	819	10	225	4	10	NA	NA	15	138	13	23	16	106
Englewood CDP	90	1,437	D	D	5	10	7	43	38	304	52	89	51	211
Ensley CDP	77	1,663	27	216	D	D	D	D	D	D	25	75	32	415
Estero village	246	4,718	18	66	9	17	9	163	61	587	113	1,022	120	534
Eustis city	115	1,723	11	50	7	129	D	D	42	357	37	137	40	171
Fairview Shores CDP	65	750	5	40	D	D	D	D	17	62	17	60	53	388
Fernandina Beach city	109	1,118	D	D	23	99	7	26	39	176	47	113	87	304
Ferry Pass CDP	100	1,333	38	323	16	288	D	D	D	D	52	172	58	508
Fish Hawk CDP	19	333	D	D	5	34	NA	NA	30	67	24	34	43	196
Fleming Island CDP	67	1,480	14	32	15	43	12	477	36	357	D	D	94	375
Florida City city	72	1,513	5	33	NA	NA	NA	NA	8	51	10	95	D	D
Florida Ridge CDP	29	296	D	D	3	24	NA	NA	5	21	7	6	28	65
Forest City CDP	35	351	13	167	8	44	13	64	15	41	16	30	40	174
Fort Lauderdale city	1,120	13,335	576	5,970	441	6,749	210	6,791	688	6,973	823	3,876	2,491	16,701
Fort Myers city	717	11,773	168	2,615	92	2,022	93	2,661	288	1,764	248	1,123	563	5,444
Fort Pierce city	246	3,345	40	463	D	D	D	D	60	448	60	493	149	944
Fort Walton Beach city	142	1,879	39	226	20	344	16	194	51	553	55	425	105	1,288
Fountainebleau CDP	121	3,240	40	96	42	114	23	1,613	74	531	63	D	125	419
Four Corners CDP	59	1,199	D	D	13	28	3	5	16	36	101	947	33	79
Fruit Cove CDP	35	504	13	17	8	14	3	7	23	101	37	46	93	185
Fruitville CDP	98	1,596	55	568	15	54	20	644	61	420	39	74	108	1,377
Fuller Heights CDP	4	D	NA	NA	NA	NA	NA	NA	4	9	3	7	4	7
Gainesville city	549	9,697	109	1,224	50	799	84	1,719	186	2,742	228	1,375	477	3,104
Gateway CDP	9	53	5	24	D	D	D	D	D	D	18	20	38	218
Gibsonton CDP	26	547	6	244	10	36	NA	NA	20	25	11	21	13	68
Gifford CDP	36	357	D	D	7	220	NA	NA	5	10	D	D	14	39
Gladeview CDP	42	802	65	1,222	24	526	D	D	D	D	6	21	7	205
Glenvar Heights CDP	153	1,892	111	443	22	556	17	180	49	171	82	177	231	1,236
Golden Gate CDP	51	456	NA	NA	11	12	D	D	22	96	12	43	30	134
Golden Glades CDP	68	622	12	86	11	16	6	25	12	47	20	59	27	59
Goldenrod CDP	25	348	10	96	D	D	6	38	14	125	10	27	23	157
Gonzalez CDP	13	51	8	35	D	D	NA	NA	D	D	6	10	11	15
Goulds CDP	23	370	NA	NA	NA	NA	NA	NA	NA	NA	6	22	NA	NA
Greenacres city	105	1,684	18	39	17	42	6	36	47	210	31	283	110	367
Groveland city	32	297	D	D	14	40	D	D	6	23	14	25	14	45
Gulf Gate Estates CDP	92	1,500	D	D	NA	NA	D	D	32	175	27	51	54	276
Gulfport city	31	142	9	71	NA	NA	NA	NA	9	44	19	37	26	62
Haines City city	67	1,191	13	135	19	423	4	13	19	115	32	142	15	44
Hallandale Beach city	154	1,816	87	436	30	102	D	D	78	442	123	519	186	973
Hialeah city	1,000	11,423	534	4,518	264	3,122	66	998	240	1,131	240	702	383	1,282
Hialeah Gardens city	102	1,494	58	332	57	279	D	D	23	66	22	91	47	430
Highland City CDP	10	40	5	31	D	D	NA	NA	7	23	4	9	23	76

1 Merchant wholesalers, except manufacturers' sales branches and offices.

Table C. Incorporated Places, Census Designated Places (CDPs), and Minor Civil Divisions (MCDs) of 10,000 or More Population — **Economic Census**

STATE City, town, township, borough, or CDP (county if applicable)	Administration and support and waste management and mediation services		Educational services		Health care and social assistance		Arts, entertainment, and recreation		Accommodation and food services		Other services (except public administration)	
	Number of establishments	Number of employees	Number of establishments	Number of employees	Number of establishments	Number of employees	Number of establishments	Number of employees	Number of establishments	Number of employees	Number of establishments	Number of employees
	15	16	17	18	19	20	21	22	23	24	25	26
FLORIDA—Con.												
Bonita Springs city	116	1,844	22	173	164	1,572	48	1,813	135	3,366	137	632
Boynton Beach city	164	2,076	19	165	363	6,057	38	765	207	4,508	201	1,520
Bradenton city	115	21,795	11	30	315	9,649	29	309	124	2,490	101	400
Brandon CDP	180	3,109	33	246	521	7,924	D	D	236	6,237	204	1,109
Brent CDP	33	3,727	3	8	54	732	4	70	33	545	45	335
Brownsville CDP	D	D	NA	NA	18	398	NA	NA	12	111	D	D
Buenaventura Lakes CDP	18	36	3	7	D	D	D	D	22	256	D	D
Callaway city	12	73	NA	NA	11	152	NA	NA	31	575	D	D
Cape Canaveral city	D	D	NA	NA	D	D	D	D	26	474	25	86
Cape Coral city	369	1,717	30	75	321	5,242	56	420	238	4,856	280	1,099
Carrollwood CDP	62	2,515	18	229	104	689	25	209	D	D	85	402
Casselberry city	62	1,092	11	54	66	558	18	179	80	1,261	71	212
Cheval CDP	17	83	NA	NA	30	1,173	8	205	8	96	D	D
Citrus Park CDP	44	347	7	46	86	712	10	57	45	991	45	329
Clearwater city	261	46,377	48	1,957	578	11,955	86	1,711	397	9,686	284	1,164
Clermont city	61	240	16	96	194	3,912	27	402	107	3,032	81	434
Cocoa city	30	242	D	D	D	D	6	78	54	722	44	269
Cocoa Beach city	21	105	4	9	45	1,158	11	196	98	2,165	64	281
Coconut Creek city	107	746	D	D	117	1,598	25	1,914	91	1,585	106	705
Conway CDP	20	125	NA	NA	25	178	NA	NA	NA	NA	8	27
Cooper City city	D	D	16	196	151	892	15	72	61	810	66	495
Coral Gables city	174	2,501	57	366	522	6,673	79	954	267	5,925	229	1,124
Coral Springs city	318	3,336	60	251	505	3,192	D	D	318	5,280	294	1,159
Coral Terrace CDP	D	D	9	56	114	5,795	3	D	D	D	43	254
Country Club CDP	D	D	NA	NA	76	690	9	14	47	699	42	148
Country Walk CDP	D	D	NA	NA	17	106	6	53	5	31	D	D
Crestview city	D	D	5	18	93	1,732	D	D	70	1,432	33	133
Cutler Bay town	D	D	10	25	94	1,220	9	64	71	1,297	D	D
Cypress Gardens CDP	7	33	NA	NA	10	224	NA	NA	14	283	D	D
Cypress Lake CDP	22	266	NA	NA	54	1,124	8	143	35	585	23	124
Dania Beach city	76	1,074	8	27	57	519	23	521	84	1,750	112	586
Davie town	255	3,009	45	293	317	3,315	69	696	257	7,377	315	1,530
Daytona Beach city	106	1,661	17	142	305	11,086	47	2,501	301	6,918	173	1,297
DeBary city	39	231	D	D	33	242	NA	NA	21	343	36	110
Deerfield Beach city	210	3,806	25	108	198	4,009	43	436	179	3,367	231	892
DeLand city	31	145	8	19	141	3,703	21	284	123	2,147	94	422
Delray Beach city	183	2,468	33	138	460	7,196	56	772	259	6,536	272	1,035
Deltona city	90	259	D	D	90	724	12	240	47	688	D	D
Destin city	56	3,055	5	7	54	507	29	412	129	4,064	81	277
Doctor Phillips CDP	54	477	12	57	D	D	19	270	82	2,671	40	307
Doral city	230	8,451	37	196	231	3,692	80	496	316	6,946	202	1,917
Dunedin city	54	616	15	63	132	2,413	22	209	D	D	78	323
East Lake CDP	56	199	8	28	87	553	10	203	37	476	30	148
East Lake-Orient Park CDP	74	2,395	11	86	54	1,558	D	D	42	3,706	54	746
East Milton CDP	10	391	D	D	D	D	NA	NA	D	D	D	D
Edgewater city	26	89	4	4	31	187	NA	NA	27	528	40	124
Egypt Lake-Leto CDP	76	18,257	12	270	138	2,344	6	17	41	499	D	D
Elfers CDP	24	174	NA	NA	D	D	NA	NA	19	197	D	D
Englewood CDP	40	87	NA	NA	D	D	D	D	57	796	65	318
Ensley CDP	29	610	D	D	29	235	6	20	52	1,138	D	D
Estero village	56	466	5	19	75	764	20	742	78	1,826	71	509
Eustis city	35	248	NA	NA	99	1,192	9	24	60	976	48	224
Fairview Shores CDP	31	247	11	145	42	1,129	4	20	30	354	38	163
Fernandina Beach city	30	188	7	59	72	752	20	204	87	1,562	43	213
Ferry Pass CDP	52	14,500	D	D	133	4,092	11	85	84	1,731	44	228
Fish Hawk CDP	17	81	3	17	27	249	3	2	15	338	9	34
Fleming Island CDP	36	194	16	46	101	1,303	D	D	49	1,273	D	D
Florida City city	7	6	4	61	24	344	NA	NA	35	722	13	48
Florida Ridge CDP	38	241	NA	NA	13	121	NA	NA	12	153	D	D
Forest City CDP	28	93	3	22	35	475	7	49	21	392	D	D
Fort Lauderdale city	764	41,101	90	677	945	15,261	187	1,572	736	18,456	793	5,081
Fort Myers city	229	5,529	32	210	456	17,839	51	1,870	353	8,181	302	1,850
Fort Pierce city	47	1,418	8	65	202	3,879	D	D	135	2,597	94	405
Fort Walton Beach city	67	3,497	4	16	82	922	12	63	85	1,479	63	314
Fountainebleau CDP	D	D	NA	NA	139	1,244	10	82	65	1,094	72	219
Four Corners CDP	57	357	6	5	19	111	14	165	84	3,534	30	241
Fruit Cove CDP	46	114	11	46	41	448	6	D	27	512	D	D
Fruitville CDP	87	3,969	8	32	69	1,123	D	D	49	1,177	75	309
Fuller Heights CDP	6	122	NA	NA	NA	NA	NA	NA	7	56	8	26
Gainesville city	179	3,270	42	405	447	18,947	58	721	421	9,768	274	2,770
Gateway CDP	D	D	NA	NA	D	D	NA	NA	3	54	D	D
Gibsonton CDP	13	46	NA	NA	9	58	9	58	11	82	11	24
Gifford CDP	23	162	NA	NA	135	4,773	4	D	9	118	11	109
Gladeview CDP	D	D	D	D	15	103	NA	NA	9	97	18	256
Glenvar Heights CDP	45	1,083	14	78	D	D	21	68	D	D	97	409
Golden Gate CDP	60	346	NA	NA	27	277	NA	NA	38	504	D	D
Golden Glades CDP	23	957	3	15	67	1,340	D	D	18	267	32	138
Goldenrod CDP	33	2,317	D	D	27	377	D	D	13	115	D	D
Gonzalez CDP	18	55	NA	NA	D	D	NA	NA	NA	NA	4	7
Goulds CDP	D	D	NA	NA	11	137	NA	NA	D	D	9	7
Greenacres city	D	D	7	23	110	807	12	127	68	1,086	66	291
Groveland city	28	217	NA	NA	D	D	NA	NA	17	262	21	81
Gulf Gate Estates CDP	18	65	NA	NA	52	952	D	D	62	950	35	108
Gulfport city	12	22	NA	NA	D	D	6	98	23	375	15	56
Haines City city	25	115	NA	NA	57	1,477	4	58	50	916	26	79
Hallandale Beach city	D	D	D	D	153	1,006	40	1,176	87	2,464	147	683
Hialeah city	D	D	41	278	796	10,440	44	D	377	6,741	442	1,790
Hialeah Gardens city	39	1,109	5	48	48	813	D	D	36	346	D	D
Highland City CDP	15	41	NA	NA	15	75	4	14	NA	NA	D	D

Table C. Incorporated Places, Census Designated Places (CDPs), and Minor Civil Divisions (MCDs) of 10,000 or More Population — **Economic Census**

STATE City, town, township, borough, or CDP (county if applicable)	Retail Trade Number of establishments	Retail Trade Number of employees	Wholesale trade[1] Number of establishments	Wholesale trade[1] Number of employees	Transportation and warehousing Number of establishments	Transportation and warehousing Number of employees	Information Number of establishments	Information Number of employees	Finance and insurance Number of establishments	Finance and insurance Number of employees	Real estate and rental and leasing Number of establishments	Real estate and rental and leasing Number of employees	Professional, scientific, and technical services Number of establishments	Professional, scientific, and technical services Number of employees
	1	2	3	4	5	6	7	8	9	10	11	12	13	14
FLORIDA—Con.														
Hobe Sound CDP	48	427	8	34	11	16	NA	NA	22	67	D	D	48	94
Holiday CDP	65	982	12	46	10	49	5	9	17	83	15	46	25	96
Holly Hill city	100	741	42	267	D	D	9	39	20	578	18	60	32	132
Hollywood city	605	7,898	293	2,731	133	2,179	81	1,212	260	2,047	346	2,367	D	D
Homestead city	182	2,610	43	307	D	D	12	110	56	304	48	144	86	526
Homosassa Springs CDP	45	706	NA	NA	7	29	NA	NA	8	44	12	64	16	36
Horizon West CDP	21	214	10	D	D	D	6	5	10	22	D	D	87	118
Hudson CDP	49	507	10	45	4	3	NA	NA	D	D	14	51	16	44
Hunters Creek CDP	30	400	19	44	22	41	D	D	24	119	D	D	61	111
Immokalee CDP	52	461	18	132	15	63	5	24	10	47	12	31	D	D
Iona CDP	52	570	9	35	D	D	6	50	26	98	42	84	43	117
Ives Estates CDP	42	310	68	426	15	23	D	D	9	33	21	73	39	192
Jacksonville city	3,145	50,554	1,099	22,090	1,065	29,740	512	15,113	1,686	60,334	1,333	8,415	3,058	35,882
Jacksonville Beach city	151	1,959	34	237	15	58	23	301	80	351	D	D	221	1,260
Jasmine Estates CDP	57	828	8	33	NA	NA	4	22	15	115	11	37	18	64
Jensen Beach CDP	138	2,407	7	119	10	18	D	D	28	181	34	111	57	258
Jupiter town	318	3,528	120	679	46	1,012	35	200	200	883	205	1,015	538	3,335
Jupiter Farms CDP	18	220	8	48	7	14	8	9	7	20	14	36	59	120
Kendale Lakes CDP	87	1,408	43	88	32	82	D	D	39	140	40	64	105	241
Kendall CDP	353	6,872	157	621	41	194	42	268	169	1,197	179	684	550	1,874
Kendall West CDP	38	701	13	21	14	25	3	6	21	76	13	29	47	72
Key Biscayne village	51	379	28	79	6	12	11	29	44	166	95	154	126	272
Keystone CDP	51	408	28	203	10	31	12	18	32	81	D	D	171	715
Key West city	296	2,785	D	D	42	513	20	174	40	328	131	546	154	404
Kissimmee city	370	5,535	58	305	86	445	26	128	106	636	190	1,028	196	889
Lady Lake town	107	2,098	7	72	3	117	7	336	29	149	D	D	21	93
Lake Butler CDP	18	250	12	19	10	12	5	11	15	46	D	D	90	223
Lake City city	172	2,189	32	581	16	955	13	86	49	412	34	110	73	358
Lakeland city	581	10,502	156	3,245	88	5,392	57	1,196	265	6,299	207	1,135	374	2,330
Lakeland Highlands CDP	24	253	7	22	NA	NA	NA	NA	14	63	29	54	47	200
Lake Magdalene CDP	145	2,293	27	168	11	48	D	D	68	749	75	271	165	914
Lake Mary city	72	1,544	48	430	10	94	66	4,255	150	4,726	84	D	212	1,327
Lakeside CDP	110	1,725	11	80	D	D	D	D	28	103	33	112	44	183
Lake Wales city	108	2,022	8	239	11	211	D	D	44	246	19	89	46	209
Lakewood Park CDP	15	240	NA	NA	4	4	NA	NA	D	D	D	D	11	14
Lake Worth city	145	1,202	55	548	26	223	D	D	44	189	51	89	120	665
Land O' Lakes CDP	109	1,710	29	122	17	45	13	38	59	213	55	157	112	311
Lantana town	62	873	5	7	12	25	NA	NA	26	151	17	51	43	156
Largo city	350	5,260	99	1,300	28	375	36	362	146	2,226	126	511	244	2,878
Lauderdale Lakes city	83	1,183	20	145	14	272	D	D	22	110	28	432	27	48
Lauderhill city	175	1,564	39	154	35	661	D	D	38	171	50	285	96	264
Lealman CDP	86	923	31	301	16	151	D	D	10	26	27	84	27	199
Leesburg city	216	2,891	52	421	28	593	22	398	69	460	50	222	72	308
Lehigh Acres CDP	122	1,914	19	161	33	128	10	29	30	175	51	305	63	196
Leisure City CDP	31	249	NA	NA	D	D	NA	NA	D	D	9	63	8	6
Lighthouse Point city	47	722	22	56	12	29	D	D	40	147	38	44	94	233
Lockhart CDP	35	262	24	236	11	34	NA	NA	8	21	16	93	30	637
Longwood city	170	1,862	97	750	17	720	21	79	55	346	50	562	130	1,030
Lutz CDP	62	922	31	83	8	12	8	23	53	274	D	D	135	482
Lynn Haven city	50	984	9	249	7	178	11	201	32	265	18	66	28	171
Maitland city	40	511	33	708	D	D	58	3,278	208	7,316	104	717	363	4,275
Mango CDP	20	357	6	24	D	D	NA	NA	7	35	8	D	5	12
Marco Island city	97	1,086	11	30	20	63	11	71	44	173	119	853	81	249
Margate city	189	2,820	52	268	33	78	16	85	87	473	56	201	147	729
Meadow Woods CDP	24	273	D	D	27	58	NA	NA	NA	NA	D	D	26	21
Medulla CDP	31	445	7	59	NA	NA	NA	NA	20	125	11	37	25	80
Melbourne city	449	6,935	113	1,504	46	522	77	2,413	175	1,436	197	682	468	8,212
Merritt Island CDP	186	3,177	22	82	24	82	18	154	66	418	73	180	163	1,278
Miami city	2,624	32,942	1,436	9,090	567	18,059	450	5,224	1,351	20,116	1,541	6,240	4,279	28,985
Miami Beach city	551	6,909	155	519	47	183	108	997	219	1,371	564	1,981	767	2,353
Miami Gardens city	307	5,021	182	3,849	49	601	33	773	53	924	75	453	95	315
Miami Lakes town	85	1,357	101	1,402	54	1,223	23	372	119	2,037	116	492	309	1,628
Miami Shores village	19	331	14	23	D	D	9	25	16	72	D	D	97	173
Miami Springs city	34	303	15	53	18	645	8	35	20	94	26	45	47	90
Middleburg CDP	41	478	3	8	D	D	NA	NA	12	47	4	D	12	61
Midway CDP	53	453	10	16	3	6	D	D	D	D	28	42	43	164
Minneola city	23	751	10	45	17	24	NA	NA	NA	NA	7	27	19	102
Miramar city	201	3,383	199	3,278	86	2,370	62	3,295	147	2,329	135	560	339	1,882
Mount Dora city	85	1,396	D	D	D	D	7	44	39	199	30	109	61	308
Myrtle Grove CDP	30	384	NA	NA	NA	NA	NA	NA	D	D	7	24	15	71
Naples city	607	9,865	47	1,502	39	517	48	1,126	245	1,522	322	961	480	1,875
Naranja CDP	26	170	D	D	D	D	NA	NA	6	22	4	13	D	D
Navarre CDP	56	939	9	76	7	42	5	10	D	D	41	83	55	479
New Port Richey city	99	1,164	15	43	7	8	D	D	40	327	54	578	81	297
New Port Richey East CDP	26	163	8	120	9	123	NA	NA	D	D	10	101	19	89
New Smyrna Beach city	155	2,029	17	57	17	213	18	86	66	274	68	198	111	294
Niceville city	67	865	8	78	9	59	D	D	33	177	21	84	51	612
Nocatee CDP	14	276	NA	NA	5	29	NA	NA	7	27	5	11	39	68
Northdale CDP	46	1,351	18	35	14	27	D	D	34	720	D	D	93	386
North Fort Myers CDP	139	2,534	20	474	18	64	15	128	D	D	58	284	64	234
North Lauderdale city	65	1,234	6	18	16	20	D	D	10	39	18	57	37	585
North Miami city	198	2,544	71	411	26	94	31	339	59	291	120	402	192	597
North Miami Beach city	190	2,670	73	236	18	543	25	334	71	393	91	190	223	833
North Palm Beach village	47	422	12	48	9	10	5	26	45	329	48	114	138	607
North Port city	99	1,951	24	194	26	57	9	30	46	181	D	D	56	151
Oakland Park city	242	2,121	108	931	46	375	17	117	100	736	110	450	225	1,069
Oakleaf Plantation CDP	11	135	3	D	D	D	NA	NA	D	D	11	13	16	47
Oak Ridge CDP	55	767	11	713	15	159	9	133	18	396	21	163	16	158
Ocala city	629	10,971	158	2,741	91	2,806	58	932	229	1,421	194	954	400	1,912

1 Merchant wholesalers, except manufacturers' sales branches and offices.

Table C. Incorporated Places, Census Designated Places (CDPs), and Minor Civil Divisions (MCDs) of 10,000 or More Population — **Economic Census**

STATE City, town, township, borough, or CDP (county if applicable)	Administration and support and waste management and mediation services		Educational services		Health care and social assistance		Arts, entertainment, and recreation		Accommodation and food services		Other services (except public administration)	
	Number of establishments	Number of employees	Number of establishments	Number of employees	Number of establishments	Number of employees	Number of establishments	Number of employees	Number of establishments	Number of employees	Number of establishments	Number of employees
	15	16	17	18	19	20	21	22	23	24	25	26
FLORIDA—Con.												
Hobe Sound CDP	D	D	NA	NA	27	881	11	204	21	269	33	115
Holiday CDP	D	D	NA	NA	D	D	5	32	20	194	33	220
Holly Hill city	20	141	NA	NA	29	397	9	74	28	283	D	D
Hollywood city	321	3,120	48	194	550	12,593	95	811	381	6,057	351	1,913
Homestead city	59	799	13	57	182	3,867	D	D	101	2,025	71	318
Homosassa Springs CDP	18	1,916	NA	NA	17	147	NA	NA	12	147	D	D
Horizon West CDP	28	95	4	16	12	D	11	176	D	D	10	67
Hudson CDP	D	D	NA	NA	102	2,190	3	42	D	D	23	87
Hunters Creek CDP	46	192	7	22	60	900	10	46	37	677	D	D
Immokalee CDP	13	80	NA	NA	32	624	NA	NA	D	D	21	169
Iona CDP	27	556	NA	NA	27	130	7	188	31	411	38	160
Ives Estates CDP	D	D	NA	NA	26	105	4	20	10	133	20	42
Jacksonville city	1,721	81,209	212	2,010	2,601	68,647	294	6,482	1,998	41,498	1,614	11,019
Jacksonville Beach city	D	D	D	D	D	D	26	435	129	3,167	124	558
Jasmine Estates CDP	D	D	NA	NA	36	445	NA	NA	33	890	D	D
Jensen Beach CDP	37	1,305	NA	NA	50	806	14	57	D	D	40	161
Jupiter town	218	8,881	26	109	376	4,974	65	1,505	181	4,756	219	1,339
Jupiter Farms CDP	D	D	3	4	19	74	9	40	7	44	D	D
Kendale Lakes CDP	86	319	5	23	103	616	D	D	47	840	62	139
Kendall CDP	144	1,715	32	294	519	9,316	37	208	158	3,339	167	1,014
Kendall West CDP	D	D	D	D	47	167	6	4	22	238	30	79
Key Biscayne village	D	D	15	D	34	110	19	115	39	1,111	45	358
Keystone CDP	63	632	8	28	53	279	9	37	27	478	23	76
Key West city	74	384	12	59	105	1,050	55	476	278	6,071	73	276
Kissimmee city	148	2,241	25	115	310	6,050	23	1,201	236	5,337	144	758
Lady Lake town	24	781	3	9	87	1,389	NA	NA	54	1,577	D	D
Lake Butler CDP	28	73	7	13	46	117	13	331	15	174	10	19
Lake City city	15	232	NA	NA	144	3,866	11	D	90	2,105	51	196
Lakeland city	185	6,409	23	256	427	13,942	37	703	300	7,573	196	1,294
Lakeland Highlands CDP	18	987	NA	NA	24	216	NA	NA	13	303	11	52
Lake Magdalene CDP	62	705	13	92	162	1,737	7	142	61	1,127	61	479
Lake Mary city	69	2,272	25	206	159	2,329	15	D	57	1,220	51	462
Lakeside CDP	47	490	8	64	68	907	4	88	D	D	D	D
Lake Wales city	16	111	3	4	64	1,209	D	D	55	977	30	113
Lakewood Park CDP	15	36	NA	NA	3	D	5	14	6	88	D	D
Lake Worth city	D	D	3	25	102	1,362	21	107	88	1,110	86	334
Land O' Lakes CDP	D	D	10	72	96	1,517	12	104	47	930	70	398
Lantana town	D	D	NA	NA	27	433	8	D	34	639	D	D
Largo city	117	3,435	D	D	316	10,599	31	277	181	2,931	186	1,040
Lauderdale Lakes city	D	D	NA	NA	96	2,515	D	D	35	596	47	187
Lauderhill city	D	D	7	60	154	1,894	18	112	83	1,073	106	387
Lealman CDP	39	352	3	13	61	1,516	5	10	26	550	36	264
Leesburg city	49	591	5	123	225	5,512	12	D	90	1,804	71	482
Lehigh Acres CDP	125	408	4	7	101	1,505	9	100	60	813	66	185
Leisure City CDP	D	D	NA	NA	30	310	NA	NA	D	D	D	D
Lighthouse Point city	D	D	6	37	55	277	12	148	31	511	38	144
Lockhart CDP	30	113	NA	NA	17	155	NA	NA	11	124	22	96
Longwood city	97	1,609	12	50	93	2,334	16	D	D	D	106	417
Lutz CDP	60	293	7	33	81	756	9	64	31	589	39	167
Lynn Haven city	19	104	NA	NA	41	503	NA	NA	35	706	D	D
Maitland city	76	6,786	16	265	170	3,668	20	D	52	890	65	407
Mango CDP	D	D	NA	NA	D	D	NA	NA	13	116	9	36
Marco Island city	52	225	3	D	32	179	21	292	69	2,621	78	518
Margate city	110	2,062	14	101	168	2,519	18	323	93	1,221	128	411
Meadow Woods CDP	22	60	NA	NA	18	137	5	3	8	202	13	25
Medulla CDP	19	456	4	47	23	166	NA	NA	18	360	D	D
Melbourne city	194	6,278	32	437	450	12,706	36	508	265	5,501	205	1,002
Merritt Island CDP	62	401	15	69	147	2,027	D	D	86	1,646	79	410
Miami city	D	100	170	1,455	1,858	41,128	318	7,230	1,460	35,124	1,195	7,218
Miami Beach city	163	1,576	44	248	426	7,303	144	1,182	691	28,900	305	2,250
Miami Gardens city	D	D	12	43	193	2,883	D	D	104	1,440	73	226
Miami Lakes town	106	5,029	7	50	235	3,060	23	144	75	1,902	60	613
Miami Shores village	D	D	11	42	54	206	19	130	24	285	23	98
Miami Springs city	D	D	D	D	52	591	6	8	46	942	16	100
Middleburg CDP	D	D	NA	NA	24	608	NA	NA	24	316	D	D
Midway CDP	32	118	7	40	38	427	D	D	16	260	18	44
Minneola city	18	169	D	D	D	D	D	D	3	68	16	55
Miramar city	147	5,296	24	125	290	3,714	39	252	124	2,084	129	986
Mount Dora city	18	176	D	D	79	1,339	16	151	71	1,245	34	156
Myrtle Grove CDP	12	169	NA	NA	23	1,069	NA	NA	14	206	D	D
Naples city	121	1,419	17	90	408	8,443	65	1,183	337	10,177	292	1,936
Naranja CDP	4	7	NA	NA	15	111	NA	NA	D	D	9	57
Navarre CDP	31	374	NA	NA	40	366	8	80	D	D	D	D
New Port Richey city	D	D	D	D	169	3,183	D	D	58	1,059	48	177
New Port Richey East CDP	D	D	NA	NA	21	295	D	D	9	81	17	69
New Smyrna Beach city	50	452	5	2	109	1,581	31	252	115	1,987	95	427
Niceville city	15	126	4	D	61	682	6	71	42	760	D	D
Nocatee CDP	8	53	4	29	13	64	NA	NA	8	113	D	D
Northdale CDP	44	210	9	39	81	920	7	237	28	489	D	D
North Fort Myers CDP	71	428	3	6	55	737	D	D	80	1,476	70	396
North Lauderdale city	34	206	NA	NA	34	311	D	D	27	497	33	160
North Miami city	D	D	13	56	167	4,020	20	208	111	1,874	118	550
North Miami Beach city	73	1,860	30	195	222	4,407	17	85	112	1,775	96	482
North Palm Beach village	D	D	5	8	83	790	8	34	D	D	47	290
North Port city	83	5,165	D	D	80	717	5	37	53	1,031	57	225
Oakland Park city	145	2,084	23	148	197	1,963	26	231	114	2,283	194	668
Oakleaf Plantation CDP	10	23	NA	NA	D	D	NA	NA	NA	NA	D	D
Oak Ridge CDP	20	919	D	D	20	287	NA	NA	24	360	D	D
Ocala city	161	3,009	16	134	583	12,284	29	383	301	6,783	243	1,427

STATE City, town, township, borough, or CDP (county if applicable)	Retail Trade Number of establishments	Retail Trade Number of employees	Wholesale trade[1] Number of establishments	Wholesale trade[1] Number of employees	Transportation and warehousing Number of establishments	Transportation and warehousing Number of employees	Information Number of establishments	Information Number of employees	Finance and insurance Number of establishments	Finance and insurance Number of employees	Real estate and rental and leasing Number of establishments	Real estate and rental and leasing Number of employees	Professional, scientific, and technical services Number of establishments	Professional, scientific, and technical services Number of employees
	1	2	3	4	5	6	7	8	9	10	11	12	13	14
FLORIDA—Con.														
Ocoee city	139	2,224	25	660	37	241	18	324	38	268	41	327	102	612
Ojus CDP	41	93	33	87	D	D	7	4	20	167	69	155	82	182
Oldsmar city	81	989	59	852	15	191	18	325	41	971	31	99	88	5,000
Olympia Heights CDP	47	200	12	20	6	14	D	D	27	141	10	16	46	251
Opa-locka city	116	480	89	958	50	613	D	D	8	57	32	220	15	98
Orange City city	111	2,133	24	108	D	D	D	D	54	486	26	95	36	200
Orlando city	1,639	30,854	661	10,635	370	19,665	291	8,846	698	9,570	987	8,964	2,332	22,012
Ormond Beach city	219	3,105	48	355	22	102	23	202	108	899	95	D	191	1,069
Oviedo city	146	2,127	30	201	12	33	11	109	72	338	D	D	149	745
Pace CDP	63	1,422	7	D	5	12	6	63	D	D	D	D	44	165
Palatka city	98	1,231	11	65	9	169	15	105	34	224	16	63	33	92
Palm Bay city	192	3,537	33	230	53	687	17	102	62	458	67	237	128	607
Palm Beach Gardens city	374	6,904	72	550	32	275	49	1,158	260	2,066	170	765	543	3,060
Palm City CDP	43	610	24	288	16	452	D	D	55	253	D	D	123	414
Palm Coast city	169	3,177	35	187	57	135	D	D	87	486	D	D	137	342
Palmetto city	61	1,008	14	168	D	D	3	3	23	100	20	45	40	173
Palmetto Bay village	99	2,301	38	86	14	14	25	172	74	745	58	131	181	789
Palmetto Estates CDP	27	341	4	9	D	D	NA	NA	D	D	D	D	14	16
Palm Harbor CDP	189	2,713	44	210	35	183	28	180	117	553	135	430	275	2,295
Palm River-Clair Mel CDP	61	432	62	1,944	38	550	8	367	20	53	27	346	21	174
Palm Springs village	131	2,080	14	228	15	24	D	D	53	290	28	95	55	249
Palm Valley CDP	40	291	29	154	14	20	9	101	58	253	54	91	121	352
Panama City city	305	4,724	62	854	46	758	34	591	108	774	98	497	222	1,556
Panama City Beach city	184	2,954	17	127	D	D	8	163	39	218	69	200	68	335
Parkland city	32	316	56	87	9	62	D	D	D	D	D	D	189	237
Pasadena Hills CDP	11	127	NA	NA	5	14	NA	NA	NA	NA	10	24	10	22
Pebble Creek CDP	18	103	3	8	D	D	NA	NA	15	88	10	24	43	159
Pembroke Pines city	577	12,099	186	506	91	485	79	848	219	2,601	233	863	640	1,857
Pensacola city	381	6,068	72	638	43	768	50	510	207	1,657	149	768	484	5,270
Pine Castle CDP	36	186	21	109	16	50	D	D	NA	NA	16	392	D	D
Pinecrest village	67	1,225	31	101	D	D	13	87	54	491	D	D	198	426
Pine Hills CDP	111	1,111	3	D	35	75	8	34	24	174	27	91	25	89
Pinellas Park city	312	4,188	195	2,598	51	1,305	18	332	80	959	73	454	161	1,096
Pine Ridge CDP	18	266	3	4	NA	NA	3	10	10	34	7	35	7	18
Pinewood CDP	55	630	D	D	4	10	D	D	4	41	5	25	9	18
Plantation city	333	5,054	118	586	63	547	66	805	240	2,663	254	2,278	743	6,356
Plant City city	183	3,768	71	2,397	27	874	14	149	84	515	46	202	103	419
Poinciana CDP	29	760	6	6	32	30	3	9	D	D	13	27	15	30
Pompano Beach city	635	8,230	456	7,001	149	2,718	74	946	144	1,078	279	1,140	523	2,179
Port Charlotte CDP	238	3,877	30	123	D	D	D	D	64	382	63	234	118	392
Port Orange city	186	3,186	34	284	36	116	16	126	70	485	111	396	132	850
Port St. John CDP	19	386	NA	NA	5	6	NA	NA	D	D	5	6	13	39
Port St. Lucie city	371	6,893	104	614	91	443	31	298	148	757	185	385	294	1,097
Port Salerno CDP	25	341	4	6	6	18	3	7	10	56	D	D	29	66
Princeton CDP	31	233	15	66	20	347	NA	NA	5	17	6	32	8	25
Punta Gorda city	111	1,874	16	61	D	D	D	D	56	262	53	211	93	360
Richmond West CDP	47	582	29	109	21	123	6	18	13	33	14	24	45	51
Riverview CDP	171	2,814	34	486	46	123	D	D	111	365	70	201	163	4,397
Riviera Beach city	126	1,376	97	2,769	49	1,807	17	138	24	98	50	271	80	319
Rockledge city	99	1,215	38	295	17	219	5	23	42	237	34	151	80	525
Royal Palm Beach village	161	3,605	24	166	33	822	16	143	46	247	37	62	119	467
Ruskin CDP	D	D	15	109	9	20	5	39	21	73	23	68	18	53
Safety Harbor city	36	277	21	56	D	D	12	46	29	577	37	70	123	403
St. Augustine city	302	3,251	23	156	D	D	17	64	60	321	78	337	146	753
St. Cloud city	132	2,369	11	90	16	18	17	73	35	187	52	124	64	192
St. Petersburg city	911	15,594	184	2,380	115	544	158	7,219	589	13,306	467	2,667	1,312	12,571
San Carlos Park CDP	32	244	7	41	D	D	3	4	10	34	11	18	22	67
Sanford city	364	6,148	97	1,476	48	1,063	24	322	67	381	92	443	145	1,222
Sarasota city	451	4,662	80	678	32	626	48	807	293	2,331	262	708	656	4,895
Sarasota Springs CDP	29	227	7	31	7	12	4	12	17	103	D	D	47	136
Satellite Beach city	21	266	10	42	NA	NA	NA	NA	17	46	24	74	55	269
Sebastian city	47	887	D	D	13	37	6	11	26	127	34	72	57	178
Sebring city	145	2,619	15	69	9	37	13	126	50	236	27	109	59	289
Seminole city	104	1,938	12	42	5	7	12	197	61	234	40	143	80	223
Shady Hills CDP	15	66	3	D	5	10	NA	NA	NA	NA	4	10	17	53
South Bradenton CDP	113	1,825	10	64	8	42	10	85	30	121	30	178	35	133
Southchase CDP	69	1,262	27	373	26	146	7	187	8	40	30	210	21	54
South Daytona city	54	389	11	92	D	D	5	70	15	71	17	44	23	75
South Miami city	102	815	18	51	6	10	D	D	45	284	62	108	172	844
South Miami Heights CDP	51	883	16	48	16	18	4	10	D	D	16	163	21	33
South Venice CDP	55	657	5	21	5	12	6	98	23	79	10	20	26	158
Spring Hill CDP	225	4,118	43	193	43	112	28	106	105	444	95	232	174	755
Stuart city	273	4,136	59	345	15	101	30	474	135	1,375	100	809	278	1,655
Sun City Center CDP	38	825	NA	NA	4	6	3	4	36	153	16	283	36	100
Sunny Isles Beach city	71	702	35	96	19	54	8	44	35	117	97	237	140	227
Sunrise city	557	11,840	257	2,861	61	785	70	2,060	141	3,739	137	763	396	2,528
Sunset CDP	43	467	25	58	7	18	D	D	41	274	D	D	144	481
Sweetwater city	68	735	71	377	38	151	3	15	30	216	21	121	42	193
Tallahassee city	877	13,577	153	2,117	78	864	200	3,562	418	4,575	376	2,652	1,194	9,135
Tamarac city	126	2,934	71	1,522	35	54	22	234	77	621	74	217	203	683
Tamiami CDP	114	1,110	57	112	40	87	17	36	49	188	D	D	160	356
Tampa city	1,867	25,775	642	10,930	336	9,930	331	10,594	1,290	27,969	1,110	5,982	2,971	41,022
Tarpon Springs city	138	1,634	34	219	15	87	20	220	46	167	54	312	96	334
Tavares city	60	706	6	73	8	82	6	32	19	98	D	D	64	255
Temple Terrace city	88	1,339	26	390	13	216	D	D	60	950	45	109	126	1,254
The Acreage CDP	34	287	26	46	41	106	6	10	12	21	23	53	89	150
The Crossings CDP	45	563	27	41	13	15	D	D	20	90	27	81	74	122
The Hammocks CDP	67	1,035	50	102	18	14	4	4	39	102	38	75	108	180
The Villages CDP	92	2,074	D	D	D	D	7	24	67	467	72	400	106	452
Thonotosassa CDP	30	819	10	67	10	382	D	D	NA	NA	10	67	15	126

1 Merchant wholesalers, except manufacturers' sales branches and offices.

Table C. Incorporated Places, Census Designated Places (CDPs), and Minor Civil Divisions (MCDs) of 10,000 or More Population — Economic Census

STATE City, town, township, borough, or CDP (county if applicable)	Administration and support and waste management and mediation services		Educational services		Health care and social assistance		Arts, entertainment, and recreation		Accommodation and food services		Other services (except public administration)	
	Number of establishments	Number of employees	Number of establishments	Number of employees	Number of establishments	Number of employees	Number of establishments	Number of employees	Number of establishments	Number of employees	Number of establishments	Number of employees
	15	16	17	18	19	20	21	22	23	24	25	26
FLORIDA—Con.												
Ocoee city	64	1,083	D	D	127	3,085	22	113	80	1,191	D	D
Ojus CDP	D	D	6	10	56	700	11	64	D	D	47	179
Oldsmar city	54	1,565	11	26	59	649	6	187	54	1,195	D	D
Olympia Heights CDP	D	D	3	D	35	241	5	12	17	259	18	60
Opa-locka city	D	D	10	98	22	187	NA	NA	D	D	52	430
Orange City city	22	298	5	42	137	2,957	10	294	76	1,682	40	138
Orlando city	754	31,801	116	2,942	1,144	38,074	242	28,497	1,129	33,869	729	6,858
Ormond Beach city	101	728	13	55	234	3,595	31	396	147	2,991	108	536
Oviedo city	65	671	12	156	128	1,279	20	189	D	D	D	D
Pace CDP	24	128	3	9	29	238	D	D	39	1,015	27	121
Palatka city	14	239	D	D	99	1,538	5	33	44	792	45	196
Palm Bay city	159	826	4	49	151	2,335	16	92	118	1,954	101	441
Palm Beach Gardens city	134	2,423	41	275	409	4,790	62	1,313	165	4,965	184	1,754
Palm City CDP	45	453	9	46	72	1,019	20	501	36	703	56	210
Palm Coast city	126	1,264	10	41	194	3,467	D	D	110	2,182	89	407
Palmetto city	22	197	4	11	37	462	9	117	35	478	44	235
Palmetto Bay village	D	D	16	99	132	2,108	17	92	D	D	54	291
Palmetto Estates CDP	D	D	3	D	26	308	NA	NA	15	148	11	59
Palm Harbor CDP	137	924	18	86	264	3,362	27	305	117	2,624	147	654
Palm River-Clair Mel CDP	19	2,293	NA	NA	13	138	NA	NA	19	179	37	316
Palm Springs village	59	1,509	6	37	156	1,932	NA	NA	47	636	73	287
Palm Valley CDP	52	810	7	30	78	963	21	D	26	831	D	D
Panama City city	58	858	10	46	354	8,121	14	152	166	3,534	106	677
Panama City Beach city	36	439	NA	NA	D	D	D	D	150	4,577	58	531
Parkland city	D	D	11	20	87	274	10	39	22	356	29	91
Pasadena Hills CDP	D	D	NA	NA	20	1,050	4	19	8	170	D	D
Pebble Creek CDP	D	D	4	21	13	110	NA	NA	12	127	5	27
Pembroke Pines city	236	5,238	58	233	638	9,390	76	536	324	7,639	255	1,522
Pensacola city	134	5,906	23	115	456	14,133	34	736	195	5,482	149	1,205
Pine Castle CDP	21	405	4	22	13	109	NA	NA	17	278	23	170
Pinecrest village	D	D	17	169	84	2,871	17	69	47	956	35	190
Pine Hills CDP	43	92	10	45	127	1,003	D	D	51	965	42	124
Pinellas Park city	152	3,895	19	161	183	3,189	22	232	133	2,501	182	1,202
Pine Ridge CDP	8	33	NA	NA	18	316	NA	NA	7	41	D	D
Pinewood CDP	D	D	NA	NA	51	2,037	NA	NA	11	196	D	D
Plantation city	266	18,122	43	354	611	7,486	42	555	212	3,869	195	875
Plant City city	45	916	7	21	134	2,237	10	714	84	1,927	67	314
Poinciana CDP	29	57	NA	NA	20	109	NA	NA	D	D	D	D
Pompano Beach city	293	4,816	33	150	335	5,819	73	1,567	279	4,425	396	2,075
Port Charlotte CDP	66	733	10	32	261	4,307	16	304	92	2,411	102	377
Port Orange city	109	2,311	D	D	182	1,915	20	393	126	2,714	104	386
Port St. John CDP	16	68	NA	NA	21	275	NA	NA	25	399	12	29
Port St. Lucie city	310	2,376	D	D	488	7,881	48	379	239	4,613	234	828
Port Salerno CDP	17	40	NA	NA	D	D	4	8	19	459	21	143
Princeton CDP	18	97	NA	NA	17	214	NA	NA	8	40	D	D
Punta Gorda city	35	1,560	D	D	95	1,337	11	178	47	1,385	41	163
Richmond West CDP	D	D	NA	NA	41	214	3	3	20	292	34	82
Riverview CDP	99	723	D	D	141	2,711	23	106	100	2,066	83	422
Riviera Beach city	D	D	11	113	72	3,543	5	361	37	886	90	648
Rockledge city	60	1,103	6	19	131	3,319	11	205	64	1,200	49	109
Royal Palm Beach village	D	D	13	226	154	1,544	11	98	105	2,109	90	488
Ruskin CDP	26	170	NA	NA	27	397	NA	NA	30	461	D	D
Safety Harbor city	44	304	4	6	109	3,239	3	9	47	842	51	240
St. Augustine city	42	516	8	10	114	1,326	34	369	229	4,344	D	D
St. Cloud city	62	235	6	13	98	1,643	D	D	82	1,475	D	D
St. Petersburg city	477	140,648	86	535	1,021	20,818	116	2,201	568	10,140	531	3,176
San Carlos Park CDP	49	255	NA	NA	D	D	NA	NA	D	D	19	56
Sanford city	80	3,067	17	353	144	2,690	15	262	150	3,039	125	655
Sarasota city	173	3,887	22	76	470	11,452	70	1,573	272	6,120	258	1,373
Sarasota Springs CDP	44	1,748	3	10	63	1,155	NA	NA	22	208	32	169
Satellite Beach city	22	42	NA	NA	D	D	5	D	23	317	15	33
Sebastian city	50	166	5	16	D	D	9	35	D	D	36	166
Sebring city	22	1,104	NA	NA	119	1,848	10	118	64	1,269	47	139
Seminole city	44	172	6	28	100	5,474	10	153	67	1,138	59	285
Shady Hills CDP	21	184	NA	NA	D	D	NA	NA	3	8	20	66
South Bradenton CDP	37	1,160	4	14	53	647	6	91	D	D	44	197
Southchase CDP	30	291	5	27	22	120	10	186	25	742	33	254
South Daytona city	22	209	NA	NA	28	587	7	37	30	289	35	102
South Miami city	33	829	12	94	239	2,959	10	44	50	975	78	442
South Miami Heights CDP	D	D	NA	NA	31	431	NA	NA	24	288	31	71
South Venice CDP	40	82	NA	NA	50	446	D	D	D	D	D	D
Spring Hill CDP	D	D	15	89	335	4,909	23	253	144	2,766	113	540
Stuart city	69	460	14	76	307	5,656	22	377	152	2,865	121	790
Sun City Center CDP	D	D	D	D	90	1,994	8	227	20	572	21	220
Sunny Isles Beach city	D	D	8	10	42	131	14	80	74	2,223	66	497
Sunrise city	D	D	40	170	289	7,051	38	D	203	4,158	148	760
Sunset CDP	27	445	D	D	158	1,291	D	D	35	384	D	D
Sweetwater city	D	D	4	32	41	246	3	3	44	604	D	D
Tallahassee city	293	4,895	83	620	680	17,885	84	1,268	647	14,587	524	4,124
Tamarac city	96	1,586	11	78	230	3,849	21	269	67	1,053	93	274
Tamiami CDP	D	D	10	19	216	1,260	9	52	61	953	81	202
Tampa city	881	45,052	161	1,467	1,526	38,844	213	10,239	1,130	28,032	1,043	9,738
Tarpon Springs city	60	520	D	D	81	1,757	20	200	75	1,375	62	221
Tavares city	19	150	D	D	99	4,075	8	129	32	379	39	131
Temple Terrace city	D	D	11	35	104	1,501	11	61	73	1,378	32	140
The Acreage CDP	D	D	5	5	42	166	D	D	14	235	55	124
The Crossings CDP	D	D	15	39	44	135	9	78	D	D	D	D
The Hammocks CDP	D	D	9	27	94	1,995	11	98	D	D	D	D
The Villages CDP	21	51	4	11	116	3,046	8	80	58	2,282	D	D
Thonotosassa CDP	36	479	NA	NA	D	D	NA	NA	7	190	D	D

Items 15–26

Table C. Incorporated Places, Census Designated Places (CDPs), and Minor Civil Divisions (MCDs) of 10,000 or More Population — Economic Census

STATE City, town, township, borough, or CDP (county if applicable)	Retail Trade Number of establishments	Retail Trade Number of employees	Wholesale trade[1] Number of establishments	Wholesale trade[1] Number of employees	Transportation and warehousing Number of establishments	Transportation and warehousing Number of employees	Information Number of establishments	Information Number of employees	Finance and insurance Number of establishments	Finance and insurance Number of employees	Real estate and rental and leasing Number of establishments	Real estate and rental and leasing Number of employees	Professional, scientific, and technical services Number of establishments	Professional, scientific, and technical services Number of employees
	1	2	3	4	5	6	7	8	9	10	11	12	13	14
FLORIDA—Con.														
Three Lakes CDP	100	598	196	1,451	29	307	16	102	51	344	80	439	214	857
Titusville city	176	2,893	20	105	19	255	14	145	55	278	39	141	102	521
Town 'n' Country CDP	271	3,668	178	2,914	88	1,331	49	2,665	95	4,500	101	646	253	1,940
Trinity CDP	16	102	10	23	6	7	NA	NA	24	75	19	78	44	91
Union Park CDP	28	269	3	D	5	7	NA	NA	D	D	9	55	9	42
University CDP (Hillsborough County)	159	2,323	22	141	7	36	8	220	15	93	51	392	38	213
University CDP (Orange County)	49	789	D	D	D	D	29	1,537	48	1,931	40	D	180	6,341
University Park CDP	99	1,394	18	39	13	31	8	19	33	148	39	87	64	250
Upper Grand Lagoon CDP	50	382	11	24	23	107	D	D	16	87	35	90	43	1,436
Valrico CDP	61	925	16	51	9	37	6	11	42	65	D	D	92	195
Venice city	140	1,663	34	184	11	104	12	159	77	398	93	293	129	421
Vero Beach city	224	1,822	D	D	22	144	24	307	135	1,039	90	538	243	1,009
Vero Beach South CDP	111	2,282	D	D	7	19	7	122	33	133	46	141	61	484
Viera East CDP	15	96	4	24	NA	NA	NA	NA	20	481	11	20	35	293
Viera West CDP	24	562	NA	NA	3	15	D	D	9	24	13	16	19	15
Villas CDP	82	1,606	30	234	8	65	11	173	39	261	49	133	86	353
Warrington CDP	50	507	NA	NA	4	11	6	21	D	D	10	64	20	22
Wekiwa Springs CDP	26	208	25	80	6	5	7	30	46	457	43	74	148	412
Wellington village	260	3,485	85	311	32	68	27	168	110	319	168	1,070	383	915
Wesley Chapel CDP	156	4,309	27	122	29	64	17	187	62	237	53	116	153	620
Westchase CDP	32	357	23	243	D	D	7	13	33	113	38	105	131	459
Westchester CDP	103	1,260	39	83	28	108	10	140	54	268	41	114	112	311
West Lealman CDP	46	328	9	34	NA	NA	NA	NA	9	22	14	21	14	22
West Little River CDP	117	844	31	260	24	107	NA	NA	14	91	8	46	D	D
West Melbourne city	159	2,720	35	231	8	33	17	298	33	153	27	108	65	453
Weston city	138	1,834	234	1,705	47	147	D	D	174	820	252	472	D	D
West Palm Beach city	595	9,297	144	1,668	123	2,555	99	2,548	308	2,836	333	1,462	1,190	7,989
West Park city	36	415	24	123	12	54	NA	NA	D	D	7	26	6	9
West Pensacola CDP	91	1,218	10	142	4	10	8	150	D	D	15	58	25	97
Westview CDP	23	233	33	1,679	21	449	NA	NA	NA	NA	5	11	D	D
Westwood Lakes CDP	12	57	4	2	8	13	NA	NA	NA	NA	5	14	13	19
Wilton Manors city	80	706	14	34	D	D	D	D	D	D	48	91	108	306
Winter Garden city	202	3,678	57	637	54	437	23	102	63	290	103	334	165	598
Winter Haven city	219	3,493	37	481	34	1,052	21	178	105	3,727	60	346	124	670
Winter Park city	250	2,871	47	443	9	28	51	814	205	1,377	171	604	525	3,559
Winter Springs city	49	424	27	128	19	75	10	41	40	80	55	98	116	659
World Golf Village CDP	17	347	9	663	7	11	4	32	14	33	17	140	38	89
Wright CDP	94	1,769	14	70	D	D	10	53	14	63	27	102	43	319
Yulee CDP	49	828	D	D	D	D	NA	NA	9	35	14	42	11	50
Zephyrhills city	81	1,495	5	8	7	136	9	84	31	160	17	54	25	137
GEORGIA	34,100	485,505	10,832	165,088	6,961	194,654	4,705	129,292	14,991	187,894	12,426	63,935	29,737	266,523
Acworth city	98	1,945	21	142	11	227	12	189	62	254	17	37	71	437
Albany city	407	5,724	103	1,804	58	1,232	D	D	157	1,093	109	451	191	1,391
Alpharetta city	406	7,575	173	3,956	54	2,729	202	18,814	451	14,827	226	1,549	907	15,625
Americus city	107	1,299	14	277	4	63	D	D	D	D	18	45	32	292
Athens-Clarke County unified government	513	8,212	94	2,042	45	1,049	52	1,392	170	1,066	202	1,392	321	1,530
Atlanta city	1,991	28,468	671	11,052	332	44,481	806	30,644	1,428	35,030	1,461	13,207	3,987	68,768
Augusta-Richmond County consolidated government	752	10,886	D	D	98	2,565	D	D	D	D	D	D	465	4,947
Bainbridge city	101	1,237	15	149	13	84	9	71	48	D	23	65	27	94
Belvedere Park CDP	58	509	NA	NA	D	D	D	D	19	78	12	33	30	98
Braselton town	47	1,190	17	733	16	3,052	D	D	29	154	25	132	44	362
Brookhaven city	111	1,796	35	269	8	20	53	6,010	92	3,304	172	1,286	377	3,665
Brunswick city	147	2,478	21	181	18	748	16	145	56	320	29	123	89	342
Buford city	248	5,704	108	2,198	32	670	21	192	68	347	60	213	127	1,098
Calhoun city	126	1,519	42	811	14	259	D	D	54	278	23	60	32	331
Candler-McAfee CDP	59	293	NA	NA	NA	NA	NA	NA	7	42	10	26	16	22
Canton city	145	2,859	30	125	15	118	16	252	66	342	37	80	104	629
Carrollton city	189	2,723	38	376	15	310	18	636	100	521	45	224	75	356
Cartersville city	187	2,709	63	875	28	858	19	335	112	581	70	225	104	670
Cedartown city	64	811	D	D	D	D	D	D	27	93	5	28	16	49
Chamblee city	218	3,776	86	676	40	470	36	638	62	471	67	312	237	2,252
Clarkston city	45	194	12	92	5	5	NA	NA	D	D	4	D	12	34
College Park city	62	381	22	1,253	72	2,629	D	D	20	218	34	1,031	66	425
Columbus city	794	11,547	152	1,978	77	1,157	59	1,082	337	15,411	242	1,314	330	2,613
Conyers city	166	3,465	32	344	18	296	D	D	75	739	44	318	74	324
Cordele city	94	1,109	18	216	11	207	9	64	D	D	17	191	20	146
Covington city	124	1,838	D	D	13	112	21	398	60	473	37	155	50	218
Cusseta-Chattahoochee County unified government	16	94	NA	NA	D	D	NA	NA	5	19	NA	NA	43	1,189
Dallas city	70	1,347	20	102	6	73	D	D	33	138	17	72	43	211
Dalton city	230	2,748	124	2,737	33	634	D	D	107	548	32	115	136	1,108
Decatur city	68	450	14	67	D	D	34	242	44	253	D	D	347	1,146
Doraville city	157	2,432	143	1,767	46	747	12	65	45	235	40	275	61	314
Douglas city	137	1,617	29	397	14	1,359	D	D	51	288	24	69	42	217
Douglasville city	243	4,655	26	879	30	575	19	118	73	482	53	171	107	552
Dublin city	159	1,914	23	214	11	284	D	D	61	458	30	152	47	349
Duluth city	191	3,017	172	3,427	39	746	53	1,534	159	4,096	111	487	305	4,196
Dunwoody city	242	5,137	53	1,559	17	239	54	2,331	173	2,822	167	699	523	7,645
East Point city	108	1,686	27	768	30	1,685	D	D	23	105	38	322	55	466
Evans CDP	90	2,305	21	209	5	17	10	451	52	241	38	111	88	473
Fairburn city	37	312	21	959	45	1,407	NA	NA	D	D	D	D	19	47
Fayetteville city	167	3,434	21	357	18	113	20	287	77	446	46	145	108	474

1 Merchant wholesalers, except manufacturers' sales branches and offices.

STATE City, town, township, borough, or CDP (county if applicable)	Administration and support and waste management and mediation services		Educational services		Health care and social assistance		Arts, entertainment, and recreation		Accommodation and food services		Other services (except public administration)	
	Number of establishments	Number of employees	Number of establishments	Number of employees	Number of establishments	Number of employees	Number of establishments	Number of employees	Number of establishments	Number of employees	Number of establishments	Number of employees
	15	16	17	18	19	20	21	22	23	24	25	26
FLORIDA—Con.												
Three Lakes CDP	D	D	16	100	91	581	15	56	D	D	89	293
Titusville city	67	1,076	6	107	147	2,868	12	177	102	2,018	80	406
Town 'n' Country CDP	159	5,899	18	152	224	4,143	26	318	125	2,425	127	550
Trinity CDP	20	37	4	5	D	D	4	D	11	193	10	34
Union Park CDP	D	D	NA	NA	11	59	4	128	13	138	9	28
University CDP (Hillsborough County)	27	594	5	17	166	9,804	D	D	61	851	61	265
University CDP (Orange County)	60	6,389	19	525	41	1,038	5	68	99	2,667	D	D
University Park CDP	D	D	D	D	115	779	D	D	61	1,052	40	145
Upper Grand Lagoon CDP	20	83	NA	NA	23	357	7	30	32	763	25	106
Valrico CDP	54	154	7	44	36	224	7	112	18	338	31	143
Venice city	52	473	7	21	142	3,601	17	159	100	2,004	82	467
Vero Beach city	65	1,129	16	167	167	1,708	19	398	119	2,577	113	513
Vero Beach South CDP	52	140	NA	NA	D	D	D	D	42	790	D	D
Viera East CDP	9	45	NA	NA	58	1,112	NA	NA	8	256	7	19
Viera West CDP	7	10	D	D	14	69	6	55	D	D	D	D
Villas CDP	35	874	NA	NA	63	867	7	64	D	D	50	305
Warrington CDP	9	26	NA	NA	D	D	NA	NA	28	587	14	54
Wekiwa Springs CDP	35	1,663	9	30	40	477	6	45	18	334	28	141
Wellington village	149	582	39	225	264	2,789	81	956	120	2,830	129	582
Wesley Chapel CDP	D	D	16	62	142	2,026	16	84	74	2,483	49	343
Westchase CDP	35	347	7	31	80	412	12	105	40	779	D	D
Westchester CDP	48	406	9	79	179	881	8	14	49	764	54	163
West Lealman CDP	20	86	3	17	30	351	NA	NA	23	383	24	136
West Little River CDP	D	D	NA	NA	27	291	NA	NA	D	D	18	50
West Melbourne city	43	699	5	28	68	1,310	6	63	59	1,492	67	283
Weston city	D	D	43	181	291	3,950	32	685	118	2,530	123	483
West Palm Beach city	301	8,014	43	255	621	13,961	81	1,945	389	8,290	383	2,254
West Park city	20	199	NA	NA	9	93	NA	NA	12	94	31	56
West Pensacola CDP	11	42	NA	NA	25	144	5	42	40	587	D	D
Westview CDP	D	D	NA	NA	D	D	NA	NA	10	104	6	15
Westwood Lakes CDP	17	23	NA	NA	20	39	NA	NA	NA	NA	12	20
Wilton Manors city	31	90	7	44	70	1,139	D	D	67	1,060	52	174
Winter Garden city	88	640	21	187	106	1,272	35	271	102	2,328	90	581
Winter Haven city	54	2,692	19	63	191	5,761	18	1,971	117	2,369	81	317
Winter Park city	94	6,480	30	174	357	5,942	50	937	163	4,692	159	878
Winter Springs city	45	245	8	22	62	323	19	145	29	263	39	99
World Golf Village CDP	30	157	6	45	23	343	D	D	D	D	D	D
Wright CDP	D	D	NA	NA	120	2,615	3	3	31	483	50	169
Yulee CDP	17	102	NA	NA	D	D	5	D	D	D	27	110
Zephyrhills city	D	D	D	D	78	1,811	5	89	41	745	34	234
GEORGIA	12,732	384,328	2,313	16,007	25,260	521,146	3,452	50,796	21,201	426,884	14,976	97,721
Acworth city	33	613	12	33	64	622	4	D	81	1,980	45	604
Albany city	89	3,192	D	D	295	8,386	23	258	D	D	123	851
Alpharetta city	307	20,709	37	985	478	5,378	53	1,536	350	7,192	179	1,439
Americus city	10	365	NA	NA	69	2,050	3	13	44	762	39	143
Athens-Clarke County unified government	138	3,096	35	169	456	10,263	66	959	360	7,878	196	1,403
Atlanta city	1,017	58,254	214	1,598	1,798	43,378	469	9,271	1,896	54,165	1,345	15,249
Augusta-Richmond County consolidated government	191	7,973	31	297	605	24,637	53	1,298	461	10,227	287	1,789
Bainbridge city	15	261	NA	NA	45	788	D	D	41	574	30	124
Belvedere Park CDP	10	16	3	2	35	323	D	D	34	706	16	52
Braselton town	21	433	6	28	D	D	8	87	59	1,516	24	243
Brookhaven city	88	2,933	19	156	175	3,685	30	416	139	2,468	84	737
Brunswick city	29	2,844	D	D	117	3,634	11	D	75	1,400	44	327
Buford city	53	883	18	145	88	797	23	D	127	2,849	102	756
Calhoun city	19	1,091	4	16	65	2,248	D	D	61	1,222	30	174
Candler-McAfee CDP	6	33	NA	NA	20	397	NA	NA	22	492	D	D
Canton city	37	372	5	10	127	3,136	15	195	108	2,290	60	340
Carrollton city	35	2,350	4	13	132	3,606	D	D	114	2,371	D	D
Cartersville city	40	1,631	11	98	128	2,395	19	324	121	2,380	83	528
Cedartown city	8	50	NA	NA	41	846	6	23	D	D	14	65
Chamblee city	70	3,181	14	62	123	1,920	14	117	128	1,559	122	634
Clarkston city	9	103	NA	NA	20	292	NA	NA	12	111	D	D
College Park city	27	1,568	D	D	65	1,754	5	7	85	2,307	27	622
Columbus city	202	4,127	34	291	666	15,924	50	1,047	474	10,818	D	D
Conyers city	41	2,597	7	44	146	2,969	8	74	123	2,794	D	D
Cordele city	12	267	NA	NA	D	D	NA	NA	44	993	20	77
Covington city	19	279	NA	NA	98	2,084	D	D	96	1,702	38	157
Cusseta-Chattahoochee County unified government	6	229	NA	NA	D	D	NA	NA	6	73	D	D
Dallas city	27	182	4	26	D	D	D	D	D	D	33	177
Dalton city	44	2,244	8	51	164	D	15	275	134	2,741	76	624
Decatur city	38	899	25	132	148	1,652	28	238	98	1,969	62	250
Doraville city	74	1,597	6	21	46	334	11	D	103	932	82	677
Douglas city	D	D	NA	NA	98	2,273	4	35	53	1,558	33	164
Douglasville city	36	1,583	D	D	146	2,754	16	D	152	3,226	D	D
Dublin city	14	1,139	D	D	109	2,357	4	25	75	1,590	41	202
Duluth city	103	4,207	45	312	D	D	27	310	186	2,349	162	852
Dunwoody city	D	D	38	323	230	3,485	25	527	149	3,804	108	557
East Point city	34	4,174	D	D	90	1,815	13	12	98	2,035	D	D
Evans CDP	46	644	10	97	121	2,157	14	238	92	2,153	D	D
Fairburn city	18	120	NA	NA	17	298	5	19	37	607	22	180
Fayetteville city	45	330	6	51	176	4,195	15	70	100	2,358	D	D

Table C. Incorporated Places, Census Designated Places (CDPs), and Minor Civil Divisions (MCDs) of 10,000 or More Population — **Economic Census**

STATE City, town, township, borough, or CDP (county if applicable)	Retail Trade Number of establishments	Number of employees	Wholesale trade[1] Number of establishments	Number of employees	Transportation and warehousing Number of establishments	Number of employees	Information Number of establishments	Number of employees	Finance and insurance Number of establishments	Number of employees	Real estate and rental and leasing Number of establishments	Number of employees	Professional, scientific, and technical services Number of establishments	Number of employees
	1	2	3	4	5	6	7	8	9	10	11	12	13	14
GEORGIA—Con.														
Forest Park city	75	629	74	2,157	78	3,185	D	D	22	189	21	199	28	130
Gainesville city	306	5,089	97	1,874	46	1,559	24	476	178	1,325	88	261	177	846
Georgetown CDP	24	312	3	633	6	17	NA	NA	D	D	11	30	12	131
Griffin city	169	2,428	33	505	12	116	D	D	70	416	25	90	57	305
Grovetown city	24	240	4	23	NA	NA	NA	NA	6	19	4	27	5	12
Hinesville city	123	1,765	6	28	D	D	D	D	41	309	41	136	33	220
Holly Springs city	28	795	18	104	7	148	3	13	13	31	5	4	22	106
Jefferson city	52	537	11	215	25	732	D	D	15	78	18	75	18	56
Johns Creek city	160	2,089	73	395	25	106	29	371	D	D	129	291	638	2,987
Kennesaw city	250	4,989	93	1,646	38	640	23	655	67	871	65	471	138	975
Kingsland city	64	917	4	D	NA	NA	4	21	D	D	8	40	13	83
LaGrange city	172	2,453	33	387	24	1,646	10	200	79	979	52	152	69	307
Lawrenceville city	292	4,128	105	3,086	42	1,178	29	685	104	754	68	399	219	1,194
Lilburn city	106	1,598	29	170	12	82	18	87	54	230	21	73	48	181
Lithia Springs CDP	64	1,708	45	1,026	22	880	D	D	18	75	27	250	14	82
Loganville city	82	1,861	14	75	13	56	D	D	35	132	19	111	35	172
Mableton CDP	75	750	41	1,059	D	D	7	26	26	101	26	95	66	109
McDonough city	140	3,089	37	1,198	55	2,782	10	102	71	341	35	99	87	589
Macon-Bibb County	D	D	178	2,913	118	2,293	83	1,482	D	D	203	1,050	356	2,611
Marietta city	428	5,858	237	3,882	65	2,575	68	1,264	198	2,200	190	958	537	5,093
Martinez CDP	137	2,629	22	111	13	94	D	D	70	385	49	225	80	635
Milledgeville city	140	2,138	14	58	6	11	D	D	53	368	26	83	49	180
Milton city	70	892	31	150	D	D	D	D	60	457	56	132	244	1,356
Monroe city	89	1,162	14	407	D	D	8	60	36	202	25	64	32	122
Moultrie city	146	1,665	26	202	D	D	D	D	D	D	25	74	47	188
Mountain Park CDP	41	787	15	55	9	22	5	44	D	D	16	45	40	145
Newnan city	220	4,095	37	513	35	747	20	366	105	508	81	212	103	781
Norcross city	208	2,726	234	4,290	59	1,611	57	2,323	114	1,393	72	634	237	3,116
North Decatur CDP	90	1,739	8	16	NA	NA	8	49	24	119	31	140	84	207
North Druid Hills CDP	61	1,107	9	66	NA	NA	D	D	32	259	40	155	113	359
Panthersville CDP	66	689	NA	NA	4	7	4	46	10	58	4	10	5	20
Peachtree City city	170	3,335	79	1,377	29	1,053	28	383	88	529	101	225	D	D
Peachtree Corners city	91	789	149	3,019	34	683	71	3,905	126	1,304	117	1,034	345	7,505
Perry city	79	1,120	9	64	6	268	5	59	34	224	18	52	36	392
Pooler city	167	2,677	41	756	34	788	8	108	35	202	30	223	40	264
Powder Springs city	41	656	14	220	8	23	D	D	11	65	9	11	24	67
Redan CDP	32	400	NA	NA	8	41	NA	NA	8	58	NA	NA	9	17
Richmond Hill city	65	933	D	D	D	D	D	D	30	128	24	82	39	161
Rincon town	42	1,139	NA	NA	D	D	D	D	26	105	12	51	17	93
Riverdale city	90	1,397	NA	NA	D	D	5	39	26	210	20	77	11	59
Rome city	295	3,723	48	899	19	523	23	304	110	718	58	207	139	706
Roswell city	340	5,875	169	2,445	39	1,038	93	1,252	269	1,607	227	1,071	764	5,455
St. Marys city	57	805	D	D	D	D	D	D	25	114	12	41	30	405
St. Simons CDP	103	681	14	205	9	34	8	42	43	146	D	D	90	336
Sandy Springs city	271	4,407	153	3,193	30	350	154	7,341	493	12,501	393	2,815	1,016	15,440
Savannah city	853	12,466	173	2,139	178	6,477	108	1,738	355	2,063	273	1,551	523	4,117
Scottdale CDP	53	692	15	992	D	D	6	28	D	D	17	147	34	194
Smyrna city	206	3,557	75	2,883	32	957	40	945	99	625	126	665	292	3,710
Snellville city	159	3,759	23	61	23	88	26	236	53	277	32	68	100	434
Statesboro city	180	2,793	20	130	12	69	16	270	87	474	55	253	91	468
Stockbridge city	97	1,738	7	58	27	291	11	313	57	509	34	141	61	324
Stonecrest city	180	3,293	39	491	46	2,865	13	137	26	125	24	172	38	205
Sugar Hill city	41	583	19	79	17	39	7	87	23	86	28	75	64	142
Suwanee city	117	2,069	105	1,496	26	955	23	293	88	916	60	160	197	1,037
Thomasville city	157	1,924	41	451	16	173	D	D	69	723	39	120	50	310
Tifton city	168	2,013	25	525	15	500	D	D	82	403	29	130	63	401
Tucker city	171	2,674	177	2,850	55	1,938	36	2,987	80	554	78	201	217	1,928
Union City city	63	2,164	8	149	30	1,855	D	D	20	104	24	134	13	77
Valdosta city	387	5,792	71	820	44	2,074	19	318	131	932	109	552	176	903
Vidalia city	D	D	D	D	7	219	7	66	41	197	11	24	44	180
Villa Rica city	67	1,200	20	309	17	169	D	D	33	281	20	66	29	144
Vinings CDP	37	985	17	540	D	D	27	408	69	819	D	D	125	1,397
Warner Robins city	314	4,805	20	210	13	67	13	180	114	801	75	318	195	2,855
Waycross city	168	2,298	24	162	17	426	9	119	48	399	29	94	49	256
Wilmington Island CDP	25	374	D	D	13	105	NA	NA	12	60	D	D	37	73
Winder city	80	1,446	16	473	13	1,100	D	D	43	210	22	45	38	283
Woodstock city	229	3,902	58	576	17	140	14	134	99	690	66	265	197	1,070
HAWAII	4,644	72,908	1,423	16,829	935	31,863	533	8,218	1,482	19,718	2,069	13,101	3,380	22,668
East Honolulu CDP	48	894	29	61	12	39	10	198	32	115	56	122	101	300
Ewa Beach CDP	12	166	NA	NA	NA	NA	NA	NA	D	D	5	8	D	D
Ewa Gentry CDP	8	122	NA	NA	3	12	NA	NA	NA	NA	4	17	3	3
Halawa CDP	16	86	24	214	4	35	NA	NA	5	22	10	43	19	45
Hilo CDP	213	4,395	61	800	46	763	15	275	75	601	87	337	98	602
Kahului CDP	191	4,485	57	836	55	2,283	23	486	51	337	47	379	47	259
Kailua CDP (Hawaii County)	123	1,924	27	233	27	480	15	187	41	230	41	162	55	202
Kailua CDP (Honolulu County)	96	1,571	19	57	8	60	11	26	43	279	55	173	101	313
Kalaoa CDP	27	681	19	248	29	278	D	D	NA	NA	11	25	27	136
Kaneohe CDP	104	1,743	15	78	8	61	13	145	24	141	31	145	51	190
Kaneohe Station CDP	9	40	NA	NA	NA	NA	NA	NA	NA	NA	NA	NA	14	64
Kapaa CDP	57	583	6	49	NA	NA	D	D	7	93	11	40	18	30
Kapolei CDP	74	2,402	10	237	12	247	D	D	33	1,135	D	D	13	106
Kihei CDP	73	755	7	35	D	D	9	41	21	110	60	270	64	344
Lahaina CDP	176	1,372	6	75	28	399	7	24	12	67	45	311	25	85
Maili CDP	5	30	NA	NA	3	38	NA	NA	NA	NA	NA	NA	NA	NA
Makakilo CDP	D	D	5	11	NA	NA	NA	NA	NA	NA	7	5	11	23
Mililani Mauka CDP	5	86	8	130	D	D	D	D	8	203	D	D	14	59

1 Merchant wholesalers, except manufacturers' sales branches and offices.

Table C. Incorporated Places, Census Designated Places (CDPs), and Minor Civil Divisions (MCDs) of 10,000 or More Population — **Economic Census**

	Economic activity by sector, 2017											
	Administration and support and waste management and mediation services		Educational services		Health care and social assistance		Arts, entertainment, and recreation		Accommodation and food services		Other services (except public administration)	
STATE City, town, township, borough, or CDP (county if applicable)	Number of establishments	Number of employees	Number of establishments	Number of employees	Number of establishments	Number of employees	Number of establishments	Number of employees	Number of establishments	Number of employees	Number of establishments	Number of employees
	15	16	17	18	19	20	21	22	23	24	25	26
GEORGIA—Con.												
Forest Park city	26	851	NA	NA	39	962	5	71	44	601	37	154
Gainesville city	90	3,852	10	70	309	11,054	24	D	157	3,290	125	613
Georgetown CDP	7	74	NA	NA	8	88	NA	NA	12	297	5	25
Griffin city	21	1,933	7	50	119	1,905	D	D	96	1,697	D	D
Grovetown city	7	31	NA	NA	8	80	D	D	21	428	10	23
Hinesville city	13	59	NA	NA	69	1,137	3	15	91	1,757	47	355
Holly Springs city	14	103	6	58	22	239	4	28	D	D	D	D
Jefferson city	15	1,658	NA	NA	29	346	NA	NA	28	582	20	112
Johns Creek city	118	5,264	81	555	216	2,864	43	1,131	162	2,402	D	D
Kennesaw city	69	2,172	22	174	111	1,687	24	467	168	3,962	121	1,099
Kingsland city	7	19	NA	NA	31	205	NA	NA	56	1,196	23	123
LaGrange city	47	3,848	D	D	D	D	D	D	90	1,742	62	286
Lawrenceville city	92	6,737	11	66	281	8,469	24	492	130	2,173	153	1,135
Lilburn city	36	639	11	61	73	624	11	111	80	1,158	D	D
Lithia Springs CDP	38	1,598	D	D	34	381	D	D	38	758	D	D
Loganville city	28	270	5	23	63	429	4	10	63	1,271	D	D
Mableton CDP	36	510	4	40	44	298	D	D	51	648	40	293
McDonough city	52	3,222	3	6	100	1,426	5	38	94	1,988	D	D
Macon-Bibb County	193	4,285	31	227	619	16,894	39	630	D	D	D	D
Marietta city	200	5,042	33	228	434	12,131	49	929	269	4,571	248	1,352
Martinez CDP	59	2,385	18	155	95	1,426	14	174	66	1,319	86	503
Milledgeville city	D	D	NA	NA	79	3,065	D	D	86	1,805	45	234
Milton city	66	6,261	19	105	45	412	18	225	58	925	55	362
Monroe city	21	117	D	D	58	1,154	7	69	56	962	26	74
Moultrie city	18	149	3	17	80	1,474	D	D	60	949	27	126
Mountain Park CDP	28	155	7	15	34	234	D	D	28	544	D	D
Newnan city	41	1,336	10	142	124	2,881	20	251	118	3,262	D	D
Norcross city	105	3,694	16	79	110	2,203	19	162	137	2,433	99	555
North Decatur CDP	22	146	18	64	185	4,408	14	89	58	920	47	231
North Druid Hills CDP	31	204	23	87	84	4,823	20	205	57	1,229	48	615
Panthersville CDP	6	102	NA	NA	22	262	NA	NA	27	376	6	34
Peachtree City city	58	690	28	204	146	1,473	35	488	120	2,937	107	968
Peachtree Corners city	109	4,441	7	66	93	1,452	25	725	86	1,467	62	330
Perry city	15	405	NA	NA	56	1,084	4	58	70	1,163	D	D
Pooler city	49	2,004	D	D	48	470	14	191	126	3,144	41	337
Powder Springs city	21	197	7	30	37	627	D	D	26	698	D	D
Redan CDP	7	28	NA	NA	28	152	NA	NA	14	243	8	15
Richmond Hill city	15	149	NA	NA	D	D	8	31	67	1,069	34	458
Rincon town	NA	NA	NA	NA	32	239	NA	NA	D	D	17	339
Riverdale city	10	134	NA	NA	75	1,201	D	D	50	954	36	178
Rome city	62	1,665	12	80	268	7,906	20	177	156	3,639	D	D
Roswell city	212	2,989	68	487	432	6,894	70	634	276	5,642	D	D
St. Marys city	12	78	D	D	56	744	D	D	47	612	27	116
St. Simons CDP	39	186	4	16	54	577	D	D	70	1,473	44	149
Sandy Springs city	262	20,013	61	401	689	22,581	60	1,153	297	5,436	251	1,914
Savannah city	216	9,789	D	D	580	19,038	75	872	638	14,866	287	1,976
Scottdale CDP	8	77	8	13	23	193	D	D	13	212	42	263
Smyrna city	116	1,749	23	196	233	2,981	8	96	188	3,573	131	598
Snellville city	40	143	8	49	206	3,467	D	D	D	D	D	D
Statesboro city	D	D	7	34	167	3,121	D	D	137	3,679	D	D
Stockbridge city	41	211	5	18	151	2,390	10	D	71	1,258	56	251
Stonecrest city	35	647	10	11	133	2,046	8	71	104	2,109	D	D
Sugar Hill city	48	186	8	36	33	325	7	9	20	325	34	136
Suwanee city	84	3,330	26	172	119	1,261	23	330	137	2,235	87	433
Thomasville city	36	1,669	D	D	113	3,459	D	D	88	1,492	46	419
Tifton city	16	759	3	6	83	3,042	D	D	80	1,977	D	D
Tucker city	105	4,757	12	86	167	3,936	23	223	134	2,415	126	842
Union City city	16	1,372	NA	NA	43	777	NA	NA	40	798	D	D
Valdosta city	75	2,007	13	47	362	7,379	17	213	204	4,588	99	458
Vidalia city	18	1,028	NA	NA	84	2,058	D	D	50	923	24	160
Villa Rica city	10	98	D	D	67	1,303	8	80	55	1,102	D	D
Vinings CDP	44	2,477	11	159	42	1,725	9	10	41	985	44	413
Warner Robins city	55	862	D	D	227	5,750	D	D	201	4,703	112	658
Waycross city	18	401	D	D	116	2,677	4	88	67	1,494	D	D
Wilmington Island CDP	19	68	NA	NA	D	D	5	67	23	320	D	D
Winder city	21	111	3	5	65	891	7	137	D	D	D	D
Woodstock city	67	1,111	20	178	152	1,764	D	D	120	2,998	84	444
HAWAII	1,894	55,555	368	2,923	3,677	73,551	510	11,912	3,865	112,743	2,912	20,219
East Honolulu CDP	D	D	12	23	82	990	23	526	66	1,189	60	290
Ewa Beach CDP	11	39	NA	NA	29	1,338	D	D	14	252	14	58
Ewa Gentry CDP	8	73	NA	NA	4	14	NA	NA	5	77	10	42
Halawa CDP	22	278	NA	NA	18	1,199	NA	NA	14	188	12	70
Hilo CDP	52	1,066	D	D	233	4,621	12	132	153	2,711	89	392
Kahului CDP	44	2,229	6	15	97	1,757	D	D	D	D	56	659
Kailua CDP (Hawaii County)	50	3,021	6	D	64	694	12	209	101	3,594	55	371
Kailua CDP (Honolulu County)	38	263	11	92	147	2,022	15	205	106	1,784	74	518
Kalaoa CDP	42	409	NA	NA	9	76	6	18	D	D	9	23
Kaneohe CDP	D	D	6	62	109	2,232	D	D	87	1,483	73	325
Kaneohe Station CDP	NA	NA	NA	NA	NA	NA	NA	NA	NA	NA	6	20
Kapaa CDP	16	612	D	D	32	321	5	247	45	848	19	59
Kapolei CDP	15	305	6	26	31	1,550	11	403	78	2,177	29	225
Kihei CDP	60	475	D	D	39	302	14	185	97	1,709	82	265
Lahaina CDP	24	528	4	D	29	192	D	D	102	4,001	43	172
Maili CDP	NA	NA	NA	NA	6	85	NA	NA	D	D	NA	NA
Makakilo CDP	13	116	NA	NA	D	D	NA	NA	4	19	D	D
Mililani Mauka CDP	10	29	4	44	D	D	NA	NA	10	173	15	67

Table C. Incorporated Places, Census Designated Places (CDPs), and Minor Civil Divisions (MCDs) of 10,000 or More Population — **Economic Census**

	Economic activity by sector, 2017													
	Retail Trade		Wholesale trade[1]		Transportation and warehousing		Information		Finance and insurance		Real estate and rental and leasing		Professional, scientific, and technical services	
STATE City, town, township, borough, or CDP (county if applicable)	Number of establishments	Number of employees	Number of establishments	Number of employees	Number of establishments	Number of employees	Number of establishments	Number of employees	Number of establishments	Number of employees	Number of establishments	Number of employees	Number of establishments	Number of employees
	1	2	3	4	5	6	7	8	9	10	11	12	13	14
HAWAII—Con.														
Mililani Town CDP............	32	1,062	5	10	3	2	D	D	24	156	10	36	24	70
Nanakuli CDP.................	D	D	NA	NA	D	D	NA	NA	NA	NA	NA	NA	NA	NA
Ocean Pointe CDP	12	352	NA	NA	NA	NA	4	23	8	38	6	12	12	47
Pearl City CDP..............	67	2,136	24	372	10	808	D	D	31	150	21	95	45	313
Royal Kunia CDP............	10	424	4	6	4	15	3	20	6	36	NA	NA	D	D
Schofield Barracks CDP ...	5	28	NA	NA	NA	NA	NA	NA	NA	NA	NA	NA	17	261
Urban Honolulu CDP.......	1,763	26,810	674	8,497	343	20,483	256	4,498	749	14,312	858	6,154	1,725	13,894
Wahiawa CDP	44	522	6	26	NA	NA	3	34	13	68	18	56	31	310
Waianae CDP	28	512	NA	NA	6	66	NA	NA	6	33	9	28	11	42
Wailuku CDP	59	697	27	233	11	197	9	52	26	155	D	D	112	511
Waimalu CDP	94	1,469	5	20	NA	NA	6	110	21	164	D	D	22	110
Waimea CDP	20	344	D	D	7	46	3	4	11	64	D	D	37	287
Waipahu CDP	98	1,585	42	624	18	195	5	73	22	124	29	152	17	549
Waipio CDP	20	979	27	802	6	102	NA	NA	12	95	8	26	20	162
IDAHO......................	6,133	82,312	1,870	23,878	1,791	19,059	793	13,410	2,923	23,040	2,644	7,521	4,686	33,246
Ammon city....................	69	1,375	D	D	9	9	D	D	28	119	23	64	D	D
Blackfoot city.................	58	772	13	291	D	D	8	44	34	167	19	49	33	161
Boise City city...............	920	15,803	383	5,346	191	3,960	238	5,933	632	5,797	555	2,156	1,298	9,518
Burley city....................	94	1,362	19	320	D	D	D	D	38	230	21	33	34	133
Caldwell city..................	110	1,626	34	388	36	743	D	D	56	287	41	215	43	212
Chubbuck city................	69	1,279	11	109	D	D	D	D	D	D	D	D	19	113
Coeur d'Alene city	289	4,457	45	485	20	253	39	1,097	150	1,678	153	456	265	1,505
Eagle city.....................	80	1,147	28	271	6	23	19	299	101	544	D	D	146	611
Garden City city.............	106	1,190	43	494	13	503	8	32	44	257	48	198	42	341
Hayden city...................	80	1,152	20	433	11	210	8	138	34	178	27	35	64	248
Idaho Falls city..............	353	5,664	114	1,243	54	583	38	819	199	1,184	105	366	305	7,969
Jerome city...................	52	674	D	D	30	339	D	D	D	D	8	13	16	57
Kuna city.....................	28	207	NA	NA	7	28	3	8	13	28	6	6	22	62
Lewiston city.................	194	2,478	43	489	28	759	19	389	77	D	D	D	71	518
Meridian city.................	310	5,788	104	2,882	60	815	36	1,210	244	3,551	177	527	268	3,002
Moscow city..................	103	1,660	9	181	NA	NA	D	D	44	207	40	144	58	444
Mountain Home city........	53	874	D	D	14	86	D	D	21	170	10	20	18	84
Nampa city...................	310	5,758	89	1,098	72	944	36	688	143	869	87	230	152	885
Pocatello city................	226	3,127	67	704	30	359	23	209	124	1,178	78	D	D	D
Post Falls city...............	109	2,133	24	365	15	116	12	64	60	271	54	129	65	549
Rexburg city.................	167	1,590	25	456	22	420	13	88	45	259	45	230	D	D
Twin Falls city..............	307	4,694	84	904	70	772	D	D	126	877	104	278	D	D
ILLINOIS......................	38,189	629,878	15,409	272,391	16,223	260,488	6,010	130,749	21,302	309,134	13,589	82,763	38,805	404,450
Addison village	108	1,738	193	4,874	157	2,739	16	210	46	291	48	167	90	480
Algonquin village	151	3,470	17	108	42	129	12	51	45	183	30	55	97	258
Alsip village..................	60	1,008	80	1,653	66	1,044	9	137	15	94	19	124	22	376
Alton city.....................	141	2,175	21	192	8	18	12	99	50	297	32	126	57	303
Antioch village	57	1,425	16	203	11	61	7	28	24	131	19	48	35	90
Arlington Heights village...	219	4,147	155	2,334	120	201	56	1,720	187	1,296	118	3,547	480	3,446
Aurora city....................	568	9,559	164	4,319	162	2,257	56	342	191	2,744	140	544	494	2,379
Barrington village............	69	1,206	26	90	11	253	15	568	81	622	39	240	143	889
Bartlett village...............	45	383	62	1,409	70	114	8	21	36	175	26	161	144	444
Batavia city...................	91	1,890	70	1,431	24	594	17	209	40	176	26	77	139	555
Beach Park village...........	22	91	NA	NA	9	81	NA	NA	D	D	3	5	8	15
Belleville city.................	178	2,788	41	517	19	548	21	463	92	791	50	233	150	1,025
Bellwood village..............	21	104	8	126	27	439	NA	NA	9	45	10	22	D	D
Belvidere city.................	72	1,083	11	89	35	550	D	D	37	169	14	45	28	240
Bensenville village...........	81	1,020	152	2,159	231	3,125	D	D	23	101	29	465	63	1,422
Berwyn city...................	102	1,273	10	67	66	104	8	29	37	194	30	60	80	278
Bloomingdale village........	156	2,909	50	848	82	574	11	110	53	338	31	150	120	535
Bloomington city.............	323	5,767	72	1,180	41	1,008	35	589	D	D	106	455	232	1,584
Blue Island city..............	39	250	26	490	15	51	D	D	15	68	11	49	22	135
Bolingbrook village	216	5,336	117	5,995	164	2,809	29	1,032	63	305	48	229	190	1,455
Boulder Hill CDP............	4	17	NA	NA	9	9	NA	NA	NA	NA	NA	NA	NA	NA
Bourbonnais village	56	1,316	10	108	8	81	D	D	46	335	20	62	36	188
Bradley village................	132	2,609	17	139	NA	NA	11	106	22	115	12	73	15	100
Bridgeview village............	84	1,803	77	745	70	672	7	131	25	189	11	225	36	142
Brookfield village.............	28	217	D	D	D	D	4	7	14	72	12	22	49	120
Buffalo Grove village........	101	1,282	125	2,881	79	359	19	156	79	657	57	269	308	2,571
Burbank city..................	90	1,504	9	25	84	112	D	D	25	126	12	30	32	96
Burr Ridge village...........	55	814	71	856	35	164	9	18	67	1,071	38	458	103	2,218
Cahokia village...............	33	483	6	277	9	146	NA	NA	15	60	7	28	6	50
Calumet City city............	136	2,172	D	D	22	94	D	D	34	228	18	126	22	66
Campton Hills village.......	6	15	10	17	D	D	D	D	13	51	D	D	57	117
Canton city...................	64	956	D	D	9	36	6	25	23	156	9	32	22	164
Carbondale city..............	156	2,777	12	152	8	144	D	D	54	635	53	279	61	618
Carol Stream village	101	2,073	105	3,112	102	2,165	18	761	38	258	36	278	96	503
Carpentersville village	49	1,151	11	42	81	69	D	D	21	101	21	94	28	67
Cary village...................	34	418	26	247	16	104	6	46	24	88	14	16	63	171
Centralia city.................	66	916	D	D	D	D	D	D	D	D	14	82	23	110
Champaign city...............	389	6,358	67	1,404	43	1,667	80	1,994	186	2,371	136	1,541	257	1,783
Channahon village...........	19	157	7	182	D	D	4	28	11	52	15	104	20	93
Charleston city...............	68	955	8	39	D	D	D	D	D	D	27	76	28	147
Chatham village..............	20	297	5	8	D	D	D	D	20	112	8	11	18	106
Chicago city..................	6,945	97,034	2,245	39,863	2,210	60,314	1,778	55,938	4,635	122,765	3,684	28,995	10,735	174,661
Chicago Heights city........	63	639	36	746	31	1,234	D	D	31	161	14	96	27	203
Chicago Ridge village.......	107	2,065	12	51	53	375	D	D	D	D	12	39	11	26
Cicero town..................	133	2,454	34	947	101	162	D	D	49	312	28	98	41	299
Collinsville city	80	1,588	20	206	14	302	D	D	55	365	21	97	74	520
Columbia city................	40	458	7	194	6	49	NA	NA	D	D	21	124	34	491
Country Club Hills city	31	530	NA	NA	9	28	D	D	12	63	NA	NA	6	15

1 Merchant wholesalers, except manufacturers' sales branches and offices.

Table C. Incorporated Places, Census Designated Places (CDPs), and Minor Civil Divisions (MCDs) of 10,000 or More Population — **Economic Census**

STATE City, town, township, borough, or CDP (county if applicable)	Administration and support and waste management and mediation services		Educational services		Health care and social assistance		Arts, entertainment, and recreation		Accommodation and food services		Other services (except public administration)	
	Number of establishments	Number of employees	Number of establishments	Number of employees	Number of establishments	Number of employees	Number of establishments	Number of employees	Number of establishments	Number of employees	Number of establishments	Number of employees
	15	16	17	18	19	20	21	22	23	24	25	26
HAWAII—Con.												
Mililani Town CDP	25	148	4	17	30	306	5	238	45	1,002	32	486
Nanakuli CDP	4	18	NA	NA	5	29	NA	NA	NA	NA	5	17
Ocean Pointe CDP	3	9	NA	NA	13	140	NA	NA	18	561	8	77
Pearl City CDP	42	656	6	61	71	909	D	D	79	1,608	69	329
Royal Kunia CDP	4	13	NA	NA	D	D	NA	NA	21	302	7	17
Schofield Barracks CDP	D	D	NA	NA	NA	NA	NA	NA	4	259	3	22
Urban Honolulu CDP	684	27,248	168	1,737	1,529	34,983	124	2,727	1,575	45,827	1,333	11,192
Wahiawa CDP	19	258	6	21	D	D	NA	NA	46	841	31	148
Waianae CDP	D	D	NA	NA	33	917	NA	NA	26	485	15	73
Wailuku CDP	43	1,023	5	16	138	4,217	13	54	55	577	58	263
Waimalu CDP	12	151	6	61	90	2,156	6	172	55	1,067	35	260
Waimea CDP	17	56	NA	NA	30	608	5	13	30	296	15	53
Waipahu CDP	28	505	4	35	92	1,074	NA	NA	63	1,183	72	459
Waipio CDP	12	219	8	54	19	224	NA	NA	25	575	23	167
IDAHO	2,480	43,125	365	2,303	5,310	98,100	804	9,644	3,856	65,463	2,749	14,016
Ammon city	D	D	NA	NA	72	1,222	3	72	31	992	19	137
Blackfoot city	12	70	D	D	70	1,688	D	D	34	553	23	171
Boise City city	478	13,101	90	647	979	26,996	115	2,511	663	13,262	531	3,282
Burley city	11	250	D	D	74	1,301	D	D	D	D	D	D
Caldwell city	37	514	6	29	126	1,977	12	220	68	1,358	52	315
Chubbuck city	15	60	D	D	51	450	D	D	27	659	22	81
Coeur d'Alene city	93	1,371	21	87	293	7,752	45	286	210	4,714	110	653
Eagle city	55	2,877	7	47	99	885	18	196	59	1,082	53	327
Garden City city	35	1,238	D	D	37	614	10	75	53	952	87	487
Hayden city	28	189	6	18	50	572	7	130	47	545	46	244
Idaho Falls city	88	5,081	18	95	455	7,585	25	571	184	3,892	122	556
Jerome city	9	24	NA	NA	32	487	NA	NA	D	D	D	D
Kuna city	21	103	NA	NA	26	298	NA	NA	21	369	D	D
Lewiston city	56	1,041	D	D	139	3,288	D	D	D	D	D	D
Meridian city	175	2,684	29	183	355	6,486	42	610	220	5,201	134	709
Moscow city	23	146	D	D	78	1,507	D	D	102	1,806	49	363
Mountain Home city	13	26	NA	NA	D	D	D	D	38	542	D	D
Nampa city	97	1,175	D	D	219	4,737	21	555	180	3,676	124	748
Pocatello city	53	1,014	7	40	314	5,003	21	296	146	2,608	D	D
Post Falls city	42	380	7	102	123	1,982	12	94	D	D	59	334
Rexburg city	29	389	6	75	D	D	8	84	60	1,141	27	144
Twin Falls city	D	D	9	37	321	5,857	32	234	165	3,406	115	802
ILLINOIS	17,158	501,964	3,228	29,986	34,235	817,733	5,218	91,647	29,025	536,245	24,296	171,261
Addison village	66	4,173	14	103	80	1,252	10	429	87	1,503	133	892
Algonquin village	37	570	15	90	102	799	17	407	93	1,984	70	324
Alsip village	41	2,809	NA	NA	35	657	8	106	46	815	D	D
Alton city	24	538	D	D	125	4,265	D	D	96	1,734	55	279
Antioch village	19	116	NA	NA	D	D	6	D	34	596	36	191
Arlington Heights village	108	1,304	36	374	414	10,686	42	594	176	3,295	201	1,262
Aurora city	219	14,670	D	D	390	9,379	57	1,398	287	4,738	236	1,387
Barrington village	30	457	15	101	92	1,240	13	D	52	746	72	584
Bartlett village	45	2,475	12	95	63	787	7	44	42	807	D	D
Batavia city	55	651	15	87	69	928	10	145	62	1,197	77	642
Beach Park village	29	33	NA	NA	9	114	NA	NA	8	155	D	D
Belleville city	46	668	12	96	190	5,448	14	412	D	D	100	629
Bellwood village	10	205	NA	NA	20	271	NA	NA	21	162	20	78
Belvidere city	21	269	D	D	46	800	D	D	40	578	44	210
Bensenville village	45	3,624	D	D	31	383	8	47	46	358	D	D
Berwyn city	35	811	4	19	146	4,445	11	74	111	1,977	71	425
Bloomingdale village	34	500	15	106	150	2,024	D	D	71	1,555	63	462
Bloomington city	122	3,426	31	311	243	5,071	38	1,163	248	4,975	176	1,706
Blue Island city	23	646	NA	NA	42	1,249	3	D	43	622	38	208
Bolingbrook village	115	8,181	21	63	175	2,527	17	363	150	3,362	99	530
Boulder Hill CDP	3	3	NA	NA	NA	NA	NA	NA	NA	NA	NA	NA
Bourbonnais village	23	866	NA	NA	92	1,249	4	84	45	1,074	D	D
Bradley village	21	180	6	D	35	1,025	5	10	66	1,615	D	D
Bridgeview village	41	655	NA	NA	33	715	13	276	60	1,018	D	D
Brookfield village	22	225	NA	NA	33	548	D	D	D	D	D	D
Buffalo Grove village	67	2,904	25	209	172	1,810	25	459	D	D	83	504
Burbank city	21	120	3	6	50	683	4	D	63	871	D	D
Burr Ridge village	44	1,113	11	D	111	1,431	17	892	24	562	24	243
Cahokia village	3	56	NA	NA	10	325	NA	NA	22	344	14	87
Calumet City city	13	47	NA	NA	58	2,316	6	58	74	1,113	46	155
Campton Hills village	19	89	NA	NA	D	D	D	D	6	78	15	71
Canton city	5	29	NA	NA	52	1,457	7	127	33	464	20	83
Carbondale city	D	D	4	33	112	3,511	D	D	104	2,152	48	289
Carol Stream village	57	1,177	15	111	62	998	14	113	69	1,320	80	425
Carpentersville village	72	459	NA	NA	28	246	5	15	43	677	D	D
Cary village	36	352	7	37	29	318	9	15	34	478	D	D
Centralia city	8	19	NA	NA	66	1,828	D	D	35	525	29	136
Champaign city	89	1,751	27	141	204	3,952	42	367	357	7,960	168	1,360
Channahon village	13	92	NA	NA	D	D	D	D	21	260	23	168
Charleston city	16	283	NA	NA	D	D	D	D	51	823	34	149
Chatham village	10	45	D	D	17	198	6	20	19	259	D	D
Chicago city	3,093	138,668	782	10,141	6,778	186,215	1,101	25,651	6,770	142,220	5,308	48,556
Chicago Heights city	28	292	NA	NA	72	2,582	4	83	42	491	38	175
Chicago Ridge village	15	429	NA	NA	35	610	5	114	33	529	D	D
Cicero town	75	2,797	NA	NA	91	1,575	10	40	104	1,255	82	310
Collinsville city	29	170	6	45	56	400	14	238	66	1,555	45	256
Columbia city	15	606	D	D	44	565	7	130	28	573	35	240
Country Club Hills city	6	3	NA	NA	19	327	NA	NA	18	184	19	335

Table C. Incorporated Places, Census Designated Places (CDPs), and Minor Civil Divisions (MCDs) of 10,000 or More Population — **Economic Census**

STATE City, town, township, borough, or CDP (county if applicable)	Retail Trade Number of establishments	Number of employees	Wholesale trade[1] Number of establishments	Number of employees	Transportation and warehousing Number of establishments	Number of employees	Information Number of establishments	Number of employees	Finance and insurance Number of establishments	Number of employees	Real estate and rental and leasing Number of establishments	Number of employees	Professional, scientific, and technical services Number of establishments	Number of employees
	1	2	3	4	5	6	7	8	9	10	11	12	13	14
ILLINOIS—Con.														
Crest Hill city................	55	701	8	26	39	833	NA	NA	19	75	14	74	27	289
Crestwood village............	69	1,635	28	367	24	1,045	D	D	18	61	11	134	18	123
Crystal Lake city............	208	3,792	D	D	43	414	21	266	108	686	54	228	191	947
Danville city.................	151	2,587	35	1,528	19	809	11	66	D	D	33	93	54	323
Darien city..................	43	1,365	27	163	75	169	6	24	42	285	17	47	84	704
Decatur city.................	285	4,159	69	1,085	58	2,215	27	385	137	1,496	72	433	114	919
Deerfield village............	76	1,265	32	D	9	140	29	1,072	92	1,779	67	283	198	2,936
DeKalb city..................	113	2,387	21	263	20	1,459	23	516	42	331	47	326	42	146
Des Plaines city.............	178	3,134	125	3,192	217	3,923	27	1,181	120	1,095	82	1,248	254	2,276
Dixon city...................	68	1,048	D	D	D	D	D	D	D	D	11	43	17	163
Dolton village...............	47	514	NA	NA	11	14	NA	NA	11	44	NA	NA	7	9
Downers Grove village......	228	5,096	116	2,557	70	1,566	49	2,444	220	4,869	119	816	347	4,485
East Moline city.............	39	780	D	D	D	D	4	32	15	103	D	D	21	503
East Peoria city.............	94	2,000	43	1,040	18	423	D	D	32	296	28	121	39	543
East St. Louis city..........	52	312	18	199	24	1,000	D	D	10	56	16	77	7	53
Edwardsville city............	105	1,800	18	924	31	7,148	20	253	81	1,047	49	141	140	1,198
Effingham city...............	134	2,521	26	994	21	524	18	125	59	310	23	165	49	366
Elgin city...................	208	3,703	176	4,035	216	796	34	649	155	3,588	90	474	276	1,678
Elk Grove Village village...	131	2,463	426	8,055	428	5,399	32	602	72	1,186	57	630	164	2,308
Elmhurst city................	154	2,963	126	4,038	51	727	23	992	109	814	85	364	259	1,457
Elmwood Park village.......	35	478	D	D	42	104	D	D	24	132	22	46	29	127
Evanston city................	205	4,000	41	298	25	431	76	1,219	112	866	120	408	410	3,350
Evergreen Park village......	74	2,173	8	32	9	22	D	D	50	474	D	D	27	119
Fairview Heights city........	233	4,570	19	177	7	20	13	211	D	D	22	114	45	692
Forest Park village..........	55	1,153	23	443	7	61	3	7	20	141	15	51	37	212
Fox Lake village.............	44	965	D	D	7	37	7	42	16	76	9	32	19	115
Frankfort village............	89	1,905	36	227	27	126	D	D	66	361	32	93	95	411
Franklin Park village........	50	672	65	1,418	90	1,586	10	232	17	107	28	119	22	90
Freeport city................	110	1,563	19	218	10	71	12	80	D	D	25	72	50	282
Gages Lake CDP.............	8	40	D	D	9	27	NA	NA	3	6	4	D	11	14
Galesburg city...............	142	3,326	21	450	19	419	D	D	60	320	29	102	49	246
Geneva city..................	193	2,519	38	430	13	494	14	235	88	549	37	129	171	616
Glen Carbon village.........	26	1,001	NA	NA	6	192	3	15	D	D	5	4	32	259
Glendale Heights village...	85	2,212	73	1,386	65	259	8	45	30	126	22	103	46	295
Glen Ellyn village...........	92	1,226	33	210	22	272	16	113	75	502	55	214	163	632
Glenview village.............	159	4,446	92	1,690	41	189	27	1,129	139	6,560	106	244	288	1,900
Godfrey village..............	39	722	D	D	11	226	D	D	29	122	14	101	26	84
Granite City city............	81	1,293	26	391	21	554	6	73	40	210	25	145	39	261
Grayslake village............	55	760	23	227	21	426	12	47	35	131	24	53	88	365
Gurnee village...............	241	5,817	61	634	23	276	17	239	63	636	34	202	139	592
Hanover Park village........	66	962	28	1,390	73	342	5	5	34	217	16	51	36	113
Harvey city..................	60	280	20	274	25	506	NA	NA	11	44	7	63	D	D
Hazel Crest village..........	21	142	4	37	12	155	D	D	D	D	7	167	12	22
Herrin city..................	61	1,041	10	130	6	127	NA	NA	D	D	13	45	21	113
Hickory Hills city...........	30	758	16	110	50	379	D	D	26	457	12	55	39	145
Highland city................	54	785	D	D	9	163	10	90	36	146	15	92	25	104
Highland Park city..........	159	2,623	46	160	D	D	25	82	87	609	78	385	221	1,146
Hinsdale village	68	557	24	109	19	448	7	15	81	423	D	D	158	524
Hoffman Estates village....	118	2,755	68	1,016	75	141	42	1,405	73	1,490	51	139	208	1,576
Homer Glen village..........	42	1,303	16	62	68	152	6	33	36	120	23	53	63	202
Homewood village	81	2,330	D	D	D	D	18	596	43	173	24	63	65	301
Huntley village..............	52	1,168	36	421	24	49	9	15	21	110	19	205	54	293
Jacksonville city............	114	1,692	16	178	15	235	13	174	D	D	D	D	28	591
Joliet city...................	392	8,204	91	2,124	242	8,277	35	363	138	1,364	99	464	223	1,370
Justice village..............	23	117	7	46	57	90	NA	NA	3	15	5	D	10	27
Kankakee city...............	89	1,249	30	454	21	600	14	408	41	226	24	71	49	253
Kewanee city................	50	879	10	35	D	D	D	D	28	302	D	D	12	61
La Grange village...........	50	544	23	133	12	314	10	127	42	204	D	D	89	370
La Grange Park village.....	10	290	6	D	10	13	NA	NA	17	45	10	24	38	71
Lake Forest city............	74	753	39	5,967	8	35	9	42	100	1,687	53	152	166	589
Lake in the Hills village.....	55	817	19	197	45	176	D	D	25	97	9	23	62	219
Lake Zurich village..........	92	2,612	66	863	18	87	13	243	61	1,503	25	71	129	792
Lansing village..............	96	1,894	25	210	41	177	8	65	27	159	24	86	37	161
Lemont village..............	45	756	19	113	76	557	7	90	46	249	33	99	D	D
Libertyville village	111	1,916	64	1,787	12	93	9	44	66	1,116	59	212	191	911
Lincoln city.................	65	912	D	D	7	118	D	D	D	D	16	56	24	167
Lincolnwood village	97	1,576	35	379	19	107	13	188	40	195	42	137	100	736
Lindenhurst village..........	18	211	6	44	12	9	D	D	12	45	6	21	28	86
Lisle village.................	71	1,117	63	1,169	37	455	35	1,495	109	2,630	59	373	224	4,635
Lockport city................	60	921	18	78	47	307	D	D	34	140	16	23	42	172
Lombard village.............	236	4,109	122	1,888	55	841	42	1,247	126	2,559	82	433	250	2,556
Loves Park city..............	D	D	56	803	20	284	9	577	48	288	29	119	50	320
Lyons village................	31	411	18	181	47	208	D	D	10	38	8	19	19	240
McHenry city................	122	2,138	42	1,859	21	398	13	462	69	333	26	102	73	461
Machesney Park village....	74	1,597	30	406	17	165	11	249	18	119	D	D	27	235
Macomb city.................	82	1,292	D	D	6	93	D	D	36	230	24	102	34	196
Marion city.................	114	2,216	26	370	25	417	14	152	87	921	29	102	75	377
Markham city................	28	278	14	313	35	1,855	NA	NA	7	35	11	224	4	47
Matteson village............	56	1,730	D	D	13	51	D	D	29	117	11	44	27	126
Mattoon city................	103	1,815	22	222	8	137	D	D	58	482	18	97	25	243
Maywood village............	41	174	7	115	12	368	NA	NA	9	32	7	15	10	23
Melrose Park village........	102	2,641	51	787	67	2,637	D	D	32	253	21	157	24	77
Midlothian village...........	42	358	D	D	13	20	D	D	22	94	7	21	9	32
Minooka village..............	23	521	11	135	28	764	NA	NA	12	37	5	14	18	160
Mokena village..............	77	1,207	70	834	35	260	11	121	52	397	36	117	131	763
Moline city..................	213	4,452	38	711	22	976	19	532	D	D	62	291	101	1,114
Montgomery village.........	48	1,334	27	1,288	39	418	NA	NA	14	55	5	14	21	95
Morris city..................	87	1,553	17	214	15	547	D	D	38	221	20	45	41	235
Morton village...............	60	1,214	D	D	28	1,916	3	5	40	300	18	94	42	365
Morton Grove village	97	1,352	59	729	32	160	17	81	39	222	D	D	82	421

1 Merchant wholesalers, except manufacturers' sales branches and offices.

Table C. Incorporated Places, Census Designated Places (CDPs), and Minor Civil Divisions (MCDs) of 10,000 or More Population — **Economic Census**

STATE City, town, township, borough, or CDP (county if applicable)	Administration and support and waste management and mediation services		Educational services		Health care and social assistance		Arts, entertainment, and recreation		Accommodation and food services		Other services (except public administration)	
	Number of establishments	Number of employees	Number of establishments	Number of employees	Number of establishments	Number of employees	Number of establishments	Number of employees	Number of establishments	Number of employees	Number of establishments	Number of employees
	15	16	17	18	19	20	21	22	23	24	25	26
ILLINOIS—Con.												
Crest Hill city	21	1,414	NA	NA	42	415	7	38	33	422	50	233
Crestwood village	28	1,238	NA	NA	19	672	9	144	44	1,115	D	D
Crystal Lake city	82	1,320	22	166	220	2,851	26	711	116	2,992	134	797
Danville city	27	486	D	D	114	4,311	13	152	95	1,663	57	281
Darien city	35	323	6	66	72	340	11	106	45	813	D	D
Decatur city	68	957	D	D	240	7,644	35	622	199	3,342	121	843
Deerfield village	58	6,422	26	162	123	1,636	13	112	64	1,296	42	301
DeKalb city	33	328	D	D	65	2,360	14	88	103	1,843	58	323
Des Plaines city	166	2,763	27	193	265	8,581	D	D	180	3,881	175	1,145
Dixon city	15	365	NA	NA	62	1,885	8	135	45	658	37	198
Dolton village	10	209	4	26	24	635	4	21	27	302	D	D
Downers Grove village	142	8,370	31	254	265	5,695	26	463	168	3,000	129	1,512
East Moline city	11	45	D	D	33	476	D	D	41	630	24	215
East Peoria city	35	459	D	D	42	775	12	43	108	2,991	42	276
East St. Louis city	12	80	D	D	39	636	NA	NA	D	D	14	100
Edwardsville city	34	1,604	17	73	77	890	17	560	87	2,365	53	377
Effingham city	33	459	4	33	109	2,369	D	D	87	1,821	67	881
Elgin city	209	7,556	19	97	294	7,370	26	1,037	180	3,329	187	1,566
Elk Grove Village village	100	5,738	11	498	147	5,466	16	92	123	2,556	125	1,240
Elmhurst city	80	1,319	22	173	218	7,388	30	505	128	2,135	116	730
Elmwood Park village	18	63	D	D	56	583	7	37	38	467	26	87
Evanston city	95	1,092	57	506	365	10,751	53	728	249	4,741	202	1,705
Evergreen Park village	16	127	D	D	95	3,069	D	D	46	1,018	D	D
Fairview Heights city	29	473	NA	NA	60	997	9	77	86	2,416	51	370
Forest Park village	19	2,898	9	63	41	763	D	D	60	790	45	271
Fox Lake village	18	114	D	D	14	86	11	71	40	503	D	D
Frankfort village	51	2,208	10	160	105	819	21	222	70	1,340	55	447
Franklin Park village	32	1,049	3	8	40	470	4	11	38	444	D	D
Freeport city	21	482	4	20	90	2,408	10	279	65	1,248	49	241
Gages Lake CDP	12	16	3	14	12	97	6	5	8	93	11	120
Galesburg city	29	283	4	5	122	3,375	14	146	97	1,498	51	369
Geneva city	31	404	17	134	138	2,955	18	387	106	2,264	74	524
Glen Carbon village	12	691	4	33	56	997	9	102	19	451	24	158
Glendale Heights village	34	415	5	D	45	871	10	184	60	1,015	33	253
Glen Ellyn village	38	806	27	152	109	1,338	10	367	D	D	64	423
Glenview village	109	1,404	31	360	288	5,687	41	688	170	3,400	169	969
Godfrey village	8	18	3	25	42	999	5	76	D	D	30	147
Granite City city	19	381	NA	NA	81	2,083	5	67	74	1,132	51	345
Grayslake village	46	635	15	79	84	935	13	38	50	769	56	198
Gurnee village	68	1,884	12	65	173	2,452	15	1,622	123	3,378	67	421
Hanover Park village	37	2,407	6	31	41	618	3	D	52	481	D	D
Harvey city	14	442	NA	NA	52	2,960	NA	NA	44	684	D	D
Hazel Crest village	10	125	NA	NA	54	2,575	NA	NA	24	260	D	D
Herrin city	8	69	NA	NA	58	2,392	6	46	31	381	19	98
Hickory Hills city	22	402	4	56	25	288	6	72	D	D	D	D
Highland city	11	82	4	38	46	931	D	D	34	621	33	301
Highland Park city	93	1,266	22	245	163	3,022	43	721	87	1,525	122	590
Hinsdale village	37	1,482	17	102	226	5,367	13	209	37	747	51	420
Hoffman Estates village	83	913	26	767	237	5,751	17	173	105	2,032	72	349
Homer Glen village	46	188	3	9	53	620	11	86	34	468	39	252
Homewood village	23	200	14	66	83	3,224	11	92	57	1,814	45	265
Huntley village	34	309	4	32	58	645	7	227	29	526	46	205
Jacksonville city	27	488	NA	NA	94	2,541	D	D	64	1,254	D	D
Joliet city	171	3,405	16	107	366	8,710	31	832	268	6,012	187	1,167
Justice village	11	16	NA	NA	17	119	NA	NA	21	156	29	223
Kankakee city	21	177	NA	NA	102	4,202	D	D	56	726	48	226
Kewanee city	7	27	NA	NA	37	634	D	D	25	408	23	57
La Grange village	19	296	12	138	101	1,906	13	51	D	D	52	391
La Grange Park village	12	20	4	54	31	746	8	91	8	175	14	162
Lake Forest city	33	238	14	83	100	2,877	28	1,170	D	D	57	453
Lake in the Hills village	41	562	11	96	47	402	9	91	29	548	D	D
Lake Zurich village	46	1,435	13	77	73	851	14	329	68	1,174	59	465
Lansing village	42	472	D	D	59	635	9	91	58	1,127	46	514
Lemont village	22	585	8	69	73	1,246	D	D	42	651	D	D
Libertyville village	45	718	14	121	209	3,996	16	304	90	1,683	95	659
Lincoln city	6	29	D	D	49	1,409	D	D	44	869	D	D
Lincolnwood village	32	3,711	3	D	105	2,378	7	95	44	1,115	45	228
Lindenhurst village	11	37	NA	NA	40	655	NA	NA	12	259	8	9
Lisle village	64	522	13	189	94	1,880	10	54	74	1,291	70	369
Lockport city	30	335	8	44	D	D	D	D	49	594	57	249
Lombard village	125	5,520	15	153	172	2,853	D	D	147	3,286	124	1,253
Loves Park city	42	1,303	7	58	59	1,429	21	475	73	1,104	54	296
Lyons village	11	64	D	D	9	45	6	132	33	369	20	146
McHenry city	53	1,859	4	13	112	3,918	8	72	D	D	76	390
Machesney Park village	30	280	NA	NA	20	133	4	15	40	818	D	D
Macomb city	13	145	NA	NA	60	1,686	4	128	73	1,218	40	124
Marion city	23	1,102	D	D	113	3,838	14	89	88	2,091	37	275
Markham city	16	184	NA	NA	11	59	NA	NA	21	250	21	92
Matteson village	15	333	6	32	48	599	D	D	45	1,179	17	92
Mattoon city	22	519	4	39	D	D	7	166	68	1,265	44	198
Maywood village	18	379	NA	NA	D	D	4	D	24	211	17	179
Melrose Park village	41	3,759	NA	NA	100	2,851	12	217	78	984	D	D
Midlothian village	11	112	NA	NA	26	181	5	240	39	409	D	D
Minooka village	13	310	3	10	D	D	3	24	27	481	D	D
Mokena village	48	978	18	902	75	1,428	18	105	49	1,113	70	589
Moline city	58	3,653	11	52	201	3,886	16	507	149	3,051	91	642
Montgomery village	30	205	NA	NA	D	D	7	37	36	460	27	103
Morris city	15	56	7	40	85	1,950	D	D	59	894	53	816
Morton village	25	267	D	D	D	D	10	69	48	947	39	194
Morton Grove village	30	379	7	66	80	771	12	188	63	826	55	297

Items 15–26

STATE City, town, township, borough, or CDP (county if applicable)	Retail Trade		Wholesale trade¹		Transportation and warehousing		Information		Finance and insurance		Real estate and rental and leasing		Professional, scientific, and technical services	
	Number of establishments	Number of employees	Number of establishments	Number of employees	Number of establishments	Number of employees	Number of establishments	Number of employees	Number of establishments	Number of employees	Number of establishments	Number of employees	Number of establishments	Number of employees
	1	2	3	4	5	6	7	8	9	10	11	12	13	14
ILLINOIS—Con.														
Mount Prospect village	151	2,723	79	1,334	122	757	D	D	93	721	44	168	175	652
Mount Vernon city	135	2,026	33	596	16	1,492	D	D	60	416	22	69	49	345
Mundelein village	95	1,044	55	612	37	364	10	46	34	181	23	50	105	3,090
Naperville city	460	10,909	243	2,458	179	2,411	110	3,783	411	7,112	235	931	1,149	9,144
New Lenox village	76	1,922	19	259	20	635	11	81	53	252	27	48	54	296
Niles village	248	6,140	93	2,154	56	1,123	22	233	72	415	44	280	80	286
Normal town	129	3,210	D	D	28	880	17	186	D	D	D	D	59	515
Norridge village	114	2,071	10	79	46	56	D	D	22	151	D	D	16	52
North Aurora village	49	1,239	18	315	17	260	3	47	30	229	D	D	37	124
Northbrook village	219	4,044	169	3,492	47	974	41	631	252	2,029	174	643	586	5,959
North Chicago city	33	125	8	273	15	95	3	3	7	128	6	27	15	156
Northlake city	33	1,057	19	529	35	757	D	D	12	53	12	221	12	271
Oak Forest city	55	637	23	96	28	261	D	D	33	246	20	81	43	177
Oak Lawn village	172	3,707	28	80	79	127	D	D	103	762	40	146	90	324
Oak Park village	146	1,736	D	D	19	269	30	147	72	351	86	378	306	1,168
O'Fallon city	92	2,537	11	47	15	207	9	111	82	432	46	160	91	1,064
Orland Park village	342	8,662	52	292	119	619	31	382	170	1,674	108	337	258	1,358
Oswego village	96	2,497	D	D	32	266	11	133	44	361	33	92	88	285
Ottawa city	105	1,523	17	673	25	954	15	155	43	412	23	80	56	477
Palatine village	179	3,328	61	401	118	1,985	24	166	117	760	83	271	328	1,360
Palos Heights city	31	427	12	69	18	165	5	26	53	297	20	60	87	302
Palos Hills city	36	296	10	18	104	160	4	3	23	97	17	24	58	826
Park Forest village	8	59	4	12	6	10	NA	NA	7	34	5	30	8	10
Park Ridge city	72	1,245	43	192	57	124	23	203	102	722	87	387	243	792
Pekin city	110	1,992	18	300	14	89	18	139	64	1,061	22	52	40	238
Peoria city	509	8,716	129	2,216	56	930	69	1,343	274	2,775	146	859	341	4,342
Plainfield village	111	2,443	25	236	89	339	15	58	64	273	37	88	143	924
Plano city	25	160	NA	NA	D	D	D	D	14	78	NA	NA	9	47
Pontiac city	50	850	8	89	D	D	D	D	D	D	8	46	17	65
Prospect Heights city	26	804	22	284	46	64	NA	NA	19	111	15	67	60	161
Quincy city	250	4,591	67	1,366	14	273	D	D	123	887	51	184	105	685
Rantoul city	37	594	5	26	NA	NA	10	303	D	D	11	54	12	39
Richton Park village	18	472	NA	NA	7	6	NA	NA	NA	NA	D	D	6	17
Riverdale village	18	123	5	97	7	162	3	11	4	20	NA	NA	6	25
River Forest village	24	869	7	22	NA	NA	4	14	23	109	16	35	62	108
River Grove village	23	598	5	176	48	101	NA	NA	7	51	4	D	16	57
Rockford city	517	8,093	167	2,509	126	3,714	56	2,613	264	2,413	151	1,051	384	4,093
Rock Island city	75	887	48	1,021	27	1,045	12	209	39	950	30	129	103	1,232
Rolling Meadows city	62	1,297	90	1,193	53	148	21	1,476	92	2,577	37	190	244	4,117
Romeoville village	68	1,695	68	2,516	160	3,689	15	548	28	159	25	252	44	259
Roscoe village	29	408	6	113	5	4	3	8	16	115	13	21	15	58
Roselle village	52	598	45	952	71	245	8	193	36	222	31	153	94	322
Round Lake village	20	215	7	6	34	58	4	3	D	D	7	58	29	56
Round Lake Beach village	57	1,703	6	25	35	42	D	D	20	168	10	19	17	52
St. Charles city	146	3,705	113	1,307	31	581	29	541	131	852	75	579	D	D
Sauk Village village	9	93	D	D	13	2,088	NA	NA	3	9	NA	NA	D	D
Schaumburg village	465	12,304	263	4,993	189	1,301	109	4,675	290	6,684	151	1,460	683	12,555
Schiller Park village	41	556	30	568	92	933	NA	NA	D	D	16	145	24	133
Shiloh village	31	686	NA	NA	3	7	NA	NA	D	D	11	19	15	217
Shorewood village	50	1,411	13	364	22	122	D	D	23	125	16	33	36	228
Skokie village	334	6,593	112	971	77	974	31	432	151	912	111	506	366	10,099
South Elgin village	87	1,793	44	282	26	118	7	35	34	181	16	28	52	202
South Holland village	35	603	46	471	29	2,257	3	6	38	169	23	121	39	262
Springfield city	570	10,751	116	1,917	54	1,487	77	1,503	284	4,750	186	762	391	4,850
Sterling city	86	1,682	17	180	D	D	D	D	D	D	11	43	24	137
Streamwood village	78	1,673	18	118	76	339	9	31	35	144	19	212	75	241
Streator city	51	749	D	D	12	260	7	38	32	226	D	D	14	63
Summit village	27	154	9	79	42	676	D	D	12	49	5	26	6	49
Swansea village	36	391	5	7	8	45	7	75	45	337	D	D	54	406
Sycamore city	62	1,332	14	245	13	240	6	59	38	264	17	31	56	709
Taylorville city	66	948	7	184	4	72	D	D	39	179	12	73	28	466
Tinley Park village	161	3,816	52	779	79	385	15	661	86	521	39	146	140	866
Troy city	28	421	8	226	D	D	NA	NA	D	D	NA	NA	11	73
Urbana city	76	1,430	22	797	13	294	12	166	34	247	30	197	71	560
Vernon Hills village	193	4,474	66	3,002	D	D	23	367	65	434	33	138	153	1,971
Villa Park village	105	1,970	32	642	34	373	D	D	34	155	20	276	61	177
Warrenville city	33	653	30	1,592	7	12	D	D	54	1,224	16	42	77	1,236
Washington city	54	1,372	D	D	D	D	9	56	26	119	13	27	21	95
Waterloo city	40	746	5	14	4	117	D	D	29	183	10	21	23	110
Wauconda village	38	486	45	528	D	D	5	3	14	59	15	55	40	225
Waukegan city	222	3,120	74	2,909	69	837	16	560	75	562	59	268	161	861
Westchester village	19	384	13	791	18	29	4	12	51	700	20	61	68	854
West Chicago city	70	1,191	74	1,591	49	381	16	68	27	76	19	101	80	869
Western Springs village	18	420	NA	NA	D	D	4	7	25	84	D	D	79	138
Westmont village	97	2,409	56	633	64	535	26	686	57	1,286	43	238	117	1,271
Wheaton city	157	3,182	42	145	25	104	37	607	133	1,537	82	272	372	1,716
Wheeling village	89	1,293	D	D	120	1,177	13	415	42	524	34	115	127	882
Wilmette village	87	1,202	27	93	NA	NA	15	57	51	204	52	333	168	359
Winnetka village	45	307	6	12	NA	NA	6	78	37	270	31	62	73	128
Wood Dale city	48	800	112	2,560	158	1,575	5	219	19	113	15	32	51	261
Woodridge village	103	2,534	68	2,848	116	1,703	8	485	47	716	37	397	D	D
Wood River city	51	976	D	D	11	230	D	D	22	107	10	56	16	60
Woodstock city	80	1,639	27	503	24	27	12	135	28	200	28	92	75	303
Worth village	34	284	8	18	35	30	NA	NA	17	161	12	13	20	60
Yorkville city	61	1,191	D	D	14	46	7	120	28	156	17	31	46	306
Zion city	44	902	D	D	13	205	NA	NA	12	62	7	29	12	35
INDIANA	21,327	336,615	6,271	96,880	5,416	128,442	2,440	47,015	9,477	102,822	6,686	34,736	13,061	121,821
Anderson city	206	3,634	39	576	27	1,481	30	901	82	457	65	303	87	395
Auburn city	57	1,043	9	89	D	D	D	D	41	191	22	74	41	263
Avon town	113	2,859	D	D	19	320	D	D	44	187	26	79	36	200

1 Merchant wholesalers, except manufacturers' sales branches and offices.

Table C. Incorporated Places, Census Designated Places (CDPs), and Minor Civil Divisions (MCDs) of 10,000 or More Population — **Economic Census**

	Economic activity by sector, 2017											
	Administration and support and waste management and mediation services		Educational services		Health care and social assistance		Arts, entertainment, and recreation		Accommodation and food services		Other services (except public administration)	
STATE City, town, township, borough, or CDP (county if applicable)	Number of establish-ments	Number of employees	Number of establish-ments	Number of employees	Number of establish-ments	Number of employees	Number of establish-ments	Number of employees	Number of establish-ments	Number of employees	Number of establish-ments	Number of employees
	15	16	17	18	19	20	21	22	23	24	25	26
ILLINOIS—Con.												
Mount Prospect village	49	380	9	40	134	1,161	13	276	110	1,621	107	735
Mount Vernon city............	20	1,178	NA	NA	125	3,847	D	D	70	1,568	49	421
Mundelein village.............	64	412	13	108	61	306	9	106	83	1,110	69	322
Naperville city.................	254	4,461	113	721	691	12,766	86	2,147	372	9,203	297	2,529
New Lenox village............	44	234	7	90	91	5,513	8	100	49	1,256	69	341
Niles village	43	393	12	141	148	3,735	13	243	120	1,551	88	515
Normal town	35	523	7	64	106	3,133	D	D	119	3,146	59	515
Norridge village...............	25	7,630	NA	NA	28	672	4	28	52	981	D	D
North Aurora village.........	27	235	4	18	D	D	4	8	25	546	D	D
Northbrook village	156	4,401	39	236	273	5,498	40	700	99	2,121	131	684
North Chicago city	29	321	3	19	D	D	3	22	31	372	21	86
Northlake city..................	17	767	3	2	D	D	NA	NA	21	258	20	63
Oak Forest city	26	425	5	85	53	1,068	7	48	D	D	D	D
Oak Lawn village	62	2,788	7	46	240	9,338	12	142	120	2,905	108	682
Oak Park village	58	627	35	380	312	5,360	38	412	108	1,834	130	646
O'Fallon city...................	28	326	7	44	85	1,828	10	421	70	1,491	56	340
Orland Park village	72	516	24	136	339	3,934	45	1,176	D	D	133	1,063
Oswego village	48	236	10	105	82	911	10	117	78	1,851	68	353
Ottawa city.....................	22	345	4	30	81	1,782	14	41	63	955	46	286
Palatine village................	122	1,198	31	185	161	1,761	28	583	116	1,571	155	765
Palos Heights city	18	96	5	23	148	5,584	5	36	39	576	41	221
Palos Hills city	33	683	4	16	67	869	5	30	37	277	28	66
Park Forest village...........	10	197	NA	NA	34	498	D	D	8	49	16	75
Park Ridge city	73	913	20	142	243	11,564	21	206	70	1,121	97	677
Pekin city.......................	30	337	D	D	101	1,882	14	107	71	1,275	60	287
Peoria city......................	142	3,626	23	191	439	23,741	51	1,391	315	6,046	198	3,953
Plainfield village..............	70	618	23	162	161	1,449	21	496	D	D	78	531
Plano city.......................	11	314	NA	NA	D	D	NA	NA	23	182	17	55
Pontiac city	10	333	NA	NA	35	948	3	D	35	445	28	179
Prospect Heights city........	38	3,113	7	47	23	187	5	33	22	434	27	105
Quincy city......................	58	759	D	D	129	5,782	29	366	128	2,568	109	525
Rantoul village.................	7	137	NA	NA	24	292	4	15	24	320	D	D
Richton Park village.........	D	D	NA	NA	18	374	NA	NA	14	231	8	28
Riverdale village	D	D	NA	NA	11	256	NA	NA	3	D	7	30
River Forest village	7	38	D	D	61	359	D	D	19	384	D	D
River Grove village	14	59	5	28	D	D	D	D	D	D	D	D
Rockford city...................	164	7,599	27	206	480	17,434	58	926	342	7,811	282	2,023
Rock Island city	34	757	D	D	114	3,488	D	D	75	1,686	59	388
Rolling Meadows city.......	70	2,551	15	45	85	1,128	11	341	82	1,447	48	573
Romeoville village............	69	2,856	4	20	40	892	16	625	60	1,324	64	450
Roscoe village	14	94	NA	NA	D	D	8	270	26	540	D	D
Roselle village	51	1,411	7	40	49	2,135	10	54	D	D	54	297
Round Lake village	31	111	NA	NA	17	91	D	D	22	518	D	D
Round Lake Beach village	59	98	NA	NA	39	414	5	90	43	798	28	130
St. Charles city................	71	1,221	D	D	184	2,229	30	374	133	3,305	113	738
Sauk Village village..........	7	23	NA	NA	8	144	NA	NA	8	190	3	2
Schaumburg village..........	209	8,358	38	262	330	4,671	43	1,320	305	8,473	245	2,381
Schiller Park village	D	D	NA	NA	11	68	NA	NA	48	1,691	D	D
Shiloh village	11	54	3	25	32	1,012	5	30	D	D	8	44
Shorewood village	20	286	5	30	29	488	NA	NA	D	D	27	324
Skokie village	125	1,615	33	230	435	8,878	33	697	176	4,284	189	1,522
South Elgin village...........	28	623	6	52	48	860	D	D	50	1,022	D	D
South Holland village........	27	396	NA	NA	75	1,143	NA	NA	34	540	D	D
Springfield city	164	2,976	34	285	401	21,292	67	1,124	420	8,603	355	2,754
Sterling city....................	11	478	NA	NA	46	1,725	5	49	47	761	26	213
Streamwood village	63	1,776	9	31	56	979	D	D	74	1,063	73	320
Streator city	12	965	NA	NA	36	364	D	D	46	441	26	108
Summit village.................	13	493	NA	NA	11	54	D	D	28	391	D	D
Swansea village..............	14	141	3	D	81	1,838	D	D	D	D	28	248
Sycamore city.................	31	271	7	54	D	D	8	319	46	935	40	236
Taylorville city................	11	280	NA	NA	34	938	NA	NA	D	D	37	194
Tinley Park village............	60	2,599	13	182	169	2,923	19	385	122	2,781	74	397
Troy city.........................	D	D	NA	NA	D	D	4	19	18	336	18	175
Urbana city	21	652	8	63	75	7,531	15	141	108	1,969	53	570
Vernon Hills village	29	412	18	152	139	1,320	21	619	97	2,048	65	543
Villa Park village	31	582	5	63	43	421	10	D	59	930	79	435
Warrenville city...............	45	633	D	D	42	1,681	NA	NA	42	862	35	152
Washington city...............	12	42	3	27	D	D	5	180	39	572	23	112
Waterloo city...................	17	102	NA	NA	D	D	D	D	38	D	21	77
Wauconda village	42	2,594	6	22	20	297	6	20	35	545	36	185
Waukegan city	163	5,493	8	34	154	3,066	25	401	169	2,522	114	478
Westchester village	54	8,515	4	D	79	909	4	32	34	314	32	429
West Chicago city............	91	4,596	9	58	39	529	10	93	58	679	46	251
Western Springs village....	D	D	8	68	40	524	10	64	23	319	18	158
Westmont village	53	6,556	16	161	109	1,400	12	132	74	1,123	85	568
Wheaton city...................	85	1,748	24	108	215	4,709	37	464	D	D	118	762
Wheeling village..............	101	2,999	20	63	77	2,002	12	45	76	2,017	83	404
Wilmette village	39	270	13	72	115	829	22	151	54	848	77	550
Winnetka village	14	99	9	145	56	303	12	30	24	418	34	157
Wood Dale city................	45	2,302	NA	NA	28	1,041	6	218	29	476	38	256
Woodridge village............	50	3,301	6	173	D	D	15	254	56	1,439	55	368
Wood River city...............	D	D	NA	NA	23	715	NA	NA	33	602	19	129
Woodstock city................	37	834	NA	NA	85	2,065	8	45	57	805	63	245
Worth village...................	4	17	NA	NA	18	131	4	37	25	433	24	100
Yorkville city...................	19	556	6	14	D	D	8	52	44	741	32	174
Zion city.........................	28	300	NA	NA	31	2,119	D	D	39	599	D	D
INDIANA	7,561	210,631	1,204	9,661	16,668	436,616	2,320	37,937	13,647	280,340	10,777	75,446
Anderson city..................	47	1,473	10	69	191	5,536	D	D	138	3,244	86	599
Auburn city.....................	22	672	3	2	56	1,435	11	302	61	1,160	34	128
Avon town	22	432	5	42	78	2,474	15	73	75	2,288	46	403

Table C. Incorporated Places, Census Designated Places (CDPs), and Minor Civil Divisions (MCDs) of 10,000 or More Population — **Economic Census**

STATE City, town, township, borough, or CDP (county if applicable)	Retail Trade — Number of establishments	Retail Trade — Number of employees	Wholesale trade¹ — Number of establishments	Wholesale trade¹ — Number of employees	Transportation and warehousing — Number of establishments	Transportation and warehousing — Number of employees	Information — Number of establishments	Information — Number of employees	Finance and insurance — Number of establishments	Finance and insurance — Number of employees	Real estate and rental and leasing — Number of establishments	Real estate and rental and leasing — Number of employees	Professional, scientific, and technical services — Number of establishments	Professional, scientific, and technical services — Number of employees
	1	2	3	4	5	6	7	8	9	10	11	12	13	14
INDIANA—Con.														
Bedford city	106	1,395	12	113	11	81	D	D	44	343	18	70	48	625
Beech Grove city	39	860	39	669	D	D	D	D	D	D	13	160	D	D
Bloomington city	361	5,762	37	401	20	271	50	985	138	997	158	848	213	1,555
Bluffton city	57	854	14	295	D	D	D	D	28	111	20	81	24	204
Brownsburg town	87	2,007	25	142	21	2,084	D	D	59	272	35	94	71	273
Carmel city	291	6,092	130	1,337	28	212	76	1,233	420	14,640	247	1,808	645	7,416
Cedar Lake town	31	415	NA	NA	D	D	NA	NA	6	25	10	30	16	43
Chesterton town	61	863	9	160	17	412	8	45	42	205	10	58	49	206
Clarksville town	182	4,216	16	161	22	472	D	D	41	274	29	118	30	138
Columbus city	193	3,525	46	734	28	526	D	D	119	950	58	216	128	2,145
Connersville city	64	924	D	D	10	78	D	D	29	147	16	46	23	138
Crawfordsville city	99	1,490	16	116	D	D	11	81	44	217	25	102	32	124
Crown Point city	86	1,091	34	200	21	135	13	148	72	474	39	191	104	661
Dyer town	39	779	D	D	14	104	NA	NA	25	116	12	23	36	233
East Chicago city	53	397	29	400	24	317	D	D	17	129	13	95	15	187
Elkhart city	286	4,227	168	3,845	58	1,316	20	300	112	996	67	428	131	885
Evansville city	698	11,649	211	3,167	111	3,266	70	2,681	279	4,604	186	1,083	366	3,391
Fishers city	206	4,188	96	1,758	47	879	47	927	194	3,161	127	468	396	2,434
Fort Wayne city	1,081	20,457	372	6,095	201	4,891	D	D	542	7,974	352	2,004	660	4,865
Frankfort city	67	790	13	104	12	466	7	46	32	181	D	D	22	59
Franklin city	69	1,546	30	547	12	437	13	92	42	212	20	61	55	434
Gary city	173	1,393	34	624	58	1,921	8	51	31	145	35	193	33	157
Goshen city	158	3,272	27	623	16	431	12	81	61	666	46	161	71	434
Granger CDP	70	1,177	25	152	D	D	D	D	29	105	19	36	66	329
Greencastle city	54	857	4	10	D	D	D	D	27	138	17	43	24	117
Greenfield city	85	1,628	15	545	10	206	D	D	42	254	26	71	D	D
Greensburg city	84	1,133	16	239	13	140	D	D	D	D	D	D	20	90
Greenwood city	321	7,324	31	1,547	62	863	25	270	144	719	96	339	117	807
Griffith town	43	616	21	269	30	344	D	D	19	82	13	92	15	75
Hammond city	210	3,522	73	1,109	97	2,128	18	199	57	292	45	201	87	926
Highland town	137	2,812	19	91	21	449	D	D	52	283	24	161	78	349
Hobart city	206	4,367	27	299	20	197	D	D	40	196	28	124	48	345
Huntington city	85	1,029	12	153	14	102	D	D	39	223	21	62	28	161
Indianapolis city (balance)	2,711	46,121	D	D	D	D	540	17,408	1,413	27,233	D	D	D	D
Jasper city	128	2,412	40	899	20	805	15	161	53	462	21	85	59	262
Jeffersonville city	131	5,105	50	917	49	3,045	10	685	81	993	61	271	101	765
Kokomo city	308	4,935	45	439	31	504	25	271	109	731	68	288	100	626
Lafayette city	425	7,654	76	1,217	61	1,158	40	474	D	D	138	821	190	1,584
Lake Station city	31	343	D	D	12	34	NA	NA	7	D	3	3	9	55
La Porte city	97	1,404	22	213	17	331	9	155	47	300	22	84	38	170
Lawrence city	118	1,767	41	797	18	451	D	D	52	374	47	277	112	2,460
Lebanon city	75	1,129	27	599	22	321	8	487	29	129	21	77	31	181
Logansport city	84	1,256	15	255	D	D	D	D	32	212	12	D	25	132
Madison city	90	1,029	D	D	4	26	D	D	32	163	21	60	D	D
Marion city	153	2,291	24	243	20	1,074	11	409	D	D	37	139	44	229
Martinsville city	72	1,114	D	D	NA	NA	D	D	31	174	15	34	27	179
Merrillville town	207	3,834	32	242	22	228	17	485	121	1,477	66	406	179	1,382
Michigan City city	230	3,803	30	638	14	240	18	174	42	518	36	180	48	265
Mishawaka city	366	7,700	52	569	27	453	31	633	118	1,376	71	488	100	1,765
Muncie city	348	5,310	55	580	25	406	D	D	D	D	74	272	108	1,105
Munster town	57	971	16	268	23	484	D	D	43	436	26	64	85	771
New Albany city	135	2,381	36	465	22	221	17	132	85	432	45	187	121	1,035
New Castle city	76	833	D	D	D	D	8	67	31	233	22	56	22	48
New Haven city	54	771	33	1,225	18	388	D	D	27	109	10	45	26	171
Noblesville city	230	4,502	81	766	20	73	30	391	102	803	77	250	220	799
Peru city	61	669	13	106	D	D	D	D	D	D	11	27	18	69
Plainfield town	136	5,233	39	2,742	88	6,660	10	105	49	205	36	144	53	671
Plymouth city	89	1,508	13	305	7	86	13	77	D	D	15	73	38	194
Portage city	93	2,016	27	727	39	305	7	169	38	207	32	165	42	252
Richmond city	198	3,313	32	542	26	357	23	173	70	675	41	180	53	303
St. John town	43	809	14	65	13	89	D	D	31	120	15	24	22	71
Schererville town	122	2,717	25	101	36	160	D	D	59	313	41	204	108	551
Seymour city	125	1,701	17	310	23	1,619	D	D	55	332	35	122	33	190
Shelbyville city	92	1,399	12	255	8	913	D	D	43	197	27	86	31	198
South Bend city	322	5,303	148	2,801	86	2,168	49	2,275	168	1,957	93	956	259	2,208
Speedway town	48	809	11	146	D	D	D	D	20	102	D	D	29	189
Terre Haute city	311	4,366	76	1,081	39	719	D	D	114	1,119	65	428	147	969
Valparaiso city	193	3,755	44	621	23	677	20	246	95	518	67	360	166	810
Vincennes city	119	1,691	15	97	9	81	D	D	45	348	D	D	31	191
Wabash city	74	979	11	221	3	3	7	45	29	239	19	98	28	132
Warsaw city	141	2,667	27	523	8	112	20	181	84	620	30	80	66	299
Washington city	62	633	4	41	7	249	8	63	36	174	13	42	26	127
Westfield city	99	2,256	46	1,071	12	214	D	D	42	583	41	100	119	1,864
West Lafayette city	86	1,845	D	D	D	D	D	D	36	510	40	321	89	814
Yorktown town	17	94	D	D	D	D	NA	NA	10	34	13	82	12	55
Zionsville town	D	D	20	140	14	750	D	D	D	D	50	118	125	466
IOWA	11,479	181,416	4,426	62,658	3,677	57,161	1,618	29,753	6,357	96,808	3,130	13,999	6,460	52,607
Altoona city	67	1,844	15	623	D	D	6	135	28	116	16	46	28	105
Ames city	208	4,362	33	855	22	322	37	1,027	83	551	84	358	145	912
Ankeny city	157	4,450	46	1,458	36	684	11	100	100	469	84	236	115	574
Bettendorf city	95	1,514	48	619	21	71	10	193	86	600	50	222	102	493
Boone city	48	824	4	13	9	720	8	385	24	130	13	46	19	97
Burlington city	112	1,440	24	399	21	153	7	144	53	416	34	600	42	248
Cedar Falls city	168	3,444	42	920	27	1,290	27	507	95	830	52	248	95	2,158
Cedar Rapids city	479	11,763	204	3,953	112	5,952	89	3,578	310	9,561	185	925	385	5,043
Clinton city	119	2,023	16	120	21	152	15	363	46	327	26	91	41	192
Clive city	105	2,265	33	211	11	70	11	113	90	881	47	215	111	834
Coralville city	164	4,081	23	271	15	233	D	D	54	1,057	36	184	70	1,515

1 Merchant wholesalers, except manufacturers' sales branches and offices.

Table C. Incorporated Places, Census Designated Places (CDPs), and Minor Civil Divisions (MCDs) of 10,000 or More Population — **Economic Census**

STATE City, town, township, borough, or CDP (county if applicable)	Administration and support and waste management and mediation services — Number of establishments	Number of employees	Educational services — Number of establishments	Number of employees	Health care and social assistance — Number of establishments	Number of employees	Arts, entertainment, and recreation — Number of establishments	Number of employees	Accommodation and food services — Number of establishments	Number of employees	Other services (except public administration) — Number of establishments	Number of employees
	15	16	17	18	19	20	21	22	23	24	25	26
INDIANA—Con.												
Bedford city	15	166	NA	NA	92	2,186	9	23	45	1,028	40	240
Beech Grove city	19	492	NA	NA	19	441	D	D	D	D	D	D
Bloomington city	81	1,290	34	199	356	9,307	36	688	363	7,661	150	1,205
Bluffton city	13	566	NA	NA	43	851	D	D	D	D	37	186
Brownsburg town	26	115	D	D	67	1,361	27	337	69	1,645	59	304
Carmel city	176	7,385	63	882	509	11,468	74	1,025	240	6,795	195	1,598
Cedar Lake town	6	48	NA	NA	D	D	D	D	D	D	D	D
Chesterton town	D	D	5	15	53	902	D	D	62	1,032	37	223
Clarksville town	15	281	D	D	47	980	13	303	78	2,810	47	282
Columbus city	58	2,771	D	D	203	5,011	23	171	140	3,536	92	659
Connersville city	12	129	NA	NA	44	1,193	5	35	D	D	D	D
Crawfordsville city	29	590	5	11	79	1,275	D	D	64	1,218	47	203
Crown Point city	35	612	15	104	116	3,782	17	238	79	1,494	76	506
Dyer town	20	185	D	D	59	1,911	8	170	46	899	29	146
East Chicago city	36	934	NA	NA	39	1,597	NA	NA	46	1,748	37	169
Elkhart city	62	3,585	13	119	166	5,527	19	210	185	3,470	130	1,151
Evansville city	175	5,678	34	283	542	18,755	66	1,379	411	9,952	303	2,498
Fishers city	137	4,187	41	336	280	4,402	52	831	207	4,614	136	1,146
Fort Wayne city	361	10,155	69	629	876	28,627	103	2,232	649	15,505	538	4,331
Frankfort city	13	913	D	D	50	733	NA	NA	D	D	D	D
Franklin city	22	754	D	D	76	2,372	D	D	72	1,394	39	242
Gary city	40	1,441	D	D	121	3,033	D	D	72	959	73	375
Goshen city	25	442	D	D	110	4,120	10	99	100	2,019	67	463
Granger CDP	32	138	D	D	38	534	16	325	36	789	40	188
Greencastle city	12	630	D	D	D	D	3	15	56	965	36	170
Greenfield city	25	704	7	D	96	1,940	D	D	73	1,755	D	D
Greensburg city	15	2,307	3	18	D	D	D	D	35	723	D	D
Greenwood city	81	8,815	D	D	187	4,900	17	183	163	4,298	123	848
Griffith town	16	252	3	D	D	D	D	D	39	437	D	D
Hammond city	58	1,299	8	38	99	4,089	D	D	145	2,194	116	896
Highland town	37	1,393	9	95	106	1,405	D	D	74	1,345	64	400
Hobart city	32	662	4	D	63	2,130	D	D	67	1,461	65	425
Huntington city	14	443	NA	NA	50	837	12	151	58	939	D	D
Indianapolis city (balance)	1,344	56,884	223	2,227	2,700	88,524	336	8,487	2,138	50,367	1,518	16,940
Jasper city	23	344	D	D	92	3,070	6	64	54	1,236	41	208
Jeffersonville city	65	2,131	12	51	157	4,457	D	D	108	2,090	76	731
Kokomo city	57	837	16	101	222	5,155	D	D	183	3,933	D	D
Lafayette city	99	4,517	13	113	377	10,181	44	436	244	5,346	D	D
Lake Station city	NA	NA	NA	NA	D	D	NA	NA	17	288	D	D
La Porte city	27	364	D	D	77	2,207	15	244	62	1,039	64	360
Lawrence city	81	898	9	98	75	1,167	D	D	D	D	73	443
Lebanon city	21	393	D	D	47	1,575	D	D	52	808	28	227
Logansport city	15	524	NA	NA	63	2,585	D	D	60	976	D	D
Madison city	14	317	NA	NA	63	D	D	D	53	890	D	D
Marion city	32	1,509	D	D	139	4,305	D	D	83	1,629	63	316
Martinsville city	9	87	D	D	57	917	4	D	31	712	27	150
Merrillville town	65	1,190	13	98	266	4,964	13	192	135	3,233	81	685
Michigan City city	42	884	D	D	97	2,617	13	126	99	3,042	70	369
Mishawaka city	74	2,722	21	225	193	5,793	D	D	204	4,544	112	709
Muncie city	92	2,756	14	132	327	9,324	32	449	177	4,511	124	874
Munster town	22	183	9	66	190	6,854	D	D	63	1,430	46	1,342
New Albany city	44	779	6	74	182	5,619	13	231	99	1,995	76	415
New Castle city	17	687	NA	NA	D	D	8	140	37	884	D	D
New Haven city	16	157	NA	NA	D	D	3	14	31	515	30	188
Noblesville city	82	1,186	15	189	179	3,425	32	347	138	3,573	102	755
Peru city	4	7	NA	NA	27	659	8	104	D	D	D	D
Plainfield town	49	4,901	10	88	78	1,144	11	109	109	2,540	59	742
Plymouth city	16	1,016	3	10	54	1,537	D	D	45	917	35	208
Portage city	32	522	D	D	68	1,121	10	222	86	1,955	62	465
Richmond city	38	1,988	8	49	136	4,518	14	70	108	2,400	64	392
St. John town	15	105	7	126	34	581	D	D	25	462	30	176
Schererville town	28	304	D	D	104	2,013	12	416	102	2,466	78	676
Seymour city	D	D	NA	NA	81	2,509	D	D	66	1,197	53	341
Shelbyville city	20	338	NA	NA	70	1,765	D	D	63	1,391	38	306
South Bend city	120	3,262	18	102	312	10,192	35	664	245	4,627	192	1,595
Speedway town	D	D	D	D	D	D	D	D	39	755	29	336
Terre Haute city	D	D	17	102	266	7,482	26	174	235	4,807	121	761
Valparaiso city	58	573	14	97	192	4,102	13	412	128	2,707	108	745
Vincennes city	29	403	D	D	63	2,858	D	D	68	1,439	42	216
Wabash city	14	281	NA	NA	52	1,217	D	D	40	686	27	222
Warsaw city	32	2,013	D	D	107	3,467	16	D	91	1,770	50	554
Washington city	15	224	NA	NA	60	1,104	D	D	37	598	30	279
Westfield city	39	1,135	17	66	77	892	25	324	76	1,747	55	340
West Lafayette city	13	62	3	29	70	2,193	11	72	165	3,249	40	626
Yorktown town	7	24	D	D	24	338	5	67	10	142	D	D
Zionsville town	55	339	9	23	66	754	24	98	47	757	44	308
IOWA	3,793	79,387	535	5,285	8,610	216,965	1,451	18,336	7,283	123,866	5,975	31,306
Altoona city	7	43	NA	NA	38	770	8	D	50	2,517	30	268
Ames city	68	1,277	17	D	165	4,962	27	376	205	4,628	110	1,006
Ankeny city	68	594	17	142	134	2,049	22	441	137	3,252	98	911
Bettendorf city	52	1,054	D	D	143	3,423	14	211	75	2,058	69	395
Boone city	8	38	NA	NA	33	1,074	11	99	27	448	25	85
Burlington city	32	430	3	20	100	1,205	D	D	86	1,848	D	D
Cedar Falls city	41	1,037	12	65	115	2,687	19	132	125	2,838	59	449
Cedar Rapids city	189	5,592	39	381	467	13,259	60	1,504	417	8,001	248	2,058
Clinton city	34	878	NA	NA	93	2,370	13	165	81	1,583	57	199
Clive city	59	1,353	8	36	111	1,197	14	279	77	1,683	77	584
Coralville city	32	585	D	D	102	1,464	12	118	117	3,067	D	D

Table C. Incorporated Places, Census Designated Places (CDPs), and Minor Civil Divisions (MCDs) of 10,000 or More Population — **Economic Census**

STATE City, town, township, borough, or CDP (county if applicable)	Retail Trade Number of establishments	Retail Trade Number of employees	Wholesale trade[1] Number of establishments	Wholesale trade[1] Number of employees	Transportation and warehousing Number of establishments	Transportation and warehousing Number of employees	Information Number of establishments	Information Number of employees	Finance and insurance Number of establishments	Finance and insurance Number of employees	Real estate and rental and leasing Number of establishments	Real estate and rental and leasing Number of employees	Professional, scientific, and technical services Number of establishments	Professional, scientific, and technical services Number of employees
	1	2	3	4	5	6	7	8	9	10	11	12	13	14
IOWA—Con.														
Council Bluffs city	200	5,265	57	926	55	822	D	D	103	550	64	279	100	634
Davenport city	472	9,446	162	2,646	64	1,345	50	1,127	196	2,013	125	552	253	2,116
Des Moines city	597	9,699	272	5,365	164	7,414	163	5,297	460	25,240	239	1,505	638	6,647
Dubuque city	326	6,228	81	991	52	2,585	40	1,597	149	3,185	83	329	144	1,941
Fairfield city	67	833	D	D	D	D	18	47	D	D	D	D	106	463
Fort Dodge city	137	2,431	37	466	22	1,899	D	D	57	342	37	221	D	D
Fort Madison city	44	762	D	D	7	78	4	31	23	150	D	D	13	49
Grimes city	36	886	37	715	19	528	D	D	D	D	14	67	25	126
Indianola city	54	1,124	D	D	D	D	6	46	36	178	15	56	30	153
Iowa City city	216	4,292	35	508	18	258	26	1,945	84	724	79	379	147	961
Johnston city	41	811	D	D	13	131	8	78	68	2,483	26	65	89	807
Keokuk city	49	914	11	82	8	119	D	D	25	129	11	36	17	83
Marion city	108	1,896	36	582	13	130	13	434	59	380	D	D	55	385
Marshalltown city	115	1,879	22	291	16	122	D	D	48	285	24	473	35	311
Mason City city	165	3,105	50	630	29	646	17	280	87	814	49	132	71	421
Muscatine city	93	1,614	D	D	27	791	7	79	40	325	34	138	40	630
Newton city	61	1,082	D	D	5	57	D	D	34	168	17	45	30	406
North Liberty city	36	402	14	237	D	D	7	118	29	423	11	45	33	217
Norwalk city	13	297	D	D	NA	NA	D	D	15	93	13	20	16	63
Oskaloosa city	74	951	15	292	D	D	9	86	31	161	12	38	24	128
Ottumwa city	114	2,123	21	136	22	308	D	D	52	411	23	119	30	161
Pella city	66	822	18	172	10	96	6	81	25	183	18	39	28	231
Sioux City city	363	7,005	140	2,129	60	1,084	D	D	139	1,054	87	479	181	994
Spencer city	88	1,307	34	435	17	221	10	156	32	239	D	D	32	172
Storm Lake city	62	966	8	55	9	47	11	87	37	244	D	D	28	187
Urbandale city	148	3,533	107	1,588	28	946	55	962	162	1,970	84	624	203	3,499
Waterloo city	281	4,867	77	1,226	63	1,249	19	378	139	1,215	90	524	96	807
Waukee city	25	895	13	499	8	70	8	48	25	105	D	D	51	143
Waverly city	46	950	D	D	D	D	8	75	44	801	D	D	17	159
West Des Moines city	385	8,858	56	623	26	450	58	1,804	361	20,154	164	1,550	424	4,496
KANSAS	10,095	149,845	3,755	52,611	2,637	57,920	1,445	30,009	5,997	61,278	3,415	14,532	7,201	65,648
Andover city	39	598	D	D	5	67	NA	NA	29	98	12	20	29	192
Arkansas City city	53	737	6	65	D	D	7	113	22	189	11	19	22	75
Atchison city	40	547	D	D	D	D	7	31	24	120	8	27	D	D
Derby city	79	1,677	D	D	D	D	11	65	46	183	21	66	26	94
Dodge City city	102	1,651	44	547	28	401	D	D	54	243	D	D	D	D
El Dorado city	56	764	D	D	12	114	D	D	35	154	29	54	35	193
Emporia city	129	1,671	16	368	20	297	D	D	D	D	41	D	D	D
Garden City city	149	2,653	26	128	49	343	D	D	60	445	31	115	45	249
Gardner city	35	695	D	D	9	1,200	NA	NA	23	127	7	12	19	70
Great Bend city	97	1,364	28	175	10	159	D	D	52	588	29	107	43	262
Hays city	148	1,932	35	358	29	313	D	D	60	367	44	121	52	275
Haysville city	23	236	NA	NA	3	2	NA	NA	10	35	7	32	4	15
Hutchinson city	182	2,715	54	805	31	1,189	20	452	103	739	55	193	77	551
Junction City city	80	1,295	D	D	34	640	D	D	D	D	D	D	27	158
Kansas City city	399	7,034	194	5,554	165	6,037	D	D	121	1,036	123	652	178	1,464
Lansing city	14	128	D	D	D	D	NA	NA	14	51	11	19	D	D
Lawrence city	333	6,119	57	375	30	886	D	D	176	1,296	140	691	259	4,867
Leavenworth city	97	1,615	D	D	12	175	11	335	49	465	37	172	D	D
Leawood city	148	2,427	35	281	11	379	14	317	196	2,576	104	566	256	1,435
Lenexa city	202	4,112	312	5,800	74	9,037	66	2,371	114	1,413	133	881	337	6,854
Liberal city	D	D	33	231	22	647	D	D	D	D	21	60	D	D
McPherson city	70	932	22	168	D	D	D	D	38	428	22	48	41	217
Manhattan city	238	4,998	35	610	21	215	D	D	124	814	122	483	D	D
Merriam city	67	2,546	32	202	6	524	8	191	22	1,328	20	76	37	312
Newton city	65	1,127	8	84	10	54	D	D	37	259	19	41	30	208
Olathe city	331	7,589	145	3,415	100	3,034	43	618	197	3,154	156	517	355	2,571
Ottawa city	66	1,085	D	D	9	309	7	62	D	D	19	42	16	90
Overland Park city	712	13,744	228	4,117	98	2,098	184	9,035	954	18,036	439	2,325	D	D
Pittsburg city	98	1,649	28	673	D	D	D	D	39	214	30	89	45	242
Prairie Village city	50	921	14	54	5	7	D	D	68	460	D	D	101	659
Salina city	229	3,997	73	1,047	47	802	27	372	109	881	59	181	105	1,064
Shawnee city	193	3,527	63	939	50	1,471	21	96	98	585	81	323	158	752
Topeka city	525	8,881	124	1,441	68	1,612	62	1,377	323	6,214	189	882	343	3,527
Wichita city	1,467	26,178	510	7,717	244	7,462	227	5,491	860	8,014	527	2,896	1,050	10,366
Winfield city	49	637	D	D	D	D	D	D	27	162	12	35	28	99
KENTUCKY	15,021	225,127	3,646	55,784	2,951	93,363	1,801	29,021	6,355	78,417	3,902	18,070	8,125	67,615
Ashland city	170	2,775	33	403	D	D	19	227	60	474	28	114	60	499
Bardstown city	111	1,772	21	350	D	D	D	D	59	313	22	74	36	177
Berea city	58	798	NA	NA	D	D	D	D	29	178	9	16	19	99
Bowling Green city	460	7,420	125	1,516	53	2,047	34	450	187	1,427	116	484	175	1,610
Burlington CDP	18	566	D	D	5	46	NA	NA	D	D	12	21	12	88
Campbellsville city	88	1,292	10	78	NA	NA	12	77	40	207	11	66	41	92
Covington city	121	1,526	30	1,023	17	437	19	324	69	4,983	34	246	119	1,104
Danville city	108	1,690	13	129	D	D	12	241	57	332	D	D	45	293
Elizabethtown city	255	4,735	40	489	29	574	23	679	92	939	62	403	87	430
Erlanger city	38	847	37	579	58	2,745	D	D	18	66	27	222	46	279
Florence city	301	6,867	D	D	D	D	18	651	109	3,042	51	198	105	955
Fort Thomas city	22	183	D	D	D	D	7	18	24	158	19	40	36	231
Frankfort city	143	1,960	43	440	D	D	17	259	66	768	29	142	100	957
Georgetown city	97	1,653	14	93	D	D	D	D	D	D	41	115	62	324
Glasgow city	133	2,079	18	328	D	D	14	222	D	D	20	69	31	200
Henderson city	134	1,866	31	418	17	217	13	224	D	D	45	182	64	382
Hopkinsville city	168	2,320	44	620	24	1,669	16	234	74	566	50	147	50	305
Independence city	39	1,006	D	D	20	1,003	6	14	16	74	5	9	D	D
Jeffersontown city	157	2,869	152	3,127	42	1,629	40	1,176	104	2,162	97	574	170	3,063

1 Merchant wholesalers, except manufacturers' sales branches and offices.

Table C. Incorporated Places, Census Designated Places (CDPs), and Minor Civil Divisions (MCDs) of 10,000 or More Population — **Economic Census**

	Economic activity by sector, 2017											
	Administration and support and waste management and mediation services		Educational services		Health care and social assistance		Arts, entertainment, and recreation		Accommodation and food services		Other services (except public administration)	
STATE City, town, township, borough, or CDP (county if applicable)	Number of establishments	Number of employees	Number of establishments	Number of employees	Number of establishments	Number of employees	Number of establishments	Number of employees	Number of establishments	Number of employees	Number of establishments	Number of employees
	15	16	17	18	19	20	21	22	23	24	25	26
IOWA—Con.												
Council Bluffs city	61	555	10	56	209	4,863	D	D	157	5,186	107	544
Davenport city	138	4,148	19	166	331	8,939	47	863	301	6,766	189	1,495
Des Moines city	303	7,797	43	341	528	22,243	78	1,608	562	9,920	447	3,030
Dubuque city	75	1,909	15	122	229	7,792	42	1,279	194	4,323	144	873
Fairfield city	D	D	D	D	D	D	8	49	34	405	33	145
Fort Dodge city	34	312	NA	NA	108	2,649	D	D	84	1,361	D	D
Fort Madison city	9	278	D	D	32	933	3	40	36	443	29	117
Grimes city	22	304	7	75	24	247	5	69	25	302	D	D
Indianola city	20	139	D	D	44	806	D	D	42	591	34	156
Iowa City city	76	1,469	D	D	271	16,070	23	295	240	4,078	118	883
Johnston city	35	255	7	50	51	1,246	D	D	46	821	39	249
Keokuk city	12	430	NA	NA	47	1,024	D	D	41	558	D	D
Marion city	37	345	D	D	91	1,037	8	127	56	898	56	389
Marshalltown city	21	437	D	D	D	D	D	D	70	993	D	D
Mason City city	53	669	3	15	110	2,935	D	D	86	1,472	72	352
Muscatine city	D	D	NA	NA	76	1,635	D	D	80	1,130	44	300
Newton city	20	153	NA	NA	53	1,304	5	136	43	618	34	126
North Liberty city	13	135	D	D	36	451	9	102	43	733	D	D
Norwalk city	12	38	NA	NA	20	297	5	71	12	147	D	D
Oskaloosa city	15	58	NA	NA	41	967	8	104	32	468	24	106
Ottumwa city	21	553	3	9	89	2,851	D	D	D	D	37	180
Pella city	16	109	D	D	52	1,361	11	88	36	687	D	D
Sioux City city	106	2,713	D	D	301	9,030	41	553	D	D	D	D
Spencer city	15	277	NA	NA	D	D	D	D	48	716	33	208
Storm Lake city	13	251	NA	NA	38	1,071	D	D	35	652	24	106
Urbandale city	84	2,265	24	229	110	2,848	23	644	93	1,833	112	776
Waterloo city	99	2,745	7	82	238	8,396	35	578	174	3,672	117	929
Waukee city	D	D	D	D	39	477	10	373	21	292	D	D
Waverly city	D	D	NA	NA	40	1,339	D	D	36	488	D	D
West Des Moines city	143	22,061	29	238	322	6,055	38	660	246	5,390	161	1,498
KANSAS	3,728	84,131	495	4,822	8,104	195,941	1,092	17,313	6,253	118,905	5,069	27,987
Andover city	18	78	D	D	55	1,113	5	277	30	480	19	54
Arkansas City city	6	16	NA	NA	28	707	D	D	33	648	22	87
Atchison city	7	43	NA	NA	D	D	9	74	28	469	21	64
Derby city	17	227	3	16	50	615	D	D	56	1,362	D	D
Dodge City city	D	D	NA	NA	D	D	4	72	88	1,503	44	243
El Dorado city	9	183	NA	NA	D	D	D	D	46	746	30	134
Emporia city	33	408	D	D	101	2,019	D	D	D	D	50	203
Garden City city	30	233	D	D	D	D	7	D	82	1,519	53	243
Gardner city	20	217	4	8	27	422	D	D	28	546	D	D
Great Bend city	17	186	NA	NA	85	1,301	8	D	47	758	44	157
Hays city	D	D	5	29	114	2,873	9	61	92	1,856	62	314
Haysville city	11	81	NA	NA	10	202	NA	NA	D	D	10	47
Hutchinson city	56	1,004	4	9	144	3,807	11	339	106	2,245	78	405
Junction City city	16	94	NA	NA	D	D	7	80	69	1,456	44	201
Kansas City city	159	5,994	10	71	280	15,926	30	D	243	5,600	190	1,349
Lansing city	8	23	NA	NA	D	D	D	D	23	628	D	D
Lawrence city	101	1,266	36	240	283	6,166	44	652	296	6,936	178	1,198
Leavenworth city	27	402	3	34	75	2,375	D	D	61	1,044	59	313
Leawood city	71	2,636	15	D	192	2,377	17	279	68	2,908	77	1,039
Lenexa city	161	14,345	D	D	162	5,278	32	727	122	3,094	84	722
Liberal city	D	D	NA	NA	D	D	D	D	D	D	D	D
McPherson city	20	66	NA	NA	60	1,266	8	198	45	732	39	133
Manhattan city	62	501	16	188	212	3,714	18	233	D	D	107	1,081
Merriam city	26	731	D	D	77	4,303	NA	NA	31	536	40	283
Newton city	D	D	NA	NA	84	2,391	D	D	47	769	35	147
Olathe city	202	5,955	35	484	294	6,486	42	939	236	5,655	197	1,292
Ottawa city	11	43	NA	NA	55	1,223	D	D	42	696	31	160
Overland Park city	453	11,705	95	980	804	17,310	103	2,758	486	11,539	401	2,392
Pittsburg city	19	173	D	D	96	2,199	D	D	68	1,752	40	172
Prairie Village city	36	214	D	D	102	1,203	16	135	37	865	42	437
Salina city	58	2,035	D	D	D	D	D	D	135	2,800	95	535
Shawnee city	100	1,286	14	117	143	1,480	22	353	120	2,614	93	605
Topeka city	169	4,271	27	D	454	15,708	51	976	326	6,472	312	2,171
Wichita city	605	19,296	D	D	1,336	34,913	133	2,702	1,011	21,150	659	4,761
Winfield city	9	157	NA	NA	72	1,172	NA	NA	D	D	22	99
KENTUCKY	4,139	108,832	589	3,736	11,597	268,711	1,406	19,605	8,228	174,910	5,900	38,040
Ashland city	19	417	3	9	163	6,436	D	D	100	2,535	D	D
Bardstown city	21	745	NA	NA	89	1,266	D	D	65	1,219	32	150
Berea city	11	383	D	D	53	879	7	29	39	750	27	137
Bowling Green city	110	6,182	25	167	351	8,704	33	633	259	6,307	179	1,128
Burlington CDP	7	103	NA	NA	20	141	D	D	24	459	16	135
Campbellsville city	19	885	NA	NA	62	1,366	D	D	38	782	D	D
Covington city	39	839	D	D	95	2,049	13	106	126	2,329	71	527
Danville city	22	657	6	23	126	2,635	10	113	D	D	D	D
Elizabethtown city	44	1,957	D	D	225	6,032	12	100	122	3,322	74	458
Erlanger city	19	615	D	D	26	702	5	232	35	886	39	552
Florence city	60	3,261	13	41	179	3,864	23	577	168	4,045	74	514
Fort Thomas city	D	D	4	25	43	1,866	9	381	12	141	D	D
Frankfort city	22	613	5	31	131	1,920	10	96	87	1,870	76	436
Georgetown city	32	2,008	NA	NA	98	1,312	11	81	100	2,138	D	D
Glasgow city	17	981	4	19	85	2,296	D	D	62	1,432	46	189
Henderson city	30	356	NA	NA	140	2,463	D	D	72	1,350	D	D
Hopkinsville city	31	1,241	D	D	136	3,051	D	D	76	1,614	54	258
Independence city	11	27	NA	NA	21	192	3	D	19	370	13	65
Jeffersontown city	122	3,375	21	196	138	2,322	25	451	124	3,215	100	787

Table C. Incorporated Places, Census Designated Places (CDPs), and Minor Civil Divisions (MCDs) of 10,000 or More Population — **Economic Census**

STATE City, town, township, borough, or CDP (county if applicable)	Retail Trade Number of establishments	Retail Trade Number of employees	Wholesale trade¹ Number of establishments	Wholesale trade¹ Number of employees	Transportation and warehousing Number of establishments	Transportation and warehousing Number of employees	Information Number of establishments	Information Number of employees	Finance and insurance Number of establishments	Finance and insurance Number of employees	Real estate and rental and leasing Number of establishments	Real estate and rental and leasing Number of employees	Professional, scientific, and technical services Number of establishments	Professional, scientific, and technical services Number of employees
	1	2	3	4	5	6	7	8	9	10	11	12	13	14
KENTUCKY—Con.														
Lawrenceburg city	50	756	4	48	NA	NA	D	D	D	D	12	60	20	81
Lexington-Fayette urban county	1,211	23,102	328	4,645	157	6,085	197	4,558	578	5,524	486	2,223	1,163	11,126
Louisville/Jefferson County metro government	1,987	32,443	682	10,313	483	30,633	453	6,836	1,113	28,466	766	4,023	1,697	17,890
Lyndon city	37	958	19	252	D	D	20	2,493	112	2,879	D	D	81	981
Madisonville city	117	1,919	24	206	13	198	D	D	65	367	28	100	44	302
Mount Washington city	39	475	NA	NA	D	D	NA	NA	21	107	6	11	21	72
Murray city	129	1,734	16	180	D	D	D	D	56	313	D	D	51	247
Newport city	85	1,626	D	D	7	303	8	128	15	52	23	132	46	323
Nicholasville city	111	2,003	31	878	9	27	8	238	45	189	25	106	55	515
Owensboro city	329	4,867	60	853	33	828	D	D	167	3,099	76	453	128	734
Paducah city	307	5,255	72	1,161	43	2,314	28	713	103	1,041	49	341	126	959
Radcliff city	76	1,044	D	D	D	D	D	D	27	198	26	109	17	109
Richmond city	196	3,220	23	180	D	D	24	282	81	335	54	197	82	507
St. Matthews city	254	5,075	25	299	D	D	13	143	77	629	64	284	110	504
Shelbyville city	78	1,356	9	112	5	90	8	42	42	226	22	102	38	158
Shepherdsville city	74	4,263	10	837	20	2,069	5	23	33	153	22	145	30	97
Shively city	62	626	D	D	D	D	D	D	23	78	D	D	12	157
Somerset city	164	2,820	26	457	D	D	9	87	74	505	27	159	71	289
Winchester city	105	1,415	17	449	13	293	D	D	D	D	21	94	40	1,162
LOUISIANA	16,564	233,385	4,673	63,503	3,834	67,721	1,537	24,091	7,542	65,556	5,121	29,345	12,072	95,652
Abbeville city	78	1,100	15	162	9	92	D	D	44	223	8	34	46	144
Alexandria city	340	5,180	76	971	24	256	31	392	172	1,137	108	423	196	1,345
Baker city	53	735	6	140	6	65	NA	NA	21	81	16	54	7	29
Bastrop city	49	500	6	118	5	39	D	D	41	213	16	34	16	67
Baton Rouge city	1,211	18,219	305	3,987	138	2,126	131	2,614	563	6,536	384	2,005	1,137	14,263
Bayou Blue CDP	14	82	D	D	7	25	NA	NA	D	D	D	D	6	17
Bayou Cane CDP	179	3,266	22	153	9	49	17	160	69	428	27	115	39	360
Belle Chasse CDP	34	258	42	876	58	899	D	D	D	D	22	276	D	D
Bogalusa city	59	748	4	24	NA	NA	NA	NA	38	201	7	19	D	D
Bossier City city	368	6,775	74	1,354	51	553	D	D	134	991	104	546	126	1,093
Broussard city	63	1,003	89	1,561	21	375	5	44	19	95	45	659	48	559
Central city	44	910	9	37	D	D	3	9	24	104	15	30	27	90
Chalmette CDP	86	1,329	12	160	D	D	D	D	28	160	15	32	39	163
Claiborne CDP	30	326	4	D	5	43	NA	NA	15	76	4	6	13	57
Covington city	148	2,882	D	D	11	257	23	471	99	1,336	27	143	158	1,007
Crowley city	72	1,410	14	177	D	D	9	100	40	216	16	65	49	136
DeRidder city	82	1,172	6	25	D	D	D	D	46	707	17	43	35	125
Destrehan CDP	19	316	7	88	9	246	D	D	18	61	9	12	31	126
Estelle CDP	16	193	NA	NA	4	21	NA	NA	8	24	NA	NA	10	31
Eunice city	74	962	14	75	11	154	6	98	33	164	12	43	28	143
Gardere CDP	16	82	NA	NA	NA	NA	NA	NA	4	7	3	D	4	58
Gonzales city	158	2,944	35	436	8	151	9	97	51	271	26	144	45	286
Gretna city	140	2,017	D	D	14	308	10	133	36	217	22	168	65	432
Hammond city	216	3,338	38	1,272	24	301	18	372	109	2,294	59	336	103	630
Harvey CDP	133	2,677	56	827	27	829	9	150	54	280	25	162	D	D
Houma city	157	2,072	63	552	58	1,076	D	D	83	529	61	382	134	1,429
Jefferson CDP	39	464	27	723	18	297	NA	NA	10	46	18	147	23	360
Kenner city	274	4,419	94	974	104	2,527	17	238	95	680	99	868	150	803
Lafayette city	822	13,685	263	3,325	119	3,686	97	2,115	457	3,373	341	1,792	1,018	6,933
Lake Charles city	469	7,026	79	978	63	1,184	34	543	220	1,548	141	642	303	1,789
Laplace CDP	86	1,472	13	D	19	278	D	D	49	308	D	D	35	183
Luling CDP	26	294	5	120	8	104	NA	NA	20	92	6	9	25	181
Mandeville city	139	2,293	26	170	16	104	16	86	74	734	36	71	139	939
Marrero CDP	129	1,766	D	D	18	153	D	D	39	177	24	113	29	197
Metairie CDP	648	11,973	184	1,823	123	1,259	79	1,332	498	6,598	277	1,658	781	5,869
Minden city	86	1,307	D	D	10	41	D	D	40	212	19	59	25	112
Monroe city	361	5,912	74	1,270	43	669	D	D	198	2,904	137	747	289	1,854
Morgan City city	77	950	31	447	18	163	8	89	45	283	35	217	49	273
Moss Bluff CDP	36	455	4	16	6	14	NA	NA	20	100	6	14	6	58
Natchitoches city	108	1,526	D	D	D	D	D	D	64	407	39	191	46	200
New Iberia city	193	2,601	49	795	17	50	D	D	97	689	55	339	89	426
New Orleans city	1,327	14,795	255	3,124	227	8,614	217	2,412	566	7,675	470	2,327	1,622	15,845
Opelousas city	116	1,802	9	253	10	1,193	12	68	70	446	19	63	65	294
Pineville city	82	1,392	7	150	D	D	D	D	38	183	18	62	29	258
Prairieville CDP	56	1,191	23	289	8	32	D	D	32	186	46	112	62	318
Raceland CDP	27	202	D	D	9	122	NA	NA	14	83	NA	NA	10	23
River Ridge CDP	23	377	8	73	4	7	3	2	15	35	12	102	37	85
Ruston city	137	2,253	27	470	9	95	D	D	82	578	46	344	76	662
Shenandoah CDP	39	527	9	25	D	D	D	D	37	186	18	35	46	118
Shreveport city	799	12,031	283	3,848	150	2,696	97	1,509	421	2,836	321	1,780	598	4,408
Slidell city	277	4,972	D	D	24	302	22	345	121	627	41	235	131	584
Sulphur city	105	1,708	29	332	27	368	D	D	45	234	34	275	55	1,154
Terrytown CDP	73	715	NA	NA	9	130	D	D	36	216	17	48	44	516
Thibodaux city	118	1,807	15	321	7	17	D	D	72	406	25	74	77	360
Waggaman CDP	D	D	NA	NA	D	D	NA	NA	NA	NA	NA	NA	4	51
West Monroe city	148	2,100	54	414	20	165	D	D	67	434	32	238	64	536
Woodmere CDP	20	380	NA	NA	D	D	NA	NA	D	D	NA	NA	6	32
Youngsville city	30	336	9	319	12	156	NA	NA	16	47	25	87	40	149
Zachary city	70	1,303	9	114	8	70	6	52	38	215	D	D	35	125
MAINE	6,250	81,733	1,309	15,527	1,238	17,202	817	11,461	1,900	27,150	1,821	7,138	3,543	23,381
Auburn city	152	3,082	44	506	24	960	D	D	53	1,088	47	161	65	662
Augusta city	155	3,642	23	802	17	219	22	511	55	677	30	193	85	632
Bangor city	283	5,699	66	888	49	1,755	36	956	98	1,237	105	622	141	993
Biddeford city	96	1,914	21	196	13	134	12	205	30	325	22	64	42	223

1 Merchant wholesalers, except manufacturers' sales branches and offices.

Table C. Incorporated Places, Census Designated Places (CDPs), and Minor Civil Divisions (MCDs) of 10,000 or More Population — **Economic Census**

	Economic activity by sector, 2017											
	Administration and support and waste management and mediation services		Educational services		Health care and social assistance		Arts, entertainment, and recreation		Accommodation and food services		Other services (except public administration)	
STATE City, town, township, borough, or CDP (county if applicable)	Number of establish-ments	Number of employees	Number of establish-ments	Number of employees	Number of establish-ments	Number of employees	Number of establish-ments	Number of employees	Number of establish-ments	Number of employees	Number of establish-ments	Number of employees
	15	16	17	18	19	20	21	22	23	24	25	26
KENTUCKY—Con.												
Lawrenceburg city.............	NA	NA	4	8	27	296	NA	NA	D	D	21	81
Lexington-Fayette urban county	455	11,554	90	604	1,154	32,976	173	3,186	849	20,035	595	4,860
Louisville/Jefferson County metro government.........	865	22,263	121	855	1,703	50,488	261	5,035	1,397	32,702	969	8,330
Lyndon city	43	1,150	6	38	69	2,427	9	301	34	422	36	290
Madisonville city	20	335	4	5	126	2,977	7	118	D	D	D	D
Mount Washington city	14	94	NA	NA	D	D	D	D	22	434	23	99
Murray city	17	128	D	D	82	1,678	6	22	72	1,559	D	D
Newport city..................	19	584	3	D	43	631	10	421	98	2,245	D	D
Nicholasville city..............	33	488	7	179	81	912	D	D	64	1,424	59	234
Owensboro city................	66	2,970	D	D	286	9,004	24	460	160	3,623	D	D
Paducah city.................	40	1,386	D	D	213	6,571	19	309	175	3,931	D	D
Radcliff city..................	D	D	NA	NA	D	D	8	36	D	D	D	D
Richmond city.................	26	1,032	13	62	157	2,773	12	158	111	2,903	50	247
St. Matthews city.............	51	757	13	110	347	11,619	18	340	120	3,194	95	668
Shelbyville city...............	21	679	NA	NA	D	D	7	27	D	D	43	170
Shepherdsville city...........	20	988	NA	NA	47	560	7	147	40	914	D	D
Shively city...................	15	88	NA	NA	40	671	NA	NA	29	960	D	D
Somerset city................	29	2,227	5	15	161	3,872	D	D	53	1,516	33	175
Winchester city	12	1,480	NA	NA	96	1,396	D	D	D	D	37	175
LOUISIANA	4,811	104,254	783	6,174	12,685	302,408	1,526	25,649	9,877	215,048	6,531	43,472
Abbeville city.................	12	126	4	25	56	1,087	D	D	39	586	28	145
Alexandria city...............	78	1,652	11	66	381	8,649	D	D	179	3,685	92	571
Baker city....................	D	D	NA	NA	29	470	3	15	20	312	11	32
Bastrop city..................	4	14	NA	NA	62	1,447	4	24	27	D	D	D
Baton Rouge city.............	362	8,316	85	643	857	25,744	97	2,389	755	18,801	570	4,281
Bayou Blue CDP.............	8	153	NA	NA	NA	NA	NA	NA	NA	NA	5	36
Bayou Cane CDP	24	512	9	60	56	1,089	7	65	93	2,601	D	D
Belle Chasse CDP	27	247	D	D	D	D	7	106	35	685	D	D
Bogalusa city................	NA	NA	NA	NA	38	782	D	D	34	508	11	67
Bossier City city..............	66	619	13	99	189	4,194	28	778	222	8,315	105	897
Broussard city................	D	D	4	38	33	523	8	84	D	D	34	261
Central city..................	21	168	NA	NA	40	585	D	D	D	D	D	D
Chalmette CDP...............	21	247	D	D	48	890	D	D	53	910	D	D
Claiborne CDP	14	49	NA	NA	31	513	5	27	20	311	12	45
Covington city................	43	362	8	51	208	5,247	D	D	120	2,681	57	327
Crowley city..................	10	106	NA	NA	58	1,213	D	D	38	645	15	109
DeRidder city.................	8	52	NA	NA	56	1,228	NA	NA	40	665	D	D
Destrehan CDP	11	56	NA	NA	D	D	7	85	17	272	13	160
Estelle CDP	6	26	NA	NA	5	63	NA	NA	13	173	14	40
Eunice city	7	58	NA	NA	56	594	4	44	34	513	D	D
Gardere CDP	D	D	NA	NA	5	49	NA	NA	4	D	6	16
Gonzales city................	30	750	4	52	71	1,988	6	49	102	1,991	35	427
Gretna city	17	281	NA	NA	D	D	D	D	76	1,114	50	188
Hammond city................	22	300	7	33	177	5,722	D	D	129	2,974	73	720
Harvey CDP..................	26	529	5	59	D	D	7	118	72	1,668	68	370
Houma city...................	47	1,324	13	130	154	4,240	8	34	99	1,395	57	593
Jefferson CDP	24	466	NA	NA	D	D	D	D	28	797	20	103
Kenner city...................	98	1,847	16	94	173	3,184	23	972	182	3,541	121	793
Lafayette city................	233	4,028	50	528	978	22,460	66	1,296	606	13,551	316	2,479
Lake Charles city.............	112	2,365	16	96	391	11,114	36	335	263	9,425	139	970
Laplace CDP.................	D	D	D	D	D	D	8	82	70	1,130	D	D
Luling CDP	12	253	NA	NA	29	801	D	D	24	223	10	48
Mandeville city...............	29	210	8	90	128	1,396	D	D	86	1,418	50	386
Marrero CDP.................	12	162	NA	NA	139	3,317	D	D	D	D	35	137
Metairie CDP	305	15,278	38	418	699	10,887	70	1,283	438	7,756	315	2,091
Minden city	16	73	NA	NA	65	1,567	D	D	37	461	D	D
Monroe city..................	89	2,891	11	93	420	9,475	26	483	168	3,769	104	708
Morgan City city..............	26	445	NA	NA	53	853	D	D	56	739	D	D
Moss Bluff CDP	4	20	NA	NA	21	159	NA	NA	24	321	11	74
Natchitoches city	15	434	D	D	89	2,002	D	D	D	D	D	D
New Iberia city...............	37	668	D	D	171	3,524	D	D	92	1,605	64	282
New Orleans city	475	12,141	110	921	994	26,020	234	6,789	1,510	42,732	722	5,256
Opelousas city...............	16	92	4	22	144	4,080	D	D	47	838	28	153
Pineville city..................	21	635	4	16	62	2,286	D	D	44	695	31	189
Prairieville CDP	36	1,251	4	29	D	D	11	64	52	1,029	48	202
Raceland CDP................	8	55	NA	NA	D	D	NA	NA	12	116	12	36
River Ridge CDP	11	40	D	D	D	D	4	19	22	193	D	D
Ruston city...................	22	342	5	39	105	2,626	D	D	81	1,954	42	202
Shenandoah CDP............	25	292	5	19	25	376	7	44	23	467	D	D
Shreveport city...............	241	7,862	D	D	843	28,006	74	1,014	474	11,625	330	2,326
Slidell city...................	47	467	D	D	187	5,057	9	106	194	3,884	105	416
Sulphur city..................	23	832	D	D	64	1,454	D	D	D	D	49	495
Terrytown CDP	20	553	4	33	59	1,120	D	D	53	752	32	195
Thibodaux city	18	228	4	21	107	2,574	D	D	72	1,408	45	261
Waggaman CDP..............	D	D	NA	NA	NA	NA	NA	NA	NA	NA	NA	NA
West Monroe city.............	36	1,037	8	66	137	3,485	D	D	85	2,164	57	389
Woodmere CDP..............	10	538	NA	NA	4	D	NA	NA	5	31	7	36
Youngsville city...............	11	129	5	22	46	289	9	36	30	477	15	37
Zachary city..................	15	72	6	36	66	1,660	6	162	44	1,078	D	D
MAINE.........................	2,228	24,383	366	2,630	4,771	112,594	887	8,027	4,257	55,746	2,921	14,477
Auburn city...................	44	1,368	NA	NA	121	2,479	D	D	85	1,558	72	389
Augusta city..................	50	958	14	204	163	6,187	11	141	91	2,241	109	773
Bangor city...................	64	1,489	15	229	286	11,651	22	211	146	3,659	93	687
Biddeford city.................	37	336	5	24	98	2,785	9	46	75	1,090	44	214

Table C. Incorporated Places, Census Designated Places (CDPs), and Minor Civil Divisions (MCDs) of 10,000 or More Population — **Economic Census**

STATE City, town, township, borough, or CDP (county if applicable)	Retail Trade Number of establishments	Retail Trade Number of employees	Wholesale trade¹ Number of establishments	Wholesale trade¹ Number of employees	Transportation and warehousing Number of establishments	Transportation and warehousing Number of employees	Information Number of establishments	Information Number of employees	Finance and insurance Number of establishments	Finance and insurance Number of employees	Real estate and rental and leasing Number of establishments	Real estate and rental and leasing Number of employees	Professional, scientific, and technical services Number of establishments	Professional, scientific, and technical services Number of employees
	1	2	3	4	5	6	7	8	9	10	11	12	13	14
MAINE—Con.														
Brunswick town	117	1,946	12	50	11	143	14	206	43	335	41	150	103	412
Falmouth town	51	797	10	103	D	D	11	122	45	1,012	D	D	74	485
Gorham town	49	497	17	437	5	79	NA	NA	17	154	22	38	45	181
Kennebunk town	55	516	14	79	NA	NA	8	60	32	324	19	45	55	280
Lewiston city	150	1,731	39	702	25	1,158	24	833	58	1,897	54	226	78	1,014
Orono town	14	150	3	4	NA	NA	D	D	12	84	9	63	17	86
Portland city	388	5,340	173	2,580	101	1,842	140	2,415	318	7,837	303	1,577	677	6,052
Saco city	61	1,288	18	338	18	189	8	131	29	282	36	94	74	320
Sanford city	85	1,423	11	92	7	28	7	32	30	259	22	100	37	144
Scarborough town	120	2,631	48	428	D	D	18	125	49	410	47	238	89	630
South Portland city	253	4,674	45	714	30	903	25	636	91	3,348	55	346	96	1,283
Standish town	15	305	NA	NA	D	D	4	8	3	25	6	10	16	43
Waterville city	109	2,083	10	55	9	148	D	D	30	227	20	150	43	181
Wells town	56	387	6	33	D	D	NA	NA	12	56	22	42	19	94
Westbrook city	77	1,267	43	979	21	299	13	378	35	414	19	95	67	532
Windham town	92	1,486	14	62	10	45	4	87	28	124	20	45	47	170
York town	67	655	13	123	5	45	4	16	26	115	D	D	57	163
MARYLAND	17,911	291,814	4,598	73,388	3,504	73,564	2,550	54,141	7,422	102,326	6,811	49,157	20,974	283,999
Aberdeen city	65	1,399	18	601	14	862	6	85	16	134	20	117	58	1,360
Accokeek CDP	13	179	D	D	D	D	NA	NA	NA	NA	5	4	18	68
Adelphi CDP	16	247	NA	NA	3	6	NA	NA	5	35	8	32	18	31
Annapolis city	423	6,433	75	621	33	668	46	802	134	1,115	101	557	368	2,338
Annapolis Neck CDP	20	268	D	D	NA	NA	3	10	11	23	D	D	48	157
Arbutus CDP	63	1,451	64	984	34	1,401	D	D	12	69	17	163	67	692
Arnold CDP	31	586	13	31	3	6	6	78	23	83	20	33	66	262
Aspen Hill CDP	44	1,161	4	5	16	69	15	41	26	141	D	D	72	133
Ballenger Creek CDP	169	4,300	60	772	26	720	17	239	43	650	43	280	110	1,477
Baltimore city	1,912	21,064	508	7,678	337	10,401	319	6,431	699	21,031	748	5,107	1,698	25,853
Bel Air town	151	3,015	12	70	D	D	D	D	76	679	40	157	146	975
Bel Air North CDP	47	852	14	71	9	40	D	D	31	200	23	78	70	313
Bel Air South CDP	87	2,255	D	D	14	63	16	165	54	221	D	D	92	739
Beltsville CDP	107	1,488	107	1,519	39	667	21	843	31	219	42	332	113	5,192
Bensville CDP	4	8	NA	NA	3	2	NA	NA	NA	NA	NA	NA	13	33
Bethesda CDP	251	4,748	52	376	13	51	86	3,167	324	8,739	304	3,919	832	12,418
Bowie city	157	4,235	18	100	18	79	19	130	66	576	38	110	198	2,443
Brock Hall CDP	16	270	18	1,287	9	845	7	153	D	D	11	75	33	156
Brooklyn Park CDP	35	430	D	D	D	D	NA	NA	NA	NA	7	39	8	70
California CDP	61	2,037	NA	NA	6	55	D	D	22	215	18	65	73	2,837
Calverton CDP	26	1,530	D	D	5	17	24	1,233	20	529	21	148	40	498
Cambridge city	57	794	D	D	8	64	8	55	D	D	20	64	34	177
Camp Springs CDP	43	1,200	NA	NA	9	29	NA	NA	D	D	19	103	27	148
Carney CDP	84	2,115	8	55	4	8	D	D	30	230	18	64	42	308
Catonsville CDP	118	1,781	17	38	D	D	10	61	51	262	51	208	119	886
Chillum CDP	51	804	3	9	11	42	NA	NA	7	18	23	166	12	56
Clarksburg CDP	18	200	D	D	7	66	NA	NA	D	D	16	82	98	260
Clinton CDP	82	1,295	11	107	22	120	D	D	26	198	15	49	44	260
Cloverly CDP	13	181	NA	NA	7	20	5	5	6	15	10	16	42	66
Cockeysville CDP	139	3,777	50	1,612	6	124	37	1,731	211	5,956	57	952	166	4,469
Colesville CDP	26	284	NA	NA	NA	NA	9	33	13	91	11	39	50	152
College Park city	64	1,374	7	90	10	26	12	135	D	D	26	307	90	547
Columbia CDP	411	9,650	130	2,806	50	627	91	3,468	305	5,301	169	1,676	D	D
Crofton CDP	46	502	10	61	3	4	5	17	28	149	D	D	84	647
Cumberland city	86	1,025	23	206	22	410	18	232	52	592	30	85	53	342
Damascus CDP	31	437	D	D	D	D	NA	NA	9	34	9	16	41	167
Dundalk CDP	198	3,001	26	231	40	286	D	D	40	261	39	260	34	204
Easton city	148	2,335	33	327	13	211	14	285	D	D	35	135	95	1,011
East Riverdale CDP	21	94	NA	NA	D	D	NA	NA	3	8	5	42	5	10
Edgewood CDP	55	1,892	18	431	12	248	NA	NA	D	D	D	D	33	360
Eldersburg CDP	77	1,150	22	118	20	289	10	56	26	139	31	84	97	540
Elkridge CDP	54	315	81	3,316	54	1,672	17	1,267	17	178	30	205	96	5,180
Elkton town	83	1,644	9	38	11	216	D	D	35	182	D	D	D	D
Ellicott City CDP	182	3,418	34	139	16	200	D	D	133	847	D	D	514	2,539
Essex CDP	89	932	10	104	12	135	9	127	20	106	D	D	29	155
Fairland CDP	29	1,055	7	9	4	7	D	D	14	162	D	D	43	115
Ferndale CDP	33	756	26	543	20	331	6	48	12	56	14	104	28	540
Forestville CDP	79	1,249	25	294	14	455	4	30	12	56	14	85	9	79
Fort Meade CDP	20	231	NA	NA	NA	NA	NA	NA	D	D	D	D	86	1,595
Fort Washington CDP	41	550	3	D	9	45	3	6	15	101	D	D	55	199
Frederick city	337	6,207	89	1,048	27	733	42	661	178	2,683	121	473	390	6,056
Friendly CDP	5	31	NA	NA	NA	NA	NA	NA	NA	NA	NA	NA	10	34
Gaithersburg city	301	6,469	62	722	23	346	39	1,472	119	1,101	96	357	471	8,464
Germantown CDP	143	3,491	20	898	18	103	40	1,200	58	388	41	278	324	4,575
Glassmanor CDP	21	322	NA	NA	NA	NA	NA	NA	4	26	9	205	NA	NA
Glen Burnie CDP	312	6,011	43	745	48	1,187	25	590	72	501	59	435	162	1,179
Glenmont CDP	11	189	NA	NA	NA	NA	NA	NA	6	48	NA	NA	20	41
Glenn Dale CDP	11	58	6	D	6	10	NA	NA	9	41	7	13	51	1,108
Greenbelt city	88	1,388	7	106	D	D	18	264	44	479	24	D	198	6,561
Hagerstown city	211	4,439	52	503	40	1,798	21	440	95	3,892	62	458	112	941
Halfway CDP	89	1,883	10	270	8	101	D	D	12	75	10	49	8	72
Havre de Grace city	36	325	11	39	7	47	D	D	17	63	16	78	26	86
Hillcrest Heights CDP	46	489	NA	NA	NA	NA	4	29	4	16	13	77	NA	NA
Hyattsville city	104	2,034	9	46	12	222	8	453	D	D	24	139	48	230
Ilchester CDP	24	254	8	194	12	40	15	220	25	275	25	70	131	1,231
Joppatowne CDP	27	239	D	D	7	57	NA	NA	5	13	8	43	9	33
Kemp Mill CDP	4	D	D	D	3	4	5	4	6	10	7	51	30	271
Kettering CDP	22	709	NA	NA	3	1	NA	NA	9	55	3	19	13	67
Lake Shore CDP	41	636	5	11	13	135	3	29	13	52	14	24	34	196
Landover CDP	53	511	37	1,807	25	729	D	D	5	20	19	541	19	197

1 Merchant wholesalers, except manufacturers' sales branches and offices.

Table C. Incorporated Places, Census Designated Places (CDPs), and Minor Civil Divisions (MCDs) of 10,000 or More Population — **Economic Census**

STATE City, town, township, borough, or CDP (county if applicable)	Administration and support and waste management and mediation services		Educational services		Health care and social assistance		Arts, entertainment, and recreation		Accommodation and food services		Other services (except public administration)	
	Number of establishments	Number of employees	Number of establishments	Number of employees	Number of establishments	Number of employees	Number of establishments	Number of employees	Number of establishments	Number of employees	Number of establishments	Number of employees
	15	16	17	18	19	20	21	22	23	24	25	26
MAINE—Con.												
Brunswick town	40	1,120	6	12	138	3,225	22	167	90	1,244	58	403
Falmouth town	31	583	D	D	81	741	14	285	24	469	21	145
Gorham town	49	284	5	15	31	666	5	19	22	349	D	D
Kennebunk town	17	58	NA	NA	68	1,180	12	101	58	998	38	184
Lewiston city	53	1,522	6	14	185	7,223	14	168	90	1,258	78	429
Orono town	NA	NA	D	D	D	D	NA	NA	21	322	D	D
Portland city	224	5,497	55	861	462	15,910	75	1,058	413	7,068	286	1,905
Saco city	34	266	D	D	96	1,504	17	D	62	787	43	223
Sanford city	27	155	6	19	97	2,303	6	34	56	768	46	302
Scarborough town	68	664	8	91	113	3,708	21	172	78	1,070	58	334
South Portland city	64	1,488	14	37	136	3,289	D	D	134	2,782	84	612
Standish town	8	32	NA	NA	13	88	NA	NA	16	178	D	D
Waterville city	15	185	5	11	112	3,782	D	D	72	1,467	37	235
Wells town	28	115	NA	NA	21	204	D	D	90	882	26	77
Westbrook city	37	441	12	85	85	2,118	D	D	41	645	45	429
Windham town	45	353	D	D	55	844	5	110	31	632	52	206
York town	42	208	NA	NA	51	1,439	13	142	76	926	31	118
MARYLAND	8,438	222,648	1,697	16,897	16,800	384,096	2,172	43,573	12,139	237,730	10,355	81,469
Aberdeen city	15	547	5	17	49	434	4	60	55	1,142	D	D
Accokeek CDP	9	38	NA	NA	6	27	3	25	14	134	D	D
Adelphi CDP	14	56	NA	NA	17	388	NA	NA	20	491	11	69
Annapolis city	72	672	23	253	204	2,005	54	838	196	5,866	202	1,802
Annapolis Neck CDP	22	113	NA	NA	17	527	7	17	13	265	18	275
Arbutus CDP	57	1,455	4	34	34	2,136	NA	NA	D	D	43	332
Arnold CDP	33	278	D	D	60	1,073	14	266	27	461	24	117
Aspen Hill CDP	45	197	D	D	99	1,268	10	289	41	743	31	131
Ballenger Creek CDP	38	947	4	D	46	1,831	10	251	70	2,188	48	380
Baltimore city	620	22,063	120	2,564	1,494	77,508	203	7,484	1,542	25,190	996	9,183
Bel Air town	37	145	14	101	119	4,377	7	269	71	1,751	71	518
Bel Air North CDP	47	245	5	28	75	1,026	11	109	34	662	D	D
Bel Air South CDP	42	268	10	37	129	1,679	15	145	54	1,371	47	322
Beltsville CDP	71	2,695	6	28	50	864	NA	NA	50	553	73	1,537
Bensville CDP	D	D	NA	NA	NA	NA	NA	NA	NA	NA	D	D
Bethesda CDP	162	15,322	83	1,608	376	9,310	75	1,203	229	5,085	274	3,267
Bowie city	75	1,107	14	357	265	2,585	D	D	96	2,601	64	401
Brock Hall CDP	16	1,252	6	24	11	318	3	23	6	121	11	102
Brooklyn Park CDP	7	114	NA	NA	14	272	D	D	24	332	D	D
California CDP	D	D	D	D	D	D	8	59	54	1,562	22	150
Calverton CDP	21	312	NA	NA	NA	NA	8	211	31	810	19	152
Cambridge city	13	223	NA	NA	60	1,499	D	D	D	D	28	234
Camp Springs CDP	14	854	D	D	31	424	NA	NA	28	448	30	122
Carney CDP	29	183	D	D	58	1,758	5	89	47	968	D	D
Catonsville CDP	52	1,038	14	55	181	4,887	D	D	100	1,427	87	569
Chillum CDP	22	389	NA	NA	30	976	NA	NA	33	411	D	D
Clarksburg CDP	22	349	3	21	32	420	NA	NA	11	123	13	51
Clinton CDP	25	1,026	D	D	122	3,436	D	D	56	1,043	69	327
Cloverly CDP	22	111	9	44	21	192	NA	NA	11	90	8	64
Cockeysville CDP	88	5,077	16	566	89	2,870	D	D	105	2,593	106	1,046
Colesville CDP	24	287	NA	NA	45	465	D	D	16	182	14	74
College Park city	29	467	D	D	34	297	10	172	120	2,022	51	282
Columbia CDP	200	7,406	92	1,649	514	10,083	D	D	262	6,266	219	1,962
Crofton CDP	29	179	D	D	50	751	10	262	33	778	D	D
Cumberland city	13	1,360	D	D	D	D	7	62	D	D	54	336
Damascus CDP	21	120	4	6	25	265	D	D	24	393	D	D
Dundalk CDP	48	893	4	18	93	981	12	242	103	1,504	73	387
Easton town	34	1,443	5	D	165	4,137	16	382	90	1,745	78	403
East Riverdale CDP	7	158	NA	NA	9	113	NA	NA	11	80	6	16
Edgewood CDP	17	142	4	22	37	482	NA	NA	47	830	30	161
Eldersburg CDP	44	645	8	49	84	1,958	13	282	61	1,299	56	397
Elkridge CDP	47	1,688	D	D	38	444	10	154	37	482	D	D
Elkton town	20	121	NA	NA	113	2,583	7	123	59	1,032	58	400
Ellicott City CDP	85	983	45	329	289	3,685	26	370	161	3,392	139	916
Essex CDP	23	289	D	D	47	607	13	105	D	D	56	362
Fairland CDP	17	141	3	18	47	595	NA	NA	21	160	D	D
Ferndale CDP	24	1,034	NA	NA	26	723	NA	NA	28	491	20	233
Forestville CDP	21	581	NA	NA	16	393	NA	NA	24	248	D	D
Fort Meade CDP	7	99	NA	NA	8	151	NA	NA	24	358	D	D
Fort Washington CDP	28	660	10	76	65	1,086	5	65	33	311	D	D
Frederick city	130	4,006	34	250	440	8,565	D	D	265	5,127	205	1,639
Friendly CDP	10	178	NA	NA	4	35	NA	NA	NA	NA	3	4
Gaithersburg city	259	3,672	41	241	227	4,744	37	918	220	4,686	151	1,236
Germantown CDP	91	1,046	21	159	200	1,949	11	191	134	2,267	83	630
Glassmanor CDP	4	14	NA	NA	7	76	NA	NA	7	42	3	17
Glen Burnie CDP	89	1,336	15	88	240	6,477	10	224	157	3,108	151	1,077
Glenmont CDP	12	55	3	2	16	160	NA	NA	9	141	10	41
Glenn Dale CDP	22	253	D	D	43	284	NA	NA	7	144	D	D
Greenbelt city	45	1,206	D	D	161	1,820	6	33	53	1,390	29	223
Hagerstown city	57	1,780	8	49	210	3,935	17	362	139	2,672	106	696
Halfway CDP	13	127	NA	NA	D	D	NA	NA	35	1,026	16	80
Havre de Grace city	8	42	4	8	57	1,511	8	50	35	676	25	118
Hillcrest Heights CDP	6	46	D	D	14	88	NA	NA	D	D	14	62
Hyattsville city	22	388	D	D	87	1,260	4	53	63	1,049	32	136
Ilchester CDP	24	715	7	45	D	D	10	134	20	434	16	100
Joppatowne CDP	14	154	NA	NA	17	57	NA	NA	14	125	20	86
Kemp Mill CDP	7	26	6	56	25	247	NA	NA	D	D	12	65
Kettering CDP	5	4	NA	NA	9	194	NA	NA	16	241	12	61
Lake Shore CDP	27	144	4	D	21	296	NA	NA	26	717	37	165
Landover CDP	23	922	NA	NA	10	57	NA	NA	25	447	23	318

Table C. Incorporated Places, Census Designated Places (CDPs), and Minor Civil Divisions (MCDs) of 10,000 or More Population — **Economic Census**

STATE City, town, township, borough, or CDP (county if applicable)	Retail Trade Number of establishments	Number of employees	Wholesale trade¹ Number of establishments	Number of employees	Transportation and warehousing Number of establishments	Number of employees	Information Number of establishments	Number of employees	Finance and insurance Number of establishments	Number of employees	Real estate and rental and leasing Number of establishments	Number of employees	Professional, scientific, and technical services Number of establishments	Number of employees
	1	2	3	4	5	6	7	8	9	10	11	12	13	14
MARYLAND—Con.														
Langley Park CDP	50	637	NA	NA	8	11	3	8	7	33	14	188	11	45
Lanham CDP	58	1,500	13	248	13	137	11	327	14	141	19	97	70	1,759
Largo CDP	12	160	NA	NA	3	3	NA	NA	4	D	8	43	10	50
Laurel city	144	2,544	19	610	16	125	15	113	43	676	50	853	90	1,037
Lexington Park CDP	38	352	D	D	D	D	8	88	13	64	17	82	47	2,479
Linthicum CDP	43	592	36	777	19	590	8	194	28	1,326	21	108	79	2,522
Lochearn CDP	20	139	8	214	4	4	NA	NA	D	D	11	99	9	18
Maryland City CDP	40	1,531	6	49	8	357	NA	NA	D	D	D	D	52	759
Mays Chapel CDP	14	62	D	D	NA	NA	NA	NA	D	D	11	24	38	61
Middle River CDP	66	1,054	38	1,061	26	291	NA	NA	12	84	14	99	31	625
Milford Mill CDP	49	653	16	204	16	127	16	481	19	236	20	273	82	2,508
Mitchellville CDP	15	149	12	280	11	141	10	633	8	28	11	260	57	987
Montgomery Village CDP	55	800	7	27	NA	NA	6	15	17	89	D	D	74	517
New Carrollton city	46	1,084	NA	NA	6	16	4	31	7	35	9	71	8	59
North Bethesda CDP	197	4,068	53	559	22	271	46	970	151	1,563	148	1,544	442	6,752
North Laurel CDP	39	913	12	542	14	61	D	D	D	D	21	233	62	449
North Potomac CDP	21	262	13	24	D	D	10	81	5	D	18	38	171	690
Ocean Pines CDP	7	21	5	4	NA	NA	D	D	7	16	10	65	25	56
Odenton CDP	79	1,191	14	316	12	337	11	108	36	155	38	152	73	703
Olney CDP	53	947	14	56	4	32	7	10	28	184	29	171	136	721
Overlea CDP	46	832	5	39	D	D	D	D	D	D	D	D	17	134
Owings Mills CDP	90	1,733	47	935	16	49	21	309	97	4,492	56	782	175	4,158
Oxon Hill CDP	112	1,778	5	36	11	229	10	133	17	167	18	88	28	124
Parkville CDP	91	1,187	9	47	5	13	4	24	20	93	D	D	36	201
Parole CDP	132	2,687	23	246	10	226	25	527	110	770	52	649	216	3,963
Pasadena CDP	71	1,405	20	367	26	655	NA	NA	14	62	17	57	39	246
Perry Hall CDP	55	710	15	211	12	23	6	19	40	247	18	39	46	180
Pikesville CDP	130	1,514	24	61	11	65	15	125	93	341	D	D	283	1,226
Potomac CDP	183	3,781	19	76	4	6	36	444	71	300	84	302	338	2,404
Randallstown CDP	55	1,067	8	77	D	D	D	D	19	76	18	41	24	128
Redland CDP	20	402	8	39	7	26	NA	NA	16	60	7	49	29	158
Reisterstown CDP	66	1,002	9	71	15	49	6	28	31	167	D	D	58	349
Riviera Beach CDP	23	238	4	7	NA	NA	NA	NA	5	20	NA	NA	11	20
Rockville city	279	4,451	83	2,003	33	180	76	2,418	255	3,982	148	1,862	891	24,125
Rosaryville CDP	3	6	3	D	NA	NA	NA	NA	9	55	NA	NA	12	41
Rosedale CDP	72	928	42	977	18	558	D	D	9	55	18	136	21	118
Rossville CDP	62	1,683	29	631	12	135	5	78	13	164	21	239	22	333
Salisbury city	218	4,500	51	642	21	287	32	826	105	824	76	491	146	1,058
Seabrook CDP	21	336	NA	NA	7	12	NA	NA	D	D	4	37	16	63
Severn CDP	189	4,149	10	156	26	57	19	350	D	D	22	213	D	D
Severna Park CDP	115	1,256	30	199	10	63	23	158	96	401	58	298	188	1,108
Silver Spring CDP	183	2,521	45	471	20	47	79	2,464	80	726	124	1,051	412	5,925
South Laurel CDP	49	491	11	82	10	42	4	7	D	D	34	215	32	225
Suitland CDP	45	720	NA	NA	NA	NA	D	D	7	29	D	D	31	232
Summerfield CDP	4	47	NA	NA	D	D	NA	NA	NA	NA	6	38	10	164
Takoma Park city	63	472	6	48	4	24	14	59	17	103	15	86	75	325
Timonium CDP	123	2,291	31	262	D	D	16	236	106	1,332	D	D	104	1,440
Towson CDP	351	6,589	45	301	16	254	38	708	214	2,089	132	932	589	4,199
Travilah CDP	D	D	9	23	4	8	6	102	NA	NA	D	D	121	512
Urbana CDP	12	67	NA	NA	NA	NA	NA	NA	D	D	11	44	48	167
Waldorf CDP	332	6,323	D	D	22	568	28	334	D	D	66	324	124	1,077
Walker Mill CDP	8	30	NA	NA	NA	NA	NA	NA	NA	NA	6	34	4	16
Westminster city	150	3,041	34	403	8	188	14	82	59	349	27	109	100	482
Wheaton CDP	157	2,785	10	D	18	74	13	67	33	176	27	154	98	472
White Oak CDP	27	651	NA	NA	4	34	NA	NA	10	47	27	574	D	D
Woodlawn CDP (Baltimore County)	178	3,135	26	269	14	75	16	397	32	206	36	340	81	770
MASSACHUSETTS	23,928	364,204	6,324	120,957	3,973	91,247	3,879	127,108	9,630	198,360	7,584	52,315	21,985	310,313
Abington town	55	1,115	D	D	11	178	NA	NA	13	101	11	35	26	86
Acton town	109	1,638	26	251	7	113	18	143	33	262	20	66	134	1,162
Acushnet town	17	92	6	54	12	145	NA	NA	D	D	6	20	9	15
Agawam Town city	87	967	43	658	D	D	D	D	D	D	24	98	60	762
Amesbury Town city	39	410	21	169	5	20	5	10	D	D	12	32	56	371
Amherst town	57	894	D	D	D	D	D	D	D	D	35	212	71	326
Andover town	71	1,102	39	1,140	14	62	27	1,904	75	2,682	D	D	198	4,038
Arlington town	92	1,035	10	61	D	D	22	226	39	449	D	D	131	327
Ashland town	47	842	11	46	12	165	D	D	14	48	8	27	59	787
Athol town	42	658	D	D	7	99	D	D	12	110	9	20	7	38
Attleboro city	151	3,018	32	560	22	71	11	151	32	152	25	125	72	298
Auburn town	136	2,742	45	1,810	13	406	7	62	35	408	25	178	40	289
Barnstable Town city	355	4,187	46	602	35	902	42	579	D	D	95	303	215	999
Bedford town	50	819	24	1,146	8	179	19	2,149	32	509	20	224	102	2,350
Belchertown town	24	246	D	D	D	D	4	11	8	50	5	13	21	69
Bellingham town	84	1,985	20	2,026	D	D	7	76	11	39	D	D	21	116
Belmont town	76	695	12	43	10	113	15	98	36	243	24	53	101	263
Beverly city	141	2,006	44	364	15	236	31	375	82	1,848	50	314	174	1,961
Billerica town	108	2,082	85	2,213	50	1,014	25	1,454	21	117	29	182	125	2,801
Boston city	2,191	32,451	512	11,960	386	19,417	710	26,898	1,985	84,833	1,263	13,923	3,485	86,292
Bourne town	83	1,611	14	118	18	246	13	73	D	D	32	123	D	D
Braintree Town city	284	5,936	48	518	38	810	31	677	136	2,136	83	1,659	201	1,919
Brockton city	327	5,070	69	1,455	68	1,267	28	309	72	887	62	226	129	672
Brookline town	123	1,750	24	111	5	15	35	182	55	379	D	D	229	1,052
Burlington town	267	6,093	74	2,238	12	73	119	10,405	115	1,193	48	692	262	9,934
Cambridge city	387	5,773	82	2,489	24	212	203	13,141	166	1,737	210	1,392	983	33,024
Canton town	84	1,196	69	2,207	29	451	13	327	44	1,993	D	D	127	1,899
Carver town	28	267	D	D	5	45	4	30	8	26	6	12	8	34
Charlton town	25	181	8	86	12	109	NA	NA	D	D	3	D	23	76
Chelmsford town	115	1,869	43	610	21	2,239	25	2,395	37	195	29	165	155	2,312

1 Merchant wholesalers, except manufacturers' sales branches and offices.

Table C. Incorporated Places, Census Designated Places (CDPs), and Minor Civil Divisions (MCDs) of 10,000 or More Population — Economic Census

STATE City, town, township, borough, or CDP (county if applicable)	Administration and support and waste management and mediation services		Educational services		Health care and social assistance		Arts, entertainment, and recreation		Accommodation and food services		Other services (except public administration)	
	Number of establishments	Number of employees	Number of establishments	Number of employees	Number of establishments	Number of employees	Number of establishments	Number of employees	Number of establishments	Number of employees	Number of establishments	Number of employees
	15	16	17	18	19	20	21	22	23	24	25	26
MARYLAND—Con.												
Langley Park CDP	10	25	NA	NA	D	D	NA	NA	29	318	D	D
Lanham CDP	32	3,217	8	82	56	1,221	7	149	39	702	36	576
Largo CDP	NA	NA	NA	NA	14	109	NA	NA	14	567	D	D
Laurel city	45	1,396	5	30	131	1,517	D	D	98	2,213	65	487
Lexington Park CDP	D	D	NA	NA	D	D	NA	NA	D	D	D	D
Linthicum CDP	30	1,963	7	116	35	825	7	143	87	2,327	26	388
Lochearn CDP	15	462	NA	NA	39	524	NA	NA	11	153	D	D
Maryland City CDP	17	318	D	D	21	336	D	D	D	D	25	101
Mays Chapel CDP	10	68	3	D	18	84	5	11	5	114	8	7
Middle River CDP	31	324	NA	NA	27	560	5	106	44	651	D	D
Milford Mill CDP	28	602	6	28	89	4,109	D	D	34	406	25	121
Mitchellville CDP	22	563	8	375	46	687	NA	NA	12	307	10	56
Montgomery Village CDP	21	148	D	D	53	1,308	NA	NA	38	439	30	176
New Carrollton city	10	102	D	D	17	250	NA	NA	28	498	25	153
North Bethesda CDP	95	4,276	46	358	383	6,927	D	D	116	2,286	200	3,256
North Laurel CDP	26	369	6	37	19	100	NA	NA	22	307	D	D
North Potomac CDP	23	548	D	D	63	464	3	6	24	260	9	49
Ocean Pines CDP	14	18	NA	NA	12	104	NA	NA	8	148	14	189
Odenton CDP	29	164	10	50	87	1,079	8	277	58	1,057	47	660
Olney CDP	48	562	20	102	128	2,448	11	273	47	971	39	286
Overlea CDP	13	335	4	38	36	654	3	43	27	529	21	137
Owings Mills CDP	74	1,653	12	85	106	2,296	D	D	107	2,055	48	616
Oxon Hill CDP	15	178	NA	NA	54	369	D	D	56	6,172	35	343
Parkville CDP	29	502	D	D	75	797	7	35	47	509	55	269
Parole CDP	52	3,579	10	49	181	7,191	10	92	86	1,936	73	556
Pasadena CDP	38	405	3	19	58	628	9	247	43	761	47	249
Perry Hall CDP	37	144	10	161	84	861	7	136	50	1,067	D	D
Pikesville CDP	92	1,176	16	60	236	3,290	15	383	76	1,209	80	470
Potomac CDP	42	1,425	26	99	138	1,116	26	671	97	2,992	60	390
Randallstown CDP	22	165	4	10	106	1,619	D	D	35	370	44	207
Redland CDP	21	191	D	D	24	185	D	D	21	319	D	D
Reisterstown CDP	32	338	8	68	61	646	D	D	38	527	D	D
Riviera Beach CDP	9	52	NA	NA	11	55	4	5	21	268	D	D
Rockville city	192	13,983	39	308	374	8,387	38	1,139	268	4,157	249	3,193
Rosaryville CDP	9	33	NA	NA	10	54	NA	NA	NA	NA	NA	NA
Rosedale CDP	29	323	3	7	28	256	D	D	34	427	D	D
Rossville CDP	24	746	NA	NA	87	5,149	4	D	48	1,089	D	D
Salisbury city	48	2,822	11	52	206	6,774	12	111	142	3,017	108	920
Seabrook CDP	16	104	NA	NA	57	2,347	3	19	26	358	20	48
Severn CDP	40	2,389	D	D	39	638	9	D	82	4,887	48	357
Severna Park CDP	61	2,425	23	291	118	2,037	19	451	74	1,516	80	468
Silver Spring CDP	139	3,813	44	660	296	4,571	35	981	172	2,971	219	2,480
South Laurel CDP	19	159	NA	NA	36	477	NA	NA	14	195	30	148
Suitland CDP	8	24	NA	NA	18	137	3	32	18	347	D	D
Summerfield CDP	D	D	NA	NA	D	D	3	25	5	95	12	148
Takoma Park city	15	361	12	46	85	2,844	5	23	35	549	37	219
Timonium CDP	60	1,242	18	153	88	2,179	27	777	54	1,285	51	503
Towson CDP	110	2,734	35	291	498	15,429	37	843	226	4,732	152	1,133
Travilah CDP	16	777	4	24	28	94	NA	NA	D	D	D	D
Urbana CDP	10	83	4	10	D	D	3	D	D	D	D	D
Waldorf CDP	56	696	24	288	217	2,449	14	310	154	3,586	128	899
Walker Mill CDP	NA	NA	NA	NA	5	51	NA	NA	8	23	8	26
Westminster city	37	396	10	82	97	1,614	7	44	D	D	73	495
Wheaton CDP	53	491	17	136	144	1,883	8	50	93	999	62	350
White Oak CDP	17	206	NA	NA	86	935	5	35	16	210	10	118
Woodlawn CDP (Baltimore County)	44	1,566	5	106	109	2,189	6	95	121	1,981	D	D
MASSACHUSETTS	11,137	220,304	2,502	27,490	19,349	635,012	3,477	66,160	17,773	311,058	14,810	100,088
Abington town	28	150	4	13	26	410	10	62	36	586	44	180
Acton town	40	260	23	212	67	1,084	21	242	45	685	61	331
Acushnet town	15	42	NA	NA	D	D	NA	NA	19	235	20	64
Agawam Town city	52	424	6	39	62	1,369	12	1,715	65	769	57	385
Amesbury Town city	24	102	5	27	54	832	12	82	40	539	39	142
Amherst town	19	372	27	106	80	1,231	13	133	80	1,129	60	409
Andover town	69	2,715	14	120	119	2,361	28	543	85	1,326	64	481
Arlington town	41	430	20	117	126	2,048	26	181	87	1,177	101	438
Ashland town	29	150	7	46	29	425	3	20	42	569	47	334
Athol town	D	D	NA	NA	31	798	3	62	19	144	17	126
Attleboro city	60	676	13	118	128	4,657	15	249	85	1,813	82	320
Auburn town	39	453	9	77	64	1,599	8	55	49	1,155	42	333
Barnstable Town city	154	1,135	27	124	253	8,175	55	635	189	3,118	175	1,169
Bedford town	29	164	6	35	53	2,451	D	D	D	D	34	205
Belchertown town	14	60	D	D	27	270	NA	NA	19	285	D	D
Bellingham town	30	134	3	24	17	229	7	82	46	729	D	D
Belmont town	32	194	14	183	95	3,117	10	167	42	545	53	365
Beverly city	77	1,892	17	123	180	4,732	28	750	119	1,823	100	591
Billerica town	86	4,977	9	42	63	1,396	9	242	74	1,285	94	556
Boston city	1,133	37,427	301	5,760	1,747	133,669	361	13,163	2,456	61,705	1,852	19,411
Bourne town	42	575	11	105	46	644	D	D	63	927	50	269
Braintree Town city	95	3,269	11	334	126	3,818	21	328	123	2,746	117	808
Brockton city	101	2,968	16	43	294	12,717	15	337	168	2,447	184	1,369
Brookline town	42	385	41	345	311	3,780	32	363	175	2,683	135	969
Burlington town	108	10,376	22	281	113	6,667	21	117	139	4,593	98	884
Cambridge city	135	4,562	106	2,190	361	9,551	82	1,284	476	12,601	284	2,154
Canton town	70	780	15	161	97	3,084	19	237	69	828	69	423
Carver town	20	69	NA	NA	25	319	D	D	20	218	13	36
Charlton town	25	94	4	39	22	642	NA	NA	21	302	19	82
Chelmsford town	74	1,919	26	183	159	3,954	14	199	74	1,348	78	815

Table C. Incorporated Places, Census Designated Places (CDPs), and Minor Civil Divisions (MCDs) of 10,000 or More Population — **Economic Census**

STATE City, town, township, borough, or CDP (county if applicable)	Retail Trade		Wholesale trade[1]		Transportation and warehousing		Information		Finance and insurance		Real estate and rental and leasing		Professional, scientific, and technical services	
	Number of establishments	Number of employees	Number of establishments	Number of employees	Number of establishments	Number of employees	Number of establishments	Number of employees	Number of establishments	Number of employees	Number of establishments	Number of employees	Number of establishments	Number of employees
	1	2	3	4	5	6	7	8	9	10	11	12	13	14
MASSACHUSETTS—Con.														
Chelsea city	109	1,882	84	1,512	59	1,181	D	D	22	413	35	178	36	219
Chicopee city	166	2,576	42	1,458	32	811	12	347	D	D	41	188	43	618
Clinton town	36	370	12	142	4	53	D	D	12	120	10	51	20	126
Concord town	87	704	14	182	7	74	24	1,374	51	207	D	D	175	1,301
Danvers town	179	5,662	32	633	19	223	21	654	87	865	26	93	128	1,020
Dartmouth town	189	4,205	19	428	13	230	10	106	35	274	33	94	63	325
Dedham town	170	3,562	24	409	18	222	18	518	57	1,006	43	293	116	1,420
Dennis town	89	1,074	D	D	9	292	8	48	21	117	23	59	35	101
Dracut town	62	917	12	249	17	871	D	D	21	118	19	98	42	170
Dudley town	21	230	D	D	5	7	NA	NA	6	44	D	D	9	25
Duxbury town	35	213	12	69	D	D	5	25	23	51	17	31	56	125
East Bridgewater town	29	164	12	93	9	57	NA	NA	8	34	8	25	19	132
Easthampton Town city	46	380	D	D	D	D	6	38	11	212	14	38	43	183
East Longmeadow town	58	823	21	518	6	36	7	101	D	D	23	596	50	367
Easton town	80	1,375	24	317	31	485	12	48	46	274	D	D	70	358
Everett city	125	2,009	49	1,229	39	670	5	16	39	1,565	24	76	D	D
Fairhaven town	68	1,061	9	15	7	141	5	156	22	273	7	24	24	148
Fall River city	276	3,329	69	1,486	48	2,502	17	258	95	1,076	75	719	159	1,058
Falmouth town	158	1,979	14	37	19	138	21	270	D	D	50	106	109	1,813
Fitchburg city	122	1,643	34	349	21	760	7	52	32	537	31	155	45	303
Foxborough town	71	1,580	33	621	20	150	22	990	25	151	30	307	70	613
Franklin Town city	107	1,771	47	1,179	31	730	13	64	44	381	35	153	96	804
Gardner town	77	1,314	6	61	8	178	9	148	20	177	13	50	25	164
Gloucester city	126	1,550	37	368	24	253	13	123	29	289	27	71	85	292
Grafton town	34	306	9	65	9	68	7	11	D	D	8	13	31	254
Greenfield Town city	98	1,496	D	D	6	51	12	94	D	D	17	59	43	161
Groton town	18	213	D	D	3	32	3	4	9	52	3	4	D	D
Hanover town	151	2,169	22	117	9	89	5	81	30	499	24	157	62	309
Hanson town	25	278	8	83	9	105	NA	NA	8	32	NA	NA	15	60
Harwich town	64	693	7	25	8	93	D	D	10	64	16	28	27	46
Haverhill city	137	2,525	49	460	20	280	11	50	48	370	48	325	84	612
Hingham town	151	2,502	43	386	9	70	10	177	91	2,443	41	125	142	3,424
Holbrook town	34	186	12	256	20	121	NA	NA	7	53	D	D	11	58
Holden town	40	526	6	122	4	20	5	20	D	D	11	22	36	139
Holliston town	36	236	25	660	6	39	3	12	13	55	D	D	53	358
Holyoke city	207	3,651	19	365	14	272	8	82	43	730	42	348	64	386
Hopkinton town	26	455	D	D	6	72	7	57	26	255	23	69	D	D
Hudson town	80	2,131	26	273	7	74	11	168	23	426	16	80	50	1,249
Hull town	18	107	NA	NA	7	77	NA	NA	6	D	10	14	19	54
Ipswich town	45	432	16	358	NA	NA	D	D	17	133	12	18	39	178
Kingston town	73	1,361	9	334	NA	NA	5	78	19	156	13	29	23	61
Lakeville town	23	191	14	124	10	435	NA	NA	D	D	12	29	38	145
Lawrence city	227	1,729	53	1,319	55	376	29	636	D	D	45	318	65	390
Leicester town	22	398	6	44	NA	NA	3	2	4	22	4	38	10	25
Leominster city	213	4,390	39	439	29	367	18	158	52	477	44	476	95	577
Lexington town	67	797	D	D	D	D	30	1,042	68	431	D	D	277	7,424
Littleton town	41	1,139	18	430	D	D	9	69	10	70	10	63	48	3,388
Longmeadow town	35	512	7	33	D	D	6	19	D	D	18	52	38	80
Lowell city	229	2,591	48	622	29	352	36	1,913	75	1,278	78	553	135	1,631
Ludlow town	50	651	D	D	13	159	4	107	D	D	13	104	27	177
Lunenburg town	33	649	3	20	4	22	NA	NA	7	25	16	106	20	55
Lynn city	218	2,266	40	396	45	329	20	139	48	926	46	180	80	343
Lynnfield town	77	1,767	D	D	12	495	10	294	35	225	20	47	82	392
Malden city	129	1,184	36	623	24	483	15	419	34	231	53	374	58	204
Mansfield town	86	1,814	44	1,554	17	291	D	D	29	220	24	101	77	583
Marblehead town	73	482	D	D	D	D	13	46	33	234	25	79	81	301
Marlborough city	213	3,293	82	2,126	28	197	42	715	84	2,431	53	210	198	4,420
Marshfield town	64	940	21	235	17	70	8	54	33	210	D	D	58	171
Mashpee town	81	970	D	D	4	17	6	31	D	D	23	75	46	172
Maynard town	26	182	6	D	D	D	D	D	7	57	12	45	48	581
Medfield town	27	442	13	62	NA	NA	5	27	14	79	13	16	43	156
Medford city	143	1,810	41	578	28	300	21	748	68	1,028	46	193	144	2,803
Medway town	42	412	7	43	4	34	9	231	15	107	D	D	33	134
Melrose city	59	777	9	45	NA	NA	7	6	22	142	23	95	77	276
Methuen Town city	126	2,260	40	647	28	1,993	12	146	41	347	39	D	78	359
Middleborough town	71	825	18	465	25	393	D	D	D	D	14	27	48	256
Milford town	122	2,230	34	864	18	433	16	93	31	360	20	89	83	470
Millbury town	67	1,633	11	147	6	137	D	D	7	157	4	7	21	108
Milton town	28	307	5	18	4	4	10	34	25	105	22	88	71	260
Nantucket town	161	1,034	D	D	21	87	15	93	D	D	66	148	D	D
Natick town	304	5,975	52	483	16	202	D	D	37	791	53	300	216	1,440
Needham town	98	1,190	53	584	D	D	64	2,497	117	1,447	72	502	238	2,531
New Bedford city	291	2,945	91	2,012	76	1,166	24	178	93	568	80	452	177	1,065
Newburyport city	108	1,194	37	524	11	62	20	157	40	374	24	93	123	704
Newton city	320	4,964	92	1,205	42	262	101	3,616	180	1,861	155	3,059	606	4,535
Norfolk town	21	112	10	145	D	D	NA	NA	11	27	D	D	39	94
North Adams city	55	910	D	D	11	102	11	304	16	149	D	D	19	119
Northampton city	159	2,149	D	D	13	165	31	349	41	421	33	92	122	682
North Andover town	67	1,403	D	D	9	120	10	199	69	391	36	176	162	1,115
North Attleborough town	203	3,868	24	191	7	36	13	129	26	171	32	153	72	269
Northborough town	63	1,728	25	314	12	1,008	6	22	25	104	17	66	84	833
Northbridge town	46	840	D	D	D	D	6	3	17	255	D	D	31	120
North Reading town	50	628	17	140	D	D	D	D	27	270	12	40	78	343
Norton town	33	431	13	1,155	12	74	D	D	6	35	12	48	29	144
Norwell town	55	986	19	310	D	D	14	513	63	750	D	D	100	1,134
Norwood town	144	3,362	63	1,024	22	937	25	513	58	1,057	42	185	160	2,858
Oxford town	43	1,114	17	242	17	116	D	D	11	100	8	52	23	99
Palmer Town city	52	583	D	D	17	144	6	128	D	D	7	40	27	125
Peabody city	290	5,289	54	1,250	54	999	22	146	70	803	45	285	115	856
Pembroke town	94	1,243	33	250	6	21	3	13	16	95	15	46	45	519

1 Merchant wholesalers, except manufacturers' sales branches and offices.

Table C. Incorporated Places, Census Designated Places (CDPs), and Minor Civil Divisions (MCDs) of 10,000 or More Population — **Economic Census**

STATE City, town, township, borough, or CDP (county if applicable)	Administration and support and waste management and mediation services		Educational services		Health care and social assistance		Arts, entertainment, and recreation		Accommodation and food services		Other services (except public administration)	
	Number of establishments	Number of employees	Number of establishments	Number of employees	Number of establishments	Number of employees	Number of establishments	Number of employees	Number of establishments	Number of employees	Number of establishments	Number of employees
	15	16	17	18	19	20	21	22	23	24	25	26
MASSACHUSETTS—Con.												
Chelsea city	46	2,048	3	26	82	2,574	D	D	84	941	52	674
Chicopee city	44	523	7	94	95	1,903	9	115	101	1,665	96	536
Clinton town	19	52	3	4	14	320	NA	NA	33	322	30	163
Concord town	39	206	15	139	130	3,364	29	384	44	1,071	57	221
Danvers town	59	2,348	16	109	170	5,032	24	319	100	2,134	81	489
Dartmouth town	50	471	6	63	118	2,930	17	293	102	2,351	72	470
Dedham town	61	712	15	106	103	2,209	20	369	71	1,671	75	617
Dennis town	47	220	D	D	43	423	13	76	100	805	41	155
Dracut town	30	92	11	70	57	705	6	110	65	893	64	205
Dudley town	12	44	NA	NA	D	D	4	36	24	194	20	265
Duxbury town	D	D	D	D	50	585	8	40	26	337	15	250
East Bridgewater town	27	102	6	48	25	343	3	169	31	463	D	D
Easthampton Town city	16	47	9	33	37	695	D	D	44	552	42	210
East Longmeadow town	31	93	9	60	68	1,566	7	142	34	519	53	318
Easton town	52	1,630	8	119	74	1,229	27	371	48	1,018	67	398
Everett city	52	570	4	D	53	1,122	7	123	90	1,153	76	404
Fairhaven town	18	157	NA	NA	41	2,706	5	62	54	914	34	160
Fall River city	66	1,119	15	58	306	11,860	19	310	189	2,538	158	873
Falmouth town	80	390	13	121	125	2,767	47	363	129	2,622	86	368
Fitchburg city	46	2,345	8	45	124	3,604	7	63	81	1,032	61	316
Foxborough town	48	3,512	D	D	56	746	D	D	58	1,658	37	250
Franklin Town city	46	522	D	D	73	1,100	D	D	67	1,420	D	D
Gardner city	18	185	D	D	64	2,128	8	67	44	872	35	143
Gloucester city	54	224	6	14	87	1,783	27	336	106	1,313	80	400
Grafton town	27	88	8	62	34	529	D	D	22	268	29	140
Greenfield Town city	34	610	6	37	97	2,750	13	193	55	742	44	179
Groton town	19	412	3	D	30	658	4	3	16	370	14	61
Hanover town	40	330	9	38	54	1,008	16	293	48	847	D	D
Hanson town	19	170	3	25	D	D	NA	NA	16	248	13	42
Harwich town	61	249	NA	NA	40	581	11	53	53	836	28	134
Haverhill city	69	562	6	84	143	3,560	32	743	134	1,903	100	500
Hingham town	47	784	15	160	78	2,010	29	375	56	1,724	58	325
Holbrook town	21	280	NA	NA	D	D	D	D	20	228	D	D
Holden town	25	147	D	D	42	678	3	10	25	496	D	D
Holliston town	36	679	8	78	25	180	D	D	14	149	32	116
Holyoke city	25	304	14	126	143	5,845	15	197	98	1,603	56	397
Hopkinton town	39	848	6	77	52	821	12	115	36	367	28	165
Hudson town	44	487	NA	NA	34	491	D	D	47	764	45	289
Hull town	D	D	NA	NA	D	D	D	D	29	182	13	36
Ipswich town	25	117	9	54	24	292	9	255	38	462	35	155
Kingston town	27	84	8	49	33	675	17	556	46	1,191	38	189
Lakeville town	28	195	D	D	27	574	9	112	14	196	23	84
Lawrence city	89	1,504	15	62	190	10,384	D	D	125	1,239	131	812
Leicester town	15	154	NA	NA	15	483	5	118	15	205	15	63
Leominster city	69	1,400	9	38	129	3,902	16	127	114	2,172	71	329
Lexington town	56	1,171	29	286	169	3,413	32	405	82	1,574	71	470
Littleton town	19	135	NA	NA	27	517	4	20	21	278	18	96
Longmeadow town	13	193	4	13	59	1,113	5	87	22	429	D	D
Lowell city	104	2,437	15	92	227	10,190	22	291	207	2,972	183	906
Ludlow town	32	293	7	43	31	503	7	27	37	539	35	206
Lunenburg town	16	50	NA	NA	13	126	4	7	20	184	10	48
Lynn city	94	1,318	9	57	204	7,025	16	207	159	1,625	142	590
Lynnfield town	26	163	4	21	30	382	4	80	28	841	D	D
Malden city	54	505	18	229	118	2,984	11	111	120	1,345	119	738
Mansfield town	35	410	9	72	48	854	D	D	50	1,135	56	359
Marblehead town	36	258	19	74	48	670	19	468	44	510	50	266
Marlborough city	114	3,568	12	74	145	7,591	21	367	153	2,429	100	984
Marshfield town	38	275	7	30	49	568	19	267	57	912	52	310
Mashpee town	38	247	5	47	43	653	11	166	44	659	36	276
Maynard town	D	D	4	14	19	138	D	D	31	315	25	91
Medfield town	35	270	4	30	36	450	D	D	19	322	28	144
Medford city	73	727	18	137	128	3,305	D	D	128	2,288	115	1,034
Medway town	29	203	D	D	29	301	D	D	26	456	D	D
Melrose city	34	86	6	19	81	2,114	12	276	43	605	56	343
Methuen Town city	61	2,157	6	59	116	3,894	11	340	98	1,889	67	364
Middleborough town	42	427	NA	NA	55	1,023	D	D	48	1,005	47	338
Milford town	58	670	5	85	128	3,450	10	174	72	1,344	D	D
Millbury town	26	200	4	23	18	408	NA	NA	40	595	D	D
Milton town	22	136	4	15	79	1,574	17	179	26	541	33	206
Nantucket town	126	881	D	D	31	521	31	339	124	1,168	47	235
Natick town	71	1,192	29	322	119	1,932	26	349	101	1,953	113	642
Needham town	68	1,405	23	424	161	4,996	23	269	D	D	91	537
New Bedford city	83	4,079	15	88	226	8,588	24	361	210	2,719	161	1,036
Newburyport city	31	359	13	101	97	2,656	26	217	70	1,398	65	760
Newton city	195	5,017	88	1,306	490	11,068	79	1,401	235	4,069	241	1,967
Norfolk town	19	111	4	14	21	D	7	26	10	225	17	90
North Adams city	15	84	3	11	42	1,002	6	183	50	609	29	137
Northampton city	42	674	25	196	175	5,830	28	402	105	1,806	86	554
North Andover town	62	2,979	25	292	137	3,741	19	227	70	1,433	63	431
North Attleborough town	42	644	9	660	59	888	14	862	67	1,084	D	D
Northborough town	26	203	8	86	56	887	8	207	42	675	47	292
Northbridge town	20	229	NA	NA	38	1,025	7	132	30	299	24	95
North Reading town	37	554	10	76	47	668	11	165	39	800	57	349
Norton town	29	400	D	D	50	911	8	135	33	695	39	120
Norwell town	52	1,356	9	84	75	1,924	D	D	30	476	D	D
Norwood town	69	2,390	24	192	164	4,008	10	181	92	1,975	102	713
Oxford town	10	40	5	D	21	254	4	45	23	294	27	127
Palmer Town city	14	272	7	17	20	738	6	26	31	359	27	87
Peabody city	84	1,946	11	77	170	5,803	13	334	145	2,698	142	679
Pembroke town	D	D	5	29	31	1,121	11	133	44	821	53	265

Table C. Incorporated Places, Census Designated Places (CDPs), and Minor Civil Divisions (MCDs) of 10,000 or More Population — **Economic Census**

STATE City, town, township, borough, or CDP (county if applicable)	Retail Trade — Number of establishments	Number of employees	Wholesale trade[1] — Number of establishments	Number of employees	Transportation and warehousing — Number of establishments	Number of employees	Information — Number of establishments	Number of employees	Finance and insurance — Number of establishments	Number of employees	Real estate and rental and leasing — Number of establishments	Number of employees	Professional, scientific, and technical services — Number of establishments	Number of employees
	1	2	3	4	5	6	7	8	9	10	11	12	13	14
MASSACHUSETTS—Con.														
Pepperell town	25	181	7	33	5	22	D	D	D	D	9	17	D	D
Pittsfield city	192	3,125	46	688	28	428	24	446	D	D	43	265	134	2,709
Plymouth town	230	4,438	44	340	27	471	30	860	84	599	60	330	179	1,009
Quincy city	243	4,402	64	1,095	50	603	57	2,585	151	8,142	107	651	283	2,860
Raynham town	91	2,421	27	281	13	269	7	43	19	314	24	75	38	270
Reading town	63	2,065	8	26	10	35	7	42	37	407	21	42	75	331
Rehoboth town	23	162	10	62	D	D	4	20	6	26	6	8	18	60
Revere city	122	2,085	21	191	55	440	11	238	31	201	28	233	47	153
Rockland town	50	676	33	507	17	173	3	33	30	492	15	45	41	415
Salem city	177	2,205	33	191	16	91	18	107	53	637	42	232	159	682
Sandwich town	77	739	D	D	6	16	6	21	D	D	27	131	67	321
Saugus town	188	3,682	D	D	19	112	19	217	21	198	27	100	38	213
Scituate town	44	297	9	23	7	42	4	5	20	81	18	27	49	145
Seekonk town	126	2,847	25	188	21	480	D	D	17	75	16	44	31	227
Sharon town	26	369	19	164	10	230	6	11	13	102	D	D	86	207
Shrewsbury town	116	1,893	37	626	35	2,051	8	135	39	310	44	230	109	992
Somerset town	59	906	8	22	6	113	7	30	17	133	8	26	28	86
Somerville city	206	3,555	48	637	24	1,210	46	581	D	D	79	445	208	1,315
Southborough town	30	236	26	341	9	151	D	D	30	284	11	123	81	3,158
Southbridge Town city	56	797	13	87	3	5	5	30	D	D	11	57	19	111
South Hadley town	29	340	D	D	7	57	NA	NA	21	117	5	20	27	81
Spencer town	29	447	NA	NA	6	201	4	8	10	103	9	14	17	76
Springfield city	460	5,693	95	1,405	76	1,966	61	1,457	D	D	118	780	270	2,349
Stoneham town	75	957	8	110	17	115	5	75	27	184	17	165	83	677
Stoughton town	106	1,864	69	1,460	39	1,227	D	D	44	263	38	218	101	460
Sudbury town	63	871	22	657	4	48	16	92	28	99	D	D	120	910
Swampscott town	41	791	D	D	6	47	4	23	D	D	20	110	39	75
Swansea town	103	1,636	15	70	D	D	D	D	11	96	9	13	34	361
Taunton city	195	2,861	63	3,567	47	1,268	D	D	51	578	38	126	93	567
Tewksbury town	90	2,136	24	523	25	1,234	5	152	23	312	29	122	70	669
Tyngsborough town	28	244	19	343	7	45	5	65	8	38	11	30	36	292
Uxbridge town	40	566	14	142	10	458	NA	NA	D	D	7	13	22	97
Wakefield town	65	706	28	467	15	79	23	1,270	77	1,348	45	567	152	2,684
Walpole town	83	1,406	42	794	17	438	13	56	30	463	19	126	96	490
Waltham city	237	3,454	93	3,195	44	1,656	127	7,185	158	3,889	122	849	420	17,227
Wareham town	140	2,356	21	307	22	362	8	363	24	166	17	78	29	393
Watertown Town city	133	2,985	33	509	20	729	46	2,119	D	D	41	167	133	2,782
Wayland town	42	474	D	D	NA	NA	11	18	25	93	11	106	71	295
Webster town	58	744	15	442	15	216	3	16	D	D	19	74	21	123
Wellesley town	117	1,704	25	93	D	D	D	D	171	5,741	D	D	277	1,575
Westborough town	93	2,214	47	880	14	516	29	838	85	2,576	39	226	159	4,869
Westfield city	134	2,127	33	1,000	32	1,365	D	D	D	D	35	150	64	602
Westford town	67	1,636	23	407	9	81	20	406	32	183	21	78	117	2,690
Weston town	20	166	11	55	3	6	8	32	D	D	D	D	65	241
Westport town	61	468	10	164	13	276	NA	NA	17	93	13	22	19	80
West Springfield Town city	181	3,417	57	730	26	578	12	172	D	D	40	158	73	665
Westwood town	48	2,187	27	630	11	82	D	D	38	706	30	330	87	1,185
Weymouth Town city	192	2,735	49	473	25	447	13	108	43	361	44	127	99	544
Whitman town	36	437	11	100	6	61	NA	NA	16	121	4	10	7	9
Wilbraham town	36	636	7	32	D	D	NA	NA	D	D	12	66	36	191
Wilmington town	71	1,379	82	2,793	41	1,124	17	416	29	358	28	222	69	2,692
Winchendon town	25	207	7	63	NA	NA	NA	NA	D	D	NA	NA	4	10
Winchester town	45	529	12	192	NA	NA	11	20	37	251	D	D	111	733
Winthrop Town city	34	200	6	18	9	37	NA	NA	15	92	11	24	20	62
Woburn city	182	3,582	208	3,983	62	2,227	63	2,591	111	2,325	91	1,979	329	6,002
Worcester city	552	7,378	161	2,114	107	2,469	68	1,670	241	6,154	175	762	419	3,958
Wrentham town	172	3,026	11	51	6	18	4	63	11	55	11	120	34	149
Yarmouth town	143	2,361	D	D	17	454	15	198	D	D	37	397	62	249
MICHIGAN	34,201	469,987	9,173	147,939	6,637	118,638	3,970	70,442	12,987	169,105	8,467	54,808	21,832	282,246
Ada township	D	D	20	724	D	D	9	253	59	434	30	128	77	273
Adrian city	102	1,834	12	85	10	298	8	205	39	486	26	80	34	148
Algoma township	29	579	12	72	4	10	4	20	8	24	9	27	17	62
Allendale charter township	25	274	10	83	6	94	D	D	9	48	9	51	19	148
Allen Park city	109	2,073	12	174	11	112	12	209	35	586	D	D	54	556
Alpena city	70	1,230	15	163	8	71	10	124	32	241	10	93	30	174
Alpine township	58	1,241	23	894	D	D	D	D	19	99	3	2	19	60
Ann Arbor city	540	8,265	69	453	20	315	128	4,604	230	2,865	167	1,864	646	7,279
Antwerp township (balance)	27	152	D	D	8	45	4	50	7	21	D	D	D	D
Auburn Hills city	222	4,174	85	2,689	24	590	22	465	80	3,238	49	314	164	14,534
Bangor charter township	85	1,731	15	281	5	15	5	72	24	145	18	46	19	257
Bath charter township	15	347	NA	NA	3	6	D	D	6	34	13	43	19	135
Battle Creek city	230	3,109	33	431	27	1,240	21	798	85	679	44	271	100	2,176
Bay City city	133	1,125	29	511	D	D	12	57	56	540	21	93	81	588
Bedford township	51	734	15	247	10	32	D	D	34	139	16	60	40	294
Benton charter township	92	1,982	22	232	8	134	8	178	20	159	18	82	18	503
Berkley city	63	953	9	84	NA	NA	D	D	17	62	12	37	49	331
Beverly Hills village	26	257	10	9	NA	NA	5	18	11	85	9	27	35	155
Big Rapids city	63	944	6	22	NA	NA	D	D	28	149	17	69	27	169
Birmingham city	164	1,529	48	263	10	77	34	450	139	1,431	98	520	315	2,550
Blackman charter township	132	3,158	21	283	18	401	D	D	25	168	23	130	30	450
Bloomfield charter township	101	1,837	54	345	10	29	22	152	108	802	85	1,297	296	3,107
Brandon charter township	28	294	8	29	7	21	4	30	10	43	8	23	19	68
Brighton township	75	1,001	26	227	17	166	7	131	50	542	D	D	96	894
Brownstown charter township	50	739	11	658	51	1,858	3	20	17	134	D	D	17	130

1 Merchant wholesalers, except manufacturers' sales branches and offices.

Table C. Incorporated Places, Census Designated Places (CDPs), and Minor Civil Divisions (MCDs) of 10,000 or More Population — Economic Census

STATE City, town, township, borough, or CDP (county if applicable)	Administration and support and waste management and mediation services		Educational services		Health care and social assistance		Arts, entertainment, and recreation		Accommodation and food services		Other services (except public administration)	
	Number of establishments	Number of employees	Number of establishments	Number of employees	Number of establishments	Number of employees	Number of establishments	Number of employees	Number of establishments	Number of employees	Number of establishments	Number of employees
	15	16	17	18	19	20	21	22	23	24	25	26
MASSACHUSETTS—Con.												
Pepperell town	18	210	4	10	D	D	NA	NA	10	106	17	69
Pittsfield city	64	893	12	138	227	7,371	30	400	146	1,822	95	712
Plymouth town	119	1,778	15	351	209	6,630	33	1,053	171	3,363	124	802
Quincy city	115	2,857	27	152	287	8,035	35	892	246	3,397	214	1,482
Raynham town	40	525	3	7	54	839	D	D	48	1,038	47	282
Reading town	27	738	11	141	76	1,130	13	331	44	803	61	356
Rehoboth town	33	125	3	3	15	71	10	59	14	120	D	D
Revere city	66	662	8	45	81	1,179	D	D	105	1,463	84	364
Rockland town	25	131	12	136	22	597	7	109	45	836	39	163
Salem city	59	512	11	42	134	5,978	32	688	155	2,353	124	709
Sandwich town	54	205	D	D	D	D	14	173	57	988	30	146
Saugus town	48	252	5	20	63	1,118	16	306	97	2,099	87	467
Scituate town	23	93	D	D	32	510	15	107	37	631	38	182
Seekonk town	41	331	6	71	35	253	17	252	73	1,648	D	D
Sharon town	25	146	D	D	64	569	9	119	16	194	26	152
Shrewsbury town	44	239	25	223	74	1,608	13	263	69	1,141	69	432
Somerset town	14	61	NA	NA	38	799	6	77	49	743	D	D
Somerville city	51	945	27	148	159	4,179	32	470	243	4,058	132	1,436
Southborough town	26	485	D	D	27	757	8	32	D	D	15	107
Southbridge Town city	13	128	3	7	61	2,147	6	20	37	304	41	187
South Hadley town	21	118	5	97	35	556	6	55	D	D	35	143
Spencer town	16	60	NA	NA	16	251	3	18	19	363	D	D
Springfield city	134	3,356	29	550	445	24,004	20	349	252	4,603	227	2,584
Stoneham town	43	833	D	D	87	1,387	12	152	50	758	53	378
Stoughton town	69	768	14	95	85	25,510	14	200	78	1,357	68	336
Sudbury town	23	572	7	28	73	1,001	22	222	34	666	46	302
Swampscott town	29	85	D	D	44	706	7	25	30	606	D	D
Swansea town	28	62	D	D	44	794	15	134	41	614	32	135
Taunton city	58	891	14	32	133	3,589	13	283	118	2,103	103	462
Tewksbury town	39	157	D	D	73	2,474	10	449	70	1,516	68	382
Tyngsborough town	27	1,100	3	10	14	447	11	237	25	644	34	172
Uxbridge town	17	74	5	12	15	255	8	71	20	235	34	138
Wakefield town	75	2,194	15	123	86	1,792	7	14	68	729	99	452
Walpole town	60	330	8	117	65	1,270	D	D	D	D	64	442
Waltham city	177	12,489	29	954	219	5,244	32	581	328	4,343	176	1,075
Wareham town	26	122	6	25	55	1,911	D	D	66	1,320	44	222
Watertown Town city	44	480	16	219	119	1,585	25	310	98	1,354	101	1,116
Wayland town	29	130	5	4	44	562	D	D	D	D	25	159
Webster town	12	294	5	33	39	1,176	D	D	45	625	43	175
Wellesley town	52	1,120	26	156	189	2,131	31	558	D	D	60	371
Westborough town	60	1,756	19	236	111	2,877	16	582	84	1,477	70	456
Westfield city	44	365	D	D	96	2,421	13	324	75	1,217	64	452
Westford town	42	492	12	60	65	892	16	432	55	1,228	47	234
Weston town	20	558	4	6	44	779	10	166	D	D	12	50
Westport town	27	140	D	D	27	164	9	60	31	537	31	137
West Springfield Town city	69	1,680	10	38	116	3,126	17	399	101	2,114	61	467
Westwood town	33	1,211	7	107	55	1,785	8	357	38	497	31	344
Weymouth Town city	76	818	12	152	165	8,909	17	363	105	1,443	131	1,086
Whitman town	D	D	4	7	D	D	5	25	24	457	35	173
Wilbraham town	21	168	D	D	36	754	5	153	23	387	26	104
Wilmington town	55	1,910	11	119	55	1,675	12	91	50	892	66	410
Winchendon town	D	D	3	8	11	142	NA	NA	22	221	10	31
Winchester town	31	368	12	178	93	2,784	16	259	31	558	45	202
Winthrop Town city	12	41	5	28	33	297	9	78	35	389	32	102
Woburn city	179	6,955	29	344	178	4,761	30	615	120	2,209	143	1,188
Worcester city	180	5,556	50	451	648	33,563	44	1,661	487	7,323	358	2,286
Wrentham town	31	686	3	6	28	577	D	D	23	653	D	D
Yarmouth town	67	462	10	54	75	1,003	24	150	124	1,496	56	475
MICHIGAN	11,458	336,635	1,763	15,370	26,977	627,808	3,469	49,733	20,696	399,032	16,545	104,291
Ada township	31	810	D	D	48	464	4	D	16	279	22	112
Adrian city	24	452	D	D	113	1,793	6	133	78	1,458	43	371
Algoma township	13	382	NA	NA	D	D	NA	NA	9	164	16	85
Allendale charter township	7	75	5	34	20	250	NA	NA	27	737	D	D
Allen Park city	30	239	D	D	84	1,210	6	120	72	1,394	57	239
Alpena city	8	74	NA	NA	55	1,687	D	D	39	568	36	280
Alpine township	12	606	NA	NA	13	54	6	90	26	532	D	D
Ann Arbor city	125	2,737	52	440	372	24,404	71	849	434	10,233	235	1,855
Antwerp township (balance)	6	20	NA	NA	14	270	3	3	11	142	15	78
Auburn Hills city	74	15,044	7	43	56	1,635	15	D	152	3,861	46	532
Bangor charter township	10	79	4	18	55	1,118	6	46	42	883	D	D
Bath charter township	13	42	NA	NA	9	119	D	D	7	128	9	67
Battle Creek city	42	1,046	10	88	171	6,712	19	298	D	D	96	845
Bay City city	23	170	8	65	150	3,562	17	248	96	1,648	73	458
Bedford township	17	570	4	13	59	748	D	D	54	760	D	D
Benton charter township	17	281	NA	NA	27	832	4	53	35	872	32	270
Berkley city	20	79	5	39	51	356	D	D	40	711	43	291
Beverly Hills village	14	66	NA	NA	D	D	3	174	15	327	11	51
Big Rapids city	7	298	NA	NA	45	1,168	D	D	47	998	24	115
Birmingham city	54	483	30	550	147	1,358	35	335	77	2,043	105	951
Blackman charter township	19	261	NA	NA	48	987	D	D	57	1,557	34	189
Bloomfield charter township	64	1,396	25	439	229	2,019	25	666	83	1,550	63	499
Brandon charter township	26	68	NA	NA	D	D	3	4	19	236	D	D
Brighton township	41	492	8	37	61	1,062	9	75	34	464	67	398
Brownstown charter township	25	180	NA	NA	71	841	6	30	33	683	D	D

STATE City, town, township, borough, or CDP (county if applicable)	Retail Trade		Wholesale trade[1]		Transportation and warehousing		Information		Finance and insurance		Real estate and rental and leasing		Professional, scientific, and technical services	
	Number of establishments	Number of employees	Number of establishments	Number of employees	Number of establishments	Number of employees	Number of establishments	Number of employees	Number of establishments	Number of employees	Number of establishments	Number of employees	Number of establishments	Number of employees
	1	2	3	4	5	6	7	8	9	10	11	12	13	14
MICHIGAN—Con.														
Burton city	126	1,964	D	D	12	193	5	88	24	231	20	79	36	329
Byron township	118	1,567	54	2,046	38	2,454	9	56	38	265	25	163	58	252
Cadillac city	73	729	9	269	10	171	15	131	32	158	21	59	27	147
Caledonia township	43	858	20	298	8	88	NA	NA	D	D	12	44	39	233
Cannon township	13	93	12	43	5	20	5	5	D	D	7	7	36	73
Canton charter township	230	5,686	59	2,688	86	1,158	29	322	68	371	D	D	219	968
Cascade charter township	69	2,004	51	2,044	48	1,470	33	867	88	1,200	40	225	136	1,348
Chesterfield township	136	2,850	33	475	34	151	9	127	40	191	37	533	66	357
Clawson city	36	303	23	264	6	17	7	151	10	92	10	87	34	219
Clinton charter township	332	5,619	84	888	70	481	24	664	142	835	89	453	220	1,604
Coldwater city	66	910	13	301	13	1,287	8	58	36	323	23	63	29	501
Commerce charter township (balance)	104	2,151	48	582	D	D	17	297	47	228	40	222	121	612
Comstock charter township	50	1,034	34	506	9	259	D	D	19	83	12	74	27	815
Cooper charter township	6	25	3	4	3	28	NA	NA	NA	NA	3	2	9	19
Davison township	38	1,144	D	D	4	33	D	D	11	47	11	60	26	144
Dearborn city	556	6,600	138	1,765	334	1,372	68	511	101	4,237	D	D	271	15,810
Dearborn Heights city	214	1,846	41	123	155	426	14	130	46	213	D	D	89	291
Delhi charter township	53	719	D	D	13	137	12	86	D	D	19	111	52	427
Delta charter township	159	3,403	27	871	38	4,135	18	747	79	3,745	47	281	76	717
Detroit city	1,945	13,065	377	7,476	298	6,388	250	7,045	475	27,792	268	1,832	764	16,904
DeWitt charter township	25	124	D	D	D	D	NA	NA	21	69	16	53	30	174
East Bay township	28	623	7	46	NA	NA	NA	NA	12	180	7	44	23	159
East Grand Rapids city	22	196	9	13	NA	NA	5	9	D	D	13	30	51	205
East Lansing city	85	1,588	10	30	D	D	24	432	97	2,441	44	398	125	1,551
Eastpointe city	111	934	10	39	7	10	7	29	18	97	14	56	33	182
Egelston township	19	130	3	18	D	D	NA	NA	3	11	3	11	8	55
Emmett charter township	52	1,241	D	D	5	154	3	46	16	65	6	19	21	64
Escanaba city	114	1,754	27	218	20	362	14	172	44	608	19	43	48	313
Farmington city	55	421	7	85	NA	NA	D	D	35	387	14	59	61	401
Farmington Hills city	270	3,983	168	3,414	44	519	71	2,009	246	3,905	193	1,998	724	14,791
Fenton city	97	1,623	19	155	6	47	D	D	40	364	21	107	36	146
Fenton charter township	25	514	D	D	5	5	3	10	8	40	12	526	32	81
Ferndale city	94	845	46	847	12	53	19	163	17	239	24	68	68	305
Flint city	331	3,025	61	948	49	1,496	32	520	67	879	66	519	123	631
Flint charter township	233	3,929	24	358	22	732	15	185	65	1,021	46	309	100	603
Flushing charter township	17	108	D	D	4	23	NA	NA	D	D	6	14	16	69
Fort Gratiot charter township	117	2,519	D	D	9	43	4	55	30	140	17	76	20	120
Fraser city	45	700	43	628	11	50	3	14	16	82	13	44	34	191
Frenchtown township	85	2,042	D	D	7	63	5	70	16	61	D	D	D	D
Fruitport charter township	84	1,423	5	25	4	46	D	D	11	59	7	39	14	94
Gaines charter township	33	362	21	500	D	D	10	91	D	D	15	42	32	172
Garden City city	106	744	17	123	D	D	D	D	D	D	D	D	24	72
Garfield charter township	167	3,282	48	434	21	306	D	D	32	151	38	121	69	588
Genesee charter township	25	195	D	D	8	39	NA	NA	D	D	10	28	13	141
Genoa township	54	699	31	165	10	188	D	D	27	128	D	D	84	536
Georgetown charter township	90	1,294	39	248	22	242	14	37	47	379	D	D	75	403
Grand Blanc charter township	77	1,586	22	449	14	43	12	168	56	462	29	114	70	354
Grand Haven city	103	1,404	18	225	4	20	14	185	40	211	28	262	70	305
Grand Haven charter township	26	641	5	9	3	52	4	51	15	48	D	D	24	51
Grand Rapids city	575	7,642	209	4,832	82	1,121	103	2,169	375	5,619	197	1,401	635	8,130
Grand Rapids charter township	65	826	23	369	4	11	16	483	94	2,128	63	660	106	784
Grandville city	215	4,472	51	642	14	311	15	189	63	638	36	146	78	475
Green Oak township	83	1,269	30	509	12	598	6	93	17	82	D	D	53	221
Grosse Ile township	7	137	D	D	5	10	NA	NA	D	D	D	D	14	31
Grosse Pointe Park city	12	61	6	14	NA	NA	3	5	D	D	D	D	35	179
Grosse Pointe Woods city	53	488	5	13	3	1	D	D	28	186	D	D	54	140
Hamburg township	16	112	D	D	7	11	NA	NA	12	19	D	D	41	83
Hamtramck city	116	470	5	24	42	251	3	3	D	D	5	19	9	61
Harper Woods city	74	1,298	7	48	NA	NA	4	4	16	77	12	56	23	160
Harrison charter township	47	422	10	200	14	101	6	7	13	41	26	67	37	442
Hartland township	27	584	D	D	3	2	D	D	20	88	6	36	23	40
Hazel Park city	63	530	21	275	NA	NA	D	D	10	45	11	24	20	94
Highland charter township	54	1,088	7	46	D	D	5	26	20	80	17	40	47	260
Highland Park city	71	559	8	218	5	217	NA	NA	D	D	D	D	D	D
Holland city	156	2,218	40	618	23	857	11	444	77	603	57	274	90	2,365
Holland charter township	203	3,682	71	1,030	26	425	14	230	74	684	44	390	82	1,020
Holly township (balance)	7	25	NA	NA	6	56	NA	NA	NA	NA	7	21	6	4
Huron charter township	22	139	6	252	20	628	NA	NA	6	16	D	D	9	52
Independence charter township	80	1,423	29	290	5	20	17	55	60	348	44	170	94	374
Inkster city	51	291	7	89	6	9	NA	NA	5	14	D	D	10	42
Ionia city	27	222	D	D	NA	NA	NA	NA	17	211	7	29	9	26
Jackson city	152	1,606	52	743	10	231	17	253	63	708	36	163	70	1,108
Kalamazoo city	264	2,768	84	1,564	41	1,209	36	779	108	1,048	87	639	195	1,686
Kalamazoo charter township	52	393	18	273	4	30	D	D	D	D	13	69	20	90
Kentwood city	285	4,828	133	3,588	63	1,048	27	220	91	2,215	51	188	115	1,431
Lansing city	450	6,257	115	1,800	40	2,935	79	1,300	110	4,643	98	690	250	2,760
Lenox township (balance)	11	304	D	D	6	40	NA	NA	NA	NA	NA	NA	3	2
Leoni township	51	865	20	94	11	197	4	19	D	D	D	D	D	D
Lincoln charter township	34	658	D	D	5	38	NA	NA	17	68	D	D	25	137
Lincoln Park city	125	1,319	D	D	16	72	D	D	D	D	D	D	34	317
Livonia city	434	7,510	242	4,365	122	2,501	69	1,785	197	2,660	96	808	368	7,825

1 Merchant wholesalers, except manufacturers' sales branches and offices.

Table C. Incorporated Places, Census Designated Places (CDPs), and Minor Civil Divisions (MCDs) of 10,000 or More Population — **Economic Census**

STATE City, town, township, borough, or CDP (county if applicable)	Administration and support and waste management and mediation services		Educational services		Health care and social assistance		Arts, entertainment, and recreation		Accommodation and food services		Other services (except public administration)	
	Number of establish-ments	Number of employees	Number of establish-ments	Number of employees	Number of establish-ments	Number of employees	Number of establish-ments	Number of employees	Number of establish-ments	Number of employees	Number of establish-ments	Number of employees
	15	16	17	18	19	20	21	22	23	24	25	26
MICHIGAN—Con.												
Burton city	35	5,445	5	D	90	1,564	7	57	57	985	D	D
Byron township	45	855	NA	NA	39	710	9	93	39	615	56	418
Cadillac city	14	672	D	D	61	1,625	9	120	39	600	31	128
Caledonia township	22	3,937	3	26	D	D	8	23	34	778	24	178
Cannon township	16	81	D	D	D	D	6	61	D	D	D	D
Canton charter township	85	3,500	31	259	230	2,494	D	D	163	3,667	118	689
Cascade charter township	63	1,924	14	161	D	D	21	287	65	1,596	55	877
Chesterfield township	50	728	8	79	102	1,566	11	74	87	1,878	D	D
Clawson city	25	656	NA	NA	40	452	D	D	36	473	D	D
Clinton charter township	112	4,256	15	58	443	7,701	22	410	D	D	219	1,194
Coldwater city	8	136	NA	NA	64	1,364	D	D	53	867	D	D
Commerce charter township (balance)	76	1,552	9	106	112	2,392	18	378	91	1,678	68	375
Comstock charter township	25	533	NA	NA	24	482	D	D	46	990	21	103
Cooper charter township	5	32	NA	NA	10	135	D	D	4	91	D	D
Davison township	12	204	NA	NA	48	610	5	47	20	533	D	D
Dearborn city	148	7,861	26	295	464	9,746	28	D	293	4,836	227	1,444
Dearborn Heights city	52	435	6	27	133	1,287	8	73	117	1,739	110	365
Delhi charter township	32	547	7	24	71	1,044	D	D	35	655	35	132
Delta charter township	49	1,448	11	80	D	D	16	139	105	2,760	81	825
Detroit city	465	16,575	75	561	982	50,181	92	4,307	963	25,115	785	5,867
DeWitt charter township	18	254	NA	NA	D	D	4	62	33	465	D	D
East Bay township	13	129	NA	NA	20	261	4	6	41	1,373	15	87
East Grand Rapids city	9	9	3	D	D	D	3	5	13	297	10	40
East Lansing city	36	1,093	D	D	130	2,818	10	149	136	2,704	57	682
Eastpointe city	25	287	NA	NA	94	432	4	19	54	848	57	215
Egelston township	5	16	NA	NA	7	193	NA	NA	12	98	D	D
Emmett charter township	8	26	NA	NA	D	D	4	9	28	2,478	D	D
Escanaba city	17	522	D	D	65	1,226	7	85	61	874	D	D
Farmington city	14	78	7	93	52	546	9	188	43	552	33	148
Farmington Hills city	177	11,323	21	401	421	15,018	40	675	182	3,003	168	2,344
Fenton city	21	303	6	23	64	785	6	36	64	1,577	46	221
Fenton charter township	14	355	3	D	25	237	3	39	16	380	D	D
Ferndale city	33	281	7	31	37	273	18	106	D	D	56	248
Flint city	50	1,387	12	50	201	9,385	15	547	171	2,787	116	1,227
Flint charter township	55	4,773	6	29	319	4,453	9	29	96	2,200	57	453
Flushing charter township	10	20	NA	NA	D	D	NA	NA	5	9	15	94
Fort Gratiot charter township	7	58	NA	NA	43	752	5	39	D	D	23	77
Fraser city	33	351	3	17	35	496	8	105	33	431	D	D
Frenchtown township	14	198	NA	NA	63	896	8	53	53	1,071	18	109
Fruitport charter township	12	176	3	21	21	285	5	27	46	1,021	D	D
Gaines charter township	32	844	6	9	D	D	3	3	26	721	D	D
Garden City city	22	189	NA	NA	81	1,990	D	D	45	623	D	D
Garfield charter township	48	451	D	D	92	1,544	9	143	41	664	57	365
Genesee charter township	12	245	NA	NA	D	D	NA	NA	18	119	19	117
Genoa township	20	158	4	22	58	899	15	608	12	217	D	D
Georgetown charter township	52	1,311	9	38	58	1,322	13	132	40	975	69	324
Grand Blanc charter township	42	1,210	4	31	177	5,980	16	228	57	1,113	41	218
Grand Haven city	14	272	6	23	62	1,441	9	235	85	1,393	39	231
Grand Haven charter township	23	521	NA	NA	22	183	D	D	10	128	9	28
Grand Rapids city	243	14,406	41	505	559	30,484	75	1,717	477	11,352	382	2,679
Grand Rapids charter township	47	962	7	38	166	3,806	D	D	44	1,002	49	453
Grandville city	37	853	9	70	67	1,428	17	133	78	2,291	61	753
Green Oak township	37	207	3	17	19	146	5	44	D	D	D	D
Grosse Ile township	14	31	NA	NA	13	203	8	116	15	139	D	D
Grosse Pointe Park city	6	64	NA	NA	D	D	D	D	28	303	14	86
Grosse Pointe Woods city	21	54	4	12	79	1,150	6	83	42	735	31	218
Hamburg township	33	137	4	21	21	245	8	94	D	D	19	78
Hamtramck city	11	121	3	48	35	444	NA	NA	45	381	28	51
Harper Woods city	13	394	NA	NA	39	739	D	D	17	282	D	D
Harrison charter township	25	60	4	47	D	D	17	110	32	520	D	D
Hartland township	19	158	5	69	35	375	D	D	31	787	16	207
Hazel Park city	12	82	NA	NA	D	D	D	D	32	397	34	140
Highland charter township	33	136	3	19	D	D	5	D	25	416	41	180
Highland Park city	D	D	NA	NA	27	698	NA	NA	D	D	D	D
Holland city	37	1,706	D	D	135	4,238	9	238	79	2,118	72	575
Holland charter township	58	3,581	9	150	103	1,855	12	123	99	2,440	97	579
Holly township (balance)	19	1,102	NA	NA	D	D	NA	NA	4	17	4	19
Huron charter township	15	129	NA	NA	D	D	3	D	10	83	D	D
Independence charter township	41	226	8	60	160	1,493	21	387	65	1,492	47	510
Inkster city	10	268	NA	NA	38	691	NA	NA	17	140	19	65
Ionia city	NA	NA	NA	NA	28	571	NA	NA	19	348	11	43
Jackson city	31	912	7	45	178	7,385	19	118	86	1,392	74	484
Kalamazoo city	87	3,410	24	188	232	13,832	41	912	228	5,225	162	1,809
Kalamazoo charter township	25	241	NA	NA	57	1,151	5	31	31	453	22	95
Kentwood city	89	22,329	7	61	147	4,146	19	549	103	2,415	83	1,052
Lansing city	110	3,889	27	248	271	14,168	30	786	226	4,437	266	2,122
Lenox township (balance)	D	D	NA	NA	8	64	4	31	4	D	4	41
Leoni township	D	D	NA	NA	15	230	4	26	23	387	24	167
Lincoln charter township	15	200	5	14	26	280	NA	NA	31	764	D	D
Lincoln Park city	18	815	NA	NA	60	1,048	3	27	67	1,066	75	323
Livonia city	224	10,791	30	313	492	11,622	40	635	282	6,259	245	1,811

Table C. Incorporated Places, Census Designated Places (CDPs), and Minor Civil Divisions (MCDs) of 10,000 or More Population — **Economic Census**

STATE City, town, township, borough, or CDP (county if applicable)	Retail Trade Number of establish-ments	Number of employees	Wholesale trade[1] Number of establish-ments	Number of employees	Transportation and warehousing Number of establish-ments	Number of employees	Information Number of establish-ments	Number of employees	Finance and insurance Number of establish-ments	Number of employees	Real estate and rental and leasing Number of establish-ments	Number of employees	Professional, scientific, and technical services Number of establish-ments	Number of employees
	1	2	3	4	5	6	7	8	9	10	11	12	13	14
MICHIGAN—Con.														
Lyon charter township	57	1,115	31	838	15	86	7	16	D	D	18	54	44	545
Macomb township............	118	1,868	31	155	64	189	14	77	68	333	33	85	97	340
Madison Heights city	168	3,126	118	2,526	20	852	28	459	33	176	40	491	119	1,663
Marion township	10	48	8	57	7	11	D	D	NA	NA	3	2	11	21
Marquette city.................	131	2,010	12	93	9	80	15	155	65	708	34	188	74	411
Melvindale city................	37	202	13	124	34	406	D	D	D	D	D	D	12	143
Meridian charter township	187	3,584	D	D	13	100	15	88	85	997	47	360	155	698
Midland city....................	200	3,468	35	612	9	160	23	182	84	1,223	51	316	125	2,298
Milford charter township (balance)...................	12	733	21	128	6	140	NA	NA	10	116	13	446	D	D
Monitor charter township ..	29	738	4	D	D	D	NA	NA	15	119	5	6	8	165
Monroe city....................	79	677	17	317	10	144	D	D	35	415	13	42	45	216
Monroe charter township ..	36	586	D	D	6	88	NA	NA	20	91	12	31	13	248
Mount Clemens city	73	460	11	84	13	81	D	D	32	174	D	D	112	415
Mount Morris township	63	518	D	D	9	68	D	D	18	109	15	63	12	61
Mount Pleasant city	117	2,444	22	294	8	187	15	205	57	423	39	1,015	61	470
Mundy township..............	45	829	23	170	11	179	7	44	30	137	13	40	27	389
Muskegon city.................	117	1,699	34	473	22	542	11	75	42	288	19	126	83	768
Muskegon charter township...................	62	1,127	11	87	10	54	7	26	28	145	10	33	18	67
Muskegon Heights city	31	168	D	D	NA	NA	5	61	4	13	NA	NA	7	31
New Baltimore city...........	28	244	7	97	NA	NA	NA	NA	11	50	5	7	12	35
Niles city	41	512	5	77	D	D	4	58	25	163	13	43	D	D
Niles township	40	883	11	76	9	83	D	D	19	143	14	92	14	46
Northville township	59	1,769	D	D	8	35	8	47	35	141	D	D	115	709
Norton Shores city...........	105	1,852	25	331	11	129	14	174	41	273	18	270	41	282
Novi city........................	343	7,145	171	3,161	42	2,129	31	714	129	1,125	79	321	350	5,183
Oakland charter township.	13	197	15	32	D	D	3	2	18	104	17	31	47	121
Oak Park city..................	114	1,166	48	588	14	423	11	145	22	72	23	461	26	250
Oceola township	7	40	6	13	4	22	NA	NA	3	4	4	3	18	50
Orion charter township (balance)...................	80	1,665	35	891	18	179	5	28	29	150	D	D	72	548
Oshtemo charter township	87	2,822	22	354	D	D	12	115	67	402	23	143	66	483
Owosso city	39	311	11	100	NA	NA	D	D	21	113	12	45	23	145
Oxford charter township (balance)...................	26	463	15	56	4	28	5	53	16	96	10	48	35	75
Park township (Ottawa County)	13	68	10	63	8	109	NA	NA	D	D	13	26	37	67
Pittsfield charter township	106	2,709	69	1,433	28	788	32	877	40	303	D	D	142	2,499
Plainfield charter township	114	1,721	37	361	12	76	8	33	75	510	42	145	89	814
Plymouth charter township	66	1,543	74	1,896	26	435	16	172	48	1,135	D	D	136	2,380
Pontiac city	197	1,966	41	774	30	1,027	D	D	D	D	37	198	48	3,042
Portage city....................	296	5,658	50	1,213	24	352	18	323	141	2,264	56	1,375	136	1,453
Port Huron city................	100	1,168	22	247	26	367	19	235	46	736	19	708	68	400
Port Huron charter township...................	44	635	16	244	14	285	NA	NA	6	33	D	D	6	36
Redford charter township .	169	1,473	51	570	13	56	11	186	37	178	D	D	45	476
Riverview city..................	30	191	12	149	9	109	NA	NA	D	D	D	D	12	51
Rochester city.................	69	574	13	58	6	171	8	285	54	338	34	147	108	1,650
Rochester Hills city..........	252	5,660	86	861	21	103	26	187	90	476	54	318	236	3,533
Romulus city...................	79	814	71	1,806	203	17,603	D	D	D	D	41	898	16	173
Roseville city..................	233	4,877	44	780	23	166	D	D	33	261	35	231	44	212
Royal Oak city.................	210	2,419	50	312	19	220	40	588	82	553	81	412	292	2,200
Saginaw city...................	133	738	30	548	20	292	20	744	35	557	20	97	75	693
Saginaw charter township	231	3,982	32	378	11	277	19	372	112	759	46	285	121	983
St. Clair Shores city	171	1,880	33	183	8	55	8	61	76	494	44	137	168	766
Sault Ste. Marie city.........	92	1,335	16	239	13	28	D	D	34	256	13	46	26	176
Scio township (balance) ...	68	1,603	41	572	8	150	15	1,228	28	146	D	D	114	692
Shelby charter township ...	283	4,924	80	1,186	60	333	20	110	124	667	70	325	197	3,036
Southfield city	362	5,298	124	2,349	56	1,162	177	6,338	308	9,416	233	2,549	720	14,277
Southgate city.................	123	2,586	9	29	23	223	6	238	43	253	D	D	27	235
South Lyon city	30	374	NA	NA	NA	NA	5	12	19	73	7	21	14	40
Springfield charter township...................	16	153	11	37	3	11	NA	NA	3	7	7	12	26	69
Spring Lake township	29	292	D	D	7	21	D	D	12	41	7	14	31	112
Sterling Heights city.........	458	6,921	153	1,877	198	889	54	1,787	153	1,767	105	693	255	7,854
Sturgis city.....................	67	1,081	14	206	8	37	D	D	29	195	8	30	28	720
Summit township	43	527	7	27	8	99	D	D	D	D	15	85	40	305
Superior charter township	10	56	6	9	NA	NA	NA	NA	D	D	D	D	30	261
Taylor city......................	290	4,978	61	962	93	1,617	25	297	44	235	52	359	81	791
Texas charter township.....	27	228	10	78	D	D	NA	NA	D	D	10	70	34	74
Thomas township	36	796	4	D	5	37	NA	NA	D	D	4	13	13	45
Traverse City city	263	3,382	43	457	23	342	48	439	125	1,932	90	370	217	1,190
Trenton city	57	385	7	69	D	D	6	14	25	104	D	D	27	97
Troy city.........................	582	12,256	320	7,383	71	970	135	5,427	438	10,189	181	1,354	902	16,472
Tyrone township (Livingston County).......	7	47	NA	NA	8	80	NA	NA	NA	NA	6	8	11	20
Union charter township.....	40	690	8	68	8	128	8	85	11	100	14	92	11	83
Van Buren charter township...................	68	1,619	24	822	39	1,478	D	D	24	1,401	D	D	28	567
Vienna charter township...	37	1,012	D	D	NA	NA	6	32	13	53	5	16	8	37
Walker city.....................	120	2,445	79	2,531	43	1,536	14	698	51	400	31	126	54	433
Warren city.....................	463	5,697	180	4,105	162	3,636	36	609	97	757	95	982	172	21,392
Washington township........	61	1,075	9	73	11	71	9	30	34	149	D	D	52	1,149
Waterford charter township	255	3,090	58	495	52	905	21	184	82	519	71	287	130	584
Wayne city......................	74	640	14	217	22	1,091	D	D	D	D	D	D	14	69
West Bloomfield charter township...................	180	1,830	50	87	30	72	29	348	77	424	87	1,697	246	793
Westland city..................	277	4,331	52	507	48	354	21	290	52	275	D	D	64	285

1   Merchant wholesalers, except manufacturers' sales branches and offices.

Table C. Incorporated Places, Census Designated Places (CDPs), and Minor Civil Divisions (MCDs) of 10,000 or More Population — **Economic Census**

STATE City, town, township, borough, or CDP (county if applicable)	Administration and support and waste management and mediation services		Educational services		Health care and social assistance		Arts, entertainment, and recreation		Accommodation and food services		Other services (except public administration)	
	Number of establishments	Number of employees	Number of establishments	Number of employees	Number of establishments	Number of employees	Number of establishments	Number of employees	Number of establishments	Number of employees	Number of establishments	Number of employees
	15	16	17	18	19	20	21	22	23	24	25	26
MICHIGAN—Con.												
Lyon charter township	35	217	D	D	31	336	11	181	36	514	D	D
Macomb township	97	836	9	42	168	1,023	D	D	85	1,600	69	501
Madison Heights city	64	3,461	12	184	115	2,645	10	74	114	1,890	88	543
Marion township	12	52	NA	NA	7	75	NA	NA	6	37	17	83
Marquette city	32	258	D	D	154	4,267	13	87	88	2,008	59	295
Melvindale city	10	315	NA	NA	D	D	NA	NA	25	266	D	D
Meridian charter township	41	453	20	136	155	2,383	17	537	118	2,167	74	483
Midland city	52	1,102	D	D	249	6,583	24	394	126	2,973	104	845
Milford charter township (balance)	32	406	NA	NA	34	540	NA	NA	8	84	18	58
Monitor charter township	12	85	NA	NA	26	413	D	D	15	338	8	24
Monroe city	24	779	NA	NA	98	1,924	4	152	55	991	38	158
Monroe charter township	9	80	D	D	29	931	D	D	18	259	15	91
Mount Clemens city	29	640	NA	NA	89	3,250	D	D	D	D	56	410
Mount Morris township	18	409	5	12	47	634	D	D	30	864	31	170
Mount Pleasant city	14	128	D	D	159	2,200	D	D	D	D	50	317
Mundy township	27	1,481	NA	NA	36	662	NA	NA	30	859	17	83
Muskegon city	22	275	5	16	118	7,161	14	260	85	1,442	58	428
Muskegon charter township	13	1,615	NA	NA	34	533	5	47	44	837	24	140
Muskegon Heights city	3	25	NA	NA	15	417	NA	NA	13	188	13	66
New Baltimore city	6	12	NA	NA	40	855	8	9	21	362	28	125
Niles city	11	270	NA	NA	42	474	D	D	34	528	25	170
Niles township	13	83	NA	NA	21	407	5	31	D	D	19	62
Northville township	30	120	10	41	64	1,226	14	117	49	1,075	39	212
Norton Shores city	17	1,771	4	34	91	1,352	10	100	48	1,115	38	280
Novi city	101	2,206	24	192	296	7,623	32	847	187	4,586	119	1,192
Oakland charter township	13	45	6	13	D	D	6	91	11	157	9	41
Oak Park city	42	614	D	D	98	827	4	26	45	551	D	D
Oceola township	10	42	3	2	8	91	NA	NA	3	42	D	D
Orion charter township (balance)	56	767	8	72	87	1,003	13	245	41	1,049	52	335
Oshtemo charter township	33	1,419	6	32	90	1,969	6	25	53	1,440	38	274
Owosso city	11	119	NA	NA	51	1,811	9	73	33	536	33	187
Oxford charter township (balance)	26	99	4	D	31	447	5	62	16	293	D	D
Park township (Ottawa County)	NA	NA	3	7	17	192	9	161	12	172	11	46
Pittsfield charter township	51	1,892	15	123	D	D	16	169	78	1,772	48	427
Plainfield charter township	42	1,017	14	102	76	866	13	451	58	1,415	55	311
Plymouth charter township	35	577	5	D	65	525	15	259	59	1,460	44	244
Pontiac city	58	1,065	D	D	140	6,071	14	66	98	1,458	68	577
Portage city	74	1,286	16	310	198	2,769	15	288	152	3,547	101	795
Port Huron city	25	666	5	32	158	4,564	D	D	53	967	38	197
Port Huron charter township	16	217	4	61	19	495	4	32	22	513	21	104
Redford charter township	39	1,858	D	D	85	2,727	9	134	75	1,123	80	322
Riverview city	5	14	3	53	45	1,328	NA	NA	16	232	D	D
Rochester city	35	339	16	191	94	2,227	11	464	60	1,554	69	422
Rochester Hills city	103	2,173	19	132	327	3,839	28	239	154	3,301	111	774
Romulus city	43	1,899	NA	NA	53	850	NA	NA	82	3,020	51	633
Roseville city	49	610	5	118	143	1,479	6	98	105	2,898	83	411
Royal Oak city	82	1,202	19	201	221	11,738	27	204	177	3,633	138	774
Saginaw city	43	1,048	4	28	173	10,734	10	204	75	1,356	60	436
Saginaw charter township	45	5,787	12	126	245	4,409	19	235	105	2,571	94	576
St. Clair Shores city	64	1,325	7	D	261	3,285	23	179	D	D	117	716
Sault Ste. Marie city	8	56	NA	NA	70	2,032	11	99	58	3,353	D	D
Scio township (balance)	46	3,044	D	D	D	D	D	D	D	D	41	387
Shelby charter township	118	2,021	21	258	263	2,422	27	552	197	3,786	153	874
Southfield city	277	22,837	33	390	719	13,913	24	337	244	4,307	177	1,164
Southgate city	19	410	4	92	99	1,513	8	159	86	2,135	D	D
South Lyon city	12	25	3	13	36	343	5	75	34	490	25	122
Springfield charter township	23	287	NA	NA	D	D	4	24	4	23	D	D
Spring Lake township	14	135	4	28	27	470	D	D	25	490	D	D
Sterling Heights city	182	7,053	20	198	453	6,039	28	295	262	5,168	215	1,092
Sturgis city	8	205	NA	NA	30	771	3	33	33	474	23	101
Summit township	10	679	3	20	D	D	D	D	37	726	21	125
Superior charter township	17	159	NA	NA	37	622	NA	NA	7	42	12	162
Taylor city	68	3,188	13	136	141	3,198	17	218	151	2,919	109	1,028
Texas charter township	8	51	3	23	18	163	6	193	26	584	D	D
Thomas township	10	115	4	9	18	339	7	81	22	498	D	D
Traverse City city	66	673	12	105	236	7,250	26	382	145	2,671	117	836
Trenton city	17	153	NA	NA	77	1,891	NA	NA	39	687	28	152
Troy city	443	21,054	51	852	499	12,559	38	626	319	7,054	243	2,000
Tyrone township (Livingston County)	8	26	NA	NA	5	93	4	12	NA	NA	4	2
Union charter township	8	596	NA	NA	26	620	7	121	D	D	21	139
Van Buren charter township	26	764	3	11	31	327	D	D	44	1,150	23	167
Vienna charter township	8	72	NA	NA	35	504	7	53	24	486	D	D
Walker city	50	1,053	7	56	70	1,198	D	D	76	2,247	67	761
Warren city	142	3,650	8	43	447	7,385	24	301	295	5,414	260	1,305
Washington township	33	395	NA	NA	52	345	6	36	40	691	D	D
Waterford charter township	100	1,057	18	76	179	2,837	D	D	134	2,631	179	885
Wayne city	17	626	NA	NA	52	2,577	NA	NA	33	528	D	D
West Bloomfield charter township	71	522	26	132	290	6,132	36	608	96	1,637	105	422
Westland city	68	874	3	D	190	2,733	15	236	153	2,911	129	851

Table C. Incorporated Places, Census Designated Places (CDPs), and Minor Civil Divisions (MCDs) of 10,000 or More Population — Economic Census

	Economic activity by sector, 2017													
STATE City, town, township, borough, or CDP (county if applicable)	Retail Trade		Wholesale trade¹		Transportation and warehousing		Information		Finance and insurance		Real estate and rental and leasing		Professional, scientific, and technical services	
	Number of establish-ments	Number of employees	Number of establish-ments	Number of employees	Number of establish-ments	Number of employees	Number of establish-ments	Number of employees	Number of establish-ments	Number of employees	Number of establish-ments	Number of employees	Number of establish-ments	Number of employees
	1	2	3	4	5	6	7	8	9	10	11	12	13	14
MICHIGAN—Con.													
White Lake charter township	75	1,977	11	25	12	75	NA	NA	22	83	D	D	41	150
Wixom city	47	1,268	135	2,973	23	287	9	191	26	271	20	171	84	1,318
Woodhaven city	64	2,199	D	D	14	95	D	D	18	100	D	D	8	31
Wyandotte city	76	510	7	36	12	541	8	31	19	262	D	D	40	149
Wyoming city	251	4,629	176	4,245	85	3,418	29	188	101	870	60	540	117	822
Ypsilanti city	56	383	5	50	17	1,341	5	5	20	61	D	D	35	440
Ypsilanti charter township	114	1,542	15	672	24	345	D	D	32	113	D	D	46	461
Zeeland charter township	19	178	17	357	18	497	NA	NA	D	D	5	8	13	34
MINNESOTA	18,827	302,886	6,397	108,895	4,835	88,812	2,788	61,911	9,584	166,181	7,218	38,077	16,689	186,597
Albert Lea city	104	1,777	20	345	26	276	D	D	40	345	D	D	31	148
Alexandria city	140	2,376	19	432	20	127	13	184	68	326	31	127	59	352
Andover city	47	949	17	62	15	259	NA	NA	D	D	60	184	66	157
Anoka city	58	624	20	507	16	286	D	D	44	350	D	D	57	309
Apple Valley city	118	3,478	23	121	22	136	18	154	D	D	67	176	160	469
Arden Hills city	24	416	28	466	NA	NA	10	180	34	530	18	35	52	568
Austin city	87	1,517	7	38	14	368	10	107	41	231	17	215	D	D
Bemidji city	158	2,667	21	304	19	286	13	323	55	380	D	D	48	382
Big Lake city	29	375	3	D	7	67	D	D	D	D	9	38	10	38
Blaine city	227	4,730	69	1,107	67	995	D	D	D	D	80	198	D	D
Bloomington city	529	11,577	193	5,285	87	1,664	87	3,370	408	9,754	199	4,618	542	9,590
Brainerd city	113	1,116	21	286	19	224	D	D	41	807	23	80	D	D
Brooklyn Center city	64	2,053	23	597	D	D	11	80	16	104	34	148	60	490
Brooklyn Park city	153	4,081	89	1,645	56	1,796	18	315	D	D	70	395	135	738
Buffalo city	77	1,514	7	86	6	17	D	D	33	159	22	31	50	224
Burnsville city	325	6,637	151	2,570	40	1,285	29	541	116	965	124	675	268	1,786
Champlin city	32	641	15	231	D	D	6	52	D	D	33	99	64	204
Chanhassen city	69	1,462	51	1,773	7	36	21	397	D	D	43	358	136	3,125
Chaska city	45	814	25	315	7	205	8	105	D	D	D	D	83	678
Cloquet city	47	636	D	D	D	D	D	D	26	188	6	67	17	68
Columbia Heights city	41	521	9	78	11	76	D	D	D	D	11	42	D	D
Coon Rapids city	192	4,948	33	405	33	759	17	195	83	549	70	241	118	866
Cottage Grove city	49	1,136	11	339	21	296	D	D	D	D	D	D	47	103
Crystal city	64	836	11	91	D	D	D	D	11	65	15	94	25	77
Duluth city	405	6,344	94	1,041	61	1,415	52	1,223	162	2,807	137	638	D	D
Eagan city	265	5,074	146	2,657	143	5,672	60	5,872	137	7,780	141	770	346	3,219
East Bethel city	16	99	8	47	9	45	NA	NA	5	25	18	15	16	12
Eden Prairie city	224	6,654	170	4,053	42	1,317	86	2,255	202	6,748	131	820	436	4,273
Edina city	277	5,064	108	934	18	200	57	1,262	238	2,148	225	1,665	D	D
Elk River city	93	1,778	23	140	28	428	D	D	51	301	43	110	79	436
Fairmont city	68	1,096	D	D	9	105	3	49	35	247	D	D	30	153
Faribault city	96	1,618	10	231	22	643	10	131	37	531	24	81	44	331
Farmington city	25	246	10	89	16	378	D	D	D	D	13	13	43	159
Fergus Falls city	84	1,544	20	181	15	257	D	D	50	230	17	42	41	217
Forest Lake city	91	1,954	D	D	9	55	9	61	D	D	35	242	44	188
Fridley city	81	2,035	67	1,923	24	1,476	D	D	D	D	32	415	65	282
Golden Valley city	81	2,051	75	1,291	14	1,507	40	838	118	4,711	63	481	D	D
Grand Rapids city	100	1,581	15	66	8	183	10	99	51	285	19	80	54	435
Ham Lake city	31	225	19	154	17	112	D	D	D	D	21	44	58	142
Hastings city	59	1,263	11	110	11	602	D	D	D	D	D	D	41	174
Hibbing city	70	1,103	32	388	14	645	8	90	35	177	14	55	40	282
Hopkins city	74	880	42	1,026	D	D	12	258	D	D	38	483	76	1,942
Hugo city	17	322	12	174	9	11	NA	NA	13	54	13	20	26	68
Hutchinson city	83	1,524	15	380	10	176	6	123	45	208	19	84	34	184
Inver Grove Heights city	74	1,979	18	152	24	415	D	D	D	D	34	134	81	445
Lakeville city	108	2,799	59	856	40	600	D	D	94	565	91	308	196	556
Lino Lakes city	34	550	24	475	13	273	4	23	D	D	35	79	65	182
Little Canada city	34	721	16	226	D	D	4	24	D	D	26	195	45	602
Mankato city	267	5,849	53	915	35	886	D	D	117	948	72	561	D	D
Maple Grove city	229	5,183	97	2,632	34	1,408	32	720	149	884	117	265	314	1,435
Maplewood city	215	4,384	37	379	17	276	D	D	D	D	D	D	85	351
Marshall city	90	1,579	22	409	16	519	10	199	D	D	D	D	34	299
Mendota Heights city	22	233	40	855	15	287	11	111	59	1,392	16	82	103	1,309
Minneapolis city	1,135	13,609	466	7,907	185	16,037	435	12,832	933	43,011	794	5,194	2,555	36,745
Minnetonka city	288	6,346	115	1,814	D	D	74	3,133	269	11,623	160	1,085	436	4,098
Monticello city	56	1,566	13	329	5	84	D	D	D	D	22	52	32	106
Moorhead city	107	2,123	27	569	26	176	10	81	65	269	33	149	D	D
Mounds View city	24	375	14	803	7	308	NA	NA	D	D	D	D	25	312
New Brighton city	41	607	35	855	20	661	10	102	D	D	D	D	88	1,163
New Hope city	51	1,389	52	966	D	D	8	22	37	223	36	229	58	300
New Ulm city	63	1,270	12	89	25	981	8	152	34	286	15	163	36	391
North Branch city	60	776	12	171	D	D	NA	NA	15	69	11	27	D	D
Northfield city	56	853	12	675	8	151	5	17	25	200	21	132	47	229
North Mankato city	23	468	17	272	14	355	D	D	19	92	14	110	16	298
North St. Paul city	20	271	6	39	8	29	5	50	10	97	8	12	D	D
Oakdale city	60	1,891	38	728	14	546	13	393	77	840	32	71	89	1,107
Otsego city	18	404	8	36	16	204	NA	NA	11	39	14	27	26	104
Owatonna city	106	2,014	16	305	19	376	16	932	D	D	20	253	37	158
Plymouth city	186	3,574	186	5,545	D	D	58	1,101	207	4,773	167	976	489	7,686
Prior Lake city	48	431	14	55	14	97	8	13	46	149	30	77	97	261
Ramsey city	64	563	30	504	20	293	4	70	D	D	29	37	42	178
Red Wing city	98	1,357	11	90	17	178	6	81	35	634	22	108	36	670
Richfield city	110	3,253	12	77	D	D	16	135	D	D	32	162	96	601
Robbinsdale city	35	234	6	28	NA	NA	4	9	D	D	24	39	32	119
Rochester city	493	10,464	72	790	63	1,500	55	2,076	204	1,662	155	716	D	D
Rogers city	58	1,255	41	1,295	24	397	D	D	D	D	30	67	58	731
Rosemount city	39	397	17	150	24	898	D	D	D	D	17	36	71	986
Roseville city	281	6,334	78	1,157	49	1,849	40	2,181	83	1,457	65	391	187	1,787

1 Merchant wholesalers, except manufacturers' sales branches and offices.

Table C. Incorporated Places, Census Designated Places (CDPs), and Minor Civil Divisions (MCDs) of 10,000 or More Population — Economic Census

	Economic activity by sector, 2017											
	Administration and support and waste management and mediation services		Educational services		Health care and social assistance		Arts, entertainment, and recreation		Accommodation and food services		Other services (except public administration)	
STATE City, town, township, borough, or CDP (county if applicable)	Number of establishments	Number of employees	Number of establishments	Number of employees	Number of establishments	Number of employees	Number of establishments	Number of employees	Number of establishments	Number of employees	Number of establishments	Number of employees
	15	16	17	18	19	20	21	22	23	24	25	26
MICHIGAN—Con.												
White Lake charter township	51	168	7	78	35	340	7	43	33	684	D	D
Wixom city	51	807	D	D	23	130	10	140	36	596	35	258
Woodhaven city	7	44	NA	NA	47	587	7	131	48	1,443	D	D
Wyandotte city	25	300	5	17	58	2,832	6	31	67	846	50	238
Wyoming city	91	3,356	11	330	149	5,085	19	665	143	2,763	119	1,167
Ypsilanti city	19	342	D	D	54	6,331	6	43	64	1,125	26	96
Ypsilanti charter township	49	442	6	33	94	1,211	10	114	85	1,536	52	288
Zeeland charter township	18	254	NA	NA	D	D	NA	NA	7	117	D	D
MINNESOTA	7,787	172,358	1,408	17,321	17,066	473,338	3,012	48,380	12,022	239,194	11,339	77,400
Albert Lea city	20	329	NA	NA	62	2,137	D	D	53	853	45	270
Alexandria city	28	398	NA	NA	125	3,401	19	140	61	1,183	62	336
Andover city	36	412	D	D	59	717	12	362	34	582	D	D
Anoka city	29	654	D	D	56	1,580	9	108	44	860	37	313
Apple Valley city	66	466	16	889	147	2,011	20	D	81	2,022	66	629
Arden Hills city	18	873	D	D	25	849	D	D	26	547	17	87
Austin city	27	453	D	D	82	2,369	8	176	54	870	57	329
Bemidji city	18	217	7	38	115	2,451	21	101	74	1,725	54	309
Big Lake city	17	29	NA	NA	27	449	5	31	18	357	D	D
Blaine city	99	13,550	18	261	135	2,826	25	480	D	D	136	1,068
Bloomington city	272	15,774	43	749	296	7,142	52	1,329	286	8,771	200	2,179
Brainerd city	19	483	NA	NA	98	3,430	9	144	43	602	48	286
Brooklyn Center city	41	1,719	D	D	141	2,781	6	115	59	1,067	27	344
Brooklyn Park city	119	3,351	17	305	176	4,282	18	159	101	1,675	93	638
Buffalo city	28	232	3	32	75	2,288	D	D	43	787	36	222
Burnsville city	114	1,423	22	211	269	6,896	46	1,166	134	2,830	133	821
Champlin city	22	109	D	D	49	566	10	179	32	720	D	D
Chanhassen city	43	718	18	235	76	1,324	17	847	56	1,132	65	482
Chaska city	31	328	9	58	76	1,330	6	167	41	700	34	222
Cloquet city	11	76	NA	NA	54	1,120	9	50	28	435	33	132
Columbia Heights city	30	625	NA	NA	49	787	NA	NA	37	569	25	102
Coon Rapids city	64	3,303	5	35	200	7,113	22	454	115	2,968	104	896
Cottage Grove city	27	259	5	31	63	729	4	17	42	667	43	265
Crystal city	24	726	6	27	79	1,025	4	23	34	557	48	338
Duluth city	74	1,644	28	147	470	17,433	63	950	254	6,157	185	1,372
Eagan city	99	2,050	29	709	206	5,045	28	D	176	3,519	155	1,725
East Bethel city	19	35	NA	NA	D	D	3	43	5	134	D	D
Eden Prairie city	110	2,027	39	346	186	3,152	50	1,066	154	3,507	148	1,152
Edina city	122	8,302	43	374	424	9,300	34	1,153	127	3,340	141	1,451
Elk River city	43	800	5	26	83	2,006	D	D	D	D	50	316
Fairmont city	13	203	NA	NA	64	1,392	11	60	38	712	33	88
Faribault city	21	178	D	D	94	1,923	12	122	54	983	51	271
Farmington city	24	121	3	38	D	D	D	D	21	439	23	103
Fergus Falls city	15	81	D	D	104	2,770	12	137	49	782	48	247
Forest Lake city	26	230	4	38	59	763	15	898	43	1,175	56	428
Fridley city	46	2,208	6	21	95	3,034	8	513	D	D	59	486
Golden Valley city	84	2,478	12	D	174	4,992	15	340	73	1,458	67	853
Grand Rapids city	16	436	D	D	117	2,468	D	D	52	996	46	287
Ham Lake city	33	433	NA	NA	23	118	10	178	16	223	D	D
Hastings city	22	256	7	33	55	1,215	D	D	44	790	48	326
Hibbing city	18	312	NA	NA	64	2,641	8	21	27	587	31	300
Hopkins city	36	790	7	25	61	6,892	17	303	52	967	68	413
Hugo city	23	147	NA	NA	34	294	NA	NA	14	233	D	D
Hutchinson city	9	236	D	D	75	1,808	D	D	40	779	29	218
Inver Grove Heights city	66	557	D	D	75	1,454	D	D	47	959	54	405
Lakeville city	93	1,241	23	177	120	1,685	17	585	73	2,040	89	599
Lino Lakes city	11	51	D	D	33	329	NA	NA	16	573	26	130
Little Canada city	29	979	4	59	37	855	D	D	23	352	36	237
Mankato city	42	964	8	71	228	7,128	33	564	151	4,014	85	806
Maple Grove city	101	1,007	28	219	212	4,452	25	476	122	3,673	147	1,617
Maplewood city	37	804	8	78	212	5,254	20	241	98	2,028	74	450
Marshall city	21	199	4	16	67	1,652	9	150	47	937	37	179
Mendota Heights city	43	958	7	71	D	D	8	138	20	1,231	27	236
Minneapolis city	724	25,558	204	3,873	1,392	60,986	313	6,730	1,298	30,932	1,033	10,041
Minnetonka city	178	4,651	38	323	233	4,100	31	788	101	2,445	123	837
Monticello city	12	486	NA	NA	50	1,151	5	48	39	872	39	250
Moorhead city	35	545	D	D	151	4,001	D	D	71	1,425	78	386
Mounds View city	8	85	NA	NA	28	347	5	128	20	324	D	D
New Brighton city	26	547	7	25	98	2,104	12	146	27	643	53	327
New Hope city	22	278	4	D	72	1,925	D	D	44	826	29	142
New Ulm city	17	109	4	23	52	1,653	15	160	41	759	39	156
North Branch city	12	70	NA	NA	52	910	6	30	24	439	21	95
Northfield city	19	156	7	49	D	D	9	177	52	990	39	231
North Mankato city	17	455	D	D	42	676	D	D	16	310	D	D
North St. Paul city	16	789	NA	NA	31	619	6	48	23	167	25	125
Oakdale city	36	378	6	67	81	1,102	15	487	44	1,459	38	138
Otsego city	22	185	3	D	16	203	7	42	11	234	D	D
Owatonna city	24	287	D	D	120	2,457	12	132	72	1,448	63	422
Plymouth city	148	5,788	33	736	286	5,263	34	729	127	2,954	131	1,101
Prior Lake city	50	349	5	9	45	590	D	D	D	D	D	D
Ramsey city	33	604	6	23	D	D	8	73	21	362	29	180
Red Wing city	20	630	8	59	84	2,197	11	247	51	2,328	42	225
Richfield city	55	735	11	49	124	2,753	10	111	69	1,357	66	742
Robbinsdale city	D	D	8	58	64	5,459	5	54	21	338	D	D
Rochester city	132	2,660	33	346	431	20,978	54	979	308	7,631	216	1,850
Rogers city	45	811	5	37	35	591	8	64	36	881	D	D
Rosemount city	25	163	7	105	D	D	10	49	28	600	37	225
Roseville city	66	1,295	14	136	202	3,857	19	289	121	3,509	112	1,143

Table C. Incorporated Places, Census Designated Places (CDPs), and Minor Civil Divisions (MCDs) of 10,000 or More Population — **Economic Census**

STATE City, town, township, borough, or CDP (county if applicable)	Retail Trade		Wholesale trade[1]		Transportation and warehousing		Information		Finance and insurance		Real estate and rental and leasing		Professional, scientific, and technical services	
	Number of establishments	Number of employees	Number of establishments	Number of employees	Number of establishments	Number of employees	Number of establishments	Number of employees	Number of establishments	Number of employees	Number of establishments	Number of employees	Number of establishments	Number of employees
	1	2	3	4	5	6	7	8	9	10	11	12	13	14
MINNESOTA—Con.														
St. Cloud city	326	6,467	84	2,399	49	3,323	43	1,295	155	2,750	117	606	D	D
St. Louis Park city	183	4,203	89	1,412	D	D	56	887	149	2,466	148	1,005	352	3,666
St. Michael city	31	375	D	D	14	134	NA	NA	16	51	19	29	54	123
St. Paul city	725	9,284	246	6,243	132	1,915	149	5,505	276	12,836	393	2,413	939	7,440
St. Peter city	41	472	D	D	5	6	NA	NA	16	108	9	12	16	126
Sartell city	36	355	5	18	D	D	D	D	31	250	14	41	29	307
Sauk Rapids city	39	638	13	667	D	D	3	27	16	97	8	25	26	141
Savage city	70	991	49	894	19	135	7	23	31	126	45	155	111	268
Shakopee city	109	2,354	56	1,566	27	2,545	12	309	43	206	52	151	96	1,003
Shoreview city	32	620	16	567	D	D	9	228	46	1,933	D	D	100	425
South St. Paul city	42	1,007	24	460	16	213	NA	NA	D	D	21	84	31	210
Stillwater city	90	1,079	22	330	D	D	9	24	47	290	D	D	120	442
Vadnais Heights city	33	1,196	30	507	10	126	D	D	D	D	D	D	40	472
Waconia city	33	782	12	61	D	D	9	46	D	D	D	D	38	218
West St. Paul city	95	1,719	7	37	9	136	D	D	35	148	D	D	51	154
White Bear township	11	295	15	323	NA	NA	NA	NA	D	D	14	220	33	93
White Bear Lake city	85	1,516	28	216	9	25	10	82	62	358	D	D	85	610
Willmar city	127	2,394	45	713	14	213	14	275	46	376	26	68	D	D
Winona city	104	2,126	27	301	25	751	D	D	41	435	28	89	52	232
Woodbury city	255	5,566	33	303	20	327	23	722	126	1,394	98	585	279	1,119
Worthington city	71	1,264	18	205	11	259	8	82	27	181	D	D	D	D
MISSISSIPPI	11,525	141,410	2,347	32,051	2,121	39,819	1,019	14,262	4,715	33,499	2,403	9,683	4,746	30,477
Bay St. Louis city	38	205	D	D	D	D	6	40	22	104	12	27	29	187
Biloxi city	205	2,578	32	226	19	114	19	254	77	630	56	231	138	984
Brandon city	96	1,580	18	384	D	D	8	50	53	467	33	69	75	273
Brookhaven city	145	1,716	D	D	11	1,139	D	D	59	329	D	D	40	267
Byram city	43	1,053	D	D	7	52	NA	NA	21	103	6	10	20	181
Canton city	78	966	20	248	18	1,510	5	26	23	103	14	59	22	72
Clarksdale city	93	875	21	226	14	116	11	68	D	D	30	84	27	161
Cleveland city	104	1,213	10	107	10	177	D	D	D	D	24	73	38	140
Clinton city	89	1,236	14	49	D	D	D	D	50	254	37	117	56	256
Columbus city	236	3,095	52	940	37	418	17	341	103	489	45	161	70	366
Corinth city	136	1,633	29	486	10	109	D	D	61	257	17	138	39	791
D'Iberville city	88	2,126	10	47	4	9	D	D	35	160	17	61	18	85
Gautier city	52	640	5	13	3	94	D	D	25	136	D	D	17	76
Greenville city	166	2,238	30	336	32	464	D	D	67	305	31	113	59	250
Greenwood city	144	1,588	D	D	11	124	12	124	D	D	29	96	D	D
Grenada city	98	1,200	D	D	14	130	D	D	48	192	21	71	D	D
Gulfport city	382	5,972	78	868	59	1,147	42	510	150	1,601	111	575	183	1,154
Hattiesburg city	454	6,900	73	822	40	652	40	535	183	1,352	104	507	163	1,519
Hernando city	66	993	13	115	13	146	D	D	30	162	9	23	37	131
Horn Lake city	84	1,341	D	D	D	D	D	D	24	116	23	83	14	65
Jackson city	624	8,303	216	2,962	97	2,780	125	2,490	379	5,041	222	1,037	576	4,964
Laurel city	183	2,415	39	495	D	D	D	D	86	457	35	118	54	339
Long Beach city	38	308	6	60	NA	NA	NA	NA	14	68	12	32	19	69
McComb city	147	2,143	19	135	NA	NA	D	D	73	366	29	130	46	162
Madison city	97	2,097	20	102	9	82	14	1,219	78	454	D	D	138	592
Meridian city	314	4,497	50	1,315	33	813	D	D	149	961	66	321	112	870
Moss Point city	42	352	7	56	5	14	D	D	15	153	NA	NA	12	243
Natchez city	122	1,767	26	180	11	568	15	147	64	377	33	111	46	220
Ocean Springs city	113	1,482	11	82	4	19	D	D	44	208	38	185	74	430
Olive Branch city	148	2,660	55	1,592	71	4,231	D	D	60	302	27	81	39	151
Oxford city	195	2,866	14	222	9	44	D	D	D	D	55	219	115	896
Pascagoula city	115	1,792	25	171	14	190	D	D	58	414	27	116	77	653
Pearl city	172	2,756	52	680	25	351	8	113	55	489	37	216	25	147
Petal city	52	753	4	53	7	79	NA	NA	D	D	12	44	23	81
Picayune city	97	1,452	8	64	4	47	7	39	52	252	16	52	27	241
Ridgeland city	282	3,621	68	1,059	15	518	51	1,954	214	2,663	89	398	197	2,341
Southaven city	274	4,680	33	1,381	58	2,852	13	167	86	553	50	208	79	497
Starkville city	150	2,088	13	822	9	26	D	D	D	D	50	229	65	428
Tupelo city	380	6,235	113	1,633	65	1,355	D	D	158	1,841	78	340	160	983
Vicksburg city	178	2,366	28	218	20	759	D	D	D	D	31	128	73	404
West Point city	71	715	D	D	D	D	D	D	30	157	10	23	D	D
Yazoo City city	68	853	16	187	D	D	D	D	26	146	13	48	14	167
MISSOURI	20,694	312,616	6,293	95,156	4,884	88,413	2,701	60,546	10,747	141,494	6,644	37,144	14,171	161,595
Affton CDP	34	386	15	288	19	137	D	D	D	D	9	62	21	119
Arnold city	87	2,043	19	224	20	169	D	D	60	364	29	88	45	260
Ballwin city	83	1,667	12	49	13	44	D	D	D	D	29	82	69	111
Bellefontaine Neighbors city	11	128	D	D	3	26	NA	NA	NA	NA	D	D	5	18
Belton city	72	1,546	17	225	7	291	8	78	30	124	27	137	31	234
Blue Springs city	157	3,621	39	355	22	196	17	353	D	D	70	656	119	464
Bolivar city	62	904	8	472	7	13	D	D	26	173	11	49	35	1,383
Branson city	302	4,019	D	D	7	110	22	280	46	375	D	D	65	328
Bridgeton city	93	2,506	54	823	48	2,064	D	D	44	872	34	203	41	528
Cape Girardeau city	286	4,769	67	793	D	D	D	D	132	1,010	89	264	120	864
Carthage city	53	1,004	7	76	D	D	D	D	47	287	14	60	21	126
Chesterfield city	380	5,835	137	1,932	40	528	46	852	362	5,883	129	852	403	14,366
Clayton city	70	521	27	1,037	12	54	24	577	275	6,498	113	1,134	D	D
Columbia city	494	10,223	112	1,441	55	1,233	82	1,538	274	7,510	228	1,163	367	4,365
Concord CDP	65	1,422	8	39	17	365	D	D	D	D	21	41	44	223
Crestwood city	44	713	12	360	3	15	D	D	D	D	21	54	57	416
Creve Coeur city	108	2,504	50	738	25	255	32	1,580	211	3,184	102	1,419	250	3,710
Dardenne Prairie city	8	356	8	34	4	7	D	D	D	D	10	12	26	64
Eureka city	48	745	14	58	5	4	6	19	D	D	11	24	40	165
Excelsior Springs city	50	828	7	25	7	363	5	47	22	79	D	D	D	D

1 Merchant wholesalers, except manufacturers' sales branches and offices.

Table C. Incorporated Places, Census Designated Places (CDPs), and Minor Civil Divisions (MCDs) of 10,000 or More Population — **Economic Census**

STATE City, town, township, borough, or CDP (county if applicable)	Administration and support and waste management and mediation services		Educational services		Health care and social assistance		Arts, entertainment, and recreation		Accommodation and food services		Other services (except public administration)	
	Number of establishments	Number of employees	Number of establishments	Number of employees	Number of establishments	Number of employees	Number of establishments	Number of employees	Number of establishments	Number of employees	Number of establishments	Number of employees
	15	16	17	18	19	20	21	22	23	24	25	26
MINNESOTA—Con.												
St. Cloud city	86	2,333	18	134	284	13,312	41	529	180	4,324	142	1,217
St. Louis Park city	107	3,159	D	D	234	9,950	34	668	96	2,412	143	1,088
St. Michael city	32	342	NA	NA	27	221	9	41	12	174	D	D
St. Paul city	327	9,692	97	1,218	1,112	45,769	152	4,543	674	13,422	634	5,191
St. Peter city	5	69	NA	NA	40	1,807	NA	NA	23	381	17	243
Sartell city	D	D	5	19	72	2,420	11	154	18	377	13	59
Sauk Rapids city	D	D	NA	NA	46	1,043	6	D	16	337	D	D
Savage city	45	402	11	104	67	836	11	226	D	D	57	604
Shakopee city	56	856	9	52	89	2,666	25	949	D	D	67	383
Shoreview city	45	1,233	8	72	98	1,325	13	317	29	571	27	152
South St. Paul city	35	245	D	D	D	D	8	D	26	336	39	220
Stillwater city	19	81	6	44	75	2,210	16	156	70	1,246	56	347
Vadnais Heights city	16	674	4	21	45	1,006	8	73	D	D	23	388
Waconia city	16	80	3	22	47	3,344	D	D	29	477	29	130
West St. Paul city	27	249	3	9	77	1,580	7	264	56	1,061	59	406
White Bear township	23	190	NA	NA	21	135	NA	NA	D	D	13	75
White Bear Lake city	27	1,168	12	165	102	1,506	19	530	56	1,021	79	1,875
Willmar city	31	512	NA	NA	155	4,953	D	D	56	1,001	51	329
Winona city	23	422	NA	NA	103	2,794	25	363	96	2,017	43	204
Woodbury city	76	965	28	419	235	3,797	33	741	130	3,497	122	998
Worthington city	9	228	3	7	59	D	D	D	30	515	D	D
MISSISSIPPI	2,296	52,891	307	2,036	6,391	169,010	694	8,203	5,651	129,836	3,417	18,345
Bay St. Louis city	11	45	NA	NA	D	D	D	D	44	1,183	11	43
Biloxi city	39	1,302	D	D	150	5,455	23	771	156	12,235	66	326
Brandon city	32	178	7	14	D	D	7	126	73	1,251	37	137
Brookhaven city	10	59	D	D	69	1,746	5	16	59	1,120	34	243
Byram city	8	37	NA	NA	18	311	NA	NA	34	612	D	D
Canton city	11	921	NA	NA	49	964	NA	NA	39	625	D	D
Clarksdale city	D	D	NA	NA	71	1,502	D	D	D	D	26	96
Cleveland city	12	479	3	D	61	1,277	8	108	52	1,013	D	D
Clinton city	20	363	D	D	53	1,285	13	144	65	1,295	41	246
Columbus city	42	992	8	28	142	3,085	16	170	108	2,289	67	364
Corinth city	14	665	D	D	91	2,277	D	D	52	900	37	124
D'Iberville city	4	144	5	6	28	423	8	126	73	2,871	32	142
Gautier city	13	437	NA	NA	32	282	D	D	29	523	D	D
Greenville city	27	448	NA	NA	126	2,934	11	90	78	2,140	D	D
Greenwood city	8	61	4	22	D	D	8	68	67	1,262	D	D
Grenada city	D	D	4	10	D	D	D	D	D	D	D	D
Gulfport city	89	2,458	D	D	252	7,631	20	274	205	5,964	114	767
Hattiesburg city	68	2,095	15	89	229	9,360	21	355	254	6,028	106	746
Hernando city	9	38	D	D	D	D	D	D	D	D	27	127
Horn Lake city	9	64	NA	NA	D	D	5	D	59	1,561	20	121
Jackson city	212	9,249	D	D	624	30,160	46	813	374	8,801	312	2,097
Laurel city	15	186	D	D	80	3,015	8	77	D	D	47	251
Long Beach city	5	32	NA	NA	20	189	NA	NA	39	493	D	D
McComb city	7	46	4	31	86	2,043	D	D	67	1,487	D	D
Madison city	42	486	D	D	93	5,051	25	413	D	D	36	217
Meridian city	52	982	D	D	200	6,596	D	D	162	3,874	D	D
Moss Point city	10	170	NA	NA	26	356	NA	NA	35	639	D	D
Natchez city	D	D	NA	NA	89	1,859	D	D	81	1,711	27	128
Ocean Springs city	16	151	3	D	118	2,231	12	181	84	1,402	37	162
Olive Branch city	52	2,814	D	D	74	1,183	D	D	95	2,241	D	D
Oxford city	28	287	D	D	134	2,720	D	D	167	3,644	48	318
Pascagoula city	25	599	7	21	83	2,287	D	D	67	1,148	43	327
Pearl city	27	434	6	23	D	D	8	23	80	1,715	46	299
Petal city	9	237	NA	NA	29	310	D	D	23	483	D	D
Picayune city	7	124	NA	NA	63	962	D	D	D	D	D	D
Ridgeland city	53	3,548	16	159	130	2,441	D	D	131	3,342	91	690
Southaven city	53	1,685	6	29	159	3,613	D	D	154	3,728	59	389
Starkville city	25	806	D	D	79	1,945	10	79	109	2,678	49	227
Tupelo city	95	6,165	9	29	245	8,839	25	173	182	3,932	D	D
Vicksburg city	37	546	D	D	113	2,180	D	D	114	3,676	45	215
West Point city	7	20	NA	NA	28	658	NA	NA	D	D	D	D
Yazoo City city	3	3	NA	NA	D	D	NA	NA	D	D	D	D
MISSOURI	7,561	175,544	1,077	8,825	19,097	423,057	2,274	40,484	12,896	263,644	10,513	68,206
Affton CDP	24	144	3	D	27	369	5	55	27	742	26	131
Arnold city	41	1,649	4	43	60	986	5	101	84	2,254	52	306
Ballwin city	44	160	8	34	44	553	14	516	52	1,128	47	287
Bellefontaine Neighbors city	5	68	NA	NA	24	218	NA	NA	5	96	5	33
Belton city	35	288	4	6	60	1,018	4	D	53	1,308	D	D
Blue Springs city	77	652	18	160	144	1,868	22	231	123	2,659	110	540
Bolivar city	8	37	NA	NA	48	1,954	D	D	33	460	D	D
Branson city	43	1,000	NA	NA	72	1,531	88	1,620	244	5,288	45	271
Bridgeton city	45	2,337	6	44	141	4,442	NA	NA	70	1,773	54	3,271
Cape Girardeau city	63	1,345	4	D	272	9,492	D	D	141	3,417	99	594
Carthage city	7	98	NA	NA	52	930	7	89	43	628	29	94
Chesterfield city	122	5,046	43	416	281	7,862	47	639	199	4,217	151	1,213
Clayton city	59	1,851	8	486	129	1,744	19	230	105	2,576	106	1,090
Columbia city	169	3,096	36	207	584	18,346	60	923	417	9,877	289	1,947
Concord CDP	26	103	NA	NA	74	790	8	227	37	903	44	318
Crestwood city	19	361	8	54	20	139	11	109	20	521	31	164
Creve Coeur city	134	10,435	19	148	447	13,642	18	D	89	1,883	94	1,040
Dardenne Prairie city	11	75	NA	NA	D	D	NA	NA	8	216	6	48
Eureka city	13	42	3	12	36	462	10	1,579	29	545	D	D
Excelsior Springs city	7	282	NA	NA	29	811	3	D	31	684	25	110

STATE City, town, township, borough, or CDP (county if applicable)	Retail Trade		Wholesale trade[1]		Transportation and warehousing		Information		Finance and insurance		Real estate and rental and leasing		Professional, scientific, and technical services	
	Number of establishments	Number of employees	Number of establishments	Number of employees	Number of establishments	Number of employees	Number of establishments	Number of employees	Number of establishments	Number of employees	Number of establishments	Number of employees	Number of establishments	Number of employees
	1	2	3	4	5	6	7	8	9	10	11	12	13	14
MISSOURI—Con.														
Farmington city	112	1,851	14	360	12	137	18	172	D	D	27	116	51	255
Ferguson city	58	1,437	13	683	5	64	D	D	D	D	9	30	16	58
Festus city	43	1,080	5	21	8	108	D	D	41	249	18	156	30	165
Florissant city	157	3,510	10	33	17	326	D	D	D	D	31	112	57	260
Fort Leonard Wood CDP	13	87	NA	NA	NA	NA	NA	NA	D	D	NA	NA	24	135
Fulton city	55	696	NA	NA	D	D	D	D	35	247	11	37	19	76
Gladstone city	74	1,853	13	49	11	35	D	D	75	357	47	162	D	D
Grain Valley city	22	315	16	99	D	D	D	D	15	240	13	60	15	113
Grandview city	80	1,017	34	424	17	660	D	D	24	197	31	285	D	D
Hannibal city	94	1,453	12	209	D	D	10	679	49	263	16	32	37	221
Harrisonville city	59	974	9	64	13	952	5	17	32	145	15	42	28	129
Hazelwood city	97	1,873	58	1,472	51	1,331	10	114	34	682	34	136	49	620
Independence city	400	8,576	73	483	58	527	45	612	170	1,588	94	426	224	894
Jackson city	79	940	22	158	11	111	D	D	48	196	12	50	35	272
Jefferson City city	243	5,176	60	926	26	487	D	D	158	1,679	64	221	212	1,425
Jennings city	35	343	NA	NA	NA	NA	NA	NA	D	D	10	28	NA	NA
Joplin city	360	6,311	85	1,715	49	3,872	30	734	138	853	85	449	137	940
Kansas City city	1,456	25,405	590	11,714	368	12,404	335	11,116	879	26,329	631	4,863	1,957	32,540
Kearney city	32	529	10	82	D	D	D	D	19	128	13	24	D	D
Kennett city	60	764	9	94	12	57	6	48	33	167	D	D	18	67
Kirksville city	90	1,470	12	128	14	121	D	D	D	D	D	D	39	135
Kirkwood city	110	2,386	31	172	12	182	20	325	72	420	49	152	133	576
Lake St. Louis city	63	1,342	D	D	7	74	9	225	42	212	19	48	45	118
Lebanon city	132	1,762	21	165	D	D	10	92	D	D	21	107	33	147
Lee's Summit city	288	5,910	104	1,522	46	560	37	708	238	1,851	143	382	349	1,816
Lemay CDP	37	355	7	47	9	57	NA	NA	D	D	6	28	10	36
Liberty city	96	1,881	20	206	21	104	7	46	86	359	37	161	D	D
Manchester city	77	1,919	16	51	11	44	4	15	D	D	12	59	51	336
Marshall city	60	758	23	293	7	68	D	D	39	217	6	14	D	D
Maryland Heights city	115	1,536	204	5,207	37	992	48	3,186	90	6,485	66	391	146	2,268
Maryville city	51	949	9	52	NA	NA	D	D	28	174	10	20	23	147
Mehlville CDP	179	3,805	12	189	35	78	D	D	D	D	D	D	43	204
Mexico city	58	537	8	112	7	202	D	D	34	201	7	29	24	128
Moberly city	86	1,127	10	237	10	851	D	D	D	D	15	84	D	D
Neosho city	71	1,030	11	750	22	255	11	333	47	274	21	71	28	131
Nixa city	71	930	24	277	15	99	D	D	40	175	D	D	46	194
Oakville CDP	45	637	26	163	32	129	NA	NA	D	D	D	D	54	223
O'Fallon city	227	3,670	78	1,183	36	697	27	574	D	D	88	488	146	591
Old Jamestown CDP	10	86	3	4	9	35	NA	NA	D	D	NA	NA	11	25
Overland city	63	782	45	1,057	14	359	D	D	15	70	15	92	30	525
Ozark city	101	1,463	10	184	13	87	15	113	51	230	D	D	49	278
Poplar Bluff city	152	2,550	23	162	17	129	D	D	70	632	33	124	39	246
Raymore city	37	925	3	D	7	25	D	D	31	155	15	31	36	84
Raytown city	86	1,449	18	153	5	13	4	44	36	164	17	73	D	D
Republic city	51	953	D	D	D	D	D	D	30	133	13	54	23	64
Rolla city	132	2,113	24	252	15	280	D	D	58	350	26	131	52	313
St. Ann city	27	339	D	D	6	72	NA	NA	15	82	10	84	6	17
St. Charles city	267	4,163	78	1,584	45	947	25	450	158	914	96	546	265	3,046
St. Joseph city	287	5,638	90	1,162	74	1,586	37	811	152	1,784	100	393	132	1,246
St. Louis city	878	9,928	401	6,973	210	7,287	203	5,891	385	15,596	412	2,388	1,114	18,010
St. Peters city	337	6,893	73	846	40	511	21	379	D	D	84	273	D	D
Sedalia city	131	2,248	28	296	19	342	D	D	57	312	35	300	58	1,459
Sikeston city	119	1,569	29	768	27	377	D	D	63	394	22	79	42	306
Spanish Lake CDP	17	296	NA	NA	6	10	NA	NA	D	D	14	66	7	21
Springfield city	940	16,834	320	7,221	173	8,614	123	4,702	539	7,114	380	2,844	681	6,162
Town and Country city	25	552	20	388	4	53	D	D	115	1,618	D	D	107	1,596
Troy city	77	1,167	D	D	5	354	6	91	D	D	15	41	24	99
Union city	43	764	9	63	9	187	D	D	30	220	10	42	40	265
University City city	82	770	20	236	D	D	13	249	33	95	46	762	90	257
Warrensburg city	79	1,253	8	15	D	D	D	D	48	223	22	59	35	145
Washington city	114	2,017	24	173	18	435	D	D	73	445	16	46	52	331
Webb City city	38	650	9	155	D	D	D	D	24	90	4	20	18	83
Webster Groves city	69	837	23	174	4	10	11	66	53	202	D	D	121	1,059
Wentzville city	118	2,967	35	280	25	1,128	19	175	50	353	D	D	48	1,695
West Plains city	136	1,567	22	252	7	40	11	68	55	250	30	129	45	202
Wildwood city	39	475	33	53	5	222	14	139	40	107	D	D	115	421
MONTANA	4,754	59,032	1,366	13,078	1,370	11,939	693	8,637	1,971	15,804	2,036	5,951	3,836	17,711
Billings city	606	9,384	247	3,468	128	2,688	89	1,460	362	4,108	277	1,033	520	3,536
Bozeman city	363	5,443	65	830	32	654	D	D	167	1,358	219	526	490	2,309
Butte-Silver Bow	162	2,175	D	D	33	387	19	162	56	315	57	156	107	546
Great Falls city	325	5,075	88	970	48	716	32	448	158	1,086	103	353	170	1,088
Helena city	223	3,525	44	401	34	422	45	557	114	1,398	91	226	215	1,569
Kalispell city	180	3,543	31	415	19	195	28	310	87	1,395	72	294	144	661
Missoula city	459	6,865	108	1,298	58	974	77	1,787	219	1,613	196	718	481	2,940
NEBRASKA	7,154	109,729	2,782	35,143	2,497	29,722	983	20,967	4,420	68,117	2,354	11,293	4,699	39,566
Beatrice city	81	975	19	302	21	110	8	95	33	169	16	30	27	118
Bellevue city	98	2,325	18	90	15	73	16	559	57	263	51	189	90	1,172
Chalco CDP	22	581	25	513	11	184	D	D	D	D	9	43	14	161
Columbus city	138	2,071	22	201	32	304	D	D	D	D	31	133	52	358
Fremont city	115	2,209	31	592	19	434	9	85	59	326	38	168	34	168
Grand Island city	279	4,879	73	1,084	64	1,920	D	D	139	1,147	66	249	91	640
Hastings city	126	1,853	36	444	25	124	D	D	D	D	45	110	56	266
Kearney city	191	3,604	49	763	34	583	D	D	102	572	57	144	85	967
La Vista city	41	1,169	48	881	17	302	6	256	36	D	19	70	28	190
Lexington city	55	697	8	51	9	23	D	D	22	97	5	14	12	60
Lincoln city	951	18,008	251	3,847	183	4,272	134	4,692	636	13,704	391	1,957	835	8,293
Norfolk city	180	2,725	32	1,218	36	292	D	D	92	652	56	79	70	611
North Platte city	162	2,077	25	312	29	874	D	D	71	437	40	147	64	328

1 Merchant wholesalers, except manufacturers' sales branches and offices.

Table C. Incorporated Places, Census Designated Places (CDPs), and Minor Civil Divisions (MCDs) of 10,000 or More Population — **Economic Census**

STATE City, town, township, borough, or CDP (county if applicable)	Administration and support and waste management and mediation services		Educational services		Health care and social assistance		Arts, entertainment, and recreation		Accommodation and food services		Other services (except public administration)	
	Number of establishments	Number of employees	Number of establishments	Number of employees	Number of establishments	Number of employees	Number of establishments	Number of employees	Number of establishments	Number of employees	Number of establishments	Number of employees
	15	16	17	18	19	20	21	22	23	24	25	26
MISSOURI—Con.												
Farmington city	20	1,359	3	28	129	3,658	5	37	62	1,378	41	186
Ferguson city	13	27	NA	NA	93	922	3	148	42	672	23	86
Festus city	18	164	3	21	49	611	D	D	38	1,093	27	190
Florissant city	37	456	10	49	211	2,589	D	D	D	D	93	516
Fort Leonard Wood CDP	5	324	NA	NA	D	D	NA	NA	4	D	3	14
Fulton city	8	150	NA	NA	47	2,027	7	71	37	558	30	105
Gladstone city	39	892	6	36	76	776	4	D	44	946	54	279
Grain Valley city	26	139	D	D	20	177	NA	NA	9	169	17	49
Grandview city	46	663	3	4	64	531	3	13	45	1,026	34	191
Hannibal city	15	321	D	D	D	D	D	D	D	D	36	139
Harrisonville city	13	28	3	9	48	1,244	D	D	33	608	24	69
Hazelwood city	48	1,374	NA	NA	111	984	4	6	55	949	46	279
Independence city	110	878	20	131	342	6,465	26	333	229	5,721	179	1,005
Jackson city	16	170	4	35	45	653	D	D	D	D	25	82
Jefferson City city	75	1,870	18	126	254	6,697	20	426	151	3,194	192	1,151
Jennings city	7	113	NA	NA	68	318	NA	NA	13	269	D	D
Joplin city	54	6,489	D	D	276	10,140	23	354	193	4,606	111	890
Kansas City city	682	20,776	101	712	1,770	45,482	221	6,819	1,186	30,485	860	7,708
Kearney city	14	345	3	15	24	221	4	51	24	428	D	D
Kennett city	7	26	NA	NA	66	1,469	NA	NA	27	415	19	49
Kirksville city	16	107	6	31	95	1,961	5	65	59	1,169	D	D
Kirkwood city	54	455	19	122	120	1,915	21	515	71	1,877	61	459
Lake St. Louis city	21	636	5	4	56	1,723	12	97	34	778	27	277
Lebanon city	10	453	4	10	61	1,133	5	89	60	1,111	36	137
Lee's Summit city	136	1,837	29	188	330	6,882	40	423	198	4,846	171	1,052
Lemay CDP	26	445	NA	NA	D	D	NA	NA	27	517	D	D
Liberty city	47	1,038	17	153	134	3,209	13	64	76	1,747	55	336
Manchester city	31	292	11	74	40	591	11	110	29	581	D	D
Marshall city	13	55	NA	NA	49	1,159	4	D	31	452	29	90
Maryland Heights city	102	6,309	9	122	96	3,886	20	544	96	3,063	64	632
Maryville city	11	13	3	16	38	1,038	D	D	35	814	21	80
Mehlville CDP	31	283	NA	NA	74	642	7	103	70	1,700	D	D
Mexico city	17	525	NA	NA	54	1,005	6	84	30	494	33	188
Moberly city	11	168	NA	NA	59	1,233	D	D	39	627	29	114
Neosho city	11	378	NA	NA	D	D	D	D	31	568	D	D
Nixa city	29	321	4	51	43	384	7	25	38	721	D	D
Oakville CDP	53	393	D	D	D	D	9	60	39	747	39	221
O'Fallon city	91	1,971	19	125	226	3,365	25	673	169	3,947	142	1,225
Old Jamestown CDP	16	158	NA	NA	50	395	NA	NA	6	49	8	32
Overland city	33	544	3	4	60	1,044	5	69	43	789	53	246
Ozark city	25	159	NA	NA	51	852	9	D	53	1,063	31	171
Poplar Bluff city	7	930	NA	NA	133	3,507	9	50	72	1,619	42	171
Raymore city	31	131	4	20	49	581	3	2	23	473	24	131
Raytown city	31	747	7	23	88	966	4	41	51	1,169	48	396
Republic city	19	107	D	D	25	283	3	11	D	D	D	D
Rolla city	18	202	5	22	108	3,312	D	D	104	2,114	43	214
St. Ann city	12	101	NA	NA	29	106	NA	NA	32	393	D	D
St. Charles city	105	2,141	15	133	261	5,464	33	343	228	7,324	162	1,035
St. Joseph city	D	D	14	113	D	D	20	566	192	3,990	148	1,175
St. Louis city	424	19,850	70	877	1,554	39,629	148	4,609	1,002	22,623	625	5,377
St. Peters city	89	1,970	18	139	299	4,540	35	712	171	3,748	166	1,255
Sedalia city	33	2,142	D	D	121	3,019	D	D	60	1,472	D	D
Sikeston city	28	506	3	D	108	2,653	7	37	D	D	35	202
Spanish Lake CDP	7	13	NA	NA	48	727	NA	NA	D	D	15	48
Springfield city	278	10,330	59	461	768	28,280	75	1,334	702	14,999	476	4,094
Town and Country city	29	1,783	6	50	202	6,141	10	423	D	D	21	210
Troy city	12	48	NA	NA	39	862	5	56	37	884	D	D
Union city	10	330	NA	NA	36	608	D	D	33	618	26	138
University City city	25	199	12	270	169	1,682	12	D	85	1,439	57	513
Warrensburg city	14	54	D	D	71	1,871	NA	NA	74	1,701	D	D
Washington city	24	857	NA	NA	105	2,518	11	D	61	1,294	40	231
Webb City city	7	48	NA	NA	23	525	NA	NA	34	537	D	D
Webster Groves city	40	389	9	134	92	3,103	D	D	57	1,075	43	235
Wentzville city	61	5,268	9	61	88	1,292	9	113	84	1,954	56	379
West Plains city	8	274	D	D	104	2,613	8	53	47	852	34	177
Wildwood city	50	331	8	23	58	581	9	330	26	664	24	111
MONTANA	1,857	29,275	287	1,733	3,716	73,254	1,234	10,492	3,568	52,415	2,409	12,077
Billings city	243	17,054	D	D	534	13,921	148	1,550	347	8,420	302	1,927
Bozeman city	137	712	43	255	305	4,646	83	462	241	4,553	183	1,103
Butte-Silver Bow	57	337	9	64	169	3,114	46	328	137	2,184	65	277
Great Falls city	D	D	12	80	269	6,664	72	689	208	3,739	D	D
Helena city	55	696	19	71	D	D	55	756	157	3,072	170	1,022
Kalispell city	52	2,231	D	D	201	5,827	33	406	123	2,236	83	525
Missoula city	155	2,047	45	314	453	9,689	84	1,299	293	6,180	252	2,039
NEBRASKA	2,780	64,557	359	2,849	5,817	135,691	913	14,879	4,621	76,386	4,107	21,757
Beatrice city	20	140	NA	NA	46	1,541	7	108	40	556	D	D
Bellevue city	51	361	8	48	131	2,384	D	D	119	2,415	85	474
Chalco CDP	16	82	NA	NA	D	D	7	84	D	D	D	D
Columbus city	35	1,055	D	D	89	2,063	D	D	67	1,110	D	D
Fremont city	41	975	D	D	106	2,629	12	414	69	1,132	62	258
Grand Island city	77	1,202	D	D	182	4,408	25	464	151	2,565	136	920
Hastings city	45	380	4	23	103	2,826	D	D	80	1,400	D	D
Kearney city	45	528	7	52	183	3,892	22	490	129	2,613	98	554
La Vista city	28	265	4	76	47	420	10	138	42	977	20	149
Lexington city	D	D	NA	NA	29	605	5	60	27	281	D	D
Lincoln city	408	6,074	83	666	1,012	24,568	129	2,878	746	14,706	678	4,126
Norfolk city	47	733	D	D	149	3,041	D	D	76	1,530	74	433
North Platte city	26	184	D	D	135	2,873	15	113	87	1,763	D	D

Table C. Incorporated Places, Census Designated Places (CDPs), and Minor Civil Divisions (MCDs) of 10,000 or More Population — **Economic Census**

STATE / City, town, township, borough, or CDP (county if applicable)	Retail Trade — Number of establishments	Retail Trade — Number of employees	Wholesale trade¹ — Number of establishments	Wholesale trade¹ — Number of employees	Transportation and warehousing — Number of establishments	Transportation and warehousing — Number of employees	Information — Number of establishments	Information — Number of employees	Finance and insurance — Number of establishments	Finance and insurance — Number of employees	Real estate and rental and leasing — Number of establishments	Real estate and rental and leasing — Number of employees	Professional, scientific, and technical services — Number of establishments	Professional, scientific, and technical services — Number of employees
	1	2	3	4	5	6	7	8	9	10	11	12	13	14
NEBRASKA—Con.														
Omaha city	1,597	33,315	677	10,090	367	9,683	303	9,281	1,327	36,370	803	5,999	1,672	19,019
Papillion city	100	2,811	17	157	19	337	D	D	63	623	23	77	44	510
Scottsbluff city	122	1,979	31	294	22	182	D	D	51	678	29	76	49	300
South Sioux City city	60	952	D	D	14	1,188	D	D	D	D	D	D	21	125
NEVADA	8,745	145,773	2,665	32,879	1,647	55,100	1,424	17,896	4,192	37,906	4,684	30,562	9,018	60,168
Boulder City city	42	259	9	33	10	428	D	D	16	84	D	D	47	199
Carson City	220	3,141	81	620	30	235	40	384	120	1,007	118	361	246	1,126
Elko city	115	1,886	54	631	31	523	D	D	51	249	38	257	76	371
Enterprise CDP	406	6,596	98	1,852	62	2,613	55	1,086	91	1,084	181	4,454	346	2,083
Fernley city	31	716	D	D	15	1,270	D	D	20	64	17	42	21	96
Gardnerville Ranchos CDP	13	68	NA	NA	NA	NA	NA	NA	NA	NA	7	3	11	27
Henderson city	768	14,462	240	1,925	120	2,340	131	1,100	478	4,323	513	1,719	1,020	4,993
Las Vegas city	1,923	35,708	409	2,708	204	5,048	349	5,071	1,055	12,200	1,081	5,775	2,610	17,301
Mesquite city	55	747	8	85	12	228	7	76	26	118	D	D	40	131
North Las Vegas city	344	7,295	191	4,000	134	6,825	41	445	110	613	131	839	153	2,526
Pahrump CDP	91	1,313	D	D	19	62	D	D	D	D	35	72	D	D
Paradise CDP	1,648	25,035	534	6,751	265	15,946	208	2,560	483	3,622	654	6,503	1,067	10,969
Reno city	1,015	17,305	306	5,519	189	5,292	177	2,984	577	5,000	540	2,960	1,270	8,428
Spanish Springs CDP	16	225	14	312	11	43	D	D	D	D	11	9	28	72
Sparks city	322	5,258	226	3,757	153	5,869	D	D	109	530	132	817	136	920
Spring Creek CDP	16	200	NA	NA	D	D	NA	NA	6	D	3	3	D	D
Spring Valley CDP	479	7,802	121	773	67	2,104	100	1,083	411	5,492	453	1,657	686	4,547
Summerlin South CDP	18	56	D	D	4	10	17	149	30	262	56	113	126	327
Sunrise Manor CDP	230	3,663	65	974	76	1,414	27	947	56	471	141	641	72	286
Sun Valley CDP	21	184	NA	NA	5	10	NA	NA	6	39	5	18	6	20
Whitney CDP	48	505	6	18	8	256	NA	NA	11	57	26	182	19	24
Winchester CDP	106	1,840	16	44	9	45	28	281	158	476	78	2,264	138	979
NEW HAMPSHIRE	6,032	96,591	1,509	22,314	814	13,901	773	16,782	2,035	29,386	1,523	7,920	3,674	32,387
Amherst town	73	1,081	22	259	5	45	D	D	D	D	10	24	75	389
Bedford town	78	2,071	35	351	13	260	20	440	151	1,415	47	D	144	1,396
Berlin city	35	301	D	D	3	19	D	D	D	D	5	18	6	47
Claremont city	80	1,480	16	400	7	45	6	47	D	D	18	267	18	135
Concord city	278	5,108	55	1,075	25	477	36	541	123	2,074	D	D	207	2,034
Conway town	188	2,257	13	105	10	78	18	181	D	D	37	132	31	219
Derry town	103	1,239	23	171	19	203	11	48	D	D	23	104	44	506
Dover city	91	1,369	32	500	12	462	15	142	D	D	32	122	86	469
Durham town	18	178	NA	NA	NA	NA	6	27	D	D	17	73	28	118
Exeter town	74	776	26	430	15	132	11	42	D	D	15	98	D	D
Goffstown town	46	649	9	85	D	D	NA	NA	D	D	D	D	24	82
Hampton town	66	439	19	136	6	10	5	10	33	195	27	87	52	441
Hanover town	37	377	D	D	NA	NA	11	85	D	D	16	48	25	299
Hooksett town	85	1,997	35	587	10	158	D	D	25	1,056	D	D	22	180
Hudson town	75	1,602	42	526	17	161	D	D	D	D	17	40	52	551
Keene city	152	2,710	31	273	D	D	21	335	58	1,031	35	156	87	392
Laconia city	80	843	14	78	5	155	D	D	D	D	D	D	44	290
Lebanon city	164	2,929	33	368	18	314	30	780	36	252	42	119	85	1,384
Londonderry town	70	1,860	45	700	45	1,690	9	144	32	259	40	441	87	587
Manchester city	419	7,274	195	3,163	62	1,240	135	4,313	280	4,353	156	1,589	457	4,859
Merrimack town	157	2,649	33	516	15	194	14	166	D	D	D	D	73	844
Milford town	75	1,137	13	127	D	D	D	D	D	D	15	53	27	256
Nashua city	464	9,984	119	1,527	50	912	74	2,234	D	D	124	505	306	3,316
Pelham town	38	322	13	135	5	16	NA	NA	D	D	10	56	22	123
Portsmouth city	260	3,699	68	1,315	25	772	52	3,451	169	4,113	69	541	284	3,141
Raymond town	28	476	6	61	D	D	NA	NA	D	D	4	12	8	66
Rochester city	131	2,897	11	167	D	D	12	191	D	D	25	76	36	295
Salem town	312	6,602	85	1,671	23	191	20	444	67	1,051	38	169	120	1,680
Somersworth city	81	1,470	10	134	NA	NA	NA	NA	D	D	10	22	19	155
Windham town	45	405	16	93	9	45	13	60	23	83	D	D	35	188
NEW JERSEY	31,200	469,615	12,289	230,006	7,573	177,147	3,885	96,288	11,601	198,542	9,622	61,052	28,962	325,516
Aberdeen township	50	898	17	168	13	151	11	192	28	152	11	137	51	325
Asbury Park city	63	400	7	33	6	30	11	42	6	35	20	161	29	160
Atlantic City city	275	2,970	5	D	10	197	D	D	23	120	45	452	D	D
Barnegat township	32	327	D	D	5	23	5	13	15	76	14	124	13	64
Bayonne city	178	2,011	55	905	91	2,377	D	D	51	D	37	182	71	492
Beachwood borough	17	94	6	18	4	11	NA	NA	NA	NA	NA	NA	8	48
Belleville township	86	1,155	37	322	36	275	D	D	13	91	25	198	35	115
Bellmawr borough	29	247	18	166	11	634	NA	NA	D	D	12	64	16	133
Bergenfield borough	84	818	33	234	19	145	4	18	D	D	D	D	42	228
Berkeley township	55	707	17	197	11	130	D	D	19	108	15	47	26	83
Berkeley Heights township	32	311	D	D	9	117	6	128	23	462	10	D	50	645
Bernards township	38	752	25	938	D	D	D	D	55	1,455	D	D	133	1,846
Bloomfield township	130	2,034	28	470	33	139	13	85	37	429	58	281	108	2,704
Bordentown township	44	617	11	686	14	242	D	D	14	68	10	63	29	132
Bound Brook borough	30	513	D	D	13	38	NA	NA	D	D	10	28	28	142
Branchburg township	26	159	59	1,245	14	781	D	D	D	D	14	121	68	2,016
Brick township	214	4,215	38	353	32	175	25	288	67	426	53	195	142	738
Bridgeton city	90	594	23	366	8	54	D	D	D	D	14	123	29	112
Bridgewater township	257	6,121	68	3,053	43	1,432	24	2,142	89	2,628	50	260	300	4,088
Burlington township	70	2,073	20	929	40	1,685	5	106	20	269	25	131	27	289
Camden city	190	940	50	1,214	35	605	18	75	28	187	41	198	58	1,013
Carteret borough	43	3,101	35	1,147	78	3,072	8	32	14	70	12	51	28	432
Cedar Grove township	30	324	23	257	NA	NA	3	10	23	116	11	21	42	242
Chatham township	24	357	D	D	D	D	4	24	14	46	6	67	28	81

1 Merchant wholesalers, except manufacturers' sales branches and offices.

Table C. Incorporated Places, Census Designated Places (CDPs), and Minor Civil Divisions (MCDs) of 10,000 or More Population — **Economic Census**

STATE City, town, township, borough, or CDP (county if applicable)	Administration and support and waste management and mediation services		Educational services		Health care and social assistance		Arts, entertainment, and recreation		Accommodation and food services		Other services (except public administration)	
	Number of establishments	Number of employees	Number of establishments	Number of employees	Number of establishments	Number of employees	Number of establishments	Number of employees	Number of establishments	Number of employees	Number of establishments	Number of employees
	15	16	17	18	19	20	21	22	23	24	25	26
NEBRASKA—Con.												
Omaha city	880	42,965	134	1,274	1,828	51,418	244	6,172	1,340	27,002	1,043	7,314
Papillion city	28	836	7	89	90	1,532	8	416	59	1,393	57	351
Scottsbluff city	26	338	NA	NA	98	2,514	11	133	70	1,062	53	329
South Sioux City city	10	149	NA	NA	27	434	6	124	35	596	D	D
NEVADA	4,562	119,626	655	6,324	7,372	132,093	1,635	31,918	6,810	319,584	4,032	28,825
Boulder City city	22	204	6	32	37	625	D	D	46	864	32	110
Carson City	132	1,283	D	D	215	3,865	51	1,019	170	3,036	132	618
Elko city	31	447	D	D	97	1,393	D	D	99	1,715	D	D
Enterprise CDP	173	9,279	22	153	D	D	97	2,439	290	9,562	D	D
Fernley city	14	304	NA	NA	25	196	16	340	33	537	13	87
Gardnerville Ranchos CDP	16	61	NA	NA	10	111	NA	NA	11	83	4	12
Henderson city	442	5,167	84	601	879	12,658	197	3,474	535	16,075	423	3,209
Las Vegas city	1,009	25,413	162	1,148	2,077	39,266	332	6,476	1,403	45,459	921	6,955
Mesquite city	19	283	NA	NA	44	722	D	D	37	2,369	29	43
North Las Vegas city	206	7,608	26	435	274	6,983	D	D	270	7,756	182	2,045
Pahrump CDP	27	378	D	D	65	875	D	D	55	1,141	51	298
Paradise CDP	788	31,004	75	1,060	706	11,172	237	4,340	1,210	150,441	554	4,575
Reno city	557	18,842	88	768	1,019	22,180	151	3,008	821	23,651	523	3,845
Spanish Springs CDP	22	72	NA	NA	D	D	NA	NA	12	159	8	47
Sparks city	167	2,040	18	196	182	3,102	46	1,317	210	5,393	172	1,071
Spring Creek CDP	8	18	NA	NA	D	D	NA	NA	15	166	D	D
Spring Valley CDP	274	10,383	71	455	780	13,299	132	1,288	570	8,731	300	1,903
Summerlin South CDP	29	210	9	17	D	D	D	D	30	3,143	D	D
Sunrise Manor CDP	113	1,867	7	36	66	675	11	61	179	5,018	102	426
Sun Valley CDP	14	40	NA	NA	6	65	D	D	9	137	3	4
Whitney CDP	14	205	NA	NA	D	D	D	D	36	1,194	D	D
Winchester CDP	79	614	7	34	200	5,316	20	332	108	7,391	32	152
NEW HAMPSHIRE	2,393	56,346	460	4,369	3,737	94,594	815	12,442	3,784	59,531	3,011	17,864
Amherst town	19	88	10	83	D	D	8	70	23	439	32	156
Bedford town	83	1,347	17	141	113	3,155	D	D	48	1,182	46	380
Berlin city	D	D	NA	NA	33	939	D	D	14	134	17	63
Claremont city	12	43	NA	NA	47	755	D	D	29	433	26	82
Concord city	66	1,067	25	253	237	9,984	25	401	131	2,877	222	1,356
Conway town	24	116	D	D	55	1,298	16	455	105	1,769	36	164
Derry town	45	342	6	82	89	1,981	10	130	D	D	71	414
Dover city	62	1,286	D	D	139	4,200	17	179	110	1,905	74	467
Durham town	D	D	D	D	12	173	5	23	39	493	D	D
Exeter town	34	842	12	52	87	3,313	12	187	50	642	D	D
Goffstown town	30	184	NA	NA	27	202	D	D	27	333	43	146
Hampton town	34	311	D	D	29	368	17	57	115	1,116	33	171
Hanover town	12	61	15	15	39	762	5	13	35	692	15	72
Hooksett town	25	405	7	60	31	275	11	164	D	D	50	305
Hudson town	42	217	11	105	32	603	11	141	45	650	69	301
Keene city	38	612	9	79	109	3,645	15	279	95	1,659	63	611
Laconia city	30	438	3	28	70	3,045	D	D	89	780	54	200
Lebanon city	33	447	D	D	84	7,208	12	386	57	1,089	46	426
Londonderry town	60	2,562	7	29	D	D	10	302	55	1,035	D	D
Manchester city	213	27,899	50	471	350	14,010	49	1,035	307	6,151	284	2,389
Merrimack town	56	795	10	33	58	960	11	234	63	1,043	59	525
Milford town	33	450	NA	NA	37	407	NA	NA	43	677	41	213
Nashua city	134	2,731	35	926	370	9,314	45	592	228	4,686	191	1,645
Pelham town	25	259	NA	NA	18	164	4	14	17	211	D	D
Portsmouth city	77	2,332	D	D	216	4,417	57	711	176	3,896	113	803
Raymond town	15	85	NA	NA	20	181	NA	NA	18	367	26	109
Rochester city	36	454	D	D	74	1,883	8	133	73	1,164	63	349
Salem town	71	3,153	12	116	117	1,823	24	448	113	2,477	97	612
Somersworth city	13	85	NA	NA	45	956	5	240	26	293	24	267
Windham town	16	379	7	49	D	D	10	135	31	481	28	174
NEW JERSEY	14,211	350,711	2,980	37,081	28,005	613,406	3,842	65,529	21,495	318,734	19,162	113,846
Aberdeen township	26	74	9	42	37	404	11	112	37	538	D	D
Asbury Park city	12	321	NA	NA	24	416	11	267	92	1,781	41	534
Atlantic City city	25	773	D	D	68	3,300	D	D	199	26,558	64	844
Barnegat township	28	157	D	D	28	385	6	17	24	269	28	110
Bayonne city	35	291	9	36	170	2,708	17	300	D	D	131	491
Beachwood borough	6	10	NA	NA	D	D	NA	NA	7	83	11	32
Belleville township	43	477	3	5	D	D	9	169	62	707	71	433
Bellmawr borough	15	723	D	D	11	149	3	24	24	286	18	146
Bergenfield borough	35	186	D	D	77	643	D	D	41	370	63	149
Berkeley township	46	113	3	33	59	1,301	D	D	52	531	53	246
Berkeley Heights township	26	573	10	136	40	1,978	8	180	32	470	27	155
Bernards township	42	221	13	440	84	3,285	8	451	53	1,500	34	521
Bloomfield township	66	963	14	111	143	2,603	13	85	D	D	101	376
Bordentown township	7	82	D	D	21	538	8	179	34	580	21	167
Bound Brook borough	22	924	D	D	D	D	NA	NA	27	244	26	123
Branchburg township	31	926	6	26	D	D	8	170	45	514	38	275
Brick township	116	716	21	160	279	8,931	33	263	143	2,363	160	830
Bridgeton city	12	182	NA	NA	40	1,397	D	D	30	216	17	86
Bridgewater township	106	2,998	29	306	171	2,701	D	D	123	2,789	97	694
Burlington township	18	886	D	D	62	1,891	D	D	45	709	37	219
Camden city	44	1,446	D	D	161	13,231	10	357	90	482	54	393
Carteret borough	16	615	NA	NA	D	D	NA	NA	22	268	23	89
Cedar Grove township	31	310	4	D	52	1,325	10	60	19	320	D	D
Chatham township	11	96	7	59	28	480	6	172	21	223	23	187

Table C. Incorporated Places, Census Designated Places (CDPs), and Minor Civil Divisions (MCDs) of 10,000 or More Population — **Economic Census**

STATE City, town, township, borough, or CDP (county if applicable)	Retail Trade Number of establishments	Number of employees	Wholesale trade¹ Number of establishments	Number of employees	Transportation and warehousing Number of establishments	Number of employees	Information Number of establishments	Number of employees	Finance and insurance Number of establishments	Number of employees	Real estate and rental and leasing Number of establishments	Number of employees	Professional, scientific, and technical services Number of establishments	Number of employees
	1	2	3	4	5	6	7	8	9	10	11	12	13	14
NEW JERSEY—Con.														
Cherry Hill township	439	9,086	99	1,059	40	678	53	1,825	175	2,657	119	641	502	6,397
Cinnaminson township	67	1,212	44	826	17	359	D	D	23	121	14	59	46	716
City of Orange township	119	656	16	221	19	416	D	D	D	D	30	84	15	50
Clark township	53	1,560	14	D	17	422	3	27	38	304	D	D	68	959
Cliffside Park borough	53	167	25	43	15	62	6	9	D	D	D	D	50	206
Clifton city	300	4,875	178	1,802	89	1,287	30	412	94	1,020	107	596	242	1,413
Clinton township	21	332	10	46	6	124	9	157	D	D	14	72	59	1,160
Collingswood borough	46	230	D	D	4	191	D	D	19	79	11	97	56	538
Cranford township	44	462	50	1,101	23	208	D	D	67	811	D	D	133	1,115
Delran township	81	1,376	D	D	17	177	4	6	8	45	12	216	19	65
Denville township	101	1,344	36	363	6	185	6	62	31	178	D	D	98	674
Deptford township	218	5,228	19	D	18	127	15	143	24	249	11	58	29	155
Dover town	71	815	20	160	30	462	4	37	22	115	D	D	29	177
Dumont borough	23	249	10	40	7	19	NA	NA	21	74	9	15	29	106
East Brunswick township	227	3,906	111	1,035	60	922	36	556	76	1,161	48	258	317	2,647
East Greenwich township	13	52	13	141	6	58	NA	NA	9	27	D	D	14	37
East Hanover township	96	2,300	47	701	12	279	12	138	37	268	24	152	82	2,528
East Orange city	151	1,275	18	140	35	223	6	41	13	84	49	248	47	147
East Windsor township	78	1,684	23	869	D	D	15	216	23	176	D	D	105	923
Eatontown borough	156	2,970	42	663	13	210	13	282	32	295	36	643	90	2,561
Edgewater borough	77	1,700	25	128	4	10	12	108	9	80	32	102	76	315
Edison township	415	7,794	345	7,596	198	5,572	59	1,756	147	2,216	127	1,772	800	16,435
Egg Harbor township	139	3,091	41	385	25	760	20	316	32	344	44	178	83	1,605
Elizabeth city	532	7,489	106	3,450	250	9,272	21	155	73	405	100	434	D	D
Elmwood Park borough	54	614	39	993	41	389	D	D	D	D	21	102	55	445
Englewood city	156	2,084	93	1,303	19	223	16	189	D	D	63	236	130	649
Evesham township	199	3,699	49	521	15	74	30	276	148	2,864	60	287	236	2,404
Ewing township	126	1,735	35	683	22	451	22	496	33	5,073	35	160	101	1,289
Fair Lawn borough	88	872	56	589	22	402	13	36	51	596	D	D	209	1,168
Fairview borough	60	485	35	370	16	91	NA	NA	D	D	12	50	9	33
Florence township	18	83	D	D	D	D	NA	NA	NA	NA	5	37	14	103
Florham Park borough	31	396	29	1,470	D	D	16	267	107	2,483	D	D	135	5,364
Fort Lee borough	135	1,340	153	1,109	48	213	35	848	105	926	135	610	248	1,554
Franklin township (Gloucester County)	43	479	15	143	16	82	NA	NA	8	98	5	14	18	341
Franklin township (Somerset County)	125	1,632	124	6,807	55	779	31	1,314	72	596	48	235	340	5,672
Franklin Lakes borough	26	450	29	165	5	61	3	3	D	D	20	77	52	247
Freehold borough	103	2,025	12	265	5	14	7	64	32	207	18	224	90	514
Freehold township	199	4,581	36	204	22	453	34	434	72	468	32	187	142	704
Galloway township	72	1,031	D	D	14	342	D	D	21	130	23	178	47	269
Garfield city	71	912	41	477	33	63	NA	NA	19	145	16	68	31	209
Glassboro borough	77	1,165	15	150	D	D	6	50	14	87	8	36	15	84
Glen Rock borough	35	315	23	512	4	32	NA	NA	27	268	16	86	68	353
Gloucester township	184	2,520	30	301	26	199	10	100	36	176	36	193	77	276
Gloucester City city	26	181	15	217	12	723	NA	NA	D	D	5	14	11	51
Guttenberg town	D	D	D	D	D	D	NA	NA	6	80	9	10	26	70
Hackensack city	260	3,615	181	1,562	64	554	32	330	92	937	138	615	411	2,870
Haddon township	48	662	8	51	NA	NA	NA	NA	D	D	6	54	19	58
Haddonfield borough	53	310	D	D	D	D	13	35	30	172	20	47	134	1,289
Hamilton township (Atlantic County)	157	3,587	10	188	4	44	D	D	12	55	7	38	36	308
Hamilton township (Mercer County)	279	5,146	86	1,010	69	1,587	34	2,051	124	1,726	68	379	252	3,153
Hammonton town	84	1,119	22	370	16	77	D	D	30	653	15	61	31	254
Hanover township	46	1,149	51	1,343	23	346	28	275	39	634	37	304	97	11,222
Harrison township	28	625	D	D	6	85	D	D	D	D	14	43	29	240
Harrison town	39	200	18	479	19	414	D	D	D	D	10	28	22	61
Hasbrouck Heights borough	39	316	35	399	21	370	12	132	D	D	19	76	52	362
Hawthorne borough	65	633	37	627	15	255	D	D	24	98	18	453	50	195
Hazlet township	77	1,457	15	107	16	260	D	D	30	131	15	53	76	1,059
Highland Park borough	38	284	D	D	D	D	NA	NA	D	D	23	202	40	204
Hillsborough township	75	1,390	58	1,002	23	509	20	128	D	D	29	140	169	596
Hillsdale borough	34	450	D	D	4	18	4	15	D	D	10	34	25	40
Hillside township	65	745	65	1,245	53	552	NA	NA	9	66	15	52	D	D
Hoboken city	167	1,480	34	229	33	1,887	51	1,745	77	1,082	112	529	225	1,286
Holmdel township	64	1,209	22	93	12	56	17	1,801	42	393	22	114	103	594
Hopatcong borough	20	116	4	6	15	66	NA	NA	NA	NA	NA	NA	12	69
Hopewell township (Mercer County)	26	321	D	D	D	D	6	82	D	D	12	140	62	3,196
Howell township	192	3,292	65	441	34	631	16	925	46	324	28	192	108	596
Irvington township	172	895	28	372	31	211	D	D	14	101	25	126	22	126
Jackson township	153	2,043	22	115	31	161	6	21	35	162	47	245	100	367
Jefferson township	52	747	19	D	9	117	D	D	17	232	3	D	43	339
Jersey City city	818	12,319	189	5,929	242	6,288	125	3,452	359	31,471	263	1,583	655	8,057
Kearny town	98	1,838	49	904	133	2,399	8	105	D	D	33	238	54	264
Kinnelon borough	13	240	D	D	D	D	D	D	8	36	D	D	38	126
Lacey township	80	1,427	20	69	19	103	7	34	23	163	17	67	57	333
Lakewood township	474	4,462	202	2,495	53	1,873	25	191	102	524	324	1,395	275	2,788
Lawrence township (Mercer County)	195	4,245	D	D	D	D	21	627	65	837	41	377	192	3,157
Lincoln Park borough	20	429	23	136	13	250	NA	NA	11	68	D	D	27	72
Linden city	196	2,696	113	1,948	147	1,817	D	D	30	236	39	209	55	934
Lindenwold borough	22	176	D	D	5	13	NA	NA	NA	NA	13	92	9	37
Little Egg Harbor township	32	471	5	32	9	123	A	13	8	37	12	25	12	35
Little Falls township	55	1,513	17	125	12	60	4	191	24	340	18	63	52	379
Little Ferry borough	46	238	51	825	25	221	NA	NA	D	D	14	107	16	142
Livingston township	197	2,835	31	186	16	130	22	1,404	84	1,515	64	474	196	1,456
Lodi borough	92	1,107	48	530	29	125	7	232	21	122	27	126	25	90

1 Merchant wholesalers, except manufacturers' sales branches and offices.

Items 1–14

STATE City, town, township, borough, or CDP (county if applicable)	Administration and support and waste management and mediation services		Educational services		Health care and social assistance		Arts, entertainment, and recreation		Accommodation and food services		Other services (except public administration)	
	Number of establish-ments	Number of employees	Number of establish-ments	Number of employees	Number of establish-ments	Number of employees	Number of establish-ments	Number of employees	Number of establish-ments	Number of employees	Number of establish-ments	Number of employees
	15	16	17	18	19	20	21	22	23	24	25	26
NEW JERSEY—Con.												
Cherry Hill township.........	181	26,443	37	300	400	10,584	45	686	202	4,690	214	1,848
Cinnaminson township	40	451	3	19	47	539	D	D	46	708	D	D
City of Orange township ...	31	1,265	3	13	62	750	NA	NA	48	483	50	193
Clark township.................	21	2,168	5	8	69	906	10	178	D	D	39	223
Cliffside Park borough	29	91	5	45	61	359	4	108	56	372	55	161
Clifton city......................	106	2,603	22	227	442	5,344	26	314	D	D	209	1,103
Clinton township	34	371	7	30	49	778	D	D	20	335	D	D
Collingswood borough	14	42	D	D	40	545	4	44	54	805	D	D
Cranford township............	43	1,239	13	57	83	2,077	16	102	D	D	60	332
Delran township................	33	290	4	9	34	479	5	39	38	843	D	D
Denville township.............	40	363	D	D	112	2,701	11	108	58	845	67	490
Deptford township............	38	494	3	20	D	D	10	225	73	2,270	53	266
Dover town......................	D	D	4	46	46	1,750	NA	NA	50	387	D	D
Dumont borough...............	26	95	4	39	37	225	NA	NA	35	219	30	84
East Brunswick township..	96	6,714	32	256	275	4,956	27	410	102	1,820	107	694
East Greenwich township .	9	59	3	19	14	93	D	D	8	97	D	D
East Hanover township.....	67	848	D	D	33	694	9	D	73	1,198	60	344
East Orange city	22	129	14	184	150	6,677	D	D	55	681	69	309
East Windsor township	36	788	D	D	64	580	14	198	55	1,053	51	287
Eatontown borough	28	692	6	78	93	2,078	17	569	61	1,278	49	405
Edgewater borough	13	231	5	10	59	398	13	D	67	1,135	60	651
Edison township	198	14,755	41	589	428	11,089	23	826	279	4,232	196	1,115
Egg Harbor township........	89	732	D	D	121	2,905	22	333	91	1,441	77	327
Elizabeth city..................	107	6,445	19	293	219	6,377	10	101	260	3,291	208	1,671
Elmwood Park borough	40	1,298	D	D	47	5,483	6	68	43	489	48	236
Englewood city................	45	641	19	191	242	5,205	24	359	59	776	112	652
Evesham township............	95	2,992	D	D	254	5,351	D	D	98	1,990	102	963
Ewing township................	62	17,225	D	D	101	2,123	D	D	100	1,415	77	542
Fair Lawn borough............	49	663	14	146	202	3,115	15	143	76	891	90	463
Fairview borough	19	210	3	6	12	126	D	D	43	302	40	162
Florence township	12	16	NA	NA	12	164	NA	NA	D	D	D	D
Florham Park borough......	41	11,221	5	95	94	1,246	15	D	43	842	35	758
Fort Lee borough	83	722	26	115	214	1,504	16	95	136	1,364	153	663
Franklin township (Gloucester County)......	23	719	NA	NA	18	230	4	14	30	320	33	178
Franklin township (Somerset County)......	100	2,991	23	196	256	3,631	D	D	160	1,853	D	D
Franklin Lakes borough	30	135	D	D	D	D	15	224	21	212	32	163
Freehold borough	26	208	3	D	48	776	9	73	48	692	39	159
Freehold township	58	1,730	10	74	227	6,158	D	D	99	2,023	84	753
Galloway township............	38	148	D	D	119	4,587	D	D	93	1,710	63	415
Garfield city.....................	27	296	6	27	34	501	NA	NA	49	575	D	D
Glassboro borough...........	15	291	D	D	42	938	8	133	D	D	35	270
Glen Rock borough...........	17	110	7	38	47	631	D	D	31	295	D	D
Gloucester township.........	78	608	D	D	83	1,421	13	162	88	1,467	90	694
Gloucester City city..........	D	D	NA	NA	9	57	NA	NA	31	216	14	64
Guttenberg town...............	10	30	3	D	27	246	NA	NA	20	96	29	162
Hackensack city...............	119	2,942	19	124	373	18,335	15	448	137	2,313	151	916
Haddon township..............	13	39	4	25	17	253	8	D	40	577	D	D
Haddonfield borough	25	269	6	D	64	756	D	D	32	228	31	139
Hamilton township (Atlantic County)	24	238	4	51	54	744	8	92	70	1,329	47	200
Hamilton township (Mercer County)	162	2,614	36	223	316	7,491	25	870	D	D	240	1,304
Hammonton town	29	429	NA	NA	45	413	D	D	35	821	D	D
Hanover township.............	61	1,500	12	419	65	1,919	18	355	35	821	38	570
Harrison township.............	24	251	5	D	59	682	7	114	29	399	D	D
Harrison town	10	47	D	D	D	D	3	271	40	624	20	55
Hasbrouck Heights borough.........................	15	232	6	D	36	316	8	152	39	714	D	D
Hawthorne borough..........	37	192	4	64	58	808	8	24	43	332	50	233
Hazlet township................	19	100	7	95	79	794	8	121	57	741	41	178
Highland Park borough......	D	D	11	85	69	802	NA	NA	31	226	39	127
Hillsborough township	71	1,491	24	232	151	2,243	19	414	69	988	82	474
Hillsdale borough.............	25	115	5	53	20	146	NA	NA	23	345	32	140
Hillside township..............	18	179	NA	NA	16	310	NA	NA	27	295	D	D
Hoboken city....................	40	512	32	1,671	153	2,674	D	D	260	4,079	150	980
Holmdel township.............	24	451	7	43	124	2,522	13	171	34	664	20	200
Hopatcong borough..........	D	D	NA	NA	8	113	D	D	11	68	D	D
Hopewell township (Mercer County)	42	289	D	D	38	2,236	16	140	13	197	30	168
Howell township...............	117	1,056	25	149	118	2,369	21	306	98	1,198	100	767
Irvington township............	22	1,025	NA	NA	89	787	D	D	D	D	D	D
Jackson township	93	612	10	43	77	1,417	17	1,985	52	440	75	419
Jefferson township...........	27	141	D	D	42	372	18	171	47	669	35	144
Jersey City city	183	13,295	62	515	532	11,874	81	1,057	564	7,109	419	1,860
Kearny town.....................	41	1,376	7	12	67	1,016	D	D	68	743	D	D
Kinnelon borough	19	42	3	12	D	D	NA	NA	6	78	14	121
Lacey township................	45	203	D	D	81	1,047	13	87	50	750	D	D
Lakewood township	164	1,763	41	1,338	338	9,397	D	D	112	1,266	158	952
Lawrence township (Mercer County)	73	3,720	D	D	198	3,371	16	452	104	2,024	73	648
Lincoln Park borough........	20	124	NA	NA	25	968	5	9	16	149	D	D
Linden city......................	59	982	6	66	72	1,801	D	D	D	D	105	951
Lindenwold borough	14	47	NA	NA	16	167	NA	NA	13	157	D	D
Little Egg Harbor township	14	66	D	D	17	573	8	67	19	218	29	110
Little Falls township.........	29	296	NA	NA	47	512	4	D	51	663	50	318
Little Ferry borough	D	D	NA	NA	D	D	NA	NA	24	286	D	D
Livingston township	62	2,150	36	360	252	6,917	15	400	D	D	84	709
Lodi borough....................	25	206	NA	NA	33	207	7	20	57	501	D	D

Table C. Incorporated Places, Census Designated Places (CDPs), and Minor Civil Divisions (MCDs) of 10,000 or More Population — **Economic Census**

STATE City, town, township, borough, or CDP (county if applicable)	Retail Trade Number of establishments	Number of employees	Wholesale trade[1] Number of establishments	Number of employees	Transportation and warehousing Number of establishments	Number of employees	Information Number of establishments	Number of employees	Finance and insurance Number of establishments	Number of employees	Real estate and rental and leasing Number of establishments	Number of employees	Professional, scientific, and technical services Number of establishments	Number of employees
	1	2	3	4	5	6	7	8	9	10	11	12	13	14
NEW JERSEY—Con.														
Long Branch city..............	86	1,112	28	125	12	41	6	25	18	104	D	D	53	155
Lower township................	43	615	D	D	11	28	NA	NA	14	52	D	D	15	79
Lumberton township........	32	635	19	1,313	17	279	NA	NA	7	44	12	182	18	70
Lyndhurst township..........	71	1,818	51	1,091	25	740	14	279	D	D	23	149	74	1,166
Madison borough.............	64	797	12	D	4	15	6	21	D	D	D	D	59	257
Mahwah township............	65	1,677	97	2,665	D	D	17	155	49	908	31	94	107	1,609
Manalapan township.........	121	1,529	67	474	37	206	12	171	49	264	30	141	167	842
Manchester township.......	42	595	6	18	13	50	NA	NA	D	D	14	82	19	108
Mantua township	39	966	14	97	14	565	5	17	14	136	5	16	35	243
Manville borough.............	27	422	NA	NA	5	14	NA	NA	D	D	NA	NA	8	19
Maple Shade township	78	1,402	D	D	8	25	D	D	12	93	26	205	22	316
Maplewood township........	74	587	14	99	16	135	15	75	17	73	19	95	73	220
Marlboro township	85	1,361	81	697	32	222	14	60	46	370	33	109	237	1,975
Medford township............	82	1,892	D	D	13	84	8	83	48	228	29	62	86	607
Metuchen borough...........	58	461	23	350	10	263	6	20	41	308	D	D	118	910
Middle township..............	116	2,944	16	115	D	D	14	176	39	212	21	85	40	192
Middlesex borough...........	56	521	D	D	20	174	NA	NA	8	45	12	90	46	337
Middletown township........	158	2,420	35	211	24	608	11	85	95	1,787	43	142	178	1,457
Millburn township............	204	4,890	28	432	D	D	14	131	90	1,949	68	685	167	1,883
Millstone township	26	96	17	194	9	23	6	29	13	79	6	20	47	364
Millville city....................	86	1,703	25	545	10	850	9	128	D	D	16	78	37	240
Monroe township (Gloucester County)......	83	1,396	19	110	12	318	D	D	19	133	15	126	48	170
Monroe township (Middlesex County).......	68	626	53	1,497	50	3,005	7	44	38	237	25	328	178	471
Montclair township...........	157	1,255	23	106	9	152	37	218	44	286	77	289	215	784
Montgomery township.......	46	548	30	92	D	D	D	D	D	D	21	286	212	1,795
Montville township..........	54	511	90	1,787	20	316	D	D	42	170	D	D	153	1,059
Moorestown township.......	116	1,848	58	1,601	19	330	16	490	91	1,456	53	271	217	2,390
Morris township	31	559	20	D	D	D	11	326	46	2,232	24	150	93	2,832
Morristown town	113	1,339	27	201	16	281	21	546	100	728	53	496	255	3,265
Mount Laurel township	128	4,077	76	1,884	24	456	34	1,711	156	13,353	66	2,013	266	5,131
Mount Olive township	80	1,686	44	804	26	1,380	D	D	23	206	19	127	97	858
Neptune township............	86	1,633	29	384	9	169	17	639	D	D	19	142	57	359
Newark city	903	7,325	333	6,003	402	30,896	168	5,939	396	16,905	227	2,413	473	8,271
New Brunswick city..........	123	679	62	840	33	650	20	362	40	381	58	395	125	1,084
New Milford borough.........	24	297	7	41	NA	NA	8	55	D	D	10	23	25	58
New Providence borough .	28	437	12	D	D	D	14	301	32	434	7	37	61	1,100
North Arlington borough....	40	312	15	502	24	417	NA	NA	16	91	11	37	17	39
North Bergen township.....	177	3,289	113	2,602	118	1,746	22	228	D	D	66	362	86	281
North Brunswick township	148	3,168	62	1,109	33	646	16	186	D	D	46	389	225	2,043
North Plainfield borough...	55	859	4	28	19	57	D	D	D	D	5	16	13	70
Nutley township	70	749	22	168	9	41	D	D	35	255	24	94	78	822
Oakland borough..............	45	811	18	294	11	261	D	D	D	D	8	33	48	531
Ocean township (Monmouth County)......	138	2,858	37	271	10	267	7	90	33	384	D	D	89	548
Ocean City city................	101	972	D	D	8	29	14	73	26	306	41	129	49	203
Old Bridge township	149	2,109	D	D	58	358	14	47	56	469	41	297	154	765
Palisades Park borough....	101	503	68	311	13	40	9	129	D	D	29	82	64	164
Paramus borough	586	14,840	93	1,476	38	1,211	53	1,939	139	2,361	70	470	206	2,412
Parsippany-Troy Hills township..................	159	2,275	127	4,721	63	2,380	62	2,996	204	6,533	125	1,323	475	11,785
Passaic city....................	252	2,189	86	1,104	56	427	19	204	34	205	51	157	68	350
Paterson city...................	555	3,641	185	2,284	120	1,552	23	175	52	372	84	402	89	368
Pemberton township........	35	452	NA	NA	4	12	4	7	4	19	D	D	13	47
Pennsauken township.......	121	1,592	114	3,405	49	945	8	33	16	69	32	315	56	763
Pennsville township	48	711	D	D	NA	NA	NA	NA	11	95	D	D	19	62
Pequannock township.......	63	884	32	348	8	119	NA	NA	25	107	11	56	41	148
Perth Amboy city.............	208	1,353	39	1,152	82	792	D	D	D	D	32	158	58	211
Phillipsburg town	47	823	15	98	D	D	NA	NA	8	51	3	7	23	198
Pine Hill borough	14	102	D	D	NA	NA	NA	NA	NA	NA	NA	NA	D	D
Piscataway township	84	1,359	111	2,848	48	1,077	57	2,253	D	D	33	688	287	8,700
Plainfield city..................	124	615	21	D	32	143	D	D	16	55	26	84	D	D
Plainsboro township	22	152	30	6,151	D	D	22	1,022	47	1,905	25	549	310	5,597
Pleasantville city.............	59	962	29	411	12	344	D	D	8	45	16	217	36	173
Point Pleasant borough	61	594	12	36	7	26	6	68	23	111	17	45	51	222
Pompton Lakes borough...	35	139	11	51	D	D	NA	NA	16	63	5	13	32	118
Princeton.......................	137	3,170	D	D	7	10	22	229	101	1,148	48	323	238	1,592
Rahway city	72	578	64	791	30	216	NA	NA	10	111	23	197	D	D
Ramsey borough..............	97	2,549	44	1,167	12	69	10	58	38	324	D	D	98	516
Randolph township..........	61	677	56	986	14	237	D	D	25	117	29	88	115	558
Raritan township..............	80	2,529	27	245	7	68	6	34	30	223	16	30	79	433
Readington township........	44	741	27	334	14	286	D	D	D	D	18	82	74	610
Red Bank borough...........	113	864	11	57	10	226	18	206	107	932	37	126	159	1,078
Ridgefield borough	72	511	76	563	23	109	5	22	D	D	16	25	50	172
Ridgefield Park village	29	191	D	D	24	128	7	198	D	D	23	150	39	700
Ridgewood village	97	1,031	29	111	7	42	14	75	48	315	50	229	130	389
Ringwood borough...........	19	169	16	78	5	15	7	22	9	40	D	D	35	61
River Edge borough..........	22	244	11	33	NA	NA	5	23	D	D	13	135	43	309
River Vale township	22	93	8	18	NA	NA	D	D	7	25	17	29	42	111
Robbinsville township.......	39	5,162	23	1,692	18	589	8	208	D	D	17	145	77	505
Rockaway township..........	124	2,443	35	1,739	19	299	11	270	13	113	18	89	57	462
Roselle borough	59	260	D	D	26	355	3	10	9	77	7	35	D	D
Roselle Park borough	38	184	13	D	7	17	NA	NA	8	90	13	33	D	D
Roxbury township............	108	2,308	36	369	18	326	15	200	24	148	D	D	57	191
Rutherford borough..........	50	534	34	200	19	236	D	D	38	471	35	112	94	919
Saddle Brook township.....	55	748	58	860	32	1,247	10	259	47	655	35	339	62	763
Sayreville borough...........	107	1,316	59	652	57	541	9	74	D	D	32	130	88	1,149
Scotch Plains township.....	39	149	22	D	D	D	4	15	26	123	20	61	D	D
Secaucus town	97	3,339	129	5,610	109	8,452	48	2,390	31	494	48	686	89	1,065

1 Merchant wholesalers, except manufacturers' sales branches and offices.

Table C. Incorporated Places, Census Designated Places (CDPs), and Minor Civil Divisions (MCDs) of 10,000 or More Population — **Economic Census**

STATE City, town, township, borough, or CDP (county if applicable)	Administration and support and waste management and mediation services		Educational services		Health care and social assistance		Arts, entertainment, and recreation		Accommodation and food services		Other services (except public administration)	
	Number of establishments	Number of employees	Number of establishments	Number of employees	Number of establishments	Number of employees	Number of establishments	Number of employees	Number of establishments	Number of employees	Number of establishments	Number of employees
	15	16	17	18	19	20	21	22	23	24	25	26
NEW JERSEY—Con.												
Long Branch city	38	163	NA	NA	94	5,100	12	92	102	1,456	63	255
Lower township	34	123	D	D	30	632	14	86	55	820	36	151
Lumberton township	22	251	5	23	51	883	5	39	16	113	D	D
Lyndhurst township	44	1,952	D	D	D	D	7	299	67	489	D	D
Madison borough	29	198	15	73	53	717	18	532	48	723	48	200
Mahwah township	69	946	9	82	63	555	15	466	60	1,058	59	460
Manalapan township	81	966	8	41	154	1,461	40	467	78	1,069	96	696
Manchester township	34	233	NA	NA	68	2,035	NA	NA	27	307	39	295
Mantua township	28	256	D	D	45	805	3	3	26	586	41	199
Manville borough	20	97	NA	NA	D	D	NA	NA	23	159	25	138
Maple Shade township	25	145	8	37	24	268	6	205	42	866	D	D
Maplewood township	25	153	12	56	80	1,232	22	104	D	D	51	292
Marlboro township	73	1,046	34	316	161	1,550	24	406	57	756	82	414
Medford township	57	1,018	D	D	107	1,379	21	435	60	834	67	411
Metuchen borough	33	184	16	231	85	1,695	10	60	42	400	D	D
Middle township	57	301	NA	NA	112	2,572	21	173	73	670	62	279
Middlesex borough	27	274	3	15	33	286	D	D	30	225	54	252
Middletown township	86	2,360	22	190	166	2,086	41	503	112	1,558	119	780
Millburn township	35	994	15	117	133	923	21	831	66	1,436	77	611
Millstone township	35	307	NA	NA	D	D	12	99	D	D	24	240
Millville city	15	50	D	D	93	1,688	10	D	58	803	52	229
Monroe township (Gloucester County)	47	566	D	D	51	723	9	126	46	798	65	385
Monroe township (Middlesex County)	52	293	12	178	124	1,768	13	68	52	393	58	376
Montclair township	51	608	24	259	226	4,752	56	784	175	2,058	138	801
Montgomery township	58	418	20	163	D	D	13	448	39	469	44	499
Montville township	67	703	11	64	77	532	23	D	53	733	45	303
Moorestown township	66	1,397	D	D	157	3,967	16	232	60	1,343	55	323
Morris township	38	974	8	75	63	1,224	16	238	30	790	24	238
Morristown town	82	723	13	114	200	12,851	12	D	114	1,860	98	584
Mount Laurel township	99	3,873	D	D	153	3,146	21	1,302	133	3,070	75	500
Mount Olive township	44	592	14	96	70	849	D	D	59	771	49	209
Neptune township	35	179	10	83	102	7,034	D	D	74	1,084	61	462
Newark city	332	12,692	44	408	471	18,615	36	2,295	582	9,177	563	3,527
New Brunswick city	73	2,084	D	D	123	9,944	13	448	182	2,307	92	975
New Milford borough	24	93	NA	NA	17	314	3	10	28	273	D	D
New Providence borough	41	529	D	D	48	901	D	D	D	D	D	D
North Arlington borough	14	203	NA	NA	37	254	NA	NA	39	323	D	D
North Bergen township	59	1,178	D	D	111	2,567	D	D	116	1,414	108	586
North Brunswick township	64	7,441	15	96	144	2,752	D	D	91	1,460	93	490
North Plainfield borough	40	135	D	D	D	D	3	12	26	203	35	156
Nutley township	44	213	9	88	110	769	7	38	68	601	85	306
Oakland borough	40	365	5	28	50	492	5	95	32	348	D	D
Ocean township (Monmouth County)	55	326	16	64	128	1,505	18	406	78	889	D	D
Ocean City city	20	69	D	D	D	D	21	260	145	643	49	152
Old Bridge township	68	727	20	103	167	2,771	15	287	91	1,200	D	D
Palisades Park borough	32	85	12	116	D	D	13	80	90	509	74	227
Paramus borough	108	1,763	20	236	273	6,281	26	785	154	3,653	79	669
Parsippany-Troy Hills township	185	10,922	30	294	205	4,255	26	D	180	2,878	95	758
Passaic city	56	1,384	10	86	131	2,776	8	D	D	D	91	426
Paterson city	132	5,224	13	93	238	8,526	14	186	D	D	232	1,348
Pemberton township	11	21	NA	NA	22	1,585	NA	NA	D	D	18	89
Pennsauken township	50	979	3	13	84	1,385	NA	NA	63	915	D	D
Pennsville township	8	38	NA	NA	34	223	NA	NA	25	569	D	D
Pequannock township	23	660	11	82	52	2,478	D	D	29	378	D	D
Perth Amboy city	41	1,163	7	64	80	1,375	6	15	111	670	D	D
Phillipsburg town	10	107	NA	NA	57	1,402	6	50	30	397	D	D
Pine Hill borough	4	27	NA	NA	13	179	NA	NA	14	172	D	D
Piscataway township	95	3,470	22	174	109	2,899	17	137	93	1,522	62	1,560
Plainfield city	53	281	9	61	106	1,964	D	D	D	D	87	325
Plainsboro township	36	2,026	16	152	86	3,425	8	279	51	1,087	25	255
Pleasantville city	29	214	NA	NA	46	1,204	NA	NA	34	361	43	453
Point Pleasant borough	32	231	3	11	D	D	8	86	D	D	50	237
Pompton Lakes borough	17	38	4	50	39	397	5	33	27	261	D	D
Princeton	51	541	D	D	140	2,371	37	850	102	2,101	103	973
Rahway city	28	788	NA	NA	52	1,479	6	106	59	603	D	D
Ramsey borough	161	880	11	29	D	D	26	389	D	D	61	585
Randolph township	56	532	20	147	85	920	22	534	46	560	56	410
Raritan township	40	542	14	140	118	6,890	17	450	48	661	D	D
Readington township	44	392	5	5	D	D	11	175	32	320	D	D
Red Bank borough	45	854	17	159	122	3,230	19	715	93	1,666	80	490
Ridgefield borough	24	109	7	19	35	195	8	23	37	377	D	D
Ridgefield Park village	17	105	D	D	17	84	NA	NA	25	215	21	53
Ridgewood village	35	485	D	D	216	5,958	14	199	89	1,117	85	590
Ringwood borough	31	462	NA	NA	30	240	9	26	16	169	26	67
River Edge borough	24	565	5	17	30	753	3	11	22	223	D	D
River Vale township	26	227	D	D	16	391	D	D	20	140	D	D
Robbinsville township	36	1,599	D	D	D	D	D	D	D	D	37	491
Rockaway township	38	545	NA	NA	31	347	4	13	45	739	39	375
Roselle borough	20	174	NA	NA	23	648	NA	NA	32	404	D	D
Roselle Park borough	D	D	6	64	39	345	4	38	30	343	24	80
Roxbury township	47	563	15	107	80	992	15	122	62	1,070	69	376
Rutherford borough	32	1,675	D	D	73	801	D	D	62	801	49	169
Saddle Brook township	28	1,188	7	D	56	1,037	7	93	48	693	D	D
Sayreville borough	41	418	18	124	65	524	12	196	D	D	D	D
Scotch Plains township	59	869	14	89	69	881	15	528	35	630	51	183
Secaucus town	61	2,312	D	D	72	1,604	15	724	95	1,946	43	259

Table C. Incorporated Places, Census Designated Places (CDPs), and Minor Civil Divisions (MCDs) of 10,000 or More Population — **Economic Census**

Economic activity by sector, 2017

STATE City, town, township, borough, or CDP (county if applicable)	Retail Trade Number of establishments	Retail Trade Number of employees	Wholesale trade[1] Number of establishments	Wholesale trade[1] Number of employees	Transportation and warehousing Number of establishments	Transportation and warehousing Number of employees	Information Number of establishments	Information Number of employees	Finance and insurance Number of establishments	Finance and insurance Number of employees	Real estate and rental and leasing Number of establishments	Real estate and rental and leasing Number of employees	Professional, scientific, and technical services Number of establishments	Professional, scientific, and technical services Number of employees
	1	2	3	4	5	6	7	8	9	10	11	12	13	14
NEW JERSEY—Con.														
Somers Point city	64	1,376	7	D	NA	NA	5	20	12	61	7	23	23	138
Somerville borough	57	804	13	241	6	151	6	51	40	201	17	55	112	717
Southampton township	28	252	9	57	9	357	D	D	5	22	4	16	18	108
South Brunswick township	79	1,377	144	4,714	90	3,795	37	1,849	47	374	40	393	406	4,577
South Orange Village township	35	355	D	D	6	23	10	36	19	96	27	163	88	227
South Plainfield borough	119	2,348	121	2,910	59	1,589	17	284	24	243	31	274	150	3,720
South River borough	32	210	D	D	23	158	NA	NA	D	D	7	21	24	100
Sparta township	48	520	23	272	13	141	D	D	D	D	D	D	98	497
Springfield township (Union County)	91	1,764	42	769	12	186	6	30	40	510	27	134	124	748
Stafford township	116	2,952	8	23	9	60	14	196	26	150	20	103	48	215
Summit city	99	852	D	D	7	9	15	140	103	1,213	46	210	129	1,113
Teaneck township	88	579	54	759	21	74	19	486	47	399	63	362	140	4,583
Tenafly borough	40	624	30	78	5	12	8	15	21	147	D	D	57	154
Tinton Falls borough	143	2,072	23	263	11	628	16	1,329	D	D	23	142	82	2,202
Toms River township	386	8,012	56	354	31	168	35	541	131	1,248	97	346	302	1,723
Totowa borough	80	2,272	57	1,738	16	780	20	320	D	D	35	215	98	1,106
Trenton city	233	1,343	42	610	18	144	33	327	D	D	58	310	125	840
Union township (Union County)	256	5,722	97	1,922	62	868	23	987	66	467	62	417	169	1,136
Union City city	271	1,269	39	182	63	195	14	120	45	D	54	138	108	357
Upper township	42	749	D	D	D	D	D	D	14	95	14	75	32	188
Ventnor City city	25	313	3	D	D	D	NA	NA	6	19	9	18	16	52
Vernon township	29	340	15	68	7	63	NA	NA	D	D	7	41	27	65
Verona township	39	436	10	35	D	D	7	106	27	161	21	58	62	235
Vineland city	261	3,815	71	1,999	42	1,771	22	383	63	535	57	252	104	580
Voorhees township	85	1,473	D	D	14	127	17	987	58	318	30	124	139	936
Wall township	115	1,857	61	632	25	186	27	183	108	1,088	49	352	186	1,679
Wallington borough	26	404	10	173	13	139	NA	NA	D	D	9	24	9	19
Wanaque borough	24	263	D	D	D	D	NA	NA	3	16	NA	NA	12	26
Wantage township	29	482	NA	NA	9	63	NA	NA	D	D	NA	NA	13	28
Warren township	37	349	30	331	11	99	25	1,497	79	1,634	27	113	135	3,065
Washington township (Gloucester County)	177	3,581	32	483	16	316	18	212	60	362	45	167	107	647
Washington township (Morris County)	22	319	D	D	8	123	NA	NA	10	33	12	33	72	219
Waterford township	14	96	10	49	5	150	NA	NA	6	33	6	D	11	36
Wayne township	320	8,850	74	1,287	38	1,269	23	398	111	1,175	72	313	224	2,138
Weehawken township	30	334	7	29	13	47	13	143	D	D	23	79	25	57
West Caldwell township	43	988	40	1,873	5	16	9	85	47	320	37	211	95	746
West Deptford township	38	758	38	2,028	22	705	5	565	24	101	11	50	28	624
Westfield town	109	1,352	15	D	12	92	10	57	61	380	30	107	142	822
West Milford township	63	607	D	D	11	88	D	D	17	220	D	D	45	243
West New York town	215	1,287	24	166	41	89	D	D	D	D	51	234	79	219
West Orange township	94	1,188	31	172	19	161	27	307	55	357	57	177	147	952
West Windsor township	72	1,684	58	604	D	D	25	1,467	97	1,207	39	168	406	9,813
Westwood borough	66	623	20	141	D	D	7	149	D	D	20	81	48	193
Willingboro township	42	484	7	26	D	D	7	167	12	104	10	183	12	92
Winslow township	74	1,011	22	473	20	320	D	D	16	78	16	50	39	219
Woodbridge township	472	11,468	125	3,306	178	4,685	58	1,509	169	4,486	141	872	493	7,738
Woodland Park borough	28	459	27	197	D	D	D	D	17	760	17	132	41	154
Woolwich township	11	163	D	D	D	D	NA	NA	4	23	11	100	21	27
Wyckoff township	66	763	30	143	D	D	5	33	35	128	21	44	78	222
NEW MEXICO	6,335	92,557	1,507	16,914	1,404	18,165	825	12,619	2,715	25,035	2,408	9,229	4,728	56,695
Alamogordo city	123	2,084	8	42	17	154	D	D	D	D	35	138	D	D
Albuquerque city	1,806	32,482	633	8,376	296	5,660	301	8,164	978	14,121	897	3,942	D	D
Artesia city	53	799	D	D	20	135	9	120	26	325	16	69	25	166
Carlsbad city	111	1,805	D	D	34	461	18	103	D	D	30	147	52	386
Chaparral CDP	14	140	NA	NA	D	D	NA	NA	5	15	3	D	D	D
Clovis city	163	2,240	25	277	28	419	D	D	72	418	57	190	66	302
Deming city	56	866	D	D	18	164	D	D	D	D	16	43	D	D
Espanola city	52	939	D	D	6	44	D	D	D	D	11	17	D	D
Farmington city	298	4,754	91	764	47	783	D	D	103	662	79	433	157	897
Gallup city	164	2,832	36	461	20	573	D	D	D	D	36	160	D	D
Hobbs city	151	2,682	66	965	60	694	18	191	59	409	62	408	55	348
Las Cruces city	394	7,221	71	665	52	981	D	D	205	1,622	D	D	251	2,801
Las Vegas city	61	823	D	D	D	D	D	D	31	195	11	31	D	D
Los Alamos CDP	24	413	NA	NA	NA	NA	10	46	D	D	D	D	D	D
Los Lunas village	65	1,451	NA	NA	10	736	D	D	39	168	21	38	38	191
Lovington city	38	339	D	D	24	275	8	48	17	80	11	76	D	D
North Valley CDP	28	376	41	1,089	22	359	D	D	D	D	17	79	D	D
Portales city	39	601	D	D	D	D	D	D	D	D	D	D	D	D
Rio Rancho city	112	2,859	24	154	25	285	D	D	D	D	63	214	106	457
Roswell city	179	2,985	33	335	33	531	D	D	D	D	64	164	88	691
Santa Fe city	710	8,126	72	695	43	518	74	644	D	D	224	703	516	2,060
South Valley CDP	62	688	25	343	D	D	NA	NA	25	146	10	13	D	D
Sunland Park city	14	110	D	D	D	D	NA	NA	D	D	12	41	D	D
NEW YORK	78,260	945,360	26,900	330,990	13,083	259,694	11,769	298,902	26,296	564,569	34,076	193,442	61,744	668,196
Albany city	468	6,947	98	1,373	61	1,330	93	2,281	174	4,869	143	882	451	10,628
Amherst town (balance)	467	11,894	133	3,584	58	760	65	781	357	13,507	166	1,154	436	4,685
Amsterdam city	72	1,328	12	48	15	815	4	58	20	79	11	45	28	146
Arcadia town (balance)	14	359	NA	NA	D	D	NA	NA	NA	NA	5	12	NA	NA
Auburn city	114	1,893	D	D	12	173	14	460	36	191	35	84	46	258
Aurora town (balance)	4	10	9	68	D	D	NA	NA	D	D	6	23	14	67
Babylon village	62	396	10	92	11	81	D	D	D	D	21	81	93	510

1 Merchant wholesalers, except manufacturers' sales branches and offices.

Table C. Incorporated Places, Census Designated Places (CDPs), and Minor Civil Divisions (MCDs) of 10,000 or More Population — Economic Census

STATE City, town, township, borough, or CDP (county if applicable)	Administration and support and waste management and mediation services Number of establishments (15)	Number of employees (16)	Educational services Number of establishments (17)	Number of employees (18)	Health care and social assistance Number of establishments (19)	Number of employees (20)	Arts, entertainment, and recreation Number of establishments (21)	Number of employees (22)	Accommodation and food services Number of establishments (23)	Number of employees (24)	Other services (except public administration) Number of establishments (25)	Number of employees (26)
NEW JERSEY—Con.												
Somers Point city	D	D	NA	NA	D	D	7	96	53	1,074	34	191
Somerville borough	43	460	7	93	90	3,490	8	166	54	585	43	212
Southampton township	23	203	NA	NA	8	72	4	16	13	289	D	D
South Brunswick township	91	1,563	23	129	119	1,209	21	188	84	926	76	397
South Orange Village township	17	249	14	137	81	1,551	16	105	D	D	33	123
South Plainfield borough	64	2,170	12	108	103	1,795	D	D	72	1,184	D	D
South River borough	D	D	NA	NA	14	196	D	D	18	167	29	133
Sparta township	38	306	15	123	103	2,049	8	124	43	656	47	327
Springfield township (Union County)	42	863	8	60	100	1,249	12	251	D	D	61	430
Stafford township	40	201	7	44	113	2,712	13	183	D	D	59	351
Summit city	51	1,402	22	246	135	6,238	21	802	D	D	79	665
Teaneck township	34	331	13	106	241	5,237	13	146	89	1,008	65	213
Tenafly borough	21	107	10	100	84	1,152	14	153	36	403	43	194
Tinton Falls borough	60	973	10	70	101	1,989	16	153	44	773	D	D
Toms River township	180	1,265	36	273	495	9,879	46	727	232	3,331	256	1,449
Totowa borough	41	1,096	4	26	74	1,598	8	66	37	850	40	248
Trenton city	68	513	D	D	160	8,046	13	177	142	916	139	805
Union township (Union County)	102	4,878	11	147	212	3,481	17	401	150	D	146	937
Union City city	56	1,665	14	67	193	2,147	D	D	154	1,144	117	308
Upper township	23	87	D	D	D	D	10	41	42	467	36	112
Ventnor City city	9	51	NA	NA	21	277	NA	NA	D	D	31	169
Vernon township	42	335	6	145	31	D	4	30	29	1,120	31	114
Verona township	26	129	D	D	65	1,078	9	148	33	346	49	446
Vineland city	75	2,189	D	D	219	7,064	13	90	118	2,099	121	731
Voorhees township	34	1,038	10	79	201	7,057	17	287	95	1,765	63	440
Wall township	84	2,230	15	132	168	3,291	D	D	72	824	82	690
Wallington borough	12	130	NA	NA	D	D	4	73	24	111	D	D
Wanaque borough	14	137	4	37	14	400	D	D	D	D	D	D
Wantage township	17	92	NA	NA	D	D	3	14	15	122	13	36
Warren township	49	178	D	D	D	D	20	149	60	630	48	328
Washington township (Gloucester County)	65	489	17	190	206	4,910	29	504	107	1,827	115	812
Washington township (Morris County)	43	475	4	14	D	D	8	75	23	207	D	D
Waterford township	18	178	4	45	20	314	D	D	19	270	13	55
Wayne township	146	5,034	20	220	291	4,747	38	828	164	2,966	124	673
Weehawken township	8	150	3	29	D	D	11	59	28	574	18	91
West Caldwell township	30	269	4	33	66	861	8	158	28	555	D	D
West Deptford township	36	1,360	NA	NA	47	1,194	10	162	28	525	28	160
Westfield town	50	178	19	92	146	2,125	21	436	D	D	100	561
West Milford township	64	219	5	11	61	600	12	55	D	D	57	182
West New York town	44	682	13	162	117	3,153	13	53	95	756	86	262
West Orange township	69	992	10	52	279	4,952	22	433	94	1,482	86	261
West Windsor township	56	1,636	D	D	90	2,835	14	183	74	1,870	47	528
Westwood borough	35	387	9	75	104	1,637	12	187	35	479	48	165
Willingboro township	10	25	NA	NA	66	1,730	D	D	D	D	34	81
Winslow township	47	283	D	D	82	2,858	6	17	56	727	D	D
Woodbridge township	174	15,103	27	126	225	4,772	D	D	240	3,780	216	1,244
Woodland Park borough	22	123	NA	NA	51	518	9	104	28	326	D	D
Woolwich township	6	60	4	14	33	300	4	24	7	57	D	D
Wyckoff township	44	277	10	130	70	1,762	5	D	33	452	D	D
NEW MEXICO	1,963	34,659	422	2,624	5,134	127,808	700	12,062	4,392	91,601	2,963	17,547
Alamogordo city	23	256	D	D	98	2,501	D	D	D	D	54	288
Albuquerque city	712	17,531	173	1,173	1,818	50,897	215	3,659	1,399	31,062	1,004	6,871
Artesia city	D	D	6	D	37	871	5	47	42	777	25	107
Carlsbad city	D	D	D	D	73	1,920	D	D	77	1,565	47	462
Chaparral CDP	D	D	NA	NA	13	775	NA	NA	4	16	D	D
Clovis city	31	381	D	D	D	D	12	50	D	D	71	404
Deming city	8	35	NA	NA	44	1,047	3	51	59	783	D	D
Espa ola city	8	64	3	11	53	1,491	D	D	D	D	20	116
Farmington city	61	471	D	D	237	6,045	15	179	169	3,710	145	959
Gallup city	8	134	NA	NA	103	4,247	10	39	D	D	58	370
Hobbs city	42	1,034	4	16	D	D	D	D	104	2,236	57	500
Las Cruces city	121	2,724	19	243	453	11,917	24	237	283	6,408	176	908
Las Vegas city	5	7	NA	NA	D	D	NA	NA	57	906	23	62
Los Alamos CDP	19	405	NA	NA	59	909	D	D	26	421	D	D
Los Lunas village	6	35	NA	NA	53	842	NA	NA	D	D	D	D
Lovington city	7	62	NA	NA	D	D	D	D	28	363	15	53
North Valley CDP	29	860	NA	NA	18	334	D	D	15	317	39	308
Portales city	D	D	NA	NA	D	D	NA	NA	34	559	D	D
Rio Rancho city	87	3,075	13	93	174	3,483	D	D	108	2,640	89	500
Roswell city	38	155	5	79	163	3,997	16	132	119	2,359	64	443
Santa Fe city	161	1,043	60	304	426	7,348	115	1,524	370	8,091	306	1,752
South Valley CDP	31	329	NA	NA	49	633	NA	NA	32	464	23	100
Sunland Park city	6	99	NA	NA	19	763	D	D	D	D	D	D
NEW YORK	27,508	670,441	6,246	66,107	58,902	1,654,593	13,019	185,076	54,797	824,806	48,436	299,209
Albany city	136	2,970	29	237	356	23,957	53	1,159	446	6,343	289	1,909
Amherst town (balance)	344	15,847	44	316	619	13,359	59	1,033	363	7,433	256	2,090
Amsterdam city	12	86	NA	NA	100	2,343	5	7	41	314	D	D
Arcadia town (balance)	7	31	NA	NA	D	D	NA	NA	NA	NA	D	D
Auburn city	27	382	D	D	157	3,631	18	478	83	1,189	59	254
Aurora town (balance)	15	58	NA	NA	D	D	D	D	8	110	13	30
Babylon village	32	1,487	5	14	82	1,412	6	91	53	1,142	55	338

Table C. Incorporated Places, Census Designated Places (CDPs), and Minor Civil Divisions (MCDs) of 10,000 or More Population — **Economic Census**

STATE City, town, township, borough, or CDP (county if applicable)	Retail Trade Number of establishments	Number of employees	Wholesale trade[1] Number of establishments	Number of employees	Transportation and warehousing Number of establishments	Number of employees	Information Number of establishments	Number of employees	Finance and insurance Number of establishments	Number of employees	Real estate and rental and leasing Number of establishments	Number of employees	Professional, scientific, and technical services Number of establishments	Number of employees
	1	2	3	4	5	6	7	8	9	10	11	12	13	14
NEW YORK—Con.														
Babylon town (balance)	819	11,561	594	8,436	210	4,527	66	970	140	815	191	1,227	420	3,672
Ballston town (balance)	27	511	11	209	NA	NA	NA	NA	17	138	9	14	38	268
Batavia city	80	1,194	30	341	5	93	D	D	37	268	16	57	30	137
Bath town (balance)..........	27	297	NA	NA	6	65	NA	NA	D	D	3	11	4	12
Beacon city	52	307	8	35	NA	NA	6	29	10	70	14	40	42	126
Bedford town.................	113	1,053	36	198	9	122	20	278	46	197	D	D	112	310
Beekman town	16	193	3	3	6	12	NA	NA	5	15	3	9	14	14
Bethlehem town	95	1,759	22	277	24	468	D	D	47	875	32	174	86	354
Binghamton city	169	1,745	54	621	26	492	15	393	64	1,011	53	217	115	1,485
Blooming Grove town (balance)	13	110	7	40	5	15	3	4	D	D	9	23	11	31
Brighton town.................	92	939	43	628	13	188	30	581	140	1,963	75	694	183	2,508
Brookhaven town (balance)	1,309	17,230	415	5,583	231	3,864	112	2,160	378	1,934	293	967	965	9,014
Brunswick town.................	34	891	11	43	D	D	D	D	D	D	5	17	21	63
Buffalo city	877	8,134	233	4,611	141	3,926	118	3,450	255	9,489	275	2,354	717	14,519
Camillus town	83	1,995	12	28	D	D	12	322	33	142	16	51	40	180
Canandaigua city	64	1,369	7	67	NA	NA	7	124	19	294	18	60	42	115
Canandaigua town	45	800	8	40	6	87	D	D	10	72	13	42	23	117
Canton town (balance)	16	171	4	143	NA	NA	NA	NA	NA	NA	NA	NA	NA	NA
Carmel town	127	1,226	37	113	21	66	D	D	51	250	36	95	103	332
Catskill town (balance)	16	171	D	D	4	30	D	D	NA	NA	7	20	D	D
Cheektowaga town (balance)	344	7,181	139	3,107	105	2,965	37	708	93	1,191	81	942	120	1,167
Chenango town	42	787	D	D	7	85	4	12	15	71	6	50	D	D
Chester town (balance)	15	245	17	107	D	D	D	D	NA	NA	4	3	14	36
Chili town	68	1,391	32	692	31	761	6	35	D	D	23	210	45	437
Cicero town (balance).......	120	3,020	34	465	25	1,457	D	D	49	250	32	118	55	973
Clarence town.................	187	3,548	40	337	16	68	11	54	77	414	37	276	109	725
Clarkstown (balance)	454	7,633	134	1,306	55	1,058	70	1,069	138	852	134	611	487	2,087
Clay town (balance)..........	150	3,661	45	942	27	1,374	14	274	46	214	42	258	59	288
Clifton Park town..............	146	2,470	41	772	11	122	22	668	87	544	42	217	164	1,189
Cohoes city	41	438	11	97	5	20	NA	NA	D	D	D	D	23	68
Colonie town (balance).....	413	8,821	165	2,581	81	2,770	63	2,662	296	5,538	159	1,276	409	5,166
Corning city	49	732	4	13	NA	NA	7	113	30	420	11	68	30	263
Cornwall town (balance)...	16	116	7	40	11	55	4	39	12	49	9	36	30	178
Cortland city	63	520	D	D	6	93	9	95	26	277	20	74	38	337
Cortlandt town (balance) ..	85	1,618	22	D	20	128	20	190	D	D	32	121	85	529
Depew village	76	1,456	30	683	14	155	NA	NA	D	D	10	53	19	122
De Witt town	186	3,765	162	3,727	58	1,292	39	1,363	141	3,820	64	587	D	D
Dobbs Ferry village..........	25	220	8	D	D	D	5	17	D	D	D	D	44	151
Dryden town	43	335	7	101	12	95	8	99	D	D	8	68	28	131
Dunkirk city	41	368	5	134	8	157	NA	NA	14	107	9	88	20	88
Eastchester town (balance)	109	1,891	20	D	11	107	D	D	40	238	D	D	113	296
East Fishkill town	71	653	17	87	15	45	6	56	30	144	26	73	100	647
East Greenbush town	64	1,316	D	D	10	257	D	D	24	279	17	106	64	1,869
East Hampton town (balance)	141	780	17	169	27	83	14	115	D	D	56	197	D	D
Elma town....................	26	350	10	72	6	46	NA	NA	8	17	7	51	22	140
Elmira city	80	1,115	36	442	12	212	9	186	41	746	28	102	46	239
Endicott village	56	450	15	85	5	79	8	197	24	154	10	194	34	255
Evans town	35	408	6	201	7	39	D	D	10	51	8	20	11	30
Fallsburg town	35	167	9	427	12	146	NA	NA	7	66	24	66	13	32
Farmington town..............	22	324	14	275	14	398	NA	NA	5	22	10	89	18	56
Fishkill town (balance)......	38	1,054	6	20	D	D	15	183	21	328	13	68	50	232
Floral Park village	54	322	27	144	15	51	6	28	33	222	43	155	94	793
Fredonia village	26	581	4	D	NA	NA	D	D	20	72	11	36	18	84
Freeport village	186	1,904	74	589	43	688	13	290	40	307	47	233	123	377
Fulton city	63	531	D	D	6	79	D	D	16	157	14	47	23	50
Garden City village	199	3,357	62	905	9	590	20	444	188	2,889	D	D	586	3,563
Gates town	95	2,108	54	793	33	1,632	12	265	30	294	48	363	54	2,477
Geddes town (balance)	35	969	15	208	7	390	NA	NA	8	72	9	18	18	71
Geneva city.................	61	1,165	10	184	5	143	D	D	19	217	11	27	22	142
Glen Cove city	101	1,146	49	594	11	58	14	33	26	165	25	99	85	310
Glens Falls city	57	873	21	246	9	135	12	401	37	959	18	51	62	491
Glenville town (balance) ..	58	1,689	D	D	7	195	NA	NA	D	D	15	26	D	D
Gloversville city	59	719	14	170	7	122	D	D	13	59	7	45	25	130
Goshen town (balance)	17	233	17	232	6	348	NA	NA	6	22	7	11	15	59
Grand Island town	36	482	16	108	13	44	D	D	D	D	13	67	42	257
Great Neck village	43	859	47	185	D	D	NA	NA	15	74	D	D	52	229
Greece town	279	6,263	31	331	29	133	D	D	75	500	68	293	123	822
Greenburgh town (balance)	213	3,804	114	1,848	49	1,218	56	1,058	111	1,023	99	887	230	1,546
Guilderland town.............	117	1,256	34	523	17	87	D	D	55	311	41	149	160	777
Halfmoon town.................	50	1,195	30	709	D	D	D	D	D	D	29	231	60	795
Hamburg town (balance) ..	171	3,980	18	224	23	198	D	D	27	172	37	184	55	275
Harrison village	53	352	56	1,030	D	D	D	D	133	5,743	82	933	166	2,225
Haverstraw village	20	73	5	48	4	223	D	D	7	16	4	11	D	D
Haverstraw town (balance)	22	291	D	D	7	23	NA	NA	8	27	6	19	20	42
Hempstead village	208	2,482	34	245	26	88	15	357	41	273	53	278	D	D
Hempstead town (balance)	1,935	29,337	577	4,537	402	7,625	180	3,786	648	7,900	548	1,952	1,692	8,311
Henrietta town	275	7,399	112	4,194	47	1,000	47	2,736	71	794	58	634	167	3,566
Highlands town (balance) .	14	85	NA	NA	NA	NA	NA	NA	NA	NA	D	D	12	16
Horseheads town (balance)	40	840	14	363	D	D	NA	NA	D	D	7	28	7	49
Huntington town (balance)	895	11,347	368	6,133	169	2,534	120	3,564	677	10,919	338	1,448	1,439	11,032
Hyde Park town	56	523	9	41	6	32	D	D	16	86	16	36	25	126
Irondequoit town	107	2,232	13	65	19	267	6	32	D	D	49	252	67	339
Islip town (balance)..........	1,132	13,499	690	10,948	328	6,188	105	2,548	406	3,474	315	1,365	999	8,346

1 Merchant wholesalers, except manufacturers' sales branches and offices.

Table C. Incorporated Places, Census Designated Places (CDPs), and Minor Civil Divisions (MCDs) of 10,000 or More Population — **Economic Census**

	Economic activity by sector, 2017											
	Administration and support and waste management and mediation services		Educational services		Health care and social assistance		Arts, entertainment, and recreation		Accommodation and food services		Other services (except public administration)	
STATE City, town, township, borough, or CDP (county if applicable)	Number of establishments	Number of employees	Number of establishments	Number of employees	Number of establishments	Number of employees	Number of establishments	Number of employees	Number of establishments	Number of employees	Number of establishments	Number of employees
	15	16	17	18	19	20	21	22	23	24	25	26
NEW YORK—Con.												
Babylon town (balance)....	365	5,167	60	512	346	5,674	80	1,080	333	4,686	522	3,420
Ballston town (balance)....	20	282	5	11	14	185	NA	NA	16	195	20	88
Batavia city	10	101	5	D	87	2,260	9	523	50	947	42	304
Bath town (balance)..........	5	18	NA	NA	15	1,296	NA	NA	8	55	D	D
Beacon city	20	118	6	23	26	453	10	70	48	655	27	125
Bedford town	75	492	17	76	97	1,381	31	166	51	929	75	510
Beekman town	17	32	3	8	15	86	NA	NA	18	104	23	41
Bethlehem town	50	187	11	81	99	1,714	21	309	74	945	71	353
Binghamton city	48	1,467	8	50	154	7,381	22	355	176	3,255	108	652
Blooming Grove town (balance)	8	30	6	11	11	96	NA	NA	7	42	D	D
Brighton town	78	2,531	21	182	293	6,793	14	168	76	1,132	71	587
Brookhaven town (balance)	735	5,389	118	756	1,252	29,298	169	1,960	922	12,801	988	4,630
Brunswick town	9	20	NA	NA	23	127	NA	NA	20	251	21	86
Buffalo city	325	7,018	47	311	687	38,916	104	2,974	697	13,799	431	3,135
Camillus town	20	76	5	11	82	909	13	80	D	D	D	D
Canandaigua city	19	238	5	110	69	3,243	12	70	61	866	35	317
Canandaigua town	16	64	D	D	24	497	12	109	21	233	19	123
Canton town (balance)	5	7	NA	NA	4	59	NA	NA	D	D	D	D
Carmel town	83	389	23	85	117	2,851	28	246	100	861	127	480
Catskill town (balance)	8	9	NA	NA	23	489	D	D	19	55	D	D
Cheektowaga town (balance)	133	3,075	13	77	166	5,168	27	384	207	5,621	133	1,121
Chenango town	13	441	NA	NA	21	367	8	47	24	319	D	D
Chester town (balance)	12	238	NA	NA	9	56	3	D	4	D	9	29
Chili town	41	458	5	28	66	1,156	10	88	57	724	41	186
Cicero town (balance).......	59	408	D	D	44	683	24	383	78	1,415	D	D
Clarence town	67	622	26	178	107	1,352	21	200	85	1,740	103	494
Clarkstown town (balance)	232	2,628	56	294	397	7,651	64	1,232	251	3,415	255	1,268
Clay town (balance)	69	1,615	14	135	129	1,923	9	314	67	1,644	D	D
Clifton Park town	55	649	D	D	134	2,175	18	492	106	2,002	70	519
Cohoes city	8	88	NA	NA	29	700	6	38	29	189	D	D
Colonie town (balance).....	177	7,589	47	458	249	5,088	49	1,041	284	5,794	275	2,450
Corning city	18	993	NA	NA	71	2,475	D	D	57	744	35	290
Cornwall town (balance) ...	17	528	NA	NA	D	D	5	62	22	219	D	D
Cortland city	14	310	NA	NA	76	2,736	10	108	83	2,084	43	238
Cortlandt town (balance) ..	61	602	10	55	76	3,795	D	D	55	478	64	222
Depew village	36	497	3	19	35	812	4	27	D	D	57	389
De Witt town	94	10,403	19	163	131	2,701	26	303	124	2,572	115	1,356
Dobbs Ferry village..........	22	57	D	D	48	1,578	11	119	39	533	28	143
Dryden town	22	57	NA	NA	30	678	8	6	18	218	18	157
Dunkirk city	10	450	3	5	36	1,003	8	53	24	198	35	234
Eastchester town (balance)	40	307	22	211	96	866	16	304	51	713	123	663
East Fishkill town	43	378	12	88	72	1,027	11	65	62	473	D	D
East Greenbush town	23	189	4	5	45	848	4	209	57	925	39	431
East Hampton town (balance)	179	1,225	12	32	58	546	54	582	142	1,698	69	331
Elma town	16	66	D	D	23	347	D	D	19	303	33	148
Elmira city	27	529	4	D	127	4,622	14	238	D	D	39	216
Endicott village	19	227	4	12	43	879	4	35	D	D	D	D
Evans town	20	85	NA	NA	58	560	D	D	36	451	D	D
Fallsburg town	8	58	NA	NA	47	812	D	D	27	99	32	102
Farmington town	20	162	NA	NA	18	122	D	D	20	430	15	103
Fishkill town (balance)	21	122	NA	NA	52	812	D	D	43	780	35	158
Floral Park village	34	848	13	20	57	1,202	10	157	45	355	57	203
Fredonia village	8	144	4	24	21	339	D	D	28	742	14	40
Freeport village	85	517	9	110	159	1,902	18	54	108	848	130	773
Fulton city	8	123	NA	NA	56	1,353	6	115	41	463	D	D
Garden City village	81	2,437	15	179	188	2,603	26	674	115	3,298	100	854
Gates town	72	1,347	8	67	89	2,298	16	418	92	1,491	68	582
Geddes town (balance)	10	47	4	22	22	744	6	14	31	539	20	146
Geneva city	11	197	NA	NA	NA	NA	3	85	70	1,062	29	110
Glen Cove city	101	308	7	17	112	2,819	19	396	D	D	79	292
Glens Falls city	29	2,110	D	D	122	3,914	13	358	57	668	26	261
Glenville town (balance) ...	D	D	D	D	47	882	D	D	D	D	30	170
Gloversville city	12	199	NA	NA	62	1,686	NA	NA	31	190	24	238
Goshen town (balance)	14	135	5	15	19	290	7	D	9	85	14	77
Grand Island town	20	87	NA	NA	43	482	9	47	39	605	D	D
Great Neck village	25	291	7	46	D	D	6	80	15	88	42	223
Greece town	105	820	D	D	219	8,370	28	611	155	3,306	124	623
Greenburgh town (balance)	86	1,808	28	225	236	2,885	51	837	142	2,080	160	917
Guilderland town	55	879	11	27	137	2,641	16	435	100	1,602	75	453
Halfmoon town	35	545	6	53	35	281	10	136	38	553	48	292
Hamburg town (balance) ..	57	532	6	21	102	1,783	22	D	119	2,170	77	446
Harrison village	100	953	27	661	127	3,331	27	985	D	D	66	1,415
Haverstraw village	16	34	NA	NA	26	576	NA	NA	33	153	D	D
Haverstraw town (balance)	15	58	3	3	27	346	9	130	20	112	16	56
Hempstead village	73	501	8	48	203	4,169	8	151	134	2,710	125	752
Hempstead town (balance)	990	7,518	167	1,155	1,622	26,974	253	4,609	1,190	15,521	1,323	6,625
Henrietta town	75	11,178	20	463	77	2,932	28	840	176	3,778	102	715
Highlands town (balance) .	7	23	D	D	D	D	NA	NA	8	259	7	324
Horseheads town (balance)	9	449	NA	NA	10	598	NA	NA	20	488	D	D
Huntington town (balance)	615	16,476	125	908	869	16,815	157	1,950	501	7,672	657	3,500
Hyde Park town	22	125	3	5	52	807	D	D	46	593	39	151
Irondequoit town	51	984	10	174	102	2,259	14	151	93	1,503	68	373
Islip town (balance)	682	10,484	91	608	881	23,617	136	1,783	665	9,147	782	3,689

STATE City, town, township, borough, or CDP (county if applicable)	Retail Trade Number of establishments	Number of employees	Wholesale trade[1] Number of establishments	Number of employees	Transportation and warehousing Number of establishments	Number of employees	Information Number of establishments	Number of employees	Finance and insurance Number of establishments	Number of employees	Real estate and rental and leasing Number of establishments	Number of employees	Professional, scientific, and technical services Number of establishments	Number of employees
	1	2	3	4	5	6	7	8	9	10	11	12	13	14
NEW YORK—Con.														
Ithaca city	173	3,000	14	111	9	215	26	329	53	678	55	412	133	991
Ithaca town	17	366	D	D	NA	NA	D	D	D	D	14	45	34	129
Jamestown city	106	1,411	33	236	12	120	13	178	50	285	28	110	57	280
Johnson City village	115	2,553	15	121	NA	NA	6	193	30	150	11	36	16	213
Kenmore village	41	415	D	D	3	5	D	D	D	D	5	7	26	73
Kent town	21	93	D	D	8	13	NA	NA	7	25	3	3	25	40
Kingsbury town (balance)	23	270	D	D	5	50	NA	NA	4	35	NA	NA	7	58
Kingston city	117	1,845	23	237	16	352	22	293	61	671	44	162	119	441
Kirkland town	23	226	7	71	4	23	3	20	D	D	6	7	18	82
Kiryas Joel village	152	926	59	229	19	64	11	31	D	D	47	114	101	383
Lackawanna city	53	501	12	209	16	446	NA	NA	9	40	10	26	13	88
La Grange town	40	410	24	281	18	346	4	39	16	141	D	D	34	151
Lake Grove village	163	3,689	10	D	4	5	D	D	D	D	14	40	26	58
Lancaster village	20	178	14	193	6	97	D	D	13	135	6	18	16	73
Lancaster town (balance)	55	1,468	30	538	23	681	7	148	D	D	20	423	46	522
Lansing town (balance)	11	90	NA	NA	7	86	D	D	NA	NA	8	12	21	326
Le Ray town	30	518	4	17	D	D	NA	NA	D	D	10	156	25	166
Lewisboro town	34	292	17	D	D	D	11	28	8	24	12	16	65	239
Lewiston town	9	77	D	D	6	17	NA	NA	D	D	8	31	17	23
Lindenhurst village	91	516	41	290	D	D	D	D	D	D	16	33	58	161
Lloyd town	31	415	13	179	D	D	D	D	22	98	13	28	30	131
Lockport city	62	551	19	224	18	550	8	185	28	130	21	78	64	205
Lockport town	82	1,851	D	D	11	210	D	D	24	280	17	87	17	72
Long Beach city	84	906	28	98	12	51	11	29	30	406	49	129	105	195
Lynbrook village	96	697	50	291	37	259	11	59	54	328	33	74	104	661
Lysander town (balance)	21	145	D	D	17	621	3	4	D	D	11	34	30	122
Malone town (balance)	25	476	3	78	5	13	NA	NA	D	D	4	16	D	D
Malta town	24	288	14	275	9	142	9	76	D	D	7	41	47	354
Mamakating town	20	112	NA	NA	10	342	NA	NA	D	D	7	12	17	99
Mamaroneck village	97	680	31	180	10	15	13	117	32	278	D	D	88	290
Mamaroneck town (balance)	27	540	9	D	5	111	9	50	15	49	14	47	66	130
Manlius town	40	932	D	D	3	14	NA	NA	27	98	23	86	42	168
Massapequa Park village	43	350	13	27	D	D	D	D	24	115	16	24	50	77
Massena village	74	1,284	D	D	3	12	7	56	19	164	7	18	16	58
Mastic Beach village	16	82	NA	NA	8	93	NA	NA	NA	NA	D	D	7	6
Middletown city	115	1,509	27	210	10	69	10	443	20	203	26	95	45	165
Milton town (balance)	28	300	5	16	D	D	NA	NA	D	D	7	25	20	140
Mineola village	128	865	52	500	18	214	11	226	58	268	43	168	231	1,459
Monroe town (balance)	40	1,033	D	D	NA	NA	D	D	5	D	9	35	22	53
Montgomery town (balance)	35	444	22	767	33	1,148	NA	NA	12	153	15	201	21	91
Moreau town	22	92	4	14	D	D	NA	NA	NA	NA	8	27	9	49
Mount Kisco village	120	1,696	27	232	11	116	16	194	51	584	D	D	80	382
Mount Pleasant town (balance)	88	1,721	72	1,449	31	432	26	797	64	1,025	51	248	191	1,384
Mount Vernon city	226	2,264	86	962	37	1,039	13	125	28	130	127	549	101	377
Newburgh city	84	756	34	271	32	302	8	53	16	78	18	81	56	416
Newburgh town	157	3,387	47	1,175	35	1,055	21	340	60	352	32	193	98	859
New Castle town	49	450	15	D	6	196	11	24	33	109	24	53	91	418
New Hartford town	145	3,116	16	171	D	D	D	D	48	1,147	18	83	48	270
New Paltz town (balance)	34	513	D	D	D	D	NA	NA	8	22	4	4	25	124
New Rochelle city	237	3,025	70	382	39	185	30	711	76	299	200	692	215	719
New Windsor town	85	1,062	28	435	29	722	14	158	31	253	43	473	55	2,065
New York city	35,488	353,094	13,813	150,295	5,643	121,685	6,628	208,759	10,913	373,260	20,435	127,520	28,631	406,156
Niagara Falls city	287	4,335	D	D	38	580	11	92	33	254	46	306	79	391
Niskayuna town	55	1,663	D	D	D	D	D	D	D	D	16	67	55	2,279
North Castle town	68	608	39	436	27	600	14	105	D	D	44	294	128	1,003
North Greenbush town	29	364	8	182	D	D	10	598	D	D	8	19	33	529
North Hempstead town (balance)	726	11,170	392	5,635	112	1,497	87	1,409	314	3,758	389	2,305	844	6,103
North Tonawanda city	75	1,166	D	D	18	364	D	D	30	133	8	20	31	151
Ogden town	17	70	13	241	6	9	3	33	D	D	10	21	18	68
Ogdensburg city	40	786	13	275	D	D	6	48	14	108	5	19	13	80
Olean city	108	1,679	13	91	6	121	12	162	29	449	23	123	36	443
Oneida city	52	1,088	D	D	5	35	7	90	16	177	14	68	21	114
Oneonta city	64	496	D	D	5	90	6	51	17	170	D	D	37	262
Onondaga town	28	322	D	D	7	180	5	46	11	56	13	30	26	134
Ontario town	36	378	15	105	3	2	NA	NA	9	27	10	33	10	162
Orangetown town (balance)	85	1,149	58	1,415	26	527	36	1,110	62	289	53	127	151	1,558
Orchard Park town	95	2,692	42	356	D	D	7	244	41	230	19	153	72	509
Ossining village	75	609	12	D	12	60	10	56	29	145	29	101	52	166
Ossining village (balance)	7	50	D	D	NA	NA	7	29	D	D	8	19	34	215
Oswego city	96	1,400	D	D	4	26	10	114	32	259	23	79	42	133
Owego town (balance)	30	283	9	77	5	56	D	D	8	61	5	7	D	D
Oyster Bay town (balance)	1,211	16,074	776	11,229	231	5,305	190	5,478	631	12,615	477	2,728	1,635	12,532
Parma town (balance)	27	263	4	8	5	11	NA	NA	3	3	D	D	9	31
Patchogue village	142	1,479	12	42	5	19	11	86	D	D	D	D	59	306
Patterson town	29	191	D	D	7	220	D	D	8	27	7	22	23	110
Peekskill city	95	916	27	318	22	43	9	103	19	95	31	176	53	207
Penfield town	111	2,796	20	235	11	14	11	66	D	D	34	182	111	895
Perinton town (balance)	57	1,110	54	480	8	37	28	280	144	1,805	45	349	188	1,964
Pittsford town (balance)	63	1,844	26	178	5	13	19	243	84	961	43	254	124	1,296
Plattekill town	15	161	5	19	NA	NA	D	D	NA	NA	NA	NA	10	16
Plattsburgh city	90	1,037	15	169	14	98	D	D	45	210	34	92	72	387
Plattsburgh town	148	2,832	22	396	17	393	6	168	23	151	26	150	16	103
Pomfret town (balance)	18	187	NA	NA	4	7	NA	NA	3	13	NA	NA	4	14
Port Chester village	155	2,397	39	484	19	109	14	115	23	99	31	107	72	229
Potsdam town (balance)	33	600	3	19	4	32	6	40	D	D	10	31	6	69

1 Merchant wholesalers, except manufacturers' sales branches and offices.

Table C. Incorporated Places, Census Designated Places (CDPs), and Minor Civil Divisions (MCDs) of 10,000 or More Population — **Economic Census**

NEW YORK—Con.

STATE City, town, township, borough, or CDP (county if applicable)	Administration and support and waste management and mediation services — Number of establishments	Number of employees	Educational services — Number of establishments	Number of employees	Health care and social assistance — Number of establishments	Number of employees	Arts, entertainment, and recreation — Number of establishments	Number of employees	Accommodation and food services — Number of establishments	Number of employees	Other services (except public administration) — Number of establishments	Number of employees
	15	16	17	18	19	20	21	22	23	24	25	26
Ithaca city	26	387	14	76	104	1,510	25	191	204	3,447	86	575
Ithaca town	14	46	D	D	48	2,348	4	75	27	484	7	35
Jamestown city	17	532	6	122	91	2,870	18	275	79	895	64	360
Johnson City village	16	177	NA	NA	81	4,191	5	73	56	835	40	214
Kenmore village	31	578	4	42	27	411	D	D	32	349	37	177
Kent town	16	40	NA	NA	17	253	7	43	14	73	D	D
Kingsbury town (balance)	10	79	NA	NA	9	78	4	9	12	72	9	37
Kingston city	41	386	10	20	187	4,719	22	382	116	1,130	68	320
Kirkland town	11	35	D	D	28	717	6	34	D	D	25	124
Kiryas Joel village	35	260	NA	NA	23	1,213	9	22	17	61	17	71
Lackawanna city	17	225	NA	NA	36	907	5	27	47	692	36	177
La Grange town	35	177	6	13	58	1,436	6	192	36	412	D	D
Lake Grove village	10	33	6	35	22	168	3	D	33	713	16	77
Lancaster village	11	38	NA	NA	18	197	5	77	19	258	17	108
Lancaster town (balance)	57	479	7	69	73	1,608	14	231	58	1,368	D	D
Lansing town (balance)	13	62	NA	NA	7	60	5	26	9	81	D	D
Le Ray town	7	39	NA	NA	13	118	NA	NA	31	469	17	87
Lewisboro town	37	505	8	15	39	246	15	78	14	157	36	155
Lewiston town	D	D	NA	NA	25	1,216	5	D	D	D	D	D
Lindenhurst village	56	952	7	39	49	386	D	D	68	848	103	345
Lloyd town	11	83	D	D	40	751	5	18	29	247	D	D
Lockport city	34	515	NA	NA	89	1,786	13	184	54	651	39	132
Lockport town	29	130	6	47	41	827	D	D	33	742	D	D
Long Beach city	45	187	9	48	88	1,205	19	170	96	927	104	318
Lynbrook village	56	433	9	76	111	1,857	12	169	75	836	91	440
Lysander town (balance)	20	79	NA	NA	D	D	8	32	17	83	21	74
Malone town (balance)	5	20	NA	NA	16	330	D	D	15	D	6	25
Malta town	15	104	5	36	51	828	13	105	39	828	19	123
Mamakating town	20	69	NA	NA	10	58	NA	NA	19	115	7	16
Mamaroneck village	80	600	18	95	87	1,318	28	468	81	800	109	518
Mamaroneck town (balance)	15	57	5	21	D	D	10	169	10	206	25	114
Manlius town	21	122	4	21	80	1,021	9	423	22	561	D	D
Massapequa Park village	29	127	8	50	40	780	D	D	D	D	D	D
Massena village	7	61	NA	NA	35	946	3	28	39	591	31	132
Mastic Beach village	12	23	NA	NA	D	D	NA	NA	19	156	12	45
Middletown city	20	202	9	163	92	2,064	D	D	72	659	55	301
Milton town (balance)	18	97	3	18	26	179	3	10	18	181	11	57
Mineola village	69	1,006	11	99	80	9,829	D	D	62	769	108	487
Monroe town (balance)	13	103	D	D	D	D	5	27	D	D	12	92
Montgomery town (balance)	21	224	D	D	21	317	3	9	17	168	39	225
Moreau town	12	74	NA	NA	12	193	4	11	10	76	8	24
Mount Kisco village	43	252	12	56	116	3,915	14	419	75	726	75	339
Mount Pleasant town (balance)	81	2,511	15	D	115	6,916	D	D	77	1,538	79	406
Mount Vernon city	80	508	12	267	150	3,251	14	170	100	1,009	151	677
Newburgh city	23	330	NA	NA	112	3,323	7	45	79	904	59	540
Newburgh town	67	1,045	11	91	97	1,303	D	D	103	1,422	68	461
New Castle town	31	469	9	85	49	363	33	144	D	D	52	233
New Hartford town	22	611	D	D	97	2,697	9	76	D	D	33	238
New Paltz town (balance)	15	184	5	14	38	538	12	61	22	836	18	127
New Rochelle city	196	1,095	26	174	272	5,879	41	641	213	2,172	214	1,034
New Windsor town	44	778	10	46	83	1,164	13	185	71	550	69	366
New York city	9,172	378,217	NA	NA	NA	NA	6,771	96,960	24,871	396,907	23,119	159,346
Niagara Falls city	40	1,422	5	17	103	2,607	17	175	202	5,417	73	425
Niskayuna town	D	D	D	D	81	1,812	5	137	32	466	D	D
North Castle town	44	526	14	152	50	742	19	318	64	803	47	209
North Greenbush town	16	55	NA	NA	31	895	3	17	28	446	23	72
North Hempstead town (balance)	283	4,178	78	984	732	19,475	92	1,611	361	5,755	484	3,543
North Tonawanda city	29	274	5	31	61	1,165	18	78	55	751	59	186
Ogden town	26	466	4	19	19	287	3	21	8	132	18	46
Ogdensburg city	11	118	NA	NA	48	1,760	NA	NA	33	298	21	102
Olean city	10	344	4	D	94	2,165	6	166	71	885	33	199
Oneida city	13	140	NA	NA	77	1,739	5	28	35	412	24	88
Oneonta city	9	24	D	D	62	1,475	10	D	75	989	32	134
Onondaga town	32	200	4	12	45	2,079	8	143	22	414	15	40
Ontario town	14	166	NA	NA	12	93	3	1	D	D	18	60
Orangetown town (balance)	73	809	15	114	127	3,319	40	574	126	1,375	102	440
Orchard Park town	55	806	D	D	121	3,317	D	D	50	1,208	60	361
Ossining village	74	1,796	10	102	44	900	7	28	50	321	60	207
Ossining town (balance)	16	127	4	18	18	351	D	D	D	D	20	99
Oswego city	11	30	5	22	85	2,856	14	117	90	1,313	44	187
Owego town (balance)	17	186	NA	NA	28	289	D	D	30	473	13	28
Oyster Bay town (balance)	639	13,986	152	938	1,187	19,421	226	2,904	750	10,645	808	4,413
Parma town (balance)	13	162	NA	NA	D	D	D	D	8	88	D	D
Patchogue village	27	487	5	62	76	1,250	16	286	90	2,255	82	373
Patterson town	23	88	NA	NA	12	160	7	159	17	205	23	178
Peekskill city	53	288	8	65	61	866	11	55	70	753	80	938
Penfield town	66	477	22	175	145	2,254	18	753	89	1,573	D	D
Perinton town (balance)	65	3,250	15	85	142	1,926	20	248	69	1,388	71	458
Pittsford town (balance)	34	2,460	D	D	75	1,465	18	723	43	1,248	38	393
Plattekill town	23	68	NA	NA	8	157	3	10	9	387	4	6
Plattsburgh city	17	884	4	11	116	4,281	8	136	82	1,327	33	164
Plattsburgh town	15	100	NA	NA	63	787	D	D	55	982	31	189
Pomfret town (balance)	3	11	NA	NA	8	169	3	9	13	216	3	12
Port Chester village	74	441	13	125	49	1,233	12	375	109	1,073	97	398
Potsdam town (balance)	NA	NA	NA	NA	16	256	NA	NA	9	76	D	D

Table C. Incorporated Places, Census Designated Places (CDPs), and Minor Civil Divisions (MCDs) of 10,000 or More Population — **Economic Census**

STATE City, town, township, borough, or CDP (county if applicable)	Retail Trade — Number of establishments	Retail Trade — Number of employees	Wholesale trade[1] — Number of establishments	Wholesale trade[1] — Number of employees	Transportation and warehousing — Number of establishments	Transportation and warehousing — Number of employees	Information — Number of establishments	Information — Number of employees	Finance and insurance — Number of establishments	Finance and insurance — Number of employees	Real estate and rental and leasing — Number of establishments	Real estate and rental and leasing — Number of employees	Professional, scientific, and technical services — Number of establishments	Professional, scientific, and technical services — Number of employees
	1	2	3	4	5	6	7	8	9	10	11	12	13	14
NEW YORK—Con.														
Poughkeepsie city	125	1,649	23	219	18	123	D	D	32	305	47	198	121	921
Poughkeepsie town (balance)	241	4,513	32	289	23	515	23	274	60	817	59	198	113	3,844
Putnam Valley town	12	36	NA	NA	7	15	D	D	5	13	6	8	29	35
Queensbury town	211	3,826	24	272	14	836	14	906	36	198	30	157	53	269
Ramapo town (balance)	246	1,454	84	340	20	49	11	69	59	274	121	374	172	587
Red Hook town	37	407	6	16	3	4	13	86	13	59	16	58	35	100
Riverhead town	368	6,203	50	715	27	256	25	323	70	955	53	204	110	629
Rochester city	743	7,184	242	3,356	119	3,629	101	4,480	207	3,871	286	2,481	637	9,109
Rockville Centre village	120	1,163	35	259	17	176	12	93	68	418	89	180	206	710
Rome city	117	2,083	19	215	29	1,416	13	230	D	D	33	97	85	1,444
Rotterdam town	102	1,606	20	171	23	1,228	14	571	26	D	22	142	D	D
Rye city	61	453	18	183	D	D	11	217	49	724	39	243	88	299
Salina town	89	1,420	52	1,412	24	570	14	156	44	996	45	363	87	2,918
Saratoga Springs city	146	1,947	24	554	15	307	29	443	85	828	83	380	184	1,294
Saugerties town	40	353	13	342	8	94	D	D	5	21	9	69	24	46
Scarsdale village	59	521	22	D	NA	NA	10	45	35	141	43	132	81	267
Schenectady city	197	1,520	38	362	28	230	22	383	62	1,168	59	264	125	1,234
Schodack town	32	254	12	110	7	406	NA	NA	D	D	6	18	18	132
Shawangunk town	14	47	7	D	11	305	NA	NA	D	D	9	25	13	50
Sleepy Hollow village	28	77	8	D	D	D	3	2	D	D	D	D	33	83
Smithtown town (balance)	419	7,275	303	5,532	84	1,172	49	1,142	233	1,763	156	427	D	D
Somers town	35	490	11	D	7	44	9	43	33	130	D	D	80	230
Southampton town (balance)	317	2,954	61	383	33	320	34	253	D	D	131	289	225	771
Southeast town (balance)	87	1,155	45	853	23	118	15	114	38	193	22	85	73	565
Southold town	137	831	25	92	12	187	18	175	D	D	47	149	75	238
Southport town	23	242	6	73	NA	NA	NA	NA	4	26	NA	NA	D	D
Spring Valley village	164	1,380	45	371	18	683	16	167	43	375	104	567	89	245
Stony Point town	41	433	15	91	D	D	D	D	D	D	9	19	27	108
Suffern village	29	502	23	198	D	D	6	88	27	128	16	42	38	303
Sullivan town	15	115	D	D	7	21	NA	NA	NA	NA	3	6	13	42
Sweden town (balance)	34	1,215	6	238	D	D	D	D	D	D	7	18	5	25
Syracuse city	593	7,219	120	1,855	50	990	80	1,212	219	3,807	209	1,615	462	7,318
Tarrytown village	26	260	22	D	D	D	15	116	D	D	D	D	111	809
Thompson town (balance)	39	668	NA	NA	8	30	NA	NA	9	113	12	65	10	15
Tonawanda city	46	554	29	723	22	712	D	D	D	D	23	81	35	193
Tonawanda town (balance)	188	1,836	79	1,093	73	2,234	11	249	59	626	49	406	89	1,523
Troy city	142	1,338	26	347	17	364	20	219	32	276	40	235	98	754
Ulster town	138	2,788	18	90	10	295	8	79	22	304	25	92	23	148
Union town (balance)	66	849	24	194	9	228	D	D	19	392	25	114	33	430
Utica city	186	2,619	54	846	21	669	26	560	66	1,720	52	177	137	1,238
Valley Stream village	178	2,151	59	432	148	1,392	12	67	66	432	52	227	146	1,574
Van Buren town (balance)	23	399	7	926	13	563	NA	NA	6	35	10	36	D	D
Vestal town	139	3,209	25	286	11	207	26	788	38	274	30	179	44	397
Victor town (balance)	129	2,700	33	447	4	35	D	D	16	73	20	54	61	748
Wallkill town	222	3,915	42	765	33	486	19	778	43	879	42	141	47	213
Wappinger town (balance)	73	2,201	22	581	16	58	7	112	20	106	D	D	47	219
Warwick town (balance)	26	598	19	153	10	36	D	D	7	15	9	26	36	108
Watertown city	157	2,045	18	322	18	343	18	598	55	405	42	260	50	427
Watervliet city	27	242	5	39	5	133	NA	NA	7	44	8	31	D	D
Wawarsing town (balance)	17	305	4	D	4	5	NA	NA	5	20	NA	NA	D	D
Webster town (balance)	94	2,972	35	144	14	53	16	567	D	D	25	91	68	461
Westbury village	93	865	30	139	12	157	12	46	37	448	30	130	96	508
West Haverstraw village	34	264	D	D	4	13	D	D	7	28	8	32	11	36
West Seneca town	142	2,874	17	445	20	882	19	324	58	594	34	153	75	344
Wheatfield town	49	656	20	302	20	208	NA	NA	20	62	16	88	31	443
White Plains city	396	7,271	105	1,757	38	555	76	1,513	269	5,313	203	771	690	5,859
Whitestown town	21	542	5	38	D	D	D	D	13	2,050	12	52	11	74
Wilton town	117	2,433	19	537	10	754	8	101	D	D	14	40	35	167
Woodbury village	216	5,194	9	31	5	5	NA	NA	D	D	21	101	23	63
Yonkers city	715	10,095	149	1,270	106	4,336	54	1,461	146	1,104	345	1,475	264	1,596
Yorktown town	169	2,739	25	D	20	408	21	429	54	315	D	D	117	2,071
NORTH CAROLINA	34,926	496,081	9,831	154,877	6,110	125,437	3,920	94,977	13,543	190,259	12,450	56,360	24,766	221,438
Albemarle city	141	1,802	15	189	5	15	D	D	42	255	25	130	35	163
Apex town	148	3,034	46	451	14	110	22	112	62	371	D	D	196	617
Archdale city	46	450	21	574	12	200	NA	NA	19	99	12	41	19	64
Asheboro city	187	2,619	33	323	11	127	17	227	74	594	35	174	62	334
Asheville city	872	14,168	160	1,660	50	962	110	1,920	302	2,391	354	1,204	693	3,657
Belmont city	60	1,223	15	146	7	101	6	14	34	131	15	46	41	137
Boone town	167	2,607	12	62	D	D	20	346	48	301	D	D	81	341
Burlington city	354	5,770	74	1,213	30	819	28	526	126	1,257	78	289	94	774
Carrboro town	58	765	9	175	3	16	10	143	15	58	33	129	107	287
Cary town	544	9,914	158	3,619	42	276	151	14,001	298	3,331	292	1,138	1,049	11,172
Chapel Hill town	168	2,741	25	141	6	37	54	738	145	1,042	D	D	D	D
Charlotte city	2,758	46,761	1,606	27,225	811	31,860	663	24,733	2,123	81,731	1,936	11,022	3,655	47,392
Clayton town	84	1,412	14	208	D	D	D	D	41	178	25	67	60	259
Clemmons village	78	1,017	15	249	D	D	9	77	D	D	D	D	69	308
Concord city	507	10,139	109	1,785	67	1,591	43	943	116	646	151	629	254	993
Cornelius town	112	1,603	46	515	19	120	28	189	87	655	114	470	188	720
Davidson town	26	244	14	88	D	D	11	85	39	174	D	D	D	D
Durham city	867	14,593	216	5,244	121	2,788	D	D	374	9,930	337	2,013	D	D
Eden city	88	1,079	D	D	9	433	D	D	24	135	24	83	23	132
Elizabeth City city	150	2,111	13	234	D	D	D	D	D	D	24	141	51	198
Elon town	9	44	NA	NA	NA	NA	NA	NA	4	18	3	3	12	31
Fayetteville city	861	14,319	95	1,710	69	856	64	1,298	248	1,614	249	1,457	434	5,417
Fuquay-Varina town	118	2,158	16	208	10	142	D	D	46	301	26	55	68	266
Garner town	156	3,136	66	1,411	20	438	21	329	58	329	35	145	87	1,302

1 Merchant wholesalers, except manufacturers' sales branches and offices.

Table C. Incorporated Places, Census Designated Places (CDPs), and Minor Civil Divisions (MCDs) of 10,000 or More Population — **Economic Census**

	Economic activity by sector, 2017											
	Administration and support and waste management and mediation services		Educational services		Health care and social assistance		Arts, entertainment, and recreation		Accommodation and food services		Other services (except public administration)	
STATE City, town, township, borough, or CDP (county if applicable)	Number of establishments	Number of employees	Number of establishments	Number of employees	Number of establishments	Number of employees	Number of establishments	Number of employees	Number of establishments	Number of employees	Number of establishments	Number of employees
	15	16	17	18	19	20	21	22	23	24	25	26
NEW YORK—Con.												
Poughkeepsie city............	30	2,751	7	129	145	5,520	13	227	102	1,540	90	519
Poughkeepsie town (balance)	57	2,046	12	69	169	4,409	25	261	147	2,362	101	521
Putnam Valley town	20	178	4	3	18	144	11	37	10	90	D	D
Queensbury town	47	733	6	28	125	1,931	28	723	117	2,399	71	423
Ramapo town (balance) ...	80	692	D	D	164	3,779	12	102	78	1,201	94	380
Red Hook town................	14	955	3	10	38	818	14	30	46	415	14	41
Riverhead town................	93	928	10	57	202	3,919	34	669	159	2,104	111	673
Rochester city.................	243	7,854	51	554	484	37,839	100	2,162	590	7,749	376	2,559
Rockville Centre village	45	2,489	19	133	209	2,823	24	187	127	1,943	117	635
Rome city......................	22	439	D	D	108	2,528	14	63	87	1,273	68	412
Rotterdam town	39	297	5	7	49	702	9	170	67	957	51	278
Rye city........................	31	189	15	588	56	1,612	25	646	D	D	46	329
Salina town....................	48	4,485	5	D	63	2,348	10	137	75	1,227	63	642
Saratoga Springs city	47	1,094	14	80	165	4,024	51	1,085	169	3,889	94	496
Saugerties town	18	51	6	44	16	170	18	91	31	349	D	D
Scarsdale village	15	130	10	155	80	456	13	79	27	217	40	146
Schenectady city	64	977	11	78	212	8,001	25	1,859	170	2,208	105	776
Schodack town	22	170	NA	NA	28	390	NA	NA	16	255	D	D
Shawangunk town	12	20	NA	NA	13	115	NA	NA	16	74	D	D
Sleepy Hollow village........	17	23	6	35	D	D	6	33	D	D	25	54
Smithtown town (balance)	269	4,460	65	454	386	10,202	50	713	280	4,396	341	1,667
Somers town...................	56	321	D	D	61	1,182	11	150	43	437	29	101
Southampton town (balance)	366	2,201	25	106	135	1,841	79	724	195	2,158	153	732
Southeast town (balance).	59	294	D	D	67	1,687	15	193	48	574	52	268
Southold town.................	93	494	7	18	69	1,362	40	363	124	861	70	238
Southport town................	6	22	NA	NA	14	207	NA	NA	15	165	7	25
Spring Valley village.........	51	649	D	D	71	4,054	D	D	D	D	62	207
Stony Point town..............	28	330	NA	NA	D	D	D	D	36	406	D	D
Suffern village................	23	188	D	D	59	2,692	3	14	39	343	D	D
Sullivan town..................	14	62	NA	NA	5	63	D	D	4	12	7	53
Sweden town (balance)	10	17	NA	NA	10	94	3	23	D	D	17	89
Syracuse city..................	162	7,466	33	287	446	26,170	47	1,243	425	7,156	258	1,642
Tarrytown village.............	29	550	8	261	62	1,208	23	232	57	1,261	42	193
Thompson town (balance)	11	161	NA	NA	34	2,292	D	D	28	404	21	61
Tonawanda city...............	25	335	NA	NA	30	368	NA	NA	41	766	D	D
Tonawanda town (balance)	102	2,154	15	140	168	3,916	23	323	129	1,831	131	741
Troy city........................	35	220	10	D	187	5,567	12	239	166	2,298	81	497
Ulster town.....................	20	516	4	14	40	1,615	11	97	60	886	46	306
Union town (balance)........	17	363	4	25	53	937	9	165	50	617	38	138
Utica city.......................	56	1,202	D	D	221	10,854	20	D	D	D	106	3,141
Valley Stream village	63	1,378	11	44	171	5,562	19	343	91	1,444	D	D
Van Buren town (balance)	10	81	NA	NA	4	21	D	D	19	263	11	45
Vestal town....................	38	1,508	3	26	85	1,613	15	221	92	2,429	55	356
Victor town (balance)........	23	503	NA	NA	33	419	9	91	51	D	27	204
Wallkill town...................	50	495	7	34	110	7,512	16	159	99	2,044	83	711
Wappinger town (balance)	32	701	D	D	49	394	8	117	47	380	47	184
Warwick town (balance)....	37	147	4	14	38	625	9	336	26	206	32	114
Watertown city................	31	830	4	D	160	4,587	16	100	107	2,156	63	330
Watervliet city.................	9	24	NA	NA	18	105	NA	NA	24	213	D	D
Wawarsing town (balance)	D	D	NA	NA	D	D	NA	NA	23	204	D	D
Webster town (balance)....	56	436	8	32	76	1,723	16	174	63	1,473	60	260
Westbury village.............	90	492	9	101	85	833	4	38	64	2,074	57	401
West Haverstraw village ...	13	26	NA	NA	32	885	3	17	31	277	D	D
West Seneca town...........	87	1,700	11	83	151	2,203	D	D	86	1,475	96	618
Wheatfield town	D	D	5	35	75	1,736	3	13	35	433	D	D
White Plains city	198	5,386	55	499	391	13,062	44	778	231	3,544	243	1,590
Whitestown town	9	24	NA	NA	8	574	7	17	8	42	17	78
Wilton town	23	160	6	12	41	1,121	D	D	38	836	D	D
Woodbury village	20	97	NA	NA	20	189	5	23	44	768	21	52
Yonkers city...................	175	3,362	25	588	493	10,893	56	1,491	387	4,822	442	1,635
Yorktown town................	79	576	21	120	172	1,971	20	475	109	1,126	98	536
NORTH CAROLINA.........	13,101	280,437	2,225	20,442	24,080	602,444	3,868	69,027	21,437	429,125	15,118	93,642
Albemarle city................	18	297	D	D	122	2,450	11	249	D	D	D	D
Apex town......................	61	1,128	22	127	128	1,143	19	202	96	2,156	D	D
Archdale city..................	15	344	NA	NA	D	D	4	91	31	548	D	D
Asheboro city.................	33	992	5	23	143	3,276	11	188	108	2,391	45	325
Asheville city..................	210	4,234	89	537	739	24,227	126	2,342	646	15,437	334	2,077
Belmont city...................	D	D	6	12	49	740	D	D	42	902	26	150
Boone town....................	24	182	D	D	D	D	19	195	107	2,650	54	311
Burlington city................	56	1,910	17	78	247	10,615	24	492	196	4,568	105	696
Carrboro town.................	15	95	14	84	56	D	D	D	47	920	36	206
Cary town......................	245	5,161	118	2,243	D	D	81	2,675	432	9,309	305	2,251
Chapel Hill town..............	58	774	51	441	274	15,270	39	471	221	4,537	102	1,334
Charlotte city..................	1,699	67,395	305	2,715	2,288	60,916	413	12,043	2,214	50,810	1,608	14,437
Clayton town...................	32	264	8	49	90	1,326	D	D	65	1,376	D	D
Clemmons village	34	237	D	D	63	1,064	13	228	69	1,513	D	D
Concord city...................	122	2,397	29	192	271	7,600	56	2,328	265	7,952	178	1,070
Cornelius town................	61	1,555	21	285	D	D	38	704	86	1,401	75	467
Davidson town	19	201	12	62	45	587	10	27	45	777	19	54
Durham city....................	367	8,218	116	1,620	823	27,001	106	2,162	709	15,662	445	5,545
Eden city.......................	20	425	NA	NA	45	1,025	7	77	50	815	21	98
Elizabeth City city...........	23	222	NA	NA	125	2,209	7	141	D	D	D	D
Elon town.......................	5	37	NA	NA	17	242	NA	NA	D	D	NA	NA
Fayetteville city...............	163	4,116	34	332	612	18,776	56	661	534	12,325	304	1,788
Fuquay-Varina town.........	30	220	5	27	63	1,313	10	167	82	1,737	51	319
Garner town....................	55	793	13	190	100	1,375	8	130	86	2,259	D	D

Table C. Incorporated Places, Census Designated Places (CDPs), and Minor Civil Divisions (MCDs) of 10,000 or More Population — **Economic Census**

| | Economic activity by sector, 2017 | | | | | | | | | | | | | |
| | Retail Trade | | Wholesale trade[1] | | Transportation and warehousing | | Information | | Finance and insurance | | Real estate and rental and leasing | | Professional, scientific, and technical services | |
STATE City, town, township, borough, or CDP (county if applicable)	Number of establish-ments	Number of employees	Number of establish-ments	Number of employees	Number of establish-ments	Number of employees	Number of establish-ments	Number of employees	Number of establish-ments	Number of employees	Number of establish-ments	Number of employees	Number of establish-ments	Number of employees
	1	2	3	4	5	6	7	8	9	10	11	12	13	14
NORTH CAROLINA—Con.														
Gastonia city	365	5,816	84	882	49	893	23	495	116	726	106	470	154	1,040
Goldsboro city	296	4,265	61	1,302	17	247	15	230	97	806	48	287	87	523
Graham city	70	769	10	250	NA	NA	3	18	28	131	16	83	36	258
Greensboro city	1,246	20,654	538	9,612	201	8,811	159	4,938	612	9,961	508	3,933	965	7,972
Greenville city	414	6,765	54	503	42	406	48	725	186	1,168	130	559	238	1,182
Harrisburg town	45	937	24	302	D	D	D	D	28	138	17	17	40	168
Havelock city	67	669	NA	NA	D	D	D	D	15	95	24	76	33	478
Henderson city	139	1,863	17	401	D	D	14	509	43	217	39	168	40	268
Hendersonville city	218	3,487	33	221	D	D	16	235	85	497	49	110	101	515
Hickory city	410	7,136	118	4,143	37	936	42	1,466	155	764	110	472	197	1,712
High Point city	388	5,018	307	4,428	57	1,049	43	1,391	173	2,643	125	708	289	2,867
Holly Springs town	67	1,289	15	63	3	43	4	10	45	188	D	D	106	470
Hope Mills town	48	1,132	D	D	8	327	3	84	21	95	12	45	16	125
Huntersville town	173	3,872	53	924	22	123	24	299	108	848	109	306	217	1,715
Indian Trail town	107	2,226	88	927	42	732	10	179	41	141	45	111	72	341
Jacksonville city	329	6,247	27	139	24	295	D	D	94	816	118	450	139	943
Kannapolis city	155	1,807	21	297	26	898	D	D	48	255	45	153	53	463
Kernersville town	157	3,315	65	839	43	2,225	17	103	57	312	44	102	91	465
Kings Mountain city	54	766	D	D	9	164	NA	NA	22	93	15	65	20	325
Kinston city	150	1,969	28	280	17	340	D	D	53	471	33	172	46	258
Knightdale town	68	1,538	6	37	9	78	D	D	23	119	18	88	38	159
Laurinburg city	102	1,369	8	51	NA	NA	13	70	D	D	19	42	21	77
Leland town	54	1,125	8	55	10	86	D	D	23	107	24	148	37	137
Lenoir city	115	1,560	D	D	14	231	D	D	48	247	27	70	36	147
Lewisville town	23	534	5	43	4	31	NA	NA	D	D	4	8	27	69
Lexington city	150	2,259	26	307	14	497	5	68	58	404	39	193	63	271
Lincolnton city	89	1,651	12	134	D	D	10	91	40	236	25	62	30	189
Lumberton city	207	2,866	31	321	15	228	D	D	64	864	35	108	59	258
Matthews town	164	3,091	54	944	22	109	26	448	67	282	63	385	141	771
Mebane city	117	1,751	9	375	14	821	D	D	19	88	D	D	22	119
Mint Hill town	66	949	26	124	22	135	9	45	38	214	35	59	61	627
Monroe city	226	3,026	63	1,077	36	269	21	208	81	429	39	147	107	745
Mooresville town	258	4,663	105	998	21	140	25	338	124	629	96	263	179	1,812
Morganton city	151	2,466	21	241	7	28	D	D	55	290	30	72	58	256
Morrisville town	106	1,782	88	4,185	57	2,372	39	3,076	D	D	59	624	200	7,841
Mount Airy city	151	1,799	20	316	14	326	14	166	41	290	26	123	37	254
Mount Holly city	23	248	7	22	7	107	4	4	D	D	15	38	21	76
Murraysville CDP	20	245	D	D	8	34	NA	NA	5	7	15	31	18	72
Myrtle Grove CDP	19	316	6	54	D	D	NA	NA	16	62	11	40	34	71
New Bern city	205	3,162	28	307	14	209	25	350	72	435	59	193	101	615
Newton city	61	578	11	337	10	616	10	91	31	275	18	46	28	92
Pinehurst village	37	365	7	18	D	D	NA	NA	D	D	23	42	44	91
Piney Green CDP	8	31	NA	NA	NA	NA	NA	NA	NA	NA	6	30	NA	NA
Raleigh city	1,798	29,789	596	10,466	221	5,404	295	8,823	1,016	18,387	962	6,090	2,494	33,853
Reidsville city	93	1,233	D	D	D	D	D	D	40	224	22	50	23	96
Roanoke Rapids city	117	1,557	8	122	9	81	D	D	38	226	22	91	21	127
Rocky Mount city	300	4,016	83	1,534	31	1,245	D	D	106	1,300	68	440	110	730
Salisbury city	200	3,193	53	844	22	1,029	D	D	87	512	44	134	90	548
Sanford city	210	2,741	33	550	13	230	D	D	61	289	31	91	71	322
Shelby city	175	2,334	24	225	D	D	D	D	63	374	51	254	77	498
Smithfield town	187	3,042	18	196	8	2	15	92	63	366	30	257	49	220
Southern Pines town	121	1,677	7	37	8	172	13	344	D	D	45	133	81	791
Spring Lake town	49	657	5	21	NA	NA	D	D	14	82	11	53	15	365
Stallings town	47	839	26	217	9	63	NA	NA	9	17	16	26	33	83
Statesville city	204	3,062	59	835	24	534	16	172	94	570	46	184	83	533
Summerfield town	24	219	13	37	3	6	3	6	10	26	14	42	39	80
Tarboro town	58	922	D	D	10	97	D	D	D	D	14	27	16	75
Thomasville city	131	1,350	31	711	24	767	6	30	33	296	D	D	35	165
Wake Forest town	D	D	31	296	20	78	18	81	D	D	52	158	154	1,530
Waxhaw town	37	629	11	70	9	34	D	D	23	126	24	32	52	126
Weddington town	8	102	7	16	5	8	7	21	14	35	11	7	55	188
Wilmington city	801	11,925	138	1,385	97	1,361	89	2,978	359	2,743	305	1,117	674	4,243
Wilson city	272	3,456	80	811	29	386	18	290	91	2,743	71	258	90	542
Winston-Salem city	1,009	16,801	236	3,954	112	2,283	93	1,724	444	9,537	351	1,687	694	5,556
NORTH DAKOTA	3,277	49,579	1,563	20,075	1,467	17,380	353	7,284	1,738	17,896	1,100	5,440	1,821	14,880
Bismarck city	388	7,549	132	2,460	78	1,685	45	949	207	1,557	140	446	261	2,335
Dickinson city	139	2,054	54	623	48	450	D	D	47	358	43	180	74	443
Fargo city	539	11,419	253	5,174	161	3,053	88	3,003	388	9,142	277	1,716	449	5,007
Grand Forks city	282	5,846	57	953	69	1,070	D	D	107	848	80	569	119	1,301
Jamestown city	89	1,455	21	275	25	320	D	D	44	410	23	50	29	217
Mandan city	79	1,356	31	272	35	169	D	D	40	341	D	D	64	1,231
Minot city	268	5,160	79	1,305	81	707	16	452	113	974	D	D	121	737
West Fargo city	101	1,531	52	546	40	828	D	D	44	310	D	D	48	821
Williston city	112	1,857	76	1,034	72	1,012	D	D	48	324	96	421	98	403
OHIO	35,500	588,060	11,430	193,412	7,698	189,666	4,295	102,069	17,229	260,044	10,782	62,902	23,854	250,438
Akron city	549	7,127	229	3,602	109	1,732	73	1,951	198	3,546	165	977	440	4,411
Alliance city	108	1,760	12	267	4	18	9	71	38	192	14	63	28	156
Amherst city	61	876	D	D	NA	NA	5	20	24	134	12	33	23	59
Ashland city	77	1,513	24	234	17	168	9	106	44	238	23	120	41	886
Ashtabula city	72	741	11	84	13	163	NA	NA	34	138	13	36	23	113
Athens city	100	1,856	D	D	5	78	14	436	45	310	38	176	42	412
Aurora city	99	2,668	36	1,296	4	55	7	69	27	97	11	39	55	467
Austintown CDP	111	2,091	33	532	17	384	D	D	46	285	22	124	24	118
Avon city	88	2,591	36	991	10	85	8	26	52	370	22	95	70	426
Avon Lake city	39	440	16	66	10	296	8	31	34	103	18	63	50	115
Barberton city	61	718	22	228	10	25	5	43	22	109	12	37	D	D

1 Merchant wholesalers, except manufacturers' sales branches and offices.

Table C. Incorporated Places, Census Designated Places (CDPs), and Minor Civil Divisions (MCDs) of 10,000 or More Population — Economic Census

STATE City, town, township, borough, or CDP (county if applicable)	Administration and support and waste management and mediation services		Educational services		Health care and social assistance		Arts, entertainment, and recreation		Accommodation and food services		Other services (except public administration)	
	Number of establishments	Number of employees	Number of establishments	Number of employees	Number of establishments	Number of employees	Number of establishments	Number of employees	Number of establishments	Number of employees	Number of establishments	Number of employees
	15	16	17	18	19	20	21	22	23	24	25	26
NORTH CAROLINA—Con.												
Gastonia city	86	2,298	8	101	311	9,322	23	447	209	4,659	150	931
Goldsboro city	30	383	5	70	186	6,299	12	214	161	3,371	90	596
Graham city	14	258	4	18	32	341	4	63	46	911	D	D
Greensboro city	455	22,218	84	1,176	890	24,398	122	2,541	884	20,121	564	3,979
Greenville city	73	1,503	21	228	386	14,873	27	396	298	7,275	138	859
Harrisburg town	29	524	3	17	35	633	D	D	44	906	39	288
Havelock city	13	68	3	5	D	D	D	D	48	753	21	97
Henderson city	12	215	NA	NA	78	2,284	D	D	D	D	32	180
Hendersonville city	31	267	5	27	143	3,686	D	D	129	2,597	81	469
Hickory city	82	2,669	16	79	286	9,735	27	551	193	4,176	123	754
High Point city	126	3,029	18	167	274	8,440	31	526	236	5,662	196	1,743
Holly Springs town	40	459	D	D	94	732	21	285	63	1,336	46	189
Hope Mills town	5	55	NA	NA	23	413	6	179	49	1,164	D	D
Huntersville town	115	2,939	41	312	181	3,106	D	D	121	3,005	95	525
Indian Trail town	79	887	6	7	D	D	D	D	83	1,371	D	D
Jacksonville city	62	1,955	14	146	198	4,155	15	263	246	5,373	106	702
Kannapolis city	25	563	NA	NA	63	907	D	D	82	1,591	D	D
Kernersville town	49	1,466	5	D	81	1,011	21	239	93	1,914	75	491
Kings Mountain city	17	182	NA	NA	43	840	4	83	37	666	9	24
Kinston city	28	2,478	D	D	129	3,429	6	124	79	1,666	49	395
Knightdale town	22	447	9	37	39	807	3	47	48	950	D	D
Laurinburg city	18	422	NA	NA	88	2,147	D	D	D	D	24	80
Leland town	18	160	4	18	37	597	7	67	45	874	D	D
Lenoir city	10	46	4	23	77	1,733	D	D	D	D	D	D
Lewisville town	16	31	D	D	20	206	D	D	12	134	D	D
Lexington city	14	1,590	4	27	79	2,094	D	D	101	1,827	50	270
Lincolnton city	D	D	NA	NA	72	1,671	4	142	54	1,065	44	145
Lumberton city	22	1,648	D	D	144	4,659	D	D	104	2,358	40	209
Matthews town	62	1,338	16	125	144	3,779	31	684	112	2,578	85	465
Mebane city	11	101	4	10	33	373	D	D	49	1,044	D	D
Mint Hill town	43	246	7	33	44	567	11	67	40	648	D	D
Monroe city	49	1,079	6	19	158	4,048	11	135	115	2,384	90	496
Mooresville town	85	1,269	27	340	206	3,055	57	1,341	190	3,895	118	653
Morganton city	19	400	D	D	107	3,922	D	D	86	2,097	41	159
Morrisville town	88	3,738	23	194	64	848	11	142	124	2,441	47	289
Mount Airy city	20	648	NA	NA	72	1,803	D	D	79	1,556	29	182
Mount Holly city	D	D	4	7	D	D	NA	NA	24	327	D	D
Murraysville CDP	16	78	NA	NA	5	34	NA	NA	9	140	16	43
Myrtle Grove CDP	11	70	3	2	D	D	5	8	15	441	D	D
New Bern city	38	1,310	D	D	187	5,467	D	D	124	2,588	74	287
Newton city	13	246	NA	NA	31	960	7	D	26	392	D	D
Pinehurst village	11	67	NA	NA	78	5,867	7	311	28	1,785	18	73
Piney Green CDP	5	27	NA	NA	NA	NA	NA	NA	NA	NA	4	17
Raleigh city	916	31,228	180	1,390	1,635	43,361	244	7,406	1,259	29,257	1,106	8,160
Reidsville city	15	168	D	D	72	1,414	7	80	50	825	D	D
Roanoke Rapids city	18	504	D	D	62	1,057	D	D	47	980	44	247
Rocky Mount city	79	1,539	D	D	219	6,098	24	397	149	3,372	76	458
Salisbury city	D	D	8	48	187	7,950	19	300	143	3,027	62	330
Sanford city	39	758	D	D	145	2,519	11	121	105	1,915	71	366
Shelby city	23	531	D	D	151	4,013	8	169	87	1,863	52	354
Smithfield town	23	360	NA	NA	91	2,521	D	D	69	1,712	35	132
Southern Pines town	23	602	11	183	98	2,117	19	407	85	1,798	56	388
Spring Lake town	5	121	NA	NA	16	122	NA	NA	49	750	D	D
Stallings town	25	184	3	14	13	160	7	57	D	D	D	D
Statesville city	D	D	6	22	181	4,835	11	129	123	2,452	70	446
Summerfield town	27	155	NA	NA	15	106	3	D	14	248	D	D
Tarboro town	D	D	NA	NA	43	1,776	D	D	33	593	D	D
Thomasville city	40	1,282	NA	NA	49	1,568	4	122	72	1,137	D	D
Wake Forest town	53	353	18	138	D	D	26	278	100	2,045	80	473
Waxhaw town	19	90	6	13	27	331	D	D	D	D	28	174
Weddington town	20	100	3	33	18	105	8	53	D	D	D	D
Wilmington city	237	3,452	50	340	673	16,330	88	1,467	525	11,091	317	2,137
Wilson city	44	1,118	D	D	206	4,782	D	D	144	3,010	91	565
Winston-Salem city	307	15,263	51	355	631	32,573	91	2,611	578	13,249	418	2,661
NORTH DAKOTA	1,138	13,921	122	926	2,057	62,455	470	5,418	2,080	36,648	1,763	9,706
Bismarck city	136	2,735	D	D	292	10,316	42	914	197	5,353	248	1,656
Dickinson city	43	276	5	19	90	1,809	D	D	72	1,288	D	D
Fargo city	243	4,766	33	303	426	19,053	79	1,717	371	8,857	307	2,393
Grand Forks city	89	1,264	D	D	147	7,143	45	938	182	4,165	109	656
Jamestown city	21	180	4	35	65	2,620	11	31	46	822	D	D
Mandan city	31	390	D	D	59	1,182	9	183	D	D	64	282
Minot city	68	868	16	98	144	4,809	36	440	164	3,558	121	710
West Fargo city	57	547	4	29	66	942	15	62	46	969	66	506
Williston city	55	621	4	25	66	1,194	13	49	D	D	72	431
OHIO	13,485	380,754	2,041	18,776	29,595	856,794	3,999	76,914	24,346	474,616	18,425	126,378
Akron city	185	5,430	25	214	492	31,388	48	1,348	414	6,196	337	2,022
Alliance city	6	201	NA	NA	NA	NA	8	125	74	1,377	46	329
Amherst city	11	299	NA	NA	46	880	6	33	49	1,072	32	200
Ashland city	28	338	3	D	85	2,400	D	D	55	1,128	48	338
Ashtabula city	20	146	NA	NA	69	2,110	8	159	53	716	35	141
Athens city	16	159	6	23	119	2,537	D	D	113	2,348	45	204
Aurora city	21	71	3	12	30	658	D	D	37	727	26	172
Austintown CDP	22	951	D	D	92	1,846	7	52	79	1,475	49	312
Avon city	42	985	8	64	81	2,888	18	280	67	1,499	D	D
Avon Lake city	32	650	5	74	45	525	11	114	45	536	35	224
Barberton city	18	94	NA	NA	78	2,110	NA	NA	42	682	D	D

Table C.   Incorporated Places, Census Designated Places (CDPs), and Minor Civil Divisions (MCDs) of 10,000 or More Population — **Economic Census**

	Economic activity by sector, 2017													
	Retail Trade		Wholesale trade[1]		Transportation and warehousing		Information		Finance and insurance		Real estate and rental and leasing		Professional, scientific, and technical services	
STATE City, town, township, borough, or CDP (county if applicable)	Number of establish-ments	Number of employees	Number of establish-ments	Number of employees	Number of establish-ments	Number of employees	Number of establish-ments	Number of employees	Number of establish-ments	Number of employees	Number of establish-ments	Number of employees	Number of establish-ments	Number of employees
	1	2	3	4	5	6	7	8	9	10	11	12	13	14
OHIO—Con.														
Bay Village city	12	248	14	38	NA	NA	3	8	D	D	10	10	40	117
Beachwood city	144	2,727	52	467	D	D	27	436	144	1,315	99	1,541	217	1,805
Beavercreek city	270	6,178	25	265	10	23	21	316	85	600	47	171	229	5,170
Bedford city	60	1,605	19	168	D	D	NA	NA	D	D	16	78	18	72
Bedford Heights city	33	465	58	1,171	18	773	NA	NA	D	D	24	291	19	333
Bellefontaine city	88	911	D	D	4	22	D	D	31	174	16	93	24	145
Berea city	42	614	23	159	15	122	D	D	D	D	12	79	41	318
Bexley city	24	212	4	3	3	7	4	24	24	99	D	D	41	78
Blue Ash city	82	1,316	117	2,156	22	1,311	40	1,540	143	1,531	58	629	245	4,866
Boardman CDP	278	4,982	30	447	28	455	17	322	91	649	46	187	117	608
Bowling Green city	92	1,780	12	78	D	D	14	199	57	260	40	168	49	273
Brecksville city	33	477	34	865	11	163	17	658	50	1,822	28	159	88	740
Bridgetown CDP	54	1,196	9	87	7	72	D	D	38	176	25	103	24	133
Broadview Heights city	31	505	29	405	13	20	12	226	35	271	22	44	72	307
Brooklyn city	45	1,786	20	858	D	D	D	D	25	936	14	89	10	19
Brook Park city	54	988	35	471	37	1,334	D	D	18	173	12	100	28	924
Brunswick city	83	1,487	45	401	22	408	9	115	D	D	29	85	62	298
Bucyrus city	54	702	D	D	7	98	D	D	28	414	10	58	20	106
Cambridge city	75	916	9	265	8	185	D	D	34	203	24	83	24	139
Canton city	281	3,843	79	1,257	20	223	19	380	93	1,560	66	307	127	677
Celina city	74	1,072	8	208	5	166	D	D	32	353	15	65	18	148
Centerville city	105	2,525	14	81	D	D	3	23	D	D	37	189	88	509
Chillicothe city	165	3,351	23	204	7	432	D	D	55	366	34	124	45	225
Cincinnati city	866	15,048	309	5,562	183	4,974	201	8,161	510	24,247	435	2,689	1,115	20,598
Circleville city	58	619	D	D	NA	NA	D	D	D	D	17	61	29	136
Clayton city	23	672	D	D	D	D	NA	NA	13	26	9	19	11	51
Cleveland city	1,136	9,648	511	9,019	241	5,958	177	4,781	509	16,138	395	2,997	1,091	20,238
Cleveland Heights city	91	1,201	13	65	4	61	14	102	51	131	52	226	95	259
Columbus city	2,600	48,299	788	18,425	572	29,206	611	12,717	1,195	55,807	1,040	8,225	2,259	30,953
Conneaut city	29	305	NA	NA	NA	NA	NA	NA	11	111	4	13	15	51
Coshocton city	73	777	3	19	6	119	12	81	32	180	8	19	18	75
Cuyahoga Falls city	168	3,559	44	643	15	194	22	253	66	348	45	209	96	578
Dayton city	346	3,707	141	2,405	83	2,271	50	1,189	123	4,364	113	501	290	3,387
Defiance city	99	1,847	7	63	11	231	12	220	39	393	22	79	37	171
Delaware city	112	1,940	20	191	26	1,851	19	89	50	D	34	210	79	429
Dent CDP	22	663	4	15	D	D	4	49	19	130	15	37	18	37
Dover city	66	1,044	14	94	NA	NA	4	42	30	247	13	55	30	293
Dublin city	107	2,358	90	1,815	34	877	62	3,580	243	6,589	113	698	443	7,332
East Cleveland city	52	261	D	D	5	31	NA	NA	D	D	11	46	D	D
Eastlake city	53	756	25	337	6	155	NA	NA	39	82	16	66	34	229
East Liverpool city	39	298	7	27	8	118	NA	NA	5	26	NA	NA	7	39
Elyria city	198	3,164	53	296	19	278	D	D	67	364	56	258	77	440
Englewood city	54	967	12	100	D	D	NA	NA	24	114	16	46	28	284
Euclid city	83	1,034	37	453	16	200	12	115	91	229	45	287	48	326
Fairborn city	69	878	D	D	8	327	D	D	28	177	31	105	73	2,138
Fairfield city	167	4,069	75	2,299	38	1,028	16	165	D	D	57	340	81	912
Fairview Park city	56	1,168	9	19	3	15	7	78	22	215	15	79	68	642
Findlay city	201	3,900	43	772	33	1,423	17	377	104	574	49	419	86	1,241
Finneytown CDP	43	681	NA	NA	NA	NA	3	6	D	D	3	6	11	23
Forest Park city	57	1,619	38	1,105	5	49	NA	NA	20	777	15	121	24	582
Forestville CDP	45	1,368	6	11	3	6	6	21	49	226	28	104	53	190
Fostoria city	37	446	7	87	6	272	5	20	22	126	5	13	17	78
Franklin city	35	605	16	208	NA	NA	NA	NA	19	155	12	69	21	599
Fremont city	102	1,500	16	189	17	311	D	D	47	307	21	64	31	149
Gahanna city	91	1,468	48	904	25	385	21	192	68	501	46	401	141	1,278
Galion city	40	423	6	67	NA	NA	D	D	D	D	7	20	15	492
Garfield Heights city	66	876	31	413	19	224	8	43	D	D	22	87	31	328
Green city	62	1,869	39	645	40	1,715	8	174	61	458	27	195	73	802
Greenville city	90	1,432	15	153	9	151	D	D	39	301	16	50	26	160
Grove City city	121	3,115	29	936	40	3,968	17	151	63	553	43	152	51	366
Hamilton city	190	3,518	40	769	23	411	13	304	71	420	39	194	86	353
Harrison city	58	1,546	15	660	NA	NA	4	11	23	129	16	54	15	59
Heath city	112	2,348	12	129	13	239	10	94	32	171	14	43	20	255
Hilliard city	87	1,613	44	724	15	228	24	3,001	57	671	51	217	112	796
Huber Heights city	111	2,553	23	516	18	1,323	D	D	D	D	26	136	30	377
Hudson city	72	1,215	51	460	11	695	20	448	91	1,938	33	398	129	644
Ironton city	46	500	7	74	4	36	D	D	21	115	9	47	19	94
Kent city	74	940	10	91	4	47	9	112	26	157	30	153	37	234
Kettering city	150	4,391	28	196	8	77	19	1,036	D	D	60	324	108	2,721
Lakewood city	114	1,067	20	366	17	98	13	92	53	480	46	160	125	470
Lancaster city	188	2,858	28	231	24	225	19	172	80	530	49	143	70	416
Lebanon city	84	1,766	22	429	12	286	11	35	40	332	24	90	60	425
Lima city	109	1,374	42	528	26	379	17	286	60	555	23	114	71	529
Lincoln Village CDP	37	564	NA	NA	NA	NA	NA	NA	D	D	11	29	7	4
London city	42	1,289	D	D	NA	NA	D	D	16	76	9	15	20	100
Lorain city	124	1,894	25	397	18	236	D	D	43	543	39	143	52	185
Loveland city	42	1,168	23	687	D	D	5	10	22	82	D	D	42	138
Lyndhurst city	66	1,188	8	27	NA	NA	D	D	D	D	17	98	41	105
Macedonia city	60	1,313	34	679	D	D	6	46	D	D	8	34	25	130
Mack CDP	6	118	3	D	3	15	NA	NA	D	D	8	18	10	42
Mansfield city	172	2,288	52	677	30	744	24	424	95	580	55	314	117	576
Maple Heights city	75	1,071	21	600	15	143	NA	NA	31	398	9	45	12	71
Marietta city	108	1,606	17	270	8	139	D	D	47	512	22	109	51	299
Marion city	71	684	16	202	11	168	D	D	44	248	17	50	33	116
Marysville city	79	1,923	20	189	16	288	11	64	44	183	28	127	36	1,089
Mason city	125	2,143	55	3,326	25	537	D	D	57	501	45	214	126	784
Massillon city	111	2,561	22	391	17	361	7	191	45	329	22	177	51	242
Maumee city	101	2,667	43	2,651	23	1,864	12	151	90	1,181	31	161	86	2,469
Mayfield Heights city	105	2,133	22	1,019	NA	NA	17	209	98	1,937	35	423	67	978
Medina city	108	1,677	45	463	18	197	10	156	46	226	41	155	101	639
Mentor city	276	5,755	88	717	22	376	D	D	169	592	52	201	147	1,330
Miamisburg city	69	1,826	26	465	7	99	16	626	29	287	17	69	39	453

1   Merchant wholesalers, except manufacturers' sales branches and offices.

Table C. Incorporated Places, Census Designated Places (CDPs), and Minor Civil Divisions (MCDs) of 10,000 or More Population — **Economic Census**

STATE City, town, township, borough, or CDP (county if applicable)	Administration and support and waste management and mediation services		Educational services		Health care and social assistance		Arts, entertainment, and recreation		Accommodation and food services		Other services (except public administration)	
	Number of establishments	Number of employees	Number of establishments	Number of employees	Number of establishments	Number of employees	Number of establishments	Number of employees	Number of establishments	Number of employees	Number of establishments	Number of employees
	15	16	17	18	19	20	21	22	23	24	25	26
OHIO—Con.												
Bay Village city	14	59	4	60	27	347	4	31	14	153	24	105
Beachwood city	61	3,216	19	180	192	6,569	10	296	64	2,069	55	599
Beavercreek city	52	255	19	107	154	3,520	13	221	136	4,131	69	460
Bedford city	18	135	NA	NA	41	1,158	NA	NA	D	D	D	D
Bedford Heights city	25	599	NA	NA	31	1,043	D	D	19	322	24	162
Bellefontaine city	11	1,199	NA	NA	66	1,462	10	97	46	1,842	30	317
Berea city	22	105	D	D	45	1,222	D	D	41	588	43	218
Bexley city	5	18	4	12	15	113	D	D	25	500	24	106
Blue Ash city	134	9,972	19	191	138	3,390	7	196	85	1,598	78	1,018
Boardman CDP	68	2,698	11	82	213	5,077	D	D	101	2,453	80	432
Bowling Green city	22	481	D	D	105	2,853	10	106	106	2,628	46	237
Brecksville city	21	553	6	42	40	600	10	34	22	463	30	171
Bridgetown CDP	11	65	5	57	44	699	3	38	49	1,409	30	269
Broadview Heights city	42	746	7	102	67	902	12	99	33	549	36	245
Brooklyn city	10	47	NA	NA	27	493	4	110	49	1,119	D	D
Brook Park city	21	406	NA	NA	25	530	9	111	37	552	29	508
Brunswick city	32	444	7	46	59	1,095	13	82	69	1,309	62	359
Bucyrus city	12	161	NA	NA	D	D	7	22	34	623	30	128
Cambridge city	17	338	D	D	91	2,809	NA	NA	52	1,203	36	169
Canton city	58	956	12	94	205	10,591	23	470	155	2,735	125	909
Celina city	8	93	NA	NA	35	543	NA	NA	42	795	34	182
Centerville city	36	322	NA	NA	NA	NA	16	185	62	1,567	50	498
Chillicothe city	25	420	NA	NA	111	1,938	D	D	93	2,575	54	328
Cincinnati city	392	12,262	64	513	896	55,181	146	6,496	813	17,343	542	4,633
Circleville city	15	360	NA	NA	63	1,722	D	D	29	505	23	79
Clayton city	18	93	NA	NA	60	939	NA	NA	18	352	D	D
Cleveland city	403	13,824	53	1,040	758	79,004	127	8,202	1,014	17,408	705	5,805
Cleveland Heights city	26	68	10	47	99	1,182	16	58	79	1,137	54	308
Columbus city	997	42,274	NA	NA	NA	NA	238	6,805	2,072	46,502	1,251	11,396
Conneaut city	D	D	NA	NA	24	407	4	10	34	359	17	77
Coshocton city	D	D	NA	NA	61	1,302	9	D	D	D	D	D
Cuyahoga Falls city	59	1,861	13	80	143	4,101	15	123	138	3,002	107	706
Dayton city	139	4,499	NA	NA	NA	NA	33	1,165	266	5,041	197	1,667
Defiance city	8	165	3	19	66	1,562	D	D	57	1,149	42	304
Delaware city	33	1,402	4	19	140	3,088	12	299	91	1,709	56	273
Dent CDP	9	42	NA	NA	22	480	4	6	16	532	D	D
Dover city	6	47	3	13	74	2,577	8	140	31	590	27	260
Dublin city	143	7,765	NA	NA	NA	NA	32	745	136	3,437	65	1,445
East Cleveland city	6	114	NA	NA	24	719	NA	NA	22	212	8	51
Eastlake city	19	151	D	D	18	105	11	88	32	371	D	D
East Liverpool city	D	D	NA	NA	38	958	3	37	14	221	27	92
Elyria city	43	893	D	D	144	4,257	D	D	112	2,125	76	382
Englewood city	9	247	NA	NA	41	874	7	181	46	940	D	D
Euclid city	30	326	NA	NA	98	3,581	7	125	61	665	52	266
Fairborn city	29	699	8	80	53	919	4	103	72	1,326	39	263
Fairfield city	59	3,689	NA	NA	NA	NA	10	94	103	2,241	86	669
Fairview Park city	28	241	7	59	72	697	4	21	D	D	40	261
Findlay city	61	1,875	12	83	159	4,521	19	309	152	3,994	113	837
Finneytown CDP	12	34	NA	NA	24	270	D	D	25	624	D	D
Forest Park city	17	297	4	39	48	859	4	40	D	D	31	179
Forestville CDP	14	248	4	21	93	2,630	D	D	44	1,111	29	295
Fostoria city	12	43	NA	NA	NA	NA	4	79	25	429	26	125
Franklin city	11	176	NA	NA	27	784	4	73	19	452	26	278
Fremont city	26	762	NA	NA	79	1,349	7	144	53	871	41	181
Gahanna city	66	1,676	15	196	170	3,722	17	299	97	2,017	67	594
Galion city	D	D	NA	NA	NA	NA	NA	NA	26	410	19	106
Garfield Heights city	31	381	NA	NA	73	2,580	NA	NA	39	654	D	D
Green city	57	1,987	8	52	89	2,108	D	D	55	1,124	D	D
Greenville city	15	237	NA	NA	56	1,524	10	110	54	779	43	204
Grove City city	53	1,556	10	62	127	1,910	17	403	123	3,348	65	809
Hamilton city	38	1,255	5	99	173	3,561	16	167	141	2,958	85	637
Harrison city	4	13	NA	NA	26	251	4	24	41	1,164	D	D
Heath city	13	488	D	D	26	462	D	D	59	1,368	D	D
Hilliard city	58	1,011	13	77	138	1,738	20	375	78	1,651	58	381
Huber Heights city	26	2,870	NA	NA	NA	NA	9	215	82	1,754	61	313
Hudson city	57	1,211	20	89	87	1,563	18	301	52	946	D	D
Ironton city	10	89	NA	NA	44	722	3	D	24	496	D	D
Kent city	26	601	6	9	57	1,044	D	D	91	1,921	46	311
Kettering city	54	1,256	NA	NA	NA	NA	20	628	D	D	87	688
Lakewood city	55	1,162	14	88	110	1,415	19	340	138	2,031	71	443
Lancaster city	36	776	6	D	182	5,043	18	266	105	2,235	78	537
Lebanon city	19	350	4	14	72	1,804	D	D	48	875	40	203
Lima city	43	1,338	8	73	162	8,181	14	205	73	1,304	64	435
Lincoln Village CDP	6	98	NA	NA	D	D	NA	NA	21	517	4	18
London city	8	94	3	3	31	805	4	10	21	417	11	42
Lorain city	32	446	4	120	145	4,186	D	D	D	D	74	494
Loveland city	16	252	NA	NA	NA	NA	D	D	38	574	26	135
Lyndhurst city	22	123	NA	NA	73	941	D	D	D	D	D	D
Macedonia city	16	373	NA	NA	30	491	D	D	42	1,004	D	D
Mack CDP	17	66	NA	NA	9	103	NA	NA	5	112	10	37
Mansfield city	63	2,738	6	47	248	6,291	12	256	104	1,960	107	629
Maple Heights city	15	347	NA	NA	45	748	NA	NA	32	342	31	108
Marietta city	17	657	3	D	80	4,573	10	113	77	1,573	54	259
Marion city	25	861	NA	NA	141	3,495	9	51	48	926	46	374
Marysville city	21	2,275	D	D	68	1,716	D	D	59	1,440	D	D
Mason city	45	1,019	22	164	131	2,596	20	303	105	2,460	70	642
Massillon city	23	858	7	28	87	2,931	9	82	80	1,352	64	484
Maumee city	39	1,766	6	30	102	2,501	18	D	94	2,231	59	507
Mayfield Heights city	39	2,740	NA	NA	D	D	10	14	61	1,449	44	372
Medina city	60	5,354	6	30	87	2,210	7	29	61	1,182	64	406
Mentor city	106	3,271	11	126	178	3,056	15	132	163	3,824	125	830
Miamisburg city	27	1,891	5	77	43	1,971	8	58	63	1,721	D	D

Table C. Incorporated Places, Census Designated Places (CDPs), and Minor Civil Divisions (MCDs) of 10,000 or More Population — **Economic Census**

STATE City, town, township, borough, or CDP (county if applicable)	Retail Trade Number of establishments	Retail Trade Number of employees	Wholesale trade[1] Number of establishments	Wholesale trade[1] Number of employees	Transportation and warehousing Number of establishments	Transportation and warehousing Number of employees	Information Number of establishments	Information Number of employees	Finance and insurance Number of establishments	Finance and insurance Number of employees	Real estate and rental and leasing Number of establishments	Real estate and rental and leasing Number of employees	Professional, scientific, and technical services Number of establishments	Professional, scientific, and technical services Number of employees
	1	2	3	4	5	6	7	8	9	10	11	12	13	14
OHIO—Con.														
Middleburg Heights city	95	2,504	43	504	82	2,559	16	833	54	290	27	297	96	1,117
Middletown city	124	3,340	D	D	19	315	D	D	61	295	43	153	70	413
Monfort Heights CDP	20	626	8	21	NA	NA	NA	NA	20	209	D	D	18	55
Monroe city	106	1,932	32	480	19	881	D	D	D	D	17	160	D	D
Montgomery city	41	798	11	64	NA	NA	D	D	D	D	30	155	58	198
Mount Vernon city	91	1,530	19	159	5	30	12	158	47	266	24	96	28	228
New Albany city	13	D	D	D	10	623	8	96	46	3,660	17	102	56	240
Newark city	136	1,828	25	296	19	275	15	217	78	2,653	50	203	D	D
New Franklin city	21	119	6	58	5	47	NA	NA	15	54	7	49	17	49
New Philadelphia city	116	2,001	24	172	9	37	11	217	36	177	24	127	46	366
Niles city	140	2,348	10	124	D	D	D	D	30	176	22	85	32	794
Northbrook CDP	21	478	5	36	NA	NA	D	D	13	74	D	D	5	26
North Canton city	58	1,019	10	241	11	60	6	12	49	466	D	D	59	372
North Olmsted city	241	5,236	18	163	14	53	20	287	66	711	50	185	66	284
North Ridgeville city	50	592	29	180	20	200	5	8	26	102	12	57	40	212
North Royalton city	69	606	33	537	32	146	17	166	48	320	27	177	79	288
Norton city	45	765	16	123	11	86	4	14	D	D	8	41	18	82
Norwalk city	69	1,079	18	203	10	119	14	145	33	183	16	61	40	260
Norwood city	98	2,208	13	175	5	19	20	402	62	649	19	135	48	878
Oregon city	63	1,864	9	118	15	89	6	45	32	191	17	84	16	54
Oxford city	46	1,003	D	D	NA	NA	3	7	22	123	D	D	20	62
Painesville city	50	307	20	274	6	20	4	6	37	122	12	38	42	368
Parma city	219	3,650	58	1,095	47	579	15	193	123	616	55	316	102	632
Parma Heights city	42	436	NA	NA	D	D	D	D	D	D	16	98	31	222
Pataskala city	33	622	10	181	17	724	12	52	22	93	9	43	20	445
Perrysburg city	89	1,735	46	725	15	222	12	108	67	392	25	126	78	1,094
Pickerington city	50	989	D	D	3	20	9	92	30	135	26	88	48	210
Piqua city	107	1,787	13	184	9	298	8	45	31	212	17	55	19	74
Portsmouth city	102	1,344	D	D	11	112	12	163	43	264	30	109	51	222
Powell city	44	501	22	99	4	6	6	57	35	125	19	29	94	421
Ravenna city	44	860	9	69	8	123	5	29	28	197	10	41	30	119
Reading city	38	407	16	152	6	113	NA	NA	13	64	13	60	22	440
Reynoldsburg city	118	2,455	10	36	13	37	7	71	53	313	36	D	79	498
Richmond Heights city	59	578	7	38	9	259	4	45	20	132	12	D	29	94
Riverside city	51	473	8	46	6	275	NA	NA	10	43	17	97	29	492
Rocky River city	80	1,145	29	211	15	340	9	73	76	474	D	D	109	333
Salem city	76	1,288	12	87	5	84	D	D	32	164	6	25	23	126
Sandusky city	93	1,184	21	819	8	69	D	D	47	268	D	D	51	270
Seven Hills city	14	188	D	D	8	20	D	D	40	701	5	5	25	498
Shaker Heights city	44	522	12	25	NA	NA	9	29	42	209	31	75	102	461
Sharonville city	78	1,347	123	3,350	56	2,462	8	194	62	693	61	806	95	1,869
Sidney city	89	1,631	16	697	17	555	D	D	43	272	24	52	34	276
Solon city	97	1,695	125	3,226	25	380	21	236	104	599	53	175	131	1,835
South Euclid city	60	1,031	10	72	8	45	6	23	D	D	12	82	31	101
Springboro city	53	1,066	26	1,088	D	D	5	13	47	259	26	45	64	578
Springdale city	151	3,287	D	D	14	322	15	1,398	47	1,045	24	91	64	1,431
Springfield city	224	4,171	46	1,044	27	2,081	D	D	95	2,351	55	222	85	508
Steubenville city	93	1,939	17	228	D	D	18	302	38	237	20	106	45	158
Stow city	98	2,294	49	400	13	164	9	59	58	270	D	D	79	801
Streetsboro city	64	1,799	24	759	16	423	5	19	24	101	22	81	20	126
Strongsville city	240	5,320	71	1,897	35	349	23	855	98	1,695	54	295	130	718
Struthers city	17	231	NA	NA	D	D	NA	NA	D	D	D	D	11	43
Sylvania city	66	1,318	12	56	6	58	5	18	44	358	6	19	57	525
Tallmadge city	46	1,919	21	176	20	243	5	23	23	103	D	D	38	660
Tiffin city	75	999	10	552	8	69	D	D	36	216	D	D	31	168
Toledo city	880	13,410	242	3,619	152	3,670	92	1,677	298	2,976	247	2,232	412	4,285
Trenton city	17	134	D	D	D	D	NA	NA	D	D	NA	NA	7	17
Trotwood city	58	771	5	49	D	D	D	D	13	46	16	46	9	53
Troy city	87	2,451	20	573	9	474	D	D	61	304	19	104	51	350
Twinsburg city	53	1,005	104	2,703	18	1,124	19	1,245	51	879	27	95	76	786
University Heights city	39	985	3	2	D	D	D	D	D	D	10	33	25	79
Upper Arlington city	83	1,065	15	34	D	D	14	269	108	686	62	385	153	647
Urbana city	43	549	7	64	5	162	5	33	25	159	13	29	22	206
Vandalia city	54	1,339	24	619	21	633	D	D	38	233	23	340	36	434
Van Wert city	63	901	10	136	8	157	4	15	30	776	8	26	19	85
Vermilion city	33	461	5	19	D	D	5	8	13	45	D	D	14	36
Wadsworth city	72	1,987	15	182	10	216	8	36	D	D	16	37	40	292
Warren city	142	3,681	25	448	20	755	10	166	48	218	26	104	76	322
Warrensville Heights city ..	48	682	56	841	14	207	D	D	D	D	27	230	33	692
Washington Court House city	68	1,033	D	D	5	7	D	D	32	138	D	D	13	43
West Carrollton city	40	530	17	241	NA	NA	NA	NA	15	74	14	101	6	53
Westerville city	121	2,156	50	475	23	237	24	295	161	6,291	69	673	224	2,691
Westlake city	182	2,658	81	1,018	24	282	24	11,186	174	1,246	80	289	244	2,136
Whitehall city	89	1,947	11	1,266	5	18	8	25	37	987	33	145	36	271
White Oak CDP	39	491	5	11	7	118	NA	NA	35	225	12	38	32	147
Wickliffe city	29	311	17	179	9	114	NA	NA	D	D	D	D	26	117
Willoughby city	95	1,575	62	676	17	227	10	254	74	250	40	203	87	678
Willowick city	35	532	4	7	NA	NA	NA	NA	38	78	3	5	14	74
Wilmington city	78	1,236	9	140	D	D	10	97	34	313	21	76	19	461
Wooster city	169	2,864	32	439	16	349	10	172	75	744	28	114	68	555
Worthington city	71	1,149	42	490	17	291	15	124	101	1,386	56	196	136	2,079
Xenia city	75	1,837	11	83	9	308	9	79	36	167	18	54	21	96
Youngstown city	162	1,441	83	1,223	17	244	18	728	43	471	D	D	85	724
Zanesville city	168	2,937	26	245	16	1,259	15	599	75	636	34	180	64	374
OKLAHOMA	12,963	180,451	3,859	50,233	2,736	51,368	1,593	28,623	6,867	59,479	4,461	22,135	9,736	70,920
Ada city	136	1,607	29	279	12	86	D	D	68	1,006	33	148	68	290
Altus city	95	1,176	13	99	17	142	D	D	44	319	21	128	33	237

1 Merchant wholesalers, except manufacturers' sales branches and offices.

Table C. Incorporated Places, Census Designated Places (CDPs), and Minor Civil Divisions (MCDs) of 10,000 or More Population — **Economic Census**

STATE City, town, township, borough, or CDP (county if applicable)	Administration and support and waste management and mediation services		Educational services		Health care and social assistance		Arts, entertainment, and recreation		Accommodation and food services		Other services (except public administration)	
	Number of establish-ments	Number of employees	Number of establish-ments	Number of employees	Number of establish-ments	Number of employees	Number of establish-ments	Number of employees	Number of establish-ments	Number of employees	Number of establish-ments	Number of employees
	15	16	17	18	19	20	21	22	23	24	25	26
OHIO—Con.												
Middleburg Heights city	44	1,743	6	27	130	6,938	6	72	70	1,560	43	225
Middletown city	39	1,672	NA	NA	NA	NA	15	131	94	2,103	81	551
Monfort Heights CDP	13	365	NA	NA	44	924	3	8	13	349	D	D
Monroe city	16	302	NA	NA	NA	NA	3	69	28	370	14	210
Montgomery city	16	1,606	D	D	110	4,431	4	149	34	854	39	253
Mount Vernon city	13	292	D	D	98	2,327	D	D	63	1,363	46	340
New Albany city	20	3,562	NA	NA	NA	NA	12	327	D	D	11	60
Newark city	59	848	7	70	159	5,008	19	220	97	1,474	77	493
New Franklin city	15	29	NA	NA	19	178	D	D	12	183	D	D
New Philadelphia city	28	460	3	15	61	964	9	36	60	1,065	58	339
Niles city	22	1,273	D	D	49	804	7	80	65	1,563	33	140
Northbrook CDP	9	169	NA	NA	13	431	3	4	15	435	6	27
North Canton city	26	476	5	19	73	2,263	6	185	D	D	41	412
North Olmsted city	50	894	10	94	85	1,468	9	66	120	2,547	94	682
North Ridgeville city	45	254	5	6	39	555	9	74	42	765	44	240
North Royalton city	57	436	11	62	68	1,174	10	163	D	D	65	289
Norton city	26	492	NA	NA	NA	NA	9	43	23	373	D	D
Norwalk city	18	350	3	21	56	1,919	6	13	49	766	37	228
Norwood city	41	1,940	6	14	58	1,391	D	D	65	1,722	36	406
Oregon city	21	169	D	D	97	2,585	D	D	59	1,232	39	246
Oxford city	8	147	D	D	31	617	D	D	74	2,067	36	281
Painesville city	26	193	NA	NA	38	555	4	D	31	527	37	293
Parma city	93	2,152	6	11	202	5,401	17	216	169	2,827	125	822
Parma Heights city	9	238	NA	NA	57	814	D	D	38	533	D	D
Pataskala city	21	88	NA	NA	21	140	10	66	32	459	D	D
Perrysburg city	36	345	8	106	113	1,910	15	D	79	2,188	57	413
Pickerington city	20	146	NA	NA	NA	NA	8	192	79	1,745	D	D
Piqua city	13	587	NA	NA	42	721	8	23	52	1,021	31	128
Portsmouth city	21	275	4	41	133	5,615	7	D	66	1,284	D	D
Powell city	23	145	12	D	81	849	D	D	45	918	48	208
Ravenna city	10	26	NA	NA	70	2,653	4	5	31	453	30	402
Reading city	D	D	NA	NA	19	194	4	5	24	215	21	91
Reynoldsburg city	40	1,476	NA	NA	NA	NA	4	22	77	1,854	45	238
Richmond Heights city	25	93	NA	NA	38	1,320	NA	NA	24	277	17	88
Riverside city	13	787	NA	NA	36	749	5	79	56	966	24	110
Rocky River city	34	369	6	52	92	920	11	278	63	1,278	66	643
Salem city	15	230	NA	NA	NA	NA	D	D	49	756	38	278
Sandusky city	24	314	4	3	93	3,513	D	D	83	1,106	43	175
Seven Hills city	26	2,701	D	D	33	349	D	D	18	340	16	63
Shaker Heights city	32	368	8	36	70	2,223	8	194	32	400	39	122
Sharonville city	59	3,441	NA	NA	NA	NA	D	D	82	1,631	56	416
Sidney city	21	1,458	D	D	68	1,547	9	144	51	1,066	34	236
Solon city	78	1,684	16	136	97	1,132	10	127	68	1,161	50	786
South Euclid city	20	69	7	30	67	862	6	D	42	734	38	238
Springboro city	19	140	NA	NA	NA	NA	10	366	43	1,024	41	248
Springdale city	35	10,155	8	62	90	1,768	D	D	64	1,698	30	269
Springfield city	42	2,666	D	D	229	5,888	16	286	162	3,487	113	860
Steubenville city	16	227	NA	NA	101	2,894	6	81	53	1,074	42	242
Stow city	47	834	9	77	84	1,603	18	156	97	1,951	69	385
Streetsboro city	21	352	NA	NA	30	615	6	123	59	1,159	33	194
Strongsville city	41	436	D	D	113	1,939	22	306	124	2,812	96	870
Struthers city	4	5	NA	NA	13	225	3	32	14	232	D	D
Sylvania city	24	980	7	100	123	4,155	12	175	50	888	50	417
Tallmadge city	37	378	NA	NA	NA	NA	3	14	27	472	D	D
Tiffin city	14	299	D	D	83	1,453	7	134	59	1,395	46	166
Toledo city	273	9,157	44	254	739	24,505	90	4,552	649	11,380	387	2,543
Trenton city	3	31	NA	NA	26	D	3	D	11	186	D	D
Trotwood city	8	92	NA	NA	26	D	3	D	12	207	D	D
Troy city	30	1,981	4	54	97	1,542	8	102	75	1,897	60	307
Twinsburg city	37	727	16	123	56	2,555	D	D	52	1,095	D	D
University Heights city	10	24	3	D	30	206	5	11	26	569	20	99
Upper Arlington city	28	466	14	77	97	2,137	13	269	69	1,524	40	293
Urbana city	D	D	NA	NA	35	736	D	D	37	559	D	D
Vandalia city	24	737	9	122	50	1,167	D	D	35	829	37	388
Van Wert city	9	397	NA	NA	57	1,355	D	D	30	638	33	207
Vermilion city	D	D	NA	NA	NA	NA	13	71	30	328	20	73
Wadsworth city	18	158	6	20	72	1,747	6	34	59	1,241	43	235
Warren city	41	1,073	4	42	164	5,512	14	134	69	1,061	69	323
Warrensville Heights city	15	565	D	D	61	2,531	6	87	25	544	D	D
Washington Court House city	17	451	NA	NA	39	1,061	D	D	39	859	33	137
West Carrollton city	21	669	NA	NA	29	706	3	D	32	698	D	D
Westerville city	66	5,130	NA	NA	NA	NA	19	163	117	2,767	84	1,100
Westlake city	115	2,508	14	91	236	4,520	23	445	105	2,656	80	714
Whitehall city	17	298	D	D	86	2,322	6	83	49	921	37	215
White Oak CDP	22	183	5	13	52	569	8	89	28	476	27	161
Wickliffe city	18	741	NA	NA	19	480	6	80	32	497	D	D
Willoughby city	48	1,356	5	122	118	3,390	7	271	95	1,924	74	376
Willowick city	9	58	NA	NA	12	70	NA	NA	24	399	D	D
Wilmington city	D	D	3	2	72	1,557	D	D	42	961	D	D
Wooster city	42	600	D	D	139	3,869	11	187	92	2,023	52	335
Worthington city	52	3,825	13	111	129	2,976	12	95	44	1,026	45	213
Xenia city	8	131	3	D	87	1,586	7	106	45	1,053	39	270
Youngstown city	44	751	NA	NA	NA	NA	D	D	D	D	99	1,165
Zanesville city	27	764	D	D	131	5,352	13	177	113	2,450	87	712
OKLAHOMA	4,568	102,699	568	4,039	11,035	226,462	1,152	26,523	8,397	159,826	5,565	31,947
Ada city	28	741	4	8	D	D	D	D	D	D	D	D
Altus city	12	140	D	D	D	D	D	D	50	1,060	D	D

Table C. Incorporated Places, Census Designated Places (CDPs), and Minor Civil Divisions (MCDs) of 10,000 or More Population — **Economic Census**

STATE City, town, township, borough, or CDP (county if applicable)	Retail Trade Number of establishments	Retail Trade Number of employees	Wholesale trade[1] Number of establishments	Wholesale trade[1] Number of employees	Transportation and warehousing Number of establishments	Transportation and warehousing Number of employees	Information Number of establishments	Information Number of employees	Finance and insurance Number of establishments	Finance and insurance Number of employees	Real estate and rental and leasing Number of establishments	Real estate and rental and leasing Number of employees	Professional, scientific, and technical services Number of establishments	Professional, scientific, and technical services Number of employees
	1	2	3	4	5	6	7	8	9	10	11	12	13	14
OKLAHOMA—Con.														
Ardmore city	203	2,569	45	769	29	1,203	19	206	D	D	54	192	110	499
Bartlesville city	148	2,237	18	72	8	217	D	D	D	D	D	D	82	1,557
Bethany city	47	282	15	91	D	D	D	D	29	141	20	43	39	89
Bixby city	67	873	27	168	7	63	D	D	D	D	D	D	55	139
Broken Arrow city	264	5,160	141	1,577	38	425	42	696	D	D	97	324	257	1,640
Chickasha city	92	1,133	31	437	20	105	D	D	49	309	27	126	57	197
Choctaw city	24	484	4	15	NA	NA	NA	NA	D	D	6	6	15	56
Claremore city	116	1,714	16	75	D	D	9	50	D	D	29	79	47	225
Del City city	64	1,106	8	49	D	D	NA	NA	38	225	15	80	24	88
Duncan city	129	1,557	29	229	23	652	13	117	68	627	21	64	67	360
Durant city	86	1,340	21	595	D	D	D	D	55	476	21	D	48	255
Edmond city	355	5,653	113	1,196	43	351	52	319	D	D	233	561	510	2,554
Elk City city	86	1,144	22	170	26	519	D	D	29	223	30	248	45	179
El Reno city	59	867	18	166	17	196	D	D	32	186	21	164	23	88
Enid city	244	3,628	55	679	46	1,236	D	D	105	717	83	337	108	560
Glenpool city	27	582	D	D	NA	NA	NA	NA	10	41	4	7	17	39
Guthrie city	59	914	D	D	NA	NA	D	D	39	148	23	83	28	120
Guymon city	61	695	D	D	D	D	D	D	D	D	11	22	D	D
Jenks city	41	501	D	D	9	258	9	10	D	D	D	D	67	310
Lawton city	336	4,833	D	D	34	523	D	D	151	1,263	122	431	124	1,288
McAlester city	119	1,678	27	292	18	245	D	D	61	358	33	D	76	284
Miami city	45	441	11	77	NA	NA	D	D	33	194	16	39	28	143
Midwest City city	170	4,077	11	81	D	D	7	67	87	568	65	257	88	615
Moore city	167	2,913	D	D	19	111	15	625	D	D	56	248	76	374
Muskogee city	204	3,027	46	594	24	624	D	D	101	594	43	164	64	499
Mustang city	46	899	D	D	D	D	8	30	35	161	22	215	46	255
Norman city	434	7,673	64	943	52	663	49	945	D	D	224	1,006	464	2,302
Oklahoma City city	2,234	33,933	1,026	16,717	512	13,513	339	8,105	1,413	17,852	1,058	6,008	2,577	25,695
Okmulgee city	55	716	10	63	NA	NA	6	31	D	D	9	27	22	65
Owasso city	121	3,206	19	99	D	D	11	181	D	D	55	190	74	200
Ponca City city	121	1,598	30	142	16	481	12	127	68	296	27	86	53	359
Sand Springs city	69	1,256	15	217	9	38	D	D	D	D	D	D	42	178
Sapulpa city	73	1,064	28	1,199	15	226	D	D	44	348	22	81	41	160
Shawnee city	184	2,590	20	151	7	89	D	D	81	580	38	167	72	577
Stillwater city	198	3,294	26	178	20	161	D	D	87	663	68	344	108	973
Tahlequah city	107	1,556	D	D	D	D	D	D	56	277	21	122	38	118
Tulsa city	1,664	28,067	694	11,740	310	9,873	288	9,497	D	D	773	6,322	1,854	17,646
Warr Acres city	50	553	6	20	D	D	D	D	32	175	18	329	28	104
Weatherford city	70	1,006	9	D	10	101	D	D	31	196	24	171	D	D
Woodward city	106	1,162	31	236	31	388	D	D	48	275	D	D	42	159
Yukon city	96	1,844	18	130	18	70	9	75	64	409	52	135	79	249
OREGON	14,318	211,222	4,452	67,900	3,225	60,206	2,388	39,690	6,121	63,459	6,771	29,773	12,620	92,358
Albany city	191	3,094	50	493	23	662	15	236	96	756	67	226	114	701
Aloha CDP	69	740	D	D	15	95	13	36	26	92	33	64	48	150
Altamont CDP	57	543	7	92	15	127	NA	NA	D	D	20	71	23	112
Ashland city	140	1,150	21	156	6	37	28	164	48	213	D	D	119	400
Beaverton city	409	9,745	163	3,933	65	1,516	99	3,332	237	4,500	281	1,150	D	D
Bend city	597	8,285	141	1,204	74	776	119	1,718	251	1,817	323	808	638	2,520
Bethany CDP	19	239	4	7	NA	NA	9	25	11	23	16	208	65	232
Bull Mountain CDP	7	10	NA	NA	3	6	4	2	D	D	13	37	25	40
Canby city	56	918	20	502	15	153	9	169	30	119	D	D	38	117
Cedar Mill CDP	18	329	3	2	5	84	9	98	D	D	22	52	58	322
Central Point city	35	491	12	73	15	214	5	154	25	84	14	84	30	102
Coos Bay city	82	1,475	11	136	27	609	15	185	28	185	21	111	43	229
Cornelius city	22	684	D	D	4	30	4	72	D	D	5	14	7	19
Corvallis city	217	3,632	25	213	15	220	37	328	88	747	D	D	195	1,555
Cottage Grove city	58	843	4	14	6	24	D	D	20	82	D	D	19	84
Dallas city	37	603	D	D	8	64	10	42	22	84	14	38	17	88
Damascus city	18	226	D	D	10	65	NA	NA	6	18	17	37	26	83
Eugene city	747	11,990	251	3,325	91	1,293	122	1,805	357	3,598	355	1,469	720	4,231
Forest Grove city	40	483	9	104	9	38	6	20	24	124	28	82	35	166
Four Corners CDP	52	545	6	36	8	39	D	D	15	73	16	31	10	58
Gladstone city	30	815	D	D	5	32	NA	NA	16	48	8	45	25	93
Grants Pass city	237	3,701	36	244	16	246	28	225	97	604	79	365	93	739
Gresham city	279	4,385	53	1,756	69	1,297	47	856	111	2,095	118	442	123	458
Happy Valley city	21	511	13	28	D	D	4	13	16	43	D	D	D	D
Hayesville CDP	28	379	6	34	9	35	NA	NA	12	56	11	34	3	9
Hermiston city	74	1,409	23	312	21	1,592	11	81	35	197	29	145	32	131
Hillsboro city	328	6,986	109	2,182	55	1,331	70	3,165	144	2,978	152	603	255	9,104
Independence city	17	189	5	63	6	11	NA	NA	8	11	6	19	8	29
Keizer city	88	1,425	17	45	D	D	13	78	46	213	32	151	54	259
Klamath Falls city	115	1,944	21	181	22	183	D	D	45	346	40	104	78	570
La Grande city	75	1,061	D	D	12	117	D	D	34	191	14	63	45	218
Lake Oswego city	108	1,168	90	1,643	10	97	40	1,218	317	3,175	167	909	D	D
Lebanon city	61	896	D	D	D	D	D	D	28	181	15	32	21	155
McMinnville city	146	2,296	17	143	19	194	21	202	53	490	35	107	83	338
Medford city	473	8,072	115	1,223	86	1,991	55	851	213	1,789	191	745	257	1,493
Milwaukie city	61	995	45	782	16	262	19	329	28	566	32	126	76	377
Monmouth city	10	115	NA	NA	NA	NA	NA	NA	D	D	11	37	10	25
Newberg city	69	1,116	D	D	10	72	14	40	35	183	D	D	48	186
Newport city	97	1,386	13	77	11	80	11	86	26	262	D	D	42	153
Oak Grove CDP	76	1,049	13	84	6	28	8	36	17	90	18	49	31	156
Oak Hills CDP	NA	NA	NA	NA	NA	NA	5	15	D	D	8	30	24	48
Oatfield CDP	7	129	4	7	5	11	D	D	17	159	17	346	23	41
Ontario city	86	1,664	18	312	13	191	D	D	28	189	17	61	28	172
Oregon City city	123	1,919	16	239	21	164	16	101	52	269	D	D	106	515
Pendleton city	65	878	11	234	15	625	14	122	40	209	20	68	40	184
Portland city	2,703	37,084	1,103	22,237	671	20,921	660	12,270	1,214	21,055	1,527	10,487	3,934	35,617
Prineville city	58	546	12	93	D	D	D	D	D	D	D	D	25	105
Redmond city	126	2,090	42	253	26	564	21	511	58	240	54	126	54	308

1 Merchant wholesalers, except manufacturers' sales branches and offices.

Table C. Incorporated Places, Census Designated Places (CDPs), and Minor Civil Divisions (MCDs) of 10,000 or More Population — **Economic Census**

STATE City, town, township, borough, or CDP (county if applicable)	Administration and support and waste management and mediation services — Number of establishments	Number of employees	Educational services — Number of establishments	Number of employees	Health care and social assistance — Number of establishments	Number of employees	Arts, entertainment, and recreation — Number of establishments	Number of employees	Accommodation and food services — Number of establishments	Number of employees	Other services (except public administration) — Number of establishments	Number of employees
	15	16	17	18	19	20	21	22	23	24	25	26
OKLAHOMA—Con.												
Ardmore city	53	743	D	D	197	3,543	D	D	95	1,914	63	695
Bartlesville city	38	931	D	D	153	2,874	D	D	98	1,749	68	428
Bethany city	D	D	NA	NA	47	1,247	4	76	31	375	37	154
Bixby city	36	2,740	D	D	45	311	10	115	36	686	D	D
Broken Arrow city	147	2,724	29	183	244	4,451	36	554	221	4,732	167	1,188
Chickasha city	18	201	NA	NA	D	D	6	38	56	960	35	157
Choctaw city	14	42	NA	NA	14	96	NA	NA	18	333	D	D
Claremore city	23	549	D	D	100	2,037	D	D	68	1,215	46	225
Del City city	D	D	NA	NA	31	474	NA	NA	42	864	36	214
Duncan city	28	339	3	D	97	1,708	D	D	66	919	47	216
Durant city	16	701	D	D	114	1,857	D	D	58	1,162	21	107
Edmond city	186	2,295	44	299	510	5,338	54	1,095	262	5,149	206	996
Elk City city	D	D	NA	NA	66	858	D	D	53	666	19	88
El Reno city	9	36	NA	NA	43	574	D	D	43	593	23	86
Enid city	55	919	D	D	D	D	21	244	124	2,396	101	530
Glenpool city	6	31	NA	NA	18	185	NA	NA	21	316	12	100
Guthrie city	D	D	D	D	33	854	D	D	38	500	D	D
Guymon city	14	453	NA	NA	36	498	D	D	41	591	D	D
Jenks city	21	472	6	59	61	578	7	190	30	617	21	81
Lawton city	80	1,824	11	192	232	5,609	D	D	217	4,576	D	D
McAlester city	21	308	D	D	107	2,288	D	D	71	1,177	39	171
Miami city	D	D	NA	NA	55	1,155	NA	NA	32	771	D	D
Midwest City city	45	500	5	25	196	2,732	11	228	133	2,792	58	338
Moore city	62	441	11	87	104	924	14	112	139	3,063	74	331
Muskogee city	34	869	D	D	191	5,417	D	D	112	2,125	D	D
Mustang city	D	D	3	35	49	417	NA	NA	44	979	D	D
Norman city	150	12,585	47	301	486	8,811	D	D	363	7,908	170	984
Oklahoma City city	1,154	35,117	128	1,148	2,436	54,538	195	5,273	1,597	33,987	1,140	8,064
Okmulgee city	10	86	NA	NA	55	990	NA	NA	35	584	20	108
Owasso city	40	307	D	D	105	1,984	9	214	101	2,601	D	D
Ponca City city	23	406	3	4	99	1,785	D	D	63	1,113	41	228
Sand Springs city	23	245	NA	NA	39	589	D	D	57	944	24	135
Sapulpa city	D	D	5	23	57	1,381	D	D	68	1,132	31	159
Shawnee city	33	820	3	5	139	2,639	12	196	117	2,546	53	275
Stillwater city	46	503	D	D	126	3,016	15	151	188	3,600	81	753
Tahlequah city	17	358	4	D	89	2,772	4	68	68	1,105	30	185
Tulsa city	763	21,917	111	914	1,588	45,593	172	3,351	1,205	25,731	900	6,379
Warr Acres city	D	D	NA	NA	32	356	NA	NA	38	769	27	85
Weatherford city	11	53	NA	NA	50	798	D	D	40	751	22	122
Woodward city	D	D	4	14	72	850	D	D	53	753	D	D
Yukon city	D	D	D	D	88	941	D	D	85	1,822	D	D
OREGON	5,947	107,631	1,153	9,412	13,948	263,278	1,992	29,222	11,708	182,613	7,414	43,543
Albany city	77	1,506	5	43	138	3,041	16	135	133	2,191	82	612
Aloha CDP	75	635	D	D	126	834	10	40	D	D	46	199
Altamont CDP	19	199	NA	NA	45	289	NA	NA	43	590	D	D
Ashland city	27	147	18	73	161	1,373	35	934	155	2,567	39	209
Beaverton city	207	4,677	60	566	473	6,216	76	1,544	341	5,608	203	1,350
Bend city	239	3,959	51	399	533	9,929	87	1,770	382	6,525	260	1,326
Bethany CDP	20	59	18	154	D	D	D	D	26	334	D	D
Bull Mountain CDP	5	17	NA	NA	3	6	D	D	3	8	6	15
Canby city	17	61	NA	NA	53	563	9	87	39	511	42	345
Cedar Mill CDP	16	108	5	49	D	D	3	5	14	200	7	53
Central Point city	14	110	NA	NA	34	557	4	20	30	547	20	90
Coos Bay city	27	1,215	NA	NA	100	2,766	7	D	57	833	39	245
Cornelius city	23	179	NA	NA	D	D	NA	NA	15	185	D	D
Corvallis city	45	476	26	184	251	5,425	23	329	193	3,535	118	899
Cottage Grove city	11	59	6	21	D	D	7	21	43	624	21	87
Dallas city	11	21	NA	NA	63	896	6	20	D	D	D	D
Damascus city	22	120	NA	NA	15	44	NA	NA	9	111	16	68
Eugene city	212	6,373	77	521	829	12,879	96	1,793	576	9,516	381	2,529
Forest Grove city	23	139	4	7	D	D	7	34	49	795	31	117
Four Corners CDP	17	180	NA	NA	D	D	3	40	40	776	18	107
Gladstone city	8	38	NA	NA	28	458	D	D	22	267	D	D
Grants Pass city	55	1,386	D	D	253	4,939	19	348	162	2,499	80	377
Gresham city	120	1,721	D	D	413	5,934	37	510	237	4,217	145	753
Happy Valley city	22	104	7	24	35	301	11	64	45	471	23	113
Hayesville CDP	16	321	NA	NA	D	D	NA	NA	16	255	13	39
Hermiston city	20	527	NA	NA	78	1,304	3	51	55	931	D	D
Hillsboro city	187	4,319	30	408	350	7,724	48	952	293	5,784	165	2,021
Independence city	15	285	D	D	24	293	3	D	D	D	9	36
Keizer city	56	464	8	39	111	1,536	16	178	74	1,187	43	176
Klamath Falls city	25	855	D	D	126	3,054	D	D	94	1,428	53	195
La Grande city	19	87	NA	NA	67	1,316	D	D	51	665	33	127
Lake Oswego city	D	D	20	148	240	2,419	42	429	114	2,189	102	526
Lebanon city	6	23	NA	NA	50	1,780	5	44	46	793	29	168
McMinnville city	36	586	D	D	155	2,634	D	D	94	1,534	54	289
Medford city	142	3,368	26	160	435	12,307	41	539	278	4,872	163	1,169
Milwaukie city	48	899	6	35	108	3,886	13	186	50	636	40	184
Monmouth city	7	20	3	D	52	631	D	D	D	D	D	D
Newberg city	29	146	8	50	106	2,031	7	54	66	1,333	37	148
Newport city	19	332	D	D	53	1,067	D	D	98	1,419	42	178
Oak Grove CDP	20	497	3	24	52	865	NA	NA	38	492	39	175
Oak Hills CDP	7	21	NA	NA	D	D	NA	NA	D	D	5	15
Oatfield CDP	11	29	NA	NA	43	524	NA	NA	3	35	D	D
Ontario city	12	65	NA	NA	76	1,535	D	D	64	961	36	177
Oregon City city	55	501	6	34	157	2,617	16	145	D	D	75	404
Pendleton city	19	193	NA	NA	96	1,416	11	115	D	D	40	194
Portland city	1,093	24,883	327	3,821	2,906	67,025	494	7,257	2,882	47,324	1,926	13,837
Prineville city	14	91	3	4	27	521	5	8	37	442	35	167
Redmond city	49	607	6	40	126	1,884	9	30	104	1,452	55	431

Table C. Incorporated Places, Census Designated Places (CDPs), and Minor Civil Divisions (MCDs) of 10,000 or More Population — **Economic Census**

STATE City, town, township, borough, or CDP (county if applicable)	Retail Trade Number of establishments	Number of employees	Wholesale trade[1] Number of establishments	Number of employees	Transportation and warehousing Number of establishments	Number of employees	Information Number of establishments	Number of employees	Finance and insurance Number of establishments	Number of employees	Real estate and rental and leasing Number of establishments	Number of employees	Professional, scientific, and technical services Number of establishments	Number of employees
	1	2	3	4	5	6	7	8	9	10	11	12	13	14
OREGON—Con.														
Roseburg city	194	3,229	26	207	12	448	D	D	91	794	54	207	90	625
St. Helens city	34	607	NA	NA	9	49	6	31	17	132	17	38	25	101
Salem city	621	10,944	155	1,722	77	1,522	83	1,999	301	2,591	311	1,335	500	2,972
Sandy city	42	932	7	22	8	109	4	93	13	103	13	43	17	89
Sherwood city	43	961	20	213	10	86	6	58	30	120	D	D	59	188
Silverton city	25	364	7	146	7	67	4	21	25	87	17	30	26	87
Springfield city	211	3,698	49	1,024	35	798	22	1,207	74	874	71	272	95	671
The Dalles city	86	1,278	D	D	7	26	13	287	37	320	32	73	29	193
Tigard city	321	7,553	170	2,629	42	502	67	2,016	253	3,970	132	614	347	3,296
Troutdale city	69	1,221	9	84	34	1,465	D	D	16	51	11	102	19	87
Tualatin city	105	2,130	114	1,860	34	982	33	787	49	356	78	326	107	1,264
West Linn city	40	568	20	73	6	103	8	22	65	289	D	D	131	415
Wilsonville city	79	1,824	79	2,237	33	801	20	447	54	327	62	282	91	2,260
Woodburn city	179	2,867	16	231	15	656	D	D	29	130	16	76	31	134
PENNSYLVANIA	42,514	662,560	12,071	204,256	8,822	230,350	5,562	113,792	17,607	282,836	10,662	66,715	29,991	340,361
Abington township	246	4,842	35	212	20	129	21	118	68	371	48	306	130	605
Adams township (Butler County)	26	325	20	146	3	88	NA	NA	13	142	D	D	45	396
Allentown city	374	5,997	124	2,582	61	769	29	602	113	1,038	102	509	215	1,282
Altoona city	228	4,940	46	791	23	341	20	333	83	599	48	213	84	659
Amity township	28	371	12	164	10	150	NA	NA	9	52	9	28	16	253
Antrim township	18	421	11	207	10	43	D	D	8	17	4	2	12	141
Aston township	34	553	24	302	11	205	D	D	D	D	12	92	42	354
Baldwin borough	17	103	NA	NA	D	D	D	D	D	D	4	7	16	257
Bensalem township	336	5,754	124	1,909	73	938	31	830	89	1,124	84	597	168	1,291
Berwick borough	52	626	8	184	D	D	D	D	D	D	10	31	15	119
Bethel Park municipality	101	2,627	37	272	6	310	13	113	53	340	27	97	95	504
Bethlehem city	219	3,576	73	3,434	56	2,376	37	956	145	3,178	70	520	187	1,481
Bethlehem township	59	1,265	23	417	38	1,380	7	87	25	260	19	65	45	512
Bloomsburg town	48	1,081	9	141	4	24	D	D	D	D	16	47	39	209
Bristol township	141	1,624	110	2,353	70	1,779	13	326	49	240	36	163	55	408
Buckingham township	80	523	19	150	9	191	10	168	38	291	18	141	128	832
Butler city	62	939	11	120	6	257	D	D	25	164	19	51	54	300
Butler township (Butler County)	94	2,500	10	243	NA	NA	10	191	33	256	19	80	26	228
Cain township	44	1,102	12	198	NA	NA	D	D	20	116	D	D	27	65
Carlisle borough	105	2,406	13	301	25	1,724	10	163	D	D	33	99	70	412
Cecil township	9	15	23	959	8	129	9	132	29	297	27	223	74	1,793
Center township (Beaver County)	54	1,204	3	9	3	5	NA	NA	12	63	5	33	18	73
Chambersburg borough	135	2,333	33	642	21	1,718	21	286	58	625	37	141	83	926
Cheltenham township	108	1,418	29	184	5	219	9	40	61	468	29	136	121	505
Chester city	63	341	20	201	14	112	7	16	3	21	15	44	16	262
Chestnuthill township	52	976	D	D	7	14	5	30	14	75	11	20	23	106
Coal township	22	512	D	D	NA	NA	NA	NA	D	D	4	19	D	D
Coatesville city	31	211	4	18	D	D	NA	NA	5	37	9	45	12	20
College township	99	1,854	26	205	9	180	23	301	40	242	20	156	72	625
Columbia borough	27	284	11	223	6	21	NA	NA	9	36	4	6	10	50
Concord township	108	3,207	17	336	7	112	D	D	D	D	21	84	69	397
Coolbaugh township	11	69	NA	NA	D	D	NA	NA	D	D	D	D	D	D
Cranberry township (Butler County)	173	4,125	81	1,356	23	533	27	1,110	75	627	48	244	122	7,918
Cumru township	25	370	5	33	6	68	NA	NA	14	133	10	28	33	387
Darby borough	13	267	D	D	D	D	NA	NA	3	16	5	38	NA	NA
Derry township (Dauphin County)	115	1,893	14	47	5	57	12	93	38	231	35	145	59	417
Derry township (Westmoreland County)	12	74	11	54	8	120	NA	NA	3	7	D	D	5	17
Dingman township	6	31	NA	NA	NA	NA	NA	NA	NA	NA	D	D	8	23
Douglass township (Montgomery County)	41	662	7	63	D	D	NA	NA	5	D	8	27	21	215
Dover township	31	500	7	68	D	D	NA	NA	D	D	8	15	17	100
Doylestown township	36	899	12	D	9	24	8	61	42	279	D	D	95	481
Dunmore borough	50	597	25	380	14	824	7	208	25	340	9	37	37	261
East Cocalico township	23	207	16	2,512	D	D	NA	NA	9	77	8	57	19	141
East Goshen township	23	355	13	54	D	D	D	D	23	130	18	94	54	555
East Hempfield township	100	2,349	68	1,154	27	995	22	141	43	293	26	161	71	440
East Lampeter township	216	3,361	40	816	21	343	11	163	38	527	18	147	44	253
East Norriton township	61	1,161	16	131	6	29	D	D	35	245	12	146	44	1,263
Easton city	136	1,859	27	401	21	811	11	109	37	342	24	70	76	531
East Pennsboro township	37	303	8	44	NA	NA	5	65	46	587	D	D	56	2,334
East Stroudsburg borough	69	1,413	D	D	8	50	5	66	18	81	17	43	35	477
Easttown township	38	755	9	35	D	D	4	16	32	289	23	377	68	1,228
East Whiteland township	67	1,312	66	4,080	14	336	31	2,523	56	803	37	240	178	6,386
Elizabeth township (Allegheny County)	24	277	D	D	4	24	NA	NA	D	D	3	4	12	68
Elizabethtown borough	28	250	6	98	D	D	D	D	15	62	6	16	22	91
Emmaus borough	49	831	7	29	D	D	D	D	15	88	5	28	27	183
Ephrata borough	45	577	5	70	7	105	11	228	23	312	11	34	34	241
Ephrata township	64	1,327	23	593	D	D	NA	NA	D	D	NA	NA	8	54
Erie city	339	4,889	102	1,741	46	616	30	340	158	4,368	54	284	181	1,735
Exeter township	59	1,656	11	169	D	D	D	D	29	151	12	68	42	287
Fairview township (Erie County)	20	171	10	127	8	167	NA	NA	D	D	9	29	12	36
Fairview township (York County)	26	532	19	176	19	1,084	3	37	D	D	12	64	33	198
Falls township	116	1,751	53	1,111	54	1,450	7	308	21	183	27	153	66	500
Ferguson township	44	1,043	6	50	NA	NA	10	393	35	177	D	D	86	1,351

1 Merchant wholesalers, except manufacturers' sales branches and offices.

Table C. Incorporated Places, Census Designated Places (CDPs), and Minor Civil Divisions (MCDs) of 10,000 or More Population — **Economic Census**

STATE City, town, township, borough, or CDP (county if applicable)	Administration and support and waste management and mediation services		Educational services		Health care and social assistance		Arts, entertainment, and recreation		Accommodation and food services		Other services (except public administration)	
	Number of establish-ments	Number of employees	Number of establish-ments	Number of employees	Number of establish-ments	Number of employees	Number of establish-ments	Number of employees	Number of establish-ments	Number of employees	Number of establish-ments	Number of employees
	15	16	17	18	19	20	21	22	23	24	25	26
OREGON—Con.												
Roseburg city..................	58	1,792	D	D	218	5,618	11	289	120	2,233	71	416
St. Helens city.................	D	D	NA	NA	62	931	D	D	41	500	14	127
Salem city.......................	225	4,950	43	306	724	15,658	74	984	457	7,454	322	1,811
Sandy city.......................	9	20	NA	NA	33	399	D	D	38	508	21	212
Sherwood city.................	34	412	8	50	59	617	D	D	51	887	38	284
Silverton city...................	14	21	4	13	56	1,063	8	80	31	477	21	88
Springfield city................	72	1,503	15	79	216	8,193	20	248	178	3,149	96	538
The Dalles city................	20	967	D	D	73	2,019	4	44	54	811	41	196
Tigard city.......................	171	8,650	37	299	277	3,308	32	359	181	3,223	155	1,116
Troutdale city..................	16	99	4	60	26	219	6	32	42	991	D	D
Tualatin city....................	83	5,785	8	132	D	D	D	D	87	1,691	97	561
West Linn city.................	35	185	9	85	114	870	8	39	53	767	46	185
Wilsonville city................	57	1,836	9	40	76	2,999	D	D	87	1,607	52	312
Woodburn city.................	23	419	NA	NA	D	D	7	75	72	1,144	25	121
PENNSYLVANIA...............	16,004	338,211	2,539	24,289	37,699	1,035,971	4,862	101,095	28,843	481,682	26,075	161,337
Abington township	87	527	16	87	236	12,287	27	629	117	2,007	98	552
Adams township (Butler County)	17	401	3	16	31	1,061	9	91	12	441	D	D
Allentown city..................	117	3,594	19	362	340	9,317	38	696	278	4,016	247	1,606
Altoona city.....................	70	1,422	13	96	231	7,152	19	188	136	2,437	118	613
Amity township	22	93	NA	NA	22	457	8	27	D	D	D	D
Antrim township	9	108	NA	NA	D	D	3	15	D	D	D	D
Aston township	39	4,670	9	38	38	408	6	183	39	663	43	248
Baldwin borough..............	18	77	4	27	24	983	NA	NA	17	163	26	134
Bensalem township	115	1,292	9	45	166	2,739	D	D	180	3,735	141	751
Berwick borough..............	6	24	NA	NA	D	D	4	7	26	300	27	112
Bethel Park municipality ...	51	1,025	6	50	142	1,850	D	D	74	1,865	85	561
Bethlehem city.................	84	3,593	NA	NA	NA	NA	26	444	232	5,777	157	1,163
Bethlehem township	30	1,107	5	34	89	1,598	7	135	44	680	27	151
Bloomsburg town..............	D	D	5	18	63	1,046	8	116	53	1,164	41	275
Bristol township	55	1,321	7	50	113	2,349	12	336	94	893	112	632
Buckingham township.......	39	188	6	26	43	469	13	179	32	532	D	D
Butler city.......................	18	242	3	9	102	1,937	5	D	37	445	45	240
Butler township (Butler County)	19	359	4	116	82	2,961	15	94	47	1,273	39	220
Caln township	13	77	3	D	57	2,941	NA	NA	38	577	D	D
Carlisle borough..............	28	1,037	5	47	79	2,047	D	D	87	1,682	60	440
Cecil township	33	1,167	3	49	22	268	8	140	23	335	D	D
Center township (Beaver County)	20	152	D	D	49	1,043	3	18	30	771	24	145
Chambersburg borough....	30	1,434	D	D	177	5,743	10	194	98	2,027	82	473
Cheltenham township	63	415	17	106	123	2,472	18	138	D	D	D	D
Chester city.....................	17	299	D	D	75	2,020	4	1,605	31	452	D	D
Chestnuthill township.......	17	133	NA	NA	34	422	6	28	D	D	21	64
Coal township	9	108	NA	NA	16	855	NA	NA	13	278	5	21
Coatesville city................	6	25	NA	NA	23	260	5	58	15	59	D	D
College township	31	825	4	59	63	1,689	D	D	29	797	37	272
Columbia borough	7	44	NA	NA	19	218	NA	NA	17	157	23	121
Concord township	54	2,267	6	56	71	1,343	D	D	70	1,737	49	614
Coolbaugh township.........	12	403	NA	NA	12	74	NA	NA	D	D	10	33
Cranberry township (Butler County)..................	67	2,752	9	120	150	2,373	14	386	85	2,360	91	1,316
Cumru township...............	D	D	NA	NA	37	735	5	61	20	348	D	D
Darby borough.................	NA	NA	NA	NA	28	1,582	NA	NA	18	105	6	17
Derry township (Dauphin County)	24	753	6	37	107	10,323	D	D	88	2,964	53	427
Derry township (Westmoreland County)	6	93	NA	NA	21	1,113	5	39	10	69	26	111
Dingman township	7	34	NA	NA	D	D	D	D	NA	NA	9	29
Douglass township (Montgomery County) ...	14	182	NA	NA	15	342	4	82	D	D	D	D
Dover township...............	16	197	NA	NA	23	369	4	74	17	261	D	D
Doylestown township........	36	551	6	15	98	3,933	10	163	26	353	32	430
Dunmore borough............	34	884	NA	NA	69	1,383	D	D	47	610	33	193
East Cocalico township	14	174	NA	NA	19	173	NA	NA	20	302	27	217
East Goshen township......	34	255	D	D	31	752	5	117	18	282	D	D
East Hempfield township..	53	1,504	9	128	148	3,411	14	652	59	1,132	47	336
East Lampeter township...	41	687	6	23	46	1,182	D	D	123	2,492	42	253
East Norriton township	44	276	6	84	83	3,561	8	155	44	671	42	276
Easton city......................	31	603	6	42	75	1,993	11	399	114	1,558	71	391
East Pennsboro township.	19	597	D	D	88	5,256	D	D	44	876	27	154
East Stroudsburg borough	23	95	D	D	86	2,922	8	25	57	988	49	228
Easttown township...........	17	120	11	74	48	2,844	8	378	31	428	D	D
East Whiteland township ..	62	1,521	8	106	43	679	15	263	75	1,190	D	D
Elizabeth township (Allegheny County)	13	125	NA	NA	27	233	8	50	16	156	21	96
Elizabethtown borough.....	5	115	NA	NA	23	1,912	7	30	21	224	20	102
Emmaus borough............	24	738	NA	NA	D	D	4	25	27	351	D	D
Ephrata borough..............	17	160	3	2	49	2,035	5	D	37	562	41	248
Ephrata township.............	13	247	NA	NA	18	667	NA	NA	23	277	D	D
Erie city..........................	82	2,435	17	144	458	16,369	43	962	211	4,197	215	1,446
Exeter township...............	37	628	4	7	48	1,069	8	63	43	1,007	D	D
Fairview township (Erie County)	10	47	NA	NA	29	746	3	117	16	180	19	93
Fairview township (York County)	32	431	NA	NA	14	270	10	56	30	406	26	102
Falls township.................	67	444	10	88	68	822	13	306	68	905	D	D
Ferguson township	21	262	D	D	62	1,054	9	50	34	791	34	261

Table C. Incorporated Places, Census Designated Places (CDPs), and Minor Civil Divisions (MCDs) of 10,000 or More Population — **Economic Census**

STATE City, town, township, borough, or CDP (county if applicable)	Retail Trade Number of establishments	Number of employees	Wholesale trade[1] Number of establishments	Number of employees	Transportation and warehousing Number of establishments	Number of employees	Information Number of establishments	Number of employees	Finance and insurance Number of establishments	Number of employees	Real estate and rental and leasing Number of establishments	Number of employees	Professional, scientific, and technical services Number of establishments	Number of employees
	1	2	3	4	5	6	7	8	9	10	11	12	13	14
PENNSYLVANIA—Con.														
Forks township	29	670	D	D	8	215	D	D	D	D	9	36	16	113
Franconia township	16	151	16	179	8	261	D	D	8	55	13	92	28	158
Franklin Park borough	10	160	15	51	4	3	NA	NA	44	311	9	72	48	201
Greene township (Franklin County)	40	276	D	D	8	126	D	D	D	D	7	33	20	186
Greensburg city	201	3,539	30	425	11	135	19	370	70	534	40	175	117	624
Guilford township	74	1,455	19	238	16	740	3	5	14	78	7	41	15	108
Hamilton township (Franklin County)	19	279	D	D	11	152	NA	NA	4	21	4	24	10	128
Hampden township	139	2,660	41	453	43	3,041	15	398	64	1,546	53	184	139	1,172
Hampton township	55	626	21	177	D	D	D	D	31	182	26	110	50	495
Hanover township (Luzerne County)	42	1,133	20	615	10	299	D	D	D	D	10	24	D	D
Hanover township (Northampton County)	18	453	19	547	D	D	12	419	28	626	14	219	43	918
Hanover borough	141	2,688	14	125	D	D	9	89	44	290	19	84	54	241
Harborcreek township	46	1,145	8	133	9	135	D	D	D	D	15	49	12	185
Harrisburg city	181	2,266	60	1,502	44	735	35	790	86	2,791	57	263	250	3,168
Harrison township	46	862	NA	NA	D	D	NA	NA	19	103	5	9	16	84
Hatfield township	76	1,787	59	1,752	14	878	10	100	25	145	23	119	46	501
Haverford township	90	1,532	33	188	10	103	21	173	D	D	41	246	126	468
Hazleton city	110	1,055	32	482	30	1,369	14	199	32	161	15	38	42	139
Hempfield township (Westmoreland County)	89	1,886	34	1,166	17	195	14	116	44	193	22	94	68	546
Hermitage city	110	2,580	12	171	D	D	7	99	49	860	27	109	39	216
Hilltown township	58	2,338	31	190	13	57	3	15	15	107	10	18	26	75
Hopewell township (Beaver County)	38	509	D	D	D	D	NA	NA	7	18	4	11	8	359
Horsham township	81	1,483	63	2,004	D	D	24	2,942	101	3,631	39	388	138	3,087
Indiana borough	55	772	8	46	NA	NA	D	D	36	1,051	18	60	42	286
Jefferson Hills borough	7	34	10	56	NA	NA	NA	NA	8	24	8	13	16	72
Johnstown city	114	1,842	27	218	6	122	10	563	56	624	22	227	70	967
Kingston borough	74	698	20	208	6	53	3	26	38	220	24	99	72	388
Lancaster city	345	5,430	53	869	25	1,975	32	1,406	64	1,626	49	328	225	2,087
Lancaster township (Lancaster County)	35	621	5	164	5	13	D	D	D	D	16	79	27	138
Lansdale borough	58	724	39	500	9	512	12	250	34	217	14	49	52	403
Lansdowne borough	28	247	8	52	D	D	NA	NA	D	D	3	7	19	38
Lebanon city	99	1,396	17	116	8	128	12	179	47	480	29	170	47	325
Lehigh township	20	112	5	27	NA	NA	NA	NA	4	13	NA	NA	11	72
Lehman township (Pike County)	NA	NA	NA	NA	NA	NA	NA	NA	NA	NA	D	D	D	D
Limerick township	196	3,403	30	604	21	1,065	D	D	35	175	16	51	54	491
Logan township	67	942	16	287	8	338	D	D	12	54	18	89	22	140
Lower Allen township	115	2,538	27	359	15	404	D	D	54	2,124	29	318	89	1,299
Lower Burrell city	35	332	4	D	NA	NA	NA	NA	14	75	9	41	19	52
Lower Gwynedd township	21	291	23	131	NA	NA	11	139	32	143	15	54	63	1,995
Lower Macungie township	68	1,125	20	258	12	154	14	76	35	180	33	88	72	369
Lower Makefield township	31	396	22	156	8	30	9	22	45	266	22	51	119	949
Lower Merion township	288	4,732	64	684	18	142	73	1,767	238	4,593	144	1,014	430	2,541
Lower Moreland township	56	474	46	1,181	33	122	10	68	45	200	26	102	96	336
Lower Paxton township	193	4,345	41	449	31	251	31	678	85	758	59	251	135	2,074
Lower Pottsgrove township	20	495	5	53	NA	NA	NA	NA	16	293	6	47	27	266
Lower Providence township	55	871	22	202	13	177	18	252	29	152	16	76	93	1,221
Lower Salford township	39	814	D	D	5	79	D	D	35	242	18	66	60	932
Lower Saucon township	23	310	D	D	D	D	3	13	D	D	4	5	18	72
Lower Southampton township	143	1,805	75	904	78	272	24	509	81	544	52	354	171	1,110
Loyalsock township	60	1,000	18	95	5	42	7	77	29	262	24	291	24	264
McCandless township	68	1,250	18	182	6	51	8	165	59	275	38	198	82	678
McKeesport city	65	618	17	169	D	D	NA	NA	21	74	6	36	15	39
Manchester township	45	664	42	1,026	20	759	7	114	D	D	23	195	34	443
Manheim township (Lancaster County)	146	2,897	59	639	20	256	15	237	143	1,502	78	425	D	D
Manor township (Lancaster County)	25	157	7	926	5	14	NA	NA	14	65	21	171	28	237
Marple township	76	1,299	37	407	4	14	12	179	D	D	20	170	89	624
Meadville city	76	758	8	82	4	76	10	129	39	248	17	145	42	235
Middle Smithfield township	16	76	NA	NA	D	D	NA	NA	D	D	D	D	7	5
Middletown township (Bucks County)	124	3,835	33	262	26	309	20	210	60	349	52	328	116	1,066
Middletown township (Delaware County)	29	366	6	13	D	D	D	D	D	D	16	35	44	128
Milford township	14	135	15	145	6	8	NA	NA	6	30	5	10	27	284
Millcreek township (Erie County)	209	4,255	63	963	26	643	19	302	86	649	72	375	111	825
Monroeville municipality	268	5,533	38	317	10	28	22	312	D	D	60	409	89	1,291
Montgomery township (Montgomery County)	107	2,923	46	674	12	249	14	100	35	237	25	126	94	386
Moon township	74	1,947	32	509	44	2,473	25	309	51	1,149	53	605	103	2,112
Mount Joy township (Lancaster County)	36	784	7	312	11	207	NA	NA	11	46	6	13	13	108
Mount Lebanon township	77	779	16	52	7	54	10	72	43	208	33	88	130	431
Mount Pleasant township (Westmoreland County)	40	556	14	182	8	304	NA	NA	10	33	D	D	12	93
Muhlenberg township	98	2,199	44	758	22	855	5	50	29	168	17	54	17	134
Munhall borough	19	147	D	D	3	4	D	D	8	62	6	50	9	104
Murrysville municipality	67	751	19	370	6	59	9	107	36	365	19	63	86	460
Nanticoke city	17	191	NA	NA	NA	NA	NA	NA	14	49	4	9	6	27

1 Merchant wholesalers, except manufacturers' sales branches and offices.

Table C. Incorporated Places, Census Designated Places (CDPs), and Minor Civil Divisions (MCDs) of 10,000 or More Population — **Economic Census**

	Economic activity by sector, 2017											
	Administration and support and waste management and mediation services		Educational services		Health care and social assistance		Arts, entertainment, and recreation		Accommodation and food services		Other services (except public administration)	
STATE City, town, township, borough, or CDP (county if applicable)	Number of establish-ments	Number of employees	Number of establish-ments	Number of employees	Number of establish-ments	Number of employees	Number of establish-ments	Number of employees	Number of establish-ments	Number of employees	Number of establish-ments	Number of employees
	15	16	17	18	19	20	21	22	23	24	25	26
PENNSYLVANIA—Con.												
Forks township	21	360	NA	NA	23	609	6	49	28	261	D	D
Franconia township...........	25	379	3	6	23	903	4	51	13	188	D	D
Franklin Park borough	15	428	3	D	38	367	6	192	5	56	D	D
Greene township (Franklin County)	23	198	NA	NA	18	319	6	44	17	298	D	D
Greensburg city	24	539	5	11	157	5,071	23	351	96	2,368	76	464
Guilford township	20	134	NA	NA	21	439	6	78	29	361	D	D
Hamilton township (Franklin County).........	8	52	NA	NA	9	224	3	7	12	225	16	57
Hampden township...........	46	1,550	16	76	96	2,193	13	226	89	1,814	61	483
Hampton township...........	30	206	5	52	65	669	11	197	40	739	D	D
Hanover township (Luzerne County)	23	1,107	NA	NA	24	290	3	D	27	246	D	D
Hanover township (Northampton County) ..	15	940	6	45	81	2,087	NA	NA	20	482	11	102
Hanover borough	18	782	3	15	122	2,853	7	284	68	1,580	70	460
Harborcreek township.......	15	212	NA	NA	33	636	8	213	33	710	D	D
Harrisburg city	90	1,884	15	84	207	8,012	31	334	180	2,571	185	1,394
Harrison township............	7	43	NA	NA	63	1,466	D	D	25	414	29	120
Hatfield township	25	434	6	48	75	1,793	7	96	29	450	D	D
Haverford township...........	64	340	20	52	183	4,435	29	381	77	1,035	92	445
Hazleton city...................	31	1,516	4	62	103	2,938	7	16	63	722	48	194
Hempfield township (Westmoreland County)	43	576	8	32	119	2,291	9	104	57	1,294	69	361
Hermitage city	29	517	NA	NA	173	3,341	12	351	70	1,563	49	251
Hilltown township.............	45	492	3	20	32	406	D	D	27	290	D	D
Hopewell township (Beaver County)...........	11	105	NA	NA	32	385	4	6	27	440	19	115
Horsham township............	88	4,212	6	54	77	3,014	20	366	93	1,534	82	526
Indiana borough...............	13	187	NA	NA	60	994	8	16	39	1,076	37	222
Jefferson Hills borough.....	16	73	NA	NA	48	2,441	4	13	18	242	D	D
Johnstown city	24	1,043	5	17	109	5,045	9	144	69	894	59	349
Kingston borough	25	122	3	21	130	2,685	5	27	45	562	46	481
Lancaster city	63	930	15	120	201	10,120	27	572	193	4,075	148	1,295
Lancaster township (Lancaster County)	12	62	4	22	34	1,473	4	65	23	766	16	113
Lansdale borough............	27	371	9	64	62	2,940	6	257	43	468	D	D
Lansdowne borough.........	10	129	NA	NA	26	345	D	D	11	194	D	D
Lebanon city	23	840	NA	NA	90	2,944	D	D	D	D	63	255
Lehigh township...............	15	59	NA	NA	10	101	D	D	8	101	D	D
Lehman township (Pike County)	9	51	NA	NA	NA	NA	6	118	7	96	D	D
Limerick township............	45	608	6	51	60	802	13	621	70	1,143	D	D
Logan township................	15	358	NA	NA	34	1,286	9	148	36	642	27	223
Lower Allen township.......	34	466	D	D	67	1,751	9	90	56	905	56	478
Lower Burrell city.............	11	38	NA	NA	40	403	NA	NA	25	260	37	184
Lower Gwynedd township	25	249	D	D	45	1,404	11	596	29	591	D	D
Lower Macungie township	49	529	8	60	65	922	10	141	35	475	43	275
Lower Makefield township	30	105	14	23	74	987	9	94	19	416	D	D
Lower Merion township.....	110	1,492	50	1,003	483	13,671	55	1,004	D	D	233	2,061
Lower Moreland township.	28	328	7	19	88	1,674	8	162	33	361	46	307
Lower Paxton township.....	80	2,907	19	139	195	5,445	D	D	108	2,757	111	698
Lower Pottsgrove township	14	480	5	37	50	779	3	42	18	255	20	107
Lower Providence township	48	990	6	56	41	1,860	12	104	52	646	D	D
Lower Salford township	D	D	5	48	44	847	4	244	36	420	D	D
Lower Saucon township....	25	72	NA	NA	9	115	4	19	19	175	D	D
Lower Southampton township	74	1,335	15	104	125	5,503	19	248	64	1,297	112	558
Loyalsock township..........	23	281	NA	NA	69	1,676	3	D	47	1,128	D	D
McCandless township.......	29	880	11	114	136	4,185	11	70	44	1,098	64	429
McKeesport city	13	129	NA	NA	107	2,448	6	17	D	D	34	180
Manchester township........	31	1,180	3	D	29	533	9	135	39	1,028	33	286
Manheim township (Lancaster County)	87	4,704	16	142	203	6,428	20	485	117	2,888	95	891
Manor township (Lancaster County)	24	134	NA	NA	25	842	D	D	17	276	D	D
Marple township	42	882	8	83	102	2,754	14	187	43	689	60	383
Meadville city..................	16	125	D	D	123	3,508	6	252	D	D	43	254
Middle Smithfield township	6	146	NA	NA	3	53	NA	NA	D	D	7	44
Middletown township (Bucks County)............	71	785	10	150	187	7,049	D	D	75	1,578	67	458
Middletown township (Delaware County).......	24	210	NA	NA	76	4,068	5	432	21	384	D	D
Milford township...............	14	42	NA	NA	20	398	NA	NA	9	167	D	D
Millcreek township (Erie County)	72	2,712	14	136	191	4,994	D	D	142	2,722	127	778
Monroeville municipality....	52	999	13	118	236	6,094	20	296	118	2,580	91	599
Montgomery township (Montgomery County) ...	39	694	5	10	46	469	D	D	58	1,448	D	D
Moon township	47	2,243	3	32	127	1,731	9	116	88	2,139	44	349
Mount Joy township (Lancaster County)	12	157	NA	NA	14	298	6	36	D	D	D	D
Mount Lebanon township .	30	249	10	127	134	2,073	13	96	64	1,294	56	322
Mount Pleasant township (Westmoreland County)	11	79	NA	NA	20	130	6	8	D	D	32	228
Muhlenberg township	25	1,026	NA	NA	43	579	10	59	47	852	55	334
Munhall borough..............	5	173	NA	NA	29	430	NA	NA	24	173	D	D
Murrysville municipality.....	33	310	4	14	73	852	13	61	38	1,030	53	305
Nanticoke city	NA	NA	NA	NA	26	417	NA	NA	13	110	13	44

Table C. Incorporated Places, Census Designated Places (CDPs), and Minor Civil Divisions (MCDs) of 10,000 or More Population — **Economic Census**

STATE City, town, township, borough, or CDP (county if applicable)	Retail Trade Number of establishments	Number of employees	Wholesale trade[1] Number of establishments	Number of employees	Transportation and warehousing Number of establishments	Number of employees	Information Number of establishments	Number of employees	Finance and insurance Number of establishments	Number of employees	Real estate and rental and leasing Number of establishments	Number of employees	Professional, scientific, and technical services Number of establishments	Number of employees
	1	2	3	4	5	6	7	8	9	10	11	12	13	14
PENNSYLVANIA—Con.														
Nether Providence township	16	601	4	6	D	D	D	D	11	30	14	45	60	298
Newberry township	15	98	5	D	9	40	NA	NA	D	D	9	D	8	21
New Britain township	21	182	11	264	NA	NA	NA	NA	21	444	5	8	39	170
New Castle city	70	593	D	D	10	183	D	D	24	212	19	212	42	236
New Garden township	21	325	25	744	11	239	NA	NA	D	D	5	8	26	294
New Hanover township	11	104	5	11	NA	NA	NA	NA	11	D	NA	NA	21	52
New Kensington city	43	738	16	192	NA	NA	11	163	16	69	8	23	D	D
Newtown township (Bucks County)	63	1,027	34	508	9	72	14	118	70	997	29	123	150	2,373
Newtown township (Delaware County)	68	915	29	325	NA	NA	D	D	68	710	D	D	101	804
Norristown borough	90	627	35	399	D	D	6	117	16	67	25	139	77	491
Northampton township	88	1,024	68	867	48	106	14	184	56	280	30	88	183	505
North Fayette township	27	488	17	361	6	16	3	26	D	D	10	15	21	59
North Huntingdon township	95	2,330	21	337	11	354	D	D	D	D	28	100	69	408
North Lebanon township	48	876	D	D	11	608	6	252	9	D	4	19	6	44
North Middleton township	17	255	D	D	9	306	D	D	D	D	5	34	D	D
North Strabane township	28	280	18	273	10	165	4	7	14	67	14	123	36	275
North Union township	44	341	11	91	15	369	NA	NA	12	39	11	76	18	259
North Versailles township	43	1,122	10	43	10	210	D	D	10	39	6	48	15	87
North Whitehall township	33	420	18	148	14	330	D	D	16	94	5	6	25	169
Palmer township	44	779	16	191	8	2,432	6	60	17	80	15	62	32	151
Patton township	42	1,481	D	D	3	34	D	D	20	105	19	149	28	217
Penn township (Westmoreland County)	20	224	14	298	11	39	4	7	23	87	6	8	35	147
Penn township (York County)	50	997	8	195	9	234	D	D	24	118	7	26	15	79
Penn Hills township	90	1,507	26	216	11	55	D	D	D	D	37	123	43	189
Peters township (Washington County)	95	1,640	36	163	7	200	D	D	66	296	25	95	89	466
Philadelphia city	4,540	53,157	1,006	17,207	720	26,354	913	19,163	1,547	43,786	1,293	10,704	3,123	58,180
Phoenixville borough	54	1,041	16	130	5	102	7	59	23	286	24	84	47	175
Pine township (Allegheny County)	80	1,613	17	152	NA	NA	10	90	83	941	23	125	124	958
Pittsburgh city	1,121	17,273	380	7,665	143	4,512	325	10,969	725	41,161	453	4,909	1,569	30,512
Plum borough	50	572	29	217	9	594	9	79	16	101	18	48	35	502
Plumstead township	51	1,469	23	629	6	66	NA	NA	21	61	10	49	38	140
Plymouth township	142	4,169	52	959	19	600	27	917	105	2,728	57	611	167	3,371
Pocono township	144	2,502	13	124	8	91	4	24	18	88	14	86	19	74
Pottstown borough	104	1,358	37	262	9	207	17	283	27	299	14	75	49	244
Pottsville city	78	1,100	14	132	D	D	11	253	38	286	13	50	58	575
Radnor township	118	1,453	33	221	D	D	32	1,041	169	4,208	54	271	213	1,318
Rapho township	19	338	18	372	11	137	NA	NA	7	57	3	11	20	157
Reading city	226	3,225	51	1,282	62	927	22	664	47	1,357	137	D	125	1,973
Richland township (Allegheny County)	49	1,353	12	64	11	662	D	D	D	D	10	186	21	84
Richland township (Bucks County)	80	1,602	22	440	7	165	NA	NA	13	90	5	33	20	111
Richland township (Cambria County)	109	1,903	17	154	14	459	16	181	51	527	19	122	38	699
Ridley township	90	1,534	16	75	6	19	7	122	D	D	11	37	39	515
Robinson township	107	2,102	43	572	18	380	9	79	D	D	22	103	59	1,033
Ross township (Allegheny County)	264	4,973	35	321	6	21	20	166	67	277	33	297	109	567
Rostraver township	56	1,443	7	82	13	295	D	D	14	95	14	59	14	86
St. Marys city	64	642	18	104	11	170	5	47	25	158	10	23	25	175
Salisbury township (Lancaster County)	39	323	12	105	10	242	NA	NA	5	33	5	13	16	120
Salisbury township (Lehigh County)	39	699	6	59	5	85	D	D	D	D	8	18	26	179
Sandy township	63	1,347	11	118	9	143	D	D	18	71	7	49	13	116
Scott township (Allegheny County)	31	282	10	63	3	12	5	24	32	263	D	D	50	334
Scranton city	303	3,802	76	1,235	31	821	28	561	109	2,113	60	334	206	1,237
Shaler township	46	849	16	136	7	248	D	D	20	198	26	109	31	132
Sharon city	39	454	11	169	4	42	3	23	19	150	8	31	26	135
Silver Spring township	82	3,238	18	312	32	927	8	92	25	261	13	61	38	245
Skippack township	31	162	10	115	D	D	NA	NA	18	D	8	D	48	270
Somerset township (Somerset County)	61	1,096	21	127	D	D	NA	NA	13	60	7	27	14	293
South Fayette township	24	416	35	422	4	70	D	D	14	75	12	93	53	263
South Middleton township	38	1,316	9	56	10	1,178	NA	NA	D	D	8	29	28	208
South Park township	14	205	8	34	D	D	NA	NA	D	D	5	13	28	73
South Union township	74	1,321	4	37	4	59	D	D	11	65	11	66	19	79
South Whitehall township	86	1,755	17	261	D	D	11	185	78	1,382	45	274	83	1,466
Spring township (Berks County)	40	1,128	19	735	D	D	6	79	65	1,076	37	149	75	721
Springettsbury township	177	4,138	26	726	11	185	13	75	68	595	41	241	62	711
Springfield township (Delaware County)	111	2,990	18	126	NA	NA	D	D	D	D	24	184	51	170
Springfield township (Montgomery County)	51	810	16	69	7	25	12	274	31	130	D	D	79	238
Spring Garden township	32	322	13	356	16	679	6	55	D	D	12	57	27	319
State College borough	115	1,654	8	51	6	52	19	214	56	335	D	D	85	551
Stroud township	39	708	13	91	D	D	6	76	11	67	12	36	17	90
Susquehanna township	79	1,139	18	980	16	174	23	1,331	72	4,302	26	152	106	1,429
Swatara township (Dauphin County)	108	2,223	72	1,923	37	2,559	D	D	32	461	34	189	40	751

1 Merchant wholesalers, except manufacturers' sales branches and offices.

Table C. Incorporated Places, Census Designated Places (CDPs), and Minor Civil Divisions (MCDs) of 10,000 or More Population — **Economic Census**

STATE City, town, township, borough, or CDP (county if applicable)	Administration and support and waste management and mediation services		Educational services		Health care and social assistance		Arts, entertainment, and recreation		Accommodation and food services		Other services (except public administration)	
	Number of establishments	Number of employees	Number of establishments	Number of employees	Number of establishments	Number of employees	Number of establishments	Number of employees	Number of establishments	Number of employees	Number of establishments	Number of employees
	15	16	17	18	19	20	21	22	23	24	25	26
PENNSYLVANIA—Con.												
Nether Providence township	18	709	NA	NA	49	1,101	D	D	7	130	D	D
Newberry township	11	15	NA	NA	D	D	D	D	12	188	18	64
New Britain township	27	120	7	51	25	484	D	D	21	297	D	D
New Castle city	21	717	D	D	92	3,485	5	98	43	514	58	256
New Garden township	21	498	D	D	13	227	D	D	9	159	22	134
New Hanover township	19	105	NA	NA	17	147	5	97	8	68	D	D
New Kensington city	15	242	NA	NA	57	622	6	100	38	498	26	356
Newtown township (Bucks County)	54	430	D	D	104	2,719	12	538	47	772	40	222
Newtown township (Delaware County)	55	3,100	18	160	87	2,193	15	201	34	730	55	786
Norristown borough	41	1,068	D	D	106	2,563	12	128	68	416	D	D
Northampton township	69	519	13	43	114	928	14	215	63	1,025	68	360
North Fayette township	16	102	NA	NA	20	318	4	16	31	452	D	D
North Huntingdon township	52	545	NA	NA	81	1,293	10	41	45	1,106	53	331
North Lebanon township	D	D	3	28	D	D	D	D	13	224	D	D
North Middleton township	11	395	NA	NA	D	D	NA	NA	13	62	D	D
North Strabane township	23	441	6	42	44	947	D	D	23	499	D	D
North Union township	9	54	D	D	34	823	3	33	17	98	26	125
North Versailles township	13	128	3	8	24	361	5	99	33	416	D	D
North Whitehall township	28	104	3	D	35	1,621	8	97	22	229	D	D
Palmer township	19	109	D	D	51	815	9	95	D	D	D	D
Patton township	9	24	D	D	30	375	6	32	D	D	D	D
Penn township (Westmoreland County)	34	197	3	6	35	777	11	52	26	229	27	102
Penn township (York County)	12	94	NA	NA	36	906	7	170	34	680	D	D
Penn Hills township	57	1,035	D	D	122	1,768	11	255	52	675	79	318
Peters township (Washington County)	44	434	16	116	134	1,689	D	D	62	1,325	69	475
Philadelphia city	1,231	33,043	276	4,295	3,992	161,976	451	15,371	3,953	61,893	2,687	20,004
Phoenixville borough	25	93	5	6	57	1,318	D	D	55	812	39	182
Pine township (Allegheny County)	29	436	16	132	144	2,155	13	214	61	1,162	59	502
Pittsburgh city	469	20,510	117	1,110	1,383	60,636	209	9,309	1,311	26,134	912	7,796
Plum borough	49	179	NA	NA	35	727	7	9	35	588	44	232
Plumstead township	33	257	8	232	39	576	3	16	33	430	D	D
Plymouth township	74	3,389	16	164	108	2,234	13	287	64	1,559	D	D
Pocono township	15	704	D	D	41	743	6	42	71	3,482	29	166
Pottstown borough	28	475	6	239	79	2,842	7	296	59	911	D	D
Pottsville city	19	372	D	D	130	4,069	3	5	46	696	38	212
Radnor township	77	2,229	29	216	140	2,118	32	761	126	2,577	82	582
Rapho township	19	89	NA	NA	4	94	5	119	23	336	19	117
Reading city	40	1,663	6	37	159	4,881	22	769	146	1,910	107	738
Richland township (Allegheny County)	25	265	3	13	51	1,037	D	D	34	715	D	D
Richland township (Bucks County)	19	89	NA	NA	19	157	4	19	17	384	D	D
Richland township (Cambria County)	29	472	NA	NA	91	1,725	D	D	60	1,338	42	192
Ridley township	32	278	7	33	55	840	5	62	72	1,078	72	359
Robinson township	32	2,095	NA	NA	81	1,040	3	23	52	1,247	54	357
Ross township (Allegheny County)	59	688	10	68	86	2,045	D	D	91	2,112	D	D
Rostraver township	14	89	NA	NA	36	384	8	44	43	956	27	134
St. Marys city	20	180	NA	NA	56	1,158	D	D	42	564	39	179
Salisbury township (Lancaster County)	8	80	NA	NA	12	167	NA	NA	20	155	17	79
Salisbury township (Lehigh County)	16	370	NA	NA	124	10,723	6	35	21	506	D	D
Sandy township	13	190	NA	NA	26	566	NA	NA	26	601	22	155
Scott township (Allegheny County)	17	738	4	37	72	3,779	3	63	39	528	35	224
Scranton city	56	1,212	13	39	337	11,865	D	D	209	2,681	148	771
Shaler township	39	198	NA	NA	38	328	6	25	36	456	57	253
Sharon city	15	209	NA	NA	51	1,701	4	70	24	330	33	191
Silver Spring township	27	175	5	18	D	D	3	D	38	771	40	282
Skippack township	23	262	D	D	37	1,273	5	39	29	351	D	D
Somerset township (Somerset County)	13	79	NA	NA	37	629	4	28	22	293	28	178
South Fayette township	26	460	D	D	50	951	7	48	D	D	33	1,173
South Middleton township	27	411	4	63	D	D	9	125	26	285	27	150
South Park township	7	29	5	8	19	362	D	D	17	192	15	59
South Union township	9	436	NA	NA	77	1,754	7	120	35	774	D	D
South Whitehall township	34	4,593	D	D	133	2,463	13	734	76	1,717	60	405
Spring township (Berks County)	30	299	12	132	66	1,998	5	18	26	565	37	252
Springettsbury township	35	1,247	9	107	98	2,379	14	552	104	2,247	63	410
Springfield township (Delaware County)	44	264	7	96	84	1,838	10	369	56	1,790	D	D
Springfield township (Montgomery County)	32	190	6	19	88	3,266	13	376	35	496	D	D
Spring Garden township	19	456	D	D	D	D	6	368	25	348	D	D
State College borough	21	465	8	92	120	3,795	18	343	143	3,014	53	285
Stroud township	8	22	NA	NA	21	652	7	172	26	416	20	87
Susquehanna township	46	1,679	4	23	119	7,099	D	D	68	1,310	66	416
Swatara township (Dauphin County)	34	1,425	3	14	52	1,527	7	85	74	1,331	71	516

STATE City, town, township, borough, or CDP (county if applicable)	Retail Trade Number of establishments	Number of employees	Wholesale trade[1] Number of establishments	Number of employees	Transportation and warehousing Number of establishments	Number of employees	Information Number of establishments	Number of employees	Finance and insurance Number of establishments	Number of employees	Real estate and rental and leasing Number of establishments	Number of employees	Professional, scientific, and technical services Number of establishments	Number of employees
	1	2	3	4	5	6	7	8	9	10	11	12	13	14
PENNSYLVANIA—Con.														
Towamencin township......	20	363	22	215	D	D	3	17	21	110	16	110	34	289
Tredyffrin township...........	102	1,948	60	1,690	9	127	67	4,128	222	18,340	85	1,047	333	4,567
Unity township	40	1,109	10	38	8	41	NA	NA	18	73	5	29	35	329
Upper Allen township........	30	1,512	15	645	D	D	D	D	D	D	14	43	78	1,044
Upper Chichester township................	62	956	28	938	18	324	7	54	17	140	16	189	26	311
Upper Darby township.......	232	3,085	36	346	16	21	D	64	338	47	275	104	415	
Upper Dublin township......	63	1,347	38	361	9	217	25	829	98	4,298	34	420	159	2,588
Upper Gwynedd township	31	506	22	196	7	62	D	D	22	166	17	114	62	389
Upper Macungie township	83	3,951	74	2,875	75	3,714	12	288	40	918	31	193	107	1,684
Upper Merion township.....	387	8,439	111	3,194	43	755	69	2,874	189	6,133	97	1,185	317	9,410
Upper Moreland township.	108	2,748	56	731	11	280	9	153	41	200	30	323	93	495
Upper Providence township (Delaware County)	18	72	7	96	D	D	D	D	22	237	17	87	59	249
Upper Providence township (Montgomery County)	41	1,058	31	644	13	761	9	277	D	D	22	265	86	619
Upper St. Clair township...	125	2,378	23	72	D	D	14	298	44	347	27	112	88	512
Upper Saucon township ...	62	810	D	D	D	D	11	97	39	225	17	37	54	499
Upper Southampton township..................	63	719	22	237	26	70	11	37	62	430	38	109	97	359
Upper Uwchlan township..	15	647	11	162	4	27	4	7	16	81	7	6	87	545
Uwchlan township............	49	925	31	1,107	D	D	18	703	65	1,453	15	224	118	1,317
Warminster township	107	2,345	76	1,461	33	149	17	112	60	484	32	136	70	721
Warrington township (Bucks County)	95	2,433	26	405	8	22	19	253	42	927	D	D	83	1,089
Warwick township (Bucks County)	30	340	38	357	24	167	NA	NA	28	132	7	21	60	312
Warwick township (Lancaster County)	46	980	12	403	16	206	10	35	14	53	11	307	18	341
Washington township (Franklin County)............	39	407	D	D	4	126	5	38	6	33	9	18	17	107
Washington city	82	1,067	15	115	12	295	D	D	37	328	18	94	84	569
Waynesboro borough	41	936	NA	NA	NA	NA	5	62	16	83	11	31	25	134
West Bradford township....	8	41	D	D	D	D	D	D	D	D	6	8	40	121
West Chester borough......	65	551	35	257	5	40	19	341	64	625	45	204	166	1,118
West Deer township..........	21	136	13	138	6	50	NA	NA	5	12	8	65	15	57
West Goshen township......	89	4,258	91	1,207	29	3,169	22	136	76	414	45	209	147	1,678
West Hanover township.....	21	447	11	198	9	50	NA	NA	7	29	4	77	14	81
West Hempfield township .	39	709	14	393	12	452	NA	NA	14	93	9	33	30	1,216
West Lampeter township ..	49	794	6	20	6	269	4	13	24	98	6	59	22	210
West Manchester township	90	1,847	25	226	20	1,970	9	298	41	276	13	57	19	55
West Mifflin borough.........	128	3,107	13	375	13	284	11	95	18	133	10	169	D	D
West Norriton township	42	788	40	1,699	8	77	13	143	9	D	14	50	34	226
Westtown township	22	318	8	14	D	D	NA	NA	20	127	8	10	48	208
West Whiteland township .	194	3,445	60	717	7	442	25	1,142	83	928	44	326	187	3,238
White township	105	3,020	21	217	10	211	9	106	27	215	15	53	36	362
Whitehall borough............	13	118	6	15	4	41	NA	NA	D	D	13	77	23	89
Whitehall township...........	275	5,414	29	220	26	329	D	D	37	255	33	227	34	181
Whitemarsh township	42	686	31	208	8	130	14	462	51	956	40	187	115	3,560
Whitpain township	56	844	36	243	14	98	14	413	126	2,661	60	461	219	4,920
Wilkes-Barre city..............	242	4,820	41	313	20	428	30	992	72	1,848	48	312	109	1,356
Wilkinsburg borough	26	215	7	97	4	43	NA	NA	D	D	15	87	17	43
Williamsport city	98	1,410	35	938	27	884	15	343	62	790	34	260	74	661
Willistown township	15	84	17	130	NA	NA	7	27	26	120	11	29	67	320
Windsor township	17	524	D	D	D	D	4	16	D	D	8	22	13	40
Worcester township	13	186	15	336	4	11	8	70	11	D	11	32	48	211
Wyomissing borough	148	2,948	18	454	5	46	16	369	80	1,520	D	D	87	906
Yeadon borough	22	96	11	109	NA	NA	NA	NA	3	15	3	6	D	D
York city	128	1,482	54	901	9	282	20	804	60	389	33	296	136	1,913
York township	104	2,052	23	379	11	104	14	305	52	1,011	37	337	53	443
RHODE ISLAND..............	3,769	48,753	1,107	16,847	700	11,082	456	6,863	1,452	27,061	1,110	5,287	3,026	23,910
Barrington town	33	284	4	7	NA	NA	5	13	D	D	D	D	43	105
Bristol town.....................	57	552	31	436	D	D	5	20	20	103	D	D	35	135
Burrillville town................	23	146	8	51	D	D	D	D	NA	NA	7	10	D	D
Central Falls city	43	197	3	31	11	30	NA	NA	D	D	7	37	9	34
Coventry town..................	83	1,633	19	233	D	D	D	D	16	115	16	58	38	241
Cranston city...................	300	5,101	122	2,081	58	652	29	348	128	2,754	83	333	227	1,775
Cumberland town	69	783	30	645	21	593	D	D	D	D	38	172	72	649
East Greenwich town.......	58	690	20	840	D	D	8	105	D	D	D	D	90	370
East Providence city	132	1,884	68	1,363	29	239	17	262	D	D	47	231	130	1,099
Glocester town................	23	175	NA	NA	10	79	NA	NA	D	D	7	8	D	D
Johnston town	134	1,716	29	311	45	845	D	D	26	1,553	39	212	52	196
Lincoln town	53	775	44	811	18	306	8	164	37	2,898	D	D	72	1,151
Middletown town..............	97	1,511	15	168	9	695	9	158	37	989	31	178	83	2,807
Narragansett town	49	660	19	206	8	21	NA	NA	D	D	32	107	31	102
Newport city....................	207	1,482	22	70	34	184	17	241	41	375	51	275	125	677
North Kingstown town.......	110	2,081	50	538	41	665	20	269	D	D	21	61	109	455
North Providence town.....	96	1,192	10	79	17	72	D	D	D	D	32	112	40	170
North Smithfield town	46	1,188	13	86	9	207	NA	NA	D	D	12	28	36	163
Pawtucket city.................	195	1,783	64	2,278	68	583	22	74	D	D	64	225	111	819
Portsmouth town..............	49	436	11	203	7	75	7	59	D	D	18	56	55	216
Providence city	649	6,659	179	1,926	109	1,050	152	2,704	382	4,600	213	1,354	792	6,865
Scituate town..................	18	163	8	33	D	D	3	27	D	D	D	D	20	98
Smithfield town	101	1,817	40	536	13	85	14	244	66	2,349	16	83	68	444
South Kingstown town......	109	1,440	D	D	8	16	13	56	D	D	D	D	86	375
Tiverton town..................	57	511	D	D	D	D	NA	NA	D	D	6	24	33	91

1 Merchant wholesalers, except manufacturers' sales branches and offices.

STATE City, town, township, borough, or CDP (county if applicable)	Administration and support and waste management and mediation services		Educational services		Health care and social assistance		Arts, entertainment, and recreation		Accommodation and food services		Other services (except public administration)	
	Number of establishments	Number of employees	Number of establishments	Number of employees	Number of establishments	Number of employees	Number of establishments	Number of employees	Number of establishments	Number of employees	Number of establishments	Number of employees
	15	16	17	18	19	20	21	22	23	24	25	26
PENNSYLVANIA—Con.												
Towamencin township	12	284	NA	NA	32	576	NA	NA	15	250	D	D
Tredyffrin township	116	5,385	25	194	136	3,264	22	343	72	1,026	97	881
Unity township	23	251	NA	NA	72	934	10	84	28	603	31	139
Upper Allen township	28	631	NA	NA	44	1,336	D	D	28	641	35	184
Upper Chichester township	29	242	D	D	31	376	5	56	44	673	D	D
Upper Darby township	88	1,813	5	20	208	4,235	D	D	D	D	131	529
Upper Dublin township	91	3,228	15	332	87	1,855	D	D	51	528	40	369
Upper Gwynedd township	17	90	7	61	55	1,110	6	75	43	576	D	D
Upper Macungie township	58	4,606	8	39	63	920	12	159	70	1,364	46	367
Upper Merion township	157	9,691	24	222	164	3,578	27	309	146	4,931	106	1,081
Upper Moreland township	58	1,967	8	48	116	2,682	7	120	61	1,113	66	374
Upper Providence township (Delaware County)	21	128	4	D	31	369	3	D	6	82	19	150
Upper Providence township (Montgomery County)	38	1,393	8	24	55	1,202	14	426	38	761	29	247
Upper St. Clair township	20	182	7	42	60	1,102	12	217	D	D	32	177
Upper Saucon township	21	195	D	D	38	679	12	262	D	D	11	73
Upper Southampton township	54	1,069	D	D	82	1,474	D	D	37	617	D	D
Upper Uwchlan township	10	107	5	11	20	295	3	13	9	134	16	128
Uwchlan township	33	1,143	D	D	57	604	11	245	41	821	38	247
Warminster township	52	333	9	76	92	2,424	10	95	67	993	D	D
Warrington township (Bucks County)	54	511	10	52	67	1,262	D	D	74	1,521	49	465
Warwick township (Bucks County)	28	632	3	38	32	529	D	D	16	258	D	D
Warwick township (Lancaster County)	19	109	NA	NA	50	1,148	D	D	28	509	25	106
Washington township (Franklin County)	16	64	NA	NA	D	D	6	70	D	D	24	109
Washington city	22	429	NA	NA	156	4,307	D	D	68	1,222	54	247
Waynesboro borough	5	95	3	14	44	904	NA	NA	D	D	28	187
West Bradford township	13	121	4	26	D	D	7	127	4	D	13	41
West Chester borough	33	484	6	16	54	1,032	11	255	102	1,860	65	401
West Deer township	27	99	NA	NA	14	277	5	22	8	28	D	D
West Goshen township	73	7,153	12	37	141	5,638	21	529	53	1,016	D	D
West Hanover township	18	192	NA	NA	13	168	D	D	22	432	15	107
West Hempfield township	18	101	D	D	25	1,015	5	58	23	341	D	D
West Lampeter township	25	104	D	D	29	1,564	5	88	23	725	24	116
West Manchester township	22	972	NA	NA	61	1,743	D	D	D	D	64	345
West Mifflin borough	17	733	4	65	53	902	D	D	51	813	31	168
West Norriton township	37	385	D	D	33	918	3	D	24	305	33	160
Westtown township	13	406	3	D	35	310	D	D	10	86	D	D
West Whiteland township	62	2,794	D	D	168	2,527	13	317	96	1,710	72	603
White township	17	151	D	D	113	3,037	6	204	40	926	49	382
Whitehall borough	12	1,094	NA	NA	23	476	4	54	14	245	12	54
Whitehall township	22	278	8	40	58	1,469	7	120	81	2,167	74	446
Whitemarsh township	55	958	D	D	80	2,183	16	392	50	1,135	49	306
Whitpain township	80	1,802	13	62	101	2,826	10	186	63	1,091	43	283
Wilkes-Barre city	55	1,169	6	37	146	7,076	13	511	140	2,407	91	540
Wilkinsburg borough	12	69	NA	NA	46	1,397	NA	NA	12	202	15	57
Williamsport city	26	377	D	D	113	5,462	13	139	88	1,792	73	728
Willistown township	25	165	D	D	120	3,767	7	50	15	266	D	D
Windsor township	24	77	NA	NA	26	382	D	D	15	222	16	75
Worcester township	20	83	NA	NA	14	469	8	92	15	149	D	D
Wyomissing borough	32	1,754	D	D	138	3,256	10	294	77	2,303	58	450
Yeadon borough	5	131	NA	NA	11	815	4	12	10	94	D	D
York city	35	1,074	9	157	129	7,828	17	363	95	1,533	77	681
York township	31	822	D	D	142	4,311	7	50	82	1,848	36	254
RHODE ISLAND	1,760	23,189	285	2,134	3,177	87,546	575	8,673	3,167	50,642	2,318	13,882
Barrington town	27	104	D	D	50	1,904	17	245	21	273	D	D
Bristol town	34	146	6	56	42	724	D	D	67	708	56	291
Burrillville town	D	D	3	17	18	518	6	12	27	461	D	D
Central Falls city	D	D	NA	NA	24	408	NA	NA	35	237	18	49
Coventry town	40	271	D	D	48	1,211	9	145	58	898	58	175
Cranston city	153	2,548	26	154	293	5,980	D	D	209	3,249	181	1,300
Cumberland town	59	575	8	33	86	1,208	12	118	64	899	75	466
East Greenwich town	27	160	7	57	103	1,776	10	146	78	1,451	49	276
East Providence city	67	855	13	89	160	4,521	26	546	D	D	103	576
Glocester town	11	28	NA	NA	16	270	5	13	D	D	D	D
Johnston town	110	1,580	7	23	106	2,328	D	D	87	1,201	88	451
Lincoln town	39	261	5	D	76	885	19	483	57	2,787	42	233
Middletown town	40	154	7	17	76	1,844	12	151	92	1,550	50	289
Narragansett town	24	86	4	3	38	420	D	D	79	1,126	34	131
Newport city	55	424	9	103	62	1,726	46	619	192	3,595	80	552
North Kingstown town	53	557	15	104	73	1,671	32	288	62	864	60	601
North Providence town	47	574	5	9	91	2,120	5	52	75	795	58	258
North Smithfield town	19	145	3	7	54	886	D	D	25	624	D	D
Pawtucket city	97	2,047	15	158	160	4,131	21	448	D	D	140	787
Portsmouth town	28	177	6	50	34	806	D	D	41	343	39	282
Providence city	236	7,005	57	609	577	29,944	60	2,110	642	11,268	421	3,336
Scituate town	16	44	NA	NA	15	98	NA	NA	D	D	D	D
Smithfield town	53	554	10	69	74	1,815	16	169	D	D	47	241
South Kingstown town	68	391	D	D	104	2,784	33	382	102	1,660	70	395
Tiverton town	26	148	D	D	29	465	4	17	34	396	D	D

Table C. Incorporated Places, Census Designated Places (CDPs), and Minor Civil Divisions (MCDs) of 10,000 or More Population — **Economic Census**

STATE City, town, township, borough, or CDP (county if applicable)	Retail Trade Number of establishments (1)	Number of employees (2)	Wholesale trade¹ Number of establishments (3)	Number of employees (4)	Transportation and warehousing Number of establishments (5)	Number of employees (6)	Information Number of establishments (7)	Number of employees (8)	Finance and insurance Number of establishments (9)	Number of employees (10)	Real estate and rental and leasing Number of establishments (11)	Number of employees (12)	Professional, scientific, and technical services Number of establishments (13)	Number of employees (14)
RHODE ISLAND—Con.														
Warren town	48	318	15	141	6	201	9	203	14	47	D	D	27	153
Warwick city	417	8,259	133	1,845	77	2,171	38	588	170	3,715	118	939	353	3,072
Westerly town	124	1,990	15	221	9	36	7	63	32	455	28	71	57	266
West Warwick town	90	877	20	363	12	327	D	D	D	D	D	D	38	161
Woonsocket city	131	1,372	39	658	18	779	9	38	D	D	35	135	39	302
SOUTH CAROLINA	17,700	253,384	4,360	61,421	2,805	63,980	1,639	37,970	7,449	73,990	5,890	26,764	10,859	100,377
Aiken city	209	3,610	20	94	D	D	17	385	105	559	45	162	112	1,291
Anderson city	243	3,951	25	202	6	60	25	169	116	660	55	162	124	711
Beaufort city	115	1,633	10	74	6	26	D	D	46	184	42	111	109	406
Berea CDP	40	471	NA	NA	D	D	5	8	16	71	7	15	9	39
Bluffton town	94	1,292	24	132	D	D	12	107	53	765	44	118	100	491
Cayce city	D	D	23	361	15	171	7	106	33	454	16	98	47	418
Charleston city	784	11,100	138	2,180	120	3,211	96	7,033	371	2,628	434	1,617	855	6,668
Clemson city	50	899	NA	NA	NA	NA	D	D	27	99	D	D	31	151
Columbia city	670	11,864	140	3,118	58	1,133	101	2,229	441	14,446	254	1,548	825	8,579
Conway city	156	2,130	28	247	8	124	12	182	68	442	35	125	102	417
Dentsville CDP	97	1,479	13	316	6	16	D	D	37	430	23	568	32	248
Easley city	128	2,097	20	161	9	27	D	D	56	252	27	56	45	314
Five Forks CDP	20	426	13	87	NA	NA	6	9	16	38	19	21	41	87
Florence city	365	6,543	55	1,006	13	261	28	300	173	3,125	64	304	140	1,111
Forest Acres city	79	1,577	5	D	5	28	8	84	60	283	19	42	49	661
Fort Mill town (York County)	58	1,179	21	1,082	15	412	17	45	38	458	D	D	58	4,788
Gaffney city	142	2,259	9	55	D	D	7	121	53	251	25	113	28	131
Gantt CDP	34	419	39	545	19	410	NA	NA	7	36	10	101	7	23
Garden City CDP	39	440	3	D	NA	NA	NA	NA	17	52	D	D	18	44
Goose Creek city	83	1,944	D	D	D	D	D	D	41	253	27	105	65	838
Greenville city	684	11,380	233	3,016	66	1,888	162	3,801	596	10,317	333	1,878	954	15,341
Greenwood city	164	2,933	16	284	7	32	11	177	75	428	33	122	66	432
Greer city	148	3,210	45	418	31	929	14	69	81	644	42	162	87	638
Hanahan city	20	247	19	246	21	846	NA	NA	5	13	19	92	37	683
Hilton Head Island town	262	2,722	55	299	45	278	30	240	101	701	252	1,119	249	982
Irmo town	79	1,658	D	D	9	49	D	D	61	279	23	83	61	298
James Island town	28	250	D	D	3	5	5	27	8	19	9	11	30	96
Ladson CDP	35	418	26	303	21	306	D	D	5	10	13	83	12	104
Lake Wylie CDP	31	650	D	D	6	26	5	13	26	79	D	D	33	77
Lexington town	158	3,182	34	570	11	84	17	142	93	589	46	175	142	722
Mauldin city	78	958	37	488	8	47	D	D	45	765	30	147	60	405
Moncks Corner town	70	1,185	8	29	NA	NA	D	D	42	220	10	44	30	137
Mount Pleasant town	390	6,224	84	428	66	1,655	55	899	254	1,809	323	818	530	3,244
Myrtle Beach city	668	10,778	82	795	32	484	38	1,322	156	1,189	242	1,712	258	1,452
Newberry city	69	908	7	58	D	D	D	D	D	D	8	32	29	106
North Augusta city	107	2,166	6	44	15	599	12	199	54	409	20	80	35	256
North Charleston city	570	9,439	211	3,594	202	3,326	78	2,746	157	2,325	191	1,412	376	7,183
North Myrtle Beach city	183	2,763	12	73	11	32	10	68	54	263	74	1,148	58	224
Oak Grove CDP	25	193	9	73	6	88	NA	NA	4	9	13	39	4	8
Orangeburg city	123	1,239	17	261	12	133	D	D	61	441	18	65	42	167
Parker CDP	49	594	9	165	4	38	5	72	14	38	7	22	D	D
Port Royal town	26	328	4	36	NA	NA	NA	NA	7	27	10	34	19	74
Red Bank CDP	31	783	3	D	NA	NA	D	D	14	58	D	D	9	31
Red Hill CDP	18	387	8	27	5	62	NA	NA	4	20	9	47	11	47
Rock Hill city	322	5,741	80	1,453	30	1,541	40	888	146	821	106	433	173	1,204
St. Andrews CDP	59	644	13	106	D	D	15	168	44	206	34	199	43	198
Seven Oaks CDP	61	1,043	10	108	D	D	D	D	64	391	D	D	60	606
Simpsonville city	92	2,105	22	168	9	221	7	50	49	201	35	82	41	131
Socastee CDP	58	488	4	8	6	24	7	101	16	89	17	45	27	63
Spartanburg city	344	6,234	58	432	23	951	34	1,962	184	1,868	91	403	187	1,269
Summerville town	223	4,891	35	409	26	522	D	D	115	638	84	305	142	1,498
Sumter city	250	3,754	29	269	17	321	D	D	97	697	52	271	100	581
Taylors CDP	34	250	18	127	8	23	5	107	16	60	21	56	33	66
Tega Cay city	11	358	D	D	NA	NA	D	D	8	42	14	19	34	97
Wade Hampton CDP	101	1,411	19	128	5	11	8	52	52	233	38	74	77	344
West Columbia city	158	4,133	48	751	16	310	D	D	65	323	30	158	69	420
SOUTH DAKOTA	3,884	53,134	1,392	16,630	1,259	10,207	478	7,254	1,981	26,270	1,143	4,330	1,967	13,063
Aberdeen city	160	2,746	41	714	31	250	D	D	84	990	54	280	54	340
Brandon city	24	336	12	67	D	D	D	D	D	D	13	37	13	39
Brookings city	95	1,679	24	246	12	109	D	D	44	532	38	173	62	523
Huron city	69	951	23	367	15	126	D	D	38	434	25	87	D	D
Mitchell city	122	1,842	29	374	14	92	9	309	55	348	D	D	D	D
Pierre city	87	1,402	21	181	19	328	D	D	D	D	D	D	49	329
Rapid City city	478	8,423	127	1,514	82	795	47	1,076	216	2,714	193	598	273	1,863
Sioux Falls city	783	16,116	326	5,479	242	3,412	136	3,434	582	14,274	297	1,649	577	5,461
Spearfish city	89	1,161	D	D	12	180	D	D	38	247	D	D	40	153
Vermillion city	39	675	5	35	D	D	6	28	D	D	D	D	15	158
Watertown city	176	2,620	54	637	35	226	11	185	66	779	58	113	67	266
Yankton city	102	1,565	23	162	15	107	16	185	49	618	25	D	D	D
TENNESSEE	22,593	322,218	5,864	100,044	4,324	148,152	2,788	49,464	10,210	128,741	6,048	36,212	11,411	116,205
Arlington town	29	320	9	814	12	343	D	D	14	52	5	26	22	124
Athens city	116	1,760	11	171	6	83	D	D	62	359	25	72	32	191
Bartlett city	127	1,869	61	857	19	970	20	294	71	427	36	189	115	2,305
Brentwood city	169	3,386	67	644	18	579	75	1,963	295	5,537	125	674	333	4,095
Bristol city	152	2,932	41	303	12	105	18	443	91	392	36	99	65	624
Chattanooga city	1,084	20,026	375	5,996	216	10,169	136	3,369	508	13,075	316	1,802	650	7,162
Clarksville city	491	8,241	70	915	45	432	32	441	200	1,274	162	728	174	1,777

1 Merchant wholesalers, except manufacturers' sales branches and offices.

Table C. Incorporated Places, Census Designated Places (CDPs), and Minor Civil Divisions (MCDs) of 10,000 or More Population — Economic Census

	Economic activity by sector, 2017											
STATE City, town, township, borough, or CDP (county if applicable)	Administration and support and waste management and mediation services		Educational services		Health care and social assistance		Arts, entertainment, and recreation		Accommodation and food services		Other services (except public administration)	
	Number of establish-ments	Number of employees	Number of establish-ments	Number of employees	Number of establish-ments	Number of employees	Number of establish-ments	Number of employees	Number of establish-ments	Number of employees	Number of establish-ments	Number of employees
	15	16	17	18	19	20	21	22	23	24	25	26
RHODE ISLAND—Con.												
Warren town	21	56	D	D	38	574	D	D	42	637	D	D
Warwick city	170	3,052	16	129	357	8,635	41	746	258	5,497	229	1,598
Westerly town	33	87	7	36	101	1,867	33	301	116	1,445	61	264
West Warwick town	25	154	7	143	42	775	8	D	61	730	56	230
Woonsocket city	25	310	3	39	139	4,136	7	107	85	1,200	62	242
SOUTH CAROLINA	6,155	276,277	817	4,746	10,588	244,198	1,687	28,317	10,847	223,081	7,068	46,847
Aiken city	D	D	6	43	205	4,442	27	350	158	3,200	70	366
Anderson city	38	738	NA	NA	189	5,932	13	327	155	2,959	72	444
Beaufort city	29	114	5	21	75	2,718	8	38	94	2,042	48	267
Berea CDP	9	105	NA	NA	17	365	NA	NA	26	321	7	54
Bluffton town	48	381	10	24	89	1,305	D	D	64	1,817	D	D
Cayce city	13	315	5	18	D	D	6	72	48	913	D	D
Charleston city	255	5,625	44	280	540	17,068	122	2,001	641	16,356	320	2,118
Clemson city	10	134	D	D	41	556	5	37	86	2,267	21	140
Columbia city	215	9,425	48	283	563	24,289	60	766	573	13,902	358	3,793
Conway city	21	248	6	106	77	2,673	9	89	105	1,772	54	234
Dentsville CDP	38	1,042	D	D	63	1,119	D	D	50	1,066	36	193
Easley city	18	341	NA	NA	85	1,924	D	D	70	1,491	D	D
Five Forks CDP	17	109	7	44	41	399	5	140	27	262	16	70
Florence city	79	3,467	7	32	267	12,687	16	330	211	4,806	90	694
Forest Acres city	27	709	3	11	D	D	11	379	45	1,057	D	D
Fort Mill town (York County)	D	D	6	9	46	654	13	D	47	862	43	317
Gaffney city	12	715	NA	NA	36	477	8	119	60	1,313	D	D
Gantt CDP	15	161	NA	NA	21	302	D	D	17	187	11	228
Garden City CDP	14	150	NA	NA	25	298	9	116	60	1,027	13	48
Goose Creek city	31	365	6	46	52	562	6	103	74	1,570	48	282
Greenville city	342	25,206	52	268	478	16,083	69	1,338	471	12,028	262	1,810
Greenwood city	15	263	NA	NA	91	4,165	D	D	92	2,238	47	240
Greer city	45	566	5	41	82	1,403	11	73	99	1,843	61	341
Hanahan city	25	258	5	44	11	434	D	D	16	143	D	D
Hilton Head Island town	166	2,471	19	118	186	2,655	61	1,358	259	6,802	133	1,144
Irmo town	20	145	6	24	83	850	9	167	58	1,276	66	431
James Island town	23	118	4	7	13	132	NA	NA	29	457	D	D
Ladson CDP	D	D	NA	NA	D	D	D	D	15	346	D	D
Lake Wylie CDP	D	D	3	9	19	264	9	165	27	541	D	D
Lexington town	30	846	7	61	D	D	13	183	107	2,604	69	520
Mauldin city	39	3,206	6	63	86	990	7	275	58	783	D	D
Moncks Corner town	7	13	NA	NA	53	708	D	D	46	861	D	D
Mount Pleasant town	196	15,929	47	204	D	D	81	913	254	5,290	190	1,122
Myrtle Beach city	119	1,658	13	76	260	3,600	100	2,325	585	15,481	186	1,284
Newberry city	D	D	NA	NA	42	1,199	NA	NA	48	753	22	110
North Augusta city	D	D	5	35	60	1,031	12	193	63	1,140	37	145
North Charleston city	237	9,653	24	317	363	8,192	24	852	363	8,051	235	2,101
North Myrtle Beach city	33	481	NA	NA	D	D	28	568	184	5,009	53	466
Oak Grove CDP	9	28	NA	NA	D	D	NA	NA	4	69	D	D
Orangeburg city	D	D	D	D	82	959	D	D	65	1,271	36	162
Parker CDP	D	D	NA	NA	10	329	NA	NA	21	282	D	D
Port Royal town	8	71	NA	NA	33	402	NA	NA	24	325	D	D
Red Bank CDP	8	39	NA	NA	D	D	4	60	18	381	16	100
Red Hill CDP	17	139	NA	NA	42	1,103	3	D	5	32	12	44
Rock Hill city	D	D	10	137	298	7,059	28	369	199	5,221	118	865
St. Andrews CDP	24	1,022	NA	NA	36	560	NA	NA	48	789	35	219
Seven Oaks CDP	52	2,315	9	88	50	566	NA	NA	38	837	38	275
Simpsonville city	19	1,579	8	41	D	D	D	D	63	1,352	D	D
Socastee CDP	27	134	4	D	22	236	4	14	27	288	22	76
Spartanburg city	69	5,746	17	132	208	9,385	23	301	216	4,658	129	1,077
Summerville town	51	739	9	37	190	3,165	D	D	167	3,571	117	669
Sumter city	39	2,017	D	D	162	4,648	10	223	140	2,999	81	541
Taylors CDP	29	204	4	18	21	212	7	162	19	100	24	97
Tega Cay city	D	D	NA	NA	12	105	NA	NA	8	143	8	30
Wade Hampton CDP	52	2,161	10	47	67	1,089	4	33	61	1,001	D	D
West Columbia city	D	D	NA	NA	67	2,094	4	D	78	1,311	63	444
SOUTH DAKOTA	1,166	11,887	145	823	2,420	71,821	697	6,799	2,495	40,704	1,860	8,713
Aberdeen city	51	356	NA	NA	102	3,072	27	270	88	1,873	65	296
Brandon city	13	63	D	D	17	375	6	21	18	385	12	39
Brookings city	29	181	D	D	85	1,485	25	204	74	1,713	52	291
Huron city	13	93	NA	NA	D	D	D	D	37	508	35	127
Mitchell city	D	D	NA	NA	66	2,090	D	D	44	832	40	183
Pierre city	32	134	D	D	D	D	D	D	65	263		
Rapid City city	131	1,606	D	D	365	10,448	86	659	263	6,179	257	1,486
Sioux Falls city	294	4,978	D	D	560	29,192	159	2,761	466	11,856	368	2,769
Spearfish city	20	212	5	19	70	1,607	D	D	66	1,126	47	138
Vermillion city	7	25	NA	NA	D	D	D	D	43	832	17	74
Watertown city	35	382	NA	NA	D	D	30	109	D	D	71	326
Yankton city	28	213	4	31	D	D	8	76	62	962	44	186
TENNESSEE	7,170	255,284	971	10,734	15,891	414,598	2,824	37,967	13,518	287,534	8,570	61,744
Arlington town	25	308	NA	NA	14	111	5	52	20	416	D	D
Athens city	21	337	NA	NA	86	1,952	D	D	68	1,447	D	D
Bartlett city	76	1,422	D	D	134	4,208	16	163	98	1,613	D	D
Brentwood city	153	11,476	24	330	261	7,021	64	931	115	2,905	110	904
Bristol city	42	1,608	NA	NA	134	3,617	17	254	101	2,124	52	276
Chattanooga city	309	16,353	50	370	915	27,089	110	2,533	730	17,030	464	3,310
Clarksville city	97	2,723	26	266	335	8,076	38	407	350	7,637	D	D

Table C. Incorporated Places, Census Designated Places (CDPs), and Minor Civil Divisions (MCDs) of 10,000 or More Population — **Economic Census**

STATE City, town, township, borough, or CDP (county if applicable)	Retail Trade — Number of establishments	Retail Trade — Number of employees	Wholesale trade¹ — Number of establishments	Wholesale trade¹ — Number of employees	Transportation and warehousing — Number of establishments	Transportation and warehousing — Number of employees	Information — Number of establishments	Information — Number of employees	Finance and insurance — Number of establishments	Finance and insurance — Number of employees	Real estate and rental and leasing — Number of establishments	Real estate and rental and leasing — Number of employees	Professional, scientific, and technical services — Number of establishments	Professional, scientific, and technical services — Number of employees
	1	2	3	4	5	6	7	8	9	10	11	12	13	14
TENNESSEE—Con.														
Cleveland city	280	4,265	46	556	32	1,981	17	326	144	1,577	59	212	114	652
Collegedale city	23	662	4	58	NA	NA	3	10	16	107	12	34	14	90
Collierville town	207	3,877	43	894	33	284	14	155	77	505	48	170	107	482
Columbia city	214	2,597	47	540	21	219	18	323	100	1,649	50	199	59	471
Cookeville city	282	4,187	54	551	36	998	D	D	118	1,038	53	207	102	594
Crossville city	175	2,258	D	D	20	1,116	D	D	D	D	24	86	47	156
Dickson city	116	1,694	21	555	6	122	D	D	54	396	15	71	35	142
Dyersburg city	139	1,703	29	445	10	231	D	D	D	D	20	D	34	169
East Ridge city	84	820	9	31	D	D	3	53	46	176	17	42	25	121
Elizabethton city	89	1,584	D	D	8	149	D	D	51	298	D	D	26	116
Farragut town	90	1,657	12	173	10	43	15	138	71	480	37	96	77	448
Franklin city	481	8,792	153	2,437	45	490	123	2,888	359	7,627	163	804	480	5,922
Gallatin city	145	2,411	35	530	30	1,379	16	245	87	430	47	618	63	444
Germantown city	147	2,120	33	937	16	662	10	94	93	530	45	325	110	602
Goodlettsville city	129	1,809	31	667	13	316	D	D	50	703	25	118	49	342
Greeneville town	160	2,457	15	240	18	1,261	D	D	87	524	31	134	60	252
Hartsville/Trousdale County	26	222	NA	NA	NA	NA	NA	NA	5	46	NA	NA	6	57
Hendersonville city	203	3,222	53	487	18	179	32	237	130	688	85	312	126	2,199
Jackson city	439	6,871	122	2,199	45	1,254	D	D	182	1,305	105	513	146	1,117
Johnson City city	436	7,718	83	1,527	32	296	51	1,385	D	D	117	737	155	1,070
Kingsport city	317	5,487	71	989	46	805	19	504	149	1,522	60	311	123	834
Knoxville city	1,264	21,652	395	6,266	156	5,628	172	4,241	600	8,710	389	2,840	732	6,824
Lakeland city	22	190	D	D	3	15	4	9	5	13	11	33	17	194
La Vergne city	65	898	62	2,827	65	2,848	D	D	D	D	17	108	22	858
Lawrenceburg city	117	1,206	20	221	D	D	D	D	53	245	18	51	22	170
Lebanon city	222	2,979	57	1,265	48	3,430	16	200	86	664	58	259	91	478
Lewisburg city	78	932	D	D	10	199	D	D	D	D	10	31	20	86
McMinnville city	116	1,338	12	143	8	18	13	199	51	317	14	33	28	85
Manchester city	94	1,145	6	25	D	D	D	D	D	D	14	134	28	155
Martin city	50	754	10	146	5	39	D	D	29	224	12	36	11	54
Maryville city	173	2,686	33	334	18	457	D	D	97	633	37	120	D	D
Memphis city	2,306	35,216	906	22,618	874	52,767	263	5,555	1,098	16,211	753	7,045	1,243	14,880
Middle Valley CDP	10	142	NA	NA	NA	NA	NA	NA	3	7	NA	NA	4	14
Millington city	69	1,137	D	D	6	35	D	D	32	153	18	112	36	394
Morristown city	249	4,054	40	788	D	D	17	307	D	D	D	D	58	233
Mount Juliet city	152	2,666	21	280	29	730	16	139	69	472	42	D	61	632
Murfreesboro city	575	11,809	101	974	77	1,593	54	1,774	260	3,370	169	1,164	D	D
Nashville-Davidson metropolitan government	2,426	36,463	907	18,710	486	21,923	678	14,993	1,365	33,159	1,032	8,141	2,094	29,524
Oak Ridge city	107	1,535	27	203	7	60	20	285	61	1,106	40	134	153	8,104
Paris city	106	1,449	16	476	D	D	D	D	D	D	D	D	32	287
Portland city	41	355	9	307	16	959	4	21	20	160	8	24	6	55
Red Bank city	35	346	D	D	NA	NA	3	13	15	55	6	9	15	78
Sevierville city	302	5,052	D	D	8	152	13	171	77	520	58	343	63	277
Seymour CDP	D	D	6	15	D	D	3	14	18	76	D	D	17	62
Shelbyville city	120	1,411	D	D	24	2,041	D	D	D	D	27	82	34	149
Smyrna town	157	2,569	29	860	37	1,054	19	128	D	D	43	179	48	730
Soddy-Daisy city	39	543	13	154	4	30	D	D	14	64	6	41	D	D
Springfield city	81	1,356	19	689	D	D	D	D	49	220	23	81	40	237
Spring Hill city	89	1,613	D	D	19	1,536	12	65	42	169	26	115	46	156
Tullahoma city	137	1,571	16	188	D	D	D	D	D	D	22	82	41	630
Union City city	88	1,293	24	388	12	105	D	D	43	331	15	72	15	94
White House city	35	669	NA	NA	5	72	D	D	20	102	9	30	14	170
TEXAS	80,874	1,304,540	28,861	435,728	19,943	485,957	10,473	248,765	40,589	551,228	32,290	198,712	70,033	735,744
Abilene city	503	7,962	D	D	91	1,952	D	D	248	2,293	167	776	256	1,600
Addison town	124	1,974	116	2,062	66	1,021	60	2,854	231	8,115	162	1,316	423	6,228
Alamo city	53	920	24	182	13	103	D	D	18	94	11	145	14	56
Aldine CDP	61	350	46	561	16	93	NA	NA	11	40	17	139	9	62
Alice city	95	1,308	25	192	21	320	D	D	55	267	20	95	38	248
Allen city	325	6,374	D	D	D	D	42	1,694	D	D	106	347	372	1,706
Alton city	19	303	NA	NA	5	21	NA	NA	8	32	NA	NA	NA	NA
Alvin city	107	1,969	D	D	15	171	D	D	44	194	41	297	31	188
Amarillo city	777	13,450	211	3,039	152	2,044	74	1,220	442	5,349	289	1,246	478	2,665
Andrews city	D	D	D	D	25	340	D	D	19	116	18	98	D	D
Angleton city	64	1,220	D	D	13	222	6	50	41	221	24	171	48	244
Anna city	19	290	NA	NA	NA	NA	NA	NA	D	D	3	7	6	40
Arlington city	1,196	21,315	332	5,236	175	2,045	113	2,535	464	9,650	370	2,014	784	6,083
Atascocita CDP	32	343	8	37	16	40	3	14	29	107	15	27	71	234
Athens city	75	964	16	154	5	17	D	D	41	227	26	215	35	551
Austin city	3,359	57,095	1,028	21,202	398	11,348	1,028	34,334	2,056	27,761	2,089	14,255	6,026	84,531
Azle city	45	880	8	117	D	D	D	D	20	D	18	54	25	128
Bacliff CDP	16	102	NA	NA	NA	NA	NA	NA	D	D	4	3	3	14
Balch Springs city	82	1,307	12	291	D	D	7	55	D	D	13	41	7	43
Bay City city	79	1,059	13	64	18	137	10	53	33	179	21	126	D	D
Baytown city	287	5,915	54	612	57	2,017	16	275	88	643	87	607	107	1,685
Beaumont city	599	9,023	178	2,276	99	2,043	54	779	226	1,709	202	1,513	349	4,657
Bedford city	128	1,982	31	140	32	446	17	521	94	1,957	70	353	155	731
Beeville city	66	996	6	69	8	21	9	117	35	168	15	49	25	72
Bellaire city	45	426	30	151	11	381	D	D	78	1,251	50	201	197	996
Bellmead city	45	1,258	NA	NA	D	D	NA	NA	11	103	3	19	8	35
Belton city	75	1,088	12	158	9	590	8	55	30	174	25	82	42	433
Benbrook city	42	663	12	81	7	31	D	D	33	122	13	25	68	448
Big Spring city	103	1,392	24	151	16	114	D	D	D	D	32	109	34	155
Boerne city	115	2,386	26	208	9	59	16	84	50	319	43	85	D	D
Bonham city	39	418	D	D	NA	NA	5	33	22	128	6	21	15	55
Borger city	53	809	17	130	D	D	6	35	D	D	D	D	19	170

1 Merchant wholesalers, except manufacturers' sales branches and offices.

Table C. Incorporated Places, Census Designated Places (CDPs), and Minor Civil Divisions (MCDs) of 10,000 or More Population — **Economic Census**

STATE City, town, township, borough, or CDP (county if applicable)	Administration and support and waste management and mediation services — Number of establishments	Number of employees	Educational services — Number of establishments	Number of employees	Health care and social assistance — Number of establishments	Number of employees	Arts, entertainment, and recreation — Number of establishments	Number of employees	Accommodation and food services — Number of establishments	Number of employees	Other services (except public administration) — Number of establishments	Number of employees
	15	16	17	18	19	20	21	22	23	24	25	26
TENNESSEE—Con.												
Cleveland city	58	3,531	5	24	211	4,578	D	D	182	3,941	D	D
Collegedale city	7	86	NA	NA	34	632	5	D	18	209	12	209
Collierville town	65	982	D	D	119	1,715	D	D	124	2,595	70	509
Columbia city	47	808	D	D	181	4,691	12	106	101	2,042	D	D
Cookeville city	49	1,263	10	74	217	5,820	17	203	154	3,745	D	D
Crossville city	16	745	NA	NA	116	2,458	4	D	77	1,453	D	D
Dickson city	20	1,092	D	D	108	1,875	10	101	76	1,479	D	D
Dyersburg city	23	383	D	D	97	1,966	D	D	56	1,090	35	143
East Ridge city	17	397	NA	NA	49	810	NA	NA	57	950	26	206
Elizabethton city	D	D	NA	NA	69	1,551	D	D	D	D	23	170
Farragut town	31	770	9	63	96	1,428	12	250	79	1,681	34	221
Franklin city	195	5,712	47	362	387	8,667	176	1,379	321	8,352	197	1,716
Gallatin city	35	1,143	7	27	120	2,937	16	181	84	1,658	75	390
Germantown city	60	595	14	120	213	7,539	D	D	89	2,112	72	575
Goodlettsville city	31	1,022	D	D	83	1,940	10	90	81	1,535	D	D
Greeneville town	33	2,715	D	D	117	3,716	8	D	83	1,594	41	251
Hartsville/Trousdale County	D	D	NA	NA	22	273	NA	NA	9	188	9	37
Hendersonville city	66	1,111	D	D	188	2,791	D	D	123	2,797	102	540
Jackson city	103	5,063	D	D	320	13,468	26	330	216	5,218	D	D
Johnson City city	89	4,787	22	124	334	13,174	32	261	269	6,674	161	920
Kingsport city	60	1,149	D	D	277	7,487	22	383	210	4,926	110	960
Knoxville city	332	25,829	54	511	969	32,083	108	1,985	777	19,947	493	3,430
Lakeland city	13	77	NA	NA	18	142	7	108	16	341	D	D
La Vergne city	32	1,146	D	D	21	174	D	D	35	531	27	868
Lawrenceburg city	D	D	NA	NA	71	1,148	D	D	42	707	20	74
Lebanon city	54	2,439	7	104	170	2,573	16	124	123	2,597	78	1,065
Lewisburg city	12	561	NA	NA	47	666	D	D	D	D	17	109
McMinnville city	16	898	D	D	90	1,295	D	D	49	828	33	124
Manchester city	14	323	D	D	64	1,013	NA	NA	61	1,116	27	86
Martin city	9	554	NA	NA	50	1,177	NA	NA	39	697	D	D
Maryville city	33	891	14	137	162	4,624	12	85	87	1,866	72	375
Memphis city	774	41,697	106	3,442	1,667	55,489	148	4,111	1,399	31,459	904	8,775
Middle Valley CDP	11	48	NA	NA	NA	NA	NA	NA	D	D	NA	NA
Millington city	21	543	D	D	26	354	D	D	52	919	30	252
Morristown city	56	2,635	D	D	169	4,246	D	D	D	D	73	449
Mount Juliet city	37	405	6	44	103	1,060	15	177	102	2,340	63	436
Murfreesboro city	126	3,896	34	311	446	11,923	46	624	397	9,538	231	1,510
Nashville-Davidson metropolitan government	1,163	40,719	179	2,195	1,912	75,503	827	9,720	1,982	50,360	1,293	13,383
Oak Ridge city	61	20,345	D	D	152	3,707	11	130	75	1,567	58	268
Paris city	14	772	3	12	72	D	D	D	47	844	27	141
Portland city	10	548	NA	NA	32	334	3	5	D	D	D	D
Red Bank city	13	98	NA	NA	D	D	NA	NA	16	298	D	D
Sevierville city	37	529	D	D	97	1,844	16	264	136	4,117	48	288
Seymour CDP	14	99	NA	NA	D	D	NA	NA	31	491	D	D
Shelbyville city	14	640	NA	NA	84	1,099	D	D	55	860	33	139
Smyrna city	62	4,437	11	108	148	2,214	14	270	123	2,887	D	D
Soddy-Daisy city	14	220	NA	NA	15	212	3	D	D	D	D	D
Springfield city	14	896	D	D	78	1,393	5	111	D	D	D	D
Spring Hill city	51	1,852	9	52	65	677	11	76	78	1,814	42	233
Tullahoma city	19	925	NA	NA	123	1,969	13	131	D	D	41	148
Union City city	D	D	NA	NA	64	951	D	D	D	D	21	72
White House city	14	254	NA	NA	32	405	6	22	39	866	D	D
TEXAS	29,171	1,013,362	5,558	51,738	69,952	1,581,577	7,620	153,566	57,098	1,201,419	37,506	285,777
Abilene city	158	2,641	30	151	382	11,855	D	D	295	6,704	D	D
Addison town	132	4,984	35	529	144	2,688	25	278	214	5,735	90	855
Alamo city	5	23	NA	NA	30	859	NA	NA	30	701	11	55
Aldine CDP	22	241	NA	NA	6	96	NA	NA	13	153	30	159
Alice city	D	D	NA	NA	99	5,282	D	D	60	910	D	D
Allen city	93	1,163	40	311	363	3,832	35	672	214	4,572	118	912
Alton city	NA	NA	NA	NA	21	193	NA	NA	3	17	NA	NA
Alvin city	28	1,459	3	6	59	1,054	7	122	77	1,360	43	274
Amarillo city	234	5,041	37	307	679	17,186	68	957	530	11,165	376	2,926
Andrews city	D	D	NA	NA	D	D	NA	NA	32	399	D	D
Angleton city	12	63	NA	NA	77	992	D	D	41	736	28	161
Anna city	4	6	NA	NA	15	62	3	10	15	213	D	D
Arlington city	347	12,493	61	664	1,011	22,351	85	5,408	774	19,755	476	3,291
Atascocita CDP	35	194	6	19	48	532	8	276	36	536	D	D
Athens city	15	100	NA	NA	86	1,692	D	D	62	982	32	162
Austin city	1,533	46,340	472	7,347	3,150	71,118	545	9,671	2,981	73,697	2,203	19,625
Azle city	8	58	NA	NA	53	779	4	15	29	616	D	D
Bacliff CDP	D	D	NA	NA	NA	NA	NA	NA	17	230	7	22
Balch Springs city	16	505	NA	NA	11	122	D	D	41	721	36	216
Bay City city	13	69	NA	NA	62	999	D	D	54	720	47	343
Baytown city	50	1,250	8	56	226	4,800	14	194	206	4,458	116	1,119
Beaumont city	162	4,885	20	134	618	13,552	43	561	299	6,662	225	2,630
Bedford city	57	1,795	16	127	232	6,185	10	95	116	2,380	63	508
Beeville city	4	17	NA	NA	57	739	NA	NA	46	658	D	D
Bellaire city	50	1,328	12	88	D	D	6	11	53	595	43	151
Bellmead city	D	D	NA	NA	21	325	NA	NA	30	638	D	D
Belton city	20	150	4	18	55	1,092	D	D	63	1,195	49	313
Benbrook city	26	190	NA	NA	D	D	4	17	38	705	27	232
Big Spring city	13	113	NA	NA	D	D	D	D	81	1,295	37	286
Boerne city	35	267	9	50	116	1,596	12	143	71	1,158	52	292
Bonham city	4	156	NA	NA	32	1,417	D	D	D	D	D	D
Borger city	17	269	NA	NA	D	D	6	53	44	680	22	157

Table C. Incorporated Places, Census Designated Places (CDPs), and Minor Civil Divisions (MCDs) of 10,000 or More Population — **Economic Census**

STATE City, town, township, borough, or CDP (county if applicable)	Retail Trade Number of establishments	Number of employees	Wholesale trade[1] Number of establishments	Number of employees	Transportation and warehousing Number of establishments	Number of employees	Information Number of establishments	Number of employees	Finance and insurance Number of establishments	Number of employees	Real estate and rental and leasing Number of establishments	Number of employees	Professional, scientific, and technical services Number of establishments	Number of employees
	1	2	3	4	5	6	7	8	9	10	11	12	13	14
TEXAS—Con.														
Brenham city	116	1,911	27	409	8	237	13	136	53	796	31	97	42	300
Brownsville city	513	9,075	184	1,317	170	1,841	37	503	230	1,365	138	621	271	1,956
Brownwood city	111	1,518	18	350	10	116	D	D	49	322	25	79	36	147
Brushy Creek CDP	13	341	D	D	D	D	3	4	4	13	16	43	D	D
Bryan city	301	4,049	82	1,574	46	934	38	913	113	751	111	632	196	1,050
Buda city	38	1,293	28	701	5	32	NA	NA	25	100	25	128	40	181
Burkburnett city	22	318	6	41	6	74	3	17	12	70	D	D	6	22
Burleson city	181	3,925	28	228	28	272	13	116	80	361	50	224	65	255
Canyon city	34	548	D	D	5	23	3	7	26	191	14	40	19	69
Canyon Lake CDP	46	433	D	D	12	24	D	D	16	62	23	133	54	312
Carrollton city	442	6,032	404	6,804	128	1,973	79	2,421	198	2,195	179	1,544	430	3,556
Cedar Hill city	147	3,360	15	242	28	412	14	146	D	D	27	92	58	177
Cedar Park city	278	4,438	50	469	24	77	32	301	122	1,147	97	356	241	1,310
Celina city	24	170	4	10	NA	NA	NA	NA	D	D	9	8	17	30
Channelview CDP	56	475	26	490	57	1,676	NA	NA	13	81	22	125	22	254
Cibolo city	24	440	D	D	4	28	NA	NA	15	44	10	26	16	38
Cinco Ranch CDP	18	178	12	19	7	32	NA	NA	21	75	18	35	52	101
Cleburne city	139	2,469	36	417	25	1,261	D	D	58	277	43	260	73	298
Cloverleaf CDP	12	82	NA	NA	9	20	NA	NA	7	29	5	14	10	16
Clute city	40	517	19	159	D	D	NA	NA	26	152	20	117	11	283
College Station city	311	6,258	38	277	24	1,154	D	D	131	1,151	149	726	205	2,008
Colleyville city	86	1,051	34	103	18	383	10	172	99	556	68	149	183	686
Conroe city	385	7,488	123	1,557	52	1,309	18	363	173	926	111	515	227	1,007
Converse city	34	706	13	299	12	484	D	D	12	40	15	50	16	56
Coppell city	89	3,727	94	2,704	82	5,849	34	1,008	89	2,429	85	829	278	5,864
Copperas Cove city	76	1,169	D	D	8	51	D	D	34	223	32	119	26	117
Corinth city	35	684	D	D	5	3	D	D	17	54	17	25	53	170
Corpus Christi city	978	17,527	355	5,276	196	2,990	117	1,860	533	3,834	413	2,647	786	7,070
Corsicana city	131	2,032	25	425	21	446	D	D	D	D	45	118	52	245
Crowley city	30	372	NA	NA	9	59	NA	NA	13	78	11	24	14	359
Dallas city	4,129	65,708	1,969	32,922	718	42,128	824	23,279	2,948	47,008	2,555	24,594	5,875	83,897
Deer Park city	68	1,379	45	794	21	348	D	D	37	326	39	476	73	2,057
Del Rio city	140	2,078	D	D	45	414	20	183	66	467	35	105	35	213
Denison city	94	1,171	15	263	5	35	D	D	45	1,100	22	71	40	271
Denton city	445	7,546	93	1,158	51	5,275	35	645	186	1,247	187	990	292	1,417
DeSoto city	87	2,484	31	338	32	1,527	10	73	50	266	44	225	42	240
Dickinson city	72	947	D	D	11	27	6	30	D	D	27	113	29	104
Donna city	47	769	18	205	6	25	NA	NA	15	112	11	101	8	42
Dumas city	53	827	10	84	12	57	D	D	D	D	13	40	16	72
Duncanville city	112	1,606	20	276	D	D	D	D	D	D	40	D	55	286
Eagle Pass city	148	2,641	33	165	91	707	D	D	60	411	D	D	34	196
Edinburg city	220	4,634	79	1,692	49	945	16	275	132	910	69	204	154	1,195
El Campo city	69	1,118	29	323	18	101	6	64	43	202	20	100	20	111
Elgin city	41	649	D	D	D	D	D	D	14	76	3	12	13	42
El Paso city	1,984	34,562	852	9,401	761	11,742	205	8,145	888	6,960	793	3,791	1,211	9,756
Ennis city	72	1,196	D	D	16	639	D	D	35	178	21	60	23	119
Euless city	171	2,506	40	734	33	397	21	215	35	134	D	D	92	839
Farmers Branch city	192	3,002	214	6,108	73	2,048	74	3,006	161	6,126	101	1,235	395	6,430
Fate city	7	63	7	50	D	D	NA	NA	NA	NA	5	9	11	41
Flower Mound town	155	3,358	87	1,922	24	84	23	425	136	721	D	D	334	1,949
Forest Hill city	42	520	7	50	D	D	NA	NA	D	D	NA	NA	5	24
Forney city	50	1,211	D	D	D	D	6	66	21	112	17	34	35	341
Fort Bliss CDP	18	159	NA	NA	NA	NA	NA	NA	NA	NA	NA	NA	45	417
Fort Hood CDP	19	141	NA	NA	NA	NA	NA	NA	D	D	NA	NA	59	975
Fort Worth city	2,246	39,925	699	17,277	581	27,519	284	6,064	1,248	21,744	910	5,596	1,891	20,570
Four Corners CDP	13	31	6	37	4	24	NA	NA	NA	NA	NA	NA	13	14
Fredericksburg city	144	1,485	20	194	15	85	D	D	46	303	33	83	53	213
Freeport city	30	290	23	201	26	496	NA	NA	10	53	18	131	19	228
Fresno CDP	16	115	NA	NA	8	56	NA	NA	3	2	NA	NA	5	4
Friendswood city	90	1,292	20	127	14	111	12	41	D	D	48	122	142	551
Frisco city	540	11,660	131	2,676	56	881	80	2,858	329	17,571	251	946	954	5,484
Fulshear city	14	99	D	D	D	D	NA	NA	6	7	7	17	40	77
Gainesville city	110	1,500	24	416	12	590	D	D	D	D	18	54	32	182
Galena Park city	11	72	7	75	29	793	NA	NA	NA	NA	NA	NA	4	52
Galveston city	217	2,707	34	298	47	1,737	18	230	D	D	75	334	111	606
Garland city	612	9,410	182	3,339	114	2,192	42	610	219	1,191	175	1,385	298	2,261
Gatesville city	49	696	NA	NA	D	D	D	D	16	164	D	D	12	104
Georgetown city	205	3,806	48	408	36	265	29	305	D	D	87	319	203	807
Glenn Heights city	29	245	4	5	5	7	NA	NA	D	D	4	2	4	38
Grand Prairie city	371	5,732	295	6,961	211	7,418	38	807	132	1,273	144	1,367	187	1,289
Grapevine city	312	5,614	101	2,152	173	3,477	35	419	111	962	115	1,177	253	1,725
Greenville city	139	2,540	D	D	8	46	23	572	51	211	39	167	45	501
Groves city	30	280	7	57	15	63	NA	NA	11	111	8	55	8	47
Haltom City city	147	1,545	111	1,524	21	145	D	D	44	240	31	197	53	276
Harker Heights city	57	1,246	3	D	D	D	D	D	24	130	27	89	27	139
Harlingen city	289	5,440	73	716	38	867	41	1,851	163	1,478	113	552	151	941
Henderson city	72	912	14	321	7	84	D	D	38	392	14	58	39	205
Hereford city	D	D	18	255	23	217	D	D	D	D	15	60	D	D
Hewitt city	25	489	18	149	10	98	NA	NA	14	58	12	26	12	56
Hidalgo city	53	782	60	368	62	605	NA	NA	24	188	16	38	14	51
Highland Village city	61	1,018	14	29	NA	NA	5	57	D	D	23	565	74	269
Horizon City city	23	553	6	121	18	344	D	D	15	76	10	18	9	36
Houston city	9,493	159,513	4,721	81,680	2,075	77,317	1,317	34,541	5,336	93,483	4,321	35,135	10,488	153,689
Humble city	319	6,830	53	626	37	289	26	549	92	608	52	212	92	659
Huntsville city	144	2,490	22	224	11	36	D	D	64	384	52	161	65	412
Hurst city	274	5,553	27	173	19	123	20	409	81	436	41	222	143	747
Hutto city	29	574	7	55	D	D	NA	NA	D	D	9	18	16	59
Ingleside city (Nueces and San Patricio Counties)	9	51	NA	NA	D	D	NA	NA	7	30	11	38	13	74
Irving city	668	12,263	351	12,141	207	10,157	227	15,523	643	25,046	381	4,869	1,235	25,765

1 Merchant wholesalers, except manufacturers' sales branches and offices.

Table C. Incorporated Places, Census Designated Places (CDPs), and Minor Civil Divisions (MCDs) of 10,000 or More Population — **Economic Census**

STATE City, town, township, borough, or CDP (county if applicable)	Administration and support and waste management and mediation services		Educational services		Health care and social assistance		Arts, entertainment, and recreation		Accommodation and food services		Other services (except public administration)	
	Number of establishments	Number of employees	Number of establishments	Number of employees	Number of establishments	Number of employees	Number of establishments	Number of employees	Number of establishments	Number of employees	Number of establishments	Number of employees
	15	16	17	18	19	20	21	22	23	24	25	26
TEXAS—Con.												
Brenham city	19	411	D	D	82	1,853	8	71	66	969	D	D
Brownsville city	98	3,186	16	172	479	17,053	30	441	342	6,555	139	625
Brownwood city	13	337	4	13	106	2,924	D	D	64	1,278	47	217
Brushy Creek CDP	9	25	D	D	42	607	5	11	10	212	D	D
Bryan city	100	2,247	D	D	242	4,796	24	645	175	3,446	150	962
Buda city	21	386	9	65	27	382	D	D	41	1,035	27	174
Burkburnett city	3	7	NA	NA	16	234	NA	NA	D	D	13	40
Burleson city	41	165	13	52	108	1,308	13	D	109	2,547	D	D
Canyon city	14	149	NA	NA	D	D	D	D	46	845	D	D
Canyon Lake CDP	22	280	NA	NA	19	210	8	D	36	470	33	117
Carrollton city	260	16,489	63	457	427	6,935	40	984	351	4,655	234	1,673
Cedar Hill city	25	230	10	63	100	1,309	D	D	91	2,145	D	D
Cedar Park city	70	1,037	39	262	261	3,764	36	785	185	3,925	161	1,034
Celina city	16	113	NA	NA	13	183	3	10	11	133	10	29
Channelview CDP	17	483	NA	NA	18	504	NA	NA	41	517	27	236
Cibolo city	13	46	D	D	D	D	4	52	16	147	D	D
Cinco Ranch CDP	12	36	11	66	40	253	D	D	13	284	24	128
Cleburne city	31	810	D	D	119	1,774	D	D	88	1,594	71	442
Cloverleaf CDP	8	442	NA	NA	13	164	NA	NA	6	109	D	D
Clute city	7	239	3	D	10	179	NA	NA	38	856	32	252
College Station city	98	2,013	36	236	180	5,705	37	698	339	9,157	111	1,071
Colleyville city	54	459	12	82	D	D	18	398	65	1,119	81	657
Conroe city	120	18,458	17	102	278	4,808	27	542	196	4,483	152	1,014
Converse city	11	47	5	16	29	552	D	D	28	673	D	D
Coppell city	149	5,995	25	273	173	1,685	12	293	78	1,927	80	1,046
Copperas Cove city	D	D	D	D	34	461	D	D	57	1,002	52	296
Corinth city	23	171	D	D	46	773	NA	NA	30	473	D	D
Corpus Christi city	348	12,556	D	D	1,071	27,875	86	1,963	827	18,020	487	3,837
Corsicana city	19	491	NA	NA	124	2,554	D	D	60	1,214	50	187
Crowley city	6	28	NA	NA	22	193	4	30	21	312	D	D
Dallas city	2,025	86,246	320	3,375	4,386	121,052	433	12,428	3,172	73,679	1,883	18,163
Deer Park city	43	1,970	3	25	52	787	D	D	66	1,786	D	D
Del Rio city	22	782	NA	NA	D	D	7	D	82	1,767	D	D
Denison city	15	132	NA	NA	85	3,515	7	37	60	1,044	32	115
Denton city	164	2,977	30	287	480	8,327	D	D	325	7,433	205	1,328
DeSoto city	28	549	6	39	175	4,565	7	85	76	1,638	52	214
Dickinson city	22	107	3	D	D	D	D	D	39	753	32	223
Donna city	5	19	NA	NA	49	786	NA	NA	23	364	D	D
Dumas city	D	D	NA	NA	D	D	D	D	37	462	31	114
Duncanville city	34	423	6	16	131	1,970	D	D	67	1,788	68	445
Eagle Pass city	13	241	NA	NA	101	3,998	D	D	72	1,407	33	149
Edinburg city	46	1,720	11	32	332	10,504	D	D	142	2,768	80	339
El Campo city	14	94	NA	NA	28	603	D	D	40	569	D	D
Elgin city	5	43	NA	NA	16	210	NA	NA	D	D	D	D
El Paso city	596	27,421	103	895	1,635	45,067	148	2,663	1,448	32,400	D	D
Ennis city	13	586	D	D	64	1,002	D	D	48	987	42	284
Euless city	49	1,226	10	50	85	1,191	15	417	96	1,756	67	522
Farmers Branch city	214	29,882	27	164	191	5,030	18	474	106	2,964	85	1,144
Fate city	9	32	NA	NA	8	110	NA	NA	NA	NA	5	42
Flower Mound town	92	1,186	52	646	274	3,895	29	494	D	D	110	959
Forest Hill city	13	203	NA	NA	8	68	NA	NA	36	655	13	61
Forney city	11	202	6	27	46	594	5	38	54	D	42	261
Fort Bliss CDP	6	629	NA	NA	NA	NA	NA	NA	7	153	D	D
Fort Hood CDP	10	180	NA	NA	D	D	NA	NA	D	D	13	105
Fort Worth city	805	38,455	139	1,512	2,113	59,067	205	6,153	1,644	37,634	1,001	9,263
Four Corners CDP	7	102	NA	NA	16	149	NA	NA	D	D	7	24
Fredericksburg city	32	154	D	D	94	1,765	12	136	100	1,655	49	237
Freeport city	14	830	NA	NA	D	D	NA	NA	25	315	D	D
Fresno CDP	12	211	3	27	21	170	NA	NA	6	190	4	30
Friendswood city	31	201	17	121	139	1,243	13	113	66	1,136	59	297
Frisco city	229	4,734	99	777	647	7,966	98	2,919	434	9,494	237	1,660
Fulshear city	9	12	NA	NA	D	D	NA	NA	12	153	D	D
Gainesville city	13	130	D	D	59	842	D	D	73	1,411	38	247
Galena Park city	5	58	NA	NA	NA	NA	NA	NA	11	94	5	46
Galveston city	61	1,002	12	48	128	8,418	36	546	240	7,318	116	650
Garland city	199	4,897	31	300	492	10,093	34	678	364	6,701	265	1,418
Gatesville city	NA	NA	NA	NA	22	671	NA	NA	29	380	D	D
Georgetown city	54	853	22	144	197	4,577	23	344	127	2,822	118	654
Glenn Heights city	D	D	NA	NA	D	D	NA	NA	D	D	7	28
Grand Prairie city	159	6,391	18	166	282	4,994	25	628	249	4,808	202	1,382
Grapevine city	97	2,649	27	155	254	3,640	27	736	217	9,464	101	1,418
Greenville city	14	184	D	D	130	2,922	9	84	80	1,770	41	206
Groves city	D	D	NA	NA	D	D	D	D	26	342	D	D
Haltom City city	56	2,512	5	77	43	489	D	D	72	905	81	540
Harker Heights city	14	62	9	190	D	D	8	35	62	912	34	198
Harlingen city	56	2,140	16	139	375	15,455	20	D	173	4,065	113	698
Henderson city	15	345	NA	NA	D	D	5	24	44	630	32	164
Hereford city	D	D	NA	NA	D	D	4	47	33	432	28	101
Hewitt city	11	73	NA	NA	18	515	NA	NA	D	D	20	180
Hidalgo city	9	79	NA	NA	9	262	NA	NA	17	380	D	D
Highland Village city	23	94	8	61	53	600	D	D	43	1,383	D	D
Horizon City city	4	10	NA	NA	17	163	D	D	24	483	8	19
Houston city	3,910	232,360	648	7,029	8,402	220,087	783	25,027	7,240	159,256	4,429	40,422
Humble city	34	654	7	75	185	3,213	14	400	172	4,577	D	D
Huntsville city	22	574	D	D	96	2,188	D	D	D	D	48	316
Hurst city	76	1,398	18	105	152	1,581	17	208	136	4,142	85	537
Hutto city	21	241	4	16	D	D	D	D	25	468	17	69
Ingleside city (Nueces and San Patricio Counties)	9	86	NA	NA	10	62	NA	NA	27	303	12	47
Irving city	419	40,819	49	575	676	12,494	62	773	656	13,735	324	6,050

Items 15–26

Table C. Incorporated Places, Census Designated Places (CDPs), and Minor Civil Divisions (MCDs) of 10,000 or More Population — **Economic Census**

STATE City, town, township, borough, or CDP (county if applicable)	Retail Trade Number of establishments	Number of employees	Wholesale trade[1] Number of establishments	Number of employees	Transportation and warehousing Number of establishments	Number of employees	Information Number of establishments	Number of employees	Finance and insurance Number of establishments	Number of employees	Real estate and rental and leasing Number of establishments	Number of employees	Professional, scientific, and technical services Number of establishments	Number of employees
	1	2	3	4	5	6	7	8	9	10	11	12	13	14
TEXAS—Con.														
Jacinto City city	28	244	6	255	8	134	NA	NA	9	44	NA	NA	8	38
Jacksonville city	81	1,447	8	45	9	370	D	D	38	230	16	32	27	79
Katy city	302	6,621	73	660	33	283	32	263	91	1,483	72	332	185	2,492
Keller city	103	1,689	25	74	16	89	13	200	76	299	62	172	177	604
Kerrville city	165	2,506	22	115	18	163	D	D	65	422	55	156	104	529
Kilgore city	73	1,032	68	919	D	D	D	D	37	208	24	278	28	215
Killeen city	402	6,892	D	D	43	418	31	600	119	1,269	152	630	110	984
Kingsville city	88	1,310	D	D	D	D	D	D	D	D	29	116	D	D
Kyle city	68	1,872	12	118	D	D	8	59	38	160	D	D	26	89
La Homa CDP	8	49	NA	NA	5	27	NA	NA	NA	NA	NA	NA	3	10
Lake Jackson city	104	2,664	7	20	8	14	10	161	59	622	31	136	39	204
Lakeway city	50	709	19	84	6	12	10	40	72	331	44	199	134	605
La Marque city	52	912	8	125	6	231	7	76	D	D	12	25	9	90
Lancaster city	64	1,075	23	900	37	2,226	10	357	D	D	19	78	18	62
La Porte city	72	576	46	1,422	73	2,755	4	29	24	195	33	370	68	2,355
Laredo city	795	13,447	D	D	1,323	15,615	73	846	D	D	247	890	D	D
League City city	213	4,426	61	590	34	419	18	258	124	1,365	86	295	189	1,921
Leander city	58	835	13	57	9	31	12	99	26	79	35	63	87	281
Leon Valley city	65	1,177	14	95	6	97	5	75	31	188	17	64	26	317
Levelland city	49	720	17	105	12	169	D	D	41	204	D	D	19	72
Lewisville city	438	7,375	126	3,335	62	2,755	50	1,193	161	7,872	141	746	248	2,665
Little Elm city	52	985	17	114	11	37	10	91	15	73	19	51	65	141
Live Oak city	29	540	5	27	D	D	NA	NA	D	D	9	25	13	73
Lockhart city	40	600	D	D	8	249	4	37	24	153	14	32	19	42
Longview city	490	7,419	165	2,129	70	1,515	45	707	214	1,669	146	683	306	2,240
Lubbock city	889	17,441	312	4,860	160	3,731	110	2,772	521	5,599	412	1,912	606	4,324
Lufkin city	254	4,462	45	589	40	750	20	310	109	619	64	314	116	659
Lumberton city	45	786	4	9	NA	NA	NA	NA	30	192	14	30	11	51
McAllen city	847	14,186	360	3,343	161	2,390	69	1,444	337	3,792	242	858	502	3,860
McKinney city	395	8,136	130	1,730	63	1,333	55	803	272	3,084	214	755	514	2,206
Mansfield city	160	3,527	58	2,147	44	504	13	159	103	520	58	207	129	505
Manvel city	20	256	8	113	7	90	D	D	D	D	6	7	13	32
Marshall city	125	1,547	26	133	16	184	D	D	68	635	29	79	69	264
Mercedes city	145	2,400	12	151	NA	NA	D	D	17	70	14	123	15	177
Mesquite city	435	7,849	71	642	74	3,671	31	481	116	650	98	452	112	736
Midland city	463	8,368	168	2,646	156	1,995	59	857	320	2,052	293	1,719	443	2,948
Midlothian city	60	848	D	D	31	900	D	D	32	142	29	111	42	177
Mineral Wells city	62	823	19	202	10	78	D	D	25	132	18	89	38	157
Mission city	208	3,852	85	613	44	194	D	D	121	615	73	208	86	366
Mission Bend CDP	13	48	D	D	D	D	NA	NA	NA	NA	NA	NA	22	38
Missouri City city	176	3,402	71	851	23	573	13	295	80	446	62	221	183	781
Mount Pleasant city	103	1,626	24	196	D	D	D	D	54	374	22	61	D	D
Murphy city	52	763	D	D	14	21	D	D	D	D	D	D	71	155
Nacogdoches city	193	2,640	29	286	17	191	18	127	84	546	47	184	73	367
Nederland city	85	728	16	262	19	304	D	D	36	246	20	183	37	262
New Braunfels city	321	5,707	D	D	37	1,905	25	274	153	759	149	540	199	1,126
North Richland Hills city	171	3,994	37	371	23	282	12	119	95	2,646	64	501	151	460
Odessa city	407	7,700	188	2,973	121	1,699	39	672	219	1,529	154	1,446	213	1,549
Orange city	104	1,247	D	D	18	474	D	D	53	484	23	86	48	225
Palestine city	129	1,752	25	381	23	1,940	D	D	53	213	33	105	47	132
Pampa city	79	987	24	292	18	207	D	D	D	D	D	D	32	225
Paris city	173	2,417	38	250	29	331	D	D	D	D	39	161	50	297
Pasadena city	419	6,655	159	2,859	102	1,564	30	382	158	1,068	134	892	185	4,077
Pearland city	300	6,635	66	546	39	204	22	163	140	763	108	380	236	1,286
Pearsall city	34	448	6	51	D	D	D	D	17	89	4	10	8	70
Pecan Grove CDP	6	127	D	D	NA	NA	NA	NA	D	D	5	13	30	129
Pecos city	D	D	D	D	34	360	D	D	D	D	D	D	D	D
Pflugerville city	120	1,970	48	672	23	771	16	292	46	159	39	114	93	540
Pharr city	174	2,543	130	1,514	144	2,249	D	D	87	612	46	251	69	831
Plainview city	88	1,279	25	325	25	1,437	D	D	45	188	21	55	40	181
Plano city	1,085	23,966	402	6,240	103	1,088	235	8,403	825	22,329	570	5,611	1,750	31,565
Pleasanton city	59	962	20	159	12	666	D	D	33	178	21	108	21	74
Port Arthur city	181	3,235	31	577	39	925	D	D	58	351	33	343	41	365
Portland city (Nueces and San Patricio Counties)	43	935	5	14	7	47	6	88	33	159	D	D	29	164
Port Lavaca city	48	938	10	76	9	40	D	D	D	D	12	144	19	405
Port Neches city	21	164	12	111	6	50	D	D	23	258	14	36	21	190
Princeton city	20	368	3	10	NA	NA	NA	NA	D	D	NA	NA	D	D
Prosper town	36	600	D	D	D	D	D	D	D	D	29	85	62	156
Raymondville city	22	256	NA	NA	6	18	D	D	D	D	5	11	D	D
Red Oak city	24	474	D	D	10	78	3	9	15	119	6	17	11	37
Rendon CDP	22	106	13	79	13	53	3	D	13	D	5	9	12	29
Richardson city	351	5,337	231	5,702	50	1,193	183	11,062	329	22,149	201	1,275	D	D
Richmond city	97	1,631	19	117	10	25	8	21	23	88	D	D	92	319
Rio Grande City city	68	901	8	51	12	86	D	D	32	187	8	16	37	142
Robinson city	26	322	7	113	9	136	3	22	5	17	4	5	8	21
Robstown city	35	340	13	250	8	250	NA	NA	23	108	D	D	D	D
Rockport city	54	786	4	14	D	D	D	D	23	147	20	71	32	133
Rockwall city	223	4,656	42	316	39	607	21	211	94	578	73	235	198	923
Roma city	25	216	D	D	4	20	NA	NA	20	107	NA	NA	3	9
Rosenberg city	184	3,544	25	420	14	323	18	219	70	353	34	459	52	194
Round Rock city	426	10,564	98	912	51	977	43	701	201	1,859	165	555	444	13,529
Rowlett city	98	1,903	33	144	25	176	D	D	D	D	22	44	92	480
Royse City city	19	396	7	84	D	D	NA	NA	7	35	6	21	8	37
Sachse city	25	619	6	7	12	46	NA	NA	D	D	11	28	35	119
Saginaw city	47	982	20	456	16	707	D	D	D	D	D	D	18	53
San Angelo city	406	6,498	97	1,194	57	681	D	D	192	1,599	136	557	189	1,231
San Antonio city	4,419	81,646	1,280	25,669	684	20,987	532	16,607	2,182	58,213	1,783	12,132	3,644	46,677
San Benito city	75	1,370	12	58	13	202	D	D	45	261	13	53	20	84
San Juan city	55	990	14	182	14	593	D	D	23	107	9	40	10	24

1 Merchant wholesalers, except manufacturers' sales branches and offices.

TX(Jacinto City city)—TX(San Juan city)

Table C. Incorporated Places, Census Designated Places (CDPs), and Minor Civil Divisions (MCDs) of 10,000 or More Population — Economic Census

STATE City, town, township, borough, or CDP (county if applicable)	Administration and support and waste management and mediation services		Educational services		Health care and social assistance		Arts, entertainment, and recreation		Accommodation and food services		Other services (except public administration)	
	Number of establishments	Number of employees	Number of establishments	Number of employees	Number of establishments	Number of employees	Number of establishments	Number of employees	Number of establishments	Number of employees	Number of establishments	Number of employees
	15	16	17	18	19	20	21	22	23	24	25	26
TEXAS—Con.												
Jacinto City city	NA	NA	NA	NA	21	307	NA	NA	D	D	8	38
Jacksonville city	15	417	NA	NA	54	1,353	NA	NA	40	713	D	D
Katy city	87	2,999	30	274	260	4,110	28	801	206	4,667	D	D
Keller city	56	559	18	140	153	1,670	19	199	78	1,384	72	434
Kerrville city	48	236	NA	NA	172	3,344	17	144	101	1,985	79	561
Kilgore city	29	848	NA	NA	37	619	D	D	65	889	30	161
Killeen city	71	937	16	100	211	2,898	D	D	274	6,252	182	1,068
Kingsville city	18	291	D	D	72	1,305	3	D	68	1,238	36	155
Kyle city	19	200	7	49	82	1,950	8	145	59	1,337	35	221
La Homa CDP	D	D	NA	NA	6	201	NA	NA	4	14	NA	NA
Lake Jackson city	20	171	8	50	145	2,214	D	D	83	1,943	33	229
Lakeway city	39	271	15	81	83	899	13	186	D	D	D	D
La Marque city	12	72	NA	NA	21	236	D	D	32	744	D	D
Lancaster city	12	236	3	D	47	1,304	3	19	46	862	26	170
La Porte city	39	1,064	3	32	44	448	NA	NA	68	1,391	D	D
Laredo city	195	5,991	27	177	D	D	D	D	D	D	D	D
League City city	82	675	24	171	200	2,907	D	D	169	3,453	117	802
Leander city	40	338	D	D	57	407	D	D	D	D	43	172
Leon Valley city	22	200	3	49	45	1,343	8	161	D	D	D	D
Levelland city	NA	NA	NA	NA	41	1,038	D	D	38	680	D	D
Lewisville city	200	5,021	29	149	284	5,698	44	1,023	275	5,161	178	1,131
Little Elm city	26	176	D	D	36	294	15	83	56	949	29	154
Live Oak city	13	143	NA	NA	94	1,640	4	140	D	D	10	72
Lockhart city	D	D	3	6	43	526	NA	NA	33	623	17	90
Longview city	121	2,980	18	93	393	10,308	30	328	274	5,630	183	1,531
Lubbock city	299	6,000	62	542	819	23,907	84	1,923	668	15,930	405	3,610
Lufkin city	46	1,107	8	41	263	7,245	15	184	124	2,849	96	628
Lumberton city	9	43	NA	NA	22	262	5	31	D	D	D	D
McAllen city	152	5,474	35	358	821	18,470	46	574	439	10,773	195	1,286
McKinney city	178	2,766	53	276	516	7,979	55	1,078	288	6,578	193	1,398
Mansfield city	75	1,574	33	214	D	D	25	693	139	3,622	93	771
Manvel city	NA	NA	NA	NA	8	192	NA	NA	D	D	10	73
Marshall city	17	267	NA	NA	88	1,630	7	43	D	D	D	D
Mercedes city	5	167	NA	NA	24	406	NA	NA	24	500	10	87
Mesquite city	105	1,901	15	97	355	8,370	D	D	236	5,700	115	823
Midland city	194	3,576	24	98	393	7,444	48	D	333	7,990	252	2,152
Midlothian city	32	165	6	39	56	773	5	31	52	936	30	242
Mineral Wells city	11	1,098	NA	NA	48	810	NA	NA	47	655	D	D
Mission city	45	241	14	51	306	10,015	13	266	142	2,593	78	391
Mission Bend CDP	18	109	NA	NA	29	222	NA	NA	11	91	12	39
Missouri City city	52	499	27	236	230	2,249	18	261	125	1,889	D	D
Mount Pleasant city	13	425	D	D	D	D	D	D	65	1,075	D	D
Murphy city	17	174	7	76	60	454	4	162	53	951	D	D
Nacogdoches city	37	1,049	4	D	179	3,196	13	92	108	2,168	D	D
Nederland city	23	788	4	44	D	D	6	50	39	722	37	182
New Braunfels city	97	1,710	26	152	285	5,296	47	1,173	260	6,136	147	1,096
North Richland Hills city	91	1,507	11	27	175	2,577	21	296	145	3,074	93	487
Odessa city	D	D	D	D	290	8,055	33	483	264	6,443	193	1,687
Orange city	18	1,276	6	28	69	775	D	D	70	1,044	32	470
Palestine city	26	282	D	D	121	2,061	4	105	67	1,145	41	225
Pampa city	14	81	NA	NA	D	D	D	D	42	647	33	126
Paris city	28	520	3	41	187	3,588	D	D	100	1,840	D	D
Pasadena city	91	3,569	10	51	352	7,459	17	330	238	5,473	167	2,056
Pearland city	85	2,110	46	421	372	4,937	25	499	236	5,726	165	1,227
Pearsall city	NA	NA	NA	NA	21	549	NA	NA	29	368	D	D
Pecan Grove CDP	7	22	NA	NA	11	72	D	D	4	102	D	D
Pecos city	D	D	NA	NA	D	D	3	15	D	D	14	45
Pflugerville city	46	299	16	168	94	1,025	D	D	93	2,267	64	449
Pharr city	35	1,786	7	93	162	5,088	8	63	109	2,209	64	487
Plainview city	D	D	NA	NA	64	1,069	D	D	57	1,158	45	296
Plano city	521	19,124	154	1,324	1,632	29,943	117	2,399	922	19,346	524	4,256
Pleasanton city	D	D	NA	NA	49	690	4	64	43	698	D	D
Port Arthur city	44	1,166	6	37	D	D	D	D	117	2,263	52	248
Portland city (Nueces and San Patricio Counties)	9	71	D	D	41	648	5	49	36	799	D	D
Port Lavaca city	7	295	NA	NA	28	586	4	115	41	557	18	138
Port Neches city	9	317	D	D	25	131	D	D	D	D	16	126
Princeton city	NA	NA	NA	NA	14	109	3	11	17	250	D	D
Prosper town	29	188	5	27	51	231	11	42	D	D	20	114
Raymondville city	D	D	NA	NA	D	D	NA	NA	18	280	D	D
Red Oak city	10	228	D	D	19	310	4	7	20	389	D	D
Rendon CDP	17	113	NA	NA	8	50	4	D	D	D	D	D
Richardson city	265	9,389	48	343	599	8,892	68	716	459	7,531	201	1,718
Richmond city	30	215	9	22	124	2,377	20	279	65	798	57	255
Rio Grande City city	7	37	NA	NA	71	3,738	NA	NA	25	358	D	D
Robinson city	11	138	3	11	D	D	NA	NA	17	190	8	34
Robstown city	D	D	NA	NA	16	2,874	D	D	23	326	11	41
Rockport city	11	63	NA	NA	42	493	D	D	65	806	28	91
Rockwall city	96	15,008	23	191	224	2,933	21	369	153	3,973	92	639
Roma city	D	D	NA	NA	16	263	NA	NA	D	D	NA	NA
Rosenberg city	29	391	3	7	76	850	8	37	120	2,461	61	269
Round Rock city	131	2,862	51	324	364	8,980	42	1,317	333	7,804	211	1,942
Rowlett city	49	262	13	63	120	2,283	13	153	85	1,455	77	399
Royse City city	9	77	NA	NA	21	267	3	D	D	D	D	D
Sachse city	22	104	8	30	D	D	D	D	26	401	D	D
Saginaw city	13	84	4	13	28	277	5	D	47	983	D	D
San Angelo city	106	2,008	D	D	263	7,868	32	597	248	4,816	191	1,052
San Antonio city	1,576	79,741	285	4,640	4,263	113,846	D	D	3,546	93,890	2,132	16,568
San Benito city	13	454	NA	NA	55	1,827	5	31	39	751	15	56
San Juan city	D	D	NA	NA	55	1,382	D	D	23	428	12	99

Table C. Incorporated Places, Census Designated Places (CDPs), and Minor Civil Divisions (MCDs) of 10,000 or More Population — **Economic Census**

Economic activity by sector, 2017

STATE City, town, township, borough, or CDP (county if applicable)	Retail Trade Number of establishments	Retail Trade Number of employees	Wholesale trade[1] Number of establishments	Wholesale trade[1] Number of employees	Transportation and warehousing Number of establishments	Transportation and warehousing Number of employees	Information Number of establishments	Information Number of employees	Finance and insurance Number of establishments	Finance and insurance Number of employees	Real estate and rental and leasing Number of establishments	Real estate and rental and leasing Number of employees	Professional, scientific, and technical services Number of establishments	Professional, scientific, and technical services Number of employees
	1	2	3	4	5	6	7	8	9	10	11	12	13	14
TEXAS—Con.														
San Marcos city	397	10,611	26	183	27	1,541	30	923	104	483	92	612	94	799
Santa Fe city	35	233	D	D	3	49	NA	NA	D	D	8	17	16	57
Schertz city	55	1,464	52	1,602	19	1,494	D	D	38	246	38	211	51	466
Seabrook city (Chambers.	50	484	4	50	12	418	D	D	18	65	25	116	39	378
Seagoville city	32	590	4	52	D	D	5	49	D	D	13	33	8	44
Seguin city	124	1,959	23	322	18	126	D	D	70	336	34	134	45	255
Selma city	77	2,069	8	88	7	436	6	113	8	53	D	D	21	168
Sherman city	217	4,035	40	372	21	478	17	399	80	635	46	171	105	400
Sienna Plantation CDP	5	17	NA	NA	D	D	D	D	7	6	11	19	40	88
Snyder city	52	678	D	D	D	D	6	54	D	D	15	44	D	D
Socorro city	61	716	15	103	43	575	NA	NA	24	137	16	31	18	121
South Houston city	83	911	46	354	13	43	NA	NA	29	116	8	18	7	49
Southlake city	216	4,760	66	731	23	599	26	468	168	1,023	105	800	243	1,572
Spring CDP	169	2,105	38	296	29	589	D	D	59	255	53	332	D	D
Stafford city	158	2,631	167	2,689	26	1,499	17	668	64	309	44	174	146	1,478
Stephenville city	128	1,760	14	173	D	D	11	101	45	271	27	96	48	213
Sugar Land city	546	8,629	203	2,947	61	815	58	1,174	294	3,895	212	516	643	9,908
Sulphur Springs city	123	1,563	24	929	20	237	D	D	56	516	24	104	37	137
Sweetwater city	54	730	12	44	9	43	D	D	25	124	10	51	D	D
Taylor city	63	792	9	99	9	56	11	84	D	D	11	26	20	65
Temple city	269	4,836	62	2,208	38	1,297	30	902	147	1,635	85	450	103	652
Terrell city	136	1,930	D	D	30	2,382	13	76	39	353	16	100	24	151
Texarkana city	292	5,078	52	579	32	305	29	274	158	1,105	81	395	123	2,248
Texas City city	189	2,747	36	504	24	449	9	78	D	D	41	910	54	671
The Colony city	76	2,811	19	339	12	25	D	D	D	D	32	104	80	480
The Woodlands CDP	349	8,603	120	1,218	44	467	45	778	385	3,461	225	981	578	5,377
Timberwood Park CDP	21	59	17	33	8	19	D	D	11	13	27	58	51	144
Tomball city	159	4,013	49	716	11	162	17	487	97	442	56	308	100	631
Trophy Club town	9	150	4	6	4	7	4	4	17	55	12	36	44	102
Tyler city	634	10,870	121	1,503	71	1,163	66	1,902	367	2,894	226	911	450	3,518
Universal City city	59	1,082	11	51	NA	NA	D	D	31	161	20	111	23	146
University Park city	99	1,116	16	45	5	7	D	D	D	D	64	117	113	282
Uvalde city	79	1,318	21	201	26	270	8	77	D	D	31	117	26	242
Vernon city	D	D	D	D	D	D	D	D	D	D	D	D	17	63
Victoria city	342	5,539	81	1,133	53	817	D	D	160	862	107	792	140	1,016
Vidor city	61	756	D	D	10	145	NA	NA	24	99	15	98	8	34
Waco city	564	8,748	148	1,864	71	1,824	61	923	288	5,049	182	1,462	278	2,307
Watauga city	81	1,049	4	7	4	11	8	70	D	D	11	31	24	119
Waxahachie city	156	2,946	D	D	24	1,259	20	265	68	424	48	179	81	402
Weatherford city	196	3,561	D	D	24	350	12	92	73	457	52	230	106	551
Webster city	136	1,936	30	601	12	222	16	596	62	347	47	318	111	2,661
Wells Branch CDP	22	104	27	322	12	71	D	D	D	D	14	101	27	1,112
Weslaco city	158	3,378	29	444	17	223	20	341	101	483	41	194	52	404
West Odessa CDP	30	317	19	188	60	342	NA	NA	D	D	11	194	16	52
West University Place city	20	296	6	9	NA	NA	D	D	28	98	21	37	78	155
White Settlement city	34	241	10	170	5	38	D	D	15	118	7	26	14	142
Wichita Falls city	417	6,438	125	1,116	59	960	48	957	188	1,435	150	756	193	1,279
Wylie city	83	1,893	19	166	D	D	D	D	D	D	40	123	64	213
UTAH	9,995	153,633	3,109	46,631	2,342	61,942	1,746	52,159	5,289	67,500	5,577	19,457	10,873	92,444
Alpine city	24	50	8	23	D	D	9	20	19	109	27	43	74	741
American Fork city	159	3,079	32	821	15	420	36	2,426	66	673	67	216	143	1,229
Bluffdale city	19	83	17	258	D	D	8	100	D	D	32	56	58	298
Bountiful city	144	2,207	D	D	25	1,007	24	174	116	551	93	170	223	1,003
Brigham City city	73	1,002	9	93	24	265	5	26	36	223	25	38	25	116
Cedar City city	161	2,091	23	165	26	165	D	D	65	431	83	151	116	429
Cedar Hills city	15	234	D	D	6	43	4	4	14	41	17	17	39	53
Centerville city	69	1,353	21	152	6	44	11	184	35	199	D	D	66	220
Clearfield city	66	571	18	245	20	207	8	97	48	223	27	82	67	1,198
Clinton city	34	979	NA	NA	9	21	3	16	15	102	5	45	13	42
Cottonwood Heights city	74	1,778	41	709	18	217	24	1,423	157	1,996	172	600	228	1,497
Draper city	212	4,439	68	1,995	24	241	55	2,458	179	5,457	142	499	307	2,099
Eagle Mountain city	19	182	6	27	12	47	D	D	8	7	28	35	48	100
Farmington city	88	1,618	D	D	6	20	20	143	58	241	40	97	105	525
Grantsville city	9	153	D	D	15	48	NA	NA	6	29	12	12	10	17
Heber city	63	849	D	D	17	85	12	48	31	131	42	54	72	275
Herriman city	34	385	8	8	19	95	D	D	D	D	51	66	66	132
Highland city	56	245	11	25	8	25	6	17	29	72	D	D	106	129
Holladay city	68	609	21	83	NA	NA	21	196	82	707	D	D	199	1,638
Hurricane city	51	643	23	472	22	1,074	7	57	18	87	26	60	37	79
Kaysville city	84	1,019	24	250	11	130	16	561	45	300	43	75	130	872
Kearns CDP	34	441	4	23	9	64	6	40	D	D	11	35	7	11
Layton city	294	5,222	46	338	47	1,236	25	473	128	800	127	512	213	1,552
Lehi city	178	2,707	36	1,233	24	123	67	5,524	95	722	D	D	325	3,937
Lindon city	80	1,353	38	699	D	D	18	1,042	15	475	30	138	61	835
Logan city	275	4,271	71	691	22	363	41	368	121	644	124	361	189	1,868
Magna CDP	26	439	5	36	12	92	NA	NA	D	D	12	19	D	D
Midvale city	157	3,646	52	577	21	1,693	11	345	101	766	83	534	127	3,481
Millcreek city	174	2,573	69	634	D	D	25	141	141	1,179	143	590	295	1,843
Murray city	340	6,394	93	868	56	680	42	935	200	4,031	169	1,143	D	D
North Logan city	56	812	10	140	10	187	D	D	20	264	13	22	61	181
North Ogden city	24	487	D	D	D	D	4	21	21	73	24	38	28	80
North Salt Lake city	48	318	30	312	29	1,300	7	21	24	70	43	169	67	1,164
Ogden city	349	4,272	96	1,835	53	2,488	37	906	155	1,623	114	381	275	2,689
Orem city	478	7,756	103	1,203	54	696	94	2,142	175	1,282	210	724	D	D
Payson city	59	1,393	11	213	11	54	6	39	24	99	13	10	33	159
Pleasant Grove city	97	1,144	30	135	15	116	20	137	50	276	D	D	140	985
Pleasant View city	16	74	D	D	6	27	NA	NA	10	17	13	20	16	63
Provo city	396	4,673	60	1,983	27	237	103	5,614	162	1,700	136	556	415	2,798

1 Merchant wholesalers, except manufacturers' sales branches and offices.

Table C. Incorporated Places, Census Designated Places (CDPs), and Minor Civil Divisions (MCDs) of 10,000 or More Population — **Economic Census**

STATE City, town, township, borough, or CDP (county if applicable)	Administration and support and waste management and mediation services		Educational services		Health care and social assistance		Arts, entertainment, and recreation		Accommodation and food services		Other services (except public administration)	
	Number of establishments	Number of employees	Number of establishments	Number of employees	Number of establishments	Number of employees	Number of establishments	Number of employees	Number of establishments	Number of employees	Number of establishments	Number of employees
	15	16	17	18	19	20	21	22	23	24	25	26
TEXAS—Con.												
San Marcos city	46	1,454	11	67	169	3,732	22	156	256	5,899	92	529
Santa Fe city	10	75	NA	NA	12	75	NA	NA	27	349	17	65
Schertz city	36	490	9	83	69	1,042	4	162	59	1,596	D	D
Seabrook city (Chambers)	15	163	NA	NA	22	232	11	123	47	1,078	22	97
Seagoville city	8	82	NA	NA	11	154	NA	NA	23	423	D	D
Seguin city	25	356	8	26	101	1,914	D	D	88	1,569	51	351
Selma city	11	205	NA	NA	11	102	3	10	37	1,018	D	D
Sherman city	54	1,271	D	D	213	3,898	D	D	112	2,739	59	387
Sienna Plantation CDP	6	8	NA	NA	13	93	4	39	NA	NA	D	D
Snyder city	D	D	NA	NA	23	581	D	D	D	D	D	D
Socorro city	14	71	NA	NA	15	293	NA	NA	29	499	18	101
South Houston city	8	79	NA	NA	8	38	5	40	D	D	D	D
Southlake city	82	1,115	38	520	269	2,900	29	588	128	3,408	91	733
Spring CDP	45	258	10	53	99	875	12	479	131	2,592	D	D
Stafford city	60	4,996	12	58	137	2,859	D	D	78	2,023	66	700
Stephenville city	37	569	NA	NA	69	1,461	11	65	78	1,538	54	269
Sugar Land city	145	4,148	79	679	740	12,100	45	D	377	8,118	190	1,559
Sulphur Springs city	24	372	NA	NA	D	D	D	D	56	970	44	172
Sweetwater city	D	D	NA	NA	D	D	D	D	38	573	D	D
Taylor city	11	231	NA	NA	26	497	NA	NA	36	537	18	90
Temple city	75	1,181	12	150	199	21,426	25	353	187	4,019	132	876
Terrell city	14	266	NA	NA	51	1,617	D	D	67	1,275	D	D
Texarkana city	63	2,023	9	35	247	6,804	D	D	148	3,886	108	788
Texas City city	30	523	5	75	103	2,264	6	50	88	1,518	48	281
The Colony city	39	565	11	21	61	632	12	485	83	1,919	53	242
The Woodlands CDP	151	15,744	56	358	464	7,295	45	2,048	303	8,196	181	1,616
Timberwood Park CDP	28	432	4	6	D	D	D	D	10	162	13	50
Tomball city	36	540	9	48	171	3,441	D	D	130	2,665	D	D
Trophy Club town	6	23	NA	NA	31	346	D	D	D	D	D	D
Tyler city	151	2,843	31	215	569	20,676	44	768	358	8,501	244	1,569
Universal City city	19	153	4	D	23	160	8	90	D	D	51	252
University Park city	22	237	7	45	72	419	D	D	61	1,619	28	222
Uvalde city	10	59	NA	NA	71	1,732	D	D	52	845	D	D
Vernon city	D	D	NA	NA	33	1,153	D	D	31	394	D	D
Victoria city	93	1,345	D	D	277	6,721	D	D	185	3,663	128	889
Vidor city	7	108	3	4	20	379	D	D	D	D	D	D
Waco city	167	6,394	29	365	454	16,024	53	1,382	367	8,862	253	1,621
Watauga city	16	344	5	59	38	333	D	D	61	1,200	30	176
Waxahachie city	37	1,021	D	D	116	2,078	10	138	100	2,669	61	352
Weatherford city	40	511	5	63	150	2,414	D	D	121	2,541	64	444
Webster city	44	2,078	10	153	271	6,692	11	979	123	3,669	62	532
Wells Branch CDP	26	365	4	3	16	754	3	58	18	180	23	111
Weslaco city	26	348	5	59	195	7,892	8	64	91	2,073	61	517
West Odessa CDP	11	111	NA	NA	D	D	NA	NA	14	240	29	188
West University Place city	12	104	3	13	D	D	4	4	20	408	8	44
White Settlement city	13	49	NA	NA	16	397	D	D	18	300	D	D
Wichita Falls city	89	2,495	20	D	365	10,507	33	440	260	5,438	189	970
Wylie city	38	356	3	32	69	1,074	D	D	49	985	D	D
UTAH	4,561	144,067	949	9,457	8,254	146,365	1,180	28,240	5,931	118,734	4,763	29,903
Alpine city	14	50	8	40	23	166	4	35	NA	NA	D	D
American Fork city	51	1,681	17	460	152	2,603	15	122	89	1,968	69	413
Bluffdale city	31	481	3	24	10	34	NA	NA	NA	NA	D	D
Bountiful city	76	1,387	18	170	223	3,291	15	98	74	1,562	79	565
Brigham City city	20	1,299	D	D	D	D	8	35	42	780	23	124
Cedar City city	53	708	D	D	144	2,182	16	86	D	D	63	222
Cedar Hills city	D	D	3	7	D	D	4	4	D	D	6	10
Centerville city	21	105	D	D	44	221	5	90	26	676	32	121
Clearfield city	32	1,475	NA	NA	61	1,672	NA	NA	D	D	D	D
Clinton city	21	191	NA	NA	D	D	NA	NA	27	563	D	D
Cottonwood Heights city	54	2,777	23	234	147	1,559	13	165	D	D	34	190
Draper city	117	1,964	29	276	174	1,671	D	D	117	2,066	95	693
Eagle Mountain city	D	D	4	2	16	68	NA	NA	8	112	10	20
Farmington city	29	104	8	26	68	338	D	D	36	723	D	D
Grantsville city	12	382	NA	NA	D	D	NA	NA	5	41	D	D
Heber city	44	192	6	D	D	D	8	112	D	D	D	D
Herriman city	39	87	6	D	38	338	6	11	19	431	18	124
Highland city	26	176	D	D	47	227	10	66	26	702	D	D
Holladay city	38	294	19	237	126	934	D	D	55	803	55	260
Hurricane city	21	61	NA	NA	33	670	6	25	35	457	27	114
Kaysville city	40	228	15	104	77	668	11	190	24	508	36	210
Kearns CDP	15	97	NA	NA	9	130	NA	NA	18	232	16	63
Layton city	98	799	19	114	214	3,915	19	296	166	3,673	123	825
Lehi city	78	3,902	25	411	114	1,058	25	674	98	2,154	60	527
Lindon city	D	D	16	764	34	396	8	52	18	331	33	132
Logan city	64	700	19	207	220	3,667	28	248	128	3,069	115	586
Magna CDP	16	501	NA	NA	23	391	NA	NA	23	343	D	D
Midvale city	66	1,707	9	76	81	781	13	451	109	1,961	77	447
Millcreek city	117	6,992	25	165	371	5,110	33	290	D	D	115	742
Murray city	126	3,428	19	200	370	10,971	19	384	125	2,927	165	1,220
North Logan city	13	462	4	25	62	894	D	D	15	283	D	D
North Ogden city	22	85	3	5	34	475	D	D	13	317	15	51
North Salt Lake city	32	1,600	6	56	D	D	9	66	23	296	22	155
Ogden city	116	4,762	16	91	309	7,156	D	D	216	3,798	141	1,120
Orem city	159	9,063	43	332	314	5,771	57	522	186	3,680	172	1,007
Payson city	D	D	D	D	66	898	5	17	31	544	29	84
Pleasant Grove city	47	382	22	221	82	660	14	49	34	654	50	214
Pleasant View city	8	45	NA	NA	24	216	NA	NA	NA	NA	7	37
Provo city	150	18,614	36	354	323	10,535	47	305	202	4,386	141	727

Table C. Incorporated Places, Census Designated Places (CDPs), and Minor Civil Divisions (MCDs) of 10,000 or More Population — **Economic Census**

STATE City, town, township, borough, or CDP (county if applicable)	Retail Trade		Wholesale trade[1]		Transportation and warehousing		Information		Finance and insurance		Real estate and rental and leasing		Professional, scientific, and technical services	
	Number of establish-ments	Number of employees	Number of establish-ments	Number of employees	Number of establish-ments	Number of employees	Number of establish-ments	Number of employees	Number of establish-ments	Number of employees	Number of establish-ments	Number of employees	Number of establish-ments	Number of employees
	1	2	3	4	5	6	7	8	9	10	11	12	13	14
UTAH—Con.														
Riverton city	64	1,283	16	43	16	61	12	35	D	D	D	D	111	241
Roy city	71	1,056	D	D	D	D	D	D	43	749	24	45	29	176
St. George city	436	6,553	108	743	69	2,170	77	1,098	228	1,179	262	607	447	2,103
Salt Lake City city	919	15,363	601	13,791	331	30,880	332	8,410	694	17,021	608	3,524	1,616	20,088
Sandy city	405	7,001	120	1,177	51	491	74	2,613	305	3,128	276	1,350	D	D
Santaquin city	11	62	D	D	NA	NA	NA	NA	5	15	5	4	8	9
Saratoga Springs city	39	293	5	5	10	31	5	7	22	67	24	25	61	114
Smithfield city	31	418	5	23	8	28	NA	NA	17	71	14	16	28	60
South Jordan city	174	4,012	41	122	21	327	42	2,650	146	2,471	173	454	323	1,951
South Ogden city	72	1,160	D	D	5	11	NA	NA	52	486	D	D	44	508
South Salt Lake city	223	3,239	226	4,226	40	525	D	D	43	353	70	421	134	1,694
Spanish Fork city	112	1,783	23	210	18	177	14	67	52	312	48	81	108	358
Springville city	96	1,213	23	320	D	D	14	91	29	174	30	D	82	342
Syracuse city	21	587	7	49	13	22	D	D	15	44	33	32	63	118
Taylorsville city	79	1,388	21	99	D	D	D	D	D	D	D	D	115	7,775
Tooele city	70	1,365	9	60	D	D	D	D	32	139	30	74	43	190
Vernal city	83	1,041	16	150	29	279	D	D	34	194	26	87	44	216
Washington city	70	1,174	18	80	16	79	7	12	24	111	65	142	62	133
West Haven city	24	211	D	D	7	30	NA	NA	8	27	27	112	31	206
West Jordan city	210	4,371	73	1,496	53	283	21	340	117	1,192	93	211	160	601
West Point city	D	D	NA	NA	3	6	NA	NA	NA	NA	3	4	10	13
West Valley City city	291	5,682	145	2,504	112	4,591	64	3,596	110	8,067	94	462	149	2,326
Woods Cross city	40	697	24	257	22	253	6	32	17	87	12	25	44	305
VERMONT	3,219	38,390	671	9,395	491	6,082	513	8,052	945	8,535	784	2,938	2,096	12,563
Bennington town	104	1,487	D	D	10	94	16	201	24	145	18	83	35	146
Brattleboro town	104	1,233	21	647	11	202	16	124	30	437	28	108	56	308
Burlington city	213	2,856	43	477	19	189	74	2,110	124	932	66	334	308	3,009
Colchester town	56	942	27	608	9	140	15	729	36	357	34	106	55	506
Essex town (balance)	57	895	15	591	4	42	5	186	18	66	16	82	49	244
Essex Junction village	41	356	3	11	NA	NA	D	D	16	77	5	10	33	152
Milton town	27	349	D	D	13	233	NA	NA	5	22	7	22	15	105
Rutland city	138	1,713	29	141	7	99	12	112	48	385	25	93	81	381
South Burlington city	175	3,384	50	878	26	569	41	1,126	71	651	66	333	113	1,288
VIRGINIA	27,134	429,072	5,937	86,698	5,062	104,497	4,113	105,182	11,404	154,331	10,051	55,778	31,431	470,265
Alexandria city	475	7,862	72	872	60	1,365	104	1,799	236	2,902	282	1,580	1,211	19,170
Annandale CDP	115	1,116	22	331	10	15	30	320	D	D	61	510	264	3,141
Arlington CDP	559	9,693	74	568	72	6,166	195	8,644	262	4,185	474	4,227	1,915	48,270
Ashburn CDP	86	2,447	32	845	30	217	113	5,696	76	877	D	D	458	5,938
Bailey's Crossroads CDP	102	2,123	D	D	11	26	13	281	26	215	38	179	122	1,861
Blacksburg town	96	1,468	9	310	7	34	D	D	51	384	42	346	146	1,499
Bon Air CDP	146	2,407	8	24	4	7	12	135	69	465	29	89	86	926
Brambleton CDP	13	183	6	4	NA	NA	6	54	NA	NA	7	D	215	315
Brandermill CDP	63	1,482	15	136	5	49	10	122	39	622	17	55	58	345
Bristol city	139	1,845	28	350	10	302	13	292	48	229	21	91	34	164
Broadlands CDP	15	375	NA	NA	NA	NA	4	8	8	32	9	23	108	426
Buckhall CDP	9	379	9	96	5	9	NA	NA	5	23	15	23	43	104
Bull Run CDP	93	1,856	NA	NA	D	D	3	19	27	168	39	173	36	279
Burke CDP	42	635	11	27	7	24	8	23	34	133	D	D	130	371
Burke Centre CDP	29	692	NA	NA	NA	NA	3	8	11	52	14	34	44	215
Cascades CDP	35	1,203	NA	NA	D	D	D	D	17	75	16	47	95	482
Cave Spring CDP	120	2,001	30	251	9	40	D	D	107	1,024	50	301	106	787
Centreville CDP	86	1,217	D	D	19	58	20	491	60	306	D	D	317	2,094
Chantilly CDP	147	3,444	105	2,071	34	1,468	43	1,425	D	D	83	934	614	26,389
Charlottesville city	281	3,282	44	451	12	122	72	1,724	119	1,023	84	555	334	2,763
Cherry Hill CDP	12	546	NA	NA	6	17	NA	NA	9	34	3	6	D	D
Chesapeake city	785	14,925	241	3,552	218	3,662	75	2,506	281	4,340	307	1,421	519	9,596
Chester CDP	85	1,942	7	85	D	D	D	D	30	141	33	148	44	229
Christiansburg town	165	3,350	D	D	11	222	D	D	55	277	32	123	68	420
Colonial Heights city	169	3,283	9	58	4	14	D	D	D	D	35	164	45	435
Culpeper town	113	1,830	7	161	10	52	D	D	D	D	23	75	41	255
Dale City CDP	71	1,086	8	20	17	36	8	130	30	104	18	91	83	448
Danville city	302	4,558	45	560	23	353	22	273	103	861	53	237	64	393
Dranesville CDP	4	32	NA	NA	NA	NA	3	11	D	D	6	10	70	139
East Highland Park CDP	46	493	9	188	8	92	NA	NA	D	D	8	34	10	60
Fairfax city	217	4,681	27	250	12	108	40	327	159	1,201	62	242	552	4,932
Fairfax Station CDP	8	231	D	D	5	8	NA	NA	D	D	14	63	59	170
Fair Oaks CDP	162	4,099	9	D	9	142	27	580	85	1,742	49	396	366	10,170
Falls Church city	103	1,304	16	126	12	157	23	313	43	D	38	176	164	1,847
Forest CDP	66	898	10	189	3	43	4	27	42	257	D	D	75	580
Fort Hunt CDP	13	171	4	14	NA	NA	D	D	D	D	10	13	70	214
Franconia CDP	23	234	D	D	9	228	NA	NA	D	D	22	212	93	2,073
Franklin Farm CDP	19	349	D	D	3	24	6	6	D	D	D	D	156	351
Fredericksburg city	261	4,326	24	254	10	126	22	447	93	620	75	314	181	1,401
Front Royal town	85	886	D	D	11	234	D	D	41	203	14	40	47	248
Gainesville CDP	84	2,338	11	412	9	76	D	D	26	253	21	58	92	679
Glen Allen CDP	118	2,695	D	D	7	29	D	D	24	1,002	13	52	52	1,856
Great Falls CDP	32	287	12	28	NA	NA	13	66	28	184	D	D	171	776
Groveton CDP	24	689	NA	NA	NA	NA	D	D	D	D	8	37	27	84
Hampton city	423	6,748	60	921	45	418	36	976	119	827	123	784	290	4,585
Harrisonburg city	325	5,341	58	864	32	268	32	931	132	926	71	373	140	1,091
Herndon town	79	957	D	D	19	1,074	66	5,749	63	2,825	69	351	340	7,765
Highland Springs CDP	31	241	7	41	7	179	NA	NA	13	37	11	43	8	118
Hollins CDP	D	D	19	426	8	200	D	D	31	2,445	18	104	39	348
Hopewell city	72	636	D	D	6	22	NA	NA	D	D	19	71	41	293
Huntington CDP	26	458	NA	NA	6	38	NA	NA	NA	NA	8	69	29	479
Hybla Valley CDP	70	1,618	D	D	NA	NA	D	D	D	D	15	86	22	219

1 Merchant wholesalers, except manufacturers' sales branches and offices.

Table C. Incorporated Places, Census Designated Places (CDPs), and Minor Civil Divisions (MCDs) of 10,000 or More Population — **Economic Census**

STATE City, town, township, borough, or CDP (county if applicable)	Administration and support and waste management and mediation services		Educational services		Health care and social assistance		Arts, entertainment, and recreation		Accommodation and food services		Other services (except public administration)	
	Number of establishments	Number of employees	Number of establishments	Number of employees	Number of establishments	Number of employees	Number of establishments	Number of employees	Number of establishments	Number of employees	Number of establishments	Number of employees
	15	16	17	18	19	20	21	22	23	24	25	26
UTAH—Con.												
Riverton city	64	298	18	86	100	1,672	11	167	53	1,111	D	D
Roy city	20	451	4	D	56	595	4	D	41	674	D	D
St. George city	216	1,596	25	170	479	7,927	50	594	241	5,083	182	1,092
Salt Lake City city	470	25,396	105	1,459	741	25,849	143	3,336	835	19,340	699	5,916
Sandy city	211	11,373	41	346	315	3,567	47	1,217	213	3,892	169	1,079
Santaquin city	6	18	NA	NA	10	90	NA	NA	8	108	D	D
Saratoga Springs city	20	58	5	27	30	297	9	42	16	310	D	D
Smithfield city	24	219	D	D	D	D	6	13	11	140	15	75
South Jordan city	110	2,334	28	240	174	2,436	24	434	111	2,570	81	505
South Ogden city	30	505	3	27	82	954	D	D	33	666	31	249
South Salt Lake city	78	2,273	D	D	65	1,542	14	160	93	1,079	143	924
Spanish Fork city	53	847	18	59	D	D	4	71	54	1,179	D	D
Springville city	D	D	6	209	83	773	D	D	41	837	D	D
Syracuse city	20	89	D	D	D	D	D	D	19	269	15	71
Taylorsville city	63	2,394	5	26	110	1,444	11	165	D	D	41	272
Tooele city	D	D	D	D	D	D	9	72	51	905	D	D
Vernal city	17	69	D	D	D	D	NA	NA	52	834	37	144
Washington city	46	213	NA	NA	36	159	D	D	D	D	31	127
West Haven city	26	263	3	D	14	199	3	106	17	243	29	191
West Jordan city	142	2,147	24	229	209	4,575	13	171	133	2,622	125	815
West Point city	12	61	NA	NA	11	81	NA	NA	3	0	4	8
West Valley City city	147	4,238	30	504	140	4,106	D	D	226	4,126	130	741
Woods Cross city	26	257	8	107	15	335	3	10	11	171	D	D
VERMONT	1,195	8,724	281	2,005	2,102	48,285	457	7,739	1,979	32,891	1,603	7,339
Bennington town	22	366	4	49	97	2,702	11	63	54	688	39	181
Brattleboro town	21	324	23	268	100	2,392	15	82	86	1,042	56	239
Burlington city	76	637	26	191	176	8,863	37	794	172	3,588	128	814
Colchester town	39	263	6	34	51	1,605	12	100	36	733	31	179
Essex town (balance)	27	247	7	107	30	379	11	297	19	409	26	108
Essex Junction village	14	148	6	31	36	449	5	108	34	352	24	81
Milton town	11	35	NA	NA	D	D	3	7	13	172	D	D
Rutland city	41	365	8	20	136	3,946	16	131	92	1,196	70	381
South Burlington city	53	1,190	22	150	148	2,417	17	343	93	2,259	91	550
VIRGINIA	11,056	270,301	2,419	21,690	20,522	454,501	3,071	61,703	18,199	358,010	15,700	118,537
Alexandria city	287	16,111	78	586	426	7,386	75	1,283	402	8,518	611	9,983
Annandale CDP	77	3,444	22	108	173	3,136	17	117	136	1,458	108	434
Arlington CDP	D	D	110	1,996	516	11,848	104	2,398	665	18,101	715	14,016
Ashburn CDP	57	3,615	52	530	151	2,835	27	1,305	135	2,607	78	803
Bailey's Crossroads CDP	34	1,287	10	159	48	958	3	174	86	1,286	62	301
Blacksburg town	24	272	13	59	D	D	22	202	112	2,249	54	382
Bon Air CDP	30	542	D	D	99	1,901	11	274	60	1,608	47	267
Brambleton CDP	13	112	8	32	D	D	NA	NA	18	293	12	150
Brandermill CDP	22	347	8	56	59	823	6	257	D	D	35	232
Bristol city	D	D	D	D	51	987	D	D	79	1,955	41	243
Broadlands CDP	8	43	8	33	11	73	D	D	25	627	14	83
Buckhall CDP	25	145	7	5	9	81	5	75	4	89	D	D
Bull Run CDP	23	308	NA	NA	61	695	6	114	41	640	D	D
Burke CDP	38	185	D	D	97	1,014	D	D	39	620	47	280
Burke Centre CDP	11	110	4	D	30	765	3	267	24	423	21	172
Cascades CDP	13	189	5	D	72	724	NA	NA	23	619	20	144
Cave Spring CDP	43	1,055	D	D	129	1,704	D	D	63	1,476	59	276
Centreville CDP	71	578	26	122	130	1,174	14	395	136	2,146	79	438
Chantilly CDP	116	9,426	28	242	116	3,314	25	406	136	2,098	123	1,317
Charlottesville city	90	2,561	38	417	158	9,293	53	750	292	5,491	158	1,729
Cherry Hill CDP	8	30	NA	NA	9	101	D	D	14	177	5	19
Chesapeake city	341	11,643	66	837	514	10,002	54	1,280	486	10,068	438	3,057
Chester CDP	33	625	5	51	D	D	D	D	69	1,620	D	D
Christiansburg town	32	345	D	D	D	D	D	D	83	2,265	D	D
Colonial Heights city	20	126	6	31	91	1,616	9	292	84	2,221	63	517
Culpeper town	24	174	D	D	61	1,523	D	D	79	1,558	53	481
Dale City CDP	69	367	4	14	86	1,015	D	D	D	D	42	188
Danville city	49	1,775	D	D	180	5,096	15	189	143	2,925	89	424
Dranesville CDP	13	49	NA	NA	12	127	3	3	NA	NA	11	31
East Highland Park CDP	10	71	NA	NA	21	252	4	41	15	252	15	60
Fairfax city	79	2,256	31	472	265	4,300	25	603	183	3,332	166	1,258
Fairfax Station CDP	18	271	D	D	D	D	5	92	NA	NA	11	83
Fair Oaks CDP	44	1,819	22	174	169	4,513	9	123	70	1,655	55	1,254
Falls Church city	42	844	14	128	123	2,335	18	236	114	1,213	94	573
Forest CDP	27	608	D	D	63	988	7	36	31	441	39	220
Fort Hunt CDP	10	71	5	15	16	277	D	D	6	91	14	51
Franconia CDP	30	825	5	28	67	887	3	D	30	439	47	411
Franklin Farm CDP	14	91	D	D	23	217	D	D	27	403	18	126
Fredericksburg city	41	528	14	70	225	5,189	19	447	186	4,460	113	762
Front Royal town	12	22	NA	NA	55	1,523	D	D	60	792	46	359
Gainesville CDP	24	670	12	90	75	875	16	215	76	1,938	D	D
Glen Allen CDP	22	427	5	31	35	329	D	D	71	2,009	D	D
Great Falls CDP	27	348	15	91	38	371	13	181	28	446	31	171
Groveton CDP	25	159	NA	NA	17	221	NA	NA	22	499	D	D
Hampton city	120	4,656	19	148	281	7,833	D	D	256	5,902	169	953
Harrisonburg city	56	738	13	81	185	3,080	24	234	208	5,138	131	715
Herndon town	66	2,504	NA	NA	NA	NA	9	177	128	1,903	89	731
Highland Springs CDP	D	D	NA	NA	15	273	NA	NA	10	133	17	207
Hollins CDP	16	349	NA	NA	NA	NA	3	19	38	611	D	D
Hopewell city	14	87	NA	NA	45	1,183	7	24	50	771	38	231
Huntington CDP	6	80	3	1	D	D	NA	NA	21	260	22	161
Hybla Valley CDP	15	115	NA	NA	68	2,060	D	D	39	709	17	109

Table C. Incorporated Places, Census Designated Places (CDPs), and Minor Civil Divisions (MCDs) of 10,000 or More Population — **Economic Census**

STATE City, town, township, borough, or CDP (county if applicable)	Retail Trade Number of establishments	Number of employees	Wholesale trade[1] Number of establishments	Number of employees	Transportation and warehousing Number of establishments	Number of employees	Information Number of establishments	Number of employees	Finance and insurance Number of establishments	Number of employees	Real estate and rental and leasing Number of establishments	Number of employees	Professional, scientific, and technical services Number of establishments	Number of employees
	1	2	3	4	5	6	7	8	9	10	11	12	13	14
VIRGINIA—Con.														
Idylwood CDP	16	210	3	3	D	D	9	21	D	D	18	95	82	1,308
Kings Park West CDP	18	278	3	4	NA	NA	7	32	9	27	8	17	44	108
Kingstowne CDP	27	1,071	4	34	NA	NA	NA	NA	9	111	9	60	76	2,213
Lake Monticello CDP	12	140	NA	NA	NA	NA	NA	NA	5	20	12	20	14	14
Lake Ridge CDP	42	566	4	10	5	20	5	12	31	351	28	204	108	664
Lakeside CDP	44	477	20	562	13	169	D	D	20	104	14	79	36	286
Lansdowne CDP	11	149	NA	NA	D	D	D	D	13	65	12	47	85	1,448
Laurel CDP	62	1,236	23	174	9	103	D	D	24	607	21	129	47	662
Leesburg town	279	5,980	17	277	19	129	35	557	107	925	60	252	371	3,208
Lincolnia CDP	62	804	36	618	24	449	13	274	26	153	26	257	108	1,440
Linton Hall CDP	21	198	15	256	D	D	4	5	10	79	18	35	115	406
Lorton CDP	41	480	40	372	19	454	5	14	11	40	22	D	64	834
Lowes Island CDP	6	95	4	4	NA	NA	D	D	7	10	8	10	78	249
Lynchburg city	355	6,890	74	898	35	1,029	51	633	171	2,473	119	458	192	2,919
McLean CDP	238	4,580	36	296	11	62	38	920	107	567	D	D	520	5,389
McNair CDP	23	328	24	3,133	6	5	43	4,483	D	D	26	241	379	18,325
Madison Heights CDP	53	726	D	D	9	140	NA	NA	17	83	7	13	14	60
Manassas city	176	2,153	47	458	46	455	15	92	75	553	45	226	216	1,693
Manassas Park city	24	143	21	257	6	41	5	19	D	D	9	51	19	152
Manchester CDP	73	955	9	58	14	157	D	D	D	D	26	81	64	1,371
Martinsville city	91	1,432	18	154	6	646	13	118	40	228	22	83	46	183
Marumsco CDP	82	1,600	13	40	33	428	8	98	15	80	22	129	26	127
Meadowbrook CDP	36	582	NA	NA	12	54	NA	NA	8	44	5	11	13	49
Mechanicsville CDP	151	3,868	41	534	26	569	9	304	71	389	52	180	88	477
Merrifield CDP	108	2,649	30	243	18	250	25	2,536	D	D	49	452	221	7,480
Montclair CDP	14	327	D	D	NA	NA	NA	NA	5	46	6	19	35	112
Mount Vernon CDP	18	105	NA	NA	4	22	NA	NA	D	D	5	18	44	179
Neabsco CDP	48	1,222	D	D	8	50	D	D	13	97	8	7	27	100
New Baltimore CDP	20	121	6	74	NA	NA	NA	NA	5	12	7	39	39	353
Newington CDP	41	1,026	64	822	29	949	9	752	12	50	27	183	128	3,429
Newington Forest CDP	D	D	NA	NA	4	5	NA	NA	NA	NA	4	6	23	38
Newport News city	648	10,091	112	1,887	83	1,181	52	1,624	224	1,721	280	1,419	363	5,003
Norfolk city	830	11,729	187	2,714	184	7,500	164	2,352	268	3,992	317	3,133	707	10,576
Oakton CDP	30	288	7	7	D	D	D	D	37	424	46	282	225	4,380
Petersburg city	141	2,454	D	D	18	227	7	57	D	D	37	163	36	239
Poquoson city	27	307	NA	NA	3	18	NA	NA	8	38	8	16	16	67
Portsmouth city	261	3,060	43	659	62	1,917	D	D	72	476	77	388	144	1,450
Purcellville town	44	580	8	63	8	201	6	22	16	72	D	D	48	963
Radford city	42	500	9	36	NA	NA	D	D	25	139	24	121	25	139
Reston CDP	105	2,327	40	2,157	D	D	165	11,757	195	3,266	D	D	925	28,994
Richmond city	790	9,088	253	3,815	126	3,856	134	2,310	390	9,554	329	2,197	910	11,464
Roanoke city	533	8,966	155	2,211	95	3,866	49	929	216	3,344	174	938	308	2,688
Rose Hill CDP	23	207	NA	NA	11	37	5	35	D	D	8	45	46	125
Salem city	151	1,995	68	1,552	27	497	20	315	79	583	43	199	78	450
Short Pump CDP	196	4,796	12	41	6	6	21	1,107	57	517	45	325	147	663
South Riding CDP	29	740	D	D	7	6	9	116	17	48	29	81	264	830
Springfield CDP	216	4,460	21	642	30	628	25	332	48	361	50	281	161	3,513
Staunton city	133	1,834	21	227	13	211	20	142	58	403	38	142	64	298
Sterling CDP	103	1,807	18	185	41	778	15	92	19	76	D	D	88	697
Stone Ridge CDP	10	202	NA	NA	D	D	NA	NA	NA	NA	4	10	74	128
Sudley CDP	63	1,059	NA	NA	10	16	6	35	20	114	5	40	23	783
Suffolk city	238	3,997	36	1,117	75	1,382	24	247	84	879	74	279	145	923
Sugarland Run CDP	14	174	4	9	4	5	NA	NA	4	17	NA	NA	37	122
Timberlake CDP	48	521	14	183	D	D	D	D	24	138	D	D	31	178
Tuckahoe CDP	144	1,861	21	82	10	42	10	112	93	489	D	D	151	697
Tysons CDP	221	4,968	61	822	13	337	158	8,519	265	11,146	217	2,765	972	45,229
Vienna town	94	1,215	D	D	NA	NA	7	33	D	D	D	D	159	1,042
Virginia Beach city	1,506	24,023	351	4,770	206	1,822	233	6,050	849	17,385	761	5,451	1,494	21,755
Wakefield CDP	D	D	NA	NA	NA	NA	NA	NA	NA	NA	7	6	37	96
Waynesboro city	122	2,161	14	229	20	225	19	426	39	424	35	91	43	320
West Falls Church CDP	58	857	8	30	D	D	7	28	D	D	18	229	114	2,013
West Springfield CDP	26	469	5	9	NA	NA	5	12	D	D	21	611	85	496
Williamsburg city	121	1,658	8	68	NA	NA	7	77	33	162	D	D	28	129
Winchester city	284	4,317	36	459	18	139	16	202	104	722	66	306	142	995
Wolf Trap CDP	6	39	5	4	NA	NA	6	38	D	D	26	35	115	271
Woodlawn CDP	25	343	NA	NA	4	3	NA	NA	7	28	10	45	12	33
Wyndham CDP	D	D	6	7	NA	NA	NA	NA	4	2	9	25	39	77
WASHINGTON	21,751	347,728	7,755	120,320	5,474	100,012	3,864	139,868	9,992	104,294	11,826	53,706	22,144	214,628
Aberdeen city	95	1,716	17	233	12	164	12	131	24	220	20	90	35	200
Anacortes city	89	804	10	134	21	86	9	30	40	181	29	105	63	285
Arlington city	78	1,437	26	448	28	612	5	10	D	D	46	164	33	189
Artondale CDP	11	41	5	13	4	5	NA	NA	D	D	14	14	22	51
Auburn city	291	5,174	180	4,529	121	3,053	D	D	72	377	95	380	151	707
Bainbridge Island city	74	796	17	126	12	40	28	156	51	172	59	124	197	555
Battle Ground city	48	1,014	12	47	14	286	8	51	D	D	20	42	33	183
Bellevue city	653	14,690	281	4,021	65	847	241	23,683	636	9,988	613	3,693	1,361	22,379
Bellingham city	515	8,719	146	1,497	49	590	70	1,790	200	1,808	234	993	446	2,086
Bonney Lake city	55	1,593	NA	NA	12	30	7	59	D	D	20	33	28	85
Bothell city	110	1,725	54	1,754	12	213	61	3,766	112	1,862	99	249	273	4,074
Bothell East CDP	4	14	5	7	NA	NA	NA	NA	NA	NA	10	23	25	37
Bothell West CDP	15	103	4	4	NA	NA	D	D	D	D	8	15	31	61
Bremerton city	151	2,050	22	190	16	442	19	484	38	355	67	242	75	798
Bryn Mawr-Skyway CDP	16	160	4	13	4	15	NA	NA	D	D	19	55	12	91
Burien city	151	2,055	23	128	34	261	D	D	43	264	75	232	95	484
Camano CDP	19	141	D	D	7	13	3	4	6	17	18	27	30	49
Camas city	52	417	20	324	9	42	12	56	D	D	26	107	79	939
Centralia city	118	1,393	14	105	7	145	10	98	35	213	33	101	37	207
Cheney city	25	354	NA	NA	NA	NA	D	D	D	D	D	D	9	29

1 Merchant wholesalers, except manufacturers' sales branches and offices.

Table C. Incorporated Places, Census Designated Places (CDPs), and Minor Civil Divisions (MCDs) of 10,000 or More Population — **Economic Census**

	Economic activity by sector, 2017											
	Administration and support and waste management and mediation services		Educational services		Health care and social assistance		Arts, entertainment, and recreation		Accommodation and food services		Other services (except public administration)	
STATE City, town, township, borough, or CDP (county if applicable)	Number of establishments	Number of employees	Number of establishments	Number of employees	Number of establishments	Number of employees	Number of establishments	Number of employees	Number of establishments	Number of employees	Number of establishments	Number of employees
	15	16	17	18	19	20	21	22	23	24	25	26
VIRGINIA—Con.												
Idylwood CDP...............	18	2,647	8	109	27	538	3	8	16	350	25	168
Kings Park West CDP......	11	142	5	29	19	201	NA	NA	21	450	14	54
Kingstowne CDP............	17	508	NA	NA	19	248	NA	NA	33	723	16	135
Lake Monticello CDP.......	11	55	NA	NA	D	D	D	D	8	114	8	82
Lake Ridge CDP.............	34	355	9	47	67	1,357	12	144	40	702	39	339
Lakeside CDP................	16	276	3	9	38	565	10	376	23	353	49	341
Lansdowne CDP.............	14	427	D	D	D	D	NA	NA	25	483	19	339
Laurel CDP...................	19	601	D	D	76	1,776	4	50	D	D	D	D
Leesburg town...............	60	458	25	242	182	3,129	25	364	142	2,924	114	658
Lincolnia CDP................	44	1,162	10	76	60	1,209	D	D	42	529	46	331
Linton Hall CDP.............	22	100	6	40	24	375	11	33	24	292	D	D
Lorton CDP..................	39	701	5	25	49	781	5	126	21	470	D	D
Lowes Island CDP..........	7	31	NA	NA	14	92	D	D	12	182	7	36
Lynchburg city..............	103	2,338	28	235	289	10,123	35	567	270	6,023	171	1,013
McLean CDP.................	72	1,087	30	579	226	1,643	35	747	D	D	110	618
McNair CDP.................	39	1,088	12	613	D	D	6	31	45	788	18	164
Madison Heights CDP......	11	98	NA	NA	D	D	D	D	31	429	D	D
Manassas city...............	102	1,586	14	164	177	3,231	17	184	126	1,947	137	902
Manassas Park city.........	40	281	D	D	D	D	4	25	14	118	D	D
Manchester CDP............	37	1,664	3	D	69	1,638	7	192	D	D	D	D
Martinsville city.............	26	1,305	NA	NA	107	2,190	9	178	45	710	37	178
Marumsco CDP.............	39	190	4	2	106	2,433	3	35	61	1,106	73	358
Meadowbrook CDP........	D	D	NA	NA	31	440	D	D	D	D	D	D
Mechanicsville CDP........	55	882	13	76	179	4,892	16	317	104	2,156	112	745
Merrifield CDP..............	63	3,212	16	225	151	2,606	D	D	81	2,164	74	598
Montclair CDP..............	15	109	5	27	D	D	3	44	22	490	14	92
Mount Vernon CDP.........	14	134	5	32	23	277	NA	NA	19	206	24	78
Neabsco CDP...............	7	47	5	31	36	D	7	129	23	534	D	D
New Baltimore CDP........	22	107	D	D	D	D	NA	NA	6	76	11	106
Newington CDP.............	43	1,144	11	92	D	D	NA	NA	26	319	68	496
Newington Forest CDP.....	4	25	NA	NA	8	96	NA	NA	3	18	7	29
Newport News city..........	204	6,814	40	314	452	15,710	52	1,025	411	7,516	283	1,731
Norfolk city..................	248	12,810	53	462	582	20,755	75	1,558	612	11,326	396	3,023
Oakton CDP.................	37	798	17	24	66	2,358	6	10	34	418	49	306
Petersburg city.............	23	550	NA	NA	126	4,361	10	72	94	930	75	576
Poquoson city...............	22	105	NA	NA	16	180	3	3	21	292	D	D
Portsmouth city.............	87	3,672	D	D	227	7,627	D	D	163	2,414	143	1,143
Purcellville town............	13	85	D	D	34	266	8	D	39	753	45	228
Radford city.................	13	81	NA	NA	41	561	NA	NA	41	993	23	66
Reston CDP.................	121	8,437	42	1,161	261	5,509	41	1,206	141	3,888	137	2,138
Richmond city...............	287	9,853	69	398	607	27,376	114	2,455	677	14,306	520	4,950
Roanoke city................	147	4,580	26	249	316	13,827	49	545	302	7,205	252	1,629
Rose Hill CDP..............	32	186	4	17	23	146	7	242	9	150	D	D
Salem city...................	D	D	7	D	143	5,424	13	195	97	1,885	88	474
Short Pump CDP...........	31	354	15	171	46	416	D	D	114	3,348	67	610
South Riding CDP..........	26	455	12	149	119	2,858	8	225	129	2,674	86	672
Springfield CDP.............	81	2,086	D	D	95	2,486	12	241	84	1,333	86	456
Staunton city................	21	223	8	99	42	507	8	77	75	1,139	57	302
Sterling CDP.................	65	500	11	59	18	245	6	112	D	D	16	73
Stone Ridge CDP...........	8	19	5	28	240	4,979	16	348	150	3,029	137	715
Sudley CDP..................	22	160	D	D	D	D	NA	NA	13	138	7	41
Suffolk city..................	85	1,650	15	94	37	392	7	31	25	357	D	D
Sugarland Run CDP........	10	55	3	5	156	3,144	22	431	74	1,195	90	509
Timberlake CDP............	21	193	NA	NA	209	3,002	31	3,328	189	4,760	140	1,417
Tuckahoe CDP..............	53	428	16	126	123	863	15	402	103	1,467	88	456
Tysons CDP.................	141	13,706	52	881	1,162	21,729	202	3,598	1,292	25,108	943	5,762
Vienna town.................	24	405	24	157	D	D	4	3	NA	NA	D	D
Virginia Beach city..........	741	16,510	143	1,020	47	630	10	109	77	1,678	59	413
Wakefield CDP..............	14	111	5	29	88	1,243	4	4	D	D	49	381
Waynesboro city............	24	299	5	28	58	651	9	184	26	459	21	173
West Falls Church CDP....	47	1,227	12	87	42	666	D	D	155	3,667	36	379
West Springfield CDP......	13	54	6	77	269	7,080	18	258	144	3,320	92	536
Williamsburg city...........	18	447	5	39	12	83	D	D	5	31	12	18
Winchester city.............	42	2,241	13	110	18	254	NA	NA	D	D	26	135
Wolf Trap CDP..............	14	156	4	11	18	172	D	D	6	151	D	D
Woodlawn CDP.............	17	54	NA	NA								
Wyndham CDP..............	7	27	NA	NA								
WASHINGTON	10,128	162,436	2,428	20,215	21,264	438,835	3,097	65,091	17,828	289,371	13,444	78,480
Aberdeen city...............	22	441	4	7	94	1,597	D	D	54	638	38	161
Anacortes city..............	30	185	3	21	78	1,573	12	79	60	855	63	332
Arlington city................	22	68	9	31	D	D	10	73	73	981	53	206
Artondale CDP..............	18	50	3	3	D	D	4	19	NA	NA	D	D
Auburn city..................	102	1,871	13	106	215	3,917	D	D	159	2,514	162	1,180
Bainbridge Island city......	47	255	22	101	106	1,092	32	347	63	769	52	403
Battle Ground city..........	23	93	4	15	60	675	4	32	54	912	40	211
Bellevue city................	350	18,795	175	1,683	1,053	15,245	89	2,418	512	10,576	443	3,020
Bellingham city.............	146	2,115	53	382	519	9,046	76	1,058	359	6,023	276	1,771
Bonney Lake city...........	17	102	4	34	46	546	5	34	51	1,022	D	D
Bothell city..................	78	1,412	22	226	174	2,487	17	414	143	2,270	82	500
Bothell East CDP...........	8	59	NA	NA	11	96	NA	NA	5	40	7	26
Bothell West CDP..........	17	39	NA	NA	23	103	NA	NA	D	D	10	50
Bremerton city..............	37	594	D	D	138	4,816	15	370	114	2,053	90	440
Bryn Mawr-Skyway CDP ..	7	42	NA	NA	19	150	D	D	9	91	12	26
Burien city..................	69	328	15	114	194	2,908	18	278	D	D	107	598
Camano CDP...............	21	45	NA	NA	D	D	3	39	16	107	15	39
Camas city..................	28	123	D	D	53	370	D	D	39	456	30	96
Centralia city...............	25	353	D	D	95	2,353	7	97	71	1,047	42	198
Cheney city.................	NA	NA	NA	NA	D	D	NA	NA	33	346	D	D

Table C. Incorporated Places, Census Designated Places (CDPs), and Minor Civil Divisions (MCDs) of 10,000 or More Population — **Economic Census**

STATE City, town, township, borough, or CDP (county if applicable)	Retail Trade — Number of establishments	Retail Trade — Number of employees	Wholesale trade[1] — Number of establishments	Wholesale trade[1] — Number of employees	Transportation and warehousing — Number of establishments	Transportation and warehousing — Number of employees	Information — Number of establishments	Information — Number of employees	Finance and insurance — Number of establishments	Finance and insurance — Number of employees	Real estate and rental and leasing — Number of establishments	Real estate and rental and leasing — Number of employees	Professional, scientific, and technical services — Number of establishments	Professional, scientific, and technical services — Number of employees
	1	2	3	4	5	6	7	8	9	10	11	12	13	14
WASHINGTON—Con.														
Cottage Lake CDP	18	241	23	53	NA	NA	D	D	D	D	38	46	98	196
Covington city	61	1,603	10	87	9	40	D	D	12	45	D	D	30	129
Des Moines city	40	303	12	237	22	109	D	D	21	87	30	71	31	123
Eastmont CDP	9	28	4	16	5	27	NA	NA	7	11	13	24	30	69
East Renton Highlands CDP	8	33	7	13	5	18	NA	NA	3	2	15	30	13	32
East Wenatchee city	71	1,548	11	154	6	23	5	156	27	138	19	55	20	132
Edgewood city	13	78	6	33	D	D	NA	NA	D	D	14	43	19	82
Edmonds city	132	1,902	43	176	21	69	22	156	99	521	D	D	213	1,061
Elk Plain CDP	7	192	NA	NA	3	3	NA	NA	NA	NA	NA	NA	D	D
Ellensburg city	106	1,411	22	133	19	94	10	122	40	192	39	90	41	207
Enumclaw city	59	748	10	69	10	40	D	D	D	D	19	79	29	106
Everett city	439	7,422	132	2,680	75	1,583	49	1,765	191	1,596	173	1,115	323	3,467
Fairwood CDP (King County)	15	233	7	12	3	3	D	D	10	54	D	D	28	57
Federal Way city	260	4,913	57	433	81	286	D	D	152	1,191	130	597	188	1,621
Ferndale city	45	489	23	287	14	222	5	10	18	91	19	51	23	166
Fife city	74	2,237	80	2,517	59	1,431	D	D	D	D	28	243	31	606
Five Corners CDP	31	537	D	D	D	D	3	5	D	D	9	17	17	39
Fort Lewis CDP	12	69	NA	NA	NA	NA	NA	NA	5	27	NA	NA	30	297
Frederickson CDP	18	260	6	36	17	71	NA	NA	D	D	8	32	11	38
Graham CDP	21	273	9	134	D	D	D	D	10	24	20	25	12	18
Grandview city	29	363	7	109	D	D	NA	NA	10	47	12	26	7	12
Hazel Dell CDP	82	1,532	13	95	20	172	11	91	D	D	41	167	73	574
Issaquah city	160	3,736	50	532	12	341	D	D	88	381	96	392	207	1,232
Kelso city	59	836	17	203	10	260	D	D	11	56	D	D	17	183
Kenmore city	39	446	19	108	D	D	D	D	21	66	30	53	74	171
Kennewick city	378	6,713	78	749	32	327	41	624	156	968	173	729	190	1,342
Kent city	343	7,603	407	10,147	268	5,971	D	D	119	1,324	196	985	246	2,534
Kirkland city	250	4,905	130	1,405	35	267	100	4,129	237	1,742	272	1,159	594	6,422
Lacey city	158	3,697	30	538	24	739	26	940	89	832	62	241	82	1,729
Lake Forest Park city	28	176	10	14	D	D	D	D	D	D	D	D	37	233
Lakeland North CDP	7	26	D	D	D	D	NA	NA	NA	NA	8	D	14	108
Lakeland South CDP	6	11	8	24	15	18	NA	NA	NA	NA	D	D	8	23
Lake Morton-Berrydale CDP	8	12	5	5	9	23	NA	NA	NA	NA	D	D	19	54
Lake Stevens city	46	893	13	48	11	38	8	32	D	D	38	167	29	85
Lake Stickney CDP	14	94	D	D	8	56	NA	NA	NA	NA	8	141	11	85
Lake Tapps CDP	13	74	7	29	D	D	NA	NA	6	7	27	46	16	21
Lakewood city	242	3,016	68	1,157	40	759	18	216	D	D	117	686	106	710
Longview city	174	3,223	42	568	23	308	20	202	71	644	70	263	71	448
Lynden city	68	813	14	376	14	163	4	39	36	249	26	115	53	211
Lynnwood city	411	8,806	84	822	21	80	37	1,185	169	1,531	103	398	191	2,320
Maltby CDP	24	455	29	513	10	40	NA	NA	D	D	15	180	38	112
Maple Valley city	49	923	10	59	15	122	D	D	26	105	22	32	47	174
Martha Lake CDP	23	108	4	34	8	25	NA	NA	D	D	19	54	27	54
Marysville city	179	3,699	38	355	14	72	23	250	55	325	72	240	67	281
Mercer Island city	36	488	30	115	8	38	D	D	75	980	D	D	150	510
Midland CDP	29	355	13	177	5	25	NA	NA	D	D	10	45	8	44
Mill Creek city	51	917	16	32	7	50	3	9	47	202	D	D	81	242
Mill Creek East CDP	17	109	9	47	D	D	D	D	D	D	D	D	40	120
Minnehaha CDP	10	143	6	53	11	22	D	D	3	10	6	18	15	63
Monroe city	90	1,446	31	350	D	D	8	64	D	D	21	67	36	161
Moses Lake city	135	2,036	47	436	26	387	15	150	55	289	45	128	57	266
Mountlake Terrace city	34	429	9	58	10	240	NA	NA	D	D	18	42	44	410
Mount Vernon city	132	2,168	40	604	19	315	15	156	63	361	53	148	103	540
Mukilteo city	35	287	65	640	11	107	10	55	33	196	35	D	90	662
Newcastle city	11	250	11	47	4	45	NA	NA	16	49	21	51	45	135
North Lynnwood CDP	35	489	15	55	7	14	3	9	D	D	22	64	29	101
Oak Harbor city	74	1,224	NA	NA	4	34	10	55	35	228	42	158	41	392
Olympia city	362	5,504	47	329	12	181	58	804	139	1,499	109	425	D	D
Orchards CDP	28	486	29	301	19	72	D	D	14	60	17	62	47	371
Parkland CDP	61	947	14	94	35	68	4	13	D	D	26	109	16	47
Pasco city	161	2,708	74	1,064	105	1,342	16	169	40	290	69	D	80	505
Port Angeles city	106	999	D	D	23	206	D	D	41	316	23	84	D	D
Port Orchard city	91	1,786	8	40	8	63	9	80	35	334	32	99	61	314
Poulsbo city	76	1,471	11	134	6	29	9	97	41	236	34	114	67	640
Pullman city	50	1,209	10	177	10	126	11	113	22	115	43	252	41	273
Puyallup city	216	5,482	42	571	39	2,019	17	614	88	741	112	431	118	885
Redmond city	249	4,497	154	3,422	20	1,707	D	D	109	1,069	171	1,051	487	11,054
Renton city	297	5,735	113	3,949	96	1,061	22	97	143	1,371	157	548	246	1,705
Richland city	162	2,726	26	298	25	473	22	97	63	770	102	298	203	6,935
Salmon Creek CDP	48	835	28	228	12	34	12	119	D	D	41	92	64	363
Sammamish city	60	680	43	84	D	D	D	D	47	120	D	D	255	701
SeaTac city	84	866	31	296	109	5,055	D	D	20	183	58	823	31	279
Seattle city	2,502	39,883	1,041	19,093	461	28,414	1,010	34,925	1,484	25,787	2,133	12,440	5,375	82,213
Sedro-Woolley city	36	340	6	55	D	D	NA	NA	9	D	24	46	15	73
Shelton city	49	928	5	46	5	15	6	47	24	226	18	49	24	105
Shoreline city	128	2,759	31	124	10	75	D	D	54	312	84	268	128	516
Silverdale CDP	183	3,586	9	68	D	D	15	139	81	484	D	D	90	797
Silver Firs CDP	10	66	D	D	NA	NA	NA	NA	D	D	22	54	25	90
Snohomish city	81	1,317	16	139	4	112	11	48	D	D	33	147	50	253
Snoqualmie city	24	115	8	88	NA	NA	D	D	14	50	D	D	52	192
South Hill CDP	76	1,890	12	75	40	73	11	57	D	D	62	147	44	225
Spanaway CDP	52	835	8	29	21	296	NA	NA	D	D	26	61	11	54
Spokane city	849	13,695	276	3,988	131	2,228	139	2,979	547	6,962	342	1,885	786	6,065
Spokane Valley city	482	8,405	212	3,496	90	1,800	50	420	193	1,751	147	892	200	1,291
Sumner city	53	2,280	55	1,980	49	2,558	NA	NA	D	D	26	181	32	256
Sunnyside city	73	1,079	16	248	16	165	10	75	19	154	20	64	21	130
Tacoma city	752	12,652	202	2,949	177	3,785	67	849	299	3,758	301	1,573	529	3,905

1 Merchant wholesalers, except manufacturers' sales branches and offices.

Table C. Incorporated Places, Census Designated Places (CDPs), and Minor Civil Divisions (MCDs) of 10,000 or More Population — **Economic Census**

STATE City, town, township, borough, or CDP (county if applicable)	Administration and support and waste management and mediation services — Number of establishments	Number of employees	Educational services — Number of establishments	Number of employees	Health care and social assistance — Number of establishments	Number of employees	Arts, entertainment, and recreation — Number of establishments	Number of employees	Accommodation and food services — Number of establishments	Number of employees	Other services (except public administration) — Number of establishments	Number of employees
	15	16	17	18	19	20	21	22	23	24	25	26
WASHINGTON—Con.												
Cottage Lake CDP	37	222	11	61	D	D	9	94	10	106	26	239
Covington city	16	94	NA	NA	54	425	NA	NA	45	844	34	223
Des Moines city	30	331	5	30	80	1,389	6	59	55	831	35	150
Eastmont CDP	15	31	NA	NA	25	100	NA	NA	4	17	D	D
East Renton Highlands CDP	16	59	4	35	14	64	D	D	D	D	7	23
East Wenatchee city	22	315	D	D	50	550	D	D	47	1,020	D	D
Edgewood city	21	168	NA	NA	15	154	NA	NA	7	100	14	72
Edmonds city	79	809	21	69	219	4,195	18	251	133	2,032	115	531
Elk Plain CDP	9	29	NA	NA	6	86	NA	NA	4	94	7	42
Ellensburg city	21	151	D	D	74	1,687	12	80	94	1,512	42	225
Enumclaw city	15	64	5	42	53	544	8	48	49	696	38	136
Everett city	156	3,864	D	D	444	14,553	39	645	377	5,036	253	1,966
Fairwood CDP (King County)	11	25	3	112	26	132	4	127	23	307	D	D
Federal Way city	129	1,431	31	227	367	6,243	37	693	242	3,796	154	694
Ferndale city	19	151	D	D	42	419	7	124	36	501	D	D
Fife city	37	951	NA	NA	D	D	D	D	50	1,940	D	D
Five Corners CDP	27	623	NA	NA	D	D	3	D	11	147	28	86
Fort Lewis CDP	7	86	NA	NA	D	D	NA	NA	11	141	8	61
Frederickson CDP	14	70	NA	NA	11	67	NA	NA	15	230	D	D
Graham CDP	19	44	3	15	24	194	3	38	19	192	20	74
Grandview city	4	21	NA	NA	15	340	NA	NA	15	124	D	D
Hazel Dell CDP	25	167	8	45	69	998	7	90	70	1,065	72	448
Issaquah city	59	1,891	43	324	234	4,383	25	828	130	2,324	106	828
Kelso city	14	104	D	D	36	593	7	D	32	639	23	123
Kenmore city	41	214	7	29	48	318	7	160	34	351	33	138
Kennewick city	111	2,806	17	169	302	5,911	28	584	214	3,894	160	963
Kent city	198	4,824	33	217	336	4,085	28	411	290	3,799	242	1,449
Kirkland city	159	2,689	61	466	427	9,426	59	1,002	240	4,007	237	1,286
Lacey city	56	744	10	121	148	2,832	D	D	139	2,366	100	685
Lake Forest Park city	18	66	4	12	26	158	4	D	12	199	15	86
Lakeland North CDP	20	105	NA	NA	15	40	NA	NA	5	36	4	17
Lakeland South CDP	13	61	NA	NA	11	97	NA	NA	3	37	7	19
Lake Morton-Berrydale CDP	14	83	4	6	6	53	3	67	3	37	4	21
Lake Stevens city	25	114	9	36	44	407	D	D	40	724	D	D
Lake Stickney CDP	13	155	NA	NA	9	197	NA	NA	D	D	4	18
Lake Tapps CDP	15	96	NA	NA	8	31	NA	NA	7	54	10	66
Lakewood city	77	708	14	106	218	5,847	24	875	180	2,568	131	801
Longview city	35	1,463	12	63	159	4,602	D	D	110	1,694	82	547
Lynden city	34	125	5	25	37	699	11	135	46	517	29	164
Lynnwood city	109	2,199	29	127	242	2,899	15	204	220	3,626	153	1,066
Maltby CDP	38	879	3	6	21	54	D	D	D	D	18	160
Maple Valley city	18	89	16	73	55	493	14	201	53	861	50	213
Martha Lake CDP	17	57	NA	NA	29	198	4	62	16	247	12	62
Marysville city	56	485	14	90	134	1,625	14	201	123	1,795	113	505
Mercer Island city	41	131	32	141	93	959	20	390	36	581	48	170
Midland CDP	21	785	NA	NA	11	91	NA	NA	23	308	31	162
Mill Creek city	34	407	6	44	90	1,056	13	160	D	D	D	D
Mill Creek East CDP	19	118	8	25	13	108	D	D	D	D	D	D
Minnehaha CDP	14	184	NA	NA	D	D	NA	NA	6	55	D	D
Monroe city	23	126	6	41	D	D	8	145	D	D	55	244
Moses Lake city	29	851	6	80	103	2,159	10	208	83	1,471	66	271
Mountlake Terrace city	28	202	8	D	53	679	11	630	D	D	24	95
Mount Vernon city	47	742	16	128	151	4,991	16	359	94	1,312	83	352
Mukilteo city	35	260	8	91	64	581	10	146	61	753	48	214
Newcastle city	18	59	5	14	23	158	6	D	D	D	12	62
North Lynnwood CDP	13	93	NA	NA	20	354	NA	NA	25	300	31	237
Oak Harbor city	26	160	D	D	77	953	D	D	64	966	48	236
Olympia city	83	1,364	31	220	475	10,295	31	505	221	3,978	205	1,473
Orchards CDP	28	171	4	37	40	417	4	5	20	279	D	D
Parkland CDP	28	416	6	24	49	448	5	83	D	D	D	D
Pasco city	75	882	D	D	126	1,987	D	D	105	1,625	D	D
Port Angeles city	32	167	D	D	122	2,759	15	74	90	1,126	57	287
Port Orchard city	13	93	7	39	75	1,364	6	93	79	1,053	50	240
Poulsbo city	25	159	D	D	77	1,647	D	D	62	902	38	155
Pullman city	13	92	5	50	72	1,467	D	D	98	1,651	40	179
Puyallup city	55	858	17	130	213	5,725	20	640	149	3,139	118	918
Redmond city	106	3,148	60	427	250	3,359	37	692	295	5,942	162	1,043
Renton city	143	2,992	38	383	362	8,124	24	904	282	4,099	189	1,039
Richland city	61	4,525	20	144	242	5,653	32	652	156	3,019	89	553
Salmon Creek CDP	39	309	7	159	64	678	8	36	47	718	D	D
Sammamish city	60	454	43	390	99	700	23	463	40	658	37	182
SeaTac city	46	1,012	NA	NA	42	1,090	3	599	113	3,690	73	836
Seattle city	1,307	23,589	502	5,610	2,912	85,733	591	12,795	3,159	58,136	2,080	15,523
Sedro-Woolley city	6	39	D	D	36	703	NA	NA	32	350	18	82
Shelton city	8	8	D	D	61	1,274	D	D	D	D	28	126
Shoreline city	74	678	22	153	217	2,973	31	823	102	1,139	89	448
Silverdale CDP	32	305	8	68	161	2,221	9	508	100	2,070	61	425
Silver Firs CDP	29	145	NA	NA	18	111	D	D	14	194	9	39
Snohomish city	27	270	5	63	56	635	6	11	64	890	49	272
Snoqualmie city	18	95	10	131	D	D	9	220	33	490	19	86
South Hill CDP	39	238	D	D	106	1,393	D	D	67	1,758	D	D
Spanaway CDP	18	75	NA	NA	32	207	3	42	32	544	D	D
Spokane city	290	4,667	77	545	956	29,351	95	1,696	642	12,036	458	2,736
Spokane Valley city	209	4,606	23	194	374	7,637	32	463	226	3,918	207	1,477
Sumner city	28	1,611	D	D	32	420	D	D	44	698	D	D
Sunnyside city	15	118	6	23	67	1,513	D	D	38	540	21	90
Tacoma city	360	7,576	46	386	673	27,464	77	2,714	541	9,576	453	3,393

STATE City, town, township, borough, or CDP (county if applicable)	Retail Trade Number of establishments	Number of employees	Wholesale trade[1] Number of establishments	Number of employees	Transportation and warehousing Number of establishments	Number of employees	Information Number of establishments	Number of employees	Finance and insurance Number of establishments	Number of employees	Real estate and rental and leasing Number of establishments	Number of employees	Professional, scientific, and technical services Number of establishments	Number of employees
	1	2	3	4	5	6	7	8	9	10	11	12	13	14
WASHINGTON—Con.														
Tukwila city	289	7,430	175	3,192	94	2,582	D	D	62	1,377	99	1,162	136	1,964
Tumwater city	87	1,843	46	692	20	519	10	103	48	281	53	164	71	356
Union Hill-Novelty Hill CDP	17	195	9	27	NA	NA	D	D	15	61	29	D	96	262
University Place city	45	848	7	57	12	19	4	16	D	D	D	D	73	243
Vancouver city	588	12,125	203	2,268	171	2,115	137	2,793	411	3,461	347	1,708	608	4,989
Vashon CDP	37	429	3	7	6	40	D	D	11	43	13	36	69	158
Walla Walla city	132	1,505	30	161	11	83	16	277	65	582	44	154	81	412
Washougal city	30	379	12	196	12	95	3	3	13	54	D	D	31	113
Wenatchee city	199	2,992	64	1,157	22	246	28	327	87	548	62	264	127	812
West Richland city	12	146	D	D	3	26	NA	NA	D	D	D	D	28	54
White Center CDP	37	490	5	23	D	D	NA	NA	D	D	8	18	13	66
Woodinville city	86	1,563	70	1,667	10	119	D	D	39	149	43	102	96	921
Yakima city	344	5,794	103	2,417	60	463	40	652	160	1,158	163	746	215	1,522
WEST VIRGINIA	5,963	82,985	1,205	14,578	1,181	15,094	677	10,196	2,087	16,270	1,432	6,061	2,813	22,856
Beckley city	145	2,652	31	264	13	128	D	D	51	299	29	145	60	277
Charleston city	302	5,318	101	1,097	32	886	88	1,927	253	3,232	129	607	368	3,580
Clarksburg city	95	1,920	31	418	14	188	11	235	40	221	12	25	66	616
Fairmont city	87	940	26	270	D	D	D	D	45	279	23	59	81	768
Huntington city	209	2,884	65	901	15	155	28	1,058	96	855	72	358	138	1,534
Martinsburg city	106	2,416	10	116	D	D	14	240	47	338	32	93	80	325
Morgantown city	233	4,421	24	218	16	118	28	403	82	593	73	342	131	1,879
Parkersburg city	183	3,194	39	357	26	268	21	480	76	628	48	212	80	524
St. Albans city	47	794	D	D	3	19	D	D	21	120	14	41	21	118
South Charleston city	82	1,387	26	314	10	429	D	D	33	323	10	54	42	385
Teays Valley CDP	24	431	8	159	NA	NA	3	139	20	119	9	21	26	215
Vienna city	86	2,011	4	35	NA	NA	D	D	21	203	10	45	15	46
Weirton city	67	1,101	D	D	D	D	D	D	D	D	18	89	37	298
Wheeling city	138	1,595	57	1,099	D	D	D	D	72	1,230	48	D	128	1,957
WISCONSIN	18,908	317,668	5,934	104,382	5,635	104,143	2,634	59,134	8,972	146,594	4,956	27,163	11,553	106,041
Allouez village	14	208	D	D	9	137	3	14	D	D	16	135	30	350
Appleton city	278	4,874	96	1,479	41	787	41	1,372	190	5,000	D	D	166	1,617
Ashwaubenon village	220	4,032	82	1,970	58	1,295	17	333	90	1,972	31	294	86	1,035
Baraboo city	111	1,868	D	D	11	138	12	69	29	222	18	80	39	429
Beaver Dam city	82	1,606	9	118	13	942	12	120	46	281	17	45	28	212
Bellevue village	56	1,744	8	62	17	436	D	D	32	219	11	29	30	274
Beloit city	104	1,761	19	352	21	669	16	344	37	440	19	141	41	1,084
Brookfield city	271	5,303	109	1,689	22	1,136	55	3,688	278	5,250	111	1,494	314	4,513
Brown Deer village	31	861	14	393	10	23	D	D	16	307	7	20	22	133
Burlington city	57	1,292	17	183	8	155	D	D	34	183	9	17	28	267
Caledonia village	45	556	14	165	24	236	3	3	21	96	12	54	35	133
Cedarburg city	60	658	12	132	NA	NA	8	30	D	D	14	38	47	359
Chippewa Falls city	82	2,390	13	221	D	D	9	90	37	212	D	D	47	430
Cudahy city	34	487	14	124	42	837	NA	NA	14	95	16	40	16	43
DeForest village	19	364	18	238	7	982	D	D	15	112	5	28	21	79
De Pere city	64	1,327	43	1,034	21	380	7	51	D	D	22	122	72	733
Eau Claire city	318	6,459	88	1,472	51	831	40	951	161	2,694	96	541	151	1,328
Fitchburg city	52	999	28	1,002	14	97	D	D	53	326	44	233	86	567
Fond du Lac city	197	4,289	47	858	29	452	D	D	92	1,315	28	228	74	1,201
Fort Atkinson city	46	680	13	540	17	267	13	401	29	204	13	40	24	181
Fox Crossing village	13	128	17	126	19	815	D	D	D	D	7	20	18	315
Franklin city	79	2,312	41	409	41	723	12	130	34	138	29	130	61	416
Germantown village	52	1,410	53	1,637	17	239	D	D	D	D	D	D	59	375
Glendale city	110	2,445	26	742	11	250	20	251	54	698	D	D	110	1,653
Grafton village	52	1,207	11	68	5	25	5	69	D	D	D	D	35	146
Grand Chute town	292	6,376	65	839	23	297	21	369	71	877	42	269	107	1,154
Green Bay city	313	5,673	114	3,378	87	6,455	48	1,028	193	2,124	87	637	212	2,075
Greendale village	105	2,062	8	54	6	23	D	D	16	93	D	D	23	141
Greenfield city	152	3,181	13	80	22	112	D	D	63	520	44	198	77	707
Greenville town	24	191	26	461	18	1,475	4	17	D	D	13	63	25	195
Harrison village	4	21	D	D	4	24	NA	NA	4	9	4	2	11	22
Hartford city	48	795	D	D	13	202	10	90	D	D	6	16	18	374
Howard village	61	1,085	26	284	20	393	D	D	D	D	16	112	32	307
Hudson city	86	2,383	32	651	14	678	16	170	D	D	29	68	74	452
Janesville city	276	6,749	71	1,740	54	1,532	36	1,080	104	662	62	225	101	837
Kaukauna city	36	785	23	459	15	368	NA	NA	19	154	11	98	15	150
Kenosha city	290	9,394	53	897	68	1,770	18	177	126	676	72	375	136	717
La Crosse city	243	4,846	56	1,406	48	1,640	45	1,588	110	1,036	87	915	152	1,406
Lisbon town	7	42	D	D	12	123	NA	NA	17	130	7	13	14	54
Little Chute village	29	271	14	209	NA	NA	NA	NA	17	130	5	20	11	406
Madison city	946	19,081	271	5,246	91	2,597	248	6,015	492	18,410	416	3,311	1,074	15,405
Manitowoc city	142	2,614	23	364	22	220	16	145	64	549	D	D	53	400
Marinette city	88	1,350	10	73	12	374	7	104	29	226	8	18	30	174
Marshfield city	116	2,366	24	662	D	D	D	D	59	876	20	66	36	331
Menasha city	43	401	9	93	5	291	D	D	D	D	9	54	26	202
Menomonee Falls village	124	2,867	90	1,597	31	705	16	698	67	1,438	23	422	96	891
Menomonie city	74	1,573	11	348	20	1,321	D	D	44	369	21	104	42	298
Mequon city	92	1,297	62	915	12	113	18	207	101	1,434	D	D	148	823
Middleton city	103	2,876	53	955	10	580	35	1,170	104	1,640	59	521	147	3,210
Milwaukee city	D	D	439	11,197	327	7,615	252	6,526	710	33,362	471	3,767	1,148	17,420
Monroe city	82	1,985	18	219	18	117	D	D	36	209	20	41	27	288
Mount Pleasant village	81	1,782	17	262	18	247	D	D	54	781	27	135	59	414
Muskego city	42	808	30	352	18	268	NA	NA	30	170	18	50	53	145
Neenah city	83	1,904	17	561	12	206	8	47	52	969	24	167	50	562
New Berlin city	99	2,076	112	2,516	41	1,214	20	527	60	921	39	125	122	2,110
Oak Creek city	88	2,244	39	2,298	73	2,617	9	104	48	436	27	358	48	399

1 Merchant wholesalers, except manufacturers' sales branches and offices.

Table C. Incorporated Places, Census Designated Places (CDPs), and Minor Civil Divisions (MCDs) of 10,000 or More Population — Economic Census

STATE City, town, township, borough, or CDP (county if applicable)	Administration and support and waste management and mediation services — Number of establishments	Number of employees	Educational services — Number of establishments	Number of employees	Health care and social assistance — Number of establishments	Number of employees	Arts, entertainment, and recreation — Number of establishments	Number of employees	Accommodation and food services — Number of establishments	Number of employees	Other services (except public administration) — Number of establishments	Number of employees
	15	16	17	18	19	20	21	22	23	24	25	26
WASHINGTON—Con.												
Tukwila city	72	2,593	11	165	111	2,014	17	1,047	147	4,003	74	562
Tumwater city	33	279	7	66	105	1,179	11	231	71	1,107	64	401
Union Hill-Novelty Hill CDP	31	850	5	59	35	443	10	67	16	173	D	D
University Place city	35	225	11	73	100	1,095	D	D	40	697	60	262
Vancouver city	289	12,395	61	563	693	15,603	62	1,091	494	8,677	404	2,443
Vashon CDP	29	103	8	49	38	266	17	141	21	330	32	93
Walla Walla city	41	265	NA	NA	127	4,493	16	319	112	1,801	71	324
Washougal city	D	D	5	22	22	189	5	38	25	265	18	94
Wenatchee city	54	432	17	110	154	5,506	19	245	129	1,974	109	452
West Richland city	11	32	NA	NA	17	171	3	29	13	81	8	22
White Center CDP	19	228	NA	NA	38	393	7	163	39	305	36	134
Woodinville city	47	1,550	24	255	D	D	11	197	77	1,503	68	391
Yakima city	83	2,129	D	D	374	10,187	40	816	244	4,118	177	1,101
WEST VIRGINIA	1,473	33,540	181	1,136	4,869	132,627	775	6,681	3,614	68,102	2,524	14,894
Beckley city	25	1,486	D	D	177	4,615	13	165	87	1,932	D	D
Charleston city	149	4,505	22	153	369	12,200	43	803	222	4,558	205	1,383
Clarksburg city	20	339	D	D	62	1,704	14	109	75	1,432	42	269
Fairmont city	17	481	10	D	88	1,903	D	D	65	1,041	51	362
Huntington city	64	2,442	NA	NA	NA	NA	28	561	189	3,616	86	503
Martinsburg city	29	338	NA	NA	116	3,065	D	D	88	1,965	47	322
Morgantown city	49	2,124	9	58	135	10,407	31	279	225	4,566	81	652
Parkersburg city	47	1,446	D	D	176	5,377	27	348	120	2,298	97	604
St. Albans city	D	D	NA	NA	33	287	7	24	29	450	D	D
South Charleston city	29	1,074	4	21	104	2,889	7	36	65	1,287	D	D
Teays Valley CDP	11	112	NA	NA	28	722	NA	NA	17	230	13	48
Vienna city	10	71	NA	NA	43	770	8	32	39	869	D	D
Weirton city	22	195	NA	NA	NA	NA	D	D	59	935	25	112
Wheeling city	44	1,786	NA	NA	NA	NA	31	358	97	2,162	98	893
WISCONSIN	7,372	158,452	1,161	9,782	15,983	417,365	2,809	47,048	14,840	244,099	10,351	63,120
Allouez village	12	233	NA	NA	56	1,590	7	D	21	317	21	144
Appleton city	88	3,667	24	237	296	9,061	31	1,106	217	4,163	139	1,292
Ashwaubenon village	52	2,457	17	210	91	2,358	23	1,008	105	2,790	74	735
Baraboo city	15	260	NA	NA	48	1,534	7	30	44	1,909	39	138
Beaver Dam city	15	257	D	D	77	1,784	12	290	52	880	32	124
Bellevue village	18	148	NA	NA	49	891	9	D	35	609	D	D
Beloit city	19	664	4	D	63	2,108	D	D	95	1,738	50	254
Brookfield city	113	2,813	25	323	388	5,085	33	709	130	3,419	136	1,163
Brown Deer village	16	754	NA	NA	61	963	D	D	30	549	D	D
Burlington city	15	137	4	15	64	1,655	7	48	45	709	D	D
Caledonia village	26	228	NA	NA	28	359	9	66	D	D	30	244
Cedarburg city	20	177	7	64	D	D	14	97	38	568	D	D
Chippewa Falls city	22	288	D	D	67	1,420	9	196	67	870	D	D
Cudahy city	21	428	NA	NA	31	1,028	6	107	28	329	D	D
DeForest village	10	76	4	28	16	187	3	15	15	271	D	D
De Pere city	28	515	9	30	51	850	D	D	70	1,062	41	313
Eau Claire city	117	2,992	D	D	269	8,306	41	1,034	229	4,861	141	1,045
Fitchburg city	33	305	15	243	59	2,084	19	403	45	984	41	471
Fond du Lac city	44	1,465	D	D	199	5,515	19	473	116	2,144	92	634
Fort Atkinson city	15	447	NA	NA	71	2,518	10	329	38	457	33	166
Fox Crossing village	22	846	NA	NA	27	711	6	89	8	100	D	D
Franklin city	41	386	D	D	115	2,156	19	196	64	1,110	52	568
Germantown village	47	648	7	63	42	755	9	17	47	970	36	253
Glendale city	48	643	11	76	154	3,408	10	395	57	1,478	48	361
Grafton village	15	56	D	D	39	618	9	116	32	594	24	122
Grand Chute town	D	D	15	110	90	1,966	D	D	118	2,948	83	627
Green Bay city	124	2,489	16	91	331	16,466	44	D	255	5,340	164	1,003
Greendale village	8	1,749	NA	NA	22	397	D	D	36	551	D	D
Greenfield city	46	878	4	83	154	2,823	14	418	70	1,987	76	451
Greenville town	17	311	5	46	D	D	5	D	12	208	21	368
Harrison village	13	113	NA	NA	5	12	D	D	7	208	D	D
Hartford city	12	86	5	55	38	1,140	D	D	37	641	D	D
Howard village	39	443	NA	NA	48	587	D	D	43	900	46	196
Hudson city	28	777	9	41	88	1,101	D	D	75	1,867	52	363
Janesville city	66	1,440	12	46	186	5,385	27	436	165	3,467	121	685
Kaukauna city	19	146	3	D	25	552	D	D	28	333	31	164
Kenosha city	78	2,920	8	42	345	7,213	23	495	229	4,304	153	1,037
La Crosse city	70	1,846	14	61	186	9,192	45	912	227	4,549	121	989
Lisbon town	10	158	NA	NA	4	50	7	131	NA	NA	12	47
Little Chute village	7	473	NA	NA	D	D	D	D	29	473	15	82
Madison city	342	9,189	113	1,026	741	39,689	156	2,474	808	17,393	645	5,782
Manitowoc city	38	973	D	D	124	3,288	15	341	99	1,559	72	310
Marinette city	12	183	NA	NA	65	1,585	4	64	50	681	29	132
Marshfield city	15	326	NA	NA	95	5,819	D	D	71	1,087	48	323
Menasha city	22	500	NA	NA	39	1,031	8	D	40	497	21	281
Menomonee Falls village	69	1,025	D	D	82	4,159	22	486	72	1,570	71	672
Menomonie city	13	712	D	D	72	2,038	11	26	68	1,229	39	244
Mequon city	73	610	D	D	149	3,427	28	519	49	1,144	69	452
Middleton city	46	1,863	14	138	82	1,100	13	360	85	1,958	51	361
Milwaukee city	971	29,621	104	1,241	1,744	61,852	164	6,049	1,229	26,656	846	6,350
Monroe city	20	444	D	D	47	1,746	12	144	44	616	D	D
Mount Pleasant village	33	440	4	28	124	2,099	6	155	64	1,435	D	D
Muskego city	53	790	7	63	39	642	11	105	42	643	51	243
Neenah city	27	2,017	6	D	93	1,554	17	479	87	1,283	55	370
New Berlin city	73	1,743	D	D	105	2,009	21	593	63	1,410	76	834
Oak Creek city	32	316	8	89	71	714	12	80	73	1,672	50	303

Table C. Incorporated Places, Census Designated Places (CDPs), and Minor Civil Divisions (MCDs) of 10,000 or More Population — **Economic Census**

STATE City, town, township, borough, or CDP (county if applicable)	Retail Trade — Number of establishments (1)	Number of employees (2)	Wholesale trade[1] — Number of establishments (3)	Number of employees (4)	Transportation and warehousing — Number of establishments (5)	Number of employees (6)	Information — Number of establishments (7)	Number of employees (8)	Finance and insurance — Number of establishments (9)	Number of employees (10)	Real estate and rental and leasing — Number of establishments (11)	Number of employees (12)	Professional, scientific, and technical services — Number of establishments (13)	Number of employees (14)
WISCONSIN—Con.														
Oconomowoc city	77	1,240	21	185	12	1,377	6	26	43	460	23	98	47	162
Onalaska city	91	2,998	D	D	12	91	D	D	70	866	20	66	34	230
Oregon village	24	354	6	17	NA	NA	D	D	14	119	11	35	22	93
Oshkosh city	259	5,404	50	1,091	41	1,073	31	832	97	1,265	60	366	95	1,604
Pewaukee city	42	391	102	1,660	17	293	20	843	80	2,403	37	329	129	1,675
Platteville city	56	1,209	D	D	D	D	8	85	27	275	23	81	13	263
Pleasant Prairie village	133	2,663	24	701	29	648	D	D	8	73	18	67	46	273
Plover village	69	1,799	14	298	15	406	D	D	29	110	D	D	19	176
Portage city	57	946	13	141	10	91	8	101	29	117	13	115	28	281
Port Washington city	26	288	7	D	9	73	D	D	18	201	10	14	29	549
Racine city	240	3,126	47	411	28	780	18	344	50	606	D	D	101	657
Richfield village	28	461	14	122	D	D	4	5	D	D	10	25	26	61
River Falls city	42	608	5	94	5	3	6	44	D	D	D	D	36	399
Sheboygan city	171	3,226	42	889	16	327	13	191	87	1,709	31	112	85	690
Shorewood village	35	547	D	D	3	20	NA	NA	20	74	19	116	39	160
South Milwaukee city	23	440	5	10	16	31	NA	NA	12	67	9	42	14	45
Stevens Point city	113	1,947	24	372	22	1,143	25	292	78	5,332	27	122	61	451
Stoughton city	41	546	16	243	6	135	D	D	23	83	17	66	25	154
Suamico village	23	535	7	20	13	97	D	D	8	49	6	25	15	35
Sun Prairie city	78	1,923	32	901	18	429	D	D	59	379	38	155	89	516
Superior city	117	2,027	38	652	33	1,163	D	D	48	353	31	D	58	365
Sussex village	25	756	20	497	8	128	NA	NA	15	174	4	8	19	189
Two Rivers city	38	472	4	75	8	143	NA	NA	18	93	7	20	9	19
Verona city	32	495	23	587	8	128	D	D	27	115	4	4	63	482
Watertown city	79	1,402	19	521	17	307	D	D	45	209	14	82	29	193
Waukesha city	233	5,326	103	2,200	47	2,097	28	560	119	1,093	58	539	170	1,218
Waunakee village	33	342	13	441	8	144	D	D	19	98	15	45	57	234
Waupun city	31	386	4	61	D	D	NA	NA	20	99	10	14	12	65
Wausau city	175	5,863	47	692	71	2,002	22	391	126	4,293	42	208	121	865
Wauwatosa city	291	5,783	56	1,110	24	543	38	934	141	2,135	51	222	240	2,106
West Allis city	228	4,008	99	2,156	39	691	31	335	83	1,344	50	255	86	863
West Bend city	132	2,525	29	218	23	369	16	102	D	D	D	D	58	534
Weston village	46	621	31	701	17	199	3	13	D	D	14	69	20	84
Whitefish Bay village	26	366	6	11	NA	NA	6	29	15	79	15	33	36	67
Whitewater city	35	560	9	344	5	15	5	15	20	159	13	114	21	85
Wisconsin Rapids city	110	1,742	11	85	15	286	D	D	D	D	27	121	49	251
WYOMING	2,583	29,786	696	5,967	943	9,892	401	4,268	1,070	7,015	1,199	4,777	2,395	9,589
Casper city	291	4,198	92	1,039	79	716	26	395	137	908	138	551	216	1,190
Cheyenne city	324	5,039	95	626	89	2,709	88	1,400	220	1,834	145	577	520	2,272
Evanston city	63	838	10	85	17	217	D	D	23	130	23	79	32	159
Gillette city	151	2,171	60	699	54	845	D	D	43	354	72	328	103	486
Green River city	33	300	4	23	6	50	7	62	D	D	11	35	28	98
Jackson town	200	1,660	14	70	25	184	38	274	76	472	119	385	235	735
Laramie city	117	1,647	16	147	15	133	18	83	D	D	D	D	117	656
Riverton city	71	1,057	22	141	17	133	14	170	37	196	33	108	49	261
Rock Springs city	122	1,886	41	330	45	643	15	91	37	214	50	554	71	285
Sheridan city	136	1,639	18	83	14	106	D	D	D	D	46	136	136	696

1 Merchant wholesalers, except manufacturers' sales branches and offices.

Table C. Incorporated Places, Census Designated Places (CDPs), and Minor Civil Divisions (MCDs) of 10,000 or More Population — **Economic Census**

	Economic activity by sector, 2017											
	Administration and support and waste management and mediation services		Educational services		Health care and social assistance		Arts, entertainment, and recreation		Accommodation and food services		Other services (except public administration)	
STATE City, town, township, borough, or CDP (county if applicable)	Number of establish-ments	Number of employees	Number of establish-ments	Number of employees	Number of establish-ments	Number of employees	Number of establish-ments	Number of employees	Number of establish-ments	Number of employees	Number of establish-ments	Number of employees
	15	16	17	18	19	20	21	22	23	24	25	26
WISCONSIN—Con.												
Oconomowoc city	15	49	8	52	101	2,764	13	511	61	999	30	146
Onalaska city	19	850	6	83	84	2,100	9	374	54	1,515	46	402
Oregon village	10	39	5	41	28	320	6	54	19	303	17	65
Oshkosh city	49	1,180	13	121	201	5,961	34	606	200	4,194	100	870
Pewaukee city	37	877	9	159	65	1,320	12	171	33	759	36	589
Platteville city	14	260	NA	NA	39	877	NA	NA	42	805	29	92
Pleasant Prairie village	27	523	6	55	41	1,762	4	23	41	1,027	12	105
Plover village	13	169	3	10	37	458	7	26	43	835	D	D
Portage city	15	211	NA	NA	52	1,558	5	24	48	690	36	176
Port Washington city	13	136	D	D	D	D	7	D	35	600	D	D
Racine city	63	1,573	D	D	207	5,788	35	294	D	D	119	786
Richfield village...............	16	256	NA	NA	8	85	8	77	19	417	D	D
River Falls city	11	260	D	D	45	854	8	44	49	747	31	142
Sheboygan city	48	1,088	5	15	196	4,863	22	491	140	2,347	100	523
Shorewood village	11	329	4	25	39	475	12	46	33	679	22	111
South Milwaukee city	16	153	NA	NA	41	868	NA	NA	39	375	D	D
Stevens Point city	41	717	D	D	133	3,890	20	611	121	1,912	63	384
Stoughton city.................	18	92	4	37	43	1,094	8	94	35	507	34	185
Suamico village	18	111	NA	NA	24	203	5	D	D	D	D	D
Sun Prairie city	34	307	11	70	75	1,486	D	D	73	1,429	64	391
Superior city	29	389	D	D	94	1,776	D	D	100	1,528	D	D
Sussex village.................	11	50	D	D	28	484	6	54	18	282	D	D
Two Rivers city................	6	29	NA	NA	22	787	D	D	22	D	D	D
Verona city	24	435	7	50	37	603	9	44	41	677	25	105
Watertown city	24	333	NA	NA	91	1,581	15	148	59	770	51	617
Waukesha city.................	101	2,792	20	188	275	6,515	37	807	163	2,998	138	957
Waunakee village	25	354	10	103	32	413	14	84	27	497	27	96
Waupun city	NA	NA	NA	NA	29	556	D	D	22	350	D	D
Wausau city	46	1,168	17	110	232	7,274	27	476	117	2,122	75	425
Wauwatosa city	127	14,686	21	254	384	12,197	26	674	155	3,902	104	808
West Allis city	95	7,243	12	72	233	8,225	11	345	163	2,383	119	828
West Bend city	31	934	5	D	120	1,658	18	459	72	1,479	84	582
Weston village	21	766	NA	NA	49	1,750	10	312	34	460	D	D
Whitefish Bay village	D	D	D	D	35	659	7	18	13	214	25	116
Whitewater city	D	D	NA	NA	25	426	4	10	44	892	22	66
Wisconsin Rapids city.......	24	355	D	D	99	2,204	D	D	68	944	54	366
WYOMING......................	1,080	6,893	159	1,115	2,001	33,540	445	4,791	1,839	27,248	1,368	6,245
Casper city.....................	131	1,065	19	D	317	5,458	35	327	158	3,086	160	826
Cheyenne city	172	1,459	24	96	322	6,534	31	448	181	3,277	176	1,042
Evanston city	6	36	NA	NA	57	1,210	D	D	40	517	21	48
Gillette city	50	484	D	D	107	2,083	16	148	99	1,713	86	475
Green River city	D	D	NA	NA	18	237	D	D	26	409	19	98
Jackson town..................	90	567	21	D	110	1,366	50	393	111	2,518	89	436
Laramie city....................	40	264	D	D	D	D	D	D	95	1,617	70	326
Riverton city....................	14	41	NA	NA	60	600	4	25	54	679	D	D
Rock Springs city.............	32	229	D	D	84	1,245	D	D	81	1,296	45	244
Sheridan city...................	36	118	D	D	D	D	14	191	78	1,277	63	223

APPENDIX A
GEOGRAPHIC CONCEPTS

This volume presents data for places and Minor Civil Divisions (MCDs). These two types of geographic areas are similar and often represent the same location. Although they are presented separately in most data sources, this volume combines them to simplify analysis in the twelve states where MCDs serve as general-purpose local governments.

Table A includes data for all places and MCDs, regardless of size. Table B and Table C include incorporated places, census designated places (CDPs) and MCDs with a 2010 census population of 10,000 or more, or a population of 10,000 or more as estimated in the 5-year American Community Survey (ACS)

The places for which data are presented in this volume include incorporated places, Census Designated Places (CDPs), consolidated cities, minor civil divisions (MCDs), and Economic Census Places.

Incorporated Places

Incorporated places included in this volume are generally those reported to the Census Bureau as being legally in existence on January 1, 2019, under the laws of their respective states as cities, boroughs, municipalities, towns, and villages, with the following exceptions: the towns in the New England states, New York, and Wisconsin and the boroughs in New York are recognized as minor civil divisions (MCDs) for decennial census purposes; the boroughs in Alaska are county equivalents for decennial census statistical presentation purposes. There are a few incorporated places that do not have a legal description. An incorporated place is established to provide governmental functions for a concentration of people, as opposed to a minor civil division, which generally is created to provide services or administer a geographic area without regard, necessarily, to population. Places always are within a single state or equivalent entity, but may extend across county and county subdivision boundaries. MCDs are sometimes called County Subdivisions and each MCD is wholly within a named county. When an incorporated place extends across county boundaries, there are several MCDs within that single incorporated city, sometimes with zero populations.

Census Designated Place (CDP)

Census designated places (CDPs) are delineated for each decennial census as the statistical counterparts of incorporated places. CDPs are delineated to provide census data for concentrations of population, housing, and commercial structures that are identifiable by name but not legally incorporated under the laws of the state in which they are located. CDP boundaries usually are defined in cooperation with state, local, and tribal officials. These boundaries, which usually coincide with visible features or the boundary of an adjacent incorporated place or other legal entity boundary, have no legal status, nor any officials elected to serve traditional municipal functions. CDP boundaries may change from one decennial census to the next with changes in the settlement pattern; a CDP with the same name as a CDP in an earlier census does not necessarily have the same boundary. The ACS includes CDPs, generally the same as those in the 2010 census, but some have become incorporated places.[1] Other data sources sometimes have different definitions of places and towns and may include places that the Census Bureau has categorized as CDPs. However, CDPs are generally not included in other data sources.

Beginning with the 2000 census, CDPs did not need to meet a minimum population threshold to qualify for tabulation of census data. For the 1990 census and earlier censuses, the Census Bureau required CDPs to qualify on the basis of various minimum population size criteria.

Hawaii is the only state that has no incorporated places recognized by the U.S. Census Bureau. All places shown in the data products for Hawaii are CDPs. Honolulu county was divided into Urban Honolulu CDP and East Honolulu CDP for the first time in the 2010 census.

Consolidated City

A consolidated city is a unit of local government for which the functions of an incorporated place and its county or MCD have merged. The legal aspects of this action may result in both the primary incorporated place and the county or MCD continuing to exist as legal entities, even though the county or MCD performs few or no governmental functions and has few or no elected officials. In places where this occurs, and in places where one or more other incorporated places in the county or MCD continue to function as separate governments (even though they have been included

---

1 For lists of places that have changed since the 2010 census, see https://www.census.gov/programs-surveys/acs/technical-documentation/table-and-geography-changes.html

in the consolidated government), the primary incorporated place is referred to as a consolidated city.

This volume contains data for eight consolidated cities: Milford, CT; Athens-Clarke County, GA; Augusta-Richmond County, GA; Greeley County Unified Government, KS; Indianapolis, IN; Louisville/Jefferson County, KY; Butte-Silver Bow, MT; and Nashville-Davidson, TN.

Within the consolidated city, there is usually a large core city that is the principal city of the consolidated city. This principal city is referred to as the "balance" in census tabulations. Table A and Table B include both the consolidated city and the "balance". Some data sources include both, while others are not clear about which entity is identified.

Minor Civil Division (MCD)

The primary political divisions of most states are termed counties. Minor civil divisions (MCDs) are the primary governmental or administrative divisions of a county in many states (parish in Louisiana). MCDs represent many different kinds of legal entities with a wide variety of governmental and/or administrative functions. MCDs are variously designated as American Indian reservations, assessment districts, boroughs, charter townships, election districts, election precincts, gores, grants, locations, magisterial districts, parish governing authority districts, plantations, precincts, purchases, road districts, supervisors' districts, towns, townships, and unorganized territories. In some states, all or some incorporated places are not located in any MCD (independent places) and thus serve as MCDs in their own right. In other states, incorporated places are part of the MCDs in which they are located (dependent places), or the pattern is mixed—some incorporated places are independent of MCDs and others are included within one or more MCDs. In Maine and New York, there are American Indian reservations and off-reservation trust lands that serve

as MCD equivalents; a separate MCD is created when the American Indian area crosses a county boundary.

The MCDs in 12 states (Connecticut, Maine, Massachusetts, Michigan, Minnesota, New Hampshire, New Jersey, New York, Pennsylvania, Rhode Island, Vermont, and Wisconsin) also serve as general-purpose local governments that typically can perform the same governmental functions as incorporated places. The Census Bureau presents data for these MCDs in all data products providing information for places. In this volume, MCDs are included for these 12 states.

The name of each MCD is followed by its county name in parentheses. Where an MCD is co-extensive with an incorporated place or a CDP, only a single listing is included, with the county name in parentheses and a notation that specifies the two types of entities.

Economic Place

Table C includes data from the 2017 Economic Census. The Economic Census uses a concept called the "Economic Place" that includes incorporated places, census designated places, and minor civil divisions with populations of 2,500 or more. Table B includes only those Economic Places with populations of 10,000 or more. In some states, incorporated cities or villages are within towns or MCDs. In the Economic Census data, the "balance" of the town that is outside of incorporated cities or villages is identified as a separate place.[2] In the decennial census, the American Community Survey, and other sources, data represent these entire towns, while the Economic Census data represent only the portion of the town that is not within an incorporated place inside the town. The component incorporated places are not in Table B if their populations are below 10,000.

---

2 Details about specific places in the Economic Census can be found at https://www.census.gov/programs-surveys/economic-census/geographies.html

APPENDIX B
SOURCE NOTES AND EXPLANATIONS

TABLE A
ALL PLACES

Table A presents data from the 2010 Census of Population and Housing, the annual Population Estimates Program, and the American Community Survey. Data are included for the United States, the 50 states and the District of Columbia, all incorporated places, consolidated cities, and census designated places (CDPs), as well as for minor civil divisions (MCDs) in the 12 states where MCDs serve as general purpose local governments. This table includes 19,781 incorporated places; 8 consolidated cities; 9,792 CDPs, and 12,047 MCDs (in the 12 applicable states). In Table A, the number of geographic entities has been reduced to 38,143 by eliminating duplicate entities. Where an MCD is co-extensive with an incorporated place or a CDP, only a single listing is included.

All data were retrieved through the Census Bureau's online platform at data.census.gov, or from the downloadable datasets of the Population Estimates Program.

POPULATION, Item 1 through 4
Source: U.S. Census Bureau—Population Estimates Program, Incorporated Places and Minor Civil Divisions Datasets: Subcounty Resident Population Estimates: April 1, 2010 to July 1, 2019; American Community Survey, 2015-2019 5-year estimates; 2010 SF1, Table P1

The population total for 2010 is from the decennial census and represents the resident population as of April 1 in the census year. However, where possible, item 1 shows the 2010 census *base* population, rather than the actual enumerated population. The base population may differ from the census count due to legal boundary updates, other geographic program changes, and Count Question Resolution actions. The base population serves as the starting point for the annual estimates. The 2019 annual estimates and the percent change since 2010 are shown in items 2 and 3. All Census Designated Places and some Minor Civil Divisions are not available in the 2019 Population Estimates dataset. Their 2010 population totals are from the 2010 SF1 data

and there is no measure of population change from 2010 to 2019.

Column 4 shows the total population estimate for each area from the American Community Survey 5-year file for the years 2015 through 2019. This total is derived from the census and the population estimates and represents the population over that 5-year time period. The population characteristics in columns 5 through 16 are based on this total population.

POPULATION BY RACE AND HISPANIC ORIGIN, Items 5 through 9
Source: U.S. Census Bureau— American Community Survey, 2015-2019 5-year estimates, Table DP05

The U.S. Census Bureau collects race data in accordance with guidelines provided by the U.S. Office of Management and Budget (OMB), and these data are based on self-identification. The racial categories included in the census questionnaire generally reflect a social definition of race recognized in this country and not an attempt to define race biologically, anthropologically, or genetically. In addition, it is recognized that the categories of the race item include racial and national origin or sociocultural groups. People may choose to report more than one race to indicate their racial mixture, such as "American Indian" and "White." People who identify their origin as Hispanic, Latino, or Spanish may be any race.

Respondents were offered the option of selecting one or more races. In this table, Columns 5 through 7 refer to individuals who identified with only one racial category and who were not Hispanic or Latino. Column 8 combines the racial categories American Indian and Alaska native alone; Native Hawaiian and Other Pacific Islander alone; some other race alone; and two or more races, all not Hispanic or Latino. Column 9 includes all persons who were of Hispanic or Latino origin.

The **White** population is defined as persons having origins in any of the original peoples of Europe, the Middle East, or North Africa. It includes those who indicated their race as White, as well as persons who did not classify themselves in one of the specific race categories listed on the questionnaire but entered a nationality such as Irish, German, Italian, Lebanese, Near Easterner, Arab, or Polish.

The **Black** population includes persons having origins in any of the Black racial groups of Africa. It includes those who indicated their race as "Black, African Am., or Negro", as well as persons who did not classify themselves in one of the specific race categories but reported entries such as African American, Afro American, Kenyan, Nigerian, or Haitian.

The **Asian** population includes persons having origins in any of the original peoples of the Far East, Southeast Asia, or the Indian subcontinent, including, for example, Cambodia, China, India, Japan, Korea, Malaysia, Pakistan, the Philippine Islands, Thailand, and Vietnam. It includes persons who indicated their race as Asian Indian, Chinese, Filipino, Japanese, Korean, Vietnamese, or "Other Asian," as well as persons who provided write-in entries of such groups as Cambodian, Laotian, Hmong, Pakistani, or Taiwanese.

The **American Indian or Alaska Native** population includes persons having origins in any of the original peoples of North and South America (including Central America) and who maintain tribal affiliation or community attachment. It includes those who indicated their race as American Indian or Alaska Native, as well as persons who did not classify themselves in one of the specific race categories but reported entries such as Canadian Indian, French-American Indian, Spanish-American Indian, Eskimo, Aleut, Alaska Indian, or any of the American Indian or Alaska Native tribes.

The **Native Hawaiian or Other Pacific Islander** population includes persons having origins in any of the original peoples of Hawaii, Guam, Samoa, or other Pacific Islands. It includes those who indicated their race as "Native Hawaiian", "Guamanian or Chamorro", "Samoan," or "Other Pacific Islander", as well as persons who reported entries such as Part Hawaiian, American Samoan, Fijian, Melanesian, or Tahitian.

The Hispanic population is based on a question that asked respondents "Is this person Spanish/Hispanic/Latino?" Persons marking any one of the four Hispanic categories (i.e., Mexican, Puerto Rican, Cuban, or other Hispanic, Latino, or Spanish origin) are collectively referred to as Hispanic.

In the American Community Survey, people who identify with the terms "Hispanic" or "Latino" are those who classify themselves in one of the specific Hispanic or Latino categories listed on the ACS questionnaire - "Mexican," "Puerto Rican," or "Cuban" - as well as those who indicate that they are "other Spanish, Hispanic, or Latino." Origin can be viewed as the heritage, nationality group, lineage, or country of birth of the person or the person's parents or ancestors before their arrival in the United States. People who identify their origin as Spanish, Hispanic, or Latino may be of any race.

AGE, Items 10 through 12
Source: U.S. Census Bureau— American Community Survey, 2015-2019 5-year estimates, Table DP05

Age is defined as age at last birthday, as of the date of the ACS interview or questionnaire. The ACS also asked for the specific date of birth of the respondent, and ACS procedures used the birth date for deriving age data.

The median age is the age that divides the population into two equal-size groups. Half of the population is older than the median age and half is younger. Median age is based on a standard distribution of the population by single years of age and is shown to the nearest tenth of a year.

EDUCATIONAL ATTAINMENT, Items 13 and 14
Source: U.S. Census Bureau— American Community Survey, 2015-2019 5-year estimates, Table DP02

Educational attainment data are tabulated for people 25 years old and over. Respondents are classified according to the highest degree or the highest level of school completed. The question included instructions for persons currently enrolled in school to report the level of the previous grade attended or the highest degree received.

High School Diploma or less: this category includes people whose highest degree was a high school diploma or its equivalent, people who reported completing the 12th grade but not receiving a diploma, people whose highest grade attended was less than 12th grade, and people who never attended school.

Bachelor's degree or more: this category includes people who have received a bachelor's, master's, or professional or doctorate degree.

HOUSEHOLD COMPUTER USE, Items 15 and 16
Source: U.S. Census Bureau— American Community Survey, 2015-2019 5-year estimates, Table DP02

A household consists of persons occupying a single housing unit. A housing unit is a house, an apartment, a group of rooms, or a single room occupied as separate living quarters. The occupants may be a single family, one person living alone, two or more families living together, or any other group of related or unrelated persons who share a housing unit. The number of households is the same as the number of year-round occupied housing units.

The **computer use** question asked if anyone in the household owned or used a computer and included three response categories for a desktop/laptop, a handheld computer, or some other type of computer. Respondents could select all categories that applied.

TABLE B
PLACES AND MINOR CIVIL DIVISIONS OF 10,000 OR MORE POPULATION.

Table B presents data from several sources for incorporated places, consolidated cities, census designated places, and minor civil divisions (in the 12 states where MCDs serve as general purpose local governments) with 10,000 or more population. There are 4,924 geographic entities in Table B, including the United States, the states, and the District of Columbia. Where an MCD is co-extensive with a place, only a single listing is included.

LAND AREA, Items 1 and 5
Source: U.S. Census Bureau—2019 U.S. Gazetteer Files

Land area measurements are shown to the nearest square mile. Land area includes dry land and land temporarily or partially covered by water, such as marshlands, swamps, and river floodplains. Square miles may be multiplied by 2.59 to convert these area measurements into square kilometers.

POPULATION, Item 2 through 4
Source: U.S. Census Bureau—Population Estimates Program, Incorporated Places and Minor Civil Divisions Datasets: Subcounty Resident Population Estimates: April 1, 2010 to July 1, 2019; 2010 SF1, Table P1

The population total for 2010 is from the decennial census and represents the resident population as of April 1 in the census year. However, where possible, item 2 shows the 2010 census *base* population, rather than the actual enumerated population. The base population may differ from the census count due to legal boundary updates, other geographic program changes, and Count Question Resolution actions. The base population serves as the starting point for the annual estimates. All Census Designated Places and some Minor Civil Divisions are not available in the 2019 Population Estimates dataset. Their 2010 population totals are from the 2010 SF1 data and there is no measure of population change from 2010 to 2019.

The 2019 annual estimates and the percent change since 2010 are shown in items 3 and 4.

FOREIGN-BORN POPULATION, 2015-2019, Item 6
Source: U.S. Census Bureau—2015-2019 American Community Survey 5-year estimates, Table B05002

The **foreign-born population** includes anyone who was not a U.S. citizen or a U.S. national at birth. This includes respondents who indicated they were a U.S. citizen by naturalization or not a U.S. citizen.

RESIDENCE ONE YEAR AGO, 2015-2019, Item 7
Source: U.S. Census Bureau—2015-2019 American Community Survey 5-year estimates, Table B07003

The data on residence 1 year ago were derived from answers to a question that was asked of the population 1 year and older. People who had moved from another residence in the United States or Puerto Rico 1 year earlier were asked to report the exact address (number and street name); the name of the city, town, or post office; the name of the U.S. county or municipio in Puerto Rico; state or Puerto Rico; and the ZIP Code where they lived 1 year ago. People living outside the United States and Puerto Rico were asked to report the name of the foreign country or U.S. Island Area where they were living 1 year ago. Column 7 shows the proportion of all residents 1 year and older who lived in the same house where they had lived one year before the interview date.

HOUSEHOLD INCOME, 2015-2019, Items 8 through 10.
Source: U.S. Census Bureau—2015-2019 American Community Survey 5-year estimates, Tables B17017 and B19013

Household Income includes the income of the householder and all other individuals 15 years old and over in the household, whether they are related to the householder or not. Because many households consist of only one person, average household income is usually less than average family income. Although the household income statistics cover the past 12 months, the characteristics of individuals and the composition of households refer to the time of interview. Thus, the income of the household does not include amounts received by individuals who were members of the household during all or part of the past 12 months if these individuals no longer resided in the household at the time of interview. Similarly, income amounts reported by individuals who did not reside in the household during the past 12 months but who were members of the household at the time of interview are included. However, the composition of most households was the same during the past 12 months as at the time of interview.

Total income is the sum of the amounts reported separately for wage or salary income; net self-employment income; interest, dividends, or net rental or royalty income or income from estates and trusts; Social Security or railroad retirement income; Supplemental Security Income (SSI); public assistance or welfare payments; retirement, survivor, or disability pensions; and all other income.

Receipts from the following sources are not included as income: capital gains, money received from the sale of property (unless the recipient was engaged in the business of selling such property); the value of income "in kind" from food stamps, public housing subsidies, medical care, employer contributions for individuals; withdrawal of bank deposits; money borrowed; tax refunds; exchange of money between relatives living in the same household; and gifts and lump-sum inheritances, insurance payments, and other types of lump-sum receipts.

Median income. The median divides the income distribution into two equal parts: half of the cases fall below the median income and half above the median. For households, the median income is based on the distribution of the total number of households including those with no income. Median income for households is computed on the basis of a standard distribution with the minimum value less than $2,500 and the maximum value $250,000 or more. Median income is rounded to the nearest whole dollar. Median income figures are calculated using linear interpolation if the width of the interval containing the estimate is $2,500 or less. If the width of the interval containing the estimate is greater than $2,500, Pareto interpolation is used.

Income components were reported for the 12 months preceding the interview month. Monthly Consumer Price Indices (CPI) factors were used to inflation-adjust these components to a reference calendar year (January through December). For example, a household interviewed in March 2010 reports their income for March 2009 through February 2010. Their income is adjusted to the 2010 reference calendar year by multiplying their reported income by 2010 average annual CPI (January-December 2010) and then dividing by the average CPI for March 2009-February2010.

In order to inflate income amounts from previous years, the dollar values on individual records are inflated to the latest year's dollar values by multiplying by a factor equal to the average annual CPI-U-RS factor for the current year, divided by the average annual CPI-U-RS factor for the earlier/earliest year

Poverty statistics in ACS products adhere to the standards specified by the Office of Management and Budget in Statistical Policy Directive 14. The Census Bureau uses a set of dollar value thresholds that vary by family size and composition to determine who is in poverty

The data on poverty status of households were derived from answers to the income questions. Since poverty is defined at the family level and not the household level, the poverty status of the household is determined by the poverty status of the householder. Households are classified as poor when the total income of the householder's family is below the appropriate poverty threshold. (For nonfamily householders, their own income is compared with the appropriate threshold.) The income of people living in the household who are unrelated to the householder is not considered when determining the poverty status of a household, nor does their presence affect the family size in determining the appropriate threshold. The poverty thresholds vary depending on three criteria: size of family, number of related children, and, for 1- and 2-person families, age of householder.

Since ACS is a continuous survey, people respond throughout the year. Because the income questions specify a period covering the last 12 months, the appropriate poverty thresholds are adjusted with monthly inflation factors for the 12 months preceding the data collection, and further adjusted to represent the 5-year period covered by the 2015-2019 data.

HOUSING VALUE, Item 11
Source: U.S. Census Bureau—2015-2019 American Community Survey 5-year estimates, Table B25077

Median value is the dollar amount that divides the distribution of specified owner-occupied housing units into two equal parts, with half of all units below the median value and half above the median value. Value is defined as the respondent's estimate of what the house would sell for if it were for sale. Data are presented for single-family units on fewer than 10 acres of land that have no business or medical office on the property.

Poverty Thresholds for 2019 by Size of Family and Number of Related Children Under 18 Years

Size of family unit	Weighted average thresholds	Related children under 18 years								
		None	One	Two	Three	Four	Five	Six	Seven	Eight or more
One person (unrelated individual)	13,011									
Under 65 years	13,300	13,300								
Aged 65 and older	12,261	12,261								
Two people	16,521									
Householder under age 65	17,196	17,120	17,622							
Householder aged 65 and older	15,468	15,453	17,555							
Three people	20,335	19,998	20,578	20,598						
Four people	26,172	26,370	26,801	25,926	26,017					
Five people...	31,021	31,800	32,263	31,275	30,510	30,044				
Six people..	35,129	36,576	36,721	35,965	35,239	34,161	33,522			
Seven people...	40,016	42,085	42,348	41,442	40,811	39,635	38,262	36,757		
Eight people	44,461	47,069	47,485	46,630	45,881	44,818	43,470	42,066	41,709	
Nine people or more................................	52,875	56,621	56,895	56,139	55,503	54,460	53,025	51,727	51,406	49,426

Source: U.S. Census Bureau.

EMPLOYMENT STATUS, 2015-2019, Items 12 and 13
Source: U.S. Census Bureau—2015-2019 American Community Survey 5-year estimates, , Table B23025

The data on **employment status** refer to work during the week preceding the interview. The employment status data tabulations include people 16 years old and over.

Employed. All civilians 16 years old and over who were either (1) "at work" — those who did any work at all during the reference week as paid employees, worked in their own business or profession, worked on their own farm, or worked 15 hours or more as unpaid workers on a family farm or in a family business; or (2) were "with a job but not at work" — those who did not work during the reference week, but who had jobs or businesses from which they were temporarily absent because of illness, bad weather, industrial dispute, vacation, or other personal reasons. Excluded from the employed are people whose only activity consisted of work around their own house (e.g., painting, repairing, or housework) or unpaid volunteer work for religious, charitable, and similar organizations. Also excluded are all institutionalized people and people on active duty in the United States Armed Forces.

Unemployed. All civilians 16 years old and over were classified as unemployed if they were neither "at work" nor "with a job but not at work" during the reference week, were looking for work during the last 4 weeks, and were available to start a job. Also included as unemployed were civilians 16 years old and over who: did not work at all during the reference week, were on temporary layoff from a job, had been informed that they would be recalled to work within the next 6 months or had been given a date to return to work, and were available to return to work during the reference week, except for temporary illness. Examples of job seeking activities were:

- Registering at a public or private employment office
- Meeting with prospective employers
- Investigating possibilities for starting a professional practice or opening a business
- Placing or answering advertisements
- Writing letters of application
- Being on a union or professional register

Civilian Labor force. All people classified as "employed" and "unemployed".

Not in labor force. All people 16 years old and over who are not classified as members of the labor force. This category consists mainly of students, individuals taking care of home or family, retired workers, seasonal workers enumerated in an off-season who were not looking for work, institutionalized people (all institutionalized people are placed in this category regardless of any work activities they may have done in the reference week), and people doing only incidental unpaid family work (fewer than 15 hours during the reference week).

HOUSEHOLDS, 2015-2019, Items 14 and 15.
Source: U.S. Census Bureau—2015-2019 American Community Survey 5-year estimates, Table B11001

A **household** includes all of the people who occupy a housing unit. (People not living in households are classified as living in group quarters.) A housing unit is a house, an apartment, a mobile home, a group of rooms, or a single room occupied (or if vacant, intended for occupancy) as separate living quarters. Separate living quarters are those in which the occupants live separately from any other people in the building and that have direct access from the outside of the building or through a common hall. The occupants may be a single family, one person living alone, two or more families living together, or any other group of related or unrelated people who share living quarters.

A family includes a householder and one or more other people living in the same household who are related to the householder by birth, marriage, or adoption. All people in a household who are related to the householder are regarded as members of his or her family. A **family household** may contain people not related to the householder. Thus, family households may include more members than do families. A household can contain only one family for purposes of census tabulations. Not all households contain families since a household may comprise a group of unrelated people or of one person living alone.

CRIME, Items 16 through 19
Source: U.S. Federal Bureau of
Investigation—Uniform Crime Reports

Crime data are as reported to the FBI by law enforcement agencies and have not been adjusted for under-reporting. This may affect comparability between geographic areas or over time.

Through the voluntary contribution of crime statistics by law enforcement agencies across the United States, the Uniform Crime Reporting (UCR) Program provides periodic assessments of crime in the nation as measured by those offenses that come to the attention of the law enforcement community. The Committee on Uniform Crime Records of the International Association of Chiefs of Police initiated this voluntary national data-collection effort in 1930. UCR Program contributors compile and submit their crime data in one of two manners: either directly to the FBI or through the State UCR Programs.

Seven offenses, because of their seriousness, frequency of occurrence, and likelihood of being reported to police, were initially selected to serve as an index for evaluating fluctuations in the volume of crime. These serious crimes were murder and nonnegligent manslaughter, forcible rape, robbery, aggravated assault, burglary, larceny-theft, and motor vehicle theft. By congressional mandate, arson was added as the eighth index offense in 1979. The totals shown in this volume do not include arson.

In 2004, the FBI discontinued the use of the Crime Index in the UCR Program and its publications, stating that the Crime Index was driven upward by the offense with the highest number of cases (in this case, larceny-theft) creating a bias against jurisdictions with a high number of larceny-thefts but a low number of other serious crimes, such as murder and forcible rape. The FBI is currently publishing

a violent crime total and a property crime total until a more viable index is developed.

In 2013, the FBI adopted a new definition of rape. Rape is now defined as, "Penetration, no matter how slight, of the vagina or anus with any body part or object, or oral penetration by a sex organ of another person, without the consent of the victim." The new definition updated the 80-year-old historical definition of rape which was "carnal knowledge of a female forcibly and against her will." Effectively, the revised definition expands rape to include both male and female victims and offenders, and reflects the various forms of sexual penetration understood to be rape, especially nonconsenting acts of sodomy, and sexual assaults with objects.

Violent crimes include four categories of offenses: (1) Murder and nonnegligent manslaughter, as defined in the UCR Program, is the willful (nonnegligent) killing of one human being by another. This offense excludes deaths caused by negligence, suicide, or accident; justifiable homicides; and attempts to murder or assaults to murder. (2) Rape is the penetration, no matter how slight, of the vagina or anus with any body part or object, or oral penetration by a sex organ of another person, without the consent of the victim. Assaults or attempts to commit rape by force or threat of force are also included; however, statutory rape (without force) and other sex offenses are excluded. (3) Robbery is the taking or attempting to take anything of value from the care, custody, or control of a person or persons by force or threat of force or violence and/or by putting the victim in fear. (4) Aggravated assault is an unlawful attack by one person upon another for the purpose of inflicting severe or aggravated bodily injury. This type of assault is usually accompanied by the use of a weapon or by other means likely to produce death or great bodily harm. Attempts are included, since injury does not necessarily have to result when a gun, knife, or other weapon is used, as these incidents could and probably would result in a serious personal injury if the crime were successfully completed.

Property crimes include three categories: (1) Burglary, or breaking and entering, is the unlawful entry of a structure to commit a felony or theft, even though no force was used to gain entrance. (2) Larceny/theft is the unauthorized taking of the personal property of another, without the use of force. (3) Motor vehicle theft is the unauthorized taking of any motor vehicle.

Rates are based on population estimates provided by the FBI. Data were obtained from *Crime in the United States*, Table 8 for city agencies. Data are not available for cities that do not have police departments. This includes all census designated places as well as cities where the police function is provided by the county or a separate agency. **https://ucr.fbi.gov/crime-in-the-u.s/2018/crime-in-the-u.s.-2018/tables/table-8/table-8.xls/view**

CONSTRUCTION—BUILDING PERMITS, Items 20 through 22
Source: U. S. Census Bureau—Building Permits Survey

Figures represent private residential construction authorized by building permits in approximately 19,000 places in the United States. Valuation represents the cost of construction as recorded on the building permit. This figure usually excludes the cost of on-site and off-site development and improvements and the cost of heating, plumbing, electrical, and elevator installations.

Most of the permit-issuing jurisdictions are municipalities; the remainder are counties, townships, or unincorporated towns. For the municipalities, and townships or towns, the area subject to building permit requirements to which the figures pertain is normally that of the governmental jurisdictions. A small number of municipalities have authority to issue building or zoning permits for areas extending beyond their corporate limits. In such cases, the data relate to the entire area within which the permit-issuing authority is exercised. Similarly, a small number of townships issue permits for only a part of the township and the data normally cover only the area subject to the township's permit system. The portion of construction measurable from building permit records is inherently limited since such records obviously do not reflect construction activity outside of the area subject to local permit requirements. For the nation as a whole, less than 2 percent of all privately owned housing units built are construction in areas that do not require building permits.

If a city or town was not matched as a permit-issuing place covered by the Census Bureau, an "NA" is shown. Cities that are permit-issuing places but that issued no permits during the period are represented by a "0." State totals were obtained by summing the data for permit-issuing places within each jurisdiction.

Residential building permits include buildings with any number of housing units. Hotels, apartment hotels, dormitories, fraternity houses, and other non-housekeeping residential buildings are not included.

The building permits data were compiled from the place level files available from the Census Bureau at https://www.census.gov/construction/bps/

LOCAL GOVERNMENT FINANCES, Items 23 through 30
Source: U. S. Census Bureau—2017 Census of Governments

Total **general revenue** includes all governmental revenue except utility, liquor store, and employee-retirement or other insurance trust revenue. It includes all tax collections and intergovernmental revenue, even if designated for employee-retirement or local utility purposes.

Intergovernmental revenue consists of amounts received from other governments as fiscal aid in the form of shared revenues and grants-in-ad, as reimbursements for performance of general expenditure functions, and specific services for the paying government (e.g., care of prisoners or contractual research) of amounts in lieu of taxes. It excludes amounts received from other governments for sale of property, commodities, and utility services. All intergovernmental revenue is classified as general revenue. Intergovernmental revenue from the state government includes amounts originally from the federal government but channeled through the state.

Taxes are compulsory contributions exacted by a government for public purposes, and exclude employee and employer assessments for retirement and social insurance purposes, which are classified as insurance trust revenue. All tax revenue is classified as general revenue and comprises amounts received (including interest and penalties but excluding protested amounts and refunds) from all taxes imposed by a government Note that local government tax revenue excludes any amounts from shares of state-imposed and collected taxes, which are classified as intergovernmental revenue.

Total **general expenditure** includes all city expenditure other than the specifically enumerated kinds of expenditure classified as utility, liquor store, and employee retirement and other insurance trust expenditures.

Capital outlays are direct expenditures for contract of force account construction of buildings, roads, and other improvements, and for purchases of equipment, land, and existing structures. They include amounts for additions, replacements, and major alterations to fixed works and structures. However, expenditure for repair to such works and structures is classified as current operation expenditure.

A major portion of capital outlay is commonly financed by borrowing, while government revenue does not include receipts from borrowing. Among other things, this distorts the relationship between the totals presented for revenue and expenditure and renders this relationship useless as a direct measure of the degree of budgetary "balance," as that term is generally applied.

Total **debt** outstanding is the total of all debt obligations remaining unpaid on the date specified.

Information about the 2017 Census of Governments is available at https://www.census.gov/programs-surveys/cog.html , The data in this volume were compiled from the

Individual Units files of the State and Local Governments Finance data at https://www.census.gov/data/tables/2017/econ/gov-finances/summary-tables.html

TABLE C
PLACES AND MINOR CIVIL DIVISIONS OF 10,000 OR MORE POPULATION

ECONOMIC ACTIVITY BY SECTOR, Items 1 through 30
Source: U.S. Census Bureau, 2012 Economic Census

Table C presents data from the 2017 Economic Census for Economic Census Places with populations of 10,000 or more. These are generally the same places that were included in Table B.

The Economic Census provides a detailed portrait of the nation's economy once every five years, from the national to the local level. The 2017 Economic Census covers nearly all of the U.S. economy in its basic collection of establishment statistics. In 1997, it began use of the new North American Industry Classification System (NAICS) and therefore data are not comparable to economic data from prior years, which were based on the Standard Industrial Classification (SIC) system.

NAICS, developed in cooperation with Canada and Mexico, classifies North America's economic activities at 2-, 3-, 4-, and 5-digit levels of detail, and the U.S. version of NAICS further defines industries to a sixth digit. The Economic Census takes advantage of this hierarchy to publish data at these successive levels of detail: sector (2-digit); subsector (3-digit); industry group (4-digit); industry (5-digit); and U.S. industry (6-digit). This volume includes data at the 2-digit (sector) level.

The following industry categories are not included in the Economic Census: Agriculture, Forestry, Fishing and Hunting; Rail Transportation; Postal Service; Funds, Trusts, and Other Financial Vehicles; Elementary and Secondary Schools; Junior Colleges; Colleges, Universities, and Professional Schools; Religious Organizations; Labor Unions and Similar Labor Organizations; Political Organizations; Private Households; and Public Administration.

The economic census does not generally include government-owned establishments, even when their primary activity would be classified in industries covered by the economic census. Because of these exclusions, economic census data for industries in many sectors might appear to be incomplete, as illustrated below.

At the same time, exceptions have been made to *include* the following governmental activities in the economic census: Hospitals; Government-owned liquor stores; University press publishers; and Federal Reserve Banks. In addition, the economic census does *include* the activities of private contractors that may be carrying out governmental functions on contract. Examples are highway construction contractors; privately operated prisons; private firms contracting to provide services to government; and Government-owned/contractor-operated (GOCO) plants.

Aside from the above exceptions, the 2017 Economic Census includes private nonfarm establishments in 18 sectors. Four sectors are not published at the place level: Manufacturing; Mining, quarrying, and oil and gas extraction; Construction; and Management of companies and enterprises. A fourth sector—Utilities—is not included in this volume because it exists in very few places. For the remaining 13 sectors, Table C shows the number of establishments and the number of employees in each sector.

Number of establishments. An establishment is a single physical location at which business is conducted and/or services are provided. It is not necessarily identical with a company or enterprise, which may consist of one establishment or more.

Economic census figures represent a summary of reports for individual establishments rather than companies. For cases where a census report was received, separate information was obtained for each location where business was conducted. When administrative records of other federal agencies were used instead of a census report, no information

Sector	Illustrative Governmental Activities Excluded
Utilities	Public electric, gas, water and sewer utilities
Construction	Highway construction performed by government employees
Retail Trade	Post exchanges, ship stores and similar establishments operated on military posts by agencies of the federal government
Transportation and Warehousing	Publicly-operated buses and subway systems
Information	Public libraries
Administrative and Support and Waste Management and Remediation Services	Municipal trash removal
Health Care and Social Assistance	Municipal ambulance services and County or city nursing care services
Arts, Entertainment, and Recreation	Public museums or zoos

was available on the number of locations operated. Each economic census establishment was tabulated according to the physical location at which the business was conducted. The count of establishments represents those in business at any time during the census year.

When two activities or more were carried on at a single location under a single ownership, all activities generally were grouped together as a single establishment. The entire establishment was classified on the basis of its major activity and all data for it were included in that classification. However, when distinct and separate economic activities (for which different industry classification codes were appropriate) were conducted at a single location under a single ownership, separate establishment reports for each of the different activities were obtained in the census.

Number of Employees. Paid employees consist of full- and part-time employees. Included are employees on paid sick leave, paid holidays, and paid vacations; not included are full- and part-time leased employees whose payroll was filed under an employee leasing company's Employer Identification Number (EIN), and temporary staffing obtained from a staffing service. The definition of paid employees is the same as that used by the Internal Revenue Service (IRS) on Form 941.

The following sectors are included in Table C:

Wholesale Trade. The Wholesale Trade sector comprises establishments engaged in wholesaling merchandise, generally without transformation, and rendering services incidental to the sale of merchandise. The merchandise described in this sector includes the outputs of agriculture, mining, manufacturing, and certain information industries, such as publishing.

The wholesaling process is an intermediate step in the distribution of merchandise. Wholesalers are organized to sell or arrange the purchase or sale of (a) goods for resale (i.e., goods sold to other wholesalers or retailers), (b) capital or durable nonconsumer goods, and (c) raw and intermediate materials and supplies used in production.

Wholesalers sell merchandise to other businesses and normally operate from a warehouse or office. These warehouses and offices are characterized by having little or no display of merchandise. In addition, neither the design nor the location of the premises is intended to solicit walk-in traffic. Wholesalers do not normally use advertising directed to the general public. Customers are generally reached initially via telephone, in-person marketing, or by specialized advertising that may include Internet and other electronic means. Follow-up orders are either vendor-initiated or client-initiated, generally based on previous sales, and typically exhibit strong ties between sellers and buyers. In fact,

transactions are often conducted between wholesalers and clients that have long-standing business relationships.

This sector comprises two main types of wholesalers: merchant wholesalers that sell goods on their own account and business-to-business electronic markets, agents, and brokers that arrange sales and purchases for others generally for a commission or fee.

In this book, only the merchant wholesalers are included.

(1) *Merchant wholesalers.* Establishments that sell goods on their own account are known as wholesale merchants, distributors, jobbers, drop shippers, and import/export merchants. Also included as wholesale merchants are sales offices and sales branches (but not retail stores) maintained by manufacturing, refining, or mining enterprises apart from their plants or mines for the purpose of marketing their products. Merchant wholesale establishments typically maintain their own warehouse, where they receive and handle goods for their customers. Goods are generally sold without transformation, but may include integral functions, such as sorting, packaging, labeling, and other marketing services.

(2) (*not included in this book*) *Manufacturers' sales branches and offices.* Establishments arranging for the purchase or sale of goods owned by others or purchasing goods, generally on a commission basis are known as business-to-business electronic markets, agents and brokers, commission merchants, import/export agents and brokers, auction companies, and manufacturers' representatives. These establishments operate from offices and generally do not own or handle the goods they sell.

Some wholesale establishments may be connected with a single manufacturer and promote and sell the particular manufacturers' products to a wide range of other wholesalers or retailers. Other wholesalers may be connected to a retail chain, or limited number of retail chains, and only provide a variety of products needed by that particular retail operation(s). These wholesalers may obtain the products from a wide range of manufacturers. Still other wholesalers may not take title to the goods, but act as agents and brokers for a commission.

Retail trade. The Retail Trade sector comprises establishments engaged in retailing merchandise, generally without transformation, and rendering services incidental to the sale of merchandise.

The retailing process is the final step in the distribution of merchandise; retailers are, therefore, organized to sell merchandise in small quantities to the general public. This sector comprises two main types of retailers: store and non-store retailers.

1. Store retailers operate fixed point-of-sale locations, located and designed to attract a high volume of walk-in customers. In general, retail stores have extensive displays of merchandise and use mass-media advertising to attract customers. They typically sell merchandise to the general public for personal or household consumption, but some also serve business and institutional clients. These include establishments, such as office supply stores, computer and software stores, building materials dealers, plumbing supply stores, and electrical supply stores. Catalog showrooms, gasoline stations, automotive dealers, and mobile home dealers are treated as store retailers.

In addition to retailing merchandise, some types of store retailers are also engaged in the provision of after-sales services, such as repair and installation. For example, new automobile dealers, electronics and appliance stores, and musical instrument and supplies stores often provide repair services. As a general rule, establishments engaged in retailing merchandise and providing after-sales services are classified in this sector.

The first eleven subsectors of retail trade are store retailers. The establishments are grouped into industries and industry groups typically based on one or more of the following criteria:

(a) The merchandise line or lines carried by the store; for example, specialty stores are distinguished from general-line stores.

(b) The usual trade designation of the establishments. This criterion applies in cases where a store type is well recognized by the industry and the public, but difficult to define strictly in terms of merchandise lines carried; for example, pharmacies, hardware stores, and department stores.

(c) Capital requirements in terms of display equipment; for example, food stores have equipment requirements not found in other retail industries.

(d) Human resource requirements in terms of expertise; for example, the staff of an automobile dealer requires knowledge in financing, registering, and licensing issues that are not necessary in other retail industries.

2. Nonstore retailers, like store retailers, are organized to serve the general public, but their retailing methods differ. The establishments of this subsector reach customers and market merchandise with methods, such as the broadcasting of "infomercials," the broadcasting and publishing of direct-response advertising, the publishing of paper and electronic catalogs, door-to-door solicitation, in-home demonstration, selling from portable stalls (street vendors, except food), and distribution through vending machines. Establishments engaged in the direct sale (nonstore) of products, such as

home heating oil dealers and home delivery newspaper routes are included here.

The buying of goods for resale is a characteristic of retail trade establishments that particularly distinguishes them from establishments in the agriculture, manufacturing, and construction industries. For example, farms that sell their products at or from the point of production are not classified in retail, but rather in agriculture. Similarly, establishments that both manufacture and sell their products to the general public are not classified in retail, but rather in manufacturing. However, establishments that engage in processing activities incidental to retailing are classified in retail. This includes establishments, such as optical goods stores that do in-store grinding of lenses, and meat and seafood markets.

Wholesalers also engage in the buying of goods for resale, but they are not usually organized to serve the general public. They typically operate from a warehouse or office and neither the design nor the location of these premises is intended to solicit a high volume of walk-in traffic. Wholesalers supply institutional, industrial, wholesale, and retail clients; their operations are, therefore, generally organized to purchase, sell, and deliver merchandise in larger quantities. However, dealers of durable nonconsumer goods, such as farm machinery and heavy duty trucks, are included in wholesale trade even if they often sell these products in single units.

Retail establishments operated by agencies of the federal government, such as military post exchanges and ship stores, are not included.

Transportation and Warehousing. The Transportation and Warehousing sector includes industries providing transportation of passengers and cargo, warehousing and storage for goods, scenic and sightseeing transportation, and support activities related to modes of transportation. Establishments in these industries use transportation equipment or transportation related facilities as a productive asset. The type of equipment depends on the mode of transportation. The modes of transportation are air, rail, water, road, and pipeline.

The Transportation and Warehousing sector distinguishes three basic types of activities: subsectors for each mode of transportation, a subsector for warehousing and storage, and a subsector for establishments providing support activities for transportation. In addition, there are subsectors for establishments that provide passenger transportation for scenic and sightseeing purposes, postal services, and courier services.

A separate subsector for support activities is established in the sector because, first, support activities for transportation are inherently multimodal, such as freight transportation arrangement, or have multimodal aspects. Secondly, there are production process similarities among the support activity industries.

One of the support activities identified in the support activity subsector is the routine repair and maintenance of transportation equipment (e.g., aircraft at an airport, railroad rolling stock at a railroad terminal, or ships at a harbor or port facility). Such establishments do not perform complete overhauling or rebuilding of transportation equipment (i.e., periodic restoration of transportation equipment to original design specifications) or transportation equipment conversion (i.e., major modification to systems). An establishment that primarily performs factory (or shipyard) overhauls, rebuilding, or conversions of aircraft, railroad rolling stock, or a ship is classified in Subsector 336, Transportation Equipment Manufacturing according to the type of equipment.

Many of the establishments in this sector often operate on networks, with physical facilities, labor forces, and equipment spread over an extensive geographic area.

Warehousing establishments in this sector are distinguished from merchant wholesaling in that the warehouse establishments do not sell the goods.

Excluded from this sector are establishments primarily engaged in providing travel agent services that support transportation and other establishments, such as hotels, businesses, and government agencies. These establishments are classified in Administrative and Support and Waste Management and Remediation Services. Also, establishments primarily engaged in providing rental and leasing of transportation equipment without operator are classified in Rental and Leasing Services.

For the 2012 Economic Census, Rail Transportation and Postal Service are not included. Publicly-operated buses and subway systems are not included.

Information. The Information sector comprises establishments engaged in the following processes: (a) producing and distributing information and cultural products, (b) providing the means to transmit or distribute these products as well as data or communications, and (c) processing data.

The main components of this sector are the publishing industries, including software publishing, and both traditional publishing and publishing exclusively on the Internet; the motion picture and sound recording industries; the broadcasting industries, including traditional broadcasting and those broadcasting exclusively over the Internet; the telecommunications industries; web search portals, data processing industries, and the information services industries.

The expressions "information age" and "global information economy" are used with considerable frequency today.

The general idea of an "information economy" includes both the notion of industries primarily producing, processing, and distributing information, as well as the idea that every industry is using available information and information technology to reorganize and make themselves more productive.

For the purposes of NAICS, it is the transformation of information into a commodity that is produced and distributed by a number of growing industries that is at issue. The Information sector groups three types of establishments: (1) those engaged in producing and distributing information and cultural products; (2) those that provide the means to transmit or distribute these products as well as data or communications; and (3) those that process data. Cultural products are those that directly express attitudes, opinions, ideas, values, and artistic creativity; provide entertainment; or offer information and analysis concerning the past and present. Included in this definition are popular, mass-produced products as well as cultural products that normally have a more limited audience, such as poetry books, literary magazines, or classical records.

The unique characteristics of information and cultural products, and of the processes involved in their production and distribution, distinguish the Information sector from the goods-producing and service-producing sectors. Some of these characteristics are:

1. Unlike traditional goods, an "information or cultural product," such as a newspaper on-line or television program, does not necessarily have tangible qualities, nor is it necessarily associated with a particular form. A movie can be shown at a movie theater, on a television broadcast, through video-on-demand or rented at a local video store. A sound recording can be aired on radio, embedded in multimedia products, or sold at a record store.
2. Unlike traditional services, the delivery of these products does not require direct contact between the supplier and the consumer.
3. The value of these products to the consumer lies in their informational, educational, cultural, or entertainment content, not in the format in which they are distributed. Most of these products are protected from unlawful reproduction by copyright laws.
4. The intangible property aspect of information and cultural products makes the processes involved in their production and distribution very different from goods and services. Only those possessing the rights to these works are authorized to reproduce, alter, improve, and distribute them. Acquiring and using these rights often involves significant costs. In addition, technology is revolutionizing the distribution of these products. It is possible to distribute them in a physical form, via broadcast, or on-line.
5. Distributors of information and cultural products can easily add value to the products they distribute. For

instance, broadcasters add advertising not contained in the original product. This capacity means that unlike traditional distributors, they derive revenue not from sale of the distributed product to the final consumer, but from those who pay for the privilege of adding information to the original product. Similarly, a directory and mailing list publisher can acquire the rights to thousands of previously published newspaper and periodical articles and add new value by providing search and software and organizing the information in a way that facilitates research and retrieval. These products often command a much higher price than the original information.

The distribution modes for information commodities may either eliminate the necessity for traditional manufacture, or reverse the conventional order of manufacture-distribute: A newspaper distributed on-line, for example, can be printed locally or by the final consumer. Similarly, packaged software, which at the time of the 2012 Economic Census was mainly bought through the traditional retail channels, is already becoming available mainly on-line. The NAICS Information sector is designed to make such economic changes transparent as they occur, or to facilitate designing surveys that will monitor the new phenomena and provide data to analyze the changes.

Many of the industries in the NAICS Information sector are engaged in producing products protected by copyright law, or in distributing them (other than distribution by traditional wholesale and retail methods). Examples are traditional publishing industries, software and directory and mailing list publishing industries, and film and sound industries. Broadcasting and telecommunications industries and information providers and processors are also included in the Information sector, because their technologies are so closely linked to other industries in the Information sector.

Public libraries are not included.

Finance and Insurance. The Finance and Insurance sector comprises establishments primarily engaged in financial transactions (transactions involving the creation, liquidation, or change in ownership of financial assets) and/or in facilitating financial transactions. Three principal types of activities are identified:

1. Raising funds by taking deposits and/or issuing securities and, in the process, incurring liabilities. Establishments engaged in this activity use raised funds to acquire financial assets by making loans and/or purchasing securities. Putting themselves at risk, they channel funds from lenders to borrowers and transform or repackage the funds with respect to maturity, scale, and risk. This activity is known as financial intermediation.
2. Pooling of risk by underwriting insurance and annuities. Establishments engaged in this activity collect fees,

insurance premiums, or annuity considerations; build up reserves; invest those reserves; and make contractual payments. Fees are based on the expected incidence of the insured risk and the expected return on investment.
3. Providing specialized services facilitating or supporting financial intermediation, insurance, and employee benefit programs.

In addition, monetary authorities charged with monetary control are included in this sector.

The subsectors, industry groups, and industries within the NAICS Finance and Insurance sector are defined on the basis of their unique production processes. As with all industries, the production processes are distinguished by their use of specialized human resources and specialized physical capital. In addition, the way in which these establishments acquire and allocate financial capital, their source of funds, and the use of those funds provides a third basis for distinguishing characteristics of the production process. For instance, the production process in raising funds through deposit-taking is different from the process of raising funds in bond or money markets. The process of making loans to individuals also requires different production processes than does the creation of investment pools or the underwriting of securities.

Most of the Finance and Insurance subsectors contain one or more industry groups of (1) intermediaries with similar patterns of raising and using funds and (2) establishments engaged in activities that facilitate, or are otherwise related to, that type of financial or insurance intermediation. Industries within this sector are defined in terms of activities for which a production process can be specified, and many of these activities are not exclusive to a particular type of financial institution. To deal with the varied activities taking place within existing financial institutions, the approach is to split these institutions into components performing specialized services. This requires defining the units engaged in providing those services and developing procedures that allow for their delineation. These units are the equivalents for finance and insurance of the establishments defined for other industries.

The output of many financial services, as well as the inputs and the processes by which they are combined, cannot be observed at a single location and can only be defined at a higher level of the organizational structure of the enterprise. Additionally, a number of independent activities that represent separate and distinct production processes may take place at a single location belonging to a multilocation financial firm. Activities are more likely to be homogeneous with respect to production characteristics than are locations, at least in financial services. The classification defines activities broadly enough that it can be used both by those classifying by location and by those employing a more top-down approach to the delineation of the establishment.

Establishments engaged in activities that facilitate, or are otherwise related to, the various types of intermediation have been included in individual subsectors, rather than in a separate subsector dedicated to services alone because these services are performed by intermediaries, as well as by specialist establishments, the extent to which the activity of the intermediaries can be separately identified is not clear.

The Finance and Insurance sector has been defined to encompass establishments primarily engaged in financial transactions; that is, transactions involving the creation, liquidation, change in ownership of financial assets; or in facilitating financial transactions. Financial industries are extensive users of electronic means for facilitating the verification of financial balances, authorizing transactions, transferring funds to and from transactors' accounts, notifying banks (or credit card issuers) of the individual transactions, and providing daily summaries. Since these transaction processing activities are integral to the production of finance and insurance services, establishments that principally provide a financial transaction processing service are classified to this sector, rather than to the data processing industry in the Information sector.

Legal entities that hold portfolios of assets on behalf of others are significant and data on them are required for a variety of purposes. Thus for NAICS, these funds, trusts, and other financial vehicles are the fifth subsector of the Finance and Insurance sector. These entities earn interest, dividends, and other property income, but have little or no employment and no revenue from the sale of services. Separate establishments and employees devoted to the management of funds are classified in Other Financial Investment Activities.

Real Estate and Rental and Leasing. The Real Estate and Rental and Leasing sector comprises establishments primarily engaged in renting, leasing, or otherwise allowing the use of tangible or intangible assets, and establishments providing related services. The major portion of this sector comprises establishments that rent, lease, or otherwise allow the use of their own assets by others. The assets may be tangible, as is the case of real estate and equipment, or intangible, as is the case with patents and trademarks.

This sector also includes establishments primarily engaged in managing real estate for others, selling, renting and/or buying real estate for others, and appraising real estate. These activities are closely related to this sector's main activity, and it was felt that from a production basis they would best be included here. In addition, a substantial proportion of property management is self-performed by lessors.

The main components of this sector are the real estate lessors industries (including equity real estate investment trusts (REITs)); equipment lessors industries (including motor vehicles, computers, and consumer goods); and lessors of nonfinancial intangible assets (except copyrighted works).

Excluded from this sector are establishments primarily engaged in renting or leasing equipment with operators. Establishments renting or leasing equipment with operators are classified in various subsectors of NAICS depending on the nature of the services provided (e.g., transportation, construction, agriculture). These activities are excluded from this sector because the client is paying for the expertise and knowledge of the equipment operator, in addition to the rental of the equipment. In many cases, such as the rental of heavy construction equipment, the operator is essential to operate the equipment.

Professional, Scientific, and Technical Services. The Professional, Scientific, and Technical Services sector comprises establishments that specialize in performing professional, scientific, and technical activities for others. These activities require a high degree of expertise and training. The establishments in this sector specialize according to expertise and provide these services to clients in a variety of industries and, in some cases, to households. Activities performed include: legal advice and representation; accounting, bookkeeping, and payroll services; architectural, engineering, and specialized design services; computer services; consulting services; research services; advertising services; photographic services; translation and interpretation services; veterinary services; and other professional, scientific, and technical services.

This sector excludes establishments primarily engaged in providing a range of day-to-day office administrative services, such as financial planning, billing and recordkeeping, personnel, and physical distribution and logistics. These establishments are classified in Administrative and Support and Waste Management and Remediation Services.

Administrative and Support and Waste Management and Remediation Services. The Administrative and Support and Waste Management and Remediation Services sector comprises establishments performing routine support activities for the day-to-day operations of other organizations. These essential activities are often undertaken in-house by establishments in many sectors of the economy. The establishments in this sector specialize in one or more of these support activities and provide these services to clients in a variety of industries and, in some cases, to households. Activities performed include: office administration, hiring and placing of personnel, document preparation and similar clerical services, solicitation, collection, security and surveillance services, cleaning, and waste disposal services.

The administrative and management activities performed by establishments in this sector are typically on a contract or fee basis. These activities may also be performed by establishments that are part of the company or enterprise. However, establishments involved in administering, overseeing, and managing other establishments of the company or enterprise, are classified in Management of Companies and Enterprises. Those establishments normally undertake the strategic and organizational planning and decision making role of the company or enterprise.

Municipal trash removal is not included.

Educational Services. The Educational Services sector comprises establishments that provide instruction and training in a wide variety of subjects. This instruction and training is provided by specialized establishments, such as schools, colleges, universities, and training centers. These establishments may be privately owned and operated for profit or not for profit, or they may be publicly owned and operated. They may also offer food and/or accommodation services to their students.

Educational services are usually delivered by teachers or instructors that explain, tell, demonstrate, supervise, and direct learning. Instruction is imparted in diverse settings, such as educational institutions, the workplace, or the home, and through diverse means, such as correspondence, television, the Internet, or other electronic and distance-learning methods. The training provided by these establishments may include the use of simulators and simulation methods. It can be adapted to the particular needs of the students, for example sign language can replace verbal language for teaching students with hearing impairments. All industries in the sector share this commonality of process, namely, labor inputs of instructors with the requisite subject matter expertise and teaching ability.

For the 2012 Economic Census, Elementary and Secondary Schools; Junior Colleges; and Colleges, Universities, and Professional Schools are not included.

Health Care and Social Assistance. The Health Care and Social Assistance sector comprises establishments providing health care and social assistance for individuals. The sector includes both health care and social assistance because it is sometimes difficult to distinguish between the boundaries of these two activities. The industries in this sector are arranged on a continuum starting with those establishments providing medical care exclusively, continuing with those providing health care and social assistance, and finally finishing with those providing only social assistance. The services provided by establishments in this sector are delivered by trained professionals. All industries in the sector share this commonality of process, namely, labor inputs of health practitioners or social workers with the requisite expertise. Many of the industries in the sector are defined based on the educational degree held by the practitioners included in the industry.

Excluded from this sector are aerobic classes in Amusement, Gambling and Recreation Industries and nonmedical diet and weight reducing centers Personal and Laundry Services. Although these can be viewed as health services, these services are not typically delivered by health practitioners.

Municipal ambulance services, and county or city nursing care services are not included.

Arts, Entertainment, and Recreation. The Arts, Entertainment, and Recreation sector includes a wide range of establishments that operate facilities or provide services to meet varied cultural, entertainment, and recreational interests of their patrons. This sector comprises (1) establishments that are involved in producing, promoting, or participating in live performances, events, or exhibits intended for public viewing; (2) establishments that preserve and exhibit objects and sites of historical, cultural, or educational interest; and (3) establishments that operate facilities or provide services that enable patrons to participate in recreational activities or pursue amusement, hobby, and leisure-time interests.

Some establishments that provide cultural, entertainment, or recreational facilities and services are classified in other sectors. Excluded from this sector are: (1) establishments that provide both accommodations and recreational facilities, such as hunting and fishing camps and resort and casino hotels are classified in Accommodation; (2) restaurants and night clubs that provide live entertainment in addition to the sale of food and beverages are classified in Food Services and Drinking Places; (3) motion picture theaters, libraries and archives, and publishers of newspapers, magazines, books, periodicals, and computer software are classified in Information; and (4) establishments using transportation equipment to provide recreational and entertainment services, such as those operating sightseeing buses, dinner cruises, or helicopter rides, are classified in Scenic and Sightseeing Transportation.

Public museums and zoos are not included.

Accommodation and Food Services. The Accommodation and Food Services sector comprises establishments providing customers with lodging and/or preparing meals, snacks, and beverages for immediate consumption. The sector includes both accommodation and food services establishments because the two activities are often combined at the same establishment.

Excluded from this sector are civic and social organizations; amusement and recreation parks; theaters; and other recreation or entertainment facilities providing food and beverage services.

Other Services (except Public Administration). The Other Services (except Public Administration) sector comprises establishments engaged in providing services not specifically provided for elsewhere in the classification system. Establishments in this sector are primarily engaged in activities, such as equipment and machinery repairing, promoting or administering religious activities, grantmaking, advocacy, and providing drycleaning and laundry services, personal care services, death care services, pet care services, photofinishing services, temporary parking services, and dating services.

Private households that engage in employing workers on or about the premises in activities primarily concerned with the operation of the household are included in this sector.

Excluded from this sector are establishments primarily engaged in retailing new equipment and also performing repairs and general maintenance on equipment. These establishments are classified Retail Trade.

The following sectors are not included in Table C because they are only available at the state level. The definitions are included because they are in Table 4 in the Introduction. In a few states, these sectors represent significant numbers of employees.

Utilities. The Utilities sector comprises establishments engaged in the provision of the following utility services: electric power, natural gas, steam supply, water supply, and sewage removal. Within this sector, the specific activities associated with the utility services provided vary by utility: electric power includes generation, transmission, and distribution; natural gas includes distribution; steam supply includes provision and/or distribution; water supply includes treatment and distribution; and sewage removal includes collection, treatment, and disposal of waste through sewer systems and sewage treatment facilities.

Excluded from this sector are establishments primarily engaged in waste management services classified in Waste Management and Remediation Services. These establishments also collect, treat, and dispose of waste materials; however, they do not use sewer systems or sewage treatment facilities.

Public electric, gas, water, and sewer utilities are not included.

Manufacturing. The Manufacturing sector comprises establishments engaged in the mechanical, physical, or chemical transformation of materials, substances, or components into new products. The assembling of component parts of manufactured products is considered manufacturing, except in cases where the activity is appropriately classified in Construction.

Establishments in the Manufacturing sector are often described as plants, factories, or mills and characteristically use power-driven machines and materials-handling equipment. However, establishments that transform materials or substances into new products by hand or in the worker's home and those engaged in selling to the general public products made on the same premises from which they are sold, such as bakeries, candy stores, and custom tailors, may also be included in this sector. Manufacturing establishments may process materials or may contract with other establishments to process their materials for them. Both types of establishments are included in manufacturing.

The materials, substances, or components transformed by manufacturing establishments are raw materials that are products of agriculture, forestry, fishing, mining, or quarrying as well as products of other manufacturing establishments. The materials used may be purchased directly from producers, obtained through customary trade channels, or secured without recourse to the market by transferring the product from one establishment to another, under the same ownership.

The new product of a manufacturing establishment may be finished in the sense that it is ready for utilization or consumption, or it may be semifinished to become an input for an establishment engaged in further manufacturing. For example, the product of the alumina refinery is the input used in the primary production of aluminum; primary aluminum is the input to an aluminum wire drawing plant; and aluminum wire is the input for a fabricated wire product manufacturing establishment.

The subsectors in the Manufacturing sector generally reflect distinct production processes related to material inputs, production equipment, and employee skills. In the machinery area, where assembling is a key activity, parts and accessories for manufactured products are classified in the industry of the finished manufactured item when they are made for separate sale. For example, a replacement refrigerator door would be classified with refrigerators and an attachment for a piece of metal working machinery would be classified with metal working machinery. However, components, input from other manufacturing establishments, are classified based on the production function of the component manufacturer. For example, electronic components are classified in Computer and Electronic Product Manufacturing and stampings are classified in Fabricated Metal Product Manufacturing.

Manufacturing establishments often perform one or more activities that are classified outside the Manufacturing sector of NAICS. For instance, almost all manufacturing has some captive research and development or administrative operations, such as accounting, payroll, or management. These captive services are treated the same as captive manufacturing activities. When the services are provided by separate establishments, they are classified to the NAICS sector where such services are primary, not in manufacturing.

Mining, Quarrying, and Oil and Gas Extraction. The Mining, Quarrying, and Oil and Gas Extraction sector comprises establishments that extract naturally occurring mineral solids, such as coal and ores; liquid minerals, such as crude petroleum; and gases, such as natural gas. The term mining is used in the broad sense to include quarrying, well operations, beneficiating (e.g., crushing, screening, washing, and flotation), and other preparation customarily performed at the mine site, or as a part of mining activity.

The Mining, Quarrying, and Oil and Gas Extraction sector distinguishes two basic activities: mine operation and mining support activities. Mine operation includes establishments operating mines, quarries, or oil and gas wells on their own account or for others on a contract or fee basis. Mining support activities include establishments that perform exploration (except geophysical surveying) and/or other mining services on a contract or fee basis (except mine site preparation and construction of oil/gas pipelines).

Establishments in the Mining, Quarrying, and Oil and Gas Extraction sector are grouped and classified according to the natural resource mined or to be mined. Industries include establishments that develop the mine site, extract the natural resources, and/or those that beneficiate (i.e., prepare) the mineral mined. Beneficiation is the process whereby the extracted material is reduced to particles that can be separated into mineral and waste, the former suitable for further processing or direct use. The operations that take place in beneficiation are primarily mechanical, such as grinding, washing, magnetic separation, and centrifugal separation. In contrast, manufacturing operations primarily use chemical and electrochemical processes, such as electrolysis and distillation. However, some treatments, such as heat treatments, take place in both the beneficiation and the manufacturing (i.e., smelting/refining) stages. The range of preparation activities varies by mineral and the purity of any given ore deposit. While some minerals, such as petroleum and natural gas, require little or no preparation, others are washed and screened, while yet others, such as gold and silver, can be transformed into bullion before leaving the mine site.

Mining, beneficiating, and manufacturing activities often occur in a single location. Separate receipts will be collected for these activities whenever possible. When receipts cannot be broken out between mining and manufacturing, establishments that mine or quarry nonmetallic minerals, and then beneficiate the nonmetallic minerals into more finished manufactured products are classified based on the primary activity of the establishment. A mine that

manufactures a small amount of finished products will be classified in Mining, Quarrying, and Oil and Gas Extraction. An establishment that mines whose primary output is a more finished manufactured product will be classified in Manufacturing.

Construction. The Construction sector comprises establishments primarily engaged in the construction of buildings or engineering projects (e.g., highways and utility systems). Establishments primarily engaged in the preparation of sites for new construction and establishments primarily engaged in subdividing land for sale as building sites also are included in this sector.

Construction work done may include new work, additions, alterations, or maintenance and repairs. Activities of these establishments generally are managed at a fixed place of business, but they usually perform construction activities at multiple project sites. Production responsibilities for establishments in this sector are usually specified in (1) contracts with the owners of construction projects (prime contracts) or (2) contracts with other construction establishments (subcontracts).

Establishments primarily engaged in contracts that include responsibility for all aspects of individual construction projects are commonly known as general contractors, but also may be known as design-builders, construction managers, turnkey contractors, or (in cases where two or more establishments jointly secure a general contract) joint-venture contractors. Construction managers that provide oversight and scheduling only (i.e., agency) as well as construction managers that are responsible for the entire project (i.e., at risk) are included as general contractor type establishments. Establishments of the "general contractor type" frequently arrange construction of separate parts of their projects through subcontracts with other construction establishments.

Establishments primarily engaged in activities to produce a specific component (e.g., masonry, painting, and electrical work) of a construction project are commonly known as specialty trade contractors. Activities of specialty trade contractors are usually subcontracted from other construction establishments, but especially in remodeling and repair construction, the work may be done directly for the owner of the property.

Establishments primarily engaged in activities to construct buildings to be sold on sites that they own are known as for-sale builders, but also may be known as speculative builders or merchant builders. For-sale builders produce buildings in a manner similar to general contractors, but their production processes also include site acquisition and securing of financial backing. For-sale builders are most often associated with the construction of residential buildings. Like general contractors, they may subcontract all or part of the actual construction work on their buildings.

There are substantial differences in the types of equipment, work force skills, and other inputs required by establishments in this sector. To highlight these differences and variations in the underlying production functions, this sector is divided into three subsectors.

Construction of Buildings, comprises establishments of the general contractor type and for-sale builders involved in the construction of buildings. Heavy and Civil Engineering Construction, comprises establishments involved in the construction of engineering projects. Specialty Trade Contractors, comprises establishments engaged in specialty trade activities generally needed in the construction of all types of buildings.

Force account construction is construction work performed by an enterprise primarily engaged in some business other than construction for its own account, using employees of the enterprise. This activity is not included in the construction sector unless the construction work performed is the primary activity of a separate establishment of the enterprise. The installation and the ongoing repair and maintenance of telecommunications and utility networks is excluded from construction when the establishments performing the work are not independent contractors. Although a growing proportion of this work is subcontracted to independent contractors in the Construction Sector, the operating units of telecommunications and utility companies performing this work are included with the telecommunications or utility activities.

Management of Companies and Enterprises. The Management of Companies and Enterprises sector comprises (1) establishments that hold the securities of (or other equity interests in) companies and enterprises for the purpose of owning a controlling interest or influencing management decisions or (2) establishments (except government establishments) that administer, oversee, and manage establishments of the company or enterprise and that normally undertake the strategic or organizational planning and decision making role of the company or enterprise. Establishments that administer, oversee, and manage may hold the securities of the company or enterprise.

Establishments in this sector perform essential activities that are often undertaken in-house by establishments in many sectors of the economy. By consolidating the performance of these activities of the enterprise at one establishment, economies of scale are achieved.

Government establishments primarily engaged in administering, overseeing, and managing governmental programs are classified in Public Administration and are not included in the Economic Census. Establishments primarily engaged in providing a range of day-to-day office administrative services, such as financial planning, billing and recordkeeping, personnel, and physical distribution and logistics are classified in Office Administrative Services.

CPSIA information can be obtained
at www.ICGtesting.com
Printed in the USA
BVHW092326060921
616182BV00005B/6